All Music Guide to

THE BLUES

THE DEFINITIVE GUIDE

TO THE BLUES

3RD EDITION

Edited by

Vladimir Bogdanov

Chris Woodstra

Stephen Thomas Erlewine

AMG
All Media Guide

Backbeat
Books

All Media Guide has created the world's largest and most comprehensive information databases for music, videos, DVDs, and video games. With coverage of both in-print and out-of-print titles, the massive AMG archive includes reviews, plot synopses, biographies, ratings, images, titles, credits, essays, and thousands of descriptive categories. All content is original, written expressly for AMG by a worldwide network of professional staff and freelance writers specializing in music, movies, and games. The AMG databases – **All Music Guide®, All Movie Guide®,** and **All Game Guide™**—are licensed by major retailers and Internet content sites and are available to the public through its websites (www.allmusic.com, www.allmovie.com, www.allgame.com) and through its series of books: *All Music Guide, All Music Guide to Rock, All Music Guide to Country, All Music Guide to Jazz, All Music Guide to Blues,* and *All Music Guide to Electronica.*

All Media Guide 301 E. Liberty Street, Suite 400, Ann Arbor, MI 48104
T: 734/887-5600 F: 734/827-2492
www. allmediaguide.com email: feedback@allmediaguide.com

Published by **Backbeat Books**
600 Harrison Street, San Francisco, CA 94105
www.backbeatbooks.com
Email: books@musicplayer.com
An imprint of the Music Player Group
Publishers of Guitar Player, Bass Player, Keyboard, and other magazines
United Entertainment Media, Inc.
A CMP Information company

CMP
United Business Media

Distributed to the book trade in the U.S. and Canada by
Publishers Group West, 1700 Fourth Street, Berkeley, CA 94710

Distributed to the music trade in the U.S. and Canada by
Hal Leonard Publishing, PO Box 13819, Milwaukee, WI 53213

Cover Design: Wagner Design, Ann Arbor, MI
AMG–All Music Guide Founder: Michael Erlewine
Text Composition: Interactive Composition Corporation

Library of Congress Cataloging-in-Publication Data

All music guide to the blues: the definitive guide to the blues/edited by Vladmir Bogdanov,
    Chris Woodstra, and Stephen Thomas Erlewine.–3rd ed.
        p. cm.
Includes index.
ISBN: 0-87930-736-6 (alk. paper)
1. Blues (Music)–Discography. 2. Sound recordings–Reviews. I. Bogdanov, Vladimir, 1965-
II. Woodstra, Chris. III. Erlewine, Stephen Thomas.

ML156.4.B6A45 2003
016.781643'0266–dc21

2003040408

Printed in the United States of America
03 04 05 06 07   5 4 3 2 1

Contents

How to Use this Book

ARTIST NAME

VITAL STATISTICS: For groups, **f.** indicates date and place of formation; **db.** indicated date disbanded. For individual performers, date, and place of birth (**b.**) and death (**d.**), if known, are given.

INSTRUMENT(S) / STYLE(S): Indicates the instruments played if the artist is an individual, followed by the styles of music associated with the performer or group.

BIOGRAPHY: A quick view of the artist's life and musical career. For major performers, proportionately longer biographies are provided.

ALBUM REVIEWS: These are the albums selected by our editors and contributors.

KEY TO SYMBOLS: ● ☆ ★

ESSENTIAL RECORDINGS: Albums marked with a star should be part of any good collection of the genre. Often, these are also a good first purchase (filled star). By hearing these albums, you can get a good overview of the entire genre. These are must-hear and must-have recordings. You can't go wrong with them.

FIRST PURCHASE: Albums marked with either a filled circle or a filled star should be your first purchase. This is where to begin to find out if you like this particular artist. These albums are representative of the best this artist has to offer. If you don't like these picks, chances are this artist is not for you. In the case of an artist who has a number of distinct periods, you will find an essential pick marked for each period. Albums are listed chronologically when possible.

ALBUM TITLE: The name of the album is listed in bold as it appears on the original when possible. Very long titles have been abbreviated, or repeated in full as part of the comment, where needed.

DATE: The year of an album's first recording or release, if known.

RECORD LABEL: Record labels indicate the current (or most recent) release of this recording. Label numbers are not included because they change frequently.

ALBUM RATINGS: ✦ TO ✦✦✦✦✦ In addition to the stars and circles used to distinguish exceptional noteworthy albums, as explained above, all albums are rated on a scale from one to five diamonds.

REVIEWERS: The name of each review's author is given at the end of the review.

Little Brother Montgomery

b. Apr. 18, 1906, Kentwood, LA, **d.** Sep. 6, 1985, Champaign, IL
Vocals, Piano / Piano Blues

A notable influence to the likes of Sunnyland Slim and Otis Spann, pianist "Little Brother" Montgomery's lengthy career spanned both the earliest years of blues history and the electrified Chicago scene of the 1950s.

By age 11, Montgomery had given up on attending school to instead play in Louisiana juke joints. He came to Chicago as early as 1926 and made his first 78s in 1930 for Paramount (the booty that day in Grafton, WI, included two of Montgomery's enduring signature items, "Vicksburg Blues" and "No Special Rider"). Bluebird recorded Montgomery more prolifically in 1935-1936 in New Orleans.

In 1942, Little Brother Montgomery settled down to a life of steady club gigs in Chicago, his repertoire alternating between blues and traditional jazz (he played Carnegie Hall with Kid Ory's Dixieland band in 1949). Otis Rush benefitted from his sensitive accompaniment on several of his 1957-1958 Cobra dates, while Buddy Guy recruited him for similar duties when he nailed Montgomery's "First Time I Met the Blues" in a supercharged revival for Chess in 1960. That same year, Montgomery cut a fine album for Bluesville with guitarist Lafayette "Thing" Thomas that remains one of his most satisfying sets.

With his second wife, Janet Floberg, Montgomery formed his own little record company, FM, in 1969. The first 45 on the logo, fittingly enough, was a reprise of "Vicksburg Blues," with a vocal by Chicago chanteuse Jeanne Carroll (her daughter Karen is following in her footsteps around the Windy City). —*Bill Dahl*

Tasty Blues / 1960 / Prestige/Original Blues Classics ✦✦✦✦
Here's a very attractive example of a pianist with roots dug deep in prewar tradition updating his style just enough to sound contemporary for 1960. With a little help from bassist Julian Euell and Lafayette Thomas (better-known as Jimmy McCracklin's guitarist), Montgomery swoops through his seminal "Vicksburg Blues" and "No Special Rider" with enthusiasm and élan. —*Bill Dahl*

Little Brother Montgomery / 1961 / Decca ✦✦
● **Chicago: The Living Legends** / 1961 / Riverside/Original Blues Classics ✦✦✦✦✦
Chicago: The Living Legends was recorded live at the Birdhouse in Chicago. Much of the record is performed by Montgomery solo, although there's a handful of wonderful cuts that feature him with a small group of traditional jazz musicians. Most of the album is devoted to classic songs from the likes of Duke Ellington and Jelly Roll Morton, yet there are a couple of originals thrown in the mix as well. It's all distinguished by Montgomery's wonderful, laidback performances, which make this a little gem. —*Thom Owens*

Piano, Vocal, and Band Blues / Jul. 1962 / Riverside ✦✦✦

No Special Rider / 1968 / Genes/Adelphi ✦✦✦
Barrelhouse piano player Eurreal "Little Brother" Montgomery played boogie from the crowds as a touring, pre-teen performer. Also a vocalist, Montgomery began his half-century of recording in the Depression with such songs of loss as "Vicksburg Blues" and "No Special Rider." On these 1969 recordings, rich, full-throated Jeanne Carroll ("Penny Pinching Blues") appears on four of the 12 tracks. She carefully enunciates her way through a rendition of Ma Rainey's "You Gotta See Your Mama Every Night." The excellent blues vocalist and pianist Little Brother Montgomery, an influence to Willie Dixon, Otis Spann, and Skip James, here guides us from his home through the tradition of classic early, post-ragtime piano blues. —*Tom Schulte*

☆ **Complete Recorded Works (1930–1936)** / 1992 / Document ✦✦✦✦✦
This single CD from the European Document label has all of Montgomery's 26 prewar recordings as a leader. Two solo numbers are from 1930, including "Vicksburg Blues"; there are a couple songs from 1931 and four duets with guitarist Walter Vincson from 1935. The remainder of this release features Montgomery during a marathon session on Oct. 16, 1936 that resulted in 18 solo selections. All the numbers except the final three on this CD have vocals by Montgomery, but the most rewarding selections are those three instrumentals. On "Farish Street Jive," "Crescent City Blues" and "Shreveport Farewell," Little Brother Montgomery shows just how talented a pianist he was, making one regret that he felt compelled to sing (in a likable but not particularly distinctive voice) on all of the other numbers. A very complete and historic set. —*Scott Yanow*

Complete Recorded Works (1930-1954) / Jun. 2, 1994 / Document ✦✦✦✦

Contributors

All Music Guide

Vladimir Bogdanov, President
Chris Woodstra, Vice President of Content
    Development
Stephen Thomas Erlewine, Director of Pop
    Content
John Bush, Senior Pop Editor
Joslyn Layne, Associate Pop Editor

Assistant Pop Editors

Al Campbell
Andy Kellman
Greg McIntosh
Heather Phares
Stacia Proefrock
Tim Sendra
Brad Torreano
Sean Westergaard
MacKenzie Wilson

Technical Editors

Shakey "Mark" Donkers, Data Processing
    Manager
Zac Johnson, Data Processing Supervisor
Maeve Sullivan, Data Processing Supervisor
Jonathan Ball
Matt Collar
George Davis
Eileen Donis-Forster
Heather Humphrey
Jack L.V. Isles
Aaron Latham
Skyler Miller
Corwin Moore
Suky Morita
David Serra
Donn Stroud
Ryan Sult
Rob Theakston
Chris M True

Copy Editors

Jason Birchmeier
Amy Cloud
Meg Erlewine
David Lynch
Rachel Sprovtsoff-Mangus
Amber Melosi
Aaron Warshaw

Contributors

Bret Adams
Greg Adams
Donnie Addison
David R. Adler
Mark Allan
Jason Anderson
Rick Anderson
Jason Ankeny
William Ashford
Glenn Astarita
Jon Azpiri
Kenneth Bays
Brian Beatty
George Bedard
Larry Belanger
Michael Berick
Jason Birchmeier
Myles Boisen
Ross Boissoneau
Rob Bowman
Adam Bregman
Sandra Brennan
Brian Briscoe
Keith Brown
Jeff Burger
Brandon Burke
John Bush
Nathan Bush
Becky Byrkit
Al Campbell
Bil Carpenter
Kenneth M. Cassidy
Evan Cater
Nate Cavalieri

Eugene Chadbourne
Ken Chang
James Chrispell
Jim Coffin
Paul Collins
Stephen Cook
Scott Cooper
Erik Crawford
Jeff Crooke
Zachary Curd
Bill Dahl
Peter J. D'Angelo
Mike DaRonco
Ben Davies
Hank Davis
Michael P. Dawson
Todd Deery
Mike DeGagne
Mark Deming
Charlotte Dillon
Scott Dirks
Robert L. Doerschuk
Chuck Donkers
John Dougan
Travis Drageset
Ken Dryden
John Duffy
Paula Edelstein
Bruce Eder
Kurt Edwards
Jason Elias
Michael Erlewine
Stephen Thomas Erlewine
Kathleen C. Fennessy
Rob Ferrier
Matt Fink
Sigmund Finman
John Floyd
Dan Forte
Richard Foss
John Franck
Niles J. Frantz
David Freedlander
Michael Gallucci
Bob Gendron
Brandon Gentry

Richard S. Ginell
Daniel Gioffre
Rev. Keith A. Gordon
Robert Gordon
Bob Gottlieb
Karen E. Graves
Tom Graves
Adam Greenberg
Matthew Greenwald
JT Griffith
Tim Griggs
Erik Hage
Char Ham
Andrew Hamilton
Chris Handyside
Shawn Haney
Jeff Hannusch
Amy Hanson
Craig Harris
Brett Hartenbach
Ralph Heibutzki
Dan Heilman
Alex Henderson
Robert Hicks
Matthew Hilburn
Gary Hill
Larry Hoffman
Steve Hoffman
Ed Hogan
Hal Horowitz
Stephen Howell
Steve Huey
Mark A. Humphrey
Vik Iyengar
Jimmy James
Steve James
Jesse Jarnow
Vincent Jeffries
David Jehnzen
Zac Johnson
Liana Jonas
Thom Jurek
Chris Kelsey
Mark Kirschenmann
Cub Koda
Jeffrey Konkel
Todd Kristel
Peter Kurtz
Steve Kurutz
Keir Langley
Ronnie D. Lankford, Jr.
Peggy Latkovich

David Lavin
Joslyn Layne
Uncle Dave Lewis
Richard Lieberson
Steven Loewy
Kip Lornell
Bret Love
Lars Lovén
John Lowe
Craig Lytle
Dennis MacDonald
Jason MacNeil
Dave Marsh
Stewart Mason
Burgin Mathews
Steve Matteo
David L. Mayers
Michael McCall
Wilson McCloy
Steven E. McDonald
Dean McFarlane
Steve McMullen
Bill Meredith
Bill Meyer
Richard Meyer
William Meyer
Michael G. Nastos
Dave Nathan
Opal Louis Nations
Jim Newsom
Shawn Nicholls
Chris Nickson
Christine Ohlman
Brian Olewnick
J.P. Ollio
Jim O'Neal
Brian O'Neill
Thom Owens
Richard Pack
Roch Parisien
Barry Lee Pearson
Paul Pearson
Jana Pendragon
Keith Pettipas
Heather Phares
Lindsay Planer
Bob Porter
Frank Powers
Jim Powers
Greg Prato
Stacia Proefrock
Jack Rabid

Bruce Boyd Raeburn
Chip Renner
Vince Ripol
Ed Rivadavia
Pemberton Roach
Joel Roberts
John Storm Roberts
Matthew Robinson
Jeffrey Pepper Rodgers
William Ruhlmann
Thomas Schulte
Jeff Schwachter
Linda Seida
Tim Sendra
Tim Sheridan
Earl Simmons
Richard Skelly
Chris Slawecki
Dave Sleger
Jim Smith
Michael Smith
Don Snowden
Leo Stanley
Denise Sullivan
Kim Summers
Brendan Swift
Stanton Swihart
David Szatmary
Jeff Tamarkin
Bryan Thomas
Dave Thompson
Bradley Torreano
John Uhl
Richie Unterberger
Mark Vanderhoff
Philip Van Vleck
Joe Viglione
Sean Westergaard
Brian Whitener
Ann Wickstrom
Jonathan Widran
MacKenzie Wilson
Billy C. Wirtz
Rose of Sharon Witmer
Cary Wolfson
Jan Mark Wolkin
Chris Woodstra
Jim Worbois
Ron Wynn
Scott Yanow
Curtis Zimmermann

Introduction

Cub Koda played an integral role at AMG since the first edition of All Music Guide *was published in 1992 until his untimely death in 2000. He wrote many pieces for AMG, but the one project he was proudest of was the* All Music Guide to the Blues. *Cub worked hard on capturing what he loved about the blues in his introduction to the book, and it stands as a vibrant, exciting piece of writing that crystalizes how Cub not only made you want to read more, but made you want to go out immediately and listen to what he was talking about. It was the perfect introduction for the first edition and it remains an ideal overview for the* All Music Guide to the Blues *as it reaches its third edition.*

"I live across the street from a juke box, baby—All night long it plays the blues."

I was recently talking to a friend of mine and was telling them about the project you now hold in your hands, the blues entry into the *All Music Guide* series of reference books. As I was explaining to him about the avalanche of information to be checked and crosschecked, the myriad essays highlighting the music's history, the thousands of albums and compilations to be listened to and the blues maps to show how all the different styles came together and who influenced who, my buddy put his index finger up to his pursed lips, like he always does when I'm yammering on and on and he wants me to shut up. Then he smiled and said, "So, is this another blues revival we're going through?" I smiled back and thought to myself, blues explosion is more like it.

The blues is big business these days—bigger than ever—and if you don't believe me, just turn on your TV set or radio; the sound and style is seemingly everywhere. The blues—in all its myriad strains—has become party music for the millennium. Just look at the short list of irrefutable facts in the last decade of the 20th century: A chain franchise of blues clubs with weekly syndicated TV broadcasts emanating from them? Howlin' Wolf and Muddy Waters' faces emblazoned on the front of T-shirts that you can order out of catalogs? A blues chart in *Billboard* magazine? The Pillsbury Dough Boy selling blueberry muffins on TV with a honking blues riff in the background? Robert Johnson guitar picks and polishing cloths with a facsimile of his autograph on one and his picture on the other? Instructional videos for aspiring guitarists and harmonica blowers by the carload? John Lee Hooker doing Pepsi commercials? Do you think any of this could have happened—or even have been conceivable—30 years ago? No way. The days of the blues as a growth industry have definitely arrived. If you've come to this guide from a rock & roll background, we certainly have no intentions of making you feel stupid or ashamed of it, quite the contrary. To be honest, that's where most of us came in. As a matter of fact, one of the really cool things about the blues is its inclusionary nature; there's room for everybody. You don't have to be a walking blues encyclopedia to hear and get its basic message. That rock & roll comes straight from the blues is one of the few facts about its history that you can get a room full of critics, musicians, or fans to agree on. Now whether you define the moment of its mass acceptance as Elvis cutting loose in the Sun studios or Eric Clapton recycling Robert Johnson for the first time, and whether or not you believe that they (and myriad others) took the music somewhere the originators couldn't have imagined, is usually where the arguments start up.

But the blues are far more than just your standard "seminal" genre influence, like comparing Louis Armstrong's recordings from the '20s to some contemporary, horn-tooting be-bopper and saying, "This is where it came from!" The music is now so interwoven into the fabric of rock and popular music, we take something like hearing the music of Muddy Waters in a TV commercial or a bunch of child actors attempting to sing the blues while extolling the virtues of Kraft Macaroni and Cheese—a couple of notions that would have been unthinkable just a few years back—as nothing out of the ordinary. As rock and country music become more manufactured and fragmented, the blues as a popular music force becomes stronger and stronger. This still surprises some folks, who—while changing channels on their remote control–watch John Lee Hooker picking up Grammy awards while singing duets with Bonnie Raitt, listen to slide guitar and harmonica wailings in beer commercials, gaze at B.B. King and Buddy Guy duking it out on the *Tonight Show* while ZZ Top does the endless boogie on MTV, then usually say something profound along the lines of, "Wow, the blues are really gettin' popular!" These poor, misguided people react as if the music just

pitched a tent in their back yard, moving in while they were asleep. But to quote Lord Chesterfield, "An honest mistake is to be pitied, not ridiculed."

Because the blues has *always* been here. Part of its resiliency stems from it being such a bedrock musical form. The other part of the equation is the fact that blues can run the emotional roller coaster from sounding sad and lonesome one minute to the rockinest party you've ever been to the next, and every place in between. It'll definitely go through surges of popularity, but it originally found its way onto records (big, clunky 10 inch ones that went around the turntable at 78 RPM and broke in half if you sat on them) because it was popular music. It sounded good, it sounded different. It was like hearing the same song over and over again, but all with their own distinct flavor. The familiarity of its basic structure—and how far you could go with it—made it sound as comfortable as the music felt. But no matter how familiar the form was, it was always developing, going different places. And like all evolving American art forms infused by commerce (in this case, the recording industry), the blues kept on changing, splintering off into new permutations, reinventing itself to keep pace with the modern world. Of course, like any other self-respecting branch of indigenous American music, it's a genre filled with absolutely great songs. Most of these numbers have stood the test of time, becoming part and parcel of everyone's set list, from the legendary greats that spawned them to the local bar band playing down the street. Now a great song can always come back and find a new audience, sometimes without changing a single note and other times just dressing it up in contemporary clothes, not unlike an audio Mary Kay makeover. If you think this theory doesn't really hold water, then how else do you explain David Lee Roth having a hit with Louis Prima material? (A man who made so many records for so many different labels, by the way, that he could easily qualify for his *own* All Music Guide.) Most of the music's originators didn't live long enough to reap the big paycheck from all this, but it is all of one piece, a taut connecting thread that links it all together. Elmore James may not have lived long enough to jam on MTV with Eric Clapton and the Rolling Stones, but it all comes from *somewhere*, and Henri Cartier Bresson, famous art photographer from the '40s and '50s, perhaps said it best; "There are no new ideas in the world, only new ways of doing them." That's pretty good, but maybe President Harry S. Truman said it even better; "The only thing new is the history you don't know." And *that*, dear reader, is where this book comes in.

What you are now holding in your hands is a very real collection of American musical history, something that leaps boundaries between blues and its bastard child, rock & roll with stops along the way between jazz, jump, New Orleans zydeco and sweet soul music. If you're an old hardliner, who has done more than your fair share of excavating into the dark past of American roots music, most of these artists and their work will be as plain as the nose on your face. If you're coming to this guide with an interest in the blues that outweighs your knowledge of its history (which roughly parallels the history of recorded music), you're fully expected to keep smacking the side of your head and exclaiming, "So *that's* where that came from!" while you wade through it all, using our handy little maps to tie it all together. We'll do our best to turn you on to the good stuff. Then it's up to you to decide which ones you want to add to your collection.

But in the final analysis, it really doesn't matter who you are or what you know or don't know, because the blues are for *everybody*, from old hippies who were there when Howlin' Wolf and Son House had their first encounters playing to a sea of white faces to young affluent yuppies to whom Howlin' Wolf is just a black face on a postage stamp. This volume does not purport to be the "ultimate" blues book and considering the raft of other books currently out there (a long way down the research highway from 30 years ago when Robert Johnson was more a fictional romantic vision than a set of cold facts with a couple of photographs to go along with it), the notion of there even *being* such an animal is at best subjective. As a famous bluesman once told me backstage at a genre mixed pop festival back in the '70s, "You can't be the best, you just try to be a good 'un" and that's what we have honestly strived for here. A lot of sweat, hard work and a steady diet of warmed over coffee and even colder pizza have gone into these pages. And a lot of love for the music and the people that make it, too. There's no didactic axe to grind out of any of the writers contributing to this book; if there was, their revisionist historical opinions would be promptly filed by the editors into the round file cabinet next to their respective desks, if you get my drift. We've tried to keep the bios and essays unclouded by romantic projection while still being infused with verve, wit and style and we certainly make no apologies for our various contributors' unabashed passion for certain artists. After all, this is a music of and about passion and when the blues hits you hard, it's easy to get swept up in that passion, too.

While the book definitely tips its hat to the music's pioneers and originators—the true giants of the blues in a very spiritual sense–we also haven't tried to make too many distinctions about what is and isn't the blues. Long before the Blues Brothers were doing their own brand of minstrel show for folks who thought Lightnin' Slim was a weight loss program, the old critical saw of "can white men sing the blues?" had been raging at full throttle. We don't make those kind of decisions here, that's somebody else's book. We don't care what color somebody's skin is, their point of ethnic origin or their economic strata. If they can sing and play the blues and sound good doing it, you're going to be reading about it here. While perhaps not quite adopting a "let it all in and let 'em sort it out later" attitude, we've tried to illustrate the depth and wide breadth of the music, while giving current artists of substantive worth their moment in the sun as well. Just don't expect to find a listing for the *101 Strings Play the Blues* album anywhere between these covers, ok?

What we have done is try to assemble the definitive picks on every artist and compilation listed. Walking into any new disc emporium these days can be a fairly daunting task. Most well stocked stores have a decent sized blues section. But there's a hundred Lightnin' Hopkins CDs here; which ones are the good

ones? Which one do I buy first? That's where we come in; if it's good, we want to steer you straight to it. Also along the way, you'll see the occasional "buyer beware" alert review listed as well. If it's a stinkburger, no sense in you getting stuck with it. We also realize that not everybody has the financial outlay to go purchasing multi-disc box sets just because that's the definitive statement on a particular artist or genre. So wherever possible we've listed single disc best-of's as well. If you're coming to an artist for the very first time, that 12-song midline priced compilation just might be the perfect one to start with. And if your old favorite moth eaten vinyl album that you've had since Kennedy was President isn't listed here, don't despair. Now that record companies have figured out a way to sell us back our own record collections, eventually *everything* will get reissued on compact disc sooner or later.

So in putting this book to bed, we here at the All Music Guide are struck with the inescapable conclusion that the blues continue to roll on, its history continuing to be rewritten at every turn. While sadly most of the originators are gone (and wouldn't it be nice to watch that Robert Johnson video that never got made right about now?), their achievements have outlasted the vagaries of fads and fashion and will undoubtedly continue to do so into the next century. This is a music of great substance. We've done our best to steer you to the best of it, while giving it a sense of place and time. So please enjoy this book and don't let anybody tell you different; until time travel is perfected and we can all go back and watch Charley Patton and Son House jamming in a Mississippi juke joint, *these* are the good old days for the music. Just listen to these blues.   *—Cub Koda*

Style Descriptions

ACOUSTIC BLUES

Acoustic Blues is a general catchall term describing virtually every type of blues that can be played on a non-electric musical instrument. It embraces a wide range of guitar and musical styles including folk, the songster tradition, slide, fingerpicking, ragtime, and all of the myriad regional strains (Chicago, Delta, Louisiana, Mississippi, Texas, Piedmont, etc.) that thrived in the early days of the genre's gestation. But acoustic blues is not limited to merely guitar music; its "acoustic" appellation is an elastic-enough term to also include mandolin, banjo, piano, harmonica, jug, and other non-electric instruments including homemade ones, like the one-string monochord bottleneck diddleybow. —*Cub Koda*

ACOUSTIC CHICAGO BLUES

Acoustic Chicago Blues describes the version of music emanating from the Windy City in the years before the twin arrivals of Muddy Waters and electric guitars changed everything. Chicago was recording central for most blues recording artists of the 1930s and '40s, and most performers were plugged into what has become known as "the Bluebird Beat," an acoustic-based progenitor of the later electric Chicago blues band lineup. Its music is earmarked by what is usually described as a "hokum style"—heavy on lyrics that promote a lighthearted atmosphere, and propelled by a jazz-influenced beat and a more city-derived slant. —*Cub Koda*

ACOUSTIC LOUISIANA BLUES

While arguably more of a geographical than a singular stylistic distinction, Acoustic Louisiana Blues nonetheless has a flavor all its own. With distinctly folk leanings to its basic makeup, the form imparts a sometimes backwoods-front porch ambience to both its sound and its stylings. Rough and informal by nature, the genre pays no particular homage to any specific influences, yet is reflective of the spirit and ambience of its country surroundings. Its lyrical content can vacillate between common folk themes (some dating back to the turn of the century) and surprisingly confessional and personal ones as well, often imparting a taut emotional atmosphere to the music. —*Cub Koda*

ACOUSTIC MEMPHIS BLUES

The Memphis style of acoustic country blues is a most distinctive form, and is historically important for the rise of two distinct changes it brought to the music. First was the rise in popularity of the jug band, a style of lighthearted blues played on homemade instruments with a pronounced Dixieland jazz feel. The second influence—and perhaps most important—was the beginnings of assigning parts to guitarists for solo (lead) and rhythm work, a now-commonplace form of arranging that is part and parcel of all modern-day blues bands. This version of Memphis blues was heavily tied to the local medicine show and vaudeville traditions, lasting well into the late '30s. Because of its proximity to Mississippi and the Delta, slide guitar work also crops up in acoustic Memphis blues from time to time, though in nowhere the proportion that it does in other genres. —*Cub Koda*

ACOUSTIC NEW ORLEANS BLUES

Although New Orleans is generally thought of as more of a jazz and rhythm & blues town—with its clubs and dance halls filled with professional bands and singers—the streets of the Crescent City gave birth to a quite different strain of the music. The Acoustic New Orleans Blues style, therefore, embraces everything from itinerant street singers and guitarists to rag-tag "spasm" bands (themselves an offshoot of the jug band) to house frolic piano players. The music also reflects the tastes of the patrons on the street, including jazz, boogie woogie, ballads, rhythm & blues, and pop tunes, all of them interfacing with the most serious of blues. —*Cub Koda*

ACOUSTIC TEXAS BLUES

Earmarked by a lazier, more relaxed approach than its nearby Delta neighbor, the earliest incarnation of Acoustic Texas Blues occurred in the mid-'20s, scoring some of the very first guitar-driven blues hits in the marketplace. Featuring acoustic guitar work rich in filigree patterns—almost an extension of the vocals rather than merely a strict accompaniment to it—the music was already working out defined lead solo patterns and embellishments, even in an unaccompanied context. This ground floor version of the Texas style embraced both the songster and country blues traditions, with its lyrics relying less on affairs of the heart than in other forms. It's also a lyrical tradition that spawned many of the now-commonplace blues metaphors (mean black snake, etc.) and its songbook can boast of some of the hardest indictments on life in prison ever etched into black phonograph records. —*Cub Koda*

BLACK GOSPEL

While many white musicians gravitated toward country, folk, and old-timey music to express their spirituality outside of traditional Christian hymns, Black Gospel music drew heavily upon the traditional spirituals that had been passed down from the days of slavery, picking up its more driving rhythmic emphasis from blues and early jazz. Composer and singer Thomas A. Dorsey crystallized the style in 1932 with his epochal "Take My Hand, Precious Lord," and went on to compose a great many songs that later became standards. When performed in the churches, the music was traditionally sung by a choir, with individual soloists sometimes taking the spotlight; this often happened in a form known as "call and response," in which either the choir or the soloist would repeat and/or answer the lyric that had just been sung by the other, with the soloist improvising embellishments of the melody for greater emphasis. As the music developed, these soloists became more and more virtuosic, performing with wild emotion (and, in the South, physicality) in order to properly express the spiritual ecstasy the music was meant to evoke. The music was quite egalitarian in terms of gender, as both male and female performers—Brother Joe May, Rev. James Cleveland, Mahalia Jackson, the Clara Ward Singers, etc.—gained wide renown among both black and white audiences. The small-group format was also prevalent, with major figures including the Five Blind Boys of Mississippi, the Soul Stirrers, the Swan Silvertones, and the Dixie Hummingbirds; in general, these groups placed a greater premium on smooth vocal harmonies, although some performances could approach the raucous energy (if not quite the huge sound) of a choir-with-soloist group. As the years progressed, black gospel and black popular music influenced and borrowed from one another, reflecting the gradual change of emphasis toward R&B; black gospel also had an enormous impact on the development of soul music, which directed gospel's spiritual intensity into more secular concerns, and included a great many performers whose musical skills were developed in the church. As a recognizable style unto itself, black gospel music largely ceased to develop around the 1970s; progressing racial attitudes had helped black popular music reach wider audiences (and become more lucrative) than ever before, and tastes had turned towards the earthy hedonism of funk and the highly arranged, sophisticated Philly soul sound. The former wasn't quite appropriate for worship, and it wasn't all that practical to duplicate the latter in church services. However, the traditional black gospel sound survived intact and was eventually augmented by contemporary gospel (an '80s/'90s variation strongly influenced by latter-day urban R&B); plus, singers like Whitney Houston continued to develop within its ranks.

BLUES GOSPEL

There has always been a point, both stylistically and philosophically, where the sacred (gospel music) and the profane (blues, the devil's music) strike an uneasy alliance. Consisting almost entirely of performers who are lay preachers or street-corner evangelists, Blues Gospel features use of blues guitar patterns that are tightly interwoven to the most heartfelt statements of religious conviction. Embracing everything from ragtime fingerpicking and knife-edged slide techniques to crudely strummed rhythm patterns, the style owes less allegiance to a particular kind of guitar than to using the instrument's possibilities to propel its lyrical message. Though its proponents are scarce, there are few sounds in the blues that are as alternately spiritual or as bone-chilling as blues gospel music. —*Cub Koda*

BLUES REVIVAL

During the '60s, the blues were rediscovered by a new generation of young listeners. A number of older country blues artists, like Son House and Furry Lewis, experienced a dramatic upsurge in popularity, as their older records became popular and they became in-demand performers. Many of these artists recorded prolifically during the Blues Revival of the '60s, and these records became quite popular. At times, these recordings were the only opportunity the musicians had to record extensively since the '20s or '30s (or were the only chance to record at all).

BRITISH BLUES

More than a mere geographical distinction, the early British Blues of the late '50s and early '60s paid strict adherence to replicating American blues genres, with an admiration for its originators bordering on reverence. But by the time of the blues revival of the mid-'60s, British guitarists—in the main led by Eric Clapton—were starting to bend the form to create their own amalgam. Wedding the string-bending fervor of the B.B., Albert, and Freddie King styles to the extreme volume produced by large amplifiers, British blues largely coalesced into blues rock, with formerly traditional blues artists like the Rolling Stones and Clapton becoming rock stars. The British style has perhaps the closest ties to rock music as opposed to rock & roll, a distinct stylistic descendant of the 1950s. It is this constant shift between preserving older styles and mainstreaming it into the pop marketplace that is the hallmark of British blues. —*Cub Koda*

CHICAGO BLUES

What is now referred to as the classic Chicago Blues style was developed in the late '40s and early '50s, taking Delta blues, fully amplifying it and putting it into a small-band context. Adding drums, bass, and piano (sometimes saxophones) to the basic string band and harmonica aggregation, the style created the now-standard blues band lineup. The form was (and is) flexible to accommodate singers, guitarists, pianists, and harmonica players as the featured performer in front of the standard instrumentation. Later permutations of the style took place in the late '50s and early '60s, with new blood taking their cue from the lead guitar work of B.B. King and T-Bone Walker, creating the popular Westside subgenre (which usually featured a horn section appended to the basic rhythm section). Although the form has also embraced rock beats, it has generally stayed within the guidelines developed in the 1950s and early '60s. —*Cub Koda*

CLASSIC FEMALE BLUES

"Classic Female Blues" or more accurately "Vaudeville Blues," was a field dominated by women singers that enjoyed its heyday in the 1920s. Although officially introduced by Mamie Smith with her hit OKeh recording of "Crazy Blues" in 1920, vaudeville entertainers such as "coon shouter" Sophie Tucker and comedienne Marie Cahill, anticipated some aspects of the style on record prior to World War I. Mamie Smith, an educated city girl from the West End of Cincinnati, was something of an anomaly among Classic Female Blues singers; most of the women were from the South and toured on the T.O.B.A. booking circuit. A few of these artists, including Ethel Waters, the unrecorded Florence Mills, and the unopposed mistress of the genre, Bessie Smith, made the transition to "legitimate" venues. Some singers led their own bands, and several key figures in jazz, such as Coleman Hawkins, made their way into the business playing in these groups. After 1930, with the advent of popular singers in a non-"Classic Blues" vein, the genre went into a slow decline, although its impact on jazz was still felt in 1942 when Peggy Lee adopted Lil Green's race market hit "Why Don't You Do Right," As R&B shouters came to dominate the field, Classic Female Blues singers disappeared altogether, however the example of Bessie Smith is still felt strongly in the work of 1960s rock artist Janis Joplin. —*Uncle Dave Lewis*

CONTEMPORARY BLUES

Contemporary Blues draws upon traditional acoustic and electric blues, but offers a more smoothed-out take on the genre that incorporates the influences of rock, pop, R&B, and/or folk. As such, contemporary blues is most often (though not always) electric, and rarely (though once in a while) purist. Because of its up-to-date production and mellower audience sensibility, the style tends to be more polished and sometimes even a bit genteel; it's still definitely soulful, but not quite as earthy or gritty as the music that predates it, and not as aggressive or fiery as modern-day electric blues from Chicago or Texas. Since it's informed by other types of music, contemporary blues has a greater chance of crossing over to pop, album rock, or adult-contemporary radio formats. Artists like Robert Cray, Keb' Mo', and prodigies like Kenny Wayne Shepherd and Jonny Lang epitomize the contemporary blues sound.

COUNTRY BLUES

Country Blues is a catchall term that delineates the depth and breadth of the first flowering of guitar-driven blues, embracing both solo, duo, and string band performers. The term also provides a convenient general heading for all the multiple regional styles and variations (Piedmont, Atlanta, Memphis, Texas, acoustic Chicago, Delta, ragtime, folk, songster, etc.) of the form. It is primarily—but not exclusively—a genre filled with acoustic guitarists, embracing a multiplicity of techniques from elaborate fingerpicking to the early roots of slide playing. But some country blues performers like Lightnin' Hopkins and John Lee Hooker later switched over to electric guitars without having to drastically change or alter their styles. —*Cub Koda*

DELTA BLUES

The Delta Blues style comes from a region in the southern part of Mississippi, a place romantically referred to as "the land where the blues were born." In its earliest form, the style became the first black guitar-dominated music to make it onto phonograph records back in the late '20s. Although many original Delta blues performers worked in a string-band context for live appearances, very few of them recorded in this manner. Consequently, the recordings from the late '20s through mid-'30s consist primarily of performers working in a solo, self-accompanied context. The form is dominated by fiery slide guitar and passionate vocalizing, with the deepest of feelings being applied directly to the music. Its lyrics are passionate as well, and in some instances remain the highest flowering of blues songwriting as stark poetry. The form continues to the present time with new performers working in the older solo artist traditions and style. —*Cub Koda*

DIRTY BLUES

The Dirty Blues is a bit of a cliché in some areas, and to many modern ears, it seems more a joke than a legitimate form. But the dirty blues has a long tradition in the blues, and it often resurfaces in modern blues and rock. During the early days of recorded blues, raunchy songs were recorded nearly as often as love songs and laments. These songs were distinguished by their often humorous double entendres and metaphors; in performance, the songs could actually flirt with the vulgar, but on wax, the meanings were suggested. The dirty blues primarily were about sex, but there were many songs about drugs and reefer that were essentially dirty blues—namely, simple country blues with taboo lyrics.

The dirty blues thrived in the days before World War II. After the war, many record labels concentrated on records that were commercially viable, and the dirty blues faded away, only to be resurrected during the blues revival of the '60s, when many white collegiates discovered the form.

EARLY AMERICAN BLUES

Early American Blues delineates the sound of the raw African-American song being put into a recognizable form of a commercial context. Starting with the work songs of slaves in the plantation fields down South and following it to the development of "floating verses" used by them to form actual songs, there was no written structure involved. But the strength—and popularity—of the music could not go unnoticed by other African-American musicians of more professional standing. This development brought with it the very first attempts to put the blues into the standard 12-bar form, utilizing three basic-chord changes and the AAB verse stanzas indigenous to the genre. —*Cub Koda*

EAST COAST BLUES

East Coast Blues essentially falls into two categories: Piedmont Blues and Jump Blues and its variations. Musically, Piedmont Blues describes the shared style of musicians from Georgia, the Carolinas, and Virginia as well as others from as far afield as Florida, West Virginia, Maryland, and Delaware. It refers to a wide assortment of aesthetic values, performance techniques, and shared repertoire rooted in common geographical, historical, and sociological circumstances. The Piedmont guitar style employs a complex fingerpicking method in which a regular, alternating-thumb bass pattern supports a melody on treble strings. The guitar style is highly syncopated and connects closely with an earlier string-band tradition integrating ragtime, blues, and country dance songs. It's excellent party music with a full, rock-solid sound.

Jump Blues is an uptempo, jazz-tinged style of blues that first came to prominence in the mid- to late 1940s. Usually featuring a vocalist in front of a large, horn-driven orchestra or medium sized combo with multiple horns, the style is earmarked by a driving rhythm, intensely shouted vocals, and honking tenor saxophone solos, all of those very elements a precursor to rock & roll. The lyrics are almost always celebratory in nature, full of braggadocio and swagger. With less reliance on guitar work (the instrument usually being confined to rhythm section status) than other styles, jump blues was the bridge between the older styles of blues—primarily those in a small band context—and the big band jazz sound of the 1940s. —*Barry Lee Pearson & Cub Koda*

ELECTRIC BLUES

Electric Blues is an eclectic genre that embraces just about every kind of blues that can be played on an amplified instrument. Its principal component is that of the electric guitar, but its amplified aspect can extend to the bass (usually a solid body Fender-type model, but sometimes merely an old "slappin'" acoustic with a pickup attached), harmonica, and keyboard instruments. Stylistically, the form is a wide-open field, accessible to just about every permutation possible—embracing both the old, the new, and sometimes futuristic, and something that falls between the two. Some forms of it copy the older styles of urban blues (primarily the Chicago, Texas, and Louisiana variants) usually in a small-combo format, while others head into funk and soul territory. Yet electric blues is elastic enough to include artists who pay homage to those vintage styles of playing while simultaneously recasting them in contemporary fashion. It is lastly a genre that provides a convenient umbrella for original artists of late '40s and early '50s derivation who seemingly resist neat classifications. —*Cub Koda*

ELECTRIC CHICAGO BLUES

Electric Chicago Blues was developed in the late '40s and early '50s, taking what was essentially Delta blues, amplifying it, and putting it into a small-band context. Taking the basic guitar and harmonica lineup and fortifying it with drums, bass, and piano (sometimes saxophones), the form created what we now know as the standard blues band. Over the years, the electric Chicago style has been flexible enough to accommodate singers, guitarists, pianists, and harmonica players as the featured performer in front of the standard instrumentation. It has developed over the decades as well, with later versions of the style moving away from the strict Delta guitar patterns and embracing the lead guitar work of B.B. King and T-Bone Walker, creating the popular West Side subgenre which usually featured a horn section appended to the basic rhythm section. Although Electric Chicago Blues has also embraced rock beats and modern funk rhythms in the last decade or so, its most avid practitioners have generally stayed within the guidelines developed in the 1950s and early '60s. —*Cub Koda*

ELECTRIC DELTA BLUES

When electric guitars became the staple sound of blues, the Mississippi Delta area was one of the first to react and adapt quickly. Harnessing the rawness and emotional passion of Mississippi blues to this technological development—largely an outgrowth of the necessity of being heard over the din in noisy taverns and juke joints—gave Electric Delta Blues a primordial thump all its own. Often distorted and played at high volumes, its guitar work shares many of the patterns that occur in the electric Chicago style—its spiritual cousin—while imparting the cruder, more down-home flavor of the region. —*Cub Koda*

ELECTRIC HARMONICA BLUES

It's unclear who was the first bluesman to blow his harp into a cheap microphone plugged into an equally cheap public address system and distort it beyond belief, but the artist who made the genre known as Electric Harmonica Blues come to life was none other than Little Walter Jacobs. Its greatest single innovator, greatest-selling artist, and the wellspring of the entire genre, Jacobs' tone became the sound to emulate, and his legacy has persisted in defining the sound and style of the genre decades after his death. Not unlike Charlie Parker's shadow in modern jazz and Hank Williams, Sr.'s in country, Walter's influence has so saturated the genre that it has only been in the last decade or so that new players have turned to the other geniuses of the form (most notably Walter Horton) for inspiration, finding new and innovative ways to express themselves on this humble instrument. *—Cub Koda*

ELECTRIC MEMPHIS BLUES

The later, post-World War II version of Electric Memphis Blues featured explosive, distorted electric guitar work, thunderous drumming, and fierce, declamatory vocals. This wonderfully animated music was largely captured for posterity by Sam Phillips at the Memphis Recording Service studio, later issuing much of it on his Sun Records label. *—Cub Koda*

ELECTRIC TEXAS BLUES

The geographical subgenre known as Texas blues has encompassed a number of style variations over the decades, but its longest-lasting and most developed is its electric incarnation. This change in the region's sound came after World War II, bringing with it a fully electric style—largely pioneered by T-Bone Walker—that featured jazzy, single-string soloing over predominantly horn-driven backing. The style stayed much the same throughout the 1950s, but started moving toward a smaller combo, sans horn section, as the decade moved on. But as much of an uptown sound as Electric Texas Blues represented, its juke-joint roadhouse roots were never too far below the surface, with artists like Lightnin' Hopkins, Juke Boy Bonner, Hop Wilson, and Frankie Lee Sims rocking the joint in duo and trio formats with a frightening intensity. The style moved away from the larger horn-led sounds to smaller and smaller combo formats, eventually embracing much of the same instrumentation as the electric Chicago style, with even more emphasis placed on the lead guitar work. The genre stays current and thriving with a spate of regional performers primarily working in small-combo contexts, with a great many of them hailing from the Austin area. *—Cub Koda*

FOLK-BLUES

Folk-Blues describes a type of blues usually played on non-electric musical instruments. It embraces a wide range of guitar and musical styles that thrived in the early days of the music style's gestation. But folk-blues is not limited to merely guitar music; its "folk" appellation is an elastic-enough term to also include down-home, no-frills music played on mandolin, banjo, harmonica, and other non-electric instruments, with its group sound being projected through the jug bands. Folk-blues evokes the sound and image of a rough-hewn, somewhat informal music, a sound and style born of southern plantations, house frolics, and juke joints; it is true folk music, played by and for the people. The term also provides a convenient general heading for all the multiple regional styles and variations (Piedmont, Atlanta, Memphis, Texas, Delta, ragtime, songster, etc.) embraced by the form. *—Cub Koda*

HARMONICA BLUES

Harmonica Blues refers to any style of blues where the harmonica plays a central figure. Although the harmonica was present in many country blues recordings, it became a dominant force in the '50s, when the instrument was amplified. *—Cub Koda*

JUMP BLUES

Jump Blues refers to an uptempo, jazz-tinged style of blues that first came to prominence in the mid- to late '40s. Usually featuring a vocalist in front of a large, horn-driven orchestra or medium sized combo with multiple horns, the style is earmarked by a driving rhythm, intensely shouted vocals, and honking tenor saxophone solos—all of those very elements a precursor to rock & roll. The lyrics are almost always celebratory in nature, full of braggadocio and swagger. With less reliance on guitar work (the instrument usually being confined to rhythm section status) than other styles, jump blues was the bridge between the older styles of blues—primarily those in a small-band context—and the big band jazz sound of the 1940s. *—Cub Koda*

LOUISIANA BLUES

A looser, more laid-back, and percussive version of the Jimmy Reed side of the Chicago sound, Louisiana Blues has several distinctive stylistic elements to distinguish it from other genres. The guitar work is simple but effective, heavily influenced by the boogie patterns used on Jimmy Reed singles, with liberal doses of Lightnin' Hopkins and Muddy Waters thrown in for good measure. Unlike the heavy backbeat of the Chicago style, its rhythm can be best described as "plodding," making even uptempo tunes sound like slow blues simply played a bit faster. The production techniques on most of the recordings utilize massive amounts of echo, giving the performances a darkened sound and feel, thus coining the genre's alternate description as "swamp blues." *—Cub Koda*

MEMPHIS BLUES

A strain of country blues all its own, Memphis Blues gives the rise to two distinct forms: the jug band (playing and singing a humorous, jazz-style of blues played on homemade instruments) and the beginnings of assigning parts to guitarists for solo (lead) and rhythm, a tradition that is now part and parcel of all modern day blues—and rock & roll—bands. The earliest version of the genre was heavily tied to the local medicine show and vaudeville traditions, lasting well into the late '30s. The later, post-World War II version of this genre featured explosive, distorted electric guitar work, thunderous drumming, and fierce, declamatory vocals. *—Cub Koda*

MODERN ACOUSTIC BLUES

Modern Acoustic Blues finds contemporary artists reviving the older, more country-derived styles of blues in its myriad strains. The form places a great deal of emphasis on instrumental expertise, providing the genre with some astounding players who do more than merely replicate older styles. An outgrowth of the folk music boom and original blues revival of the mid-'60s, its emotional makeup can encompass everything from provincialism to intense personal statements. While clearly honoring traditional forms, the style also has room for original material, providing a forum for new ideas as well as extending the genre's musical repertoire into the future. *—Cub Koda*

MODERN ELECTRIC BLUES

Modern Electric Blues began in the late '70s and early '80s, after blues-rock ran its course and most major labels had given up on the blues. As a musical form, electric blues had not changed significantly since the mid-'60s, once the British blues bands invaded America. As a result, the music sounded essentially the same, blending classic electrified Chicago and Texas blues with a distinct rock influence. This new generation of blues musicians received support through new independent labels like Alligator, which provided a crucial outlet of modern electric blues. As the '80s progressed, modern electric blues found its audience, and it continued to thrive through the late '90s.

MODERN ELECTRIC CHICAGO BLUES

Modern Electric Chicago Blues keeps the same structure and sound as Chicago blues, so the term is primarily a distinction of eras. The modern era begins in the late '60s, as a new generation began to play the blues. Some of these players displayed rock influences, mainly in terms of loud amplification, but they kept the spirit of Chicago blues alive.

NEW ORLEANS BLUES

Primarily (but not exclusively) piano- and horn-driven, New Orleans Blues is enlivened by Caribbean rhythms, an unrelenting party atmosphere, and the "second-line" strut of the Dixieland music so indigenous to the area. There's a cheerful good-naturedness to the style that infuses the music with a good-time feel, no matter how somber the lyrical text. The music itself uses a distinctively "lazy" feel, with all of its somewhat complex rhythms falling just a hair behind the beat. But the vocals can run the full emotional gamut from laid-back crooning to full-throated gospel shouting, making for some interesting juxtapositions, both in style and execution. *—Cub Koda*

NEW ORLEANS R&B

Primarily a piano- and horn-driven style, New Orleans R&B is the next step over from its more bluesier practitioners. There's a cheerful good-naturedness to the style that infuses the music with a good-time feel, no matter how somber the lyrical text. The music itself uses a distinctively "lazy" feel, with all of its somewhat complex rhythms falling just a hair behind the beat, making for what is known as "the sway." The vocals can run the full emotional gamut, from laid-back crooning to full-throated gospel shouting, while the horn lines provide a perfect droning backdrop. Enlivened by Caribbean rhythms, an unrelenting party atmosphere, and the distinctive "second-line" strut of the Dixieland music so indigenous to the area, there's nothing quite as intoxicating as the sound of Crescent City R&B. *—Cub Koda*

PIANO BLUES

Piano Blues runs through the entire history of the music itself, embracing everything from ragtime, barrelhouse, boogie woogie, and smooth West Coast jazz stylings to the hard-rocking rhythms of Chicago blues. *—Cub Koda*

PIEDMONT BLUES

Piedmont Blues refers to a regional substyle characteristic of black musicians of the southeastern United States. Geographically, the Piedmont means the foothills of the Appalachians west of the tidewater region and Atlantic coastal plain stretching roughly from Richmond, VA, to Atlanta, GA. Musically, Piedmont blues describes the shared style of musicians from Georgia, the Carolinas, and Virginia, as well as others from as far afield as Florida, West Virginia, Maryland, and Delaware. It refers to a wide assortment of aesthetic values, performance techniques, and shared repertoire rooted in common geographical, historical, and sociological circumstances; to put it more simply, Piedmont blues means a constellation of musical preferences typical of the Piedmont region. The Piedmont guitar style employs a complex fingerpicking method in which a regular, alternating-thumb bass pattern supports a melody on treble strings. The guitar style is highly syncopated and connects closely with an earlier string band tradition, integrating ragtime, blues, and country dance songs. It's excellent party music with a full, rock-solid sound. *—Barry Lee Pearson*

PREWAR BLUES

Prewar Blues is country blues recorded before World War II. Prewar blues is entirely acoustic, but there are variations to the style—it could be acoustic guitars, piano blues, solo singers, string bands, or jug bands. The primary unifying factors are that the music is all acoustic, is usually a folk song, and was recorded prior to World War II.

PREWAR GOSPEL BLUES

Prewar Gospel Blues is gospel blues recorded prior to World War II. There has always been a point, both stylistically and philosophically, where the sacred (gospel music) and the profane (blues, the devil's music) have had an uneasy alliance, and this genre strain is it. Consisting almost entirely of performers who are lay preachers or streetcorner evangelists, their use of blues guitar patterns are tightly interwoven to the most heartfelt statements of religious conviction. Embracing everything from ragtime fingerpicking and knife-edged slide techniques to crudely strummed rhythm patterns, the style owes less allegiance to a particular style of guitar than to using the instrument's possibilities to propel its lyrical message. Though its proponents are few, there are few sounds in the blues that are as alternately spiritual or as bone-chilling as gospel blues music. —*Cub Koda*

R&B

Evolving out of jump blues in the late '40s, R&B laid the groundwork for rock & roll. R&B kept the tempo and the drive of jump blues, but its instrumentation was sparer and the emphasis was on the song, not improvisation. It was blues chord changes played with an insistent backbeat. During the '50s, R&B was dominated by vocalists like Ray Charles and Ruth Brown, as well as vocal groups like the Drifters and the Coasters. Eventually, R&B metamorphosed into soul, which was funkier and looser than the pile-driving rhythms of R&B.

SLIDE GUITAR BLUES

Slide guitar blues is produced when a player uses some kind of tubular finger covering (usually made of metal or glass, like a bottleneck) to depress the strings of a guitar over the frets so that the strings are stretched and bent, producing a wavering tone. Traditionally slide guitar blues was played on resonator guitars, but a variety of acoustic and electric guitars have also been used. Blues slide guitar originated in the Mississippi Delta region where it was popularized by a number of blues players, including Robert Johnson. Electric slide guitar blues developed along with other electric blues styles with the migration of African-Americans north to Chicago in the 1940s.

SOUL-BLUES

Perhaps one of the most modern forms of blues, Soul-Blues fuses disparate elements of black popular music to create a wholly urban amalgam of its own. Artists who wanted to move stylistically beyond the three-chord confines of conventional blues forms found the rhythm & blues strain of the 1950s and the southern soul style of the mid-'60s far more to their creative liking. Soul-blues combines the best elements of the two and blends that with the standard blues band instrumentation—sometimes augmented with an R&B-styled horn section. The genre also provides more traditional blues artists with a style to visit on occasion, injecting some contemporary life into their recordings. —*Cub Koda*

SWAMP BLUES

Swamp Blues, the looser, more rhythmic variation of the standard Louisiana sound, also brings more contemporary elements of New Orleans, zydeco, soul music, and Cajun to bear on its style. The guitar work is simple but effective, and is heavily influenced by the boogie patterns used on Jimmy Reed records, with liberal doses of Lightnin' Hopkins and Muddy Waters. Unlike the heavy backbeat of the more popular urban styles, its rhythm can be best described as laid-back, making even its most uptempo offerings share the same mood and ambience of the most desultory of slow blues. —*Cub Koda*

TEXAS BLUES

A geographical subgenre earmarked by a more relaxed, swinging feel than other styles of blues, Texas Blues encompasses a number of style variations and has a long, distinguished history. Its earliest incarnation occurred in the mid-'20s, featuring acoustic guitar work rich in filigree patterns—almost an extension of the vocals rather than merely a strict accompaniment to it. This version of Texas blues embraced both the songster and

country blues traditions, with its lyrics relying less on affairs of the heart than other forms. The next stage of development in the region's sound came after World War II, bringing forth a fully electric style that featured jazzy, single-string soloing over predominantly horn-driven backing. The style stays current with a raft of regional performers primarily working in a small combo context. —*Cub Koda*

URBAN BLUES

The descriptive phrase Urban Blues was first used in the early part of the 20th century to differentiate between the more uptown sentiments pervasive to the style and the cruder, more rural stylings of country blues artists. This term was later used in the 1940s to describe a type of sophisticated blues written about the vagaries of city life, its lyrics alternately dealing with romantic strife and the innumerable good times to be easily obtained in an urban area. Always city-derived, the music is earmarked by a pronounced uptown emphasis, embracing everything from jump blues to jazz-influenced stylings to smooth, supper-club-style vocals. —*Cub Koda*

VAUDEVILLE BLUES

On the African-American T.O.B.A. vaudeville circuit of the 1920s and early '30s, the headlining acts were the blues singers. Even the minstrel shows, with their emphasis on group performance, gave precedence to the blues performer—more often than not a female firmly rooted in the then-popular classic style of shouting. But the Vaudeville Blues singers had to put on a show with their singing, and many, like the husband and wife team of Butterbeans and Susie, used the blues as a blueprint for their myriad comedy routines. Others, like Coot Grant and Kid Sox Wilson, were prolific songwriters, using their special material in their stage act while farming out some of the best of it to other singers who worked the same circuit, like Bessie Smith. —*Cub Koda*

WEST COAST BLUES

More piano-based and jazz-influenced than anything else, West Coast Blues is—in actuality—the California style, with all of the genre's main practitioners coming to prominence there, if not actual natives of the state in particular. In fact, the state and the style played host to a great many post-war Texas guitar expatriates, and their jazzy, T-Bone Walker style of soloing would become an earmark of the genre. West Coast blues also features smooth, honey-toned vocals, frequently crossing into urban blues territory. The West Coast style was also home to numerous jump blues practitioners, as many traveling bands of the 1940s ended up taking permanent residence there. Its current practitioners work almost exclusively in the standard small-combo format. —*Cub Koda*

WORK SONGS

Handed down from the days of slavery, work songs helped black field workers pass the time under oppressive social and environmental conditions. They were usually simple, repetitive chants and melodies, easily remembered and modified. Some work songs had a spiritual focus, while others were carefully coded metaphors containing social commentary and/or guidelines for escape. After slavery was abolished, work songs continued to be passed along, especially in black sharecropper families who still worked in the South. The field recordings by the father/son team of John and Alan Lomax, most made during the first half of the 20th century, constitute the primary modern-day source for work songs.

Marion Abernathy

Vocals / R&B

Marion Abernathy, otherwise known as "the Blues Woman," was one of a handful of artists who played a key role in starting Specialty Records. In 1944, founder Art Rupe, having felt cheated in his first partnership in a record label, put together what was then known as Juke Box Records. Abernathy, who he dubbed "the Blues Woman," was the second artist ever released on the label (backed by the Buddy Banks Sextet) doing "Voo-It! Voo-It!," co-written by saxman Banks and guitarist William "Frosty" Pyles. She may have left behind as many as a dozen tracks from this period. *—Bruce Eder*

● **1947–1949** / Jun. 5, 2001 / Classics ♦♦♦

"Peg Leg" Ben Abney

b. Sep. 7, 1883, **d.** Feb. 1970, Fayetteville, NC

Piano / Piano Blues

"Peg Leg" Ben Abney was one of less than a half-dozen blues pianists from Charlotte, NC, to make records during the 78 rpm era. Abney's total recorded output consists of six sides made in Charlotte on June 22, 1936. If his birth date as listed in the Social Security Death Index is to be trusted, then Abney was 52 at the time of these sessions, making him one of the oldest blues pianists on record. However this does not mean that Abney's is one of the oldest blues styles represented; his elementary stride basses and fragments of Earl Hines-like "trumpet piano" phrases suggests a manner of playing that was developed in the mid- to late '20s. Ben Abney's piano playing is dense, clotted, and highly discordant, suggesting that he was a latecomer to the instrument. Abney's age, style and nickname suggests that he may have started out as a general laborer, suffered a debilitating injury in middle age, and learned to play blues as a means to support himself afterward. He is listed as a musician in the Charlotte City directories throughout the '30s. Abney was a fine singer, and his six surviving blues contain lyrics that may refer to personal experiences. Bluebird was being polite when they titled his third selection as "Way Down in Town," for the lyric as sung is "Way Down in Polack Town," and the song refers to panhandling in a predominantly white neighborhood. Abney sings "Some people give me a nickel, others a lousy dime/Anyone who'd give me that much, you guys ain't no friend of mine." Abney refers to faraway places such as Tennessee and St. Louis in his blues, but among the scant evidence that exists in reference to him there is nothing to suggest that he ever left North Carolina. But his piano playing suggests some awareness of Chicago style, not only that of Hines but in particular the approach of Jimmy Yancey. Like Yancey, Abney has an eccentric pet phrase, a substituted chord in the turn back that reads like something out of Thelonious Monk. This figure is found in three of Abney's six recorded selections. Bluebird waited a long time to release the last coupling from this session; it didn't appear until 1938, and this is the only one of his records to contain the full billing of " 'Peg Leg' Ben Abney." The originals of these Bluebirds must be rare in the extreme, as even the Document Records reissue of them is taken from a poor and deteriorating tape copy, rather than the original 78 rpm shellacs. *—David N. Lewis*

Mick Abrahams

b. Apr. 7, 1943, Luton, Bedfordshire, England

Vocals, Guitar / Prog-Rock/Art Rock, Singer/Songwriter, Blues-Rock, R&B

Mick Abrahams was one of the more unfortunate hard-luck stories in rock music. Best known for his work on Jethro Tull's debut album, *This Was*, where he played blues licks that had critics comparing him favorably to Eric Clapton, he left the group, and since then has never managed to achieve lasting success as a recording artist, or the world-class fame of his former bandmates. Leading various incarnations of his best known band, Blodwyn Pig, he has persevered over the last quarter century, and achieved some major cult recognition, especially in England.

Abrahams joined his first band, the Crusaders, in 1964, alongside pianist Graham Waller, drummer (and Screaming Lord Sutch/Cyril Davies veteran) Carlo Little, and bassist Alex Dmochowski, all backing singer Neil Christian. Abrahams' musical hero was Alexis Korner, the man who—with Cyril Davies—brought blues to England. He was one of that legion of young guitarists, which included Brian Jones and Keith Richards, who found their way into music through Korner's groundbreaking work with Blues Incorporated. In 1965, Abrahams and Waller joined the Toggery Five, a septet whose members included drummer Clive Bunker. That group had a momentary brush with the record books when they cut a Mick Jagger-Keith Richards song as a failed single, but otherwise failed to make any lasting impression.

In the summer of 1967, while playing in his next group, McGregor's Engine with Bunker, Abrahams met Ian Anderson and bassist Glenn Cornick, who were playing in a group called the John Evan Smash. After comparing notes on their shared enthusiasm for blues, they decided to form Jethro Tull. Abrahams remained with the group until November of 1968, and his guitar was very prominent in the group's sound during this period, revealing him to be one of the best among England's legions of bluesmen. Evidence of his skill, passion, and persuasiveness are all over their second single, "A Song

For Jeffrey," and the album *This Was*. Anderson's voice and flute, however, quickly challenged Abrahams for primacy, and by the fall of 1968 Anderson had won that battle; in November, Abrahams was gone.

Early in 1969, Abrahams formed his own group, Blodwyn Pig, with Jack Lancaster on saxophone, ex-McGregor's Engine member Andy Pyle on bass, and Ron Berg on drums. This was a blues band through-and-through, and even arriving on the scene in a time when London was filled with white blues players, Blodwyn Pig quickly became a critical favorite with its performances and its first album, *Ahead Rings Out*. Considered a classic progressive blues album, the record found a small audience in the United States, while in England it was a Top Ten album. The group's second long-player, *Getting To This*, released a year later, was received with enthusiasm as well, and also made the British Top Ten.

The group was riven by internal conflicts, however, as Lancaster and the other members expressed a desire to go in a somewhat different direction in their music, and for Lancaster's sax to become more prominent. Abrahams left the band in 1970, to be replaced by ex-Yes guitarist Peter Banks and guitarist/singer Larry Wallis. The group continued on under the leadership of Lancaster, although it was eventually renamed Lancaster's Bomber. Initially Abrahams formed a new group called Wommet; it was very short-lived, however, so he reorganized his career around the Mick Abrahams Band, with Walter Monaghan on bass, Bob Sargeant on guitar, keyboards and vocals, and Ritchie Dharma on drums. He released two albums on Chrysalis, *Mick Abrahams* and *At Last*, with his former Blodwyn Pig bandmate Lancaster expanding the lineup to a quintet. Neither sold very well, although Abrahams was never at a loss for paying gigs.

In 1974, Abrahams reformed Blodwyn Pig with his ex-Tull bandmate Bunker, and Pyle and Lancaster, but the group only lasted a few gigs before breaking up. Meanwhile, Abrahams virtually left the music business, but not before he recorded what proved to be his biggest selling solo album of all, an instruction record entitled *Learning To Play Guitar With Mick Abrahams*. He continued to play occasional shows, but made his living outside of music, working as a driver, lifeguard, and financial consultant. He seemed content to play the odd impromptu show at the local pub, or for causes that mattered to him in his home town of Dunstable.

Finally, in 1988, however, he reformed Blodwyn Pig with Andy Pyle back in the lineup on bass, ex-Bonzo Dog Band member Dick Heckstall-Smith and Bernie Hetherington on saxes, Bruce Boardman on keyboards, and Clive Bunker on drums. The reformed group was a success, releasing a well received album called *All Said And Done*. Their 1993 lineup, including new keyboardist Dave Lennox, Mike Summerland on bass, and Graham Walker on drums, released the album *Lies (A New Day)*, Blodwyn Pig's most accomplished album ever. The group later issued a live recording from their 1993 tour (where Abrahams was reunited with Ian Anderson at one gig), entitled *All Tore Down*. Abrahams continues to play and record regularly, with a following in England and America with Blodwyn Pig. As of the mid-'90s, the group consisted of a quartet of Abrahams, Walker, Lennox, and Summerland, with vocalist Jackie Challoner and saxplayer Nick Payne augmenting their membership in the studio. *—Bruce Eder*

● **Mick Abrahams** / 1971 / BGO ♦♦♦

Abrahams' first formal solo album is more focused on blues and blues-rock, and far less on jazz, than his work with Blodwyn Pig, and it is a better record for it. For first time listeners, much of this record will recall Clapton's first post-Cream solo LP, *Eric Clapton*, in its generally laid back sound and the presence of a fairly strong country blues influence. Abrahams' vocals here are a little more mournful than soulful—his playing (especially when he picks up an acoustic guitar) is up to his usual standard, however, and Ritchie Dharma's drumming is dizzying in its speed and complexity. Much of the material is substandard, however, and one number in particular, "Seasons," is especially annoying—evidently Abrahams couldn't decide whether he wanted to invade Yes territory (especially Steve Howe's solo noodlings) or the Allman Bros. turf on this 15-minute extended track (which, as a piece of psychedelia, is several years late), which ultimately goes nowhere. "Winds of Change," an unassuming four-minute acoustic blues, is far more to the point. *—Bruce Eder*

At Last / 1972 / Edsel ♦♦

Lies / 1995 / A New Day ♦♦♦

One / 1996 / A New Day ♦♦♦

Mick's Back / Jul. 30, 1996 / Indigo ♦♦♦

Nathan Abshire

b. Jun. 23, 1913, Gueydan, LA, **d.** May 13, 1981, Basile, LA

Vocals, Accordion / Traditional Cajun, Swamp Blues, Louisiana Blues, Zydeco

Nathan Abshire helped bring the blues and honky tonk to Cajun music and repopularized the accordion with his recordings during the '50s and '60s, but still never managed to make a living from his music. Born in Gueydan, LA, on June 23, 1913, Abshire began playing professionally in the '20s, and he first recorded in the early '30s with Happy Fats & the Rainbow Ramblers. Abshire went to work at the Basile, LA, town dump around that time, and he held the job for most of his working life.

His fortunes began looking bright by 1936, however, when the Rainbow Ramblers began backing him on sides for Bluebird. After serving in World War II, Abshire cut "Pine Grove Blues"—his most famous single and later his signature song—for D.T. Records. He recorded for Khoury/Lyric, Swallow and Kajun during the '50s and '60s; meanwhile playing local dances and appearing on sessions by the Balfa Brothers. A renewal of interest in Cajun and folk music during the '70s gave Abshire a chance to play several festivals and colleges, and star in the 1975 PBS-TV Cajun documentary, *Good Times Are Killing Me*. The title proved prophetic, however, as Abshire fought alcoholism during his last years. Several sessions for Folkways and La Louisienne followed in the late '70s, but he died on May 13, 1981. —*John Bush*

Pine Grove Blues / 1979 / Swallow ✦✦✦
According to the liner notes on the original LP, this was Abshire's first album, although he had previously had some tracks on several various-artists collections. The Balfa Brothers back him on most of the songs on this jovial, none-too-slick-sounding Cajun recording, devoted mostly to Abshire originals. Actually the bottom end of "La Valse De Holly Beach" is a little muddily recorded by the standards of the '70s, but if anything that adds to the appeal of music that wasn't meant to sound too finely honed in the recording studio. Joe South's "Games People Play" makes for an unexpected cover choice, though it's slotted into a standard upbeat Cajun rhythm, with infectious ensemble "la-la" backup vocals, steel guitar, accordion, and fiddle. Is there a drawback to a well-executed set by a major veteran Cajun musician in which the performers sound like they're having fun? Well, it's one that bugs many a non-Cajun obsessive: by the time you get late in the program of these 12 songs, you wish for a little more variety in this standard mix of cheery uptempo tunes and lazy, drawling slower ones. *Pine Grove Blues* was paired with another Abshire album originally issued on Swallow, *The Good Times Are Killing Me*, on a single-disc Ace CD reissue (see below). —*Richie Unterberger*

The Good Times Are Killing Me / 1979 / Swallow ✦✦✦
As on Abshire's prior Swallow album *Pine Grove Blues*, the Balfa Brothers take a prominent role as accompanists. It differs from the previous record, though, in that Abshire takes just five of the lead vocals on the twelve selections. The lead singing is distributed much as it would be in a leaderless band, some vocals taken by Rodney Balfa, others by Dewey Balfa, and some by Thomas Langley. Also, the production is usually crisper this time around, and the percussion more to the forefront in the mix. In respects to repertoire and performance, though, it's pretty much the same traditionally based mix of two-steps and waltzes, uptempo and slow tempo. The alternation of different lead singers helps alleviate the similarity that causes the attention of many to drag over the course of a Cajun album. The slower, more lugubrious numbers have a welcome honky-tonk country feel. The closing "La Noce a Rosalie" is the most atypical piece, sounding a little like an unplugged front-porch toss-off, with spoken sections from Abshire. *The Good Times Are Killing Me* was paired with another Abshire album originally issued on Swallow, *Pine Grove Blues*, on a single-disc Ace CD reissue in 2002. —*Richie Unterberger*

The Cajun Legend: Best of Nathan Abshire / 1991 / Swallow ✦✦✦✦✦
With "The Good Times Are Killing Me" emblazoned on his accordion case, Abshire embodied the Cajun musician's ethos. There are 20 two-steps and waltzes here, some with the Balfa Brothers, including a remake of the great "Pine Grove Blues" and a heartfelt "Tramp Sur La Rue" with wailing vocals from Nathan. —*Mark A. Humphrey*

★ **French Blues** / 1993 / Arhoolie ✦✦✦✦✦
Recorded between 1949 and 1956, this is prime Cajun music. The fidelity is slightly better than the best Cajun discs of the '30s, but the approach is still satisfyingly raw and spontaneous, with waltzes, boogies, and blues. A steel guitar is present to varying degrees on most of the tracks, giving the fiddle/accordion-dominated arrangements a bit more flavor. This has a great spontaneous feel that stops short (but not that short) of raggedness, highlighted by Abshire's joyous calls and asides. Includes his big "hit," "Pine Grove Blues," although a hit by the standards of this regional style only constituted about three thousand copies sold. With 28 tracks and 78 minutes running time, it's the usual excellent value for an Arhoolie reissue. —*Richie Unterberger*

The Great Cajun Accordionist / Dec. 12, 1995 / Ace ✦✦✦✦
One time through this CD and the listener will know why Nathan Abshire was called great. The accordionist, born in 1913, was a huge force in the music of his culture from the '30s until his death in 1981, and his influence continues to this day. It was he who incorporated the blues of Creole tradition into Cajun music. His signature tune, "Pine Groves Blues," was a regional hit and made an impact on every Cajun musician thereafter. The man was ahead of his time. Cajun music would not hit the mainstream scene until shortly before his death, so he never got the acclaim that was really his due. Still, listeners have his recordings. This one contains both traditional selections and those written by Abshire himself. As always, the music is meant for dancing. Abshire's virtuosity shines on "Le Two Step de l'Acadian," as well as his own "Le Two Step de Choupique." He is in turn lyrical on waltzes such as "Le Valse du Kaplan" and his "Le Valse de Bayou Teche," hard driving on "Le Blues Francais," and poignant on "Pauvre Hobo." The songs are played with all the heart and soul of the man with "the good times are killing me" as his personal motto. The CD is worthy of this giant of Cajun accordion music. —*Rose of Sharon Witmer*

Pine Grove Blues/The Good Times Are Killing Me / Mar. 2002 / Ace/Kent ✦✦✦✦
This two-on-one CD reissue pairs two albums Nathan Abshire recorded for Swallow in the '70s. —*Richie Unterberger*

Johnny Ace (John Alexander)

b. Jun. 9, 1929, Memphis, TN, **d.** Dec. 25, 1954, Houston, TX
Vocals, Piano / R&B
The senseless death of young pianist Johnny Ace while indulging in a round of Russian roulette backstage at Houston's City Auditorium on Christmas Day of 1954 tends to overshadow his relatively brief but illustrious recording career on Duke Records. That's a pity, for Ace's gentle, plaintive vocal balladry deserves reverence on its own merit, not because of the scandalous fallout resulting from his tragic demise.

John Marshall Alexander was a member in good standing of the Beale Streeters, a loosely knit crew of Memphis young bloods that variously included B.B. King, Bobby Bland, and Earl Forest. Signing with local DJ David Mattis' fledgling Duke logo in 1952, the rechristened Ace hit the top of the R&B charts his very first time out with the mellow ballad "My Song." From then on, Ace could do no musical wrong, racking up hit after hit for Duke in the same smooth, urbane style. "Cross My Heart," "The Clock," "Saving My Love for You," "Please Forgive Me," and "Never Let Me Go" all dented the uppermost reaches of the charts. And then, with one fatal gunshot, all that talent was lost forever (weepy tribute records quickly emerged by Frankie Ervin, Johnny Fuller, Varetta Dillard, and the Five Wings).

Ace scored his biggest hit of all posthumously. His haunting "Pledging My Love" (cut with the Johnny Otis orchestra in support) remained atop Billboard's R&B lists for ten weeks in early 1955. One further hit, "Anymore," exhausted Duke's stockpile of Ace masters, so they tried to clone the late pianist's success by recruiting Johnny's younger brother (St. Clair Alexander) to record as Buddy Ace. When that didn't work out, Duke boss Don Robey took singer Jimmy Lee Land, renamed him Buddy Ace, and recorded him all the way into the late '60s. —*Bill Dahl*

● **Johnny Ace Memorial Album** / 1974 / MCA ✦✦✦✦✦
It's downright bizarre that Ace's catalog hasn't enjoyed a fresh reissue in 40 years. This 12-song CD is the exact same package that Don Robey rushed out following the pianist's death, with all the velvety hits ("Pledging My Love," "My Song," "The Clock," "Never Let Me Go") and a mere two blistering rockers, "How Can You Be So Mean" and "Don't You Know." A more thorough examination of Ace's discography is definitely in order! —*Bill Dahl*

Aces

f. 1945, Chicago, IL
Group / Chicago Blues
Led by brothers Louis and Dave Myers, the pioneering Chicago blues combo the Aces earned their greatest success in support of Little Walter. Natives of Byhalia, Mississippi, guitarist Louis and bassist Dave originally performed under the name the Little Boys; with the subsequent addition of harpist Junior Wells, they rechristened themselves the Three Deuces, followed by the Three Aces. The 1950 enlistment of drummer Fred Below prompted another name change, this time to the Four Aces; finally, to simplify matters once and for all, the group performed as just the Aces. Influenced in large part by jazz, they developed an urbane, sophisticated style well ahead of its time; in particular, Below's refined rhythms led to the rise of the blues shuffle beat, and helped launch the drums to a new prominence within the blues band hierarchy. In 1952, Wells quit to join the Muddy Waters band, filling the vacancy created by the recent departure of harpist Little Walter Jacobs; ironically, Walter himself quickly signed the remaining Aces as his new backing unit, renaming the trio the Jukes. A series of seminal recordings followed—"Mean Old World," "Sad Hours," "Off the Wall," and "Tell Me Mama" among them—before Louis' 1954 exit resulted in the Jukes' gradual dissolution. The Myers brothers and Below re-formed under the Aces moniker in 1970 to tour Europe before again going their separate ways. —*Jason Ankeny*

Kings of Chicago Blues / 1971 / Vogue ✦✦✦
● **Dust My Broom** / 1971 / Vogue ✦✦✦✦
Chicago Beat / 1976 / Black & Blue ✦✦

Arthur Adams

b. Dec. 25, 1940, Medon, TN
Vocals, Guitar / Electric Memphis Blues, Soul-Blues
As house bandleader at B.B. King's Los Angeles blues club, Arthur Adams cranks out searing blues for the well-heeled tourists who trod the length of Universal Studios' glitzy City Walk. But the great majority of his transient clientele can't begin to imagine the depth and variety of the guitarist's career.

The shaven-headed Tennessee native began playing guitar in the mid-'50s, taking early inspiration from the man whose name adorns the club that later employed him (Howard Carroll, axeman for gospel's Dixie Hummingbirds, also was a principal influence). He studied music at Tennessee State University, playing briefly with the school's resident jazz and blues aggregation.

Touring as a member of singer Gene Allison's band, Adams found himself stranded in Dallas, where he dazzled the locals with his fancy fretwork. Relocating to L.A. in 1964, he began to do session work for jazz great Quincy Jones, and cut singles for the Bihari Brothers' Kent label and Hugh Masekela's Motown-distributed Chisa imprint. His late-'60s R&B sides for the latter were co-produced by Stewart Levine and featured support from most of the Crusaders. Adams' 1970 debut LP for Blue Thumb, *It's Private Tonight*, was co-produced by Bonnie Raitt and Tommy Lipuma. In 1992, Adams wrote two songs for King's *There Is Always One More Time* album. 1999 saw the release of *Back on Track*, which also featured King as a guest guitarist. —*Bill Dahl*

It's Private Tonight / 1972 / Blue Thumb ✦✦✦
● **Home Brew** / 1975 / Fantasy ✦✦✦✦✦
Arthur Adams' second album *Home Brew* may boast a production that's a little too slick, but there's no disguising the fact that the record is an appealing collection of driving blues, distinguished by some unpredictable jazzy flourishes that keep things interesting, even when the songwriting is uneven. —*Thom Owens*

Midnight Serenade / 1977 / Fantasy ✦✦✦
I Love Love Love My Lady / 1979 / A&M ✦✦
Back on Track / Jun. 22, 1999 / Blind Pig ✦✦✦
Tennessee-born, Los Angeles-based singer/guitarist Adams, who has been a sideman for the better part of four decades, is billed to sing like an angel (he is from that City) and

play guitar like a man possessed. It's not hard to buy. His vocalizing has a sweet, soulful quality ala Robert Cray or at times Bobby Bland. And his electric six string takes definite cues from his idol, B.B. King, who employs Adams at his L.A. club and shows up on two of these tracks.

Adams wrote 3/4 of these slick tunes, typically ranging from straight midtempo to downhearted blues about women. "Honda Betty" is as contemporary a theme as you'll find, and there are some T-Bone Walker-like shuffles as on "Jumpin' The Gun" and the cookin' "Good, Good, Good." Some fine horn charts punctuate five cuts, backup vocals on two, and B.B. cameos on "Get You Next to Me," and the signature slow "Long Haul." A personal "Rehabilitation Song" speaks of being in a halfway house and the abuse that preceded it, pleading for forgiveness.

The final selection "Backup Man" could be a double entendre, expressing frustration about being a part-time lover or a star in the shadows. Adams has many redeeming qualities on a restrained blues and contemporary pop level. Perhaps a live recording will reveal more from this gifted musician who perfectly reflects the carefree attitude of his adopted home. *—Michael G. Nastos*

Johnny Adams

b. Jan. 5, 1932, New Orleans, LA, **d.** Sep. 14, 1998

Vocals / Retro-Soul, New Orleans R&B, New Orleans Blues, Soul-Blues, R&B, Soul

Renowned around his Crescent City home base as "the Tan Canary" for his extraordinary set of soulfully soaring pipes, veteran R&B vocalist Johnny Adams tackled an exceptionally wide variety of material for Rounder in his later years; elegantly rendered tribute albums to legendary songwriters Doc Pomus and Percy Mayfield preceded forays into mellow, jazzier pastures. But then, Adams was never particularly into the parade-beat grooves that traditionally define the New Orleans R&B sound, preferring to deliver sophisticated soul ballads draped in strings.

Adams sang gospel professionally before crossing over to the secular world in 1959. Songwriter Dorothy LaBostrie—the woman responsible for cleaning up the bawdy lyrics of Little Richard's "Tutti Frutti" enough for worldwide consumption—convinced her neighbor, Adams, to sing her tasty ballad "I Won't Cry." The track, produced by a teenaged Mac Rebennack, was released on Joe Ruffino's Ric logo, and Adams was on his way. He waxed some outstanding follow-ups for Ric, notably "A Losing Battle" (the Rebennack-penned gem proved Adams' first national R&B hit in 1962) and "Life Is a Struggle."

After a prolonged dry spell, Adams resurfaced in 1968 with an impassioned R&B revival of Jimmy Heap's country standard "Release Me" for Shelby Singleton's SSS imprint that blossomed into a national hit. Even more arresting was Adams' magnificent 1969 country-soul classic "Reconsider Me," his lone leap into the R&B Top Ten; in it, he swoops effortlessly up to a death-defying falsetto range to drive his anguished message home with fervor.

Despite several worthy SSS follow-ups ("I Can't Be All Bad" was another sizable seller), Adams never traversed those lofty commercial heights again (particularly disappointing was a short stay at Atlantic). But he found a new extended recording life at Rounder; his 1984 set, *From the Heart*, proved to the world that this Tan Canary could still chirp like a champ. With producer Scott Billington, he recorded some nine albums for the label prior to his cancer-related death on September 14, 1998. *—Bill Dahl*

Heart & Soul / 1969 / SSS ✦✦✦✦✦

This country-soul, containing all his hits from 1962-1968, was produced by Shelby Singleton. *—Richard Pack*

A Tan Nightingale / 1969 / Charly ✦✦✦

● **Reconsider Me** / 1969 / Collectables ✦✦✦✦✦

This 22-song British compilation is the only place to find a decent cross-section of Adams' SSS sides, including his two biggest hits, the stately "Release Me" and the truly stunning "Reconsider Me." Not all of Adams' late-'60s waxings were ballads; "South Side of Soul Street" is a sizzling upbeat workout. But it's as a balladeer that Adams has always excelled; some of his finest soul senders are to be found right here. *—Bill Dahl*

Stand By Me / 1976 / Chelsea ✦✦✦

This is a relaxed, live-in-the-studio recording of standards. *—Richard Pack*

After All the Good Is Gone / 1978 / Ariola ✦✦

From the Heart / 1984 / Rounder ✦✦✦✦

First-class production by Scott Billington, a delicious Crescent City combo led by longtime cohort Walter "Wolfman" Washington on guitar and Red Tyler on tenor sax, and Adams' perennially luxurious pipes tab this as one of his finest contemporary outings. Nice song selection: the pens of Tony Joe White, Percy Mayfield, Sam Cooke, and Doc Pomus were all tapped. Johnny unfurls his "mouth trombone"—an uncanny vocal 'bone imitation—on Mayfield's "We Don't See Eye to Eye." *—Bill Dahl*

After Dark / Jul. 1985 / Rounder ✦✦✦

When Adams signed with Rounder in the mid-'80s, few outside the R&B/soul and blues world were aware of his skills or eclectic range. *After Dark* was Adams' second Rounder session. It included amazing covers of Doc Pomus' "I Don't Know You" and "Give a Broken Heart a Break," John Hiatt's "Lovers Will" and the Dan Penn/Chips Moman soul classic "Do Right Woman—Do Right Man." This was one of the first records on which Adams' wondrous voice, with its extensive range at the top and bottom, was both well-produced and effectively mastered and recorded. *—Ron Wynn*

Room With a View of the Blues / Apr. 1987-May 1987 / Rounder ✦✦✦✦✦

Although calling Johnny Adams a blues singer is far too confining, he's certainly among the finest to perform in that idiom. He's equally brilliant at slow or uptempo numbers, can effectively convey irony, heartache or triumph, and is a masterful storyteller. These ten blues numbers covered every emotional base, allowing Adams a chance to show his proficiency. With great support from an instrumental corps that included guitarists Walter "Wolfman" Washington and Duke Robillard, keyboardist Dr. John, and saxophonists Red Tyler and Foots Samuel, plus Ernie Gautreau on valve trombone, Adams didn't just cut a blues album, he made unforgettable blues statements. *—Ron Wynn*

Walking on a Tightrope / Mar. 1989-May 1989 / Rounder ✦✦✦✦

Whenever Johnny Adams does a repertory album, it's as much his own showcase as a forum for the spotlighted composer. Even Percy Mayfield's lyrically brilliant works didn't hamper Adams from displaying his special magic; his treatments on the session's ten tunes ranged from excellent to magnificent. Adams was gripping on "My Heart Is Hangin' Heavy," nicely bemused on "The Lover and the Married Woman" and convincing on the title track and "Danger Zone." Although he's done numerous Rounder vehicles, Adams hasn't yet turned in a dud. *—Ron Wynn*

Johnny Adams Sings Doc Pomus: The Real Me / 1991 / Rounder ✦✦✦✦

The late Doc Pomus was one of the top songwriters in the R&B/blues tradition while Johnny Adams was one of his favorite singers; their eventual matchup was quite logical. Pomus wrote a few new songs and worked with Adams on planning this Rounder CD up until his own death. Fortunately the project was not halted and resulted in an enjoyable set. Pomus' intelligent and universal lyrics perfectly fit Adams' style which features flawless enunciation and an ability to sincerely convey a wide range of emotions. With hornlines arranged by Red Tyler, occasional brief solos contributed by pianist Dr. John and guitarist Duke Robillard, and top notch singing by Johnny Adams, Doc Pomus' music is well served on a strong set of blues and ballads. *—Scott Yanow*

● **I Won't Cry** / 1991 / Rounder ✦✦✦✦✦

Even on his earliest singles, Adams already had developed a velvety crooning style seemingly at odds with his raucous hometown. This 14-track collection of Adams' 1959-1963 work for Ric Records contains some stunning stuff, most of it in the big-voiced ballad mode (with an occasional nod to Ray Charles). "I Won't Cry," "A Losing Battle," and "Lonely Drifter" capture Adams' tender, mellifluous delivery beautifully. *—Bill Dahl*

Good Morning Heartache / 1993 / Rounder ✦✦✦

Adams could sing the phone book and make it sound sweet, so his personalized rendition of the title track and several more jazz standards on this collection shouldn't come as too much of a surprise. Nevertheless, it's a long way from "Reconsider Me," and perhaps a bit too jazzy for some R&B fans. *—Bill Dahl*

The Verdict / 1995 / Rounder ✦✦

Fans of Adams' R&B dusties may not find everything on this jazz-based collection to their taste, but Adams' vocal ease within the jazz idiom is undeniable. Noteworthy sidemen include Harry Connick, Jr., and Houston Person. *—Bill Dahl*

One Foot in the Blues / 1996 / Rounder ✦✦✦✦

Johnny Adams is renowned for his smoky but smooth voice, but *One Foot in the Blues* is as much a showcase for Lonnie Smith's Hammond B-3 organ, which sounds like a living, breathing creature. The spare, mostly live-in-the-studio production allows plenty of wide open sonic space for Smith's expressive organ (including his pulsating bass pedal), Ed Peterson's after-hours tenor sax, and Jimmy Ponder's gentle guitar fills. While Adams' most fervent champions thrill to his every note, others may find his singing mannered on the ballads that dominate this session, and his voice is certainly huskier than in the days when he earned the sobriquet "the Tan Canary." As the title suggests, the CD is only partly blues; Adams' other "foot" here, as on his previous '90s recordings, is placed squarely between the cabaret-jazz crooning of Johnny Hartman and the soul-pop styling of Lou Rawls. *—Steve Hoffman*

Man of My Word / Aug. 18, 1998 / Rounder ✦✦✦✦✦

Adams kept cranking out solo albums for the Rounder imprint and this one was the ninth such effort, finding him in tip-top shape vocally and in full command of his consummate powers. In addition to top-notch new material from Dan Penn ("It Ain't the Same Thing"), Carson Whitsett ("Bulldog Break His Chain"), Bobby Charles ("I Don't Want to Know") and Jonnie Barnett ("Going Out of My Mind Sale"), Adams takes on William Bell's "You Don't Miss Your Water," Brook Benton's "Looking Back" and Percy Sledge's "It Tears Me Up." Closing out the album is a duet with Aaron Neville on the gospel chestnut "Never Alone." *—Cub Koda*

The Immortal Soul of Johnny Adams / Apr. 20, 1999 / Aim ✦✦✦✦

A wonderful introduction to the astonishing voice of Johnny Adams, this disc is culled from material (the liner notes aren't explicit about dates) he recorded from the mid-'70s to the early '80s. This is the period when he was recording for Senator Jones before he signed with Rounder Records. These tracks were for the large part recorded in his hometown of New Orleans, with some of the top session men available, such as Walter Washington, Allen Toussaint, George Porter and Leo Nocentelli, to name but a few. This leads to one of the criticisms of this disc: there are no credits as to writers of the songs or who was playing on which cuts. However, you are getting 61-plus minutes of vintage Adams with excellent backing musicians and great sound quality for an exceedingly low price. The sound quality is very good however. We have the music and that is the important thing. If you don't know Adams' voice you have been deprived of a musical treat. He was well-known and loved in his native New Orleans as "The Tan Canary," and he was respected by all who knew him and his music. Aaron Neville, for one, credits him as a leading inspiration toward the evolution of his singing style. Listen to what this man does with a song. The delivery is smooth as silk without the feeling of overpolished studio production. He works a song and makes it his own. Listen to his disco-ish version of that Ben E. King standard, "Spanish Harlem"—it should be a disaster with the excessive production, but his timing, falsetto voice and phrasing don't let the song sink, and it in fact became a hit! There are strings on a couple tracks that give the sound an overproduced effect, and several endings are rather abrupt. Yet when his voice soars and plummets (like on "Share Your Love") he takes your mind away from the distractions and flaws that are inherent in this release from this *Louisiana* mid-price music series. You are receiving more than ample recompense. These songs are good, hard to find, and gathered together on one disc. Just kick back and close your eyes and listen to what he does with the gospel-influenced "Stairway to Heaven." His voice reaches and rises, but never strains as it reaches new plateaus. It alone is worth the price of admission. *—Bob Gottlieb*

There Is Always One More Time / Oct. 31, 2000 / Rounder ♦♦♦
There Is Always One More Time is a compilation of the recordings Johnny Adams made for Rounder Records in the '80s and '90s. The compilation was put together by Scott Billington, who produced all of Adams' Rounder albums. In his liner notes, Billington acknowledges that he had never produced an R&B singer before, so it may not be surprising that he was quick to have Adams sing in styles other than R&B. It was precisely this eclecticism that caused fans and reviewers to reserve their judgment on the Rounder recordings, and Billington has carried it over to the compilation. Drawing from all the albums as well as discs by Ruth Brown and Alvin "Red" Tyler on which Adams guested, he emphasizes novelty material. With Brown, Adams is heard joshing his way through Willie Mabon's "I Don't Know"; "A Lot of Living to Do" (aka "A Lot of Livin' to Do"), on which Adams is accompanied by Harry Connick Jr., at the piano and on which he imitates a horn, is from the Broadway musical *Bye Bye Birdie*; "But Not for Me," also featuring a horn imitation, is the Gershwin standard; and "Never Alone" is an a cappella gospel tune. Of course, there are some bluesy numbers, such as "One Foot in the Blues," and several R&B songs. *There Is Always One More Time* is representative of Adams' later work in that it tries to broaden him stylistically. Clearly, he went along gamely with whatever Billington brought him and added his soulful sound to it. But that didn't mean he did his best work. *—William Ruhlmann*

Released: A Memorial Album / Feb. 1, 2001 / RPM ♦♦♦
The chronological span of this anthology is given in its subtitle, "The Big Voice, The Big Songs 1968-1983." Unfortunately, the year of release is not given for individual songs in the track listing, although the (actually rather lengthy) liner notes do at least admit that the "latter half" of this CD covers 1976-1983. It can be reasonably inferred that the first half thus covers material starting in the late '60s and dating from no later than the mid-'70s, particularly as it definitely does include his 1968-1970 singles "Reconsider Me," "Release Me," and "I Won't Cry." It's the earlier half of the CD—probably mostly or wholly from the late '60s and early '70s, from the sound of things—that commands the most attention, comprising accomplished, though not quite godhead, Nashville soul. These cuts are a bit (but not much) poppier than deep Southern soul, crossing gospel, swamp pop, R&B, blues, and even some country, funk, and New Orleans influences in an easygoing, warm fashion. Adams' likable vocals, which convey passion without breaking out in a sweat, retain their charm on the later material, the arrangements ranging from decently down-home to too sweet-and-slick urban soul flourishes, particularly in the keyboards. *—Richie Unterberger*

Greatest Performances / Nov. 1993 / Ace ♦♦♦
Greatest Performances collects recordings Johnny Adams made for the Hep Me label in the early '80s. Although Adams himself is in fine form, the production is too slick and has dated poorly. For many of the songs, Adams simply sang to pre-recorded rhythm tracks, which gives the material a flat, processed ambience. Furthermore, the material is not suited to his style—though he tries hard, Adams simply can't breathe life into "Feelings." When he does have a song he can sink his teeth into, such as "The Greatest Love," the results are quite good. Unfortunately, he doesn't get enough of those kinds of songs on *Greatest Performances*. *—Thom Owens*

C.C. Adcock

Guitar / Zydeco
Being raised in southwest Louisiana with zydeco bursting out of every juke joint has given C.C. Adcock a different take on standard four-bar blues. The Lafayette-raised Adcock, a guitarist, singer and songwriter, doesn't play straight-ahead blues; his music is heavily laden with unconventional blues-rock melodies and zydeco rhythms. The many thousands of miles he has logged touring with the likes of Bo Diddley and Stanley Dural (better known as Buckwheat Zydeco) show through in his playing, which is fiery, intense and, most of all, danceable.

Charles Clinton Adcock spent his teen years supporting musicians like Dural, Diddley and Bobby Charles, touring with them when he could. His demo tapes with British producer Tarka Cordell caught the ears of some executives at Island Records, and he was signed to a deal. Adcock recorded most of his debut album in his native Lafayette and in studios in Los Angeles, featuring local musicians like Tommy McLain and Warren Storm. On his self-titled major-label debut for Island Records, a 1994 album, Adcock fuses a smorgasbord of styles, including Louisiana blues, zydeco, Cajun and classic R&B into a musical gumbo that is uniquely his own. He puts his own musical stamp on songs by Art Neville ("Fool to Care"), Arthur Alexander ("Sally Sue Brown"), and Gene Terry ("Cindy Lou"). Released when he was just 23, Adcock hasn't recorded anything since, but he continues to tour regionally. Six years after his first album, Adcock resurfaced with his sophomore effort *House Rocker*.

An industrious songwriter and guitarist, it's likely that Adcock and his band will continue to carve a broader fan base for themselves in coming years. He is young yet, and so is his band, so that makes him an artist to watch in the future, and one who will no doubt help to expand the parameters of blues music. *—Richard Skelly*

● **C.C. Adcock** / 1994 / Island ♦♦♦
"It's been a lifetime mean from drinkin'/Cheatin' and shankin' man dead," sings C.C. Adcock on "Couchemal," the first track from his debut eponymous album. This line pretty well sums up this record, with its Louisiana swamp blues grooves and gritty lyrics. Any record that has a song called "Kissin' Kouzans" on it (a lovely ode to small-town intermarriage) is liable to have a distinctive vibe to it, and *C.C. Adcock* does not disappoint. In addition to having a great drawling vocal delivery, Adcock is also a fine guitarist, in a sloppy bayou kind of way. He has included two instrumentals on this record, "Beaux's Bounce" and "Good Lovin'," that both delight and entertain. Roots music enthusiasts will certainly be entertained by the raw guitar tones, primitive drumming, and confidently delivered vocals. The sexuality displayed on this record is somewhere between middle school and five to ten in the county prison, but it's good for drinking beers to, and really is quite captivating when taken on its own terms. Well-executed sleaze, even if the record (although it is not much over a half-hour) feels like it goes on for too long. Dirty in every sense of the word. *—Daniel Gioffre*

House Rocker / Oct. 17, 2000 / Evangeline ♦♦♦

Gaye Adegbalola

b. Mar. 21, 1944, Fredericksburg, VA
Vocals, Guitar / Contemporary Blues, Modern Electric Blues
Best known as a member of the acoustic blues trio Saffire—The Uppity Blues Women, singer/guitarist Gaye Adegbalola was born March 21, 1944, and raised in Virginia. She played flute during high school but initially pursued a career outside of the arts, following a stint as a biochemical researcher by teaching eighth-grade science and winning Virginia Teacher of the Year honors in 1982. With her friend and guitar teacher Ann Rabson, she formed Saffire. The group issued its debut album on Alligator in 1990, with Adegbalola's composition, "The Middle Age Boogie Blues," proceeding to win a W.C. Handy Award for Song of the Year. A series of acclaimed Saffire albums followed, and in 1999 Adegbalola made her solo debut with *Bitter Sweet Blues*. *—Jason Ankeny*

● **Bitter Sweet Blues** / Oct. 12, 1999 / Alligator ♦♦♦
With *Bitter Sweet Blues*, Gaye Adegbalola has produced an album that starts off where her work with Saffire—The Uppity Blues Women left off, and jumps into a new, adventurous space. An expanded cast of musicians and more personal lyrics are some of the benefits to going solo, and Adegbalola makes use of both well. Each song has either humor or power, sometimes both. The only thing that seems incongruous is the mixture of songs with wildly varying moods and topics. While satirical woman-power songs like "Big Ovaries" are empowering and funny, when paired with "Nightmare"—a powerful, personal song about child molestation—the effect is somewhat gross. The feminist politics of both songs mesh rather well, but it is difficult for the listener to shift from laughing at bawdy sexuality to somber empathy in just a few tracks. Overall, though, this is a fine first solo effort that resonates with spirit and emotion. *—Stacia Proefrock*

Ray Agee

b. Apr. 10, 1930, Dixons Mills, AL, **d.** 1990
Vocals, Guitar / West Coast Blues
Known primarily for his tough 1963 remake of the blues standard "Tin Pan Alley" (featuring the moaning lead guitar of Johnny Heartsman) for the tiny Sahara logo, vocalist Ray Agee recorded for myriad labels both large and small during the '50s and '60s without much in the way of national recognition outside his Los Angeles home base. That's a pity—he was a fine, versatile blues singer whose work deserves a wider audience (not to mention CD reissue).

The Alabama native was stricken with polio at age four, leaving Agee with a permanent handicap. After moving to L.A. with his family, he apprenticed with his brothers in a gospel quartet before striking out in the R&B field with a 1952 single for Eddie Mesner's Aladdin Records (backed by saxist Maxwell Davis' band). From there, his discography assumes daunting proportions; he appeared on far too many logos to list (Elko, Spark, Ebb, and Cash among them).

Ray Agee slowly slipped away from the music business in the early '70s. Reportedly, he died around 1990. *—Bill Dahl*

● **Tin Pan Alley** / 1960-1968 / Diving Duck ♦♦♦♦
This obscure Dutch LP is the only collection of Agee's vintage singles you're likely to encounter until someone decides to do some serious cross-licensing. Yes, the doom-laden "Tin Pan Alley" is aboard, along with the distinctive "You Hit Me Where It Hurts" and "The Gamble." *—Bill Dahl*

Garfield Akers

b. 1901, Bates, Mississippi, **d.** 1959
Guitar, Vocals / Delta Blues, Prewar Blues
The throbbing guitar sound of Garfield Akers was a primary influence on subsequent generations of Mississippi bluesmen, with the likes of John Lee Hooker and Robert Wilkins citing him as an influence. Born around 1901 in Bates, MS, Akers remains a shadowy figure; after honing his skills at local dances and house parties, he relocated to the Hernando area, where he worked by day as a sharecropper. After moving on to Memphis, in 1929 he made his first Vocalion label recordings at the Peabody, accompanied by guitarist Joe Callicott; between this first date and a 1930 session for Brunswick, four Akers' performances still exist—his two-part signature "Cottonfield Blues," "Jumpin' and Shoutin' Blues," and "Dough Roller Blues," one of the first variations on Hambone Willie Newbern's seminal "Roll and Tumble." All reflect a distinctively insistent guitar style, and also reveal a high-pitched, almost otherworldly voice. Akers remained an active presence on the south Memphis circuit throughout the '30s, briefly resurfacing in the early '50s before fading back into obscurity; he is believed to have died around 1959. *—Jason Ankeny*

Dave Alexander

b. Mar. 10, 1938, Shreveport, LA
Trumpet, Piano, Bass / West Coast Blues, Piano Blues
Pianist and drummer Dave Alexander is both an effective vocalist and outstanding instrumentalist, who's best known for many festival and club appearances and his Arhoolie albums. Also known as Omar Hakim Khayyam, Alexander's an articulate writer and

advocate for the blues and African-American music. He's written several articles for *Living Blues*. A self-taught pianist, Alexander's played with LC Robinson, Big Mama Thornton, Jimmy McCracklin, and Lafayette Thomas. *—Ron Wynn*

- **The Rattler/Dirt on the Ground** / Aug. 1, 1972+Dec. 5, 1972 / Arhoolie ♦♦♦♦

The compact disc *The Rattler / Dirt on the Ground* contains two of Dave Alexander's early '70s albums, offering a good portrait of Alexander's eclectic, entertaining blues. *—Thom Owens*

Alger "Texas" Alexander

b. Sep. 12, 1900, Jowett, TX, **d.** Apr. 16, 1954, Richard, TX

Vocals / Prewar Country Blues, Country Blues, Acoustic Texas Blues, Texas Blues, Acoustic Blues

A primal, stirring blues voice, Alexander was well known in the Brazos River bottomlands when he started recording in 1927. From bluesmen like Lightnin' Hopkins and Lowell Fulson comes a verbal image of this big-voiced master of blues song craft standing on a wagon bed at a country fair or picnic. His vibrant tenor, one step away from a field holler, rang out over the revelry as he improvised verse after verse.

His early records for OKeh are notable not only for the personal originality of his songs, but for the musical motifs against which they are set. Unable to play himself, Alexander used a variety of accompanists. On disc these range from the brilliant guitar work of Little Hat Jones, Lonnie Johnson and Eddie Lang to the string-band blues of the Mississippi Sheiks and the full on jazz of King Oliver's New Orleans band.

Alexander's performing and recording career continued into the '30s with sessions for Vocalion. In 1940, he was sent to the state pen at Paris, TX, for killing his wife. After his release in 1945 he spent time in Houston, joining his cousin Lightnin' Hopkins for live shows and recording for the Freedom label with pianist Buster Pickens. By 1954 he was back in the bottomlands where he died a debilitated victim of the ravages of syphillis. His recordings—titles like "Corn Bread Blues" or "Frisco Train"—are an express ticket back to days before records and radio, when the blues were young and lived way up country. *—Steve James*

- **Texas Alexander, Vol. 1 (1927)** / Dec. 1, 1995 / Document ♦♦♦♦

Texas Alexander, Vol. 1 (1927) is the first installment of Document's multi-volume series of his complete recorded works. The first disc contains many of his classics, including a number of recordings with Lonnie Johnson that rank among his very best work. *—Thom Owens*

Texas Alexander, Vol. 2: 1928–1930 / Sep. 8, 2000 / Document ♦♦♦

Texas Alexander, Vol. 3: 1930–1950 / Sep. 8, 2000 / Document ♦♦♦♦

Dave Allen

Bass / Texas Blues

The odd man out on the otherwise freaky and psychedelic International Artists label, Dave Allen was a straightforward Texas blues guitarist rather in the mold of Houston's own Johnny Winters. Based in the small hill country town of San Marcos, TX, Allen first made a local name for himself in the nearby college town of Austin, where his unpretentious blues-rock style led International Artists head Lelan Rogers to ask him to record an album. Although 1969's *Color Blind* is a fairly solid example of Texas blues-rock, it's primarily of interest to collectors because of its status as one of the original 12 albums released on the highly regarded International Artists label. Allen dropped from sight shortly after the album's release. *—Stewart Mason*

- **Color Blind** / 1969 / International Artist ♦♦♦

Everything about Dave Allen's sole album is slightly off, from the somewhat defensive title (Allen is a blues guitarist who happens to be white) to the naff cover photo and lame graphics, all the way down to the fact that *Color Blind* is a completely straightforward slice of Texas blues-rock that happens to be on International Artists, the label that was otherwise home to the freaky likes of the 13th Floor Elevators, the Red Krayola, and Endle St. Cloud. *Color Blind* may be many things—and foremost, it's a surprisingly enjoyable slab of unpretentious Texas blues-rock, the sort of thing one might hear in a roadhouse in San Angelo on any given weekend—but freaky it ain't. This has undoubtedly angered many psychedelic completists who finally tracked down this album in expectation of it sounding like *God Bless the Red Krayola & All Who Sail With It* and who summarily dismissed it as a result. Listened to with open ears, however, *Color Blind* is really quite good, gathering up the best parts of Texas-style blues-rock while staying clear of pitfalls like excessively flashy solos, endless and plodding jams, or misogynistic lyrics. Tunes like "Poor Soul" and "Baby Please Don't Try to Tell Me What to Do" are solid, rocking blues well worth seeking out by any fans of early Johnny Winter or the like. *—Stewart Mason*

Lee Allen

b. Jul. 2, 1926, Sewanee, TN, **d.** Oct. 18, 1994, Los Angeles, CA

Saxophone / Instrumental Rock, R&B, New Orleans R&B

The blasting tenor saxophone of Lee Allen was every bit as integral a factor in the sizzling sound of the '50s New Orleans R&B as were the well-documented contributions of Fats Domino, Lloyd Price, and Little Richard. As a key member of the studio band at Cosimo's, Allen played his searing solos that sparked hundreds of Crescent City classics. Allen's wallpaper-peeling sax solos are instantly identifiable—check out Richard's "Slippin' and Slidin'" and "Tutti Frutti" for irrefutably exciting evidence.

But despite his sax mastery, Allen failed to sustain a brief solo career. Signing with Al Silver's New York-based Ember label, he managed one decent-sized hit in 1958, the rocking instrumental "Walkin' With Mr. Lee," while the second-line scorcher "Boppin' at the Hop" inexplicably never received any national airplay.

When the New Orleans sound shifted to a funkier beat, Allen's muscular sound fell out of favor on the local recording scene. Nevertheless, Allen remained active until his death in 1994, touring extensively with Domino, as well as working with a variety of young rockers (including The Blasters) who revered his blistering sound. *—Bill Dahl*

- **Walkin' With Mr. Lee** / 1958 / Collectables ♦♦♦♦♦

New Orleans' favorite tenor sax player had a modest hit with the title track, a bouncy instrumental tailor-made for his honkin' style. The resulting album issued on the Ember label and a stray 45 are collected up here, a loose batch of blues, rockers, smoky jazz ballads, and jumpers. All of these are assigned quaint malt-shop titles like "Teen Dream," "Hot Rod Special," "Boppin' at the Hop," and "Bee Hive." But corny titles aside, here's some classic New Orleans blowing in a variety of settings, all of which work, making for a solid sax album that's grade-A listening all the way. *—Cub Koda*

Bernard Allison

b. Nov. 26, 1965

Guitar, Vocals, Producer / Modern Electric Blues

Bernard Allison is the guitar-playing, singing and songwriting son of the late, legendary blues guitarist Luther Allison. True to form for this chip off the old block, the young Allison injects every bit as much energy into his live shows as his late father did. Bernard counts among his influences icons like Albert King, Muddy Waters and Freddie King, and later, Stevie Ray Vaughan and Johnny Winter.

Allison began accompanying his famous father to blues festivals in the early '70s. There, he was introduced to a who's-who of Chicago blues stars: Muddy Waters, Hound Dog Taylor and Albert King, among others. When he was seven or eight, he began having aspirations of becoming a guitar slinger like his father. Allison's father was more than just a casual record collector, and so Bernard benefited from his father and brothers' collections of classic blues and gospel.

After graduating from high school, Allison began playing with Koko Taylor in her touring band. He stayed with Taylor's band until 1985, when he left to hustle up his own gigs as Bernard Allison and Back Talk. Allison spent a lot of time in Canada with his first band, and later rejoined Taylor and her Blues Machine for another two years in the late '80s. After joining his father in Europe for a live recording, Bernard was asked to join Luther's touring band and become his European bandleader. Allison's father helped his son along with the finer points of showmanship for several years until he was good enough to lead his own trio or quartet. At Christmas, 1989, while both were living together in Paris, the elder Allison arranged to give his son the most precious gift for budding musicians: studio time to record his first album. Allison's debut, *Next Generation*, was recorded for Mondo Records using musicians from his dad's band. His other foreign-label releases include *Hang On!*, *No Mercy*, and *Funkifino*.

In December 1996, Allison was contacted by Cannonball Records founder Ron Levy. Allison was home in Chicago visiting family at Christmas, and hadn't brought any of his guitars or other equipment with him. Levy wanted something based in traditional electric blues, with a few bones for newer fans of the idiom who have jumped on the blues bandwagon since 1990. Allison released his stunning U.S. debut, *Keepin' the Blues Alive* in early 1997, receiving a great deal of critical acclaim. On his successful tour of clubs around the U.S. in the latter half of 1997, Allison was joined by drummer Ray "Killer" Allison (no relation) and Buddy Guy bassist Greg Rzab, among others. *Times Are Changing* followed a year later. In mid-2000, *Across the Water* was released. Based in Paris full-time, he has the comfort and security that the multitude of blues clubs and festivals around Europe can provide. *—Richard Skelly*

Hang On! / 1994 / Ruf ♦♦

One of the earliest Bernard Allison albums, recorded in 1992 and reissued in late 2001 (unfortunately complete with its original tacky cover art), is a middling effort from a talented bluesman who hadn't found his niche. Recorded live in the studio with his dad Luther's band in Paris, where they were living at the time, Bernard compensates for his lack of direction by playing very loud and very fast. While the band of pros keeps the music simmering, Allison's gruff voice and aggressive approach make the songs often seem like bluesy Southern rock instead of the electrified Chicago blues that his dad epitomized. Certainly the younger Allison was grieving the then-recent death of Stevie Ray Vaughan, as tunes like "Missing Stevie," the title track (which edges dangerously close to Deep Purple territory), and the closing ten-minute "Voodoo Chile Medley" (which includes excerpts from Lonnie Mack's "Wham" and Vaughan's "Testify") attest. Even his rugged but not totally successful version of "Rockin' Robin" sounds like it was run through the SRV blender, all tough shards of solos and husky vocals twisting the twee radio hit into a boogie-fied romp. There's no doubt the man can play his guitar, as evidenced on the slow blues of "You're Hurting Me," and there are moments of startling intensity here. But the whole doesn't cohere as anything more than a talented guitarist who loves his blues-rawk but hasn't found his own voice yet. Oddly, this quickie reissue with almost no liner notes misspells Don Nix's name (the writer of "Going Down") and more shockingly leaves in a typo that omits a "t" in dad Luther's first name, showing that there was shamefully little time or effort put into this reissue. Still, fans of either father or son of the Allison surname will want to own this, if only as an indication of the raw talent that Bernard would later harness with more skill, creativity, and aplomb. *—Hal Horowitz*

No Mercy / Feb. 21, 1996 / Inakustik ♦♦♦

- **Keepin' the Blues Alive** / Jul. 1, 1997 / Cannonball ♦♦♦♦

Using a group of hand-picked Chicago musicians he was friendly with, and borrowed equipment, Bernard Allison recorded his stunning U.S. debut, *Keepin' the Blues Alive*. The album was released early in 1997, perfectly blending traditional post-WWII Chicago blues with a few blues-rock riffs from the '70s and '80s thrown in. Songs like "Young Boy's Blues," "When I'm Lonely" and "Tell Me Why" demonstrate a refreshing approach to blues songwriting reminiscent of Louisiana bluesman Larry Garner. *—Richard Skelly*

Next Generation / Jun. 9, 1998 / Celluloid ♦♦♦

Bernard Allison's inaugural effort bristled with the urgency and blues-rock guitar chops that distinguished his late father, Luther Allison. The pair played together for much of the

'80s before Bernard recorded this album with his father's musicians—including keyboardist Michel Carras, who pulls down some good barrelhouse piano parts. The mood is feisty and assertive, especially on "B.A.'s Knockin' at Your Door" and "Low Down and Dirty," which poses the gleeful question, "And you think I'd change my style?" Of course not; fans knew exactly what they were getting, such as the Hendrix-flecked string-bending that drives "Help." (Bernard even dabbles on drums and keyboards.) Other highlights include the title track's party blues, complete with sassy horns; "Baby Child," a hilarious recounting of how Bernard began his career; and "Travlin'," a slower, yet frank look at the road's ups and downs. While hardly the deftest lyricist, Bernard's breezy self-assurance on guitar and can-do musical ethic should overcome most objections. —*Ralph Heibutzki*

Times Are Changing / Oct. 6, 1998 / Ruf/Platinum ✦✦✦✦

Across the Water / Aug. 8, 2000 / Tone-Cool ✦✦✦

Rock, funk, and straight-ahead blues are all covered with ease on *Across the Water*, guitarist Bernard Allison's first release on the Tone-Cool label. Allison is the son of blues guitarist Luther Allison and while the blues was a constant in his early listening, the rock and funk influences of his generation also played a natural part in his musical upbringing. Allison employs producer Jim Gaines who has worked with Santana, Stevie Ray Vaughan, and Albert Collins, helping to achieve the right blend of musical influences without getting away from the blues focus. —*Al Campbell*

Luther Allison

b. Aug. 17, 1939, Widener, AR, **d.** Aug. 12, 1997, Madison, WI

Vocals, Guitar / Modern Electric Chicago Blues, Modern Electric Blues, Chicago Blues
An American-born guitarist, singer and songwriter who had lived in France since 1980, Luther Allison was the man to book at blues festivals in the mid-'90s. Allison's comeback into the mainstream was ushered in by a recording contract with an American record company, Chicago-based Alligator Records. After he signed with Alligator in 1994, Allison's popularity grew exponentially and he worked steadily until his death in 1997. Born August 17, 1939, in Widener, AR, Allison was the fourteenth of 15 children, the son of cotton farmers. His parents moved to Chicago when he was in his early teens, but he had a solid awareness of blues before he left Arkansas, as he played organ in the church and learned to sing gospel in Widener as well. Allison recalled that his earliest awareness of blues came via the family radio in Arkansas, which his dad would play at night. Allison recalls listening to both the Grand Ole Opry and B.B. King on the King Biscuit Show on Memphis' WDIA. Although he was a talented baseball player and had begun to learn the shoemaking trade in Chicago after high school, it wasn't long before Allison began to focus more of his attention on playing blues guitar. Allison had been hanging out in blues clubs all through high school, and with his brother's encouragement, he honed his string bending skills and powerful, soul-filled vocal technique.

It was while living with his family on Chicago's West Side that he had his first awareness of wanting to become a full-time bluesman, and he played bass behind guitarist Jimmy Dawkins, who Allison grew up with. Also in Allison's neighborhood were established blues greats like Freddie King, Magic Sam and Otis Rush. He distinctly remembers everyone talking about Buddy Guy when he came to town from his native Louisiana. After the Allison household moved to the South Side, they lived a few blocks away from Muddy Waters, and Allison and Waters' son Charles became friends. When he was 18 years old, his brother showed him basic chords and notes on the guitar, and the super bright Allison made rapid progress after that. Allison went on to "blues college" by sitting in with some of the most legendary names in blues in Chicago's local venues: Muddy Waters, Elmore James and Howlin' Wolf among them.

His first chance to record came with Bob Koester's then-tiny Delmark Record label, and his first album, *Love Me Mama*, was released in 1969. But like anyone else with a record out on a small label, it was up to him to go out and promote it, and he did, putting in stellar, show-stopping performances at the Ann Arbor Blues festivals in 1969, 1970 and 1971. After that, people began to pay attention to Luther Allison, and in 1972 he signed with Motown Records. Meanwhile, a growing group of rock & roll fans began showing up at Allison's shows, because his style seemed so reminiscent of Jimi Hendrix and his live shows clocked in at just under four hours!

Although his Motown albums got him to places he'd never been before, like Japan and new venues in Europe, the recordings didn't sell well. He does have the distinction of being one of a few blues musicians to record for Motown. Allison stayed busy in Europe through the rest of the '70s and '80s, and recorded *Love Me Papa* for the French Black and Blue label in 1977. He followed with a number of live recordings from Paris, and, in 1984, he settled outside of Paris, since France and Germany were such major markets for him. At home in the U.S., Allison continued to perform sporadically, when knowledgeable blues festival organizers or blues societies would book him.

As accomplished a guitarist as he was, Allison wasn't a straight-ahead Chicago blues musician. He learned the blues long before he got to Chicago. What he did so successfully is take his base of Chicago blues and add touches of rock, soul, reggae, funk and jazz. Allison's first two albums for Alligator, *Soul Fixin' Man* and *Blue Streak*, are arguably two of his strongest. His talents as a songwriter are fully developed, and he's well recorded and well produced, often with horns backing his band. Another one to look for is a 1992 reissue on Evidence, *Love Me Papa*. In 1996, Motown reissued some of the three albums worth of material he recorded for that label (between 1972 and 1976), on compact disc.

Well into his mid-fifties, Allison continued to delight club and festival audiences around the world with his lengthy, sweat-drenched, high energy shows, complete with dazzling guitar playing and inspired, soulful vocals. He continued to tour and record until July of 1997, when he was diagnosed with inoperable lung cancer. Just over a month later, he died in a hospital in Madison, Wisconsin—a tragic end to one of the great blues comeback stories. 1998's posthumous *Live in Paradise* captured one of his final shows, recorded on La Reunion Island in April 1997. —*Richard Skelly*

Love Me Mama / Jun. 24, 1969-Jun. 25, 1969 / Delmark ✦✦✦

Although it has its moments—particularly on the title track—Luther Allison's debut album, *Love Me Mama*, is on the whole uneven, featuring more mediocre tracks than killer cuts. Nevertheless, it offers intriguing glimpses of the style he would later develop. —*Thom Owens*

Bad News Is Coming / 1973 / Motown ✦✦✦✦✦

The very thing that made Luther Allison noteworthy became an albatross around his neck. Years after his initial run of records in the '70s, he was known for the same thing he was at the time—he was the only blues artist on Gordy, or any Motown affiliated label. This was true and novel, but many focused on the novelty, not the truth, ignoring Allison's status as a terrific torchbearer of raw Chicago blues. Some of material illustrates some contemporary influence—dig that funky groove and organ on "Raggedy and Dirty," or the rock-oriented slow burn of Mel London's "Cut You A-Loose"—but as his original title track illustrates, he can also deliver a torturous, impassioned slow grind. Still, this isn't an album about originality, it's a record how tradition can remain alive in a contemporary setting. Apart from the slightly cleaner production and the extended running time, this could have been released 15 years earlier, since its heart is in classic Chicago blues, particularly Chess. He draws on Willie Dixon via Howlin' Wolf for the first two tracks, dipping into Elmore James and B.B. King's catalogs later on in the record. This accounts for over half of the album's running time, and every one of these tunes are familiar—and, for good measure, he dips into "Spoonful" on "Cut You A-Loose"—but what matters is Allison's performance, which is never less than committed and usually gripping. And that's what makes this record work—it's firmly on familiar territory, but Allison gives it his own personality through the sheer strength of his love for this music. Perhaps that doesn't make for a revolutionary debut—it's not a visionary record the way, say, Magic Sam's *West Side Soul* is—but that would come later. With *Bad News Is Coming*, Luther Allison just delivered one of the best straight-ahead Chicago blues records of the early '70s. Too bad everybody thought of it as a little folly on Motown. [Allison and producer Joe Peraino cut a lot of material during these sessions, and four of the best of these outtakes—the original "It's Been a Long Time," plus versions of "The Stumble," "Sweet Home Chicago," and "Take My Love (I Want to Give It All to You)"—appeared on Universal/Motown's excellent 2001 reissue. There's really no difference in quality with these cuts; they simply couldn't fit on the original, but thanks to the expanded time of a CD, there's four other first-class cuts to savor on this fine modern blues platter.] —*Stephen Thomas Erlewine*

● **Luther's Blues** / 1974 / Motown ✦✦✦✦✦

Luther's Blues is where Luther Allison began to come into his own, developing a fluid, gutsy style full of soulful string bending. There are still a few weak spots, but the album remains an effective slice of contemporary Chicago blues. —*Thom Owens*

Night Life / Oct. 1975 / Gordy ✦

On *Night Life*, Luther Allison tried to make soul crossover album but the slick production fails to provide a suitable bed for his bluesy guitars and vocals. Occasionally, he spits out a good solo, but only the most devoted listeners will be able to dig them out, since they're buried beneath a glossy varnish. —*Thom Owens*

Love Me Papa / Dec. 13, 1977 / Evidence ✦✦✦✦

Luther Allison is the blues' proverbial little boy with the curl; when he's good, he's great. When he's bad, he's awful. Allison was on throughout most of the nine tracks (three bonus cuts) on this 1977 date recently reissued by Evidence on CD, playing with the ferocity, direction, and inventiveness that is often missing from his more uneven efforts. His covers of Little Walter Jacobs' "Last Night" and "Blues With a Feeling" are not reverential or respectful but are launching pads for high-octane, barreling riffs, snappy phrases, and exciting solos. His vocals are not always that keen, but Allison at least stretches them out and adds verbal embellishments, yells, and shouts of encouragement. —*Ron Wynn*

Live in Paris / 1979 / Platinum ✦✦✦

Live in Paris was recorded in the late '70s, shortly before Luther Allison decided to leave America for France because the U.S. blues scene was faltering. And, as *Live in Paris* attests, Allison was at his best when he played straight blues with a bit of a wild, electric edge. The album isn't perfect by any means, but there's energy and fire to his playing that holds your attention throughout the record. —*Stephen Thomas Erlewine*

Power Wire Blues / Apr. 18, 1979-Apr. 19, 1979 / Charly ✦

Power Wire Blues is a collection of outtakes from his uneven *Rumble* album. Since the best takes of these sessions were pretty weak, these lesser tracks have even less to distinguish—much less recommend—them. It's one to be avoided. —*Thom Owens*

Gonna Be a Live One in Here Tonight / Apr. 18, 1979-Apr. 19, 1979 / Rumble ✦✦

Gonna Be a Live One in Here Tonight is a solid, no-frills documentation of a late-'70s club show from Luther Allison. Though it's not an exceptional performance, it certainly isn't a disappointing one and dedicated fans will find it worth their time. —*Thom Owens*

Southside Safari / 1983 / M.I.L. Multimedia ✦✦

Life Is a Bitch / 1984 / Encore! ✦✦✦

Here I Come / 1985 / Encore! ✦✦✦

Serious / 1987 / Blind Pig ✦✦✦✦✦

Serious marks the beginning of Luther Allison's late-'80s/early-'90s hot streak. The more streamlined, rock-oriented approach actually is a benefit, since it gives Allison a shot of energy that makes his guitar simply burn all the way through the record. —*Thom Owens*

Hand Me Down My Moonshine / 1994 / Ruf ✦✦✦

Hand Me Down My Moonshine is a refreshing all-acoustic session from Allison that demonstrates a previously hidden side of his talent. Though there are some hard-rocking stomps, his playing reveals new grace and subtlety, making it a necessary purchase for all diehard fans. —*Thom Owens*

Soul Fixin' Man / 1994 / Alligator ✦✦✦✦✦

Soul Fixin' Man was blues guitarist/vocalist Luther Allison's first American recording in nearly 20 years. However, his domestic inactivity was not because Allison had stopped playing music. Far from it, since he was based in Paris and worked constantly on the European continent. A powerful player whose intensity on this set sometimes borders on rock (although remaining quite grounded in blues), Luther Allison (who contributed eight of the dozen songs) displays the large amount of musical growth he had experienced since the mid-'70s. Joined by his quintet, the Memphis Horns, and (on "Freedom") a choir, Allison is heard throughout in top form. *—Scott Yanow*

Blue Streak / Oct. 1995 / Alligator ✦✦✦✦
A follow-up to his previous *Soul Fixin' Man* (which uses the same personnel and may be from the same sessions), bluesman guitarist/singer Luther Allison is in top form throughout this well-rounded set. Allison wrote (or co-wrote with guitarist James Solberg) all but one of the dozen songs, and these range from heated blues struts to blues ballads. Recommended to fans of lowdown, intense Chicago blues. *—Scott Yanow*

Sweet Home Chicago / Nov. 2, 1995 / Charly ✦✦✦
This so-so board tape from the mid-'70s catches Luther and an unnamed band playing for a small club crowd. It's a typically exuberant Luther performance, as he runs through a set of staples like "Dust My Broom," "You Don't Love Me," and "Sweet Home Chicago." But what ultimately sinks this set is the sound, which is bootleg quality at best. Pass it by. *—Cub Koda*

The Motown Years 1972–1976 / 1996 / Motown ✦✦✦
Allison's reign as Motown's only bluesman saw the guitarist offer competently executed, but basically unmemorable, blues with some soul and rock influences. This 17-track compilation includes selections from all three of the LPs he issued on the label (drawing most heavily from his second, *Luther's Blues*), and adds a previously unreleased live cut from the 1972 Ann Arbor Blues Festival. Pop influences can be heard in the occasional wah-wah guitar and brass-conscious production; Berry Gordy even co-wrote one of the tracks ("Someday Pretty Baby"), and Randy Brecker arranged the horns on Allison's final Motown full-length. *—Richie Unterberger*

Where Have You Been? Live in Montreux 1976–1994 / 1997 / A&M ✦✦✦✦
This CD features the exciting blues guitarist/singer Luther Allison on selections taken from four appearances at the Montreux Jazz Festival. Although the title says 1974-1994, the earliest numbers are actually from 1976, and these are the most memorable cuts on the CD. Even when sticking to cover tunes throughout the powerhouse performance (such as "Sweet Home Chicago" and "Little Red Rooster"), Allison plays with such enthusiasm and ferocity that he sounds as if he wrote the songs himself. Among the other highlights, Allison is heard on his 1983 set closer "Sky Is Crying," shouting out a Memphis soul-type ballad ("Memories") in 1984 and sounding remarkably close to B.B. King at times during 1994's "Bad Love" (which has background riffs from the Memphis Horns). This is a strong (and easily recommended) all-around overview that can serve as a perfect introduction to the talented Luther Allison. *—Scott Yanow*

Reckless / Mar. 25, 1997 / Alligator ✦✦✦
Luther's third album for Alligator finds the fifty-something bluesman truly at the peak of his powers. His superb guitar playing has never been more focused, and his singing shows a fervent shouter in full command. But Allison's songwriting has made giant strides as well, and ten of the 14 tracks aboard feature him as a co-writer as well. The production by Jim Gaines delivers a modern-sounding album that stays firmly in the blues tradition while giving full vent to Luther's penchant for blending soul, rock and funk grooves into his musical stew. There are really no duff tracks aboard, but special attention should be paid to the sloppy but right slide guitar-meets-rock & roll groove of "Low Down and Dirty," and Allison's incredibly hot minor key soloing (at full rock volume) on "Drowning at the Bottom," an acoustic duet with his son Bernard on "Playin' a Losing Game," and the grinding social commentary of "Pain in the Streets." If Allison had made albums like this for Motown some 20 years previously, it would be very interesting to speculate on how the blues history books just might have been rewritten. *—Cub Koda*

Live in Chicago / Aug. 24, 1999 / Alligator ✦✦✦✦
Pulled from performances at the Chicago Blues Festival, Buddy Guy's Legends club with a couple of strays recorded in Lincoln, NE, that were too good not to include, this two-disc set captures Allison at the absolute peak of his powers. Disc one is the Chicago Blues Festival in its entirety with a bonus track of Luther jamming on the finale with Otis Rush and Eddie C. Campbell on a medley of two B.B. King tunes. Disc two is equally potent, a combination of performances pulled from Buddy Guy's Legends club and the Zoo Bar in Lincoln, NE. Luther simply played his heart and spirit out right to the end and these recordings spotlight it in a very fine manner. One of the label's best. *—Cub Koda*

Mose Allison

b. Nov. 11, 1927, Tippo, MS
Lyricist, Vocals, Piano / Vocal Jazz, Jazz Blues, Hard Bop
Not unlike his namesake, Luther Allison, pianist Mose Allison has suffered from "categorization problem," given his equally brilliant career. Although his boogie woogie and bebop-laden piano style is innovative and fresh sounding when it comes to blues and jazz, it is as a songwriter that Allison really shines. Allison's songs have been recorded by the Who ("Young Man Blues"), Leon Russell ("I'm Smashed"), and Bonnie Raitt ("Everybody's Cryin' Mercy"). Other admirers include Tom Waits, John Mayall, Georgie Fame, the Rolling Stones and Van Morrison. But because he's always played both blues and jazz, and not one to the exclusion of the other, his career has suffered. As he himself admits, he has a "category" problem that lingers to this day. "There's a lot of places I don't work because they're confused about what I do," he explained in a 1990 interview in *Goldmine* magazine. Despite the lingering confusion, Allison remains one of the finest songwriters in 20th-century blues.

Born in Tippo, MS, on November 11, 1927, Allison's first exposure to blues on record was through Louis Jordan recordings, including "Outskirts of Town" and "Pinetop Blues." Allison credits Jordan as being a major influence on him, and also credits Nat "King" Cole, Louis Armstrong and Fats Waller. He started out on trumpet but later switched to piano. In his youth, he had easy access, via the radio, to the music of Pete Johnson, Albert Ammons and Meade Lux Lewis. Allison also credits the songwriter Percy Mayfield, "The Poet Laureate of the Blues," as being a major inspiration on his songwriting. After a stint in college and the Army, Allison's first professional gig was in Lake Charles, LA, in 1950. He returned to college to finish up at Louisiana State University in Baton Rouge, where he studied English and Philosophy, a far cry from his initial path as a chemical engineering major.

Allison began his recording career with the Prestige label in 1956, shortly after he moved to New York City. He recorded an album with Al Cohn and Bobby Brookmeyer, and then in 1957 got his own record contract. A big break was the opportunity to play with Cohn and Zoot Sims shortly after his arrival in New York, but he later became more well-known after playing with saxophonist Stan Getz. After leaving Prestige Records, where he recorded now classic albums like *Back Country Suite* (1957), *Young Man Mose* (1958), and *Seventh Son* (1958-1959), he moved to Columbia for two years before meeting up with Nesuhi Ertegun of Atlantic Records. He recalled that he signed his contract with Atlantic after about ten minutes in Nesuhi's office. Allison spent a big part of his recording career at Atlantic Records, where he became most friendly with Ertegun. After the company saw substantial growth and Allison was no longer working directly with him, he became discouraged and left. Allison has also recorded for Columbia (before he began his long relationship with Atlantic), and the Epic and Prestige labels.

Allison's discography is a lengthy one, and there are gems to be found on all of his albums, many of which can be found in vinyl shops. His output since 1957 has averaged at least one album a year until 1976, when he finished up at Atlantic with the classic *Your Mind Is On Vacation*. There was a gap of six years before he recorded again, this time for Elektra's Musician subsidiary in 1982, when he recorded *Middle Class White Boy*. Since 1987, he's been with Bluenote/Capitol. His debut for that label was *Ever Since the World Ended*. Allison has recorded some of the most creative material of his career with the Bluenote subsidiary of Capitol Records, including *My Backyard* (1990) and *The Earth Wants You* (1994), both produced by Ben Sidran. Also in 1994, Rhino Records released a boxed set, *Allison Wonderland*. *—Richard Skelly*

Back Country Suite / Mar. 7, 1957 / Prestige/OJC ✦✦✦✦
Mose Allison's very first recording finds the 29-year-old pianist taking just two vocals (on his "Young Man Blues" and "One Room Country Shack") but those are actually the most memorable selections. The centerpiece of this trio outing with bassist Taylor LaFargue and drummer Frank Isola (which has been reissued on CD) is Allison's ten-part "Back Country Suite," a series of short concise folk melodies that puts the focus on his somewhat unique piano style which, although boppish, also looked back toward the country blues tradition. Very interesting music. *—Scott Yanow*

● **Greatest Hits** / Mar. 7, 1957-Feb. 13, 1959 / Prestige/OJC ✦✦✦✦✦
Basic, no-frills anthology of 13 of his better late-'50s Prestige sides, all of which feature his vocals. It has most of his most famous songs, particularly to listeners from a rock background, including his versions of "The Seventh Son," "Eyesight to the Blind" (covered by the Who on *Tommy*, though Sonny Boy Williamson II did it before Allison), "Parchman Farm" (done by John Mayall), and "Young Man's Blues" (also covered by the Who). Were it not for the significant omission of "I'm Not Talking" (retooled by the Yardbirds), this would qualify as the basic collection for most listeners, although more thorough retrospectives are available (particularly Rhino's *Anthology*). *Greatest Hits* does include liner notes by Pete Townshend, originally penned for a 1972 collection. *—Richie Unterberger*

Local Color / Nov. 8, 1957 / Prestige/OJC ✦✦✦
This CD reissue brings back Mose Allison's second of six Prestige recordings. Allison performs eight instrumentals in a trio with bassist Addison Farmer and drummer Nick Stabulas, displaying his unusual mixture of country blues and bebop and even taking an effective trumpet solo on "Trouble In Mind." However it is his vocals on "Lost Mind" and particularly the classic "Parchman Farm" that are most memorable. *—Scott Yanow*

Creek Bank / 1959 / Prestige ✦✦✦✦
When Mose Allison recorded his six early albums for Prestige, he was best-known as a bop-based pianist who occasionally sang. This single CD (which reissues in full *Young Man Mose* and *Creek Bank*) has 15 instrumentals including a rare appearance by Allison on trumpet ("Stroll") but it is his five typically ironic vocals that are most memorable, particularly Allison's classic "The Seventh Son" and "If You Live." His piano playing, even with the Bud Powell influence, was beginning to become original and he successfully performs both revived swing songs and moody originals. *—Scott Yanow*

Autumn Song / Feb. 13, 1959 / Prestige/OJC ✦✦✦✦
Mose Allison recorded six albums as a leader for Prestige during 1957-59, an era when he was better known as a jazz pianist than as a folk/country blues vocalist and masterful lyricist. On this CD reissue of his final Prestige date, Allison (in a trio with bassist Addison Farmer and drummer Ronnie Free) performs seven instrumentals (including "It's Crazy," "Autumn Song" and "Groovin' High") but it is the three vocals ("Eyesight to the Blind," "That's All Right" and Duke Ellington's "Do Nothin' Till You Hear From Me") that are most memorable. One realizes why Allison was soon emphasizing his vocals; he was a much more distinctive singer than pianist although his piano playing was actually pretty inventive. This is an excellent all-round set. *—Scott Yanow*

Transfiguration of Hiram Brown / 1960 / Columbia/Legacy ✦✦✦✦
Mostly instrumental, this ingratiating release features outstanding playing by this exceptionally talented yet largely unknown songwriter/singer/pianist. The album begins with the eight-part "Hiram Brown" suite, in which a naïve country boy loses his illusions and optimism in the big city. Five standards complete the album in fine style. "Baby Please Don't Go" and "'Deed I Do" offer Mose's unique, smoky singing at its most touching. This

album was released with *I Love the Life I Live* and *V-8 Ford Blues* in a delightful 1994 collection called *High Jinks*. *—Mark Allan*

I Love the Life I Live / 1960 / Columbia/Legacy ✦✦✦✦✦
When this album was recorded in 1960, this laconic Mississippian wasn't the brilliant lyricist he would later become. But he had great taste. The title track, written by Willie Dixon, sure sounds like a Mose song; "Fool's Paradise" is another gem. Mose's four tunes are instrumentals. The production by Teo Macero makes it feel like you're perched on one end of the piano bench. This album was released with *Transfiguration of Hiram Brown* and *V-8 Ford Blues* in a delightful 1994 collection called *High Jinks*. *—Mark Allan*

V-8 Ford Blues / Apr. 1961 / Epic/Legacy ✦✦✦✦
Besides cool playing and his uniquely smoky singing, Mose has great taste in material. "Hey Good Lookin'" fits right in with revisited versions of "I Love the Life I Live," "I Ain't Got Nobody" and "Baby Please Don't Go," complete with what the singer himself calls his distinctive "involuntary groan" during the piano solo. Teo Macero's intimate production makes it feel like you're right there in the studio. This album was released with *Transfiguration of Hiram Brown* and *I Love the Life I Live* in a delightful 1994 collection called *High Jinks*. *—Mark Allan*

Swingin' Machine / 1962 / Collectables ✦✦✦
Jazz fans may find this Mose Allison session unique among scads of releases from this laid-back, witty and original singer and pianist. Almost never found recording outside of the piano trio context, this album perhaps reveals the reason why: on a whole, adding horns to Allison's band just doesn't work that well. The trombonist Jimmy Knepper is of particular interest, in that he most often recorded under the intense leadership of Charles Mingus, a far cry from the loose and relaxed sound of Allison. His fellow hornman here is tenor saxophonist Jimmy Reider; not a very well-known jazzman but certainly competent in a swing style. If the leader had stuck to all vocal numbers this might have been a top drawer album. All the vocal tracks here are fine, with the song "Stop This World" rating among the best things this artist has recorded in a long career. It's the instrumental tracks that drag, however, since like any respectable pianist bandleader, Allison chooses to put the two horns out front for theme-solo-theme arrangements that would only be worth repeated listening if every other jazz performance ever recorded happened to vanish off the face of the earth. Allison's piano playing picked up some steam as the '60s wore on, so it is a shame he didn't revisit this concept at a later date. In all, an enjoyable album but a bit disappointing. *—Eugene Chadbourne*

I Don't Worry About a Thing / Mar. 15, 1962 / Rhino ✦✦✦✦✦
Mose Allison was already 34 and had recorded nine records as a leader before cutting his debut for Atlantic (which has been reissued on CD by Rhino) but this was his breakthrough date. One of jazz's greatest lyricists, at the time, Allison was making the transition from being a pianist who occasionally sang to becoming a vocalist who also played his own unusual brand of piano. In addition to the original versions of "Your Mind Is on Vacation," "I Don't Worry About a Thing (Because I Know Nothing Will Turn out Right)" and "It Didn't Turn out That Way," he sings bluish versions of two standards ("Meet Me at No Special Place" and "The Song Is Ended") and plays five instrumentals with his trio. There are only 33 1/2 minutes of music on this straight reissue of the orignal LP, but the set is one of Mose Allison's most significant recordings. *—Scott Yanow*

The Best of Mose Allison / 1962-1970 / Atlantic ✦✦✦✦✦
The Mose Allison installment in Atlantic's Jazz Anthology series of 1970 is superior to most in that line simply on the grounds of time. Since Mose's songs were usually brief, Atlantic was able to fit 12 of them onto a single LP and thus provide a wider selection of his output, unlike others in that series which included only five or six tracks, making it serve as a pretty good capsule introduction to one of American music's most idiosyncratic individualists. Many of his most famous songs are here—"Your Mind Is on Vacation," "New Parchman," "I'm the Wild Man," "I Don't Worry About a Thing," "Your Molecular Structure," etc., along with covers like "Rollin' Stone" and a rushed live remake of his biggest "hit," Willie Dixon's "Seventh Son." For a more comprehensive—and well-packaged—overview of most of his career, turn to the double-CD box *Allison Wonderland* on Rhino/Atlantic. *—Richard S. Ginell*

The Word from Mose / Mar. 10, 1964 / Collectables ✦✦✦
This iconoclastic performer has sometimes been described as a country blues player, perhaps leading to images of a blind man standing on a corner playing a guitar with a bottleneck slide. In reality, Mose Allison is from a much more cosmopolitan tradition, and the country blues adage comes from attempts to describe the sound he gets playing light, swinging jazz with a distinctly rural, Southern influence. This album, from one of many he recorded for Atlantic, actually contains examples of him taking material from the real country blues heritage and reworking it into his own style, to brilliant effect. His "New Parchman Farm" is a fantastic piece, as he changes what was once a stark, depressing prison blues into something else again. Perhaps this version would be more suited to white-collar criminals such as the Watergate mob, basking in upper-class prisons complete with tennis courts. At any rate, this is a performance that only the most hardened individual would be able to listen to without a smile cracking their face. Like most of Allison's releases, this one suffers from a handful of tracks that although not quite throwaway, surely lack the substance of the best songs here. *—Eugene Chadbourne*

Wild Man on the Loose / Jan. 28, 1965 / 32 Jazz ✦✦✦
The lion's share of recordings by this artist are in a piano trio setting, and this mid-'60s session finds him working with one of the best combinations he ever had. Bassist Earl May is a solid, inventive player who is beautifully recorded here with a sound that can have the soulfulness of a classical guitar at times. On drums, Paul Motian is something of a legend, and here is heard at his most straight-ahead, simple and swinging with some nice touches from the brushes. He is also recorded extremely well, giving the pianist a really beautiful base to take off from, as well as making the overall tracks sound brilliant. The art of recording piano trios in this manner, with such a clear and immediate sound, seems to have been lost unfortunately. Sometimes a weak link on his records, even the Allison instrumentals come across forcefully. Is there a Cecil Taylor influence, or is it just the same Duke Ellington touches heard in Taylor's music? The instrumental track "Power House" is one of the finest numbers of this sort Allison has recorded. Vocal performances are smooth as always, although the set does not contain any totally classic numbers. *—Eugene Chadbourne*

I've Been Doin' Some Thinkin' / Jul. 9, 1968 / 32 Jazz ✦✦✦✦
Three years had gone by between this release and the previous Mose Allison outing on Atlantic, perhaps giving the artist time to concoct some of the really tasty lyrics he came up with. The opening track, "Just Like Livin'," alternates between absurd satire and to-the-point cynicism in a way that is completely unique to Allison, although many other artists have tried to imitate it. How many songwriters can sum up life in less than two minutes, after all? There are many other highlights as well, including the memorable structure of "City Home" and a rococo reworking of "You Are My Sunshine" that might cause a riot at a wedding if played as a request. A peak perhaps not only of this album but the entire Allison career is the ballad "Everybody's Cryin' Mercy," as powerful an indictment of hypocrisy as has ever been recorded. Bassist Red Mitchell is on hand with his fat but easy-to-digest sound, and he seems to prompt Allison to play aggressively. Some of the piano solos sound like they were rendered with various martial arts techniques. *—Eugene Chadbourne*

Your Mind Is on Vacation / 1976 / Koch ✦✦✦✦✦
It seems strange to realize that this was Mose Allison's only recording during the 1973-1981 period. In addition to his trio with bassist Jack Hannah and drummer Jerry Granelli, such guests as altoist David Sanborn, Al Cohn, and Joe Farrell on tenors and trumpeter Al Porcino pop up on a few selections. However, Mose Allison is easily the main star, performing ten of his originals (including a remake of the famous title cut, "What Do You Do After You Ruin Your Life," and "Swingin' Machine") plus renditions of the standards "Foolin' Myself" and "I Can't See for Lookin'." *—Scott Yanow*

Mose in Your Ear / 1977 / Atlantic ✦✦✦✦
This live session from 1972 features Mose Allison at his best. Performing with his working trio (bassist Clyde Flowers and drummer Eddie Charlton), Allison sounds quite inspired on such tunes as "Fool's Paradise," "I Don't Worry About a Thing," "Hey Good Lookin'," "I Ain't Got Nothin' But The Blues" and "The Seventh Son." Most memorable is his minor-toned downbeat ballad version of "You Are My Sunshine" which casts new meaning on the usually optimistic lyrics. This near-classic set is long overdue to be reissued on CD. *—Scott Yanow*

Pure Mose / 1978 / 32 Jazz ✦✦✦
This 1997 CD features pianist/vocalist/composer Mose Allison on a previously unreleased live session from San Francisco's legendary Keystone Korner, playing his usual repertoire in a trio with bassist Tom Rutley and drummer Jerry Granelli. Since Allison only recorded one album during 1973-1981, this decently recorded live set is quite valuable; the year (1978) is an estimate. Most of the material is fairly familiar, but the singer's spirited delivery and interplay with the audience make this a CD well worth getting by his fans. Highlights include "Wildman on the Loose," "Swinging Machine," "I Live the Life I Love," "I Ain't Got Nothin' But the Blues" and "Your Mind Is on Vacation." *—Scott Yanow*

Sage of Tippo / 1981 / 32 Jazz ✦✦✦
Perhaps the best way to organize a box set by a great recording artist is just not to organize too much, to simply collect the work together and put it in a box. This is what has been done here with four fine Mose Allison albums done originally for Atlantic. They are presented in their original form, in the original sequence, and you even get the original liner notes although there are of course enjoyable and typically succinct comments from 32 Jazz honcho and longtime Allison booster Joel Dorn. The drawback in the case of Allison is that each of these albums had a few disposable tracks, which multiplied times four adds up to a big chunk of material the listener may feel no desire to return to ever again. The playing by three different trios and one quintet is generally on a very high level, although the latter group proves that less is more in the case of backup for Allison. The listener might be better advised to seek out smaller packages of this totally original and extremely enjoyable recording artist. *—Eugene Chadbourne*

Middle Class White Boy / Feb. 2, 1982 / Discovery ✦✦✦✦
This Elektra issue finds the unique Mose Allison well-featured in a sextet also including Joe Farrell on tenor and flute and guitarist Phil Upchurch. Allison's unusual mixture of bop, country blues and his own eccentric personality have long given him a distinctive sound on piano but it is his ironic vocals and superb lyric-writing abilities that make him a major figure. In addition to such originals as "How Does It Feel? (To Be Good Looking)," "I Don't Want Much" and "I'm Nobody Today," Allison brings new life to such standards as "When My Dreamboat Comes Home," "I'm Just a Lucky So-and-So" and "The Tennessee Waltz." *—Scott Yanow*

Lesson in Living / Jul. 21, 1982 / Elektra ✦✦✦
On the second of two albums cut in 1982 (which were his only recordings from the 1977-1986 period), vocalist/pianist Mose Allison is saddled with an unnecessary and not always complementary all-star group consisting of guitarist Eric Gale, bassist Jack Bruce, drummer Billy Cobham, and (on "You Are My Sunshine") altoist Lou Donaldson. However for this live set (recorded at the Montreux Jazz Festival), Mose is in fine form performing mostly remakes of his songs. Highlights include "Your Mind Is On Vacation," "Lost Mind," "Seventh Son," "I Don't Worry About a Thing" and the definitive rendition of his unusual minor-toned version of "You Are My Sunshine." *—Scott Yanow*

Jazz Profile / May 11, 1987-Sep. 8, 1993 / Blue Note ♦♦♦
This single CD has highlights from Mose Allison's three Blue Note albums of 1987-1993 (*Ever Since the World Ended, My Backyard* and *The Earth Wants You*). Although it would be preferable to acquire the complete records instead (and Allison's greatest material was actually recorded in earlier years), there are plenty of gems on this set, including "Ever Since the World Ended," "I Looked in the Mirror," "Ever Since I Stole the Blues" and "Certified Senior Citizen." Joined by a variety of all-star players (including Bennie Wallace on tenor, altoist Arthur Blythe and guitarist John Scofield), Allison's singing, witty delivery, piano playing and insightful (yet humorous) lyrics easily steal the show. *—Scott Yanow*

Ever Since the World Ended / Oct. 28, 1987 / Blue Note ♦♦♦♦
Mose Allison, who was a musical institution long before 1987, had not run out of creative juices after 30 years of major league performances. This set finds him introducing such ironically truthful songs as "Ever Since the World Ended," "Top Forty," "I Looked In the Mirror" and "What's Your Movie." The many guest artists (including altoist Arthur Blythe, tenor saxophonist Bennie Wallace, Bob Malach on both alto and tenor and guitarist Kenny Burrell) are unnecessary frivolities but Allison's trio (with bassist Dennis Irwin and drummer Tom Whaley) is tight and ably backs the unique singer/pianist. *—Scott Yanow*

My Backyard / 1990 / Blue Note ♦♦♦
For this New Orleans session, vocalist/pianist/lyricist Mose Allison utilized several top local but world-class musicians: tenor saxophonist Tony Dagradi, guitarist Steve Masakowski, bassist Bill Huntington and drummer John Vidacovich. Among the new songs introduced at the session were "Ever Since I Stole The Blues," "You Call It Joggin'," "The Gettin' Paid Waltz" and "My Backyard." Allison, who is heard in top form, revived "That's Your Red Wagon" and "Sleepy Lagoon" and sounds in good spirits throughout this enjoyable and typically philosophical outing. *—Scott Yanow*

★ **Allison Wonderland: Anthology** / 1994 / Rhino ♦♦♦♦♦
Only Dave Frishberg and possibly Mark Murphy can rival Mose Allison when it comes to creative use of irony in lyric writing, and neither compares as an instrumentalist. He's a fine bop pianist able to play challenging instrumentals and eclectic enough to integrate country blues and gospel elements into his style. Allison's unique mix of down-home and uptown styles has made him a standout since the '50s. He's one of the few jazz musicians on Atlantic's roster ideally suited for Rhino's two-disc anthology format. Allison recorded many different kinds of songs and was always as much, if not more, a singles than an album artist. In addition, Rhino thankfully sequenced the selected songs—which span over 40 years, from 1957 to 1989, and include all of his best-known songs—chronologically. Allison does reflective duo and trio pieces, moves into uptempo combo numbers with a jump beat, then returns to the intimate small-group sound. His ability to highlight key lyrics, delivery, timing, and pacing is superb. The set includes such classics as "Back Country Blues," "Parchman Farm," "Western Man," and "Ever Since the World Ended," plus definitive covers of Willie Dixon's "The Seventh Son" and Sonny Boy Williamson II's "Eyesight to the Blind." It's an essential introduction to Allison's catalog. *—Ron Wynn*

The Earth Wants You / 1994 / Blue Note ♦♦♦
Mose Allison, one of the top lyricists of the '90s, shows throughout this entertaining CD that his powers as a pianist and singer are also very much intact. The album introduces a few new classics in "Certified Senior Citizen," "This Ain't Me" and "Who's in, Who's Out." His voice is still in prime form and his piano playing remains quite unique. It is true that the guests on the set (guitarist John Scofield, altoist Joe Lovano, Bob Malach on tenor and trumpeter Randy Brecker) are not all that necessary but Allison's performance makes this an excellent showcase for his music. *—Scott Yanow*

Gimcracks and Gewgaws / 1997 / Blue Note ♦♦♦♦♦
The older Mose Allison gets, the sharper his mind becomes, the more idiosyncratic his music sounds, and the more pleasure the aficionado gets for spending the better part of an hour with his latest stuff. By this time, the 70-year-old philosopher from Tippo, Miss. had sharpened his wit and insight on life to an even keener edge, musing wryly on materialism, technology, aging, death, even his own name ("MJA, Jr."). The tunes seem to have disappeared almost entirely but it doesn't matter; the lyrics are so damned clever and as hilarious as ever, even when they are obviously sequels to previous masterworks like "Your Mind Is on Vacation" ("What's With You") or "Young Man's Blues" ("Old Man Blues"). Mose's piano style by now has been pared down to its unique essentials, a ceaseless, swinging linear flow drawing from the three Bs—Bach, Bartok and bop—and his voice has barely aged since his Prestige days. Mark Shim muses ably on tenor sax now and then, and guitarist Russell Malone ranges all over the stylistic lot between R&B and jazz. At this rate, waiting four years or so between albums in the '90s, Allison has kept his creative batteries fresh every time out. *—Richard S. Ginell*

Mose Allison Trilogy: High Jinks! / Dec. 21, 1959-May 23, 1961 / Columbia/Legacy ♦♦♦♦
Three formerly rare Mose Allison albums originally cut for Columbia and Epic between 1959 and 1961 (*Transfiguration of Hiram Brown, I Love the Life I Live* and *V-8 Ford Blues*) are reissued in full on this attractive three-CD set plus six previously unreleased numbers. During this period (which dates between his associations with the Prestige and Atlantic labels), Mose Allison was making the transition from being a pianist/vocalist to a vocalist/pianist. He sings on roughly half the selections including "Baby, Please Don't Go," "'Deed I Do," "Fool's Paradise" and "I Love The Life I Live." The instrumentals (which also feature Addison Farmer, Henry Grimes, Bill Crow or Aaron Bell on bass, and Jerry Segal, Paul Motian, Gus Johnson or Osie Johnson on drums) are highlighted by the interesting eight-song "Hiram Brown Suite." Mose Allison fans will want to go out of their way to get this set. *—Scott Yanow*

The Mose Chronicles: Live in London, Vol. 1 / Mar. 13, 2001 / Blue Note ♦♦♦♦
Few if any white performers have captured the soul, heart, and emotion of the blues better than Jack Teagarden and Mose Allison. Allison has the added distinction of singing songs with words that sometimes remind the listener of situations where those words would have come in real handy if thought of at the time. *Vol. 1*—hopefully the first of many—was recorded over a three-day period at a gig at the Pizza Express in London, England. The play list is made up of songs Allison likes to sing, whether he composed them or they were written by others. "You Call It Joggin'" and "What's Your Movie" have shown up on other Allison recordings for Blue Note, and "Middle Class White Boy" was the title of one of his most popular albums. All of these compositions, with their often sardonic lyrics, tell stories real people can relate to. There's no pie in the sky, wide-eyed romanticism in Allison's material. Some songs have a hopeful outlook—some would call it wishful thinking—such as "Ever Since the World Ended" (when "there was no more difference between black and white"). He acknowledges the influence of Nat "King" Cole with a song Cole used to sing with his trio, "Meet Me at No Special Place." Even after all these years, Allison still has that imitable style, a mixture of blues and country delivered in a soft understated manner, and always swinging. Still another feature of an Allison performance is that one must be ready and willing to be surprised. For example, "You Are My Sunshine" is done in an unusually slow tempo and possesses a somber, regretful spirit replete with arpeggios and Allison dramatically pounding the keys. He indulges in some pianistic flights of fancy on "Entruption." The members of the trio are in total sync with Allison's way of doing things. Roy Babbington's bass and especially Mark Taylor's drums chip in with accents at just the right places, italicizing the impressions Allison is creating. A Mose Allison album requires close listening to catch the meaning of the message and to appreciate the good humor of Allison's playing and singing. This is not background music, and is strongly recommended. *—Dave Nathan*

The Mose Chronicles: Live in London, Vol. 2 / Jan. 8, 2002 / Blue Note ♦♦♦♦
The second volume drawn from Mose Allison's January 2000 run at London's Pizza Express presents the artist in a professional, if relaxed, form. *Vol. 1* was billed as an in-concert look at Allison's early, oft-covered material, but actually included a healthy number of selections from his prime later-career output. This second installment comes closer to that stated goal, as every single song dates back to the '50s and '60s. As a result, it's even more remarkable that Allison finds ways to make them sound vital and fresh; "Tell Me Something" features a piano solo that's alternately gentle and dramatic, while "Just Like Livin'" is revealed as an underappreciated summation of Allison's lyrical outlook. The rhythm section anticipates the bandleader's every twist, displaying particular synergy on an offhandedly cool "Molecular Structure" taken at a near-breakneck pace. That's not surprising considering that bassist Roy Babbington and drummer Mark Taylor are longtime Allison associates estimated to have accompanied him for more than 1,000 dates. Better yet, *Vol. 2* supplements Allison's standard jazz trio format with a guitarist, Jim Mullen, who proves a master of improvisation, most notably on the riveting extended jam during "You Can Count on Me." As the years go by, tricky moves like Allison's held-note vocal on "One of These Days" feel less like gimmicks and more like personal statements, and *The Mose Chronicles: Live in London, Vol. 2* is full of that kind of crowd-pleasing detail. The album succeeds both as an introduction to Allison's weighty song catalog and as a glimpse of his latter-day live act. *—Kenneth Bays*

The Allman Brothers Band

f. 1969, Macon, GA, **db.** 1982

Group / Slide Guitar Blues, Album Rock, Boogie Rock, Southern Rock, Hard Rock, Blues-Rock

The story of the Allman Brothers Band is one of triumph, tragedy, redemption, dissolution, and a new redemption. Over nearly 30 years, they've gone from being America's single most influential band to a has-been group trading on past glories, to reach the '90s as one of the most respected rock acts of their era.

For the first half of the '70s, the Allman Brothers Band was the most influential rock group in America, redefining rock music and its boundaries. The band's mix of blues, country, jazz, and even classical influences, and their powerful, extended onstage jamming altered the standards of concert performance—other groups were known for their onstage jamming, but when the Allman Brothers stretched a song out for 30 or 40 minutes, at their best they were exciting, never self-indulgent. They gave it all a distinctly Southern voice and, in the process, opened the way for a wave of '70s rock acts from south of the Mason-Dixon Line, including the Marshall Tucker Band, Lynyrd Skynyrd, and Blackfoot, whose music, at least initially, celebrated their roots. And for a time, almost single-handedly, they also made Capricorn Records into a major independent label.

The group was founded in 1969 by Duane Allman (Nov. 20, 1946-Oct. 29, 1971) on guitar and Gregg Allman (b. Dec. 8, 1947) on vocals and organ; Forrest Richard ("Dickey") Betts (b. Dec. 12, 1943) on guitar; Berry Oakley (b. Apr. 4, 1948-d. Nov. 12, 1972) on bass; and Butch Trucks and Jai Johanny ("Jaimoe") Johanson (b. July 8, 1944) on drums. Duane and Gregg Allman loved soul and R&B, although they listened to their share of rock & roll, especially as it sounded coming out of England in the mid-'60s. Their first group was a local Daytona Beach garage band called the Escorts, which sounded a lot like the early Beatles and Rolling Stones; they later became the Allman Joys and plunged into Cream-style British blues, and then the Hour Glass, a more soul-oriented outfit. The group landed a contract with Liberty Records with help from the Nitty Gritty Dirt Band, but the company wasted the opportunity on a pair of overproduced albums that failed to capture the Hour Glass' sound. The group split up after Liberty rejected a proposed third LP steeped in blues and R&B.

Duane Allman began working as a session guitarist at Fame Studios in Muscle Shoals, Alabama, and it was there, appearing on records by Wilson Pickett, Aretha Franklin, John Hammond, and King Curtis, among others, that he made his reputation. In 1969, at the coaxing of ex-Otis Redding manager Phil Walden, Allman gave up session work and began putting together a new band—Jaimoe (Johnny Lee Johnson) Johanson came aboard, and then Allman's longtime friend Butch Trucks, and another Allman friend, Berry

Oakley joined, along with Dickey Betts, with whom Oakley was playing in a group called Second Coming. A marathon jam session ensued, at the end of which Allman had his band, except for a singer—that came later, when his brother Gregg agreed to join. They were duly signed to Walden's new Capricorn label.

The band didn't record their first album until after they'd worked their sound out on the road, playing heavily around Florida and Georgia. The self-titled debut album was a solid blues-rock album and one of the better showcases for guitar pyrotechnics in a year with more than its share, amid albums by the Cream, Blind Faith, the Jeff Beck Group, and Led Zeppelin. It didn't sell 50,000 copies on its initial release, but *The Allman Brothers Band* impressed everyone who heard it and nearly everyone who reviewed it. Coming out at the end of the '60s, it could have passed for a follow-up to the kind of blues-rock coming out of England from acts like Cream, except that it had a sharper edge—the Allmans were American and Southern, and their understanding of blues (not to mention elements of jazz, mostly courtesy of Jaimoe) was as natural as breathing. The album also introduced one of the band's most popular concert numbers, "Whipping Post."

Their debut album attracted good reviews and a cult following with its mix of assured dual lead guitars by Duane Allman and Dickey Betts, soulful singing by Gregg Allman, and a rhythm section that was nearly as busy as the lead instruments, between Oakley's rock-hard bass and the dual drumming of Trucks and Johanson. Their second album, 1970's *Idlewild South*, recorded at Capricorn's studios in Macon, Georgia, was produced by Tom Dowd, who had previously recorded Cream. This was a magical combination—Dowd was completely attuned to the group's sound and goals, and *Idlewild South* broadened that sound, adding a softer acoustic texture to their music and introducing Dickey Betts as a composer (including the original studio version of "In Memory of Elizabeth Reed," an instrumental tribute to Miles Davis that would become a highlight of their shows, in many different forms, for the next 30 years). It also had a Gregg Allman number, "Midnight Rider," which became one of the band's more widely covered originals and the composer's signature tune.

By this time, the band's concerts were becoming legendary for the extraordinarily complex yet coherent interplay between the two guitarists and Gregg Allman's keyboards, sometimes in jams of 40 minutes or more to a single song without wasting a note. And unlike the art rock bands of the era, they weren't interested in impressing anyone with how they played scales, how many different tunings they knew, or which classical riffs they could quote. Rather, the Allmans incorporated the techniques and structures of jazz and classical into their playing. In March of 1971, the band played a series of shows at the Fillmore East that were recorded for posterity and subsequently transformed into their third album, *At Fillmore East*. This double LP, issued in July of 1971, became an instant classic, rivaling the previous blues-rock touchstone cut at the Fillmore, Cream's *Wheels of Fire*. Duane Allman and his band were suddenly the new heroes to millions of mostly older teenage fans. Although it never cracked the Top Ten, *At Fillmore East* was certified as a gold record on October 15, 1971.

Fourteen days later, Duane Allman was killed in a motorcycle accident. The band had been midway through work on their next album, *Eat a Peach*, which they completed as a five-piece, with Dickey Betts playing all of the lead and slide guitar parts. Their second double album in a row became another instant classic, and their first album to reach the Top Ten, peaking at number five.

Despite having completed *Eat a Peach*, the group was intact in name only. Rather than try and replace Duane Allman as a guitarist, they contrived to add a second solo instrument in the form of a piano, played by Chuck Leavell. The group had already begun work on a long-delayed follow-up to *Eat a Peach*, when Oakley was killed in a motorcycle accident only a few blocks from Allman's accident site.

Lamar Williams (b. Jan. 15, 1949-d. Jan. 25, 1983) was recruited on bass, and the new lineup continued the group's concert activities, as well as eventually finishing their next album, *Brothers and Sisters*, which was released on August 1, 1973. During the extended gap in releases following *Eat a Peach*, Atco reissued *The Allman Brothers Band* and *Idlewild South* together as the double LP *Beginnings*, which charted higher than either individual release.

Brothers and Sisters marked the beginning of a new era. The album had a more easygoing and freewheeling sound, less bluesy and more country-ish. This was partly a result of Capricorn's losing the services of Tom Dowd, who had produced their three previous albums. Additionally, Dickey Betts' full emergence as a songwriter and singer as well as the group's only guitarist, playing all of the lead and slide parts, altered the balance of the group's sound, pushing forth his distinct interest in country-rock. Betts also became the reluctant *de facto* leader of the band during this period, not from a desire for control as much as because he was the only one with the comparative stability and creative input to take on the responsibility.

The record occupied the number one spot for six weeks, spurred by the number two single "Ramblin' Man," and became their most well-known album. It was an odd reversal of the usual order of success for a rock band—usually, it was the release of the album that drew the crowds to concerts, but in this case, the months of touring the band had done paved the way for the album. The fact that it kept getting pushed back only heightened the fans' interest.

Ironically, *Brothers and Sisters* was a less challenging record than the group's earlier releases, with a relatively laidback sound, relaxed compared to the groundbreaking work on the group's previous four albums. But all of this hardly mattered; based on the reputation they'd established with their first four albums, and the crowd-pleasing nature of "Ramblin' Man" and the Dickey Betts-composed instrumental "Jessica," the group was playing larger halls and bigger crowds than ever.

An entire range of Southern-based rock acts had started to make serious inroads into the charts in the wake of the Allman Brothers. Labels such as MCA and even Island Records began looking for this same audience, signing acts like Lynyrd Skynyrd and Blackfoot, respectively, among others. For the first time since the mid-'50s, the heyday of the rockabilly era, a major part of the country was listening to rock & roll with a distinctly Southern twang.

The band began showing cracks in 1974, as Gregg Allman and Dickey Betts both began solo careers, recording albums separately from the group. Allman married Cher

(twice), an event that set him up in a Hollywood-based lifestyle that created a schism with the rest of the band. They might have survived all of this, but for the increasing strain of the members' other personal habits—drugs and alcohol had always been a significant part of the lives of each of the members, except perhaps for Jaimoe, but as the strain and exhaustion of touring continued, coupled with the need to produce new music, these indulgences began to get out of control, and Betts' leadership of the group created a further strain for him.

The band's difficulties were showcased by their next album, the highly uneven *Win, Lose or Draw*, which lacked the intensity and sharpness of their prior work. The whole band wasn't present for some of the album, and Gregg Allman's involvement with Cher, coupled with his serious drug problems, prevented him from participating with the rest of the group—his vocals were added separately, on the other side of the country.

The band finally came apart in 1976 when Allman found himself in the midst of a federal drug case against a supplier and agreed to testify against a friend and band employee. Leavell, Johanson, and Williams split to form Sea Level, which became a moderately successful band, cutting four Capricorn over the next four years, while Betts pursued a solo career. All of them vowed never to work with Gregg Allman again.

Amid this split, Capricorn Records, reaching ever deeper into its vaults for anything that could generate income, issued two collections, double-LP live collection called *Wipe the Windows, Check the Oil, Dollar Gas*, showcasing the *Brothers and Sisters*-era band at various concerts, and a double-LP best-of package, *The Road Goes On Forever*. *Wipe the Windows* was a modest seller, appearing as it did when the group's sales had already fallen off, and it was compared unfavorably with the legendary work on *At Fillmore East*. The studio compilation passed with barely a ripple, however, because most fans already had the stuff on the original albums.

They were all back together by 1978, however, and over the next four years the group issued a somewhat uneven series of albums. *Enlightened Rogues* (1979) somewhat redeemed their reputations—produced by Tom Dowd, who had always managed to get the very best work out of the group, it had more energy than any record they'd issued in at least six years. It also restored the two-guitar lineup, courtesy of Dan Toler (from Dickey Betts' solo band), who was brought in when Chuck Leavell (along with Lamar Williams) refused to return to the Allmans. By that time, however, the Allmans were fighting against time and musical trends. Disco, punk, and power-pop had pretty much stolen a march on the arena acts epitomized by the Allmans; whatever interest they attracted was a matter of nostalgia for their earlier releases. The group was in danger of becoming arena rock's third big oldies act (after the Moody Blues and Paul McCartney's Wings).

Additionally, their business affairs were in a shambles, owing to the bankruptcy of Capricorn Records in late 1979. When the fallout from the Capricorn collapse settled, PolyGram Records, the company's biggest creditor, took over the label's library, and the Allman Brothers were cut loose from their contract.

Their signing to Arista enabled the group to resume recording. What they released, however, was safe, unambitious, routinely commercial pop-rock, closer in spirit to the Doobie Brothers than their own classic work, and a shadow of that work, without any of the invention and daring upon which they'd built their reputations. The group's fortunes hit a further downturn when Jaimoe was fired, breaking up one of the best rhythm sections in rock. For most of the '80s, the group was on hiatus, while the individual members sorted out their personal and professional situations. During those years, only Dickey Betts seemed to be in a position to do much with his music, and most of that wasn't selling.

In 1989, the band was reactivated again, partly owing to the PolyGram's decision to issue the four-CD box set retrospective *Dreams*. That set, coupled with the reissue of their entire Capricorn catalog on compact disc in the years leading up to the box's release, reminded millions of older listeners of the band's greatness, and introduced the group to millions of people too young to have been around for Watkins Glen, much less the Fillmore shows.

They reunited and also restored the band's original double-lead-guitar configuration, adding Warren Haynes on lead guitar alongside Dickey Betts, with Allen Woody playing bass; Chuck Leavell was gone, however, having agreed to join the Rolling Stones on tour as their resident keyboard player, and Lamar Williams had succumbed to cancer in 1983. The new lineup reinvigorated the band, which signed with Epic Records and surprised everyone with their first release, *Seven Turns*. Issued in 1990, it got some of the best reviews and healthiest sales they'd had in more than a decade. Their subsequent studio albums failed to attract as much enthusiasm, and their two live albums, *An Evening With the Allman Brothers Band* and *2nd Set*, released in 1992 and 1995, respectively, were steady but not massive sellers. Much of this isn't the fault of the material so much as a natural result of the passage of time, which has left the Allmans competing with two decades' worth of successors and rivals.

The group has stayed together since 1989, overcoming continuing health and drug problems, which have occasionally battered their efforts at new music. They remain a top concert attraction 25 years-plus after their last historically important album, easily drawing more than 20,000 fans at a time to outdoor venues, or booking 2,000-seat theaters for three weeks at a time. Their back catalog, especially the first five albums, remain consistent sellers on compact disc and recently returned to the reconstituted Capricorn label (still a home for Southern rockers, including the latter-day Lynyrd Skynyrd, as well as reissues of Elmore James and other classic bluesmen) under a 1997 licensing agreement that has resulted in their third round of digital remastering.

Apart from their Arista releases, the Allman Brothers Band has remained remarkably consistent, altering their music only gradually over 30 years. They sound more country than they did in their early days, and they're a bit more varied in the vocal department, but the band still soars at their concerts and on most of their records for the last ten years.
—*Bruce Eder*

The Allman Brothers Band / 1969 / Polydor ✦✦✦✦✦
This might be the best debut album ever delivered by an American blues band, a bold, powerful, hard-edged, soulful essay in electric blues with a native Southern ambience. Some lingering elements of the psychedelic era then drawing to a close can be found in

"Dreams," along with the template for the group's onstage workouts with "Whipping Post," and a solid cover of Muddy Waters' "Trouble No More." There isn't a bad song here, and only the fact that the group did even better the next time out keeps this from getting the highest possible rating. *—Bruce Eder*

☆ **Idlewild South** / 1970 / Polydor ✦✦✦✦✦

The best studio album in the group's history, electric blues with an acoustic texture, virtuoso lead, slide, and organ playing, and a killer selection of songs, including "Midnight Rider," "Revival," "Don't Keep Me Wonderin'," and "In Memory of Elizabeth Reed" in its embryonic studio version, which is pretty impressive even at a mere six minutes and change. They also do the best white cover of Willie Dixon's "Hoochie Coochie Man" anyone's ever likely to hear. *—Bruce Eder*

☆ **At Fillmore East** / Jul. 1971 / Polydor ✦✦✦✦✦

Whereas most great live rock albums are about energy, *At Fillmore East* is like a great live jazz session, where the pleasure comes from the musicians' interaction and playing. The great thing about that is, the original album that brought the Allmans so much acclaim is as notable for its clever studio editing as it is for its performances. Producer Tom Dowd skillfully trimmed some of the performances down to relatively concise running time (edits later restored on the double-disc set *The Fillmore Concerts*), at times condensing several performances into one track. Far from being a sacrilege, this tactic helps present the Allmans in their best light, since even if the music isn't necessarily concise (three tracks run over ten minutes, with two in the 20-minute range), it does showcase the group's terrific instrumental interplay, letting each member (but particularly guitarist Duane and keyboardist/vocalist Gregg) shine. Even after the release of the unedited concerts, this original double album (single CD) remains the pinnacle of the Allmans and Southern rock at its most elastic, bluesy, and jazzy. *—Stephen Thomas Erlewine*

★ **Eat a Peach** / 1972 / Polydor ✦✦✦✦✦

A tribute to the dearly departed Duane, *Eat a Peach* rambles through two albums, running through a side of new songs, recorded post-Duane, spending a full album on live cuts from the *Fillmore East* sessions, then offering a round of studio tracks Duane completed before his death. On the first side, they do suggest the mellowness of the Dickey Betts-led *Brothers and Sisters*, particularly on the lovely "Melissa," and this stands in direct contrast with the monumental live cuts that dominate the album. They're at the best on the punchier covers of "One Way Out" and "Trouble No More," both proof of the group's exceptional talents as a roadhouse blues-rock band, but Duane does get his needed showcase on "Mountain Jam," a sprawling 33-minute jam that may feature a lot of great playing, but is certainly a little hard for anyone outside of diehards to sit through. Apart from that cut, the record showcases the Allmans at their peak, and it's hard not to feel sad as the acoustic guitars of "Little Martha" conclude the record, since this tribute isn't just heartfelt, it offers proof of Duane Allman's immense talents and contribution to the band. *—Stephen Thomas Erlewine*

Brothers and Sisters / 1973 / Polydor ✦✦✦✦

The group's first new studio album in two years shows off a leaner, brand of musicianship, which, coupled with a pair of serious crowd-pleasers, "Ramblin' Man" and "Jessica," helped drive it to the top of the charts for a month and a half, and platinum record sales. This was the first album to feature the group's new lineup, with Chuck Leavell on keyboards and Lamar Williams on bass, as well as Dickey Betts' emergence as a singer alongside Gregg Allman. The tracks appear on the album in the order in which they were recorded, and the first three, up through "Ramblin' Man," feature Berry Oakley—their sound is rock hard and crisp. The subsequent songs with Williams have the bass buried in the mix, and an overall muddier sound. The interplay between Leavell and Betts is beautiful on some songs, and Betts' slide on "Pony Boy" is a dazzling showcase that surprised everybody. Despite its sales, *Brothers and Sisters* is not quite a classic album (although it was their best for the next 17 years), especially in the wake of the four that had appeared previously, but it served as a template for some killer stage performances, and it proved that the band could survive the deaths of two key members. Capricorn's 1997 reissue has a brighter sound than the older PolyGram CD, but the Mobile Fidelity audiophile disc has the best sound, a richer, broader tone. *—Bruce Eder*

☆ **Beginnings** / 1973 / Polydor ✦✦✦✦✦

This is where the group's CD release history gets complicated. *Beginnings* was originally put together by Atco as a double-LP to encourage new fans who'd missed them to buy the group's first two albums, and proved so successful that it was kept in print on CD by Polydor when it acquired the group's catalog. Polydor's single-CD version of this double-LP, however, was substandard in audio quality, digitized from an LP production master, and their individual CDs of *The Allman Brothers Band* and *Idlewild South* were far superior. But when Capricorn got the library back in 1997, they remastered *Beginnings* along with the rest of the library, and the Capricorn version of this CD is one of the better bargains going. *—Bruce Eder*

Win, Lose or Draw / 1975 / Polydor ✦✦

An unexpectedly poor showing from the group, considering the two-year lag between albums and what had come before. Despite a good cover of Muddy Waters' "Can't Lose What You Never Had"—highlighted by a great Dickey Betts solo—as an opener, there's not much here that's first-rate. The band sounds lethargic, although they still play decently. The title track and Dickey Betts' instrumental "High Falls" are among the few highlights, decent but unexceptional performances sparked by Betts' playing (which is engaging even on the loser tracks like "Louisiana Lou"). The album's main fault lies not with what it is, but what it could have been, and who it's from—as a debut album from a new band, it would be excusable and acceptable. *—Bruce Eder*

Wipe the Windows, Check the Oil, Dollar Gas / 1976 / Polydor ✦✦✦

This live album was released by Capricorn Records largely as a way of raising money in a hurry, but it fares surprisingly well musically. The 1973-1974 Allman Brothers Band featured here is the one that most fans actually saw, since most listeners didn't discover them or get to their concerts until after the deaths of Duane Allman and Berry Oakley. *Wipe the Windows* isn't a landmark release like the Fillmore tapes—a collection of rock's greatest guitar albums could be complete without it. But no Allman Brothers Band fan should pass up *Wipe the Windows*, which is a most solid live album, and, in particular, a better representation of the songs off of *Brothers and Sisters* and *Win, Lose or Draw* than the original studio versions. "Southbound," "Ramblin' Man," "Jessica," and, to a lesser degree, "Wasted Words," come off exceptionally well. This second-generation band, with Dickey Betts as the sole lead guitar and Gregg Allman and Chuck Leavell sharing the keyboards, also performs a reconceived version of "In Memory of Elizabeth Reed"—they could never spark more fire than the version from the Fillmore, so they transform it into a moodier piece with more space for the keyboards to open up. Compiled from shows in New Orleans, San Francisco, Bakersfield, Oakland, and Watkins Glen (New York). *—Bruce Eder*

Enlightened Rogues / 1979 / Polydor ✦✦✦

The group's best studio album since *Brothers and Sisters* is a loud, brash, hard-rocking collection of consistently solid if not first-rate songs. The singing is some of the best since *Idlewild South*, and although they would do better once they brought in Warren Haynes, the dual guitar lineup of Dickey Betts and Dan Toler is a reminder of what the group had been missing since Duane Allman's death. The music isn't earth-shattering, but it is exciting through and through. *—Bruce Eder*

Reach for the Sky / 1980 / Razor & Tie ✦✦

The second album from *Allmans Mach Two* shows them holding their own, wearing their influences (especially gospel) a bit more on their sleeves, and even coming up with a minor single in "Angeline." *—William Ruhlmann*

Brothers of the Road / 1981 / Razor & Tie ✦✦

"Straight from the Heart" (number 39), written by Dickey Betts and Johnny Cobb and sung by Gregg Allman, is one of the group's better accommodations to pop music, and on the whole, this is an accessible version of their trademark sound: call it Allmans Lite. The ruling influence here may be Arista president Clive Davis, who also oversaw the pop-oriented Grateful Dead albums of the same period. But the main duty of pop music is to sell, and when this album petered out at number 44, The Allmans called it quits for the second time. *—William Ruhlmann*

Dreams / Jun. 1989 / Polydor ✦✦✦✦✦

Spanning four discs and nearly 100 tracks, *Dreams* is one of those rare box sets that tells a story while delivering the definitive word on its subject. Its success has a lot to do with its status as Polygram/Bill Levinson's sequel to the acclaimed hit *Crossroads*, which summarized Eric Clapton's winding career perfectly. They follow the same approach here, gathering pre-Allman's recordings from the clan, including cuts by the Allman Joys, selecting the hits from the classic years, and adding stray cuts by solo projects to the mix. It's a smart move and it results in a terrific box that truly offers the definitive word on one of the longest-running dramas in Southern rock. Yes, the Allmans reunited rather successfully after this box, so none of that material is here, but it's not missed—this is the story of the band. *—Stephen Thomas Erlewine*

Seven Turns / Oct. 1990 / Epic ✦✦✦✦✦

The group's comeback album, their best blues-based outing since *Idlewild South*, and one that restored a lot of their reputation. With Tom Dowd running the session, and the group free to make the music they wanted to, they ended up producing this bold, rock-hard album, made up mostly of songs by Dickey Betts (with contributions by new keyboardman Johnny Neel and lead guitarist Warren Haynes), almost every one of them a winner. Apart from the rippling opening number, "Good Clean Fun," and which he co-authored, Gregg Allman's contribution is limited to singing and the organ, but the band seems more confident than ever, ripping through numbers like "Low Down Dirty Mean," "Shine It On," and "Let Me Ride" like they were inventing blues-rock here, and the Ornette Coleman-inspired "True Gravity" is their best instrumental since "Jessica." *—Bruce Eder*

Live at Ludlow Garage: 1970 / 1991 / Polydor ✦✦✦✦✦

Ninety-one minutes of the Allman Brothers Band in concert from a Cincinnati venue that they loved, nearly a year before their legendary Fillmore shows. The acoustics are good, though a little shaky—the tape was made at 7 1/2 ips, the bare minimum professional standard, which leaves more hiss than one might like, and a bit less clarity than a fully professional live album might show; on the other hand, the group's sound imparts its own punch and clarity, and it was done in stereo, and if not for the existence of the Fillmore tapes, and the fact that the albums they yielded sold a kajillion copies, this show might well have been released in the '70s. It isn't as intense as the Fillmore shows, but it does capture the group as a little known working band with but a single album out and building a reputation—and with Dickey Betts yet to emerge as either a singer or composer, and their sound still being worked out ("Statesboro Blues" gets a startlingly subdued performance, anticipating the acoustic version of "In Memory of Elizabeth Reed" from the the '90s recording *2nd Set*). They build their set on ambitious reinterpretations of songs by Blind Willie McTell, Muddy Waters ("Trouble In Mind"), John Lee Hooker ("Dimples"), and Willie Dixon, whose "Hoochie Coochie Man" is a soaring highlight of this two-disc set, in a version that makes every other white band's cover seem wimpy by comparison, climaxing with a searing, though somewhat disjointed 44-minute version of "Mountain Jam." *—Bruce Eder*

Shades of Two Worlds / Jul. 1991 / Epic ✦✦✦✦

The group's follow-up to their comeback album is a major step forward, with more mature songs, more improvisation than the group had featured in their work since the early '70s, and more confidence than they'd shown since *Brothers and Sisters*. It's all here, from acoustic bottleneck playing ("Come on in My Kitchen") to jazz improvisation

("Kind of Bird"), with the most reflective songwriting ("Nobody Knows") in their history. —*Bruce Eder*

A Decade of Hits 1969–1979 / Oct. 1991 / Polydor ✦✦✦✦
The record industry's blatantly greedy ploy of remastering and "upgrading" CDs is shameful. The sonics are usually improved, but the CDs could have been mastered properly the first time. But then fans wouldn't buy the same titles twice. The Allman Brothers Band's indispensable compilation *A Decade of Hits 1969-1979* was reissued in 2000, just nine years after the original release. The remastered 2000 edition still features the same 16 songs, but the packaging and liner notes include an essay by *Guitar World* journalist Alan Paul, photos, and detailed recording credits. It would be easy to argue that individual albums like *Idlewild South, At Fillmore East, Eat a Peach,* or *Brothers and Sisters* are more cohesive artistic statements, but no self-respecting rock & roll fan should be without a copy of *A Decade of Hits 1969-1979,* which includes the cream of those albums. It's impossible to go wrong with one CD featuring Gregg Allman's harrowing "Whipping Post" and gorgeous "Midnight Rider," Dickey Betts' soaring "Ramblin' Man," and the lovely instrumentals "Jessica" and "In Memory of Elizabeth Reed," let alone the blues covers "Statesboro Blues" and "One Way Out," which many people probably don't realize are covers because the band embodies them so much. Fans shouldn't have much of a problem recognizing the 2000 version. The cover featuring the band logo stitched on the denim jacket is still intact, but the white lettering is laid out a little differently on both the front and back covers. Plus, the shrink-wrap has an identifying sticker. Better still, just look at the copyright date. The first pressing's liner notes include a typographical error; there's a noticeable gap within the essay text where the *Enlightened Rogues* title is missing. —*Bret Adams*

An Evening With the Allman Brothers Band: First Set / Mar. 1992 / Epic ✦✦✦✦
A good live album, but not quite the worthy successor to the Fillmore shows in their various forms—the band is on form throughout this more than one-hour distillation of shows in Boston and New York from their 1992 tour, covering old and new repertory, but there are no surprises. The song lineup wastes some opportunities, however, and there isn't any serious new ground covered, which may be par for the course for a band in its 22nd year. On the up side, very much, the crispness of the recording helps one fully appreciate the power and articulation of the playing by everyone, but especially Dickey Betts and Warren Haynes. —*Bruce Eder*

The Fillmore Concerts / Oct. 20, 1992 / Polydor ✦✦✦✦✦
A good idea that worked out even better, with one small caveat. *The Fillmore Concerts* is made up of performances from the two Fillmore shows that originally comprised *At the Fillmore East* and the concert portions of *Eat a Peach,* plus one track ("One Way Out") from a Fillmore show from a couple of months later, the 16-track masters from each show transferred to digital and remixed by original producer Tom Dowd. The sound is sterling and the two hour-plus running time makes this a dream for fans of the band, as well as an improvement on the original releases of this material. It is also a slightly less honest release, where "In Memory of Elizabeth Reed" is concerned—Dowd edited the version here together from two different performances, first and second shows, the dividing line being where Duane Allman's solo comes in. Not that this is the only concert album where this kind of editing has been done, but the original *Live at the Fillmore* contained a single take of the song, and some purists may prefer that. Otherwise, this set runs circles around more than 99 percent of the guitar albums ever released, with breathtaking sound (which, unlike the similarly conceived but less effective *Derek and the Dominos Live at the Fillmore,* loses none of its bite), and most fans might as well start here. —*Bruce Eder*

Where It All Begins / May 3, 1994 / Epic ✦✦✦
After a year of personal and personnel problems, the group got back together to record this surprisingly consistent live-in-the-studio venture. It lacks the ambition and stretch of *Seven Turns* or *Shades of Two Worlds,* along with their peaks, but it is still a solidly consistent album, driven by some of the virtues of live spontaneity. Highlights include Gregg Allman's frank drug song "All Night Train," the Bo Diddley-beat-driven "No One to Run With," and the glorious dual guitar workout "Back Where It All Begins." —*Bruce Eder*

An Evening With the Allman Brothers Band: 2nd Set / 1995 / Epic ✦✦✦✦
The Allman Brothers Band's fifth live release in 25 years, cut during 1994 in Raleigh, NC, and at the Garden State Arts Center in New Jersey, is a high-water mark in their Epic Records catalog. If anything, they're even better here than they were on the earlier *Evening With the Allman Brothers Band,* the old material getting fresh new approaches—the band was *on* for both nights, and presented sets, including an acoustic version of "In Memory of Elizabeth Reed" and "Jessica" (which won a Grammy Award) that soared and flowed, especially Dickey Betts' and Warren Haynes' guitars. What's more, the clarity of the recording and the volume at which it was recorded make this a most rewarding 70 minutes of live music on a purely technical level—you can practically hear the action on the guitars during the acoustic set. It won't replace *At Fillmore East* or the live portions of *Eat a Peach,* but it deserves a place on the shelf not very far from them. —*Bruce Eder*

Fillmore East, February 1970 / 1996 / Grateful Dead ✦✦✦✦
The Allman Brothers shared the bill with the Grateful Dead on several notable occasions. This release recalls the Brothers in support of the Dead and Love in February 1970 at the fabulous Fillmore East. No specific dates for the performances are noted, so it is presumed this release is a composite from recordings made at some point during the two sets per night that the Allmans performed on February 11th through the 14th. There is no mistaking the unbridled fervor of the original lineup of the band. Rising to the challenge of exploratory psychedelia—while remaining ever faithful to their Southern blues roots—blues standards such as "(I'm Gonna Move To The) Outskirts of Town" and "Hoochie Coochie Man" are strengthened and extended beyond their typical assertions. No longer are they relegated to the inadequately rendered thrashings of garage rock.

Betts and the Allmans understand the dynamics of blues. It is out of this respect for the art form that the band is able to pull off such authentic psychedelia-tinged Delta sounds. Likewise, the Allman Brothers were beginning to ascend as not only premier interpreters, but purveyors of a revolutionary new electric guitar-driven blues movement including the likes of Led Zeppelin, Eric Clapton's various outings, as well as the Ron "Pigpen" McKernan-led Grateful Dead. The early originals and performance staples "Whipping Post," "In Memory of Elizabeth Reed," and "Mountain Jam"—which is based on the Donovan Leitch song—are nothing short of revelatory. The band gels instantly into a symbiotic instrument with each member both playing and listening in equal measure. The recording also bears mentioning. Stanley Owsley—the Grateful Dead's very own sonic solution—recorded this music the same way that he documented the Dead night after night. His theories on live recording are unique and capture aural insights that are lost to some. *Fillmore East, February 1970* is available exclusively through Grateful Dead Production. —*Lindsay Planer*

Mycology: An Anthology / Jun. 9, 1998 / Epic ✦✦✦
Mycology: An Anthology collects highlights from the Allman Brothers' '90s recordings for Epic Records. Although these latter-day recordings didn't quite reach the heights of the group's '70s heyday, they were surprisingly strong and *Mycology* is the best way for the curious fan to discover that. By rounding up the best moments from *Seven Turns, Shades of Two Worlds, An Evening With the Allman Brothers Band* and *Where It All Begins,* the collection offers a good distillation of an underrated portion of the group's career, thereby making it of equal interest to casual and hardcore fans alike. —*Stephen Thomas Erlewine*

Peakin' at the Beacon / Nov. 14, 2000 / Epic ✦✦✦
When Gregg Allman was asked why Dickey Betts was kicked out of the Allman Brothers Band in the spring of 2000, he is reported to have suggested the answer lay in the tapes from the group's two-week stand at the Beacon Theatre in New York. That makes it surprising that the Allmans would turn to those tapes to assemble their first new album release in five and a half years, *Peakin' at the Beacon.* Happily, however, there is no evidence of Betts' alleged shortcomings on the disc, though it must be admitted that, since he is one of two lead guitarists (the other being Derek Trucks, making his recorded debut with the band), it isn't always easy to tell who is playing. There is plenty of guitar work, and it is up to the Allmans' usual standard. Following the instrumental opener, Gregg Allman sings lead on seven straight songs, all of which come from the band's first three studio albums. Betts finally appears as a vocalist on the ninth track, the 1990 folk-country tune "Seven Turns." Finally, there is a 27-and-a-half-minute version of the 1975 Betts instrumental "High Falls," a typical extended workout complete with jazzy interludes and a lengthy percussion section. The Allmans may not have been due for another live album (two of their last three releases being concert recordings), but the series of Beacon shows has become an annual event, and the disc serves as a souvenir from the March 2000 shows. Fans who attended those shows, or who just want to be reassured that the Allmans sound much the same as ever, may enjoy the album; less devoted listeners probably shouldn't bother. —*William Ruhlmann*

● **The Road Goes on Forever [Expanded]** / Oct. 23, 2001 / Universal ✦✦✦✦✦
The initial release of *The Road Goes on Forever* was solid, containing the simple basics of the Allmans' Capricorn recordings. The expanded version that Mercury released in 2001 improves it considerably by almost doubling its running length with 13 bonus tracks and sprawling over two full CDs. This gives plenty of space to showcase the Allmans at their unrestrained best, capturing some of their finest concert jams while sketching a full portrait of their time at Capricorn. As a historic document, the box *Dreams* still can't be beat, but for listeners who want a thorough anthology that's not exhaustive, this is an excellent choice. —*Stephen Thomas Erlewine*

Duane Allman

b. Nov. 20, 1946, Nashville, TN, d. Oct. 29, 1971, Macon, GA

Slide Guitar, Sitar, Guitar (Electric), Guitar / Slide Guitar Blues, Southern Rock, Blues-Rock, Album Rock

Duane Allman went from musical unknown to become one of rock's most revered guitar virtuosos, only to die a legend, all in about 24 months. He barely had time to establish his legacy, much less his name—two finished studio albums with his band, a live album and lots of shows with them (some of which, off radio, are starting to surface on bootlegs), and session work in which he played behind other artists, along with songs off of a busted solo album project. The bulk of his reputation and legacy rests, understandably, with the Allman Brothers Band, but there were enough outside projects to justify a pair of anthology collections. Either one is the place to start musically, with the first set also containing a wonderful extended essay on his life and career, but serious fans will obviously want the entire albums from which a lot of those tracks, even the session work, were pulled. —*Bruce Eder*

● **Anthology** / 1972 / Polydor ✦✦✦✦✦
This double album was the first fully annotated rock anthology, complete with biographical essay and song analysis. It probably would have succeeded regardless, but the presence of Derek and the Dominos' "Layla," at just the point that it was becoming a rock standard, helped push the sales even higher. The highlights, electric and acoustic, are too numerous to detail—"Goin' Down Slow," a glorious finished fragment from Duane Allman's attempted solo album; the B.B. King medley played by the pre-Allman Brothers Band, and the Hour Glass in one of their few unfettered trips into the studio. There are also shining moments playing behind others, including "The Weight" by Aretha Franklin and "Hey Jude" by Wilson Pickett, plus work with King Curtis (on whose "Games People Play" listeners hear Allman playing an electric sitar). Other highlights include Cowboy, Johnny Jenkins ("Rollin' Stone"), John Hammond ("Shake for Me"), Boz Scaggs (the

13-minute epic "Loan Me a Dime"), and Delaney & Bonnie & Friends, rounded out by some great moments with the Allman Brothers Band. *—Bruce Eder*

An Anthology, Vol. 2 / 1974 / Polydor ✦✦✦✦✦

The session work with other players here isn't quite as good as the material on the first anthology, but *Volume Two* does feature a live cut by Delaney & Bonnie, plus a pair of what were then previously unissued Allman Brothers Band live tracks (among them "Midnight Rider" from the Fillmore East in June 1971). There's another good Duane Allman solo number and a good Hour Glass track ("Been Gone Too Long"), more session work with Aretha Franklin and King Curtis, Ronnie Hawkins ("Matchbox"), Wilson Pickett ("Born to Be Wild"), Johnny Jenkins, Boz Scaggs, Sam Samudio, and Otis Rush. The annotation here isn't as thorough as it was on the first volume, but anyone who owns the first double-CD set will almost certainly have to own this one as well, and for a mid-priced set there's a lot of very good music. *—Bruce Eder*

Gregg Allman

b. Dec. 8, 1947, Nashville, TN

Vocals, Keyboards, Piano, Guitar (Acoustic), Organ / Southern Rock, Blues-Rock, Album Rock, Boogie Rock

Gregg Allman's most visible contribution to rock music is as lead singer, organist, and songwriter within the Allman Brothers Band, founded by his brother Duane (d. 1971) in 1969. He has never threatened to eclipse the band that carries his family name, but he has found occasional success and popularity with his solo work, which is distinctly different, more soulful and less focused on high-wattage virtuosity.

Allman's instrument is the organ, and he is most effective, when he is in top form, as a singer. His first instrument, ironically enough, was the guitar, and he took it up before his older brother Duane did. But Duane learned it better and quickly eclipsed Gregg. Where Gregg did excel was on the organ and as a singer (a role Duane was never comfortable with), which proved important but not at the center of a group that became famous for its 40-minute instrumental jams and three-hour sets. Through their early efforts, in bands like the Allman Joys and the Hour Glass, they shared the spotlight, with Duane taking the lengthy solos and Gregg fronting the band and offering Booker T. Jones-type keyboard playing. Liberty Records signed the Hour Glass and tried making Gregg into the focus of their efforts during the late '60s, but it never quite worked.

When the Allman Brothers Band was organized, the flashy (and vital) instrumental moments belonged to his brother and Dickey Betts and, later still, Warren Haynes. Gregg's songs, however, including "Whipping Post" and "Midnight Rider," were among the group's notable originals during their classic period, 1969-1972. Beginning with *Brothers and Sisters*, Betts' songwriting and singing came to increasing prominence.

It was during the period that *Brothers and Sisters* was burning up the charts that Gregg Allman emerged as a solo artist with his first album, the critically well-received hit *Laid Back*, which put the softer, more serious, soul- and gospel-tinged side of his work in sharper focus. A tour followed, which yielded a live album that was also a success. This first period of solo popularity was interrupted by a combination of professional and personal conflicts; the Allman Brothers Band toured extensively and struggled to come up with a follow-up to *Brothers and Sisters*, and Gregg Allman began a relationship with Cher, the ex-wife and singing partner of Sonny Bono, which resulted in a tumultuous series of marriages and divorces for the two. These activities were played out amid Allman's well-publicized drug problems that culminated with his testifying against a band employee in a federal drug case, which, in turn, led to the temporary but extended dissolution of the Allman Brothers Band.

Ironically, it was during this period, in 1977, that he delivered *Playin' Up a Storm*, a pop-soul effort that proved to be his most accomplished and successful album. Alas, this was to be the peak of his career away from the band. His next two albums, *I'm No Angel* and *Just Before the Bullets Fly*, released at the end of the '80s, were quickly eclipsed by the re-formed and reinvigorated Allman Brothers Band's success on stage and on record. His 1997 release *Searching for Simplicity* and the double-CD anthology *One More Try* had none of the urgency or success of the band's activities. *—Bruce Eder*

Laid Back / 1973 / Polydor ✦✦✦✦✦

Recorded in the same year as the *Brothers and Sisters* album, this solo debut release is a beautiful amalgam of R&B, folk, and gospel sounds, with the best singing on any of Gregg Allman's solo releases. He covers his own "Midnight Rider" in a more mournful, dirge-like manner, and Jackson Browne's "These Days" gets its most touching and tragic-sounding rendition as well. Although Chuck Leavell and Jaimoe are here, there's very little that sounds like the Allman Brothers Band—prominent guitars, apart from a few licks by Tommy Talton (Cowboy, ex-We The People) are overlooked in favor of gospel-tinged organ and choruses behind Allman's soulful singing. *—Bruce Eder*

The Gregg Allman Tour / 1974 / Polygram ✦✦✦✦

Gregg Allman's tour in support of his debut solo LP, *Laid Back*, led to the recording of this album (originally two LPs) at Carnegie Hall in New York and the Capitol Theatre in Passaic, NJ. It's a match for *Laid Back* in musical value and then some, with a good, wide range of repertory and great performances throughout by all concerned, plunging head-first and deep into blues, R&B, honky tonk, and gospel. Strangely enough, the album contains only three of *Laid Back*'s songs—"Don't Mess Up a Good Thing" opens the show in a properly spirited, earthy manner, but it's the second song, "Queen of Hearts," in a soaring rendition, with gorgeous backing by Annie Sutton, Erin Dickins, and Lynn Rubin, and superb sax work by Randall Bramblett and David Brown, that shows Allman in his glory as a singer and bandleader. Allman gives a lively, raucous, honky tonk-style rendition of the Elvis Presley hit "I Feel So Bad," complete with a killer guitar solo by Tommy Talton, and "Turn on Your Lovelight" gets an extended treatment worthy of the Allman Brothers Band. One would expect that, with Chuck Leavell and Jaimoe present in the band, there would be more similarity to the Allmans' sound, and that they'd be prominently featured, but Tommy Talton and bassist Kenny Tibbetts get more of a spotlight. Several Allman Brothers songs are present here, in more laid-back and lyrical versions, and the Capricorn Records band Cowboy—essentially serving as the core of Allman's touring band—gets a featured spot with two songs, "Time Will Take Us" and "Where Can You Go," that leave one wanting to hear a lot more concert material from them, and from Talton as a singer. *The Gregg Allman Tour* was reissued on CD in late 2001 by Polydor in a clearer, sharper remastered edition that contains Martin Mull's complete introduction of the band. *—Bruce Eder*

Playin' Up a Storm / 1977 / Razor & Tie ✦✦✦✦✦

In a way, *Playin' Up a Storm* doesn't really highlight Gregg Allman's strengths, since it's a little smoother and soul-inflected than his work with the Allman Brothers. Then again, that's not a problem; after all, why make a solo album that's exactly like your full-time gig? Consequently, *Playin' Up a Storm* is a well-made, expertly performed set of blues-rock, soul-pop, and straight-ahead rock & roll. There aren't any true classics here, but the thing that makes it one of Allman's best solo efforts is the terrific performances. Not only is he in fine voice, delivering each song with conviction, but his supporting band—featuring such luminaries as Dr. John and Bill Payne—is sterling. All the grooves are in the pocket, the sound is enticing, and the overall effect is just right. Not an earth-shattering record, but it will please true Allman fans. *—Stephen Thomas Erlewine*

I'm No Angel / 1986 / Epic ✦✦✦

Nearly ten years separate Gregg Allman's third and fourth solo albums (not counting *Allman & Woman*), which is quite a long stretch by anyone's standards. Of course, there were a number of reasons why Allman didn't release an album between 1977's *Playin' Up a Storm* and 1986's *I'm No Angel*—various substance addictions, bad marriage, disappearing bands. By 1986, he had pulled it all together and crafted *I'm No Angel*, an album designed to be a comeback. After all, the title track alone was a statement of purpose, a declaration of his bad-boy ways. Since this album was released in the midst of the Reagan era, it's not only a little musically tame—slick surfaces and keyboards dominate—but the attitude is a little lax, too. On the title track, a song that justifiably became one of his signature tunes, the lyrics say "darn" instead of "damn," which is a little tame for someone like Allman. Still, what matters is the tune, and it's a corker—so much so that it overshadows many of the other cuts on the record. However, *I'm No Angel* is, by and large, a solid and thoroughly enjoyable set of songs. The main problem is the production, which is a bit too much of its time. However, that's an easy flaw to overlook, especially for hard-core fans, because Allman rarely delivered a solo album as solid as this. *—Stephen Thomas Erlewine*

Just Before the Bullets Fly / 1988 / Epic ✦✦

I'm No Angel was such a success that Gregg Allman wasted no time delivering its follow-up, 1988's *Just Before the Bullets Fly*. Essentially, the album is *I'm No Angel, Part 2*, with the same glossy mixes and straight-ahead rock & roll. This isn't a bad thing, in theory, and the execution is solid. It's just that the songs aren't there. There are a couple of moments that work—namely, the opening punch of "Demons" and "Before the Bullets Fly"—but most of the tunes aren't terribly memorable, and the ultra-slick production doesn't help matters. Given this tepid effort, it's little wonder that it took Allman nearly ten years to deliver a sequel. *—Stephen Thomas Erlewine*

● **One More Try: An Anthology** / Sep. 23, 1997 / Polygram ✦✦✦✦✦

Although it may be a little too comprehensive for some tastes, *One More Try: An Anthology* is the definitive Gregg Allman collection. Spanning two discs and 34 songs, the collection touches upon every phase of his career. Of course, it concentrates on his solo career—all of his hits, key album tracks, and AOR staples are here—but it also contains a couple of Allman Brothers cuts for good measure. The end result is a weighty anthology that winds up as the final statement on Gregg Allman's career. *—Thom Owens*

Searching for Simplicity / Nov. 11, 1997 / 550 Music ✦✦✦

In his initial solo recordings, Gregg Allman tried for a more eclectic pop approach than the Southern blues-rock of his day job with the Allman Brothers Band. His later solo work, done during breaks in the Brothers' career, was much closer to the traditional ABB sound. On his first solo album since the Allmans' reformation in 1989, he again makes what is essentially an Allman Brothers Band record without the other members, except new guitarist Jack Pearson, whose Duane Allman/Dickey Betts-style slide work is all over the disc. Allman signals the same-but-different approach by opening the album with an "unplugged" version of the Allmans' signature song, "Whipping Post," and though he adds horns to some tracks for a more R&B feel, the rest of the album finds him growling through standard-issue blues-rock, some of the songs originals, some covers, among them an excellent version of "Dark End of the Street" and an arrangement of John Hiatt's "Memphis in the Meantime" that makes it sound like a Betts country-rocker. Recovering from personnel changes, the Allman Brothers Band didn't release an album in 1997; this record should help tide their fans over. *—William Ruhlmann*

20th Century Masters—The Millennium Collection: The Best of Gregg Allman / Mar. 26, 2002 / Mercury ✦✦✦

This midline-priced best-of surveys Gregg Allman's stop-and-start solo career of the '70s, which he conducted during hiatuses in the career of the Allman Brothers Band that, at the time, were thought of either as temporary or permanent. The first track, "Melissa," actually is an Allmans recording from the 1972 *Eat a Peach* album that was a minor singles chart entry and that serves as a good introduction to the set, since it is a Gregg Allman-written and -sung ballad. Following the success of 1973's *Brothers and Sisters*, Allman cut a solo album, the aptly titled *Laid Back*, from which five tracks have been excerpted, among them his remake of the Allman Brothers song "Midnight Rider," which became a Top 20 hit. On his own, Allman is a much more mellow performer, contrasting the rock & roll drive of the band with a ballad style that invites in strings and horns, as well as the occasional steel guitar, which turns up in his cover of Jackson Browne's "These Days." The version of the Allmans' "Dreams" comes from *The Gregg Allman Tour*, a live track that re-conceives the song, even finding room for a lengthy saxophone solo. The last three tracks come from the only moderately successful 1977 solo album *Playin' Up a Storm*, recorded at a time when the Allman Brothers had broken up and Allman had formed his own backup band. The compilation rescues three appealing ballads from it, and they are in keeping with the soft tones of the rest of the disc. Gregg Allman's solo forays have proven to be a sidelight to the career of his main band, but if you are a lover of his voice who has always wished you didn't have to sit through all those guitar solos, this is the collection for you. *—William Ruhlmann*

No Stranger to the Dark: The Best of Gregg Allman / Jun. 11, 2002 / Epic/Legacy ✦✦✦
Even if you accept that a best-of for Gregg Allman can focus wholly on his solo career (as this one does) and not include any of his work with the Allman Brothers, this could not by any stretch be considered "the best of Gregg Allman." It's really the best of what he's recorded for Sony, which is really an entirely different animal. That means there's nothing from his three '70s albums, which most listeners would view as containing his best solo work; the chronological stretch on this comp only covers the last half of the '80s and the '90s. Like, say, Rod Stewart, this was a time in which his recordings had really only a shadow of their old power, although (like Stewart) his voice was still in good shape and he didn't stoop to levels as low as Stewart did. Given the pool of what it has to work with, this disc is a reasonable selection, evenly spread between highlights of the *I'm No Angel*, *Just Before the Bullets Fly*, and *Searching for Simplicity* albums. And there are a few extras that might make this worth getting for Allman completists: previously unreleased live cuts from 1987 ("Melissa") and 1998 (his long-lived staple cover of Jackson Browne's "These Days"), a studio outtake from 1985, and "Brother to Brother," a duet with Lori Yates that was on the 1989 *Next of Kin* soundtrack. Overall, though, it's hardly a guide to even some of his best work, the '80s tracks suffering from slick period production and unmemorable AOR material. His voice is certainly operating at a level above the quality of many of the songs, and is better served by the occasional cuts on which the blues-soul elements come more to the foreground, like "I've Got News for You" and the cover of "Dark End of the Street." *—Richie Unterberger*

American Blues Exchange

f. 1968

Group / Garage Rock, Blues-Rock

American Blues Exchange was started in the spring of 1968 by a group of students at Trinity College in Hartford, Connecticut. Like many of their young contemporaries, the band members were enamored with the progressive blues of some of Britain's heaviest rock bands, who themselves were paying homage to American heroes like Muddy Waters, Elmore James, and Chuck Berry. Initially formed by Peter Hartman (bass) and Roger Briggs (guitar) as a duo, American Blues Exchange quickly morphed into a band with the additions of classmates Roy Dudley (vocals, harmonica) and Dale Reed (drums) and they began playing together at area coffeehouses, clubs, and frat parties. Dan Mixter (guitar, vocals) joined in the fall of the year, completing the lineup that would remain together for the next two-and-a-half years. American Blues Exchange played mostly on weekends, due to its members' school commitments, and for the most part were limited to the Connecticut/western Massachusetts region. Dudley developed into the band's strongest original writer, and his songs gradually began to be incorporated into the band's live shows. By 1969, there were enough original songs to record an album, and the band entered the studio to make *Blueprints*, pressed in a run of a thousand LPs, about half of which actually sold. *—Stanton Swihart*

● **Blueprints** / 1969 / Gear Fab ✦✦✦
Blueprints is a sort of second- or third-generation go at the blues. American Blues Exchange, it seems, were influenced more by the British blues-based bands and American rock bands of the San Francisco acid-rock variety, which were spinning blues changes in completely new, non-blues directions, than by straight blues itself. More than competent players, the band had a burning dual-guitar attack in Roger Briggs and Dan Mixter, and when used as the foundation of the songs such as "Ode to the Lost Legs of John Bean" and the fabulous blues rave-ups that explode in the middle of "On Solitude" and "The Taker," American Blues Exchange create excellent, tension-filled rock full of an intensity that doesn't have to stand in comparison to the blues because it is removed from the genre. "Burlington Letter," too, is a beautiful ballad that draws from the San Francisco sound of the times, though it would have greatly benefitted from distinct vocal personalities on the order of a Grace Slick or Marty Balin. Roy Dudley's voice is the weakest component of the band's studio cuts and occasionally causes the music to drag. As it is, "Burlington Letter" is full of dynamic atmospherics, but they never completely take off into the ether. Still, it shows a band that could certainly play. The rhythm section is perfectly capable of holding down a groove (the Canned Heat facsimile, "Recorder Thing") or whipping into a frenzy beneath the guitars. There is plenty to listen to on *Blueprints*, but when American Blues Exchange tries to play it straight, the album falters. The Gear Fab reissue adds three additional blues covers that show the band can indeed be impressive—much stronger than on the studio cuts—including a raw vocal by Dudley on "One Sunny Day" that destroys all his studio vocals. On the evidence of those live cuts, *Blueprints* is perhaps not entirely indicative of the band's prowess and that lessens its musical value. *—Stanton Swihart*

Albert Ammons

b. Sep. 23, 1907, Chicago, IL, **d.** Dec. 2, 1949, Chicago, IL

Piano / Swing, Boogie-Woogie, Piano Blues

Albert Ammons was one of the big three of late-'30s boogie-woogie, along with Pete Johnson and Meade "Lux" Lewis. Arguably the most powerful of the three, Ammons was also flexible enough to play swing music. Ammons played in Chicago clubs from the '20s on, although he also worked as a cab driver for a time. Starting in 1934, he led his own band in Chicago, and he made his first records in 1936. In 1938, Ammons appeared at Carnegie Hall with Pete Johnson and Meade "Lux" Lewis, an event that really helped launch the boogie-woogie craze. Ammons recorded with the other pianists in duets and trios, fit right in with the Port of Harlem Jazzmen on their Blue Note session, appeared regularly at Cafe Society, recorded as a sideman with Sippie Wallace in the '40s, and he even cut a session with his son, the great tenorman Gene Ammons. Albert Ammons worked steadily throughout the '40s, playing at President Harry Truman's inauguration in 1949; he died later that year. Many of his recordings are currently available on CD. *—Scott Yanow*

☆ **Complete Blue Note Recordings of Albert Ammons and Meade Lux Lewis** / Nov. 21, 1935-Apr. 22, 1944 / Mosaic ✦✦✦✦✦
This magnificent three-LP box set was issued as part of the first release by the Mosaic label. The out of print collection has all of the music recorded during Blue Note's first session (nine piano solos by Albert Ammons, eight including a five-part "The Blues" by Meade "Lux" Lewis, and a pair of Ammons-Lewis duets) plus Lewis' 1935 version of "Honky Tonk Train Blues" and his complete sessions of October 4, 1940, April 9, 1941 (four songs on harpsichord), and August 22, 1944. The music emphasizes boogie-woogie and both Ammons (quite memorable on "Boogie Woogie Stomp") and Lewis are heard in prime form. Incidentally, one of their duets (which is mistakenly titled "The Sheik of Araby") is actually "Nagasaki." This box is well worth bidding on at an auction. *—Scott Yanow*

Blues & Boogie Woogie King: 1936–1947 / Feb. 13, 1936-Aug. 6, 1947 / EPM Musique ✦✦✦✦
This fine import brings together some of Albert Ammons' best work. Cut during his prime years, the 20 tracks include two of the boogie-woogie master's classic piano solos, "Boogie Woogie Stomp" and the nicely gauged blues "Chicago in Mind." The band material is not quite as captivating, but still delivers enough in the way of quality to keep things on the right track. In addition to his regular band, the Rhythm Kings, Ammons gets sympathetic support from tenor saxophonist Don Byas, trumpeter Hot Lips Page, trombonist Vic Dickenson, and his son and future tenor great, Gene Ammons. Big Joe Turner is also on hand to add a little Kansas City fire. A perfect entrée for Ammons newcomers. *—Stephen Cook*

1936–1939 / 1936-1939 / Classics ✦✦✦✦✦

Master of Boogie / 1936-1939 / Milan ✦✦
This is the type of CD that frustrates completists and veteran collectors; the 13 selections are taken from a variety of sessions and the recording dates that are given are often incorrect. The great boogie-woogie pianist Albert Ammons is heard on five of the nine piano solos he recorded at Blue Note's debut session in 1939 along with a solo number apiece that were cut for Columbia and Storyville. In addition Ammons plays "Two And Fews" in duet with Meade "Lux" Lewis (from the Blue Note date), leads a hot group on two of the four numbers from his relatively rare debut session (dating from 1936, not 1939 as it states on the back cover) and is heard at the famous Spirituals To Swing concert of 1938 backing blues singer-guitarist Big Bill Broonzy and jamming with Meade "Lux" Lewis and Pete Johnson on three pianos. Great music, inexcusably lousy packaging. *—Scott Yanow*

Boogie Woogie Stomp / 1938-1939 / Delmark ✦✦✦
The classic boogie-woogie performances of Albert Ammons, Meade "Lux" Lewis and Pete Johnson have never been put out completely and in chronological order, although some sessions have been reissued many times. This 1998 Delmark CD confuses the matter a bit because some of the live recordings that it includes formerly came out on Euphonic LPs, and some are unknown. The selections alternate between solo tracks by Ammons (nine), Lewis (six) and Johnson (two); there is also a lone piano duet ("Saturday Night") by Ammons and Lewis. Because the performances (recorded at the Hotel Sherman in 1939 and in an obscure studio session in 1938 that adds bassist Herbert Marshall) are not issued in chronological order, and since the music switches between the pianists, it can be a bit confusing trying to figure out who is playing when. Musically, the three pianists are quite consistent and since the music is taken from their prime period, it is easily recommended to boogie-woogie collectors despite one's reservations about the order of the performances. *—Scott Yanow*

● **The First Day** / Jan. 6, 1939 / Blue Note ✦✦✦✦✦
Producer Alfred Lion was very impressed when he attended John Hammond's *Spirituals to Swing* concert of Dec. 23, 1938, which had introduced boogie-woogie pianists Albert Ammons and Meade "Lux" Lewis to New York audiences. Two weeks later, he started the Blue Note label by recording nine Ammons solos, eight by Lewis, and a pair of heated duets during a single day. All of the music (except an untitled original by Meade "Lux" Lewis slated to be issued by Blue Note in the future) is on this single CD. Ammons, the more forceful (relatively speaking) of the two pianists, generally takes honors, but there are plenty of rewarding performances, including Lewis' five-part "The Blues," Ammons' "Boogie Woogie Stomp," and their duet on "Nagasaki." Highly recommended to collectors who do not already own Mosaic's more extensive three-LP limited-edition Ammons/Lewis set. *—Scott Yanow*

King of Boogie Woogie (1939–1949) / Jan. 6, 1939-Jan. 4, 1948 / Blues Classics ✦✦✦
Albert Ammons is featured on six piano solos from two sessions in 1939, leading a quartet in 1946 and jamming with his sextet during 1947-1948 on this LP sampler. His boogie-woogie music is consistently exciting in all the formats even if one regrets that these performances have been reissued in a somewhat hodge-podge fashion; the selections are drawn from the catalogs of Blue Note, Solo Art and Mercury. Highlights include "Boogie Woogie Stomp," "Boogie Woogie at the Civic Opera," "Baltimore Breakdown" and "Swanee River Boogie." *—Scott Yanow*

1939–1946 / Apr. 8, 1939-Jul. 2, 1946 / Classics ♦♦♦♦♦
This CD offers three distinct periods in the development of boogie-woogie pianist Albert Ammons. Kicking off with solo tracks recorded in 1939 and 1944 for the Solo-Art and Commodore labels, the next batch follows him into a small-band format with Hop Lips Page practically stealing the show in his demonstrative style. The final ten selections emanate from Chicago sessions for Mercury—again with a small group—featuring vocals from Sippie Wallace and Mildred Anderson. Ammons was a giant in his chosen field of endeavor, and these sides make a marvelous addition to his too-short discography. *—Cub Koda*

Boogie Woogie Trio, Vol. 2 / Sep. 17, 1939-Oct. 31, 1939 / Storyville ♦♦♦♦
The 23 selections on this generous CD feature boogie-woogie pianists Albert Ammons, Pete Johnson, and Meade "Lux" Lewis broadcasting from Chicago's Sherman Hotel in September and October of 1939. There are eight piano solos by Ammons, six from Johnson, and six by Lewis, plus a version of "Saturday Night Struggle" by the duo of Ammons and Lewis and two cuts with all three pianists. It is very good to have this music available again (along with two previously unreleased Lewis tracks), although one wonders why the music was shuffled around instead of having separate parts of the CD featuring individual pianists. All three players were in their prime in 1939 and quite enthusiastic about having finally been discovered. Easily recommended to boogie-woogie fans. *—Scott Yanow*

Boogie Woogie Trio, Vol. 1 / Apr. 10, 1944-Sep. 11, 1954 / Storyville ♦♦♦♦♦
In the late '30s, a boogie-woogie craze was launched, helped greatly by the exciting recordings and performances of pianists Albert Ammons, Pete Johnson, and Meade "Lux" Lewis, both as soloists and in various combinations. On the first of two CD volumes released by Storyville, there are ten exciting selections (five previously unreleased) from 1944 featuring the three pianists as a trio (including "Boogie Woogie Prayer," "Jumpin' the Boogie," "St. Louis Blues," and "Lady Be Good"), four solos by Pete Johnson from 1947 (including "Swanee River" and "Yancey Special"), and eight solos by Meade "Lux" Lewis that were broadcast from San Francisco's Hangover Club during 1953-1954. The recording quality is pretty decent and the playing by the three boogie-woogie masters is consistently heated and swinging. *—Scott Yanow*

1946–1948 / Nov. 12, 1946-1948 / Classics ♦♦♦

Kip Anderson

b. 193?, Anderson, SC
Vocals / Retro-Soul, Soul-Blues, R&B, Southern Soul
Without benefit of anything resembling a chart hit, Kip Anderson has amassed an impressive Southern soul legacy over the last three-plus decades. And how many other R&B artists were named after Rudyard Kipling, anyway?

Anderson still lives in the same rural region of South Carolina where he grew up. The singer learned his way around his folks' upright piano as a youth, composing his first tune in 1959. Anderson later bounced from label to label, cutting "I Will Cry" for producer Bobby Robinson in 1963; "That's When the Crying Begins" for ABC-Paramount the following year, and several gems for Checker in 1965-1966 (including one of his best-known numbers, "A Knife and a Fork," in Muscle Shoals under the supervision of Rick Hall and Gene "Daddy G" Barge). By 1969, Anderson was inked to Nashville-based Excello, where he waxed the impassioned deep soul gem "I Went Off and Cried."

Anderson's hearty vocal talents have popped up most recently on Ichiban Records. He's cut two albums for the Atlanta firm—*A Dog Don't Wear No Shoes* and *A Knife and a Fork*—and contributed the jolliest track of all, "Gonna Have a Merry Christmas," to the label's 1994 anthology *Ichiban Blues at Christmas Volume Three. —Bill Dahl*

● **A Dog Don't Wear No Shoes** / 1992 / Ichiban ♦♦♦♦
A Dog Don't Wear No Shoes is an energetic latter-day record from Kip Anderson that proves that the vocalist has lost very little of his power or charisma over the years. All of the music is in the deep soul tradition and he doesn't alter the formula much at all, but with a vocalist as gritty and impassioned as Anderson, that doesn't matter. *—Thom Owens*

A Knife & A Fork / 1993 / Ichiban ♦♦♦
A Knife & A Fork is nearly a carbon copy of its predecessor, *A Dog Don't Wear No Shoes*, but that's not necessarily a bad thing. Though the material is slightly weaker than the previous album, Kip Anderson makes the weakest songs somewhat convincing with his wonderful voice. *—Thom Owens*

Little Willie Anderson

b. May 21, 1920, West Memphis, AR, **d.** Jun. 20, 1991, Chicago, IL
Vocals, Harmonica / Modern Electric Chicago Blues, Electric Harmonica Blues, Electric Chicago Blues, Chicago Blues
Some folks called Chicago harpist Little Willie Anderson "Little Walter Jr.," so faithfully did Anderson's style follow that of the legendary harp wizard. But Anderson was already quite familiar with the rudiments of the harmonica before he ever hit the Windy City, having heard Sonny Boy Williamson, Robert Nighthawk, and Robert Jr. Lockwood around West Memphis.

Anderson came to Chicago in 1939, eventually turning pro as a sideman with Johnny Young. Anderson served as Walter's valet, chauffeur, and pal during the latter's heyday, but his slavish imitations probably doomed any recording possibilities for Anderson—until 1979, that is, when Blues On Blues label boss Bob Corritore escorted him into a Chicago studio and emerged with what amounts to Anderson's entire recorded legacy. *—Bill Dahl*

● **Swinging the Blues** / Jul. 1979 / Earwig ♦♦♦♦
Blues on Blues has been defunct for quite some time, but Earwig recently restored Anderson's only album to digital print. It's a loose, informal affair, Anderson's raw vocals and swinging harp backed by an all-star crew: guitarists Robert Jr. Lockwood, Sammy Lawhorn, and Jimmie Lee Robinson; bassist Willie Black, and drummer Fred Below. Anderson only revived one Walter standard, having brought a sheaf of his own intermittently derivative material to the session (although he does take a stab at bluesifying Lester Young's jazz classic "Lester Leaps In"). *—Bill Dahl*

Pink Anderson

b. Feb. 12, 1900, Spartanburg, SC, **d.** Oct. 12, 1974, Spartanburg, SC
Vocals, Guitar / Piedmont Blues, Country Blues, Acoustic Blues
A good-natured fingerpicking guitarist, Anderson played for about 30 years as part of a medicine show. He did make a couple of sides for Columbia in the late '20s with Simmie Dooley, but otherwise didn't record until a 1950 session, the results of which were issued on a Riverside LP that also included tracks by Gary Davis. Anderson went on to make some albums on his own after the blues revival commenced in the early '60s, establishing him as a minor but worthy exponent of the Piedmont school, versed in blues, ragtime, and folk songs. Anderson also became an unusual footnote in rock history when Syd Barrett, a young man in Cambridge, England, combined Pink's first name with the first name of another obscure bluesman (Floyd Council) to name his rock group, Pink Floyd, in the mid-'60s. *—Richie Unterberger*

Gospel, Blues and Street Songs / 1961 / Original Blues Classics ♦♦♦

● **Carolina Blues Man, Vol. 1** / Apr. 12, 1961 / Prestige/Bluesville ♦♦♦♦♦
A vast majority of the known professional recordings of Piedmont blues legend Pink Anderson were documented during 1961, the notable exception being the platter he split with Rev. Gary Davis—*Gospel, Blues and Street Songs*—which was documented in the spring of 1950. This is the first of three volumes that were cut for the Prestige Records subsidiary Bluesville. *Carolina Blues Man* finds Anderson performing solo—with his own acoustic guitar accompaniment—during a session cut on his home turf of Spartanburg, SC. Much—if not all—of the material Anderson plays has been filtered through and tempered by the unspoken blues edict of taking a familiar (read: traditional) standard and individualizing it enough to make it uniquely one's own creation. Anderson's approach is wholly inventive, as is the attention to detail in his vocal inflections, lyrical alterations, and, perhaps more importantly, Anderson's highly sophisticated implementation of tricky fretwork. His trademark style incorporates a combination of picking and strumming chords interchangeably. This nets Anderson an advanced, seemingly electronically enhanced sound. "Baby I'm Going Away"—with its walkin' blues rhythms—contains several notable examples of this technique, as does the introduction to "Every Day of the Week." The track also includes some of the most novel chord changes and progressions to be incorporated into the generally simple style of the street singer/minstrel tradition from which Pink Anderson participated in during the first half of the 20th century. Listeners can practically hear Anderson crack a smile as he weaves an arid humor with overtly sexual connotations into his storytelling—especially evident on "Try Some of That" and "Mama Where Did You Stay Last Night." Aficionados and most all students of the blues will inevitably consider this release an invaluable primer into the oft-overlooked southern East Coast Piedmont blues. *—Lindsay Planer*

Medicine Show Man, Vol. 2 / 1962 / Prestige ♦♦♦♦♦
Like Vols. 1 and 3 of the series of LPs Anderson did for Bluesville, this was recorded in 1961 (though it was recorded in New York City whereas the others were recorded in Spartanburg, SC). Vols. 1 and 3 were mostly traditional songs; this is *all* traditional songs in the public domain. It follows that if you liked Vols. 1 and 3, you'd probably like this too; if you want to choose just one, you're about as well off with any of the individual volumes. If you had to split hairs, it seems that Anderson sounds a bit more comfortable in the studio/recording setting on this one than on the others, and a tad less countrified and more urbane. The tone is cheerful and easygoing, like that of a well-loved man entertaining his neighbors. Which is not to say this is a throwaway; the phrasing and rhythms are crisp, and the ragtime-speckled folk/blues guitar accomplished. *—Richie Unterberger*

Ballad & Folksinger, Vol. 3 / 1963 / Prestige/Bluesville ♦♦♦♦
This release contains what is sadly the final volume in Bluesville's trilogy of long-players featuring the highly original Piedmont blues of Pink Anderson. As with the two previous discs, *Ballad & Folksinger* was recorded in 1961. It is also notable that Anderson returns to his native South Carolina to document this set. The second installment—*Medicine Show Man*—had been compiled from a New York City session held earlier the same year. Astute listeners will note that three of the titles—"The Titanic," "John Henry," and "The Wreck of the Old 97"—were duplicated from Anderson's side-long contribution to *Gospel, Blues and Street Songs*. The other side featured another Piedmont native, Rev. Gary Davis. However, Anderson's delivery is notably different when comparing the two performances. One of the primary discrepancies lies in the pacing. Here, the readings are more definite and seemingly less rushed. The same is true for the phrasing of Anderson's vocals, most notably on "John Henry." The intricate and somewhat advanced guitar-playing—that became one of Anderson's trademarks—is arguably more pronounced on these recordings as well. Again, "John Henry" displays the picking and strumming techniques that give his decidedly un-amplified vintage Martin acoustic guitar such a full resonance that it practically sounds electric. The instrumental introduction to "Betty and Dupree" exemplifies the walking blues or stride motif particularly evident and notable among Piedmont blues artists. Enthusiasts should also note that in addition to these latter recordings, Anderson also performed on four tracks with his mentor Simmie Dooley in the late '20s for Columbia Records. Those pieces can be found on the compilation *Georgia String Bands (1928-1930)*. Anderson actively toured until a debilitating stroke forced him to retire in 1964. *—Lindsay Planer*

Jake Andrews

Guitar, Vocals / Blues-Rock

Austin, TX, guitar phenom Jake Andrews began performing on the local club circuit while still a pre-teen, releasing his 1999 debut *Time to Burn* at age 19. *—Jason Ankeny*

• **Time to Burn** / May 11, 1999 / Jericho ♦♦♦

Like many Austin musicians, Jake Andrews is a child of the blues, but he's also the child of John "Toad" Andrews, who played with Mother Earth in the '60s. That gave him an edge in the cutthroat music business, but it's just as likely that the reason why he secured a record contract at the age of 19 was the fact that teenage blues prodigies were a hot commodity in the '90s. Ever since Jonny Lang and Kenny Wayne Shepherd, other labels were clamoring for their own hot shot, and Andrews was well-suited for the part, since he can play and has a weathered voice that sounds much older than 19. He also has a tendency to veer away from straight-ahead blues, favoring blues-rock, as well as the occasional soul song. Clearly, his biggest influence is fellow Texan Stevie Ray Vaughan, whose big, blustery guitar tone and throaty voice provides the template for Andrews' debut *Time to Burn*. While Andrews isn't nearly as developed or as skilled at emulation as SRV was on his debut, he is considerably younger and his technical acumen is something to behold. However, *Time to Burn* suffers from the same problem that plagues albums from young bluesmen—it's impressive on the surface and even quite enjoyable, but it's not particularly nuanced or deep. Depending on your view, that may be a minor thing, since Andrews keeps it rawer than Lang and he already shows signs of branching past SRV-styled blues-rock and developing his own style. It may be a fairly conventional '90s blues-rock album on the surface, but *Time to Burn* nevertheless does announce the arrival of a guitarist that has the potential to become one of the leading lights of Texas blues-rock, once he matures a bit. *—Stephen Thomas Erlewine*

Jake Andrews / Feb. 19, 2002 / Emusic ♦♦♦

One listen to "Better Start Now" or "Matters of the Heart" will be enough to convince anyone that young axeman Jake Andrews owes a debt to the late Stevie Ray Vaughan. However, he's definitely not cut completely from the same Texas cloth—Andrews' music doesn't have the same swing, and on tracks like "They'll Never Know" it's apparent that his tastes run outside the blues, too, to something a little heavier. He also loves his riffs—not to mention the careful neo-'50s retro styling of his clothes. That he can play guitar is beyond question, and music's always going to have room for another good guitar slinger. His problem, at least for now, is that he's yet to really develop any individuality. His compositions here are pretty anonymous, and sometimes ponderous, such as the lengthy "In Your Sunshine," which comes across like a not particularly good Free outtake. His voice, too, could almost be anyone, although you sense he'd love to be Paul Rodgers. Just listen to "Prince of This World" and the influence of that band and singer are crystal clear; however, Andrews hasn't managed their use of space and dynamics. And while the song should always be thing, by focusing more on the song than his fretwork, Andrews isn't playing to his strengths. Even the boogie of "2 Dirty Dogs," which Vaughan would have sent to the stratosphere, never properly ignites—although you suspect it could be a killer live. There's plenty of time for improvement, though—Andrews is still young, and the blues lasts a lifetime. *—Chris Nickson*

The Animals

f. 1964, Newcastle upon Tyne, England, **db.** 1968

Group / British Blues, Psychedelic, British Invasion, Blues-Rock, Rock & Roll

One of the most important bands originating from England's R&B scene during the early '60s, the Animals were second only to the Rolling Stones in influence among R&B-based bands in the first wave of the British Invasion. The Animals had their origins in a Newcastle-based group called the Kansas City Five, whose membership included pianist Alan Price, drummer John Steel, and vocalist Eric Burdon. Price exited to join the Kontours in 1962, while Burdon went off to London. The Kontours, whose membership included Bryan "Chas" Chandler, eventually were transmuted into the Alan Price R&B Combo, with John Steel joining on drums. Burdon's return to Newcastle in early 1963 heralded his return to the lineup. The final member of the combo, guitarist Hilton Valentine, joined just in time for the recording of a self-produced EP under the band's new name, the Animals. That record alerted Graham Bond to the Animals; he was likely responsible for pointing impresario Giorgio Gomelsky to the group.

Gomelsky booked the band into his Crawdaddy Club in London, and they were subsequently signed by Mickie Most, an independent producer who secured a contract with EMI's Columbia imprint. A studio session in February 1964 yielded their Columbia debut single, "Baby Let Me Take You Home" (adapted from "Baby Let Me Follow You Down"), which rose to number 21 on the British charts. For years, it was rumored incorrectly that the Animals got their next single, "House of the Rising Sun," from Bob Dylan's first album, but it has been revealed that, like "Baby Let Me Take You Home," the song came to them courtesy of Josh White. In any event, the song—given a new guitar riff by Valentine and a soulful organ accompaniment devised by Price—shot to the top of the U.K. and U.S. charts early that summer. This success led to a follow-up session that summer, yielding their first long-playing record, *The Animals*. Their third single, "I'm Crying," rose to number eight on the British charts. The group compiled an enviable record of Top Ten successes, including "Don't Let Me Be Misunderstood" and "We've Gotta Get Out of This Place," along with a second album, *Animal Tracks*.

In May of 1965, immediately after recording "We've Gotta Get Out of This Place," Alan Price left the band, citing fear of flying as the reason; subsequent biographies of the band have indicated that the reasons were less psychological. When "House of the Rising Sun" was recorded, using what was essentially a group arrangement, the management persuaded the band to put one person's name down as arranger. Price came up the lucky one, supposedly with the intention that the money from the arranger credit would be divided later on. The money was never divided, however, and as soon as it began rolling in, Price suddenly developed his fear of flying and exited the band. Others cite the increasing contentiousness between Burdon and Price over leadership of the group as the latter's reason for leaving. In any case, a replacement was recruited in the person of Dave Rowberry.

In the meantime, the group was growing increasingly unhappy with the material they were being given to record by manager Mickie Most. Not only were the majority of these songs much too commercial for their taste, but they represented a false image of the band, even if many were successful. "It's My Life," a number seven British hit and a similar smash in America, caused the Animals to terminate their association with Most and with EMI Records. They moved over to Decca/London Records and came up with a more forceful, powerful sound on their first album for the new label, *Animalisms*. The lineup shifts continued, however: Steel exited in 1966, after recording *Animalisms*, and was replaced by Barry Jenkins, formerly of the Nashville Teens. Chandler left in mid-1966 after recording "Don't Bring Me Down" and Valentine remained until the end of 1966, but essentially "Don't Bring Me Down" marked the end of the original Animals.

Burdon re-formed the group under the aegis of Eric Burdon and the New Animals, with Jenkins on drums, John Weider on guitar and violin, Danny McCulloch on bass, and Vic Briggs on guitar. He remained officially a solo act for a time, releasing a collection of material called *Eric Is Here* in 1967. As soon as the contract with English Decca was up, Burdon signed with MGM directly for worldwide distribution, and the new lineup made their debut in mid-1967. Eric Burdon and the New Animals embraced psychedelica to the hilt amid the full bloom of the Summer of Love. By the end of 1968, Briggs and McCulloch were gone, to be replaced by Burdon's old friend, keyboard player/vocalist Zoot Money, and his longtime stablemate, guitarist Andy Summers, while Weider switched to bass. Finally, in 1969, Burdon pulled the plug on what was left of the Animals. He hooked up with a Los Angeles-based group called War, and started a subsequent solo career.

The original Animals reunited in 1976 for a superb album called *Before We Were So Rudely Interrupted*, which picked up right where *Animalisms* had left off a decade earlier and which was well-received critically but failed to capture the public's attention. In 1983, a somewhat longer-lasting reunion came about between the original members, augmented with the presence of Zoot Money on keyboards. The resulting album, *Ark*, consisting of entirely new material, was well received by critics and charted surprisingly high, and a world tour followed. By the end of the year and the heavy touring schedule, however, it was clear that this reunion was not going to be a lasting event. The quintet split up again, having finally let the other shoe drop on their careers and history, and walked away with some financial rewards, along with memories of two generations of rock fans cheering their every note. *—Bruce Eder*

The Animals [US] / 1964 / MGM ♦♦♦

Early blues-oriented material rounded out by a few more commercial tracks—this album is stronger than the British version, as it includes several more tracks off of their singles. *—Bruce Eder*

The Animals [UK] / 1964 / Columbia ♦♦♦

The group's U.K. debut long-player, containing—in the custom of the time in England—not one of their singles up to that point, including "House of the Rising Sun." Apart from "Story of Bo Diddley" (which is, itself, heavily steeped in conventions out of Bo Diddley's repertory), everything here is a cover of traditional blues and R&B material, and a bit on the dry side, as though the band was trying too hard to prove themselves. This is one of the more serious and dour British Invasion-era albums, with none of the cheerfulness evident on the work of the Liverpool, Birmingham, or Manchester-based bands of the period—the Chuck Berry covers, in particular, seem rather joyless compared to rival versions by the Rolling Stones, et al. For adult orientation, *The Animals* is roughly on a par with the Rolling Stones' debut LP (though that album is also more fun). The group would do better in the future in a less stiff and intense posture, but this is a strong debut. In 1998, *The Animals* was reissued in remastered form as part of EMI's 100th Anniversary series, and all of its tracks also appear on EMI's *Complete Animals* double-CD set as well. *—Bruce Eder*

The Animals on Tour / 1965 / MGM ♦♦♦

Pay no attention to the title "on tour"—this isn't a live album (MGM records loved to use that phrase, incorporating it onto a Herman's Hermits album of the same era). This is actually the American version of the British *Animal Tracks* LP, released two months earlier than the U.K. version and with "Boom Boom," "I'm Crying," "Dimples," and "She Said Yeah" replacing "Roberta," "For Miss Caulker," and "Mess Around." The latter is no loss, but the other two deserved to be heard—otherwise, the essentials of the better album are here and the replacement tracks are enjoyable, to be sure. *—Bruce Eder*

Animal Tracks / 1965 / Columbia ♦♦♦

The band's second British album, recorded just before Alan Price exited the lineup, displays far more energy and confidence than its predecessor, and it's fascinating to speculate where they might've gone from here had the original lineup held together. There are a few lightweight tunes here, such as "Let the Good Times Roll" and the rollicking opener, "Mess Around," that capture the Animals loosening up and having fun, but much of *Animal Tracks"* is pretty intense R&B-based rock. "How You've Changed" is a reflective, downbeat Chuck Berry number that Eric Burdon turns into a dark romantic confessional/inquisition, matched by Hilton Valentine's chopped out, crunchy lead work over the break, while Alan Price does his best to impersonate Johnnie Johnson. The group doesn't do as well with their cover of Billy Boy Arnold's "I Ain't Got You" as the Yardbirds did with the same number, treating it in a little too upbeat a fashion, and Hilton Valentine and Alan Price failing to add very much that's interesting to the break (especially in comparison to Eric Clapton's solo on the Yardbirds' version). "Roberta," by contrast, is a great rock & roll number, and their version of "Bright Lights, Big City," sparked by Burdon's surging, angry performance and Price's hard-driving organ solo. Price's playing opens what is easily the best blues cut on the album, "Worried Life Blues," where Hilton Valentine steps out in front for his most prominent guitar solo in the early history of the band, backed by Price's surging organ. Burdon and company also excell on a pair of Ray

Charles covers, turning in a jauntily cheerful, euphoric performance of "Hallelujah I Love Her So," his jubilation matched by Price's ebullient organ work; and a slow, pain-racked performance by Burdon and company on the slow blues "I Believe To My Soul," arguably—along with "Worried Life Blues"—the singer's best performance on either of the group's EMI long-players, and matched by Price's quick-fingered yet equally ominous piano playing. *—Bruce Eder*

In the Beginning / 1965 / Sundazed ♦♦♦
Recorded in December of 1963 at a live concert, this CD captures the Animals at their rawest and most animated on record, ripping ferociously through a bunch of standards (by Chuck Berry, James B. Odom, et al.), playing the crowd and making snide comments about their London rivals the Rolling Stones, all with Sonny Boy Williamson II hanging somewhere around the stage. Sundazed has actually found the original master to this oft-bootlegged piece of rock/blues history. *—Bruce Eder*

Animalism / 1966 / MGM ♦♦♦♦♦
If the Animals had never recorded another album except for *Animalism*, their musical reputation would have been assured—none of the participants had ever participated on, or would ever work on, a better long-player. The irony was that *Animalism* (not to be confused with the group's earlier, British-issued *Animalisms*, or its American counterpart, *Animalization*) was only ever issued in America, and came out after the group had ceased to exist, and, thus, was scarcely noticed by anybody (which made it a choice occupant of cut-out bins for decades). Recorded mostly during the spring and summer of 1966 by the lineup of Eric Burdon, Hilton Valentine, Chas Chandler, Dave Rowberry, and Barry Jenkins, *Animalism* proved to be a glorious musical high point, as well as an end point for the band. Even as they were playing out their string, all of the members had begun growing in their musicianship, with guitarist Hilton Valentine taking on a much bolder, bluesier voice on his instrument and keyboardist Dave Rowberry developing a sound as distinctive as that of his predecessor Alan Price. Part of *Animalism* was cut in Los Angeles under the aegis of Frank Zappa, who arranged (and probably played on) the opening number, "All Night Long," a surging traditional blues song, and who also worked on the album's ominous rendition of "The Other Side of This Life." Sam Cooke's "Shake" is treated to a restrained Burdon vocal and superb musical acrobatics by Valentine and Rowberry, while B.B. King's "Rock Me Baby" becomes the vehicle for a virtuoso workout by Valentine, and a thunderous performance by Chandler and Jenkins. "Smokestack Lightning" is the most successful cover the group ever did of a Chicago blues number (unless you count their version of Donovan's "Hey Gyp," which is also here in all of its Bo Diddley-inspired glory), and "Hit the Road, Jack" represents the best work that Burdon ever did with a Ray Charles number. The vinyl is worth hunting down, and the fact that Polygram has never re-released *Animalism* is astonishing. *—Bruce Eder*

Animalisms / Jun. 1966 / Decca ♦♦♦♦
During their first two years of recording, the Animals had never quite succeeded when it came to recording LPs—good as some of the songs on their first two albums, done for EMI, had been, there was this sense that single were what this band was really about. Then, newly signed to English Decca, they delivered *Animalisms*, a truly transcendent collection of a dozen songs, mostly superb covers interspersed with some good originals, principally by Eric Burdon and Dave Rowberry. Burdon was never singing better and the group had developed a bold, tight sound that seemed to lift his soul shouting to ever higher levels of passion and conviction. "Outcast," "Maudie," "You're on My Mind," "Clapping," "That's All I Am to You," "Squeeze Her—Tease Her," "I Put a Spell on You," "She'll Return It," and "Gin House Blues" all rate among the best work the band ever did, passionate, gorgeous, and exciting R&B down to the last note, with Burdon at the peak of his career; and "Sweet Little Sixteen," though a relatively minor song here, was their best Chuck Berry cover to date, highlighted by Rowberry's flashy piano (doing some Jerry Lee Lewis arpeggios) and Hilton Valentine's boldest guitar work yet, combining the lead and rhythm parts in a hard chopping, twanging virtuoso performance. Ironically, the *Animalisms* album (which was issued in America two months later in somewhat altered form, as *Animalization*) appeared just as the group was about to enter its final phase of existence—they'd switched drummers from John Steel to Barry Jenkins during the period in which these tracks were recorded, and Burdon would soon decide to dissolve the lineup. *—Bruce Eder*

Animalization / 1966 / Polydor ♦♦♦♦
The U.S. version of the British *Animalisms* album removed the loose jam "Clapping," and the superb "Squeeze Her—Tease Her" and "That's All I Am to You" are removed in favor of the hits "Don't Bring Me Down," "See See Rider," and "Inside—Looking Out"—it's still a great record, if not as cohesive as the U.K. version, and was the last original Animals LP to attract many buyers in the U.S. The song content of both versions has been assembled on Repertoire's 2000 release of *Animalisms*. *—Bruce Eder*

Eric Is Here / Mar. 1967 / One Way ♦♦
During the months after Eric Burdon and the remaining members of the original Animals split, the singer cut this album backed by an orchestra and doing songs by Randy Newman, Barry Mann and Cynthia Weil, and other pop-music fixtures—quite a turnaround for the blues purist Burdon, and also very effective as mainstream pop music, including the U.S. hit "Help Me Girl." To add to the general confusion surrounding this material, some of it seems to have been recorded with the original Animals, or at sessions conducted while they were still together. Several songs, including "Help Me Girl," show up on Sequel Records' *Inside Looking Out*. *—Bruce Eder*

Winds of Change / Sep. 1967 / One Way ♦♦♦
This album marked the debut of Eric Burdon and the New Animals, a decidedly looser, more psychedelic outfit than any the blues-singing idol had previously been associated with. "San Franciscan Nights," "Paint It Black," and "Yes I'm Experienced" (Burdon's answer to Jimi Hendrix's "Are You Experienced?") were moody and pulsating, and also fiercely experimental—one can get a glimpse of this band at work in the D.A. Pennebaker movie *Monterey Pop*, doing "Paint It Black" on stage. It was a logical extension of the later work of the original Animals into the Summer of Love. *—Bruce Eder*

The Twain Shall Meet / Mar. 1968 / One Way ♦♦♦
The Twain Shall Meet was a more lopsidedly experimental album—even its major hit, "Sky Pilot," a venture into anti-war politicking on an epic level, marked a new level of sophistication for the band, which played hard and became well-known for their ability to jam on stage. *—Bruce Eder*

Every One of Us / Jul. 1968 / One Way ♦♦
A rather spare and disappointing album, recorded amid the splintering of the original New Animals. Keyboard player Zoot Money arrived to fill up the lineup even as guitarist Vic Briggs and bassist Danny McCulloch prepared to leave. *—Bruce Eder*

Love Is / Dec. 1968 / One Way ♦♦
One can get an idea of the confusion that fans must have felt by virtue of the fact that *Love Is* was the third album by Eric Burdon and the Animals to be issued in 1968, even with a major lineup change taking place. Future Police-man Andy Somers, aka Summers, arrived on guitar to join his longtime stablemate Zoot Money, while John Weider moved over to bass. This album marked the end of the Animals as a continually operating music unit, and betrays an understandable lack of direction and enthusiasm. *—Bruce Eder*

The Best of Eric Burdon & the Animals, Vol. 2 / 1969 / MGM ♦♦♦
Actually the third Animals hits LP to be released by MGM in the '60s, this collection is the work of lead singer Eric Burdon with the backup group he assembled upon the breakup of the original Animals. The recordings all come from 1967 and 1968, Burdon's psychedelicized period, when he was penning praises of the Monterey Pop Festival ("Monterey," number 15) and San Francisco ("San Franciscan Nights," number nine). The only other Top 40 hit on the album was the antiwar epic "Sky Pilot" (number 15), in its full seven-and-a-half-minute glory. Burdon had come a long way from his Manchester roots and his blues records, and this was the last album in his second phase; in fact, the New Animals had split by the time it was released. *—William Ruhlmann*

Before We Were So Rudely Interrupted / 1976 / Repertoire ♦♦♦♦
Cut 11 years after the Animals' original lineup recorded their last LP and six years before their more well-remembered reunion tour, this oft-overlooked album is just short of a lost classic; it lacks the intensity of their 1983 studio effort, *Ark*, but it is more substantial musically than that album and fits in very neatly with their preceding work, as though they'd scarcely skipped a beat. Recorded under the auspices of the late Chas Chandler's Barn Productions, the album was highlighted by a dramatically bluesy rendition of "It's All Over Now, Baby Blue," boasting superb playing by Alan Price. Hilton Valentine's soaring guitar pyrotechnics light up "Fire on the Sun," perhaps the flashiest performance of his career for this most introspective of '60s British blues axemen, and "As the Crow Flies" has the group returning to its roots, as a dark, brooding rendition of the Jimmy Reed song that gives room for Chandler, Valentine, Price, and John Steel to show off their '60s-era blues chops in a more expansive form. After a promising start, the gospel number "Many Rivers to Cross" falls apart a bit, but "Just a Little Bit," with its rippling organ break, the group's original "Riverside County," and the pounding finale, "The Fool," make the rest of side two eminently enjoyable, although, coming out in the midst of the punk and disco booms, the LP never had a chance to be heard by more than the most dedicated fans. The album was remastered and reissued on CD in the spring of 2000 by Repertoire Records. *—Bruce Eder*

Ark / 1983 / Castle ♦♦
The group's formal reunion, complete with a new repertory and a well-financed recording. The album has its dark, moody moments, and sometimes bogs down in the sheer heaviness of the sound and sensibilities, but where Burdon is on target as a singer, which is 70 percent of the time, the group sounds amazingly good. *—Bruce Eder*

Rip It to Shreds: Their Greatest Hits Live / Aug. 20, 1984 / IRS ♦♦
A document of the group's 1983 reunion tour. They played better shows along this tour than the one they actually taped—some of the balances (especially on the guitars) are a little off, and the band's sound and overall performance are somewhat creaky and anemic at times, but it is a fair representation of a largely successful attempt at recapturing past glories. *—Bruce Eder*

★ **The Best of the Animals** / 1988 / ABKCO ♦♦♦♦♦
The original Animals' American hits, including "House of the Rising Sun," "Don't Let Me Be Misunderstood," "It's My Life," and "We Gotta Get Out of This Place," in a compilation originally released in 1965. The lineup of songs is strong, but the sound is indifferent—the British *Complete Animals* covers the same territory and a lot more to much greater effect, at only twice the cost with three times the music and infinitely superior sound and notes. *—Bruce Eder*

The EP Collection / 1989 / See for Miles ♦♦♦♦♦
This 20-track CD, running just under an hour, is a good bargain. The real value behind these *See for Miles* EP collections is that, particularly where British invasion bands are concerned, they allow the listener to truly track the group's progress and the real advancement of their sound. The Animals, in their years on EMI, only released two LPs but got out five EPs in the same period. This is prime material, a good balance between the group's blues and R&B influences on the one hand and producer Mickie Most's more pop-oriented leanings, and it shows just how powerful this band was, whatever kind of music they chose to play. Their key hits represented here, including "House of the Rising Sun," "Baby Let Me Take You Home," "Don't Let Me Be Misunderstood," and "We've Gotta Get Out of This Place," surrounded by very strong tracks which show the members gaining confidence and extending themselves musically, month by month. The only drawback for the more casual listener is the focus of the collection, which is limited to the band's

stay on EMI, which lasted barely two years, if that, so later hits like "It's My Life" are not present. Everything here does appear on the label's *Complete Animals* double-CD set, but that's where the 1999 reissue of this disc is important—*The EP Collection* offers state of the art digital sound, better than that on EMI's late-'80s set, and it also easily runs circles around ABKCO Records' *Best of the Animals*. The instruments all have startling presence, and Eric Burdon's voice practically booms out on "We've Gotta Get Out of This Place." The notes are very informative as well, explaining how the formative Animals managed to cross paths with (and later diverge paths from) producer Mickie Most. *—Bruce Eder*

Inside Looking Out: The 1965–1966 Sessions / 1990 / Sequel ♦♦♦♦♦

Together with the double-CD *The Complete Animals, Inside Looking Out* forms a complete retrospective of the great British Invasion band. This 22-song compilation features all of the essential recordings cut by the group in 1965 and 1966 after they broke with their original producer Mickie Most, and before Eric Burdon dissolved the core of the original lineup to pursue solo stardom with an Animals group featuring entirely different musicians. These tracks were perhaps more soul-oriented than their previous recordings, but the group still burns on the hits "Inside Looking Out" and "Don't Bring Me Down." Despite the absence of original keyboardist Alan Price, the group continued to showcase Burdon's passionate vocals and burning, vibrant organ (by Price's replacement Dave Rowberry) on both renowned and obscure R&B tunes, with an occasional original thrown in. Besides the entirety of their final British LP *Animalisms* (from 1966) and the above-mentioned singles, the CD includes the hits "Help Me Girl" and "See See Rider" (credited to "Eric Burdon and the Animals," these were possibly Burdon solo records). The four tracks from their first release, an independently released 1963 EP featuring primitive R&B standards, are small but noteworthy bonus cuts that close this collection. [Re-released in 2000 by Repertoire Records as *Animalisms* with four extra stereo-mixed tracks]. *—Richie Unterberger*

Roadrunners! / 1990 / Raven ♦♦♦

A 19-track collection of otherwise unavailable live performances from 1966-1968, taken from shows in Melbourne, Stockholm, London, and the 1967 Monterey Pop Festival, as well as radio and television broadcasts. Most of this dates from the psychedelic version of the band, which will disappoint those who are primarily interested in the group's rock/R&B prime. It's quite a good relic, though, with rough and ready execution by both Burdon and the band, and some unusual R&B and psychedelic material alongside the versions of hits like "Inside Looking Out," "Monterey," "San Franciscan Nights," and "When I Was Young." Sound ranges from fair to very good. *—Richie Unterberger*

☆ **The Complete Animals** / Jul. 1990 / EMI ♦♦♦♦♦

The title is a bit of a misnomer; this double CD does include the complete sessions that the Animals recorded with producer Mickie Most in 1964 and 1965. The 40 songs capture the band at their peak, including most of their best and biggest hits: "House of the Rising Sun," "Don't Let Me Be Misunderstood," "Bring It on Home to Me," "We Gotta Get Out of This Place," "I'm Crying," "It's My Life," and "Boom Boom." Most of the rest of the tunes don't match the excellence of these smashes, though they're solid. The great majority of them are covers of vintage R&B/rock tunes by Chuck Berry, Fats Domino, and the like, which aren't quite as durable as reinterpretations from the same era by the Stones and Yardbirds. When they hit the mark, though, the Animals produced some great album tracks that have been mostly forgotten by time, such as "I'm Mad Again" (originally by John Lee Hooker), "Worried Life Blues," and "Bury My Body." After leaving Most, the group would maintain their peak for another year or so (this period is represented on the fine import collection *Inside Looking Out*) despite the departure of one of rock's all-time finest organists, Alan Price. This compilation has everything that Price recorded with the group, including four previously unreleased cuts and the non-LP Eric Burdon original on the B-side of "It's My Life," "I'm Gonna Change the World." *—Richie Unterberger*

The Best of Eric Burdon & the Animals, 1966–1968 / 1991 / Polydor ♦♦♦

Despite its being credited to Eric Burdon & the Animals, this hour-long compilation may prove to be of equal interest to serious fans of the original Animals (i.e., the quintet that recorded "House of the Rising Sun," "It's My Life," etc.). The first four cuts, at least—"Don't Bring Me Down," "See See Rider," "Inside Looking Out," and "Hey Gyp"—were done by the classic second lineup, featuring Burdon and original members Hilton Valentine, Chas Chandler, and John Steel, along with Dave Rowberry on keyboards, and those tracks all sprang from the original Animals' R&B roots. They also happen to be first-rate recordings and, indeed, are superior to many of the tracks off of the original band's first two LPs. As for the rest, overlooking "Help Me Girl"—an Eric Burdon solo release on which it isn't clear who played, other than drummer Barry Jenkins—it's all the work of Eric Burdon & the Animals, the psychedelic outfit that Burdon and his management assembled in 1966 around Jenkins; and John Weider on guitar, bass, violin, and keyboards; Vic Briggs on guitar, vibes, keyboards, and saxophone; and Danny McCulloch on bass, with Andy Summers showing up late in the day on "River Deep, Mountain High." Their material is surprisingly engaging, even if it isn't what anyone really wants to remember Burdon for—in contrast to the typical British psychedelic music of the period, which tended to sound very fey and elegant, the "new Animals" played a hard, ballsy kind of psychedelia that never lost sight of the rhythm (and, at its best, didn't stray too far from the blues) of their R&B roots. The sides represented here are played more than competently and show occasional inspiration in the writing, arrangements, and performance. Though their sound is more of an acquired taste than that of the original Animals, they were a talented band, and perhaps if they could have pulled together one album that was as inspired as the singles "When I Was Young," "Monterey," or "Sky Pilot," they might have sustained some success. Instead, their albums tended toward the self-consciously heavy, spaced-out noodling that we hear on "Winds of Change," where Burdon sounds as though he's doing a burlesque of Jim Morrison. This disc lives up to its name, however, distilling down the best elements of the group's various facets, so you get their most accessible single sides and the best of the album noodling (the sitar and violin on "Winds of Change" are beautifully played, even if they don't go anywhere). The disc could have been extended to include cuts like "Shake" by the early transitional lineup, and "Paint It Black," which would have come close to making it definitive, but those did turn up later on Polygram Special Products' budget-priced best-of on the group. The sound is very good for a 1991 CD release, and the notes are reasonably thorough. *—Bruce Eder*

The Arc Angels

f. 1990, Texas

Group / Blues-Rock

Formed shortly after the death of Texas guitar hero Stevie Ray Vaughan, the Arc Angels may have been too good a story to be true. The quartet paired Vaughan's outstanding rhythm section of bassist Tommy Shannon and drummer Chris Layton with lead-singing guitarists and Texas Vaughan protégés Charlie Sexton and Doyle Bramhall II. Taking their name from the initials of the Austin Rehearsal Complex where they originally started jamming, the group released its self-titled debut album in 1992, with the thought that it would be the first of many. *Arc Angels* came closer than any other album at the time to carrying on Vaughan's incredible torch of blues, rock, and post-Jimi Hendrix guitar pyrotechnics. Tracks like "Living in a Dream," "Good Time," "Spanish Moon," and the Vaughan dedication "Sent by Angels," all bore the late guitar legend's influence, but without mimicry. For Shannon (who'd also worked previously with another Texas guitar-slinger in Johnny Winter) and Layton, the album was a catharsis after losing their friend and bandmate; for Sexton and Bramhall II it proved that two lead-singing lead guitarists could suppress their egos enough to function together. Trading vocal lines during verses recalled another Texas band, ZZ Top; former Faces keyboardist Ian McLagan added tasty work on piano and Hammond organ, and the Arc Angels seemed poised for the blues/rock summit as they toured in support of their debut until late 1993. But the perhaps inevitable competition between the throaty voiced Bramhall II and smooth-singing Sexton would eventually surface, and even more so during extending guitar solos of one-upmanship. Worse—especially for Shannon and Layton, who had seen Vaughan nearly kill himself before getting straight—was the increasing frequency of Bramhall II's substance abuse. By October of 1993, this ascending band decided to concentrate its efforts elsewhere, and separately. The exception was Shannon and Layton, who'd created such a stylistic rhythmic impact with Vaughan and worked so perfectly together that they were essentially a package deal. The two recorded through the '90s on Vaughan tribute projects and with another group that showed the late master's influence, Storyville, while Bramhall II went through treatment and Sexton continued on a solo career that had begun when he was a teenager in the mid-'80s. By 1998, a clean and sober Bramhall II started a band called the Mighty Zor, with Shannon and Layton as his rhythm section. When Sexton showed up for a few gigs to jam with the trio, a series of unofficial Arc Angels reunion gigs—mostly in Texas—was born. Whether a second CD will ever be recorded, or if the Arc Angels will remain one of those one-album comets like Hendrix's Band of Gypsys, remains to be seen. Shannon and Layton continue to get hired together in the new millennium, while both Bramhall II and Sexton release solo CDs and likewise get work as session men with major artists (former Pink Floyd leader Roger Waters and Bob Dylan, respectively). Regardless of whether it's followed up or not, *Arc Angels* provides lasting proof that the spirit of Vaughan lives on. *—Bill Meredith*

● **Arc Angels** / 1992 / Geffen ♦♦♦♦

There are one-hit wonders throughout the history of music, but very few one-album wonders like the Arc Angels. After the death of blues-rock guitar hero Stevie Ray Vaughan, fellow singing guitarists, Texans, and Vaughan devotees Doyle Bramhall II and Charlie Sexton formed the quartet with Vaughan's rhythm section of bassist Tommy Shannon and drummer Chris Layton. Their 1992 debut release would also be their swan song, but the self-titled album would prove to be one of the best rock/pop/blues recordings of the decade as well. The opening "Living in a Dream" is the only tune Sexton and Bramhall II co-composed, and is perhaps the closest that the Arc Angels come to re-creating Vaughan's signature sound. "Paradise Cafe" is one of a handful of tracks Sexton co-wrote with pop composer Tonio K., but he and Bramhall II engage in some ZZ Top-like call-and-response vocals, and Bramhall II's Vaughan dedication, "Sent by Angels," features some of the album's most impassioned singing. Funky tunes like "Sweet Nadine," "Good Time," and "Carry Me On" lighten the mood, and Shannon, Layton, and guest keyboardist Ian McLagan play brilliantly throughout in setting up the singing guitarists. The spirit of Vaughan permeates the recording, from the production of Little Steven to the liner notes ("Dedicated to our friend, Stevie Ray Vaughan. We miss you"), yet never sounds forced, purposeful, or contrived. Alas, the final two songs—the rocking "Shape I'm In" and epic "Too Many Ways to Fall"—sport titles that point toward the Arc Angels being a Vaughan-like comet rather than a future veteran group. Sexton's solo recording career had started as a teenager; Bramhall II and his father Doyle Bramhall were friends of Vaughan's (the elder Bramhall even composing and co-composing tunes with the guitar giant). But the two frontmen who complemented each other so well nonetheless couldn't blend their egos as easily. *Arc Angels* stands as testimony that a band needn't have a long career to have a lasting legacy. *—Bill Meredith*

Fernest Arceneaux

b. Aug. 27, 1940, Lafayette, LA

Accordion, Vocals, Arranger / Zydeco

A torch-bearer for the classic zydeco traditions personified by Clifton Chenier, Fernest Arceneaux earned the title "The New Prince of Accordion" for his virtuosic prowess. Born August 27, 1940 to a large sharecropping family based in Lafayette, Louisiana, he first picked up his brother-in-law's accordion while working the fields as a child, and learned his craft by copying his father, himself a rural musician whom the youngster often backed at local house parties. However, by the '60s, Arceneaux had abandoned his zydeco roots to play guitar in a rock & roll band, a group which originally featured two drummers and created such a mighty racket that they were dubbed Fernest and the Thunders. Only during the late '70s—and only at the behest of his hero Chenier himself—did Arceneaux return to the accordion, and soon the Thunders made the move from rock to zydeco. Discovered in 1978 by Belgian blues aficionado Robert Sacre, the group—also featuring singer/bassist Victor Walker, guitarist Chester Chevalier and drummer Clarence "Jockey" Etienne—mounted the first of many European tours, and within months they recorded their debut LP *Fernest and the Thunders*; albums like 1979's *Rockin' Pneumonia* and 1981 *Zydeco Stomp* followed, but shortly after recording the latter, Walker was killed in a barroom brawl. Arceneaux himself then assumed vocal duties, although as a result of asthma his presence failed to pack the same punch; still, the Thunders remained a popular live attraction, especially on the Gulf Coast crawfish circuit, and continued issuing LPs including 1985's *Zydeco Thunder*, 1987's *Gumbo Special* and 1994's *Zydeco Blues Party*. *Gumbo Special* was reissued in 2000. *—Jason Ankeny*

● **Zydeco Stomp** / 1981 / JSP ✦✦✦✦
Working with his longtime backing band the Thunders, Fernest Arceneaux turns in a wonderful zydeco blues collection with *Zydeco Stomp*. Arceneaux and the Thunders cut the album in London in 1981, playing a set of covers and originals that don't stray far from the zydeco-blues formula. That's hardly a bad thing, however, since the group packs musical muscle and bassist Victor Walker is a powerful vocalist—he's equally powerful on uptempo rockers and slow blues. Arceneaux isn't as strong vocally, but he's still enjoyable. More importantly, he packs quite a punch on the accordion, driving *Zydeco Stomp* into the realm of ecstatic party music with his propulsive style. *—Thom Owens*

Old School Zydeco / Nov. 7, 2000 / Mardi Gras ✦✦✦

Gumbo Special / Dec. 12, 2000 / Chrisly ✦✦✦

Tom Archia

b. Nov. 16, 1919, Groveton, TX, **d.** Jan. 16, 1977, Houston, TX
Sax (Tenor) / Hard Bop

Tom Archia is a Texas tenor man that has been somewhat overlooked under the shadow of giants such as Herschel Evans, Illinois Jacquet, Arnett Cobb, or Booker Ervin. He was born Ernest Alvin Archia, Jr. and was generally known as "Sonny." "Tom," however, was the only thing that sounded right in terms of a name for a professional musician, and for a while he was even billed as Texas Tom. He started music lessons on violin, demonstrating an aptitude for picking up melodies by ear that must have impressed his mother enough so that she went the price of a saxophone when asked to. By his teenage years, the family was living in Houston in the district called the Fifth Ward, with Illinois and Russell Jacquet living right down the street. In high school, Archia studied under one Percy McDavid, who later became the Supervisor of Music in the Los Angeles school system. McDavid taught an eclectic repertoire to his orchestra classes, including Duke Ellington compositions. Archia's bandmates included Richie Dell on piano, the Jacquet brothers and Arnett Cobb on tenor saxophone, and others—in other words, not the typical high school band. The high point for this group came in 1935 when Ellington himself visited the school to hear the orchestra.

Archia's college days added up to gaps between road tours. A band would come to town, and the eager tenor man would take off with it, only to have his father take off across Texas in order to track him down. He finally shipped out for good with Milt Larkin's band, a top Houston swing aggregation. In the reed section, Archia sat alongside Eddie "Cleanhead" Vinson, Jacquet, and Cobb. This band took on an epic run at Chicago's Rumboogie club, where big-shot bandleaders such as Lionel Hampton and Cootie Williams came in and began picking off sidemen to join their own groups until Larkin finally had no choice but to disband in 1943. In the meantime, Archia had become settled in Chicago, where he stayed put. He got his first recording opportunity with a Roy Eldridge octet shortly after the Larkin job was finished. Archia came out to Los Angeles in the mid-'40s, meeting up once again with the Jacquet brothers. Archia's first collaboration on the West Coast was in bebop trumpeter Howard McGhee's combo. Members of the McGhee band also recorded behind blues shouter Wynonie Harris for Philo. In 1946, Archia led a band behind singer Dinah Washington. He returned to Chicago in the late '40s and continued recording in several different lineups for labels such as Chess and Aristocrat, including his own sessions under the name of Tom Archia and His All Stars, which sometimes combined him with fellow tenor blaster Gene Ammons. He both toured and recorded with trumpeter Oran "Hot Lips" Page, including sessions backing up vocalists such as blues-great Lonnie Johnson and further work with Harris. His playing was more and more taken up with rhythm and blues gigs, yet he demonstrated plenty of jazz influence in his blowing, particularly that of Lester Young. In 1952, following a hiatus of several years, he returned to the studio to backup Dinah Washington in a group that also featured pianist Wynton Kelly and drummer Jimmy Cobb. He continued working with this vocalist for several years. Playing as the hornman in various Chicago organ trios began to be his scene in the late '50s, but he found it tougher to keep working in the '60s and by 1967, Archia was supposedly in dire straits. His sister brought him back to Houston to recuperate, and by the end of the decade, Archia was gigging all over town, even acquiring a new nickname, "the Devil." In 1973 he played in the Sonny Franklin Big Band, rejoining his old pal Arnett Cobb in the reed section. Tom Archia died in January 1977, at age 57, at Houston's St. Elizabeth Hospital. *—Eugene Chadbourne*

● **1947–1948** / Aug. 7, 2001 / Classics ✦✦✦✦

Archibald (Leon T. Gross)

b. Sep. 14, 1912, New Orleans, LA, **d.** Jan. 8, 1973, New Orleans, LA
Vocals, Piano / Piano Blues

When most people think of the song "Stagger Lee," as it's usually spelled, they think of Lloyd Price and his 1958 chart-topping single. Eight years before Price's version, however, a single on Imperial Records (spelled "Stack-a-Lee"), credited to and featuring the pounding piano of Archibald, reached the R&B Top Ten and gave the song its first unified national exposure in a single rendition. If Archibald never followed this up, it wasn't for lack of talent or a lot of years in the business of making music. He was born Leon T. Gross in New Orleans, LA, in 1912 and took up the piano as a child, initially entertaining at parties under the name "Archie Boy," which became Archibald. His major influences included Burnell Santiago, Tuts Washington, and Eileen Dufeau, among his barrelhouse piano predecessors. Gross enjoyed a healthy career into his late thirties, despite the interruption of military service during World War II, happily playing at the bars in New Orleans and earning a living and a lot of local respect.

In 1950, he was signed to Imperial Records, part of the same wave that brought Dave Bartholomew and Fats Domino onto the company's roster, and Archibald made his first recordings in March 1950. During the summer of that year, he enjoyed his only national hit with the single "Stack-a-Lee," produced by Dave Bartholomew. He never saw the national charts again with any of his sides, recording for Imperial until 1952, and his subsequent attempts at making records were undermined by poor health, union disputes, and record-company difficulties. Ironically, though Archibald's early-'50s sides, such as "Ballin' With Archie," "Shake Baby Shake," and "Crescent City Bounce"—all of which featured Bartholomew's brash trumpet playing, Joe Harris, and Clarence Hall, respectively, on alto and tenor sax, and as solid a rock & roll beat as anything on Imperial—could have found an audience as late as 1958, they were forgotten and mostly overlooked after their initial release; and despite the fact that his playing and sound were clearly an influence on the work of such figures as Huey "Piano" Smith and Dr. John, Archibald wasn't even on the periphery of the rock & roll boom and never participated in recording even as an elder statesman in the manner of his slightly younger contemporary Professor Longhair (who cut whole albums for Paul McCartney's MPL imprint and for Alligator in the '70s). Archibald never had a comeback, but he enjoyed long residences at such venues as the Poodle Patio Club, the Court of Two Sisters, and the Balloy Club. He died of a heart attack at the age of 60, mostly remembered by R&B scholars for his handful of sides for Imperial, and by his audience in New Orleans. *—Bruce Eder*

Alphonse "Bois Sec" Ardoin

b. Nov. 16, 1915, Duralde, LA
Accordion / Zydeco, Creole

Singer and accordionist Alphonse "Bois Sec" Ardoin was a crucial link to the musique Creole traditions of a bygone era—his music kept alive the Cajun "la la" music which developed in the African-American communities of his native southwestern Louisiana, and which was a clear antecedent of the contemporary zydeco sound. Born in rural Duralde, Ardoin was tagged with his nickname—translating as "Dry Wood"—because as a child he was always the first one in the fields to seek shelter during a rainstorm; born and raised as a sharecropper, farming remained the primary focus of his life even as an adult, often at the expense of his musical pursuits. He taught himself the accordion at the age of 12, inspired by the exploits of his older cousin, the famed Creole virtuoso Amédé Ardoin, who in the years to follow he regularly backed at house parties and club dates. However, unlike his cousin, Bois Sec never became a professional player—his mother was dead set against a career in music. In 1948, Ardoin teamed with fiddler Canray Fontenot, his principal collaborator in the years to follow; as the Duralde Ramblers, they became a fixture at local house parties and dances, and earned such tremendous regional success that they even played the Newport Folk Festival in 1966, the same year they cut their classic album *Les Blues de Bayou* for the Melodeon label. By the early '70s, Ardoin was fronting the Ardoin Brothers Band, which featured his sons Morris, Gustave and Lawrence (later the frontman of the French Zydeco Band), as well as Fontenot; after Gustave was killed in a 1974 auto accident, Ardoin appeared to lose much of his passion for music, and the following year retired from playing dances, although he continued making the infrequent live appearance for years to come. *—Jason Ankeny*

● **Musique Creole** / 1966 / Arhoolie ✦✦✦✦✦
The superb *La Musique Creole* is most notable for its inclusion of the rare 1966 Alphonse "Bois Sec" Ardoin and Canray Fontenot LP *Les Blues du Bayou*, the record cut in the wake of the duo's triumphant appearance at that year's Newport Folk Festival. Long renowned as among the finest Creole records ever made, its 16 tracks capture Ardoin and Fontenot at the peak of their powers; their interplay on cuts like "Les Blues du Voyager," "Duralde Ramble," and the bluesy instrumental "La Danse de la Misere" borders on the telepathic. The inclusion of eight tracks from a 1971 Arhoolie LP also titled *La Musique Creole*, as well the Ardoin Family Orchestra's previously unreleased "Ardoin Two-Step," is just the icing on the cake. A must for all Creole fans. *—Jason Ankeny*

Allons Danser / Jul. 14, 1998 / Rounder ✦✦✦✦✦
This is another in the long line (these musical families go back to the 19th century) of joinings of these two families. The Balfa family is from the Cajun tradition, while the Ardoins stem from the Creole tradition (they were playing back when it was called "French music"). The music on this disc evolved out of friendship and mutual admiration for the music that they share; it is a special album that not only has the latest band from the Balfa family group playing with the 82-year-old elder of the Ardoins, but it has Steve Riley playing the drums. This disc is about as close as you are going to get to the pure music of this region before it was "discovered," its children introduced to VH-1 and MTV, and the hybrids formed when the "French music" was mixed with rock & roll and R&B. Balfa Toujours have two very good discs out on Rounder and play around the country, but Bois Sec Ardoin was 82 years old and not traveling the club circuit any longer. He and his former partner, legendary fiddler Canray Fontenot, who died in 1995, earned several National Heritage Awards for their music. This is music that will inspire one to turn to one's partner and say, "Allons danser!" ("let's dance"). *—Bob Gottlieb*

Amédé Ardoin

b. Mar. 11, 1896, L'Anse des Rougeau, LA, **d.** Nov. 9, 1941, Alexandria, LA
Vocals, Accordion / Zydeco, Creole

Amédé Ardoin is to zydeco music as Robert Johnson is to the blues and Buddy Bolden is to jazz. Like Johnson and Bolden, Ardoin not only died under still mysterious conditions, but also shares the potency of their musical influence, having laid the foundation for southwest Louisiana's zydeco music.

The first Creole to be recorded, Ardoin is best remembered for his resonating, high-pitched vocals and sizzling-hot accordion playing. Although he recorded only 30 tunes, his compositions have been included in the repertoire of Cajun and zydeco artists ranging from Austin Pitre and Dewey Balfa to Beausoleil and C.J. Chenier. Iry LeJeune helped to launch a revival in Cajun music in the '50s, when he recorded twelve of Ardoin's tunes.

The great-grandson of a slave, Ardoin moved, as a child, with his family to work on the Rougeau farm in L'Anse des Rougeau near Basile. While there, he frequented the homes of his friends Adam Fontenot, who played accordion and was later the father of fiddler Canray Fontenot, and Alphonse LaFleur, who played fiddle. Together with LaFleur or Douglas Bellard, a black fiddler from Bellaire Cove, Ardoin became a frequent performer at dances, playing mostly for white audiences who paid him $2.50 per night.

In his teens, Ardoin moved frequently, working for room and board. For a while, he worked as a sharecropper on Oscar Comeaux's farm near Chataignier. While there, he met Dennis McGee, a white fiddler from Eunice. One of the first biracial Cajun duos, Ardoin and McGee began to play at house parties, often attended by Ardoin's cousin, Bois Sec Ardoin. When Comeaux sold the farm, the two musicians moved to Eunice, where they worked at Celestin Marcantel's farm. A lover of music, Marcantel often transported Ardoin and McGee to performances in his horse-drawn buggy.

Ardoin and McGee's recording debut came on December 9, 1929 when they cut seven tunes at a studio in New Orleans. They returned to the studio to record six songs on November 20 and 21, 1930. On August 8, 1934, they recorded six tunes at the Texas Hotel in San Antonio. Their fourth and final recording session, recorded at a New York studio on December 22, 1934, produced twelve new tunes. Their recordings were issued on the Brunswick, Vocalion, Decca, Melotone and Bluebird labels.

Ardoin often performed with fiddler Sady Courville of Eunice. In the late '30s, they played every Saturday night at Abe's Palace in Eunice. Courville's mother, however, prevented them from recording together.

Ardoin's death remains shrouded in mystery. One report has him being brutally beaten after wiping his brow with a handkerchief handed to him by the daughter of a white farm owner. According to McGee, Ardoin was poisoned by a jealous fiddler. More recent studies have concluded that Ardoin died of venereal disease at the Pineville Mental Institution. *—Craig Harris*

★ **Louisiana Cajun Music, Vol. 6: Amédé Ardoin—His Original Recordings** / Mar. 1983 / Old Timey ✦✦✦✦✦

Amédé Ardoin's *His Original Recordings* is divided between seven songs Ardoin recorded with Dennis McGee and seven solo tracks. The duets with McGee are among the most legendary Cajun recordings; McGee's fiddle perfectly meshes with Ardoin's accordion and raw, bluesy voice. These are the recordings that laid the foundation on contemporary Cajun and Zydeco. Ardoin's solo recordings are nearly as influential and exciting, capturing him alone with his accordion. While these aren't quite as kinetic as the duets, they are nevertheless enjoyable. *—Thom Owens*

☆ **The Roots of Zydeco** / 1995 / Arhoolie ✦✦✦✦✦

Amédé Ardoin was arguably the founder of zydeco music, incorporating blues into French folk. The songs on this collection were recorded in 1930 and 1934. Though the sound might be a bit harsh for some—these were taken from 78s, after all—these are important recordings and they continue to sound fresh and vital. *—Thom Owens*

First Black Cajun Recording Artist / Arhoolie ✦✦✦✦

Violinist Dennis McGee is featured on this 14-track album, which contains recordings from 1929, 1930, and 1934. *—AMG*

Chris Ardoin

b. 1981, Louisiana

Accordion, Vocals, Arranger / Zydeco

A third generation product of the southwestern Louisiana region's most famed musical dynasty, nouveau zydeco accordionist Chris Ardoin followed in the traditions established by his father, French Zydeco Band frontman Lawrence "Black" Ardoin; his grandfather, Cajun "la la" legend Alphonse "Bois Sec" Ardoin; and his distant cousin, Creole virtuoso Amédé Ardoin. Born in 1981, Chris made his public debut at the age of four, playing with his father at a Texas gumbo cook-off; just five years later, he backed his grandfather during an appearance at Carnegie Hall. The child prodigy also soon joined his father's new band Lagniappe as a full-time member, but like Lawrence before him, Ardoin eventually rejected the confines of traditional zydeco to pursue his own muse; with his older brother Sean, cousin Alphonse and family friend Peter Jacobs, he formed the band Double Clutchin', the name representative of the kind of repeated bass drum kicks which define the funky "new zydeco" sound. Double Clutchin' debuted with 1994's *That's Da Lick*, recorded when bandleader Ardoin was just 13; *Lick It Up!* followed a year later, and in 1997 the group signed to Rounder for *Gon' Be Jus' ine. Turn the Page* followed in 1998 and *Best Kept Secrets* arrived two years later. *—Jason Ankeny*

That's Da Lick / 1994 / Maison de Soul ✦✦✦

Lick It Up! / 1995 / Maison de Soul ✦✦✦

● **Gon' Be Jus' Fine** / Jul. 8, 1997 / Rounder ✦✦✦✦

Although only a mere 15 years old at the time of this 1997 release, Chris Ardoin was already somewhat of a veteran of zydeco music with two previous albums for local Louisiana labels to his credit. He's also a member of one of zydeco's most established musical families: he's the grandnephew of Amédé Ardoin—the first Cajun or Creole musician to record in the '20s—and the grandson of Alphonse "Bois Sec" Ardoin. With his brother Sean on drums and vocals and Gabriel "Pandy" Perrodin, Jr. on guitar (son of bayou guitarist Gabriel "Fats" Perrodin, aka Guitar Gable, who played the buzzing riff on Slim Harpo's "I'm a King Bee"), Tammy Ledet on rub board and Derek "Dee" Greenwood on bass, they forge a new chapter in zydeco with a sound that mines new beats and grooves from reggae to hip-hop while keeping all firmly grounded in their Creole roots. The Ardoin brothers' harmony vocals add a fresh twist to the sound as well, sounding especially fine on the title track, "I Don't Want What I Can't Keep" and the blues-rocker "I Believe In You." There are traditional numbers here, including the frantic workout of "Ardoin Two Step" (a version of the family's "Amede Two Step") and the old-time waltz "Dimanche apres midi (Sunday Afternoon Waltz)," which Sean sings in the original French. But the true highlights are the more forward-looking pieces, like the college chant stomp of "We Are the Boys" (which appears in a special "Bad Boys Dance Mix" version at the end as a bonus track), "Lake Charles Connection" (sporting a wild guitar solo from Perrodin) and "When I'm Dead and Gone," perhaps zydeco's first song about the apocalypse. This is dance music of the highest order, wedding modern funk grooves to the basic fun core of the music's roots. If the Ardoin brothers and their band are truly the future of zydeco, then the future is in very good hands and the dance floor was never fuller. *—Cub Koda*

Turn the Page / Oct. 6, 1998 / Rounder ✦✦✦✦

Chris Ardoin & Double Clutchin' continue to be the most forward-looking of all the young zydeco bands coming up. Their use of modern beats merging with the oldest of musical traditions in the genre makes for a what's-old-is-new mix that's hard to ignore. From the rap modal style of "Fever for Your Flavor," with superb soulful guitar interplay from Bobby Broussard and Nathaniel Fontenot, to Canray Fontenot's ancient-sounding (by comparison) "Barres de la Prison," this album snares a pretty wide musical net with big-time results. Brothers Chris and Sean Ardoin's intuitive relationship between their respective accordion and drums is seamless and highlighted superbly on "Talk Talk," "Early One Morning," "Acting the Devil," a great medley of "Stay In or Stay Out" and "Pass the Dutchie," "Double Clutchin' Old Style" and the title track. Equally as seamless is the groove laid down by bassist Dee Greenwood and rub-board gal Tammy Ledet, making the whole band sound one of constant motion. When they talk about zydeco being irresistible dance music, *this* is what they're talking about. *—Cub Koda*

Best Kept Secrets / Jul. 18, 2000 / Rounder ✦✦✦✦

Chris Ardoin & Double Clutchin' gained the reputation as being one of the most exciting live zydeco bands around. They also posses the ability to transfer their energetic live shows onto their studio recordings and *Best Kept Secret* is no exception. Switching between accordion and guitar duties, Ardoin leads Double Clutchin' through a mix of modern influences with traditional Louisiana Cajun music. Highlights include the zydeco cover versions of the Temptations "Papa Was a Rollin' Stone" and Sheryl Crow's "If It Makes You Happy." *—Al Campbell*

Lawrence "Black" Ardoin

b. Nov. 17, 1946, Duralde, LA

Drums, Accordion / Zydeco, Creole

The son of Creole accordion legend Alphonse "Bois Sec" Ardoin, Lawrence "Black" Ardoin not only carried on the family's musical traditions, but he later passed on the torch to his own son Chris, one of the most acclaimed proponents of the nouvelle zydeco sound. Born in Duralde, Louisiana in 1946, Ardoin was the second of Bois Sec's sons, joining his father and siblings Morris and Gustave in the Ardoin Brothers Band; originally a drummer, he took over accordion duties when Gustave was killed in a 1974 auto accident, and upon his father's mid-'70s retirement, assumed full leadership of the group. However, over time the confines of traditional Creole music stifled Ardoin, and in the early '80s he formed a new combo, the French Zydeco Band, which also allowed him to pursue his interests in Cajun and swamp pop sounds. In 1984, the group debuted with the LP *Lawrence "Black" Ardoin & His French Zydeco Band*; a long recording hiatus preceded the release of 1992's follow-up, *Hot & Spicy Zydeco*. Following its release, Ardoin formed a new group, Lagniappe, which included his son Chris on accordion; as the youngster continued his creative evolution, he began leading his own unit, Double Clutchin', which Lawrence also managed. *—Jason Ankeny*

● **Lawrence "Black" Ardoin & His French Band** / 1984 / Arhoolie ✦✦✦✦

Hot & Spicy Zydeco / 1992 / Maison de Soul ✦✦✦✦

Although it doesn't match the heights of Lawrence "Black" Ardoin's 1984 album for Arhoolie, *Hot & Spicy Zydeco* nevertheless cooks, boasting some hot zydeco jams that carry the album through some uneven material. *—Leo Stanley*

Howard Armstrong

b. Mar. 4, 1909, La Follette, TN

Vocals, Violin, Mandolin, Guitar / Prewar Country Blues, Country Blues, Acoustic Blues, Songster

Country bluesman Howard Armstrong was born March 4, 1909 in La Follette, Tennessee; one of 11 children, as a youngster he fashioned his first fiddle out of a goods box strung with horsehair. Honing his musical skills in his family band, as a teen he began performing alongside Knoxville performers Ted Bogan and Carl Martin in groups like the Tennessee Chocolate Drops and the Four Aces. Armstrong's groups were exceptions to the rule of the era which dictated that black performers perform only material from the segregated "race music catalogs"; their repertoire included not only old-time jigs, reels, waltzes, rags and minstrel show favorites, but also current jazz, blues and Tin Pan Alley hits.

In 1930, the Chocolate Drops made their radio debut and cut their first sides for the Vocalion label. During the Depression, the trio of Howard, Bogan and Martin lived on the road, playing throughout the Appalachian circuit and appearing with a medicine show headed by one Dr. Leon D. Bondara. By the early '30s they found themselves in Chicago, regularly playing the city's South Side and Maxwell Street flea market area; living on tips left them in dire financial straits, however, and they soon began "pullin' doors"—playing stores and taverns in the white immigrant areas, where the Italian, Polish and German which Armstrong learned to speak as a child growing up in multi-ethnic La Follette opened doors that most other black performers found barred.

By the end of the decade, the popularity of radio and the emergence of the jukebox brought Armstrong's professional playing days to a halt; however, during the '70s his few recordings were rediscovered by folk music scholars, and he reunited with Bogan and Martin to tour college campuses, coffeehouses and festivals. After Martin's 1978 death, the surviving duo forged on, and in 1985 they became the subject of the feature documentary *Louie Bluie*, a film directed by Terry Zwigoff. The accompanying soundtrack also introduced Armstrong's music to new fans through its mix of new recordings and vintage sides dating back to the '30s. *—Jason Ankeny*

● **Louie Bluie** / 1985 / Arhoolie ✦✦✦

The soundtrack to the *Louie Bluie* film has Armstrong in informal settings with various musicians, including Ted Bogan, Ikey Robinson, Yank Rachell, and Tom Armstrong. The selection of material gives a good indication of the breadth of the songster's repertoire, with ragtime, songs in German and Polish, blues, and a bawdy version of "Darktown Strutter's Ball" with much explicit profanity. If you're a casual blues fan and want a representative disc of the songster genre, you could do a lot worse than this, especially as the clear fidelity is far superior to what's possible from remastered 78s. And if you need some of those remastered 78s, the disc isn't a total loss either, as it has the 1934 single he issued under the name "Louie Bluie," "Ted's Stomp"/"State Street Rag," which has some expert, speedy violin (on "Ted's Stomp") and mandolin (on "State Street Rag") by Armstrong. The CD reissue adds four songs from 1929-1938 not on the original Arhoolie LP: "Vine Street Drag" by the Tennessee Chocolate Drops, two sides by Sleepy John Estes with Yank Rachell (including the famous "Milk Cow Blues"), and a 1938 single by Yank Rachell. *—Richie Unterberger*

James Armstrong

b. Apr. 22, 1957, Los Angeles, CA

Vocals / Modern Electric Blues, Soul-Blues

Guitarist, singer and songwriter James Armstrong has a bright future in blues music. However, this is in spite of the fact that as of summer 1997, he is still recovering from a brutal stabbing attack by an unknown assailant who broke into his apartment in Sunnyvale, California.

Armstrong's debut album for Hightone Records, *Sleeping with a Stranger*, got him noticed by clubs and festivals around the U.S. and Europe. He was supposed to tour in support of his album in the spring and summer of 1997, but it was canceled owing to his injuries in the brutal attack. (The assailant was arrested.)

Armstrong, the son of a guitarist, began playing guitar at age nine and joined his first band at 13. He began writing and performing his own songs shortly after that. He spent his early childhood in the L.A. area. Jimi Hendrix changed his life, and he credits the *Are You Experienced?* album with having a particularly big impact on his guitar playing. From the time of his first band at 13, Armstrong always insisted he and his bandmates do no covers, only their own tunes; however, later on, his band would work a few Hendrix covers into their sets. Armstrong counts among his other influences more conventional bluesmen like Albert and Freddie King, as well as B.B. King.

Over the years in the Los Angeles area, before he moved to northern California, Armstrong backed up the likes of Big Joe Turner, Sam Taylor, Albert Collins and Rickie Lee Jones. He issued the solo *Dark Night* in 1998 and returned two years later with *Got It Goin' On*. *—Richard Skelly*

● **Sleeping With a Stranger** / Oct. 17, 1995 / Hightone ✦✦✦✦

One listen to his *Sleeping With a Stranger* and one might be inclined to compare James Armstrong with Robert Cray, but the similarities end after the obvious comparison: young, talented black songwriters who believe in incorporating elements of soul and R&B into their blues playing. The truth is, Armstrong is a supremely talented songwriter, a guitarist who has no need to be overly flashy, and a more than adequate singer. As *Sleeping with a Stranger* shows, Armstrong has a bright future, and he'll continue to broaden the parameters of modern blues for some time to come. *—Richard Skelly*

Dark Night / Oct. 6, 1998 / Hightone ✦✦✦✦

After miraculously coming out alive from being attacked and nearly stabbed to death, Armstrong came back strong with this wonderful collection of tunes featuring solid performances on every one. Armstrong turns over the lion's share of lead guitar duties to Michael Ross here, and his silky leads blend with Armstrong's still very potent singing voice quite sympathetically. Highlights include the soulful "Too Many Misses for Me," "Trouble On the Homefront," the Texas shuffle of "The Bank of Love," the proud daddy rock of "Lil' James" and the title track. Guest lead guitar turns from Doug MacLeod and Joe Louis Walker on two tracks apiece make for some nice guitar fireworks as well to spice things up. There are inspired sessions, and there are *inspired* sessions; these come from a place where a man says no to death, yes to life and stands tall to tell about it and fight another day. *—Cub Koda*

Got It Goin' On / Sep. 19, 2000 / Hightone ✦✦✦

Got It Goin' On is an apt title for this third release from California bluesman James Armstrong. While his previous release, *Dark Night*, was steeped in a soul/blues vein, this album is a solid, stripped-down blues session. Armstrong's guitar chops (especially on slide guitar) and impassioned vocals continue to gain strength following the horrendous attack on his life in 1997. Making an encore appearance is guitarist Michael Ross, who blends in with the dominant role Armstrong assumes, while the keyboard work is provided by Jimmy Pugh of the Robert Cray Band. The majority of cuts were written or co-written by Armstrong, including the heartfelt ballad "Another Dream," the funky rocker "2 Sides," included in the movie *Speechless*, and the New Orleans-influenced "Mr. B's." *—Al Campbell*

Billy Boy Arnold

b. Sep. 16, 1935, Chicago, IL

Vocals, Harmonica / Harmonica Blues, Electric Chicago Blues, Electric Harmonica Blues

Talk about a comeback. After too many years away from the studio, Chicago harpist Billy Boy Arnold returned to action in a big way with two fine albums for Alligator: 1993's *Back Where I Belong* and 1995's *Eldorado Cadillac*. Retaining his youthful demeanor despite more than four decades of blues experience, Arnold's wailing harp and sturdy vocals remained in top-flight shape following the lengthy recording layoff.

Born in Chicago rather than in Mississippi (as many of his musical forefathers were), young Arnold gravitated right to the source in 1948. He summoned up the courage to knock on the front door of his idol, harmonica great John Lee "Sonny Boy" Williamson, who resided nearby. Sonny Boy kindly gave the lad a couple of harp lessons, but their relationship was quickly severed when Williamson was tragically murdered. Still in his teens, Arnold cut his debut 78 for the extremely obscure Cool logo in 1952. "Hello Stranger" went nowhere but gave him his nickname when its label unexpectedly read "Billy Boy Arnold."

Arnold made an auspicious connection when he joined forces with Bo Diddley and played on the shave-and-a-haircut beat specialist's two-sided 1955 debut smash "Bo Diddley"/"I'm a Man" for Checker. That led, in a roundabout way, to Billy Boy's signing with rival Vee-Jay Records (the harpist mistakenly believed Leonard Chess didn't like him). Arnold's "I Wish You Would," utilizing that familiar Bo Diddley beat, sold well and inspired a later famous cover by the Yardbirds. That renowned British blues-rock group also took a liking to another Arnold classic on Vee-Jay, "I Ain't Got You." Other Vee-Jay standouts by Arnold included "Prisoner's Plea" and "Rockinitis," but by 1958, his tenure at the label was over.

Other than an excellent Samuel Charters-produced 1963 album for Prestige, *More Blues on the South Side*, Arnold's profile diminished over the years in his hometown (though European audiences enjoyed him regularly) and he first ended up driving a bus in his hometown of Chicago, then working as a parole officer for the state of Illinois. Fortunately, that changed: *Back Where I Belong* restored this Chicago harp master to prominence, and *Eldorado Cadillac* drove him into the winner's circle a second time. After a six year lull between recordings, 2001's *Boogie 'n' Shuffle* on Stony Plain found Arnold still in fine form, backed by Duke Robillard and his band on a set of rough and ready blues.*—Bill Dahl*

Blow the Back off It / 1953-Sep. 1957 / Red Lightnin' ✦

Bootleg vinyl collection of the harpist's Vee-Jay stuff suffering from truly rotten sound quality. Its only saving grace is the appearance of Arnold's ultra-rare 1953 debut 78, "Hello Stranger," but its aural reproduction is worst of all (you can barely discern the music from the scratches and noise). *—Bill Dahl*

● **I Wish You Would** / Apr. 1955-Sep. 1957 / Charly ✦✦✦✦✦

The harpist's indispensable dozen 1955-1957 waxings for Vee-Jay, including the classic "I Wish You Would" and its blues-soaked flip "I Was Fooled" (stinging guitar by Jody Williams), the often-covered (but never bettered, except maybe by Jimmy Reed) "I Ain't Got You," and the vicious "Don't Stay Out All Night" and "You've Got Me Wrong." Also included are a pair of rarities Arnold cut for Chess prior to his exit as Diddley's sideman; "Sweet on You Baby" and "You Got to Love Me" feature big bad Bo on guitar and the ever-dynamic Jerome Green shakin' the maraccas. *—Bill Dahl*

Crying and Pleading / Apr. 1955-Sep. 1957 / Charly ✦✦✦✦

This vinyl collection of Arnold's complete Vee-Jay output is mid-'50s Chicago blues at its best. Includes "I Wish You Would," "I Was Fooled," "Rockinitis" and the original "I Ain't Got You," later covered by The Yardbirds. *—Cub Koda*

More Blues on the South Side / Dec. 30, 1963 / Prestige/Original Blues Classics ✦✦✦✦

Over half a decade away from the studio didn't hinder Arnold one bit on this 1963 session. His still-youthful vocals, strong harp, and imaginative songs are very effectively spotlighted, backed by a mean little Chicago combo anchored by guitarist Mighty Joe Young and pianist Lafayette Leake. The CD reissue adds a previously unreleased instrumental, "Playing with the Blues." *—Bill Dahl*

Going to Chicago / Jun. 1966 / Testament ✦✦✦

Uneven but intriguing 1966 collection, most of it previously unreleased. The first half-dozen sides are the best, full of ringing West Side-styled guitar licks by Mighty Joe Young and Jody Williams and Arnold's insinuating vocals (he rocks "Baby Jane" with a Chuck Berry-inspired fury). An odd drumless trio backs Arnold on the next seven selections, which get a little sloppy at times but retain period interest nonetheless. *—Bill Dahl*

King of Chicago Blues, Vol. 3 / 1975 / Vogue ✦✦✦

Sinner's Prayer / 1976 / Red Lightnin' ✦✦✦

Checkin' It Out / 1979 / Quicksilver ✦✦

Ten Million Dollars / Dec. 15, 1984 / Evidence ✦✦

Recording opportunities were scarce for Arnold stateside in 1984. But over in France, Black & Blue welcomed the harpist into their studios to cut this set, backed by guitarist Jimmy Johnson's professional outfit. Only a handful of originals here; the set is predominated by hoary standards such as "My Babe," "Just a Little Bit," "Last Night," and "I Done Got Over It" (but at least they're played with a bit more panache than usual). *—Bill Dahl*

Back Where I Belong / 1993 / Alligator ✦✦✦✦

Indeed he is. Recorded in Los Angeles with a crew of young acolytes offering spot-on backing (guitarists Zach Zunis and Rick Holmstrom acquit themselves well), Arnold eases back into harness with a remake of "I Wish You Would" before exposing some fine new originals (the Chuck Berry-styled rocker "Move on Down the Road" is a stomping standout) and an homage to his old mentor Sonny Boy (a romping "Shake the Boogie"). *—Bill Dahl*

Eldorado Cadillac / Nov. 1995 / Alligator ♦♦♦♦
Billy Boy Arnold, a fluent blues harmonica player and an expressive singer, made his initial impact in the '50s/early '60s, but then went three decades between American records. The second recording from his comeback, *Eldorado Cadillac*, finds Arnold (who worked many yeas earlier with Bo Diddley) in enthusiastic form while utilizing a top-notch group that includes guitarists Bob Margolin and James Wheeler, pianist Sonny Leyland, bassist Steve Hunt, drummer Chuck Cotton, and (for three numbers) David Zielinski on tenor. Arnold contributes such originals as "Don't Stay out All Night," "Mama's Bitter Seed," "Man of Considerable Taste," "Too Many Old Flames," and "Slick Chick." A fun set of passionate Chicago blues. *—Scott Yanow*

Blowin' the Blues Away / Apr. 7, 1998 / Culture Press ♦♦♦

Boogie 'n' Shuffle / Apr. 10, 2001 / Stony Plain ♦♦♦♦
At this point in his career, harmonica legend Billy Boy Arnold could just coast on his Chicago blues laurels, rehashing his old tunes and tricks whenever he decides to cut a new album. But fortunately, Arnold doesn't buy into shortcuts, and neither does his producer for this session, Duke Robillard. On *Boogie 'n' Shuffle*, Arnold really lets it rip—not only in the John Lee Williamson tradition he's well-known for, but also in the R&B traditions of Ray Charles and Jimmy McCracklin. Robillard's band is certainly up to the task, seamlessly switching from flashy soul grooves ("Home in Your Heart") to lazy Jimmy Reed-styled boogies ("Come Here Baby") to Delta blues barrelhouse ("Greenville"). As for Arnold, he's still yet to prove himself a singer of much power or range (he gets a bit overwhelmed by the busy arrangements on "Just Your Fool" and "Greenback"), but he makes up for it with classy phrasing that can turn a run-of-the-mill 12-bar shuffle into a masterpiece—the swinging "Let's Work It Out" being the best example here. While Arnold does show off some nice harmonica riffs, this isn't exactly a blues harp extravaganza; three of the tunes are harpless, and the emphasis is clearly on Arnold's singing and songwriting. The bonus track interview offers a colorful, anecdotal history of the Chicago blues scene according to Arnold, with glimpses of John Lee Williamson, Willie Dixon, and the hallowed '50s Chess sessions that produced the Bo Diddley beat. *—Ken Chang*

Kokomo Arnold (James Arnold)

b. Feb. 15, 1901, Lovejoys Station, GA, **d.** Nov. 8, 1968, Chicago, IL
Vocals, Guitar / Prewar Blues, Acoustic Chicago Blues, Acoustic Blues, Slide Guitar Blues
"Kokomo" was a popular brand of coffee early in the 20th century, and was the subject of Francis "Scrapper" Blackwell's first recorded blues in 1928. When slide guitar specialist James Arnold revamped this number as "Old Original Kokomo Blues" for Decca in 1934, little did he know that this would soon become his permanent handle—Kokomo Arnold.

Kokomo Arnold was born in Georgia, and began his musical career in Buffalo, New York in the early '20s. During prohibition, Kokomo Arnold worked primarily as a bootlegger, and performing music was a only sideline to him. Nonetheless he worked out a distinctive style of bottleneck slide guitar and blues singing that set him apart from his contemporaries. In the late '20s, Arnold settled for a short time in Mississippi, making his first recordings in May 1930 for Victor in Memphis under the name of "Gitfiddle Jim." Arnold moved to Chicago in order to be near to where the action was as a bootlegger, but the repeal of the Volstead Act put him out of business, so he turned instead to music as a full-time vocation.

From his first Decca session of September 10, 1934 until he finally called it quits after his session of May 12, 1938, Kokomo Arnold made 88 sides under his own name for Decca, which rejected only nine of them—two of the rejected titles have since been recovered. On some sides he was joined on piano by Peetie Wheatstraw, although most of Kokomo Arnold's records were made solo. Arnold also played guitar on two tunes cut in July 1936 by Oscar's Chicago Swingers, a dance band led by singer Sam Theard. Judging from the overall size of his recorded output, you might suspect that he was a success as a recording artist, and this was true; along with Peetie Wheatstraw and Amos Easton (Bumble Bee Slim), Kokomo Arnold was a predominant figure among blues singers in the Decca Race catalogues of the '30s. He was also well-known as a live performer as well, appearing mainly in Chicago, but also on at least a couple of occasions in New York.

Some of Kokomo Arnold's songs proved highly influential on other musicians. His first issued coupling on Decca 7026 paired "Old Original Kokomo Blues" with "Milk Cow Blues." Delta Blues legend Robert Johnson must've known this record, as he re-invented both sides of it into songs for his own use—"Old Original Kokomo Blues" became "Sweet Home Chicago," and "Milk Cow Blues" became "Milkcow's Calf Blues." "Milk Cow Blues" ultimately proved of use, more or less, in its original form with some "real gone" modifications, to another artist a little further down the line: Elvis Presley.

As for Kokomo Arnold himself, he quit the music business in disgust in 1938 and went into factory work in Chicago. He was rediscovered there by blues researchers in 1962, but didn't show much enthusiasm for reviving his musical career, and certainly did not resume recording. Kokomo Arnold died of a heart attack at the age of 67.

Some blues pundits have drawn a direct qualitative value between Peetie Wheatstraw and Kokomo Arnold, with Arnold coming out on top. There was a popular re-issue album in the '60s featuring eight songs by each artist which seemed to support this conclusion. This has no real relevance however; although they were personally acquainted and recorded together, Kokomo Arnold and Peetie Wheatstraw were really working different ends of the '30s blues spectrum. Their main connection to one another is their combined influence on Robert Johnson, and in this respect Wheatstraw seems to have had the upper hand. *—Uncle Dave Lewis*

Complete Recorded Works, Vol. 1 (1930–1935) / 1930-1935 / Document ♦♦♦
All of Kokomo Arnold's '30s recordings have been made available on four Document CDs. *Vol. 1* features the singer/guitarist on two songs from 1930 (recorded in Memphis, TN, as "Gitfiddle Jim") and then the first 22 selections that he cut in Chicago during 1934-1935, two of which were previously unreleased. Best known is "Milk Cow Blues," but the memorable and sometimes haunting blues singer also performs such numbers as "Old Original Kokomo Blues," "Front Door Blues," "Back Door Blues," "Chain Gang Blues," and "Hobo Blues." Blues collectors will definitely want all four CDs in this perfectly done series. *—Scott Yanow*

King of the Bottleneck Guitar (1934–1937) / 1934-1937 / Black & Blue ♦♦♦♦♦

Blues Classics by Kokomo Arnold & Peetie Wheatstraw / 1934-1938 / Blues Classics ♦♦♦♦♦
Eight tracks each by Kokomo Arnold and Peetie Wheatstraw. Includes "Milk Cow Blues." *—Michael Erlewine*

★ **Bottleneck Guitar Trendsetters of the 1930s** / 1934-1938 / Yazoo ♦♦♦♦♦
Bottleneck Guitar of the 1930s collects all of Kokomo Arnold's classic tracks from the '30s, including the classic "Milk Cow Blues." It's an essential item for a blues library—within these sides lay the groundwork for the Delta and Chicago blues to come, from Robert Johnson to Elmore James. *—Thom Owens*

Complete Recorded Works, Vol. 2 (1935–1936) / 1935-1936 / Document ♦♦♦
For completists, specialists, and academics, Document's *Complete Recorded Works, Vol. 3 (1936-1937)* is invaluable, offering an exhaustive overview of Kokomo Arnold's early recordings. For less-dedicated listeners, the disc is a mixed blessing. There are some absolutely wonderful, classic performances on the collection—"Policy Wheel Blues" and "'Cause You're Dirty" to name just two—but the long running time, exacting chronological sequencing, and poor fidelity (all cuts are transferred from original acetates and 78s) are hard to digest. The serious blues listener will find all these factors to be positive, but casual listeners will find the collection of marginal interest for the very same reasons. *—Thom Owens*

Complete Recorded Works, Vol. 3 (1936–1937) / 1936-1937 / Document ♦♦♦
Another invaluable offering from the blues archivists at Document, Kokomo Arnold's *Complete Recorded Works, Vol. 3 (1936-1937)* compiles 22 performances, recorded between May 1936 and March 1937. Despite the inclusions of a few Arnold classics, including "Dark Angel" and "Wild Water Blues," the disc is a mixed blessing. The combination of a long running time, chronological sequencing, and poor fidelity make for a difficult listen. While serious blues listeners won't have a problem with any of these factors, beginners are advised to look elsewhere first. *—Thom Owens*

Complete Recorded Works, Vol. 4 (1937–1938) / 1937-1938 / Document ♦♦♦
Like its predecessors, the final volume in Document's *Complete Recorded Works* series alternates a few excellent performances with many more additions intended for collectors only. Drawn from Kokomo Arnold's last few sessions, from the 14-month period between March 1937 and May 1938, the collection does include a few classics, like "Mean Old Twister" and "Red Beans and Rice." Still, many of the rest are period material with poor fidelity, of only marginal interest to most blues fans. *—Thom Owens*

Blues Classics, Vol. 1 / Nov. 4, 1997 / Blues Classics ♦♦♦♦♦

Asylum Street Spankers

f. 1995, Austin, TX
Group / Americana, Contemporary Folk, Acoustic Blues, Neo-Traditional Folk
The Asylum Street Spankers, from Austin, Texas, are a unique band led by vocalist/washboard player/poet Wammo and vocalist Christina Marrs. They're finding a growing cult following for their unique brand of acoustic blues and early jazz. While much of their material is blues from the '20s and '30s, the band also performs original songs in their live shows and on their debut album for Watermelon Records, *Spanks for the Memories*. The band's live shows are performed without amplifiers or microphones, usually including tunes from Bessie Smith, Robert Johnson and other standard, traditional blues tunes. In addition to Wammo and Marrs, members of the Asylum Street Spankers have included guitarist Colonel Josh, guitarist Jeff Ross, banjo and mandolin player Pops Bayless, drummer Jimmie Dean, guitarist and saw player Olivier, kazoo player Mysterious John, Guy Forsyth, and bassist Kevin Smith.

The genesis of the eight-member band occurred in the early '90s at a hotel outside of Austin. After an all-night acoustic tune swap, the musicians realized they were on to something, getting back to basics and playing acoustic music. After several phone calls and circulated tapes, the band met again for a rehearsal, and the chemistry took over from there.

The band began attracting growing crowds after playing steady Wednesdays at the Electric Lounge, a bar in Austin, and from that following, they took the next step and recorded their debut album for a local label, Watermelon Records. While many of the melodies and progressions on *Spanks for the Memories* are old, some of the band's lyrics are straight out of contemporary America. Songs like "Funny Cigarette," "Trade Winds," "Lee Harvey" and "Hometown Boy" are funny and entertaining to most audiences. This was proven by the following live album, which chronicled a 1996 show and showcased their charm and charisma in a live setting. The *Nasty Novelties* EP provided fans with one great song title ("Rotten Cocksucker's Ball"), but it was the following year's full length *Hot Lunch* that brought the real goods. Another fine set of old-fashioned pop, the record won rave reviews and set them apart from other, more gimmick-oriented revivalists.

The next year, *Spanker Madness* took fans by surprise with its hootenanny-style structure and heavy cast of guest musicians. Every song revolved around the merits of marijuana, and the humorous approach and loose vibe drafted a new set of fans that were enticed by the band's liberal politics. A clever Christmas album and an EP of more dirty songs (highlighted by the hilarious "Everybody's Fucking But Me") held over fans until 2002, when *My Favorite Record* was released on their own Spanks-A-Lot Records. *—Richard Skelly and Bradley Torreano*

Spanks for the Memories / Nov. 5, 1996 / Watermelon ♦♦♦♦
Sometimes there's a thin line between tribute and parody, and Austin's acoustic Asylum Street Spankers walk that line with more grace and dignity than most. On their debut album, the Austin-based collective borrows classic jug band instrumentation, vocal

mannerisms, and in some cases even repertoire, imbuing songs like Lucille Bogan's "Shave 'Em Dry" and Robert Johnson's seminal blues "If I Had Possession Over Judgement Day" with both authenticity and irony. For the most part, it works well, largely due to the fact that the Asylum Street Spankers know when to go for camp appeal and when to play it straight. The contributions of co-frontman Wammo take the former route, with originals "Lee Harvey" and "Startin' to Hate Country" dependent on humor for their effectiveness; covers of pop standards "I'll See You in My Dreams" and "Brazil" are less affected. More surprising is the album's emotional range. How many groups could get away with sequencing a whimsical ode to marijuana ("Funny Cigarette," which succeeds based on its attention to vaudevillian detail, even though the band bettered it in 2000 with "Beer," which was essentially a rewrite) back to back with a darkly earnest glimpse at the underbelly of small-town America (Guy Forsyth's devastating "Hometown Boy")? Not many, and that boldness is the greatest strength of *Spanks for the Memories*, an album that's among the rawest yet most nuanced in the group's catalog. —*Kenneth Bays*

Live / Jun. 24, 1997 / Watermelon ♦♦♦
Live captures the wackiness and musical acumen of the Asylum Street Spankers equally well. Their humor—which can make the music sound near-parodic—may frustrate some purists, but their talent for folk-blues, string band music and jump blues may win them over yet. There's a bit more energy and flair on *Live* than their studio albums, which helps make it their best record to date.—*Stephen Thomas Erlewine*

● **Hot Lunch** / Feb. 23, 1999 / Cold Spring ♦♦♦♦
This, Asylum Street Spankers' sophomore recording, breezes in on acoustic guitar and ukulele strains and the words "Life ain't a cakewalk, it's a waltz/And they're playing my music out of time"—and it only gets better from there. Indeed, the Asylum Street Spankers, a loose, unplugged collective of Austin, TX, pickers and *bon vivants*, seem to have little trouble, on *Hot Lunch*'s 16 cuts, deftly blending virtuosic musicianship with seemingly effortless musical and lyrical wit. The band flits between ragtime, country, old-style AM radio pop tunes, swing, and country blues with equal ease. The Spankers are—particularly on such puckish, narrative cuts as "Trippin' Over You," "Sad Bomber," and others—manage to walk the razor thin line between novelty and just plain fun-lovin' jamboree frolics. It's this graceful self-awareness that separates Asylum Street Spankers from such less graceful musical revivalists as the Squirrel Nut Zippers. In fact, on the cut "Smells Like Thirty-Something," the Spankers seem to, well, spank the mid-'90s swing revival craze on its rump, chiding, atop a rollicking, bluesy riff, "I like martinis/and I like cigars/But I hate martini and cigar bars." Somewhere between that sense of humor and vocalist/instrumentalist (for every Spanker is a multi-instrumentalist) Christina Marrs' sublime vocals lies the charm of Asylum Street Spankers as expressed in these grooves. A beautiful, rocking, and rollicking unplugged beer-and-pot party populated with the most unpretentious, heartbreaking characters you're ever likely to meet. —*Chris Handyside*

Spanker Madness / Mar. 21, 2000 / Bloodshot ♦♦♦
If you're ever flipping through the discs in your local record shop wondering "where might I find the perfect soundtrack for my weekend backyard hash get-down," the cover of *Spanker Madness*, a parody of the propaganda posters associated with the 1938 cult film classic *Reefer Madness*, should be enough to answer your question. Otherwise, here's the skinny on the disc: This latest Asylum Street Spankers hootenanny consists of 15-some people singing and playing up the wonders of cannabis with everything from guitars, ukuleles, and harmonicas to washboards, bells, and "various pieces of metal piled in the back of Leroy's '67 Ford F100 parked in the studio driveway." The songs are usually trite country blues and old-style jazz ditties: "Wake and Bake" is a love duet about a couple bonding over the morning's first toke of tea, and odd man out and executive producer Wammo stands up for his drug of choice on "Beer." All the tomfoolery (one of the record's more memorable lyrics goes "Marijuana makes me wanna eat candy and screw

Madonna/With her hair bleached by peroxide/Huffin' on some nitrous oxide") and the lighthearted jam-session atmosphere makes it tough to take the Spankers seriously, but the album has its solemn moments. On "Take the Heat," for instance, Guy Forsyth sings about a busted woman battling to keep custody of her daughter. Like the doobies they sing about, the lead vocal duties are passed around from song to song, as are the instrumental solos. Wammo and fellow executive producer Christina Marrs share most of the singing duties, although other notable performances include Forsyth on "Orion" and Stanley Smith keening like Randy Newman back in the day on "Another Blade of Grass." Other than maybe Dr. Dre's *The Chronic*, there's probably never been an album dedicated to the use of narcotics that has been too commercially successful, which quickly dispels the notion that the 13 retro-sounding tunes on this disc are some kind of sellout-throwback gimmick. Coming on the heels of the derivative Big Bad Voodoo Daddy/Cherry Poppin' Daddies neo-swing trend, when suddenly any punk with a zoot suit who knew how to snap and pronounce that word (say it…"dad-dio") was hip, this disc's relative lack of contrivance was a breath of fresh air. —*John Uhl*

Spanks for the Memories [Expanded] / Apr. 30, 2002 / Ass ♦♦♦♦
The 2002 reissue of *Spanks for the Memories* adds "Drunkard's Wave," a lurching barroom anthem, and "Black Eyed Blues," a comic tale of revenge that slyly echoes the bawdy early blues numbers the band holds dear. —*Kenneth Bays*

Lynn August

b. Aug. 7, 1948, Lafayette, LA
Vocals, Accordion / Zydeco
One of zydeco's most versatile performers, Lynn August spiked his native southwestern Louisiana sound with elements of pop, gospel and R&B. Born in Lafayette on August 7, 1948, the blind August was encouraged by his mother to pursue a career in music, and he was raised on a steady diet of zydeco, New Orleans rhythm and blues and swamp pop. After learning to play drums on an old wash basin, at the age of 12 he was recruited to play percussion with the legendary Esquerita, who convinced him to also take up the piano; a few years later, August made the switch to the Hammond B-3 organ as well. During the mid-'60s, he played with a young Stanley "Buckwheat" Dural, later mounting a solo career as well as sitting in with a variety of local swamp pop combos; he also led a big band, and even directed a church choir. In 1988, August turned to the accordion and began his zydeco career in earnest; forming the Hot August Knights with tenor saxophonist John Hart. He also studied field recordings made in 1934 by archivist Alan Lomax to absorb the original Creole style of "jure" singing into his own contemporary aesthetic. After signing to the Maison de Soul label, August debuted with *It's Party Time*, followed in 1989 by *Zydeco Groove*; a move to Black Top heralded the release of 1992's *Creole Cruiser*, with the acclaimed *Sauce Piquante* appearing a year later. —*Jason Ankeny*

It's Party Time / 1988 / Maison de Soul ♦♦♦

Zydeco Groove / 1989 / Maison de Soul ♦♦♦

● **Creole Cruiser** / Jan. 1992 / Black Top ♦♦♦♦
Creole Cruiser is Lynn August's first effort for Black Top Records, and like his pair of records for Maison de Soul, it's rollicking, energetic zydeco. Backed by a band that features Meters bassist George Porter, Jr. and keyboardist Sammy Berfect, August tears through a set of New Orleans standards, augmenting the play list with such fine originals as "'58 Pink Cadillac" and several traditional jures. He and his band really cook up a head of steam during these 16 numbers, making *Creole Cruser* an excellent party record of neo-traditional New Orleans zydeco. —*Thom Owens*

Sauce Piquante / Jul. 1, 1993 / Black Top ♦♦♦

Creole People / Feb. 9, 1999 / Aim ♦♦♦

B

Smoky Babe (Robert Brown)

b. 1927, Itta Bena, MS, **d.** 1975
Vocals, Guitar / Blues Revival, Louisiana Blues, Piedmont Blues, Acoustic Louisiana Blues

Robert Brown, aka Smoky Babe, is a shadowy figure from the early days of the '60s folk-blues revival. The scant details of his life read like a prototypical country bluesman's bio; born in Itta Bena, MS, in 1927, raised on a plantation, had a hard life of sharecropping, picked up the guitar along the way, spent several years hoboing throughout the South, moved to the big city and found life no better there. He apparently only worked sporadically as a semi-pro musician for a spell in New Orleans in the '50s, returning to his adopted home base of Scotlandville to work as a garage mechanic at the time of his discovery. His brief recording career was limited to a pair of album-length releases recorded as "in the field" location sessions in 1960 and 1961 for the Folk Lyric and Bluesville labels. His few recordings display a strong rhythmic sense in his guitar playing with a strong thumping bass line with the occasional foray into slide guitar. His vocals were nothing less than rich, strong and authoritative. After a few years of playing at picnics and local parties for friends around Baton Rouge in the early '60s, he seemingly disappeared, never to be seen or heard from again. He is thought to have died in 1975. —*Cub Koda*

● **Louisiana Country Blues** / 1996 / Arhoolie ✦✦✦✦
A reissue (on compact disc) of a reissue (on Arhoolie) of an album originally released on the Folk Lyric label, this combines two albums of Louisiana country blues material on one CD. Smoky Babe may have been a semi-pro musician, but the feel of the 12 sides suggests that he was full command of his powers when folklorist Dr. Harry Oster hit the "record" button. Combined with another album's worth of material from the equally obscure Herman E. Johnson (who performs four tracks on electric guitar in a most chaotic manner), this is back porch country blues of the highest order. Just because neither is a "famous name," don't let that keep you from checking out this superlative release. —*Cub Koda*

Hottest Brand Goin' / Aug. 7, 2001 / Original Blues Classics ✦✦✦✦
In an ideal world, singer/acoustic guitarist Smoky Babe would have left behind a huge catalog. But, regrettably, the southern bluesman wasn't well known, and he only recorded a few albums. One of them was *Hottest Brand Goin'*, which was recorded for Prestige's Bluesville label in Baton Rouge, LA, in 1961, and was reissued on CD for Fantasy's Original Blues Classics (OBC) series in 2001. Everything on this album is pure, unadulterated acoustic country blues; however, Babe doesn't embrace any one style of country blues exclusively. A Mississippi native who moved to Louisiana, Babe gets his inspiration from a variety of southern sources. The Louisiana influence is present, but his approach also owes something to Mississippi Delta blues (Robert Johnson, Mississippi John Hurt) as well as Piedmont blues (Sonny Terry & Brownie McGhee) and Texas blues (Lightnin' Hopkins). The Hopkins influence is prominent—"Long Way from Home," "Cold Cold Snow," and "Insect Blues" are the sort of moody, dusky gems that Hopkins would have embraced—and yet, you can't overlook the Louisiana, Mississippi, and Georgia influences that also do their part to enrich this CD. Babe's vocals are soulful and authoritative, his acoustic guitar playing rugged and gritty. Most of the time, Babe is unaccompanied, although three selections find him joined by either Clyde Causey or Henry Thomas on harmonica. Again, it's most regrettable that Babe didn't do a lot more recording, but it's better to have only a few albums by him than none at all—and *Hottest Brand Goin'* is enthusiastically recommended to lovers of earthy, unpretentious southern country blues. —*Alex Henderson*

Back Porch Blues

f. 1988, **db.** 1995
Group / Modern Delta Blues

Back Porch Blues, an acoustic Delta blues-styled band, consisted of founding members Sheila Wilcoxson (vocals), Jeffrey Dawkins (harp), and Whit Draper (guitar). The trio (no drums) created quite a stir in the northwest corner of America from 1988 to 1995 by serving up down-home, traditional blues with gobs of soul. The Portland, OR-based band played select dates throughout the States, including the Riverbend Festivals of Chattanooga, TN; the Mississippi Crossroads Blues Festival; and the Centrum Hot Jazz Festival of Port Townsend, WA, but burnt brightest in the NW area. Their seven-year itch for success produced only one CD, *Back to Basics*, on Burnside Records, and a spot on a live recording of the Portland Waterfront Blues Festival. (The CD was released in 1993 by Burnside.) Recipients of accolades galore, the band garnered the Cascade Blues Association's Muddy Award for Best Traditional Blues Act (five years straight from 1989 to 1993), induction into the CBA Hall of Fame for Best Traditional Blues Act in 1991, a Muddy for Best New Blues Band in 1989, another for Best New Blues Album in 1990, and a Crystal Award from the Portland Music Association for Outstanding Blues Act in 1992. Never completely focused on music, Wilcoxson earned a bachelor's degree from the University

of Michigan and a doctorate from Williamette during the BPB experience. But mad support from a vociferous legion of fans wasn't enough to keep the fire burning. Failing to secure a deal with a major recording company nailed the coffin shut for BPB. They disbanded in 1995, leaving only a morsel of recorded material to remember them by. Wilcoxson—who also sang with the acoustic blues band Sheila & Backwater Blues toward the end of BPB—now performs solo. —*Andrew Hamilton*

● **Back to Basics** / 1992 / Burnside ✦✦✦✦
Sheila Wilcoxson's strong, dirty, and downtrodden "I've been to hell and back" vocals are the centerpiece of Back Porch Blues' setup of guitar, drums, percussions, and two basses. Whit Draper's earsplitting guitar captivates throughout on uptempo jams like "Boogie Woman" and slow, nasty crawlers like "Mean Old Man," with its orgasmic rhythm. A musician doubles on harp (uncredited) and blows it like he/she is hemorrhaging, especially on "NW Line." The baker's dozen tracks are compelling and the sound full and satisfying, even without the presence of a drummer. —*Andrew Hamilton*

Mildred Bailey (Mildred Rinker)

b. Feb. 27, 1907, Tekoa, WA, **d.** Dec. 12, 1951, Poughkeepsie, WA
Vocals / Traditional Pop, Standards, Swing, Classic Female Blues

An early jazz singer with a sweet voice that belied her plump physique, Mildred Bailey balanced a good deal of popular success with a hot jazz-slanted career that saw her billed as Mrs. Swing (her husband, Red Norvo, was Mr. Swing). Born Mildred Rinker in Washington state in 1907, Bailey began performing at an early age, playing piano and singing in movie theaters during the early '20s. By 1925, she was the headlining act at a club in Hollywood, doing a mixture of pop, early jazz tunes, and vaudeville standards. Influenced by Ethel Waters, Bessie Smith, and Connie Boswell, she developed a soft, swinging delivery that pleased all kinds of nightclub audiences in the area. After sending a demonstration disc in to Paul Whiteman in 1929, she gained a spot with one of the most popular dance orchestras of the day.

The added exposure with Whiteman soon gave Bailey her own radio program. She had already debuted on a recording date with guitarist Eddie Lang in 1929, but in 1932 she gained fame by recording what became her signature song, "Rockin' Chair"—written especially for her by Hoagie Carmichael—with a Whiteman small group. Recording for Vocalion during the '30s, Bailey often utilized her husband, xylophonist Red Norvo. She also appeared on his recordings of the late '30s, and the arrangements of Eddie Sauter proved a perfect accompaniment to her vocals.

Though she and Norvo later divorced, Bailey continued to perform and record during the '40s. She appeared on Benny Goodman's Camel Caravan radio program, and gained her own series again during the mid-'40s. Hampered by health problems during the late '40s, she spent time in the hospital suffering from diabetes and died of a heart attack in 1951. —*John Bush*

Volume 1 / Oct. 5, 1929-Mar. 2, 1932 / The Old Masters ✦✦✦
The first of two Mildred Bailey CDs from the TOM label contains 21 of the vocalist's first 23 recordings; the two bypassed selections are included on the second volume. The superior swing singer is mostly heard on ballads (some of which are a bit dated) with orchestras led by Eddie Lang ("What Kind o' Man Is You?"), Frankie Trumbauer ("I Like to Do Things for You"), Jimmie Noone, Glen Gray and Paul Whiteman in addition to her initial sessions as a leader; this release is accurately subtitled "Sweet Beginnings" and the jazz content is generally not all that high. Although there are fairly long liner notes (the same ones are used on both volumes), the personnel for these early recordings are not included. Despite that inexcusable omission, fans of Mildred Bailey should be delighted to have these interesting sides reissued; highlights include "Concentratin' on You," "Home," "All of Me" and her original version of "Georgia on My Mind." —*Scott Yanow*

☆ **The Complete Columbia Recordings of Mildred Bailey** / Oct. 5, 1929-Mar. 5, 1942 / Mosaic ✦✦✦✦✦

★ **Her Greatest Performances (1929–1946)** / 1929-1946 / Columbia ✦✦✦✦✦
This three-LP box set (which deserves to be reissued on CD) lives up to its name. Bailey was one of the top singers of the '30s and this package, which features highlights from her career (mostly dating from 1933-1939), shows why. She holds her own with a variety of all-star groups which include such classic players as trumpeters Bunny Berigan, Buck Clayton, Charlie Shavers, and Roy Eldridge (the latter is great on "I'm Nobody's Baby"), trombonist Tommy Dorsey, clarinetist Benny Goodman, altoist Johnny Hodges, tenors Coleman Hawkins and Chu Berry, pianists Teddy Wilson and Mary Lou Williams, and her husband, xylophonist Red Norvo. There are lots of gems on this definitive set. —*Scott Yanow*

● **1932–1936** / Aug. 18, 1932-Nov. 9, 1936 / Classics ✦✦✦✦
Two dozen recordings made by Bailey between 1932 and 1936 form this important chapter in the chronological review of her best work. This is right at the time she left

Paul Whiteman's band and started recording on her own, often in the company of top-notch jazz artists like the Dorsey Brothers, Bunny Berigan, Teddy Wilson, Johnny Hodges, Artie Shaw, and future husband Red Norvo. As always, Bailey's timing is impeccable, her intonation nigh perfect, and the songs—even the poppier offerings—all swing like crazy. *—Cub Koda*

The Legendary V-Disc Series / 1940-1951 / Vintage Jazz ♦♦♦♦
Mildred Bailey fans will find this to be a very interesting CD, for the talented swing singer is heard on some previously unavailable V-Disc sessions from the war years (including a few false starts) along with some radio appearances. There is a complete radio show with her guests The Delta Rhythm Boys, four duets with pianist Teddy Wilson, three selections with vibraphonist Red Norvo's quintet, a few songs with either Paul Baron's studio orchestra or the Ellis Larkins Trio, one number ("There'll Be a Jubilee") with Benny Goodman's big band and two selections ("Lover, Come Back to Me" and "It's So Peaceful in the Country") from a 1951 radio aircheck that ended up being her last recordings. Any listener who wonders why Mildred Bailey was awarded her own postage stamp should be required to get this CD. *—Scott Yanow*

The Blue Angel Years 1945–1947 / 1945-1947 / Baldwin Street Music ♦♦♦♦
In 1944, Mildred Bailey was getting back on track after a disastrous recording ban that held up her career as well as those of other jazz and popular music performers. Then things started going her way. Bailey was offered a radio show by CBS and, when Max Gordon opened his new Blue Angel jazz club, Bailey signed on with a trio headed by young pianist Ellis Larkins. She remained there until 1947. Baldwin Street Music has found several recordings from this period of Bailey's life, as well as a few with groups aside from the Larkins trio. Of the 22 tracks, three are previously unreleased and nine have never been reissued on CD. Bailey harbored a small feathery voice in a big body, which some say made her look matronly and therefore prevented her from achieving the popularity she deserved. Nevertheless, few could sing in as natural and unaffected a manner as Bailey could. A great admirer (and friend) of Bessie Smith, she was one of the few white singers who understood the blues as sung by the black masters of the genre, and this understanding is reflected in the way she developed and honed her craft. She was intense without resorting to being overly emotional. "I'll Close My Eyes" makes the listener feel privy to an intimate conversation that Bailey is having. Her version of "Can't Help Lovin' That Man of Mine" rivals Billie Holiday's as the archetypical rendition of this classic. Of the tunes she cut with Larkins, "Can't We Be Friends" epitomizes the musical relation they built during the few years they were together. Larkins' work with Bailey presaged a career that made him a highly sought-after partner by singers, like Ella Fitzgerald and Sylvia Sims, whose voices were not that dissimilar from Bailey's. This album is typical of the excellence Baldwin Street Music builds into its releases. The sound is superior, the liner notes are interesting and intelligently written, and there's a bonus track with snippets of other releases from the label. Highly recommended. *—Dave Nathan*

Majestic Mildred Bailey / Mar. 5, 1946-Nov. 20, 1947 / Savoy ♦♦♦♦
During 1946-1947, singer Mildred Bailey recorded four sessions for the Majestic label; these later sides were among her finest recordings. This Savoy LP reissues most of the music from these sessions, including several previously unreleased alternate takes. In fact, of the five songs left out, three are heard in previously unreleased alternate versions. Bailey is featured with Ted Dale's orchestra (with arrangements by Eddie Sauter), a septet with pianist Ellis Larkins and trumpeter Irving "Mouse" Randolph, Julian Work's string orchestra, and (best of all) the Ellis Larkins Trio. Among the more memorable selections are "I'll Close My Eyes," "Lover Come Back to Me," "You Started Something," and "Almost Like Being in Love." Hopefully, this delightful music will eventually be reissued (with all of the performances) on CD. *—Scott Yanow*

The Rockin' Chair Lady / Mar. 1947 / Decca ♦♦♦♦
The superior swing singer is heard on 20 studio performances throughout this diverse CD which spans virtually her entire recording career. The best selections are the first four, a complete session from 1935 that has Bailey joined by an all-star quartet comprised of trumpeter Bunny Berigan, altoist Johnny Hodges, pianist Teddy Wilson and bassist Grachan Moncur. In addition she sings four ballads from 1931 with The Casa Loma Orchestra and is accompanied on ten songs by The Delta Rhythm Boys, a quartet led by pianist Herman Chittison or Harry Sosnick's octet in 1941-1942. This interesting CD concludes with Mildred Bailey's final studio session, two numbers ("Cry, Cry, Cry" and "Blue Prelude") from 1950. Some of the material was formerly rare, making this an essential CD for swing collectors. *—Scott Yanow*

Music Til Midnight / Oct. 6, 1994+Oct. 13, 1994 / Mr. Music ♦♦♦♦
Mildred Bailey's weekly half-hour radio series of 1944-1945 (which had 34 shows in all) is long overdue to be released on CD. Two of the programs are on this enjoyable CD. Bailey is heard with Paul Baron's Orchestra, and among the musical guests are clarinetist Ernie Caceres (featured on "Cherry"), an all-star sextet (pianist Teddy Wilson, trumpeter Charlie Shavers, vibraphonist Red Norvo, guitarist Remo Palmieri, bassist Billy Taylor, and drummer Specs Powell), trombonist Trummy Young (who sings "I'm Living for Today"), trumpeter Billy Butterfield (showcased on Alec Wilder's "I'm Seeing Her Tonight"), and pianist Hazel Scott (featured on "Soon"). As for Bailey, she sounds in happy form on "Someday Sweetheart," "There's Be a Jubilee," and "More Than You Know." A special bonus is a five-minute section in which Bailey reminisces with her former boss, Paul Whiteman. *—Scott Yanow*

Volume 2 / 1995 / The Old Masters ♦♦♦
The second of two CDs from the TOM ("The Old Masters") label finishes the documentation of singer Mildred Bailey's earliest recordings. Bailey is featured with Paul Whiteman, the Dorsey Brothers Big Band, the Casa Loma Orchestra ("Heat Wave"), an all-star group with Benny Goodman (and tenor-great Coleman Hawkins) and on a her few of her own sessions. Although the emphasis is on ballads, the program generally holds on to one's interest (despite a few songs with racist lyrics, notably "Snowball") and the Goodman session (which is rounded off with an instrumental version of "Georgia Jubilee") is a near-classic. Other highlights include "I'll Never Be the Same," "Love Me Tonight," a touching "There's a Cabin in the Pines" and Bailey's earliest version of her future theme song "Rockin' Chair." *—Scott Yanow*

American Legends No. 4: Mildred Bailey / 1996 / LaserLight ♦♦♦
The almost complete lack of documentation on this low-priced disc makes it difficult to place in Mildred Bailey's discography, but the performances on many of which Bailey is backed by Red Norvo or Ellis Larkins, are typically accomplished. Her hit "Thanks for the Memory" (now remembered as Bob Hope's theme song) is included, as are some excellent offbeat arrangements of such songs as "The Lamp Is Low" and "Smoke Dreams" (the latter featuring a delightful Norvo xylophone solo). Sound quality is adequate, and with a running time for the 12 tracks of over 36 minutes, you will get what you pay for if you only pay in the vicinity of $5 for this disc. *—William Ruhlmann*

Etta Baker

b. Mar. 31, 1913, Caldwell County, NC
Vocals, Piano, Guitar, Fiddle, Banjo / Piedmont Blues, Country Blues, Acoustic Blues
Guitarist Etta Baker quietly enjoyed one of the blues' most enduring careers, working in almost total obscurity and recording only on the rarest of occasions while honing her craft throughout the greater part of the 20th century. Born in Caldwell County, NC, on March 31, 1913, she was the product of a musical family, taking up the guitar as a child and learning from her father and other relatives traditional blues and folk songs. Over time, Baker emerged among the foremost practitioners of acoustic Piedmont guitar fingerpicking, an open-tuned style not far removed from bluegrass banjo picking; however, for decades only relatives and friends ever heard her play, as she confined her performances solely to family gatherings and parties. She finally made her initial recordings in 1956, joining her father and other family members on a field recording titled *Instrumental Music of the Southern Appalachians*; she again faded into willful obscurity, however, raising her nine children and toiling in a textile mill. Finally, while in her sixties—at an age at which most performers consider retirement—Baker finally began pursuing music professionally, hitting the folk and blues festival circuit. In 1991—35 years after her debut recording—she issued the album *One-Dime Blues*, and continued performing live throughout the decade to follow, returning in 1999 with *Railroad Bill*. *—Jason Ankeny*

● **One-Dime Blues** / 1991 / Rounder ♦♦♦♦♦
Guitarist/vocalist Etta Baker hadn't made any recordings or even been in a studio since 1956 before making the 20 numbers comprising this CD. But judging from the arresting vocals, prickly accompaniment and commanding presence she displayed on each song, it seemed as if she had been cutting tracks daily. Baker moved from sassy and combative blues tunes like "Never Let Your Deal Go Down" and "But on the Other Hand Baby" to chilling numbers like "Police Dog Blues," novelty tunes, double entendre cuts, folk pieces, and even country-flavored material. Singing and playing in vintage Piedmont style with a two- and three-finger technique, Etta Baker offered timeless, memorable performances. *—Ron Wynn*

Railroad Bill / Jun. 8, 1999 / Music Maker ♦♦♦♦
The "premier woman Piedmont blues guitar instrumentalist" is a wordy but accurate description of 87-year-old Etta Baker of Morganton, NC. One of the last pickers who was around when the music was first being recorded, Baker's 83 years of practice is manifested in these wonderful recordings of traditional folk ballads. One highlight follows another, and although "Brown's Boogie" trips up the album's gentle flow, the rest is front-porch perfect. This is music you never get tired of listening to. Newcomers to guitar should buy this album, both to marvel at the intricate technique and to amuse themselves with how frustratingly difficult it can be. *—Jim Smith*

LaVern Baker (Delores Williams)

b. Nov. 11, 1929, Chicago, IL, **d.** Mar. 10, 1997, New York, NY [Manhattan]
Bass, Vocals / Jump Blues, R&B
LaVern Baker was one of the sexiest divas gracing the mid-'50s rock & roll circuit, boasting a brashly seductive vocal delivery tailor-made for belting the catchy novelties "Tweedlee Dee," "Bop-Ting-a-Ling," and "Tra La La" for Atlantic Records during rock's first wave of prominence.

Born Delores Williams, she was singing at the Club DeLisa on Chicago's south side at age 17, decked out in raggedy attire and billed as "Little Miss Sharecropper" (the same handle that she made her recording debut under for RCA Victor with Eddie "Sugarman" Penigar's band in 1949). She changed her name briefly to Bea Baker when recording for OKeh in 1951 with Maurice King's Wolverines, then settled on the first name of LaVern when she joined Todd Rhodes' band as featured vocalist in 1952 (she fronted Rhodes' aggregation on the impassioned ballad "Trying" for Cincinnati's King Records).

LaVern signed with Atlantic as a solo in 1953, debuting with the incendiary "Soul on Fire." The coy, Latin tempo "Tweedlee Dee" was a smash in 1955 on both the R&B and pop charts, although her impact on the latter was blunted when squeaky-clean Georgia Gibbs covered it for Mercury. An infuriated Baker filed suit over the whitewashing, but she lost. By that time, though, her star had ascended: Baker's "Bop-Ting-A-Ling," "Play It Fair," "Still," and the rocking "Jim Dandy" all vaulted into the R&B Top Ten over the next couple of years.

Baker's statuesque figure and charismatic persona made her a natural for TV and movies. She co-starred on the historic R&B revue segment on Ed Sullivan's TV program in November of 1955 and did memorable numbers in Alan Freed's rock movies *Rock, Rock, Rock* and *Mr. Rock & Roll*. Her Atlantic records remained popular throughout the decade: she hit big in 1958 with the ballad "I Cried a Tear," adopted a pseudo-sanctified bellow for the rousing Leiber & Stoller-penned gospel sendup "Saved" in 1960, and cut a

Bessie Smith tribute album before leaving Atlantic in 1964. A brief stop at Brunswick Records (where she did a sassy duet with Jackie Wilson, "Think Twice") preceded a late-'60s jaunt to entertain the troops in Vietnam. She became seriously ill after the trip and was hospitalized, eventually settling far out of the limelight in the Philippines. She remained there for 22 years, running an NCO club on Subic Bay for the U.S. government.

Finally, in 1988, Baker returned stateside to star in Atlantic's 40th anniversary bash at New York's Madison Square Garden. That led to a soundtrack appearance in the film *Dick Tracy*, a starring role in the Broadway musical *Black & Blue* (replacing her ex-Atlantic labelmate Ruth Brown), a nice comeback disc for DRG (*Woke Up This Mornin'*), and a memorable appearance at the Chicago Blues Festival. Baker died on March 10, 1997. *—Bill Dahl*

LaVern / 1956 / Atlantic ✦✦✦

LaVern Baker / 1957 / Atlantic ✦✦✦✦✦
It includes her hits "Tweedlee Dee" and "Jim Dandy." Some formulaic material (like "Tra-La-La," an obvious attempt at recapturing "Tweedly Dee") is included, but there's some good stuff too. *—George Bedard*

LaVern Sings Bessie Smith / Jan. 27, 1958 / Atlantic ✦✦✦✦✦
This is an album that should not have worked. LaVern Baker (a fine R&B singer) was joined by all-stars from mainstream jazz (including trumpeter Buck Clayton, trombonist Vic Dickenson, tenor saxophonist Paul Quinichette and pianist Nat Pierce) for twelve songs associated with the great '20s blues singer Bessie Smith. Despite the potentially conflicting styles, this project is quite successful and often exciting. The arrangements by Phil Moore, Nat Pierce, and Ernie Wilkins do not attempt to re-create the original recordings; Baker sings in her own style (rather than trying to emulate Bessie Smith), and the hot solos work well with her vocals. *—Scott Yanow*

Blues Ballads / 1959 / Atlantic ✦✦✦
Before she became a successful rock and roll vocalist, LaVern Baker did straight jazz and gutbucket blues, and that's what she's singing here. These tunes didn't have any crossover appeal, but they're gritty, unpolished, and sung with the intensity and energy that made Baker's later material so memorable. *—Ron Wynn*

Precious Memories / Jun. 4, 1959 / Atlantic ✦✦✦
LaVern Baker sang gospel with passion, exuberance, and reverence on this 1959 session. She was backed by a small combo with the Alex Bradford singers and sounded more magnificent and moving than at any time she had done jazz, blues or R&B. This one is very hard to find and has not as of yet been reissued on CD. *—Ron Wynn*

See See Rider / 1963 / Atlantic ✦✦✦

★ **Soul on Fire: The Best of LaVern Baker** / 1991 / Atlantic ✦✦✦✦✦
The cream of this vivacious '50s R&B belter's Atlantic catalog comprises this 20-track hits collection. Includes Baker's bouncy "Tweedlee Dee," and the storming rockers "Jim Dandy" and "Bop-Ting-a-Ling," the pseudo-gospel raveup "Saved," and Baker's torchy blues ballads "Soul on Fire" and "I Cried a Tear." She imparts "See See Rider" with a lighthearted reading that contrasts starkly with Chuck Willis' Atlantic smash of a few years before. *—Bill Dahl*

Woke Up This Mornin' / Apr. 1992 / DRG ✦✦✦
Credible comeback effort that spotlights Baker's still-seductive pipes on a program of mostly familiar standards—everything from the straight-ahead blues "Rock Me Baby" to the Stax-era "Knock on Wood" and "I Can't Turn You Loose" to the Bee Gees' "To Love Somebody" and Carole King's sappy "You've Got a Friend." Supple backing by a cadre of New York session aces—guitarist Cornell Dupree, drummer Bernard Purdie, keyboardist Paul Griffin, bassist Chuck Rainey—adds the proper grooves for each. *—Bill Dahl*

Blues Side of Rock 'n' Roll / 1993 / Star Club ✦✦✦✦✦
This import may be of slightly dubious origins (sounds like everything was dubbed from vinyl, though the sound quality is quite acceptable), but it delves a lot deeper into LaVern Baker's Atlantic discography (26 cuts) and picks up a few essential sides ignored by Atlantic's own CD: "Tra La La," "Voodoo Voodoo," "Hey Memphis" (Baker's sequel to Elvis' "Little Sister"), and a hellacious version of "He's a Real Gone Guy" sporting a vicious King Curtis sax break. *—Bill Dahl*

LaVern/LaVern Baker / Jul. 28, 1998 / Collectables ✦✦✦✦✦
This Collectables CD contains LaVern Baker's first two albums, *LaVern* and *LaVern Baker*, on disc. Both records are excellent—even if a couple of cuts fall a little flat, most of the material is first-rate and Baker is in terrific form, singing with power and grace. The remastering and packaging aren't quite up to the standard of the music itself, but serious Baker fans will want this disc regardless, since it contains so many fine recordings that aren't available anywhere else. *—Stephen Thomas Erlewine*

See See Rider/Blues Ballads / Jul. 28, 1998 / Collectables ✦✦✦✦✦
Like its companion disc *LaVern/LaVern Baker*, this Collectables CD contains two early LaVern Baker albums, *See See Rider* and *Blues Ballads*, on one disc. There are a couple of minor flaws with each album, but for the most part, they each are dominated by great songs and performances, illustrating what a terrific, powerful vocalist Baker was. The remastering and packaging aren't quite up to the standard of the music itself, but serious Baker fans will want this disc regardless, since it contains so many fine recordings that aren't available anywhere else. *—Stephen Thomas Erlewine*

Precious Memories/LaVern Sings Bessie Smith / Jul. 11, 2000 / Collectables ✦✦✦✦
LaVern Baker praises the Lord on one hand ("Journey to the Sky" and "Just a Closer Walk With Thee") and tributes Bessie Smith on the other ("Empty Bed Blues" and "Gimme a Pigfoot [And a Bottle of Beer]") on the same CD. Baker's splendid vocals and superlative productions and arrangements make this contrasting gospel and blues union work. *—Andrew Hamilton*

Mickey Baker

b. Oct. 15, 1925, Louisville, KY

Guitar / East Coast Blues, Rock & Roll, R&B

Of all the guitarists who helped transform rhythm & blues into rock & roll, Mickey Baker is one of the very most important, ranking almost on the level of Chuck Berry and Bo Diddley. The reason he isn't nearly as well known as those legends is that a great deal of his work wasn't issued under his own name, but as a backing guitarist for many R&B and rock & roll musicians. Baker originally aspired to be a jazz musician, but turned to calypso, mambo, and then R&B, where the most work could be found. In the early and mid-'50s, he did countless sessions for Atlantic, King, RCA, Decca, and OKeh, playing on such classics as the Drifters' "Money Honey" and "Such a Night," Joe Turner's "Shake Rattle & Roll," Ruth Brown's "Mama, He Treats Your Daughter Mean," and Big Maybelle's "Whole Lot of Shakin' Going On." He also released a few singles under his own name, and made a Latin jazz-tinged solo album, *Guitar Mambo*. Baker's best work, though, was recorded as half of the duo Mickey & Sylvia. Their hit "Love Is Strange," as well as several other unknown but nearly equally strong tracks, featured Baker's keening, bluesy guitar riffs, which were gutsier and more piercing than most anything else around in the late '50s. Mickey & Sylvia split in the late '50s (though they recorded off and on until the middle of the next decade), and Baker recorded his best solo album, the all-instrumental *The Wildest Guitar*. In 1961, he took the male spoken part (usually assumed to be Ike Turner) on Ike & Tina Turner's first hit, "It's Gonna Work Out Fine." Shortly afterwards he moved to France, making a few hard-to-find solo records and working with a lot of French pop and rock performers, including Ronnie Bird, the best '60s French rock singer. He's recorded only sporadically since the mid-'60s. *—Richie Unterberger*

The Wildest Guitar / 1959 / Atlantic ✦✦✦✦✦
Despite Baker's well-deserved reputation as one of the most influential guitar players of early rock & roll, *The Wildest Guitar* was one of the few chances he really got to strut his stuff as a solo artist. This entirely instrumental set features keening, sharp bluesy riffs in much the same distinctive style that gained him fame on "Love Is Strange" and other tunes with Mickey & Sylvia. The choice of material, though, is a bit surprising, favoring some surprisingly cornball standards: "Third Man Theme," "Autumn Leaves," "Lullaby of the Leaves," and Cole Porter's "Night and Day." Baker (who also arranged the album) manages to invest all of these with a snazzy R&B feel and biting solos. And he does actually write four of the twelve tunes himself, on which he fashions the kind of straightforward R&B that one would be more likely to expect. This is a pretty good showcase to hear Baker's unadorned virtuosity. But he's really better appreciated within the context of stronger material, either as half of Mickey & Sylvia or on the innumerable '50s R&B cuts (many on Atlantic) that feature his session work. *—Richie Unterberger*

● **Rock With a Sock** / Jun. 28, 1994 / Bear Family ✦✦✦✦✦
This 28-cut single disc covers several early and mid-'50s tracks with Baker finding creative ways to perform on period-piece rock and R&B/novelty material. His playing is uniformly impressive, even when fitting into less-than-outstanding productions and compositions. There are five Mickey & Sylvia tracks that conclude the session; they range from the interesting "Hello Stranger" to the odd "Woe, Woe Is Me," but really take away from the disc's purpose—to showcase Mickey Baker the player and demonstrate why he has such a sterling reputation among guitar fans and musicians. *—Ron Wynn*

Long John Baldry

b. Jan. 12, 1941, London, England

Vocals / British Blues, British Invasion, Blues-Rock

Like Cliff Richard, Chris Farlowe, Slade, Blur, and eel pie, Long John Baldry is one of those peculiarly British phenomenons that doggedly resists American translation. As a historical figure, he has undeniable importance. When he began singing as a teenager in the '50s, he was one of the first British vocalists to perform folk and blues music. In the early '60s, he sang in the band of British blues godfather Alexis Korner, Blues Incorporated, which also served as a starting point for future rock stars Mick Jagger, Jack Bruce, and others. As a member of Blues Incorporated, he contributed to the first British blues album, *R&B at the Marquee* (1962). He then joined the Cyril Davies R&B All Stars, taking over the group (renamed Long John Baldry and His Hoochie Coochie Men) after Davies' death in early 1964. This band featured Rod Stewart as a second vocalist, and also employed Geoff Bradford (who had been in an embryonic version of the Rolling Stones) on guitar.

In the mid-'60s, he helped form Steampacket, a proto-supergroup that also featured Stewart, Julie Driscoll, and Brian Auger. When Steampacket broke up, he fronted Bluesology, the band that gave keyboardist Reg Dwight—soon to become Elton John—his first prestigious gig. He was a well-liked figure on the London club circuit, and in fact the Beatles took him on as a guest on one of their 1964 British TV specials, at a time when the Fab Four could have been no bigger, and Baldry was virtually unknown.

All of these famous associations, alas, don't change the hard fact that Baldry wasn't much of a singer. His dry-as-dust, charmless croak approximated what Manfred Mann's Paul Jones (whom Baldry resembled slightly physically) may have sounded like while recovering from a tonsillectomy. His greatest commercial success came not with blues, but unbearably gloppy orchestrated pop ballads that echoed Engelbert Humperdinck. The 1967 single "Let the Heartaches Begin" reached number one in Britain, and Baldry had several other small British hits in the late '60s, the biggest of which was "Mexico" (1968). (None of these made an impression in the U.S.)

The commercial success of his ballads led Baldry to forsake the blues on record for a few years. Cruel as it may be to say, it wasn't much of a loss to the blues world; Baldry's early blues recordings don't hold a candle even to second-tier acts like Graham Bond, let alone the Stones or the Bluesbreakers. He returned to blues and rock in 1971 on *It Ain't Easy*, for which Rod Stewart and Elton John shared the production duties. The album contained a tiny American chart item, "Don't Try to Lay No Boogie-Woogie on the King of Rock 'n' Roll," and Stewart and John split the production once again on the 1972 follow-up,

Everything Stops for Tea. Baldry never caught on as an international figure, though, and by 1980 had become a Canadian citizen. He continued to record, and did commercial voice-overs as well as the voice of Captain Robotnick in children's cartoons. *—Richie Unterberger*

● **Long John's Blues** / Aug. 1964 / Ascot ✦✦✦✦
Stacked up against other British blues/R&B albums of the time, this is a distinctly lower-echelon effort, much stiffer and more routine than the recordings of the Rolling Stones, John Mayall, Graham Bond, Duffy Power, and others. What made early British efforts in this style exciting was the sense of risk-taking, even recklessness. Baldry and the Hoochie Coochie Men are totally lacking in that department, displaying a by-the-numbers approach in arrangements (particularly in the trad piano rolls) and material selection, which consists almost entirely of overdone standards like "My Babe," "Got My Mojo Working," and "Goin' Down Slow." Stacked up against Baldry's own work, though, this qualifies as his most "essential" effort, if only because it is for his contributions to the British blues scene that he is most remembered. This is the most accurate reflection of his work in that field, and Baldry is in better voice here than he is on much of his later '60s work. The album is still mediocre or worse, although it does feature Geoff Bradford (who played in a very early precursor to the Rolling Stones) on guitar. The BGO CD reissue combines *Long John's Blues* and the 1966 LP *Looking at Long John* on one disc. *—Richie Unterberger*

Looking at Long John / 1966 / United Artists ✦✦✦
Baldry's move from blues into pop/soul for his second album may have been viewed as something of a loss in integrity, given his purist blues stance on his debut. Maybe it wasn't such a bad idea, though, given that the debut LP wasn't very good, and the British blues-rock field was crowded with many greater talents in the mid-'60s. *Looking at Long John*, with a sub-Righteous Brothers sort of approach, is certainly a change in style, but the result really isn't any better. Baldry's vocal limitations are a big handicap whether applied to white-boy blues or blue-eyed soul, and the production is thin in comparison with the American soul/pop it's clearly trying to emulate. If you wanted this kind of stuff, the Righteous Brothers did it many times better. Not only that, if you were British at the time and weren't aware of the Righteous Brothers, you weren't about to turn to John Baldry; the Walker Brothers (American, but based in Britain) also did this kind of stuff much better. The BGO CD reissue combines this and the 1964 LP *Long John's Blues* on one disc. *—Richie Unterberger*

Let the Heartaches Begin / 1968 / Sequel ✦✦
With "Let the Heartaches Begin," Baldry abandoned all pretenses at blues or soul for treacly MOR pop of the worst sort. The marketplace did not respond with the emphatic veto that cosmic justice demanded; on the contrary, the single went to number one in Britain and was the singer's greatest commercial success by far. The album offered material in the same vein: over-orchestrated, sentimental ballads with female backup vocals supporting Long John's hoarse wall of gravel, many written by the same Tony Macaulay-John Macleod team that was responsible for "Heartaches." Even if you've got a yen for MOR British pop of the period, you're much better off with Tom Jones, or even Engelbert Humperdinck. The BGO CD reissue combines this and the 1969 LP *Wait for Me* on one disc. *—Richie Unterberger*

Let There Be Long John / 1968 / Pye ✦✦

Wait for Me / 1969 / Janus ✦✦✦
For his last album of the '60s, Baldry took a marginally more soulful approach than he had on *Let the Heartaches Begin*, although Tony Macaulay (co-writer of the "Let the Heartaches Begin" single) was still around to feed him a few mainstream pop tunes. The result was more bearable than the previous effort, but not much. No one's going to highly value Baldry's soul-revue interpretations of "Sunshine of Your Love," "Cry Like a Baby," or other soul and rock hits of the period, even for camp or nostalgia value. The more pop-oriented selections are still the sort of cabaret-ish hack jobs that induce grimaces, and Baldry's vocals are still lacking in basic chops. The CD reissue adds the bonus tracks "Mexico" and "When the Sun Comes Shining Thru'," which were both British Top 30 hits for Baldry in the late '60s. The BGO CD reissue combines *Wait for Me* and the 1967 LP *Let the Heartaches Begin* on one disc. *—Richie Unterberger*

Golden Hour of Long John Baldry / 1969 / Knight-Castle ✦✦✦
A 20-song CD built around Baldry's number one British smash "Let the Heartaches Begin" and songs from that session and related ones. None of it works terribly well, as Baldry tries for a Stax/Volt-type ambience on half the material ("Sunshine of Your Love," "River Deep Mountain High") only to fall way short of anyone ever associated with the Memphis outfit—the presence of string-laden dreck like "For All We Know" (not the Carpenters song) and what may be the worst cover of "MacArthur Park" ever done by anybody, in his best (i.e., worst) Engelbert Humperdinck manner, only destroys whatever value resided in the livelier R&B-based songs. It's all pretty horrendous, considering that Baldry was still cool enough in late 1966 to be introducing the Rolling Stones for the principal gig captured on *Got Live If You Want It*. Still, this stuff does represent the peak of Baldry's commercial career, so it should appeal to someone, and the mastering is decent, though the annotation is nonexistent. *—Bruce Eder*

It Ain't Easy / 1971 / Warner Brothers ✦✦✦
It Ain't Easy features a British blues/rock lineup befitting the man behind the Long John Baldry moniker. This album returns Baldry to a decidedly edgier and hipper audience, with a literal cast of all-stars on some of the more adventurous material he had covered to date. This is no doubt due, at least in part, to the involvement of rock superstars Rod Stewart and Elton John. In fact, John confesses to have taken the last name in his stage moniker from Baldry's first. Among their contributions to the project, Stewart and Elton divided the production tasks—each taking a side of the original album. Immediately, Baldry sheds the MOR blue-eyed pop soul image. The backing band on Stewart's side include fellow Face and future Rolling Stone, Ron Wood, on electric guitar and acoustic guitarist Sam Mitchell, who appeared on many of Stewart's early-'70s solo albums. His contributions to this side are numerous, including an especially potent solo on Leadbelly's "Black Girl." This authentic duet featuring Maggie Bell on co-lead vocals is a definite return to the Mississippi Delta for the song which is also known as the bluegrass standard "In the Pines." Other highlights from Stewart's sector include the humorous and self-biographical lead-off track "Conditional Discharge," which is paired with the full-tilt boogie of "Don't Try to Lay No Boogie-Woogie on the King of Rock & Roll." Arguably the oddest cover version on this album is also among the best; "Morning Morning" from head Fug Tuli Kupferberg is given new and surprisingly fresh life by Baldry. Highlights from Elton John's side include Randy Newman's "Let's Burn Down the Cornfield," which would have fit perfectly on John's Tumbleweed Connection album. Additionally, "Rock Me When He's Gone" was actually recorded by John, although his version remained unissued until the 1992 odds and sods compilation *Rare Masters*. *—Lindsay Planer*

On Stage Tonight–Baldry's Out! / 1979 / EMI ✦✦✦
On Stage Tonight—Baldry's Out! nicely rectifies a 30-year oversight: the gentleman has never previously released a live recording. Captured in Germany, the disc blends the strongest tracks from Baldry's *It Still Ain't Easy* comeback album with updated past greats. And it just wouldn't be Baldry (especially live) without the ferocious backing of longtime soulmate Kathi McDonald. While Baldry's blues can sometimes be a tad too "polite," *On Stage Tonight* captures that unique smoky growl in top form. *—Roch Parisien*

It Still Ain't Easy / 1991 / Stony Plain ✦✦✦✦
Baldry's deep, rough-edged vocals have not changed over the years. The band is tight, with Mike Kalanj's Hammond B-3 and Bill Rogers' sax standing out. There are no flaws on this one, just great music. *—Chip Renner*

Right to Sing the Blues / 1996 / Stony Plain ✦✦✦
One of the founding fathers of the '60s British Blues scene, Long John Baldry owns one of the great white blues voices, a power that remains undiminished for *Right to Sing the Blues*. The disc forms another consistent Baldry primer visiting the rich diversity of blues styles, from the quiet folk-blues of "Whoa Back Buck" (longtime colleague Papa John King tearing up his slide guitar) to jump blues party tunes like opener "They Raided the Joint." Vocal sidekick Kathi McDonald also carries the torch, especially on an incendiary title track already highlighted by a scorching Colin James guitar riff. On occasion, the tall one is too much the mannered gentleman for the good of his muse. I would love to hear him bust loose more frequently—as he does on "I'm Shakin'," his pipes sounding like gargled nails with an Irish Cream chaser. It would also be nice to find him writing again. While mostly recognized as a judicious interpreter, Baldry has proven his capability over the years, and the complete absence of self-penned material strikes one as borderline laziness. He even dips back to a tune already covered on a previous release—Bonnie Dobson's classic "Morning Dew"—albeit giving it a fresh Cajun/Zydeco coat of paint. In case dependable, honorable music isn't enough incentive on its own, the disc earns bonus points by concluding with a 23-minute interview in which Baldry recounts his take on the British Blues scene. Not exactly flashy multimedia, but a nice addition for fans of pop music history. *—Roch Parisien*

A Thrill's a Thrill: The Canadian Years / 1996 / EMI ✦✦✦✦
Two-CD set *A Thrill's a Thrill—The Canadian Years* distills the best from Baldry's seven Canadian releases, recorded between 1979 and 1993. I would have been happier with a complete career retrospective, but the highlights here hold up elegantly in their own right: "Baldry's Out," "It Still Ain't Easy," and a definitive covers of "Morning Dew" among them. Besides, an eight-minute live rendition of signature song "Don't Try to Lay No Boogie-Woogie on the King of Rock & Roll" captures the old days nicely. *—Roch Parisien*

Live / 2000 / Stony Plain ✦✦✦
Brit blues legend Baldry recorded this live album during his 1999 European tour on a Hamburg stop. During the '60s blues resurgence, Baldry had musicians such as Charlie Watts, Rod Stewart, and Jack Bruce pass through his bands. His sound still echoes the tough, power blues that led to the development of such groups as Cream and Led Zeppelin. Baldry chooses to do much of his classic material while leading the group from his 12-string acoustic guitar. Long John is a potent, gravel-voiced blues man. His tough, exaggerated blues-rock is guaranteed to wow a crowd. Capturing this in a live setting makes for an excellent document of Long John's time-tested talent. An added bonus is a shining new star on the blues scene and new member to Baldry's trio, guitarist Matt Taylor. The liner notes include an overview of Baldry's entire career with photos going back to the '60s. *—Tom Schulte*

Remembering Leadbelly / Nov. 6, 2001 / Stony Plain ✦✦✦
Long John Baldry came of age as a singer during the British blues boom, and it's obvious that his love of the music hasn't left him. As he explains in the interview track at the end, Leadbelly was his first musical inspiration, and here he has his chance to pay homage to the man. In his sixties at the time of this recording, Baldry's voice has improved with age, deepening a little and sounding more gravelly—just perfect for the grittiness of Leadbelly's songs, which ran the gamut from blues to folk, gospel, and beyond. It's an intelligent selection, ignoring the obvious "Goodnight Irene" and "In the Pines," while keeping defining moments like "Rock Island Line" (the tune that launched skiffle in England), "Birmingham Jail," and "We're in the Same Boat Brother"—it's remarkable just how familiar so much of the material is. The version of "Gallows Pole" (much better known for its subsequent incarnation as a Led Zeppelin piece) roars with power and urgency, "Lining Track" and "John Hardy" (whose unusual arrangement centers around pump organ) are definitive railroad songs, while the hymns "Mary Don't You Weep" and

"We Shall Walk Through the Valley," though springing from an older well, were very much a part of the Huddie Leadbetter repertoire. There's even a children's song, "On a Christmas Day," showing yet another facet of the big man. Add in an interview with Alan Lomax, the folklorist who discovered Leadbelly and helped his career, and you have something that stands as more than a tribute, but a full portrait of a seminal American artist. *—Chris Nickson*

Marcia Ball

b. Mar. 20, 1949, Orange, TX

Vocals, Piano / Swamp Blues, Louisiana Blues, Piano Blues, Modern Electric Blues

Pianist and singer/songwriter Marcia Ball is a living example of how East Texas blues meets southwest Louisiana swamp rock. Ball was born March 20, 1949, in Orange, TX, but grew up across the border in Vinton, LA. That town is squarely in the heart of "the Texas triangle," an area that includes portions of both states and has produced some of the country's greatest blues talents: Janis Joplin, Johnny and Edgar Winter, Queen Ida Guillory, Lonnie Brooks, Zachary Richard, Clifton Chenier, and Kenny Neal, to name a few. Ball's earliest awareness of blues came over the radio, where she heard people like Irma Thomas, Professor Longhair, and Etta James, all of whom she now credits as influences. She began playing piano at age five, learning from her grandmother and aunt and also taking formal lessons from a teacher.

Ball entered Louisiana State University in the late '60s as an English major. In college, she played in the psychedelic rock & roll band Gum. In 1970, Ball and her first husband were headed West in their car to San Francisco, but the car needed repairs in Austin, where they had stopped off to visit one of their former bandmates. After hearing, seeing, and tasting some of the music, sights, and food in Austin, the two decided to stay there. Ball has been based in Austin ever since.

Her piano style, which mixes equal parts boogie woogie with zydeco and Louisiana swamp rock, is best-exemplified on her series of excellent recordings for the Rounder label. They include *Soulful Dress* (1983), *Hot Tamale Baby* (1985), *Gatorhythms* (1989), and *Blue House* (1994). Also worthy of checking out is her collaboration with Angela Strehli and Lou Ann Barton on Antone's *Dreams Come True* (1990). Ball, like her peer Strehli, is an educated business woman fully aware of all the realities of the record business. Ball never records until she feels she's got a batch of top-notch, quality songs. Most of the songs on her albums are her own creations, so songwriting is a big part of her job description. Although Ball is a splendid piano player and a more than adequate vocalist, "the songwriting process is the most fulfilling part of the whole deal for me," she said in a 1994 interview, "so I always keep my ears and eyes open for things I might hear or see.... I like my songs to go back to blues in some fashion." As much a student of the music as she is a player, some of Ball's albums include covers of material by O.V. Wright, Dr. John, Joe Ely, Clifton Chenier, and Shirley & Lee.

In the late '90s, Ball released her final discs to be released under the Rounder banner, *Let Me Play With Your Poodle* (1997) and *Sing It!* (1998). The latter featured Ball with Irma Thomas and Tracy Nelson utilizing both solo and combined energy that generated much exposure for all three women as it was nominated for both a Grammy and a W.C. Handy Blues Award as Best Contemporary Blues Album. Ironically, while both of Ball's final Rounder releases were critically acclaimed, she signed with Alligator Records in 2000 and released her first album for the label, *Presumed Innocent*, in 2001. Ball, who's established herself as an important player in the club scenes in both New Orleans and Austin, continues to work at festivals and clubs throughout the U.S., Canada, and Europe. *—Richard Skelly & Al Campbell*

Soulful Dress / 1983 / Rounder ✦✦✦

Marcia Ball got things started in a celebratory fashion on her debut Rounder release, doing the title track in a taunting, challenging manner aided by flashy guitar riffs from Stevie Ray Vaughan. From there, she artfully displayed other sides of her personality, from dismayed to defiant and assured. Her rendition of "Soul On Fire" was heartfelt, but didn't approach the majestic quality of LaVern Baker's original. She did much better on "I Don't Want No Man," striking the air of disdain and dissatisfaction that Bobby "Blue" Bland immortalized on "I Don't Want No Woman"; guitarist Kenny Ray even got the Wayne Bennett licks down perfectly. *—Ron Wynn*

Hot Tamale Baby / Apr. 1985 / Rounder ✦✦✦✦✦

Marcia Ball solidifed the favorable impression made with her debut Rounder effort with this rousing second outing. She dedicated it to the late King of Zydeco, Clifton Chenier, and was backed by a fine band of veteran pros that included saxophonist Alvin Tyler. Ball ripped through Booker T. Jones' soul gem "Never Like This Before" and Chenier's title composition, while also demonstrating her own facility with R&B on "That's Enough of That Stuff" and "Love's Spell." She came close, but didn't quite hit the mark on O.V. Wright's "I'm Gonna Forget About You," turning in a more than acceptable rendition that still didn't approach the original. But other than that one misstep, which she compensated for with a charged version of "I Don't Know," Marcia Ball proved that her debut was no fluke. *—Ron Wynn*

● **Gatorhythms** / 1989 / Rounder ✦✦✦✦✦

Marcia Ball explored R&B and honky-tonk country on this album, keeping her blues chops in order while expanding her repertoire. She included a pair of tunes by country vocalist Lee Roy Parnell, "What's A Girl To Do" and "Red Hot," doing both in a feisty, attacking fashion. She also was challenging and upbeat on Dr. John's "How You Carry On" and "Find Another Fool." Her third Rounder album was her most entertaining and dynamic, as Ball became less of an interpreter and more of an individualist. *—Ron Wynn*

Dreams Come True / 1990 / Antone's ✦✦✦

Dreams Come True is an all-star session by vocalists Marcia Ball, Lou Ann Barton and Angela Strehli. The three women sing with a band led by Dr. John and the session features guest appearances by such luminaries as David "Fathead" Newman and Jimmie Vaughan. The music is straight out of the Texas school of roadhouse R&B and blues boogie but it's delivered with a gritty, hearfelt edge, particularly on the part of the three vocalists. *Dreams Come True* may follow formula, but it's followed with style and affection, which makes it a very enjoyable listen. *—Thom Owens*

Blue House / 1994 / Rounder ✦✦✦✦

Though purists may quibble about her interpretations of classic material, just about everyone acknowledges that Marcia Ball is one fine songwriter. *Blue House* contains eight gems of swamp boogie fusion, delivered in Ball's supple, slinky voice. Listen to "The Facts of Life", a slow, sensual, worldly piece of Louisiana soul with an irresistible melody. It takes some living to write this kind of song, and considerable skill to give it this memorable delivery. Consider "St. Gabriel," a song that sounds so much like a lost blues classic that you'll check the credits to see what Delta legend penned it. Surprise! It's Marcia Ball. Her covers on *Blue House* are unusually well chosen—"Fingernails" fits her so well that it's hard to believe it's a Joe Ely tune, and her piano work on "Red Beans" does the song proud. And if her slightly subdued performance on "If This Is Love" isn't quite up to the energy level that the song deserves, it's one cut out of twelve, and the other eleven are stellar. *Blue House* is a marvelous album with plenty of personality and character, and highly recommended. *—Richard Foss*

Let Me Play With Your Poodle / Jun. 24, 1997 / Rounder ✦✦✦✦✦

This album of snaky swamp rock is one of Ball's best recordings. Great choice of songs (she wrote 5 of the 13) that let her show all her talents, both vocally and instrumentally. Slow tempo songs display the force of her voice, as in "I Still Love You," and another of the many gems, "For the Love of a Man." Meanwhile, the playfulness of the title cut and "The Right Tool for the Job" allow her to have fun and let the band air it out. Then there is the perfect song to end the disc and an absolute *tour de force*, Randy Newman's "Louisiana 1927."

Ball has again assembled another top-notch cast of characters who more than hold up their end of the bargain. A few of the many who shine are George Rains on drums, Mark Kazanoff, who does double duty as a co-producer and excels on various saxes, and Derek O'Brien, who also co-produced and shares much of the guitar work with Steve Williams. If you don't know Marcia Ball, this is a fantastic introduction, and if you liked her past work this is a gem you won't want to miss. *—Bob Gottlieb*

Sing It! / Jan. 13, 1998 / Rounder ✦✦✦

As a matter of fact we are docking into past ports a bit here on this retro excursion into protofeminist diva rock. *Sing It!* is a blessed event, too—and a great excuse to visit New Orleans for this "summit meeting" of major minds and throats of three of the most formidable female voices on at least three musical maps today. Other triple threat records take heed: this is exactly how its done, a perfect collaboration done with honor, grace, and deep within the southern traditions of vocal licks-trading, which makes this artifact timeproof. Tracy Nelson has that earth-mother caterwaul as she summons, and we recall, the depths of the '60s as only Nelson can remind us. Irma Thomas growls ferociously from under a streetlamp and will not let us walk on by. Her sass is matched by Marcia Ball's downtown attitude and hunker-down suggestiveness. Spinetinglers to the core, each one. These tunes romp as well as they stomp and successfully mark territories among soul singers, blues artists, country strutters and just plain funky womanity, they way we love our Memphis gals (and how they can scare the crawfish out of a fella). The songs themselves sing of familiar old territories—deadbeat dads and old lovers, less than rosy rolling in the clover, releasing those Saturday night ya-yas—but the intensity of each of these hardcore principals bring a resonance to each small moment on the record. Their backup reads like a veritable roster of first-chair Memphis originals, installing that swampy-deep backwoods, diggin-it groove. This is a fine, fine record by three brilliant, completely authentic women: a gem of backwater to runneth over. *—Becky Byrkit*

Presumed Innocent / Apr. 24, 2001 / Alligator ✦✦✦

Hank Ballard

b. Nov. 18, 1936, Detroit, MI

Vocals, Leader, Songwriter / R&B

In the world of early rhythm & blues and doo wop, Hank Ballard was the very definition of earthiness. Though influenced by high-energy gospel vocal groups, Ballard's music with the Midnighters couldn't have been more diametrically opposed in terms of subject matter: his lyrics were filled with raunchy double entendres that left little to the imagination, pushing the envelope of what was considered acceptable in the '50s. His songs were sometimes banned on the radio, but that only made him an even bigger jukebox favorite among black audiences. Ballard's hard-driving, rhythmic style was also an underappreciated influence on the rawer side of R&B, particularly on a young James Brown; plus, his composition "The Twist"—recorded for a hit by Chubby Checker—became one of the biggest hits in rock & roll history.

Hank Ballard was born November 18, 1936, in Detroit, but moved to Bessemer, AL, as a young child following his father's death. There he began singing in church and when he returned to Detroit at age 15, he set about forming a doo wop group while working on the Ford assembly line. Around the same time, singers Henry Booth and Charles Sutton were organizing a doo wop outfit called the Royals, which reputedly at one time also featured Jackie Wilson and future Four Top Levi Stubbs; it eventually grew to include vocalists Lawson Smith and Sonny Woods, plus gritty guitarist Alonzo Tucker. Initially copying the smooth style of Sonny Til & the Orioles, the Royals were discovered by Johnny Otis in 1952 and signed with Federal Records. However, when Hank Ballard replaced Smith in 1953, they adopted a rougher, more hepped-up sound in keeping with Ballard's numerous original compositions and Clyde McPhatter influence. Ballard's first recording with the group was 1953's "Get It," which hit the Top Ten on the R&B charts, but it was the following year's ribald "Work With Me Annie" that really broke the group (they changed their name to the Midnighters around this time, to avoid confusion with the Five Royales). "Work With Me Annie" topped the R&B charts and nearly reached the pop Top 20, despite a number of radio stations refusing to air the song. It inspired a number of answer records and the Midnighters themselves entered the fray with the sequels "Annie Had a Baby" (another R&B chart-topper) and "Annie's Aunt Fannie." They also scored another major smash with the Ballard-penned "Sexy Ways," which solidified their reputation as R&B's most risqué act.

However, after the momentum of "Work With Me Annie" slowed, the Midnighters seemed at a loss as to how to recapture it. They went nearly three and a half years without another big hit, and with the decline in their fortunes came numerous personnel shifts. Lawson Smith returned to the fold to replace Sutton, Norman Thrasher replaced Sonny Woods, and Tucker's guitar post was taken first by Arthur Porter, then Cal Green. Ballard attempted to take his 1958 composition "The Twist" to Vee-Jay, which declined to release the version they recorded; King, Federal's parent label, issued it as the B-side of the Midnighters' R&B comeback ballad hit "Teardrops on Your Letter" in 1959. Still, "The Twist" gained some notice and found a fan in *American Bandstand* host Dick Clark, who brought the song to Chubby Checker's attention; the rest was history, as "The Twist" became the first song to hit number one during two completely separate chart runs. Ballard and the Midnighters benefited from the exposure, scoring their first Top Ten pop singles in 1960 with "Finger Poppin' Time" and "Let's Go, Let's Go, Let's Go." A few more R&B hits followed, generally dance-oriented songs in the vein of "The Twist," before the well dried up for a second time. The Midnighters gradually disintegrated and Ballard became a solo act; by the end of the '60s, he was working with longtime fan James Brown, who produced several singles for Ballard during the late '60s and early '70s. After a lengthy absence from music, Ballard re-formed the Midnighters during the mid-'80s, first as a female group, then male, and began touring once again. In 1990, Ballard received his due as an R&B innovator with his election into the Rock & Roll Hall of Fame. —*Steve Huey*

Singin' & Swingin' / Jun. 1959 / King ◆◆◆◆◆

Vintage red-hot R&B, shouting vocals, and frenzied instrumentals. Hank Ballard led one of the finest R&B orchestras on the '50s circuit, and his King albums are masterpieces. His singing was usually steamy, his lyrics laden with innuendo, and he kept up a furious pace throughout each album. This is one of about ten Ballard albums that have been reissued on CD and is certainly well worth getting in any configuration. —*Ron Wynn*

Mr. Rhythm & Blues (Finger Poppin' Time) / 1960 / King ◆◆◆

While Hank Ballard & the Midnighters scored their biggest hits in the mid-'50s ("Work With Me Annie," "Sexy Ways"), they certainly didn't stop making the charts and cutting quality sides in the years that followed. And while many newcomers will want to first check out one of the fine retrospectives available, like Rhino's *Sexy Ways: The Best of Hank Ballard & the Midnighters*, seasoned listeners will not be disappointed by this circa-1960 release on the group's longtime label, King. Featuring the Top Ten smash "Finger Poppin' Time" and the infectious "The Coffee Grind," *Mr. Rhythm & Blues* rolls out the group's patented blend of gospel, R&B, and pop on 12 quality tracks. —*Stephen Cook*

★ Sexy Ways: The Best of Hank Ballard & the Midnighters / Nov. 16, 1993 / Rhino ◆◆◆◆◆

Hank Ballard & the Midnighters were the 2 Live Crew of the early '50s, burning up the airwaves and black jukeboxes with lascivious-for-the-time period tunes like "Work with Me Annie," "Annie Had a Baby," and the title track. Although Ballard would go on to write dance hits, including the original version of "The Twist," the Midnighters at their best ("Open Up the Back Door") were Black doo wop at the end of a dark alley. Forget all previous compilations on these guys, this is the one you want. —*Cub Koda*

The EP Collection . . . Plus / Sep. 12, 2000 / See for Miles ◆◆◆◆

See for Miles' *EP Collection*, like most of the series, is a greatest-hits collection from Hank Ballard containing almost all of his biggest hits, plus a bunch of notable B-sides and covers. There are a few nifty rarities here, but also a couple of obscurities that aren't all that interesting either (the instrumental "The Big Frog"), and just because there are a generous 24 tracks doesn't necessarily mean that this is preferable to tighter collections. All the same, it's a fine collection of Ballard's best recordings and, while Rhino's set may be preferable, you'll still understand Ballard's greatness if you get this instead. —*Stephen Thomas Erlewine*

Dancin' and Twistin' / Oct. 31, 2000 / Ace ◆◆◆

Since Ballard & the Midnighters remain most known for their mid-'50s R&B/early rock & roll hits, it has sometimes been overlooked that they actually reached their crossover pop peak in the early '60s. In 1960 and 1961, they had seven Top 40 hits in the pop charts, and two Top Ten hits with "Finger Poppin' Time" and "Let's Go, Let's Go, Let's Go." All of those hits are on this 24-song anthology, which is devoted almost exclusively to Ballard's '60s output. Ballard's original version of "The Twist," recorded in 1958 (and a Top 30 hit in 1960, although Chubby Checker's cover went to number one) is here, and its success laid the foundation for an endless series of dance records over the next few years. "The Coffee Grind," "The Continental Walk," "The Switch-a-Roo," "It's Twistin' Time," "Good Twistin' Tonight," "Do You Know How to Twist?," even "The Float": all are on board. (And how could one resist calling "The Float" a dance bound to be dead on the water, even if it did make number ten R&B?) Ballard may have been more earthy, more funky, and more authentic in every way than Chubby Checker, but in this era he was really pursuing a similar formula: twist and dance records, the themes recycled ad infinitum. And it must be conceded that the formula, in Ballard's hands, wears out its welcome when the singles are heard bang right after each other. It's competent dance rock bridging '50s R&B and early soul, without nearly enough variation or innovation to sustain interest. Really, "Finger Poppin' Time," "Let's Go, Let's Go, Let's Go," and "The Twist" are all you need to hear from this era, and you can probably find them on various-artists anthologies without breaking too heavy a sweat. —*Richie Unterberger*

The Very Best of Hank Ballard and the Midnighters / Oct. 9, 2001 / Collectables ◆◆◆

Though it bills itself *The Very Best of Hank Ballard and the Midnighters*, Collectables' compilation doesn't quite live up to that title, since it's missing several definitive singles,

including "Sexy Ways," "Work With Me Annie," and "Annie Had a Baby." However, it does feature some of Ballard's more pop-oriented songs, such as "Teardrops on Your Letter," "Let's Go, Let's Go, Let's Go," "Finger Poppin' Time," and "The Twist." The inclusion of songs like "Work With Me Annie" would have made this album almost as good of a retrospective as *Sexy Ways: The Best of Hank Ballard and the Midnighters*; as it stands, it's just a decent collection of Ballard's mid-career work. —*Heather Phares*

Chico Banks

Guitar / Contemporary Blues, Modern Electric Chicago Blues, Soul-Blues

Along with Bernard Allison, Melvin Taylor and a handful of others, guitarist, singer and songwriter Chico Banks is part of the new generation of Chicago blues players who are expanding the boundaries of this often maligned, misunderstood music. Like Allison and Taylor, and even older Southern musicians like Larry Garner and Sherman Robertson, Banks focuses on good-time, upbeat blues.

Banks' music may not impress blues purists—he freely mixes in elements of soul, funk and rock—but when a musical form remains too static, as the late Luther Allison would say, it loses its vibrancy. He credits influences from a mixed bag of artists from the '60s and '70s: "Magic Sam" Maghett, Buddy Guy, Albert King, Jimi Hendrix, Otis Clay, George Benson and Tyrone Davis. But his playing also reflects the contribution of jazz pianist Ahmad Jamal, and the funk of Prince, the Isley Brothers, the Ohio Players and Parliament/Funkadelic. Also not to be overlooked is his father, Jessie Banks, who played with the gospel group the Mighty Clouds of Joy.

Since joining his first band, a Top 40 cover group, at 14, Banks has performed with Johnny Christian, Evidence labelmate Melvin Taylor, Buddy Guy, Otis Clay, James Cotton, Artie "Blues Boy" White, Little Milton, Magic Slim, Big Time Sarah, Chick Rogers and most recently, Mavis Staples. Banks' sessionography includes albums by Willie Kent, Freddie Roulette and Pops Staples.

On his 1997 debut, *Candy Lickin' Man*, Banks is joined by the great gospel singer Mavis Staples, who also contributes liner notes. Although only in his twenties, Banks is already a veteran song interpreter; he covers classics like "Groove Me," "Got to Be Some Changes Made" and "The Sky Is Crying," putting his own individual stamp on each tune. —*Richard Skelly*

● Candy Lickin' Man / Oct. 14, 1997 / Evidence ◆◆◆◆

When Chico Banks played guitar with the Staple Singers, his playing was hard, uncluttered, and straight to the point, yet it was tempered to fit right in with the Staples' sound. Banks' father Jessie was with the Mighty Clouds of Joy and also a bluesman, and his brother Stanley Banks is a keyboardist, with whom he co-wrote two of these songs. His playing is influenced by blues, rhythm & blues, gospel, and the psychedelia of Jimi Hendrix, especially on his tasty, never burdensome use of the wah-wah pedal. His voice is more than adequate for the job, but the cuts that stand out are those on which he concentrates on his guitar. On "It Must Be Love," Mavis Staples does the vocals, and you can feel the electricity between the two born of a mutual respect for excellence. On "All Your Love," he has "Big James" Montgomery handling the vocals and lets loose some fine playing through that wah-wah pedal. This is one of the finest guitar players to come down the avenue in a good stretch, and he can only mature from here. This is no throwaway first album, with one good cut and lots of dross; its nearly 70 minutes are filled with some mighty fine playing. —*Bob Gottlieb*

Barbecue Bob (Robert Hicks)

b. Sep. 11, 1902, Walnut Grove, GA, **d.** Oct. 21, 1931, Lithonia, GA

Vocals, Guitar / Prewar Country Blues, Country Blues

Barbecue Bob was the name given by Columbia Records talent scout Don Hornsby to Atlanta blues singer Robert Hicks. Hicks is widely credited as being the singer who more than any helped to popularize Atlanta blues in its formative period. Born to a family of sharecroppers in Walnut Grove, GA, Robert Hicks and his brother, Charlie "Lincoln" Hicks relocated with them to Newton County. There the Hicks brothers came in contact with Savannah "Dip" Weaver and her son, Curley Weaver. With the Weavers, the Hicks boys learned to play guitar and sing. Another local kid, Eddie Mapp, arrived in the area around 1922 and began to play harmonica with Robert and Charley Hicks and Curley Weaver. For several years in the early to mid-'20s, this group, or some group derived from this nucleus of musicians, would play parties and dances all around Atlanta and the surrounding territory.

Robert Hicks was the first of this group to "break out"; by 1926, Hicks was working at Tidwell's Barbecue Place in the affluent Atlanta suburb of Buckhead. Hicks would cook for, serve, and sing for the patrons. Robert Hicks proved a local sensation, and somehow attracted the notice of Columbia's Don Hornsby. Hornsby made publicity photographs of Hicks in chef's whites and devised the moniker Barbecue Bob to put on Hicks' first Columbia record, "Barbecue Blues," recorded in Atlanta on March 25, 1927. It proved a strong seller, and Hicks traveled to New York to make its follow-up, "Mississippi Heavy Water Blues," in addition to seven other titles on June 15 and 16. Lightning struck twice, and Columbia realized they had a hit artist in Barbecue Bob. Over the next three years the Columbia remote truck stopped in Atlanta on numerous occasions primarily to make records with Hicks, and altogether he made 62 sides for Columbia. Only six of these were rejected, one title being remade and three others having since been found and issued. Robert Hicks was joined by his brother, Charley Lincoln Hicks, on four of these sides; one pair recorded on November 9, 1927 ("It Won't Be Long Now Parts 1 & 2") was issued as by Barbecue Bob and Laughing Charley. This highly influential coupling is regarded as a classic and is one of the most frequently anthologized blues recordings from the '20s. Robert Hicks also participated in a pseudonymous session for QRS in December, 1930 issued as by the Georgia Cotton Pickers. This session also resulting in records being issued involving Hicks' longtime friends Curley Weaver, Eddie Mapp, and possibly a younger friend, Buddy Moss. Hicks had already completed his last session as Barbecue Bob for Columbia on the fifth of that month. Earlier that year his wife had died of pneumonia, and less than a year later Hicks himself succumbed to the same illness, brought on by a bout with influenza. He was only 29.

Robert Hicks played a 12-string Stella guitar on his recordings, but in person he was just as likely to play a 6-string. He also made some use of bottleneck techniques. Hicks was a consummate stylist of older material, and contributed textbook versions of such blues standards as "Poor Boy a Long Ways from Home," "Fo' day Creep," and "Goin' Up the Country." Eric Clapton has adopted Hicks' version of "Motherless Chile Blues." Hicks' influence extends to the whole of early Atlanta blues, and he is considered second, if not equal to Blind Willie McTell in this respect. *—Uncle Dave Lewis*

Brownskin Gal / 1927-1930 / Agram ♦♦♦
A boxed import set with a variety of blues, hokum, and comedy routines. Includes an 80-page bio and transcription book. Unfortunately, this compilation is marred by weak sound quality. *—Barry Lee Pearson*

● **Chocolate to the Bone** / 1927-1930 / Yazoo ♦♦♦♦♦
Although Robert "Barbecue Bob" Hicks recorded over 65 extant sides (three are not known to have survived) in a three-year stretch starting in 1927 up to his death in 1931, the 20 collected here make a perfect introduction to the work of this Atlanta-based artist. He may have played a big-city acoustic 12-string guitar, but Hicks' playing was provincial, down-home, and often modal, reducing any chord progression down to one or two chords. He also played embellishments on this instrument with a bottleneck, a rarity then and a rarity now. Usually tuned to an open chord, Barbecue Bob's playing nonetheless shows great diversity and musical flexibility. The 20 sides collected here (all off of old, scratchy 78s and cleaned up as well as can be expected) give a nice cross-section of that diversity as a solo artist, along with a pair of sides showcasing Bob in a small band context with Buddy Moss on harmonica and Curley Weaver on second guitar and another with Hicks backing up former gal pal Nellie Florence on a raucous "Jacksonville Blues." Of special merit for collectors is the inclusion of two previously unissued sides struck from slightly better sounding test pressings, "Twistin' Your Stuff" and "She Shook Her Gin." This expanded collection replaces the 14-track vinyl collection of the same name. *—Cub Koda*

Complete Recorded Works, Vol. 1 (1927–1928) / 1991 / Document ♦♦♦♦
"Barbecue Bob," who was born Robert Hicks, gained his nickname because he worked as a chef at a barbecue place. A warm singer and extroverted guitarist, Barbecue Bob has had his entire output (recorded during 1927-1930) reissued on three Document CDs. *Vol. 1* has 21 unaccompanied performances (all of the sessions except two from New York were recorded in Atlanta) plus the two-part "It Won't Be Long Now," which teams Hicks with hs brother, guitarist/vocalist "Laughing Charley" Hicks. Other highlights include "Barbecue Blues," "Mississippi Heavy Water Blues," "Poor Boy a Long Ways From Home," "Brown-Skin Gal," an early version of "When the Saints Go Marching In" (from 1927), "Fo Day Creep," and "Chocolate to the Bone." *—Scott Yanow*

Complete Recorded Works, Vol. 2 (1928–1929) / 1991 / Document ♦♦♦♦
"Barbecue Bob," whose complete output has been reissued on three Document CDs, was a fairly big star by the time he recorded the 23 numbers on *Vol. 2*. Based in Atlanta (where all of these performances, including a previously unreleased "Unnamed Blues," were recorded), Barbecue Bob (Robert Hicks) performed a friendly repertoire ranging from country blues to the new-fangled hokum music. Among the more memorable selections on this disc are "Mississippi Low-Levee Blues," "Midnight Weeping Blues" (one of two numbers that find him backing singer Nellie Florence), "Beggin' for Love," "It Just Won't Hay," "Black Skunk Blues," and "Me and My Whiskey." *—Scott Yanow*

Complete Recorded Works, Vol. 3 (1929–1930) / 1991 / Document ♦♦♦♦♦
"Barbecue Bob"'s final recordings are on this third of three discs. Bob (whose name was actually Robert Hicks) died on October 21, 1931, at the age of just 29, from pneumonia. Since his last solo records were made during November 6, 1929, and April 17-December 5, 1930, there is no decline heard in his singing or playing. Barbecue Bob is heard on 13 unaccompanied numbers (including "She Move It Just Right," "Yo Yo Blues No. 2," "We Sure Got Hard Times," and "Atlanta Moan") and interacting with his brother Charlie Lincoln on the amusing two-part "Darktown Gamblin'." Barbecue Bob's final four recordings were made as part of the Georgia Cotton Pickers on December 7-8, 1930, a trio with guitarist/singer Curley Weaver and Buddy Moss on harmonica. Recommended, as are all three volumes of this valuable series. *—Scott Yanow*

Barbecue Bob: The Essential / Aug. 7, 2001 / Classic Blues ♦♦♦♦

John Henry Barbee

b. Nov. 14, 1905, Henning, TN, **d.** Nov. 3, 1964, Chicago, IL
Vocals, Guitar / Delta Blues, Country Blues
A strong storyteller and good guitarist, John Henry Barbee learned music playing in various homes throughout Henning, Tennessee, as a youth. He worked for a short time with John Lee Williamson (Sonny Boy Williamson I) in 1934, then began playing with Sunnyland Slim. They made appearances across the Mississippi Delta. Barbee later moved to Chicago, where he recorded for Vocalion in 1938. He played with Moody Jones' group on Maxwell Street in the '40s, but then left the music business for several years. Barbee recorded for Spivey and Storyville in the mid-'60s, and toured Europe as part of the American Folk Blues Festival. A portion of the tour's concert in Hamburg, Germany was issued by Fontana. Barbee was involved in an auto accident in 1964, and suffered a heart attack while in jail waiting for the case to come to court. *—Ron Wynn*

● **Blues Masters, Vol. 3: I Ain't Gonna Pick No More Cotton** / Oct. 8, 1964 / Storyville ♦♦♦♦
Storyville recorded a session from John Henry Barbee during the blues revival of the early '60s, which was released as *Blues Masters, Vol. 3: I Ain't Gonna Pick No More Cotton*. The country bluesman hauled out several of his old songs, plus a handful of classics, ranging from "John Henry" and "That's Alright Mama" to "Dust My Broom." Barbee's performances are direct and unadorned, similar in style to his late-'20s/early-'30s recordings but, if anything, they're a little bit better. His playing may not be quite as raw, but his voice has grown deeper and more powerful with age, giving the music an unexpected resonance. Barbee wasn't much more than a minor country blues player, but his music was quite enjoyable, and this 16-track collection is the best way to hear his modest talents. *—Thom Owens*

Barkin' Bill

b. Mississippi
Vocals / Contemporary Blues, Modern Electric Chicago Blues, Electric Chicago Blues
Blessed with a lush, deeply burnished baritone that's seemingly the antithesis of the rough-hewn Chicago blues sound, Barkin' Bill Smith finally broke through in 1994 with his own debut album for Delmark. Influenced by the likes of Joe Williams (Count Basie's smooth crooner, not the gruff nine-string guitarist), Brook Benton, and Jimmy Witherspoon, the natty dresser grew up in Mississippi and stopped off to sing in East St. Louis and Detroit before settling in the Windy City.

Slide guitarist Homesick James anointed Smith with his enduring stage handle in 1958 when the two shared a stage. After scuffling for decades on the South and West sides, Smith finally hooked up with young guitarist Dave Specter & the Bluebirds and made his recorded debut on the band's 1991 Delmark release, *Bluebird Blues*. After leaving Specter's employ, Smith's own album bow, *Gotcha!*, emerged three years later. *—Bill Dahl*

● **Gotcha!** / 1994 / Delmark ♦♦♦♦
The veteran vocalist wraps his suave, bottomless pipes around a well-chosen cross-section of covers, from Duke Henderson's jump blues "Get Your Kicks" and Johnny "Guitar" Watson's "I Love to Love You" to tougher straightforward blues originally cut by Freddy King, Guitar Slim, Jimmy Rogers, and Little Walter. A cadre of local session aces provides fine support, especially guitarist Steve Freund (who receives a couple of instrumental showcases). *—Bill Dahl*

Roosevelt "Booba" Barnes

b. Sep. 25, 1936, Longwood, MS, **d.** Apr. 2, 1996, Chicago, IL
Vocals, Guitar / Modern Delta Blues, Electric Delta Blues, Modern Electric Blues
Booba Barnes and his Playboys band rocked the hardest of all the juke-joint combos in the Mississippi delta during the '80s, and after the release of his debut album (*The Heartbroken Man*, 1990), "Booba" took his act and his band north to Chicago, following the trail of his idols Howlin' Wolf and Little Milton. In a *Guitar Player* review, Jas Obrecht called Barnes "a wonderfully idiosyncratic guitar player and an extraordinary vocalist by any standard."

Roosevelt "Booba" Barnes began playing music professionally in 1960, playing guitar in a Mississippi band named the Swinging Gold Coasters. Four years later, he moved to Chicago, where he performed in blues clubs whenever he could get work. Barnes returned to his home state of Mississippi in 1971, where he began playing bars and clubs around Greenville.

Barnes continued to play the juke joints of Mississippi for the next decade. In 1985, he opened his own joint, the Playboy Club. With Barnes and his backing band, the Playboys, acting as the house band, the bar became one of the most popular in the Delta. Soon, the band was popular enough to have a record contract with Rooster Blues. Their first album, *The Heartbroken Man*, was released in 1990. After its release, Barnes and the Playboys toured the United States and Europe. They continued to tour, as well as occasionally record, until Barnes died of cancer in April 1996. *—Jim O'Neal & Stephen Thomas Erlewine*

★ **The Heartbroken Man** / 1990 / Rooster Blues ♦♦♦♦♦
Roosevelt "Booba" Barnes didn't record his first album, *Heartbroken Man*, until 1990. By that point, he had become a seasoned blueman, and was well-known in the South as a tough, hard-rocking guitarist. *Heartbroken Man* delivers on the promise of his reputation. It's an astonishing record, filled with gutsy vocals and gnarled, unpredictable guitar. Unlike most modern blues, it's teeming with life, and its raw, unvarnished production is a welcome, bracing contrast to the sterile atmosphere of most modern blues records. But what really counts is the music itself, and Barnes proves to be the heir to such classic bluesmen as Howlin' Wolf and Slim Harpo (both of whom he covers here), as both a performer and songwriter. An instant modern classic. *—Thom Owens*

The Barrett Sisters

Group / Traditional Gospel, Black Gospel
Delois, Billie, and Rodessa Barrett began singing as children in the Chicago-based Morning Star Baptist Church in the '40s. Under the direction of their aunt, Mattie Dacus, they were originally known as The Barrett and Hudson Singers before becoming The Barrett Sisters. Delois was recruited for The Roberta Martin Singers while a high school senior at Englewood High. After graduation, she joined Martin's group full time and remained a member for 18 years. Rodessa Barrett became a choral director of Galileo Baptist church and Billie Barrett became a church soloist after taking voice lessons at the American Music Conservatory. They formed The Barrett Sisters in 1962 and have remained together ever since. Their first LP was recorded for Savoy in 1963. They currently record for I Am Records in Chicago. *—Ron Wynn*

What Shall I Render (Unto God) / Dec. 1, 1995 / Sony Special Products ♦♦♦♦
Originally released in 1985, *What Shall I Render (Unto God)* captures the Barrett Sisters at the peak of their formidable powers, delivering electrifying renditions of "He Shall Feed His Flock" and "Waiting for the Lord's Return." *—Chuck Donkers*

Best of the Barrett Sisters / Jun. 25, 1996 / Intersound ♦♦♦♦

What a Wonderful World / 1998 / Un-d-nyable ♦♦♦
A more contemporary production, geared toward fans of a modern approach. *—Ron Wynn*

Nobody Does It Better / Word ♦♦♦♦

- **What Will You Do With Your Life** / Savoy ♦♦♦♦♦

What Will You Do With Your Life is a fine collection of the Barrett Sisters' Savoy recordings that showcases the gospel group at their very best. *—Leo Stanley*

The Best of the Barrett Sisters / MCA ♦♦♦♦♦

Great sides by one of today's leading female aggregations. Nashboro sides. *—Opal Louis Nations*

Sweet Emma Barrett

b. Mar. 25, 1897, New Orleans, LA, **d.** Jan. 28, 1983, New Orleans, LA

Vocals, Piano / New Orleans Jazz

Sweet Emma Barrett, who was at her most powerful in the early '60s, became a symbolic figure with the Preservation Hall Jazz Band, playing in a joyous but obviously weakened and past-her-prime style on world tours. Barrett spent most of her career living and playing in New Orleans, including gigs with Oscar "Papa" Celestin in the '20s and later with Armand Piron. Sweet Emma, who gained the nickname of "the bell gal" because she wore a hat and red garters with bells that made sounds while she played, was purely a local figure until 1961 when she made her finest recording, a Riverside set with the future members of the Preservation Hall Jazz Band. Ironically, as Barrett (through the group's well-received tours) became better known, her playing and singing swiftly declined due to her age, and after a 1967 stroke, she continued to perform despite having a largely paralyzed left hand. In addition to the recommended Riverside set (reissued on CD), Barrett led less significant sessions for GHB (1963-1964), Preservation Hall, Nobility, and a 1978 album for Smoky Mary. *—Scott Yanow*

- **New Orleans: The Living Legends** / Jan. 1961 / Riverside/OJC ♦♦♦♦♦

This CD reissue of the future members of the Preservation Hall Jazz Band is at such a high level it makes one wonder why this group had so many erratic recordings. Pianist Emma Barrett (who also takes four vocals) is in fine form and trombonist Jim Robinson was always a major asset to any New Orleans jazz band, but it is the performances of trumpeter Percy Humphrey (who never sounded better on record) and his brother, clarinetist Willie, that really make this music special. Together the septet plays such songs as "Bill Bailey," "Just a Little While to Stay Here," and "The Saints" with drive, enthusiasm, and surprising musicianship. It's essential music for all New Orleans jazz fans. *—Scott Yanow*

Sweet Emma Barrett and Her New Orleans Music / Sep. 1963 / Southland ♦♦♦

For her second album as a leader, pianist Sweet Emma Barrett (who sings on four of the eight songs) heads two overlapping groups. While she is joined throughout by banjoist Emanuel Sayles, bassist Placide Adams and drummer Paul Barbarin, the frontlines change, with four songs featuring trumpeter Alvin Alcorn, trombonist Jim Robinson and clarinetist Louis Cottrell; the remaining four numbers have trumpeter Don Albert, trombonist Frog Joseph and clarinetist Raymond Burke. Overall, this set gives listeners a good sampling of the state of New Orleans jazz circa 1963 and is one of the few recordings of Barrett mostly without the regular members of what would become the Preservation Hall Jazz Band (Robinson and Sayles excepted). The ensemble-oriented renditions of such numbers as "Big Butter and Egg Man," "Bogalusa Strut" and "Take Me Out to the Ball Game" are fun and joyful. *—Scott Yanow*

Sweet Emma and Her Preservation Hall Jazz Band / Oct. 18, 1964 / Preservation Hall ♦♦♦

This LP features The Preservation Hall Jazz Band in its early days, when pianist/vocalist Sweet Emma Barrett was the leader. Clarinetist Willie Humphrey and trumpeter Percy Humphrey, although not up to the level they attained on the Riverside CD, are in better than usual form, and trombonist Jim Robinson is his usual consistent self. This band clearly enjoys themselves jamming mostly on warhorses, making this a high-spirited set of New Orleans jazz. *—Scott Yanow*

New Orleans Traditional Jazz Legends / 1992 / Mardi Gras ♦♦♦

A 1992 reissue featuring noted classic blues and traditional New Orleans jazz vocalist Sweet Emma Barrett. She lived up to her reputation, belting out the one-liners, double entendres, and innuendo with gusto, then turning poignant or bemused when necessary. Her fine vocals were backed by fairly routine support, but hearing Sweet Emma Barrett made everything worthwhile. *—Ron Wynn*

The Bell Gal and Her Dixieland Boys / 1994 / Riverside ♦♦♦♦

When this album was originally issued in the early '60s, Herb Friedwald observed in its liner that "the days of New Orleans jazz are now clearly numbered." (He was wrong, but it was an easy mistake to make at that point.) Friedwald tempered his pessimism by expressing enthusiasm for the group led by the then-64-year-old pianist and singer Sweet Emma Barrett, who had once played for the Old Original Tuxedo Jazz Band and had adopted an idiosyncratic stage attire consisting of a bright red dress with a hat and garters all festooned with bells. Her band at this time included trumpeter Percy Humphrey, clarinetist Willie Humphrey, and the legendary trombone player Jim Robinson, among others, and it swings and shouts mightily. Standards like "Bill Bailey" and the inevitable "When the Saints Come Marching In" are on the program, as well as the bawdy "I Ain't Gonne Give Nobody None of This Jelly Roll" (on which Barrett sings, wonderfully) and a foot-stomping rendition of "Down in Honky-Tonk Town." The CD reissue includes three bonus tracks, all of them taken from the two-LP Riverside collection entitled *New Orleans: The Living Legends*. Though in places you might wish for a slightly better-defined sound, this album is a joy from beginning to end. *—Rick Anderson*

Dave Bartholomew

b. Dec. 24, 1920, Edgard, LA

Vocals, Trumpet, Songwriter / New Orleans R&B, Rock & Roll, R&B

Dave Bartholomew is the multi-talented figure behind a majority of classic New Orleans R&B of the '50s and the self-proclaimed inventor of the "Big Beat." Bartholomew has over 4000 songs in his enormous catalog and is responsible for arranging and producing timeless records by Shirley & Lee, Lloyd Price, Smiley Lewis, and especially Fats Domino. Bartholomew was born in Edgard, LA, on December 24, 1920. His first instruments were tuba and trumpet. He fronted several bands in the Crescent City before being drafted into the army. His military time brought scoring and arranging experience which came in handy following World War II. After his stint in the service, Bartholomew returned to New Orleans and put together a group of musicians that would comprise the bedrock of R&B in the city, including saxophonists Alvin "Red" Tyler, Lee Allen, and drummer Earl Palmer. This became the band that backed up the majority of solo talent traveling through New Orleans. Bartholomew led his first studio session under his own name in 1947 for Deluxe, but the label went out of business shortly thereafter and the sessions went unnoticed. In 1949, Bartholomew met Lew Chudd who was forming a new label, Imperial Records. Chudd hired Bartholomew as house arranger, bandleader, and talent scout, and he immediately started cranking out numerous hits through the '50s for Fats Domino, Shirley & Lee, Smiley Lewis, Earl King, Chris Kenner, Tommy Ridgley, Frankie Ford, Robert Parker, and a host of others. Bartholomew stayed with Imperial until the hits dried up in the mid-'60s, followed by short stays at Trumpet, Mercury, and his own Broadmoor label. In the '70s and '80s, he took various behind-the-scenes musical jobs while living off his many song royalties and formed a Dixieland jazz band that continues to play around the Crescent City. The '90s found Bartholomew being inducted into the Rock and Roll Hall of Fame in 1991 and releasing two discs: *Dave Bartholomew and the Maryland Jazz Band* in 1995 and *New Orleans Big Beat* three years later. *—Al Campbell*

In the Alley / 1991 / Charly ♦♦♦♦

Dave Bartholomew is best known for producing and arranging classic New Orleans R&B sides from the '50s, especially for Fats Domino. It's curious that success eluded him on sessions released under his own name. Recorded between 1949 and 1952, the jump blues tracks on *In the Alley* were originally released on Deluxe and King, separate from Bartholomew's work with the Imperial label. King signed Bartholomew as a name artist, and ten of this compilation's 20 tracks find him backed up by the Todd Rhodes Orchestra. The remaining tracks are credited to the Dave Bartholomew Orchestra and feature some of the greatest Crescent City R&B session men from the period, including drummer Earl Palmer, bassist Frank Fields, and pianist Salvador Doucette. Six of the titles, including the excellent "Basin Street Breakdown," are previously unissued takes. Also included is the original song for which Bartholomew is most widely known, though again not for his version of it: "My Ding-a-Ling," which became a huge hit for Chuck Berry in 1972. Bartholomew was more of a Louis Jordan-style vocalist than a Joe Turner blues shouter, and that influence is prevalent throughout this disc. While this is a highly recommended set, there are a few clunkers here and there, including a strained and soulless "Stormy Weather" and the lengthy call-and-response vamp "Lawdy Lawdy Lord, Pt. 1 and 2," which would have been sufficient concluding with part one. *—Al Campbell*

★ **The Spirit of New Orleans: The Genius of Dave Bartholomew** / 1993 / EMI ♦♦♦♦♦

Released as part of EMI's *Legends of Rock N' Roll* series in 1992, there has been no better retrospective of Dave Bartholomew's music than the double-disc set, *The Spirit of New Orleans: The Genius of Dave Bartholomew*. That's partially because at 50 tracks, it's the most comprehensive collection ever assembled on Bartholomew, but its real genius is that it doesn't shine a spotlight solely on his solo recordings. Instead, those are interspersed among the numerous hits he wrote and produced for such New Orleans legends as Fats Domino, Smiley Lewis, Earl King, Bobby Mitchell, Snooks Eaglin, Shirley & Lee, Pee Wee Crayton, Tommy Ridgley, Chris Kenner and many others (including sides by T-Bone Walker). There are plenty of classics here—"Stack A Lee," "Ain't It a shame," "Bo Weevil," "I Hear You Knocking," "I'm Gonna Be a Wheel Someday," "One Night," "Come On, Pts 1 & 2," "Walking to New Orleans," "Trick Bag" among them—plus numerous singles and songs known only to collectors. There has since been a dynamite single-disc collection of Bartholomew recordings issued, but any serious collector of New Orleans music needs to have this, pure and simple. *—Stephen Thomas Erlewine*

1947-1950 / Jul. 10, 2001 / Classics ♦♦♦♦

☆ **The Big Beat of Dave Bartholomew: 20 of His Milestone Productions 1949–1960** / Mar. 12, 2002 / Capitol ♦♦♦♦♦

The last time EMI/Capitol's reissue division prepared a large reissue series of Imperial's rich catalog of New Orleans R&B it was in the early '90s, and Dave Bartholomew was given a generous double-disc set that showcased his productions, songwriting, and performing. That set was used as the basis for 2002's *The Big Beat of Dave Bartholomew*, a single-disc, 20-track collection (released as part of EMI/Capitol's *Crescent City Soul* series) that does the job of that double-disc somewhat better, largely because of its conciseness. With only 20 tracks to work with, the compilers are forced to put the best of the hits and cult favorites on one disc, and the results are dynamite. Apart from Smiley Lewis' hit "One Night" and Bartholomew's record-collector favorites "The Monkey" and "That's How You Got Killed Before," there aren't that many acknowledged classics here—there are songs better known by other performers (Smiley Lewis and Fats Domino's "I Hear You Knocking" and "Blue Monday" are performed by the respective other artist, Bobby Mitchell's "I'm Gonna Be a Wheel Someday" is better known by Fats), but much of this is known primarily to fanatics of the scene, and it's great that they're given an airing such as this. Perhaps there aren't songs that should have been hits, but many of these songs stand as excellent sides from the peak of New Orleans R&B and any serious collector should pick this disc up—even if they already own *The Spirit of New Orleans*. *—Stephen Thomas Erlewine*

Lou Ann Barton

b. Feb. 17, 1954, Fort Worth, TX

Vocals / Electric Texas Blues, Blues-Rock

Although she doesn't tour nearly as much as she probably could, Austin-based vocalist Lou Ann Barton is one of the finest purveyors of raw, unadulterated roadhouse blues from the female gender that you'll ever hear. Like Delbert McClinton, she can belt out a lyric so that she can be heard over a two-guitar band with horns. Born February 17, 1954, in Fort Worth, she's a veteran of thousands of dance hall and club shows all over Texas. Barton moved to Austin in the '70s and later performed with the Fabulous Thunderbirds and Stevie Ray Vaughan and Double Trouble.

Although she has a few great recordings out, notably *Old Enough* produced by Jerry Wexler and Glenn Frey, Barton has to be seen live to be fully appreciated. She belts out her lyrics in a twangy voice so full of Texas that you can smell the barbecue sauce. She swaggers confidently about the stage, casually tossing her cigarette to the floor as the band kicks in on its first number. The grace, poise and confidence she projects on stage is part of a long tradition for women blues singers. The blues world still needs more good female blues singers like Barton, to help to broaden the appeal of the music to diverse audiences and to further its evolution.

Barton has several other excellent albums out on the Austin-based Antone's Records, *Read My Lips* (1989) and her cooperative effort with fellow Texas blues women Marcia Ball and Angela Strehli, *Dreams Come True* (1990). *Old Enough* was reissued on compact disc in 1992 on the Antone's label. The only criticism one could level at Barton—and it may be unfair because of business complications—is that she hasn't recorded much. Here's hoping that this premier interpreter of Texas roadhouse blues will be well recorded in the future. *—Richard Skelly*

Old Enough / 1982 / Discovery ✦✦✦

The debut album by Austin-based blues-rock singer Lou Ann Barton didn't sound like many major-label releases of 1982. Produced by Atlantic Records veteran Jerry Wexler (with, worryingly, some help from ex-Eagles schlockmeister Glenn Frey) and recorded at the legendary Muscle Shoals Sound Studios, *Old Enough* is a solid piece of soulful Texas-style blues-rock. Barton reveals herself to be an exceptional singer, sassy and sly but with a welcome tendency toward restraint. (Many singers in this style try too hard to prove their soulfulness and end up sounding ridiculous.) She's also got a keen eye for songs, investing the old standard "Finger Poppin' Time" with enough relish to make it sound fresh and turning Marshall Crenshaw's rockabilly-tinged "Brand New Lover" into a full-on Wanda Jackson-style barnburner. There are a few missteps, like the too-slick-by-half radio-friendly ballad "It's Raining," but overall, *Old Enough* is an unpretentious, timeless-sounding set. It all but disappeared upon its 1982 release and remained out of print until the Austin blues label Antone reissued it on CD in 1997. *—Stewart Mason*

Forbidden Tones / 1986 / Spindletop ✦✦✦✦

In most cases, *Forbidden Tones* would be a recipe for disaster: After a disappointing major label stint with her Jerry Wexler-produced 1982 debut *Old Enough*, Austin-based R&B singer Lou Ann Barton came home, hooked up with a small local indie, and recorded a synthesizer-heavy, new wave-influenced pop album. It shouldn't work, but it does. Of course, this is largely due to Barton's tremendous voice—she's one of the finest R&B singers of her generation—but also to the better than average musicianship and largely excellent song selection. Barton, who produced the album herself, called in various highly regarded pals to help, including Los Angeles session legends Jerry Marotta, Dean Parks, and Larry Knetchel, and fellow Austinites like Fabulous Thunderbirds guitarist Jimmie Vaughan. The entirely pop song selection is interesting, featuring Beatles and Mink DeVille covers and tunes from AOR hit machines Will Jennings and Billy Steinberg. It's hard to tell if Barton is consciously trying to play up the non-R&B elements of her music in an attempt to seem more well-rounded as a performer or what, but—whatever the motivation—it sounds terrific. The album's highlight is an absolutely scorching version of John Hiatt's "Pink Bedroom," an acid portrait of a pregnant teenage trendoid that in Barton's hands maintains a certain level of sympathy even as its lyrics draw blood (literally, in the last verse). It sounds like *Get Happy*-era Elvis Costello & the Attractions fronted by a roadhouse belter, and it's one of the great lost tracks of the mid-'80s. Although nothing else on *Forbidden Tones* matches that song and the album's near-EP length makes it slightly frustrating, it's still an impressive comeback. *—Stewart Mason*

● **Read My Lips** / 1989 / Discovery ✦✦✦✦✦

Lou Ann Barton didn't have the best of luck in her early career. Incongruously signed to a major label for 1982's *Old Enough*, she delivered a fine debut that was utterly out of step with the times. Shunted to a tiny indie in her adopted hometown of Austin, she recorded 1986's oddly poppy *Forbidden Tones*, an album of John Hiatt and Beatles covers that recalled Marti Jones' albums from the same period; it was a fine record, but it was a complete stylistic aberration. Barton returned to her blues-rock roots for 1989's *Read My Lips*. Cutting out the synthesizers and pop gloss of *Forbidden Tones* for a more traditional sound and recording with longtime friends like the Fabulous Thunderbirds' Kim Wilson and Jimmie Vaughan, Barton delivers her strongest set of tunes. As always, the song selection is heavy on the covers, including a new, heart-wrenching version of Irma Thomas' "It's Raining" that beats the pants off the too-slick version she recorded on *Old Enough*. Barton also salutes her influences on solid covers of Barbara Lynn's "You'll Lose a Good Thing" and a rave-up rendition of Wanda Jackson's rockabilly anthem "Let's Have a Party," not to mention the tough-chick standby "You Can Have My Husband." Wisely free of attempts to update or modernize her timeless Texas-style blues-rock, *Read My Lips* is a rockin' good time. *—Stewart Mason*

Dreams Come True / 1990 / Antone's ✦✦✦

Dreams Come True is an all-star session by vocalists Marcia Ball, Lou Ann Barton and Angela Strehli. The three women sing with a band led by Dr. John and the session features guest appearances by such luminaries as David "Fathead" Newman and Jimmie

Vaughan. The music is straight out of the Texas school of roadhouse R&B and blues boogie but it's delivered with a gritty, hearfelt edge, particularly on the part of the three vocalists. *Dreams Come True* may follow formula, but it's followed with style and affection, which makes it a very enjoyable listen. *—Thom Owens*

Sugar Coated Love / Dec. 8, 1998 / M.I.L. Multimedia ✦✦✦

Thunderbroad / Apr. 3, 2001 / Blues Factory ✦✦✦

Someday / Sep. 3, 2002 / Catfish ✦✦✦

Paul Bascomb

b. Feb. 12, 1912, Birmingham, AL, **d.** Dec. 2, 1986, Chicago, IL

Sax (Tenor) / Jump Blues, Swing

It is easy to divide Paul Bascomb's career into two, for he was a top soloist with Erskine Hawkins' swing orchestra and later on recorded a popular series of early rhythm & blues records. The brother of trumpeter Dud Bascomb (another star of the Hawkins band), the tenorman was one of the founding members of the 'Bama State Collegians (which eventually became the Erskine Hawkins big band) in the early '30s and, except for a period in 1938-1939 when he replaced the late Herschel Evans with Count Basie's orchestra, he was with Hawkins until 1944. Bascomb co-led groups with Dud (1944-1947) and in the early '50s recorded extensively for the United label; the accessible performances have been partially reissued by Delmark. Paul Bascomb was active (if maintaining a low profile) into the mid-'80s. *—Scott Yanow*

● **Bad Bascomb!** / Mar. 3, 1952-Aug. 30, 1952 / Delmark ✦✦✦✦

This CD collects together tenor saxophonist Paul Bascomb's United recordings of 1952. The material is pretty basic and R&B-ish, but fun, with the highlights including "Blues and the Beat," "Pink Cadillac," "Soul and Body," and "Indiana." The backup group includes trumpeter Eddie Lewis and pianist Duke Jordan, and the CD reissue adds four alternate takes to the original 13 selections. Recommended. *—Scott Yanow*

Johnnie Bassett

b. Oct. 9, 1935, Marianna, FL

Vocals, Guitar / Urban Blues, Modern Electric Blues

Guitarist, singer and songwriter Johnnie Bassett grew up with blues music all around him in his native Florida. His unique ability to combine jump blues and Delta stylings gives his playing a distinctive sound.

The self-taught guitarist recalls seeing Tampa Red, Arthur "Big Boy" Crudup and other classic blues artists at fish fries in his grandmother's backyard. Bassett cites Aaron "T-Bone" Walker as a major influence, as well as B.B. and Albert King, Tiny Grimes and Billy Butler.

After Bassett's family moved to Detroit in 1944, he made his debut as a guitarist with Joe Weaver and the Bluenotes, a teenage R&B band. The group won local talent contests and were hired to backup Big Joe Turner, Ruth Brown and others on their tour stops in Detroit. Bassett went into the Army in 1958 and played in a country & western group while stationed in Washington state.

After returning to Detroit, he found work as a session guitarist for Fortune Records by day and in nightclubs at night. In the studios, he played backup to musicians and groups like Nolan Strong and the Diablos, Andre Williams and the Don Juans and the Five Dollars. He also played guitar on the first recording by Smokey Robinson and the Miracles while traveling to Chicago to record as a session man for the Chess Records label. During his Detroit days, he also accompanied John Lee Hooker, Eddie Burns, Alberta Adams, Lowell Fulson and the T.J. Fowler Band at their live shows, as well as Dinah Washington.

In the '60s, Bassett moved to Seattle, where he backed up Tina Turner, Little Willie John and others. Jimi Hendrix was a frequent guest at the bluesman's club gigs around Seattle. Before the decade ended, he moved back to Detroit, where he's been based ever since.

In 1994, Bassett received a lifetime achievement award from the Detroit Blues Society. He later recorded an album for the Dutch Black Magic label, *I Gave My Life to the Blues* (1996). Bassett and his band, the Blues Insurgents—which he's been fronting since the early '90s—have made several U.S., Canadian and European tours in support of LPs including 1997's *Bassett Hound* and 1998's *Cadillac Blues*. *—Richard Skelly*

● **Cadillac Blues** / Jan. 20, 1998 / Cannonball ✦✦✦✦

Two in a row for Johnny Bassett and his fine band, the Blues Insurgents. They are the keepers of the flame of straight-ahead, postwar blues. Bassett, musically, is a direct descendant of B.B. King circa 1965, with his pure, clean tone and long, flowing guitar lines uncluttered by electronic devices. Vocally, he sounds like Mose Allison and Johnny Adams in an untrained way. His band is very tight and unusual because, along with trumpet, tenor sax and drums, it includes organ, which also plays the bass parts. If this disc has any faults, it may be that Bassett delivers a couple of the hurting songs with too much positive emotion, which seems at odds with his lyrics. A very satisfying disc of shuffles, down-in-the-alley slow blues and funk. *—Sigmund Finman*

Lefty Bates (William Bates)

b. May 7, 1924, Pelahatchie, MS, **d.** Mar. 2, 1991, Indianapolis, IN

Guitar / Chicago Blues

It is no great mystery where the nickname for this Chicago blues rhythm guitarist came from. Obviously, Lefty Bates played his guitar upside down, in the manner of many southpaw pickers. He was born William Bates with both May 7, 1924, and the somewhat earlier date of March 9, 1920, provided by various sources for his entry into the world. He is claimed as a native son of Mississippi as well as Alabama, as there is some speculation that he was really born in the latter state's prosperous village of Leighton. He was raised in St. Louis and, while still in high school, formed a vocal and string band of the kind that was quite popular in the black community during the '30s and '40s. The group was called the Hi-De-Ho Boys, and consisted of vocalist and dancer Tommy Powell, bassist and vocalist James Crosby, and a threesome of guitarists and vocalists: Bill Williams, Walter

Jones, and Cleo Roberts. This group migrated to Chicago in 1936, recorded on Decca, and worked several clubs regularly up until 1950. During this period, Bates served in World War II and formed his own combo when he got out. This led to a stint in the combo Aristo-Kats, who cut a series of sides for RCA Victor. Bates once again became one of the Hi-De-Ho Boys when the Aristo-Kats called it quits.

Early in the '50s, Bates formed a trio with bassist Quinn Wilson, a former member of the Aristo-Kats, and the legendary Chicago pianist Horace Palm. This group gigged for much of the '50s, sometimes expanding to a quartet by adding a horn player. There were very few recordings released under his own name, including a solitary release on Boxer in 1955, another on United several years later, and two sides done on Apex at the close of the '50s. He also did a record with his group for the Mad label in 1958, a company whose name summed up the disposition of most people in the independent record business as well as the feelings of artists once the sides are released and go nowhere. This was certainly the case with Bates: none of these sides achieved any notoriety, but that apparently did not matter to Bates. The lion's share of his bread came from club gigs and session guitar work on other people's recordings. For many years he was a stalwart at Chicago blues-scene clubs such as the legendary Theresa's, and appeared in the second guitar position on many records by blues giants such as Jimmy Reed and Buddy Guy.

Playing rhythm guitar on a blues record is not the fastest path to glory, as listeners sometimes emphasize the lead guitar in rhythm & blues and forget about the rhythm being so expertly provided by this type of player. Bates was versatile, able to handle the laid-back shuffle of Reed as well as the aggressive, sometimes mind-numbing assault of Guy. He also shows up on a variety of sessions by lesser-known players such as Larry Birdsong and Honey Brown. He was also one of the few rhythm guitarists who could follow John Lee Hooker off into the one-chord ozone. This ability to adapt to a variety of settings within the blues genre was the main reason he was chosen as a member of what would become the house band for the famous Vee-Jay label; along with other players such as bassist, bandleader and manager Al Smith, and the juicy, honking saxophonist Red Holloway. This group of players began working under the auspices of the Chance record label, a precursor to Vee-Jay, whose motto and philosophy was summed up in its name: once cut, there was a chance that a side might end up getting released, and yes, just a chance the musicians involved might get paid, although holding one's breath awaiting the check was not a smart idea. The label operated out of a garage and developed some of the earliest Jimmy Reed sides with the doggy backup band entitled the Spaniels. Meanwhile, Vee-Jay apparently upped the ante and lured away some of the session players by offering the rich sum of 41.25 dollars per man per session, although Holloway admitted in an interview the musicians "...might have to wait a couple of months before you got that." Typical arrangements for these sessions were thrown together with no preparation, or waiting time on the other hand. The players had to be ready to put something together behind whatever lead singer the company was recording, whether it was a gut-bucket country bluesman gone electric or a more sophisticated doo wop group.

Bates got into a similar jack-of-all-trades situation with the upstart Club 51 label, another Chicago outfit that recorded the fascinating mixture of blues, R&B, doo wop, and jazz that was going on during this period. At Club 51, however, the left-handed axeman was the honcho, leading up the studio bands under names such as the Lefty Bates Orchestra. Some of the records for this label combined Bates and his sidemen—often the same players that were on the Vee-Jay sides—with vocal groups such as the Five Buddies or solid Chicago bluesmen such as pianist Sunnyland Slim. In the '70s, Bates took over leadership of the Ink Spots, at that point more of a franchise than a group. Following a long stretch in Chicago, Bates migrated to the quiet Hoosier scene of Indianapolis, where he finished out his days, playing the blues right up 'til the end. Precisely when that was is once again in some dispute, as his death is sometimes listed as 1996 rather than five years earlier. *—Eugene Chadbourne*

The Beale Street Sheiks

f. 1927, **db.** 1929

Group / Country Blues, Acoustic Memphis Blues

The Beale Street Sheiks was the name used by Memphis musicians Frank Stokes and Dan Sane for their blues duo on Paramount Records releases from sessions held in 1927 and 1929. It is likely that they also used this moniker in the field, but they did not employ it on the duo records they made for Victor. *—Uncle Dave Lewis*

Complete Recorded Works (1927–1929) / Document ♦♦♦♦

Chris Beard

b. Aug. 29, 1957, Rochester, NY

Guitar, Vocals / Modern Electric Blues

Guitarist, singer and songwriter Chris Beard is the son of Rochester-area blues guitarist Joe Beard. He has been patiently paying his dues on the club circuit around the Northeast for the last 20 years. Beard, who goes by the nickname "Prince of the Blues," is one of the Young Lions of blues in the '90s. He can be safely grouped with other idiom-expanding artists like Larry Garner, Tutu Jones and Michael Hill.

Beard began playing guitar at age five, inspired by all the blues talent his father had over to the house—artists like Buddy Guy and Matt "Guitar" Murphy. He learned to play "Green Onions" as a 6-year-old, and at 15 he began playing with a local classic rhythm & blues ensemble. He continued playing in local bands and sitting in with his father's band through high school. After graduation, he began fronting his own group and writing his own songs, taking inspiration from people like Albert King and Johnny "Guitar" Watson.

Beard's debut album, *Barwalkin'*, for the London-based JSP Records, is a 12-track showcase of style and songwriting virtuosity. Produced by Johnny Rawls, who also plays guitar on the recording, Beard is accompanied by Hammond B-3 organist Brian Charette, former Johnny Copeland Band bassist Randy Lippincott, and drummer Barry Harrison. The Nutmeg Horns, consisting of Bruce and Robert Feiner on saxophones and Jim Hunt on trumpet, add body to some songs. *—Richard Skelly*

● **Barwalkin'** / Jun. 24, 1997 / JSP ♦♦♦♦

Born to Play the Blues / Apr. 10, 2001 / JSP ♦♦♦

Joe Beard

b. Feb. 4, 1938, Ashland, MS

Guitar / Modern Electric Blues

Born and raised in Ashland, Mississippi, guitarist Joe Beard grew up with the Murphy brothers, one of whom later found an international following as Matt "Guitar" Murphy. Guitarist Nathan Beauregard lived with Beard's cousin, so he was surrounded by aspiring and veteran blues musicians while growing up, and he began singing at an early age. Beard became interested in playing guitar via the Murphy brothers, who sat in with a young B.B. King when he played at the Roosevelt Lake Club. Beard began to learn guitar at age 17 from Ernest Scruggs, a neighbor, before heading to Chicago.

Beard moved to Rochester, N.Y., and from time to time would visit one of his brothers in Chicago. He quickly became enamored of the blues being played in clubs there by people like Jimmy Reed and Sonny Boy Williamson. Beard sat in with John Lee Hooker one night and received encouraging words from Hooker, and also later sat in with his idol, Muddy Waters.

While in Rochester, he formed the Soul Brothers Six, playing bass and singing, but he didn't perform in public on guitar until 1965. Beard befriended classic blues guitarist Son House, who was a neighbor in Rochester, and played a concert for students at the University of Rochester in 1968. Beard worked as an electrician by day and would occasionally play out at night and on weekends for most of the '60s on through to the '80s. He has a reputation as one of the best local players around Rochester, and though he may not be a household name in other parts of the U.S., he toured Europe in 1983 and did studio and stage work that same year with Buster Benton, Lafayette Leake and Memphis Slim. At the famed BK Lounge, Beard and his backing bands opened for Bobby Bland, Albert King and others. Beard also performed at President H. W. George Bush's inaugural gala. In 1990, he recorded an album for Kingsnake Records, *No More Cherry Rose*, which was well received by the blues radio community.

Beard recorded an album with Ronnie Earl's band for the California-based AudioQuest label, *Blues Union* (1996). Accompanying him are Hammond B-3 organist Bruce Katz and tenor saxophonist David "Fathead" Newman. The album was a critical success, winning *Offbeat Magazine*'s Blues Album of the Year award. He followed it up with 1998's *For Real* and 2000's *Dealin'*, both records featuring Duke Robillard—*Richard Skelly*

No More Cherry Rose / 1990 / Kingsnake ♦♦♦

Joe Beard was 52 when he recorded *No More Cherry Rose* in 1990, an enjoyable electric blues date that employs Lucky Peterson on piano, Ernie Lancaster on guitar, Bob Greenlee on bass, and John Dubuc on harmonica (among others). Not a bad cast of players, and this isn't a bad album at all. Except for a likable interpretation of Lightnin' Hopkins' "Papa's Little Angel," the singer/guitarist concentrates on his own songs, which range from the humorous "When I Get Drunk" and the playful "Let Me Love You" to the lonely "Heaven on My Own" and the haunting title song. Beard favors a relaxed, laid-back style of singing that clearly owes a debt to Jimmy Reed, and he has also been influenced by Texas blues great Lightnin' Hopkins. However, it's equally clear that the singer/guitarist is very much his own man. Not a gem but generally pleasing, this album went out of print after several years but will hopefully be reissued someday. *—Alex Henderson*

● **Blues Union** / Aug. 18, 1995-Aug. 19, 1995 / AudioQuest ♦♦♦♦

Although Joe Beard is a country-based bluesman and fellow guitarist Ronnie Earl (who brought along his Broadcasters for this set) is strictly city, they work together quite well. The emphasis is often on Beard's expressive vocals (which sometimes look toward John Lee Hooker and Lightnin' Hopkins but display their own personality). Beard and Earl contribute contrasting guitar solos, pianist-organist Bruce Katz fuels a grooving rhythm section, tenor saxophonist David "Fathead" Newman has a couple of cameos and the harmonica of John Dubuc is a strong asset on three songs. Even with its nods toward the past, this release is a fine example of blues in the mid-'90s. *—Scott Yanow*

For Real / Mar. 24, 1998 / AudioQuest ♦♦♦

This has well-presented variations of old-style blues, from acoustic ("Dirty Groundhog"), to slow burners ("Elem"), to Chicago/Muddy Waters style ("Who's Using Who"). Duke Robillard graciously acts in his role as a team player, although he stands out with a hip solo on "If That's What Pleases Her." Jerry Portnoy's harp on "She's Wonderful" is slow and easy, reminiscent of a hot summer's day in the country. *—Char Ham*

Dealin' / Aug. 15, 2000 / AudioQuest ♦♦♦♦

In the blues world it's OK to be a late bloomer, and when it came to recording, Joe Beard was exactly that. The charismatic singer/guitarist, whose influences range from Jimmy Reed to Lightnin' Hopkins, worked "day gigs" when his kids were growing up and didn't start to build a catalog until he was in his fifties. Blues lovers who heard Beard's AudioQuest dates of the '90s found themselves saying, "Hey, this guy is very talented; why haven't I heard of him until now?" And, of course, the answer to that question is that his nine-to-fives and family life had kept him from being a full-time bluesman. But when his kids reached adulthood, the Mississippi native turned Rochester, NY, resident had more time to devote to music. Recorded in April 2000 (when he was 62), *Dealin'* is Beard's third CD for AudioQuest and underscores his ability to handle a variety of electric blues styles. Beard's appreciation of Reed and the Chicago blues is evident on gutsy, rough-and-tumble tracks like "Give Me Up and Let Me Go," "My Eyes Keep Me in Trouble," and "The Bitter Seed," a Jimmy Reed classic. Like Reed, Beard favors a gentle and laid-back style of singing but still has plenty of grit and doesn't mind having a tough, hard-driving band behind him. Meanwhile, "Holding a Losing Hand" and "If I Get Lucky" (both Beard originals) go for the sort of moody, shadowy, haunting ambiance that often worked so well for Hopkins and John Lee Hooker. This isn't to say that Beard is going out of his way to emulate Reed, Hopkins, Hooker, or anyone else. *Dealin'* shows who some of his influences are, but it also reminds you that Beard is an appealing bluesman in his own right. *—Alex Henderson*

Elder Charles D. Beck

b. 1900, Georgia, USA, **d.** ca 1972, Africa

Vocals, Clapping, Drums, Trumpet, Organ (Hammond) / Prewar Gospel Blues, Traditional Gospel, Black Gospel, Southern Gospel

The conventional wisdom is that modern African-American gospel springs from Thomas A. Dorsey and begins during the depression. However, there are figures from the formative years of contemporary gospel that appear equally important in terms of its development that have gained little, if any recognition. One such artist was the Elder Charles D. Beck, responsible for more than 60 recordings over his lifetime for every little label under the sun. As a singing evangelist, Elder Beck appeared in tent revivals and in black churches all over the United States during his long career, and in a live context, Beck was a famous performer. He viewed recording as an essential part of his work, both as a means to spread the gospel and to establish his name. He literally recorded whenever he could get into a studio, and also appeared extensively on radio, although little is known of his activities there.

Elder Beck was born in Mobile, Alabama around 1900. He first turns up on record in December 1930, recording at the King Edward Hotel in Jackson, Mississippi for OKeh along with Elder Curry and his Congregation (including the great track "Memphis Flu," sometimes cited as a pioneer rock & roll record.) He turns up again in New York in the summer of 1937, recording solo for Decca with his own piano as "The Singing Evangelist." His piano playing is swinging and pumping in a barrelhouse idiom, but makes use of a lighter touch than had Arizona Dranes on her recordings of the '20s. Elder Beck closed out his prewar recording career with a Bluebird session featuring a full compliment of congregation in July 1939.

After World War II, with the rise of independent record labels, Elder Beck really hit his stride. Between 1946 and 1956, he recorded for Eagle, Gotham, King, Chart and possibly other small labels which have fallen under the radar of gospel and blues researchers. These records are all classics: "Jesus, I Love You," which he recorded twice, bears such a strong resemblance to Elvis Presley's ballad style that it supports the idea that Beck may have been one of the preachers that Presley himself heard sing while attending black tent revival services as a child. "There's a Dead Cat on the Line," which had been recorded by the Rev F.W. McGee back in 1930, shows that Elder Beck was aware of the gospel records made by his predecessors and attempted to reinvent them in his own style—a crucial method of operation that would become central to later gospel recording artists. Some of his recordings, such as "Wine Head Willie Put That Bottle Down" are theatrical set pieces where Beck interacts with members of his congregation in a sort of morality play. This reaches a feverish pitch in his final 78-era release, "Rock and Roll Sermon," where Elder Beck lectures on the evils of rock & roll music to the accompaniment of a blistering rock-guitar solo and a congregation on the brink of ecstasy. There's literally nothing else like it on this earth.

Elder Beck's final recording was a full-length LP, *Urban Holiness Service*, made in December 1957 for Folkways. This was an entire service recorded at the Church of God in Christ in Buffalo, NY. The folk collectors who recorded it may not have been aware of how well-entrenched already the Elder was in terms of recording, but during this service Elder Beck literally pulls out all the stops, playing piano, trumpet, vibes, organ and drums at various times. As in his 78 records like "Shouting With Elder Beck" and "What Do You Think About Jesus," Elder Beck maintains a tremendously exciting pace and keeps the congregation at a level of high energy and involvement. He must've been an extremely compelling performer in person.

After 1960, Americans saw increasingly less of Elder Beck, as he was involved in overseas missionary work, primarily in Ghana. He is believed to have died there sometime around 1972. Two of his documented recordings, issued on Eagle 101 and 104, have still not been located. While Elder Beck is still all but unknown to experts on blues and gospel, within his own milieu he remains a celebrity artist, and sales of his reissued recordings remain strong to this day. *—Uncle Dave Lewis*

● **Complete Recorded Works (1946–1947)** / Dec. 3, 1997 / Document ♦♦♦♦
One of the most exciting preachers of his day. *—Opal Louis Nations*

Jeff Beck

b. Jun. 24, 1944, Wallington, Surrey, England

Leader, Guitar (Electric), Guitar, Bass / Album Rock, Guitar Virtuoso, British Blues, Fusion, Hard Rock, Blues-Rock, Rock & Roll

While he was as innovative as Jimmy Page, as tasteful as Eric Clapton, and nearly as visionary as Jimi Hendrix, Jeff Beck never achieved the same commercial success as any of his contemporaries, primarily because of the haphazard way he approached his career. After Rod Stewart left the Jeff Beck Group in 1971, Beck never worked with a charismatic lead singer who could have helped sell his music to a wide audience. Furthermore, he was simply too idiosyncratic, moving from heavy metal to jazz-fusion within a blink of an eye. As his career progressed, he became more fascinated by automobiles than guitars, releasing only one album during the course of the '90s. All the while, Beck retained the respect of fellow guitarists, who found his reclusiveness all the more alluring.

Jeff Beck began his musical career following a short stint at London's Wimbledon Art College. He earned a reputation by supporting Lord Sutch, which helped him land the job as the Yardbirds' lead guitarist following the departure of Eric Clapton. Beck stayed with the Yardbirds for nearly two years, leaving in late in 1966 with the pretense that he was retiring from music. He returned several months later with "Love Is Blue," a single he played poorly because he detested the song. Later in 1967, he formed the Jeff Beck Group with vocalist Rod Stewart, bassist Ron Wood and drummer Aynsley Dunbar, who was quickly replaced by Mickey Waller; keyboardist Nicky Hopkins joined in early 1968. With their crushingly loud reworkings of blues songs and vocal and guitar interplay, the Jeff Beck Group established the template for heavy metal. Neither of the band's records, *Truth* (1968) or *Beck-Ola* (a 1969 album that was recorded with new drummer Tony Newman), were particularly successful, and the band tended to fight regularly, especially on their frequent tours of the US. In 1970, Stewart and Wood left to join the Faces, and Beck broke up the group.

Beck had intended to form a power trio with Vanilla Fudge members Carmine Appice (drums) and Tim Bogert (bass), but those plans were derailed when he suffered a serious car crash in 1970. By the time he recuperated in 1971, Bogart and Appice were playing in Cactus, so the guitarist formed a new version of the Jeff Beck Group. Featuring keyboardist Max Middleton, drummer Cozy Powell, bassist Clive Chaman, and vocalist Bobby Tench, the new band recorded *Rough and Ready* (1971) and *Jeff Beck Group* (1972). Neither album attracted much attention. Cactus dissolved in late 1972, and Beck, Bogert and Appice formed a power trio the following year. The group's lone studio album—a live record was released in Japan but never in the U.K. or U.S.—was widely panned due to its plodding arrangements and weak vocals, and the group disbanded the following year.

For about 18 months, Beck remained quiet, re-emerging in 1975 with *Blow By Blow*. Produced by George Martin, *Blow By Blow* was an all-instrumental jazz-fusion album that received strong reviews. Beck collaborated with Jan Hammer, a former keyboardist for the Mahavishnu Orchestra, for 1976's *Wired*, and supported the album with a co-headlining tour with Hammer's band. The tour was documented on the 1977 album, *Jeff Beck With the Jan Hammer Group—Live*.

After the Hammer tour, Beck retired to his estate outside of London and remained quiet for three years. He returned in 1980 with *There and Back*, which featured contributions from Hammer. Following the tour for *There and Back*, Beck retired again, returning five years later with the slick, Nile Rodgers-produced *Flash*. A pop-rock album recorded with a variety of vocalists, *Flash* featured Beck's only hit single, the Stewart-sung "People Get Ready," and also boasted "Escape," which won the Grammy for Best Rock instrumental. During 1987, he played lead guitar on Mick Jagger's second solo album, *Primitive Cool*. There was another long wait between *Flash* and 1989's *Jeff Beck's Guitar Shop* with Terry Bozzio and Tony Hymas. Though the album sold only moderately well, *Guitar Shop* received uniformly strong reviews and won the Grammy for Best Rock Instrumental. Beck supported the album with a tour, this time co-headlining with guitarist Stevie Ray Vaughan. Again, Beck entered semi-retirement upon the completion of the tour.

In 1992, Beck played lead guitar on Roger Waters' comeback album, *Amused to Death*. A year later, he released *Crazy Legs*, a tribute to Gene Vincent and his lead guitarist Cliff Gallup, which was recorded with the Big Town Playboys. Beck remained quiet after the album's release prior to resurfacing in 1999 with *Who Else!*. *You Had It Coming* followed two years later. *—Stephen Thomas Erlewine*

☆ **Truth** / Aug. 1968 / Epic ♦♦♦♦♦
Despite being the premiere of heavy metal, Jeff Beck's *Truth* has never quite carried its reputation the way the early albums by Led Zeppelin did, or even Cream's two most popular LPs, mostly as a result of the erratic nature of the guitarist's subsequent work. Time has muted some of its daring, radical nature, elements of which were appropriated by practically every metal band (and most arena rock bands) that followed. *Truth* was almost as groundbreaking and influential a record as the first Beatles, Rolling Stones, or Who albums. Its attributes weren't all new—Cream and Jimi Hendrix had been moving in similar directions—but the combination was: the wailing, heart-stoppingly dramatic vocalizing by Rod Stewart, the thunderous rhythm section of Ron Wood's bass and Mickey Waller's drums, and Beck's blistering lead guitar, which sounds like his amp is turned up to 13 and ready to short out. Beck opens the proceedings in a strikingly bold manner, using his old Yardbirds hit "Shapes of Things" as a jumping-off point, deliberately rebuilding the song from the ground up so it sounds closer to Howlin' Wolf. There are lots of unexpected moments on this record: a bone-pounding version of Willie Dixon's "You Shook Me"; a version of Jerome Kern's "Ol' Man River" done as a slow electric blues; a brief plunge into folk territory with a solo acoustic guitar version of "Greensleeves" (which was intended as filler but audiences loved); the progressive blues of "Beck's Bolero"; the extended live "Blues Deluxe"; and "I Ain't Superstitious," a blazing reworking of another Willie Dixon song. It was a triumph—a number 15 album in America, astoundingly good for a band that had been utterly unknown in the U.S. just six months earlier—and a very improbable success. *—Bruce Eder*

Beck-Ola / Jun. 1969 / Epic ♦♦♦♦♦
When it was originally released in June 1969, *Beck-Ola*, the Jeff Beck Group's second album, featured a famous sleeve note on its back cover: "Today, with all the hard competition in the music business, it's almost impossible to come up with anything totally original. So we haven't. However, this disc was made with the accent on heavy music. So sit back and listen and try and decide if you can find a small place in your heads for it." Beck was reacting to the success of peers and competitors like Cream and Led Zeppelin here, bands that had been all over the charts with a hard rock sound soon to be dubbed heavy metal, and indeed, his sound employs much the same brand of "heavy music" as theirs, with deliberate rhythms anchoring the beat, over which the guitar solos fiercely and the lead singer emotes. But he was also preparing listeners for the weakness of the material on an album that sounds somewhat thrown together. Two songs are rehauls of Elvis Presley standards ("All Shook Up" and "Jailhouse Rock") and one is an instrumental interlude contributed by pianist Nicky Hopkins, promoted from sideman to group member, with the rest being band-written songs that serve basically as platforms for Beck's improvisations. But that doesn't detract from the album's overall quality, due both to the guitar work and the distinctive vocals of Rod Stewart, and *Beck-Ola* easily could have been the album to establish the Jeff Beck Group as the equal of the other heavy bands of the day. Unfortunately, a series of misfortunes occurred. Beck canceled out of a scheduled appearance at Woodstock; he was in a car accident that sidelined him for over a year; and Stewart and bass player Ron Wood decamped to join Faces, breaking up the group. Nevertheless, *Beck-Ola* stands as a prime example of late-'60s British blues-rock and one of Beck's best records. [Epic Records remastered the album and reissued it on CD on July 4, 2000.] *—William Ruhlmann*

Rough and Ready / Oct. 1971 / Epic ♦♦♦
Recouping after a car crash and faced with the loss of Rod Stewart and Ron Wood, Jeff Beck redefined what the Jeff Beck Group was about, deciding to tone down the bluesy

bombast, adding keyboardist Max Middleton for a jazz edge, then having Bob Tench sing to give it an overblown early-'70s AOR edge. As expected, these two sides are in conflict and Tench can be a little overbearing, but there are moments here that bring out the best in Beck. Namely, these are the times when the group ventures into extended, funk-inflected, reflective jazzy instrumental sections. These are the moments that point the way toward the success of *Blow by Blow*, yet this remains an unabashed rock record of its time, and it falls prey to many of its era's excesses, particularly lack of focus. Still, there are moments that are as fine as anything Beck played here. — *Stephen Thomas Erlewine*

Jeff Beck Group / Apr. 1972 / Epic ✦✦✦

Continuing with the same group lineup as on *Rough and Ready*, *Jeff Beck Group* was slagged off by critics for Steve Cropper's admittedly lazy production. However, several of the songs hold up masterfully, including the skronky "Ice Cream Cakes," the superlative redo of Don Nix's "Going Down," and the beautifully sad and wistful instrumental, "Definitely Maybe." Beware of early, poor-sounding versions. — *Tom Graves*

Blow by Blow / Mar. 1975 / Epic ✦✦✦✦✦

Blow by Blow typifies Jeff Beck's wonderfully unpredictable career. Released in 1975, Beck's fifth effort as a leader and first instrumental album was a marked departure from its more rock-based predecessors. Only composer/keyboardist Max Middleton returned from Beck's previous lineups. To Beck's credit, *Blow by Blow* features a tremendous supporting cast. Middleton's tasteful use of the Fender Rhodes, clavinet, and analog synthesizers leaves a soulful imprint. Drummer Richard Bailey is in equal measure supportive and propulsive as he deftly combines elements of jazz and funk with contemporary mixed meters. Much of the album's success is also attributable to the excellent material, which includes Middleton's two originals and two collaborations with Beck, a clever arrangement of Lennon and McCartney's "She's a Woman," and two originals by Stevie Wonder. George Martin's ingenious production and string arrangements rival his greatest work. Beck's versatile soloing and diverse tones are clearly the album's focus, and he proves to be an adept rhythm player. *Blow by Blow* is balanced by open-ended jamming and crisp ensemble interaction as it sidesteps the bombast that sank much of the jazz-rock fusion of the period. One of the album's unique qualities is the sense of fun that permeates the performances. On the opening "You Know What I Mean," Beck's stinging, blues-based soloing is full of imaginative shapes and daring leaps. On "Air Blower," elaborate layers of rhythm, duel lead, and solo guitars find their place in the mix. Propelled by the galvanic rhythm section, Beck slashes his way into "Scatterbrain," where a dizzying keyboard and guitar line leads to more energetic soloing from Beck and Middleton. In Stevie Wonder's ballad "Cause We've Ended as Lovers," Beck variously coaxes and unleashes sighs and screams from his guitar in an aching dedication to Roy Buchanan. Middleton's aptly titled "Freeway Jam" best exemplifies the album's loose and fun-loving qualities, with Beck again riding high atop the rhythm section's wave. As with "Scatterbrain," Martin's impeccable string arrangements enhance the subtle harmonic shades of the closing "Diamond Dust." *Blow by Blow* signaled a new creative peak for Beck, and it proved to be a difficult act to follow. It is a testament to the power of effective collaboration and, given the circumstances, Beck clearly rose to the occasion. In addition to being a personal milestone, *Blow by Blow* ranks as one of the premiere recordings in the canon of instrumental rock music. — *Mark Kirschenmann*

Wired / May 1976 / Epic ✦✦✦✦

Released in 1976, Jeff Beck's *Wired* contains some of the best jazz-rock fusion of the period. *Wired* is generally more muscular, albeit less-unique than its predecessor, *Blow by Blow*. Joining keyboardist Max Middleton, drummer Richard Bailey, and producer George Martin from the *Blow by Blow* sessions are drummer Narada Michael Walden, bassist Wilbur Bascomb, and keyboardist Jan Hammer. Beck contributed no original material to *Wired*, instead relying on the considerable talents of his supporting cast. Perhaps this explains why *Wired* is not as cohesive as *Blow by Blow*, seemingly more assembled from component parts. Walden's powerful drumming propels much of *Wired*, particularly Middleton's explosive opener, "Led Boots," where Beck erupts into a stunning solo of volcanic intensity. Walden also contributes four compositions, including the funk-infused "Come Dancing," which adds an unnamed horn section. While Walden's "Sophie" is overly long and marred by Hammer's arena rock clichés, his "Play With Me" is spirited and Hammer's soloing more melodic. Acoustic guitar and piano predominate the closing ballad, "Love Is Green"; Beck's electric solo gracefully massages the quiet timbres. *Wired* is well balanced by looser, riff-oriented material and Walden's more intricate compositions. Walden and Hammer give *Wired* a '70s-era jazz-rock flavor that is indicative of their work with the Mahavishnu Orchestra. Bascomb's throw-down, "Head for Backstage Pass," finds Bailey skillfully navigating the mixed meters while Beck counters with a dazzling, gritty solo. Hammer's "Blue Wind" features an infectious riff over which Beck and Hammer trade heated salvos. As good as "Blue Wind" is, it would have benefited from the Walden/Bascomb rhythm section and a horn arrangement by Martin. One of *Wired*'s finest tracks is an arrangement of Charles Mingus' "Goodbye Pork Pie Hat." Beck's playing is particularly alluring: cleanly ringing tones, weeping bends, and sculpted feedback form a resonant palette. Bailey and Middleton lend supple support. Within a two-year span, the twin towers *Blow by Blow* and *Wired* set a standard for instrumental rock that even Beck has found difficult to match. On Wired, with first-rate material and collaborators on hand, one of rock's most compelling guitarists is in top form. — *Mark Kirschenmann*

Jeff Beck With the Jan Hammer Group Live / Mar. 1977 / Epic ✦✦

Jeff Beck toured to promote *Wired*, backed by a jazz-fusion group led by synthesizer player Jan Hammer. This straightforward live souvenir combines songs from *Blow by Blow* and *Wired*, plus a few other things, and while it features typically fiery playing from Beck, the backup is a bit too heavy-handed and the occasional vocals (by Hammer and drummer Tony Smith) are embarrassing. — *William Ruhlmann*

There and Back / Jun. 1980 / Epic ✦✦✦

Jeff Beck's first new studio album in four years found him moving from old keyboard partner Jan Hammer (three tracks) to new one Tony Hymas (five), which turned out to be the difference between competition and support. Hence, the second side of this instrumental album is more engaging and less of a funk-fusion extravaganza than most of the first. If it were anybody else, you'd say that this was a transitional album, but this was the only studio album Beck released between 1976 and 1985, which makes it more like an unexpected Christmas letter from an old friend: "Everything's fine, still playing guitar." — *William Ruhlmann*

Flash / Jul. 1985 / Epic ✦✦✦

Produced by Nile Rodgers and Arthur Baker, *Flash* is Beck's surprisingly successful stab at a pop album, featuring a fine performance with Rod Stewart on "People Get Ready." — *Stephen Thomas Erlewine*

Jeff Beck's Guitar Shop / Oct. 1989 / Epic ✦✦✦✦

Guitar Shop represents guitar hero Jeff Beck's return to the scene following his 1985 pop/rock-based recording, *Flash*, an outing that featured his one time lead vocalist, Rod Stewart. Essentially, this 1989 release provides Beck's ardent admirers with a power-packed outing, brimming with memorable melodies, drummer Terry Bozzio's often blistering rock drumming, and keyboardist Tony Hymas' effective synth textures. Here, Beck surges onward in altogether stunning fashion via his quirky lead lines, sweet-tempered slide guitar work, disfigured extended notes and deterministic mode of execution. With "Behind the Veil," the band delves into a reggae groove, featuring Beck's lower register thematic statements and well-placed notes. Otherwise, the ensemble tackles the blues and hard rock motifs amid Beck's crunching chord clusters, animated lines, and soaring heavenward soloing on the lovely and somewhat ethereal ballad titled "Two Rivers." Simply put, this is a wonderfully produced effort and a significant entry into the artist's extensive recorded legacy. — *Glenn Astarita*

Beckology / Nov. 19, 1991 / Epic/Legacy ✦✦✦✦✦

Jeff Beck is a genius, arguably the greatest rock guitarist of his generation (and, yes, that includes Hendrix), but never has such a gifted musician had such a spotty discography. Beck did some of his best work on his solo albums, yet he only cut a few terrific albums, with the rest of the albums being remarkably uneven. Often, he had inspired work as a sideman or as part of a band, such as the Yardbirds. This means that even the dedicated fans have had to sort through a lot of dreck, not to mention the casual fans that wanted a way to explore his vast, at times, confusing discography. The triple-disc box set *Beckology* performs its duty exceedingly well, drawing a history from his earliest recordings with his first band, the Tridents, right up to 1989's *Jeff Beck's Guitar Shop*. Some great moments are missing (there always are on a box), but it's impossible to argue with what's here, which not only offers everything essential he recorded, but winds up summarizing his career brilliantly. This is the one necessary Beck album, the one that makes the case that he is indeed a genius. — *Stephen Thomas Erlewine*

Frankie's House / Jan. 5, 1992 / Epic ✦✦

Beck fans will find his playing here mesmerizing, surpassing the technical mastery of *Guitar Shop*. Apart from a sizzling instrumental version of "High Heeled Sneakers," less devoted listeners will find *Frankie's House* as captivating as most other incidental film music. — *Stephen Thomas Erlewine*

Crazy Legs / Jun. 29, 1993 / Epic ✦✦

Jeff Beck has made many strange albums, but none were ever quite as strange as this. With the Big Town Playboys offering support, Beck rips through 18 Gene Vincent numbers (not "Be-Bop-a-Lula," however), paying tribute to Vincent's guitarist, Cliff Gallup. Beck sounds terrific as he reconstructs Gallup's parts, but he doesn't add anything to the originals. Still, *Crazy Legs* is a fun listen and offers many insights into Beck's playing, if not Gallup's. — *Stephen Thomas Erlewine*

● The Best of Beck / Aug. 15, 1995 / Epic ✦✦✦✦✦

Basically this record exists because the record company wanted to have some product on the shelf while Beck was touring. The 14 tracks do contain some of his most often-played (by radio, at any rate) recordings, including "Shapes of Things," "Plynth," and "Beck's Bolero" from the original Jeff Beck Group days in the late '60s, and the vocoder showcase "She's a Woman" and fusion landmark "Freeway Jam" from *Blow by Blow*. It may do for casual listeners who only want one Beck CD, although more serious fans would be better off with the *Beckology* box. — *Richie Unterberger*

Best of Jeff Beck / 1995 / Columbia ✦✦

The chief appeal of this European import, a skimpy nine-song survey of Beck's late-'60s work, is the inclusion of three tracks from rare solo singles that weren't featured on the first two Jeff Beck Group albums: "Hi Ho Silver Lining," "Tallyman," and "Love Is Blue." Beck takes lead vocals on the first two of these, and though "Hi Ho Silver Lining" actually made the British Top 20, Beck and/or those around him quickly realized that a strong lead vocal presence (i.e., someone other than Beck) was in order. These are typical British pop/rock tunes of the era, but the real curiosity is "Love Is Blue," a cheesy rendition of the Paul Mauriat megasmash that sets Beck's stinging guitar against a near-Muzak arrangement. — *Richie Unterberger*

Who Else! / Mar. 16, 1999 / Epic ✦✦✦✦

Jeff Beck has never shied away from following trends, at least as far as the musical styles he uses to back up his signature guitar sound. Back in 1969, in a sleeve note on *Beck-Ola*, he noted that he hadn't come up with "anything totally original," and instead made an album "with the accent on heavy music" at a time when the "heavy music" of the Jimi Hendrix Experience and Led Zeppelin was all the rage. In 1975, at the height of the jazz fusion movement, he made a jazz fusion album, and a good one, too. In both cases, however, the fashionable genres only provided a contemporary-sounding context in which his playing could flourish. If anyone has ever needed to be inspired to work, it's this recluse. So on his first regular studio album of new material in ten years, Beck, on at least a few tracks, solos over heavily percussive techno tracks reminiscent of Prodigy. But whether he's piercing such a rhythmic wall, rearranging the blues on the live "Blast from the East," or floating over an ambient soundscape on "Angel (Footsteps)," it's the same old Beck, with his stinging and sustained single-note melodies, his harmonics, his contrasting tones, his drive. And the man who played "Greensleeves" straight on *Truth* in 1968 is the same one who is faithful to the Irish air "Declan" here. Older fans who haven't been spending time at raves in recent years may want to program their CDs to avoid the electronica, but they should at least give those tunes a listen—are they any heavier than the "heavy music" of 1969? *—William Ruhlmann*

You Had It Coming / Feb. 6, 2001 / Epic ✦✦✦

Jeff Beck returns two years after the ten-years-in-the-making *Who Else!*, and *You Had It Coming* isn't surprising just for its rapidity, but for its music. From the moment the electronicized, post-rave beats of "Earthquake" kick off the record, it's clear that Beck isn't content to stay in place—he's trying to adapt to the modern world. To a certain extent, this isn't an entirely new phenomenon, since each of his records is clearly, inextricably of its time, from the crunching metal of *Truth* through the breezy jazz fusion of *Blow By Blow* to the modernized album rock of *Guitar Shop*. This is just another side of that, as Beck works with electronic music, both noisy and new age introspective. It's a bit clever, actually, since Beck's playing has always been otherworldly, dipping, bending, and sounding like anything other than a normal guitar. The problem is, when he's surrounded by lockstep, processed beats and gurgling synths, his guitar doesn't leap to the forefront and capture attention the way it does on his best recordings. Still, there's something to be said for the effort, because even if it doesn't sound like a Beck record, it isn't a bad record, and it's certainly a helluva lot more successful than Clapton's similar forays into these waters. Besides, knowing that he knocked this out so quickly makes it a little endearing. *—Stephen Thomas Erlewine*

Robert "Wolfman" Belfour

b. Sep. 11, 1940, Holly Springs, MS

Vocals, Guitar / Blues Revival, Delta Blues, Country Blues

Robert "Wolfman" Belfour is a little-known but very powerful blues guitarist and singer based in Memphis, Tennessee. Born to sharecropper parents on a farm in Holly Springs, Mississippi, he began playing guitar in the late '40s after the death of his father who left the instrument to him. He learned by emulating the sounds of such greats as John Lee Hooker, Muddy Waters, and his idol, Howlin' Wolf, as they were being broadcast on his mother's battery-operated radio. He was also influenced to some extent by his neighbor, Junior Kimbrough. Belfour's style is deeply-rooted in the sounds of his North Mississippi birthplace. It is a highly rhythmic and riff-oriented type of playing that can also be heard in the work of other players from the region, like Jessie Mae Hemphill, R.L. Burnside, and the late Fred McDowell.

Belfour moved to Memphis in 1968 and started playing on Beale Street in the early '80s at the suggestion of his wife. He was recorded by musicologist David Evans in 1994 for the German-based Hot Fox label, playing eight songs on a 20-song compilation, *The Spirit Lives On, Deep South Country Blues and Spirituals in the 1990s*. The record also features selections from veteran barrelhouse piano player and long-time Memphis resident Mose Vinson, who is also a native of Holly Springs. Although Belfour is virtually unkown in the United States, he makes yearly trips to Europe to perform for enthusiastic and very appreciative crowds who have a deep reverence for authentic country blues, releasing *What's Wrong With You* in mid-2000. *—Keith Brown*

● **What's Wrong With You** / May 23, 2000 / Epitaph ✦✦✦✦

There's a certain honesty about people like Robert Belfour. Just by listening to *What's Wrong With You* one can immediately tell that he had a back-breaking life in Memphis, TN. Blues enthusiasts are fortunate enough to hear all about it on his first album.

Belfour was 60 years old by the time that *What's Wrong With You* came out. Over forty years of guitar playing is clearly heard throughout this record, as he bears his soul of all the heartbreak and hard times in his life. And through his vintage of country-based blues that looks back into the '20s and '30s, you can tell that there's not a fake bone in Belfour's body. *—Mike DaRonco*

Carey Bell

b. Nov. 14, 1936, Macon, MS

Vocals, Drums, Harmonica, Guitar, Bass / Modern Electric Chicago Blues, Harmonica Blues, Electric Chicago Blues

His place on the honor roll of Chicago blues harpists long ago assured, Carey Bell has truly come into his own as a bandleader with terrific discs for Alligator and Blind Pig. He learned his distinctive harmonica riffs from the Windy City's very best (both Walters—Little and Big—as well as Sonny Boy Williamson II), adding his own signature effects for good measure (an other-worldly moan immediately identifies many of his more memorable harp rides). He was already playing the harp when he was eight and working professionally with his godfather, pianist Lovie Lee, at 13. The older and more experienced Lee brought Carey with him to Chicago in search of steady musical opportunities in 1956. Finally, in 1969, Bell made his debut album (on harp) for Delmark, and he was on his way. He served invaluable early-'70s stints in the bands of Muddy Waters and Willie Dixon, touring extensively and recording with both legends. The 1990 harmonica summit meeting *Harp Attack!* brought him into the studio with fellow greats James Cotton, Junior Wells, and Billy Branch, while the solo set *Deep Down* rates as his finest album to date. *—Bill Dahl*

Carey Bell's Blues Harp / Feb. 12, 1969+May 6, 1969 / Delmark ✦✦✦✦

It's a mite ragged around the edges, but Bell's 1969 debut session certainly sports the proper ambience—and no wonder, with guitarists Eddie Taylor and Jimmy Dawkins and pianist Pinetop Perkins on hand to help out. No less than four Little Walter covers and two more from Muddy Waters' songbook dot the set, but many of the best moments occur on the original numbers. Delmark's CD reissue includes three previously unissued items. *—Bill Dahl*

Last Night / 1973 / One Way ✦✦✦

Nothing flashy or outrageous here, just a meat-and-potatoes session produced by Al Smith that satisfyingly showcases Bell's charms. Once again, there are hearty tributes to Little Walter ("Last Night") and Muddy Waters ("She's 19 Years Old"), but there's some original stuff too, backed by a combo that boasted a daunting collective experience level: Taylor and Perkins return, along with bassist David Myers and drummer Willie "Big Eyes" Smith. *—Bill Dahl*

Heartaches and Pain / 1977 / Delmark ✦✦✦

Legendary producer Ralph Bass supervised this quickie session back in 1977, but it failed to see the light of day domestically until Delmark rescued it from oblivion. They did the blues world a favor: it's a worthwhile session, Bell storming through a mostly original setlist (the omnipresent Little Walter cover this time is "Everything's Gonna Be Alright"). Aron Burton and Sam Lay comprise the rhythm section, and son Lurrie contributes lead guitar. *—Bill Dahl*

Goin' on Main Street / 1982 / Evidence ✦✦✦

Originally recorded for Germany's L+R label in 1982, this studio date for Carey Bell's Blues Harp Band finds the group stretching out on seven lengthy blues jams. Son Lurrie Bell contributes some nice licks, including a tortured solo to close out a nearly ten-minute version of "I Am Worried," and other son Carey Bell Jr. anchors the rhythm section on electric bass. *—John Bush*

Son of a Gun / 1984 / Rooster Blues ✦✦✦✦

Lurrie and his dear old dad democratically split the vocals and most of the solo space on this LP to generally winning effect. Nothing overly polished or endlessly rehearsed; just solid mainstream Chicago blues. *—Bill Dahl*

Harpslinger / 1988 / JSP ✦✦

Dynasty! / 1990 / JSP ✦✦

Harp Attack! / 1990 / Alligator ✦✦✦✦

Four of Chicago's preeminent blues harpists—Bell, James Cotton, Junior Wells, and relative newcomer Billy Branch—gathered in a downtown studio to wax this historic summit meeting. Bell's vocal showcases include two originals, "Hit Man" and "Second Hand Man," and a Muddy Waters cover, "My Eyes Keep Me in Trouble." *—Bill Dahl*

Mellow Down Easy / 1991 / Blind Pig ✦✦✦✦

The harpist hooked up with a young Maryland-based band called Tough Luck for this disc, certainly one of his better outings. The traditional mindset of the combo pushed Bell back to his roots, whether on the originals "Just like You" and the Horton homage "Big Walter Strut" or revivals of Muddy Waters' "Short Dress Woman" and "Walking Thru the Park" and the classic Little Walter title cut. *—Bill Dahl*

● **Deep Down** / 1995 / Alligator ✦✦✦✦✦

More than a quarter century after he cut his debut album, Bell recently made his finest disc to date. Boasting superior material and musicianship (guitarists Carl Weathersby and Lurrie Bell and pianist Lucky Peterson are all stellar) and a goosed-up energy level that frequently reaches incendiary heights, the disc captures Bell outdoing himself vocally on the ribald "Let Me Stir in Your Pot" and a suitably loose "When I Get Drunk" and instrumentally on the torrid "Jawbreaker." For a closer, Bell settled on the atmospheric Horton classic "Easy"; he does it full justice. *—Bill Dahl*

Good Luck Man / Oct. 7, 1997 / Alligator ✦✦✦

Carey Bell is an effective and surprisingly versatile singer but it is his powerful harmonica that really stands out. One of the last of the major Chicago blues harpists, Bell (an alumnus of the Muddy Waters and Willie Dixon bands) had led his own groups for most of the previous 30 years when he came out with this disc. His longtime guitarist Steve Jacobs offers some concise and stinging comments but the leader is virtually the whole show on his CD, which finds him leading a tight six-piece group. Nothing too unusual occurs but the music definitely has plenty of spirit. *—Scott Yanow*

Brought Up the Hard Way / Mar. 10, 1998 / JSP ✦✦✦✦

Brought Up the Hard Way compiles a selection of Carey Bell's best JSP sides; featured guests are Lefty Dizz and Louisiana Red. *—Steve Huey*

Lurrie Bell

b. Dec. 13, 1958, Chicago, IL

Vocals, Guitar / Modern Electric Chicago Blues, Electric Chicago Blues

Lurrie Bell was born on December 13, 1958, in Chicago. His famous father, harpist Carey Bell, had him working out on guitar as a wee lad. By 1977, he was recording with his dad and playing behind a variety of established stars, tabbed by many observers at the time as a sure star on the rise. But personal problems took their toll on his great potential; Bell's recorded output and live performances were inconsistent in the '80s and early '90s. Among the highlights of Bell's discography are three tracks in tandem with harpist Billy Branch under the Sons of Blues banner (Bell was a founding member of the band) from Alligator's first batch of 1978 *Living Chicago Blues* anthologies and a 1984 collaboration, *Son of a Gun*, with his old man for Rooster Blues. Then there's his set for Delmark, *Mercurial Son*, as bizarre a contemporary blues album as you're likely to encounter. Bell followed *Mercurial Son* with the more straightforward *700 Blues* in spring 1997; *The Blues Had a Baby* appeared two years later. *—Bill Dahl and Al Campbell*

Everybody Wants to Win / 1989 / JSP ✦✦✦

Mercurial Son / Oct. 3, 1995 / Delmark ✦✦✦✦

Mercurial Son, Lurrie Bell's intense second album, is a searing, passionate collection of urban blues laced with the rhythmic fury of vintage '50s R&B and rock & roll. In particular, Bell works the classic Bo Diddley shuffle a number of times, tapping into the scary, menacing undertones of Diddley's primal beats. Not only is his guitar playing white hot, his vocals are gutsy and impassioned—he makes even the weaker numbers on the album sound convincing. And the songs on *Mercurial Son* are varied and intriguing, ranging from rollicking rockers and dense, funky boogie to heartfelt ballads and even an a cappella track. The variety is what makes the album stand out from the pack of contemporary blues releases—it's one of more compelling recent blues records. *—Stephen Thomas Erlewine*

700 Blues / Apr. 29, 1997 / Delmark ♦♦♦

Young Man's Blues: The Best of the JSP Sessions (1989–1990) / Nov. 18, 1997 / JSP ♦♦♦♦

Kiss of Sweet Blues / Sep. 22, 1998 / Delmark ♦♦♦

Blues Had a Baby / Nov. 23, 1999 / Delmark ♦♦♦♦

The blues of Lurrie Bell comes from a turbulent place, but there's no denying the man can play. This album brings together tracks from three different sessions, the bulk being held in 1997. Supported by a spartan rhythm section, Bell sprays kamikaze guitar licks over a bevy of old standards like "Five Long Years," "Who Do You Love," "Mean Old Frisco," and "You're the One." The last four songs on the album are the real treat; cut in 1995 at the *Mercurial Son* sessions, this is just Lurrie and his electric guitar running through raw, soulful, and sometimes whacked-out versions of everything from "Rollin' and Tumblin'" to "If I Had a Hammer." If you've wondered what all the fuss is about, grab this CD and turn on to the blues world of Lurrie Bell. *—Cub Koda*

Fred Below

b. Sep. 16, 1926, Chicago, IL, **d.** Aug. 14, 1988, Chicago, IL

Drums / Chicago Blues

Fred Below was born in Chicago on September 16, 1926. Below played drums in high school and went on to study percussion at the Roy C. Knapp School of Percussion. Primarily a jazz drummer at the time, he played bebop and joined the Army as part of the 427th Army band. After the service, he returned to Chicago in 1951 to find that blues gigs were what was happening. Jazz was in a lull.

Then Muddy Waters drummer Elgin Evans introduced Below to a group called the Three Aces—Junior Wells (vocals, harp), Louis Myers (guitar), and Dave Myers (bass)—which needed a drummer. As a jazz drummer, Below did not know blues drumming and it was a rough fit at first. The next big event came when Little Walter (on the sudden success of his instrumental "Juke") quit the Muddy Waters band and was replaced by Junior Wells. Little Walter then joined the Three Aces which he had been itching to do because Muddy Waters did not play in the uptempo style that Walter was into. Little Walter and the Four Aces (later renamed the Jukes) were a perfect fit and this four-piece electric blues combo became the hottest band in Chicago.

It is hard to estimate the effect of this band on Chicago music scene, and a large part of this success is due to the refined and elegant drumming of Below. He plays on almost all of Walter's greatest hits. He was in total demand for recording sessions. Everyone wanted him and he recorded for Muddy Waters, Willie Dixon, Chuck Berry, Otis Rush, Elmore James, Junior Wells, Buddy Guy, Dinah Washington, John Brim, the Platters, the Moonglows, the Drifters, Bo Diddley, John Lee Hooker, Howlin' Wolf, and many more. Fred Below and the Aces pretty much created the standard for the blues shuffle beat. Below also was known for his use of the ride cymbal, the wood block, tom-tom fills, and many other embellishments. Just check out his drum solo on Little Walter's classic tune "Off the Wall." *—Michael Erlewine*

Buster Bennett (Joseph Bennett)

b. Mar. 19, 1914, Pensacola, FL, **d.** Jul. 3, 1980, Houston, TX

Sax (Alto) / Jump Blues

Sure, the name Buster Bennett sounds like the name of a bluesman, so much so that the familiarity of it all leads many to answer positively when asked if they have heard of this artist. The cold, hard reality is that they probably have not. This Chicago blues saxophonist and vocalist, who appeared on more than two dozen recording sessions between 1938 and 1947, has been pretty much forgotten, except among collectors of the most obscure blues material. He was born Joseph Bennett on the Florida gulf coast, began playing professionally in Texas, and arrived in Chicago when he was 19, cutting his first recordings shortly thereafter. He got his start on blues sessions for the Melrose label, working regularly on sessions for this firm from 1938 to 1942. This included sides with the great Big Bill Broonzy, as well as much less-remembered artists such as the optimistic Yas Yas Girl and the mischievious Monkey Joe. He collaborated best with the lively Washboard Sam, whose music had a ragtime element just perfect for the alto or soprano sax to romp around in. Bennett also worked off the Melrose plantation on sessions for Jimmie Gordon under the direction of R&B legend Sammy Price. Bennett's presence on so many sessions might have been because of more than just sheer musical talent. Apparently, he was quite persuasive at getting advances out of various session producers, who would then have to schedule him on dates in order to recoup. Bennett's early recorded efforts reveal distinctive gutbucket mannerisms which throw back to the Roaring '20s, including his use of the soprano sax, temporarily out of fashion at that time. His recording career can be divided into two parts, although this may have had more to do with existing opportunities or recording trends then artistic direction. He began working in the aforementioned blues accompanist capacity, but in the second period was eventually signed as a leader, presented as a hard-edged, raunchy instrumentalist and blues singer. The American Recording Company did not have any interest in recording the blues standards by artists such as Robert Johnson that were apparently the meat of his nightclub repertoire, except for one combination of such material, recorded under the name of the "Buster Bennett Medley." Although he played on records that were hits, such as "Diggin' My Potatoes," whatever claim to fame he might have really stems from his own three-year contract with Columbia, which began in 1945. The label tried to sell him as another Louis Jordan, with whom there are superficial similarities, i.e., a frontman who plays sax. The two artists really had little in common besides this. He came across as more of an old-fashioned blues singer than Jordan, and much less polished. The differences continued on sax, where Jordan would near bebop licks, while Bennett hung with an almost quaint New Orleans tone and rhythmic feel. As a bandleader, he looked for similar musical directions in his players. An instrumental tune entitled "Leap Frog," which he did not write but adapted as something of a theme song, showed his adeptness with intricate melodic jumps on the horn and for a time, led to a double-deckered nickname for him: Buster "Leap Frog" Bennett. The end of his recording days basically coincided with the general decline of blues recording in Chicago. This included Columbia completing its race series in 1950. By the mid-'50s, Bennett suffered from health problems that required him to quit playing professionally, and he ended up leaving Chicago and retiring in Texas. Houston newspapers did absolutely nothing to commemorate his passing: there was no obituary and not even a notice in the column for area deaths. *—Eugene Chadbourne*

Duster Bennett (Anthony Bennett)

b. Sep. 23, 1946, **d.** Mar. 26, 1976, Warwickshire, England

Vocals, Drums, Harmonica, Guitar / British Blues, Blues-Rock

Duster Bennett was a British blues singer and harmonica player. He signed to Mike Vernon's Blue Horizon label in 1967 and was backed on his debut album, *Smiling Like I'm Happy* (1968), by members of Fleetwood Mac. He was a session harmonica player and a member of John Mayall's Bluesbreakers. He was killed in a car accident in 1976. *—William Ruhlmann*

● **Smiling Like I'm Happy** / Jul. 8, 1968-Sep. 9, 1968 / Blue Horizon ♦♦♦♦♦

One of the unsung heroes of British blues, this one-man band was a fine harmonica player and singer, a decent guitarist, and a soulful enough singer to make one overlook his distinctly *unbluesy* high voice. The opening "Worried Mind"—just Duster on harp, guitar, voice, high-hat and kick drum—is a marvelously sloppy shuffle romp that holds its own with the Fabulous Thunderbirds' work ten years hence. On other tracks Bennett is backed by three-fourths of the original Fleetwood Mac, who provide simple, effective support without stealing any limelight; solos are kept to a minimum. Originals "My Lucky Day" (with chromatic harmonica) and "Jumping at Shadows" which Mac would later cover) are absolutely outstanding, and Duster does justice to Magic Sam's "My Love Is Your Love." *—Dan Forte*

Bright Lights / 1969 / Blue Horizon ♦♦♦

12 Dbs / 1970 / Blue Horizon ♦♦♦♦♦

Considering his status among Britain's finest blues composers, it's always seemed somewhat galling that Duster Bennett is best known for his cover of the Kinks' "Act Nice and Gentle"—although when you hear it, you can understand why. Without deviating at all far from Ray Davies' magical prototype, Bennett imbues the song with all the emotion and joy which Davies himself buried beneath weary cynicism, while guitarist Top Topham lets rip with exactly the kind of guitar playing that ensured he remained a legend long after he left the Yardbirds. "Act Nice and Gentle" opens side two of Bennett's third album—perhaps deliberately, it is immediately followed by "Woman Without Love," a song which finds Bennett enacting an almost note-perfect Ray Davies impersonation, while strings and a superbly syrupy backing chorus build tear-blindingly up behind him. Past Bennett albums showcased the performer. *12 Dbs* showcases the artist. *12 Dbs* is Bennett's best-produced and certainly most adventurous album, although that's not to say it lacks any of the humor, spark, and verve which highlight its predecessors. "Slim's Blues" is a magnificent plod, the blues when they first wake up in the morning; "Vitamin Pills" is a 12-bar shuffle which disguises its utterly surreal lyric with an absolutely traditional soundtrack; and "That Mean Old Look" is a riotous talking blues, apologizing for a nightmarish night on the town with his girl. So it's business as idiosyncratically usual, and the best track of all has not even been mentioned. "I Chose to Sing the Blues" is a Stones-y R&B-flavored grind which outlines all the things he could have done, if he hadn't become a singer. Gambler, lover, president, or doctor, he threw them all away, and *12 Dbs* proves he made the right choice. *—Dave Thompson*

Bennett / 1970 / Blue Horizon ♦♦♦

Justa Duster / 1970 / Blue Horizon ♦♦♦♦

Of all the albums released during the British blues boom of the late '60s—a role call which includes debut albums by Savoy Brown, Ten Years After, Chicken Shack, and, of course, Peter Green's Fleetwood Mac, none have the instant effervescence and overall good-time-being-had-by-all vibe of *Justa Duster*. From the opening neo-soul lament "I'm Gonna Wind Up Ending Up or I'm Gonna End Up Winding Up With You"—described in the liner notes as "the most important track Duster Bennett has ever made," through to the closing boogie of Jimmy Reed's "Bright Lights, Big City," with the album divided neatly between anarchic studio and riotous live recordings, *Justa Duster* is the most evocative and certainly one of the most varied albums in the entire genre. As usual, Bennett lives up to his one-man billing throughout most of the record; the exceptions are the ones you'd expect—the lo-fi rhythm section which powers "Raining in My Heart," "Talk to Me," and "Bright Lights" itself. Elsewhere, however, the supercharged skiffle of "If You Could Hang Your Washing Like You Hang Your Lines" takes its accompaniment from its absolute spontaneity, while a dark, largely instrumental take on the hymn "Rock of Ages" has a spectral gospel moodiness that conjures up a chorus, though there's not another soul in sight. The in-concert tracks are less moody, more manic, painting Bennett among the most impulsive performers of his age. "Just Like a Fish" opens with near-enough the same beat that Gary Glitter would subpoena for his entire career, while producer Mike Vernon's purposefully semi-bootleg mix brings a magnificent audio vérité quality to the show. The result is a night in the best blues boom of all, and you didn't even have to be there to enjoy it. *—Dave Thompson*

Out in the Blue / 1995 / Indigo ♦♦♦♦
Odds and ends, mostly from 1966-1968, with a few tracks from 1975 and 1976, the year Bennett was killed in a car wreck. Two tracks feature fine lead guitar by Duster's longtime friend (and original Yardbird) Top Topham—home tapes worthy of inclusion if only for Top's amazing and expressive vibrato. Five tracks feature Peter Green, including a demo of his "Trying So Hard to Forget" that's especially moody, and the fascinating snippet "Two Harps" instrumental duet (unaccompanied harmonicas, as the title implies), showing the similarity in the pair's harp styles. The final cut, "Everyday," from 1976, sets one of Bennett's finest vocal performnces against a string backdrop. What a contrast to the one-man band shouting "Worried Mind"—and it works. *—Dan Forte*

Jumpin' at Shadows / 1995 / Indigo ♦♦♦

Blue Inside / 1996 / Indigo ♦♦♦

I Choose to Sing the Blues / Aug. 11, 1998 / Indigo ♦♦♦

Comin' Home / Jun. 29, 1999 / Indigo ♦♦♦

Shady Little Baby / Dec. 12, 2000 / Indigo ♦♦♦

Tab Benoit

b. Nov. 17, 1967, Baton Rouge, LA
Vocals, Guitar / Swamp Blues, Modern Electric Blues, Modern Electric Texas Blues
Guitarist, singer and songwriter Tab Benoit makes his home south of New Orleans in Houma, LA. Born November 17, 1967, he's one of a handful of bright rising stars on the modern blues scene. For most of the '90s, he worked each of his records the old fashioned way, by playing anywhere and everywhere he and his band could play. Unlike so many others before him, Benoit understands that blues is not a medium in favor with 50,000 watt commercial rock radio stations, so as a consequence, he's worked each of his releases with as many shows as he can possibly play. Since the release of his first album for Justice, Benoit has taken his brand of Cajun-influenced blues all over the U.S., Canada and Europe. *Nice & Warm*, his debut album for Houston-based Justice Records, prompted some critics to say he's reminiscent, at times, of three blues guitar gods: Albert King, Albert Collins and Jimi Hendrix.

Although the hardworking, modest guitarist scoffs at those comparisons, and doesn't think he sounds like them (and doesn't try to sound like them), Benoit doesn't appear to be one who's easily led into playing rock & roll in favor of his downhome blend of swamp blues and east Texas guitar-driven blues. Talk to Tab at one of his shows, and he'll tell you about his desire to "stay the course," and not water down his blues by playing items that could be interpreted as "alternative" rock. Despite the screaming guitar licks he coaxes from his Telecaster and his powerful songwriting and singing abilities, Benoit's laidback, down-to-earth personality off stage is the exact opposite of his live shows.

Benoit's releases include *Nice & Warm* (1992), *What I Live For* (1994), *Standing on the Bank* (1995) *Live: Swampland Jam* (1997) *These Blues Are All Mine* (1999) and Wetlands (2002). Considering many of Benoit's records have surpassed the 50,000 mark, he's well on his way to a career that could rival the kind of popularity that the late Stevie Ray Vaughan enjoyed in the late '80s. *—Richard Skelly & Al Campbell*

● **Nice & Warm** / 1992 / Vanguard ♦♦♦♦♦
Tab Benoit's debut album *Nice & Warm* is a startingly fresh debut. The guitarist has a gutsy, fuel-injected style that adds real spice to his swampy blues. Benoit draws equally from the Louisiana and Texas traditions and *Nice & Warm* proves it; not only does he carry on the tradition, he offers a fresh take on it as well. *—Thom Owens*

What I Live For / 1994 / Vanguard ♦♦♦
What I Live For is a white-hot sophomore effort by Tab Benoit, showcasing a more assured and confident guitarist. Although he hasn't changed his basic musical approach—it's all hard-driving Southern blues—his sound is fuller and more direct this time around, proving that his debut was no fluke. *—Thom Owens*

Standing on the Bank / 1995 / Vanguard ♦♦♦
On his third album, Tab Benoit stripped his sound to its bare essentials by recording live, directly to a two-track. Naturally, the process gives *Standing on the Bank* a startling immediacy, as the guitarist shreds a number of originals to pieces with his piercing solos. *—Thom Owens*

Live: Swampland Jam / Sep. 16, 1997 / Vanguard ♦♦♦♦
This is by far the best album this Louisiana blues/swamp-rocker has come up with to date. Benoit is playing with basically a three-piece, with Doug Therrien on bass and Allyn Robinson on drums. The rest of the sound is filled in by various guests, some exceedingly strong Louisiana players. Therein lives both the problem and the strength of this disc—the sound is a bit thin when there's no guest taking up some space. Only on the slow burner "Heart of Stone" and "Gone Too Long" does the basic band fill up the airwaves. The music is good, but without that fourth player, it doesn't have enough density. When there is another player, the sound is as gritty and raw as they come—Cajun-based blues with a swampy sensuality. Benoit's singing and guitar playing have taken giant steps forward and are up there with the best. *—Bob Gottlieb*

Homesick for the Road / Mar. 23, 1999 / Telarc ♦♦♦♦
Homesick for the Road provides a showcase for three fine blues singer/guitarists. The recording is clean and crisp, as is typical of the Telarc label, and the music cooks from start to finish. This disc provides an excellent introduction to each performer, with ample opportunities for each to shine. Debbie Davies brings to mind Bonnie Raitt, with her appealing vocal timbre and bluesy delivery. The youthful Benoit sings with an authority beyond his 31 years, making Screamin' Jay Hawkins' classic "I Put a Spell on You" his own. Kenny Neal has the scruffy, soulful delivery of a man who knows what the blues are all about. His "I've Been Mistreated" sounds like a late-'60s slice of Muscle Shoals soul. All three of the co-leaders are excellent guitarists, and the band is solid and tight. *Homesick for the Road* rolls down the car window for an enticing look at three relatively young performers carrying the blues torch into the future. *—Jim Newsom*

These Blues Are All Mine / Oct. 12, 1999 / Vanguard ♦♦♦
This is a strong statement by Tab Benoit announcing his true arrival; although he only wrote five of the 13 songs on this disc, he stakes a legitimate claim to all of them with some of his most inspired playing and singing ever. His backing group sounds great and keeps up with him over the entire disc. He is one of a handful of performers—Tabby Thomas and Johnny Jenkins also manage this—with that rare ability to combine aggressive blues with the rhythms and sounds of the dark standing waters and Spanish moss-draped trees of the Louisiana swamps. Listen to the spin he puts on the Hank Williams classic "Jambalaya." He injects just a tad more blues and zydeco seasoning to take the song to a different level without messing with the basic ingredients that made it a standard. He does some equally good and interesting things with songs from Albert Collins and Willie Dixon, among others. However, when he plays his own songs, he rips apart the room and leaves it all out there for us to see. Feel the anguish and pain that run rampant in the title cut, "These Blues Are All Mine." Neither his voice nor his guitar leave room for any doubt about how he is feeling. As tormented as he is in "These Blues," feel the joy of a life lived in the swamp that percolates through "Crawfishin'." Listen to him rave in "Bayou Boogie"—this is one happy and satisfied man. This is definitely one hell of a keeper. *—Bob Gottlieb*

Wetlands / Mar. 26, 2002 / Telarc ♦♦♦♦
Recorded during a month in Louisiana and sounding it, Tab Benoit's sixth album is a swampy example of the best of that state's music. Rocking, bluesy, and filled with soul, guitarist/vocalist Benoit keeps his sound stripped down to just a three-piece, giving his voice and greasy guitar plenty of room to maneuver. From obscure Professor Longhair second-line tunes ("Her Mind Is Gone") to a cover from zydeco king Boozoo Chavis ("Dog Hill") to a version of Otis Redding's "These Arms of Mine" that makes it seem like a lost New Orleans classic, Benoit traverses a lot of territory over this hour of music. Like his influences, Benoit never overdoes his approach, preferring to keep the focus on his gritty voice, lean guitar, and stark accompaniment of his backing duo. This is music caught between rootsy rock, funk, R&B, and blues, but far from sounding schizoid, it revels in its multiple inspirations. Benoit is in wonderful voice and spirits throughout, sounding loose yet in control regardless of what style he's playing. His guitar solos are taut and succinct, capturing the essence of the atmosphere without reverting to needless showboating. This is music from the heart, played with class, subtlety, and a reverence for its past squeezed into every spirited groove. Thirteen songs and not a misstep, *Wetlands* is not only Tab Benoit's best album, it's the one most representative of his upbringing and style. Like the autobiographical "Down in the Swamp," those who have never made it to Louisiana need only play this to understand how the area—and Benoit—oozes with the ambience of the muggy air, rich food, and spirits of musicians who have passed. *—Hal Horowitz*

Buster Benton

b. Jul. 19, 1932, Texarkana, AR, **d.** Jan. 20, 1996, Chicago, IL
Vocals, Guitar / Modern Electric Chicago Blues, Modern Electric Blues, Soul-Blues
Despite the amputation of parts of both his legs during the course of his career, Chicago guitarist Buster Benton never gave up playing his music—an infectious hybrid of blues and soul that he dubbed at one point "disco blues" (an unfortunate appellation in retrospect, but useful in describing its danceability). In the late '70s, when blues was at low ebb, Benton's waxings for Ronn Records were a breath of fresh air.

Inspired by the music of Sam Cooke and B.B. King, the gospel-bred Benton began playing the blues during the mid-'50s while living in Toledo, OH. By 1959, he was leading his own band in Chicago. During the '60s, he cut a series of soul-slanted singles for local concerns (Melloway, Alteen, Sonic, Twinight) before hooking up with the great Willie Dixon in 1971.

Benton was a member of Dixon's Blues All-Stars for a while, and Dixon is credited as songwriter of Benton's best-known song, the agonized slow blues "Spider in My Stew." Its release on Stan Lewis' Shreveport-based Jewel Records gave Benton a taste of fame; its follow-up, "Money Is the Name of the Game," solidified his reputation. A 1979 LP for Jewel's Ronn subsidiary (logically titled *Spider in My Stew*) stands as one of the most engaging Chicago blues LPs of its era, its contemporary grooves abetting Benton's tasty guitar work and soulful vocals.

Benton cut three albums later on for Ichiban, but compared to his Ronn output, they were disappointing. On the Chicago circuit, Benton's extreme courage in the face of physical adversity will long be cited. He was on kidney dialysis for the last few years of his life as a result of diabetes, and a portion of his right leg was amputated in 1993 due to poor circulation (he had already lost part of the other a decade earlier). Still, he continued to play his brand of uplifting blues until the end. *—Bill Dahl*

● **Spider in My Stew** / Jul. 21, 1978 / Ronn ♦♦♦♦♦
Without a doubt, this album, originally released on Ronn in 1979, stands as the best place to begin an in-depth examination of Benton's legacy. "Spider in My Stew," and obviously, is here, along with the wonderful Cooke-influenced R&B outing "Lonesome for a Dime," an irresistibly funky "Sweet 94" (Ron Scott's gurgly electric saxophone gives this cut and several others a unique feel), a driving "Funny About My Money," and the mournful minor-key blues "Sorry." Ronn has beefed the CD program up still further with three additions: the doomy, Bobby Bland-styled "Money Is the Name of the Game," a shuffling "Dangerous Woman," and Benton's happy-go-lucky cover of David Dee's "Going Fishin'." *—Bill Dahl*

Blues Buster / 1979 / Red Lightnin' ♦♦♦♦♦

Buster Benton Is the Feeling / 1980 / Ronn ♦♦♦
The guitarist's 1980 follow-up didn't pack quite the same knockout punch as its predecessor, but it's a decidedly solid encore effort nonetheless, with tight backup from a

talented unit (harpist Carey Bell, pianist Lafayette Leake, rhythm guitarist Jimmy Johnson, and saxist Scott). *—Bill Dahl*

Sweet 94 / 1980 / Charly ♦♦♦

First Time in Europe / 1983 / Blue Phoenix ♦♦♦

Why Me / 1988 / Ichiban ♦♦

The pleading title track is a worthy addition to the Benton canon, but this album isn't nearly as consistent as the guitarist's superior Ronn output. *—Bill Dahl*

I Like to Hear My Guitar Sing / 1991 / Ichiban ♦♦

Ironically, Benton's axe doesn't have much room to sing on this disappointing outing. *—Bill Dahl*

Blues at the Top / May 1993 / Evidence ♦♦♦♦

A compilation of the two albums Benton made for the French Black & Blue label in 1983 and 1985, this 15-song collection rates with his best. Two separate bands are involved, and the sound changes with them: backed by harpist Billy Branch's Sons of Blues, Benton exercises his R&B-laced chops, while the older hands behind him on "Honey Bee," "The Hawk Is Coming," and "Hole in My Head" (guitarist Johnny Littlejohn, pianist Leake, drummer Odie Payne) ensure that the grooves stay more in the mainstream. *—Bill Dahl*

That's the Reason / May 15, 1997 / Ronn ♦♦♦

Blues and Trouble / Sep. 3, 2002 / Black & Blue ♦♦♦

Rod Bernard

b. Aug. 12, 1940, Opelousas, LA

Vocals, Guitar / Rock & Roll, New Orleans R&B, Traditional Cajun

Swamp pop musician Rod Bernard was born in Opelousas, Louisiana in the early '40s and made his professional debut on KSLO Opelousas when he was only ten. Two years later, Bernard was a deejay at the station, but in 1954, his family moved to Winnie, Texas. There Bernard became acquainted with the town barber Huey Meaux, who later became a major producer of Cajun recordings. By the time he was a teenager, Bernard formed his first band (the Twisters) and cut two records on Jake Graffagnino's Carl label.

They then recorded King Karl's "This Should Go on Forever" for Floyd Soileau's Jin label (which eventually licensed the recording to Chicago's Argo label) and took the records to Huey Meaux—who was now hosting a French music show on KPAC Port Arthur. Meaux had the song played throughout East Texas and took a copy to the Big Bopper, who played it at KTRM Beaumont, Texas. It took seven months, but eventually the record made it to the Top 20 on the pop charts. Bernard then appeared on Dick Clark's *American Bandstand* (where he had to sanitize some of the lyrics for mainstream audiences) and signed with Mercury Records. After recording over 40 songs for the label, Bernard watched as only four sides were released. One of them, "One More Chance," made it to the pop charts as a minor hit.

By 1962, Bernard's Mercury contract had run out. He began working for Hall-Way Records, where many of his sessions were backed by Johnny and Edgar Winter. He achieved small success with a rocked up version of the traditional Cajun song "Colinda," before Bernard became a deejay and musical director at KVOL, and later a sales executive at KLFY-TV, both Lafayette stations. He also performed on television with the Shondells, a group he had co-founded in 1963. In 1965, a compilation of 12 songs he and the Shondells sang on the show were released as *Saturday Hop* on the La Louisianne label. The group also released a single, "Our Teenage Love" for Teardrop. Bernard and Carol Ranchou of La Louisianne founded the Arbee label. Bernard released several albums throughout the seventies and continued to work for KLFY-TV for years. In the late '90s, Rod Bernard returned to the studios and recorded *The Louisiana Tradition*. *—Sandra Brennan*

● **Essential Collection** / Jan. 27, 1998 / Jin ♦♦♦♦♦

The Louisiana Tradition / Jun. 29, 1999 / CSP ♦♦♦♦

Rod Bernard is one of the few Louisiana swamp pop musicians to have ever made the hit parade. His record, "This Should Go on Forever," made the Top 20 chart in 1959 and won the young musician an appearance on *American Bandstand*. Popular hits may come and go, but Bernard's position as one of the driving forces in the idiom has remained a constant. The man designated as a "living legend" in the Louisiana Music Hall of Fame has continued to perform his style of music at clubs and festivals and has recorded numerous CDs. *Louisiana Tradition* was made in 1999. As the name suggests, the CD is faithful to his Cajun roots, as well as to the R&B style in which he sings. The vocalist is backed by Rufus Thibodeaux on fiddle, Jimmy Breaux on accordion, Oran "Junior" Guidry on guitar, Warren Storm on drums and rub board, Richard Comeaux on steel guitar, John Kimbrough and Gene Romero on saxophones, and Gerald Melancon on drums. There is a scorching cover of Chuck Berry's "Maybelline"; most of the tunes are penned by Bernard himself. He starts right off in a Louisiana mode with "Backwater Bayou," sings in French on "Gardez Donc," describes the apprehension and camaraderie of a "Hurricane Watch," and gets melancholy with "When I Hold You in My Dreams" and "The Fantasy Is Over." The obligatory alligator song of the genre is the last on the album, with a cover of Guidry's "See You Later, Alligator." Thus do things go in the swamp. *—Rose of Sharon Witmer*

Eric Bibb

b. Aug. 16, 1951, New York, NY

Vocals, Guitar / Contemporary Blues, Modern Electric Blues, Modern Acoustic Blues, Folk-Blues

Eric Bibb's music is a rich blend of the blues with elements of folk, country, gospel, and soul, thanks in part to his being the son of New York folk singer Leon Bibb, which afforded young Eric exposure to a wide variety of music and opportunities to meet performers like Pete Seeger and Bob Dylan. Bibb launched his career in Europe, performing at blues and folk festivals in London, Cambridge, and Dublin, sometimes with a full band and sometimes with slide guitarist Goran Wennerbrandt; he eventually settled permanently in Sweden, where he works as a music and voice teacher when not performing. Bibb's debut album, *Good Stuff*, was released in Europe in 1997 and the U.S. a year later; it was followed by *Shakin' a Tailfeather* in 1998, which featured producer Linda Tillery and a guest appearance by Taj Mahal. *Home To Me* arrived in 2000 and the enchanting *Painting Signs* followed the next summer. *—Steve Huey*

Good Stuff / Apr. 15, 1997 / Rhino ♦♦♦♦

Eric Bibb's debut album, *Good Stuff*, is a clever fusion of contemporary folk and classic country blues and classic gospel that emphasizes the guitarist's skill at fusing genres, as well as his flair for writing solid bluesy songs. Not all of the material really catches hold, but it all shows promise, and the very best moments on the record confirm that he was one of the more intriguing new bluesmen during the late '90s. *—Thom Owens*

Me to You / 1998 / Code Blue ♦♦♦

Spirit and the Blues / Feb. 2, 1999 / Rhino ♦♦♦♦

Eric Bibb grew up in New York City, surrounded by a plethora of cultural variety from Leadbelly to Villa Lobos wafting in from the radio and the streets. By the time little Eric got his first guitar, his father, the eminent Leon Bibb, was making the rounds as a respected folksinger. Leon removed Eric from school in favor of packing him along to rehearsals, where he consorted with the likes of Judy Collins, Odetta, Bob Dylan, Earl Robinson and many others. *Spirit and the Blues* is a funky folk-blues delight: a bubbling pot of authentic bottleneck spirituals and memorable hum-alongs, especially for hardcore Deacons fans. Bibb blends the muddy-river vocal style of Delta gospel and the drive of white vagabond balladeers like Woody Guthrie and Pete Seeger. Choice cuts "Lonesome Valley" and "Satisified Mind" are gorgeous understated revisits of neglected gems; "Where I Shall Be" is a meditative adaption of an old field prayer recorded by Blind Lemon Jefferson. Bibb's fingerpicking technique engages the "micro-melodies" happening between melody and bass line, skillfully accompanied by the harmonica-wielding Reverend Dan Smith on "Keep Goin' On" and the traded leads with Goran's steel-bodied National Style "O" on "Lonesome Valley." Bibb's songs successfully trade visits with gospel as well as sassy, lazy blues tunes about sex and old-fashioned romance, as in "Braggin'," also a favorite cut. A modern and beautifully mixed record, graced with spirit and a real timelessness factor. *—Becky Byrkit*

Home to Me / Jul. 4, 2000 / Rhino ♦♦♦

Home to Me is the forth U.S. release from acoustic roots chameleon Eric Bibb. These 13 tracks, the majority penned by Bibbs, encompass his deep musical debt to folk (maintaining a healthy dose of his early Woody Guthrie influence), soul (a respectful cover of Sam Cooke's "Bring It on Home to Me"), and gospel, underscored by a consistent blues base, not unlike the first Keb' Mo' disc. Bibb combines his poetic flair with political concerns and universal issues on "Mandela Is Free," "World War Blues," and "Walk the Walk," while special guest Taj Mahal is featured on the concluding duet "Sing Your Song." *—Al Campbell*

● **Painting Signs** / Aug. 7, 2001 / Rhino ♦♦♦♦

With *Painting Signs*, Eric Bibb makes a fine case for blues as a music of introspection, warmth, and supreme nuance. Easily his most mature album to date, *Painting Signs* continues Bibb's formula of socially aware songs performed from an acutely personal point-of-view; standout tracks "Don't Ever Let Nobody Drag Your Spirit Down" and a cover of "Hope in a Hopeless World" hammer home his message of individual freedom and the responsibilities that accompany it. (It's no coincidence that Pops Staples, to whom Bibb dedicates this album, once recorded the latter song.) That's not to say *Painting Signs* is overly didactic or, indeed, "heavy" in any way; even the most serious songs here, like the plea for peace and unity "Got to Do Better," are leavened by a musical backdrop that's soulful and immediately accessible. Gospel-leaning backing vocals by Linda Tillery and her Cultural Heritage Choir help flesh out several cuts, and robust accordion fills by Bibb's longtime accompanist Janne Petersson add a subtle Louisiana flavor to the rolling, propulsive "Kokomo" and, to surprisingly good effect, the deep-grooved version of Jimmy Reed's "Honest I Do." Elsewhere, he keeps a minimalist tone dominated by acoustic guitar, an arrangement that's particularly mesmerizing on the chilling title track. With its emphasis on sophisticated songcraft and its gentle blend of folk, gospel, and country influences, *Painting Signs* presents Bibb as an artist intent on blurring the line between blues and "roots music" in general. *—Kenneth Bays*

Big Boy Henry (Richard Henry)

b. 1921, Beaufort, NC

Vocals / Modern Electric Blues

Born Richard Henry, this North Carolina country blues artist enjoyed a unique niche in his later life as a folk festival and club performer, bringing great pleasure to blues fans in a period when many older artists in this genre were passing away. He grew up on the North Carolina coast in the '20s and '30s, an era when bluesmen still played on street corners and juke joints were hopping at night with live music. The South Carolinian bluesman Fred Miller was one of his first big musical influences, and Henry assumed the traditional apprentice role in the country blues relationship, meaning he would "go around" with Miller to various functions where a few coins would be made and some blues would be sung. Henry quickly took over the vocal duties since his partner's singing abilities was in direct contrast to his excellent guitar technique. Miller moved to New York and Big Boy Henry began a series of journeys to the city in order to continue their relationship. This led to meetings with other Piedmont bluesmen such as the whooping harmonica player Sonny Terry and his sidekick Brownie McGhee. In 1951, Henry got the opportunity to record with backup from this famous duo, the blues equivalent of getting Rembrandt and Cezanne to help decorate. In a typical development in American blues recording history, these tracks were canned rather than released, although a release was finally arranged decades later. A defeated Henry limped back to his coastal digs in New Bern, NC, and decided to give up playing blues.

In the '50s and '60s, he worked on fishing and oystering crews and also ran a grocery store. He also did a touch of preaching in local churches, perhaps following the advice of fellow bluesman Son House as expressed in the song "Preachin' Blues": "I'm gonna become a Baptist preacher/And then I won't have to work." In 1971, he moved back to his first family home in Beaufort, not realizing that this would lead to a group of younger local musicians recognizing him. All it took was a little bit of their subsequent encouragement and he was ready to return to playing. As he got older, the guitarist's abilities were naturally hampered because of arthritis, but he still picked inventive single-string blues lines, tinkering with rhythms and bar-line blues structures with as much freedom as Lightnin' Hopkins. Younger North Carolina blues players such as the harmonica virtuoso Chris Turner and guitarist Billy Hobbs enjoyed the challenge of following the older man, who never failed to set the powerful musical mood known as "deep blues feeling." His vocal style was considered as powerful as ever in his senior years as he created his own inventive versions of blues standards and wrote his own songs as well, often touching on current events. The powerful song "Mr. President," written as an angry response to social welfare cuts undertaken by Ronald Reagan in the '80s, won him a W.C. Handy Award from the Blues Foundation. In 1995, he received the North Carolina Arts Council Folk Heritage award.

Henry's involvement with music goes well beyond performing. He has been actively involved with older members of his community in attempts to maintain and record one of the important coastal traditions, the work songs sung by himself and other African-Americans who fished on menhaden boats. His activities included organizing a group of retired fisherman into a singing group, the Menhaden Chantey Men. *—Eugene Chadbourne*

● **Poor Man's Blues** / Mar. 5, 1996 / New Moon ✦✦✦✦✦

Big Brother & the Holding Company

f. 1965, San Francisco, CA, **db.** 1972

Group / Album Rock, Acid Rock, Psychedelic, Blues-Rock

Big Brother are primarily remembered as the group that gave Janis Joplin her start. There's no denying both that Joplin was by far the band's most striking asset, and that Big Brother would never have made a significant impression if they hadn't been fortunate enough to add her to their lineup shortly after forming. But Big Brother also occupies a significant place in the history of San Francisco psychedelic rock, as one of the bands that best captured the era's loosest, reckless, and indulgent qualities in its high-energy mutations of blues and folk-rock.

Big Brother was formed in 1965 in the Haight-Ashbury; by the time Joplin joined in mid-1966, the lineup was Sam Andrew and James Gurley on guitar, Peter Albin on bass, and David Getz on drums. Joplin, a recent arrival from Texas, entered the band at the instigation of Chet Helms, who (other than Bill Graham) was the most important San Francisco rock promoter. Big Brother, like the Grateful Dead and Quicksilver Messenger Service, were not great songwriters or singers. They didn't entirely welcome Joplin's presence at first, though, and Joplin did not dominate the group right away, sharing the lead vocals with other members.

It soon became evident to both band and audience that Joplin's fiery wail—mature and emotionally wrenching, even at that early stage—had to be spotlighted to make Big Brother a contender. But Big Brother wasn't superfluous to the effort, interpreting folk and blues with an inventive (if sometimes sloppy) eclecticism that often gave way to distorted guitar jamming, and matching Joplin's passion with a high-spirited, anything-goes ethos of their own.

Big Brother catapulted themselves into national attention with their performance at the Monterey Pop Festival in June 1967, particularly with Joplin's galvanizing interpretation of "Ball and Chain" (which was a highlight of the film of the event). High-powered management and record label bids rolled in immediately, but unfortunately the group had tied themselves up in a bad contract with the small Mainstream label, at a time where they were stranded on the road and needed cash. Their one Mainstream album (released in 1967) actually isn't bad at all, containing some of their stronger cuts, such as "Down on Me" and "Coo Coo." It didn't fully capture the band's strengths, and with the help of new high-powered manager Albert Grossman (also handler of Bob Dylan, the Band, and Peter, Paul & Mary), they extricated themselves from the Mainstream deal and signed with Columbia.

The one Big Brother album for Columbia that featured Joplin, *Cheap Thrills* (1968), wasn't completed without problems of its own. John Simon found the band so difficult to work with that he withdrew his production credit from the final LP, which was assembled from both studio sessions and live material (recorded for an aborted concert album). *Cheap Thrills* nonetheless went to number one when it was finally released, and though it too was an erratic affair, it contained some of the best moments of acid rock's glory days, including "Ball and Chain," "Summertime," "Combination of the Two," and "Piece of My Heart."

Cheap Thrills made Big Brother superstars, a designation that was short-lived. By the end of 1968, Joplin had decided to go solo, a move from which neither she nor Big Brother ever fully recovered. That's putting matters too simply: Joplin never found a backing band as sympathetic, but did record some excellent material in the remaining two years of her life. Big Brother, on the other hand, had the wind totally knocked out of their sails. Although they did re-form for a while in the early '70s with different singers (indeed, they continued to perform in watered-down variations into the '90s), nothing would ever be the same. *—Richie Unterberger*

Big Brother & the Holding Company / 1967 / Columbia ✦✦✦

Big Brother's debut album was not recorded under optimum circumstances. The sessions were too rushed, and the sound thinner than the band would have liked, especially given how much more powerful some of the material (such as "Down on Me") would sound in later concerts. Still, it's not the useless throwaway some critics have portrayed it as, and it decently conveys the band's loose, sometimes reckless blend of blues, folk-rock, and psychedelia. Janis Joplin sings with soulful intensity on "Down on Me" and "Call on Me"; Peter Albin's "Light Is Faster Than Sound" is good wacked-out early Haight-Ashbury psychedelic rock; and the rock cover of Moondog's "All Is Loneliness" is spookily imaginative. The 1999 CD reissue adds the worthy single "Coo Coo"/"The Last Time" (good Eastern-influenced guitar work on the former, a good hurt hard rock vocal from Joplin on the latter) and previously unreleased alternate takes of "Call on Me" and "Bye, Bye Baby." *—Richie Unterberger*

★ **Cheap Thrills** / Aug. 1968 / Columbia ✦✦✦✦✦

Cheap Thrills, the major-label debut of Janis Joplin, was one of the most eagerly anticipated, and one of the most successful, albums of 1968. Joplin and Big Brother had earned extensive press notice ever since they played the Monterey Pop Festival in June 1967, but their only recorded work was a poorly produced, self-titled Mainstream album, and they spent a year getting out of their contract with Mainstream in order to sign with Columbia while demand built. When *Cheap Thrills* appeared in August 1968, it shot into the charts, reaching number one and going gold within a couple of months, and "Piece of My Heart" became a Top 40 hit. Joplin, with her ear- (and vocal cord-) shredding voice, was the obvious standout. Nobody had ever heard singing as emotional, as desperate, as determined, as loud as Joplin's, and *Cheap Thrills* was her greatest moment. Big Brother's backup, typical of the guitar-dominated sound of San Francisco psychedelia, made up in enthusiasm what it lacked in precision. But everybody knew who the real star was, and Joplin played her last gig with Big Brother while the album was still on top of the charts. Neither she nor the band would ever equal it. Heard today, *Cheap Thrills* is a musical time capsule and remains a showcase for one of rock's most distinctive singers. The 1999 CD reissue adds the previously unreleased outtakes "Roadblock" and "Flower in the Sun" from the *Cheap Thrills* sessions, along with previously unreleased live March 1968 versions of "Catch Me Daddy" and "Magic of Love." *—William Ruhlmann*

Be a Brother / Oct. 1970 / Acadia ✦✦

Big Brother comes back as a sextet with the additions of guitarist David Schallock and singer/songwriter/producer Nick Gravenites. Of course, it's a different band without Janis Joplin, but that psychedelic sound is still in place, albeit with a Chicago blues edge courtesy of Gravenites. There's also an amusing reply to Merle Haggard's "Okie From Muskogee," "I'll Change Your Flat Tire, Merle." *—William Ruhlmann*

How Hard It Is / 1971 / Acadia ✦✦✦

The second and final of the post-Janis Joplin Big Brother albums for Columbia looks and sounds like the closing of a chapter. A picture of Big Brother inside the gatefold has the band glowing with heavenly light; the cover photo is more telling, with faceless men standing in the shadows. To realize how good a Big Brother & the Holding Company album this is, all one has to do is play it next to *Do What You Love*, the group's release from 1998. On that disc, Lisa Battle is a commendable vocalist, but *Do What You Love* feels strained in both songwriting and performance. *How Hard It Is*, on the other hand, from 27 years earlier, is right on target. The title track feels like vintage Big Brother. Kathi McDonald is credited as a guest artist on "Black Widow Spider"; she co-sings the lead, but it sure sounds like her on "How Hard It Is" and "House on Fire" as well and, eerily, it is much like when Janis sang in unison with the band. The major difference is that they can play their instruments better here, four years after the Monterey Pop Festival brought them to the attention of Clive Davis. Nick Gravenites and McDonald were the perfect choices to step in, Gravenites having written two tracks on Joplin's *Kozmic Blues* LP and also having performed with her on *Joplin in Concert*. McDonald has sweetness, but can reach in and find some gravel to complement Gravenites. Everything on this album is listenable, and the three instrumentals—"Last Band on Side One," "Maui," and "Promise Her Anything, But Give Her Arpeggio"—are statements that the band members are real musicians, journeymen with vision. The loss of more recorded music by this group from this point in time is a tragedy. The Gravenites' version of "Buried Alive in the Blues," the song he wrote for Joplin's *Pearl* album, is chilling; her death happened hours before the scheduled session when she was to sing on the Full Tilt Boogie Band's recording. Sony would be wise to include Big Brother's rendition on future copies of *Pearl*: It completes the circle. Big Brother would do well to continue in the more bluesy direction this album pointed to rather than perform Janis Joplin's hits in small clubs. The instrumental "Maui" and the song "Shine On" are as good as anything Moby Grape and Quicksilver Messenger Service could conjure up. Sam Andrew, James Gurley, Peter Albin, and David Getz cover music from all three phases of Joplin's career. The first song on side two, "Nu Boogaloo Jam," is pure Kozmic Blues Band, which Sam Andrew was part of at the beginning; the aforementioned "Buried Alive in the Blues," as stated, was recorded by the Full Tilt Boogie Band for *Pearl*. This album covers the gamut of styles that Joplin would bring to the world between 1968 and 1970. It's a catastrophe that this band was waiting for its lead singer to come home for the inevitable reunion; Joplin's death affected many lives and the body of work this band could have amassed. Where the Doors went off into a brief and spirited rock-jazz journey for two albums—Jim Morrison's band experimenting with ideas they couldn't attempt as a superstar pop group—Big Brother had lost its Morrison and was lost without its focal point. *How Hard It Is* and the album that preceded it, *Be a Brother*, are very musical and very good albums, but they just don't have the electric majesty of *Cheap Thrills*, an album that took their wildness and used it as an incredible bed for Joplin's truly cosmic vocal work and emotion. If allowed to record as the Grateful Dead and the Jefferson Airplane had despite those bands' personnel changes, there would now be a deep catalog of San Francisco rock from this essential psychedelic/experimental ensemble. Although Janis Joplin had a guest vocal on *Be a Brother*, her only participation here consists of photos inside the album jacket, a family tree of sorts. This is a striking record by an important band, but Joplin's contributions were so overwhelming that the integrity in these grooves never got the chance to reach a wider audience when it was first released. *—Joe Viglione*

Cheaper Thrills / Apr. 1984 / Acadia ♦♦
Recorded on July 28, 1966, before the band had cut any studio material, this performance was one of Janis Joplin's first gigs with Big Brother. The sound is decent, with several famous staples of their repertoire already in place—"Down on Me," "Coo-Coo," "Ball and Chain." Yet in comparison with their best studio and live recordings from 1967 and 1968, this is a bit limp. Big Brother were never noted for their polish, but made up for that with reckless bravado; however, that's largely missing at this juncture in their development, which finds them sounding somewhat tentative in their adaptation of R&B and garage-band ethos to heavy guitar arrangements. Big Brother were never noted for their songwriting ability either, and this set is pretty reliant on R&B staples like "Let the Good Times Roll" and "I Know You Rider"; the unabashedly psychedelic workout "Gutra's Garden" hasn't aged well at all. Joplin's vocals are fairly strong, but these early versions of "Down on Me" and, especially, "Ball and Chain" don't hold a candle to her performances of the same tunes at the 1967 Monterey Pop Festival. Other members of the band take the lead vocal on a few numbers, emphatically proving—as they always did when given a chance—that Joplin was necessary to put them on the map. This recording is an interesting glimpse into the group's formative days, though, and features eight songs not on their late-'60s albums. *—Richie Unterberger*

Live at Winterland '68 / 1998 / Columbia/Legacy ♦♦♦
Recorded live in San Francisco on April 12 and April 13, this set is a snapshot of the band—with fine sound—reaching the peak of their form. All of the well-known songs from their first two albums are present: "Ball and Chain," "Down on Me," "Piece of My Heart," "Summertime," "Combination of the Two," and "Light Is Faster Than Sound," for starters. There isn't a single song that isn't available in some form on either the *Janis* box or the *Farewell Song* compilation, though. Also, these versions aren't remarkably different or better than the familiar ones, although they tend to run longer, particularly on the seven-minute "Light Is Faster Than Sound" and the ten-minute "Ball and Chain." A treat for fans to hear, with a 24-page booklet that has lots of comments from the band. *—Richie Unterberger*

Do What You Love / Feb. 11, 1999 / Cheap Thrills ♦♦
Big Brother & the Holding Company's two post-Joplin releases, *Be a Brother* and *How Hard It Is*, are two of the best recordings by bands picking up the pieces after the losses of their respective comets/focal points. Where the Billion Dollar Babies and Spiders From Mars had to move on without Alice Cooper and David Bowie, respectively, their musical genre didn't lend itself to reconstituted hard rock groups—look at the sad fate of post-Jeff Lynne ELO or BTO without Randy Bachman. Like Grace Slick, Janis Joplin joined the group in which she rose to fame after it had formed, but as the Jefferson Airplane could reinvent itself for the future as a Starship with or without Slick, Big Brother was never given the chance to continue producing its experimental psychedelic pop. The layoff results in the band's weakest effort ever. Lisa Battle has a strong voice, and is so different from Janis that the band should have developed a new sound for her. It didn't, doing a disservice to this able singer. Battle does a great job on the funky tribute to Joplin that is "Women Is Losers"; it succeeds because it is not a note-for-note copy but a new look at an original Joplin composition. On the other hand, what is the point in trying to recreate "I Need a Man to Love?" You can't possibly top the electric John Simon production from *Cheap Thrills*, or *Live at Winterland '68*'s power. The production values here are spotty as well. "Take Off" is not nearly as good an opener as "Combination of the Two," and a new interpretation of that would have been more substantial. The high points of this CD are "Save Your Love" (where Battle's voice carefully patterns itself around this slinky blues-pop, despite the low-budget surroundings); the title track; and two very short pieces, "The OK Chorale" and "Back Door Jamb." Both those musical exercises should have been expanded to give Battle the chance to identify herself as Big Brother's current singer. The band, after all, began pre-Janis by creating unorthodox sounds. Here they have abandoned what made them so special, and appear to be imitating their past. Had they continued to release records as Big Brother in the '70s and '80s, there is the possibility they could have developed a following like that which the Grateful Dead nurtured. Kathy McDonald and Nick Gravenites, who both appeared on *Be a Brother* and *How Hard It Is*, are the kind of talents who bring out the best these musicians have to offer. Seven or eight albums with that lineup would have created a formidable body of work. Put Lisa Battle into that mix as well, and the possibilities are endless. *Do What You Love* has no catalog number and no direction—even more disappointing when you realize these are super-talented journeymen wasting their time. *—Joe Viglione*

Live in San Francisco, 1966 / Apr. 30, 2002 / Varese Sarabande ♦♦♦
Recorded on July 28, 1966, before the band had cut any studio material, this performance was one of Janis Joplin's first gigs with Big Brother. The sound is decent, with several famous staples of their repertoire already in place: "Down on Me," "Coo-Coo," and "Ball and Chain." Yet, in comparison with their best studio and live recordings from 1967 and 1968, this is a bit limp. Big Brother was never noted for their polish, but made up for that with reckless bravado; however, that's largely missing at this juncture in their development, which finds them sounding somewhat tentative in their adaptation of R&B and garage band ethos to heavy guitar arrangements. Big Brother was never noted for their songwriting ability either, and this set is pretty reliant on R&B staples like "Let the Good Times Roll" and "I Know You Rider"; the unabashedly psychedelic workout "Gutra's Garden" hasn't aged well at all. Joplin's vocals are fairly strong, but these early versions of "Down on Me" and, especially, "Ball and Chain" don't hold a candle to her performances of the same tunes at the 1967 Monterey Pop Festival. Other members of the band take the lead vocal on a few numbers, emphatically proving—as they always did when given a chance—that Joplin was necessary to put them on the map. This show is an interesting glimpse into the group's formative days, though, and features eight songs not on their late-'60s albums. This set of material was first released in 1984 as *Cheaper Thrills*, and since then it's been around on various labels under various titles. The 2002 Varese Sarabande edition differs from previous iterations only in that it adds a live version of "Hall of the Mountain King," recorded at television station KQED in San Francisco on April 25, 1967 (a pretty cool cut, though it's been long available as part of the *Ball and Chain* video, which includes the entire half-hour set). *—Richie Unterberger*

The Big DooWopper (Cornell H. Williams)

b. Nov. 13, 1953, Grenada, MS
Piano / Modern Electric Blues, Soul-Blues
Cornell Williams, aka The Big DooWopper, was born on November 13, 1953, in Grenada, MS. Born partially blind, he completely lost his sight at the age of 17 due to cataracts. When he was six years old he started taking piano lessons before moving to Chicago with his parents. Chicago exposed him to the thriving blues scene and earned him his nickname DooWopper, singing with his mother, father, and some friends in a street corner doo wop group. His mother was a backup singer who toured with B.B. King, who was a big influence musically and personally to DooWopper. While growing up, DooWopper was enrolled in Illinois School for the Visually Handicapped, and he continued to build his singing and keyboard ability. After high school graduation in the early '70s, he played live music sporadically throughout the decade. By the early '80s, he was shopping around crude demos with little response, while continually performing on the sidewalks and train stations of Chicago, occasionally gaining the odd paying club gig. When his demo finally reached the right hands in 1999, he was given studio time to cut his impressive version of Prince's "Purple Rain," overdubbing his gospelized keyboards and five part doo wop harmony! This break finally allowed the release of his first full length recording *All in the Joy* on the Chicago-based Delmark label in 2000. *—Al Campbell*

• **All in the Joy** / May 30, 2000 / Delmark ♦♦♦♦
Since its inception, Delmark Records has consistently released blues and jazz recordings that are filled with passion and fury, and they usually prove to be timeless. This tradition continues with the first release from the blind street musician from Chicago, Cornell H. Williams, aka the Big DooWopper. *All in the Joy* is not only extraordinary in its honesty but also in the high-quality production that went into it. This is not a "field recording" taken live from an "eccentric street performance" but an impressive first release from this vocalist and keyboardist backed by a full rhythm section of guitar, drums, and bass, and even strings on one cut. Featuring nine originals and four covers, including a gospel-inspired rendition of Prince's "Purple Rain" on which DooWopper overdubs his own complex harmony arrangement. Also included is a five-minute interview with DooWopper in which his shared insights bring to mind the similar cosmic revelations of Sun Ra. *—Al Campbell*

Big Maybelle (Mabel Louise Smith)

b. May 1, 1924, Jackson, TN, **d.** Jan. 23, 1972, Cleveland, OH
Vocals / New York Blues, East Coast Blues, Jump Blues, R&B
Her mountainous stature matching the sheer soulful power of her massive vocal talent, Big Maybelle was one of the premier R&B chanteuses of the '50s. Her deep, gravelly voice was as singular as her recorded output for OKeh and Savoy, which ranged from down-in-the-alley blues to pop-slanted ballads. In 1967, she even covered ? & the Mysterians' "96 Tears" (it was her final chart appearance). Alleged drug addiction leveled the mighty belter at the premature age of 47, but Maybelle packed a lot of living into her shortened lifespan.

Born Mabel Louise Smith, the singer strolled off with top honors at a Memphis amateur contest at the precocious age of eight. Gospel music was an important element in Maybelle's intense vocal style, but the church wasn't big enough to hold her talent. In 1936, she hooked up with Memphis bandleader Dave Clark; a few years later, Maybelle toured with the International Sweethearts of Rhythm. She debuted on wax with pianist Christine Chatman's combo on Decca in 1944, before signing with Cincinnati's King Records in 1947 for three singles of her own backed by trumpeter Oran "Hot Lips" Page's band.

Producer Fred Mendelsohn discovered Smith in the Queen City, re-christened her Big Maybelle, and signed her to Columbia's OKeh R&B subsidiary in 1952. Her first OKeh platter, the unusual "Gabbin' Blues" (written by tunesmith Rose Marie McCoy and arranger Leroy Kirkland) swiftly hit, climbing to the upper reaches of the R&B charts. "Way Back Home" and "My Country Man" made it a 1953 hat trick for Maybelle and OKeh. In 1955, she cut a rendition of "Whole Lot of Shakin' Goin' On" a full two years before Louisiana piano pumper Jerry Lee Lewis got his hands and feet on it. Mendelsohn soon brought her over to Herman Lubinsky's Savoy diskery, where her tender rendition of the pop chestnut "Candy" proved another solid R&B hit in 1956. Maybelle rocked harder than ever at Savoy, her "Ring Dang Dilly," "That's a Pretty Good Love," and "Tell Me Who" benefiting from blistering backing by New York's top sessioneers. Her last Savoy date in 1959 reflected the changing trends in R&B; Howard Biggs' stately arrangements encompassed four violins. Director Bert Stern immortalized her vivid blues-belting image in his documentary *Jazz on a Summer's Day*, filmed in color at the 1958 Newport Jazz Festival.

Maybelle persevered throughout the '60s, recording for Brunswick, Scepter (her "Yesterday's Kisses" found her coping admirably with the uptown soul sound), Chess, Rojac (source of "96 Tears"), and other labels. But the good years were long gone when she slipped into a diabetic coma and passed away in a Cleveland hospital in 1972. *—Bill Dahl*

Candy / May 14, 1956-Nov. 26, 1957 / Savoy Jazz ♦♦♦♦♦
The belter moved over to Newark, NJ-based Savoy midway through the decade and continued to prosper: "Candy," "Ramblin' Blues," and the intense "Blues Early, Early" rate with her finest cuts. "Ring Dang Dilly" and "Tell Me Who" rock with the seemingly effortless swing peculiar to New York's R&B scene at the time, thanks to the presence of saxists Warren Lucky and Jerome Richardson and guitarists Mickey Baker and Kenny Burrell, among others. *—Bill Dahl*

Blues, Candy and Big Maybelle / 1956-1957 / Savoy Jazz ♦♦♦
Two vinyl albums of Maybelle's Savoy recordings on one compact disc makes for a nice 28-track retrospective of her prime work. First up is the album originally issued as *Blues, Candy and Big Maybelle*, a chunk of session work from 1956-1957, with a three-song date from 1959 to round things up. Her takes on "Rockhouse," "Ramblin' Blues," and the title track are the big tickets here. The second anthology, titled simply *Big Maybelle*, features her recordings from 1956-1959, with the balance of it leaning toward her later output for the label. A 1957 session with Kenny Burrell on guitar yields interesting stabs at "White Christmas" and "Silent Night," while a 1959 session finds her big voice framed with a string section on a great read of "Until the Real Thing Comes Along." A very underrated singer, Big Maybelle is a total delight and deserves a much wider hearing. *—Cub Koda*

Big Maybelle Sings / 1958 / Savoy ♦♦♦♦♦

The Last of Big Maybelle / 1973 / Muse ♦♦
This may be late in her career recordings, chock full of wah-wah pedals and other dated devices, but make no mistake about it, this is Big Maybelle still singing her heart out on each and every track. Moving effortlessly between rockers, R&B ballads, pop lightweights, Hank Williams country, and the blues, Big Maybelle's voice inhabits this material with a warmth and husk that most female singers today can only hint at. Not the place to start, but a good place to end up. *—Cub Koda*

Big Maybelle / 1988 / Savoy ♦♦♦♦♦
The collections of Big Maybelle's sides for the OKeh (*The Complete OKeh Sessions 1952-55*) and Savoy labels are the most complete and best representative of her career. They are definitely the place to begin a collection of her stunning and powerful body of work. Where the fantastic OKeh disc covers her material from the first half of the '50s, this one compiles her Savoy sides from 1956-1959. While not entirely different from one another, these sessions featured some outstanding sidemen who were not unfamiliar with the Savoy label. Tenormen Frank Rehak and Jerome Richardson, multi-instrumentalist Sahib Shihab, guitarist Kenny Burrell, pianist Hank Jones, and baritone player George Barrow all appeared on bebop dates for the label during this period. The result finds Maybelle's powerful vocals matched by musicianship of a similar order. Every song in this collection is a standard. All are just dripping with feeling and none of them disappoint. While this release's subtitle (*Roots of R'n'R, Blues and Early Soul, Vol. 13*) might lead one to expect an album of barn-burning scorchers, it actually has a fair number of ballads and even two Christmas tunes. Make no mistake, however; the material on this volume of the very successful Savoy *Roots* series is tough and hot. Even "White Christmas" is sexy. This is a highly recommended album for fans of early R&B and soul. *—Brandon Burke*

● **The Complete OKeh Sessions 1952–55** / 1994 / Epic/Legacy ♦♦♦♦♦
Maybelle's entire OKeh output—26 tracks—including her three R&B chart items, "Whole Lotta Shakin' Goin' On," and the risqué slow blues "I'm Getting 'Long Alright." "Gabbin' Blues," her 1952 OKeh debut smash, is a humorous dialogue between Maybelle and gossiping rival Rose Marie McCoy, the tune's co-writer. Maybelle was no mere copyist; her sandpapery vocals stood in sharp contrast to the many interchangeable thrushes then populating the R&B world. Great support from New York session wizards such as tenor saxist Sam "The Man" Taylor and guitarist Mickey Baker throughout. *—Bill Dahl*

Very Best of Big Maybelle: That's All / Jan. 5, 1998 / Collectables ♦♦♦
Collectables' *The Very Best of Big Maybelle: That's All* features 12 songs that she recorded for Sceptor Records in the '60s. This wasn't the most particularly distinguished period of Maybelle's career, and this collection doesn't put it in perspective, leaving out some of the best records she made for the label, including the minor hit "Yesterday's Kisses." That said, this does have its moments—enough to make it worthwhile to dedictated soul collectors willing to sort the wheat from the chaff. It just isn't a definitive collection, not even of her Scepter recordings. *—Stephen Thomas Erlewine*

Half Heaven, Half Heartache: The Brunswick Recordings / May 22, 2001 / West Side ♦♦♦♦

Big Miller (Clarence Horatius Miller)

b. Dec. 18, 1922, Sioux City, IA, **d.** Jun. 9, 1992
Vocals / Urban Blues, Jump Blues

It will have to be a big statue, because he wasn't called Big Miller for nothing—although he did look pint-size when standing alongside his fellow blues shouter Big Joe Turner during a reunion tour in the '70s. The plan is to unveil a life-sized statue of Miller by the year 2003 in one of Edmonton, Alberta's city parks. It is a long way from the Kansas City jazz scene that welcomed Miller as a singer beginning in his teenage years. But Edmonton was this artist's adopted home from the '70s up until his death in the early '90s. It is said that he lived in the backseat of the car he'd driven into Edmonton in for several months before becoming established enough to afford his own place, which seems a bit harsh for a fellow who had already paid dues performing with the likes of Duke Ellington and Count Basie. Hopefully this didn't take place in the winter, when that northern city's temperatures can dip to 30 below zero and stay that way for weeks. If so, they might have wound up calling him "Frozen Miller" and a statue would not have been needed. He was born Clarence Horatius Miller, and perhaps his most defining career moment came in the '50s with his participation in the Jon Hendricks revue entitled *Evolution of the Blues*. Miller's size, vocal power, and intense stage presence combined to drive home the legend of the blues shouters, men who could sing over an entire big band without using a microphone. The success of this show led to a recording contract with Columbia, for whom the artist cut several albums, a pair of which were reissued on a CD package in 2000. The earlier stages of his recording career included a stint with Savoy, which was one of the first jazz labels to record him. A group led by Clifford Curry known as the Clovers, which would later change its name to the Five Pennies, provided backup on some of the Savoy sessions. The singer also doubled on trombone, sometimes playing in a big band section and later using this instrument for special solo features, although his range was limited. Miller also had a sideline movie career, including a cameo in the star-packed comedy *It's a Mad, Mad, Mad, Mad World*. Cinematic activities also continued in the frozen North, where one of Miller's strangest projects was a role in the surrealistic film *Big Meat Eater*, directed by Chris Windsor. From the script synopsis: "Bob's life is thrown into turmoil when he decides to hire Abdullah (The Big Meat Eater)—a massive human blockhouse of a man—as an apprentice in his butcher shop. Unbeknownst to Bob, Abdullah has just murdered the Mayor of Burquitlam in a fit of pique—and the corpse is hidden in Bob's freezer... Abdullah sings the blues while he charcoal grills gangsters and turns dalmatian dogs into spotted spam..." OK.

Miller's Edmonton activities more normally included collaborations with the city's top local artists such as the bandleader Tommy Banks, with whom Miller performed a highly acclaimed concert at the Montreux Pop Festival. Although the singer's repertoire was of course focused around standards and blues numbers from the Kansas City days, he kept an ear to the ground in the '70s and wound up doing a fine cover version of "Big Yellow Taxi" by Alberta native Joni Mitchell. In 1987, the National Film Board of Canada chose Miller as the subject of a documentary short, no doubt presenting a better image of the man than in his role as Abdullah. Miller was also closely involved with the formation and growth of his adopted city's jazz society. The Edmonton Jazz Society first began organizing events a few years after the singer had moved to the city, a period in which the last major appearances by jazz artists was a tour by Louis Armstrong in the '40s. At first the new jazz organization was only throwing small club gigs in rented venues. With Miller's frequent participation as a guest artist and enthusiastic spokesman for live jazz, the jazz society grew into the sponsors of a citywide festival presenting dozens of concerts each summer. Another music program in this area that expanded greatly during Miller's lifetime was the Banff Centre for Fine Arts located a few hundred miles to the southwest of Edmonton in the Rocky Mountains. The facility added a jazz program in the early '70s, eventually allowing an opportunity for the big singer to expand into the role of a teacher. His fellow faculty members included virtuoso jazz pianist Oscar Peterson. Miller tends to be remembered fondly by his fellow musicians, some of whom recorded tributes. These include a piano solo recorded by Kansas City old-timer Jay McShann entitled "Big Miller's Blues," as well as a track entitled "Never Be the Same: Big Miller Blues" by the Canadian Shuffle Demons. *—Eugene Chadbourne*

Did You Ever Hear the Blues? / Nov. 26, 1959 / United Artists ♦♦♦

Revelations and the Blues / Aug. 1961 / Columbia ♦♦
The first sound that is heard on this record is the solo bass of Red Mitchell. Now that is big. As for Big Miller, the name is based on his physical size, as anybody might guess. And in that regard, it is quite accurate. In regards to talent, it is not to say that he should have been called "tiny." He is a charismatic, warm, and bubbly personality and an energetic performer who in the right hands can become an almost gala part of a concert event. The most obvious example would be the use Jon Hendricks made of Miller in his *Evolution of the Blues* stage show, which is no doubt what led to this Columbia release. Whether he can carry an entire album on his own is not a point that would be made in his favor on the basis of listening to this album. The label itself can't be faulted, as it seems to have given him plenty of room to express himself, plus a top-flight band to back him up. These players are mostly known for jazz, which isn't the worst direction one could go in when it comes to Miller, especially if it means some tidbits from tenor master Ben Webster. The whole subject of appropriate backup for this artist is complicated, because he is kind of a "between" blues guy. He sings a blues number as if it was jazz, smoothly displaying sophisticated vocal prowess and swaying rhythmically like another Big Joe Turner. His limitations start to show when he attempts an actual jazzier number, but he always makes a valiant effort to gloss over this by getting funky, working in blues inflections, and reminding the listener where he is really coming from. Probably a lot more enjoyable was the material that was not mostly his own songs. Here is the album's insurmountable weakness, because no matter how well the band plays or how well the vocalist tries, the material is just plain boring. It might summarize a good deal of the blues repertoire to mention the subjects of wanting a woman, missing a woman, or complaining about the woman that one has. These topic titles would also serve as a good summary of what the boring drunken guy at the end of the bar has to say in the course of an evening. The effect of listening to too many of Miller's songs is more like the latter. There is no spark of invention that would make any of these songs memorable, let alone moving or even enjoyable. The most interesting track is "The Monterey Story," yet another song about a festival held in that coastal city, kind of a jazz sister to the rock track cut by the Animals. *—Eugene Chadbourne*

Big Miller Sings, Twists, Shouts and Preaches / Aug. 1962 / Columbia ♦♦♦

Last of the Blues Shouters / 1992 / Southland ♦♦♦

● **Revelations and the Blues/Sing, Twists, Shouts & Preaches** / Feb. 19, 2002 / Collectables ♦♦♦♦
Big Miller was not only similar in size to Jimmy Rushing and Big Joe Turner, but sounded like them also. These Collectables reissues from the vaults of Columbia Records show a definite kinship to Rushing and Turner in his vocal style and blend of blues and swing. Big Miller also showed his prowess on a number of instruments, including drums, harmonica, trombone, and bass. While not up to the standards of his influences, these jump blues renditions of "Am I Blue," "I Gotta Right to Sing the Blues," "Runnin Wild," and "I'm Goin Fishin" will be enjoyed by both the collector and casual listener alike. *—Al Campbell*

Live at Athabasca University / Stony Plain ♦♦♦♦♦
Big sings some great old blues numbers such as Willie Littlefield's "Kansas City," and T-Bone Walker's "Stormy Monday Blues," his own boogie-woogie-style song "Big's Boogie," and Gertrude "Ma" Rainey's "See See Rider." A real nice big-band blues release, 51 minutes in length. *—Chip Renner*

The Big Three Trio

f. 1946, Chicago, IL, **db.** 1952, Chicago, IL

Group / Acoustic Chicago Blues, Chicago Blues

For the legendary Willie Dixon, the Big Three Trio was an important launching pad for a fantastic career. Pianist Leonard "Baby Doo" Caston and guitarist Bernardo Dennis (replaced after a year by Ollie Crawford) joined upright bassist Dixon to form the popular trio in 1946. Caston was just out of the service (where he'd played on U.S.O. tours during World War II); Dixon had been a conscientious objector. Dixon had previously worked with Caston in the Five Breezes and with Dennis in the Four Jumps of Jive.

Sharing vocal (they specialized in three-part harmonies) and writing duties democratically, the trio signed with Jim Bullet's Bullet imprint in 1946 for a solitary session before making a giant jump in stature to Columbia Records in 1947. Their polished, pop-oriented presentation resulted in one national hit, "You Sure Look Good to Me," in 1948, and a slew of other releases that stretched into 1952 (toward the end, they were shuttled over to the less prestigious OKeh subsidiary).

Incidentally, Dixon dusted off two songs the trio waxed for OKeh, "Violent Love" and "My Love Will Never Die," and handed them to Otis Rush a few years later when the burly bassist was working as a producer at Eli Toscano's Cobra Records. Rush's tortured "My Love Will Never Die" was a postwar masterpiece; the corny "Violent Love" may be the worst thing the southpaw guitarist ever committed to tape.

Caston split at the end of 1952, effectively breaking up the trio. But Dixon's destiny was at Chess Records, where he was already making inroads as a session bassist and songwriter. Pretty soon, he'd be recognized as one of the most prolific and invaluable figures on the Windy City scene. —*Bill Dahl*

I Feel Like Steppin' Out / 1946-Jun. 16, 1952 / Dr. Horse ✦✦✦

I Feel Like Steppin' Out complements the Columbia release *The Big Three Trio*, gathering most of the material that was left off that disc and only duplicating "Signifying Monkey." The Big Three played the blues very loosely, adding bits of jazz and pop to their sound—unlike most blues groups of their time, they all sang in unison. Though this compilation isn't quite as strong as the Columbia disc, it's worthwhile for dedicated fans. —*Thom Owens*

● **The Willie Dixon: The Big Three Trio** / 1990 / Columbia/Legacy ✦✦✦✦✦

The only domestic compilation celebrating this trio's accomplishments is a 21-track affair containing Dixon's "dozens" diatribe "Signifying Monkey," the catchy "Tell That Woman" (later covered by Peter, Paul & Mary as "Big Boat Up the River"), and several crackling instrumentals ("Big 3 Boogie," "Hard Notch Boogie Beat") that show what fine musicianship this triumvirate purveyed. Points off, though, for not including their only legit hit, "You Sure Look Good to Me." —*Bill Dahl*

Big Time Sarah (Sarah Streeter)

b. Jan. 31, 1953, Coldwater, MS

Vocals / Modern Electric Chicago Blues, Electric Chicago Blues

A rousing vocalist and dynamic entertainer, "Big Time" Sarah Streeter's among the more enterprising contemporary blues performers. She moved to Chicago from Coldwater, MS, as a child, and sang in South Side gospel choirs before debuting as a blues vocalist on stage at Morgan's Lounge at 14. She later worked with Buddy Guy and Junior Wells, Johnny Bernard and Sunnyland Slim. A single on Slim's Airways label helped launch her solo career. Streeter's been a featured performer at many North Side clubs since the late '70s, and appeared at several blues festivals. She formed the Big Time Express in 1989, and Delmark issued *Lay It on 'Em Girls*, in 1993. *Blues in the Year One-D-One* followed in 1996. —*Ron Wynn*

Blues with the Girls / 1982 / EPM Musique ✦✦✦

● **Lay It on 'Em Girls** / 1993 / Delmark ✦✦✦✦✦

"Big Time" Sarah Streeter has the power, struttin' tone and booming voice ideal for stomping, sassy numbers. This CD spotlights the band Streeter formed in 1989, the BTS Express. Streeter's songs explore the familiar battle between the sexes, with Streeter sometimes angry, sometimes confused and often confrontational in the "classic" blues style. She covers three numbers by Willie Dixon, as well as material from Bill Withers, George Gershwin and Leonard Feather, and displays both a vibrant style and more versatility than might be expected. —*Ron Wynn*

Blues in the Year One-D-One / Jun. 4, 1996 / Delmark ✦✦✦

A Million of You / 2001 / Delmark ✦✦✦✦

Chicago barnstormer Big Time Sarah has been a sure-fire North Side draw and festival show-stealer for at least as long as she has had her tight Big Time Express band behind her, probably a lot longer. On *A Million of You*, Sarah's powerful, commanding vocal style and the arrangements of bandleader/guitarist Rico McFarland translate into a disc as exciting as one of her live performances, or as close as one can get without being there. Highlights include the traditional "Train I Ride," and standards like "Red Dress" and "The Sky Is Crying," all with fine solos from her band, and near perfect singing from Sarah: modern electric blues at its sweaty, steamy best. —*John Duffy*

Big Twist & the Mellow Fellows

f. 1970, Carbondale, IL, **db.** 1990

Group / Modern Electric Chicago Blues, Soul-Blues, Contemporary Blues

Born in Terre Haute, IN, in 1937, Larry "Big Twist" Nolan heartily epitomized the image "300 pounds of heavenly joy." Based in Chicago, the huge singer and his trusty R&B band, the Mellow Fellows, were one of the hottest draws on the Midwestern college circuit during the '80s with a slickly polished sound modeled on the soul-slanted approach of Bobby Bland, Little Milton, and Tyrone Davis.

Twist started out singing and playing drums in rough-and-tumble country bars in downstate Illinois during the late '50s and early '60s (chicken wire-enclosed stages were a necessity at this raucous scene). Young saxist Terry Ogolini jammed often with the big

man at a joint called Junior's in a Prairie State burg called Colp. Ogolini and guitarist Pete Special spearheaded the nucleus of the first edition of the Mellow Fellows in the college town of Carbondale during the early '70s, with Twist doubling on drums. After taking southern Illinois by storm, the unit relocated en masse to Chicago in 1978.

Their eponymous 1980 debut album for Flying Fish accurately captured the group's slick sound, while the 1982 follow-up, *One Track Mind*, attempted to be somewhat more contemporary without losing the band's blues/R&B base. A move to Alligator in 1983 elicited an album co-produced by Gene "Daddy G" Barge, whose sax solos previously enlivened R&B classics by Chuck Willis, Gary (U.S.) Bonds, Little Milton, and countless more. The group's final album with Twist up front was the *Live from Chicago! Bigger Than Life!!*

Numerous personnel changes over the years failed to scuttle the band, and neither did the death of Twist in 1990 from diabetes and kidney failure. Martin Allbritton, an old singing buddy of Twist's from downstate who had previously gigged around Chicago as frontman for Larry & the Ladykillers, had already been deputizing for the ailing Twist, so it fell to Allbritton to assume the role full-time. Barge shared the singing duties on selected gigs and on the band's 1990 album *Street Party*.

Special left the organization not long after that, taking the name Mellow Fellows with him when he hit the door. That's when the remaining members adopted the handle of the Chicago Rhythm & Blues Kings. With Ogolini and longtime trumpeter Don Tenuto comprising a red-hot horn section, they're still a popular, dance-friendly fixture around the Chicago scene. —*Bill Dahl*

Big Twist & The Mellow Fellows / 1980 / Flying Fish ✦✦✦✦

The upbeat rhythms and charismatic persona of Big Twist always afforded this group an accessibility greater than that of most hardcore Chicago blues acts. This debut set followed the same formula, mixing time-tested favorites such as Tyrone Davis' "Turn Back the Hands of Time" with the inevitable crowd-pleaser "The Sweet Sound of Rhythm & Blues." —*Bill Dahl*

One Track Mind / 1982 / Flying Fish ✦✦✦

This is a slicker affair than their first album, highlighted by a revival of Albert King's "Cold Women" and the rousing "Living It Up." —*Bill Dahl*

● **Playing for Keeps** / 1983 / Alligator ✦✦✦✦

Twist's adopted theme song, the Willie Dixon-penned "300 Pounds of Heavenly Joy," hails from this goodtime collection, co-produced by tenor sax legend Gene "Daddy G" Barge. —*Bill Dahl*

Live from Chicago! Bigger Than Life!! / 1987 / Alligator ✦✦✦✦

Recorded live in 1987 at Biddy Mulligan's, a longtime Chicago blues institution that fell on hard times not too long thereafter, this disc showcases the Mellow Fellows' strengths in front of a rabidly devoted crowd. "300 Pounds of Heavenly Joy," "Turning Point," and the playful "Too Much Barbeque" rate among the highlights, as Twist's onstage charisma makes the show go. —*Bill Dahl*

Big Wheeler (Golden Wheeler)

b. Dec. 15, 1929, Beaconton, GA, **d.** Jul. 20, 1998, Chicago, IL

Vocals, Harmonica / Modern Electric Chicago Blues, Electric Chicago Blues, Electric Harmonica Blues

He was part of the Chicago circuit for four decades, but Golden "Big" Wheeler waited until 1993 to release his debut album on Delmark. As befits such a veteran, Wheeler's sturdy harmonica style was a throwback to the '50s and his idol, Little Walter.

Wheeler was first turned onto the harp while driving a cab by one of his regular fares, Buster Brown. Brown's shot at "Fannie Mae"-fired stardom was still a few decades down the line, but Wheeler's was even further off. He left Georgia in 1941, eventually settling in Chicago, where he met Little Walter. The two became friends, Walter acting as something of a mentor. Wheeler began fronting his own combo in 1956 but never really sustained a musical career (he worked as a mechanic to pay the bills).

In 1993, Delmark unleashed the harpist's debut disc, *Big Wheeler's Bone Orchard*, which found him backed by a young local outfit, the Ice Cream Men. *Jump In* followed in 1997, the year before Big Wheeler's death. Wheeler's brother, guitarist James Wheeler, is also a longtime denizen of the Windy City scene; joining Mississippi Heat after spending an extended stint behind Otis Rush. —*Bill Dahl*

Chicago Blues Session, Vol. 14 / 1989 / Wolf ✦✦✦✦✦

● **Bone Orchard** / 1993 / Delmark ✦✦✦✦✦

The veteran Chicago harpist's long-overdue debut album is quite credible, but you can't help but think he's got a far more satisfying set within him yet. Dreary backing by the overly cautious Ice Cream Men is the prime reason the set only occasionally soars—with a less derivative combo, Wheeler could come up with something special before he's through. —*Bill Dahl*

Jump In / 1997 / Delmark ✦✦✦

On his second LP, Wheeler is joined by his brother James on guitar, pianist Allen Batts, bassist Bob Stroger and drummer Baldhead Pete for a traditionally minded set featuring a number of the singer/harmonica player's original compositions. —*Jason Ankeny*

Elvin Bishop

b. Oct. 21, 1942, Glendale, CA

Vocals, Guitar / Modern Electric Chicago Blues, Southern Rock, Blues-Rock, Modern Electric Blues, Album Rock

Elvin Bishop was born in Glendale, CA, on October 21, 1942. He grew up on a farm in Iowa with no electricity and no running water. His family moved to Oklahoma when he was ten. Raised in an all-white community, he had no exposure to blacks or their music except though the radio where he would listen to sounds from faraway Mexico and blues stations in Shreveport, LA; in particular, the piercing sound of Jimmy Reed's harmonica got his attention. Bishop says it was like a crossword puzzle that he had to figure out.

What is this music? Who makes it? Where and how do black people live? What is this music all about? He put the pieces together.

But it was not until he won a National Merit Scholarship to the University of Chicago in 1959 that he found the real answers to his questions. Suddenly, there he was right in the heart of the Chicago blues scene. Live. It was a dream come true. "The first thing I did when I got there was to make friends with the black guys working in the cafeteria. They took me to all the clubs. I sunk myself totally in the blues life as quick as I could," says Bishop.

After two years of college, he just dropped out and was into music full time. Howlin' Wolf guitarist Little Smokey Smothers befriended Bishop and taught him the basics of blues guitar. In the early '60s he met and teamed up with Paul Butterfield to become the core of the Butterfield Blues Band. Although only playing guitar for a few years, he practiced day and night on the blues music that he loved. He and Butterfield played together in just about every place possible—campuses, houses, parks, and clubs. They began to become well-known in 1963 when they took a job at Big John's on Chicago's North Side and the Paul Butterfield Blues Band was born. Bishop helped to create and played on the first several Butterfield albums. (The "Pigboy Crabshaw" is Bishop's countrified persona referred to in the title of the third Butterfield album.)

When he left the Butterfield band after the *In My Own Dream* album (1968), Bishop relocated to and settled in the San Francisco area where he appeared often at the Filmore with artists like Eric Clapton, B. B. King, and Jimi Hendrix. He recorded for Epic (four albums) and later signed with Capricorn in 1974. His recording of "Travelin' Shoes" (from the album *Let It Flow*) hit the charts, but he scored big with the lovely tune "Fooled Around and Fell in Love" (from his album *Struttin' My Stuff*) in 1976. He was (and is) famous for having fun on stage (putting on a great show) and letting the good times roll. Over the next few years the Elvin Bishop Group dissolved, and Bishop was not heard from much until he signed with Alligator in 1988.

Bishop then released *Big Fun* (1988) and *Don't Let the Bossman Get You Down* (1991), which were well received. He also participated in Alligator's 1992 20th anniversary cross-country tour and released *Ace in the Hole* (1995). Over the years, Bishop has graced the albums of many great bluesmen including Clifton Chenier and John Lee Hooker. He toured with B.B. King in 1995. Bishop is known for his sense of humor, his unique style of slide guitar, and fusion of blues, gospel, R&B, and country flavors. He lives with his wife and family in the San Francisco area, is a prodigious gardener, and continues to play dates in the U.S. and abroad, issuing *The Skin I'm In* in 1998 and *That's My Partner!* in 2000. —*Michael Erlewine*

Rock My Soul / Sep. 1972 / Epic ◆◆◆
The talented musician in the likable Elvin Bishop is always fighting for the upper hand with Pigboy Crabshaw, his spaced-out hayseed persona. Co-producer Delaney Bramlett helps steer the sound toward Memphis and Muscle Shoals R&B and keeps the focus on the music, not the headliner. Not a bad idea, considering his enthusiasm barely overcomes his singing limitations. This is a solid and surprisingly varied outing that, until "Fooled Around and Fell in Love," gave him his signature tune in the powerhouse title track. —*Mark Allan*

Let It Flow / May 1974 / One Way ◆◆◆◆◆
For his fourth album, Elvin Bishop organized a new backup group and switched to Capricorn Records. Capricorn was known as the standard bearer of the Southern rock movement—the Allman Brothers Band, The Marshall Tucker Band, etc.—and Bishop was able to emphasize the country blues aspects of his persona and his music in the move from Marin County, California, to Macon, Georgia. The guest artists included the Allmans' Dickey Betts, Marshall Tucker's Toy Caldwell, Charlie Daniels, and Sly Stone, and Bishop turned in one of his best sets of songs, including "Travelin' Shoes" (with its Allmans-like twin lead guitar work), which became his first charting single, just as the album was his first to make the Top 100 LPs. —*William Ruhlmann*

The Best of Elvin Bishop: Crabshaw Rising / 1975 / Epic ◆◆◆
In his first manifestation as a bandleader (1969-1972), Elvin Bishop lived in Marin County, CA, and performed under the auspices of promoter Bill Graham. Not surprisingly, the three albums he cut in that period, two for Graham's Fillmore label and the third for its parent, Epic, fit into the soul-blues-rock style of post-psychedelic San Francisco, even to the point of featuring an extended instrumental, "Hogbottom," on which Bishop takes Carlos Santana's place fronting the Santana percussion section. This ten-track compilation selects from the albums *The Elvin Bishop Group*, *Feel It!*, and *Rock My Soul*, effectively summarizing this phase in Bishop's career. Long out of print, it was superseded in 1994 by the 18-track CD *The Best of Elvin Bishop: Tulsa Shuffle*, which contained nine of its selections. Then, oddly enough, it was reissued in 1996! —*William Ruhlmann*

Juke Joint Jump / Apr. 1975 / One Way ◆◆◆
Elvin Bishop's Macon Takeover continued on his second Capricorn album, which had a slightly less country feel than *Let It Flow* but continued to be dominated by twin guitar playing (courtesy of Bishop and Johnny "V" Vernazza) and honky tonk piano playing (from Phil Aaberg). The song quality wasn't quite as consistent this time, but "Sure Feels Good" became Bishop's second singles chart entry. —*William Ruhlmann*

Struttin' My Stuff / Dec. 1975 / Capricorn ◆◆◆
Features the hit single "Fooled Around and Fell in Love," sung by Mickey Thomas. —*William Ruhlmann*

Hometown Boy Makes Good! / Oct. 1976 / Capricorn ◆◆
Elvin Bishop broke the bank with the success of "Fooled Around and Fell in Love" in the spring of 1976, so when he returned with this album in the fall, he turned up on the cover holding bags of money. The question, of course, was whether the hit would turn out to be a breakthrough or a fluke. The nearest thing to a follow-up to "Fooled Around" was "Spend Some Time," a ballad on which Mickey Thomas again sang soulfully. But it barely scraped into the charts, and the rest was typical Bishop good-time boogie (along with

trendy tastes of disco and reggae), the relatively thin songwriting reflecting a rushed recording schedule—this was Bishop's fourth new album in just over two and a half years. —*William Ruhlmann*

Raisin' Hell / Jul. 1977 / Capricorn ◆◆
Headliner Elvin Bishop's folksy, good-ole-boy charm is as much a part of this upbeat live set as the music, thanks to generous doses of good-natured banter with fans. This live best-of collection, culled from five performances over almost a year, is highly entertaining. Mickey Thomas takes the singing pressure off the boss, but the thin sound undercuts the swagger of the horn section. —*Mark Allan*

Hog Heaven / 1978 / Capricorn ◆◆◆
Capricorn Records, having switched distribution from Warner Brothers to Phondisc, was on its way out by the time it released this, its sixth Elvin Bishop album, which may help explain why, only two years after he was in the Top Ten with "Fooled Around and Fell in Love," he didn't even reach the charts with this album. It's also true that lead singer Mickey Thomas had decamped to join Jefferson Starship, leaving Bishop to reestablish his country blues boy persona. But Maria Muldaur had signed on (she sings lead on "True Love"), and with two years between studio albums, Bishop had found the time to write some good vehicles for his guitar work and Southern rock backup band. —*William Ruhlmann*

Big Fun / 1988 / Alligator ◆◆◆
In the ten years between the release of *Hog Heaven* and this comeback record, Elvin Bishop was represented in record stores by a *Best Of* on Capricorn and an album released only in Germany (*Is You Is Or Is You Ain't My Baby?* on Line Records). Then he signed with Bruce Iglauer's independent blues label Alligator and made this record, which, naturally, emphasizes his more blues-oriented guitar playing, although without sacrificing his country boy identity. Dr. John tickles some of the ivories, and harmonica player Norton Buffalo (of Commander Cody and His Lost Planet Airmen) also guests. —*William Ruhlmann*

Don't Let the Bossman Get You Down! / Jul. 1, 1991 / Alligator ◆◆◆◆
On *Don't Let the Bossman Get You Down*, Bishop projects a good-natured, humorous persona in the extended spoken-word sections of his songs, but still finds time to play a lot of tasty blues guitar. —*William Ruhlmann*

● **Sure Feels Good: The Best of Elvin Bishop** / 1992 / Polydor ◆◆◆◆◆
A fine collection of the blues-rock guitarist's best moments, which covers more material than the earlier compilation, *Best of Elvin Bishop/Crabshaw Rising*. —*Stephen Thomas Erlewine*

The Best of Elvin Bishop: Tulsa Shuffle / 1994 / Epic/Legacy ◆◆◆◆◆
This 18-track compilation selects from the early albums *The Elvin Bishop Group*, *Feel It!*, and *Rock My Soul*. The only thing wrong with it is that it would be easy to make the mistake of thinking that it covers all of his solo career rather than only the first four years, especially because there have now been four different albums released with the title *The Best of Elvin Bishop*. —*William Ruhlmann*

Ace in the Hole / Jul. 25, 1995 / Alligator ◆◆◆
On Elvin Bishop's third Alligator release, *Ace in the Hole*, his guitar playing remains as fiery as ever, but the overall quality of the songwriting has slipped somewhat, making it his least-consistent effort on the label. —*Thom Owens*

The Skin I'm In / Aug. 11, 1998 / Alligator ◆◆◆
Elvin keeps the cornpone good-ole-boy schtick down to an acceptable level on this, perhaps his most serious solo album to date. Although Bishop's good-time approach is still evident on tunes like "I'm Gone," "Right Now Is the Hour," the acoustic "Radio Boogie" (with a guest shot from Charlie Musselwhite) and "Country Blues," the playing and lyrics get much deeper and more serious with "Shady Lane," "The Skin They're In," "Middle Aged Man" and "Long Shadows." Perhaps the most cohesive album he's made to date, revealing an artist coming to grips with his muse, his age and his art, all at once. —*Cub Koda*

That's My Partner! / Jul. 25, 2000 / Alligator ◆◆◆
Every now and again you get one of those discs that picks up a few threads that have long lain dormant for various reasons, and you are more than overjoyed that someone took the time to help make the reconnections that seem to make life richer. Little Smokey took the young—and new to Chicago—Elvin Bishop under his wing in the early '60s and taught the kid everything, from playing blues guitar to how to walk the walk. It is well-documented how Bishop's career took off when he hooked up with Paul Butterfield and Mike Bloomfield in the Butterfield Blues Band (setting the stage for all the other twin lead guitar bands such as the Allman Brothers Band that followed). Smokey remained in Chicago and virtually gave up trying to make a living playing music in favor of a job to support the family. With the kids grown, by the '80s he started playing again. In January 2000, the two hooked up again for three nights that would be recorded by Alligator. Maybe this was to say thank you for the early help; more likely—judging by the playing—it was a return of the early love between the two. It was more than worth the wait to hear the interplay of Elvin and Smokey, backed by a more-than-capable band (a nod to S.E. Willis on keyboards) that provides strong, solid support while letting the two stand to the forefront and play off each other. Bishop has always been known as a fun-loving musician; however, he takes his chops seriously, his playing is crisp, and—as he shows here—he is at his best when playing off an equal (listen to his signature "Travelin' Shoes"!). The joy of playing that deep-felt Chicago blues with an old friend and colleague and the chance for teacher and pupil to stand up and show off their licks and progress shine through here. The banter between the two helps to push the music along to greater heights. Just listen to this gutter-crawling version of "Little Red Rooster." You know the Wolf would be proud. —*Bob Gottlieb*

King Biscuit Flower Hour Presents in Concert / Jan. 23, 2001 / King Biscuit ◆◆◆◆

20th Century Masters—The Millennium Collection: The Best of Elvin Bishop / Jan. 15, 2002 / Mercury ♦♦♦♦
After starting out with the Paul Butterfield Blues Band in the mid-'60s, Elvin Bishop recorded solo for the short-lived Fillmore label (later controlled by Sony) in the late '60s and early '70s, and he made several albums for the independent Alligator Records in the '80s and '90s. But he gained his greatest commercial recognition on Capricorn Records (the early catalog of which is now controlled by Universal) in the mid- to late '70s, and it is this portion of his career that is represented on this midline-priced best-of, which has been assigned to Universal's Mercury imprint. Bishop modified his basic blues-rock style for each of his affiliations: With Butterfield he played Chicago blues, on Fillmore he took on something of the San Francisco acid rock style, and on Capricorn he absorbed some of the Southern rock of labelmates like the Allman Brothers Band. Four of his five Hot 100 chart entries are found here (the missing one is the least successful, "Spend Some Time"), among them "Fooled Around and Fell in Love," the Top Five hit that has always been an anomaly for him, not only because Mickey Thomas is featured on lead vocals, but also because, even though Bishop wrote it, it sounds much more pop-oriented than one expects from him. More consistent with his style is the minor chart entry "Travelin' Shoes," which boasts a lot of Allmans-like slide guitar work, especially in the seven-minute-plus workout heard here (the single was a three-minute edit), and some politically incorrect lyrics about beating a woman with a baseball bat that probably didn't sound as objectionable back in 1974. But then, the country-blues never boasted the most enlightened lyrics, and Bishop also cheerfully admits to "Stealin' Watermelons." At a reasonable price, this collection effectively summarizes his six Capricorn albums. *—William Ruhlmann*

Billy Bizor

b. 1917, Centerville, TX, **d.** Apr. 4, 1969, Houston, TX
Vocals, Harmonica / Blues Revival, Acoustic Texas Blues
The blues revival of the '60s allowed the spotlight to finally fall on performers like Billy Bizor, an otherwise obscure harpist best known in conjunction with his recordings in support of his cousin, the renowned Lightnin' Hopkins. Born in Centerville, Texas in 1917, Bizor (also, variously, Bizer and Biser) dwelled in almost total obscurity prior to the '60s, developing a spare, haunted sound largely unaffected by the passage of time, making him a prime candidate for rediscovery by purists. Among his first recordings were a series of unheralded early-'60s dates backing Hopkins; between 1968 and 1969, Bizor cut his only solo session in Houston with producer Roy Ames, revealing him to be an intense, emotionally charged singer. Eventually issued as *Blowing My Blues Away*, the end result went unreleased for several years; tragically, Bizor himself never saw the recordings come to light—he died April 4, 1969. *—Jason Ankeny*

- **Blowing My Blues Away** / 1968-1969 / Collectables ♦♦♦♦
Blowing My Blues Away was recorded in 1968 and 1969, at the height of the blues revival. Billy Bizor wasn't very well known before the blues revival and that's part of the reason why his style didn't change very much from the '30s and '40s—his blues is still deeply indebted to the stripped-down sounds of Lightnin' Hopkins, who happens to be Bizor's cousin. All of the material on *Blowing My Blues Away* was previously unreleased, so it's designed for hardcore blues collectors, but for those listeners that are interested, this is an entertaining curiosity. *—Thom Owens*

Black Ace (Babe Turner)

b. Dec. 21, 1907, Hughes Springs, TX, **d.** Nov. 7, 1972, Fort Worth, TX
Guitar (Steel), Guitar, Vocals / Slide Guitar Blues, Prewar Country Blues, Country Blues, Acoustic Texas Blues, Texas Blues
A solid guitarist and vocalist, Babe Turner, aka Black Ace, built his own guitar as a child, then taught himself to play. He was also in a gospel choir in Hughes Springs, TX. Turner honed his skills playing at community functions during the '20s, then worked with Smokey Hogg at dances in Greenville, TX in the '30s. Hogg and Buddy Woods were frequent partners for Turner, who made several solo tours in the '30s and '40s. He appeared in the 1941 film *The Blood of Jesus* and 1962 movie *The Blues*. Turner had a show on Fort Worth radio station KFJZ from 1936-1941. He recorded for Decca in 1937. After a stint in the army during the early '40s, Turner's jobs were mostly non-musical, except for his film stints. He did make a 1960 LP for Arhoolie. Turner took his nickname from the 1936 recording "Black Ace." *—Ron Wynn*

Black Ace / 1960 / Arhoolie ♦♦♦

- **I'm the Boss Card in Your Hand, 1937–1960** / 1992 / Arhoolie ♦♦♦♦♦
I Am the Boss Card in Your Hand stands as the definitive Black Ace collection to date—not only does Arhoolie's CD reissue include the entirety of their original 1960 release, but it also appends previously unissued material from the same session and even tosses in a half dozen tracks from his 1937 Decca label debut. Thanks largely to its steadfast refusal to fit easily into any kind of regional genre pigeonhole, Ace's music possesses a beautifully timeless quality; though he's a poignant vocalist, the real treat here is his slide guitar mastery, as instrumentals like "Ace's Guitar Blues" and "Bad Times Stomp" reveal a unique hybrid sound successfully bridging the gap between the Delta and Hawaiian styles. *—Jason Ankeny*

Black Boy Shine (Harold Holiday)

d. 1948
Vocals, Piano / Prewar Blues, Country Blues, Texas Blues, Piano Blues
Almost nothing is known of Black Boy Shine, aka Harold Holiday, except that he was based in a section of Houston, TX (which may have been his home) called West Dallas. In 1936 and 1937 he recorded for Vocalion in San Antonio and Dallas, and left behind 18 sides. A smooth vocalist and pianist, his music had a surprising elegance despite the barrelhouse environment reflected in songs like "Dog House Blues" and "Back Home Blues." By 1948, he was said to have been near death from tuberculosis. *—Bruce Eder*

- **Black Boy Shine & Black Ivory King** / Nov. 4, 1994 / Document ♦♦♦♦♦
Eighteen songs by Black Boy Shine (rounded out by four more from Black Ivory King), in surprisingly good sound. Holiday had no time, in the course of two years of recordings, to deteriorate in either his sound or health on record here. Most of his songs have to do with aspects of life for his black audience, and are highlighted by inventive piano playing and a surprisingly sweet, almost sultry melodious vocal style. "Hobo Blues" and "Ice Pick and Pistol Woman Blues" depict some of the more brutal and vivid sides of the life that Holiday or his audience lived. *—Bruce Eder*

Black Ivory King (Dave Alexander)

Vocals, Piano / Piano Blues
Black Ivory King, aka Dave Alexander, rather sadly, didn't spend a big part of his career recording—only four songs survived him on record. He cut these for American Decca in Dallas early in 1937, and may have been based in Dallas-Fort Worth during this period. He was evidently a traveller of the rails, and gave an account of this part of his life in his finest song, "The Flying Crow," named for the rail line he took out of Shreveport through Port Arthur, TX and Ashdown, AR, and through Oklahoma into Kansas City, MO. Almost nothing more is known of the man, except that he was familiar with the work of Blind Lemon Jefferson, cutting a version of "Match Box Blues" that incorporates some of the latter's verses. *—Bruce Eder*

- **Black Boy Shine & Black Ivory King** / Nov. 4, 1994 / Document ♦♦♦♦♦
Black Ivory King's four songs are appended to 18 tracks by Black Boy Shine, and they're worth it, as a unique perspective (especially "The Flying Crow") on black life in the Southern and border states during the mid-'30s. As a vocalist he was bold and confident, and the results are compelling, if a little frustrating for the limited number of songs left behind. *—Bruce Eder*

Otis Blackwell

b. 1931, Brooklyn, NY, **d.** May 6, 2002, Nashville, TN
Songwriter, Piano / East Coast Blues, Urban Blues, Rock & Roll, R&B
Few '50s rock & roll tunesmiths were as prolifically talented as Otis Blackwell. His immortal compositions include Little Willie John's "Fever," Elvis Presley's "Don't Be Cruel" and "All Shook Up," Jerry Lee Lewis' "Great Balls of Fire" and "Breathless," and Jimmy Jones' "Handy Man" (just for starters).

Though he often collaborated with various partners on the thriving '50s New York R&B scene (Winfield Scott, Eddie Cooley, and Jack Hammer, to name three), Blackwell's songwriting style is as identifiable as that of Willie Dixon or Jerry Leiber and Mike Stoller. He helped formulate the musical vocabulary of rock & roll when the genre was barely breathing on its own.

Befitting a true innovator, Blackwell's early influences were a tad out of the ordinary. As a lad growing up in Brooklyn, he dug the Westerns that his favorite nearby cinema screened. At that point, Tex Ritter was Otis Blackwell's main man. Smooth blues singers Chuck Willis and Larry Darnell also made an impression. By 1952, Blackwell parlayed a victory at an Apollo Theater talent show into a recording deal with veteran producer Joe Davis for RCA, switching to Davis' own Jay-Dee logo the next year. He was fairly prolific at Jay-Dee, enjoying success with the throbbing "Daddy Rollin' Stone" (later covered by the Who). From 1955 on, though, Blackwell concentrated primarily on songwriting (Atlantic, Date, Cub, and MGM later issued scattered Blackwell singles).

"Fever," co-written by Cooley, was Blackwell's first winner (he used the pen name of John Davenport, since he was still contractually obligated to Jay-Dee). Blackwell never met Elvis in person, but his material traveled a direct pipeline to the rock icon; "Return to Sender," "One Broken Heart for Sale," and "Easy Question" also came from his pen. Dee Clark ("Just Keep It Up" and "Hey Little Girl"), Thurston Harris, Wade Flemons, Clyde McPhatter, Brook Benton, Ben E. King, the Drifters, Bobby Darin, Ral Donner, Gene Vincent, and plenty more of rock's primordial royalty benefited from Blackwell's compositional largesse before the British Invasion forever altered the Brill Building scene.

In 1976, Blackwell returned to recording with a Herb Abramson-produced set for Inner City comprised of his own renditions of the songs that made him famous. A 1991 stroke paralyzed the legendary song scribe, but his influence remained so enduring that it inspired *Brace Yourself!*, an all-star 1994 tribute album that included contributions by Dave Edmunds, Joe Ely, Deborah Harry, Chrissie Hynde, Kris Kristofferson, Graham Parker, and bluesman Joe Louis Walker. He died on May 6, 2002 in his Nashville home. *—Bill Dahl*

- **Otis Blackwell 1953-55** / 1953-Feb. 9, 1955 / Flyright ♦♦♦♦♦
The British Flyright logo has neatly compiled all 17 known titles that Blackwell cut for Jay-Dee, including "Daddy Rollin' Stone," and the equally ominous "On That Power Line," and four sides with a killer New York combo featuring tenor sax wailer Sam "The Man" Taylor and guitarist Mickey Baker. *—Bill Dahl*

All Shook Up / 1995 / Shanachie ♦♦♦♦
Blackwell's "comeback" album, originally cut in 1976 for Herb Abramson's Inner City label, is a successful effort at reclaiming the songs of his that made people like Elvis, Jerry Lee Lewis ("Great Balls of Fire," "Breathless"), Dee Clark ("Hey Little Girl"), et al. famous. For some listeners this album won't offer any real revelation, alas—the backings seem a little too smooth (one suspects that the original demos on "Fever," "All Shook Up," etc., had some rough edges that made them more interesting). They're all played well, however, and Blackwell's singing is impeccable. Anyone else might be accused of mimicking Elvis' style on "All Shook Up" and related numbers, except that history tells us different, and the performances are genuine and honest. Blackwell shows off a surprisingly wide range, most notably on the lullaby "Sleep Is Just Around the Corner" and the ballad "Clinging to a Dream," all of which makes this far more than just an Elvis Presley-related curio. Also included is Blackwell's credible rendition of "Searchin'," a song authored by his contemporary rivals Leiber and Stoller. *—Bruce Eder*

Scrapper Blackwell (Francis Hillman Blackwell)

b. Feb. 21, 1903, Syracuse, NC, d. Oct. 27, 1962, Indianapolis, IN

Vocals, Guitar / Prewar Blues, Piedmont Blues, Acoustic Chicago Blues, Acoustic Blues
Scrapper Blackwell was best known for his work with pianist Leroy Carr during the early and mid-'30s, but he also recorded many solo sides between 1928 and 1935. A distinctive stylist whose work was closer to jazz than blues, Blackwell was an exceptional player with a technique, built around single-note picking, that anticipated the electric blues of the '40s and '50s. He abandoned music for more than 20 years after Carr's death in 1935, but re-emerged at the end of the '50s and began his career anew, before his life was taken in an apparent robbery attempt.

Francis Hillman "Scrapper" Blackwell was of part-Cherokee Indian descent, one of 16 children born to Payton and Elizabeth Blackwell in Syracuse, NC. His father played the fiddle, and Blackwell himself was a self-taught guitarist, having started out by building his own instrument out of cigar boxes, wood, and wire. He also took up the piano, an instrument that he played professionally on occasion. By the time he was a teenager, Blackwell was working as a part-time musician, and traveled as far away as Chicago. By most accounts, as an adult Blackwell had a withdrawn personality, and could be difficult to work with, although he had an exceptionally good working relationship with Nashville-born pianist Leroy Carr, whom he met in Indianapolis in the mid-'20s. They made a natural team, for Carr's piano playing emphasized the bass, and liberated Blackwell to explore the treble strings of his instrument to the fullest.

Carr and Blackwell performed together throughout the midwest and parts of the south, including Louisville, St. Louis, Cincinnati, and Nashville, and were notably successful. With Blackwell's help, Carr became one of the top blues stars of the early '30s, and the two recorded well over 100 sides together between 1928 and 1935. They might've had major success going into the war years and beyond. It was not to be, however, as Carr's heavy drinking and a nephritis condition caused his death in Indianapolis on April 29, 1935.

Blackwell also recorded without Carr, both as a solo and also occasionally with other partners, including Georgia Tom Dorsey and an obscure singer named Black Bottom McPhail, and had occasionally worked with blues bands such as Robinson's Knights of Rest. His biggest success and greatest effectiveness, however, lay in his work with Carr, and after the latter's death he continued working long enough to cut a tribute to his late partner. His withdrawn personality didn't lend itself to an extended solo career, and he gave up the music business before the end of the '30s.

Blackwell's career might've ended there, preserved only in memory and a hundred or so sides recorded mostly with Carr. At the end of the '50s, however, with the folk/blues revival gradually coming into full swing, he was rediscovered living in Indianapolis, and prevailed upon to resume playing and recording. This he did, for the Prestige/Bluesville label, at least one album's worth of material that showed his singing and playing unmarred by age or other abuse. Blackwell appeared ready to resume his career without missing a beat, and almost certainly would've been a prime candidate for stardom before the burgeoning young White audience of college students and folk enthusiasts that embraced the likes of Furry Lewis, the Rev. Gary Davis, and Mississippi Fred McDowell. In 1962, however, soon after finishing his work on his first Prestige/Bluesville long-player (which, for reasons best understood by the label's current parent company, Fantasy Records, has never been re-released on CD), Blackwell was shot to death in a back alley in Indianapolis, the victim of a mugging. The crime was never solved.

Scrapper Blackwell was one of the most important guitar players of the '20s and early '30s, with a clean, dazzlingly articulate style that anticipated the kind of prominent solo work that would emerge in Chicago as electric blues in the '40s and '50s, in the persons of Robert Nighthawk and the young Muddy Waters. His "string-snapping" solos transcend musical genres and defy the limitations of his period. Although Blackwell's recordings were done entirely on acoustic guitar, the playing on virtually every extant track is—and this is no joke—electrifying in its clarity and intensity. Along with Tampa Red (who also had some respect in jazz circles, and who was a more derivative figure, especially as a singer), Blackwell was one of a handful of prewar blues guitarists whose work should be known by every kid who thinks it all started with Chuck Berry or even Muddy Waters.

Note: In addition to the albums credited to Scrapper Blackwell, his recordings can also be found on collections of Leroy Carr's work (virtually all of which features Blackwell) including such releases as Magpie Records' *The Piano Blues: Leroy Carr 1930-1935*; and one Carr/Blackwell duet, "Papa's on the Housetop," which is not on *The Virtuoso Guitar of Scrapper Blackwell*, but shows up on Yazoo's *Uptown Blues: Guitar Piano Duets* anthology. —*Bruce Eder*

★ **Virtuoso Guitar 1925-1934** / 1925-1934 / Yazoo ✦✦✦✦✦
It's for recordings like this that a lot of blues guitar fans started listening to the music in the first place. The definitive Blackwell collection to date, featuring not only his best extant solo sides, but also his work in association with Leroy Carr, Black Bottom McPhail, and Tommy Bradley. The 14 songs here all have something to offer in the playing—and generally the singing as well—that will give the listener pause, a run, an arpeggio, a solo passage that makes you say, "Whoa, what was that?" The sound is surprisingly good, and one only wishes there were more than 14 songs here, although it's hard to imagine anything that could follow the last track, Leroy Carr's "Barrelhouse Woman No. 2." —*Bruce Eder*

1928-1939, Vol. 1 / Jun. 16, 1928-Mar. 17, 1939 / Document ✦✦✦✦
Scrapper Blackwell will always be best remembered for playing the guitar on a lengthy set of duets released under the name of pianist/singer Leroy Carr. His own solo recordings from the same era did not make him famous but they are certainly worthy. This CD is the first of two Document discs that have all of Blackwell's dates as a leader from the era. Blackwell is showcased on unaccompanied solos, playing on one song apiece with singer Bertha "Chippie" Hill, Leroy Carr (though this time Blackwell is the vocalist and leader), Robinson's Knights of Rest (a trio also including clarinetist Arnett Nelson), and singer Teddy Moss, plus four songs backing the vocals of Black Bottom McPhail.

Highlights include "Penal Farm Blues," "Mr. Scrapper's Blues," the two-part "Trouble Blues," "Be-Da-Da-Bum," "Hard Time Blues," and "Mix That Thing." Excellent music that shows just how underrated Scrapper Blackwell continues to be. —*Scott Yanow*

Scrapper Blackwell, Vol. 2 (1934-1958) / 1934-1958 / Document ✦✦✦✦
The second volume of Scrapper Blackwell sides features material he cut solo in 1934, accompanying himself on the piano, and as a solo guitarist from 1935 ("D Blues," "A Blues"), as well as songs cut as part of Pinewood Tom and His Blues Hounds, teamed as a guitarist with Josh White (on vocals and guitar) and pianist Leroy Carr; under the name Frankie Black accompanied by pianist Dot Rice, and some in association with Bumble Bee Slim. These are all first-rate sides, equal to the best of his work with Leroy Carr and among the finest guitar playing in any category of music that you're ever likely to hear. Among the songs, "My Old Pal Blues (Dedicated to the Memory of Leroy Carr)" is a beautiful and poignant piece of personal, topical blues songwriting dealing with Carr's death in April of 1935, with Dot Rice providing excellent, fluid piano accompaniment to Blackwell's voice and guitar. Rice and Blackwell are teamed together again, backing Bumble Bee Slim on "Hey Lawdy Mama," the song that Willie Dixon later transformed into the classic "Meet Me in the Bottom" for Howlin' Wolf. The real treat, however, is the first release on CD of the four songs that Blackwell recorded in 1958, at the outset of his comeback—these little-known tracks are dark, moody, and utterly dazzling. Most of the masters are in surprisingly good condition ("Mean Mistreater Mama" and "She's Alright with Me" from 1934, and "Hey Lawdy Mama" from 1935 are notable and unfortunate exceptions), and this is an indispensable release for any serious fan of blues guitar, or guitar-piano duets. Neither gets any better than this. —*Bruce Eder*

Scrapper Blackwell, Vol. 3 (1959-1960) / 1959-1960 / Document ✦✦✦✦✦
Austria's Document Records apparently had this 22-track, 75-minute CD out in 1994, but it only started coming into the U.S. in 1996, and doesn't even show up in some reference sources. Scrapper Blackwell's all-too-brief comeback at the end of the '50s is well represented by a dozen songs from a live concert at Indianapolis' 1444 Gallery from September 20, 1959, some teaming Blackwell with singer Brooks Berry, paired off with ten tracks from Blackwell's 1960 British-only album on Dave Dobell's 77 label. Blackwell's technique on the guitar had not suffered at all from his nearly 20-year layoff from performing—he finesses sounds from his acoustic instrument that are soft and glittering, utilizing melody notes and carefully varied rhythms, and six of the tracks here are guitar solos, all of which are fascinating on repeated listening. His piano playing is also represented on one track. Blackwell's voice lacks some of the resonance that it had on his '30s recordings, and, if anything, the sadness in his persona is even more pronounced this late in his career, but he imbues his work with an intense passion that makes it compelling to hear. The worth of these performances makes his death, during an apparent mugging in 1962, all the more tragic, for more than almost any blues figure—including Memphis Minnie and Big Bill Broonzy—who almost made it to the folk/blues revival, Blackwell shows here how he could have reached millions with his work had he lived only a couple of years longer. Oh, and the apology made by the producers for the sound quality of the 1959 concert tape (provided by Duncan Schmidt, who also appears on a track or two) is utterly unnecessary. —*Bruce Eder*

Blues Before Sunrise / Jan. 1962 / 77 ✦✦✦

Mr. Scrapper's Blues / Sep. 1962 / Prestige/Original Blues Classics ✦✦✦
Blackwell, it's not always remembered, was rediscovered in the late '50s, though he didn't have much chance to make a new career out of the blues revival before his death a few years later. He performs well, but not wonderfully, on this July 1961 session in Indianapolis, accompanied only by his guitar (although he uses piano on one song, "Little Girl Blues"). His guitar playing is in better shape than his vocals, and, in fact, his instrumental work is sparkling on tunes like "Blues Before Sunrise," where the pacing and alternation of chords and single-note runs is immaculate. The instrumental "'A' Blues" is also a standout in its tradeoffs between high and low notes. It's mostly blues of a slow and deliberate, if varied, pace, though "Little Boy Blues" picks up the mood into a charging, swinging rhythm. —*Richie Unterberger*

Bobby "Blue" Bland

b. Jan. 27, 1930, Rosemark, TN

Vocals, Leader / Retro-Soul, Electric Texas Blues, Soul-Blues, R&B, Soul, Texas Blues
Bobby Bland earned his enduring blues superstar status the hard way: without a guitar, harmonica, or any other instrument to fall back upon. All Bland had to offer was his magnificent voice, a tremendously powerful instrument in his early heyday, injected with charisma and melisma to spare. Just ask his legion of female fans, who deemed him a sex symbol late into his career.

For all his promise, Bland's musical career ignited slowly. He was a founding member of the Beale Streeters, the fabled Memphis aggregation that also included B.B. King and Johnny Ace. Singles for Chess in 1951 (produced by Sam Phillips) and Modern the next year bombed, but that didn't stop local DJ David Mattis from cutting Bland on a couple of 1952 singles for his fledgling Duke logo.

Bland's tormented crying style was still pretty rough around the edges before he entered the Army in late 1952. But his progress upon his 1955 return was remarkable; with saxist Bill Harvey's band (featuring guitarist Roy Gaines and trumpeter Joe Scott) providing sizzling support, Bland's assured vocal on the swaggering "It's My Life Baby" sounds like the work of a new man. By now, Duke was headed by hard-boiled Houston entrepreneur Don Robey, who provided top-flight bands for his artists. Scott soon became Bland's mentor, patiently teaching him the intricacies of phrasing when singing sophisticated fare (by 1962, Bland was credibly crooning "Blue Moon," a long way from Beale Street).

Most of Bland's savage Texas blues sides during the mid- to late '50s featured the slashing guitar of Clarence Hollimon, notably "I Smell Trouble," "I Don't Believe," "Don't Want No Woman," "You Got Me (Where You Want Me)," and the torrid "Loan a Helping Hand"

and "Teach Me (How to Love You)." But the insistent guitar riffs guiding Bland's first national hit, 1957's driving "Farther Up the Road," were contributed by Pat Hare, another vicious picker who would eventually die in prison after murdering his girlfriend and a cop. Later, Wayne Bennett took over on guitar, his elegant fretwork prominent on Bland's Duke waxings throughout much of the '60s.

The gospel underpinnings inherent to Bland's powerhouse delivery were never more apparent than on the 1958 outing "Little Boy Blue," a vocal *tour de force* that wrings every ounce of emotion out of the grinding ballad. Scott steered his charge into smoother material as the decade turned: the seminal mixtures of blues, R&B, and primordial soul on "I Pity the Fool," the Brook Benton-penned "I'll Take Care of You," and "Two Steps From the Blues" were tremendously influential to a legion of up-and-coming Southern soulsters.

Scott's blazing brass arrangements upped the excitement ante on Bland's frantic rockers "Turn on Your Love Light" in 1961 and "Yield Not to Temptation" the next year. But the vocalist was learning his lessons so well that he sounded just as conversant on soulful R&B rhumbas (1963's "Call on Me") and polished ballads ("That's the Way Love Is," "Share Your Love With Me") as with an after-hours blues revival of T-Bone Walker's "Stormy Monday Blues" that proved a most unlikely pop hit for him in 1962. With "Ain't Nothing You Can Do," "Ain't Doing Too Bad," and "Poverty," Bland rolled through the mid-'60s, his superstar status diminishing not a whit.

In 1973, Robey sold his labels to ABC Records, and Bland was part of the deal. Without Scott and his familiar surroundings to lean on, Bland's releases grew less consistent artistically, though *His California Album* in 1973 and *Dreamer* the next year boasted some nice moments (there was even an album's worth of country standards). The singer re-teamed with his old pal B.B. King for a couple of mid-'70s albums that broke no new ground but further heightened Bland's profile, while his solo work for MCA teetered closer and closer to MOR (Bland has often expressed his admiration for ultra-mellow pop singer Perry Como).

Since the mid-'80s, Bland has mainly recorded for Jackson, Ms' Malaco Records. His pipes undeniably reflect the ravages of time, and those phlegm-flecked "snorts" he habitually emits become annoying in large doses. But Bobby "Blue" Bland endures as a blues superstar of the loftiest order. —*Bill Dahl*

Blues Consolidated / May 1958 / Duke ✦✦✦✦✦
An album split between Bland and his Blues Consolidated touring partner Junior Parker, featuring great early-'50s sides by these two Houston-based performers. —*Cub Koda & Hank Davis*

Like Er Red Hot / 1960 / Duke ✦✦✦
This anthology presents a cross-section of early Duke/Peacock hits. —*Bill Dahl*

☆ **Two Steps from the Blues** / 1961 / Duke/Peacock ✦✦✦✦✦
Without a doubt, *Two Steps from the Blues* is the definitive Bobby Blue Bland album, and one of the great records in electric blues and soul-blues. In fact, it's one of the key albums in modern blues, marking a turning point when juke-joint blues was seamlessly blended with gospel and southern soul, creating a distinctly Southern sound where all of these styles blended so thoroughly it was impossible to tell where one began and one ended. Given his Memphis background, Bobby Bland was perfectly suited for this kind of amalgam as envisioned by producer/arranger Joe Scott, who crafted these wailing horn arrangements that sounded as impassioned as Bland's full-throated, anguished vocals. It helped, of course, that the songs were uniformly brilliant. Primarily from the pen of Deadric Malone, along with Duke head Don Robey and Scott (among others), these are the tunes that form the core of Bobby Blue Bland's legend and the foundation of soul-blues: "Two Steps from the Blues," "I Don't Want No Woman," "Cry, Cry, Cry," "I'm Not Ashamed," "Lead Me On," "Little Boy Blue"—songs so good they overshadow standards like "St. James Infirmary." These are songs that blur the division between Ray Charles soul and Chess blues, opening the doors for numerous soul and blues sounds, from Muscle Shoals and Stax through the modern-day soul-bluesman. Since this, like many blues albums from the late '50s/early '60s, was a collection of singles, it's possible to find the key tracks, even the entire album, on the numerous Bobby Blue Bland collections released over the years, but this remains an excellent, essential blues album on its own terms—one of the greatest ever released. —*Stephen Thomas Erlewine*

Call on Me / 1963 / MCA ✦✦✦✦✦
A near-perfect collection of early-'60s sides documents the man at his best. —*Hank Davis*

Ain't Nothing You Can Do / 1964-1965 / MCA ✦✦✦✦
Fine soulful mid-'60s sides, including the title track, "Loneliness Hurts," and a cathartic reading of the soul classic "Blind Man." —*Cub Koda & Hank Davis*

The Soul of the Man / 1966 / MCA ✦✦✦✦✦
Like his two other seminal '60s titles on the Duke label, *Here's the Man* and *Two Steps From the Blues*, Bobby Bland's *The Soul of the Man* features the powerful and gravelly voiced singer mixing it up with a bluesy, soul-tinged blend of swingers and slower, after-hours material. While the uptempo blues "Reach Right Out" finds Bland vocally playing it cool, ballad cuts like "I Can't Stop" show him seamlessly working his dynamic range of hushed tones and throaty cries. Bland's varied approach is reflected in the album's diverse material, which includes the Stax-inspired groover "Back in the Same Old Bag"; a driving, horns-aplenty instrumental "Soul Stretch"; and the breezy, Northern soul sounding gem "Let's Get Together." Adding to the album's appeal are fine covers of the Jimmy Witherspoon standard "Ain't Nobody's Business If I Do" and Peggy Lee's signature tune "Fever." Bland's longstanding musical director Joe Scott provides his standard mix of tight rhythmic backing and urbane horn and guitar charts, perfectly framing the singer's robust voice with a toasty and slightly rough-hewn backdrop. While *The Soul of the Man* is essential listening for Bland fans, it also serves as a fine introduction to the great blues singer's catalog. —*Stephen Cook*

Touch of the Blues / 1967 / Duke ✦✦✦✦✦
During his Duke tenure, Bobby "Blue" Bland's rich, creamy voice was at its stark, dramatic peak. Like his other label releases, even when he got overly sentimental or just plain corny material, or the songs were overarranged, Bland's smashing leads made everything work. —*Ron Wynn*

Touch of the Blues/Spotlighting the Man / 1967 / MCA ✦✦✦✦
Two of Bland's better albums for Duke coupled on one great-sounding CD. Both LPs were issued originally in 1969 but contained tracks from as far back as his 1967 Top Ten R&B hit "That Did It" and its immediate follow-up, "Touch of the Blues." Bland never turned his back on the style that brought him to prominence (he digs into Charles Brown's "Driftin' Blues" aggressively, Wayne Bennett providing luscious chording behind him), even if his stately reading of Joe Turner's "Chains of Love" is sweetened considerably by strings. On the other hand, the husky singer's unwise whack at Anthony Newley's Broadway showstopper "Who Can I Turn To" is about as far removed from blues tradition as is imaginable. —*Bill Dahl*

The Best of Bobby Bland, Vol. 2 / Mar. 1968 / Duke ✦✦✦

Spotlight the Man / 1969 / Duke ✦✦✦

Here's the Man! / 1969 / Duke ✦✦✦
Here's the Man! contains recordings Bland cut for the Duke label in the early '60s. It has the same intensity and variety of his late-'50s breakthrough album, *Two Steps From the Blues*, and mimics that album's program of big band-blues swingers, straight blues, and ballads. Bland displays his vocal power throughout *Here's the Man!* using his volcanic, guttural delivery to easily work through Joe Scott's galvanizing arrangements, especially on "Twistin' up the Road" and "Turn on Your Love Light." He shows stylistic flexibility as well, expertly handling both T-Bone Walker's after-hours classic "Stormy Monday Blues" and the honky tonk-style ballad "You're the One (That I Adore)." In the '70s, Bland would even record an entire album of country standards. Along with Little Milton, Bland took the swinging, soulful blues of Roy Brown and B.B. King and updated it to fit the more polished, yet no less driving soul sound that was emerging around 1960; *Here's the Man!* is a prime document of Bland's explorations. Since it is out of print, though, look for these fine tracks on Bland's many MCA compilations. —*Stephen Cook*

If Loving You Is Wrong / 1970 / Duke ✦✦✦

His California Album / 1973 / BGO ✦✦✦
And his first for ABC-Dunhill in 1973 after more than two decades with Duke (Don Robey's still represented, though, under his songwriting alias of Deadric Malone on four cuts, including the album's biggest hit, "This Time I'm Gone for Good"). Producer Steve Barri contemporized Bland by having him cover Leon Russell's "Help Me Make It Through the Day," Luther Ingram's "(If Loving You Is Wrong) I Don't Want to Be Right," and Gladys Knight & the Pips' "I've Got to Use My Imagination." —*Bill Dahl*

Blues Consolidated (Barefoot Rock & You Got Me) / 1973 / Duke ✦✦✦
Half Jr. Parker, half Bobby Bland, and all classic '50s R&B. —*Bill Dahl*

Woke Up Screaming / 1974 / Duke ✦✦✦✦✦
This is a 16-track import anthology of Bland's earliest Duke sides from 1952 to 1957, at which point the *Blues Consolidated* album takes over. —*Hank Davis*

Dreamer / 1974 / BGO ✦✦✦
Barri's slightly antiseptic production style and Michael Omartian's arrangements weren't the equivalent of Joe Scott's immaculate collaborations with Bland, but this 1974 album's "Ain't No Love in the Heart of the City" and a meaty "I Wouldn't Treat a Dog (The Way You Treated Me)" were both huge hits. —*Bill Dahl*

☆ **The Best of Bobby Bland** / 1974 / MCA ✦✦✦✦✦
There have been many Bobby Blue Bland collections over the years, and 1974's *The Best of Bobby Bland* has been eclipsed by several of them in terms of comprehensiveness and completeness. Still, in terms of a listening experience, this is one of the great blues greatest hits collections, providing 12 of Bland's greatest songs, including "I Smell Trouble," "I Pity the Fool," "Cry, Cry, Cry," "Turn on Your Love Light," "Farther Up the Road" and "Stormy Monday." Best of all, there's only three tunes that overlap with his seminal *Two Steps from the Blues*, which makes this an excellent supplement to that album, as well as a great concise introduction to this blues titan. —*Stephen Thomas Erlewine*

Introspective of the Early Years / 1974 / Duke ✦✦✦

Get on Down With Bobby Bland / 1975 / ABC ✦✦✦

Together Again . . . Live / 1976 / MCA ✦✦✦
This not-so-exciting second Bobby "Blue" Bland and B.B. King pairing was recorded in Los Angeles Coconut Grove. There were more show business theatrics and less solid, soulful blues vocalizing than on their acclaimed debut, but there were still enough good moments to make it acceptable. —*Ron Wynn*

Reflections in Blue / 1977 / MCA ✦✦✦

Come Fly with Me / 1978 / MCA ✦✦

I Feel Good, I Feel Fine / 1979 / MCA ✦✦✦

Sweet Vibrations / 1980 / MCA ✦✦✦
Slick and smooth. —*Bill Dahl*

Here We Go Again / 1982 / MCA ✦✦✦

Tell Mr. Bland / 1983 / MCA ✦✦
Laid back and slickly produced. —*Bill Dahl*

Members Only / 1985 / Malaco ✦✦✦
After some fairly soporific early-'80s releases for MCA, this album re-energized Bland's recording fortunes. The Larry Addison-penned title track caught on with blues-soul fans, making it to the middle reaches of the R&B charts as a single. —*Bill Dahl*

After All / 1986 / Malaco ✦✦

First Class Blues / 1987 / Malaco ✦✦✦✦

Blues You Can Use / 1987 / Malaco ✦✦✦

Blues You Can Use could have accurately been titled *Blues and Soul You Can Use* because it offers a generous dose of R&B along with straight-ahead electric blues. But then, that title wouldn't have been as catchy. More important than the title, of course, is the music itself—and Bobby "Blue" Bland is in decent form on this album, which came out when the singer was 56 or 57. To be sure, *Blues You Can Use* isn't in a class with Bland's classic Duke output of the '50s and '60s—and his voice is undeniably thinner than it was in his younger days. But Bland demonstrates that he could still be expressive and charismatic on 12-bar ditties like "I've Got a Problem" and "For the Last Time" as well as laid-back soul numbers such as "Restless Feelin's," "There's No Easy Way to Say Goodbye" and the tear-jerker "Let's Part as Friends." Produced by Malaco founders Tommy Couch and Wolf Stephenson, *Blues You Can Use* isn't essential. But it's enjoyable, and it's a good example of the fact that Malaco often did well by Bland in the '80s and '90s. *—Alex Henderson*

Midnight Run / 1989 / Malaco ✦✦✦

When Bobby "Blue" Bland was recording for Malaco in the '80s and '90s, many blues experts asserted that he was past his prime—and they were right. Bland had done his best work for Duke in the '50s and '60s, and his voice wasn't what it once was. But the blues/soul singer was still capable of delivering a worthwhile album, and he still had a loyal fan base. In fact, the singer was a consistent seller for Malaco, which could generally be counted on to give him good or excellent material to work with. Recorded when Bland was in his late fifties, *Midnight Run* isn't remarkable but is generally decent. The production of Tommy Couch and Wolf Stephenson is rock solid, and Bland is soulful and satisfying on the amusing "Take Off Your Shoes," the reggae-influenced title song and arrangements of Bill Withers' "Ain't No Sunshine" and the Mel & Tim hit "Starting All Over Again." Although casual listeners would be better off with a collection of Bland's Duke material, *Midnight Run* is a CD that his hardcore fans will enjoy. *—Alex Henderson*

Portrait of the Blues / 1991 / Malaco ✦✦✦

The 3B Blues Boy—The Blues Years: 1952–59 / 1991 / Ace ✦✦✦

25-track compilation of bluesy material that Bland recorded for Duke between 1952 and 1959. Bland had previously released a few sides for Chess and Modern in the early '50s, but these sides represent the era in which he began to find his voice. It still catches him at a relatively early stage in his development, concentrating on jump blues-oriented material, sometimes with horn sections, showing the considerable influence of B.B. King. There's some sharp guitar on these sides (including some by Roy Gaines, who also played with Chuck Willis and Hound Dog Thornton), and the vocals are full and confident, if a bit overripe. But neophytes should begin with his early- and mid-'60s sides, when his blend of blues and soul reached a much higher level of maturity. *—Richie Unterberger*

The Voice: Duke Recordings 1959–69 / 1991 / Ace ✦✦✦✦✦

A 26-track compilation of Duke sides from Bland's peak decade (1959-1969). MCA's two-volume *The Duke Recordings* covers this period in greater depth, and will be more readily available to most North American consumers. On its own terms, though, it's an excellent collection. Contains most of his biggest R&B hits ("Turn On Your Love Light," "Stormy Monday Blues," "Call On Me," "Ain't Nothing You Can Do"), as well as some cuts that didn't make it onto *The Duke Recordings*. *—Richie Unterberger*

☆ **I Pity the Fool: The Duke Recordings, Vol. 1** / 1992 / MCA ✦✦✦✦✦

Everything the young Bland waxed for Duke between 1952 and the 1960 date that produced "Cry, Cry, Cry" and the R&B-laced "Don't Cry No More" is included in this album. From 1955 on, this is uniformly seminal stuff, Bland's vocal confidence growing by the session and buttressed by the consistently innovative riffs and solos of guitarists Clarence Hollimon, Wayne Bennett (he's amazing on a torrid "You Did Me Wrong"), Roy Gaines and Pat Hare. "Farther Up the Road," the exotic ballad "Hold Me Tenderly," "Little Boy Blue," and the title track are but few of the two-disc collection's many standouts. No blues fan should be minus this set! *—Bill Dahl*

Years of Tears / 1993 / Malaco ✦✦✦✦

Perhaps no artist has flourished at Malaco more than Bobby "Blue" Bland. Bland's animated, raw voice, though not as wide-ranging, still has a character and quality unmatched in blues, soul or vintage R&B. This CD is his finest for the label since *Members Only*. The opening number "Somewhere Between Right & Wrong" has a simmering track, Bland's mournful, explosive leads, tasty organ, tight drumming, and on-the-money lyrics from composers Johnny Barranco and George Jackson. It sets the stage for nine additional country-tinged and bluesy soul tunes, including three from Frederick Knight, who also produced his compositions. It's not his Duke material, but it's close enough to satisfy. *—Ron Wynn*

☆ **Turn on Your Love Light: The Duke Recordings, Vols. 1–2** / 1994 / MCA ✦✦✦✦✦

Picking up right where the first volume left off and continuing into 1964, this two-disc compilation (50 tracks!) showcases one of Bland's most appealing periods at Duke. Joe Scott was experimenting boldly with his protégé's repertoire, his brass-powered arrangements urging Bland to increased heights of incendiary energy on "Turn on Your Love Light" and "Yield Not to Temptation" (driven by future James Brown drummer Jabo Starks' funky traps) and advanced sophistication levels for the honey-smooth "Share Your Love with Me" and "That's the Way Love Is." Wayne Bennett's crackling blues licks invest "Stormy Monday Blues," "The Feeling Is Gone," and "Black Night" with T-Bone-derived tradition, while Bland handles Charlie Rich's "Who Will the Next Fool Be" with just the right amount of bluesy resignation. *—Bill Dahl*

Sad Street / Oct. 24, 1995 / Malaco ✦✦

Malaco's well-oiled, violin-enriched studio sound fits Bland's laidback contemporary approach just fine these days (even if his voice admittedly ain't what it used to be). With top-flight songwriters George Jackson, Robert Johnson, and Sam Mosley contributing material to the project, the results are agreeable if less than earthshaking. Why Bland chose to cover Rod Stewart's "Tonight's the Night" remains a mystery, however. *—Bill Dahl*

That Did It!: The Duke Recordings, Vol. 3 / Jun. 18, 1996 / MCA ✦✦✦

That Did It! is the third and final installment in MCA's series of double-disc compilations of Bobby Blue Bland's Duke recordings. This set collects everything he recorded between 1965 and 1972, including two unreleased tracks and several alternate takes. Although the music on *That Did It!* isn't quite as strong as the songs on the first two installments of the series, it does collect a full 16 singles that have never appeared on an album before, as well as featuring several top-notch album tracks. For Bland fans, the collection remains a necessary purchase—this is Bland's final set of essential recordings. *—Thom Owens*

Live on Beale Street / Feb. 17, 1998 / Malaco ✦✦✦

Recorded live at the New Daisy Theater with Bland's regular working road band, this captures him in fine form, bringing together old favorites with some other numbers for a heady blend. When called for, the old Joe Scott heavy horn-laden arrangements are summoned up on tunes like "St. James Infirmary," "Farther On Up the Road," "That's the Way Love Is," "I Pity the Fool" and "I'll Take Care of You," with consummate ease. But even more telling are how effortlessly and seamlessly material like Buddy Ace's "Love of Mine," "Members Only," "Soon as the Weather Breaks," and Bill Withers' "Ain't No Sunshine" and "Get Your Money Where You Spend Your Time" meshes with the old standbys. A lengthy slow-blues medley brings guest appearances from Johnnie Taylor and Bobby Rush on "Stormy Monday," but the real star here is Bland himself. He's in good voice and good humor, and this makes a fine addition to his stack of latter day recordings. *—Cub Koda*

★ **Greatest Hits, Vol. 1: The Duke Recordings** / Jun. 16, 1998 / Duke/Peacock ✦✦✦✦✦

This single-disc compilation cherry-picks through MCA's three two-disc anthology sets and puts together 16 tracks of essential Bland, starting with 1957's "Farther up the Road" and ending up with his 1969 reading of Big Joe Turner's "Chains of Love." It gathers up all the biggies: "Turn on Your Lovelight," "I Pity the Fool," "Stormy Monday Blues," "Call On Me," "I'll Take Care of You," and the transfers are exemplary. While it obviously leaves off a few of the early favorites—"Little Boy Blue" is almost inexcusable in its absence—this and its companion volume will be the best introduction for anyone wanting to explore the Bobby Bland collection. *—Cub Koda*

Greatest Hits, Vol. 2: The ABC-Dunhill/MCA Recordings / Jul. 14, 1998 / MCA ✦✦✦✦✦

Subtitled *The ABC-Dunhill/MCA Recordings*, this picks up the last tenure of Bland working under the corporate MCA umbrella. With tunes aboard from various albums and singles, this 16-track collection covers the highlights from his '70s period, with only 1982's "Recess in Heaven" falling outside the time frame. Bland was a much different vocalist by now, and if anything, these tracks, some of them flirting outright with disco, spearheaded the easy-listening-blues style that he still spearheads. Highlights include "This Time I'm Gone for Good," an uncharacteristically funky "Goin' Down Slow," "I Wouldn't Treat a Dog (The Way You Treated Me)," "Ain't No Love in the Heart of the City," "Yolanda" and Bland's own "The Soul of a Man." Experiments with country show up on "Today I Started Loving You Again" and "I Hate You," and yet Bland's duet with B.B. King on Louis Jordan's "Let the Good Times Roll" still shows that his blues roots were always close at hand. Not the place to start, but his last hurrah before going over to Malaco, and a solid collection to investigate nonetheless. *—Cub Koda*

Blues & Ballads / May 18, 1999 / MCA ✦✦✦

A 16-track collection that draws on his Duke and Dunhill recordings from the '60s, '70s, and '80s. Kicking off with the 1960 single "I've Been Wrong So Long" (featuring barn-burning guitar work from Wayne Bennett) and continuing right to the Al Bell productions from the early '80s, Bland's seamless command of the material at hand makes for a smooth listening ride all the way. A perfect companion set to any greatest-hits collection you might want to assemble. *—Cub Koda*

Get on Down with Bobby Bland/Reflections in Blue / Jul. 14, 1999 / BGO ✦✦✦

20th Century Masters—The Millennium Collection: The Best of Bobby "Blue" Bland / Jan. 25, 2000 / MCA ✦✦✦✦

20th Century Masters—The Millennium Collection: The Best of Bobby "Blue" Bland collects a dozen of his definitive performances, including "I Pity the Fool," "Stormy Monday Blues," and "Who Will the Next Fool Be?" Within a dozen songs, the collection spans Bland's most aching, plaintive moments, such as "I'm Too Far Gone (To Turn Around)," as well as more uptempo fare like "That's the Way Love Is" and "Ain't Nothing You Can Do." While this collection can't compete with more complete best-ofs like *Greatest Hits, Vol. 1* or *The Anthology*, *The Millennium Collection* is still a decent introduction to Bland's powerful, influential style. *—Heather Phares*

☆ **The Anthology** / Jun. 5, 2001 / MCA ✦✦✦✦✦

As the quintessential chitlin circuit R&B/blues star, Memphis-based singer Bobby "Blue" Bland's career has been relatively well-documented on CD. Still, until this 2001 double set, all 25 of his Top Ten R&B hits have not been available in one package. *The Anthology* is still not a complete career overview though, as it ends in 1982 before his prolific years at Malaco. It does, however, cover a remarkably prolific 30-year period, starting with his first recordings for Duke in 1952 and touching base at Dunhill and MCA, all conveniently located under the current Universal Music label umbrella. Die-hard fans of Bland during this period likely own the three double-disc sets MCA released in the mid-'90s but, for those who don't need the warts-and-all treatment yet want something more in depth than skimpy single-disc collections, this is certainly the way to go. Soul expert Bill Dahl's excellent liner notes provide anecdotes along with the major events that shaped Bland's life and ultimately these recordings. The 16-page book lists detailed and comprehensive individual track information, noting specific musicians on each of the 50 cuts. The overall effect is startling in its consistency. Bland's style and voice are immediately identifiable throughout, and the songwriting—even on the later tracks—typically suits his grits-and-honey approach. A previously unreleased live eight-minute 1973 version of "This Time I'm Gone for Good," which demonstrates how effectively Bland extended his songs in concert, is the only collectable track here, but this chronologically arranged set is not geared toward that segment of the audience. Sonically, *The Anthology* is the best this material has ever sounded, with the '60s songs absolutely stunning in their remastered definition. While he experienced a significant career resurgence in the '80s, which is where this sets stops, these are the classic songs that form the basis of any serious blues collection. As such, it's an essential document of one of America's most talented, and creative, blues singers. *—Hal Horowitz*

The Blazers

f. 1990

Group / Roots Rock

The Blazers, who play a guitar-heavy blend of blues, surf-rock, country, rocked-up norteño, cumbia, and other Mexican styles, are often compared with their East Los Angeles counterparts, Los Lobos. Like Los Lobos, the Gourds, or Doug Sahm's Texas Tornados, the Blazers perform a rousing, danceable mix of North American musical styles. The group is driven by two guitarist-singers, Manuel Gonzales and Ruben Guaderamma, who have been playing together since high school, rocking the beer joints of East L.A. Their fiery guitar playing and bluesy, soulful singing are given a strong, driving beat by bassist Lee Stuart and drummer Raul Medrano. The Blazers' infectious Ameri-Mex rock grooves and dual guitar action have prompted comparisons with Santana, the Kinks, the Rolling Stones, Chuck Berry and the Allman Brothers. Their 1994 debut album, *Short Fuse*, was hailed as one of the best rock records of the year by many critics. Already, the group has made several overseas tours and been well-received by roots-starved European audiences. The band's albums also include *East Side Soul* (1995), *Just For You* (1997) and *Puro Blazers* (2000). All of them should find favor with any fan of hard-driving blues-rock and rockabilly. *—Richard Skelly*

Short Fuse / 1994 / Rounder ✦✦✦

The Blazers come out of the same milieu—indeed, the same Los Angeles neighborhood—as Los Lobos, and they share the same mixture of '50s rock, blues, and country styles in their music. *Short Fuse*, their debut album, was produced by Cesar Rosas of Los Lobos, and that's appropriate, because The Blazers lean toward his more traditional side of Los Lobos' music. There's nobody in the band who writes songs with the depth and imaginativeness of Los Lobos' team of David Hidalgo and Louis Perez, but that doesn't keep them from playing up a storm on a combination of English-language rock ravers and Spanish-language folk-based tunes. If you love Los Lobos, you will at least like The Blazers. *—William Ruhlmann*

● **East Side Soul** / Oct. 17, 1995 / Rounder ✦✦✦✦

Few bands have ever combined gutsy blues-rock and sheer joyous energy the way the Blazers did on *East Side Soul*, much less created such a successful and interesting fusion of musical cultures. Many critics have remarked on the richness that their Latin rhythms brings to straight-ahead rock numbers, but not on the tasteful way those influences go the other way. You can hear traces of Little Feat and John Fogerty on the cumbias and other numbers which are sung in Spanish. On this album everything mixes perfectly, and the material is of uniformly high quality. Manuel Gonzales contributes stinging guitar leads throughout, notably on "Let Me Go," which has a distinct hint of Stevie Ray Vaughan in the tone and phrasing. The band plays with precision and passion, and the production on *East Side Soul* is more polished than on their first album. This is definitely the one to get if you're interested in hearing the Blazers in full cry. *—Richard Foss*

Just for You / Aug. 5, 1997 / Rounder ✦✦✦✦

Twenty years of rocking them in East L.A. has made Mex-pop masters out of the Blazers. "Just for You" offers dual-guitar roots rock action pumped up with help from Lee Thornburg and Greg Smith (Tower of Power). This is definite party music with an especially strong title track. Tossing Mexican cumbias into their blend of rockin' blues, their full music includes organ and a horn section. *—Tom Schulte*

Puro Blazers / May 16, 2000 / Rounder ✦✦✦

Blind Blake (Arthur Blake)

b. 1895?, Jacksonville, FL, **d.** 1937?, Jacksonville, FL

Vocals, Guitar / Piedmont Blues, Prewar Country Blues, Country Blues, Acoustic Blues, Ragtime

What happened to Blind Blake? His disappearance in 1932 from the Chicago blues scene, where he was undisputed king of the string and recorded 81 solo sides for Paramount, is one of the unresolved mysteries of early blues. Similarly mysterious is Blake's prodigious fingerstyle guitar technique which has plank spankers to this day asking: "How the hell did he do that!?"

Like many early blues recording artists, Blake was regionally well-known, if not legendary, before he began making records. His peregrinations through the Southeast and Midwest were those of the itinerant songster; his repertoire included everything from blues to rags to music hall novelties. On Paramount records he broke out in 1926 with his debut release, a finger-buster called "West Coast Blues." Through the late '20s he performed and recorded with banjoists Papa Charlie Jackson and Gus Cannon, chanteuses Ma Rainey and Ida Cox, pianist Charlie Spand and a host of others as first-call guitar on Paramount's studio A-team. His best playing, however, was reserved for solo outings like "Diddie-Wah-Diddie" or "Police Dog Blues." On these he spun off guitar variations so dense they were dubbed "piano sounding" by his label. The hot licks framed lyrics often laced with suggestive double entendre. His hypermetabolic instrumentals were full of diffident spoken asides in an accent that gave credence to his supposed Southern seaboard origins.

Blake spent part of 1930 and 1931 touring with the vaudeville show "Happy-Go-Lucky" and returned to the Paramount studios in Grafton, WI, for his final session in 1932. His subsequent whereabouts, including rumors of his murder or death by mishap, have never been substantiated. It's commonly supposed that, as the Depression knocked the bottom out of the race record industry, Blake simply moved back to the South so beloved in his song lyrics, and died there soon after.

Blake's influence, especially in the folk/blues revival, was pervasive. His brilliant playing was touted by guitar godfathers like Josh White and Gary Davis; his songs covered by contemporary acousticians including Dave Van Ronk, Leon Redbone and Ry Cooder. On guitar, he's still the one to beat ... probably always will be. As he says himself, "Here's somethin' gonna make you feel good!" *—Steve James*

Rope Stretchin' Blues (1926–1931), Vol. 4 / 1966 / Document ✦✦✦✦

This album was the final installment of a four volume set comprising the entire known output of this blues picker's blues picker. Like any of Blake's too few collections, it shows off the vast range of his repertoire, including ragtime and country shuffle numbers as well as blues. There are some solo numbers as well as duets with a pianist, little bits of minstrel show-style accompaniment from rattlebones and xylophone, and several female guest vocal spots that definately have the required funk. There are glitches in the recording that sound like someone went after the master with a Boy Scout knife, but listening past this the antique sound was quite capable of picking up enough of Blake's playing to send most guitarists into finger-counting exercises. *—Eugene Chadbourne*

★ **Ragtime Guitar's Foremost Fingerpicker** / 1990 / Yazoo ✦✦✦✦✦

Ragtime Guitar's Foremost Fingerpicker contains a total of 28 prime tracks from Blind Blake. Alternating between solo acoustic numbers and songs recorded with a string band, the set demonstrates how exceptionally gifted the guitarist was—he's playing arrangements and rhythms that several subsequent generations were never able to completely figure out. Blind Blake was one of the finest acoustic guitarists of the '20s and '30s and this is the definitive compilation. *—Thom Owens*

Complete Recorded Works, Vol. 1 (1926–1927) / 1991 / Document ✦✦✦✦

Blind Blake, one of the top blues guitarists and singers of the '20s, is a mystery figure whose birth and death dates are not definitively known. He recorded 84 selections in six years (1926-1932), and fortunately all have been reissued on four Document CDs. *Vol. 1* mostly features Blake in unaccompanied performances other than six numbers backing singer Leola Wilson, one song in which he is joined by a kazoo player and two in which someone plays rattlebones behind his guitar. Among the classics heard on this CD are "Early Morning Blues," "Too Tight," "Come on Boys Let's Do That Messin' Around," and "Seabord Stomp." All four of Blind Blake's Document CDs are essential for every serious blues collection. *—Scott Yanow*

Complete Recorded Works, Vol. 2 (1927–1928) / 1991 / Document ✦✦✦

Guitarist/singer Blind Blake's entire recorded output has been made available on four Document CDs. *Vol. 2* covers a busy seven-month period and features Blake in several different diverse but equally rewarding settings. He performs solo; backs singers Elzadie Robinson, Bertha Henderson, and Daniel Brown; and holds his own with clarinetist Johnny Dodds and percussionist/xylophonist JImmy Bertrand in a jazz set. There are many memorable numbers among the 25 songs on this CD, including "Southern Rag," "He's in the Jailhouse Now," "Hot Potatoes" (an exuberant instrumental with Dodds), "Southbound Rag," and "No Dough Blues." Blind Blake at his best, but get all four volumes. *—Scott Yanow*

Complete Recorded Works, Vol. 3 (1928–1929) / 1991 / Document ✦✦✦

The third volume in the series opens with a pair of mid-1928 tracks featuring Blind Blake in the role of sideman, lending his brilliant guitar leads in support of Elzadie Robinson on "Elzadie's Policy Blues" and "Pay Day Daddy Blues." Blake's next session, from later that same year, returns him to the fore, yielding the mesmerizing "Notoriety Woman," one of the most menacingly violent tracks he ever cut; the same date also produced the comparatively lighthearted "Sweet Papa Low Down," a seeming attempt to cash in on the Charleston dance craze. The real jewel of the set, however, is a 1929 session teaming him with pianist Charlie Spand; "Hastings St." is a lively, swinging guitar and piano duet, while "Police Dog Blues" is among Blake's most vividly lyrical efforts, further galvanized by his haunting instrumental work. *—Jason Ankeny*

Complete Recorded Works, Vol. 4 (1929–1932) / 1991 / Document ✦✦✦

The fourth and final volume in Document's series assembles a wide range of Blind Blake material, from sides cut under the name Blind Arthur ("Guitar Chimes" and "Blind Arthur's Breakdown"), collaborations with vaudeville singer Chocolate Brown, aka Irene Scruggs, and even his sole two-part blues, the morbid "Rope Stretchin' Blues." Among the final pair of tracks, from mid-1932, the first, "Champagne Charlie Is My Name," is so atypical that some question whether it is even Blake at all; however, his last known side, "Depression's Gone from Me Blues," is a career-capping triumph—just why he never recorded again is just one of the many mysteries which continue to swirl about this legendary figure. *—Jason Ankeny*

The Master of Ragtime Guitar: The Essential Recordings / 1996 / Indigo ✦✦✦✦

The Best of Blind Blake / Oct. 10, 2000 / Yazoo ✦✦✦✦

Little is known about Blind Blake, including the date of his birth and death. His recording career lasted six years, from 1926-1932, and included 79 titles. After this, he disappeared. His music, however, has survived. Blake's a distinguished vocalist, with a steady medium range reminiscent of Big Bill Broonzy. His easy delivery on "Too Tight Blues, No. 2" and "Georgia Bound" is immediately accessible. The ragtime flavor of many of the tunes creates a light and happy blues. Even when the songs occasionally turn bare and graphic, covering everything from suicide to sex to murder, Blake's spry delivery comes off as joyful. There are also a number of ragtime-influenced instrumentals like "Southern Rag," "Blind Arthur's Breakdown," and "West Coast Blues" that feature his complicated guitar work. "Blind Arthur's Breakdown" is a *tour de force* in ragtime guitar that features complicated fingerpicking and multiple changes in pacing. Blake is accompanied on several cuts by other unidentified musicians, including a harmonica player on "Panther Squall Blues" and vibraphonist on "Doggin' Me Mamma Blues." It would have been helpful to know a little more about these musicians, though this information may not be available. The liner notes provide a good overview of Blake's music and try to sort out the fact and fiction of his scant biography. These recordings have been transferred from 78s, scratches, surface noise, and all. This is particularly noticeable on songs like "Ice Man Blues" and "Guitar Chimes," but both Blake's vocals and guitar picking remain discernable, and it's probably fortunate that these recordings have been preserved at all. With *The Best of Blind Blake,* Yazoo has released another fine recording of vintage blues. *—Ronnie D. Lankford, Jr.*

Blind Faith

f. May 1969, England, **db.** Nov. 1969

Group / Album Rock, British Blues, Hard Rock, Blues-Rock

Blind Faith was either one of the great successes of the late '60s, a culmination of the decade's efforts by three legendary musicians—or it was a disaster of monumental proportions, and a symbol of everything that had gone wrong with the business of rock at the close of the decade. In actual fact, Blind Faith was probably both.

By any ordinary reckoning, the quartet compiled an enviable record. They generated some great songs, two of them ("Sea of Joy," "Presence of the Lord") still regarded as classics 30-plus years later; sold hundreds of thousands of concert tickets and perhaps a million more albums at the time; and they were so powerful a force in the music industry that they were indirectly responsible for helping facilitate the merger of two major record companies that evolved into Time Warner, before they'd released a note of music on record. And they did it all in under seven months together.

Blind Faith's beginnings dated from 1968 and the break-up of Cream. That band had sold millions of records and eventually achieved a status akin to that of the Beatles or the Rolling Stones. Cream's internal structure was as stressful as it was musically potent, however, as a result of the genuine personal dislike between bassist/singer Jack Bruce and drummer Ginger Baker, which occasionally overwhelmed the respect they had for each other as musicians, leaving guitarist/singer Eric Clapton to serve as mediator. After two years of service as a referee, spent all the while in an unremitting spotlight, the public seemingly hanging on every note he played, Clapton was only too happy to leave that situation behind.

The initial spark for Blind Faith came from Clapton and Steve Winwood, whose band Traffic had split up in January of 1969, amid acrimonious disputes over songwriting and direction. Winwood at age 20 was some three years younger than Clapton, and had emerged as a rock star at 17 as a member of the Spencer Davis Group, spending three years as their lead singer on a string of enviable R&B-based hits. His concerns were musical—he wanted to work with the best musicians, and wanted to experiment with jazz, which led him to leave the Spencer Davis Group and form Traffic, which proved riven by egos nearly as strong as the members' musical impulses. The January 1969 break-up would be the first of several temporary splits in the band's lineup.

The two musicians had long admired and respected each other—they shared an enthusiasm for and dedication to the blues, and complemented each other in the sense that Clapton's work was more oriented toward Mississippi Delta blues and its urban descendants, while Winwood came out of more of an R&B sound and had the voice to make that work, and both were interested in experimenting in a group situation without any pressure. It had even occurred to Clapton during the months of Cream's disintegration that the addition of a fourth member on keyboards might have stabilized the band, in terms of both its music and its internal dynamics.

As it turned out, nothing could have saved Cream, but he looked up Winwood anyway after the band's demise, in late December of 1968, and the two found that they genuinely liked working together. The notion of forming a band took shape as an eventual goal during jams between the two that lasted for hours. At one point, Clapton even considered forming another trio, between himself and Winwood and a third member as drummer. These ideas took a sharp, new, more immediate turn when Ginger Baker turned up to sit in with them in January of 1969. The results were impressive to all concerned, and the drummer was eager to be let into the group they were planning.

Clapton found himself in a personal bind, having promised Baker on Cream's demise that they would work together on their next project, but he was not looking forward to reuniting with him just nine weeks after the old group's final show, with all of the expectations that their link-up would engender from outsiders. Apart from his resentment at being the buffer between Baker and Bruce, Clapton had felt straightjacketed in Cream, required by the demands of fans and, by extension, the record company, to write, play, and sing blues-based rock in a certain way; and he'd also felt trapped in the band's experimental departures from blues. Winwood, who failed to appreciate the dangers that Clapton saw or the seriousnness of the guitarist's resistance, finally persuaded him, largely on the basis on the fact that Baker's presence only strengthened them musically, and that they would be hard put upon to find anyone his equal.

They began working out songs early in 1969, and in February and March the trio was in London at Morgan Studios, preparing the beginnings of basic tracks for an album, which began seriously taking shape as songs at Olympic Studios in April and May under the direction of producer Jimmy Miller. The music community was already onto the link-up, despite Clapton's claim that he was cutting an album of his own on which Winwood would play. The rock press wasn't buying any of it, knowing that Baker was involved as well, and then the promoters and record companies got involved, pushing those concerned for an album and a tour.

What's more, they were offering more money than ever, for what seemed, from a business standpoint, a very good reason. Beginning with the *Disraeli Gears* album in 1967 and running thru *Wheels of Fire* in late 1968, Cream had been virtually a money-machine for their record labels, music publishers, and concert promoters alike. Their break-up had been a blow to the music business akin to the death of a top performer; it was hard for their record labels, Atlantic in America and Polydor in Europe, or the promoters prepared to book their tours, who or what could replace them on the ledger books. (It was true that Atlantic had at least one other major blues-rock iron in the fire at the time, in the guise of a new band called Led Zeppelin, but in early 1969 no one yet had an inkling of precisely how big that quartet was going to become).

Thus, the idea, coming along just three months later, of Eric Clapton reuniting with Ginger Baker and performing with Steve Winwood, who was, himself, a major star in England, was like a resurrection. And given a new bite at the apple, the record labels were salivating as they opened their checkbooks to write out big advances, and every concert promoter who could tried to get in on the money to be made, offering huge sums for the chance to profit from a tour by such a band.

It was all impossible to resist. In May, the final version of the band came together with the addition of Rick Grech, a talented musician but hardly a star, on bass. A member of the band Family (which he abandoned in the middle of their U.S. tour), Grech took the bassist's spot in the new group in preparation for going out on the road. By then the group was known as Blind Faith, a slyly cynical reference that reflected Clapton's outlook on the new group. His doubts might've been taken more seriously if anyone had stopped to dwell on the fact that they'd hardly had time to work out any songs beyond those that were going onto the album—at least, none that were not associated with other bands. Tours were booked, first of northern Europe and then America, with millions of dollars promised for the latter, contracts signed, and advances paid. The band made its debut at a concert in London's Hyde Park on June 7, 1969, in front of 100,000 fans who'd been primed by weeks of press reports heralding Blind Faith as "super Cream" and their tour as an event akin to the Second Coming.

From that first show, there was trouble over the split between the adulation accorded the band and Clapton's misgivings over the quality of the group's work. A perfectionist by nature, he reportedly left the stage at Hyde Park shaken over the ragged quality of the show they'd given, while 100,000 people roared with approval over their performance. He could already see the same pattern that had made his stay with Cream utterly enervating as a musical experience re-emerging with Blind Faith—the fans could cheer all they wanted, but he had musicianship to care about and worry over, and it was a lousy show. The tour had already been booked, however, and there was more involved than Clapton's musical sensibilities to consider. And, in a sense, maybe the promoters knew more than Clapton did—it turned out that all the quartet had to do was show up to please the crowds that they found.

Unbeknownst to Clapton as he pondered going out on the road with an unprepared, under-rehearsed band—and it would have boggled his mind had he known—on the other side of the Atlantic, the hype surrounding Blind Faith had already affected a much bigger part of the record industry than any aspect of the group's impending tour ever would. In early 1969, Warner-Seven Arts, previously known as the Kinney Corporation (a company that made millions in the parking garage business), was in the process of acquiring record companies. Under the guidance of their president, Steve Ross, they'd already bought Warner Bros. studios, which included Warner-Reprise Records, and had arranged to purchase Atlantic Records late in 1968.

Ross knew, however, that Atlantic was worth acquiring only if its president, founder, and chief guiding personality, Ahmet Ertegun, stayed with the company—but Ertegun, a true music enthusiast as well as a superb businessman, wasn't convinced that he wanted to work for a corporate owner. He'd founded Atlantic with his brother and a partner, and liked being his own boss and calling the musical shots as he'd seen them, rather than reporting to anyone else.

Ross saw his investment in jeopardy and scheduled a meeting with Ertegun to try and convince the man to stay on. The problem for Ross was that Atlantic was practically a part of Ertegun, and Ertegun was almost as much an artist as a businessman, all of which was part of the secret of his success in holding together a team of creative production and engineering geniuses like Jerry Wexler and Tom Dowd, not to mention the stable of artists they worked with.

A few nights before the meeting, he'd been at home when his teenage son passed through with a friend, who'd heard that Ross was in the process of buying Atlantic Records. The friend had started telling Ross about how hot Atlantic Records looked to be, and about the break-up of Cream; he enthused over Clapton's hook-up with Winwood and Baker, and the notion being floated in the press of the Blind Faith tour and album, the latter to be released by Atlantic, and how every rock listener in America was just waiting to grab up that album and pay to see the group.

Ross, who was of an age that made him part of Vaughn Monroe's or Patti Page's audience, hadn't a clue what the teenager was talking about, and knew nothing about Cream, Clapton, or Blind Faith. As he later recounted it, however, when he met with Ertegun, the matter of Blind Faith came up in the conversation, as Ertegun was trying to explain what Atlantic was involved in musically. Ross saw his opening and tried his best to run with it, desperately attempting to recall, as he stood there talking, everything that his son's friend had told him about Cream, Clapton, Baker, and Winwood, even though he knew nothing of the music involved. Ertegun, who was at least impressed with Ross' attempt to communicate with him about music, agreed to remain with the new management of Atlantic, which prospered in the '70s and '80s under his guidance even more than it had in the '50s and '60s. Thus marked the beginning of what soon became Warner-Elektra-Atlantic and, more recently, Warner-EMI Records.

The brief Blind Faith tour of northern Europe in June of 1969 went well. These were out-of-the-spotlight events in small clubs, before serious audiences that were there to listen to music—northern Europe had (and has) a long tradition for offering this kind of audience, which allowed bluesmen of lesser stature than Clapton et al. to earn decent livings playing in that part of the world.

From there, however, they moved on to the United States, making their debut at Madison Square Garden on July 12 in front of more than 20,000 people. A riot developed when fans charged the stage, only to be repulsed by the police; in the half-hour melee that ensued, Ginger Baker was clubbed on the head by a policeman who thought he was an interloper, and Winwood's piano was destroyed. The environment and that sort of passion placed the group in a ridiculous situation—in truth, they didn't sound that good and they knew it, and the nature of sound systems in 1969 destroyed whatever panache they might've brought to their performance, as an under-rehearsed group; yet audiences roared and demanded more music, and rioted at their shows.

It was that way along the entire tour, seven weeks across the United States and Canada ending in Hawaii, marred by particularly angry confrontations between fans and police in Los Angeles. Even as they made their way across the country, the band was questioned about why Clapton seemed to be placing himself on the periphery and giving center-stage to Winwood, who was far less well-known in America at that time. The band's repertory also seemed very light, their new material—even allowing for the inevitable Ginger Baker drum solo on "Do What You Like"—amounting to barely an hour's worth of music. The way the band had been marketed, the requests for performances of earlier hits by each of the star members, especially Clapton and Baker's work with Cream, were inevitable, and the group obliged them.

Clapton was now trapped in a kind of "mega-Cream" situation, only worse—there hadn't been any riots at the trio's shows—and seemed as though he'd rather have been somewhere else. To him, it must have seemed as though he'd sold his soul to the Devil; there was no backing out on the tour, just enduring it, and hoping that when the smoke cleared the monetary reward would mitigate the miseries he'd suffered. Where the music they were playing should have been the highlight, it was a chore and an obligation. He did find a haven in music along the tour, but not Blind Faith's—one of the opening acts was a country- and blues-based rock act called Delaney & Bonnie, who had a fun, freewheeling approach to performing and a surprisingly soulful sound. He began spending more time hanging out with them than with the members of Blind Faith, listening to what they were doing and enjoying it, and comparing notes on the blues with Delaney Bramlett.

Blind Faith's tour ended on August 24, 1969. By that time, the self-titled album—which ran into controversy over its cover, of a topless pre-pubescent girl, and was repackaged in America with a photo of the group—had been out for almost a month, and had already sold more than half-a-million copies in America alone, hitting number one on the charts in England and America. The money was rolling in to all concerned even as they realized that the album showcased one of the fundamental flaws in the band's conception. There was very good music on *Blind Faith*, but there wasn't a lot of it—barely 40 minutes' worth, which was hardly a body of music worthy of a international-class act. It was a good album, but those six songs didn't constitute a repertory, much less a defined sound.

In a more logical sequence of events, the group would've spent more weeks rehearsing, and played some more small gigs in England or northern Europe, perfecting their sound and working out material. They would've had time to become a group, with the debut album issued in the midst of that; and then prepared a second LP, recorded and ready to go when their international bookings began, shows for which they would've had at least a dozen songs that they could claim as their own.

Instead, the logic collapsed like a row of dominoes falling: Baker joining, which got the press excited about a reconstituted Cream, which raised the stakes and the pressure for an immediate tour and an even more immediate album. In the end, Blind Faith was like a baby removed too soon from the womb and asked to grow and thrive.

The group returned to England amid alternate rumors of a U.K. tour or a breakup. By October, what was already a forgone conclusion to the members became official—there would be no second Blind Faith album, not from the studio or even a live album (though a couple of live tracks surfaced on the 1995 Steve Winwood retrospective set *The Finer Things*), nor any release of the film they'd made of the Hyde Park show.

Blind Faith ultimately proved too little and too much all at once. The band had left its members a bit shell-shocked, Clapton most of all, but even he had lots of money to show for it (and more coming in, the Blind Faith tour and album helping stimulate sales of Cream's old albums as well). He retreated to the safety of Delaney & Bonnie, where he began playing some of the best blues of his entire career; no longer in a leadership position, or expected to step into the spotlight at every turn, he got his wish for anonymity on tour with the group from December of 1969 until early 1970, in the course of which he also met the sidemen—Carl Radle, Jim Gordon, and Bobby Whitlock—that would finally give him the kind of safe, anonymous showcase for his work that he'd hoped Blind Faith would be, in Derek & the Dominoes, who did exactly what he'd hoped Blind Faith would do, play small clubs very quietly and work out their music out of the spotlight.

Ginger Baker, however, found the Blind Faith experience to be no worse than a mixed blessing. There'd been little new musical discovery, but the money had been very good, and it had proved that audiences would turn out for an offshoot of Cream. Additionally, he'd liked working with Winwood and Grech, and decided to try and keep them together. This led to the formation, in late November of 1969, of Ginger Baker's Air Force, a big-band ensemble whose sound embraced rock, jazz, R&B, folk, African music, and blues.

Winwood and Grech would only remain with that group long enough to play at a pair of shows debuting the band in England during January of 1970. It was understood that, at the behest of Chris Blackwell, the head of Island Records (to which Winwood was signed), Winwood was to begin work on a projected solo album and was taking Rick Grech with him, into what would become the Traffic reunion album *John Barleycorn Must Die*. Meanwhile, the memory of Blind Faith lingered with the album, which became a perennial favorite in Clapton's, Winwood's, and Baker's catalogs. Clapton and Winwood later came to appreciate the record. For all of their musical merits, which were considerable, Blind Faith's short life-span made them virtually a symbol of the tail-end of the '60s and what those years were about: Too much too soon in that overheated cultural, psychic, and business environment, even for the prodigious talents and personalities involved, resulting in a quick burnout. *—Bruce Eder*

● **Blind Faith** / Jul. 1969 / Polydor ♦♦♦♦

Blind Faith's first and last album, more than 30 years old and counting, remains one of the jewels of the Eric Clapton, Steve Winwood, and Ginger Baker catalogs, despite the crash-and-burn history of the band itself, which scarcely lasted six months. As much a follow-up to Traffic's self-titled second album as it is to Cream's final output, it merges the soulful blues of the former with the heavy riffing and outsized song lengths of the latter for a very compelling sound unique to this band. Not all of it works—between the virtuoso electric blues of "Had to Cry Today," the acoustic-textured "Can't Find My Way Home," the soaring "Presence of the Lord" (Eric Clapton's one contribution here as a songwriter, and the first great song he ever authored) and "Sea of Joy," the band doesn't do much with the Buddy Holly song "Well All Right"; and Ginger Baker's "Do What You Like" was a little weak to take up 15 minutes of space on an LP that might have been better used for a shorter drum solo and more songs. Unfortunately, the group was never *that* together as a band and evidently had just the 42 minutes of new music here ready to tour behind. *—Bruce Eder*

Blind Faith [Deluxe Edition] / Jan. 9, 2000 / Polydor ♦♦♦♦

Blind Faith's lone album is often considered vivid proof as to why superstar collaborations simply don't work but, in retrospect, it does have something to offer. For a number of years, partisans have trumpeted that the album was "not all that bad," and though they may overcompensate with their affection for this messy affair, it does have two songs that are classics of classic rock: "Can't Find My Way Home" and "Presence of the Lord." "Had to Cry Today" is also pretty effective, as is the Buddy Holly cover "Well All Right." Still, for those who subscribe to conventional rock critic doctrine, it may seem a little strange that an album as muddied as *Blind Faith* was given this lavish *2001 Deluxe Edition*, containing basically everything capable of release that the group cut during these sessions. This expanded edition will not change any minds; just on principle, it may even sour some open-minded listeners who have a distaste for meandering, endless jams. They may be right, since the four jams that comprise the nearly hourlong second disc just aren't that interesting, even if fleeting moments work well. The bonus tracks on the first disc are interesting (apart from the winding 15-minute "Acoustic Jam"), including two previously unreleased versions of "Sleeping in the Ground" (the one on *Crossroads* is missing), an electric version of "Can't Find My Way Home," and "Time Winds." The fact remains that—even with these new tracks and the lavish presentation—this is a muddled album, but it's still a hell of a set for the dedicated, filled with unheard music, good liners, and beautiful packaging. Those who do love the album will not be disappointed by this. [The two bonus tracks that appeared on the initial CD release of *Blind Faith* are not here, since they apparently were not recordings of the group.] *—Stephen Thomas Erlewine*

Blind Percy & His Blind Band

Vocals / Prewar Country Blues, Prewar Blues

It is unknown who the members of Blind Percy & His Blind Band were, and in fact one can question whether any or all of them were even blind. An expert on the topic of blues singers with the prefix of "Blind" before their name was blues and folk performer Josh White. He paid his dues—and the concept is certainly understandable in this case—as a lead boy for more than 60 different blind singers. Among them was Blind Joe Taggart, a blues gospel performer, who like the similar and much better known Blind Willie Johnson, often gigged and recorded with female accompaniment. According to White, Taggart suffered from cataracts but was hardly blind. Taggart definitely recorded some non-gospel blues numbers under the name of Blind Joe Amos, and may have also cut tracks such as "Pennsylvania Woman Blues" under the name of Six Cylinder Smith. There is much evidence that the latter artist was the same man who recorded under the name of Blind Percy, so by connecting the Braille dots one might even come to the conclusion that Blind Percy is actually Blind Joe Taggart. This is not a theory that every blues scholar agrees with, however. Harmonica enthusiasts see Six Cylinder Smith and possibly Blind Percy as some of the extremely few proponents of a style of harmonica playing known as "rack harmonica." This is the way Bob Dylan plays harmonica, on a wire rack that fits over the performer's head and rests on his shoulders. In blues, the common harmonica style involves a performer playing the harmonica and only the harmonica, cupping the instrument in the hand and adding important adjustments to the sound with various exotic hand motions. None of this is possible with a rack mount, although scraping the inner part of the ear while putting the thing on certainly is. No photographs exist of Smith or Blind Percy; if they did, sophisticated photo editing technology might be able to locate such ear scrapes and help establish who is who and how whoever it was played the harmonica and the guitar at the same time, if they actually did. White has never acknowledged that his former boss Taggart could be either Smith or Percy. The Chicago blues guitarist Jimmie Lee Robinson indicated in an interview that "a man named Blind Percy" taught him guitar rudiments. This would place Blind Percy, possibly Six Cylinder Smith, in Chicago in the '30s and '40s. His recordings from the decade before have been anthologized in collections of music from Texas/Louisiana/Arkansas bluesmen, as well as in complete collections of Taggart because of the identity questions. Tracks attributed to Blind Percy include "Coal River Blues" and "Fourteenth Street Blues." *—Eugene Chadbourne*

Rory Block

b. Nov. 6, 1949, New York, NY

Slide Guitar, Vocals, Guitar / Contemporary Blues

Aurora "Rory" Block has staked her claim to be one of America's top acoustic blueswomen, an interpreter of the great Delta blues singers, a slide guitarist par excellence, and also a talented songwriter on her own account. Born and raised in Manhattan by a family that had Bohemian leanings, she spent her formative years hanging out with musicians like Peter Rowan, John Sebastian, and Geoff Muldaur, who hung out in her father's sandal shop, before picking up the guitar at the age of ten. Her record debut came two years later, backing her father on the *Elektra String Band Project*, a concept album. She met guitarist Stefan Grossman, who, like her, was in love with the blues. The pair would often travel to the Bronx to visit the Reverend Gary Davis, one of the greatest living bluesmen. At the tender age of 15 she left home, hitting the road in true '60s fashion and traveling through the South, where she learned her blues trade at the feet of Skip

James and Mississippi John Hurt, her greatest influence, before ending up in Berkeley. It was there that she developed her slide technique (she uses a socket wrench as her slide), but she didn't record until 1975, when she released *I'm in Love* (a compilation of earlier material, *The Early Tapes 1975-1976*, appeared later). After two records for Chrysalis, she recorded the instructional *How to Play Blues Guitar* for Grossman's Kicking Mule label, and later moved to then-fledgling Rounder, with whom she's had an ongoing relationship. She toured constantly, often playing as many as 250 dates in a year, which kept her away from her family—she'd married and begun having children in the early '70s—but developed her reputation as a strong, vibrant live performer, and one of the best players of old country blues in America. In 1987 the best of her Rounder cuts were compiled on *Best Blues and Originals*, which, as it said, featured her interpretations of blues classics and some of her own material. Two of the tracks, released as singles in Belgium and Holland, became gold record hits. In addition to her regular albums, Block made a series of instructional records and videos, as well as a children's record, *Color Me Wild*. Although she had been performing for a long time, the plaudits didn't really begin until 1992, when she won a NAIRD Award for *Ain't I a Woman*, a feat repeated in 1994 and 1997. In 1996 she began winning W.C. Handy Awards, first for Best Traditional Album (*When a Woman Gets the Blues*), and in 1997 and 1998 for Best Traditional Blues Female Artist. In 1997 she was elected to the CAMA Hall of Fame, and in 1999 she received yet another Handy Award, for Best Acoustic Blues Album (*Confessions of a Blues Singer*). She stills tours, although not as heavily as in earlier times, and she's often accompanied by her grown son Jordan Block Valdina who also plays on her albums. *—Chris Nickson*

Intoxication So Bitter Sweet / 1977 / Chrysalis ♦♦

You're the One / 1978 / Chrysalis ♦♦

High Heeled Blues / 1981 / Rounder ♦♦♦♦♦
This was the most blues-oriented release of the three sessions Block issued in the early '80s for Rounder; it was also the most concentrated and successful. There were none of the experimental or tentative qualities that sometimes marred the other two dates; Block was in command from the opening moments of her cover of "Walkin' Blues" to the final bars of "Uncloudy Day." Her voice had fire, soul and grit, and she never sounded maudlin or unconvincing, whether doing "Hilarity Rag" or "Devil Got My Man." Her playing was also dynamic and focused, and John Sebastian obviously made a good production partner, as Block got back on track after making records that contained some good cuts but weren't as consistent. *—Ron Wynn*

Blue Horizon / 1983 / Rounder ♦♦♦
Block bounced all over the musical lot on this session. She did vintage folk tunes such as "Frankie and Johnny" effectively and covered Rev. Gary Davis' "Feel Just Like Goin' On" and the spiritual "Swing Low" with vigor, but wasn't as compelling on "Catastrophe Rag" or the bittersweet/satiric "Just Like a Man." Block's voice and talents are versatile enough to handle multiple styles, but she remains first and foremost a fine interpreter of classic blues and gospel. When she opts for the singer/songwriter bit or folk/country mode, she's professional enough to bring it off, but lacks the flair or distinctiveness to make it sound anything except competent. *—Ron Wynn*

Rhinestones & Steel Strings / 1983 / Rounder ♦♦♦♦
Guitarist/vocalist Rory Block's mix of traditional blues covers, originals, satirical and folk/country material was featured on this album mixing mid-'80s and early-'90s tracks. Her versions of Robert Wilkins' "No Way for Me to Get Along" and Rev. Gary Davis' "Sit Down on the Banks" were among the high points, as well as Block's "Dr. Make It Right" and "I Might Find a Way." For the most part, the songs were nicely performed and varied between upbeat and somber themes. Block's vocals were frequently outstanding and never less than convincing, while her playing was strong and steady. *—Ron Wynn*

I've Got a Rock in My Sock / 1986 / Rounder ♦♦
Rory Block was combative, poignant, energetic and laidback on this record. She did a good cover of Charley Patton's "Moon's Going Down," awhich changed things considerably from the strident mood established on the opening selection "Send the Man Back Home." She handled the melancholy title track, was playful on "Lovin' Whiskey" and introspective on the final song "Highland Overture," a guitar/synthesizer duet that almost, but didn't quite plunge into the New Age/background music abyss. This seemed like an experimental/searching session for Block, who sometimes was enjoyable, but overall didn't fare as well as on most of her other releases. *—Ron Wynn*

• **Best Blues & Originals** / 1987 / Rounder ♦♦♦♦♦
Best Blues & Originals collects the highlights from Rory Block's '80s albums for Rounder, saving a bunch of fine tracks from otherwise spotty releases. It's a nice overview and, consequently, a solid introduction to her catalog. *—Thom Owens*

House of Hearts / 1987 / Rounder ♦♦♦
A somber, morose mood permeated this album dedicated to Block's son, guitarist Thiele David Biehusen, who died in a car crash at age 20 and whose voice can be heard on the answering machine in the lengthy final cut "House of Hearts." There are also other equally gripping tunes, like "Farewell Young Man," "Heavenly Bird" and "Bonnie Boy." Block's voice was at its most mournful, and this is both a deeply moving work and a downer of an album. It's impossible not to be affected hearing Block's singing or these lyrics; anyone who's been through any remotely similar experience will feel the pain, and even those who haven't can't help but share in her sadness. *—Ron Wynn*

The Early Tapes 1975–1976 / 1989 / Alcazar ♦♦
On *The Early Tapes 1975-1976*, Rory Block is still trying to find a distinctive style. She samples from her idols—Robert Johnson, Charley Patton, and several others—adding slight blues and folk influences to her solo acoustic blues. However, she hasn't arrived at an original sound on any of these takes. Consequently, *Early Tapes* is of interest to historians and Rory Block completists, but few other listeners. *—Thom Owens*

Mama's Blues / 1991 / Rounder ♦♦♦♦♦
Rory Block is quite impressive. Ignoring the fact that she is a white woman singing older-style blues in the '90s, Block compares favorably to many of the top country blues artists of the '30s. Highlights of her very enjoyable set include Robert Johnson's "Terraplane Blues," a pair of Tommy Johnson classics and two songs recorded by Bessie Smith ("Do Your Duty" and "Weepin' Willow Blues"). Block's own originals (which have intelligent lyrics) sound more contemporary (with the influences of R&B, pop and gospel being felt), which alters the general mood of the release a bit. However, even with its brief playing time (38 minutes), her CD is highly recommended as a fine example of the work of this talented blues performer. *—Scott Yanow*

Ain't I a Woman / 1992 / Rounder ♦♦♦♦♦
Rory Block's 11th album marked both a personal and professional milestone. Now a thoroughly experienced singer, Block sounded much more confident and assured doing traditional blues tunes. Her performance on the title cut was both assertive and definitive, while she also displayed her customary versatility, doing country and folk-flavored numbers such as "Silver Wings" and "Rolling Log" in addition to a stunning gospel number, "Walk In Jerusalem." Block's vocals and guitar work have blossomed, toughened and greatly improved over her career, and were in prime form here. *—Ron Wynn*

Angel of Mercy / Feb. 28, 1994 / Rounder ♦♦♦
Block moves completely away from the blues form on this release, doing original pieces that evoke the familiar themes of alienation, anguish and romantic conflicts, but in a production climate geared more toward folk and singer/songwriter arrangements than 12-bar settings. She still plays excellent guitar solos and accompaniment, but her vocals are now powerful or mournful, questioning or declarative, and she's unconcerned with trying to capture the quality of someone else's compositions. The disc's final selection, the nine-minute-plus "A Father and Two Sons," reworks the biblical Prodigal son tale with a contemporary focus, featuring wonderful vocal interaction between Block and her son Jordan. This album showcases Rory Block's own sound and vision and deserves widespread praise and attention. *—Ron Wynn*

When a Woman Gets the Blues / 1995 / Rounder ♦♦♦♦
What does a woman do when she gets the blues? If she is blues wizard Rory Block, she gets out her guitar and starts singing and playing until her spirits lift. That is exactly what she does on this 1995 Rounder recording. The CD features her son, Jordan Block Valdina, on vocals with her, along with Annie Raines on harmonica and Warren Bernhardt on piano and harmonica. Together, they reach back in time for some tried-and-true blues, as well as one original from the pen of the blues diva. "Take My Heart Away" is Block's own contribution to the recording, which won her a W.C. Handy award in 1996 for Best Traditional Blues Album. The jury was impressed with her form on songs that like Blind Willie McTell's "T'aint Long for Day," which sounds as fresh as when it was first recorded over half a century ago. Block's unique voice shines on a cappella pieces, such as "Sweet Sunny South" and "Be Ready When He Comes." The latter is a beautiful gospel tune which finds mother and son harmonizing and trading leads. As sonorous and sweet as some of the cuts are, others are hard-driving country blues. Block gets in a scorching cover of Son House's "Preaching Blues" and turns plaintive on "Tallahatchie Blues" and "Peavine Blues," then bitter for "Joliet Blues." This is Rory Block at her best. *—Rose of Sharon Witmer*

Turning Point / 1996 / Munich ♦♦
Recorded in 1989, this wasn't released in the United States until 1996. Block sounds like she's trying to capture the AOR market on most of this all-original set, in somewhat the same vein as Bonnie Raitt, but less effectively so. Glimpses of her acoustic and blues roots are no more than fleeting, as on "Leavin' Here" or the acoustic guitar instrumental, "Down the Hiway." It's not arresting enough to capture the pop audience, and Block fans who like her bluesy stuff the best might find the slick approach downright alienating. *—Richie Unterberger*

Tornado / Mar. 19, 1996 / Rounder ♦♦♦
After establishing her blues credentials with the traditional "Mississippi Bottom Blues," Rory Block turns to a set of original folk-rock songs on which she is joined by a band and such guests as David Lindley (who plays a guitar solo on "Pictures of You") and Mary-Chapin Carpenter (who sings harmony on "You Didn't Mind"). Block brings a blues simplicity and directness to her music and lyrics, which helps ease her transition from folk-blues interpreter to folk-rock singer/songwriter. *—William Ruhlmann*

Gone Woman Blues / 1997 / Rounder ♦♦♦♦♦
Subtitled "The Country Blues Collection," Rory Block sticks to what she may do better than any other contemporary player around. These cuts have all been heard scattered about on various other albums going back to *High Heeled Blues* from 1989; here they are pulled together into one comprehensive whole. She explores the wide variety of country blues, and even at 69-plus minutes this disc never gets repetitive. Except for five cuts, she is unaccompanied, and when she is, it only enhances what she does. Her youngest son, Jordan Block Valdina, helps out by doing the male vocal on a stunning a cappella version of "Be Ready When He Comes." The harmonica backing by Little Annie Raines (a frequent collaborator with Paul Rishell) just perfectly walks that line of being enhancing without intruding. If you like country blues, this is one you don't want to miss. *—Bob Gottlieb*

Confessions of a Blues Singer / Oct. 6, 1998 / Rounder ♦♦♦
Those who adore Block's work as a preservationist in reinterpreting classic Delta blues from the '20s and '30s will delight in this outing, another return to her solo acoustic roots. Block wanted to approach this album as an attempt to capture the spirit of the one-take recordings of the classic bluesmen, settling for rough mixes and not worrying about endings and other modern-day recording niceties. The result is an album that's the loosest of

her career and one that's squarely focused on her guitar and vocals. Breaking things up are guest appearances from Bonnie Raitt playing slide on "Rambling On My Mind" and her son Jordan Block Valdina on piano and vocals on "I Am In the Heavenly Way" and "Long Way From Home." Bringing a sense of full circle to the project are the two originals that Block chooses to close the album with. Both "Mother Marian" (a tribute to mentor Marian Van Ness) and the autobiographical "Life Song" feature a full band behind her poignant lyrics. Other highlights include takes on Charlie Patton's "Bo Weavil Blues," Furry Lewis' "Kassie Lee," Robert Johnson's "If I Had Possession Over Judgment Day" and Block's own "Silver Slide Moan." Far less overwrought than her usual offerings but still full of much inspired feeling, this is Block's most solid outing to date. *—Cub Koda*

I'm Every Woman / Jan. 2002 / Rounder ✦✦

After listening to the opening track of *I'm Every Woman*, one might be inclined to expect 45 minutes of acoustic blues to follow. "Guitar Ditty" features no more than a girl and her guitar with a great big sound. It's quite surprising, then, when Rory Block cuts loose on the title cut, a pastiche of slide guitar, disco beat, and funky '70s orchestra. Clearly, the listener isn't in the Delta anymore. Indeed, Block pretty much keeps her guitar in the corner of the studio for most of the album, trading her deep blues for a healthy dose of soul, a bit of gospel, and few other odds and ends. It's probably impossible to compare *I'm Every Woman* to *Confessions of a Blues Singer*, Block's 1998 recording. One features songs by Robert Johnson, Charlie Patton, and Blind Willie McTell; the other, by Al Green and Ashford-Simpson. One maintains a fairly straightforward production, centering on acoustic guitar and vocals; the other jumps from guitar ditties to a cappella gospel to full-tilt boogie. Kelly Joe Phelps lends his vocals and a nice bit of guitar to "Pretty Polly," while Annie Raines and Paul Rishell help out on a stirring vocal version of "Rock Island Line." Block also successfully tackles Bonnie Raitt/Toni Price territory with the vibrant "I Feel Like Breaking Up Somebody's Home." While there are several memorable moments on *I'm Every Woman*, the overall approach seems more scattershot than eclectic, and will confuse and perhaps anger Block's fans. *—Ronnie D. Lankford, Jr.*

Blodwyn Pig

f. 1968, England

Group / Blues-Rock, Prog-Rock/Art Rock

A quirky detour of late-'60s British progressive/blues rock, Blodwyn Pig was founded by former Jethro Tull guitarist Mick Abrahams, who left Tull after the *This Was* album. Abrahams was joined by bassist Andy Pyle, drummer Ron Berg, and Jack Lancaster, who gave the outfit their most distinctive colorings via his saxophone and flute. On their two albums, they explored a jazz/blues/progressive style somewhat in the mold of (unsurprisingly) Jethro Tull, but with a lighter feel. They also bore some similarities to John Mayall's jazzy late-'60s versions of the Bluesbreakers, or perhaps Colosseum, but with more eclectic material. Both of their LPs made the British Top Ten, though the players' instrumental skills were handicapped by thin vocals and erratic (though oft-imaginative) material. The group were effectively finished by Abrahams' departure after 1970's *Getting to This*. They briefly reunited in the mid-'70s, and Abrahams was part of a different lineup that re-formed in the late '80s; they have since issued a couple of albums in the '90s. *—Richie Unterberger*

● **Ahead Rings Out** / Aug. 1969 / BGO ✦✦✦✦

None of Jethro Tull's progressive rock tendencies or classical influences followed Mick Abrahams into his creation of Blodwyn Pig, even with the inclusion Jack Lancaster's sax- and flute-playing prowess. Instead, Abrahams built up a sturdy British blues-rock sound and used Lancaster's horn work to add some fire to the band's jazzy repertoire. *Ahead Rings Out* is a stellar concoction of gritty yet flamboyant blues-rock tunes and open-ended jazz centered around Mick Abrahams' cool-handed guitar playing, but it's the non-stop infusion of the other styles that makes the album such a solid listen. After only one album with Jethro Tull, Abrahams left to form this band, and it's evident that he had a lot of pent-up energy inside him when he recorded each of the album's tracks. With a barrage of electrifying rhythms and fleeting saxophone and woodwind excursions, cuts like "Sing Me a Song That I Know," "Up and Coming," and "Backwash" whip up highly energetic sprees of rock and blues. Most of the tracks have a hearty shot of rock up the middle, but in cuts like "The Change Song" and "Backwash," the explosive riffs are accompanied by a big band style of enthusiasm, adding even more depth to the material. Andy Pyle's bass playing is definitely distinct throughout each track and is used for anything but a steady background, while labeling Ron Berg's drumming as freewheeling and intemperate would be an understatement. It's apparent that Blodwyn Pig's style is indeed distinct, releasing a liberated and devil-may-care intensity while still managing to stay on track, but the fact that each cut convokes a different type of instrumental spiritedness is where the album really gains its reputation. Wonderfully busy and even a tad motley in some places, *Ahead Rings Out* shows off the power and vitality that can be channeled by combining a number of classic styles without sounding pretentious or overly inflated. A year later, Blodwyn Pig recorded *Getting to This* before Abrahams left the band, and although it's a solid effort, it falls just a smidgen short of *Ahead Rings Out*'s bluesy dynamism. *—Mike DeGagne*

Getting to This / Apr. 1970 / BGO ✦✦✦

The group explored similar avenues as they did on *Ahead Rings Out* on their follow-up. It took a more pile-driving approach than their first effort, but the material wasn't as strong. *—Richie Unterberger*

Lies / 1993 / Viceroy ✦✦✦✦✦

The reconstituted Blodwyn Pig, consisting of Mick Abrahams (lead vocals, guitars), Graham Walker (drums), Dave Lennox (keyboards, vocals), and Mike Summerland (bass, vocals), with Jackie Challoner (backing vocals) and Nick Payne (harmonica, saxes). This is more of a soul band than the original Blodwyn Pig, and thankfully they've left jazz and progressive rock behind on this album. Apart from the superb title track, there's a ton of R&B-styled material here, all played and sung hard but well, with a level of maturity that only adds to the depth of the performances. In addition to originals by Abrahams, there are covers of songs by Doc Pomus and Dr. John ("The Victim") and Alexis Korner ("I Wonder Who"), the latter one of a pair of live tracks reuniting Abrahams with his former bandmates Clive Bunker and Andy Pyle. *—Bruce Eder*

All Tore Down (Blodwyn Pig Live) / 1994 / Indigo ✦✦✦✦✦

It would be difficult to imagine a better live album coming from the likes of the Blodwyn Pig. The music is pure R&B, mid-'60s British style only more soulful than most of those bands ever got—Abrahams and company perform dazzling, passionate renditions of their best songs, including "Lies," a tribute to Alexis Korner ("I Wonder Who"), and even an extended (17 minutes, no less) version of "Cat's Squirrel," a song that Abrahams brought to Jethro Tull's *This Was* back in 1968. One of those rare cases—you might say a unique example—of a revamped, reformed sixties/seventies band outdoing its original incarnation on every count. *—Bruce Eder*

Modern Alchemist / May 5, 1997 / Indigo ✦✦✦

Michael Bloomfield

b. Jul. 28, 1943, Chicago, IL, **d.** Feb. 15, 1981, San Francisco, CA

Vocals, Keyboards, Guitar / Modern Electric Chicago Blues, Blues-Rock, Electric Chicago Blues, Jazz-Rock, Psychedelic

Michael Bloomfield was one of America's first great white blues guitarists, earning his reputation on the strength of his work in the Paul Butterfield Blues Band. His expressive, fluid solo lines and prodigious technique graced many other projects—most notably Bob Dylan's earliest electric forays—and he also pursued a solo career, with variable results. Uncomfortable with the reverential treatment afforded a guitar hero, Bloomfield tended to shy away from the spotlight after spending just a few years in it; he maintained a lower-visibility career during the '70s due to his distaste for fame and his worsening drug problems, which claimed his life in 1981.

Michael Bernard Bloomfield was born July 28, 1943, into a well-off Jewish family on Chicago's North Side. A shy, awkward loner as a child, he became interested in music through the Southern radio stations he was able to pick up at night, which gave him a regular source for rockabilly, R&B, and blues. He received his first guitar at his bar mitzvah and he and his friends began sneaking out (with the help of their families' maids) to hear electric blues on the South Side's fertile club scene. The young Bloomfield sometimes jumped on-stage to jam with the musicians and the novelty of such a spectacle soon made him a prominent scenester. Dismayed with the turn his education was taking, his parents sent him to a private boarding school on the East Coast in 1958 and he eventually graduated from a Chicago school for troubled youth. By this time, he'd embraced the beatnik subculture, frequenting hangout spots near the University of Chicago. He got a job managing a folk club and frequently booked veteran acoustic bluesmen; in the meantime, he was also playing guitar as a session man and around the Chicago club scene with several different bands.

In 1964, Bloomfield was discovered through his session work by the legendary John Hammond, who signed him to CBS; however, several recordings from 1964 went unreleased as the label wasn't sure how to market a white American blues guitarist. In early 1965, Bloomfield joined several associates in the Paul Butterfield Blues Band, a racially integrated outfit with a storming, rock-tinged take on Chicago's urban electric blues sound. The group's self-titled debut for Elektra, released later that year, made them a sensation in the blues community and helped introduce white audiences to a less watered-down version of the blues. Individually, Bloomfield's lead guitar work was acclaimed as a perfectly logical bridge between Chicago blues and contemporary rock. Later, in 1965, Bloomfield was recruited for Bob Dylan's new electrified backing band; he was a prominent presence on the groundbreaking classic *Highway 61 Revisited* and he was also part of Dylan's epochal plugged-in performance at the 1965 Newport Folk Festival. In the meantime, Bloomfield was developing an interest in Eastern music, particularly the Indian raga form, and his preoccupation exerted a major influence on the next Butterfield album, 1966's *East-West*. Driven by Bloomfield's jaw-dropping extended solos on his instrumental title cut, *East-West* merged blues, jazz, world music, and psychedelic rock in an unprecedented fashion. The Butterfield band became a favorite live act on the emerging San Francisco music scene and in 1967, Bloomfield quit the group to permanently relocate there and pursue new projects.

Bloomfield quickly formed a new band called the Electric Flag with longtime Chicago cohort Nick Gravenites on vocals. The Electric Flag was supposed to build on the innovations of *East-West* and accordingly featured an expanded lineup complete with a horn section, which allowed the group to add soul music to their laundry list of influences. The Electric Flag debuted at the 1967 Monterey Pop Festival and issued a proper debut album, *A Long Time Comin'*, in 1968. Critics complimented the group's distinctive, intriguing sound, but found the record itself somewhat uneven. Unfortunately, the band was already disintegrating; rivalries between members and shortsighted management—not to mention heroin abuse—all took their toll. Bloomfield himself left the band he'd formed before their album was even released. He next hooked up with organist Al Kooper, whom he'd played with in the Dylan band, and cut *Super Session*, a jam-oriented record that spotlighted his own guitar skills on one half and those of Stephen Stills on the other. Issued in 1968, it received excellent reviews and moreover became the best-selling album of Bloomfield's career. *Super Session*'s success led to a sequel, *The Live Adventures of Mike Bloomfield and Al Kooper*, which was recorded over three shows at the Fillmore West in 1968 and released the following year; it featured Bloomfield's on-record singing debut.

Bloomfield, however, was wary of his commercial success and growing disenchanted with fame. He was also tired of touring and after recording the second album with Kooper, he effectively retired for a while, at least from high-profile activities. He did, however, continue to work as a session guitarist and producer, and also began writing and playing on movie soundtracks (including some pornographic films by the Mitchell Brothers). He played locally and occasionally toured with Bloomfield and Friends, which included Nick Gravenites and ex-Butterfield mate Mark Naftalin. Additionally, he returned to the studio in 1973 for a session with John Hammond and New Orleans pianist Dr. John; the result, *Triumvirate*, was released on Columbia, but didn't make much of a splash. Neither did Bloomfield's 1974 reunion with Electric Flag and neither did KGB, a short-lived supergroup with Barry Goldberg, Rick Grech (Traffic), and Carmine Appice that recorded for MCA in 1976. During the late '70s, Bloomfield recorded for several smaller labels (including Takoma), usually in predominantly acoustic settings; through *Guitar Player* magazine, he also put out an instructional album with a vast array of blues guitar styles, titled *If You Love These Blues, Play 'Em as You Please*.

Unfortunately, Bloomfield was also plagued by alcoholism and heroin addiction for much of the '70s, which made him an unreliable concert presence and slowly cost him some of his longtime musical associations (as well as his marriage). By 1980, he had seemingly recovered enough to tour in Europe; that November, he also appeared on-stage in San Francisco with Bob Dylan for a rendition of "Like a Rolling Stone." However, on February 15, 1981, Bloomfield was found dead in his car of a drug overdose; he was only 37. *—Steve Huey*

Don't Say That I Ain't Your Man / 1964-1969 / Columbia/Legacy ✦✦✦✦✦
Fifteen tracks covering the pioneering blues-rock guitarist's '60s work, which was by far his best and most influential. Bloomfield worked with a bunch of bands during the decade, and the compilation flits rather hurriedly from his contributions to the Paul Butterfield Blues Band and Electric Flag to his collaborations with Al Kooper and some late-'60s solo tracks (none of his groundbreaking mid-'60s work with Dylan is here). Collectors will be interested in the first five songs, which date from previously unreleased sessions produced by John Hammond in late 1964 and early 1965. Featuring Charlie Musselwhite on harmonica, this pre-Butterfield Blues Band outfit plays convincingly, but the material is standard-issue, and Bloomfield's vocals are thin and weak (they didn't improve much over time). As befits Bloomfield's considerable but erratic talent, this is an interesting but erratic compilation; seek out the first two Paul Butterfield albums for a more cohesive showcase of his skills. *—Richie Unterberger*

● **Super Session** / 1968 / Columbia ✦✦✦✦✦
In the wake of groups like Cream, Blind Faith, and Crosby, Stills, Nash & Young, among many others, the era of the supergroup flowered well into the '70s. Although billed as *Super Session: Mike Bloomfield, Al Kooper, Steve Stills*, this rock classic was not initially conceived as the all-star lineup it ended up becoming. When Bloomfield was not physically prepared for the first sessions due to insomnia, Kooper, at the last minute, enlisted Steve Stills, who had just left Buffalo Springfield. Employing the talents of Barry Goldberg (who played with Bloomfield in the Electric Flag) on piano for two cuts, Harvey Brooks (another Bloomfield cohort from the Electric Flag) on bass, and Eddie Hoh, one of the key drummers for the Mamas & the Papas, the album Al Kooper ended up making was really two. Side one featured Bloomfield and Kooper, and was highlighted by "Albert's Shuffle" and a fine reworking of the Ragovoy-Shuman song "Stop." Side two was billed as Steve Stills and Al Kooper, and included the 11-minute watershed, late-'60s jam "Season of the Witch." Oddly enough, the inspiration came not from the original Donovan version but from the Brian Auger version, which featured vocals by Julie Driscoll. One of those albums that seems to get better with age and that gets the full reissue treatment every time a new audio format comes out, this is a super session indeed. *—Steve Matteo*

Live at Bill Graham's Fillmore West / 1969 / Columbia ✦✦✦✦✦
This session from early 1969 featured Nick Gravenites, Mark Naftalin, John Kahn, and Snooky Flowers (among others), with cameos from Taj Mahal and Jesse Ed Davis, but it's clear from the opening notes who the real star is. Over the years, Bloomfield's titanic solos on "Blues on a Westside" have dwarfed the rest of the album in my memory, but the truth is his playing just burns across every track. (More of Michael's great guitar work from these shows is on Nick Gravenites' *My Labors* on Columbia.) *—Cary Wolfson*

The Live Adventures of Mike Bloomfield and Al Kooper / 1969 / Columbia ✦✦
Recorded over three nights in 1968 at the Fillmore Auditorium in San Francisco, the follow-up to the acclaimed *Super Session* has its moments, but is mostly long on '60s noodly grooviness and lacking in focus and inspiration. It's notable (sort of) for Bloomfield's singing debut. *—Cary Wolfson*

It's Not Killing Me / 1969 / Columbia ✦✦
Let's see. For his first solo album, take a brilliant young guitarist who can barely sing and put the emphasis on... his vocals. Well, somebody thought it was a good idea. Too bad they were wrong. There are just a few examples of that B.B. King-inflected guitar style among the rock and country-flavored throwaways. *—Cary Wolfson*

Triumvirate / 1973 / Columbia ✦✦✦
In 1973 someone at Columbia evidently decided to try and recoup some of the investment the label had made in Bloomfield and John Hammond—they were thrown into a recording studio along with Dr. John, who had recently scored a hit with "Right Place, Wrong Time." It probably sounded like a good idea at the time, but the results were uninspired. Pass by this CD and pick up any one of their solo recordings instead. *—Jan Mark Wolkin*

Try It Before You Buy It / 1975 / One Way ✦✦
Try It Before You Buy It is one of Michael Bloomfield's neglected albums, and there's a reason why—although there's some very fine playing scattered throughout the album, the performances are uneven and unfocused. Furthermore, the album leans too close to a straight rock & roll direction for blues purists. If you dig hard, there are some rewards on *Try It Before You Buy It*, but on the whole, it's one that should be left on the shelf. *—Thom Owens*

The Root of Blues / 1976 / LaserLight ✦✦✦
A budget-label reissue of the instructional blues LP released by *Guitar Player* magazine in 1976, this CD includes most of the songs but omits Michael's spoken passages about each track. Bloomfield pays tribute to his influences and favorites: acoustic and electric, solo and with a band. Standout tracks include "Death in My Family," played in the style of Guitar Slim, "WDIA," a tribute to B.B. King, "City Girl," dedicated to T-Bone Walker, and an acoustic version of "Kansas City," played, in Bloomfield's words, "in a style I would call 'Travis Picking', after Merle Travis. It seems an anomaly to use a modern style for such an old song, but the method of syncopated contrapuntal fingerpicking is well suited to the song because the key of E has so many open strings." *—Jan Mark Wolkin*

Analine / 1977 / Takoma ✦✦✦✦
On this album, Michael Bloomfield continued the country blues and folk explorations of his Grammy-nominated instructional outing, *If You Love These Blues Play 'Em As You Please* (1976). For *Analine*, he worked in an acoustic, often single-handed mode, being the only musician on seven of its nine tracks (and writing just over half the material, too). Such one-man efforts often carry an air of sterility about them, but not here; Bloomfield's version of Duke Ellington's "Mood Indigo" retains the jaunty swing feel associated with its composer. The solo guitar pieces are equally well executed, particularly "Effinonna Rag" and the tribute to "Mr. Johnson and Mr. Dunn," where Bloomfield plays dueling guitar parts in the blues pioneers' style. Along the way, Bloomfield taps into folk ("Frankie and Johnny"), gospel ("At the Cross"), and even Hawaiian idioms ("Hilo Waltz"). He also sings two stirring originals about cancer ("Big 'C' Blues") and a hapless voyeur (the hilarious "Peepin' an' a Moanin' Blues"). Former Electric Flag singer and cohort Nick Gravenites contributes and sings the title track, whose mandolin and accordion runs close the album on an epic note. This is a well-executed labor of love that shows Bloomfield in a different context than many listeners will associate with him. *—Ralph Heibutzki*

I'm With You Always / 1977 / Demon ✦✦✦
This release, recorded at McCabe's Guitar Shop in Santa Monica, CA, in 1977, captures a superb live show, with Bloomfield in top form as he performs before an appreciative audience in an intimate setting. Michael's singing is spirited and his guitar playing is precise and inventive as he plays favorite songs from his repertoire. Highlights include solo acoustic performances of two songs written by Shelton Brooks in the early 1900s, a piano/guitar duet demonstrating the rapport he had with pianist Mark Naftalin, and hot performances by Bloomfield, Naftalin and a rhythm section of Buddy Helm on drums and Buell Neidlinger on bass. Bloomfield shows what he had been doing all those years out of the spotlight—refining his technique and researching the music he loved. *—Jan Mark Wolkin*

Count Talent & the Originals / 1978 / Clouds ✦✦✦
This album is a mixed bag, though not without its share of agreeably sleazy charms. The title refers to Bloomfield and the "usual suspects" who often played with him, including keyboardist Mark Naftalin, bassist David Shorey, drummer-vocalist Bob Jones, bassist-singer Roger "Jellyroll" Troy, and singer Nick Gravenites, among others. They're all here, with plenty of raunchy horns and keyboards for company. Gravenites' vehicle, "Bad Man"—a somber recounting of the street life's ups and downs—provides one of the undisputed highlights, as well as "You Was Wrong," a mournful lament where Bloomfield lays down some truly stinging guitar. Bloomfield's slide guitar prowess also shines on "Peach Tree Man," sung in his characteristic warble about a '30s-era hermaphrodite blues guitarist. How's that for an unlikely topic? Jones' vocal cameos open and close the proceedings with the agreeable R&B swagger of "Love Walk" and "Let the People Dance," which are lesser songs, but well performed. The same goes for "Sammy Knows How to Party," which won't win any lyrical prizes, and there's little reason for an instrumental remake of Leo Sayer's soft pop ballad "When I Need You." This album makes enjoyable listening, but will likely please Bloomfield completists most. Non-initiates should seek out his more definitive solo work, such as *Between the Hard Place and the Ground*. *—Ralph Heibutzki*

Michael Bloomfield / 1978 / Takoma ✦✦✦✦
This self-titled effort found Bloomfield reaching back to his nightclub roots, following forays into acoustic music (*Analine*), sleazy R&B-derived rock (*Count Talent & the Originals*), and instructional albums (*If You Love These Blues Play 'Em as You Please*). Six of the eight tracks here are blues standards that Bloomfield tailored to his aggressive and in-your-face guitar style. The sound mirrors *Count Talent*'s barroom lurch, only with a smaller cast. This time, the bedrock is drummer-vocalist Bob Jones and bassist "Gashouse Dave" Shorey, with Bloomfield shouldering the multi-instrumental load. Bloomfield adds some deft touches, such as lead acoustic guitar and six-string banjo on "Knockin' Myself Out," a darkly humorous look at self-destruction. "Sloppy Drunk" sketches the alcoholic's life from a lighter standpoint, while "Women Loving Each Other" is a frank examination of lesbianism, from the jilted man's side. (Pianist Ira Kamin and bassist Doug Kilmer make crucial contributions on the latter two songs.) Bloomfield and friends also nod to their roots on a haunting rendition of "See That My Grave Is Kept Clean," which glows from his accordion, piano, and acoustic slide guitar. The funky "My Children, My Children" gives matters a more contemporary sheen, as does "The Gospel Truth," an instrumental by producer Norman Dayron where Bloomfield's guitar gets plenty of flying time. Having long abandoned the major-label rat race, independent labels became Bloomfield's major professional outlet, ensuring that his work remained relatively low profile (like the man himself). This album is among his most consistent efforts; needless to say, it's also extremely scarce, so snatch it up before another knowledgeable person gets there first. *—Ralph Heibutzki*

Between a Hard Place and the Ground / 1979 / Takoma ✦✦✦✦
Bloomfield and friends have always been able to get it together on record, and this effort is one more example of seasoned pros putting out music which appears to magically flow from them. "Big Chief from New Orleans" and "Lights Out" show Bloomfield in a lighter frame of mind. Of course, by this time, the public was generally ignoring his output,

which is a shame, because *Between a Hard Place and the Ground* is well worth seeking out to experience Mike Bloomfield in the later stages of his career. *—James Chrispell*

Living in the Fast Lane / 1980 / ERA ♦♦♦
Michael Bloomfield was a pioneer in blues-rock, one of the performers who found a way to maintain his own sound while paying tribute to the blues greats that created the music he idolized. The 10 tracks presented on *Living in the Fast Lane* weren't as vital as his earlier material, but were done with the same intensity and passion that marked all his numbers. They were backed on several cuts by Duke Tito and the Marin Country Playboys, while on "When I Get Home," the Singers of The Church of God in Christ joined lead vocalist Roger Troy for a rousing, spirit-filled performance that was the album's high point. *—Ron Wynn*

Bloomfield/Harris / 1980 / Kicking Mule ♦♦♦♦
Michael Bloomfield's love of gospel music is well-known; it anchored his solo acoustic sets, and also inspired these duets with classical guitarist Woody Harris (who accompanied him on his last European tour, in the summer of 1980). A more intimate recording situation could not have been devised, with Harris anchoring the chords on his acoustic guitar while Bloomfield solos on acoustic or electric slide guitar. The exception is "Great Dreams From Heaven," which was Harris' song choice and on which he solos, according to Norman Dayron's back-cover liner notes. The notes serve as interesting reminders of Bloomfield's ever-inquisitive musicological bent. For example, "I'll Overcome" is cited as a song from Bloomfield's earliest playing days in Chicago, not the version associated with America's civil rights movement. This record carries the power of two topflight guitarists in relaxed form, with only their favorite songs for company. Bloomfield, at times, coaxes some otherworldly, ethereal sounds from his guitar. When he does, the results are truly stunning, such as on the closing treatment of "Peace in the Valley," or "Gonna Need Somebody on My Bond." Such intimate acquaintance with American idioms paid great dividends. This album is another example of Bloomfield's ability to assimilate other styles and make them his own; it is well worth the trouble to find. *—Ralph Heibutzki*

Best of Michael Bloomfield / 1987 / Takoma ♦♦♦♦
While the title's accuracy is debatable, this CD contains ten fine tracks drawn from three albums produced by Norman Dayron for Takoma between 1978 and 1980. Arrangements are spare (with one horn-powered exception) and Bloomfield's vocals are greatly improved over his early attempts. Running-time, as on all the Takoma releases, is short at 43:30. *—Cary Wolfson*

Blues Gospel & Ragtime Guitar Instrumentals / Nov. 19, 1993 / Shanachie ♦♦
Another uneven set of Norman Dayron leftovers, this one shows the guitar hero in exile, running through a set of tunes pulled from both electric and acoustic sessions. Michael "Bloomers" Bloomfield plays slide on "When I Need You," "Just a Closer Walk With Thee," and "At the Cross," opting for his better-known single-string work on "Memphis Radio Blues" and "Blues for Norman." While this is certainly not the place to start a Bloomfield collection by any stretch, it's worth checking out after you've assembled the essentials of the man's work. *—Cub Koda*

Live at the Old Waldorf / 1998 / Columbia/Legacy ♦♦♦♦
If you've never really experienced Mike Bloomfield just letting loose and playing ripping and inspired guitar, this is a darn good starting point. Recorded live in 1976 and 1977 by producer Norman Dayron at the Old Waldorf nightclub on Bloomfield's home turf in San Francisco with a hand-picked band, the results are startling to say the least. Bloomfield plays with assurance and authority throughout, exploring new ideas with each new chorus from his guitar, arguably at his best since his early Butterfield/Dylan days. He plays a lot of slide guitar here, too, and tracks like "Bad Luck Baby," "The Sky Is Crying," "Dancin' Fool," and "Buried Alive In the Blues" showcase his mighty talents with the bottleneck, taking the lessons learned first hand from Robert Nighthawk to places new and wild. Bloomfield was never much of a singer, and everybody from old pal Nick Gravenites to bassist Roger Troy to drummer Bob Jones end up handling all the vocals on this disc. But one listen to the "Blues Medley" that kicks off the proceedings is reason enough to know why Bloomfield's reputation on his chosen instrument ranks up there with the greats. Consider this disc validation of that rep. *—Cub Koda*

I'm Cutting Out / Sep. 4, 2001 / Sundazed ♦♦♦
In late 1964 and early 1965, around or just prior to the time he joined the Paul Butterfield Blues Band, Mike Bloomfield cut some unreleased solo sides for Columbia. Mostly produced by John Hammond, these featured backing by an electric band that included Charlie Musselwhite on harmonica. Five of those songs came out on the 1994 Bloomfield CD compilation *Don't Say That I Ain't Your Man!*. This LP has all five of those tracks, plus five additional ones that didn't make it onto the 1994 CD. For that reason alone, this is essential for Bloomfield fans, even if you already have that previous disc. At this point, Bloomfield was rawer and less imaginative than the guitarist he would develop into with Butterfield and as a Bob Dylan accompanist, and he was never much of a singer. Nonetheless, there's a good brash early blues-rock energy to these sides, which mix straightforward covers of Chicago blues giants like Little Walter and Muddy Waters with a few Bloomfield originals. The good news is that the previously unissued cuts (including alternate versions of "I Got My Mojo Working" and "I Feel So Good") are not disreputable leftovers, but up to the same level of the ones that showed up on *Don't Say That I Ain't Your Man!*. Certainly one of the new finds, "I'm Cutting Out," is the best of the three Bloomfield originals on the collection, as a nice, bouncy no-nonsense blues tune with a superb stinging guitar solo and a raunchier vocal than was Bloomfield's wont. The alternate version of "I Got My Mojo Working" is less frenetic than the one on *Don't Say That I Ain't Your Man!*, and for that reason a bit better. Liner notes with an appreciation by Al Kooper and a 1966 Bloomfield interview add to the desirability of this vinyl-only release. *—Richie Unterberger*

Little Joe Blue (Joseph Valery, Jr.)

b. Sep. 23, 1934, Vicksburg, MS, **d.** Apr. 22, 1990, Reno, NV
Vocals, Guitar / West Coast Blues, Modern Electric Blues, Soul-Blues
Little Joe Blue, born Joseph Valery, Jr., was a relatively late starter as a blues artist. Born in Mississippi in 1934, his musical sensibilities were heavily influenced by the work of Louis Jordan, Joe Liggins, and B.B. King, which he encountered from his teens into his twenties. He didn't turn to music as a profession until the late '50s, when he was well into his twenties, forming his band the Midnighters in Detroit at the end of the decade. By the early '60s, Valery had moved to Reno, Nevada, where he began recording as an adjunct to his performances in local clubs, before moving on to Los Angeles. He recorded for various labels, including Kent and Chess' Checker Records division during the early to mid-'60s, and never entirely escaped the criticism that he was a B.B. King imitator, which dogged him right into the '80s. The style that King popularized also happened to suit Valery, however, and he gained some credibility in 1966 when he racked up a modest hit in 1966 with the song "Dirty Work Is Going On," which has since become a blues standard. He had extended stints with Jewel Records and Chess from the late '60s into the early '70s, and recorded until the end of the '80s. Valery performed throughout the south, and later Texas and California, during that decade, and later toured Europe, including performances as part of the International Jazz Fest during the '80s. There is current one CD of his work in print, the Evejim disc *Little Joe Blue's Greatest Hits*, a reissue of two LPs, *I'm Doing Alright* and *Dirty Work Going On*, that he cut in the '80s. His "Standing on the Threshold," featuring a powerful vocal performance and some beautifully soaring horns behind some lean, mean guitar and piano, also appears on *Jewel Spotlights the Blues, Vol. 1*. *—Bruce Eder*

• **The Very Best of Little Joe Blue** / Aug. 27, 1996 / Collectables ♦♦♦♦

The Blues Band

f. 1979, England
Group / Modern Electric Blues
England's the Blues Band is led by guitarist/singer Dave Kelly, who, before forming the group in 1979, had been a member of the John Dummer Blues Band and issued several solo recordings on his own (Kelly had also received praise for his playing by such blues legends as Howlin' Wolf and John Lee Hooker). After hooking up with friend/bassist Gary Fletcher, the seeds for the Blues Band were sown, resulting in countless albums (including such titles as 1980's *Official Bootleg Album* and *Ready*, 1981's *Itchy Feet*, 1982's *Brand Loyalty*, 1983's *Bye Bye Blues*, 1986's *These Kind of Blues*, 1989's *Back for More*, 1991's *Fat City*, 1993's *Homage*, and 1995's *Wire Less*, among others). In addition, Kelly formed the Dave Kelly Band in the mid-'80s (issuing four albums), penned music for commercials and such projects as BBC TV's *King of the Ghetto* and *The Comic Strip Presents Strike!*, was voted Best Acoustic Artist by BBC polls throughout the '90s, and is an honorary patron of the London Guitar College with Hank Marvin. *—Greg Prato*

• **The Best of the Blues Band** / Aug. 24, 1999 / Varese Sarabande ♦♦♦♦
Varese's *The Best of the Blues Band* collects 16 highlights from the Blues Band, the group vocalist Paul Jones formed with Dave Kelly after leaving Manfred Mann. This music is pretty much straight-ahead British blues, but since it was recorded after the peak of British blues, it's a little slicker and more commercial, and it also boasts some hints of album rock. As such, it's primarily of interest to either British blues fetishists or Manfred Mann collectors. *—Stephen Thomas Erlewine*

• **The Official Bootleg Album/Ready** / 2001 / BGO ♦♦♦♦♦
The Blues Band is a virtual who's who of the British blues scene. An '80s supergroup of sorts, the band consists of Paul Jones, solo artist and former member of Manfred Mann (lead vocals and harmonica); Dave Kelly, solo artist and former member of the John Dummer Blues Band (lead vocals and slide guitar); Tom McGuinness, former member of Manfred Mann and McGuinness Flint (lead guitar and backup vocals); Hughie Flint, also former McGuinness Flint (drums); and Gary Fletcher, formerly of Sam Apple Pie (bass and backup vocals). Although formed in 1979, the band released its debut album, *The Bootleg Album*, in 1980 as supposedly a one-time live project. The album was originally a private pressing, recorded live and released by the band themselves, but it sold so well it was re-released intact by Arista after signing the band to a contract. The Blues Band became so popular that they got together as a permanent unit and recorded another album in 1980 called *Ready*. This release is a part of BGO's reissue program of the Blues Band's original albums in the *2 on 1* CD series. This two-CD set has been remastered from original master tapes and features the original artwork of both albums and additional sleeve notes written by noted British rock writer John Tobler and bandmember Tom McGuinness detailing the history of the band and the albums. The track listing for "Ready" also contains two bonus tracks recorded live by the band. A superb package and a must for any fan of British blues music. *—Keith Pettipas*

Itchy Feet/Brand Loyalty / Mar. 20, 2001 / BGO ♦♦♦
The Blues Band's third and fourth albums, *Itchy Feet* and *Brand Loyalty*, were originally released in 1981 and 1982, respectively. The lineup on each album is the same as on the first two with the exception that Rob Townsend of the band Family replaced Hughie Flint on drums. *Itchy Feet* was in the U.K. Top 60 album chart for three weeks and was the band's third album to chart within an 18-month period. This release is a part of BGO's continuing reissue program of the Blues Band's original albums in the two on one CD series. This two-CD set has been remastered from original master tapes and features the original artwork of both albums and additional sleeve notes written by noted British rock writer John Tobler and bandmember Tom McGuinness detailing the history of the band and the albums. Both albums contain two bonus tracks taken from rare singles EPs and live tracks that were released around the same time as the original albums. Another superb package and a must for any fan of British blues music. In 2001, the band's profile is still high in England, with them working very hard gig-wise, and with Paul Jones having a weekly blues program on one of Britain's most popular radio stations, BBC Radio 2. *—Keith Pettipas*

Greenstuff: Live at the BBC 1982 / 2002 / Hux ♦♦♦
All but one of the 15 songs were recorded in concert for the BBC on December 8, 1982 (the one remaining track, a cover of Bob Dylan's "Maggie's Farm," was recorded on March 23, 1981 for a separate BBC broadcast). The Blues Band were, in limited respects, a big deal in Britain in this era: a blues-rock group with integrity and pedigree that had a reputation as an excellent live act. On this record, it must be said, they come across more like an above-average blues-rock bar band, one that happens to feature a singer (Paul Jones) who's much, much better than the typical bloke you'll see fronting a bunch of geezers doing Chess covers at the local pub. Did it make for a good night out? Maybe. Does it make for enlightening listening? No, to be harsh. Even if they know their chops and are enjoying what they're doing, the repertoire is stuffed with unimaginative covers of chestnuts by Muddy Waters, Willie Dixon, Little Walter, and the like, as well as some originals quite derivative of same. It's stating the obvious, perhaps, but Jones (and fellow ex-Manfred Manner Tom McGuinness) are not exactly stretching their creative capacities here; even their blues covers in Manfred Mann were much more exciting. And there's no excuse for Dave Kelly taking the occasional lead vocal, so inferior is he to Jones. There are some bright spots here and there—the Jones original "I Can't Hold on Much Longer" is a decent tough blues-soul ballad, and the cover of Roy Head's "Treat Her Right" pretty heated for an overplayed standard. Overall, though, it's only fair treadmill blues-rock (accent on the blues) that makes those of us who weren't in the appreciative crowds wonder what all the fuss was about. *—Richie Unterberger*

Blues Boy Willie (Willie McFalls)

b. Nov. 28, 1946, Memphis, TX
Vocals, Harmonica / Contemporary Blues, Modern Electric Blues, Soul-Blues
Willie McFalls, a native Memphian from Texas, not Tennessee, took the chitlin circuit by surprise in 1990 when the comical blues dialog of "Be-Who?" put his second album on the *Billboard* charts and his act on the road. Blues Boy Willie came to Ichiban Records courtesy of his boyhood friend from Texas, bluesman-producer Gary B. B. Coleman. Willie's three albums to date all bear the typical Coleman touch—competent but predictable blues tracks with a small studio band. It has been the spunky spoken repartee between Willie and his wife Miss Lee on the novelty numbers that has earned Willie an unexpected niche on the Southern soul-blues scene. *—Jim O'Neal*

Strange Things Happening / 1989 / Ichiban ♦♦♦♦
Blues Boy Willie's debut album, *Strange Things Happening*, is an excellent collection of classic Southern soul and electric blues, given a modern edge. While the production may be a little too slick for fans of classic '60s grit, there's no doubting that Willie's heart is in the right place, and he keeps things engaging even when the material gets a little predictable. *—Thom Owens*

Be Who? 2 / 1990 / Ichiban ♦♦♦

I Got the Blues / 1992 / Ichiban ♦♦♦

Don't Look Down / 1993 / Ichiban ♦♦

Juke Joint Blues / 1995 / Ichiban ♦♦♦♦

● **American Roots: Blues** / Mar. 12, 2002 / Ichiban ♦♦♦♦

The Blues Project

f. 1965, New York, NY, **db.** 1973, New York, NY
Group / Folk-Rock, Blues-Rock, Modern Electric Blues
One of the first album-oriented, "underground" groups in the United States, the Blues Project offered an electric brew of rock, blues, folk, pop, and even some jazz, classical, and psychedelia during their brief heyday in the mid-'60s. It's not quite accurate to categorize them as a blues-rock group, although they did plenty of that kind of material; they were more like a Jewish-American equivalent to British bands like the Yardbirds, who used a blues and R&B base to explore any music that interested them. Erratic songwriting talent and a lack of a truly outstanding vocalist prevented them from rising to the front line of '60s bands, but they recorded plenty of interesting material over the course of their first three albums, before the departure of their most creative members took its toll.

The Blues Project was formed in Greenwich Village in the mid-'60s by guitarist Danny Kalb (who had played sessions for various Elektra folk and folk-rock albums), Steve Katz (a guitarist with Elektra's Even Dozen Jug Band), flutist/bassist Andy Kulberg, drummer Roy Blumenfeld, and singer Tommy Flanders. Al Kooper, in his early twenties a seasoned vet of rock sessions, joined after sitting in on the band's Columbia Records audition, although they ended up signing to Verve, an MGM subsidiary. Early member Artie Traum (guitar) dropped out during early rehearsals; Flanders would leave after their first LP, *Live at the Cafe Au-Go-Go* (1966).

The eclectic resumés of the musicians, who came from folk, jazz, blues, and rock backgrounds, were reflected in their choice of material. Blues by Muddy Waters and Chuck Berry tunes ran alongside covers of contemporary folk-rock songs by Eric Anderson and Patrick Sky, as well as the group's own originals. These were usually penned by Kooper, who had already built songwriting credentials as the co-writer of Gary Lewis' huge smash "This Diamond Ring," and established a reputation as a major folk-rock shaker with his contributions to Dylan's mid-'60s records. Kooper also provided the band's instrumental highlights with his glowing organ riffs.

The live debut sounds rather tame and derivative; the group truly hit their stride on *Projections* (late 1966), which was, disappointingly, their only full-length studio recording. While they went through straight blues numbers with respectable energy, they really shone best on the folk and jazz-influenced tracks, like "Fly Away," Katz's lilting "Steve's Song," Kooper's jazz instrumental "Flute Thing" (an underground radio standard that's probably their most famous track), and Kooper's fierce adaptation of an old Blind Willie Johnson number, "I Can't Keep from Crying." A non-LP single from this era, the pop-psychedelic "No Time Like the Right Time," was their greatest achievement and one of the best "great hit singles that never were" of the decade.

The band's very eclecticism didn't augur well for their long-term stability, and in 1967 Kooper left in a dispute over musical direction (he has recalled that Kalb opposed his wishes to add a horn section). Then Kalb mysteriously disappeared for months after a bad acid trip, which effectively finished the original incarnation of the band. A third album, *Live at Town Hall*, was a particularly half-assed project given the band's stature, pasted together from live tapes and studio outtakes, some of which were overdubbed with applause to give the impression that they had been recorded in concert.

Kooper got to fulfill his ambitions for soulful horn rock as the leader of the original Blood, Sweat & Tears, although he left that band after their first album; BS&T also included Katz (who stayed onboard for a long time). Blumenfeld and Kulberg kept the Blues Project going for a fourth album before forming Seatrain, and the group re-formed in the early '70s with various lineups, Kooper rejoining for a live 1973 album, *Reunion in Central Park*. The first three albums from the Kooper days are the only ones that count, though; the best material from these is on Rhino's best-of compilation. *—Richie Unterberger*

Live at the Cafe Au-Go-Go / May 1966 / Verve/Forecast ♦♦♦
Although Tommy Flanders (who'd already left the band by the time this debut hit the streets) is credited as sole vocalist, four of the then-sextet's members sang; in fact, Danny Kalb handles as many leads as Flanders (four each), Steve Katz takes center stage on Donovan's "Catch the Wind," and Al Kooper is featured on "I Want to Be Your Driver." The band could be lowdown when appropriate (Kalb's reading of "Jelly, Jelly"), high energy (Muddy Waters' "Goin' Down Louisiana" sounds closer to Chuck Berry or Bo Diddley), and unabashedly eclectic (tossing in Donovan or Eric Andersen with no apologies). Kalb's moody take on "Alberta" is transcendent, and the uptempo arrangement of "Spoonful" is surprisingly effective. *—Dan Forte*

Projections / Nov. 1966 / Verve/Forecast ♦♦♦♦♦
Produced by Tom Wilson (Dylan, Zappa), the Blues Project's second effort was their finest hour. In less than a year the enthusiastic live band had matured into a seasoned studio ensemble. Steve Katz's features are lightweight folk but Al Kooper reworks two gospel themes ("Wake Me, Shake Me," "I Can't Keep from Crying") into ambitious blues-rock compositions, and Danny Kalb proves he's no mere folkie on extended versions of "Two Trains Running" and "Caress Me Baby." Bassist Andy Kulberg switches to flute and Kalb gets psychedelic on the jazzy "Flute Thing," penned by Kooper. *—Dan Forte*

The Best of the Blues Project / 1966-1967 / Rhino ♦♦♦♦♦
With the exception of a live version of "Flute Thing" from the Blues Project's 1973 reunion concert included only on the CD version, this compilation is culled entirely from the albums *Live at the Cafe Au-Go-Go*, *Projections*, and *The Blues Project Live at Town Hall*, all recorded and released in the period 1966-1967. Just as those individual albums do, it confirms the acclaim accorded the Blues Project at the time. The group's sophistication and ability to create a hybrid of musical styles keeps the music from sounding dated. In fact, this music not only stands as among the best of its time, but it continues to appeal where much of the music made simultaneously fails to escape its era. (Not to be confused with *Best of the Blues Project*, Verve Forecast FTS 3077 [1969 07], which is an earlier compilation with a different selection of songs.) *—William Ruhlmann*

The Blues Project Live at Town Hall / Sep. 1967 / One Way ♦♦♦
Released just after Al Kooper left the band, one imagines that neither he nor the other members of the group were pleased with this LP. According to Kooper, it was a pastiche of studio outtakes and a few live performances, and only one of the songs was actually recorded at New York City's Town Hall. Anyway, this has a meandering, ten-minute "Flute Thing" and decent live versions of "Wake Me, Shake Me" and "I Can't Keep from Crying" which, despite a somewhat rawer feel, are not necessary supplements to the fine studio takes. "Where There's Smoke, There's Fire" and the great "No Time Like the Right Time" had already been released as singles; to hear them without canned applause, you only need to turn to Rhino's first-rate *Best of the Blues Project* instead. That compilation also contains the other cut of note on this album, an outtake-sounding cover of Patrick Sky's "Love Will Endure." *—Richie Unterberger*

Planned Obsolescence / Dec. 1968 / One Way ♦♦♦

Lazarus / 1971 / Capitol ♦♦♦

The Blues Project / 1972 / Capitol ♦♦♦

Original Blues Project Reunion in Central Park / 1973 / One Way ♦♦♦
Considering that the original lineup had broken up six years earlier, this ranks as one of the most artistically successful reunions in blues or rock. If there were any ego problems, they don't show; typically Kalb and Kooper shine, but all five are playing as a team. Most important, the members seem to respect their own past—and re-create it with spontaneity and energy. *—Dan Forte*

Projections from the Past / 1989 / Hablabel ♦♦♦
A double album of dubious legality, but fairly easy availability. This captures the Blues Project's best lineup—Kooper, Katz, Kalb, Kulberg, and Blumenfeld—live at the Matrix club in San Francisco on September 1, 1966. If there's any revelation to be had from these fair-quality tapes, it's that there's not much of a revelation at all. The group performs a lot of the stronger material from their first and second albums in versions very close to the records. They shine brightest on the more adventurous material with jazz and folk tangents, like "Steve's Song," "Flute Thing," "Catch the Wind," and "Cheryl's Going Home." Most of the rest is competent but not especially brilliant white-boy blues renditions of numbers like "Hoochie Coochie Man," "You Can't Catch Me," and "You Can't Judge a Book By the Cover"; the swaggering "Shake That Baby" is about the best of these. Essential only for serious collectors. Be warned that there are a few (not many) clumsy edits, and that the entire fourth side is simply tracks lifted from their *Live at Town Hall* LP. *—Richie Unterberger*

● **Anthology** / Jan. 28, 1997 / Polydor/Chronicles ✦✦✦✦✦

The most complete Blues Project collection ever assembled, the two-disc *Anthology* compiles 36 tracks taken from their three albums on Verve and their two records on Capitol as well as rare singles, previously unreleased songs and alternate versions, and material from solo projects. —*Jason Ankeny*

The Blues Train

Group / Blues-Rock

Closely related to fellow Canadian band and labelmates, the Crazy People, the Blues Train may very well have arisen from the same stable of studio musicians and songwriters for the exploit rock label Condor that gave life to that band. Who exactly the musicians were that made up the Blues Train, however, remains an unknown, since all the performances were uncredited and the little history that is known about the band mimics the story of the Crazy People almost exactly. Formed in the late '60s, the band was part of the outstanding psychedelic ballroom scene that emerged at the time in Vancouver. They were bluesier than most other bands on the circuit, but just as interesting. As with the Crazy People, several rumors surround the band, adding to their mystery. The most plausible theory, however, holds that obscure but prodigious itinerant songwriter Johnny Kitchen was a member. He was certainly involved in some capacity, owing to his songwriting credit on their eponymous 1970 album. He also had a hand in two other Condor releases, including the Crazy People's *Bedlam*, before heading to the U.S. and becoming involved in a plethora of underground psychedelic releases on tiny and private labels. Still, although his song copyrights through BMI number over 200, virtually nothing is known about Kitchen. Prominent Vancouver personality and local television weatherman Jack Millman, who was also involved in several of the other rock-oriented efforts on the label, produced the album. And despite the loose threads, *The Blues Train* is one of the most musically intriguing works to emerge from Canada during the era. —*Stanton Swihart*

● **The Blues Train** / Nov. 14, 2000 / Gear Fab ✦✦✦✦

If most people's appreciation of Canadian rock during the late '60s and early '70s begins and ends with the Guess Who, they are missing out on a host of great lesser-known bands. One of the most intriguing of those bands is the Blues Train, a sensational psychedelic blues combo that, like the Crazy People, put out an album on the Vancouver exploit label Condor. That immediately brings into question who exactly played on the album, since one theory holds that the same studio house band was responsible for all the label's product. Regardless of band makeup, though, *The Blues Train* is valuable on its own considerable merits. It houses some truly excellent music, and if it is not a proper band, it certainly comes across as the work of a legitimate unit—and a pretty outstanding one at that. As the band moniker implies and in keeping with perhaps the primary influence on the rock & roll scene of the era, there is a heavy identification with blues, including covers of Willie Dixon's "Hootchie Kootchie Man" and the traditional "Mojo" alongside convincing, likeminded originals like "Ride the Train" and "Busted in Chicago." There is some scorching guitar throughout, and a bass drum pulse that frequently mimics the chug of a train, an enduring symbol that holds romantic sway over the music (as the band itself articulates in the original liner notes). Joe Sanchez is (presumably) the main songwriter in the band, having contributed four of the 11 songs, and he turns out a few sensational tunes in "Missin' You," "A&R Man," and "Coast to Coast." The former song, with its chugging, jostling roadhouse groove and Tin Pan Alley piano, is Harry Nilsson on a prescription of the blues, while "Coast to Coast" is flawless honky-tonk blues with a dollop of sarcastic whimsy, again reimagining Nilsson as a grizzled old bluesman. If the Blues Train sounds like a bar-band version of the Grass Roots on occasion (which isn't even a bad thing, come to think of it) or overly emotes at others to pound home its love of the blues, the group never sounds like a pale imitation of the real thing. *The Blues Train* is a surprising delight—scraggly, robust, and catchy with a wonderful sense of its place and purpose. It is perhaps even one of the strongest still unknown (and likely to remain so) blues-rock albums of the era. —*Stanton Swihart*

Blues Traveler

f. 1988

Group / Jam Bands, American Trad Rock, Pop/Rock, Blues-Rock

A New York-based blues-rock quartet formed in 1988 by singer/harmonica player John Popper, guitarist Chan Kinchla, bassist Bobby Sheehan, and drummer Brendan Hill, Blues Traveler was part of a revival of the extended jamming style of '60s and '70s groups like the Grateful Dead and Led Zeppelin. Signed to A&M, they released their first album, *Blues Traveler*, in May 1990 and followed it with *Travelers & Thieves* in September 1991. Popper was in a serious car accident in 1992, leaving him unable to perform for a number of months. Fortunately, he recovered, yet he still had to perform in a wheelchair for a period of time. In April 1993, Blues Traveler released its third album, *Save His Soul*, which became its first to make the Top 100. Blues Traveler's aptly named fourth album, *Four*, released in September 1994, at first looked like a sales disappointment, but it rebounded in 1995 when "Run-Around," a single taken from it, became the group's first chart hit. "Run-Around" became one of the biggest singles of 1995, spending nearly a full year on the charts and sending *Four* into quintuple platinum status.

As the group prepared the follow-up to *Four*, Blues Traveler released the live doublealbum *Live From the Fall* in the summer of 1996. The group returned in the summer of 1997 with its fifth studio album, *Straight on Till Morning*. After completing his 1999 debut solo effort *Zygote*, Popper—who'd been experiencing chest pains for months—was forced to undergo an angioplasty; weeks later, tragedy struck on August 20, 1999, when Sheehan was found dead in his New Orleans home. He was just 31 years old. The new millennium saw a newly charged Blues Traveler, and their sixth record, *Bridge*, appeared in May 2001. —*William Ruhlmann*

● **Blues Traveler** / May 1990 / A&M ✦✦✦✦✦

Blues Traveler's loose jam structures on basic blues riffs mark them as a band in the tradition of such predecessors as the Grateful Dead. Unlike that communal effort, however,

this group has a distinct focal point in virtuoso harmonica player and vocalist John Popper, who keeps things from meandering too much. —*William Ruhlmann*

Travelers & Thieves / Sep. 1991 / A&M ✦✦✦

"I have my moments," John Popper declares, and many of them, as harmonica player, singer, and lyricist are here, on an album that finds Blues Traveler stretching out much as they do onstage. Popper is a man with a lot on his mind, but when he reaches "The Best Part," his verbosity approaches a Walt Whitman-like exuberance, and guitarist Chan Kinchla is right with him, contributing sweet fills here, Pete Townshend-style strumming there. And as for the rhythm work of bassist Bobby Sheehan and drummer Brendan Hill, as Popper says, "It's all in the groove." —*William Ruhlmann*

Save His Soul / Apr. 1993 / A&M ✦✦✦

Led by the guttural vocals and incisive harmonica of imposing frontman John Popper, *Save His Soul* is a savory package that dresses obvious influences in a fresh suit of clothes. While six and 12 strings rule, the true inspiration here is Popper's delivery on harmonica and other wind instruments, which spits in machine-gun-rapid fire or carries a piercing, emotive melody line with equal ease. Having restrained themselves for most of *Save His Soul*, Blues Traveler close with the seven-minute opus "Fledgling," flowing from epic, orchestral ballad mode to angst-ridden wall-of-noise. —*Roch Parisien*

Four / Sep. 13, 1994 / A&M ✦✦✦

Lacking the rootsier edge of *Save His Soul*, *Four* finds Blues Traveler retreating to their standard blues-boogie formula, with mixed results. Of course, there are some fine songs here—including their breakthrough hit single "Run-Around"—but too often the band sounds like they're coasting. *Four* is a solid record, but it shows signs that the band's formula may be wearing thin. —*Stephen Thomas Erlewine*

Live From the Fall / Jul. 1996 / A&M ✦✦✦✦✦

Like any jam-oriented band, Blues Traveler has a reputation for being better in concert than they are in the studio. Therefore, it would make sense that the double-disc *Live From the Fall* would be the ideal Blues Traveler album, since it allows the band to stretch out and demonstrate their true talents. In a sense, that is true. The two discs—which were recorded in the fall of 1995, as the band was supporting the surprise success of *Four*—do give the band room to improvise, and they exploit the extra space for all of its worth. Initially, Blues Traveler wanted to release without track indexes, so the listener could hear how each song flowed into the next. And the album does sound like that—like a neverending medley, where melodic themes pop in and out of the long solos. Occasionally, they detour into covers (War's "Low Rider," John Lennon's "Imagine"), but they mainly weave a tapestry of their own material, including rarities like the B-side "Regarding Steven" and the unreleased "Closing Down the Park." For fans of pop hits like "Run-Around" and "Hook," this can be a little irritating, but for those who have been with the band since the beginning, *Live From the Fall* is a priceless document—more than any other album, this showcases what Blues Traveler is about. —*Stephen Thomas Erlewine*

Straight on Till Morning / Jul. 1, 1997 / A&M ✦✦✦✦

The commercial success of *Four* was a mixed blessing for Blues Traveler. It did give them a wider audience, but it also put them in the delicate position of pleasing their new, hookhappy fans while retaining their hardcore, jam-oriented cult following. They skillfully manage to do just that on *Straight on Till Morning*, the bluesy, ambitious follow-up to *Four*. On the whole, *Straight on Till Morning* is a tougher album than any of its predecessors, boasting a gritty sound and several full-on jams. But the key to the album is its length and its sprawling collection of songs, which find Blues Traveler trying anything from country-rock to jangling pop/rock. They manage to be simultaneously succinct and eclectic, and they occasionally throw in a good pop hook or two. Blues Traveler is still too loose to be a true pop/rock band, and John Popper would still benefit from a sense of meter, but *Straight On Till Morning* is the first studio record that captures the essence of the band. —*Stephen Thomas Erlewine*

Bridge / Apr. 2001 / Interscope ✦✦✦✦

Blues Traveler went through a lot after their sequel to *Four*, *Straight on Till Morning*, stiffed in 1997. John Popper went through a severe health scare after cutting a schizophrenic solo album and, not long afterward, bassist Bob Sheehan died from a drug overdose. Reeling on both the personal and professional fronts, they took some time off, resurfacing mid-way through 2001 with *Bridge*, the album they should have released as the sequel to *Four*. This cuts back significantly on winding jams, upping the ante with tight songs and performances, a clean muscular production, and a lack of vocal histrionics from Popper. Melodically, they've rarely been stronger, and there's a sense of peace and maturity to the record that's appealing, especially since it's weighted with an undercurrent of loss and experience. This doesn't surface all that often, yet it's enough to provide a substantive center to one of the group's strongest records. They may not be in the public spotlight anymore, but the return to relative anonymity, along with the decade of experience underneath their belt, has mellowed and enriched their music, and while this may not be a record that will win new fans, it's certainly one that satisfies anyone who's taken the journey with them. —*Stephen Thomas Erlewine*

Louie Bluie (Howard Armstrong)

b. 1909, Dayton, TN

Violin, Vocals, Mandolin / Prewar Country Blues, Blues Revival, Songster, Vaudeville Blues

A violinist, mandolinist, and guitarist in the black string-band style who made a few recordings in the twenties and thirties, Howard Armstrong, aka "Louie Bluie," was rescued from the obscurity of specialist record collections when he was the subject of the *Louie Bluie* film documentary in the '80s, produced by Terry Zwigoff (more famous for his film *Crumb*). (Armstrong was also known as "Louie Bluie" as he issued a single under that nickname in 1934.) In his youth he was in bands with Carl Martin and guitarist Ted Bo-gan, including the Four Aces and the Tennessee Chocolate Drops, the latter of whom recorded "Vine Street Drag" in 1930. The traveling entertainers settled for a while in Chi-cago in the '30s, but stopped playing professionally by the late '30s, although Armstrong and Bogan got a new life in the '70s on the folk and festival circuit. A lively if not espe-cially innovative entertainer, Armstrong was one of the last exponents of the black string band style by the time of the *Louie Bluie* film. For its soundtrack, he did some recording with two veterans of the idiom, mandolinist Yank Rachell and banjoist Ikey Robinson, as well as other musicians. The soundtrack, plus some sides from the '20s and '30s that Arm-strong and Rachell had a hand in, is available as a CD. —*Richie Unterberger*

● **Louie Bluie** / 1998 / Arhoolie ◆◆◆
The soundtrack to the *Louie Bluie* film has Howard Armstrong, aka "Louie Bluie," in informal settings with various musicians, including Ted Bogan, Ikey Robinson, Yank Rachell, and Tom Armstrong. The selection of material gives a good indication of the breadth of the songster's repertoire, with ragtime, songs in German and Polish, blues, and a bawdy version of "Darktown Strutter's Ball" with much explicit profanity. If you're a ca-sual blues fan and want a representative disc of the songster genre, you could do a lot worse than this, especially as the clear fidelity is far superior to what's possible from re-mastered 78s. And if you need some of those remastered 78s, the disc isn't a total loss ei-ther, as it has the 1934 single he issued under the name "Louie Bluie," "Ted's Stomp"/"State Street Rag," which has some expert, speedy violin (on "Ted's Stomp") and mandolin (on "State Street Rag") by Armstrong. The CD reissue adds four songs from 1929-1938 not on the original Arhoolie LP: "Vine Street Drag" by the Tennessee Choco-late Drops, two sides by Sleepy John Estes with Yank Rachell (including the famous "Milk Cow Blues"), and a 1938 single by Yank Rachell. —*Richie Unterberger*

Eddie Bo (Edwin J. Bocage)
b. Sep. 20, 1930, New Orleans, LA
Vocals, Piano / New Orleans R&B, R&B
Singer/pianist/producer Eddie Bo was a session musician and recording artist in New Or-leans, starting with Ace in 1954. In 1969, he scored a Top 40 R&B hit with "Hook and Sling—Part I." —*William Ruhlmann*

● **Check Mr. Popeye** / 1988 / Rounder ◆◆◆◆
Engaging early-'60s New Orleans R&B from a prolific pianist, with a classic title track that spawned a local "Popeye" dance craze. —*Bill Dahl*

I Love to Rock 'N' Roll / 1994 / Famous Groove ◆◆◆◆
There is no sessionography, no discography, no indication of when the 29 tracks on Fa-mous Groove's Eddie Bo compilation *I Love Rock 'N' Roll* were recorded, but it's clear that these are all from the early and mid-'50s, prior to his stint at Ric in 1959. Most of them come from his time with Apollo, along with singles earlier and later. It would have been nice to have more detail in the notes, but this provides a thorough overview of his pre-hit years, while serving up some raw, stinging R&B and blues, as well as some sweet bal-lads. Though there are a couple of cuts that fall flat over the course of the collection, much of this is top-drawer New Orleans R&B, whether it's rocking or swinging (witness "I'm Wise," an easy swinger that Little Richard turned into the hard-charging "Slippin' and Slidin'"). There's a heavier blues element here than a lot of New Orleans R&B, which helps give it some depth, and the surprising variety in the material—ballads, mambos, rockers, swing and shuffles—will make up for the lo-fidelity and slightly uneven mate-rial. All of this makes *I Love to Rock 'N' Roll* a good choice for those serious about their New Orleans R&B, even if it doesn't have the hits of "Check Mr. Popeye" or 1969's "Hook and Sling." —*Stephen Thomas Erlewine*

Hook & Sling / Feb. 27, 1997 / Funky Delicacies ◆◆◆◆◆
A mover and shaker behind the New Orleans music scene, Eddie Bo had regional success in the late '50s with piano stroll-era novelties like "Check Mr. Popeye," but hit his stride a decade later with a brand of funk and soul that could only have originated in his home-town. "The Hook & Sling" was an R&B hit in 1969, propelled by Bo's good-natured ex-hortations and the undeniable groove from drummer James Black. The follow-up single, "(If It's Good to You) It's Good for You," did not achieve the same kind of chart success but is just as tough. *Hook & Sling* collects Bo's output for a number of small New Orleans la-bels, as well as tracks previously unreleased. Primarily heavy funk instrumentals, with plenty of wah-wah guitars and drum breaks, there are connections to Bo's musical past, including "Love Has Been Good" and "Come to Me," two blues-based ballads that lean hard on Bo's piano. Despite the contrasting styles, *Hook & Sling*'s material is impressively strong throughout, including good advice on love ("Check Your Bucket") and dance crazes "The Thang"). This is a life-changing release from the vaults. —*Kurt Edwards*

Lucille Bogan (Lucille Anderson)
b. Apr. 1, 1897, Amory, MS, d. Aug. 10, 1948, Los Angeles, CA
Vocals / Prewar Blues, Prewar Country Blues, Country Blues, Classic Female Blues
Bessie Jackson was a pseudonym of Lucille Bogan, a classic female blues artist from the '20s and '30s. Her outspoken lyrics deal with sexuality in a manner that manages to raise eyebrows even within a genre that is about as nasty as recorded music ever got prior to the emergence of artists such as 2 Live Crew or Ludacris. The name change seems to be quite different in her case than the usual pattern among blues artists who recorded under other names simply to make an end run around pre-existing recording contracts. Jackson/Bogan seemed to be looking for something more substantial, in that she not only changed her name but her performance style as well, and never recorded again under the name of Lucille Bogan once the Jackson persona had emerged. This was despite having enjoyed a hit record in the so-called "race market" in 1927 with the song "Sweet Petunia" as Bogan, but perhaps this was a scent she was trying to hide from.
This performer came out of the extremely active blues scene of Birmingham, AL, in

the '20s. She was born Lucille Anderson in Mississippi, picking up Bogan as a married name. She was the aunt of pianist and trumpet player Thomas "Big Music" Anderson. Bogan made her first recordings of the tunes "Lonesome Daddy Blues" and "Pawnshop Blues," in 1923, in New York City for the OKeh label. Despite the blues references in the titles, these were more vaudeville numbers. She moved to Chicago a year or two later and developed a huge following in the Windy City, before relocating to New York City in the early '30s, where she began a long collaborative relationship with pianist Walter Roland. This was the type of musical combination that many songwriters and singers only dream about; he was a perfect foil, knew what to play on the piano to bring out the best in her voice, and was such a sympathetic partner that it is hard to know where her ideas start and his end, no matter what name she was using. The pair made more than 100 records together before Bogan stopped recording in 1935.
One of the most infamous of the Jackson sides is the song "B.D. Woman's Blues," which 75 years later packs more of a punch than the lesbian-themed material of artists such as Holly Near or the Indigo Girls. "B.D." was short for "bull dykes," after all, and the blues singer lays it right on the line with the opening verse: "Comin' a time/women ain't gonna need no men." Well, except for a good piano player such as Walter Roland or some of her other hotshot accompanists such as guitarists Tampa Red and Josh White, or banjo picker Papa Charlie Jackson. She herself gets an accordion credit on one early recording, quite unusual for this genre. Certainly one of Bogan's greatest talents was as a songwriter, and she copyrighted dozens of titles, many of them so original that other blues artists were forced to give credit where credit was due instead of whipping up "matcher" imitations as was more than the norm. She still wrote songs during her later years living in California, and her final composition was "Gonna Leave Town," which turned out to be quite a prophetic title. By the time Smokey Hogg cut the tune in 1949, Jackson really had left town, having passed away the previous year from coronary sclerosis. While the ma-terial of some artists from this period has become largely forgotten, this is hardly the case for her; Saffire—The Uppity Blues Women have recorded several of her songs, as has bandmember Ann Rabson on her solo projects, as well as the naughty novelty band the Asylum Street Spankers. —*Eugene Chadbourne*

Lucille Bogan (1923-1935) / 1923-1935 / Story of the Blues ◆◆◆◆◆
A solid 18-track compilation of Lucille's best sides from her peak period. —*Cub Koda*

● **Lucille Bogan & Walter Roland, 1927-1935** / Mar. 1927-Mar. 7, 1935 / Yazoo ◆◆◆◆◆
This 14-track compilation is split evenly down the middle between Bogan and her main piano accompanist, Roland, who also doubles on guitar on some tracks. The Bogan sides are a particular delight, featuring a version of "Barbecue Bess" that is nothing short of sublime. As all of these tracks are rescued off highly battered 78s, the fidelity is about what you would expect. But that's no reason to deter you from enjoying this timeless music. —*Cub Koda*

Complete Recorded Works, Vol. 1 / Jun. 2, 1994 / Document ◆◆◆
Complete Recorded Works, Vol. 2 (1930-1933) / Jun. 2, 1994 / Document ◆◆◆
Complete Recorded Works, Vol. 3 (1934-1935) / Jun. 2, 1994 / Document ◆◆◆
Reckless Woman: 1927-1935 / Feb. 6, 2001 / EPM Musique ◆◆◆◆◆
It is very hard to overestimate the importance of Lucille Bogan's recordings to the genre of female blues. Her blunt, charismatic lyrics dealt with issues honestly, going against the grain of the typical sugarcoated female singers of the time. From her hilariously porno-graphic "Shave 'Em Dry" to her many songs about the trials and tribulations of adult womanhood ("Baking Powder Blues," "Pig Iron Sally"), she paved the way for a more honest, emotional release in the genre that only men had really explored before her. Most of these tracks were recorded under the name Bessie Jackson, and several of them fea-ture frequent collaborator Walter Roland. The songs are definitely a bit dated, and the sound quality varies from average to bad from track to track, but as a historical document of one woman's brilliant career as a lyricist, it is hard to beat *Reckless Woman: 1927-1935.* —*Bradley Torreano*

Lucille Bogan and Walter Roland: The Essential / Aug. 6, 2002 / Classic Blues ◆◆◆◆

Ted Bogan
b. May 10, 1910, Spartanburg, SC, d. Jan. 29, 1990, Detroit, MI
Guitar, Vocals / Prewar Country Blues
Ted Bogan was one of the greatest musical artists to ever emerge from Spartanburg, SC, or "South Cackalacky," as the natives would describe it. Bogan was something like a growth from a massive tulip bulb, a bloom that for some reason was never allowed to fully open. He performed and recorded beautifully throughout a career that spanned more than half a century, but was mostly known as a member of the string bands vari-ously known as Martin, Bogan & Armstrong or Martin, Bogan & the Armstrongs. The var-ious members played in many other formations, including the New Mississippi Sheiks, over the years, but at the crux of it all was a strange relationship between Bogan and Howard Armstrong, aka "Louie Bluie," that seems to have rivaled the hate-fest of Brownie McGhee and Sonny Terry. Most important, however, is that Bogan was not just a country bluesman, but a skilled and versatile purveyor of a variety of classic styles who appar-ently held his own up against no less a genius guitarist than Les Paul. Bogan wasn't just a fancy picker, though he could do that, but an interpreter of songs who apparently should have known much greater glory from this aspect of his talent. The many new fans Bogan played for during this period may not have realized the man could indeed outdo Janis Joplin, Jimmy Stewart, and Ethel Waters in his rendition of "Summertime." Bogan learned guitar as a child, beginning with fingerpicking. His early efforts were in humble imitation of Leroy Carr and Blind Blake, artists he had heard on records. A Canadian huckster who called himself Dr. Mines hired Bogan to play in his medicine show, the story goes, and like all the details involved with Martin, Bogan & Armstrong, there is also the possibility of fiction baked in with fact. Bogan in his later years was always happy to ex-plain the many inaccuracies or outright lies in the details of Armstrong's life story, as Armstrong was always telling it. He criticized the flamboyant Armstrong to concert

organizers, backstage help, and hipsters who happened to be standing around, all part of a relationship that lasted for almost 70 years. Armstrong also would have been happy to talk about Bogan, but never found the time in his full schedule of talking about himself. Bogan's performing experiences were from the beginning ones in which diverse music played a strong part, as the medicine show also featured comedians and dancers, including historic early performers such as Ham Bone and Leroy and Bozo Brown. Dance music of the era included themes associated with the "Bucking Wing" and the "Possum Walk." Bogan's flair with this material led to live broadcast exposure in Spartanburg, traditionally a strong border location with access to North and South Cackalackears, as well as Georgians. Hooking up with fiddler and guitarist Carl Martin, Bogan relocated to Knoxville, TN, where he would become such a local institution that when it came time to paint the Knoxville Music History Mural, there was no question that Howard Armstrong, Ted Bogan, and Carl Martin would be included; after all, the trio had performed for years on Knoxville street corners as well as on radio and local television. It was during the extended Knoxville stay that Bogan strongly advanced his guitar technique, including the development of a system he called "octahaves," basically doubling one or both of the chord's lowest notes on the high strings. Bogan's style also shifted to flatpicking during this period, part of the sonic demands of playing in a group and projecting in venues such as street corners. One of the groups these players had in the '40s was the Four Keys, which toured throughout West Virginia, Pennsylvania, Ohio, Indiana, and Michigan. In Chicago, the group recorded as a backup unit for bluesman Bumble Bee Slim and this enjoyable material has been reissued in a series of three volumes or a complete box. The group then changed its name to the Tennessee Chocolate Drops in a shrewd move that cashed in on both the race record market as well as the fanatic interest in hillbilly music on radio and records. For many years, the group worked quite successfully until the advent of jukeboxes and amplified bands eroded public support for traditional acoustic string bands. The revival of the band began in the late '70s, with Bogan and Martin still based out of Chicago. *Louie Bluie*, a film based on one of Armstrong's stage and recording pseudonyms, features plenty of footage of Bogan in action. *—Eugene Chadbourne*

Deanna Bogart

b. 1960, Detroit, MI

Vocals, Saxophone, Piano / Piano Blues, Modern Electric Blues, Boogie-Woogie, Rock & Roll, New Orleans R&B

Drawing on a variety of musical sources ranging from boogie-woogie to New Orleans R&B to swing to rock & roll, singer and barrelhouse pianist Deanna Bogart emerged as one of the most eclectic performers in contemporary blues. Born in Detroit in 1960, she cut her teeth on the Maryland blues circuit, developing a crowd-pleasing style which often found her leaping up from her piano bench to chat with the audience; clad in her trademark black fedora, Bogart was also known to blow a mean tenor saxophone. A gifted composer as well, her debut LP *Out to Get You* appeared in 1991, followed in 1992 by *Crossing Borders*; a four-year hiatus preceded the release of *New Address*. *—Jason Ankeny*

● **Out to Get You** / May 1991 / Blind Pig ♦♦♦♦♦

Debut album by this delightful two-fisted boogie-woogie pianist, saxophonist, and songster. Highlights abound everywhere, but of particular note is her striking originals "Over Thirty" and "Morning Glory." *—Cub Koda*

Crossing Borders / 1992 / Flying Fish ♦♦♦

The follow-up album to Bogart's debut effort is chock full of the kind of wonderful crossbreeding of styles this artist brings to her work. "Don't Know a Thing About Love" is a slice of low-down funk 'n' nasty while the kickoff track, "Tell Me," rocks as hard as anything on the album. Of course, Deanna's specialty—the piano boogie—is represented nicely by the tracks "Eclectic Boogie" and "Backstage Boogie." *—Cub Koda*

New Address / Oct. 29, 1996 / Lightyear ♦♦♦

The Great Unknown / Jun. 16, 1998 / Shanachie ♦♦♦♦

On her fourth album, 1999's *The Great Unknown*, Deanna Bogart serves up some more of her heartfelt, bluesy piano and vocals. Bogart's wide-ranging sound embraces rock, soul, swing and R&B, but keeps its roots in the blues. *The Great Unknown* includes Bogart originals like "Adam Bomb Boogie," "Love Funk" and the title track. *—Heather Phares*

Spencer Bohren

b. Wyoming

Vocals, Guitar / Folk-Blues

Guitarist, singer and songwriter Spencer Bohren is from Wyoming but is often associated with the Crescent City, as he lived there for a number of years and continues to prove a popular club attraction there. Brought up in a strict Baptist family, Bohren sang harmonies in church, and it was his passion for gospel music that led him to become an equally diligent student of blues. He left Wyoming in 1968 for the folk scene around Denver. At the Denver Folklore Center and in coffeehouses, he learned acoustic folk-blues firsthand from people like Reverend Gary Davis before moving to Seattle, where he played with a series of blues bands and continued to hone his songwriting abilities. In 1973, he moved back to Colorado to play with folk-blues singer Judy Roderick, and after talking extensively with Dr. John (Mac Rebennack) one night, he decided to move to New Orleans, where Rebennack was born and raised. Bohren spent a decade there, playing clubs like Tipitinas and the Absinthe Bar. In 1983, Bohren and his family began a seven-year journey on the road in an Airstream RV; Bohren performed all over the U.S., and later began to tour extensively in Europe and Japan. In 1989, Bohren had a Top 40 hit in Sweden. Although his discography is quite extensive and Bohren has been presented at many large festivals around the U.S. and Europe, a major-label deal in the U.S. still eludes him. Bohren's albums include *Born In Biscayne* (1984) for Great Southern Records, *Down in Mississippi* (1986) for New Blues Records, 1989's *Live In New Orleans* for Great Southern Records, *Snap Your Fingers* for Loft Records (a French label) and *Totta and Hot 'n' Tots* (a Swedish group featuring Bohren); *Spencer Bohren* for Alpha Records of Japan in 1991, *Full Moon* for Virgin Records of France in 1992, and *Present Tense* for Loft Records in France, a 1995 release. His most recent recordings on U.S. labels include *Vintage*, a 1994 release for New Blues of New Orleans, and *Dirt Roads*, a 1996 release on his own Zephyr label out of Casper, Wyoming. In 1990, Bohren moved back to Casper until returning to New Orleans in 1997. Bohren continues to tour Europe three or four times a year, and beginning in 1996, Bohren's album *Present Tense* was available in Europe on Sony and on his own Zephyr label in the U.S. *Carry the Word* followed in 2000, and *Solitaire* in 2002. *—Richard Skelly*

Down in Mississippi / 1986 / New Blues ♦♦♦

● **Live in New Orleans** / Mar. 5, 1989 / Great Southern ♦♦♦♦

Spencer Bohren, a folk-blues singer and guitarist who was 39 at the time of this recording, gives life and vitality to some older styles throughout *Live In New Orleans*. A throwback in some ways to the early '60s, Bohren explores country blues, Bo Diddley's "Hoodoo You Love," and a few folk songs, a brief throwaway version of "Maple Leaf Rag," and even an a cappella version of the gospel song "This Body Is a Prison." His duo partner Jab Wilson gives the date a little extra color with his harmonica and Bohren's guitar is particularly expressive on "Mindin' My Business" and "The Sky Is Crying," but the emphasis here is on Spencer Bohren the singer and storyteller. This is a pleasing set that should satisfy fans of the folkish side of the blues legacy. *—Scott Yanow*

Vintage / 1994 / Zephyr Artists ♦♦♦♦

Dirt Roads / Nov. 26, 1996 / Last Call ♦♦♦♦

Way out in the country where the pavement ends is where the dirt roads begin. Don't be fooled by the title—this is contemporary but laid-back blues played from the heart. It is definitely a country blues-feeling disc, with much the same kind of feel as Taj Mahal or maybe Keb' Mo', but played with a distinctive, very spare touch. What notes he doesn't play are as important as the ones he does. Just listen to the traditional "The Water Is Wide"; it is done as sparse as can be, and yet it is perhaps one of the richest and most emotional versions you will hear. Grab at his version of "The Wild Ox Moan"; you may never hear it done with such heart and feeling. The one shortcoming of the disc is the lack of noting which instruments he is playing at a particular time. In fact, he is listed on vocals, stringed instruments, and percussion. You can pick out the lap steel, mandolin, guitar, and slide guitar, but there is a haunting feeling there are either more instruments, or he is doing something unheard of. A too-brief note on Jab Wilson's harmonica playing is the perfect complement to the mood and style of the disc—the right shoe to go with the left. The most pleasant surprise was the beautiful emotional quality of his vocals. You can hear the influence of a southern raising in the gospel-singing family tradition. The years of living in the ripe blues country of the Mississippi Delta have given a decided blues phrasing to his vocals, and then there is the influence of the New Orleans folk and rhythm scene. The songs he wrote, half of the 12, fit in style so perfectly you know this is his music—like that beautiful, old, but so well-broken-in pair of boots you just can't bear to part with. This is a gem you are going to have to do some work to find, but your efforts will be well rewarded. The sheer mystic magic this disc contains will more than pay back the effort spent. *—Bob Gottlieb*

Carry the Word / Jun. 6, 2000 / Last Call ♦♦♦♦

Quiet passion and intensity infuse this disc from the opening cut to the ending, which you hate to see approaching. This is a disc of traditional spiritual/gospel songs played in the very spare and understated manner Mr. Bohren is gaining attention with at festivals and club appearances. He is one of those guitar/slide guitar players who is eloquent within his sparcity. The disc has a rich, full sound that he accomplishes with a minimum of additional accompaniment, but when it is there it is placed strategically so that it has maximum impact. The perspicacious use of the backup enhances the disc and never detracts, always letting the focus fall one what is important to the song. Both the Nott Brothers Quartet and Teresa Albury know their roles and stay right there, never trying to steal the spotlight, their singing supports and enhances the lead vocals. Jab Wilson, whose wonderful harmonica playing does such a perfect job of supporting and urging Mr. Bohren to push the singing and guitar playing to new heights. This is at the other extreme end of the spectrum from the Sacred Steel Series that Arhoolie has done, and there is room enough in this world for the various aspects and quite frankly it is enlightening to hear such a different perspective. Spencer was raised in the gospel church, so it was almost a forgone conclusion that he would one day return to his roots after exploration of different tentacles of them. He has used his decades of probing into the blues and folk music to enhances his understanding of his own roots, and thus able to take it to new heights. *—Bob Gottlieb*

Solitaire / 2002 / Valve ♦♦♦

This disc presents Spencer Bohren playing solo using a variety of instruments—including his voice, which is getting stronger and more expressive with each outing. His singing is enhanced and supported by his often understated and outstanding handling of his instruments. These include electric and acoustic lap steel, electric and acoustic guitar, and a variety of rhythm instruments. He wrote or co-wrote five of the 11 songs featured here, combining his originals with the others he has selected into a cohesive whole. Both his selection of songs written by others and what he does with them are extraordinary. There is a version here of the Jagger-Richards classic "No Expectations" that brings whole new dimensions to this gem of a song. His restrained but eerie electric lap steel augments his expressive and haunting phrasing, bringing a level of agony and distress to the song that was only hinted at prior to this. His version of Hank Williams' oft-done "Long Gone Lonesome Blues" holds to a very country feel and shows another dimension that his voice can hold with authority. There are times when his big Guild guitar seems to whisper behind his vocals as if it were another voice. At other times, he cuts loose with some dazzling bottleneck guitar ("Been 'Round This World"), and he uses the lap steel to heighten the tension created by the vocals in a song like "Witch Doctor." This disc gives listeners a wide range of styles held together by the sense of mood and space Bohren creates with his music and the spaces he uses to frame that music. *—Bob Gottlieb*

Zuzu Bollin (A.D. Bollin)

b. Sep. 5, 1922, Frisco, TX, **d.** Oct. 2, 1990, Dallas, TX

Vocals, Guitar / Texas Blues

Two 78s in the early '50s and a 1989 rediscovery album don't add up to much of a recorded legacy. But Zuzu Bollin's contribution to the Texas blues legacy shouldn't be overlooked—his T-Bone Walker-influenced sound typified postwar Lone Star blues guitar.

Born A.D. Bollin, Zuzu listened to everyone from Blind Lemon Jefferson and Leroy Carr (on records) to Joe Turner and Count Basie. He picked up his nickname while in the band of Texan E.X. Brooks; seems he had a sweet tooth for a brand of gingersnap cookies called ZuZus. Bollin formed his own combo in 1949, featuring young saxist David "Fathead" Newman. After a stint with Percy Mayfield's band, Bollin resumed playing around Dallas. In late 1951, he made his recording debut for Bob Sutton's Torch logo. Newman and saxist Leroy Cooper, both future members of Ray Charles' band, played on Bollin's "Why Don't You Eat Where You Slept Last Night" and "Headlight Blues." A Torch follow-up, "Stavin' Chain"/"Cry, Cry, Cry," found Bollin backed by Jimmy McCracklin's combo.

No more recording ensued after that, though Bollin toured with bandleaders Ernie Fields and Joe Morris before chucking the music biz in 1964 to go into a more stable profession: dry cleaning. Bollin's 1987 rediscovery was the Dallas Blues Society's doing: they engineered a series of gigs and eventually a fine 1989 album, *Texas Bluesman*, that beautifully showcased Bollin's approach. Their efforts were barely in time—Bollin died in 1990. *—Bill Dahl*

● **Texas Bluesman** / 1989 / Antone's ✦✦✦✦✦

Zuzu's principal contribution to Texas blues history is an immaculately realized collection that includes remakes of both sides of his debut 78 (the original version of "Why Don't You Eat Where You Slept Last Night" is available on *Vol. 3* of Rhino's *Blues Masters* series, "Texas Blues") and a uniformly tasty lineup of jump blues goodies. The sterling band includes guitarist Duke Robillard (who co-produced), drummer George Rains, and saxists David Newman and Kaz Kazanoff. *—Bill Dahl*

Graham Bond

b. Oct. 28, 1937, Romford, Essex, England, **d.** May 8, 1974, London, England

Vocals, Saxophone, Organ / British Blues, British Invasion, Blues-Rock

An important, underappreciated figure of early British R&B, Graham Bond is known in the U.S., if at all, for heading the group that Jack Bruce and Ginger Baker played in before they joined Cream. Originally an alto sax jazz player—in fact, he was voted Britain's New Jazz Star in 1961—he met Bruce and Baker in 1962 after joining Alexis Korner's Blues Incorporated, the finishing school for numerous British rock and blues musicians. By the time he, Bruce, and Baker split to form their own band in 1963, Bond was mostly playing the Hammond organ, as well as handling the lion's share of the vocals. John McLaughlin was a member of the Graham Bond Organization in the early days for a few months, and some live material that he recorded with the group was eventually issued after most of their members had achieved stardom in other contexts. Saxophonist Dick Heckstall-Smith completed Bond's most stable lineup, who cut a couple of decent albums and a few singles in the mid-'60s.

In their prime, the Graham Bond Organization played rhythm & blues with a strong jazzy flavor, emphasizing Bond's demonic organ and gruff vocals. The band arguably would have been better served to feature Bruce as their lead singer—he is featured surprisingly rarely on their recordings. Nevertheless, their best records were admirably tough British R&B/rock/jazz/soul, and though Bond has sometimes been labeled as a pioneer of jazz-rock, in reality it was much closer to rock than jazz. The band performed imaginative covers and fairly strong original material, and Bond was also perhaps the very first rock musician to record with the Mellotron synthesizer. Hit singles, though, were necessary for British bands to thrive in the mid-'60s, and Bond's group began to fall apart in 1966, when Bruce and Baker joined forces with Eric Clapton to form Cream. Bond attempted to carry on with the Organization for a while with Heckstall-Smith and drummer Jon Hiseman, both of whom went on to John Mayall's Bluesbreakers and Colosseum.

Bond never recaptured the heights of his work with the Organization. In the late '60s he moved to the U.S., recording albums with musicians including Harvey Brooks, Harvey Mandel, and Hal Blaine. Moving back to Britain, he worked with Ginger Baker's Airforce, the Jack Bruce Band, and Cream lyricist Pete Brown, as well as forming the band Holy Magick, who recorded a couple albums. Bond's demise was more tragic than most: he developed serious drug and alcohol problems and an obsession with the occult, and it has even been posthumously speculated (in the British Bond biography *Mighty Shadow*) that he sexually abused his stepdaughter. He committed suicide by throwing himself into the path of a London Underground train in 1974. *—Richie Unterberger*

Live at Klooks Kleek / 1964 / Charly ✦✦✦

This nine-track concert gig has appeared in various guises and through various labels (most notoriously Springboard International in the U.S. in the late '70s), and it has a dubious reputation on vinyl. In 1988, however, it appeared on CD under this title, and it finally seemed to justify the trouble it took to record. The Graham Bond Organization's studio recordings were admirable, sometimes impressive, but never essential parts of the British blues boom, leading one to wonder precisely what—apart from the presence of two future members of Cream—the group's reputation was based on. The answer is on these sides, recorded by Giorgio Gomelsky "under extreme difficulty." Listening to the band rumble and surge through standards like "Wade In the Water," "Big Boss Man," "Stormy Monday," and "Early In the Morning," it's easy to understand how they got signed and what the record companies were looking for, and also why they didn't get it—this is gritty stuff, loud R&B with some jazz elements, Dick Heckstall-Smith blowing up a storm on sax, and more than a little stretching out (especially by Baker, whose solos here (check out "Early In the Morning") are more enjoyable than most of what he did with Cream), all of it pretty intense and none of it easy to capture in the studio. The audience and the urgency of concert work were both essential to the group's functioning. On the techincal side, there's some distortion, even some overload, and Jack Bruce's bass isn't captured in its more resonant form (and what electric bass on any live recording before about 1968 ever was?), but the electricity is here, along with the immediacy, and this CD may be the way to best appreciate this band. *—Bruce Eder*

● **The Sound of 65** / Mar. 1965 / Edsel ✦✦✦✦✦

Although the Organization's first album was recorded a mere year or two before Cream's debut, it bears little resemblance to Cream's pioneering hard blues-rock. Instead, it's taut British R&B with a considerable jazz influence. That influence comes not so much from the rhythm section as saxophonist Dick Heckstall-Smith and lead singer/organist Bond himself. This LP is not as exciting or rock-oriented as those of contemporaries like the Rolling Stones or John Mayall, but is respectably gritty, mostly original material, with an occasionally nasty edge. There are some obscure treasures of the British R&B explosion to be found here, including the original version of "Train Time" (later performed by Cream), the thrilling bass runs on "Baby Be Good to Me," and the group's hardboiled rearrangements of such traditional standards as "Wade in the Water" and "Early in the Morning." Even their blatant stab at commercialism (the ballad "Tammy") has its charm. *—Richie Unterberger*

There's a Bond Between Us / Nov. 1965 / Edsel ✦✦✦✦✦

Bond's second album stakes out similar territory as his debut in a more polished but slightly less exciting fashion. Some of the covers are a bit routine and hackneyed, and the original material isn't quite as strong (or frequent) as on the first effort. On a few tunes, the group expands from rave-ups to mellower, jazzier ballads that retain an R&B base. Highlights include the early Jack Bruce composition "Hear Me Calling Your Name" (to which he also contributes a fine lead vocal) and the excellent Bond tune "Walkin' in the Park," which holds up to the best early British R&B numbers. The album is also notable for being one of the very first rock LPs to feature the Mellotron, which Bond uses subtly and well. *—Richie Unterberger*

Mighty Grahame Bond / 1969 / Pulsar ✦✦

Despite the presence of high-profile musicians Harvey Brooks and Harvey Mandel, Bond's second album from his stay in the U.S. in the late '60s was a lukewarm, half-inspired affair. It's average blues-rock with light gospel and funk overtones, and a few of the songs are pretty shapeless. It's best when Bond brings out the demonic tones of both his organ (or, occasionally, mellotron) and vocals, but these are flashed infrequently. The label made it clear that Graham was not a top priority in their promotion department by misspelling his first name on the record itself. *—Richie Unterberger*

Solid Bond / May 1970 / Warner Brothers ✦✦✦

This rather odd double LP is a patchy, yet good assortment of '60s material that Bond did not put out during that decade, and which remains unavailable on any other release. Nine of the 12 tracks date from 1966, with Bond accompanied by Dick Heckstall-Smith on sax and Jon Hiseman on drums (Jack Bruce and Ginger Baker had by this time left to join Cream). Most of those nine songs are not on the two proper albums he issued in the '60s (*The Sound of 65* and *There's a Bond Between Us*), and though a few did appear on those albums and non-LP singles, these recordings are different versions. While not up to the level of the best cuts waxed by the Bruce/Baker lineup, these Hiseman/Heckstall-Smith-backed numbers are still solid jazzy R&B with that aura of faint menace unique to Bond's mid-'60s work. His singing is particularly effective in its drawn-out anguish on "It's Not Goodbye" and "Springtime in the City" has those uneasy descending chord progressions and creepy R&B black-mass organ that were Bond specialties. "Neighbour Neighbour" and "Walkin' in the Park" aren't as good as the versions he did with Bond and Baker on the first two Graham Bond Organization LPs, but they're different enough to merit hearing. The three remaining songs were done in 1963 with Bruce, Baker, Heckstall-Smith, and John McLaughlin, and are long, straight jazz pieces that are much different in nature. Historically they're interesting, particularly in their documentation of the period in which McLaughlin (who solos well, though his free jazz style was a long way off in coming) was in the band. However, Bond's outfit became much more distinguished as an R&B group than they were as an average jazz one, making the 1963 material more of a curiosity than a highlight of his discography. *—Richie Unterberger*

Graham Bond Organization / 1984 / Charly ✦✦

This live 1964 gig is one of Giorgio Gomelsky's innumerable tapes of British club acts of the period, several of which would be released many years later in attempts to cash in on some big names who were present. These historical documents, never intended for release, ranged from superb to wretched. This LP (which, like most of these Gomelsky projects, has been reissued under numerous different covers and titles) falls about right in the middle of this scale. Bond led an erratic, interesting group that incorporated elements of jazz and improvisation into its blend of blues, R&B, and rock. Future Cream members Jack Bruce and Ginger Baker were his rhythm section in his prime, and Dick Heckstall-Smith handled horns; this is the lineup featured on this set. But it's not deathless stuff. The fidelity, for one, is muddy, especially the bottom, Bruce's bass suffering the most. The better tunes—"Wade in the Water," "Early in the Morning," "Train Time," and "Spanish Blues"—are available in better performances and much clearer fidelity on the group's first studio album, *The Sound of 65*. The rest is routine, even below average in spots, early British R&B. The Organization may have been among the most accomplished players on the scene, but they couldn't hold a candle to the Stones or Yardbirds in terms of imagination and excitement. A better introduction to the sound of this lineup is the fine Edsel reissue of *The Sound of 65* and *There's a Bond Between Us*, which have been combined into one package. *—Richie Unterberger*

Sound of 65/There's a Bond Between Us / Dec. 14, 1999 / BGO ✦✦✦✦✦

This two-LPs-on-one-CD package is essential listening for anyone who is seriously interested in either British blues, the Rolling Stones' early sound, or the history of popular music, in England or America, during the late '50s and early '60s. In England during the years 1957-1962, jazz and blues used to intermix freely, especially among younger blues enthusiasts and more open-minded jazzmen—by 1963, most of the former had gone off to form bands like the Rolling Stones, the Yardbirds, the Pretty Things, etc., with guitars a the forefront of their sound, while the latter (most notably British blues godfather Alexis Korner) kept some jazz elements in their work. The Graham Bond Organization (along with Zoot Money's Big Roll Band and other, similar outfits) represented the jazzier side of the British blues boom, less charismatic and sexually provocative than blues-rock bands like the Stones or the Yardbirds, but no less potent a product of the same inspiration, sax and organ being much more prominent in their sound. Indeed, Bond's playing on the organ as represented on this CD is the distant antecedent to Keith Emerson's more ambitious keyboard excursions of 3-4 years later, without the incessant copping of classical riffs. The playing and singing (by Graham Bond and a young Jack Bruce) are curiously soulful, and when Ginger Baker takes a solo on "Oh Baby," it's a beautiful, powerful, even lyrical experience (as drum solos go), and one of those bold, transcendant, virtuoso moments, akin to Brian Jones' harmonica solo on the Stones' version of "Hi Heel Sneakers." The band was more exciting on stage, as the evidence of their one surviving early live performance indicates, but they were worth hearing on record as well. In a universe that was fair and idealized, this CD and the two albums contained on it would rank right up there in sales with anything (including the Bluesbreakers with Eric Clapton album) that John Mayall ever released, and Bond also proves himself a more fervent and exciting figure here than Mayall ever seemed on his records. *—Bruce Eder*

Holy Magick/We Put Our Magick on You / Mar. 21, 2000 / BGO ✦✦

One of the founding fathers of the British blues movement, Graham Bond released two spectacular albums in 1965 as the Graham Bond Organization. *The Sound of 65* and *There's a Bond Between Us* (also re-released on BGO Records) are essential jazz/blues albums for any music fan. When Bond broke up the Organization, he moved to the United States where he recorded two "solo" albums in 1965. In 1966, he returned to England where he became a member of Ginger Baker's Air Force for a time then left and formed the band Magick with his wife Diane Stewart. *Holy Magick*, the band's debut album, was originally released on the "progressive" Vertigo label in 1970. The album was based on Bond's interest in white magic and Druid and Celtic mysticism. *Holy Magick* consists of two parts containing 18 songs based around mantras, rituals, and improvisational pieces. The band, a flexible unit, featured some of the top musicians Britain had to offer in 1970 including Rick Grech (Blind Faith), Victor Bronx, Alex Dmochowski, Jon Moreshead from the Aynsley Dunbar Retaliation, and a host of session performers. While barely accessible to a rock audience, this album has been both dismissed and praised by critics and fans, depending on one's musical taste. The music was very much jazz oriented. When it was originally released it did not sell well and became a collector's item. In 1971 Bond released the second Magick album which was intended to be the second part of his Magick trilogy. The theme behind this album was Eastern mysticism, in particular the Hindu and Aquarian philosophy. The lineup for this album had changed, but the sound was an extension of the debut only with different themes and more of a blues direction. Again the album was released on Vertigo but did not sell well so Bond postponed the third part of the trilogy and took a break from the music business. Unfortunately, he died a tragic death in 1974, and the trilogy was never completed. This set by BGO Records contains both albums on a single CD. It has been remastered from original master tapes, and the package contains an in-depth essay on the history of Bond and both projects along with photos and reproductions of the original album graphics. *—Keith Pettipas*

"Brownsville" Son Bonds

b. Mar. 16, 1909, Brownsville, TN, **d.** Aug. 31, 1947, Dyersburg, TN

Vocals, Kazoo, Guitar / Country Blues

An associate of Sleepy John Estes and Hammie Nixon, Bonds played very much in the same rural Brownsville style that the Estes-Nixon team popularized in the '20s and '30s. Curiously, either Estes or Nixon (but never both of them together) played on all of Bonds' recordings. The music to one of Bonds' songs, "Back and Side Blues" (1934), became a standard blues melody when John Lee "Sonny Boy" Williamson from nearby Jackson, TN, used it in his classic "Good Morning, (Little) School Girl" (1937). According to Nixon, Bonds was shot to death, while sitting on his front porch, by a nearsighted neighbor who mistook him for another man. *—Jim O'Neal*

● **Complete Recorded Works in Chronological Order** / Sep. 6, 1934-Sep. 24, 1941 / Wolf ✦✦✦✦✦

This is an above average collection from Wolf Records in Vienna, both in terms of audio quality and content. The 18 songs by "Brownsville" Son Bonds, recorded between 1934 and 1941, are in surprisingly decent sound, for the most part, with no horrendous flaws to mar the collection. The songs are all good and the playing generally inspired, especially on the later tracks, where Bonds added a kazoo to his sound and really takes off, in a more rocking and freewheeling way than even Tampa Red. The diversity of the material is also a surprise—four of the songs are rough, fervent gospel numbers, including the extraordinarily beautiful "I Want to Live So God Can Use Me," "Ain't That News," and "Give Me That Old Time Religion," cut by Bonds working as "Brother Son Bonds" (with Hammie Nixon backing him up on vocals and jug). They fit in well with their raw quality amid the lusty country blues numbers ("All Night Long," "She Walks Like My Woman," etc.) that make up the rest of this disc. The guitar-harmonica duets between Bonds and Nixon are especially pleasing, but Bonds' voice, surging and soaring, is the real show, especially on the early numbers, where the recordings really don't do justice to his guitar. The last four songs on this disc feature Charlie Pickett on vocals and guitar, and were recorded in 1937, with Nixon linking one of Pickett's songs with the rest of this collection. *—Bruce Eder*

Juke Boy Bonner (Weldon Bonner)

b. Mar. 22, 1932, Bellville, TX, **d.** Jun. 29, 1978, Houston, TX

Vocals, Harmonica, Guitar / West Coast Blues, Texas Blues

One-man bands weren't any too common on the postwar blues scene. Joe Hill Louis and Dr. Ross come to mind as greats who plied their trade all by their lonesome—and so did Juke Boy Bonner, a Texan whose talent never really earned him much in the way of tangible reward.

Born into impoverished circumstances in the Lone Star State during the Depression, Weldon Bonner took up the guitar in his teens. He caught a break in 1947 in Houston, winning a talent contest that led to a spot on a local radio outlet. He journeyed to Oakland in 1956, cutting his debut single for Bob Geddins' Irma imprint ("Rock With Me Baby"/"Well Baby") with Lafayette "Thing" Thomas supplying the lead guitar. Goldband Records boss Eddie Shuler was next to take a chance in 1960; Bonner recorded for him in Lake Charles, LA, with Katie Webster on piano, but once again, nothing happened career-wise.

Troubled by stomach problems during the '60s, Bonner utilized his hospital downtime to write poems that he later turned into songs. He cut his best work during the late '60s for Arhoolie Records, accompanying himself on both guitar and racked harmonica as he weaved extremely personal tales of his rough life in Houston. A few European tours ensued, but they didn't really lead to much. Toward the end of his life, he toiled in a chicken processing plant to make ends meet. Bonner died of cirrhosis of the liver in 1978. *—Bill Dahl*

One Man Trio / Feb. 1967 / Flyright ✦✦✦✦✦

Going Back to the Country / Dec. 20, 1967-Jan. 23, 1968 / Arhoolie ✦✦✦✦✦

Part of a stellar run of '60s recordings cut in his native Texas, *Going Back to the Country* was the first of Juke Boy Bonner's three particularly fine dates for the Arhoolie label. Accompanying himself on electric guitar and harmonica, Bonner reels off a set of originals that range from dusky slow blues ("Sad, Sad Sound") to stomping uptempo sides ("Stay Off Lyons Avenue"). Bonner shows the influence of both Jimmy Reed and fellow Texan Lightnin' Hopkins in his approach, but he always delivers inimitable work, thanks to a sophisticated lyrical bent (Bonner wrote poetry, too) and a beat tailor-made for the many juke joints where he cut his teeth and got his name. A solid sampling from Bonner's prime. *—Stephen Cook*

● **Life Gave Me a Dirty Deal** / Nov. 30, 1968-May 5, 1969 / Arhoolie ✦✦✦✦✦

Likely the most consistent and affecting collection you'll encounter by this singular Texas bluesman, whose strikingly personal approach was stunningly captured by Arhoolie's Chris Strachwitz during the late '60s in Houston. Twenty-three utter originals include "Stay Off Lyons Avenue," "Struggle Here in Houston," "I Got My Passport," and the title track. Bonner sang movingly of his painfully impoverished existence for Arhoolie, and the results still resound triumphantly today. *—Bill Dahl*

☆ **The Struggle** / Nov. 30, 1968-May 5, 1969 / Arhoolie ✦✦✦✦✦

Recorded in extreme stereo, with drums on one channel and Bonner's guitar on the other, this is Juke Boy Bonner's most cohesive album. Great songwriting and performances throughout. *—Cub Koda*

Things Ain't Right / Nov. 4, 1969-Nov. 28, 1969 / Sequel ✦✦

This set is somewhat disappointing compared to the Arhoolie sides. *—Bill Dahl*

Legacy of the Blues, Vol. 5 / 1972 / GNP Crescendo ✦✦✦

Juke Boy Bonner remains one of the great hidden treasures of the blues. He was a one-man band who had serious lyrical concerns in all of his blues, creating stark and moving poetry out of the simplest of forms. Working in a Jimmy Reed-style of guitar boogie patterns and blowing an expressive neck-rack harmonica, he never saw much in the way of fame or fortune, but every single session produced music of considerable worth. Add this solo session, produced by Chris Strachwitz for Sonet's *Legacy of the Blues* series, to the list of essential albums to put into your shopping cart, as it's the blues at its most personal and moving. In tracks like "I'm a Bluesman," "Problems All Around," "Tired of the Greyhound Bus," and "Funny Money," you'll hear a bluesman laying his heart on the line for the music—something that should happen every time the "record" button goes on, but rarely does. *—Cub Koda*

Adventures of Juke Boy Bonner / 1980 / Collectables ✦

Juke Boy was one of the most forward-thinking of all the unreconstructed Texas bluesmen, his lyrics touching on modern themes while staying totally rooted to down-home juke-joint blues. But this album takes his music and turns it inside out with a full band, overdubbed female backup vocals, synthesizers galore, and plenty of fuzz-toned guitar licks not played by Bonner, making for a musical mish-mosh that isn't even laughable. There's even a clarinet popping up in the mix! This travesty never should have been recorded, much less reissued; shame on this label for doing so. Even if you already have plenty of Juke Boy Bonner in your collection (and there really isn't all *that* much to collect), avoid this piece of crap like the plague it is. *—Cub Koda*

The Texas Blues Troubadours / 1990 / Collectables ✦✦✦

Juke Boy Bonner, 1960–1967 / 1991 / Flyright ✦✦✦

Jumpin' With Juke Boy / Sep. 14, 1993 / Collectables ✦✦✦

Boogie Woogie Red (Vernon Harrison)

b. Oct. 18, 1925, Rayville, LA, **d.** 1985, Detroit, MI

Vocals, Piano / Piano Blues, Detroit Blues, Boogie-Woogie

Though a Louisiana native, Vernon Harrison has been associated with the Detroit blues sound as long as anyone. A Motor City resident since 1927, he began performing in the local clubs as a teenager. As a sideman he worked locally with Sonny Boy Williamson, Baby Boy Warren, and John Lee Hooker. Despite Red's renown for the blues and boogie-woogie style that earned him his nickname, he recorded only a few times as a featured artist, and aside from a bit of European touring in the '70s, he remained a local Detroit treasure, rarely appearing outside the area. *—Jim O'Neal*

- **Live at the Blind Pig** / 1974 / Blind Pig ♦♦♦♦

A crudely recorded but fun live album, it captures the somewhat demented 80-proof charm of this Detroit pianist. Recorded in the basement of the Blind Pig in Ann Arbor, MI, this album features guest appearances by John Nicholas, Fran Christina, and Bill Heid. *—George Bedard*

Red Hot / 1977 / Blind Pig ♦♦♦♦

Roy Book Binder

b. Oct. 5, 1941, New York, NY

Vocals, Guitar / Modern Acoustic Blues, Folk-Blues

An often stirring folk/blues guitarist and vocalist, Roy Book Binder's been playing country blues since the mid-'60s, when he began recording for Blue Goose. Greatly influenced by Rev. Gary Davis and Pink Anderson, Book Binder played in East Coast coffeehouses in the early '60s, then began accompanying Rev. Davis on tours in the mid-'60s. He also played with Larry Johnson, Arthur "Big Boy" Crudup and Homesick James. Besides constant concerts and tours, Book Binder's made additional recordings for Blue Goose, as well as Adelphi and Rounder.

Book Binder began playing blues guitar while he was enlisted in the navy. Following his discharge from the military, he enrolled in Rhode Island Junior College. After a brief spell there, he attended New York's New School for Social Research. Book Binder quit school in 1967, after he met the Rev. Gary Davis. Roy became Davis' chauffeur, during which he took extensive lessons from the blind guitarist. Book Binder started his recording career slowly, cutting some singles for Kicking Mule and Blue Goose in 1968. In 1969, he toured England with Arthur "Big Boy" Crudup and Homesick James. The following year, he released his first album, *Travelin' Man*, on Adelphi. After the release of *Travelin' Man*, he began touring America extensively.

Book Binder began playing with fiddler Fats Kaplin in 1973, recording *Git Fiddle Shuffle* the same year. Roy and Fats were a duo for three years, playing numerous concerts and recording a second album, *Ragtime Millionaire* in 1976. Following the release of *Ragtime Millionaire*, the duo stopped performing together and Book Binder bought a motor home, which became his permanent residence. Live performances became his primary concern after the release of *Goin' Back to Tampa* in 1979. For nearly ten years, he toured the country in the motor home, driving himself from club to club, hitting numerous coffeehouses and festivals along the way.

Book Binder returned to recording in 1988, releasing *Bookaroo!* on Rounder Records. During the '80s, he recorded regularly—releasing an album every two to four years—in addition to his constant touring. *—Ron Wynn & Stephen Thomas Erlewine*

Travelin' Man / 1970 / Genes/Adelphi ♦♦♦

Git Fiddle Shuffle / 1975 / Blue Goose ♦♦♦

Goin' Back to Tampa / Mar. 1979 / Flying Fish ♦♦♦

Although Roy Book Binder doesn't put a new spin on acoustic Delta blues, he is passionate about the music and, as his debut *Goin' Back to Tampa* proves, he can replicate the sound of the genre exactly. *Goin' Back to Tampa* didn't exactly launch his recording career—it would take him a decade to release another album—but it captured the spirit of his music quite effectively. *—Thom Owens*

Bookeroo! / 1988 / Rounder ♦♦♦

The line between sincere appreciation and blind imitation is a thin one, and too often contemporary blues or country musicians cross it when covering classic songs. Roy Book Binder avoids the problem by refusing to become overwhelmed by idolatry, and instead enjoying himself while doing vintage material. That was evident on the 12 songs that comprised this session. While Book Binder's convivial vocals made his versions of Jesse Thomas' "Friend Like Me," Merle Haggard's "Nobody Knows I'm Hurtin'," or Jimmie Rodgers' "Waiting for a Train" appealing, his guitar solos and band interaction gave the songs a vital, modern kick. *—Ron Wynn*

- **The Hillbilly Blues Cats** / Jun. 15, 1992 / Rounder ♦♦♦♦

A solid, if a bit uninspired, effort, *The Hillbilly Blues Cats* teams Book Binder with harp player Rock Bottom and bassist Billy Ochoa. Together the trio make their way through oft-forgotten blues chestnuts such as "One Meatball" and "Tired of Bein' Mistreated," as well as the occasional Binder composition thrown in for good measure. A talented guitarist who studied under Rev. Gary Davis and Arthur "Big Boy" Crudup, Binder's music on this album suffers the fate of many modern day blues traditionalists—that is, allowing the audience to ask the question "Why not just listen to the original?" Recording a song like "Statesboro Blues," which everyone from the Allman Brothers to Taj Mahal has done better, only furthers the point. Though he is a fine reproducer of old-time country blues, on *Hillbilly Blues Cats* Binder has yet to find the key to making his music sound like more than just a reproduction. *—Steve Kurutz*

Live Book . . . Don't Start Me Talkin' . . . / May 2, 1994 / Rounder ♦♦♦

Live Book . . . Don't Start Me Talkin' . . . captures Roy Book Binder in concert, playing a selection of standards and originals with conviction and energy. In fact, the record is frequently more compelling and exciting than his studio efforts, which tend to sound a bit too clean and studied. Here, he just plays the blues and the results are always engaging. *—Thom Owens*

Polk City Ramble / Jan. 13, 1998 / Rounder ♦♦♦♦

On *Polk City Ramble*, Roy Book Binder toughens his acoustic blues sound with the addition of bass and drums; while primarily comprised of originals, the LP also sports intriguing covers from artists ranging from Blind Lemon Jefferson to Billy Joe Shaver. *—Jason Ankeny*

James Booker

b. Dec. 17, 1939, New Orleans, LA, **d.** Nov. 8, 1983, New Orleans, LA

Vocals, Piano / New Orleans R&B, New Orleans Blues, Boogie-Woogie, Acoustic New Orleans Blues, Piano Blues

Certainly one of the most flamboyant New Orleans pianists in recent memory, James Carroll Booker III was a major influence on the local rhythm & blues scene in the '50s and '60s. Booker's training included classical instruction until age 12, by which time he had already begun to gain recognition as a blues and gospel organist on radio station WMRY every Sunday. By the time he was out of high school he had recorded on several occasions, including his own first release, "Doing the Hambone" in 1953. In 1960 he made the national charts with "Gonzo," an organ instrumental, and over the course of the next two decades played and recorded with artists as varied as Lloyd Price, Aretha Franklin, Ringo Starr, the Doobie Brothers, and B.B. King. In 1967 he was convicted of possession of heroin and served a one-year sentence at Angola Penitentiary (referred to as the "Ponderosa"), which took the momentum out of an otherwise promising career. The rediscovery of "roots" music by college students during the '70s (focusing primarily on "Fess"—Professor Longhair) provided the opportunity for a comeback by 1974, with numerous engagements at local clubs like Tipitina's, The Maple Leaf, and Snug Harbor. As with "Fess," Booker's performances at the New Orleans Jazz & Heritage Festivals took on the trappings of legendary "happenings," and he often spent his festival earnings to arrive in style, pulling up to the stage in a rented Rolls-Royce and attired in costumes befitting the "Piano Prince of New Orleans," complete with a cape. Such performances tended to be unpredictable: he might easily plant some Chopin into a blues tune or launch into a jeremiad on the CIA with all the fervor of a "Reverend Ike-meets-Moms Mabley" tag-team match.

Booker's left hand was simply phenomenal, often a problem for bass players who found themselves running for cover in an attempt to stay out of the way; with it he successfully amalgamated the jazz and rhythm & blues idioms of New Orleans, adding more than a touch of gospel thrown in for good measure. His playing was also highly improvisational, reinventing a progression (usually his own) so that a single piece would evolve into a medley of itself. In addition, he had a plaintive and seering vocal style which was equally comfortable with gospel, jazz standards, blues, or popular songs. Despite his personal eccentricities, Booker had the respect of New Orleans' best musicians, and elements of his influence are still very much apparent in the playing of pianists like Henry Butler and Harry Connick, Jr. *—Bruce Boyd Raeburn*

King of the New Orleans Keyboard / 1976 / Junco Partner ♦♦♦♦♦

Spectacular date by a great New Orleans pianist whose personal difficulties prevented him from both long life and sustained career achievement. Booker was cited as inspiration by everyone from Dr. John to Harry Connick, Jr., and played with array of performers, from Lloyd Price to Aretha Franklin, B.B. King, Ringo Starr, and the Doobie Brothers. He seamlessly fused a blues base, jazz touches, and R&B/gospel feeling, and this was among his best (and few) recordings. *—Ron Wynn*

Junco Partner / Oct. 22, 1976 / Hannibal ♦♦♦♦♦

This solo disc by arguably the most brilliant of New Orleans' resplendent pianists shows off all the edge and genius he possessed. There may be moments on other discs of slightly more inspired playing (and this is arguable), but for a whole disc this one stands far from the crowd. You can hear some of the most awe-inspiring playing here that reflects the extremely broad background that he could, and did, draw from. You can hear his classical training and the brilliance of his interpretive skills in "Black Minute Waltz." He follows this with a version of Leadbelly's "Good Night Irene," which shows off his raucous bordello style of playing and voice. The disc goes on showing off the eclectic variety of influences that make up this man's music. This disc also displays the man's prodigious composing and arranging talents. Though he was regarded as eccentric and crazy, even by New Orleans' accepting standards (he was a flamboyant, black substance abuser, and a homosexual, who spent time both in Angola State Prison and a mental institution), he was considered a musical genius and thus given a certain amount of leeway. Very informative notes by Booker himself (some insight), Joe Boyd (the producer), and George Winston on Booker and his styling. An absolute must if you like New Orleans music. *—Bob Gottlieb*

New Orleans Piano Wizard: Live! / Nov. 27, 1977 / Rounder ♦♦♦♦

Why so much of what pianist/vocalist James Booker recorded in the '70s didn't surface until the '90s is a mystery, but that's secondary compared to the greatness routinely presented on this CD. It contains nine Booker selections which he performed at the 1977 Boogie Woogie and Ragtime Piano Contest held in Zurich. His relentless, driving style, ability to switch from a hard-hitting tune to a light, soft one without skipping a beat, and wild mix of sizzling keyboard licks and bemused, manic vocals is uniformly impressive. It's a bit short for a CD at 37 minutes, but it has so much flamboyant music and singing that it shouldn't be missed. *—Ron Wynn*

★ **Classified** / Oct. 18, 1982+Oct. 20, 1982 / Rounder ♦♦♦♦♦

While there has suddenly been a flood of CDs featuring masterful New Orleans keyboard wizard and vocalist James Booker, his best release arguably remains *Classified*. The 12-track set was a landmark album, as Booker displayed every facet of his distinctive style. He did uptempo blues, quasi-classical, rock and R&B, making them all sound easy while performing frequently awesome keyboard feats. His "Professor Longhair Medley: Bald Head/Tipitina" pays homage to a legend while also demonstrating how much farther Booker's pianistic skills had developed. While his vocals sometimes aren't the equal of his brilliant playing, they're never less than effective and are sometimes almost frightening in their intensity. *—Ron Wynn*

Spiders on the Keys / 1993 / Rounder ♦♦♦

This aptly named disc showcases James Booker's piano playing; his stretches and runs are breathtaking in their fluidity. This disc (along with its Rounder partner, *Resurrection of the Bayou Maharajah*) was culled from some 60 or so hours of tapes that John Parsons recorded at the Maple Leaf Bar from 1977 to 1982. The main difference in the music on the two discs is that this one is purely instrumental. In fact listen to this version of "Papa Was a Rascal," and then listen to the rendition on *Resurrection*, and what you have is two almost entirely different entities. This disc is made up roughly of what might be called piano bar standards, such as "Sunny Side of the Street" and "Eleanor Rigby," but regardless of how many times you have heard this fare, Booker manages to make each song sound fresh and vital. A special debt of gratitude must go to both Scott Billington and John Parsons for the care taken with this recorded legacy. *—Bob Gottlieb*

Resurrection of the Bayou Maharajah / Jul. 22, 1993 / Rounder ♦♦♦♦
For a man of such talent and influence, New Orleans piano legend James Booker is amazingly underrecorded. This disc, along with its partner (*Spiders on the Keys*) offer up some measure of what the folks of the Big Easy might have heard if they caught James Booker on one of his "on" nights (he was a known drug user and inconsistent in his playing). He is at his best here (recorded at the Maple Leaf between 1972-1982), focused and intense in his playing, wildly passionate on both keyboards and vocals. Some songs are repeated on the companion disc, but each treatment makes the songs new again, so that even his standards are always fresh and vital. Sheer genius at the keyboards and unrestrained, heartfelt vocals on such highlights as Fats Domino's "All By Myself," "The Fat Man," and "St. James Infirmary." *—Bob Gottlieb*

Gonzo: More Than All the 45's / Jun. 11, 1996 / Night Train ♦♦♦♦
Numerous discs are available featuring the eccentric and tragic New Orleans R&B pianist James Booker usually performing solo, recorded during live gigs from the '70s and early '80s. This disc provides an amazing collection of the earliest Booker on piano and organ backed by a full band. Booker made his recording debut in 1954 with the Imperial single "Doing the Hambone," backed with "Thinking About My Baby." During the next few years he would release equally exciting, although sporadic, singles on Chess, Ace, Peacock, and Duke, supported by some of New Orleans finest R&B musicians, including the sax section of Lee Allen, Robert Parker, and Red Tyler, drummer Earl Palmer, and bassist Frank Fields. The 1956 Chess singles "You're Near Me" and "Heavenly Angel" find Booker paired up on doo wop vocal duets with Arthur Booker (no relation). The remaining tracks are scorching dance numbers tied in with novelty/twist themes with catchy names such as "Teenage Rock," "Gonzo" (providing a national hit), "Cool Turkey," "The Duck," "The Crown," and "Beale Street Popeye." This is exceptional New Orleans R&B that provides an important piece of the James Booker musical puzzle. *—Al Campbell*

Lost Paramount Tapes / Mar. 11, 1997 / DJM ♦♦♦
This is a disc made by one of the best piano players to come out of New Orleans, James Booker, playing with an all-star band of New Orleans musicians, most of whom Booker befriended during his days with Dr. John. The music sparkles, all the more amazing because it was recorded live in the L.A. area with no overdubs in 1973, and is just being released in 1997 because it was lost for 20 years. This disc hits a groove and does not quit, shifting from straight-ahead blues to an R&B beat, drifting into some complex Caribbean rhythms, moving off into some jazz riffs, but all the time maintaining the original blues feel it started with. All the players get to shine, but it is definitely James Booker's disc. *—Bob Gottlieb*

A Taste of Honey / 2000 / Night Train ♦♦♦
New Orleans pianist James Booker is captured live on these previously unreleased 1977 solo tracks recorded in the Crescent City. Many of these titles were standards in Booker's repertoire and similar versions have previously been released on disc by Rounder. Spread out over two discs are multiple versions of "A Taste of Honey," "Junco Partner," "Please Send Me Someone to Love," and "Tico Tico/Papa Was a Rascal." The revealing "Classified ('Version 1')" contains almost ten minutes worth of the bizarre rants Booker became known for on "bad" nights. While it provides insight into the unfortunate mental condition of this brilliant pianist, it becomes thoroughly depressing with repeated listening. Throughout his career, Booker consistently demonstrated a capacity to provide emotional renditions of these songs no matter how many times he had played them or what his mental shape happened to be at the time. This disc doesn't provide any revelatory renditions of these songs; it simply uncovers another sampling of this genius of New Orleans piano. *—Al Campbell*

Earl Bostic

b. Apr. 25, 1913, Tulsa, OK, **d.** Oct. 28, 1965, Rochester, NY
Sax (Alto) / Soul-Jazz, R&B
Alto saxophonist Earl Bostic was a technical master of his instrument, yet remained somewhat underappreciated by jazz fans due to the string of simple, popular R&B/jump blues hits he recorded during his heyday in the '50s. Born Eugene Earl Bostic in Tulsa, OK, on April 25, 1913, Bostic played around the Midwest during the early '30s, studied at Xavier University, and toured with several bands before moving to New York in 1938. There he played for Don Redman, Edgar Hayes, and Lionel Hampton, making his record debut with the latter in 1939. In the early '40s, he worked as an arranger and session musician, and began leading his own regular large group in 1945. Cutting back to a septet the next year, Bostic began recording regularly, scoring his first big hit with 1948's "Temptation." He soon signed with the King label, the home of most of his biggest jukebox hits, which usually featured a driving, heavy, R&B-ish beat and an alto sound that could be smooth and romantic or aggressive and bluesy.

In 1951, Bostic landed a number one R&B hit with "Flamingo," plus another Top Ten in "Sleep." Subsequent hits included "You Go to My Head" and "Cherokee." Bostic's bands became important training grounds for up-and-coming jazzmen like John Coltrane, Blue Mitchell, Stanley Turrentine, Benny Golson, Jaki Byard, and others. Unfortunately, Bostic suffered a heart attack in the late '50s, which kept him away from music for two years. He returned to performing in 1959, but didn't record quite as extensively; when he did record in the '60s, his sessions were more soul-jazz than the proto-R&B of old. On October 28, 1965, Bostic suffered a fatal heart attack while playing a hotel in Rochester, NY. *—Steve Huey*

☆ **That's Earl, Brother** / 1943-Dec. 1945 / Spotlite ♦♦♦♦♦
Earl Bostic was one of the most technically gifted of all saxophonists, having complete control of his alto including a huge range. Because he became famous for his R&B hits of the '50s, Bostic has tended to be underrated in jazz circles, but this set from the British Spotlite label shows how powerfully he could play in swing settings. Bostic is featured on four rare numbers apiece with Lionel Hampton's big band (broadcasts from 1943-1944), a studio set with an octet headed by cornetist Rex Stewart in 1945, and with his own ensemble in concert in late 1945; the latter numbers are the earliest documented examples of Bostic leading a band. This set is highly recommended to swing and bop collectors and even to fans of R&B; Bostic's brilliant playing crossed many musical boundaries. *—Scott Yanow*

1945–1948 / Dec. 1945-1947 / Classics ♦♦♦♦

● **All His Hits** / Jul. 1946-Jul. 17, 1964 / King ♦♦♦♦
This definitive recording is not entirely made of altoist Earl Bostic's hits; in fact, "Arrivederci Roma" was never previously released. However, virtually all of Bostic's best-selling numbers are here, including the two-part "That's the Groovy Thing," "Flamingo," "Sleep," and "845 Stomp," plus later tunes taken from albums. 1964's "Walk on the Wild Side" is from Bostic's final King record, cut a year before his death. Listeners wanting to be introduced to Earl Bostic's popular R&B-ish music cannot do better than picking up this album. *—Scott Yanow*

Wild, Man / 1946-1948 / Grand Prix ♦♦♦
Prior to signing with King, the brilliant altoist Earl Bostic recorded 33 selections as a leader, most for Gotham; some of these titles would later be acquired by King. At this relatively early point, Bostic (who was in his mid-thirties) had his sound and technique down, along with a melodic and showy way of interpreting standards and jam tunes. Mostly ignoring the harmonic innovations of bebop, Bostic opted to extend his swing playing into R&B. Although this budget LP does not give the personnel or even the recording dates, most of the selections are relatively rare and quite enjoyable. Highlights include the two-part "Let's Ball," "Barfly Baby," "Tippin' In" and "Temptation," which was very much in the style of Bostic's upcoming King hits. *—Scott Yanow*

Earl Blows a Fuse / 1946-Jan. 30, 1958 / Charly ♦♦♦♦
This English import has a fine cross section of altoist Earl Bostic's recordings for King, starting with 1946's two-part "That's the Groovy Thing" and his huge hit version of "Flamingo" and continuing up until 1958. Although Bostic generally had impressive names in his backup groups (including on this set clarinetist Tony Scott, pianist Jaki Byard, guitarist Al Casey, trumpeter Blue Mitchell, tenors Stanley Turrentine and Benny Golson and even John Coltrane on "Moonglow"), the spotlight is entirely on the altoist. Romps alternate with ballads, and the repertoire ranges from jumping originals to swing-era standards. A fine sampling of Earl Bostic's music. *—Scott Yanow*

1948–1949 / 1948+May 28, 1949 / Classics ♦♦♦♦

The Best of Earl Bostic / 1951-1956 / King ♦♦♦♦
A nice cross-section of this fiery alto saxist's '50s output, it includes his hits "Sleep" and "Flamingo." *—Bill Dahl*

For You / 1956 / Deluxe ♦♦♦♦♦
Although primarily known as a smoothly raucous R&B bandleader, Earl Bostic has jazz credentials that go deep, with records that reveal a technique as good as Charlie Parker's. While Parker made history, and the honker "walked the bar," Bostic still deserves kudos for producing some of the most urbane early-'50s jump blues. And, like Art Blakey after him, he should be remembered for mentoring a slew of up-and-coming hard bop stars—at various times his roster included John Coltrane, Benny Golson, Tommy Turrentine, Blue Mitchell, Stanley Turrentine, and Teddy Charles. In the post-bebop era where jazz combos dominated, many of these musicians might have missed invaluable lessons in ensemble playing and soloing economy that swing era musicians learned routinely in the big band-rich '30s. The outfits of Bostic, King Kolax, and Johnny Otis helped fill the gap, and this particular Bostic album, with its super-tight arrangements and incredible playing, proves the point. Coltrane might not be heard working out an early version of his "sheets of sound," but there's a wealth of top-quality material to be heard. Hits like "Sleep" and "Cherokee" (one of Bostic's best solo vehicles) only make "misses" like the nostalgic, after-hours rendition of "Smoke Gets in Your Eyes" and the heavenly swinging "Night and Day" that much more of a treat. A definite must for fans who like a little pop in their jazz and R&B mix. *—Stephen Cook*

Let's Dance With Earl Bostic / 1957 / King ♦♦♦
Take this alto sax legend up on the invitation! *—Bill Dahl*

Dance Music from the Bostic Workshop / Oct. 10, 1958-Dec. 3, 1958 / King ♦♦♦
Includes an astonishing display of sax technique over a torrid R&B beat on the breathtaking "Up There in Orbit." *—Bill Dahl*

EP Collection / Jun. 23, 1999 / See for Miles ♦♦♦♦

Lillian Boutte

b. Aug. 6, 1949, New Orleans, LA
Vocals / Standards, New Orleans Jazz
A versatile singer based in New Orleans, Lillian Boutte is capable of singing both New Orleans dixieland standards and New Orleans R&B, swing era tunes and contemporary originals. She sang as a child (winning a vocal contest when she was 11), performed with her college's gospel choir and then in 1973 was hired by Allen Toussaint as a backup singer for the many projects recorded in his studio. Boutte appeared as an actress and

singer in the musical *One Mo' Time* during 1979-1984, recorded a gospel album with the Olympia Brass Band in 1980 and in 1982 made her first jazz album. Boutte has spent time alternating between living and performing in Europe and New Orleans, and she has been closely associated with reed player Thomas L'Etienne, who usually leads her backup groups. Through the years Lillian Boutte has recorded for many labels (mostly in Europe) including Herman, Feel The Jazz, High Society, Turning Point, Timeless, Southland, Storyville, GHB, Calligraph (with Humphrey Lyttelton), Blues Beacon and Dinosaur Entertainment. *—Scott Yanow*

● **Lipstick Traces** / Apr. 27, 1992 / Blues Beacon ✦✦✦✦
Lillian Boutte's debut album, *Lipstick Traces*, is an appealing blend of classy New Orleans R&B, Southern soul, classic female blues and jazzy pop, all performed with a signature sense of swing. Boutte doesn't belt these songs out—she caresses them and delivers them with style. Her phrasing is closer to jazz than blues, but her music is inarguably blues, which means that her singing, her music and her album have a classy, sophisticated flavor that is quite alluring. *—Leo Stanley*

Jazz Book / Feb. 1993 / Blues Beacon ✦✦✦✦
Lillian Boutte is a talented veteran singer from New Orleans who is quite credible in a variety of musical styles. For this fairly definitive outing, she mostly sticks to jazz standards and swings her way through such songs as "Now Baby or Never," "Comes Love," "Love Come Back to Me" and even the "Tennessee Waltz." Boutte is assisted by Thomas L'Etienne (her husband) on tenor and clarinet, trumpeter Leroy Jones (heard throughout in top form), pianist Edward Frank, bassist Lloyd Lambert and drummer Soren Frost. Dr. John, a longtime friend, guests instrumentally on four selections, playing either guitar, organ or piano. An excellent outing, easily recommended to listeners wanting to discover a "new" spirited singer. *—Scott Yanow*

Gospel Book / Dec. 16, 1993 / Blues Beacon ✦✦✦

But . . . Beautiful / 1995 / Dinosaur ✦✦✦
Lillian Boutte is a versatile singer who can swing. This particular CD is really more of a middle-of-the-road soulful pop recording than a jazz date (no real improvising takes place) but Boutte's appealing voice and easygoing style sound fine throughout the diverse program, even if the background musicians are given little to do. Highlights include "Be Glad You Ain't Dead" (which has a guest vocal from the date's producer, Dr. John), "You'd Be So Nice to Come Home To," "When Sunny Gets Blue" and "Tomorrow Night." *—Scott Yanow*

I Sing Because I'm Happy / Jan. 1, 2000 / Timeless ✦✦✦
Vocalist Lillian Boutte chose a line from one of gospel music's best-loved songs for the title of her CD, *I Sing Because I'm Happy*. It comes from "His Eye Is on the Sparrow," which is among the selections that Boutte sings on the recording. The New Orleans-born singer went back to her roots in the gospel tradition to make this record. Boutte grew up in a Creole neighborhood in which an integral part of the cultural fabric was the church. She was raised singing in a choir. In fact, her friend Dr. Martin Luther King, Jr., once likened her voice to the great Mahalia Jackson. Boutte speaks of having a recommitment of faith after a life-threatening illness. She often performs gospel when she returns to the city of her birth from her home in Germany. It is with her German musician husband, Thomas L'Etienne, that she made this record of gospel favorites. The singer is renowned in Europe; the decision to make the record reflects the great interest that Europeans have in the jazz and gospel traditions of New Orleans. The jazz singer lifts her voice in praise on a number of gospel favorites, such as "Precious Lord," "In the Sweet by and By," and "What a Friend We Have in Jesus." She is exudes joy on "That Old Time Religion" and shows reverence on "Were You There When They Crucified My Lord?." The CD shows that while Lillian Boutte may be an international star of jazz, she is still a daughter of the church. *—Rose of Sharon Witmer*

Music Is My Life / Jan. 1, 2000 / Timeless ✦✦✦
The title of this CD, *Music Is My Life*, is an apt summation of the life of songstress Lillian Boutte. She and her husband, Thomas L'Etienne, who plays alto and tenor saxophone and clarinet in her band, have spent thousands of hours on the road in Europe, performing gospel and traditional jazz. Boutte, who is from New Orleans, was born and bred in that tradition. She first toured Europe as a star in the musical *One Mo' Time*, married a German musician, and settled in Hamburg, Germany. Her husband, like many Europeans, holds traditional jazz and its makers in reverence. The other members of her music friends, as she calls them, are also Europeans. They include Hans Knudsenon piano, Arild Holm on banjo, Bob Culverhouse on bass, and Loren Houlind on drums. The play list on this CD is a mix of popular standards, blues, and gospel, all done up in Boutte's jazzy style. She takes a song like "All of Me" and turns it into a work of jazz art. Her rendition of "He Touched Me" reflects the depth of her feeling for her gospel roots. The ballads "I Cried for You" and "For All We Know" are perfect vehicles for showcasing the soft and subtle way that the vocalist engages in a song. "Go Back Where You Stayed Last Night" shows her bluesy side. One can understand upon hearing Lillian Boutte sing why music is her life. *—Rose of Sharon Witmer*

Pat Boyack

b. Jun. 26, 1967, Helper, UT
Guitar / Blues-Rock, Modern Electric Blues
Like so many guitarists of his generation, Pat Boyack traced his initial fascination with the blues back to his early admiration of Stevie Ray Vaughan. Born June 26, 1967, in Helper, Utah, Boyack's tastes as a teen originally ran more along the lines of Van Halen and Kiss, but soon he became so immersed in the contemporary Texas blues sound that he eventually relocated to Dallas to pursue a musical career of his own. In 1993, he relocated to the Phoenix area, where he formed the bar band Rocket 88s with vocalist/harpist Jimmy Morello; after the group dissolved, Boyack returned to Dallas, where he eventually formed the blues-rock unit the Prowlers with bassist John Garza and drummer Doug Swancy. After issuing their debut effort *Armed and Dangerous* in 1993, the Prowlers welcomed Morello into their ranks, and *Breakin' In* followed in late 1994. After 1996's *On the Prowl*, the band fell apart, and Boyack assembled a new supporting cast for his 1997 solo debut, *Super Blue & Funky*. *—Jason Ankeny*

Breakin' In / 1994 / Bullseye Blues ✦✦✦

On the Prowl / Mar. 19, 1996 / Bullseye Blues ✦✦✦
Overall, this is not quite in the top echelon but is a solid entry in the increasingly crowded sub-genre of greasy, white-hipster, roadhouse blues—a retro-blend of Texas and Chicago blues sensibilities with dirty-toned guitar, danceable jump and shuffle rhythms, and soul-inflected vocals. The band is a guitar-bass-drums trio, plus singer Jimmy Morello (who brings to mind Kim Wilson and Sugar Ray Norcia, sans harp). Boyack displays flashes of wit on guitar. Producer Ron Levy thickens the sound with his own Hammond B-3, although mixed very much in the background, and with horns on a few cuts. The tunes are all originals, a majority written or co-written by Morello (who has since left the band). Best cuts are the upbeat "Sugar," with its catchy "wo-wo-wo-wo" hook; the minor key "I Know It's Over"; and the Albert King-style "Cleanin' Out My Closet." *—Steve Hoffman*

● **Super Blue & Funky** / Jul. 8, 1997 / Bullseye Blues ✦✦✦✦
Pat Boyack shows up with a new and different sound from his previous efforts on this, his third album for the Bullseye Blues label. When the nucleus of the Prowlers fell apart after the release of their second album, *On the Prowl*, it left Boyack without a band. But producer Mark Kazanoff encouraged him to keep honing his craft, and the result is a disc that shows much growth, both in the writing and the playing. Boyack penned ten of the 14 songs on this, and catchy numbers like "I'll Be the Joker" and the two ballads, "Sweet Redemption" and "Why Must I Suffer?" show a real maturation of his tunesmithing skills. Departing vocalist Jimmy Morello is ably replaced by new singer Spencer Thomas, who brings a mellower and more relaxed feel to the band on tracks like "Think (Before You Do)," Jimmy Nolan's "The Way You Do" and "Can't You See." W.C. Clark also contributes guest vocals on "Righteous Love" and "Why Must I Suffer?," while Boyack literally blazes on guitar showcases like "Poppa Stoppa," "Mexican Vodka" and his own "Longwallin'." With great tunes, solid playing and crisp production all in place, this is Boyack's most realized effort to date. *—Cub Koda*

Eddie Boyd

b. Nov. 25, 1914, Stovall, MS, **d.** Jul. 13, 1994, Helsinki, Finland
Vocals, Songwriter, Piano / Piano Blues, Electric Chicago Blues, Chicago Blues
Few postwar blues standards have retained the universal appeal of Eddie Boyd's "Five Long Years." Cut in 1951, Boyd's masterpiece has attracted faithful covers by B.B. King, Muddy Waters, Jimmy Reed, Buddy Guy, and too many other bluesmen to recount here. But Boyd's discography is filled with evocative compositions, often full of after-hours ambience.

Like so many Chicago blues stalwarts, Boyd hailed from the fertile Mississippi Delta. The segregationist policies that had a stranglehold on much of the South didn't appeal to the youngster, so he migrated up to Memphis (where he began to play the piano, influenced by Roosevelt Sykes and Leroy Carr). In 1941, Boyd settled in Chicago, falling in with the "Bluebird beat" crowd that recorded for producer Lester Melrose. He backed harp legend Sonny Boy Williamson on his 1945 classic "Elevator Woman," also accompanying Bluebird stars Jazz Gillum, and Tampa Red, on wax. Melrose produced Boyd's own 1947 recording debut for RCA as well; the pianist stayed with Victor through 1949.

Boyd reportedly paid for the date that produced "Five Long Years" himself, peddling the track to JOB Records (where the stolid blues topped the R&B charts during 1952). Powerful DJ Al Benson signed Boyd to a contract with his Parrot imprint and promptly sold the pact to Chess, inaugurating a stormy few years with Chicago's top blues outlet. There he waxed "24 Hours" and "Third Degree," both huge R&B hits in 1953, and a host of other Chicago blues gems. But Boyd and Leonard Chess were often at loggerheads, so it was on to Narvel "Cadillac Baby" Eatmon's Bea & Baby imprint in 1959 for eight solid sides with Robert Jr. Lockwood on guitar, and a slew of lesser labels after that. A serious auto wreck in 1957 had stalled his career for a spell.

Sick of the discrimination he perceived toward African Americans in this country, Boyd became enamored of Europe during his tour with the 1965 American Folk Blues Festival, so he moved to Belgium. The recording opportunities long denied him in his native land were plentiful overseas; Boyd cut prolifically during the late '60s, including two LPs for producer Mike Vernon. In the early '70s, he settled in Helsinki, Finland, where he played often and lived comfortably until his death. *—Bill Dahl*

Rattin' and Running Around / 1947-1956 / Crown Prince ✦✦✦✦
Import vinyl containing a nice cross-section of Boyd's RCA and Chess efforts, including three sides from 1947 with Bill Casimir on tenor sax; the doomy Chess entries "The Nightmare Is Over," and a rocking "Driftin'," and "Life Gets to Be a Burden," and the bouncy 1956 rhumba "Don't." *—Bill Dahl*

Five Long Years / Oct. 20, 1965 / Evidence ✦✦✦✦
One of the first and best of Boyd's many overseas recordings, cut while he was in the midst of that auspicious 1965 American Folk Blues Festival tour of Europe. While the caravan was ensconced in London, young producer Mike Vernon spirited Boyd and a rhythm section (guitarist Buddy Guy, bassist Jimmie Lee Robinson, and drummer Fred Below) off to the studio, where Boyd ran through some of his classics ("I'm Comin' Home," "24 Hours," the title track) and a few less familiar items while alternating between piano and organ. *—Bill Dahl*

Eddie Boyd & His Blues Band / 1967 / Deram ✦✦✦

Live / 1968 / Storyville ✦✦✦

7936 South Rhodes / Jan. 25, 1968 / BGO ✦✦✦
Recorded in London in January 1968 with three members of the early lineup of

Fleetwood Mac (the one that played blues, not pop/rock): Peter Green (guitar), John McVie (bass), and Mick Fleetwood (drums). It's an adequate setting for Boyd's straight Chicago piano blues, going heavier on the slow-to-midtempo numbers than the high-spirited ones, though Green is a far more sympathetic accompanist than the rhythm section. *—Richie Unterberger*

Legacy of the Blues, Vol. 10 / 1974 / GNP Crescendo ♦♦♦

Vacation from the Blues / 1976 / Jefferson ♦♦♦

Lovers Playground / 1985 / Stockholm ♦♦

● **Third Degree** / 1993 / Charly ♦♦♦♦♦

Amazingly, the only comprehensive overview of Boyd's 1951-1959 Chess stint available on CD. Both "Third Degree" and "24 Hours" are aboard this 20-track compilation, along with the lesser-known standouts "I Got the Blues," "Nothing but Trouble," and "Cool Kind Treatment." Boyd's sturdy, concise piano work and darkly introspective vocals were brilliantly captured on tape by Leonard Chess, even if the two weren't exactly the best of pals. *—Bill Dahl*

Live in Switzerland / May 30, 1995 / Storyville ♦♦♦

1947–1950 Complete Recordings / Aug. 7, 2001 / EPM Musique ♦♦♦♦♦

Ishman Bracey

b. Jan. 9, 1901, Byram, MS, **d.** Feb. 12, 1970, Jackson, MS

Vocals, Guitar / Delta Blues, Prewar Country Blues

Ishman Bracey (certain 78 rpm record labels are incorrectly spelled "Ishmon," and this has carried over in some sources) was an early figure in Mississippi Delta blues and an associate of singer Tommy Johnson. Bracey learned guitar from "Mississippi" Ruben Lacy, and starting in the 1910s he played local dances, juke joints, fish fries and other local events in rural Mississippi. Bracey first recorded for Victor in Memphis in February, 1928 with Charlie McCoy on second guitar, and the two returned to Memphis for a second batch of records on August 31 of that year. Ishman Bracey finished out his recording career at Paramount with a group called the New Orleans Nehi Boys featuring Kid Ernest Michall on clarinet and Charley Taylor on piano. Bracey also accompanied Taylor on four selections of his own. As in the case of his close friend Tommy Johnson, Ishman Bracey's recording output is small; only 16 titles in all, although four of them are known in alternate takes. Two additional titles, "Low Down Blues" and "Run to Me at Night," were apparently issued by Paramount, but have never been found. Original copies of Ishman Bracey's 78-rpm records are among the most valued items sought by blues collectors. Of Bracey's songs, "Trouble Hearted Blues" and "Left Alone Blues" are very highly regarded, but in general his work is quite consistent and listening to his small output in its complete form certainly has its rewards. After his recording career ended, Bracey continued to perform, again with Tommy Johnson, on the medicine-show circuit. After World War II Bracey "got religion," and wasn't even interested in discussing his career as a bluesman when rediscovered in the late '50s. However, he did provide advice to researchers that led to the rediscovery of Skip James, and it is worth noting that Ishman Bracey continued to perform sacred material in local churches up until the day he died. *—Uncle Dave Lewis*

● **Complete Recorded Works (1928–1929)** / Feb. 4, 1928-Dec. 1929 / Document ♦♦♦♦♦

Bracey's complete recorded works (1928-1929) are presented in chronological order on this single disc, with the bonus of four tracks by the elusive Charley Taylor. Since Bracey only recorded a handful of sides, this compilation is far more accessible than most of Document's *Complete Recorded Works* discs. Furthermore, Bracey was one of the best Delta blues artists of the '20s and his work is consistently engaging. *Complete Recorded Works (1928-1929)* is the best compilation available on Bracey—not only does it work as a concise introduction, it has everything completists will need. *—Cub Koda & Stephen Thomas Erlewine*

Prof. Alex Bradford

b. 1926, Bessemer, AL, **d.** Feb. 15, 1978, Newark, NJ

Vocals, Leader, Composer, Arranger, Piano / Traditional Gospel, Black Gospel

"Singing Rage of the Gospel Age," Professor Alex Bradford, who has been called "Gospel's Little Richard," arguably stands as the most influential male artist of gospel's post-World War II Golden Age. Important as composer ("I'm Too Close to Heaven and I Can't Turn Around"), singer (alternating between a rough, husky chest voice and a falsetto that turned him into a male soprano), stage (and altar) performer, record producer, and group and choir leader, Bradford also pioneered the extension of gospel to secular contexts, particularly with his world tour with Marion Williams in *Black Nativity* (1960), based on texts by Langston Hughes. He was, rare among important gospel performers, both instrumentalist and vocalist. As choir director of Newark's Abyssinian Baptist Church, he proved a fine talent scout into the bargain, giving a start to, among others, Cissy Houston and the Sweet Inspirations, Dionne and Dee Dee Warwick, C and the Shells, and Judy Clay, all of whom went on to have important careers in soul and pop, none of whom ever strayed far from the gospel basis of their singing. Bradford made important recordings on his own, and he wrote hit material for Roberta Martin, Sallie Martin, and Mahalia Jackson, all of whom he also served as accompanist. His Bradford Specials, with whom he made his most important records in the mid-'50s, were the first male group to adopt the innovations brought to gospel by female quartets such as those of Roberta Martin and Clara Ward.

In addition to his influence on the Newark soul singers, Bradford also played a role in shaping the styles of Little Richard, Ray Charles, and even Sam Cooke, all of whose work reflects careful study of his aptitudes and antics.

Bradford grew up in Bessemer, a coal town just outside Birmingham, AL. Bessemer's sizable black population produced some of the earliest gospel quartets, notably the Famous Blue Jays and the Swan Silvertones, which were deeply influential on young Bradford, although he'd later revolutionize the male gospel style by converting "quartets" to "groups." Bradford began performing at age four, singing and dancing in black vaudeville, and, while training in dance and music with a great local jazz pianist, Mildred Belle Hall, proved precociously proficient, enough to have a grand future in popular music.

But Bradford had joined the Holiness Church at age six (over the objection of his father, a Southern Baptist), and by the time he was in his teens, he'd become a follower of Prophet Jones, a Church of God in Christ minister (and flamboyant pianist) who went on to found the Christ Universal Dominion Kingdom of God and Temple of Christ, International Fellowship in Detroit, for a time an influential force in the African-American world.

After a tangle with a racist cop, his parents sent him to New York, where he formed a quartet, the Bronx Gospelaires. On his return to Alabama, he went to a private school and later taught himself, thus earning the "Professor" tag. But his calling was to preach and sing, and he did so prolifically, eventually becoming ordained in three churches and serving as a lay minister in two others.

While still a teen, he served in the Army and entertained at camp shows. He returned to the Birmingham area and preached at the Mother Hargrove Bishop Universal Spiritual Church but soon moved to Chicago. There he was taken up by Roberta Martin and Mahalia Jackson, respectively the most important group leader and solo singer in gospel. (Both Martin and Jackson had known him as a boy in Birmingham.) They were both encouraging and inhibiting and Bradford was eventually compelled to make a break. When he finally formed his first important group, the Bradfordettes, Bradford did so distinctively, drawing equally from gospel and show biz choreography.

Bradford continued to write prolifically for others, coming up with two significant hits for the Roberta Martin Singers, "Since I Met Jesus" and "Let God Abide," while making his first forays into recording for New York's Apollo label, in 1951. Like most gospel journeymen during the Golden Age, he traveled and did shows at churches and revival programs much more than he recorded, and Bradford was always welcome because he had a near-riotous act, heavily arranged and choreographed but finally as spontaneous as gospel must be, that wrecked houses (as the saying goes) all over the gospel circuit.

His breakthrough came when he began recording in Los Angeles for the great producer Art Rupe's Speciality Records. In 1954, "I'm Too Close to Heaven" sold more than a million copies. He recorded for Specialty for six years, at one point serving as director of its gospel line, which meant producing such esteemed colleagues as Bessie Griffin, Princess Stewart, and the Argo Singers.

After leaving Specialty in 1959, he toured England with *Black Nativity* (the recording on Vee-Jay is important but a mere shadow of the stage show). In 1959 and 1960, he recorded in New York for the Savoy and Gospel labels, but made more important recordings for Vee-Jay where he recorded from 1962-1964. It was during this period that he became an international star, touring Europe, principally England, and even going as far as Australia, with a group that included future Rolling Stones diva Madeline Bell (that's her on "Gimme Shelter"). He made some records, mainly unreleased, for Chess' Checker subsidiary in 1966, and rounded out his recording career with sessions for Nashboro in 1967 and 1968, which are fine of their kind but not as dynamic as the best of what he had done earlier.

Gospel styles changed and Bradford's popularity dwindled, which is perhaps why he agreed to take the choir director position at Abyssinian Baptist. He'd already made one recording with the 120-voice choir, for Columbia in 1960 (which includes a definitive performance of his song, "I Want to Ride That Glory Train"), and made another for Jubilee in 1969. But Bradford's interests outside church in the late '60s and '70s were more taken up with a series of gospel-influenced off-Broadway plays directed by Vinnette Carroll, who'd done *Black Nativity*. He toured the nation with the comedic *Don't Bother Me, I Can't Cope*. In 1978, he was in the mist of a struggle with another hit, *Your Arms Too Short to Box With God*, when he had a stroke and died, aged only 51. *—Dave Marsh*

★ **Shakin' the Rafters** / 1960 / Columbia/Legacy ♦♦♦♦♦

A massive 120-voice group led by one of gospel's greatest creative figures, and featuring some of Bradford's greatest songs ("I Want to Ride That Train to Glory," "Said I Wasn't Gonna Tell Nobody," "He Stays in My Room," "The Lord Will Make a Way [Somehow]"), plus a fabulous "The Lord's Prayer." Extensive annotation by Leonard Goines. Produced by John Hammond but that meant he left Bradford alone to get the sounds down his way. And it worked, big time. *—Dave Marsh*

He Lifted Me / 1970 / Specialty ♦♦♦

A good "hard gospel" outing, spiced with animated leads from Bradford. *—Ron Wynn*

The Best of Alex Bradford / 1982 / Specialty ♦♦♦♦♦

A comprehensive selection of his fiery, stomping cuts with the Bradford Specials all-male quintet on Specialty Records. *—Ron Wynn*

Rainbow in the Sky / 1992 / Specialty ♦♦♦♦♦

Only "What Makes a Man Turn His Back on God?," which features Bessie Griffin, has been previously released. But any number of those 23 sides could have been issued with success (only "Dinner, Mr. Rupe?," a half-minute of studio byplay, wouldn't). The earlier, slightly longer take of "Too Close to Heaven" is especially interesting to compare to the hit; too sweet how Bradford whittled almost 30 seconds out of a performance already in fine fighting trim. Superb annotation by gospel historian Anthony Heilbut offers an insightful history of Bradford and his sound and also gets down to cases about various tracks. *—Dave Marsh*

☆ **Too Close** / 1993 / Specialty ♦♦♦♦♦

These are the hits, to the extent that gospel has hits. "Too Close to Heaven," the opener and title track, did sell a million copies in the mid-'50s, when not even many pop records did that. Other highlights: "He Lifted Me," "He Leads Me Surely Through," "Right Now," "Don't Let Satan Turn You 'Round," plus "He'll Wash You Whiter Than Snow," with the great Sallie Martin, and the previously unreleased "Move Upstairs," with the equally great Bessie Griffin. Plus four more outtakes. Very interesting liner notes but they spell out very few musical specifics. *—Dave Marsh*

One Step/Angel on Vacation / 1993 / Collectables ♦♦♦♦

Two 1962 Vee-Jay sessions that feature the Professor working with such stalwarts of the Bradford recording groups as Willie James McPhatter (also a great organist), Calvin

White, and Madeline Bell, who is actually the focus of many tracks. Check "They Came Out Shouting" and "Daniel Is a Prayin' Man" and you'll hear what the Rolling Stones were seeking when they added Bell to "Gimme Shelter." Bradford's own vocals are not his best but the overall quality of songs is very high. Liner notes mainly trace Bradford history. *—Dave Marsh*

Too Close to Heaven / Sep. 1, 1995 / Charly ✦✦✦✦
Fine '60s Vee-Jay collection with Bradford and his singers. *—Opal Louis Nations*

Don't Blame God and Other Gospel Hits / Apr. 23, 1996 / Nashboro ✦✦✦✦✦
Hits is pushing it quite a bit: This is a tribute album from just after Bradford died in 1978, and it features the material he had been working on for his next Nashboro set. It includes a trio of songs added for the CD release. Better yet, it concludes with a previously unissued live medley of "I Believe," "I've Been Dipped in the Water," and "Jesus Gave It to Me" that captures the wholeness of Bradford's appeal like nothing since his Specialty records. Worth it for that alone, as well as Tony Heilbut's loving memorial notes. *—Dave Marsh*

Pop Gospel With Chris Barber/The Soul of Alex Bradford / Jul. 10, 2001 / Collectables ✦✦✦
These two Vee-Jay albums are a study in contrast. *Pop Gospel* shows Bradford adrift from gospel and pursuing his showbiz ambitions, always a better idea on-stage than in the more coldly analytical atmosphere of the recording studio, where all the seams show. At times it verges on unlistenable and it's never far from corny. But *The Soul of Alex Bradford* is a fine piece of work, even if it lacks the chills and thrills of his Specialty heyday. Annotation reproduces the original LP notes. For completists only. *—Dave Marsh*

A Lifetime Believing/Black Man's Lament / Jul. 31, 2001 / Collectables ✦✦✦✦
A pair of albums made in 1971-1972 for Atlantic Records' Cotillion subsidiary. The songs are longer, in the fashion of the day, so two discs are required, but the extra time still isn't enough to let Bradford rock the studio the way he does a church. He seems caught up as much in the mechanics of record making as in the spirit. Still, the songs remain strong—"Letter to the U.N.," from *A Lifetime* even turns over some new ground, and "Something Happened Today" offers historian Anthony Heilbut a chance to try his hand at lyric writing. Notes and packaging are generic Collectables stuff. *—Dave Marsh*

Walking With the King / Savgos ✦✦✦
Prof. Alex Bradford delivered a series of smashing, aggressive, animated hard gospel anthems here, singing with the fire and fury normally associated with Golden Age material, yet also incorporating some elements of modern production. While not quite as majestic as Brother Joe May, Bradford could moan, shout, and holler with almost any singing evangelist, and he demonstrated that on these numbers. *—Ron Wynn*

Tiny Bradshaw

b. Sep. 23, 1905, Youngstown, OH, **d.** Nov. 26, 1958, Cincinnati, OH
Vocals, Leader, Drums, Piano / Jump Blues, Swing, R&B
Tiny Bradshaw really had a two-part career, in the '30s in swing and from the mid-'40s on as a best-selling R&B artist. He majored in psychology at Wilberforce University but chose music as his career. Bradshaw sang early on with Horace Henderson's Orchestra (in addition to playing drums), Marion Hardy's Alabamians, the Savoy Bearcats, The Mills Blue Rhythm Band, and Luis Russell. In 1934 he put together his own orchestra and they recorded eight spirited numbers for Decca later that year. A decade of struggle lay ahead and, when Bradshaw's big band recorded again in 1944, the music was more R&B and jump-oriented. The majority of Bradshaw's recordings were cut during 1950-1954, although there would be one session apiece made in 1955 and 1958. All of his post-1947 output was made for King including the seminal "Train Kept A-Rollin'" in 1951. For several decades, that song became a staple of numerous garage bands along with notable recorded versions by the Yardbirds in the '60s and Aerosmith in the '70s. In 1954, Bradshaw suffered the first of two strokes; the second would be two years later. He spent the next few years recovering in a Florida hospital. In the meantime, King tried to keep his name from disappearing altogether by releasing a single made up of previous sessions. By early 1958, Bradshaw slowly returned to touring and leading his band. A final single was released by King "Bushes" backed with "Short Shorts," which failed to gain any interest. Essentially, Tiny Bradshaw's career was over. The record-buying public, led by teenagers, had already discovered Little Richard, Chuck Berry, and Elvis. While trying to make the transistion to the rock & roll market, Bradshaw passed away from a third stroke on November 26, 1958, at his home in Cincinnati. He was 53 years old. Bradshaw is remembered not only as a fine jump blues shouter, but a bandleader who employed some of the greatest jazz players as sidemen along the way, including Shad Collins, Russell Procope, and Happy Caldwell (all in 1934), Sonny Stitt (who recorded with Bradshaw in 1944), Big Nick Nicholas, Red Prysock, Bill Hardman, and Sil Austin. *—Scott Yanow & Al Campbell*

Off and on / 1950-1952 / King ✦✦✦✦✦

● **Breakin' Up the House** / 1950-1952 / Charly ✦✦✦✦✦
Sixteen of Tiny Bradshaw's biggest and hardest-swinging King label waxings from 1950-1952, notably "The Train Kept A-Rollin'," "Well, Oh Well," "Two Dry Bones on the Pantry Shelf," "Walkin' the Chalk Line," and the jiving title item. Unfortunately, the torrid big band-styled instrumental arrangements that also defined Bradshaw's output are nowhere to be found on this collection. *—Bill Dahl*

Selections / 1957 / King ✦✦✦✦✦

The Great Composer / 1959 / King ✦✦✦
Domestic CD collection that duplicates one of the popular jump blues bandleader's early albums from the King catalog. *—Bill Dahl*

24 Great Songs / 1966 / King ✦✦✦

Walk That Mess!: The Best of the King Years / Dec. 15, 1998 / West Side ✦✦✦✦

EP Collection . . . Plus / Dec. 14, 1999 / See for Miles ✦✦✦✦
Another excellent entry in See for Miles' EP series, here are 24 of Bradshaw's sides for the King label pulled from various extended-play 45 albums along with five bonus tracks. By and large, it's a wild collection of honkin' sax-driven big band sides that trot the fine line between big band stomps and jump blues rockers with a few stray pop things (the corny "Butterfly") thrown in to round things out. An excellent introduction to this highly underrated bandleader's work. *—Cub Koda*

1934–1947 / Feb. 5, 2002 / Classics ✦✦✦✦

Johnny Bragg

b. Jan. 18, 1926, Nashville, TN
Vocals / Doo Wop, R&B
Johnny Bragg came to the music business by a stranger route than most other artists. When he formed his first group and began to write songs, he was doing serious time for rape in a Tennessee prison. Falsely accused of numerous counts of the crime at the age of 16 and convicted at 17, Bragg had already begun serving six sentences of 99 years each when he began singing. The court had ordered that he serve his sentences consecutively. While singing with a group of other inmates that he called the Prisonaires, and with a decade of time served already under his belt, he came to the attention of a reform-minded governor and eventually to the notice of Sam Phillips, who recorded Bragg on his Sun label. Many evenings, Bragg and his fellow bandmates left prison walls behind to perform at concerts held in such esteemed venues as the governor's mansion. Bragg and the Prisonaires also sang on television. Their list of appearances also included the home of Al Gore, Sr. All the while they were performing, they were held under armed guard before being transported back to their tiny cells.

In retrospect, it seems Bragg might not have received the big musical break with Phillips if he hadn't also gotten one of the worst breaks of his life by being wrongly accused and convicted. *Just Walkin' in the Rain*, a book about Bragg and his group of musical prisoners written by Jay Warner, was published in 2001 by Renaissance Books. A CD titled *The Johnny Bragg Story: Just Walkin' in the Rain* was also issued that year by Relentless. Bragg led the Prisonaires during the '50s. Later he sang with two other groups, the Solotones and the Marigolds, who recorded on the label Excello. He also recorded as a solo act for ElBeJay and Tree Music in 1959. His greatest claim to fame, however, came when he wrote the best-selling "Just Walkin' in the Rain." Bragg and the Prisonaires first recorded the song in 1953. Three years later, Johnnie Ray's version soared up the charts, barely missing the top spot. Jim Reeves also made a cover of the song. BMI acknowledged Bragg with honors in 1988 when the number of times "Just Walkin' in the Rain" had been played on the radio topped a million.

While Bragg surely got a bad break when he was sent off to prison, the periods of his life that bracket his time behind bars weren't much easier. A native of Nashville, he was blind from the time of his birth in 1926. His affliction suddenly disappeared when he was around the age of six or seven. His teen years were marked by small-time scrapes with local authorities. Bragg eventually was released from prison when Tennessee's governor, before leaving office, commuted his sentence early in 1959. Bragg landed back in jail a few more times before finally leaving prison life behind for good in 1977. *—Linda Seida*

● **The Johnny Bragg Story: Just Walkin' in the Rain** / Feb. 13, 2001 / Madacy ✦✦✦
The music contained on this disc is as compelling as the stories that are behind it. Both bear out the old saying that truth is stranger than fiction. Fiction has certain rules it has to obey, and it has to be "believable," while there are no constraints or regulations whatsoever on the truth. This music is from the seminal stages of rock & roll, and this group is straight from the Tennessee State Penitentiary system, thanks to a Governor who appreciated music. This group was not just released, but still incarcerated and having to go back there each night after the recording sessions, which for the most part were done at Sun Studios, the same studio where Elvis Presley, Johnny Cash, Carl Perkins, and all those other pioneers made their starts. Rumor has it that Elvis and Johnny Bragg became a great admirer of the work the other was doing and often traded musical ideas. They did sing with each other at various state functions of the time. This is work that is reminiscent of some of the recordings of the Ink Spots, Louis Jordan, and the Mills Brothers, and yet at times has the raw energy of the early Elvis and Hank Williams. The fact that we have it is due to the forward thinking of the Governor of Tennessee at the time, Frank Clement (a story in his own right). The music comes from the harmonies of the gospel groups, the street corners, and all the music that was available on the radio at the time. Music that stretched the whole gamut, all the way from the groups previously mentioned to Perry Como, and all the pioneers at the Grand Ole Opry. The man who put it all together was Johnny Bragg, who never sang until he was falsely incarcerated for rape. Stories held in abeyance, this is music that should not be missed, and contained here is the original version of "Just Walkin' in the Rain," and this version is capable of bringing tears to your eyes. This is rock & roll at its most primal. *—Bob Gottlieb*

Doyle Bramhall

b. Feb. 17, 1949, Dallas, TX
Vocals, Drums, Guitar / Texas Blues, Electric Texas Blues, Modern Electric Blues
Born in Dallas in 1949, this singer/songwriter/drummer grew up listening to Dallas radio (with heavy doses of Jimmy Reed, Ray Charles and Bobby Blue Bland on rock & roll stations) and locals the Nightcaps, one of the country's first White electric blues bands. In high school he joined the Chessmen, which soon included a young Jimmie Vaughan on guitar; they opened in Dallas on Jimi Hendrix's first U.S. tour. Moving to Austin in 1970, he and Vaughan formed Texas Storm, which later shortened its name to Storm and occasionally included Jimmie's younger brother Stevie on bass. Doyle next formed the Nightcrawlers with Stevie (now on lead guitar), who later credited Bramhall as a primary vocal influence. During this time the two also co-wrote "Dirty Pool," which Vaughan included on his debut, *Texas Flood*. Doyle wrote or co-wrote seven more songs on subsequent Stevie Ray albums, and collaborated on three for *Family Style* by the Vaughan

Brothers (which also featured Bramhall on drums). While drumming with Marcia Ball and Mason Ruffner in the early '80s, Bramhall began stockpiling solo recordings, which eventually comprised his long-awaited debut on CD, featuring both Vaughan's and Doyle's son, guitarist Doyle Bramhall, II, formerly of the Arc Angels. He also began a collaboration that proved interesting—with pop singer Jennifer Warnes. *—Dan Forte*

• **Bird Nest on the Ground** / 1994 / Discovery ✦✦✦✦✦

Well, they say the best things in life are worth waiting for—drummer Bramhall started recording this tasty blues-rock album in 1980, wrapping it up in 1992—here it is, out on Antone's in 1994. Not a shabby effort, either—Bramhall has that big smoky Bob Seger kind of voice, and the music is muscular and warm, a friendly, welcome bar-rock kind of sound. Good stuff, I say. *—Steven McDonald*

Billy Branch

b. Oct. 3, 1951, Great Lakes, IL

Vocals, Harmonica / Harmonica Blues, Electric Harmonica Blues, Chicago Blues, Modern Electric Blues

If blues harmonica has a long-term future on the Chicago circuit, Billy Branch will likely play a leading role in shaping its direction. Educator as well as musician, Branch has led the Sons of the Blues, his skin-tight quartet, since the late '70s. Despite numerous personnel changes, the SOBs have never wavered in their dedication to pure, unadulterated Chicago blues.

Although he was born just north of the Windy City, Branch grew up in Los Angeles, only to return to Chicago in 1969 to attend the University of Illinois. Spurred on by the entrancing riffs of mouth-organ masters Carey Bell, Big Walter Horton, and Junior Wells, Branch began to make a name for himself. He replaced Bell in Willie Dixon's Chicago Blues All-Stars, recording with the prolific legend and touring extensively.

The SOBs really were dominated by second-generation talent at the start—guitarist Lurrie Bell was Carey Bell's son, while bassist Freddie Dixon was the offspring of Willie Dixon. They contributed three tunes to Alligator's first batch of *Living Chicago Blues* anthologies in 1978. The SOBs waxed *Where's My Money?*, their Red Beans Records LP, in 1984; by then, personnel included guitarist Carlos Johnson, bassist J.W. Williams, and drummer Mose Rutues. Shortly after that album was completed, guitarist Carl Weathersby was installed as co-frontman, where he remains (as does Rutues; bass is now handled by Nick Charles).

Other than co-headlining Alligator's 1990 summit meeting *Harp Attack!* with fellow harp masters Junior Wells, Carey Bell, and James Cotton, Branch largely busied himself with extensive sideman work (he's first-call session harpist around the Windy City) and teaching an innovative "Blues in the Schools" program until 1995. Verve issued his *The Blues Keep Following Me Around*, an impressive showcase for his gravelly vocals and spellbinding harp. *Satisfy Me* followed in 1999. *Chicago's Young Blues Generation* was issued on Evidence in 2001. *—Bill Dahl*

Where's My Money? / 1984 / Evidence ✦✦✦

Slightly scattershot 1984 LP, originally released on the now-defunct Red Beans logo, that hits more than it misses. At its best—the sardonic title track, a couple of vocals by veteran pianist Jimmy Walker, a stunning "Son of Juke" that spotlights Branch's harp wizardry—it's a fine introduction to the SOBs' multi-faceted attack. *—Bill Dahl*

Harp Attack! / 1990 / Alligator ✦✦✦✦

Four of the Windy City's undisputed harmonica masters in the same studio, trading solos and vocals with good-natured abandon. Billy's showcases are the apt original "New Kid on the Block" and a deft cover of Little Walter's "Who." *—Bill Dahl*

Chicago Blues Session, Vol. 22 / Oct. 8, 1990-Oct. 7, 1992 / Wolf ✦✦✦✦✦

This disc is a fine portrait of Chicago blues—past and present. Award-winning harpist Billy Branch and legendary giant of the famed Howlin' Wolf Band, Hubert Sumlin, here join hands with some of the finest contemporary musicians in the Windy City—among them: Willie Kent, John Primer, Johnny B. Moore, and Carl Weathersby. Sumlin offers two superb band tracks as well as five acoustic duets with guitarist John Primer. In addition, there are four Billy Branch numbers that recast the work of Jimmy Rogers, Jimmy Reed, and Little Walter without ever becoming slavish. The dual-guitar work of Johnny B. Moore and John Primer is exceptional. *—Larry Hoffman*

Mississippi Flashback / Jan. 1992 / GBW ✦✦✦

Live '82 / 1994 / Evidence ✦✦✦

The fact that Billy Branch's backing band for this live date from 1982 is called the SOBs gives listeners hope that this will be a nasty, biting concert. For the most part, that's incorrect, since this wasn't a performance that reached a rolling boil—it was one that kept a low simmer. Nearly all of the songs are taken at slow tempos, and the band lays back greatly; even when they get a little bit of steam, as on "Eyesight to the Blind," they're relaxed. This isn't a bad thing, and the group—including not just Branch, but Lurrie Bell, Eli Murray, J. W. Williams, and Carey Bell, all held in place by drummer Mose Rutues—works well together, creating some nice off-hand moments in nearly every track. Still, nothing here is particularly compelling, even with the addition of two bonus tracks on the CD reissue, and it's primarily only of interest to completists. *—Stephen Thomas Erlewine*

• **The Blues Keep Following Me Around** / 1995 / Verve ✦✦✦✦✦

Branch and Carl Weathersby ventured down to Maurice, LA, to cut this impressive disc with a home-grown rhythm section, but only Branch's name appears on its front. Certainly the harpist is the star of the show, growling covers of dusties by Sonny Boy Williamson, Willie Dixon, and Howlin' Wolf. Nevertheless, guitarist Weathersby provides two of the set's highlights, passionately singing his own "Should Have Been Gone" and "Should Have Known Better." *—Bill Dahl*

Chicago's Young Blues Generation / Jun. 12, 2001 / Evidence ✦✦✦

Jackie Brenston

b. Aug. 15, 1930, Clarksdale, MS, **d.** Dec. 15, 1979, Memphis, TN

Vocals, Saxophone / Jump Blues, R&B, Electric Memphis Blues

Determining the first actual rock & roll record is a truly impossible task. But you can't go too far wrong citing Jackie Brenston's 1951 Chess waxing of "Rocket 88," a seminal piece of rock's fascinating history with all the prerequisite elements firmly in place: practically indecipherable lyrics about cars, booze, and women; Raymond Hill's booting tenor sax, and a churning, beat-heavy rhythmic bottom.

Sam Phillips, then a fledgling in the record business, produced "Rocket 88," Brenston's debut waxing, in Memphis. The singer/saxist was backed by Ike Turner's Kings of Rhythm, an aggregation that Brenston had joined the previous year. Turner played piano on the tune; Willie Kizart supplied dirty, distorted guitar. Billed as by Jackie Brenston & His Delta Cats, "Rocket 88" drove up to the top slot on the R&B charts and remained there for more than a month. But none of his Chess follow-ups sported the same high-octane performance, though "Real Gone Rocket" was certainly a deserving candidate.

Brenston's slide from the spotlight was swift. After a few more Chess singles stiffed (including a duet with Edna McRaney, "Hi-Ho Baby"), Brenston reunited with Turner in 1955, holding down the baritone sax chair until 1962. He cut a series of terrific sides fronting Turner's Kings of Rhythm along the way: "Gonna Wait for My Chance" and "Much Later" for Federal in 1956, "You've Got to Lose" for Chicago's Cobra label in 1958 (also doing session work there with Otis Rush and Buddy Guy), and "You Ain't the One" for Sue in 1961. After a final single for Mel London's Mel-Lon imprint, Brenston was through; he worked as a truck driver and showed little interest in reliving his glory years. *—Bill Dahl*

• **Rocket 88** / Mar. 5, 1951-Apr. 17, 1953 / Charly ✦✦✦✦✦

If Brenston's "Rocket 88" was in actuality the very first rock & roll record, as many experts claim, the rest of his brief Chess legacy adds up to quite a definitive rockin' statement. Among these 16 sides dating from 1951-1953 are his amazing sequel "My Real Gone Rocket," which probably rocks even harder than "Rocket 88" as Ike Turner pounds the keys; "Tuckered Out," the evocative "Fat Meat Is Greasy" (one of several items only out in Japan before the advent of this British CD), and seven sides Brenston cut in Chicago without Sam Phillips to guide him, nor Turner's Kings of Rhythm to back him up. Great stuff. *—Bill Dahl*

Clarence Brewer

b. 1950

Guitar, Vocals / Electric Delta Blues

Clarence Brewer, better known as King Clarentz around the Ozark mountain area where he's a fixture of the local scene, mixes the infectious boogie rhythms of John Lee Hooker with the edgier juke joint modalism of R.L. Burnside and up-to-the-minute lyrics for a blend that's both irresistible and unique in modern blues. Born in 1950, Brewer has developed a strong local following in the Ozarks as a blues performer, sculptor and folk artist. (His woodcuts adorn the cover art of his debut album.) Playing slide on a Sears and Roebuck Silvertone guitar while spinning tales of voodoo, politics gone wrong, the devil's den, fast food killing the populace, and bad women and whiskey, King Clarentz is a totally modern-thinking, cutting-edge bluesman who produces a sound that is positively crude and archaic. In 1998, Brewer cut his debut album, released the following year on HMG and produced by Lou Whitney of the Skeletons and featuring the Skeletons as a backing band. More than just a good-time performer with a backwoods style, Clarence Brewer is a modern artist with much to say and a beautifully raucous way of saying it. *—Cub Koda*

• **King Clarentz** / Feb. 23, 1999 / HMG

John Brim

b. Apr. 10, 1922, Hopkinsville, KY

Vocals, Harmonica, Guitar / Electric Chicago Blues, Chicago Blues

One of the last still-active links to the classic '50s Chicago blues sound that once thrived at Chess Records (only one of Brim's several label associations during the '50s), John Brim may be best-known for writing and cutting the original "Ice Cream Man" that David Lee Roth and Van Halen covered on their first album. That's a pity, for the seriously under-recorded Brim made some exceptionally hard-nosed waxings.

Brim picked up his early guitar licks from the 78s of Tampa Red and Big Bill Broonzy before venturing first to Indianapolis in 1941 and Chicago four years later. He met his wife Grace in 1947; fortuitously, she was a capable drummer who played on several of John's records. In fact, she was the vocalist on a 1950 single for Detroit-based Fortune Records that signaled the beginning of her hubby's discography.

Brim recorded for Random, JOB, Al Benson's Parrot logo (the socially aware "Tough Times"), and Chess ("Rattlesnake," his answer to Big Mama Thornton's "Hound Dog," was pulled from the shelves by Chess for fear of a plagiarism suit). Cut in 1953, the suggestive "Ice Cream Man" had to wait until 1969 to enjoy a very belated release. Brim's last Chess single, "I Would Hate to See You Go," was waxed in 1956 with a stellar combo consisting of harpist Little Walter, guitarist Robert Jr. Lockwood, bassist Willie Dixon, and drummer Fred Below (clearly, Chess had high hopes for Brim, but to no avail).

After a hiatus of a few decades, Brim made a welcome return to studio action with a set for Tone-Cool Records, *The Ice Cream Man.* He still plays occasionally around Chicago. *—Bill Dahl*

• **Whose Muddy Shoes** / 1991 / MCA/Chess ✦✦✦✦✦

First unleashed back in 1969 on vinyl as part of the Chess Vintage Series, this hard-hitting disc couples six of Brim's meanest Parrot and Chess sides with nine Elmore James gems. Brim is at his toughest on the threatening "Be Careful" and "Lifetime Baby." *—Bill Dahl*

Ice Cream Man / 1994 / Tone-Cool ✦✦✦

Brim's vocals don't quite possess the same snap, crackle, and pop that they did in the mid-'50s, but thanks to a savvy song selection and sympathetic backing by the likes of guitarist Bob Margolin and harpist Jerry Portnoy, Brim's comeback album is a generally successful project. *—Bill Dahl*

Joe Britton

b. Nov. 28, 1903, Birmingham, AL, **d.** Aug. 12, 1972, New York, NY

Trombone / Classic Jazz, Swing

A sweet home Alabama fellow, this trombonist was among the second generation of professional American jazz musicians and also straddled the worlds of blues and R&B, poking the long slide of his trombone into any combo that was lucky enough to have him. His credits are lengthy following his student days under the guidance of Fess Whatley. Classic blues singer Bessie Smith took him on the road from 1924 through 1926 as a member of her backing group, at first the Fred Longshaw Orchestra and then the Bill Woods Orchestra. The next year, he jumped to an outfit called Frank Bunch & the Fuzzy Wuzzies, most likely the most obscure name in the list of the groups he played for. He settled in New York in the '30s and fastened a grip on that city's fast-moving and faster-growing jazz scene, working with Ellsworth Reynold's Bostonians, Teddy Hill, the band of classic jazz drummer Kaiser Marshall, Charlie Johnson, Edgar Hayes, and the Vernon Andrade Orchestra. Positions with bigger jazz names were his in the '40s: he worked with saxophonist and composer Benny Carter from 1940-1941 and modern trumpet maestro Dizzy Gillespie, while at the same time collaborating on older styles of jazz. It was his chance to finally work with Jelly Roll Morton, with whom he also gigged and recorded in that decade, and Kansas City jazz pioneer Jay McShann. He also worked with Lucky Millinder for three years beginning in 1942. Blues shouter Wynonie Harris was also a frequent employer, and although this was not always a gig that provided a trombonist with a lot of solo space, Britton shows up on a half-dozen of Harris' raunchy R&B records, not to mention compact disc box set reissues. He also plays in a similar vein on recordings by Sister Rosetta Tharpe. Britton also performed and recorded with the great jazz pianist Earl Hines. The trombonist dabbled into orchestra arrangements and his work in this field is spotlighted on the album *Breaks, Blues and Boogies* by fellow bone-man Vic Dickenson. Britton retired from full-time professional playing in the '50s, but gigged off and on into the '60s, including a regular stint in a band led by saxophonist Wesley Fagan. *—Eugene Chadbourne*

Brooklyn All-Stars

f. 1950

Group / Traditional Gospel, Black Gospel

The Brooklyn All-Stars are an internationally recognized male gospel group who have been performing since 1950. Over their long, fruitful careers, they have won numerous awards and racked up two gold albums. Original members include the group's founder, Thomas J. Spann, Hardy Clifton, and Sam Thomas. They recorded several cuts for Peacock in 1959, including "Rest Awhile" and "Meet Me in Galilee." Their early years were difficult ones; with little money for touring, they often traveled to engagements stuffed into a single car, relying on parishioners' hospitality for food and lodging because they were not permitted inside restaurants and motels. Things improved over the '60s, and they established themselves as a fine traditional gospel act. Between 1971 and 1978, they were annually voted the number one gospel group in the U.S. Their biggest-selling hits are "When I Stood on the Banks of Jordan" and "He Touched Me and Made Me Whole," on the Jewel label. During the '80s, the All-Stars embarked upon a series of world tours. *—Sandra Brennan*

Family Prayer / 1964 / HOB ✦✦✦✦✦

Tight harmonies, fine lead work from Hardie Clifton and Thomas J. Spann. *—Opal Louis Nations*

I've Got My Ticket / Sep. 23, 1994 / Jewel ✦✦✦✦✦

Good strong quartet singing with power-packed delivery. *—Opal Louis Nations*

The Best of the Brooklyn All-Stars / 1995 / Nashboro ✦✦✦✦✦

As the title suggests, truly the quartet's finest moments on Nashboro. *—Opal Louis Nations*

● **Our Greatest Hits** / Nashboro ✦✦✦✦✦

Powerful material drawn from a variety of '60s and '70s Nashboro albums, it's led principally by the soaring tenor of the underrated Hardie Clifton. *—Opal Louis Nations*

Hadda Brooks

b. Oct. 29, 1916, Los Angeles, CA

Vocals, Piano / Boogie-Woogie, Piano Blues

In the mid- to late '40s, black popular music began to mutate from swing jazz and boogie-woogie into the sort of rhythm & blues that helped lay the foundation for rock & roll. Singer and pianist Hadda Brooks was one of the many figures who was significant in aiding that transition, although she's largely forgotten today. While her torch song delivery was rooted in the big band era, her boogie-woogie piano looked forward to jump blues and R&B. Ironically, the same qualities that made her briefly successful—her elegant vocals and jazzy arrangements—left her ill-equipped to compete when harder-driving forms of rhythm & blues, and then early rock & roll, began to dominate the marketplace in the early '50s.

Brooks got a recording deal through a chance meeting with jukebox operator Jules Bihari, who was looking to record some boogie-woogie. The Los Angeles-based Bihari, along with his brother Joe, would become major players in early R&B via their Modern label, which issued sides by B.B. King, John Lee Hooker, Etta James, Jesse Belvin, and other stars. Brooks actually preferred ballads to boogie-woogies, but worked up her style by listening to Pete Johnson, Albert Ammons, and Meade "Lux" Lewis records. Her first record, the pounding "Swingin' the Boogie," was a sizable regional hit in 1945. Joe Bihari would later tell author Arnold Shaw that the single was instrumental in establishing the Biharis' in the record business.

Brooks' first records were instrumental, but by 1946 she was singing as well. She had a fair amount of success for Modern in the late '40s, reaching the R&B Top Ten with "Out of the Blue" and her most famous song, "That's My Desire" (which was covered for a big pop hit by Frankie Laine). Her success on record led to some roles in films, most notably in a scene from *In a Lonely Place,* which starred Humphrey Bogart.

Brooks briefly left Modern for an unsuccessful stint with major label London in 1950. After a similarly unrewarding return to Modern in the early '50s, and a brief stay at OKeh, she largely withdrew from recording into the nightclub circuit. For most of the '60s, in fact, she was based in Australia, where she hosted her own TV show. Her profile was boosted in the mid-'90s by her induction into the Rhythm & Blues Foundation Hall of Fame, and by the inclusion of her recording of "Anytime, Anyplace, Anywhere" in the film *The Crossing Guard.* A new album on Pointblank, *Time Was When,* was released in early 1996. *—Richie Unterberger*

Femme Fatale / 1956 / Modern ✦✦✦

Boogie / 1958 / Crown ✦✦✦

Sings & Swings / 1963 / Crown ✦✦✦

● **That's My Desire** / 1994 / Virgin ✦✦✦✦✦

Twenty-five tracks from her prime, recorded for Modern in the '40s and '50s, including her hits "That's My Desire" and "Out of the Blue," as well as "Anytime, Anyplace, Anywhere." While Brooks was an important figure of the L.A. '40s R&B scene, latter-day listeners may find this rather tame. Vocally she owed much more to pop-jazz stylings than gritty R&B influences. Her most durable and influential performances were her instrumental ones at the piano bench, especially on the pounding "Swingin' the Boogie," which leads off this collection. *—Richie Unterberger*

Anytime, Anyplace, Anywhere / Sep. 25, 1994 / DRG ✦✦✦✦

Time Was When / Feb. 20, 1996 / Virgin ✦✦✦

Jump Back Honey: The Complete OKeh Sessions / Feb. 11, 1997 / Columbia ✦✦✦✦✦

She was best known as a boogie-woogie piano player in the late '40s, but this first-time CD reissue focuses on Hadda Brooks' brilliantly sophisticated, laidback vocal material in the '50s. These songs don't carry the dirgelike sentiments of most blues, but more of a euphoric look at life and love. There are rocking dancers such as "Jump Back Honey" and "Brooks Boogie" among tasteful ballads such as "I Went To Your Wedding" and saucy midtempos like "Time Was When." *—Bill Carpenter*

I've Got News for You / Mar. 9, 1999 / Virgin ✦✦✦

This two-CD set spans Brooks' career from 1945 to 1998 and does a fine job of gathering bits and pieces from the veteran singer/pianist's catalog. Divided into two sections—"Hadda Sings" and "Hadda Swings"—which unsuccessfully tries to separate essentially similar patterns in Brooks' style and manner, this amounts to a representative, if incomplete, compilation of progressing, artistic achievement. The '90s recordings featured here aren't bad, but it's the late-'40s material—particularly Brooks' sublime take on "That's My Desire"—that gives *I've Got News for You* something to shout about. *—Michael Gallucci*

Lonnie Brooks (Lee Baker Jr.)

b. Dec. 18, 1933, Dubuisson, LA

Vocals, Guitar / Modern Electric Chicago Blues, Electric Chicago Blues, Modern Electric Blues

Having forged a unique Louisiana/Chicago blues synthesis unlike anyone else's on the competitive Windy City scene, charismatic guitarist Lonnie Brooks has long reigned as one of the town's top bluesmen. A masterful showman, the good-natured Brooks puts on a show equal to his recordings (and that's saying a lot, considering there are four decades of wax to choose from).

Born Lee Baker Jr. in Louisiana, Brooks took his time when choosing his vocation; he didn't play guitar seriously until he was in his early twenties and living in Port Arthur, TX. Rapidly assimilating the licks of B.B. King and Long John Hunter, he landed a gig with zydeco pioneer Clifton Chenier (not a bad way to break into the business) before inaugurating his own recording career in 1957 with the influential swamp pop ballad "Family Rules" for Eddie Shuler's Lake Charles, LA-based Goldband Records. The young rock & roller—then billed as Guitar Junior—enjoyed more regional success on Goldband with the rocking dance number "The Crawl" (covered much later by the Fabulous Thunderbirds). Mercury also issued two 45s by Guitar Junior.

When Sam Cooke offered the young rocker a chance to accompany him to Chicago, he gladly accepted. But two problems faced him once he arrived: there was another Guitar Junior in town (precipitating the birth of Lonnie Brooks), and the bayou blues that so enthralled Gulf Coast crowds didn't cut it up north. Scattered session work (he played on Jimmy Reed's Vee-Jay classic "Big Boss Man") and a series of R&B-oriented 45s for Midas, USA, Chirrup, and Chess ensued during the '60s, as Brooks learned a new style of blues. The Guitar Junior sobriquet was briefly dusted off in 1969 for his Capitol album debut, *Broke & Hungry,* but its lack of success buried the alias for good.

By the late '70s, Brooks was gaining a deserved reputation as an exceptionally dynamic Chicago bluesman with a fresh perspective. He cut four outstanding sides for Alligator's first batch of *Living Chicago Blues* anthologies in 1978 that quickly led to his own Alligator debut LP, *Bayou Lightning,* the next year. Five more albums of his own for the firm and extensive touring cemented Brooks' standing as a Chicago blues giant. Son Ronnie Baker Brooks is a chip off the proverbial block, playing rhythm guitar in his old man's band and duetting on "Like Father, Like Son" on Lonnie's 1991 album *Satisfaction Guaranteed.* Brooks long association with Alligator Records continued into the late '90s with the release of *Roadhouse Rules* in 1996, which focused more on R&B than down-home blues, and *Lone Star Shootout* in 1999. The disc featured Brooks with fellow guitar slingers Long John Hunter and Phillip Walker playing together and solo in varied combinations of bluespower. *—Bill Dahl & Al Campbell*

The Crawl / 1955-1959 / Charly ✦✦✦✦✦

Lonnie Brooks' pervasive '50s bayou blues roots, laid bare and rocking hard. "Family Rules" was highly influential to the blossoming swamp pop movement soon sweeping southern Louisiana; "The Crawl," "I Got It Made (When I Marry Shirley Mae)," "Roll, Roll, Roll," and "Knocks Me Out" (the latter one of his Mercury singles) drive with youthful abandon. The youngster's ears were wide-open—he even covered Harlan Howard's country ditty "Pick Me Up on Your Way Down," investing it with serious swamp angst. *—Bill Dahl*

Broke & Hungry / Oct. 6, 1969+Oct. 8, 1969 / Capitol ♦♦♦
A momentary 1969 return to the Guitar Junior monicker—for Capitol Records, no less—was produced by Eddie Shuler's son Wayne and focuses on Lonnie Brooks' enduring swamp blues roots (long after he'd jettisoned the style). Unavailable on CD (Crosscut reissued it on vinyl), the LP consists of interpretations of oldies first rendered by Guitar Slim, Lightnin' Slim, Elton Anderson, Larry Davis, Hop Wilson, and Professor Longhair (along with Brooks' own "The Train and the Horse"). *—Bill Dahl*

Sweet Home Chicago / Dec. 8, 1975 / Evidence ♦♦
The French Black & Blue label was savvy enough to spirit Brooks into a studio when he was touring the continent in 1975 as part of Chicago Blues Festival '75. As befits the jam-session ambience of the date (pianist Willie Mabon, harpist Mack Simmons, and two-thirds of the Aces are on hand), hoary standards predominate: "Crosscut Saw," "Things I Used to Do," "Mama Talk to Your Daughter," and the ubiquitous title track (which remains a signature song). The omnipresent "The Train and the Horse" returns as well. *—Bill Dahl*

Let's Talk It Over / Mar. 24, 1977 / Delmark ♦♦♦
Of all the quickie dates produced by Ralph Bass in 1977 for a project that never came to real fruition, Lonnie Brooks' contribution to the series is likely the most satisfying—thanks to a tight band (his working unit at the time) and a sheaf of imaginative originals (notably "Crash Head on into Love," "Greasy Man," and the title cut). An ingenious reworking of Lowell Fulson's "Reconsider Baby" doesn't hurt either. *—Bill Dahl*

● **Bayou Lightning** / Mar. 1979 / Alligator ♦♦♦♦♦
All the promise that Lonnie Brooks possessed was realized on this album, his finest and most consistent to date. The churning bayou groove of "Voodoo Daddy," and a soul-steeped "Watch What You Got," a bone-chilling remake of Junior Parker's "In the Dark," rollicking covers of Tommy Tucker's "Alimony" and Brooks' own "Figure Head," and the swaggering originals "You Know What My Body Needs" and "Watchdog" are among the set's many incendiary highlights. *—Bill Dahl*

Turn on the Night / 1981 / Alligator ♦♦♦
Inconsistent in comparison to its illustrious predecessor, his encore Alligator offering still contains some goodies. Chief among them are the infectious originals "Eyeballin'" and "Don't Go to Sleep on Me," along with a delicious revival of Bobby "Blue" Bland's "I'll Take Care of You." *—Bill Dahl*

Hot Shot / 1983 / Alligator ♦♦♦♦
A return to rollicking good-time form, boasting the roaring "Don't Take Advantage of Me" and "I Want All My Money Back," relentless rocking revivals of Otis Blackwell's "Back Trail" and J.B. Lenoir's "One More Shot," and a faithful remake of Lonnie Brooks' own "Family Rules" from the Guitar Junior era. *—Bill Dahl*

Live at Pepper's 1968 / 1984 / Black Top ♦♦♦
Lonnie Brooks in his jukebox bluesman mode, playing the hits of the day for an appreciative crowd at one of Chicago's legendary blues joints. First issued on the European Black Magic label, the set captures his showmanship effectively as he attacks "You Don't Have to Go," "Sweet Little Angel," "Hide Away," and Johnnie Taylor's soul workout "Who's Making Love." Even in 1968, he was stockpiling originals—a rocking "Shakin' Little Mama" and a distinctive "The Train & the Horse" are all his. *—Bill Dahl*

Wound Up Tight / 1986 / Alligator ♦♦♦
More energetic efforts with a decidedly rocked-up edge. Johnny Winter, long an ardent admirer of Brooks back to the Guitar Junior days, drops by with a passel of fiery guitar licks for the title track and "Got Lucky Last Night." *—Bill Dahl*

Live from Chicago / 1988 / Alligator ♦♦♦
Cut live at Chicago's B.L.U.E.S. Etcetera nightclub, the disc captures the high-energy excitement of Lonnie Brooks' live show. Many familiar titles from his Alligator catalog, along with a handful of never-before released tunes and a marathon "Hide Away" where Brooks pulls out all the guitaristic tricks at his command. *—Bill Dahl*

Satisfaction Guaranteed / 1991 / Alligator ♦♦
Only intermittently satisfying, contrary to its title: a little more subtlety would have benefitted drummer Kevin Mitchell, and some of the material is a bit makeweight. Nevertheless, there are some nice moments, especially on the tunes Brooks penned himself. "Like Father, like Son," the duet between Lonnie and son Ronnie, seems a mite contrived. *—Bill Dahl*

Roadhouse Rules / Feb. 27, 1996 / Alligator ♦♦♦
Lonnie Brooks' music comes from the R&B side of the blues. Brooks is a passionate singer with an intense rockish guitar style. With the exception of "Roll of the Tumbling Dice" (a relaxed duet featuring the harmonica of Sugar Blue), the music on this CD is generally unrelenting in its ferocity, blues-oriented but also quite open to the influences of Stax-type soul and rock. The impressive musicianship and sincerity of Lonnie Brooks' music is probably easier to respect than to love; this release gives listeners a good sampling of his playing. *—Scott Yanow*

Deluxe Edition / Oct. 28, 1997 / Alligator ♦♦♦♦♦
Deluxe Edition rounds up 15 highlights from Lonnie Brooks' late-'70s and '80s recordings for Alligator. Like many Alligator artists, Brooks made records that were just a little too slick to demonstrate the depth of his talents and the grittiness of his playing, yet they still remained solid, rock-inflected contemporary blues albums. The bulk of the highlights from his records are here, making it a fine introduction to Brooks' most popular recordings. *—Stephen Thomas Erlewine*

Lone Star Shootout / May 25, 1999 / Alligator ♦♦♦♦
Louisiana-born and Texas-toughened, Brooks (66), Long John Hunter (68), and Phillip Walker (62) show what blues peers can do in what seem to be peaking years. There are three numbers where all three go full tilt together; the rest of the material varies in personnel, group and solo emphasis. The distinctive, gutsy voice of Brooks, Walker's loping guitar lines with his slighly rough, seasoned voice, and the riveting presence of Walker on all counts, musically and vocally, are showcased to consistently satisfying levels. Of the 15 cuts, there are a handful of rockers and boogies, a few pure soul tunes and ballads, a jump blues, a Cajun calypso, and some straight blues—something for everyone. The hard-swinging "Street Walking Woman" and the slower shuffle "Feel Good Doin' Bad" are great musically, if lacking in message. Walker gets a back-to-back showcase on "I Can't Stand It No More/I Met the Blues in Person," and he tears it up. Brooks pleads and shouts on "This Should Go On Forever," while Hunter's highlights are the cautious "Alligators Around My Door" and the B.B. King cop on "Quit My Baby." Score some plus points for Kaz Kazanoff's sax and harp playing, and the horn charts are mighty fine throughout. Speaking of unsung heroes and heroines, credit pianist Marcia Ball on three cuts, Riley Osbourn playing keys on the others, and Ervin Charles, who does yeomanlike vocal and guitar work and gets two showcase cuts on his own, the best being the Muddy Waters closer "Two Trains Running." This is a historic joining of three blues legends, with so much talent you have to give huge props. Also, buy this simply for Bruce Iglauer's info-laden song notes, worth the price of the CD alone. *—Michael G. Nastos*

Big Bill Broonzy

b. Jun. 26, 1893, Scott, MS, **d.** Aug. 15, 1958, Chicago, IL
Vocals, Leader, Songwriter, Mandolin, Guitar / Prewar Blues, Country Blues, Acoustic Chicago Blues, Acoustic Blues

In terms of his musical skill, the sheer size of his repertoire, the length and variety of his career and his influence on contemporaries and musicians who would follow, Big Bill Broonzy is among a select few of the most important figures in recorded blues history. Among his hundreds of titles are standards like "All by Myself" and "Key to the Highway." In this country he was instrumental in the growth of the Chicago Blues sound, and his travels abroad rank him as one of the leading blues ambassadors.

Literally born on the banks of the Mississippi, he was one of a family of 17 and learned to fiddle on a homemade instrument. Taught by his uncle, he was performing by age ten at social functions and in church. After brief stints on the pulpit and in the Army, he moved to Chicago where he switched his attention from violin to guitar, playing with elders like Papa Charlie Jackson. Broonzy began his recording career with Paramount in 1927. In the early '30s he waxed some brilliant blues and hokum and worked Chicago and the road with great players like pianist Black Bob, guitarist Will Weldon, and Memphis Minnie.

During the Depression years Big Bill Broonzy continued full steam ahead, doing some acrobatic label-hopping (Paramount to Bluebird to Columbia to OKeh!). In addition to solo efforts, he contributed his muscular guitar licks to recordings by Bumble Bee Slim, John Lee (Sonny Boy) Williamson and others who were forging a powerful new Chicago sound.

In 1938, Broonzy was at Carnegie Hall (ostensibly filling in for the fallen Robert Johnson) for John Hammond's revolutionary *Spirituals to Swing* series. The following year he appeared with Benny Goodman and Louis Armstrong in George Seldes' film production *Swingin' the Dream*. After his initial brush with the East Coast cognoscenti, however, Broonzy spent a good part of the early '40s barnstorming the South with Lil Green's road show or kicking back in Chicago with Memphis Slim.

He continued alternating stints in Chicago and New York with coast-to-coast road work until 1951 when live performances and recording dates overseas earned him considerable notoriety in Europe and led to worldwide touring. Back in the States he recorded for Chess, Columbia and Folkways, working with a spectrum of artists from Blind John Davis to Pete Seeger. In 1955, *Big Bill Blues*, his life as told to Danish writer Yannick Bruynoghe, was published.

In 1957, after one more British tour, the pace began to catch up with Broonzy. He spent the last year of his life in and out of hospitals and succumbed to cancer in 1958. He survives though; not only in his music, but in the remembrances of people who knew him... from Muddy Waters to Studs Terkel. A gentle giant they say... tough enough to survive the blues world... but not so tough he wouldn't give a struggling young musician the shirt off his back. His music, of course, is absolutely basic to the blues experience, and was celebrated in 1999 with the release of the three-disc retrospective *The Bill Broonzy Story*. *—Steve James*

★ **The Young Big Bill Broonzy (1928–1935)** / 1928-1935 / Yazoo ♦♦♦♦♦
Big Bill Broonzy was one of the few country blues musicians of the '20s and '30s to find success when the music evolved into an electric, urbanized form. From his initial sides with Paramount in 1927, he followed the music's development closely. Switching to electric guitar and adding drums to his music in the late '30s, he helped pave the way for the Chicago bluesmen that followed him. Even though his music continued to contain echoes of his rural background, Broonzy's reversion to a folk-blues style (popular amongst white audiences) in the '50s was viewed by purists as an inauthentic stance. The truth is that experts have always had a difficult time classifying Broonzy's music. Even on the early sides collected on *The Young Bill Broonzy (1928-1935)*, the guitarist alternates between standard 12-bar fare, brisk rag numbers, guitar and piano duets, and showcases of his flatpicking prowess. Regardless of the setting, however, one thing remains certain: Broonzy's guitar skills are superb. He was an exceptional flatpicker, capable of dazzling with rapid, single-note runs. Proof is provided on "I Can't Be Satisfied" (with Hokum Boy Frank Braswell on second guitar) and the classic "How You Want It Done?" Broonzy was also criticized for relying, more than most, on the key of C (favored by ragtime musicians), though a song like "Skoodle Do Do" demonstrates the guitarist's ability to construct an unconventional arrangement regardless. In addition to Brasswell, Broonzy is

joined by Steel Smith (six-string banjo) and Georgia Tom Dorsey (piano) on various selections. Along with the companion set *Do That Guitar Rag*, this is quite simply the finest collection of Broonzy's timeless, early sides available. *—Nathan Bush*

☆ **Do That Guitar Rag (1928–1935)** / 1928-1935 / Yazoo ✦✦✦✦✦
This a marvelous little companion piece to *Young Big Bill Broonzy (1928-1935)* on Yazoo. Broonzy's ragtime guitar picking is textbook in its scope and his vocals are as warm as can be. Dubbed from old 78s, the ultra high quality of the music make any audiophile nitpicking a moot point indeed. Broonzy at his youngest and full of pep. *—Cub Koda*

Vol. 1, 1934–1947 / Oct. 19, 1934-Sep. 29, 1947 / Document ✦✦✦
This Document LP from 1986 collects 18 formerly very rare Big Bill Broonzy studio performances, 17 of which had never been on LP previously. As it is, Document reissued all of this music on CD in more complete fashion in the '90s. However, if one runs across this LP, there is much to enjoy here. The 18 cuts are from 15 different sessions, with a test pressing of "C-C Rider" being the lone entry from 1934 and "San Antonio Blues" and "Just Rocking" representing Broonzy's postwar years; otherwise, the performances are from 1937-1941. With fine backup work from such players as pianists Black Bob, Blind John Davis, Joshua Altheimer and Memphis Slim, plus either bass or drums and (on four occasions) one or two horns, Broonzy is heard throughout in excellent form. Highlights include "Made a Date With an Angel," "Good Time Tonight," "What Is That She Got" and "Just Rocking." Not essential, but a good gap-filler. *—Scott Yanow*

Vol. 2, 1935–1949 / Jun. 20, 1935-Jan. 4, 1949 / Document ✦✦✦
Unlike Document's Big Bill Broonzy CDs, this LP (the second of two albums) is a sampler of Broonzy's work, a very generous 20-selection program. The emphasis is on rarity rather than necessarily quality (all but one tune had never been out on album when this 1988 LP was released). But in general, the consistent vocalist/guitarist is in typically excellent form. With the exception of three later tracks, the music dates from 1935-1941. Broonzy's accompanists included pianists Black Bob, Blind John Davis, Joshua Altheimer and Memphis Slim and various bassists or drummers; trumpeter Punch Miller guests on "Why Do You Do That to Me." Among the other selections included in this hour-long LP are "I'm a Southern Man," "I Want My Hands On It," a test pressing of "Flat Foot Susie With Her Flat Yes Yes," "Don't You Want to Ride" and "Let's Have a Little Fun." However, since all of the music is available in more complete form on Document CDs, that is a preferable way to acquire these recordings. *—Scott Yanow*

Blues in the Mississippi Night / 1946 / Rykodisc ✦✦✦✦✦
In 1946, the day after a successful Town Hall concert was given by guitarist Big Bill Broonzy, pianist Memphis Slim and harmonica wizard Sonny Boy Williamson, Alan Lomax met the trio at the Decca studios in New York. Armed with just a single microphone and a disc recorder, Lomax persuaded Memphis Slim to play a blues and then he said "Listen, you all have lived with the blues all your life, but nobody here understands them. Tell me what the blues are all about." For the next two hours the three bluesmen talked about their lives, the day-to-day struggles with racism and about the constant battle to avoid prisons and lynch mobs in the South. Broonzy did the majority of the storytelling and there are many interesting (and sometimes scary) anectodes, some dark humor and demonstrations about how anger toward the White man could be safely expressed in music. After hearing the playback of the candid conversations, the bluesmen begged Lomax not to release them because they were fearful that their families and relatives in the South would be murdered if their frank comments ever came out. One hour of the discussions was finally released in 1991 on this single CD along with an accompanying booklet which contains the complete transcription of the meeting. Although there are only three brief songs on this set, the important release (recorded 19 years before the Civil Rights Act made anti-racism protests a bit safer) should be of great interest to blues historians and those concerned with the history of race relations. *—Scott Yanow*

In Concert / Sep. 15, 1951 / Raretone ✦✦✦✦
This double LP from 1988 released for the first time a Big Bill Broonzy concert made in Dusseldorf, Germany, with Graeme Bell's Australian Jazz Band. Bell's hot Dixieland band (an octet that includes trumpeter Roger Bell, trombonist Derick Bentley, Don Roberts on clarinet and tenor, pianist Bell, and the remarkable Lazy Ade Monsborough on trumpet, clarinet and alto) is well featured on half of the program, playing such numbers as "Muskrat Ramble," Jelly Roll Morton's "Kansas City Stomp" and "It Don't Mean a Thing." Broonzy, who at the time was portrayed as a folk and country blues artist (never mind that he was really a sophisticated guitarist based in Chicago), mostly plays familiar standards including "John Henry," "Trouble In Mind" and "Mama Don't Allow"; on three of his seven songs he is joined by some of Bell's musicians. The proceedings end with everyone coming together for a spirited "When the Saints Go Marching In." Overall, the unique combination of Big Bill Broonzy (who usually worked as an unaccompanied solo act during this period) and Graeme Bell works quite well. *—Scott Yanow*

Big Bill Broonzy & Washboard Sam / 1953 / MCA/Chess ✦✦✦
Although Chess didn't bother to anthologize these sides into album form until the early '60s, this marvelous collection actually dates from 1953. Broonzy and Sam are both in great form here, sharing the vocals throughout and recalling their earlier days as Bluebird label and session mates. The sound is fleshed out by the addition of guitarist Lee Cooper (who at times almost sounds a bit too modern for the genre being explored here, throwing in what can only be described as Chuck Berry licks) and Big Crawford on upright bass. *—Cub Koda*

1955 London Sessions / 1955 / Collectables ✦✦✦
There's no shortage of late-era Big Bill Broonzy recordings, as the blues legend appeared throughout Europe and cut numerous sessions during the final five years of his life. The ten songs assembled here—taken from various Pye/Nixa EPs and 10" LPs cut during October of 1955—are unusual in that they're more diverse and intense than much of what Broonzy cut in America. "When Do I Get to Be Called a Man," which is practically a sung demand for civil rights, opens the CD on a dignified but impassioned note. "St. Louis Blues" is done by Broonzy as a solo guitar instrumental, and benefits from his dazzling (and often underrated) dexterity on the guitar. "Southbound Train" finds him playing in front of a band (including Phil Seaman on drums) that lends a slow, "Chattanooga Choo-Choo"-style accompaniment to his singing and playing. "It Feels So Good" is another band number, this time with saxmen Bruce Turner (alto) and Kenny Graham (tenor) and trumpeter Leslie Hutchinson given more room to stretch out. The performances are first-rate, as is the recording, the cutting of which was assisted by a young (and not yet famous) Joe Meek. One of Broonzy's more interesting and diverse later recordings. *—Bruce Eder*

Big Bill Broonzy Sings Folk Songs / 1956 / Smithsonian/Folkways ✦✦✦✦✦
Often ranked with such blues greats as Robert Johnson, Son House, and Elmore James, Big Bill Broonzy was for many years the last surviving practitioner of the "Delta" style of blues. This record, cut for Smithsonian/Folkways in 1956, captures Broonzy late in his career but still during the peak of his power. Indeed, a more magisterial performance could not be imagined. While born and raised on the Mississippi, Broonzy takes this opportunity to demonstrate the range of musical influences he's successfully mastered over the course of his career. Proving to be equally at home in both country-folk and straight blues idioms, Broonzy offers sparkling renditions of both "Alberta" and "John Henry," where Broonzy sings an interesting set of uncommon lyrics, bending the melody with an inspired blues shift. On "This Train," Broonzy works the call and response with a gospel choir and scathingly delivers the line, "This train carries both white and black now." Perhaps simply to prove a point, he closes with the slightly more contemporary standard "Glory of Love," sweetly inflecting the chorus with a tender bit of jazz lyricism. While this is not considered "the" Broonzy album to own, it is, nonetheless, a very good one, and has the obvious advantage of being kept continually in print by Smithsonian/Folkways. *—Brian Whitener*

Historic Concert Recordings / 1957 / Southland ✦✦

Blues With Big Bill Broonzy, Sonny Terry, Brownie McGhee / 1959 / Folkways ✦✦✦✦
Taped live on the air at WFMT Chicago in 1959, this Folkways recording is an extremely entertaining collection. With 12 outstanding performances scattered between questions from interviewer Studs Terkel, the session has a very live and impromptu feeling. The material itself is first-rate, with Broonzy, McGhee, and Terry all taking separate turns with their own selections, as well as trading off verses in songs on which all three play. From McGhee's "Blood River Blues" to Broonzy's guitar workout on "Shuffle Rag," the material is consistently engaging. Even better, we get to hear each of the blues legends give their own definitions of the blues as well as their earliest memories and experiences with the music. In addition to this, each explains his connection to the songs before he sings them. The listener is even treated to an impromptu jam session during which all three trade off-the-cuff verses. At Broonzy's urging the three decide to show what they consider an essential link between spirituals and the blues, and each closes out the set with a spiritual, with all of them joining in on "When the Saints Go Marching In." Overall, this is an extremely interesting and entertaining blues document and resource. *—Matt Fink*

The Bill Broonzy Story / 1960 / Verve ✦✦✦
This three-CD set (originally five LPs) was a product of three recording sessions, held on July 12 and 13, 1957, immediately before Broonzy entered the hospital for surgery on the lung cancer that would end his career and take his life just a year later. He sounds in good enough spirits, and the voice and guitar are still in excellent form as he runs through the songs that evidently mattered most to him on those two days: "Key to the Highway," "Take This Hammer," "See See Rider," "Alberta," "Frankie and Johnny," "In the Evening (When the Sun Goes Down)," "Swing Low, Sweet Chariot," and more than two dozen others. Producer Bill Randle didn't get a lot of the songs he'd hoped to record, such as "Stack O Lee" and "Night Time Is the Right Time," which Broonzy didn't want to sing, but he got enough for five LPs' worth of music out of the ten hours of recordings. (Did the rest survive, one wonders, and might there be anything that was left off that's worth hearing?) The sound is state of the art, with the singer and his solo acoustic guitar clean and close. The set is a vital and important document, as well as great listening, not only for the music but for Broonzy's between-song banter—he was one of the great raconteurs of the blues—although it isn't quite as indispensable as one might think. *—Bruce Eder*

★ **Good Time Tonight** / 1990 / Columbia/Legacy ✦✦✦✦✦
If you're following the 30-plus year career of Bill Broonzy and already have the two early compilations available on Yazoo, here's where you go next. These are basically ensemble works covering the time frame between 1930 to 1940 and Broonzy sounds very comfortable in the company of Blind John Davis and Joshua Altheimer. The 20 tracks compiled here (culled from various Vocalion, ARC and Columbia sessions) sound pretty great, benefitting mightily from modern sound restoration devices. *—Cub Koda*

Complete Recorded Works (1927–1942) / 1991 / Document ✦✦✦
If having it *all* is your ultimate goal as a blues collector, this 11-CD set will certainly aid and abet in that pursuit. On this exhaustive collection from 1927-1942 you *will* find a plethora of great sides, including "C-C Rider," "Milkcow Blues," and his finest instrumental, "House Rent Stomp." Collecting up 15 years of recorded works and running them in strict chronological order is a most laudable effort, but this certainly is not the place to start in building up a great Big Bill Broonzy collection. For completists only. *—Cub Koda*

Complete Recorded Works, Vol. 1 (1927–1932) / 1991 / Document ✦✦✦✦✦
This is a particularly fascinating CD, for it has the first 26 selections ever recorded by Big Bill Broonzy as a leader. The beginning of Document's complete reissuance of all of Broonzy's early recordings, the set starts with four duet numbers that Broonzy cut during 1927-1928 with fellow guitarist John Thomas. Although his style was already a bit recognizable, the young guitarist/vocalist really started coming into his own in 1930. There

are 15 selections from that year included on this set, with Big Bill often using the pseudonyms of Sammy Sampson or Big Bill Johnson; in fact, even the final seven numbers (from 1932) had him billed as the latter. The CD finds Broonzy evolving from a country blues musician who already had strong technique into a star of hokum records. Among the many highlights are "Big Bill Blues" (different versions in 1928 and 1932), "I Can't Be Satisfied," "Pig Meat Strut," "Beedle Um Bum" and "Selling That Stuff." Pianist Georgia Tom Dorsey helps out on three numbers. Big Bill Broonzy fans have a right to rejoice about the existence of this wonderful series. —*Scott Yanow*

Complete Recorded Works, Vol. 2 (1932–1934) / 1991 / Document ✦✦✦
By early 1932, the point at which this second volume in Document's series begins, Big Bill Broonzy was well established on the Chicago music scene; although his music was beginning to take on an urbanized flavor, his forte was still country blues, and the opening tracks here—"Mr. Conductor Man," "Too-Too Train Blues" and "Bull Cow Blues" among them—are among his finest examples of the form. Of equal interest are the sides he subsequently recorded with his Jug Busters, a rather mysterious group which yielded just two tracks—"Rukus Juice Blues" and "M and O Blues"—but which pushed Broonzy further away from his rural roots; in all likelihood, the group also inaugurated his collaboration with the enigmatic yet renowned Black Bob, with whom he would cut a series of classic guitar and piano duets in the months to follow. —*Jason Ankeny*

Complete Recorded Works, Vol. 3 (1934–1935) / 1991 / Document ✦✦✦
Big Bill Broonzy's absorption of the urbanized Chicago blues style was essentially complete by the time of the 1934-1935 recordings assembled here. The highlight is a highly productive session featuring the State Street Boys, a group featuring Broonzy alongside harpist Jazz Gillum, guitarist Carl Martin, pianist Black Bob, and violinist Zeb Wright, whose dissonant, scraping style lends the combo a highly distinctive sound; their material is fascinatingly diverse, ranging from the train songs "Midnight Special" and "Mobile and Western Line" to the saucy "She Caught the Train" and the much-covered "Don't Tear My Clothes." Also with Black Bob, Broonzy continued recording more simplified guitar/piano duets—their "Southern Blues" is a lovely and nostalgic reminiscence about life on the other side of the Mason-Dixon line, while "Good Jelly" ranks among his most lyrically inventive efforts. —*Jason Ankeny*

1934–1947 / Jan. 1991 / Wolf ✦✦✦

Unissued Test Pressings / 1992 / Milan ✦✦✦
Unissued Test Pressings compiles 15 alternate versions of Big Bill Broonzy classics like "WPA Blues," "Married Life Is a Pain" and "Unemployed Stomp," released here with their spoken introductions intact; that alone makes these sides invaluable for scholars, as the intros not only run down the other musicians on the session but also provide additional track information. Unfortunately, scholars and Broonzy fanatics are about the only listeners to whom the collection will appeal—the overall sound quality is simply too poor for casual fans to endure. —*Jason Ankeny*

Complete Recorded Works, Vol. 4 (1935–1936) / 1992 / Document ✦✦✦✦✦
Swing might have been king by 1935-1936, but Big Bill Broonzy was a different type of royalty, one of the major bluesmen in Chicago. Always a technically skilled guitarist, Broonzy's vocalizing had grown in maturity and depth during the first half of the '30s. On the fourth of 11 Document CDs that contain all of Big Bill's prewar recordings as a leader (and many as a sideman), Broonzy is heard on two religious numbers with the Chicago Sanctified Singers, one tune ("Keep Your Mind on It") with the Hokum Boys, and 21 songs either in duets with pianist Black Bob or trios with Black Bob and bassist Bill Settles. Among the more memorable selections are "Bad Luck Blues," "I'm Just a Bum," "Keep Your Hands Off Her," "The Sun Gonna Shine In My Door Someday" and "Match Box Blues." —*Scott Yanow*

Complete Recorded Works, Vol. 5 (1936–1937) / 1992 / Document ✦✦✦✦
Big Bill Broonzy recorded a great deal in Chicago during the '30s, and fortunately, every one of the selections (except for a few that cannot be located) have been reissued on CD by the Austrian Document label in this "complete" series. In addition to selections with a trio (which includes pianist Black Bob and bassist Bill Settles), Broonzy is heard on this fifth volume with the Hokum Boys (on "Nancy Jane"), the Midnight Ramblers (including Washboard Sam), and the Chicago Black Swans (a band similar to the Harlem Hamfats that adds guitarist Tampa Red). The final four numbers return to the trio format but add trumpeter Punch Miller to two of the songs. Throughout, Broonzy is heard in prime form. Among the selections are "Big Bill's Milk Cow No. 2," "Nancy Jane," "Detroit Special," "Out With the Wrong Woman," "Southern Flood Blues," and "Let's Reel and Rock." —*Scott Yanow*

Complete Recorded Works, Vol. 6 (1937) / 1992 / Document ✦✦✦✦
1937 was a busy year for Big Bill Broonzy, who was turning 44. A greatly in-demand blues guitarist in Chicago, Broonzy was also an underrated singer and a major solo artist. This CD from the Austrian Document label (the sixth of 11 that trace his entire prewar recording career) includes 26 selections with plenty of alternate takes and nine previously unreleased performances. Broonzy is joined by either Black Bob, Leeford or Aletha Robinson or Joshua Altheimer on piano (Blind John Davis joins up for the final session), and sometimes bassist Bill Settles, drummer Fred Williams, unidentified players and (on three occasions) trumpeter Punch Miller. Although not quite essential, this CD will be desired by Broonzy's greatest fans, along with all of the releases in this very valuable series. Among the more notable selections are "Mean Old World," "Down in the Alley," "Louise, Louise Blues" and "It's Too Late Now." —*Scott Yanow*

Complete Recorded Works, Vol. 7 (1937–1938) / 1992 / Document ✦✦✦✦
Big Bill Broonzy's '30s recordings (reissued in full on this extensive series of Document CDs) are remarkably consistent and have an impressive amount of variety within the blues idiom. During the 11 months covered by this seventh volume, Broonzy recorded as

part of three different trios with either Blind John Davis or Joshua Altheimer on piano and Fred Williams, Bill Settles or Ransom Knowling on bass; a "modern" quartet with tenorman Bill Owsley and the pioneering electric guitar of George Barnes (on Mar. 1, 1938); and with a few slightly expanded groups, including one with trumpeter Punch Miller. Broonzy was open to the influence of swing (thus the occasional horns) while sticking to his Chicago blues base. Such numbers as "Hattie Blues," "Somebody's Got to Go," "It's a Low Down Dirty Shame," "Unemployment Stomp," "Night Time Is the Right Time No. 2" and "W.P.A. Rag" show off his versatility and talents. —*Scott Yanow*

Complete Recorded Works, Vol. 8 (1938–1939) / 1992 / Document ✦✦✦✦✦
Big Bill Broonzy's popularity continued to rise during the five months covered by this CD (the eighth of 11) in Document's "complete" Broonzy series. In addition to 21 studio sides (five previously unissued) made in Chicago, Broonzy is heard performing "Done Got Wise" and "Louise, Louise" at John Hammond's "Spirituals to Swing" concert at Carnegie Hall (with the backing of pianist Albert Ammons and bassist Walter Page). Otherwise, the influential guitarist/singer is featured with the Memphis Five (a group including trumpeter Walter Williams and altoist Buster Bennett) and various trio/quartets with his regular pianist of the period, Joshua Altheimer. This CD is particularly notable for including the original version of "Just a Dream," which became a standard. Otherwise, Broonzy shows off the influence of both swing and country blues in varying combinations; his repertoire here includes "Trouble and Lying Woman," "Flat-Foot Susie With Her Flat Yes Yes," "Preachin' the Blues" and "Fightin' Little Rooster." —*Scott Yanow*

Complete Recorded Works, Vol. 9 (1939) / 1992 / Document ✦✦✦✦
During the latter half of 1939, blues guitarist/singer Big Bill Broonzy was near the height of his fame and was recording quite prolifically. For the ninth of 11 Document CDs in the comprehensive Broonzy series, he is joined throughout by pianist Joshua Altheimer and either bassist Ransom Knowling (the first nine numbers) or drummer Fred Williams. The erratic clarinetist Odell Rand (who also plays some alto sax) is on the first session and does not help things much, but Broonzy is so strong that it really does not matter. Among the more notable numbers are "She Never," "Too Many Drivers," "That's All Right Baby" and "Dreamy Eyed Baby," while "Just a Dream No. 2" is a remake/continuation of his hit from earlier in the year. —*Scott Yanow*

Complete Recorded Works, Vol. 10 (1940) / 1992 / Document ✦✦✦✦
The tenth of 11 Document CDs covering all of Big Bill Broonzy's prewar sessions as a leader has three dates (resulting in 14 songs) in which Broonzy is joined by the reliable pianist Joshua Altheimer and either drummer Fred Williams or Washboard Sam on washboard. Altheimer died unexpectedly later that summer; the other two sets included on this CD have either Blind John Davis or Memphis Slim in Altheimer's place, and the trio is rounded off by either drummer Williams or bassist Ransom Knowling. Although Big Bill did not evolve much during 1940, he was near the peak of his popularity and very much in prime form. Among the high points of the 26 selections (including three previously unreleased alternate takes) in this collection are "Jivin' Mr. Fuller Blues," "Leap Year Blues," "What Is That She Got," "Lonesome Road Blues" and "I'll Never Dream Again." Recommended to Broonzy's many fans. —*Scott Yanow*

Complete Recorded Works, Vol. 11 (1940–1942) / 1992 / Document ✦✦✦✦✦
The final of Document's prewar Big Bill Broonzy CDs (documenting all of his 1927-1942 recordings) features Broonzy playing in a timeless style. Most of the performances could be considered goodtime music, with Broonzy sounding as if he were ready to party. On three of the four complete sessions that are included (plus "Rockin' Chair Blues," left over from the 1940 date otherwise included on *Vol. 10*), Broonzy is joined by either Memphis Slim, Horace Malcolm or Blind John Davis on piano, plus Washboard Sam (his half-brother) on washboard; Jazz Gillum sits in on harmonica during "Key to the Highway." The final set has Broonzy, pianist Memphis Slim and drummer Judge Riley joined by trumpeter Punch Miller and altoist Buster Bennett. Overall, this is a pretty strong program, with such numbers as "Sweet Honey Bee," "When I Been Drinking," "Key to the Highway," "Conversation With the Blues," "All By Myself," "I Feel So Good," "I'm Gonna Move to the Outskirts of Town" and "I'm Woke Up Now" being among the 25 selections. Big Bill Broonzy fans will want all of the releases in this remarkable series. —*Scott Yanow*

Black, Brown and White / 1995 / Evidence ✦✦✦
Black, Brown and White includes live tracks recorded in Belgium in March 1952 (three featuring pianist Blind John Davis) and December 1955 during Europe's discovery of Big Bill Broonzy. The highlight of the disc is the laid-back atmosphere in the living room setting recorded at Broonzy biographer Yannick Bruynoghes' house in Brussels. Several Broonzy classics are revisited, along with traditional blues standards "Nobody's Business," "Alberta," and "Careless Love." —*Al Campbell*

I Feel So Good / 1995 / Indigo ✦✦✦✦✦

Complete Recorded Works, Vol. 12 (1945–1947) / Sep. 1, 1995 / Document ✦✦✦

☆ **Big Bill's Blues** / 1996 / Pearl ✦✦✦✦✦
If you're going to sweat a Big Bill Broonzy collection down to only one disc, this is the one to keep in the collection. It's really his most representative work, highlighting most of the best-known numbers from his extensive repertoire and the highlights (including a hilarious "When I've Been Drinkin'," in which he supposedly downs several shots on microphone during the take) are numerous. —*Cub Koda*

Treat Me Right / Feb. 6, 1996 / Rykodisc/Tradition ✦✦✦✦
This midpriced reissue of the Archive of Folk Music recording Big Bill Broonzy (FS-213) chronicles the blues singer-guitarist's European comeback of the early '50s, when he was in his late fifties. He is assured and comfortable with the material, which includes such standards as "Baby Please Don't Go," "See Rider," and even "Sixteen Tons" (the last

suggesting his eclecticism). His performance of "St. Louis Blues" should serve as a lesson to guitar players everywhere, and "Ridin' On Down," which he speak-sings in a deadpan manner, is hilarious. Complete with warmups and coughs, this is hardly a professional session, but a pro like Broonzy doesn't require much more than a microphone and a tape recorder to make a good record. *—William Ruhlmann*

In Chicago 1932–1937 / Feb. 20, 1996 / EPM Musique ♦♦♦♦

The indomitable Big Bill Broonzy would have already passed his 100th birthday, and hardcore blues enthusiasts are of course ever grateful for the many, many great records made by Big Bill and his century's worth of influence. His high old time in Chicago spanned a far longer period than *In Chicago 1932-1937* documents, although these are without question choice and demonstrative cuts performed at a distinct and motivated peak in the man's career. All of these spare but full-tilt blues classics can be found on numerous other collections, although there is a well-knit and sequenced quality to these live versions that distinguishes this record from even other live Windy City shows. "Long Tall Mama," "You Know I Got a Reason" and "Little Bug" are the kind of sweet-smiling, affectionately home-cooked blues songs that bring to mind and heart an almost fatherly Big Bill. "Oh Babe" is a plaintive but convincing suitor's song, and "Come Up to My House" is pure mischief. Regardless of the selection, there is zero doubt found here or anywhere else that Chicago is this man's town, and 1932 to 1937 was more like a great blues weekend there. *—Becky Byrkit*

Warm, Witty & Wise / 1998 / Columbia/Legacy ♦♦♦♦

The title is apt. Warmth, wit, and wisdom spring from these 16 blues recordings from 1930-1941, as does a clever, ribald sense of humor, jocularity, and juicy, expressive guitar playing. At least Broonzy had the satisfaction before his passing of knowing the abundant inspiration he provided to the later famed generation of '50s Chicago blues legends. You can hear plenty of Broonzy's earnest, confident-just-shy-of-cocky, appealing attitude about sex, booze, bars, and Depression-era hard times in the recordings of other later Chess masters such as Sonny Boy Williamson, Bo Diddley, and Howlin' Wolf. This tall Southern gent vet left the South of his birth for the more fertile black playing grounds of Chi-town in the jazz age '20s, and lit up the South Side clubs once he added a band. In fact, to get to the good stuff, save the 1930-1932 New York recordings that open this disc for last. These are excellent, thoroughly picked, folk-blues recordings, just his smooth voice and working fingers, nearly as fast and as flavorful as '20s and '30s masters Mississippi John Hurt, Robert Johnson, Blind Lemon Jefferson, and Leadbelly. But move instead to the drums/bass/piano/guitar work on the 1938-1939 Chicago recordings, where the sizzle and wordplay just grow. Listeners would chuckle over the double entendres in songs like "Too Many Drivers" or the drunken hilarity of "When I Been Drinking" if they weren't so entranced by the pumping piano, some of the earliest electric guitar blues solos, and Broonzy's rich, surprisingly sunny singing. The string bass, shuffling drums, and occasional sax, clarinet, or trumpet are similarly first-rate, but it's the unfettered piano of Joshua Altheimer that steals the show. Blues in this case makes for mischievous grins, not frowns and bleeding hearts, and for that Broonzy's work will always inspire successive generations of blues lovers. *—Jack Rabid, The Big Takeover*

Chicago Calling / May 4, 1999 / Culture Press ♦♦♦♦♦

Before the rise of Muddy Waters in the '40s, no artist was more important to the Chicago blues than Big Bill Broonzy. His roots were the country blues of the Mississippi Delta, but when he moved to the Windy City, the singer/guitarist developed a tougher, more muscular and robust approach that had a major impact on Waters and many other Chicago residents. Spanning 1935-1941, *Chicago Calling* boasts 25 of the classic sides Broonzy recorded in Chicago during the Depression and World War II. If you want to hear where a lot of Waters' inspiration came from, take a close listen to Broonzy's spirited performances on such acoustic gems as "Night Time is the Right Time," "Detroit Special," "Trucking Little Woman" and "Just A Dream (On My Mind)." Overall, the sound quality is good for 78-era recordings—some of the material is a bit scratchy, but nonetheless, digital remastering works wonders on these sides and filters out a lot of noise, pops, ticks, etc. Released in France on Culture Press' Blue Boar label, this collection made it to North American stores as an import. *—Alex Henderson*

Trouble in Mind / Feb. 22, 2000 / Smithsonian/Folkways ♦♦♦♦

This is something of a best-of for Broonzy's Folkways recordings, done in 1956-1957 near the end of his life, all featuring just his voice and his acoustic guitar (although Pete Seeger adds banjo to a live version of "This Train (Bound for Glory)"). Although Broonzy, who died in 1958 of throat cancer, was likely not in peak physical shape by this time, you wouldn't suspect that from the quality of the performances. His vocals are still rich and moving on a relaxed selection of originals and standards, including such well-known favorites as "Trouble in Mind," "Key to the Highway," "Digging My Potatoes," "It Hurts Me Too," and "C.C. Rider." Especially good is his version of "Louise," where the intensity rises to a level higher than most of the other tracks approach. Occasionally Broonzy gets into racial and social comment, as on "When Will I Get to Be Called a Man" and the more controversial "Black, Brown and White Blues." *—Richie Unterberger*

The Post War Years: 1945–1949, Vol. 2 / Aug. 15, 2000 / EPM Musique ♦♦♦♦

Absolutely the Best / Dec. 5, 2000 / Fuel 2000 ♦♦♦

A very affordable collection of Big Bill Broonzy's better-known songs, Fuel Records' 15-song collection *Absolutely the Best* serves as a good overview and an excellent starting point for curious blues fans. The album is an assortment of traditional folksongs, reworked blues standards, and eight Broonzy originals. The liner notes give a brief look into the life of this legendary bluesman, and the music deals with his bouncing brand of bare-bones acoustic country blues, omitting his late career foray into horn-driven R&B. The only complaint with this collection is that the recording quality from the earlier recordings is a little brash and raspy, which is to be expected but is quite noticeable when sequenced right next to cleaner tracks. *—Zac Johnson*

Van Broussard

b. Mar. 29, 1937, Prairieville, LA

Guitar / Traditional Cajun, Louisiana Blues, Swamp Pop, New Orleans R&B, Zydeco, Traditional Country

Although he is not a household name nationally, Van Broussard is almost legendary in the Cajun bayou areas of Southern Louisiana for helping forge the way for swamp pop music. At various times, he has performed as a solo act, as half of the team Van & Titus, and more recently with the Bayou Boogie Band. Before his sister, Grace Broussard, had a hit record in 1963 with Dale Houston in the pairing Dale & Grace, she also performed frequently with her older brother in their hometown of Prairieville, LA, at a nightspot called Cal's Club. During the early years of Broussard's career, his music revolved around Dixieland as he performed in the region of Ascension Parish. A turning point came in the mid-'50s, when Elvis Presley's early recordings caught Broussard's attention and he started leaning toward the sounds of R&B and, later, straight-ahead into swamp pop. Broussard's long career includes releases for a number of different labels, among them CSP, Red Stick, Rex, and Bayou Boogie. During his later years, Broussard put out more than half a dozen albums with CSP, amassing approximately 100 recorded songs for that label alone. His popular singles include "Lord I Need Somebody Bad Tonight" in 1977 and "Feed the Flame" in 1958. The Louisiana Hall of Fame inducted the artist in 1997. *—Linda Seida*

Early Years / 1993 / CSP ♦♦♦♦

Legendary Bayou Boogie / Nov. 27, 2001 / CSP ♦♦♦

Andrew Brown

b. Feb. 25, 1937, Jackson, MS, **d.** Dec. 11, 1985

Vocals, Guitar / Modern Electric Chicago Blues, Electric Chicago Blues

Tragically under-recorded until late in his career, Chicago blues guitarist Andrew Brown still had time enough to wax a handful of great singles during the mid-'60s and two '80s albums (unfortunately, both of them were only available as imports) that beautifully showcased his fluid, concise lead guitar and hearty vocals.

The Mississippi native moved to Chicago in 1946. With Earl Hooker teaching him a few key licks, Brown matured quickly; he was playing in south suburban clubs—his main circuit—by the early '50s. His 45s for USA (1962's "You Better Stop") and 4 Brothers (the mid-'60s sides "You Ought to Be Ashamed" and "Can't Let You Go") were well-done urban blues. But it wasn't until 1980, when Alligator issued three of his songs on its second batch of *Living Chicago Blues* anthologies, that Brown's name began to resonate outside the Windy City.

Producer Dick Shurman was responsible for Brown's only two albums: the Handy Award-winning *Big Brown's Chicago Blues* for Black Magic in 1982 and *On the Case* for Double Trouble three years later. But Brown was already suffering from lung cancer when the second LP emerged. He died a short time later. *—Bill Dahl*

● **Big Brown's Chicago Blues** / Oct. 5, 1981+Oct. 25, 1981 / Black Magic ♦♦♦♦♦

Quite an impressive full-length debut, even if American audiences were hard-pressed to locate a copy. Well-chosen covers—Joe Tex's "I Want To (Do Everything for You)," Betty Everett's "Your Love Is Important to Me," Bobby Rush's "Mary Jane"—mingle with six attractive originals. *—Bill Dahl*

On the Case / Aug. 9, 1983-Oct. 26, 1984 / Double Trouble ♦♦♦♦

Another classy contemporary blues album that frustratingly still awaits domestic CD reissue, just like its predecessor. Once again, the tasty guitarist exhibits intriguing taste in covers, reviving Donna Hightower's "Right Now," and Little Milton's "Losing Hand," and the immortal Birdlegs & Pauline's "Spring." But the majority of the set consists of well-conceived originals. Jimmy Johnson is on board as rhythm guitarist. *—Bill Dahl*

Buster Brown

b. Aug. 15, 1911, Cordele, GA, **d.** Jan. 31, 1976, Brooklyn, NY

Vocals, Harmonica / Electric Harmonica Blues, R&B

Whooping blues harpists nearing the age of 50 with number one R&B hits to their credit were predictably scarce in 1959. Nevertheless, that's the happy predicament Buster Brown found himself in when his infectious "Fannie Mae" paced the charts. Even more amazingly, the driving number made serious inroads on the pop airwaves as well.

The Georgian, whose harp style was clearly influenced by Sonny Terry, had never made a professional recording (there was a 1943 Library of Congress session that laid unissued at the time) before Fire Records boss Bobby Robinson brought the short, stockily built Brown into a New York studio in June of 1959 to wax "Fannie Mae."

Brown's reign as an unlikely star was short-lived. He managed minor follow-up hits on Fire with a rather ragged 1960 revival of Louis Jordan's "Is You Is or Is You Ain't My Baby" and his 1962 farewell bow, the effervescent rocker "Sugar Babe." A subsequent 1964 stop at Chicago's Checker Records produced a glistening update of the old blues "Crawlin' Kingsnake" that sank without a trace. *—Bill Dahl*

● **The New King of the Blues** / 1960-1961 / Collectables ♦♦♦♦♦

If blues musicians took up residency in Vegas during the late '50s, it might come out sounding like this. Brown's gleeful run through myriad blues-related styles (gospel, R&B, doo wop, New Orleans, early rock & roll) casts a vaudevillian sheen over many of the 16 tracks here, placing the performance squarely in the realm of Louis Jordan's own showy style. The fact Brown had a very brief hour in the sun with his unexpected 1959 hit "Fannie Mae" further indicates his pop approach to blues probably was better suited to the lounges of the chitlin circuit than the main venues of blues and rock & roll. His almost perfunctory versions of war horses like "St. Louis Blues" and "Blueberry Hill" reveal the downside the situation. But he does have his moments, particularly when he plies a hard, Chicago blues groove à la Little Walter on cuts like "Don't Dog Your Woman"; his harmonica sound borrows from both Walter and Sonny Terry while his singing is punctuated with timely whoops taken straight from Terry's animated vocal style. Even with more than just a few bright moments here, the good amount of watered down material ultimately makes this Brown collection a secondary choice next to prime titles by Muddy Waters, Howlin' Wolf, Wynonie Harris, and even Big Jay McNeely. *—Stephen Cook*

Raise a Ruckus Tonight / 1976 / Relic ♦♦♦♦♦

Here are 21 Fire Records masters by the whooping harmonica ace, including his classic "Fannie Mae" (in crystal-clear stereo), the irresistible "Sugar Babe," and a load of similar stompers that should have been hits but weren't—"Good News," "Doctor Brown," the previously unissued "No More," "Lost in a Dream." Brown occasionally made an unwise stab at something other than 12-bar fare; "Blueberry Hill," "St. Louis Blues," and the Moonglows' "Sincerely" definitely didn't suit Brown's raucous, untutored approach. *—Bill Dahl*

Good News / 1996 / Charly ♦♦♦

The Very Best of Buster Brown / Oct. 26, 1999 / Collectables ♦♦♦♦♦

The Very Best of Buster Brown features 22 original classics by Brown, the blues harpist/singer who hit the number one R&B spot with "Fannie Mae" (number 38 pop). Brown was the archetypal R&B singer who came on the scene five years too late. When he scored his big hit, popular music was switching to sounds more accessible to a younger populace, like "The Twist." The wailing harp player sang with the same intensity. His strident tenor was similar to '60s soul man Howard Tate, but more powerful. "Madison Shuffle" is a harp lover's delight; Brown blows the mouth organ as if he's falling off a cliff yelling help—but transforms to Mr. Happy Harp on the melodic "Lost in a Dream." The selections include "Dr. Brown," "John Henry," "Is You Is or Is You Ain't My Baby?," "Fannie Mae," a "Fannie Mae" outtake, "Fannie Mae is Back," and a super soulful rendition of the Moonglows' "Sincerely." With the exception of the Moonglows' tune and a few others, Brown wrote most of the material. Even if you don't normally buy CDs of this genre, you'll love this one. Buster Brown made everything he did essential, and influenced many '60s singers such as Wilson Pickett and Joe Stubbs. It's a shame he wasn't more successful. *—Andrew Hamilton*

Charles Brown

b. Sep. 13, 1922, Texas City, TX, **d.** Jan. 21, 1999, Oakland, CA

Vocals, Piano / Urban Blues, West Coast Blues, Piano Blues

How many blues artists remained at the absolute top of their game after more than a half-century of performing? One immediately leaps to mind: Charles Brown. His incredible piano skills and laid-back vocal delivery remained every bit as mesmerizing at the end of his life as they were way back in 1945, when his groundbreaking waxing of "Drifting Blues" with guitarist Johnny Moore's Three Blazers invented an entirely new blues genre for sophisticated postwar revelers: an ultra-mellow, jazz-inflected sound perfect for sipping a late-night libation in some hip after-hours joint. Brown's smooth trio format was tremendously influential to a host of high-profile disciples—Ray Charles, Amos Milburn, and Floyd Dixon, for starters.

Classically trained on the ivories, Brown earned a degree in chemistry before moving to Los Angeles in 1943. He soon hooked up with the Blazers (Moore and bassist Eddie Williams), who modeled themselves after Nat "King" Cole's trio but retained a bluesier tone within their ballad-heavy repertoire. With Brown installed as their vocalist and pianist, the Blazers' "Drifting Blues" for Philo Records remained on Billboard's R&B charts for 23 weeks, peaking at number two. Follow-ups for Exclusive and Modern (including "Sunny Road," "So Long," "New Orleans Blues," and their immortal 1947 Yuletide classic "Merry Christmas Baby") kept the Blazers around the top of the R&B listings from 1946 through 1948, until Brown opted to go solo.

If anything, Brown was even more successful on his own. Signing with Eddie Mesner's Aladdin logo, he visited the R&B Top Ten no less than ten times from 1949 to 1952, retaining his mournful, sparsely arranged sound for the smashes "Get Yourself Another Fool," the chart-topping "Trouble Blues" and "Black Night," and "Hard Times." Despite a 1956 jaunt to New Orleans to record with the Cosimo's studio band, Brown's mellow approach failed to make the transition to rock's brasher rhythms, and he soon faded from national prominence (other than when his second holiday perennial, "Please Come Home for Christmas," hit in 1960 on the King label). Occasionally recording without causing much of a stir during the '60s and '70s, Brown began to regroup by the mid-'80s. *One More for the Road*, a set cut in 1986 for the short-lived Blue Side logo, announced to anyone within earshot that Brown's talents hadn't diminished at all while he was gone (the set later re-emerged on Alligator). Bonnie Raitt took an encouraging interest in Brown's comeback bid, bringing him on tour with her as her opening act (thus introducing the blues vet to a whole new generation or two of fans). His recording career took off too, with a series of albums for Bullseye Blues (the first entry, 1990's *All My Life*, is especially pleasing), and more recently, a disc for Verve.

In his last years, Brown finally received at least a portion of the recognition he deserved for so long as a genuine rhythm and blues pioneer. But the suave, elegant Brown was by no means a relic, as anyone who witnessed his thundering boogie piano style will gladly attest; he returned in 1998 with *So Goes Love* before dying on January 21, 1999. *—Bill Dahl*

☆ **The Complete Aladdin Recordings of Charles Brown** / Sep. 11, 1945-Sep. 4, 1956 / Mosaic ♦♦♦♦♦

Every single brilliant side—some 109 in all—that this elegant, tremendously influential pianist cut for the Mesner brothers' Philo and Aladdin imprints from 1945 to 1956 is housed in this lavishly produced five-disc box set. Mosaic's customary attention to detail is evident in the packaging and the sound; Brown's brilliance makes the entire box a delight, from his earliest sessions with the Three Blazers through his hitmaking run as a solo star during the late '40s and early '50s. The genesis of the entire West Coast club blues style resides in this box; its expense is well worth it. *—Bill Dahl*

Snuff Dippin' Mama / 1946-1947 / Night Train ♦♦♦♦♦

Even with the above box, you won't own all of Brown's seminal work. In 1946, he and the Blazers landed at Exclusive Records, which is the era that this collection examines via 19 fine sides including the jivey "Juke Box Lil" and "C.O.D.," a mournful "Sunny Road," and the jazzy "B-Sharp You'll See." Guitarist Johnny Moore and bassist Eddie Williams were indeed sharp in smooth support. *—Bill Dahl*

★ **Driftin' Blues: The Best of Charles Brown** / 1948-1956 / Collectables ♦♦♦♦♦

Originally put out by EMI in 1992, this roundup of Charles Brown's 1945-1956 Aladdin sides is essential listening for all R&B fans—and that goes for jazz and pop lovers as well. Sticking mostly to an exquisite after-hours mode, Brown delivers one smooth blues gem after another until this 20-track disc comes to a close. Backed for the most part by guitarist Johnny Moore and his Three Blazers, Brown effortlessly lays down such standouts as the title track, "Black Night," and "Get Yourself Another Fool." Yes, the mood here is evocative of Nat Cole's classic trio sides, but Brown and Moore—unlike Cole—infuse their lush surroundings with a healthy dose of sophisticated West Coast blues. Capped off with the original version of Brown's classic Yuletide cut "Merry Christmas Baby," *Driftin' Blues* is the perfect way to get cozy with this venerable blues performer. *—Stephen Cook*

Driftin' Blues / 1963 / DCC ♦♦

Brown's balladeer leanings come heavily to the fore on these lushly arranged 1963 sides, originally produced by Bob Shad for issue on his Mainstream logo. He croons Steve Lawrence's "Go Away Little Girl," and Ruby & the Romantics' "Our Day Will Come," and Henry Mancini's "Days of Wine and Roses" in his mellowest supper-club style—which simply doesn't match up to what came before. Charles plays organ on this album, contributing to the lounge-like ambience. *—Bill Dahl*

The Boss of the Blues / 1963 / Mainstream ♦♦

More 1963-1964 Mainstream sides with some duplication—the first six tracks here also appear on the DCC compilation. Tracks seven through sixteen find Brown surrounded by strings as he smoothly intones "Pledging My Love," "Blueberry Hill," and "Cottage for Sale" (they didn't even let him sit down at the keyboard at all for these dates!). *—Bill Dahl*

Sunny Land / 1979 / Route 66 ♦♦♦♦♦

This is a nice cross-section of the pianist's smooth early work for a variety of labels. *—Bill Dahl*

One More for the Road / Aug. 6, 1986-Aug. 8, 1986 / Alligator ♦♦♦

One of the first comeback salvos that the veteran pianist fired after suffering the slings and arrows of anonymity for much too long. Typically delectable in a subtle, understated manner, Brown eases through a very attractive program. *—Bill Dahl*

Let's Have a Ball / 1989 / Route 66 ♦♦♦♦♦

Charles Brown's smooth, West Coast blues sound of the '40s and '50s was similar to Nat Cole's own streamlined style. Brown's velvety vocal tone and fluid piano playing provided an alternative to the rawer performances on Chicago blues records and eventually inspired R&B singers like Johnny Ace and Sam Cooke. The out of print Brown title *Let's Have a Ball* is a fine showcase of his unique talent and a nice B-sides companion to EMI's Aladdin hits collection, *Driftin' Blues*. The 17 tracks here were all recorded in Los Angeles between 1945-1961 (some with his usual trio, Johnny Moore's Three Blazers, and some with expanded outfits featuring horns). The album not only contains a few of Brown's more famous numbers, like "In the Evening When the Sun Goes Down," but also rare cuts such as "It's Nothing" and "Tonight I'm Alone." There is a nice variety of styles here as well, like the blues swinger "Soothe Me," a doo wop style number called "My Little Baby," and the mambo novelty "Hot Lips and Seven Kisses." With his assured and even vocal phrasing, Brown handles all the tracks here with aplomb. To get all the tracks on both *Let's Have a Ball* and *Driftin' Blues*, along with all the rest of Brown's Aladdin and Philo sides, order Mosaic Record's mammoth box set. If you just want a good introduction to Brown's music, though, get the EMI disc and keep looking in the used record bins for a copy of the excellent *Let's Have a Ball*. *—Stephen Cook*

All My Life / 1990 / Bullseye Blues ♦♦♦♦♦

By far Brown's best contemporary effort (and the set that really got his recording career back in high gear). Cameos by Dr. John and Ruth Brown certainly didn't hurt the set's chances, but it's the eternally suave pianist and his excellent road band (especially guitarist Danny Caron and saxist Clifford Solomon) that make this such a delightful collection. *—Bill Dahl*

Blues and Other Love Songs / 1992 / 32 Jazz ♦♦♦

This Charles Brown session from early 1992 finds the singer sounding just as natural as he did in the early '50s. *Blues and Other Love Songs* was originally released on Muse records and is available as a budget title from the excellent reissue label 32 Jazz. Brown is in a typically soulful mood, crooning like a gritty modern day Nat "King" Cole. Backing up the piano and vocals of Brown are soul-groove saxophonist Houston Person, whose smokey tenor chops were an excellent match for Brown's blues. Danny Caron on guitar, Ruth Davies on bass, and Gaylord Birch round out the rhythm section. These ten tracks consist of five originals and five covers featuring a brief version of Thelonious Monk's "Round Midnight," showing off Brown's ability to play straight jazz. Person is also heard with Brown on the 32 jazz reissue *Lost and Found*, which combines the albums *Sweet Slumber* and *Wildflower* on one disc. *—Al Campbell*

Someone to Love / 1992 / Bullseye Blues ♦♦♦

Bonnie Raitt, who played such an integral role in Brown's successful comeback, guests on two tracks on the pianist's *Bullseye Blues* encore, which isn't quite the *tour de force* that his previous outing was but is eminently solid nonetheless. Caron and Solomon once again shine in support of their leader. *—Bill Dahl*

Cool Christmas Blues / 1994 / Rounder ♦♦♦
Long recognized as the perennial top contender when it comes to Yuletide R&B, Brown salutes the holiday season in his own inimitable manner. Naturally, there's the umpteenth remake of his seminal "Merry Christmas Baby," along with several more that he's been crooning every December since before most of us were born. But nobody does 'em better. *—Bill Dahl*

Just a Lucky So and So / Jan. 24, 1994 / Bullseye Blues ♦♦♦
Charles Brown's casual, yet stunning phrasing, inventive voicings and piano accompaniment are wonderfully presented on this 10-song set. Ron Levy's production and the arrangements of Wardell Quezergue and Brown are tasteful, breezy and geared for his carefully constructed, teasing solos and rich, creamy leads. Such numbers as Brown's classic "Drifting Blues," as well as "Gloomy Sunday" and "I Won't Cry Anymore," convey despair and hurt, yet retain a certain appeal and charm. Brown keeps making fine records, sounding as convincing in the '90s as he did at the start of his career. *—Ron Wynn*

These Blues / 1995 / Verve ♦♦♦♦

Honey Dripper / Nov. 5, 1996 / Verve ♦♦♦♦
"Soothing" is not a word normally associated with blues, but it's the word that best captures the experience of listening to Charles Brown, and *Honey Dripper* is no exception. Listening to it is like sipping a fine bottle of cognac. Seventy-two years old at the time of this recording session, Brown sounds agile, almost ageless. Indeed, time seems to stand still when he plays and sings in that same understated, urbane manner he popularized with Johnny Moore's Three Blazers back in the '40s. Like his other recordings this decade, *Honey Dripper* features Brown's regular working combo, led by guitarist Danny Caron and including saxophonist Clifford Solomon. The songs range from straight-ahead blues to jazz ballads, with some straddling the line. *—Steve Hoffman*

1944–1945 / 1997 / Classics ♦♦♦♦♦
This Classics CD features pianist/vocalist Charles Brown on his first 22 recordings, when he was a sideman with guitarist Johnny Moore's Three Blazers. Brown already sounded quite distinctive, and as it turned out, the 21st song ("Drifting Blues") was his biggest hit. Due to the instrumentation (a trio/quartet with bassist Eddie Williams and sometimes Oscar Moore on second guitar), the music is a bit reminiscent at times of the Nat King Cole Trio, but it had a special soul and feeling of its own. Frankie Laine makes a couple of early appearances, but Brown takes care of the bulk of the vocals, and there are also eight excellent instrumentals. Recommended. *—Scott Yanow*

1946 / Feb. 3, 1998 / Classics ♦♦♦♦
With the great success of the slow blues ballad "Driftin' Blues," Johnny Moore's Three Blazers emphasized laidback material on record after record in 1946, looking for another hit. Ironically the main star of virtually all of the records, pianist-vocalist Charles Brown, was given second billing if he was mentioned at all, while guitarist Moore (who is joined by bassist Eddie Williams) was often mistaken as the singer. Brown would stick with Moore into 1947 and was largely responsible for the group's success. The second Classics CD to reissue all of the trio's recordings includes 23 enjoyable titles that mostly have a sameness to them in tempo and mood. All are vocal showcases for Brown except for the two-part "Warsaw Concerto" and "Nutmeg," the lone instrumentals. A worthwhile set but not as essential a release as the earlier volume in this series. *—Scott Yanow*

In a Grand Style / Jul. 20, 1999 / Bullseye Blues ♦♦♦♦
This posthumously released material—mostly classic and classy love songs—puts an exclamation point on the career of a true American music legend, a legitimate grand master in more ways than one. It is not, as the back cover states, a "solo piano album." Charles Brown does, in fact, sing on all the cuts save one, but there's no rhythm section or soloist to help. It's simply Charles Brown, all soulful, with light-colored blues, gently swinging but by himself. There are classics like "Black Night," "Stumbled and Fell in Love," the curious "One Never Knows, Does One?" and Little Walter's slightly raucous "Give Me a Woman." Brown's classical background on "Charles' Chopin Liszt" unleashes a cascading, tinkling, arpeggiated side rarely heard. Other intros also showcase this part of Brown's musicianship. Everything on the record, except for "Liszt," is a slow, cigarette-type smoldering blues that is sometimes downhearted, other times hopeful. But the lyrics of Brown's original "Wouldn't It Be Grand" speaks volumes about his hope for our future: "Wouldn't that be grand, if and when we die, we unite together in the sky/Get together, take our stand, glory land/Wouldn't that be grand." *—Michael G. Nastos*

Since I Fell for You / Oct. 12, 1999 / Garland ♦♦♦♦
So much of Charles Brown's work is available on CD that novices can have a hard time knowing where to begin. Ideally, novices should start out with his most essential stuff, and *Since I Fell for You* falls short of essential even though it is quite rewarding. This 1999 reissue focuses on a 1963 date that Bob Shad produced for Mainstream. With Brown on vocals and organ, Roy Coleman on electric guitar, Freddie Simon on tenor sax, and Charles Brady on drums, *Since I Fell for You* emphasizes torch singing. Brown revisits the classic "Driftin' Blues," but most of the time he sticks to ballads—and the end result is a thoroughly pleasing collection of mood music. From Steve Lawrence's "Go Away, Little Girl" (which subsequently became a hit for Donny Osmond and Marlena Shaw in the '70s) and Ruby & the Romantics' "Our Day Will Come" to Henry Mancini's "Days of Wine and Roses," a smoky jazz-noir ambience prevails. So why would a novice not want to start out with a CD that is so pleasing? Because as strong as these 1963 performances are, Brown's Aladdin output of the '40s and '50s is even stronger. Nonetheless, *Since I Fell for You* is well worth acquiring if you're a confirmed Brown addict who already has his essential work and wants to dig deeper. *—Alex Henderson*

Blue Over You: The Ace Recordings / Oct. 26, 1999 / West Side ♦♦♦
An entire album of unissued Charles Brown, recorded for Johnny Vincent's Ace label between 1959 and 1960, yields a treasure trove of tracks in this collection. There are nice remakes of "Black Night" and "Driftin' Blues," but even better are tracks like "Please Come Home for Christmas, blues ballads like "Blue Over You," and the old standard "There Is No Greater Love." Many tracks recorded in extreme late-'50s stereo make for fascinating listening to go along with some fascinating music. *—Cub Koda*

1946–1947 / Mar. 14, 2000 / Classics ♦♦♦♦♦
The 24 selections on this Classics CD (their third Charles Brown release) were all recorded by Johnny Moore's Three Blazers, a trio consisting of guitarist Moore, bassist Eddie Williams, and the real star, pianist-vocalist Charles Brown. The final three numbers add Moore's brother, Oscar Moore (formerly with the Nat King Cole Trio), on second guitar. Unlike with their earlier pre-"Driftin' Blues" material, the emphasis is generally on slower tempos with Brown having a vocal on every selection. Most notable is the hit version of "Merry Christmas Baby"; other highlights include "Was I to Blame for Falling in Love With You," "Huggin' Bug," "St. Louis Blues," "Juke Box Lil," and "New Orleans Blues." The Blazers' style, a more bluish version of the Nat King Cole Trio, is always pleasing. However, since Charles Brown was getting very little recognition for his talents (audience members often thought that he was Johnny Moore!), he would not be sticking around in the group much longer. *—Scott Yanow*

The Very Best of Charles Brown / Jul. 25, 2000 / Cleopatra ♦♦♦
The title *The Very Best of Charles Brown* is a definite exaggeration. This reissue, which Stardust put out in 2000, *does* contain some of the best and most famous songs associated with the late blues/jazz vocalist, including "Merry Christmas, Baby," "Trouble Blues," "Driftin' Blues," and "Black Night." However, it doesn't offer the definitive versions of those gems, which Brown originally recorded for Aladdin back in the '40s and '50s; instead, it contains remakes that he provided for Johnny Otis' Blues Spectrum label in the early '70s (possibly in 1973). Produced by Johnny Otis in Brown's adopted home of Los Angeles, these recordings find the singer/pianist joined by Otis on drums and son Shuggie Otis on guitar and bass. On "Getting to Be Evening," the late Leonard Feather—who was the world's most famous jazz critic—is heard on piano. Brown's accompaniment is solid, and his performances are pleasing, if less than essential. Were this a collection of his essential Aladdin output, the title *The Very Best of Charles Brown* would have been justified; but this disc should have had a more accurate and modest title like *The Blues Spectrum Sessions.* However, it isn't a bad CD, far from it. Although not recommended to casual listeners—who would be better off searching for a collection of Brown's classic Aladdin work—this is a reissue that collectors and hardcore Brown fans will enjoy. *—Alex Henderson*

Driftin' & Dreamin' / Mar. 27, 2001 / Ace ♦♦♦♦

1947–1948 / Apr. 3, 2001 / Classics ♦♦♦♦
Although the 24 selections on this CD have been reissued under pianist/vocalist Charles Brown's name, he is actually the featured sideman with Johnny Moore's Three Blazers, a band also including guitarists Johnny Moore and Oscar Moore, plus bassist Eddie Williams. However, putting it under Brown's name is only fitting because he has vocals on all but one of the selections (the instrumental "Scratch Street") and is the most impressive soloist. These performances, cut for the small Los Angeles-based Exclusive label, are mostly little-known (making them formerly rare collector's items), and the set overall has more tempo and mood variation than the earlier classics; the band was not trying as hard to duplicate the success of "Driftin' Blues." Recommended. *—Scott Yanow*

1948–1949 / May 7, 2002 / Classics ♦♦♦
Pianist/singer Charles Brown left Johnny Moore's Three Blazers in 1948 since Brown's vocals were chiefly responsible for the group's success, but he was receiving no credit; people thought that he was Johnny Moore. His first 24 records as a leader, with Chuck Norris or Tiny Mitchell on guitar and bassist Eddie Williams, are reissued on this disc. The music was all recorded for the Aladdin label and nine of the selections were previously unreleased. "Trouble Blues" and "Get Yourself Another Fool" were minor hits. The main problem with the music is that virtually every song is at the same medium-slow tempo, so listening to this set straight through can be a little tedious. But it is very good to have this formerly rare material available in such comprehensive form. *—Scott Yanow*

Clarence "Gatemouth" Brown

b. Apr. 18, 1924, Vinton, LA
Vocals, Drums, Violin, Mandolin, Harmonica, Guitar, Bass / Modern Electric Texas Blues, Texas Blues, Electric Texas Blues

Whatever you do, don't refer to multi-instrumentalist Clarence "Gatemouth" Brown as a bluesman, although his imprimatur on the development of Texas blues is enormous. You're liable to get him riled. If you must pigeonhole the legend, just call him an eclectic Texas musical master whose interests encompass virtually every roots genre imaginable. Brown learned the value of versatility while growing up in Orange, TX. His dad was a locally popular musician who specialized in country, Cajun, and bluegrass—but not blues. Later, Gate was entranced by the big bands of Count Basie, Lionel Hampton, and Duke Ellington (a torrid arrangement of "Take the 'A' Train" remains a centerpiece of Brown's repertoire). Tagged with the "Gatemouth" handle by a high school instructor who accused Brown of having a "voice like a gate," Brown has used it to his advantage throughout his illustrious career. (His guitar-wielding brother, James "Widemouth" Brown, recorded "Boogie Woogie Nighthawk" for Jax in 1951.)

In 1947, Gate's impromptu fill-in for an ailing T-Bone Walker at Houston entrepreneur Don Robey's Bronze Peacock nightclub convinced Robey to assume control of Brown's career. After two singles for Aladdin stiffed, Robey inaugurated his own Peacock label in 1949 to showcase Brown's blistering riffs, which proved influential to a legion of Houston string-benders (Albert Collins, Johnny Copeland, Johnny "Guitar" Watson, Cal Green, and many more have pledged allegiance to Brown's riffs). Peacock and its sister label Duke prospered through the '50s and '60s.

Gate stayed with Peacock through 1960. The R&B charts didn't reflect Brown's importance (he hit only once nationwide with 1949's two-sided smash "Mary Is Fine"/"My Time Is Expensive"). But his blazing instrumentals ("Boogie Uproar," "Gate Walks to Board," 1954's seminal "Okie Dokie Stomp"), horn-enriched rockers ("She Walked Right In," "Rock My Blues Away"), and lowdown Lone Star blues ("Dirty Work at the Crossroads") are a major component of the rich Texas postwar blues legacy. Brown broke new ground often—even in the '50s, he insisted on sawing his fiddle at live performances, although Robey wasn't interested in capturing Gate's violin talent until "Just Before Dawn" (his final Peacock platter in 1959).

The '60s weren't all that kind to Brown. His cover of Little Jimmy Dickens' country novelty "May the Bird of Paradise Fly Up Your Nose" for tiny Hermitage Records made a little noise in 1965 (and presaged things to come stylistically). But the decade was chiefly memorable for Brown's 1966 stint as house bandleader for *The!!!!Beat*, a groundbreaking syndicated R&B television program out of Dallas hosted by WLAC DJ Bill "Hoss" Allen. When Gate began to rebuild his career in the '70s, he was determined to do things his way. Country, jazz, even calypso now played a prominent role in his concerts; he became as likely to launch into an old-time fiddle hoedown as a swinging guitar blues. He turned up on *Hee Haw* with pickin' and grinnin' pal Roy Clark after they cut a sizzling 1979 duet album for MCA, *Makin' Music*. Acclaimed discs for Rounder, Alligator, Verve, and Blue Thumb in the '80s, '90s, and 2000s have proven that Gatemouth Brown is a steadfastly unclassifiable American original. —*Bill Dahl*

San Antonio Ballbuster / Dec. 1948-Sep. 1959 / Drive ✦✦✦✦
Considering how sub-par the sound quality is on this disc (it's a CD reproduction of an old Red Lightnin' bootleg), it wouldn't rate a recommendation if the material therein were otherwise available. But many of these Peacock masters aren't obtainable anywhere else—the stunning 1953 instrumental "Boogie Uproar," and storming rockers "Win with Me Baby," "You Got Money," and "Just Got Lucky," and the after-hours hit "I've Been Mistreated," for starters. So until something better comes along ... —*Bill Dahl*

San Antonio Ballbuster / 1965 / Charly ✦✦✦
It's 1965, and Gate's guitar sound is different—not so brash and trebly but smoother, with more of a jazz and occasional country kick. Most of these sides were never issued after being acquired by Chess. There are two takes of Little Jimmy Dickens' C&W novelty hit "May the Bird of Paradise," both of 'em swinging easy. Gate was in a Sonny Boy Williamson mood that day, reviving three of the harpist's oldies along with a few of his own and the ominous blues "Long Way Home," which threatens mayhem most charmingly. —*Bill Dahl*

The Blues Ain't Nothin' / 1972 / Black & Blue ✦✦✦

Just Got Lucky / Mar. 22, 1973-Jul. 1, 1973 / Evidence ✦✦✦✦
More goodies from the same French 1973 dates (originally issued on Black & Blue). Lots of Jordan covers, along with Brown's own "Here Am I" and "Long Way Home," three Peacock remakes, and a sizzling revival of Bill Doggett's "Honey Boy." The last three titles date from a 1977 session, again cut in France, and are all Brown originals. —*Bill Dahl*

Sings Louis Jordan / Jul. 22, 1973-Jul. 24, 1973 / Black & Blue ✦✦✦
Enjoyable foray through Jordan's songbook by a master guitarist. —*Bill Dahl*

Pressure Cooker / Jul. 23, 1973-Aug. 1, 1973 / Alligator ✦✦✦✦
Before Gate was able to rebuild a following stateside, he frequently toured Europe. He recorded the contents of this inexorably swinging set in France in 1973 with all-star backing by keyboardists Milt Buckner and Jay McShann, saxists Arnett Cobb and Hal Singer, among others. Brown indulges his passion for Louis Jordan by ripping through "Ain't That Just like a Woman" and "Ain't Nobody Here but Us Chickens" and exhibits his immaculate fretwork on the torrid title item. —*Bill Dahl*

Cold Strange / Jul. 31, 1973-Aug. 1, 1973 / Black & Blue ✦✦✦
Swinging guitar and tasty vocals. —*Bill Dahl*

Gate's on the Heat / 1975 / Barclay ✦
The worst Brown album currently on the shelves. Cut back in the '70s with a band that wouldn't know how to swing if it were permanently marooned on a playground (the rhythm guitarist is particularly abominable), this one's a must to avoid. —*Bill Dahl*

Blackjack / 1977 / Music Is Medicine ✦✦✦
There aren't many 75-year-old entertainers who rock with the intensity of Gatemouth Brown, a multi-instrumentalist from Louisiana who is a master of guitar, fiddle, viola, mandolin and harmonica. A look into Brown's history shows him leading a 23-piece orchestra in the late '40s, after a stint during the '20s and '30s as a Peacock Records recording artist. During the '60s, Brown traded in his guitar for a gun, signing on as a deputy sheriff in New Mexico. In 1974, at the age of 50, he jumped headfirst back into his music, and the rest is history. *Blackjack* was originally released on the Music Is Medicine label in 1977, and explores the versatile Brown's love for Texas swing, featuring outstanding tracks laced with swing, big band, R&B and straight-up blues. Alternating between a smoking guitar and a fiery fiddle, Brown drives these 12 songs like a stock-car at NASCAR's Darlington, fast as he can go, but still in absolute control of the vehicle. From the funky guitar picking of "Chickenshift," to the bluesy title cut, "Blackjack," Brown burns brightly. The soulful "Dark End of the Hallway" is another standout track, as is the intense closing instrumental, "Up Jumped the Devil." For anyone who had previously tacked the blues label on Clarence "Gatemouth" Brown's considerable cowboy hat, now is the time to reconsider. While Brown is indeed a master bluesman, he is equally adept at handling Texas swing, country, jazz and rock & roll. A man of many talents who shows absolutely zero signs of slowing down. —*Michael B. Smith*

Alright Again! / Jun. 2, 1981-Jun. 8, 1981 / Rounder ✦✦✦✦✦
One of the most satisfying contemporary Brown discs of all for the discerning blues fan. Nothing but swinging, horn-abetted blues adorn this album, as Gate pays tribute to an influence and a protégé by covering T-Bone Walker's "Strollin' with Bones" and Albert Collins' "Frosty." Brown's jauntily revives Junior Parker's "I Feel Alright Again" and Percy Mayfield's "Give Me Time to Explain," while his own numbers—a funky "Dollar Got the Blues," the luxurious blues "Sometimes I Slip"—are truly brilliant. —*Bill Dahl*

One More Mile / Oct. 1982 / Rounder ✦✦✦
Considerably more varied than its predecessor, with nods toward the Louisiana swamp ("Sunrise Cajun Style," complete with pedal steel guitar), sentimental ballads (Cecil Gant's "I Wonder"), and jazz ("Big Yard"). Blues purists will perk up for revivals of Junior Parker's "Stranded" and Roy Milton's "Information Blues." —*Bill Dahl*

Atomic Energy / 1984 / Blues Boy ✦✦✦✦✦
Another cross-section of old Peacock efforts, there is some sound quality. —*Bill Dahl*

Real Life (Live) / Sep. 4, 1985-Sep. 7, 1985 / Rounder ✦✦✦
Live set cut in Fort Worth, TX, that presents an accurate depiction of the breadth and scope of a Gatemouth Brown concert. Switching between guitar and violin, Gate offers everything from a reprise of "Okie Dokie Stomp" to a tender "Please Send Me Someone to Love" from Percy Mayfield's songbook and personalized renditions of "St. Louis Blues" and "Frankie and Johnny." —*Bill Dahl*

Texas Swing / 1988 / Rounder ✦✦✦✦✦
When Clarence "Gatemouth" Brown walked into the studio in the early '80s to record *Alright Again!*, he had already had an illustrious career by most standards. Yet, much of Gate's best output had been behind him by more than two decades; with *Alright Again!*, he set out to prove he was still a relevant artist. The album won Brown a Grammy, and its follow-up, *One More Mile*, was a Grammy-nominated record as well. *Texas Swing* combines the two records, culling 17 tracks from the sessions. Listening to this album, it is easy to see why the songs had such impact. Never one to be pigeonholed, Brown and his backup band move from slick blues on "Frosty" and "One More Mile" to breezy swing reminiscent of the best big bands on Roy Milton's "Information Blues" and Brown's own "Dollar Got the Blues." As a listener, it is fascinating to hear Brown pull the tiny nuances out of his guitar, giving the instrumentals and solos previously unheard depth and confirming his position as a master musician. —*Steve Kurutz*

Standing My Ground / 1989 / Alligator ✦✦✦✦
A delightfully eclectic program spotlighting nearly all of Gate's musical leanings—blues, jazz, country, even a hearty taste of "Louisiana Zydeco"—and a revealing glimpse of his multi-instrumental abilities: he plays guitar, violin, drums, and piano! There's a tender remake of the Chuck Willis R&B ballad and a funk-tinged update of "Got My Mojo Working," but everything else is from Brown's own pen. —*Bill Dahl*

★ **The Original Peacock Recordings** / 1990 / Rounder ✦✦✦✦✦
Only 12 songs long, this collection remains the best place to begin appreciating why so many young Texas blues guitarists fell in love with Gatemouth Brown's style (until MCA decides to compile the ultimate Brown package, anyway). Listen to the way his blazing axe darts and weaves through trombonist Pluma Davis' jazzy horn chart on 1954's "Okie Dokie Stomp," and or the stratospheric licks drenching "Dirty Work at the Crossroads." Brown proves that a violin can adapt marvelously to the blues (in the right hands, anyway) on "Just Before Dawn," and blows a little atmospheric harp on "Gate's Salty Blues." —*Bill Dahl*

No Looking Back / 1992 / Alligator ✦✦✦
Clarence "Gatemouth" Brown was one of the most jazz-oriented of bluesmen, a colorful guitarist and a primitive but swinging fiddler. On this release he includes many instrumental sections in his performances including four all-out boppish jazz jams ("Digging New Ground," "C-Jam Blues," "The Peeper" and the stomping "We're Outta Here"). Brown's vocals, which feature consistently intelligent lyrics ("Better Off With the Blues" is particularly memorable), are part of the music rather than the entire show; he even gives his obscure backup horns chances to solo. The set is a particularly strong example of Gatemouth Brown's music with each of the 11 selections (except perhaps for "I Will Be Your Friend," a poppish vocal duet with Michelle Shocked) being well worth hearing. —*Scott Yanow*

Live 1980 / Dec. 6, 1994 / Charly ✦✦✦
This distorted board tape captures Clarence "Gatemouth" Brown and an anonymous band, circa 1980, working a small club date. The playing is wonderful and Gatemouth is at the top of his game, both on guitar and violin. However, the bootleg quality of the sound is so off-putting that one can't imagine listening to this disc more than once. For completists only. —*Cub Koda*

The Man / 1995 / Verve ✦✦✦
Brown made the big jump to major-label stature for this typically unclassifiable set, which feistily sweeps through zydeco ("Big Mammou"), country ("Up Jumped the Devil"), Louis Jordan ("Early in the Morning"), and even a little blues along its unpredictable course. Cajun accordionist Jo-El Sonnier receives several solos in a guest-starring role. —*Bill Dahl*

A Long Way Home / Apr. 1996 / Verve ✦✦
This is one of the few lousy recordings of this determinedly eclectic multi-instrumentalist's lengthy career. He's stuck going the superstar cameo route à la John Lee Hooker (there's less Gate on this disc than on any other Gate set), welcoming Eric Clapton aboard for some amazingly generic guitar solos, vocally duetting with frog-voiced Leon Russell and chirpy Maria Muldaur, and backing Loudermilk as he sings his own composition "Tobacco Road" (where's Lou Rawls when you need him?). A handful of acoustic numbers add depth, but there's not much here at all that's likely to satisfy Gate's legion of blues fans. —*Bill Dahl*

Gate Swings / Jul. 15, 1997 / Verve ✦✦✦

American Music, Texas Style / Jun. 29, 1999 / Verve ♦♦♦
Clarence "Gatemouth" Brown was 74 when he recorded *American Music, Texas Style*, and the Texas bluesman made it clear that he still had plenty of energy. On this CD, Brown really emphasizes his love of jazz. Young hard bop players like trumpeter Nicholas Payton and alto saxman Wes Anderson are on board, and the veteran singer/guitarist offers no less than three standards from Duke Ellington's repertoire ("I'm Beginning to See the Light," "Don't Get Around Much Anymore," and son Mercer Ellington's "Things Ain't What They Used to Be") and two classics from Charlie Parker's years with Jay McShann ("Hootie Blues," "Jumpin' the Blues"). Meanwhile, the jazz influence is hard to miss on such fast jump blues as "Rock My Blues Away" and "Without Me Baby." Brown's voice is thinner than it used to be, but his guitar playing is as energetic as ever. While this CD isn't definitive, it's a good, solid effort that Brown can be proud of. *—Alex Henderson*

Okie Dokie Stomp / Jul. 13, 1999 / Bullseye Blues & Jazz ♦♦♦
A budget, 12-song collection taken from Gatemouth's three '80s-era Rounder albums with an added bonus of a 10-minute version of "The Drifter," recorded live in Switzerland in 1982. A good starting point for anyone coming to this multi-talented artist. *—Cub Koda*

Definitive Black and Blue Sessions / Apr. 10, 2001 / Black & Blue

Back to Bogalusa / Jul. 24, 2001 / Blue Thumb ♦♦♦♦
In 1995, septuagenarian Clarence "Gatemouth" Brown moved from the independent blues label Alligator to Verve, then the jazz division of PolyGram now part of Universal. In his five albums for the label (the last two of them released on the Blue Thumb subsidiary)—*The Man* (1995), *Long Way Home* (1996), *Gate Swings* (1997), *American Music, Texas Style* (1999), and now *Back to Bogalusa*—he has been able to pursue his eclectic inclinations more fully than he did when his label bosses were trying to emphasize his blues guitar playing. The center of Brown's taste is post-World War II jump blues and R&B with a distinctly Southwestern feel. Tasty as his guitar playing is, he likes to add horns and even a bit of country fiddle to the mix. As its title indicates, *Back to Bogalusa* particularly investigates the Louisiana influences on this Pelican State native, notably on the tracks "Going Back to Louisiana," "Breaux Bridge Rag," "Bogalusa Boogie Man," and the Cajun-styled "Louisian'." He adds in some sympathetic songs by writers of a later generation, notably "Lie No Better," co-written by Delbert McClinton and Little Feat's "Dixie Chicken," co-written by Lowell George. And he sounds most at home in the funky instrumentals "Grape Jelly" and "Slap It." Brown has taken hits from blues critics for the perceived apostasy of his golden years, but with a singing and playing ability that belies his years he sounds like he's having a wonderful time. *—William Ruhlmann*

Cleo Brown

b. Dec. 8, 1903, Mississippi, **d.** Apr. 15, 1995, Denver, CO
Piano, Vocals / Boogie-Woogie, Jive, Stride
The singer Cleo Brown, known in later years as C. Patra Brown, made recordings in the '30s and '40s, then entered the studios once again in the late '80s after being rediscovered living in the hinterlands of Colorado. Judging from the titles of compilation albums she appears on, Brown seems like she'd be a lot of fun, lumped in a class with other slick chicks, hot mamas, queens of boogie-woogie, female jivers, and rockin' piano ladies. Even amongst this peer group, Brown had some particularly endearing characteristics, especially in her choice of material. Reefer songs are a dime bag a dozen but how many tributes to swollen feet have been recorded? Her "Breakin' in a New Pair of Shoes" is a link with the great Fats Waller, with whom she was frequently compared. He recorded "Your Feet's Too Big," his own tribute to feet, big if not swollen. Another of Brown's greatest and most unusual songs is "When Hollywood Goes Black and Tan," celebrating black performers in the movie business.

Born into a musical household in Mississippi, she started singing in her father's church as a youngster. Following the family move to Chicago in 1919, she began formal studies music on piano. By the early '20s, she was working professionally in clubs and tent shows as well as broadcasting live with her own regular radio show. By the early '30s, she was well-established and for the next two decades she worked almost non-stop, performing in cities across the United States and holding forth regularly in clubs such as New York's Three Deuces. Opinions vary widely as to her talents, but there is no doubt that she was a great communicator. In fact, some listeners may wind up wishing they had a more personal relationship with Brown once they have heard such personal messages as "Mama Don't Want No Peas and Rice and Coconut Oil," or better yet "The Stuff Is Here and It's Mellow." On the strength of the latter number, originally cut in 1935 for Decca, Brown was ceremoniously welcomed into the fraternity of "artists who have recorded songs about reefer," meaning that her music is available on a variety of compilations collecting such material.

There were two sides to her musical performances: her voice and her piano playing. As for the former, the previously mentioned range of opinion veers from those who describe her as a "female Fats Waller," which definitely should be taken as a compliment unless one is describing taste in clothing; to the other end of the spectrum, in which Brown is considered to have a "tiny and twee" voice that gets across completely on the strength of her personality. As for the keyboard, she is more evenly appreciated in this regard, considered along with players such as Freddie Slack and Bob Zurke as the most prominent of the second generation of boogie-woogie players. "It's coming with us to that Desert Island," one critic said of a Cleo Brown performance; while another writer, singling out her efforts from amongst the large cast of a four-CD set, wrote "Cleo Brown was an absolute revelation on "Lookie Lookie Lookie (Here Comes Cookie)," her piano chops easily the equal of her sly vocals." The influences of the major players from the original boogie-woogie craze can be heard in her playing, of course, including Pinetop Smith, whose piece "Pinetop's Boogie" she recorded, as well as Albert Ammons, Jimmy Yancey, Joe Sullivan, Clarence Lofton, Pete Johnson, and Meade "Lux" Lewis. Some jazz writers also hand out some of the credit for the popularity of her records to her accompanists, which included leading jazzmen of the day.

By the late '40s, the rowdy content of her music was beginning to bother her. Brown was going through a religious experience that made singing about the usual tawdry classic blues themes a bit unsettling. She retired from music in 1953 and took up nursing. This was a short-lived career, winding up in a decision to return to music, but only of the religious variety. It was pianist Marian McPartland, a fine player as well as the host of the wonderful National Public Radio show Piano Jazz, that came upon Brown living in the Denver, CO, area under not much of a professional spotlight. She was persuaded to visit New York in order to tape an appearance for Piano Jazz, resulting in a superb article on her by jazz writer Whitney Balliett, eventually reprinted in his book *American Singers.* A new spate of recordings and performances followed, the final chapters of a legend that had gone from the lore of the viper to the gospel, and back again. Although hipsters no doubt wish somebody a bit less of a square had come up with the song, Dave Brubeck's "Sweet Cleo Brown" is a charming tribute. *—Eugene Chadbourne*

Living in the Afterglow / Jun. 11, 1996 / Audiophile ♦♦♦♦
Cleo Brown was a singing boogie-woogie pianist active from the '30s into the '50s who was one of Dave Brubeck's early influences. She retired from music and she stuck to playing exclusively for her church in Denver as the jazz world lost track of her—until Marian McPartland sought Brown for an appearance on her Piano Jazz series in the '80s. This studio session followed the taping of the program, with McPartland as a guest on several tracks. Many of the numbers are original gospel compositions by Brown, some sung in a very friendly manner, such as her "I'm a Little Old Woman," the charming "Afterglow," and the very bluesy "I've Been 'Buked and Scorned." Brown's chops show no signs of slipping as she plays wonderful two-fisted piano on standards such as "Without a Song," and her stimulating duets with McPartland include the spiritual "Down by the Riverside," the surprising choice of "Silent Night," "Marian's Mood" (possibly worked out on the spot in the studio by the pianists), and the old hymn "Just a Closer Walk With Thee." Sadly, this was Cleo Brown's final recording prior to her death in 1995. *—Ken Dryden*

The Legendary Cleo Brown / Apr. 27, 1999 / President ♦♦♦

● **Here Comes Cleo** / Aug. 14, 2001 / Hep ♦♦♦♦

J.T. Brown

b. Apr. 2, 1918, Mississippi, **d.** Nov. 24, 1969, Chicago, IL
Vocals, Sax (Tenor) / Electric Blues, Chicago Blues, Electric Chicago Blues
His braying tenor sax tone earned J.T. Brown the dubious distinction of being told his horn sounded like a "nanny goat." That didn't stop the likes of Elmore James from hiring Brown for some of his most important sessions for Meteor and Modern, though; Brown's style was truly distinctive.

Mississippi-born John T. Brown was a member of the Rabbit Foot Minstrels down south before arriving in the Windy City. By 1945, Brown was recording behind pianist Roosevelt Sykes and singer St. Louis Jimmy Oden, later backing Eddie Boyd and Washboard Sam for RCA Victor. He debuted on wax as a bandleader in 1950 on the Harlem label, subsequently cutting sessions in 1951 and 1952 for Chicago's United logo as well as JOB.

Brown's sideman credentials included wailing riffs beside slide guitarist Elmore James and pianist Little Johnny Jones for the Bihari brothers' Meteor and Flair logos in 1952 and 1953. Meteor issued a couple of singles under Brown's own name (well, sort of) during the same timeframe: "Round House Boogie"/"Kickin' the Blues Around" was credited to the Bep Brown Orcehestra, while "Sax-ony Boogie" was listed as by Saxman Brown and its flip, the vocal "Dumb Woman Blues," as by J.T. (Big Boy) Brown! All four are available on Flair's four-disc James box set, incidentally.

After a final 1956 date for United that laid unissued at the time, Brown's studio activities were limited to sideman roles. In January of 1969, he was part of Fleetwood Mac's *Blues Jam at Chess* album, even singing a tune for the project, but he died before the close of that year. *—Bill Dahl*

Rockin' With J.T. / 1984 / Krazy Kat ♦♦♦♦
Rockin' With J.T. collects a number of tracks J.T. Brown recorded during the late '40s and early '50s. Unfortunately, many of these songs—some of which were changed upon the 1984 reissue, so that the collection could feature songs that weren't on *Windy City Boogie*—feature Brown only as a sideman, working with the likes of Washboard Sam, Roosevelt Sykes and Booker T. Washington. That said, the cuts with him as a sideman positively smoke, and his jumping saxophone is a good reason why. There are also a handful of songs he cut with his own band that round out this imperfect but quite valuable collection. *—Thom Owens*

● **Windy City Boogie** / 1998 / Delmark ♦♦♦♦
J.T. Brown had a long career as Chicago's preeminent blues tenor saxophonist with his unique "nanny goat" vibrato, and these sides collected in this 20-track collection spotlight his stays with the United, JOB and Atomic H labels spread out between 1951 to 1960. Brown wasn't a brilliant instrumentalist, but unique he certainly was, and even paint-by-the-numbers instrumental studio jams like "Use That Spot," "Rock-em," "Windy City Boogie," "House Party Groove," "Blues for JOB" all sparkle with his enthusiasm and a tone that cuts through just about anything. The presence on these tracks of Little Brother Montgomery, Big Crawford, Lafayette Leake, Willie Dixon, Jody Williams, Fred Below, Jump Jackson, Sunnyland Slim and Matt "Guitar" Murphy makes this early Chicago blues that skirts into jazzy territory from time to time but never leaves the alley. A nice, fairly complete collection of one of bluesdom's greatly unsung instrumentalists. *—Cub Koda*

James Brown

b. May 3, 1933, Macon, GA
Vocals, Leader, Arranger, Piano, Organ / Blaxploitation, R&B, Funk, Soul
Soul Brother Number One, the Godfather of Soul, the Hardest Working Man in Show Business, Mr. Dynamite—those are mighty titles, but no one can question that James

Brown has earned them more than any other performer. Other singers were more popular, others were equally skilled, but no other African-American musician has been so influential on the course of popular music in the past several decades. And no other musician, pop or otherwise, put on a more exciting, exhilarating stage show—Brown's performances were marvels of athletic stamina and split-second timing.

Through the gospel-impassioned fury of his vocals and the complex polyrhythms of his beats, Brown was a crucial midwife in not just one, but two revolutions in American Black music. He was one of the figures most responsible for turning R&B into soul; he was, most would agree, *the* figure most responsible for turning soul music into the funk of the late '60s and early '70s. Since the mid-'70s, he's done little more than tread water artistically; his financial and drug problems eventually got him a controversial prison sentence. Yet in a sense his music is now more influential than ever, as his voice and rhythms are sampled on innumerable rap and hip-hop recordings, and critics have belatedly hailed his innovations as among the most important in all of rock or soul.

Brown's rags-to-riches-to-rags story has heroic and tragic dimensions of mythic resonance. Born into poverty in the South, he ran afoul of the law by the late '40s on an armed robbery conviction. With the help of singer Bobby Byrd's family, Brown gained parole, and started a gospel group with Byrd, changing their focus to R&B as the rock revolution gained steam. The Flames, as the Georgian group were known in the mid-'50s, were signed by Federal/King, and had a huge R&B hit right off the bat with the wrenching, churchy ballad "Please, Please, Please." By now the Flames had become James Brown and the Famous Flames, the charisma, energy, and talent of Brown making him the natural star attraction.

All of Brown's singles over the next two years flopped, as he sought to establish his own style, recording material that was obviously derivative of heroes like Roy Brown, Hank Ballard, Little Richard, and Ray Charles. In retrospect, it can be seen that Brown was in the same position as dozens of other R&B one-shots—talented singers in need of better songs, or not fully on the road to a truly original sound. What made Brown succeed where hundreds of others failed was his superhuman determination, working the chitlin circuit to death, sharpening his band, and keeping an eye on new trends. He was on the verge of being dropped from King in late 1958 when his perseverance finally paid off, as "Try Me" became a number one R&B (and small pop) hit, and several follow-ups established him as a regular visitor to the R&B charts.

Brown's style of R&B got harder as the '60s began, as he added more complex, Latin- and jazz-influenced rhythms on hits like "Good Good Lovin'," "I'll Go Crazy," "Think," and "Night Train," alternating these with torturous ballads that featured some of the most frayed screaming to be heard outside of the church. Black audiences already knew that Brown had the most exciting live act around, but he truly started to become a phenomenon with the release of *Live at the Apollo* in 1963. Capturing a James Brown concert in all its whirling-dervish energy and calculated spontaneity, it reached number two in the album charts, an unprecedented feat for a hardcore R&B LP.

Live at the Apollo was recorded and released against the wishes of the King label. It was these kinds of artistic standoffs that led Brown to seek better opportunities elsewhere. In 1964, he ignored his King contract to record "Out of Sight" for Smash, igniting a lengthy legal battle that prevented him from issuing vocal recordings for about a year. When he finally resumed recording for King in 1965, he had a new contract that granted him far more artistic control over his releases.

Brown's new era had truly begun, however, with "Out of Sight," which topped the R&B charts and made the pop Top 30. For some time, Brown had been moving toward more elemental lyrics which threw in as many chants and screams as words, and more intricate beats and horn charts that took some of their cues from the ensemble work of jazz outfits. "Out of Sight" wasn't called funk when it came out, but it had most of the essential ingredients. These were amplified and perfected on 1965's "Papa's Got a Brand New Bag," a monster that finally broke Brown to the White audience, reaching the Top Ten. The even more adventurous follow-up, "I Got You (I Feel Good)," did even better, making number three.

These hits kicked off Brown's period of greatest commercial success and public visibility. From 1965 to the end of the decade, he was rarely off the R&B charts, often on the pop listings, and all over the concert circuit and national television, even meeting with Vice-President Hubert Humphrey and other important politicians as a representative of the Black community. His music became even bolder and funkier, as melody was dispensed with almost altogether in favor of chunky rhythms and magnetic interplay between his vocals, horns, drums, and scratching electric guitar (heard to best advantage on his like "Cold Sweat," "I Got the Feelin'," and "There Was a Time"). The lyrics were now not so much words as chanted, stream-of-consciousness slogans, often aligning themselves with Black pride as well as good old-fashioned (or new-fashioned) sex. Much of the credit for the sound he devised belonged to (and has now been belatedly attributed) his top-notch supporting musicians, such as saxophonists Maceo Parker, St. Clair Pinckney, and Pee Wee Ellis; guitarist Jimmy Nolen; backup singer and longtime loyal associate Bobby Byrd; and drummer Clyde Stubblefield.

Brown was both a brilliant bandleader and a stern taskmaster, leading his band to walk out on him in late 1969. Amazingly, he turned the crisis to his advantage by recruiting a young Cincinnati outfit called the Pacemakers, featuring guitarist Catfish Collins and bassist Bootsy Collins. Although they only stayed with him for about a year, they were crucial to Brown's evolution into even harder funk, emphasizing the rhythm and the bottom even more. The Collins brothers, for their part, put their apprenticeship to good use, helping define '70s funk as members of the Parliament/Funkadelic axis.

In the early '70s, many of the most important members of Brown's late-'60s band returned to the fold, to be billed as the J.B's (they also made records on their own). Brown continued to score heavily on the R&B charts throughout the first half of the '70s, the music becoming even more and more elemental and beat-driven. At the same time, he was retreating from the White audience he had cultivated during the mid- to late '60s; records like "Make It Funky," "Hot Pants," "Get on the Good Foot," and "The Payback" were huge soul sellers, but only modest pop ones. Critics charged, with some justification, that the Godfather was starting to repeat and recycle himself too many times. It must be remembered, though, that these songs were made for the singles-radio-jukebox market and not meant to be played one after the other on CD compilations (as they are today).

By the mid-'70s, Brown was beginning to burn out artistically. He seemed shorn of new ideas, was being outgunned on the charts by disco, and was running into problems with the IRS and his financial empire. There were sporadic hits, and he could always count on enthusiastic live audiences, but by the '80s, he didn't have a label. With the explosion of rap, however, which frequently sampled vintage JB records, Brown was now hipper than ever. He collaborated with Afrika Bambaataa on the critical smash single "Unity," and re-entered the Top Ten in 1986 with "Living in America." Rock critics, who had always ranked Brown considerably below Otis Redding and Aretha Franklin in the soul canon, began to reevaluate his output, particularly his funk years, sometimes anointing him not just as Soul Brother Number One, but as *the* most important Black musician of the rock era.

In 1988, Brown's personal life came crashing down in a well-publicized incident in which he was accused by his wife of assault and battery. After a year skirting hazy legal and personal troubles, he led the police on an interstate car chase after allegedly threatening people with a handgun. The episode ended in a six-year prison sentence that many felt excessive; he was paroled after serving two years.

It's probably safe to assume that, given his advancing age, Brown will not make any more important recordings, although he continues to perform and release new material like 1998's *I'm Back*. Yet his music is probably more popular in the American mainstream today than it's been in over 20 years, and not just among young rappers and samplers. For a long time his cumbersome, byzantine discography was mostly out of print, with pieces available only on skimpy greatest-hits collections. A series of exceptionally well-packaged reissues on PolyGram has changed the situation; the *Star Time* box set is the best overview, with other superb compilations devoted to specific phases of his lengthy career, from '50s R&B to '70s funk. *—Richie Unterberger*

Please, Please, Please / 1959 / Polydor ♦♦♦
Though James Brown and His Famous Flames had scored an R&B Top Ten hit in 1956 with "Please, Please, Please," and Brown's next nine singles for Federal Records flopped until "Try Me," his third single of 1958, scored. That was when King Records (Federal's parent label) assembled this, Brown's debut album, out of some of those singles sessions. You can hear the sound of a group and its enthusiastic singer looking for a hit, sometimes in the rock & roll of "Chonnie-On-Chon" (1957) or the 1956 B-side "I Feel That Old Feeling Coming On," sometimes by remaking "Please, Please, Please" under another name, such as "I Don't Know" (1956), sometimes by tackling Coasters-like novelty material such as "That Dood It" (1958), sometimes by aping the smooth Sam Cooke, as on the 1958 B-side "That's When I Lost My Heart," and once by rewriting "My Bonnie (Lies Over The Ocean)" as the 1958 B-side "Baby Cries Over The Ocean." Only the two hits were really memorable, but the album presented the sound of a major star-to-be in search of his sound. *—William Ruhlmann*

Try Me! / 1959 / King ♦♦♦
When James Brown and His Famous Flames finally scored a second hit with their 11th single, "Try Me," King Records constructed this 16-track LP, including the hit along with both sides of three of its follow-ups, "I Want You So Bad"/"There Must Be a Reason," "I've Got to Change"/"It Hurts to Tell You," and "Got to Cry"/"It Was You"; the B-side of a fourth follow-up, "Don't Let It Happen to Me"; the 1957 single "Can't Be the Same"/"Gonna Try"; the 1957 B-sides "I Won't Plead No More" and "Messing With the Blues"; the B-side of Brown's first hit ("Please Please Please"), "Why Do You Do Me"; and three other stray tracks. The earliest work especially sounded more like that of a doo wop group rather than that of a gritty R&B solo singer. None of it measured up to "Try Me," but you could see what Brown had been aiming at, and if the set list comprised what were in effect James Brown's greatest flops, circa 1959, it demonstrated that he possessed as much promise as fervor. (*Try Me!* was reissued in 1964 under the title *The Unbeatable James Brown: 16 Hits*.) *—William Ruhlmann*

Think / 1960 / Polydor ♦♦♦
James' third album (his first for King), gets a straight-up reissue on compact disc, right down to the booklet featuring both original covers on either side—a nice touch. This is 1960 James Brown, moving from King's Federal subsidiary to the parent label with the hits "Bewildered," "If You Want Me," "You've Got the Power," "I'll Go Crazy," "Baby You're Right" (co-written with Joe Tex), and "I'll Never, Never Let You Go." Although Brown's albums would soon be interchangeable, the same cuts reappearing again and again, this is one of his better efforts as well as a pivotal point in his career. *—Cub Koda*

The Amazing James Brown / 1961 / King ♦♦♦♦
Well on his way to becoming soul-brother number one, James Brown's recordings are exhilarative, which can be attributed to his urgent delivery. His uptempo numbers illuminate with the Georgia native's trademark baritone, while his ballads are impressively as smooth as silk. The two singles to see chart action from this album are "Just You and Me, Darling" and "Lost Someone." The former has that locomotive rhythm, and chanting background vocals complemented by the Godfather's wailing cry—vintage James Brown. The single peaked on the Billboard R&B charts at number 17 after ten weeks. The latter, a pleading ballad, has its tender moments charged with Brown's weeping sighs. It topped off on the Billboard R&B charts at number two, holding down that slot for four consecutive weeks. Brown's ability to bring excitement to his upbeat songs goes without saying, but his serenading side is as majestic as some of the best melo-dramatic groups of the day. He goes from his stalwart vocals to a silky tone. This album houses quite a few of those recordings. *—Craig Lytle*

James Browns Presents His Band & Five Other Great Artists / Oct. 1961 / King ♦♦♦
James Brown on organ, along with Henry Moore, Hank Marr, Clifford Scott, Jimmy Forrest, and Herb Hardesty, explodes on 12 scorching R&B instrumentals. King Records reissued these same tracks, the same year (1961), under the same catalog number as

Jump Around. "Hold It" b/w "The Scratch," a "Night Train" sound-alike, was the first single; it was followed by "Suds," "Cross Firing" (the B-side of "Lost Someone"), and "Night Train." These tracks have held up well and are as invigorating as ever. A sax, Brown's organ, and a bop-influenced bass dominate. Four of these tracks are available on the CD *Soul Pride: The Instrumentals (1960-69)*. —*Andrew Hamilton*

Shout and Shimmy / 1962 / King ✦✦✦
On an album named after the R&B Top 40 title hit and featuring the 1961 Top Ten R&B hit "I Don't Mind," James Brown and His Famous Flames can be heard making music in the variety of styles—blues, Little Richard-style rock, doo wop—out of which they eventually would develop the James Brown funk sound of the mid-'60s. (Actually, the music is older than the copyright date, since King cobbled the LP together from non-charting singles and B-sides dating back to 1958.) It's a more primitive sound than they would later achieve, but remains infectious. (*Shout And Shimmy* was reissued in 1963 under the title *Excitement—Mr. Dynamite*.) —*William Ruhlmann*

★ **Live at the Apollo** / Jan. 1963 / Polydor ✦✦✦✦✦
An astonishing record of James and the Flames tearing the roof off the sucker at the mecca of R&B theatres, New York's Apollo. When King Records owner Syd Nathan refused to fund the recording, thinking it commercial folly, Brown single-mindedly proceeded anyway, paying for it out of his own pocket. He had been out on the road night after night for a while, and he knew that the magic that was part and parcel of a James Brown show was something no record had ever caught. Hit follows hit without a pause—"I'll Go Crazy," "Try Me," "Think," "Please Please Please," "I Don't Mind," "Night Train," and more. The affirmative screams and cries of the audience are something you've never experienced unless you've seen the Brown Revue in a Black theater. If you have, I need not say more; if you haven't, suffice to say that this should be one of the very first records you ever own. —*Rob Bowman*

Roots of a Revolution / 1984 / Polydor ✦✦✦✦✦
A double-CD retrospective of 1956-1964 recordings that charts Brown's progress from doo wop and Little Richard-influenced R&B to the verge of his groundbreaking mid-'60s funk. It doesn't include his biggest hits of the era (which are found on *Star Time*), but these are by and large equally exciting. Many fine overlooked R&B hits and B-sides are included like "Shout and Shimmy," "I've Got Money," the gospel-influenced "Oh Baby Don't You Weep," and "Maybe the Last Time," which inspired the Rolling Stones' "The Last Time." —*Richie Unterberger*

Messing With the Blues / 1991 / Polydor ✦✦✦
Although he is most famous for his innovations in soul and funk music, James Brown never lost sight of his blues and R&B roots. His albums often placed surprisingly rootsy covers of old chestnuts alongside his groundbreaking polyrhythmic workouts. This double CD compiles thirty of the bluesiest items from his vast recorded legacy. Cut between 1957 and 1985, most of the tracks actually date from the '60s; many of these, in turn, were laid down in the early part of the decade, when J.B. was gradually evolving from his more conventional beginnings. The artists whose songs are covered here read like a *Who's Who* of R&B pioneers: Louis Jordan, Roy Brown, Memphis Slim, Ivory Joe Hunter, Fats Domino, Chuck Willis, Little Willie John, Billy Ward, Guitar Slim, and Bobby Bland. It's quite an instructive insight into Brown's not-always-visible roots. It would be fair to say that this does not rank among his most exciting material, finding him in a smoother and more conventional style than his most innovative work. It is nonetheless always entertaining and accomplished, with Brown's love for this material shining through strongly in his committed interpretations. Especially intriguing are an 11-minute cover of Chuck Willis' "Don't Deceive Me" and a two-part, blues-based rap vamp from the early '70s, "Like It Is, Like It Was (The Blues)." The disc includes several unreleased cuts, alternate takes, and unedited versions of previously released songs. —*Richie Unterberger*

☆ **Star Time** / Jun. 1991 / Polydor ✦✦✦✦✦
One of the great box sets of all time; over four CDs, Brown's recorded legacy is traced from "Please Please Please" in 1956 through his 1984 duet with Afrika Bambaataa, "Unity Pt. 1." With 71 tracks in all, the set places the number one R&B artist ever in his proper perspective as the prime progenitor of funk, one of the architects of soul, and the Godfather of Rap. To have done any one of these things would have been a bid for immortality; having done all three makes him a god. Four CDs at once is virtually too rich for one sitting. The well-written liner notes provide three different perspectives on Brown's career. A cornerstone of any great collection. —*Rob Bowman*

● **20 All-Time Greatest Hits!** / Oct. 1991 / Polydor ✦✦✦✦✦
While Brown's 30-track *Solid Gold* collection would be the first-pick introductory disc if it made it to CD, this fine hits package certainly won't disappoint Brown neophytes looking for a way in. Covering his prime stretch from the late '50s through the early '70s, *20 All-Time Greatest Hits!* includes early R&B milestones ("Please, Please, Please"), epochal '60s sides ("Papa's Got a Brand New Bag, Pt. 1"), and latter-day funk classics ("Papa Don't Take No Mess, Pt. 1"). And that's not to mention such perennials as "Mother Popcorn," "Hot Pants," "Cold Sweat," and "Think." Start your Brown obsession here. —*Stephen Cook*

★ **JB40: 40th Anniversary Collection** / Oct. 8, 1996 / Polydor ✦✦✦✦✦
Brown's catalog was in a shambles for years, but the CD age has reversed the situation to such an extent that you now have a wide variety of greatest-hits options to choose from. On the whole, this might be the best buy, cramming 40 of his biggest hit singles from 1956-1979 onto two discs. It's perhaps a little too weighted toward the '70s (which comprise all of disc two), and some decent moderate-size hits are omitted, like "Oh Baby Don't You Weep," "Bring It Up," and "Get It Together." But it does have the core classics. If you don't want to spring for the *Star Time* box, but want more than a single-disc collection, this is the one to have. —*Richie Unterberger*

Nappy Brown (Napoleon Brown Goodson Culp)
b. Oct. 12, 1929, Charlotte, NC
Vocals / Jump Blues, R&B
Nobody sounded much like Nappy Brown during the mid-'50s. Exotically rolling his consonants with sing-song impunity (allegedly, Savoy Records boss Herman Lubinsky thought Brown was singing in Yiddish), bellowing the blues with gospel-inspired ferocity, Brown rode rock & roll's first wave for a few glorious years before his records stopped selling. But in the early '80s, Brown seemingly rose from the dead to stage a comeback bid. He became ensconced once again as a venerable blues veteran who'd stop at nothing (including rolling around the stage in sexual simulation) to enthrall his audience. Napoleon Brown's sanctified screams come naturally—he grew up in Charlotte, NC, singing gospel as well as blues. He was fronting a spiritual aggregation, the Heavenly Lights, who were signed to the roster of Newark, NJ's Savoy Records when Lubinsky convinced the leather-lunged shouter to cross the secular line in 1954. Voilà, Nappy Brown the R&B singer was born.

Brown brought hellfire intensity to his blues-soaked Savoy debut, "Is It True," but it was "Don't Be Angry" the next year that caused his fortunes to skyrocket. The sizzling rocker sported loads of Brown's unique vocal gimmicks and a hair-raising tenor sax solo by Sam "The Man" Taylor, becoming his first national smash. Those onboard New York session aces didn't hurt the overall ambience of Brown's Savoy dates—Taylor's scorching horn further enlivened "Open Up That Door," while Budd Johnson or Al Sears took over on other equally raucous efforts. Novelty-tinged upbeat items such as "Little by Little" and "Piddily Patter Patter" defined Brown's output, but his throat-busting turn on the 1957 blues number "The Right Time" (borrowed by Ray Charles in short order) remains a highlight of Brown's early heyday.

After decades away from the limelight, Brown resurfaced in 1984 with a very credible album for Landslide Records, *Tore Up*, with guitarist Tinsley Ellis' band, the Heartfixers. Later, he recorded a fine set for Black Top (*Something Gonna Jump Out the Bushes*) with Anson Funderburgh, Ronnie Earl, and Earl King sharing guitar duties, and some not-so-fine CDs for other logos. —*Bill Dahl*

That Man / Mar. 31, 1954-Aug. 21, 1961 / Swift ✦✦✦✦✦
That Man collects 17 songs Nappy Brown recorded for Savoy Records between 1954 and 1961, including "The Right Time," "Down in the Alley," and "Is It True." The compilation spotlights his lesser-known recordings, not his hits, but these songs are every bit as good as his more popular material from the same era. —*Thom Owens*

Nappy Brown Sings / 1955 / Savoy ✦✦✦✦✦
Scorching N.Y. R&B from the '50s. —*Bill Dahl*

Don't Be Angry! / Feb. 1, 1955-Oct. 4, 1956 / Savoy Jazz ✦✦✦✦
Rolling his consonants like a crazed cantor, shouter Nappy Brown brought a gospel-imbued fervor to his rocking mid-'50s R&B that few of his peers could match. Backed by some of New York's finest sessioneers, Brown roars 16 of his best early Savoy sides on this essential purchase. "Don't Be Angry," "Just a Little Love," "Open Up That Door," and "Bye Bye Baby" rate with his hottest jump efforts, "I Cried like a Baby" and "It's Really You" are hair-raising blues, and "Little by Little" rides a bouncy, pop-accessible groove. Now where's volume two?? —*Bill Dahl*

The Right Time / 1958 / Savoy ✦✦✦✦✦
More scorching N.Y. R&B from the '50s. —*Bill Dahl*

I Done Got Over / Feb. 26, 1983-Apr. 1983 / Stockholm ✦✦
I Done Got Over features some good vocal performances from Nappy Brown, but this album—which essentially runs through his '50s hits, with a couple new tracks thrown in for good measure—is one of his lesser works. Brown is supported by the Roosters, a stiff Swedish band that can't get the music cooking. Consequently, Brown never puts forth much of an effort. The result is a disappointingly uninspired record. —*Thom Owens*

Tore Up / Aug. 1984 / Alligator ✦✦✦
After too many years during which he was missing and presumed forever lost in action, Brown returned to prominence with this very credible album, cut with backing by guitarist Tinsley Ellis and the Heartfixers and originally issued on the tiny Landslide logo. He reprises his salacious blues "Lemon Squeezin' Daddy" and rolls his R's like the good old days on dusties by Little Walter, the Midnighters, Howlin' Wolf, and even Bob Dylan and the Allmans. —*Bill Dahl*

Something Gonna Jump out the Bushes / Apr. 1987 / Black Top ✦✦✦✦
Ultra-solid support from guitarists Anson Funderburgh, Eugene Ross, Ronnie Earl, and Earl King and Black Top's superb house horn section make this Dallas-cut set Brown's best contemporary album to date. His lusty shouting style works well on covers of the Dominoes' "Have Mercy Baby," the "5" Royales' title track, a pair of Earl King-penned numbers, and Robert Ward's "Your Love Is Real." —*Bill Dahl*

Just for Me / 1988 / JSP ✦✦

Deep Sea Diver / 1989 / Meltone ✦✦
Deep Sea Diver is a competent, but not particularly inspiring, live album recorded in 1989. Occasionally, Nappy Brown turns in a fiery performance—particularly on "Things Have Changed" and the title track—but just as often, his singing is workmanlike. There are enough good moments to make the album worthwhile for fans, but it is not an essential purchase. —*Thom Owens*

Apples & Lemons / 1990 / Ichiban ✦✦✦
Early-'90s jump blues, shouting R&B, and gospel-edged soul from Nappy Brown, who made his finest material in the '50s and '60s, but has done some exuberant material during the '80s and '90s. While his voice doesn't have the swagger or ferocity it did in its heyday, it's still impressive enough to give this the residue of authenticity. —*Ron Wynn*

Aw! Shucks / Jan. 1991-Feb. 1991 / Ichiban ✦✦

Aw! Shucks is one of Nappy Brown's most uninspired efforts. Out of the nine songs, only one was written by Brown; the remaining eight were written by various songwriters, including members of the Ichiban staff. None of the songs are engaging and they're made even worse by flat, uninspired performances. The musicians may be accomplished professionals, but they can't breathe life into any of these songs. *—Thom Owens*

I'm a Wild Man / Jun. 1, 1995 / New Moon ✦✦✦

Who's Been Foolin' You / May 20, 1997 / New Moon ✦✦✦

★ **Night Time Is the Right Time** / Jul. 18, 2000 / Savoy Jazz ✦✦✦✦✦

Night Time Is the Right Time is a two disc collection of 36 gems recorded by R&B singer Nappy Brown. With one foot grounded in the blues and the other stepping toward soul, Brown's mid- to late-'50s recordings are exciting and impressive. The first disc, with classics like "Don't Be Angry," "That Man," and "Two-Faced Woman (And a Lyin' Man)," is probably the best. The tight arrangements, filled with saxophone, piano, and electric guitar, place Brown's voice in the best light. He shouts, croons, and bends words playfully on upbeat numbers like "Just a Little Love" and "Piddily Patter Patter." While his voice is distinctive, it is the exuberant punch of his delivery that keeps his music vibrant some forty years after it was recorded. Even slower numbers, such as "Is that Really You?," find Brown building a soulful intensity, or the "slow burn" as it was called. There are several songs like "I've Had My Fun" on the second disc that fall more comfortably into the blues category. These are fine recordings, but straight R B seemed to work best for his style. It should also be noted that whatever you call his music—R&B, soul, jump blues—much of it would have fit comfortably into '50s rock & roll, though it is certainly rawer and more exciting than the average Top 40 radio. This is fine R&B and a good collection for Brown fans. A great place to learn more about the roots of soul music. *—Ronnie Lankford, Jr.*

Richard Rabbit Brown

b. 1880, Louisiana, **d.** 1937, New Orleans, LA

Vocals, Guitar / Acoustic Blues, Acoustic Louisiana Blues

A New Orleans songster who lived in the city's roughest section and composed songs about several of its most notorious murders, Richard Rabbit Brown was born in 1880, probably in rural Louisiana. It's not known when he turned up in New Orleans, but after arriving he migrated to the portion of Jane's Alley (later home to Louis Armstrong) known as the Battlefield (even the police force often refused to enter to stop disputes). Two of his most popular songs were "The Downfall of the Lion" (concerning the shotgun murder of the police chief on Basin Street) and "Gyp the Blood" (about a New York gangster who sparked a near-riot, and the closing of Storyville as it was known, by killing a bar owner). Brown sang on streetcorners and nightclubs, and earned extra money as a singing boatman. He recorded six sides for Victor in 1927, including the story songs "Mystery of the Dunbar's Child" and "Sinking of the Titanic." Little else is known about the rest of his life, though it is known that he died in 1937. Five of his recordings were included on the Document collection *The Greatest Songsters: Complete Works (1927-1929)*, along with tracks by Mississippi John Hurt and Hambone Willie Newbern. *—John Bush*

● **The Greatest Songsters: Complete Works (1927–1929)** / 1990 / Document ✦✦✦

Roy Brown

b. Sep. 10, 1925, New Orleans, LA, **d.** May 25, 1981, San Fernando, CA

Vocals, Leader, Songwriter, Piano / Jump Blues, West Coast Blues, R&B

When you draw up a short list of the R&B pioneers who exerted a primary influence on the development of rock & roll, respectfully place singer Roy Brown's name near its very top. His seminal 1947 DeLuxe Records waxing of "Good Rockin' Tonight" was immediately ridden to the peak of the R&B charts by shouter Wynonie Harris and subsequently covered by Elvis Presley, Ricky Nelson, Jerry Lee Lewis, and many more early rock icons (even Pat Boone). In addition, Brown's melismatical pleading, gospel-steeped delivery impacted the vocal styles of B.B. King, Bobby Bland, and Little Richard (among a plethora of important singers). Clearly, Roy Brown was an innovator—and from 1948-1951, an R&B star whose wild output directly presaged rock's rise.

Born in the Crescent City, Brown grew up all over the place: Eunice, LA (where he sang in church and worked in the sugarcane fields); Houston, TX; and finally Los Angeles by age 17. Back then, Bing Crosby was Brown's favorite singer—but a nine-month stint at a Shreveport, LA, nightclub exposed him to the blues for the first time. He conjured up "Good Rockin' Tonight" while fronting a band in Galveston, TX. Ironically, Harris wanted no part of the song when Brown first tried to hand it to him. When pianist Cecil Gant heard Brown's knockout rendition of the tune in New Orleans, he had Brown sing it over the phone to a sleepy DeLuxe boss, Jules Braun, in the wee hours of the morning. Though Brown's original waxing (with Bob Ogden's band in support) was a solid hit, Harris' cover beat him out for top chart honors.

Roy Brown didn't have to wait long to dominate the R&B lists himself. He scored 15 hits from mid-1948 to late 1951 for DeLuxe, ranging from the emotionally wracked crying blues of "Hard Luck Blues" (his biggest seller of all in 1950) to the party-time rockers "Rockin' at Midnight," "Boogie at Midnight," "Miss Fanny Brown," and "Cadillac Baby." Strangely, his sales slumped badly from 1952 on, even though his frantic "Hurry Hurry Baby," "Ain't No Rockin' No More," "Black Diamond," and "Gal From Kokomo" for Cincinnati's King Records rate among his hottest house rockers.

Brown was unable to cash in on the rock & roll idiom he helped to invent, though he briefly rejuvenated his commercial fortunes at Imperial Records in 1957. Working with New Orleans producer Dave Bartholomew, then riding high with Fats Domino, Brown returned to the charts with the original version of "Let the Four Winds Blow" (later a hit for Domino) and cut the sizzling sax-powered rockers "Diddy-Y-Diddy-O," "Saturday Night," and "Ain't Gonna Do It." Not everything was an artistic triumph; Brown's utterly lifeless cover of Buddy Knox's "Party Doll"—amazingly, a chart entry for Brown—may well be the worst thing he ever committed to wax (rivaled only by a puerile "School Bell Rock" cut during a momentary return to King in 1959).

After a long dry spell, Brown's acclaimed performance as part of Johnny Otis' troupe at the 1970 Monterey Jazz Festival and a 1973 LP for ABC-BluesWay began to rebuild his long-lost momentum. But it came too late; Brown died of a heart attack in 1981 at age 56, his role as a crucial link between postwar R&B and rock's initial rise still underappreciated by the masses. *—Bill Dahl*

☆ **Blues Deluxe** / 1991 / Charly ✦✦✦✦✦

More tracks (two dozen in all) from Brown's voluminous DeLuxe and King catalogs make this British import well worth searching around for. Hellacious jumps—"Cadillac Baby," "Good Rockin' Man"—and plenty of rarities distinguish this collection by one of the true pioneers of R&B. *—Bill Dahl*

Mighty Mighty Man! / 1993 / Ace ✦✦✦✦✦

Another British import that really delivers the rocking goods! This time zeroing in on Brown's 1953-1959 King sides exclusively, the 22-cut CD shows that Brown actually picked up his tempos to meet rock's rise head on. The clever sequel "Ain't No Rocking No More," "Black Diamond," "Gal from Kokomo," and "Shake 'Em Up Baby" rate with his hottest rockers, with great support from a crew of Crescent City stalwarts. *—Bill Dahl*

★ **Good Rocking Tonight: The Best of Roy Brown** / 1994 / Rhino ✦✦✦✦✦

An unassailable 18-cut cross-section of the monstrously popular and influential New Orleans jump blues shouter's sides for DeLuxe, King, and Imperial labels that spans 1947-1957 and takes in his seminal "Good Rocking Tonight" (where it all began!), "Rockin' at Midnight," "Boogie at Midnight," and "Love Don't Love Nobody"; the almost unbearably tortured "Hard Luck Blues," and the unbelievably raunchy two-parter "Butcher Pete." Looking for the origins of rock? Here they are! *—Bill Dahl*

The Complete Imperial Recordings / Jun. 20, 1995 / Capitol ✦✦✦

Like many other early R&B pioneers, Brown was a bit lost at sea amid the rock & roll explosion in the mid-'50s. From 1956 to 1958, he recorded these 20 tracks for Imperial under the direction of legendary New Orleans R&B producer Dave Bartholomew. Brown and Bartholomew were attempting to update Brown's jump blues/R&B hybrid with a lot of Fats Domino-type Crescent City influence on these sides. The results weren't bad, but with Bartholomew co-writing most of the tunes and using local musicians like saxophonist Lee Allen, Brown sounded more like a journeyman New Orleans R&B singer than an innovative, bluesy forefather of rock & roll. There were a couple of commercial successes; his cover of Buddy Knox's "Party Doll" made the R&B Top 20, and "Let the Four Winds Blow" actually made the pop Top 40, although Fats Domino would have much greater success with the same song when he covered it a few years later. Diluted by occasional pop and rock influences, as well as a substandard variation of "Good Rockin' Tonight," this compilation shouldn't be the first Brown on your shelf. But for those who want to go a little further, it's packaged very well, with thorough liner notes and seven previously unissued cuts. *—Richie Unterberger*

1947–1949 / May 7, 2002 / Classics ✦✦✦✦

Hard Luck and Good Rocking 1947–1950 / Jun. 4, 2002 / EPM Musique ✦✦✦✦

Ruth Brown

b. Jan. 12, 1928, Portsmouth, VA

Vocals / Jump Blues, R&B

They called Atlantic Records "the house that Ruth built" during the '50s, and they weren't referring to the Sultan of Swat. Ruth Brown's regal hitmaking reign from 1949 to the close of the '50s helped tremendously to establish the New York label's predominance in the R&B field. Later, the business all but forgot her—she was forced to toil as domestic help for a time—but she returned to the top, her status as a postwar R&B pioneer (and tireless advocate for the rights and royalties of her peers) recognized worldwide.

Young Ruth Weston was inspired initially by jazz chanteuses Sarah Vaughan, Billie Holiday, and Dinah Washington. She ran away from her Portsmouth home in 1945 to hit the road with trumpeter Jimmy Brown, whom she soon married. A month with bandleader Lucky Millinder's orchestra in 1947 ended abruptly in Washington, D.C., when she was canned for delivering a round of drinks to members of the band. Cab Calloway's sister Blanche gave Ruth a gig at her Crystal Caverns nightclub and assumed a managerial role in the young singer's life. DJ Willis Conover dug Brown's act and recommended her to Ahmet Ertegun and Herb Abramson, bosses of a fledgling imprint named Atlantic.

Unfortunately, Brown's debut session for the firm was delayed by a nine-month hospital stay caused by a serious auto accident en route to New York that badly injured her leg. When she finally made it to her first date in May of 1949, she made up for lost time by waxing the torch ballad "So Long" (backed by guitarist Eddie Condon's band), which proved to be her first hit.

Brown's seductive vocal delivery shone incandescently on her Atlantic smashes "Teardrops in My Eyes" (an R&B chart-topper for 11 weeks in 1950), "I'll Wait for You" and "I Know" in 1951, 1952's "5-10-15 Hours" (another number-one rocker), the seminal "(Mama) He Treats Your Daughter Mean" in 1953, and a tender Chuck Willis-penned "Oh What a Dream" and the timely "Mambo Baby" the next year. Along the way, Frankie Laine tagged her "Miss Rhythm" during an engagement in Philly. Brown belted a series of her hits on the groundbreaking TV program *Showtime at the Apollo* in 1955, exhibiting delicious comic timing while trading sly one-liners with MC Willie Bryant (ironically, ex-husband Jimmy Brown was a member of the show's house band).

After an even two-dozen R&B chart appearances for Atlantic that ended in 1960 with "Don't Deceive Me" (many of them featuring hell-raising tenor sax solos by Willis "Gator" Jackson, who many mistakenly believed to be Brown's husband), Brown faded from view. After raising her two sons and working a nine-to-five job, Brown began to rebuild her musical career in the mid-'70s. Her comedic sense served her well during a TV sitcom stint co-starring with McLean Stevenson in *Hello, Larry*, in a meaty role in director John

Waters' 1985 sock-hop satire film *Hairspray*, and during her 1989 Broadway starring turn in *Black and Blue* (which won her a Tony Award).

There were more records for Fantasy in the '80s and '90s (notably 1991's jumping *Fine and Mellow*), and a lengthy tenure as host of National Public Radio's "Harlem Hit Parade" and "BluesStage." Brown's nine-year ordeal to recoup her share of royalties from all those Atlantic platters led to the formation of the nonprofit Rhythm & Blues Foundation, an organization dedicated to helping others in the same frustrating situation.

Factor in all those time-consuming activities, and it's a wonder Ruth Brown has time to sing anymore. But she does (quite royally, too), her pipes mellowed but not frayed by the ensuing decades that have seen her rise to stardom not once, but twice. *—Bill Dahl*

Sweet Baby of Mine (1949–1956) / Apr. 6, 1949-Mar. 2, 1956 / Route 66 ♦♦♦♦♦
Excellent collection covering blues and R&B songs Brown did prior to becoming a huge hit artist for Atlantic in the late '50s. These were R&B gems, but such artists as Patti Page and Georgia Gibbs were covering them for the white market and Brown was locked out until 1957. But she enjoyed 11 Top Ten R&B hits, which are contained on this anthology. *—Ron Wynn*

Ruth Brown Sings Favorites / 1956 / Atlantic ♦♦♦
Ruth Brown had extensive gospel and jazz roots, which Atlantic honed to perfection, turning her into an R&B queen. These songs aren't quite the same, but they show her full stylistic range and also how powerful and strong her voice was in the '50s. *—Ron Wynn*

Ruth Brown / 1957 / Atlantic ♦♦♦
Ruth Brown at her stinging, assertive, bawdy best, doing the sizzling, innuendo-laden R&B that helped make Atlantic the nation's prime independent during the early days of rock and roll. There's also plenty of equally fiery, hot musical accompaniment, with Willis Jackson sometimes featured on tenor sax. *—Ron Wynn*

Late Date With Ruth Brown / Jan. 27, 1959-Feb. 5, 1959 / Atlantic ♦♦♦♦
Good after-hours, smoky blues and R&B session featuring Ruth Brown in prime form. Nobody, male or female, sang with more spirit, sass, and vigor than Brown during the '50s, and this session reminded those who had forgotten that Brown could also hold her own with sophisticated material as well as sexy stuff. *—Ron Wynn*

Gospel Time / 1962 / Polygram ♦♦♦

Fine Brown Frame / Jun. 18, 1968+Jul. 2, 1968 / Koch ♦♦
In the late '60s, veteran singer Ruth Brown recorded two albums with the Thad Jones/Mel Lewis Orchestra, but neither one was all that classic. Brown sounds fine on this CD reissue, but the big band has little to do except be supportive. The opening "Yes Sir, That's My Baby" is pretty weak, and "Sonny Boy" certainly did not need to be revived. Much better are "Trouble in Mind," "Black Coffee" and "Fine Brown Frame," but Ruth Brown's earlier (and later) recordings are superior to this historical curiosity. *—Scott Yanow*

Black Is Brown and Brown Is Beautiful / 1969 / DCC ♦♦
Veteran R&B/jazz singer Ruth Brown is in strong voice for this audiophile CD reissue but she occasionally goes over the top. The Gary McFarland arrangements for an expanded rhythm section (with guitarist Eric Gale) and the Howard Roberts Chorale are quite predictable and the material has few surprises except for a soulful version of "Yesterday." Closer to soul than to jazz, the set is enjoyable enough but nothing happens to raise it above the average album of the period. Ruth Brown has recorded more significant music elsewhere. *—Scott Yanow*

Have a Good Time / Jun. 10, 1988-Jun. 11, 1988 / Fantasy ♦♦♦♦
Ruth Brown, a top-selling artist in the '50s, endured over two decades of relative obscurity before she began to be noticed again in 1988. Recorded live at the Cinegrill in Hollywood, Brown is assisted by a fine quintet (which includes tenor great Red Holloway, altoist Charles Williams and organist Bobby Forrester) for fresh remakes of some of her hits, along with some newer material. All of Brown's Fantasy CDs feature a mature singer still in her prime. Highlights of this particular release (her debut for the label) include "Gee Baby, Ain't I Good to You," "Teardrops From My Eyes," "When I Fall in Love" and "Mama He Treats Your Daughter Mean." *—Scott Yanow*

Blues on Broadway / Jun. 12, 1989-Jun. 13, 1989 / Fantasy ♦♦♦♦♦
Ruth Brown was starring on Broadway in *Black and Blue* when she recorded her second Fantasy set. The emphasis is on ancient standards (mostly from the '20s) that predated Brown's rise as an R&B star in the '50s. Assisted by trumpeter Spanky Davis, tenorman Red Holloway, trombonist Britt Woodman, a rhythm section led by pianist/organist Bobby Forrester and (on three numbers) altoist Hank Crawford, Brown makes such songs as "Nobody Knows You When You're Down and Out," "If I Can't Sell It, I'll Keep Sittin' on It" and "Am I Blue" sound as if they were written for her. *—Scott Yanow*

★ **Miss Rhythm (Greatest Hits and More)** / 1990 / Rhino ♦♦♦♦♦
Before Aretha Franklin was exalted as the Queen of Soul, Ruth Brown was dubbed "Miss Rhythm"—and with good reason. A gritty, aggressive belter with an impressive range and a powerhouse of a voice, Brown was the top female R&B singer of the early to mid-'50s, and would directly or indirectly have an influence on such greats as Etta James and LaVern Baker. A two-CD set ranging from Brown's early hits to engaging obscurities and rarities, *Miss Rhythm* offers a fine overview of her Atlantic years. Early hits like "Mama, He Treats Your Daughter Mean," "Teardrops From My Eyes," "Mambo Baby," and "5-10-15 Hours" point to the fact that a lot of early R&B was essentially blues at a fast tempo. The set also reminds of early R&B's connection to jazz—in fact, classics like 1949's "So Long" (her first single) and "Have a Good Time" are examples of first-class torch singing. There are numerous Brown albums that are well worth acquiring, but for those interested in exploring her early music for the first time, *Miss Rhythm* is an excellent place to start. *—Alex Henderson*

Fine and Mellow / Apr. 1, 1991-Aug. 13, 1991 / Fantasy ♦♦♦♦
Nice contemporary effort with a strongly swinging R&B flavor running throughout. Ruth Brown goes back to the '40s (Louis Jordan's "Knock Me a Kiss," Dinah Washington's "Salty Papa Blues") and '50s (Brook Benton's "It's Just a Matter of Time," Jackie Wilson's "I'll Be Satisfied," the Lula Reed/Ray Charles dirge "Drown in My Own Tears") for much of the disc, paying loving tribute to her main lady Billie Holiday with the tasty title cut and delivering a pair of Duke Ellington numbers along the way. *—Bill Dahl*

The Songs of My Life / Mar. 1993 / Fantasy ♦♦♦
Before Ruth Brown became an R&B and rock legend in the '50s, she was a jazz, blues, and gospel stylist. She shows that aspect of her talent on *The Songs of My Life*, a fine set produced by guitarist Rodney Jones, who also did the arrangements and conducted the backing band. While she displays her timing, interpretive skills, and still-impressive delivery and enunciation throughout, Brown also demonstrates on her rendition of Eric Clapton's "Tears In Heaven" that she retains an interest in and awareness of contemporary songs that fit her style. Ruth Brown proves that it's not the song or the lyric but the singer who makes a tune work. *—Ron Wynn*

★ **The Best of Ruth Brown** / Jun. 18, 1996 / Rhino ♦♦♦♦♦
For those who want a cheaper and more concise collection of her best Atlantic cuts than the two-CD *Miss Rhythm*, this superb 23-track CD has the cream of her '50s work, including no less than 19 Top Ten R&B singles. Charting her evolution from her jazzy debut, "So Long," through jump blues and early rock & roll, it also adds a bonus of two previously unissued live cuts from 1959. *—Richie Unterberger*

R+B = Ruth Brown / Jan. 20, 1997-Feb. 28, 1997 / Bullseye Blues ♦♦♦♦
Ms. Brown's lengthy career has taken her from the Apollo Theater to Broadway. One of the original rhythm & blues superstars, she has emerged on the other side as one of the genre's most beloved singers. On this outing, producer Scott Billington returns Ruth to her roots in the company of a superb New Orleans band, surrounds her with stellar arrangements of new and old songs and just lets her rip. The kickoff track, "That Train Don't Stop Here," finds her in a bluesy groove with a lengthy rap at the end that extends the running time to almost seven minutes. Tunes like "In Another World," "Too Little Too Late" and "Break It to Me Gently" mine classic soul ballad territory, while Brown's jazzy side comes to the fore on "Sold My Heart to the Junkman" and "Love Letters." In the blues department, fine versions of Ivory Joe Hunter's "False Friend Blues" and Willie Mabon's "I Don't Know" strengthen the song selection, while Ruth teams up with Bonnie Raitt on a conversational "Outskirts of Town." On the last tune, Sarah Brown's "Can't Get Excited," Ruth starts out militant and winds up flirtatious, making a fitting closer for this great little album. Ms. Brown is in fine form here, and this is one terrific modern-day roots recording. *—Cub Koda*

A Good Day for the Blues / Mar. 2, 1999 / Bullseye Blues ♦♦♦
At age 70, Ruth Brown was still in full command of her powers when she cut this beaut of an album in 1998. Fueled by an all-star band featuring Duke Robillard on guitar and New Orleans session stalwarts like James Singleton on bass, keyboardist Davell Crawford, alto saxophonist Ray Moore and a core group that also serves as her touring group, this record was cut live with all the musicians (including a full horn section) playing at once with no overdubs, a throwback to her recording modus operandi at Atlantic back in the '50s. The songs are first rate, featuring new compositions from soul tunesmith Dan Penn ("Can't Stand a Broke Man," "Be Good to Me Tonight"), torchy ballads ("Never Let Me Go," "A Lover Is Forever," "The Richest One," "I Believe I Can Fly" and "True"), riotous spoken word fables ("Cabbage Head" and "H.B.'s Funky Fable"), and solid rhythm numbers ("Hangin' by a Shoestring," "Ice Water in Your Veins"), all expertly played and sung. Far from being on the downhill side of things, Brown demonstrated that there was still plenty of gas left in the tank when she cut this one. *—Cub Koda*

Ruth Brown/Miss Rhythm (Greatest Hits and More) / Jun. 22, 1999 / Collectables ♦♦♦♦
Comprised of two prior Atlantic collections, this 26-track disc features the cream from Brown's hitmaking stretch for the label during most of the '50s. Along with such smashes as "(Mama) He Treats Your Daughter Mean," "Lucky Lips," and "Teardrops From My Eyes," there are plenty of minor gems to be had like "Somebody Touched Me" and "I Can See Everybody's Baby." And adding a bit of '50s pop verve, there are rockin' novelties like the Bobby Darin-penned "This Little Girls Gone Rockin'" and Lieber and Stoller's "I Can't Hear a Word You Say" (all told, the Coasters' hitmaking duo contribute three cuts to the mix). Along with a balanced mix of A- and B-sides, the disc features a support crew that includes tenor saxophonists Budd Johnson and Willis Jackson, trumpeter Taft Jordan, guitarist Mickey Baker, and drummer Connie Kay. This Collectables title might not beat out Rhino's two-disc retrospective, but it certainly will suit those in the market for a less-exhaustive introductory collection. *—Stephen Cook*

1949–1950 / Jul. 10, 2001 / Classics ♦♦♦

Walter Brown

b. Aug. 1917, Dallas, TX, **d.** Jun. 1956, Lawton, OK
Vocals / Jazz Blues, Jump Blues
Blues singer Walter Brown fronted the roaring Jay McShann Orchestra (which included young alto saxist Charlie Parker) in 1941, when the roaring Kansas City aggregation cut their classic "Confessin' The Blues" and "Hootie Blues" for Decca. The Dallas native remained with McShann from 1941 to '45 before going solo (with less successful results). *—Bill Dahl*

● **Confessin' the Blues** / Apr. 22, 1949-Nov. 1, 1949 / Affinity ♦♦♦♦♦
Confessin' the Blues collects a number of tracks Walter Brown recorded with Jay McShann during 1949. Although this is an imperfect collection, spotlighting only a small portion of Brown's recorded legacy, it nevertheless is a terrific jump blues record that proves Brown was a fine blues shouter. *—Leo Stanley*

Blues Everywhere / Oct. 17, 2000 / West Side ✦✦✦
1945–1947 / Oct. 2, 2001 / Classics ✦✦✦✦

Willie Brown

b. Aug. 6, 1900, Clarksdale, MS, **d.** Dec. 30, 1952, Tunica, MS
Guitar, Vocals / Delta Blues
One of the most influential of the early Delta blues guitarists, Willie Brown was arguably the quintessential accompanist of his era, most notably backing legends including Charley Patton and Son House. Born August 6, 1900 in Clarksdale, Mississippi, Brown was an affecting singer and extraordinary guitarist, but spent the vast majority of his career as a sideman, with his ability to "second" other players much celebrated among his peers. In addition to performing alongside Robert Johnson, he appeared on many of the seminal sides cut by Patton between 1929 and 1934, including a legendary 1930 Paramount label session which also yielded two of the three existing Brown solo cuts, "M & O Blues" and "Future Blues," as well as material with barrelhouse pianist Louise Johnson. His final solo performance, "Make Me a Pallet on the Floor," originated from a 1941 Alan Lomax Library of Congress field recording; during the same session, Brown also backed Son House. (In regards to Brown's own discography, it should be noted that among blues scholars there is some debate over the origins of a 1929 track called "Rowdy Blues"; credited to one Kid Bailey, it's believed in some quarters that it is in fact Brown under an assumed name, while others contend that he merely played second guitar on the date instead.) Little to nothing is known of Brown's later years, and he died in Tunica, Mississippi on December 30, 1952. —*Jason Ankeny*

Bob Brozman

b. Mar. 8, 1954, New York, NY
Slide Guitar, Vocals, Ukulele, Guitar (Steel), Guitar / Country Blues, Electric Blues, Worldbeat
Multi-intrumentalist, historian and educator Bob Brozman was born in New York on March 8, 1954. His uncle, Barney Josephson, was a prominent clubowner who ran Cafe Society in Greenwich Village, one of the first places in New York, or anywhere, where Black and White musicians played on stage together.

Brozman studied music and ethnomusicology at Washington University in St. Louis. Brozman is not only a master of classic blues from the '20s and '30s, but also a competent performer of early jazz and ragtime. In the mid-'70s while still in college, he would make trips down south to find, interview and play with the older blues artists from the '20s and '30s whom he admired.

Brozman recorded several fine albums in the early and mid-'80s for the Kicking Mule and Rounder labels, and for students of early, vintage blues and vintage guitar aficionados, they're well worth looking for. In 1985, he recorded *Hello Central ... Give Me Dr. Jazz* for the Massachusetts-based Rounder label and followed up in 1988 with *Devil's Slide*. For die-hard blues fans who seek an album devoid of any of the other genres Brozman so easily interprets (like ragtime and calypso), the album to get is *A Truckload of Blues*, a 1992 Rounder release. He has also collaborated with a number of musicians from around the world, including Hawaiian music legends the Tau Moe Family, with whom Brozman recorded *Remembering the Songs of Our Youth*.

He has his own website at: www.bobbrozman.com. —*Richard Skelly*

Blue Hula Stomp / 1981 / Kicking Mule ✦✦✦
There's little doubt that Bob Brozman's a virtuoso on all plucked string instruments, but his specialty is the National Resophonic guitar, and he can make that do anything, as he shows on this collection, which, like much of his work, has a decidedly Hawaiian lilt. The bulk of the material on *Blue Hula Stomp* dates from the '20s and '30s, rejigged in his own idiosyncratic style, whether it's the unusual, bluesy "Do You Call That a Buddy?" or the lightning fast hula, "Hano Hano Hanalei." He's not just someone who can play with remarkable speed and precision, as he does on "Chili Blues," but also with moving expression, as on the 1916 "hesitation" waltz, "Paauau Waltz," a tune that demands a lot of the player, but which Brozman pulls off with moving panache. Perhaps the most unusual, however, is "Ukulele Spaghetti," played on a National ukulele, the kind of piece to make every guitarist—and uke player—pick his or her jaw up off the floor in complete awe. And when he really takes off on the title track, it becomes explosive, as Brozman handles wooden and National Hawaiian guitars, rhythm and duet guitars, wooden ukulele, saxophones, *and* a vocal. A work of genuine joy and complete genius. —*Chris Nickson*

Hello Central ... Give Me Dr. Jazz / Sep. 1985 / Rounder ✦✦✦
Bob enlists George Winston and others to faithfully re-create the 78-rpm era, focusing on early-jazz standards, hokum and blues. —*Myles Boisen*

● **Devil's Slide** / 1988 / Rounder ✦✦✦✦✦
Blues, Hawaiian, calypso, hot jazz—slide-wizard Bob can do it all with startling authenticity and humor. This CD compilation has five cuts from his *Hello Central* album to boot. —*Myles Boisen*

A Truckload of Blues / 1992 / Rounder ✦✦✦✦✦
Guitarist Bob Brozman's long-awaited all-blues album covers similar territory as others who have turned in heartfelt treatments of traditional and Delta blues tunes. But the difference between Brozman and many of his predecessors is that he has fun doing these songs. He's wise enough to understand that there are only so many ways one can sing "Old Dog Blues" or "Kitchen Man," and that many of the great veterans really enjoyed what they sang. Brozman is also a technical marvel, particularly on bottleneck. But just as his vocals aren't simply replications, he doesn't merely whip out licks and display flash; there's thought in the soloing, creativity in the riffs and plenty of heart in the grooves. Brozman emerges with one of the better and more memorable repertory projects, one that seems more like his take on traditional blues rather than one more museum piece. —*Ron Wynn*

Kika Kila Meets Ki Ho'Alu / Apr. 15, 1997 / Dancing Cat ✦✦✦
This is one of the better and livelier entries in Dancing Cat's extensive slack-key guitar series, for reasons of variety alone. The title of the album is roughly translated as Hawaiian acoustic steel meets slack-key, and the disc, logically, is comprised of duets between steel player Brozman and slack guitarist Kaapana. Brozman, noted as both a Hawaiian-style steel virtuoso and archivist of vintage Hawaiian recordings, tends to dominate the arrangements, with Kaapana acting more as a second foil. Brozman goes for a circa 1920 sound, reminiscent of the time when the Hawaiian guitar was in transition from its purely acoustic origins to the louder sound created by resonator guitars. The pair mostly cover Hawaiian songs from the late-19th and early-20th centuries, often from early Hawaiian recording artists such as Tau Moe, Sol Hoopii, and Kalama's Quartet. —*Richie Unterberger*

Jack Bruce

b. May 14, 1943, Lanarkshire, Scotland
Vocals, Leader, Keyboards, Harmonica, Bass / British Blues, Prog-Rock/Art Rock, Album Rock, Jazz-Rock
Although some may be tempted to call multi-instrumentalist, songwriter and composer Jack Bruce a rock & roll musician, blues and jazz are what this innovative musician really loves. As a result, these two genres are at the base of most of the recorded output from a career that goes back to the beginning of London's blues scene in 1962. In that year, he joined Alexis Korner's Blues Incorporated.

Bruce's most famous songs are, in essence, blues tunes: "Sunshine of Your Love," "Strange Brew," "Politician," and "White Room." Bruce's best-known songs remain those he penned for Cream, the legendary blues-rock trio he formed with drummer Ginger Baker and guitarist Eric Clapton in July 1966. Baker and Bruce played together for five years before Clapton came along, and although their trio only lasted until November 1968, the group is credited with changing the face of rock & roll and bringing blues to a worldwide audience. Through their creative arrangements of classic blues tunes like Robert Johnson's "Crossroads," Skip James' "I'm So Glad," Willie Dixon's "Spoonful," and Albert King's "Born Under a Bad Sign," the group helped popularize blues-rock and led the way for similar groups that came about later on, like Led Zeppelin.

John Simon Asher Bruce was born May 14, 1943, in Lanarkshire, near Glasgow, Scotland. His father was a big jazz fan, and so he credits people like Louis Armstrong and Fats Waller among his earliest influences. He grew up listening to jazz and took up bass and cello as a teen. After three months at the Royal Scottish Academy of Music, he left, disgusted with the politics of music school. After travelling around Europe for a while, he settled into the early blues scene in 1962 in London, where he eventually met drummer Ginger Baker. He played with British blues pioneers Alexis Korner and Graham Bond before leaving in 1965 to join John Mayall's Bluesbreakers, whose guitarist was Eric Clapton. This gave him time to get his chops together without having to practice. With Manfred Mann, who he also played with before forming Cream, Bruce learned about the business of making hit songs. The group's reputation for long, extended blues jams began at the Fillmore in San Francisco at a concert organized by impressario Bill Graham. Bruce later realized that Cream gave him a chance to succeed as a musician, and admitted that if it weren't for that group, he might never have escaped London. After Cream split up in November 1968, Bruce formed Jack Bruce and Friends with drummer Mitch Mitchell and guitarist Larry Coryell. Recording-wise, Bruce took a different tack away from blues and blues-rock, leaning more in a folk-rock direction with his solo albums *Songs for a Tailor* (1969), *Harmony Row* (1971) and *Out of the Storm* (1974).

In 1970 and 1971, he worked with Tony Williams Lifetime before putting together another power trio with guitarist Leslie West and drummer Corky Laing in 1972, simply called West, Bruce & Laing. After working with Frank Zappa on his album *Apostrophe* in 1974, Bruce was at it again in 1975 with the Jack Bruce Band, where members included keyboardist Carla Bley and guitarist Mick Taylor. Again on the road in 1980 with Jack Bruce and Friends, the latter version of the group included drummer Billy Cobham, keyboardist David Sancious and guitarist Clem Clempson, formerly of Humble Pie. In the early '80s, he formed another trio, B.L.T., this time with guitarist Robin Trower before working with Kip Hanrahan on his three solo albums.

Through three and a half decades, Bruce has always been a supreme innovator, pushing himself into uncharted waters with his jazz and folk-rock compositions. Bruce's bluesiest albums would have to include all of his work with Cream, the albums *B.L.T.* and *Truce* with Robin Trower, some of his West, Bruce and Laing recordings, and several of his albums from the '80s and early '90s. These include *Willpower* (PolyGram, 1989), *A Question of Time* (Epic Records, 1989), which includes guest performances by Albert Collins, Nicky Hopkins and Baker, as well as his CMP Records live career retrospective album, recorded in Cologne, France, *Cities of the Heart* (1993). —*Richard Skelly*

Songs for a Tailor / 1969 / Polygram ✦✦✦✦
With a live version of "Crossroads" going Top 30 for Cream, *Songs for a Tailor* was released in 1969, showing many more sides of Jack Bruce. George Harrison (again using his L'Angelo Misterioso moniker) appears on the first track, "Never Tell Your Mother She's Out of Tune," though his guitar is not as prominent as the performance on "Badge." The song is bass heavy with Colosseum members Dick Heckstall-Smith and Jon Hiseman providing a different flavor to what Bruce fans had become accustomed to. Hiseman drums on eight of the ten compositions, including "Theme From an Imaginary Western," the second track, and Jack Bruce's greatest hit that never charted. With "just" Chris Spedding on guitar and Jon Hiseman on drums, Bruce paints a masterpiece performing the bass, piano, organ, and vocals. The song is so significant it was covered by Mountain, Colosseum, and a Colosseum spin-off, Greenslade. One has to keep in mind that the influential *Blind Faith* album was being recorded this same year (and according to the late Jimmy Miller, producer of that disc, Jack Bruce filled in for Rick Grech on some of the Blind Faith material). Bruce's omnipresence on the charts and in the studio gives the diversity on *Songs for a Tailor* that much more intrigue. "Tickets to Water

Falls" and "Weird of Hermiston" feature the Hiseman/Spedding/Bruce trio, and though the wild abandon of Ginger Baker is replaced by Hiseman's jazz undercurrents, these are still basically two- to three-and-a-half-minute songs, not as extended as the material on Bruce's work on his McLaughlin/Heckstall-Smith/Hiseman disc *Things We Like* recorded a year before this, but released two years after *Songs for a Tailor* in 1971. The history is important because this album is one of the most unique fusions of jazz with pop and contains less emphasis on the blues, a genre so essential to Bruce's career. Indeed, "Theme From an Imaginary Western" is total pop. It is to Jack Bruce what "Midnight Rider" is to Gregg Allman, a real defining moment. "Rope Ladder to the Moon" has that refreshing sparkle found on "Tickets to Water Falls" and "Weird of Hermiston," but Bruce has only John Marshall on drums and producer Felix Pappalardi adding some vocals while he provides cellos, vocals, guitar, piano, and bass. Side two goes back to the thick progressive sound of the first track on side one, and has a lot in common with another important album from this year, Janis Joplin's *I Got Dem Ol' Kozmic Blues Again Mama!* Jack Bruce and Janis Joplin were two of the most familiar superstar voices on radio performing hard blues-pop. Joplin added horns to augment her expression the same time Jack Bruce was mixing saxes and trumpets to three tracks of this jazz/pop exploration. "He the Richmond" deviates from that, throwing a curve with Bruce on acoustic guitar, Pappalardi on percussion, and Marshall slipping in again on drums. But the short one minute and 44 second "Boston Ball Game, 1967" proves the point about the pop/jazz fusion succinctly and is a nice little burst of creativity. "To Isengard" has Chris Spedding, Felix Pappalardi, and Jack Bruce on acoustic guitars, a dreamy folk tune until Hiseman's drums kick in on some freeform journey, Spedding's guitar sounding more like the group Roxy Music, which he would eventually join as a sideman, over the total jazz of the bass and drums. "The Clearout" has Spedding, Hiseman, and Bruce end the album with progressive pop slightly different from the other recordings here. As with 1971's *Harmony Row*, Peter Brown composed all the lyrics on *Songs for a Tailor* with Jack Bruce writing the music. A lyric sheet is enclosed and displays the serious nature of this project. It is picture perfect in construction, performance, and presentation. *—Joe Viglione*

Things We Like / 1970 / Atco ✦✦

Recorded in 1968, this is a semi-acoustic, semi-electric jazz set with all the acoustically "clean" instruments interacting with the sometimes fiery tone of John McLaughlin's guitar. McLaughlin thrives in cohesive and sympathetic groupings, and his playing with old London chums Jack Bruce, Dick Heckstall-Smith, and Jon Hiseman is reminiscent of his classic work with Miroslav Vitous, Tony Williams, and Miles Davis. Most of the compositions are by Bruce and are grooving, well-crafted avant-garde jazz with appropriately mystical/mystifying titles like "Over the Cliff," "Hckkh Blues," "Statues," and "Sam Enchanted Dick" (a Heckstall-Smith addition that fades into the standard "Sam's Sack" by Milt Jackson). The players push themselves expressively as is evidenced throughout and notably in Heckstall-Smith's crafty overtone manipulation and simultaneous, multi-saxophone playing (like a mentor, Rashaan Roland Kirk, had done before him). This album may be too unpredictable for fans of Bruce's rock and blues sides, but it is an important historical recording that sets many moods from reflective and meditative to kinetic and ecstatic. Not to be missed by McLaughlin's jazz fans. *—Wilson McCloy*

Harmony Row / 1971 / Atco ✦✦✦

Harmony Row is the legitimate follow-up to Jack Bruce's excellent *Songs for a Tailor,* although 1971 also saw the almost simultaneous release of 1968 jazz tapes entitled *Things We Like* by this artist. An elaborate gatefold package has a shadow photo of the artist from the back overlooking a golden sun on the waters. The self-produced disc begins with the pop excursion "Can You Follow" that blends into "Escape to the Royal Wood (On Ice)." Bruce provides the voice, keyboards, bass and some percussion, making this very much a solo project. "You Burned the Tables on Me" takes things into a progressive rock meets jazz arena. The only reference to blues here is Bruce's voice, but guitarist Chris Spedding's scratchy guitar and the percussion—either by Bruce or drummer Jim Marshall; who plays on what is not specified—make the track sound almost like Cream without Clapton. There's a rare photo of Peter Brown in the second cardboard gatefold, and one of Bruce, while all of Brown's lyrics are spread out for public consumption. A nice touch, as Peter Brown is to Jack Bruce what Keith Reid is to Procol Harum, and the cleverly obscured words are sometimes the only foundation to grasp while rock & roll's innovative bassist goes from genre to genre, combining rhythms and melodies that defy commercial categorization. *Harmony Row* is the album that combines many flavors of Bruce's experimentations, making it courageous, adventurous, and hardly the product for a mass audience. "Folk Song" is barely a folk song; it is a progressive pop tune with that elegant Procol Harum sweeping mystical statement–pretty piano against church-like organ and vocals, with amazing guitar embellishments by Chris Spedding. "Folk Song" has elements Bruce would examine again on the album *Monkjack,* and which should have made him the darling of underground FM radio. It's a far cry from the all-out assault of his forthcoming power trio, West, Bruce & Laing, which emerged a year after this. The delicacy of "Smiles and Grins"' hard jazz is what would have given the project with Leslie West a much-needed diversion. But what happened was Bruce embracing the trail Mountain stampeded down, while a purer blending of the two would have been re-readings of this *Harmony Row* material. "Post War" is a good example of how the under-appreciated Leslie West could have expanded his influence—Spedding's contributions are enormous, and like West, he is the only other musician save the drummer on Bruce's essential projects in 1971 and 1972, the albums *Harmony Row* and *Why Dontcha.* Drummer Jim Marshall appeared on the previous *Songs for a Tailor,* as did Spedding, though they didn't perform together on that disc. Here Bruce takes two players from that solo album and moves them into another head space. His use of the talents around him is impeccable, and another reason why fans should have embraced this quirky and intelligent troubadour. "A Letter of Thanks" is so complex it borders on the Mothers of Invention-style of non-groove while Victoria Sage is more in line with the ideas set forth on *Songs for a Tailor,* with exquisite vocals by this tremendous singer. The final track, the tasty Spanish-influenced "The Consul At Sunset," utilizes multiple percussive ideas with piano and guitars overlapping Peter Brown's words, those words as important as the contributions from Marshall, Spedding, and Bruce. It's actually quite an amazing transition when set against the other discs released in this four-year period, and a stunning output from a major artist without yielding a Top 40 hit. *—Joe Viglione*

Out of the Storm / 1974 / RSO ✦✦✦

Out of the Storm is Jack Bruce yet again taking a different path. No one can accuse this man of being redundant as he leaves behind the hard rock of *Whatever Turns You On* from his 1973 work with West, Bruce & Laing and takes on Steely Dan with a track like "Keep on Wondering." The problem with West, Bruce & Laing is that they should have been the backup band providing Bruce the vehicle to express his artistry. "Keep It Down" would have been a tremendous track for WBL, and Lou Reed/Alice Cooper guitarist Steve Hunter provides the tasteful licks that Leslie West would've used a sledgehammer to find. The title track is real introspection with more "I" references than found on a page in a Marie Osmond autobiography. Bruce uses the rock format to sing the poetry that he and long-time collaborator Peter Brown have crafted here. When played next to his other albums, from *Things We Like* to *Monkjack,* as well as the aforementioned Leslie West collaborations, the indelible voice of Bruce is found to belong, not to a chameleon, but to a true changeling. In an industry that resists change, his music evolves in relentless fashion, switching formats as efficiently and quickly as he switches record labels. While Eric Clapton achieves the acclaim, it is Jack Bruce who delivers a novel and totally original title like "One," with a vocal that moves from cabaret to blues to soul. The man has one of the most powerful and identifiable rock & roll voices, and his body of work is overpowering. "One" has the drums of Jim Gordon and another venture into the Procol Harum sound Bruce has toyed with over various albums in different ways. *Out of the Storm* is another excellent chapter with Steve Hunter showing proficiency and remarkable restraint. Robin Trower, Mick Taylor, Leslie West, Eric Clapton, and so many other guitar greats have put their sound next to Jack Bruce's voice, and this is Steve Hunter aiding and abetting, but not getting in the way of Bruce's creative pop/jazz. *—Joe Viglione*

How's Tricks / 1977 / RSO ✦✦✦✦

A wonderfully tortured Jack Bruce vocal on the song "Without a Word" opens up *How's Tricks,* the second LP for RSO Records by the journeyman bassist/vocalist. Produced by Bill Halverson, who engineered Cream as well as solo Eric Clapton recordings, the material further fuses the all-out jazz of *Things We Like* with the pop found on *Songs for a Tailor.* "Johnny B'77" has the quartet driving the melody onto the fringes of rock, while "Time" bares elements Bruce brought to *Disraeli Gears,* defining his third of the Cream saga. As former bandmate Leslie West had his Leslie West Band out and about in the mid-'70s, this quartet is listed as the Jack Bruce Band. It is yet another about-face for Bruce, singing nine more sets of lyrics by Peter Brown, with guitarist Hughie Burns and keyboardist Tony Hymas getting their chance to participate in the songwriting; it's basically well-performed pop with jazz overtones that has the voice of Bruce adding the blues. The reggae of the title track, and the accompanying album art, may have made for some marketing confusion. There's a magician with cards and old-world glitz permeating this show, the band holding a crystal ball on the back-cover photograph. Having left Atlantic for Robert Stigwood's imprint, a bit more direction could have been in store for this important artist. The packaging doesn't have the elegance of *Harmony Row,* nor does it show respect for the music inside the package. Hughie Burns takes the lead vocal on "Baby Jane," his own composition, and it sounds out of place, disrupting the flow that returns on the exquisite "Lost Inside a Song," where Bruce picks up where he left off. The Steely Dan comparisons are harder to make here, songs like "Madhouse" more hardcore jazz-rock than Fagen and Becker would care to indulge in. "Waiting for the Call" is perhaps the album's bluesiest track, with magnificent harmonica-playing by the vocalist/rock legend. "Outsiders" sounds like Roxy Music gone jazz, while the final track, written by keyboardist Tony Hymas and lyricist Peter Brown, is a nice melodic vehicle for Bruce's voice to conclude the album with. Simon Phillips provides solid drumming throughout, and the well-crafted lyrics are included on the inner sleeve. A strange but highly musical and important outing in the Jack Bruce catalog. *—Joe Viglione*

I've Always Wanted to Do This / 1980 / Epic ✦✦✦

Truce / 1982 / One Way ✦✦✦

● **Willpower: A Twenty-Year Retrospective** / 1989 / Polygram ✦✦✦✦✦

Willpower was really designed to be Jack Bruce's *Crossroads*—it followed Clapton's monumental box by a year, had similar artwork, a similar approach that blended selections from throughout his various projects, and the same remastering/production team. Thing is, Bruce didn't have the commercial success of Clapton, nor did he have the same sizable following (although his fans were indeed devoted), and critics just sorta gave up paying attention around 1970, so there wasn't much of an audience for *Willpower* upon its release in 1989. Nevertheless, it's a pretty terrific summary of Bruce's career, never staying too long in one particular period (even the selections from Cream lack such heavy hitters as "Sunshine of Your Love" or "I Feel Free"), and encapsulating how unpredictable and adventurous Bruce's career has been. This is not heavy on hits, even if it has such signature songs as "White Room," "Theme for an Imaginary Western," "Never Tell Your Mother She's Out of Tune," "How's Tricks," and "As You Said," because Bruce never had that many hits, even radio hits. But it does provide a through, representative introduction. *—Stephen Thomas Erlewine*

Roy Buchanan

b. Sep. 23, 1939, Ozark, AL, d. Aug. 14, 1988, Fairfax, VA
Vocals, Guitar / Blues-Rock, Modern Electric Blues

Roy Buchanan has long been considered one of the finest, yet criminally overlooked guitarists of the blues-rock genre whose lyrical leads and use of harmonics would later influence such guitar greats as Jeff Beck, his one-time student Robbie Robertson, and ZZ Top's Billy Gibbons. Although born in Ozark, AL, on September 23, 1939, Buchanan grew up in the small town of Pixley, CA. His father was both a farmer and Pentecostal preacher, which would bring the youngster his first exposure to gospel music when his family would attend racially mixed revival meetings. But it was when Buchanan came across late-night R&B radio shows that he became smitten by the blues, leading to Buchanan picking up the guitar at the age of seven. First learning steel guitar, he switched to electric guitar by the age of 13, finding the instrument that would one day become his trademark: a Fender Telecaster. By 15, Buchanan knew he wanted to concentrate on music full-time and relocated to Los Angeles, which contained a thriving blues/R&B scene at the time. Shortly after his arrival in L.A., Buchanan was taken under the wing by multi-talented bluesman Johnny Otis, before studying blues with such players as Jimmy Nolen (later with James Brown), Pete Lewis, and Johnny "Guitar" Watson. During the mid- to late '50s, Buchanan led his own rock band, the Heartbeats, which soon after began backing rockabilly great Dale ("Suzy Q") Hawkins.

By the dawn of the '60s, Buchanan had relocated once more, this time to Canada, where he signed on with rockabilly singer Ronnie Hawkins (no relation to Dale Hawkins). The bass player of Ronnie Hawkins' backing band, the Hawks, studied guitar with Buchanan during his tenure with the band. Upon Buchanan's exit, the bassist-turned-guitarist would become the leader of the group, which would eventually become popular roots rockers the Band: Robbie Robertson. Buchanan spent the '60s as a sideman with obscure acts, as well as working as a session guitarist for such varied artists as pop idol Freddy Cannon, country artist Merle Kilgore, and drummer Bobby Gregg, among others, before Buchanan settled down in the Washington, D.C., area in the mid- to late '60s and founded his own outfit, the Snakestretchers. Despite not having appeared on any recordings of his own, word of Buchanan's exceptional playing skills began to spread among musicians as he received accolades from the likes of John Lennon, Eric Clapton, and Merle Haggard, as well as supposedly receiving and declining an invitation to join the Rolling Stones at one point.

The praise eventually led to an hour-long public television documentary on Buchanan in 1971, the appropriately titled *The Best Unknown Guitarist in the World*, and a recording contract with Polydor Records shortly thereafter. Buchanan spent the remainder of the decade issuing solo albums, including such guitar classics as his 1972 self-titled debut (which contained one of Buchanan's best-known tracks, "The Messiah Will Come Again"), 1974's *That's What I Am Here For*, and 1975's *Live Stock*, before switching to Atlantic for several releases. But by the '80s, Buchanan had grown disillusioned by the music business due to the record company's attempts to mold the guitarist into a more mainstream artist, which led to a four-year exile from music between 1981 and 1985.

Luckily, the blues label Alligator convinced Buchanan to begin recording again by the middle of the decade, issuing such solid and critically acclaimed releases as 1985's *When a Guitar Plays the Blues*, 1986's *Dancing on the Edge*, and 1987's *Hot Wires*. But just as his career seemed to be on the upswing once more, tragedy struck on August 14, 1988, when Buchanan was picked up by police in Fairfax, VA, for public intoxication. Shortly after being arrested and placed in a holding cell, a policeman performed a routine check on Buchanan and was shocked to discover that he had hung himself in his cell. Buchanan's stature as one of blues-rock's all-time great guitarists grew even greater after his tragic death, resulting in such posthumous collections as *Sweet Dreams: The Anthology*, *Guitar on Fire: The Atlantic Sessions*, *Deluxe Edition*, and *20th Century Masters*. —*Greg Prato*

Roy Buchanan / Aug. 1972 / Polydor ✦✦✦✦✦

The recording and production on this, Roy Buchanan's first record for Polydor, is delightfully bare, sparse in ornamentation, and full of bum notes and aborted ideas that would be deleted on most commercial releases. It is a loose, highly improvised affair that amply demonstrates why the leader is one of the underappreciated giants of rootsy guitar. Straddling country, blues, and traditional rock & roll, Buchanan's playing is fiery and unpremeditated. His tone is delightfully raw and piercing, his solo ideas impetuous and uncluttered. On the instrumental tracks, such as his famous reading of "Sweet Dreams" or Buchanan's own "The Messiah Will Come Again," one can see why he was such an influence on Jeff Beck, another master of the instrument known for his genre-blending and ragged spontaneity. There is a slight Michael Bloomfield influence felt in Buchanan's blues playing, most evident in the first chorus of "John's Blues" and the quasi-Eastern ornamentations on "Pete's Blue." He plays with pitch, placing notes in unexpected places, constantly keeping the listener guessing. The country tracks, such as "I am a Lonesome Fugitive" and Hank Williams' "Hey, Good Lookin'," benefit greatly from Chuck Tilley's understated vocals. Despite Tilley's presence, the main focus on this record is Buchanan's wailing guitar, which punctuating the vocals with bluesy cries and country moans. The strongest track on *Roy Buchanan* is "The Messiah Will Come Again." This song opens with Buchanan's mumbled spoken word intro over quiet organ and then yields to spine-tingling, sorrow-laden Telecaster that cries and screams in existential torment before giving way in turn to percussive flurries that make less sense as melodic improvisation than as cries of passion. This is raw guitar playing and music making, not for the faint of heart. Fans of blues or country guitar, or those just curious why Jeff Beck would dedicate "'Cause We've Ended As Lovers" from *Blow By Blow* to Buchanan, would do themselves a favor by picking up this album. —*Daniel Gioffre*

Second Album / 1973 / Polydor ✦✦✦

More blues-based than his debut, with great stretched-out jams showcasing some of his best playing. —*Cub Koda*

That's What I Am Here For / Feb. 1974 / Polydor ✦✦✦✦

The late Roy Buchanan is a sadly underrated cult figure in the world of hard rock guitar. His aggressive attack, soulful selection of notes, and general playing attitude made him one of the most respected players of his generation. With heavy competition from musicians such as Eric Clapton, Duane Allman, and Jimi Hendrix, this is quite a feat. *That's What I Am Here For*, one of his earlier Polydor albums, illustrates all of the above artists in fine style. The extended reading of "Hey Joe" is enough to seal Buchanan's reputation, with some lightning-fast and super-heavy blues runs. Overall, the album suffers from some weak songwriting, but there are some gems, such as an extremely sad "Home Is Where I Lost Her," a tale of the death of a lady friend. Billy Price's vocals are a bit mannered and somewhat dated, but effective nonetheless. Another of the album's highlights is "Rodney's Song," a soulful Southern rocker that would have been at home on an early Allman Brothers album. Buchanan really rips on this one, and proves what an awesome player he really was. —*Matthew Greenwald*

Live Stock / Aug. 1975 / Polydor ✦✦✦✦✦

Brilliant live blues-rock guitar by the legend who supposedly turned down a spot in the the Rolling Stones. A must for guitar-hero fans. —*David Szatmary*

A Street Called Straight / Apr. 1976 / Wounded Bird ✦✦

Loading Zone / May 1977 / Atlantic ✦✦

You're Not Alone / Apr. 1978 / Wounded Bird ✦✦✦

Piercing guitar solos explode in a spacey atmosphere. —*David Szatmary*

My Babe / 1981 / ERA ✦✦

Buchanan was a terrific guitarist, but *My Babe* is not the place to hear him in his glory. Too often, the album is dragged down by slick production and Paul Jacobs' overbearing vocals. Buchanan's playing is fairly good, but he sounds a little uninspired, which is understandable, considering his surroundings. —*Stephen Thomas Erlewine*

When a Guitar Plays the Blues / Jul. 1985 / Alligator ✦✦✦✦

Roy Buchanan was always one of the most respected guitarists in his field, ever since the '70s. However, he hit a rough patch in the early '80s, falling out of favor and finding record contracts hard to find. He made a startling comeback in 1985 with *When a Guitar Plays the Blues*, his first record for Alligator Records. Though the record still suffers the slightly antiseptic formula of Alligator Records, Buchanan shines throughout, making it clear why this brought him back to the spotlight in 1985. —*Stephen Thomas Erlewine*

Dancing on the Edge / Jun. 1986 / Alligator ✦✦✦

Hot Wires / 1987 / Alligator ✦✦✦

Another stinging effort. —*David Szatmary*

● **Sweet Dreams: The Anthology** / Sep. 22, 1992 / Polydor/Chronicles ✦✦✦✦✦

Over two CDs, *Sweet Dreams* collects the finest moments from Buchanan's '70s albums, including nine unreleased tracks; as a career retrospective, it's the finest collection available. —*Stephen Thomas Erlewine*

Guitar on Fire: The Atlantic Sessions / Apr. 20, 1993 / Rhino ✦✦✦

Rhino's *Guitar on Fire: The Atlantic Sessions* is a terrific 16-track overview of Buchanan's Atlantic recordings, containing nearly all of the material he cut for the label. This may not capture Buchanan at his very best, but it's a near-peak, and anyone who wants to delve into this portion of his career is advised to pick this up. —*Stephen Thomas Erlewine*

Deluxe Edition / Jan. 30, 2001 / Alligator ✦✦✦✦✦

The third non-crossed licensed anthology from the master guitarist focuses on his three-album stint at Chicago's blues-based Alligator Records. The artist considered the music he made during his 1985-1987 association with the label the most honest of his career. Since he received complete creative control on these discs, his 1988 suicide, a short year after *Hot Wires*—one of Roy Buchanan's best albums ever—was released, makes his untimely death even more shocking. With its 16 tracks—two previously unreleased—almost evenly divided between instrumentals and (predominantly) guest vocals shared by Otis Clay, Delbert McClinton, and Johnny Sayles (Buchanan tentatively and gruffly talks/sings three selections), this is not only a terrific overview of the musician's astounding guitar virtuosity, but a sad coda to a short yet intense career that never broke him through to a wide audience. "You know I ain't broke, but I'm badly bent" are not only lyrics to "Ain't No Business," but also the sad state of affairs the artist found himself in as he was recording his final disc. With a completely unique guitar style that effortlessly shifted from a crying moan (as in the opening bars) to his cover of Otis Redding's "These Arms of Mine" to a raging howl—exemplified by the thumping take on Willie Dixon's "You Can't Judge a Book by the Cover"—Buchanan effectively covered all the blues-soul-rock bases with passion, integrity, and class. His economy of style is obvious in the concentrated 2:29 track (and appropriately titled) instrumental "Whiplash." Although the guitarist's material was often subpar on his two previous labels, the music he recorded during these three years was top-notch, and consistently throbbed with his trademarked rugged, steely tone. While he occasionally stooped to slinging out a wild flurry of fret-shredding cacophony, as in the middle of "Peter Gunn," just to provide proof of his jaw-dropping abilities, Buchanan more frequently kept those more ostentatious impulses in check. There's none of the gospel and low-key country he often dipped into during his Polydor years, yet the essence of those genres is imbedded in his blues and R&B work here. This Alligator *Deluxe Edition* features rare photos, adequate track information, and a heartfelt remembrance penned by label boss Bruce Iglauer. At 61 minutes, only its playing time is questionable, since there easily could have been another quarter-hour of music added. Still, for those who need a concise compilation of Roy Buchanan's phenomenal skills with no filler, this handy disc fits the bill. —*Hal Horowitz*

20th Century Masters—The Millennium Collection: The Best of Roy Buchanan / Mar. 26, 2002 / Polydor ✦✦✦✦
Roy Buchanan's five albums for Polydor, released between 1972 and 1975 and excerpted on this midline-priced best-of, were a worthy compromise between artistic expression and commercial considerations. In the late '60s and early '70s, record companies and music journalists beat the bushes looking for guitar heroes on the scale of Eric Clapton and Jimi Hendrix and came up with at least a couple, Johnny Winter in Texas and Buchanan in Washington, D.C. Polydor no doubt signed Buchanan hoping it had a Clapton/Hendrix-size star, but he lacked the temperament for the big time and merely fulfilled his contract, though he was then scooped up by Atlantic for another try. The tracks here, a good if brief summary of the Polydor years, illustrate both his strengths and weaknesses. The major, perhaps sole strength is the guitar work, which is utterly distinctive within a blues context and at times overwhelming. Buchanan can wring tremendously emotional runs from his axe and then, as in the version of "Hey Joe" here, let forth a sonic assault that rivals any Hendrix ever managed. To listen to this album is to hear a great blues guitarist inventing his art before you. On the tracks from the early albums (the compilation is sequenced chronologically), producer Peter Kieve Siegel was mostly content with that, but on the later albums, more of an attempt was made to turn Buchanan into a singer (his voice was limited and hesitant), or to add other elements, including horn sections and backup singers, to expand the music's appeal beyond blues aficionados. The results are less interesting, but that's what you expect at a major label. So, while not actually the best of Roy Buchanan, this compilation encapsulates his tenure at Polydor and provides a taste for the neophyte of what he sounded like. *—William Ruhlmann*

Roy Buchanan/Second Album / Apr. 23, 2002 / Bang On ✦✦✦✦

Buckwheat Zydeco (Stanley Dural Jr.)

b. Nov. 14, 1947, Lafayette, LA

Keyboards, Accordion, Piano, Organ / Zydeco, Creole

Contemporary zydeco's most popular performer, accordionist Stanley "Buckwheat" Dural Jr. was the natural successor to the throne vacated by the death of his mentor Clifton Chenier; infusing his propulsive party music with strains of rock and R&B, his urbanized sound—complete with touches of synthesizer and trumpet—married traditional and contemporary zydeco with uncommon flair, in the process reaching a wider mainstream audience than any artist before him. Dural was born in Lafayette, Louisiana on November 14, 1947; with his braided hair, he soon acquired the nickname "Buckwheat" (an homage to the *Our Gang* character), and by the age of four was already touted as a piano prodigy. Although often exposed to traditional zydeco as a child, he preferred R&B, and by the mid-'50s was playing professionally with Lynn August; Dural's notoriety as a keyboardist quickly spread, and he also backed notables including Joe Tex and Clarence "Gatemouth" Brown.

In 1971, Dural founded Buckwheat and the Hitchhikers, a 16-piece funk band which he led for the next half-decade; however, in 1976 he finally fell under zydeco's sway when recruited to back Chenier—a friend of his father—on tour. Originally brought on as an organist, Dural picked up the accordion within two years and began learning from the master himself; rechristening himself Buckwheat Zydeco, he formed his own combo by 1979, the Ils Sont Partis Band (translated as "They're off!," so named in honor of the cry heard at the beginning of each horse race at the Lafayette track). Upon signing to the Blues Unlimited label, the group debuted in 1979 with *One for the Road*, followed in 1980 by *Take It Easy, Baby*. After 1983's *100% Fortified Zydeco*, the group moved to the Rounder label, where they issued the Grammy-nominated *Turning Point*; its 1985 follow-up, *Waitin' for My Ya Ya*, was similarly honored.

In 1986, New York-based music critic Ted Fox helped Buckwheat Zydeco land a deal with Island Records, in the process becoming the first zydeco act ever signed to a major label; Fox subsequently acted as their producer as well. The group made their Island debut in 1987 with the acclaimed *On a Night Like This*, another Grammy nominee; that same year they also appeared in the hit movie *The Big Easy*, further increasing their public visibility. *Taking It Home* followed in 1988, but after 1990's *Where There's Smoke There's Fire*, Buckwheat Zydeco was dropped by Island, signing to Charisma for 1992's *On Track*. The years to follow saw the band drifting from one label to another, signing to Warner for 1994's *Choo Choo Boogaloo*, then hopping to Atlantic for 1997's *Trouble*; although their commercial fortunes may have dipped, they remained hugely popular as a live attraction, despite purists' charges of commercialism, and celebrated two decades of music in 1999 with *The Buckwheat Zydeco Story: A 20 Year Party*. *—Jason Ankeny*

★ **100% Fortified Zydeco** / 1983 / Black Top ✦✦✦✦✦
Currently the most visible zydeco artist nationally, this mid-'80s effort is his best, as the material recorded is more inventive. The sound is great and the song selection is superior. *—Jeff Hannusch*

Turning Point / 1983 / Rounder ✦✦✦
This is a good sampling of modern zydeco. *—Jeff Hannusch*

Waitin' for My Ya-Ya / 1985 / Rounder ✦✦✦
Buckwheat Zydeco came closest on this 1985 session to balancing his R&B and pop tendencies with a zydeco authenticity missing from his releases on other labels. The Ils Sont Partis Band, especially guitarist Jimmy Reed, rub board man Elijah Cudges, and trumpeter Calvin Landry put some spark and drive behind the arrangements on the covers of Fats Domino's "Walkin' to New Orleans" and Percy Sledge's "Warm and Tender Love," while Zydeco's singing on these and other numbers like "Lache Pas La Patate" and "Tee Nah Nah" was more focused, less gimmicky and more on target than at any time before or since. Although he never was as talented as some of his supporters claimed, Buckwheat Zydeco was closer to a serious zydeco performer than merely another copyist here. *—Ron Wynn*

Buckwheat's Zydeco Party / 1987 / Rounder ✦✦✦✦✦

On a Night Like This / 1987 / Island ✦✦✦✦
A relatively basic album of party-based zydeco from the heir apparent to the throne after the death of Clifton Chenier. The nice thing about Buckwheat Zydeco's (Stanley Dural's) albums is the broader diversity that he uses as far as the compositions are concerned. Along with his own compositions on this album are bits from Booker T ("Time Is Tight"), the Blasters ("Marie Marie"), and Bob Dylan ("On a Night Like This"). To accompany his own band, a portion of the Dirty Dozen Brass Band fills in on horns throughout the album, much to the credit of the finished sound. The album is jumping, just the way it's supposed to. This is certainly one of Buckwheat's best albums, right in with *Where There's Smoke, There's Fire*. Pick it up for a high energy album of Louisiana's party music. *—Adam Greenberg*

Taking It Home / 1988 / Polygram ✦✦✦
On his second album for Island Records, Buckwheat Zydeco continues to mix things up, adding some rock and pop covers to his trademark zydeco gumbo. Like its predecessor, *On a Night Like This*, the results on *Taking It Home* are a little mixed—the production is a little slick, covers like Derek & the Dominos' "Why Does Love Got to Be So Sad" (featuring none other than Eric Clapton on guitar) are ill-advised, and there simply isn't the fire that distinguished his independent work. That said, no Buckwheat Zydeco album is a complete waste, and hearing him run through gritty, funky originals like "These Things You Do" and "Down Dallas Alley" makes *Taking It Home* worthwhile for long-term fans. *—Thom Owens*

On Track / 1992 / Charisma ✦✦✦
When Stanley "Buckwheat" Dural laces on the accordion, you can bet that it's well past Lawrence Welk's bedtime. *On Track* is party-time zydeco, the indigenous dance music of southwest Louisiana's black Creoles spiced with contemporary rock, soul, and blues. Dural throws just about everything into the gumbo, from the funky bass and driving horns of "Won't You Let Me Go?" to the bayou lullaby "There Will Always Be Tomorrow." The most soulful version ever of "The Midnight Special" is also well worth checking out. Lovers of down-to-earth, good-time music will find themselves right *On Track* with Buckwheat's latest. *—Roch Parisien*

Menagerie: The Essential Zydeco Collection / 1993 / Mango ✦✦✦✦
Menagerie: The Essential Zydeco Collection collects highlights from Buckwheat Zydeco's three albums for Island Records between 1987 and 1990. There are a number of really good songs here ("Ma 'Tit Fille," "Hey Good Lookin'," "Where There's Smoke There's Fire"), and the compilation actually distills his uneven Island albums into a strong single-disc collection. However, if you're looking for Buckwheat at his best, stick to the Rounder and Black Top releases. *—Thom Owens*

Trouble / Apr. 29, 1997 / Tomorrow Recordings ✦✦✦
Since 1979, Buckwheat Zydeco has been synonymous with good vibes, party music and zydeco itself. *Trouble* is far more than just an example of an artist of his reputation coasting on his laurels. This album was originally released in 1997 by Mesa/Atlantic. That release and Mesa's corporate structure were, to say the least, problematic, and it was good fortune that "Buckwheat" Dural was able to retain rights to the master, as it has now been properly released. From the smoking meltdown of "It's So Hard to Stop" to the title track (which is as good as a New Orleans R&B-based dance track as you'll ever hear), this album is easily one of Buckwheat Zydeco's finest efforts. This CD also includes a super-funky version of the Robert Johnson classic "Crossroads," which gives a great new spin on one of the greatest blues-rock warhorses of all time. This record is infectious, fun (like that's new for this band), and one of their most worthwhile discs. *—Matthew Greenwald*

The Buckwheat Zydeco Story: A 20-Year Party / Jul. 6, 1999 / Tomorrow Recordings ✦✦✦✦✦
The Buckwheat Zydeco Story: A 20-Year Party paints a nice portrait of Buckwheat Zydeco's rise from independent labels to stardom, following him from *Turning Point*, his first record for Rounder in 1983, to 1997's *Trouble*, the last record he cut for a major label. In the years separating those two albums, he recorded a wealth of great music, more than can fit on a 15-track collection, but *The Buckwheat Zydeco Story* is nevertheless a good, concise sampler that works as an excellent introduction for neophytes. Yes, long-time followers will probably have a few favorites missing, but they'll only need to turn here for the previously unreleased 1998 live recording of "Hey Baby," which is really good. Curious listeners, however, will find that this gives a nice feeling for the arc of Buckwheat Zydeco's career, and that it gives a good idea of where to turn to next—whether that would be the early Rounder material or the Island albums that made him a near-household name. That makes the compilation a good introduction to Buckwheat, even if it may not be definitive. *—Stephen Thomas Erlewine*

● **Ultimate Collection** / Jul. 18, 2000 / Hip-O ✦✦✦✦✦
Hip-O's 2000 retrospective *The Ultimate Collection* may fall short of the promise of the title, but it comes damn close, offering 19 tracks of prime Buckwheat from the late '70s, '80s, and '90s. Sure, there are some great tracks missing, and it could be argued the label-specific compilations give a more focused listening experience, but this is the best available overview of his entire career, and nearly as good as an overview as could be hoped for. *—Stephen Thomas Erlewine*

Down Home Live / Apr. 24, 2001 / Tomorrow Recordings ✦✦✦
Stanley "Buckwheat" Dural Jr. returned to his hometown of Lafayette, LA, to celebrate Thanksgiving 2000. The band played a three-hour-plus set of hot zydeco at El Sid O's Zydeco & Blues Club, 73 minutes of which are captured here. Everyone should have as much fun at his or her job as Buckwheat Zydeco does. Relentlessly upbeat, the band puts out a raucous, brassy wall of sound that impels the listener to dance. This is a band who will let no groove go before their time. Though the release includes a scant nine tracks, none is shorter than five and a half minutes and the longest is 13. Dural uses his piano

accordion like a handheld orchestra, playing thick chords and rippling riffs. Michael Melchione's stadium rock guitar work would sound out of place if it weren't for the level of intensity maintained by the rest of the band. They bring the pace down only twice on the disc, both times with the only non-Dural-penned tunes. They stroll majestically on Fats Domino's "Walking to New Orleans." They end their set with a heartfelt rendition of the Stones' "Beast of Burden" that sounds like it was written for them. The only drawback to the release is that which plagues many live recordings—a little too much repetitive stage patter. If listeners can get past that and the feeling of regret over missing the actual concert, *Down Home Live* will find a place in their party music collection. —*Peggy Latkovich*

Norton Buffalo

b. Sep. 28, 1951, Oakland, CA

Vocals, Harmonica / Modern Electric Blues, Blues-Rock, Contemporary Blues
One of the most versatile harpists in contemporary music, Norton Buffalo earned his greatest success in blues circles, but also proved himself adept in areas ranging from rock to country to even new age. Born September 28, 1951 in Oakland, California, he earned perhaps his greatest success as a member of the Steve Miller Band, a position he held for over two decades beginning in the mid-'70s; as a session player, Buffalo also lent his harmonica skills to records from performers including the Doobie Brothers, Bonnie Raitt, Johnny Cash and Elvin Bishop. He issued his solo debut, *Lovin' in the Valley of the Moon*, on Capitol in 1977, followed a year later by *Desert Horizon*. After spending the '80s primarily as a sideman, Buffalo teamed with blues slide guitarist Roy Rogers in 1991 for *R&B*, which earned a Grammy nomination for the track "Song for Jessica"; the duo's follow-up, *Travellin' Tracks*, appeared a year later. Additionally, Buffalo led his own band, the Knockouts. —*Jason Ankeny*

Lovin' in the Valley of The Moon / 1977 / Capitol ✦✦

Desert Horizon / 1978 / Capitol ✦✦✦

● **Lovin' in the Valley of the Moon/Desert Horizon** / Nov. 1995 / Edsel ✦✦✦✦
Lovin' in the Valley of the Moon/Desert Horizon combines Norton Buffalo's two late-'70s albums on one compact disc. While both albums are quite uneven, Buffalo has some fine solos on each records, and this is a nice bargain for diehard blues-rock collectors and serious harp fans.—*Stephen Thomas Erlewine*

King of the Highway / Sep. 26, 2000 / Blind Pig ✦✦✦
King of the Highway is the first solo release from blues harp wailer Norton Buffalo and his band, the Knockouts, since the release of 1978's *Desert Horizon*. Norton Buffalo is an in-demand studio musician who has played on numerous sessions in all genres of music, highlighted by his involvement with blues slide guitarist Roy Rogers. The majority of *King of the Highway* is enjoyable (while occasionally predictable) straight-ahead modern blues mixed at times with an occasional hint of New Orleans zydeco rhythm courtesy of Buffalo's unamplified harmonica. One of the main strengths of this 13-track Blind Pig date is the loose feeling brought by friends including Elvin Bishop, Steve Miller (Buffalo has been a member of his band for 25 years), and Merl Saunders, gathering together simply to jam. —*Al Campbell*

George "Mojo" Buford

b. Nov. 10, 1929, Hernando, MS

Harmonica / Harmonica Blues, Electric Chicago Blues, Electric Harmonica Blues
When Muddy Waters deemed a harp player talented enough to follow Little Walter and James Cotton into his peerless combo, he must have been someone special. Mojo Buford spent several stints in the employ of the Chicago blues legend, and was his harpist of choice in the final edition of the Waters band.

George Buford left Mississippi for Memphis while still young, learning his early blues lessons there. He relocated to Chicago in 1952, eventually forming a band called the Savage Boys that mutated into the Muddy Waters Jr. Band (no, they weren't fronted by a Waters imitator; they subbed for their mighty sponsor at local clubs when he was on the road). Buford played with Muddy Waters as early as 1959, but a 1962 uprooting to Minneapolis to front his own combo, and cut a couple of solid but extremely obscure LPs for Vernon and Folk-Art, removed him from the Windy City scene for a while. Buford returned to Waters' combo in 1967 for a year, put in a longer stint with him during the early '70s, and came back for the last time after Jerry Portnoy exited with the rest of his mates to form the Legendary Blues Band. Buford recorded as a bandleader for Mr. Blues (later reissued on Rooster Blues) and the British JSP logo, never drifting far from his enduring Chicago blues roots. —*Bill Dahl*

Exciting Harmonica Sound of Mojo Buford / 1963 / BluesRecordSoc ✦✦✦✦
One of his best and earliest LPs. —*Bill Dahl*

● **Mojo Buford's Blues Summit** / Feb. 17, 1979 / Rooster Blues ✦✦✦✦✦
Buford in the company of guitarists Little Smokey Smothers, Pee Wee Madison, Sammy Lawhorn, and Sonny Rogers, with a rhythm section pounding it out like crazy. —*Cub Koda*

Still Blowin' Strong / Feb. 14, 1996 / Blue Loon ✦✦✦

Harpslinger / Apr. 16, 1996 / Blue Loon ✦✦✦

State of the Blues Harp / Jun. 9, 1998 / JSP ✦✦✦

Home Is Where My Harps Is / Jul. 7, 1998 / Blue Loon ✦✦✦
No, that's not a typo in the title. Those with personal knowledge of former Muddy Waters sideman Mojo Buford will tell you that this was a perfectly fitting title for his third Blue Loon release. All tunes were recorded at New Moon Studio in Mpls., half with the Senders and half with harp player Curtis Blake, several members of the Rough Cuts, and piano man Mike "Hook" Deutsch—all from Minneapolis. Buford wrote all but two of the 13 songs, from the Hooker-influenced opener, "Mo's Boogie," to the swingin' "Harp Breaker."

The lyrics are classic Mojo, enough to crack up anyone who's listened to their share of ol' time style blues vocals. In the fifth track, he sings "You can steal my chickens, but you sho can't make 'em lay; you can steal my woman, but you sure can't make her stay." Or how about this one: "We gonna boogie 'til my hair turn wet." (That's not a typo either). Mojo's harp sounds particularly sweet and catchy when paired with Curtis Blake's. Dave "Cool Breeze" Brown does a sweet, T-Bone style guitar solo on "Cool & Mo Better Blues", Mark Asche is wonderful throughout on piano, and Bill Black lays down a very funky bass solo on "I Want You to Be My Girl." It is the tracks with Blake and the Roughcuts that stand out, however. Blake's engaging harp lines actually bring to mind a visual of squawking, pecking chickens on "You Can Steal My Chicken." Dan Schwalbe's guitar playing is mighty tasty on all tracks, but is especially ear-catching on "Memphis Bound." —*Ann Wickstrom*

Built for Comfort Blues Band

f. Syracuse, NY

Group / Modern Electric Blues, Bar Band, Blues-Rock
Built for Comfort was a short-lived Syracuse, NY, group featuring two brothers on guitar and harmonica/vocals. But the real stars were the rhythm section of Mark Tiffault on drums and Paul "Big Daddy" LaRonde on bass, the two most in-demand musicians in that area of the country. Adept in a number of styles, LaRonde and Tiffault are currently the rhythm section for the New Orleans-inspired group Lil Georgie & the Shuffling Hungarians. —*AMG*

Be Cool / 1992 / Blue Wave ✦✦✦
Local Syracuse blues quartet running through a typical set of Chicago standards. No new ground broken here, but the rhythm section of Paul LaRonde and drummer Mark Tiffault swings admirably. —*AMG*

● **Keep Cool** / Nov. 1992 / Blue Wave ✦✦✦✦
Central New York bar band blues is what BFC serves up on this 14-track set, featuring members of local groups the Kingsnakes and the Corvairs. The song lineup is split down the middle between genre faithful originals and bar staples like Little Walter's "Too Late" and Jimmy Reed's "I Ain't Got You." —*Cub Koda*

High Ballin' / Jun. 16, 1996 / Blue Wave ✦✦✦

Bull City Red (George Washington)

Washboard, Vocals, Guitar / East Coast Blues, Country Blues
Bull City Red, whose real name was George Washington, is best known as a sometimes sideman on washboard to the likes of Blind Boy Fuller, Sonny Terry, and Blind Gary Davis. He was a partial albino, and he came from Durham, North Carolina, a town best known for W.T. Blackwell's "Genuine Durham Smoking Tobacco," which carried a bull trademark image. The town earned the nickname of "Bull City," which became attached to guitarist/washboard man George Washington. He wasn't an especially gifted guitarist, his strongest skill being his ability to imitate Blind Boy Fuller.

His strongest talent lay with the washboard, which he played extremely well, backing up any number of other players. Red led an otherwise blind group that included Fuller, Sonny Terry and, for a time, Blind Gary Davis as well, and with help from their manager, department store owner J.B. Long, landed a contract with Vocalion. At one point in their history, Red, Fuller, Terry, and guitarist Sonny Jones performed together as "Brother George and His Sanctified Singers," and made several recordings of gospel-themed material.

Red was later responsible for hooking Terry up with Brownie McGhee, whom he met while on a trip to Burlington. McGhee was partnered with a blues harpist and one-man band named Jordan Webb at the time, and Red introduced the two to Fuller and Terry as well as their manager. Eventually a musical relationship developed between Terry and McGhee, and following Fuller's death after surgery in 1941, Long began recording McGhee with Webb, Terry, washboard man Robert Young (who had previously played with McGhee), and Red.

He cut more than a dozen sides showing off his skills as a singer and guitarist as well as on the washboard, between 1935 and 1939. The material as such wasn't too impressive, at least as far as Red's guitar work, but his performance on washboard was lively and his singing most expressive. —*Bruce Eder*

● **1935–1939** / Jul. 24, 1935-Jul. 13, 1939 / Story of the Blues ✦✦✦✦
Not a bad compilation—13 songs cut by Bull City Red over a four-year stretch, which include gospel-tinged songs as well as country blues in the Blind Boy Fuller mode. The sound is reasonably good throughout, given the rarity of some of the records, and the analog-to-digital transfer fairly clean given the age of the source material—Red's guitar comes through in startling clarity, and surface noise is generally held in check, or at least to manageable levels. Among the highlights here is Red's version of "I Saw the Light," and which, in another form, entered the repertory of Hank Williams, among others. His singing, however, is actually much better on more traditional blues numbers like "I Won't Be Dogged Around" and the grimly amusing "Pick and Shovel Blues." The last five numbers here, from July of 1939 (four years later than the next oldest cuts), were credited to "Brother George and His Sanctified Singers," and have a strong religious content, although they still play out OK as blues. Sonny Terry also sings on those, and Sonny Jones plays some of the guitar, while Red goes back to washboard. —*Bruce Eder*

Bumble Bee Slim (Amos Easton)

b. May 7, 1905, Brunswick, GA, **d.** 1968, Los Angeles, CA

Vocals, Guitar / Piedmont Blues, Prewar Country Blues, Acoustic Chicago Blues, West Coast Blues
Popular and prolific, Bumble Bee Slim parlayed a familiar but rudimentary style into one of the earliest flowerings of the Chicago style. Much of what he performed he adapted from the groundbreaking duo Leroy Carr and Scrapper Blackwell—Slim built on Carr's laconic, relaxed vocal style and Blackwell's guitar technique. During the mid-'30s,

Bumble Bee Slim recorded a number of sides for a variety of labels, including Bluebird, Vocalion, and Decca, becoming one of the most-recorded bluesmen of the decade.

Born in Georgia, Bumble Bee Slim left his home when he was a teenager. He joined a circus and travelled throughout the south and the Midwest for much of his adolescence and early adulthood. Eventually, he made a home in Indianapolis, where he played local parties and dance halls.

Bumble Bee Slim moved to Chicago in the early '30s. After a few years in the city, he began a recording career; his first singles appeared on Bluebird. Slim wrote and recorded frequently during the mid-'30s, selling more records than most of his contemporaries. In addition to cutting his own sides, he played on records by Big Bill Broonzy and Cripple Clarence Lofton, among others.

Bumble Bee Slim moved back to Georgia in the late '30s. After a few years, he left the state once again, relocating to Los Angeles in the early '40s. During the '50s, Slim cut some West Coast blues for Specialty and Pacific Jazz, which failed to gain much interest. For the rest of his career, he kept a low profile, playing various California clubs. Bumble Bee Slim died in 1968. *—Cub Koda & Stephen Thomas Erlewine*

● **1931–1937** / 1931-1937 / Document ✦✦✦✦✦

Document's *1931-1937* rounds up 18 of Bumble Bee Slim's best sides. The collection highlights Slim's easygoing style—even when the tempo starts rocking, his vocals are relaxed—which he had based on Leroy Carr and Scrapper Blackwell. He found great success because he was happy to follow expectations, turning in side after side of laidback country blues. These 18 songs contain many of his best—including "No Woman No Nickel," "Bye Bye Baby Blues," "Deep Bass Boogie," "Can't You Trust Me No More," "I Done Lost My Baby," "Steady Roll Mama Blues," "How Long, How Long Blues" and "Going Back to Florida"—making it the best available overview of his peak years. *—Thom Owens*

Bumble Bee Slim (1931–1937) / Mar. 1991 / Story of the Blues ✦✦✦✦

Released on CD as part of DA Music's *Story of the Blues* series, this CD features Bumble Bee Slim, aka Amos Easton, one of the more popular blues vocalists of the '30s. This is an excellent overview of his early work. With the assistance of pianists Jimmy Gordon, Myrtle Jackson and Black Bob, guitarist Big Bill Broonzy and many unknown musicians, Slim (who also plays guitar on the solo "No Woman No Nickel") dispalys a likable delivery and an easy-to-understand enunciation on the set of vintage acoustic Chicago blues. A fine sampling. *—Scott Yanow*

1934–1937 / Jun. 16, 1994 / Wolf ✦✦✦✦

Like many other Southern blues musicians looking for work during the Depression, Bumble Bee Slim made his way to the industrial cities of the northern Mississippi. From Chicago to Detroit, Slim and his contemporaries molded the easygoing sound of Southern, rural blues to the complex and sonorous backdrop of the metropolis, and, in the process, laid the groundwork for the electric blues revolution of the '40s and '50s. Wolf Records' compilation *1934-1937* includes many of the Georgia native's prime cuts from this time, and spotlights the blues luminaries who backed him up. Big Bill Broonzy, Tampa Red, Memphis Minnie, and Black Bob standout on fine tracks like "When Somebody Loses" and "New Orleans Stop Time," producing an ensemble sound that combines the rough feel of Delta blues with the tighter sound of the Chicago style. This sophisticated blend reaches an apex in the excellent work of boogie-woogie piano master Albert Ammons and guitarist Lonnie Johnson on "I'm Having So Much Trouble." With his Leroy Carr-inspired, easygoing voice, Slim expertly oversees the fine backing, infusing his many tales of a rough and rambling life with humor and even a sense of detachment ("When The Music Sounds Good" includes a parody of the kind of uptight, white producer Slim, no doubt, ran into). In addition to Document Records' *1931-1937*, this Wolf title provides a nice introduction to the music of Bumble Bee Slim. For fans who want all of Slim's sides, there's Document's *Complete Recorded Works* series. *—Stephen Cook*

Complete Recorded Works, Vol. 1: (1931–1934) / Sep. 1, 1994 / Document ✦✦✦✦

The first of nine releases devoted to Slim's music. As with many Document releases, the sound is pretty uneven. But considering that "Rough Rugged Road Blues," and recorded in October of 1931, was one of the last sides ever issued by Paramount, and that no copies were known to exist until 1992, one has to live with the considerable surface noise on that number, and on "Honey Bee Blues," and the even worse sound on "Stumbling Block Blues" and "Yo Yo String Blues" (on which one can barely tell that a song is there beneath the scratchiness). "Chain Gang Bound," by comparison, sounds almost like a modern recording, despite dating from exactly the same era. The six Paramount sides here are the only recordings here on which Slim played his own guitar, and his style is clean and engaging, with some very deft slide playing in evidence. The other cuts, mostly for Vocalion, generally sound considerably better and were recorded with piano accompaniment, or a band with piano and guitars, and they have a more sophisticated urban sound, anticipating R&B more than they resemble Slim's earlier rural-style songs. His vocals are also considerably more expressive and show a far greater range. Slim's Vocalion debut, "Greasy Greens" and "I'm Waiting on You," cut in New York, are remarkable performances for 1932. His subsequent sides were all cut in Chicago, and are more readily identifiable with that city's then-burgeoning blues tradition—none of the Chicago sides are quite as unexpected as the four New York sides, but they're all eminently listenable. The eight sides cut by Bumble Bee Slim & His Three Sharks—a pretty fair band featuring piano, guitar, and mandolin—features "Someday Things Will Be Breaking My Way," a song more familiar to modern listeners as "Sitting on Top of the World" and immortalized by Albert King and Cream. "Runnin' Drunk Blues" is a delightful, sprightly rag; and on the latest songs on this volume, the guitar returns to the fore, most notably on "Dead and Gone Mother," which features three guitars. *—Bruce Eder*

Complete Recorded Works, Vol. 2: (1934) / Sep. 1, 1994 / Document ✦✦✦✦

Complete Recorded Works, Vol. 3: (1934–1935) / Sep. 1, 1994 / Document ✦✦✦✦

The opening six songs on this volume, which covers the period from November 1934 until April 1935, are decidedly different in texture from much of the material that preceded them in Slim's output. With no more than a guitar or two and perhaps a mandolin backing him up, his music leans less toward the kind of urban R&B sound that his early Vocalion tracks did. The playing is superb, with Carl Martin and Ted Bogan showing off a special virtuosity, while Slim's vocals are brilliantly expressive. The sound is rather rough on some of the material here, leading one to believe that there aren't many copies around of several of these songs—"Way Down In Georgia" and "There You Stand" would not pass muster for release on most labels, being nearly inaudible amid their extreme surface noise. When Slim resumed his piano-based recording in early 1935, he took on a more sophisticated and less rural sound, and his voice became stronger in this mode, far more expressive and involved, alternately playful, sly, or mournful. The guitar accompaniment on some of the late February 1935 tracks, however, are notable as they include Big Bill Broonzy in the session—one of these, "Milk Cow Blues," will prove a major frustration, a magnificent, classic piece of Chicago blues with great playing all around, but almost unlistenable because of the surface noise on the master source, which, one assumes, was irreplaceable. But "Everybody's Fishin'," which follows, is so clean and delightful that it almost makes up for the sonic sins of the earlier song. *—Bruce Eder*

Complete Recorded Works, Vol. 4: (1935) / Sep. 1, 1994 / Document ✦✦✦✦

Complete Recorded Works, Vol. 5: (1935–1936) / Sep. 1, 1994 / Document ✦✦✦✦

Complete Recorded Works, Vol. 6: (1936) / Sep. 1, 1994 / Document ✦✦✦✦

Complete Recorded Works, Vol. 7: (1936–1937) / Sep. 1, 1994 / Document ✦✦✦✦

Complete Recorded Works, Vol. 8: (1937–1951) / Sep. 1, 1994 / Document ✦✦✦✦

Complete Recorded Works, Vol. 9: (1934–1951) / Jan. 2, 1998 / Document ✦✦✦✦

Eddie "Guitar" Burns

b. Feb. 8, 1928, Belzoni, MS

Vocals, Harmonica, Guitar / Modern Electric Blues, Detroit Blues

Detroit boasted a vibrant blues scene during the postwar era, headed by John Lee Hooker and prominently featuring Eddie Burns, who hit the Motor City in 1948 and musically flourished there. While still in Mississippi, Burns picked up his early blues training from the 78s of Sonny Boy Williamson, Tommy McClennan, and Big Bill Broonzy. When he hit Detroit, Burns was exclusively a harp player. He cut "Notoriety Woman," his first single for Holiday in 1948, with partner John T. Smith on guitar. Burns added guitar to his personal arsenal the next year, cutting sessions with Hooker. Burns' own discography was slim but select—he cut singles for DeLuxe in 1952 ("Hello Miss Jessie Lee"), Checker in 1954 ("Biscuit Baking Mama"), JVB, and Chess in 1957 ("Treat Me Like I Treat You"). In 1961, Burns waxed the slashing "Orange Driver" and several more R&B-slanted sides for Harvey Fuqua's Harvey Records.

Later, Burns made a fine album for Blue Suit Records, *Detroit*, that showed his versatility on two instruments to good advantage. Incidentally, blues talent runs in the Burns family: brother Jimmy is a blues-soul performer based in Chicago, with his own impressive discography stretching back to the '60s. *—Bill Dahl*

● **Treat Me Like I Treat You** / 1948-1965 / Moonshine ✦✦✦✦✦

With everything dubbed from vinyl onto vinyl, the sound quality on this LP won't be top-notch—but as it contains Burns' rough-edged 1948-1965 Detroit blues and boogies, it's the best cross-section of his early work compiled thus far. The guitarist/harpist's first few singles were marvelously raw affairs—"Treat Me like I Treat You" and "Biscuit Baking Mama" drip Hastings Street ambience—while Burns' 1961 sides for Harvey Fuqua's Harvey logo—"Messin' With My Bread," "Orange Driver"—are driving R&B. *—Bill Dahl*

Bottle Up & Go / 1972 / Action Replay ✦✦

Detroit / 1989 / Evidence ✦✦✦✦

Impressive contemporary outing that captures Burns' traditional leanings very effectively. Backed by a mean little combo that includes ex-Motown staff pianist Joe Hunter, Burns revives his classic "Orange Driver" and offers a few fresh compositions as well. Originally issued on Toledo, OH-based Blue Suit Records. *—Bill Dahl*

Eddie Burns / 1989 / Blue Suit ✦✦✦✦✦

Eddie Burns features solid, contemporary backing against Burns' impassioned vocals. *—Cub Koda*

Eddie Burns Blues Band / 1993 / Evidence ✦✦✦

Eddie Burns is not an especially attractive vocalist, but when you listen closely to his weary sighs, straining delivery, and anguished inflections, it's hard not to be swayed by his expressiveness. His playing is not loaded with catchy hooks, spinning lines, distorted fills, or other rock/blues devices, but is simple, tight, and nicely executed. Burns' band includes keyboardist Joe Hunter, bassist Frank Bryant, and drummer Bobby Smith, all of whom are also straightforward, no-frills types. These are lean, direct, unsophisticated tunes. Burns' music won't appeal to those seeking innovation or flair, but it is a good outing of conventional, often derivative blues material. *—Ron Wynn*

Snake Eyes / May 28, 2002 / Delmark ✦✦✦

Lonesome Feeling / Sep. 3, 2002 / Black & Blue ✦✦✦

Jimmy Burns

b. Feb. 27, 1943, Dublin, MS

Vocals, Guitar / Modern Electric Blues, Soul-Blues, Contemporary Blues

The younger brother of bluesman Eddie Burns, singer/guitarist Jimmy Burns followed in the family tradition, becoming a staple of Chicago's West Side club circuit after a long absence from the spotlight. Born February 27, 1943 in Dublin, MS, he cut a handful of singles early in his career, but upon marrying and starting a family, he largely applied the brakes to his musical aspirations to focus on domestic life. Burns performed only rarely in the decades to follow; however, with his children all grown in the early '90s, he rekindled his career, following up a hard day of operating his barbecue stand by cutting loose with a set of soulful blues at the Smokedaddy, his regular venue. In 1996, at the age of 53, Burns finally issued his long-awaited full-length debut, *Leaving Here Walking.* —*Jason Ankeny*

Leaving Here Walking / Nov. 26, 1996 / Delmark ✦✦✦

● **Night Time Again** / Jul. 27, 1999 / Delmark ✦✦✦✦

A second CD for Burns follows on the heels of his National Association Of Independent Record Distributors Blues CD of 1998 "*Leaving Here Walking.*" It's as good as the previous award winner, with Burns presenting the complete package of commercially appealing, blues faithful tunes, mostly written by Burns. His guitar playing is economical but not sparse, tinged with excitable phrases but never over the top, the perfect cool-burning balance. Burns also has a fine band of veteran keyboardist Allen Batts, bassist Sho Komiya and drummer Kenny Smith (from Rockin' Johnny's band) and second guitarist Michael Dotson, whose taste and supportive nature is the perfect foil for the leader. Of these 14 cuts, three are some pretty convincing soul blues ala Robert Cray, the best being "Spend Some Time With Me," including a outstanding piano solo by Batts. The easy rocker kicking off the CD "No Consideration" has Burns at his emotional edge, frustrated by his woman, a great modern blues song. "Shake For Me" and "You Say You Need Lovin'" are crackling fiery, horns accentuate "Baby Don't Do It," and "Too Much Loving," quieter heat is prevalent during the shuffle "Hard Road" or the twelve bar guitar instrumental work out "Don't Be Late." Burns changes up the program for the Major Lance hit "Monkey Time," and "1959 Revisited," a doo wop tribute with multi-part vocal harmonies and minimal guitar. This is a bluesman who has a style all his own, free of clichés and influences, with a controlled feeling for the blues that bubbles over when called upon. He could be the premier blues exponent of today, one that the public better be paying close attention to. This recording is highly recommended and, like the previous date, is a legitimate Blues CD of the Year candidate. —*Michael G. Nastos*

R.L. Burnside

b. Nov. 23, 1926, Oxford, MS

Vocals, Guitar / Juke Joint Blues, Modern Delta Blues, Delta Blues, Electric Delta Blues, Modern Electric Blues

North Mississippi guitarist R.L. Burnside is one of the paragons of state-of-the-art Delta juke joint blues. The guitarist, singer and songwriter was born November 23, 1926 in Oxford, MS, and makes his home in Holly Springs, in the hill country above the Delta. He's lived most of his life in the Mississippi hill country, which, unlike the Delta region, consists mainly of a lot of small farms. He learned his music from his neighbor, Fred McDowell, and the highly rhythmic style that Burnside plays is evident in McDowell's recording as well. Despite the otherworldly country blues sounds put down by Burnside and his family band, known as the Sound Machine, his other influences are surprisingly contemporary: Muddy Waters, John Lee Hooker and Lightnin' Hopkins. But Burnside's music is pure country Delta juke joint blues, heavily rhythm-oriented and played with a slide.

It's only recently that he's been hitting full stride with his tours and his music, thanks to the efforts of Fat Possum Records. In recent years, the label has issued recordings made by a group of Burnside's peers, including Junior Kimbrough, Dave Thompson and others.

Up until the mid-'80s, Burnside was primarily a farmer and fisherman. After getting some attention in the late '60s via folklorists David Evans and George Mitchell (Mitchell recorded him for the Arhoolie label), he recorded for the Vogue, Swingmaster and Highwater record labels. Although he had done short tours, it wasn't until the late '80s that he was invited to perform at several European blues festivals. In 1992, he was featured alongside his friend Junior Kimbrough (whose Holly Spings juke joint Burnside lives next to), in a documentary film, *Deep Blues.* His debut recording, *Bad Luck City,* was released that same year on Fat Possum Records. Burnside has a second record out on the Oxford-based Fat Possum label, *Too Bad Jim* (1994).

These recordings showcase the raw, barebones electric guitar stylings of Burnside, and on both recordings he's accompanied by a small band, which includes his son Dwayne on bass and son-in-law Calvin Jackson on drums, as well as guitarist Kenny Brown. Both recordings also adequately capture the feeling of what it must be like to be in Junior Kimbrough's juke joint, where both men have been playing this kind if raw, unadulterated blues for over 30 years. This is the kind of downhome, backporch blues played today as it has been for many decades. In 1996, Burnside teamed with indierocker Jon Spencer to cut *A Ass Pocket of Whiskey* for the hip Matador label; he returned to Fat Possum in 1998 for the more conventional *Come on In. My Black Name A-Ringin'* followed a year later and *Mississippi Hill Country Blues* and *Wish I Was in Heaven Sitting Down* were released in 2000. *Well Well Well* and *Goin' Down South* both appeared in 2001. —*Richard Skelly*

Bad Luck City / 1992 / Fat Possum ✦✦✦✦✦

Welcome to Mississippi. This is the sound you would be likely to hear in any juke joint hosting the talents of the real-life Burnside family band. What you can't see on this disc is the picture of them grinning ear-to-ear as they play—or the sight of R.L.'s son Dwayne duck-walking while his dad smiles and nods to friends across the floor. His other son, Joseph, would likely be pounding out the solid bass line, while his son-in-law Calvin Jackson proudly presided over the drums. No, you can't see it but you can hear it if you listen closely. This set was recorded live at Syd's in Oxford, MS. As for the music, it's rough, real, and one-of-a-kind… the way blues should be. —*Larry Hoffman*

● **Too Bad Jim** / 1994 / Fat Possum ✦✦✦✦✦

Too Bad Jim is cut from the same cloth as its predecessor, *Bad Luck City.* It features R.L. Burnside fronting a small juke joint combo, tearing through some greasy blues. However, *Too Bad Jim* is the better album, simply from a performance standpoint. Burnside sounds

more relaxed and the band steps back from the spotlight slightly, letting the guitarist burn brightly on his own, showcasing his deep blues roots. —*Thom Owens*

A Ass Pocket of Whiskey / Jun. 25, 1996 / Matador ✦✦✦✦

Although he had been playing for years, it wasn't until the '90s that R.L. Burnside's raw electrified Delta blues was heard by a wide audience. His new fans celebrated his wild, unbridled energy, so it made sense for him to team with the Jon Spencer Blues Explosion, the warped indie-rock band that's all about energy. However, the very purists who celebrate Burnside hate Spencer, believing that he mocks the blues. As the blistering *A Ass Pocket of Whiskey* proves, Spencer may not treat the blues with reverence, but he and his band capture the wild essence of juke-joint blues. And that makes them the perfect match for Burnside, who knows his history but isn't burdened by it. Together, Burnside and the Blues Explosion make raw, scintillating, unvarnished blues that positively burns. —*Thom Owens*

Mr. Wizard / Mar. 11, 1997 / Fat Possum ✦✦✦

While it's not quite as relentlessly exciting as *A Ass Pocket of Whiskey,* primarily because the Jon Spencer Blues Explosion isn't along to provide support, *Mr. Wizard* is another set of blistering electric blues from R.L. Burnside, highlighted by his stomping guitar, powerful voice and cheerfully vulgar lyrics. —*Thom Owens*

Sound Machine Groove / Jul. 22, 1997 / HMG ✦✦✦

Recorded by folklorist David Evans in 1979 and 1980, these are Burnside's first recordings with electric guitar and also his first with a band. That band was the Sound Machine, a band he literally created himself out of members of his own family, blending raw Mississippi blues with soul, funk, R&B and other urban flavors to make a marvelous amalgam of his own. Contemporary beats and modern themes like "Bad Luck City," "Searching for My Baby," "Can't Let You Go" and "Sound Machine Groove" sit nicely alongside slower, traditional material like "Going Down South" and "Begged for a Nickel," while R.L.'s duets with drummer Calvin Jackson on "Goin' Away Baby" and "Long Haired Doney" show a marvelous empathy and interplay. Especially notable is a version of "Sitting on Top of the World" with Burnside on slide guitar that, with Jackson's help, neatly evokes the sound and feel of a fife and drum band. Although R.L. is presently the darling of the blues crowd and hailed as something of an overnight success, one listen to this disc tells you he was already forging a new chapter in the Mississippi blues tradition with these recordings. —*Cub Koda*

Acoustic Stories / Sep. 23, 1997 / M.C. ✦✦✦

R.L. Burnside is notorious for his gritty, greasy Delta blues, as each of his records since his 1991 discovery have been blistering electric recordings. That's what makes *Acoustic Stories* so refreshing. Recorded at New York City in 1988 with harp player John Neremberg, the album balances originals with a handful of well-selected covers, including three John Lee Hooker tunes: "When My First Wife Left Me," "Hobo Blues" and "Meet Me in the Bottom." Burnside is more exciting when he's electric, but these are unexpectedly haunting recordings that prove he's not just about rocking the joint. —*Thom Owens*

Come on In / Aug. 11, 1998 / Fat Possum ✦✦✦

You have to give a guy credit for trying. In an age when most of the old blues players are either dead or too old to play, R.L. Burnside, the 71 year-old Mississippi native, can still rip dirty, juke-joint blues in convincing fashion. *Come on In* attempts, to some success, to bring one of America's oldest musical forms into the 21st century by adding sampling and looping techniques to Delta blues. *Come on In* is a collaboration with Beck mixmaster Tom Rothrock and Alec Empire of Digital Hardcore. Seldom does one see the words "dub", "remix" and "programming" on a Delta blues album, but R.L. Burnside is no ordinary bluesman. *Come on In* is a risky move to say the least, and unfortunately, it doesn't always pay off. The best tracks in the album are the least techno-fied. "Come on In," a live solo shot, and the down'n'dirty "Just Like a Woman" has a non-trip-hopped Burnside mining tough riffs for all their emotion. "Let My Baby Ride" with a stomping, looped beat, is still recognizable as Burnside and works well. On the other hand, "Don't Stop Honey" and "It's Bad You Know" take the techno tampering too far, and the results are feckless shells of what were once gritty blues. Next time out, if Burnside gets his ass pocket o' whiskey, turns down the techno a bit and cranks those amps up, he could be onto something. —*Matthew Hilburn*

My Black Name A-Ringin' / 1999 / Genes ✦✦✦

R.L. Burnside has been playing the blues since the '50s, but providing for his large family (he would eventually have 13 children) and his love for his hometown kept him from supporting himself with his music until the '80s. These recordings were made in 1969 when blues musician Big Joe Williams led a carload of Adelphi Records filmmakers and sound engineers on a tour through the blues country from Chicago south to Mississippi. Burnside was one of the highlights of the trip, and the crew ended up setting up camp near his home for some time to record. *My Black Name A-Ringin'* presents Burnside in a stripped-down, acoustic form and shows his native north-hill country style as well as some early influences. Each song shows off a different facet of his style: "Goin' Down South" is a hypnotic drone with short, repetitive rhythmic sections; "Two Trains Runnin'" features more of a traditional Delta style with its deep, sad harmonica; and "My Black Name A-Ringin'" shows what Burnside could do with a traditional song dating as far back as slavery. Overall, this album presents an interesting prequel to Burnside's recordings with Fat Possum Records and his experimentalism in the '90s. —*Stacia Proefrock*

Mississippi Hill Country Blues / Jul. 11, 2000 / Swingmaster ✦✦✦

It's a pleasure to hear R.L. Burnside's early acoustic blues played the way he learned them in the hill country of northern Mississippi. Three of these tracks date from 1967 and were recorded in Coldwater, MS, by folklorist George Mitchell, while the remaining 16 were recorded in the early '80s by Swingmaster operator Leo Bruin in Groningen, Netherlands. This is Burnside playing solo (and mainly) acoustic country blues with the only addition to his guitar and voice being the harmonica of Red Ramsey on "Rolling and Tumbling." While you can't go wrong with the purchase of any Burnside recording, these Swingmaster sessions portray a natural relaxed unaccompanied Burnside, recorded long before the Fat Possum releases that, beginning in the '90s, would find him playing in an electric band with his son and son-in-law and occasionally experimenting with sampling and indie rock leanings. *—Al Campbell*

Wish I Was in Heaven Sitting Down / Oct. 24, 2000 / Fat Possum ♦♦♦

Like jazz, the blues has its share of late bloomers—artists who didn't start recording or didn't become well-known until they were well into their fifties or sixties. R.L. Burnside is very much a late bloomer; the Mississippi bluesman was born in 1926, but it wasn't until the '90s that he started to enjoy the publicity he deserved. Recorded in 2000, *Wish I Was in Heaven Sitting Down* finds the veteran singer continuing to be fairly unpredictable at 73. Essentially, this CD falls into the Mississippi blues category—Burnside maintains the earthy, down-home rawness that people expect from Mississippi country blues. But Burnside certainly isn't without urban influences, and this CD illustrates his appreciation of John Lee Hooker and early Muddy Waters as well as the Texas blues of Lightnin' Hopkins. Burnside has also been influenced by R&B; one of the few tracks that he didn't write or co-write is a cover of Aretha Franklin's '60s smash "Chain of Fools." The producers (who include Andy Kaulkin, John Porter, and Brad Cook) try to make that track and others relevant to hip-hop by adding sampling and scratching—and when they do, it sounds forced and unnatural. Some of the producing is simply too high-tech for an artist as raw as Burnside, but that doesn't make his vocals any less impressive. Despite its imperfections, *Wish I Was in Heaven Sitting Down* is a generally appealing document of Burnside at 73. *—Alex Henderson*

Well Well Well / Mar. 27, 2001 / M.C. ♦♦♦♦

At first glance, this archival collection may appear to be too much of a hodgepodge. The recording dates range from 1986 to 1993; the locations range from a large theater in The Hague to a shotgun house in New Orleans; the lineups range from solo performances by Burnside to trio sessions with Jon Morris and Calvin Jackson; and the songs range from Burnside originals to blues classics by Muddy Waters ("Can't Be Satisfied"), John Lee Hooker ("Boogie Chillen'"), Big Joe Williams ("Mellow Peaches"), and others. However, the material coheres fairly well despite the scattershot nature of this collection. Burnside's performances are relatively consistent in both quality and musical style; he sticks to straightforward blues without the hip-hop and techno elements found on some of his other recordings, and his dry sense of humor helps unify the music with the spoken word portions of the album. The one-minute interview segment (in which Burnside discusses fishing and guitar playing) and 93-second in-concert monologue (about a girl who saw him eat grass from her front lawn) fit comfortably next to the songs, and the bull-session atmosphere of "Bad Luck Money Rap" (in which he tells Morris and vocalist/harp player Curtis Salgado about certain things that make him so mad he could eat fried chicken) is compatible with the relaxed, informal feel of the album, although at six minutes and 30 seconds it's too long of an intermission from the music. Some of the album's highlights include a powerful rendition of "Staggolee" with explicit lyrics that ensure that this traditional tune is "not suitable for airplay"; a short but sweet performance of the Lightnin' Hopkins song "Mojo Hand"; a live version of Burnside's own ".44 Pistol" recorded at the Queen Street Playhouse in Charleston, SC; a recording of his signature song, "Goin' Down South," with Morris and Jackson at a shed in Gieterveen, Holland; and a performance of "How Many More Years" in Athens, Greece, that proves that Burnside really can sing and play the blues, even though his vocals don't have the overpowering intensity of Howlin' Wolf's original version. *—Todd Kristel*

Burnside on Burnside / Oct. 23, 2001 / Fat Possum ♦♦♦♦

Like jazz, blues music has faced a problem of attrition, with its major names dying off and younger artists having trouble establishing themselves at anything like an equal level of recognition. One way out of this dilemma has been the discovery of new-old bluesmen, musicians who have reached an advanced age without becoming stars, who can now be trotted out as performers in the tradition of the lost heroes. Of course, the practice of discovering or rediscovering old bluesmen dates back at least to the folk boom, but it is given impetus by the dire state of blues music. R.L. Burnside owes his breakthrough to the 1992 documentary *Deep Blues*, which led to his signing to Fat Possum Records when he was already in his sixties. Since then, he has been taken up by such hip figures as Jon Spencer and Beck producer Tom Rothrock, resulting in albums that have broadened his popularity but irritated purists with their contemporary gimmicks. The purists should be pleased by the live album *Burnside on Burnside*, recorded on a West Coast tour in the winter of 2001, which finds the Mississippi musician in Portland and San Francisco, backed only by second guitarist Kenny Brown and drummer Cedric Burnside, Burnside's grandson. The 74-year-old singer/guitarist rocks out furiously for the better part of the set, evoking obvious predecessors such as Muddy Waters and John Lee Hooker. He's no match for them, of course, not only because he lacks their distinctiveness, but because of his ingratiating attitude, complete with corny jokes. But that has its appeal, too. Has there ever been a Delta bluesman as friendly as R.L. Burnside? Probably not, but if your hobby suddenly became a paying profession just as you hit retirement age, you'd be happy about it, too. *—William Ruhlmann*

Harold Burrage

b. Mar. 30, 1931, Chicago, IL, **d.** Nov. 26, 1966, Chicago, IL

Vocals, Piano / R&B, Soul

Pianist Harold Burrage started out singing blues and R&B during the '50s and ended up as a linchpin of the emerging Chicago soul sound of the '60s; he made recordings in both styles and more than a few idiomatic shades in between. Burrage mentored young soul singers Otis Clay and Tyrone Davis, but never had a chance to see them fully blossom; he died young in 1966.

Burrage debuted on wax in 1950 with a jumping "Hi-Yo Silver" for Decca with Horace Henderson's band in support. Singles for Aladdin and States preceded one of his most prolific studio periods with Eli Toscano's Cobra imprint. In 1956, Burrage cut the amusing "You Eat Too Much" for Cobra, backed by a solid combo featuring guitarist Wayne Bennett and bassist Willie Dixon. Jody Williams added stinging guitar to Burrage's 1957 Cobra offering "Messed Up," while "Stop for the Red Light," his third Cobra 45, was a novelty complete with auto wreck sound effects. "Betty Jean," his last Cobra single, is unabashed rock & roll, with Otis Rush on guitar. Burrage also served as a session pianist for the firm, backing up Magic Sam and Charles Clark.

After a romping 1960 effort for Vee-Jay, "Crying for My Baby," Burrage revamped his vocal approach considerably when recording rather prolifically for One-derful's M-Pac! subsidiary during the early to mid-'60s. There he sang in a very credible soul style, enjoying his only national R&B hit in 1965 with the driving "Got to Find a Way" (later revived by one of Burrage's protégés, Otis Clay). *—Bill Dahl*

She Knocks Me Out! / 1956-1958 / Flyright ♦♦♦♦♦

Only showcases one facet of the late piano-playing singer's multi-faceted discography, but it's one of the most fascinating—his 1956-1958 stay at Chicago's Cobra Records. Under Willie Dixon's supervision, Burrage recorded in a variety of styles—rockin' blues ("Satisfied," the amusing "You Eat Too Much"), novelty stuff ("Stop for the Red Light," complete with crashing sound effects reminiscent of Nervous Norvus), and straight-ahead rock & roll ("Betty Jean"). *—Bill Dahl*

● **Messed Up: Complete Cobra Recordings** / Jun. 26, 2002 / West Side ♦♦♦♦♦

Charlie "Uke Kid" Burse

b. Aug. 25, 1901, Decatur, AL, **d.** Dec. 20, 1965, Memphis, TN

Ukulele / Acoustic Memphis Blues, Prewar Country Blues

When a musician is described by biographers as "obnoxious and abusive at times," it naturally makes the individual in question seem all the more fascinating, especially if the person was armed with a ukulele. Such is the case with the "Uke Kid," eventually best-known by his real name, Charlie Burse. He was not an original member of the historic Memphis Jug Band, but he became part of the loose roster of players associated with this group around 1928, only a couple of years after the group had begun recording. With Memphis as hot and sticky as it is, staying close to the shade seems to be a smart idea and in the case of Burse, that meant none other than Will Shade, the fascinating Memphis multi-instrumentalist who learned about jug band music in Kentucky and then brought the new sound to Memphis where it went over like a good fireworks display.

Although they were lifelong associates and continued playing together for nearly four decades, Shade and Burse were not at all alike personally. The former man was all business; indeed, he was the business manager of the Memphis Jug Band, hired all the musicians, and was one of the first Memphis players to become a full-time musician and buy his own home with the proceeds. Burse, on the other hand, seems to have established a reputation as a hell-raiser and nothing but, although the term "egotist" is sometimes tossed in for good luck. Keeping the Uke Kid in line was just another of Shade's shady responsibilities, but it doesn't seem to have caused any serious friction because the two men kept up a happy musical relationship right up until Burse's death in the mid-'60s.

One of their last recording efforts together was the wonderful *Beale St. Mess Around* album on Rounder, although it unfortunately was not released commercially until almost ten years after Burse died. This was a gathering of Memphis country blues and jug band vets, getting together in house to frolic around with the music they loved. Other members of the Memphis Jug Band at one time or another included Hattie Hart, Charlie Polk, Walter Horton, Memphis blues scene stalwart Furry Lewis, Memphis Minnie and her husband Kansas Joe McCoy, Dewey Corley, and Vol Stevens. Burse seems to have played more instruments than all these folks combined. In the true jug band tradition, he came to a session or gig loaded for bear, handling just about every instrument with strings on it that is normally used in country or country blues music, including tenor guitar, banjo, ukulele banjo, regular guitar, and mandolin. Ironically, he may have never actually played a normal ukulele, although jug band music scholars are still engaged in fisticuffs on this subject. In addition, he was a master rhythm keeper on the spoons and an enjoyable vocalist.

In 1939, Burse put together his own band, the Memphis Mudcats. The Memphis Jug Band had at that point been stuck in low gear since the mid-'30s, when the public's taste in recordings began shifting and leaving the old-time jug band music at the bottom of the hill. Perhaps in reaction to these changing trends, the new Burse project boasted what was thought to be a more modern sound than the traditional jug band. This included an actual bass replacing the jug and the more sophisticated saxophone taking the place of the whining harmonica. This group may not have lasted long, but there was at least the opportunity to cut some sides for Vocalion. Burse went at it with relish in the late '30s, coming up with an especially enjoyable set of sides that included the promise of "Good Potatoes on the Hill," the pleasure of finding a "Weed Smoking Mama," and the gut-ache of "Too Much Beef." His song "Bottle Up and Go," itself based on a long strain of traditional material, seems to have been influential in the later progress of this particular lyric, often recorded as "Step It Up and Go" blues players will sometimes to be said to be doing the Charlie Burse or "Memphis" version of the song.

With this and other cultural accomplishments under his belt, along with whatever else was required to be abusive and obnoxious, Burse got the solo thing out of his system and went back into partnership with Shade, the two of them continuing to find performing opportunities around Memphis, although the gigs were not always on the level they might have wanted. The two bluesmen kept busy with Memphis house parties and playing for donations on street corners. As the Memphis music scene revitalized itself in the '60s and '70s, traditional players such as this became local heroes. Shade and Burse were first rediscovered and recorded by blues researcher Samuel Charters in 1956, during a period when Memphis' reputation for murders was running far ahead of music. Unfortunately, Burse passed away before too much of this newfound glory could trickle down his way. *—Eugene Chadbourne*

Aron Burton

b. Jun. 15, 1938, Senatobia, MS
Vocals, Bass / Electric Chicago Blues
Long recognized as a rock-solid bassist (and a master landscaper for the Chicago Park District), Aron Burton has begun to emphasize his vocal talents more prominently of late. His 1993 Earwig album *Past, Present, & Future* showcased both of Burton's specialties, establishing him as bandleader instead of bandsman. Burton left Mississippi for Chicago in 1955. He got his feet wet as a singer and bassist in the late '50s with Freddy King at Walton's Corner on the West Side (King bought Aron his first bass). He got drafted in 1961, came out four years later, and got back into playing with various rock (notably Baby Huey & the Babysitters) and blues (Junior Wells, Fenton Robinson) groups. Burton did sessions with Wild Child Butler, Jackie Ross, Carey Bell, and a 45 of his own for Eddy Clearwater's Cleartone logo ("Garbage Man"), but it was his signing on as a charter member of Albert Collins' Icebreakers in 1978 (Aron's brother Larry was the band's rhythm guitarist) that catapulted him into the spotlight. He played on Collins' landmark Alligator LP *Ice Pickin'* and toured extensively with the Master of the Telecaster before getting restless and leaving the band. Burton did sessions with Johnny Littlejohn, James Cotton, and Fenton Robinson before taking a three-year European hiatus in the late '80s. That's where he cut his debut LP, *Usual Dangerous Guy*, with Champion Jack Dupree guesting on piano. Since returning to Chicago, Burton has picked up where he left off—he's playing, singing, and leading his own band instead of backing others. *—Bill Dahl*

● **Past, Present, & Future** / 1993 / Earwig ✦✦✦✦
A compendium of tracks cut back in the '80s (some with the late pianist Champion Jack Dupree) over in Europe (the "past" part of the title) and a few more recent sides waxed in his Chicago hometown, this collection effectively spotlights bassist Aron Burton's talents as a front man. *—Bill Dahl*

Aron Burton Live / 1996 / Earwig ✦✦✦✦
Veteran bassist Aron Burton, after nearly four decades as a greatly in-demand sideman in the blues world, finally put together his own band in the early '90s. This CD, his third recording as a leader, is very much a blues revue in the spirit of Johnny Otis. Burton sings on six of the 13 songs, sharing the vocal mike with guitarist Michael Dotson, keyboardist Allen Batts, drummer Kenny Smith, the fine harmonica player Lester Davenport and (on extroverted versions of "Fever" and "Hound Dog") Liz Mandville-Greeson. Instrumentally, Burton sounds quite happy to liberally feature his sidemen and play a supportive role. Although all of the players fare well, each one displaying a strong musical personality, the high-powered guitarist Dotson often takes honors, demonstrating that he is a highly expressive and up-and-coming bluesman. Whether it be warhorses or newer material, the Aron Burton show keeps moving and never loses one's interest. Recommended. *—Scott Yanow*

Good Blues to You / Mar. 9, 1999 / Delmark ✦✦✦
In the tradition of Willie Dixon and Willie Kent, Burton leads his blues band from the electric bass guitar chair. He's an excellent singer—like a more pronounced, forceful B.B. King—and his musical foundation on the bottom is immaculate. Brother Larry co-leads on guitar, Dave Specter and Lurrie Bell play seconds, and Lester Davenport and Billy Branch split duties on harmonica, as do drummers Tino Cortez and Vern Rodgers. The Chicago Horns are in on two cuts, and the marvelous pianist Allen Batts jams throughout. Larry Burton wrote two of the 11 numbers; the best is the definitive anthem "Stuck in Chicago," with the lyric "everyday it's the same/I work six nights a week/still no one knows my name" sung deliberately and frustratingly slow. "Good Idea at the Time" features group vocals over Batts' exceptional boogie-woogie piano and a slight New Orleans shuffle boil. The six Aaron Burton tunes are highlighted by the horn-fired funky title track "Too Late to Apologize," the 12-bar "Southbound Train," and the totally downhearted "The Woman I Met Out in the Rain." Branch stirs souls with his spine-shivering harmonica licks during the funky, horn-driven "Good Blues" and the much slower "Marryin' Game." Classics like the Albert King evergreen "I'll Play the Blues for You," "Next Time You See Me," and the tone-setting, feel-good kicker "No More Draggin'" prove Burton's dedication to his idiom by recognizing and adding to these immortal blues tunes. This is Burton's third album as a leader, after decades of backing up Junior Wells, Fenton Robinson, Albert Collins, James Cotton, and others. It may be hard to be a star behind a bass, but Burton has succeeded, as evidenced by these "good blues." *—Michael G. Nastos*

Sam Butera

b. Aug. 17, 1927, New Orleans, LA
Bandleader, Vocals, Sax (Tenor), Saxophone / Cocktail, New Orleans Jazz, Rock & Roll, R&B
Sam Butera spent much of his career leading Louis Prima's band, but his career continued long after Prima's death, coming to include sounds and styles far beyond Prima's brand of New Orleans jazz. A rock, R&B, and jazz legend, Butera is a towering crossover figure at the saxophone and as a band leader.

He was born in New Orleans to Italian-American parents. His father Joseph owned a butcher shop in a Black section of the city, and played the guitar and the concertina in his spare time. At a wedding he was taken to at age seven, Sam Butera first saw and heard a saxophone, and, with his father's blessings, asked to take lessons. He studied the clarinet at school but eventually returned to the sax, and at age 18 was featured in *Look* magazine (*Life*'s major competitor) as one of the top young jazzmen in the country. He got a gig with Ray McKinley right out of high school, and also played with the bands of Tommy Dorsey and Joe Reichman. His major influences in those years included Charlie Ventura, Lester Young, Gene Ammons, Charlie Parker, and Big Jay McNeely—he seemed to gravitate naturally to swing and bebop. Ultimately, however, the biggest influence on his playing was Lee Allen, a member of Paul Gayten's band, with which he frequently played.

Butera formed his own group—inspired by Gayten's band—after returning to New Orleans, and they quickly began a four-year engagement at the 500 Club, which was owned by Louis Prima's brother. His sound reflected a vast range of influences, including modern jazz and R&B, and in 1951 Butera cut a pair of raunchy R&B instrumental sides that might have figured in the early history of white rock & roll if only they'd gotten out at the time. He also had a featured spot in a Woody Herman concert that yielded both a chance for a new tour and a recording contract with RCA. The resulting sessions in the fall of 1953 gave Butera a chance to rock out in an alternately soft and sweet, or hard and playful manner. There weren't any significant sales, but RCA had him back in early 1954 for a series of sessions of its R&B-oriented Groove label (home of Piano Red, amongst others), and his version of "I Don't Want to Set the World on Fire" was a modest regional hit.

He played some R&B shows, including a celebrated tour as part of Alan Freed's first East Coast rock & roll showcase, and Butera's loud, wild sax sound won him an enthusiastic following. However, he was soon back doing jazz with Ella Fitzgerald and Louie Bellson. He finally hooked up with Louis Prima in 1954 and spent the next 20 years leading his band, the Witnesses. Butera's own record releases were cut short, with only a handful of his Groove sides (including a vocal performance, "Giddyap Baby") ever issued at the time.

Butera achieved financial security over the next 20 years working for Prima, and only then, in the mid-'70s, began re-emerging as a performer in his own right. *—Bruce Eder*

● **Hot New Orleans Nights** / 1989 / Bear Family ✦✦✦✦✦
Nineteen tracks cut by Sam Butera for RCA between September 1953 and July 1954. Highlights include the hot rocking "Chicken Scratch," "Shine the Buckle," "Sam's Clan," and "Easy Rocking," the superb vocal performance "Giddyap Baby," the sultry yet raunchy "Ooh," and the soft, soulful "Sam's Reverie," adapted from a piece by Debussy. *—Bruce Eder*

The Whole World Loves Italians / Oct. 29, 1996 / USA Music Group ✦✦✦
Although he had already worked gigs as a member of such outfits as Ray McKinley's big band, Sam Butera's long career really began in 1954 when he joined Louis Prima. Using the same formula that was so successful when he was with the raucous, R&B-hyped Prima, Butera has continued to record and perform extensively. With his band the Wildest, this album highlights Butera's vocals and honking tenor sax. A nod to the album's Italian theme comes with the inclusion of such Butera workhorses as the wild, tongue-in-cheek "Che-La-Luna" and a gentler "Come Back to Sorrento," as well as an Italian phrase thrown in now and then. But this recording session was not limited to ethnic material. Butera's New Orleans roots are revisited with an R&B—rather than traditional jazz—version of "When the Saints Go Marchin' In." There are some classic standards on the play list as well, such as "I'm Confessin'," which Butera plays and sings straight with a raspy voice and style not unlike that of Louis Armstrong, and a string-enhanced, earnestly delivered "Unforgettable." "Misty" provides an opportunity for Butera to show that his sax need not always be strident, but can be sweet as well. So while this album is pitched toward the popularity of pseudo-Italian music and conventions, it has much more to offer, presenting the full range of Butera's skills as a musician. *—Dave Nathan*

Louis Prima Presents the Wildest / Nov. 24, 1998 / Jasmine ✦✦✦

Plays Music from the Rat Race / Oct. 26, 1999 / Jasmine ✦✦✦

On Stage / Jul. 22, 2000 / Get Hip ✦✦✦
Louis Prima's long time bandleader keeps the torch burning brightly on this live outing, blowing the roof off of some unnamed lounge with a vengeance. The band is a strong match for any of the classic versions of the Witnesses (the band that Butera led on all the Prima recordings and Sam does a nice stand in for Louis on "Just a Gigolo/I Ain't Got Nobody," "I'm Confessin'," and the closer, a medley of "Cella Luna/When the Saints Go Marching In." The kind of album that if you saw the show live, you'd buy one at the merchandising tent that night. One for the Prima completists. *—Cub Koda*

The Butler Twins

b. Jan. 21, 1942, Florence, AL
Group / Modern Electric Blues
Clarence and Curtis Butler are two longtime beacons on the Detroit-area blues scene, and with two recently recorded albums for the London-based JSP Records, they may finally begin to garner a wider following outside of Detroit. The brothers' albums for JSP include *Pursue Your Dreams* (1996) and *Not Gonna Worry About Tomorrow* (1995).

Guitarist Clarence and harmonica player Curtis Butler grew up near W.C. Handy's birthplace of Florence, Alabama, about 30 miles from the Mississippi Delta. They took their earliest musical cues from their father, guitarist Willie "Butch" Butler, who was famous in the region but never recorded.

The twins moved to Detroit in the 1960 and quickly found work in Motor City auto plants. The club scene at the time was booming, with the music of John Lee Hooker, Little Sonny, Bo Collins, Bobo Jenkins and dozens of others spilling out of the city's juke joints. The twins continued working and sitting in as much as they could, but by the late '60s, the blues scene in Detroit had dried up. Civil unrest and the rise of the Motown sound didn't leave much room for a flourishing blues scene, but by the early '80s, when the blues began a resurgence again nationally, the Butler Twins were still on the scene. More importantly, they were celebrated as survivors and veterans.

The twins' two JSP releases may allow them to tour more extensively in the U.S., Canada and Europe. *—Richard Skelly*

● **Not Gonna Worry About Tomorrow** / May 2, 1995 / JSP ✦✦✦✦
The Butler Twins turned in a fine debut with *I Ain't Gonna Worry About Tomorrow*. The pair specialize in hard-driving urban blues, straight out of the '60s. There are no innovations here, but there don't need to be, since the duo slams home this blistering electric blues with passion and energy. *—Thom Owens*

Pursue Your Dreams / May 7, 1996 / JSP ✦✦✦

The Butler's Boogie / May 16, 2000 / Orchard ✦✦✦✦
Detroit city, year 2000, Hastings street has been obliterated by the highways and some question whether Detroit still maintains its place as one of the nations blues capitals. Surprisingly enough, the scene still exists, not in the inner city, but out in the suburbs.

Recorded live at the Attic bar in Hamtramck, MI, *Butlers Boogie* is a testament to the strength of Detroit blues 60 years after its heyday. Clarence and Curtis Bulter have lived the blues life: The brothers were born in Alabama then emigrated to Michigan in the '50s and worked in the factories most of their lives, playing music on the side. The duo brings their story to life with songs like "Goin' Down to the Juke Joint" and "Goin' Back Home." Clarence's lead vocals still have a powerful resonance expressing a true blues passion with every note. Occasionally, since this is a live album, the group's jams get a bit repetitive. Still, this isn't a fault to the music, in fact, the album only increases the desire to see the Bulter Twins live. *—Curtis Zimmermann*

George "Wild Child" Butler

b. Oct. 1, 1936, Hernando, MS

Vocals, Harmonica, Guitar / Electric Chicago Blues, Modern Electric Blues

From all accounts, George Butler was indeed a "wild child." But he found time between the youthful shenanigans that inspired his mom to bestow his descriptive nickname to learn some harp basics at age 12. He was gigging professionally as a bandleader by the late '50s, but Butler's recording career didn't blossom until he moved to Chicago in 1966 and signed with Shreveport, LA-based Jewel Records (his sidemen on these sessions included bassist Willie Dixon and guitarist Jimmy Dawkins).

The harpist didn't have much luck in the recording wars: his 1969 Mercury album sank with little trace, while a 1976 LP for T.K., *Funky Butt Lover*, did equally little for his fortunes (it was later reissued in slightly altered form on Rooster Blues as *Lickin' Gravy*). Around 1981, Butler moved up north to Ontario, Canada, and continued his career. A decade later, he cut the first of two albums for British producer Mike Vernon; *These Mean Old Blues* was an engaging set of original material cut in London. *Stranger*, the fruits of another English session, emerged in 1994. *—Bill Dahl*

● **Open Up Baby** / 1966-1967 / Charly ✦✦✦✦✦

Charly's *Open Up Baby* rounds up several singles George "Wild Child" Butler recorded for Jewel between 1966 and 1968. All of the sessions were produced by Willie Dixon, and the great majority of the songs were written either by Butler or Dixon. Some of the material has dated a bit ("Hippy Playground," for instance), but there's no denying the down and dirty grit in Butler's performances, as he's backed by such well-known musicians as Big Walter Horton and Jimmy Dawkins. Butler rarely did straight-ahead Chicago blues any better than he did here. *—Thom Owens*

Keep on Doing What You're Doing / Nov. 11, 1969 / Mercury ✦✦✦

Lickin' Gravy / Feb. 7, 1976 / M.C. ✦✦✦

Before it finally saw the light of day, this 1976 album had to undergo some overdubbing touchups a full decade later that replaced certain guitar tracks with Pinetop Perkins' keyboards. Not the best way to make an album, but the results are nevertheless pretty decent, as Butler dishes up a set of his own material, a couple of Willie Dixon copyrights, and Lightnin' Slim's "Rooster Blues." *—Bill Dahl*

These Mean Old Blues / Feb. 15, 1992 / Bullseye Blues ✦✦✦✦

Considering his nickname and near-anonymity at the time, it is surprising to realize that Wild Child Butler was already 55 when he made this CD. Although he had recorded very few released sessions before this album, Butler had been active most of the time since settling in Ontario, Canada. A talented harmonica player, he also possesses a deep and very expressive voice. With a first-rate combo that features the intense guitar of Pete Boss, Butler performs most of his best material for his Bullseye Blues debut. Among the highpoints are the title cut, the topical "Crack House Woman," an unaccompanied "Walkin' The Little Girl Home" and the minor-toned "It's A Pity." Recommended. *—Scott Yanow*

Stranger / 1994 / Bullseye Blues ✦✦✦✦

Another set of impressive originals cut in England and produced by Mike Vernon with the same attention to traditional detail as their fine previous collaboration. Butler's understated approach reeks of an authenticity that grows harder to find with every passing year, whether on his own "Weak in the Knees" and "Face It Baby" or the Vernon-generated "High I.Q." and "I'm Not Guilty." *—Bill Dahl*

Sho' 'Nuff / Aug. 14, 2001 / APO ✦✦✦

Henry Butler

b. New Orleans, LA

Vocals, Piano / Piano Blues, New Orleans Blues, New Orleans R&B

Henry Butler's blues-based, New Orleans funk-style piano playing is not for every blues fan, to be sure. Butler is a local legend in New Orleans, but rarely tours other parts of the country; most any time of the year, he can be found playing in one of New Orleans' famous nightspots. It's not an exaggeration to say Butler is a piano genius who has yet to be discovered by the masses. His recordings demonstrate that he can do it all: he writes his own songs, does his own arrangements of classic tunes by Professor Longhair and others, and can play with as much passion as a soloist as he can with a band. What makes him great—but admittedly difficult for record companies to market—is that he constantly pushes himself in new directions as a musician. He can't be pigeonholed as blues, jazz, or even rock & roll, though he performs all three genres with impeccable taste, depth of understanding and freshness of appreciation. Butler's playing also reflects influences like gospel and classic R&B.

Butler was born in New Orleans and first began playing piano at a neighbor's house when he was six. While attending the Louisiana State School for the Blind in Baton Rouge, he began taking piano lessons, also studying drums, baritone saxophone and valve trombone. He began playing professionally when he was 14 in Baton Rouge clubs, and then attended college at Southern University in Baton Rouge. He later did post-graduate work at Michigan State University. Before graduating from college, Butler received a National Endowment for the Arts grant to study with Cannonball Adderley and his group of veteran musicians; he learned a lot from all of them, including pianist George Duke.

In the mid-'70s, he returned to New Orleans and found work as a voice teacher at the New Orleans Center for the Creative Arts. Butler then lived in Los Angeles and New York City for several periods of time, pursuing record deals.

Butler credits jazz clarinetist Alvin Batiste with being a major influence on his career. When Butler was listening to Jimi Hendrix and Chicago, Batiste advised him to begin studying the music of John Coltrane and Charlie Parker, which enabled Butler to develop the great improvisational abilities he demonstrates in his performances today.

Butler has several albums to his credit: *Fivin' Around* (MCA/Impulse!, 1986), *The Village* (MCA/Impulse!, 1988), *Orleans Inspiration* (1990,) album for the now-defunct Windham Hill Jazz label; a 1992 independent release, *Blues & More, Vol. 1*; and 1996's *For All Seasons* on the Atlantic Jazz label. Butler continues to support himself through private lessons and performances around the Crescent City; in 2000, he teamed with Corey Harris for the album *Vu-Du Menz*. *—Richard Skelly*

Fivin' Around / 1985-1986 / MCA ✦✦✦✦

Pianist Henry Butler's recording debut as a leader was also the first record released by the "new" Impulse label. Cut in the mid-'80s when MCA was directly involved with Impulse, the program features Butler with some rather notable musicians—bassist Charlie Haden, drummer Billy Higgins, trumpeter Freddie Hubbard and tenorman Azar Lawrence plus occasional color provided by flutist Steve Kujala and the oboe of Jeff Clayton. Two selections (including "Giant Steps") add a string quartet, and Butler sings "I Want Jesus to Walk With Me." The wide-ranging repertoire (which also has seven diverse originals and the standard "Old Folks") and the inventive frameworks make this a memorable and very successful set. *—Scott Yanow*

The Village / Feb. 1987-Mar. 1987 / MCA ✦✦✦✦✦

Henry Butler's second Impulse! recording is a two-LP set (not yet reissued on CD) that is essentially a post-bop performance. The influence of the pianist's New Orleans heritage (which is partly felt on his version of Scott Joplin's "The Entertainer") and gospel music would be explored more fully in the future. Butler is joined by bassist Ron Carter, drummer Jack DeJohnette and occasionally by clarinetist Alvin Batiste, John Purcell (on soprano, flute, oboe and English horn) and (for "The Entertainer") Bob Stewart on tuba. Butler sings "Music Came," but essentially this is an advanced trio set that shows how fine a pianist he is. *—Scott Yanow*

● **Orleans Inspiration** / Jul. 27, 1989-Jul. 28, 1989 / Windham Hill ✦✦✦✦✦

Henry Butler, who had recorded a pair of post-bop sets for MCA/Impulse, switches to New Orleans R&B on this spirited program, cut live at Tipitina's in New Orleans. Assisted by guitarist Leo Nocentelli, bassist Chris Severin, drummer Herman Jackson, and the synthesizer of Michael Goods, Butler puts on a fine show. He plays and sings (in a gospel-ish baritone voice) a variety of originals, plus Leonard Bernstein's "Somewhere," "Goin' Down Slow," and Professor Longhair's "Tipitina's" and "Mardi Gras in New Orleans." *—Scott Yanow*

Blues & More, Vol. 1 / 1992 / Windham Hill ✦✦✦✦

A versatile pianist with a passionate voice, Henry Butler emphasizes the bluesy side of his musical personality throughout this CD of unaccompanied solos. Most of the selections on the date (other than "Down by the Riverside," "That Lucky Old Sun" and "Jamaica Farewell") are his own and Butler puts plenty of feeling and soulful swing into the music. An accessible and generally creative outing. *—Scott Yanow*

For All Seasons / Jun. 14, 1995-Jun. 16, 1995 / Atlantic ✦✦✦✦

On some of his recordings, Henry Butler has performed gospel music and/or New Orleans funk, taken soulful vocals, and played some electric keyboard. This trio outing, however, is purely acoustic and mostly in the straight-ahead vein. With assistance from bassist Dave Holland and drummer Herman Jackson (trombonist Steve Turre dropped by to play the romantic melody on "Souvenir d'un Amour"), Butler explores such numbers as "St. Louis Blues," "How Insensitive," "Without a Song," and several of his originals. This is one of Butler's strongest jazz dates and finds him displaying his individuality on basic but viable chord structures. *—Scott Yanow*

Blues After Sunset / Apr. 21, 1998 / Black Top ✦✦✦✦

The line of innovative New Orleans piano players who serve as conduits for fusing genres is continued with this release by Henry Butler. Here he approaches his music for the first time primarily as a blues performer, rather than as a jazz musician playing blues. He is an extraordinary performer who has put together all the years of growing up in the Crescent City, with its diverse musical heritage, his training in piano and voice from the Louisiana State School for the Blind, his continued musical education at Southern University, and the post-graduate work in voice (singing German lieder) at Michigan State, and fused it into one cohesive whole. All the flavors are there and distinct when you look for them, but put together they form a cohesive whole that provokes more thought than the individual parts would. Listen to his terrifying vocals and the support his piano provides for them on his version of "Death Has No Mercy." The tune has always had a chill, but he puts it into another realm that brings up vivid images of the Angels of Death swooping on down. He is joined on several cuts by Snooks Eaglin on guitar and Mark Kazanoff on harmonica, who provide an empathetic support that enhances and helps carry these tunes to further reaches. On "Tetherball," he and Kazanoff play off each other, whirl around each other in an orbit that at times stretches way out there before coming back to this plane at the end of the song, just as the ball rolls up tight against the pole. Henry Butler does it all on this superlative disc—he co-produced it, wrote eight of the 12 songs, did all of the arranging, and provided vocals and piano. This is a disc that should not be missed at any cost. *—Bob Gottlieb*

The Game Has Just Begun / May 7, 2002 / Basin Street ✦✦✦

Henry Butler goes all-out electric on his first Basin Street release, outfitting his rootsy brand of blues-rock with synth textures, keyboard bass, even drum machine on a few tracks. Raymond Weber lays down real drums most of the time; the guitar solos by June Yamagishi and Shane Theriot are often blistering. Artistically, however, the results are mixed. The disc gets off to a strong start with four hard-hitting originals, then loses its way until track eight, a grooving rendition of "High-Heeled Sneakers" featuring Butler's superb piano. But the rock covers ("Great Balls of Fire," "Riders on the Storm") are listless, the pop arrangements ("You Are My Sunshine," "When You Listen With Your Eyes") are middle of the road, and the three electronic mood instrumentals are interesting only up to a point. (A 15-minute question-and-answer session with Butler ends the disc.) This is definitely not the best starting point for anyone new to Butler's music. *—David R. Adler*

Lester Butler

b. Nov. 12, 1959, Virginia **d.** May 9, 1998, Los Angeles, CA

Harmonica, Vocals / Modern Electric Blues, Blues-Rock

Musical visionaries in their lifetime are often criticized for blasphemously blending musical styles. Such was the case with Lester Butler. His last album, *13*, melded the roots of American music, blues and alternative rock. Yet Butler could also get down and blow some hardcore blues, backing luminaries Billy Boy Arnold, King Ernest and Finis Tasby.

His first band, the Red Devils, received the attention of producer Rick Rubin (Red Hot Chili Peppers, Mick Jagger, Tom Petty) while playing their favorite haunt, the King King. With Rubin, they released their only album, which was named after that haunt. Their sound attracted the likes of Jagger, who took them into the studio, but the tracks were never used for Jagger's album *Wandering Spirit*.

Alex Schultz, fresh from Rod Piazza and the Mighty Flyers, teamed with Butler to form 13. Though abhorred by blues purists, the group broke ground, especially in Europe where they drew high praise from rock bands, who in turn gave 13 opening slots for their shows. 13 was a step away from stardom when Butler died unexpectedly at age 38. *—Char Ham*

• **13 Featuring Lester Butler** / 1997 / Hightone ♦♦♦♦

From the opening harp honk of "So Low Down," and one is immediately struck by the fact that this is one dirty-sounding, forward-looking blues album, entering into territories usually unexplored by the pleated pants and berets hardliners intent on regurgitating their own record collections. There is not one slickly played, sung, or produced note to be found anywhere on this disc, making it stand out from the rest of the pack right from the beginning. Harmonica man/vocalist Lester Butler's songwriting pen comes up with nine of the 13 tracks on this disc, and all of them are every bit as finely wrought as the classics covered elsewhere on the album. With burning, solid guitar work from Alex Shultz, Paul Bryant, and someone named Smokey Hormel, a trio of revolving bassists and a pair of revolving drummers (Tom Levy, James Moore, and James Intveld doing the plunking with Steven Hodges and Johnny Morgan doing the skin-beating) and Andy Kaulkin on piano, this is one lowdown, lo-fi sounding ("grungy" would not be too descriptive a phrase here) album that immediately sucks you in with its sheer honesty alone. Even hackneyed titles like Howlin' Wolf's "Smokestack Lightning," Elmore James' "So Mean To Me," and Doctor Ross' "The Boogie Disease" sound reasonably fresh here, no mean accomplishment for anybody. Although Butler overdubs his vocals on this session, thus utilizing his harp lines as a member of the band rather than the traditional vocal-harp fill-vocal method used in a true "live" recording, things sound so alarmingly natural, it's a very minor, niggling point at best. Is this the greatest White juke joint record ever made? Belly up to the bar, turn up the volume and you'll sure find out; it's a hard one to ignore. *—Cub Koda*

Butterbeans & Susie

Group / Vaudeville Blues, Prewar Blues, Dirty Blues

Joe and Susie Edwards were never household names—at least not in many white households—but from the early '20s through the '50s, they were one of the top comedic music acts on the black vaudeville circuit, from New York to Chicago to Detroit. Working as Butterbeans & Susie, they were masters of comic timing and the double entendre in their interaction. In her stage and recorded persona, Susie Edwards was the model for dozens of other dominant, but frustrated, wives throughout the history of stage and recorded entertainment in the 20th century, while Joe Edwards made the role of the inadequate husband sing with laughter. The comic setup was a common one in entertainment, in the white as well as the black community, but they were considered too raunchy for white audiences. Despite this, they recorded extensively during the '20s, principally for the OKeh label. With the onset of the Great Depression, which crippled the recording industry, they kept busy mainly on the stage, and made one last record at the end of the '50s. *—Bruce Eder*

• **Complete Recorded Works, Vol. 1 (1924–1925)** / Sep. 23, 1997 / Document ♦♦♦♦

Complete Recorded Works, Vol. 2 (1926–1927) / Sep. 23, 1997 / Document ♦♦♦♦

Paul Butterfield

b. Dec. 17, 1942, Chicago, IL, **d.** May 4, 1987, Hollywood, CA

Vocals, Leader, Harmonica, Guitar, Flute / Modern Electric Chicago Blues, Harmonica Blues, Blues-Rock, Electric Chicago Blues, Chicago Blues, Electric Harmonica Blues

Paul Butterfield was the first white harmonica player to develop a style original and powerful enough to place him in the pantheon of true blues greats. It's impossible to underestimate the importance of the doors Butterfield opened: before he came to prominence, white American musicians treated the blues with cautious respect, afraid of coming off as inauthentic. Not only did Butterfield clear the way for white musicians to build upon blues tradition (instead of merely replicating it), but his storming sound was a major catalyst in bringing electric Chicago blues to white audiences who'd previously considered acoustic Delta blues the only really genuine article. His initial recordings from the mid-'60s—featuring the legendary, racially integrated first edition of the Paul Butterfield Blues Band—were eclectic, groundbreaking offerings that fused electric blues with rock & roll, psychedelia, jazz, and even (on the classic *East-West*) Indian classical music. As members of that band—which included Michael Bloomfield and Elvin Bishop—drifted away, the overall impact of Butterfield's music lessened, even if his amplified harp playing was still beyond reproach. He had largely faded from the scene by the mid-'70s, and fell prey to health problems and drug addiction that sadly claimed his life prematurely. Even so, the enormity of Butterfield's initial impact ensured that his legacy was already secure.

Paul Butterfield was born December 17, 1942 in Chicago and grew up in Hyde Park, a liberal, integrated area on the city's South Side. His father, a lawyer, and mother, a painter, encouraged Butterfield's musical studies from a young age, and he took flute lessons up through high school, with the first-chair flautist in the Chicago Symphony Orchestra serving as his private tutor for a time. By this time, however, Butterfield was growing interested in the blues music that permeated the South Side; he and college-age friend Nick Gravenites (a future singer, guitarist, and songwriter in his own right) began hitting the area blues clubs in 1957. Butterfield was inspired to take up guitar and harmonica, and he and Gravenites began playing together at college campuses around the Midwest. After being forced to turn down a track scholarship to Brown University because of a knee injury, Butterfield entered the University of Illinois-Chicago, where he met a fellow white blues fan in guitarist Elvin Bishop. Butterfield was evolving into a decent singer, and not long after meeting Bishop, he focused all his musical energy on the harmonica, developing his technique (mostly on diatonic harp, not chromatic) and tone; he soon dropped out of college to pursue music full-time.

After some intense woodshedding, Butterfield and Bishop began making the rounds of the South Side's blues clubs, sitting in whenever they could. They were often the only whites present, but were quickly accepted because of their enthusiasm and skill. In 1963, the North Side club Big John's offered Butterfield's band a residency; he'd already recruited Howlin' Wolf's rhythm section—bassist Jerome Arnold and drummer Sam Lay—by offering more money, and replaced original guitarist Smokey Smothers with his friend Bishop. The new quartet made an instant splash with their hard-driving versions of Chicago blues standards. In late 1964, the Paul Butterfield Blues Band was discovered by producer Paul Rothchild, and after adding lead guitarist Michael Bloomfield, they signed to Elektra and recorded several sessions for a debut album, the results of which were later scrapped.

At first, there was friction between Butterfield and Bloomfield, since the harmonica man patterned his bandleading style after taskmasters like Howlin' Wolf and Little Walter; after a few months, though, their respect for each other's musical skills won out, and they began sitting in together at blues clubs around the city. A song from their aborted first session, the Nick Gravenites-penned "Born in Chicago," was included on the Elektra sampler *Folksong '65* and created a strong buzz about the band. In the summer of 1965, they re-entered the studio for a second crack at their debut album, adding organist Mark Naftalin as a permanent sixth member during the sessions. In the meantime, they were booked to play that year's Newport Folk Festival. When Bob Dylan witnessed their well-received performance at an urban blues workshop during the festival, he recruited Butterfield's band to back him for part of his own set later that evening. Roundly booed by acoustic purists, Dylan's plugged-in performance with the Butterfield Band ultimately shook the folk world to its foundations, kickstarting an electric folk-rock movement that effectively spelled the end of the traditionalist folk revival.

On the heels of their historic performance at Newport, the Paul Butterfield Blues Band released their self-titled debut album later in 1965. Now regarded as a classic, the LP caused quite a stir among white blues fans who had never heard electric Chicago-style blues performed by anyone besides British blues-rock groups. Not only did it sow the seeds of a thousand bar bands, but it also helped introduce more white listeners to the band's influences, especially Muddy Waters and B.B. King. Toward the end of 1965, drummer Sam Lay fell ill and was replaced by the jazz-trained Billy Davenport, whose rhythmic agility and sophistication soon made him a permanent member. He was particularly useful since Butterfield was pushing to expand the band's sound, aided by Bloomfield's growing interest in Eastern music, especially Ravi Shankar. Their growing eclecticism manifested itself on their second album, 1966's *East-West*, which remains their greatest achievement. The title cut was a lengthy instrumental suite incorporating blues, jazz, rock, psychedelia, and raga; although it became their signature statement, the rest of the album was equally inspired, perhaps due in part to Butterfield's more relaxed, democratic approach to bandleading.

Unfortunately, Mike Bloomfield left the band at the height of its success in 1967, and formed a new group called the Electric Flag with Nick Gravenites, which aspired to take *East-West*'s eclecticism even further. Bishop moved into the lead guitar slot for the band's third album, 1967's *The Resurrection of Pigboy Crabshaw* (a reference to Bishop's nickname). Displaying a greater soul influence, the album also featured a new rhythm section in bassist Bugsy Maugh and drummer Phil Wilson, plus a horn section that included a young David Sanborn. *Pigboy Crabshaw* proved to be the closing point of the Butterfield Band's glory days; the 1968 follow-up *In My Own Dream* was uneven in its songwriting and focus, and both Elvin Bishop and Mark Naftalin left the band before year's end. Still hoping for a breakout commercial hit, Elektra brought in producer/songwriter Jerry Ragovoy, a longtime R&B professional, which marked the first time they'd asserted control over a Butterfield recording. That didn't sit well with Butterfield, who wanted to move in a jazzier direction than Ragovoy's radio-friendly style allowed; the result, 1969's *Keep on Moving*, was another inconsistent outing, despite the return of Billy Davenport and an injection of energy from the band's new guitarist, 19-year-old Buzzy Feiten. 1969 wasn't a washout for Butterfield, though; his band was still popular enough to make the bill at Woodstock, and he also took part in an all-star Muddy Waters session dubbed *Fathers and Sons*, which showcased the Chicago giant's influence on the new generation of bluesmen and greatly broadened his audience.

After 1970's *Live* and the following year's studio effort *Sometimes I Just Feel Like Smilin'*, Butterfield broke up his band and parted ways with Elektra. Tired of all the touring and personnel turnover, he retreated to the communal atmosphere of Woodstock, still a musicians' haven in the early '70s, and in 1971 formed a new group eventually dubbed Better Days. Guitarist Amos Garrett and drummer Chris Parker were the first to join, and with folk duo Geoff and Maria Muldaur in tow, the band was initially fleshed out by organist Merl Saunders and bassist John Kahn, both from San Francisco. Sans Geoff Muldaur, this aggregation worked on the soundtrack of the film *Steelyard Blues*, but Saunders and Kahn soon returned to the Bay Area, and were replaced by New Orleans pianist Ronnie Barron and Taj Mahal bassist Billy Rich. This lineup—with Geoff Muldaur back, plus contributions from singer/songwriter Bobby Charles—released the group's first album, *Better Days*, in 1972 on Butterfield manager Albert Grossman's new Bearsville label. While it didn't quite matchup to Butterfield's earliest efforts, it did return him to critical favor. A follow-up, *It All Comes Back*, was released in 1973 to positive response, and in 1975 he backed Muddy Waters once again on *The Woodstock Album*, the last LP release ever on Chess.

Butterfield subsequently pursued a solo career, with diminishing returns. His Henry Glover-produced solo debut *Put It in Your Ear* appeared in 1976, but failed to impress many: his harmonica playing was pushed away from the spotlight, and the material was erratic at best. The same year, he appeared in the Band's farewell concert film *The Last Waltz*. Over the next few years, Butterfield mostly confined himself to session work; he attempted a comeback in 1981 with legendary Memphis soul producer Willie Mitchell, but the sessions—released as *North-South*—were burdened by synthesizers and weak material. By this time, Butterfield's health was in decline; years of heavy drinking were beginning to catch up to him, and he also contracted peritonitis, a painful intestinal condition. At some point—none of his friends knew quite when—Butterfield also developed an addiction to heroin; he'd been stridently opposed to it as a bandleader, leading to speculation that he was trying to ease his peritonitis symptoms. He began to play more gigs in Los Angeles during the early '80s, and eventually relocated there permanently; he also toured on a limited basis during the mid-'80s, and in 1986 released his final album, *The Legendary Paul Butterfield Rides Again*. However, his addiction was bankrupting him, and in the past half decade he'd seen Mike Bloomfield, Muddy Waters, and manager Albert Grossman pass away, each loss leaving him shaken. On May 4, 1987, Butterfield himself died of a drug overdose; he was not quite 45 years old. —*Steve Huey*

An Offer You Can't Refuse / 1963 / M.I.L. Multimedia ◆◆◆
An album released on the Red Lightnin' label in 1972 consisting of one side of Big Walter Horton and the other side with very early Paul Butterfield (1963). Contains six tracks with Butterfield, Smokey Smothers on guitar, Jerome Arnold on bass, and Sam Lay on drums. This was recorded at Big Johns, the North side Chicago club where the Butterfield Band first played in 1963—some two years before the material on the first Paul Butterfield Blues Band album, which was released in 1965. The six tracks include two instrumentals, "Got My Mojo Working" and the Butterfield-authored tune "Loaded." Although this is very early Butterfield, the harp playing is excellent and already in his own unique style. The singing is a little rough and heavy sounding. Butterfield fans will want to find this rare vinyl for musical and historical reasons. —*Michael Erlewine*

The Original Lost Elektra Sessions / Dec. 1964 / Rhino ◆◆◆◆◆
All but one of these 19 tracks were recorded in December, 1964, as Butterfield's projected first LP; the results were scrapped and replaced by their official self-titled debut, cut a few months later. With both Bloomfield and Bishop already in tow, these sessions rank among the earliest blues-rock ever laid down. Extremely similar in feel to the first album, it's perhaps a bit rawer in production and performance, but not appreciably worse or different than what ended up on the actual debut LP. Dedicated primarily to electric Chicago blues standards, Butterfield fans will find this well worth acquiring, as most of the selections were never officially recorded by the first lineup (although different renditions of five tracks showed up on the first album and the *What's Shakin'* compilation). —*Richie Unterberger*

☆ **Paul Butterfield Blues Band** / 1965 / Elektra ◆◆◆◆
Even after his death, Paul Butterfield's music didn't receive the accolades that were so deserved. Outputting styles adopted from Howlin' Wolf and Muddy Waters among other blues greats, Butterfield became one of the first white singers to rekindle blues music through the course of the mid-'60s. His debut album, *The Paul Butterfield Blues Band*, saw him teaming up with guitarists Elvin Bishop and Mike Bloomfield, with Jerome Arnold on bass, Sam Lay on drums, and Mark Naftalin playing organ. The result was a wonderfully messy and boisterous display of American-styled blues, with intensity and pure passion derived from every bent note. In front of all these instruments is Butterfield's harmonica, beautifully dictating a mood and a genuine feel that is no longer existent, even in today's blues music. Each song captures the essence of Chicago blues in a different way, from the back-alley feel of "Born in Chicago" to the melting ease of Willie Dixon's "Mellow Down Easy" to the authentic devotion that emanates from Bishop and Butterfield's "Our Love Is Drifting." "Shake Your Money Maker," "Blues With a Feeling," and "I Got My Mojo Working" (with Lay on vocals) are all equally moving pieces performed with a raw adoration for blues music. Best of all, the music that pours from this album is unfiltered... blared, clamored, and let loose, like blues music is supposed to be released. A year later, 1966's *East West* carried on with the same type of brash blues sound partnered with a jazzier feel, giving greater to attention to Bishop's and Bloomfield's instrumental talents. —*Mike DeGagne*

★ **East-West** / 1966 / Elektra ◆◆◆◆◆
The second Butterfield album had an even greater effect on music history, paving the way for experimentation that is still being explored today. This came in the form of an extended blues-rock solo (some 13 minutes)—a real fusion of jazz and blues inspired by the Indian raga. This ground-breaking instrumental was the first of its kind and marks the root from which the acid rock tradition emerged. —*Jeff Tarmarkin and Michael Erlewine*

East-West Live / 1966-1967 / Winner ◆◆◆◆
The tune "East-West" from the second Butterfield Blues Band album of the same name made music history. It is arguably the first extended rock solo, a fusing of blues-rock

with Eastern scales and tone. Here is the root of psychedelic—acid rock. Now, thanks to Mark Naftalin (the original Butterfield keyboardist), we have three live recordings of "East-West" recorded in 1966-1967 that capture the origin and development of this classic tune. The first example (some 12 minutes) was taped prior to the edited studio version; the second (16 minutes) and third (28 minutes) were recorded after the album cut. There is some great music (and music history) here. —*Michael Erlewine*

The Resurrection of Pigboy Crabshaw / 1967 / Elektra ◆◆◆◆◆
In his third album, Butterfield adds a horn section and the direction of the group has started to veer away from straight Chicago-style blues toward a sound more influenced by R&B. By this time, Bloomfield has left the group and Elvin Bishop, aka Pigboy Crabshaw, takes over on lead guitar. A lot of great tunes here, like "Driftin' and Driftin'." —*Michael Erlewine*

In My Own Dream / 1968 / Wounded Bird ◆◆◆

Keep on Moving / 1969 / Wounded Bird ◆◆◆

Sometimes I Just Feel Like Smilin' / 1971 / Wounded Bird ◆◆◆

Better Days / 1973 / Bearsville ◆◆◆◆
Included is Paul Butterfield with Geoff Muldaur, Howard Johnson, Ronnie Barron, Bobby Charles, and others. —*AMG*

It All Comes / 1973 / Bearsville ◆◆◆

The Legendary Paul Butterfield Rides Again / 1986 / Amherst ◆◆◆

Strawberry Jam / 1996 / Winner ◆◆◆
These nine cuts are from various live performances of the Paul Butterfield Blues Band during their heyday in the mid- to late '60s. This album was put together by Mark Naftalin, who played keyboards on those first few incredible Butterfield albums. Don't look for the clearest sound (it's adequate) because these are live tunes recorded at clubs, often with minimal equipment. It is the music that is in focus here—a window into that incredible band at a time when they were hot. Those of us who were on the scene at the time know that, although the original Butterfield albums are great, the band was a total knockout when heard live. Featuring Butterfield's harmonica, here are glimpses into that time and music. Most of the tunes have appeared elsewhere, but the extended instrumental "Strawberry Jam" (written by Naftalin) is unique to this album—worth hearing. It features great guitar by Elvin Bishop. —*Michael Erlewine*

An Anthology—The Elektra Years / Oct. 28, 1997 / Elektra ◆◆◆◆◆
An Anthology—The Elektra Years is a double-disc, 33-song set that offers a comprehensive overview of Paul Butterfield's eight years with the label. His first two albums, *Paul Butterfield Blues Band* and *East-West*, were seminal, groundbreaking records that blurred the boundaries between blues, jazz and rock, suggesting everything from blues-rock to psychedelia. They were stunning achievements which proved to be difficult to match, but Butterfield's remaining albums for the label all had a few good cuts. *An Anthology* does a nice job of rounding up those highlights, picking the best moments from uneven records; consequently, it's quite a valuable package for listeners who simply want a sampling from those later albums instead of purchasing them individually. Butterfield's first two albums remain necessary listens in their own right, but this set offers an excellent summary of his entire stint with Elektra. —*Stephen Thomas Erlewine*

John Byrd

b. Mississippi

Vocals, Guitar / Piedmont Blues, Prewar Country Blues, Prewar Gospel Blues
John Byrd was born in Mississippi in the 1890s, or possibly earlier. After an early career spent mostly in Mississippi, Byrd moved to Louisville, Kentucky, in the '20s and '30s, and made much of his living playing 12-string guitar in a band led by Walter Taylor (who may also have worked as "Washboard Walter"). He recorded blues under his own name and also cut gospel music as the Rev. George Jones during the late '20s and the beginning of the '30s. Byrd's voice could be rough and raspy, somewhere midway between Louis Armstrong and Howlin' Wolf, and when he did gospel, as on "That White Mule of Sin" or "The Heavenly Airplane," his debut recordings from 1929, the effect is spellbinding (especially when he worked in tandem with Sister Jones, aka Mae Glover). Walter Taylor had the more flexible and aesthetically pleasing voice between the two, but even on recordings on which Taylor sang, Byrd's guitar playing displays the kind of dexterity, in its runs and fills, that gives him equal footing and them some (on the break—check out "Narrow Face Blues." As a singer, Byrd had a narrower range than Taylor, but his guitar more than made up for any shortcomings, often sounding like the work of two good players rather than a single extraordinary one. Had he been able to remain active after World War II, and come from a city with more of a blues reputation than Louisville, he might've been remembered at least as well and widely as Blind Willie McTell. —*Bruce Eder*

● **John Byrd & Walter Taylor** / Oct. 1991 / Story of the Blues ◆◆◆
These Kentuckians were prominent in the Louisville area, where they played a wide range of material including hillbilly, jug band, gospel, blues, and general hokum. The set is a mixed bag featuring two truly unforgettable comic (?) sermons, "The White Mule of Sin" and "The Heavenly Airplane," along with the hillbilly classic "Don't Let Your Deal Go Down." If you're looking for a unique ear-opener, this is it. —*Larry Hoffman*

The Cadets

f. Los Angeles, CA, **db.** 1958
Group / Doo Wop, R&B

This West Coast group used two names for recording sessions. They called themselves "The Jacks" when doing dates for Modern and "The Cadets" on RPM. They began as a gospel group during the late '40s in Los Angeles. Ted Taylor, Aaron Collins, Lloyd Mc-Craw, and Will Jones were the original lineup, and the Cadets were among the more popular bands doing R&B covers. The Cadets' lone hit was "Stranded in the Jungle," which they recorded for Modern as the Jacks in 1956. It peaked at number eight R&B and number 15 pop. Davis and Collins would later join the Flares in 1961, while Taylor would enjoy solo success as a blues, soul, and gospel vocalist. Jones joined the Coasters in 1958 and remained there for over a decade. Collins' sisters, Betty and Rose, also recorded for Modern/RPM as "The Teen Queens." —*Ron Wynn*

Rockin' n' Reelin' / 1957 / Crown ✦✦✦✦
Yes, those rockin' and reelin' Cadets were also those jumping Jacks, and vice versa; a simple side-by-side comparison of the cover of this and the cover of *Jumping With the Jacks* (their original and sole albums for Crown) confirms that it's obviously the same group. The general idea was that all the smooth ballad material would be issued as the Jacks and all the uptempo sides would be issued under the Cadets banner. And that's pretty much the edict that's largely offered here, with only the bluesy "So Will I," and covers of "Fools Rush In," Johnnie and Joe's "I'll Be Spinning," and—improbably enough—"Heartbreak Hotel" heading into doo wop ballad territory. The rest of the album consists of first-rate covers (how the group got on the charts in the first place, covering the Jayhawks' "Stranded in the Jungle" as the Cadets and the Feathers' "Why Don't You Write Me" as the Jacks) like Peppermint Harris' "I Got Loaded," "Smack Dab in the Middle," the Marigolds' "Rollin' Stone," the Willows' "Church Bells May Ring," and the Dominoes' "Sixty Minute Man," here presented with the cleaned-up title change, "Dancin' Dan." This is one of the all-time great doo wop albums, wacky behind-the-scenes rock & roll record company chicanery and all. —*Cub Koda*

The Cadets Meet the Jacks / 1958 / Ace ✦✦✦✦
Recording frequently as the Jacks, the Cadets produced some of the greatest doo wop rockers of the '50s, many of which are featured here as companions to 1956's huge novelty hit, "Stranded in the Jungle." Blessed with one of doo wop's most distinctive vocalists in Dub Jones, the disc also features many of the Cadets' best covers, including Nappy Brown's "Don't Be Angry" and an English version of the French cabaret hit "Hands Across the Table." Some great originals include the sweaty "Baby Ya Know" and "Let's Rock'n'Roll," one of the era's awesome lost anthems. —*Jim Smith*

● **Stranded in the Jungle** / 1994 / Ace ✦✦✦✦

Shirley Caesar

b. Oct. 13, 1938, Durham, NC
Vocals / Traditional Gospel, Contemporary Gospel, Black Gospel

A popular gospel singer who often shouts her music in order for her messages to be received, Shirley Caesar performed with the Caravans in the '60s before pursuing a professional solo career in 1966. Born in North Carolina, Caesar is known as the First Lady of Gospel. At the age of ten she began singing and performing for family and friends. She graduated from Shaw University with a Bachelor of Science degree in Business Administration in 1984. She also received honorary doctorates from Shaw University and Southeastern University. Her professional career began in the '60s when she was with the Caravans. In 1966 she began making a name for herself on the gospel music circuit.

Shirley Caesar performs with an energetic and boisterous style. She believes that with all the suffering and hardships in the world people will listen to her recordings and be encouraged. Her live album, *He Will Come*, is a testimony to her philosophy of life. The album was recorded with the choir, band and congregation of her church. In the title song "He Will Come," Shirley Caesar transcends the message of hope, that although society is getting worse, the Lord will save us and is coming. Among her other gospel hits with inspiring messages include "God Is Good," "Revive Us Again" and "Time to Be Blessed." Shirley Caesar's hope is that her messages will be listened to and people will be encouraged to lead good lives. Her 1987 hit, "Hold My Mule," was written to encourage people to "fight the good fight." All her songs combine music with ministry to convey her messages.

Shirley Caesar has received numerous awards for her gospel albums. She received Grammy Awards for *Stand Still, Shirley Caesar Live…He Will Come, Sailin', Rejoice, Celebration* and *He's Working It Out For You*. Between 1981 and 1995 she received seven Dove Awards for Black Gospel Album of the Year for *Live at the G.M.W.A., Live…in Chicago, Celebration, Christmasing, Sailin', Go,* and *Rejoice*. She also received two Black Gospel Song of the Year Awards for "He's Working It Out For You" and "Hold My Mule."

Besides being the minister of her church in North Carolina and performing concerts nationwide, Shirley Caesar has performed on Broadway. Her Broadway performances include roles in *Born to Sing: Mama 3, Mama I Want to Sing* and *Sing: Mama 2*. She made a guest appearance at the 25th anniversary of Walt Disney World with fellow artists Peabo Bryson, CeCe Winans, Regis Philbin and Kathie Lee Gifford. Her activities include performing for President Clinton and Hillary Rodham Clinton at a campaign function. Despite her busy schedule, Shirley Caesar constantly finds time to get her messages of encouragement and peace to people. —*Kim Summers*

★ **The Best of Shirley Caesar With the Caravans** / 1966 / Savoy ✦✦✦✦✦
A truncated but very potent ten-song selection of Caesar's best work with the Caravans. Before going on as a solo artist, Caesar was the group's lead singer, and these are the performances that established her reputation on the gospel music circuit. It's full-blooded, energetic music with Shirley pouring her heart and soul into numbers like "I Feel Good," "Lord Do Something for Me," "Roll On," "Soul Salvation," and "Choose Ye This Day." The running time may be short on this one, but every track is a winner. This best-of makes for a marvelous introduction to the artist. —*Cub Koda*

First Lady / 1977 / HOB ✦✦✦
Secular songs and Christian themes are mixed here. —*Bil Carpenter*

Shirley Caesar Sings Her Gospel Favorites, Vol. 2 / 1978 / Spire ✦✦✦✦✦
More fervent singing with Caesar Singers & Choir. —*Opal Louis Nations*

Rejoice / 1980 / Myrrh ✦✦✦✦✦
The title track featured Shirley Caesar in peak form, soaring, shouting, and declaring her love for God. The LP overall wasn't quite as strong as some other Caesar releases, lacking consistent material or top performances. Still, Caesar often managed to salvage things solely with her vocal power and personality. —*Ron Wynn*

Sailin' / 1984 / Word ✦✦✦✦✦
Shirley Caesar and Rev. Al Green made a magnificent team on the title track, which helped win each a Grammy. Caesar's evocative leads and Green's shimmering harmonies and equally spectacular leads were a session highlight, although there were some other fine numbers spotlighting Caesar as well. —*Ron Wynn*

Live … in Chicago / 1988 / Word ✦✦✦
Including traditional black gospel testifying, singing, and storytelling, this album was recorded with The Thompson Community Singers and Albertina Walker. —*Bil Carpenter*

Celebration / 1990 / Myrrh ✦✦✦

☆ **Her Very Best** / 1991 / Word ✦✦✦✦✦
Her Very Best collects highlights from four of Shirley Caesar's albums for Word in the '80s, selecting two from each album and adding two unreleased cuts as incentives for hardcore fans that already have the original albums. The result is a representative introduction to her latter-day recordings. These aren't necessarily her best work, but they're nevertheless strong, offering further proof that Shirley Caesar is one of the great voices in recorded gospel history. —*Leo Stanley*

I Remember Mama / Feb. 25, 1992 / Word ✦✦✦✦✦
Shirley Caesar's poignant remembrances of her mother set the stage for this album that mixed sentimental fare with rocking evangelism and surging performances. No Golden Age gospel artists have been more successful at retaining their zeal while adapting to contemporary production and arranging tendencies than Caesar. She doesn't compromise her lyrical message, but will hold still for electronics, strings, and even an occasional funk backbeat. This resulted in another hit album for a gospel legend. —*Ron Wynn*

Jesus, I Love Calling Your Name / Apr. 28, 1992 / Word ✦✦✦
More fervent lyrical material from Shirley Caesar, backed by both choral and contemporary production and arrangements. The results weren't always successful, but when they clicked, they were masterful. The title track was a sizable hit on gospel radio, and Caesar continued her string of successful LPs that blended traditional vocals and modern/mainstream voicings and backing. —*Ron Wynn*

No Charge / Mar. 14, 1995 / HOB ✦✦✦✦
More gospel pyrotechnics from this queen of the revival circuit. —*Opal Louis Nations*

Don't Drive Your Mama Away / Oct. 24, 1995 / HOB ✦✦✦✦✦
Some of Caesar's finest work was cut for HOB, and this collection proves it. —*Opal Louis Nations*

Just a Word / Jul. 1996 / Word ✦✦✦✦
Not strictly a Shirley Caesar album, *Just a Word* nevertheless is a good showcase of mid-'90s contemporary gospel music. Recorded on the final day of the Outreach Convention, *Just a Word* features four songs with Caesar's lead vocals and a host of other gospel vocalists and musicians, singing both standards and new gospel songs. The

performances are energetic and invigorating, demonstrating that traditional gospel is nearly always best heard in a live setting. Makes you wish you were there… —*Leo Stanley*

A Miracle in Harlem / Apr. 29, 1997 / Word ✦✦✦

To Be Like Him: The Very Best of Shirley Caesar / Mar. 3, 1998 / Collectables ✦✦✦✦

Hallelujah: A Collection of Her Finest Recordings / Aug. 17, 1999 / Music Club ✦✦✦
The recordings compiled here are drawn from HOB Records sessions spanning from 1967 to 1975. On these, a variety of choirs join Shirley Caesar in spreading the gospel, stirring the revival, and joyously praising. This great lady of gospel has a husky preacher's sound and a devout believer's anointment. Her voice is extraordinary, calling to mind the better-known voice of Aretha Franklin and the lesser-known voice of Sister Wynona Carr. The choirs and congregations sing in stirring harmonies and with enough energy to be thrilling. Amazing church organ, piano, and clapping all add to the live service experience. "Satan, We're Gonna Tear Your Kingdom Down" and "Jordan River (I'm Bound to Cross)" are the absolute standouts, with Caesar and different choirs delivering exciting versions of these. The most secular-styled tunes found here are from the later recordings: songs one through three provide moral stories of love and faith and warning, and track number five is wrapped in the music of a classic Marvin Gaye arrangement. This album is a great collection of soul gospel as sung by the tremendous Shirley Caesar. —*Joslyn Layne*

The First Lady of Gospel / Feb. 8, 2000 / Frank Music ✦✦✦✦
Heard here are three CDs' worth of Shirley Caesar, including live congregational recordings, studio tracks, songs with and without choirs, songs with sermonizing openings, topical songs ("King Heroin"), prayerful tunes, and many of her most famous recordings, such as "No Charge," "The World Didn't Give It to Me," "Don't Be Afraid," "Millennial Reign," and "Faded Rose." Listen and be moved by the soulful songs and faith of Shirley Caesar. Many of these selections were reissued in 2002 on a two-disc collection also titled *The First Lady of Gospel.* —*Joslyn Layne*

Faded Rose / May 16, 2000 / Frank Music ✦✦✦✦
More memorable moments by this ex-Caravan soloist. —*Opal Louis Nations*

You Can Make It / Sep. 5, 2000 / Myrrh ✦✦✦
Shirley Caesar has a masterful command of gospel praise song, and "Lift Him Up," which comes right in the middle of *You Can Make It,* is a practically generic example of the style, with its frantic tempo, excited chorus, and repeated exhortations to "Praise His name!" Caesar, of course, both leads the choir and provides emotive variations. You might say that the album breaks down into two types of songs, ones like "Lift Him Up" that start out at a pitch of excitement and stay there throughout, and others like the title song that proceed at a slower pace and begin more quietly, only to build to a fervent climax. But within the strictures of the form, Caesar demonstrates a willingness to incorporate elements of other pop music styles, sometimes ones that are known for being influenced by gospel. You could listen to the first part of the opening track, "Rejoice," and almost think you had put a James Brown record on by mistake, as the music takes a funky turn. *You Can Make It* sounds like a Patti LaBelle ballad for much of its run, while the horn-filled "Nicodemus" has a '70s pop sound that recalls the rock band Chicago. But Caesar's throaty, impassioned voice is unmistakable, and she's at her best on more traditional gospel tunes like "What Joy," a duet with Bobby Jones. Nevertheless, the subtle varying of styles serves to broaden the appeal of a music that often finds itself preaching, however joyfully, to the choir. —*William Ruhlmann*

Chris Cain

b. Nov. 19, 1955, San Jose, CA
Vocals, Guitar / Modern Electric Blues, Jazz Blues
Chris Cain's crisp lead guitar and gravelly vocals have brought him national recognition. Influenced by B. B. and Albert King as well as various jazz players, Cain has cooked up a jumping sound on the Bay Area circuit.

A native of San Jose, CA, Cain began playing California blues clubs in the mid-'80s, most notable the JJ's Cafe and JJ's Lounge South Bay circuit. Soon, his following was large enough to earn him a contract with an independent record label, Blue Rock'it. Cain's debut album, *Late Night City Blues,* was released in 1987. By this time, his backing band featured lead tenor saxophonist Noel Catura, bassist Ron Torbensen, saxophonist Mark Whitney, and drummer Robert Higgins. The album received good reviews, which led to national bookings for Cain and his band, as well as several European dates. In 1988, Cain and his band received a handful of W.C. Handy Award nominations, including Blues Band of the Year and Guitarist of the Year. Cain signed to Blind Pig in 1990, releasing his second album, *Cuttin' Loose,* the same year. The guitarist stayed at Blind Pig for the next few years, releasing *Can't Buy A Break* in 1992 and *Somewhere Along the Way* in 1995. Cain and his band remained a popular concert attraction throughout the '90s. —*Bill Dahl & Stephen Thomas Erlewine*

Late Night City Blues / 1987 / Blue Rock'it ✦✦✦
This debut album was rewarded with four Handy Award nominations. —*Bill Dahl*

● **Cuttin' Loose** / 1990 / Blind Pig ✦✦✦✦✦
This is a wonderful, big-voiced, contemporary West Coast bluesman and superb guitar player. There are several horns in the band, giving it a great, huge sound. Even better things will be coming. —*Niles J. Frantz*

Can't Buy a Break / 1992 / Blind Pig ✦✦✦✦✦
Can't Buy a Break is a slow-burning, laidback contemporary blues record that positively swings. Cain's licks are clean, warm and fluid—he's able to seamlessly bounce back and forth between R&B, funk, jazz, jump blues, and Chicago blues. Furthermore, he proves himself to be an adept saxophonist, keyboardist and vocalist, as well as songwriter—the album is a true *tour de force.* His backing band is tight and sympathetic, giving the

impression that Cain is fronting a much larger band than he is. It's a refreshing, diverse, and relaxed record that shows there is more to contemporary blues than wailing blues-rock. —*Thom Owens*

Somewhere Along the Way / Nov. 1995 / Blind Pig ✦✦✦

Unscheduled Flight / Nov. 18, 1997 / Blue Rock'it ✦✦✦

Cain Does King / Apr. 24, 2001 / Blue Rock'it ✦✦✦✦

J.J. Cale

b. Dec. 5, 1938, Oklahoma City, OK
Vocals, Guitar / Singer/Songwriter, Blues-Rock
Notorious for his laid-back, rootsy style, J.J. Cale (b. Jean Jacques Cale) is best-known for writing "After Midnight" and "Cocaine," songs that Eric Clapton later made into hits. But Cale's influence wasn't only through songwriting—his distinctly loping sense of rhythm and shuffling boogie became the blueprint for the adult-oriented roots-rock of Clapton and Mark Knopfler, among others. Cale's refusal to vary the sound of his music over the course of his career caused some critics to label him as a one-trick pony, but he managed to build a dedicated cult following with his sporadically released recordings.

Born in Oklahoma City but raised in Tulsa, OK, Cale played in a variety of rock & roll bands and Western swing groups as a teenager, including one outfit that also featured Leon Russell. In 1959, at the age of 21, he moved to Nashville, where he was hired by the Grand Ole Opry's touring company. After a few years, he returned to Tulsa, where he re-united with Russell and began playing local clubs. In 1964, Cale and Russell moved to Los Angeles with another local Oklahoma musician, Carl Radle.

Shortly after he arrived in Los Angeles, Cale began playing with Delaney & Bonnie. He only played with the duo for a brief time, beginning a solo career in 1965. That year, he cut the first version of "After Midnight," which would become his most famous song. Around 1966, Cale formed the Leathercoated Minds with songwriter Roger Tillison. The group released a psychedelic album called *A Trip Down Sunset Strip* the same year. Deciding that he wouldn't be able to forge a career in Los Angeles, Cale returned to Tulsa in 1967. Upon his return, he set about playing local clubs. Within a year, he had recorded a set of demos. Radle obtained a copy of the demos and forwarded it to Denny Cordell, who was founding a record label called Shelter with Leon Russell. Shelter signed Cale in 1969. The following year, Eric Clapton recorded "After Midnight," taking it to the American Top 20 and thereby providing Cale with needed exposure and royalties. In December of 1971, Cale released his debut album, *Naturally,* on Shelter Records; the album featured the Top 40 hit "Crazy Mama," as well as a re-recorded version of "After Midnight," which nearly reached the Top 40, and "Call Me the Breeze," which Lynyrd Skynyrd later covered. Cale followed *Naturally* with *Really,* which featured the minor hit "Lies," in 1972.

Following the release of *Really,* J.J. Cale adopted a slow work schedule, releasing an album every other year or so. *Okie,* his third album, appeared in 1974. Two years later, he released *Troubadour,* which yielded "Hey Baby," his last minor hit, as well as the original version of "Cocaine," a song that Clapton would later cover. By this point, Cale had settled into a comfortable career as a cult artist and he rarely made any attempt to break into the mainstream. One more album on Shelter Records, *5,* appeared in 1979 and then he switched labels, signing with MCA in 1981. MCA only released one album (1981's *Shades*) and Cale moved to Mercury Records the following year, releasing *Grasshopper.* In 1983, Cale released his eighth album, *8.* The album became his first not to chart. Following its release, Cale left Mercury and he entered a long period of seclusion, reappearing in late 1990 with *Travel Log,* which was released on the British independent label Silvertone; the album appeared in America the following year. *10* was released in 1992. The album failed to chart, but it re-established his power as a cult artist. He moved to the major label Virgin in 1994, releasing *Close to You* the same year. It was followed by *Guitar Man* in 1996. —*Stephen Thomas Erlewine*

Naturally / Dec. 1971 / Mercury ✦✦✦
J.J. Cale's debut album, *Naturally,* was recorded after Eric Clapton made "After Midnight" a huge success. Instead of following Slowhand's cue and constructing a slick blues-rock album, Cale recruited a number of his Oklahoma friends and made a laid-back country-rock record that firmly established his distinctive, relaxed style. Cale included a new version of "After Midnight" on the album, but the true meat of the record lay in songs like "Crazy Mama," which became a hit single, and "Call Me the Breeze," which Lynyrd Skynyrd later covered. On these songs and many others on *Naturally,* Cale effortlessly captured a lazy, rolling boogie that contradicted all the commercial styles of boogie, blues and country rock at the time. Where his contemporaries concentrated on solos, Cale worked the song and its rhythm, and the result was a pleasant, engaging album that was in no danger of raising anybody's temperature. —*Thom Owens*

Really / Dec. 1972 / Mercury ✦✦✦
Cale's guitar work manages to be both understated and intense here. The same is true of his seemingly offhand singing, which finds him drawling lines like "You get your gun, I'll get mine" with disarming casualness. But he has trouble coming up with original material as strong as that on his debut, and for some, his approach will be too casual; there are many times, when the band is percolating along and Cale is muttering into the microphone, that the music seems to be all background and no foreground. You may find yourself waiting for a payoff that never comes. —*William Ruhlmann*

Okie / May 1974 / Mercury ✦✦✦
Cale moves toward country and gospel on some songs here, but since those are two of his primary influences, the movement is slight. And longtime producer Audie Ashworth attempts to place more emphasis on Cale's vocals on some songs by double-tracking them and pushing them up in the mix. But much of this is still low-key and bluesy in what was becoming Cale's patented style. —*William Ruhlmann*

Troubadour / Sep. 1976 / Mercury ✦✦✦✦✦
Producer Audie Ashworth introduced some different instruments, notably vibes and what sound like horns (although none are credited), for a slightly altered sound here. But Cale's

albums are so steeped in his introspective style that they become interchangeable. If you like one of them, chances are you'll want to have them all. This one is notable for introducing "Cocaine," which Eric Clapton covered on his *Slowhand* album a year later. —*William Ruhlmann*

5 / Aug. 1979 / Mercury ✦✦
As Cale's influence on others expanded, he just continued to turn out the occasional album of bluesy, minor-key tunes. This one was even sparer than usual, with the artist handling bass as well as guitar on many tracks. Listened to today, it sounds so much like a Dire Straits album, it's scary. (Mark Knopfler & Co. had appeared in 1978, seven years after Cale.) —*William Ruhlmann*

Shades / Feb. 1981 / Mercury ✦✦

Grasshopper / Mar. 1982 / Mercury ✦✦
J.J. Cale drifts toward a more pop approach on this album, starting with the lead-off track, "City Girls," which could almost but not quite be a hit single. The usual blues and country shuffle approach is in effect, but Audie Ashworth's production is unusually sharp, the playing has more bite than usual, and Cale, whose vocals are for the most part up in the mix, sounds more engaged. It's not clear, however, that this is an improvement over his usual laidback approach, and, in any case, it shouldn't be over-emphasized—this is still a J.J. Cale album, with its cantering tempos and single-note guitar runs. It's just that, when you have a style as defined as Cale's, little movements in style loom larger. —*William Ruhlmann*

8 / 1983 / Mercury ✦✦
At 12 years and eight albums into his recording career, Cale's approach has changed little, and here is another collection of groove tunes that act as platforms for the artist's intricate guitar playing. He is sometimes accompanied by a female vocalist, co-writer Christine Lakeland. —*William Ruhlmann*

Special Edition / 1984 / Mercury ✦✦✦✦✦
Sinuous rhythms, conversational singing, and, most of all, intricate, bluesy guitar playing characterize Cale's performances of his own songs. This compilation, covering over a decade of recording, includes the songs Eric Clapton, who borrowed heavily from Cale's style in his '70s solo work, made famous: "After Midnight" and "Cocaine." —*William Ruhlmann*

Travel Log / Feb. 1990 / Silvertone ✦✦✦✦✦
Cale's first album in six years finds him taking a more aggressive stance in terms of tempos and playing, although he remains a man with a profound sense of the groove and, especially as a singer, a minimalist. But as he says, "Shuffle or die." —*William Ruhlmann*

Number 10 / Nov. 10, 1992 / Silvertone ✦✦✦
There are no major surprises on Cale's tenth outing; fans get the same dependable, unassuming, comfy results, like a well-worn but form-fitting pair of slippers. Subtle licks percolate and resonate from the front-porch jam session on "Jailer" and "Low Rider." "Lonesome Train" and "Shady Grove" choogle along, as amiable as they are hypnotic. The closest thing to a twist comes with the phased vocals and spiralling guitar runs of "Digital Blues." It would be easy to imagine *Number 10* getting completely buried behind a wash of '90s white noise, but for those prepared to kick off their boots and sit a spell, Cale's latest offers up some seductive rewards. —*Roch Parisien*

Closer to You / Aug. 23, 1994 / Virgin ✦✦

Guitar Man / Jun. 25, 1996 / Virgin ✦✦✦
J.J. Cale's albums usually sound interchangeable, and his twelfth release, *Guitar Man*, is no exception. Although he has recorded *Guitar Man* as a one-man band effort, it sounds remarkably relaxed and laid-back, like it was made with a seasoned bar band. That doesn't mean there's much excitement on the album, but Cale's music has never been about excitement—it's more about laying back and letting the music flow. Of course, that approach results in remarkably uneven records, and *Guitar Man* is no exception. There's a handful of very good songs, but there's nothing on the level of his previous classics. It's just another pleasant J.J. Cale album, nothing more but nothing less, either. —*Thom Owens*

Anyway the Wind Blows: The Anthology / Jun. 17, 1997 / Mercury ✦✦✦✦✦
Although it is a little too extensive for casual fans, the double-disc, 50-track *Anyway the Wind Blows—The Anthology* is a definitive retrospective of J.J. Cale's career, featuring all the highlights from his career. Cale's albums often sounded similar, but they were remarkably uneven in terms of quality, which is what makes *Anyway the Wind Blows* essential for both neophytes and collectors. Not only is it a perfect introduction, containing such essentials as "Cocaine," "Call Me the Breeze" and "After Midnight," but it is one of his most consistently listenable and enjoyable discs. —*Stephen Thomas Erlewine*

● **The Very Best of J.J. Cale** / Jun. 9, 1998 / Mercury ✦✦✦✦✦
The Very Best of J.J. Cale is an excellent single-disc collection of the music from one of the most influential singer-songwriters that emerged out of America during the '70s. Just as Townes Van Zandt and Guy Clark define Texas songwriting, Cale is the epitome of the Oklahoma writers. Although most people know him as the writer of Eric Clapton's hit "Cocaine," Cale constantly offered up other quality material that could only be defined by his vocal style, which can accurately be described as "reclining in the groove." Popular tunes such as "Call Me the Breeze," "Hey Baby" and "Crazy Mama" have a deceptively laid-back intensity that to a large degree influenced such rockers as Lowell George of Little Feat and the previously mentioned Clapton. Cale's guitar work proved to be influential as well (again on Clapton), but also popular swamp-rockers such as Delaney Bramlett. *The Very Best of J.J. Cale* offers a comprehensive collection from Cale's early-'70s recordings in Nashville, to Muscle Shoals in Alabama, to his later work on Hollywood. If you're going to explore Cale's groove, this is the place to start. —*Matthew Greenwald*

J.J. Cale Live / Jun. 5, 2001 / Narada ✦✦✦✦
Cale's live performance style does nothing to quell his reputation for laid-back but pristine guitar playing and reserved "Mississippi John Hurt"-style delivery. A man who truly appreciates the value of restraint, Cale leaves plenty of room for his immaculate guitar lines, even to the point of irony on an ambling version of the previously insistent "Mama Don't." This collection, which was gleaned from an assortment of live shows dating from 1990-1996, finds Cale allowing his songs to unfold organically. Of particular note is the lilting "Magnolia." Less nostalgic than when it first appeared on 1971's *Naturally*, this version, recorded at Carnegie Hall in 1996, is crisper and more clipped, replacing the original's sense of longing with the resigned confidence that permeates this entire set. —*Travis Drageset*

20th Century Masters: Millennium Collection / Jul. 23, 2002 / Mercury ✦✦✦✦
J.J. Cale's *20th Century Masters: The Millennium Collection* gathers a dozen of his best-known songs, including "Magnolia," "Crazy Mama," and "Call Me the Breeze," as well as "Cocaine" and "After Midnight." The collection focuses on his '70s work, featuring not only singles, but album tracks from *Naturally, Really, 5*, and *Okie*, among others. Though it's not as extensive a collection as *Anyway the Wind Blows: The Anthology* or *The Very Best of J.J. Cale*, this compilation does provide a good, concise primer on Cale's influential mix of earthy blues-rock and finely crafted songwriting. —*Heather Phares*

Bob Call

Piano / Jump Blues, Piano Blues
Early blues pianist Bob Call was known for recording with vocalist Elzadie Robinson in Chicago during the '20s, even though he recorded as an accompanist after WWII. Call was believed to come from Texas, but by the late '20s he was residing in Chicago and befriended pianist Will Ezell. Both alternately accompanied singer Elzadie Robinson during her Paramount recordings. Bob Call also recorded the song "31 Blues" solo for the Brunswick label in late 1929, and accompanied blues vocalist James "Boodle It" Wiggins during that time. Among Call's late-'20s recordings are these; several for Vocalion that went unissued; and his own featured dates for Paramount, which included his take on "Keep a-Knockin' an You Can't Get In." The '30s found Call studying music in Chicago. He went back to recording as accompanist after WWII, and still resided in Chicago as of the late '60s. —*Joslyn Layne*

Blind James Campbell

b. Sep. 17, 1906, Nashville, TN
Guitar, Vocals / Blues Revival, Acoustic Blues, Jug Band, String Bands
Among the last of a dying breed of Southern street musicians, bluesman Blind James Campbell and his Friendly Five were a staple of the Nashville musical landscape for decades. Campbell was born in Music City on September 17, 1906; although he played guitar from the age of 13, he did not pursue performing as a livelihood until the age of 30, when he was left permanently blind following an accident at the fertilizer plant where he worked. He then formed a group dubbed the Nashville Washboard Band, a loose-knit aggregation which consisted of himself on vocals and guitar, mandolin, lard can (or tub bass), and a washboard; they honed their skills not only on the streets but also at area parties, typically playing to white audiences but also sitting in at black roadhouses. Campbell followed much the same path in the years and decades which followed, later informally rechristening the band the Friendly Five; in 1962 he was discovered by Arhoolie Records chief Chris Strachwitz, who recorded him with a backing group consisting of multi-instrumentalist Beauford Clay, trumpeter George Bell, second guitarist Bell Ray and tuba player Ralph Robinson. Unhappy with the quality of the recordings, Strachwitz returned to Nashville a year later and recorded Campbell again; the best selections were then assembled for release as the LP *Blind James Campbell and His Nashville Street Band*. —*Jason Ankeny*

● **Blind James Campbell and His Nashville Street Band** / 1995 / Arhoolie ✦✦✦✦✦
On their lone release, Blind James Campbell and His Nashville Street Band serve up a singular blend of blues, jazz, old-time, skiffle and jug band music; while their material is traditional, the presentation is anything but, with a tuba taking the place of bass guitar and Campbell's gravelly voice going lower and deeper than either. —*Jason Ankeny*

Eddie C. Campbell

b. May 6, 1939, Duncan, MS
Vocals, Guitar / Modern Electric Chicago Blues, Modern Electric Blues
Happily, Eddie C. Campbell returned to Chicago after spending a decade entrenched in Europe. His shimmering West Side-styled guitar playing and unusually introspective songwriting have been a breath of fresh air on the Windy City circuit, reuniting the veteran bluesman with fans he left behind in 1984.

Campbell left rural Mississippi for the bright lights of Chicago at age ten, sneaking a peek at Muddy Waters at the 1125 Club soon after he arrived and jamming with his idol when he was only 12. He fell in with some West Side young bloods—Luther Allison, Magic Sam—and honed a guitar attack rooted deep in the ringing style. Campbell paid his sideman dues on the bandstand with everyone from Howlin' Wolf and Little Walter to Little Johnny Taylor and Jimmy Reed. Koko Taylor recommended Campbell to Willie Dixon, who hired him as a Chicago Blues All-Star in 1976.

Campbell cut his own debut album, the rousing *King of the Jungle*, in 1977 for the Steve Wisner's short-lived Mr. Blues logo (now available on Rooster Blues, it includes the guitarist's lighthearted Yuletide perennial "Santa's Been Messin' With the Kid"). But he split the country for calmer European climates, recording a nice 1984 album, *Let's Pick It!*, with a Dutch group that first came out on Black Magic and now adorns the Evidence catalog.

When Eddie C. Campbell finally returned stateside for the birth of his son, he made up for lost time by gigging steadily around Chicago and making a comeback album for Blind Pig, *That's When I Know*, that contained some very distinctive originals. *Gonna Be Alright* followed in 1999. —*Bill Dahl*

- **King of the Jungle** / 1977 / Rooster Blues ✦✦✦✦✦
Flamboyant West Side-styled guitarist's debut album, first issued on the short-lived Mr. Blues logo, remains his best, with his slashing guitarist and lowdown vocals beautifully presented on covers of material by Magic Sam, Muddy Waters, Percy Mayfield, Willie Mabon, and his own Yuletide perennial "Santa's Messin' with the Kid." Great band, too: harpist Carey Bell, pianist Lafayette Leake, bassist Bob Stroger, and drummer Clifton James. *—Bill Dahl*

Let's Pick It! / Oct. 1984 / Evidence ✦✦✦✦
Recorded while Eddie Campbell was on a European sojourn that lasted a decade or so, this disc, cut back in 1984 for Black Magic with an overseas combo, is a very convincing effort mixing Campbell's own "Cold and Hungry," "Dream," and "Messin' with My Pride" with songs by Albert King, Jimmy Reed, Jimmie Lee Robinson, and Magic Sam. *—Bill Dahl*

The Baddest Cat on the Block / 1985 / JSP ✦✦
This is not his best album. *—Bill Dahl*

Mind Trouble / 1988 / Double Trouble ✦✦✦

That's When I Know / 1994 / Blind Pig ✦✦✦✦
During that long decade away from home, Eddie C.'s skills as a unique blues songwriter certainly blossomed. His triumphant homecoming set contains some highly distinctive material—a homespun "Sister Taught Me Guitar," and the incandescent title track, a forceful "Sleep," and "Busted," and a decidedly mystical "Son of Sons." *—Bill Dahl*

Gonna Be Alright / Sep. 14, 1999 / Icehouse ✦✦✦

John Campbell

b. Jan. 20, 1952, Shreveport, LA, **d.** Jun. 13, 1993
Slide Guitar, Guitar / Modern Electric Blues
Guitarist, singer and songwriter John Campbell had the potential of turning a whole new generation of people onto the blues in the '90s, much the same way Stevie Ray Vaughan did in the '80s. His vocals were so powerful and his guitar playing so fiery, you couldn't help but stop what you were doing and pay attention to what you were hearing. But unfortunately, because of frail health and a rough European tour, he suffered a heart attack while sleeping on June 13, 1993, at the age of 41.

Campbell was born in Shreveport, LA, on January 20, 1952, and grew up in Center, TX. Although he got his own guitar at age eight and began playing professionally when he was 13, he didn't get serious about playing blues for a living until he was involved in a near-fatal drag racing accident that broke several ribs, collapsed a lung and took his right eye. In his teens, Campbell opened for people like Clarence "Gatemouth" Brown, Albert Collins and Son Seals, but he later got sidetracked by drag racing, and it was while he was recuperating from his near-death drag racing accident that he re-learned guitar, developing his own distinctive, rhythm and slide-heavy style, based in some measure on the music of Lightnin' Hopkins.

In 1985, after playing a variety of clubs between east Texas and New Orleans, Campbell moved to New York. One night in New York, guitarist Ronnie Earl happened upon Campbell in a club, playing with Johnny Littlejohn. Earl was so impressed that he offered to produce an album by Campbell, and the result was *A Man and His Blues* (Crosscut 1019), a Germany-only release that has since been made available in the U.S. That album earned Campbell a W.C. Handy Award nomination in 1989, and not long after that, the rock & roll world started to take notice of him. Although he never sent a tape to a record company in his life, after drawing ever-growing crowds to the downtown New York clubs where he played, executives at Elektra Records took notice of him and signed him to a contract. Both of his albums for Elektra, *One Believer* (1991) and *Howlin' Mercy* (1993) are brilliant, well-produced recordings, yet they only hint at Campbell's potential for greatness, had he lived longer. *—Richard Skelly*

One Believer / 1991 / Elektra ✦✦✦✦✦
The Elektra debut by the late bluesman John Campbell is a curious affair in more than one respect—despite its obvious excellence and original voice. The first is that he was signed at all. Clearly, in 1990 when Campbell signed his deal, record company executives were still interested inn finding new and original talent and developing them over a period of time. *One Believer* was outside of virtually every trend on major labels and in pop at the time. Other than Chris Whitley's *Living with the Law*, it was the only roots record issued on a major label in 1991. The other thing is that *One Believer* is an oddity even for Campbell. It's a deeply atmospheric record full of subtle shimmering organs and warm guitar textures that accent the dreamy spooky side of the blues more than the crunchy stomp and roll that Campbell was known for in the clubs—and displayed on his follow-up *Howlin' Mercy*. Tracks like "Angel of Sorrow," "World of Trouble," and "Wild Streak" offer shimmering ambient textures from which the blues emanate from the ether, tonally and melodically challenging all acceptable notions of what Texas blues should sound like—but then, Mr. Campbell was living and working in New York and his music was certainly influenced by that late-night environment. These are beautiful songs, tempered in shadow and restraint while baring their teeth at all the right moments. Other places the roadhouse magic comes out of the closet as on "Couldn't Do Nothin'," "Devil in My Closet," and "Person to Person." On "Voodoo Edge," the slowhand blues meets a crisscross New Orleans second-line backbeat à la Dr. John and comes up with chunky honky-tonk piano and shakers to give the piece an "I Walk on Gilded Splinters" feel, extending Campbell's sound over a deeper, darker shade of roots music. This in underlined by the album's last two tracks—"Take Me Down" and the title track—which are menacing in their conviction and creepy swampy in execution. This is a fine, fine debut that remains in print. *—Thom Jurek*

- **Howlin' Mercy** / 1993 / Elektra ✦✦✦✦✦
Slide guitarist and songwriter John Campbell was a man driven. Before his untimely death, he had pulled out all the stops to play a music that was full of mystery, pathos, dark energy, and plenty of rock & roll strut 'n' growl; it could be frightening in its intensity. *Howlin' Mercy* was the last of two recordings for Elektra, and is by far the heavier of the two. As displayed by its opening track, "Ain't Afraid of Midnight," Campbell was a considerable slide guitarist who owed his skill to the bluesmen like Lightnin' Hopkins (from his home state of Texas), Fred McDowell, and a few others. His solos are wrangling, loose, and shambolic; they are undeniably dark and heavy. They cut with elegance across the rhythms and melodies in his songs. This is followed by a version of "When the Levee Breaks" that is a direct counter to and traditional reclamation of the Led Zep version and places it back firmly in the blues canon. As evidenced by "Saddle Up My Pony," Campbell was equally skilled at transmuting the Delta blues and framing them in a very modern context without taking anything away from their chilling, spare power and poetry. And in the modern rock and blues idiom, he was a master, as evidenced by the stomp and roll of "Firin' Line"; "Written in Stone"; and the epic, swamp blues cum overdriven scorcher "Wolf Among the Lambs." This final moment is perhaps Campbell's greatest on record in that it embodies all of his strengths and reveals none of them to be contradictions. Campbell was living and playing in New York at the end of his life, and that city's conflicting energies are reflected in his playing and writing. They needed each other, it seems, and if ever there were a Delta blues record that visited the Texas roadhouse and settled on the streetcorners of NYC, this is it. Awesome. *—Thom Jurek*

Canned Heat

f. 1966, Los Angeles, CA
Group / Boogie Rock, Blues-Rock, Modern Electric Blues
A hard-luck blues band of the '60s, Canned Heat was founded by blues historians and record collectors Alan Wilson and Bob Hite. They seemed to be on the right track and played all the right festivals (including Monterey and Woodstock, making it very prominently into the documentaries about both) but somehow never found a lasting audience. Certainly their hearts were in the right place. Canned Heat's debut album—released shortly after their appearance at Monterey—was every bit as deep into the roots of the blues as any other combo of the time mining similar turf, with the exception of the original Paul Butterfield band. Hite was nicknamed "The Bear" and stalked the stage in the time-honored tradition of Howlin' Wolf and other large-proportioned bluesmen. Wilson was an extraordinary harmonica player, with a fat tone and great vibrato. His work on guitar, especially in open tunings (he played on Son House's rediscovery recordings of the mid-'60s, incidentally), gave the band a depth and texture that most other rhythm players could only aspire to. Henry Vestine—another dyed-in-the-wool record collector—was the West Coast's answer to Michael Bloomfield and capable of fretboard fireworks at a moment's notice.

Canned Heat's breakthrough moment occurred with the release of their second album, establishing them with hippie ballroom audiences as the "kings of the boogie." As a way of paying homage to the musician they got the idea from in the first place, they later collaborated on an album with John Lee Hooker that was one of the elder bluesman's most successful outings with a young white (or black, for that matter) combo backing him up. After two big chart hits with "Going Up the Country" and an explosive version of Wilbert Harrison's "Let's Work Together," Wilson died under mysterious (probably drug-related) circumstances in 1970, and Hite carried on with various reconstituted versions of the band until his death just before a show in 1981, from a heart seizure.

Still, the surviving members—led by drummer Adolfo "Fito" de la Parra—continued touring and recording, recruiting new vocalist Walter Trout; he was replaced in 1985 by James Thornbury, who fronted the band for the next decade. After Thornbury exited in 1995, Canned Heat tapped Robert Lucas to assume lead vocal duties; they soon recorded *The Canned Heat Blues Band*, which sadly was Vestine's last recording with the group—he died in Paris in December 1997 in the wake of the band's recent tour. *Boogie 2000* followed two years later. *—Cub Koda & Bruce Eder*

Canned Heat / 1967 / Liberty ✦✦
Canned Heat is a good stopping off point when following the blues path through rock in the '60s. With such blues staples as "Rollin' & Tumblin'," "Dust My Broom" and "Goin' Down Slow," this album presents White boys in L.A., authenticating their blues alongside such original material as "Catfish Blues," "Rich Woman" and "Big Road Blues." Although the production sounds outdated, many of the cuts here could almost pass for the real thing (that is, if you didn't know who these guys were). A nice touchstone between yesterday and today. *—James Chrispell*

Boogie With Canned Heat / Feb. 1968 / Liberty ✦✦✦
With *Boogie With...* Canned Heat hit the Top 40 and became so-called stars with the road classic "On the Road Again." While they began as a blues band and still serve up a mean blues on "Marie Laveau," they got caught up in the boogie craze that swept through in the late '60s, hence the track "Tried Hockey Boogie," which while not the best of cuts, does boogie along. Elsewhere, they warn of the hazards of using speed on "Amphetamine Annie" and rock out on the staple classic "Evil Woman." *Boogie with Canned Heat* isn't the best Canned Heat album, but it is good enough to seek out. *—James Chrispell*

Living the Blues / Nov. 1968 / Liberty ✦✦✦
Living the Blues would have made a rather fine one-record set, but with the inclusion of the 41-minute "Refried Boogie," things get blown way out of proportion. "Refried" isn't what you want to listen to more than once, if that, for it is best known for some of the most boring soloing ever set to vinyl in the '60s, and that says quite a bit. If you omit that lengthy cut, the rest of *Living the Blues* is pretty interesting. It includes the smash Top 40 hit "Going Up the Country" and has other cuts such as "Boogie Music" and "Sandy's Blues" that do not detract from Canned Heat's rise in popularity. The strangest cut, "Parthenogenesis" (which supposedly meant "the development of an unfertilized egg"), could have been pared down to a fine six-minute cut, but at over 19 minutes, the development gets pretty drawn out. As was the case with many releases in the late '60s, *Living*

the Blues has more than its share of padding, but the music held within much of the grooves here is worth a listen. *—James Chrispell*

The Canned Heat Cookbook / 1969 / Liberty ✦✦✦
The inclusion of Canned Heat's two best-known tracks, "Going Up the Country" and "On the Road Again," make this set worthwhile. The track listing is for the 1981 abridged reissue. *—J.P. Ollio*

Hallelujah / 1969 / Liberty ✦✦✦
Although *Hallelujah* added nothing new to Canned Heat's established blues 'n' boogie formula, "Same All Over" was a classic song of the genre, and "Sic 'Em Pigs" an entertaining era-specific goof. Larry Taylor's bass and Henry Vestine's guitar highlight this album. *—Jim Newsom*

Future Blues / 1970 / BGO ✦✦✦✦✦
The final Canned Heat album to feature co-founder Alan Wilson, *Future Blues* was also one of their best, surprisingly restrained as a studio creation by the band, the whole thing clocking in at under 36 minutes, as long as some single jams on their live discs. It was also one of their most stylistically diverse efforts. Most of what's here is very concise and accessible, even the one group-composed jam—Alan Wilson's "Shake It and Break It" and his prophetically titled "My Time Ain't Long" (he would be dead the year this record was issued), which also sounds a lot like a follow-up to "Going Up the Country" until its final, very heavy and up-close guitar coda. Other songs are a little self-consciously heavy, especially their version of Arthur "Big Boy" Crudup's "That's All Right, Mama." Dr. John appears playing piano on the dark, ominous "London Blues," and arranges the horns on "Skat," which tries for a completely different kind of sound—late-'40s-style jump blues—than that for which the group was usually known. And the band also turns in a powerhouse heavy guitar version of Wilbert Harrison's "Let's Work Together." The Beat Goes On reissue is very clean and extremely loud. *—Bruce Eder*

Hooker 'n' Heat / 1971 / EMI ✦✦✦✦
John Lee Hooker's simple boogie was something Canned Heat mastered early on in their career. It could be argued that it was the only thing they mastered—they simply knew how to amplify it really loudly. They never found the subtle variations that Hooker did, but that doesn't mean they were a hindrance to the legend on this jam session. If anything, Hooker spurs the group to some of their grittiest, low-down boogie on record. The jams get a little lethargic and lengthy at times, especially since the album meanders its way through two discs, but this is certainly some of the best blues Canned Heat ever recorded. *—Stephen Thomas Erlewine*

Canned Heat Concert (Recorded Live in Europe) / 1971 / United Artists ✦✦✦
Canned Heat's greatest strength was their feel for boogie, but aside from a couple singles, their music never seemed to translate well to the studio. Live performances showed them off best (witness their brief Monterey Pop film cameo). This album lacks the rawness and vigor of the earlier *Live at Topanga Corral*, but it has its moments. Al Wilson sounds positively spooky on two quiet numbers that he penned between tour dressing rooms and hotels (on "Pulling Hair Blues" he laments his inability to get laid!). Bob Hite cuts loose on Wilbert Harrison's buoyant "Let's Work Together," their last hit single. His good-timey on-stage patter is a hoot, especially when he name-drops with the London audience. OK, this isn't quite *Live at the Regal*. But where else can you hear a 300 pound blues singer lampoon Jim Morrison?! *—Peter Kurtz*

Historical Figures & Ancient Heads / 1972 / Repertoire ✦✦✦
Adding Joel Scott Hill to the band, Canned Heat was infused with a bit of much-needed new blood. While nothing here found favor with AM radio, FM saw fit to include such cuts as "Cherokee Dance," "Utah" and the Heat's collaboration with Little Richard, "Rockin' With the King." Full of the usual boogie, *Historical Figures & Ancient Heads* still comes of as a rather pale reminder of just how bluesy this band once was. New blood or not, this disc didn't do much in the way of revitalizing Canned Heat's faltering career—they appear to have become old before their time. *—James Chrispell*

● **The Best of Canned Heat** / 1972 / EMI ✦✦✦✦✦
All of Canned Heat's best tracks and biggest hits ("Going Up the Country," "On the Road Again") are included on this single-disc collection. *—Stephen Thomas Erlewine*

Reheated / 1989 / Varese Sarabande ✦✦✦✦
Originally released in Europe, this features a reconstituted Canned Heat lineup from 1988. Drummer Fito de la Parra and bassist Larry Taylor are the only two left over from the old days, but that doesn't seem much of a problem here, as top-flight guitar work from Junior Watson and James Thornbury drives these songs right along. There's a nice, organic feel to many of the tracks, with minimal production on some providing a welcome rough touch. There's a fine remake of "Bull Frog Blues" aboard, but tracks like "Hucklebuck," "(So Fine) Betty Jean," "I Love to Rock and Roll," and "Mercury Blues" are the big tickets here. One of the group's best latter-day albums. *—Cub Koda*

On the Road / 1989 / EMI ✦✦✦✦
On the Road is a compilation concentrating entirely on Canned Heat's earliest recordings, hitting all the highlights ("On the Road Again," "Going Up the Country") from their biggest albums and offering most casual fans a definitive—if not a little too comprehensive—overview. *—Stephen Thomas Erlewine*

Uncanned! The Best of Canned Heat / May 17, 1994 / EMI ✦✦✦✦✦
Uncanned! The Best of Canned Heat is exactly what it claims to be—the definitive portrait of the blues-soaked hippie boogie band. Spreading 41 tracks (including numerous rarities, alternate takes, and Levi commercials) over two CDs, the set is perfect for the hardcore Canned Heat collector. For casual fans, the collection simply contains too much music; they would be better served by the single-disc collection, *The Best of Canned Heat*. *—Stephen Thomas Erlewine*

Canned Heat 1967–1976: The Boogie House Tapes / Jun. 27, 2000 / Ruf ✦✦✦
This double disc assembled by drummer Fito de la Parra, the only remaining member of the original '60s band, and Canned Heat collector Walter de Paduwa is a compilation of some previously "lost" studio and live performances of the indefatigable boogie band. While hardcore fans will rejoice hearing the great Alan Wilson, who appears on roughly half of these tracks, in his prime, it's still a very mixed bag. Guitarists Harvey Mandel and Henry Vestine are featured prominently, as is vocalist Bob "The Bear" Hite who, along with drummer de la Parra, is the only constant band member across these two CDs. Many of these tunes were never intended for release, and as such they are sub-par blues workouts that might have been fun at the time but lay lifeless on album. Still, there are some stunning moments, mostly provided by bird-voiced Wilson, that make this worth the bargain price. Two tunes recorded for the *Playboy After Dark* TV show in 1969 and 1970, a frustratingly clipped "On the Road Again" and a chilling "My Time Ain't Long" (incorrectly credited to Harvey Mandel, it's actually a Wilson composition) sung by Wilson shortly before his death are certainly of interest to collectors, although neither eclipses the studio version. The same holds for Wilson's stunning turn on his "London Blues" recorded live at Montreux in 1970. Disc two features six Wilson tracks, and although he isn't singing on every one, his presence is felt. Guitarist Vestine is fired up on "You Know I Love You" and there are other tracks that find him in incredible form spitting out psychedelic liquid leads, making the late guitarist, who passed away in 1998, one of the stars of this set. His sterling work on "I Love My Baby" (mysteriously credited to de la Parra as are other jams here) is remarkable, and the band in general locks together like a well-oiled boogie machine with Wilson's trebly slide stinging like a hornet. Sound quality ranges from just above bootleg to fairly good, sometimes wavering in the same tune, and the skimpy liner notes are barely adequate. Although the information is useful, it's split between pages, forcing the reader to flip back and forth to see who is playing on which track and where the performance was originally recorded. Clearly this is not the place for a Canned Heat novice to begin, and even more established fans might find its few gems slim pickings among the unfocused, extended, you-had-to-be-there tracks. It's an intermittently interesting, warts-and-all document of a blues band with good intentions that had some inspired moments, but this inconsistent collection does not show them at their best. *—Hal Horowitz*

Live at the Kaleidoscope 1969 / Oct. 3, 2000 / Varese Sarabande ✦✦✦
Live at the Kaleidoscope highlights Canned Heat while they were still in their prime in 1969 at the Kaleidoscope in L.A., featuring Bob Hite on vocals and Alan Wilson on guitar. Originally released under the title *Live at Topanga Corral*, which had been out of print for a number of years, featuring inspired cover versions of "Sweet Sixteen," "Dust My Broom," and "Wish You Would." While *Live at the Kaleidoscope* doesn't include the hits "On the Road Again" or "Going' Up the Country," it is a decent representation of the blues/rock boogie this band was known for. *—Al Campbell*

Don't Forget to Boogie: Vintage Heat / Jun. 4, 2002 / Varese Sarabande ✦✦✦
This is actually a CD repackage of the 1966 recordings that appeared back in 1970 on the Janus LP *Vintage Canned Heat*. Produced by Johnny Otis, this was the group in their early formative stage with the lineup that would play on their official 1967 debut album: Bob Hite, Alan Wilson, Henry Vestine, Larry Taylor, and Frank Cook. All but two of the songs are covers of well-worn blues staples, mostly from the classic electric Chess catalog, including "Spoonful," "Rollin' and Tumblin'," "Pretty Thing," "Got My Mojo Working," and "Louise," with John Lee Hooker's "Dimples" as well. Though more basic and tentative and than the late-'60s recordings for which they're well known, these are pretty brisk, concise performances that mark Canned Heat as one of the few enduring white American blues-rock bands of the era. Indeed, this lacks the jam-prone bombast that afflicted many of their famous releases, and even those who dismiss their familiar stuff for that reason might find themselves enjoying this. One of the two group originals, "Straight Head," sounds like they might have been trying, if just slightly, to aim a little closer to the pop market in the manner of some of the tracks recorded around the same time by the Rising Sons (the L.A. folk-rock/blues group with Taj Mahal and Ry Cooder). It's only 24 minutes long, and one song, "Rollin' and Tumblin'," is presented twice (once with harmonica, once without), but it's a worthy archival collection. *—Richie Unterberger*

Cannon's Jug Stompers

Group / Jug Band, Prewar Country Blues, Acoustic Memphis Blues
Gus Cannon was the best known of all the jug band musicians and a seminal figure on the Memphis blues scene. His recollections have also provided us with much of our knowledge of the earliest days of the blues in the Mississippi Delta. Cannon led his Jug Stompers on banjo and jug in a historic series of dates for the Victor label in 1928-1930. The ensemble usually included a second banjoist or guitarist, one of whom often doubled on kazoo, and the legendary Noah Lewis on harmonica. The jug band style enjoyed a revival during the folk boom of the '50s and '60s, resulting in an ultra-rare Gus Cannon album on Stax, of all labels, after his "Walk Right In" became the nation's best-selling record for the Rooftop Singers in 1963. Cannon's Victor output was also a favorite source of early blues material for the Grateful Dead. *—Jim O'Neal*

Ace Cannon

b. May 5, 1934, Grenada, MS
Session Musician, Saxophone, Instrumental / Memphis Soul, Nashville Sound/Countrypolitan, Country-Pop, R&B, Soul
One of Nashville's premier session men from the late '50s through the early '70s, alto saxophonist Ace Cannon began playing at the age of ten and signed with Sun Records during the early days of rock & roll. He performed with Billy Lee Riley and Brad Suggs but then in 1959 joined the original Bill Black Combo, recording for the Hi label. He stayed with the band until 1961, when he made his solo chart debut with the instrumental "Tuff,"

which made it to the country Top 20. This in turn was followed by a Top 40 hit, "Blues (Stay Away from Me)," and a minor hit for the Santos label, "Sugar Blues." He had two more hits in the mid-'60s with "Cotton Fields" and "Searchin'," both recorded for Hi. A decade later, he became the subject of the 1974 documentary film, *Ace's High*. After moving to Nashville in the mid-'70s, Cannon's version of "Blue Eyes Crying in the Rain" became a minor hit and was nominated for the Best Country Instrumental Performance Grammy that year. Cannon continued to perform into the '90s and frequently toured with such legends of early rock & roll as Carl Perkins. *—Sandra Brennan*

Aces High/Plays the Great Show Tunes / Nov. 20, 1995 / Hi ♦♦♦♦
Two early albums from Ace Cannon, *Aces High* and *Plays the Great Show Tunes*, were reissued on one CD by HI Records in 1995. Although each record has its share of weak spots, they remain infectious and enjoyable, and this disc is worth seeking out for any hardcore fan of Cannon or early-'60s rock & roll and R&B. *—Stephen Thomas Erlewine*

Tuff Sax/Moanin' Sax / Nov. 20, 1995 / Hi ♦♦♦
An early album from Ace Cannon, *Moanin' Sax*, was reissued on the same CD with a latter-day record, *Ruff Sax*, by HI Records in 1995. Although each record has its share of weak spots, they remain infectious and enjoyable, with the former leaning toward early-'60s rock & roll and R&B and the latter leaning toward '70s funk, disco and soul. The two musical styles on the disc don't necessarily sit well together, but both albums have been out of print for years, so their reappearance on disc is welcome. *—Stephen Thomas Erlewine*

Unsafe Sax / Jan. 1, 1996 / King ♦♦
Ace Cannon's *Unsafe Sax* contains several familiar sax hits—including "Tuff," "Fever," "Honky Tonk" and "Raunchy"—but at eight tracks, it's too skimpy even to justify its budget price. *—Stephen Thomas Erlewine*

The Best of Ace Cannon / Nov. 19, 1996 / Curb ♦♦♦
The Best of Ace Cannon contains pleasant but unexceptional '90s re-recordings of Ace Cannon's biggest hits, including "Tuff" and "Blue Eyes Crying in the Rain," plus versions of standards like "Tennessee Waltz" and "Georgia On My Mind." *—Stephen Thomas Erlewine*

Hi Masters / Sep. 15, 1998 / Hi ♦♦♦♦

● **Best of Ace Cannon: The Hi Records Years** / Apr. 10, 2001 / Capitol ♦♦♦♦
On this 18-song best-of, the chronological and stylistic breadth is a little—not much—greater than you'd suspect, starting with his biggest single, 1961's "Tuff," and going all the way up to 1971. Most of the time, the saxophonist was content to grind out slow to medium shuffles with repetitive riffs and simple R&B-pop hooks, occasionally using organ, much in the style of his labelmates Bill Black's Combo (with whom Cannon sometimes played sax). Like Black, Cannon's singles were good jukebox fare, sometimes selling a lot to the specific jukebox market even when they didn't chart. (Often they didn't chart; only three singles besides "Tuff" made the Top 100, all of them included here.) The formula was simplistic and sometimes monotonous, especially when piled right after the other. However, his grooves were tight, and in the unavoidable Cannon-Black comparisons, Cannon comes out on top, simply because his instrumentals were more soulful and just a bit grittier. Toward the end of the '60s, too, he unexpectedly got into a tougher bag that was explicitly derivative of fellow Memphians Booker T. & the MG's, but was actually pretty well done. It made for an improved sound, anyway, on cuts like "Funny (How Time Slips Away)," the downright funky "Soul for Sale," and "If I Had a Hammer" (yes, the old Peter, Paul & Mary folk hit). The 1971 cover of Joe Liggins' "Drunk" is, again unexpectedly, quite creditable funk, and the only number here to feature vocals, done in a suitably phlegmy manner. *—Richie Unterberger*

Gus Cannon

b. Sep. 12, 1883, Red Banks, MS, **d.** Oct. 15, 1979, Memphis, TN
Jug, Kazoo, Piano, Guitar, Fiddle, Banjo / Jug Band, Prewar Blues, Prewar Country Blues, Country Blues, Acoustic Memphis Blues, Acoustic Blues

A remarkable musician (he could play five-string banjo and jug simultaneously!), Gus Cannon bridged the gap between early blues and the minstrel and folk styles which preceded it. His band of the '20s and '30s, Cannon's Jug Stompers, represents the apogee of jug band style. Songs they recorded, notably the raggy "Walk Right In," were staples of the folk repertoire decades later; and Cannon himself continued to record and perform into the '70s.

Self-taught on an instrument made from a frying pan and a raccoon skin, he learned early repertoire in the 1890s from older musicians, notably Mississipian Alec Lee. The early 1900s found him playing around Memphis with songster Jim Jackson and forming a partnership with Noah Lewis whose harmonica wizardry would be basic to the Jug Stompers sound. In 1914, Cannon began working with a succession of medicine shows, and would continue to do so into the '40s, as he further developed his style and repertoire.

His recording career began with Paramount sessions in 1927. He continued to record into the '30s as a soloist and with his incredible trio which included Noah Lewis along with guitarists Hosea Wood or Ashley Thompson. (Side projects included duets with Blind Blake and the first ever recordings of slide banjo!) Often obliged to find employment in other fields than music, Cannon continued to play anyway, mostly around Memphis. He resumed his stalled recording efforts in 1956 with sessions for Folkways. Subsequent sessions paired him with other Memphis survivors like Furry Lewis. Advancing age curtailed his activities in the '70s, but he still played the occasional cameo, sometimes from a wheelchair, until shortly before his death. *—Steve James*

Walk Right In / 1963 / Stax ♦♦♦
In June of 1963, 79-year-old Gus Cannon went into the studio in Memphis to cut his first recording in close to seven years, all a result of the Roofttop Singers having made his "Walk Right In" into a number one single. The producers didn't ask for too much out of Cannon, to judge from the results—just that he sit there with his banjo and old friends Will Shade (jug) and Milton Roby (washboard) backing him, and do his favorite songs. He introduces a few of them in separately indexed spoken passages, and runs through them in leisurely if dedicated fashion: the title track (which is much bluesier than the hit in Cannon's hands), "Salty Dog" (the best track here), "Gonna Raise a Ruckus Tonight," "Make Me a Pallet on Your Floor," and "Crawdad Hole." The album is almost an audio documentary tour through different corners of Cannon's life and career that, ideally, might've run to several volumes. *—Bruce Eder*

The Complete Works: 1927–1930 / 1989 / Yazoo ♦♦♦♦♦
Complete Works compiles all of the recordings Cannon's Jug Stompers made in the late '20s. Gus Cannon and the Jug Stompers were the definitive jug band and all of their classic tracks, including "Walk Right In," are featured on this essential single-disc collection. *—Thom Owens*

Complete Recorded Works, Vol. 1 (1927–1928) / 1990 / Document ♦♦♦

Complete Recorded Works, Vol. 2 (1929–1930) / 1990 / Document ♦♦♦
Highlighted by Gus Cannon's signature "Walk Right In"—popularized in the early '60s by The Rooftop Singers—the second volume in Document's series is a jumble of prime recordings by Cannon and longtime partner Noah Lewis, collecting both solo sides and various group outings. The first tracks come from the Beale Street Boys, a duo comprising Cannon and vocalist/banjoist Hosea Woods, and are followed by a handful of solo harmonica recordings by Lewis; despite their extracurricular activities, by the time all three come together as Cannon's Jug Stompers they're in peak form, shifting easily from the ribald "Tired Chicken" to the plaintive "Going to Germany." With an ad hoc jug band including guitarist Sleepy John Estes and mandolinist Yank Rachell, Lewis then headlines four more sides before rejoining Cannon for one final session which brought their recording career together to a close. *—Jason Ankeny*

Legendary 1928–30 Recordings / 1994 / JSP ♦♦♦♦

★ **The Best of Cannon's Jug Stompers** / Aug. 14, 2001 / Yazoo ♦♦♦♦♦
When listening to blues singers from another era, many are turned off by the music's rustic simplicity. Just a guy or gal with a guitar, singing in a whiny voice. Compared to your average country blues singer, a band like Cannon's Jug Stompers is downright accessible. Equipped with a guitar, banjo, harmonica, and, of course, a jug, these folks were bona fide noise makers. If the listener happens to be a Deadhead, he or she will be familiar with songs like "Minglewood Blues," "Viola Lee Blues," and "Big Railroad Blues." As one can also divine from the song titles, banjoist Gus Cannon, harmonica player Noah Lewis, and a number of bandmates stick close to the blues. There's a relaxed laziness to pieces like "Wolf River Blues" and "The Rooster's Crowing Blues" that separate the group from noisier, more boisterous bands like the Skillet Lickers. There's a great version of "Walk Right In," a song that became a big hit for the Rooftop Singers in 1963. A disclaimer on the back of the CD case mentions that it is impossible to completely clean up these old recordings. Nonetheless, considering the 70-75-year-old records Yazoo had to work with, the end product sounds pretty darn good. The liner notes include a nice long essay on the history of the band by Don Kent. *The Best of Cannon's Jug Stompers* delivers 70 minutes of traditional jug band music, offering a fine introduction to both the band and the musical style. In other words, it's a classic. *—Ronnie D. Lankford, Jr.*

Captain Beefheart (Don Glen Vliet)

b. Jan. 15, 1941, Glendale, CA
Vocals, Keyboards, Harmonica, Guitar / Experimental Rock, Proto-Punk, Experimental, Psychedelic, Prog-Rock/Art Rock, Blues-Rock

Born Don Glen Vliet, Captain Beefheart was one of modern music's true innovators. The owner of a remarkable four-and-one-half octave vocal range, he employed idiosyncratic rhythms, absurdist lyrics and an unholy alliance of free jazz, Delta blues, latter-day classical music and rock & roll to create a singular body of work virtually unrivalled in its daring and fluid creativity. While he never came even remotely close to mainstream success, Beefheart's impact was incalculable, and his fingerprints were all over punk, new wave and post-rock.

Don Vliet was born January 15, 1941 in Glendale, CA (he changed his name to Van Vliet in the early '60s). At the age of four, his artwork brought him to the attention of Portuguese sculptor Augustinio Rodriguez, and Vliet was declared a child prodigy. In 1954, he was offered a scholarship to study in Europe; his parents declined the proposal, however, and the family instead moved to the Mojave Desert, where the teen was befriended by a young Frank Zappa. In time Vliet taught himself saxophone and harmonica, and joined a pair of local R&B groups, the Omens and the Blackouts.

After a semester at college, he and Zappa moved to Cucamonga, California, where they planned to shoot a film, *Captain Beefheart Meets the Grunt People*. As the project remained in limbo, Zappa finally moved to Los Angeles, where he founded the Mothers of Invention; Van Vliet later returned to the Mojave area, adopted the Beefheart name and formed the first lineup of his backing group the Magic Band with guitarists Alex St. Clair and Doug Moon, bassist Jerry Handley and drummer Paul Blakely in 1964.

In their original incarnation, the Magic Band was a blues-rock outfit which became staples of the teen-dance circuit; they quickly signed to A&M Records, where the success of the single "Diddy Wah Diddy" earned them the opportunity to record a full-length album. Comprised of Van Vliet compositions like "Frying Pan," "Electricity" and "Zig Zag Wanderer," label president Jerry Moss rejected the completed record as "too negative," and a crushed Beefheart went into seclusion. After replacing Moon and Blakely with guitarist Antennae Jimmy Semens (born Jeff Cotton) and drummer John "Drumbo" French, the group (fleshed out by guitarist Ry Cooder) recut the songs in 1967 as *Safe as Milk*.

After producer Bob Krasnow radically remixed 1968's hallucinatory *Strictly Personal* without Beefheart's approval, he again retired. At the same time, however, Zappa formed his own company, Straight Records, and he soon approached Van Vliet with the promise of complete creative control; a deal was struck and after writing 28 songs in a nine-hour frenzy, Beefheart formed the definitive lineup of the Magic Band—made up of Semens, Drumbo, guitarist Zoot Horn Rollo (born Bill Harkleroad), bassist Rockette Morton (Mark Boston) and bass clarinetist the Mascara Snake (Victor Fleming)—to record the seminal 1969 double album *Trout Mask Replica*.

Following 1970's similarly outre *Lick My Decals Off, Baby*, Beefheart adopted an almost commercial sound for the 1972 releases *The Spotlight Kid* and *Clear Spot*. Shortly thereafter, the Magic Band broke off to form Mallard, and Beefheart was dropped by his label, Reprise. After a two-year layoff, he released a pair of pop-blues albums, *Unconditionally Guaranteed* and *Bluejeans & Moonbeams*, with a new, short-lived Magic Band; following another fallow period, 1978's *Shiny Beast (Bat Chain Puller)* marked a return to the eccentricities of his finest work.

After 1982's *Ice Cream for Crow*, Van Vliet again retired from music, this time for good; he returned to the desert, took up residence in a trailer and focused on painting. In 1985, he mounted the first major exhibit of his work, done in an abstract, primitive style reminiscent of Francis Bacon. Like his music, his art won wide acclaim, and some of his paintings sold for as much as $25,000. In the '90s Van Vliet dropped completely from sight when he fell prey to multiple sclerosis; however, releases like 1999's five-disc *Grow Fins* box set and the two-disc anthology *The Dust Blows Forward* maintained his prominence. *—Jason Ankeny*

☆ **Safe as Milk** / 1967 / Buddha ♦♦♦♦♦

Beefheart's first proper studio album is a much more accessible, pop-inflected brand of blues-rock than the efforts that followed in the late '60s—which isn't to say that it's exactly normal and straightforward. Featuring Ry Cooder on guitar, this is blues-rock gone slightly askew, with jagged, fractured rhythms, soulful, twisting vocals from Van Vliet, and more doo wop, soul, straight blues, and folk-rock influences than he would employ on his more avant-garde outings. "Zig Zag Wanderer," "Call on Me," and "Yellow Brick Road" are some of his most enduring and riff-driven songs, although there's plenty of weirdness on tracks like "Electricity" and "Abba Zaba." [Buddha's 1999 reissue of *Safe as Milk* contained restored artwork and seven bonus tracks.] *—Richie Unterberger*

Strictly Personal / 1968 / Blue Thumb ♦♦♦♦

Considered by many to be a substandard effort due to the circumstances of its release (producer Bob Krasnow, the owner of Blue Thumb, the label which debuted with this album, remixed the album while Don Van Vliet and crew were off on a European tour, adding extraneous sound effects like heartbeats and excessive use of psychedelic-era clichés like out-of-phase stereo panning and flanging), 1968's *Strictly Personal* is actually a terrific album, every bit the equal of *Safe As Milk* and *Trout Mask Replica*. Opening with "Ah Feel Like Ahcid," an a cappella blues workout with its roots in Son House's "Death Letter," the brief (barely 35 minutes) album is at the same time simpler and weirder than *Safe As Milk* had been. Working without another songwriter or arranger for the first time, Captain Beefheart strips his idiosyncratic blues down to the bone, with several of the songs (especially "Son of Mirror Man/Mere Man") having little in the way of lyrics or chords beyond the most primeval stomp. Krasnow's unfortunate sound effects and phasing do detract from the album at points, but the strength of the performances, especially those of drummer John French, make his efforts little more than superfluous window dressing. *Strictly Personal* is a fascinating, underrated release. *—Stewart Mason*

☆ **Trout Mask Replica** / 1969 / Reprise ♦♦♦♦♦

Trout Mask Replica is Captain Beefheart's masterpiece, a fascinating, stunningly imaginative work that still sounds like little else in the rock & roll canon. Given total creative control by producer and friend Frank Zappa, Beefheart and his Magic Band rehearsed the material for this 28-song double album for over a year, wedding minimalistic R&B, blues, and garage rock to free jazz and avant-garde experimentalism. Atonal, sometimes singsong melodies; jagged, intricately constructed dual-guitar parts; stuttering, complicated rhythmic interaction—all of these elements float out seemingly at random, often without completely interlocking, while Beefheart groans his surrealist poetry in a throaty Howlin' Wolf growl. The disjointedness is perhaps partly unintentional—reportedly, Beefheart's refusal to wear headphones while recording his vocals caused him to sing in time with studio reverberations, not the actual backing tracks—but by all accounts, the music and arrangements were carefully scripted and notated by the Captain, which makes the results even more remarkable. As one might expect from music so complex and, to many ears, inaccessible, the influence of *Trout Mask Replica* was felt more in spirit than in direct copycatting, as a catalyst rather than a literal musical starting point. However, its inspiring reimagining of what was possible in a rock context laid the groundwork for countless future experiments in rock surrealism, especially during the punk/new wave era. *—Steve Huey*

The Spotlight Kid/Clear Spot / 1972 / Reprise ♦♦♦♦♦

This two-fer compiles two Beefheart albums originally released in 1972. *The Spotlight Kid* was a stripped-down, slide guitar-filled move toward Beefheart's beloved Delta blues, dark in outlook and more traditional in approach, although it was still distinctly Beefheart's take on the blues. *Clear Spot* was more typical of Beefheart's earlier work with the Magic Band, although it too was musically simpler, as well as thematically brighter. *—Steve Huey*

Legendary A&M Sessions / 1984 / A&M ♦♦♦

Before gaining a cult with his avant-garde excursions in the late '60s, Captain Beefheart wielded a much more traditional sort of blues-rock. That's not to say that these two obscure mid-'60s A&M singles (packaged together on this five-song EP, which adds a previously unreleased track from the same era) aren't well worth hearing. The Captain's Howlin' Wolf-like growl led a tough outfit that ranked among the best early American blues-rock groups, and among the few that could reasonably emulate the Rolling Stones' toughness. Produced, unbelievably enough, by future Bread leader David Gates, this reissue includes their regional hit cover of Bo Diddley's "Diddy Wah Diddy." The best track, though, is "Moonchild," their shameless derivation of Howlin' Wolf's "Smokestack Lightning." Featuring wailing harmonica, stomping riffs and adventurous, quasi-psychedelic production, it was actually written by Gates himself. To think that the same man was also responsible for "If" and "Baby I'm A-Want You" blows the mind. *—Richie Unterberger*

The Mirror Man Sessions / Jun. 1, 1999 / Buddha ♦♦♦

The Mirror Man Sessions features the complete remastered contents of *Mirror Man*, albeit in a resequenced running order, and fills out the rest of the CD with a number of bonus tracks taken from additional recordings, both finished and unfinished, made around the same time for what would have been a *double* album titled *It Comes to You in a Plain Brown Wrapper*. As a listening experience, the package will appeal more to those who value the instrumental Beefheart; the *Mirror Man* album is, of course, essentially a 50-plus-minute jam session, containing as it does only four songs, and the bonus tracks—many of which appeared on the One Way label's reissue of *Safe as Milk*—mostly consist of jams and instrumentals which push the boundaries of conventional blues-rock, with a Beefheart vocal tossed in here and there. Some may miss Beefheart's surreal poetry, gruff vocals, and/or free jazz influence, while others may find it fascinating to hear the Magic Band simply letting go and cutting loose. *—Steve Huey*

● **The Dust Blows Forward: An Anthology** / Aug. 17, 1999 / Rhino ♦♦♦♦♦

Leaving alone the obvious condition that Captain Beefheart's numerous experimental albums aren't as prime for a "best-of" treatment as the discographies of most artists are, this is a pretty good overview of career highlights. The two CDs span his 1966 "Diddy Wah Diddy" single to his final album (1982's *Ice Cream for Crow*), each disc weighing in at about 75 minutes. With so much material to draw from (not even counting that mammoth five-CD box set of unreleased stuff), there will be inevitable disagreements among fans as to which songs were selected; there are seven from *Clear Spot*, for instance, but only two from *Safe as Milk*. Every period is sampled, however, and his weakest albums (*Unconditionally Guaranteed* and *Bluejeans & Moonbeams*) are judiciously represented by just one cut each. A few rarities do crop up, including a quite good and bluesy previously unreleased *Clear Spot* outtake ("Little Scratch"), "Hard Workin' Man" (from the soundtrack to *Blue Collar*), and the 1982 instrumental B-side "Light Reflected off the Oceands [sic] of the Moon." There are also little detours from Beefheart's albums for two tracks from 1966 singles and two collaborations with Frank Zappa from Zappa's *Bongo Fury*. It's not for the collector, but it's a decent package for someone who wants to get familiar with the Captain or doesn't need more than a few of his regular albums. Comprehensive notes in a 60-page booklet offer a good straightforward cruise through his oft-confusing history and shifting Magic Band personnel. *—Richie Unterberger*

Grow Fins: Rarities (1965–1982) / 1999 / Revenant ♦♦♦

An unprecedented project in the rock field: a five-CD box set of unreleased material by a cult artist that never had anything close to a chart hit. Of course Captain Beefheart is the ultimate cult artist, and one with a following so rabid (if limited) that the compilation has a wider audience than many would anticipate. Despite the impressive chronological span and variety of demos, live performances, backing tracks, and outtakes, be cautioned that this is *not* a best-of or ad hoc career overview. A good deal of the tracks (some of which have long been available on bootleg) are of slightly substandard or low fidelity, and Beefheart's most significant work is ultimately contained on his numerous official releases. However, this is an important addition to his catalog, and one that many of his fanatics will find essential, though it won't do much to convert the casual fan due to the difficult nature of much of the material. Disc one, with live cuts and demos from 1966-1967 that include a few songs recorded on *Safe as Milk*, is certainly the most interesting and accessible of the quintet. Disc two is more shambling and experimental, with its assortment of 1968 live performances. Disc three is for the hardcore: home-recorded (though in OK fidelity) run-throughs of *Trout Mask Replica* material from 1969, without vocals. Disc four is for the harder core: 12 more minutes of *Trout Mask* home sessions, plus enhanced-CD live performance footage from 1968-1973. CD five is an interesting, erratic assortment of live, radio, demo, and work tape material from 1969-1982, fidelity varying from good to poor. The liner notes are exceptionally detailed, with many first-hand quotes by bandmembers and much historical narrative by frequent Magic Band drummer John French. *—Richie Unterberger*

Grow Fins, Vol. 2: Trout Mask House Sessions / Sep. 21, 1999 / XERIC ♦♦♦♦

This double-LP set is the second of three limited-edition double LPs on XERIC/Table of the Elements which came out in conjunction with the *Grow Fins* CD box set to satisfy the vinyl collectors' market. These four sides of audiophile vinyl packaged in elaborate color gatefold sleeves are surely among the most beautifully designed Captain Beefheart objects in existence. The set features a 24-page booklet and poster, unpublished photos, and extensive liner notes by John French, David Fricke, and John Corbett. The collection is largely instrumental and takes tracks from the legendary *Trout Mask Replica* album, when Don Van Vliet put the band up to the extraordinary task of learning to play the sounds inside his head. While holed up in a California villa, the group developed the extraordinary instrumental vocabulary that makes *Trout Mask Replica* one of the most noteworthy albums in the history of rock, and here that process is documented with alternate versions, outtakes, and general disciplinary studies under the direction of the mad captain. The ideas were no less unhinged prior to the studio sessions that made the extraordinary album, making this album an essential compendium to the album, even if the sound quality is poor in places. Even with repeated listens, however, this still sheds little light on the mystery of one of the most fascinating and bizarre recordings of the '60s, and these rehearsal tapes are equally as compelling as the end results. With all tracks previously unissued, *Grow Fins, Vol. 2: Trout Mask Home Sessions* is as essential as any of the Magic Band's live recordings. *—Skip Jansen*

London 1974 / Aug. 21, 2001 / MPG ✦✦✦

This live recording of Captain Beefheart & the Magic Band was taken from a London date during one of the more fierce peaks of the band's existence, the same period that produced the overlooked classic masterpiece *Clear Spot*. Though the session was intended to produce a live album for Virgin, the release never materialized, though the versions of "Mirror Man" and "Upon the Me Oh My" came out of the 1975 Virgin sampler *V*. Thanks to the obscure Portuguese imprint Movie Play Gold, highlights from the concert made it onto CD at a concise 40 minutes. The disc features nine tracks of full-tilt Magic Band mayhem on "Full Moon Hot Sun," "Sugar Bowl," "Crazy Little Thing," "This Is the Day," "New Electric Ride," as well as older '60s classics like "Abba Zabba" and "Peaches." The CD has exceptional sound quality, while some other live Captain Beefheart from the same period fares a little rough in recording quality. This comes highly recommended as an opportunity to hear the Magic Band at an all-time high. —*Skip Jansen*

The Caravans

f. 1952, Chicago, IL

Group / Traditional Gospel, Black Gospel

During the period stretching from the late '50s to the mid-'60s, the Caravans went unrivaled as the nation's most popular touring gospel group; acclaimed as one of the greatest female acts ever to arrive on the spiritual music front, their fluctuating roster was unparalleled as a launching pad for future superstars—Shirley Caesar, Inez Andrews, Bessie Griffin and James Cleveland were just a few of the ensemble's alumni who later went on to solo fame. The Caravans were formed in Chicago in 1952 by contralto Albertina Walker and other onetime members of the Robert Anderson Singers, among them Ora Lee Hopkins, Elyse Yancey and Nellie Grace Daniels; virtually from the outset, their lineup shifted regularly, but in addition to longtime mainstay Walker, the recordings the group made for the States label between 1952 and 1956 include Griffin, Dorothy Norwood and Cassietta George, who enlisted in 1954. Also present was Cleveland, who not only accompanied the group on piano but also narrated hymns, his relaxed monologues a stark contrast to the fervent group vocals behind him.

By 1956, the Caravans were among the most popular acts in all of gospel music, famed for their uncanny—almost telepathic—teamwork. They moved to Savoy in 1958, where their lineup now included both Andrews and Caesar as well as Dolores Washington; the combination of the young soprano phenom Caesar and the shrieking contralto Andrews was a powerhouse one-two punch, and as the decade drew to a close, the Caravans were the queens of the gospel circuit. Although Andrews had exited by 1962, the group continued to ride high, signing to Vee-Jay to record the LP *Seek Ye the Lord*. Their Vee-Jay tenure proved their most stable, with a consistent roster of Walker, Caesar, George, Washington, Josephine Howard and pianist James Herndon appearing on all of their output for the label. However, when Caesar exited in 1966 to go solo, the Caravans' run at the top ended, and within months only Walker remained. She set about forming a new edition which included future disco diva Loleatta Holloway, but the venture proved short-lived; Caravans reunion concerts, however, were common in the years to follow. —*Jason Ankeny*

The Best of the Caravans / 1977 / Savoy ✦✦✦

This doesn't necessarily contain their best material, only those songs that garnered either chart success or radio airplay during the '50s and early '60s. Like all Savoy releases, there's almost no discographical information, although Walker, Andrews, and Caesar are the artists featured most prominently. —*Ron Wynn*

Soul Salvation / 1978 / Fairway ✦✦✦✦✦

More soul-searing songs led by Cassietta George, Inez Andrews, Albertina Walker and Shirley Caesar. —*Opal Louis Nations*

Seek Ye the Lord/The Soul of the Caravans / Oct. 1993 / Collectables ✦✦✦✦✦

1962's *Seek Ye the Lord* and the following year's *The Soul of the Caravans*, the group's first two LPs for the Vee-Jay label, are compiled on this fine two-fer set featuring the incendiary vocals of Shirley Caesar. It's Caravans leader Albertina Walker, however, who most frequently commands the spotlight, taking over the first five tracks for solo performances; while Caesar chimes in with scorching originals including "Jesus Will Save," "One of These Old Days" and "I'm Going Thru," Cassietta George also assumes control for typically elegant readings of "I'm Ready to Save the Lord," "Lord, Don't Leave Us Now" and "My Religion." —*Jason Ankeny*

Amazing Grace / May 30, 1995 / Charly ✦✦✦✦✦

Best of the Vee-Jay output with Albertina Walker, Shirley Caesar, and Inez Andrews. —*Opal Louis Nations*

Carry Me Home / Oct. 24, 1995 / HOB ✦✦✦✦✦

Fabulous gospel from the golden age. —*Opal Louis Nations*

Jesus & Me: The Very Best of the Caravans / Mar. 3, 1998 / Collectables ✦✦✦

Fine Vee-Jay sides led by one of today's major soloists. —*Opal Louis Nations*

★ **Till I Meet the Lord** / ✦✦✦✦✦

Chuck Carbo

Vocals / New Orleans R&B, R&B

The mellifluous vocal tones of Chuck Carbo was a principal ingredient in the success of the Spiders, the premier R&B vocal group around New Orleans during the '50s. He mounted a strong comeback bid as a smooth solo artist, cutting two albums for Rounder: *Drawers Trouble* in 1993 and 1996's *The Barber Blues*.

The gospel-steeped Carbo (whose actual first name is Hayward) and his brother Chick (real first name: Leonard) shared frontman duties for the Spiders, whose hits for Imperial included the two-sided smash "I Didn't Want to Do It"/"You're the One," a ribald "I'm Slippin' In" in 1954, and "Witchcraft" (later covered by Elvis Presley) the next year. Imperial's main man in the Crescent City, Dave Bartholomew, produced the quintet's 1954-1956 output, as well as writing many of their best numbers (notably a risqué "The

Real Thing"). Carbo cut a few 45s under his own name for Imperial, Rex, and Ace after going solo; Chick waxed 45s of his own for Atlantic, Vee-Jay, and Instant.

Chuck Carbo never stopped performing entirely, although he made his living as a lumber truck driver when gigs got scarce. In 1989, he scored a local hit with his cover of Jeannie & Jimmy Cheatham's "Meet Me With Your Black Drawers On." It was reprised on *Drawers Trouble*, a comeback set reuniting Carbo with pianists Mac "Dr. John" Rebennack and Edward Frank. *The Barber's Blues* ensured Carbo's return to the spotlight with two more Cheatham copyrights and a second-line "Hey, Mardi Gras! (Here I Am)." —*Bill Dahl*

● **Drawers Trouble** / 1993 / Rounder ✦✦✦✦

Veteran New Orleans R&B singer Carbo proves he's a capable front man even without the presence of his '50s vocal group, the Spiders, on this infectious comeback set. With Crescent City vet Edward Frank handling piano and arranging duties, Carbo smoothly intones a mostly original lineup of songs (Jeannie & Jimmy Cheatham's lascivious standard "Meet Me with Your Black Drawers On" being one of the few exceptions). Dr. John contributes his considerable skills on keyboard and guitar to the project. —*Bill Dahl*

The Barber's Blues / 1996 / Rounder ✦✦✦

Ex-Spiders lead Carbo returns with a Rounder encore that eschews Dr. John but brings back Edward Frank as co-producer and pianist. Some of the selections are a little on the hackneyed side (a permanent moratorium on "Everyday I Have the Blues," please!), but Carbo's second line-based "Hey, Mardi Gras! (Here I Am)," the title item, and a easy-on-the-ears reprise of the Cheathams' "Don't Boogie with Your Black Drawers On" hit the spot. —*Bill Dahl*

Carolina Slim (Edward P. Harris)

b. Aug. 22, 1923, Leasburg, NC, *d.* Oct. 22, 1953, Newark, NJ

Guitar / Piedmont Blues, Acoustic Blues

The blues guitarist, best known as Carolina Slim, was born in Leasburg, NC, on August 22, 1923. His real name is Edward P. Harris. He never performed or recorded under that name though, using a number of nicknames instead, including Country Paul, Georgia Pine, Jammin' Jim, and Lazy Slim Jim. Though much about his life is unknown, not even the reason for working under different names, it is said that Harris learned to play the guitar from his father. Blues artists like Lightnin' Hopkins and Blind Boy Fuller influenced the style of music Harris played.

Around 1950, Harris moved to Newark, NJ. It was there that he made his first recording for the Savoy label as Carolina Slim. A year later he was working for the King label and using the name Country Paul. During about a two-year span, Harris recorded 27 songs. Some of the tracks fans can find on albums by Harris are "Worry You off My Mind," "Mama's Boogie," "I'll Never Walk in Your Door," "Wine Head Baby," "Black Chariot Blues," and "Mother Dear Mother."

In 1953, at only 30 years of age, Edward Harris died from a heart attack. Since then, some of his recordings have been released on albums like *Carolina Blues & Boogie* and *The Complete Recorded Works in Chronological Order, 1950-1952*. —*Charlotte Dillon*

● **Complete Recorded Works 1950–1952** / Jun. 2, 1994 / Document ✦✦✦✦

Barbara Carr

b. Jan. 9, 1941, St. Louis, MO

Vocals / Chicago Soul, Retro-Soul, Soul-Blues

Folks only familiar with her more recent work may be mildly surprised that alluring singer Barbara Carr recorded for Chess back in 1966. Carr's "Don't Knock Love" was a delicious slice of Chicago soul arranged by Phil Wright that got dusted off and released by Chess a second time in 1970 when she came back to the company and cut "Think About It Baby" (written, arranged, and produced by St. Louis saxist Oliver Sain). After a lengthy fallow period, Carr returned with an infectious "Good Woman Go Bad" for (presumably) her own Bar-Car logo. Carr also did a credible job on "Messin' with My Mind," a George Jackson number that both Otis Clay and Clarence Carter have also cut. Stan Lewis' Shreveport-based Paula Records later issued an album of Carr material from this era that deftly mixes blues and soul genres. —*Bill Dahl*

● **Good Woman Go Bad** / Oct. 18, 1994 / Paula ✦✦✦✦✦

Barbara Carr had a number of good Chess singles during the late '60s, but she never received the opportunity to record a full album for the label. She didn't make a full-length album until the '90s, when all kinds of underappreciated blues veterans were given a second chance. Carr was one of the more deserving of that breed, as *Good Woman Go Bad* proves. She's a dynamic, energetic vocalist who invests true passion to even mediocre songs. Unfortunately, there are a few too many average tunes on the record, but Carr saves the day with her storming performances. —*Thom Owens*

Footprints on the Ceiling / Mar. 4, 1997 / Ecko ✦✦✦✦

Bone Me Like You Own Me / May 5, 1998 / Ecko ✦✦✦✦

Adults Only Please! Barbara Carr's hot, risqué Southern soul tales are too explicit for the kiddies and will shock most adults. The titles—"Long on Talk, Short on Love," "Bone Me Like You Own Me," and "If the Lord Keeps the Thought of You out of Mind, I'll Keep Your Booty out of My Bed"—speak volumes. On "Livin' a Lie," Carr is miserable because her husband supplies but doesn't satisfy; she's totally off the wall on "Bit Off More Than You Could Chew" and "Show Me No Mercy." Every song is delivered in Barbara's tough-as-nails style; she's ably assisted by a crack production crew. —*Andrew Hamilton*

Leroy Carr

b. Mar. 27, 1905, Nashville, TN, *d.* Apr. 29, 1935, Indianapolis, IN

Vocals, Songwriter, Piano / Piano Blues, Urban Blues

The term "urban blues" is usually applied to post-World War II blues-band music, but one of the forefathers of the genre in its pre-electric format was pianist Leroy Carr. Teamed with the exemplary guitarist Scrapper Blackwell in Indianapolis, Carr became one of the top blues stars of his day, composing and recording almost 200 sides during his short lifetime, including such classics as "How Long, How Long," "Prison Bound Blues," "When the Sun Goes Down," and "Blues Before Sunrise." His blues were expressive and evocative, recorded only with piano and guitar, yet as author Sam Charters has noted, Carr was "a city man" whose singing was never as rough or intense as the country bluesmen's; and as reissue producer Francis Smith put it, "He, perhaps more than any other single artist, was responsible for transforming the rural blues patterns of the '20s into the more city-oriented blues of the '30s."

Born in Nashville, Leroy Carr moved to Indianapolis as a child. While he was still in his teens, he taught himself how to play piano. Carr quit school in his mid-teens, heading out for a life on the road. For the next few years, he would play piano at various parties and dances in the midwest and south. During this time, he held a number of odd jobs—he joined a circus, he was in the army for a while, and he was briefly a bootlegger. In addition to his string of jobs, he was married for a short time.

Carr wandered back toward Indianapolis, where he met guitarist Scrapper Blackwell in 1928. The duo began performing and shortly afterward they were recording for Vocalion, releasing "How Long How Long Blues" before the year was finished. The song was an instant, surprise hit. For the next seven years, Carr and Blackwell would record a number of classic songs for Vocalion, including "Midnight Hour Blues," "Blues Before Sunrise," "Hurry Down Sunshine," "Shady Lane Blues" and many others.

Throughout the early '30s, Carr was one of the most popular bluesmen in America. While his professional career was successful, his personal life was spinning out of control, as he sunk deeper and deeper into alcoholism. His addiction eventually cut his life short—he died in April 1935. Carr left behind a enormous catalog of blues and his influence could be heard throughout successive generation of blues musicians, as evidenced by artists like T-Bone Walker, Otis Spann, and Champion Jack Dupree. *—Jim O'Neal & Stephen Thomas Erlewine*

★ **Blues Before Sunrise** / 1962 / Portrait ♦♦♦♦♦

Despite minimal sound quality, this reissue contains some prime Leroy Carr/Scrapper Blackwell material. They were arguably the greatest piano and guitar duo to emerge in the late '20s and early '30s. You can find these tracks on other import collections, but this was among the first reissues available on a domestic label. *—Ron Wynn*

Singin' the Blues, 1934 / 1973 / Biograph ♦♦♦

The Biograph folks got ahold of original CBS test pressings of this classic blues material to try to improve sound quality possibilities, but as can be imagined with recordings from the early '30s there is a lot missing and the performers sound like they are coming at you from the house around the corner. And the mighty blues licks might have been struck with a toothpick. Of course no matter what the quality of the recording, certain things about these tracks still jump right out, such as the rhythm feel, always easy and unforced, never too fast or too slow, and the equally unstrained but compelling vocals. These tracks are all among the last recorded by Carr and sidekick Scrapper Blackwell; they include sideman appearances by the young Josh White, who went on to a succesful career as a folk blues artist but never recorded anything as down to earth as this again. *—Eugene Chadbourne*

☆ **Naptown Blues (1929–1934)** / 1988 / Yazoo ♦♦♦♦♦

A seminal piano/guitar duo, Leroy Carr was among the most influential early blues singer/pianists, and Scrapper Blackwell was a remarkably fluid guitarist. *—Mark A. Humphrey*

The Piano Blues 1930–1935 / 1990 / Magpie ♦♦♦♦

It's an incomplete collection, but *1930-1935* collects the great majority of Leroy Carr and Scrapper Blackwell's duets from the early '30s and provides a good introduction to one of the seminal Chicago blues guitar and piano duos. *—Thom Owens*

Complete Recorded Works, Vol. 1 (1928–1929) / 1992 / Document ♦♦♦

Completists, specialists and academics take note—Document's *Complete Recorded Works, Vol. 1 (1928-1929)* offers an exhaustive overview of Leroy Carr's early recordings. Less dedicated listeners will probably find the long running time, exacting chronological sequencing, poor fidelity (all cuts are transferred from original acetates and 78s), and number of performances a bit off-putting, even though the serious blues listener will find all these factors to be positive. *—Thom Owens*

The Piano Blues, Vol. 2 / 1992 / Magpie ♦♦♦

Complete Recorded Works, Vol. 2 (1929–1930) / 1992 / Document ♦♦♦

Southbound Blues / 1994 / Drive ♦♦♦

Complete Recorded Works, Vol. 3 (1930–1932) / 1994 / Document ♦♦♦

Complete Recorded Works, Vol. 3 (1930-1932) continues Document's exhaustive overview of Leroy Carr's recordings for Vocalion between 1928 and his death in 1935. Though Carr produced a few classics during the year and a half covered by this volume (including "Alabama Women Blues" and "New How Long How Long Blues, Pt. 2"), the vast majority of listeners will have trouble working through this material, much of which sounds very similar. Still, it's the only way to hear the complete work of this important bluesman, which is more than enough for serious blues fans. *—Thom Owens*

Complete Recorded Works, Vol. 4 (1932–34) / Jan. 10, 1996 / Document ♦♦♦♦♦

Complete Recorded Works, Vol. 5 (1934) / Jan. 10, 1996 / Document ♦♦♦♦

Complete Recorded Works, Vol. 6 (1934–35) / Jan. 10, 1996 / Document ♦♦♦♦

Unissued Test Pressings & Alternate Takes (1934–37) / Sep. 10, 1996 / Document ♦♦♦♦

How Long Blues 1928–1935 / Feb. 1998 / EPM Musique ♦♦♦

American Blues Legend / Jul. 1, 1999 / Charly ♦♦♦♦♦

Leroy Carr remains one of the shadowy figures of the blues; enormously successful but with a musical cannonade that has not worn well with the intervening decades, classically doomed and dead at an early age from the evils of alcohol, Carr should actually have more of a rep in blues history than he currently maintains. Reissues of his classic work are not as plentiful as one would think, and this one is one of the best. With over an hour of play time packed into 20 tracks, this highlights Carr—usually in the company of guitar partner Scrapper Blackwell—in a collection of his best-known tunes like "How Long Has That Evening Train Been Gone," "Blues Before Sunrise," "When the Sun Goes Down," and "Mean Mistreater Mama." Josh White adds guitar work to five tracks, including "It's Too Short," "Shining Pistol," and "Hustler's Blues." A great little collection to start with. *—Cub Koda*

Leroy Carr & Scrapper Blackwell (1929–1935) / 2000 / Story of the Blues ♦♦♦

Sister Wynona Carr

b. Aug. 23, 1924, Cleveland, OH, **d.** May 12, 1976, Cleveland, OH

Vocals / Traditional Gospel, Jump Blues, Black Gospel, R&B

Though largely unrecognized during her own lifetime, singer and composer Sister Wynona Carr was among the truly pioneering artists of gospel's golden era; while her music—sophisticated and sensual, distinguished by lyrics of rare metaphorical depth and a progressive sound drawing heavily on jazz and blues—was simply too radical for contemporary listeners, in hindsight she stands as one of the great innovators of her day. Born in Cleveland, Ohio on August 23, 1924, Carr began learning piano at the age of eight; at 13, she entered the Cleveland Music College to study voice, harmony and arranging, and a short time later began performing in Baptist churches across the region. In 1944, she relocated to Detroit to direct a local choir, and in the months to follow also formed her own group, the Carr Singers, to tour the Midwest and the South.

While touring with the Wilson Jubilee Singers, an offshoot of Cleveland's renowned Wings Over Jordan Choir, Carr caught the attention of the Pilgrim Travelers' J.W. Alexander, who was so impressed by her talents that he funded her first demo recording and sent it to Specialty Records founder Art Rupe. The label quickly snapped her up, and in early 1949 Carr traveled to Los Angeles to record her first session, backed by a jump combo helmed by ace session pianist Austin McCoy. Her debut 78, pairing the swinging "Each Day" with the torch-like ballad "Lord Jesus," served as an immediate indication of her versatility; produced in the vein of Sister Rosetta Tharpe's recordings of the era, Rupe sought to further emphasize the comparisons between the two vocalists by appending "Sister" to Carr's name, a ploy which reportedly made her bristle.

Carr's next studio date followed in Philadelphia later in 1949; a revolutionary session, it yielded "I'm a Pilgrim Traveler," a reworking of the blues standard "St. James Infirmary," as well as "I Heard the News (Jesus Is Coming Again)," which updated the 1948 Roy Brown and Wynonie Harris hit "Good Rockin' Tonight." Other material, like the Carr original "Our Father," suggested a strong jazz influence; however, while all of the tracks recorded during the session promised to push the singer into new stylistic directions, Rupe apparently felt the songs were all too daring, and none of them were released. Carr's next return to the studio, in 1950, was far more traditional, and included a new rendition of "Our Father," recorded as a duet with Brother Joe May; it too went unreleased, although the song was later covered as a May solo side as well as in a version by the Five Blind Boys of Mississippi.

Despite all of the frustration and setbacks, Carr forged on; she toured relentlessly, but did not go back into the studio until mid-1952. With "The Ball Game," a vividly metaphorical tale of a showdown between Jesus and Satan, she finally scored a major gospel hit, yet her career continued to flounder—another two years passed prior to her next Specialty session, recorded in Detroit (where she was serving as choir director at the New Bethel Baptist Church under the Rev. C.L. Franklin). Although she recorded rarely, Carr nevertheless remained a highly prolific songwriter, composing poetic, topical material often inspired by headlines of the day; she cut dozens of demos for Specialty, and ironically enough earned more money from sales of her sheet music than from her actual recordings.

After successfully touring white nightclubs in 1954 with Sister Rosetta Tharpe and Marie Knight, Carr finally broke her ties with gospel to pursue a career singing R&B; in 1957, she scored with the hit ballad "Should I Ever Love Again," but again fate was against her—at the same time the record was rising on the chart, she was stricken with tuberculosis, and spent the next two years on the sidelines, convalescing at her parents' home. A number of booking agencies sought Carr out, but she was simply too ill to perform; her career never recovered from the loss of momentum, and after leaving Specialty in 1959 she briefly signed to Reprise before spending the remainder of the '60s performing on the Cleveland supper club circuit. As the '70s dawned, Carr went into seclusion; her health continued to decline, and she died on May 12, 1976. *—Jason Ankeny*

Jump Jack Jump! / 1955 / Specialty ♦♦♦♦♦

This 24-track set covers Carr's R&B tunes, with many unissued but fine tunes such as "If These Walls Could Speak," "Finders Keepers," and "Weather Man" finally getting out of the vault. The CD also includes her trademark upbeat, sassy songs, "Jump Jack Jump," "Boppity Bop (Boogity Boop)," "Ding Dong Daddy" and "Nursery Rhyme Rock." Thematic variety wasn't her label's strong suit when it came to material, and they might have done better with more numbers like "Please Mr. Jailer" and "It's Raining Outside" and a few less boogies and jump pieces. *—Ron Wynn*

★ **Dragnet for Jesus** / 1992 / Specialty ♦♦♦♦♦

A must for every fan of soul gospel, *Dragnet for Jesus* compiles all of the gospel songs—many (previously) unreleased—that Wynona Carr recorded for the Specialty label. Spanning 1949 to1954, are many of Carr's original compositions including "I'm a Pilgrim Traveler" and "Nobody But Jesus," as well as her efforts at incorporating pop culture into God's message with the sports-themed "15 Rounds for Jesus" and her most-recognized song, "the Ball Game." The title track is based around a popular TV show of the time, *Dragnet*, opening with a detective office scene. But don't imagine that Carr was making light of, or trying to secularize, the message of salvation. One listen to her earnest, soulful voice and there's no doubt that the woman's heart was in it. Imagine the smoke-and-scotch hoarse edge of Janis Joplin's voice, pour Aretha Franklin's soulful inflections all over it, and you're close to the powerful delivery of Wynona Carr. Carr was, in fact, the gospel choir director of Rev. C.L. Franklin's church (Aretha's father) when Aretha was young. Most of the song's feature a quartet of piano, bass, drums, and either organ or guitar, with Carr usually on the piano. At the end of the disc is a bonus of two demos and a live recording of her leading the previously mentioned church choir in a stunning, hair-raising arrangement of "Our Father." With her out-of-this-world sultry voice, Carr incorporated blues and jazz elements and popular themes, yet she never really took off with the gospel audiences. Regardless, she remains one of the leading ladies of gospel. *—Joslyn Layne*

Chubby Carrier (Roy Carrier Jr.)

Vocals, Accordion / Contemporary Blues, Zydeco

The traditional two-steps and blues-inspired rhythms of zydeco are transformed into the modern dance-inspiring music of Roy "Chubby" Carrier Jr. and his group, the Bayou Swamp Band. While the *Chicago Tribune* referred to Carrier as "one of the finer standard bearers of the classic zydeco sound among the new generation of Louisiana bands," the *Worcester Telegram and Gazette* praised Carrier for his "unbridled enthusiasm and the ability to make a party happen whether he's playing for five people or five hundred" and the *Atlanta Daily News* wrote that Carrier "knows how to let the good times roll with the power and precision of a seasoned musician."

Carrier hails from one of zydeco's most important families. His grandfather was one of zydeco's first musicians. His father, Roy Carrier Sr. has balanced his work on an oil rig with performances with his own band. Several of his cousins toured and recorded as the Carrier Brothers.

Taught the accordion by his father, Carrier made his debut with his father's band at the age of 12. For most of his teens, however, he played drums in the band, taking over the accordion when his father's work prevented him from playing with the group.

After playing accordion in a series of high school bands, Carrier accepted an invitation to play the frottoir (washboard) for Terrance Simien & the Mallet Playboys in 1986. He remained with the band until 1989 when he left to form his own group with his brothers, Troy "Dikki Du" Carrier and Kevin Carrier, sharing washboard responsibilities. The original band, which also included lead guitarist David LeJeune and bassist Rodney Dural, recorded their debut album, *Go Zydeco Go*, shortly after being formed. Their first nationally distributed album, *Boogie Woogie Zydeco*, followed in 1991. Carrier's breakthrough came with his third album, *Dance All Night*. Released in 1993, the album received a *Living Blues* critics award as best zydeco album of the year. Carrier's fourth album, *Who Stole the Hot Sauce*, featured impressive renditions of War's "The Cisco Kid" and Pete Townshend's "Squeeze Box." *—Craig Harris*

★ **Boogie Woogie Zydeco** / 1991 / Flying Fish ♦♦♦♦♦

After building a resumé in zydeco circles playing with Terrance Simien & the Mallet Playboys, singer/accordion player Chubby Carrier struck out on his own in 1990 and soon signed with the Chicago-based Flying Fish label as a solo artist. *Boogie Woogie Zydeco* may have been recorded in the Chicago suburb of Evanston, but sweaty, exuberant originals like "Allons Dancez," "Hey Barbariba" and "Bernadette" are pure Louisiana. Carrier slows down the tempo for the '60s-type soul numbers "Be Fair to the People" and "Sherrie," both of which are so appealing that they make one wish he embraced slower tempos more often. On the whole, however, the Louisiana native favors zydeco that is unrelenting in its energy. Zydeco fans should make a point of hunting for this CD. *—Alex Henderson*

Dance All Night / 1993 / Blind Pig ♦♦♦♦

Who Stole the Hot Sauce? / 1996 / Blind Pig ♦♦♦♦♦

It's Party Time / 1999 / Right Click ♦♦♦

Chubby Carrier and the Bayou Swamp Band's album *It's Party Time!* offers a good amount of variety. The album opens up with "Bernadette," which is a traditional number with a classic zydeco sound. This album celebrates the way that the Cajuns partied years back, gathering friends and family for house parties. "They Wanna Party Now" adds a unique sound to the guitar work with the use of a voice box. It also uses a great bass riff on the uptempo beat of the tune. On "Funky BSB" the listener is treated to some of Chubby Carrier's signature swamp-funk sound. The listener is going to want to get up and cut a rug on this jazzy boogie tune. The title track "It's Party Time" kicks off with a fantastic lead guitar intro, then moves into a zydeco-flavored "Soul Train." As this tune builds, an urge to shout "Come on everybody climb aboard the zydeco train, it's party time!" might rise—a symptom of the Chubby Carrier and the Bayou Swamp Band fever. "I Don't Want to Leave You" is a harmonious, romantic number. Overall this is a great party album with funk and variety. It does stray from the traditional Cajun roots music, moving into the swamp-funk sound and beyond. Some may be surprised on how far from their roots the band has wandered while maintaining their quality party style. A search for traditional Cajun music should lead one to other sources, but for listeners looking for some refreshingly new music from Louisiana by musicians cranking out their own, original sound, then it would be safe to say *It's Party Time*. *—Larry Belanger*

Too Hot to Handle / Mar. 23, 1999 / Louisiana Red Hot ♦♦♦

This is a disc that shows great promise—this man and his band can stir it up and hit a groove that is incandescent. One problem, though, is that this live disc lacks the fire and energy of their live performances. Part of that missing energy is the sound, which seems dull—almost dead. When this band plays live, the sound is raw and alive, and everyone, including the lame and the dead, rise up and dance. As a band, they are tight and hold together well, each member is more than capable on his instrument and the sum is greater than the parts would seem to be capable of adding up to. They have one of the best bass players heard in a long time—he is not only good but incredibly inventive, ranking up there with players such as Victor Wooten and Ron Carter. On this disc he never really gets a chance to shine. Chubby has a way of picking songs that showcase the band's strengths; "Fire on the Mountain" is an extended dub version that outshines the other versions, which shows the versatility of this band in mixing up the tempos. Chubby is writing some good new songs he has three on this disc, and they fit right into the zydeco pattern, yet at the same time add some new wrinkles. Listen to and catch the time stops, horn arrangements and wah-wah guitar of "Wasting Time." This is truly a new level of "swamp funk" that is going to start rising from the mists of the bayous and taking the country by insidious invasion. Overall, the disc cooks and shows off a band that is definitely on the rise. Dancing is mandatory. *—Bob Gottlieb*

Roy Carrier

Accordion / Zydeco

While not as well-known as his son Chubby, accordionist Roy Carrier enjoyed a successful zydeco career in his own right. A native of Lawtell, Louisiana, he learned to play in the traditional Cajun style from his own father, and later formed his own band which he fronted when not working as an offshore oil-driller or operating his own small farm. At the age of 12, Chubby Carrier joined the band as a drummer, later going on to significant success as a solo performer; Roy continued on as a popular regional attraction, eventually opening his own Lawtell area zydeco club, the Offshore Lounge. During the late '80s, he signed to the Lanor Records label, scoring a pair of local hits with "I Found My Woman Doing the Zydeco" and "I'm Coming Home to Stay"; in 1991 he recorded *The Soulful Side of Zydeco* (a split release with Joe Walker), followed in 1995 by *Zydeco Strokin'*. *—Jason Ankeny*

Soulful Side of Zydeco / Nov. 21, 1995 / Zane ♦♦♦♦

Zydeco Strokin' / Nov. 1995 / Paula ♦♦♦

● **At His Best** / Feb. 20, 1996 / Zane ♦♦♦♦

At His Best collects many of Roy Carrier's greatest songs, even if they're not necessarily in their original versions. Nevertheless, these are really good versions of such staples as "You Better Watch Out," "Strokin'," "She's Naked," and "Leaving Lawtell," making it an excellent introduction to the zydeco accordionist. *—Thom Owens*

Karen Carroll

b. Jan. 30, 1958, Chicago, IL

Vocals / Modern Electric Chicago Blues, Soul-Blues, Contemporary Blues, Blues-Rock

Blues singer Karen Carroll was seemingly destined for a career in music: not only was her mother Jeanne Carroll a blues and jazz vocalist as well, but her godparents were guitarist George Freeman and singer Bonnie Lee. Born in Chicago on January 30, 1958, Carroll started performing at the age of nine, joining her mother's band as a guitarist five years later; at 18 she struck out on her own, cutting her teeth in tiny South Side blues joints and developing a deep vocal style heavily influenced by jazz phrasing as well as the intensity of gospel. She made her recorded debut on Carey Bell's 1984 outing *Son of a Gun*, followed by the 1989 Eddie Lusk LP *Professor Strut*; Carroll made her solo debut with 1995's *Had My Fun*, returning two years later with *Talk to the Hand*. *—Jason Ankeny*

● **Had My Fun** / Oct. 3, 1995 / Delmark ♦♦♦♦

Karen Carroll has plenty of opportunity to strut her stuff on her debut, *Had My Fun*. Unlike many contemporary blues albums, which are highly polished blasts of blues-rock, *Had My Fun* takes its time. Many of the songs are torchy slow blues or down-and-dirty Chicago blues—either way, they sound natural, never forced. That's appropriate, since Carroll sings like a natural, caressing the ballads and growling the nastier numbers. Best of all, there's actual grit in the production—four of the songs were recorded live—and that allows Carroll to achieve her full potential on this impressive debut. *—Thom Owens*

Talk to the Hand / 1997 / Delmark ♦♦♦

While her debut *Had My Fun* featured Carroll's thunderous, gospel-influenced vocals in a live setting, this studio recording also spotlights her burgeoning songwriting skills. *—Jason Ankeny*

Carter Brothers

Group / Electric Blues, Soul-Blues, Soul

This electric blues act with a soul bent recorded for Jewel Records, among other labels. Roman Carter (lead vocals, bass), Albert Carter (guitar), and Jerry Carter (vocals, piano) came from Garland, AL, and began recording in 1964 for producer/songwriter Duke Coleman's local label. Stan Lewis' Jewel Records licensed a pair of their singles, of which "Southern Country Boy" got to number 21 on the R&B charts nationally. They never cut an album, but before splitting up in 1967 (when Albert and Jerry Carter were said to have been drafted) the trio recorded more than a dozen single sides, which might make a great album someday. Lead singer Roman Carter, who also cut solo singles for Jewel, endured as a solo performer over the next 30 years and was given an award as Best Male Blues Vocalist at the Fifth Annual Real Blues Awards, sponsored by *Real Blues* magazine in 1999. *—Bruce Eder*

● **Blues on Tour: 1965-1969** / Jun. 26, 2002 / West Side ♦♦♦♦

Bo Carter (Armenter Chatmon)

b. Mar. 21, 1893, Bolton, MS, **d.** Sep. 21, 1964, Memphis, TN

Vocals, Guitar, Clarinet, Bass, Banjo / Dirty Blues, Country Blues, Acoustic Blues

Bo Carter (Armenter "Bo" Chatmon) had an unequaled capacity for creating sexual metaphors in his songs, specializing in such ribald imagery as "Banana in Your Fruit Basket," "Pin in Your Cushion," and "Your Biscuits Are Big Enough for Me." One of the most popular bluesmen of the '30s, he recorded enough material for several reissue albums, and he was quite an original guitar picker, or else three of those albums wouldn't have been released by Yazoo. (Carter employed a number of different keys and tunings on his records, most of which were solo vocal and guitar performances.) Carter's facility extended beyond the risqué business to more serious blues themes, and he was also the first to record the standard "Corrine Corrina" (1928). Bo and his brothers Lonnie and Sam Chatmon also recorded as members of the Mississippi Sheiks with singer/guitarist Walter Vinson. *—Jim O'Neal*

Bo Carter, Vols. 1-5 (1928–1940) / 1928-1940 / Document ✦✦✦

Document's five-disc series—sold individually, not as a package—cover everything Bo Carter recorded between 1928-1940. Although there is plenty of fine music on these discs, only a historian or a completist needs to listen to the entire series—any of Carter's single-disc collections give a better, more concise overview of his music. However, musicologists and diehard fans will find each of the five essential. *—Stephen Thomas Erlewine*

● **Greatest Hits, 1930–1940** / Feb. 1970 / Yazoo ✦✦✦✦✦

With mostly solo selections by Carter, plus a couple of Mississippi Sheiks songs, it features very fine and distinctive country blues guitar playing and singing. Most of the songs are of the double entendre variety—a possible reason why he's not as well-known as he deserves to be, since some blues researchers did not deem his material worthy. As with most Yazoo releases, the liner notes include various guitar tunings and chord progressions for each song—fascinating for guitarists. *—George Bedard*

Twist It, Babe / 1974 / Yazoo ✦✦✦✦

Singer/guitarist Bo Chatmon lived something of a double musical life. One had him playing country blues with the Mississippi Sheiks, one of the most popular African-American string bands of the '20s and '30s, while, as Bo Carter, he became a highly successful solo performer, peddling his popular brand of double entendre blues. The first of two Yazoo Bo Carter anthologies (the companion to *Banana in Your Fruit Basket*), *Twist It, Babe* collects sides the guitarist recorded between 1931 and 1938. Carter himself, though he may lack significant spark as a performer, remains a competent fingerpicker, with a smooth, pleasant singing tone. Combined with relatively clean fidelity, the sentiments of his songs have been preserved, loud and clear. Much of the material here is comprised of Carter's one-dimensional sexual metaphors (the title track, "Doubled in a Knot," "Let Me Roll Your Lemon," etc.). Yet while the concerns on *Twist It, Babe* are largely the same ones that occupied Carter throughout the greater part of his career, they are often less blatant. While "Twist It, Babe" repeats a simple vocal pattern over some graceful guitar work with little variation, songs like "Some Day," "The Law Gonna Step on You," and "I Get the Blues" reveal more complex melodies and greater subtlety in dealing with his subject matter. "Rolling Blues" is a fine version of Jim Jackson's hit "Kansas City Blues" (a song also reworked by Charlie Patton as "Going to Move to Alabama"). "Policy Man Blues" even manages to break the mold with its tale of a familiar roustabout, prone to losing his earnings in card games. *Twist It, Babe* presents an accurate portrait of Carter and is a more well-rounded collection than its companion volume. *—Nathan Bush*

Banana in Your Fruit Basket / 1978 / Yazoo ✦✦✦✦

Bo Carter is the alias for singer/guitarist Bo Chatmon, a member of the famous Chatmon family from Mississippi (which produced 13 musically capable children). Notorious for his double entendre blues, Carter based his songs around sexual metaphors and the results were, unsurprisingly, widely popular. If there were such a thing as parental warning stickers in the '30s, they would have been applied liberally to Carter's releases. On *Banana in Your Fruit Basket* (the companion to *Twist It Baby*), Yazoo brings together 14 more Carter sides from the '30s. A cursory glance at track titles alone tells a great deal: "Mashing That Thing," "Don't Mash My Digger So Deep," "Pin in Your Cushion," "My Pencil Won't Write Anymore." The themes in Carter's music were certainly pervasive in the country blues of the period, but they were rarely as explicit. Whereas one singer might ask "Baby, where'd you stay last night? You got the hair all tangled and you ain't talkin' right" (a stock blues verse), few would ask the same woman "Baby, what kind of scent is that?" when she walks through the door. Often, Carter's metaphors are so thin that the results have little value beyond their novelty. Musically, Carter has a relaxed, clear, and fairly indistinct singing style and a fluid, fingerpicking guitar attack to match it. While *Banana in Your Fruit Basket* paints an accurate picture of Bo Chatmon's alter ego, the music is very much a product of its time. Giving insight into what people appreciated in their entertainment, it also feels like proof that not much has changed. *—Nathan Bush*

Bo Carter, Vol. 1 (1928–1931) / 1991 / Document ✦✦✦

Bo Carter, Vol. 2 (1931–1934) / 1991 / Document ✦✦✦

Here are 22 songs (with three still missing) cut by Carter, solo with guitar or with Lonnie Chatmon on fiddle, over a three-year period. Document has had unusual luck with the quality on this release, as there's relatively little surface noise on much of it. This helps bring out the richness, dexterity, and playfulness of Carter's playing, as well as the expressiveness of his voice in extraordinary detail. Perhaps the most surprising element of these sides are the two unissued OKeh tracks from 1931, "The Law Is Gonna Step On You" and "Pig Meat Is What I Crave," which are the equal of anything that the label did put out from those same sessions, and show Carter's playing to great advantage and in extraordinarily high-quality sound. His music was probably closest in spirit to the early work of Tampa Red and Georgia Tom Dorsey, with its mixture of double entendre lyrics and hokum influences. The three-year gap in Carter's recordings, caused by the crunch that hit the blues business with the Great Depression, show him re-emerging at the end (for Bluebird) with a more sophisticated sound, less stripped-down than his early sides but just as playful in its risqué way ("Banana In Your Fruit Basket," etc.). *—Bruce Eder*

Bo Carter, Vol. 3 (1934–1936) / 1991 / Document ✦✦✦

Bo Carter, Vol. 4 (1936–1938) / 1991 / Document ✦✦✦

Bo Carter, Vol. 5 (1938–1940) / 1991 / Document ✦✦✦

Bo Carter: The Essential / Aug. 7, 2001 / Classic Blues ✦✦✦✦

Goree Carter

b. Dec. 31, 1930, Houston, TX, **d.** Dec. 29, 1990, Houston, TX

Vocals, Guitar / Electric Texas Blues

T-Bone Walker inspired a legion of young Texas blues guitarists during the years following World War II with his elegant electrified riffs and fat chords. Among his legion of disciples was Houston's Goree Carter, whose big break came when Solomon Kahal signed him to Houston's Freedom Records circa 1949.

Carter's best-known waxing, the torrid "Rock Awhile" (billed to Goree Carter & His Hepcats) emerged not long thereafter, its sizzling opening lick sounding quite a bit like primordial Chuck Berry. Freedom issued plenty of Carter platters over the next few years, and he later recorded for Imperial/Bayou, Sittin' in With, Coral, Jade, and Modern without denting the national charts. Eventually, he left music behind altogether. *—Bill Dahl*

● **Unsung Hero** / 1992 / Collectables ✦✦✦✦

Houston guitarist Goree Carter's slashing late-'40s/early-'50s sides for Freedom display a strong T-Bone Walker influence, though his best-known effort, the storming "Rock Awhile," kicks a lot harder than Walker's elegant output. These 14 sides are fine examples of the horn-leavened Lone Star sound of the early '50s; while derivative, Carter was a very competent axe-handler. *—Bill Dahl*

Joe Carter

b. Nov. 6, 1927, Midland, GA

Slide Guitar, Vocals / Slide Guitar Blues, Harmonica Blues, Blues-Rock, Electric Chicago Blues

One of the truly great unsung heroes of the Chicago club scene of the '50s, Joe Carter was a slide-playing twin disciple of Elmore James and Muddy Waters. Born in Georgia, Carter came under the early tutelage of local player Lee Willis, who showed the youngster various tunings and how to use a thumb pick. Arriving in Chicago by 1952, Joe made a beeline to the area's club scene to see his idols Muddy Waters and Elmore James. It was Muddy who lent Carter the money to purchase his first electric guitar. Shortly thereafter, Joe started up his first group with guitarist Smokey Smothers and Lester Davenport on harmonica, quickly establishing himself as a club favorite throughout Chicago. Sadly, Carter never recorded with this group—or any other configuration—during his heyday. A contract with Cobra Records was offered (with a young Freddie King being added in the studio to his regular group), but Joe declined as he felt the money would in no way equal what he was pulling down in club work. A true shame and a moment of blues history forever lost as Carter didn't end up being documented until he returned to active playing in the '70s, recording his lone album for the Barrelhouse label in 1976. The intervening years hadn't changed his approach one bit, still full of biting guitar and hoarse, shouted vocals over a bedrock simple foundation. The hoarseness of the vocals, unfortunately, were a portent of the future, as Carter retired from playing in the '80s after a bout with throat cancer. Joe Carter clearly worked in the mode of Elmore and Muddy—seldom contributing much in the way of original material—but it was all delivered with a passion that was 100 percent genuine, easily making him an emblematic figure of '50s-style Chicago blues in its heyday. *—Cub Koda*

● **Mean & Evil Blues** / Jan. 1978 / Barrelhouse ✦✦✦✦✦

Joe Carter's lone recorded effort for the tiny Barrelhouse label remains to this day one of the great lost blues albums of the '70s, if not at the top of the list. On the surface, its content could not be more at odds with the standard blues album of that decade; a two guitars-drums-no bass combo running through a set of Chicago staples largely plucked from the repertoires of Muddy Waters and Elmore James, minus any modern embellishments, recorded in studio environs that could best be described as crude. But the intensity and emotional commitment radiates off of Carter like laser beams on every single track, making the starkness of this album all the more appealing. With a guitar tone from his massive Epiphone hollow body that cuts like a knife coupled with a voice that wavers between phlegmatic, stentorian and utterly agonized (the second verse of "Treat Me the Way You Do"), Carter creates a mood on these sides so loaded with ambience that the listener is immediately sucked in from beginning to end. As real as any Hound Dog Taylor Alligator album of the period minus the good time slant, this is eerie, late-night, juke-joint music of the highest order. Currently MIA on compact disc (as of press time), its non-appearance is one of the great tragedies of the reissue field, considering the dearth of lesser albums from this period being re-released. Needless to say, its appearance in any form is a worthwhile addition to any blues collection. *—Cub Koda*

Original Chicago Blues / 1982 / JSP ✦✦✦

Tommy Castro

b. 1955, San Jose, CA

Slide Guitar / Contemporary Blues, Blues-Rock, Soul-Blues

According to all the press and hype and hoopla, Tommy Castro is pegged as the next big star of the blues. Long a favorite among Bay Area music fans, Castro—in the space of two album releases—has taken his music around the world and back again with a sheaf of praise from critics and old-time blues musicians alike. His music is a combination of soul-inflected rockers with the occasional slow blues or shuffle thrown into the mix to keep it honest. His vocals are laidback and always a hair behind the beat, while his scorching guitar tone is Stevie Ray Stratocaster-approved. Crossover success does not seem out of the question.

Born and raised in San Jose, California, Castro started playing guitar at the tender age of ten. Initially inspired by Mike Bloomfield, Eric Clapton and Elvin Bishop, he started the inevitable journey into the roots of his heroes and discovered and quickly became enamored of B.B. King, Buddy Guy, Elmore James, Muddy Waters and Freddie King. His vocal styling came from constant listening to Ray Charles, Wilson Pickett, James Brown and Otis Redding. After playing with numerous Bay Area groups honing his chops, he landed a gig playing guitar for the San Francisco band the Dynatones, who were then signed to Warner Brothers. The two-year stint augured well for Castro, playing to the biggest crowds he had seen up to that point and backing artists as diverse as Carla Thomas and Albert King.

Returning to San Francisco, Castro formed his own group and released his first self-produced album in 1993, *No Foolin'*, on the dime-sized Saloon label. That same year also saw him winning the Bay Area Music Award for best club band, an honor he duplicated the following year. In 1997, he won "Bammies" for "Outstanding Blues Musician" and for "Outstanding Blues Album" for his debut release on Blind Pig Records, *Exception to the Rule*. Also in 1997 Castro and his band began a three year stint working as the house band on NBC's *Comedy Showcase*, which aired after *Saturday Night Live*. *Live at the Fillmore* was released in early 2000, and with everyone from industry insiders to B.B. King singing his praises, Castro appeared to be headed for bigger and better things. It was not to be however, as in 2001 he left Blind Pig Records and recorded *Guilty of Love* for the small 33rd Street label. Blind Pig closed the books on their association with Castro in 2002 by releasing the career retrospective *The Essential Tommy Castro*. *—Cub Koda*

Exception to the Rule / 1995 / Blind Pig ♦♦♦

Can't Keep a Good Man Down / May 5, 1997 / Blind Pig ♦♦♦♦

There's a clean San Francisco sheen to Tommy Castro's second album for Blind Pig, and it's not just the glossy production work of Jim Gaines (Santana, Huey Lewis and Stevie Ray Vaughan) that's responsible for it. Castro and his band have long been local favorites of the Bay area bar crowd, and his blues-rock/soul-pop synthesis with the occasional slow blues thrown in makes him another young contender for the yuppie throne of modern bluesdom. From the opening rock strut of "Can't Keep a Good Man Down" and "You Knew the Job Was Dangerous," Castro lays down lazy, in-the-pocket vocals (the only time he hits scream territory is on the closer, Albert King's "Can't You See What You're Doing to Me") pitted against in your face guitar blasts à la Stevie Ray Vaughan. These Texas-approved Stratocaster tones reach their apex on a five-minute-plus workout of Buddy Guy's "My Time After Awhile," where Castro literally wrenches every textbook tone and volume setting out of his instrument and makes this perhaps the most blues-approved moment of the set. A large quotient of varied originals abound, and the soulful strut of "I Want to Show You," "Take the Highway Down" and the funk jive of "High on the Hog" and "You Gotta Do What You Gotta Do" play off against the simplistic shuffle "You Only Go Around Once" and the lowdown blues instrumental "Hycodan," an atmospheric duet between Castro's guitar and saxophonist Keith Crossan's late-night mood blowing. But the real blues moments are few and far between here—this is blues-rock, no doubt about it, and the end result is music with crossover written all over it. If Huey Lewis and the News were to cut a blues album with a hotter guitar player in tow, it might end up sounding very much like this. *—Cub Koda*

Right as Rain / Feb. 9, 1999 / Blind Pig ♦♦♦♦

Young guitar slinger Tommy Castro came back with his third Blind Pig album in early 1999, again produced by veteran Jim Gaines (Stevie Ray, Santana, Huey Lewis, etc.), and it's another bid for mainstream blues-rock success. From the opening notes of the kickoff tune, "Lucky In Love," Castro is in the driver's seat with a set of blues-rock originals that give him plenty of room to spray his Stevie Ray-inspired guitar licks in between his soul-man vocals. Dr. John makes guest keyboard appearances on "I've Got to Love Somebody's Baby" and "Don't Turn Your Heater Down," the latter also sporting a guest vocal turn from Delbert McClinton. An off-the-wall cover choice is "Chairman of the Board," sandwiched in between solid originals like the ballad "Just a Man" and the funky "My Kind of Woman." There isn't much hard blues on this outing, but Castro continues to define his own spin on the form without being just another pretty-boy Stevie Ray Vaughanabee in the process, this being a very good thing. *—Cub Koda*

Live at the Fillmore / Feb. 22, 2000 / Blind Pig ♦♦♦

Blues-rock guitarist Castro brings us his fourth recording, an enhanced CD recorded live at his hometown, San Francisco-based Fillmore Auditorium. Castro is a good guitarist who is not hung up on pyrotechnics; he plays clean, undistorted licks in the basic tradition. Vocally, he is quite reminiscent of Tower of Power singer Emilio Castillo (check out "What Is Hip?" for the similarities.) This 11-song set starts off rocking on the straight-laced, organ-fired (by Jimmy Pugh) "Right as Rain," one of several tracks from previous discs. Castro is also into hot funk with horn help from trumpeter Tom Poole and tenor saxophonist Keith Crossan for "Like an Angel" and the 12-bar R&B-ish "Nasty Habits," all of which are Castro's tunes. "My Time After Awhile" is the most straight-blues-oriented number of the lot, slow and quietly sizzling. "Lucky in Love" and "I Got to Change" are more pop-oriented, the former in rock territory, the latter à la Otis Redding. Albert King's "Can't You See What You're Doing to Me?" is a loping blues-rock tune with Castro's best guitar improvs and most animated, feverish vocal. Even more into Otis Redding's bag, "Just a Man" is a sweet, slow soul sender, followed by the good, old-time type, midtempo, high-energy-injected rocker "Can't Keep a Good Man Down." Castro's rhythm section of bassist Randy McDonald and drummer Billy Lee Lewis finally doubles the time on the fastest tune, the typical '60s dance ditty "The Girl Can't Help It" with background vocals, and Castro exclaims, "it's not my thing, but we'll borrow it" before posing the strut of James Brown's "Sex Machine" in extended fashion for band intros and some enjoyable jamming. Every musician should put out a live club or concert date, yet few do these days. Castro's confidence is evident, his band is tight, and this CD produces a pretty good representation of what you hear in any given short set of Castro's performances. Three sets, or at least the best moments of that long night of party music, would have been even better. *—Michael G. Nastos*

● **The Essential Tommy Castro** / Aug. 14, 2001 / Blind Pig ♦♦♦♦

Blind Pig closes out their four-album Tommy Castro association with this adequate collection of his recorded highlights for the San Francisco-based label. Not the best guitar slinger in town, Castro compensates by writing tunes that mix good-time soul, R&B, funk, and roots rock together with blues to produce a swampy, wholly satisfying mix that goes down easy. Songs like "Right as Rain," "Can't Keep a Good Man Down," and "Lucky in Love" crackle with Chuck Berry by way of the Stones' basic rock & roll simplicity. However, this compilation seemed to be rushed out in 2001 in order to compete with Castro's *Guilty of Love* album of new material for another label, and it shows. There is no indication of which release the songs originate from in the skimpy notes, and Castro had no say in choosing the tracks. The 50-minute playing time is too brief for an artist with a four-CD catalog, and even though the enhanced concert CD-ROM video for "Nobody Loves Me Like My Baby" is a welcome addition and gives a visceral demonstration of how tough the band rocks live, it's also duplicated as an audio only selection on the disc. Regardless, the music holds up as rugged, bluesy rock with strong connections to Memphis soul with the Stax-styled ballad "Just a Man" and James Brown funk in "Nasty Habits" tempering the Stevie Ray Vaughn-isms of Castro's meat-and-potatoes playing. He also boasts a distinctly gritty voice that works perfectly with his original material and the previously unavailable version of Little Richard's "The Girl Can't Help It," added here as one of two unreleased tracks. As it is, *The Essential* is a satisfactory collection for those who want a taste of the Castro experience, but one that could—and should—have been a lot better. *—Hal Horowitz*

Guilty of Love / Aug. 28, 2001 / 33rd Street ♦♦♦

Dedicated to late San Francisco blues heroes Stu Blank and John Lee Hooker and featuring Hooker's final vocal appearance, *Guilty of Love* holds the promise of something special. Unfortunately, it's a bit flat, lacking the fire you might expect. While Castro's material is eclectic and clever, incorporating rock, soul, R&B, and roots, it's not always above cliché. Also, some tracks are given a subdued, if not sluggish treatment. "Face of Love," for example, is more low key than low down. The Otis Redding-styled "Whole Lot of Soul" doesn't pack a wallop, either. Castro does turn it up on the roots rocker "Shakin' the Good Hard Times Loose," sounding like a cross between Delbert McClinton and James Brown. And the good-time closer, "If You Aint Lovin', You Aint Livin'," bringing to mind Bobby Bland, is genuinely fun and cool. Fittingly, Stu Blank, who sadly succumbed to cancer in 2001, gives the most memorable performance with his "Dirt Road Blues." This charged final performance on tape between Blank and Castro finally has some of the emotion and intensity that Castro brings to his famous club dates. *—Bill Meyer*

Catfish Keith (Keith Daniel Kozachik)

b. Feb. 9, 1962, East Chicago, IN

Slide Guitar, Vocals / Modern Acoustic Blues, Slide Guitar Blues

A cutting-edge blues singer, songwriter, and slide guitarist, Catfish Keith was born Keith Daniel Kozachik on February 9, 1962, in East Chicago, IN. As a child he first heard the blues while living in "The Harbor," a working class steel mill town. Listening to Muddy Waters, Howlin' Wolf, and Buddy Guy on the radio gave him a love of the blues. When he first picked up the guitar as a teenager, he was inspired to aim for the deep Delta blues after hearing songs by Son House.

Following high school in Davenport, Iowa, Catfish Keith hit the road embarking on his lifelong quest as a solo performer of American roots music. His many travels took him to the Caribbean, where in the Virgin Islands he crewed briefly on a sailboat. He absorbed the rhythms of jazz, calypso, and reggae, and the music of Joseph Spence. This music gave Catfish Keith inspiration to reach new musical heights. Though he grew up on the Mississippi River, Catfish Keith earned his nickname from a West Indian lobster diving partner who, after seeing him swim, dubbed him "Catfish-Swimmin'-Around," and "Catfish-Steel-Guitar-Man."

In 1984, at age 22, Catfish Keith recorded his first album on the Kicking Mule label, *Catfish Blues*. The all-solo debut established him as a new force in acoustic blues. It reached number one on independent worldwide radio charts. This enabled Catfish Keith to play and tour heartily. He was constantly learning directly from legends such as Johnny Shines, David Honeyboy Edwards, Jessie Mae Hemphill, and Henry Townsend. Catfish Keith and Penny Cahill married in 1988 and they soon formed Fish Tail Records. In 1991, *Pepper in My Shoe!* was released to rave reviews, sparking international interest and extensive touring in the U.K. and Europe. Catfish Keith was embraced as a true blues star. The *Guardian* called Catfish Keith "a solo revelation" who was "breaking new ground for blues." Catfish Keith, headlining major festivals and concerts, was featured on the covers of *Blues Life* of Austria/Germany, *Blueprint* in the U.K. and *Block* in the Netherlands. *Pepper in My Shoe!* was followed by *Jitterbug Swing*, which was nominated for a W.C. Handy Award for Best Acoustic Blues Album of 1992. Catfish Keith was also honored to perform at the W.C. Handy Awards show, where he appeared alongside Robert Cray, Billy Gibbons of ZZ Top, Buddy Guy, Johnny Copeland, Delbert McClinton, and others. The British Blues Connection nominated Catfish Keith for Best Overseas Artist, naming him "the new slide king of the National steel guitar." *Cherry Ball* was released in 1993, further exploring Catfish's string-twanging style to the delight of an ever-growing following of devoted fans. James Jensen in *Dirty Linen* wrote: "Catfish will give you goose bumps and leave you howling for more!" Catfish Keith's fifth solo album, *Fresh Catfish*, was nominated for a W. C. Handy Award for Best Acoustic Blues Album of 1995. This disc displayed the drive and swing of a true blues performer on the vanguard of the era's music scene. Mark E. Gallo of the *Blues Review* was quoted as saying, "Catfish Keith is hands down one of the finest acoustic bluesmen in America." In 1999, Catfish Keith released *Pony Run*, another amazing compilation of guitar genius. *—Larry Belanger*

Pony Run / 1999 / Fish Tail ♦♦♦♦

Catfish Keith is joined on a couple of tunes here by pianist Radoslav Lorkovic; all the other songs are solo ventures. Keith has excellent guitar skills and a very powerful voice that is well suited to the genre. He pours his entire heart and soul into each and every song, making the end product very magnetic and touching. His guitar playing and singing take the listener back in time to when barrelhouse music was at its prime. He gives the listener a chance to feel the music that Delta blues masters played many decades ago. The strength of Delta blues was the emotional tie between the artists and their songs;

their music was a window to their souls. Keith has managed to capture this feeling on his album, allowing listeners to take a trip without ever leaving the easy chair. The 1999 National Reso-Phonic Baritone Polychrome Tricone steel-bodied guitar in the hands of this amazing guitarist is featured on two standout tracks. The first, "Butt Dance," features humorous lyrics that some might find offensive, but the guitar playing on this number is sure to drop a few jaws, as Keith does a little second-line slide guitar on the baritone. The second standout tune is actually the last piece on the album, "Doggone My Bad Luck Soul." The baritone guitar gives this instrumental a powerful presence; the tune also has strains of the Robert Johnson classic "Crossroads," with its powerful energy and dynamic melody. The energy level of the album never drops, from the first song, "I Just Can't Help It," to the very last. On "I Just Can't Help It," Keith is joined by Lorkovic on the piano; the strong rhythm guitar work, with accentuations from the piano blending with Keith's powerful vocals, makes this a solid, soulful groove tune. Keith is an amazing solo artist who is keeping a uniquely American style of music alive with his own Midas touch. Although this is not a genre that is at its highest in terms of popularity, this truly unique guitarist and singer delivers some timeless pieces of musical genius that will delight those who give them a listen. *—Larry Belanger*

● **A Fist Full of Riffs** / Sep. 25, 2001 / Solid Air ✦✦✦✦✦
Some people fill a record with personality. Catfish Keith is one. Not only is his guitar picking out of this world, but a real sense of the pleasure he gets from playing comes through the speakers. Mixing it up with blues, New Orleans tunes, Caribbean music, Hawaiian picking, and a smidgen of ragtime on his eighth album, he's all over the place—but a delight to follow. That's he's world class is beyond question, but there's more going in his work than just expansive technique. There's true thought and heart behind his moving version of "Motherless Children," just as there's a playful spirit inhabiting "12th Street Rag," with its jaw-dropping harmonics, or the title cut. Perhaps the best track, however, is "Dark Was the Night, Cold Was the Ground," with its deep, gorgeous slide work. Coming as it does after the bouncy "Way Out West," an instrumental reworking of a song Keith has recorded before, it's a stark change of mood that works well. He's superb on his interpretations of the Hawaiian pieces, with both "Kohala March" and "Hawaiian Cowboy" splendid exercises in frantic slack-key playing. Even if he chooses not to act the part, Catfish Keith is a guitar star. In a more perfect world, he'd be feted and his records would sell in huge quantities. As it is, though, just be grateful he puts out wonderful albums like this and enjoy them to the fullest. *—Chris Nickson*

Cephas & Wiggins

f. 1984, Bowling Green, VA
Group / East Coast Blues, Modern Acoustic Blues, Acoustic Blues, Piedmont Blues
The duo of acoustic guitarist John Cephas and harpist Phil Wiggins enjoyed a partnership spanning across several decades, during which time they emerged among contemporary music's most visible exponents of the Piedmont blues tradition. Both were born in Washington, D.C., although Wiggins was a quarter century younger than his partner; they met at a jam session in 1977, and both performed as regular members of Wilbert "Big Chief" Ellis' Barrelhouse Rockers for a time prior to Ellis' death. Their music, rooted in the rural African-American dance music of Virginia and North Carolina, showed the influence of Blind Boy Fuller, Gary Davis, and Sonny Terry, with a broad repertoire consisting of Piedmont blues standards as well as an eclectic sampling of Delta stylings, R&B, ballads, ragtime, gospel, and country & western; from their 1984 debut onward, *Sweet Bitter Blues*, Cephas & Wiggins' sound applied sophisticated traditional instrumentation and modern gospel-edged vocals to both traditional standards and their own hard-hitting compositions, offering a soulful acoustic option to electric blues. A popular festival act, they also issued LPs including 1986's W.C. Handy Award-winning *Dog Days of August*, 1988's *Walking Blues*, 1992's *Flip, Flop, & Fly*, and 1996's *Cool Down*. They kept going strong and in 1999 released their ninth album, *Homemade*, on the legendary Alligator label. In 2000 Bullseye Blues issued *From Richmond to Atlanta*, a compilation of tracks from Cephas & Wiggins' three Flying Fish albums recorded between 1984 and 1992. The duo continued to tour and play festivals, helping to keep the Piedmont sound alive. In the summer of 2002, they released *Somebody Told the Truth*, a mixture of old and new tracks that reintroduced them to the next generation of blues fans. *—Barry Lee Pearson & Richard Skelly*

Sweet Bitter Blues / 1984 / L&R ✦✦✦
This German import, released by Evidence Music in 1994 on compact disc, is notable for seven live tracks, the rest being studio cuts, many from previous releases. While the live recording quality is a little muddy at times, the stage energy of this Piedmont acoustic blues duo is unmistakable on such tracks as their own "Burn Your Bridges" and an inspired version of Jimmy Reed's "Running and Hiding." *—Jeff Crooke*

Let It Roll: Bowling Green / 1985 / Marimac ✦✦✦
Similar to *Dog Days of August*, but includes five other cuts. *—Barry Lee Pearson*

● **Dog Days of August** / 1986 / Flying Fish ✦✦✦✦✦
Handy Award-winning acoustic guitar and harmonica Piedmont blues. Includes ballads "John Henry," "Staggerlee, " and ten original compositions. *—Barry Lee Pearson*

Guitar Man / 1987 / Flying Fish ✦✦✦
Their second Handy Award winner includes slide guitar, Piedmont fingerpicking, and wonderful harmonica. *—Barry Lee Pearson*

Walking Blues / 1988 / Marimac ✦✦✦✦✦
A fine assortment of Piedmont blues, ragtime, and country. Includes "Walking Blues." *—Barry Lee Pearson*

Flip, Flop, & Fly / 1992 / Flying Fish ✦✦✦
Similar to the songsters of the '20s and '30s, Cephas & Wiggins are able to move easily between ragtime, blues, jazz and Piedmont-style folk music. *Flip, Flop, & Fly*, the title track being the old Joe Turner hit, treads ground on all the above genres and styles. In particular "Darkness on the Delta" and "Banks of the River" showcase the emotional depth capable in Cephas' voice, and the original composition "The Backbiter" is modern acoustic blues at its best. *—Steve Kurutz*

Bluesmen / 1993 / Chesky ✦✦✦

Cool Down / Jan. 30, 1996 / Alligator ✦✦✦✦
Cool Down is the first album the acoustic blues duo Cephas & Wiggins have recorded for Alligator Records and it ranks among their best. The spirit of the session is laidback and eclectic, as the pair draws on everyone from Blind Lemon Jefferson and Blind Boy Fuller to Fats Domino and Merle Travis. There are also a half-dozen originals that might not be as captivating as the covers, but they certainly elicit engaging performances from the pair. Throughout *Cool Down*, Cephas dominates the music but Wiggins' harmonica steals the show whenever he pops through the cracks. *Cool Down* is the kind of album that demonstrates how some blues musicians simply get better with age. *—Thom Owens*

Goin' Down the Road Feelin' Bad / Jun. 23, 1998 / Evidence ✦✦✦
John Cephas and Phil Wiggins don't provide any surprises on this date, *Goin' Down the Road Feelin' Bad*. That doesn't mean this is a disc to ignore. They have remained faithful to the Piedmont blues sound and to their credit haven't incorporated any modern twists or foisted an attempt at soul-blues, for instance. They play what they love and continue in the tradition of Brownie McGhee and Sonny Terry or Blind Blake. Among the 14 tracks, two—"Burn Your Bridges" and "Guitar and Harmonica Rag"—are Cephas & Wiggins originals; the rest are mainly traditional. *—Al Campbell*

Homemade / Jan. 26, 1999 / Alligator ✦✦✦
Homemade might fall just short of the peaks of *Cool Down*, Cephas & Wiggins' first album for Alligator Records, but it has a similiar rustic, laidback charm that is equally engaging. The duo may not be breaking any new ground with this record, but they're performing at a high standard, which is enough to make *Homemade* enticing for any fan of Cephas & Wiggins. *—Thom Owens*

From Richmond to Atlanta / Oct. 10, 2000 / Rounder ✦✦✦
From Richmond to Atlanta collects selections from Cephas & Wiggins' three Flying Fish albums recorded between 1984 and 1992, *Dog Days of August*, *Guitar Man*, and *Flip, Flop, & Fly*. Guitarist John Cephas and harmonica man Phil Wiggins have been playing acoustic Piedmont-inspired blues together for enthusiastic audiences for over three decades. This 12-song set captures an engaging mixture of ragtime, Delta, country, gospel, and folk originals and classics, with 24-bit remastering at a mid-line price from Bullseye Blues. *—Al Campbell*

Eddie Chamblee

b. Feb. 24, 1920, Atlanta, GA
Sax (Tenor) / Swing, R&B
Good, sometimes inspirational player who made contributions in both big-band and small-combo settings as well as early R&B. Chamblee studied law at Chicago State University, then played with several army bands from 1941 to 1946. He headed a small group in Chicago from 1946 until the mid-'50s, then worked for two years with Lionel Hampton, recording and touring in Europe in 1956. Chamblee went back to small combos, and backed vocalist Dinah Washington on many superb dates in 1957, 1958 and 1963. He and Washington were also briefly married. Chamblee worked with Milt Buckner and Hampton in the '70s, returning with them to Europe in 1976, 1977 and 1978. He also recorded with each musician, and did some sessions with his own band in '76. Chamblee played for a short period in Count Basie's orchestra in 1982. *—Ron Wynn*

● **The Rocking Tenor Sax of Eddie Chamblee** / Feb. 27, 1964 / Prestige ✦✦✦
Though by no means an innovator or virtuoso on par with the great tenor saxophonists of the mid-'60s, Eddie Chamblee deserved better than the relative obscurity which proved his fate; issued in conjunction with Victor Japan's excellent *Soul Jazz Collection* campaign, with any luck the re-release of his aptly titled 1964 Prestige label debut *The Rocking Tenor Sax of Eddie Chamblee* will retroactively earn him some notice. Chamblee blows with a leering, bump-and-grind swagger more ideally suited to a roadhouse strip joint than an uptown jazz club (fittingly enough, he performed in the Brigitte Bardot opus *And God Created Woman*), and in tandem with organist Dayton Selby and drummer Al Griffin, he tears through scintillating readings of "The Honeydripper" and "Champin'." The trio fares less successfully on downtempo material like "Softly As I Leave You" and the closing "Little Things Mean a Lot"—it's not without good reason that the cover spells out "Rocking" entirely in capital letters. *—Jason Ankeny*

Bobby Charles (Robert Charles Guidry)

b. Feb. 21, 1938, Abbeville, LA
Vocals, Songwriter / New Orleans R&B, Traditional Cajun
More successful as a songwriter than a singer, Bobby Charles was nonetheless an important contributor to Louisiana music in both respects. He authored several hits for key artists in the early days of rock & roll (including Bill Haley and Fats Domino), and although he recorded mostly in obscurity, he emerged as one of the founding fathers of swamp pop.

Robert Charles Guidry was born February 21, 1938, in the Cajun-country town of Abbeville, LA, and grew up listening to traditional Cajun music. As a teenager, he discovered rock & roll and rhythm & blues, and began singing with a band called the Cardinals, who performed at local dances. During this period, he wrote a song called "See You Later, Alligator," which particularly impressed a Crowley, LA, record store owner who happened to know Chess Records founder Leonard Chess. The young singer auditioned over the phone and was rewarded with a recording session at the legendary Cosimo's studio in New Orleans. After hearing the single version of "See You Later, Alligator," Chess signed Guidry (by some accounts, not realizing he was a white Cajun) and soon shortened his name to the less regional Bobby Charles. Chess released "See You Later, Alligator" as Charles' debut single in 1955, and he toured behind it after graduating from high school. While it connected with R&B audiences, the song didn't become a big pop hit until 1956, when Bill Haley covered it for a national best-seller. Charles scored another minor hit that year with "Time Will Tell," and stayed with Chess through 1957, recording R&B singles that even at this stage were already infused with a Cajun musical sensibility.

In 1958, Charles moved to Imperial and cut several more singles through the next year. Although he was silent for a few years after cutting a one-off cover of "Goodnight Irene" for Farie in 1959, Charles' reputation as a songwriter continued to grow. In 1960, Fats Domino took "Walking to New Orleans" into the Top Ten, and Clarence "Frogman" Henry did likewise early the following year with "(I Don't Know Why I Love You) But I Do." Charles subsequently recorded sides for Hub City (1963), Jewel (1964), and Paula (1965), by which time he was experimenting with country music.

With little commercial success of his own, Charles drifted away from the music business for a while. He returned in 1972 on the Bearsville label and cut a self-titled album (his first full-length) that was co-produced by the Band's Rick Danko. In fact, the majority of the Band appeared on the record as supporting musicians, as did Dr. John, David Sanborn, and Amos Garrett. In spite of considerable critical acclaim, *Bobby Charles* didn't sell very well, and after recording with Paul Butterfield in 1973, a disenchanted Charles again retreated from music. He appeared with the Band in their 1976 concert film *The Last Waltz*, joining them onstage for one song of their final performance. The following year, he returned to Bearsville and recorded another album with Spooner Oldham on piano, but the project was never released.

Charles kept quiet for most of the next decade, returning in 1986 with a couple of singles on the Rice n' Gravy label, plus a European-only album called *Clean Water* in 1987. In the meantime, his songs had been recorded by numerous artists from the worlds of blues, rock, country, and soul; a partial list includes Joe Cocker, Delbert McClinton, Lou Rawls, Ray Charles, Tom Jones, Kris Kristofferson, Rita Coolidge, Etta James, Junior Wells, Clarence "Gatemouth" Brown, Bo Diddley, David Allan Coe, and even UB40. In 1995, Charles signed with the Canadian blues'n'roots label Stony Plain and released a new album, *Wish You Were Here Right Now*, which consisted of sessions from 1992-1993 plus selections from a 1984 jam session at Willie Nelson's studio. In addition to Nelson, guests included Neil Young, Fats Domino, and slide ace Sonny Landreth. A follow-up, *Secrets of the Heart*, appeared in 1998, but Charles has since returned to rural Cajun country to live the quiet life, supported by his songwriting royalties; he's also become a local environmental activist. His excellent *Bobby Charles* album has been reissued several times (including once in 1988 under the title *Small Town Talk*, its most famous composition). *—Steve Huey*

● **Bobby Charles** / 1972 / Stony Plain ✦✦✦✦✦

Hooking up with the Band, specifically Rick Danko and their producer John Simon, was one of the smartest moves Bobby Charles ever made. His subsequent eponymous album on Bearsville not only gave him a bigger audience, but lead to the perfect production for his sly, subtle blend of New Orleans R&B, rock & roll and country. Partially, that's because the production is fuller, richer than his sides for Chess, Jewel and Paula, boasting not just some grit, but a sweetness on ballads like "I Must be In a Good Place Now," a tune every bit as good as those from the singer/songwriters that dominated the charts in 1972. This gives the album an earthier quality than anything else he recorded; it also makes the album feel like a perfect companion piece to other roots-rock albums from the time like, of course, the Band. Still, there's a special charm to this record, largely because while it sounds contemporary, it retains Charles' mellow vibe, and his sharp songwriting. The songs come on slow—"Street People," "He's Got All the Whiskey," "Small Town Talk" all slowly unwind—but the slow build is friendly, welcoming you into the song. This isn't lazy music, but it takes its time, and it's better for it; it's perfect music for a hot summer afternoon. It's a true hidden gem of both blue-eyed soul, Southern R&B, and early-'70s roots-rock (and early-'70s singer/songwriterism for that matter). *—Stephen Thomas Erlewine*

Wish You Were Here Right Now / 1995 / Stony Plain ✦✦✦

Secrets of the Heart / Jan. 27, 1998 / Stony Plain ✦✦✦✦

Hopefully, this disc will prevent the writer of such songs as "Walking to New Orleans," "See You Later Alligator," "I Can't Quit You," and "The Jealous Kind" from being known only as a songwriter. Bobby Charles is a writer of superb talent and stylistic versatility. This disc includes the R&B smash for Delbert McClinton, "I Can't Quit You," the south of the border "Angel Eyes," the "loungey" (in the best sense) "But I Do," and the second-line soul of "Party Town" standing out; several new tracks, like "You" and "I Don't Want to Know," have the potential to join the ranks of Charles classics. To bring out the best in these songs, he has received the support of a stellar cast of players from New Orleans and beyond, who treat the songs with the respect that their writer deserves. There are no mediocre songs on this disc; some may not be to your taste, but each is well crafted and performed with care. There is also a bonus at the end of the disc after a two-minute pause—a better-than-average interview that lasts about 15 minutes. It's nice the first time, but it is a pain when it comes up on shuffle mode. *—Bob Gottlieb*

Walking to New Orleans (The Jewel & Paula Recordings 1964–1965) / Dec. 12, 2000 / West Side ✦✦✦✦✦

Bobby Charles could write a hit, as "Walking to New Orleans" and "See You Later Alligator" proved, but he wasn't necessarily the one to *have* the hit. Others would come along and record perfect, definitive versions of the songs, while Bobby remained behind the scenes—or, perhaps more accurately, down in New Orleans, recording singles for independent labels without ever breaking out the region. It's not that hard to see why he remained a local favorite, not a star. He had a relaxed delivery that was too idiosyncratic and laid-back, something that was perfect for New Orleans and R&B connoisseurs back then, and right now. These are the sides that are often overlooked in Charles' career—he had more success with Chess in the '50s, his band-sponsored Bearsville record in 1972 brought him to a new audience—but they're as good as anything he ever did. This has a light, easy touch, not just in his delivery but in the nimble rhythms and the no-frills production (never gritty, always friendly). Some of the sides are a little generic but in a good way: They deliver what they should. But the best is smart, funny, warm New Orleans R&B that anyone who truly loves the genre should seek out. *—Stephen Thomas Erlewine*

Ray Charles (Ray Charles Robinson)

b. Sep. 23, 1930, Albany, GA

Vocals, Leader, Piano / Pop-Soul, Country-Soul, Jazz Blues, Urban Blues, Piano Blues, R&B, Soul

Ray Charles was the musician most responsible for developing soul music. Singers like Sam Cooke and Jackie Wilson also did a great deal to pioneer the form, but Charles did even more to devise a new form of Black pop by merging '50s R&B with gospel-powered vocals, adding plenty of flavor from contemporary jazz, blues, and (in the '60s) country. Then there is his singing—his style is among the most emotional and easily identifiable of any 20th century performer, up there with the likes of Elvis and Billie Holiday. He's also a superb keyboard player, arranger, and bandleader. The brilliance of his '50s and '60s work, however, can't obscure the fact that he's made few classic tracks since the mid-'60s, though he's recorded often and tours to this day.

Blind since the age of six (from glaucoma), Charles studied composition and learned many instruments at the St. Augustine School for the Deaf and the Blind. His parents had died by his early teens, and he worked as a musician in Florida for a while before using his savings to move to Seattle in 1947. By the late '40s, he was recording in a smooth pop/R&B style derivative of Nat "King" Cole and Charles Brown. He got his first Top Ten R&B hit with "Baby, Let Me Hold Your Hand" in 1951. Charles' first recordings have come in for their fair share of criticism, as they are much milder and less original than the classics that would follow, although they're actually fairly enjoyable, showing strong hints of the skills that were to flower in a few years.

In the early '50s, Charles' sound started to toughen as he toured with Lowell Fulson, went to New Orleans to work with Guitar Slim (playing piano on and arranging Slim's huge R&B hit, "The Things That I Used to Do"), and got a band together for R&B star Ruth Brown. It was at Atlantic Records that Ray truly found his voice, consolidating the gains of recent years and then some with "I Got a Woman," a number two R&B hit in 1955. This is the song most frequently singled out as his pivotal performance, on which Charles first truly let go with his unmistakable gospelish moan, backed by a tight, bouncy horn-driven arrangement.

Throughout the '50s, Charles ran off a series of R&B hits that, although they weren't called "soul" at the time, did a lot to pave the way for soul by presenting a form of R&B that was sophisticated without sacrificing any emotional grit. "This Little Girl of Mine," "Drown in My Own Tears," "Hallelujah I Love Her So," "Lonely Avenue," and "The Right Time" were all big hits. But Charles didn't really capture the pop audience until "What'd I Say," which caught the fervor of the church with its pleading vocals, as well as the spirit of rock & roll with its classic electric piano line. It was his first Top Ten pop hit, and one of his final Atlantic singles, as he left the label at the end of the '50s for ABC.

One of the chief attractions of the ABC deal for Charles was a much greater degree of artistic control of his recordings. He put it to good use on early-'60s hits like "Unchain My Heart" and "Hit the Road Jack," which solidified his pop stardom with only a modicum of polish attached to the R&B he had perfected at Atlantic. In 1962, he surprised the pop world by turning his attention to country & western music, topping the charts with the "I Can't Stop Loving You" single, and making a hugely popular album (in an era in which R&B/soul LPs rarely scored high on the charts) with *Modern Sounds in Country and Western Music*. Perhaps it shouldn't have been so surprising; Charles had always been eclectic, recording quite a bit of straight jazz at Atlantic, with noted jazz musicians like David "Fathead" Newman and Milt Jackson.

Charles remained extremely popular through the mid-'60s, scoring big hits like "Busted," "You Are My Sunshine," "Take These Chains from My Heart," and "Crying Time," although his momentum was slowed by a 1965 bust for heroin. This led to a year-long absence from performing, but he picked up where he left off with "Let's Go Get Stoned" in 1966. Yet by this time Charles was focusing increasingly less on rock and soul, in favor of pop tunes, often with string arrangements, that seemed aimed more at the easy listening audience than anyone else. Charles' influence on the rock mainstream was as apparent as ever; Joe Cocker and Steve Winwood in particular owe a great deal of their style to him, and echoes of his phrasing can be heard more subtly in the work of greats like Van Morrison.

One approaches sweeping criticism of Charles with hesitation; he's an American institution, after all, and his vocal powers have barely diminished over the years. The fact remains, though, that his work since the late '60s on record has been very disappointing. Millions of listeners yearned for a return to the all-out soul of his 1955-1965 classics, but Charles had actually never been committed to soul above all else. Like Aretha Franklin and Elvis Presley, his focus is more upon all-around pop than many realize; his love of jazz, country, and pop standards is evident, even if his more earthy offerings are the ones that truly broke ground and will stand the test of time. He's dented the charts (sometimes the country ones) occasionally, and can command devoted international concert audiences whenever he feels like it. For good or ill, he's ensured his imprint upon the American mass consciousness in the '90s by singing several ads for Diet Pepsi. The CD era has seen several excellent packages that focus on various chronological/thematic phases of the legend's career. *—Richie Unterberger*

The Great Ray Charles / 1956 / Atlantic ✦✦✦

This set is rather unusual, for it is strictly instrumental, allowing Ray Charles a rare opportunity to be a jazz-oriented pianist. Two selections are with a trio (bassist Oscar Pettiford joins Charles on "Black Coffee"), while the other six are with a septet taken from his big band of the period. Key among the sidemen are David Newman (soloing on both tenor and alto) and trumpeter Joseph Bridgewater; highlights include Quincy Jones' "The

Ray," "My Melancholy Baby," "Doodlin'," and "Undecided." Ray Charles should have recorded in this setting more often in his later years. *—Scott Yanow*

The Genius After Hours / 1956 / Rhino ✦✦✦✦✦
Taken from the same three sessions as *The Great Ray Charles* but not duplicating any of the performances, this set casts Charles as a jazz-oriented pianist in an instrumental setting. Brother Ray has five numbers with a trio (three songs have Oscar Pettiford on bass) and jams on three other tunes ("Hornful Soul," "Ain't Misbehavin'" and "Joy Ride") with a septet arranged by Quincy Jones; solo space is given to David "Fathead" Newman on tenor and alto and trumpeter Joseph Bridgewater. Fine music; definitely a change of pace for Ray Charles. *—Scott Yanow*

The Genius Hits the Road / 1956-1972 / Rhino ✦✦✦
In keeping with his jazz/pop crossover ambitions, Charles decided to record a concept album of sorts with a dozen songs devoted to various parts of the U.S.—"Alabamy Bound," "Georgia On My Mind," "Moonlight in Vermont," "California, Here I Come," "Blue Hawaii," etc. The crossover vibe is further heightened by the brassy big-band arrangements, and material from the likes of Al Jolson and Hoagy Carmichael. It sounds a bit corny now, with an in-your-face gung-ho cheer. But it did what Charles wanted it to do, reaching the Top Ten of the album charts, and spinning off a big hit with "Georgia On My Mind." The 1997 CD reissue on Rhino adds seven bonus tracks from 1956-1972 that also had a travel/geographic theme, and the best of these are actually the highlights of the record, most notably "Hit the Road Jack," "Lonely Avenue," and his cover of Hank Snow's "I'm Movin' On." *—Richie Unterberger*

Ray Charles / Jul. 1957 / Atlantic ✦✦✦
These are animated soul and R&B recordings, although the rock & roll links are pretty obvious as well. The songs, vocals, arrangements, and production are great; only the sound quality falters. But they can also be obtained on many other anthologies with far superior sound. *—Ron Wynn*

Ray Charles at Newport / Jul. 5, 1958 / Atlantic ✦✦✦✦✦
For his appearance at the Newport Jazz Festival on July 5, 1958, Charles pulled out all the stops, performing raucous versions of "The Right Time," "I Got a Woman," and "Talkin' 'Bout You." This album was reissued in 1973 as a two-record set, packaged with *Ray Charles in Person* under the title *Ray Charles Live*. *— William Ruhlmann*

The Genius of Ray Charles / 1959 / Atlantic ✦✦✦✦✦
Some players from Ray Charles' big band are joined by many ringers from the Count Basie and Duke Ellington bands for the first half of this program, featuring Charles belting out six songs arranged by Quincy Jones. "Let the Good Times Roll" and "Deed I Do" are highlights, and there are solos by tenorman David "Fathead" Newman, trumpeter Marcus Belgrave and (on "Two Years of Torture") tenor Paul Gonsalves. The remaining six numbers are ballads, with Charles backed by a string orchestra arranged by Ralph Burns (including "Come Rain or Come Shine" and "Don't Let the Sun Catch You Cryin'"). Ray Charles' voice is heard throughout in peak form, giving soul to even the veteran standards. *—Scott Yanow*

What'd I Say / May 28, 1959 / Atlantic ✦✦✦
At a concert held at Herndon Stadium in Atlanta on May 28, 1959, Ray Charles turns in a blistering version of "What'd I Say" and takes on the big-band era with versions of Tommy Dorsey's "Yes Indeed!" and Artie Shaw's "Frenesi," not to mention performances of "The Right Time" and "Tell the Truth." This album was reissued in 1960 under the title *Ray Charles in Person* and again in 1973 as a part of a two-record set, packaged with *Ray Charles at Newport* under the title *Ray Charles Live*. *— William Ruhlmann*

Genius + Soul = Jazz / 1960 / DCC ✦✦✦
One of the best early-'60s examples of soul/jazz crossover, this record, like several of his dates from the period, featured big-band arrangements (played by the Count Basie band). This fared better than some of Charles' similar outings, however, if only because it muted some of his straight pop aspirations in favor of some pretty mean and lean, cut-to-the-heart-of-the-matter B-3 Hammond organ licks. Most of the album is instrumental and swings pretty vivaciously, although Charles does take a couple of vocals with "I'm Gonna Move to the Outskirts of Town" and "I've Got News for You." Yet one of those instrumentals, a cover of the Clovers' "One Mint Julep," would give Charles one of his most unpredictable (and best) early-'60s hits. In 1997, it was combined with the much later *My Kind of Jazz* album (from 1970) onto a single-disc CD reissue by Rhino. *—Richie Unterberger*

Dedicated to You / Jan. 1961 / ABC/Paramount ✦✦✦

Ray Charles and Betty Carter / Jun. 13, 1961-1966 / ABC/Paramount ✦✦✦✦
This pairing of two totally idiosyncratic vocalists acquired legendary status over the decades in which it had been out of print. But the proof is in the listening, and frankly it doesn't represent either artist's best work. There is certainly a powerful, often sexy rapport between the two—Charles in his sweet balladeering mode, Carter with her uniquely keening, drifting high register—and they definitely create sparks in the justly famous rendition of "Baby, It's Cold Outside." The main problem is in Marty Paich's string/choir arrangements, which too often cross over the line into treacle, whereas his charts for big band are far more listenable. Moreover, Charles' sweetness can get a bit cloying too, although some of the old grit emerges on "Takes Two to Tango." On the CD reissue—remixed by Charles himself—Dunhill adds the great, rare B-side to the "Unchain My Heart" single, "But On The Other Hand Baby," and two excellent if unrelated album cuts, "I Never See Maggie Alone" (1964) and "I Like To Hear It Sometime" (1966). *—Richard S. Ginell*

The Genius Sings the Blues / Oct. 1961 / Atlantic ✦✦✦✦✦
Down-home, anguished laments and moody ballads were turned into triumphs by Ray Charles. He sang these songs with the same conviction, passion, and energy that made his country and soul vocals so majestic. This has not as of yet turned up in the reissue bins, but is probably headed in that direction. *—Ron Wynn*

Modern Sounds in Country and Western Music, Vol. 1 / 1962 / ABC/Paramount ✦✦✦✦✦
Less modern for its country-R&B blend (Elvis Presley & company did it in 1955) and lushly produced C&W tone (the Nashville sound cropped up in the late '50s) than for its place as a high-profile crossover hit, *Modern Sounds in Country and Western Music* fit right in with Ray Charles' expansive musical ways while on the Atlantic label in the '50s. In need of even more room to explore, Charles signed with ABC/Paramount and eventually took full advantage of his contract's "full artistic freedom clause" with this collection of revamped country classics. Covering a period from 1939 to the early '60s, the 12 tracks here touch on old-timey fare (Floyd Tillman's "It Makes No Difference to Me Now"), honky tonk (three Hank Williams songs), and early countrypolitan (Don Gibson's "I Can't Stop Loving You"). Along with a Top Ten go at Eddy Arnold's "You Don't Know Me," the Gibson cover helped the album remain at the top of the pop charts for nearly three months and brought Charles international fame. Above a mix of swinging big band charts by Gerald Wilson and strings and choir backdrops from Marty Paich, Charles' intones the sleepy-blue nuances of country crooners while still giving the songs a needed kick with his gospel outbursts. No pedal-steel or fiddles here, just a fine store of inimitable interpretations. The 1988 Rhino reissue adds three bonus tracks: "You Are My Sunshine," "Here We Go Again," and "That Lucky Old Sun." *—Stephen Cook*

☆ **Modern Sounds in Country and Western Music, Vol. 2** / 1962 / ABC/Paramount ✦✦✦✦✦
Having struck the mother lode with *Vol. 1* of this genre-busting concept, "Brother Ray," producer Sid Feller, and ABC-Paramount went for another helping and put it out immediately. The idea was basically the same—raid the then-plentiful coffers of Nashville for songs and turn them into Ray Charles material with either a big band or a carpet of strings and choir. This time, though, instead of a random mix of backgrounds, the big band tracks—again arranged by Gerald Wilson in New York—went on side one, and the strings/choir numbers—again arranged by Marty Paich in Hollywood—were placed on side two. Saleswise, it couldn't miss, but, more importantly, *Vol. 2* defied the curse of the sequel and was just as much of an artistic triumph as its predecessor, if not as immediately startling. Charles' transfiguration of "You Are My Sunshine" sets the tone, and, as before, there's a good quota of Don Gibson material; "Don't Tell Me Your Troubles" becomes a fast gospel rouser and "Oh Lonesome Me" a frantic big band number. Paich lays on the '50s and early-'60s Muzak with an almost gleeful, over-the-top commercial slickness that with an ordinary artist would have been embarrassing. But the miracle is that Charles' hurt, tortured, soulfully twisting voice transforms the backgrounds as well as the material; you believe what he's singing. It appealed across the board, from the teenage singles-buying crowd to adult consumers of easy listening albums and Charles' core black audience—and even those who cried "sellout" probably took some secret guilty pleasures from these recordings. While Charles didn't get a number one chartbuster à la "I Can't Stop Loving You" out of this package, "Sunshine" got up to number seven, and "Take These Chains From My Heart," with its Shearing-like piano solo and big string chart, made it to number eight—which wasn't shabby at all. *—Richard S. Ginell*

Ingredients in a Recipe for Soul / Jul. 1963 / ABC ✦✦✦✦
Although it was a big commercial success, reaching number two on the LP charts, this record would typify the erratic nature of much of Charles' '60s output. It's too eclectic for its own good, really, encompassing pop standards, lowdown blues, Mel Torme songs, and after-hours ballads. The high points are very high—"Busted," his hit reworking of a composition by country songwriter Harlan Howard, is jazzy and tough, and one of his best early-'60s singles. And the low points are pretty low, especially when he adds the snow-white backup vocals of the Jack Halloran Singers to "Over the Rainbow" and "Ol' Man River." A number of the remaining cuts are pretty respectable, like the tight big-band arrangement of "Ol' Man Time" and the ominously urbane "Where Can I Go?" In 1997, it was paired with the 1964 LP *Have a Smile With Me* on a two-for-one CD reissue on Rhino, with the addition of historical liner notes. *—Richie Unterberger*

Have a Smile With Me / 1964 / ABC/Paramount ✦✦
The idea behind this LP was to offer a lighthearted sequel to its quasi-concept predecessor, *Sweet and Sour Tears*. There's nothing wrong with the idea of letting Ray just kick back and have fun, but "The Thing" and "The Man with the Weird Beard" transcend the boundaries of humor into silliness and, worse, stupidity. On the other hand, he also turns out a good jazzy version of Hank Williams' "Move It On Over" (the record's highlight), and manages to swing through fairly superficial fare like "Ma (She's Making Eyes at Me)" and "Two Ton Tessie" with solid flair. It was another inconsistent '60s set, the shortage of top-notch tunes disguised by a flimsy concept, though he elevates the material with soulful vocals and good arrangements, particularly when the Raelettes back him up (as they do on half the tracks). In 1997, it was paired with the 1963 LP *Ingredients in a Recipe for Soul* on a two-for-one CD reissue on Rhino, with the addition of historical liner notes. *—Richie Unterberger*

Sweet & Sour Tears / Mar. 1964 / Rhino ✦✦✦
One of a series of ultra-loose concept albums Charles cut in the '60s, this one dedicated entirely to songs with titles or lyrical references to crying and tears. It's an excuse for Ray to choose his usual varied menu of upbeat jumpers, slow countrified weepers, and proudly saccharine pop standards. The production, as one might fear, also tends to the lachrymose side on the slow tunes, with the thick strings and backup vocals straight out of TV variety shows. One is almost tempted to think that Charles was toying with audience expectations by mixing unabashedly sentimental slow tunes with the far more bluesy, satisfying, and upbeat numbers, such as "Don't Cry, Baby" and "Baby, Don't You

Cry," as well as his surprisingly brassy, punchy treatment of "Cry Me a River." These out-ings have always played much better with critics than the gloppy pop tunes, and for good reason—they are much better. The Rhino CD reissue adds seven bonus tracks from throughout his early career (1956-1971) that also tapped into the "crying" motif. These threaten to steal the show from the *Sweet & Sour Tears* album it's supposedly embel-lishing, including the Bacharach-David penned 1964 single "I Wake Up Crying," the smol-dering 1966 album track "No Use Crying," and the 1956 R&B chart-topper "Drown in My Own Tears," next to which much of the rest of the program sounds positively hokey. —*Richie Unterberger*

Country & Western Meets Rhythm & Blues / Aug. 1965 / ABC/Paramount ✦✦✦
A partially successful revisiting by Charles of his country sessions of the early '60s. These songs weren't quite as transcendent as those on the prior dates, but he showed once again that the lines between country, R&B, and soul weren't as rigid as many in the various camps thought. —*Ron Wynn*

My Kind of Jazz / Apr. 1970 / Tangerine ✦✦✦✦
This LP came seemingly out of the blue as a showcase for the Ray Charles big band, spawning two little-known sequels later on in the '70s. It's a roaring, solid band, too, play-ing jazz standards like "This Here," "The Sidewinder," "Bluesette" and "Senor Blues," comfortable at slow, loping tempos as well as in the rousers, with excellent mainstream soloists (none of whom are identified) and good conventional charts (also uncredited). The sole exception to the pattern—and a hit single in its own right—is a catchy, funky, Charles gospel/blues called "Booty Butt," where Ray adds multi-tracked gospel moans for his sole vocal contribution, and the band chimes in only on the very last chord. Clearly, the title and the appalling lack of credits say volumes about Charles' reputation as a control freak; this is his kind of jazz and nobody else's. In 1997, it was combined with the much earlier *Genius + Soul* album onto a single-disc CD reissue by Rhino. —*Richard S. Ginell & Richie Unterberger*

Greatest Hits, Vol. 1 / 1987 / DCC ✦✦✦✦
The first of two DCC compilations to collect the best of Brother Ray's '60s stint at ABC-Paramount Records, when he flew off in a dozen different stylistic directions. Included on this 20-track disc are Charles' immortal rendering of "Georgia on My Mind," and the sin-uously bluesy "Unchain My Heart," the Latin-beat instrumental "One Mint Julep," per-sonalized remakes of the country standards "Born to Lose," "Your Cheating Heart," and "Crying Time," and his exultant rendition of the soulful "Let's Go Get Stoned." —*Bill Dahl*

Greatest Hits, Vol. 2 / 1987 / DCC ✦✦✦✦✦
More seminal performances from the '60s ABC catalog of the Genius (DCC split the clas-sics evenly between the two discs, making both of them indispensable). His beloved "Hit the Road Jack" (one of several Percy Mayfield copyrights dotting Charles' repertoire), the daring country crossover "I Can't Stop Loving You," an electric-piano powered "Sticks and Stones," a wise "Them That Got," and a wonderfully mellow "At the Club" rank with the 20-song disc's standouts (though versions of the Beatles' "Yesterday" and the corny "Look What They Done to My Song, Ma" end the set on a bummer note). —*Bill Dahl*

☆ **Greatest Country and Western Hits** / 1988 / DCC ✦✦✦✦✦
Collecting the highlights from Charles' two *Modern Sounds in Country and Western Mu-sic* albums, *Greatest Country and Western Hits* features some of the most essential country-soul material ever recorded. —*Stephen Thomas Erlewine*

Anthology / 1989 / Rhino ✦✦✦✦✦
Perhaps the best single CD collection of Ray Charles' '60s and '70s ABC/Paramount ma-terial. They've also been issued on two separate anthologies, but for someone who only wants the essential items, this disc has them all over its 20 tracks. —*Ron Wynn*

Soul Brothers/Soul Meeting / 1989 / Atlantic ✦✦✦✦
This brings together all of the extant takes recorded for two albums that Milt Jackson made with Ray Charles for Atlantic in 1957 and 1958. With Oscar Pettiford, Connie Kay, and Kenny Burrell in the various lineups, this is bluesy jazz in a laid-back manner; it sur-prised many hardcore R&B fans when these albums were originally issued. Jackson moves from vibes to piano, and even guitar (on "Bag's Guitar Blues"), while Ray jumps between piano and alto sax on these sessions. A rare glimpse of Charles' jazz soul com-ing up for air. —*Cub Koda*

☆ **The Birth of Soul** / 1991 / Atlantic ✦✦✦✦✦
The title isn't just hype—this absolutely essential three-disc box is where soul music first took shape and soared, courtesy of Ray Charles' church-soaked pipes and bedrock piano work. Brother Ray's formula for inventing the genre was disarmingly simple: he brought gospel intensity to the R&B world with his seminal "I Got a Woman," "Hallelujah I Love Her So," "Leave My Woman Alone," "You Be My Baby," and the primal 1959 call-and-response classic "What'd I Say." There's plenty of brilliant blues content within these 53 historic sides: Charles' mournful "Losing Hand," "Feelin' Sad," "Hard Times," and "Black-jack" ooze after-hours desperation. No blues collection should be without this boxed set, which comes with well-researched notes by Robert Palmer, a nicely illustrated accompa-nying booklet, and discographical info aplenty. —*Bill Dahl*

The Birth of a Legend / 1992 / Valley Vue ✦✦✦✦✦
Of all the countless compilations that have been stitched together of Ray Charles' early sides for Jack Lauderdale's Swing Time Records, this two-disc box is the only CD pack-age that treats these enormously important works with the reverent respect that they de-serve (meaning decent mono sound quality instead of murky electronic reprocessed stereo dubbed from vinyl, cogent liner notes, and full discographical annotation). This is where the genius began, imitating Charles Brown at the very start (1949) and sounding like nobody but Brother Ray by 1952 (when he defected to Atlantic and hit the real big time). Forty-one tracks in all. —*Bill Dahl*

Blues + Jazz / 1993 / Rhino ✦✦✦✦✦
Another easy access point for Charles' seminal Atlantic catalog. This two-disc set is evenly split between his bluesiest sides on the first disc and a selection of his greatest jazz sides on disc two (gorgeously showcasing the sax work of David "Fathead" Newman on sev-eral pieces). Charles was a masterful blues purveyor; his "I Believe to My Soul" is simul-taneously invested with heartbreak and humor, while the earlier "Sinner's Prayer," "The Sun's Gonna Shine Again," and the gospel-based "A Fool for You" emanate both hope and deep pain. —*Bill Dahl*

The Early Years / 1994 / Fat Boy/Tomato ✦✦✦
In the late '40s and early '50s, Charles recorded several dozen sides for the Swing Time/Down Beat label, 30 of which are presented here. As has been noted many times by critics, these usually found Charles in a Nat "King" Cole swing-blues groove that was much smoother than the gritty R&B/soul he'd record for Atlantic in the later '50s; the in-fluence of urban blues balladeer Charles Brown is also evident. Some critical essays, in fact, may lead you to believe that this work is trivial, but while it's undeniably derivative, it's enjoyable on its own terms, and not without strong hints of the searing soulfulness that was to come. Some of the selections are delivered with such refined polish that it doesn't even sound like Charles. But on the more anguished and fast tempoed cuts in par-ticular, you can hear him starting to arrive at the phrasing and emotion that would flower in the mid-'50s. Unfortunately, like most Tomato reissues, the sound is substandard; even assuming that the master tapes can't be located, a better job was probably possible, and a couple of cuts even duplicate skips from the vinyl. Exact dates and songwriting credits are also missing, although Pete Welding's essay does at least discuss the material on the discs in some detail, unlike many of Tomato's liner notes. —*Richie Unterberger*

★ **The Best of Atlantic** / Jul. 19, 1994 / Rhino ✦✦✦✦
The 20-track compilation (only 12 tracks on cassette) *The Best of Atlantic* compiles all of Ray Charles' Top Ten R&B hits for Atlantic Records, from "I've Got a Woman" and "This Little Girl of Mine" to "Drown in My Own Tears," "Hallelujah I Love Her So," "Lonely Av-enue," "(Night Time Is) The Right Time," and "What'd I Say (Pt. 1)." In addition to the big hits, there are minor hits that nevertheless showcase Charles at his peak, like "Swanee River Rock" and "Just for a Thrill." For fans who only want the hits and don't want to in-vest in the splendid three-disc set *The Birth of Soul, The Best of Atlantic* is an essential purchase. —*Stephen Thomas Erlewine*

Berlin, 1962 / Apr. 1996 / Pablo ✦✦✦
An hour of previously unreleased live music from Ray Charles in his prime. During this era he was touring with a big band including saxophonists David "Fathead" Newman and Hank Crawford, as well as background singers the Raelettes. The fidelity is excellent, and the set includes Charles standards like "One Mint Julep," "I Got a Woman," "Georgia on My Mind," "Hallelujah I Love Her So," "I Believe to My Soul," "Hit the Road, Jack," "Un-chain My Heart," and "What'd I Say." Yet most fans will probably much prefer the more compact, small-combo arrangements of the studio versions. The horn charts offer an in-teresting contrast, but these live performances may be a little too stagey for optimum re-sults, with some detours from hard R&B into popular standards. —*Richie Unterberger*

Complete Swing Time & Down Beat Recordings 1949–1952 / Feb. 21, 1997 / Night Train ✦✦✦
The light blues and jazz of Ray Charles' early recordings were heavily influenced by Nat King Cole, and Charles frequently recorded in a similar trio format. His sound changed dramatically soon after he signed to Atlantic in 1952: His singing became more forceful and confident, and his rock 'n' soul performances were unlike anything he had done ear-lier for the Swing Time or Down Beat labels. Night Train's two-disc set collects 45 of Charles' rare recordings for the aforementioned independent labels, including several al-ternate takes, all of which find him in an imitative mode that pales beside his later trail-blazing sides. It is interesting to hear a reserved Ray Charles croon his way through these arrangements, many of which are frankly lackluster despite the presence of supporting players like Stanley Turrentine (a situation not improved by the slightly murky sound quality and sometimes wobbly pitch of the source material). As a historical document, this is a comprehensive look at Charles' early output, with session information and cur-sory notes, but without songwriting or publishing information. Buyers looking for early, raw R&B won't find it here, but serious devotees of Ray Charles will appreciate this archival release. —*Greg Adams*

Genius + Soul = Jazz/My Kind of Jazz / Jun. 10, 1997 / Rhino ✦✦✦✦✦
Single-disc CD reissue combines two of Charles' more jazz-oriented outings, though *Ge-nius + Soul* (from 1961) enjoys a much more sterling reputation than the comparatively obscure *My Kind of Jazz* (1970). Question: if genius plus soul equals jazz, does that mean genius minus soul equals fusion? —*Richie Unterberger*

Ingredients in a Recipe for Soul/Have a Smile With Me / Aug. 19, 1997 / Rhino ✦✦✦
A two-for-one pairing of albums from 1963 (*Ingredients in a Recipe for Soul*) and 1964 (*Have a Smile With Me*), with the addition of historical liner notes. Neither rate among his better albums—both are inconsistent mixtures of hard-edged jazz/pop/soul and main-stream pop standards. Each, though, has some fine cuts, notably the Top Ten hit "Busted" (on *Recipe*) and a jazzy cover of Hank Williams' "Move It On Over" (on *Have a Smile With Me*). The CD also adds two bonus tracks: both parts of the orchestral pop "Without a Song" single from 1965. —*Richie Unterberger*

Genius & Soul: The 50th Anniversary Collection / Sep. 16, 1997 / Rhino ✦✦✦✦✦
As the first comprehensive, multi-label box set assembled on Ray Charles, the five-disc, 101-song *Genius & Soul: The 50th Anniversary Collection* is an extensive overview of one of the greatest musicians of the 20th century. Charles produced a body of work so rich and diverse that even five CDs only scratches the surface of his accomplishments. None of his instrumentals are on *Genius & Soul*, nor are his jazz and traditional pop

efforts spotlighted. Instead, the box traces the evolution of his career, as he moves from an R&B pioneer to a mainstream pop crooner to a country-pop vocalist to a contemporary soul singer. Charles was a gripping, captivating vocalist, capable of making even bland music sound vital, but the fact is, his '70s and '80s recordings pale in comparison to his seminal '50s and '60s sides. Which means that the set becomes less compelling as it reaches the fifth disc, but the first three and a half discs are filled with timeless music that remains exciting, vital and altogether wondrous. *—Stephen Thomas Erlewine*

Ray Charles and Betty Carter/Dedicated to You / 1998 / Rhino ✦✦✦✦✦
Rhino's reissue of Ray Charles' 1961 duet album with Betty Carter, *Dedicated to You*, combined the terrific original album with their other great duet album, *Ray Charles and Betty Carter*. Both records were recorded the same year and were produced by Sid Feller and arranged by Marty Paitch. Both are stellar albums, showcasing their astonishing range and wonderful, empathetic interplay. *—Leo Stanley*

Standards / Mar. 3, 1998 / Rhino ✦✦✦✦
Standards is a 17-track collection of Ray Charles' versions of classic pop songs, culled recordings he made for Atlantic, ABC/Paramount, ABC/TRC and Crossover/Atlantic between 1959 and 1977. There are a handful of hits—"Georgia on My Mind," "Ruby," "That Lucky Old Sun," "Without Love (There Is Nothing)," "Makin' Whoopee"—but the collection concentrates on little-known album tracks and live cuts. Although the steady stream of repackages from Rhino can be a little overwhelming, the idea behind *Standards* is attractive, and it's executed well—it's nice to have all these songs on one collection, even if the live cuts can be a little distracting. Certainly, anyone looking for a collection of mellow ballads from Charles will not be disappointed by this set. *—Stephen Thomas Erlewine*

Complete Country & Western Recordings 1959–1986 / Oct. 27, 1998 / Rhino ✦✦✦✦
Ray Charles' explorations into country music were no mere dalliance. They have their genesis in "I'm Movin' On," the last record he made for Atlantic before moving on to ABC Paramount in 1960. But it was with the enormously successful *Modern Sounds in Country and Western Music* series of albums in 1962 (and the career-making single "I Can't Stop Lovin' You") that made their mark, crossing over genre boundaries that were unthinkable at the time. An African-American doing hillbilly music was not a first, nor were uptown arrangements of hillbilly songs, but here was the Genius of Soul validating the music of the white working class, plain and simple. He was putting his own spin to it (hence the *Modern Sounds*), not merely a black voice singing Gene Autry songs, investing them with pain, emotion, and sorrow. It was an unprecedented achievement, both commercially and artistically, and now—decades later—it's viewed as just another genre-bender in the grand Ray Charles tradition. But this 92-track, four-CD box set is the first to gather them all in one place and view it as a consistent piece of work spread over a career as a stylist that's second to none. The first disc combines both volumes of the *Modern Sounds* albums; the rest of the anthology moves through singles, various returns to the concept over the years, and stray tracks from his later stretch at Columbia to spice it all up. This multi-disc set contains some very special music, nicely packaged—a moment in American music well worth investigating. *—Cub Koda*

★ **Ultimate Hits Collection** / Mar. 16, 1999 / Rhino ✦✦✦✦✦
James Brown may be "the hardest working man in show business," Aretha Franklin may be the Queen of Soul, but as *Ultimate Hits Collection* proves, the most apt nickname in all of music may belong to Ray Charles: the Genius. Forget for a moment that fitting all of Charles' hits on a mere two CDs is not remotely possible. Almost any Ray Charles greatest-hits compilation is going to be excellent, and this one is better than most, if only because it's two-discs long. *Ultimate Hits Collection* follows the path of Charles' work as it cruises through the genres he so richly influenced: R&B, pop, jazz, blues, and country. The standard favorites are here from Charles' repertoire, but what sets this compilation apart are the lesser-known tracks. "Mess Around" and "Hide 'Nor Hair" are certainly not as popular as "Hit the Road Jack," but they are no less enjoyable. The most welcome inclusion is Charles' version of the country classic "You Don't Know Me," which is often left off of other Charles retrospectives. Of the multitude of duets he has recorded, two appear here. "Seven Spanish Angels" with Willie Nelson and "I'll Be Good to You" with Quincy Jones and Chaka Khan are fine choices, but adding "Baby Grand" with Billy Joel could have pushed the collection from great to superb. The liner notes are lengthy and compelling, featuring some great photos, and the packaging, with each disc in its own jewel box, is functional. The sound quality is also superb, considering some of the recordings were almost 50 years old at the time of this release. *—Mark Vanderhoff*

The Very Best of Ray Charles / Mar. 14, 2000 / Rhino ✦✦✦✦
This 16-track budget package hits all the high notes of Brother Ray's rise to greatness. Starting in the '50s with classic Atlantic sides like "I've Got a Woman," "Hallelujah I Love Her So," "Night Time (Is the Right Time)," and "What'd I Say," the set also includes his landmark ABC country sides of the '60s ("I Can't Stop Loving You," "Georgia on My Mind"), finishing up with a duet with Willie Nelson on "Seven Spanish Angels." A perfect introduction to an American musical treasure. *—Cub Koda*

The Best of Ray Charles, Vol. 2 / Sep. 19, 2000 / Rhino ✦✦✦✦
Another round of great tracks compiled in typical Rhino fashion: the best recordings of the best tracks by some of the best artists. Chock-full of soul, this compilation features "Brother Ray" classics like "Hide 'Nor Hair," "Take These Chains From My Heart," and the one-two punch of the Beatles' "Yesterday" and "Eleanor Rigby." The only complaint about this fine collection is that the first volume really packed in the well-known songs, leaving volume two with what almost feels like second-string hits. A fine second step into the world of Ray Charles' music, especially for the price. *—Zac Johnson*

Rockie Charles (Charles Merick)

b. Nov. 14, 1942, Boothville, LA
Vocals, Guitar / Modern Electric Blues
Although a longtime veteran of the music industry, singer/guitarist Rockie Charles and his soulful blues sound only began attracting attention during the mid-'90s. Born Charles Merick in Boothville, LA, on November 14, 1942, he first emerged during the early '60s in a series of New Orleans R&B bands, taking inspiration from Earl King and Chuck Berry; auditions for the Minit and Imperial labels went nowhere, but during the middle of the decade Charles cut a handful of sides for Black Patch, including "Sinking Like a Ship." He soon relocated to Nashville, where he backed performers including O.V. Wright, Little Johnny Taylor and Roscoe Shelton. Upon returning to New Orleans in 1970, Charles established his own label, Soulgate, scoring a local hit with the single "The President of Soul"; however, with the rise of disco, his fortunes dwindled, and he spent the better part of the next two decades working as a tugboat captain and oyster fisherman. In 1994, however, Orleans Records producer Carlo Ditta responded to an advertisement Charles had placed in a local entertainment magazine, and two years later the singer finally released his debut solo LP, *Born for You*. *—Jason Ankeny*

● **Born for You** / Dec. 17, 1996 / Orleans ✦✦✦

Sam Chatmon

b. Jan. 10, 1897, Boltmon, MS, **d.** Feb. 2, 1983, Hollandale, MS
Vocals, Arranger, Guitar / Dirty Blues, Blues Revival, Acoustic Blues, Country Blues
A product of the prodigious Chatmon family that included not only Lonnie of the famous Mississippi Sheiks but also the prolific Bo Carter and several other blues-playing brothers, Sam Chatmon survived to be hailed as a modern-day blues guru when he began performing and recording again in the '60s. Sam continued brother Bo's tradition of sly double entendre blues to entertain a new generation of aficionados, but he also showed a more serious side on songs like the title track of the early Arhoolie anthology *I Have to Paint My Face*.

Chatmon began playing music as a child, occasionally with his family's string band, as well as the Mississippi Sheiks. Sam launched his own solo career in the early '30s. While he performed and recorded as a solo act, he would still record with the Mississippi Sheiks and with his brother Lonnie. Throughout the '30s, Sam traveled throughout the South, playing with a variety of minstrel and medicine shows. He stopped traveling in the early '40s, making himself a home in Hollandale, MS, where he worked on plantations.

For the next two decades, Sam Chatmon was essentially retired from music and only worked on the plantations. When the blues revival arrived in the late '50s, he managed to capitalize on the genre's resurgent popularity. In 1960, he signed a contract with Arhoolie and he recorded a number of songs for the label. Throughout the '60s and '70s, he recorded for a variety of labels, as well as playing clubs and blues and folk festivals across America. Chatmon was an active performer and recording artist until his death in 1983. *—Jim O'Neal & Stephen Thomas Erlewine*

Mississippi Sheik / 1970 / Blue Goose ✦✦✦✦✦

● **Sam Chatmon's Advice** / 1979 / Rounder ✦✦✦✦✦
Sam Chatmon's Advice is an excellent collection that features many of his greatest sides from the early '30s, making it the best available distillation of Chatmon's numerous solo recordings. *—Thom Owens*

Sam Chatmon & His Barbecue Boys / 1987 / Flying Fish ✦✦✦
An excellent set of trio recordings by this underrated performer. *—Ron Wynn*

1970–1974 / Oct. 12, 1999 / Flyright ✦✦✦
This selection of good-natured hokum and traditional country blues offers fans of the genres more than an hour's worth of enjoyable, if not particularly essential, listening. Though Chatmon's singing and whistling is hampered by some missing teeth, the guitarist's fingerpicking still proves engaging, especially on "Prowlin' Groundhog" and the uptempo "Chatmon Family Rag." But like so many other rediscovered acoustic blues artists to be recorded decades after their heyday, Chatmon sounds tired at times, possibly even lost during a couple of the midtempo numbers. Backed by a full string band, including jug, at the album's end, Chatmon sounds more focused, singing with genuine energy and calling out spry encouragement to his bandmates during their solos. The disc notes include an interview with Chatmon that recounts—how accurately, who knows?—tales of the guitarist's early recording career and his amazingly talented family. *—Brian Beatty*

Rev. Julius Cheeks

b. Aug. 7, 1929, Spartanburg, SC, **d.** Jan. 27, 1981, Miami, FL
Vocals, Leader / Traditional Gospel, Southern Gospel, Black Gospel
At the peak of his career, the Rev. Julius Cheeks was the definitive hard gospel singer, famed for a gritty, powerful baritone which influenced not only the next generation of gospel performers but also secular stars including James Brown and Wilson Pickett. Born into abject poverty on August 7, 1929 in Spartanburg, SC, as a child Cheeks was enamored of the recordings of the Dixie Hummingbirds, the Soul Stirrers and others; he began singing in the second grade, quitting school that same year to pick cotton. Later joining a local gospel group dubbed the Baronets, in 1946 he was spotted by the Rev. B.L. Parks, a former Dixie Hummingbird in the process of forming a new group called the Nightingales; upon Cheeks' arrival, he became infamous across the gospel circuit for playing the clown, while each night pushing his voice to its breaking point.

The Nightingales enjoyed considerable success on the road, but they made virtually no money; to make ends meet Cheeks briefly joined the Soul Stirrers, rejoining the Nightingales during the early '50s. Upon signing to Peacock, the group rattled off a string of hits, among them "Somewhere to Lay My Head" and "The Last Mile of the Way"; they were in fact so popular, and so often the subject of acclaim, that they eventually rechristened themselves the Sensational Nightingales. In 1954, Cheeks offically became a preacher, but he remained a performer, emerging as a gifted writer and arranger as well; a temperamental man, he left the group on numerous occasions, finally quitting for good in 1960 and going into semi-retirement. He soon returned to action with a new group, the Sensational Knights. Cheeks died in Miami on January 27, 1981. —*Jason Ankeny*

At the Gate I Know / 1981 / Savoy ✦✦✦

The late Rev. Julius Cheeks is well-known throughout the quartet music industry as one of the hardest quartet lead vocalists during gospel music's Golden Age. His rock-solid baritone voice was at one time able to destroy the best of sound systems. This 1981 release, which is alternately titled "The Legend Lives On," represents another era in the great recording career of Rev. Cheeks. By this time, his voice was damaged beyond repair as a result of both overexertion and improper care. Rev. Cheeks shows his ability to convey powerful messages in song with remakes of his classic recordings and rearrangements of gospel standards. His enlistment of choral background on most of the selections is a surprising success from a lifelong quartet icon. Though his lead singing is at times abrasive, his ability to conduct, arrange, and allow for flawless vocal exchanges with auxiliary singers shows his many years of experience. For example, alternate lead vocalist George McAllister is not only a powerful addition to this project but represents a younger version of Rev. Cheeks. Though his clean, crisp baritone was long gone, Cheeks is able to put his seal of approval on many of his original compositions and arrangements like "At the Gate I Know," "Crying in the Chapel," and "I Want to Go Where Jesus Is." The definite highlight of this project is the powerful yet chilling story of "There's a Man Going Around Taking Names." This mournful selection brings to the forefront the ever-present reminder of mortality that became synonymous with the later compositions of Rev. Cheeks. On the whole, this recording is a powerful look at one of gospel music's legends shortly before his untimely death. —*Minister Donnie Addison*

How Far is Heaven / Jul. 1, 1991 / Savoy ✦✦✦✦✦

A collection of the best Knights sides headed by this great, late dynamic lead singer. —*Opal Louis Nations*

● Somebody Left on That Morning Train / Nov. 6, 2001 / Savoy ✦✦✦✦✦

Marvelous leads and a good production. This is the best album Cheeks has made as a solo singer. —*Ron Wynn*

Family / Savoy ✦✦✦

Nice vocals and more midtempo song sermons. —*Ron Wynn*

We'll Lay Down Our Lives / Savoy ✦✦✦

Representative, but a cut below his best single sessions. —*Ron Wynn*

Clifton Chenier

b. Jun. 25, 1925, Opelousas, LA, d. Dec. 12, 1987, Lafayette, LA
Vocals, Accordion / Zydeco, Creole

The undisputed "King of Zydeco," Clifton Chenier was the first Creole to be presented a Grammy award on national television. Blending the French and Cajun two-steps and waltzes of southwest Louisiana with New Orleans R&B, Texas blues and big band jazz, Chenier created the modern, dance-inspiring, sounds of zydeco. A flamboyant personality, remembered for his gold tooth and the cape and crown that he wore during concerts, Chenier set the standard for all the zydeco players who have followed in his footsteps. In an interview from Ann Savoy's book, *Cajun Music: Reflection of a People*, Chenier explained, "Zydeco is rock and French mixed together, you know, like French music and rock with a beat to it. It's the same thing as rock and roll but it's different because I'm singing in French." The son of sharecropper and amateur accordion player, Joe Chenier, and the nephew of a guitarist, fiddler and dance club owner, Maurice "Big" Chenier, Chenier found his earliest influences in the blues of Muddy Waters, Peetie Wheatstraw and Lightnin' Hopkins, the New Orleans R&B of Fats Domino and Professor Longhair, the '20s and '30s recordings by zydeco accordionist Amédé Ardoin and the playing of childhood friends Claude Faulk and Jesse and Zozo Reynolds. Acquiring his first accordion from a neighbor, Isaie (easy) Blasa in 1947, Chenier was taught the basics of the instruments by his father. By 1944, Chenier was performing, with his brother Cleveland on frottoir (rub board) in the dance halls of Lake Charles.

Moving to New Iberia in the mid-'40s, Chenier worked in the sugar fields, cutting sugar cane. After moving to Port Arthur, TX, in 1947, he divided his time between driving a refinery truck and hauling pipe for Gulf and Texaco and playing with his brother. In 1954, Chenier signed with Elko Records. His first recording session, at Lake Charles radio station KAOK, yielded seven tunes including the regional hit single "Cliston Blues" and "Louisiana Stomp."

Chenier's first national attention came with his first single for the Specialty record label, "Ay Tete Fille (Hey, Little Girl)," a cover of a Professor Longhair tune, released in May 1955. The song was one of 12 that he recorded during two sessions produced by Bumps Blackwell, best known for his work with Little Richard. By 1956, Chenier had left his day job to devote his full-time attention to music, touring with his band, the Zydeco Ramblers, which included blues guitarist Phillip Walker. The following year, Chenier left Specialty and signed with the Chess label in Chicago. Although he toured, along with Etta James, throughout the United States, Chenier's career suffered when the popularity of ethnic and regional music styles began to decline. Although he recorded thirteen songs for the Crowley, Louisiana-based Zynn label, between 1958 and 1960, none charted.

The turning point in Chenier's career came when Lightnin' Hopkins' wife, who was a cousin, introduced Chris Strachwitz, owner of the roots music label, Arhoolie, to his early recordings. Strachwitz quickly signed Chenier to Arhoolie, producing his first single, "Ay Yi Yi"/"Why Did You Go Last Night?," in four years. Although they continued to work together until the early '70s, Chenier and Strachwitz differed artistically. While Chenier wanted to record commercial-minded R&B, Strachwitz encouraged him to focus on traditional zydeco. Chenier's first album for Arhoolie, *Louisiana Blues & Zydeco*, featured one side of blues and R&B and one side of French two-steps and waltzes.

In 1976, Chenier recorded one of his best albums, *Bogalusa Boogie*, and formed a new

group, the Red Hot Louisiana Band, featuring tenor saxophonist "Blind" John Hart and guitarist Paul Senegal.

Chenier reached the peak of his popularity in the '80s. In 1983, he received a Grammy award for his album, *I'm Here!*, recorded in eight hours in Bogalusa, Louisiana. The following year, he performed at the White House. Although he suffered from kidney disease and a partially amputated foot and was required to undergo dialysis treatment every three days, Chenier continued to perform until one week before his death on December 12, 1987. Following his death, his son, C.J. Chenier, took over leadership of the Red Hot Louisiana Band.

A documentary video of Chenier's performances at the San Francisco Blues Festival, the New Orleans Jazz and Heritage Festival, and on Louisiana television was released by Arhoolie. —*Craig Harris*

Zodico Blues & Boogie / 1955 / Specialty ✦✦✦✦✦

Clifton Chenier's mid-'50s singles for Specialty were among his rawest and simplest; they were short ditties with rippling accordion and gritty vocals on top and driving rhythms and surging instrumental accompaniment underneath. That's the formula displayed on this 20-cut presentation of Chenier's early work, where he was often backed by guitarists Phillip Walker or Cornelius Green (Lonesome Sundown), with his brother Cleveland handling rub board duties. This is Chenier in his stylistic infancy, building and nurturing what ultimately became a signature sound. —*Ron Wynn*

Louisiana Blues & Zydeco / 1965 / Arhoolie ✦✦✦✦

This was the first full album by a zydeco artist to be released by Arhoolie. It became something of an advance scout as the Cajun accordion army began to spread its music outside of the Louisiana bayous, with Clifton Chenier winding up with a Grammy for his efforts, as well as performances all over the world. This album puts together a few different instrumental lineups for recording at Houston's Gold Star studios, a facility with an important place in Texas blues history. Nonetheless, the recording sound is a tad thin, as perhaps the engineers were frightened by some of the manic moves of a few of the instrumentalists. Although this style of music is known mostly for the accordion and rub board antics as featured on the second side, the tracks on the first side also include some ferocious piano and electric guitar playing. Some tracks just really cook and should put any listener in a good mood. The instrumental "Hot Rod" has a great drum part and accordion improvising that sounds totally relaxed, followed by an under-recorded but nasty-sounding guitar solo. Too bad it fades out so quickly. Altogether, lots of variety, plenty of creative musical ideas, and some deeply soulful singing delivered by this great zydeco artist just as his career was starting to lift off. —*Eugene Chadbourne*

Bayou Blues / 1970 / Specialty ✦✦✦✦

Bayou Blues compiles a selection of 12 tracks Clifton Chenier cut for Specialty Records in 1955, including the original versions of "Boppin' the Rock," "Eh, Petite Fille," "I'm On My Way" and "Zodico Stomp." It may not be a definitive retrospective, but it's an entertaining and necessary sampler of Chenier at the beginning of his career. —*Thom Owens*

King of the Bayous / 1970 / Arhoolie ✦✦✦✦✦

After gaining initial notoriety in the '50s and '60s on Specialty Records and a variety of small Texas and Louisiana labels, Zydeco King Clifton Chenier brought the blues-fueled Cajun music he practically invented to Chris Strachwitz's roots label Arhoolie, subsequently recording a series of fine albums including 1970's *King of the Bayous*. Featuring brother and longtime partner Cleveland Chenier on rub board, Robert St. Judy on drums, Joe Morris on bass, and Antoine Victor on guitar, *King of the Bayous* includes Chenier's standard blend of zydeco two-step, waltzes and blues, and provides an excellent taste of what the band no doubt played on countless one-niters along the Louisiana-Texas Gulf Coast. Zydeco-brand blues predominates with Chenier originals "Hard to Love Someone," "Who Can Your Good Man Be" and "I Am Coming Home," in addition to a cover of the honky-tonk weeper "Release Me." Offering a contrast to the blues and something for the dancers, the band lays down a lively two-step beat on "Tu Le Ton Son Ton," "Josephine Par Se Ma Femme" and "Zodico Two-Step." Throughout the varied set, Chenier's irrepressible vocals and accordion playing stand out. A nice sample of bayou zydeco by one of its finest and most original practitioners. —*Stephen Cook*

Out West / 1974 / Arhoolie ✦✦✦✦✦

Special guests Elvin Bishop and Steve Miller joined Chenier for an excellent outing blending blues and rock influences with zydeco. Chenier's vocals were tough and convincing, while Bishop and Miller, along with saxophonist Jon Hart, were outstanding. —*Ron Wynn*

Cajun Swamp Music Live / Aug. 1978 / Tomato ✦✦✦✦

By the time this album came out, Chenier & His Red Hot Louisiana Band were beginning to receive the kind of widespread acclaim they so much deserved. They had already built a firm reputation on the heels of several fine Arhoolie-released records and countless hours on the road. Now, *Cajun Swamp Music Live* finds Chenier and company taking their juicy act beyond the Gulf Coast circuit to the main stage at the Montreux Jazz Festival. Taped in the late '70s, the 18 choice cuts feature the band repaying the adoration of a charged crowed with a non-stop run of inspired performances. Mixing in his standard variety of zydeco and blues-fueled vocals and instrumentals, Chenier wows the Swiss patrons with both his fine accordion workouts and wry in-between-song banter (he alternates between English and Cajun French for the mostly French-speaking audience). Also including top-drawer contributions from his band—including brother Cleveland Chenier on rub board, Robert Pet on drums, and Paul Senegal on guitar—*Cajun Swamp Music Live* is an album all Chenier fans will definitely want to pick up. —*Stephen Cook*

And His Red Hot Louisiana Band in New Orleans / 1979 / GNP Crescendo ✦✦✦

In New Orleans was recorded in the late '70s with one of Clifton Chenier's classic bands, which featured his brother on washboard, saxophonist John Hart, and guitarist Paul

Senegal, among others. The album is textbook Chenier—it rocks & rolls, wails and shouts. It's may be a typical record for the King of Zydeco, but that means it's very, very enjoyable. *—Thom Owens*

Bon Ton Roulet / May 1981 / Arhoolie ♦♦♦♦
Great rock'em-sock'em zydeco. *—Jeff Hannusch*

I'm Here! / May 1982 / Alligator ♦♦♦
A relatively standard release from Clifton Chenier, the then reigning king of zydeco. The music bumps and grooves in all the ways it's supposed to. One of the songs dates the album a bit ("Zydeco Disco"), but aside from that one, the rest of the album is pretty much straightforward zydeco and blues. In spots it delves a little into jazz, but only in spots. In and of itself, delving into jazz wouldn't be such a bad thing, but this band's form of the genre tends to be a bit sloppy. When it comes to zydeco, there's no stopping them, but elsewhere they're more stoppable. For a basic look into Chenier's brand of zydeco, this album might not be too bad, though certainly others exist that may serve better. For a look into the style in general, one should expand into other major players (Buckwheat Zydeco, Beau Jocque, Little Nathan) as well as Chenier and his family. *—Adam Greenberg*

The King of Zydeco Live at Montreux / 1984 / Arhoolie ♦♦♦
This is a nice concert set. *—Mark A. Humphrey*

Live! at the Long Beach & San Francisco Blues Festivals / 1985 / Arhoolie ♦♦♦
The 19 selections on this disc were done in the early '80s, when Chenier was past his romping prime but still keeping the zydeco engine running. He has done them all before on other releases, but keeps them entertaining and enjoyable through sheer will and personality. *—Ron Wynn*

Sings the Blues / 1987 / Arhoolie ♦♦♦
Lots of great accordion and unique vocals come from the blues side of the bayou. *—Jeff Hannusch & Mark A. Humphrey*

Bogalusa Boogie / Jul. 1987 / Arhoolie ♦♦♦♦
The zydeco maestro assembled his roadworthy and definitely boogie-as-all-get-out combo in a studio in the Louisiana countryside and cut this entire album in one day, everything completely live except for one accordion overdub. Clifton Chenier was, of course, an undisputed master of zydeco music and listeners looking for a good example of him at his best should be eager to grab this or any of the artist's Arhoolie releases, as his work for this label is consistently top-notch. The good-natured and easy groove the band sets up should be instructive to any musicians interested in learning how to get people to dance. The medium tempo blues numbers such as "Quelque Chose Sur Mon Idee" are really beautiful, while the instrumental "Ride 'Em Cowboy" is simply lots of fun, the honking tenor sax and clickety-clacking rub board riding high in the saddle. *—Eugene Chadbourne*

Live at St. Mark's / 1988 / Arhoolie ♦♦♦
Live at St. Mark's captures a rollicking concert performed in Richmond, California. Chenier leads the band through a blend of zydeco and blues, singing with gusto and spice all along. Furthermore, he plays to the audience, telling jokes and stories, which give the album a special, intimate feel. With all the wonderful music and joy that *Live at St. Marks* radiates, there's little question that it is one of Chenier's finest live albums. *—Thom Owens*

60 Minutes With the King of Zydeco / 1988 / Arhoolie ♦♦♦♦
This album is Arhoolie's attempt to create a posthumous greatest hits compilation for the King of Zydeco, presenting the 15 best-sellers from their catalog. As such, all of the best songs from Chenier's days are available together here, ranging from slower blues to high speed party-based zydeco. Any fan of Chenier (or zydeco in general) should look into this album for its breadth over the years. Aside from that, single albums are probably better suited for most purposes. If someone just wants one comprehensive Clifton Chenier album in their collection, however, this is the one to have. *—Adam Greenberg*

★ **Zydeco Dynamite: The Clifton Chenier Anthology** / 1993 / Rhino ♦♦♦♦♦
Clifton Chenier was to zydeco what Elvis Presley was to rockabilly, only more so—the genre's founding father and tireless ambassador. Rhino has done an admirable job of collecting the accordionist's important work for this two-disc, 40-track set, harking back to a wonderfully chaotic "Louisiana Stomp" that he waxed in Lake Charles, Louisiana in 1954 for J.R. Fullbright's tiny Elko label. Whether you're in the market for one zydeco collection to summarize the entire genre or ready to delve deeply into the legacy of the idiom's pioneer, this is precisely where to begin. *—Bill Dahl*

We're Gonna Party / Oct. 25, 1994 / Collectables ♦♦♦

Zydeco Sont Pas Sale / Apr. 22, 1997 / Arhoolie ♦♦♦♦♦
Clifton Chenier is the acknowledged Little Richard of zydeco. He is the grand architect of the real, Creole French, pseudo-Caribbean blend of blues and R&B. This mid-priced sampler culls all its cuts from seven other Arhoolie releases. Chenier continually updated his sound, while retaining the royal title King of Zydeco. While condensing his nearly four-decade career into 15 cuts can scarcely do it justice, this is an excellent starting point. You should be able to identify the periods of Chenier's career that merit further investigation. Or, you have an excellent po-boy party disc that has something to satisfy every zydeco opinion. *—Thomas Schulte*

Squeezebox Boogie / Jun. 22, 1999 / Just a Memory ♦♦♦♦
Squeezebox Boogie is among the late-'90s CDs that came from Just a Memory's *Collectors Classics* series, which also gave us blues titles by Muddy Waters, the Reverend Gary Davis, James Cotton, and the Sonny Terry/Brownie McGhee team. *Collectors Classics* is an appropriate name for the series, for it was aimed at serious collectors rather than casual listeners. *Squeezebox Boogie* isn't meant to serve as an introduction to the talents of Clifton Chenier, but seasoned fans will find a lot to admire about this rare recording made in August 1978 at the long gone Rising Sun Club in Montreal. True to form, the bilingual Louisiana singer excels as a bluesman on "I'm a Hog for You," "Bon Ton Roulet," and B.B. King's "Rock Me Baby," but is equally impressive as a zydeco artist on "Zydeco Cha Cha" and his famliar "Joli Blonde." Also quite infectious is Chenier's blues/jazz/zydeco interpretation of the Glenn Miller smash "In the Mood." The sound quality is fine; those who complained about the sound quality and distorted vocals on Muddy Waters' *Hoochie Coochie Man* (another *Collectors Classics* title recorded at the Rising Sun Club in the late '70s) will find that the sound is much cleaner and sharper on this CD. Although not for novices, *Squeezebox Boogie* is easily recommended to seasoned Chenier fans. *—Alex Henderson*

Live at 1966 Berkeley Blues Festival / Jan. 25, 2000 / Arhoolie ♦♦♦♦
Recorded live on KAL radio in Berkeley, CA. on April 15, 1966, this presents roughly equal shares of material from Clifton Chenier, Mance Lipscomb, and Lightnin' Hopkins, performing at the 1966 Berkeley Blues Festival. The sound is not state-of-the-art, but decent considering the vintage. The material is not going to surprise anyone familiar with the artists: good news if you're in love with their music and want typical excerpts of their sets, bad if you think you might have enough of them and are considering whether to investigate further. Chenier's performance (lasting nine songs) might be of the greatest historical interest of the three on this disc, as it was his first appearance before a "a mostly young, white, relatively sophisticated concert audience," as Chris Strachwitz writes in the liner notes. It's just Chenier, his accordion, and drummer Francis Clay, mostly on original tunes, as well as zydeco arrangements of Slim Harpo's "Baby Scratch My Back" and Ray Charles' "What'd I Say?" Half of the material on this disc was previously available on Arhoolie LP 1030, but eleven of the 23 songs on the CD (and six of Chenier's nine contributions) were previously unreleased. *—Richie Unterberger*

Live at Grant Street / Oct. 24, 2000 / Arhoolie ♦♦♦
Clifton Chenier recorded this 73-minute performance in Lafayette, LA, on April 28, 1981, backed by the Red Hot Louisiana Band. That group featured Cleveland Chenier on rub-board, C.J. Chenier on alto sax, and Robert Peter on drums; oddly, the guitar and bass players for this specific gig remain unidentified. No surprises here—just a good energetic set by the king of zydeco, with a full-sounding band and pretty good fidelity. As usual, he varied the set between traditional-sounding zydeco and numbers with a heavier soul and blues flavor (on which the saxophone comes much more to the fore), including a cover of the old Chuck Willis hit "What Am I Living For." *—Richie Unterberger*

Roscoe Chenier

b. Nov. 6, 1941, Notleyville, LA
Vocals / Swamp Blues, Soul
A second cousin of the late zydeco/blues legend Clifton Chenier, Roscoe Chenier is an expressive blues/R&B singer and guitarist who isn't nearly as well known as his famous relative. Roscoe Chenier was born and raised in Louisiana, where he joined a band called Rockin' CD and the Blues Runners as a teenager in 1957. Chenier formed his own band in 1959, and in 1961, he recorded the 45-rpm single "Born for Bad Luck" and its B side "Annie Mae's Yo-Yo" for Reynaud. The single didn't do a lot nationally, although it was played on local jukeboxes in southern Louisiana and eventually became a collector's item. Chenier (whose influences range from B.B. King to Fats Domino) continued to play the Louisiana circuit into the '90s, but not until 1993 would he record again—and not until 1993 would he actually record an album. That year, a 52-year-old Chenier recorded his self-titled debut album for Avenue Jazz. The CD was good enough to make one wish that Chenier wasn't so obscure, but when the '90s were coming to a close, he had yet to come out with a second album or become better known outside of Louisiana. *—Alex Henderson*

● **Roscoe Chenier** / 1993 / Avenue Jazz ♦♦♦♦
Although Roscoe Chenier's self-titled debut album came out on Avenue Jazz and ended up in some jazz bins, the fact is that this isn't a jazz release—it's really a collection of electric blues, Fats Domino-influenced R&B, and classic '60s-type soul. The CD contains no jazz whatsoever, and it doesn't contain any zydeco either, despite the fact that the singer/guitarist is the second cousin of the late zydeco/blues great Clifton Chenier. But Roscoe Chenier doesn't need to embrace zydeco to make it clear that he's from Louisiana—the bayou influence comes through whether he's providing 12-bar blues on "Home Wrecker," "Losing the Only One You Love," and "Come on Home" or getting into a classic soul sound on "Just Because" and "You Don't Understand." As good as the album is, it didn't make Chenier well-known. But *Roscoe Chenier* is worth picking up if you come across a copy. *—Alex Henderson*

Roscoe Style / Oct. 16, 2001 / Black & Tan ♦♦♦

The Chicago Blue Stars

f. Chicago, IL
Group / Electric Chicago Blues
This was in actuality Charlie Musselwhite's band circa 1969, but because of his Vanguard contract he could not sing or be pictured on the sextet's only LP—although his harp playing is credited. Boasting perhaps the greatest Chicago rhythm section ever (drummer Fred Below and bass monster Jack Myers), the group showcased steel guitarist Freddie Roulette, pianist Skip Rose, and Aces guitarist Louis Myers. *—Dan Forte*

● **Coming Home** / Mar. 1970 / Blue Thumb ♦♦♦
Because Musselwhite's contract forbid him to sing and Roulette had yet to develop into a strong vocalist, Louis Myers bears most of the vocal weight, and Rose and Below make one rather weak attempt each. But instrumentally—two Roulette spotlights and Musselwhite's jazzy arrangement of the title track—the group backed up their legendary status. As welcome as this "group" effort is, it's a shame the unit never recorded in the context it was formed—as Musselwhite's stellar backup band. *—Dan Forte*

Chicken Shack

f. 1966, Birmingham, England, **db.** 1973

Group / British Blues, Blues-Rock

This British blues-rock group is remembered mostly for their keyboard player, Christine Perfect, who would join Fleetwood Mac after marrying John McVie and changing her last name. Although they were one of the more pedestrian acts of the British blues boom, Chicken Shack was quite popular for a time in the late '60s, placing two albums in the British Top 20. The frontperson of Chicken was not Perfect/McVie, but guitarist Stan Webb, who would excite British audiences by entering the crowds at performances, courtesy of his 100-meter-long guitar lead. They were signed to Mike Vernon's Blue Horizon label, a British blues pillar that had its biggest success with early Fleetwood Mac.

Chicken Shack was actually not far behind Mac in popularity in the late '60s, purveying a more traditional brand of Chicago blues, heavily influenced by Freddie King. Although Webb took most of the songwriting and vocal duties, Christine Perfect also chipped in with occasional compositions and lead singing. In fact, she sang lead on their only British Top 20 single, "I'd Rather Go Blind" (1969). But around that time, she quit the music business to marry John McVie and become a housewife, although, as the world knows, that didn't last too long. Chicken Shack never recovered from Christine's loss, commercially or musically. Stan Webb kept Chicken Shack going, with a revolving door of other musicians, all the way into the '80s, though he briefly disbanded the group to join Savoy Brown for a while in the mid-'70s. *—Richie Unterberger*

40 Blue Fingers, Freshly Packed and Ready to Serve / 1968 / Epic ✦✦✦✦

If one can overlook Stan Webb's hyperventilating vocal excesses (which ain't easy), this is a promising debut, especially noteworthy for Webb's Freddie King-inspired guitar sting and Christine Perfect's understated vocals (only two, unfortunately compared to Webb's six). Webb does justice to his mentor with two instrumentals, King's "San-Ho-Zay" and his own "Webbed Feet." and Perfect proves the ideal counterpart—one of the few pianists paying homage to King's longtime collaborator Sonny Thompson. Nice spare sound, typical of Mike Vernon's Blue Horizon Label. *—Dan Forte*

O.K. Ken? / 1969 / BGO ✦✦

This was Chicken Shack's most popular album, making the British Top Ten. If you're looking for relics of the British Blues Boom, however, you'd be much better off with Ten Years After, to say nothing of legitimate artists such as Fleetwood Mac and John Mayall. British blues at its best could be exciting (if usually derivative), but it's difficult to fathom how this relentlessly plodding, monotonous effort met with such success. Stan Webb took most of the songwriting and vocal chores, emulating the slow-burning Chicago boogie with little skill or subtlety (though he wasn't a bad guitarist). Christine Perfect did write and sing a few songs, but these unfortunately found both her compositional and vocal chops at a most callow stage of development. To nail the coffin, most of the songs were preceded by excruciating comic dialog that made Cheech & Chong sound sophisticated in comparison. *—Richie Unterberger*

100 Ton Chicken / 1969 / Blue Horizon ✦✦

Lethargic blues, sounding like an opening act recorded at the blues bar down the street. This record literally screams for a competent singer, as Stan Webb's lazy, mumbling vocals are almost laughable (did he intend it that way?). Sorry, but this chicken laid a 20-ton rotten egg. *—Peter Kurtz*

Accept Chicken Shack / 1970 / Blue Horizon ✦✦

Imagination Lady / 1972 / Indigo ✦✦✦✦

Imagination Lady is the fifth long-player for Stan Webb's Chicken Shack. Much in the same tradition as the great British bluesmen Alexis Korner and John Mayall, Webb's revolving-door personnel landed the band several notable members, including: John Almond (tenor/alto sax), Hughie Flint (drums), and Christine Perfect (keyboards/vocals). For this album, Webb (guitar/vocals) gathered a trio consisting of himself, future Gods and Jethro Tull member John Glascock (bass), and Paul Hancox (drums). Enthusiasts of the more traditional *40 Blue Fingers, Freshly Packed and Ready to Serve* and *OK Ken* albums have been quick to dismiss the latter-era band, often citing the whole over amplified power-metal trip as detracting from their blues origins. While certainly valid assessments, the power trio featured on *Imagination Lady* brings more than sheer volume to this release. As with the previous Chicken Shack long-players, this disc features several Webb originals augmented with some well-chosen cover tunes. The album opens with a ferocious cover of B.B. King's "Crying Won't Help You." This version is highlighted by Glascock's thrashing bass lines and Webb's wah-wah driven lead guitar and gin-soaked vocals. In a style akin to the Faces or even some of the rowdier moments from the Peter Green-led Fleetwood Mac, this trio grinds out the blues with a decidedly English edge. The folkie "If I Were a Carpenter" is speared with searing electric guitar leads that rip throughout the likewise spirited contributions from Glascock and Hancox. The tune is also afforded an unexpected sensitivity that contrasts well between the all-out sonic onslaught of the chorus and the restrained polyrhythms of the verses. In regards to original material, "Daughter of the Hillside" is without a doubt Webb's most impressive contribution to the album. It is arguably the strongest side on the disc. This straight-ahead rocker is an ideal trio effort with equal contributions from all three recalling the intense instrumentality of Cream or early Led Zeppelin. With so much potential, it's unfortunate that the 11-minute epic "Telling Your Fortune"—which is nothing more than a 12-bar blues platform for solos from Webb and Hancox—is so erratic. In an ironic contrast, the closing number "The Loser" is upbeat and almost pop-oriented, again displaying the immense strength of this short-lived incarnation of Chicken Shack. *—Lindsay Planer*

Unlucky Boy / 1973 / London ✦✦✦

● **Collection** / 1988 / Castle ✦✦✦✦

Collection contains the cream of Chicken Shack's uneven albums and provides a perfect introduction to the British blues band. *—Thom Owens*

On Air / May 1998 / Strange Fruit ✦✦✦

Chosen Gospel Singers

f. 1950, Houston, TX

Group / Traditional Gospel, Black Gospel

Despite notching a series of hits between the early '50s and early '60s, the Chosen Gospel Singers remain one of the most elusive groups of gospel's golden era—plagued by constant lineup changes, the ensemble's proper history remains sketchy at best, and even the exact involvement of their most famous alumnus, Lou Rawls, is something of a mystery. It's known that the Chosen Gospel Singers were formed in Houston in 1950, and originally consisted of J.B. Randall, Aaron Wyatt, Willie Rose and two shadowy figures later recalled by their surnames of Sheridan and Files. On the advice of manager Joe Johnson, himself a founding member of the Pilgrim Travelers, the group soon relocated to Los Angeles; upon arriving on the West Coast, the first of countless roster fluctuations struck, and in seemingly no time Randall was the only surviving original member.

Tenors E.J. Brumfield, George Butler, and Fred Sims, in addition to baritone Oscar Cook, were soon recruited to flesh out the Chosen lineup, and in November 1952 this quintet made their first recordings for the Specialty label, yielding the hit single "One-Two-Three." (Ted Taylor, later a soul singer of some renown, was also briefly a member during this same period, although he did not appear on record.) The steady personnel shifts have been attributed in large part to the group's status as a semi-professional venture—the Chosen's grueling weekend touring schedules played havoc with the individual members' day jobs, and for many the frustrations of constant firings ultimately ended in rejecting music in favor of finding steady work. Additionally, many had family commitments which made touring outside of the West Coast impossible.

When the Chosen went back into the studio in mid-1953, then, only Randall remained from the previous incarnation; his new collaborators included low tenor John Evans, tenors J.T. "Rattler" Ratley and Preston Whitted, and baritone Sam Thomas. During a subsequent tourstop in Chicago, they recruited 17-year-old lead vocalist Lou Rawls, already a gospel veteran through his work with the Teenage Kings of Harmony, the Holy Wonders and the Highway QC's. In February 1954, Rawls made his first recordings as a Chosen Gospel Singer; another session followed just two months later, but in the interim both Evans and Ratley apparently exited the ranks. Also gone was Randall, the sole remaining link to the group's origins; he was replaced by Raeford Blair. There is some evidence that E.J. Booker, later of the Pilgrim Travelers, was also in the group at this juncture, although other accounts deny such a claim.

Rawls joined the Army prior to the Chosen's final Specialty session, recorded in early 1955; he was replaced by Brooklyn native Bob Crutcher for the studio date, which generated the hit "Prayer for the Doomed." Later that year, the Chosen signed with the Nashboro label; Crutcher remained in the lead slot, with Tommy Ellison of the Harmonizing Four soon joining him at the helm. Rawls resurfaced on their fourth Nashboro single, "Walk with Me," which may or may not have been first cut prior to his military tenure; both Sims and Brumfield definitely returned to action, however, with the latter fronting the final incarnation of the Chosen, a lineup which also included the members of a Tyler, Texas, quartet led by singer Willie Neal Johnson known as the Gospel Keynotes. When Brumfield quit soon after, he handed the reins to Johnson, who restored the name to the Gospel Keynotes, bringing the Chosen's convoluted story to a close. *—Jason Ankeny*

● **The Lifeboat** / 1954 / Specialty ✦✦✦✦✦

Featured are previously unreleased tracks, alternate takes, and long-out-of-print gems by this major gospel quartet, led at times by Lou Rawls. *—Opal Louis Nations*

Meet the Selah Jubilees / ✦✦✦

Popa Chubby (Theodore Joseph Horowitz)

b. 1960, Bronx, NY

Vocals / Contemporary Blues, Modern Electric Blues

Born Theodore Joseph (Ted) Horowitz in the Bronx, NY, Popa Chubby was the son of a candy store owner. At 13, Chubby began playing drums; shortly thereafter, he discovered the music of the Rolling Stones and began playing guitar. Although he grew up in the '70s, Chubby took his cue from artists of the '60s, including Sly & the Family Stone, Jimi Hendrix and Eric Clapton, among others. By the time he was in his early twenties, he enjoyed and played blues music, but also worked for a while backing up punk poet Richard Hell. Chubby's first big break was winning a national blues talent search sponsored by KLON, a public radio station in Long Beach, CA. He won New Artist of the Year Award and opened at the Long Beach Blues Festival in 1992. Chubby has continued to play more than 200 club dates a year through the '90s. His Sony/OKeh debut, *Booty and the Beast*, was produced by longtime Atlantic Records engineer/producer Tom Dowd, whose recordings by Aretha Franklin, Ray Charles, Wilson Pickett and others are legendary. In 1994, Chubby released several albums on his own Laughing Bear label, *It's Chubby Time* and *Gas Money*, before landing his deal with Sony Music/OKeh Records for *Booty and the Beast*, his major label debut, released in 1995. In 1996, the Prime CD label released a live recording of Chubby's, *Hit the High Hard One*. Two years later, *One Million Broken Guitars* was released on Lightyear Records; *Brooklyn Basement Blues* followed in 1999. In 2000 Chubby signed with the Blind Pig label and released *How'd a White Boy Get the Blues?* in 2001. The disc turned out to be a slight departure, incorporating elements of contemporary pop and hip hop. *—Richard Skelly & Al Campbell*

Gas Money / 1994 / Prime ✦✦✦

It's Chubby Time / 1994 / Prime ✦✦✦✦

Booty and the Beast / 1995 / OKeh/550 Music ✦✦✦✦

Popa Chubby's major-label debut album is an inspiring set of energetic, gut-bucket blues-rock, filled with exceptional playing. Chubby has soul, even if he doesn't quite cut it as a songwriter; there aren't many songs that are inventive or memorable. But as an instrumental workout, *Booty and the Beast* is terrific. Using the blues as a basic foundation, Popa Chubby spins off into new directions, incorporating bits of rock and jazz to his forceful playing. His guitar playing is what makes the album a promising debut. —*Stephen Thomas Erlewine*

Hit the High Hard One / 1996 / Prime/Laughing Bear ✦✦✦

One Million Broken Guitars / Jun. 2, 1998 / Lightyear ✦✦✦
Over the course of his career, Popa Chubby hasn't exactly grown. Instead, he's found his formula and he's sticking to it, thank you, no matter what anybody else might say. That's probably why he didn't quite cut it as a major-label artist—there is a market for his competent, muscular blues-rock, just not a large one. That cult audience is the reason why he's better suited for the indies, but on *One Million Broken Guitar Strings*—unbelievably, his fifth album (only one was a live effort)—he's not distinctive enough to be a true cult artist. He turns out amiable post-SRV blues-rock, spiked with a couple of jazz flourishes, and while the end result is enjoyable, it's not necessarily memorable. Even the better moments are usually instrumental highlights, not actual songs, which fade immediately after they're played. Again, it confirms that Chubby is a fine guitarist, but his weakness as a songwriter is beginning to overwhelm him, and *One Million Broken Guitar Strings* is a testament to this Achilles heel. —*Stephen Thomas Erlewine*

Brooklyn Basement Blues / Sep. 21, 1999 / Shanachie ✦✦✦
Popa Chubby plays loud blues-rock, plain and simple. The songs on this 1999 outing are almost all originals from his pen with Otis Redding's "I've Been Loving You Too Long"and Jimi Hendrix' "The Wind Cries Mary" being the only covers aboard. While blues purists will no doubt find his playing and demeanor rock-excessive, fans of burning bluesy guitar will actually find a lot to savor here. Chubby never really overplays (given the parameters of the genre he's working in, mind you) and the tunes show a stronger sense of melody this time out. There's a nice selection of grooves and all of them exist as songs first, and as frameworks second. Fans of high-powered blues-rock will love this one. —*Cub Koda*

How'd a White Boy Get the Blues? / Aug. 14, 2001 / Blind Pig ✦✦✦
Influenced by blues greats Stevie Ray Vaughn, Buddy Guy, Willie Dixon, and the three Kings (all of whom he name-checks in the aptly titled "Carrying on the Torch of the Blues"), Popa Chubby, aka Ted Horowitz, brazenly ventures into more contemporary waters while remaining true to his rootsy influences and the spirit of the genre. While the hip-hop beats and Chubby's rapping are a little awkward on the album's opening "Daddy Played the Guitar and Mama Was a Disco Queen" (a video of the track is also included as the enhanced CD-ROM portion of the disc), especially as he injects them into a song that starts out as an acoustic ballad, his ragged and incisive slide keep it grounded in familiar territory. Chubby's fifth release for his fifth label commendably takes chances to break out of the strict electric blues-rock genre that he's worked so well in the past. That it doesn't always click is forgivable since he's at least aiming to expand his typically limited palette. Not quite a one-man band, Chubby at various times plays bass, drums, harmonica, dobro, and sitar in addition to his six-string duties, often overdubbing himself. The process lends a slightly claustrophobic sound to the disc that becomes particularly wearing on the nine-minute "Since I Lost My Leg" (where Chubby plays everything) with the track getting bogged down in endless repetition of its one greasy riff. With a sufficiently gruff, world-weary voice, the singer/guitarist delivers his down-and-out rockers like "No Comfort" with its blatant Hendrix attack and the slow, wiry funk of "Savin' My Love Up for My Lover" with knowing intensity. While the jaunty tack-piano drive of the clumsily titled "It's a Sad Day in New York City When There Ain't No Room for the Blues" pushes the tune into cheery territory, the self-explanatory downbeat lyrics belie the song's more lighthearted approach. The guitarist even shifts into the fast-tempo, Southern rock, chicken-pickin' route on "Goin' Down to Willies," one of the album's least bluesy tracks. He also dips into the Memphis midtempo R&B swamps with "Time Is Killing Me," the album's most melodic pop track. Although he's not entirely successful, Popa Chubby hits enough stylistic bases to make this a listenable and often invigorating album which gets extra points for attempting to push past the stereotypical blues clichés and into more experimental waters. —*Hal Horowitz*

● **The Good, the Bad and the Chubby** / Jul. 9, 2002 / Blind Pig ✦✦✦✦
Against all odds, Popa Chubby has turned into a distinctive, strong modern bluesman. He's still saddled with that ridiculous name, which makes it hard to take him seriously, and he has a tendency to indulge in easy, vulgar jokes, but that's just part of who he is. If that annoys you, look past it and concentrate on the music on *The Good, the Bad and the Chubby*, which is lean and adventurous, solidly within the postmodern blues-rock tradition, but breaking free of the Stevie Ray fixations that distinguished his earlier work by adding bits of jazz and an ever-so-subtle hip-hop underpinning. Plus, there's Chubby's insistence on relying on original material—a welcome turn of events, since it gives his album character even when the songs aren't first rate. Fortunately, through much of *The Good*, the music is good and he tackles a number of different kinds of songs, from topical tunes about 9-11 to joke songs, knowing relationship songs, and much more. Perhaps there are a couple of songs that stretch out a little bit too long, and maybe the album could use a little more grit in the production, but these, overall, are minor quibbles, since *The Good, the Bad and the Chubby* is one of the strongest, most distinctive modern blues albums of 2002, proving that Popa has come a long way in his decade of recording. —*Stephen Thomas Erlewine*

Eric Clapton (Eric Patrick Clapp)

b. Mar. 30, 1945, Ripley, England
Vocals, Guitar (Electric), Guitar / Album Rock, British Blues, Pop/Rock, Adult Contemporary, Hard Rock, Blues-Rock
By the time Eric Clapton launched his solo career with the release of his self-titled debut album in mid-1970, he was long established as one of the world's major rock stars due to

his group affiliations—the Yardbirds, John Mayall's Bluesbreakers, Cream, and Blind Faith—affiliations that had demonstrated his claim to being the best rock guitarist of his generation. That it took Clapton so long to go out on his own, however, was evidence of a degree of reticence unusual for one of his stature. And his debut album, though it spawned the Top 40 hit "After Midnight," was typical of his self-effacing approach: it was, in effect, an album by the group he had lately been featured in, Delaney & Bonnie & Friends.

Not surprisingly, before his solo debut had even been released, Clapton had retreated from his solo stance, assembling from the D&B&F ranks the personnel for a group, Derek & the Dominos, with which he played for most of 1970. Clapton was largely inactive in 1971 and 1972, due to heroin addiction, but he performed a comeback concert at the Rainbow Theatre in London on January 13, 1973, resulting in the album *Eric Clapton's Rainbow Concert* (September 1973).

But Clapton did not launch a sustained solo career until July 1974, when he released *461 Ocean Boulevard*, which topped the charts and spawned the number one single "I Shot the Sheriff."

The persona Clapton established over the next decade was less that of guitar hero than arena rock star with a weakness for ballads. The follow-ups to *461 Ocean Boulevard*, *There's One in Every Crowd* (March 1975), the live *E.C. Was Here* (August 1975), and *No Reason to Cry* (August 1976), were less successful. But *Slowhand* (November 1977), which featured both the powerful "Cocaine" (written by J.J. Cale, who had also written "After Midnight") and the hit singles "Lay Down Sally" and "Wonderful Tonight," was a million-seller. Its follow-ups, *Backless* (November 1978), featuring the Top Ten hit "Promises," the live *Just One Night* (April 1980), and *Another Ticket* (February 1981), featuring the Top Ten hit "I Can't Stand It," were all big sellers.

Clapton's popularity waned somewhat in the first half of the '80s, as the albums *Money and Cigarettes* (February 1983), *Behind the Sun* (March 1985), and *August* (November 1986) indicated a certain career stasis. But he was buoyed up by the release of the box set retrospective *Crossroads* (April 1988), which seemed to remind his fans of how great he was. *Journeyman* (November 1989) was a return to form.

It would be his last new studio album for nearly five years, though in the interim he would suffer greatly and enjoy surprising triumph. On March 20, 1991, Clapton's four-year-old son was killed in a fall. While he mourned, he released a live album, *24 Nights* (October 1991), culled from his annual concert series at the Royal Albert Hall in London, and prepared a movie soundtrack, *Rush* (January 1992). The soundtrack featured a song written for his son, "Tears in Heaven," that became a massive hit single.

In March 1992, Clapton recorded a concert for *MTV Unplugged* that, when released on an album in August, became his biggest-selling record ever. Two years later, Clapton returned with a blues album, *From the Cradle*, which became one of his most successful albums, both commercially and critically. *Crossroads 2: Live in the Seventies*, a box set chronicling his live work from the '70s, was released to mixed reviews. In early 1997, Clapton, billing himself by the pseudonym "x-sample," collaborated with keyboardist/producer Simon Climie as the ambient new age and trip-hop duo T.D.F. The duo released *Retail Therapy* to mixed reviews in early 1997.

Clapton retained Climie as his collaborator for *Pilgrim*, his first album of new material since 1989's *Journeyman*. *Pilgrim* was greeted with decidedly mixed reviews upon its spring 1998 release, but the album debuted at number four and stayed in the Top Ten for several weeks on the success of the single "My Father's Eyes." In 2000, Clapton teamed up with old friend BB King on *Riding With the King*, a set of blues standards and material from contemporary singer/songwriters. Another solo outing entitled *Reptile* followed in early 2001. —*William Ruhlmann*

Eric Clapton / Jul. 1970 / Polydor ✦✦✦✦✦
Eric Clapton's eponymous solo debut was recorded after he completed a tour with Delaney & Bonnie. Clapton used the core of the duo's backing band and co-wrote the majority of the songs with Delaney Bramlett—accordingly, *Eric Clapton* sounds more laid-back and straightforward than any of the guitarist's previous recordings. There are still elements of blues and rock & roll, but they're hidden beneath layers of gospel, R&B, country, and pop flourishes. And the pop element of the record is the strongest of the album's many elements—"Blues Power" isn't a blues song and only "Let It Rain," the album's closer, features extended solos. Throughout the album, Clapton turns out concise solos that de-emphasize his status as guitar god, even when they display astonishing musicality and technique. That is both a good and a bad thing—it's encouraging to hear him grow and become a more fully rounded musician, but too often the album needs the spark that some long guitar solos would have given it. In short, it needs a little more of Clapton's personality. —*Stephen Thomas Erlewine*

461 Ocean Boulevard / Jul. 1974 / Polydor ✦✦✦✦✦
461 Ocean Boulevard is Eric Clapton's second studio solo album, arriving after his side project of Derek & the Dominos and a long struggle with heroin addiction. Although there are some new reggae influences, the album doesn't sound all that different from the rock, pop, blues, country, and R&B amalgam of *Eric Clapton*. However, *461 Ocean Boulevard* is a tighter, more focused outing that enables Clapton to stretch out instrumentally. Furthermore, the pop concessions on the album—the sleek production, the concise running times—don't detract from the rootsy origins of the material, whether it's Johnny Otis' "Willie and the Hand Jive," the traditional blues "Motherless Children," Bob Marley's "I Shot the Sheriff," or Clapton's emotional originals, "Let It Grow" and "Better Make It Through Today" (the latter included only on several reissues of the album). With its relaxed, friendly atmosphere and strong bluesy roots, *461 Ocean Boulevard* set the template for Clapton's '70s albums. Though he tried hard to make an album exactly like it, he never quite managed to replicate its charms. —*Stephen Thomas Erlewine*

There's One in Every Crowd / Mar. 1975 / Polydor ✦✦
Having stayed out of the recording studio for four years prior to making his comeback album, *461 Ocean Boulevard*, Eric Clapton returned to recording only a few months later to make its follow-up, *There's One in Every Crowd*. Perhaps he hadn't had time to write

or gather sufficient material to make a similarly effective album, since the result is a scattershot mixture of styles, leading off with two gospel tunes, one a reggae version of "Swing Low, Sweet Chariot." Clapton and his second guitarist, George Terry, had written a sequel to "I Shot the Sheriff," "Don't Blame Me," which Clapton sang in his best impersonation of Bob Marley's voice. The album's best track, naturally, was the blues cover, Clapton's take on Elmore James' "The Sky Is Crying." But *There's One in Every Crowd* was a disappointing follow-up to *461 Ocean Boulevard*, and fans let Clapton know it: While the former album had topped the charts and gone gold, the latter didn't even make the Top Ten. *—William Ruhlmann*

E.C. Was Here / Aug. 1975 / Polydor ✦✦✦

Following Eric Clapton's recovery from heroin addition in 1974 and subsequent comeback (announced by *461 Ocean Boulevard*), the guitar legend retained his fine band and toured extensively, and this live album is a souvenir of that period. Despite having such pop-oriented hits as "I Shot the Sheriff," *E.C. Was Here* makes it clear that Clapton was and always would be a blues man. The opening cut, "Have You Ever Loved a Woman," clearly illustrates this, and underlines the fact that Clapton had a firm grasp on his blues guitar ability, with some sterling, emotionally charged and sustained lines and riffs. A short version of "Drifting Blues" also drives the point home, with a lazy, Delta blues feel that is intoxicating. Aside from these standout blues workouts, Clapton provides a surprise with two songs from his Blind Faith period. "Presence of the Lord" and Steve Winwood's classic "Can't Find My Way Home" are given great readings here and highlight Clapton's fine touring band, particularly co-vocalist Yvonne Elliman, whose singing adds a mellifluousness to Clapton's blues vocal inflections. The market was a bit oversaturated with Clapton and Cream reissue products at the time, and this fine record got lost in the shuffle, but it remains an excellent document of the period. *—Matthew Greenwald*

No Reason to Cry / Aug. 1976 / Polydor ✦✦✦

When he gave a speech inducting the Band into the Rock & Roll Hall of Fame, Eric Clapton said that after he heard their debut album, *Music from Big Pink*, he wanted to join the group, the fact that they already had a guitarist in Robbie Robertson notwithstanding. In the winter of 1975-1976, when he cut *No Reason to Cry* at the Band's Shangri-la Studio in Malibu, California, he came as close as he ever would to realizing that desire. Clapton is a musical chameleon; though some of *No Reason to Cry* is identifiable as the kind of pop/rock Clapton had been making since the start of his solo career (the best of it being "Hello Old Friend," which became his first Top 40 single in two years), the most memorable music on the album occurs when Clapton is collaborating with members of the Band and other guests. He duets with Band bassist Rick Danko on Danko's "All Our Past Times," and with Bob Dylan on Dylan's "Sign Language," as Robertson's distinctive lead guitar is heard rather than Clapton's. As a result, the album is a good purchase for fans of Bob Dylan and the Band, but not necessarily for those of Eric Clapton. The CD reissue adds a bonus track, "Last Night," which is a traditional 12-bar blues song credited to Clapton. *—William Ruhlmann*

Slowhand / Nov. 1977 / Polydor ✦✦✦✦✦

After the guest-star-drenched *No Reason to Cry* failed to make much of an impact commerically, Eric Clapton returned to using his own band for *Slowhand*. The difference is substantial—where *No Reason to Cry* struggled hard to find the right tone, *Slowhand* opens with the relaxed, bluesy shuffle of J.J. Cale's "Cocaine" and sustains it throughout the course of the album. Alternating between straight blues ("Mean Old Frisco"), country ("Lay Down Sally"), mainstream rock ("Cocaine," "The Core"), and pop ("Wonderful Tonight"), *Slowhand* doesn't sound schizophrenic because of the band's grasp of the material. This is laid-back virtuosity—although Clapton and his band are never flashy, their playing is masterful and assured. That assurance and the album's eclectic material make *Slowhand* rank with *461 Ocean Boulevard* as Eric Clapton's best albums. *—Stephen Thomas Erlewine*

Backless / Nov. 1978 / Polydor ✦✦✦

Having made his best album since *461 Ocean Boulevard* with *Slowhand*, Eric Clapton followed with *Backless*, which took the same authoritative, no-nonsense approach. If it wasn't quite the masterpiece, or the sales monster, that *Slowhand* had been, this probably was because of that usual Clapton problem—material. Once again, he returned to those Oklahoma hills for another song from J.J. Cale, but "I'll Make Love to You Anytime" wasn't quite up to "Cocaine" or "After Midnight." Bob Dylan contributed two songs, but you could see why he hadn't saved them for his own album, and Clapton's own writing contributions were mediocre. Clapton did earn a Top Ten hit with Richard Feldman and Roger Linn's understated pop shuffle "Promises," but it was not one of his more memorable recordings. Of course, Clapton's blues playing on the lone obligatory blues cut, "Early in the Morning" (presented in its full eight-minute version on the CD reissue), was stellar. *Backless* was his last album to feature the backup group that had been with him since 1974. *—William Ruhlmann*

Just One Night / Apr. 1980 / Polydor ✦✦✦✦✦

Although Eric Clapton has released a bevy of live albums, none of them have ever quite captured the guitarist's raw energy and dazzling virtuosity. The double-live album *Just One Night* may have gotten closer to that elusive goal than most of its predecessors, but it is still lacking in many ways. The most notable difference between *Just One Night* and Clapton's other live albums is his backing band. Led by guitarist Albert Lee, the group is a collective of accomplished professionals that have managed to keep some grit in their playing. They help push Clapton along, forcing him to spit out crackling solos throughout the album. However, the performances aren't consistent on *Just One Night*—there are plenty of dynamic moments like "Double Trouble" and "Rambling on My Mind," but they are weighed down by pedestrian renditions of songs like "All Our Past Times." Nevertheless, more than any other Clapton live album, *Just One Night* suggests the guitarist's in-concert potential. It's just too bad that the recording didn't occur on a night when he *did* fulfill all of that potential. *—Stephen Thomas Erlewine*

Another Ticket / Feb. 1981 / Polydor ✦✦✦

Now, here's a star-crossed album. Polydor rejected the first version of it, produced by Glyn Johns, and Eric Clapton was forced to cut it all over again with Tom Dowd. Then, a few dates into a US promotional tour coinciding with its release, Clapton collapsed and was found to be near death from ulcers due to his alcoholism. Finally, it turned out to be the final record of his 15-year association with Polydor, which therefore had no reason to promote it. Nevertheless, the album made the Top Ten, went gold, and spawned a Top Ten single in "I Can't Stand It." And the rest of it wasn't too shabby, either. The first and last Clapton studio album to feature his all-British band of the early '80s, it gave considerable prominence to second guitarist Albert Lee and especially to keyboard player/singer Gary Brooker (formerly leader of Procol Harum), and they gave it more of a blues-rock feel than the country-funk brewed up by the Tulsa shuffle crew Clapton had used throughout the '70s. Best of all, Clapton had taken the time to write some songs—he's credited on six of the nine selections—and tunes such as the title track and "I Can't Stand It" held up well. This wasn't great Clapton, but it was good, and it deserved more recognition than conditions allowed it at the time. *—William Ruhlmann*

Time Pieces: Best of Eric Clapton / May 1982 / Polydor ✦✦✦✦✦

Time Pieces is a good single-disc collection of Eric Clapton's solo hits—including "I Shot the Sheriff," "After Midnight," "Wonderful Tonight," Derek & the Dominos' "Layla," and "Cocaine"—that has since been supplanted by the more thorough *The Cream of Eric Clapton*, which combines his solo work with selections of his Cream and Blind Faith work. Nevertheless, the compilation still provides a good introduction for neophyte Clapton fans, especially those that just want copies of his '70s hits. *—Stephen Thomas Erlewine*

Money and Cigarettes / Feb. 1983 / Warner Brothers ✦✦✦

Money and Cigarettes marked several important turning points in Eric Clapton's recording career. It was his debut release on his own Duck imprint within Warner Bros.' Reprise Records subsidiary. It was also the first album he made after coming to terms with his drinking problem by giving up alcohol. Newly focused and having written a batch of new songs, he became dissatisfied with his longtime band and fired them, with the exception of second guitarist Albert Lee. In their place, he hired session pros like Stax Records veteran bassist Donald "Duck" Dunn and Muscle Shoals drummer Roger Hawkins, also bringing in guest guitarist Ry Cooder. His new songs reflected on his changed condition, with "Ain't Going Down," a thinly veiled musical rewrite of the Jimi Hendrix arrangement of "All Along the Watchtower," serving as a statement of purpose that declared, "I've still got something left to say." "The Shape You're In" was a criticism of his wife for her alcoholism that concluded, "I'm just telling you baby 'cause I've been there myself," while the lengthy acoustic ballad "Pretty Girl" and "Man in Love" reaffirmed his feelings for her. The album's single was the relatively slight pop tune "I've Got a Rock n' Roll Heart," but Clapton's many blues fans must have been most pleased with the covers of Sleepy John Estes' "Everybody Oughta Make a Change" (significantly placed as the album's leadoff track), Albert King's "Crosscut Saw," and Johnny Otis' "Crazy Country Hop." For all the changes and the high-powered sidemen, though, *Money and Cigarettes* ended up being just an average effort from Clapton, which his audience seems to have sensed since, despite the Top 20 placement for the single, it became his first album in more than six years to miss the Top Ten and fail to go gold. *—William Ruhlmann*

Time Pieces, Vol. 2: 'Live' in the Seventies / 1985 / Polydor ✦✦✦

Neither a career retrospective nor a rarities collection, *Time Pieces, Vol. 2: 'Live' in the Seventies* is an odd record. Featuring a selection of material recorded in concert at various points in the '70s, the album never gives an accurate impression of Clapton's progression as a guitarist—it's sequenced haphazardly, with tracks falling outside of strict chronological order. Nevertheless, there are a number of fine performances here, especially on album tracks like "Tulsa Time" and "If I Don't Be There by Morning," as well as the extended solos of "Rambling on My Mind." Diehard fans will find things of interest on *Time Pieces, Vol. 2*, but the album can be safely ignored by most listeners. *—Stephen Thomas Erlewine*

Behind the Sun / Mar. 1985 / Warner Brothers ✦✦✦

Clapton's career was in decline in the early '80s when he switched record labels from Polydor to Warner Bros. and his debut Warner album, *Money and Cigarettes*, became his first to fall below gold-record status in more than six years. As a result, Warner looked critically at his follow-up, the Phil Collins-produced *Behind the Sun*, in the fall of 1984 and rejected the first version submitted, insisting that he record several new songs written by Jerry Williams, backed by Los Angeles session players under the auspices of company producers Lenny Waronker and Ted Templeman. Warner then emphasized the new tracks, releasing two of them, "Forever Man" (which reached the Top 40) and "See What Love Can Do," as singles. The resulting album, not surprisingly, was somewhat schizophrenic, though the company may have been correct in thinking that the album as a whole was competent without being very exciting. The added tracks were not bad, but they were not the surefire hits they were supposed to be. As usual, there was some effective guitar soloing (notably on "Same Old Blues"), but despite the tinkering, *Behind the Sun* was not one of Clapton's better albums. It went gold after nearly two years in release. *—William Ruhlmann*

August / Nov. 1986 / Warner Brothers ✦✦

Eric Clapton adopted a new, tougher, hard R&B approach on *August*, employing a stripped-down band featuring keyboard player Greg Phillinganes, bassist Nathan East, and drummer/producer Phil Collins, plus, on several tracks, a horn section and, on a couple of tracks, backup vocals by Tina Turner, and performing songs written by old Motown hand Lamont Dozier, among others. The excellent, but incongruous, leadoff track, however, was "It's in the Way That You Use It," which Clapton and Robbie Robertson had written for Robertson's score to the film *The Color of Money*. Elsewhere, Clapton sang and played fiercely on songs like "Tearing Us Apart," "Run," and "Miss You," all of which earned AOR radio play. That radio support may have helped the album to achieve gold status in less than six months, Clapton's best commercial showing since 1981's *Another Ticket*, despite the album's failure to generate a hit single. The title commemorates the birth in August 1986 of Clapton's son Conor. The CD version of the album contains the bonus track "Grand Illusion." *—William Ruhlmann*

☆ **Crossroads** / Apr. 1988 / Polydor ✦✦✦✦✦
A four-disc box set spanning Eric Clapton's entire career—running from the Yardbirds to his '80s solo recordings—*Crossroads* not only revitalized Clapton's commerical standing, but it established the rock & roll multi-disc box set retrospective as a commercially viable proposition. Bob Dylan's *Biograph* was successful two years before the release of *Crossroads*, but Clapton's set was a bonafide blockbuster. And it's easy to see why. *Crossroads* manages to sum up Clapton's career succinctly and thoroughly, touching upon all of his hits and adding a bevy of first-rate unreleased material (most notably selections from the scrapped second Derek & the Dominos album). Although not all of his greatest performances are included on the set—none of his work as a session musician or guest artist is included, for instance—every truly essential item he recorded is present on these four discs. No other Clapton album accurately explains why the guitarist was so influential, or demonstrates exactly what he accomplished. *—Stephen Thomas Erlewine*

Journeyman / Nov. 1989 / Reprise ✦✦✦✦✦
For most of the '80s, Eric Clapton seemed rather lost, uncertain of whether he should return to his blues roots or pander to AOR radio. By the mid-'80s, he appeared to have made the decision to revamp himself as a glossy mainstream rocker, working with synthesizers and drum machines. Instead of expanding his audience, it only reduced it. Then came the career retrospective *Crossroads*, which helped revitalize his career, not only commercially, but also creatively, as *Journeyman*—the first album he recorded after the success of *Crossroads*—proved. Although *Journeyman* still suffers from an overly slick production, Clapton sounds more convincing than he has since the early '70s. Not only is his guitar playing muscular and forceful, his singing is soulful and gritty. Furthermore, the songwriting is consistently strong, alternating between fine mainstream rock originals ("Pretending") and covers ("Before You Accuse Me," "Hound Dog"). Like any of Clapton's best albums, there is no grandstanding to be found on *Journeyman*—it's simply a laid-back and thoroughly engaging display of Clapton's virtuosity. On the whole, it's the best studio album he's released since *Slowhand*. *—Stephen Thomas Erlewine*

24 Nights / Oct. 8, 1991 / Reprise ✦✦✦
Eric Clapton, who had not released a live album since 1980, had several good reasons to release one in the early '90s. For one thing, his spare backup band of keyboardist Greg Phillinganes, bassist Nathan East, and drummer Steve Ferrone, was his best live unit ever, and its powerful live versions of Cream classics like "White Room" and "Sunshine of Your Love" deserved to be documented. For another, since 1987, Clapton had been playing an annual series of concerts at the Royal Albert Hall in London, putting together various special shows—blues nights, orchestral nights, etc. *24 Nights*, a double album, was culled from two years of such shows, 1990 and 1991, and it demonstrated the breadth of Clapton's work, from his hot regular band to assemblages of bluesmen like Buddy Guy and Robert Cray to examples of his soundtrack work with an orchestra led by Michael Kamen. The result was an album that came across as a lavishly constructed retrospective and a testament to Clapton's musical stature. But it made little impact upon release (though it quickly went gold), perhaps because events overcame it—three months later, Clapton's elegy for his baby son, "Tears In Heaven," was all over the radio, and a few months after that he was redefining himself on *Unplugged*—a live show as austere as *24 Nights* was grand. Still, it would be hard to find a more thorough demonstration of Clapton's abilities than the one presented here. *—William Ruhlmann*

Rush / Jan. 14, 1992 / Reprise ✦✦✦
An excellent dark blues score written by Clapton (with help on the three songs) and performed by an augmented version of his band. This soundtrack album produced one big hit for Clapton with "Tears In Heaven," but it's a wonderfully intense piece of work all the way through, with some terrific guitar work from Clapton himself. Buddy Guy turns up to add lead vocals and guitar on the 11-minute version of Willie Dixon's "Don't Know Which Way to Go," and that's more than all right too. There's a very good chance that the dark intensity of this music was as much informed by the tragedies in Clapton's life ("Tears In Heaven" is about his son) as the film itself. Whatever the cause, this album has far more impact than you might expect from the score to a movie—there's a sense of the music here working something out in Clapton's heart, a sense given a lot of power thanks to the intense, heart-wrenching passion invoked by some of the turns taken here. At its best, Clapton's music can speak of the pain he feels—and Clapton has rarely been better than he is here. *—Steven McDonald*

Unplugged / Aug. 18, 1992 / Reprise ✦✦✦✦✦
Clapton's *Unplugged* was responsible for making acoustic-based music, and *Unplugged* albums in particular, a hot trend in the early '90s. Clapton's concert was not only one of the finest *Unplugged* episodes, but was also some of the finest music he had recorded in years. Instead of the slick productions that tainted his '80s albums, the music was straightforward and direct, alternating between his pop numbers and traditional blues songs. The result was some of the most genuine, heartfelt music the guitarist has ever committed to tape. And some of his most popular—the album sold over seven million copies in the U.S. and won several Grammies. *—Stephen Thomas Erlewine*

From the Cradle / Sep. 13, 1994 / Reprise ✦✦✦✦✦
For years, fans craved an all-blues album from Clapton; he waited until 1994 to deliver *From the Cradle*. The album manages to recreate the ambience of postwar electric blues, right down to the bottomless thump of the rhythm section. If it wasn't for Clapton's labored vocals, everything would be perfect. As long as he plays his guitar, he can't fail—his solos are white-hot and evocative, original and captivating. When he sings, Clapton loses that sense of originality, choosing to mimic the vocals of the original recordings. At times, his overemotive singing is painful; he doesn't have the strength to pull off Howlin' Wolf's growl or the confidence to replicate Muddy Waters' assured phrasing. Yet, whenever he plays, it's easier to forget his vocal shortcomings. Even with its faults, *From the Cradle* is one of Clapton's finest moments. *—Stephen Thomas Erlewine*

● **The Cream of Clapton** / Mar. 7, 1995 / Polydor/Chronicles ✦✦✦✦✦
Eric Clapton was contracted to Polydor Records from 1966 to 1981, first as a member of Cream, then Blind Faith, and later as a solo artist and as the leader of Derek & the Dominos. This 19-track, 79-minute disc surveys his career, presenting an excellent selection from the period, including the Cream hits "Sunshine of Your Love," "White Room," and "Crossroads"; "Presence of the Lord," Clapton's finest moment with Blind Faith; "Bell Bottom Blues" and "Layla" from Derek & the Dominos; and 11 songs from Clapton's solo work, among them the hits "I Shot The Sheriff," "Promises," and "I Can't Stand It." The selection is thus broader and better than that found on 1982's *Time Pieces* collection, and with excellent sound and liner notes by Clapton biographer Ray Coleman, *The Cream of Clapton* stands as the single-disc best-of to own for Clapton's greatest recordings. [Not to be confused with the popular 1987 Polydor (U.K.) compilation *The Cream of Eric Clapton*, which has since been retitled *The Best of Eric Clapton*.] *—William Ruhlmann*

Eric Clapton's Rainbow Concert [Expanded] / Jul. 25, 1995 / Polydor/Chronicles ✦✦✦
In these days of CD expansion, it is not unusual for a record company to reissue an old album with a bonus track or two. This reconstruction of the January 13, 1973, comeback concert by Eric Clapton is something else again, however. The original six-track LP ran less than 27 minutes; the new 14-track CD runs almost 74 minutes. The eight additions—"Layla," "Blues Power," "Bottle of Red Wine," "Bell Bottom Blues," "Tell the Truth," "Key to the Highway," "Let It Rain," and "Crossroads"—make the disc an effective recapitulation of Clapton's career over the previous seven years, including his solo work and his appearances with John Mayall's Bluesbreakers, Cream, and Derek & the Dominos. Despite the addiction that had kept him largely homebound for almost two years, Clapton played well, though the all-star backup band was as ragged as it was spirited. The loose feel of the evening was brought out in the stage announcements, many by Pete Townshend, who even mentioned a social disease just before introducing "Presence of the Lord." This still isn't a great Eric Clapton show, but it has been transformed from a historical curiosity to a historical document. *—William Ruhlmann*

Crossroads 2: Live in the Seventies / Apr. 2, 1996 / Polydor/Chronicles ✦✦✦
Crossroads was a box set that appealed to both beginners and fanatics. *Crossroads 2 (Live in the Seventies)* only appeals to fanatics. Spanning four discs and consisting almost entirely of live material (there are a handful of studio outtakes), this is music that will only enthrall completists and archivists. For those listeners, there is a wealth of fascinating, compelling performances here, as well as a fair share of mediocre, uninspired tracks. The key word for the entire album is detail—it is an album for studying the intricacies of Clapton's playing and how it evolved. For example, it's easy to hear the differences and progressions between the four versions of Robert Johnson's "Rambling on My Mind." And it is Clapton that evolves, not his supporting band—although they are proficient, they are hardly exciting. However, their static, professional support provides a nice bed to chart Slowhand's growth over the course of the decade, simply because he is always the focal point. *Crossroads 2* may only be for a collector, but for those collectors, it is a treasure, even if some of the tracks are fool's gold. *—Stephen Thomas Erlewine*

Pilgrim / Mar. 10, 1998 / Reprise ✦✦
One strange thing about Eric Clapton's '90s success is that it relied almost entirely on covers and new versions of classic hits; he released no albums of new material between 1989's *Journeyman* and 1998's *Pilgrim*. In the decade between the two albums, he had two new hits—his moving elegy to his deceased son, "Tears in Heaven," and the slick contemporary soul of the Babyface-written "Change the World"—and *Pilgrim* tries to reach a middle ground between these two extremes, balancing tortured lyrics with smooth sonic surfaces. Working with producer Simon Climie, his collaborator on the TDF side project, Clapton has created a numbingly calm record that, for all of its lyrical torment, displays no emotion whatsoever. Much of the problem lies in the production, which relies entirely on stiff mechanical drumbeats, gauzy synthesizers, and meandering instrumental interludes. These ingredients could result in a good record, as "Change the World" demonstrated, but not here, due to *Pilgrim*'s monotonous production. Unfortunately, Clapton doesn't want to shake things up—his singing is startlingly mannered, even on emotionally turbulent numbers like "My Father's Eyes" or "Circus." Even worse, he's content to take a back seat instrumentally, playing slight solos and fills as colorless as the electronic backdrops. The deadened sonics would make *Pilgrim* a chore even if there were strong songs on the record, but only a handful of tunes break through the murk. Considering that *Journeyman*, his last album of original material, was a fine workmanlike effort and that *From the Cradle* and *Unplugged* crackled with vitality, the blandness of *Pilgrim* is all the more disappointing. *—Stephen Thomas Erlewine*

The Blues / Jul. 27, 1999 / Polygram ✦✦✦✦
Eric Clapton earned a reputation as a blues guitarist early in his career, and while he frequently returned to the blues—usually recording at least one blues tune per album—he never recorded a full-fledged blues album until 1994's *From the Cradle*. It became one of the most popular records of his career. Not long afterward, MCA assembled a collection of Jimi Hendrix's blues recordings, and that compilation also proved quite successful. Those two releases provided the blueprint for *Blues*, Polygram's double-disc collection of

blues highlights from Clapton's RSO recordings of the '70s. On each of those albums, Clapton dabbled in the blues, and all of those moments, along with five previously unreleased tracks (both live and studio cuts), are featured here. Given that it's a compilation spanning ten years, it's not entirely surprising that *Blues* isn't entirely cohesive, but the quality of the songs and performances is better than the majority of his RSO albums. As a matter of fact, nearly every performance on this set offers proof that Clapton could still dazzle as a guitarist during the '70s, even if his life was plagued with personal problems that ultimately affected his recording career. *Blues* may not appeal to listeners that just want hits, but even serious fans that have most of the tunes here may find this a revelatory listening experience. *—Stephen Thomas Erlewine*

Clapton Chronicles: Best of 1981–1999 / Oct. 12, 1999 / Reprise ♦♦♦♦
Clapton Chronicles ignores Clapton's 1983 Reprise debut, *Money and Cigarettes* (which sounded more like an RSO album, anyway), starting with the pair of Phil Collins-produced mid-'80s albums, *Behind the Sun* and *August*. Though these had a pop sheen, they were album-rock holdovers. Clapton didn't get the balance between hard rock and commercial gloss right until 1989's *Journeyman*, whose featured songs—"Before You Accuse Me," "Bad Love," and "Pretending"—form the heart of this compilation. *Journeyman* was overshadowed by the phenomenal success of "Tears in Heaven" and 1992's *Unplugged*. Not only did *Unplugged* go platinum ten times, it established a new public image—classy, stylish, and substantial. That's the image that prevails on *Clapton Chronicles*. His triple-platinum blues album *From the Cradle* is written out of the picture, with songs from movie soundtracks taking its place. Apart from the Babyface-produced "Change the World," these tunes are a little too self-conscious and subdued, as are selections from 1998's *Pilgrim*. However, this deliberate move to paint Clapton's '80s and '90s recordings as adult-contemporary fare is accurate. Clapton's musical journey from 1985 to 1999 was taken mostly in the middle of the road, and *Clapton Chronicles* certainly captures that journey, missing no major hits from the late '80s and '90s. Whether it's a necessary addition to a Clapton collection is a matter of taste. It's certainly an excellent complement to *Unplugged* and *Time Pieces*, his two most popular and pop-oriented albums, but that might not be what every fan wants. *—Stephen Thomas Erlewine*

Riding With the King / Jun. 13, 2000 / Reprise ♦♦♦♦
The potential for a collaboration between B.B. King and Eric Clapton is enormous, of course, and the real questions concern how it is organized and executed. This first recorded pairing between the 74-year-old King and the 55-year-old Clapton was put together in the most obvious way: Clapton arranged the session using many of his regular musicians, picked the songs, and co-produced with his partner Simon Climie. That ought to mean that King would be a virtual guest star rather than earning a co-billing, but because of Clapton's respect for his elder, it nearly works the other way around. The set list includes lots of King specialties—"Ten Long Years," "Three O'Clock Blues," "Days of Old," "When My Heart Beats Like a Hammer"—as well as standards like "Hold on I'm Coming" and "Come Rain or Come Shine," with some specially written and appropriate recent material thrown in, so King has reason to be comfortable without being complacent. The real danger is that Clapton will defer too much; though he can be inspired by a competing guitarist such as Duane Allman, he has sometimes tended to lean too heavily on accompanists such as Albert Lee and Mark Knopfler when working with them in concert. That danger is partially realized; as its title indicates, *Riding With the King* is more about King than it is about Clapton. But the two players turn out to have sufficiently complementary, if distinct, styles so that Clapton's supportive role fills out and surrounds King's stinging single-string playing. (It's also worth noting that there are usually another two or three guitarists on each track.) The result is an effective, if never really stunning, work. *—William Ruhlmann*

Reptile / Mar. 13, 2001 / Reprise ♦♦♦
For a musician known to strive for authenticity, Eric Clapton has always been curiously obsessed with appearances, seemingly as interested in sartorial details and hairstyles as in the perfect guitar lick. It's hard to find two photographs of him from the '60s and early '70s that appear to be the same person, and even after he formally launched his solo career he switched looks frequently. Thus, the album sleeve of his 13th solo studio album of new material, *Reptile*, its "concept" credited to the recording artist, seems significant. The album cover shows a smiling Clapton as a child, and there are family photographs on the back cover and in the booklet, along with a current photograph of the artist, who turned 56 in the weeks following the album's release, in an image that does nothing to hide the wrinkles of late middle age. This photograph faces a sleeve note by Clapton that begins with his explanation of the album title: "Where I come from, the word 'reptile' is a term of endearment, used in much the same way as 'toe rag' or 'moosh.'" (Thanks, Eric. Now, all listeners have to do is find out what "toe rag" and "moosh" mean!) The note then goes on to dedicate the album warmly to Clapton's uncle. All of this might lead you to expect an unusually personal recording from a man who has always spoken most eloquently with his guitar. If so, you'd be disappointed. *Reptile* seems conceived as an album to address all the disparate audiences Clapton has assembled over the years. His core audience may think of him as the premier blues guitarist of his generation, but especially as a solo artist, he has also sought a broader pop identity, and in the '90s, with the hits "Tears in Heaven" and "Change the World," he achieved it. The fans he earned then will recognize the largely acoustic sound of such songs as "Believe in Life," "Second Nature," and "Modern Girl." But those who think of Clapton as the guy who plays "Cocaine" will be pleased with his cover of another J.J. Cale song, "Travelin' Light," and by the time the album was in record stores mainstream rock radio had already found "Superman Inside," which sounds like many of his midtempo rock hits of the '80s. This diversity is continued on less familiar material, especially the many interesting cover songs. Somebody, perhaps the artist himself, has been busy looking for old chestnuts, since *Reptile* contains a wide variety of them: the 1930 jazz song "I Want a Little Girl," recorded by McKinney's Cotton Pickers among others; John Greer's 1952 R&B hit "Got You on My Mind"; Ray Charles' 1955 R&B hit "Come Back Baby"; James Taylor's 1972 hit "Don't Let Me Be Lonely Tonight"; and Stevie Wonder's 1980 hit "I Ain't Gonna Stand for It." The two earliest of these songs are old and obscure enough that Clapton is able to make them his own, and he recasts the Taylor song enough to re-invent it, but remaking songs by Charles and Wonder means competing with them vocally, and as a singer Clapton isn't up to the challenge. He is assisted by the current five-man version of the Impressions, who do much to shore up his vocal weaknesses, but he still isn't a disciplined or thoughtful singer. Of course, when that distinctive electric guitar sound kicks in, all is forgiven. Still, *Reptile* looks like an album that started out to be more ambitious than it ended up being. There may be a song here for each of the artist's constituencies (and, more important to its commercial impact, for every major radio format except talk and country), but as a whole the album doesn't add up to the statement Clapton seems to have been hoping to make. *—William Ruhlmann*

W.C. Clark

b. Nov. 16, 1939, Austin, TX
Vocals, Guitar / Retro-Soul, Texas Blues, Modern Electric Blues
Guitarist, singer and songwriter W.C. Clark was one of Austin's original blues musicians, and he is considered the godfather of that city's blues scene.

Wesley Curley Clark was born and raised in Austin and grew up surrounded by music, since his father was a guitar player and his mother and grandmother sang in the choir at St. John's College Baptist Church. By the time he was 16, he played his first show at Victory Grill and was introduced to local legends T.D. Bell and Erbie Bowser. He began playing bass with Bell's band, honing his blues chops on guitar on his own time. While East Austin's club scene flourished in the late '50s and early '60s, white students from the nearby University of Texas campus began to patronize the blues clubs, and after taking a regular gig at Charlie's Playhouse, Clark made music his full-time occupation. After six years at the playhouse, he met R&B singer Joe Tex and joined his band as guitarist. After leaving Tex's band and returning to Austin, Clark was surprised and encouraged by the infusion of young white blues players on the local scene. Bill Campbell, Angela Strehli, Lewis Cowdrey and Paul Ray and the Vaughan brothers were attracting growing crowds to their shows and forming close bonds with the black blues players who had already been on the scene.

In the early '70s, Clark teamed up with guitarist and piano player Denny Freeman and vocalist Angela Strehli to form a group called Southern Feeling. With this group, Clark was able to blossom as a songwriter, but after a record deal fell apart, he took a job as a mechanic at a local Ford dealership. However, a young guitarist named Stevie Ray Vaughan kept visiting him at the garage. Vaughan was putting his own band together and insisted that Clark be a part of it. Calling themselves the Triple Threat Revue, they eventually took to the road with Lou Ann Barton as lead vocalist. Clark and keyboardist Mike Kindred wrote "Cold Shot," which went on to become one of Vaughan's biggest hits in the mid-'80s.

Clark has recorded three albums—*Something for Everybody* (1986), released independently on his own label, and two albums for the New Orleans-based Black Top label, 1994's *Heart of Gold* and 1996's *Texas Soul*. On *Texas Soul*, Clark is accompanied by a band of Austin-area blues veterans, including Chris Layton and Tommy Shannon of Vaughan's Double Trouble, producer and guitarist Derek O'Brien, and saxophonist Mark "Kaz" Kazanoff.

In March 1997, Clark and his band had an accident while returning to Austin in their van; he lost his fiancee and drummer. Clark was uninjured, but the experience slowed him down for a while. However, Clark continues to be active on the Austin blues scene, of which he is affectionately referred to as "the godfather," releasing *Lover's Plea* in 1998. He hit the road to promote the album around the same time that the PBS show *Austin City Limits* began showing a rare performance with Stevie Ray Vaughan as a part of their best-of series. After the tour, he went back to the studio and didn't return until 2002, when *From Austin With Soul* was released. *—Richard Skelly*

● **Heart of Gold** / May 2, 1994 / Black Top ♦♦♦♦♦
Heart of Gold is an impressive showcase for W.C. Clark's deep talents, giving him the opportunity to flaunt his chops and prove that he can play nearly anything. Clark's foundation is in greasy roadhouse Texas blues and while there's a number of wonderful cuts in that style here, he doesn't limit himself to Texas shuffles. Instead, he turns out some sweaty soul—including a seductive, passionate reading of Latimore's "Let's Straighten It Out"—and some organ-drenched Tex-Mex workouts which not only give the album diversity, they also give the album depth. And that's the reason why *Heart of Gold* is the definitive W.C. Clark release—it's the first (and arguably only) time he's gotten it completely right on record. *—Thom Owens*

Texas Soul / 1996 / Black Top ♦♦♦
Although W.C. Clark does perform a few blues, this CD is essentially an R&B/soul session which puts the emphasis on Clark's calm but emotional vocals (some of the lyrics are somewhat philosophical) and stinging guitar. The five-piece Kamikaze Horns are restricted to ensemble fills and riffs. Even if a certain predictability pervades the set, Clark (who in spots reminds one slightly of both Ray Charles and B.B. King) is a skilled perfomer in the idiom, making this a date recommended to fans of the Stax sound of the '60s. *—Scott Yanow*

Lover's Plea / May 5, 1998 / Black Top ♦♦♦♦
Long a fixture on the Austin, Texas music scene, W.C. Clark has been both mentor and band mate to Stevie Ray Vaughan, Marcia Ball and Lou Ann Barton. With an all-star Austin cast of Double Trouble's Chris Layton and Tommy Shannon, Sarah Brown, Derek O'Brien and Mark Kazanoff, Clark spreads his musical palette wide on this disc. Equal parts Texas blues and the kind of soul/R&B music as exemplified by O.V. Wright, Al Green and Sam Cooke, Clark's vocals here are nothing short of eloquent while his guitar

stings and stabs with the best of them. W.C.'s ode to his deceased girlfriend ("Are You Here, Are You There?") is one of the numerous highlights aboard along with "Pretty Little Mama," "Changing My Life With Your Love" and the closer, "That's a Good Idea." With tight playing, great songs and solid arrangements, this is Clark's most realized album to date. *—Cub Koda*

From Austin With Soul / Apr. 23, 2002 / Alligator ♦♦♦♦
Although he records for Alligator—Chicago's home of "house-rocking music"—this long-awaited return from Austin's founding father of the blues might just as well have been waxed during the glory years of Hi Records. As on his last release, guitarist/vocalist Clark meshes R&B with gospel, funk, and blues in a greasy Memphis soul stew that bubbles with passion. The delight Clark exudes in playing this music is evident on every track. His lead guitar playing sparkles, but is mostly reduced to fills and takes a back seat to the jaw-dropping singing that reaches out and grabs the listener. Like Al Green, with whom he shares a similar vocal approach, Clark testifies with every phrase. Not religious-based, this is still music grounded in the church no matter how funky and bluesy it is. When Clark states he's a "Real Live Livin' Hurtin' Man," he might as well be preaching from the pulpit and saving souls. Divided halfway between covers and originals, Clark's versions of Clarence Carter's "Snatching It Back," Allen Toussaint by way of Lee Dorsey's "Get out of My Life Woman," O.V. Wright's "I've Been Searching," and even Oliver Sain's warhorse "Don't Mess Up a Good Thing" (with Marcia Ball providing the female duet part) find new life in this setting. He even rescues "How Long Is a Heartache Supposed to Last?" from obscure soulman Jimmy Lewis and makes it sound like the lost classic it is. Longtime associate Mark Kazanoff's tenor sax and production keep the album focused while playing to Clark's strengths: his searing voice and supple guitar work. When he does let loose on six-string during "I'm Gonna Disappear," it's obvious he's got the chops to do more. But it's that restraint that makes this such a satisfying comeback. Anyone who experiences *From Austin With Soul* is going to want to hear more from this magnificent and classy soul/bluesman. *—Hal Horowitz*

William Clarke

b. Mar. 29, 1951, Inglewood, CA, **d.** Nov. 2, 1996, Fresno, CA

Vocals, Harmonica / Modern Electric Chicago Blues, Electric Chicago Blues, Electric Harmonica Blues

The heir apparent to Chicago's legacy of amplified blues harmonica, William Clarke was the first original new voice on his instrument to come along in quite some time; he became a sensation in blues circles during the late '80s and early '90s, stopped short by an untimely death in 1996. A pupil and devotee of George Harmonica Smith, Clarke was a technical virtuoso and master of both the diatonic harp and the more difficult chromatic harp (the signature instrument of both Smith and Little Walter). Where many new harmonica players had become content to cop licks from the Chicago masters, Clarke developed his own style and vocabulary, building on everything he learned from Smith and moving beyond it. His four '90s albums for Alligator earned wide critical acclaim and remain his signature showcases.

William Clarke was born March 29, 1951, in the South Central L.A. suburb of Inglewood; his parents had moved there from Kentucky and lived a blue-collar life. Clarke dabbled in guitar and drums as a youth, and grew up listening to rock & roll, but eventually found his way to the blues by way of the Rolling Stones' early albums. He took up the harmonica in 1967, and soon found his way onto the Los Angeles blues scene while working a day job as a machinist. Clarke's early style was influenced by Big Walter Horton, Junior Wells, James Cotton, and Sonny Boy Williamson II, but he soon began to incorporate the influence of '60s soul-jazz, mimicking the lines of the genre's top sax and organ players. He was a regular in South Central L.A.'s blues clubs, often hopping from one venue to another in order to keep playing all night. In this manner, he met quite a few West Coast blues luminaries, including—among others—T-Bone Walker, Pee Wee Crayton, Lowell Fulson, Big Mama Thornton, and George "Harmonica" Smith (who ultimately became his teacher and mentor).

Smith and Clarke first began to perform and record together in 1977, and kept up their relationship until Smith's death in 1983. In the meantime, Clarke guested on sessions by West Coast artists like Smokey Wilson and Shakey Jake Harris, and released several of his own LPs, all recorded for small labels. The first was 1978's *Hittin' Heavy*, which was followed by 1980's *Blues from Los Angeles*; both were released on tiny local labels. 1983's *Can't You Hear Me Calling* was more of a proper debut, though Clarke still hadn't quite hit his stride yet. That would start to happen with 1987's *Tip of the Top*, a tribute to Smith that was issued by Satch and earned a W.C. Handy Award nomination. Clarke finally quit his job as a machinist that year, and followed *Tip of the Top* with a live album, *Rockin' the Boat*, in 1988. By this time, his reputation was beginning to spread beyond Los Angeles, despite the fact that none of his albums had yet achieved full national distribution.

Clarke subsequently sent a demo tape to Alligator Records, and was immediately offered a contract. His label debut was the galvanizing *Blowin' Like Hell*, which earned rave reviews upon its release in 1990 and established him as a new, fully formed voice on amplified harmonica. Clarke hit the road hard, touring America and Europe over the next year; he also won the 1991 Handy Award for Blues Song of the Year, thanks to "Must Be Jelly." His follow-up, 1992's *Serious Intentions*, was equally blistering in its intensity. 1994's *Groove Time* added a horn section, bringing some of the jazz and swing undercurrents in Clarke's music forward. He pursued that direction even further on 1996's *The Hard Way*, his jazziest and most ambitious outing yet, which earned strong reviews once again.

Unfortunately, Clarke's health was deteriorating; always a large man, hard living on the road was taking its toll on his body. He collapsed on-stage in Indianapolis in March 1996 and was diagnosed with congestive heart failure. Despite losing weight and living clean and sober from then on, the damage had been done; Clarke resumed his heavy touring schedule a few months later and seemed to have recovered, until he collapsed on-stage again in Fresno. He was admitted to the hospital with a bleeding ulcer and died the next day, November 2, 1996, when surgical attempts to save his life failed. He was only 45 and in the prime of his career. Posthumously, Clarke won three W. C. Handy Awards stemming from *The Hard Way*: Album of the Year, Song of the Year ("Fishing Blues"), and Instrumentalist of the Year for harmonica. In 1999, Alligator released a best-of compilation titled *Deluxe Edition*. *—Steve Huey*

Hittin' Heavy / 1978 / Good Times ♦♦

Blues from Los Angeles / 1980 / Hittin' Heavy ♦♦

Can't You Hear Me Calling / 1983 / Rivera ♦♦♦
Can't You Hear Me Calling only gives a glimmer of what's to come from this new genius of the blues, but it is enjoyable nonetheless. *—Cub Koda*

Tip of the Top / 1987 / King Ace ♦♦♦
Tip of the Top is a loose tribute to William Clarke's mentor, George "Harmonica" Smith, who taught Clarke many of his tricks. Clarke plays a selection of tracks that were staples in Smith's catalog (including a version of "Hard Times," which features Smith himself), as well as newer songs written in the same style. But what really makes *Tip of the Top* notable is how William Clarke begins to develop his distinctive, idiosyncratic sound on the record. Unlike his debut *Can't You Hear Me Calling*, *Tip of the Top* explores some new sounds, which would come to fruition in his next few albums. *—Thom Owens*

Rockin' the Boat / 1988 / Rivera ♦♦♦♦
Recorded live in 1987, this features Clarke and his regular working band on a wide variety of material showcasing his formidable talents as a vocalist and harmonica man extraordinaire. *—Cub Koda*

★ **Blowin' Like Hell** / 1990 / Alligator ♦♦♦♦♦
The title says it all. William Clarke cooks on this one, his first CD. And these are new sounds. Songs like "Lollipop Mama," "Gambling for My Bread," and "Lonesome Bedroom Blues" (all written by Clarke) are just great tunes. "Must Be Jelly" won Clarke a W.C. Handy Award for Song of the Year in 1991. Clarke's timing and music are right on the money. With the great Alex Schultz on lead guitar. There is no doubt that Clarke is one of the few modern bluesmen who are exploring and extending the amplified blues harp tradition without violating any of its principles. No one plays chromatic blues harp with this kind of passion and sheer conviction. Hear for yourself. *—Michael Erlewine*

Serious Intentions / 1992 / Alligator ♦♦♦♦♦
His follow-up to *Blowin' Like Hell* burns with a ferocious intensity, particularly for his groundbreaking work on chromatic harp and his ability to cover all styles with remarkable elan. Again, he wrote most of the songs, and "Pawnshop Bound," "Trying to Stretch My Money," and "With a Tear in My Eye" are real songs. Instrumentals like "Chasin' the Gator" feature Clarke with Alex Schultz on lead guitar. *—Cub Koda and Michael Erlewine*

Groove Time / 1994 / Alligator ♦♦♦♦
Here is Clarke, hot again. This time he has added a horn section on some cuts for this recording. No problem. Alex Schultz is there on lead guitar to make sure that this album rocks. Clarke once again writes most of the songs—all 15 fat tracks. By this time, his Alligator albums have a style and feel (all his own) that one looks forward to. Plenty of high-impact amplified chromatic harmonica here of the push-the-band-hard variety that Clarke does so well plus some tasty acoustic thrown in too. *—Michael Erlewine*

The Hard Way / 1996 / Alligator ♦♦♦♦
His fourth CD from Alligator is his jazziest and bluesist recording to date. Clarke has written half of the compositions and put his own sound and style on those he did not write. Highlights include "The Boss" (inspired by saxophonist Willis Jackson) which is a fast jump that finds chromatic harp riffing along with a horn section—some interesting ideas. Other tunes are the Benny Moten tune "Moten Swing," "My Mind is Working Overtime," (a Latin-tinged tune written by Clarke), and "Letter from Home." *—Michael Erlewine*

Deluxe Edition / Feb. 23, 1999 / Alligator ♦♦♦♦
Clarke was the new harmonica genius for the millennium when his heart gave out on tour in 1996 and he passed away at age 45. This deluxe edition brings together 16 tracks culled primarily from his four Alligator albums along with three previously unreleased tracks from sessions conducted in 1986 and 1995, every track a winner. Clarke's tone is massive and only outdone by the wealth of ideas he constantly poured into his instrument. While others were still trying to imitate Little Walter, Clarke took the lessons he learned from George "Harmonica" Smith and built one of the most original and truly breathtaking styles in modern blues. Consider this disc his lasting legacy. *—Cub Koda*

Francis Clay

b. Nov. 16, 1923, Rock Island, IL

Drums / Chicago Blues

Drummer Francis Clay was born in Rock Island, IL, on November 16, 1923. Learning music from his family, Clay was playing some guitar and entering amateur contests at the age of five. But it was drums that fascinated him and he would create his own drum set from things around the house. He turned professional when he was 15 years old. In 1941 Clay formed his first band—Francis Clay and His Syncopated Rhythm playing behind acts like Gypsy Rose Lee, in circuses, on riverboats, etc. This lasted until around 1944. He returned to his home in 1946 and ran a booking office, recording studio, and taught drums. Around 1947 Clay was playing with George "Harmonica" Smith in Chicago. In the early '50s he toured with jazz organist Jack McDuff.

In 1957, Clay took a fill-in job with Muddy Waters and, since he had only played jazz, had no idea how to play the blues. Muddy Waters taught him and in several days they had the thing together. Waters asked him to stay on and Clay was there for the next four years.

In 1962, Clay left Muddy Waters and formed a band with James Cotton, which lasted about a year. Clay then worked with Otis Rush, Buddy Guy, Bobby Fields, and others. In 1965, Clay rejoined Muddy Waters for a stint of almost two years.

In the late '60s, Clay worked and recorded with a number of artists including James

Cotton, Muddy Waters, Lightnin' Hopkins, John Lee Hooker, Big Mama Thornton, Victoria Spivey, George "Harmonica" Smith, Shakey Jake Harris, Sunnyland Slim and others. Due to knee problems, Clay has not done much playing in recent years. Francis Clay has been called "the definitive Muddy Waters drummer." He resides in San Francisco. *—Michael Erlewine*

Peter J. "Doctor" Clayton (Peter Cleighton)

b. Apr. 19, 1898, Georgia, **d.** Jan. 7, 1947, Chicago, IL
Vocals, Piano, Composer / St. Louis Blues, Prewar Blues
A mainstay of the mid-'30s to late-'40s Chicago circuit, Clayton was a great songwriter with a fierce, declamatory style of his own. *—Cub Koda*

Doctor Clayton and His Buddy (1935–1947) / 1989 / DA Music ✦✦✦✦
A collection of tracks from Peter J. "Doctor" Clayton and "Doctor Clayton's Buddy," Sunnyland Slim. Recorded from 1935 to 1947, this is two-fisted, barrelhouse piano at its finest and tracks like Clayton's "Yo Yo Jive," "Slick Man Blues," and "Black Snake Blues" and Sunnyland's "Broke and Hungry," "Nappy Head Woman," "Illinois Central," and "Sweet Lucy Blues" are absolutely amazing in their conversational tones. A great little set. *—Cub Koda*

● **Complete Recorded Works (1935–1942)** / Jun. 2, 1994 / Document ✦✦✦

Willie Clayton

b. Mar. 29, 1955, Indianola, MS
Vocals / Retro-Soul, Chicago Soul, Soul-Blues
As long as he's been recording (from 1969 through the 2000s), one might think that Willie Clayton is an old geezer. No way—he was just past the age of 40 when he hit his commercial stride with a couple of blues-soul albums for Ace that sold well to the Southern market (where the two interrelated idioms have never been deemed mutually exclusive). After his debut single for Duplex, "That's the Way Daddy Did," went nowhere, Clayton left Mississippi for Chicago in 1971. Like his older Windy City compatriots Otis Clay and Syl Johnson, the young singer ended up contracted to Hi Records in Memphis, where he worked with producer Willie Mitchell and the vaunted Hi rhythm section. Hi issued a series of fine Clayton efforts on its Pawn subsidiary, including "I Must Be Losin' You," "It's Time You Made Up Your Mind," and "Baby You're Ready," but none of them hit. Finally, in 1984, Clayton enjoyed a taste of soul success when his "Tell Me" (produced by General Crook) and "What a Way to Put It" for Compleat Records nudged on to the R&B charts. *Let's Get Together*, Clayton's 1993 album for Johnny Vincent's Ace logo, was a smooth soul-blues hybrid dominated by originals but titled after Al Green's immortal hit. *Simply Beautiful*, his Ace follow-up, found Clayton mixing dusties by Rev. Al, Aretha Franklin, and Arthur Crudup with his own stuff. *It's About Love* followed in 1999. *—Bill Dahl*

Forever / 1988 / P-Vine ✦✦✦

Never Too Late / 1989 / Polydor ✦✦✦
Southern soul singer Willie Clayton shortened his first name and cut one late-'80s album for Polydor. It was a well-produced and nicely sung date, but the songs, focus, and approach were so "deep" soul-oriented that it didn't get any attention from the urban contemporary types at major record companies. Nor did the company pick a single and push it. Clayton soon returned to the Kirstee label. *—Ron Wynn*

Feels Like Love / 1992 / Kirstee/Ichiban ✦✦✦
Emotive soul singer Willie Clayton is still a well-kept secret north of the Mason-Dixon Line and west of the Mississippi River. You got a hole in your soul if you can't get into Clayton's heart-on-the-sleeve, gut-wrenching renditions of David Ruffin's "Walk Away from Love" and Bobby Womack's "That's the Way I Feel About You." His resonant, razor-edged tenor also does supreme justice to seven originals. To single out a few would be dogging the rest; they're all top-shelf, direct declarations, requests, and whiskey-induced flights in fantasy, of which "Suspended Animation" is but one example. *—Andrew Hamilton*

Let's Get Together / 1993 / Ace ✦✦✦
This is contemporary Southern deep soul with a strong taste of underlying blues. The clever "Three People (Sleeping in My Bed)" and "Back Street Love Affair," along with the self-penned "Feels like Love" and "Let Me Love You," are attractive showcases for Clayton's warm, assured vocal delivery. *—Bill Dahl*

Simply Beautiful / 1994 / Ace ✦✦✦
More of the same—Clayton's intimate confident vocals framed in terms midway between deep soul and contemporary blues. His own "Lose What You Got" and "Crazy for You" rate highly, along with Frank Johnson's "Love Stealing Ain't Worth Stealing" and the singer's delicate revival of Al Green's title cut. *—Bill Dahl*

No Getting Over Me / 1995 / Ichiban ✦✦✦✦✦
Worth the price of admission for Clayton's soulful remake of country crooner Ronnie Milsap's title track alone—but there's plenty more contemporary deep soul to be found on this exceptionally solid set. *—Bill Dahl*

● **Chicago Soul Greats** / Jul. 18, 1995 / Hi ✦✦✦✦

At His Best / Nov. 21, 1995 / Ichiban ✦✦✦
You can pick any one of the sensational Willie Clayton's CDs at random and come up with a winner every time. *At His Best* is not a greatest-hits compilation; the title signifies Clayton at his best, or in his best voice. His golden tenor is like a Porsche engine: well-tuned, powerful, and smooth as Jack Daniels. You forget the originals when Clayton remakes a song, and he does many here, excelling on timeless deep soul classics like "I've Been Loving You Too Long," "Open the Door to Your Heart," "Shining Star," "In the Mood," and the Independents' "Leaving Me." There are also two choking compositions by Sam Dees: "What a Way to Put It" and "So Tied Up." *—Andrew Hamilton*

Ace in the Hole / Feb. 13, 1996 / Ace ✦✦✦✦
The most consistent and satisfying of Clayton's contemporary output for Johnny Vincent's reactivated Ace imprint, thanks to top-flight soul-blues items like "Hurt by Love" and "My Baby's Cheating on Me," the Bob Jones-penned "Equal Opportunity" and "Bartender's Blues," and the singer's own "Happy." *—Bill Dahl*

Chapter One / Apr. 22, 1997 / Gamma ✦✦✦

Something to Talk About / Jun. 2, 1998 / Avanti ✦✦✦
Since 1992, Willie Clayton has recorded a steady stream of excellent albums comprising Southern soul, R&B, and blues. *Something to Talk About*, while less essential than previous efforts, continues the amazing string. The 14 songs here are mostly originals—quite different from previous releases, where his engaging tenor enhanced a slew of remakes. Laid-back but effective, the standouts include "Mine All Mine," "One Last Kiss," "Are You Married," the title track, and "Heart of the City," though you won't be unhappy with any of these. *—Andrew Hamilton*

Eddy Clearwater

b. Jan. 10, 1935, Macon, MS
Vocals, Guitar / Electric Chicago Blues, Chicago Blues, Modern Electric Blues, R&B
Once dismissed by purists as a Chuck Berry imitator (and an accurate one at that), tall, lean, and lanky Chicago southpaw Eddy Clearwater is now recognized as a prime progenitor of West Side-style blues guitar. That's not to say he won't liven up a gig with a little duck-walking or a frat party rendition of "Shout"; after all, Clearwater brings a wide array of influences to the party. Gospel, country, '50s rock, and deep-down blues are all incorporated into his slashing guitar attack. But when he puts his mind to it, "The Chief" (a nickname accrued from his penchant for donning Native American headdresses onstage) is one of the Windy City's finest bluesmen.

Eddy Harrington split Birmingham, AL, for Chicago in 1950, initially billing himself on the city's South and West sides as Guitar Eddy. His uncle, Rev. Houston H. Harrington, handed his nephew his initial recording opportunity; the good reverend operated a small label, Atomic-H. Eddy made the most of it, laying down a shimmering minor-key instrumental, "A-Minor Cha Cha," and the Berry-derived "Hillbilly Blues" (both on Delmark's *Chicago Ain't Nothin' but a Blues Band* anthology).

Drummer Jump Jackson invented Eddy's stage moniker as a takeoff on the name of Muddy Waters. As Clear Waters, he waxed another terrific Berry knock-off, "Cool Water," for Jackson's LaSalle logo. By the time he journeyed to Cincinnati in 1961 to cut the glorious auto rocker "I Was Gone," a joyous "A Real Good Time," and the timely "Twist Like This" for Federal Records producer Sonny Thompson, he was officially Eddy Clearwater. Things were sparse for quite a while after that; Clearwater occasionally secured a live gig dishing out rock and country ditties when blues jobs dried up.

But Rooster Blues' 1980 release of *The Chief*, an extraordinarily strong album by any standards, announced to the world that Eddy Clearwater's ascendancy to Chicago blues stardom was officially underway. Two encores for Rooster Blues, a set for Blind Pig (1992's *Help Yourself*), and *Mean Case of the Blues*, released in 1996 on his reactivated Cleartone Records, along with consistently exciting live performances, cemented Clearwater's reputation. He became known as a masterful blues showman whose principal goal is to provide his fans with a real good time. *Cool Blues Walk* followed in 1998, followed by *Chicago Daily Blues* the next year, and *Reservation Blues* in mid-2000. *—Bill Dahl*

● **The Chief** / 1980 / Rooster Blues ✦✦✦✦✦
This was the charismatic southpaw's debut album back in 1980, and remains his best to date. He rocks like Chuck Berry used to (but no longer can) on "I Wouldn't Lay My Guitar Down," and tears up the West Side-based "Bad Dream" and "Blues for a Living," imparts a hard-driving Chi-town shuffle to "Find You a Job" and "I'm Tore Up," and gives "Lazy Woman" a decidedly un-lazy Latin tempo. One of the best Chicago blues LPs of the '80s. *—Bill Dahl*

Two Times Nine / 1981 / New Rose ✦✦✦
Recorded originally for Clearwater's own Cleartone label and later leased to Ron Bartolucci's Baron imprint, these late-'70s sides were potent indicators of his maturing blues style. These weren't homemade sessions; all-star sidemen include drummer Casey Jones, guitarist Jimmy Johnson, and saxist Abb Locke. The title cut is a blistering Chuck Berry-styled rocker, "Came Up the Hard Way" displays a firm grasp of the West Side sound, and "A Little Bit of Blues, A Little Bit of Rock & Roll" utilizes a funky groove to foot-stomping advantage. *—Bill Dahl*

Flimdoozie / 1986 / Rooster Blues ✦✦✦
As yet unavailable on compact disc, Clearwater's encore LP for Rooster Blues wasn't quite the equal of its predecessor but registered as a solid enough outing nonetheless. The Chief coined a new term for the rollicking title track, engaged in some harrowing blues during a lengthy "Black Night" medley, and rocked the house with a '50s-styled "Do This Town Tonight." *—Bill Dahl*

Blues Hang Out / Dec. 3, 1989 / Evidence ✦✦✦
Eddy Clearwater has had a tough time shaking his "Chuck Berry imitator" label, and he includes Berry-tinged numbers at the halfway point and end of this nice, if thoroughly derivative, urban blues set recorded in 1989 for Black and Blue and recently reissued by Evidence on CD, with the familiar country boogie shuffle and tinkling licks. Clearwater could not do a set without the signature "Lay My Guitar Down," and this rendition is surging and enjoyable although inferior to the definitive one. Otherwise, it is a pile-driving and urgently performed date; Clearwater and Will Crosby swap slashing lines, crackling phrases, and answering fills. Clearwater's session contains several robust, entertaining passages, even if there is absolutely nothing you have not heard before. *—Ron Wynn*

Real Good Time: Live! / 1990 / Rooster Blues ✦✦✦✦
Eddy Clearwater delivers on the promise of this set's title on his best concert recording to date, recorded at a couple of Indiana nightspots. Those enduring (and endearing) Berry roots surface anew on a storming medley of "A Real Good Time" and "Cool Water," and there are more '50s-style rockers in "Hi-Yo Silver" and "Party at My House." But he

exhibits a social conscience on the decided departure "Tear Down the Wall of Hate." *—Bill Dahl*

Chicago Blues Session, Vol. 23 / 1990 / Wolf ✦✦
This OK live set isn't the equivalent of his later *Rooster Blues* concert set, though. *—Bill Dahl*

Help Yourself / 1992 / Blind Pig ✦✦✦
Clearwater wrote the lion's share of this well-produced collection, reaching back for material by Jimmy Reed, Otis Rush, and Willie Mabon to round it out. The usual infectious mix of shimmering West Side blues, hauling rockabilly, and even a touch of funk on "Little Bit of Blues." Guitarist Will Crosby shares lead chores with his boss, and Carey Bell (Eddy's cousin) handles the harp work. *—Bill Dahl*

Boogie My Blues Away / 1995 / Delmark ✦✦✦
Veteran producer Ralph Bass produced this collection back in 1977 for a blues album series that never materialized; Delmark finally brought it to domestic light recently. Solid, unpretentious package that shows both Clearwater's West Side-styled southpaw guitar sound and his Chuck Berry-oriented capacity for rocking the house. *—Bill Dahl*

Mean Case of the Blues / 1996 / Bullseye Blues ✦✦✦
Clearwater comes up with a compelling mix of tunes on this 10-track outing, his first for the Bullseye Blues imprint. The southpaw guitarist covers a wide range of styles (as befitting a true West Side guitarist, where versatility is a badge of merit) including Magic Sam's "Look Whatcha Done," Nat King Cole's "Send for Me," Gene Allison's "You Can Make It If You Try," and Clearwater originals like "Party at My House," "Don't Take My Blues," "Hard Way to Make an Easy Living," "Love Being Loved By You," and the title track. Produced by Eddy and utilizing his regular working band with guest appearances from Jerry Soto on keyboards, Mike Peavey on saxophone, Steven Frost on trumpet and Billy Branch on harmonica, this is the Chief just laying it down simple and hard, doing what he does best—delivering taut and shimmering West Side guitar and vocals with a vengeance. *—Cub Koda*

Cool Blues Walk / Oct. 6, 1998 / Bullseye Blues ✦✦✦✦
Produced by Duke Robillard and utilizing his band as the backing unit, this record is tightly focused from note one, making a marvelous framework for "The Chief" to do exactly what he does best. With the exception of the covers "Sen-Say-Shun," "Stranded" and "I Just Want to Make Love to You," Clearwater wrote every tune aboard in his usual wide range of styles from the rocking "Very Good Condition" to the country-ish "Nashville Road" to the shuffling "Boppin' at the Top of the Rock." Eddie continues to surprise with a rare appearance playing piano and singing the decidedly non-blues-like ballad "I Love You" which also features Marilyn Mair and Mark Davis adding mandocello and mandola to this distinctive tune. Duke shares solo space with Clearwater throughout the album, and their exchanges on the moody "Blues for a Living" is solid blues playing in two contrasting styles. Perhaps Clearwater's most focused album to date, this 1998 outing captures a '50s West Side bluesman still at the peak of his abilities. *—Cub Koda*

Reservation Blues / Sep. 12, 2000 / Bullseye Blues ✦✦✦✦✦
Eddy Clearwater is equally talented as a bluish singer and as an improvising guitarist. On *Reservation Blues*, he ranges from Chicago blues to rock & roll, throwing in a couple instrumentals too. His repertoire includes both socially relevant lyrics and good-time music, featuring some of the latter when the former gets a bit too somber. Although there are some solid solos from his supporting players (including three guitar spots for Duke Robillard, two fine solos from tenor saxophonist Dennis Taylor, and a guest appearance by Carey Bell on harmonica during "Find Yourself"), Clearwater is the main star throughout. Fortunately, he is heard in prime form, whether happily jamming "I Wouldn't Lay My Guitar Down" and "Blues Cruise" or singing in a more serious mood on "Winds of Change" and "Everything to Gain." A gem. *—Scott Yanow*

Jon Cleary

b. 1964, Kent, England
Organ (Hammond), Keyboards, Piano / Contemporary Blues, New Orleans Blues, Piano Blues, Soul-Blues

A respected session and sideman, British blues pianist and composer Jon Cleary has worked with rock, blues, and soul artists like Bonnie Raitt, D'Angelo, Maria Muldaur, Taj Mahal, and Eric Clapton.

Originally a guitarist, Cleary began playing at age five, and started his first band at 15. Raised on blues, jazz, and soul records, his love of New Orleans blues and jazz in particular took him across the ocean after he graduated from art school.

Upon arriving in New Orleans, Cleary started hanging out at one of the city's most storied venues—the Maple Leaf Club. The bar's owner offered him a job painting the Maple Leaf's exterior; free admission and beer were Cleary's wages. He soaked up the bar's atmosphere, realizing that blues piano was his calling; the house he lived in had a piano, on which he spent hours practicing each day.

Returning to London culminated in forming a six-piece traditional New Orleans R&B band, with which he developed a reputation as a talented and gentlemanly musician. However, the Big Easy called to Cleary again. He moved back and got bookings in clubs as a featured and side performer, playing with bluesmen like Smokey Johnson, James Singleton, and George Porter. One of these gigs included Walter "Wolfman" Washington in the audience; taken with Cleary's playing, Washington offered Cleary a spot in his own band. Cleary played with Washington for two years, continuing his introduction to more sophisticated forms of R&B and blues, as well as incorporating Latin influences into his style.

At this point, Cleary began writing his own material and formed his own band, the Absolute Monster Gentlemen, with bassist Cornell Williams and guitarist Derwin "Big D" Perkins from the gospel group the Friendly Travelers, and drummer Jeffrey "Jellybean" Alexander. Just as the Absolute Monster Gentlemen achieved a reputation as one of New Orleans' finest combos, Cleary encountered visa problems and had to return to the U.K. immediately.

Back in England, Cleary continued refining and expanding his vision of the blues, when he received a call from producer John Porter, a fellow Englishman who had seen some of Cleary's performances at the Maple Leaf and wanted to introduce him to the blues scene at large. Recording with Taj Mahal and a gig at the Hollywood Athletic Club followed, as well as a collaboration between Cleary and Porter on his 1999 solo debut album, *Moonburn*. Three years would go by until a new album would be prepared, but by 2002 he had an eponymous album ready with the Absolute Monster Gentlemen. *—Heather Phares*

Alligator Lips & Dirty Rice / Mar. 1, 1994 / Ace ✦✦✦

Moonburn / Apr. 20, 1999 / Virgin ✦✦✦
Jon Cleary is one of those rare artists that is capable of transcending his geographical background to seamlessly embody a completely foreign musical style. In Cleary's case, the roots are England and the style is New Orleans blues. On *Moonburn*, the pianist comes off as Dr. John's long lost musical soulmate, blending country blues phrasing with the lazy piano rhythms of the bayou. "Unnecessarily Mercenary" and "Fool's Game," in particular, sparkle with a mischievous gleam that shows Cleary to be a musical peer of the New Orleans style rather than a imitator. *—Steven Kurutz*

● **Jon Cleary and the Absolute Monster Gentlemen** / May 7, 2002 / Basin Street ✦✦✦
Jon Cleary, the New Orleans-based multi-instrumentalist and singer, cooks up a batch of funky music on his first Basin Street release. Backed by a small core band and a smattering of guests (including Bonnie Raitt on slide guitar), Cleary delivers hard-hitting urban blues and soul that can bring to mind Tower of Power, Bill Withers, and even a little Steely Dan. His singing can be a bit generic, but his organ and Wurlitzer flourishes are quite tasty, as is the dead-on rhythm guitar of Derwin "Big D" Perkins and the bass-and-drum lock-up of Cornell Williams and Jeffrey "Jellybean" Alexander. *—David R. Adler*

Rev. James Cleveland

b. Dec. 5, 1932, Chicago, IL, **d.** Feb. 9, 1991, Culver City, CA
Vocals, Leader, Trombone, Piano / Traditional Gospel, Contemporary Gospel, Black Gospel

The visionary behind the contemporary gospel sound, the Reverend James Cleveland was a pioneering composer and choral director whose progressive arrangements—jazzy and soulful, complete with odd time signatures—helped push the music past the confines of the traditional Baptist hymnal into new and unexpected directions, infusing elements of the sanctified church style and secular pop to alter the face of gospel forever. Born in Chicago on December 5, 1932, Cleveland was a boy soprano at Pilgrim Baptist Church, the home of minister of music Thomas A. Dorsey; as his parents were unable to afford a piano, he crafted a makeshift keyboard out of a windowsill, somehow learning to play without ever producing an actual note. When his voice changed, becoming gruff and harsh, Cleveland continued singing, developing into an expressive crooner; for the most part, however, he focused on piano, becoming a top-notch accompanist.

In 1950, Cleveland signed on as a pianist and occasional third lead with the Gospelaires, a trio led by Norsalus McKissick and Bessie Folk; although the group was short-lived, it brought him to the attention of pianist Roberta Martin, for whom he began composing. Even his earliest material reflects a bluesy, funkified style well ahead of its time, while his arrangements of traditional spirituals like "Old Time Religion" and "It's Me O Lord" were highly stylized, almost unrecognizable from their usual interpretations. By the mid-'50s, Cleveland was a member of the Caravans, not only playing piano but also narrating hymns in his rough yet relaxing voice; despite the group's success, however, he kept quitting and rejoining their ranks, earning a reputation as a highly temperamental character. He also played briefly with groups including the Meditation Singers and the Gospel All-Stars; in 1959, he also cut a rendition of Ray Charles' "Hallelujah I Love Her So," his first overt attempt to bridge gospel and R&B.

Although Cleveland kept drifting from group to group, his reputation continued to grow—with the Gospel Chimes, he cut a series of records which veered sharply from pop-inflected ballads to fiery shouters, arranging harmonies which straddled the line between the current group style and the rapidly developing choir sound. By 1960, he was clearly well ahead of the pack; "The Love of God," a cover of a Soul Stirrers number he cut with the Detroit choir the Voices of Tabernacle, was a breakthough hit, his fusion of pop balladry and choir spirit finally reaching its apotheosis. After years of struggle, Cleveland was now a major star, and across the country, choir directors began mimicking his style; he soon signed to Savoy, where he recorded with the All-Stars and Chimes as well as his own group, the Cleveland Singers, which featured on organ a young Billy Preston. His third Savoy LP, 1962's live *Peace Be Still*, made history, selling an astonishing 800,000 copies to an almost exclusively black audience without the benefit of mainstream promotion.

The success of *Peace Be Still* established Cleveland as arguably the most crucial figure to emerge in gospel since Mahalia Jackson; throughout the '60s, when hit status for spiritual records typically reflected sales of five thousand copies, his LPs regularly sold five times that amount. Additionally, his annual Gospel Singers Workshop Convention—an outgrowth of his organization the Gospel Workshop of America—helped launch the careers of numerous younger talents, a generation of artists largely inspired by the modernized sound pioneered by Cleveland himself. During the '70s, he remained a towering figure, leading his latest creation, the Southern California Community Choir, and recording prolifically; although his pace began to slow in the decade that followed—and despite his death on February 9, 1991—Cleveland's shadow continues to loom large across the gospel landscape. *—Jason Ankeny*

☆ **The Best of James Cleveland** / 1960 / HOB ✦✦✦✦✦
Great material with the Voices of the Tabernacle of Detroit. *—Opal Louis Nations*

★ **Peace Be Still** / 1962 / Savoy ✦✦✦✦✦
A set of original Cleveland tunes and traditional hymns done in the choir format he

pioneered with The Angelic Choir of New Jersey. This live recording, done with crude technology, is helped somewhat by the high-fidelity pressing. It includes "I Had a Talk with God" and "I'll Wear a Crown." Cleveland's gruff vocals appear on most cuts. —*Bil Carpenter*

I Stood on the Banks of the Jordan / 1964 / Savoy ◆◆◆◆
Some of his finest live in-church sides. —*Opal Louis Nations*

Lord, Let Me Be an Instrument / 1966 / Savoy ◆◆
Amazing vocal acrobatics from soloist Rosetta Davis. —*Opal Louis Nations*

In the Beginning / 1978 / Kenwood ◆◆◆
Great early-'50s Apollo sides with the Gospelaires and the Gospel All Stars. —*Opal Louis Nations*

Gospel Music Workshop of America / 1990 / Savoy ◆◆◆◆◆
A typically strong Cleveland performance with an all-star choir. —*Kip Lornell*

Having Church / 1990 / Savoy Gospel ◆◆◆◆◆

Victory Shall Be Mine / 1991 / Savoy ◆◆◆
This is among Cleveland's best later works. —*Kip Lornell*

King & Queen of Gospel / 1992 / HOB ◆◆◆
Fine examples of good gospel by both soloists at budget price. —*Opal Louis Nations*

Crown Price of Gospel / Nov. 19, 1993 / HOB ◆◆◆◆◆
Some of Cleveland's finest moments. —*Opal Louis Nations*

Old Time Religion / 1994 / HOB ◆◆◆◆◆
Good, best-selling collection of this important innovator's work. —*Opal Louis Nations*

In Times Like These / Mar. 14, 1995 / HOB ◆◆◆◆◆
More classic material by this singer, composer, arranger, and choirmaster of immense influence. —*Opal Louis Nations*

Get Right Church / Jul. 18, 1996 / Liquid 8 ◆◆◆◆◆
More joy and live church feeling from the man who revolutionized choral singing. —*Opal Louis Nations*

Great Day: The Very Best of Rev. James Cleveland / Mar. 3, 1998 / Collectables ◆◆◆◆
Rev. James Cleveland changed the sound of gospel music. Some of his best sides. —*Opal Louis Nations*

★ **Hallelujah: A Collection of His Finest Recordings** / Aug. 17, 1999 / Music Club ◆◆◆◆◆
This release compiles selections of the gospel performances that Rev. James Cleveland cut for Hob Records between 1958 and 1967. Cleveland is backed up on most songs by either the Voices of the Tabernacle or the Gospel Chimes, and both Detroit vocal groups add much life and sincerity to the tunes—particularly the Voices, whose large-choir praises round out the songs with an impressive depth. Album standouts are the tunes "It Is Well (With My Soul)" with Rev. Charles Craig, Jr. and "Love of God" with the Voices of the Tabernacle. Cleveland powerfully leads these soul gospel tunes through energetic renditions, and a terrific shoutin' organ adds its musical "amens" throughout. All come together to give the listener a dose of a decently powerful church service. —*Joslyn Layne*

Climax Blues Band

f. 1969, Stafford, England
Group / Pop/Rock, Soft Rock, Blues-Rock
Led by Colin Cooper, the former frontman of the R&B unit the Hipster Image, the Stafford, England-based Climax Chicago Blues Band was one of the leading lights of the late-'60s blues boom. A sextet also comprised of guitarists Derek Holt and Peter Haycock, keyboardist Arthur Wood, bassist Richard Jones and drummer George Newsome, the group debuted in 1969 with a self-titled effort recalling the work of John Mayall.

Prior to the release of 1969's *Plays On*, Jones left the group, prompting Holt to move to bass. In 1970 the Climax Chicago Blues Band moved to the Harvest label, at the same time shifting towards a more rock-oriented sound on the LP *A Lot of Bottle*. Around the release of 1971's *Tightly Knit*, Newsome was replaced by drummer John Holt; upon Wood's exit in the wake of 1972's *Rich Man*, the unit decided to continue on as a quartet, also dropping the "Chicago" portion of its name to avoid confusion with the American band of the same name.

In 1974 the Climax Blues Band issued *FM/Live*, a document of a New York radio concert. 1975's *Stamp* was their commercial breakthrough, and 1976's *Gold Plated* fared even better, spurred on by the success of the hit "Couldn't Get It Right." However, the rise of punk effectively stopped the group in their tracks, although they continued recording prolifically well into the '80s; after 1988's *Drastic Steps*, the Climax Blues Band was silent for a number of years, but resurfaced in 1994 with *Blues From the Attic*. —*Jason Ankeny*

The Climax Chicago Blues Band / 1969 / See for Miles ◆◆◆◆
The debut album of the Climax Chicago Blues Band (they'd later drop the "Chicago" part of the name) was recorded on two days separated by a couple of months in 1968. As British blues revivalists, Climax was better than most, featuring strong playing from guitarist Peter Haycock and keyboardist Arthur Wood. The selections run the gamut from Chicago retreads ("Mean Old World," "Insurance," "Wee Baby Blues," "Don't Start Me to Talkin'") to band originals ("And Lonely," "Looking for My Baby," "Going Down This Road" and "You've Been Drinking." If one can make it past Colin Cooper's mannered vocals, there's much for Brit blues fans to enjoy here. —*Cub Koda*

Plays On / 1969 / C-Five ◆◆◆
The second album by the group showed the band starting to expand from their strictly blues format and taking on more pronounced rock affectations. Haycock's is more to the fore, and Cooper's harmonica takes a back seat to this saxophone work. This album also marks the band dabbling in crediting songs to themselves that were actually written by

other older, Blacker blues musicians, a common practice with many British blues groups. —*Cub Koda*

#3 / 1970 / Sire ◆◆◆◆

A Lot of Bottle / 1970 / C-Five ◆◆◆
This album starts out promisingly (and interestingly, and misleadingly) with a cool acoustic number, "Country Hat," before the amplification gets cranked up and a lot of subtlety goes out the window. Still, this is generally an exciting album, if not always an interesting one. The band plays hard enough on grinding, crunchy shouters like "Reap What I've Sowed" (which features a wondering, soaring solo by Peter Haycock, and a spellbinding performance by Derek Holt on bass), which also parallels Mountain's contemporary release "Mississippi Queen"; and they bring back in that oft-overlooked instrument, the saxophone (played by Colin Cooper), on "Brief Case." Much of the rest is on the bland side, "Alright Blue?" being a tedious workout for the harmonica as lead instrument. A couple of Willie Dixon and Muddy Waters covers are more engaging than most of the originals that follow, until the pleasantly loose-limbed closer, "Cut You Loose." —*Bruce Eder*

Tightly Knit / 1971 / See for Miles ◆◆◆◆
This 1998 disc is a straight-up, no-bonus-track reissue of the group's 1971 Chrysalis album. By now, the group has settled into a very comfortable groove and suddenly don't seem to be trying so hard, instead letting the music speak for itself. This newfound confidence is also mirrored in the fact that eight of the ten tunes aboard are group-penned originals. While they show some versatility on tunes like "Little Link" and "Shoot Her if She Runs" (both exhibiting a strong country rock flavor), they still manage to sound like no one else but the Climax Blues Band on such familiar warhorses as "Spoonful" and Robert Johnson's "Come on in My Kitchen." Peter Haycock's lead guitar reaches scorching levels on the almost-ten-minute-long "St. Michael's Blues"; "Who Killed McSwiggin" explores the Bo Diddley beat for all its worth, and the closing "That's All" takes the pan-flute New Orleans groove into folk-singalong territory, making a top-notch finish for the group's most varied outing. —*Cub Koda*

Rich Man / 1972 / See for Miles ◆◆◆

FM/Live / 1973 / Sire ◆◆◆◆
Heavy on the kind of blues rock favored by Humble Pie, this is a live outing in front of a too-loud New York audience. Sax player Colin Cooper helps to separate these English midland lads from the heads-down no-nonsense boogie competition, although the emphasis is squarely on guitarist Peter Haycock. His solo electric slide showcase "Country Hat" is a marvel. The band's pop leanings featured so strongly on their studio recordings come through in "I Am Constant." It's a solid outing, and much meatier than subsequent offerings. —*Mark Allan*

Gold Plated / 1976 / See for Miles ◆◆◆
The smash hit "Couldn't Get it Right" is a perfect synthesis of Peter Haycock's guitar and Colin Cooper's sax that leaped out of radio speakers. But the music is starting to drift away from blues toward a soul-pop sound that would later sap the band of its vitality. —*Mark Allan*

Shine On / 1978 / Sire ◆◆◆
By the late '70s, the members of this veteran English group knew they didn't want to be a blues band, but they didn't know where they wanted to go. The first three songs point the way toward low-key pop epitomized by "When Talking Is Too Much Trouble." There's a bit of funk here and an album-closing nod to the band's blues-based past with "Champagne and Rock & Roll." The guitar of Colin Haycock and sax of band founder Colin Cooper are underused, a problem that would continue to dog the band as they sought a new identity. —*Mark Allan*

Real to Reel / 1979 / Warner Brothers ◆◆◆

Flying the Flag / 1980 / Warner Brothers ◆◆
A veteran outfit as the '80s dawned, this British quartet can't seem to decide what to play: blues, soul, or pop. "I Love You," written by bassist Derek Holt, is an AM-ready charmer in the manner of Badfinger or Paul McCartney that points toward pop. But, by abandoning their blues roots, they sound like just another average white band. —*Mark Allan*

● **Couldn't Get It Right** / 1987 / See for Miles ◆◆◆◆◆
This 22-track compilation makes for a commendable jaunt through some of the Climax Blues Band's best material. It may not be the most comprehensive set available, but it does manage to excerpt songs from some of the group's better albums. Led by the number nine hit "Couldn't Get It Right" (number ten in the U.K.), this compilation package takes the essential cuts from their most significant releases, including their self-titled debut album from 1968, when they were known as the Climax Chicago Blues Band, as well as 1971's *Tightly Knit*; 1972's *Rich Man*; and 1976's *Gold Plated*, which heralded both "Berlin Blues" and "Everyday." The band gained prominence with the fiery saxophone playing of Colin Cooper and the slick but resounding guitar work of Peter Haycock, making tracks like "Reap What I Sowed," "Looking for My Baby," and the ever-so-strange "Mole in the Dole" standouts on this set. The added bonuses are worthwhile as well, especially both of the B-side cuts, "Milwaukee Truckin' Blues" and "Loving Machine." Collectors and fans will appreciate the single version of "Using the Power," incorporating their streamlined blues-rock sound to perfection. Some notable omissions from this package are indeed important ones. Missing is the jazz-tinged song entitled "Flight" from early in the band's career, and the sugary but well-done ballad "I Love You," a number 12 hit for them in 1981 off of the *Fly the Flag* album. But even so, *Couldn't Get It Right* still makes for a favorable listen, proving that the band's chosen title for this compilation couldn't be farther from the truth. —*Mike DeGagne*

25 Years 1968–1993 / 1994 / Repertoire ✦✦✦✦✦
Most casual fans know the Climax Blues Band through "Couldn't Get It Right" and "I Love You," a pair of slick pop and soft rock hits from the late '70s and early '80s. Anyone who heard those two hits probably was puzzled by the "Blues" in the group's name, since they were in no way bluesy. But, as shown by the double-disc, 32-track set *25 Years*, they started out as a British blues band in the late '60s. Unfortunately, they just weren't very good, slogging through the same three chords without much inspiration for nearly ten years. That decade is represented on the first disc, and while the group does show signs of improvement over those 16 songs, the music is still unbelievably dull (and, in the case of "Shoot Her If She Runs," offensive). By the late '70s, the band was in desperate need of a hit, so they changed their tune, incorporating pop, disco, and soft rock. "Couldn't Get It Right" was an excellent song, far catchier than any of their early blues tunes, and it deservedly became a Top Ten hit. The group subsequently tried to replicate its success, but they couldn't get it right until 1981, when the appealingly schmaltzy "I Love You" almost went Top Ten. Afterward, they played soft rock until they broke down and returned to the blues, with only a handful of memorable songs along the way. *25 Years* is a little tedious to anyone who just wants the hits, but, unfortunately, it's the only readily available compilation from the group. It will suit anyone who really wants to dig into the Climax Blues Band, since it accurately sketches the progression of their career, but it doesn't have enough good music to warrant such an extensive compilation. *—Stephen Thomas Erlewine*

Harvest Years 1969–1972 / Apr. 29, 1998 / See for Miles ✦✦✦✦

Dorothy Love Coates (Dorothy McGriff)

b. Jan. 30, 1928, Birmingham, AL, **d.** Apr. 9, 2002, Birmingham, AL
Vocals, Leader / Traditional Gospel, Black Gospel
Perhaps the most underrated gospel vocalist and songwriter of black gospel's golden age, Dorothy Love Coates represented, in the words of Craig Werner's *A Change Is Gonna Come: Music, Race and the Soul of America*, "the best of what the early '60s offered: a model of call and response rooted in an unflinching engagement with history; an understanding of the world that sends pulses of energy back and forth between gospel and the blues; an unwavering commitment to the beloved community; a refusal to be seduced into a mainstream where the value of life is measured in money; and music so powerful it can change your life."

It changed the fortunes of many more famous music stars. Holland-Dozier-Holland based the Supremes' "You Can't Hurry Love" on Coates' "(You Can't Hurry God) He's Right on Time"; Wilson Pickett used the Gospel Harmonettes' version of the classic theme "99 and a Half Won't Do" as the model for his soul hit; Little Richard, among others, copied Coates' stentorian vocal leads. In addition, Coates was one of the few gospel stars to vocally oppose segregation, often appearing at civil rights rallies during the late '50s and early '60s. ("The Lord has blessed our going out and our coming in. He's blessed our sitting in, too.") This was all the more brave because Coates lived in Birmingham, AL, the most dangerous city in the U.S. for such activists, and she was not then singing professionally. "At night I'd sing for the people, days I'd work for the white man," as she put it to gospel historian Tony Heilbut.

The Gospel Harmonettes—Mildred Miller Howard, mezzo-soprano; Odessa Edwards, contralto and sermonizer; Willie May Newberry, contralto; and pianist Evelyn Starks—were already Birmingham radio celebrities in the '40s when the several years younger Dorothy McGriff joined them. After winning on *Arthur Godfrey's Talent Scouts* TV program, the Harmonettes made some less than stellar sides for RCA in 1949. With Dorothy taking over more forcefully, they became national gospel stars soon after they began recording for Specialty Records in 1951.

That July, they traveled to Hollywood and made "I'm Sealed" and "Get Away Jordan," both of which became standards. Dorothy soon married Willie Love, the great lead voice of the Fairfield Four, although that marriage didn't last long. (She later married Carl Coates, bass voice and guitarist with the Sensational Nightingales, thus becoming Dorothy Love Coates.) The group's summer 1953 Specialty session produced "No Hiding Place," another classic; their 1956 date, "You Must Be Born Again"; and in August 1956, the group's two greatest recordings, "99 and a Half Won't Do" and, above all, "That's Enough."

They traveled the "gospel highway" from church to church and town to town, all through the South, Midwest, and in such northern cities as Philadelphia, New York, and Newark (where her childhood friend, Alex Bradford, was also established as a gospel star). In 1959, they began recording for Savoy Records in Newark. From later in 1959 to 1961, Dorothy retired to care for a newborn daughter with epilepsy and cerebral palsy. In 1961, the group, which adjusted its membership to include Cleo Kennedy (later a backup singer for Bob Dylan and Bruce Springsteen), recorded for Savoy, and then in 1964 for Vee-Jay, an affiliation that lasted until 1968, when they did a few songs for OKeh/Columbia (including the remarkable "Strange Man") and made some discs for Nashboro. Neither Coates nor her group recorded since about 1970, although Coates was intermittently active in live performance during subsequent years.

As a vocalist, Dorothy Love Coates stood out from any previous female lead in gospel because she was as much preacher as singer. Her vocals were always hoarse, sometimes sounding as if she'd actually damaged her throat shouting and testifying. But she swung behind all that hammering, and her records have power and drive that is virtually unmatched in any American music. *—Dave Marsh*

☆ **Get on Board** / 1956 / Specialty ✦✦✦✦✦
Two dozen stunning leftovers from the *Best Of* albums. The material here is less famous, but the best of it—"Peace Be Still," "Get on Board," "These Are They," plus the many alternate takes of Coates' best-known numbers—ranks with the finest material produced in gospel's '50s golden age. Coates, at this point, had taken her testifying, preaching vocal style to a new height that imbues even the tracks originally tossed aside with fierce spirit and an unquenchable thirst for freedom. Anthony Heilbut's notes are an excellent combination of informative and enraptured. *—Dave Marsh*

The Original Gospel, Vols. 1–2 / 1970 / Specialty ✦✦✦
Dorothy singing ragged with the group on fire circa 1951-1957. *—Opal Louis Nations*

★ **The Best of Dorothy Love Coates & the Original Gospel, Vols. 1-2** / 1991 / Specialty ✦✦✦✦✦
One of the cornerstones of golden age gospel, this set compiles two vinyl discs originally compiled by Barret Hansen (Dr. Demento). It includes all of the famous Dorothy Love Coates songs: "That's Enough," with a searing vocal that makes Aretha sound like a poetry reciter; "99 and a Half," the model for Wilson Pickett's secular version; "Get Away Jordan" and "I'm Sealed," which kicked off the group's career; "No Hiding Place," a purely fearsome blues; and "(You Can't Hurry God) He's Right on Time," later to become the Supremes' "You Can't Hurry Love." As a writer and performer, Coates expresses complete conviction in the message of the social gospel; she literally believes that her musical ministry has a crucial role in saving souls and the world. (No one who hears her can doubt it much.) Remastered by Kirk Felton in 1991. The cover art and Hansen's rudimentary notes, unchanged since the late '60s when the LPs came out, could use an update, but those are minor flaws next to music of such great emotional power and lyric intelligence. *—Dave Marsh*

● **Camp Meeting/The Soul of the Gospel Harmonettes** / Jul. 1993 / Vee-Jay ✦✦✦✦✦
Two mid-'60s albums that show Coates during the height of her crusade for salvation and at the high tide of her hopes for creating "the beloved community" of the civil rights movement as a direct outgrowth of Christian faith, as reflected in such songs as "The Righteous on the March," "Step By Step," and "Now I'm Ready." She has described her mission as "writing about a changing condition, a changing world," and often, her lyrics and delivery ("I'm sort of a hedge and highway singer") reflect exactly that. The liner notes are good as to commentary, completely confusing as to who sings what—they credit Coates as the lead singer on 16 tracks, no lead singer for "Is Your All on the Altar," the debut track and one of the best, and lead vocals by others on 16 tracks—although listeners will have little trouble figuring out which are sung by Coates with nothing more than their ears. *—Dave Marsh*

Charly Gospel Greats: Love Lifted Me / Charly UK ✦✦✦✦
Another compilation of the Vee-Jay Records material the band recorded from 1964 to 1968, much of it overlapping with the Vee-Jay gospel two-fer. That means its highlights are "The Righteous on the March," "Step By Step," and "Now I'm Ready." It has only 20 tracks and is poorly annotated. Nevertheless, the music's great. *—Dave Marsh*

The Best of Dorothy Love Coates & the Gospel Harmonettes / Jan. 31, 1995 / Nashboro ✦✦✦✦
Here are 14 of the final sides Coates recorded with her group—now including Dylan/Springsteen singer Cleo Kennedy—in Nashville in 1968-1969. It includes arguably the greatest of all her civil rights-oriented songs, "The Separation Line," and a tremendously moving rendition of "God Shall Wipe Away All Tears" that makes up what it lacks in finesse with some potent staccato embellishments. "Heaven, I've Heard So Much About It" is sufficiently rousing to raise the spirits of the dead. While not at the same level as her masterful Specialty recordings, this is further evidence why Dorothy Love Coates ranks as one of the greatest singers in American history. Opal Louis Nations contributes very solid notes. *—Dave Marsh*

Willie Cobbs

b. Jul. 15, 1932, Monroe, AR
Vocals, Harmonica / Modern Electric Blues, Modern Electric Chicago Blues, Soul-Blues
If for nothing else, the name of Willie Cobbs will always ring immortal for the prominence of his composition "You Don't Love Me," covered by everyone from Junior Wells to the Allman Brothers. But Cobbs' own discography is dotted with other triumphs, including a 1994 album for Rooster Blues, *Down to Earth*, that made it clear that Cobbs was alive, well, and committed to playing the blues.

Cobbs decided the prospect of rice farming didn't appeal to him enough to stick around his native Arkansas, so he migrated to Chicago in 1947. He hung out with Little Walter and Eddie Boyd while honing his harp chops on Maxwell Street. But Cobbs' recording career didn't fully blossom until 1960, when his waxing of "You Don't Love Me" for Billy Lee Riley's Memphis-based Mojo logo made him something of a regional star (one previous 45 for Joe Brown's Ruler imprint back in Chicago had stiffed instantly). "You Don't Love Me" eventually was leased to Vee-Jay—no doubt warming Cobbs' heart, since Vee-Jay boss Jimmy Bracken had once turned down Cobbs' audition, explaining that he sounded too much like Vee-Jay breadwinner Jimmy Reed.

Throughout the '60s, '70s, and '80s, Cobbs recorded a slew of obscure singles, often for his own labels (Riceland, Ricebelt, C&F), and operated nightclubs in Arkansas and Mississippi before cutting a long-overdue album for Rooster Blues (backed by labelmates Johnny Rawls and L.C. Luckett). He's also managed to slip in a little cinematic action into his schedule, appearing in the films *Mississippi Masala* and *Memphis*. *—Bill Dahl*

Hey Little Girl / 1991 / Wilco ✦✦✦
Underrated blues and soul composer and vocalist Willie Cobbs got rare time in the spotlight with this early-'90s release. Although things were erratic production and sound quality-wise, Cobbs' warm, soulful delivery made it consistently entertaining, if not always satisfying. *—Ron Wynn*

● **Down to Earth** / 1994 / Rooster Blues ✦✦✦✦✦
The only CD widely available by the Arkansas harpist whose chief claim to blues fame resides with his classic composition "You Don't Love Me" (later revived by Junior Wells and the Allman Brothers, among many others). With tasty backing by labelmates Johnny Rawls and L.C. Luckett adding luster to Cobbs' sturdy vocals and harp, the disc is a strong reminder that blues is alive and well in its southern birthplace. And yes, there's an accurate remake of his hit (segued with another of his gems, "Hey Little Girl"). *—Bill Dahl*

Jukin' / May 16, 2000 / Bullseye Blues ♦♦♦
This Bullseye release from blues harpist Willie Cobbs puts his unmistakable Memphis soul mixed with Mississippi Delta hybrid into action. *Jukin'* (not to be confused with Little Walter's *Juke*) succeeds as Cobbs mission statement to keep soul-blues alive as a vital part of the musical landscape into the new millennium. Cobbs voice is similar to Little Walter and much like his harmonica playing: gritty, and seasoned. Versions of "Reconsider Baby," "You're So Fine," "Mean Old World," and "Please Send Me Someone to Love" are combined with tight horn arrangements and consistently engaging guitar and organ work. *—Al Campbell*

Joe Cocker (John Robert Cocker)

b. May 20, 1944, Sheffield, Yorkshire, England
Vocals / Pop/Rock, Soft Rock, Adult Contemporary, Blues-Rock
After starting out as an unsuccessful pop singer (working under the name Vance Arnold), Joe Cocker found his niche singing rock and soul in the pubs of England with his superb backing group, the Grease Band. He hit number one in the U.K. in November 1968 with his version of the Beatles' "A Little Help From My Friends." His career really took off after he sang that song at the Woodstock festival in August 1969. A second British hit came with a version of Leon Russell's "Delta Lady" in the fall of 1969 (by then, Russell was Cocker's musical director) and both of his albums, *With a Little Help From My Friends* (April 1969) and *Joe Cocker!* (November 1969), went gold in America. In 1970, his cover of the Box Tops' hit "The Letter" became his first U.S. Top Ten. Cocker's first peak of success came when Russell organized the "Mad Dogs & Englishmen" tour of 1970, featuring Cocker and over 40 others, and resulting in a third gold album and a concert film. Subsequent efforts were less popular, and problems with alcohol (both on-stage and off-) reduced Cocker's once-powerful voice to a croaking rasp. But he returned to the U.S. Top Ten with the romantic ballad "You Are So Beautiful" in 1975 and topped the charts in a duet with Jennifer Warnes on "Up Where We Belong," the theme from the 1982 film *An Officer and a Gentleman.* He has survived, still charting into the '90s, albeit with less frequency than he did in the '70s and '80s. He also continued to work throughout the new millennium. *No Ordinary World* was his first release since 1997's *Across from Midnight. Respect Yourself* appeared in 2002. *—Cub Koda & William Ruhlmann*

With a Little Help from My Friends / Apr. 1969 / A&M ♦♦♦♦♦
The album that foisted Joe Cocker on an unsuspecting public is full of tasteful, raucous covers, Cocker's trademark hysterical vocals, and outstanding studio backing by pros like Jimmy Page and Steve Winwood. *—Tom Graves*

Joe Cocker! / Nov. 1969 / A&M ♦♦♦♦
Joe Cocker's first three A&M albums form the bedrock of a career that spans over three decades. While Cocker certainly wasn't always in top form during this stretch—thanks to alcohol problems and questionable comeback moves in the '80s and '90s—his early records did inform the classic pub rock sound later credited to proto-punk figures like Graham Parker and Brinsley Schwarz. On those early records, Cocker mixed elements of late-'60s English blues revival recordings (John Mayall, et al.) with the more contemporary sounds of soul and pop; a sound fused in no small part by producer and arranger Leon Russell, whose gumbo mix figures prominently on this eponymous release and the infamous *Mad Dogs & Englishmen* live set. Russell's sophisticated swamp blues aesthetic is felt directly with versions of his gospel ballad "Hello, Little Friend" and Beatles-inspired bit of New Orleans pop—and one of Cocker's biggest hits—"Delta Lady." Following up on the huge success of an earlier cover of "With a Little Help From My Friends," Cocker mines more Beatles gold with very respectable renditions of "She Came in Through the Bathroom Window" and "Something." And rounding out this impressive set are equally astute takes on Dylan's "Dear Landlord," Leonard Cohen's "Bird on the Wire," and John Sebastian's "Darling Be Home Soon." Throughout, Cocker gets superb support from his regular backing group of the time, the Grease Band. A fine introduction to the singer's classic, late-'60s and early-'70s period. *—Stephen Cook*

Mad Dogs & Englishmen / Aug. 1970 / A&M ♦♦♦♦♦
A superb document of Cocker's high-energy 1970 tour, it included about a zillion musicians and hangers-on. All the goods are here, and many consider this Cocker's last great moment. *—Tom Graves*

● **The Anthology** / Aug. 17, 1999 / A&M ♦♦♦♦♦
A&M's double-disc *Anthology* may be too much for casual fans that just want the hits, but anyone else will find this exhaustive 37-track chronicle of Joe Cocker's prime years definitive. The first disc concentrates on his first three albums, buttressed by a rare 1964 single of the Beatles' "I'll Cry Instead" and his 1970 non-LP single "The Letter"/"Space Captain." Disc two features highlights of all the albums he recorded between 1972 and 1982, selecting not only hits, but key album tracks. The end result is a collection that is concise and definitive. It may be missing such latter day hits as "When the Night Comes" and doesn't cover as much ground as the box set *Long Voyage Home*, but anyone looking for a comprehensive collection of Cocker's classic recordings will be satisfied by *Anthology. —Stephen Thomas Erlewine*

Porky Cohen

b. Jun. 2, 1924, Springfield, MA
Trombone / Swing, R&B
Best-known for his years as trombonist with Roomful of Blues, Porky Cohen finally had his recording debut as a leader in 1996, a highly enjoyable outing for Bullseye Blues with many of the members of the group. He started playing trombone at 13 and considers Jack Teagarden his most important early influence. Cohen worked local engagements from age 15 and took lessons from Miff Mole after graduating from high school in 1941. After a tryout with Benny Goodman, Cohen played with Tony Pastor's band, Charlie Barnet (off and on during 1943-1948), the Casa Loma Orchestra, Lucky Millinder, Tommy Dorsey, Boyd Raeburn, Artie Shaw (1949-1950), with a variety of Dixieland bands in the '50s, Bob Wilber & the Six, and the Jewels of Dixie (from the late '50s to the late '70s). Porky Cohen was a strong asset to Roomful of Blues from 1979-1988 before choosing to semi-retire. *—Scott Yanow*

● **Rhythm & Bones** / 1996 / Bullseye Blues ♦♦♦♦
Although trombonist Porky Cohen has played in the jazz major leagues since the early '40s (including periods with Tony Pastor, Charlie Barnet, the Casa Loma Orchestra, Lucky Millinder, Boyd Raeburn, Tommy Dorsey, Artie Shaw, Bobby Hackett, the Six with Bob Wilber, and various Dixieland bands) and toured regularly with Roomful of Blues during 1979-1988, this CD was his first opportunity to lead his own date. Seventy at the time, Cohen is heard in prime form leading a romping session featuring some of the members of Roomful of Blues, along with his successor trombonist Carl Querfurth. The joyous music, which only has two vocals among the 13 numbers (updates of Jimmy Rushing and Bessie Smith songs featuring Sugar Ray Norcia and Michelle Willson), mixes together heated swing and '50s style R&B blues to exhilarating effect; Illinois Jacquet would feel quite comfortable in this setting. There are plenty of opportunities for not only Cohen to solo, but all of the other horn players. An added plus is the lengthy and definitive liner notes, which fully relate (along with many photos) the Porky Cohen story. Highly recommended. *—Scott Yanow*

Deborah Coleman

b. Oct. 3, 1956, Portsmouth, VA
Vocals, Guitar / Contemporary Blues, Modern Electric Blues
Although she's a powerful blues guitarist, songwriter and singer, Deborah Coleman got her first inspiration from an unlikely place: seeing the pop group the Monkees on TV. Born in Portsmouth, Virginia and raised in a military family, Coleman took to music easily enough, since her dad played piano, two brothers played guitar, and a sister played guitar and keyboards. She picked up the guitar at age eight after seeing the Monkees and began to play professionally at 15, playing bass with a series of Portsmouth-area R&B and rock bands. She later switched to guitar after hearing Jimi Hendrix, also taking to James Brown and the Beatles. Coleman began buying records by blues-rock groups like Cream and Led Zeppelin, and slowly followed the music's origins back to basic blues. When she was 25, she got married and focused on raising her daughter while working day jobs as a nurse and electrician. After her daughter grew old enough to leave home alone, Coleman began to play out again, locally at first. In 1985, she began working with an all-female group, Moxxie. When that group split up in 1988, she got her blues chops together as part of an R&B trio. After two years of touring with the trio, Coleman did some woodshedding, seeing as many blues acts as she could live and studying blues recordings. Coleman got the break she was looking for in 1993 when she entered the Charleston (S.C.) Blues Festival's National Talent Search. Leading her own band, she took first place. She immediately put together her own touring group, the Thrillseekers, beginning a solo career as a bandleader. Coleman used her contest prize of free studio time to record a demo and secure a record deal with New Moon Records out of Chapel Hill, N.C. Her debut, *Takin' a Stand*, was released in 1995 on that label, and she followed it up two years later with *I Can't Lose*, her first album for Blind Pig. Coleman returned in 1998 with *Where Blue Begins*; *Soft Place to Fall* followed in the spring of 2000. She released her fifth album for Blind Big *Livin' on Love* in 2001, further consolidating her position as one of the top active blueswomen. Making this designation somewhat official, Coleman won the Orville Gibson Award for "Best Blues Guitarist, Female" in 2001. Also that year she was nominated for a W.C. Handy award for the fourth time. *—Richard Skelly*

Takin' a Stand / Jun. 1, 1995 / New Moon ♦♦♦

● **I Can't Lose** / Feb. 4, 1997 / Blind Pig ♦♦♦♦
Deborah Coleman's Blind Pig debut, *I Can't Lose*, is a powerful album of great ballads and blues stories, and of course, great guitar playing and singing. Her version of Billie Holiday's "Fine and Mellow" got her a lot of airplay on college and public radio stations around the U.S. *—Richard Skelly*

Where Blue Begins / Sep. 15, 1998 / Blind Pig ♦♦♦
Deborah Coleman is a double rarity in the male-dominated world of contemporary blues: she's a female lead singer who's not imitating the bellowing "blues mama" persona so familiar to the genre, and she's one hell of a lead guitar player. Using Luther Allison's backing band, *Where Blue Begins* is a smooth blend of Coleman's furious fretwork and pussycat purr of a voice. Coleman's slide shreds up "Goodbye Misery" while her buoyant licks carry the Texas blues of "Travelin' South." Even when her lyrics come close to cliché, like on "Beside Myself" and "Hain't It Funny" she saves the songs with some wicked playing and her Joan Armatrading vocal stylings. This album proves Coleman's not a novelty but a rare talent in a genre that desperately needs some new blood. *—Todd Deery*

Soft Place to Fall / Mar. 21, 2000 / Blind Pig ♦♦♦
For her third recording, Coleman continues to show the promise that her previous CDs gave a glimpse of. While still not as much of a blues devotee as she could be, she gives all indications of being a solid performer, a steadily improving vocalist, and a decent guitarist. She wrote three of the 11 cuts here, and they're the best of the lot. "What Goes Around" is a good 12-bar tune about cheatin' and messin' around; "Another Hoping Fool" is a slinky blues number about waiting by the telephone for that reassuring late-night call; and the title track sounds much like a Dire Straits tune, especially in the spare guitar playing of Coleman and Jack Holder. Coleman interprets Little Johnny Taylor's "If You Love Me Like You Say" in a cool funk mode, jumps into the direct blues of the adapted classic "I'm a Woman," and rocks the Jerry Williams number "Nothin' to Do With Love," which has all the potential to be a legitimate hit. On the boogie beat of "Don't Lie to Me" and the hard swing of the getting-back-to-love statement "So Damn Easy," Coleman changes up a bit to a more authentic blues style. She rocks on the simple "Look What You Do to Me," rocks even harder for "Confused," and goes into a more Southern-rock area

on "The Day It Comes." She also uses pop/R&B-ish background vocals on "Look What You Do," "The Day," and "So Damn Easy." Deborah Coleman is still on the trail of eclipsing Sue Foley, Debbie Davies, and Susan Tedeschi to take her place as the high priestess of contemporary blues. While not there yet, she has all the tools and musical ability to reach that lofty perch. *—Michael G. Nastos*

Livin' on Love / May 22, 2001 / Blind Pig ♦♦♦
Deborah Coleman detected a void in the music stratum and successfully filled it: A lead guitarist/vocalist playing the in the male dominated world of blues-rock. Others like Bonnie Raitt and Marie Muldaur have contributed to varying degrees in the contemporary blues scene (and other styles) but Coleman with her string of five consistently strong albums in only seven years demonstrates that she is serious about her craft and knows her calling as a blueswoman. *Livin' on Love* combines slow-grind blues pieces, R&B and gutsy rockers with a soulful voice and exemplary guitar playing proving that she's here to stay, not merely passing through. *—Dave Sleger*

Gary B.B. Coleman

b. 1947, Paris, TX, **d.** 1994
Vocals, Keyboards, Guitar, Bass / Modern Electric Blues, Soul-Blues
After a career as a local bluesman and blues promoter in Texas and Oklahoma, Gary Coleman found his niche when he signed over his first album, a self-produced outing originally issued on his own label, to the fledgling Ichiban company out of Atlanta in 1986. Since that time, both Coleman and Ichiban made their marks in the blues field—not only did Coleman release half a dozen of his own albums, he also oversaw production of the bulk of Ichiban's hefty blues catalog, bringing to the studio a number of artists he'd booked or toured with in his previous career (Chick Willis, Buster Benton, and Blues Boy Willie, among others). A singer/guitarist onstage, Coleman often took on a multi-instrumentalist's role in the studio. His music remained true to the blues and to the King legacy saluted in his "B.B." moniker and in his acknowledged debt to fellow-Texan Freddie King.

Coleman began listening to the blues as a child and by the time he was 15, he was working with Freddie King. Following his association with King, Coleman supported Lightnin' Hopkins and formed his own band, which played around Texas. Gary also began booking blues musicians into clubs in Texas, Oklahoma, and Coloradio. He continued to play gigs and book concerts for nearly two decades. In 1985, he formed Mr. B's Records, his own independent label. Coleman released his debut album, *Nothin' But the Blues*, the following year. The album was popular and gained the attention of Ichiban Records, who signed Coleman and re-released *Nothin' But the Blues* in 1987.

If You Can Beat Me Rockin', Coleman's second album, was released in 1988. That same year, he began producing albums for a number of other artists, as well as writing songs for other musicians and acting as an A&R scout for Ichiban. Between 1988 and 1992, he released six records and produced another 30, including albums for Little Johnny Taylor and Buster Benton. Coleman continued to be active both as a performing and recording artist, as well as a producer, until his untimely death in the mid-'90s. *—Jim O'Neal & Stephen Thomas Erlewine*

Nothin' But the Blues / 1987 / Ichiban ♦♦♦♦♦
With a darker overall tone, it's sadder and more introspective, and one of his more consistent records. It includes two very good slow blues, "Let Me Love You Baby" and "Shame on You." *—Niles J. Frantz*

If You Can Beat Me Rockin'... / 1988 / Ichiban ♦♦♦♦♦
He was influenced by Jimmy Reed, T-Bone Walker, B.B. King, and Lightnin' Hopkins, along with country & western, cajun, and early rock & roll. *—Niles J. Frantz*

One Night Stand / 1989 / Ichiban ♦♦♦

Dancin' My Blues Away / 1990 / Ichiban ♦♦♦

Romance Without Finance Is a Nuisance / 1991 / Ichiban ♦♦♦
It was no coincidence that Gary Coleman had "B.B." in his name. One of Coleman's main influences was B.B. King, and he was happy to acknowledge King's inspiration (although he's also learned a thing or two from Bobby "Blue" Bland, Jimmy Reed and the late Albert Collins). *Romance Without Finance* underscores the fact that while Coleman may not be the most original artist in the world, his Ichiban output has been consistent and enjoyable. The singer/electric guitarist's sense of humor serves him quite well on such amusing cuts as "Food Stamp Annie," "If You See My One-Eyed Woman" and "She Ain't Ugly (She Just Don't Look Like Nobody Else)." But he's equally appealing when embracing a somber minor-key groove à la Bland, and "Dealing from the Bottom of the Deck" is a fine example of Coleman's brooding side. Whether Coleman is being remorseful or humorous, this CD was a welcome addition to his catalog. *—Alex Henderson*

• **The Best of Gary B.B. Coleman** / 1991 / Ichiban ♦♦♦♦♦
This is a good career overview, though it does expose a certain lack of originality and diversity. *—Niles J. Frantz*

Too Much Weekend / 1992 / Ichiban ♦♦♦

Cocaine Annie / Apr. 1996 / Icehouse ♦♦

Retrospectives / Jun. 30, 1998 / Ichiban ♦♦♦
Gary B.B. Coleman's premature death in 1994 was quite a loss for the blues world. In 1998, Ichiban looked back on Coleman's years with the label with *Retrospectives*. This CD (which spans 1987-1992) was part of Ichiban's blues-oriented *Retrospectives* series, which also included collections by Jerry McCain, Trudy Lynn, and Luther "Houserocker" Johnson. This CD points to the fact that while Coleman was never an innovator, he was a soulful electric bluesman who often put a lot of heart into his stories. Ichiban provides a well-rounded picture of the singer/guitarist; humorous offerings like "Welfare Cadillac," "Romance Without Finance Is a Nuisance," and "Don't Give That Recipe Away" are heard along with brooding, dark performances of "St. James Infirmary" and Elmore James' "The Sky Is Cryin'." For listeners wanting to explore Coleman's Ichiban output, *Retrospectives* would be an appropriate starting point. *—Alex Henderson*

Jaybird Coleman

b. May 20, 1896, Gainesville, AL, **d.** Jan. 28, 1950, Tuskegee, AL
Jug, Vocals, Harmonica, Guitar / Piedmont Blues, Harmonica Blues, Jug Band, Country Blues
Jaybird Coleman was an early blues harmonica player. Although he only recorded a handful of sides and his technique wasn't particularly groundbreaking, his music was strong and a good representation of the sound of country blues harmonica in the early '30s.

Coleman was the son of sharecroppers. As a child, he taught himself how to play harmonica. He would perform at parties, both for his family and friends. Coleman served in the Army during World War I. After his discharge, he moved to the Birmingham, AL, area. While he lived in Birmingham, he would perform on street corners and occasionally play with the Birmingham Jug Band.

Jaybird made his first recordings in 1927—the results were released on Gennett, Silvertone, and Black Patti. For the next few years, he simply played on street corners. Coleman cut his final sessions in 1930, supported by the Birmingham Jug Band. These recordings appeared on the OKeh record label.

During the '30s and '40s, Coleman played on street corners throughout Alabama. By the end of the '40s, he had disappeared from the state's blues scene. In 1950, Jaybird Coleman died of cancer. *—Stephen Thomas Erlewine*

• **1927–1930** / 1993 / Document ♦♦♦♦
Jaybird Coleman wasn't one of the most distinctive early country blues harmonica players, but he nevertheless made engaging, entertaining music. All of his recordings—which only totalled 11 sides—are collected on Document's *1927-1930*. For fans of the genre, there are some cuts of interest here, but the music doesn't have enough weight to be of interest to anyone but country blues fanatics. *—Thom Owens*

Michael Coleman

Guitar / Chicago Blues, Soul, Funk
Before becoming one of Chicago's hottest electric blues guitarists, Michael Coleman began his career playing alongside James Cotton for nearly a decade. The guitarist joined Cotton's band in 1979 at the age of 23. For the next seven years, he remained by Cotton's side before eventually going on to work with Eddy Clearwater and Syl Johnson, among others. Later, Coleman embarked on a solo career. He recorded his American debut release, *Do Your Thing!*, for Delmark Records, who released the album in 2000. *Do Your Thing!* featured Coleman performing mostly covers—Jimmy Reed's "You Don't Have to Go," Otis Redding's "Dock of the Bay," Isaac Hayes' "Do Your Thing," Robert Geddins' "Tin Pan Alley," and more—along with a couple of Coleman's own compositions. In addition to playing guitar on the album, Coleman also sang. The result was an album very much his own, a testament to his talents and abilities as a blues guitarist of the highest order. *—Jason Birchmeier*

• **Do Your Thing!** / 2000 / Delmark ♦♦♦
Do Your Thing! demonstrates that a bluesman doesn't have to be a fantastic vocalist to provide a meaningful album. Best known in Chicago blues circles for his ten years as James Cotton's guitarist, Michael Coleman isn't a singer's singer. He is an adequate singer with a relaxed, laid-back vocal style that owes a lot to Jimmy Reed, but as a guitarist, Coleman obviously has sizable chops. And thankfully, he takes a lot of guitar solos on *Do Your Thing!*, which has as much to do with pre-1980 soul and funk as it does with electric Chicago blues. Not that Coleman (who was 44 when this CD was recorded in July 2000) isn't an expressive singer—he doesn't have massive pipes, but he still gets his points across on 12-bar blues numbers (including Reed's "You Don't Have to Go" and Robert Geddins' "Tin Pan Alley") as well as soul classics like Otis Redding's "Dock of the Bay," Isaac Hayes' "Do Your Thing," and Latimore's "Let's Straighten It Out." Meanwhile, Coleman pleasantly surprises the listener with an instrumental version of Fleetwood Mac's "Black Magic Woman," which was also recorded by Santana—and which really gives him a chance to stretch out on guitar. And equally surprising is Coleman's interpretation of Jimi Hendrix's "Message of Love," which he changes from crunching hard rock to bluesy, rock-influenced soul. *Do Your Thing!* isn't a masterpiece, but it's a decent effort from an impressive guitarist who is also a likable, if limited, singer. *—Alex Henderson*

Wallace Coleman

b. 1936, Morristown, TN
Harmonica / Harmonica Blues
If the name doesn't ring a bell, don't go searching for a copy of *Blues for Dummies*. Wallace Coleman entered the blues fray after retiring from the Cleveland, OH, bakery where he unloaded trucks. He was born in 1936 in Morristown, TN, where he fell for the blues listening to Howlin' Wolf, Sonny Boy Williamson, and Little Walter recordings on WLAC late night broadcasts out of Nashville. Jimmy Reed and Little Walter records inspired him to play the harmonica. Coleman taught himself to play on a 50 cent harp and developed lung power by imitating freight trains.

He followed his mother, who remarried and moved, to Cleveland, OH, in 1956; Wallace arrived a year later and found a career-lasting job at Hough Bakery where he played the harp during his breaks, honing his skills. He befriended the blues artists who came to town which wasn't difficult to do since most played small clubs seating less than 100 patrons. So blues notables like Jimmy Reed, Muddy Waters, Elmore James, and others were accessible to aspiring musicians and fans. Amazingly, he didn't perform in public until he was 51.

Guitar Slim (known for his playing as well as his prowess with the ladies) was introduced to Coleman by one of Wallace's co-workers; an impromptu audition resulted in Coleman regularly playing with Slim's band at the Cascade Lounge located at 79th & St. Clair. Renowned blues singer and guitar player Robert Jr. Lockwood resided near the

Cascade on Lawnview Avenue and went to hear the band one evening and came away impressed with Coleman's traditional blues playing. So much so that he offered him a position with his band, Coleman nixed the offer because he was two years from retirement; as events unfolded, he retired early anyway for a chance to pursue the music blooming from his soul. Ironically, the bakery closed for good four years after he left.

Upon retiring, he contacted Lockwood in 1987 to see if the offer still stood, it did, and he began a 10-year association with the Godfather of Cleveland Blues. A guy he emulated as a teen in Morristown without even knowing it; Lockwood played guitar on many of the blues records that he admired; Coleman even created harmonica parts for some of Robert Johnson's songs redid by Lockwood—Johnson's stepson. The 10 years were eventful as Lockwood's band gigged all over the U.S., Canada, and overseas. In 1996 he formed his own band: the Wallace Coleman Blues Band. A year later he left Lockwood for good and recorded his first CD, *Wallace Coleman* on Fishhead Records.

The critically acclaimed album received rave reviews from blues critics; it included one of his finest efforts "Black Spider." Career highlights include the Lockwood years, playing the Rose Center in his birthplace, Morristown, TN, and his enterprise: Pinto Blues Music where he has released a second CD entitled *Stretch My Money*. When not touring he played regularly at the Main Street Cafe in Medina, and Pepper Joe's Bar and Grill in Lakewood, OH. And has also performed at the East Cleveland Library, many private parties, and at the Rock & Roll Hall of Fame's Tribute to Muddy Waters. He married happily to Jody Getz. *—Andrew Hamilton*

● **Stretch My Money** / 2000 / Pinto Blues Music ♦♦♦♦
Harpsman Wallace Coleman waxed this second CD on his own Pinto Blues Music label and builds on the momentum established by his Fishhead Records debut. Coleman blows a traditional blues harp with plenty of hot ear-cleaning solos to accent his storytelling vocal delivery. Prime examples of the style are "Stretch My Money," "Bring It on Home," the cattish "Spare Woman" (which is about infidelity), "Shake Me," and "Off the Hook." *—Andrew Hamilton*

Wallace Coleman / Jun. 26, 2000 / Fishhead ♦♦♦
A harmonica player/vocalist schooled at Little Walter University, a traditionalist with little affinity for contemporary sounds or flavor, as well as an underrated vocalist, Wallace Coleman excels on the humorous "Big Dog Blues" and "Black Spider": the former is about a dog whom food bills exceed the entire family's, and the latter is about a wicked woman with spiderish ways. Furthermore, "So Long" finds Coleman in good spirits despite the hurt on a midtempo drinking number, the super-cool "101 Blues" epitomizes the word "sweet," and "Off the Wall" is a tough instrumental fueled by Coleman's spirited harping. *—Andrew Hamilton*

Albert Collins

b. Oct. 3, 1932, Leona, TX, **d.** Nov. 24, 1993, Las Vegas, NV
Vocals, Leader, Songwriter, Guitar / Modern Electric Texas Blues, Electric Texas Blues
Albert Collins, "The Master of the Telecaster," "The Iceman," and "The Razor Blade" was robbed of his best years as a blues performer by a bout with liver cancer that ended with his premature death on November 24, 1993. He was just 61 years old. The highly influential, totally original Collins, like the late John Campbell, was on the cusp of a much wider worldwide following via his deal with Virgin Records' Pointblank subsidiary. However, unlike Campbell, Collins had performed for many more years, in obscurity, before finally finding a following in the mid-'80s.

Collins was born October 1, 1932, in Leona, TX. His family moved to Houston when he was seven. Growing up in the city's Third Ward area with the likes of Johnny "Guitar" Watson and Johnny "Clyde" Copeland, Collins started out taking keyboard lessons. His idol when he was a teen was Hammond B-3 organist Jimmy McGriff. But by the time he was 18 years old, he switched to guitar, and hung out and heard his heroes, Clarence "Gatemouth" Brown, John Lee Hooker, T-Bone Walker and Lightnin' Hopkins (his cousin) in Houston-area nightclubs. Collins began performing in these same clubs, going after his own style, characterized by his use of minor tunings and a capo, by the mid-'50s. It was also at this point that he began his "guitar walks" through the audience, which made him wildly popular with the younger White audiences he played for years later in the '80s. He led a ten-piece band, the Rhythm Rockers, and cut his first single in 1958 for the Houston-based Kangaroo label, "The Freeze." The single was followed by a slew of other instrumental singles with catchy titles, including "Sno-Cone," "Icy Blue," and "Don't Lose Your Cool." All of these singles brought Collins a regional following. After recording "De-Frost" b/w "Albert's Alley" for Hall-Way Records of Beaumont, TX, he hit it big in 1962 with "Frosty," a million-selling single. Teenagers Janis Joplin and Johnny Winter, both raised in Beaumont, were in the studio when he recorded the song. According to Collins, Joplin correctly predicted that the single would become a hit. The tune quickly became part of his ongoing repertoire, and was still part of his live shows more than 30 years later, in the mid-'80s. Collins' percussive, ringing guitar style became his trademark, as he would use his right hand to pluck the strings. Blues-rock guitarist Jimi Hendrix cited Collins as an influence in any number of interviews he gave.

Through the rest of the '60s, Collins continued to work day jobs while pursuing his music with short regional tours and on weekends. He recorded for a other small Texas labels, including Great Scott, Brylen and TFC. In 1968, Bob "The Bear" Hite from the blues-rock group Canned Heat took an interest in the guitarist's music, traveling to Houston to hear him live. Hite took Collins to California, where he was immediately signed to Imperial Records. By later 1968 and 1969, the '60s blues revival was still going on, and Collins got wider exposure opening for groups like the Allman Brothers at the Fillmore West in San Francisco. Collins based his operations for many years in Los Angeles before moving to Las Vegas in the late '80s.

He recorded three albums for the Imperial label before jumping to Tumbleweed Records. There, several singles were produced by Joe Walsh, since the label was owned by Eagles' producer Bill Szymczyk. The label folded in 1973. Despite the fact that he didn't record much through the '70s and into the early '80s, he had gotten sufficient airplay around the U.S. with his singles to be able to continue touring, and so he did, piloting his own bus from gig to gig until at least 1988, when he and his backing band were finally able to use a driver. Collins' big break came about in 1977, when he was signed to the Chicago-based Alligator Records, and he released his brilliant debut for the label in 1978, *Ice Pickin'*. Collins recorded six more albums for the label, culminating in 1986's *Cold Snap*, on which organist Jimmy McGriff performs. It was at Alligator Records that Collins began to realize that he could sing adequately, and working with his wife Gwen, he co-wrote many of his classic songs, including items like "Mastercharge," and "Conversation With Collins."

His other albums for Alligator include *Live in Japan*, *Don't Lose Your Cool*, *Frozen Alive!*, and *Frostbite*. An album he recorded with fellow guitarists Robert Cray and Johnny "Clyde" Copeland for Alligator in 1985, *Showdown!* brought a Grammy award for all three musicians. His *Cold Snap*, released in 1986, was nominated for a Grammy award.

In 1989, Collins signed with the Pointblank subsidiary of major label Virgin Records, and his debut, *Iceman*, was released in 1991. The label released the compilation *Collins Mix* in 1993. Other compact disc reissues of his early recordings were produced by other record companies who saw Collins' newfound popularity on the festival and theater circuit, and they include *The Complete Imperial Recordings* on EMI Records (1991) and *Truckin' With Albert Collins* (1992) on MCA Records. Collins' sessionography is also quite extensive. The albums he performs on include David Bowie's *Labyrinth*, John Zorn's *Spillane*, Jack Bruce's *A Question of Time*, John Mayall's *Wake Up Call*, B.B. King's *Blues Summit*, Robert Cray's *Shame and a Sin*, and Branford Marsalis' *Super Models in Deep Conversation*.

Although he'd spent far too much time in the '70s without recording, Collins could sense that the blues were coming back stronger in the mid-'80s, with interest in Stevie Ray Vaughan at an all-time high. Collins enjoyed some media celebrity in the last few years of his life, via concert appearances at Carnegie Hall, on *Late Night With David Letterman*, in the Touchstone film *Adventures in Babysitting*, and in a classy Seagram's Wine Cooler commercial with Bruce Willis. The blues revival that Collins, Vaughan, and the Fabulous Thunderbirds helped bring about in the mid-'80s continued into the '90s. But sadly, Collins was not able to take part in the ongoing evolution of the music. *—Richard Skelly*

The Cool Sound of Albert Collins / 1965 / TCF Hall ♦♦♦♦♦

Love Can Be Found Anywhere / 1969 / BGO ♦♦♦

Trash Talkin' / 1969 / Imperial ♦♦♦

Truckin' With Albert Collins / 1969 / MCA ♦♦♦♦♦
Truckin' With Albert Collins is a 1969 Blue Thumb reissue of *The Cool Sound of Albert Collins*, which was originally released on TCF Hall Records in 1965. These are the earliest recordings that Collins made and already his trademark sound is in place—his leads are stinging, piercing and direct. The album features a set of blistering instrumentals (with the exception of the vocal "Dyin' Flu") that would eventually become his signature tunes, including "Frosty" and "Frostbite." Collins doesn't just stick to blues, he adds elements of surf, rock, jazz, and R&B. These songs may not have been hits at the time, but they helped establish his reputation as the Master of the Telecaster. *—Thom Owens*

The Complete Albert Collins / 1970 / Imperial ♦♦♦
This inconsistent set is worthwhile nonetheless. *—Bill Dahl*

There's Gotta Be a Change / 1971 / Tumbleweed ♦♦
Although this probably isn't Albert Collins' best album, it is significant for several reasons. Producer Bill Szymczyk, who had great commercial success with B.B. King on *Indianola Mississippi Seeds* obviously hoped to duplicate that for his own Tumbleweed label. To that end, an all-star assemblage of players were present for these sessions at the famed Record Plant West in Los Angeles. Highlights include a slashing guitar duel between Collins and Jessie Ed Davis. *—William Ashford*

Alive & Cool / 1971 / Red Lightnin' ♦

★ **Ice Pickin'** / 1978 / Alligator ♦♦♦♦♦
Ice Pickin' is the album that brought Albert Collins directly back into the limelight, and for good reason, too. The record captures the wild, unrestrained side of his playing that had never quite been documented before. Though his singing doesn't quite have the fire or power of his playing, the album doesn't suffer at all because of that—he simply burns throughout the album. *Ice Pickin'* was his first release for Alligator Records and it set the pace for all the albums that followed. No matter how much he tried, Collins never completely regained the pure energy that made *Ice Pickin'* such a revelation. *—Thom Owens*

Frostbite / 1980 / Alligator ♦♦♦
Frostbite was the first indication that Albert Collins' Alligator albums were going to follow something of a formula. The album replicated all of the styles and sounds of *Ice Pickin'*, but the music lacked the power of its predecessor. Nevertheless, there was a wealth of fine playing on the album, even if the quality of the songs themselves is uneven. *—Thom Owens*

Frozen Alive! / 1981 / Alligator ♦♦♦
Frozen Alive! demonstrates the exuberant power of Albert Collins in concert and contains enough first-rate solos to make it a worthwhile listen for fans of his icy style. *—Thom Owens*

Don't Lose Your Cool / 1983 / Alligator ♦♦♦♦
Keeping up with his "Iceman" moniker, Albert Collins delivers with his fourth Alligator release *Don't Lose Your Cool*. The title cut was one of his first instrumental hits back in the late '50s and here it's given a gritty, organ-driven workout à la one of his heroes and onetime collaborators, Jimmy McGriff. Forging on in this impressively diverse set, Collins revels in the humorous, spoken commentary of Oscar Brown Jr.'s "But I Was Cool" (reminiscent of Collins' spoken interludes on the John Zorn piece "Spillane"), updates the jump blues antics of Big Walter Price's "Get to Gettin'," and closes the set out with a faithful take on Guitar Slim's "Quicksand." He also adds a few of his own impressive cuts here, including the funky, syncopated New Orleans groove "Melt Down" and the Stax 'n' blues cut "Ego Trip." Throughout, of course, Collins comes up with plenty of his grating, barbed

wire guitar licks and rough-hewn vocals. Riding atop his crack, seven-piece Ice Breakers band (including a fine horn section), Collins certainly keeps things burnin' on this set, while still living up to all the icy allusions with some of the most cool and urbane modern blues on record. —*Stephen Cook*

Live in Japan / 1984 / Alligator ✦✦✦
Compared to *Frozen Alive!*, *Live in Japan* is a little more drawn-out and funky, featuring extended jamming on several songs. That isn't necessarily a bad thing—Collins and his bandmates can work a groove pretty damn well. Of course, the main reason to listen to an Albert Collins album is to hear the man play. And play he does throughout *Live in Japan*, spitting out piercing leads with glee. On the whole, it's not quite as consistent as *Frozen Alive!*, but that's only by a slight margin. —*Thom Owens*

Showdown / 1985 / Alligator ✦✦✦✦
A summit meeting between Texas guitar veterans Collins and Johnny Copeland and newcomer Robert Cray, the set is scorching all the way. —*Bill Dahl*

Cold Snap / 1986 / Alligator ✦✦✦
Cold Snap has a stronger R&B direction than Collins' previous Alligator releases, most notably in the presence of a slicker production. That approach doesn't suit him particularly well—he's at his best when he's just playing the blues, not when he's trying to sing. Nevertheless, he turns out a number of gripping solos, and that is what prevents *Cold Snap* from being too much of a disappointment. —*Thom Owens*

Ice Cold Blues / 1986 / Charly ✦✦✦

Iceman / 1991 / Virgin ✦✦✦
Albert Collins doesn't change anything for his major label debut, *Iceman*. Like its predecessors, it is slick and professional, featuring a variety of shuffles, R&B tunes, and slow blues, all stamped with Collins' trademark icy wail. None of the songs or performances are particularly noteworthy, but *Iceman* is a solid set that delivers the goods for fans of his style. —*Thom Owens*

☆ **The Complete Imperial Recordings** / 1991 / EMI ✦✦✦✦✦
Texan Albert Collins was in the very first rank of post-war blues guitarists. This two-CD set is a reissue of all 36 sides he cut for Imperial from 1968 to 1970—representing this artist's second major recording stint. Instrumentals comprise roughly three-fourths of the material. They frame his distinctive guitar work with a tight ensemble of organ, bass, and drums, adding at times a piano and/or second guitar, punctuated by a horn section. About ten of these tunes are as great as anything Collins ever did. They are riddled with the biting, incisive, dramatic, and economical playing that made him a legend. There are also some outstanding vocals. Although this set is not without its clinkers, it is a solid package and a must for any Collins fan. —*Larry Hoffman*

Molten Ice / 1992 / Cass ✦✦✦
Reissued domestically in 1998, *Molten Ice* captures Albert Collins live in Toronto in 1973 with backing by that city's Moe Peters Band. —*Steve Huey*

Collins Mix: The Best / Oct. 5, 1993 / Pointblank ✦✦✦✦
This provided fresh looks at 11 Collins classics, among them such epic numbers as "Don't Lose Your Cool," "Frosty," "Honey Hush" and "Tired Man." There were slow, wailing ballads with blistering solos, electrifying uptempo wailers with a great horn section answering Collins' phrases with their own bleats, and first-rate mastering and production. Guest stars included B.B. King, Branford Marsalis, Kim Wilson and Gary Moore, while Collins injected vitality into numbers he'd already made standards years ago. This set is a wonderful tribute to an incredible guitarist and musician. —*Ron Wynn*

Live '92/'93 / Sep. 12, 1995 / Pointblank ✦✦✦
Compiling a number of performances recorded shortly before Albert Collins' death, *Live '92-'93* offers definitive proof that the guitarist remained vital until his last days. —*Thom Owens*

Live / 1996 / Munich ✦✦✦
Collins is backed by a Dutch band on this recording of a December 1978 show in Alkmaar, Holland. Dividing his attention between originals and covers of tunes by the likes of Lowell Fulson and Guitar Slim, it's a typically energetic set with long solos, the backup musicians playing competently, and female singer Tineke Schoemaker taking the vocals on "Blue River Rising." But it's not particularly an essential addition, or preferable, to his more widely known live albums of the '80s and '90s. —*Richie Unterberger*

Deluxe Edition / 1997 / Alligator ✦✦✦✦✦
Deluxe Edition is a solid, albeit imperfect, 13-track collection of highlights from Albert Collins' latter-day recordings for Alligator. There are only a handful of genuine classics, but there are a lot of great performances that spotlight Collins' stinging guitar work and impassioned vocals. Nevertheless, it's only adequate as an introduction, since *Ice Pickin'* remains the place to become acquainted with Collins' blistering blues. —*Stephen Thomas Erlewine*

The Hot "Cool" Sound of Albert Collins / Jun. 23, 1998 / M.I.L. Multimedia ✦✦✦
Recorded live at a 1973 Toronto club date, *The Hot "Cool" Sound of Albert Collins* offers a rather lackluster portrait of the Iceman. Backed by a subpar local backing group, he simply goes through the motions on tracks like "All About My Girl" and "Frosty." —*Jason Ankeny*

Love Can Be Found Anywhere/Trash Talkin' / Sep. 26, 2000 / Collectables ✦✦✦

Sam Collins
b. Aug. 11, 1887, Louisiana, d. Oct. 20, 1949, Chicago, IL
Vocals, Guitar / Prewar Country Blues, Country Blues
One of the earliest generation of blues performers, Collins developed his style in South Mississippi (as opposed to the Delta). His recording debut single ("The Jail House Blues,"

1927) predated those of legendary Mississippians such as Charley Patton and Tommy Johnson and was advertised as "Crying Sam Collins and his Git-Fiddle." Collins did not become a major name in blues—in fact his later records appeared under several different pseudonyms, most notably the name Jim Foster—but his rural bottleneck guitar pieces were among the first to be compiled on LP when the country blues reissue era was just beginning. Sam Charters wrote in *The Bluesmen*: "Although Collins was not one of the stylistic innovators within the Mississippi blues idiom, he was enough part of it that, in blues like 'Signifying Blues' and 'Slow Mama Slow,' he had some of the intensity of the Mississippi music at its most creative level." —*Jim O'Neal*

Complete Recorded Works (1927–1931) / 1927-1931 / Document ✦✦✦
Every track that Sam Collins recorded at the end of the '20s and early in the '30s is included on Document's *Complete Recorded Works (1927-1931)*. Although the comprehensiveness of the set is a little intimidating for casual listeners—they should stick with the better-sequenced *Jailhouse Blues*—historians will find the collection invaluable. —*Thom Owens*

● **Jailhouse Blues** / 1990 / Yazoo ✦✦✦✦
Known as "Crying" Sam Collins, after the eerie, falsetto quality of his voice, the artist in fact had many nicknames. A rather prolific recording artist, less than half of the 50 sides he cut saw release. Often the same tune would crop up on different labels necessitating a variety of pseudonyms (including "Bunny Carter," "Big Boy Woods," and "Salty Dog Sam"). *Jailhouse Blues* collects the bulk of the guitarist's commercially released output. Perhaps not as expressive or emotionally exhilarating as the "hard" Mississippi Delta singers, Collins' voice has an accessible, undeniable beauty. His guitar accompaniment proves a mastery of the basic slide and fingerpicking skills, delivered with a rough but pleasant style. These elements were combined with a compelling set of influences (intentional or otherwise) that came together in his music. For one, Collins probably picked up a lot from listening to recordings and performers from the area. His songs are filled with common, stock blues phrases delivered without a great degree of personal reconfiguring. "Hesitation Blues," a popular song from the period, is given a raw, swift rendition. The guitar line follows his singing, but he ends his phrases with deep, hard chords that contrast his high vocal. Other songs are approached in a similar manner. On "Midnight Special," the pace is almost rushed. Collins' vocals on both songs bear a striking resemblance to Skip James (at times, Collins actually sounds strikingly like a woman). The connection is made stronger by the fact that Collins' "Lead Me All the Way" has been performed by James as "Jesus Is a Mighty Good Leader." More unusual, however, are the strains of white music that run through Collins' style of Mississippi blues. On "It Won't Be Long," for instance, his characteristic vibrato and natural blues phrasing are less prominent, creating a bizarre mix of white and black delivery. —*Nathan Bush*

King of the Blues 11 / 1992 / Pea Vine ✦✦✦✦
The 22 songs here, mostly clean and well transferred, make this one of the better bargains among Japanese imports, especially at a $14 list price. The first 15 songs date from 1927, and most of them feature Collins solo, playing some lively and dexterous blues accompanied by some very expressive vocals. "Lion's Den Blues," "Yellow Dog Blues," "Riverside Blues," and "I'm Still Sitting on Top of the World" (just two of the songs that refer to more familiar later songs) are highlights on this very fine disc, which includes some major surprises—on "Lovely Lady Blues," for instance, one actually gets a real sense of room ambience from the 1927 disc, done for the Gennett label; and there are places where Collins' playing is so animated that it sounds like two guys. The notes are in Japanese, but it's the music that counts here. —*Bruce Eder*

Joanna Connor
b. Aug. 31, 1962, Brooklyn, NY
Vocals, Guitar / Blues-Rock, Modern Electric Blues
What sets Joanna Connor apart from the rest of the pack of guitar-playing female blues singers is her skill on the instrument. Even though Connor has become an accomplished singer over time, her first love was guitar playing, and it shows in her live shows and on her recordings.

Brooklyn-born, Massachusetts-raised Joanna Connor was drawn to the Chicago blues scene like a bee to a half-full soda can. Connor, a fiery musician raised in the '70s—when rock & roll was all over the mass media—just wanted to play blues. She was born August 31, 1962, in Brooklyn, NY, and raised by her mother in Worcester, MA. She benefited from her mother's huge collection of blues and jazz recordings, and a young Connor was taken to see people like Taj Mahal, Bonnie Raitt, Ry Cooder and Buddy Guy in concert.

Connor got her first guitar at age seven. When she was 16, she began singing in Worcester-area bands, and when she was 22, she moved to Chicago. Soon after her arrival in 1984, she began sitting in with Chicago regulars like James Cotton, Junior Wells, Buddy Guy and A.C. Reed. She hooked up with Johnny Littlejohn's group for a short time before being asked by Dion Payton to join his 43rd Street Blues Band. She performed with Payton at the 1987 Chicago Blues Festival. Later that year, she was ready to put her own band together.

Her 1989 debut for the Blind Pig label, *Believe It!*, got her out of Chicago clubs and into clubs and festivals around the U.S., Canada and Europe. Her other albums include 1992's *Fight* for Blind Pig (the title track a Luther Allison tune), *Living on the Road* (1993), and *Rock and Roll Gypsy* (1995), the latter two for the Ruf Records label. *Slidetime* on Blind Pig followed in 1998 and *Nothing But the Blues*, a live recording of a 1999 show in Germany, appeared on the German Inakustik label in 2001. Connor left Blind Pig and signed to small indie label M.C. in 2002. Her first release for her new label, *The Joanna Connor Band*, finds Connor expanding her sound a bit in an attempt to reach a more mainstream audience.

Connor has blossomed into a gifted blues songwriter. Her songwriting talents, strongly influenced by greats like Luther Allison, will insure that she stays in the blues spotlight for years to come. *—Richard Skelly*

• **Believe It!** / 1989 / Blind Pig ♦♦♦♦♦
On the surface, *Believe It!* is standard-issue bar-band blues-rock, but it is distinguished by Joanna Connor's passion for the music. Connor believes in the music so much, it can't help but appear in the grooves every once in a while. In particular, her guitar playing is noteworthy—it's tough, greasy, and powerful. *Believe It!* suffers from a lack of memorable songs—she's still trying to develop a distinctive songwriting voice—but Connor's strong performances carry the album through any weak moments. *—Thom Owens*

Fight / 1992 / Blind Pig ♦♦♦
To date, Joanna Connor's studio work has not lived up the live-wire energy of her personal performances. *Fight* takes a major step toward setting this right. This stuff wails, especially Robert Johnson's "Walking Blues" which Connor reinvents courtesy of some stinging slidework. While Connor's lack of dependence on cover material rates bonus points, not all her songs are memorable—even if the guitar playing is. *—Roch Parisien*

Living on the Road / 1993 / Peter Pan ♦♦♦

Rock and Roll Gypsy / Oct. 17, 1995 / Ruf ♦♦♦

Big Girl Blues / 1996 / Ruf ♦♦♦♦
The comparison of Connor to Bonnie Raitt is unavoidable, considering the similarities of their vocal style and skill at slide guitar. But Connor offers a more savage guitar approach, akin to George Thorogood, and she comes on as a bit nastier. The album is filled with impressive guitar work, but the bad-girl pose wears thin after a while. *—Tim Sheridan*

Slidetime / May 19, 1998 / Blind Pig ♦♦♦
Joanna Connor's fourth album for Blind Pig finds her still working solidly in blues-rock territory with plenty of her blistering slide guitar work well to the fore. Connor penned all 11 of the tunes here, co-writing one of them with guitarist Ron Johnson and the other with drummer Boyd Martin; her songwriting chops show considerable added depth and improvement on this go round. Still keeping her sound in the time-honored road-band format of two guitars, bass and drums. She brings aboard background vocals on "Slide It In," "Got To Have You" and "Pea Vine Blues," the latter also featuring some nice finger-picked guitar from Ron Johnson. Connors' guitar positively blisters on "My Man," "Free Free Woman" and others, making this one of her strongest outings. *—Cub Koda*

Nothing but the Blues / Apr. 3, 2001 / Inakustik ♦♦♦♦
Brooklyn, NY-born vocalist/composer/electric slide guitarist Joanna Connor honed her craft, shedding and learning in Chicago's blues clubs. However, with several albums to her credit along with a seemingly hefty touring schedule, the artist has attained prominence in Europe and abroad, as the high-octane "Nothing but the Blues" was recorded live in Bamberg, Germany. Essentially, Ms. Connor once again demonstrates her exuberant blues-based convictions via her spirited vocals, electrified crunch chords and scorching slide guitar lines. Supported by a rock solid band, featuring bassist Darnell Wilcher, drummer Lance Lewis and guitarist Tony Palmer, Ms. Connor belts out a series of standard and original compositions amid a '70s-style hard rock groove, brimming with fiery dynamics and strong soloing. And while the author of the CD liners boldly states "This is the future of blues-rock," admirers of sizzling blues-drenched guitar licks, impacting opuses, and bone-crushing interplay might reap huge benefits here. *—Glenn Astarita*

The Joanna Connor Band / May 28, 2002 / M.C. ♦♦♦
If Joanna Connor has trouble breaking from the indie world into the big leagues, she could no doubt thrive as a songwriter for Bonnie Raitt, whose inspiration informs Connor's vocal style, blues-rock guitar approach, and attitude. Raitt's producers often add a lot of slickness and polish, while Connor scores points by keeping things slightly more raw. "Fine and Sublime" is romantic blues-rock at its best, but Connor goes beyond this at times, thinking globally on more than a few occasions. "No Black and White" is a global unity message set to a blend of rock and Irish jig rhythms. "Afrisippi," a colorful tribute to the place where humanity first reared its head, has a South African rolling guitar vibe; it would be better sung than spoken, but Connor's message is what counts—all music derives from the same basic spiritual and human source. While Connor is a solid songwriter, she's also a clever interpreter of soul standards ranging from "Fever" to "Somebody Have Mercy" by Sam Cooke. *—Jonathan Widran*

Ry Cooder

b. Mar. 15, 1947, Los Angeles, CA

Slide Guitar, Vocals, Mandolin, Guitar / Slide Guitar Blues, Cuban Pop, Contemporary Blues, Roots Rock, Worldbeat, Ethnic Fusion, Country-Rock, Blues-Rock, Modern Electric Blues, Album Rock, Film Music, Instrumental Rock, Original Score

Whether serving as a session musician, solo artist, or soundtrack composer, Ry Cooder's chameleon-like fretted instrument virtuosity, songwriting, and choices of material encompass an incredibly eclectic range of North American musical styles, including rock & roll, blues, reggae, Tex-Mex, Hawaiian, Dixieland jazz, country, folk, R&B, gospel, and vaudeville. The 16-year-old Cooder began his career in 1963 in a blues band with Jackie DeShannon and then formed the short-lived Rising Sons in 1965 with Taj Mahal and Spirit drummer Ed Cassidy. Cooder met producer Terry Melcher through the Rising Sons and was invited to perform at several sessions with Paul Revere and the Raiders. During his subsequent career as a session musician, Cooder's trademark slide guitar work graced the recordings of such artists as Captain Beefheart (*Safe As Milk*), Randy Newman, Little Feat, Van Dyke Parks, the Rolling Stones (*Let It Bleed*, *Sticky Fingers*), Taj Mahal, and Gordon Lightfoot. He also appeared on the soundtracks of *Candy* and *Performance*.

Cooder made his debut as a solo artist in 1970 with a self-titled album featuring songs by Leadbelly, Blind Willie Johnson, Sleepy John Estes, and Woody Guthrie. The follow-up, *Into the Purple Valley*, introduced longtime cohorts Jim Keltner on drums and Jim Dickinson on bass, and it and *Boomer's Story* largely repeated and refined the syncopated style and mood of the first. In 1974, Cooder produced what is generally regarded as his best album, *Paradise and Lunch*, and its follow-up, *Chicken Skin Music*, showcased a potent blend of Tex-Mex, Hawaiian, gospel, and soul music, and featured contributions from Flaco Jimenez and Gabby Pahinui. In 1979, *Bop Till You Drop* was the first major-label album to be recorded digitally. In the early '80s, Cooder began to augment his solo output with soundtrack work on such films as *Blue Collar*, *The Long Riders*, and *The Border*, he has gone on to compose music for *Southern Comfort*, *Goin' South*, *Paris, Texas*, *Streets of Fire*, *Alamo Bay*, *Blue City*, *Crossroads*, *Cocktail*, *Johnny Handsome*, *Steel Magnolias*, and *Geronimo*. *Music By Ry Cooder* (1995) compiled two discs' worth of highlights from Cooder's film work.

In 1992, Cooder joined Keltner, John Hiatt, and renowned British tunesmith Nick Lowe, all of whom had played on Hiatt's *Bring the Family*, to form Little Village, which toured and recorded one album. Cooder next turned his attention to world music, recording the album *A Meeting by the River* with Indian musician V.M. Bhatt. Cooder's next project, a duet album with renowned African guitarist Ali Farka Toure titled *Talking Timbuktu*, won the 1994 Grammy for Best World Music Recording. *—Steve Huey*

Ry Cooder / 1970 / Reprise ♦♦♦♦
Already a seasoned music business veteran at the age of 22, Ry Cooder stepped out from behind the shadows of the likes of Jackie DeShannon, Taj Mahal, the Rolling Stones, and Captain Beefheart, signing his own deal with Warner Brothers records in 1969. Released the following year, Cooder's eponymous debut creates an intriguing fusion of blues, folk, rock & roll, and pop, filtered through his own intricate, syncopated guitar; Van Dyke Parks and Lenny Waronker's idiosyncratic production; and Parks and Kirby Johnson's string arrangements. And while he's still finding his feet as a singer, Cooder puts this unique blend across with a combination of terrific songs, virtuosic playing, and quirky, yet imaginative, arrangements. For material, Cooder, the son of folklorist parents, unearths ten gems—spanning six decades dating back to the '20s—by legends such as Woody Guthrie, Blind Blake, Sleepy John Estes, and Leadbelly, as well as a current Randy Newman composition. Still, as great as his outside choices are, it's the exuberant charm of his own instrumental "Available Space" that nearly steals the show. Its joyful interplay between Cooder's slide, Van Dyke Parks' music hall piano, and the street-corner drumming creates a piece that is both loose and sophisticated. If "Available Space" is the record's most playful moment, its closer, "Dark Is the Night," is the converse, with Cooder's stark, acoustic slide extracting every ounce of torment from Blind Willie Johnson's mournful masterpiece. Some of the eccentric arrangements may prove to be a bit much for both purists and pop audiences alike, but still, Cooder's need to stretch, tempered with a reverence for the past, helps to create a completely original work that should reward adventurous listeners. *—Brett Hartenbach*

Into the Purple Valley / 1971 / Reprise ♦♦♦♦♦
First there are no other credits for musicians; because of his reputation for honesty in music, I will assume that he plays all the instruments, including the ones with no strings. He is known as a virtuoso on almost every stringed instrument and on this CD he demonstrates this ability on a wide variety of instruments. The main focus of the music here is on the era of the Dust Bowl, and what was happening in America at the time, socially and musically. Songs by Woody Guthrie, Leadbelly, and a variety of other people show Ry's encyclopedic knowledge of the music of this time, combined with an instinctive feel for the songs. "Phenomenal" is the descriptive word to describe his playing, whether it is on guitar, Hawaiian "slack key" guitar, mandolin, or more arcane instruments he has found. This is a must for those who love instrumental virtuosity, authentic reworkings of an era, or just plain good music. *—Bob Gottlieb*

Boomer's Story / 1972 / Reprise ♦♦♦♦♦
Largely laidback and bluesy, this album features a number of paeans to an America long lost. *—Jeff Tamarkin*

• **Paradise and Lunch** / 1974 / Reprise ♦♦♦♦♦
Ry Cooder understands that a great song is a great song, whether it was written before the Depression or last week. Still, at the same time he isn't afraid to explore new avenues and possibilities for the material. Like his three previous records, *Paradise and Lunch* is filled with treasures which become part of a world where eras and styles converge without ever sounding forced or contrived. One may think that an album that contains a traditional railroad song, tunes by assorted blues greats, and a Negro spiritual alongside selections by the likes of Bobby Womack, Burt Bacharach, and Little Milton may lack cohesiveness or merely come across as a history lesson, but to Cooder this music is all part of the same fabric and is as relevant and accessible as anything else that may be happening at the time. No matter when it was written or how it may have been done in the past, the tracks, led by Cooder's brilliant guitar, are taken to new territory where they can coexist. It's as if Washington Phillips' "Tattler" could have shared a place on the charts with Womack's "It's All Over Now" or Little Milton's "If Walls Could Talk." That he's successful on these, as well as the Salvation Army march of "Jesus on the Mainline" or the funky, gospel feel of Blind Willie McTell's "Married Man's a Fool," is not only a credit to Cooder's talent and ingenuity as an arranger and bandleader, but also to the songs themselves. The album closes with its most stripped-down track, an acoustic guitar and piano duet with jazz legend Earl "Fatha" Hines on the Blind Blake classic "Ditty Wah Ditty." Here both musicians are given plenty of room to showcase their instrumental prowess, and the results are nothing short of stunning. Eclectic, intelligent, and thoroughly entertaining, *Paradise and Lunch* remains Ry Cooder's masterpiece. *—Brett Hartenbach*

Chicken Skin Music / 1976 / Reprise ♦♦♦♦♦
Hawaiian traditional music meets Leadbelly and Ben E. King on Cooder's gospelization of rock & soul. *—Jeff Tamarkin*

Show Time / 1976 / WEA International ♦♦♦
Recorded live in 1976, Cooder cooks and struts his stuff on this grand tour of his abilities. The great Flaco Jimenez is on accordion. *—Jeff Tamarkin*

Jazz / 1978 / Reprise ♦♦♦
A tribute to Dixieland, with a stopover at the blues hotel. Joseph Byrd's arrangements on tunes by Bix Beiderbecke, Joseph Spence, et al., are inspired. *—Jeff Tamarkin*

Bop Till You Drop / 1979 / Reprise ♦♦
Cooder has disowned this early digital recording, and he's right; not only is the sound dry, but the music is rather lifeless. Although it has some bright moments, it's not his best. *—Jeff Tamarkin*

Borderline / 1980 / Reprise ♦
Ry is off track here on covers of old rock & roll songs. The warmth of the earlier recordings is missing, and his already indistinguished vocals are hopeless here. *—Jeff Tamarkin*

The Long Riders / 1980 / WEA International ♦♦♦
Ry Cooder's soundtrack for *The Long Riders* received a top-notch treatment from Warner Bros. (Japan), who not only did an excellent remastering job, but backed it up with English lyrics to the songs, notes, and a Japanese insert. Cooder was in fine form with this score, using original material, unusual and anachronistic instruments (saz, tamboura, electric guitar), and elements of traditional songs from the Civil War period. As a result, the album can be appreciated as a unique entity, away from the film—and bonded to the film, the music provides grace and power to the onscreen events. *—Steven McDonald*

The Slide Area / 1982 / Reprise ♦♦♦
This CD opens with an outrageous and exceedingly funky "UFO Has Landed in the Ghetto," and which seems so out of place with the other material. Yes, it is a rhythm & blues, bordering at times on funk album, and rap is one direction R&B took, but.... Listen to the groove on "Which Came First," and try to keep your body from bobbing to the strong rhythm laid down by Jim Keltner, Tim Drummond, and the background vocalists. While we are on the subject of vocals, this is one of Ry Cooder's best efforts, and his backup vocalists are key here and deserve special recognition: Bobby King, John Hiatt, Willie Greene, and Herman Johnson for most of the CD. The two gems on this are the phenomenal treatments of both "Blue Suede Shoes" and Bob Dylan's "I Need a Woman." Two songs as different in the original forms as pigs and gerbils are converted to R&B hit status. Both contain some memorable slide guitar work, but isn't that what we expect from this master of the guitar family. The album is very good but those two songs make it a gem. *—Bob Gottlieb*

Ry Cooder Live / 1982 / Warner Brothers ♦♦♦

Crossroads / 1986 / Reprise ♦♦♦
The ersatz blues story of the film gives Ry Cooder leeway to turn in an impressive blues-derived soundtrack featuring Sonny Terry along with his usual collaborators Van Dyke Parks, Jim Keltner, Nathan East, and others. But it's Cooder's guitar playing that highlights the album. *— William Ruhlmann*

Get Rhythm / 1987 / Reprise ♦♦♦
"The Musician's Musician." "The Master of the Eclectic." There are probably a dozen more titles by which this "guitar player" is known. To even refer to him as a guitar player is probably a gross mislabeling of this musician. He defies any sort of categorization; this is his greatest strength and for some his weakness. The theme for these nine cuts is rhythm of all different ilk. I won't even give the parameters because he seems to have none. I wondered how many different instruments he played on this album (I thought I counted five different types of guitar); it only says guitar and vocal for his credits. Listen to his version of "All Shook Up," more bop and rhythm than Elvis could put into four of his songs. It seems musicians line up to play with him, and they feel he did them a favor by letting them play on his albums. He always gives them plenty of space to do what they do. This CD will make the dead start tapping their toes. *—Bob Gottlieb*

Music By Ry Cooder / Jul. 11, 1995 / Reprise ♦♦♦♦♦
Since he's a limited vocalist with erratic songwriting skills, one could justifiably argue that the soundtrack medium is the best vehicle for Cooder's talents, allowing him to construct eclectic, chiefly instrumental pieces drawing upon all sorts of roots music and ethnic flavors (often, but not always, employing his excellent blues and slide guitar). This two-CD, 34-song compilation gathers excerpts from eleven of the soundtracks he worked on between 1980 and 1993 (three of the cuts, from the 1981 film *Southern Comfort*, are previously unreleased). As few listeners (even Cooder fans) are dedicated enough to go to the trouble of finding all of his individual soundtracks, this is a good distillation of many of his more notable contributions in this idiom, although it inevitably leaves out some fine moments. Still, it's well programmed and evocative, often conjuring visions of ghostly landscapes and funky border towns. *—Richie Unterberger*

Robert Cooksey

d. Nov. 14, 1969
Harmonica, Vocals / Vaudeville Blues, Prewar Blues, Folk-Blues
The City of Brotherly Love claims this early blues artist as one of its own, yet birth records for Robert Cooksey are a trifle sketchy. Not so his harmonica style, which was pretty much his own and quite a contrast to the country blues norm. Foregoing the wail of wahs-wahs and the shrieks of overblown high notes, Cooksey cooked up a simple-and-clear folk broth that some critics have identified as the source of Bob Dylan's harmonica technique, while others resent the presence of Dylan's name and the words "harmonica" and "technique" in the same sentence. Clearly, Dylan was inspired by the duo of Cooksey and guitarist Bobby Leecan, one of the main settings that the harmonica player recorded in during the '20s. Cooksey and Leecan created a musical blend between blues, vaudeville, and jazz on a series of tracks cut for the Victor label. There is a wonderful blend between the harmonica and the cornet of Thomas Morris on some of the recordings from this period, musical magic that literally glows with its symbolic mingling of jazz and blues styles.

Cooksey also recorded some duo numbers with guitarist Alfred Martin which have been mistakenly credited to Leecan. The earliest dates for the harmonica man in the studio was the spring of 1924, when he backed up blues singer Viola McCoy on sessions for Vocalion. That puts him within months of the very first recording of harmonica ever made, the Clara Smith recording "My Doggone Lazy Man," which featured harmonica player Herbert Leonard. "West Indies Blues" was the memorable title Cooksey cut with the dramatic but very real McCoy. The following year, he backed up Sara Martin on an OKeh day in the studio. It was two years later when he finally teamed up with Leecan, who also played some guitar and even a bit of kazoo. One of their records has been chosen as a kind of anthem for blues record collectors, who always think they "Need More Blues." Cooksey's several recorded features on harmonica have found their way into compilation collections of early recordings on the tiny axe, such as *Harmonica Blues* and *Harmonica Masters*. *—Eugene Chadbourne*

Johnny Copeland

b. Mar. 27, 1937, Haynesville, LA, **d.** Jul. 3, 1997, New York, NY
Vocals, Guitar / Modern Electric Texas Blues, Electric Texas Blues, Texas Blues
Considering the amount of time he spent steadily rolling from gig to gig, Johnny "Clyde" Copeland's rise to prominence in the blues world in the early '90s wasn't all that surprising. A contract with the PolyGram/Verve label put his '90s recordings into the hands of thousands of blues lovers around the world. It's not that Copeland's talent changed all that much since he recorded for Rounder Records in the '80s; it's just that major companies began to see the potential of great, hardworking blues musicians like Copeland. Unfortunately, Copeland was forced to slow down in 1995-1996 by heart-related complications, yet he continued to perform shows until his death in July of 1997.

Johnny Copeland was born March 27, 1937, in Haynesville, LA, about 15 miles south of Magnolia, AR (formerly Texarkana, a hotbed of blues activity in the '20s and '30s). The son of sharecroppers, his father died when he was very young, but Copeland was given his father's guitar. His first gig was with his friend Joe "Guitar" Hughes. Soon after, Hughes "took sick" for a week and the young Copeland discovered he could be a front man and deliver vocals as well as anyone else around Houston at that time.

His music, by his own reasoning, fell somewhere between the funky R&B of New Orleans and the swing and jump blues of Kansas City. After his family (sans his father) moved to Houston, Copeland was exposed, as a teen, to musicians from both cities. While he was becoming interested in music, he also pursued boxing, mostly as an avocation, and it is from his days as a boxer that he got his nickname "Clyde."

Copeland and Hughes fell under the spell of T-Bone Walker, whom Copeland first saw perform when he was 13 years old. As a teenager he played at locales such as Shady's Playhouse—Houston's leading blues club, host to most of the city's best bluesmen during the '50s—and the Eldorado Ballroom. Copeland and Hughes subsequently formed The Dukes of Rhythm, which became the house band at the Shady's Playhouse. After that, he spent time playing on tour with Albert Collins (himself a fellow T-Bone Walker devotee) during the '50s, and also played on stage with Sonny Boy Williamson [II], Big Mama Thornton, and Freddie King. He began recording in 1958 with "Rock 'n' Roll Lily" for Mercury, and moved between various labels during the '60s, including All Boy and Golden Eagle in Houston, where he had regional successes with "Please Let Me Know" and "Down on Bending Knees," and later for Wand and Atlantic in New York. In 1965, he displayed a surprising prescience in terms of the pop market by cutting a version of Bob Dylan's "Blowin' in the Wind" for Wand.

After touring around the "Texas triangle" of Louisiana, Texas and Arkansas, he relocated to New York City in 1974, at the height of the disco boom. It seems moving to New York City was the best career move Copeland ever made, for he had easy access to clubs in Washington, D.C., New York, Philadelphia, New Jersey, and Boston, all of which still had a place for blues musicians like him. Meanwhile, back in Houston, the club scene was hurting, owing partly to the oil-related recession of the mid-'70s. Copeland took a day job at a Brew 'n' Burger restaurant in New York and played his blues at night, finding receptive audiences at clubs in Harlem and Greenwich Village.

Copeland recorded seven albums for Rounder Records, beginning in 1981 and including *Copeland Special, Make My Home Where I Hang My Hat, Texas Twister, Bringing It All Back Home, When the Rain Starts Fallin', Ain't Nothing But a Party* (live, nominated for a Grammy), and *Boom Boom*; he also won a Grammy award in 1986 for his efforts on an Alligator album, *Showdown!* with Robert Cray and the late Albert Collins. Although Copeland had a booming, shouting voice and was a powerful guitarist and live performer, what most people don't realize is just how clever a songwriter he was. His latter-day releases for the PolyGram/Verve/Gitanes label, including *Flyin' High* (1992) and *Catch Up With the Blues*, provide ample evidence of this on "Life's Rainbow (Nature Song)" (from the latter album) and "Circumstances" (from the former album).

Because Copeland was only six months old when his parents split up and he only saw his father a few times before he passed away, Copeland never realized he had inherited a congenital heart defect from his father. He disovered this in the midst of another typically hectic tour in late 1994, when he had to go into the hospital in Colorado. After he was diagnosed with heart disease, he spent the next few years in and out of hospitals, undertaking a number of costly heart surgeries. Early in 1997, he was waiting for a heart transplant at Columbia Presbyterian Medical Center in New York City. As he was waiting, he was put on the L-VAD, a recent innovation for patients suffering from congenital heart defects. In 1995, Copeland appeared on CNN and ABC-TV's *Good Morning America*, wearing his L-VAD, offering the invention valuable publicity.

Despite his health problems, Copeland continued to perform and his always spirited concerts did not diminished all that much. After living 20 months on the L-VAD—the longest anyone had lived on the device—he received a heart transplant on January 1, 1997, and for a few months, the heart worked fine and he continued to tour. However, the heart developed a defective valve, necessitating heart surgery in the summer. Copeland died of complications during heart surgery on July 3, 1997. *—Richard Skelly & Bruce Eder*

● **Copeland Special** / 1981 / Rounder ✦✦✦✦✦
This immaculate collection put the veteran Houston axeman among the blues elite; it features searing guitar and soulful vocals. —*Bill Dahl*

Make My Home Where I Hang My Hat / 1982 / Rounder ✦✦✦
This second Rounder Records album has its share of incendiary moments. —*Bill Dahl*

Texas Twister / 1983 / Rounder ✦✦✦✦✦
Johnny Copeland's tenure on Rounder Records was mostly productive. He made several albums that ranged from decent to very good, increased his audience and name recognition and got better recording facilities and company support than at most times in his career. The 15 numbers on this anthology cover four Rounder sessions, and include competent renditions of familiar numbers. But what makes things special are the final three selections; these were part of Copeland's superb and unjustly underrated *Bringing It Back Home* album, recorded in Africa, which matched Texas shuffle licks with swaying, riveting African rhythms. —*Ron Wynn*

I'll Be Around / 1984 / Mr. R&B ✦✦✦✦✦
Exceptional collection of Copeland's primordial work. —*Bill Dahl*

Showdown [A Collins & R Cray] / 1985 / Alligator ✦✦✦✦✦
A summit meeting between Texas guitar veterans Collins and Johnny Copeland and newcomer Robert Cray, the set is scorching all the way. —*Bill Dahl*

Down on Bending Knee / 1985 / Mr. R&B ✦✦✦✦✦
This second volume of his early sides is equally impressive. —*Bill Dahl*

Bringin' It All Back Home / 1986 / Rounder ✦✦✦✦
Imaginative hybrid of blues and African idioms. —*Bill Dahl*

Houston Roots / 1988 / Ace ✦✦✦✦✦

When the Rain Starts Fallin' / 1988 / Rounder ✦✦✦
More highlights from his Rounder Records material. —*Bill Dahl*

Ain't Nothing but a Party / 1988 / Rounder ✦✦✦
Texas guitarist and vocalist Johnny Copeland didn't turn in a formula job on these six tunes recorded live at the 1987 Juneteenth festival. Indeed, the concert setting seems to put some juice in Copeland's singing; his voice isn't raspy or detached, and he actually seems exuberant about doing the umpteenth version of "Big Time" and "Baby, Please Don't Go." His band, especially saxophonist Bert McGowan, also seem to get new life from the crowd reaction and dig in behind Copeland with renewed vigor. Even Copeland's shuffle licks and patterns, which can become awfully predictable, were executed with some sharp twists and surprising turns. —*Ron Wynn*

Collection, Vol. 1 / 1988 / Collectables ✦✦✦
Fifteen mostly early Johnny Copeland sides, originally released on the Golden Eagle, All Boy, Paradise, and Suave labels, recorded between 1960 and the summer of 1967, including the hit singles "Please Let Me Know" and "Down On Bending Knees" (from 1960 and 1963, respectively). Some of the previously unissued numbers, such as the instrumental "Late Hours," are showcases for Copeland (and especially for his guitar) as good as the released stuff. A close listen reveals Copeland developing great confidence, mostly as a singer but also as a guitarist, between 1960 and 1963 on sides like "Working Man's Blues," while other songs, such as "There's a Blessing," show him turning into a top soul shouter, in keeping with the changing times—"It Must Be Love" and "I've Gotta Go Home" are two great unheralded jewels in the latter category on this collection. The B-side "Wella Wella Baby" clocks in at a near-epic-length five minutes, none of it wasted. His heart-stopping vocal workout on the 1967 Paradise single "(The Night Time Is) The Right Time" is also some of the most worthwhile music from this decade of Copeland's career. His never-issued solo acoustic demo of Arthur Crudup's "That's All Right Mama" is followed by the finished single—on electric instruments, with a girl chorus and a full piano and rhythm section—released on Suave in late 1964. All pretty cool, and good sound all the way through, too. —*Bruce Eder*

Boom Boom / 1990 / Rounder ✦✦
Sometimes Copeland's Texas shuffle blues just don't have any bite. He came perilously close on this set to having to depend on gimmicks and experience. Copeland couldn't find anyway to refresh material like "Beat the Boom Boom Baby" and "Pie In The Sky," although he tried hard with shouts, cries and moans. He was more successful on "Nobody But You," "I Was Born All Over" and "Blues Ain't Nothin'," where his soul and gospel roots helped inject some life into the lyrics. His band tried to help matters, but really couldn't elevate the proceedings. If you're only a warm to casual fan, this wasn't one of Copeland's greatest. —*Ron Wynn*

Collection, Vol. 2 / 1990 / Collectables ✦✦✦
Another 14 Johnny Copeland sides, filling in more holes in his history from before and even during his Rounder Records tenure. "Love Song," which opens the set, is from 1990 and shows him in exceptionally good vocal and instrumental form, while "Daily Bread" dates from 1984. All of the rest is attributed to the late '60s and early '70s (although there's an unreleased version of his 1963 single "Please Let Me Know" here as well), which sounds about right. "May the Best Man Win" is a fine piece of late-'60s soul, with a few dissonant edges and a very active horn section that make it doubly interesting. "Heebie Jeebies" is one of the best dance tunes in Copeland's entire output, while his raunchy cover of B.B. King's "Rock Me Baby" is a killer guitar/piano workout, clocking in at over five minutes and worth every second. The rest lurches between '60s soul influences ("Mama Told Me," "Soul Power") and a slicker '70s sound, but it's all enjoyable if one can adjust to the sudden shifts in style and sound. —*Bruce Eder*

Flyin' High / Sep. 1992 / Verve ✦✦
Johnny Copeland's patented "Texas twister" style isn't as flamboyant or forceful on this 10-cut CD as on past occasions (at least instrumentally), but his vocals were in fairly good

shape. Copeland was at his best on tunes where the emphasis was on style rather than lyric meaning and elaboration. He seemed ill at ease on other tunes, notably the cover of "Jambalaya," where he never got comfortable with the bayou beat and plowed on through, concluding the number compentently, but never offering anything distinctive. The album doesn't cook or boil like Copeland's regional singles, or even his best Alligator material. Instead, it simmers, but winds up just slightly missing the mark. —*Ron Wynn*

Further Up the Road / 1993 / Aim ✦✦✦
This live Australian import is a no-frills Texas guitar feast. —*Bill Dahl*

Catch Up With the Blues / 1994 / Verve ✦✦✦

Jungle Swing / May 1996 / Verve ✦✦
Johnny Copeland's eclectic nature is on display on *Jungle Swing*, an ambitious collaboration with jazz pianist Randy Weston. Weston brings a selection of African rhythms and melodic textures to the table, which are incorporated subtly into the rhythmic underpinnings of each song. In no sense is *Jungle Swing* a worldbeat experiment—it's just a small, affectionate tribute. Even so, the African flourishes don't dominate the sound of the record. Like always, Copeland takes center stage with his clean, precise licks. At this point in his career, he knows exactly what to play and the guitarist never overplays throughout the course of the disc. There are a few weak moments on the disc, but the sheer strength of Copeland's musicianship—and his willingness to stretch out ever so slightly—make it worth the time for any of his fans. —*Thom Owens*

Live in Australia 1990 / Mar. 18, 1997 / Black Top ✦✦✦
This is no hastily assembled disc to cash in on the late Johnny Copeland's unfortunately early demise, but one of his finest recordings. Whether in the studio or live, Copeland always pours a lot of sweat into his playing and singing, yet also proved capable of a subtler range of emotions. From the devastation of "Cut Off My Right Arm" to the joy in Nappy Brown's signature tune "Wella Wella Baby," all of the songs are filled with amazingly good vocals and tasteful guitar fills. This album is a fitting tribute to a man who gave his all to every performance. —*Bob Gottlieb*

Crazy Cajun Recordings / Feb. 18, 1999 / Edsel ✦✦✦✦

Honky Tonkin' / Jul. 13, 1999 / Bullseye Blues & Jazz ✦✦✦
A budget sampling from Copeland's five Rounder albums from the '80s. All in all, a nice cross-section and a good introduction to this artist's later work. Special bonus points for including his collaboration with African musicians on their closer, "Kasavubu." —*Cub Koda*

Gulf Coast Guitars / Oct. 9, 2001 / Music Club ✦✦✦

Shemekia Copeland

b. 1979, New York, NY [Harlem]
Vocals / Modern Electric Blues, Soul-Blues
The daughter of renowned Texas blues guitarist Johnny Copeland, Shemekia Copeland began making a splash in her own right before she was even out of her teens. Projecting a maturity beyond her years, Copeland fashioned herself a powerful, soul-inflected shouter in the tradition of Koko Taylor and Etta James, yet also proved capable of a subtler range of emotions. Copeland was born in Harlem in 1979 and her father encouraged her to sing right from the beginning, even bringing her up on-stage at the Cotton Club when she was just eight years old. She began to pursue a singing career in earnest at age 16, when her father's health began to decline due to heart disease; he took Shemekia on tour with him as his opening act, which helped establish her name on the blues circuit. She landed a record deal with Alligator, which issued her debut album *Turn the Heat Up!* in 1998, when she was just 19 years old (sadly, her father didn't live to see the occasion). While the influences on Copeland's style were crystal clear, the record was met with enthusiastic reviews praising its energy and passion. Marked as a hot young newcomer to watch, Copeland toured the blues festival circuit in America and Europe, and landed a fair amount of publicity. Her second album, *Wicked*, was released in 2000 and featured a duet with one of her heroes, early R&B diva Ruth Brown. *Wicked* earned Copeland a slew of W.C. Handy Blues Award nominations and she walked off with three: Song of the Year, Blues Album of the Year, and Contemporary Female Artist of the Year. The follow-up record, *Talking to Strangers*, was produced by legendary pianist Dr. John and featured songs that she proudly claimed were her best yet. —*Steve Huey*

● **Turn the Heat Up!** / May 5, 1998 / Alligator ✦✦✦✦✦
The daughter of the late bluesman Johnny Copeland steps up to the plate with this, her debut album for the Alligator imprint. Although only 19 at the time of this recording, Copeland comes to this album with a mature style and vast amounts of assuredness. While comparisons to Koko Taylor and Etta James will be plentiful, Shemekia has enough tricks up her sleeve to make this a disc well worth checking out. Eight of the 14 tunes aboard are co-written by producer John Hahn and strong musical support is summoned up from guitarist Jimmy Vivino, with guest turns from Joe Louis Walker and "Monster" Mike Welch, while the Uptown Horns show up on three tunes, including the title track. Highlights are numerous on this disc, but special attention should be paid to Copeland's "Ghetto Child," a nice cover of Don Covay's "Have Mercy"; Walker's "Your Mama's Talking"; and the strutting "I Always Get My Man." This is one very impressive debut. —*Cub Koda*

Wicked / Sep. 12, 2000 / Alligator ✦✦✦✦
Copeland continues to prove herself as one of the strongest young talents in the blues on this disc. While the material itself isn't as strong as that on her stellar first album, she still invests her all in tunes like the blasting "Not Tonight" and the romantic "Love Scene." —*Tim Sheridan*

Talking to Strangers / Sep. 17, 2002 / Alligator ✦✦✦✦
This disc, which has Dr. John at the controls as a producer, brings together a mix that

brings out the best for all those concerned and involved with this project. There is no weakness here, it is a straight-ahead use of all the strengths of this daughter of Johnny Copeland. The songs were well selected to effectively show off all her potency as a vocalist. There are some many good writers that are also players on this disc that the tunes fit like gloves. There are strong contributions by Fingers Hahn, Mac Rebennack, and Shemekia herself. The tunes, varied in style, are all based in the deep blues, and were selected for their capability to push her vocal talents to constant new personal pinnacles. She keeps it interesting by varying the pace and on "The Push I Need," she sounds right at home singing this funky tune as a duet with Dr. John. She stays with the good Doctor through the tune as if she were doing this every day. Then she turns around and seems just as comfortable singing "Happy Valentine's Day," as a slow bluesy torch-burner, with minimal accompaniment. This disc shows us some new sides of this fine singer, while she stretches her limits and she more than holds her own while being in the company of such luminous musicians as accompany her on this disc. This disc seems a return to the blues burner she is capable of being. She does her daddy proud on this stellar disc. *—Bob Gottlieb*

Al Copley

b. 1952, Buffalo, NY

Piano / Jump Blues, Piano Blues, Modern Electric Blues, Boogie-Woogie

Blues pianist and singer Al Copley was born in 1952 in Buffalo, NY. Although his family moved several times while Copley was a youngster (first to San Francisco, CA, then Westerly, RI), he was able to take piano lessons on a regular basis. Inspired by the boogie-woogie style of playing, Copley formed his first band in 1965, Ponce de Leon & the Young Ones, before forming Roomful of Blues three years later. Copley spent the early '70s attending the Berklee School of Music in Boston, while still playing with Roomful of Blues. The group began issuing albums in the later part of the decade, as Copley could be heard on such releases as 1977's self-titled debut, 1979's *Let's Have a Party*, 1981's *Hot Little Mama*, and 1984's *Dressed Up to Get Messed Up*. But it was also in 1984 that Copley left the group to move to Europe. The move led to numerous appearances at jazz and blues festivals, as Copley embarked on a solo career later in the decade that resulted in such releases as 1986's *A Handful of Key* and 1989's *Automatic Overdrive*.

Although there was a brief Roomful of Blues reunion around this time, Copley returned back to solo work, which led to Copley joining guitarist Jimmie Vaughan for a series of highly prestigious gigs at Royal Albert Hall in England opening for Eric Clapton. Copley would strike up a friendship with Clapton, which led to Copley himself opening several shows for him in 1997. Throughout the '90s, Copley issued solo releases (including *Good Understanding*, *Live at Montreaux*, and his swinging pairing with Hal Singer *Blue Paris Nights*), while also forming the seven-piece outfit Al Copley's Prophet Motive in 1999. In addition to his recording with Roomful of Blues and as a solo artist, Copley has guested on other artist's albums, including releases by the Fabulous Thunderbirds, Eddie C. Campbell, and Duke Robillard, among others. 2000 marked the release of his ninth record, *Rainy Summer* on One Mind records. *—Greg Prato*

A Handful of Key / 1986 / Off-Beat ✦✦

Automatic Overdrive / 1989 / Black Top ✦✦✦

Royal Blue / 1991 / Black Top ✦✦✦✦✦

Royal Blue pairs Al Copley, an original member of Roomful of Blues, with Hal Singer, who worked with Duke Ellington, Wynonie Harris and T-Bone Walker and notched some hits during the '40s. Recorded in New Orleans with Duke Robillard and Snooks Eaglin on guitar, the record flirts with both small-band, jazzy tunes like "That's Hal" and "Morning, Noon and Night" and grittier ensemble material like "Sittin' in the Barber's Chair." *—Jason Ankeny*

● **Good Understanding** / Sep. 27, 1994 / Bullseye Blues ✦✦✦✦

Some things refuse to die, they just morph endlessly. While few of the original members of the Fabulous Thunderbirds are present for this effort, two founding members of Roomful of Blues are leading the charge. The results are commendable. Duke Robillard's expert guitar lines ride along on Al Copley's true-blue piano and smoky vocals for a very fine trip. The trademark Texas blues of Jimmie Vaughan is replaced here with some of the swampiest Louisiana R&B you can find. You'll boogie, you'll stroll, you'll pass out in your whiskey, but you'll have a good time. *—Tim Sheridan*

Dewey Corley

b. Jun. 18, 1898, Halley, AR, **d.** Apr. 15, 1974, Memphis, TN

Washtub Bass, Kazoo, Vocals, Jug / Delta Blues

There's not much chance of making jug band music without a jug, although a few have tried. A washtub bass doesn't hurt, either. In fact, one of the main concepts of this tricky, goofy, and spirited style of music is to create a bass line out of something that basically sounds like a pile of junk. Perhaps it was supposed to be called "junk band music." There would be no more expert opinion than that of Dewey Corley, who was not only the leader of the Beale Street Jug Band from the '30s onward, but also one of the great players on all manner of jug band ordnance: including, of course, jug, and ranging from the depth-charge of the washtub bass to the insect-like whine of the kazoo, upon which he is considered one of the great soloists. In his later years, he also turned out to be one of the great A&R men, helping record companies such as Adelphi scout out missing Memphis blues legends such as the elusive Hacksaw Harney and the superb guitarist Willie Morris.

Corley picked up the interest in music from his father and began playing the harmonica as a child growing up in Arkansas. He started hoboing around the country at the age of 18 and became highly influenced by Will Shade, the charismatic and superbly organized founder of the original Memphis Jug Band. It was Shade who introduced the genre in the river city after hearing a jug band holding forth over the hill in Kentucky. Corley came in and out of Shade's Memphis Jug Band, as did many other Memphis blues players such as Furry Lewis and Memphis Minnie. He was also a member of Jack Kelly's South Memphis Jug Band and also backed quite a few of the city's diverse bluesmen in duo and trio settings. His own Beale Street Jug Band was a most successful venture and became a fixture in Memphis for nearly three decades. A series of 1950 photographs of a ceremony honoring W.C. Handy at the Beale Street Auditorium shows the aged blues composer standing at the entrance to the building, holding the sheet music for his "Memphis Blues and surrounded by many V.I.P.s. Seated in front of this group are the seven members of the Beale Street Jug Band with a broadly grinning Corley. In the end, he would be the last surviving member of both the Memphis Jug Band and the Beale Street Jug Band.

In terms of his career, getting older just meant getting better for this artist. While he was busily involved in the blues scene in the '30s and '40s, he managed to keep out of the recording studio almost completely; inevitably, somebody else is tooting kazoo, thumbing washtub, or huffing clouds of feted breath across the top of a jug on vintage recordings by the Memphis Jug Band, or at least this is what the credits indicate on reissues. Corley himself refuted this information, stating on several occasions that he played jug with the Memphis Jug Band during a two-day recording session in 1934 for OKeh, and not Jab Jones. It was not a fact deemed worthy of a headline in *Variety* magazine such as "Jab No Jug." Perhaps Corley was actually busy at another engagement by the same band in another part of town because in its heyday, leader Shade employed so many players that he was able to keep two different versions of the group going simultaneously. Then there was the rock & roll era and at first it seemed like there were no bookings at all for the Memphis jug bands anymore. But while some older bluesmen balked at the onset of new record labels and enthusiastic young white listeners in the '60s, this was Corley's ticket into the recording studio, where he shined with enthusiasm and, needless to say, solos that sound like Charlie Parker might have, if he had played kazoo. *—Eugene Chadbourne*

Murali Coryell

Guitar, Vocals, Producer / Contemporary Blues

Although he's the son of fusion guitarist Larry Coryell, Murali Coryell chose not to follow in the same style of music as his father—he specializes in blues and soul. Coryell issued his debut album in 1995, *Eyes Wide Open*, following it up four years later with *2120*. Recorded at Todd Rundgren's Bearsville Studios in Woodstock, NY, it became the first ever album issued by new label Czyz, created by the sons of original Chess Records founders Leonard and Phil—Marshall and Kevin Chess. In addition to Coryell, *2120* features Rod Gross (drums) and Bill Foster (bass). In 2000, Coryell teamed with his father and brother Julian, to record the collaboration album *Coryells*. *—Greg Prato*

● **2120** / Sep. 21, 1999 / Czyz ✦✦✦✦

Coryell's fiery debut, and the first release from Czyz Records, resounds with echoes: Singer-guitarist Murali's father is jazz-rock fusion guitarist Larry Coryell; the album title refers to the Chess Studios' South Michigan Street address; Czyz is the original Polish surname that became Americanized into "Chess"; and Marshall Chess, who served as co-producer with Murali, heads up this label just like his famous Chess family elders did theirs. But *2120* offers no grounds for nepotism charges because Coryell's electric blues trio, with bassist Bill Foster and drummer Rod Gross, charge out of the gate positively smokin'. The leader's slashing and burning, raw guitar style often sounds like Otis Rush and Buddy Guy. His smoldering and sexy presentation of R&B, blues, soul, and rock (including covers of Bo Diddley and Marvin Gaye) frequently sets off fireworks of Jimi Hendrix proportions, yet, apparently wiser than his years, Coryell never makes the young bluesman's mistake of overplaying. *—Chris Slawecki*

Ike Cosse

Vocals, Harmonica, Guitar / Modern Electric Blues

Guitarist and vocalist Issac "Ike" Cosse led a band called the Coldbloods around the San Francisco Bay area for 20 years. Cosse took his earliest musical inspiration from guitarists like Eric Clapton, Jimmy Page and Jimi Hendrix, and he played jazz and fusion for some time before settling on the blues.

Cosse joined the band of saxophonist Joe Puttley in 1983 and learned the finer points of blues playing from him, as well as the need to be an entertainer when on the bandstand. After working with Puttley for a number of years, Cosse was given the chance to sing; "Crosscut Saw" and "Further On Up the Road" were the first two blues songs he performed on stage.

After forming his own band, Ike and the Coldbloods, in 1987, he began to work the clubs around the San Francisco Bay area, where he had relocated some years earlier. Ike and the Coldbloods played at Slim's in San Francisco, Moe's Alley in Santa Cruz, and other venues around the Bay area. After several years of interpreting cover songs in Bay area clubs, Cosse realized if he was going to take his music anywhere, he would need to perform original compositions.

After dropping a copy of his self-released album off at B.B. King's Club in Los Angeles, Cosse got a booking there, opening for Coco Montoya and Johnny Johnson. Cosse's first album, *The Spot Is Hot*, was released on his own label in 1995. Since then, he's recorded an album for JSP Records of London, *The Lowdown Throwdown*. Cosse currently lives in Santa Clara, California. *—Richard Skelly*

The Lowdown Throwdown / Apr. 8, 1997 / JSP ✦✦✦

Ike Cosse's debut for London-based JSP came about after the label's owner heard a copy of the bluesman's self-produced cassette. With *The Lowdown Throwdown*, Cosse proved capable of attacking the full range of blues styles; "Dog Dang Shoot" is straight Chicago material, while "Hell to Pay" offers James Brown-style funk and "Let It Happen" recalls classic R&B balladry. What's most appealing about *The Lowdown Throwdown* is Cosse's lyrical directness; he prefers plain speech over metaphor, describing experiences with past romantic conquests ("I Just Wanna Rent") and strip club employees ("Bang Bang Girls") with humor and frankness. Cosse's vocals are a bit on the thin side, which is especially troublesome when he writes above his range, as on "My Baby's So Cynical." But after all, Cosse isn't setting out to be the next Bobby "Blue" Bland; he comes across on *The Lowdown Throwdown* as a highly individual entertainer confident in his ability to make the audience relate to his songs. Each time you start to think he's sounding too full of himself, he lets loose with a brilliant bit of self-deprecating humor. And he's not above completely hamming it up when necessary, as on one perfect couplet from "You're the Man," which recounts his attempt to move back home after leaving his father's house: "My door is always open to you for dinner/But your room is now the aerobics center." *—Kenneth Bays*

● **Cold Blooded World** / Oct. 17, 2000 / JSP ♦♦♦♦
Santa Monica blues artist Ike Cosse dropped his backing band for his second album for JSP. *Cold Blooded World* is unmistakably a portrait of one man and his outlook on the world. Where other modern practitioners of his genre often seem pressured by their record companies to buff out any idiosyncrasies, Cosse isn't afraid to come across as exactly what he is: a performer who's as natural a storyteller as he is a bluesman, using simple guitar textures and spare harmonica to support tales filled with humor, heartbreak, and wry observation. He recalls John Lee Hooker on "Brothers Gittin' on With Others," while "That's the Blues" explores the issue of gun violence over a guitar figure straightforward enough to have come from Lightnin' Hopkins or any number of early postwar legends. Novelties such as "Nothing You Can Do or Say" help keep the tone light, though even the potentially heavy numbers ("Black Cowboy," in which the singer laments the absence of his fellow African-Americans in movie Westerns) are mitigated by an observational, man-on-the-street lyrical bent. In Cosse's world, it's raw charisma and the ability to put forth quality songs that matters, not technical prowess. Granted, Cosse's material might not always follow traditional blues in structure. But in manner and mood, he's arguably more authentic than contemporary blues acts who emphasize slickness but lack a personal creative vision. *Cold Blooded World*, as unpretentious as a night at a juke joint, is a document of a bluesman on the rise. *—Kenneth Bays*

Sean Costello

b. 1979, Philadelphia, PA
Vocals / Blues-Rock, Modern Electric Blues
Teen blues phenom Sean Costello was born in Philadephia and raised in Atlanta, receiving his first guitar for his ninth birthday. A primarily self-taught player, he initially gravitated towards hard rock but soon discovered Stevie Ray Vaughan, moving on from there to Howlin' Wolf; under the wing of local bluesman Felix Reyes, a 14-year-old Costello won the Beale Street Blues Society's talent award in 1994. Another contestant was Susan Tedeschi and soon Costello began touring as her lead guitarist and stayed with her band for a couple years. He also provided guitar on Tedeschi's 1998 album *Just Won't Burn*. Soon after leaving Tedeschi's band, Costello assembled backing outfit the Jivebombers—bassist Carl Shankle, keyboardist and harpist Paul Linden and drummer Terrence Prather—and issued his debut album *Call the Cops* in 1996. After touring extensively and revamping his band by replacing Shankle with Melvin Zachary on bass and adding keyboardist Matt Wauchope, Costello released *Cuttin' In* in early 2000. The album was a success in the blues community gaining him a W.C. Handy Award nomination for "Best New Artist Debut." In 2001 Costello released his third album *Moanin' for Molasses* and further cemented his reputation as one of the best young blues guitarists on the scene. *—Jason Ankeny*

Call the Cops / 1996 / Blue Wave ♦♦♦
Young fretburner Sean Costello was a mere 16 years old when he recorded this debut opus in 1996 but was already showing class A chops and a deep knowledge of the blues. With over half of the material on here emanating from his pen, Costello also takes on some classic tunes like "Anna Lee," "Take A Little Walk With Me," Willie Dixon's "Sit Down Baby," and Little Walter's "One More Chance With You" and turns in solid versions that show his understanding of the material. This 1999 reissue clearly shows that not all young guitarists are merely Stevie Ray Vaughan-abees. *—Cub Koda*

● **Cuttin' In** / Jan. 25, 2000 / Landslide ♦♦♦♦♦
This is Costello's second solo album, his first since his appearance on Susan Tedeschi's hit CD *Just Won't Burn*. Costello is only 20 years old, but his guitar work is in a completely different league from that of the other kid blues guitarists currently causing a fuss in bluesland. Costello comes from a remarkably well-informed place as a player. This is reflected not only in his guitar style, but also in the choice of material on *Cuttin' In*. He has a nice feel for jump blues, as we hear on his cover of Sonny Boy Williamson's "Mellow Chick Swing," and he can do the hard-edged Chicago blues with the requisite skill and fury—check out his Butterfield-esque original "Who's Been Cheatin' Who." The R&B influence has not eluded Costello either—his cover of Otis Rush's "Double Trouble" is handled with a soulful feel that belies his age. And Costello's not afraid to take a flyer, either, which brings us to the calypso funkiness of "Goombay Rock," a song worthy of the Squirrel Nut Zippers' attention. Costello the guitarist has snatched the key to the blues kingdom. His playing is shockingly deep for a 20-year-old. And his vocal work is nearly a match for his guitar chops; given time, that too will become very real. Of all the young blues lions out there brandishing their electric guitars, Costello is the one who's got his head and heart into the deep blues. *—Philip Van Vleck*

Moanin' for Molasses / May 15, 2001 / Landslide ♦♦♦♦
The third time's the charm for this young Atlanta bluesman. Not only is *Moanin'* his most accomplished and evocative album, it is also the one that took him from being a little-known but promising up-and-comer who once backed Susan Tedeschi to a prominent solo artist who landed W.C. Handy award nominations and was featured on the cover of national blues magazine Blues Revue. Combining stunning covers of obscure soul (James Brown's "I Want You So Bad" and Johnnie Taylor's "You Can't Win With a Losing Hand"), blues (Otis Rush's "It Takes Time" and Willie Dixon's "One Kiss"), and R&B (Mike Bloomfield's "You're Killing My Love," likely picked up from Atlanta's Theodis Ealey, who also covered it) along with his own sturdy originals, the album crackles with excitement. Costello's soulful voice has matured, and his singing is authoritative, although without the pretentiousness that often mars many young blues musicians. Most importantly, Costello owns these songs and makes his points concisely, with most tracks running under four minutes, and some under three, a rarity for blues albums. His solos are classy, crisp, and succinct, supporting the songs without overwhelming them, and the occasional horns perfectly punctuate the tracks, adding emphasis but never overshadowing Costello's finesse and charm. He sounds absolutely inspired here, helped by tough and sparkling originals like "You're a Part of Me" that easily hold their own with the covers. Costello also shares the spotlight here, especially with harp player Paul Linden, who co-wrote a few tracks and plays solid solos throughout. Costello's natural charisma and obvious delight in performing, along with his ability to mesh blues, R&B, and soul, make this album one of the roots highlights of 2001, and a terrific listen anytime. *—Hal Horowitz*

Elizabeth Cotten

b. Jan. 5, 1895, Chapel Hill, NC, **d.** Jun. 29, 1987, Syracuse, NY
Vocals, Composer, Guitar / Blues Revival, Folk Revival, Traditional Folk
Elizabeth Cotten was among the most influential guitarists to surface during the roots music revival era, her wonderfully expressive and dexterous fingerpicking style a major inspiration to the generations of players who followed in her wake. Cotten was born in Chapel Hill, NC, in January 1895; after first picking up the banjo at the age of eight, she soon moved on to her brother's guitar, laying it flat on her lap and over time developing her picking pattern and eventually her chording. By the age of 12 she was working as a domestic, and three years later gave birth to her first child; upon joining the church, she gave up the guitar, playing it only on the rarest of occasions over the course of the next quarter century. By the early '40s, Cotten had relocated to Washington, D.C., where she eventually began working for the legendary Charles Seeger family and caring for children Pete, Peggy, and Mike.

When the Seegers learned of Cotten's guitar skills a decade later, they recorded her for Folkways, and in 1957 she issued her debut LP, *Folksongs and Instrumentals With Guitar*. The track "Freight Train," written when she was 12, became a Top Five hit in the U.K., and its success ensured her a handful of concert performances. The great interest in her music spurred her to write new material, which appeared on her second album, *Shake Sugaree*. As Cotten became increasingly comfortable performing live, her presentation evolved, and in addition to playing guitar she told stories about her life and even led her audiences in singing her songs; over the years, she recalled more and more tunes from her childhood, and in the course of tours also learned new material. Cotten did not retire from domestic work until 1970, and did not tour actively until the end of the decade; the winner of a National Endowment for the Arts National Heritage Fellowship Award as well as a Grammy—both earned during the final years of her life—she died on June 29, 1987. *—Jason Ankeny*

★ **Folksongs and Instrumentals With Guitar** / 1957 / Smithsonian/Folkways ♦♦♦♦♦
This first LP collection by a widely influential guitarist includes her classic "Freight Train." *—William Ruhlmann*

When I'm Gone / 1965 / Smithsonian/Folkways ♦♦♦♦
The third volume in the original Folkways series of albums by this master fingerpicker and acoustic music legend was actually pieced together from recordings made hither, thither, and yonder over nearly a decade. From the first notes of the opening instrumental, "New Year's Eve," the listener will know they are in presence of greatness. The best way to describe her playing would perhaps be some kind of symbolic contrast to other well-known artists. For example, she is a Rembrandt painting while John Fahey is a picture postcard, no slight to Fahey intended. Some might assume that it took ten years to put together a new Cotten album, but this decision most likely had more to do with the label's scaredy-cat approach to marketing or producer Mike Seeger's reputation for perfectionism, or both. The latter trait was certainly one Cotten didn't share, and the fact that so many different recordings were done in situations such as people's living rooms is no surprise as the grand dame simply had to have a guitar in her hand whenever she sat down, and would often go home from a two or even three hour gig and play guitar all night in her motel room. This album features several songs with lyrics by her granddaughter Johnine Rankin. It also came originally with an insert that despite a horribly Xeroxed cover picture has much to offer in the way of anecdotes and historical information as well as printed lyrics. She revives "Freight Train" here, but of more interest are numbers such as "Willie," "Jenny," and "Gaslight Blues," all played with a delicate, precise touch, as if the guitar was speaking to her of its own power. *—Eugene Chadbourne*

Shake Sugaree, Vol. 2 / 1965 / Smithsonian/Folkways ♦♦♦♦♦
Many listeners are familiar with the saga of Elizabeth Cotten, and how she was discovered doing domestic work for the Seeger dynasty—practically the equivalent of Shakespeare working as a copy runner at the local newspaper office. Her first album was done when the idea of being a recording artist was still something that startled her, whereas, by the time this second volume came along, she was already thinking like a performer and coming up with lots of new material. The opening track is "Shake Sugaree," with her daughter Brenda Evans singing, and what a classic track this is. There really isn't a letdown after that, and in many ways this is the ultimate Cotten album. Both her guitar and banjo playing are featured, and although she is hardly as well-known for her work on the five-banger, her style is great and she is really one of a handful of artists that play the banjo with a real country blues feeling. The collection of short, traditional pieces involving banjo on the second side is such a sparkling collection of miniatures that it wouldn't be out of place in a jeweler's display case. There never seemed to be any reason to put this artist in a recording studio, as she played guitar all day anyway, and all anyone had to do was point a microphone in her direction. Nonetheless, the producer, Mike Seeger, proudly points out that some of the tracks were recorded in a freezing high-school gym,

not that any of this ambience makes its way onto the vinyl. Cotten could hardly be accused of having frozen fingers here. She is in contrast one of the most accurate guitarists to ever record, partially because she never saw a need to do anything too show-offy. She never plays a note that isn't directly connected to the development of the melody or variations thereof, much in the manner of a skilled Indian classical musician. The multi-part "Fox Chase" is a masterpiece. —*Eugene Chadbourne*

Live! / 1984 / Arhoolie ♦♦♦

No dates are given for this live disc, although according to the liners, "this album is a sampler of performances during her ninth decade" (which would be roughly the early '70s to the early '80s). She does some of the most popular items from her repertoire over the course of this 50-minute recording, including "Freight Train," "Shake Sugaree," and "Oh Babe, It Ain't No Lie" (which was covered by the Grateful Dead). The guitar playing is good, the vocals are less impressive; there's plenty of storytelling between the numbers, and audience participation on some of the choruses during the songs. —*Richie Unterberger*

Freight Train and Other North Carolina Folk Songs and Tunes / 1989 / Smithsonian/Folkways ♦♦♦♦

Elizabeth Cotten was born in January of 1895 in Chapel Hill, NC, where her father worked in the mines and her mother was a maid servant and laundress. She began playing guitar at the age of eight, secretly practicing on her older brother's instrument. At the age of 12, she began to work with her mother in helping the family to scrape by, though she continued to play music with her family, in particular her siblings. Sometime around 1912 she was married and joined the church, which occasioned her to give up playing music for the next 25 years. Through a series of strange accidents (she once found the daughter of Peggy and Pete Seeger in a department store and came to work for them) this led to her re-involvement with music. She played frequently during the '60s and '70s, often with Mike Seeger; the recordings collected here were made during 1957 and 1958 at her home in Washington. Cotten has a very distinctive picking style and a beautifully fragile and off-key voice; both make these recordings a pleasure. Included are a mix of originals and personal versions. Of note are "Vastopol," which sounds nothing like the John Fahey version, and "Sweet Bye and Bye," of which this version might be specific to North Carolina. Also enjoyable is "Honey Babe Your Papa Cares for You," whose melodically vague style is characteristic of Cotten's ear and unique way of suppressing melody. If this album intrigues you, you might want to check out her live album on Arhoolie, which some believe to be even better. —*Brian Whitener*

James Cotton

b. Jul. 1, 1935, Tunica, MS

Vocals, Leader, Drums, Harmonica, Guitar / Modern Electric Chicago Blues, Harmonica Blues, Electric Chicago Blues

At his high-energy '70s peak as a bandleader, James Cotton was a bouncing, sweaty, whirling dervish of a bluesman, roaring his vocals and all but sucking the reeds right out of his defenseless metal harmonicas with his prodigious lungpower. Due to throat problems, Cotton's vocals are no longer what they used to be, but he remains a masterful instrumentalist.

Cotton had some gargantuan shoes to fill when he stepped into Little Walter's slot as Muddy Waters' harp ace in 1954, but for the next dozen years, the young Mississippian filled the integral role beside Chicago's blues king with power and precision. Of course, Cotton prepared for such a career move for a long time, having learned how to wail on harp from none other than Sonny Boy Williamson himself.

Cotton was only a child when he first heard Williamson's fabled radio broadcasts for *King Biscuit Time* over KFFA out of Helena, AR. So sure was Cotton of his future that he ended up moving into Williamson's home at age nine, soaking up the intricacies of blues harpdom from one of its reigning masters. Six years later, Cotton was ready to unleash a sound of his own.

Gigging with area notables Joe Willie Wilkins and Willie Nix, Cotton built a sterling reputation around West Memphis, following in his mentor's footsteps by landing his own radio show in 1952 over KWEM. Sam Phillips, whose Sun label was still a fledgling operation, invited Cotton to record for him, and two singles commenced: "Straighten Up Baby" in 1953 and "Cotton Crop Blues" the next year. Legend has it Cotton played drums instead of harp on the first platter.

When Waters rolled through Memphis minus his latest harpist (Junior Wells), Cotton hired on with the legend and came to Chicago. Unfortunately for the youngster, Chess Records insisted on using Little Walter on the great majority of Waters' waxings until 1958, when Cotton blew behind Waters on "She's Nineteen Years Old" and "Close to You." At Cotton's instigation, Waters had added an Ann Cole tune called "Got My Mojo Working" to his repertoire. Walter played on Muddy Waters' first studio crack at it, but that's Cotton wailing on the definitive 1960 reading (cut live at the Newport Jazz Festival).

By 1966, Cotton was primed to make it on his own. Waxings for Vanguard, Prestige, and Loma preceded his official full-length album debut for Verve Records in 1967. His own unit then included fleet-fingered guitarist Luther Tucker and hard-hitting drummer Sam Lay. Throwing a touch of soul into his eponymous debut set, Cotton ventured into the burgeoning blues-rock field as he remained with Verve through the end of the decade.

In 1974, Cotton signed with Buddah and released *100% Cotton*, one of his most relentless LPs, with Matt "Guitar" Murphy sizzlingly backing him up. A decade later, Alligator issued another standout Cotton LP, *High Compression*, that was split evenly between traditional-style Chicago blues and funkier, horn-driven material. *Harp Attack!*, a 1990 summit meeting on Alligator, paired Cotton with three exalted peers: Wells, Carey Bell, and comparative newcomer Billy Branch. Antone's Records was responsible for a pair of gems: a live 1988 set reuniting the harpist with Murphy and Tucker and a stellar 1991 studio project, *Mighty Long Time*.

Cotton still commands a huge following, even though serious throat problems (he sometimes sounds as though he's been gargling Drano) have tragically robbed him of his

once-ferocious roar. That malady ruined parts of his Grammy-nominated album for Verve, *Living the Blues*; only when he stuck to playing harp was the customary Cotton energy still evident. —*Bill Dahl*

The James Cotton Blues Band / 1967 / Verve ♦♦♦

Upbeat, soul-influenced mid-'60s work by Cotton's initial solo aggregation. —*Bill Dahl*

Cut You Loose! / 1967 / Vanguard ♦♦♦

One of Cotton's earlier solo efforts. —*Bill Dahl*

Pure Cotton / 1968 / Verve ♦♦♦

Cotton in Your Ears / 1968 / Verve ♦♦♦

Taking Care of Business / 1970 / Capitol ♦♦

100% Cotton / Mar. 1974 / Sequel ♦♦♦♦

The ebullient, roly-poly Chicago harp wizard was at his zenith in 1974, when this cooking album was issued on Buddah. Matt "Guitar" Murphy matched Cotton note for zealous note back then, leading to fireworks aplenty on the non-stop "Boogie Thing," a driving "How Long Can a Fool Go Wrong," and the fastest "Rocket 88" you'll ever take a spin in. —*Bill Dahl*

High Energy / 1975 / One Way ♦♦

Shipping Cotton off to New Orleans during the mid-'70s to work with producer Allen Toussaint wasn't a good idea at all. The end result can for the most part be described as disco blues with a Crescent City funk tinge, without much to recommend it on any level. —*Bill Dahl*

Live & on the Move / 1976 / Sequel ♦♦♦

Originally released on two vinyl platters in 1976 by Buddah, this set was digitally unleashed anew by the British Sequel label. It faithfully captures the boogie-burning capabilities of the mid-'70s Cotton outfit, fired by its leader's incendiary harp wizardry and Murphy's scintillating licks. —*Bill Dahl*

Dealing With the Devil / 1984 / Aim ♦♦♦♦♦

Two Sides of the Blues / 1984 / Intermedia ♦♦♦

High Compression / 1984 / Alligator ♦♦♦♦♦

This is the best contemporary Cotton album gracing the shelves today, thanks to its ingenious formatting: half the set places Cotton in a traditional setting beside guitarist Magic Slim and pianist Pinetop Perkins, and a solid rhythm section; the other half pairs him with a contemporary combo featuring guitarist Michael Coleman's swift licks and a three-piece horn section. Both combinations click on all burners. Includes scorching theme song, "Superharp." —*Bill Dahl*

Live from Chicago Mr. Superharp Himself / 1986 / Alligator ♦♦

Thoroughly disappointing live collection taped at a Chicago nightspot called Biddy Mulligan's. Band is sloppy (especially horn section), and the harpist himself sounds uninspired. —*Bill Dahl*

Live & on the Move, Vol. 2 / 1986 / Buddah ♦♦♦

Take Me Back / 1987 / Blind Pig ♦♦♦

Another back-to-the-roots campaign for the powerhouse harmonica ace, powered by guitarists Sammy Lawhorn and John Primer and piano patriarch Pinetop Perkins. Cotton attacks nothing but covers, largely of the Chicago subspecies: Little Walter's "My Babe," Jimmy Reed's "Take Out Some Insurance" and "Honest I Do," Muddy Waters' "Clouds in My Heart." Hardly indispensable, but heartfelt. —*Bill Dahl*

Live at Antone's / 1988 / Antone's ♦♦♦♦

Reuniting Cotton with his former guitarists Matt Murphy and Luther Tucker, pianist Pinetop Perkins, and Muddy Waters' ex-rhythm section (bassist Calvin Jones and drummer Willie Smith) looks like a great idea on paper, and it worked equally well in the flesh, when this set was cut live at Antone's Night Club in Austin, TX. —*Bill Dahl*

Harp Attack! / 1990 / Alligator ♦♦♦♦

Four Chicago harmonica greats, one eminently solid album. Teamed with Junior Wells, Billy Branch, and Carey Bell, Cotton sings Willie Love's Delta classic "Little Car Blues" and Charles Brown's "Black Night" and plays along with his cohorts on most of the rest of the set. —*Bill Dahl*

Mighty Long Time / 1991 / Discovery ♦♦♦♦

Although the titles are all familiar (most of them a little too much so), Cotton and his all-star cohorts (guitarists Jimmie Vaughan, Matt Murphy, Luther Tucker, Hubert Sumlin, and Wayne Bennett, the omnipresent Perkins on keys) pull the whole thing off beautifully. Cotton's cover of Wolf's "Moanin' at Midnight" is remarkably eerie in its own right, and he romps through Muddy Waters' "Blow Wind Blow" and "Sugar Sweet" with joyous alacrity. —*Bill Dahl*

3 Harp Boogie / 1994 / Tomato ♦♦

The music on this set is actually all right; it gets a low rating because of its odd patchwork assembly. Five of the tracks come from a 1963 acoustic session recorded at an apartment on the South Side, featuring Elvin Bishop on guitar, Cotton on vocals and harmonica, Paul Butterfield on harmonica, and Billy Boy Arnold on harmonica (hence the title *3 Harp Boogie*). The other four selections are taken from his 1967 Verve album *James Cotton Blues Band*, available in its entirety on the *Best of the Verve Years* compilation. That means you probably only want this for the rarer acoustic cuts, which are good, but short value for a CD purchase, unless you're a very big Cotton fan. —*Richie Unterberger*

Living the Blues / 1994 / Verve ♦♦

All the guest stars in the world (Joe Louis Walker, Dr. John, Lucky Peterson, Larry McCray) can't mask the simple fact that Cotton's voice was thoroughly shot when he made this disc (apparently the Grammy nominating committee gratuitously overlooked this). The instrumentals, obviously, aren't affected by this malady; they're typically rousing. But whenever Cotton opens his mouth, he sounds as though he's been gargling Drano. *—Bill Dahl*

● **The Best of the Verve Years** / 1995 / Verve ✦✦✦✦✦
Taken from the high-energy harpist's first three albums for Verve following his split from Muddy Waters (including the entirety of his fine eponymous 1967 debut), this 20-track anthology is a fine spot to begin any serious Cotton collection. In those days, Cotton was into soul as well as blues—witness his raucous versions of "Knock on Wood" and "Turn on Your Lovelight," backed by a large horn complement. Compiler Dick Shurman has chose judiciously from his uneven pair of Verve follow-ups, making for a very consistent compilation. *—Bill Dahl*

Feelin' Good / Jan. 1, 1996 / Eclipse Music Group ✦✦✦
Pulled off of vinyl from various mid-'60s albums, here are ten tracks of Cotton in fine form, backed by his regular working band. Cotton storms through classics like "Off the Wall," "Don't Start Me to Talkin'," "Sweet Sixteen," and the title cut. The tracks are literally swimming in reverb, but the band blows hard and heavy; for a budget set, you could do a lot worse. *—Cub Koda*

Deep in the Blues / Aug. 1996 / Verve ✦✦✦
Deep in the Blues is a fascinating jam session between James Cotton, guitarist Joe Louis Walker, and jazz bassist Charlie Haden. The trio runs through a number of classic blues songs written by Muddy Waters, Percy Mayfield, and Sonny Boy Williamson and a few originals by Walker and Cotton. The sound is intimate and raw, which is a welcome change from Cotton's usual overproduced records. *—Thom Owens*

The Best of the Vanguard Years / Jun. 22, 1999 / Vanguard ✦✦✦✦

Superharps / Oct. 26, 1999 / Telarc ✦✦✦✦✦
Four great blues harmonica players (James Cotton, Billy Branch, Charlie Musselwhite, and Sugar Ray Norcia) are featured in various combinations on this spirited disc, backed by a four-piece rhythm section (with guitarist Kid Bangham and pianist Anthony Geraci). Cotton and Norcia have solo pieces, seven numbers feature two harmonicas, and the lengthy low-down blues "Harp to Harp" has all four of the harmonica players taking turns soloing. Much of the material is jazz-oriented, including "The Hucklebuck," "TD's Boogie Woogie," and "Route 66," and the majority of the selections are instrumentals. Each of the harmonica players sounds inspired and the results are consistently exciting and swinging. *—Scott Yanow*

Fire Down Under the Hill / 2000 / Telarc ✦✦✦

It Was a Very Good Year / Feb. 13, 2001 / Justin Time ✦✦✦✦
James Cotton's *It Was a Very Good Year* is a tribute CD that has been restored from its "live" performance in Montreal's the New Penelope Cafe in the late '60s. The benefit of today's technology has assisted in capturing the chomaticism inherent in the harmonica playing of James Cotton, excitement of Albert Gianquito's piano (you may remember him from his stints with Santana), Bobby Anderson on bass, Francis Clay on drums, and Luther Tucker on guitar. This blues band features a broad selection of tunes that range from the opener, "It Was a Very Good Year," in a sultry Latinized version to "The Midnight Creeper," a number loosely based on Little Walter Jacobs' "Juke." Cotton performs excellent covers of Muddy Waters' famous "Hoochie Coochie Man" and Otis Rush's big hit, "I Can't Quit You Baby." The highlight of this great set is the Paul Butterfield Blues Band hit "One More Mile," written by Cotton and featuring a dark elemental blues, which is a stark contrast to Cotton's well-known style. This is a great find for those that may have thrown out their Cotton LPs, and this newly restored CD is a nice treasure for blues fans. *—Paula Edelstein*

35th Anniversary Jam of the James Cotton Blues Band / May 28, 2002 / Telarc ✦✦✦
Don't complain that there are too many guests here—that's what this jam was all *about*, inviting a bunch of friends and kindred spirits to jam in the studio during June of 2001. These musicians were here to salute not just the great James Cotton and his songs, but the long life of his classic James Cotton Blues Band, by playing some of their greatest songs and having a good time. And that's what this is—a good jam session, performed with heart and vigor. Some of the guests might be a bit better than others, but the band is lively, there's more grit than you'd expect for an all-digital production, and Cotton has moments where he simply *smokes*. He's constantly a joy to hear; listen to how he breaks into "Jingle Bells" during "The Creeper" and try not to smile. Sure, this isn't the first James Cotton album you should get, or even the fifth, but if you've been a longtime fan, you'll have fun with this. *—Stephen Thomas Erlewine*

Robert Covington

b. Dec. 13, 1941, Yazoo City, MS, **d.** Jan. 17, 1996, Chicago, IL
Vocals, Drums / Modern Electric Blues

Robert Covington, born in Yazoo City, MS, on December 13, 1941, grew up taking music and voice lessons. Active as a teenager in drum and bugle corps, Covington played in a number of bands, including Little Melvin and the Downbeats. About to go to college (what became Alcorn State University in Lorman, MS), he chose instead to join Big Joe Turner's group when that player passed through town looking for a drummer. Turner's stage presence and vocal technique became a major inspiration and mentor for him, and they toured the South all that summer and fall.

In 1962, Covington had some small success with the Lee Covington Review and his single, "I Know." His group had a horn section, female backup signers, and backed groups like Ernie K-Doe and Ted Taylor.

Covington moved to Chicago in 1965 and played with Little Walter, Fenton Robinson, Buddy Guy, Junior Wells, and Lonnie "Guitar Junior" Brooks. He sat in with Sunnyland Slim at the Flying Fox and they began to work together on a regular basis. In 1983 he became a full-time member of the Sunnyland Slim Band. As Slim's frequency of performing declined (in his later years), Covington fronted his own band and established his own reputation. He was a hot act at Kingston Mines in Chicago, where he served as the swing singer; he even headlined one night a week. Covington's smooth delivery and big-band style voice has earned him the nickname, "golden voice." Robert Covington died on January 17, 1996, in Chicago. *—Michael Erlewine*

● **The Golden Voice of Robert Covington** / 1988 / Evidence ✦✦✦✦
Covington wrote six of the nine songs on this album (formerly released in 1988 on Red Beans). Covington's strong reassuring voice is in good form, in particular on "Trust in Me." With Carl Weathersby on guitar. *—Michael Erlewine*

Ida Cox (Ida Prather)

b. Feb. 25, 1896, Toccoa, GA, **d.** Nov. 10, 1967, Knoxville, TN
Vocals / Classic Female Blues

One of the finest classic blues singers of the '20s, Ida Cox was singing in theaters by the time she was 14. She recorded regularly during 1923-1929 (her "Wild Woman Don't Have the Blues" and "Death Letter Blues" are her best-known songs). Although she was off-record during much of the '30s, Cox was able to continue working and in 1939 she sang at Cafe Society, appeared at John Hammond's Spirituals to Swing concert, and made some new records. Cox toured with shows until a 1944 stroke pushed her into retirement; she came back for an impressive final recording in 1961.

Cox left her hometown of Toccoa, GA, as a teenager, traveling the south in vaudeville and tent shows, performing both as a singer and a comedienne. In the early '20s, she performed with Jelly Roll Morton, but she had severed her ties with the pianist by the time she signed her first record contract with Paramount in 1923. Cox stayed with Paramount for six years and recorded 78 songs, which usually featured accompaniment by Lovie Austin and trumpeter Tommy Ladnier. During that time, she also cut tracks for a variety of labels, including Silvertone, using several different pseudonyms, including Velma Bradley, Kate Lewis, and Julia Powers.

During the '30s, Cox didn't record often, but she continued to perform frequently, highlighted by an appearance at John Hammond's 1939 Spirituals to Swing concert at Carnegie Hall. The concert increased her visibility, particularly in jazz circles. Following the concert, she recorded with a number of jazz artists, including Charlie Christian, Lionel Hampton, Fletcher Henderson, and Hot Lips Page. She toured with a number of different shows in the early '40s until she suffered a stroke in 1944. Cox was retired for most of the '50s, but she was coaxed out of retirement in 1961 to record a final session with Coleman Hawkins. In 1967, Ida Cox died of cancer. *—Scott Yanow & Stephen Thomas Erlewine*

☆ **Complete Recorded Works, Vol. 1 (1923)** / Jun. 1923-Dec. 1923 / Document ✦✦✦✦✦
Ida Cox was one of the most powerful blues singers of the '20s, ranking just below Bessie Smith. The Document label has reissued all of Cox's '20s recordings on four CDs, leaving out many of the alternate takes (since there are a great deal from 1923-1924) to be put out on a later series. The first CD has the master takes of all of Cox's recordings from 1923, plus four alternates. Except for the closing "Bear-Mash Blues," which finds the singer joined by her future husband Jesse Crump on piano, the music either features accompaniment by pianist Lovie Austin (an underrated blues player) or assistance from Austin, the great cornetist Tommy Ladnier and clarinetist Jimmy O'Bryant. Cox was one of the few singers from this early period who could overcome the technical limitations of the primitive recording equipment and really communicate with the listener. Among the highlights from her first year on records are "Any Woman's Blues," "Graveyard Dream Blues" (which is heard in three versions), "Ida Cox's Lawdy, Lawdy Blues," "Moanin' Groanin' Blues," "Come Right In" (which has some lines that would become quite familiar in later songs) and "I've Got the Blues for Rampart Street." Highly recommended. *—Scott Yanow*

The Uncrowned Queen of the Blues / Jun. 1923-Aug. 1924 / Black Swan ✦✦✦✦✦
Ida Cox was one of the most talented of the classic blues singers of the '20s. This Black Swan CD has 20 of her first 32 recordings and, although one regrets that it is not a "complete" series (hopefully the dozen other titles will be reissued by Black Swan eventually), the music is consistently enjoyable and timeless. In fact, quite a few of the lyrics (many of which were written by Cox) were later permanently "borrowed" by Jimmy Rushing and Joe Williams; the first stanza of "Goin' to Chicago" was taken from "Chicago Monkey Man Blues" and "Bear-Mash Blues" has a couple of Williams' best lines. When one considers that the music on this CD is taken from 1923-24, it can certainly be considered ahead of its time! Most of the musicians backing Ida Cox are excellent, particularly pianist Lovie Austin and (on five numbers) cornetist Tommy Ladnier and clarinetist Jimmy O'Bryant. The recording quality (even with some surface noise) has been greatly cleaned up for this reissue and Cox's singing is very easy to understand. Although uncrowned, Ida Cox (who after retiring in 1945 came back for a final recording in 1961) can still communicate to today's listeners, something than can be said about very few other singers from 1923. *—Scott Yanow*

Complete Recorded Works, Vol. 2 (1924–1925) / 1924-1925 / Document ✦✦✦✦✦
Unlike most of her contemporaries, who spent at least part of their time singing vaudeville-type material and pop songs, Ida Cox stuck throughout her career to the blues. On the second of four Document CDs that reissue all of her '20s material (although some of the many alternate takes are bypassed), Cox is mostly accompanied by either Lovie Austin's Blues Serenaders (which usually includes cornetist Tommy Ladnier and clarinetist Jimmy O'Bryant, although the great Johnny Dodds is on six selections) or, on one date, members of Fletcher Henderson's Orchestra. The recording quality of these Paramount 78s (which cover a 13-month period) is erratic, but there are a few classics here, including "Chicago Monkey Man Blues" (which has some lyrics that would later be used for "Going to Chicago"), "Blues Ain't Nothin' Else But," "Wild Women Don't Have the Blues" and "Death Letter Blues." Throughout, Ida Cox (who was second to Bessie Smith at the time) is quite consistent, making the most of her limitations. Recommended. *—Scott Yanow*

Complete Recorded Works, Vol. 3 (1925–1927) / 1925-1927 / Document ♦♦♦♦
The third of four "complete" Ida Cox CDs from Document has 14 selections from 1925, six from 1926 and four from 1927. Most of the sessions feature the masterful blues singer assisted by Lovie Austin's Blues Serenaders, whose personnel was changing during this era—they featured either Tommy Ladnier, the underrated Bob Shoffner, Bernie Young or Shirley Clay on cornet, Jimmy O'Bryant or (on two songs) Johnny Dodds on clarinet, and other unidentified musicians, including a trombonist. In addition, there are three duets with banjoist Papa Charlie Jackson, a couple of numbers in which Cox is joined by cornetist Dave Nelson and Jesse Crump on reed organ, and the first four tunes from a lengthy 1927 set that has Cox accompanied only by Crump's piano. Most interesting is "How Long Daddy, How Long," which was the basis of Leroy Carr's famous "How Long Blues." Other highlights include "Long Distance Blues," "Southern Woman's Blues," "Coffin Blues" and Cox's famous "'Fore Day Creep." All four of the discs in this valuable series are easily recommended to serious blues collectors. *—Scott Yanow*

Complete Recorded Works, Vol. 4 (1927–1938) / 1927-1938 / Document ♦♦♦♦
The fourth and final CD in Document's extensive Ida Cox series features the classic blues singer in a variety of settings: backed by her future husband Jesse Crump on eight selections from 1927; accompanied by a variety of mostly unknown players on a dozen numbers from 1928; joined by a trio (including trombonist Roy Palmer) on two 1929 sides; and, finally, assisted by five Count Basie sidemen (trumpeter Shad Collins, trombonist Dickie Wells, tenorman Buddy Tate, bassist Walter Page and drummer Jo Jones) and pianist James P. Johnson during her two songs at the 1938 Spirituals to Swing Concert. Unfortunately, Document did not put out a *Vol. 5* to cover Cox's 1939-1940 recordings (which were reissued by Affinity). Although none of these individual selections became that famous, she is heard in prime form throughout, and she is at her best during the duets with Crump. In fact, Cox is in such fine form during her 1938 concert appearance that it makes one wonder why she was not more active on records during the '30s and '40s. The first two CDs in this series get the edge, but all four will be wanted by vintage blues fans. *—Scott Yanow*

Complete Recorded Works, Vol. 5 (1939–1940) / 1939-1940 / Document ♦♦♦♦
Other than an album from 1961, this CD has blues singer Ida Cox's final recordings. The first seven selections (which include a previously unreleased "One Hour Mama") has four additional alternate takes. Cox is heard in 1939 backed by an accurately titled "all-star band" that consists of trumpeter Hot Lips Page, trombonist J.C. Higginbotham, clarinetist Edmond Hall, either James P. Johnson or Fletcher Henderson on piano, guitarist Charlie Christian, bassist Artie Bernstein and Lionel Hampton on drums. Although her prime was considered the '20s, Ida Cox on "Death Letter Blues" and "Four Day Creep" still sounds pretty strong. The remainder of this CD is taken from a 1940 session with trumpeter Red Allen, Higginbotham, Hall, pianist Cliff Jackson, bassist Billy Taylor, and drummer Jimmy Hoskins that resulted in four titles and four alternate takes; only two performances were released previously, but Cox's singing is excellent. It is a pity that because musical styles had changed, Ida Cox was largely forgotten during this period. *—Scott Yanow*

★ **Blues for Rampart Street** / Apr. 11, 1961+Apr. 12, 1961 / Riverside/Original Blues Classics ♦♦♦♦♦
Classic blues singer Ida Cox had not recorded since 1940 nor performed regularly since the mid-'40s when she was coaxed out of retirement to record a date for Riverside in 1961. At 65 years old (some books list her as being 72), Cox's voice was a bit rusty and past its prime, but she still had the feeling, phrasing, and enough tricks to perform a strong program. With assistance from trumpeter Roy Eldridge, tenor saxophonist Coleman Hawkins, pianist Sammy Price, bassist Milt Hinton, and drummer Jo Jones (swing-era veterans who came up after Cox was already a major name), the singer does her best on such numbers as "Wild Women Don't Have the Blues," "Blues for Rampart Street," "St. Louis Blues," and "Death Letter Blues." Since she passed away in 1967, this final effort (reissued on CD) was made just in time and is well worth acquiring by '20s jazz and blues collectors. *—Scott Yanow*

Wild Women Don't Have the Blues / Apr. 11, 1961+Apr. 12, 1961 / Rosetta ♦♦♦♦
Ida Cox's *Wild Women Don't Have the Blues* was recorded at the end of her career. Surprisingly, Cox's voice hadn't faded away—she could belt out a song with nearly as much power as she did in her early career. In fact, *Wild Women Don't Have the Blues* ranks as one of her finest albums. Not only is Cox in fine voice, the support Coleman Hawkins and his small group lends is strong and sympathetic, making this album one to treasure. *—Thom Owens*

Ida Cox: The Essential / Jun. 5, 2001 / Classic Blues

Harry "Fats" Crafton

Vocals, Guitar / Jump Blues
Harry Crafton was one of the better—and, ultimately, unfairly neglected—guitarists to come out of the postwar era. He carved a small but special niche for himself in Philadelphia beginning soon after World War II, cutting for a string of independent labels with a guitar sound that was heavily influenced by Tiny Grimes and a singing style reminiscent of Eddie "Cleanhead" Vinson. What little anyone seems to know about Harry "Fats" Crafton mostly concerns his career. In addition to being signed to Ivin Ballen's Gotham Records as an artist in 1949, he had a relationship with the company as a songwriter starting early in 1950, which was how he was most visible within the company. Crafton's songwriting credits often appear in confunction with bandleader and talent scout Doc Bagby and composer Don Keene. He led a group of his own, known first as the Jivetones and later on as the Craft Tones, and also played in bands led by Doc Bagby. He was prominently featured with Bagby's band on sides credited to the leader. In 1950, Crafton cut an instrumental, "Guitar Boogie"—dominated by his guitar and an unknown saxman (maybe Tiny Grimes band alumnus Joe Sewell)—that was five years ahead of its time as a piece of primordial rock & roll. In 1951, Crafton began recording for the Jarman label in East Newark, NJ, with a band called the Sonotones, which included jazz organist Jimmy Smith (just out of music school at the time) in its lineup. By 1954, he was leading the Craft Tones, whose lineup, at least at one point, included Sewell on tenor sax, Jimmy Johnson on drums, and Doc Starkes on bass, as well as Agnes Riley as vocalist with Crafton. Those sides rock even harder than Crafton's early-'50s jump blues numbers, and one can only wonder at their failure to find at least a cult audience, although titles like "Big Fat Hot Dog," sung by Riley, were probably too risqué for any radio station in the country to play heavily. Crafton, Sewell, Starkes, and Johnson subsequently joined R&B singer (and RCA-Victor alumnus) Melvin Smith in the Nite Riders Orchestra, who cut sides for M-G-M, Swan, and Sue Records, among other labels, during the late '50s and early '60s. Nothing is known of Crafton's whereabouts in music or anywhere else since the mid-'60s, although it is said that he ran a record store in Philadelphia at some point. *—Bruce Eder*

● **Harry Crafton: 1949–54** / 1987 / Collectables ♦♦
Ever wonder what Louis Jordan might've sounded like had he been in his prime in the '50s instead of the early '40s? This 14 song CD answers that question-it's as fun and entertaining as anything of Jordan's, and it's a fine showcase for some excellent singing and solid guitar-based r&b by Harry Crafton. The Jarman sides are left out, but the rest of his solo recording career is represented, including a few cuts credited to Doc Bagby's band but featuring the guitarist so prominently as to be Crafton numbers. The highlights also include three previously unissued cuts, an outtake of "It's Been A Long Time Baby," "Rusty Dusty," which is a Crafton outtake of "Get Off, Mama," itself a reworking of the 1942 Louis Jordan song "Rusty Dusty"; and "Guitar Boogie," a hot ax-and-sax instrumental. "Let Me Tell You Baby" is a tribute to the sexual prowess of fat men, covering similar ground to Willie Dixon's "Built For Comfort," reminding its women listeners that "there's more love in every pound"—the backing chorus behind Crafton's lines about being "big as a bear" is a subtle but brilliantly effective moment. He shines across several years worth of hot jump blues, from 1949's "Roly Poly Mama" to 1954's "She Got A Mule Kick"—it falls to Agnes Riley, however, to deliver the raunchiest lyrics on this disc, on "Big Fat Hot Dog," from 1954. The sound is amazingly good throughout, even on the outtakes, with Crafton's guitar clean and out in front everywhere it should be—the only track that disappoints is the 1950 Christmas song "Bring That Cadillac Back," on which the band sounds muted. *—Bruce Eder*

Hank Crawford (Bennie Ross Crawford, Jr.)

b. Dec. 21, 1934, Memphis, TN
Sax (Alto) / Hard Bop, Soul-Jazz, R&B
With an unmistakable blues wail, full of emotion and poignancy, altoist Hank Crawford bridges the gap between that tradition and that of jazz more completely than any other living horn player. Born in Memphis, Crawford was steeped in the blues tradition from an early age. He began playing piano but switched to alto when his father brought one home from the army. He claims his early influences as Louis Jordan, Earl Bostic, and Johnny Hodges. Crawford hung out with Phineas Newborn Jr., Booker Little, and George Coleman in high school. Upon graduating, Crawford played in bands fronted by Ike Turner, B.B. King, Junior Parker, and Bobby "Blue" Bland at Memphis Palace Theater and Club Paradise. In 1958 Crawford went to college in Nashville where he met Ray Charles. Charles hired Crawford originally as a baritone saxophonist. Crawford switched to alto in 1959 and remained with Charles' band—becoming its musical director—until 1963. The phrasing and voicings he learned there proved invaluable to him as the hallmark of his own sound. He also wrote and arranged a tune for Charles. The cut, "Sherry," his first for the band, was put on the *Live at Newport* album. Crawford cut a slew solo albums for Atlantic while with the band, and when he formed his group, he remained with the label until 1970. He signed with Creed Taylor's Kudu in 1971 and cut a series of fusion-y groove jazz dates through 1982. In 1983 he moved to Milestone and returned to form as a premier arranger, soloist, and composer, writing for small bands—that included guitarist Melvin Sparks, organist Jimmy McGriff, and Dr. John—as well as large. Crawford has been constantly active since then, as a leader and sideman, recording the best music of his long career. *—Thom Jurek*

After Hours / 1967 / Atlantic ♦♦♦
The most unusual aspect to this straight CD reissue of a Hank Crawford Atlantic LP is that the altoist plays some very effective piano on two numbers including a lengthy feature on "After Hours." Fortunately his alto playing is not neglected and he really shows off his appealing tone on "Who Can I Turn To," "Makin' Whoopee" and "When Did You Leave Heaven." A fine soulful crossover set that is quite accessible and melodic. *—Scott Yanow*

● **Heart and Soul: The Hank Crawford Anthology** / May 17, 1994 / Rhino ♦♦♦♦♦
This is one of the better of Rhino's two-CD samplers of Atlantic jazz artists. Altoist Hank Crawford, one of the most soulful stylists to emerge during the '60s, is heard on 31 of his best recordings, 27 as a leader plus sideman appearances with Ray Charles, David "Fathead" Newman, B.B. King and Etta James. Crawford's sound and style were virtually the same in the '90s as they were in the '60s although the settings changed a bit. Highlights of this well-conceived introduction include "Please Send Me Someone to Love," "Two Years of Torture," "Don't Get Around Much Anymore," "The Very Thought of You," "Trouble in Mind" and "Hank's Groove." Recommended to listeners not familiar with the beauty of Hank Crawford's playing. *—Scott Yanow*

Memphis, Ray and a Touch of Moody / Feb. 24, 1998 / 32 Jazz ♦♦♦
Altoist Hank Crawford is not quite at peak form on the LPs which comprise this two-fer reissue, but it contains enough moments of excitement to ensure that serious fans will want to add *Memphis Ray/Touch of Moody* to their collections anyway. *—Jason Ankeny*

Robert Cray

b. Aug. 1, 1953, Columbus, GA

Vocals, Guitar / Retro-Soul, Contemporary Blues, Modern Electric Blues

Tin-eared critics have frequently damned him as a yuppie blues wanna-be whose slickly soulful offerings bear scant resemblance to the real downhome item. In reality, Robert Cray is one of a precious few young (at this stage, that translates to under 50 years of age) blues artists with the talent and vision to successfully usher the idiom into the 21st century without resorting either to slavish imitation or simply playing rock while passing it off as blues. Just as importantly, his immensely popular records helped immeasurably to jump-start the contemporary blues boom that still holds sway to this day. Blessed with a soulful voice that sometimes recalls '60s-great O.V. Wright and a concise lead guitar approach that never wastes notes, Cray's ascendancy was amazingly swift—in 1986 his breakthrough *Strong Persuader* album for Mercury (containing "Smoking Gun") won him a Grammy and shot his asking price for a night's work skyward. Unlike too many of his peers, Cray continues to experiment within his two presiding genres, blues and soul. Sets such as *Midnight Stroll*, *I Was Warned* and *Shame + a Sin* for Mercury show that the "bluenatics" (as he amusedly labels his purist detractors) have nothing to fear and plenty to anticipate from this innovative, laudably accessible guitarist. *—Bill Dahl*

Who's Been Talkin' / 1980 / Mercury ♦♦♦♦

The Pacific Northwest-based blues savior's first album in 1980 boded well for his immediate future. Unfurling a sterling vocal delivery equally conversant with blues and soul, Cray offers fine remakes of the Willie Dixon-penned title tune, O.V. Wright's deep soul romp "I'm Gonna Forget About You," and Freddy King's "The Welfare (Turns Its Back on You)," along with his own "Nice as a Fool Can Be" and "That's What I'll Do." *—Bill Dahl*

☆ **Bad Influence** / 1983 / Hightone ♦♦♦♦♦

One of Cray's best albums ever, and the one that etched him into the consciousness of blues aficionados prior to his mainstream explosion. Produced beautifully by Bruce Bromberg and Dennis Walker, the set sports some gorgeous originals ("Phone Booth," "Bad Influence," "So Many Women, So Little Time") and two well-chosen covers, Johnny "Guitar" Watson's "Don't Touch Me" and Eddie Floyd's Stax-era "Got to Make a Comeback." Few albums portend greatness the way this one did. *—Bill Dahl*

False Accusations / 1985 / Hightone ♦♦♦♦

If its predecessor hadn't been so powerful, this collection might have been a little more striking in its own right. As it is, a solid if not overwhelming album sporting the memorable "Playin' in the Dirt" and "I've Slipped Her Mind." *—Bill Dahl*

Showdown [A Collins & J Copeland] / 1985 / Alligator ♦♦♦♦♦

Cray found himself in some pretty intimidating company for this Grammy-winning blues guitar summit meeting, but he wasn't deterred, holding his own alongside his idol Albert Collins and Texas great Johnny Copeland. Cray's delivery of Muddy Waters' rhumba-rocking "She's into Something" was one of the set's many highlights. *—Bill Dahl*

★ **Strong Persuader** / 1986 / Mercury ♦♦♦♦♦

The set that made Cray a pop star, despite its enduring blues base. Cray's smoldering stance on "Smoking Gun" and "Right Next Door" rendered him the first sex symbol to emerge from the blues field in decades, but it was his innovative expansion of the genre itself that makes this album a genuine '80s classic. "Nothing but a Woman" boasts an irresistible groove pushed by the Memphis Horns and some metaphorically inspired lyrics, while "I Wonder" and "Guess I Showed Her" sizzle with sensuality. *—Bill Dahl*

Don't Be Afraid of the Dark / 1988 / Mercury ♦♦♦

With 1986's *Strong Persuader*, guitarist and vocalist Robert Cray stepped to the front of the line as a smooth and intelligent practitioner of the blues genre. *Strong Persuader* almost worked as well as a greatest hits set, with the brilliant Willie Mitchell-influenced "I Guess I Showed Her" being best of a perfect ten. With that standard being set, *Don't Be Afraid of the Dark* is marred by it's lack of potent material and a tired-sounding band and Cray. The title is a steamy track punctuated by the Memphis Horns. The edgy and methodical "Don't You Even Care" finds Cray again on the losing end of a relationship. Although the relationship blues are stinging here, this album's best effort strays far from the formula. The oddly humorous "Night Patrol" has Cray playing armchair therapist wondering what went wrong with a drunk and a 17-year-old girl on the corner. By song's end he can also wonder about himself, as he too hits the streets a potentially dangerous wandering psycho. For the most part *Don't Be Afraid of the Dark* has the sly work Cray is famous for. The sprite "Gotta Change Rules" the country/Memphis sound influenced has Cray doing some strong vocalizations and taut guitar riffs. "At Last" and "Laugh Out Loud," while not horrible, do come off like uninspired filler. This is one of those albums that might not be exciting at first, but if it is listened to intently some of the songs do become worthwhile. *—Jason Elias*

Midnight Stroll / Jun. 1990 / Mercury ♦♦♦

Cray went into a more soul-slanted direction for this solid collection, coarsening his vocal cords for "The Forecast (Calls for Pain)" and the rest of the set. *—Bill Dahl*

Too Many Cooks / Sep. 1990 / Tomato ♦♦♦♦

Bluesman Robert Cray has occasionally been critized for mixing pop and funk elements in his music but no such criticism can be made about this CD reissue of his recording debut. It seems obvious in hindsight from the music that Cray would become a star for his appealing voice and strong guitar playing manage to both update and reinforce the blues tradition. This superior if brief (under 36-minute) session is recommended to all lovers of the blues. *—Scott Yanow*

I Was Warned / Apr. 1992 / Mercury ♦♦♦

Robert Cray's soulful vocals and spanky, sustainless guitar enliven the fairly by-the-numbers blues-influenced R&B on *I Was Warned*. The band itself is solid (especially tough-as-nails drummer Kevin Hayes), if unexceptional; the addition of the Memphis Horns (Andrew Love on tenor sax and Wayne Jackson on trumpet and trombone) on many of these tracks is a definite step in the right direction. However, the tracks are devoid of any kind of dirt whatsoever, which prevents them from really kicking the listener the way that they should. Granted, Cray isn't R.L. Burnside or even Buddy Guy, but a little more grit to the band performances, arrangements, tones, and recording would go a long way toward aiding the emotional kick of his admittedly great set of pipes. Cray is also not aided by the writing, which is hit or miss throughout. Such standout tracks as the anguish-laden "He Don't Live Here Anymore" and the swinging "Our Last Time" serve to offset missteps such as the title track. The production even actually helps the Steve Cropper co-written "On the Road Down," which features a great vocal performance from the leader. In addition to his wonderful singing voice, Cray's unique guitar sound and approach, one of the most distinctive in blues, is on full display on *I Was Warned*. Take a listen to the beginning of his solo on "Just a Loser," to the way that the phrase just flows out of his guitar in a way that suggests the blues without being overtly bluesy, for a good indication of his extremely effective instrumental skills. His playing is powerful and idiosyncratic, but his intensity and focus are unfortunately not matched by other aspects of this recording. *I Was Warned* is not a bad Cray album by any means; it just lacks the sort of fire that would make it really take off. *—Daniel Gioffre*

Shame + a Sin / Oct. 5, 1993 / Mercury ♦♦♦♦

This time, Cray veered back toward the blues (most convincingly, too), even covering Albert King's "You're Gonna Need Me" and bemoaning paying taxes on the humorous "1040 Blues." Unlike his previous efforts, Cray produced this one himself. Also, longtime bassist Richard Cousins was history, replaced by Karl Sevareid. *—Bill Dahl*

Some Rainy Morning / May 9, 1995 / Mercury ♦♦♦

Typically well-produced and well-played outing—mostly originals, with smoldering covers of Syl Johnson's "Steppin' Out" and Wilson Pickett's "Jealous Love" for good measure. Cray's crisp, concise guitar work and subtly soulful vocals remain honed to a sharp edge. *—Bill Dahl*

Sweet Potato Pie / May 5, 1997 / Mercury ♦♦♦

Robert Cray always flirted with gritty Southern soul, but it wasn't until *Sweet Potato Pie* that he made a full-fledged soul-blues record in Memphis. Cray hasn't abandoned blues, but he's woven punchy horns and sexy rhythms into the mix, resulting in one of his stronger records of the '90s. The material remains a bit uneven, but his taste is impeccable—few blues guitarists are as succinct and memorable as he, and the soul settings of *Sweet Potato Pie* only confirm that fact. *—Thom Owens*

Take Your Shoes Off / Apr. 27, 1999 / Rykodisc ♦♦♦♦

It's evident right from the start that Robert Cray's aiming for a Memphis soul groove on *Take Your Shoes Off*. Willie Mitchell of Hi Records fame co-wrote and did the horn arrangements for the lead-off cut, "Love Gone to Waste," and Jim Pugh's burbling organ would have fit snugly into the mix of an early-'70s Al Green record. The blues is not missing from this effort, but is most present in Cray's usual assertive blues guitar lines. Otherwise, this is far more appropriately pegged as a blues-soul album, or even just a retro-soul album, than a straight blues one. Cray, indeed, only writes about half of the songs, covering soul classics identified with Mack Rice's "24-7 Man" and Solomon Burke's "Won't You Give Him (One More Chance)," as well as Willie Dixon's "Tollin' Bells." No one would be claiming that this disc plows new territory, but to Cray's credit, he fits the quasi-Hi and (less frequently) Stax-type grooves with an unforced ease. It's a lot harder to do than it sounds—for Cray or anyone in the late '90s—and it's frankly more interesting than a straight-ahead blues album from the singer-guitarist would have been. *—Richie Unterberger*

Heavy Picks: The Robert Cray Collection / Nov. 16, 1999 / Mercury ♦♦♦♦♦

Robert Cray left his longtime home Mercury Records following the release of 1997's *Sweet Potato Pie*, moving to Rykodisc in 1999. Not long after his Ryko debut *Take Your Shoes Off*—just a little over six months, actually—Mercury released *Heavy Picks: The Robert Cray Collection*. It wasn't really an attempt to steal the thunder from *Take Your Shoes Off*, since that album had eased into the catalog by that point; it was merely a welcome compilation of Cray's first 17 years of recording. Almost all of his albums, from 1980's *Who's Been Talkin'* to *Sweet Potato Pie*, are represented (1995's *Some Rainy Morning* is conspicuously missing, perhaps because of its slick soul direction), and the selections are by and large on the money—the crossover hits "Smoking Gun," "Right Next Door (Because of Me)," and "I Guess I Showed Her" are here, but so are some straight-ahead blues cuts too, including the Albert Collins duet "The Dream." The only real fault with *Heavy Picks* is that the collection feels haphazardly assembled, bouncing from era to era. Ultimately, however, that doesn't matter, since this captures the highlights from his Tomato and Mercury recordings quite well. *—Stephen Thomas Erlewine*

Shoulda Been Home / May 15, 2001 / Rykodisc ♦♦♦♦♦

Perhaps the most telling tune on *Shoulda Been Home* is the T-Bone Walker-influenced "Renew Blues," not because of the style, but because the slow blues fades out after just one tiny minute. By contrast, the mellow soul sway of "Out of Eden" stretches out to over nine minutes. Robert Cray has been heralded as a savior of modern blues, but the truth is Cray's music is much closer to the vintage soul of O.V. Wright and Otis Redding than the 12-bar form of B.B. King or Albert King. Granted, his punctuating Stratocaster guitar riffs borrow from the books of all the blues masters, but his songwriting and arranging don't. Often backed by arpeggiated guitar chords, Cray's vocals are front and center here, passionately leaning into these predominantly slow or midtempo tunes. By contrast, only a couple of cuts are upbeat enough to really get the knees a-shakin'. The infectious opening cut "Baby's Arms"—the best tune on the record—could have been a hit single for Stax Records, and Sir Mack Rice's upbeat "Love Sickness" *was* a hit for Stax Records. Meanwhile, "Help Me Forget," with its mellow, candlelight mood, could have been a hit for

Barry White. In fact, most of the tunes on *Shoulda Been Home* are the perfect compliment for sharing a big can of Schlitz Malt Liquor with the one you love in a dimly lit room. Ironically, three of the 12 tunes herein are much more standard blues forms than Cray may have ever released: the aforementioned "Renew Blues," as well as a pair of Elmore James covers. Robert Cray may be the savior of vintage soul, but he does just enough to warrant the label of "blues savior" as well. *—Scott Cooper*

Pee Wee Crayton (Connie C. Crayton)

b. Dec. 18, 1914, Rockdale, TX, **d.** Jun. 25, 1985, Los Angeles, CA

Vocals, Guitar / West Coast Blues, Electric Texas Blues, Texas Blues

Although he was certainly inexorably influenced by the pioneering electric guitar conception of T-Bone Walker (what axe-handler wasn't during the immediate postwar era?), Pee Wee Crayton brought enough daring innovation to his playing to avoid being labeled as a mere T-Bone imitator. Crayton's recorded output for Modern, Imperial, and Vee-Jay contains plenty of dazzling, marvelously imaginative guitar work, especially on stunning instrumentals such as "Texas Hop," "Pee Wee's Boogie," and "Poppa Stoppa," all far more aggressive performances than Walker usually indulged in.

Like Walker, Connie Crayton was a transplanted Texan. He relocated to Los Angeles in 1935, later moving north to the Bay Area. He signed with the Bihari brothers' L.A.-based Modern logo in 1948, quickly hitting pay dirt with the lowdown instrumental "Blues After Hours" (a kissin' cousin to Erskine Hawkins' anthem "After Hours"), which topped the R&B charts in late 1948. The steaming "Texas Hop" trailed it up the lists shortly thereafter, followed the next year by "I Love You So." But Crayton's brief hitmaking reign was over, through no fault of his own.

After recording prolifically at Modern to no further commercial avail, Crayton moved on to Aladdin and, in 1954, Imperial. Under Dave Bartholomew's savvy production, Crayton made some of his best waxings in New Orleans: "Every Dog Has His Day," "You Know Yeah," and "Runnin' Wild" found Crayton's guitar turned up to the boiling point over the fat cushion of saxes characterizing the Crescent City sound.

From there, Crayton tried to regain his momentum at Vee-Jay in Chicago; 1957's "I Found My Peace of Mind," a Ray Charles-tinged gem, should have done the trick, but no dice. After one-off 45s for Jamie, Guyden, and Smash during the early '60s, Crayton largely faded from view until Vanguard unleashed his LP, *Things I Used to Do*, in 1971. After that, Pee Wee Crayton's profile was raised somewhat; he toured and made a few more albums prior to his passing in 1985. *—Bill Dahl*

Pee Wee Crayton / 1959 / Crown ♦♦♦♦♦

An ancient but indispensable collection of his Modern label output, it includes the instrumentals "Texas Hop" and "Blues After Hours." *—Bill Dahl*

The Things I Used to Do / 1971 / Vanguard ♦♦♦♦

Pee Wee Crayton, a popular L.A.-based blues singer and guitarist, recorded frequently between 1947-1957 but this 1970 session was his first full album and ended an eight-year drought in the studios. At 55, Crayton performed some country-flavored tunes and soul ballads but is at his best on the simpler straight-ahead blues such as a spirited "Let the Good Times Roll," the atmospheric instrumental "Blues After Hours," "Things I Used to Do" and "S.K. Blues" which at 6:24 is easily the longest performance of the brief 41-minute set. Although not a major stylist, Crayton is in good form throughout his date. *—Scott Yanow*

Rocking Down on Central Avenue / 1982 / Ace ♦♦♦♦

Nice vinyl selection of Crayton's Modern output, split between mellow vocals and blistering instrumentals. *—Bill Dahl*

Blues After Hours / 1993 / P-Vine ♦♦♦♦

There are much better annotated Pee Wee Crayton anthologies out there, but the dark horse import *Blues After Hours* offers an extremely well-rounded collection of material, compiling sides from Crayton's memorable stints at both the Modern and Imperial labels (a feat that has yet to be accomplished by any domestic single-CD reissue of Crayton's work). This is a great starting point for blues guitar fans—especially Texas- and West Coast-style enthusiasts—who may be unfamiliar with Crayton's often overlooked career. The seven instrumentals alone (including the classics "Blues After Hours," "Texas Hop," and "Poppa Stoppa") are worth the price of admission, and the vocal cuts are just as impressive, with a young Crayton showing off his keen ability to switch from "over the top blues shouter" mode to "dapper R&B crooner" mode at the drop of a downbeat. In addition to the tracks culled from the Modern and Imperial sessions (originally recorded between 1947 and 1955), *Blues After Hours* includes "The Telephone Is Ringing," a slow blues that Crayton cut for Vee-Jay in 1956. Ignore the skimpy liner notes and the cheap cover art; the songs assembled in this package are all first-rate, and they represent an essential chapter in postwar electric blues. *—Ken Chang*

● **The Modern Legacy Vol. 1** / 1996 / Ace ♦♦♦♦♦

As an overview of Crayton's work for Modern from 1948-1951, this might not be ideal, as only about half of it appeared on singles during that time; the rest was mostly unissued until the '80s and '90s, some making their first appearance on this CD. It also means that some of his Modern singles, including his biggest hit for the label (the ballad "I Love You So"), aren't here, as they were saved for another Ace volume of Crayton's Modern sides. Those considerations aside, this is superior Los Angeles jump blues, with the rare vault sides holding up about as well as what came out on singles. Were this the only anthology to appear of Crayton's Modern material—heck, were it the only Crayton material, period—it would still offer convincing proof of his stature as a significant bluesman, one who (like several Modern labelmates) was instrumental in the transition from the earliest electric blues to a harder R&B style. Although his singing and songwriting are good, what really makes this stand out is his incendiary guitar playing. In addition to taking good single-note solos, he made use of insistent, sometimes machine-gun-like jazzy chords that unpredictably shifted keys and pushed the limits of the day's amplification technology. That really comes to the fore on some of the uptempo instrumentals, like the nearly out-of-control "Pee Wee's Wild." Unlike many blues guitar heroes, though, he doesn't have to wait for the fast tunes to strut his stuff, as the crazily descending solo of the bump-and-grind "Please Come Back" demonstrates. On top of being a quality early electric blues anthology on its own merits, the CD makes a good case for Crayton being one of the more overlooked pioneers of the electric guitar as a whole. *—Richie Unterberger*

Complete Aladdin & Imperial Recordings / Mar. 19, 1996 / Capitol ♦♦♦♦♦

Crayton was fading fast commercially by the time he cut these sides in the '50s, though his vocal and instrumental skills, particularly his stinging guitar, were undimmed. Aside from two 1951 tracks cut for Aladdin in 1951, this 20-song compilation is devoted to his mid-'50s hitch with Imperial. The label had him record in New Orleans with Dave Bartholomew and other local musicians, giving many of these sides a hybrid jump blues/New Orleans R&B feel (Imperial would use the same approach with Roy Brown around this time). It's not his very best work, but even at its slightest this is pleasant. It's most effective, however, when the Crescent City touches are muted in favor of slicing straight-ahead blues riffing, as on the instrumental "Blues Before Dawn." Another obscure cut, "Do Unto Others," is nothing less than a revelation, boasting a light-years-ahead-of-its-time opening riff that sounds almost identical to the blast of notes that opens the Beatles' "Revolution," cut nearly 15 years later. *—Richie Unterberger*

Early Hour Blues / Jun. 22, 1999 / Blind Pig ♦♦♦♦

A West Coast blues guitar hero, Crayton died shortly after these sessions, done primarily with Rod and Honey Piazza's band, or with jazz pianist Llew Matthews' quartet. The two dates show Crayton could do it all. Jump blues, hard or straight blues, and boogie were all easily played. It's that unmistakable T-Bone Walker influence, a stinging, swinging single line or chunky, chortling chord progressions that made Crayton stand out among the crowded blues guitar landscape. He was a one-of-a kind player, and this CD is not only his final testament, but a solid exclamation point on the career of a true American music legend. Crayton also proved to be a pretty good singer. His soulful rendering of the hit "Send for Me" is sincere and believable. "Barefootin'" might be a throwaway, but he really sends up the B.B. King evergreen "When I'm Wrong." Steaming instrumentals with big horn charts swing hard as on "You Know Yeah," Eddie Taylor's "E.T. Blues," "Red Rose Boogie," and the short horn-fired rave-up "Head'n'Home." The Piazzas and Matthews really know how to support a star, and their work is as credible as any. Additional kudos to Crayton's wife, Esther, who wrote six of these 11 cuts, and was always a major factor in his repertoire. On some of his solos, Crayton is astounding; on the rest, his guitar is merely spectacular. Though 14 years late (Crayton died in 1985) and only 45 minutes short on this CD, this is a precious document of one of originals of blues guitar, and a reminder that although he was relatively obscure, he had many fans who knew what the real deal was. For blues scholars, this is an artist, like Freddie King, Otis Rush, and T-Bone, well worth studying and relishing. *—Michael G. Nastos*

Modern Legacy, Vol. 2: Blues Guitar Magic / Jun. 26, 2000 / Ace ♦♦♦♦

As a companion volume to *The Modern Legacy Vol. 1* (also on Ace), this wraps up the label's comprehensive overview of Crayton's stint with Modern Records. With material from the end of the '40s and the early '50s, about half of the 25-track CD was drawn from 1949-1952 singles, filled out by LP cuts and four previously unreleased items. This might not be quite as good as volume one, recycling some of the same ideas a few times (something, of course, found on many blues albums). But it's in the same league, showing Crayton to be a capable and often exciting performer in both the uptempo and ballad styles, and on both vocal and instrumental tracks. The highlights, naturally, are the guitar solos, as fiery and innovative as any being done in blues and R&B at the time, even if Crayton has not received the wide recognition granted some of his peers. There's the exhilarating staccato picks on the high end of the neck on the instrumental "Poppa Stoppa," for instance, and his facility for alternating speedy solo lines with crunching, thick chords that rapidly changed keys. "Long After Hours" starts off with an unholy burst of thick distorted chords that no doubt caused some turntable needles to shudder violently upon its first release. Crayton was not just about boogying blues, as demonstrated here by his biggest hit, "I Love You So," a ballad that made the R&B Top Ten in 1949, and "Have You Lost Your Love for Me," which has an almost doo wop-pop influence. Sound quality varies—sometimes this sounds right off the master tape, at other times there's surface noise—but is about as good as could be given the condition of the source materials. *—Richie Unterberger*

Cream

f. 1966, England, **db.** 1968, London, England

Group / British Psychedelia, British Blues, Psychedelic, Hard Rock, Blues-Rock

Although Cream were only together for a little more than two years, their influence was immense, both during their late-'60s peak and in the years following their breakup. Cream were the first top group to truly exploit the power-trio format, in the process laying the foundation for much blues-rock and hard rock of the '60s and '70s. It was with Cream, too, that guitarist Eric Clapton truly became an international superstar. Critical revisionists have tagged the band as overrated, citing the musicians' emphasis upon flash, virtuosity, and showmanship at the expense of taste and focus. This was sometimes true of their live shows in particular, but in reality the best of their studio recordings were excellent fusions of blues, pop, and psychedelia, with concise original material outnumbering the bloated blues jams and overlong solos.

Cream could be viewed as the first rock supergroup to become superstars, although none of the three members were that well-known when the band formed in mid-1966. Eric Clapton had the biggest reputation, having established himself as a guitar hero first with the Yardbirds, and then in a more blues-intensive environment with John Mayall's Bluesbreakers. (In the States, however, he was all but unknown, having left the Yardbirds before "For Your Love" made the American Top Ten.) Bassist/singer Jack Bruce and drummer Ginger Baker had both been in the Graham Bond Organization, an underrated British R&B combo that drew extensively upon the jazz backgrounds of the musicians. Bruce had also been, very briefly, a member of the Bluesbreakers along with Clapton, and also briefly a member of Manfred Mann, when he became especially eager to pay the rent.

All three of the musicians yearned to break free of the confines of the standard rock/R&B/blues group, in a unit that would allow them greater instrumental and improvisational freedom, somewhat in the mold of a jazz outfit. Eric Clapton's stunning guitar solos would get much of the adulation, yet Bruce was at least as responsible for shaping the group's sound, singing most of the material in his rich voice. He also wrote their best original compositions, sometimes in collaboration with outside lyricist Pete Brown.

At first Cream's focus was electrified and amped-up traditional blues, which dominated their first album, *Fresh Cream*, which made the British Top Ten in early 1967. Originals like "N.S.U." and "I Feel Free" gave notice that the band was capable of moving beyond the blues, and they truly found their voice on *Disraeli Gears* in late 1967, which consisted mostly of group-penned songs. Here they fashioned invigorating, sometimes beguiling hard-driving psychedelic pop, which included plenty of memorable melodies and effective harmonies along with the expected crunching riffs. "Strange Brew," "Dance the Night Away," "Tales of Brave Ulysses," and "S.W.L.A.B.R." are all among their best tracks, and the album broke the band bigtime in the States, reaching the Top Five. It also generated their first big U.S. hit single, "Sunshine of Your Love," which was based around one of the most popular hard-rock riffs of the '60s.

With the double album *Wheels of Fire*, Cream topped the American charts in 1968, establishing themselves alongside the Beatles and Hendrix as one of the biggest rock acts in the world. The record itself was a more erratic affair than *Disraeli Gears*, perhaps dogged by the decision to present separate discs of studio and live material; the concert tracks in particular did much to establish their reputation, for good or ill, for stretching songs way past the ten-minute mark on-stage. The majestically doomy "White Room" gave Cream another huge American single, and the group were firmly established as one of the biggest live draws of any kind. Their decision to disband in late 1968—at a time when they were seemingly on top of the world—came as a shock to most of the rock audience.

Cream's short lifespan, however, was in hindsight unsurprising given the considerable talents, ambitions, and egos of each of its members. Clapton in particular was tired of blowing away listeners with sheer power, and wanted to explore more subtle directions. After a farewell tour of the States, the band broke up in November 1968. In 1969, however, they were in a sense bigger than ever—a posthumous album featuring both studio and live material, *Goodbye*, made number two, highlighted by the haunting Eric Clapton-George Harrison composition "Badge," which remains one of Cream's most beloved tracks.

Clapton and Baker would quickly resurface in 1969 as half of another short-lived supergroup, Blind Faith, and Clapton of course went on to one of the longest and most successful careers of anyone in the rock business. Bruce and Baker never attained nearly as high a profile after leaving Cream, but both have kept busy in the ensuing decades with various interesting projects in the fields of rock, jazz, and experimental music. —*Richie Unterberger*

Fresh Cream / Dec. 1966 / Polydor ✦✦✦✦

All of the raw material that would make Cream one of the finest bands of their era is present here on this, their debut release. *Fresh Cream* contains the band's signature mixture of psychedelic pop songs and blues-rock improvisations. The best of one extreme is the opener "I Feel Free" (absent on the original, British release of the record). It is a '60s pop gem, with a catchy opening and a haunting verse. This excellent track was made present on the American release of *Fresh Cream* in January of 1967 at the expense of the omission of "Spoonful." An excellent example of Eric Clapton's blues mastery, this reading of the Willie Dixon classic is ultimately the high point of the record. Not to downplay the contributions of Jack Bruce and Ginger Baker, but it is Clapton's incendiary playing that really makes this blues come alive. This is where his (and, by extension, Cream's) muse really lies: in the extended, high-energy, improvised explorations of traditional blues tunes. However, Clapton seems a bit lost on some of the more pop-oriented fare; his rhythm guitar playing especially is often atrocious. Jack Bruce not only handles most of the vocal chores with panache, but also plays very innovative bass, using it both more aggressively and more melodically than most players of his generation were accustomed to doing. Also not to be missed is Bruce's harmonica playing, showcased on the bass-less "Rollin' and Tumblin'." Ginger Baker's heavy drumming is notable throughout. His distinct, idiosyncratic style is best demonstrated by the drum solo on his own "Toad," wherein he gives his drums such a primal pounding that the listener is not sure whether to laugh at his caveman-like intensity or to sit back in awe at the unrelenting assault. Either way, it is extremely entertaining, and is one of the best moments of the record. All in all, *Fresh Cream* is a fine first album, but Baker, Bruce, and Clapton would all go on to bigger and better, both together with Cream and separately with other projects. —*Daniel Gioffre*

Disraeli Gears / Nov. 1967 / Polydor ✦✦✦✦✦

The threesome of Jack Bruce, Ginger Baker, and legendary guitarist Eric Clapton forming the band Cream was a monumental effort of jazz, blues, and psychedelic rock during the British rock period of the late '60s. Cream, with their raw fury of intense sound, was renowned for their rare talent of taking songs of complex arrangements and making them an act of spontaneous beauty during live shows. *Disraeli Gears*, their second release, was an essential landmark recording that brought listeners to the direction they were soon to take with *Wheels of Fire*. Taking on a circus-spinning arsenal of sounds and effects, Cream's fashionable art is a blend of highly sustained drenched distortion, rampant percussion, and a kaleidoscope of various musical textures and colors, both in melody and rhythm. Each of *Disraeli Gears'* list of 11 tunes is original in format, con-

taining it own unique brands of dashing blues-laden guitar riffs by Clapton, as well as thick bass lines and smashing drum leads. Highlights of the record feature Clapton's awe-inspiring and soul-gripping guitar leads, including hits such as "Sunshine of Your Love" and "Tales of Brave Ulysses." The latter is a magical poem laced into a line of mesmerizing chordal changes. *Disraeli Gears* is a definitive staple of early British rock and a sensational addition to the avid classic rock listener. —*Shawn Haney*

Wheels of Fire / Jun. 1968 / Polydor ✦✦✦✦

Wheels of Fire was a two-album set, one disc recorded in the studio, the second disc recorded on stage in San Francisco. Side three contains the definitive live version of what became Clapton's signature piece, Robert Johnson's "Crossroads," plus a version of "Spoonful" that clocks in just short of 17 minutes. On such pieces, Cream approached blues-based rock with a jazz aesthetic, using the song as a framework to begin and end a performance. The strength of the performance is in the improvisation. When it worked, as it does on "Spoonful," they were brilliant. When it didn't, as on "Traintime" and "Toad," the band became excess incarnate. The studio disc contained their second Top Ten single, Jack Bruce's "White Room," as well as a stunning cover of Albert King's "Born Under a Bad Sign." Other tracks, particularly those written by Ginger Baker, do not hold up. —*Rob Bowman*

Goodbye / Jan. 1969 / Polydor ✦✦✦

Like *Wheels of Fire* before it, *Goodbye* showcases both sides of Cream: that of a late-'60s pop band and that of an unchained blues-rock powerhouse. The live tracks on side one are highly improvised affairs, with even "I'm So Glad" receiving an extended guitar solo from Clapton. How he is able to play such laid-back and tasty blues over the relentlessly aggressive Jack Bruce and Ginger Baker is a mystery. In fact, the real superstar of these recordings is Bruce, whose upfront, distorted bass playing kicks Baker along as much as it challenges Clapton. At times it sounds more like a battle than anything else, battles that Bruce, with his tenacity and pure drive, almost always wins. The ominous neo-blues of "Politician" and the more traditional "Sitting on Top of the World" close out this extraordinary selection of live material. Side two opens with one of Cream's finest pop songs: "Badge." Co-written by George Harrison, this track features more great bass from Bruce as well as some phenomenal singing. The remaining tracks on side two, "Doing That Scrapyard Thing" and "What a Bringdown," aren't quite up to the standards of the other material, but what would a Cream album be without some throwaways? Luckily the other tracks are so strong as to raise it to the status of a must-have. A fitting way to go out, *Goodbye* captures all that is good about Cream, and is one of the band's proudest moments. —*Daniel Gioffre*

Live Cream, Vol. 1 / Apr. 1970 / Polydor ✦✦✦

Cream was a band born to the stage. This is their most consistently brilliant album. Four of the five cuts appeared on *Fresh Cream*. The fifth, "Lawdy Mama," is a traditional blues piece that makes its first appearance here. All but "Lawdy Mama" are given extended jazz-based treatment. The dialogue among the three musicians as the jams develop is fascinating. Foreground and background seem to dissolve as all three musicians take charge, using the full range of their instruments. Performances like this single-handedly raised the stakes of musicianship in rock. —*Rob Bowman*

Live Cream, Vol. 2 / Mar. 1972 / Polydor ✦✦✦

A great lost curio, *Live Cream, Vol. 2* is not only vastly superior to its volume one predecessor in every way, it is also one of the greatest Cream albums in their slim catalog. Utilizing—for the time—state-of-the-art mobile recording equipment, the sonic excellence on this album surely must be acknowledged to the engineers: Tom Dowd and Bill Halverson. The feeling that you are in the front row is very much in evidence, and this is largely due to their ability to capture the band's live fury with clarity. As for the performances, this record captures the band at their peak. The group made their reputation as a live act with epic, lengthy jams that verged on jazz, and indeed there is one example of this on the 13-plus-minute closing cut, "Steppin' Out." On record, this occasionally made for tough listening. But on the rest of this album, compact, four- to five-minute versions of "Deserted Cities of the Heart" and "Tales of Brave Ulysses," among others, make it a vital, intense, and enjoyable listen that is ultimately rewarding. —*Matthew Greenwald*

Klook's Kleet '66 / 1995 / (no label) ✦✦✦✦✦

A significant addition to the pool of unreleased Cream material, this has eight alternate versions/outtakes from their earliest sessions in the summer of 1966, as well as a different version of "Lawdy Mama" from 1967, a Falstaff beer commercial, and seven songs recorded live at the Klook's Kleet club in 1966. It's the studio outtakes that you'd want this for; the fidelity is phenomenal, at the same level of an official release. Contains alternate versions of many of the songs from their first album, with differences ranging from minor to major. "Sweet Wine," with a long extended feedback solo from Clapton, is particularly noteworthy, and "You Make Me Feel," an odd and frankly none too impressive bit of English pop, is an original that would never be released by the group. The liner notes say that the Kloot's Kleet acetates were recorded for consideration as a live album, but it's hard to see how that would have happened, as the fidelity is tinny and the vocals muffled. More in line with the standards of typical live bootlegs of the era, it does offer serious fans the chance to hear (approximately) how they sounded on-stage at their inception, with a few staples of their early repertoire ("N.S.U.," "Crossroads") and a couple less done-to-death numbers ("Meet Me in the Bottom," "Steppin' Out"). —*Richie Unterberger*

★ **The Very Best of Cream** / May 9, 1995 / Polydor/Chronicles ✦✦✦✦✦

There have been many compilations drawn from the four albums Cream originally released between 1966 and 1969. But the one most commonly available since the early '80s was the ten-track *Strange Brew: The Very Best of Cream* (1983) (Polydor 811 639), a bare-bones collection focusing on the group's hit singles. Note, then, that this album, despite the similar title, is a newly compiled 1995 CD/cassette containing all of the recordings on *Strange Brew*, plus ten more. It is thus the most comprehensive Cream anthology on the market, including all the group's essential tracks on a single disc with superior sound in a package containing good annotations. *—William Ruhlmann*

Those Were the Days / Sep. 23, 1997 / Polydor ♦♦♦♦
Those Were the Days is an ambitious four-disc, 63-track box set that divides Cream's career into two halves. The first two discs feature every studio track the group ever released, plus a handful of unreleased cuts, alternate takes and rarities. The other two discs are devoted to live material, which is segued together in an attempt to recreate the "ideal" Cream concert. It's a remarkably comprehensive collection, complete with an extensive booklet and remastered sound, yet it doesn't reveal any new insights about Cream, nor does it offer any invaluable rarities. Therefore, it's only for diehard collectors or listeners wanting to acquire the entire Cream catalog at once; casual fans will be satisfied with individual albums or greatest-hits collections. *—Stephen Thomas Erlewine*

Steppin' Out / Invasion Unlimited ♦♦♦
The best unreleased Cream to circulate widely, this collects 18 performances for the BBC between 1966 and 1968. Mostly very good sound, these fine straight-ahead renditions include most of the best tracks from their early albums, with the notable absence of their two biggest hits, "White Room" and "Sunshine Of Your Love." The two versions of the instrumental title track, one of Clapton's prime showcases in his Bluesbreakers days, are special highlights. These BBC sessions are available under a number of different guises; this particular package is the most thorough. *—Richie Unterberger*

Arthur "Big Boy" Crudup

b. Aug. 24, 1905, Forest, MS, **d.** Mar. 28, 1974, Nassawadox, VA
Vocals, Songwriter, Guitar / Delta Blues, Electric Delta Blues, Electric Blues, R&B
Arthur Crudup may well have been Elvis Presley's favorite bluesman. The swivel-hipped rock god recorded no less than three of "Big Boy's" Victor classics during his seminal rockabilly heyday: "That's All Right Mama" (Elvis' Sun debut in 1954), "So Glad You're Mine," and "My Baby Left Me." Often lost in all the hubbub surrounding Presley's classic covers are Crudup's own contributions to the blues lexicon. He didn't sound much like anyone else, and that makes him an innovator, albeit a rather rudimentary guitarist (he didn't even pick up the instrument until he was 30 years old).

Around 1940, Crudup migrated to Chicago from Mississippi. Times were tough at first; he was playing for spare change on the streets and living in a packing crate underneath an elevated train track when powerful RCA/Bluebird producer Lester Melrose dropped a few coins in Crudup's hat. Melrose hired Crudup to play a party that 1941 night at Tampa Red's house attended by the cream of Melrose's stable: Big Bill Broonzy, Lonnie Johnson, Lil Green. A decidedly tough crowd to impress—but Crudup overcame his nervousness with flying colors. By September of 1941, he was himself an RCA artist.

Crudup pierced the uppermost reaches of the R&B lists during the mid-'40s with "Rock Me Mama," "Who's Been Foolin' You," "Keep Your Arms Around Me," "So Glad You're Mine," and "Ethel Mae." He cut the original "That's All Right" in 1946 backed by his usual rhythm section of bassist Ransom Knowling and drummer Judge Riley, but it wasn't a national hit at the time. Crudup remained a loyal and prolific employee of Victor until 1954, when a lack of tangible rewards for his efforts soured Crudup on Nipper (he had already cut singles in 1952 for Trumpet disguised as Elmer James and for Checker as Percy Lee Crudup).

In 1961, Crudup surfaced after a long layoff with an album for Bobby Robinson's Harlem-based Fire logo dominated by remakes of his Bluebird hits. Another lengthy hiatus preceded Delmark boss Bob Koester's following the tip of Big Joe Williams to track down the elusive legend (Crudup had drifted into contract farm labor work in the interim). Happily, the guitarist's sound hadn't been dimmed by Father Time: his late-'60s work for Delmark rang true as he was reunited with Knowling (Willie Dixon also handled bass duties on some of his sides). Finally, Crudup began to make some decent money, playing various blues and folk festivals for appreciative crowds for a few years prior to his 1974 death. *—Bill Dahl*

That's All Right Mama / 1961 / Relic ♦♦♦
After a long studio hiatus, Crudup reentered the studio in 1961 at the behest of producer Bobby Robinson of Fire/Fury Records. The results of their brief liaison show that Crudup hadn't altered his approach one whit during the layoff—these remakes of his RCA classics sound amazingly similar to the originals. There are a few unfamiliar titles aboard this 18-song collection to make it all the more worthwhile. *—Bill Dahl*

Mean Ol' Frisco / 1962 / Collectables ♦♦♦♦♦
These are his '60s Fire sessions. It fits into the second stage of his recording career, with *Look on Yonder's Wall* and *Coal Black Mare*. *—Barry Lee Pearson*

Look on Yonder's Wall / 1969 / Delmark ♦♦♦
This late-'60s Delmark session represents the third stage of his career history. *—Barry Lee Pearson*

☆ **The Father of Rock & Roll** / 1972 / RCA ♦♦♦♦♦
The best collection of Crudup's seminal '40s and '50s Bluebird recordings, including the original version of "That's All Right Mama." *—Barry Lee Pearson*

★ **That's All Right Mama** / 1992 / Bluebird/RCA ♦♦♦♦♦
This may not have been where rock & roll all started, but it's very likely where Elvis Presley's knowledge of blues began: 22 tracks dating from 1941 to 1954 by the guitarist whose "That's All Right" proved Presley's ticket to Sun Records stardom. Crudup was fairly limited on guitar—his accompaniment is rudimentary at best—but his songs were uncommonly sturdy (Elvis also covered "So Glad You're Mine" and "My Baby Left Me," both here in their original incarnations) and his vocals strong. *—Bill Dahl*

Meets the Master Blues Bassists / 1994 / Delmark ♦♦♦
Delmark boss Bob Koester brought Crudup back from obscurity one more time during the late '60s, and by golly, he still sounded pretty much the same. The 1968-1969 waxings comprising this disc date from 1968-1969 and team the veteran guitarist with two upright bassists of legendary status: Willie Dixon and Crudup's longtime cohort Ransom Knowling. A few remakes are aboard, but plenty of new material as well. *—Bill Dahl*

Complete Recorded Works, Vol. 1 (1941–1946) / Jun. 2, 1994 / Document ♦♦♦♦
Arthur "Big Boy" Crudup was an important transition figure between '30s Chicago blues, early R&B, and rock & roll, being an early influence on Elvis Presley. On this first of four Document CDs that reissue all of his recordings from the '40s and '50s, Crudup mostly performs duets with either Joe McCoy or Ransom Knowling on bass or Melvin Draper, Charles Saunders, or Jump Jackson on drums. The first session is unusual in that Crudup is heard on acoustic guitar, but he was playing electric by 1942 and was largely distinctive from the start. Among the more memorable of the 24 numbers (which conclude with a pair of trio selections with Ransom Knowling and drummer Judge Riley) are "Black Pony Blues," "Standing at My Window," "Gonna Follow My Baby," "Give Me a 32-20," "Mean Old Frisco," "Raised to My Hand," "Cool Disposition," and "That's Your Red Wagon." All four of these Crudup discs are easily recommended to blues collectors. *—Scott Yanow*

Complete Recorded Works, Vol. 2 (1946–1949) / Jun. 2, 1994 / Document ♦♦♦♦♦
Arthur "Big Boy" Crudup's "That's All Right" (which he first recorded in 1946) became a hit for Elvis Presley eight years later. Strangely enough, three of the four songs that Crudup recorded on Sept. 6, 1946 all have the same "That's All Right" melody, although each utilize different lyrics. (Crudup was clearly more talented as a lyricist than as a composer.) Nevertheless, he is heard in prime form on the five sessions from 1946-1949, all of which have him joined by the driving bassist Ransom Knowling and drummer Judge Riley. The trio digs into such numbers (in addition to "That's All Right") as Crudup's "After Hours," "Gonna Be Some Changes Made" (which has Big Boy using the words of the standard "There'll Be Some Changes Made" but turning the song into a blues), "Hey Mama, Everything's All Right," "Dust My Broom," and "Shout Sister Shout." Timeless blues. *—Scott Yanow*

Complete Recorded Works, Vol. 3 (1949–1952) / Jun. 2, 1994 / Document ♦♦♦♦
The third of four Arthur "Big Boy" Crudup Document CDs (which completely reissue his recordings from the '40s and '50s) features the singer/guitarist in trio settings, mostly with bassist Ransom Knowling and drummer Judge Riley. Crudup's expressive vocals and the driving rhythm section make such songs as "She's Just Like Caldenia," "Oo-Wee Darling," "Anytime Is the Right Time," "Love Me Mama," "Where Did You Stay Last Night," and "Goin' Back to Georgia" quite memorable. Listening to these consistently exciting performances gives listeners strong clues as to where rock & roll came from. *—Scott Yanow*

Complete Recorded Works, Vol. 4 (1952–1954) / Jun. 2, 1994 / Document ♦♦♦

After Hours / 1997 / Camden ♦♦♦
After Hours is an uneven collection that combines Crudup's RCA material (recorded between 1941 and 1954) with material he recorded for Fire in the '60s. There's a few essential items here, but in general it's an ill-conceived collection that doesn't serve as a good overview of Crudup's career. *—Stephen Thomas Erlewine*

Arthur Crudup: The Essential / Aug. 7, 2001 / Classic Blues ♦♦♦♦

Cuby & the Blizzards

f. 1965, Grollo, Holland
Group / Blues-Rock
Although unknown to the English-speaking market, Cuby & the Blizzards have been one of Holland's top blues bands since the mid-'60s. Some of their early singles had a beat/punk orientation, particularly "Stumble & Fall" and "Your Body Not Your Soul," both of which would be reissued on various Dutch beat compilations a few decades later. They quickly settled into a straighter blues groove, however. Their claims to fame in the larger rock/pop world are that they briefly backed Van Morrison in the gap between his departure from Them and the beginning of his solo career, although details of the association remain murky; also, at one point lead guitarist Eelco Gelling was asked to join John Mayall's Bluebreakers, although he declined. *—Richie Unterberger*

Desolation / 1966 / Philips ♦♦♦
By the time of their first LP, the group were already sliding toward a straighter blues outlook than had been explored on their more R&B/pop-flavored early singles. For that reason, it might disappoint mid-'60s beat fans looking for something wilder and catchier. As a blues group they were competent, but the execution here is kind of lugubrious, and not up to the level of the best British blues acts with a similar repertoire. *—Richie Unterberger*

Best of 66–68 / 1968 / Philips ♦♦♦♦
The Best of 66-68 is a solid collection of Cuby & the Blizzards' best material from the mid-'60s. Although the material was fairly uneven, lead guitarist Eelco Gelling often shines, and the collection may be of interest to hardcore British blues fans. *—Thom Owens*

● **Universal Masters Collection** / Aug. 27, 2002 / Universal International ♦♦♦♦

Shannon Curfman

b. Jul. 31, 1985, Fargo, ND
Vocals, Guitar / Contemporary Blues, Blues-Rock
Teen blues-rock phenom Shannon Curfman was born July 31, 1985, in Fargo, ND. After picking up the guitar she began her performing career at age seven, forming her own band three years later; opening stints for acts including Tab Benoit, Delbert McClinton, the Fabulous Thunderbirds and the Steve Miller Band earned Curfman a growing following throughout the midwest, and after relocating to Minneapolis she released her

debut album, *Loud Guitars, Big Suspicions*, in 1998. Major label Arista reissued the disc a year later. —*Jason Ankeny*

● **Loud Guitars, Big Suspicions** / Sep. 28, 1999 / Arista ✦✦✦

It's easy to call Shannon Curfman the female equivalent of such hot-shot guitar-slingers as Johnny Lang, especially since Lang not only appears on her debut *Loud Guitars, Big Suspicions*, he co-wrote a few songs with her as well. And it is true that Curfman does play modern blues-rock that recalls Lang's, but it's not a direct copy, it's simply informed by the same influences. After all, *Loud Guitars, Big Suspicions* makes it clear that Curfman has her own voice, one that's a little bolder and gutsier than Lang's. Throughout the record, her singing is impassioned and playing is firey. She does take the occasional stumble, but that's usually because the material is a little weak or undistinguished. That doesn't happen too often, though, and even when it does, it's not enough to make *Loud Guitars* anything less than a top-notch debut. [*Loud Guitars, Big Suspicions* was initially released as an independent album. It was re-released by Arista in September 1999 with a different cover and mix, along with some new songs.] —*Stephen Thomas Erlewine*

Daddy Stovepipe (Johnny Watson)

b. Apr. 12, 1867, Mobile, AL, **d.** Nov. 1, 1963

Guitar / Prewar Blues, Acoustic Chicago Blues

The given name of Daddy Stovepipe was Johnny Watson; among other aliases he worked under during his long life were "Jimmy Watson" and the "Rev. Alfred Pitts." Born in Mobile, AL in 1867, Daddy Stovepipe may well have been the earliest-born blues performer to record. His career began around 1900 in Mexico as a twelve-string guitarist in early mariachi bands. Ultimately Daddy Stovepipe established himself as an entertainer with the Rabbit's Foot Minstrels, a southern traveling tent show that also gave rise to the careers of Ma Rainey, Jaybird Coleman, Brownie McGhee, Louis Jordan, Jim Jackson, and others. Settling into the role of a one-man band, Daddy Stovepipe worked as an itinerant street musician, centering around Maxwell Street in Chicago. On May 10, 1924 Daddy Stovepipe made his way to Richmond, Indiana and cut the first pair of 16 extant tracks that he would record in the 78 era. These are indeed among the most primitive blues performances on record, with "Sundown Blues" played in a jaunty 6/8 time. In July 1927 Gennett's mobile unit recorded Daddy Stovepipe in Birmingham, Alabama, with a whistler named Whistlin' Pete, about whom nothing else is known. Issued as by "Sunny Jim and Whistlin' Joe," these sides are even more of a guilty pleasure than the first two, despite their extreme rarity.

In 1931 Daddy Stovepipe was recorded by the ARC mobile facility in Chicago for Vocalion's race series. Here he was partnered by Mississippi Sarah, in real life Sarah Watson and "Mrs." Daddy Stovepipe. She was a good singer and an expert jug player, and the married couple's humorous back and forth banter make the 12 sides they made together a very special side attraction in recorded blues. Eight titles were made by the duo in Chicago in 1931, and the remaining four followed in 1935 for Bluebird. Afterward, the "Stovepipes" settled down in Greenville, Mississippi and Daddy Stovepipe went to work away from music, but Sarah Watson's unexpected death in 1937 sent her husband back out on the road.

In subsequent years it appears that Daddy Stovepipe was playing in the American Southwest and in Mexico. For a time in the '40s Daddy Stovepipe played in zydeco bands in Louisiana and Texas, and by 1948 he was back up on Maxwell Street, where he was working at the time of his rediscovery. He reappears once again before the microphone in 1960, recording such unpromising fare as his versions of "Tennessee Waltz" and the jump tune "Monkey and the Baboon." By that point he was 93 years old and not sounding particularly great. Daddy Stovepipe died just three years later after surgery to remove his gall bladder led to bronchial pneumonia. He had been born during the first days of reconstruction, and died the same month as President John F. Kennedy.

Johnny "Daddy Stovepipe" Watson should not be confused with Cincinnati-based one-man-band Sam Jones, who recorded under the odd name of Stovepipe No. 1. Nor should he be confused with McKinley Peebles, who recorded as Sweet Papa Stovepipe. — *Uncle Dave Lewis*

Larry Dale

b. 1923, Texas

Guitar / East Coast Blues, Electric Blues, R&B

A New York session guitarist who's backed some of the city's top artists, Larry Dale also made a handful of fine singles as a singer during the '50s and early '60s.

Taking initial inspiration on his guitar from B.B. King during the early '50s, Dale made some solid sides as a leader for Groove in 1954 (including "You Better Heed My Warning"/"Please Tell Me") with a band that included another local guitar great, Mickey Baker, and pianist Champion Jack Dupree. Dale was a frequent studio cohort of the rollicking pianist, playing his axe on all four of Dupree's 1956-1958 sessions for RCA's Groove and Vik subsidiaries, and under his legal handle of Ennis Lowery, on the definitive Dupree LP, 1958's *Blues from the Gutter*, for Atlantic. Dale also recorded with saxist Paul Williams during the mid-'50s for Jax, providing the vocal on "Shame Shame Shame."

Dale worked the New York club circuit during the '50s with pianist Bob Gaddy, who had a fairly successful single for Old Town in 1955, "Operator." From 1956 to 1958, Dale played with bandleader Cootie Williams before rejoining Gaddy. At last report, the two still played together.

Dale made most of his best sides as a leader when the decade turned. For "Glover Records," he waxed the storming party blues "Let the Doorbell Ring" and an equally potent "Big Muddy" in 1960, then revived Sticks McGhee's "Drinkin' Wine-Spo-Dee-O-Dee" in 1962 on Atlantic. Alas, none of those worthy sides made much of a splash. — *Bill Dahl*

Dallas String Band

Group / Prewar Country Blues

The music of the Dallas String Band has been called pre-blues as well as proto-blues. The group has been referred to as the only black string band in history and an early Texas country band, sometimes in the same paragraph, often after being credited with erasing all color lines in American musical history. Enough lies are told about the group to resemble another great cover-up in Dallas history, the one with the grassy knoll and the book depository. Left behind as key evidence are the dozen recordings the group made for Columbia beginning in the late '20s, as well as the solo activities of three key members. The auxiliary membership of the group is where the action really is in terms of impressive history, as the names of both Blind Lemon Jefferson and T-Bone Walker can be dropped. Although neither of these artists show up anywhere near a Dallas String Band recording, the group's place in Texas blues history is as secure as the crown jewels. And the mighty state of Texas takes its blues history seriously, perhaps as seriously as the Brits take their royalty's sparkling goodies. Texas blues fans will be happy to brag that independent studios and labels in Dallas were busy recording blues before anyone ever heard of the Delta or Chicago. Flashing back through Dallas blues history, one runs into the Dallas String Band before the year 1927 is out. In 1929, the year Blind Lemon Jefferson died and was buried in Wortham, TX, the Dallas String Band was still cutting records in their hometown. Meanwhile, T-Bone Walker was recording his first sides under the name of Oak Cliff T-Bone. The Dallas String Band provided a link between Jefferson and Walker, considered two of the state's great blues artists from the acoustic and electric eras, respectively. The group, which was billed as Coley Jones & the Dallas String Band on at least one of the original 78s, also included Sam Harris on guitar and Marco Washington on bass.

While Jones did the most extensive recordings on his own of the members, his material is also the most uneven. He began his career on guitar with a background in minstrel shows, but is considered something of a hack on this somewhat typical blues instrument. Switching to the mandolin, he kicked up quite a stir and developed a highly original style in the context of the Dallas String Band. The rarity of black blues- and swing-flavored mandolin playing is part of the attraction; other blues mandolinists include Yank Rachell, Johnny Shines, and Johnny Young. Washington and Harris had played together in the Tennessee-based band of Sonny Boy Williamson I (or John Lee Williamson), and the former artist was one of the originators of a blues bass style in which the instrument was more felt than articulated.

The Dallas String Band also had other rotating members and played on the streets of many North Texas towns. Like the similar East Texas Serenaders, the Dallas String Band probed outside the norm of square dance keys such as G, D, and A, playing in technically more difficult keys such as F. Recorded documentation of the group is wonderful, but apparently only hints at the group's full power. Their lineup on record of two mandolins, guitar, and bass omits the violin, clarinet, and trumpet that were reported to have been included on most of the band's live dates.

By the time the group had evolved into the plain and simple Coley Jones String Band in the early '30s, Harris was out, replaced by none other than Walker—and this was essentially the group where the axeman really got his start. But that doesn't make it the only connection between the Dallas String Band and Walker. There was a family connection with Washington as well, although exactly what seems in dispute. The bassist is sometimes identified as Walker's uncle and sometimes as his stepfather. The young Walker also used to work as a lead boy for Jefferson, sometimes leading him to Dallas String Band jam sessions where he was spotted playing from time to time. The Dallas String Band's most well-known tunes are "Dallas Rag," which is a popular number among fancy-pants guitar pickers such as Stefan Grossman, and "Hokum Blues"; indeed, the latter title represents the first use of the word "hokum" in a blues song title and as for what exactly "hokum" is, a good example can be found within the song itself in the form of this joke involving Jones. "Say Coley, can you sing?" one of the other bandmembers asks. To which Coley Jones responds, "No, I lost my voice in jail. I'm always behind a few bars and can never get a key." "Chasin' Rainbows" is yet another classic original from the band and a song that has been used as an album title by both Robert Crumb and the Double Decker String Band. Jones can be heard on one of his better solo efforts on Harry Smith's 1952 folk song collection *Anthology of American Folk Music*. — *Eugene Chadbourne*

● **Tell Her** / 1992 / EMI Latin ✦✦✦✦

Julius Daniels

b. 1903, Denmark, SC, **d.** 1947

Vocals, Guitar / Piedmont Blues, Acoustic Blues

A South Carolina bluesmen who may have been the first in the Piedmont to record, Julius Daniels appeared on at least four sides for Victor during the late '20s. Born in Denmark, SC, Daniels lived in the Piedmont region his entire life, later in Pineville and then in Charlotte, NC. As was typical in the area, his concerns were rural ("Can't Put the Bridle on the Mule This Time") and nautical ("My Mama Was a Sailor"). His songs are scattered across several compilations, including Harry Smith's spellbinding 1952 folksong compendium *Anthology of American Folk Music* as well as *Raggin' the Blues: Essential East Coast Blues* on Indigo and *Songsters & Saints: Vocal Traditions on Race Records* on Matchbox Bluesmasters. — *John Bush*

Billy Davenport

b. Apr. 23, 1931, **d.** Dec. 24, 1999

Drums / Chicago Blues

Drummer Billy Davenport was born April 23, 1931, in Chicago. His parents were sharecroppers from rural Alabama who migrated to Chicago in 1928. He began learning drums at the age of six, after finding an old pair of drumsticks in an alley behind the Twin Door Lounge on the South side of Chicago. A natural musician, his parents soon recognized his gift and encouraged him. He started out playing on tin cans after seeing a movie about Gene Krupa. He also admired Sid Catlett. He took drum lessons while in the Boy Scouts and went on to play jazz in high school, in the R.O.T.C., in swing bands, and various venues in the Chicago area. In 1949, he studied music for one year at Midwestern School of Music in Chicago. He played with Bob Hadley, Leo Parker, Slam Stewart, Neal Anderson, Tampa Red, Sonny Stitt, and others. He got to hear everyone live—Billie Holiday, Charlie Parker, Billy Eckstine, Gene Ammons—all the greats. His drum influences included Art Blakey, Louis Bellson, and Max Roach.

From 1951 to 1955, Davenport was in the U.S. Navy, in the Mechanic Drum and Bugle Corps. In the mid-'50s, the jazz scene was on the decline and Davenport turned to blues gigs to pay the rent. In the late '50s, he played with Billy Boy Arnold, Dusty Brown, and Freddy King. In 1960 he played with the Ernie Fields Orchestra and joined Otis Rush in 1961, working with him for about a year. He also worked with harp player Little Mack Simmons, Syl Johnson, Junior Wells, Mighty Joe Young, James Cotton, Muddy Waters, and Howlin' Wolf.

He met Paul Butterfield at Pepper's Lounge in 1964 and sat in with them at their gig at Big Johns on Chicago's North side. When Butterfield's drummer Sam Lay became ill late in 1965, Butterfield called on Davenport to join the group and tour with them. Davenport's jazz background brought a different quality to the Butterfield group. It was at this time that Bloomfield was absorbing Eastern scales and with the more sophisticated drumming of Davenport, they began to work on a tune they called "The Raga." This resulted in the tune "East/West," the extended tune that was to have such an impact on rock music history. Much of this success was due to Davenport's ability to add color and tone to the composition, something not generally found in straight-ahead blues drummers. Davenport retired from music in 1968 due to illness, but was playing again from 1972-1974 with Jimmy Dawkins, Willie Dixon, and Buster Benton. He again retired from 1974 to 1981, after which he joined the Pete Baron Jazztet. Davenport described his own drumming as a combination of his two idols: the two base drums of Louis Bellson and the unique drum roll of Art Blakey. *—Michael Erlewine*

Charles "Cow Cow" Davenport

b. Apr. 23, 1894, Anniston, AL, **d.** Dec. 3, 1955, Cleveland, OH

Songwriter, Piano, Organ / Piano Blues, Boogie-Woogie

Charles "Cow Cow" Davenport is one of those seldom-remembered names in the annals of early blues history. But a little investigation will unearth the salient fact that he played an important part in developing one of the most enduring strains of the music; yes, "Cow Cow" Davenport was one hell of a boogie-woogie piano player. Davenport worked on numerous vaudeville tours on the TOBA circuit in the '20s and early '30s, usually in the company of vocalist Dora Carr. While he's principally noted as the composer of his signature tune, "The Cow Cow Boogie," which would be revived by jazz band vocalist Ella Mae Morse during the boogie woogie craze of the early '40s, he also claimed to have written Louis Armstrong's "I'll Be Glad When You're Dead, You Rascal You," selling the tune outright and receiving no royalties or composer credits. He recorded for a variety of labels from 1929 to 1946, eventually settling in Cleveland, Ohio, where he died in 1955 of hardening of the arteries. *—Cub Koda*

Alabama Strut / 1979 / Magpie ♦♦♦♦♦

Alabama Strut largely consists of solo instrumental tracks Cow Cow Davenport recorded in the late '20s and early '30s. The centerpiece of the collection are three different versions of "Cow Cow Blues"—including a vocal with Dora Carr and one with a cornet—but what really captivates is the fludity of Davenport's infectious boogie-woogie style. This is one of the best places to hear him play, but unfortunately it's a difficult record to find. *—Thom Owens*

Accompanist / Jun. 2, 1994 / Document ♦♦♦

★ **Complete Recorded Works, Vol. 1** / Jun. 2, 1994 / Document ♦♦♦♦♦

The complete output of pianist/singer Cow Cow Davenport as a leader has been made available on two CDs by Europe's Document CD; his sideman dates are also available on two other CDs. Because Cow Cow (named after his famous "Cow Cow Blues") is often categorized as a member of the blues world, it is sometimes overlooked how strong a jazz/blues pianist he was. On this first volume, Davenport is heard collaborating with singer Dora Carr, playing duets with cornetist B.T. Wingfield, interacting with singer Sam Theard, and performing heated solos which are sometimes commented upon by his partner Ivy Smith; in addition, there are a few solo instrumentals that really show what Davenport could do. The highlights include "Chimes Blues," "Atlanta Rag," "Back In the Alley" and four versions of "Cow Cow Blues." *—Scott Yanow*

Complete Recorded Works, Vol. 2 (1929–1945) / Jun. 2, 1994 / Document ♦♦♦♦♦

The second half of the Cow Cow Davenport story (the two Document CDs in this series have all of his recordings as a leader) features Davenport in a variety of settings: solo in 1929; sharing vocal duets with Sam Tarpley and Ivy Smith during 1929-1930; sticking to vocalizing on a lone date from 1938; and performing eight selections (six of which are piano solos) in 1945 for what would be his final recordings. Although Cow Cow Davenport ended up quite destitute and forgotten, his music was generally quite joyous, and he was certainly a fine, underrated pianist. Among the more memorable selections on this recommended disc are "Mama Don't Allow No Easy Riders," "Everybody Likes That Thing," "The Mess Is Here," "Jeep Boogie" and "Hobson City Stomp." *—Scott Yanow*

Complete Recorded Works, Vol. 3 / Mar. 2, 1998 / Document ♦♦♦♦

Charles "Cow Cow" Davenport 1926–1938 / Jun. 13, 2000 / Wolf ♦♦♦♦♦

The material ranges from magnificent Cow Cow Davenport solo tunes to good and not-so-good duets with a host of performers. Ivy Smith and Dora Carr are the artists with whom Davenport works best. Since these were dubbed from 78s, don't expect pristine sound. *—Ron Wynn*

Cow Cow Davenport: The Essential / Aug. 6, 2002 / Classic Blues ♦♦♦♦

"Mad Dog" Lester Davenport

b. Jan. 16, 1932, Tchula, MS

Vocals, Harmonica / Electric Chicago Blues

Until 1992, Lester Davenport's chief claims to blues fame were the 1955 Bo Diddley Chess session he played harp on (it produced "Pretty Thing" and "Bring It to Jerome") and a lengthy, much more recent stint holding down the harmonica slot with the multi-generational Gary, IN, band, the Kinsey Report. That instantly changed with the issue of Davenport's own album for Earwig, *When the Blues Hit You*; now this Chicago blues veteran had something on the shelves to call his very own.

Davenport hit Chicago in 1945 at age 14. He quickly soaked up the sights and sounds so prevalent on the local blues scene, checking out Arthur "Big Boy" Spires, Snooky Pryor, and Homesick James, who invited the youngster to jam sessions and tutored him on the intricacies of the idiom. Gigs with Spires and James preceded his brief hookup with Bo Diddley (which included a booking behind Diddley at New York's famous Apollo Theater). Davenport led his own band while holding down a day job as a paint sprayer during the '60s, remaining active on the West side prior to joining forces with the Kinseys during the '80s.

Now, about that "Mad Dog" handle: it seems that Davenport liked to prowl the stage while playing a few notes on every instrument on the bandstand during his younger days. The shtick earned him the name; his tenacious playing did the rest. *—Bill Dahl*

● **When the Blues Hit You** / Aug. 1991 / Earwig ♦♦♦♦♦

Although he'd been on the Chicago scene since the '50s, backing Bo Diddley on some of his earliest Chess waxings, this was harpist "Mad Dog" Lester Davenport's long-overdue debut album. And a fine one it was, too, filled with mainstream Windy City blues immersed in the '50s tradition. His band for the project included pianist Sunnyland Slim and guitarist John Primer. *—Bill Dahl*

Cyril Davies

b. 1932, Denham, Buckinghamshire, England, **d.** Jan. 7, 1964, England

Vocals, Harmonica / British Blues

The Cyril Davies R&B All-Stars were, after the Rolling Stones, the best British blues band of the early '60s—and if they'd gotten to stay together a little longer under Davies, they might even have given Mick Jagger, Brian Jones, and company a real run for their money. This regrettably short-lived blues band was assembled by harpist/singer Cyril Davies (1932-1964) in 1963, following his exit from Blues Incorporated. The group's original lineup, featuring Davies on harp and vocals, had Bernie Watson on guitar, Nicky Hopkins on piano, Ricky Brown playing bass, and Carlo Little on the drums—all four had been recruited from the ranks of Screaming Lord Sutch's Savages. This quintet recorded an initial single, "Country Line Special," driven by Davies' wailing harp and vocals, that was sufficiently authentic to get it placed alongside the British releases of songs by Muddy Waters, Howlin' Wolf, and the rest of the Chess Record luminaries in England's Pye Records catalog.

Watson and Brown went their separate ways during the summer of 1963, and Jeff Bradford and Cliff Barton came in on guitar and bass, respectively, with Long John Baldry—another Blues Incorporated alumnus—occasionally sitting in on vocals. Their second single, "Preachin' the Blues," was released in September to modest but promising success, and for a time it looked like Davies and company were going to be a major force on the burgeoning R&B scene. But Davies collapsed late in 1963, and was diagnosed as suffering from acute leukemia; he died in January of 1964.

Long John Baldry kept Hopkins, Bradford, Barton, and Little together as his backup band, the Hoochie Coochie Men, but the moment had passed. Davies' vocals, though hardly overly impressive, had a character to them that made the group's records competitive during the early blues boom of 1962-1963, and his harp playing was second to no one in England, a powerful, alternately mournful or exultant sound. Baldry, by contrast, never became more than a middle-level success in England, though it wasn't for lack of talent—he was a good singer, but by 1966 the audience for British blues was looking for flash along with the talent, and guitar players with charisma were more important than vocalists; witness the talent that Eric Clapton parlayed into international superstardom while John Mayall was left behind as a cult figure. Ironically, Baldry's biggest single exposure on record to international audiences may have been as the speaker introducing the Rolling Stones on their 1966 concert album *Got Live if You Want It*. Nicky Hopkins subsequently emerged as a star session player in his own right, recording and performing with various bands (including the Rolling Stones) during the late '60s and '70s, and members of the All-Stars/Hoochie Coochie Men also turned up on Screaming Lord Sutch's recordings during this period, most notably his *Heavy Friends* album.

The Cyril Davies R&B All-Stars remain an impressive footnote in the history of British blues, however, for their handful of recordings, including "Country Line Special," "Preachin' the Blues," and a hard-rocking rendition of Buddy Holly's "Not Fade Away." They never recorded an album, but their songs appear on numerous anthologies including: *A Shot of Rhythm and Blues* (Sequel Records), *Stroll On* (Sony Music), and *Dealing With the Devil* (Sony Music). *—Bruce Eder*

The Legendary Cyril Davies / 1970 / Folklore ♦♦♦

Early acoustic sides by Davies and Korner, reissued in 1970 on the Folklore label. The two hadn't found their way yet, and while the playing is raw and interesting, the work is a little too unfinished to be truly representative of either artist. The Marquee Club album is more representative. *—Bruce Eder*

● **R&B from the Marquee** / 1971 / Decca ♦♦♦♦

The most important of Blues Incorporated's albums, this record features Davies all over it, and is his one reasonably representative album. He may be the best thing here, his blues harp the most accomplished and authentic sounding instrument, and his vocals are quite convincing and natural as well. *—Bruce Eder*

Dealing With the Devil: Immediate Blues, Vol. 2 / 1972 / Immediate ♦♦♦♦
A multi-artist compilation that includes Davies' & the All-Stars' cover of "Someday Baby." The rest ain't bad, neither. *—Bruce Eder*

Stroll On / 1992 / Sony ♦♦♦♦
Another compilation, this time featuring "Not Fade Away" and worthwhile on that basis alone. *—Bruce Eder*

Debbie Davies

b. Aug. 22, 1952, Los Angeles, CA
Vocals, Guitar / Modern Electric Blues
Like Joanna Connor and Sue Foley, Debbie Davies' first love was playing guitar. Writing good songs and developing her vocal chops came about later for this Los Angeles native now living in Connecticut. Born August 22, 1952, to musician parents in Los Angeles, Davies cut her teeth in the San Francisco Bay area, playing blues and rock & roll for a time in college. Back in Los Angeles in 1986, she joined Maggie Mayall and the Cadillacs, an all-female R&B band led by John Mayall's wife before joining Albert Collins' Icebreakers in the late '80s. Collins used Davies to open his shows, and as part of Collins' band for three years, she got to travel throughout the U.S., Europe and Canada, playing dueling guitars nightly with Collins.

In 1991, Davies became lead guitarist for Fingers Taylor and the Ladyfingers Revue, a band made up with many of the nation's best female musicans. This group opened for Jimmy Buffett's "Outpost Tour."

Davies takes most of her inspiration from two blues guitar masters she's paid the most attention to, her late boss Albert Collins, and Eric Clapton. A talented songwriter, vocalist, and most importantly, ensemble guitar player, Davies has been leading her own band since September, 1991. She has two excellent albums for the San Francisco-based Blind Pig label, *Picture This* (1993) and *Loose Tonight* (1994); *Round Every Corner* appeared on Shanachie in 1998, and the following year Davies released *Tales From The Austin Motel*. *Love the Game* appeared in early 2001. *—Richard Skelly*

● **Picture This** / 1993 / Blind Pig ♦♦♦♦
Debbie Davies played with Albert Collins and that experience carries her through her debut album, *Picture This*. All the way through the album, she plays and sings with a barely restrained energy, spitting out burning leads and positively wailing her vocals. The album is a mixture of solid originals and classic covers, including a version of "I Wonder Why" that features a cameo from Collins. On the whole, *Picture This* is an exciting debut. *—Thom Owens*

Loose Tonight / 1994 / Blind Pig ♦♦♦
Davies' second album, *Loose Tonight*, contains the same high-octane blues, R&B and rock & roll as her first, only delivered with a slightly rougher edge. The roughness kick-starts the record into high gear, which means *Loose Tonight* delivers just as much thrills as *Picture This*. *—Thom Owens*

I Got That Feeling / 1996 / Blind Pig ♦♦♦♦
Davies' third album finds this artist moving in a much more "pop" direction, proving that she can both stretch her wings artistically and has far more to offer than merely recycled riffs and motifs filtered through a women's perspective. Her social consciousness raising quickly comes up for air on the opening track, "Howlin' At The Moon," one of only three Davies originals aboard this outing. But her interpretations of gospel pop ballad material like Lenny McDaniel's beautiful "Tired Angels," and duets with Coco Montoya on Albert Collins' title track and Tab Benoit on "Let The Heartaches Begin" are every bit as strong, her vocal skills showing more maturity and assuredness with each album. Her solo work is spot on, always paying homage to a wide variety of stylistic lessons well learned and solidly in the blues pocket with no added rock affectations to bog it down. But tracks like "Homework" (not the Otis Rush classic) make it clear that this is Debbie Davies being mainstreamed into Bonnie Raitt territory and she doesn't sound uncomfortable there at all, making this a most ambitious effort. *—Cub Koda*

Round Every Corner / May 19, 1998 / Shanachie ♦♦♦
Debbie Davies' fourth album, 1998's *Round Every Corner*, display her bluesy singing, writing and playing talents on 11 songs, including originals by Davies, some traditional songs, and covers. Davies' own songs range from the romantic "Such a Fine Man" to the upbeat "A.C. Strut," and she performs accomplished versions of Creedence Clearwater Revival's "Who'll Stop the Rain" and the traditional "Blue and Lonesome." Davies' skillful, soulful take on the blues grows richer with time. *—Heather Phares*

Tales from the Austin Motel / Jun. 22, 1999 / Shanachie ♦♦♦♦
For *Tales from the Austin Motel*, Debbie Davies temporarily ditched her touring band and teamed up with drummer Chris Layton and bassist Tommy Shannon, better known as the rhythm section of Stevie Ray Vaughan's legendary supporting group, Double Trouble. The intention was to craft a tribute album to their influences and collegues—namely, the Texas blues giants Albert Collins, Stevie Ray Vaughan. The trio tackles a number of covers, including such standards as "I Want to Be Loved" and "I Just Want to Make Love to You," but the majority of the album is devoted to Davies' originals. They're all solid, journeyman songs—nothing too special, but nothing bad, either. (Although these ears did hear something out of the ordinary—a lift from "Remember You're a Womble" on the instrumental "Percolatin." But that probably wasn't intentional.) The main reason to hear *Tales from the Austin Motel* is to listen to Davies play with Double Trouble, and the results do not disappoint. Some may quibble that the recording is a little too crystal clear to really capture the nasty Austin sound they strive to achieve, but the trio does have a dynamic interplay. It serves as a reminder of what a good rhythm section Layton and Shannon are—they make an already excellent guitarist sound like a successor to SRV, which is no mean feat. But that's not to take anything away from Davies. Over the course of her four previous albums, she established herself as a formidible talent, but her work on *Tales* affirms that she holds a prime place in the modern electric Texas blues pantheon. *—Stephen Thomas Erlewine*

Love the Game / Mar. 13, 2001 / Shanachie ♦♦♦

Blind John Davis

b. Dec. 7, 1913, Hattiesburg, MS, **d.** Oct. 12, 1985, Chicago, IL
Vocals, Piano / Piano Blues, Boogie-Woogie
The piano work of John Davis was featured on blues records by the score during the '30s and '40s. His accompaniments to Tampa Red, Sonny Boy Williamson, Big Bill Broonzy, and others brought him fame as a blues musician, but like his piano compatriot Little Brother Montgomery, Davis did not care to be typecast as such and often expressed a preference for the sweet, sentimental favorites he played in countless piano lounges. But as with Montgomery, most of Davis' own recording opportunities came from blues companies, and he never failed to acquit himself well when it came to blues and boogie-woogie. He was the first pianist to do a European blues tour (with Broonzy in 1952), returning to the continent frequently as a solo act during the '70s and '80s. With blues-piano appreciation in Europe being what it is and has been, it's not surprising that most of the albums of Blind John Davis were recorded there and not in Chicago, his home from the age of two until his death. *—Jim O'Neal*

1938–1939 / 1938 / Story of the Blues ♦♦♦♦

Alive "Live" and Well / 1976 / Chrischaa ♦♦♦

Stompin' on a Saturday Night / 1978 / Alligator ♦♦♦♦♦
Stompin' on a Saturday Night is a propulsive live set recorded in Germany in 1976 that captures the pianist late in his career. While he may be past his prime, he remains a terrific, instinctive pianist, and the record goes a long way toward proving his influence. *—Thom Owens*

Blind John Davis / Apr. 3, 1983 / Evidence ♦♦♦

You Better Cut That Out / 1985 / Red Beans ♦♦♦
His final session, with hot piano licks and failing vocals. *—Ron Wynn*

● **1938–1952, Vol. 1** / Oct. 12, 1999 / Document ♦♦♦♦♦

CeDell Davis

b. Jun. 9, 1927, Helena, AR
Vocals, Guitar / Electric Country Blues, Electric Delta Blues
CeDell Davis was born in 1927 in Helena, AR. His right hand was crippled by polio at the age of ten, so he switched his guitar to a left-handed bottleneck style, which makes for a unique, atonal sound. He played locally throughout the '50s and '60s, with friends such as Robert Nighthawk, Big Joe Williams and Charlie Jordan. After a series of compilation appearances and several live dates in New York, Fat Possum Records signed Davis. Noted blues journalist Robert Palmer produced his debut, *Feel like Doin' Something Wrong* (1994). *The Best of CeDell Davis* (1995) was also released, with help from Col. Bruce Hampton & the Aquarium Rescue Unit. *The Horror of It All* followed in 1998. Davis took time away from recording after these releases, and spent the next four years writing and performing. When he returned to the studio, he drafted musicians like R.E.M.'s Peter Buck and the Screaming Trees' Barrett Martin into his sessions. The final results, *When Lightnin' Struck the Pine*, arrived in stores that summer. *—John Bush*

Feel Like Doin' Something Wrong / 1994 / Fat Possum ♦♦♦♦
Produced by blues historian and journalist Robert Palmer, *Feel Like Doin' Something Wrong* captures the haunted, otherworldly blues of CeDell Davis. Using a knife for a guitar slide, Davis creates strange, unpredictable sounds and matches them with his gnarled voice. Even better, there's hardly a bad song in the bunch, and his versions of "Murder My Baby," "Boogie Chillen," "Every Day Every Way" and "If You Like Fat Women" rank among the finest contemporary blues in the '80s. *—Stephen Thomas Erlewine*

● **The Best of CeDell Davis** / Jan. 24, 1995 / Fat Possum ♦♦♦♦
CeDell Davis' guitar tunings are quite unique—he seems to have some sort of internal scale that makes for brilliant blues guitar and very difficult band performances (for this album he's backed up by Col. Bruce Hampton and members of the Aquarium Rescue Unit). What's amazing is that the sometimes atonal result works beautifully—it's a razor-like mix in that it's cutting and makes for tense social situations, but it's a standout blues album, with Davis' busted-up voice being pushed along by the ARU/Davis music train. A quirky surprise. *—Steven McDonald*

The Horror of It All / May 19, 1998 / Fat Possum ♦♦♦
Those who have fallen under the spell of the Fat Possum label's brand of raw, rocking Delta blues are bound to find plenty to like in the music of CeDell Davis. That said, Davis doesn't really sound like anyone else on the label . . . nor any other for that matter. His angular, atonal bottleneck guitar playing and garbled vocals are bound to offend many fans of slick, contemporary urban blues, but for a raw taste of the Delta you need not look further. Although the songs and performances on *The Horror of It All* rank a notch below those on 1994's *Feel Like Doin' Something Wrong*, it's still a strong outing. Davis goes it alone with his guitar on most of the tracks; joined only by drums on one song; and drums, bass, and second guitar on another. Yet, despite the sparseness of the instrumentation, the album offers more variety than most of the contemporaneous releases on the label. Davis veers comfortably from the type of hypnotic, droning blues favored by deceased label-mate Junior Kimbrough on tracks like "The Horror" to John Lee Hooker-like boogies such as "I Want You." Mostly, though, Davis sounds like no one so much as himself. As per usual with Fat Possum Records releases, even the most familiar blues on the album (e.g., "Keep on Snatchin' It Back, "Coon Can Mattie") are listed as originals, and one song ("If You Like Fat Women") is reprised from the earlier album. None of which matters, of

course, when the performances are this spirited. Davis manages to make each of these songs his own. *The Horror of It All* makes a nice addition to any Delta blues collection. *—Jeffrey Konkel*

Reverend Gary Davis

b. Apr. 30, 1896, Laurens, SC, **d.** May 5, 1972, Hammonton, NJ

Vocals, Arranger, Guitar / Piedmont Blues, Country Blues, Blues Gospel, Acoustic Blues, Folk-Blues

In his prime of life, which is to say the late '20s, the Reverend Gary Davis was one of the two most renowned practitioners of the East Coast school of ragtime guitar; 35 years later, despite two decades spent playing on the streets of Harlem in New York, he was still one of the giants in his field, playing before thousands of people at a time, and an inspiration to dozens of modern guitarist/singers including Bob Dylan, Taj Mahal, and Donovan, and Jorma Kaukonen, David Bromberg, and Ry Cooder, who studied with Davis.

Davis was partially blind at birth, and lost what little sight he had before he was an adult. He was self-taught on the guitar, beginning at age six, and by the time he was in his twenties he had one of the most advanced guitar techniques of anyone in blues—his only peers among ragtime-based players were Blind Arthur Blake, Blind Lemon Jefferson, and Blind Willie Johnson. Davis himself was a major influence on Blind Boy Fuller.

Davis' influences included gospel, marches, ragtime, jazz, and minstrel hokum, and he integrated them into a style that was his own. In 1911, when Davis was a still teenager, the family moved to Greenville, SC, and he fell under the influence of such local guitar virtuosi as Willie Walker, Sam Brooks and Baby Brooks. Davis moved to Durham, NC, in the mid-'20s, by which time he was a full-time street musician, and celebrated not only for the diversity of styles that his playing embraced, but also for his skills with the guitar, which were already virtually unmatched in the blues field.

Davis went into the recording studio for the first time in the '30s with the backing of a local businessman. Davis cut a mixture of blues and spirituals for the American Record Company label, but there was never an equitable agreement about payment for the recordings, and following these sessions, it was 19 years before he entered the studio again. During that period, he went through many changes. Like many other street buskers, Davis always interspersed gospel songs amid his blues and ragtime numbers, to make it harder for the police to interrupt him. He began taking the gospel material more seriously, and in 1937 he became an ordained minister. After that, he usually refused to perform any blues.

Davis moved to New York in the early '40s and began preaching and playing on street-corners in Harlem. He recorded again at the end of the '40s, with a pair of gospel songs, but it wasn't until the mid-'50s that a real following for his work began developing anew. His music, all of it now of a spiritual nature, began showing up on labels such as Stinson, Folkways, and Riverside, where he recorded seven songs in early 1956. Davis was "rediscovered" by the folk revival movement, and after some initial reticence, he agreed to perform as part of the budding folk music revival, appearing at the Newport Folk Festival, where his raspy voiced sung sermons, most notably his transcendent "Samson and Delilah (If I Had My Way)"—a song most closely associated with Blind Willie Johnson—and "Twelve Gates to the City," were highlights of the procedings for several years. He also recorded a live album for the Vanguard label at one such concert, as well as appearing on several Newport live anthology collections. He was also the subject of two television documentaries, one in 1967 and one in 1970.

Davis became one of the most popular players on the folk revival and blues revival scenes, playing before large and enthusiastic audiences—most of the songs that he performed were spirituals, but they weren't that far removed from the blues that he'd recorded in the '30s, and his guitar technique was intact. Davis' skills as a player, on the jumbo Gibson acoustic models that he favored, were undiminished, and he was a startling figure to hear, picking and strumming complicated rhythms and countermelodies. Davis became a teacher during this period, and his students included some very prominent white guitar players, including David Bromberg and the Jefferson Airplane's Jorma Kaukonen (who later recorded Davis' "I'll Be Alright" on his acclaimed solo album *Quah!*).

The Reverend Gary Davis left behind a fairly large body of modern (i.e., post-World War II) recordings, well into the '60s, taking the revival of his career in his stride as a way of carrying the message of the gospel to a new generation. He even recorded anew some of his blues and ragtime standards in the studio, for the benefit of his students. *—Bruce Eder*

American Street Songs / Aug. 8, 1956 / Riverside ♦♦♦

Pure Religion & Bad Company / 1957 / Smithsonian/Folkways ♦♦♦♦

Moses Asch became the first producer to record Davis in a full-length album release, showcasing his dazzling guitar style more fully than ever before. *—Bruce Eder*

Say No to the Devil / 1958 / Bluesville/Original Blues Classics ♦♦♦♦

Say No to the Devil is Rev. Gary Davis' third Bluesville album and it was originally released in 1961. Davis was in fine form throughout the session, playing some startlingly intricate 12-string guitar licks, blowing some rootsy harp, and singing with conviction. Between the songs, Davis tells some rambling stories, which are just as gripping and fascinating as the music itself. *—Thom Owens*

Rev. Gary Davis at Newport / 1959 / Vanguard ♦♦♦♦

One of the finest single artist albums to come out of Newport, not quite in the league of Muddy Waters' performance but a superb introduction to the range of his repertory, from ragtime and novelty tunes to gospel numbers. *—Bruce Eder*

Harlem Street Singer / Aug. 1960 / Bluesville/Original Blues Classics ♦♦♦♦♦

Recorded during a three hour session on August 24, 1960, Gary Davis laid down 12 of his most impassioned spirituals for *Harlem Street Singer.* Starting off the session with a version of Blind Willie Johnson's "If I Had My Way I'd Tear That Building Down," here renamed "Samson and Delilah," Davis is in fine form. His vocals are as expressive as Ray Charles' while similar in richness to Richie Havens' work. *Harlem Street Singer* features his inspired country blues fingerpicking as well. Many moods color the selections, from the gentle "I Belong to the Band" to the mournful "Death Don't Have No Mercy," only to be followed by the joyous shouting of "Goin' to Sit Down on the Banks of the River." Overall, the collection is well worth the purchase and should be considered essential listening for fans of country blues or gospel. *—Matt Fink*

Gospel, Blues & Street Songs / Jul. 1961 / Riverside/Original Blues Classics ♦♦♦♦♦

This first edition title—later renamed *Gospel, Blues & Street Songs*—is one of the cornerstones of Riverside Records' *Original Blues Classics* series. Regardless of the moniker, these sides loom large in the available works of seminal blues icons Pink Anderson and Rev. Gary Davis. Both performers hail from the largely underappreciated Piedmont blues scene—which first began to flourish in the late 19th and early 20th centuries—near the North/South Carolina state border. Anderson's seven tracks were recorded in Charlottesville, VA, on May 29, 1950—while he was literally on the road. His highly sophisticated and self-accompanied style of simultaneously picking and sliding—accomplished using a half-opened jackknife—could pass for an electronic effect. The folk ballad "John Henry" contains the most evident example of this unique fretwork. His lyrically smug prankster edict is revealed on tracks such as "I Got Mine" and "He's in the Jailhouse Now." The Rev. Gary Davis side—which appropriately contains all spirituals—was recorded in N.Y.C. on January 28, 1956. However, Davis' delivery is steeped in the minstrel and street blues of his native Carolinas. Here is where the worlds of Davis and Anderson sonically intersect. As a performer, his clean and intricate acoustic picking and guttural vocalization stand as his trademark. Included here are several of the Reverend's most revered works, including "Samson and Delilah"—which became a performance staple for the Grateful Dead, as well as "Keep Your Lamp Trimmed and Burning." This was covered to great effect by Hot Tuna, whose lead guitarist, Jorma Kaukonen, took lessons from the Reverend in the early '60s. *—Lindsay Planer*

At "Al Matthes" / 1966 / ♦♦♦

At "Al Matthes" is taken from a collection of private acetates from 1966 and the sound suffers somewhat, but not the performances. Rev. Gary Davis runs through a selection of blues and rags—his performances are divided equally between instrumentals and vocals. Davis is relaxed and engaging, making this a small rough gem in his catalog. *—Thom Owens*

New Blues & Gospel / 1971 / ♦♦♦

As the title suggests, *New Blues & Gospel* is equally divided between blues and gospel recordings. Recorded in 1971, Gary Davis was past his prime when these tracks were cut, but he still manages to invest the songs with grit and passion. It's a minor entry in his catalog, but completists will find the album of interest. *—Thom Owens*

From Blues to Gospel / Mar. 1971 / Biograph ♦♦♦

This particular set was recorded one year before Davis' death, when he was 76 years old. Producer Arnold Caplin has combined two LPs to create this package and believes these to be the artist's very last recordings. Although the master-picker pulls off some prodigious playing here—on both the six- and 12-string guitars—he is no match for his own earlier work recorded between 1935-1960. Listeners already familiar with the younger Davis' playing will feel great affection and gratitude for these last recordings. *—Larry Hoffman*

When I Die I'll Live Again / 1972 / Fantasy ♦♦♦

This two-fer offers Davis' best work of the '60s. *—Richard Lieberson*

At the Sign of the Sun / 1973 / Gospel Heritage ♦♦♦

Fine later performances are included on this CD. *—Richard Lieberson*

Blind Gary Davis / 1974 / Document ♦♦♦♦♦

All of Davis' stunning early recordings (1935-1949). *—Kip Lornell*

O Glory / Jan. 1974 / Adelphi ♦♦

The Guitar & Banjo of Reverend Gary Davis / 1978 / Prestige/Original Blues Classics ♦♦♦

Because this is an all-instrumental recording, it's an offbeat entry into the catalog of a performer known both as an important guitarist and as a singer. Some might miss Davis' vocals on this 1964 recording, but on the other hand there are plenty of records with him singing around. This gives listeners a chance to hone in on his dexterous guitar skills, blending ragtime, folk, and blues, usually on guitar (though he plays banjo on a couple of songs, and harmonica on one). "Maple Leaf Rag" is a natural showcase for Davis' talents, and "Candy Man," which may be his most well-known song, is here presented without words, making for an interesting juxtaposition with more commonly heard versions on which he (or others) sings. As further evidence of his eclecticism, there's a version of "United States March aka Soldier's Drill"—not the best format for his strengths, certainly, but an illustration of his ability to adapt his style to unexpected material. *—Richie Unterberger*

Blues & Ragtime / 1993 / Shanachie ♦♦♦♦♦

The Rev. Gary Davis forsook his gospel calling for a little while between 1962 and 1966 to set down formal studio versions of many of his most important blues and ragtime repertory. Some of the material here runs over ten minutes, as Davis lays out his best playing and singing voice. The booklet includes a fairly detailed biography as well as musical annotation. *—Bruce Eder*

★ **Complete Works (1935–1949)** / 1994 / Document ♦♦♦♦♦

Bull City Red, who played with the Reverend Gary Davis at various times, turns up on vocals for "I Saw the Light," but the rest of *1935-1949* is all Davis' show. Given the quality of what is here; the quality and inventiveness of the playing alone is astonishing, a youthful version of the technique that was still dazzling players 30 years later after Davis' rediscovery. Some of the tracks are a little noisy but generally the quality is better than decent for blues of this vintage, and it's startling to hear the '30s versions of numbers like "Twelve Gates to the City," which Davis was still performing better than anyone else in the mid-'60s. On "You Can Go Home," he really does get the guitar to sound like an orchestra, rippling through melodic and harmonic flourishes with the kind of assurance that would have made many a would-be bluesman of the '50s just throw away the guitar in despair. The Document disc overlaps Yazoo Records' *Complete Early Recordings* and includes three cuts not found there. "Civil War March," a guitar transcription of military marches that Davis cut for Moe Asch in 1945, is by itself worth the purchase price of this disc; one of the most humbling examples of a lighthearted virtuoso piece that one is ever likely to run into, its presence alone makes the disc a potentially better choice than the Yazoo version. However, the two subsequent tracks dating from 1949, "I Cannot Bear My Burden By Myself" and "I'm Gonna Meet You at the Station," are just as alluring, showing Davis still playing and singing brilliantly, patiently waiting to be rediscovered a few years later. —*Bruce Eder*

Complete Early Recordings / 1994 / Yazoo ✦✦✦✦✦
One can't possibly own too much of the Reverend Gary Davis' music from any era, but he made so few recordings in the '30s that the material is represented on several overlapping CDs. The Yazoo collection of his sides cut for the American Record Company is good as far as it goes—which is a long way—giving as complete a picture as one will ever find of Davis' output during that decade, with good sound and a superb set of sleeve notes on his life and work. It is not, unfortunately, as full an account of Davis' pre-'50s career as other discs that are available (especially from Document Records), and purchasers should be aware of one thing that they can be sure of concerning Davis—they will want more of his music. —*Bruce Eder*

O, Glory: The Apostolic Studio Sessions / 1996 / Genes ✦✦✦
Recorded in 1969, *O, Glory: The Apostolic Studio Sessions* is the Rev. Gary Davis' final studio LP, but he went out in style, working under the most state-of-the-art studio conditions of his career. The result is perhaps the best-sounding record in his catalog, even if the performances don't quite capture all the fire of his peak period; equally interesting is another break in tradition—rarely recorded with other artists (outside of a few early-'50s sides cut with Sonny Terry), here Davis is backed by vocalist Sister Annie Davis, harpist Larry Johnson and the Apostolic Family Chorus. Also worth noting is that Davis performs on a pair of instruments he'd never before recorded with, the piano and the five-string banjo. The cumulative result makes *O Glory* a must for historians, but casual fans will undoubtedly be better served by his earlier material. —*Jason Ankeny*

Have a Little Faith / 1999 / Bluesville ✦✦✦✦✦
A good sharp set of a dozen numbers, Davis getting into numbers relatively well-known ("Motherless Children," "You Got to Move") and more obscure. His guitar playing is in fine form throughout, though at least as good are his hoarse, spirited vocals. Listen to the rich, urgent upper-register moans that punctuate "Crucifixion" for proof. The jubilant "I'll Fly Away" is an outstanding example of country-gospel-blues' potential to uplift and inspire. —*Richie Unterberger*

I Am the True Vine / 1999 / Catfish ✦✦✦✦
Gary Davis (1896-1972) was a decided and acknowledged influence on a number of early rockers, including Bob Dylan, the Grateful Dead, and the Rolling Stones, and this sampler of works from 1935-1949 shows ample reasons why. The pieces are almost all religious blues, but of an extremely earthy and rough sort, the type of things Davis sang to crowds on street corners from North Carolina to Harlem. His voice is gravelly and casual, sometimes slurring entire lines, yet he manages to strike the right tone with satisfying consistency. What may cause the contemporary listener to really sit up and take notice, however, is his astonishing and intricate guitar playing. If extracted and heard out of context, one might well imagine he's listening to John Fahey from 30 years hence. The album, in fact, closes with an instrumental that incorporates various march themes. There are a bunch of killer songs here, including the title track and "I Am the Light of the World," which have both lost none of their power over the years. The disc comes with excellent historical and critical liner notes by Robert Tilling. Highly recommended. —*Brian Olewnick*

Little More Faith / Jul. 13, 1999 / Prestige/Original Blues Classics ✦✦✦✦

Live at Cambridge 1971 / Apr. 18, 2000 / Catfish ✦✦
Substandard home recording of Davis playing in Cambridge in the early '70s. Five very long performances stretched out to nearly 40 minutes, complete with tuning up and rapping to the crowd. While any recordings of Davis' intricate playing is always welcome, this is a pretty substandard outing and the sound quality quickly gets annoying after a few minutes. —*Cub Koda*

Demons and Angels: The Ultimate Collection / Mar. 13, 2001 / Shanachie ✦✦✦✦
This three-disc "ultimate collection" is an impressive compilation of recordings made featuring Rev. Gary Davis during a period spanning 1956 to 1966. An obvious labor of love, *Demons and Angels* was compiled and produced by one of Rev. Davis' former students—Stefan Grossman who paid Davis five dollars a lesson "regardless whether it would last an hour or several days." Going beyond gathering various performances, this set examines Rev. Davis' unique fingerpickin' acoustic guitar style from several distinctive points of view. Unfortunately the liner notes booklet sheds no light into the nature, exact recording dates, or venues of these performances. Presenting Davis in such varied settings allows enthusiast and student alike the unique perspective of hearing one of America's premier folk musicians in a most intimate situation. Disc one features songs recorded at Columbia University in 1958 and 1959 by student John Gibson. Judging from the occasional verbal instruction, as well as the lack of an audible audience, it is surmised that Davis is participating in some degree of formal instruction. Disc two includes home recordings, presumably documented by Grossman during his one-on-one

mentoring sessions between 1964 and 1966. Disc three rounds off *Demons and Angles* with various live performances from 1962-1966. The impact that Rev. Gary Davis had on musicians such as folk icon Dave Van Ronk and guitarist Jorma Kaukonen is obvious. The profound influence affected not only their choice of material, but more insidiously performance and delivery styles as well. Nowhere is this more evident than the live readings of "Let Us Get Together," "Lord, Search My Heart," and "Cocaine Blues." Rev. Davis' liquefied fretwork foreshadows Kaukonen's stunning virtuosity, while his sly, talking-blues delivery seems tailor made for Van Ronk's decidedly Greenwich Village approach. —*Lindsay Planer*

Live at Newport / Mar. 13, 2001 / Vanguard ✦✦✦✦✦
Long before Christian rockers were using so-called "Devil's music" to promote a religious message, the Rev. Gary Davis demonstrated that acoustic blues and folk didn't have to be about matters of the flesh. Davis, a fascinating cult figure, was as authentic a blues/ folk singer as Leadbelly, but he was also a Baptist minister—and he managed to bring Christian-oriented lyrics to people who weren't necessarily religious. Davis didn't believe in preaching to the choir exclusively; blues and folk venues often became his "pulpit." This reissue focuses on Davis' appearance at the 1965 Newport Folk Festival; by that time, he was 69, and many of the people who were attending his live performances weren't even born when he made his first recordings in 1935. *Live at Newport* isn't for gospel purists any more than it is for blues purists. Most of the performances (which find Davis accompanying himself on acoustic guitar and harp) are acoustic folk rather than actual 12-bar blues, and even though Davis picks a lot of songs that reflect his Christian beliefs (including "I've Done All My Singing for My Lord," "Twelve Gates to the City," and "Samson and Delilah"), he doesn't exclude secular material altogether. Eleven of the CD's 13 tracks originally appeared on Davis' old *At Newport* LP of 1967, although collectors will be glad to know that "Get Along Cindy" (a humorous vocal duet with Barry Kornfeld) and the instrumental "Soldiers Drill" are previously unreleased bonus tracks. *Live at Newport* is a highly soulful and rewarding document of Davis' late period. —*Alex Henderson*

Guy Davis

b. May 12, 1952, New York, NY [Manhattan]
Vocals, Guitar / Contemporary Blues, Modern Acoustic Blues, Soul-Blues
Updating the rural blues tradition for the modern era, Guy Davis was among the most prominent ambassadors of African-American art and culture of his generation, additionally winning great acclaim for his work in the theater. The son of the noted actors, directors and activists Ossie Davis and Ruby Dee, he was born in New York City on May 12, 1952; though raised in the city, Davis was frequently regaled with stories of Southern country life as a child, and over time became so enamored of the music of Blind Willie McTell, Skip James, Mississippi John Hurt and others that he taught himself guitar. As a 13-year-old experiencing his first Buddy Guy concert, Davis' own fate as a bluesman was sealed, especially after he learned his distinctive fingerpicking style from a nine-fingered guitarist he met on a train traveling from Boston to New York some years later.

In 1978, Davis recorded his debut LP *Dreams About Life*, produced for the Folkways label with the assistance of the legendary Moses Asch; around the same time he also began pursuing a career as an actor, landing a recurring role on the daytime soap *One Life to Live* and also appearing in the 1984 hip-hop film *Beat Street*. Long seeking to combine his shared love of music and acting, in 1991 Davis finally found a project that fulfilled all of his ambitions—*Mulebone*, the Broadway production of a Zora Neale Hurston and Langston Hughes collaboration which included a score by Taj Mahal. Two years later, Davis earned rave reviews for his work in the title role of the off-Broadway production *Robert Johnson: Trick the Devil*, with his portrayal later winning the Blues Foundation's W.C. Handy "Keeping the Blues Alive" Award.

In 1994, Davis wrote and starred in the one-man show *In Bed with the Blues: The Adventures of Fishy Waters*, another blues-based off-Broadway drama which played to strong critical notice. A year later, he collaborated with his parents on *Two Hah Hahs and a Homeboy*, which combined original material with African-American folklore and history. Around the same time, he also composed the music for the PBS series *The American Promise*; his score for an earlier telefilm, *To Be a Man*, won an Emmy. During the fall of 1995, Davis returned to writing and performing in the acoustic country blues tradition with renewed force, issuing the live LP *Stomp Down Rider* on the Red House label; a year later, he returned with *Call Down the Thunder. You Don't Know My Mind* followed in 1998 and was nominated for two W.C Handy Awards: Best Traditional Blues Album and Best Acoustic Blues Album. Davis himself was nominated for Best Acoustic Blues Artist. In early 2000 Davis issued *Butt Naked Free*. He spent much of 2001 contributing songs to tribute albums; "Soulful Wind" appeared on *Labour of Love: The Music of Nick Lowe*, "Some of These Days" on *Down the Dirt Road: The Songs of Charley Patton* and "Sweetheart Like You" on *Nod to Bob: An Artist's Tribute to Bob Dylan. Give in Kind*, Davis' sixth album, followed in 2002.—*Jason Ankeny*

Stomp Down the Rider / Oct. 17, 1995 / Red House ✦✦✦✦
Guy Davis' debut, *Stomp Down the Rider*, is a surprisingly fresh collection of acoustic blues, entirely comprised of original material. Davis already sounds like a seasoned pro, delivering crisp, intelligent and passionate songs that suggest he's only beginning to achieve his potential. —*Thom Owens*

Call Down the Thunder / Oct. 15, 1996 / Red House ✦✦✦
From the infectious opening notes of "Georgia Jelly Roll" through the stomping sounds of the closing "New Shoes," this is honest, raw, from-the-gut blues music, imbued with the joy of a gospel meeting. Guy Davis is a master storyteller, penning ten of the 13 songs included here. His slide playing is exceptional and at times very reminiscent of Robert Johnson. —*Bob Gottlieb*

You Don't Know My Mind / Apr. 21, 1998 / Red House ◆◆◆◆

This disc brings back the familiar friendly growl of modern-day traditionalist Guy Davis, with a pipin' hot baker's dozen of his compositions. Again, on this disc he has some extremely able players to help augment his songs and support his vision of them, never overplaying or getting in the way, but providing that constant base of support from which the performer can extend his inspiration. His voice wraps around the lyric and infiltrates it and gives it that heartfelt feeling that makes it his song. This is a consummate performer who loves his music and knows its roots and origins. —*Bob Gottlieb*

Butt Naked Free / Mar. 14, 2000 / Red House ◆◆◆◆◆

Making sure that country blues starts the 21st century off on the right foot, Guy Davis' *Butt Naked Free*, whose title was inspired by the comments of Davis' young son, is one of the most accomplished statements the genre has offered in a few years. Picking up where 1998's *You Don't Know My Mind* left off, Davis once again has decided to fill out his sound, but this time adding touches of mandolin, organ and accordion, with the results being altogether more satisfying and never sounding even slightly overproduced. Where Davis on his previous album sounded, at times, unsure of his new direction, *Butt Naked Free* rocks with a loose liveliness, still allowing Davis' derivative yet idiosyncratic sound to shine through. "Waiting on the Cards to Fall" and "Never Met No Woman Treats Me Like You Do," the latter with Levon Helm contributing drums and mandolin, showcase how well Davis' sound fills out and offers the unique experience of hearing what it might have sounded like if Mance Lipscomb or Reverend Gary Davis had ever recorded with full-band accompaniment. Ballads like "Let Me Stay a While" and the narrative "Sugar Belle Blue" are some of the strongest Davis has written and, if anything, benefit considerably from the more filled out sound. Of course, Davis still delivers more than a few of his stripped-down solo country blues tunes with the humorous "High Flying Rocket," the mean slide playing on "Come On Sally Hitch a Ride," and the gorgeous instrumental "The Place Where I'm From (Butt Naked Free)." More than anything, *Butt Naked Free* shows that Guy Davis is still more than happy to carry the banner of country blues, yet remains able to add to the dialogue of the genre and put his own stamp on it in the process. —*Matt Fink*

● **Give in Kind** / Apr. 9, 2002 / Red House ◆◆◆◆◆

Guy Davis has developed into a consummate bluesman. He's listened hard to classic Delta blues and based his style on it, without ever becoming a carbon copy of the greats. Instead they're his jumping-off point into something as individual as "Layla, Layla," where didgeridoo makes an appearance, or the poignant "Joppatowne." Equally adept on guitar, banjo, and harmonica, he's become a force of nature, with the ability to write a song like "I Don't Know" that sounds as if it had come directly from the '30s, alongside covers of Fred McDowell, Big Bill Broonzy, and Sleepy John Estes. The originals and older work mesh perfectly, the sign of a real bluesman. And, of course, he's capable of working the other side of the coin to blues, in gospel, as the closer, "God's Unchanging Hand," clearly shows. This is the tradition reborn and revitalized. Davis' support is wonderfully sympathetic, but he's completely at the center of things, the motivator and mover of this music, and a purveyor of the real blues. His lineage is obvious, and he's the new generation, doing it right and keeping it real. —*Chris Nickson*

James "Thunderbird" Davis

b. Nov. 10, 1938, Prichard, AL, d. Jan. 24, 1992, St. Paul, MN
Vocals / Modern Electric Blues

James Davis went out the way entertainers often dream of. While performing at the Blues Saloon in St. Paul, MN, he suffered a fatal heart attack in mid-set and died on-stage. The tragic event ended a comeback bid that warmed the heart of blues aficionados; Davis' whereabouts were so unknown prior to his triumphant re-emergence that he was rumored to be dead.

His melismatic vocal delivery betraying strong gospel roots, Davis secured his first pro gig in 1957 as opening act for Guitar Slim. The flamboyant guitarist was responsible for tagging Davis with his "Thunderbird" moniker. Davis lost a drinking contest to his boss that sent him to the hospital; the singer's libation of choice that fateful day was Thunderbird wine (which Davis swore off for life).

Davis signed on with Don Robey's Houston-based Duke Records in 1961. Robey utilized his new discovery as a demo singer for Bobby Bland when Davis wasn't cutting his own singles. Two of Davis' Duke offerings, the tortured blues numbers "Blue Monday" and "Your Turn to Cry," rank with finest blues 45s of the early '60s, but did little for Davis at the time. He left Duke in 1966, opening for Joe Tex and O.V. Wright on the road before settling down.

After just about giving up entirely on show biz, Davis was tracked down in Houma, LA, by Black Top Records boss Hammond Scott and two cohorts. A 1989 album called *Check Out Time* was the happy result; sidemen on the date included two former cohorts, bassist Lloyd Lambert (Guitar Slim's bandleader) and guitarist Clarence Hollimon. The resultant acclaim catapulted Davis back into the limelight for the last years of his life. —*Bill Dahl*

● **Check Out Time** / 1989 / Black Top ◆◆◆◆◆

Thought by many to be deceased, singer James Davis returned from musical invisibility to make this sparkling comeback set for Black Top. His hearty pipes sounding anything but over-the-hill, Davis roared a combination of his own fine tunes and remakes of songs first done by Bobby Bland, James Carr, and Wynonie Harris in front of a terrific combo (guitarists Anson Funderburgh and Clarence Hollimon, saxist Grady Gaines). A revival of his own slow blues "Your Turn to Cry" recalled Davis' early-'60s glory days. —*Bill Dahl*

Katherine Davis

Vocals / Vocal Jazz, Standards, Jazz Blues

Listening to them on radio as a youngster, Katherine Davis was enamored with the life style of the early great blues singers like Bessie Smith and Ma Rainey. She was determined to make singing her career since the clothes, cars and other accouterments of the high life of her role models fascinated her. Like many singers of Afro-American ethnicity and with family roots in the South before emigrating to Chicago, Katherine Davis first "public" performances came when she was a youngster singing Gospel in a church choir. In the early '80s, Davis moved on to study classical voice and voice literature at the Sherwood Conservatory of Music in Chicago. Davis stayed with gospel, stinting with the Reuben Lightfoot Gospel Choral in 1981 and acting in the gospel opera *Second Chance* the same year. She got her first opportunity to sing jazz and blues in small clubs in and around Chicago in 1982. But the defining moment which settled her on a jazz career was her appearance in the Kuumba's Theater's production of *In the House of the Blues* during 1984-1985, where she portrayed both her childhood heroines, Ma Rainey and Bessie Smith.

Some of the jazz performers Davis appeared with early in her career in the Chicago area included trombonist Jim Beebe, bass players Eddie Calhoun and the venerable Truck Parham, and pianist Joe Johnson. Davis has appeared at such jazz events as the Chicago Blues and Montreal Blues Festival She has toured Europe as part of the Erwin Helfer group and with her own aggregation. Jazz club gigs include stays at Andy's, Joe's Be-Bop Café, where she continues to perform, and Iron Miles in Chicago as well as at Warmdaddy's in Philadelphia.

Although Davis has appeared on several albums as a side person, she didn't record as a leader until 2000 when her inaugural album, *Dream Shoes*, was released on the Southport label. This session is a fortuitous array of blues, Motown, gospel, and standards, all wrapped up in a jazz setting. Currently Ms. Davis continues to perform at jazz festivals, tour, and work at Joe's Be-Bop Café. She is also artist-in-residence in Chicago public school system, teaching children about the blues. —*Dave Nathan*

● **Dream Shoes** / 1999 / Southport ◆◆◆

Davis is a singer who evenly combines jazz and blues (even posing the question if there really is any difference between the two on "You Choose"). Her strong, rich voice holds an attractive, dramatic quality that suggests she's also a stage actress, a storyteller, and a person who lives life to the fullest. Pianist Joe Johnson is here on several tracks—with a trio, larger band, or in duets with Davis—and he covers the stride/swing/down-home blues continuum with deft aplomb and witty depth. The 14 selections are programmed to offer something varied and definitely in the tradition. The piano-voice duets include the old-timey light stride of "Try a Little Tenderness," the suggestive 12-bar howler "Press My Button," and a laconic rendition of "I Let a Song Go Out of My Heart." Trio takes include another, sweeter version of "I Let a Song Go Out," the straight, bluesy swing of "Don't You Know," the campy "You Can't Ride This Train," and the evergreen "Honeysuckle Rose." Pianist Erwin Helfer replaces Johnson for two classics: "Darktown Strutter's Ball" (which features an unidentified saxophonist) and the Sippie Wallace chestnut "You Got to Know How." There are also two a cappella numbers: "He Is That Kind of Friend" and "Java Jive," on which Davis expresses her love/need for coffee. Whether it's on the loosey-goosey "Blues & Bulls" or the daring "You Choose" (with bassist Tatsu Aoki), Davis shows she cares not about definitions, just good ol' authentic American music. Though she's something of a late bloomer, the 40-something Davis proves on her debut disc that she truly is the last of the Chicago-based red hot mamas. —*Michael G. Nastos*

Larry Davis

b. Dec. 4, 1936, Kansas City, MO, d. Apr. 19, 1994, Los Angeles, CA
Vocals, Guitar / Electric Texas Blues, Soul-Blues

Anyone who associates "Texas Flood" only with Stevie Ray Vaughan has never auditioned Larry Davis' version. Davis debuted on vinyl in 1958 with the song, his superlative Duke Records original remaining definitive to this day despite Vaughan's impassioned revival many years down the road.

Davis grew up in Little Rock, AR, giving up the drums to play bass. Forging an intermittent partnership with guitarist Fenton Robinson during the mid-'50s, the pair signed with Don Robey's Duke label on the recommendation of Bobby Bland. Three Davis 45s resulted, including "Texas Flood" and "Angels in Houston," before Robey cut Davis loose. From there, Davis was forced to make the most of limited opportunities in the studio. He lived in St. Louis for a spell and took up the guitar under Albert King's tutelage while playing bass in King's band.

A handful of singles for Virgo and Kent and a serious 1972 motorcycle accident that temporarily paralyzed Davis' left side preceded an impressive 1982 album for Rooster Blues, *Funny Stuff*, produced by Gateway City mainstay Oliver Sain. But follow-up options remained hard to come by: Few blues fans could find a copy of the guitarist's 1987 Pulsar LP *I Ain't Beggin' Nobody*.

Finally, in 1992, Ron Levy's Bulleye Blues logo issued a first-class Davis set, *Sooner or Later*, that skillfully showcased his rich, booming vocals and concise, Albert King-influenced guitar. Unfortunately, it came later rather than sooner: Davis died of cancer in the spring of 1994. —*Bill Dahl*

Funny Stuff / 1982 / Rooster Blues ◆◆◆◆

Larry Davis didn't record all that often, but when he did, he certainly made it count. That's the case with this fine St. Louis recording, not available yet on CD but well worth searching for at your favorite used vinyl emporium. Produced by Oliver Sain (who handled all sax work) and featuring Billy Gayles on drums and pianist Johnnie Johnson, the set is a ringing endorsement of Davis' slashing, tremolo-enriched guitar and booming vocals. —*Bill Dahl*

I Ain't Beggin' Nobody / 1987 / Evidence ◆◆◆◆◆

Only bad luck and the follies of the record industry have prevented Larry Davis from being the well-known blues star he should be. Davis has never received either sustained label support or concentrated marketing and thus is only a footnote when he should be a full chapter. His playing is energetic and varied, while his vocals are animated, soulful, and expressive. He recorded the nine tracks on this '85 date (newly reissued on CD by Evidence) with longtime blues and soul producer and instrumentalist Oliver Sain at the controls, and Davis demonstrated his convincing appeal on Sain's title track, as well as the defiant "I'm A Rolling Stone" (another Sain original), Davis' own anguished "Giving Up on Love," and "Please Don't Go," a Chuck Willis composition. *—Ron Wynn*

● **Sooner or Later** / 1992 / Bullseye Blues ♦♦♦♦♦
Unless someone has the ultimate Larry Davis album still awaiting release somewhere, the late guitarist's final album also looks to be his best. Sumptuously produced by organist/Bullseye Blues boss Ron Levy with the Memphis Horns providing punchy interjections, Davis roars a finely conceived concoction of covers and his own material ("Goin' Out West," "Little Rock") that represent contemporary blues at its finest. *—Bill Dahl*

Blues Knights / 1994 / Evidence ♦♦♦
This, despite the appearance, is not a duet album. Instead, this captures a session from November 20, 1985, with guitarists Larry Davis and Byther Smith fronting the same studio band consisting of guitarist Maurice John Vaughn, bassist Douglas Watson, drummer Julian Vaughn, and tenor saxophonist A.C. Reed. As Bill Dahl points out in the liner notes to the 1994 Evidence reissue *Blues Knights*, the two frontmen keep true to their essential style, with their supple supporting band following suit. As such, the four Davis cuts are pretty relaxed and jazzy, usually quite alluring but at times a little sleepy. The Smith sessions drive harder with some uptempo shuffles and swinging grooves offering a nice change of pace (and it sounds like the band welcomes shifting the tempo a little bit, too), but that doesn't necessarily make it a greater session; both musicians acquit themselves well by offering a bit of what they do best. This does not mean that they're at their best—they simply are doing what they do, and since they're good at it, it's pretty enjoyable. Ultimately, this is just a curiosity for fans of either Davis or Smith, and while it's nice to spin once or twice, it's not something they'll put on a whole lot, either. *—Stephen Thomas Erlewine*

Little Sammy Davis

b. Nov. 28, 1928, Winona, MS
Vocals, Harmonica / Harmonica Blues, Electric Blues
No, he never hung out with the Rat Pack on the martini-stained Vegas strip, and it's highly doubtful that he honors requests for "The Candy Man." This Little Sammy Davis is a veteran harp blower with a discography dating back to 1952 and a fine '90s debut album on Delmark, *I Ain't Lyin'*. Where's he been all these years? Poughkeepsie, NY, of course. Davis learned his way around a harmonica at age eight. He eventually exited Mississippi for Florida, where he worked in the orange groves and met immaculate guitarist Earl Hooker. Davis cut four sides in 1952 for Henry Stone's Rockin' label in Miami as Little Sam Davis (with Hooker providing classy accompaniment) that comprised the bulk of his discography until many years later. He visited Chicago in 1953, hanging out with harp genius Little Walter, Jimmy Reed, and Muddy Waters. But Davis rambled on, eventually settling in Poughkeepsie.

Other than a 45 for Pete Lowry's Trix logo, things were pretty quiet for the hero until 1995, when he joined forces with guitarist Fred Scribner and got back into playing. He became a favorite guest of popular New York morning radio personality Don Imus, had his own band and an album on the shelves, and hopefully, nobody mistook him for another diminutively proportioned entertainer by the same name. *—Bill Dahl*

● **I Ain't Lyin** / Oct. 3, 1995 / Delmark ♦♦♦♦♦
From out of nowhere came Little Sam Davis with this sterling set, making it clear that at least a few blues harpists of postwar vintage are still roaming around out there, just waiting to be rediscovered. Backed by a sharp rhythm section, Davis shows that he's been keeping his ear to the ground over the decades. His harp mastery and enthusiastic vocals are equally arresting. *—Bill Dahl*

Mamie "Galore" Davis

b. Sep. 24, 1940, **d.** Oct. 6, 2001
Vocals / Delta Blues, Soul-Blues
Mamie Galore was a leading component of Mississippi Delta blues along with Lil' Bill Wallace, Robert Jr. Lockwood, Eddie Cusic, Po Henry, Willie Foster, and others. Born Mamie Louise Davis, September 24, 1940, in Erwin, MS, the music bug struck early and she sang in school and church before embarking on a music career by joining a local band after graduating from high school. She soon began performing with traveling bands, such as Little Milton, Ike & Tina Turner, Buddy Hicks, and Johnny Burton.

When the Little Milton tour rolled into Chicago, she landed a deal with St. Lawrence Records that resulted in her first single, "Special Agent 34-24-38" b/w "I Wanna Be Your Radio" (1965); the song was a female spy tale reminiscent of Edwin Starr's "Agent OO Soul." However, something was amiss as Mamie's second single, "Mistaken Wedding" b/w "You Got the Power," dropped on Thomas Records February 1966. St. Lawrence countered with "It Ain't Necessary" (March 1966). It became a local hit and Davis' biggest record, the impromptu songwriting team of Jerry Butler and two of the Contours.

She followed Higgins, aka Milton Bland, to California in 1968 and wrote songs for Sweet River Music, collaborating mainly with Dee Irwin, Virginia Bland, aka Vee Pea Smith, and Higgins on more than 30 titles including "Come on in My Kitchen," "Meanest Man I've Ever Seen," "You Know I Know You Know," and "World Don't Care but I Do." Besides the previously mentioned, Davis' significant recordings were "No Right to Cry," "I Can Feel Him Slipping Way," and a duet with Dee Irwin "By the Time I Get to Phoenix"/"I Say a Little Prayer" b/w "All I Want for Christmas" on Imperial Records.

She returned south to Greenville, MS, in 1972 where she taught blues and performed—as Mamie Davis—in blues festivals and local clubs—the Meeting Place, Flowing Fountain, Bud's Café, and Little Blues Caffa—billed as the Soul Queen of Greenville. Delta blues fans lost a thoroughbred October 6, 2001, when the vivacious singer succumbed to a fatal stroke. She was 61. *—Andrew Hamilton*

Maxwell Davis

b. Jan. 14, 1916, Independence, KS, **d.** Sep. 18, 1970, Los Angeles, CA
Sax (Tenor), Songwriter / West Coast Blues, R&B, Jump Blues
As a prolific all-purpose producer/songwriter/sideman, tenor saxman Maxwell Davis filled some of the same pivotal roles on the '50s Los Angeles R&B scene that Willie Dixon handled so skillfully in Chicago. Davis arranged and produced myriad West Coast sessions for Modern, Aladdin, and other postwar R&B indies from the late '40s on, lending his husky sax to scads of waxings.

Davis left Kansas for L.A. in 1937, working in Fletcher Henderson's orchestra before being bitten by the R&B bug. Modern/Kent probably kept him employed the steadiest throughout the '50s and '60s; he worked with Pee Wee Crayton, Etta James, Johnny "Guitar" Watson, Lowell Fulson, Z.Z. Hill, and plenty more on the Bihari brothers' star-studded roster. Over at Aladdin, he worked closely with Amos Milburn and Peppermint Harris, among others. Davis didn't have much luck recording as a bandleader, although his instrumentals "Look Sharp—Be Sharp" (an R&B adaptation of the Gillette march) for Aladdin and "Tempo Rock"/"Cool Diggin'" on RPM packed a wallop. *—Bill Dahl*

A Tribute to Charlie Barnet / 2000 / Crown ♦♦♦
One of the differing ways jazz artists are commemorated is through a tribute album. There are albums honoring Louis Armstrong, Duke Ellington, Charlie Parker, and many others. Often the musicians are former playing associates, other times they are a group of musicians showing their respect. West Coast tenor man, arranger, and orchestra leader Maxwell Davis heads a large group of excellent big band veterans to pay tribute to Charlie Barnet, who led one of the most enduring and talented outfits of the big band era. Most of the players were with Barnet at one time or another for varying lengths of time, but there are also some ringers like Plas Johnson and Don Fagerquist. Nonetheless, under Davis' leadership, listeners are treated to replays of staples from the Barnet band like "Cherokee" and "Pompton Turnpike," plus some head arrangements Barnet was noted for. Given Barnet's adulation for Duke Ellington, it's surprising Ellington's music or the Barnet tunes he dedicated to the Duke have been ignored. Also, the presence of one of Ellington's favorite singers, Bunny Briggs, might have dictated that some musical reference to Ellington be included. Instead, the singer reprises "East Side West Side," which he did with Barnet in August of 1947. To Davis' credit, he avoids slavishly regurgitating Barnet's arrangements, at the same time, he doesn't stray all that far from the original. This is the bane of tribute albums, finding the right balance between the work of the person being honored and making the album interesting enough for big band fans to purchase, even though they may have the original. Davis does a reasonably good job in striking this balance to the point that this long out of print LP should be considered for transfer to CD. *—Dave Nathan*

● **Father of West Coast R&B** / Ace ♦♦♦♦♦
Ace's *Father of West Coast R&B* is an excellent 14 track collection of the tenor saxophonist's '50s and '60s records. There are several solo sides, plus cuts featuring him with Lloyd Glenn and Gene Phillips' orchestras. Since it features Maxwell Davis as both a leader and a sideman, the collection is a nice overview of his peak years. *—Thom Owens*

Maxwell Street Jimmy Davis (Charles W. Thompson)

b. Mar. 2, 1925, Tippo, Mississippi, **d.** Dec. 28, 1995
Guitar, Vocals / Modern Electric Blues
A protégé of John Lee Hooker, Maxwell Street Jimmy Davis was a Chicago blues institution throughout the latter half of the 20th century. Born Charles W. Thompson on March 2, 1925, in Tippo, MS, he learned to play guitar from Hooker while still a teenager, developing an insistent single-chord technique similar to that of his mentor; Davis and Hooker regularly gigged together in Detroit throughout the '40s, with the former settling in Chicago early the next decade. There he became a fixture of the West Side's Maxwell Street marketplace area, performing his distinctive brand of traditional Mississippi blues amidst the daily hustle-and-bustle of local merchants and shoppers; in the wake of the folk-blues revival of the early '60s, he recorded the LP *Maxwell Street Jimmy Davis* for Elektra, and although a fine showcase for his powerful guitar skills and provocative vocals, it failed to make much impact outside of purist circles. Davis continued to record sporadically in the decades that followed, and remained a constant West Side presence prior to his death on December 28, 1995. *—Jason Ankeny*

● **Chicago Blues Session, Vol. 11** / Jul. 29, 1994 / Wolf ♦♦♦♦

Walter Davis

b. Mar. 1, 1912, Grenada, MS, **d.** Oct. 22, 1963, St. Louis, MO
Composer, Piano / Piano Blues, St. Louis Blues
While never a contemporary superstar or latter-day legend on a par with many of his peers, singer/pianist Walter Davis was among the most prolific blues performers to emerge from the prewar St. Louis scene, cutting over 150 sides between 1930 and 1952. Born March 1, 1912, in Grenada, MS, Davis' two-fisted piano style bore the heavy influence of Leroy Carr, although he was better known for his funereal vocal style; he first attracted attention upon relocating to St. Louis during the mid-'20s, and soon made the first of his many recordings for the Victor label. Despite its abundance, his work—much of it recorded in conjunction with guitarist Henry Townsend—was solid but unspectacular, eclipsed by the likes of associates including Roosevelt Sykes and Peetie Wheatstraw; still, he enjoyed a fair amount of success before a stroke prompted him to move from music to the ministry during the early '50s. Davis was still preaching at the time of his death on October 22, 1963. *—Jason Ankeny*

● **The Bullet Sides** / 1986 / Krazy Kat ✦✦✦✦✦
Simply the best collection available, including the incredible "Tears Came Rollin' Down," one of Davis' best. (Import) —*Cub Koda*

First Recordings (1930–1932) / 1992 / JSP ✦✦✦

Complete Works in Chronological Order, Vol. 1 (1933–35) / Feb. 15, 1995 / Document ✦✦✦

Complete Works in Chronological Order, Vol. 2 (1935–37) / Feb. 15, 1995 / Document ✦✦✦

Complete Works in Chronological Order, Vol. 3 (1937–38) / Feb. 15, 1995 / Document ✦✦✦

Complete Works in Chronological Order, Vol. 4 (1938–39) / Feb. 15, 1995 / Document ✦✦✦

Complete Works in Chronological Order, Vol. 5 (1939–40) / Feb. 15, 1995 / Document ✦✦✦

Complete Works in Chronological Order, Vol. 6 (1940–46) / Feb. 15, 1995 / Document ✦✦✦

Complete Works in Chronological Order, Vol. 7 (1946–52) / Feb. 15, 1995 / Document ✦✦✦

● **Please Remember Me: 1930–1947** / Oct. 12, 1999 / EPM Musique ✦✦✦✦✦

The Essential / May 1, 2001 / Classic Blues ✦✦✦✦

Jimmy Dawkins

b. Oct. 24, 1936, Tchula, MS
Vocals, Guitar / Chicago Blues, Modern Electric Blues
Chicago guitarist Jimmy Dawkins would just as soon leave his longtime nickname "Fast Fingers" behind. It was always something of a stylistic misnomer anyway; Dawkins' West Side-styled guitar slashes and surges, but seldom burns with incendiary speed. Dawkins' blues are generally of the brooding, introspective variety—he doesn't engage in flashy pyrotechnics or outrageous showmanship.

It took a long time for Dawkins to progress from West Side fixture to nationally known recording artist. He rode a Greyhound bus out of Mississippi in 1955, dressed warm to ward off the Windy City's infamous chill factor. Only trouble was, he arrived on a sweltering July day! Harpist Billy Boy Arnold offered the newcomer encouragement, and he eventually carved out a niche on the competitive West Side scene (his peers included Magic Sam and Luther Allison).

Sam introduced Dawkins to Delmark Records boss Bob Koester. *Fast Fingers,* Dawkins' 1969 debut LP for Delmark—still his best album to date—was a taut, uncompromising piece of work that won the Grand Prix du Disque de Jazz from the Hot Club of France in 1971 as the year's top album. Andrew "Big Voice" Odom shared the singing and Otis Rush the second guitar duties on Dawkins' 1971 encore *All for Business.* But after his Delmark LP *Blisterstring,* Dawkins' subsequent recordings lacked intensity until 1991's oddly titled *Kant Sheck Dees Bluze* for Chicago's Earwig Records. Since then, Dawkins has waxed discs for Ichiban and continues to tour extensively. —*Bill Dahl*

● **Fast Fingers** / 1969 / Delmark ✦✦✦✦✦
Still his toughest and most satisfying album to date, finally released on CD in 1998. Dawkins burst onto the blues scene with this album at the dawn of the '70s, his slashing, angular guitar lines and reserved vocal style beautifully captured throughout the set. —*Bill Dahl*

All for Business / 1971 / Delmark ✦✦✦
This time around, Dawkins handed the majority of the vocal duties to Andrew "Big Voice" Odom and concentrated on his guitar (actually, he had some potent help in that department, too: Otis Rush was on second guitar). A generally solid but not overly enthralling set, with two bonus cuts and an alternate take of "Moon Man" added to the CD version. —*Bill Dahl*

Tribute to Orange / Nov. 30, 1971-Nov. 2, 1974 / Evidence ✦✦✦
Jimmy Dawkins' infrequent albums are always a joy, and that was the case when he made his first sojourn to Europe in 1970 and recorded LPs for Black & Blue, Vogue, and Excello in France and England. This disc features eight numbers pairing Dawkins and the great "Gatemouth" Brown and another four matching him with equally sensational Otis Rush. The Brown/Dawkins tandem duel, match, and challenge each other as Dawkins' sometimes enigmatic, sometimes bemused and often compelling vocals set the stage for their instrumental encounters. The same holds true on the Rush/Dawkins cuts. While Rush provides searing licks and twisting solos, Dawkins' singing sets the tone with its urgent inflections and weary, resigned quality. —*Ron Wynn*

Blisterstring / Jun. 1977 / Delmark ✦✦✦
Not as impressive as either of his previous outings for Delmark, but still a great deal better than some of what would follow over the course of the next few years. —*Bill Dahl*

Hot Wire / 1981 / Isabel ✦✦
Low key, but still worthwhile. —*Bill Dahl*

Hot Wire 81 / Mar. 1981 / Evidence ✦✦
Actually, more like tepid—Dawkins wasn't exactly tearing up the strings on this low-key set, which positively pales in comparison to his previous Delmark releases. —*Bill Dahl*

Feel the Blues / 1985 / JSP ✦✦
Originally released on vinyl in 1985, this captures Dawkins with a regular working band blasting through a set of his original tunes. The set has been remixed, putting some much-needed life into Dawkins' flabby guitar sound but still unable to get his vocals out far enough to compete with his guitar. The tunes are good, though, and the band blows in tune, giving Dawkins one of the more focused sessions he's ever turned in. This was

re-released by JSP in 2000 as part of a three-disc box set (with separate albums by Lefty Dizz and Brewer Phillips) entitled *Bad Avenue.* —*Cub Koda*

All Blues / 1986 / JSP ✦✦

Kant Sheck Dees Bluze / Jun. 1991 / Earwig ✦✦✦✦
Incredibly weird title (many of the songs sport equally bizarre spellings), but a major step back in the right direction for the guitarist, whose dirty, distorted tone won't thrill the purists. —*Bill Dahl*

Blues & Pain / 1994 / Wild Dog ✦✦✦
Dawkins is back on the right track now, making solid if less than earthshaking recordings that at least hint at why he once was billed "Fast Fingers." —*Bill Dahl*

B Phur Real / 1995 / Wild Dog ✦✦✦
Here we go again with the off-the-wall spellings…more listenable modern work from the Chicago guitarist, who's found his groove again after quite a few years of less than enthralling releases. —*Bill Dahl*

Blues from Iceland / 1995 / Evidence ✦✦✦

Me, My Gitar & the Blues / Aug. 26, 1997 / Ichiban ✦✦✦

American Roots: Blues / May 14, 2002 / Ichiban ✦✦✦✦

Deep River Boys

Group / Southern Gospel, Black Gospel, R&B, Harmony Vocal Group
The Deep River Boys left a legacy of fine recordings during their 50 years of performing, setting a standard for professionalism and longevity that is to be envied. They began recording as a gospel act in the late '40s and later switched over and became an R&B act and were more popular in Europe for periods of time before coming home to the States for triumphant return engagements.

Their story begins in 1936, when all of the Boys—Harry Douglas (baritone), Vernon Gardner (first tenor), George Lawson (second tenor), Jimmy Lundy, and Edward Ware (bass)—were still students at Hampton Institute in Virginia in the mid-30s, singing in the school choir. In 1936, the Deep River Boys traveled to New York, where they found their first success by taking first place by singing spirituals on the Major Bowes Amateur Hour. This led to opportunities to appear on stage and in radio and during World War II, they performed extensively for the USO and provided entertainment for American troops overseas.

In 1937, they landed a job on CBS radio replacing the Oleanders (whose lead singer, Billy Williams, had left to form the Charioteers) and in the late '40s, they toured with Bill Robinson, aka "Mr. Bojangles," and made some very early TV appearances on the Ed Sullivan Show and Milton Berle's first television program.

The Deep River Boys signed with Bluebird Records in 1940. A year later they had already released eight singles, including "By the Light of the Silvery Moon," which featured Fats Waller on piano. When Harry Douglas went into the Army, he was replaced by Leroy Wayman, who in turn was replaced by Rhett Butler. Douglas returned to the group in 1946 and the Deep River Boys began enjoying their biggest success, appearing on Milton Berle's and Kate Smith's shows and touring again with Bill Robinson.

Like many vocal groups in their day, the Deep River Boys had more success with their live performances than with record sales, and although their label kept up a steady stream of recordings, it wasn't until 1948, when Bluebird issued "Recess in Heaven," that they enjoyed their first hit. Unfortunately, the newer R&B sound was just then emerging and their gospel sound was being pushed aside by popular vocal groups like the Dominoes, the Orioles, the Cardinals, and the Ravens. Unlike the Five Royales (a gospel group from North Carolina who called the Royal Suns before they came to New York to record R&B sides for Apollo Records), the Deep River Boys were reluctant to change; instead, they followed the path of another great gospel group of the '40s—the Delta Rhythm Boys—and moved to Europe to find work.

By 1950, however, the Deep River Boys had returned to the U.S. and Canada, where they performed an extended engagement in Montreal. Soon, they were in demand again and returned to New York to appear on The Ed Sullivan Show to premier their new recording for RCA. They continued to tour and record (they worked with the Count Basie Band early in 1951 and Erskine Hawkins). The group eventually returned to Europe, where they received a citation naming them as the Most Popular Entertainers for American Service Personnel in England. The Deep River Boys signed on for a record-breaking ten-week engagement at the London Palladium, but they were being called back home just as soon as it was over.

After a second triumphant return from England, the group began the new year—1952—by performing in Montreal once again, where they remained popular throughout their career. They later left RCA for the independent Beacon Records label, which had been reactivated by owner Joe Davis.

However, several singles for Beacon failed to generate any new interest and the Boys returned to RCA. In September of 1953, Cam Williams replaced Jim Lundy and the newly configured Deep River Boys returned to England and signed on for a nine-week appearance at the London Palladium. In the springtime of 1954, they once again found themselves back on Davis' Beacon Records for a second time. Throughout the rest of their career, the Deep River Boys continued to have sporadic releases on labels such as the RCA-subsidiary Vik Records, as well as Gallant and Wand.

George Lawson retired in 1950, followed six years later by Ed Ware in 1956 (he died shortly after). Vernon Gardner also left in 1956. Bass vocalist Ronnie Bright replaced Ware (he'd previously been in the Cadillacs). In 1963, Bright had a hit of his own, "Mr. Bass Man" (number 16) with Johnny Cymbal. He later joined Carl Gardner's lineup of the Coasters. Amazingly, a Harry Douglas-led Deep River Boys (with a revolving lineup of new members) continued to make appearances well into the '80s, 50 years after their founding. Douglas would continue to perform occasionally into his eighties. —*Bryan Thomas*

The Deep River Boys / 1943 / Langworth Transcriptions ✦✦✦✦✦
Some of the finest traditional a cappella gospel on wax. —*Opal Louis Nations*

- **Rock-A-Beatin' Boogie** / 1954-1962 / ♦♦♦♦♦

Geno Delafose

b. 1972, Eunice, LA

Vocals, Drums / Zydeco

The son of the great accordionist John Delafose, Geno Delafose carried on the family name with his own distinctive sound spanning from traditional Creole and Cajun music to contemporary R&B. Born in Eunice, LA, in 1972, he began his career at the age of eight, playing rub board and drums in his father's band the Eunice Playboys; he eventually adopted the accordion as well, and was among the few zydeco performers of his era to play both the button and piano models of the instrument. Over the years Delafose's prominence in the group grew, and he and his father often traded lead vocals; when John retired in the months prior to his 1994 death, Geno took over the band, and that same year he recorded his debut LP *French Rockin' Boogie*; *That's What I'm Talkin' About!* followed in 1996, and in 1998 he returned with *La Chanson Perdue*. *—Jason Ankeny*

French Rockin' Boogie / 1994 / Rounder ♦♦♦♦

This is the first CD by zydeco accordionist Geno Delafose. The name of the record, *French Rockin' Boogie*, is also the name of his backup group, a fine array of musicians including several family members. For as is often true in Louisiana, playing music is a family affair. Such is the case for Geno Delafose, who got his start at the age of eight in his father's band. When the great John Delafose retired, his son took over the band. By then, the younger Delafose was adept at making music on both the button and piano accordions. The sound of this musical artist is unique. In some ways, it is quite traditional Creole music, but it is pepped up with influences from the R&B and country-rock traditions. It is, above all, dance music. And Geno Delafose, with his country cowboy persona, has them smiling and dancing wherever he goes. The recording gives the listener a good sampling of the range of this master accordionist's capabilities. The title cut takes off fast to let you know the man can rock. But, as with the horses that Delafose raises, there are many changes of pace. Stirring waltzes such as "Wedding Day Waltz" are interspersed with ballads and traditional jures. Standout tunes include "Ris et la Gres" (Rice and Gravy) and "One Lie (Leads to Another)." There's nothing like a good two-step to get the blood pumping, and there are plenty of those dance favorites on the record. As Delafose admonishes on the last track, "Watch Your Step." *—Rose of Sharon Witmer*

- **That's What I'm Talkin' About!** / Jun. 1996 / Rounder ♦♦♦♦♦

This will stand as one of the finest zydeco albums of the decade. Young Geno (age 24) plays in a more tuneful and traditional style than competitors on the '90s South Louisiana zydeco circuit like Beau Jocque and Keith Frank, whose thumping dance-beats, one-chord riffs, and grunted lyrics constitute a sort of zydeco/hip-hop synthesis. Geno instead draws inspiration from the older Creole songs of his father, John Delafose. But he hasn't merely followed in his father's footsteps; he's outpaced him. His music has just the right combination of lilt and kick to it, thanks in large part to his cousin Jermaine Jack's drum work. *That's What I'm Talkin' About!* is like a zydeco carousel that whirls you delightedly round and round. Geno handles button and piano-accordion proficiently, and his voice, used to better advantage here than on his 1994 debut album *French Rockin' Boogie*, possesses that lovely "key of heartbreak" quality that characterizes the best South Louisiana music. *—Steve Hoffman*

La Chanson Perdue / Jun. 9, 1998 / Rounder ♦♦♦♦♦

Delafose's devotion and consuming interest in traditional Creole and Cajun material is brought to full fruition on this delightful platter. English translations are right alongside their French counterparts in the booklet, but the message comes through loud and clear in either language. With his regular working band French Rockin' Boogie, contributing trance-like grooves ("Bon soir Moreau"), Delafose digs deep for his roots on every track. He brings aboard Steve Riley for a couple numbers (his fiddle is particularly effective on "Joilie Basette/Quo faire"), then cuts a four-song acoustic session with Christine Balfa on acoustic guitar and fiddler Dirk Powell. The overall effect is an album that looks forward and backward for its inspiration and never disappoints for a second. *—Cub Koda*

John Delafose

b. Apr. 16, 1939, Duralde, LA, **d.** Sep. 17, 1994, Lawtell, LA

Vocals, Accordion / Zydeco

John Delafose and his band the Eunice Playboys bridged the gap between zydeco's roots and its contemporary sound with a mastery matched by few of their peers; despite an affinity for early Creole styles, French lyrics and two-step waltz rhythms, they played with all of the fiery intensity demanded by modern-day audiences, tapping into a wide array of sources—blues, Cajun, even country—to forge a propulsive traditionalist sound all their own. Born April 16, 1939, in Duralde, LA, Delafose as a child crafted fiddles and guitars out of old boards and cigar boxes fitted with window-screen wire; he eventually took up the harmonica, and at the age of 18 learned the button accordion. He soon turned to farming, and as a result did not seriously pursue music until during the early '70s, at which time he served as an accordionist and harpist with a variety of local zydeco bands. By the middle of the decade his formed his own combo, the Eunice Playboys; originally featuring guitarist Charles Prudhomme and his bassist brother Slim, the group's lineup swelled over time to also include Delafose's sons John "T.T." on rub board and Tony on drums. Another son, Geno, later joined as well, trading vocal and accordion leads with his father. Delafose and the Eunice Playboys debuted in 1980 with the regional hit "Joe Pete Got Two Women," from the LP *Zydeco Man*; *Uncle Bud Zydeco* followed in 1982, and as interest in traditional Creole culture swelled, the group became one of the hottest attractions on the Gulf Coast circuit. They returned in 1984 with *Heartaches & Hot Steps*, a year later issuing *Zydeco Excitement*; after a lengthy hiatus from the studio, Delafose resurfaced in 1992 with *Pere et Garcon Zydeco*. 1993's *Blues Stay Away from Me* was his final album; failing health forced him to curtail his touring schedule soon after, and on September 17, 1994, Delafose died. Geno succeeded his father as bandleader. *—Jason Ankeny*

Zydeco Man / 1980 / Arhoolie ♦♦♦♦

Uncle Bud Zydeco / 1982 / Arhoolie ♦♦♦

Heartaches & Hot Steps / 1984 / Maison de Soul ♦♦♦♦♦

Explosive arrangements, powerhouse vocals and accordion playing, and good band support make this a first-rate contemporary zydeco date. *—Ron Wynn*

Zydeco Excitement! / 1985 / Maison de Soul ♦♦♦

- **Joe Pete Got Two Women** / 1988 / Arhoolie ♦♦♦♦♦

Delafose's best contains his popular saga of Joe Pete. Zydeco fundamentalism from this singer/accordionist, who's so down-home, his music clearly echoes African hypnotic grooves. *—Jeff Hannusch & Mark A. Humphrey*

Pere et Garcon Zydeco / 1992 / Rounder ♦♦♦

While zydeco and Cajun-influenced hybrids have been the norm in many circles during the '80s and '90s, John Delafose & the Eunice Playboys have remained true to the classic style. This session featured predominantly hardcore material, emphasizing the two-steps, waltzes, and French lyrics at the heart of zydeco/Cajun. Delafose and his son Geno alternated lead vocals and accordion support, each singing and playing with vigor, conviction and authenticity. Meanwhile, the band backed them with equal electricity, and while such tunes as "Watch That Dog," "Morning Train" and "Go Back Where You Been" were lyrical departures, they were as fully in the zydeco framework as "Mon Coeur Fait Mal" or "Grand Mamou." *—Ron Wynn*

Delaney & Bonnie

f. 1966, **db.** 1972

Group / Album Rock, Pop/Rock, Blues-Rock

Delaney Bramlett (b. Jul. 1, 1939) and his wife Bonnie (b. Nov. 8, 1944) recorded a series of blues and country influenced albums in the late '60s and early '70s. A variety of musicians played in Delaney & Bonnie's band, including Eric Clapton, Dave Mason, Duane Allman, Leon Russell, Rita Coolidge, Jim Gordon, Bobby Whitlock, and Carl Radle; Clapton, Gordon, Whitlock, and Radle formed Derek & The Dominoes after performing together on Delaney & Bonnie's 1969-1970 tour. Delaney & Bonnie's records were a strong influence on Eric Clapton's style in the '70s. The group broke up after the Bramletts' marriage collapsed in 1972. *—Kenneth M. Cassidy*

Accept No Substitutes / 1969 / Collectors' Choice Music ♦♦♦

While Delaney & Bonnie will be forever associated with Eric Clapton and *Layla & Other Assorted Love Songs*, the couple, along with a loose association of friends, recorded a number of classics in their own right. Released in 1969, *Accept No Substitute* contained the same blend of soul and rock & roll that would show up on *Layla* the following year. While the production, as Matthew Greenwald points out in the liner notes, has a "pop sheen," Delaney & Bonnie's earthy vocals, along with the band's rhythm & blues assault, nonetheless dictate the proceedings. The horn section and expressive guitar create a lovely mix on "Get Ourselves Together" and "Someday," giving the listener a taste of what gospel might sound like if performed by a good '60s rock band. This religious connection is even more predominate on "Soldiers of the Cross," a piece of lyrical fundamentalism that would fit quite comfortably into a Baptist choir's repertoire. This isn't to infer that *Accept No Substitute* is pious in any way; only that Delaney & Bonnie and their friends add a spiritual quality to the music they perform. One also shouldn't miss the imaginative "Ghetto," a song that cleverly combines soulful piano with strings. For those unfamiliar with Delaney & Bonnie's other work, *Accept No Substitute* is a good place to start. *—Ronnie D. Lankford, Jr.*

- **Delaney & Bonnie & Friends on Tour With Eric Clapton** / Jun. 1970 / Atco ♦♦♦♦♦

This 42-minute, eight-song live album, cut at Croydon late in 1969, is not only the peak of Delaney & Bonnie's output, but also the nexus in the recording and performing careers of Eric Clapton and George Harrison. *On Tour With Eric Clapton* features the guitarist performing the same blend of country, blues, and gospel that would characterize his own early solo ventures in 1970. He rises to the occasion with dazzling displays of virtuosity throughout, highlighted by a dizzying solo on "I Don't Want to Discuss," a long, languid part on "Only You Know and I Know," and searing, soulful lead on the beautifully harmonized "Coming Home." Vocally, Delaney & Bonnie were never better than they come off on this live set, and the 11-piece band sounds tighter musically than a lot of quartets that were working at the time, whether they're playing extended blues or ripping through a medley of Little Richard songs. It's no accident that the band featured here would become Clapton's own studio outfit for his debut solo LP, or that the core of this group—Bobby Whitlock, Carl Radle, and Jim Gordon—would transform itself into Derek & the Dominos as well; or that most of the full band here would also comprise the group that played with George Harrison on *All Things Must Pass* and at the Concert for Bangladesh, except that the playing here (not to mention the recording) is better. Half the musicians on this record achieved near-superstar status less than a year later, and although the reasons behind their fame didn't last, listening to their work decades later, it all seems justified. One only wishes that Atlantic Records might check their vaults for any unreleased numbers from these shows that could fit on an extended CD. *—Bruce Eder*

To Bonnie from Delaney / 1970 / Atco ♦♦♦♦

Following *On Tour With Eric Clapton*, this disc should have been huge. Unfortunately, the Friends who backed up the Bramletts then jumped ship and became Joe Cocker's Mad Dogs & Englishmen, so the Bramletts had to recruit a whole new band. This is, then, their third "first" album, and even though it's good, there's no telling how good it could have been had things not turned out the way they did. The acoustic medley is worth the price here alone, and they did have a couple of stabs at the Top 40 with "Soul Shake" and "Free the People." Even Little Richard guests on his own "Miss Ann." But nothing seemed to go right again for Delaney & Bonnie, and they were starting to sound a little weary. Good stuff, just not the best. *—James Chrispell*

Motel Shot / 1971 / Atco ✦✦✦

Decades before the *Unplugged* phenomenon took off, Delaney & Bonnie recorded an album's worth of tunes in just that fashion. Rounding up a "cast of ???" for the event, it tries to show how musicians on the road unwind after concerts and get back to the basics. Delaney & Bonnie even got a hit single here with "Never Ending Song of Love." This is a refreshing record and one that should not be missed. It includes strains of gospel, country, blues, folk, and R&B, while never straying from the acoustic trail. *—James Chrispell*

Country Life / 1972 / Atco ✦✦

D&B Together / 1972 / Columbia ✦✦

It appears as though the Bramletts were pulling in a lot of markers here in the hopes of getting that elusive hit. On *D&B Together*, we find studio versions of "Only You Know & I Know" and "Superstar," both of which were concert highlights over two years before. Surprisingly, the best cut here is also a studio take of "Comin' Home," written with Eric Clapton and featured on the *On Tour...* album. While not as loose as the live cut, "Comin' Home" is great music nonetheless. The problem was, nobody seemed to care much anymore. *—James Chrispell*

The Best of Delaney & Bonnie / Nov. 1990 / Rhino ✦✦✦✦✦

Bonnie Bramlett released "Groupie," the song she co-wrote with Leon Russell, as an Atlantic single in December of 1969. Almost two years later in September of 1971, Karen Carpenter took it to the top of the pop and adult contemporary charts under the name "Superstar." It may not have been Bramlett's favorite rendition of one of her songs, but it was phenomenal and deserved success for the talented singer/songwriter beyond her appearances on the TV show *Roseanne*. "Groupie (Superstar)" is the highlight of a simply great collection of musical expression by the underrated and abundantly talented duo known simply as Delaney & Bonnie. Goldmine/Discoveries magazine contributor Joe Tortelli is very detailed in his six-page liner notes/track listing to this 18-song compilation. It includes their two Top 20 hits from 1971, "Never Ending Song of Love" and "Only You Know and I Know"; the excellent double-sided minor hits "Free the People" and "Soul Shake"; three tracks from their Jimmy Miller-produced legendary live *Delaney & Bonnie & Friends on Tour With Eric Clapton* (and George Harrison); a thrilling rendition of "Piece of My Heart" tracked two years after Janis Joplin but tipping the hat, no doubt, to Aretha's sister, Emma Franklin, who did it before both these gals—this best-of basically concentrates on the Elektra, Stax, and Atlantic recordings. The pity here is that this isn't a double CD containing the Leon Russell and Jackie DeShannon tapes released on GNP Crescendo as *Genesis*, some material from their final album on CBS and maybe a version of "Let It Rain," the magnificent song Bonnie Bramlett co-wrote with Eric Clapton for his 1970 solo album produced by Delaney. There are great photographs of the "friends"—saxophone player Bobby Keyes, horn player Jim Price, bassist Carl Radle, drummer Jim Keltner, and Bobby Whitlock, as well as the singers. This album contains musicianship by all of the above, plus Dave Mason, Gram Parsons, Duane Allman, Alan Estes, and so many others, especially Rita Coolidge, who performed "Superstar" on *Mad Dogs & Englishman*—the world's first taste of lovely Coolidge before she became a hit artist herself a half-dozen or so years later. Hearing "Free the People" and its revolutionary sound for rock & roll radio, along with Bonnie Bramlett's extraordinarily passionate "The Love of My Man," one wonders what it takes to get the world to recognize a diamond this polished. The plethora of name musicians aren't here for show, they are all working their tails off, and the result is a true masterpiece of rock/R&B/pop and blues clocking in at 69:39. The downside is that it really should be twice as long, and they have enough legitimate music—as stated—to fill a double CD. For now this is a unique time capsule which lives up to the title "Best Of." *—Joe Viglione*

Paul deLay

b. Jan. 31, 1952, Portland, OR

Vocals, Harmonica / Electric Harmonica Blues, Modern Electric Blues

For originality in contemporary blues with a capital "o," one need look no further than West Coast harmonica stylist, singer, and songwriter Paul deLay. DeLay is the freshest songwriting voice to come onto the West Coast blues scene since Robert Cray rose to prominence in the San Francisco Bay area in the '80s. Not surprisingly, he backs up his original songs with some very stylized chromatic harmonica playing that incorporates a sense of swing and jazz, largely based on the Chicago blues harp masters.

DeLay was born Jan. 31, 1952 in Portland, OR, but raised in the Ardenwald neighborhood of Milwaukee, in a musically inclined family. After hearing Paul Butterfield play "Good Morning Little Schoolgirl," he became hooked on blues harmonica by age eight. He took his inspiration from Big Walter "Shakey" Horton and Little Walter Jacobs, and later, George "Harmonica" Smith and Charlie Musselwhite. DeLay took lessons on piano and tried to teach himself guitar and drums, but he found his true calling when he picked up the harmonica. He began playing along with records at first, and later formed a jug band in the '60s.

DeLay led a band called Brown Sugar, which played in Portland, Oregon-area clubs for most of the '70s, and then began leading a band under his own name in 1978. DeLay toured with Chicago piano player Sunnyland Slim and guitarist Hubert Sumlin for a few months that same year. When he got off the road, he concentrated his efforts on developing his own sound while leading his own band. He began writing his own songs in 1980, and by that point he was already a veteran of the bandstand. DeLay knew he didn't want to write standard blues songs, and to this day he avoids clichéd lyrical themes.

The Paul deLay Band recorded four independent albums on their own label by 1988: *Teasin'*, *American Voodoo*, *The Paul deLay Band*, and *Burnin'*. The band toured constantly, and deLay's alcoholism turned into a major problem. When he finally quit drinking, he slowly began using cocaine instead, which he was busted for dealing. While spending three years in prison, deLay wrote a huge number of original songs and put his boozing and cocaine-snorting habits behind him for good. When he came out of prison in 1995, deLay made up for his lost time, and the results can be heard on several fine albums. Most notable are two albums for Evidence, *Take It from the Turnaround* (1996), an album that combines two independent releases he recorded locally in Portland for Criminal Records, and his more recent *Ocean of Tears* (1997). Both albums are fine examples of deLay's unique gift for telling a story and his natural sense of humor and wittiness, as well as great singing and harmonica playing. Both also showcase excellent backing bands. That's why deLay's reputation has spread out from his home base in Oregon to envelop the rest of the country, as well as parts of Canada and Europe.

In the late '80s and '90s, the Paul deLay Band performed at the San Francisco Blues Festival, the Pocono Blues Festival, the Long Beach Blues Festival, and the San Francisco Harmonica Festival, among many other large-scale gatherings. *—Richard Skelly*

Teasin' / 1970 / Criminal ✦✦

The deLay band's first recording gave birth to Criminal Records. *—Michael Erlewine*

The Blue One / 1985 / Criminal ✦✦

Six tunes with the earlier band, including "Something's Got a Hold on Me." *—Michael Erlewine*

Burnin' / 1988 / Criminal ✦✦✦✦

Reached number 20 on the *Living Blues* chart. This album was the debut of guitarist Peter Dammann. Includes hornwork by ex-Mayall sax player Chris Mercer. *—Michael Erlewine*

American Voodoo / 1988 / Criminal ✦✦✦

The standout album from the early material, this second deLay album reached number two on the Italian blues charts. Worth seeking out. *—Michael Erlewine*

Paul deLay / 1988 / Criminal ✦✦✦✦✦

Other One / 1990 / Criminal ✦✦✦

All 11 songs written by deLay plus plenty of fine harp playing. With Peter Dammann on guitar and Louis Pain on keyboards. *—Michael Erlewine*

The Best of Paul deLay: You're Fired / 1990 / Red Lightnin' ✦✦✦✦

A collection of deLay material released by the British label Red Lightnin' in May of 1990. *—Michael Erlewine*

Paulzilla / 1992 / Criminal ✦✦✦✦✦

Declared the album of the year by the Cascades Blues Association, this was completed just days before deLay's three-year visit to the pen. DeLay wrote most of the songs and there is plenty of first-rate chromatic harp playing here. With Peter Dammann on guitar and Louis Pain on keyboards. *—Michael Erlewine*

● **Take It from the Turnaround** / 1996 / Evidence ✦✦✦✦✦

Combining the best of two albums (1991's *Just This One* and 1992's *Paulzilla*) on one CD, *Take It from the Turnaround* heralds the arrival of a harp player who's been a certified blues legend in his native region of Portland, OR. DeLay blows with authenticity and a full command of his instrument and way more than a hint of reckless abandon. Traditional blues, even by modern bar-band standards, this ain't, but the high creative level of deLay's songwriting on numbers like "Second Hand Smoke," "Merry Way" and the heartfelt "Just This One" heralds the arrival of a new way of looking at things and bodes well for future recordings. As a parenthetical note, the liner notes that accompany this release are superlative, telling deLay's story in a way that's both horrifying and inspiring. The man has lived a life in the blues and not only lived to tell the tale, but has triumphed over the worst elements a road musician has to suffer through. *—Cub Koda*

Ocean of Tears / Sep. 1996 / Evidence ✦✦✦✦

To sing the blues effectively, one must sing about what they know. Paul deLay knows what it is like to win and lose love, to be confident one moment and desperate the next, and to get high, suffer from drug abuse, and eventually kick his habit triumphantly. All of these experiences are part of his Evidence CD. DeLay, a fine harmonica player who is joined by his Portland-based sextet (which also includes guitarist Peter Dammann, organist Louis Pain, Dan Fincher on tenor, bassist John Mazzocco, and drummer Mike Klobas), has a highly expressive and rather raw voice. He performs ten colorful originals on *Ocean of Tears*, the majority of which were written while he was in prison on drug charges. DeLay's lyrics consistently tell memorable stories, and it's for his sincerity, emotional intensity, and insightful words that this CD is most highly recommended to blues and folk collectors. *—Scott Yanow*

Nice & Strong / Feb. 3, 1998 / Evidence ✦✦✦✦

Nice & Strong finds Paul deLay at the top of his form, turning out a set of hard-driving Chicago-style blues. Not only does deLay sound tougher than ever, his songs are simply stunning, displaying a devilish humor and a new vulnerability. It's another winning record from one of the great contemporary blues musicians and harp players of the '90s. *—Stephen Thomas Erlewine*

deLay Does Chicago / Jan. 12, 1999 / Evidence ✦✦✦✦

After six albums of blues harmonica playing that defies all the rules, deLay comes to Chicago, hooks up with the Johnny Burgin band, and cuts a nice, relaxed record in the '50s Chicago style. But that doesn't mean that deLay turned in a bunch of old Little Walter and Muddy Waters tunes from his record collection for this one. Instead, he wrote—or co-wrote with various band members—every tune on here, with many of them ("Beautiful Bones," "Oak Street beach," "All Cried Out") tipping their stylistic hat in the direction of Junior Wells and Buddy Guy's efforts on the classic *Hoodoo Man Blues* album. Zora Young guests on "Come On Home," and Jimmy Dawkins contributes some nasty, stinging guitar on "El Train" and "What's Coming Next." But as always, deLay's stratospheric explorations on his harp (especially his swinging work with the chromatic) are the big ticket, and tracks like "Brave Woman," the Elmore-styled "Wait," "Only Me" provide plenty of harmonica fireworks. If this is a side project between albums with his regular working band, then the infusion of new blood and new surroundings combine to make this one of the most accessible albums of his career. *—Cub Koda*

Heavy Rotation / Aug. 14, 2001 / Evidence ♦♦♦

Derek & the Dominos

f. 1970, New York, NY, **db.** 1971

Group / Album Rock, British Blues, Hard Rock, Blues-Rock

Derek & the Dominos was a group formed by guitarist/singer Eric Clapton (born Eric Patrick Clapp, March 30, 1945, Ripley, Surrey, England) with other former members of Delaney & Bonnie & Friends, in the spring of 1970. The rest of the lineup was Bobby Whitlock (b. 1948, Memphis, TN) (keyboards, vocals), Carl Radle (b. 1942, Oklahoma City, OK—d. May 30, 1980) (bass), and Jim Gordon (b. 1945, Los Angeles) (drums). The group debuted at the Lyceum Ballroom in London on June 14 and undertook a summer tour of England. From late August to early October, they recorded the celebrated double album *Layla and Other Assorted Love Songs* (November 1970) with guitarist Duane Allman sitting in. They then returned to touring in England and the U.S., playing their final date on December 6.

The *Layla* album was successful in the U.S., where "Bell Bottom Blues" and the title song charted as singles in abbreviated versions, but it did not chart in the U.K. The Dominos reconvened to record a second album in May 1971, but split up without completing it. Clapton then retired from the music business, nursing a heroin addiction.

In his absence, and in the wake of Allman's death in a motorcycle accident on October 29, 1971, the Dominos and *Layla* gained in stature. Re-released as a single at its full, seven-minute length in connection with the compilation album *History of Eric Clapton* (Atco 803) (March 1972), "Layla" hit the Top Ten in the U.S. and the U.K. in the summer of 1972. (It would return to the U.K. Top Ten in 1982.) A live album, *In Concert* (January 1973), taken from the 1970 U.S. tour, was also a strong seller.

Time has only added to the renown of the group, which is now rated among Eric Clapton's most outstanding achievements. The 1988 Eric Clapton box set retrospective *Crossroads* featured material from the abortive second album sessions. *The Layla Sessions* was a 1990 box set expanding that album across three CDs/cassettes. *Live at the Fillmore* (1994) offered an expanded version of the *In Concert* album. *—William Ruhlmann*

★ **Layla and Other Assorted Love Songs** / Nov. 1970 / Polydor ♦♦♦♦♦

Wishing to escape the superstar expectations that sank Blind Faith before it was launched, Eric Clapton retreated with several sidemen from Delaney & Bonnie to record the material that would form *Layla and Other Assorted Love Songs*. From these meager beginnings grew his greatest album. Duane Allman joined the band shortly after recording began, and his spectacular slide guitar pushed Clapton to new heights. Then again, Clapton may have gotten there without him, considering the emotional turmoil he was in during the recording. He was in hopeless, unrequited love with Patti Boyd, the wife of his best friend, George Harrison, and that pain surges throughout *Layla*, especially on its epic title track. But what really makes *Layla* such a powerful record is that Clapton, ignoring the traditions that occasionally painted him into a corner, simply tears through these songs with burning, intense emotion. He makes standards like "Have You Ever Loved a Woman" and "Nobody Knows You (When You're Down and Out)" into his own, while his collaborations with Bobby Whitlock—including "Any Day" and "Why Does Love Got to Be So Sad?"—teem with passion. And, considering what a personal album *Layla* is, it's somewhat ironic that the lovely coda "Thorn Tree in the Garden" is a solo performance by Whitlock, and that the song sums up the entire album as well as "Layla" itself. *—Stephen Thomas Erlewine*

In Concert / Jan. 1973 / Polydor ♦♦♦

While it isn't nearly as intense as *Layla, In Concert* offers some fine playing by Clapton and his band and easily ranks among his best live albums. *—Stephen Thomas Erlewine*

The Layla Sessions: 20th Anniversary Edition / Sep. 1990 / Polydor ♦♦♦

Featuring two discs of outtakes and jams, the three-CD box *The Layla Sessions* manages to detract from the original by surrounding it with endless, dull instrumentals. Then again, all the unreleased material proves what a well-constructed album *Layla* is. *—Stephen Thomas Erlewine*

Live at the Fillmore / Feb. 22, 1994 / Polydor ♦♦♦

In his liner notes, Anthony DeCurtis calls *Live at the Fillmore* "a digitally remixed and remastered version of the 1973 Derek & the Dominos double album *In Concert*, with five previously unreleased performances and two tracks that have only appeared on the four-CD Clapton retrospective, *Crossroads*." But this does not adequately describe the album. *Live at the Fillmore* is not exactly an expanded version of *In Concert*; it is a different album culled from the same concerts that were used to compile the earlier album. *Live at the Fillmore* contains six of the nine recordings originally released on *In Concert*, and three of its five previously unreleased performances are different recordings of songs also featured on *In Concert*—"Why Does Love Got to Be So Sad?," "Tell the Truth," and "Let It Rain." The other two, "Nobody Knows You When You're Down and Out" and "Little Wing," have not been heard before in any concert version. Even when the same recordings are used on *Live at the Fillmore* as on *In Concert*, they have, as noted, been remixed and, as not noted, re-edited. In either form, Derek & the Dominos' October 1970 stand at the Fillmore East, a part of the group's only U.S. tour, finds them a looser aggregation than they seemed to be in the studio making their only album, *Layla and Other Assorted Love Songs*. A trio backing Eric Clapton, the Dominos leave the guitarist considerable room to solo on extended numbers, five of which run over ten minutes each. Clapton doesn't show consistent invention, but his playing is always directed, and he plays more blues than you can hear on any other Clapton live recording. *—William Ruhlmann*

The Detroiters

f. Detroit, MI

Group / Traditional Gospel

One of the most successful gospel groups of the late '40s, the Detroiters were led by Oliver Green, a native of Texas who began his career during the Depression era as a member of the Southern Wonders. Upon settling in the Motor City in 1938, he formed the Evangelist Singers of Detroit, a quartet which hosted their own local radio and earned some measure of national popularity as a result of their frequent tours with Sister Rosetta Tharpe. The Evangelists were also the first group to cut the hit topical song "Tell Me Why You Like Roosevelt," which was composed by their booking manager Otis Jackson; after signing on with the Detroit radio station WGC, bandleader Horace Heidt insisted they change their name to the Detroiters, a more secular moniker which by extension would allow the addition of pop and folk material to their repertoire. Their frequent radio appearances led to a steady schedule of live bookings, and in addition to high lead Green, their ranks grew to include lower lead Leroy Barnes, first tenor Dempsey Harrison, baritone Bill Johnson, bass Robert Thomas, and pianist Nathaniel Howard. It was this Detroiters lineup which entered the studio on August 14, 1951 to record the first of three singles for the Specialty label, "Let Jesus Lead You"; the same session also yielded a follow-up, combining "I Trust in Jesus" with "Ride On King Jesus." A second date from 1952 spawned a rousing "Old Time Religion," but it was their last Specialty effort; for reasons unknown, label chief Art Rupe did not take a shine to the group, and they were soon dropped. Although Barnes later exited to join the Flying Clouds, the Detroiters continued touring regionally into the early '60s. *—Jason Ankeny*

● **Old Time Religion** / 1992 / Specialty ♦♦♦♦♦

Old Time Religion showcases two great gospel vocal quartets from the '40s and '50s: the Detroiters and the Golden Echoes. The first half of the disc features 15 cuts from the Detroiters, 11 of which are previously unreleased songs recorded at United Sound. The Golden Echoes are represented with 11 songs recorded in 1949, ten of which have never been released. Usually, large sections of unreleased material would mean that the disc is primarily of interest to collectors, but that's not necessarily the case here. Both quartets are excellent examples of impassioned, moving and plain entertaining classic gospel, blessed with remarkable voices—the Detroiters' lineup boasted Oliver Green and Leroy Barnes, while the Golden Echoes featured Paul Foster, Sr. and Wilmer "Little Axe" Broadnax—and true spirit; it's a pleasure to hear them in any setting. Granted, some tastes may find the preponderance of alternate takes a little tedious, but if you program them out, you're left with a sterling collection of classic gospel. *—Leo Stanley*

Harry Dial

Vocals, Guitar / Modern Electric Blues, Electric Texas Blues

A journeyman musician on the Nashville scene for years, Harry Dial cut a nasty version of the Albert King classic "Born Under a Bad Sign" for an interesting compilation of contemporary Tennessee blues performances released in the late '90s by the Taxim label. Despite the Tennessee connection and roots, Dial has been more closely associated with the Texas blues scene, an inspiration that might have been behind that choice of a cover tune as well, since at least one Texas guitarist, named Stevie Ray Vaughan, used to display a preference for Albert King when it came time to pay tribute to blues royalty.

After touring with a number of bands as a hired guitar slinger, Dial formed an alliance with a band called the Paramours. The backgrounds of his sidekicks in this outfit are similar to his. Wes Starr was the house drummer at Antone's in Austin for many years, a place lovers of jumping Texas blues like to go to shake their tailfeathers. The drummer has also toured as part of Delbert McClinton's band, the star of which was his usual long-winded self in his comments about the group's first release: "I like it a lot." Gregg Wetzel, a keyboardist, was once part of endless touring blues and boogie institution the Nighthawks, while bassist Abe White stays busy doing studio sessions unless asked to leap into action on tour with Jumpin' Johnny Sansone. The group has also turned into a songwriting lab, with many of the original rockers written by various combinations of the membership. Judged by his musical output, the Tennessee/Texas Dial probably wishes he was related to namesake Harry Dial, a classic musician of the '30s and '40s who drummed for Louis Armstrong, Fats Waller, and Louis Jordan. That Dial was also a bandleader, and his '30s recordings with a combo known as the Blusicians is indeed confused with the later Dial, despite the earlier artist's attempts to avoid confusion by dropping the "e" from the word "blues." Even though the Tennessee Dial's brand of blues comes a little dirtier, it is still safe to assume he has no connection with the Harry Dial who entered *the Guinness Book of World Records* for claiming to have gone 78 years without bathing. *—Eugene Chadbourne*

Big John Dickerson

b. Ohio

Vocals, Drums / Soul-Blues, R&B

Vocalist Big John Dickerson is no stranger to blues and soul music. Dickerson's current backing band, Blue Chamber, has long been the house band at Famous Dave's BBQ and Blues in uptown Minneapolis.

Dickerson has been singing for decades; he began his career in Detroit as a session drummer for Motown Records, and worked with classic R&B singers Jerry Butler and Bettye Swann on their respective tours in the '60s. His session credits include drumming for the Temptations, Five Sharps, Marvin Gaye, James Brown and Bobby "Blue" Bland, among others.

Dickerson recorded two independently released albums with the regional band Down Right Tight prior to his 1997 debut for Cannonball. *—Richard Skelly*

● **Big John Dickerson & Blue Chamber** / Sep. 30, 1997 / Cannonball ♦♦♦♦

Vocalist Big John Dickerson is no stranger to blues and soul music, and his self-titled debut for the Minneapolis-based Cannonball Records proves that point. *Big John Dickerson*

& Blue Chamber finds him working with a seven-piece group that includes horns. Produced by organist Ron Levy, the record showcases his vocals and the band's take on classic R&B and blues like "Mother-In-Law Blues," "Homework," "Oh Pretty Woman," and the instrumentals "Okie Dokie Stomp" and "Blues In D Natural." *—Richard Skelly*

Arms of the Blues / Jan. 20, 1998 / Cannonball ♦♦♦
Blue Chamber's second disc proves to be no sophomore jinx as the band is turning into a well-oiled machine, full of solid playing and singing. Produced by blues hotshot Jim Gaines in a decidedly hands off manner, this brings several fine originals to the table along with nice renditions of B.B. King's "You Upset My Baby," Michael Bloomfield's "Reap What You Sow,"and Carey Bell's "Low Down Dirty Shame." Dickerson's vocal are warm and honeyed and gruff in all the right spots. Good club music. *—Cub Koda*

Bo Diddley

b. Dec. 30, 1928, McComb, MS
Vocals, Guitar (Electric), Violin, Guitar / Rock & Roll, R&B, Electric Chicago Blues
He only had a few hits in the '50s and early '60s, but as Bo Diddley sang, "You Can't Judge a Book by Its Cover." You can't judge an artist by his chart success, either, and Diddley produced greater and more influential music than all but a handful of the best early rockers. The Bo Diddley beat—bomp, ba-bomp-bomp, bomp-bomp—is one of rock & roll's bedrock rhythms, showing up in the work of Buddy Holly, the Rolling Stones, and even pop-garage knock-offs like the Strangeloves' 1965 hit "I Want Candy." Diddley's hypnotic rhythmic attack and declamatory, boasting vocals stretched back as far as Africa for their roots, and looked as far into the future as rap. His trademark otherworldly vibrating, fuzzy guitar style did much to expand the instrument's power and range. But even more important, Bo's bounce was fun and irresistibly rocking, with a wisecracking, jiving tone that epitomized rock & roll at its most humorously outlandish and freewheeling.

Before taking up blues and R&B, Diddley had actually studied classical violin, but shifted gears after hearing John Lee Hooker. In the early '50s, he began playing with his longtime partner, maraca player Jerome Green, to get what Bo's called "that freight train sound." Billy Boy Arnold, a fine blues harmonica player and singer in his own right, was also playing with Diddley when the guitarist got a deal with Chess in the mid-'50s (after being turned down by rival Chicago label Vee-Jay). His very first single, "Bo Diddley"/"I'm a Man" (1955), was a double-sided monster. The A-side was soaked with futuristic waves of tremolo guitar, set to an ageless nursery rhyme; the flip was a bump-and-grind, harmonica-driven shuffle, based around a devastating blues riff. But the result was not exactly blues, or even straight R&B, but a new kind of guitar-based rock & roll, soaked in the blues and R&B, but owing allegiance to neither.

Diddley was never a top seller on the order of his Chess rival Chuck Berry, but over the next half-dozen or so years, he'd produce a catalog of classics that rival Berry's in quality. "You Don't Love Me," "Diddley Daddy," "Pretty Thing," "Diddy Wah Diddy," "Who Do You Love?," "Mona," "Road Runner," "You Can't Judge a Book by Its Cover"—all are stone-cold standards of early, riff-driven rock & roll at its funkiest. Oddly enough, his only Top 20 pop hit was an atypical, absurd back-and-forth rap between him and Jerome Green, "Say Man," that came about almost by accident as the pair were fooling around in the studio.

As a live performer, Diddley was galvanizing, using his trademark square guitars and distorted amplification to produce new sounds that anticipated the innovations of '60s guitarists like Jimi Hendrix. In Great Britain, he was revered as a giant on the order of Chuck Berry and Muddy Waters. The Rolling Stones in particular borrowed a lot from Bo's rhythms and attitude in their early days, although they only officially covered a couple of his tunes, "Mona" and "I'm Alright." Other British R&B groups like the Yardbirds, Animals, and Pretty Things also covered Diddley standards in their early days. Buddy Holly covered "Bo Diddley" and used a modified Bo Diddley beat on "Not Fade Away"; when the Stones gave the song the full-on Bo treatment (complete with shaking maracas), the result was their first big British hit.

The British Invasion helped increase the public's awareness of Diddley's importance, and ever since then he's been a popular live act. Sadly, though, his career as a recording artist—in commercial and artistic terms—was over by the time the Beatles and Stones hit America. He'd record with ongoing and declining frequency, but after 1963, he'd never write or record any original material on par with his early classics. Whether he'd spent his muse, or just felt he could coast on his laurels, is hard to say. But he remains a vital part of the collective rock & roll consciousness, occasionally reaching wider visibility via a 1979 tour with the Clash, a cameo role in the film *Trading Places*, a late-'80s tour with Ronnie Wood, and a 1989 television commercial for sports shoes with star athlete Bo Jackson. *—Richie Unterberger*

Bo Diddley / 1958 / Chess ♦♦♦♦♦
For anyone who wants to play rock & roll, *real* rock & roll, this is one of the few records that you really need. Along with Chuck Berry, Elvis, Little Richard, Jerry Lee Lewis, Muddy Waters, B.B. King, and a few select others, Bo Diddley was one of the founders of the form—and he did it like no other. Diddley had only one real style, that being the "Bo Diddley beat": a syncopated, rhythmic drive, loaded with tremolo. There are 12 examples of it on this record, and that is about all you need. It's one of those records that, after listening to just a few cuts, will find you tapping the beats on every available surface. Diddley's guitar and vocals have a gruff feeling that recalls bluesmen such as Waters, yet he has his own style. Buttressed by drums, funky piano, and usually maracas, it's absolutely infectious. This is one of the greatest rock sounds that you're likely to hear, and it's all on this one record, too. *—Matthew Greenwald*

Have Guitar, Will Travel / 1960 / Chess ♦♦♦♦
Amazingly, Bo Diddley's third album—containing classics such as "Cops and Robbers," "Run Diddley Daddy," and "Mona (I Need You Baby)"—has only been reissued on vinyl, and even that's out of print. More than one British Invasion band learned what they needed to know about American rock & roll from the songs on this record (the Stones cut "Cops and Robbers" at their earliest recording session, and later released a killer version of "Mona," though the most interesting British version of the latter was done by an all-girl band with an attitude called the Liverbirds). This record is every bit as raunchy as Diddley's first two albums (the guitars may even be crunchier, and the singing shows more range), and has more than enough to recommend it to collectors and fans. This is the album that began the funny cover photos on Diddley's records. *—Bruce Eder*

Bo Diddley in the Spotlight / 1960 / Chess ♦♦♦♦
As with Bo Diddley's first five albums (except *Have Guitar, Will Travel*), the most important cuts (but not all the good ones) off of this album have been included on *The Chess Box* from MCA, which doesn't mean that this record isn't a good separate issue, just somewhat redundant if you have the box. There are surprises from these 1960-vintage recordings, including the languid, Caribbean-sounding "Limber"; the soft, romantic "Love Me"; the doo wop-style "Deed and Deed I Do"; the loping "Walkin' and Talkin'"; upbeat, gospel-tinged rockers such as "Let Me In" interspersed with the hot and raunchy "Road Runner," "The Story of Bo Diddley," "Craw-Dad" (a genuine diamond in the rough), and "Signifying Blues"; and solid instrumentals like "Scuttle Bug" (really "Live My Life" with the vocals removed and Otis Spann overdubbed on piano) that make this record more than worthwhile. *—Bruce Eder*

Bo Diddley Is a Lover / 1961 / Checker ♦♦♦♦
There's not a bad song on this long-forgotten album; in fact, it's all good, and so little of it has been reissued that it's a crime. There are a lot of familiar moments here: Diddley slips most effectively into his "Say Man" groove on "Bo's Vacation"; plays some serious Chicago blues on "Call Me (Bo's Blues)" and makes it count; invades Chuck Berry territory by way of Howlin' Wolf on the window-rattling "Hong Kong Mississippi" (a track so riveting and funny, and so rippling in superb guitar work, it makes this album worthwhile on its own); bounces back to his signature beat on the title song, the hysterically funny autobiographical "Bo Diddley Is Loose," "Quick Draw," "Back Home," and "Not Guilty" (a song that deserves enshrinement as one of Diddley's best); and slips into a romantic groove on "You're Looking Good." Find it, buy it, and savor it. *—Bruce Eder*

Hey Bo Diddley! / 1962 / Chess ♦♦♦
Bo's music was beginning to slip in sales—though he remained a popular concert act—when Chess released this album in the summer of 1962. "I Can Tell," written by Samuel Smith, showed Bo trying out a slower, more seductively soulful sound, a whole four-and-a-half-minutes long—it is different, though not very distinguished. "Bo's Twist" isn't much more impressive, a fairly standard instrumental with an unusually grungy (like you were expecting Julian Bream) guitar sound, with the first prominent appearance of an organ in the backing of a Bo Diddley record; "Sad Sack" is a somewhat more successful instrumental. "Mr. Kruschev" is one of the funniest, most delightfully nonsensical pieces of topical songwriting Bo ever engaged in, writing about wanting to go into the army and go over to see the Soviet leader and get him to stop nuclear testing, to a background of "Hut, two—three four!" "You All Green" is first-rate Bo, and deserved to be anthologized somewhere. "You Can't Judge A Book By The Cover" was the one standard from the album, but other tracks deserving of better exposure include "Bo's Bounce" and "Who May Your Lover Be," which takes off from Howlin' Wolf's "Moaning At Midnight," recasting it in a Bo Diddley beat, with Bo sounding a lot like Wolf here, and "Give Me a Break (Man)," which is a very animated impromptu guitar jam. The album filler tracks include "Mama Don't Allow No Twistin'," Bo's take on "Mama Don't Like Music," a song that was old when country-and-western/novelty singer Smiley Burnette covered it successfully in the '30s, "Babes in the Woods" (featuring a backing chorus mimicking the doo-wop parody "Get a Job") and "Diddling," a routine Bo instrumental. *—Bruce Eder*

Bo Diddley's a Twister / 1962 / Checker ♦♦♦
A lot of the material on this record was rushed out in half-finished form, in order to get an album out that cashed in on the "twist" craze of early 1962. There may well have been words intended to the opening track, "Detour," which came out of the 1961 session featuring Peggy "Lady Bo" Jones that produced the excellent "Pills" and the rather perfunctory reading of Willie Dixon's "My Babe," and some lackluster earlier instrumental material, "Shank" and "The Twister." This record also included "Here 'Tis," the soulful Bo original that would serve the Eric Clapton-era Yardbirds in very good stead on stage—Bo's version blows theirs completely away—as well as the classics "Road Runner" and "Who Do You Love." In all, it isn't half-bad for an album that nobody intended as such, though most of the best (except "Here 'Tis") has been included on various hits compilations. *—Bruce Eder*

Bo Diddley & Company / 1962 / Checker ♦♦♦♦
This album is almost worth owning just for the cover photo of Bo and the Duchess, aka Norma-Jean Wofford, each with their axe. What makes it really cool, though, is the music, which is among the best of Bo's '60s output. "Bo's A Lumberjack" is one of the most ferociously sexual and funny signature songs Bo ever cut, "(Extra, Read All About It) Ben" is a sort of sideways version of "Say Man," with a rollicking beat and very effective use of piano in the backing band, with a grim subject matter handled in a humorous manner, and "Help Out" is one of Bo's better guitar workouts, with the man getting lots of help from the Duchess. It was records like this that helped keep Bo's reputation alive in England when Americans stopped buying his stuff. "Met You On a Saturday" is an unusual slow, romantic number from Bo, very much in a late '50s style that was probably a few years late to capture anyone's imagination. Other material, like "Diana" (a reworking of "Hey Bo Diddley") and "Little Girl" is less compelling but still solid rock & roll, as are "Gimme Gimme," "Same Old Thing," "Met You on a Saturday," "Put The Shoes on Willie" (written by Earl Hooker), and "Pretty Girl." The latter has a great chorus, and turned up in the repertories of several British Invasion bands. *—Bruce Eder*

Bo Diddley Is a Gunslinger / 1963 / Chess ✦✦✦

Not only does it sport one of the most striking album covers of its era (Diddley decked out in cowboy finery, about to get the drop on some unfortunate varmint with one of his fieriest guitars lying at his feet), this 1963 album contains some fine music. The title track continues the legend of you-know-who, while "Ride on Josephine" and "Cadillac" rock like hell (and Ed Sullivan must have been glad to see that Diddley finally learned "Sixteen Tons"). Two bonus cuts, "Working Man" and "Do What I Say," make this one a must. —*Bill Dahl*

Bo Diddley's Beach Party / 1963 / Checker ✦✦✦✦✦

A blistering live album, especially in genuine mono (the re-channeled stereo is barely passable)—and quite simply the finest live rock & roll album of its era, cut live by Diddley and band at Myrtle Beach, SC, on July 5 and 6, 1963. From the opening track (erroneously listed as "Memphis" and credited to Chuck Berry as composer) to the final note, this is some of the loudest, raunchiest guitar-based rock & roll ever preserved. It also bears an uncanny resemblance to the sound that the Rolling Stones achieved on their own *Got Live If You Want It*, which only shows how much the Stones learned from Diddley. Highlights include "Gunslinger," "Hey Bo Diddley," "Road Runner," and "I'm All Right." The sound doesn't necessarily translate ideally to compact disc, but that shouldn't dissuade anyone. Currently out of print but well worth the search. —*Bruce Eder & Cub Koda*

Surfin' With Bo Diddley / 1963 / Checker ✦✦

This is where Bo—or, more properly, Chess Records—really took a wrong step, starting with the fact that The Originator himself is actually on only about half of the cuts here, the balance having been recorded by organist Jimmy Lee Riley and his group the Megatons. The idea wasn't as bad as it sounded, at least on paper—Bo had been an indirect influence on tons of surf bands, with his signature grunge guitar sound, but the surf music world wasn't ready for a Bo-style instrumental rendition of the Jerome Kern/Oscar Hammerstein II *Showboat* standard "Ol' Man River," and Bo's own inspiration behind songs like "Surfer's Love Call" was muted, to say the least. Almost as bad—although more entertaining—is "Low Tide," Bo's rewrite of Bill Justis' "Raunchy." The best tracks are "Cookie Headed Diddley" and "Surf, Sink, or Swim," which come close to matching some of Bo's solid material from earlier albums and singles. —*Bruce Eder*

Two Great Guitars / 1964 / MCA ✦✦

Diddley shared this 1964 Chess album with his labelmate Chuck Berry. They duel it out on a pair of incredibly lengthy instrumentals (brilliantly titled "Chuck's Beat" and "Bo's Beat") that get tiresome long before they run their full course. Better (and briefer) are two numbers where they don't cross paths—Diddley's rendering of "When the Saints Go Marching In" and Berry's amazing country breakdown "Liverpool Drive." A couple of bonus Bo Diddley sides ("Stay Sharp" and "Stinkey") also make this digital re-incarnation worth acquiring. —*Bill Dahl*

500% More Man / 1965 / Checker ✦✦✦✦

By the end of 1965, Bo was making a conscious effort to recapture both the Black listenership that had deserted him and the white audience that was buying all of those soul records. Unfortunately, neither he nor Chess knew exactly how to go about it, and the result was another good album largely unheard by the public. The title track marks Bo's return to the Muddy Waters beat that he appropriated for "I'm a Man" (and that Muddy took back in "Mannish Boy") a decade earlier, and is one of Bo's greatest '60s sides. "Greasy Spoon" mentions Muddy amid its comical description of the offerings of a particularly unclean eatery (it's amazing when you think of it—ten years recording in Chicago, and longer than that living there, and Bo was still nearly as much a country blues artist as he was when he started). "Let Me Pass" is a hot number with an infectious beat and some very funny lyrics, and Bo playing some delectable guitar. "Stop My Monkey," featuring Bo backed by the singing group the Cookies, has him again trying for a commercial soul sound in a Motown vein, and "Tonight Is Ours" is one of Bo's most heartfelt romantic numbers, with the Cookies singing their hearts out while Bo tries his hand at a song that might've fit well on either of the first two albums by the Miracles, while "Hey, Red Riding Hood" brought back the Bo Diddley beat for another go around, this time with delightfully raunchy lyrics amid crisper textures and a much finer sound than ever before. "Hey's So Mad" is pretty lackluster except for the guitar break, but "Root Hoot" should've been more widely heard than it was, being one of Bo's more infectious chant-based songs. "Corn Bread" has a neatly stinging, Slim Harpo-type lead guitar sound, and is overall an OK instrumental. And then there's "Soul Food," another great Bo Diddley rocker lost in the middle of the '60s soul boom—Bo is so smooth, impassioned, sexy, and raw, and the Cookies sound so good backing him to one of his best instrumental tracks ever, that the fact this song was never a hit is a crime. By 1965, however, nobody in America was buying his records, even ones like this filled to bursting with good music and good humor, and even the British were beginning to lose interest in Bo's latest records. This was among Bo's last sessions with the Duchess, and the group he's using is more or less the studio equivalent of the band he's seen with in *The Big TNT Show* (aka *That Was Rock*). —*Bruce Eder*

Hey, Good Lookin' / Apr. 1965 / Checker ✦✦✦

One of Bo's least known albums, mostly recorded in April of 1964 and released a year later, at the point when none of his records were selling in America. With an edgy, raunchy sound and modern record techniques (it's in stereo), Bo and band come up with a solid '60s version of his original sound. The title track is a real jewel, featuring Jerome Green on the maracas and Lafayette Leake on the piano. "Mama Keep Your Big Mouth Shut" isn't a bad soul-styled number, with Bo abandoning his standard beat in favor of a smoother, more Motown-like sound. He tries for a similar sound on "I Wonder Why (People Don't Like Me)" and "Brother Bear." In addition to the title track (which is not the Hank Williams tune), the Bo Diddley beat gets a workout on "La La La," "Rain Man," and "Bo Diddley's Hoot'nanny." Bo gets to have some real fun on "London Stomp," his com-

mentary on the sudden fashionability of British rock & roll, parodying the accents and attitudes of most of the bands that he encountered on his visit to England in October of 1963. Other tracks sound like they'd have worked well as part of extended jams of the kind that Bo did on stage—"Yeah Yeah Yeah," in particular, could've come from the middle of one of Bo's 15-minute shuffle-and-chant workouts, and would've been great in such a setting, although here, as a freestanding two-and-a-half-minute track it's a little weak. There is some filler here, most notably "Let's Walk A While" and "Rooster Stew," but that can be forgiven in view of the strength of the rest of the material. —*Bruce Eder*

The Originator / 1966 / Checker ✦✦✦✦

By 1966, Bo Diddley was a long way from chart success in America, and *The Originator* was to be his last official album for four years (in the interim he would appear on the two Chess "Super Blues" all-star jam albums). Strangely enough, this is also one of his best albums, mostly comprised of rare early '60s singles ("Pills") and B-sides and filled out with some fun new recordings ("Yakky Doodle"). This record is a bit of a throwback compared with *500% More Man*, which preceded it by nearly a year, representing the Bo Diddley of the early '60s—all of the material has the signature beat and guitar, or other virtues to recommend it, including some very high spirits. —*Bruce Eder*

The Black Gladiator / Jun. 1970 / Checker ✦✦

It was four years between the release of Bo's last album of all new cuts, *500% More Man*, and this album, during which time he'd spent time recording with Chess' top bluesmen, Muddy Waters and Howlin' Wolf. The death of Leonard Chess in October of 1969 resulted in the sale of the label to the GRT corporation, and cost the company what little artistic guidance it had. The result was *The Black Gladiator*, an attempt to reshape Bo into a funk artist, in the manner of Sly and the Family Stone. As an experiment it's understandable, and Bo tries very hard (even making another song-length sexual boast on "You, Bo Diddley," which also ends with a great guitar/organ duet between Bo and Bobby Alexis), but he finally fails to find a groove that works. Despite some good guitar here and there, this record falls into the same category as Muddy's *Electric Mud* and *After the Rain* albums and Howlin' Wolf's *New Album*, attempts to transform each into a psychedelic rocker. "Power House" is a pretty good cut, using a modified Muddy Waters-"I'm a Man"/"Mannish Boy" beat and lyrics. Much of the rest is for absolute completists only, however. —*Bruce Eder*

Another Dimension / 1971 / Chess ✦✦

By the end of 1970, most of Bo Diddley's income was derived from his concert work, primarily as an "oldies" act in rock & roll revival shows such as the Toronto concert where he shared a stage with the Plastic Ono Band. But he and Chess believed there was still a way for him to try and reach a wider, more contemporary audience. This album was the result, a valiant effort to update Bo Diddley's sound and image, somewhat in the vein of Muddy Waters' *Electric Mud* only a few years later and very slightly more successful in that quest, in the sense of yielding one lasting addition to Bo's repertory. Relevance was the key word, not only in the song selection, which includes three John Fogerty songs ("Lodi," "Bad Moon Rising," "Down on the Corner") and covers of numbers by the Band and Elton John, but a new song entitled "Pollution" that tries hard to integrate the Bo Diddley beat into a message piece—it's a good try, but nothing on this record (including "Pollution") was going to challenge Marvin Gaye's *What's Goin' On* for primacy or effectiveness. The record starts off well enough, with a superb, deeply soulful cover of Al Kooper's "I Love You More Than You'll Ever Know," and a decent rendition of "The Shape I'm In." But two of the Fogerty covers ("Lodi" is the only one that sort of works) are embarrassing, with the girlie chorus killing "Bad Moon Rising." And "Bad Side of the Moon" was a waste of studio time. One song from this album has remained part of Bo's concert set for decades, however—"I Said Shutup Woman," which has the most traditional sound of anything on *Another Dimension*. —*Bruce Eder*

Where It All Began / 1972 / Chess ✦✦✦

Johnny Otis and Pete Welding produced this surprisingly successful soul effort by Bo, which succeeded in reshaping his sound, not as a Sly Stewart wannabe or a lounge act covering Creedence Clearwater Revival hits. Bo at least sounds comfortable and natural doing songs like "Look At Grandma" and "Woman," and the latter is a pretty damn good song—Bo finally emerged as a soul singer in his own right, and it worked, artistically at least. "Hey Jerome" even recalled tracks like "Say Man" in a not unflattering light. Unfortunately, none of this mattered to the people who still cared about Bo Diddley—they wanted the beat and the old sound, which was present here, on "I've Had It Hard" and the extraordinary "Bo Diddley-itis," but not in the kind of quantity they craved, amid the more modern sounds; and they wanted the old songs, which he gave them in concert. And it all came so late in the day, not only in terms of Bo's identification as anything but an oldies act but the history of Chess Records (now subsumed into the GRT corporate operation, the Chess imprint having no meaning or significance), that *Where It All Began* vanished from sight leaving scarcely a trace or a ripple on the charts. —*Bruce Eder*

Got My Own Bag of Tricks / 1972 / Chess ✦✦✦✦

For a lot of years, this double album compilation—sort of the Bo Diddley equivalent to Chuck Berry's *The Great 28* or the first two Chuck Berry *Golden Decade* sets—was the best collection of Bo's stuff on the market, containing all of his best known songs and some of the best of his album tracks up through the mid-'60s. After it was deleted in America, it was available as an import from Canada and then Europe for a long time. On vinyl it is one place to start, although the double-CD *Chess Box* has supplanted it in many respects. —*Bruce Eder*

The London Bo Diddley Sessions / 1973 / Chess ✦✦✦

After Howlin' Wolf made the Billboard album charts in 1970 with his *London Sessions* release, Chess duly began preparing similarly titled albums by its remaining roster of stars—Muddy Waters and Chuck Berry followed the Wolf, and in 1973 this Bo Diddley release came along. Actually, a lot of it was done in Chicago, with the London portion of the sessions added, seemingly to justify the title. And it did sell better than Bo's other original albums of this era, and it remains in print on compact disc, one of a handful of his albums so released. As with Muddy Waters' *London Sessions* album, Bo's presence was somewhat overwhelmed by the massive number of session musicians involved (well-meaning though they may have been) and more so, because Bo was still looking for a new sound, where Muddy knew what he was about. The songs are pretty fair, a mix of soul and funk, with elements of his old sound, and this is probably the best compromise he achieved during this phase of his career, between the old and the new. *—Bruce Eder*

Big Bad Bo / 1974 / Chess ✦✦

Having tried everything else in his search for a new sound, Bo moved into a jazz vein on this record, and the results are not bad, but not really Bo either! His cover of Van Morrison's "I've Been Workin'" and the rendition of "Hit Or Miss" aren't half-bad, but they're just not really Bo—just Bo fronting some really good jazzmen in New York. For the first time the Bo Diddley beat appears nowhere on one of his albums. There is one good blues here, however, in "Evelee," the only Bo original on *Big Bad Bo*, featuring a powerful performance by The Originator, working for most of its length with a relatively stripped down band on this one number, which should've been the model for the whole album. *—Bruce Eder*

☆ **Bo Diddley/Go Bo Diddley** / 1986 / Chess ✦✦✦✦✦

There are precious few weak tracks on this combination of Bo Diddley's first two late-'50s albums for Chess/Checker, which boasts a plethora of classics ("Bo Diddley," "I'm a Man," "Before You Accuse Me," "Crackin' Up," "Little Girl," even his electric violin workout "The Clock Struck Twelve"). The only drawback: someone failed to notice that "Dearest Darling" was on both LPs, so... it's on here twice! *—Bill Dahl*

☆ **The Chess Box** / Jul. 26, 1990 / Chess ✦✦✦✦✦

Not every single track you'll ever want or need by the legendary shave-and-a-haircut rhythm R&B/rock pioneer, but a great place to begin. Two discs (45 songs) in a great big box with a nice accompanying booklet contain the groundbreaking introduction "Bo Diddley" (never again would he be referred to as Ellas McDaniel), its swaggering flipside "I'm a Man," the killer follow-ups "Diddley Daddy," "I'm Looking for a Woman," "Who Do You Love?," and "Hey Bo Diddley;" signifying street-corner humor ("Say Man"), piledriving rockers ("Road Runner," "She's Alright," "You Can't Judge a Book by Its Cover"), and numerous stunning examples of his daringly innovative guitar style. *—Bill Dahl*

Rare & Well Done / Sep. 10, 1991 / Chess ✦✦✦✦

Sixteen extreme rarities from the deepest recesses of the Chess vaults that date from 1955-1968. The grinding "She's Fine, She's Mine" and snarling "I'm Bad" are comparatively well known, at least to collectors; far more obscure are the previously unissued "Heart-O-Matic Love," "Cookie-Headed Diddley," and "Moon Baby." *—Bill Dahl*

Bo's Blues / 1993 / Ace ✦✦✦✦✦

Twenty-two of Bo Diddley's best blues-oriented sides from the Chess catalog, including some rare stuff—the rip-roaring 1959 outing "Run Diddley Daddy," a jive-loaded "Cops and Robbers" from 1956 that features maraca shaker Jerome Green more than Diddley, and a surging "Down Home Special." If you think that everything Bo Diddley ever made has that same shave-and-a-haircut beat, this collection will set you straight! *—Bill Dahl*

The Chess Years / 1993 / Charly ✦✦✦✦✦

Bringing this box set home on the train, it started gyrating to a shave-and-a-haircut-two-bits beat on my lap... no, not really, but that would be a great TV ad for this release. Charly Records' *The Chess Years* has assembled most—though not quite all—of the music that the Originator recorded for Chess Records, which, unfortunately, means a lot of his lesser work as well—282 recordings, made between 1955 and 1974, on 12 CDs; looking at it is like staring across the Grand Canyon, except you *want* to jump into this if you have any sense. If the collection seems like overkill, that's because it is, and there's some poor material here from the late '60s/early '70s, when Bo was searching for a new commercial sound, although some of that later isn't really bad—his covers of Al Kooper's "I Love You More Than You'll Ever Know" or the Band's "The Shape I'm In" from *Another Dimension* are soulful and moving, but just aren't what one buys a Bo Diddley album to hear (and we could've done without the girlie chorus on "Bad Moon Rising"). There are more than enough jewels—and jewels that are likely *never* to appear otherwise on compact disc—to attract serious rock & roll listeners, *if* you can swing the price, which is around $120. The highlights (which would be far more costly to find on vinyl today) include "Bo Meets the Monster," his catchy (and very funny) answer to "Purple People Eater"; "Here 'Tis," which became famous when covered by the Yardbirds, but only really comes to life in the hands of the originator; the comical "Bucket," "Lazy Woman" and "Run Diddley Daddy"; the rousing, slashing "Puttentang"; the side-splittingly funny biographical song "All Together," a sort of sequel to "The Story of Bo Diddley"; the complete *Bo Diddley's Beach Party* album, and a handful of demos from the late 1960 sessions that yielded tracks for the *Bo Diddley's a Twister* album. Additionally, the collection gives the listener a chance to see how Bo explored different variations on his sound, adapting it to doo wop, folk, and even calypso, all of which worked better than one would have expected, plus soul and funk, which didn't. The sessionography is very detailed and pretty cool, and the notes are among the better biographical accounts of Bo's life and career—oh, and there are lots of pictures of Bo and the Duchess recreated throughout the set. There are problems with the mastering, however—momentary gaps exist in one or two songs, and the sound quality in certain places, such as the live *Beach Party* material, leaves something to be desired. But at its best, and that is often (at least through the mid-'60s), this set presents one of the primal forces in rock & roll. *—Bruce Eder*

Bo Diddley Is a Lover... Plus / 1994 / See for Miles ✦✦✦✦

Very welcome digital British import reissue of Bo's 1961 Checker album, bolstered by a handful of bonus tracks (including his rendering of Willie Dixon's "My Babe"). On second guitar for many of these sides is Peggy Jones, one of Diddley's prize pupils. Some of the better-known titles include "Not Guilty," "Hong Kong, Mississippi," and the bragadocious title cut. *—Bill Dahl*

Let Me Pass... Plus / 1994 / See for Miles ✦✦✦

Another British import version of a vintage Checker album, with a few highly desirable bonus cuts at the end to further recommend it. Most of the CD mirrors Diddley's 1965 *500% More Man* LP (the title track obviously being a sequel to his "I'm a Man"), but the extra items include the amusing "Mama, Keep Your Big Mouth Shut" and a danceable "We're Gonna Get Married." *—Bill Dahl*

Hey Bo Diddley/In Concert / Nov. 2, 1994 / Aim ✦✦✦

Bo's music was beginning to slip in sales—though he remained a popular concert act, as captured on the second half of this two-fer from the Aim label—when Chess released *Hey Bo Diddley* in the summer of 1962. "I Can Tell," awritten by Samuel Smith, showed Bo trying out a slower, more seductively soulful sound, a whole four and a half minutes long—it is different, though not very distinguished. "Bo's Twist" isn't much more impressive, a fairly standard instrumental with an unusually grungy (like you were expecting Julian Bream) guitar sound, with the first prominent appearance of an organ in the backing of a Bo Diddley record; "Sad Sack" is a somewhat more successful instrumental. "Mr. Kruschev" is one of the funniest, most delightfully nonsensical pieces of topical songwriting Bo ever engaged in, writing about wanting to go into the army and go over to see the Soviet leader and get him to stop nuclear testing, to a background of "Hut, two—three four!" "You All Green" is first-rate Bo, and deserved to be anthologized somewhere. "You Can't Judge a Book By the Cover" was the one standard from the album, but other tracks deserving of better exposure include "Bo's Bounce" and "Who May Your Lover Be," which takes off from Howlin' Wolf's "Moaning At Midnight," recasting it in a Bo Diddley beat with Bo sounding a lot like Wolf, and "Give Me a Break (Man)," a very animated impromptu guitar jam. The album filler tracks include "Mama Don't Allow No Twistin'" is Bo's take on "Mama Don't Like Music," a song that was old when country & western/novelty singer Smiley Burnette covered it successfully in the '30s, "Babes in the Woods" (featuring a backing chorus mimicking the doo wop parody "Get a Job") and "Diddling" is a routine Bo instrumental. *—Bruce Eder*

The Mighty Bo Diddley / Jun. 27, 1995 / Triple X ✦✦

Late model Diddley recordings originally released overseas as *This Should Not Be.* While these sides show off Diddley working in contemporary grooves and doing a good of producing himself, this is a long way from his signature sound and songs like "Ain't It Good to Be Free," "Gotta Be a Change," and "I Don't Want Your Welfare" get downright preachy. Pass this one by and check out any of his Chess recordings for the real thing instead. *—Cub Koda*

Hey! Bo Diddley/Bo Diddley / 1996 / BGO ✦✦✦✦✦

Beat Goes On reissued Bo Diddley's eponymous debut and his 1962 effort *Hey! Bo Diddley* on one compact disc in 1996. Although these two records don't necessarily sit well together—the first is sublime, the second notoriously uneven—it's still a nice way to pick them up on CD, especially since the sound and packaging are first-rate. However, the Chess issue that combines *Bo Diddley* and *Go Bo Diddley* on one CD is a better bet, since those two records—his first two—work better together. *—Stephen Thomas Erlewine*

Two Great Guitars/Super Super Blues Band / 1996 / BGO ✦✦✦

The linking theme behind this two-LP-on-one-CD compilation seems to be the fact that, on both *Two Great Guitars* and *Super Super Blues Band*, Chess Records was trying to coax or force collaborations between the company's established stars. *Two Great Guitars* was the more spontaneous and inspired of the two albums, coming about on a day when Chuck Berry happened to turn up at Chess when Bo Diddley was cutting a session, and they decided to try and cut something together—the result was a pair of superb extended guitar workouts that were unique in their time; no rock & roll record had ever featured jams of this length, or showcased the bags of tricks of a pair of axe-men like this. Although the usual assumption is that the featured guitarist on each of the tracks got the spotlight, the fact is that Bo Diddley holds his own even on the Chuck Berry piece "Chuck's Beat," providing a relentless, sometimes thunderous and sometimes shimmering rhythm guitar backup to Berry's lead guitar that's a show in itself. "Bo's Beat" features the piano nearly as prominently as either of the guitarists, and Berry wanders through some intelligent variations on his most familiar licks, part of a very busy band. The *Super Super Blues Band* album was more problematic, being a company-dictated collaboration between Howlin' Wolf, Muddy Waters, and Bo Diddley that never quite fits together—Muddy and the Wolf never got along sharing their repertory, and Bo Diddley seems caught in the middle of a nasty argument a lot of the time; sadly, Chuck Berry wasn't on Chess at the time, or else he might've been here in place of the unwilling and unhappy Wolf. There's occasionally some interesting playing or singing, and it's always nice to hear more Holwin' Wolf (nothing here is as awkward as Wolf's work on the infamous *This Is Howlin' Wolf's New Album* of the same period), but it's not a prime example of the work of anyone involved. The BGO disc is a fresh remastering of the original albums, which date from the late 1980's in their American CD editions and sound a lot better here, and it may be worth owning for anyone wanting the pyrotechnics of *Two Great Guitars*—it doesn't have the two Bo Diddley bonus cuts from the U.S. version, however. *—Bruce Eder*

A Man Amongst Men / May 21, 1996 / Code Blue ✦✦✦

Bo Diddley's major-label '90s comeback effort *A Man Amongst Men* is overflowing with guest stars, but it rarely gels into something distinctive. The presence of such heavyweights as Keith Richards, Ron Wood, and Jimmie Vaughan actually weighs down the set, preventing Diddley from digging deep into the grooves. The band never quite rocks hard enough and no one tears off an inspired solo—*A Man Amongst Men* is pleasant, but it never approaches compelling listening. —*Stephen Thomas Erlewine*

★ **His Best (Chess 50th Anniversary Collection)** / Apr. 8, 1997 / Chess ♦♦♦♦♦
With his various hits and anthology packages all out of print and the multi-disc deluxe box set out of pocketbook reach for most casual consumers, MCA finally comes up with a 20-track compilation that hits the bullseye and makes this rock pioneer's best and most influential work available to everyone. The song list reads like a primer for '60s British rhythm & blues and '90s blues bands: "Bo Diddley," "I'm a Man," "Diddley Daddy," "Pretty Thing," "Before You Accuse Me," "Hey! Bo Diddley," "Who Do You Love," "Mona" and "Roadrunner" are the tracks that made the legend and put his sound on the map worldwide. The transfers used on this set are exemplary, the majority of them utilizing masters that have a few extra seconds (or more) appended to the fades, which will cause even hardliners to hear these old standards with fresh ears; especially revelatory are the "long versions" of "I Can Tell" and "You Can't Judge a Book By Its Cover." If the box set is too big a trigger to pull and you want all of Bo's influential sides in one package, this one should be first-stop shopping of the highest priority. —*Cub Koda*

20th Century Masters—The Millennium Collection: The Best of Bo Diddley / Jan. 25, 2000 / MCA ♦♦♦
This fine but brief summation of Diddley's career includes all the relevant hits ("Bo Diddley," "I'm a Man") as well as a few not-so-relevant ones ("Dearest Darling," "Say Man"). Its brevity doesn't give much opportunity to cover all of Diddley's achievements—none of the *Millennium* collections really do— but for beginners it's a good place to start. —*Michael Gallucci*

Bo Diddley Rides Again/In the Spotlight / Mar. 9, 2002 / BGO ♦♦♦♦

Varetta Dillard

b. Feb. 3, 1933, Harlem, NY, **d.** Oct. 4, 1993, Brooklyn, NY
Vocals / R&B
Varetta Dillard was a wailing, shouting mama who scored a trio of hits for Savoy in the early '50s. Dillard was born crippled, but that didn't stop her from being an excellent R&B vocalist. She had a great voice and sang flamboyant, suggestive lyrics with verve and fire. Dillard won two Amateur Night contests at the Apollo and was subsequently signed by Savoy in 1951. Her first hit was "Easy, Easy Baby" in 1952, followed by "Mercy, Mr. Percy," her trademark song, in 1953, and "Johnny Has Gone," an evocative tribute to Johnny Ace, in 1955. The latter two peaked at number six on the R&B charts. Dillard switched to gospel in the '60s, joining the Tri-Odds. She died in 1993. —*Ron Wynn*

• **Got You on My Mind: The Complete Recordings 1958–1961, Vol. 1** / 1989 / Bear Family ♦♦♦♦♦
Bear Family issued a pair of CDs in 1989 presenting 51 of Varetta Dillard's songs. This disc, which contains 29 numbers, leads off with a curious novelty, "The Square Dance Rock." The other tunes are divided between earnest covers ("See See Rider Blues" and "Pennies From Heaven"), robust stompers ("Mama Don't Want [What Poppa Don't Want]") and teen laments ("Pray For Me Mother"). There's also an intriguing tribute piece, "I Miss You Jimmy (Tribute To James Dean)," prompting speculation as to whether the song was Dillard's idea or a company ploy to exploit Dean's tragic demise in 1956. Dillard makes most of these songs entertaining, and sometimes turns in a triumph. —*Ron Wynn*

The Lovin' Bird: The Complete Recordings 1958–1961, Vol. 2 / 1989 / Bear Family ♦♦♦♦♦
Bear Family's second CD featuring songs by R&B vocalist Varetta Dillard empties their vaults with a mix of comical novelty tunes, hard-hitting tracks and heartache numbers. Dillard moves from the hip silliness of the title track and "Mercy Mr. Percy" to the anguished "What Can I Say" and "A Little Bitty Tear." She's also outstanding on "Scorched," "You Ain't Foolin' Nobody" and "Rules Of Love." The disc's 22 tracks offer a portrait of a fine vocalist who consistently sang with vigor and depth, regardless of a number's lyrical quality. —*Ron Wynn*

The Dirty Dozen Brass Band

f. 1975, New Orleans, LA
Group / New Orleans Brass Bands, New Orleans Jazz, Funk
The Dirty Dozen Brass Band in its prime successfully mixed together R&B with the instrumentation of a New Orleans brass band. Featuring Kirk Joseph on sousaphone playing with the agility of an electric bassist, the group revitalized the brass band tradition, opening up the repertoire and inspiring some younger groups to imitate its boldness. Generally featuring five horns (two trumpets, one trombone, and two saxes) along with the sousaphone, a snare drummer, and a bass drummer, the DDBB was innovative in its own way, making fine recordings for Rounder, Columbia, and the George Wein Collection (the latter released through Concord). Guest artists have included Dr. John, Dizzy Gillespie, and Danny Barker. Unfortunately, the group became much more conventional over the years, still using R&B riffs but with a standard (and less distinctive) rhythm section. The DDBB re-emerged in 1999 with John Medeski as its producer, and many called the group's *Buck Jump* release a return to classic form. The group then returned in 2002 with yet another surprising album, *Medicated Magic.* —*Scott Yanow*

★ **My Feet Can't Fail Me Now** / 1984 / Concord Jazz ♦♦♦♦♦
The Dirty Dozen Brass Band's *My Feet Can't Fail Me Now* is a rollicking, infectious set that captures the spirit of classic New Orleans R&B and jazz because it isn't enslaved to those traditions. The group is willing to play around and have fun, adding different rock, pop, and R&B influences to their sound. The result is a wonderful, unpredictable album that is as wild and rich as New Orleans itself. —*Leo Stanley*

Live: Mardi Gras in Montreux / Jul. 1985 / Rounder ♦♦♦
Not at the same level as their debut (*My Feet Can't Fail Me Now*), this second outing by the Dirty Dozen Brass Band (taken from a couple sets performed at the 1985 Montreux Jazz Festival) is overly loose in spots and has some lightweight material that was better heard live than on record. The party music does have its strong moments, the mightly sousaphone playing of Kirk Joseph (who simulates an electric bass) pushes the group and the joy of the band is not to be denied, but "The Flintstones Meets the President" is only worth hearing once. —*Scott Yanow*

Voodoo / Aug. 1987-Sep. 1987 / Columbia ♦♦♦♦
The Dirty Dozen Brass Band certainly knew how to have a good time while playing their music. Their spirited blending of New Orleans jazz parade rhythms with R&B-ish horn riffs made them flexible enough to welcome guests Dr. John (who sings and play piano on "It's All Over Now"), Dizzy Gillespie ("Oop Pop a Dah") and Branford Marsalis ("Moose the Mooche") to their Columbia debut without altering their music at all. With Gregory Davis and Efrem Towns playing strong trumpet in the ensembles and occasional solos, and with sousaphonist Kirk Joseph not letting up for a moment, this is a typically spirited set by the unique DDBB. —*Scott Yanow*

New Orleans Album / Aug. 1989-Dec. 1989 / Columbia ♦♦♦♦
A bit of a hodge-podge, this CD features the Dirty Dozen Brass Band (comprised of two trumpets, two saxes, sometimes one trombone, the sousaphone of Kirk Joseph, snare drum and bass drum) welcoming such guests as singer Eddie Bo, guitarist-vocalist Danny Barker (showcased on "Don't You Feel My Leg"), trumpeter Dave Bartholomew (heard on "The Monkey") and rock singer Elvis Costello. However it is the R&B-ish parade band that is the main star, romping through group originals plus Cannonball Adderley's "Inside Straight" and "Kidd Jordan's Second Line." —*Scott Yanow*

Open Up: Whatcha Gonna Do for the Rest of Your Life? / Jan. 1991-Apr. 1991 / Columbia ♦♦♦♦
The Dirty Dozen Brass Band sticks to originals (except for Johnny Dyani's "Eyomzi") on this fairly adventurous set. The octet (which consists of two trumpets, two saxes, one trombone, sousaphone, snare drum and bass drum) still had a unique sound in 1991 but three songs on the date only used part of the unit and the DDBB seemed to be trying to escape the sound of the brass band tradition (they had long had a more modern repertoire). Not all of the pieces work although the music in general is pretty colorful and somewhat unpredictable, even if it falls short of essential. —*Scott Yanow*

Jelly / Aug. 1992-Jan. 1993 / Columbia ♦♦♦
The Dirty Dozen Brass Band, an innovative group that combines R&B with New Orleans parade rhythms, pays tribute to the great Jelly Roll Morton on this CD. Actually the DDBB mostly ignores Morton's original recordings (and leaves out some of his themes) in an unusual set that does not find them neglecting their own individuality. A few Danny Barker monologues add to the authenticity of this music, which takes great liberties with Morton's compositions. Trumpeter Gregory Davis (who duets with guest pianist Eddie Bo on "Dead Man Blues") is the most impressive soloist, though it is the sound of the rollicking ensembles (propelled by the sousaphone of Keith Anderson) that gives this set its sense of purpose. Purists, however, should avoid this one. —*Scott Yanow*

Buck Jump / May 25, 1999 / Mammoth ♦♦♦♦
If you have been yearning for the original sound of the Dirty Dozen Brass Band to return, this is it. Produced by John Medeski, the ensemble returns to their roots, but with a twist. They remain the ultimate party group, but are fastened to the stage with a drummer, organist, the full complement of horns sounding funky and fresh with that deep tuba and baritone sax underpinning; there's some daring improvisation rooted in counterpoint and upper-atmospheric blasts that are a familiar signature of this progressive New Orleans dance machine. Everything on the nine-song CD is saturated with, as one of the titles suggests, "Old School" style. The solos are inspired, riffs fly left and right, and they aren't afraid to moan and wail. Horn charts are tight as can be, repeated figures give the others a platform to improvise, and occasionally a calypso beat creeps in, as on the classic "Run Joe" or the Latin-inflected "Pet the Kat." It's all in the name of fun ... upbeat, positive, and with nary a trace of excess. They're at their zenith on "Duff," the collective Dozen reaching out and hammering the upper registers of their instruments, and at their most soulful on "Inner City Blues," approaching it in a most unconventional way. Of course, this band needs to be heard live for full effect, but this recorded effort might be their best yet. Every cut is solid, and the high level of musicianship is clearly evident. Singular in their stance and sound, mature like never before, and bent on having a really good time, this Dirty Dozen CD sets the bar high in mixing jazz and joy—a hard combination to beat. —*Michael G. Nastos*

Medicated Magic / Apr. 23, 2002 / Rope-A-Dope ♦♦♦
New Orleans' most famous, well-traveled, and recorded brass band celebrates its 25th anniversary with its ninth release. Best known in rock circles for contributions to albums from the Black Crowes, Elvis Costello, and especially Widespread Panic (with whom they toured and whose John Bell appears as guest vocalist on a track), the hotshot horn men offer few surprises on this disc predominantly comprised of popular Crescent City classics. But why bother stretching boundaries when their sound remains unique, stimulating, and inspiring? Adding a full-time keyboardist and guitar fleshes out but doesn't dilute the seven tooting horns as they tear through an inspired if slightly obvious set of covers from hometown legends Aaron Neville ("Tell It Like It Is"), the Meters ("Africa," "Cissy Strut"), Irma Thomas ("Ruler of My Heart"), and Dr. John ("Walk on Gilded Splinters," "Junko Partner") with infectious enthusiasm. Guests range from sacred steel guitar master Robert Randolph—whose soaring, hair-raising solos on three tracks infuse even more goosebumps than the already nail-biting musicianship—to Dr. John on vocals and piano, DJ Logic (adding nifty scratching doesn't appreciably update the Dozens' down-home approach), and jazzman Olu Dara. Sexy chanteuse Norah Jones gets slinky on the most sensuous version of "Ruler of My Heart" ever recorded, and Dr. John's gritty vocals

make the slow-groove version of Allen Toussaint's "Everything I Do Gon' Be Funky" even better than Lee Dorsey's original. But no matter how often you've heard these tunes, the Dirty Dozen's crackling second-line rhythms, bumping tuba bass lines, and uncanny ability to shift from boiling low-down gumbo to cool jazz make the versions here essential listening. "It Ain't Nothin' but a Party," as they say in the appropriately titled opening track. *—Hal Horowitz*

The Dixie Hummingbirds

f. 1928, Greenville, SC

Group / Traditional Gospel, Southern Gospel, Black Gospel

A pioneering force behind the evolution of the modern gospel quartet sound, the Dixie Hummingbirds were among the longest-lived and most successful groups of their era; renowned for their imaginative arrangements, progressive harmonies and all-around versatility, they earned almost universal recognition as the greatest Southern quartet of their generation, and their influence spread not only over the world of spiritual music but also inspired secular artists ranging from Jackie Wilson to Bobby "Blue" Bland to the Temptations. Formed in Greenville, South Carolina by James B. Davis, the Dixie Hummingbirds was a jubilee-styled act by the late '30s, joined in 1938 by 13-year-old baritone phenom Ira Tucker and bass singer extraordinaire Willie Bobo, a former member of the Heavenly Gospel Singers, the group made their recorded debut a year later on Decca, where they issued singles including "Soon Will Be Done With the Troubles of This World," "Little Wooden Church," and "Joshua Journeyed to Jericho."

Upon relocating to Philadelphia in 1942, the Hummingbirds' popularity began to grow—Tucker, in particular, wowed audiences with his flamboyant theatrics, rejecting the long tradition of "flat-footed" singers rooted in place on stage in favor of running up the aisles and rocking prayerfully on his knees. By 1944, he was even regularly jumping off stages—indeed, the frenetic showmanship of soul music may have had its origins in Tucker's manic intensity, itself an emulation of country preaching. At the same time, the Hummingbirds' harmonies continued to grow more sophisticated; the addition of Paul Owens completed the quartet's development, and together he and Tucker honed a style they dubbed "trickeration," a kind of note-bending distinguished by sensual lyrical finesse and staggering vocal intricacy. Their virtuosity did not go unnoticed by audiences, and throughout the mid-'40s—an acknowledged golden age of a cappella quartet singing—the group regularly played to packed houses throughout the south.

Under names like the Swanee Quintet and the Jericho Boys, the Dixie Hummingbirds also regularly appeared on Philadephia radio station WCAU; it was as the Jericho Boys that they auditioned for the legendary producer John Hammond, who in 1942 booked them into the Cafe Society Downtown, then the Greenwich Village area's preeminent showcase for black talent. By 1946, the Hummingbirds were again recording, cutting sides for labels including Apollo and, later in the decade, Gotham and Hob. In 1952, what many consider the group's definitive lineup—a roster of Tucker, Davis, Bobo, Beachey Thompson, James Walker (replacing Owens) and ace guitarist Howard Carroll, a roster which held intact for close to a quarter century—signed to the Peacock label, where over the course of the following decade they recorded a series of masterpieces including 1952's "Trouble in My Way," 1953's "Let's Go Out to the Programs," 1954's "Christian's Testimonial," 1957's "Christian Automobile" and 1959's "Nobody Knows the Trouble I See."

After earning a standing ovation for their performance at the 1966 Newport Folk Festival (captured on the *Gospel at Newport* LP), the Hummingbirds essentially retired from mainstream appearances to focus solely on the church circuit. They did, however, burst back into the popular consciousness in 1973, backing Paul Simon on his pop smash "Loves Me Like a Rock." The death of Willie Bobo in 1976 brought to a sad end a lengthy chapter of the Hummingbirds' history—his membership in their ranks dated back to the late '30s—but the surviving members forged on; just two years later, *Ebony* magazine named them "The World's Greatest Gospel Group." After Davis retired in 1984, Tucker was the last remaining link to the quartet's formative years; despite the subsequent deaths of Walker in 1992 and Thompson in 1994, Tucker continued leading the group at the century's end, recruiting new blood to keep the Dixie Hummingbirds' spirit alive for years to follow, celebrating their seventh decade with 1999's *Music in the Air: The 70th Anniversary All-Star Tribute Celebration*. *—Jason Ankeny*

Christian Testimonial / 1959 / MCA ✦✦✦

Great Peacock sides led by James Walker and Ira Tucker. *—Opal Louis Nations*

Prayer for Peace / 1964 / Peacock ✦✦✦

More great material from this seminal group. *—Opal Louis Nations*

In the Morning / 1964 / Peacock ✦✦✦✦✦

More fine harmony and tough singing. *—Opal Louis Nations*

The Best of the Dixie Hummingbirds / 1973 / MCA Special Products ✦✦✦✦✦

The Dixie Hummingbirds are generally regarded as one of the finest gospel groups in history, and the material showcased on *The Best of the Dixie Hummingbirds* proves why. Culled from the group's '50s and '60s recordings for Peacock, the compilation contains 12 terrific songs—including "Let's Go to the Programs," "Thank You for One More Day," "What a Friend," "Bedside of a Neighbor," "The Old Time Way" and "Our Prayer for Peace"—all of which are given astonishing, moving performances by the Hummingbirds. Throughout their long career, the Hummingbirds rarely gave anything less than impressive performances, but this remains one of the very best portraits of the superior gospel sextet. *—Stephen Thomas Erlewine*

☆ **Live** / 1976 / Mobile Fidelity ✦✦✦✦✦

With 75 minutes of fine performances, good sound quality and a varied repertoire, this the one to buy. *—Kip Lornell*

The Dixie Hummingbirds / 1988 / Gospel Heritage ✦✦✦✦

Choice Gotham material with and without Margaret Allison and the Angelic Gospel Singers of Philadelphia. *—Opal Louis Nations*

In These Changing Times / 1991 / MCA ✦✦✦

Choice selections from the best on the Peacock label. Great quartet. *—Opal Louis Nations*

In the Storm Too Long / 1991 / Gospel Jubilee ✦✦✦✦✦

Essential Regis, Apollo & Decca sides from the '40s. *—Opal Louis Nations*

We Love You Like a Rock/Every Day and Every Hour / 1991 / Mobile Fidelity ✦✦✦✦✦

☆ **Complete Recorded Works (1939–1947)** / Apr. 8, 1997 / Document ✦✦✦✦✦

Essential early sides by this seminal group. *—Opal Louis Nations*

Up in Heaven: The Very Best of the Dixie Hummingbirds & The Angelics / Mar. 3, 1998 / Collectables ✦✦✦✦

Peacock/ABC Paramount sides by this leading group from Philadelphia. *—Opal Louis Nations*

★ **Thank You for One More Day** / Nov. 17, 1998 / MCA ✦✦✦✦✦

Released in conjunction with the 70th anniversary of the Dixie Hummingbirds in 1998, this brings together 14 sides recorded for the ABC label. As one of the oldest of the still-performing groups (alongside the Fairfield Four and the Soul Stirrers), these earlier sides show the group during its hard gospel phase, although still adhering to their original concept of being a five-man gospel group with four-part harmonies surrounding and supporting a lead singer. Highlights anywhere the laser beams falls here, but special note should be paid to "Loves Me Like a Rock," "Let's Go Out to the Program" (where they imitate other groups with uncanny precision), "Two Little Fishes (And Five Loaves of Bread)," "Christian's Automobile," "Mother's Prayer," and "Bedside of a Neighbor." Equally noteworthy are "Ezekial Saw the Wheel," "In the Morning," "If Anybody Asks You," "The Final Edition," "Our Prayer for Peace" and the title track. A nice, bite-sized introduction to this long-standing gospel music tradition. *—Cub Koda*

Move On Up / Mar. 19, 2002 / Liquid 8 ✦✦✦✦

This is a good selection of the beautiful music the Dixie Hummingbirds made: tight-knit harmonies, fervent soloing, and songs ranging in mood from tender and peaceful to hand-clapping, shouting joy. This earnest and lovely music demonstrates why they're one of the groups that even unbelievers love, and joining them on at least some cuts are the Angelics. The passionate title track, "Move On Up a Little Higher," kicks things off, and is followed by another intense number—a version of "In the Morning" recorded live at what must've been quite a church service. There are plenty of breathers included, too, such as the a cappella numbers "Beaming from Heaven," the heartbreaking "Young Man," and "Get Away Jordan." *—Joslyn Layne*

20th Century Masters—The Millennium Collection: The Best of the Dixie Hummingbirds / Apr. 30, 2002 / MCA ✦✦✦✦

This discount-priced compilation is an excellent brief introduction to the Dixie Hummingbirds' Peacock Records recordings. It covers a period of 22 years, from 1953's "Let's Go Out to the Programs," on which the Hummingbirds offer their impressions of several other gospel groups, to a 1975 version of "Two Little Fishes (And Five Loaves of Bread)" from the album *Thanks to Thee*. Two other '70s recordings demonstrate the group's versatility: Stevie Wonder's "Jesus Children of America," an uptempo boogie performance, and the group's own take on "Loves Me Like a Rock," the hit on which they accompanied Paul Simon. Much of the material derives from leader Ira Tucker, who wrote or arranged seven of the 12 tracks. One can hear the group's influence on blues singers like Bobby "Blue" Bland, as well as secular R&B vocal groups like the Temptations on these tracks, which are often fiercely performed. *—William Ruhlmann*

Floyd Dixon

b. Feb. 8, 1929, Marshall, TX

Vocals, Leader, Piano / Jump Blues, West Coast Blues, Piano Blues, R&B

Floyd Dixon was an unabashed admirer of Charles Brown's mellow "club blues" sound, but he added a more energetic, aggressive jump blues edge to his sound during the early '50s—a formula that made the L.A.-based pianist an R&B star. Dixon was swept up in the late '40s R&B boom, recording for Supreme in 1947 and signing with Modern Records in 1949. He nudged into the R&B Top Ten with "Dallas Blues" and just missed similar lofty stature with "Mississippi Blues" later in 1949. After cutting prolifically for Modern, he switched over to Aladdin and hit in 1950 with "Sad Journey Blues," "Telephone Blues" the next year and the mournful "Call Operator 210" in 1952. But there was a playfully ribald side to Dixon, too. The double entendre "Red Cherries," a storming "Wine, Wine, Wine," and the two-sided 1951 live waxing "Too Much Jelly Roll" (penned by a young Jerry Leiber and Mike Stoller) and "Baby, Let's Go Down to the Woods" showcased his more raucous leanings. The hits ceased, but Dixon's West Coast R&B odyssey continued. *—Bill Dahl*

Opportunity Blues / 1976 / Route 66 ✦✦✦✦

Vinyl-only examination of the pianist's early sides for several West Coast R&B indies that spans 1948-1961. Dixon's ballad style was quite reminiscent of Charles Brown's but his jump blues leanings—here typified by "Wine, Wine, Wine" and "Real Lovin' Mama"—were all his own. *—Bill Dahl*

Rockin' This Joint Tonite / 1978 / JSP ✦✦✦

Houston Jump / 1979 / Route 66 ✦✦✦✦

Another cross-section of Dixon's 1947-1960 output that hasn't made the jump to the digital age as of yet. Surveys a wide array of labels, including a 1954 date for Atlantic's short-lived Cat subsidiary that produced "Roll Baby Roll" and "Is It True." *—Bill Dahl*

Marshall Texas Is My Home / 1991 / Specialty ✦✦✦✦✦

Dixon landed at Art Rupe's Specialty label in 1953, his music jumping harder than ever. These 22 tracks rate with his best; the collection is full of rarities and previously unissued items, many featuring the wailing tenor sax of Carlos Bermudez in lusty support of the pianist. By 1957, when he momentarily paused at Ebb Records, Dixon could do a pretty fair breathless imitation of Little Richard, as the scorching "Oooh Little Girl" definitively proves. Also includes Dixon's best-known number, the often-covered rocker "Hey Bartender" (first out on Atlantic's Cat subsidiary in 1954). *—Bill Dahl*

• **Complete Aladdin Recordings** / Mar. 19, 1996 / Capitol ♦♦♦♦♦
It's a matter of opinion as to whether Dixon's Aladdin output was his peak; many would give his Specialty sides (available on the *Marshall Texas Is My Home* compilation) the nod. Still, his late-'40s and early-'50s work for the label included some of his most popular and best tracks, such as "Wine, Wine, Wine," "Call Operator 210," "Tired, Broke and Busted," "Let's Dance," "Telephone Blues," and "Too Much Jelly Roll" (the last of which was one of Leiber-Stoller's first recorded compositions). This two-CD, 48-track compilation is geared more toward the completist collector than the average fan, especially with the inclusion of five Sonny Parker sides (which Dixon now says he didn't play on, despite some reports to the contrary) and about ten songs that feature Mari Jones on vocals. The best stuff is jump blues at its best, though, with good guitar work by Johnny and Oscar Moore (the latter of who had played with Nat "King" Cole), Dixon's fine piano playing, and witty, knowing vocals and lyrics. *—Richie Unterberger*

Wake Up and Live! / May 21, 1996 / Alligator ♦♦♦♦♦
There was a time when swing-oriented jazz, R&B and blues overlapped to form an accessible yet intelligent style of music. In the late '40s Louis Jordan, Charles Brown and Amos Milburn were popular figures and Floyd Dixon (although a bit in their shadow) was not far behind. When rock & roll suddenly took over pop music in the mid-'50s, the middle-aged black performers were tossed off the charts in favor of their younger white imitators and work began to become scarce. Fortunately Floyd Dixon survived the lean years and, as with Charles Brown, he made a "comeback." This CD is a definitive Floyd Dixon release, mixing together older hits (including his signature tune "Hey, Bartender") with newer originals; all 16 selections were written or co-composed by Dixon. Joined by a jumping band that features a liberal amount of solo space for guitarist Port Barlow, tenor saxophonist Eddie Synigal and the old-time styled trombone of Danny Weinstein (plus a couple of spots for Charles Owens' baritone), Dixon sounds in excellent shape. His voice had not aged much, his enthusiasm is very much intact and his piano playing (whether on slow blues, medium tempo novelties or the closing instrumental blues "Gettin' Ready") is quite jazz-oriented. Chip Deffaa's liner notes are an added plus. Highly recommended. *—Scott Yanow*

Cow Town Blues / Jan. 25, 2000 / Ace ♦♦♦♦
There are 26 songs from Dixon's 1948-1950 sessions for Modern compiled here, mostly taken from singles that appeared on Modern between 1949 and 1951, but also including seven previously unissued tracks. These were Dixon's first recordings, but his style was already in place, both on uptempo jump blues and ballads, sounding like fellow Los Angeles-based pianist Charles Brown on the slower tunes. This would rate a little below the compilations of his later '50s sides for Specialty and Capitol, as those include his best and best-known recordings, such as "Hey Bartender," "Wine, Wine, Wine," "Call Operator 210," and "Tired, Broke and Busted." This remains quality transitional West Coast blues, from that time when jazz and blues were intersecting to shape R&B, a movement that had Modern artists such as Dixon at the forefront. Modern session musicians such as saxophonist Maxwell Davis and guitarists Tiny Webb and Chuck Norris were sympathetic and sometimes exciting accompanists for Dixon on his Modern dates. As is the case with compilations of Modern R&B from this period, though, the songs do sometimes get too close to each other in arrangement and mood when they're grouped together en masse. This includes his first R&B hit (and biggest for Modern), the slow "Dallas Blues," although the peppier jump blues are definitely more interesting. *—Richie Unterberger*

Mary Dixon

b. Texas

Vocals / Classic Female Blues, Dirty Blues, Classic Jazz

The saga of the "Dusty Stevedore" was one of her most famous songs, but rest assured, blues singer Mary Dixon was not in the business of singing about historic forms of employment. Like so many other female classic blues artists of the '20s, her stock in trade was down-and-dirty blues about sex, the lyrics about as explicit as anything released on record prior to the rap era. Whether this was her artistic vision or not will never really be known, since this limited subject matter prevented later generations of blues researchers from finding the types of clues to long-forgotten artists' hometowns, for example, that were often found in the songs of country blues artists who were allowed to sing about other subjects besides sex. Dixon worked with accompaniment from a smallish group, sometimes just the piano tinkling of boogie-woogie maestro James P. Johnson and the horn obbligati of Ed Allen. The healthy market for naughty blues compilations combined with the lack of copyright on much of her material has led to a healthy selection of her material on various collections released in several different countries, although she is often limited to one track. The most ample supply of her recordings in one place can be found on the Document Recordings *Blue Girls* series, in which she is featured on the second volume. Some of her other songs include "Daddy You've Got Everything" and "You Can't Sleep in My Bed," unnecessary instructions at best since from the thrust of her lyrics, very little sleeping seems to go on in her bed. *—Eugene Chadbourne*

Willie Dixon

b. Jul. 1, 1915, Vicksburg, MS, **d.** Jan. 29, 1992, Burbank, CA

Vocals, Leader, Songwriter, Guitar, Bass / Chicago Blues, Electric Chicago Blues, Jump Blues, Jive

Willie Dixon's life and work was virtually an embodiment of the progress of the blues, from an accidental creation of the descendants of freed slaves to a recognized and vital part of America's musical heritage. That Dixon was one of the first professional blues songwriters to benefit in a serious, material way—and that he had to fight to do it—from his work also made him an important symbol of the injustice that still informs the music industry, even at the end of this century. A producer, songwriter, bassist and singer, he helped Muddy Waters, Howlin' Wolf, Little Walter and others find their most commercially successful voices.

By the time he was a teenager, Dixon was writing songs and selling copies to the local bands. He also studied music with a local carpenter, Theo Phelps, who taught him about harmony singing. With his bass voice, Dixon later joined a group organized by Phelps, the Union Jubilee Singers, who appeared on local radio. Dixon eventually made his way to Chicago, where he won the Illinois State Golden Gloves Heavyweight Championship. He might've been a successful boxer, but he turned to music instead, thanks to Leonard "Baby Doo" Caston, a guitarist who had seen Dixon at the gym where he worked out and occasionally sang with him. The two formed a duo playing on streetcorners, and later Dixon took up the bass as an instrument. They later formed a group, the Five Breezes, who recorded for the Bluebird label. The group's success was halted, however, when Dixon refused induction into the armed forces as a consciencious objector. Dixon was eventually freed after a year, and formed another group, the Four Jumps of Jive. In 1945, however, Dixon was back working with Caston in a group called the Big Three Trio, with guitarist Bernardo Dennis (later replaced by Ollie Crawford).

During this period, Dixon would occasionally appear as a bassist at late-night jam sessions featuring members of the growing blues community, including Muddy Waters. Later on when the Chess brothers—who owned a club where Dixon occasionally played—began a new record label, Aristocrat (later Chess), they hired him, initially as a bassist on a 1948 session for Robert Nighthawk. The Chess brothers liked Dixon's playing, and his skills as a songwriter and arranger, and during the next two years he was working regularly for the Chess brothers. He got to record some of his own material, but generally Dixon was seldom featured as an artist at any of these sessions.

Dixon's real recognition as a songwriter began with Muddy Waters' recording of "Hoochie Coochie Man." The success of that single, "Evil" by Howlin' Wolf, and "My Babe" by Little Walter saw Dixon established as Chess' most reliable tunesmith, and the Chess brothers continually pushed Dixon's songs on their artists. In addition to writing songs, Dixon continued as bassist and recording manager of many of the Chess label's recording sessions, including those by Lowell Fulson, Bo Diddley and Otis Rush. Dixon's remuneration for all of this work, including the songwriting, was minimal—he was barely able to support his rapidly growing family on the $100 a week that the Chess brothers were giving him, and a short stint with the rival Cobra label at the end of the '50s didn't help him much.

During the mid-'60s, Chess gradually phased out Dixon's bass work, in favor of electric bass, thus reducing his presence at many of the sessions. At the same time, a European concert promoter named Horst Lippmann had begun a series of shows called the American Folk-Blues Festival, for which he would bring some of the top blues players in America over to tour the continent. Dixon ended up organizing the musical side of these shows for the first decade or more, recording on his own as well and earning a good deal more money than he was seeing from his work for Chess. At the same time, he began to see a growing interest in his songwriting from the British rock bands that he saw while in London—his music was getting covered regularly by artists like the Rolling Stones and the Yardbirds, and when he visited England, he even found himself cajoled into presenting his newest songs to their managements. Back at Chess, Howlin' Wolf and Muddy Waters continued to perform Dixon's songs, as did newer artists such as Koko Taylor, who had her own hit with "Wang Dang Doodle." Gradually, however, after the mid-'60s, Dixon saw his relationship with Chess Records come to a halt. Partly this was a result of time—the passing of artists such as Little Walter and Sonny Boy Williamson was part of the problem, and the death of Leonard Chess and the sale of the company called a halt to Dixon's involvement.

By the end of the '60s, Dixon was eager to try his hand as a performer again, a career that had been interrupted when he'd gone to work for Chess as a producer. He recorded an album of his best-known songs, *I Am the Blues*, for Columbia Records, and organized a touring band, the Chicago Blues All-Stars, to play concerts in Europe. Suddenly, in his fifties, he began making a major name for himself on stage for the first time in his career. Around this time, Dixon began to have grave doubts about the nature of the songwriting contract that he had with Chess' publishing arm, Arc Music. He was seeing precious little money from songwriting, despite the recording of hit versions of such Dixon songs as "Spoonful" by Cream. He had never seen as much money as he was entitled to as a songwriter, but during the '70s he began to understand just *how much* money he'd been deprived of, by design or just plain negligence on the part of the publisher doing its job on his behalf.

Arc Music had sued Led Zeppelin for copyright infringement over "Bring It on Home" on *Led Zeppelin II*, saying that it was Dixon's song, and won a settlement that Dixon never saw any part of until his manager did an audit of Arc's accounts. Dixon and Muddy Waters would later file suit against Arc Music to recover royalties and the ownership of their copyrights. Additionally, many years later Dixon brought suit against Led Zeppelin for copyright infringement over "Whole Lotta Love" and its resemblance to Dixon's "You Need Love." Both cases resulted in out-of-court settlements that were generous to the songwriter.

The '80s saw Dixon as the last survivor of the Chess blues stable and he began working with various organizations to help secure song copyrights on behalf of blues songwriters who, like himself, had been deprived of revenue during previous decades. In 1988, Dixon became the first producer/songwriter to be honored with a boxed-set collection, when MCA Records released *Willie Dixon: The Chess Box* that included several rare Dixon sides as well as the most famous recordings of his songs by Chess' stars. The following year, Dixon published *I Am the Blues* (Da Capo Press), his autobiography, written in association with Don Snowden.

Dixon continued performing, and was also called in as a producer on movie soundtracks such as *Ginger Ale Afternoon* and *La Bamba*, producing the work of his old stablemate Bo Diddley. By that time, Dixon was regarded as something of an elder statesman, composer, and spokesperson of American blues. Dixon had suffered from increasingly poor health in recent years, and lost a leg to diabetes several years earlier, which didn't slow him down very much. He died peacefully in his sleep early in 1992. *—Bruce Eder*

Willie's Blues / 1959 / Bluesville/Original Blues Classics ♦♦♦
According to the original liner notes, this 1959 Willie Dixon session was cut during a two hour span in between flights. This certainly explains the relaxed, jam session feel of the recordings. Unfortunately, the songs come out sounding sluggish and stilted at times; this is partly due, no doubt, to the makeshift nature of the date, but also, more surprisingly, because of drummer Gus Johnson's overly slick and formalized playing. On top of this, one has to contend with Dixon's less-then-inspired vocals—it's Dixon's writing talents and A&R savvy in the blues world that warrant him a place in the pantheon, not his skills at the microphone. That all said, this still is an enjoyable disc to listen to, not least of all because of the quality of Dixon's many originals and the freshness of pianist Memphis Slim's playing. And while the vaudevillian comedy of a song like "Built for Comfort" can be traced to Dixon's earlier pop R&B work with the Big Three Trio, rougher blues standouts like "Go Easy" and "Move Me" lead back to the Chicago blues world Dixon shared with Muddy Waters and Howlin' Wolf. Not a first disc for curious listeners, but certainly a pleasant enough addition to the blues lover's collection. *—Stephen Cook*

Blues Every Which Way / 1966 / Verve ♦♦

I Am the Blues / 1970 / Columbia/Legacy ♦♦♦
The material is superb, consisting of some of Dixon's best-known songs of the '60s, and the production is smoothly professional, but none of the performances here are likely to make you forget the hits by Howlin' Wolf, Muddy Waters et al. Reissued on CD by Mobile Fidelity and more recently by Sony Music—unfortunately, none of the unreleased tracks from the session seem to have survived. *—Bruce Eder*

Catalyst / 1973 / Ovation ♦♦♦♦♦
One of his better latter-day efforts. *—Bill Dahl*

Willie Dixon's Peace? / 197 / Yambo ♦♦
This unexciting set appeared on Dixon's own label. *—Bill Dahl*

Mighty Earthquake & Hurricane / 1983 / Mighty Tiger ♦♦♦
Decent modern album by the prolific legend. *—Bill Dahl*

Willie Dixon: Live (Backstage Access) / 1985 / Pausa ♦♦
Adequate but not earthshaking. *—Bill Dahl*

Hidden Charms / Sep. 28, 1988 / Bug ♦♦♦

★ **The Chess Box** / 1989 / MCA/Chess ♦♦♦♦♦
This was the most unusual, and probably the most difficult to assemble of MCA's *Chess Box* series, mostly because of the unusual nature of Willie Dixon's contribution to Chess Records. To be sure, Dixon rates a place in the history of the label right alongside that of Muddy Waters, Howlin' Wolf, and Little Walter, but his role was more subtle than that of a performer (indeed, two of the half-dozen recordings here that feature Dixon as a singer were previously unreleased). So he is all over this two-CD set, as a songwriter, producer, and bassist, and occasionally as a singer as well, but the unifying element are the Dixon songs, and he is the only blues songwriter to be honored by a major label with a retrospective of this type. Since he was not the performer on most of this material, but, rather, was working to mesh his material with the styles and sensibilities of a vast range of players, the sounds contained on these two CDs are a lot more varied than on any of the other *Chess Box* releases—amplified Delta blues, big band, Mills Brothers-style harmony blues, jazz-influenced jump blues, and near-pop style R&B are all here; guitar pyrotechnics by Muddy Waters or Hubert Sumlin (on the Wolf's records), vocal acrobatics by Little Walter, and rippling performances by Koko Taylor illuminate this set throughout. While some of it, such as Muddy Waters' single of "Hoochie Coochie Man"; Little Walter's "My Babe"; Howlin' Wolf's performances of "Evil," "Spoonful," "Little Red Rooster," and "Back Door Man"; and Lowell Fulson's version of "Do Me Right" are easily available elsewhere, a lot else of what's here is genuinely rare and most enticing—Dixon's own renditions of "Violent Love," "Crazy For My Baby," and "Pain In My Heart," in particular, are great records, lacking perhaps only a slight measure of the energy that a Muddy Waters brought to recording. Most of the set is concentrated on his blues work—a pair of hot Bo Diddley sides ("Pretty Thing," "You Can't Judge a Book by Its Cover") that Dixon wrote are represented, but since he didn't write anything for Chuck Berry, that side of Dixon's history is left out, despite his having played bass on most of Berry's early recordings. Still, it's difficult to imagine anyone complaining over an "excuse" to bring some of the best sides of Muddy, Walter, the Wolf, Diddley, Taylor, Lowell Fulson, Jimmy Witherspoon, Sonny Boy Williamson, Otis Rush, and even Dixon's own '40s outfit, the Big Three, together in one release. The sound is impeccable, holding up to standards even a dozen years later, and the set includes a well-illustrated and annotated booklet. *—Bruce Eder*

The Big Three Trio / 1990 / Columbia/Legacy ♦♦♦
The Big Three Trio was Dixon's post-World War II blues vocal trio. His songwriting talent was still developing, and there isn't much relationship between this material and his subsequent work on Chess. The smooth vocals, however, will recall the Ink Spots, among other vocal groups of the era. *—Bruce Eder*

The Original Wang Dang Doodle / 1995 / MCA/Chess ♦♦♦♦
This is a good collection of hard-to-find and previously unreleased Dixon sides, although there are several Chess tracks that were left off that would have made it much more valuable. The title track is especially worthwhile, as is "Tail Dragger," but it is also easy to see from this collection why Dixon was never quite a star in his own right as a performer—he has a good voice, but not a very memorable or powerful one, compared with Muddy Waters, Howlin' Wolf et al. *—Bruce Eder*

In Paris / Jun. 25, 1996 / Original Blues Classics ♦♦♦

Poet of the Blues / Jun. 30, 1998 / Columbia/Legacy ♦♦♦♦
Columbia/Legacy's *Poet of the Blues* is a fine 16-track collection that spotlights Willie Dixon's own recordings of such blues standards as "Back Door Man," "I Can't Quit You Babe," "Spoonful," "The Little Red Rooster" and "I Ain't Sperstitious," plus some lesser-known originals like "If the Sea Was Whiskey," "O.C. Bounce," "Money Tree Blues," "Juice-Head Bartender" and "Signifying Monkey." Many of these songs were recorded with his early trio, the Big Three, and while they're of historical interest, they're not quite as good as his Chess recordings. Nevertheless, this is a good, concise sampler of his Columbia recordings for anyone curious about this period of Dixon's career. *—Thom Owens*

Big Boss Men / 2001 / Indigo ♦♦
The six live 1971 tracks by Dixon on this disc comprise only about half of the CD; the remainder consists of live 1972 material by Jimmy Reed, recorded at the same venue (Liberty Hall in Houston). Although Dixon offers strong vocal performances (as well as playing bass) on these cuts, the sound quality isn't so hot, and adequate at best. The band's OK, the name sideman being Walter Horton on harmonica. In addition to the familiar classics "Spoonful" and "I Just Want to Make Love to You," there's also the much lesser-known emotional, minor-key slow burner "Sitting and Crying the Blues," with uncredited piano, and the instrumental "Chicago Here I Come." On the final two songs, it might be hard to even consider Dixon as the featured artist, since Johnny Winter (credited as "John Winter") takes the vocal and guitar on "Tore Down," and then lead guitar on an instrumental, the Winter composition "Roach Stew." If this was longer and in decent fidelity, it would be a good record, but its shortcomings limit its attraction to severely dedicated Chicago blues fans. And, unfortunately, the four Jimmy Reed tracks drag the album's worth to a lower level, with sluggish performances (featuring Winter on guitar throughout) and sadly past-his-peak vocalizing by Reed. *—Richie Unterberger*

Mr. Dixon's Workshop / Aug. 28, 2001 / Fuel 2000 ♦♦♦♦
As a handy compilation of the prolific producer/songwriter/musician/A&R man's work for his non-Chess label clients, *Mr. Dixon's Workshop* is a captivating exploration into how productive Willie Dixon was on the '60s Chicago blues scene. While many of these tracks have appeared on other anthologies, specifically *The Cobra Records Story* box set, and some, like Otis Rush's "I Can't Quit You Baby," are ubiquitous, others are far more rare, making this a terrific collection of some relatively difficult to find music from one of postwar blues' most essential musicians. Charles Clark's pre-Howlin' Wolf version of "Hidden Charms," along with Jessie Fortune's "Too Many Cooks"—the latter featuring young guitarist Buddy Guy and Big Walter Horton on harp—popularized later by Robert Cray, are just two of the dusty gems found here. Guy also shows up on an early, earthy 1958 solo recording of "Sit and Cry the Blues." The fascinating final track, a previously unreleased studio session, is comprised of three alternate takes and shows the development of Otis Rush's "My Love Will Never Die" from a stark, solo piano-based ballad to the raging slow blues with horns it became, which puts the listener in an intriguing fly-on-the-wall position. Magic Sam, Junior Wells, and even a young Betty Everette are here, but it's the deep catalog items from obscure bluesmen like Harold Burrage, Lee Jackson, and Buster Benton (whose fiery "Spider in My Stew," featuring Carey Bell on eerie harp, is one of the album's highlights) that are the most welcome finds. Interestingly, a very Jerry Lee Lewis-sounding Mickey Gilley romps through a rockabilly version of "My Babe." Dixon's own rubbery standup bass lines, along with his distinctive songwriting, are the constants that tie these rather diverse artists together. Liner notes from the knowledgeable Bill Dahl provide pertinent background information; however, clear notation of who plays on each song is sadly missing. You have to search through the five pages of text in the poorly designed booklet. Otherwise this is a wonderful single-disc compilation exhibiting just how multifaceted and talented Willie Dixon was, even beyond his groundbreaking and better-known work for Chess. *—Hal Horowitz*

Lefty Dizz (Walter Williams)

b. Apr. 29, 1937, Osceola, AR, **d.** Sep. 7, 1993, Chicago, IL
Vocals, Guitar / Electric Chicago Blues

In a town like Chicago, where the competition in blues clubs was tough and keen (and still is on a hot night), certain musicians quickly learned that sometimes red-hot playing and singing didn't always get the job done by themselves. You had to entertain, put on a show, because there was *always* someone looking to take your gig away from you. Only those willing to protect their bandstand—and their livelihood in the long run—by generally peppering their presentation with a small to large dollop of showmanship were smart enough to hang in for the long run, keeping both their hometown audience and their turf intact. Although blues revisionist history always seems to overlook this, the show that T-Bone Walker, Guitar Slim, Howlin' Wolf, Muddy Waters, Little Walter, Buddy Guy, and others did in front of a black audience was wilder and far more audacious than the one a more reserved white audience *ever* got to see. For wild-ass showmen in blues history, though, one would certainly have to go a far piece to beat Walter Williams, known to blues fans in Chicago and Europe as Lefty Dizz.

A regular fixture of the Chicago scene from the mid-'60s into the early '90s, Lefty was quite a sight back in those days, fronting his band, Shock Treatment, playing and singing with an unbridled enthusiasm while simultaneously putting on a show that would have oldtimers guffawing in appreciation while scaring white patrons out of their wits. As an entertainer, he was simply nothing less than a modern day Guitar Slim informed with the outrage of a Hendrix, pulling out every trick in the book to win over an audience, whether he was protecting his home turf bandstand or stealing the show while sitting in somewhere else. It was nothing for him to play a slow blues, bring the band down, and start walking through the crowd dragging his beat-up Stratocaster behind him like a sack of potatoes, playing it with one hand the entire time. Or take on some Young Turk axeman gunning for his scalp (and gig) by kicking off Freddie King's "Hideaway" at an impossibly fast tempo, calling for break after break while infusing all of them with so many eye-popping gags that the Young Turk in question was merely reduced to becoming another member of the audience. As a bluesman, he was nothing less than deep and 100 percent for real. Nobody messed with Lefty Dizz.

Born in Arkansas in 1937, Dizz (the nickname was bestowed on him by Hound Dog Taylor and the HouseRockers, appropriating it from drummer Ted Harvey, who used the name when he was "playing jazz in the alley") started playing guitar at age 19 after a four-year hitch in the Air Force. Entirely self-taught, he played a standard right-handed model flipped upside down, without reversing the strings. His sound was raw and distorted and his style owed more to the older bluesmen than to the hipper West Side players like Otis Rush and Buddy Guy working in the B.B. King mode. By the time he came to Chicago, he had honed his craft well enough to become a member of Junior Wells' band in 1964, recording and touring Africa, Europe, and Southeast Asia with him until the late '60s. At various times during the '60s and early '70s, he'd also moonlight as a guitarist with Chicago stalwarts J.B. Lenoir and Hound Dog Taylor, while sitting in everywhere and playing with seemingly everyone. While being well known around town as a "head cutter," Lefty Dizz was always welcome on anyone's bandstand. His personality, while seemingly carefree and humorous, masked a deep, highly intelligent individual who had also earned a degree in economics from Southern Illinois University.

He kept soldiering on in the blues trenches through the '90s when he was diagnosed with cancer of the esophagus. While chemotherapy helped, Lefty went back to work far too soon and far too hard to stay on top of his game for much longer. The unflappable Dizz, who could seemingly make the best out of any given situation without complaint and had friends in the blues community by the truckload, finally passed away on September 7, 1993. And with his passing, the blues lost perhaps its most flamboyant showman. —*Cub Koda*

Ain't It Nice to Be Loved / 1995 / JSP ✦✦
Dizz recorded his final outing at Sotosound studios in Evanston, IL, surrounded with a collection of players who knew his style. Therefore, that this effort falls so short of the mark is all the more puzzling. If anyone truly needed a producer, Dizz was the man. The arrangements meander, the mix (such as it is) buries Lefty's guitar and evidently nobody bothered to tune up before or during the session. JSP has never been much noted for quality releases on either audio or artistic levels, but this is just plain embarrassing. —*Cub Koda*

Lefty Dizz With Big Moose Walker / Black & Blue ✦✦
It has been argued by more than one blues critic that for all his performing acumen, Lefty Dizz never recorded an album that captured even a smidgeon of his live intensity. This poorly produced album, recorded for the French Black & Blue imprint, would certainly support that claim. While the performances are workmanlike enough, Dizz's guitar sound (apparently routed direct to the board, bypassing his amp) gives new meaning to the words flabby and lifeless. Out of print for the time being and perhaps deservedly so. —*Cub Koda*

● **Somebody Stole My Christmas** / Isabel ✦✦✦✦
Dizz fares much better on this sophomore outing. Featuring a nice take on the title cut and fairly solid playing from all parties concerned, this certainly falls short of the fervor he could produce live but is still the best of the bunch. —*Cub Koda*

Dr. John (Malcolm John Rebennack, Jr.)

b. Nov. 21, 1940, New Orleans, LA
Vocals, Keyboards, Piano, Guitar / New Orleans R&B, Piano Blues, Rock & Roll
Although he didn't become widely known until the '70s, Dr. John had been active in the music industry since the late '50s, when the teenager was still known as Mac Rebennack. A formidable boogie and blues pianist with a lovable growl of a voice, his most enduring achievements have fused New Orleans R&B, rock, and Mardi Gras craziness to come up with his own brand of "voodoo" music. He's also quite accomplished and enjoyable when sticking to purely traditional forms of blues and R&B. On record, he veers between the two approaches, making for an inconsistent and frequently frustrating legacy that often makes the listener feel as if the "Night Tripper" (as he's nicknamed himself) has been underachieving. In the late '50s, Rebennack gained prominence in the New Orleans R&B scene as a session keyboardist and guitarist, contributing to records by Professor Longhair, Frankie Ford, and Joe Tex. He also did some overlooked singles of his own, and by the '60s had expanded into production and arranging. After a gun accident damaged his hand in the early '60s, he gave up the guitar to concentrate on keyboards exclusively. Skirting trouble with the law and drugs, he left the increasingly unwelcome environs of New Orleans in the mid-'60s for Los Angeles, where he found session work with the help of fellow New Orleans expatriate Harold Battiste. Rebennack renamed himself Dr. John, The Night Tripper when he recorded his first album, *Gris-Gris*. According to legend, this was hurriedly cut with leftover studio time from a Sonny & Cher session, but it never sounded hastily conceived. In fact, its mix of New Orleans R&B with voodoo sounds and a tinge of psychedelia was downright enthralling, and may have resulted in his greatest album. He began building an underground following with both his music and his eccentric stage presence, which found him conducting ceremonial-type events in full Mardi Gras costume. Dr. John was nothing if not eclectic, and his next few albums were granted mixed critical receptions because of their unevenness and occasional excess. They certainly had their share of admirable moments, though, and Eric Clapton and Mick Jagger helped out on *The Sun, Moon & Herbs* in 1971. The following year's *Gumbo*, produced by Jerry Wexler, proved Dr. John was a master of traditional New Orleans R&B styles, in the mold of one of his heroes, Professor Longhair. In 1973, he got his sole big hit, "In the Right Place," which was produced by Allen Toussaint, with backing by the Meters. In the same year, he also recorded with Mike Bloomfield and John Hammond Jr. for the *Triumvirate* album.

The rest of the decade, unfortunately, was pretty much a waste musically. Dr. John

could always count on returning to traditional styles for a good critical reception, and he did so constantly in the '80s. There were solo piano albums, sessions with Chris Barber and Jimmy Witherspoon, and *In a Sentimental Mood* (1989), a record of pop standards. These didn't sell all that well, though. A more important problem was that he's capable of much more than recastings of old styles and material. In fact, by this time he was usually bringing in the bacon not through his own music, but via vocals for numerous commercial jingles. It continued pretty much in the same vein throughout the '90s: New Orleans supersessions for the *Bluesiana* albums, another outing with Chris Barber, an album of New Orleans standards, and *another* album of pop standards. In 1994, *Television* did at least offer some original material. At this point he began to rely more upon cover versions for the bulk of his recorded work, though his interpretive skills will always ensure that these are more interesting than most such efforts. His autobiography, *Under a Hoodoo Moon*, was published by St. Martin's Press in 1994, and in 1998 he resurfaced with *Anutha Zone*, which featured collaborations with latter-day performers including Spiritualized, Paul Weller, Supergrass, and Ocean Colour Scene. *Duke Elegant* followed in early 2000. —*Richie Unterberger*

Gris-Gris / 1968 / Collectors' Choice Music ✦✦✦✦✦
The most exploratory and psychedelic outing of Dr. John's career, a one-of-a-kind fusion of New Orleans Mardi Gras R&B and voodoo mysticism. Great rasping, bluesy vocals, soulful backup singers, and eerie melodies on flute, sax, and clarinet, as well as odd Middle Eastern-like chanting and mandolin runs. It's got the setting of a strange religious ritual, but the mood is far more joyous than solemn. —*Richie Unterberger*

Babylon / 1969 / Wounded Bird ✦✦✦
Dr. John's ambition remained undiminished on his second solo album, *Babylon*, released shortly after the groundbreaking voodoo-psychedelia-New Orleans R&B fusion of his debut, *Gris-Gris*. The results, however, were not nearly as consistent or impressive. Coolly received by critics, the album nonetheless is deserving of attention, though it pales a bit in comparison with *Gris-Gris*. The production is sparser and more reliant on female backup vocals than his debut. Dr. John remains intent on fusing voodoo and R&B, but the mood is oddly bleak and despairing, in comparison with the wild Mardi Gras-gone-amok tone of his first LP. The hushed, damned atmosphere and after-hours R&B sound a bit like Van Morrison on a bummer trip at times, as peculiar as that might seem. "The Patriotic Flag-Waiver" (sic), in keeping with the mood of the late '60s, damns social ills and hypocrisy of all sorts. An FM underground radio favorite at the time, its ambitious structure remains admirable, though its musical imperfections haven't worn well. To a degree, you could say the same about the album as a whole. But it has enough of an eerie fascination to merit investigation. —*Richie Unterberger*

Remedies / 1970 / Wounded Bird ✦✦
Remedies is not rock & roll, it is something nearly otherworldly and almost beyond comprehension. While it includes such standout Dr. John tracks as "Wash Mama Wash" and "Loop Garoo," it also includes "Angola Anthem," which is murky, mysterious and downright evil sounding. Much of this very long cut is lost without headphones, for the music floats about in a smoky fog while Dr. John and his backup singers chant, moan and cry out. Progressive radio loved this stuff, and it still sounds great during those late-night flirtations with the dark side of the psyche. *Remedies* must be heard to be believed. —*James Chrispell*

The Sun, Moon & Herbs / Sep. 1971 / Wounded Bird ✦✦✦
Originally intended as a triple album, *The Sun, Moon & Herbs* was chopped up, whittled down and re-assembled into this single-disc release, and while Dr. John never liked this version much, perhaps this single disc is testament to the "less is more" theory. The seven cuts are all quite lengthy and the spells Dr. John and his consorts weave are dark and swampy. "Black John the Conqueror" comes from old Cajun folklore which the good Dr. has modernized and given a beat. The swampy "Craney Crow" is the younger sibling of his earlier "Walk on Guilded Splinters" and has a similar effect on the listener. "Pots on Fiyo (Fils Gumbo)" combines Latin American rhythms with lots of Cajun chants and spells. The vocals are nearly incomprehensible and actually serve as another instrument in the mix. "Zu Zu Mamou" is so thick that you can almost cut the music with a knife. Here, the atmosphere takes on a whole other meaning altogether. *The Sun, Moon & Herbs* is best listened to on a hot, muggy night with the sound of thunder rumbling off in the distance like jungle drums. Dr. John was definitely on to something here, but just what is left up to the listener. —*James Chrispell*

Dr. John / 1972 / Springboard ✦✦
Dr. John did a lot of sessions during his years of obscurity in New Orleans, and after he achieved national recognition in 1971 with the release of "Dr. John, The Night Tripper" *The Sun, Moon & Herbs* on Atco/Atlantic, those early sessions began turning up on low-budget labels. This album contains nine tracks, three of them alternate versions of other tracks, two of them apparently not featuring Dr. John at all (they are credited to "The Night Trippers"), and it still runs less than 24 minutes. Needless to say, it is not representative of later Dr. John material and should be avoided by all but completists. —*William Ruhlmann*

Dr. John's Gumbo / Apr. 1972 / Atco ✦✦✦✦✦
Dr. John's Gumbo bridged the gap between post-hippie rock and early rock & roll, blues and R&B, offering a selection of classic New Orleans R&B, including "Tipitina" and "Junko Partner," updated with a gritty, funky beat. There aren't as many psychedelic flourishes as there were on his first two albums, but the ones that are present enhance his sweeping vision of American roots music. And that sly fusion of styles makes *Dr. John's Gumbo* one of Dr. John's finest albums. —*Stephen Thomas Erlewine*

In the Right Place / Mar. 1973 / Atco ✦✦✦
Dr. John finally struck paydirt here and was certainly *In the Right Place*. With the hit single "Right Place Wrong Time" bounding up the charts, this fine collection saw many

unaware listeners being initiated into New Orleans style rock. Also including Allen Toussaint's "Life" and a funky little number entitled "Traveling Mood," which shows off the good doctor's fine piano styling, and with able help from the Meters as backup group, *In the Right Place* is still a fine collection to own. —*James Chrispell*

Desitively Bonnaroo / Apr. 1974 / Label M. ♦♦♦
When you latch on to a hit formula, don't mess with it, and that is just what the doctor ordered with *Desitively Bonnaroo*. With installment number three of Dr. John's funky New Orleans styled rock & roll, trying to strike gold again proved elusive. There wasn't the big hit single this time around to help boost sales, and the tunes were starting to sound a little too familiar. While not a carbon copy of his previous releases, *Desitively Bonnaroo* was a disappointment to his fans. Good as it was, it was the end of an era for Dr. John and his type of music. —*James Chrispell*

Hollywood Be Thy Name / 1975 / One Way ♦♦♦
In 1975 Dr. John took his well-honed New Orleans musical revue on the road and made a stop in Hollywood, with the recorded highlights released as *Hollywood Be Thy Name*. This is an enjoyable combination of live New Orleans soul and barrelhouse piano mixed with studio tracks including a reworking of his psychedelic anthem "Babylon." The live cover versions range from a soulful "Yesterday," a medley of "Its All Right With Me," "Blue Skies," and "Will the Circle Be Unbroken," plus the Roy Montrell New Orleans jump classic "Mellow Saxophone" retitled here as "I Wanna Rock." The only wrong turn taken is on the title track, which dips into a flashy Las Vegas routine complete with cheesy disco beat, that needless to say didn't suit Dr. John. —*Al Campbell*

City Lights / Feb. 1978 / Horizon ♦♦♦

Tango Palace / 1979 / Horizon ♦♦
Dr. John's second and final album for the Horizon jazz subsidiary of A&M Records finds him working with producers Tommy LiPuma and Hugh McCracken on a rollicking set that emphasizes his New Orleans roots while attempting to update his sound with '70s effects such as deep, plucked bass notes and occasional disco rhythms. The album leads off with "Keep That Music Simple," a somewhat caustic admonishment to musicians and the music business whose message is disregarded elsewhere on the record, as LiPuma and McCracken seek to cover all stylistic bases from funk to fusion to second line. Dr. John emerges from the production intact, but he is not quite as swampy as when heard at his best. —*William Ruhlmann*

Dr. John Plays Mac Rebennack / 1981 / Clean Cuts ♦♦♦♦♦
Dr. John was always respected as a consummate pianist, but he didn't make a solo, un-accompanied piano record until 1981's *Dr. John Plays Mac Rebennack*. The wait was well worth it. His music had always been impressive, but this is the first time that his playing had been put on full display, and it reveals that there's even more depth and intricacies to his style than previously expected. More importantly, the music simply sounds good and gritty, as he turns out a set of New Orleans R&B (comprised of both originals and classics) that is funky, swampy and real. —*Thom Owens*

Brightest Smile in Town / 1983 / Clean Cuts ♦♦♦
Doctor John's second solo piano album finds him combining country, blues, and New Orleans standards with originals, half of them instrumentals and half of them containing vocals that sound like they were recorded off the piano microphone. This is not a high-tech recording, by any means, but in its unadorned way it does capture the flavor of Doctor John as directly as any record he's made. —*William Ruhlmann*

The Ultimate Dr. John / 1987 / Warner Brothers ♦♦♦♦
This collection is drawn from Dr. John's years on the Atlantic label. Drawing from the albums *Gris-Gris*, *Gumbo*, *Remedies*, *Desitively Bonnaroo*, and *In the Right Place*, it puts his early years as the band leader in perspective. It takes us from the hoodoo-voodoo sounds of "I Walk on Guilded Splinters" and "Iko Iko," to the more polished tunes like "Such a Night." It is a good sampling of New Orleans rhythm & blues of this phase of his recorded years. His long years as a studio musician earned him the respect of the many great "sidemen" (a virtual who's who of New Orleans musicians) that he has playing with him on this album. If you don't have early Dr. John this is a necessity. He is at his best here. —*Bob Gottlieb*

In a Sentimental Mood / Apr. 1989 / Warner Brothers ♦♦♦
On Dr. John's first major-label effort and first vocal studio album in ten years, he performs a set of pop standards including Cole Porter's "Love for Sale" and Johnny Mercer's "Accentuate the Positive." After starting out with a wild stage act and unusual costumes, Dr. John has evolved into a vocal stylist and piano virtuoso, which makes the idea of doing this sort of material appealing. And he does it well, turning out a leisurely duet with Rickie Lee Jones on "Makin' Whoopee" that won a Grammy (Best Jazz Vocal Performance, Duo or Group) and giving sad feeling to "My Buddy." Maybe he has changed since the *Gris-Gris* days, but even a mellowed Dr. John is a tasty one. —*William Ruhlmann*

Dr. John And His New Orleans Congregation / 1990 / Ace ♦♦♦
Ace's *Dr. John and His New Orleans Congregation* isn't a Dr. John compilation in the strictest sense of the term—in other words, if you're looking for nothing but his funky hippie gumbo, you'd better look elsewhere. This disc is actually a great collection of cuts Mac Rebennack either played on or produced during the late '50s. all of which were released on Ace Records. Only "Storm Warning" is a genuine Rebennack song; the rest are New Orleans R&B at its funkiest. Not all of the songs are classics—in fact, only a handful, such as Earl King's "Let the Good Times Roll" come close to that status—but many of them are quite entertaining, especially for hardcore New Orleans R&B fanatics, making this a nice addition to either Dr. John or serious New Orleans R&B collections. —*Stephen Thomas Erlewine*

On a Mardi Gras Day / 1990 / Great Southern ♦♦♦
On a Mardi Gras Day is a live recording from 1983, capturing Dr. John at London's Marquee with Chris Barber and his 11-piece band. The presence of Barber and his big band gives the music a greater sense of swing, which makes this record—which basically consists of such familiar items as "Iko Iko," "Right Place, Wrong Time," "Li'l Liza Jane," "Stack-A-Lee" and "Such a Night"—something special in Mac Rebennack's catalog. It gives longtime fans the opportunity to hear him stretch out, play with the tempo and flash his jazz chops, which are considerable. Not the definitive or most representative Dr. John live set, but a rewarding one nonetheless. —*Thom Owens*

Goin' Back to New Orleans / Jun. 23, 1992 / Warner Brothers ♦♦♦
Having cut an album of standards on his first Warner Brothers album, *In a Sentimental Mood* (1989), Dr. John turned for its follow-up to a collection of New Orleans standards. On an album he described in the liner notes as "a little history of New Orleans music," Dr. John returned to his hometown and set up shop at local Ultrasonic Studios, inviting in such local musicians as Pete Fountain, Al Hirt, and the Neville Brothers and addressing the music and styles of such local legends as Jelly Roll Morton, Huey "Piano" Smith, Fats Domino, James Booker, and Professor Longhair. The geography may have been circumscribed, but the stylistic range was extensive, from jazz and blues to folk and rock. And it was all played with festive conviction—Dr. John is the perfect archivist for the music, being one of its primary popularizers, yet he had never addressed it quite as directly as he did here. —*William Ruhlmann*

Mos' Scocious: Anthology / Oct. 19, 1993 / Rhino ♦♦♦♦♦
Over his 35 years of recording, Mac "Dr. John" Rebennack has worn many hats, from '50s greasy rock & roller to psychedelic '70s weirdo to keeper of the New Orleans music flame. All of these modes, plus more, are excellently served up on this two-disc anthology. From the early New Orleans sides featuring Rebennack's blistering guitar work ("Storm Warning" and "Morgus the Magnificent") to the fabled '70s sides as the Night Tripper to his present-day status as repository of the Crescent City's noble musical tradition, this is the one you want to have for the collection. —*Cub Koda*

Television / Mar. 29, 1994 / GRP ♦♦
Dr. John's debut for GRP doesn't deviate from any release he's made for several other labels. It's still his chunky, humorous take on New Orleans funk; these are his songs, visions and performances, and there's none of the elevator material or laidback, detached fare that's a customary GRP byproduct. Such songs as "Witchy Red," "Spaceship Relationship" and the title selection are a delicate mix of seemingly outrageous but actually quite sharp commentary and excellent musical performances from Dr. John on keyboards, Hugh McCracken on guitar, and several other veterans, among them the great Red Tyler on tenor sax. While not quite as fiery as his classic sessions for Atlantic, if anyone can bring the funk to a company that's famous for avoiding it, it's Dr. John. —*Ron Wynn*

Cut Me While I'm Hot: The Sixties Sessions / 1995 / Magnum ♦♦♦
The liner notes for this 19-song compilation are brief, but at least have the honesty to admit that "the precise details of the circumstances surrounding these recordings may be lost forever." It speculates that the first half of the outtake-sounding program was cut in New Orleans during the first half of the '60s, while the latter part dates from L.A. sessions from 1965-1967. It actually sounds like much of this postdates the mid-'60s, with a feeling not unlike his early-'70s work. Most of the titles are self-penned, and there are also a few Professor Longhair covers. The material isn't really up to the level of his better early records, and the earlier tracks boast muffled audio (though fidelity is listenable throughout). At the same time, if you like vintage Dr. John, this is not much worse than the official stuff, the jiving throaty vocals, humorous songwriting, and distinctive keyboard playing all in place. It's low on outstanding compositions, but isn't bad at all, meaning there's no need to rush out and buy it, but also that committed fans won't mind having it around. —*Richie Unterberger*

● **The Very Best of Dr. John** / Apr. 25, 1995 / Rhino ♦♦♦♦♦
The Very Best of Dr. John compiles the best moments from the comprehensive double-disc *Anthology*, making it a more effective, and cheaper, introduction for casual fans. —*Stephen Thomas Erlewine*

Afterglow / Jun. 1995 / Blue Thumb ♦♦♦
Producer and GRP Records president Tommy LiPuma, a longtime associate of Dr. John's, revived his old Blue Thumb label as an imprint of GRP/MCA with this album, which served as something of a sequel to the last Dr. John/Tommy LiPuma collaboration, *In a Sentimental Mood*. On that earlier album, the two had covered pop standards. Here, they again turned to evergreens by the likes of Irving Berlin and Duke Ellington. But if *In a Sentimental Mood* was stylistically linked to the '20s and '30s, *Afterglow* was more a recreation of the late '40s and early '50s, with its big-band arrangements and the inclusion of jump blues numbers like Louis Jordan's "I Know What I've Got." Such songs allowed Dr. John plenty of room to play his trademark New Orleans piano solos, and, in the second half of the record, some of the Doctor's own compositions were snuck in among the classics without disturbing the mood. Of course, the dominant sound remained Dr. John's gravel-and-honey voice, an even more appropriate instrument for these bluesier standards than it was for the *Sentimental* ones. —*William Ruhlmann*

Crawfish Soiree / Feb. 11, 1997 / Aim ♦♦♦

Anutha Zone / Aug. 11, 1998 / Virgin ♦♦♦♦
Dr. John has spent so much time turning out perfectly enjoyable but interchangeable records that it may be easy to forget the spooky voodoo vibes of his earliest, arguably best, records. He may have forgotten it himself, too, but there was a whole generation of British musicians, from Modfather Paul Weller to Spaceman Jason Pierce to the teenaged punks in Supergrass, who remembered the haunted vibe lurking in *Gumbo* and

Gris-Gris. Citing his name in interviews, covering his songs and enlisting him as a session musician (Mr. Rebennack played on Spiritualized's acclaimed 1997 album, *Ladies and Gentlemen, We Are Floating in Space*), they created a buzz around Dr. John and were more than willing to play on *Anutha Zone*, hopefully generating some sales for him in return. As should be expected from any project that is a marketer's dream, the collaborations occasionally seem awkward, but what is surprising is how often it works. Pierce helps Rebennack conjure the psychedelic R&B of his earlier albums, while Weller and Supergrass help keep things cooking; furthermore, members of Primal Scream and Portishead help make "Sweet Home New Orleans" a titanic workout. The Brits aren't as funky as the classic New Orleans musicians, but they are willing to push Dr. John into his best work in years. *Anutha Zone* isn't a perfect album by any means, but it's Rebennack's most ambitious and rewarding album in many a year. *—Stephen Thomas Erlewine*

Crazy Cajun Recordings / May 11, 1999 / Edsel ♦♦♦

Medical School: The Early Sessions of Mac "Dr. John" Rebennack / Jun. 22, 1999 / Music Club ♦♦♦♦

Dr. John's early work as a producer, sessionman, and songwriter for Ace Records is legendary, not only among fans of Mac Rebennack but among devotees of New Orleans R&B. Unfortunately, there was no easy way to hear this material until Music Club's 1999 release, *Medical School: The Early Sessions of Mac "Dr. John" Rebennack*. Clocking in at 18 tracks, the disc isn't complete, but it is definitive—all the best-known cuts are here, along with a generous selection of little-known gems. To anyone but scholars and aficionados, most of the names on the compilation will not be familiar (The Ends, Al Reed, Ronnie & the Delinquents, Sugar Boy Crawford, Bobby Hebb, among others), and many of these cuts have never been well-circulated, or even released, but that's what makes the compilation so special. Not only are these lost classics from Dr. John, but these are lost gems from the prime period of New Orleans R&B. And this is not hyperbole—listening to *Medical School*, it's hard not to escape the feeling that almost every song is a hit you've never heard or have forgotten about. The instrumentals are not weak, the novelties (such as "Morgus the Magnificent") are fun, and cuts like "It Ain't No Use," "Bad Neighborhood," "You Don't Leave Me No Choice," and "Keeps Dragging Me On" are simply fantastic, sounding for all the world like classics, not throwaways. And that's the reason why *Medical School* isn't simply a necessary addition to Dr. John's catalog—it's an essential addition to any New Orleans R&B library. *—Stephen Thomas Erlewine*

Duke Elegant / Feb. 1, 2000 / Blue Note ♦♦♦♦

Duke Elegant certainly wasn't the only tribute to Duke Ellington put out in honor of the 100th anniversary of the legendary bandleader, nor was it even the first time Dr. John had tackled his material. But it would be hard to find a better homage than this one. Dr. John proves a surprisingly good match for Ellington's material, placing a tremendously funky foundation under the composer's tunes. The sound is dominated by the good doctor's incomparable New Orleans piano and organ, naturally, and the best tracks are those whose melodies are carried solely by his keyboard work, such as instrumentals "Caravan" and "Things Ain't What They Used to Be." The vocal cuts are fine—his takes on the Ellington ballad "Solitude" and especially the dreamy, elegant "Mood Indigo" show off Dr. John's uniquely expressive voice as well as any of his early-era recordings—though he occasionally tends to approach self-caricature, as on "It Don't Mean a Thing (If It Ain't Got That Swing)." Any weakness, however, is more than made up for by the closing rearrangement of "Flaming Sword," one of three Ellington rarities here. Dr. John transforms the instrumental into a luminous, gorgeously melodic display of Professor Longhair-style piano over an astonishingly sexy New Orleans funk rhythm. Ultimately, *Duke Elegant* holds up both as an innovative twist on the Ellington songbook and as a solid Dr. John album in its own right. *—Kenneth Bays*

Hoodoo: The Collection / Jul. 25, 2000 / Music Club ♦♦♦♦

Essential Recordings / Jan. 9, 2001 / Purple Pyramid ♦♦

A title like *Essential Recordings* typically means one of two things: Either it's a package that brings together an artist's accepted hits or a compilation claiming to be what it is not. This Dr. John collection belongs in the latter category, containing curios for fans' enjoyment but little for newcomers to the musical world of Mac Rebennack. Many of these tracks have appeared before in similar settings: collections like *At His Best*, *Cut Me While I'm Hot: The Sixties Sessions*, *Crawfish Soiree*, and *Masters*. Comparing the track listing with the canonized Dr. John material available on the fine Rhino compilation, however, reveals one common track—the wonderfully playful "Tipitina" from *Dr. John's Gumbo*. It is, unsurprisingly, one of the best things here and it kicks off a ragbag blend of piano blues, funky psychedelic rock, R&B rhythms, and swaggering Dixieland horns. Also included are three of the Doctor's earliest recordings ("Did She Mention My Name," "The Grass Looks Greener Yonder," and "New Orleans"), which seem completely out of place with their heavily imitative style. While Jimmy Calhoun's bass and Fred Staehle's drums provide the sturdy framework for Dr. John to relax on "Tipitina," there is a general lack of focus on the selections of *Essential Recordings*. This can be oddly compelling, as on "The Ear Is on Strike," which sounds on the verge of collapse with a rhythm that rushes, slows, rushes, and stops. Dr. John sings with a late-night, stoned, cool against a loose bass, guitar, organ, and piano concoction. But most of the time the songs feel like tired jams or early rehearsals. No doubt, a few selections would bear consideration for a lengthy Dr. John retrospective, but these recordings are not essential and not the place to begin. *—Nathan Bush*

Creole Moon / Oct. 9, 2001 / Blue Note ♦♦♦

Between his various standards albums of the '90s and the heavily collaborational *Anutha Zone* from 1998, by the end of the millennium it'd been nearly a decade since Dr. John's last record of straight-ahead New Orleans R&B. *Creole Moon* rectifies that situation nicely—it's "a personal interpretation of New Orleans" (as he says in the liner notes), and these 14 vignettes of New Orleans life are soaked in Crescent City soul. *Creole Moon* is also a return to the sound of his classic mid-'70s records (*Dr. John's Gumbo*, *In the Right Place*), right from the spidery electric piano and testifying backup vocals on the opener "You Swore." Most of his band, the Lower 9-11 Musician Vocaleers, have been playing with him for close to 20 years, and provide solid accompaniment. Dr. John also invites some friends along, including David "Fathead" Newman, slide guitarist Sonny Landreth, fiddler Michael Doucet, and a tight horn section led by Fred Wesley. And there's few better than Wesley to knock out a tough James Brown groove, as he and the band do on "Food for Thot" while Dr. John vamps over the top. Most of the other songs are little more than those loose grooves, and the booklet's constant references to African-derived rhythms (or an included Creole dictionary, aka "Gumbo-izms") may be too much for most listeners, but *Creole Moon* shows Dr. John doing what he's done best for nearly 30 years. *—John Bush*

Return of the Mac / West Side ♦♦♦♦♦

This 28-track collection of Mac Rebbenack's early New Orleans sessions for Johnny Vincent duplicates much of the material on the similarly compiled *Medical School* on Music Club. This set, however, brings an extra ten tracks to the mix, along with such gems as the long version of "Storm Warning" and Gene and Al's Spacemen's "Mercy." Long before he reinvented himself as Dr. John, these sides show that Rebbenack was a first-class session player. *—Cub Koda*

Bill Doggett

b. Feb. 16, 1916, Philadelphia, PA, **d.** Nov. 13, 1996, New York, NY

Organ (Hammond), Piano, Organ / Soul-Jazz, Swing, R&B

Although he was early on known as a fine swing-based pianist, Bill Doggett found his greatest fame in the '50s as an R&B-ish organist, particularly after recording his big hit "Honky Tonk" in 1956. He led his own big band in 1938, which accompanied Lucky Millinder for a year. After stints with Jimmy Mundy's short-lived orchestra (1939) and back with Millinder (1940-1942), Doggett arranged for the Ink Spots (1942-1944) and recorded with Johnny Otis and Illinois Jacquet (1945-1947). He replaced Wild Bill Davis with Louis Jordan's Tympany Five (1948-1951) and, following Davis' example, took up the organ. After recording with Eddie "Lockjaw" Davis and Ella Fitzgerald, Doggett led his own groups, recording frequently for King throughout the '50s. He was heard in more jazz-oriented settings in the '70s on sessions for the Black & Blue label and recorded for After Hours in 1991. *—Scott Yanow*

Dance Awhile with Doggett / Dec. 15, 1953-Feb. 28, 1958 / King ♦♦♦♦♦

Dame Dreaming / 1956 / King ♦♦♦

Everybody Dance to the Honky Tonk / 1956 / King ♦♦♦♦♦

This hugely influential jazz-laced R&B quartet plays their classic two-part instrumentals and several more groovers, with guitarist Billy Butler and saxist Clifford Scott incendiary throughout the album. *—Bill Dahl*

Doggett Beat for Dancing Feet / 1958 / King ♦♦♦

Doggett's fatback organ cooks in tandem with Butler's licks and Scott's sax. *—Bill Dahl*

Wow! / 1965 / Verve ♦♦♦

This CD reissue of a 1964 set by organist Bill Doggett's band is well-played and spirited but quite lightweight. The nine selections are mostly blues-oriented jams without any memorable melodies, stirring solos, or moments that lift the program above the routine. The rather brief results are pleasant and groovin' but rather predictable. *—Scott Yanow*

● **Leaps n' Bounds** / 1991 / Charly ♦♦♦♦♦

Nineteen tracks from the '50s, including both parts of the massive hit "Honky Tonk." The packaging could be a little more coherent, and the grooves may sometimes get a little too similar for some. But it's solid instrumental organ-sax-guitar jump blues on the verge of turning into rock & roll, with occasional standouts like "Big Boy" supplying evidence that Doggett wasn't solely a one-song wonder. *—Richie Unterberger*

All His Hits / 1995 / King ♦♦♦

These 14 hits are a mere sampling of organist Bill Doggett's prolific output on King Records. On "Big Dog Blues (Part 1)" he has that keyboard humming, and on standards like "Moondust," "Sweet Lorraine," "Don't Get Around Much Anymore," and "Soft," he displays a gentler side to his genius. You get the feeling you're in a mob's speakeasy when listening to "High Heels," where Doggett's organ gurgles underneath a free-flowing sax. His organ has no defined voice, and sounds different on every tune. "As You Desire Me" has an eerie, other worldly sound, while his most known hit "Honky Tonk" is one of the '50s' best R&B jump tunes. The only knock is the omission of half of two songs: "Big Dog Blues" and "Smokie." Forget any preconceived notions you have about Doggett—his albums are essential to any music collection. *—Andrew Hamilton*

The EP Collection / Sep. 28, 1999 / See for Miles ♦♦♦♦

Fats Domino (Antoine Domino)

b. Feb. 26, 1928, New Orleans, LA

Vocals, Leader, Songwriter, Piano / New Orleans R&B, Piano Blues, Rock & Roll, R&B

The most popular exponent of the classic New Orleans R&B sound, Fats Domino sold more records than any other black rock & roll star of the '50s. His relaxed, lolling boogie-woogie piano style and easygoing, warm vocals anchored a long series of national hits from the mid-'50s to the early '60s. Through it all, his basic approach rarely changed. He may not have been one of early rock's most charismatic, innovative, or threatening figures, but he was certainly one of its most consistent.

Domino's first single, "The Fat Man" (1949), is one of the dozens of tracks that have been consistently singled out as a candidate for the first rock & roll record. As far as Fats was concerned, he was just playing what he'd already been doing in New Orleans for years, and would continue to play and sing in pretty much the same fashion even after his music was dubbed "rock & roll."

The record made number two on the R&B charts, and sold a million copies. Just as important, it established a vital partnership between Fats and Imperial A&R man Dave Bartholomew. Bartholomew, himself a trumpeter, would produce Domino's big hits, co-writing many of them with Fats. He would also usually employ New Orleans session greats like Alvin Tyler on sax and Earl Palmer on drums—musicians who were vital in establishing New Orleans R&B as a distinct entity, playing on many other local recordings as well (including hits made in New Orleans by Georgia native Little Richard).

Domino didn't cross over into the pop charts in a big way until 1955, when "Ain't That a Shame" made the Top Ten. Pat Boone's cover of the song stole some of Fats' thunder, going all the way to number one (Boone was also bowdlerizing Little Richard's early singles for pop hits during this time). Domino's long-range prospects weren't damaged, however; between 1955 and 1963, he racked up an astonishing 35 Top 40 singles. "Blueberry Hill" (1956) was probably his best (and best-remembered) single; "Walking to New Orleans," "Whole Lotta Loving," "I'm Walking," "Blue Monday," and "I'm in Love Again" were also huge successes.

After Fats left Imperial for ABC-Paramount in 1963, he would only enter the Top 40 one more time. The surprise was not that Fats fell out of fashion, but that he'd maintained his popularity so long while the essentials of his style remained unchanged. This was during an era, remember, when most of rock's biggest stars had their careers derailed by death or scandal, or were made to soften up their sound for mainstream consumption. Although an active performer in the ensuing decades, his career as an important artist was essentially over in the mid-'60s. He did stir up a bit of attention in 1968 when he covered the Beatles' "Lady Madonna" single, which had been an obvious homage to Fats' style. —*Richie Unterberger*

Here Stands Fats Domino / 1958 / Imperial ✦✦✦
As with most of Imperial Records' LP releases on Fats Domino, this one reached across a lot of time for its dozen tracks, although the centerpiece was the hit "I'm Walkin'" in its first LP appearance. Also aboard was the latter's B-side, "I'm in the Mood for Love," but a lot of the rest dated from Domino's first Imperial sessions in December of 1949, making this something of an oldies album, or at least an excursion backward to a time and a sound from a decade earlier. Among the best of those cuts were the surprisingly elegant ballad "Hideaway Blues," with its supple piano trills, and the pounding rocker "She's My Baby," which had been two sides of a single at the outset of the '50s; also of note are the slow blues "Brand New Baby," highlighted by Ernest McLean's understated lead guitar and some supremely subtle sax work, and the jaunty "Little Bee," a charmingly raunchy and suggestive number from his second Imperial session in January of 1950. —*Bruce Eder*

Fats on Fire / 1964 / Paramount ✦✦✦
Fats on Fire is the first of a two-volume series of Fats Domino's mid-'60s recordings for ABC/Paramount, both of which are mid-priced imports packed with 24 tracks each. A lot was happening in R&B in the mid-'60s with the rise of soul and Motown, etc., but Fats stuck to his guns and kept churning out his own brand of rock & roll. The production values may be slightly more lavish on these sides, but they are definitely of a piece with his earlier recordings, and well worth acquiring for those who care enough to own either of the box sets of his classic Imperial tracks. This volume includes such gems as "There Goes My Heart Again," "Bye Baby, Bye Bye," and Ted Daffan's "I'm a Fool to Care," as well as a few re-recordings of songs from his Imperial years. —*Greg Adams*

Fats Is Back / 1968 / Bullseye Blues ✦✦✦
Like many of the early legends of rock & roll, Fats Domino didn't command a lot of attention in the late '60s. Not only had the British Invasion pushed Fats, Chuck, Little Richard, and their contemporaries off the charts, but post-1965 developments like psychedelia and folk-rock made straightforward rock & roll and rolling New Orleans R&B sound a little old-fashioned. In other words, it was time for the first generation to stage a comeback. Producer Richard Perry never neglects the essentials of Fats' music—he retains the easygoing charm and endearing shuffles, just updating it slightly. In retrospect, *Fats Is Back* feels like Perry's blueprint for Ringo Starr's star-studded extravaganzas of the mid-'70s—he selects an impeccable set of songs, nearly all covers but not just relying on obvious selections, assembles a first-rate cast of musicians, and then puts on a show. After all, this is an album that begins with a roll call of Domino's greatest hits and then ends with "One More Song for You"—it's intended to be spectacular and it comes damn close to being one. Part of the reason *Fats Is Back* works is that it's designed to entertain but never oversells itself—sort of like the man himself, actually. Fats delivers tailor-made new songs, Barbara George's "I Know," a remake of his classic "I'm Ready," and two Beatles covers (McCartney's Fats tribute "Lady Madonna" and "Lovely Rita") with equal gusto. Years on from its initial release, *Fats Is Back* still sounds like a sly, endearing update of the classic Domino sound. It may not match his classic Imperial recordings, yet it will no doubt please anyone wishing to dig a little deeper. —*Stephen Thomas Erlewine*

Live at Montreux / 1974 / Atlantic ✦✦✦
Recorded in 1973, *Live in Montreux* features Fats Domino running through all of his greatest hits—"Blueberry Hill," "Ain't That A Shame," "I'm Walking," and several others. Domino is in good spirits and his band is competent, but they deliver no real sparks. It's an enjoyable live album, but it offers nothing out of the ordinary, so only dedicated fans need apply. —*Thom Owens*

★ **My Blue Heaven: The Best of Fats Domino** / Jul. 30, 1990 / EMI ✦✦✦✦✦
For the budget-minded fan, this 20-track single-disc compilation of Fats Domino's Imperial smashes will serve nicely. Not much of his early pre-rock stuff—"The Fat Man" and "Please Don't Leave Me" are all that are here—but there's plenty of his hit-laden output from 1955 on—"Ain't It a Shame," "Blue Monday," "I'm in Love Again," "Blueberry Hill," "I'm Ready," among others. One small but substantial difference between this set and the larger packages: It uses non-sped-up masters of his mid-'50s material (some of his hits

from this era were mastered slightly faster than true pitch). Even if they're not historically correct, these versions actually sound better. —*Bill Dahl*

☆ **They Call Me the Fat Man: The Legendary Imperial Recordings** / Oct. 22, 1991 / EMI ✦✦✦✦✦
If you can't quite finance the Bear Family box, this four-disc compilation is the next best thing; an even 100 of the best Imperial sides, including a great many from 1958 on that turn up in crystal-clear stereo (as they also do on the Bear Family package). All the hits are aboard, along with a nice cross section of the important non-hits. The saxes (usually including Herb Hardesty and sometimes Lee Allen) roar with typical Crescent City power, Fats rolls the ivories, and magic happens—over and over again! Another nice booklet with plenty of photos (but a less detailed discography without sideman credits). —*Bill Dahl*

Out of New Orleans / 1993 / Bear Family ✦✦✦✦✦
An amazing piece of work—a massive eight-disc boxed set that contains every one of Fats Domino's 1949-1962 Imperial waxings. That's a tremendous load of one artist, but the legacy of Domino and his partner Dave Bartholomew is so consistently innovative and infectious that it never grows tiresome for a second. From the clarion call of "The Fat Man," Domino's 1949 debut, to the storming "Dance with Mr. Domino" in 1962, he typified everything charming about Crescent City R&B, his Creole patois and boogie-based piano a non-threatening vehicle for the rise of rock & roll. A thick, photo-filled book accompanies the disc, and there's an exhaustive discography that makes sense of Domino's many visits to Cosimo Matassa's studios. If you care about Fats Domino, this is the package to purchase! —*Bill Dahl*

Early Imperial Singles 1950–1952 / Jul. 2, 1996 / Ace ✦✦✦
Fat Man: 25 Classic Performances / Aug. 20, 1996 / Capitol ✦✦✦✦
Ostensibly replacing the compact disc *My Blue Heaven* as the definitive single-disc collection of Fats Domino's biggest hit singles, *Fat Man: 25 Classic Performances* features most of Fats Domino's biggest hits, but it inexplicably neglects such hits as "Walking to New Orleans," "Be My Guest" and "I'm Gonna Be a Wheel Someday." The only justification for the omission of so many hits is that the intent of the collection is to portray Fats Domino as the R&B heavyweight that he undoubtedly is, but seldom receives credit for being. Nevertheless, *Fat Man* masquerades as a greatest hits collection, billing itself as "25 Classic Performances," which leads you to believe that it is simply another hits collection. As an R&B compilation, *Fat Man* is strong—and, like any proper R&B collection, it presents the singles at the speed they were recorded at, not the sped-up versions that became hits—but because it lacks these hits, *My Blue Heaven* remains a preferable collection and introduction to Fats. —*Stephen Thomas Erlewine*

EP Collection / Oct. 29, 1996 / See for Miles ✦✦✦
The Imperial Singles, Vol. 2 / May 20, 1997 / Ace ✦✦✦✦✦
EP Collection, Vol. 2 / Aug. 5, 1997 / See for Miles ✦✦✦✦
A Whole Lot of Trouble / 1998 / Disky ✦✦✦✦
A Whole Lot of Trouble is the second volume of Fats Domino's mid-'60s ABC/Paramount recordings, again featuring 24 tracks on one inexpensive import CD. Like the first volume, *Fats on Fire*, this set includes a few re-recordings of songs from Fats' Imperial days, and an assortment of rock, pop, and R&B songs. In addition, there are covers of Don Gibson's "Who Cares" and Howard Harlan's "Sally Was a Good Old Girl." Fats Domino may have been an anachronism when he made these recordings, but they are nearly as entertaining as his better-known hits of the '50s. —*Greg Adams*

Rock and Rollin'/This Is Fats Domino! / Jul. 28, 1998 / Collectables ✦✦✦✦
Collectables' *Rock and Rollin'/This Is Fats Domino!* contains two original albums from Fats Domino, one of the most consistent recording artists of the early rock & roll era. During his time at Imperial, he rarely recorded anything that wasn't enjoyable—not only was his choice of material first-rate, but he could make lesser songs entertaining. Fortunately, both of these albums are filled with both hits ("My Blue Heaven," "Blueberry Hill," "Blue Monday") and fine album tracks, which, along with the bonus tracks "I'm Walkin'" and "It's You I Love," results in a thoroughly entertaining CD. Of course, serious fans who want to dig deeper would be better off with either EMI or Bear Family's box sets, but listeners who don't want to invest in the box sets—and don't mind less than pristine sound quality and haphazard repackaging—will enjoy this disc. —*Stephen Thomas Erlewine*

Rock and Rollin' With Fats Domino/Million Sellers By Fats / Jul. 28, 1998 / Collectables ✦✦✦✦
Collectables' *Rock and Rollin' With Fats Domino/Million Sellers By Fats* contains two original albums from Fats Domino, one of the most consist recording artists of the early rock & roll era. During his time at Imperial, he rarely recorded anything that wasn't enjoyable—not only was his choice of material first-rate, but he could make lesser songs entertaining. Fortunately, both of these albums are filled with both hits ("The Fat Man," "Ain't It a Shame," "Walking to New Orleans," "My Girl Josephine," "Let the Four Winds Blow") and fine album tracks, which, along with the bonus tracks "Whole Lotta Lovin'" and "I'm Ready," results in a thoroughly entertaining CD. Of course, serious fans who want to dig deeper would be better off with either EMI or Bear Family's box sets, but listeners who don't want to invest in the box sets—and don't mind less than pristine sound quality and haphazard repackaging—will enjoy this disc. —*Stephen Thomas Erlewine*

Here Stands Fats Domino/This Is Fats / Jul. 28, 1998 / Collectables ✦✦✦✦
Fabulous Mr. D/Fats Domino Swings / Jul. 28, 1998 / Collectables ✦✦✦✦
Imperial Singles, Vol. 3: 1956–1958 / Jul. 28, 1998 / Ace ✦✦✦✦✦
The third of Ace's series covering all of Domino's A- and B-sides has the tops and flips of 15 singles from 1956-1959. This was Fats' commercial peak, and some of his biggest smashes are here, including "Blueberry Hill," "I'm in Love Again," "I'm Walkin'," and "Whole Lotta Loving." For those listeners who weren't around during the era, however,

many of the 30 tracks will be unfamiliar, as he had plenty of minor hits that haven't made it into oldies radio rotation; also, most of his B-sides were chart hits (almost always more on the R&B listings than the pop ones) in their own right. "Sick and Tired" and "I Want You to Know" were popular cover choices for rock acts, and while most of the sides that didn't make the pop Top Ten are not nearly as memorable as "Blueberry Hill" and the like, they're pretty solid New Orleans rock & roll. It's hard to see exactly whose collection discs like this will fit—major Domino fans will have much or all of this on box sets—but it's a good listen for those who want more prime Fats than is available on the standard greatest-hits anthologies. —*Richie Unterberger*

☆ **Walking to New Orleans** / Mar. 12, 2002 / Imperial/Capitol ✦✦✦✦✦
Of all the early rock & rollers, Fats Domino gets a short shrift. Too easygoing for rockers, too popular for New Orleans R&B devotees, he fell into a middle ground—a middle ground that was extremely popular at the time, but didn't give him the proper respect within hipster history, probably because his music is just so damn enjoyable. Few musicians have made good music sound so easy, so effortless as Fats, and that's best appreciated in an exhaustive compilation, such as EMI's 2002 box set *Walking to New Orleans*, because the sheer scope of Fats' accomplishment becomes stunning only at this scale. Sure, it's easy to appreciate the brilliance of Domino on a hits collection, even one as generous as a 20-track collection like *My Blue Heaven*, but the true scope of his accomplishments becomes clear on a set like this, since there's not a bad cut among these 100 tracks. Yes, some are greater than others, usually the hits, but the momentum never sags because the quality of the material is so strong. Of course, much of this was already heard on the great, seminal box set, 1991's *They Call Me the Fat Man*, and this collection follows the very flow, the very sequence, of that set to a tee; even the Imperial-aping artwork on the CDs and Jeff Hannusch's liner notes are replicated. There are a few song substitutions along the way, usually skewing toward R&B instead of rock & roll, but the ten or so songs that are different don't affect the overall feel of the box, which remains one of the greatest, most listenable box sets in rock & roll. The biggest difference is in the sound (remastered and bettered, but not so much so that most listeners will notice), the packaging (no longer boxed jewel cases; it's now the easy-to-wear book), and the artwork (based on the beautiful promotional photo of the original, but now uglified with an off-kilter, cartoony illustration), all attempts to modernize the set. These differences are so minimal that anyone who already has *They Call Me the Fat Man* need not bother with this set, but anyone who missed that should pick up this slightly inferior set since the music is so fresh and good, it transcends any flaws with the packaging. —*Stephen Thomas Erlewine*

★ **Fats Domino Jukebox: 20 Greatest Hits the Way You Originally Heard Them** / Mar. 12, 2002 / Capitol ✦✦✦✦✦
Released in conjunction in 2002 with the four-disc box set *Walking to New Orleans*, as well as three other titles in EMI/Capitol's *Crescent City Soul* series, *The Fats Domino Jukebox: 20 Greatest Hits the Way You Originally Heard Them* becomes the definitive single-disc Fats collection on the market nearly by default—it's remastered, it's the one in print, and it has a flawless selection of songs. It's not markedly better than, say, the '90s definitive Fats compilation, *My Blue Heaven*, since it has essentially the same track selection and even if the tapes were restored to their originally running speed, the difference is not enough for most ears to notice, but it's still a great collection of some of the greatest music of its time, and it summarizes Domino's peaks excellently. So, if you don't already have a Fats Domino collection, this surely is the one to get (despite the really ugly art). —*Stephen Thomas Erlewine*

Lee Dorsey

b. Dec. 24, 1924, New Orleans, LA, **d.** Dec. 1, 1986, New Orleans, LA
Vocals / New Orleans R&B, R&B, Soul
Lee Dorsey epitomized the loose, easygoing charm of New Orleans R&B perhaps more than any other artist of the '60s. Working with legendary Crescent City producer/writer Allen Toussaint, Dorsey typically offered good-time party tunes with a playful sense of humor and a loping, funky backbeat. Even if he's remembered chiefly for the signature hit "Working in a Coalmine," it was a remarkably consistent and winning combination for the vast majority of his recording career.

Dorsey was born in New Orleans on December 24, 1924 (although some sources list 1926), and moved to Portland, OR, at age ten. After serving in the Navy during WWII, Dorsey returned to Portland and became a successful light heavyweight boxer, fighting under the name "Kid Chocolate." He retired from boxing in 1955 and returned to his birthplace, where he eventually opened a successful auto-body shop. He pursued a singing career by night, and wound up recording singles for several different labels, most of which made little noise (although "Lottie Mo" sold respectably). In 1961, he signed with Bobby Robinson's Fury label, where he entered the studio with producer Allen Toussaint for the first time. Dorsey's nonsense ditty "Ya Ya"—reportedly inspired by a children's rhyme—became his first national hit that year, reaching the pop Top Ten and hitting number one on the R&B charts. Despite its popularity, following it up turned out to be difficult, and with a large family to support, Dorsey returned to his auto repair business after a few more singles flopped.

Still, Allen Toussaint loved Dorsey's voice, and kept him in mind for future sessions. Toussaint's hunch paid off in 1965 when, signed to the Amy label, Dorsey turned "Ride Your Pony" into a Top Ten R&B hit. The accompanying album of the same name sold respectably as well, and Dorsey began cutting a multitude of Toussaint compositions, often with the legendary New Orleans funk ensemble the Meters as his studio backing band. *The New Lee Dorsey* was released later in 1966, and supplied Dorsey's best-known song, the irresistible "Working in a Coalmine" (which he co-wrote with Toussaint). With its clanking sound effects and Dorsey's comic exclamations, "Working in a Coalmine" became his second Top Ten pop hit and signature song, and Dorsey toured internationally with the Meters backing him up. A few follow-ups, particularly "Holy Cow" and "Everything I Do Gonh Be Funky (From Now On)," met with some success, but Dorsey was once

again hard pressed to duplicate his big hit, and once again left music for the practical concern of running his business. 1970's *Yes We Can* (on Polydor) was his last album for some time, with the title track becoming his last chart single.

After guesting on the Southside Johnny & the Asbury Jukes cut "How Come You Treat Me So Bad?," Dorsey attempted a comeback in 1977 with the ABC album *Night People*, which wasn't a commercial success despite mostly positive reviews. Still, it was enough to land him supporting slots on tours by the likes of James Brown, Jerry Lee Lewis, and even the Clash, whose 1980 tour was his last major concert jaunt. In the meantime, other artists mined his back catalog for covers: "Working in a Coalmine" was redone by robotic new wavers Devo and country duo the Judds; "Ya Ya" by Ike & Tina Turner, John Lennon, and Buckwheat Zydeco; "Everything I Do Gonh Be Funky (From Now On)" by jazzman Lou Donaldson; and "Yes We Can" by the Pointer Sisters (under the new title "Yes We Can Can"). Dorsey continued to perform sporadically, as opportunities presented themselves, until he contracted emphysema; he died in New Orleans on December 1, 1986. —*Steve Huey*

The New Lee Dorsey / 1966 / Sundazed ✦✦✦✦
Less than a year had passed between this and Dorsey's previous LP *Ride Your Pony*, and Allen Toussaint was again the prime creative force, writing material and co-producing. The sound, however, had definitely taken a step in a funkier direction. It's still lighthearted, though not lightweight, soul music with a New Orleans bounce, paced by the Top Ten hit "Working in a Coal Mine" and also including the Top 30 follow-up "Holy Cow." Other than those hit singles, the songs, though not exactly throwaways, aren't up to the same level. The original LP duplicated four songs from *Ride Your Pony*, and the 2000 Sundazed CD reissue has taken intelligent liberties with the track sequence. It removes the four duplicated songs and replaces them with rare singles from the era, most notably the uncommonly moody 1967 45 "Rain Rain Go Away." Furthermore, an additional dozen tunes are added as bonus tracks, most taken from rare 1968-1970 singles, with a couple of previously unissued cuts and a 1968 recording ("Lottie Mo '68") that didn't show up until 1997. These bonus items are on the whole more worthy of investigation than the slightly earlier rarities that fill out Sundazed's *Ride Your Pony* CD, as Dorsey and Toussaint (who was, still, writing virtually everything) venturing into deeper funk, sometimes with backup by the Meters. Maybe you don't need the five-minute reading of "What Now My Love," but "Little Ba-By," the self-fulfilling prophecy "Everything I Do Gonh Be Funky (From Now On)," and "What You Want (Is What You Get)" are decent soul-funk. Of the previously unavailable songs, "A Mellow Good Time Pt. 2" is an instrumental continuation of one of the songs on *The New Lee Dorsey*, while "I'm the One" is a serviceable 1970 Toussaint number. —*Richie Unterberger*

Ride Your Pony / 1966 / Sundazed ✦✦✦✦
Aside from the title track and the oft-covered, ultra-funky "Get Out of My Life, Woman," none of the 12 songs on this early 1966 album are familiar to most listeners. As it turns out it's a quality full-length bridging early-'60s New Orleans R&B with soul, even if the songs tend to be on the light partying side. That's part of the main draw of much New Orleans music, of course, and few were better at projecting a relaxed sense of fun than Dorsey. It helped that all but two of the songs were written by co-producer Allen Toussaint; the Crescent City giant doesn't get nearly as much attention as Smokey Robinson, but as with Smokey, one wonders if Toussaint ever slept in the '60s, so prolific and generally fine was his output. The Sundazed CD reissue is recommended even if you have the (by now hard to find) original LP, since it nearly doubles the length with almost a dozen tracks from rare 1966-1968 singles. These are more rare than exciting, to be honest, but Toussaint wrote all of these (sharing songwriting credit on one tune, "My Old Car"), and they're more good-time New Orleans soul with gradually modernizing production, even if the tunes weren't memorable enough to reach classic status. Certainly the most interesting is the two-part 1968 45 "Four Corners," an unabashed "Tighten Up" take-off with bits of James Brown and the Meters rattling around the corners; there's also a 1967 duet single with Betty Harris. —*Richie Unterberger*

Golden Classics / Apr. 20, 1990 / Collectables ✦✦✦
Covers Dorsey's Allen Toussaint-produced mid-'60s soul hits as well as some earlier material on the Relic set. —*Bill Dahl*

Soul Mine / 1993 / Charly ✦✦✦
Charly's 1993 compilation *Soul Mine* has a great cover shot of Lee Dorsey pointing a pistol into the camera, no liner notes, and all the usual suspects: "Ya Ya," "Do-Re-Mi," "Great Googa Mooga," "Ride Your Pony," "Get out of My Life Woman," "Confusion," "Working in the Coal Mine," "Holy Cow," "My Old Car," and "Everything I Do Is Gonna Be Funky (From Now On)." It also has the relatively latter-day single "Sneakin' Sally Through the Alley," plus a couple of good rarities: "Love Lots of Lovin'," "Go Go Girl," "Give It Up," "Night People," "Soul Mine," "Freedom for the Stallion." The lesser-known songs are all good—during his heyday, Dorsey was never bad—but it's not necessarily enough to make this worth seeking out for anyone but completists. Still, the disc overall is good enough to satisfy the curious and the casual fan if they happen to find it at a good price. —*Stephen Thomas Erlewine*

★ **Wheelin' and Dealin': The Definitive Collection** / Aug. 26, 1997 / Arista ✦✦✦✦✦
Wheelin' and Dealin': The Definitive Collection pretty much lives up to its title, presenting 20 choice selections from one of the greatest figures of New Orleans R&B. All of his big singles are here—"Ya Ya," "Do-Re-Mi," "Ride Your Pony," "Get Out of My Life Woman," "Working in a Coal Mine," "Holy Cow," "Everything I Do Gonh Be Funky (From Now On)"—along with lots of great lesser-known singles like "Confusion," "Can You Hear Me," and "My Old Car." There are some really good songs missing, both from his prime Bell recordings and such latter-day singles as "Sneaking Sally Through the Alley," but that's primarily because everything Dorsey cut was consistently enjoyable; even when the quality of the material dipped, the band and Dorsey remained appealing. So, even if there's a

handful of songs that could have been here, it's impossible to argue with what is, since it does result in a wonderful, endlessly listenable collection. *—Stephen Thomas Erlewine*

The EP Collection / Mar. 21, 2000 / See for Miles ✦✦✦✦✦

See for Miles' series *The EP Collection* is always fascinating, since it not only provides collectors with a nifty compilation of pop artifacts, but it also provides a chance-taking, unpredictable singles collection. Such is the case with Lee Dorsey's *The EP Collection.* There's not a bad track to be found on this dynamite 26-track collection that boasts three original British EPs, two French EPs, and six A-sides from "Ya Ya" to "Sneakin' Sally Through the Alley." The very fact that there aren't any weak moments is a testament to just how damn good Lee Dorsey was. It wasn't just that he was backed by stellar musicians under the direction of Allen Toussaint—it was that he was a supremely gifted vocalist with a sly turn of phrase. He could make throwaway songs sound substantial, and he brought unexpected twists to stronger numbers. These talents are readily apparent on any Dorsey collection, but this is one of the very finest, ranking just beneath the slightly tighter Arista compilation, *Wheelin' and Dealin'.* The truth of the matter is this—Lee Dorsey sounds terrific in any context and the singles sound great in any sequence, so even if you buy this for the handful of tracks that you don't have, you'll be satisfied. And if you get this as your first Lee Dorsey album, you're bound to be converted. *—Stephen Thomas Erlewine*

Working in a Coalmine: The Very Best of Lee Dorsey / Apr. 24, 2001 / Music Club ✦✦✦✦

Music Club's *Working in a Coalmine: The Very Best of Lee Dorsey* contains a few songs that don't normally make it on Dorsey collections, from both his Bell recordings and late-'60s/early-'70s funky Allen Toussaint-produced recordings. "Hoodlum Joe," "Messed Around (And Fell in Love)," "People Sure Act Funny," "Can I Be the One?," and "If She Won't" all don't regularly make it on Dorsey collections, which means this is something more for collectors than the neophyte who the title suggests this is aimed at. On that level, it's a neat item to pick up, even if does contain the usual suspects that any Dorsey fan has many times over. If it's viewed as an introduction, however, it falls short—for that, get *Wheelin' and Dealin'* first, then move to this to fill in some holes later. *—Stephen Thomas Erlewine*

Rev. Thomas A. Dorsey

b. Jul. 1, 1899, Villa Rica, GA, **d.** Jan. 23, 1993, Chicago, IL

Vocals, Piano, Guitar / Prewar Gospel Blues, Traditional Gospel, Blues Gospel

The acknowleged father of gospel music, Thomas A. Dorsey remains arguably the most influential figure ever to impact the genre. A versatile composer whose material shifted easily from energetic hard gospel to gossamer hymns, he penned many of the best-known songs in the gospel canon, among them "Take My Hand, Precious Lord" and "Peace in the Valley"; the founder of the National Convention of Gospel Choirs and Choruses, he was also a pioneering force in the renowned Chicago gospel community, where he helped launch the careers of legends including Mahalia Jackson and Sallie Martin. Dorsey was born in Villa Rica, GA, on July 1, 1899 and raised in the Atlanta area; there, in addition to the traditional Dr. Watts hymns, he also absorbed early blues and jazz. A child prodigy, he taught himself a wide range of instruments, and was playing blues and ragtime while still in his teens; under the stage name Georgia Tom, he was a prolific composer, authoring witty, slightly racy blues songs like the underground hit "It's Tight Like That."

Dorsey settled in Chicago in 1918, where he briefly enrolled at the city's College of Composition and Arranging; within months of his arrival, he began playing with area jazz bands including Les Hite's Whispering Serenaders. Dorsey also formed his own group, the Wildcats Jazz Band, which traveled in support of Ma Rainey. He later collaborated in a duo with Tampa Red, but in 1928, after suffering his second nervous breakdown in as many years, he opted to retire from the music business. A two-year recovery period followed, during which time a minister convinced Dorsey to return to music, albeit to move from the blues to the church. His first attempt at writing a gospel song, 1921's "If I Don't Get There," had met with some success, and he now returned with a renewed sense of purpose, renouncing secular music to devote all of his talents to the church circuit. Initially, Dorsey met with little success—forced to reject blues jobs and with no gospel offers forthcoming, he soon resorted to peddling song sheets to make a living.

Dorsey's luck appeared to be on the upswing by 1932, the year he organized one of the first gospel choirs at Chicago's Pilgrim Baptist Church; his pianist, Roberta Martin, would in a few years emerge among the top talents on the church circuit. That same year, he also founded the first publishing house devoted exclusively to selling music by black gospel composers. However, a few months later—while traveling with Theodore R. Frye to organize a choir in St. Louis—tragedy struck when Dorsey discovered that his wife had died while giving birth to their son, who himself died two days later. Devastated, Dorsey locked himself inside his music room for three straight days, emerging with a completed draft of "Take My Hand, Precious Lord," a song whose popularity in the gospel community is rivaled perhaps only by "Amazing Grace." Setting his loss behind him, he enjoyed his most prolific period in the years that followed, authoring dozens of songs with a distinctively optimistic sensibility for audiences held in the grip of the Depression.

During that same fateful year of 1932, Dorsey also hired a singer named Sallie Martin to join his group at the Ebenezer Baptist Church. Despite her unrefined vocal style, she instantly connected with audiences; over time Dorsey became increasingly aware of her value not only as a performer but also as an entrepreneur, as she took over his music store and within a few months was turning a tidy profit. In 1933, Dorsey and Martin—along with Frye, Magnolia Lewis Butts and Beatrice Brown—organized the annual National Convention of Gospel Choirs and Choruses, where they introduced new songs to choir directors from across the nation. By now, Dorsey's songs were enormously popular, not only among black churchgoers but also among white Southerners; by 1939, even the leading white gospel publishers were anthologizing his music. That year, he composed "Peace in the Valley"; although written for Mahalia Jackson, his demo singer at the time, its greatest success was in the white market—both Elvis Presley and Red Foley, among others, scored major hits with the song.

After breaking through with the Singers Covention, Dorsey and Martin next hit the so-called "gospel highway," a touring circuit previously restricted to a cappella quartets. Between the early '30s and mid-'40s, he toured the nation under the banner "Evenings with Dorsey," training young singers to perform his material; between 1939 and 1944, he also toured regularly with Jackson. By the '50s, with the rise of hard gospel, Dorsey's influence began to slip a bit, although the popularity of his greatest material held on; during the middle of the decade, with the rise of R&B, his melodies began to resurface in many of the era's secular hits. As James Cleveland emerged as the undisputed king of contemporary gospel, Dorsey began to curtail his writing and traveling, essentially retiring from active duty during the '60s; however, he continued spearheading the annual NCGGG event for years to follow, and remained among the most revered figures in spiritual music until his death on January 23, 1993. *—Jason Ankeny*

Complete Recorded Works, Vol. 1 (1928–1930) / 1992 / Document ✦✦✦✦✦

Depending on the focus of the listener, Document's *Complete Recorded Works, Vol. 1 (1928-1930)* is either an important investigation into the early blues recordings of Thomas Dorsey or an overly long collection with too much substandard material. As on other volumes in the *Complete Recorded Works* series, solid performances alternate with alternate takes and novelties, while the lengthy running time and poor fidelity make for a difficult compilation. *—Thom Owens*

Complete Recorded Works, Vol. 2 (1930–1934) / 1992 / Document ✦✦✦✦✦

For completists and academics, Document's *Complete Recorded Works, Vol. 2 (1930-1934)* is an invaluable overview of Georgia Tom's early recordings. For less-dedicated listeners, the disc is a mixed blessing, with a few classic performances balanced by poor fidelity (all cuts are transferred from original acetates and 78s) and a lengthy track listing. *—Thom Owens*

Come on Mama Do That Dance 1931–1940 / 1992 / Yazoo ✦✦✦✦✦

Hard to believe that America's greatest writer of gospel songs could come up with this solid a collection of risque blues tunes in his earlier, "sinful" days. Believe it. *—Cub Koda*

★ **Precious Lord: The Great Gospel Songs of Thomas A. Dorsey** / 1994 / Columbia/Legacy ✦✦✦✦✦

Precious Lord collects 18 of Georgia Thomas Dorsey's greatest songs, offering a terrific introduction to one of the greatest gospel country blues singers of the '30s. *—Thom Owens*

Double Trouble

f. 1985

Group / Modern Electric Blues

Best-known as the late Stevie Ray Vaughan's rock-solid rhythm section, Double Trouble actually began life as a band of equals in 1978, the year vocalist Lou Ann Barton left a blues group called Triple Threat in which Vaughan was the guitarist. Accompanied by bassist Jackie Newhouse and drummer Chris "Whipper" Layton, Vaughan took over vocal duties and the band renamed itself Double Trouble after an Otis Rush song. Bassist Tommy Shannon, who learned the blues serving an apprenticeship with Johnny Winter, joined the outfit in 1980, and he and Layton would accompany Vaughan throughout the guitarist's meteoric career, from his 1983 debut album *Texas Flood* to his tragic death in 1990. Shannon and Layton regrouped as part of a blues-rock supergroup called the Arc Angels, who released a self-titled album in 1992; subsequently, the duo became an in-demand session team, backing artists like W.C. Clark, Kenny Wayne Shepherd, and Doyle Bramhall, among others. Shannon and Layton also recorded with the Austin-based blues collective Storyville during the '90s. For their first album as Double Trouble, the duo recruited a bevy of guest stars to handle vocals and guitar, including Bramhall, Lou Ann Barton, longtime Vaughan keyboardist Reese Wynans, Jonny Lang, Willie Nelson, Dr. John, and Jimmie Vaughan. The result, *Been a Long Time,* was released in early 2001 on the Tone-Cool label. *—Steve Huey*

● **Been a Long Time** / Feb. 6, 2001 / Tone-Cool ✦✦✦

K.C. Douglas

b. Nov. 21, 1913, Sharon, MS, **d.** Oct. 18, 1975, Berkeley, CA

Vocals, Guitar / Acoustic Blues, Modern Delta Blues

K.C. Douglas was a Mississippi bluesman who transplanted himself and his music, not to Chicago but to the San Francisco Bay Area in 1945. He became one of the rare Californians with such a down-home rural style, as many of his recordings were remakes of old blues he knew from Mississippi. (His first album, an obscure item on the Cook label, was entitled *K.C. Douglas, a Dead Beat Guitar and the Mississippi Blues.*) His re-creations of Tommy Johnson's blues were of particular interest to fans of prewar blues, but his own compositions attracted attention as well. (K.C.'s music was introduced to rock listeners when his "Mercury Boogie" was redone by the Steve Miller Band.) *—Jim O'Neal*

Road Recordings / 1956 / Cook ✦✦✦

● **K.C.'s Blues** / 1961 / Bluesville/Original Blues Classics ✦✦✦✦

Like *Big Road Blues, K.C. Blues* was recorded in 1961 during the peak of the blues revival. Unlike that record, which contained a number of songs he learned through Tommy Johnson, *K.C.'s Blues* consists primarily of original compositions that showcase Douglas' easy-rolling, relaxed style perfectly. *—Thom Owens*

Big Road Blues / 1961 / Bluesville/Original Blues Classics ✦✦✦

Mercury Boogie / 1975 / Oldie Blues ✦✦✦

Country Boy / 1981 / Arhoolie ✦✦✦

Mercury Blues / Oct. 20, 1998 / Arhoolie ✦✦✦

Spare electric blues from 1973-1974 with a juke-joint feel, including a version of "Mercury Blues," covered by Steve Miller and Alan Jackson. Originally released on LP on Arhoolie 1073, the CD reissue adds a dozen previously unissued bonus cuts, taken from sessions in 1960, 1963, 1973, and 1974. It's competent but unexceptional country blues with added electricity and a rhythm section, and pretty similar-sounding most of the way through. "I'm Gonna Build Me a Web," the 1963 track, stands out here as the piano and sax add some needed texture; the three 1960 songs are solo acoustic performances. —*Richie Unterberger*

Driftin' Slim (Elmon Mickle)

b. Feb. 24, 1919, Keo, AR, d. Sep. 15, 1977, Los Angeles, CA
Vocals, Drums, Harmonica, Guitar / Harmonica Blues, Folk-Blues
Elmon "Driftin' Slim" Mickle was a harmonica player from Keo, AR, a stone's throw away from Little Rock. He got his early harmonica training when he saw John Lee "Sonny Boy" Williamson and Yank Rachell perform and approached Sonny Boy to teach him the rudiments of the instrument. By the mid-'40s, he was playing the local juke joint circuit with Sonny Boy Williamson II and King Biscuit Boy drummer Peck Curtis while doing radio stints with stations KDRK and KGHI. In 1951, he had formed his first band with locals Baby Face Turner and Junior Brooks and recorded his first sides for the Modern label. By 1957, he had moved to Los Angeles, refurbishing his act as a one-man band, adding drums and guitar to his neck rack harmonica work. He recorded sporadically, issuing singles on his own and other labels through the early '60s. In the flush of the "folk-music boom" of the mid-'60s, Slim was rediscovered and recorded for a number of collectors' labels. By the turn of the decade, ill health had forced him to retire from music and when he passed away in 1977, a chapter of American music—that of the one-man band—had virtually died with him. —*Cub Koda*

● **Driftin' Slim and His Blues Band** / Dec. 1969 / Milestone ✦✦✦✦
Slim's only full album (his earlier recordings show up on several compilations) is one of the great "rediscovery" albums of the genre. Five of the 15 tracks here are with a full band, but the real treasure trove is the remaining solo performances. These range from full-stops-out one-man-band numbers ("I'm Hunting Somebody" is a true classic) to unaccompanied harmonica pieces ("Mama Blues," "Jonah") to autobiographical recitations like "A Dip of Snuff and a Narrow Escape" that are utterly charming in their simplicity. As of press time, this album was still unavailable on compact disc, but it is still well worth seeking out as it's a true gem with loads of folkish charm. —*Cub Koda*

Somebody Hoo-Doo'd the Hoo-Doo Man / Jul. 13, 1999 / Milestone/Original Blues Classics ✦✦✦
Recorded in 1966 and 1967, two-thirds of this is one-man-band country blues, with Slim playing harmonica, guitar, bass drum, and hi-hat cymbals. The other third is modern electric blues, Slim's singing and harmonica backed by a guitar, bass, and drums. Although the quality of the performances is consistent, this makes for an uneven stylistic tone; it's almost like listening to an album shared by two artists. The electric band tracks are very good, with Slim slotting into the format with an ease not always duplicated by peers with acoustic roots. These don't sound far from the kind of blues played by Junior Wells and Buddy Guy around this time; indeed, Slim does a song, "Hoo-Doo Man Blues," that Wells did much to popularize in the mid-'60s. The electric sides are more enjoyable than the one-man band cuts, which have a slightly ramshackle feel, sometimes exhibiting similarities to early Muddy Waters or John Lee Hooker. These tracks are not on the same level as work by those two giants, and Slim's vocal approach is lighter and more carefree. —*Richie Unterberger*

Chris Duarte

b. Feb. 16, 1963, San Antonio, TX
Vocals, Guitar / Blues-Rock
Austin-based guitarist, songwriter and singer Chris Duarte is such a promising young upstart in the world of modern blues that he's already being compared with the late Stevie Ray Vaughan. It's heady stuff for the musician, who plays a rhythmic style of Texas blues-rock that is at times reminiscent of Vaughan's sound, and at other times reminiscent of Johnny Winter. The truth is, Duarte has his own sound that draws on elements of jazz, blues and rock & roll. Although he is humbled by the comparisons with the late Vaughan, the San Antonio-raised musician began playing out in clubs there when he was 15 years old.

After Duarte moved to Austin when he was 16, he began taking his guitar playing much more seriously, and at that time, Vaughan was still around playing in Austin-area clubs. Duarte was one of those lucky few thousand who got to see Vaughan at the Continental Club before the late guitarist got his first break with David Bowie. After a short stint in an Austin jazz band, Duarte joined Bobby Mack and Night Train, and began getting heavily into blues at that point. He traveled all over Texas with that band before a big break came his way in 1994, when New York-based Silvertone Records released his critically praised debut album, *Texas Sugar/Strat Magik. Tailspin Headwhack* followed in 1997 and *Love Is Greater Than Me* appeared three years later. —*Richard Skelly*

● **Texas Sugar/Strat Magic** / 1994 / Silvertone ✦✦✦✦
Guitarist Chris Duarte's *Texas Sugar/Strat Magik* is an impressive debut album, showcasing his fiery, Stevie Ray Vaughan-derived blues-rock. As a songwriter, Duarte is still developing—he fails to come up with any memorable songs, although he does contribute several competent, unexceptional genre pieces—but as an instrumentalist, he's first-rate, spitting out solos with a blistering intensity or laying back with gentle, lyrical phrases. And that's what makes *Texas Sugar/Strat Magik* a successful record—it's simply a great guitar album, full of exceptional playing. —*Stephen Thomas Erlewine*

Tailspin Headwhack / Aug. 26, 1997 / Silvertone ✦✦✦✦
Chris Duarte's debut album, *Texas Sugar/Strat Magik*, promised great things, and his second album, *Tailspin Headwhack*, doesn't fail to deliver. Like its predecessor, it's a dynamic collection of hot Texas blues-rock powered by Duarte's muscular, tasteful playing. There's still a lack of distinctive original material, but that doesn't matter, because he infuses each song, from the single "Cleopatra" to a cover of B.B. King's "The Thrill Is

Gone," with energy and passion. Most importantly, Duarte is beginning to break away from his Stevie Ray and Hendrix influences and establish himself as a talented stylist in his own right, and that's what makes *Tailspin Headwhack* a successful second record. —*Thom Owens*

Love Is Greater Than Me / Sep. 26, 2000 / Zoe ✦✦✦

Al Duncan

b. Oct. 8, 1927, McKinney, TX, d. Jan. 3, 1995, Las Vegas, NV
Drums / Chicago Blues, R&B
This drummer was one of less than a half-dozen key studio legends from the '50s and '60s who have sometimes been called "the grandfathers of groove." They are basically the forefathers of all modern timekeeping in rhythm & blues music or any nuts from its branches. Chicago's Chess Records was the most famous, but not the only homeground for these drummers. It is aesthetically possible to own a superb electric blues collection with only sides on which Al Duncan plays drums. But it would be a technical impossibility, because most of the album releases of vintage material from blues giants such as Little Walter, John Lee Hooker, or Jimmy Reed were not originally recorded as full sets featuring a single band. Accordingly, our man is usually featured as one of several drummers. There is no loss in quality between an Al Duncan and a Fred Below in any case. This is blues mastery, these are the Old Testament of blues drum feels and simply the way blues drumming is supposed to sound, despite the tendencies newer generations of drummers have to get busier and busier. In the case of Duncan, it is a wide terrain indeed as it includes the agitated, aggressive punch of Buddy Guy, as well as the ultra-relaxed, swinging feel of late-period Reed, by which time the leader's son, Jimmy Reed Jr., was rounding out the rhythm section on bass. Another one of the drummer's most famous session partners is bassist Phil Upchurch. Duncan also had a presence on doo wop and gospel sessions, bringing some of this feel into his blues projects, such as the wonderful Reed track "Shame Shame Shame" cut in 1962. It is not a long way from this feel to that of the soul group the Impressions, with whom Duncan drummed in early days. Thirty years later, he was still going strong as part of the Rob Wasserman *Trios* project. Combined for an interesting track with Wasserman and yet another old rhythm section mate, bassist and songwriter Willie Dixon, it would turn out to be one of the drummer's final recordings.

He was born with the amazingly prophetic although uncommon name of Alrock Duncan; no one would deny that the one thing his drum tracks have in common is that they all rock. He was one of the regular drummers in the employ of bandleader Al Smith, an enterprising soul whose efforts spanned the imaginary barriers between blues and jazz music in Chicago in the '50s. Eventually, many of the players working for Smith defected to the new Vee-Jay label in the mid-'50s. Duncan was the first choice drummer in housebands under the direction of guitarist Lefty Bates, also featuring players such as saxophonist Red Holloway and pianist Horace Palm. There is no exaggerating the amount of musical activity that took place involving players such as this on the Chicago scene up until rock & roll's death punch. Multiple recording sessions in a day followed by a three- or four-set club gig, winding up at an after-hour's jam session; this might have been a typical day at the beach for Duncan, and as a result avoiding him on any walk along the urban blues shoreline is about as impossible as not getting any sand on your feet. Blues fans can speculate about what might represent his best grain of playing, but one choice for sessions deserving of wider recognition would be the early-'60s sides by vocalist Billy "The Kid" Emerson. The drummer's six-string-shooting sidekicks for these recordings include the late Roy Buchanan and the "Suzie Q" man, Dale Hawkins. Drummers also rave about the brushwork on sides by the not-too-well-known vocalist Camille Howard, such as "Rock and Roll Mama." Duncan also had a bit of a career off the drum set as a songwriter, including numbers such as "It's Too Late, Brother," which has remained a blues bar band staple. While he could have avoided confusion completely if he had left his first name Alrock, the drummer didn't do too badly in terms of other Al Duncans fuzzing up the details of his career. The obscure rockabilly dude who led a combo called the Twisters and made singles such as "Bawana Jinde" and "Gossip" is a different guy, as is the Al Duncan who was a background singer for the Sons of the Pioneers. —*Eugene Chadbourne*

Little Arthur Duncan

b. 1934, Indianola, MS
Harmonica, Vocals / Electric Chicago Blues, Modern Electric Blues
Chicago blues singer/harpist Little Arthur Duncan was born in Indianola, MS, in 1934 and raised on the same Woodburn Plantation as B.B. King. He relocated to the Windy City's West Side during the '50s, often playing in the company of guitar great Earl Hooker; despite the unique harmonica sound produced by his custom of playing the bass notes on the right, for decades Duncan remained little-known outside of the Chicago scene, primarily appearing at his own Back Scratcher Social Club. In 1989 he cut *Bad Reputation* for the Blues King label, and that same year was also documented alongside Robert Plunkett and Emery Williams Jr. on Cannonball's *Blues Across America—The Chicago Scene*; the Delmark release *Singin' With the Sun* followed a decade later. —*Jason Ankeny*

● **Singin' With the Sun** / Nov. 23, 1999 / Delmark ✦✦✦✦
Long a Chicago club mainstay, Duncan sings and blows harp in the time-honored '50s style of that city's rich blues tradition. Backed by the Rockin' Johnny Band, Duncan runs through a set of originals and old favorites that proves that there's still a few of the old timers left who can deliver the goods. Duncan's harp is replaced by Martin Lang on three tracks and Eddie Taylor Jr. takes over the guitar chores on two tunes, and is particularly effective on "Tribute to Jimmy Reed." Although some of Little Arthur's originals skirt the issue of copyright and his timing is suspect in spots, this is one fine album of journeyman blues sung and played with a whole lot of feeling. —*Cub Koda*

Live in Chicago / Sep. 12, 2000 / Random Chance ✦✦✦

Champion Jack Dupree

b. Jul. 23, 1909, New Orleans, LA, **d.** Jan. 21, 1992, Hanover, Germany

Vocals, Drums, Piano, Guitar / New Orleans Blues, Acoustic Chicago Blues, Piano Blues, Chicago Blues, R&B

A formidable contender in the ring before he shifted his focus to pounding the piano instead, Champion Jack Dupree often injected his lyrics with a rowdy sense of downhome humor. But there was nothing lighthearted about his rock-solid way with a boogie; when he shouted "Shake Baby Shake," the entire room had no choice but to acquiesce.

Dupree was notoriously vague about his beginnings, claiming in some interviews that his parents died in a fire set by the Ku Klux Klan, at other times saying that the blaze was accidental. Whatever the circumstances of the tragic conflagration, Dupree grew up in New Orleans' Colored Waifs' Home for Boys (Louis Armstrong also spent his formative years there). Learning his trade from barrelhouse 88s ace Willie "Drive 'Em Down" Hall, Dupree left the Crescent City in 1930 for Chicago and then Detroit. By 1935, he was boxing professionally in Indianapolis, battling in an estimated 107 bouts.

In 1940, Dupree made his recording debut for Chicago A&R man extraordinaire Lester Melrose and OKeh Records. Dupree's 1940-1941 output for the Columbia subsidiary exhibited a strong New Orleans tinge despite the Chicago surroundings; his driving "Junker's Blues" was later cleaned up as Fats Domino's 1949 debut, "The Fat Man." After a stretch in the Navy during World War II (he was a Japanese POW for two years), Dupree decided tickling the 88s beat pugilism any old day. He spent most of his time in New York and quickly became a prolific recording artist, cutting for Continental, Joe Davis, Alert, Apollo, and Red Robin (where he cut a blasting "Shim Sham Shimmy" in 1953), often in the company of Brownie McGhee. Contracts meant little—Dupree masqueraded as Brother Blues on Abbey, Lightnin' Jr. on Empire, and the truly imaginative Meat Head Johnson for Gotham and Apex.

King Records corralled Dupree in 1953 and held onto him through 1955 (the year he enjoyed his only R&B chart hit, the relaxed "Walking the Blues"). Dupree's King output rates with his very best—the romping "Mail Order Woman," "Let the Doorbell Ring," and "Big Leg Emma's" contrasting with the rural "Me and My Mule" (Dupree's vocal on the latter emphasizing a harelip speech impediment for politically incorrect pseudo-comic effect).

After a year on RCA's Groove and Vik subsidiaries, Dupree made a masterpiece LP for Atlantic. 1958's *Blues from the Gutter* is a magnificent testament to Dupree's barrelhouse background, boasting marvelous readings of "Stack-O-Lee," "Junker's Blues," and "Frankie & Johnny" beside the risque "Nasty Boogie."

Dupree was one of the first bluesmen to leave his native country for a less racially polarized European existence in 1959. He lived in a variety of countries overseas, continuing to record prolifically for Storyville, British Decca (with John Mayall and Eric Clapton lending a hand at a 1966 date), and many other firms.

Perhaps sensing his own mortality, Dupree returned to New Orleans in 1990 for his first visit in 36 years. While there, he played the Jazz & Heritage Festival and laid down a zesty album for Bullseye Blues, *Back Home in New Orleans*. Two more albums of new material were captured by the company the next year prior to the pianist's death in January of 1992. Jack Dupree was a champ to the very end. *—Bill Dahl*

★ **Blues from the Gutter** / 1958 / Atco ♦♦♦♦♦
The 1958 masterwork album of Dupree's long and prolific career. Cut in New York (in stereo!) with a blasting band that included saxist Pete Brown and guitarist Larry Dale, the Jerry Wexler-produced Atlantic collection provides eloquent testimony to Dupree's eternal place in the New Orleans blues and barrelhouse firmament. There's some decidedly down-in-the-alley subject matter—"Can't Kick The Habit," "T.B. Blues," a revival of "Junker's Blues"—along with the stomping "Nasty Boogie" and treatments of the ancient themes "Stack-O-Lee" and "Frankie & Johnny." *—Bill Dahl*

Natural and Soulful Blues / 1961 / Atlantic ♦♦♦

Champion of the Blues / 1961 / Atlantic ♦♦♦

Sings the Blues / 1961 / King ♦♦♦♦
A domestic no-frills collection of Champion Jack Dupree's aforementioned King label material, albeit containing fewer tracks and little in the way of annotation—but you can't argue with the wonderful music therein! *—Bill Dahl*

Blues at Montreux / 1973 / Atlantic ♦♦♦
Rough around the edges, this set, caught live (and lively) at the 1971 Montreux Jazz Festival, teams Texas-born sax great King Curtis with the irrepressible Dupree. Curtis' young band copes reasonably well with Dupree's unpredictable sense of time, and despite their age differences, everyone has a good time. Only three months later, Curtis would tragically be stabbed to death on his New York doorstep. *—Bill Dahl*

1944–1945: The First 16 Side from Joe Davis / 1982 / Red Pepper ♦♦♦
Journeyman blues pianist Champion Jack Dupree took his New Orleans-born, boogie-woogie style north to Chicago and Indianapolis and gave it some blues backbone via meetings with Leroy Carr and Tampa Red. The first fruits of that education were his early '40s sides for OKeh, which are available on Columbia's *New Orleans Barrelhouse Boogie*. While his OKeh sides paired Dupree with a rhythm section, Red Pepper's reissue of his later recordings for the Joe Davis label, *1944-1945*, features him alone at the piano. The 16 tracks wear a bit thin at times as Dupree recycles many of the same boogie-woogie patterns, but the intimacy of the solo setting and the energy of his swaggering vocal delivery keep these sides engaging. Dupree supplies variety by way of subject matter that takes in domestic strife ("Outside Man"), politics ("F.D.R. Blues"), and drinking ("Rum Cola Blues"). For fans of both Champion Jack Dupree and the blues, *1944-'45* is worth getting; you'll not only get some fine boogie-woogie blues, but also hear how Dupree influenced blues and rock & roll greats like Memphis Slim and Fats Domino. *—Stephen Cook*

Blues for Everybody / 1990 / Charly ♦♦♦♦♦
Although Dupree seldom paused at any one label for very long, the piano pounder did hang around at Cincinnati-based King Records from 1951 to 1955—long enough to wax the 20 sides comprising this set and a few more that regrettably aren't aboard. By this time, Dupree was a seasoned R&B artist, storming through "Let the Doorbell Ring" and "Mail Order Woman" and emphasizing his speech impediment on "Harelip Blues" (one of those not-for-the-politically correct numbers). Most of these tracks were done in New York; sidemen include guitarist Mickey Baker and saxist Willis Jackson. *—Bill Dahl*

Back Home in New Orleans / 1990 / Bullseye Blues ♦♦♦♦♦
By far the best of Dupree's three albums for Bullseye Blues, this collection was cut during the pianist's first trip home to the Crescent City in 36 long years. With his longtime accompanist Kenn Lending on guitar, Dupree sounds happy to be back in his old stomping grounds throughout the atmospheric set. *—Bill Dahl*

Forever & Ever / 1991 / Bullseye Blues ♦♦♦
Dupree's Bullseye Blues encore partly misses the mark compared to his previous effort—the material isn't quite as strong as before. *—Bill Dahl*

1945–1953 / 1992 / Krazy Kat ♦♦♦♦♦
This Krazy Kat collection of postwar sides by Champion Jack Dupree makes a nice companion to his release on the Red Pepper label, *1944-1945*. Both albums find Dupree in excellent form and singing a variety of boogie-woogie, blues selections, but they differ in their instrumentation; *1944-1945* features Dupree in an intimate, solo piano setting, while *1945-1953* includes a variety of sidemen and has a more rambling, jam-session atmosphere. Highlights from this Krazy Kat release include the electric-blues scorcher "Stumbling Block" and the New Orleans' shuffle-beat tune "Somebody Changed the Lock." Dupree also lays down some Muddy Waters-inspired blues on "Highway Blues" and gets into some early rock & roll on "Shake Baby Shake" and "Shim Sham Shimmy." Harpist Sonny Terry and guitarist Brownie McGhee provide fine support on tracks like "Number Nine Blues" and drummer Willie Jones supplies a nice, propulsive beat throughout. *1945-1953* has a very good assortment of Dupree's prime, early cuts and, like both the Red Pepper release and Columbia's *New Orleans Barrelhouse Boogie*, it offers a good introduction to his recordings. *—Stephen Cook*

One Last Time / 1993 / Bullseye Blues ♦♦♦
Dupree's last album for the label, slightly more consistent than his last but not the equivalent of his first. *—Bill Dahl*

New Orleans Barrelhouse Boogie (The Complete Champion Jack Dupree) / 1993 / Columbia/Legacy ♦♦♦♦♦
The New Orleans barrelhouse boogie piano specialist's earliest sides for OKeh, dating from 1940-1941 and in a few cases sporting some fairly groundbreaking electric guitar runs by Jesse Ellery. Dupree rocks the house like it's a decade later on two takes of "Cabbage Greens" and "Dupree Shake Dance," while his drug-oriented "Junker Blues" was later cleaned up a bit by a chubby newcomer named Fats Domino for his debut hit 78 "The Fat Man." *—Bill Dahl*

Won't Be a Fool No More . . . Plus / 1993 / See for Miles ♦♦♦♦♦
Mike Vernon brought Dupree into the studio alongside Eric Clapton (electric guitar) and John Mayall (harmonica)—two months before they recorded the classic *Bluesbreakers* album—plus Tony McPhee (acoustic guitar), Bill Short (washboard), Malcolm Pool (bass), and Keef Hartley (drums), to cut this album, originally issued by English Decca under the title *From New Orleans to Memphis*. Two additional tracks, "Calcutta Blues" and "24 Hours," cut at the same sessions and issued separately, have been added. The disc includes rocking piano boogie like "He Knows the Rules" (with killer bottleneck by Clapton) and "Shim-Sham-Shimmy," as well as New Orleans influences ("T.V. Mama," "Pigfoot and a Bottle of Beer," "Ooh-La-La"), an extraordinary piece of spoken blues ("Big Leg Emma's"), worth the price of the CD by itself, and country blues ("Ain't That a Shame"). Dupree is in excellent vocal form and even takes a turn on acoustic guitar on one track, in addition to his trademark piano blues. The new notes by Roger Dopson include one of the most detailed and entertaining accounts of Dupree's career. *—Bruce Eder*

Me and My Mule / Dec. 14, 1999 / Magnum ♦♦♦
A nice sampling of Champion Jack's King and Savoy singles, this also includes Jack's work behind Little Willie John on tracks like "All Around the World" and "Don't Leave Me My Dear." The Muddy tracks are more problematic: They're a complete hodgepodge of early Chess tracks (some dubbed from scratchy, old 78s), a ringer from the *Fathers and Sons* album, and Sonny Boy Willamson's Checker recording of "Don't Start Me to Talkin'," which features Muddy and his band backing up the harp wizard. Some great blues, but not too sensibly ordered—or very well dubbed, either. *—Cub Koda*

A Portrait of Champion Jack Dupree / Oct. 31, 2000 / Rounder ♦♦♦
A Portrait of Champion Jack Dupree is a compilation drawn from three albums Dupree recorded for Rounder Records near the end of his life, when he was in his late seventies and early eighties. The first of them, *Back Home in New Orleans*, was released in 1990, the year he turned 80, the last, *One Last Time*, came out in 1993, the year after his death. Even at his advanced age, Dupree remained a formidable barrelhouse pianist and a strong vocal presence. Backed on these sessions by sympathetic New Orleans musicians, he seems to have been simply turned loose to do as he liked. There is a noticeable informality to the recordings, with the artist occasionally stumbling over his words, stopping and starting at will. Some tracks find him playing recognizable songs, while others, such as "Skit Skat" and "Dupree Special," are jams. The album is enjoyable despite this as an expression of Dupree's personality. On several songs, notably "Give Me the Flowers While I'm Livin'" and "You Can Make It" (both of which also appeared on the posthumous *One Last Time*), Dupree makes specific references to death (the former song even pictures him in his coffin). The subject of death is not unknown in the blues, of course, but Dupree seems conscious of his advanced age here and deals with his coming death evenly and even humorously. His last sessions may not be his best work, but they show him to be as distinctive as ever. *—William Ruhlmann*

Dynatones

f. San Francisco, CA

Group / Roots Rock, Blues-Rock, Rock & Roll

The Dynatones are a San Francisco-based blues/soul band, a mainstay of the local circuit. The group worked and recorded as solid backup behind Charlie Musselwhite in the early '80s, then made the transition to a more R&B-oriented format with numerous personnel changes by the mid '80s. Continuing to write, record and tour to this day, the Dynatones are probably best experienced live, but all their recordings are worth checking out. —*Cub Koda*

Curtain Call Live / 1982 / War Bride ✦✦✦

Shameless / 1983 / Warner Brothers ✦✦✦

● **Tough to Shake** / 1985 / Rounder ✦✦✦✦

Propelled by gutsy guitar work and hard-driving rhythms, *Tough to Shake* may be the finest album the Dynatones made. Even though the songwriting is a little uneven, it captures the essence of their greasy barroom boogie better than any of their other records. —*Thom Owens*

Live It Up! / 1986 / Rounder ✦✦✦

Chopped & Channeled / 1991 / Rhino ✦✦✦

Snooks Eaglin (Ford Eaglin, Jr.)

b. Jan. 21, 1936, New Orleans, LA
Vocals, Leader, Guitar / New Orleans Blues, New Orleans R&B

When they refer to consistently amazing guitarist Snooks Eaglin as a human jukebox in his New Orleans hometown, they're not dissing him in the slightest. The blind Eaglin is a beloved figure in the Crescent City, not only for his gritty, Ray Charles-inspired vocal delivery and wholly imaginative approach to the guitar, but for the seemingly infinite storehouse of oldies that he's liable to pull out on stage at any second (often confounding his bemused band in the process!).

Born Ford Eaglin, Jr., and blind since very early childhood due to glaucoma and a brain tumor, the lad (named after radio character Baby Snooks, who shared his mischievious ways) picked up the guitar at age six and commenced to mastering every style imaginable. Gospel, blues, jazz—young Snooks Eaglin could play it all. He spent time with a Crescent City band, the Flamingoes (whose members also included pianist Allen Toussaint), played around town as Little Ray Charles, and recorded for Chess as accompanist to Sugar Boy Crawford before going it alone on the streets of the French Quarter.

His earliest recordings in 1958 for Folkways presented Eaglin as a solo acoustic folk-blues artist with an extremely eclectic repertoire. His dazzling fingerpicking was nothing short of astonishing, but Eaglin really wanted to be making R&B with a band. Imperial Records producer Dave Bartholomew granted him the opportunity in 1960, and the results were sensational. Eaglin's fluid, twisting lead guitar on the utterly infectious "Yours Truly" (a Bartholomew composition first waxed by Pee Wee Crayton) and its sequel "Cover Girl" was unique on the New Orleans R&B front, while his brokenhearted cries on "Don't Slam That Door" and "That Certain Door" were positively mesmerizing. Eaglin stuck with Imperial through 1963, when the firm closed up shop in New Orleans, without ever gaining national exposure.

There followed a dry period for the guitarist, but he came back first as accompanist to Professor Longhair (who was in the midst of a rather remarkable comeback bid himself) and then on his own. Eaglin has reasserted his brilliance in recent years with a series of magnificent albums for hometown Black Top Records (notably *Teasin' You* and *Soul's Edge*). —*Bill Dahl*

Country Boy Down in New Orleans / 1958 / Arhoolie ✦✦✦✦✦
Country Boy Down in New Orleans collects 23 tracks Snooks Eaglin recorded in the '50s. During this time, he was a street musician, playing with just one guitar or as a one-man band. On these tracks, he is accompanied by a couple of washboard players and a harpist. As expected, the sound is stripped-down, but it is exciting. Eaglin's early repertoire included a broad variety of blues, folk, and gospel songs and all of these genres are covered thoroughly on this delightful single disc. It may not be the ripping electric blues of his best-known records, but it is just as enjoyable. —*Thom Owens*

New Orleans Street Singer / 1958 / Storyville ✦✦✦✦✦

Possum Up a Simmon Tree / Oct. 1960 / Arhoolie ✦✦✦

That's All Right / 1961 / Prestige/Original Blues Classics ✦✦✦
Recorded during the time in which Eaglin was doubling as a blues/folksinger and a commercial R&B artist (for Imperial). He addresses the acoustic folk and blues side of his repertoire, performing everything solo on six- and 12-string guitars. Time will probably judge these not to be as interesting as his full-band New Orleans R&B recordings. But this is warm, good-natured acoustic blues, with interpretations of traditional tunes, early blues by Robert Johnson, and then-recent R&B hits by Ray Charles, Arthur Crudup, and Amos Milburn. —*Richie Unterberger*

Down Yonder / 1978 / GNP ✦✦✦✦
Sam Charters produced this marvelously funky collection of oldies rendered Eaglin-style with an all-star Crescent City combo: pianist Ellis Marsalis, saxist Clarence Ford, and the French brothers as rhythm section. Eaglin's revisit of "Yours Truly" floats over a rhythmic bed so supremely second-line funky that it's astonishing, while he personalizes the New Orleans classics "Oh Red," "Down Yonder," and "Let the Four Winds Blow" as only Snooks Eaglin can. —*Bill Dahl*

Baby, You Can Get Your Gun / 1987 / Black Top ✦✦✦✦✦
The first of the masterful guitarist's amazing series of albums for Black Top is an earthly delight; his utterly unpredictable guitar weaves and darts through supple rhythms provided by New Orleans vets Smokey Johnson on drums and Erving Charles, Jr. on bass (David Lastie is on sax). Few artists boast Eaglin's "human jukebox" capabilities; his amazingly vast knowledge of eclectic numbers takes in the Four Blazes' "Mary Jo," Tommy Ridgley's "Lavinia," and the Ventures' version of "Perfidia." —*Bill Dahl*

Out of Nowhere / 1988 / Black Top ✦✦✦✦
Another wonderful lineup of Eaglinized oldies ranging from Crescent City standbys by Tommy Ridgley, Benny Spellman, and Smiley Lewis to the always unexpected (Nappy Brown's "Wella Wella Baby-La," the Isleys' "It's Your Thing," the Falcons' "You're So Fine").

Guitarist Anson Funderburgh's band is utilized for backup on half the set; a combo sporting saxist Grady Gaines on most of the rest (Eaglin goes it alone on "Kiss of Fire"). —*Bill Dahl*

New Orleans 1960-1961 / 1988 / Sundown ✦✦✦✦✦
Great R&B sides for Imperial with full band. —*Bill Dahl*

☆ **Teasin' You** / 1992 / Black Top ✦✦✦✦✦
The best of Eaglin's terrific series of Black Top efforts so far—the song selection is absolutely unassailable (lots of savage New Orleans covers, from Lloyd Price and Professor Longhair to Willie Tee and Earl King), the band simmers and sizzles with spicy second-line fire (bassist George Porter, Jr. and drummer Herman Ernest III are a formidable pair indeed), and Eaglin's churchy, commanding vocals and blistering guitar work are nothing short of mind-boggling throughout the entire disc. —*Bill Dahl*

Soul's Edge / 1995 / Black Top ✦✦✦✦✦
Give this New Orleans master enough studio time, and he'll redo the entire history of postwar R&B his own way. Here he lays his mind to Joe Simon's powerhouse soul ballad "Nine Pound Steel," the Midnighters' "Let's Go, Let's Go, Let's Go," even Bill Haley & the Comets' "Skinny Minnie" and the Five Keys' loopy "Ling Ting Tong," giving each the same singular treatment that he's always brought to his recordings. Porter and Ernest return to lay down their immaculate grooves, and Fred Kemp blows sturdy sax on Eaglin's parade-beat "I Went to the Mardi Gras." —*Bill Dahl*

● **Complete Imperial Recordings** / Oct. 24, 1995 / Capitol ✦✦✦✦
Eaglin is apt to be classified as a blues singer with considerable New Orleans R&B influences. This collection of his early-'60s recordings for the Imperial label would be much more appropriately categorized as exactly the opposite. Produced by Dave Bartholomew (who also wrote over half of the material), the thrust of these recordings is most definitely in the classic-'50s/early-'60s New Orleans R&B mold, though Eaglin's vocal delivery may be bluesier than some other practitioners of the sound. It doesn't suffer for this in the least; it's solid stuff betraying the influence of Guitar Slim and Ray Charles (though Eaglin's style is sometimes compared to the latter, it isn't extremely similar, with sparer arrangements and a distinct Creole vocal slur). This compiles 26 tracks (seven previously unreleased) that he cut between 1960 and 1963, none of which were hits, perhaps because the commercial peak of classic New Orleans R&B had already passed. But it's well worth looking into if you like records from the same period by the likes of Bartholomew, Lee Dorsey, and the early Nevilles. —*Richie Unterberger*

Live in Japan / 1997 / Black Top ✦✦✦
Culled from two nights of recording at the Park Tower Hall in Tokyo in December of 1995, this album illustrates the astonishing breadth and depth to the music Snooks Eaglin chooses to interpret in a single evening. His guitar chops are impeccable, his tone clean without being thin, and his ability to whip off lick after astonishing lick in a variety of styles while still being his own man puts him at the forefront alongside any new breed innovators. With solid swinging support, Eaglin sounds relaxed and totally in command. His sideways spins on old chestnuts like "Hello Josephine" sound refreshing, with his nod to Smiley Lewis on "Down Yonder (We Go Ballin')" and "Lillie Mae" are spot-on treatments imbued with respect for an old New Orleans running buddy. His soulful reading of Dan Penn's "Nine Pound Steel" sets the stage for a couple of strange (on the surface) choices, the Isley Brothers' "It's Your Thing" and Stevie Wonder's "(Boogie On) Reggae Woman," which Eaglin totally stamps with the full-bore charm of his own personality. But if anyone truly doubts that Eaglin is not a serious bluesman to be reckoned with, one listen to the almost seven minutes of "Black Night" will dispel any such notions, even before the guitar solo hits. While many live albums exude a "guess you had to be there" quality to them, this one makes you wish you *had* been there. —*Cub Koda*

The Crescent City Collection / May 22, 2001 / Fuel 2000 ✦✦✦✦
In 1987, when Snooks Eaglin made his debut on the Black Top label with *Baby, You Can Get Your Gun*, few would have guessed that the legendary bluesman was embarking on a fruitful and creative second (or third) career at an age when others would be considering retirement. Culled from his five exceptional albums for Black Top, *The Crescent City Collection* is a fine sampling of Eaglin's unique musical gumbo of old-fashioned New Orleans R&B, second-line parade rhythms, and guitar fretboard fireworks. This makeshift best-of highlighting Eaglin's later career is a great place for the uninitiated to introduce themselves to Crescent City music. Recommended. —*Brian Beatty*

Robert Ealey

b. Dec. 6, 1925, Texarkana, TX
Vocals / Electric Texas Blues, Texas Blues
Dallas-based vocalist and songwriter Robert Ealey began singing in his local church at

age 15 with a quartet group in his native Texarkana. Influenced by the likes of Lightnin' Hopkins, Lil' Son Jackson, Frankie Lee Sims and Aaron "T-Bone" Walker, he began singing blues professionally at 20 after he moved to Dallas. In nearby Fort Worth, he joined the Boogie Chillen Boys and became a featured vocalist at the Blue Bird Club there. After singing there for 20 years, Ealey bought the Blue Bird Club and ran it for another ten years.

In 1990, Ealey hooked up with guitarist Tone Sommer and began touring outside of Texas. The band quickly found an audience for their authentic Texas urban blues in Europe, where they have toured more than a dozen times since 1990. Sommer and Ealey also did TV commercial work that made use of their music. Every September, Ealey performs in his own blues festival, held in Sundance Square, Fort Worth.

After Black Top Records purchased several master tapes from the Top Cat label in Dallas, they released Ealey's *Turn Out the Lights*. On the album, he is accompanied by a bevy of the D/FW area's best blues accompanists, including Mike Morgan and Sommer on guitars, Ty Grimes on drums and Mark Rybiski on saxophones. *I Like Music When I Party* followed in 1997. *—Richard Skelly*

Texas Bluemen / Sep. 2, 1994 / Topcat ♦♦♦♦

If You Need Me / 1995 / Topcat ♦♦♦

● **Turn out the Lights** / Jun. 1996 / Black Top ♦♦♦♦

Turn Out the Lights is Robert Ealey's best album to date, not because he's tried anything new, but because he has his best set of songs and performances to date. Supported by such luminaries as drummer Ty Grimes and guitarists Mike Morgan and Tone Summer, Ealey storms through a set of originals making them sound like classic juke-joint rockers. A few of the songs fall a little flat, but *Turn Out the Lights* is nevertheless a roaring good time. *—Thom Owens*

I Like Music When I Party / Mar. 18, 1997 / Black Top ♦♦♦

Robert Ealey is no spring chicken. After singing in local Texas bands for years, he finally started recording in the '90s—*I Like Music When I Party* was the fourth album he cut after starting his recording career. Like the others, it's a greasy collection of Texas blues, spiked with a bit of soul. Ealey's voice may be gravelly with age, but it's by no means gone, and with the support of his youthful backing band, he can really bring it home. There's nothing deep here—just party music, played good and simple. Sometimes, that's enough. *—Thom Owens*

Ronnie Earl (Ronald Horvath)

b. Mar. 10, 1953, Queens, NY

Guitar / Modern Electric Blues, Contemporary Blues, Soul-Blues, Blues-Rock, Jazz Blues

One of the finest new blues guitarists to emerge during the '80s, Ronnie Earl often straddled the line between blues and jazz, throwing in touches of soul and rock as well. His versatility made him one of the few blues guitarists capable of leading an almost entirely instrumental outfit and his backing band the Broadcasters became one of the more respected working units in contemporary blues over the course of the '90s, following Earl's departure from Roomful of Blues.

Ronnie Earl was born Ronald Horvath in Queens, NY, on March 10, 1953. He didn't start playing guitar until after he entered college at Boston University in the early '70s and became fascinated with the local blues scene. Developing his craft quickly, he landed a job in the house band of the Speakeasy Club in Cambridge, MA, and changed his last name to the bluesier-sounding Earl in tribute to Earl Hooker, one of his favorite influences. Prior to the name switch, he'd made some recordings for the small Baron label under his original moniker beginning in 1977, first backing Guitar Johnny & the Rhythm Rockers, then as a founding member of Sugar Ray & the Bluetones with harmonica player/singer Sugar Ray Norcia. In 1979, Earl was invited to replace Duke Robillard in the prominent Rhode Island band Roomful of Blues, whose swinging jump blues revivalist sound demanded a jazz sensibility as well as ample blues feeling. Earl spent the next eight years with Roomful of Blues and watched their national profile grow steadily larger.

Meanwhile, Earl also made a few recordings on his own for Black Top Records, forming the first versions of the Broadcasters in the early '80s. He released his first solo album, *Smokin'*, in 1983 and followed it with *They Call Me Mr. Earl* in 1984 (both of those albums were later compiled on the CD *Deep Blues*). Still, they were a sidelight to his main gig with Roomful of Blues, that is until he left the band in 1987 to make a go of it as a solo artist and bandleader in his own right. A new version of the Broadcasters debuted in 1988 on *Soul Searchin'*, which featured vocalist Darrell Nulisch, harmonica player Jerry Portnoy (ex-Muddy Waters), bassist Steve Gomes, and drummer Per Hanson. *Peace of Mind* followed in 1990, as did *I Like It When It Rains*, a live album on Antone's that actually dated from 1986. 1991's *Surrounded by Love* reunited Earl with Sugar Ray Norcia and also proved the last in his long string of Black Top releases.

By the early '90s, Earl had addressed and overcome his problems with alcohol and cocaine and began to rethink his approach. He formed a new version of the Broadcasters, featuring organist Bruce Katz, bassist Rod Carey, and longtime drummer Per Hanson, and boldly elected to go without a vocalist. Earl debuted his new instrumental direction—which was more informed by jazz than ever before—on 1993's *Still River* (released by AudioQuest) and embarked on a tour of Europe. He signed with the Bullseye Blues label and issued a string of acclaimed albums, including 1994's *Language of the Soul*, 1995's *Blues Guitar Virtuoso Live in Europe* (a live album from his 1993 tour originally titled *Blues and Forgiveness*), and 1996's *Grateful Heart: Blues and Ballads* (which featured David "Fathead" Newman). The latter two were particular critical favorites, with *Live in Europe* winning *Pulse* magazine's year-end poll as Best Blues Album and *Grateful Heart* doing likewise in *Down Beat*.

Thanks to all the positive attention, Earl signed a major-label deal with Verve. His label debut, *The Colour of Love*, was issued in 1997 and sold more than 65,000 copies, making it one of the biggest hits of Earl's career; that year, he also won a W.C. Handy Award as Best Blues Instrumentalist. However, feeling that he was under too much pressure to move more units, Earl soured on the deal and around the same time suffered a bout with manic depression. He wound up not only leaving Verve, but taking a break from bandleading and live performance; he disbanded the Broadcasters and signed with the smaller Telarc label as a solo act. His Telarc debut, 2000's *Healing Time*, teamed him with legendary soul-jazz organist Jimmy McGriff. The follow-up, 2001's *Ronnie Earl and Friends*, was a loose, jam session type of affair featuring a number of special guests, including the Fabulous Thunderbirds' Kim Wilson, Irma Thomas, Luther "Guitar Jr." Johnson, and the Band's Levon Helm. *—Steve Huey*

Smokin' / 1983 / Black Top ♦♦♦

They Call Me Mr. Earl / 1984 / Black Top ♦♦♦

Deep Blues / 1985 / Black Top ♦♦♦

Soul Searchin' / 1988 / Black Top ♦♦

I Like It When it Rains / 1990 / Antone's ♦♦♦♦♦

Peace of Mind / Nov. 1990 / Black Top ♦♦♦♦♦

Peace of Mind features some nice, swinging stuff. *—Bill Dahl*

Surrounded by Love / May 1991 / Black Top ♦♦♦

Ronnie Earl recorded *Surrounded by Love* with a new version of the Broadcasters. The most notable factor of the new lineup is the reappearance of Sugar Ray Norcia, the finest vocalist/harpist Earl ever recorded with. The band sounds tight and energetic, especially on the three tracks they cut with Robert Jr. Lockwood. Parts of the album are a little slow, but the album is very entertaining, even with its minor flaws. *—Thom Owens*

● **Test of Time** / 1992 / Black Top ♦♦♦♦♦

Test of Time collects the highlights from Ronnie Earl's six Black Top albums. The 18-song compilation showcases one of the finest blues guitarists of the '80s, picking nearly all of his finest material, which happen to include duets with Robert Jr. Lockwood and Hubert Sumlin. The album is an excellent introduction to Earl, as well as his most consistently entertaining release. *—Thom Owens*

Still River / 1993 / AudioQuest ♦♦♦♦

This particular version of the Broadcasters was unarguably magical, and this recording reveals why. Recorded four years after Earl dealt with his demons (alcohol, drugs, nervous collapse), it is the first of a string of all-instrumental albums by Earl, and it drips with class and soul. It's not just the exceptional skill of the players, however, that makes it so special; it was recorded on one of a handful of audiophile labels (AudioQuest), and therefore features state-of-the-art production. From the ringing opening chords of Magic Sam's "Blues for the West Side" to the beautiful acoustic guitar/piano duet of "Derek's Peace," *Still River* is thoroughly enjoyable. "Kansas City Monarch" is slow and sweet, featuring Bruce Katz tearing up the low notes, a nice sax solo by Anders Gaardmand, and some great double-string work by Earl. There is a moody version of John Coltrane's "Equinox" and a bog-dwelling rouser written by the entire band called "Chili Ba Hugh." You'll also like the greasy Hammond B3 organ on "Soul Serenade." A tempo change three minutes into the song suddenly finds the listener "getting religion" and tempted to yell "Amen!" Earl's own "Rego Park Blues" also showcases some nice B-3 and finds Earl in the place where he shines the brightest, delicately coaxing a hushed solo from his Strat. Although not as jazzy as Earl's subsequent efforts, *Still River* sows the seeds that sprouted a few years later with *Language of the Soul* and with the albums that followed. *—Ann Wickstrom*

Language of the Soul / 1994 / Bullseye Blues ♦♦♦♦

Language of the Soul is a wonderful change of pace for guitarist Ronnie Earl. The record is the first all-instrumental album Earl has recorded and, if anything, it's even more successful than his full-fledged, band-oriented records. Working without vocals has given him the freedom to try all sorts of new things, whether it's the jazzy interludes of "Indigo Burrell" or the gospel-flavored "I Am With You." Earl's compositions aren't memorable in and of themselves (he wrote all but two of the cuts), yet they give him the opportunity to play freely. He comes up with some truly remarkable solo passages, offering definitive proof that he's one of the best contemporary blues guitarists of the '90s. *—Thom Owens*

Blues and Forgiveness / 1995 / Bullseye Blues ♦♦♦

Blues Guitar Virtuoso Live in Europe / 1995 / Bullseye Blues ♦♦♦♦♦

Although not released until 1995, this CD was recorded live in 1993 in Bremen, Germany. *Live in Europe* is Earl's tribute to his major influences, and Ronnie plays his favorite guitar throughout: a 1962 red Strat. The fast, driving "San-Ho-Zay" and "Blues for the West Side" go out to Magic Sam; "The Stumble" to Freddie King; "Thank You Mr. T-Bone" to T-Bone Walker and Duke Robillard (who inspired Earl to learn T-Bone). "Thank You Mr. T-Bone" features some cool call-and-response between Earl and Bruce Katz on the Hammond B-3. It segues nicely into "Akos," where you'll find more great B-3 (check out the improvised "Summertime" riff). An all-instrumental offering, *Live in Europe* includes a handful of tunes found on its predecessor, *Still River*, including "Szeren," "Rego Park Blues," and the aforementioned "Blues for the West Side." "Contrition," a slow, soulful tune penned by Katz, has some jaw-dropping runs by Earl. One can only imagine what it must have been like to be one of the lucky souls at this show. The only fault to be found on this album is the mislabeling of several tunes on the cover. (For example, "The Stumble" is listed as "Not Now Kovitch.") Still, it's this reviewer's all-time favorite album—thank you, Mr. Earl. *—Ann Wickstrom*

Eye to Eye / 1996 / AudioQuest ♦♦♦

This CD is a fine showcase for guitarist Ronnie Earl, who is teamed with three members of the Legendary Blues Band (pianist Pinetop Perkins, bassist Calvin Jones and drummer Willie "Big Eyes" Smith), plus organist Bruce Katz. Although pianist Perkins takes vocals on most of the songs and bassist Jones sings on two of the numbers, nearly each selection has plenty of solo space for Earl and Perkins. Sticking exclusively to the blues at a variety of tempos, the fine program (which has superior instrumental playing that overshadows the personable vocals) should be of strong interest to both blues and jazz collectors. *—Scott Yanow*

Grateful Heart: Blues and Ballads / Mar. 19, 1996 / Bullseye Blues ♦♦♦♦

Perhaps the smartest move a non-singing guitar-playing virtuoso like Mister Earl could make was ditching the lame singers who permeate most of his earlier efforts and go with an all-instrumental program. On this outing, he surrounds himself with an excellent quartet of players in David "Fathead" Newman on tenor sax, Per Hanson on drums, Rod Carey on bass and Bruce Katz on keyboards, and the results are simply sublime. Instead of a bunch of Chicago retreads, we are treated to a heady mixture of blues, jazz, soul, swing, you name it, all of it infused with taste, tone and economy. When Ronnie burns, the results are jaw dropping; when he slows it down, his choice of notes is exquisite. "Welcome Home," "Still Soul Searching," "Drown in My Own Tears" and "Skyman (For Duane Allman)" are just a few of the highlights, but there really isn't a wasted note on this record to be found. Anywhere. *—Cub Koda*

Plays Big Blues / Feb. 4, 1997 / Black Top ♦♦♦

The Colour of Love / Jun. 24, 1997 / Verve ♦♦♦♦

The continuing musical saga of bluesman Ronnie Earl ventures further into jazz territory with this, his first release on the Verve imprint. As always, Earl is ably and tightly backed by the Broadcasters, featuring solid and empathetic playing from drummer Per Hanson, bassist Rod Carey, and keyboardist and co-collaborator Bruce Katz. It's Katz's "Hippology" that opens the album with a swinging bang, sporting guest appearances on alto sax from Hank Crawford and Allman Brothers alumni Jaimoe on drums. Crawford also shows up again on "Anne's Dream," while Jaimoe joins Marc Quinones for a two-drummer rhythm section guest turn on "Bonnie's Theme" and "Mother Angel." Gregg Allman plays Hammond B-3 organ and contributes the album's only vocal on "Everyday Kinda Man." But guest stars aside, this is clearly Ronnie Earl's show to direct, and his playing, as always, sports exquisite taste, economy, and tone for days. His nine-plus-minute soliloquy on Thelonious Monk's "'Round Midnight" (the only cover on this album) blasts the venerable jazz standard into new territory as Earl's passages take on almost trumpet-like tonalities, while his "I Like That Thing You Did" (dedicated to Jimmie Vaughan) creates an organ-like sound with tons of ultra-shimmering Leslie vibrato. Since adopting an all-instrumental format several albums back, Earl's music has blossomed in a multitude of directions, embracing jazz, soul, and the rockier aspects of guitarists like Carlos Santana (the title track) and Peter Green ("Heart of Glass"), and bringing new life to the organ jazz combo format ("Deep Pockets") while remaining true to his deep blues roots, like in his closing tribute to Albert Collins, "O'Yeah." This release pushes the envelope even further and breaks new ground, wrapped in the velvet glove of Tom Dowd's production. *—Cub Koda*

Healing Time / Jan. 1, 2000 / Telarc ♦♦♦♦

Guitarist Ronnie Earl continues his string of all instrumental albums with this stunning follow-up to 1997's critically acclaimed *The Colour of Love*. With sturdy yet subtle assistance from Anthony Geraci on keyboards, Mark Greenberg or Don Williams on drums, Michael "Mudcat" Ward on bass, and, for two tracks, special guest Jimmy McGriff handling the Hammond B-3 in his inimitable fashion, Earl peels off sweet and spicy jazz-blues-gospel licks with the touch of a musician whose heart and soul is intimately infused in his music. Earl's love of Muddy Waters shines on a sizzling cover of "Catfish Blues" where his guitar alternately screams and moans through the stop-start rhythm of the song as if it's singing the lyrics. But this is primarily a jazz album with a heavy blues influence, and Earl's Kenny Burrell and Grant Green roots are pervasive throughout. His tensile tone ranges from tender and sensitive to biting and majestic, with touches of Carlos Santana's unique phrasing thrown in. Whether digging deep into the achingly soulful slow groove of "Blues for Shawn" or closing out the album with a rapturous "Amazing Grace," Ronnie Earl proves himself to be a master of moods. *Healing Time* effectively moves him into the realm of the guitar greats he idolizes. *—Hal Horowitz*

Ronnie Earl and Friends / 2001 / Telarc ♦♦♦

Ronnie Earl's first album after suffering from a bout with manic depression that sidelined him from live work for a few years, is a surprisingly modest, unassuming affair. The titular friends include Fabulous Thunderbirds founder/harpist/vocalist Kim Wilson who splits the album's vocal duties with Luther "Guitar Junior" Johnson. James Cotton, Band drummer Levon Helm, keyboardist David Maxwell, and New Orleans legend Irma Thomas (who contributes her distinctive vocals to only two stunning tunes) round out the ad hoc band. Recorded live in Woodstock, NY's Bearsville studio over three days in autumn 2000 and released almost a year later, the session is a loose affair intended to emulate the old Delmark label style of rounding up blues friends, putting them together in a room and rolling tape. Of course, with musicians of this caliber, you're unlikely to go wrong, and the resulting album is a relaxed, unpretentious chronicle of these artist's interaction on blues classics and a few similarly themed originals. Most of the songs were completed in one take (you often hear the verbal cues deciding who takes a solo), and the album doesn't feature any one particular player, preferring to share the spotlight among all the "friends." Unfortunately those who come to hear Earl, one of the more tasty, understated blues guitarists, might leave disappointed since there is precious little soloing from the ex-Roomful of Blues man here. While that makes for a democratic gathering, it's also a little frustrating if you're an Earl fan. That said, there are many fine performances here. Kim Wilson is at the top of his game, shining on Little Walter's "Blue and Lonesome" and "Last Night," two of the six tracks he sings on. The former boasts Earl's longest, most passionate solo on the album along with a harp turn from Wilson that oozes with emotion. The group clicks on all the tracks, but seems to work best on the slow blues of Earl's "Twenty-Five Days," Cotton's "One More Mile," and Thomas' showcase, a languid and heartfelt medley of "I'll Take Care of You"/"Lonely Avenue," one of the disc's undisputed highlights. An album for Sunday mornings as opposed to Saturday nights, *Ronnie Earl and Friends* is a subtle and intimate blues session, whose headlining star remains only a small, but essential portion of the event. *—Hal Horowitz*

Archie Edwards

b. Sep. 4, 1918, Union Hall, VA, **d.** Jun. 1998

Vocals / Piedmont Blues

From the time of his birth in rural Virginia in 1918, Piedmont blues guitarist Archie Edwards was surrounded by music. The hard work of farm life was punctuated by musical interludes when musicians from the town of Union Hall and surrounding areas visited to make music with his father, Roy Edwards, who played the slide guitar, harmonica, and banjo. By the time he had entered his teenage years, Edwards knew that he wanted to be a guitarist. Within a few years, he had one of his instruments to play, but the guitar was one he had to share with two brothers, Willie and Robert. He built up his repertoire by listening to recordings made by such blues legends as Blind Boy Fuller and Blind Lemon Jefferson. He also increased his musical knowledge by learning at the elbow of men like his father and other musicians who occasionally traveled through town and the neighboring areas. Edwards and his brothers earned pocket money by playing local house parties. At the time, Edwards was just a boy of 12. He didn't return to school after the eighth grade, but instead sought employment alongside another brother. The Edwards siblings toiled in a sawmill, with the guitarist continuing to appease his lifelong love of music during rare downtimes by playing around the camp, where he also labored on Saturday mornings. In the evenings after work, Edwards strummed his guitar during house parties. But by 1937, the guitarist had had enough of the sawmill. He left the area and ended up in New Jersey, where he supported himself for several years by chauffeuring and cooking before heading home. Later, he found employment at an Ohio hotel.

During World War II, the guitarist enlisted and served his time as an MP overseas. When the war was over, he made his way to the nation's capital, where he undertook the trade of a mason. Dissatisfied, he left for Virginia again, this time settling in the city of Richmond where he worked as a barber. Still unsettled, he headed back to Washington where, before he retired during the early '80s, he would work as a federal security guard. He also drove a truck and opened a barbershop in the late '50s. The storefront attracted men who loved the blues as much as he did. One of Edwards' frequent visitors was a musician he had revered since his youth, Mississippi John Hurt. The two blues lovers quickly forged a bond of friendship and they played around the capital with another blues musician, Skip James. Beginning in 1966 with the death of his idol Hurt, Edwards' music was silenced for several years when he could not play, perhaps due to grief. Following this period of mourning, he went on to pen "The Road Is Rough and Rocky." He later performed at festivals and local nightspots, and he appeared during a festival sponsored by the Smithsonian. He also appeared around Washington with an ensemble known as the Travelling Blues Workshop. The outfit included Flora Molton, Mother Scott, John Jackson, Phil Wiggins, and John Cephas. Thanks to Molton, Edwards got the chance to record. She passed his name to Alex Kustner, who booked Edwards onto the American Blues Festival across Europe. L&R soon scooped him up to record *Living Country Blues, Vol. 6: The Road Is Rough and Rocky*. He also recorded for Mapleshade in the late '80s. He went on to team with Molton and Eleanor Ellis, and the three partners toured Europe and North America. *—Linda Seida*

Blues 'n Bones / 1989 / Mapleshade ♦♦♦

Guitarist Archie Edwards, one of the rare blues ukelele players and surviving Piedmont stylists, didn't have an abundance of recordings in print when he stepped to the microphone in 1989 for this session. But the few dates he made had long ago outlined his boisterous style, exuberant manner, and defiant attitude. These qualities help make *Blues 'n Bones* something more than just a respectful date; it's got a vitality and freshness that are even more apparent when harmonica player Mark Wenner steps forward and provides some youthful energy and enthusiasm, along with the resourceful drumming of Vernell Fournier. The prickly, dry, rhythmically terse sounds Richard Thomas gets from his "bones" are worth the price alone. *—Ron Wynn*

● **The Toronto Sessions** / Nov. 6, 2001 / Northern Blues ♦♦♦

Blues guitarist Archie Edwards was 68 years old in 1986 when he recorded these sessions in Toronto. Its release 15 years later was cause for blues fans' joy and sorrow. Thought it was great to finally have available, it's unfortunate that Edwards wasn't recorded more often; his natural approach to the blues is timeless. While too many blues releases at the beginning of the 21st century prefer to mask the guts and soul of the performance with glossy over-production, the spirit of Edwards' heroes, Mississippi John Hurt and Blind Lemon Jefferson, come shining through. Highlights include Edwards' reworking of "Sitting on Top of the World," "How Long Blues," "Meet Me in the Bottom," and "Poor Me." According to the informative liner notes by Barry Lee Pearson, enough material was recorded in Toronto to warrant a second disc. *—Al Campbell*

Clarence Edwards

b. Mar. 25, 1933, Lindsay, LA, **d.** May 20, 1993, Baton Rouge, LA

Vocals, Guitar / Acoustic Louisiana Blues, Swamp Blues, Louisiana Blues

Louisiana swamp blues veteran Clarence Edwards was rediscovered in the '90s after a long hiatus from recording, and began to garner some of the recognition he deserved just prior to his unfortunately timed death. Edwards was born March 25, 1933, in Lindsay, LA, as one of 14 siblings. When his family moved into Baton Rouge, the 12-year-old Edwards began to learn the guitar by listening to old Charley Patton records. Sometime in his twenties, Edwards began playing the local blues circuit, initially joining a band called the Boogie Beats, which featured his brother Cornelius, Landry Buggs, and drummer Jackson Acox. Edwards also played with the Bluebird Kings, but his most notable (or, at least, frightening) experience on the circuit came one night when he was shot in the leg during an altercation outside the Silver Moon Club in Alsen. Apart from playing music, Edwards supported himself with farm work, and eventually landed a job at Thomas Scrap, where he worked for over 30 years. Edwards' first recording sessions were undertaken from 1959-1961, when he, his brother Cornelius, and violinist James "Butch" Cage recorded together for folk chronicler Harry Oster (see the *Country Negro Jam Sessions* album). In contrast to the traditional approach of those sessions, Edwards' next recordings—done in 1970 for producer Mike Vernon—were more conscious of contemporary trends; they've been issued on compilations like *Louisiana Blues* and *Swamp Blues*. Edwards remained largely silent until the mid-'80s, when bluesman Tabby Thomas' club the Blues Box helped revive the Baton Rouge blues scene. Thanks to Thomas, Edwards began finding regular performance work again, not just locally but on the blues festival circuit as well. In 1990, Edwards finally recorded his first full-length album, an acoustic/electric affair for Sidetrack titled *Swamps the Word* (it was later remastered and reissued on CD by Red Lightnin'). 1991 saw the release of another album, *Swampin'*, this time for New Rose, and 1992 produced *Louisiana Swamp Blues, Vol. 4*, a compilation of mostly Edwards' sessions featuring him both solo and with a small group. The quality of Edwards' work earned generally high praise in blues circles, but sadly, just as he was beginning to gain wider recognition among aficionados, he died in his longtime hometown of Scotlandville, LA, in 1993, at the age of 60. *—Steve Huey*

● **Louisiana Swamp Blues, Vol. 4** / 1990-1991 / Wolf ✦✦✦✦✦

Swampin' / 1991 / New Rose ✦✦✦
An admirable attempt at reviving the swamp blues sound by the veteran Louisiana guitarist. *—Bill Dahl*

Swamps the Word / Aug. 11, 1998 / Red Lightnin' ✦✦✦✦

David "Honeyboy" Edwards

b. Jun. 28, 1915, Shaw, MS
Vocals, Harmonica, Guitar / Delta Blues, Modern Delta Blues
Living links to the immortal Robert Johnson are few. There's Robert Jr. Lockwood, of course—and David "Honeyboy" Edwards. Until relatively recently, Edwards was something of an underappreciated figure, but no longer—his slashing, Delta-drenched guitar and gruff vocals are as authentic as it gets.

Edwards had it tough growing up in Mississippi, but his blues prowess (his childhood pals included Tommy McClennan and Robert Petway) impressed Big Joe Williams enough to take him under his wing. Rambling around the south, Honeyboy experienced the great Charley Patton and played often with Robert Johnson. Musicologist Alan Lomax came to Clarksdale, MS, in 1942 and captured Edwards for Library of Congress-sponsored posterity.

Commercial prospects for the guitarist were scant, however—a 1951 78 for Artist Record Co., "Build a Cave" (as Mr. Honey), and four 1953 sides for Chess that laid unissued until "Drop Down Mama" turned up 17 years later on an anthology constituted the bulk of his early recorded legacy, although Edwards was in Chicago from the mid-'50s on.

The guitarist met young harpist/blues aficionado Michael Frank in 1972. Four years later, they formed the Honeyboy Edwards Blues Band to break into Chicago's then-fledgling North side club scene; they also worked as a duo (and continue to do so on occasion). When Frank inaugurated his Earwig label, he enlisted Honeyboy and his long-time pals Sunnyland Slim, Big Walter Horton, Floyd Jones, and Kansas City Red to cut a rather informal album, *Old Friends*, as his second release in 1979. In 1992, Earwig assembled *Delta Bluesman*, a stunning combination of unexpurgated Library of Congress masters and recent performances that show Honeyboy Edwards has lost none of his blues fire. *—Bill Dahl*

● **White Windows** / Sep. 1988 / Evidence ✦✦✦✦✦
David "Honeyboy" Edwards is one of the last surviving Delta blues warriors and is among the originators of a musical style as evocative and vibrant as any this nation has ever experienced. Edwards' voice, with its ironic, colorful, weary tonal qualities and cutting, keen delivery are contrasted by a crisp, slicing guitar approach. Edwards does not rely on slickness, inventiveness, or niceties; his riffs, lines, phrases, and licks are as aggressive and fiery as his vocals. He showed what real traditional blues singing was all about when he recorded for Blue Suit in 1988. Evidence has reissued that 13-song session in splendid digital glory, as Edwards' triumphant, resounding voice rings through each number. *—Ron Wynn*

Delta Bluesman / 1992 / Earwig ✦✦✦✦✦
Contains the most important recordings of the slide guitarist's incredibly lengthy career, which is still going strong: his 1942 Library of Congress sides for musicologist Alan Lomax. Robert Johnson's former running partner was a formidable solo Delta bluesman in his own right; "Water Coast Blues" and "Wind Howlin' Blues" are startling in their fiery intensity. But Honeyboy remains a vital blues figure—the set is rounded out by recent waxings (some with a Chicago combo) that celebrate the ongoing contributions of this living link with Delta tradition. *—Bill Dahl*

I've Been Around / 1995 / 32 Jazz ✦✦✦
This fine solo project features Edwards recorded down in Bruce Iglauer's cellar in 1974. On "Sad & Lonesome," "Take Me in Your Arms," "I Feel So Good Today," and "Big Road Blues," Edwards is backed by Big Walter Horton on amplified harmonica while Honeyboy plays electric guitar. On "Ride With Me Tonight," "Things Have Changed," and "The Woman I'm Loving," Honeyboy's idiosyncratic timing is helped out by the addition of Eddie El on second guitar. A very solid session by this seldom-recorded artist. *—Cub Koda*

Crawling Kingsnake / Jul. 22, 1997 / Testament ✦✦✦✦
Any fan of Delta blues should grab this reissue as fast they can get to it. These are vintage recordings, mostly from 1967, made by scholar-producer Pete Welding when Edwards was 51 years old. Edwards' itinerant lifestyle resulted in his missing many opportunities to record, so that this was only the fifth session he'd had in over 30 years in music, performing solo, with an acoustic guitar on eight of the 13 cuts here. Edwards cuts a daunting figure on the guitar, making the strings sing in several voices at once (check out the playing on "Love Me Over Slow"), and his singing is a match for his playing. The eight solo numbers, dating from 1967, feature the music he was most familiar with, including Robert Johnson's "Sweet Home Chicago" and the title track of this collection. The rest date from a March 1964 session on which Edwards shares the spotlight with singer-harpist John Lee Henley. As a bonus, the last track is an interview from his 1967 solo session in which Edwards talks about Robert Johnson and Tommy Johnson, both of whom he knew personally. The background ambient sound does nothing to detract from the worth of the music, which has a wonderful raw quality. *—Bruce Eder*

World Don't Owe Me Nothing / Dec. 24, 1997 / Earwig ✦✦✦
This is a companion disc to Honeyboy Edwards' autobiography of the same name. It features full-length performances along with interview segments that tell some of the great stories of the blues, particularly trenchant being Edwards' version of the night of Robert Johnson's death. Musical high points include several turns on Johnson material like "Walkin' Blues," "Sweet Home Chicago" and "Crossroads," the latter featuring some slashing slide work from Edwards. Carey Bell contributes some great harp to Edwards' lone guitar, and on other tracks Edwards is ably supported by Rick Sherry on harmonica and washboard. With his timing as idiosyncratic as ever, Edwards also brings a couple of fine originals to the table with "My Mama Told Me" and "Every Now and Then." A great lion-in-winter recording with more than its share of oddball quirks, this is one great listening experience. *—Cub Koda*

Shake 'Em on Down / May 2, 2000 / APO ✦✦✦✦
This 1999 session finds Honeyboy working his acoustic magic in the company of Madison Slim on harmonica and Jimmy D. Lane, son of the late Jimmy Rogers, on second guitar. Recorded at the Blue Heaven Studios (a converted church) in Salina, Kansas, this is a pretty inspired session with Edwards running through old classics like Charley Patton's "High Water Everywhere" and "Pony Blues," "Drop Down Mama," "Shake 'Em on Down," "Anna Lee," "Bullfrog Blues," and "Monkey Face Woman." As an added bonus, there's also an interview with this fascinating bluesman, making this session a real keeper. One of his best. *—Cub Koda*

Mississippi Delta Bluesman / Jan. 23, 2001 / Smithsonian/Folkways ✦✦✦
Edwards presented a mixture of originals and covers of songs by the likes of Tommy Johnson, Robert Johnson, Howlin' Wolf, Charley Patton, and Memphis Minnie on this solo country blues session, originally issued by Folkways in 1979. There's nothing extraordinary about this album, true, but it's solid Delta blues that feels lived in. Edwards does much to add interest and variety to the material by varying between chording and single-string playing and high and low notes, and changing the rhythms unpredictably, sometimes with a stop-start feel. His husky voice is warm and communicative, if not as distinctive as some of the legends he hung out with, which included Patton, Robert Johnson, and others. *—Richie Unterberger*

Willie Edwards

Guitar, Vocals / Modern Electric Blues
Guitarist, singer and songwriter Willie Edwards was one of the many white kids who first discovered blues and folk music in the '60s. He began playing guitar in tenth grade and became a fan of '60s soul, as well as blues and folk music, buying albums by artists like Solomon Burke and Otis Redding. From the mid-'60s, he led a bevy of soul, R&B and blues bands around his native Connecticut, always playing rhythm guitar. It wasn't until later that he began playing lead guitar, and with his smoky, throaty vocals and Albert King-inspired guitar riffs, his various bands found audiences in clubs around Connecticut and Massachusetts. Edwards' songwriting and vocals are what set him apart from other blues bands, aside from the fact that he's been leading his own bands since 1965. Edwards recorded a strong debut album for the London-based JSP Records, *Everlastin' Tears*. The album, released in 1997 and produced by Johnny Rawls, showcases his unique songwriting voice. Edwards sings songs like "Dollar In," "Company Store," "'90s Blues," and "Read Between the Lines," that contain social commentary as well as some ferocious guitar playing. He's accompanied by Johnny Rawls on guitar and the Nutmeg Horns. *—Richard Skelly*

● **Everlastin' Tears** / Feb. 25, 1997 / JSP ✦✦✦

Willie Egan

Piano / Boogie-Woogie, Piano Blues, Rock & Roll
Known by true aficionados for the handful of great boogie rockers that he cut for the L.A.-based Mambo and Vita imprints during the mid-'50s, pianist Willie Egan should have enjoyed a considerably larger share of fame than he did.

Born on the bayou outside of Shreveport, Egan was lucky to escape his rustic existence for Los Angeles at the age of nine. Piano swiftly became his passion, as he listened to and learned from the recordings of Amos Milburn, Hadda Brooks, and Camille Howard. A 1954 single for John R. Fullbright's Elko label preceded a series of 1955-1956 gems for Larry Mead's Mambo and Vita labels, notably "Wow Wow," "What a Shame," "Come On," "She's Gone Away, But," and "Wear Your Black Dress." Egan's surname was frequently misspelled on these platters as Eggins or Egans. After a stint as one of Marvin Phillips' several duet partners (billed as Marvin & Johnny), Egan largely hung it up (a 1983 European tour got him back in the studio for one fresh album, anyway). *—Bill Dahl*

Going Back to Louisiana / 1984 / Ace ✦✦✦

Willie Egan & His Friends / 1985 / Relic ✦✦✦

Rock & Roll Fever / 1988 / Krazy Kat ✦✦

● **Come On** / 1993 / Relic ✦✦✦✦✦
The R&B boogie pianist waxed some rip-roaring rockers for the tiny Los Angeles-based Vita and Mambo logos during the mid-'50s. Here are 14 of his best collected for a long-overdue airing. This guy deserved a lot more respect than he got, judging from the jumping Louisiana-tinged "Wow Wow," "Come On," and "She's Gone Away, But . . . . " Also

aboard: 11 more obscure goodies from the same labels' vaults, notably four tracks by Harmonica Slim (including "Drop Anchor") and Big Boy Groves' lament "You Can't Beat the Horses." *—Bill Dahl*

Electric Flag

f. Apr. 1967, Chicago, IL, **db.** 1974

Group / Jazz-Rock, Psychedelic, Blues-Rock

When guitarist Mike Bloomfield left the Paul Butterfield Blues Band in 1967, he wanted to form a band that combined blues, rock, soul, psychedelia, and jazz into something new. The ambitious concept didn't come off, despite some interesting moments; maybe it was *too* ambitious to hold all that weight. Bloomfield knew for sure that he wanted a horn section in the band, which he began forming with a couple of friends, keyboardist Barry Goldberg and singer Nick Gravenites. Although the trio were all veterans of the Chicago music scene, the group based themselves in the San Francisco area. They were in turn bolstered by a rhythm section of bassist Harvey Brooks (who had played on some of Bob Dylan's mid-'60s records) and drummer Buddy Miles; on top of them came a horn section.

Oddly, before even playing any live concerts, the group recorded the soundtrack for the 1967 psychedelic exploitation movie, *The Trip*, which afforded them the opportunity to experiment with some of their ideas without much pressure. Their live debut was at the 1967 Monterey Pop Festival (although they didn't make it into the documentary film of the event), but their first proper studio album didn't come out until the spring of 1968.

A Long Time Comin' was an erratic affair, predating Blood, Sweat & Tears and Chicago as a sort of attempt at a big-band rock sound. Calling it an early jazz-rock outing is not exactly accurate; it was more like late-'60s soul-rock-psychedelia that sometimes (but not always) employed prominent horns. Indeed, it sometimes didn't always sound like the work of the same band—or, at least, you could say that it seemed torn between blues-rock, soul-rock, and California psychedelic influences. The album's success is even harder to judge in light of the facts that Gravenites really wasn't a top-notch vocalist, and that the band's instrumental skills outshone their songwriting ones.

There was enough promise on the album to merit further exploration, but it had hardly been released before the Flag began to droop. Goldberg left, followed shortly by Bloomfield, the most important component of the group's vision. A fragmented band recorded an inferior follow-up, but by 1969 they had split up. They did reunite (with Bloomfield) in 1974 for a Jerry Wexler-produced album that got little notice. *—Richie Unterberger*

The Trip [Original Soundtrack] / 1967 / Curb ♦♦♦

One of the greatest exploitation movies of all time, *The Trip* was the "vision" of Peter Fonda and Jack Nicholson (who wrote the original script). The finished film didn't turn out exactly the way Jack and Peter wanted it to, but it certainly had it's moments... all in Psychedelic Color. This, the soundtrack, was pretty cool, too. It contains the first studio recordings of the Electric Flag, Michael Bloomfield's swaggering soul/jazz/rock ensemble. Writing and performing trippy music was a bit removed from this fine ensemble's area (they were, in fact, a serious and funky band), but they succeeded admirably. Considering that it came out on Mike Curb's Sidewalk Records (a Capitol subsidiary) and it was an American International film, one wonders if the Flag saw any dough from this? No matter, as some of the music is excellent. "Fine Jug Thing" and "Peter Gets Off" are wild, jazzy rockers, which perfectly score Fonda's Sunset Strip/trip adventures. The album's closer, "Gettin' Hard," is a variation on "Hoochie Coochie Man" and closes the album out in funky style. Also, there are a few early efforts from synthesizer pioneer Paul Beaver, such as "Synesthesia," which is quite similar to David Bowie's work on the *Man Who Fell to Earth/Low* projects—eight years later. *—Matthew Greenwald*

A Long Time Comin' / 1968 / Columbia ♦♦♦♦♦

Writer Jeff Tamarkin says "ex-Butterfield Band guitarist Mike Bloomfield, drummer Buddy Miles, and others put this soul-rock band together in 1967. This debut is a testament to their ability to catch fire and keep on burnin'." That The Electric Flag do quite well—they appeared at the Monterey International Pop Festival with the Blues Project, Paul Butterfield, and Janis Joplin, and all these groups had some musical connection to each other beyond that pivotal festival. *A Long Time Comin'* is the "new soul" described appropriately enough by the late critic Lillian Roxon, and tunes like "She Should Have Just" and "Over-Lovin' You" lean more toward the soul side than the pop so many radio listeners were attuned to back then. Nick Gravenites was too much of a purist to ride his blues on the Top 40 the way Felix Cavaliere gave us "Groovin'," so Janis Joplin's eventual replacement in Big Brother & the Holding Company, Gravenites, and this crew pour out "Groovin' Is Easy" on this disc. It's a classy production, intellectual ideas with lots of musical changes, a subdued version of what Joplin herself would give us on *I Got Dem Ole Kozmic Blues Again, Mama* two years later, with some of that album written by vocalist Gravenites. Though launched after Al Kooper's Blues Project, *A Long Time Comin'* itself influenced bands who would go on to sell more records. In the traditional "Wine," it is proclaimed "you know Janis Joplin, she'll tell you all about that wine, baby." As good as the album is, though, the material is pretty much composed by Mike Bloomfield and Barry Goldberg, when they're not covering Howlin' Wolf's "Killing Floor" and adding spoken-word news broadcasts to the mix. More contributions by Buddy Miles and Gravenites in the songwriting department would have been welcome here. The extended CD version has four additional tracks, Bobby Hebb's "Sunny" and "Mystery," both which appear on the self-titled *Electric Flag* outing that followed this LP, as well as other material that shows up on *Old Glory: The Best of Electric Flag*, released in 2000. "Sittin' in Circles" opens like the Doors' "Riders on the Storm," the keyboards as well as the sound effects, and a hook of "hey little girl" which would resurface as the title of a Nick Gravenites tune on the aforementioned follow-up disc, where Gravenites and Miles did pick up the songwriting slack, Bloomfield having wandered off to *Super Session* with the Blues Project's Al Kooper. Amazing stuff all in all, which could eventually comprise a boxed set of experimental blues-rock from the mid- to late '60s. Either version of this recording, original vinyl or extended CD, is fun listening and a revelation. *—Joe Viglione*

The Electric Flag: An American Music Band / 1968 / One Way ♦♦♦♦

With guitarist Hoshal Wright replacing founding member Mike Bloomfield (formerly of Paul Butterfield Blues Band) and Herbie Rich taking full control of the organ (from another ex-Paul Butterfield member Barry Goldberg, along with future Lou Reed keyboardist Mike Fonfara), you have a definite sequel to the Electric Flag's March 1968 debut LP, *A Long Time Comin'*, appearing right on its heels in December of that same year. The original album had "An American Music Band" under the group's name, and that slogan becomes the subtitle of this follow-up. Janis Joplin songwriter Nick Gravenites takes the hook out of Barry Goldberg's "Sittin' in Circles" and reinvents it for "Hey, Little Girl" on this installment. Where 60 percent of the first album was written by Paul Butterfield exiles Bloomfield and Goldberg, the songwriting is pretty evenly split at two songs each by Buddy Miles, Harvey Brooks, and Nick Gravenites, with Brooks and Gravenites co-writing an additional title, "Nothing to Do." This makes for a heavier blues recording, co-produced by Brooks and *Cheap Thrills* album producer John Simon, who doubles on piano here (which he played on Janis Joplin's "Turtle Blues" on the aforementioned Big Brother & the Holding Company disc). The big revelations, though, are the cover songs, Dr. John's "Qualified" and an unbelievable version of Bobby Hebb's "Sunny," which Buddy Miles just encompasses and devours. The blending of styles is intuitive, as Hebb and Mac Rebennack, aka Dr. John, had worked together on their own. Virgil Gonsalves' flute at the end of "Sunny" is frosting on the cake, but the key is that a song that was a smash on three formats—R&B, country, and pop charts—and captured the heart of jazz musicians from Ella Fitzgerald to Pat Martino, gets this total reinvention here. As brilliant as Nick Gravenites is as a songwriter, it is Hebb's tune that is the centerpiece of this disc. That Sony would take it and Buddy Miles' "Mystery" for the CD release of the first album is the real mystery. Alto sax player Stemsy Hunter is wonderful on lead vocals for "With Time There Is Change," written by co-producer/bassist Harvey Brooks and perhaps the most captivating original here. They all trade lead vocalist duties, from Nick Gravenites on "Nothing to Do" to Herbie Rich on the Dr. John cover. It's an amazingly dense set of recordings that, years later, forms a remarkable thread of sounds by musicians who worked with Jimi Hendrix, Janis Joplin, and the latter-day Big Brother & the Holding Company, and who were taking the original concept a step further into uncharted waters. Where the Electric Prunes were a fun psychedelic moment, the neon signs superimposed over Buddy Miles' face didn't get the same immediate recognition. Many of the core players from both discs reunited in 1974 for the Atlantic records release *The Band Kept Playing*. Real textbook material here, highly enjoyable, and very important. *—Joe Viglione*

The Band Kept Playing / 1974 / Wounded Bird ♦♦♦

● **Old Glory: The Best of Electric Flag** / Oct. 1995 / Columbia/Legacy ♦♦♦♦♦

A perfect single-disc anthology of a band with what seemed like unlimited potential, but in reality limited output and few quality studio recordings that accurately reflected its combined musicianship. Like its musical cousins, Blood, Sweat & Tears, Electric Flag was one of the first bands to combine rock with big-band jazz swagger. This concept and the fact that Electric Flag contained Michael Bloomfield on electric guitar was reason enough for the band to be one of the most anticipated aggregations of the era. Yet many of the recordings show off the band's limitations like a sore thumb. A certain over-baked production and arrangement feel permeates many of the fine songs from the band's debut (*A Long Time Comin'*, included in its entirety), such as "Groovin' Is Easy" and "She Should Have Just," rendering it somewhat top-heavy. Yet, despite these moments of excess, the band could also perform modern blues-rock like no other and, for these tracks alone, *Old Glory* is worth purchasing. "Texas" and "Goin' Down Slow" (an outtake from the first album sessions) combine the group's real strengths with a supple energy that is positively beguiling. Between Buddy Miles' drumming and vocals, Bloomfield's unparalleled skill on electric guitar, Barry Goldberg's keyboards, and Nick Gravenites' songwriting and vocals lay true magic. The fact that these moments are few and far between can make the disc a bit frustrating but, when the listener gets into cuts such as the aforementioned "Texas" and "You Don't Realize," it's well worth the wait. The five songs from the post-Bloomfield version of the group are nearly disposable, but a pair of earlier, live cuts from the band's debut at the Monterey Pop Festival (with Bloomfield) save the end of the collection. Although Electric Flag was troubled, chaotic, and disorganized, *Old Glory* proves that the band was important and had positively sterling moments, despite its foibles. *—Matthew Greenwald*

Small Town Blues / Apr. 11, 2000 / Columbia River ♦♦

Small Town Blues is a budget disc of the Electric Flag from the Columbia River label. These nine tracks aren't the cream of the crop from this late-'60s American music outfit fronted by guitarist Mike Bloomfield. The album features a hodgepodge of inferior live recordings and latter-day studio work. The track listed as "I Should Have Left Her" is actually a live version of Howlin Wolf's "Killin' Floor." For those wondering what the fuss was about check out *A Long Time Comin'* on Columbia instead. *—Al Campbell*

Robert "Mojo" Elem

b. Itta Bena, MS

Vocals, Guitar, Bass / Electric Chicago Blues

When talking about deep bluesmen who are also great entertainers, the conversation will eventually get around to the coolest bassman/singer/showman the Windy City has in its blues arsenal, Big "Mojo" Elem. As a singer, he possesses a relatively high-pitched voice that alternately drips with honey and malice. As a bassist, his unique approach to the instrument makes him virtually one of a kind. Unlike most bass players, Elem seldom plays standard walking bass patterns, instead using a single-note groove that lends to any band he's a part of a decidedly juke-joint groove. And as a showman, he possesses an energy that makes other performers half his age look like they're sitting down. Born in Itta Bena, MS, Elem grew up in fertile blues territory. Originally a guitarist, he soaked up licks and ideas by observing masters like Robert Nighthawk and a young Ike Turner first-hand. By his 20th birthday he had arrived in Chicago and was almost immediately pressed into professional service playing rhythm guitar behind Arthur "Big Boy" Spires and harmonica man Lester Davenport. By 1956 Elem had switched over to the newly arrived (in Chicago) electric bass, simply to stand out from the pack of guitar players searching the clubs looking for work. He formed a band with harp player Earl Payton and signed on a young Freddie King as their lead guitarist, playing on King's very first single for the El-Bee label in late 1956. After Freddie's success made him the bandleader, Big Mojo stayed with King off and on for the next eight years. The '50s and '60s also found him doing club work—mostly on the West side—with Magic Sam, Junior Wells, Shakey Jake Harris, Jimmy Dawkins and Luther Allison with a short stint in Otis Rush's band as well. Aside from a stray anthology cut and a now out-of-print album for a tiny European label, Elem's career has not been documented in much depth, but he remains one of the liveliest players on the scene. *—Cub Koda*

- **Mojo Boogie** / 1978 / MCM ♦♦♦♦♦

Blessed with a sweet growl of a voice and grinding out a single-note groove heavier than any ZZ Top record you've got, this thing romps like nobody's business, and is the perfect showcase for Elem's hard driving, bare-bones honest singing and bass-pumping talents. Studebaker John Grimaldi plays some nice lead and even nicer slide, and blows some fine amplified harp when needed, while Twist Turner's no-frills drumming slots in nice with Mojo's bass hunch. A nice balance between old favorites and original material, most of it co-written with producer George Paulus. *—Cub Koda*

Big Chief Ellis (Wilbert Thirkield Ellis)

b. Nov. 10, 1914, Birmingham, AL, **d.** Dec. 20, 1977, Birmingham, AL

Vocals, Piano / Piano Blues

Prickly insights and sensitive accompaniment were the stock-in-trade of pianist and vocalist Wilbert Thirkield "Big Chief" Ellis. A self-taught player, Ellis performed at house parties and dances during the '20s, then left his native Alabama. He traveled extensively for several years, working mostly in non-musical jobs. After a three-year army stint from 1939-1942, Ellis settled in New York. He accompanied many blues musicians during their visits to the New York area. He started recording for Lenox in 1945, and also did sessions for Sittin' In and Capitol in the '40s and '50s, playing with Sonny Terry and Brownie McGhee for Capitol. Though Ellis reduced his performance schedule after moving from New York to Washington D.C., his career got a final boost in the early '70s. He recorded for Trix and appeared at several folk and blues festivals until his death in 1977. *—Ron Wynn*

- **Big Chief Ellis Featuring Tarheel Slim, Brownie M** / Jun. 1977 / Trix ♦♦♦♦♦

Some rare late-period blues from two very underrated New York musicians. Big Chief Ellis and Tarheel Slim weren't the greatest technical singers, but each was a fine interpreter, and that makes this late-'70s session quite instructive. *—Ron Wynn*

Tinsley Ellis

b. Jun. 4, 1957, Atlanta, GA

Vocals, Guitar / Modern Electric Blues, Blues-Rock

A hard rocking, high-voltage blues guitarist most often compared to Stevie Ray Vaughan, Tinsley Ellis is hardly one of the legions of imitators that comparison might imply. Schooled in a variety of Southern musical styles, Ellis draws not only from fiery Vaughan-style blues-rock, but also Texas bluesmen like Freddie King and Clarence "Gatemouth" Brown, the soulful blues of B.B. King, the funky grit of Memphis soul, and numerous other electric bluesmen. Ellis has been praised in many quarters for the relentless, storming intensity of his sound, and criticized in others for his relative lack of pacing and dynamic contrast (he's also been dubbed a much stronger guitarist than vocalist). Yet no matter which side of the fence one falls on, it's generally acknowledged that Ellis remains a formidable instrumentalist and a genuine student of the blues.

Tinsley Ellis was born in Atlanta in 1957, and spent most of his childhood in southern Florida. He began playing guitar in elementary school, first discovering the blues through the flagship bands of the British blues boom: John Mayall & the Bluesbreakers, the Peter Green-led Fleetwood Mac, the Yardbirds, the Rolling Stones, and so on. He soon moved on to a wide variety of original sources, becoming especially fond of B.B. King and Freddie King. After high school, Ellis moved back to Atlanta in 1975 to attend Emory University, and soon found work on the local music scene, joining a bar band called the Alley Cats (which also featured future Fabulous Thunderbird Preston Hubbard). In 1981, Ellis co-founded the Heartfixers with singer/harmonica player Chicago Bob Nelson, and they recorded an eponymous debut album for the tiny Southland imprint. They soon signed with the slightly larger Landslide and issued *Live at the Moon Shadow* in 1983, by which point they were one of the most popular live blues acts in the South. However, Nelson left the group shortly after the album's release, and Ellis took over lead vocal chores.

The Heartfixers' first project in their new incarnation was backing up blues shouter Nappy Brown on his well-received 1984 comeback album *Tore Up*. Ellis debuted his vocals on record on the Heartfixers' 1986 LP *Cool on It*, which brought him to the attention of Alligator Records. Ellis left the Heartfixers to sign with Alligator as a solo artist in 1988, and they picked up his solo debut *Georgia Blue* for distribution. The album helped make Ellis a fixture on the blues circuit, and he toured heavily behind it, establishing a hard-working pattern he would follow for most of his career. The follow-up *Fanning the Flames* appeared in 1989 and explored similar territory. 1992's *Trouble Time* helped land Ellis on album rock radio thanks to the track "Highwayman," but it was 1994's *Storm Warning* that really broke Ellis to a wider blues-rock audience, earning more media attention than any of his previous recordings; additionally, guitar prodigy Jonny Lang later covered Ellis' "A Quitter Never Wins" on *Lie to Me*. For 1997's *Fire It Up*, Ellis worked with legendary blues-rock producer Tom Dowd (the Allman Brothers, Derek & the Dominoes), as well as Booker T. & the MG's bassist Donald "Duck" Dunn. Ellis subsequently left Alligator and signed with Capricorn; unfortunately, shortly after the release of 2000's *Kingpin*, Capricorn went bankrupt, leaving the album high and dry. Still, Ellis soon caught on with Telarc, returning with *Hell or High Water* in 2002. *—Steve Huey*

Live at the Moon Shadow / 1983 / Landslide ♦♦♦

Atlanta blues/rockers Tinsley Ellis And The Heartfixers hit in concert with vocalist Chicago Bob Nelson. *—Michael G. Nastos*

Georgia Blue / 1989 / Alligator ♦♦

Like most of Tinsley Ellis' albums, *Georgia Blue* is filled with hot, blistering guitar, mediocre songs, and flat vocals. For fans of blues guitar, there's plenty to hear on the album—the licks and solos burn with a wild, uncontrolled fury. Others might find the album a little tedious, but not without virtue. *—Thom Owens*

- **Fanning of the Flames** / 1989 / Alligator ♦♦♦♦

Fanning of the Flames is an erratic but impressive set from Tinsley Ellis. While his basic sound is indebted to Stevie Ray Vaughan, the guitarist borrows from every other major blues artist. Furthermore, he has a tendency to overplay his licks, giving the album a feeling of unfocused fury. However, that sound can be overwhelming—his technique is impressive, even if he doesn't know when to reign it in. As a consequence, *Fanning of the Flames* is of interest only to guitar fans, not general listeners, but for guitar fans, there's plenty of music to treasure here. *—Thom Owens*

Cool on It / 1991 / Alligator ♦♦♦♦

High-energy roadhouse-rock and blues-rock with the Heartfixers. *—Niles J. Frantz*

Trouble Time / 1992 / Alligator ♦♦

Storm Warning / 1994 / Alligator ♦♦♦

A powerful blues guitarist and an excellent vocalist, Tinsley Ellis dominates his fourth Alligator CD as a leader. His backup band (guitarist Oliver Wood, bassist James Ferguson, drummer Stuart Gibson and occasional organist/pianist Stuart Grimes) does a fine job of inspiring the leader, while slide guitarist Derek Trucks and Albey Scholl on harmonica make notable guest appearances. While Ellis often plays quite passionately and hints at rock, he also performs an occasional quieter piece that shows his more traditional and introspective side. There is plenty of spirit on this generally rousing set. *—Scott Yanow*

Fire It Up / May 27, 1997 / Alligator ♦♦♦

With each successive album, Ellis has moved further and further away from mainstream blues grooves and closer and closer to hard rock. While his guitar playing is as explosive as ever, it also remains unfocused, the end result being soloing that never reaches a musical climax, but is nonetheless played with an unrelenting energy that music fans who like their blues with rock muscles will appreciate. Tracks like "Diggin' My Own Grave," "One Sunny Day," "Soulful," "Just Dropped In (To See What Condition My Condition Was In)," and "I Walk Alone" sound like they could be on anybody's blues-rock/roots-rock album, and even legendary producer Tom Dowd can't do much with Ellis' consistently flat and generally lifeless vocals. Only the slow blues "Are You Sorry," the soul ballad "Change Your Mind," the Buddy Guy/Junior Wells-inspired "Break My Rule," and the laidback set closer, "Everyday," reach for higher musical goals than the mundane. Someone special to look and listen for on this album is former Booker T. & the MG's bassist, Donald "Duck" Dunn. Duck appears on seven of the 12 songs, contributing simple, unobtrusive lines that speak in their own quiet way and underpin the tracks with a groove that's beyond rock-solid. This is a well played, well produced—if unexceptional—set of modern blues-rock, and fans of the genre will find much here to celebrate. *—Cub Koda*

Kingpin / Mar. 2000 / Capricorn ♦♦♦

Ellis turns in a strong set of originals and choice covers, all fueled by his usual strong guitar work. Highlights include "Dyin' to Do Wrong," "I'll Be Loving You," and "Slingshots and Boomerangs." *—Cub Koda*

Hell or High Water / Feb. 26, 2002 / Telarc ♦♦♦

Undeterred by the lukewarm response to his last Capricorn album (due to the bad timing of it being released mere weeks before the company folded in 2000), Atlanta-based blues rocker Tinsley Ellis signed with his third label, Telarc, in early 2002 and churned out another signature effort. Bolstered by his roaring guitar shooting fiery licks, gruff singing, and no-frills approach, Ellis adds a hearty R&B edge to his music. Shortening his solos (only the slow burning eight-minute "Feelin' No Pain" stretches out into epic length), the songs never feel like vehicles for Ellis' obvious six-string prowess. Instead, the Steely Dan "Pretzel Logic" riff inspired "All Rumors Are True" and the magnificent "Mystery to Me" with its genuine soul vibe and warm electric piano set up a groove and ride it. Ellis revisits his louder, cruncher past with the wailing intro to "All I Can Do" and the ZZ Top (circa mid-'70s) swirl of "Ten Year Day," a song inspired by the events of September 11, 2001. Atlanta vocalist Donna Hopkins contributes hard-hitting backing vocals worthy of Bonnie Bramlett on three tracks, further pushing these songs into soulful territory. While the "Bell Bottom Blues"-styled ballad of "Stuck in Love" is a little too reminiscent of Clapton's writing and guitar style, as is the wah-wah churning "Strange Brew"-isms of "All I Can Do," Ellis doesn't generally ape other guitarists. Rather, he concocts his own combination of Freddie King, Peter Green, and Memphis influences. The closing James Taylor-ish acoustic ballad seems out of place with the rest of the sturdy performances, such as the strutting title track, but shows a tender side to the tough, heartfelt blues and rock that dominate this engaging album. *—Hal Horowitz*

John Ellison

b. Aug. 11, 1941, Montgomery, WV

Vocals / R&B, Soul

The sky-high level of soulful intensity John Ellison brought to his lead vocals with the Soul Brothers Six came straight from the church. No surprise there, since he grew up in a religious household. But the way Ellison harnessed that sanctified passion on the group's secular sides was anything but common.

Leaving the coal mines of West Virginia for a more musically opportune Rochester, New York at age 18, Ellison sang soul and styled hair before hooking up with four brothers named Armstrong (Sam, Charles, Harry, and Moses) and bassist Vonell Benjamin. The Soul Brothers Six were a completely self-contained unit—they played their own instruments in addition to singing. Their first 45s on Fine (1965's "Move Girl") and Lyndell ("Don't Neglect Your Baby" the following year) veritably dripped gospel-soaked inspiration but went nowhere.

The sextet decided to relocate to Philadelphia. On the way there, Ellison wrote the magnificent "Some Kind of Wonderful," the song that put the group on the map. Atlantic Records issued the irresistible soul workout in 1967, and it slipped onto the pop charts (becoming their only hit). Deserving encores on Atlantic didn't recapture the 45's success, and the original lineup broke up in 1969. Ellison assembled another band by the same name and soldiered on at Phil L.A. of Soul Records during 1972-1973. Meanwhile, Grand Funk Railroad's graceless cover of "Some Kind of Wonderful" proved a gigantic pop smash in 1974.

The John Ellison story might have ended there (he's mostly been ensconced in Canada since then). But not too long ago, After Hours Records bosses Marty Duda and Gregory Townson happened upon the long-lost legend sitting in at a Rochester ginmill with bluesman Joe Beard. The upshot was a 1993 solo Ellison disc, *Welcome Back*, that reintroduced the singer to the American market. Two tracks, including a remade "Some Kind of Wonderful," even reunited the singer with the Armstrong brothers. Pretty wonderful, eh? *—Bill Dahl*

Welcome Back / 1993 / After Hours/Ichiban ♦♦♦

John Ellison was once a member of The Soul Brothers Six, a fine group who didn't score many hits, but made one unforgettable number, the anthemic "Some Kind of Wonderful." Ellison's gritty, crisp voice doesn't sound any softer or less soulful in the '90s than it did in the '60s. This includes a good, if not quite transcendent, remake of "Some Kind of Wonderful," and also contains some heartfelt ballads, a quasi-country number in "You Ain't Ready" and a couple of decent midtempo and dance-flavored tunes. The production, sensibility, and mood are vintage '60s, which will limit its appeal and possibilities, but it's good to hear John Ellison again, even if his disc is more a nod to the past than a beacon to the future. *—Ron Wynn*

● **The Very Best of John Ellison and the Soul Brothers Six** / 1995 / Forevermore ♦♦♦♦♦

Well, not quite all their best: this gospel-rooted R&B group enjoyed one real hit in 1967 for Atlantic, the glorious "Some Kind of Wonderful." Alas, a recent remake of the tune, albeit a nice one, graces this 20-track collection. The best stuff is the chronologically earliest—a previously unissued 1966 outing "(You're Gonna) Be by Yourself" and obscure mid-'60s 45s "Move Girl" and "Don't Neglect Your Baby" that soar to the heavens with rich sanctified harmonies. Ten 1972-1973 Soul Brothers Six items for Phil L.A. of Soul are also aboard, as are five items from Ellison's recent comeback disc for After Hours. *—Bill Dahl*

Missing You / Aug. 29, 2000 / Louisiana Red Hot ♦♦♦

Billy "The Kid" Emerson

b. Dec. 21, 1925, Tarpon Springs, FL

Keyboards, Organ / R&B

Slashing blues, infectious R&B, formulaic rock & roll, moving gospel—keyboardist Billy "The Kid" Emerson played all those interrelated styles during a lengthy career that began in Florida and later transported him up to Memphis and Chicago.

Emerson had already learned his way around a piano when he entered the Navy in 1943. After the war, he began playing around Tarpon Springs, attending Florida A&M during the late '40s and early '50s. He picked up his nickname while playing a joint in St. Petersburg; the club owner dressed the band up in cowboy duds that begged comparison with a certain murderous outlaw.

A 1952-1953 stint in the Air Force found Emerson stationed in Greenville, MS. That's where he met young bandleader Ike Turner, who whipped Emerson into shape as an entertainer while he sang with Turner's Kings of Rhythm. Turner also got Emerson through the door at Sun Records in 1954, playing guitar on the Kid's debut waxing "No Teasing Around."

Emerson's songwriting skills made him a valuable commodity around Sun—but more as a source for other performers' material later on. His bluesy 1955 outing "When It Rains It Pours" elicited a cover from Elvis a few years later at RCA, while Emerson's "Red Hot" (a takeoff on an old cheerleaders chant from Emerson's school days) became a savage rockabilly anthem revived by Billy Lee Riley for Sun and Bob Luman on Imperial.

After his "Little Fine Healthy Thing" failed to sell, Emerson exited Sun to sign with Chicago's Vee-Jay Records in late 1955. Despite first-rate offerings such as the jumping "Every Woman I Know (Crazy 'Bout Automobiles)" and a sophisticated "Don't Start Me to Lying," national recognition eluded Emerson at Vee-Jay too.

It was on to Chess in 1958, recording "Holy Mackerel Baby" and the unusual novelty "Woodchuck" (a remake of an earlier Sun single) during his year or so there. 45s for Mad, USA, M-Pac! (where he waxed the dance workout "The Whip"), and Constellation preceded the formation of Emerson's own logo, Tarpon, in 1966. In addition to Emerson's own stuff, Tarpon issued Denise LaSalle's debut single.

A prolific writer, Emerson penned songs for Junior Wells, Willie Mabon, Wynonie Harris, and Buddy Guy during the early '60s, often in conjunction with Willie Dixon. When recording opportunities slowed, Emerson played jazzy R&B in lounges and supper clubs (guitarist Lacy Gibson was a member of his trio for a while). Emerson took Europe by surprise with a dynamic segment on the American Blues Legends 1979 tour. More recently, he's rumored to have reverted to playing gospel in his native state of Florida. *—Bill Dahl*

Little Healthy Thing / 1980 / Charly ♦♦♦♦♦

Since no CD reissues are easily accessible by this important Florida-born R&B pianist, this vinyl compendium of his 1954-1955 Sun catalog will have to suffice for now. Emerson's jumping proto-rock style at Sun supplied notable rockabillies with killer material—"Red Hot," as first cut by Emerson, was later done full justice by Billy Lee Riley, while Elvis found the hip-grinding "When It Rains It Pours" to his liking. Emerson's bluesy "No Teasing Around" (with Ike Turner on guitar) and the upbeat "Something for Nothing" and the title cut are among the many highlights of this enjoyable LP. *—Bill Dahl*

Crazy 'Bout Automobiles / 1982 / Charly ♦♦♦♦

Another vinyl-only collection, this one a ten-incher with only ten songs, covering Emerson's 1955-1957 stay at Chicago's Vee-Jay label. Emerson bonded well with Vee-Jay's house bands, especially on the romping "Every Woman I Know (Crazy 'Bout Automobiles)" and a sophisticated "Don't Start Me to Lying." As with his Sun Stuff, the big-voiced Emerson was a captivating performer. *—Bill Dahl*

● **Move Baby Move** / Jul. 1, 1999 / Charly ♦♦♦♦♦

This features 27 tracks from Billy's stays at both Sun and Vee-Jay Records in the '50s, pretty much covering the major portion of his recording career. The early Sun sides feature Ike Turner on blazing lead guitar with his Kings of Rhythm band in fine support on tracks like "If Lovin' Is Believin'," "No Teasin' Around," "I'm Not Going Home," "The Woodchuck" and the previously unissued "Hey Little Girl" and "When My Baby Quit Me." Elven Parr's In The Groove Boys provide the backing for the classic "When It Rains It Pours," "Move Baby Move" and "Shim Sham Shimmy," while a combo led by Phineas Newborn provides the backdrop for "No Greater Love" and Emerson's classic "Red Hot," heard here in a delightful alternate take that nonetheless keeps this set for being complete. Three unissued Sun tracks include "Satisfied" plus alternate takes of "No Greater Love" and the similarly titled but differently structured "When My Baby Quit Me." The following ten tracks all come from Emerson's stay at Vee-Jay starting in 1957 and include "Every Woman I Know (Crazy 'Bout Automobiles)," "Don't Start Me to Lying," "Do the Chicken" and "You Never Miss Your Water" as highlights. Although you'll have to look elsewhere for the issued take of his most famous song, this otherwise is the definitive Billy "The Kid" Emerson collection and a marvelous introduction to this artist. *—Cub Koda*

Sleepy John Estes

b. Jan. 25, 1899, Ripley, TN, **d.** Jun. 5, 1977, Brownsville, TN

Vocals, Guitar / Prewar Blues, Blues Revival, Memphis Blues, Prewar Country Blues, Country Blues

Big Bill Broonzy called John Estes' style of singing "crying" the blues because of its overt emotional quality. Actually his vocal style harks back to his tenure as a work-gang leader for a railroad maintenance crew, where his vocal improvisations and keen, cutting voice set the pace for work activities. Nicknamed "Sleepy" John Estes, supposedly because of his ability to sleep standing up, he teamed with mandolinist Yank Rachell and harmonica player Hammie Nixon to play the houseparty circuit in and around Brownsville in the early '20s. Forty years later, the same team reunited to record for Delmark and play the festival circuit. Never an outstanding guitarist, Estes relied on his expressive voice to carry his music, and the recordings he made from 1929 on have enormous appeal and remain remarkably accessible today.

Despite the fact that he worked to mixed Black and White audiences in string band, jug band, or medicine show format, his music retains a distinct ethnicity and has a particularly plaintive sound. Astonishingly, he recorded during six decades for Victor, Decca, Bluebird, Ora Nelle, Sun, Delmark, and others. Over the course of his career, his music remained simple yet powerful, and despite his sojourns to Memphis or Chicago he retained a traditional down-home sound. Some of his songs are deeply personal statements about his community and life, such as "Lawyer Clark" or "Floating Bridge." Other compositions have universal appeal ("Drop Down Mama" or "Someday Baby") and went on to become mainstays in the repertoires of countless musicians. One of the true masters of his idiom, he lived in poverty, yet was somehow capable of turning his experiences and the conditions of his life into compelling art. *—Barry Lee Pearson*

The Legend of Sleepy John Estes / 1962 / Delmark ♦♦♦♦

In the late '50s Sleepy John Estes wasn't nearly as visible as he had been before and during World War II—in fact, he had become so obscure that some historians wondered if he had died. But the blues veteran was still very much alive, and in 1962 a 63-year-old Estes (some claimed he was 58 or 57) made an impressive comeback with *The Legend of Sleepy John Estes*. Produced by Delmark president Bob Koester on March 24, 1962, this historic acoustic session finds singer/guitarist Estes joined by Ed Wilkinson on bass, John "Knocky" Parker on piano, and long-time ally Hammie Nixon on harmonica. *Legend* isn't much different from Estes' recordings of the '20s, '30s, and '40s, and the Tennessee native successfully revisits old favorites like "Divin' Duck Blues," "Someday Baby Blues," "Stop That Thing," "Milk Cow Blues," and "Married Woman Blues." Although not the definitive recordings of these songs, Estes' 1962 versions are captivating nonetheless. Delmark has a lot to be proud of, and getting Estes back into the studio after many years of neglect (reunited with Hammie Nixon, no less!) is certainly among the Chicago indie's greatest accomplishments. *—Alex Henderson*

Broke and Hungry / 1963 / Delmark ♦♦♦

Nothing on this set rivals his best '60s-era recordings for the Delmark label (those can be found on *The Legend of Sleepy John Estes*), but this album is still worthwhile. Estes is joined by the most sympathetic accompanists he would ever know: Hammie Nixon on harmonica and Yank Rachell on mandolin and second guitar. Michael Bloomfield, then a fiery young guitarist just appearing on the Chicago scene, joins in on a few tunes, too. But not even his presence can rouse the somnolent Estes. *—Brian Beatty*

In Europe / 1966 / Delmark ♦♦♦♦

Having only sporadically left his rural hamlet of Brownsville, TN, for recording trips in Chicago and Memphis, blues guitarist and singer Sleepy John Estes must have found it a bit of a shock to make the 1964 American Folk-Blues Festival tour of Europe. Like most contemporary country blues musicians from the South, Estes did ramble, playing country suppers and plantation parties as a solo act or with a minstrel show, but his exposure to the urban and transatlantic world was still minimal to nonexistent. As evidenced by both reportage and this document of his 1964 trip to Denmark, France, Sweden, Germany, and England, though, Estes mostly enjoyed his first trip abroad, having fun with his international hosts while still living up to his nickname by mysteriously nodding off on several occasions. Traveling with other blues luminaries such as Howlin' Wolf and Sonny Boy Williamson, Estes teamed up with longtime harmonica partner Hammie Nixon (who also plays the jug on a few tunes here) to cut a batch of numbers at studios in Copenhagen and London. The two cover classic Estes material like "Needmore Blues" and "Drop Down Mama" (most of the material here was originally recorded for Decca during the '30s), as well as newer cuts like "Denmark Blues." In fact, throughout the album, Estes updates many of the old songs with references to cities visited and friends made along the tour route. And while Estes' sinuously grainy voice and furtive guitar strumming perfectly reflect the kaleidoscopic nature of the trip, Hammie Nixon's high-lonesome harmonica makes light of the homesickness the two musicians reportedly felt. A great disc that's best heard after first checking out Estes' classic Decca sides. —*Stephen Cook*

Electric Sleep / 1966 / Delmark ♦♦♦
To a country blues purist, asking Sleepy John Estes to record an album of electric Chicago blues is an act of blasphemy. So imagine the reaction of such elitists when, in 1968, Delmark president Bob Koester united the Tennessee bluesman with an electric-oriented Chicago blues band that included Jimmy Dawkins on electric guitar, Sunnyland Slim on piano, Carey Bell on harmonica, and Earl Hooker or Joe Harper on electric bass. Purists were appalled, and they had no kind words for the resulting album, *Electric Sleep*. But if they hadn't been so close-minded, they would have realized that this is a decent album, if an uneven and unremarkable one. While Estes' vocal style is pretty much the same, the band is pure Chicago blues—and when you think it, the combination makes perfect sense. Chicago's electric blues were a logical extension of southern country blues, just as rock & roll, soul, and funk were a logical extension of electric Chicago blues and jump blues (and just as hip-hop is a logical extension of funk and soul). Hearing a 69-year-old Estes backed by Chicago bluesmen like Dawkins and Hooker offended purists, but *Electric Sleep* (which was reissued on CD in 1991) is nothing for Delmark to be ashamed of. Although not among Estes' essential recordings, *Electric Sleep* is an interesting footnote in his long career. —*Alex Henderson*

1929–1940 / 1967 / Smithsonian/Folkways ♦♦♦♦♦
Sleepy John Estes' finest period vocally was the prewar era. This LP includes several expressive and delightful numbers in which Estes' narrative skills are especially strong. He was never a great guitarist, but the accompaniment works here because it's sparse and limited. —*Ron Wynn*

Brownsville Blues / 1969 / Delmark ♦♦♦♦
Not to be confused with the *Brownsville Blues* session that Sleepy John Estes recorded for Delmark in the '60s, this *Brownsville Blues* is an Austrian release that focuses on the Tennessee bluesman's early recordings for Victor, Decca and RCA/Bluebird. Many blues experts will tell you that Estes did his most essential work before World War II, and they speak the truth. The Tennessee country blues don't get any richer than the 23 selections on this CD, which span 1929-1941 and boast Estes' definitive versions of classics like "Divin' Duck Blues," "Milk Cow Blues," "Married Woman Blues," and "Brownsville Blues." Equally valuable is 1935's "Someday Baby Blues," the gem that became the basis for Big Maceo Merriweather's famous "Worried Life Blues." On these essential recordings, Estes' acoustic guitar playing isn't fantastic—competent, although not fantastic. But then, one doesn't have to have killer chops to create meaningful music. While Estes was never a great guitarist, he was a compelling storyteller and a most expressive vocalist—and those qualities make *Brownsville Blues* a joy to listen to. For those who don't own any Estes albums and are looking for a single-CD collection of his most essential work, *Brownsville Blues* would be an excellent choice. —*Alex Henderson*

Jazz Heritage—Down South Blues (1935–1940) / 1970 / MCA ♦♦♦
Part of an '80s MCA budget blues series, this album includes "Drop Down Mama" and "Someday Baby." With Hammie Nixon on harmonica. —*Barry Lee Pearson*

Complete Works, Vol. 1 (1929–1937) / 1990 / Document ♦♦♦♦♦
For those with enough interest, Document's *Complete Works, Vol. 1 (1929-1937)* is invaluable, offering an exhaustive overview of Sleepy John Estes' early recordings. The early to mid-'30s were the most fruitful years of Estes' long career, during which he recorded most of the best songs of his career: "The Girl I Love, She Got Long Curly Hair," "Someday Baby Blues," "Milk Cow Blues," "Drop Down Mama," and "Down South Blues." Of course, these are all available on *I Ain't Gonna Be Worried No More 1929-1941*, along with a more regimented set of classic performances from the late '30s. All of which leaves *Complete Works, Vol. 1 (1929-1937)* as a mixed blessing, more intriguing and important for serious fans than those simply wishing to get a taste of what made Sleepy John Estes great. —*Thom Owens*

Complete Works, Vol. 2 (1937–1941) / 1990 / Document ♦♦♦♦
The second half of Document's two-part series covering the early recordings of Sleepy John Estes includes a few excellent performances, though it isn't quite as interesting as the first. The only real classics on tap are "Floating Bridge" and "Everybody Oughta Make a Change," which leaves the rest of this lengthy compilation a mixed blessing for any but the most dedicated of listeners. —*Thom Owens*

★ **I Ain't Gonna Be Worried No More 1929–1941** / 1992 / Yazoo ♦♦♦♦♦
I Ain't Gonna Be Worried No More compiles 23 songs Sleepy John Estes recorded between 1929 and 1941, capturing the bluesman at the height of his creative powers. Unlike many Delta bluesmen of his era, Estes worked with a full jug band, which gave his music a greater variety of textures. His music swings, with a loose, relaxed feel that isn't heard on many Delta blues records. Furthermore, his songs are inventive, featuring pseudo-autobiographical lyrics loaded with evocative imagery. Nearly all of his best material is included on *I Ain't Gonna Be Worried No More*, making it as close to a definitive retrospective of Estes' music as possible. —*Thom Owens*

Goin' to Brownsville / Feb. 24, 1998 / Testament ♦♦♦
Sleepy John Estes never really changed or altered his style during the 50-year period he recorded. The records he made for Victor in the '20s didn't sound much different than the ones he made in the late '60s and '70s for various collector's labels. This collection features 21 previously unissued solo performances from 1962 capped with a lengthy interview with Sleepy John conducted by producer Pete Welding. Estes is in fine form throughout, particularly effective on "Lost My Eyesight," "Run Around," "Floating Bridge," "Vernita's Blues" and Big Bill Broonzy's "It Was a Dream." In the 18-minute interview that closes this disc, Estes discusses making records for Decca, Victor, and other labels, coming to Chicago, and losing his eyesight. Compelling music and even more compelling conversation, all of it loaded with realism and ambience galore. —*Cub Koda*

Blues Live / Jan. 11, 2000 / Storyville ♦♦♦♦
In Europe, blues fans can be an extremely devoted bunch—many of the European blues fans are as knowledgeable as the most obsessive. So when a country blues legend like Sleepy John Estes performed at the Folk Club of Denmark during the '60s, you can be sure that the Danish blues lovers in the audience were savoring his every word. (Many Danes speak English fluently). This 2000 CD, which is a reissue of an old Storyville LP, focuses on '60s Folk Club performances by two Tennessee country blues singers/acoustic guitarists: the legendary Estes and the lesser-known John Henry Barbee. If Estes was a major-league player in the Tennessee rural blues field, Barbee was minor-league—however, calling Barbee a minor-league player isn't saying that his performances weren't enjoyable. In fact, Barbee's set (which includes performances of Elmore James' "Dust My Broom" and Arthur "Big Boy" Crudup's "That's All Right") is pleasing and memorable. Nonetheless, Estes' set is the main reason to acquire this CD. Forming a duo with his partner Hammie Nixon (who is heard on harmonica and jug), Estes is in fine form on "Diving Duck Blues," "I'd Been Well Warned," "Mountain Cat Blues," and other compelling originals. Although not quite essential, this is a rewarding reissue that's worth adding to your collection if you're a serious fan of Tennessee country blues. —*Alex Henderson*

Newport Blues / May 28, 2002 / Delmark ♦♦♦

The Legendary 1928–1930 Recordings / Jun. 11, 2002 / JSP ♦♦♦♦

The Fabulous Thunderbirds

f. 1974, Austin, TX

Group / Modern Electric Texas Blues, Electric Texas Blues, Blues-Rock, Rock & Roll
With their fusion of blues, rock & roll, and R&B, the Fabulous Thunderbirds helped popularize roadhouse Texas blues with a mass audience in the '80s and, in the process, they helped kick-start a blues revival during the mid-'80s. During their heyday in the early '80s, they were the most popular attraction on the blues bar circuit, which eventually led to a breakthrough to the pop audience in 1986 with their fifth album, *Tuff Enuff.* The mass success didn't last too long, and founding member Jimmie Vaughan left in 1990, but the Fabulous Thunderbirds remained one of the most popular blues concert acts in America during the '90s.

Guitarist Jimmie Vaughan formed the Fabulous Thunderbirds with vocalist/harpist Kim Wilson in 1974; in addition to Vaughan and Wilson, the band's original lineup included bassist Keith Ferguson and drummer Mike Buck. Initially, the group also featured vocalist Lou Ann Barton, but she left the band shortly after its formation. Within a few years, the Thunderbirds became the house band for the Austin club Antone's, where they would play regular sets and support touring blues musicians. By the end of the decade, they had built a strong fan base, which led to a record contract with the local Takoma Records.

In 1979, the Fabulous Thunderbirds released their eponymous debut on Takoma. The record was successful enough to attract the attention of major labels and Chrysalis signed the band the following year. *What's the Word*, the group's second album, was released in 1980 and it was followed in 1981 by *Butt Rockin'.* By the time the Thunderbirds recorded their 1982 album *T-Bird Rhythm*, drummer Mike Buck was replaced by Fran Christina, a former member of Roomful of Blues.

Although the Fabulous Thunderbirds had become favorites of fellow musicians—they opened shows for the Rolling Stones and Eric Clapton—and had been critically well-received, their records didn't sell particularly well. Chrysalis dropped the band following the release of *T-Bird Rhythm*, leaving the band without a record contract for four years. While they were in limbo, they continued to play concerts across the country. During this time, bassist Keith Ferguson left the band and was replaced by Preston Hubbard, another former member of Roomful of Blues. In 1985, they finally landed another record contract, signing with Epic/Associated.

After the deal with Epic/Associated was complete, the T-Birds entered a London studio and recorded their fifth album with producer Dave Edmunds. The resulting album, *Tuff Enuff*, was released in the spring of 1986 and, unexpectedly, became a major crossover success. The title track was released as a single and its accompanying video received heavy play on MTV, which helped the song reach the American Top Ten. The success of the single sent the album to number 13 on the charts; *Tuff Enuff* would eventually receive a platinum record. "Wrap It Up," a cover of an old Sam & Dave song, was the album's second single and it became a Top Ten album rock track. Later in 1986, the T-Birds won the W.C. Handy Award for best blues band.

The Fabulous Thunderbirds' follow-up to *Tuff Enuff*, *Hot Number*, arrived in the summer of 1987. Initially, the album did fairly well—peaking at number 49 on the charts and spawning the Top Ten album rock hit "Stand Back"—but it quickly fell off the charts. Furthermore, its slick, radio-ready sound alienated their hardcore following of blues fans. "Powerful Stuff," a single from the soundtrack of the Tom Cruise film *Cocktail*, became a number-three-album rock hit in the summer of 1988. It was included on the following year's *Powerful Stuff* album, which proved to be a major commercial disappointment—it only spent seven weeks on the charts.

After the two poorly received follow-ups to *Tuff Enuff*, Jimmie Vaughan left the band to play in a duo with his brother, Stevie Ray Vaughan; following Stevie Ray's death in the summer of 1990, Jimmie pursued a full-time solo career. The Fabulous Thunderbirds replaced Vaughan with two guitarists, Duke Robillard and Kid Bangham. The first album from the new lineup, *Walk That Walk, Talk That Talk*, appeared in 1991. Following the release of *Walk That Walk, Talk That Talk*, Epic/Associated dropped the Fabulous Thunderbirds from their roster.

During the early '90s, the Fabulous Thunderbirds were in limbo, as Kim Wilson recorded a pair of solo albums—*Tigerman* (1993) and *That's Life* (1994). Wilson re-assembled the band in late 1994 and the band recorded their ninth album, *Roll of the Dice*, which was released on Private Music in 1995. Following its release, the band returned to actively touring the United States. —*Stephen Thomas Erlewine*

The Fabulous Thunderbirds / 1979 / Chrysalis ✦✦✦✦✦

Their debut album, with the original lineup of Wilson, Vaughn, Buck, and Ferguson stompin' through a roadhouse set of covers and genre-worthy originals. One of the few white blues albums that works. —*Cub Koda*

What's the Word / 1980 / Benchmark ✦✦✦✦✦

Second album, equally powerful. Some of their best, including the off-kilter "Los Fabulosos Thunderbirds" and "Running Shoes." The 2000 CD reissue on Benchmark adds three bonus tracks, one of them the aforementioned "Los Fabulosos Thunderbirds," the other two recorded live in an Austin, TX, bar. —*Cub Koda*

Butt Rockin' / 1981 / Benchmark ✦✦✦✦

As with most bands who reach back into styles more than a couple of decades old for their chief inspirations, the limitations of the Fabulous Thunderbirds' approach were becoming apparent by this, their third album. Granted they were still more competent and enthusiastic at their specialty than most of their competition, and they did expand their recorded sound a bit by using some members of Roomful of Blues on sax and piano. Ultimately, though, it's an average if well-done set of roots rock with strong echoes of the blues, New Orleans R&B, and swamp pop. The program's split between Kim Wilson originals (one of which, "One's Too Many," was co-written with Nick Lowe) and covers, including an unpredictable version of "Cherry Pink and Apple Blossom White." Actually the highlight is the instrumental "In Orbit," which features excellent Little Walter-styled harmonica by Wilson. The 2000 CD reissue on Benchmark adds liner notes by producer Denny Bruce and three bonus tracks, although no details about the extra cuts are provided. —*Richie Unterberger*

T-Bird Rhythm / 1982 / Benchmark ✦✦✦✦

After using manager Denny Bruce as producer for their first three albums, the Fabulous Thunderbirds tapped Nick Lowe for their fourth outing, *T-Bird Rhythm*. It was more of the same stew of rock, blues, R&B, and lowdown swamp music for which the early Thunderbirds were known. That was a good thing for anyone just in love with the sound and who wanted more. Those for whom one Thunderbirds album is good but enough, however, might not have seen much point to investing in another similar recording. Whatever the case, *T-Bird Rhythm* is solid, though not innovative, with the usual roots sounds that alternate between Kim Wilson originals and well-chosen covers of obscure non-hit oldies. The 2000 CD reissue on Benchmark adds historical liner notes. —*Richie Unterberger*

Tuff Enuff / 1986 / Epic Associated ✦✦✦

Their breakthrough success. The title track and soul covers point the band in a new, more mainstream direction. —*Cub Koda*

Hot Number / 1987 / Epic Associated ✦✦

Powerful Stuff / 1989 / Epic Associated ✦✦

Like the previous *Hot Number*, *Powerful Stuff* is a weak collection of watered-down blues-rock that makes too many concessions to the commerical constraints of AOR radio stations. Occasionally, the band works up some energy or Jimmie Vaughan or Kim Wilson turn out a good solo, but for the most part, *Powerful Stuff* is bland, faceless mainstream rock & roll. —*Thom Owens*

The Essential / Jun. 18, 1991 / Chrysalis ✦✦✦✦

Nice compilation of the early Chrysalis albums on one CD. —*Cub Koda*

Walk That Walk, Talk That Talk / Dec. 1991 / Epic Associated ✦✦✦

Walk That Walk, Talk That Talk is the first album the Fabulous Thunderbirds recorded without Jimmie Vaughan. It takes two guitarists—two good guitarists, by the way—to fill his place and even with Duke Robillard and Kid Bangham on board, there is something missing. Though the T-birds have returned to straight-ahead blues-rock, abandoning the overly commercial production of their previous three albums, they don't sound as distinctive as the did with Vaughan. Kim Wilson blows some good harp, Robillard throws out a few stellar solos and Bangham can almost keep up with him, but on the whole, the album is a disappointment. —*Thom Owens*

● Hot Stuff: The Greatest Hits / Aug. 25, 1992 / Epic Associated ✦✦✦✦✦

The best tracks from the Fabulous Thunderbirds' more rock-oriented years at CBS Associated Records are collected on this single-disc compilation. —*Stephen Thomas Erlewine*

Roll of the Dice / Aug. 1, 1995 / Private Music ✦✦✦

The Fabulous T-Birds' second album without Jimmie Vaughan is an improvement over *Walk That Walk, Talk That Talk*, featuring a tighter, more focused band and hotter playing. Nevertheless, the band takes a couple of missteps, particularly with a limp version of "Zip-a-Dee-Doo-Dah." —*Stephen Thomas Erlewine*

Different Tacos / 1996 / Country Town Music ✦✦✦

For Fabulous Thunderbirds fanatics, or anyone longing for the raw gutbucket blues-rock of their early recordings, *Different Tacos* is something of a godsend. Essentially, the disc is a rarities collection, boasting nine outtakes from their first four studio albums, a couple of live cuts from various U.K. tours, and a nearly complete set from an Austin club gig in the late '70s. Each track is straightforward, take-no-prisoners Texas blues, played with astonishing fervor and grit. There are alternate takes and live versions of familiar T-Birds items, plus covers and songs that were reworked or abandoned for the original albums. Certainly, the nature of this live and rarities set makes *Different Tacos* primarily of interest to hardcore fans, but those fans will find it a most welcome addition to their Thunderbirds collection. —*Stephen Thomas Erlewine*

Best of the Fabulous Thunderbirds / 1997 / EMI ◆◆◆◆

The Best of the Fabulous Thunderbirds is a terrific 22-track U.K. collection hitting all the highlights of the group's first four albums and offering a nearly flawless overview of the band's bluesiest period. —*Stephen Thomas Erlewine*

High Water / Aug. 12, 1997 / High Street ◆◆

Although credited to the Fabulous Thunderbirds, *High Water* was written and performed by bandleader Kim Wilson with guitarist Danny Kortchmar and percussionist Steve Jordan, who produced the album, and it does not feature the rest of the current T-Birds lineup, which, in any case, has long since devolved into a backup band for Wilson. Kortchmar and Jordan are not exactly authentic bluesmen, of course, but instead high-priced sessionmen, and they provide a tightly arranged, somewhat antiseptic accompaniment to Wilson, whose vocals and harmonica playing are the focus. Longtime fans may miss the prominent guitar work and band feel that characterized earlier releases. —*William Ruhlmann*

Girls Go Wild / 2000 / Benchmark ◆◆◆◆◆

Although there was no Fabulous Thunderbirds album by the name of *Girls Go Wild* prior to this 2000 release, this is actually a repackaged version of their self-titled 1979 debut. It has all of the songs from *The Fabulous Thunderbirds*, in the same sequence, but adds three bonus tracks, as well as liner notes by producer Denny Bruce. Why the title change? Well, because the lettering "Girls Go Wild" was so prominent on the cover, it became unofficially known as their "*Girls Go Wild*" album, and for this reissue, the title change is official. At any rate, it's still the group at their early bluesy best. No hard info about the bonus cuts though, except that all three, oddly, were recorded *after* drummer Fran Christina (who did not play on the debut album) joined. One of those bonus songs, "Things I Forgot to Do," is an outtake from the band's third album, *Butt Rockin'*, and features members of Roomful of Blues. —*Richie Unterberger*

Live / Oct. 9, 2001 / CMC International ◆◆◆

Like spiritually similar brethren George Thorogood (only with a Tex-Mex flair, natch), the Thunderbirds have released a live disc on the CMC imprint. This appropriately monikered *Live* does a fine job of displaying the hits, namely "Wrap It Up" and "Tuff Enuff," and that alone would make it a decent primer for the band, though purists would no doubt be able to find one or a dozen missing gems from the band's vast catalog. Gearheads will appreciate the modern technology used to capture the band's set—this is outlined nicely in the liner notes, though those same liner notes refer to the disc as *This Night in L.A.*, which is bound to create confusion. —*Brian O'Neill*

The Fairfield Four

f. Nashville, TN
Group / Hymns, Traditional Gospel, Southern Gospel, Black Gospel

During the '40s, the Fairfield Four were among the top-ranked gospel quartets, along with the Dixie Hummingbirds, Five Blind Boys, and Soul Stirrers. Originally a gospel duet created in the early '20s by the pastor of Fairfield Baptist Church in Nashville to occupy his sons, Harry and Rufus Carrethers, they became a gospel trio with the addition of John Battle. The group was transformed into a jubilee quartet by the '30s and began the first of numerous personnel changes. They recorded for RCA Victor and Columbia during the decade and were known for their reinterpretations of standard hymns, featuring bright, close baritone and tenor harmonies. When the Fairfield Four sang, they utilized the full extent of their voices, moving easily from deep, rolling basslines to the staccato upper peaks of the tenor range, all executed with precise, intricate harmonies and ever-shifting leads.

The Fairfield Four reached their broadest audience when the Sunway Vitamin Company sponsored a nationally broadcast radio show for them daily at 6:45 a.m. on WLAC, Nashville. At the same time, they also continued touring; it was a grueling schedule, especially with the drive to Nashville, and often the group would be missing a member or two on the show. In 1942, the quartet recorded for the Library of Congress, but by 1950, it all became too much. Coupled with some financial trouble and a dwindling radio audience, the Fairfield Four broke up, though one member, Reverend Sam McCrary, used the group name to perform with other quartets. In 1980, the Fairfield Four from the '40s was reunited for a concert in Birmingham, Alabama, by black gospel specialist Doug Seroff. In 1989, they were designated as National Heritage Fellows by the National Endowment for the Arts. They continue to perform, though the original members are either deceased or retired. —*Sandra Brennan & Bil Carpenter*

The Famous Fairfield Four / 1960 / Old Town ◆◆◆◆

More fine singing recorded at the RCA Studios. —*Opal Louis Nations*

One Religion / 1980 / Nashboro ◆◆◆

★ **Angels Watching Over Me** / 1981 / P-Vine ◆◆◆◆◆

Angels Watching Over Me is a remarkable collection of classic material the Fairfield Four recorded in the early '50s. Each of the 26 tracks are performed a cappella, yet there's a lot of variety within the music, since the quartet positioned themselves between the classic sound of gospel choirs and the bluesier, harder-edged sound of small vocal combos. The results are stunning and moving, making *Angels Watching Over Me* an essential addition to any serious gospel library. —*Leo Stanley*

Standing in the Safety Zone / 1992 / Warner Brothers ◆◆◆◆◆

The Fairfield Four were once among the finest hard gospel ensembles around. Unfortunately, they didn't stay together as long as their comrades, disbanding in 1950 due to business problems. They reunited 30 years later, then received a National Heritage Fellowship award in 1989. This wonderful 1992 release features awesome harmonies, a guest appearance from The Nashville Bluegrass Band on "Roll, Jordan Roll," and soaring, magnificent lead vocals from Walter Settles, Isaac Freeman, and W.L. Richardson. Old-time gospel at its best, vividly presented via contemporary technology. —*Ron Wynn*

Standing on the Rock / 1995 / Nashboro ◆◆◆◆

Essential recordings of this leading influential quartet. Dot and Bullet sides. —*Opal Louis Nations*

I Couldn't Hear Nobody Pray / Sep. 9, 1997 / Warner Brothers ◆◆◆◆◆

Around the time of this album's release, the Fairfield Four reached a new peak in mainstream visibility, complete with an appearance backing Elvis Costello on *The David Letterman Show*. Elvis Costello-led cut ("That Day Is Done") appears here, and there are odd guest appearances by country singer Pam Tillis and Prairie Home Companion narrator Garrison Keillor. But the focus is usually on the singers, who perform a cappella on most of the cuts. They sing full-bodied vocal arrangements with dignified conviction; the low parts are especially vibrant. —*Richie Unterberger*

Wreckin' the House (Live at Mt. Hope) / Jul. 7, 1998 / Dead Reckoning ◆◆◆◆

Amazingly, *Wreckin' the House* is the first live recording released by the Fairfield Four over the course of a career going back to the '20s. A document of their 1989 reunion tour, it captures the group in fine form—their a cappella performances are lively, and their harmonies are impeccable as ever. —*Jason Ankeny*

● **Best of the Fairfield Four** / May 16, 2000 / MCA International ◆◆◆◆

The Bells Are Tolling / Nov. 27, 2000 / Ace ◆◆◆◆

This 1962 LP was actually made in 1960, and was the first time the group recorded with a rhythm section. At this point, the Fairfield Four's ever-changing lineup was comprised of Henry Brown, David Aaron, Willie Williams, and Joseph Henderson. At least, that's what the liner notes on the original LP say; according to the liner notes of the 2000 CD reissue on Ace, most of the leads are taken by Clarence Mills and the Reverend Sam McCrary. Bass singer Henderson, who also played guitar, was in fact the Joe Henderson who would have a Top Ten pop hit in 1962 with "Snap Your Fingers." Regardless of who sang what, *The Bells Are Tolling* is a good gospel record with some trumpet-swallowing leads, particularly on "Don't Let Nobody Turn You Around." Not many copies were pressed the first time around, and although it was reissued in 1973 as *The Famous Fairfield Four With Rev. Samuel McCrary*, it took the 2000 Ace CD reissue to make this album easy to find. —*Richie Unterberger*

Family

f. 1967, Leicester, England, **db.** 1973
Group / British Psychedelia, Prog-Rock/Art Rock, Blues-Rock

A blues-based band with art-rock inclinations, Family was one of the more interesting groups of hippie-era Britain. Fronted by the deft and frequently excellent guitar playing of John "Charlie" Whitney and the raspy, whisky-and-cigarette voice of Roger Chapman, Family was much loved in England and Europe but barely achieved cult status in America. While bands like Jethro Tull, Ten Years After, and the Keith Emerson-led Nice (and later Emerson, Lake, and Palmer) sold lots of records, Family, which frequently toured with these bands, was left in the shadows, an odd band loved by a small but rabid group of fans.

Although the band's first official release was *Music in a Doll's House* in 1968, the roots of the band go back as far as the early '60s, when Whitney started a rhythm & blues/soul band called the Farinas while at college. In 1966, Whitney met Roger Chapman, a prematurely balding singer who had a voice so powerful that, to quote Robert Christgau, "it could kill small game at a hundred yards," and the two began a creative partnership that would last through two bands and into the early '80s. With Whitney and Chapman leading the way, Family became whole with the addition of bassist Rick Grech, saxophonist Jim King, and drummer Rob Townsend. Within a year they were hyped as the next big thing, and under that pressure and intense British pop press scrutiny delivered their debut record in 1968, *Music in a Doll's House*. *Doll's House* is pop music redolent of the zeitgeist: Chapman's voice is rooted in the blues and R&B, but the record is loaded with strings, mellotrons, acoustic guitars, horns, essentially all the trappings of post-psychedelia and early art rock. Almost completely ignored in the states, *Doll's House* was a hit in Britain and Family began a string of less art-rock, more hard rock albums that ended, as did the band, with the release of *It's Only a Movie* in 1973.

After Family's demise, Whitney and Chapman formed the blues-rock Streetwalkers; other Family members (of which there were quite a few in the band's tempestuous eight years) such as John Wetton (King Crimson, Asia) and Jim Cregan (Rod Stewart) went off to find fame and fortune elsewhere. Trivia buffs note: it was Rick Grech who was the first to leave Family in 1969 to become the least well-known member of supergroup Blind Faith. Sadly, that proved to be Grech's biggest mistake, as Blind Faith imploded in a year, and Grech (whose last notable band membership was in Traffic), long plagued by drinking problems, died of liver failure in 1990. Charlie Whitney went on to play in an extremely low-key country/blues/bluegrass band called Los Rackateeros, and Roger Chapman lives in Germany, where his solo career is flourishing. A fine, occasionally great band, Family deserved more recognition (at least in America) than they received. Something that a thoughtfully compiled CD retrospective might rectify. —*John Dougan*

● **Music in a Doll's House** / 1968 / See for Miles ◆◆◆◆◆

Not the greatest psychedelic record ever made, but a damn fine one. *Doll's House* is dripping with pretension, but that doesn't make it a bad record, rather a record that reflects its time. Chapman's voice, booming and bellowing one moment, quiet and understated the next, is a revelation, as is Charlie Whitney's deft guitar playing and songwriting. As early British hippie rock goes, this is a record well worth having. —*John Dougan*

Family Entertainment / 1969 / See for Miles ◆◆◆◆

With cover art that Roger Chapman admits was an idea stolen from the Doors LP *Strange Days*, *Entertainment* leaves some of the excess of *Doll's House* behind for a more aggressive, blues-drenched assault. Chapman really lets loose on this record, especially on "Hung Up Down," and it is easy to see why rock critics were comparing him to Rod Stewart and Joe Cocker—yes, he sings that well. In England, *Entertainment* did very well as a follow-up to *Doll's House*, but in America it was greeted with almost total apathy, something that even a Family tour did little to fix. *—John Dougan*

A Song for Me / 1970 / Castle ✦✦✦
Twenty seven years after the fact, this might well be the best of the early Family recordings. A combination of hard rock (bordering on metal) and wistful folk-rock (it sounds as if Chapman and Whitney were listening to a lot of Incredible String Band), *A Song for Me* veers toward early progressive rock, but isn't as nakedly indulgent as some early prog-rock recordings (e.g., they didn't try to sound like a jazz band, they wanted to sound like a rock band screwing around with jazz). Perhaps their most experimental record, it seems as though the credo in making this disc was that anything went. And on tracks like "Drowned in Wine," it works quite well. Again, Chapman offers more proof of his vocal greatness, and again the record sells large quantities in England and nearly nothing in America. *—John Dougan*

Anyway / 1970 / Castle ✦✦✦
The first four tracks of Family's *Anyway* were recorded at Croydon's Fairfield Hall, and while their sound throughout these songs is messy, overly loud, and remarkably bottom heavy, their is an emitted energy that would change Family's persona from this point on. Aside from the piano, violin, and drum barrages, Roger Chapman's vocals are simply electrifying, even with a voice that sounds slightly stretched and flattened. It was these four cuts that transformed Family's sound into something that audiences other than their cult following could adhere to. The eight minutes of "Good News-Bad News" and the sharply written "Holding the Compass" are testimony to what the band was transforming into. And, while the studio tracks weren't as boisterous, they were indeed rough, especially the title track and the modernized feel of "Part of the Load," sounding slightly ahead of its time. Poli Palmer's percussion work is both resounding and highly inventive, as is his flute playing, taking drumming duties away from Jim King. While many critics dismiss this album, it was the first real release that merged Chapman comfortably with the band's bizarre instrumental outcrops that actually stuck. Sure, the music is off-center and follows no precise direction at times, but this is what Chapman needed in order to find a home for his quavering voice. While albums like *Bandstand*, *It's Only a Movie*, and the earlier *Family Entertainment* have received greater praise, *Anyway*'s abrasiveness is just as relevant. The CD version of *Anyway* includes both the full and edited cuts of "Today," as well as "Song for Lots." *—Mike DeGagne*

Fearless / 1971 / Castle ✦✦✦
An improvement over *Anyway*, but at this juncture Family was floundering. Grech was gone, and the other personnel changes began limiting the band's cohesiveness. Although *Fearless* is (again) saved by Chapman and Whitney, the record's eccentricities work against them, and the hard rock moves (i.e., blues/boogie nonsense) sound forced. Chapman's drunken machismo makes "Sat'd'y Barfly" a winner. *—John Dougan*

Bandstand / 1972 / Castle ✦✦✦✦✦
Now this was more like it. Kicking off with the wickedly salacious "Burlesque," *Bandstand* was the best of the late Family recordings. For a band that for the most part eschewed riffs and hooks, both are in plentiful supply here. More important, by the time of *Bandstand*'s release, Family had reconciled the war between their art-rock and hard rock tendencies; that is to say, there is more of the latter and less of the former. So, the record doesn't have the internal stress of their earlier releases, but what it does have is Chapman shouting like he could take on the world and Whitney playing like he must have when he formed the Farinas in 1962. A corker from the word go. *—John Dougan*

It's Only a Movie / 1973 / Castle ✦✦✦
For a swan song, this is a pretty good one. Generally, at this point in a band's career, when personnel changes become more frequent, live shows become more unpredictable, and substance use seems to become more central to the band than singing and songwriting, you would think that Family (a band that partied as hard as any) would simply cough up a final piece of dreck and say so long. But *Movie* is a relaxed, funny and funky record, almost sunny in disposition. The songs take a while to worm their way in, but once they do, tracks like "No Money Down" and "Boom Bang," with their swagger and sway, end up sounding as good as any of the band's previous work. Totally ignored upon release, *Movie* was one of those records that seemed to go directly into the cutout bins, a fitting end to Family's career in America. *—John Dougan*

Music in a Doll's House/Family Entertainment / Dec. 14, 1999 / See for Miles ✦✦✦✦✦
This two-CD package is a little more interesting than a typical reissue combination of two albums. Most importantly, it adds two bonus tracks, both from their pre-*Music in a Doll's House* 1967 single, "Scene Through the Eye of a Lens"/"Gypsy Woman," which had never been legitimately reissued on compact disc before. It's also enclosed in a hardback miniature CD-sized book, with 40 pages of liner notes and, for those who care about such things, remastered with super 20-bit technology. (Though, unfortunately, there are no additional tracks other than those from the 1967 single, although some interesting non-LP cuts are mentioned in the liner notes.) As for the music itself, it's good late-'60s British psychedelia, not quite in the first tier, but among the best bands below that level. On these first two albums, Family adeptly combined bits of hard rock, trippy psychedelia, blues, folk, poetic lyrics, and classical music into something fairly whole and coherent, though not as immediately memorable as some other groups the band resembled in some ways, like Procol Harum and Traffic. They were closer to Traffic than anyone else, particularly in their use of some non-conventional rock instruments, especially saxophones, Mellotron, and, above all, Rick Grech's violin. Still, they were more sinister and unsettling than Traffic, though not in a way that prohibited a wide variety of moods. As for the rare 1967 single, the A-side, "Scene Through the Eye of a Lens," is one of the best British psychedelic rarities from that year, moving from a pastoral ballad to a quirky hard psychedelic passage with disembodied vocals and inventive synthesizer effects. However, the B-side, "Gypsy Woman," is a blander affair that's indicative of Family's most blues-rock-oriented roots. *—Richie Unterberger*

● **Anthology** / May 16, 2000 / Castle ✦✦✦✦✦
Calling this an anthology is a bit of a misnomer. While it's an expansive two-disc set, it still completely ignores Family's first two albums. While their very psychedelic debut gave little indication of what was to come, the second, *Family Entertainment*, found them hitting their stride with big songs like "The Weaver's Answer" and "Second Generation Woman," where Whitney's guitar work (which has been criminally underrated) melds with horns and some prog-like arrangements for the template of the Family sound, with singer Chapman's bleating vibrato the envy of flocks of sheep everywhere. That said, this does contain its share of the bands classics in tracks like "No Mule's Fool," "A Song for Me," "Good News-Bad News," "In My Own Time," and "Sweet Desiree." As a collection, it shows that while they refined their sound, the band never altered it a great deal—but why would they need to, when they'd found something unique (except for "Drowned in Wine," which sounds like a bad Jethro Tull copy), and the chemistry remained, for the most part, quite strong. A rock & roll heart beat under it all, as on hits like "Burlesque" or "Strange Band," with its heart-quickening violin line, but overlaid with an instrumental framework that could become quite rococo at times and containing some surprising jazzy touches, exemplified on songs like "In My Own Time." They came from a time when it was still about the songs, when it was possible to be both a singles and album band, and Family did well equally both. So, while this is far from perfect introduction to their very English brand of music—and there is no good compilation that spans their whole career—it's still well worth having. *—Chris Nickson*

Deitra Farr

b. Aug. 1, 1957, Chicago, IL
Vocals / Modern Electric Blues
Chicago vocalist Dietra Farr is so versatile, it's a misnomer to call her singing soul-blues. She's equally comfortable with ballads, pop music, soul and blues, and she presents a delightful combination of all these styles on her debut record, *The Search Is Over* (1997, JSP Records).

Farr spent her childhood listening to the radio and the soul music of the late '60s and early '70s. She began singing in the choir at the Catholic grade school she attended, and by the time she was a senior in high school, she was singing with her uncle's band. Farr also sang with another local band for fun, but music was still an avocation for her.

Farr first stepped into the recording studio when she was 18 as a vocalist for Jimmy Mayes' band, Mill Street Depot. The single, "You Won't Support Me," got airplay around Chicago and sparked her enthusiasm for a career as a singer.

After she graduated from Columbia College (in Chicago) with a degree in journalism, Farr met piano player Erwin Helfer. Helfer had learned from and played with people like Willie Mabon, Little Brother Montgomery and Sunnyland Slim. Farr began sitting in with Helfer's trio before landing a gig of her own at Kingston Mines in Chicago. She began drawing crowds to her shows, helped in no small measure by the fact that she had legendary names sitting with her, people like Homesick James, Louis Meyers and Sunnyland Slim.

Farr sang on Dave Specter's debut, *Bluebird Blues*, in 1991, and a Japanese record company, DIW, included her on a compilation of Chicago blues artists called *Chicago Blues Nights*. She also can be heard on *Chicago's Finest Blues Ladies*, a compilation for the Wolf Records label, which got her noticed overseas and allowed her to tour in Europe.

Farr's career shifted into high gear after she hooked up with the band Mississippi Heat in 1993 and recorded two albums with them, *Learned the Hard Way* (1993) and *Thunder in My Heart* (1995). Her debut for the London-based JSP Records, *The Search Is Over*, produced by guitarist/impresario Johnny Rawls, was released in 1997. Her vocals were smooth and confident, and her songs covered a broad thematic landscape. *—Richard Skelly*

● **The Search Is Over** / May 20, 1997 / JSP ✦✦✦

Robert "H-Bomb" Ferguson

b. 1929, Charleston, SC
Vocals, Piano / Jump Blues, Modern Electric Blues
His extroverted antics and multi-colored fright wig might invite the instant dismissal of Cincinnati-based singer Robert "H-Bomb" Ferguson as some sort of comic lightweight. In reality, he's one of the last survivors of the jump blues era whose once-slavish Wynonie Harris imitations have mellowed into a highly distinctive vocal delivery of his own.

Ferguson's dad, a reverend, paid for piano lessons for his son, demanding he stick to sacred melodies on the 88s. Fat chance—by age 19, Bobby Ferguson was on the road with Joe Liggins & the Honeydrippers. When they hit New York, Ferguson branched off on his own. Comedian Nipsey Russell, then emcee at Harlem's Baby Grand Club, got the singer a gig at the nightspot. Back then, Ferguson was billed as "The Cobra Kid."

Singles for Derby, Atlas, and Prestige preceded a 1951-1952 hookup with Savoy Records that produced some of Ferguson's best waxings. Most of them were obvious Harris knockoffs, but eminently swinging ones with top-flight backing (blasting saxists Purvis Henson and Count Hastings were aboard the dates). Drummer Jack "The Bear" Parker, who played on the Savoy dates, allegedly bestowed the singer with his explosive monicker. Other accounts credit Savoy producer Lee Magid with coining H-Bomb's handle; either way, his dynamite vocals fulfilled the billing.

Ferguson eventually made Cincinnati his home, recording for Finch, Big Bang, ARC, and the far more prestigious Federal in 1960. H-Bomb terminated his touring schedule in the early '70s. When he returned from premature retirement, his unique wig-wearing shtick (inspired by Rick James' coiffure) was in full bloom. Backed by his fine young band, the Medicine Men, Ferguson waxed his long-overdue debut album, *Wiggin' Out*, for Chicago's Earwig logo in 1993. It showed him to be as wild as ever (witness the gloriously sleazy "Meatloaf"), a talented pianist to boot, and more his own man than ever before. *—Bill Dahl*

Life Is Hard / Nov. 1987 / Savoy ✦✦✦✦
The atomic one in his early-'50s jump blues mode, when he made a living as an unabashed Wynonie Harris clone (and a damned good one at that). Swinging New York bands and Ferguson's hearty vocals make the similarities entirely forgivable. Hopefully, this LP will be available digitally before too long. —*Bill Dahl*

● **Wiggin' Out** / Feb. 1993 / Earwig ✦✦✦✦
Somewhere over the last 40 years or so, this purple wig-wearing R&B pioneer dropped his slavish Wynonie Harris imitations and became his own man, learning how to play piano to boot. His long-overdue debut album joyously recalls the heyday of jump blues via salacious rockers like "Meatloaf" and "Shake Your Apple Tree." Ferguson's young band, the Medicine Men, do a fine job of laying down exciting grooves behind the singer. —*Bill Dahl*

Thomas "Big Hat" Fields

b. 1947, Rayne, Lousiana
Accordion, Vocals / Zydeco
One of the many new faces to arrive on the zydeco scene during the '90s, accordionist Thomas "Big Hat" Fields was born in Rayne, Lousiana in 1947. Already well-known to his fellow performers for running a zydeco club in the Grand Coteau area, he did not even pick up the accordion until the early '90s, soon after forming the Foot Stompin' Zydeco Band with his bassist wife Geneva. Fields debuted in 1994 with *The Big Hat Man*; *Come to Louisiana* followed in 1995. —*Jason Ankeny*

The Louisiana Zydeco Man / Aug. 3, 1999 / Maison de Soul ✦✦✦

● **Louisiana Is the Place to See** / Lanor ✦✦✦✦
This is zydeco music as it is meant to be played—alive and jumping, getting you out on the dance floor. Fortunately, the most competently performed songs are in English; "Bald Headed Men" is a great example of his sense of humor. Thomas Fields' music reflects a devil-may-care, fun-loving nature. This man didn't pick up an accordion until he was in his late forties, then taught his wife to play bass so he had the nucleus for his band. They may not be the most innovative band, nor the best on their instruments yet, but reflect the heart and soul of a bright, happy future for traditional zydeco, playing with a heart, a passion, and a joy that makes up for a lot of shortcomings. —*Bob Gottlieb*

The Fieldstones

f. 1974
Group / Soul-Blues, Modern Electric Blues, Memphis Blues, Blues-Rock
One of the few remnants of the homegrown Memphis blues scene since its virtual cessation at the end of the '50s, the Fieldstones made some rough-and-ready electric blues with soul and rock influences from the mid-'70s through the early '90s. Their sound was characterized by a two-guitar front line and a raw, chunky groove not too far removed from the sort of Mississippi juke joint blues that Fat Possum recorded in the '90s. The Fieldstones did some recording in the '80s for David Evans' Highwater label, but never established much of a following outside of Memphis, and disbanded in the early '90s. —*Richie Unterberger*

● **Memphis Blues Today!** / 1983 / High Water ✦✦✦
The Fieldstones are still revered in Memphis for providing some quality live blues in the '80s, when such music was almost unknown in the city. Their 1983 album is reasonably fun, but not exceptional, modern electric blues with a more spontaneous feel than most of the discs coming out on higher-profile indie labels of the time; the guitar playing especially has a higher and lighter feel than the norm. —*Richie Unterberger*

Mud Island Blues / Jan. 30, 2001 / High Water ✦✦✦

The Five Blind Boys of Alabama

f. 1937, Talladega, AL
Group / Traditional Gospel, Southern Gospel, Black Gospel
Evolving out of the Happyland Jubilee Singers, this traditional Black gospel quartet was formed in 1937 at the Talladega Institute for the Deaf and Blind in Alabama. By the '40s they became "The Blind Boys" and recorded for Specialty, Vee-Jay, Savoy, Elektra, and other labels. Their first hit was "I Can See Everybody's Mother but Mine" in 1949. Current lineup: Joe Watson, Jimmy Carter, Sam & Bobby Butler, Curtis Foster, Johnny Fields, and Clarence Fountain. They appeared on Broadway in *Gospel at Colonus*, but gained much more fame during the late '90s and early '00s while recording for Peter Gabriel's Real World label a series of albums beginning with the collaboration-heavy *Spirit of the Century*. The group also appeared on Gabriel's 2002 album *Up*. —*Bil Carpenter*

Original Five Blind Boys of Alabama / 1959 / Savoy ✦✦✦✦
Fire and fury from the late '50s. —*Opal Louis Nations*

Church Concert in New Orleans / 1967 / HOB ✦✦✦✦
Pew-burning live recording. —*Opal Louis Nations*

Oh Lord, Stand by Me / 1970 / Specialty ✦✦✦✦✦
High voltage quartet led by the fiery Fountain, circa 1952-1956. —*Opal Louis Nations*

Marching Up to Zion / 1970 / Specialty ✦✦✦✦✦
Essential Blind Boys circa 1952-1956. —*Opal Louis Nations*

Precious Memories / 1974 / MCA ✦✦✦✦✦
Impassioned vocals matched against stinging guitar and forthright chorus. —*Opal Louis Nations*

The Five Blind Boys of Alabama / 1987 / Gospel Heritage ✦✦✦✦✦
An excellent 16-track anthology, it predates their Specialty recordings by four years, with leads shared by Clarence Fountain and the legendary Paul Excano. With scholarly notes and photos, it's a must for collectors. —*Hank Davis*

Oh Lord, Stand by Me/Marching Up to Zion / 1991 / Specialty ✦✦✦✦✦
Two of this seminal gospel group's Specialty albums on one compact disc. Compiled by

musicologist Dr. Demento (under his real name Barret Hansen), this collection offers several of the group's original singles, all of them chock-full of fervent vocalizing from lead singers Clarence Fountain and the Rev. Samuel K. Lewis. This is the perfect introduction to these wonderful musicians and some of the most passionate gospel singing you're likely to encounter. —*Cub Koda*

Deep River / 1992 / Elektra/Nonesuch ✦✦✦✦✦
On their umpteenth release, the Five Blind Boys mix some modern blues and R&B into their core gospel sound. The rhythm section, led by the organ of the legendary Booker T. Jones, keeps the accompaniment simple as the group soars through some traditional material ("Closer Walk With Thee," "Every Time I Feel the Spirit, "), a few originals by lead vocalist Clarence Fountain, and a transcendent version of Bob Dylan's "I Believe in You." —*Jason Ankeny*

★ **The Sermon** / 1993 / Specialty ✦✦✦✦✦
A treasure trove of previously unreleased material, this brings together 25 new tracks, all recorded between 1953 and 1957. Only two songs, "Heaven on My Mind" and "I'm Going Through," were ever released in any form, but the quality of the material is certainly as high as any of their early sides. Here's one of gospel's greatest groups, singing their hearts out in their absolute prime. —*Cub Koda*

Swing Low, Sweet Chariot / Oct. 17, 1994 / Jewel ✦✦✦✦✦
Good hard-singing collection. —*Opal Louis Nations*

1948–1951 / Dec. 12, 1995 / Flyright ✦✦✦✦✦
Initial recordings by this leading postwar traditional quartet. —*Opal Louis Nations*

Have Faith: The Very Best of the Five Blind Boys of Alabama / Mar. 3, 1998 / Collectables ✦✦✦✦
Pew-burning Vee-Jay sides by Clarence Fountain and the boys. —*Opal Louis Nations*

Hallelujah: A Collection of Their Finest / May 18, 1999 / Music Club ✦✦✦✦
This 15-track collection brings together both live and studio recordings made for the HOB label. Both of the famous leads with the group—Clarence Fountain and Louis Dicks—are featured on tracks like "Something's Got a Hold on Me," "When I Come to the End of My Journey," "Too Close to Heaven," "Lord's Been Good to Me" and "I Got Jesus on My Mind," their two magnificent voices trading off on "Alone and Motherless," "Running for My Life," and the perennial favorite "I Saw the Light." The live tracks on here literally sweat with emotion and fervor. A nice set. —*Cub Koda*

Spirit of the Century / Apr. 24, 2001 / Real World ✦✦✦✦✦
From start to finish this album defies categorical classification. It employs the best of R&B, Afro-beat, folk, and blues while remaining true to the Blind Boys' gospel roots. And with a tasteful selection of material by Tom Waits, Mick Jagger and Keith Richards, and Ben Harper, in addition to their usual array of traditional gospel hymns and folk tunes, it will appeal to generations of listeners. Though varied in it's stylings, the album works as a whole due to the high-quality production, arrangements, and musicianship throughout. The traditional "No More," in a slow and soulful arrangement, starts off with a plaintive slide guitar sampling of "Amazing Grace" and sits comfortably beside "Run for a Long Time," which features George Scott rapping over a percussive, groove-filled (à la Danny Thompson on double bass) and harmony-laden reworking of this classic. And the Stones' "Just Wanna See His Face," which is given a jubilee-like treatment that rivals the original, follows up a somber "Motherless Child" with grace and acuity. Other guests include Charlie Musselwhite on harmonica, John Hammond on guitar and Dobro, and David Lindley on oud and electric slide. —*Travis Drageset*

You'll Never Walk Alone/True Convictions / May 8, 2001 / Collectables ✦✦✦✦
This Collectables reissue of two 1963 albums by the Original Blind Boys of Alabama (yes, the guys with Clarence Fountain) on Vee-Jay 5029 and 5048, respectively, sees the issue of two of their finest of most forgotten issues. With Fountain sounding as much like Al Hibbler as Hibbler—and never sounding like anything less than himself—and the band taking on a much more Southern soul groove and R&B rhythmic sensibility, these are also outer space records for the band. One example is the bossa nova/cha cha rhythm employed on "I've Got a Home in That Rock," with a Brazilian flute wafting in from the wings is hardly what you'd call traditional gospel, but it smokes nonetheless. Or take the doo wop sensibility in "Somebody Bigger Than You and I" that permeates the tune which sounds like the Blind Boys hanging on a Brooklyn corner! And, finally, from that album there's a deep soul/doo wop version of "Danny Boy," with Fountain outdoing any Irish tenor on the block. From *True Convictions*—made because the first album seemed to work for the label—there are numerous Fountain originals that are part of the Blind Boys' repertoire today: "What He's Done for Me" and "I'm Journeying On," among them. This record has a much more gospel feel, though there are strange moments where the Saturday night sinnin' blues—in the accompaniment—come to call as they do on "After a While" and "Tell God All About It." As for the Blind Boys, it doesn't get much more raw than this, unadorned, pure soul and grit with a message for the ages. This is certainly one to have if for no other reason than for *You'll Never Walk Alone*, which was gospel's first psychedelic album. —*Thom Jurek*

Collectors Edition / Jun. 4, 2002 / Fuel 2000 ✦✦✦✦

The Five Blind Boys of Mississippi

f. 193?, Jackson, MS
Group / Traditional Gospel, Southern Gospel, Black Gospel
The Five Blind Boys of Mississippi are among the greatest singing groups in popular music history. Their smashing harmonies and the leads of Archie Brownlee not only influenced numerous gospel ensembles, but such secular artists as Ray Charles. Their origins date back to the '30s, when Archie Brownlee (Brownley in some accounts), Joseph Ford, Lawrence Abrams, and Lloyd Woodard formed a quartet. They were students at the Piney

Woods School near Jackson, MS. They began as the Cotton Blossom Singers, and did both spiritual and secular material. The quartet sang on the school grounds in 1936, then were recorded in 1937 by Alan Lomax for the Library of Congress. After graduation, they decided to become professional singers and for a time performed under dual identities; they were the Cotton Blossom Singers for popular songs and The Jackson Harmoneers for gospel. They became a quintet when Melvin Henderson joined. When Percell Perkins replaced Henderson in the mid-'40s, they became the Five Blind Boys. Oddly, Perkins, who doubled as their manager, was not blind. They made their recording debut for Excelsior in 1946, after meeting label owner Leon Rene in Cleveland. They recorded for Coleman in 1948, the same year Joseph Ford was replaced by J.T. Clinkscales. But when they joined Don Robey's Peacock label in 1950, the Five Blind Boys became superstars. The single "Our Father" was a Top Ten R&B hit, and they became a prolific ensemble, recording 27 singles and five albums for Peacock through the '60s. Brownlee died in New Orleans in 1960. His riveting, chilling screams and yells were among gospel's most amazing. Perkins left the group soon after becoming a minister. The list of replacements included Revs. Sammy Lewis and George Warren, as well as Tiny Powell. Roscoe Robinson took over for Brownlee, and was assisted by second lead Willmer "Little Ax" Broadnax, who was also a masterful singer. The Five Blind Boys continued through the '70s and '80s and into the '90s, though Woodard died in the mid-'70s, and Lawrence Abrams in 1982. —*Ron Wynn*

Soon I'll Be Done / Apr. 1952 / Chess ✦✦✦
Reissue of the group's stunning Chess album with Little Ax and Roscoe Robinson at the helm. —*Opal Louis Nations*

★ **The Original Five Blind Boys** / 1959 / Vee-Jay ✦✦✦✦✦
Considered the finest post-war quartet album ever made. From Peacock singles, 1951-1959. —*Opal Louis Nations*

I'll Go / 1960 / Checker ✦✦✦✦✦
Archie's soaring tenor and the group's tight harmony make this album one of the best ever released. From Vee-Jay singles, 1956-1957. —*Opal Louis Nations*

Father I Stretch My Hands to Thee / 1965 / Peacock ✦✦✦✦
Strong readings by the quartet led by Little Ax and Roscoe Robinson. —*Opal Louis Nations*

Will Jesus Be Waiting / 1969 / MCA ✦✦✦
Great recordings lead by the magnificent Archie Brownlee. '50s and '60s Peacock selections. —*Opal Louis Nations*

The Best of the Blind Boys / 1973 / MCA Special Products ✦✦✦
MCA's *Best of the Blind Boys* is a good, but not exceptional, collection of 12 highlights from the group's Peacock material. There are a number of wondrous performances here—including "Love Lifted Me," "Jesus Satisfied" and "Speak for Jesus"—but in general, the recordings aren't quite as strong as their recordings for Vee-Jay. Furthermore, the album feels a little skimpy in these days of extensive reissues, making it more of interest to completists and serious fans than listeners seeking out good values or representative collections. —*Leo Stanley*

★ **The Best of the Five Blind Boys of Mississippi, Vol. 1** / 1973 / MCA ✦✦✦✦✦
These Specialty recordings truly represent some of the best by this popular group. Arguably the greatest "quartet" ever. Featuring the wondrous Archie Brownlee. —*Kip Lornell & Ron Wynn*

My Desire/There's a God Somewhere / 1974 / Mobile Fidelity ✦✦✦
My Desire/There's a God Somewhere combines two fine albums from the Peacock vaults. Also known as The Original Five Blind Boys and the Jackson Harmoneers. The lead vocals by Archie Brownlee have been known to slay souls and reduce grown men to tears. Powerful material! —*Hank Davis*

The Tide of Life / 1979 / Jewel ✦✦✦
Just about the best set recorded by the quartet on this label. —*Opal Louis Nations*

The Best of the Five Blind Boys of Mississippi, Vol. 2 / 1983 / MCA ✦✦✦

In the Hands of the Lord / 1987 / MCA ✦✦
Choice Peacock selections by this shouting quartet led by Archie Brownlee, Big Henry Johnson, and Roscoe Robinson. —*Opal Louis Nations*

You Done What the Doctor Couldn't Do / 1991 / Jubilee ✦✦✦✦✦
Quintessential "hard" gospel singing from the late '40s and early '50s. Brownlee performs most of the lead chores, with vital dynamism and occasional lead singing from Rev. Percell Perkins and Vance "Tiny" Powell. —*Kip Lornell*

The Great Lost Blind Boys Album / 1992 / Collectables ✦✦✦✦✦
The Great Lost Blind Boys Album combines two original Vee-Jay albums from the late '50s, adding a handful of alternate takes, aborted takes and chatter to the mix. While those snippets distract from the music itself, that's not enough to stop the disc from being the definitive Five Blind Boys of Mississippi collection. All of the group's greatest numbers—"My Robe Will Fit Me," "Jesus Love Me," "No Need to Cry," "Let's Have Church," and "Leave You in the Hands of the Lord," among many others—are here in their best versions, making it essential listening for any gospel fan, or anyone who wants to know the roots of doo wop. —*Thom Owens*

Counting on Jesus / 1993 / Soul Potion ✦✦✦
The name may be the same, but these are not The Original Five Blind Boys of Mississippi; Archie Brownlee has been dead for many years, and others have departed. No roster list is included here. They still harmonize with exuberance, and the eight numbers on their most recent release are steadfastly traditional in lyrics, production structure, and feel; no huge backing choirs, synthesized backdrops or bombastic settings, but simple stories about spiritual fulfillment and release. —*Ron Wynn*

Meet the Blind Boys / Oct. 17, 1994 / Jewel ✦✦✦
Good collection by the quartet before breaking up and regrouping around Sandy Foster. —*Opal Louis Nations*

I Never Heard a Man / Apr. 16, 1996 / Jewel ✦✦✦

In Concert Live in Europe / Jan. 13, 1998 / Munich ✦✦✦

The Original/Everytime I Feel the Spirit / Feb. 19, 2002 / Collectables ✦✦✦

20th Century Masters—The Millennium Collection: The Best of the Five Blind Boys / Apr. 30, 2002 / MCA ✦✦✦
Twenty-four years in the Five Blind Boys of Mississippi's career are surveyed in the 12 tracks on this discount-priced compilation of their Peacock Records recordings. The sequencing is roughly chronological, beginning with the group's Top Ten R&B hit from 1950, "Our Father (Which Art in Heaven)." Early on the group sings hard, traditional gospel, their style very much a call-and-response approach, with lead singer Archie Brownlee dominating the sound. Brownlee is a thunderous singer, throwing everything else in the shade. The chronological sequencing allows for an appreciation of the change in the group upon Brownlee's death in 1960, followed by the leadership of Lloyd Woodard who, if anything, is even more dominating, but who introduces a more contemporary, and often more uptempo style. By the two tracks that conclude the album, the cautionary recitative "Speak Gently to Your Mother" and "His Eye Is on the Sparrow," there isn't much more to hear than Woodard and the organ or piano that back him up. These are bravura performances from an act that can be heard to have changed a lot over the course of its history. —*William Ruhlmann*

The "5" Royales

f. 1952, Winston-Salem, NC, **db.** 1965
Group / R&B

The "5" Royales were a relatively unheralded, but significant, link between early R&B and early soul in their combination of doo wop, jump blues, and gospel styles. Their commercial success was relatively modest—they had seven Top Ten R&B hits in the '50s, most recorded in the span of little over a year between late 1952 and late 1953. A few of their singles would prove extremely popular in cover versions by other artists, though—James Brown and Aretha Franklin tore it up with "Think," Ray Charles covered "Tell the Truth," and the Shirelles (and later the Mamas & the Papas) had pop success with "Dedicated to the One I Love." Almost all of their material was written by guitarist Lowman Pauling, who influenced Steve Cropper with his biting and bluesy guitar lines, which at their most ferocious almost sound like a precursor to blues-rock.

Pauling's guitar is pretty muted on their early sides, though, which sometimes walk the line between gospel and R&B. The gospel elements aren't surprising, given that the Royales were originally known as the Royal Sons Quintet when they formed in Winston-Salem, NC. In fact, they were still known as the Royal Sons Quintet when they began recording for Apollo in the early '50s, although they had six members. They would change their name to the "5" Royales in 1952, although they would, confusingly, remain a six-man outfit for a while; the quotes around the 5 in their billing were designed to alleviate some of the confusion. The Apollo singles "Baby Don't Do It" and "Help Me Somebody" made number one on the R&B charts in 1953, and they had a few other hits for Apollo before being lured away to King Records in 1954.

Although the group would remain on King for the rest of the '50s, they would only enter the R&B Top Ten two more times, with "Think" and "Tears of Joy" (both in 1957). Their later sides, however, are their best, as Pauling became much more assertive on the guitar, dashing off some piercing and fluid solos. Some of these solos are among the heaviest and wildest in '50s rock, on both relatively well-known cuts like "Think," and virtually unknown numbers like "The Slummer the Slum." Greil Marcus once wrote something to the effect that a young Eric Clapton would have once paid to hold Pauling's coat. They remained primarily a harmony vocal group, though, and if their late-'50s sides are considerably more modernized than their early Apollo hits, they're still a lot closer to doo wop than soul.

Even when their records weren't selling, the "5" Royales were a popular touring band. Their constant activity at King Records, in all likelihood, had some influence on the young James Brown, then starting his career on the same label; one of Brown's first big R&B hits was a frenetic cover of "Think." They couldn't sustain themselves without more hits, though. After leaving King and recording some more sides in the early '60s, they finally broke up by 1965. —*Richie Unterberger*

Dedicated to You / 1957 / King ✦✦✦✦✦
This may be the great lost R&B record of the '50s. The "5" Royales were a fine singing group long before this release, but on these sides recorded between 1955 and 1957, guitarist Lowman Pauling cuts loose with the most fiery guitar fills this side of Ike Turner. From the opening shout of "Think" to the closing notes of "Thirty Second Lover," Dedicated to You is a guitar *tour de force*. The album's crowning moment comes on "Say It," where Clarence Paul's pleading vocal is answered with Pauling's bluesy replies. Other highlights include Bill Doggett's gospel-tinged organ on "Someone Made You For Me," several fine sax solos ("Don't Be Ashamed," "Right Around the Corner") and the straightforward rocker "Messin' Up." An overlooked classic. —*J.P. Ollio*

Five Royales Sing for You / 1959 / King ✦✦✦
An exact reproduction of their best original album, it doesn't have many hits, but the obscurities will keep you interested. —*John Floyd*

Seventeen Original Greatest Hits / 1978 / King ✦✦✦✦✦
This is a fine collection of the "5" Royales' King material. It includes the previously unreleased "I Can't Stand Losing You" along with most of their better-known tracks. —*J.P. Ollio*

Sing "Laundromat Blues" / Dec. 1987 / Relic ✦✦✦

Sing "Baby Don't Do It" / Dec. 1987 / Relic ✦✦✦✦✦

★ **Monkey Hips and Rice: The "5" Royales Anthology** / Mar. 8, 1994 / Rhino ♦♦♦♦♦

The "5" Royales certainly did their share of forgettable period-piece tunes, but they also had transcendent songs like "Think," "Just as I Am," and "Dedicated to the One I Love." They enjoyed a lengthy run, creating many hits plus a few gems, which are all available on this sparkling two-disc set. The opening disc sets the stage, showing their gospel origins and also the rather routine cuts the band did in its formative period. They began to evolve into a more substantial unit in the mid-'50s, and by the late '50s were a sterling unit cutting emphatic, appealing numbers. Most of these appear on the second disc. By the early '60s, they had run their course, but their legacy and impact was secure. This offers the most complete picture of the "5" Royales and their superb music. *—Ron Wynn*

● **The Apollo Sessions** / Sep. 1, 1995 / Collectables ♦♦♦♦♦

Although not the career-long survey of the Rhino anthology, this 23-song, 62-minute collection covers the "5" Royales' very best years, spent with Apollo Records from 1951 until 1955, first as the Royals ("Give Me One More Chance") and then as a quintet under their more familiar name. Their sound here is vocally very smooth yet passionate, but the instrumental backings are exuberant and raunchy, the kind of combination that made acts like this such a threat to the established popular music of the era. The mix of jump blues with accomplished gospel-influenced harmony singing (best represented on the delightful "What's That" or "All Righty," or, most startling of all, "Baby Take All of Me," with its abandoned wailing in the background) helped make their music some of the most expressive and satisfying of the period. Their way with a chorus and a phrase made the "5" Royales one of the top R&B acts of their era, although it wasn't until much later that they made the jump to pop stardom. Unfortunately, during the period represented here, they were one of those R&B acts whose radio play exceeded their record sales (at least, as reported by Apollo, one reason they jumped to King Records). From 1951 until 1955, they helped provide the soundtrack against which mainstream rock & roll was born and took root with the public. On that basis alone, this material is worth hearing and owning; it was the soil in which rock & roll sprouted, the stream in which other acts' commercial hits were spawned and nurtured. They later had their share of successes, but this is their real sound, raw, sweet and elegant all at the same time. *—Bruce Eder*

All Righty!: Apollo Recordings / Mar. 3, 1999 / West Side ♦♦♦♦

All Righty! is the first complete collection of the "5" Royales' recordings for Apollo Records from 1951 to 1955, including even their gospel sides (recorded as the Royal Sons Quintet). *—John Bush*

Take Me With You Baby / Mar. 14, 2000 / Purple Pyramid ♦♦♦♦

A nice collection of the group's latter-day material originally waxed for the Memphis House of Blues imprint. Some of these sides were later issued on Vee-Jay and ABC/Paramount, but the Memphis stamp of Willie Mitchell's early work is all over these tracks. Highlights include the previously unissued "Show Me," "I Got to Know," "She Did Me Wrong," and a nice stab at James Brown's "Please Please Please." Usually, latter-day sides are a load of diminished returns, but these tracks are every bit as enjoyable as their more famous counterparts. Well worth adding to the shopping cart. *—Cub Koda*

Fleetwood Mac

f. 1967, London, England

Group / Album Rock, British Blues, Pop/Rock, Soft Rock, Adult Contemporary, Blues-Rock

While most bands undergo a number of changes over the course of their career, few groups experienced such radical stylistic changes as Fleetwood Mac. Initially conceived as a hard-edged British blues combo in the late '60s, the band gradually evolved into a polished pop/rock act over the course of a decade. Throughout all of their incarnations, the only consistent members of Fleetwood Mac were drummer Mick Fleetwood and bassist John McVie—the rhythm section who provided the band with its name. Ironically, they had the least influence over the musical direction of the band. Originally, guitarists Peter Green and Jeremy Spencer provided the band with its gutsy, neo-psychedelic blues-rock sound, but as both guitarists descended into mental illness, the group began moving toward pop/rock with the songwriting of pianist Christine McVie. By the mid-'70s, Fleetwood Mac had relocated to California, where they added the soft-rock duo of Lindsey Buckingham and Stevie Nicks to their lineup. Obsessed with the meticulously arranged pop of the Beach Boys and the Beatles, Buckingham helped the band become one of the most popular groups of the late '70s. Combining soft rock with the confessional introspection of singer/songwriters, Fleetwood Mac created a slick but emotional sound that helped 1977's *Rumours* become one of the biggest-selling albums of all time. The band's retained their popularity through the early '80s, when Buckingham, Nicks, and Christine McVie all began pursuing solo careers. The band reunited for one album, 1987's *Tango in the Night*, before splintering in the late '80s. Buckingham left the group initially, but the band decided to soldier on, releasing one other album before Nicks and McVie left the band in the early '90s, hastening the group's commercial decline.

The roots of Fleetwood Mac lie in John Mayall's legendary British blues outfit, the Bluesbreakers. John McVie (bass) was one of the charter members of the Bluesbreakers, joining the group in 1963. In 1966 Peter Green replaced Eric Clapton and a year later, Mick Fleetwood (drums) joined. Inspired by the success of Cream, the Yardbirds and Jimi Hendrix, the trio decided to break away from Mayall in 1967. At their debut at the British Jazz and Blues Festival in August, Bob Brunning was playing bass in the group, since McVie was still under contract to Mayall. He joined the band a few weeks after their debut; by that time, slide guitarist Jeremy Spencer had joined the band. Fleetwood Mac soon signed with Blue Horizon, releasing their eponymous debut the following year. *Fleetwood Mac* was an enormous hit in the U.K., spending over a year in the Top Ten. Despite its British success, the album was virtually ignored in America. During 1968, the band added guitarist Danny Kirwan. The following year, they recorded *Fleetwood Mac in Chicago* with a variety of bluesmen, including Willie Dixon and Otis Spann. The set was released later that year, after the band had left Blue Horizon for a one-album deal with Immediate Records; in the US, they signed with Reprise/Warner Bros., and by 1970, Warner began releasing the band's British records as well.

Fleetwood Mac released *English Rose* and *Then Play On* during 1969, which both indicated that the band were expanding their music, moving away from their blues-purists roots. That year, Green's "Man of the World" and "Oh Well" were number two hits. Though his music was providing the backbone of the group, Peter Green was growing increasingly disturbed, due to his large ingestion of hallucinogenic drugs. After announcing that he was planning to give all of his earnings away, Green suddenly left the band in the spring of 1970; he released two solo albums over the course of the '70s, but he rarely performed after leaving Fleetwood Mac. The band replaced him with Christine Perfect, a vocalist/pianist who had earned a small but loyal following in the UK by singing with Spencer Davis and the Chicken Shack. She had already performed uncredited on *Then Play On*. Contractual difficulties prevented her from becoming a full-fledged member of Fleetwood Mac until 1971; by that time she had married John McVie.

Christine McVie didn't appear on 1970's *Kiln House*, the first album the band recorded without Peter Green. For that album, Jeremy Spencer dominated the band's musical direction, but he had also been undergoing mental problems due to heavy drug use. During the band's American tour in early 1971, Spencer disappeared; it was later discovered that he left the band to join the religious cult the Children of God. Fleetwood Mac had already been trying to determine the direction of their music, but Spencer's departure sent the band into disarray. Christine McVie and Danny Kirwan began to move the band towards mainstream rock on 1971's *Future Games*, but new guitarist Bob Welch exerted a heavy influence on 1972's *Bare Trees*. Kirwan was fired after *Bare Trees* and was replaced by guitarists Bob Weston and Dave Walker, who appeared on 1973's *Penguin*. Walker left after that album, and Weston departed after making its follow-up, *Mystery to Me* (1973). In 1974, the group's manager Clifford Davis formed a bogus Fleetwood Mac, and had the band tour the US. The real Fleetwood Mac filed and won a lawsuit against the imposters—after losing, they began performing under the name Stretch—but the lawsuit kept the band off the road for most of the year. In the interim, they released *Heroes Are Hard To Find*. Late in 1974, Fleetwood Mac moved to California, with hopes of restarting their career. Welch left the band shortly after the move to from Paris.

Early in 1975, Fleetwood and McVie were auditioning engineers for the band's new album when they heard *Buckingham-Nicks*, an album recorded by the soft rock duo Lindsey Buckingham and Stevie Nicks. The duo was asked to join the group and their addition revived the band's musical and commercial fortunes. Not only did the pair write songs, but they brought distinctive talents the band had been lacking. Buckingham was skilled pop craftsman, capable of arranging a commercial song while keeping it musically adventurous. Nicks had a husky voice and a sexy, hippie gypsy stage persona that gave the band a charismatic frontwoman. The new lineup of Fleetwood Mac released their eponymous debut in 1975 and it slowly became a huge hit, reaching number one in 1976 on the strength of the singles "Over My Head," "Rhiannon," and "Say You Love Me." The album would eventually sell over five million copies in the U.S. alone.

While Fleetwood Mac had finally attained their long-desired commercial success, the band was fraying apart behind the scenes. The McVies divorced in 1976, and Buckingham and Nicks' romance ended shortly afterward. The internal tensions formed the basis for the songs on their next album, *Rumours*. Released in the spring of 1977, *Rumours* became a blockbuster success, topping the American and British charts and generating the Top Ten singles "Go Your Own Way," "Dreams," "Don't Stop," and "You Make Loving Fun." It would eventually sell over 17 million copies in the U.S. alone, making it the second biggest-selling album of all time. Fleetwood Mac supported the album with an exhaustive, lucrative tour and then retired to the studio to record their follow-up to *Rumours*. A wildly experimental double-album conceived largely by Buckingham, *Tusk* (1979) didn't duplicate the enormous success of *Rumours*, yet it did go multi-platinum and featured the Top Ten singles "Sara" and "Tusk." In 1980, they released the double-album *Live*.

Following the *Tusk* tour, Fleetwood, Buckingham, and Nicks all recorded solo albums. Of the solo projects, Stevie Nicks' *Bella Donna* (1981) was the most successful, peaking at number one and featuring the hit singles "Stop Draggin' My Heart Around," "Leather and Lace" and "Edge of Seventeen." Buckingham's *Law and Order* (1981) was a moderate success, spawning the Top Ten "Trouble." Fleetwood, for his part, made a world music album called *The Visitor*. Fleetwood Mac reconvened in 1982 for *Mirage*. More conventional and accessible than *Tusk*, *Mirage* reached number one and featured the hit singles "Hold Me" and "Gypsy."

After *Mirage*, Buckingham, Nicks, and Christine McVie all worked on solo albums. The hiatus was due to a variety of reasons. Each member had their own manager, Nicks was becoming the group's breakaway star, Buckingham was obsessive in the studio and each member was suffering from various substance addictions. Nicks was able to maintain her popularity, with *The Wild Heart* (1983) and *Rock a Little* (1985) both reaching the Top 15. Christine McVie also had a Top Ten hit with "Got a Hold on Me" in 1984. Buckingham received the strongest reviews of all, but his 1984 album *Go Insane* failed to generate a hit. Fleetwood Mac reunited to record a new album in 1985. Buckingham, who had grown increasingly frustrated with the musical limitations of the band, decided to make it his last project with the band. When the resulting album, *Tango in the Night*, was finally released in 1987 it was greeted with mixed reviews but strong sales, reaching the Top Ten and generating the Top 20 hits "Little Lies," "Seven Wonders," and "Everywhere."

Buckingham decided to leave Fleetwood Mac after completing *Tango in the Night*, and the group replaced him with guitarists Billy Burnette and Rick Vito. The new lineup of the band recorded their first album, *Behind the Mask*, in 1990. It became the band's first album since 1975 to not go gold. Following its supporting tour, Nicks and Christine McVie announced they would continue to record with the group, but not tour. Vito left the band in 1991, and the group released the box set *25 Years—The Chain* the following year. The classic Fleetwood Mac lineup of Fleetwood, the McVies, Buckingham and Nicks reunited to play President Bill Clinton's inauguration in early 1993, but the concert did not lead to a full-fledged reunion. Later that year, Nicks left the band and was replaced by Bekka Bramlett and Dave Mason; Christine McVie left the group shortly afterward. The new lineup of Fleetwood Mac began touring in 1994, releasing *Time* the following year to little attention. While the new version of Fleetwood Mac wasn't commercially successful, neither were the solo careers of Buckingham, Nicks and McVie, prompting speculation of a full-fledged reunion in 1997. The live album *Shrine 69* was released in 1999. *—Stephen Thomas Erlewine*

Peter Green's Fleetwood Mac / Feb. 1968 / Blue Horizon ✦✦✦✦✦

Fleetwood Mac's debut LP was a highlight of the late-'60s British blues boom. Green's always inspired playing, the capable (if erratic) songwriting, and the general panache of the band as a whole placed them leagues above the overcrowded field. Elmore James is a big influence on this set, particularly on the tunes fronted by Jeremy Spencer ("Shake Your Moneymaker," "Got to Move"). Spencer's bluster, however, was outshone by the budding singing and songwriting skills of Green. The guitarist balanced humor and vulnerability on cuts like "Looking for Somebody" and "Long Grey Mare," and with "If I Loved Another Woman," he offered a glimpse of the Latin-blues fusion that he would perfect with "Black Magic Woman." The album was an unexpected smash in the U.K., reaching number four on the British charts. *—Richie Unterberger*

Mr. Wonderful / Aug. 1968 / Castle ✦✦

Although it made number ten in the U.K., Fleetwood Mac's second album was a disappointment following their promising debut. So much of the record was routine blues that it could even be said that it represented something of a regression from the first LP, despite the enlistment of a horn section and pianist Christine Perfect (the future Christine McVie) to help on the sessions. In particular, the limits of Jeremy Spencer's potential for creative contribution were badly exposed, as the tracks that featured his songwriting and/or vocals were basic Elmore James covers or derivations. Peter Green, the band's major talent at this point, did not deliver original material on the level of the classic singles he would pen for the band in 1969, or even on the level of first-album standouts like "I Loved Another Woman." The best of the lot, perhaps, is "Love That Burns," with its mournful minor-key melody and sluggish, responsive horn lines. *Mr. Wonderful*, strangely, was not issued in the U.S., although about half the songs turned up on its stateside counterpart, *English Rose*, which was fleshed out with some standout late-'60s British singles and a few new tracks penned by Danny Kirwan (who joined the band after *Mr. Wonderful* was recorded). *—Richie Unterberger*

English Rose / Jan. 1969 / Epic ✦✦✦✦✦

Under the direction of Peter Green, Fleetwood Mac is heard as a British blues group, although its most notable performances are on Green's original tunes "Black Magic Woman" and "Albatross," both British hits. *—William Ruhlmann*

● **Pious Bird of Good Omen** / Aug. 1969 / Columbia ✦✦✦✦✦

With songs taken from *Fleetwood Mac* and *Mr. Wonderful*, *Pious Bird of Good Omen* serves as a worthy 12-track compilation of the band's early Peter Green days. Climbing to number 18 in the U.K., the album managed to catapult Fleetwood Mac's version of Little Willie John's "Need Your Love So Bad" into the English charts for the third time, resting at number 42. The album itself was released by Blue Horizon after the group's contract with them had expired, making it one of the best routes in which to explore their mingling of Chicago and British blues. "Albatross," "Black Magic Woman," and "I Believe My Time Ain't Long" are timeless Fleetwood Mac standards, representing some of the band's best pre-*Rumours* work. Anyone who isn't familiar with Fleetwood Mac's origins should use *Pious Bird of Good Omen* as a starting point in investigating the first wave of the band, which will almost certainly lead to further interests into albums such as *English Rose*, *Then Play On*, and *Kiln House*, and then into later albums like *Bare Trees* and *Penguin*, which reveal subtle yet effective changes in the band's blues sound. But even aside from its purpose as a collection, *Pious Bird of Good Omen* makes for a terrific laid-back stroll through some of the best British blues music ever made. *—Mike DeGagne*

Then Play On / Oct. 1969 / Reprise ✦✦✦✦

This Peter Green-led edition of the Mac isn't just an important transition between their initial blues-based incarnation and the mega-pop band they became, it's also their most vital, exciting version. The addition of Danny Kirwan as second guitarist and songwriter foreshadows not only the soft-rock terrain of "Bare Trees" and "Kiln House" with Christine Perfect-McVie, but also predicts *Rumours*. That only pertains to roughly half of the also excellent material here, though; the rest is quintessential Green. The immortal "Oh Well," with its hard-edged, thickly layered guitars and chamber-like sections, is perhaps the band's most enduring progressive composition. "Rattlesnake Shake" is another familiar number, a down-and-dirty, even-paced funk, with clean, wall-of-sound guitars. Choogling drums and Green's fiery improvisations power "Searching for Madge," perhaps Mac's most inspired work save "Green Manalishi," and leads into an unlikely symphonic interlude and the similar, lighter boogie "Fighting for Madge." A hot Afro-Cuban rhythm with beautiful guitars from Kirwan and Green on "Coming Your Way" not only defines the Mac's sound, but the rock aesthetic of the day. Of the songs with Kirwan's stamp on them, "Closing My Eyes" is a mysterious waltz love song; haunting guitars approach surf music on the instrumental "My Dream"; while "Although the Sun Is Shining" is the ultimate pre-*Rumours* number someone should revisit. Blues roots still crop up on the spatial, loose, Hendrix-tinged "Underway," the folky blues tale of a lesbian affair on "Like Crying," and the final outcry of the ever-poignant "Show Biz Blues," with Green moaning "do you really give a damn for me?" *Then Play On* is a reminder of how pervasive and powerful Green's influence was on Mac's originality and individual stance beyond his involvement. Still highly recommended and a must-buy after all these years, it remains their magnum opus. *—Michael G. Nastos*

Kiln House / Sep. 1970 / Reprise ✦✦✦

Fleetwood Mac's first album after the departure of their nominal leader, Peter Green, finds the remaining members, Mick Fleetwood, John McVie, Jeremy Spencer, and Danny Kirwan (plus McVie's wife, Christine) trying to maintain the band's guitar-heavy, blues-rock approach, with the burden falling on Spencer and Kirwan. They don't embarrass themselves, but none of this is of the caliber of Green's work. *—William Ruhlmann*

Fleetwood Mac in Chicago / 1975 / Sire/Blue Horizon ✦✦

A two-record set culled from sessions the Peter Green/Danny Kirwan/Mick Fleetwood/John McVie edition of the band held at Chess Studios in Chicago in January 1969 with such blues legends as Otis Spann and Willie Dixon. Despite their awe, the Brits hold their own on a set of standards. (Reissued on CD under the title *In Chicago 1969* on April 26, 1994.) *—William Ruhlmann*

Original Fleetwood Mac / 1977 / Original Masters ✦✦

This collection of outtakes from the group's early days probably dates from 1967-1968, and finds the band at their most reverently bluesy. Peter Green wrote most of the material on this set, which is quite similar to the band's first couple of albums in its purist British take on traditional electric blues forms. The material, however, isn't nearly as strong as the best early Fleetwood Mac; not that the band should be faulted for that, as this is an outtake collection, after all. A couple of the tunes featuring Jeremy Spencer are actually taken from an audition that Spencer's pre-Fleetwood Mac outfit, the Levi Set, recorded for the Blue Horizon label in England. The best track is the driving instrumental "Fleetwood Mac," and has been rumored to be an outtake from Green's days with John Mayall's Bluesbreakers. *—Richie Unterberger*

Cerulean / 1985 / Shanghai ✦✦✦

From the same 1969 Boston gigs that produced *Jumping At Shadows*, this double album's appeal is more limited, with a heavier emphasis on straight blues boogie and eccentric fifties rock & roll parodies that featured Jeremy Spencer. Highlights are the 16-minute version of the British hit "Green Manalishi" and the 24-minute version of "Rattlesnake Shake." *—Richie Unterberger*

Live at the Marquee, 1967 / 1992 / Trojan ✦✦

Another CD, titled *Live at Marquee*, is listed in discographies as having been released on the legitimate Trojan and Receiver labels in the early '90s. As it has the exact same track listing as this one, it could be assumed that this bootleg probably contains the same music. Regardless, the music on this disc is a pretty low-fidelity tape of a performance at the legendary London club in 1967. The discography in the Peter Green biography *Peter Green: Founder of Fleetwood Mac*, by Martin Celmins, gives the exact date of the performance as August 15, 1967; it also lists Bob Brunning, and not John McVie, as the bass player. The band play pretty well, but the vocals in particular are half-buried, the mix is blurry, and the whole thing sounds half-submerged in mud. That's too bad because the group go through highlights of their first album-era repertoire, including "Got to Move," "Dust My Broom," "Shake Your Money Maker," and less expected songs such as "Looking for Somebody" and "Long Grey Mare." It's of historic interest, certainly, as the first live recording of the band to circulate, and would be enjoyable if it were in as high-grade fidelity as the numerous legitimate live releases of the Peter Green-era Fleetwood Mac are. But it's not, not by a longshot. *—Richie Unterberger*

Live at the BBC / 1995 / Phantom ✦✦✦✦

If you've ever wondered what the original Fleetwood Mac *really* sounded like, these BBC Recordings give a very good idea. They're one part blues band, one part oldies act, one part serious, and one part tongue very much in cheek. Any band that could play Elmore James and B.B. King blues with absolute precision and passion one minute and become a drunken lunatic rockabilly band the next had to have chops and a sense of humor and this version of the Mac had both in spades. Jeremy Spencer craziness balances out Peter Green's seriousness, while Kirwan and the rhythm section of McVie and Fleetwood rope it all in. An illuminating two disc set that any roots music or blues lover will adore. Highly recommended. *—Cub Koda*

Peter Green's Fleetwood Mac Live at the BBC / Oct. 1995 / Castle ✦✦

A substantial (and official) supplement to the band's recorded legacy with Peter Green, this double CD features 36 songs broadcast between 1967 and 1971, in mostly superlative sound. The title, though, isn't 100 percent accurate; half a dozen tracks were recorded shortly after Green left the band, and since Green is still listed as part of the lineup for all but one of these in the liner notes, Castle Communications either has the dates or personnel wrong. Anyway, the music gives a good idea of the range of the band in their earliest, and by many accounts, best incarnation. It is not, however, all blues-rock by any means; quite a few of these are given over to Jeremy Spencer-dominated parodies of '50s rock, and while these are entertaining in a modest fashion, the best moments, unsurprisingly, are when guitarists Danny Kirwan and (more particularly) Green play their own material. Some of Green's most well-known compositions from the era are here ("Man of the World," "Albatross," "Rattlesnake Shake," and "Oh Well"), and in the usual BBC tradition, these have a sparer and rougher feel than the studio versions, though they don't either match or redefine them. "Preachin'," "Preachin' Blues," and "Early Morning Come" are otherwise unavailable showcases for Spencer, Green, and Kirwan, respectively, that demonstrate their facility with no-nonsense, down-home blues when they got in a serious mood. While this isn't as essential a collection as *Then Play On* or the numerous best-of anthologies covering the Peter Green era, it presents more solid evidence of the band's skills in both blues-rock and surprisingly straight rock (a cover of Tim Hardin's "Hang on to a Dream" is the surprise find of the set), though some may find the detours into comedy and '50s rock irksome. *—Richie Unterberger*

Live at the Boston Tea Party, Pt. 1: February 1970 / Jun. 23, 1998 / Original Masters ✦✦✦✦

Recorded during a legendary extended weekend stand in 1970, these live recordings from the three-guitar lineup of Fleetwood Mac have existed in various shoddy, uneven and sometimes sloppy configurations, but were finally sorted out and released as a triple disc box, (also available individually) in 1999. First generation source tapes were utilized, approximately an hour's worth of previously unreleased tracks as well as between song patter is interspersed among the discs, and the running order is restored to match that of the original performance. *Pt. 1*, taken from the first set, is a Peter Green bonanza. Kicking off with a sharp "Black Magic Woman," then weaving his liquid guitar lines into an achingly slow cover of Duster Bennett's "Jumping at Shadows," and finally breaking into a formerly unavailable 25 minute version of "Rattlesnake Shake," the disc's centerpiece, Green sings and plays with restrained authority. The extended jam on "Shake" proves that Green was a master improviser, referencing his blues roots even when flying off on spontaneous tangents no less riveting than those of the Allman Brothers or the Grateful Dead. Jeremy Spencer takes the lead on two rollicking Elmore James covers, "I Can't Hold Out," and "Got to Move," the latter seeing the light of day after being hidden in the vaults for 29 years. The set closes with Green's proto-metal "The Green Manalishi" in a riotous 13-minute version that leaves the original four-minute single looking limp. This is the tightest, and most varied of the three albums, and is recommended for newcomers not interested in the entire set. *—Hal Horowitz*

Live at the Boston Tea Party, Pt. 2 / Aug. 25, 1998 / Original Masters ♦♦♦
Recorded during a legendary extended weekend stand in 1970, these live recordings from the three guitar lineup of Fleetwood Mac have existed in various shoddy, uneven and sometimes sloppy configurations, but were finally sorted out and released as a triple disc box, (also available individually) in 1999. First generation source tapes were utilized, approximately an hour's worth of previously unreleased tracks as well as between song patter is interspersed among the discs, and the running order is restored to match that of the original performance. *Pt. 2* starts strong with a floating "World in Harmony," the only Peter Green/Danny Kirwin co-written track in the Mac catalog, and one that interestingly never appeared on a studio album. An abbreviated but aggressive "Oh Well" (the rocking opening only) segues into a half hour "Rattlesnake Shake" that's more raucous, driving and intense than the lower key, and slightly stiffer version on *Pt. 1*. The Kirwin/Green interplay here is stunning as they push each other past previous limits, driven by the forceful rhythm section of John McVie and Mick Fleetwood. Jeremy Spencer runs through terse versions of "Stranger Blues" and "Red Hot Mama," two hot and jittery Elmore James covers. But the show becomes slipshod with his '50s doo-wop tribute "Teenage Darling" complete with faux-Elvis singing that is pandering and irritating. The band jogs through a few revved up, enthusiastic but hardly essential Little Richard covers, redeemed by Fleetwood's driving drums and Green's wiry leads weaving through ten minutes of "Jenny Jenny." It may have been a blast at the time, but the tracks don't translate well without the visual impact of the three guitarists flailing away. The set ends with a heretofore unheard twelve minute jam simply entitled "Encore," where Joe Walsh of opening band the James Gang, adds a fourth guitar. Intermittently interesting, the quadruple guitars trading leads and riffs make for some predictably cluttered and unfocused music. Followers of the band during these early years might find this of passing curiosity, but for most people, you had to be there. Still, with Green playing at the peak of his powers, at least half of this disc is essential, especially to fans, and the numerous high points more than make up for the parts that drag. *—Hal Horowitz*

The Vaudeville Years of Fleetwood Mac: 1968 to 1970 / Oct. 13, 1998 / Trojan ♦♦♦
Two long CDs' worth of outtakes, alternate versions, and full-length versions from the Peter Green era, most in exemplary sound quality. Although much of this is interesting, and it's occasionally very good, it resembles *Peter Green's Fleetwood Mac Live at the BBC* in its unevenness, both in aesthetic quality and in stylistic tone. One is struck by how much the numbers featuring Green's singing and songwriting surpass those in which the other guitarists come to the fore. When Jeremy Spencer's in charge, it means you get '50s rock pastiches and blues satires (though he does an OK Elmore James schtick with "Talk to Me Baby" and "My Baby Is Sweeter"). These aren't without their amusing points—there's the entire session of songs that would have made a bonus EP with *Then Play On*, on which Spencer does fairly humorous impressions of Alexis Korner and John Mayall—but deathless art it's not. Green shines on a live version of "Oh Well" (everything else here, incidentally, is from the studio) and alternates of "Showbiz Blues" and "Love that Burns." There are also alternates of "Man of the World" and "The Green Manalishi," though frankly these aren't so different from the familiar renditions that they'll jar you into taking notice. Some of the cuts are nothing more than shapeless jams or instrumental tracks with ideas that sometimes got pumped up into full tunes on official albums. So it's kind of like having a high-quality, easily available bootleg of the Green-era Mac, accent on the *Then Play On* era. But those who like that period of Fleetwood Mac a lot will want to hear this, its luster enhanced by a 48-page booklet with an essay by Green biographer Martin Celmins. *—Richie Unterberger*

Shrine '69 / Jun. 22, 1999 / Rykodisc ♦♦♦
A live concert from January 25, 1969, recorded in Los Angeles by soundman Dinky Dawson. The fidelity is very good (excellent, in fact, by late-'60s standards), and the band are good form on a nine-song set (a tenth track is just a "Tune Up") that sticks mostly to lesser-known originals and covers. That means you don't get classics on the order of "Black Magic Woman" or "Oh Well," but on the other hand it's nice to hear different versions of some of the lesser-known early Mac originals, like Peter Green's anguished "Before the Beginning" and one of Danny Kirwan's better tunes, "Something Inside of Me." It's getting hard to keep track because of the bumper crop of official and semi-official live late-sixties Fleetwood Mac releases now available, but this is the first appearance of "Lemon Squeezer" to my knowledge, and "My Baby Sweet" is not easy to come by (although at least one version has appeared on a hard-to-find CD). No late-'60s Fleetwood Mac live release, it seems, is deemed complete without the inclusion of a couple of comic '50s rock covers, and you have to sit through "Great Balls of Fire" and "Blue Suede Shoes" here. The latter boasts over-the-top lewd lyrics, "lick my dick" being substituted for "blue blue, blue suede shoes" for a while in the chorus—just the type of schoolboy humor that might have seemed taboo-smashing in 1969, but seems sort of stupid on disc. This release would be of more interest if there wasn't already an abundance of live and outtake early Mac available on *Peter Green's Fleetwood Mac Live at the BBC, Jumping at Shadows, Cerulean*, and *The Vaudeville Years*. *—Richie Unterberger*

The Complete Blue Horizon Sessions: 1967-1969 / Oct. 19, 1999 / Sire ♦♦♦
A six-CD set of everything Fleetwood Mac recorded for the British Blue Horizon label. Wait, you're saying, didn't they only do two albums for Blue Horizon before leaving the company in early 1969? True, but there were also the non-LP singles that comprised the bulk of the U.K. compilation *The Pious Bird of Good Omen*, the two albums of blues jams in Chicago that came out later in 1969, and the 1971 LP *The Original Fleetwood Mac*, comprised of early outtakes. Make each of those half-dozen LPs a CD, add some outtakes and alternate takes to each, and you've got a pretty full box. Unintentionally, this box makes the Mac a candidate for Most Erratic Major Rock Group of the Late '60s, ranging from the sheer brilliance of Peter Green's songs to rote blues covers that are downright mundane, particularly some of the Jeremy Spencer showcases and Chicago blues jams. If you're a committed enough fan to consider buying this box, you already know that; you're probably more concerned with whether the previously unreleased material merits the cost. Those extras are marginal, to be honest, comprised largely of false starts, incidental studio chatter, and alternate versions that are pretty close to the official takes. Certainly the highlight of those newly unearthed tracks is the 37 minutes of alternate takes of "Need Your Love So Bad." It's also nice that the Danny Kirwan tracks that appeared only on the U.S. album *English Rose* are here as well. Unfortunately, this is not a complete retrospective of the Peter Green era, whose best material was recorded for Reprise; there's also a lot of noteworthy live stuff that appeared on different labels. Looking for more reasons to get the box anyway? There are extensive notes by producer Mike Vernon, which incorporate a few comments from Green. *—Richie Unterberger*

Live at the Boston Tea Party, Pt. 3 / Feb. 22, 2000 / Original Masters ♦♦♦
Recorded during a legendary extended weekend stand in 1970, these live recordings from the three guitar lineup of Fleetwood Mac have existed in various shoddy, uneven and sometimes sloppy configurations, but were finally sorted out and released as a triple disc box, (also available individually) in 1999. First generation source tapes were utilized, approximately an hour's worth of previously unreleased tracks as well as between song patter is interspersed among the discs, and the running order is restored to match that of the original performance. *Pt. 3* is a gold mine for fans of this Mac lineup, as it features a whopping six tracks-over 35 minutes-worth of newly found material. Most importantly, almost all of this music is of exceptional quality. Unfortunately the album's centerpiece, an intense, eleven minute, slow blues cover of B.B. King's "If You Let Me Love You," is marred by Peter Green's dead microphone, giving his vocals a hollow quality. But his guitar attacks with startling clarity, as he alternately pushes and lays back with style and moderation. Green deftly massages his solo, and the band gives him plenty of room to navigate, making this one of the most impassioned performances on all three discs. An instrumental version of Danny Kirwin's "Coming Your Way" is another recent addition, and throughout its seven minutes, the dueling guitars of Kirwin and Green spar with Mick Fleetwood's tribal drums creating a rhythmic whirlwind that frustratingly fades away before it's over. Jeremy Spencer whips out four Elmore James covers with a lately discovered version of "The Sun is Shining" a highlight, as his buzz-saw slide slices through the tune. A few Little Richard oldies crop up, and a frayed but propulsive version of "Tutti Frutti" where the band relaxes and rocks with class and restraint, shows how innovative they could be even working with the most basic three chord material. A remarkably subtle, weekend closing, eight minute "On We Jam" is the final unearthed cut, and proves that even with three talented guitarists sharing leads, the improvisational skills of this band were second to none. Not the most cohesive album of the trio, *Pt. 3* is still indispensable to fans, and a reliable overview of the strengths and diverse approaches of this short-lived but renowned version of Fleetwood Mac. *—Hal Horowitz*

Show-Biz Blues: 1968 to 1970, Vol. 2 / Jun. 26, 2001 / Receiver ♦♦♦
The title of this double CD might be a bit confusing to neophytes. It's basically a second helping of rarities, all previously unreleased, from the Peter Green era from Receiver. That label also put out what might be classified as "volume one" of this series, *The Vaudeville Years of Fleetwood Mac: 1968 to 1970* (also a double CD of rarities), in 1998. Since much of this is alternate studio or live versions of songs that are available in more polished form, it's something that should primarily be investigated by early Fleetwood Mac/Peter Green buffs. If you're among that crowd, though, there's a good deal of interest and even pleasure to be had. For instance, there are the three previously unissued 1966 instrumentals in the Booker T. & the MG's mode by the Peter B's, a pre-Mac band that Green and Fleetwood played in even before their stints in John Mayall's Bluesbreakers. Other high spots take in a cover of Otis Rush's characteristically spooky minor-key blues "I Have to Laugh" (with Jeremy Spencer on piano and vocals), and working versions of "Show-Biz Blues," one of Green's most scorching, soul-baring originals. Then there's the nice alternate take of "World in Harmony," and "Leaving Town Blues," an oddity in that it has violin by Nick Pickett. Disc two is comprised entirely of live 1970 material, the first two songs from Boston February 1970, the rest from a gig simply identified as London 1970. The sound quality on the live stuff is OK and the performances good, though so much live Mac from this time has already appeared that it's not a revelation; if you've been collecting these all along, you'll already have live versions of most of the songs, though it's nice to have a seven-minute "Coming Your Way." Of course there are still too many Spencer rock & roll oldies or Spencer originals that are pastiches of rock & roll oldies, as well as a good deal of ho-hum blues tunes. The 52-page booklet, by Green biographer Martin Celmins, is certainly a vital bonus, though, with commentary on both the Peter Green era as a whole and the tracks on *Show-Biz Blues* in particular. *—Richie Unterberger*

Jumping at Shadows: The Blues Years / Jul. 23, 2002 / Sanctuary ♦♦♦
This British two-disc collection offers a rather unique look at the Peter Green-era Fleetwood Mac rather than just focusing on the band's output from 1967, immediately after leaving John Mayall's Bluesbreakers, to 1970 when Green left. The set is chock-full of fine studio material that documents the evolution of the band from a power trio to its Jeremy Spencer and Danny Kirwan incarnations. And while it's true that other collections have documented the band from this period very well, none of them has dug quite as deep into the live archives or revealed the subsequent Peter Green side projects of the time. Here are 36 tracks that offer stunning live renditions of Green's "Black Magic Woman," "Oh Well," the second part of the "Madge Sessions," and Spencer's "Stranger Blues," as well as an absolutely searing version of Kirwan's "Comin' Your Way." Given the budget price of this completely remastered set, these alone would have been worth the price, but in a sense it's only the beginning. There are numerous tracks of Green with musical running-mate Duster Bennett from the pre-Fleetwood Mac years, including a truly haunted version of the title track. Add to this four tracks of Green's work with Bob Brunning's Sunflower Blues Band, and you have an evocative and intense portrait of a band struggling to come to grips with a reluctant genius as a frontman, and the era. What is most revealing is Green's focus on execution and mood. The music has a way of getting past him, not technically, but emotionally, on the live material—the title cut, "Rattlesnake Shake," "Lazy Poker Blues"—as well as on the instrumentals. Check the versions of Kirwan's "World in Harmony," and the extremities in this version of "Green Manalishi," for evidence. Neil Slaven assembled this comp. He also wrote its confounding and labyrinthine liner notes, which are full of information but light on continuity or style. Slaven's method of creating a musical portrait, however, is virtually unassailable. The tracks wind in and out of one another, back and forth across time and partnerships as if telling a secret that can only be fully understood when the last sentence has been whispered. There is no secret in the fact that Green was a reluctant superstar, and that madness overwhelmed him at his playing peak. What isn't known, however, is the great vulnerability and tenderness he put into every performance. That side of Peter Green is well documented here, the terminally shy skinny kid who could rain down fire from the heavens and draw water from the wells of hell on a guitar. *—Thom Jurek*

Mary Flower

b. 1949, Delphi, IN
Vocals, Guitar, Dobro / Folk-Blues, Acoustic Blues
Chances are that you'll find Mary Flower in the folk section of your local record shop. She did found a folk-cum-jazz-based ensemble called Mother Folkers in Denver, which was the mile-high city's leading women's folk collective; and she could look the part of a folkie "Earth mother" type. Flower moved seriously into blues over the last decade, however, and hasn't looked back since.

Born in Delphi, IN, Flower made her way to Denver at the beginning of the '70s, when she was in her twenties, and set up shop in the city's folk community; her gigs made her a name locally, and she established Mother Folkers. She always appreciated the blues, but it was a two-week period of study with Jim Schwall and Steve James at a blues workshop in West Virginia that transformed her.

Flower described herself as "consumed" by the experience, and made the decision to devote herself to the blues. She restarted her career, but initially encountered resistance, partly because she was a white blueswoman who didn't conform to expectations—ever since Janis Joplin, white female blues performers have been expected to sound like Big Mama Thornton, which Flower didn't, Scrapper Blackwell being more of a role model. Since the early '90s, however, she has gradually achieved acceptance, and has played places like Buddy Guy's club in Chicago as well as various festivals, where she has been well received, and tours regionally and nationally.

As a folk artist, Flower played alongside Geoff Muldaur, David Bromberg, and Ramblin' Jack Elliot. Her work in blues, however, has been strongly influenced by Scrapper Blackwell, Henry Glover, and Robert Johnson, but especially Blind Lemon Jefferson. She plays with passion, none of it forced or posed, and she has a husky voice to go with the kind of stuff she covers—she could sing prettier than she does, but what she does seems honest. She also writes originals with a cutting, clever edge. Flower has been around about as long as Bonnie Raitt, only without the major-label record contracts, the arena and movie appearances, or the Grammy, and deserves to be known by at least as many people. *—Bruce Eder*

High Heeled Blues / 1991 / ReR ♦♦♦

● **Blues Jubilee** / 1994 / Resounding ♦♦♦♦♦
This record will probably be found in the folk section of your store, but don't let that fool you—it's a dazzling piece of modern acoustic blues, with its feet in the '90s and the '30s and no stretch evident. Flower covers Scrapper Blackwell's "Memphis Town," and Memphis Minnie's "Me and My Chauffeur Blues," and, most impressively, Robert Johnson's "Walking Blues" and Blind Lemon Jefferson's "Six White Horses" (which, in a fairer reality, would be the single off this album). Her playing, backed by Steve James, is dexterous and punchy, with some beautiful and subtle flourishes (Scrapper Blackwell will come to mind), and her singing is hard and deep, with none of the softness that normally betrays folkies who try to go this route. Her originals are strong, too, with "Long-Legged Daddy" the standout. She's a blueswoman and she means it. *—Bruce Eder*

Rosewood & Steel / 1996 / Bluesette ♦♦♦
Not quite as strong as it predecessor but definitely worth hearing, *Rosewood & Steel* has Flower putting her own special spin on music by Junior Parker ("Mystery Train"), Charlie Patton ("Pony Blues"), Skip James ("Cypress Grove Blues"), and Brooks Berry ("Can't Sleep For Dreaming"), along with a bunch of originals. Geoff Muldaur, Amos Garrett, Steve James, and Paul Geremia all contribute to various songs. Flower's singing is rich and husky, and her originals exploit the various sides of her musical personality, from playful to dark and moody (check out "Cock-a-Doodle Blues" and "Two Days Straight"), and all but one slots in perfectly with the covers on this collection. Her "Midnite Blue" vaguely recalls CSN's "4+20," with some gorgeous slide by Steve James, while she impresses and then some with her lap steel playing on the delightful "Roll On, Mississippi, Roll On" and Patton's searing "Pony Blues" (which also features Geremia's slide). The real surprise is "Mystery Train," which gets about the slowest, most lyrical treatment ever on record here. *—Bruce Eder*

Ladyfingers / Sep. 11, 2001 / Bluesette ♦♦♦♦
Unassuming blues heroine Mary Flowers proves once again that she's one of the nation's premier fingerstyle blues guitarists on *Ladyfingers*. More importantly, she's made a beautifully eclectic and listenable record, which can't be said of many traditionalist outings. Though primarily a purveyor of the Piedmont blues (the Delta tradition's brighter, syncopated cousin), Flower takes flight on this record, not limiting herself to scholarly ragtime reproductions. One moment, she's getting low-down and dirty on an imaginative medley of Big Joe William's "Baby, Please Don't Go" and Booker T. Jones' "Green Onions." The next, she's delivering a torchy rendition of Toots Thielemans' jazz classic "Bluesette," followed by a country spiritual and two thoughtful original instrumentals, showing off her heavyweight chops. Memphis Minnie, Jimmie Oden, and Ivory Joe Hunter also get their due. Flower's version of Hunter's "I Almost Lost My Mind" is priceless, featuring harmony from Mollie O'Brien. Thoughtful accompaniment by Pat Donohue (guitar), John Magnie (accordion), and Mark Diamond (string bass) really adds to the session. Flower's technique is exceptional throughout and, in the end, serves the highest purpose—the music. *—Bill Meyer*

Sue Foley

b. Mar. 29, 1968, Ottawa, Ontario, Canada
Vocals, Guitar / Modern Electric Blues
This highly touted vocalist/guitarist originally hails from Ottawa, Canada, although her homebase shifted to Austin, Texas when she signed with Antone's Records and cut her debut set, *Young Girl Blues*, in 1992 (an encore, *Without a Warning*, quickly followed). Foley's wicked lead guitar makes her a rarity among blueswomen.

When she was a child in Ottawa, Foley listened to rock & roll and blues-rock groups like the Rolling Stones. Although these bands sowed the seeds of her affection for the blues, her love for the music didn't blossom until she witnessed James Cotton in concert when she was 15 years old. Cotton inspired Foley to pick up the electric guitar. During her late teens and early 20s, she jammed with local Ottawa bar bands—she didn't form her own group until she moved to Vancouver in the mid-'80s.

Foley sent a demo tape of herself to Antone's Records in 1990. Impressed, the label arranged an audition for the guitarist. Sue moved to Austin and soon signed a recording contract with Antone's. In 1992, her debut album, *Young Girl Blues*, was released. It was acclaimed by a number of blues publications. Two years later she released her second album, *Without a Warning*. It was followed by *Big City Blues* in 1995. Subsequent efforts include 1996's *A Walk in the Sun*, 1998's *Ten Days in November* and 2000's *Love Comin' Down* and *Back to the Blues*. *—Bill Dahl & Stephen Thomas Erlewine*

Young Girl Blues / 1992 / Antone's ♦♦♦♦♦
Sue Foley's debut album, *Young Girl Blues*, is an impressive effort. Not only is Foley a wild, adventurous guitarist, she can write songs that don't merely rehash standard blue clichés. Her songs have an intense passion that is heightened by her array of gutsy guitar textures, which are rooted in blues tradition but never tied down to it. *—Thom Owens*

Without a Warning / 1994 / Discovery ♦♦♦

Big City Blues / 1995 / Antone's ♦♦♦♦

Walk in the Sun / Jul. 9, 1996 / Discovery ♦♦♦♦
Walk in the Sun isn't quite typical Sue Foley. With her first three albums, the guitarist demonstrated that she had a firm grasp on searingly electric Chicago blues and high-voltage blues-rock. With *Walk in the Sun*, she expands her sonic palette somewhat, taking in gritty R&B, reverb-drenched surf and down-home country, among other styles of blues and roots music. Throughout the album, she demonstrates that she is gifted enough to effortlessly bring in these other styles without losing her distinctive identity. The result is her best album since her stellar debut, *Young Girl Blues*. *—Thom Owens*

Ten Days in November / Apr. 21, 1998 / Shanachie ♦♦♦
This blond blues belter serves up some soulful original tunes on her fifth album. While her voice is a bit thin, the disc makes a strong impression with sturdy songs and a great backing band. At the forefront are Foley's fluid lead guitar lines. *—Tim Sheridan*

● **Love Comin' Down** / May 9, 2000 / Shanachie ♦♦♦♦♦
Sue Foley just keeps getting better. On her sixth album the singer/songwriter/guitarist turns in a diverse set of blues covers (a slow mournful Willie Dixon's "The Same Thing"), Stax styled, horn fueled R&B ("Be Next to You"), New Orleans party rockin' (an obscure Freddie King cover of "You're Barking Up the Wrong Tree"), and even a spooky, flamenco influenced, spaghetti Western instrumental ("Mediterranean Breakfast") which surprisingly gel into a consistently satisfying album. Foley's distinctive voice—part Bonnie Raitt, part Bessie Smith, part Memphis Minnie—has evolved and matured, tearing and tugging at the edges, flawlessly complimenting these lovelorn songs. There's an airy, effortless, unhurried, but not laid back, quality on *Love Comin' Down*, likely motivated by recording in the Tragically Hip's cushy home studio, and Foley's performances here take on a bluesy edginess, best exemplified by the acoustic tracks "Let My Tears Fall Down" and the album closing "How Strong" where she sighs and cries with a unnerving poignancy. As producer, fellow Canadian blues-rocker Colin Linden leaves breathing room for Foley's biting, snakelike guitar and heartfelt vocals, while bolstering the tunes with subtle horns and swampy, understated drums. Lucinda Williams dramatic vocals are impressive on "Empty Cup," but it's Linden's spine-chilling dobro and Foley's menacing guitar which stand out. With a rugged, uncompromising style, smooth yet earthy and wholly assured

approach, Sue Foley dexterously treads the line between commercial and rootsy, and in the process creates her most eclectic, and best, album. *—Hal Horowitz*

Back to the Blues / Oct. 24, 2000 / Antone's ♦♦♦

Where the Action Is / Jun. 11, 2002 / Shanachie ♦♦♦

Sue Foley's seventh studio album in a decade successfully follows on the heels of 2000's terrific *Love Comin' Down*. Less atmospheric and harder rocking, Foley writes or co-writes all but three tracks, and proves herself as talented a composer as singer and guitar slinger. There's a bit of a Sheryl Crow feel to lots of this, but Foley stays locked in a blues vein, even on the more melodic rockers like "Baby Where Are You," "Get Yourself Together," and the midtempo title track. Colin Linden's hands-off production lets the songs breath, and the singer sounds loose, relaxed, and in control throughout, especially on ballads like the emotional "Let It Go." "Vertigo Blues" wades into primitive and swampy Creedence waters, aided by the album's only bass-less backing, featuring Linden on eerie, slithering slide and Bryan Owings' dark, pounding drums. A lumbering stab at the Stones' "Stupid Girl" sounds too self-conscious, but versions of Etta James' sexy "Roll With Me Henry" and an acoustic version of the obscure traditional Delta tune "Down the Big Road Blues" (best known from a version by Mattie Delaney) prove that Foley can be simultaneously sensuous and tough. Veteran backing musicians like Wilco's Ken Coomer and keyboardist Richard Bell never hog the spotlight, keeping the attention on the songs and Foley's short but stinging leads. Although she's not taking many chances, those who are already fans of the Canadian blues-rocker will be thrilled to add this rugged release to their collections, and newcomers can effectively begin theirs here. *—Hal Horowitz*

The Ford Blues Band

Group / West Coast Blues

After leaving Ukiah, CA, and moving south to San Francisco to form the Charles Ford Band (named for their father) in the late '60s with harmonica player Gary Smith, brothers Pat (drums) and Robben (guitar) were enlisted by Charlie Musselwhite and were pivotal members of one of the best aggregations the harpist ever led. Leaving Musselwhite after recording Arhoolie's *Takin' My Time*, they recruited bassist Stan Poplin and younger brother Mark, then age 17, on harmonica and played under the name the Real Charles Ford Band. Heavily influenced by the original Butterfield Blues Band and the Chess catalog, the quartet was famous for their live jazz explorations—often jamming for 30 minutes or more on a John Coltrane and George Benson tune—and hear-a-pin-drop dynamics (with Mark abandoning mike and amp to play acoustically into the room or Robben turning the volume all the way off on his fat-body Gibson L-5). Muddy Waters sat in with and praised the young band, and Chess Records even came courting. Robben went on to major cult status via session work and sporadic solo releases, and after lengthy hiatuses Mark and Pat continue to gig around the Bay Area and Europe. Pat founded his own Blue Rock'it label, on which albums like *The Ford Blues Band*, *Hot Shots*, and *1999* were released. The band's influence in northern California is still enormous, particularly among guitar players who continue to ape Robben's licks. *—Dan Forte*

● **Here We Go!** / 1990 / Crosscut ♦♦♦♦

Here We Go!, the first album from the Ford Blues Band, is a propulsive, energetic collection of Chicago blues with a twist. The twist is in the group's passion for improvisation, where they can turn standard three-chord progressions into unexpectedly jazzy interludes which add real meat to their music. The result is a thrilling, exciting debut from a fresh, promising combo. *—Thom Owens*

The Ford Blues Band / 1991 / Blue Rock'it ♦♦♦

Live at Breninale 92 / Nov. 10, 1993 / Blue Rock'it ♦♦♦♦

Hotshots / Nov. 15, 1994 / Blue Rock'it ♦♦♦

Fords & Friends / Sep. 3, 1996 / Blue Rock'it ♦♦♦

1999 / Jun. 8, 1999 / Blue Rock'it ♦♦♦

Frankie Ford

b. Aug. 4, 1939, Gretna, LA

Vocals / New Orleans R&B, Rock & Roll

It's ironic that some of the greatest New Orleans R&B of the '50s was sung by a white man. Although he could have passed for a teen idol, Frankie Ford sang with as much grit as anyone of any color in the Crescent City. He recorded some fine singles for the Ace label in the late '50s, particularly the pounding "Sea Cruise," which made the Top 20 in 1959 and remains one of the hits most identified with the classic New Orleans R&B sound. "Sea Cruise" actually began life as a Huey "Piano" Smith song with Bobby Marchan on vocals, but producer Johnny Vincent had the inspired idea of dubbing Ford's singing on top of Smith's backing track. "Sea Cruise," with its bleating foghorn and irresistible piano groove, was an impossible act to follow, and Ford never approached the Top 20 again. But he cut several more gutsy sides for Ace that featured top New Orleans players like Huey Smith and saxophonist Red Tyler; one of the best, "Roberta," was covered by the Animals in the mid-'60s. A few of his singles found him following ill-advised swing jazz and teen idol directions, and he faded from view in the '60s, although he made a cameo appearance in the film version of Alan Freed's life. *—Richie Unterberger*

New Orleans Dynamo / 1984 / Ace ♦♦♦

Recorded in 1984 in London, this is a surprisingly decent effort that emulates the sound of New Orleans R&B-rock circa 1960 with reasonable accuracy. Ford's voice sounds pretty much unchanged as he goes through a set heavy on remakes of old New Orleans tunes, like "A Certain Girl," "Sick and Tired," Huey Smith's "Don't You Know Yockomo," "Lipstick Traces (On a Cigarette)," and "Bony Moronie." The album is now available as part of Ace's CD reissue *Cruisin' with Frankie Ford*, which also includes 14 songs done by the singer for Imperial from 1960-62. *—Richie Unterberger*

All Time Greatest Hits / Sep. 9, 1996 / Stardust ♦♦♦♦

A straight up reissue of Frankie's debut album. No collection of leftovers here, this original 12-song collection featured the hits "Sea Cruise," "Roberta," and "Alimony" along with bluesier material like "Cheatin' Woman," and "It Must Be Jelly." As a budget priced collection, this one's hard to turn pass up. An essential building block for any New Orleans collection. *—Cub Koda*

Ooh-Wee Baby!: The Best of Frankie Ford / 1998 / West Side ♦♦♦♦♦

Frankie Ford's one big hit, "Sea Cruise," may rank him as a one-hit wonder, but his tenure at Ace produced other material in the fine Crescent City tradition, loaded with Ford's exuberant vocals and great playing from the New Orleans '50s A-team of session stalwarts. The collection opens with take one of Ford's great hit, different enough but really great, a true hit in the making. Both sides of his first Ace single ("Cheatin' Woman" b/w "Last One to Cry") follows that in fine fashion, and of course, the issued version of his big hit is here too. The majority of Ford's later recordings find him trying for Sinatra respectability via the Bobby Darin route, but tunes like the undubbed take of "Hour of Need," "Watchdog" and "Morgus the Magnificent" (with a young Mac Rebennack on lead guitar) are fine rocking and soulful additions to complete the big picture on this 27-track collection. *—Cub Koda*

Sea Cruise: The Very Best of Frankie Ford / Jun. 16, 1998 / Music Club ♦♦♦♦

Frankie Ford's one big hit, "Sea Cruise," is one of the truly great one-shot marvels of rock & roll history, all noise and groove and a big invitation to the party. But Ford also knew how to sell a song and the efforts of his recorded legacy at Ace Records is slimmed down to essentials on this 18-track very-best-of collection. Both sides of his debut single ("Cheatin' Woman" and "Last One to Cry") are aboard, along with Ford's later recordings, where the move into nightclub respectability all but quenches the rock & roll fire out of his music. This budget package features nine less tunes than the more deluxe Westside package and duplicates everything there. But the transfers are crisp and clear and if you still want the bare bones essentials, this also makes a recommended purchase. *—Cub Koda*

Cruisin' With Frankie Ford / Nov. 24, 1998 / Ace ♦♦♦

This has both sides of all six singles Ford did for Imperial from 1960-62 and a couple of unissued tracks from the same era, as well as his 1984 Ace recording *New Orleans Dynamo*. The main attraction is the Imperial material, which was very hard to find before this reissue. Ford's association with Imperial wasn't very fruitful commercially, producing just a couple of small hits in covers of Joe Jones' "You Talk Too Much" and Boyd Bennett's "Seventeen." This batch lacks anything on the order of "Sea Cruise," but it's still pretty solid vintage New Orleans R&B, produced by Dave Bartholomew. Some of the cuts are sweetened up with strings and backup female singers, but it's mostly on the earthy side; when he slows the pace down on "Dedicated to Fats" and "One Hour," he can sound uncannily like Fats Domino. *New Orleans Dynamo* is well above average for a '80s effort by a '50s rocker; nothing new here (in fact, many of its songs are covers of old New Orleans classics), but Ford and the London musicians execute the Crescent City R&B sound convincingly. *—Richie Unterberger*

● **Let's Take a Sea Cruise** / Aug. 24, 1999 / Ace ♦♦♦♦♦

Fine collection of 18 vintage sides, including "Sea Cruise" and "Roberta," establishes Ford's claim as one of the first of the great white R&B singers. Most of this is first-rate New Orleans R&B with a swinging bounce, enhanced by Ford's cool and cocky vocals, although a few tracks are lame excursions into trad jazz or teen idol fare. For now it's the definitive Ford anthology, but there's room for improvement: documentation for when the tracks were originally released is nonexistent, and much of the music was obviously dubbed from vinyl records, not from master tapes. *—Richie Unterberger*

Robben Ford

b. Dec. 16, 1951, Ukiah, CA

Vocals, Guitar / Crossover Jazz, Fusion, Modern Electric Blues

Robben Ford has had a diverse career. He taught himself guitar when he was 13 and considered his first influence to be Mike Bloomfield. At 18, he moved to San Francisco to form the Charles Ford Band (named after his father, who was also a guitarist) and was soon hired to play with Charles Musselwhite for nine months. In 1971, the Charles Ford Blues Band was re-formed and recorded for Arhoolie in early 1972. Ford played with Jimmy Witherspoon (1972-1973), the L.A. Express with Tom Scott (1974), George Harrison, and Joni Mitchell. In 1977, he was a founding member of the Yellowjackets, which he stayed with until 1983, simultaneously having a solo career and working as a session guitarist. In 1986, Ford toured with Miles Davis and he had two separate periods (1985 and 1987) with Sadao Watanabe, but he seemed to really find himself in 1992 when he returned to his roots: the blues. Ford formed a new group, the Blue Line, and has since recorded a couple of blues-rock dates for Stretch that are among the finest of his career. In 1999, he released *Sunrise* on Rhino and *Supernatural* on Blue Thumb. *—Scott Yanow*

Discovering the Blues / 1972-1978 / Rhino ♦♦♦

Discovering the Blues is culled from a series of concerts Robben Ford gave in the early '70s at Huntington Beach's Golden Bear and Ash Grove in Hollywood. At the time, Ford was just beginning his career, and his style wasn't nearly as accomplished as it would later be. Instead, he simply burns, tearing through blues classics with a passion and vigor—there is a joy of discovery in his playing which makes the music nearly transcendent, even with its flaws. *Discovering the Blues* is rawer than most records in Ford's catalog, but any serious fan will find it a necessary addition to their collection. *—Thom Owens*

Schizophonic / 1976 / MCA ♦♦

The Inside Story / May 1979 / Elektra ♦♦

Talk to Your Daughter / 1988 / Warner Brothers ♦♦♦♦

On his 1988 solo effort *Talk to Your Daughter*, singer/guitarist Robben Ford proves himself a master of sophisticated blues-rock guitar playing. The material is quite strong, and all the musicians perform at the highest level, but it's Ford's stellar soloing that makes this release. Fans of flailing '80s rock virtuosos would do well to check out Ford's exceptional work on *Talk to Your Daughter.* The musician's colorful yet controlled improvising and harmonic mastery is a rare and beautiful sonic treat. The title track is dripping with soulful, well-placed guitar lines that play like a master lesson of uptempo blues phrasing that guitarists would do well to study. Other standouts include "Born Under a Bad Sign" and "Ain't Got Nothin' But the Blues." The fine arrangements and especially Vinnie Colaiuta's sharp drumming are all tightly wound with crisp, clear production that tops off "Talk to Your Daughter," making it a shining success. Listeners fond of Ford's work with the Yellowjackets and numerous side gigs, as well as guitarists and all musicians, should enjoy this very professional, succinctly executed offering. First rate! *—Vincent Jeffries*

Robben Ford & the Blue Line / 1992 / Stretch ✦✦✦

The debut set by guitarist Robben Ford with his Blue Line trio (a blues band with bassist Roscoe Beck and drummer Tom Brechtlein) finds Ford returning to his roots and playing the music that best fits his style. An effective singer, it is for Ford's powerful guitar playing that this CD (which has seven originals among the nine numbers) is most highly recommended to blues collectors. *—Scott Yanow*

Mystic Mile / 1993 / Stretch ✦✦✦✦

• **Handful of Blues** / Sep. 12, 1995 / Blue Thumb ✦✦✦✦

On *Handful of Blues,* Robben Ford strips his sound back to the basics, recording a set of blues with only a bassist and a drummer. The group runs through a handful of standards, including "Don't Let Me Be Misunderstood" and "I Just Want to Make Love to You," and a number of made-to-order originals. Throughout the album the musicians play well, but Ford's voice is never commanding. However, this is a minor flaw, since his guitar speaks for itself. *—Stephen Thomas Erlewine*

Blues Connotation / 1996 / ITM ✦✦✦

Tiger Walk / 1997 / Blue Thumb ✦✦✦✦

The first thing that comes to mind when listening to *Tiger Walk* is the pair of instrumental albums recorded by Jeff Beck in the mid-seventies, *Blow by Blow* and *Wired.* Like those two recordings, this outing showcases a fiery, inventive electric guitarist in a rock and jazz-rock setting. Robben Ford, known in recent years for his blues work with his band, the Blue Line, eschews vocals here, teaming up with keyboard funk master Bernie Worrell for some chunky, funky, wah-wah-laden grooves. This music, led by Ford's blazing guitar lines, is more appropriately categorized as instrumental rock than jazz, but the rhythms recall James Brown and Worrell's alma mater, the P-Funk gang, as often as they do those of a hard rock band. Tenor saxophonist Bob Malach turns in a couple of solid solos, and the rhythm section of drummer Steve Jordon and bassist Charlie Drayton cooks throughout. *—Jim Newsom*

The Authorized Bootleg / Mar. 24, 1998 / Blue Thumb ✦✦✦✦

This is a keeper from the word "go." Recorded live in 1995 (but not released until 1998) at Yoshi's in Oakland, CA, Robben Ford is joined by long-time Blue Line trio members Roscoe Beck on bass and Tom Brechtlein on drums, as well as Bill Boublitz on a baby grand piano. Although nearly all of the songs can be found on other Ford albums (most are from *Handful of Blues*), one of the things that makes this jazzy recording so special is that Ford is playing only an acoustic guitar. The Ray Charles gem "Don't Let the Sun Catch You Crying" (which you WON'T find elsewhere) is simply beautiful, and on Paul Butterfield's "Lovin' Cup," it's just Ford and his guitar. The brilliance of his playing and the reason behind why so many guitar players put him at the top of their list can be found in Ford's performance on this release, alternating between lead and rhythm. *The Authorized Bootleg* also has great (albeit laid-back) versions of "When I Leave Here" and "Tired of Talkin'." Highly, highly recommended. *—Ann Wickstrom*

Supernatural / 1999 / Blue Thumb ✦✦✦

When an artist records one type of music exclusively for years, it's always amusing to hear the artist's manager, record company or publicist claim that he/she "defies categorization." The fact is that when an artist spends his or her entire career recording a specific style of music, categorization comes easy—and it's silly and dishonest to claim otherwise. But if any artist really does defy categorization, it's Robben Ford. The eclectic singer/guitarist is a compelling bluesman, but he's equally convincing as a jazz improviser and a pop-rock singer. On *Supernatural,* Ford's primary role is that of an easygoing pop/soft rock singer—although a pop/soft rock singer who often incorporates soul, blues or jazz. Ford, who was 47 when this album was recorded, gets in some nice guitar solos on the title song and the bluesy, playful "Lovin' Cup," but *Supernatural* isn't a blowing date—it's a vocal date, and Ford's vocals often take us back to the pop world of the '70s. In fact, Steely Dan's '70s albums are a valid comparison on this CD—like Steely, Ford incorporates enough R&B, jazz and blues elements to give his relaxed, laid-back pop and soft rock a healthy amount of grit and spice. Especially enjoyable is the socially aware pop-soul item "Hey, Brother"—depending on how you arranged it, this is the type of song that would have worked for Steely Dan, El Chicano, War, Rare Earth or Donny Hathaway in the '70s. *Supernatural* isn't among Ford's essential albums, and it falls short of being a gem. But it's a decent, if slightly uneven, effort from one of the few artists who really is versatile enough to defy categorization. *—Alex Henderson*

Sunrise / Mar. 2, 1999 / Rhino ✦✦✦✦

It's ironic that some of the people who swear up and down that they don't like jazz will get into Robben Ford, whose career has as much to do with jazz as it does with blues, pop, soul and rock. Though Ford was never a "jazz snob," his jazz credentials are quite solid. Jazz, blues and rock are all primary ingredients of *Sunrise,* a CD that was released in 1999 and contains live performances at Los Angeles and London venues in 1972. Back then, the singer/guitarist was in his early twenties and hadn't yet become famous, but those who were hip to Ford knew that he was a unique young talent who had considerable promise. This unpredictable and highly enjoyable collection ranges from the hardcore instrumental jazz of Miles Davis' "Eighty One" (which finds Ford playing the sax) and jazz-rock fusion of "Miss Miss" to spirited performances of Willie Dixon's "Little Red Rooster" and Peter Chatman's "Every Day I Have the Blues." The latter finds Ford performing a vocal duet with blues singer Jimmy Witherspoon, who is the only vocalist on "Ain't Nobody's Business." The late Witherspoon thought the world of Ford, and it's easy to see why they got along so well—like Ford, Witherspoon was an eclectic, unpredictable artist who held jazz and the blues in equally high regard. Whether you're into jazz, blues or rock—or all of the above—*Sunrise* is a CD to savor. *—Alex Henderson*

Anthology: The Early Years / Mar. 6, 2001 / Rhino ✦✦✦

Robben Ford has always been a very eclectic musician; therefore, the people who get the most out of his recordings tend to have eclectic tastes themselves. If you're the sort of broad-minded listener who holds blues, rock, and jazz in equally high regard, *Anthology: The Early Years* is a musical feast. This two-CD set, which Avenue Jazz provided in 2001, looks back on recordings that the singer/guitarist/saxman made from 1972-1976 (when he was in his early to mid-twenties). Even then, Ford was difficult to categorize—those who insist on pigeonholing musicians wondered if he was really a blues-rock singer or a jazz instrumentalist at heart. And, truth be told, he wore both hats equally well. Anyone who loves down-and-dirty blues-rock cannot help but applaud his gutsy versions of Willie Dixon's "Little Red Rooster" and B.B. King's "Sweet Sixteen." But Ford is equally convincing as a jazz instrumentalist on "Softly Rolling," "Miss Miss," and Miles Davis' "Eighty One." Many of the instrumentals are shining examples of '70s fusion, but Ford favors more of a post-bop approach on the standard "You Don't Know What Love Is" (which is one of the tunes that finds him on tenor sax and is very John Coltrane-minded). *Anthology: The Early Years* isn't the last word on Ford in the '70s, but Avenue Jazz' picks are generally excellent—and it is certainly among the places to go if you're exploring his early output for the first time. *—Alex Henderson*

A Tribute to Paul Butterfield / Jul. 31, 2001 / Blue Rock'it ✦✦✦

Blue Moon / Mar. 12, 2002 / Concord Jazz ✦✦✦✦

Over the years many people have asked, "Will the real Robben Ford please stand up?" Those are the people who wonder if the singer/guitarist is really a blues-rock vocalist or a jazz fusion instrumentalist at heart. But truth be told, Ford is many different things. He is genuinely eclectic, which is why one never really knows from one album to the next what direction he will take. *Blue Moon,* Ford's first album for Concord Jazz, is primarily a vocal date. Ford gets in his share of inspired guitar solos, and he provides one instrumental: the gutsy "Indianola." But most of the time he sings. And as a vocalist, he favors an exciting blend of blues, rock, and soul on tracks like "Something for the Pain," "Don't Deny Your Love," and "The Way You Treated Me (You're Gonna Be Sorry)." Meanwhile, "It Don't Make Sense (You Can't Make Peace)" and the moody "Make Me Your Only One" are among the CD's more jazz-tinged vocal offerings. Ford does not embrace a standard 12-bar blues format on all of the material, but then, he never claimed to be a blues purist. Ford isn't a blues purist any more than he is a rock purist, a jazz purist, or an R&B purist—he is much too restless and broad-minded to be any type of purist. That isn't good news if you only like one type of music, but it is very good news if you share Ford's eclectic outlook and have admired his diversity over the years. Ford was in his late forties when he recorded *Blue Moon* in the early 2000s, and this pleasing CD is the work of a musician who is still very much on top of his game. *—Alex Henderson*

T-Model Ford

Vocals, Guitar / Modern Delta Blues, Electric Delta Blues

Like most Fat Possum artists, T-Model Ford plays raw, juke-joint blues. And like fellow Fat Possumers Junior Kimbrough and R.L. Burnside, Ford's opportunity to cut albums arrived late in life; he was around 75 when his debut *Pee-Wee Get My Gun* was recorded in 1997. Even by Fat Possum standards, Ford's sound is pretty bare and raw, usually featuring only shuffle drums and Ford's basic, buzzy chords and riffs. He returned in mid-2000 with *She Ain't None of Your'n.* *—Richie Unterberger*

Pee Wee Get My Gun / May 20, 1997 / Fat Possum ✦✦✦

Ford fits snugly into what has become the Fat Possum house sound: repetitive, raw electric guitar riffs, going off on one or two-chord vamps with stream-of-consciousness, improvised-sounding lyrics. The effect can be hypnotic or tedious, depending upon your taste. It's got more of a boogie, down-home feel that the usual Fat Possum release though, with Frank Frost adding keyboards to the usual guitar-drum duo combination on a couple of cuts. *—Richie Unterberger*

You Better Keep Still / Nov. 10, 1998 / Fat Possum ✦✦✦

It's tough to look bad-ass when you're 77 years old, but check out the sneer on T-Model Ford's face on the cover of *You Better Keep Still.* The black hat-sporting ex-con from Mississippi didn't get serious about music until he was in his late sixties and he still doesn't take anything seriously as he improvises his way through many of these songs. Musically, he keeps everything as simple and spare as can be; no solos, just jagged guitar riffs set to his partner Spam's primitively unadorned drumming. The record begins with T-Model banging on a wooden box on "If I Had Wings, Pt. 1" and talking madness about trying to get a drink of water and being attacked by various reptiles and women he attempts to hit on. Then comes the extremely catchy guitar riff from "To the Left to the Right," a frenzied, juke-joint dance number. There's also the harsh, out of tune "Here Comes Papa" and the wacked and very funny "These Eyes." Though it's not really essential to the record, producer Jim Waters' noisy remix of "Pop Pop Pop," based mostly on a riff from "Here Comes Papa," is groovy. But T-Model Ford is in no need of a club remix. He's got everything down perfect and the wild blues that flow naturally from him are as real and feisty as blues music gets. *—Adam Bregman*

- **She Ain't None of Your'n** / May 23, 2000 / Fat Possum ♦♦♦♦

With this, his third release on Fat Possum Records, T-Model Ford takes his place as one of the label's elder statesmen, quite an accomplishment on a label loaded with septuagenarians. Ford doesn't pull any punches on *She Ain't None of Your'n*. The electronic loops and beats that have slowly crept into so many of the label's recent blues releases are noticeably absent. Instead listeners are left with a strong collection of raw, timeless Delta blues. As on Ford's previous albums, tracks range from the sublime (e.g., "Sail On") to the bizarre (e.g., "Chicken Head Man"), but even the most indulgent moments here are powered by strong grooves. On most of the album's tracks, Ford's guitar and vocals are accompanied only by drums. He and longtime drummer Spam had a falling out during the recording of the album, so Bryan Barry and the legendary Sam Carr split drumming duties on about half the tracks. There is no appreciable difference in their playing styles. Frank Frost, in one of his final recording appearances, contributes keyboards on two tracks. In addition to the aforementioned "Sail On," a number of blues standards are included on the album such as "How Many More Years" and "Mother's Gone." On a whole, *She Ain't None of Your'n* is a slight improvement over 1998's *You Better Keep Still*, but the differences are fairly negligible. Those who enjoyed Ford's previous albums will like this one as well, but it is not likely to make many converts. *—Jeffrey Konkel*

Bad Man / Sep. 10, 2002 / Fat Possum ♦♦♦♦

What goes around comes around in the blues world. Although T-Model Ford is from Mississippi, not all of his influences are Mississippi Delta influences—his dusky, moody electric blues also owe something to Chicago (Muddy Waters, Howlin' Wolf), Detroit (John Lee Hooker), and Texas (Lightnin' Hopkins). Of course, Waters, Hooker and Wolf were all born in Mississippi; they were southern bluesmen who moved north, plugged in and became identified with electric post-World War II northern blues. But Hooker wasn't born in Detroit any more than Waters and Wolf were born in Chicago. So again, what goes around comes around in the blues world. Whether you describe Ford's approach as northern or southern—and truth be told, it's a combination of the two—*Bad Man* is a compelling slice of tough, gritty, genuinely lowdown blues. The things that make Ford so compelling are his soulfulness and his lack of slickness. The singer/guitarist doesn't clean things up; he just digs in, lets the emotion flow and tells you exactly how he feels. As a result, tunes like "Black Nanny," "Ask Her for Water" and "Let the Church Roll On" have the sort of rawness and honesty that are missing from some of the slicker blues albums of the 21st century. Equally memorable is Ford's performance of Wolf's "Back Door Man"; although this Chicago blues standard has been recorded countless times, Ford manages to make the tune sound vital and alive rather than worn out and overdone. *Bad Man* (which is Ford's fourth Fat Possum outing) may not be the most innovative or groundbreaking release of 2002, but it certainly doesn't come across as contrived or formulaic either. And it's a disc that is easily recommended to anyone who likes his/her electric blues rugged, unpolished and totally sincere. *—Alex Henderson*

Blind Mamie Forehand

Vocals / Classic Female Blues, Blues Gospel, Acoustic Memphis Blues

Having made only a handful of recordings in the company of her presumed husband A.C. Forehand, the '20s performer Blind Mamie Forehand joins a class of recording artists whose uniqueness is not in name only. While it many not have been that common for women to sing the blues professionally in the '20s, Forehand was one of many who did sing gospel and also one of the few who did manage to leave compelling documentation behind. She was an active singer of spirituals on the streets of Memphis, a venue that logically led to the stylistic classification of street-corner or storefront gospel. "Honey in the Rock" is one of the titles she recorded in 1927, and these tracks have endured not just because hazy copyright status has led to overlapping reissue documentation on an international level. In fact, due to the efforts of labels such as Wolf, it is easier to find a Blind Mamie Forehand recording in Austria than a jar of peanut butter. The actual music content is something that once heard is never forgotten; the robust singers accompanying themselves on cymbals so old one can imagine clouds of dust bursting forth with each crash. *—Eugene Chadbourne*

Forest City Joe (Joe Bennie Pugh)

b. Jul. 10, 1926, Hughes, Arkansas, **d.** Apr. 3, 1960

Harmonica / Electric Chicago Blues

Blues harpist Forest City Joe was heavily influenced by John Lee "Sonny Boy" Williamson. He not only played like him, but sang like him as well. Unlike his idol, however, who was murdered on June 1, 1948, Joe lived long enough to record for the Chess brothers in the early days of their activities, when Chess was known as Aristocrat. Joe was remembered as a "great harp player" by Muddy Waters, who only missed playing at Joe's one major Chess recording session on December 2, 1948, when Joe was only 21. Joe had more of a country sound than most Chicago artists of the period, so it's surprising that the Chess brothers paired him up with J.C. Coles, a jazz guitarist of no seeming special account, who added little to a session but a few barely audible chords.

Joe Bennie Pugh was born in Hughes, AR, on July 10, 1926, to Moses Pugh and Mary Walker. He was raised in the area around Hughes and West Memphis, AR, and even as a boy played the local juke joints in the area. He hoboed his way through the state working road houses and juke joints during the '40s, and late in the decade hooked up with Big Joe Williams, playing with him around St. Louis, MO. Beginning in 1947, he also began working the Chicago area, and a year later had his one and only session for the Chess brothers' Aristocrat label. He also appeared with Howlin' Wolf and Sonny Boy "Rice Miller" Williamson, aka Sonny Boy II, on radio shows in the West Memphis area.

When he returned to Chicago in 1949, he began working with the Otis Spann Combo, appearing at the Tick Tock Lounge and other clubs in the city until the mid-'50s. Pugh returned to Arkansas and gave up music, except for occasional weekend shows with Willie Cobbs, playing in pool rooms and on street corners, beginning in 1955. Pugh recorded for Atlantic Records in 1959, and was still performing until his death in 1960, in a truck accident while returning home from a dance.

Had Muddy played Forest City Joe's one and only Chess Records session, as was intended, chances are more of Joe's work would've seen the light of day, if only in an effort to scrounge up every note that Muddy ever played. But as it was, only "Memory of Sonny Boy" and "A Woman on Every Street" ever saw the light of day, and at this writing only the former has ever appeared on an American CD.

As to his extant music, "Memory of Sonny Boy" was among the first postwar tribute records from one bluesman to another (Scrapper Blackwell had done as much for Leroy Carr in the '30s), starting a trend that continued for decade. And it's a great record, at least as far as the harp playing and the singing go. Joe's playing mimics Sonny Boy Williamson's call-and-response harp playing, performing dazzling volume acrobatics, and his singing is also highly expressive. None of the rest is as strong, but "Shady Lane Woman" is a good, bluesy romantic lament, while "A Woman on Every Street" is the other side of the coin, and a better workout on the harp. "Sawdust Bottom" should have seen release, and "Ash Street Boogie" could've seen action if the accompaniment had been better realized. Alas, J.C. Coles was seemingly content to strum along almost inaudibly in the background—ah, what Muddy might've done.... *—Bruce Eder*

Guy Forsyth

Vocals, Guitar / Texas Blues, Blues-Rock

Austin, Texas-based guitarist, singer, interpreter, and songwriter Guy Forsyth is like a lot of Austin musicians. He leads his own band, as well as a group called the Asylum Street Spankers; when he's not performing with either of these groups locally, you can find Forsyth sitting in with someone else just for kicks. Forsyth is a rare combination: He's a talented guitarist, singer, and songwriter, but also a diligent, conscientious student of blues, blues-rock, and other indigenous folk music styles.

The Guy Forsyth Band issued their Discovery/Warner Bros. label debut *Needle Gun* in 1995. On it, his quartet reinvigorates the blues-rock form, taking the music into uncharted waters. Forsyth is accompanied in his band on *Needle Gun* by Gil T. on bass, Keith Bradley on guitar and Rich Chilleri on drums. The music on their debut is equal parts blues, rock & roll and Americana. Forsyth sings with conviction and plays harmonica and some smoldering guitar. Live, the band is what you'd expect from any good blues-rock conglomeration: loud, raw and raucous. *Can You Live Without* followed in 1999 and *Steak* a year later. *—Richard Skelly*

- **High Temperature** / 1994 / Lizard Disc ♦♦♦

Guy Forsyth's debut album, *High Temperature*, suffers a bit from his unfortunate tendency to deliver lyrics as if they were jokes, but there's a lot of merit to his music. Forsyth and his backing band have real energy and can turn his originals (plus a handful of covers, like Jimmy Reed's "Mr. Luck" and Elmore James' "Done Somebody Wrong") into real barn-burners. It takes a little work to get beyond the feeling that this is all a parody, however, so this may try the patience of some hardline purists. Those that can take the bad with good, however, will hear some sturdy roadhouse boogie. *—Thom Owens*

Needle Gun / Oct. 17, 1995 / Antone's ♦♦♦

Here it is: Guy Forsyth knows how to provide a damn good time by way of gutbucket blues playing. He plays a mean slide guitar himself, and backs that up with the odd burst of dirty blues harp playing, and he has a voice that's a step and a half from Tom Waits, so the vocals have *lots* of character. The 14 songs on the album are played full force, and the band is as tight as can be—the energy level is terrific, and the album as a whole produces the sort of excitement that makes for a great party record. *—Steven E. McDonald*

Can You Live Without / Mar. 16, 1999 / Antone's ♦♦♦

Steak / Sep. 26, 2000 / Antone's ♦♦♦

Traditionally speaking, Guy Forsyth isn't strictly a bluesman. True, he covers Bo Diddley and Muddy Waters, but he is more concerned with expanding the palette of the blues than paying reverence to his idols. His style varies wildly from song to song, from the straight Delta blues of "Poor Boy" to the slouching psychedelic monster "Good Time Man." Forsyth isn't a great guitarist or singer, but his energy is commanding and his delivery is natural enough to put his ideas across, especially on the jump blues workout "Makin' Money." His music isn't for everyone, but when he finds a groove, he pounds it home with all he's got. *—Jim Smith*

Jesse Fortune

b. Feb. 28, 1930, Macon, MS

Vocals / Electric Chicago Blues

Chicago vocalist Jesse Fortune's voice is as large as his discography is small. A mere handful of 45s headed by his 1963 classic "Too Many Cooks" and a 1993 album on Delmark constitute his entire catalog—but as an active artist on the Windy City circuit, he still has time to fatten it up.

Fortune grew up in Hattiesburg, Mississippi, influenced by the pleading blues vocals of B.B. King. He arrived in Chicago in 1952 and started singing professionally with guitarist Little Monroe. He also worked with Otis Rush and Buddy Guy before the prodigious Willie Dixon officially discovered him. In April of 1963, Fortune waxed four sides for USA Records under Dixon's supervision, including the Dixon-penned minor-key rhumba "Too Many Cooks" (his sidemen at the session included Guy, Big Walter Horton on harp, and pianist Lafayette Leake). Robert Cray revived the tune for his 1980 debut album on Tomato, *Who's Been Talkin'*.

Dissatisfied with the monetary return on his date, Fortune shied away from recording (he made his living as a barber) until young guitarist Dave Specter began working the club circuit with the powerful singer. The upshot was *Fortune Tellin' Man*, the singer's debut disc for Delmark, with swinging support from Specter and his Bluebirds. *—Bill Dahl*

- **Fortune Tellin' Man** / 1993 / Delmark ♦♦♦♦♦

Team one of the criminally overlooked blues vocalists inhabiting Chicago's West side with a tight young combo sporting a decidedly retro approach and you get this fine album, veteran singer Jesse Fortune's debut set. Guitarist Dave Specter & the Bluebirds admirably back the big-voiced Fortune as he recuts his Willie Dixon-penned USA label classic "Too Many Cooks," and shouts some lesser-known B.B. King gems and a few new items. Definitely a case of better late than never! —*Bill Dahl*

Leroy Foster

b. Feb. 1, 1923, Algoma, MS, **d.** May 26, 1958, Chicago, IL
Vocals, Drums, Guitar / Electric Chicago Blues

As a charter member of the Headhunters, the brash crew that also included Muddy Waters and Jimmy Rogers (so named because of their penchant for entering nightclubs featuring other musicians and blowing them off the stage with their superior musicianship), "Baby Face" Leroy Foster was on hand to help develop the postwar Chicago blues idiom. Unfortunately, he wasn't around long enough to enjoy the fruits of his labors.

The Mississippi native came to Chicago in 1945 in the star-crossed company of harpist Little Walter and pianist Johnny Jones. He worked with Sunnyland Slim and Sonny Boy Williamson before hooking up with the young and hungry Waters aggregation. Foster played drums on 1948 dates for Tempo-Tone that produced Floyd Jones' brooding "Hard Times," Little Walter's "Blue Baby," and a Sunnyland Slim-fronted "I Want My Baby." He switched to rhythm guitar to accompany Waters on several of his 1948-1949 Aristocrat 78s, notably "You're Gonna Miss Me (When I'm Dead and Gone)," "Mean Red Spider," and "Screamin' and Cryin'," as well as Johnny Jones' rolling "Big Town Playboy." Foster also recorded for Aristocrat as a front man: "Locked Out Boogie" and "Shady Grove Blues" were done at a 1948 date that produced six Muddy masters.

Waters got in some hot water with the Chess brothers when he moonlighted on Foster's rip-roaring eight-song session for Parkway in January of 1950. Though Foster's crashing drums are prominent throughout, Muddy's slashing slide and mournful moans are clearly heard on Foster's two-part "Rollin' and Tumblin'"—enough so that Waters was forced to wax his own version for Aristocrat to kill sales on Foster's rendition by his bosses.

Those Parkway masters had amazing resiliency—Foster's raunchy "Red Headed Woman" reemerged on Savoy in 1954 ("Boll Weevil" had turned up on Herald the previous year). Two singles for JOB—1950's "My Head Can't Rest Anymore"/"Take a Little Walk with Me" (with Muddy and Rogers in support, it was later released on Chess) and 1952's "Pet Rabbit"/"Louella" (with Sunnyland and guitarist Robert Jr. Lockwood lending a hand)—round out his slim vinyl legacy. Alcoholism brought Baby Face down early—he was only 35 years old when he died in 1958. —*Bill Dahl*

● **Baby Face Leroy & Floyd Jones** / 1983 / Flyright ✦✦✦✦

The Four Aces

f. Chicago, IL
Group / Chicago Blues

Common wisdom says that Muddy Waters was the man responsible for turbocharging the Delta blues and creating what we now call Chicago Blues. Muddy's importance is inestimable, but to lay all the credit at his feet is to ignore the contributions of those who quite literally used Muddy's music as a jumping off point, and blazed historical trails of their own. Of all the great musicians who passed through Muddy's bands, perhaps the most important of all was harmonica player and singer Little Walter Jacobs. Jacobs left Muddy's band at the age of 22 already a seasoned veteran of the road and the recording studio. He quickly recruited his own superb band, and came very close to eclipsing his former boss' success during the heyday of Chicago blues in the '50s, with two number one hits among his ten appearances on the nationwide *Billboard* R&B charts; Muddy himself had 12 songs reach the Billboard charts but never scored a number one hit. Much of Little Walter's success can be attributed to the fact that he was doing something new, different, and thoroughly urban; where Muddy's appeal lay heavily with southern emigrés longing for familiar sounds, Walter's swinging, modern, jazz-inflected style found favor with a younger generation of city blues fans not so closely tied to the "down-home" sounds of the South.

But Little Walter couldn't have done it alone—he needed accompanists who shared his desire to push the edge of the blues envelope, so he recruited his band from among the most accomplished and forward-thinking blues musicians available in Chicago. His first recording and touring band in 1952 was a band that he'd sometimes sat in with while still with Muddy—the Aces, featuring brothers David and Louis Myers on guitars. The Myers brothers were born in Byhalia, MS, and had learned the rudiments of guitar from their father before the family relocated to Chicago in the early '40s while both brothers were still in their early teens. There their musical tastes were formed by equal doses of the big-band swing that was popular at the time, pop ballads they heard on the radio, and the blues that was being played all around their south side neighborhood. By the late '40s they had assumed the roles they'd play for much of their musical careers: older brother Dave providing bass lines and chords into which Louis wove his tastefully jazzy blues riffing.

Their rock-solid musical foundation provided the perfect base for the veteran bluesman they soon found themselves backing, but their musical precociousness drove them to eventually form the Aces, which incorporated some of the more modern and sophisticated influences that had raised eyebrows with the older blues crowd. The Aces were rounded out by schooled jazz drummer Fred Below, a Chicago native for whom the rough southern blues rhythms were almost completely foreign; after his first gig with the group he was so musically disoriented that he decided to quit the band, but was persuaded to stick it out and adapt his jazz techniques to the blues, ultimately becoming the most in-demand blues drummer in Chicago (in addition to putting the beat to many of rock & roll pioneer Chuck Berry's early hits). Little Walter approached his harmonica like a jazz saxophone player, and the Aces provided the propulsive backing of a swinging big band. It would have been near impossible at the time to find three musicians who were better suited to providing the solid foundation for Walter's musical innovations than the Aces, who had the musical and dynamic range, swing sensibilities, and melding of individual strengths that made them the standard by which all of Little Walter's later ensembles—and most harp-led blues bands since—have been measured.

Unfortunately, this band was not to last; the Aces had been establishing their own name around town, but when their first records with Little Walter were released by the Chess Records subsidiary Checker as by "Little Walter and His Night Caps" or "...and His Jukes" (to capitalize on the popularity of his first hit "Juke," recorded during a session while he was still with Muddy), there was dissension in the ranks. The first to leave was Louis, who was replaced by Robert Jr. Lockwood in 1954. Almost 40 years old at the time, Lockwood's roots were in the Delta; as Robert Johnson's stepson, he had a firm handle on the deepest of blues, but had been studying jazz guitarists since at least the '30s, and had been recording since before WWII. He proved to be an adept foil for Walter's harp excursions, and many of Walter's jazziest adventures were supported and driven by Lockwood's sophisticated guitar riffing.

Dave Myers was the next to leave, joining his brother Louis in 1955 in a reformed Aces that featured Junior Wells (who had played with them pre-Walter) and later Otis Rush. Dave was replaced by 19-year-old guitar prodigy Luther Tucker, who had been hanging around the band and occasionally sitting in with them, as well as with other local blues acts. Although Tucker's role was initially the same as Dave's—thumping out bass lines on his guitar and providing chordal fills behind Lockwood—he soon distinguished himself as one of the flashiest of the new breed of guitarists in Chicago. When given the chance to take the lead, Tucker's fleet-fingered bursts of nervous energy helped push Little Walter's music in new and exciting directions. The first wave of rock & roll was cresting, aggressively played electric guitar was moving to the forefront of popular music, and Luther Tucker was among the blues guitarists at the leading edge.

It was around this time that Fred Below vacated the drum seat, although as was the custom at Chess/Checker Records, he continued to be brought in for recording sessions for the next several years. Replacing him on the road for a time was his old drum school classmate Odie Payne Jr., who had been playing and recording in Chicago since the late '40s with the likes of Tampa Red, Memphis Minnie, Memphis Slim and Elmore James, and later worked as the house drummer at Cobra Records, playing behind Buddy Guy, Magic Sam, Otis Rush and others. Payne's slightly more orthodox but still distinctly jazzy style was by all accounts ideally suited to Walter's music, although there's no documentation of him ever appearing on any of Walter's records.

After a short time with a still young and rambunctious Little Walter and the even younger Luther Tucker, Lockwood was began to tire of the grind, and he left Walter's band, although he continued to appear on records with him (and also notably with Sonny Boy Williamson) until the late '50s. In 1956 Jimmie Lee Robinson joined Little Walter's band, pushing Luther Tucker into the lead role that Lockwood had vacated. Robinson was another Chicago native, who had grown up around the blues-rich Maxwell Street Market area, and knew Walter from his escapades there during his earliest years in Chicago. Robinson's formative years included musical apprenticeship on Maxwell Street, followed by formal music lessons for a time, and then time spent with guitarists Freddie King, Elmore James, Eddie Taylor and others in the early '50s. His guitar style had similarities to Tucker's, and eventually their roles carrying the top and bottom of the music melded to the point where they would trade back and forth even during songs. Unfortunately there are only a few examples of Jimmie Lee's years with Walter on record, due to the record label's insistence on not tampering with the successful studio formula that had been established by the Tucker/Lockwood/Below ensemble (usually augmented by Willie Dixon on string bass).

By the end of the '50s, Little Walter's hitmaking days were behind him, and his bands soon became a revolving door through which a number of local musicians passed. In 1959 guitarist Freddy Robinson joined the band for a time (replacing Jimmie Lee Robinson, a move that has caused much confusion among discographers over the years), during which he sometimes played electric bass. Odie Payne left the band after a short time to be replaced by the solid if less musically adventurous George Hunter. During sessions over the next few years the drum throne (on sessions, at least) was also occupied by Billy Stepney, session ace Al Duncan, and even the return of Fred Below for a 1960 session. But blues tastes were changing, and his great ensembles of the past had all scattered and moved on to other pursuits with varying degrees of success. —*Scott Dirks*

● **1946–1955** / May 11, 1999 / Flyright ✦✦✦

Inez & Charlie Foxx

f. 1962, Greensboro, NC, **db.** 1968
Group / R&B, Soul

This brother/sister duo from Greensboro made a little noise on the soul scene in the '60s. They signed with Juggy Murray Jones' Symbol label in 1962. Their biggest hit was "Mockingbird," in 1963, which was a number two R&B and number seven pop smash. Their vocal tradeoffs and arrangement were primarily responsible for its appeal, though Foxx could do some sizzling numbers on her own. They continued with "Ask Me" and "Hurt by Love," then switched to Musicor. Their final moderate hit was "(1-2-3-4-5-6-7) Count the Days" in 1967 for Dynamo, which reached number 17 on the R&B charts. Inez Foxx had a solid LP on her own for Volt in 1969, *At Memphis*. But her solo songs for the label didn't generate much interest in the early and mid-'70s. James Taylor and Carly Simon later did a cover of "Mockingbird." —*Ron Wynn*

Mockingbird / 1963 / Collectables ✦✦✦✦

Inez & Charles Foxx / 1965 / Sue ✦✦✦

Inez & Charles Foxx's second album features both sides of their smash single "Mockingbird" b/w "Jaybirds"; the pair of tunes was also on their debut album on Symbol (a subsidiary of Sue Records). But it's not a problem; the mix makes the package stronger. It features "Ask Me" from 1963, the sister/brother duo's final of four singles from that prolific year, and subsequent singles: "Hurt by Love," (later ripped-off by the New Beats as "Bread & Butter"), "La De Da I Love You," "I Fancy You," and "My Mommy Told Me." For the unacquainted, Inez & Charles Foxx were like Ike & Tina Turner, with Charlie playing more of a role vocally than Ike, and Inez, while sassy and soulful, not as dynamic as Tina. —*Andrew Hamilton*

Come By Here / 1965 / Dynamo ✦✦✦

The sibling duo's third album was more consistent than the two previous Juggy Murray

Jones' productions. While there isn't a "Mockingbird," there are many solid soul cuts, including the gospel-ish "Come by Here," a remake of "I Stand Accused" (a soul classic), and a sparkling rendition of "I Love You a Thousand Times," a tune Inez co-wrote which was a hit for the Sonny Turner-led Platters. —*Andrew Hamilton*

At Memphis / 1972 / Volt ✦✦

The Inez Foxx of "Mockingbird" fame is missing in action. None of the sides approaches the magnitude of that number seven pop hit for Foxx in September 1963. Foxx's version of Mitty Collier's soulful "I Had a Talk With My Man" is simply a less compelling rehash. Inez does better on Jeanette "Baby" Washington's "The Time," injecting new life into the timeless ballad. "You Don't Want My Love (All You Want Is My Loving)" is a good match for Foxx's light voice; it has a similar groove to Johnnie Taylor's "Just Keep on Loving Me." The last track, "Mousa Muse," is not a song, but a short interview of Inez about recording in Memphis for the first time by an interviewer named Mousa. Not what it could have been, Stax failed to deliver on this one. —*Andrew Hamilton*

● **Mockingbird: The Best of Inez Foxx** / 1986 / EMI ✦✦✦✦✦

The Best of Charlie & Inez Foxx: Mockingbird / 1994 / Collectables ✦✦✦

This covers the period (probably about 1963-1966, although dates are not given for all the tracks in the liner notes) in which Inez and Charles Foxx were on Symbol Records, a subsidiary of Sue. The original hit version of "Mockingbird" leads off the 14-song disc, and it's simply a great early pop-soul song with irresistible vocal sparring between the sister and brother. Unfortunately, nothing else on the CD matches that classic, although "Hurt By Love" was a moderate hit for them in 1964 on both sides of the Atlantic. This is average, but no better than average, pop-soul of the era, albeit more R&B-oriented than many records in the genre. Sometimes they sounded like a lesser Ike & Tina Turner (who were themselves pretty spotty on record during the period). At other times, they tried to mimic the Supremes ("La De Dah I Love You"), or just tried to rework the "Mockingbird" sound, with predictably lesser results. Any compilation worthy of the name *The Best of Charlie & Inez Foxx* needs to incorporate some of their 1966-1968 material for Musicor, which is collected on the Charly anthology *Count the Days*. It also needs to have better packaging than it gets on the no-frills sleeve that Collectables gave this release. —*Richie Unterberger*

Count the Days / Oct. 17, 1995 / Charly ✦✦✦

With 20 songs from 1966-1968, this summarizes the duo's stint with Musicor/Dynamo, in which they offered fair but on the whole unremarkable New York soul. As was true of much of their prior material with Sue, their format often recalls that of Ike & Tina Turner. The production is better and more varied than their Sue sides, but the material and delivery aren't as strong as the Turners were at their best. Note that the version of "Mockingbird" which leads off the disc is not the original 1963 hit, but an inferior 1968 remake. This compilation has been superseded in value by the 2001 Kent CD anthology, *The Dynamo Duo*, which has four more tracks from this same era, although *Count the Days* does have one song not present on *The Dynamo Duo*, "I Got It." —*Richie Unterberger*

The Dynamo Duo / Mar. 13, 2001 / Kent ✦✦✦

Dynamo was the name of the Musicor subsidiary for which Inez & Charlie Foxx did most of their late-'60s recordings, and this collects a couple dozen tracks the duo cut for Musicor/Dynamo from 1966-1969. Their Dynamo output was more consistent than what they had recorded for Sue, thanks in part to input from producer Luther Dixon, who was married to Inez Foxx at the time. However, there was no outstanding single on the order of "Mockingbird" during their time with the label, and the pair still often sounded like a lesser, more pop-oriented version of Ike & Tina Turner. This is respectable but somewhat middling New York soul with, as was true of much of the city's '60s soul output, a slicker sheen to the production than soul product from most other regions. On "I Love You 1,000 Times," they seem to be trying to mimic 1963-1964 Motown, and although they don't do so badly, that's a strategy doomed to failure. The comparison to the Turners bobs higher above the surface in the bluesy and sultry "I Stand Accused"/"Guilty" medley, one of the disc's highlights. A lowlight, however, is the outrageous 1968 medley of "Vaya Con Dios"/"Fellows in Vietnam," in which the traditional song turns into a rap about the Vietnam War. Just as you're getting all set for a protest or at least moving commentary, it builds into a plea for us to encourage American soldiers to get out of their foxholes and "kill another enemy to set us free, and to keep us free"—not the sort of sentiment that could be heartily endorsed for a conflict that took so many needless lives, a disproportionate amount of whom (on the U.S. side) were African-Americans. This CD is preferable to a prior compilation of the Foxxes' Musicor/Dynamo work, *Count the Days*, as this has four more tracks, including a 1969 Inez Foxx solo effort, "You Shouldn't Have Set My Soul on Fire." Be cautioned that the version of "Mockingbird" is not the original 1963 hit single, but a 1968 remake with strings. —*Richie Unterberger*

The Complete Recordings on Sue / Sep. 11, 2001 / Connoisseur Collection ✦✦✦✦✦

Carol Fran

b. Oct. 23, 1933, Lafayette, LA

Vocals, Piano / Soul-Blues

Soul-blues diva Carol Fran was born October 23, 1933, in Lafayette, LA. After beginning her career as a teen singing jump blues with the Don Conway Orchestra, she eventually landed in New Orleans, marrying saxophonist Bob Francois. Abbreviating her married name to simply Fran, she became a constant presence on the Bourbon Street club circuit before mounting an extended tour of Mexico. In 1957, she cut her first sides for the R&B label Excello, scoring a regional smash with her debut single "Emmitt Lee." Though she recorded extensively for Excello, only three more singles were released during Fran's abbreviated tenure with the label and she soon signed on as a featured vocalist with blues legend Guitar Slim. She continued touring with the group in the wake of Slim's 1959

death, appearing alongside various substitutes, including Nappy Brown, Lee Dorsey, and Joe Tex.

In 1962, Fran signed to Lyric and released a pair of singles, including a swamp pop rendition of "The Great Pretender"; she spent two more years on the road before catching on with the Jubilee subsidiary Port for a 1964 cover of the Orioles' classic "Crying in the Chapel." The single was then reissued on the Josie label, but was lost in the shuffle when Elvis Presley scored with his own reading of the song soon after.

Undaunted, Fran remained with Port for a series of smoldering soul sides spotlighting her crystalline vocals to magnificent effect. While the follow-up "You Can't Stop Me" featured a Sammy Lowe arrangement, her third effort for the label, the lovely "A World Without You," was penned by Bobby Darin. Sadly, both failed to make any commercial headway; however, and after one more single for Port, "Any Day Love Walks In," Fran returned to touring. She did not re-enter the studio until 1967, signing to Roulette for a cover of Brook Benton's "So Close." Despite cutting a surplus of material during her Roulette stay, the sessions remained in the can—embittered by her label experiences and stung by years of ill-informed financial dealings, she returned to Louisiana and spent over a decade confining her activities to small clubs. In 1982, Fran was reunited with Clarence Hollimon, a noted studio guitarist she briefly dated a quarter century earlier; the couple eventually married and relocated to Texas, appearing live together and in 1992 signing to Black Top to issue the album *Soul Sensation*. *See There* followed two years later, and after a long studio hiatus, Fran and Holliman resurfaced on JSP with the aptly titled 2000 release *It's About Time*. —*Jason Ankeny*

Soul Sensation / 1992 / Black Top ✦✦✦

The new sweethearts of the blues' debut for Black Top is an uncommonly varied affair, the pair performing blues, jazz, and every stylistic stripe in between. Hollimon's red-hot licks are seldom short of amazing (his instrumental showcase "Gristle" is a stunner), and Fran's full-throated vocals shine on everything from a Gulf Coast-styled "My Happiness" and a reprise of Mitty Collier's emotionally charged "I Had a Talk with My Man" to the lounge-slanted "Anytime, Anyplace, Anywhere" and the rousing sanctified closer "This Little Light." —*Bill Dahl*

● **See There!** / 1994 / Black Top ✦✦✦✦✦

The duo's Black Top encore was a slightly more focused effort than their debut. They still exhibit considerable versatility on a highly infectious dance number, "Door Poppin'," and the Louisiana-rooted "Daddy, Daddy, Daddy," and soulful remakes of Tyrone Davis' "Are You Serious" and Gladys Knight & the Pips' earthy "I Don't Want to Do Wrong," but there's a more satisfying context overall. The album was waxed in New Orleans and Texas with two entirely different bands, lending laudable variety to the selections. —*Bill Dahl*

It's About Time / May 16, 2000 / JSP ✦✦✦

Panama Francis (David Albert Francis)

b. Dec. 21, 1918, Miami, FL, **d.** Nov. 11, 2001, Orlando, FL

Leader, Drums / Jump Blues, Swing

Panama Francis has had a long and versatile career, equally at home in swing and R&B sessions. Playing for church revival meetings were among his earliest gigs and he also gigged with George Kelly's group, the Cavaliers, in Florida (1934-1938) before moving to New York. The following year he worked with Roy Eldridge (making his recording debut) and this was followed by a long period at the Savoy with the Lucky Millinder big band (1940-1946) and an association with Cab Calloway (1947-1952). Francis then became a busy studio drummer, performing anonymously on many pop and rock & roll records. In 1979, when he was in danger of being forgotten, Francis formed the Savoy Sultans, a group based on the small unit that used to play opposite Millinder at the Savoy. The Sultans recorded a steady stream of exciting hot swing records for Black & Blue and Stash during 1979-1983. During the '90s, Panama Francis continued freelancing, including recording and touring with the Statesmen of Jazz (1994-1995). In November 2001, David Albert "Panama" Francis died at the age of 82. —*Scott Yanow*

● **All-Stars 1949** / 1949 / Collectables ✦✦✦✦✦

Collectables' *All-Stars 1949* is a storming swing set that drummer Panama Francisco led in 1949. —*Leo Stanley*

Savoy Sultans / Jan. 31, 1979-Feb. 11, 1979 / Classic Jazz ✦✦✦✦✦

Although their recordings do not always show it, the Savoy Sultans in the late '30s were considered one of the hottest small swing groups in existence. Decades later, drummer Panama Francis decided to revive the group's concept by putting together a new Savoy Sultans using occasional alumni but mostly utilizing other surviving veteran players. This Classic Jazz LP finds the group at their best, cooking on such numbers as "Song of the Islands," "Frenzy," "Little John Special," and "Clap Hands, Here Comes Charlie." With George Kelly contributing the arrangements as well as his tenor and such other fine soloists as trumpeters Francis Williams and Irv Stokes, altoists Norris Turney and Howard Johnson, and pianist Red Richards, this is a hot band who could out-swing the original group. This LP deserves to be reissued on CD. —*Scott Yanow*

Panama Francis and the Savoy Sultans, Vol. 1: Groovin' / Aug. 1982 / Stash ✦✦✦

The third of four albums made by Panama Francis' Savoy Sultans is not quite on the level of the first two; it was originally cut for Black and Blue and made available for a time domestically by Classic Jazz. The Sultans once again play some heated swing and feature a nonet full of top veterans, including trumpeters Irv Stokes and Francis Williams and tenor saxophonist George Kelly, but a couple of Julia Steele vocals are unnecessary, and some of the songs ("Bill Bailey," "Theme from New York, New York" and "Jada") seem a bit frivolous. Best are "Honeysuckle Rose," "Panama" and "Cotton Tail." —*Scott Yanow*

Panama Francis and the Savoy Sultans, Vol. 2 / Aug. 1982 / Classic Jazz ✦✦✦

The revival of the Savoy Sultans by drummer Panama Francis resulted in a hot five-horn nonet that was actually superior to the original group from the '30s. The second of two Classic Jazz sets from 1979 is the equal of the first. With such fine swing-era veterans as trumpeters Francis Williams and Irv Stokes, altoists Norris Turney and Howard Johnson, tenor saxophonist George Kelly (who was also in the original group), pianist Red Richards, rhythm guitarist John Smith, bassist Bill Pemberton, and the drummer/leader, this group could really swing up a storm. Highlights of this very enjoyable LP (which, with Volume One, will hopefully be reissued eventually on CD) include Lucky Millinder's "Shipyard Social Function," a couple of heated Al Cooper tunes, and a 15 1/2-minute version of "Perdido." *—Scott Yanow*

Everything Swings / Oct. 3, 1983+Oct. 10, 1983 / Stash ♦♦♦

Panama Francis' Savoy Sultans was one of the top mainstream jazz combos of the late '70s and early '80s, reviving the joy of small-group swing with its riffing and concise but heated solos. This excellent effort, its fourth and thus far final recording, finds the group expanding to ten pieces and featuring hot solos from the likes of trumpeters Irv Stokes and Spanky Davis, veteran tenor George Kelly and (in a bit of a surprise) the modern but flexible altoist Bobby Watson. Sticking mostly to swing standards, the Savoy Sultans uplift and bring joy to such songs as "Air Mail Special," "Stomping at the Savoy," "In the Mood" and "Just You, Just Me." *—Scott Yanow*

Keith Frank

b. 1972, Soileau, LA

Vocals / Zydeco

One of the leading lights of the "nouveau zydeco" movement, accordionist Keith Frank—the son of zydeco great Preston Frank—fused the traditional sound of his father's generation with latter-day influences ranging from James Brown to Bob Marley to forge his own urbanized and infectiously danceable style. Born in Soileau, LA, in 1972, Frank began playing professionally at the age of four, sitting in on a variety of instruments with his father's combo the Family Zydeco Band; despite focusing on the accordion from the age of six onward, he initially loathed zydeco and the pressures of performing, but in high school finally gave in to the music's pull and formed his own group. As Preston Frank began to ease into retirement, Keith gradually assumed leadership duties of the family band, which now also included his sister Jennifer on bass and brother Brad on drums; as he gained confidence, he began adding elements of rap to his music, a move which dismayed purists but met with wide approval from younger listeners. Frank issued his debut album *What's His Name?* in 1994 and remained a prolific force in the years to follow. *—Jason Ankeny*

What's His Name? / 1994 / Maison de Soul ♦♦♦♦

Movin' on Up! / 1995 / Maison de Soul ♦♦♦

Only the Strong Survive / Jul. 20, 1996 / Maison de Soul ♦♦♦

Get on Boy / Jul. 25, 1996 / Zydeco Hound ♦♦♦♦

You'd Be Surprised / Apr. 22, 1997 / Maison de Soul ♦♦♦

On a Mission / Jul. 21, 1998 / Maison de Soul ♦♦♦

Live at Slim's Y-Ki-Ki / Apr. 20, 1999 / Shanachie ♦♦♦

One very hot live recording of Frank in full roar in the music's heartland. Frank puts a lot of sweat and high energy to his brand of zydeco and tracks like "Hey Pretty Baby (With Your Teeth So White)," "Sometimes We Make You Move Your Feet," and "Soileau Zydeco" are classic examples of it. A dynamite party record for any celebration. *—Cub Koda*

● **Ready or Not** / Mar. 14, 2000 / Shanachie ♦♦♦♦

Accordionist Keith Frank is one of the leading figures in the nouveau zydeco movement, incorporating influences like pop and rap with traditional zydeco instrumentation. *Ready or Not* features several rowdy originals along with covers of "I Got Loaded" by Lil' Bob and the Lollipops (also covered by Los Lobos) and Katrina and the Waves' 1983 hit "Walking on Sunshine." The Soileau Zydeco Band includes Frank's sister Jen on bass and brother Brad on drums along with James "Chocolate" Ned on scrubboard and Kent Pierre August on guitar. *—Al Campbell*

The Masked Band / Feb. 27, 2001 / Louisiana Red Hot ♦♦♦

Calvin Frazier

b. Feb. 16, 1915, Osceola, AR, **d.** Sep. 23, 1972, Detroit, MI

Guitar / Prewar Country Blues

An associate of Robert Johnson, Calvin Frazier never attained the notoriety of other Johnson protégés like Johnny Shines, Robert Jr. Lockwood or Honeyboy Edwards, but his scant recorded legacy reveals a performer whose take on prewar-era blues is as unique and distinctive as any in the canon. Born February 16, 1915, in Osceola, AR, Frazier began his career performing alongside his brothers, and in the company of Shines, he traveled to Helena, Arkansas in 1930; there they met Johnson, and together the three men slowly journeyed north to Detroit, where they sang hymns on area gospel broadcasts.

Upon returning south, Frazier and Johnson also joined with drummer Peck Curtis in a string-band combo. However, in 1935 Frazier was wounded in a Memphis shootout which left another man dead; he fled back to Detroit, marrying Shines' cousin and settling into a life of quiet anonymity. Apart from gigs supporting the likes of Big Maceo Merriweather, Rice Miller, and Baby Boy Warren, he resurfaced in 1938 long enough to cut a session for folklorist Alan Lomax; while the spectre of Johnson undeniably haunts renditions of songs including "Lily Mae" (a rewrite of "Honeymoon Blues") and "Highway 51" (lifted from "Dust My Broom"), Frazier's incomprehensible vocals, menacingly surreal lyrics and exquisite slide guitar are the hallmarks of a total original. He did not record again until a 1951 date with T.J. Fowler's jump band, and entered the studio one last time in 1954 with Warren and Miller; Frazier continued performing in the Detroit area to little notice until his death on September 23, 1972. *—Jason Ankeny*

● **This Old World's in a Tangle** / 1993 / Laurie ♦♦♦♦

1938 Library of Congress field recordings, influenced by Robert Johnson. *—Bill Dahl*

Free

f. 1968, London, England, **db.** 1973

Group / Album Rock, Hard Rock, Blues-Rock

Famed for their perennial "All Right Now," Free helped lay the foundations for the rise of hard rock, stripping the earthy sound of British blues down to its raw, minimalist core to pioneer a brand of proto-metal later popularized by '70s superstars like Foreigner, Foghat and Bad Company. Free formed in London in 1968 when guitarist Paul Kossoff, then a member of the blues unit Black Cat Bones, was taken to see vocalist Paul Rodgers' group Brown Sugar by a friend, drummer Tom Mautner. After deciding to form their own band, Kossoff and Rodgers recruited drummer Simon Kirke (since Mautner was at university) and 16-year-old bass phenom Andy Fraser (from the ranks of John Mayall's Bluesbreakers); with the aid of Alexis Korner, who also suggested the name Free, the fledgling band signed to the Island label, issuing their bluesy debut *Tons of Sobs* in 1968.

Free's eponymous 1969 follow-up expanded on their roots-based sound, incorporating rockers like Albert King's "The Hunter" as well as muscular ballads like "Lying in the Sunshine" into the mix. Although both of the first two albums fared poorly on the charts, 1970's *Fire and Water* became a tremendous hit on the strength of the primal "All Right Now," a Top Five smash powered by Rodgers' gritty, visceral vocals. After headlining 1970's Isle of Wight festival, the group appeared destined for superstardom, but the LP *Highway* did not fare nearly as well as anticipated, and after a grueling tour which yielded 1971's *Free Live*, the band dissolved amidst ego clashes and recriminations.

While Rodgers went on to form Peace and Fraser founded Toby, Kossoff and Kirke teamed with bassist Tetsu Yamauchi and keyboardist John "Rabbit" Bundrick to record the album *Kossoff/Kirke/Tetsu/Rabbit.* When none of these new projects proved successful, the original lineup of Free re-formed to record 1972's *Free at Last*, which launched the hit "Little Bit of Love." However, drug problems nagged the group, as Kossoff's longtime battle with heroin continued to worsen; soon Fraser exited to form Sharks with Chris Spedding, leaving Rodgers and Kirke to record the majority of 1973's *Heartbreaker* while a drug-addled Kossoff watched from the sidelines. Soon, the group disbanded again, this time for good: while Rodgers and Kirke went on to found Bad Company, Kossoff formed Back Street Crawler before dying of a drug-induced heart attack on March 19, 1976. *—Jason Ankeny*

Tons of Sobs / 1968 / A&M ♦♦♦♦♦

Although Free was never destined to scrape the same skies as Led Zeppelin, when they first burst out of the traps in 1968, close to a year ahead of Jimmy Page and company, they set the world of British blues-rock firmly on its head, a blistering combination of youth, ambition, and, despite those tender years, experience that, across the course of their debut album, did indeed lay the groundwork for all that Zeppelin would embrace. That Free and Zeppelin were cut from the same cloth is immediately apparent, even before you start comparing the versions of "The Hunter" that highlight both bands' debut albums. Where Free streaks ahead, however, is in their refusal to compromise their own vision of the blues—even at its most commercial ("I'm a Mover" and "Worry"), *Tons of Sobs* has a density that makes Zeppelin and the rest of the era's rocky contemporaries sound like flyweights by comparison. The 2002 remaster of the album only amplifies the fledgling Free's achievements. With remastered sound that drives the record straight back to the studio master tapes, the sheer versatility of the players, and the unbridled imagination of producer Guy Stevens, rings crystal clear. Even without their visionary seer, however, Free impresses—three bonus tracks drawn from period BBC sessions are as loose as they are dynamic, and certainly make a case for a full Free-at-the-Beeb type collection. Of the other bonuses, two offer alternate versions of familiar album tracks, while "Guy Stevens Jam" is reprised from the *Songs of Yesterday* box set to further illustrate the band's improvisational abilities. As if they needed it. *—Dave Thompson*

Free / 1969 / A&M ♦♦♦♦

Free's second outing contained all original material and was less blues-based. The loping bass and snakey guitar figures appear to be a blueprint of things to come. Paul Rodgers' dynamic vocal range is pushed steadily to the fore, and cuts such as "Songs of Yesterday" and "Woman" fit well alongside introspective selections like "Mouthful of Grass" or "Mourning, Sad Mourning." A solid set from a band just beginning to hit its stride. *—James Chrispell*

Fire and Water / 1970 / A&M ♦♦♦♦♦

If Fleetwood Mac, Humble Pie, and Foghat were never formed, Free would be considered one of the greatest post-Beatles blues-rock bands to date, and this record shows why. Conceptually fresh, with a great, roots-oriented, Band-like feel, Free distinguished itself with the public like Black Sabbath and Deep Purple did (in terms of impact, only) in 1970. A lot of people thought that they were in the same league; buttressed by the FM hit "All Right Now," the entire album and group presented itself to the world as a complete band, in every sense of the word. From Paul Kossoff's exquisite and tasteful guitar work, to Paul Rodgers' soulful vocals, this was a group that was easily worthy of the Cream, Blind Faith, or Derek & the Dominos mantle. *—Matthew Greenwald*

Highway / Feb. 1971 / A&M ♦♦♦

The last and least of the original Free studio albums, *Highway* was recorded just three months after the band scored the career-redefining hit "Alright Now," with their profile at an career-topping high, but morale heading toward an all-time low. Guitarist Paul Kossoff was reeling from the death of friend Jimi Hendrix, a new single, "The Stealer"—the follow-up to The Hit—bellyflopped ignominiously and, when the album followed suit, the band itself was not far behind. Heavily influenced by their admiration of the Band, *Highway* has understandably been described as Free's answer to *Music From Big Pink*, sharing both the laid-back vibe and mellow looseness of that role model. Where it went awry, of course, was in the fact that Free was not cut out to be country-rock guitar-twangers, no matter how fiery their missionary zeal. Yet, the strutting rockers "The Stealer" and "Ride On Pony" alone shatter the brave new mood, while reflective romancers like "Love You So" and "Be My Friend" could well have been composed specifically to rid the band of the shadow of "Alright Now," and prove that underneath the coolest exterior, there beat a heart of the molten gold. Of course, Free had bathed in such waters before, and the closing "Soon I Will Be Gone" certainly bears comparison with any of their past ballads. Nevertheless, too much of *Highway* reacted to the pressures of the recent past, rather building upon the strengths that had made such events possible in the first place, and you reach the bonus tracks appended to the 2002 remaster despairing that they will ever rediscover that earlier flair. But the 1971 hit single "My Brother Jake" is a gorgeous knockabout clearly informed by the Faces' recent assault on Free's own throne, while a couple of BBC session tracks, sensibly highlighting both the best ("Ride On Pony") and the worst ("Be My Friend") of the album itself, pack a punch that was clearly absent in the studio. In fact, whatever your opinion of *Highway* itself, the bonus tracks comprise an entire new reason to pick up the album. *—Dave Thompson*

Free Live / Sep. 1971 / A&M ✦✦✦✦✦
Although Free made excellent studio records, this live album is perhaps the best way to experience the band in all its glory. Led by singer-guitarist Paul Rodgers and lead guitarist Paul Kossoff, the band swings through nine songs with power, clarity, and a dose of funk. Of course, the hit single "All Right Now" is gleefully extended, much to the audience and listener's delight. Superbly recorded by Andy Johns, this is one of the greatest live albums of the '70s. [*Free Live* was re-released in 2002 as a British import featuring seven bonus tracks.] *—Matthew Greenwald*

Kossoff/Kirke/Tetsu/Rabbit / 1971 / Island ✦✦
A side project which sounds very Free-like. Full of bluesy guitar and Free's loping rhythms, this is a suprisingly solid set. Although it doesn't include any Paul Rodgers vocals, it does contain all the elements of future Free projects. A preamble of things to come. Good. *—James Chrispell*

Free at Last / 1972 / A&M ✦✦✦
Following Paul Rodgers' unsuccessful project titled Peace and Andy Fraser's ill-fated Toby, Free rebuilt themselves and released *Free at Last* in the summer of 1972. The band went right back to what they know best, with Rodgers bearing his blues-rock soul to Kossoff's moody electric guitar. Tracks like "Sail On," "Soldier Boy," and "Travelling Man" come out on top as some of the band's most emotive material, proving that their breakup in 1971 had no real effect on their chemistry. "Little Bit of Love" was released in the U.K., peaking at number 13, while the album itself broke the Top Ten there, stalling at number 69 in the U.S. The band's mixture of laid-back blues and gritty, bare-boned rock & roll is as poignant and as expressive as it was on *Tons of Sobs* or *Fire and Water*, even though Paul Kossoff's problems with drugs were beginning to be more and more evident. Eventually, Kossoff's addiction affected the entire band, hindering Free's ability to go on tour to promote the album. After *Free at Last*, Andy Fraser left the group and created the band Sharks along with Chris Spedding, while Kossoff was busy with his own Back Street Crawler project. After Kossoff's death in 1976, John Bundrick re-joined along with Tetsu Yamauchi for 1973's *Heartbreaker*... Free's final release. *—Mike DeGagne*

Heartbreaker / 1973 / Island ✦✦✦✦
Free's return in 1972 was scarred by any number of traumas, not least of all the departure of bassist Andy Fraser and the virtual incapacity of guitarist Paul Kossoff—one-half of the original band, and the lion's share of its spirit as well. But did their erstwhile bandmates let it show? Not a jot. The hastily recruited Tetsu Yamauchi, and vocalist Paul Rodgers himself, filled the breach instrumentally, and probably 50 percent of the ensuing *Heartbreaker* ranks among Free's finest ever work. Of course, any record that can open with the sheer majesty of "Wishing Well," Rodgers' so-evocative tribute to Kossoff, is immediately going to ascend to the halls of greatness, all the more so since Kossoff himself is in such fine form across both this cut and the next three—completing side one of the original vinyl, "Come Together in the Morning," "Travellin' in Style," and "Heartbreaker" add up to the band's most convincing sequence of songs since the days of *Fire and Water*. Further into the disc, two contributions from another new recruit, keyboard player John Bundrick, fall a little flat, a fate they share with the previously unreleased "Hand Me Down/Turn Me Round," one of the 2002 remaster's six bonus tracks. But a pair of solo Rodgers songs, "Easy on My Soul" and "Seven Angels," close the album with as much emotion as it opened on, and one could well argue that, after such a treat, the aforementioned bonus tracks are all but unnecessary, especially as the first few simply offer outtakes, alternates, and B-sides from the sessions themselves. As the CD wraps up, however, two final tracks reveal what happened once the album was completed, peeping into the band's rehearsal room on the eve of their summer tour of Japan to catch "Heartbreaker" and "Easy on My Soul" in such rough but eloquently heavenly form that this most emotionally weighted of Free's albums could demand no deeper coda. *—Dave Thompson*

● **The Free Story** / 1974 / Island ✦✦✦✦✦
Although record sales never went along with it, Free were British rock at its pinnacle. Their studio albums were superb through and through, while the one live release perhaps represented the band at their peak. This best-of features the cream of Free's releases up to 1973. Extending past the easily accessible rock tracks into the realms of the bands quieter acoustic moments, as well as the more experimental areas of Free's material, *The Free Story* gives the whole picture of what Rodgers, Kirke, Fraser, and Kossoff were about. The track selection well shows off the bands musical ability, from Paul Kossoff's vibrato-laden guitar to Andy Fraser's captivating bass playing. Indeed, few bands come close to the overall musicianship of Free. "Free left a legacy of enduring music which became a role model for much of which followed... *The Free Story* is testament to that heritage," declares the album notes. Few would disagree with that statement. *—Ben Davies*

● **Molten Gold: The Anthology** / Oct. 5, 1993 / A&M ✦✦✦✦✦
With their big riffs and bluesy melodies, Free virtually defined hard rock in the early '70s, and *Molten Gold: The Anthology* shows that this wasn't such a meager achievement. Throughout the two discs, it becomes clear that the key to Free's rock & roll was their rhythm section, which powered their riffs to perfection. This is the definitive Free, two discs of pure hard rock. *—Stephen Thomas Erlewine*

Songs of Yesterday / Oct. 10, 2000 / Island ✦✦✦✦✦
It's strange that a band with a song as immediate as "All Right Now" is a bit of an acquired taste, but it's the truth. Free was a powerful, majestic hard rock band at their peak, but they were also a little obtuse; a lot of their power came from their playing, and their songwriting was epic, but often elliptical. As such, they're for hard rock connoisseurs—a band who gained a spirited, dedicated following largely because they took devotion to unlock their treasures, especially in the years following their breakup. For those fans, the five-disc *Songs of Yesterday* is a godsend. This is not a box for listeners with less than a consuming interest in the band (even if you think you want total immersion in Free, this will not be as effective as purchasing each of their albums) since this contains a wealth of unreleased material. Very few of the tracks are actual album tracks, most are alternate mixes or alternate versions, plus there are a lot of live tracks in the mix, as well. As long as you know what you're getting into, this isn't bad, especially since it refurbishes the band's canon for the dedicated, giving them fresh insights to familiar songs (even if the new mixes aren't necessarily better than the originals—they just sound a bit brighter and more modern). For anyone else, it's a bit much, and it doesn't quite tell the story in the right fashion, since it really offers a mirror image, alternate version rather than the real thing. *—Stephen Thomas Erlewine*

Denny Freeman

b. Aug. 7, 1944, Orlando, FL
Piano, Guitar / Electric Texas Blues
This Dallas native and Austin fixture was co-lead guitarist in the Cobras with Stevie Vaughan, before joining Angela Strehli (cutting two solo LPs during his stint with the songstress), contributing to *Big Guitars from Texas*, and recording with Lou Ann Barton. More original and out-on-a-limb than most textbook-blues players, he co-wrote "Baboom/Mama Said" on the Vaughan Brothers' *Family Style* and played guitar and piano on tour with Jimmie Vaughan following the latter's *Strange Pleasure*. *—Dan Forte*

Blues Cruise / 1986 / Amazing ✦✦✦✦
"Rockin' with B.B." and "Steelin' Berry's" not only reveal two of Freeman's major influences but do justice to Mr. King and Chuck Berry—the latter featuring a fine steel guitar turn by Jimmie Vaughan. The melodic "Denny's Blues" is also a standout. Three lackluster vocal numbers (one each by Angela Strehli, Kim Wilson and Bill Carter) detract from the continuity (and level) of Freeman's instrumental set. *—Dan Forte*

Out of the Blue / 1987 / Amazing ✦✦✦✦
All instrumental this time, and a bit more varied, with gospel, jazz ("My Dominique"), exotica (Freeman's "Lost Incas" from the *Big Guitars from Texas* album), and even a nod to Billy Gibbons on "Z." Jimmie Vaughan cameos again, on steel and 6-string bass, along with the usual Austin crew (George Rains, Sarah Brown, Mel Brown, Derek O'Brien, Kaz Kazanoff, etc.). *—Dan Forte*

● **Denny Freeman** / 1991 / Amazing ✦✦✦✦✦
Freeman's two LPs wedged onto one CD, with three tunes unfortunately hitting the editing room floor. Two vocals interrupt the all-instrumental proceedings, and somehow Jimmie Vaughan's steel work on "Louisiana Luau" (from *Blues Cruise*) got the axe. *—Dan Forte*

Blues Cruise / Out of the Blue / 1997 / Amazing ✦✦✦✦✦
Two of Denny Freeman's mid-'80s albums—*Blues Cruise* (1986) and *Out of the Blues* (1987)—are combined on this single disc. On these albums, Freeman has a chance to stretch out and flaunt his amazing array of Texas blues licks—he rarely plays it safe. The disc was recorded with Antone's house band and features guest vocals by Angela Strehli and Kim Wilson. *—Thom Owens*

A Tone for My Sins / Nov. 11, 1997 / Dallas Blues Society ✦✦✦

Steve Freund

b. Jul. 20, 1952, Brooklyn, NY
Guitar / Electric Chicago Blues, Modern Electric Blues
Although he's played all around the U.S. (including stops in New York, Chicago, etc.), blues guitarist Steve Freund is best-known in the San Francisco Bay Area. Born on July 20, 1952, in Brooklyn, NY, his mother (who played classical piano) initially inspired Freund, but it was around the age of 16 when he first picked up the guitar. In 1976, Freund moved to Chicago and began to play regularly with Sunnyland Slim, which then led to gigs playing alongside such blues notables as Hubert Sumlin, Big Walter Horton, Pinetop Perkins, Paul Butterfield, Luther Allison, Koko Taylor, and Little Charlie & the Nightcats. By the late '90s, Freund had begun a regular residency at the bar/club The Saloon in San Francisco, almost always playing alongside blues pianist Wendy DeWitt, while issuing several albums along the way—*Set Me Free, Romance Without Finance, "C" for Chicago*, and *I'll Be Your Mule*. *—Greg Prato*

Set Me Free / Mar. 1984 / Razor ✦✦✦

Romance Without Finance / May 1987 / Red Beans ✦✦✦

"C" for Chicago / Nov. 23, 1999 / Delmark ✦✦✦
No one will accuse Steve Freund of having the greatest voice in the blues world. While Freund is an impressive guitarist, he is merely adequate as a singer. But when you're evaluating an album, it is important to look at the big picture. Taking different things into consideration—impressive chops, adequate singing, likable songwriting—one concludes that *"C" for Chicago*, although slightly uneven, has more plusses than minuses. Freund won't blow you away with a great voice, but he still gets his points across on enjoyable (if derivative) Chicago-style blues numbers like "Everytime I Get to Drinking," "Working Man," and "Please Love Me" (which employs Boz Scaggs as a second guitarist). One of the

CD's most memorable tracks is "I Love Money," a humorous account of having champagne tastes and a beer budget. Like so many blues songs that have been recorded over the years—or, for that matter, country songs—"I Love Money" manages to laugh at life's disappointments. Freund also provides a few instrumentals—which include "Mr. Jackson's Boogie" and the jazz-influenced "Cool Dream"—and that is a good thing because they give him a chance to really stretch out on electric guitar. Although *"C" for Chicago* is a Chicago blues album first and foremost, Freund shows his appreciation of jazz at times. And that is why he was lucky to have guitarist/singer Dave Specter produce this album. A versatile musician, Specter has one foot in the blues and the other in jazz, and he serves Freund well on this generally decent but imperfect effort. *—Alex Henderson*

- **I'll Be Your Mule** / 2001 / Delmark ♦♦♦

It is quite appropriate that one of Steve Freund's albums is titled *"C" for Chicago.* Although the singer/guitarist is a native New Yorker and presently lives in San Francisco, Chicago blues is his specialty. Freund used to live in the Windy City, where he was employed by heavyweights like Sunnyland Slim and Koko Taylor—and it was where he recorded *I'll Be Your Mule* in 2000. This CD was produced by guitarist Dave Specter, a bluesman with strong jazz leanings. Specter (who also produced *"C" for Chicago*) definitely knows his jazz; he could spend hours telling you about the contributions of Charlie Parker and Thelonious Monk. And because some (though certainly not all) parts of *I'll Be Your Mule* are jazz-influenced, Specter was the perfect producer for this CD. Freund is especially jazz-minded on B.B. King's "Fine Lookin' Woman," Big Bill Broonzy's "Ramblin' Bill," and the instrumental "Bill Reed's Blues." And yet, he isn't a Jimmy Witherspoon type of artist, or a disciple of Jimmy Rushing and Joe Williams. Freund is an electric Chicago-style bluesman whose roots are Chess Records, James Cotton, Buddy Guy, etc. But that doesn't mean that Freund (who wrote or co-wrote seven of the CD's 13 tracks) can't have some non-Chicago influences. Having a Chicago blues orientation doesn't mean that he can't be influenced by Texas blues (including Albert Collins) or incorporate jazz elements occasionally. Freund doesn't have a great voice—quite honestly, he's a better guitarist than singer. But he usually gets his points across, and while *I'll Be Your Mule* isn't a masterpiece, it is a decent and sincere, if derivative, outing. *—Alex Henderson*

Frogwings

f. 1997

Group / Jam Bands, Country-Rock, Blues-Rock

Outside of Gregg Allman, drummer Butch Trucks is the only member of Georgia's venerable Allman Brothers Band who's still in the lineup and has appeared on every album. But during one of the Allman's lulls in activity during the mid-'90s, Trucks decided to put together a side project that would allow him to play with his nephew (and future Allman Brothers guitarist), Derek Trucks. The elder Trucks called the group Frogwings, additionally recruiting Aquarium Rescue Unit members Oteil Burbridge (bass, vocals), Jimmy Herring (guitar), and Count Mbutu (percussion), Allman Brothers percussionist Marc Quiñones, plus keyboardist John Herbert and vocalist/guitarist Edwin McCain. The band performed club shows through 1997, and by the next year, Mbutu had left and Herbert had been replaced by yet another Aquarium Rescue Unit member, keyboardist/flutist Kofi Burbridge. Frogwings was becoming a hit in festivals and on the jam band circuit, yet still hadn't released a CD. But when McCain departed to focus on his solo career and Trucks recruited Blues Traveler frontman John Popper, the drummer knew he had the Frogwings lineup to record for his fledgling Flying Frog Records label.

The 2000 live CD *Croakin' at Toad's* showcased Frogwings at its hard-to-categorize best. Extended instrumentals like "Kick n Bach" hint at the Georgia jazz fusion of the Aquarium Rescue Unit; jamming numbers like "Pattern" show an Allman Brothers influence, and Popper's vocals and harmonica are reminiscent of Blues Traveler on "Ganja." The blazing Herring and youthful Trucks (equally adept at slide guitar and fingerpicking) blend their strengths nicely; Popper and bassist Burbridge (also with the Allman Brothers now) provide additional firepower, and keyboardist/brother Burbridge, Quiñones, and Trucks man the foundation of an uncategorizable jam band for the new millennium. *—Bill Meredith*

- **Croakin' at Toad's** / Aug. 22, 2000 / Flying Frog ♦♦♦

Just when it seemed safe to put away the one-hitters and trim the sideburns, along comes this jam band supergroup: Blues Traveler frontman John Popper, journeymen jammers Jimmy Herring and Kofi Burbridge, and more than half of the most recent (at the time) incarnation of the Allman Brothers Band (Butch Trucks, his nephew Derek, percussionist Marc Quiñones, and bassist Oteil Burbridge). The resulting album, a live set captured before an appreciative crowd, kicks off with a 14-minute instrumental called "Kick n Bach," letting listeners know that this band's really serious about their chops, in a really humorous sort of way. Too bad the joke is on the band. None of *Croakin at Toad's'* eight songs is anything more than an excuse for extended, indulgent soloing. Imagine a Santana rehearsal from the early '70s with a stoned Toots Thielemans sitting in on harp. Oh, this project might have been a fun distraction for the participants, but for many fans it will be merely distracting. Maybe you had to be there, like back in the '70s. *—Brian Beatty*

Frank Frost

b. Apr. 15, 1936, Auvergne, AR, **d.** Oct. 12, 1999, Helena, AR

Vocals, Piano, Harmonica, Guitar / Juke Joint Blues, Electric Delta Blues, Soul-Blues

Although the atmospheric juke joint blues of Frank Frost remained steeped in unadulterated Delta funk throughout his career, his ongoing musical journey took him well outside his Mississippi homebase.

He moved to St. Louis in 1951, learning how to blow harp first from Little Willie Foster and then from the legendary Sonny Boy Williamson, who took him on the road—as a guitar player—from 1956 to 1959. Drummer Sam Carr, a longtime Frost ally, was also part of the equation, having enticed Frost to front his combo in 1954 before hooking up with Sonny Boy.

Leaving Williamson's employ in 1959, Frost and Carr settled in Lula, MS. Guitarist Jack Johnson came aboard in 1962 after sitting in with the pair at the Savoy Theatre in Clarksdale. The three meshed perfectly—enough to interest Memphis producer Sam Phillips in a short-lived back-to-the-blues campaign that same year. *Hey Boss Man!*, issued on Sun's Phillips International subsidiary as by Frank Frost and the Nighthawks, was a wonderful collection of uncompromising Southern blues (albeit totally out of step with the marketplace at the time).

Elvis Presley's ex-guitarist Scotty Moore produced Frost's next sessions in Nashville in 1966 for Jewel Records. Augmented by session bassist Chip Young, the trio's tight down-home ensemble work was once again seamless. "My Back Scratcher," Frost's takeoff on Slim Harpo's "Baby Scratch My Back," even dented the R&B charts on Shreveport-based Jewel for three weeks.

Chicago blues fan Michael Frank sought out Frost in 1975. He located Frost, Johnson, and Carr playing inside Johnson's Clarksdale tavern, the Black Fox. Mesmerized by their sound, Frost soon formed his own record label, Earwig, to capture their raw, charismatic brand of blues. 1979's *Rockin' the Juke Joint Down*, billed as by the Jelly Roll Kings (after one of the standout songs on that old Phillips International LP), showcased the trio's multi-faceted approach—echoes of R&B, soul, even Johnny & the Hurricanes permeate their Delta-based attack.

In the years following, Frost waxed his own Earwig album (1988's *Midnight Prowler*) and appeared on Atlantic's 1992 *Deep Blues* soundtrack—an acclaimed film that reinforced the fact that blues still thrives deep in its southern birthplace. Frost returned in 1996 with *Keep Yourself Together.* He died from cardiac arrest October 12, 1999, at his home in Helena, AR; he was 63. *—Bill Dahl*

- **Hey Boss Man!** / 1962 / Philips ♦♦♦♦♦

One of the last great blues recordings produced by the legendary Sam Phillips. Frost and his Mississippi cohorts Jack Johnson and Sam Carr played Southern juke joint blues rough and ready in the classic mold, with plenty of dynamic interplay and nasty, lowdown grooves. *—Bill Dahl*

Frank Frost / 1973 / Jewel ♦♦♦

More down-home eclectic blues from the harpist/keyboardist. *—Bill Dahl*

Ride With Your Daddy Tonight / 1985 / Charly ♦♦♦♦♦

Frost's best sides for the Jewel label. Some of the most down-home '60s blues ever recorded. *—Cub Koda*

Midnight Prowler / 1988 / Earwig ♦♦♦

Frost is front-and-center with a program that's decidedly down-home. This is what modern Mississippi blues sounds like—tough, uncompromising, still rooted mainly in the '50s with a few modern touches. *—Bill Dahl*

Jelly Roll King / 1990 / Charly ♦♦♦

Jelly Roll Blues / 1991 / Paula ♦♦♦♦

Same band, different producer: this time it was Elvis Presley's legendary guitarist, Scotty Moore, behind the glass as Frost and his pals dished out the lowdown sounds during the mid-'60s for Stan Lewis' Jewel logo. "My Back Scratcher" owes a stylistic debt to Slim Harpo but feels mighty good all the same. The entire 13-song disc reeks of steamy juke-joint ambience. *—Bill Dahl*

Deep Blues / 1992 / Appaloosa ♦♦♦

Originally issued on Appaloosa, this 1999 reissue teams Frost with producer-guitar hotshot Fred James, Bob Kommersmith on upright bass, and Clarence "Gatemouth" Brown alumnus Waldo Latowsky on drums. The grooves are straightforward and cleanly played with a true spark of spontaneity plainly evident to the entire session. Even recuts of his old Jewel material like "Ride With Your Daddy Tonight" and "Pocketful of Shells" sound inspired here. A keeper. *—Cub Koda*

Screamers / Sep. 2, 1994 / Appaloosa ♦♦♦

Keep Yourself Together / 1996 / Evidence ♦♦♦

This is a nicely put together—if rather unexceptional—set with Frost's vocal and harp ably supported by his long-time drummer Sam Carr, producer Fred James on guitar and Bob Kommersmith on string bass. While nothing on here burns with the smoldering intensity of his early Sun-Phillips International sides or his later sessions for Jewel, a pair of Little Walter tunes ("Everything's Gonna Be Alright," "Just a Feeling") a remake of one of his Sun-P.I. sides ("Come on Home") and a version of Jimmy Rushing's "Going to Chicago" make this an album more than worthy of a spin or two in the CD player. *—Cub Koda*

The Jelly Roll Kings / Dec. 18, 1998 / HMG ♦♦♦

Recorded in 1998 in the Sonny Boy Williamson Memorial Music Hall in Helena, Arkansas, this pares the blues down to a bare-bones sound with Frank Frost on vocals and harmonica (piano on one track) and Sam Carr on drums (vocals on one track, "Owl Head Woman"), tied together with the overdubbed guitar work of producer Fred James, who also provides the unobtrusive bass parts in the background. The result is a very modern-sounding (i.e., powerful) production that nonetheless keeps the format so astoundingly simple, it seems like a throwback to an earlier time. Even better is that all of the material on here is original; only a solid remake of "Jelly Roll King" (previously recorded by Frost for Sun) interrupts the flow of new songs, all of them firmly in the Delta juke-joint tradition. There's something very alive about these recordings, even with James' overdubbed guitar or bass work, that has as much to do with the sound of the Music Hall as the performances themselves. Highlights include "Let's Go Out Tonight," "Love I Have Is True," "Sittin' on Daddy's Knee," the low-down instrumental "Mess Around," Frost's out-of-tune piano playing behind Carr on "Owl Head Woman" and the Bo Diddley-like closer, "Done With Me," all representative of loose, wonderful, down-home blues playing captured raw, alive and exciting. *—Cub Koda*

Big Boss Man: The Very Best of Frank Frost / Feb. 2, 1999 / Collectables ♦♦♦♦♦

Harpin' on It: The Complete Jewel Recordings / Jun. 26, 2002 / West Side ✦✦✦✦✦
West Side's 13-track collection *Harpin' on It: The Complete Jewel Recordings* compiles all of the songs he cut for the Louisiana label in the mid-'60s. While these sides aren't as down-n-dirty as his earlier material for Sun, they're still enjoyable, revved-up juke-joint blues. If anything, he stretches the form a little bit here, getting a little funkier with the rhythms, a little rockier in the guitar and all the production sounds a bit more modern, more like the mid-'60s (which, ironically enough, means it doesn't sound as timeless as his earlier recordings). Throughout it all, Frost's great harp is front and center, and his playing is always first-rate, even when the material is a little pedestrian. Fortunately, he hit the mark more often than not while on Jewel—most notably on instrumentals, plus the great Slim Harpo take-off, "My Back Scratcher"—which is why this is worth hearing. *—Stephen Thomas Erlewine*

Blind Boy Fuller

b. 1908, Wadesboro, NC, **d.** Feb. 13, 1941, Durham, NC

Vocals, Guitar / Prewar Blues, East Coast Blues, Piedmont Blues, Country Blues, Acoustic Blues

Unlike blues artists like Big Bill or Memphis Minnie who recorded extensively over three or four decades, Blind Boy Fuller recorded his substantial body of work over a short, six-year span. Neverthless, he was one of the most recorded artists of his time and by far the most popular and influential Piedmont blues player of all time. Fuller could play in multiple styles: slide, ragtime, pop, and blues were all enhanced by his National steel guitar. Fuller worked with some fine sidemen, including Davis, Sonny Terry, and washboard player Bull City Red. Initially discovered and promoted by Carolina entrepreneur H.B. Long, Fuller recorded for ARC and Decca. He also served as a conduit to recording sessions, steering fellow blues musicians to the studio.

In spite of Fuller's recorded output, most of his musical life was spent as a street musician and house party favorite, and he possessed the skills to reinterpret and cover the hits of other artists as well. In this sense, he was a synthesizer of styles, parallel in many ways to Robert Johnson, his contemporary who died three years earlier. Like Johnson, Fuller lived fast and died young, only 33 years old. Fuller was a fine, expressive vocalist and a masterful guitar player best remembered for his uptempo ragtime hits "Rag Mama Rag," "Trucking My Blues Away," and "Step It Up and Go." At the same time he was capable of deeper material, and his versions of "Lost Lover Blues" or "Mamie" are as deep as most Delta blues. Because of his popularity, he may have been overexposed on records, yet most of his songs remained close to tradition and much of his repertoire and style is kept alive by North Carolina and Virginia artists today. *—Barry Lee Pearson*

★ **Truckin' My Blues Away** / 1978 / Yazoo ✦✦✦✦✦
For most listeners, Yazoo's *Truckin' My Blues Away* may be a better bet than Columbia/Legacy's *East Coast Piedmont Style*, since it actually has a higher concentration of strong material, capturing the influential bluesman at his peak. All of the 14 tracks were recorded between 1935 and 1938, and there are a number of exceptional performances here, including "Homesick and Lonesome Blues," "Truckin' My Blues Away," "I Crave My Pig Meat," "Walking My Troubles Away," and "Sweet Honey Hole." It's a nice, concise introduction and, best of all, there's no duplication between this disc and *East Coast Piedmont Style*, making the two discs wonderful, complementary collections that tell a comprehensive story when taken together. *—Thom Owens*

East Coast Piedmont Style / Aug. 1991 / Columbia/Legacy ✦✦✦✦
Blind Boy Fuller, who died when he was only 33, recorded extensively during 1935-1940. His guitar playing was in the tradition of the ragtime-influenced Blind Blake and Blind Willie McTell while his singing was simple and direct. The music on this CD reissue becomes a bit repetitive after awhile for Fuller generally lacked variety but, taken in small doses (as if one were listening to the original 78s and treasuring individual songs), Blind Boy Fuller's performances were often memorable. The reissue is a cross section of his work with the emphasis on his earliest recordings. Guitarist Blind Gary Davis, Bull City Red on washboard and harmonica wiz Sonny Terry help out on a few numbers; five of the 20 selections were previously unreleased. *—Scott Yanow*

Complete Recorded Works, Vols. 1-4 / 1992 / Document ✦✦✦✦✦
The finest collection ever of blues and ragtime. Fuller is here both solo and with Gary Davis, Sonny Terry, and Bull City Red. This is Piedmont blues at its best (1935-1940), a must for anyone interested in down-home blues. *—Barry Lee Pearson*

☆ **Complete Recorded Works, Vol. 1 (1935–1936)** / 1992 / Document ✦✦✦✦✦

Complete Recorded Works, Vol. 2 (1936–1937) / 1992 / Document ✦✦✦✦
The second volume in Document's chronological overview of Blind Boy Fuller's life and music contains some of his most popular recordings, including the 1936 sessions which yielded both "Truckin' My Blues Away" (an update of Tampa Red's "What Is It That Tastes Like Gravy?") and "Mama Let Me Lay It on You" (a rendition of Memphis Minnie and Kansas Joe's "Can I Do It for You?"), both of them definitive versions. Fuller's gift for making familiar songs his own pops again on his next session, from early February of 1937; backed by Dipper Boy Council and Bull City Red, he delivers renditions of "Mamie," "Untrue Blues" (a version of the "Crow Jane" theme) and "New Oh Red!," all of them revelatory and unforgettable. *—Jason Ankeny*

Complete Recorded Works, Vol. 3 (1937) / 1992 / Document ✦✦✦
The 22 sides which comprise the third volume in Document's Blind Boy Fuller retrospective were all culled from sessions cut in the latter half of 1937; the first session, from mid-July, was recorded under the auspices of the Decca label, a situation which left Fuller's longtime manager J.B. Long—as well as ARC Records—none too happy. As a result, at the bluesman's next session, Long insisted he re-record many of the titles earlier cut for Decca, resulting in alternate takes of "Bulldog Blues," "Throw Your Yas Yas Back in Jail" (aka "Put You Back in Jail") and "Steel Hearted Woman" (aka "Why Don't My Baby Write to Me"); for blues historians, the chance to compare and contrast the sessions will be irresistible, although more casual fans might find this particular release less engaging than the others in the series. *—Jason Ankeny*

Complete Recorded Works, Vol. 4 (1937–1938) / 1992 / Document ✦✦✦✦
Beginning with the mid-December, 1937 session which kicks off this fourth volume in Document's retrospective, Blind Boy Fuller entered into a recording partnership with the legendary harpist Sonny Terry that continued for the remainder of Fuller's studio career. Terry's blistering harmonica and falsetto interjections lent an exciting new dynamic to Fuller's sound, as classic sides like "Pistol Snapper Blues," "Mean and No Good Woman" and "Georgia Ham Mama" amply prove, each musician pushing the other to new creative heights. *—Jason Ankeny*

Complete Recorded Works, Vol. 5 (1938–1940) / 1992 / Document ✦✦✦✦
Volume five in Document's Blind Boy Fuller series is comprised primarily of two prolific sessions, the first recorded in Columbia, South Carolina on October 29, 1938 with harpist Sonny Terry and washboard player Bull City Red, the second a Memphis date from July 12, 1939 with Terry, Bull City Red (now going as Oh Red) and second guitarist Sonny Jones. The latter is perhaps the most impressive, yielding the signature song "I Want Some of Your Pie" as well as "You've Got Something There" (a rewrite of Buddy Moss' "Daddy Don't Care") and Fuller's immortal rendition of J.B. Long's "Step It Up and Go." *—Jason Ankeny*

Complete Recorded Works, Vol. 6 (1940) / 1992 / Document ✦✦✦✦
The sixth and final volume in the series assembles the fruits of Blind Boy Fuller's final studio sessions, all dating to the first half of 1940. Despite failing health, Fuller is at his most incendiary on these sides—"Shake It, Baby" is among his most galvanizing dance tunes, while "Little Woman You're So Sweet" stands as one of his finest originals. Most energetic, however, are the sanctified songs, including "No Stranger Now," "Jesus Is a Holy Man" and "Twelve Gates to the City"—with his death less than a year away, Fuller burns with spiritual intensity, clearly yearning for some kind of redemption in his final months. *—Jason Ankeny*

The Remaining Titles 1935–1940 / 1995 / Best of Blues ✦✦✦
Remaining Titles 1935-1940 collects the rest of Blind Boy Fuller's tracks recorded in the late '30s and while they're not quite as strong as other items he recorded at the same time, they're still quite good. It's worthwhile for completists. *—Thom Owens*

Get Your Yas Yas Out: The Essential Recordings of Blind Boy Fuller / Mar. 19, 1996 / Indigo ✦✦✦✦
Blind Boy Fuller packed a lot of music into his brief six-year stint as the grandest exponent of North Carolina Piedmont blues. A fixture on the streets of Durham, Fuller offered up an infectious mix of rags, blues, instrumentals, mountain-styled songs, and even a bit of pop. And while skirting from style to style, Fuller always dished up top-notch fret work on his steel-bodied guitar and sang with a warm gruffness. Along with other stellar collections on Columbia and Catfish, this Indigo disc qualifies as a fine starting place for neophytes. Even though it's more of a fine overview than necessarily an essential collection, *Get Your Yas Yas Out* still bristles with plenty of standouts like "Rattlesnakin' Daddy," "Step Up and Go," and "Lost Lover Blues." And helping out in the instrumental department are such regular Fuller cohorts as harp master Sonny Terry and washboard player Bull City Red—fellow blues guitarist Blind Gary Davis also contributes some fine work. One of just many recent imports that are setting the standard for blues retrospectives. *—Stephen Cook*

Blind Boy Fuller With Sonny Terry and Bull City Red / Blues Classics ✦✦✦✦✦
Like Robert Johnson's inexorable connection to Delta blues or Blind Lemon Jefferson's fame as a Texas originator, guitarist Blind Boy Fuller will be forever associated with the Piedmont blues of North Carolina. Whether forged or refashioned by Fuller, Carolina blues was more mobile than the Delta style—akin to Lemon's sound in that respect—featuring a rambling blend of rags, pop, and blues, with a hint of the mountain music from nearby Appalachia thrown in. This solid Blues Classics collection covers most of Fuller's rich but short recording career from 1935-1940, featuring him with regular accompanists Sonny Terry on harmonica and Bull City Red on washboard. With Terry's wailing harp and Red's steady rhythm supplying the backdrop, Fuller sings, whoops, and hollers through breakdowns like "Step Up and Go" and "Shake It Baby," while displaying his considerable pickin' skills on instrumentals like "Jitterbug Rag." Fuller is also heard solo on classic blues like "Careless Love" and his famed slice of sexual double entendre "I'm a Rattlesnakin' Daddy." Along with collections on Columbia and Yazoo, this Blues Classics title makes for a fine introduction to Fuller's music. *—Stephen Cook*

Jesse Fuller

b. Mar. 12, 1896, Jonesboro, GA, **d.** Jan. 29, 1976, Oakland, CA

Vocals, Kazoo, Harmonica, Guitar / Blues Revival, Folk-Blues, Country Blues, West Coast Blues

Equipped with a bandful of instruments operated by various parts of his anatomy, Bay Area-legend Jesse Fuller was a folk-music favorite in the '50s and '60s. His infectious rhythm and gentle charm graced old folk tunes, spirituals, and blues alike. One of his inventions was a homemade, foot-operated instrument called the "footdella" or "fotdella." Naturally, Fuller never needed other accompanists to back his one-man show. His best-known songs include "San Francisco Bay Blues" and "Beat It on Down the Line" (the first one covered by Janis Joplin, the second by The Grateful Dead).

Born and raised in Georgia, Jesse Fuller began playing guitar when he was a child, although he didn't pursue the instrument seriously. In his early twenties, Fuller wandered around the southern and western regions of the United States, eventually settling down in Los Angeles. While he was in southern California, he worked as a film extra, appearing in *The Thief of Bagdad, East of Suez, Hearts in Dixie,* and *End of the World.* After spending a few years in Los Angeles, Fuller moved to San Francisco. While he worked various odd jobs around the Bay Area, he played on street corners and parties.

Jesse's musical career didn't properly begin until the early '50s, when he decided to become a professional musician—he was 55 years old at the time. Performing as a one-man band, he began to get spots on local television shows and nightclubs. However, Fuller's career didn't take off until 1954, when he wrote "San Francisco Bay Blues." The song helped him land a record contract with the independent Cavalier label and in 1955, he recorded his first album, *Folk Blues: Working on the Railroad With Jesse Fuller.* The albums was a success and soon he was making records for a variety of labels, including Good Time Jazz and Prestige.

In the late '50s and early '60s, Jesse Fuller became one of the key figures of the blues revival, helping bring the music to a new, younger audience. Throughout the '60s and '70s, he toured America and Europe, appearing at numerous blues and folk festivals, as well as countless coffeehouse gigs across the U.S. Fuller continued performing and recording until his death in 1976. —*Jim O'Neal & Stephen Thomas Erlewine*

Jazz, Folk Songs, Spirituals & Blues / Apr. 1958 / Good Time Jazz/Original Blues Classic ✦✦✦✦✦

Jesse Fuller was among the greatest one-man bands in blues history. The title of this 1958 date adequately described the session's musical width and depth; Fuller handled everything from old spirituals such as as "I'm Going to Meet My Loving Mother" to the rollicking "Memphis Boogie" and "Fingerbuster" and the concluding "Hesitation Blues." As sole performer, melodic, rhythmic and performing focus, Fuller's energy never wanes through the CD's 11 numbers. He nicely conveys the varying moods, themes and sentiments, knowing which lyrics to emphasize, when to intensify the pace and when to lower his voice and let the music make the point. —*Ron Wynn*

Brother Lowdown / 1959 / Fantasy ✦

Originally released as the Prestige albums *San Francisco Bay Blues* and *Jesse Fuller's Favorites,* these 26 sides are fine examples of Fuller's unique one-man-band genius. As if guitar, harmonica, kazoo and washboard weren't enough to occupy his musicianship, the man also invented the "fotdella," a bass he could play with his feet. Unfortunately, a little of Fuller goes a long way and two album's worth of similar performances on a single CD ends up being too much of a good thing. —*Brian Beatty*

The Lone Cat Sings and Plays Jazz, Folk Songs, Spirituals and Blues / Aug. 1961 / Good Time Jazz/Original Blues Classic ✦✦✦

Lone Cat Sings and Plays Jazz, Folk Songs, Spirituals and Blues features a selection of oldtime blues, ragtime, and string band songs, all performed by the one-man band Jesse Fuller. With his 12-string guitar, harmonica, kazoo, cymbals, and six-string bass (which he played with his foot), Fuller created a very unique sound that surprisingly didn't sound particularly jokey—instead, it sounded like it was part of a tradition. None of his best-known songs are included on *Lone Cat,* but there is an abundance of strange, wonderful music on the record. —*Thom Owens*

● **San Francisco Bay Blues** / 1963 / Good Time Jazz/Original Blues Classic ✦✦✦✦✦

By the time *San Francisco Bay Blues* was released in 1963, the title track had long been established as a classic and Jesse Fuller's career had been revived. Nevertheless, the album may be his finest, containing wonderful versions of "San Francisco Bay Blues," "Jesse's New Midnight Special," "John Henry," "I Got a Mind to Ramble" and "Crazy About a Woman," that find Fuller at his easygoing best. —*Thom Owens*

Favorites / 1965 / Prestige/Original Blues Classics ✦✦✦

Jesse Fuller's *Favorites* is a highly enjoyable collection of the singer's favorite blues standards. Performing everything as a solo piece, he runs through classics like "Key to the Highway," "The Midnight Special," and "Brownskin Gal" with humor and warmth. It's a small, but entertaining, gem. —*Thom Owens*

Blues, Jazz, Spirituals . . . / 1965 / Good Time Jazz ✦✦✦

Frisco Bound / 1968 / Arhoolie ✦✦✦✦

A one-man band with guitar, harmonica, kazoo, and "footdella" bass, these are some of his first recordings, ca. 1955. Innocent echoes of turn-of-the-century rural America. —*Mark A. Humphrey*

Masters of the Country Blues [Video/DVD] / Apr. 16, 1995 / Yazoo ✦✦✦✦

Johnny Fuller

b. Apr. 20, 1929, Edwards, MS, d. May 20, 1985, Oakland, CA
Vocals, Piano, Guitar, Organ / West Coast Blues

Johnny Fuller was a West Coast bluesman who left behind a spate of '50s recordings that jumped all kinds of genre fences with seemingly no trace of his Mississippi born roots. He was equally at home with low down blues, gospel, R&B, and rock & roll, all of it imbued with strong vocals and a driving guitar style. Although his Mississippi roots were never far below the surface of his best work, Johnny is usually categorized as a West Coast bluesman. Making the Bay Area his home throughout his career, Fuller turned in classic sides for Heritage, Aladdin, Specialty, Flair, Checker, and Hollywood; all but one of them West Coast-based concerns. His two biggest hits, "All Night Long" and the original version of "The Haunted House," improbably found him in the late '50s on rock & roll package shows, touring with the likes of Paul Anka and Frankie Avalon! By and large retiring from the music scene in the '60s (with the exception of one excellent album in 1974), Fuller worked as a garage mechanic until his passing in 1985. —*Cub Koda*

● **Fuller's Blues** / 1974 / Diving Duck ✦✦✦✦

Recorded in 1974, *Fuller's Blues* was Johnny Fuller's much-belated full-length debut, and it also turned out to be his last record. That's too bad, because it certainly illustrates what he was capable of achieving. He runs the gauntlet here, pulling out jumping R&B numbers and acoustic blues with equal aplomb. It's an exhilarating listen—it's just too bad there weren't more like it. —*Thom Owens*

Fools Paradise / 1984 / Diving Duck ✦✦✦

Lowell Fulson

b. Mar. 31, 1921, Tulsa, OK, d. Mar. 6, 1999
Vocals, Leader, Guitar / West Coast Blues, Texas Blues, Electric Texas Blues, Soul-Blues

Lowell Fulson has recorded every shade of blues imaginable. Polished urban blues, rustic two-guitar duets with his younger brother Martin, funk-tinged grooves that pierced the mid-'60s charts, even an unwise cover of the Beatles' "Why Don't We Do It in the Road?" Clearly, the veteran guitarist, who's been at it now for more than half a century, isn't afraid to experiment. Perhaps that's why his last couple of discs for Rounder are so vital and satisfying—and why he's been an innovator for so long.

Exposed to the western swing of Bob Wills as well as indigenous blues while growing up in Oklahoma, Fulson joined up with singer Texas Alexander for a few months in 1940, touring the Lone Star state with the veteran bluesman. Fulson was drafted in 1943. The Navy let him go in 1945; after a few months back in Oklahoma, he was off to Oakland, CA, where he made his first 78s for fledgling producer Bob Geddins. Soon enough, Fulson was fronting his own band and cutting a stack of platters for Big Town, Gilt Edge, Trilon, and Down Town (where he hit big in 1948 with "Three O'Clock Blues," later covered by B.B. King).

Swing Time records prexy Jack Lauderdale snapped up Fulson in 1948, and the hits really began to flow: the immortal "Every Day I Have the Blues" (an adaptation of Memphis Slim's "Nobody Loves Me"), "Blue Shadows," the two-sided holiday perennial "Lonesome Christmas," and a groovy midtempo instrumental "Low Society Blues" that really hammers home how tremendously important pianist Lloyd Glenn and alto saxist Earl Brown were to Fulson's maturing sound (all charted in 1950!).

Fulson toured extensively from then on, his band stocked for a time with dazzling pianist Ray Charles (who later covered Lowell's "Sinner's Prayer" for Atlantic) and saxist Stanley Turrentine. After a one-off session in New Orleans in 1953 for Aladdin, Fulson inked a longterm pact with Chess in 1954. His first single for the firm was the classic "Reconsider Baby," cut in Dallas under Stan Lewis' supervision with a sax section that included David "Fathead" Newman on tenor and Leroy Cooper on baritone.

The relentless midtempo blues proved a massive hit and perennial cover item—even Elvis Presley cut it in 1960, right after he got out of the Army. But apart from "Loving You," the guitarist's subsequent Checker output failed to find widespread favor with the public. Baffling, since Fulson's crisp, concise guitar work and sturdy vocals were as effective as ever. Most of his Checker sessions were held in Chicago and L.A. (the latter his home from the turn of the '50s).

Fulson stayed with Checker into 1962, but a change of labels worked wonders when he jumped over to Los Angeles-based Kent Records. 1965's driving "Black Nights" became his first smash in a decade, and "Tramp," a loping funk-injected workout co-written by Fulson and Jimmy McCracklin, did even better, restoring the guitarist to R&B stardom, gaining plenty of pop spins, and inspiring a playful Stax cover by Otis Redding and Carla Thomas only a few months later that outsold Fulson's original.

A couple of lesser follow-up hits for Kent ensued before the guitarist was reunited with Stan Lewis at Jewel Records. That's where he took a crack at that Beatles number, though most of his outings for the firm were considerably closer to the blues bone. Fulson has never been absent for long on disc; 1992's *Hold On* and its 1995 follow-up *Them Update Blues,* both for Ron Levy's Bullseye Blues logo, are among his most recent efforts, both quite solid.

Few bluesmen have managed to remain contemporary the way Lowell Fulson has for more than five decades. And fewer still will make such a massive contribution to the idiom. —*Bill Dahl*

★ **Hung Down Head** / 1954 / MCA/Chess ✦✦✦✦✦

This is the most indispensable collection in Fulson's vast discography. He was hitting on all burners during the mid-'50s when he was with Chess, waxing the immortal "Reconsider Baby," and swinging gems like "Check Yourself," "Do Me Right," and "Trouble, Trouble," and the supremely doomy "Tollin' Bells," here in many truncated false takes before he and the band finally jell. —*Bill Dahl*

Lowell Fulson / 1959 / Chess ✦✦✦

The rest of Fulson's 1955-1962 Chess output is classic stuff. —*Bill Dahl*

Back Home Blues / 1959 / Night Train ✦✦✦

Back Home Blues collects several tracks Lowell Fulson cut early in his career for Swing Time, when he was performing jump blues. This is high-energy, enjoyable blues—even though Fulsom doesn't sound as comfortable with jump blues as he does with postwar Chicago and Southern blues, he is completely creditable on these performances. It's an essential purchase for Fulson fans that want to dig deep into his roots. —*Thom Owens*

Soul / 1966 / United ✦✦✦✦✦

Soul is funky, uncompromising guitar blues. —*Bill Dahl*

Tramp / 1967 / United ✦✦✦✦✦

Led by one of his biggest hits, this is one of Fulson's best and funkiest. —*Bill Dahl*

Now! / 1969 / United ✦✦✦

Now! was actually comprised largely of 1967-1968 singles, filled out by three cuts which made their first appearance on this LP. It's loosey-goosey late-'60s blues-soul crossover, with a sassy attitude and adroit combinations of stinging blues guitar, strutting vocals, soulful horns, and organ, never heard better than on "I'm a Drifter." Actually, the record sounds better than much of his slightly earlier '60s Kent stuff because it's not as unduly repetitious, though it's filled out with cover versions of familiar tunes like "Funky Broadway," "Let's Go Get Stoned," and "Everyday I Have the Blues." Perhaps it wasn't cutting edge as far as late-'60s soul went, but it had some of the rawness of '50s electric blues and some of the slickness of late-'60s soul brass, and B.B. King-like horn charts, and the combination usually clicked. All of the tracks from *Now!* are on the Ace CD compilation *The Final Kent Years,* which also includes his 1978 album *Lovemaker,* a 1972 single, and three previously unissued cuts from around the time of the *Now!* sessions. —*Richie Unterberger*

In a Heavy Bag / 1970 / Jewel ♦♦
Too rock-oriented for comfort. —*Bill Dahl*

Let's Go Get Stoned / 1971 / United ♦♦

I've Got the Blues / 1973 / Fuel 2000 ♦♦♦
I've Got the Blues is as simple and straightforward as its title as Lowell Fulson lays down tracks like "Teach Me," "Crying Won't Help" and "Stoned to the Bone" in his inimitable West Coast style. —*Jason Ankeny*

Ol' Blues Singer / 1975 / Indigo ♦♦

Lowell Fulson (Early Recordings) / 1975 / Arhoolie ♦♦♦
Mostly the country blues roots of the Oklahoma-born guitarist. The first ten tracks, duets with brother Martin on second guitar, are worlds apart from the swinging horn-powered R&B efforts that Fulson is famous for. The last four numbers, though, revert to that attractive format—especially the scorching instrumental closer "Lowell Jumps One." —*Bill Dahl*

Blues Masters / 1977 / Chess ♦♦♦♦♦

Lovemaker / 1978 / Big Town ♦♦♦
Lovemaker is not the most exciting Lowell Fulson album by a long shot. But it's respectable soul-blues, and not as inappropriately polished as the usual late-'70s recordings by blues veterans. Actually, Fulson was more in the straight-ahead blues bag by this time than he had been on his mid- to late-'60s soul-influenced records, including a couple of revivals of "It Hurts Me Too" (retitled "When Things Go Wrong") and "Sittin' on Top of the World" (retitled "I Am Not Worried"). The accent is on good-natured, straightforward urbane blues, the backing less passionate than Fulson's vocals, the groove sticking mostly to the midtempo, getting into mild funk here and there, particularly on the title track. All of the tracks from *Lovemaker* are on the Ace CD compilation *The Final Kent Years*, which also includes his 1968 album *Now!*, a 1972 single, and three previously unissued cuts from around the time of the *Now!* sessions. —*Richie Unterberger*

Man of Motion / 1981 / Charly ♦♦
A vinyl collection of Fulson's late-'60s stint at Shreveport's Jewel Records. In truth, not the guitarist's shining hour—some of this stuff is competent blues (some backed by the Muscle Shoals house band of the era), others abominable attempts at cracking the blues-rock market (his rendering of the Beatles' "Why Don't We Do It in the Road" stands as the worst thing Fulson ever committed to tape). —*Bill Dahl*

Everyday I Have the Blues / 1984 / Night Train ♦♦♦♦♦
The first of two extremely solid compilations of the guitarist's late-'40s/early-'50s output for Jack Lauderdale's Los Angeles-based Swing Time imprint. You'll need 'em both, since the essentials are spread across 'em about evenly—Fulson's smashes "Every Day," "Lonesome Christmas," and "Blue Shadows" regally inhabit this 20-cut disc. —*Bill Dahl*

Think Twice Before You Speak / 1984 / JSP ♦♦♦

Lowell Fulson / 1984 / Chess ♦♦♦

One More Blues / Mar. 11, 1984 / Evidence ♦♦♦
Fulson hasn't been as prolific over the last couple of decades as he was during the '50s, but when he does get a chance to enter a studio, he usually emerges with some pretty impressive work. This 1984 album, first out on Black & Blue over in France, is no exception—the band is tight (Phillip Walker is rhythm guitarist), and Fulson came prepared with a sheaf of solid originals. —*Bill Dahl*

The Blues Got Me Down / 1985 / Diving Duck ♦♦♦♦♦

Blue Days Black Nights / 1986 / Ace ♦♦♦
Blue Days Black Night collects 15 tracks Lowell Fulson recorded in the late '60s, including the classic "Tramp." During this era, he was playing Chicago blues and Southern soul, with the occasional flourish of laidback, Western blues. Although this material is first-rate, it is available on better collections, including Flair's two-fer of *Tramp* and *Soul*. —*Thom Owens*

I Don't Know My Mind / 1987 / Bear Family ♦♦♦♦

Giant of Blues Guitar 1946/57 / 1987 / Blues Boy ♦♦♦♦♦
Fulson's country blues roots are the focus on this set of recordings from his postwar-era peak. —*Jason Ankeny*

It's a Good Day / 1988 / Rounder ♦♦♦
While no one was anticipating longtime blues great Lowell Fulson to equal or even approach his masterful '50s work on this session, he turned in a pleasantly competent date of both heartache numbers and more upbeat tunes. Fulson's leads were clear and nicely phrased, his guitar work still tasty and clever. He interspersed some swamp pop, Texas shuffle and urban blues riffs into his material, and on "Blues and My Guitar" displayed the fluidity and performance magic that made his classic sides unforgettable. —*Ron Wynn*

San Francisco Blues / 1988 / Black Lion ♦♦♦♦♦
Guitarist and vocalist Lowell Fulson helped establish his reputation with a string of fine songs for the Swing Time label in the late '40s and early '50s. Fulson showed he could belt out hard-hitting blues, do sentimental ballads, double entendre novelty pieces or irony-filled laments, and also play riveting solos. This 1992 CD reissue collects 16 early Fulson numbers, all original compositions, and features Fulson leading a group with Lloyd Glenn, King Solomon or Rufus J. Russell on piano, Ralph Hamilton, Billy Hadnott or Floyd Montgomery on bass, and Bob Harvey or Asal Carson on drums. —*Ron Wynn*

Chicago Golden Years / 1988 / Vogue ♦♦♦♦♦

Tramp/Soul / 1991 / Ace ♦♦♦♦♦
The veteran guitarist's two best mid-'60s albums for Kent Records on one packed-to-the-gills CD. Fulson cannily made the leap into soul-slanted grooves while at Kent, scoring a major R&B smash with "Tramp." Also aboard is Fulson's classic "Black Nights," "Talkin'

Woman" (later revived most memorably by Albert Collins as "Honey Hush"), and a fine version of Willie "Smokey" Hogg's enduring "Too Many Drivers." —*Bill Dahl*

Hold On / May 1992 / Bullseye Blues ♦♦♦♦
Nothing dated about this fine album, produced by organist Ron Levy—Fulson sounds at once both contemporary and timeless, slashing through a mostly original set with Jimmy McCracklin helping out on piano and the sax section including Bobby Forte and Edgar Synigal. —*Bill Dahl*

Reconsider Baby / 1993 / Charly ♦♦♦♦♦
A more in-depth assessment of Fulson's Chess years (20 titles), minus a few of the most important sides nestled on *Hung Down Head* but boasting a few others of nearly equal import: "Lonely Hours," "Rollin' Blues," "Don't Drive Me Baby," and especially the insane 1957 rocker "Rock This Morning," where Fulson does his best Little Richard imitation as Eddie Chamblee blows up a tenor sax hurricane. —*Bill Dahl*

Them Update Blues / 1995 / Bullseye Blues ♦♦♦
A half century after he made his debut waxings, Fulson is still going strong—and not as some museum piece, either. Still a vital blues artist who refuses to rest on his massive laurels, Fulson's latest is a fine addition to his vast discography, comprised mostly of fresh originals and featuring his customary biting guitar and insinuating vocals. —*Bill Dahl*

Sinner's Prayer / 1995 / Night Train ♦♦♦♦♦
Here are 20 more Swing Time essentials, notably Lowell Fulson's original reading of the mournful "Sinner's Prayer" (soon revived by his onetime band pianist Ray Charles), the exultant instrumental "Low Society" (featuring Earl Brown's sturdy alto sax), and one of Fulson's wildest rockers, "Upstairs." —*Bill Dahl*

My First Recordings / Jan. 21, 1997 / Arhoolie ♦♦♦
Twenty-six tracks that Fulson cut between 1946 and 1951 for the Swing Time, Big Town, and Down Town labels. This is far more sparsely produced, and less urbane in feel, than the material Lowell would record for Chess throughout the '50s. Indeed, on ten of the cuts, he's supported only by his brother Martin on rhythm guitar; there's a small combo on the remainder of the cuts, but a fairly subdued one. Those who prefer their blues down-home might like this better than the more polished sound that Fulson moved into for the rest of his career. It's city blues just out of the country, with Fulson's high, pleading vocals and sharp, countrified electric licks to the fore. The most famous song, by far, is the original version of "Three O'Clock Blues," which was covered for a huge R&B hit by B.B. King in the early '50s. —*Richie Unterberger*

The Complete Chess Masters (50th Anniversary Collection) / Nov. 4, 1997 / MCA/Chess ♦♦♦♦♦
Two-CD, 45-song compilation covers Fulson's Chess years, which spanned 1954 to 1963. Fulson didn't have a great deal of commercial success at Chess (the big exception being "Reconsider Baby," and which leads off this set), and his jazzy West Coast form of R&B/blues was considerably more polished than the electrified Delta blues for which Chess is most renowned. Most of this, in fact, was recorded not in Chicago, but in Los Angeles, where Fulson could work with combos more sympathetic to his style. You'd have to consider this Fulson's peak, however, and the two discs' worth of material is not excessive, due to the consistency of his material and vocal confidence throughout the decade. It's not without its weird moments of rawness, either, as in "Blues Rhumba," the Bo Diddleyesque guitar that opens "Please Don't Go," Willie Dixon's classic dirge moaning blues "Tollin' Bells," and the (deliberately?) out-of-tune guitar licks that open "K.C. Bound" with a bang. "Smokey Room" and "Be On Your Merry Way" were previously unreleased in the U.S.; "Father Time" and the alternate takes of "Lonely Hours" and "Check Yourself" were previously unreleased anywhere. —*Richie Unterberger*

My Baby / 1998 / Jewel ♦♦♦♦
Lowell Fulson always moved with the times, evidenced by the fact that one of his best known tunes was the mid-'60s soul number, "Tramp." This 11-track collection of sides recorded in the late '60s for the Shreveport, LA-based Jewel label finds him moving into blues-rock territory with an eye toward a piece of B.B. and Albert King's turf to call his own. With the Muscle Shoals rhythm section in place on most of the tracks here (appearing here uncredited, as this disc features no liner notes, recording dates or personnel, songwriter and publishing information whatsoever), the accent is more on commercial breakthrough than down-home blues. From the opening slide guitar riff on "Look at You Baby," it's clear that Lowell Fulson is in full command of his blues powers when he needs them. But his stomp down, noisy version of the Beatles' "Why Don't We Do It in the Road" shares the same seemed-like-a-good-idea-at-the-time territory as Muddy Waters' version of "Let's Spend the Night Together" and is totally devoid of any blues content whatsoever. Fulson plugs in a wah-wah on a couple of tunes and on "Don't Destroy Me," comes up with a solo that recalls both Hendrix and Stevie Ray, a long stretch from Oklahoma. While his potent slide and lead guitar work pop up here and there, this is mostly Fulson letting the band do the lion's share of the work and setting the pace. Certainly not the place to start with this prolific artist, but an interesting chapter in his career nonetheless. —*Cub Koda*

Crazy Cajun Recordings / Feb. 18, 1999 / Edsel ♦♦♦

Baby, Won't You Jump With Me? / Dec. 25, 1999 / Crown Prince ♦♦♦♦
Raised in Oklahoma and schooled in the blues throughout Texas, guitarist and singer Lowell Fulson headed west after the war like many other blacks from the Midwest and the South. He spent several years in both Oakland and Los Angeles, paving the way for a long career that would peak in the mid-'50s with hits like "Reconsider Baby" and "Loving You." And while his '50s period on the Chess and Checker labels has been well-documented, Fulson's earlier sides have not. Now, the Swedish Mr. R&B label has come out with this fine 33-track collection of cuts from 1946-1951. The disc features both early acoustic blues sides with brother Martin on guitar and a combo of piano, bass, and drums,

as well as several jump blues cuts, many of which include the venerable bandleader and pianist Lloyd Glenn. An essential title for Fulson enthusiasts. *—Stephen Cook*

The Tramp Years / May 16, 2000 / Ace ✦✦✦✦✦
The first of a planned series of three compilations devoted to Fulson's '60s Kent sides, this focuses on the chronological middle (and commercial peak) of his Kent output. "Tramp" itself, possibly Fulson's most well-known song (certainly to the pop and soul audience), leads off the disc, whose 24 tracks span 1966 to 1969. Much of the material shows Fulson to be one of the masters of blues-soul crossover (and one of the first to explore that subgenre), his work the equal of somewhat more renowned artists working the field, like B.B. King, Albert King, and Little Milton. There's a loose and lean feel that sets this off—in a good way—from the beefier, more disciplined blues-soul outings recorded by Stax and some other labels. Possibly because this series is so thorough in its coverage, the material is not always top of the line; some of the outings are routine, going through the blues motions in songwriting if not performance. Still, more often than not this is a pleasure, both for Fulson's relaxed vocals and his contrasting stinging, fluid guitar licks. Half of the dozen of the tracks are previously unissued, including "It Takes Money," a song recorded right after "Tramp"; Fulson expressed annoyance in interviews that Kent withheld this from release. As another bonus for the committed collector, four songs ("I'm Sinking," "Blues Pain," "What the Heck," and "Price for Love") are presented in extended versions from their original issue. *—Richie Unterberger*

I've Got the Blues & Then Some: 1969–1971 / Mar. 13, 2001 / West Side ✦✦✦✦

Black Nights / May 8, 2001 / Ace ✦✦✦
In the trio of Ace CDs that document Fulson's stint with Kent in the '60s, *Black Nights* covers the first part of that era (although, confusingly, it was not the first of the reissues to be released). The 1965 release "Black Nights" itself was his big success of the period, stopping just outside the R&B Top Ten and even getting into the bottom of the pop charts. A brassy and sassy feel-good tune despite the sorrowful lyrics, it also features a guitar with a twang so unusual it verges on sounding rather like an electric sitar. It's the unquestioned highlight of a collection that documents a time at which Fulson was modernizing, but only slightly, his brand of urban blues. All of the material dates from the mid-'60s, much of it written by Fats Washington, though Fulson wrote a few of these numbers himself. It's well-constructed blues-R&B with adult lyrics and just a slight '60s soul influence (especially in some of the horn arrangements). It sounds like it could have been recorded in the '50s, which is not so much of a drawback as the midtempo similarity of many of the songs to each other, and the lack of many tunes on the same level as "Black Nights." The guitar still stings admirably, though. Two of the songs were previously unissued. *—Richie Unterberger*

Final Kent Years / Feb. 19, 2002 / Ace ✦✦✦✦
The last of Ace's three compilations devoted to Fulson's Kent product basically combines his late-'60s *Now!* album with his 1978 *Lovemaker* album, adding three unissued cuts and a 1972 single. *Now!* was actually comprised largely of 1967-1968 singles, and it's this material, which takes up the first half of the CD, that holds up best. It's loosey-goosey late-'60s blues/soul crossover with a sassy attitude and adroit combinations of stinging blues guitar, strutting vocals, soulful horns, and organ, never heard better than on the opening "I'm a Drifter." Actually the *Now!* cuts sound better in this grouping than much of his slightly earlier '60s Kent stuff, because they're not as unduly repetitious, though they're filled out with cover versions of familiar tunes like "Funky Broadway," "Let's Go Get Stoned," and "Everyday I Have the Blues." Perhaps it wasn't cutting edge as far as late-'60s soul went, but it had some of the rawness of '50s electric blues and some of the slickness of late-'60s soul brass and B.B. King-like horn charts, and the combination usually clicked. *Lovemaker*, actually issued on the Big Town label (which like Kent was run by the Bihari brothers), isn't as interesting. But it's respectable soul-blues, and not as inappropriately polished as the usual late-'70s recordings by blues veterans. The 1972 single "Let's Talk It Over" (aka "Come Back Baby")/"Worried Life" is passable, as are the three previously unissued tracks (including a remake of "Blue Shadows") that date from around the time of the *Now!* LP. *—Richie Unterberger*

Anson Funderburgh

b. Nov. 15, 1954, Plano, TX
Guitar / Modern Electric Texas Blues, Modern Electric Blues
In recent years, Dallas-based guitarist Anson Funderburgh has taken his band the Rockets out of the clubs and onto the festival stages with his critically acclaimed recordings for the Black Top label out of New Orleans. With Jackson, MS-native Sam Myers delivering the vocals and harmonica treatments, this band mixes up a powerful gumbo of Texas jump blues and Delta blues that can't be found anywhere else. Funderburgh and his Rockets are a particularly hard-working band, performing across the U.S. and Europe nearly 300 nights a year.

Funderburgh was born November 15, 1954, and got hooked on the blues when he got his first guitar at age seven or eight. His first musical experiences happened in the clubs in Dallas. He developed his team approach to blues music while learning from the likes of Freddie King, Jimmy Reed and Albert Collins when these great bluesmen were passing through Dallas-area clubs, but Funderburgh had already taught himself guitar mostly from listening to classic blues records. He never had the chance to see Muddy Waters, but he did get to play with Lightnin' Hopkins in the late '70s. Funderburgh formed the Rockets in 1978, but didn't meet Sam Myers until 1982.

Funderburgh recorded with the Fabulous Thunderbirds on their *Butt Rockin'* album, and went solo in 1981, when the New Orleans-based Black Top label released *Talk to You By Hand*, the label's first release. Funderburgh added Myers on harmonica and lead vocals in 1986. Myers had traveled for years on the chitlin circuit, where he had the chance to accompany people like Elmore James and Robert Jr. Lockwood. Funderburgh admits that adding Myers on vocals and harmonica was a turning point for the Rockets, partly because of the image they project from the stage, a big towering Black man and three White guys backing him up. Funderburgh continued his association in the '90s with Black Top releasing *Tell Me What I Want to Hear* (1991), *Live at Grand Emporium* (1995), and *That's What They Want* (1997). After releasing nine albums on Black Top, in 1999 Funderburgh changed record labels with the release of *Change in My Pocket* for Bullseye Blues. At the beginning of the new millennium, Funderburgh was just coming into his prime by way of his songwriting talents. His career deserves close watching in the coming years; the best is yet to come from this guitarist and bandleader. *—Richard Skelly & Al Campbell*

Talk to You By Hand / 1981 / Black Top ✦✦

She Knocks Me Out! / 1985 / Black Top ✦✦

Knock You Out / 1985 / Spindrift ✦✦✦

My Love Is Here to Stay / 1986 / Black Top ✦✦✦
This is the first record where Sam Myers (who had been performing with Robert Jr. Lockwood, Myers' latest gig in a professional career that began in the mid-'50s) joined Funderburgh's band. This successful coupling has here and since made some truly wonderful music. *—Niles J. Frantz*

Sins / 1987 / Black Top ✦✦✦✦✦
Sins is a good fusion of Texas and Delta blues, alternating between rocking shuffles and laidback ballads. Funderburgh's playing is tasteful—he has an enticing sound, but he never falls into grandstanding—and Sam Myers' voice is rich and his harp playing intoxicating. Furthermore, the selection of material is first-rate, featuring sharp originals and well-chosen covers from the likes of Percy Mayfield and Elmore James. The result? One of Anson Funderburgh's best albums. *—Thom Owens*

Black Top Blues-A-Rama Live / 1988 / Black Top ✦✦✦

Rack 'Em Up / 1989 / Black Top ✦✦✦
Rack 'Em Up is a straightforward blues album that demonstrates Anson Funderburgh's affection for the Texas shuffle. Nobody on the album, whether it's Funderburgh or the Kamikaze Horns, overplays their hand and it delivers the goods efficiently although without flair. *—Thom Owens*

Tell Me What I Want to Hear / 1991 / Black Top ✦✦✦✦✦
First-rate, contemporary Texas shuffle and blues with tasteful, biting guitar comes from Funderburgh and great vocals and harp from Mississippian Sam Myers. This is their most varied and ambitious release to date (the band seems to get better with each album). The title track was used in the movie *China Moon*. "Rent Man Blues" is a humorous dialog between Myers and guest-vocalist Carol Fran. Myers also adds an "answer" song to the blues classic "Sloppy Drunk." *—Niles J. Frantz*

● **Thru the Years: A Retrospective (1981–1992)** / 1992 / Black Top ✦✦✦✦✦
Thru the Years: A Retrospective (1981-1992) collects the highlights from Funderburgh's albums for Black Top, drawing from all the different bands he fronted in that decade or so. The best tracks remain his cuts with Sam Myers or Darrell Nulisch, but the finest songs from his lesser bands are included, making *Thru the Years* an excellent way to get acquainted with the modern blues guitar hero. *—Thom Owens*

Live at Grand Emporium / Jan. 17, 1995 / Black Top ✦✦✦

That's What They Want / Apr. 15, 1997 / Black Top ✦✦✦✦
The blues-oriented team of Anson Funderburgh and Sam Myers is a powerful and appealing combination. While Myers takes shouting, easy-to-understand and accessible vocals on most of the selections of this release (in addition to playing a bit of harmonica), the main reason to acquire the set is for Funderburgh's exciting guitar work. His showcase on the instrumental blues "Mudslide" is a definite high point. In addition, Kevin McKendree (who is best on organ) is a strong asset to the rhythm section and takes many fine solos of his own. Although each of the 13 selections on the Alligator disc is concise (clocking in between 2:18 and 4:47 with only two songs being over four minutes), the performances are quite complete and do not exit prematurely (nor overstay their welcome). The well-paced set is easily recommended to blues collectors and jazz fans who enjoy hearing a passionate and skilled guitarist. *—Scott Yanow*

Change in My Pocket / Mar. 2, 1999 / Bullseye Blues ✦✦✦
There's something sad about a club band—especially one as hard working as Anson Funderburgh and the Rockets—trying to make a commercial record and failing so miserably at it as they do here. This album starts out as disastrously as any album possibly could. On the opening title track, it's obvious that Sam Myers is singing to a prerecorded band track and that either that band track—or Myers—is woefully off time on every one of the breaks, making this group of road veterans sound like a bar band making their first record. Funderburgh's less-is-more guitar is highlighted on his "Hula Hoop" while the bulk of the originals come from Myers writing with various band members, turning in throwaway items like "Things Have Changed," "Single Again," and "Willie Jo." As the group negotiates their way through a pile of covers (Little Walter's "Little Girl," Muddy Waters' "Young Fashioned Ways," Jimmy Rogers' "What Have I Done," Buddy Guy's "$100 Bill") it's obvious that they find themselves on more familiar turf and these end up being the true highlights of the album. Oh yes, a nice version of "Key to the Highway" ends up being a "hidden" bonus track at the end of the album, too. All in all, a very uneven album that really doesn't show this band's strengths. *—Cub Koda*

G. Love & Special Sauce

f. 1992, Philadelphia, PA
Group / Alternative Rap, Post-Grunge, Indie Rock, Alternative Pop/Rock
G. Love & Special Sauce is a trio from Philadelphia, PA. Their laid-back, sloppy blues sound is quite unique, as it encompasses the sound/production of classic R&B and recent rap artists (the Beastie Boys, in particular). The group—G. Love (real name: Garrett Dutton) on guitar/vocals/harmonica, Jeff Clemens on drums, and Jim Prescott on upright bass—released their self-titled debut in 1994 on OKeh/Epic. It received enthusiastic reviews and nearly went gold on the strength of the MTV-spun video for "Cold Beverage." The group toured heavily, also landing a subsequent spot on the H.O.R.D.E. tour, and found a receptive young audience. They followed up this success with the more mature *Coast to Coast Motel* in 1995. Although it didn't sell as well as the debut, it was definitely a stronger album. On tour, the group nearly broke up due to bickering over finances. They decided to take a break from each other, while G. Love worked on a new album with three different bands (All Fellas Band, Philly Cartel, and King's Court) and special guest Dr. John. Soon, though, G. Love & Special Sauce made amends, and the next album featured Special Sauce plus combinations of the three other groups. *Yeah, It's That Easy* was released in October of 1997, and it turned out to be a soul-inflected effort, more similar to the debut than their second album. G. Love & Special Sauce soon embarked on another world tour, returning in 1999 with *Philadelphonic. The Electric Mile*, issued in spring 2001, depicted another sultry and provocative mix from G. Love. *—Greg Prato*

G. Love & Special Sauce / 1994 / Epic/OKeh ✦✦✦
Although this is G. Love & Special Sauce's most popular album (approaching gold status), it is not their best. Although there are quite a few musical surprises, the overall sound and quality of the compositions are neither as focused nor as rewarding as future releases would be. "Cold Beverage" became the band's signature tune and a fan favorite, featuring lighthearted jive lyrics and funky musical accompaniment, and its popular MTV video putting them on the map. "This Ain't Living" is a precursor to the comforting Philly soul style that would be explored more thoroughly on 1997's *Yeah, It's That Easy.* "Town to Town" adds variety to the album with its slow-as-molasses blues style. Most of the other tracks tend to blend into each other after awhile, because of their similar sound and feel ("Rhyme for the Summertime," "Shooting Hoops," etc.). Even with its mishaps, G. Love & Special Sauce's debut serves as the musical foundation on which the group would build their future sound. *—Greg Prato*

● **Coast to Coast Motel** / Sep. 19, 1995 / Epic/OKeh ✦✦✦✦
Although not as commercially successful as their self-titled debut, *Coast to Coast Motel* is a definite improvement. The band keeps their hip-hop influence (much more prevalent on the debut) in check here, concentrating more on creating a mighty instrumental groove. It's also more of a traditional rock & roll approach for the band, with the results quite often being successful. The opening "Sweet Sugar Mama" is bass-driven and funky; other highlights include the smooth "Nancy," the uplifting "Chains #3," and the startling Led Zeppelin attack (musically, anyway) of "Small Fish." "Kiss and Tell" is an obvious attempt at a hit single, while some may consider the lyrics to "Soda Pop" a bit too foolish. As mentioned earlier, however, the group achieves some great, groovy interplay which can easily suck the listener in. Jimmy Prescott's upright bass playing and Jeff Clemens' drumming are tight and locked together, as G. Love adds his scratchy blues guitar on top. These guys have found the groove. *—Greg Prato*

Yeah, It's That Easy / Oct. 28, 1997 / Epic/OKeh ✦✦✦
On G. Love's third release, he's joined by his trusty band, Special Sauce, as well as combinations of three others: The All Fellas Band, Philly Cartel, and King's Court. The reason for the joint effort was that prior to the writing/recording of *Yeah, It's That Easy,* the group split up. G. Love soldiered on with the three other bands, but there was a reconciliation with Special Sauce during the album's recording. Hence, others (including the legendary Dr. John on piano and organ) join in with Special Sauce. The group sheds its raw rock & roll vibe, gloriously present on 1995's *Coast to Coast Motel,* and replaces it with the soothing sounds of early-'70s Philly soul. The album's approach resembles their 1994 self-titled debut more than their last release, which seems like a step back for the group. Still, the band presents plenty of compositions worthy of the G. Love & Special Sauce name, and there is more consistency and maturity with the lyrics, which deal with such heavy topics as drug abuse and senseless violence, among other things. One of the best songs, "You Shall See," and sports a tribal feel, with the drums and guitar playing together percussively. And "Stepping Stones," "Lay Down the Law," and "Take You There" do a good job of introducing the listener to the band's new soul-oriented approach. The words to "I-76" are about G. Love's hometown of Philadelphia, and the title track preaches harmony between races. A solid album, but not quite as satisfying as their last. Now if the band could just mix the groove-laden music of their second album with the thoughtful lyrics of this record...*—Greg Prato*

Philadelphonic / Aug. 3, 1999 / OKeh/550 Music ✦✦✦
The title of G. Love & Special Sauce's fourth album illustrates their desire to play up their Philadelphia roots, emphasizing classic Philly soul along with their blues-rap melange. *Philadelphonic* isn't entirely unsuccessful on that front, either. The group's laid-back, groove-oriented sound benefits from the sophisticated, sultry sound of Philly soul, as the single "Rodeo Clowns" illustrates. The problem is, G. Love & Special Sauce still winds up sacrificing songs for groove and feel. That wouldn't be so bad if *Philadelphonic* was simply a series of jams, but they continue to write material that feels like songs but never gels. They turn out to be vehicles for jams and half-hearted, muttered raps, neither of which provide hooks or memorable turns of phrase. That doesn't mean *Philadelphonic* doesn't sound good, since the group does have a way with a groove—it just never really rises above the level of a groove-jam album. *—Stephen Thomas Erlewine*

The Electric Mile / Apr. 24, 2001 / OKeh/550 Music ✦✦✦
Like G. Love & Special Sauce's previous albums, *The Electric Mile* isn't easy to categorize. Is it alternative rock, psychedelic rock, retro-soul, funk, or hip-hop? Actually, this diverse, unpredictable CD is a combination of those things—and the group also shows its appreciation of reggae, blues, and folk. True to form, vocalist G. Love and his colleagues keep things unpredictable; you never know from one song to the next if they will tend to favor retro-soul ("Night of the Living Dead"), hip-hop ("Parasite," "Electric Mile"), folk-rock ("Sara's Song"), psychedelic blues-rock ("Poison"), or reggae ("Unified"). And the impressive thing is that G. Love can go in so many different directions and never fail to sound distinctive, which is something he has in common with Prince and David Bowie. But while *The Electric Mile* (which is G. Love's fifth album) has more plusses than minuses, it isn't perfect. A few of the tunes sound unfocused, and not everything that G. Love & Special Sauce try is successful—occasionally, a song will miss its mark. But more often than not, the trio's risk-taking pays off on this generally rewarding, if imperfect, CD. *—Alex Henderson*

The Best of G. Love and Special Sauce / Mar. 26, 2002 / Epic ✦✦✦✦
While major chart success has eluded G. Love for the length of his career, he has earned an impressive live following and even more impressive album sales with his uniquely '90s blend of hip-hop, blues, and chill-out funk. Assembling a worthy career compilation should have been a no-brainer, though it seems the folks at Epic spent no more time than necessary putting *The Best of G. Love and Special Sauce* together. Favorites like the smooth, name-dropping exercise "Blues Music" and "I-76," the ultimate homage to the group's hometown of Philadelphia, are of course here, but at only 11 tracks, the disc kind of leaves you hanging. What, no extra bonus tracks, new cuts, or raving live performances could be found? A good sampler for initiates, but no doubt there are way better G. Love CD-R samplers in 1,000 college dorm rooms across the Northeast. *—John Duffy*

Bob Gaddy

b. Feb. 4, 1924, Vivian, WV
Vocals, Piano / Piano Blues, R&B, East Coast Blues, Jump Blues
Both as a session man and featured recording artist, pianist Bob Gaddy made his presence known on the New York blues scene during the '50s. He's still part of that circuit today. Gaddy was drafted in 1943, and that's when he began to take the 88s seriously. He picked up a little performing experience in California clubs while stationed on the West Coast before arriving in New York in 1946. Gaddy gigged with Brownie McGhee and guitarist Larry Dale around town, McGhee often playing on Gaddy's waxings for Jackson (his 1952 debut, "Bicycle Boogie"), Jax, Dot, Harlem, and from 1955 on, Hy Weiss' Old Town label. There Gaddy stayed the longest, waxing the fine "I Love My Baby," "Paper Lady," "Rip and Run," and quite a few more into 1960. Sidemen on Gaddy's Old Town sessions included guitarists Joe Ruffin and Wild Jimmy Spruill and saxist Jimmy Wright.
Since then, Gaddy hasn't recorded anything of note for domestic consumption, but like his longtime cohort Larry Dale, he remains active around New York. *—Bill Dahl*

● **Harlem Blues Operator** / Dec. 12, 1995 / Ace ✦✦✦
Most of Gaddy's recordings were done for Old Town in 1955-1960, and this 21-track CD covers that era comprehensively, including everything from his singles and four outtakes. Gaddy was a likable but average blues and R&B pianist and singer, covering jump blues, emotional slow electric blues, uptempo R&B that crossed over into rock & roll, Jack Dupree-style piano blues (indeed Dupree wrote some of the material here), and more, although he never got to an elite class in any particular subgenre. The great Jimmy Spruill plays stinging guitar on some of the songs, which gives some of the material, like the Willie Dixon-penned "Could I," a lift, though "Could I" sounds a bit like a Howlin' Wolf track with a way-too-polite vocal. On the other hand, some tracks are clearly trying to simulate the sound of big hits, such as the "The Girl Who Promises," with its direct ripoff of Wilbert Harrison's "Kansas City" shuffle; "Gonna Be at the Station," a very close relative of Hank Ballard's "Let's Go, Let's Go, Let's Go"; and "I Love My Baby," which is close

to being "Lawdy Miss Clawdy" with another title. Perhaps when they were recorded, it was hoped that listeners not familiar with the prototypes would be taken in, but there's a problem when these show up on reissues: the people most likely to buy reissues such as these are also the most likely listeners to know what songs from which these riffs were lifted. This is a fair set of R&B-blues crossover, and one of the relatively few single-artist compilations devoted to a New York-based blues performer of the '50s, but can't qualify as a major collection. *—Richie Unterberger*

Earl Gaines

b. Aug. 19, 1935, Decatur, AL

Vocals / Modern Electric Blues, Soul-Blues

Best known for his 1955 R&B chart-topper "It's Love Baby (24 Hours a Day)," recorded with Louis Brooks & His Hi-Toppers, Earl Gaines was born August 19, 1935 in Decatur, AL. After growing up singing in church, he headed to Nashville at the age of 16, lured by the city's booming blues scene; there he signed on with local impresario Ted Jarrett, who helped book the young singer in clubs and landed him a number of demo recording sessions. Through Jarrett, Gaines was also introduced to Brooks, who soon tapped him to become the Hi-Toppers' lead vocalist; his distinctive tenor helped make "It's Love Baby" a tremendous success for the Excello label, and the group recorded a series of subsequent singles for the company before Gaines went solo. He went on to record for labels including Deluxe/King, Hanna Barbera and Sound Stage 7, but by the late '60s he was essentially out of the music business, working as a cross-country trucker throughout the next two decades. He resurfaced during the mid-'90s thanks to the efforts of Fred James, a Nashville-based producer whose affection for the classic Excello sound also resulted in the resurrection of onetime label staples including Clifford Curry and Roscoe Shelton; for Appaloosa, Gaines issued his 1995 comeback effort *I Believe in Your Love*, and in 1997 he also joined Curry and Shelton for a joint live recording. *—Jason Ankeny*

Everything's Gonna Be Alright / Oct. 20, 1998 / Black Top ✦✦✦✦✦

Earl Gaines started his career as the singer with Louis Brooks & His Hi-Toppers, scoring an R&B hit in 1955 with "It's Love Baby (24 Hours a Day)" for Excello. More solid sides followed for Champion, Deluxe, Hollywood, Ace and Sound Stage 7 into the late '70s before hanging up his spikes. Not unlike his Excello labelmate Roscoe Shelton, he was lured out of retirement and cut new albums in the mid-'90s for Appaloosa and Magnum before cutting this one for Black Top in 1998. Smartly produced by Fred James, who also contributes all the fine guitar work, this leans more toward the blues than soul side of Shelton's musical equation, but his gritty style is best illuminated on tracks like "Is It Good to You Baby," "Two Lovers Are Better Than One," "Every Night of the Week" and the title track. With his vocal chops still in platinum shape, Gaines makes a strong showing with this one. Highlights include "You Put a Spell on Me," "I'll Carry a Torch," "Sittin' Here Drinkin'" and the humorous "Your Butt's Too Big." A winner every note of the way. *—Cub Koda*

● **24 Hours a Day** / Feb. 9, 1999 / Black Magic ✦✦✦✦✦

A 20-track compilation of Gaines' early tracks for Champion and his entire album for HBR produced by Hoss Allen. This is R&B/soul/blues from the late '50s to mid-'60s and Gaines' honeyed tones sound every bit as fine as they do on his Excello sides. The numerous highlights include "Best Of Luck Baby," "Now Do You Hear," "Don't Take My Kindness For Weakness," and "Love You So." *—Cub Koda*

Lovin' Blues: The Starday-King Years 1967–1973 / Sep. 15, 1999 / West Side ✦✦✦✦✦

The years covered on West Side's 1999 compilation *Lovin' Blues: The Starday-King Years 1967-1973* are not necessarily among Earl Gaines' best-known or most-celebrated sides. The singles he cut in the late '50s and early '60s, primarily for Excello, form the core of his legacy, but this music is high-grade Southern soul all the same. It's in a similar vein as the Excello recordings, but it's clear that this is post-Stax material with the punchy horns and gritty rhythm section. The first part of the compilation is devoted to the 1969 album *Lovin' Blues*, which is a tight, passionate unheralded minor gem of soul-blues, and then the rest of the compilation is devoted to singles and unreleased tracks. Some of this material is a little generic and faceless, while others are simply serviceable covers of R&B standards like "Sixty Minute Man," but it's all listenable, and its completeness is certainly a boon to collectors. But the real reason to get this compilation (once you've already absorbed the Excello recordings, that is) is that *Lovin' Blues* is a fine Southern soul-blues record, worth seeking out by aficionados. *—Stephen Thomas Erlewine*

Grady Gaines

b. May 14, 1934, Waskom, TX

Sax (Tenor) / Electric Texas Blues

Some of the atomic energy that Little Richard emitted nightly during the mid-'50s must have spilled onto Grady Gaines. As the hardy tenor sax blaster with Richard's road band, the Upsetters, Gaines all but blew the reed out of his horn with his galvanic solos. He wails with the same unquenchable spirit today.

The perpetually ebullient Louis Jordan was Grady's main saxman while growing up in Houston (in particular, Gaines loved his "Caldonia"). Grady wasn't the only musician in the Gaines household—brother Roy was an excellent guitarist who supplied the stinging solo on Bobby Bland's 1955 Duke waxing "It's My Life Baby" before leaving to do his own thing.

Grady was working as a session saxist at Don Robey's Duke/ Peacock Records (soloing like a man possessed on Big Walter Price's "Pack Fair and Square" and proudly populating the reed section on Gatemouth Brown's searing "Dirty Work at the Crossroads") prior to getting a fateful 1955 call from Little Richard to head up his newly formed band. Gaines recorded with the piano-pounding rock icon only sparingly—that's his storming wail on "Keep a Knockin'" and "Ooh! My Soul"—but you wouldn't know it from watching Richard's show-stopping appearances in the films *Don't Knock the Rock, The Girl Can't Help It*, and *Mr. Rock and Roll*. In every flick, Gaines is seen on screen, horn-syncing Lee Allen's sax solos!

The Upsetters remained intact long after Richard flipped out and joined the ministry in 1957. They hit the road with Dee Clark (then a Richard clone himself), Little Willie John, Sam Cooke, James Brown, Jackie Wilson, and Joe Tex. The band recorded for Vee-Jay in 1958 behind Clark and with Upsetters vocalist/saxist Wilbert Smith, who went by the name of Lee Diamond and hailed from New Orleans. More sessions at Vee-Jay, Gee, Fire, and Little Star (where they briefly reunited with Richard) followed.

After the Upsetters broke up, Grady hit the road with a variety of R&B luminaries, including Millie Jackson and Curtis Mayfield, before retiring in 1980. Fortunately, he decided to strap his horn back on in 1985, playing in Houston until Black Top Records cajoled him into cutting *Full Gain*, a veritable Houston blues motherlode, in 1988. Brother Roy Gaines, pianist Teddy Reynolds, guitarist Clarence Hollimon, and singer Joe Medwick were all involved in the project. *Horn of Plenty* followed on Black Top in 1992. Gaines and his entourage continue to blow up a Texas-sized storm wherever they touch down. *—Bill Dahl*

● **Full Gain** / 1988 / Black Top ✦✦✦✦✦

A meeting of Houston-based all-stars that scorches from the first track to the last. Tenor saxman Grady Gaines is in charge of the proceedings, wailing on the instrumentals "There Is Something on Your Mind" and "Soul Twist," while pianist Teddy Reynolds, Gaines' guitar-wielding brother Roy Gaines, and Joe Medwick divvy up the vocals. Outstanding guitarist Clarence Hollimon is also on board. *—Bill Dahl*

Horn of Plenty / 1992 / Black Top ✦✦✦

Gaines is surrounded by more vocal talent this time—Carol Fran, Teddy Reynolds, and Gaines' Texas Upsetters pals Big Robert Smith and Paul David Roberts. Hollimon and Anson Funderburgh are the guitar heroes this time, as Gaines whips up another Lone Star-size sax storm with his lusty tenor. *—Bill Dahl*

The Gales Brothers

f. Memphis, TN

Group / Modern Electric Blues, Contemporary Blues

The Gales Brothers, all born and raised in the same house in Memphis, have all forged their own musical paths in the blues world, but when the three get together for a live performance or a studio outing, a treat is in store for the blues guitar aficionado. Eric and Eugene formed the Eric Gales Band, while Manuel (b. Dec. 4, 1968) took the stage name Little Jimmy King (after Jimi Hendrix and Albert King). King has recorded two albums for the Bullseye Blues/Rounder label, *Little Jimmy King and the Memphis Soul Survivors* and *Something Inside of Me*. Eric, however, was the first family member to break out; at age 15, he signed his first recording contract and released two albums, *The Eric Gales Band* and *Picture of a Thousand Faces*. By 1991, the critics were calling him the next guitar prodigy; Gales won a poll in *Guitar World* magazine as "Best New Talent," appeared several times on *The Arsenio Hall Show*, and found some prominent fans in Eric Clapton, Keith Richards and Mick Jagger. As a unit, the Gales Brothers released one album, *Left Hand Brand*, on the House of Blues/Private Music label in March, 1995. Although House of Blues has since formed an alliance with another label and Private Music was consolidated into another unit of BMG, the record should still be available. While the Gales Brothers have played together all of their lives, this remains the first time they've ever recorded together in a good studio. Recorded at House of Blues Studios in Memphis, it was produced by David Z., who has also worked with Prince, the Fine Young Cannibals and Big Head Todd and the Monsters. *—Richard Skelly*

● **Left Hand Brand** / Mar. 26, 1995 / House of Blues ✦✦✦

Rory Gallagher

b. Mar. 2, 1949, Ballyshannon, Ireland, **d.** Jun. 14, 1995, London, England

Slide Guitar, Vocals, Harmonica, Guitar / British Blues, Blues-Rock

For a career that was cut short by illness and a premature death, guitarist, singer and songwriter Rory Gallagher sure accomplished a lot in the blues music world. Although Gallagher didn't tour the U.S. nearly enough, spending most of his time in Europe, he was known for his no-holds-barred, marathon live shows at clubs and theaters around the United States.

Gallagher was born in Ballyshannon, County Donegal, Irish Republic on March 2, 1949. He passed away from complications owing to liver transplant surgery on June 14, 1995, at age 46. Shortly after his birth, his family moved to Cork City in the south, and at age nine, he became fascinated with American blues and folksingers he heard on the radio. An avid record collector, he had a wide range of influences including Leadbelly, Buddy Guy, Freddie King, Albert King, Muddy Waters and John Lee Hooker. Gallagher would always try to mix some simple country blues songs onto his recordings.

Gallagher began his recording career after moving to London, when he formed a trio called Taste. The group's self-titled debut album was released in 1969 in England and later picked up for U.S. distribution by Atco/Atlantic. Between 1969 and 1971, with producer Tony Colton behind the board, Gallagher recorded three albums with the group before they split up. Gallagher began performing under his own name in 1971, after recording his 1970 debut, *Rory Gallagher* for Polydor Records in the U.K. The album was picked up for U.S. distribution by Atlantic Records, and later that year he recorded *Deuce*, also released by Atlantic in the U.S.

His prolific output continued, as he followed up *Deuce* with *Live in Europe* (1972) and *Blueprint* and *Tattoo*, both in 1973. *Irish Tour*, like *Live in Europe*, did a good job of capturing the excitement of his live shows on tape, and he followed that with *Calling Card* for Chrysalis in 1976, and *Photo Finish* and *Jinx* for the same label in 1978 and 1982. By this point Gallagher had made several world tours, and he took a few years rest from the road. He got back into recording and performing live again with the 1987 release (in the U.K.) of *Defender*. His last album, *Fresh Evidence*, was released in 1991 on the Capo/I.R.S. label. Capo was his own record and publishing company that he set up in the hopes of eventually exposing other great blues talents.

Some of Gallagher's best work on record wasn't under his own name, it's stuff he recorded with Muddy Waters on *The London Sessions* (Chess, 1972) and with Albert King on *Live* (RCA/Utopia). Gallagher made his last U.S. tours in 1985 and 1991, and admitted in interviews that he'd always been a guitarist who fed off the instant reaction and feedback a live audience can provide.

In a 1991 interview, he said: "I try to sit down and write a Rory Gallagher song, which generally happens to be quite bluesy. I try to find different issues, different themes and different topics that haven't been covered before... I've done songs in all the different styles... train blues, drinking blues, economic blues. But I try to find a slightly different angle on all these things. The music can be very traditional, but you can sort of creep into the future with the lyrics."

For a good introduction to Gallagher's unparalleled prowess as a guitarist, singer and songwriter, pick up *Irish Tour, Calling Card* or *Fresh Evidence*, all available on compact disc. *—Richard Skelly*

Deuce / 1971 / Buddha ✦✦✦✦

Released in November 1971, just six months after his solo debut, Rory Gallagher's second album was the summation of all that he'd promised in the wake of Taste's collapse, and the blueprint for most of what he'd accomplish over the next two years of recording. Largely overlooked by posterity's haste to canonize his next album, *Live! In Europe, Deuce* finds Gallagher torn between the earthy R&B of "Used to Be," a gritty blues fed through by some viciously unrestrained guitar playing, and the jokey, country-billy badinage of "Don't Know Where I'm Going," a too-short snippet that marries Bob Dylan to Ronnie Lane and reminds us just how broad Gallagher's sense of humor was. Reflecting the laid-back feel of *Rory Gallagher*, "I'm Not Awake Yet" is a largely acoustic piece driven as much by Gerry McAvoy's gutbucket bass as by Gallagher's intricate playing; "There's a Light," too, plays to Gallagher's sensitive side, while stating his mastery of the guitar across a protracted solo that isn't simply spellbinding in its restraint, it also has the effect of adding another voice to the proceedings. But such notions of plaintive melodicism are utterly exorcized by the moments of highest drama, a sequence that peaks with the closing, broiling "Crest of a Wave." With bass set on stun, the drums a turbulent wall of sound and Gallagher's guitar a sonic switchblade, it's a masterpiece of aggressive dynamics, the sound of a band so close to its peak that you can almost touch the electricity. Of course, that peak would come during 1972-1973, with the albums upon which Gallagher's reputation is today most comfortably set. *Deuce*, however, doesn't simply set the stage for the future, it strikes the light that ignites the entire firestorm. *—Dave Thompson*

Rory Gallagher / 1971 / Buddha ✦✦✦

Rory Gallagher's solo debut picks up where his previous band's *On the Boards* left off—it's a solid, but significantly less raucous, blues-rock outing with ten original tunes that were far more than skeletons for his incisive Strat picking. "Laundromat," "Hands Up," and "Sinner Boy"'s distinctive riffs were early concert favorites, but the album's ballads were some of Gallagher's strongest. "For the Last Time," "Just the Smile" and the acoustic "I'm Not Surprised" mixed strains of Delta blues with strong melodic sensibilities into songs of rare poignancy, especially for an artist who was best known for his scorching leads. In this respect Gallagher was an early model for Eric Clapton, whose solo career followed a similar path. Interestingly, Gallagher seems rather restrained throughout his debut, holding back the fret-burning in favor of strong songs. He opens up on the album's jazzy, seven-minute finale "Can't Believe It's You" which even features an alto sax, an instrument Gallagher all but abandoned on later albums. 2000's reissued, remastered version of the disc includes two additional tunes, Muddy Waters' slow Delta blues number "Gypsy Woman" and Otis Rush's fast Chicago shuffle "It Takes Time," both cut at the same sessions. "Gypsy Woman"'s slashing slide guitar and vocals sound as impassioned any other track; shuffle "It Takes Time" isn't quite as impressive but still shows how comfortable Gallagher is with straight blues. Brother/compiler Donal Gallagher's track notes are short but illuminating, and the remastered sound, although not as vibrant as on later reissues of Gallagher's catalog, is a big improvement over any existing version of this consistently superb album. *—Hal Horowitz*

Live in Europe / 1972 / Buddha ✦✦✦✦✦

After two critically acclaimed but commercially disappointing solo studio albums, Rory Gallagher unleashed this raging live disc in 1972 at the age of 23. It not established him in the States, where he had toured only once previously (with his first band Taste, opening for Blind Faith on their brief tour), and was a worldwide hit. Gallagher blasts through rearranged versions of three Junior Wells songs ("Messin' With the Kid," "I Could've Had Religion," and "Hoodoo Man") and Muddy Waters' "Bullfrog Blues," a holdover from his Taste days, like his fingers are exploding. Even on acoustic tracks like "Going to My Home Town" where Gallagher strums his mandolin with such ferocity it sounds like the strings are going to pop, he attacks with the intensity of a talented young man with something to prove. The songs average about six minutes, but Gallagher and his two-piece never let the energy flag. More crackling than even his best studio work, you can hear the electricity in the air as the Irishman shoots solos scorching with vitality and precision. The 2000 reissue includes two slow blues cuts, "What in the World" and "Hoodoo Man" where the guitarist pulls out his slide tricks, both are worthwhile additions. The liner notes feature a 1972 interview with the guitarist, but this is the only album of Buddha's 2000 reissued Gallagher catalog that doesn't include brother Donal's track-by-track synopsis. The crisp, clear remastered sound makes this one of the best live blues-rock albums ever, and one of the finest discs in Rory Gallagher's catalog. It's not quite like seeing him live, sweating through a vigorous, non-stop set, but it's the next best thing. *—Hal Horowitz*

Blueprint / 1973 / Buddha ✦✦✦✦

Kicking off with the furious "Walk on Hot Coals" where Rory Gallagher's stinging guitar and Lou Martin's insistent piano pounding spar within the context of one of Rory's classic rockers, the album presents a well-rounded picture of Gallagher's eclectic influences. A jaunty, acoustic run through Big Bill Broonzy's "Banker's Blues" (oddly credited to Gallagher), the ragtime "Unmilitary Two-Step" as well as an unusually straightforward country tune "If I Had a Reason" with Rory on lap-steel and Martin doing his best honky-tonk, effectively break up the blues-rock that remains the soul of the album. The album's centerpiece, a brooding "Seventh Son of a Seventh Son" finds the band locked into a swampy groove for over eight minutes as Gallagher abbreviates his own solo providing room for Martin's aggressive piano. On "Hands Off" the guitarist even picks up saxophone, and he shows off his spooky Muddy Waters-inspired slide on the train chugging "Race the Breeze," one of the guitarist's best tunes. The final two bonus tracks tacked on for this reissue don't add much of interest; an early, shuffle version of "Stompin' Ground" lacks the tension of the song that later showed up as the only studio tracks on the live *Irish Tour* album, and Roy Head's "Treat Her Right" sounds like a soundcheck warm-up, which it probably was. Concise track-by-track liner notes from Rory's brother Donal provide useful background information, and the remastered sound taken from the original tapes is a revelation, with Gallagher's guitar parts and especially vocals, clear and precise in the spiffed up mix. *—Hal Horowitz*

Tattoo / 1973 / Buddha ✦✦✦✦

Gallagher's work ethic was in high gear as he somehow found time to write nine more songs in the midst of non-stop touring for his second album released in 1973. Even more astounding is that far from sounding fatigued or burnt out, his performance here is loose and impassioned, and the tunes are some of the best of his career. Lou Martin's keyboards are better integrated into the band, and drummer Rod de'Ath swings and burns with easy confidence. The double whammy of the album's two crunching leadoff tracks, "Tattoo'd Lady" and "Cradle Rock" illustrate just how comfortable Gallagher is with his backing group, and the smooth-rolling unplugged guitar and harmonica of "20-20 Vision" proves that the blues rocker is a more than adequate Delta/folk musician. Better still is the acoustic slide intro to "Who's that Comin'" that effortlessly and discretely eases its way into a Chicago styled, midtempo, electric attack. "A Million Miles Away" pushes the envelope even further with a slow, greasy swamp groove against which Gallagher picks clipped, staccato notes over a well-oiled rhythm section, thick Hammond organ overdubbed with piano from Martin, and even a multi-tracked sax section from the guitarist. The 2000 reissue adds "Tucson, Arizona" an unusual acoustic waltz-time country Link Wray cover, and a seemingly unrehearsed driving version of the blues standard "Just a Little Bit" that runs almost eight minutes, and is interesting for about half that. Short but informational track-by-track liner notes from Gallagher's brother Donal and crisp remastered sound makes this an essential purchase for established fans and an excellent place to start for new Rory Gallagher listeners. *—Hal Horowitz*

● **Irish Tour** / 1974 / Buddha ✦✦✦✦✦

The companion piece to director Tony Palmer's documentary of the same name, *Irish Tour* was recorded that January in Belfast, Dublin, and Cork at a time when precious few performers—Irish or otherwise—were even dreaming of touring the trouble-torn island. Northern Ireland, in particular, was a rock & roll no-go area, but Gallagher never turned his back on the province and was rewarded with what history recalls as some of his best-ever gigs. *Irish Tour*, in turn, captures some of his finest known live recordings and, while it's impossible to tell which songs were recorded where, across nine in-concert recordings (plus one after-hours jam session, "Back on My Stompin' Ground"), the energy crackling from stage to stalls and back again packs an intensity that few live albums—Gallagher's own others among them—can match. Highlights of a stunning set include dramatic takes on Muddy Waters' "I Wonder Who" and Tony Joe White's "As the Crow Flies," a raw acoustic rendering that is nevertheless totally electrifying. A frustratingly brief snip of the classic Shadows-style "Maritime" (aka "Just a Little Bit") plays the album out in anthemic style and then, of course, there's "Walk on Hot Coals," a marathon excursion that posterity has decreed Gallagher's most popular and accomplished statement—a status that *Irish Tour* does nothing to contradict. It's foolish playing favorites, however. Even more than Gallagher's earlier (1972) *Live in Europe* album, *Irish Tour* confirms Gallagher not simply as the greatest bluesman Ireland ever knew, but as one of the island's greatest-ever performers. The 1999 remaster adds nothing in the way of bonus material (shame), but greatly improves the sound quality. *—Dave Thompson*

Against the Grain / 1975 / Buddha ✦✦✦

After releasing two albums in 1973 and a live, contract-fulfilling disc in 1974, Gallagher returned rested and recharged in 1975 with a new record label, Chrysalis, and a band with almost three years of hard touring under their belts. With its attention to detail, *Against the Grain* sounds more practiced and intricate than most of Gallagher's previous studio discs, but still includes some of his most powerful rockers. The supercharged "Souped-Up Ford," where Rory howls and wails, with his voice and smoking slide, and "All Around Man," an urgent blues rocker that begins with Gallagher screaming and crying together with just his electric guitar until the band kicks in with a stop-start blues rhythm, are two of the definitive moments. "Bought and Sold" adds congas to the mix to bring a more rootsy and even jazzy feel to Rory's table. But it's on the acoustic tracks where the guitarist and his band really lay into the groove. Gallagher's version of Leadbelly's "Out on the Western Plain," with its combination of Indian chords, American Delta folk and cowboy "yippee-ki-yay" chorus is one of the Irishman's unheralded highlights, and "Cross Me Off Your List" is affecting in its yearning melody, subtle keyboard and minor key. A playful and forceful romp through Sam and Dave's "I Take What I Want" shows Gallagher's soul roots. Two bonus tracks from the 2000 reissue and recorded at these sessions are country based jams, but neither is particularly impressive. Not his best album, *Against the Grain* is still prime period Rory Gallagher. Its well-rounded menu of country, Delta blues, and blues-rock is indicative of his approach; though few of these songs became classics in the guitarist's extensive catalog, they're far more mature and eclectic than most blues-rock bands' best work. *—Hal Horowitz*

Calling Card / 1976 / Buddha ♦♦♦♦♦

Gallagher's second album for Chrysalis—and last with his longstanding trio of Lou Martin (keyboards), Rod De'Ath (drums) and Gerry McAvoy (bass)—was a milestone in his career. Although *Calling Card* was produced by Deep Purple bassist Roger Glover and not surprisingly contained some of his most powerfully driving rockers, tracks like the acoustic "Barley & Grape Rag" and the jazzy, soulful, finger snapping title cut—a perennial concert favorite—found the Irish rocker not only exploring other musical paths, but also caught him on one of his most consistent songwriting streaks ever. Even "Do You Read Me," the muscular opening track, is a remarkably stripped-down affair that adds subtle synths to the rugged blues rock that was Gallagher's claim to fame. While "Moonchild," "Country Mile," and "Secret Agent" displayed catchy hooks, engaging riffs, and raging guitar work (the latter adds a touch of Deep Purple's Jon Lord-styled organ to the proceedings), it's the elegant ballad "I'll Admit You're Gone" that shifts the guitarist into calmer waters and proves his melodic talent was just as cutting on quieter tunes. And it's a crime that the gorgeous "Edged in Blue," certainly one of the artist's saddest and most beautiful pop melodies, was overlooked in his catalog. The 1999 reissue sports track-by-track and first person liner notes from Gallagher's brother Donal, crisp remastered sound, and two additional songs not included on previous versions, one of which, "Public Enemy (B-Girl Version)," later appeared on the *Photo-Finish* album in an inferior performance to this. Arguably Rory Gallagher's finest studio effort, it was among his best and most varied batch of songs, and it is a perfect place for the curious to start their collection as well as an essential disc showing Gallagher at the peak of his powers. *—Hal Horowitz*

Photo-Finish / 1978 / Buddha ♦♦♦

Remixed and expanded (with two additional tracks recorded but chopped off the vinyl version) for its debut on CD in 1999, this is a sturdy, workmanlike Rory Gallagher release. Reverting back to a trio, Gallagher toughens up his sound and blazes through some robust blues rockers like "Last of the Independents," "Shadow Play," and "Brute Force & Ignorance" (one of his best hard rock riffs) with nervy energy. Gallagher's swampy side emerges on "Cloak & Dagger," another song that explores his fascination with B-movie gumshoes, a common theme for the Irish blues-rocker. His guitar work is typically excellent throughout, especially on "Overnight Bag," as he overdubs himself on acoustic. Still, the album has a samey feel due to some of the songwriting not being quite up to snuff, and a few tracks, like the moody, slow-burning "Feel to the Fire," stretched well past its breaking point to over six minutes. Of the two additional tunes, "Early Warning" is a typically rugged chunky rocker, and "Juke Box Annie" explores the guitarist's jaunty, slightly funky country style. Neither is essential, but both will be important finds for the Gallagher collector. Brother Donal's liner and track notes are short yet informative, and the sound is an enormous improvement over the original version. There is a remarkable clarity and fullness to the bass, along with a definition that exposes heretofore unheard instruments like the mandolin on "Brute Force..." and hand claps on "Cruise on Out," both previously buried in the mix. Not a great Rory Gallagher album, but a rock-solid one that won't disappoint established fans. *—Hal Horowitz*

Top Priority / 1979 / Buddha ♦♦♦

Gallagher's fourth and final studio set for Chrysalis finds the Irish blues-rocker in prime form. Arriving only a year after *Photo-Finish*, when he spent much of his time on the road, it's remarkable that Gallagher could continue to churn out the hook-heavy high-quality tunes he wrote for this album. Playing larger arenas toughened his songs and attack, almost all of which here are high-octane sweaty rockers. While that makes for some thrilling, intense music, the nonstop vibrant energy rush is never balanced out with a ballad or even the rootsy, swampy blues that Gallagher always performed with such authority. So even though the opening charging riff of "Follow Me"; the slower, urging groove of "Keychain"; and the melodic, relatively subtle hard rock of "Bad Penny" were notable inclusions to the Gallagher catalog and his concerts, the lack of acoustic tunes or less aggressive music gives the album a one-note feel. This isn't helped by the two additional tracks added for the 1999 reissue, both of which stay locked in the same basic hard-edged format. That said, Gallagher and his backing duo are in top form, churning through the songs with remarkably crisp energy. Rory is starting to shout more than sing, but his voice was still powerfully expressive, and when he gets excited on the double-time, cranked up "Just Hit Town" as he overdubs his patented guitar lines, the blues-rocker's guttural screams make it sound like he's on fire. Gallagher also blows some snarling, overdriven harp for the first time in a while on "Off the Handle," one of the album's moodier tracks, and sounds enthusiastic throughout. Except for the lack of diversity, this remains a strong set from the Irishman, and is highly recommended, especially to his less blues-oriented fans. *—Hal Horowitz*

Stage Struck / 1980 / Buddha ♦♦♦

Guitarist Gallager's third officially released live album (during his lifetime) captures him on a grinding world tour in 1979 and 1980, pumping out blues rockers with requisite aggression, yet none of the charm and subtlety that made his previous concert recordings so essential. The song selection is weak as it concentrates on lesser tracks from his late-'70s collections, but more problematically the Irishman sounds like he's rushing the tunes and generally playing too loud. The arrangements bludgeon the songs behind a wall of sound, as Rory spits, rather than sings the lyrics, shouting above the crashing fray. This is particularly true of "Bad Penny," one of two newly added tracks for the revised 2000 edition, where Gallagher growls out the words as if they had little or no meaning, then shifts into a reggae beat that adds nothing to this version of one of his better tracks. While the live shows might have gone down well on stage, when they transfers to album, the excitement is lost, and instead of Gallagher's classy, snappy, eclectic mix of blues, folk and rock, *Stage Struck* sounds like plodding, second-rate Bad Company or Foghat. Where both previous live discs added a few acoustic tunes as well as digging into deep blues to vary the sound and show Gallagher's versatility, this one stays firmly rooted in straight-forward sluggish rock, with precious little roll. All the songs push the five-minute mark, but none have the sizzle and compactness of Gallagher's best work. He sounds like he's going though the motions for the first time in his career, making this a below par, if not quite valueless document. The two additional tunes total about eleven minutes, but the disc is at least 20 minutes short of its potential playing time. Surely there must have been other tapes from this tour of better quality to tack on here. In any case, this is a disappointing reminder that even the best artists can release inferior work. For prime live Gallagher stick with either 1972's peppy *Live in Europe*, the blistering *Irish Tour* or the terrific posthumous release, *BBC Sessions*. *—Hal Horowitz*

Jinx / 1982 / Buddha ♦♦♦♦

Rory Gallagher sounds inspired throughout *Jinx*, gamely leading new drummer Brendan O'Neill and keyboardist Bob Andrews through the blues-rock paces, even though the guitarist's personal fortunes were on a downslide from which they would never recover. "Big Guns" and "Bourbon," the album's opening selections find Rory in full fiery form, tossing out muscular guitar lines and fiery solos with descriptive lyrics catering to his infatuation with American gangsters. The album also features two of his best, and least known, songs in the spooky, paranoid title track, complete with simmering sax section, boiling tom-tom drums as well as his own stealthy harmonica, and "Easy Come Easy Go," a beautiful, bluesy ballad where Rory double tracks his acoustic and electric guitars. Gallagher's tough vocals take on a new emotional depth not previously heard, and are particularly poignant throughout. Diving into the blues, Lightnin' Slims' "Nothin' but the Devil," one of the two songs added for this reissue, is an acoustic solo showpiece revealing Gallagher's delta roots and substantial slide abilities. Louisiana Red's "Ride on Red, Ride On" is a crackling double-time burner with Rory charging through with an appropriately whisky-soaked approach and a shimmering electric slide solo. Another extra track, "Lonely Mile," a finished tune previously omitted due to the time restrictions of vinyl, is a worthy addition to Gallagher's midtempo grinding rocker catalog. Although not his best album, *Jinx* is a tough and confident release, and it's 2000 reappearance after being difficult to find for almost 20 years, especially in this pristine edition, is reason to rejoice for Rory Gallagher fans. *—Hal Horowitz*

Defender / 1988 / Buddha ♦♦♦

Released five years after his last effort (an eternity for the prolific Irish blues guitar slinger who had been churning out at least an album a year throughout the '70s), *Defender* is another quality blues-rock offering. Although Gallagher is in fine tough form here and it was his debut release for his own indie label, there is little difference between this and some of his less stellar '70s albums like *Top Priority* and *Photo-Finish*. The pounding, guitar-heavy opener, "Kickback City" sounds more like hairy rockers Bad Company than anything approaching the deep Chicago and country blues Gallagher dearly loved. The quality picks up substantially as the volume subsides on "Loanshark Blues," but by-the-books crunch-rockers like "Failsafe Day" and the unfortunately titled "Road to Hell" don't bode well for Gallagher moving out from an increasingly formulaic pigeonhole. There are a few corkers here like "Continental Op," a blazing riff that stands with Gallagher's best work and revisits his familiar cloak-and-dagger theme. The swampy, less abrasive "I Ain't No Saint" also pushes the quality up a few notches, as does his gritty version of Sonny Boy Williamson's "Don't Start Me to Talking," the bluesiest song on the disc and one of the few times he pulls out his greasy slide. "Seven Days" is the lone acoustic track and it's a good one, with piano and harp accompaniment and Gallagher singing like he means it as he takes the part of a criminal fleeing from the electric chair. The 2000 reissue adds a pair of rugged bonus tracks (along with a cleaner sound mix), which are actually better, or certainly as good as the best cuts on the rest of this competent but hardly essential Rory Gallagher disc. *—Hal Horowitz*

Fresh Evidence / 1988 / IRS ♦♦♦

There was no way that Rory Gallager could have known that *Fresh Evidence* would be his last recording, but in retrospect, it is a good summary of all that is fine and some that is frustrating about his work. The first few tracks are competent but less than perfect; "'Kid' Gloves" is yet another weak song that is based on his well-known love of crime fiction, and "The King of Zydeco" shows that Gallagher may have liked zydeco music a lot, but he doesn't sound natural playing it. Things pick up on "Middle Name," which sounds a lot like the Doors' "The Wasp" but has some sharp soloing, and things really get rolling on "Ghost Blues." From this point on, it seems that Gallagher wanted to prove his mastery of every style of blues, and amazingly, he succeeds. The Delta blues of "Heaven's Gate" shows his mastery of the form, and the jazzy, swinging Chicago blues instrumental "The Loop" is a classic track. The very best was saved for last, the thundering "Slumming Angel." Everything is absolutely together here, the distinctive voice belting out a great simple lyric over a hammering rhythm section and a heaping helping of guitar, guitar, guitar. For all that, it starts slow has a few tracks that sound like filler, albeit tasty filler, *Fresh Evidence* showed that even after over 20 years of reinterpreting various strains of blues, there was plenty of spirit and creativity left in the great Irish rocker. *—Richard Foss*

The BBC Sessions / Aug. 10, 1999 / Buddha ♦♦♦♦

The resurrected Buddha acquired the rights to much of Rory Gallagher's prime material in 1999. They began their reissue program with his first two albums, then they moved to what most hardcore fans would consider the crown jewel of the series, a double-disc collection of Gallagher's BBC sessions. Like most lead guitarists (at least those of his generation), he would often expand his music when playing live, turning in vibrant, exciting versions of his material, peppered with great guitar solos. Although it lacks the kinetic spark generated whenever a musician performs in front of a live audience, *BBC Sessions* is one of the finest live sets in his catalog, thanks to its crystalline fidelity, strong performances and classy presentation. Certainly, this collection isn't for anyone that isn't already devoted to Gallagher, but for those that are, there's plenty to cherish here—individual solos, impassioned vocals and good liner notes. It's an excellent, worthy addition to his catalog, and it helps confirm Gallagher's gift as a blues-rock guitarist. —*Stephen Thomas Erlewine*

Cecil Gant

b. Apr. 4, 1913, Nashville, TN, **d.** Feb. 4, 1951, Nashville, TN
Vocals, Piano / West Coast Blues, Piano Blues, R&B

Pianist Cecil Gant seemingly materialized out of the wartime mist to create one of the most enduring blues ballads of the '40s. Gant was past age 30 when he burst onto the scene in a most unusual way—he popped up in military uniform at a Los Angeles war bonds rally sponsored by the Treasury Department. Private Gant proceeded to electrify the assembled multitude with his piano prowess, leading to his imminent 1944 debut on Oakland's Gilt-Edge Records: the mellow pop-slanted ballad "I Wonder," which topped the R&B charts despite a wartime shellac shortage that hit tiny independent companies like Gilt-Edge particularly hard. Its flip, the considerably more animated "Cecil's Boogie," was a hit in its own right.

Pvt. Gant shot to the upper reaches of the R&B charts for Gilt-Edge like a guided missile with his "Grass Is Getting Greener Every Day" and "I'm Tired" in 1945, recording prolifically for the imprint before switching over to the Bullet label for the 1948 smash "Another Day—Another Dollar" and 1949's "I'm a Good Man but a Poor Man" (in between those two, Gant also hit with "Special Delivery" for Four Star). Urbane after-hours blues, refined ballads, torrid boogies—Gant ran the gamut during a tumultuous few years in the record business (he also turned up on King, Imperial, Dot, and Swing Time/Down Beat), but it didn't last. His "We're Gonna Rock" for Decca in 1950 (as Gunter Lee Carr) presaged the rise of rock & roll later in the decade, but Gant wouldn't be around to view its ascendancy; the one-time "G.I. Sing-Sation" died in 1952 at the premature age of 38. —*Bill Dahl*

● **Rock Little Baby** / 1976 / Flyright ✦✦✦✦✦

British record collectors were hip to '40s boogie and blues pianist Cecil Gant long before American aficionados were (not that there's much recognition of him here even now). Flyright assembled this vinyl slab of Gant goodies in loving tribute, with titles like "Screwy Boogie," "Owl Stew," and the stinging "Rock Little Baby" among the upbeat highlights. Gant's "I'm a Good Man, but a Poor Man" has been adapted by many blues artists since the pianist waxed this one. —*Bill Dahl*

Cecil Boogie / 1976 / Flyright ✦✦✦✦✦

A second generous helping of boogies and blues by "the G.I. Sing-Sation," as Pvt. Gant was billed on his earliest mid-'40s sides for Gilt-Edge. His thundering boogie piano style on "We're Gonna Rock," "Nashville Jumps," and "Cecil Boogie" presaged the rise of rock & roll. —*Bill Dahl*

Killer Diller Boogie / 1979 / Magpie ✦✦✦

Cecil Gant: 1944–1945 / Oct. 7, 1997 / Fly ✦✦✦

I'm Still Singing the Blues Today / Oldie Blues ✦✦✦✦

Gant only recorded during the immediate postwar era, but he was remarkably prolific during those years. Here we have 20 more gems in the pianist's inimitable style—boogies, blues, ballads, even his personalized rendition of "Coming Round the Mountain!" —*Bill Dahl*

Randy Garibay Jr.

Vocals, Guitar / Texas Blues, Soul-Blues, Doo Wop

Getting called the "godfather" of this or that in music is almost as bad of a cliché as being dubbed a "new Bob Dylan." In the case of Randy Garibay, he has certainly paid the dues and bent the strings enough to be something of a Texas blues godfather, but more interesting is the man's extreme versatility. Blues musicians are most often known for their strict adherence to this deep yet narrow musical form; Garibay, on the other hand, splatters salsa on the mode by proving to be adept at everything from jazz to country to doo wop to a Mexican bolero. Put it all together and you have a unique style he calls his own "puro pinche blues."

His family were immigrants and he was brought up in the barrios of San Antonio and the migrant fields of the Midwest. He learned to play guitar at the age of 18 when his brother gave him a Sears and Roebuck model for his birthday, putting him in a group of many great guitarists that started out on these cheap but hardy axes. But he was a professional singer even before he was playing guitar, beginning as a teenage lead singer for two teen dream doo wop groups, the Velvets and the Pharaohs in the '50s. The latter band performed in Texas and Mexico and sang backup for Sonny Ace and Doug Sahm on some of his earliest recordings. Garibay was also a regular attraction at one of the hot San Antonio blues venues of the '50s, the Eastwood Country Club. This was one of the renowned blues clubs for touring performers. In the '60s he joined the Dell-Kings, which took him on the road, first to Los Angeles and then for an extended stay in the gambling Mecca of Las Vegas. The band became the house group at the Sahara Hotel, allowing Garibay the opportunity to work behind a variety of headline touring artists such as Jackie Wilson, Judy Garland, and Sammy Davis Jr. As the times changed the band became weary of its own name and the doo wop connotations it might have. The group was renamed los Blues as it embarked on a road trip that lasted off and on until the '70s. Garibay backed up rhythm and blues greats Curtis Mayfield and the O'Jays hitting the stage in top drawer venues as Madison Square Garden and the Waldorf Astoria hotels in New York City, Vancouver, and Honolulu.

But as the Doug Sahm song goes, "Texas calls me . . ." Garibary wound up back in his home state holding forth with his new band, Cats Don't Sleep, a nerve-wracking band name for any cat owner who also needs their rest. The group's 1997 album "Barbacoa Blues," named after a particularly tasty style of Mexican shredded barbecued beef, was praised by critics as if they were smacking over their lips on a mouthful of it. He has been a touring artist with the Texas Commission on the Arts since 1999 and a featured performer at the 1998 Chicano Music Awards. He is also winner of the 1996 West Side Rhythm and Blues Award and the Pura Vida Hispanic Music Award in 1994 and 1995. In 2001, pioneering Chicano filmmaker Efrain Gutierrez released *Lowrider Spring Break en San Quilmas*, which features eight original songs by Garibay on the soundtrack. —*Eugene Chadbourne*

Barbacoa Blues / Mar. 25, 2000 / All Star ✦✦✦

● **Invisible Society** / Feb. 5, 2002 / Angelita Mia ✦✦✦

Terry Garland

b. Jun. 3, 1953, Johnson City, TN
Guitar / Contemporary Blues

A country blues interpreter who plays a National steel-body guitar, often with a slide, in the style of Bukka White and Fred McDowell. —*Niles J. Frantz*

● **Trouble in Mind** / 1991 / Planetary ✦✦✦✦

Garland's National guitar sounds great on this CD. Mark Wenner backs him up on harmonica. Garland can sing the blues, and he chose some big-time blues artists' songs to cover (Willie Dixon, Willie McTell, Johnny Winter, Jimmy Reed). —*Chip Renner*

Edge of the Valley / 1992 / First Warning ✦✦✦

One to Blame / Aug. 20, 1996 / Planetary ✦✦✦✦

Like Terry Garland's two albums for RCA, *The One to Blame* is an engaging collection of contemporary country blues and rock & roll reconfigured to sound like country blues. Among the highlights are "Stagger Lee," "Closer Walk with Thee," "Rollin' and Tumblin'" and "It'll Be Me." —*Stephen Thomas Erlewine*

Out Where the Blue Begins / Oct. 23, 2001 / Planetary ✦✦✦

Showing a deep knowledge and impeccable feel for traditional blues forms, Terry Garland's fourth album is an impressive step forward in his artistic evolution. Joined by Mark Wenner on harmonica, Garland's voice is taking on a weathered quality not dissimilar from that of John Hiatt's, adding another layer of authenticity to his already faithful sound. Still brimming with hypnotic slide playing and primitive foot stomping and positively attacking his National guitar in covers of Johnny Winter's "Dallas" and his original, "Blues Fell This Morning," Garland nonetheless doesn't get stuck in any one gear for too long. A mournful full horn section turns up on the smoldering "Courtesy of Love" and delicate vibes and trombone combine to make a gentle soul-groove cover of Sam Cooke's "Running Back to You." Still, Garland never strays too far from the seminal blues forms that he seems to radiate so effortlessly, never presuming he should write a new chapter in blues history, just happy to trace his finger along the best of the well-worn passages. —*Matt Fink*

Larry Garner

b. Jul. 8, 1952, New Orleans, LA
Vocals, Guitar / Swamp Blues, Louisiana Blues

Folks in Europe were hip to Larry Garner long before most blues fans in the states. The Baton Rouge guitarist had already toured extensively overseas, with two British albums to his credit, before Verve issued his stunning domestic debut, *You Need to Live a Little*, in 1995. Rooted in the swamp blues tradition indigenous to his Baton Rouge environs, Garner brings a laudable contemporary sensibility and witty composing skills to his craft.

Inspired by local swamp bluesmen Silas Hogan and Clarence Edwards, Larry Garner learned how to play guitar from his uncle and a couple of gospel-playing elders. After completing his military service in Korea, he returned to Baton Rouge and embarked on a part-time musical career (he worked at a Dow chemical plant for almost two decades until his recent retirement).

The British JSP label released Garner's first two albums: *Double Blues* and *Too Blues* (the latter an ironic slap at an unidentified U.S. blues label boss who deemed Garner's demo tape "too blues"). With the emergence of *You Need to Live a Little*, where Garner delivers creative originals detailing the difficulty of keeping "Four Cars Running" and the universal pain of suffering through "Another Bad Day," Larry Garner is poised for 21st century blues stardom. Subsequent efforts include 1998's *Standing Room Only*, 1999's *Baton Rouge*, and 2000's *Once Upon the Blues*. —*Bill Dahl*

Too Blues / Oct. 31, 1994 / JSP ✦✦✦✦

On his second JSP release, Garner dishes up a variety of blues, steeped in the postwar tradition but reflecting contemporary influences. He successfully reprises his funky "Shak Bully." "She Should've Been Back" is a soul blues, while "Love Her With a Feeling" is a step-by-step narrative à la Albert Collins. Some of his songs are sprinkled with social commentary, something he's known for. On "Thought I Had the Blues," he lays his Albert King-styled guitar playing over Jimmy Johnson's minor chords and reflects on how his blues compares with others who are worse off. There's enough of his hot guitar playing and songwriting to satisfy his fans. For example, on his Lucille Award-winning "Dog House Blues," he reworks the story about how his dog won't take him in after his wife puts him out. —*Sigmund Finman*

Double Dues / 1995 / JSP ✦✦✦

● **You Need to Live a Little** / 1995 / Verve ✦✦✦✦✦

A witty, imaginative songwriter, crisply concise guitarist, and convincing singer, Baton Rouge Larry Garner is the proverbial triple-threat—and a good bet to rise to blues stardom in the immediate future. His major-label debut is a wondrous collection filled with songs that don't embrace simple cliches ("Four Cars Running," "Another Bad Day," "Shak Bully" are anything but routine). "Miracles of Time" is almost pop-soul in its structure, while "Rats and Roaches in My Kitchen," Garner's lowdown tribute to swamp blues pioneer Silas Hogan, benefits from Sonny Landreth's burrowing slide guitar. *—Bill Dahl*

Standing Room Only / May 5, 1998 / Ruf/Platinum ✦✦✦
Although his songwriting slips a little here ("PMS" was an idea that should have never been executed), *Standing Room Only* confirms Larry Garner's position as a tough blues guitarist and dynamic performer. Despite a few weak cuts, there's still a number of very strong songs, and Garner's flair for gritty, swampy performances makes the album quite enjoyable—it just falls a little short of the high quality of his previous masterworks. *—Thom Owens*

Baton Rouge / Oct. 26, 1999 / Evidence ✦✦✦✦
This was supposed to be Garner's follow-up album to his breakthrough third album, *You Need to Live a Little*, released in 1994. Due to contract problems, however, it never saw an American release until 1999. Like its predecessor, Garner's brand of blues moves between Excello swamp blues and more soulful, contemporary styles with a strong songwriting sense ingrained in all of it. A solid band, including Larry McCray on guitar and Willie Weeks on bass, drives this session right along. Highlights include "Jook Joint Woman," "The Road of Life," "Airline Blues," "The Have and the Have Nots," and "Go to Baton Rouge." A lost little classic. *—Cub Koda*

Paul Gayten

b. Jan. 29, 1920, New Orleans, LA, **d.** Mar. 26, 1991, Los Angeles, CA
Vocals, Leader, Piano / New Orleans R&B, Jump Blues
Paul Gayten, a seminal figure in New Orleans rhythm & blues, led a varied career in the music business as a bandleader, producer, label owner, and one-time overseer of the West Coast operation of Chess Records. A nephew of blues-piano legend Little Brother Montgomery, Gayten once led one of the top bands of New Orleans, but he gave up the performing life in 1956 to turn his attention to production and eventually to his own California-based Pzazz label (which featured Louis Jordan, among others). Gayten wrote Larry Darnell's 1949 classic "For You My Love" and recorded a few Top Ten hits of his own for Regal and DeLuxe (1947-1950), some of them with vocalist Annie Laurie. *—Jim O'Neal*

● **Chess King of New Orleans/The Chess Years** / 1989 / MCA/Chess ✦✦✦✦
Sizzling mid-'50s New Orleans R&B from this veteran. *—Bill Dahl*

J. Geils Band

f. 1967, Boston, MA, **db.** 1985
Group / Album Rock, Boogie Rock, Arena Rock, Pop/Rock, Hard Rock, Blues-Rock, Rock & Roll
The J. Geils Band was one of the most popular touring rock & roll bands in America during the '70s. Where their contemporaries were influenced by the heavy boogie of British blues-rock and the ear-splitting sonic adventures of psychedelia, the J. Geils Band were a bar band pure and simple, churning out greasy covers of obscure R&B, doo wop, and soul tunes, cutting them with healthy dose of Stonesy swagger. While their muscular sound and the hyper jive of frontman Peter Wolf packed arenas across America, it only rarely earned them hit singles. Seth Justman, the group's main songwriter, could turn out catchy R&B-based rockers like "Give It to Me" or "Must of Got Lost," but these hits never led to stardom, primarily because the group had trouble capturing the energy of their live sound when in the studio. In the early '80s, the group tempered their driving rock with some pop, and the makeover paid off with the massive hit single "Centerfold," which stayed at number one for six weeks. By the time the band prepared to record a follow-up, tensions between Justman and Wolf had grown considerably, resulting in Wolf's departure, which quickly led to the band's demise. After working for years to reach to top of the charts, the J. Geils couldn't stay there once they finally achieved their goal.

Guitarist Jerome Geils, bassist Danny Klein, and harpist Magic Dick (born Richard Salwitz) began performing as an acoustic blues trio sometime in the mid-'60s. In 1967, drummer Stephen Jo Bladd and vocalist Peter Wolf joined the group, and the band went electric. Before joining the J. Geils Band, Bladd and Wolf played together in the Boston-based rock revivalist band the Hallucinations. Both musicians shared a love of arcane doo-wop, blues, R&B and rock & roll, and Wolf had become well-known by spinning such obscure singles as a jive-talking WBCN DJ called Woofuh Goofuh. Wolf and Bladd's specialized tastes became a central force in the newly revamped J. Geils Band, who positioned themselves as tough '50s greasers in opposition to the colorful psychedelic rockers that dominated the East Coast in the late '60s. Soon, the band had earned a sizable local following, including Seth Justman, an organist who was studying at Boston University. Justman joined the band in 1968, and the band continued to tour for the next few years, landing a record contract with Atlantic in 1970.

The J. Geils Band was a regional hit upon its early 1970 release, and it earned favorable reviews, especially from *Rolling Stone*. The group's second album, *The Morning After*, appeared in 1971 and, thanks to the Top 40 hit "Looking for a Love," the album expanded their following. However, the band continued to win new fans primarily through their concerts, so it was no surprise that their third album, 1972's *Full House*, was a live set. It was followed by *Bloodshot*, a record that climbed into the Top Ten on the strength of the Top 40 hit, "Give It to Me." Following the relative failure of 1973's *Ladies Invited*, the band had another hit with 1974's *Nightmares*, which featured the number 12 single "Must of Got Lost." While their live shows remained popular throughout the mid-'70s, both *Hot Line* (1975) and the live *Blow Your Face Out* (1976) were significant commercial disappointments. The band revamped their sound and shortened their name to "Geils" for 1977's *Monkey Island*. While the album received good reviews, the record failed to bring the group increased sales.

In 1978, the J. Geils Band left Atlantic Records for EMI, releasing *Sanctuary* later that year. *Sanctuary* slowly gained a following, becoming their first gold album since *Bloodshot*. *Love Stinks* (1980) expanded the group's following even more, peaking at number 18 in the charts and setting the stage for 1981's *Freeze-Frame*, the band's high watermark. Supported by the infectious single "Centerfold"—which featured a memorable video that

received heavy MTV airplay—and boasting a sleek, radio-ready sound, *Freeze-Frame* climbed to number one. "Centerfold" shot to the top of the charts late in 1981, spending six weeks at number one; its followup, "Freeze-Frame," was nearly as successful, reaching number four in the spring of 1982. The live album *Showtime!* became a gold album shortly after its late 1982 release. While the band was experiencing the greatest commercial success of their career, relationships between the members, particularly writing partners Justman and Wolf, were volatile. When the band refused to record material Wolf had written with Don Covay and Michael Jonzun, he left the band in the middle of a 1983 recording session. Justman assumed lead vocals, and the group released *You're Gettin' Even While I'm Gettin' Odd* in late 1984, several months after Wolf's successful solo debut, *Lights Out*. The J. Geils Band's record was a failure, and the band broke up in 1985. Magic Dick and Geils, calling himself Jay instead of Jerome, reunited in 1993 to form the contemporary blues band Bluestime. *—Stephen Thomas Erlewine*

The J. Geils Band / 1970 / Atlantic ✦✦✦✦✦
Their debut paid homage to the likes of Otis Rush, John Lee Hooker, and Motown through blistering covers, but originals such as "Wait" and "What's Your Hurry" more than hold their own. Magic Dick steals the show on this one. *—John Floyd*

The Morning After / 1971 / Atlantic ✦✦✦
It's rare when a group's sophomore effort is as good as their debut. *The Morning After* by the J. Geils Band is that, and in some ways, even better. Tighter and more focused than their debut, the band found success on the singles charts with "Looking for a Love." Again, they laid original material alongside blues covers, but the sound was always their own—exciting, enjoyable rocking blues. *—James Chrispell*

Full House "Live" / 1972 / Atlantic ✦✦✦✦✦
Live is the way the J. Geils Band should be experienced; they put on a show like few others, and *Full House* is the proof. From start to finish, there is not one bad cut. From the opener, "First I Look at the Purse" right on through "Looking for a Love," these guys don't give up an inch. *—James Chrispell*

Bloodshot / 1973 / Atlantic ✦✦
More hot, rockin' rhythm & blues from these guys out of Boston. *Bloodshot* includes their Top 40 hit "Give It To Me," as well as the great opener, "(Ain't Nothin' But A) House Party," plus soulful struts and bluesy shuffles in between. It's a wonder these guys could tour almost constantly and still turn out great albums one after another. On *Bloodshot*, the J. Geils Band make it appear easy. *—James Chrispell*

Ladies Invited / 1973 / Atlantic ✦✦✦
On this, their first album of all original material, something appeared to be amiss. Perhaps it was road fatigue—only the band knows for sure, but *Ladies Invited* didn't burn up the charts like their previous efforts, nor did it have that all-important hit single. It's well done and worthwhile, but lacks spark. *—James Chrispell*

Nightmares . . . and Other Tales from the Vinyl Jungle / 1974 / Atlantic ✦✦✦
After a brief sidestep, the J. Geils Band came roaring back with a very urban-jungle sort of album which percolates with beat and rocks with enthusiastic excitement. Here lies the reggae-ish "Give It to Me," as well as the concert staple "Detroit Breakdown." A fertile release from some of the hardest rockers of the '70s. *—James Chrispell*

Hotline / 1975 / Atlantic ✦✦
It appears that with *Hotline* the J. Geils Band backtracked a bit by including a few new originals alongside proven R&B workouts in what one is tempted to call a formula. But *Hotline* is still well worth listening to; it includes "Love-itis," which is entirely worth the price of the rest. *—James Chrispell*

Blow Your Face Out / 1976 / Rhino ✦✦✦✦✦
Double-album live sets came into vogue in 1976 after Peter Frampton's sales went through the roof for A&M, Bob Seger found fame with *Live Bullet* on Capitol, and the J. Geils Band released its second in-concert document in four years, *Blow Your Face Out*. There is great power in these grooves recorded over two nights, November 15 and November 19, at the now deconstructed Boston Garden and in Detroit at Cobo Hall. Here's the beautiful dilemma with the Geils band: *Full House*, recorded in Detroit in April of 1972, contains five songs that became J. Geils standards, and none of them overlap on the 1982 EMI single live disc, *Showtime*, chock-full of their latter-day classics. Can you believe there is absolutely no overlap from the first or third live album on this double disc, which came in between (except for "Looking for a Love," uncredited, which they slip into the intro of "Houseparty" on side two)? The Rhino CD contains Jeff Tamarkin's liner notes, while the original Atlantic album has an exquisite gatefold chock-full of photos, and inner sleeves with priceless band memo stuff à la Grand Funk's *Live Album*. Sides one and two are great, and three and four are even better. "Detroit Breakdown" rocks and grooves, with tons of audience applause. Wolfy and the polished authority of his monologues are in command as the band oozes into "Chimes" from 1973's *Ladies Invited*. About three and a half minutes longer than the five-minute original, it is one of many highlights on this revealing pair of discs. A precursor to 1977's title track, "Monkey Island," "Chimes" gives this enigmatic band a chance to jam out slowly and lovingly over its groove. There is so much to this album: the Janis Joplin standard "Raise Your Hand" written by Eddie Floyd, Albert Collins' "Sno-Cone" from their first album, and "Truck Drivin' Man" beating Bachman-Turner Overdrive to the punch. B.B. King producer Bill Szymczyk does a masterful job bringing it all together, and the band photos on back look . . . roguish. "Must of Got Lost," "Where Did Our Love Go," and "Give It to Me" are here in all their glory, a different glory than the studio versions, on an album that should have done for Geils what *Live Bullet* and *Frampton Comes Alive* did for their respective artists. If only a legitimate release of their 1999 tour would be issued to stand next to this monster—during that tour they combined the best elements of all three of their previous live discs. The J. Geils Band is more important and influential than the boys have been given

credit for. It will be the live documents that ensure they eventually get their due, and *Blow Your Face Out* is a very worthy component that can still frazzle speakers. *—Joe Viglione*

Monkey Island / 1977 / Atlantic ✦✦✦✦✦

One of the great lost albums, *Monkey Island* is where the Geils Band make the blues their own. It's an elaborately produced, adventurous set that analyzes their commerical failure and looks for answers to hard-to-ask questions. Unlike their 1972 live album *Full House*, *Monkey Island* refuses to pander to blues conservists or boogie-rock hammerheads; the album is steeped in the kind of pathos and bitterness that infuse the Stones' *Sticky Fingers*. The album flopped, but it remains the group's most personal statement. *—John Floyd*

Sanctuary / 1978 / BGO ✦✦✦

Hot on the heels of the band's excellent but completely overlooked *Monkey Island*, the J. Geils Band severed ties with Atlantic and signed a fresh deal with EMI Records. The band's tenure with Atlantic only yielded a few successes, and on paper, teaming up with producer Joe Wissert, the man responsible for many of Earth, Wind & Fire's and Boz Scaggs' biggest hits, seemed like an odd choice. However, *Sanctuary* was a rebirth of sorts for the sextet: Wissert crystallized the band's attack, working off their leaner songwriting and simplifying their arrangements. Keeping their boogie-woogie bar band attack intact, Peter Wolf and Seth Justman delivered first-rate material, including the down and dirty opener "I Could Hurt You," the sublime title track and the lovely "One Last Kiss," which cracked the Top 40 in early 1978. The Stevie Wonder-ish "Take It Back," also a mild hit, predicted the commercial direction the band took on *Freeze Frame* three years later. The beautiful "Teresa," a heartbreaking ballad executed with help of a simple vocal/piano arrangement courtesy of the Wolf/Justman team, and "Wild Man," which sounds like a leftover from the Atlantic years, are also highlights. *Sanctuary*'s final song, the rollicking, Magic Dick-driven "Just Can't Stop Me," encapsulates everything magical (pun intended) and soulful about this band. With its effortless playing and a breakdown that'll have you on the edge of your seat, it served as the band's call into battle for the Freeze Frame tour. The Razor & Tie reissue features covers of "I Do" and "Land of a Thousand Dances" from the band's live record *Showtime*, recorded at the height of their *Freeze Frame* period. "Land of a Thousand Dances" in particular reminds you just how incredible these guys were live. *—John Franck*

● **The Best of the J. Geils Band** / 1979 / Atlantic ✦✦✦✦

Contractual obligations aside, *The Best of the J. Geils Band* is a worthy and yet somewhat disjointed collection of the band's more popular radio songs taken from their eight Atlantic records. Released just a year after J. Geils' EMI debut *Sanctuary*, one listen to these two works back to back can make an extraordinary argument for the band's growth. Or lack of it, depending on whom you ask. On their eight years with Atlantic, Peter Wolf and company released some of THE "best white R&B" records of all time. Some sold well, some sold moderately, and some just plain tanked. The one thing that remained a constant was the band's monolithically inspired live performances. Unfortunately for Atlantic, as soon as the band left the label, almost overnight, with a newly retooled, more compact sound, success would find the six-piece on 1980's *Love Stinks* and, of course, on the gigantic blockbuster *Freeze Frame*. If you want to find out just how powerful these guys were, this "best collection" is a decent starting point. Songs like joyous "Give It to Me" or the colossal "Detroit Breakdown" are just some of the highlights. For a brief overview, pick up this set, but if it's a college education that you're after, pick up the band's Rhino anthology, *Houseparty* (a much more worthy compilation replete with killer liner notes). *—John Franck*

Love Stinks / 1980 / BGO ✦✦✦

Released some two years after the band's EMI debut, *Sanctuary*, the *Love Stinks* project would see the J. Geils Band going in an even more commercial-leaning direction than its predecessor. Taking over the main production duties, keyboard player/main songwriter Seth Justman set out to better the band's gold-plus-selling *Sanctuary*. And to some degree, he wildly succeeded. Although not as consistent or diverse as *Sanctuary*, *Love Stinks* would feature one of the band's most recognizable FM songs ever—the album's infectious title track "Love Stinks." In a live setting, the track would often turn into a veritable *tour de force* only to be outdone by Peter Wolf's hilarious rap about "Adam and Eve in the Garden of Eden smoking weed together," which would introduce the song (often on a nightly basis). "Night Time" is another great, although somewhat typical "rave-on" type of J. Geils song; "No Anchovies Please" is a little strange; and closer "Till the Walls Come Tumblin' Down" is, as the song title hints, just that. Bolstered by "Just Can't Wait," another good album opener, *Love Stinks* turns out to be solid effort, but one that sounds a little outdated at times due to its acerbic, synth textures. Not one of the band's best overall records but one that would allow the band to outdo itself with the classic *Freeze Frame* a year later. *—John Franck*

Freeze Frame / 1981 / EMI ✦✦✦✦

Tempering their bar band R&B with a touch of new wave pop production, the J. Geils Band finally broke through into the big leagues with *Freeze Frame*. Fans of the hard-driving rock of the group's '70s albums will find the sleek sound of *Freeze Frame* slightly disorienting, but the production gives the album cohesion. Good-time rock & roll remains at the core of the group's music, but the sound of the record is glossier, shining with synthesizers and big pop hooks. With its singalong chorus, "Centerfold" exemplifies this trend, but it's merely the tip of the iceberg. "Freeze Frame" has a great stop-start chorus, "Flamethrower" and "Piss on the Wall" rush along on hard-boogie riffs, and "Angel in Blue" is terrific neo-doo wop. There are still a handful of throwaways, but even the filler has a stylized, synthesized flair that makes it enjoyable, and the keepers are among the band's best. *—Stephen Thomas Erlewine*

Showtime! / 1982 / BGO ✦✦

A great live band recorded on stage in a city that loves them. What could go wrong? Enough. For one thing, the material is not as strong as on the 1972 classic *Full House*, also recorded in Detroit. And this release is marred by a witless, overlong Peter Wolf intro to "Love Stinks." He was ousted not long after this album, and the band dispersed after one album without him. To hear this sextet at its crowd-pleasing best, delve back another decade and pluck *Full House*. *—Mark Allan*

You're Gettin' Even While I'm Gettin' Odd / 1984 / EMI ✦✦

This doesn't sound like the J. Geils Band folks know and love, since Peter Wolf has left the band; *You're Gettin' Even While I'm Gettin' Odd* is mainly keyboardist Seth Justman's baby, and he uses banks and banks of synths along with more traditional keyboards to come up with the palette of sounds used here. The cut "Californicating" glides along courtesy of J. Geils' guitar and there's a slow blues titled "The Bite from Inside," but other than that, much of what's here is simply ordinary. Justman and drummer Stephen Bladd cover the vocals this time out, but they are no match for Wolf's old growl. Lots of production dazzle with none of the bite of old. *—James Chrispell*

Flashback / 1988 / EMI America ✦✦✦

Featuring a hodgepodge of material taken from the band's three biggest career-selling records (all on EMI), *Flashback* is an all too brief ten-track affair which includes a handful of classics like "Love Stinks," "Centerfold," "Freeze Frame," and a couple of other essential J. Geils Band "deep" cuts like "Flamethrower" and the terrific "Just Can't Wait." Incomprehensibly, other essentials like "Sanctuary," "Teresa," "Just Can't Stop Me," "Nightime," and even the hilarious "Piss on the Wall" (not so essential) are nowhere to be found. Glancing over the track listing, it's obvious that EMI spent next to no time putting together this compilation and decided to issue it as some sort of contractual obligation (even though Peter Wolf would continue to release solo records for the label in years to come) or perhaps as a forgone catalog piece. And that's too bad. It sure would have been nice to hear the live version of "Love Stinks" from *Showtime* (which is introduced by Wolf's now legendary, "Adam and Eve were smoking weed in the Garden of Eden" rap) or perhaps some other un-released live gems from the band's Freeze Frame tour—their biggest outing ever. Wisely, the label chose to completely shun the band's god-awful post-Peter Wolf release *You're Getting Even While I'm Getting I'm Getting Odd*. As far as compilation records go, this one's the weakest of all the J. Geils Band anthologies. For a more thorough appreciation, invest in the much superior Rhino collection *Houseparty: Anthology*. Better yet, pick up one of the band's old live records like *Blow Your Face Out* or even *Full House* (both feature material from the band's superior Atlantic releases). *—John Franck*

● **Houseparty: Anthology** / 1992 / Rhino ✦✦✦✦✦

The superb two-disc anthology *Houseparty* concentrates on the rousing, full-throttle blues-boogie of their heyday, including a full album's worth of live material (ten songs from their three live albums). The pop success of *Love Stinks* and *Freeze Frame* makes sense in the context of the set, but the songs that cut the deepest are the blues-rock numbers on the first disc and the live songs. Thankfully, the compilers (*Trouser Press* editor Ira Robbins and band members Peter Wolf and Seth Justman) end *Houseparty* with three songs from *Sanctuary*, helping secure the image of the J. Geils Band as one of America's top rock & roll groups. *—Stephen Thomas Erlewine*

Barbara George

b. Aug. 16, 1942, New Orleans, LA

Vocals / New Orleans R&B, Soul

George's "I Know (You Don't Love Me No More)" topped the R&B charts in 1961 and has proven a popular cover item ever since. The New Orleans native had never been in the studio before she brought her extremely catchy melody to Harold Battiste's fledgling A.F.O. label. Benefiting from her pleasing, unpolished vocal and a melodic cornet solo by Melvin Lastie, the tune caught fire, vaulting high on pop playlists. Amazingly, nothing else George did ever dented the charts, although she waxed some listenable follow-ups for A.F.O. and Sue. *—Bill Dahl*

● **I Know (You Don't Love Me Anymore): Golden Classics** / 1962 / Collectables ✦✦✦✦✦

Part of the label's *Golden Classics* series, this is a straight-up reissue of Barbara's A.F.O. album from 1962. With her lone smash hit as the centerpiece, the album is surprisingly free of filler, almost a prerequisite in those singles-dominated times. Her follow-up hit, "Talk About Love," is also aboard, and other highlights include nice takes of "Since I Fell for You," the bouncy "Don't Ask Me No Questions," and the soulful ballad "Honest I Do." With top-notch playing from Harold Battiste and others, this is classic early-'60s New Orleans music all the way. *—Cub Koda*

Lowell George

b. Apr. 13, 1945, Hollywood, CA, **d.** Jun. 29, 1979, Arlington, VA

Slide Guitar, Vocals, Guitar / Album Rock, Boogie Rock, Southern Rock, Hard Rock, Singer/Songwriter, Blues-Rock, Rock & Roll

As Little Feat was disbanding in late 1978, their lead guitarist/songwriter Lowell George recorded a solo album, *Thanks I'll Eat It Here*, that sounded as loose and funky as the band in their prime. After its release the following year, he set out on tour to support the album. Sadly, George died of a heart attack while on the road; he left behind a body of gritty, eclectic, and funky rock & roll. On the first five Little Feat albums, his songwriting and instrumental talents are more apparent than on his solo effort, yet that doesn't detract from the record's pleasures. *—Stephen Thomas Erlewine*

● **Thanks I'll Eat It Here** / 1979 / Warner Brothers ✦✦✦✦✦

Thanks I'll Eat it Here is strikingly different from the fusion-leanings of Little Feat's last studio album, *Time Loves a Hero*. Lowell George never cared for jazz-fusion, so it should be little surprise that there's none to be heard on *Thanks*. Instead, he picks up where *Dixie Chicken* left off (he even reworks that album's standout "Two Trains"), turning in a laid-back, organic collection of tunes equal parts New Orleans R&B, country, sophisticated blues, and pop. George wasn't in good health during the sessions for *Thanks*, which you wouldn't tell by his engaging performances, but from the lack of new tunes. Out of the nine songs on the album, only three are originals, and they're all collaborations. That's a drawback only in retrospect—it's hard not to wish that the last album George completed had more of his own songs—but Lowell was a first-rate interpreter, so even covers of Allen Toussaint ("What Do You Want the Girl to Do"), Ann Peebles ("I Can't Stand the Rain"), and Rickie Lee Jones ("Easy Money") wind up sounding of a piece with the original songs. George's music rolls so easy, the album can seem a little slight at first, but it winds up being a real charmer. Yes, a few songs drift by and, yes, Jimmy Webb's vaudevellian "Himmler's Ring" feels terribly out of place, but Lowell's style is so distinctive and his performances so soulful, it's hard not to like this record if you've ever had a fondness for Little Feat. After all, it's earthier and more satisfying than any Feat album since *Feats Don't Fail Me Now* and it has the absolutely gorgeous "20 Million Things," the last great song George ever wrote. *—Stephen Thomas Erlewine*

Lightning-Rod Man / Nov. 2, 1993 / Bizarre/Straight ✦✦✦
Before emerging as a cult star in the '70s, Lowell George was a presence on the L.A. folk-rock/psychedelic scene in the '60s. With his group the Factory, he only managed to release one single during this time. *Lightning-Rod Man* rescues 15 tunes cut by this unit, including the single and over a dozen outtakes and demos. Almost exclusively original material, most of these tracks were recorded in 1966 and 1967. They show the group pursuing a slightly eccentric folk-rock vision that neither bears much similarity to George's more famous work nor matches the best work done in this genre by their L.A. peers. At times they echo Kaleidoscope in their vaguely spacy, good-natured folkish rock; just as often, they take cues from Captain Beefheart and Frank Zappa in their skewed blues-rock and obtuse songwriting. In fact, Zappa himself produced and played on a couple of the demos, and one-time Mothers of Invention members Elliot Ingber and Roy Estrada show up on a few others. A few songs cut toward the end of the decade feature a heavier, bluesier sound that show George edging in a different direction. An enjoyable vault find, but not a major revelation. *—Richie Unterberger*

Georgia Cotton Pickers

f. 1929, **db.** 1931
Group / Country Blues, String Bands
This was one of the only country blues supergroups, although the name sounds more like something an announcer on the early Grand Ole Opry show might have come up with to hang on some old-time string band. The group recorded for the Atlanta-based QRS label and featured some of that city's finest country blues artists playing together, something all of them tended to do as buskers on the street more than in front of a studio microphone. Robert Hicks, also known as Barbecue Bob, got his brother Charlie Hicks in on the band, and the other members were two brilliant harmonica players, Eddie Mapp and Buddy Moss. The latter player also recorded as a guitarist and vocalist. Ace blues guitarist Curley Weaver filled out the group, whose recorded works have been re-released on the Document label on the *Georgia Blues* collection. These recordings were well-received at the time, up to a point. The company never had very good distribution and to make matters worse, these were some of the last blues recordings done before the Depression ground most such endeavors to a halt. Group membership was partially decimated in 1931, when within one month, Barbecue Bob dropped dead and Eddie Mapp was stabbed to death on a street corner. Probably because such a band name really belongs in country music, the next decade produced another group called the Georgia Cotton Pickers, this one playing country music and under the leadership of Paul Howard. This band's main claim to fame was the presence of fine guitarist Hank Garland, one of the few players to perform with aplomb in both the country and jazz idioms. *—Eugene Chadbourne*

Clifford "Grandpappy" Gibson

b. Apr. 17, 1901, Louisville, KY, **d.** Dec. 21, 1963, St. Louis, MO
Vocals, Guitar / Prewar Country Blues, Country Blues, St. Louis Blues
Though not a particularly great singer, Clifford "Grandpappy" Gibson was an excellent guitarist, among the finest pure players in country blues. Gibson moved from Kentucky to St. Louis in the '20s, where he lived the remainder of his life. He frequently played St. Louis clubs during the '20s and '30s, and began recording for QRS and Victor in 1929. Greatly influenced by Lonnie Johnson, Gibson also accompanied Jimmie Rodgers on a Victor single in 1931, then spent parts of the next three decades playing in the streets around St. Louis. Gibson resurfaced on recordings in 1960 with a Bobbin date, and worked another three years in St. Louis' Gaslight Square before his death in 1963. *—Ron Wynn*

● **Beat You Doing It** / 1972 / Yazoo ✦✦✦✦✦
Beat You Doing It contains all of the prime tracks Clifford Gibson recorded, offering an excellent, concise overview of the country blues guitarist. *—Thom Owens*

Complete Recorded Works (1929–1931) / 1991 / Document ✦✦✦✦
Document's 23-track collection *Complete Recorded Works* presents everything Clifford Gibson recorded between 1929-1931. Since Gibson was a fine guitarist but not an exceptional vocalist, this is primarily of interest only to diehard country blues fans. And those casual fans who do want a taste of Gibson are better served by Yazoo's more concise collection, *Beat You Doing It*. *—Thom Owens*

Lacy Gibson

b. May 1, 1936, South Carolina
Vocals, Guitar / Modern Electric Chicago Blues, Electric Chicago Blues
Slowly returning to musical action following major surgery, guitarist Lacy Gibson has been an underappreciated figure on the Windy City circuit for decades.

Lacy and his family left North Carolina for Chicago in 1949. It didn't take long for Gibson to grow entranced by the local action—he learned from veterans Sunnyland Slim and Muddy Waters and picked up pointers from immaculate axemen Lefty Bates, Matt "Guitar" Murphy, and Wayne Bennett. Gibson made a name for himself as a session player in 1963, assuming rhythm guitar duties on sides by Willie Mabon for USA, Billy "The Kid" Emerson for M-Pac!, and Buddy Guy on Chess. Gibson made his vocal debut on the self-penned blues ballad "My Love Is Real" at Chess the same year, though it wasn't released at the time (when it belatedly emerged, it was mistakenly attributed to Guy).

A couple of bargain basement 45s for the remarkably obscure Repeto logo (that's precisely where they were done—in Lacy Gibson's basement!) preceded Gibson's inconsistent album debut for then-brother-in-law Sun Ra's El Saturn label. Ralph Bass produced an album by Gibson in 1977, but the results weren't issued at the time (Delmark is currently releasing the set domestically).

A stint as Son Seals' rhythm axeman (he's on Seals' *Live and Burning* LP) provided an entrée to Alligator Records, which included four fine sides by Gibson on its second batch of *Living Chicago Blues* anthologies in 1980. Best of all was a Dick Shurman-produced album for the Dutch Black Magic logo in 1982, *Switchy Titchy*, that brilliantly spotlighted Gibson's clean fretwork and hearty vocals. After he regained his health in the mid-'90s, Lacy Gibson entered the studio and recorded *Crying for My Baby*, which was released in 1996. *—Bill Dahl*

● **Switchy Titchy** / 1982 / Black Magic ✦✦✦✦
Switchy Titchy is the best record Lacy Gibson has recorded to date. Gibson's variation on Chicago blues includes some horns pinched from Southern soul-blues records, and it's a little bit more laidback than the pile-driving sound often associated with the style. He makes up for the relaxed pace with his round, clean guitar tones and big, powerful vocals, both of which are spotlighted throughout *Switchy Titchy*. Best of all, that playing is married to a strong song selection, featuring a couple of originals and a lot of forgotten classics. That unpredictable song selection makes the entire album sound fresh and lifts the record above many of its modern blues peers. *—Thom Owens*

Crying for My Baby / 1996 / Delmark ✦✦✦

Jazz Gillum (William McKinley Gillum)

b. Sep. 11, 1904, Indianola, MS, **d.** Mar. 29, 1966, Chicago, IL
Vocals, Harmonica / Acoustic Chicago Blues, Country Blues
Next to John Lee "Sonny Boy" Williamson, no harmonica player was as popular or as much in demand on recording sessions during the '30s as Jazz Gillum. His high, reedy sound meshed perfectly on dozens of hokum sides on the Bluebird label, both as a sideman and as a leader.

Born in Indianola, MS (B.B. King's birthplace as well) in 1904, Gillum was evidently teaching himself how to play harmonica by the tender age of six. After running away from home in 1911 to live with relatives in Charleston, MS, Jazz spent the next dozen or so years working a day job and spending his weekends playing for tips on local street-corners. When he visited Chicago in 1923, he found the environment very much to his liking and put down roots there.

There he met guitarist Big Bill Broonzy and the two of them started working club dates around the city as a duo. By 1934, Gillum started popping up on recording dates for ARC and later Bluebird, RCA Victor's budget label. This association would prove to be a lasting as Chicago producer Lester Melrose frequently called on Gillum as a sideman—as well as cutting sides on his own—as part of the "Bluebird beat" house band. His career seemed to screech to a halt when the label folded in the late '40s and aside from a Memphis Slim session in 1961, he seems to have been largely inactive throughout the '50s until his death from a gunshot wound as a result of an argument in 1966. *—Cub Koda*

Complete Recorded Works, Vol. 1 (1936–1938) / Jun. 2, 1994 / Document ✦✦✦✦
William McKinley "Jazz" Gillum was a good-time singer and a fine harmonica player whose style predated the first Sonny Boy Williamson but was more advanced than the players of the '20s. His complete output up to 1949 has been made available by the Austrian Document label on four CDs. The first volume has his first five sessions and one song from his sixth. Gillum is joined by guitarist Big Bill Broonzy on all of the dates with appearances by pianist John Davis, Washboard Sam and electric guitarist George Barnes (who is heard a year before Charlie Christian debuted). Highlights include "Jockey Blues," "Don't You Scandalize My Name," "Reefer Head Woman," "Good Old 51 Highway" and "You're Laughing Now." Fine blues-oriented music. *—Scott Yanow*

Complete Recorded Works, Vol. 2 (1938–1941) / Jun. 2, 1994 / Document ✦✦✦✦
Although a minor figure in blues history, Jazz Gillum recorded 100 selections during 1934-1949 as a leader plus an album in 1961. Of those 100, the first two seem to be completely lost but the other 98 have all been reissued on four Document CDs. An expressive singer and an effective harmonica player, Gillum holds his own with his better-known sidemen who on *Vol. 2* include guitarist Big Bill Broonzy, pianist Joshua Altheimer, bassist Ransom Knowling, Washboard Sam, and (on one session) a so-so tenor saxophonist. Among the better selections from these performances covering the 1938-1941 period are such numbers as "Get Away Old Woman," "Keyhole Blues," "Hard Drivin' Woman," "Key to the Highway," and "Is That a Monkey You Got?" *—Scott Yanow*

Complete Recorded Works, Vol. 3 (1941–1946) / Jun. 2, 1994 / Document ✦✦✦✦
The third of four volumes that include all of Jazz Gillum's recordings (other than a later album) features 25 more vocals by the fine '30s-style harmonica player. There are 20 selections from 1941-1942, while the final five (from 1945-1946) find him playing and singing in an unchanged style. Guitarist Big Bill Broonzy is on all but the final selection and the pianists are Horace Malcolm, Blind John Davis, Roosevelt Sykes, or Big Maceo Merriweather. Gillum was an effective if not overly distinctive singer, while his harmonica solos are fairly basic, particularly compared to Sonny Boy Williamson and the soon-to-be discovered Little Walter. The tunes include "Me and My Buddy," "War Time Blues," "I'm Gonna Leave You on the Outskirts of Town" (a different variation of "We're Going to

Move to the Outskirts of Town"), "You're Tearing Your Playhouse Down," and "Whiskey Head Buddies." —*Scott Yanow*

Complete Recorded Works, Vol. 4 (1946–1949) / Jun. 2, 1994 / Document ✦✦✦✦
The fourth and final Document volume that reissues all of Jazz Gillum's recordings (other than his first two lost numbers and a later LP) finds the singer and harmonica player performing in a style unchanged from the late '30s even as the music world changed around him. He still sounded quite enthusiastic during this last batch of good-time and lowdown blues, and the backup groups (with either Big Maceo Merriweather, James Clark, Eddie Boyd, or Bob Call on piano and the talented guitarist Willie Lacy being a major asset) are excellent. Highlights include "Roll Dem Bones," "You Got To Run Me Down," "Signifying Woman," "The Devil Blues," and "Gonna Be Some Shooting." —*Scott Yanow*

● **The Bluebird Recordings 1934–1938** / Feb. 25, 1997 / Bluebird/RCA ✦✦✦✦✦
The Bluebird Recordings 1934-1938 is the best CD retrospective yet assembled of Jazz Gillum's peak years, offering 22 tracks—including such songs as "Early in the Morning," "Don't Scandalize My Name," "Alberta Blues," "Just Like Jessie James," "Reefer Head Woman," "Worried and Bothered," and "Good Old 51 Highway"—that find him at his easygoing best. Document's multi-volume series may be a more complete overview of his works, but this remains the best summation of his strengths and talents. —*Thom Owens*

Roll Dem Bones 1938–49 / 1998 / Wolf ✦✦✦✦
Roll Dem Bones 1938-49 rounds up a number of sides not issued on the Document series, offering good insight into the final days of Jazz Gillum's career. While it isn't the first place to go—RCA's concise and comprehensive *The Bluebird Recordings 1934-1938* holds that title—it nevertheless is a welcome addition to any serious blues historian that has all the Document reissues. —*Thom Owens*

It Sure Had a Kick: The Essential Recordings of Jazz Gillum / Jun. 26, 2001 / Indigo ✦✦✦✦
While this might not be the wisest choice if you're aiming to assemble a comprehensive Gillum collection via several discs, or just to target one definitive best-of anthology, it's a pretty good 22-song survey of his output from the late '30s to the late '40s. This is underrated, formative early Chicago band blues, paced by Gillum's likable vocal persona, fine harmonica work, and sturdy arrangements. Indeed "You're Laughing Now," from 1938, finds almost all of the elements of classic Chicago electric blues in place except electricity and a full drum set (though Washboard Sam keeps time on his washboard). Big Bill Broonzy plays guitars on about half of the tracks (all dating from the late '30s and early '40s), and Big Maceo Merriweather, Eddie Boyd, and Washboard Sam are also heard on occasion. Though much of the material verges more toward the good-timey and the jazzy than "You're Laughing Now" does, it's never hokey. Gillum gets uncommonly serious on "Wartime Blues," cut just days before the bombing of Pearl Harbor, and puts an admirable stamp on the standard "I'm Gonna Leave You on the Outskirts of Town." The late-'40s tracks, not often paid attention to by historians, show him remaining on a high level, his sound not much changed save for the addition of full drums and some electric guitar. —*Richie Unterberger*

Lloyd Glenn

b. Nov. 21, 1909, San Antonio, TX, d. May 23, 1985, Los Angeles, CA
Arranger, Piano / Jump Blues, West Coast Blues, Piano Blues
As an integral behind-the-scenes fixture in the L.A. postwar blues scene, pianist/arranger/A&R man Lloyd Glenn had few equals. His rolling ivories anchored many of Lowell Fulson's best waxings for Swing Time and Checker, and he scored his own major hits on Swing Time with the imaginative instrumentals "Old Time Shuffle Blues" in 1950 and "Chica Boo" the next year. Glenn was already an experienced musician when he left the Lone Star state for sunny California in 1942. His early sessions there included backing T-Bone Walker at the 1947 Capitol date that produced the guitarist's immortal "Call It Stormy Monday." Glenn recorded for the first time under his own name the same year for Imperial with his band, the Joymakers, which included guitarist Gene Phillips, saxist Marshall Royal, and singer Geraldine Carter.

Massively constructed guitarist Tiny Webb introduced Glenn to Swing Time owner Jack Lauderdale in 1949, inaugurating a five-year stint as A&R man at the firm for Glenn. After Swing Time's demise, the pianist moved to Aladdin Records, issuing more catchy instrumentals for Eddie Mesner's firm through 1959. There was also an isolated session for Imperial in 1962 that produced "Twistville" and "Young Date." The pianist remained active into the '80s, often touring as Big Joe Turner's accompanist. —*Bill Dahl*

After Hours / 1957 / Oldie Blues ✦✦✦✦✦
A solid collection of instrumentals recorded in the mid-'70s. In and out of print. —*AMG*

Piano Styling / 1957 / Score ✦✦✦✦
Glenn's tasty piano ticklings were to the fore on his '50s sides for the Mesners' Aladdin logo. The dozen instrumentals on this LP (still not on CD) feature remakes of "Chica-Boo" and "Old Time Shuffle" and the engaging workouts "Tiddleywinks," "Glenn's Glide," "Nite-Flite," "Footloose," and "Southbound Special." —*Bill Dahl*

Honky Tonk Train / 1983 / Night Train ✦✦✦✦
In addition to waxing his own bouncy instrumentals during his late-'40s/early-'50s stay at Swing Time Records (an unissued take of "Old Time Shuffle," one of his own hits, graces this disc), pianist Lloyd Glenn also arranged and played behind several of the firm's veteran vocalists—explaining the presence of exceptional blues outings by Joe Pullum and Jesse Thomas. —*Bill Dahl*

● **Chica Boo** / 1988 / Night Train ✦✦✦✦✦
Quite a bit of duplication between this 18-song collection and Night Train's previous disc—but since this one contains both of his hits—"Old Time Shuffle" and "Chica Boo"—it wins hands down. Pullum and Thomas are back as guest vocalists on these 1947-1952

waxings. This is lightly swinging West Coast blues with an elegant, understated edge, Glenn's tasty approach to the 88s always in the pocket. —*Bill Dahl*

Lloyd Glenn / 198 / Swingtime ✦✦✦

1947–1950 / Mar. 5, 2002 / Classics ✦✦✦✦

Old Time Shuffle / Black & Blue ✦✦✦
European sessions from the late '70s. Swinging piano throughout, showing off Glenn's patented Texas-cum-West Coast lope to good advantage. —*Cub Koda*

Lillian Glinn

b. 1902, Dallas, TX
Vocals / Prewar Country Blues, Vaudeville Blues, Prewar Gospel Blues
country blues singer Lillian Glinn was born in the Dallas, TX, area circa 1902, and was discovered by fellow blueswoman Hattie Burleson while singing spirituals in a church. Burleson took Glinn under her wing, and Glinn became a successful vaudeville performer; she also signed a record deal with Columbia in 1927. Over the course of two years and six recording sessions, Glinn recorded 22 secular numbers which often matched her warm contralto voice with slow ballad tempos. However, the deeply religious Glinn soon returned to the life of the church, leaving her singing and performing career behind. —*Steve Huey*

● **Complete Recorded Works (1927–1929)** / Jun. 2, 1994 / Document ✦✦✦✦

Barry Goldberg

b. 1941, Chicago, IL
Vocals, Keyboards, Piano, Organ / Blues-Rock, Electric Chicago Blues
Barry Goldberg was a regular fixture in the white blues firmament of the mid-'60s that seemed to stretch from Chicago to New York. A keyboardist (organ seemed to be his specialty), Goldberg was an in-demand session man—he appears with Michael Bloomfield on a Mitch Ryder album, for instance—along with Al Kooper and his blues-playing contemporary from the original Butterfield band, Mark Naftalin. Goldberg was a member of Charlie Musselwhite's first band, contributing great piano and organ lines to the *Stand Back!* album (his work on "Cristo Redentor" is moody and introspective, with a strong jazz-inflected feel, while still retaining strong blues roots) and a handful of others throughout the decade. —*Cub Koda*

Blowing My Mind / 1966 / Collectables ✦✦✦

There's No Hole in My Soul / 1968 / One Way ✦✦✦✦

Two Jews Blues / 1969 / One Way ✦✦✦✦
This is one of those late-'60s collaborations where I expected the world to explode when I put it on, and felt disappointed when it didn't. However, when you get past looking at players in the band, and listen to the music, there are a number of wonderful cuts. Enough of them for me to replace the vinyl with the CD. "Blues for Barry And…" is Bloomfield at his best with a solid band behind him cranking out this slow blues you wish wouldn't end. Barry Goldberg has always played a solid organ, whether with Harvey Mandel, Charlie Musselwhite, or out on his own. This is his chance to be the leader of an all-star lineup. My regrets are that it is only 35 minutes, and most importantly I would have liked to put all the guitar players together for a cut or two; they never get to play off one another. —*Bob Gottlieb*

Streetman / 1970 / Buddah ✦✦✦✦

Barry Goldberg & Friends Recording Live / 1976 / Buddah ✦✦✦

● **Reunion/Two Jews Blues** / Mar. 3, 1994 / Unidisc ✦✦✦✦✦
Two of Barry Goldberg's best albums from the late '60s, *Reunion* and *Two Jews Blues*, are combined on this single disc. There's some very hot playing on these two albums, particularly from Mike Bloomfield on *Two Jews Blues*, but they sound a little dated and don't quite burn as hot as some blues-rock albums from the late '60s. Nevertheless, this does capture Goldberg's two best records, which makes it both a good summary of his peak and a good introduction to his sound. —*Stephen Thomas Erlewine*

Golden Echoes

f. 194?, Los Angeles, CA
Group / Traditional Gospel
One of the first gospel groups signed to the legendary Specialty label, the Los Angeles-based Golden Echoes were led by brothers William "Big Axe" and Wilmer "Little Axe" Broadnax, Houston natives who after relocating to the West Coast during the mid-'40s joined the ranks of the Southern Gospel Singers, an act led by onetime Soul Stirrers member A.L. Johnson. The group was primarily a weekends-only concern, however, and soon the Broadnax brothers' restlessness prompted them to form their own full-time vehicle, the Golden Echoes; a series of lineup changes followed as the decade drew to a close, and eventually William exited to settle in Atlanta, where he joined the Five Trumpets. At the time of the group's one and only Specialty session, recorded in Hollywood on April 5, 1949, their roster included co-leads Wilmer Broadnax and Paul Foster, tenor Eldridge Bostic, baritone Jimmy Copeland, and bass James Ricks, a longtime veteran of the gospel circuit whose career included tenures with the Birmingham Jubilees, the Famous Blue Jays and the Flying Clouds of Detroit. The session yielded the Golden Echoes' lone Specialty single, "When the Saints Go Marching In"; for reasons unknown, label chief Art Rupe dropped the group soon after, and despite a growing reputation on the live circuit they disbanded a few months later. While Foster went on to join the Soul Stirrers, Broadnax later signed on with the likes of the Spirit of Memphis, the Fairfield Four and the Five Blind Boys of Mississippi; during the mid-'60s, he also led a short-lived new group dubbed Little Ax and the Golden Echoes. —*Jason Ankeny*

● **Walk Around Heaven** / Mar. 13, 2000 / Amir ✦✦✦

Golden Gate Quartet

f. 1931, Berkeley, VA
Group / Spirituals, Traditional Gospel, Black Gospel
Pioneer Virginia gospel/pop quartet of the '30s and '40s. Calling their innovative approach to sacred hymns "jubilee" singing, the Golden Gate Quartet, propelled by Willie Johnson and William Langford, enjoyed massive acceptance far outside the church. Their smooth Mills Brothers-influenced harmonies made the Gates naturals for pop crossover success, and they began recording for Victor in 1937. National radio broadcasts and an appearance on John Hammond's 1938 "Spirituals to Swing" concert at Carnegie Hall made them coast-to-coast favorites. By 1941 the Gates were recording for Columbia minus Langford, and movie appearances were frequent: *Star Spangled Rhythm, Hollywood Canteen,* and *Hit Parade of 1943,* to name a few. Some experiments with R&B material didn't pan out during the late '40s, and Johnson defected to the Jubilaires in 1948. The group emigrated to France in 1959; led by veteran bass singer Orlando Wilson, the Golden Gate Quartet's vocal blend is as powerful as ever. —*Bill Dahl*

The Golden Gate Quartet / 1975 / Columbia ✦✦✦✦
Here are 20 of the best postwar Columbia 78s. —*Opal Louis Nations*

☆ **35 Historic Recordings** / 1983 / RCA ✦✦✦✦✦
These breathtaking sides from 1937-1939 are largely a cappella, with both gospel and pop music. The album also includes a landmark version of "Stormy Weather" that is at the root of doo wop. —*Hank Davis*

☆ **Swing Down, Chariot** / Jul. 2, 1991 / Columbia/Legacy ✦✦✦✦✦
The most influential "jubilee" quartet of the late '30s and '40s, in inspired and deftly syncopated performances, is an archetype. —*Mark A. Humphrey*

Gospel 1937–1941 / 1992 / Frémeaux & Associés ✦✦✦✦✦
Classic early sides by this group who changed the style of quartet. —*Opal Louis Nations*

★ **Travelin' Shoes** / Sep. 1992 / Bluebird/RCA ✦✦✦✦✦
Bluebird's *Travelin' Shoes* is a terrific collection that contains 25 tracks the Golden Gate Quartet recorded between 1937 and 1939. During those years, the group was at their peak, and their a cappella harmonies proved to be quite influential on successive generations of gospel singers, as they had enough foresight to add jazz and blues inflections to their harmonies. There's no better place to judge their greatness than this splendid collection. —*Leo Stanley*

Gospel Train / Apr. 26, 1994 / JSP ✦✦✦✦✦
First-known sides by this group who started out singing barbershop (1937-1939). —*Opal Louis Nations*

Meet Me at the Golden Gate / Aug. 1, 1996 / Collector's Edition ✦✦✦✦
Memorable Columbia and OKeh sides from the '40s when the group was at its peak. —*Opal Louis Nations*

Golden Years (1949–1952) / Oct. 29, 1996 / EPM Musique ✦✦✦✦✦
Gems taken from four important OKeh/Columbia sessions. —*Opal Louis Nations*

Kings of Gospel / Dec. 26, 1996 / PMF Music Factory ✦✦✦✦✦
Repertoire of Gates' golden hits and best-known songs. —*Opal Louis Nations*

Radio Transcriptions (1941–1944) / Mar. 18, 1997 / Document ✦✦✦✦
The Very Best of the Golden Gate Quartet / Apr. 8, 1997 / Blue Note ✦✦✦✦✦
The Very Best of the Golden Gate Quartet is a terrific collection of songs the group recorded in France for EMI Pathe between 1955 and 1969, including versions of "Shadrack" and "Oh Happy Day." Although these aren't the versions that made them stars, they are nevertheless quite good and offer a good sense of what the group is about. —*Thom Owens*

Complete Works in Chronological Order, Vol. 6: 1949–1952 / Jan. 25, 2000 / Document ✦✦✦✦

Golden Gate Quartet, Vol. 1: 1937–1938 / Sep. 7, 2000 / Document ✦✦✦✦
Golden Gate Quartet, Vol. 2: 1938–1939 / Sep. 7, 2000 / Document ✦✦✦✦
Golden Gate Quartet, Vol. 3: 1939 / Sep. 7, 2000 / Document ✦✦✦✦
Golden Gate Quartet, Vol. 5: 1945–1949 / Sep. 7, 2000 / Document ✦✦✦✦
Our Story: Best of the Golden Gate Quartet / Apr. 10, 2001 / Columbia ✦✦✦✦✦
Spirituals to Swing / Jazz Time ✦✦✦✦✦
An inspired effort, recorded between 1955 and 1969. —*Kip Lornell*

The Golden Gate Quartet / Carrere ✦✦✦
Carrere's *Golden Gate Quartet* is an odd record from a latter-day version of the classic gospel quartet. By this time, the original version of the group was long gone, but the new incarnation still sounded quite good. However, the choice of songs was strange. Half of the album consisted of classic gospel songs, and half was comprised of classic pop songs like "The Great Pretender," "Blue Suede Shoes" and "Only You." Granted, the group sounds quite good on those songs, but it would have been better if they had recorded an album devoted entirely to pop instead of doing it halfheartedly. As a result, the record is only fitfully entertaining, when it could have been nothing but fun. —*Leo Stanley*

Good Rockin' Charles (Charles Edwards)

b. Mar. 4, 1933, Pratts, AL, **d.** May 17, 1989, Chicago, IL
Harmonica / Electric Chicago Blues, Electric Harmonica Blues
Harpist Good Rockin' Charles is best-known for a solo he didn't play. Suffering from a bad case of studio fright, Charles chickened out of playing on guitarist Jimmy Rogers' 1956 Chess waxing of "Walking by Myself"—leaving the door wide-open for Big Walter Horton to blow a galvanic solo that rates among his very best. Charles' domestic solo discography consists of one nice album for Steve Wisner's short-lived Mr. Blues logo in 1975.

Inspired by both Sonny Boys and Little Walter, Charles Edwards began playing harp shortly after hitting Chicago in 1949. He played with a plethora of local luminaries—Johnny Young, Lee Jackson, Arthur Spires, Smokey Smothers—before joining Rogers' combo in 1955. Cobra Records also tried and failed to corral him for a session in 1957.

Bassist Hayes Ware was instrumental in finally convincing the elusive Good Rockin' into a studio for Mr. Blues, where he shook the walls with revivals of classics by both Sonny Boys, Rogers, and Jay McShann. Unfortunately, it would prove the extent of the mysterious harpist's recorded legacy. —*Bill Dahl*

● **Good Rockin' Charles** / 1976 / P-Vine Japan ✦✦✦✦
The elusive Chicago harpist's one and only full-length album, originally issued on Steve Wisner's short-lived Mr. Blues logo and later picked up by Rooster Blues and reissued on CD by P-Vine Japan in 2002. Cut in 1975, this set shows that Charles never left the '50s stylistically—backed by a nails-tough combo, he pays tribute to both Sonny Boys and his ex-boss Jimmy Rogers while betraying more than a hint of Little Walter influence. —*Bill Dahl*

Jay Gordon

b. Charlotte, NC
Guitar (Electric) / Modern Electric Blues, Blues-Rock
Electric blues guitarist Jay Gordon recorded a series of albums for Blue Ace that inspired comparisons to such legendary guitarists as Jimi Hendrix and Stevie Ray Vaughan. Beginning with *Blues Infested* (1994), Gordon won much praise from the blues community. Each successive album became increasingly successful—*Broadcasting the Blues Live* (1996), *Electric Redemption* (1998), and so on—and the guitarist soon found himself being compared to some of the most legendary guitarists to ever play electric blues. In 2000, Gordon collaborated with Phillip Walker on the *Jaywalkin* album for Blue Ace, yet another accomplishment for the celebrated guitarist. Furthermore, in addition to his guitar playing, Gordon also produces and sings on many of his own recordings. —*Jason Birchmeier*

Blues Infested / 1994 / Blue Ace ✦✦✦✦
This early effort by the electric blues guitarist/vocalist Jay Gordon is an intense affair with passionate solos and tight guitar playing. What is unusual about the set is that the eight selections are all quite concise (only one exceeds four minutes and 24 seconds) and the program is surprisingly brief. However Gordon (who dominates the music) makes every outburst count; he is ably supported by electric bassist Russ Greene and drummer Will Donovan. Highlights include "Voodoo Boogie," "Can't Shake That Feelin'," and "Boogie in the Wine." —*Scott Yanow*

Broadcasting the Blues Live / Jun. 1, 1996 / Blue Ace ✦✦✦
● **Electric Redemption** / Jun. 23, 1998 / Blue Ace ✦✦✦✦✦
This CD gives listeners a pretty strong overview of the music of Jay Gordon, a guitarist dedicated to the blues whose wide range of intense sounds at times recalls Jimi Hendrix and Stevie Ray Vaughan. The music on this disc is divided into two parts. Drippin' Blues has 11 selections taken from a variety of sources (including a television performance), and is highlighted by "Message to Collins" (dedicated to the late Albert Collins), the swinging instrumental "Jaybird Stomp," the extended "Blacktop Alley," and "47 Beers." The second part, Savage Resurrection, is dedicated to Jimi Hendrix, Miles Davis, and John Coltrane, displaying Gordon's explosive guitar on three intense instrumentals and the title cut. Highly recommended to fans of modern electric blues. —*Scott Yanow*

Rings Around the Sun, Vol. 1 / Apr. 11, 2000 / Blue Ace ✦✦✦✦
On this best-of collection, Chicago blues guitarist/singer Jay Gordon is heard on four new performances (including "Amplifier Blues" and "Savage Resurrection"), a dozen songs taken from previous albums, and a two-and-a-half-minute "Preview of Tracks," which has brief excerpts from the other selections. With such numbers as "Message to Collins," "Lucky 13," "Voodoo Boogie," and "Blues Infested," this CD is a perfect introduction to the fiery music of Jay Gordon. —*Scott Yanow*

Jaywalkin / Jun. 26, 2000 / Blue Ace ✦✦✦✦
This CD is a summit meeting between the fiery guitarist/singer Jay Gordon and veteran Phillip Walker. Walker's guitar playing and vocalizing, though a bit more traditional, holds its own with Gordon, who is properly respectful but far from restrained. They perform eight Gordon originals, and their collaboration "Jaywalkin" with either Jimmy Thomas or Russ Greene on bass and piano, and Butch Azevedo or Joey E. Covington on drums. The lyrics are often witty, the interplay between the guitarists display their contrasting styles, and high points include "Whiskey, Women & Fast Cars," "You Should Have Married a Priest," and "Strings Talkin'." —*Scott Yanow*

Extremely Dangerous Blues / 2002 / Dixiefrog ✦✦✦
A fiery Chicago blues guitarist whose style mixes together Jimi Hendrix, Johnny Winter, Albert Collins, Muddy Waters, and others with his own musical personality, Jay Gordon has recorded five explosive CDs for the Blue Ace label. *Extremely Dangerous Blues* is a "best-of" set of previously released material put together for the European market. The dozen songs are mostly concise (all but two are under five minutes) and feature some of Gordon's strongest selections, including "Boogie in the Wine," "Lucky 13," "Message to Collins," "Savage Resurrection" (dedicated to Hendrix), and "Voodoo Boogie." Veteran guitarist/singer Phillip Walker makes a welcome guest appearance on "Jaywalkin." Gordon's expressive vocals are excellent (he is quite good on "Can't Shake This Feelin'"), as is the work of his backup bands (electric bassist Russ Greene and either Will Donovan, Rick Lambert, or Butch Azevedo on drums), but it is the leader's intense yet surprisingly versatile guitar playing that is most remarkable. Although these performances are mostly fairly brief, there is no shortage of inventive ideas within the context of rockish Chicago blues, or any loss of passion. —*Scott Yanow*

Rosco Gordon

b. 1934, Memphis, TN, **d.** Jul. 11, 2002, New York, NY [Rego Park, Queens]

Vocals, Piano / R&B, Soul

Rosco Gordon was best known for being one of the progenitors of a slightly shambolic, loping style of piano shuffle called "Rosco's Rhythm." The basic elements of this sound were further developed after Jamaican musicians got a hold of 45s Gordon recorded in the early '50s—which were not available to Jamaicans until 1959—and created ska, which took its name for the sound of this particular shuffle as it sounded being played on an electric guitar (ska-ska-ska).

No less an authority than Chris Blackwell—he was the founder/president of Island Records who produced Bob Marley, the Wailers, and Peter Tosh, to name a few—has cited Gordon's importance to reggae and ska music and championed the sound he helped create.

Gordon had originally been a member of the famed Beale Streeters, a Memphis, TN-based group that also featured the considerable talents of Johnny Ace, B.B. King, and Bobby "Blue" Bland, in the late '40s. They were scouted by none other than Ike Turner for Modern Records, who recorded the Beale Streeters' first single in 1951.

Gordon was soon recording sides for Sam Phillips and his Sun Records label. Phillips later sold the master of Gordon's own "Bootin'" to two competing labels, Chess and RPM, both of whom released it as a single. This "mix-up" did not, however, prevent the song from hitting number one on the R&B chart in 1952.

The follow-up to "Bootin'," called "No More Doggin'," was the first song to feature the now-familiar shuffle rhythm of Gordon's design, with a strong accent on the off-beat that repeated the oft-monotonous guitar phrasing. Though Gordon had recorded the song in the living room of a friend's home, in fact, the sound was fully developed and unique for its time. On July 11, 2002, Gordon died of a heart attack at his home in Queens, New York. He was 74. *—Bryan Thomas*

The Best of Rosco Gordon, Vol. 1 / Nov. 1980 / Ace ♦♦♦
These primitive early-'50s Memphis-recorded tracks were originally issued on the RPM label. *—Hank Davis*

Keep on Doggin' / 1982 / Mr. R&B ♦♦♦
A scholarly compilation of Roscoe's singles from his early-'50s R&B to mid-'60s soul. *—Hank Davis*

No More Doggin' / 1983 / Charly ♦♦♦
These are Roscoe's early-'60s sides for the Vee-Jay label. *—Hank Davis*

Let's Get High / Jun. 1990 / Charly ♦♦♦♦♦
Sensational Memphis R&B by this Sun alumnus, these are the '50s recordings of this rhythmic piano-led combo. *—Hank Davis*

● **Just a Little Bit** / Oct. 1993 / Vee-Jay ♦♦♦♦♦
Gordon's late-'50s and early-'60s Vee-Jay sessions have been treasured collector's items for years, and this new disc features 16 selections (half previously unissued in America). The revival of "No More Doggin'" was even closer to ska than the original, with Gordon smoothly angling in on the offbeat. Gordon remains a hero in Jamaica for his influence on ska and bluebeat; it's great to have these recordings available once more. *—Ron Wynn*

Bootin': The Best of the RPM Years / Nov. 24, 1998 / Ace ♦♦♦♦

Memphis, Tennessee / 2000 / Stony Plain ♦♦♦
Here is one of the pioneers of the Memphis R&B movement. This man was a huge influence in Jamaica for the starting of the ska rhythms; he had a loping and relaxed style that fit right into the early propensities of early ska artists. He hasn't been popular in the states since "Just a Little Bit," his early-'60s hit, stormed the R&B charts. At this time he married and devoted himself to his wife and growing family. It was only her untimely demise from bone cancer and the growing up of his children that allowed him to get back on the road again (mostly in Europe and Canada). But here he is back in full voice, with the help of Duke Robillard and his band to reignite the flames that have lain dormant all these years. He either wrote or co-wrote all but one of the songs here, showing he has not sat idly by during his hiatus from recording. This is an exceptionally fine effort and kudos must go to Stony Plain for taking the time to make this available for our pleasure. *—Bob Gottlieb*

The Very Best of Rosco Gordon: Just a Little Bit / Jan. 30, 2001 / Collectables ♦♦♦♦♦

Sax Gordon (Gordon Beadle)

b. 1965, Detroit, MI

Saxophone / Jump Blues, Soul-Jazz, Jazz Blues

Practicing the honking, jump blues style of jazz, saxophonist Sax Gordon appeared alongside numerous well-known artists and even recorded albums of his own. Born Gordon Beadle, the Boston-based musician performed on albums by such artists as Champion Jack Dupree, Luther "Guitar Jr" Johnson, Duke Robillard, and many more during the '90s. He began recording solo albums with *Have Horn Will Travel*, which Bullseye Blues released in 1998, followed by a second album, *You Knock Me Out*, in 2000. On his solo releases, Gordon leads his bandmates through a variety of styles that variably fall somewhere between jazz and blues. He writes many of his own songs and carefully selects a few covers as well for his albums. In 2001 and again in 2002, he received W.C. Handy Award nominations. *—Jason Birchmeier*

● **Have Horn Will Travel** / Feb. 10, 1998 / Bullseye Blues ♦♦♦♦
Duke Robillard's sax player, Gordon Beadle, aka Sax Gordon, comes to the plate with his debut album and delivers a disc with some true horn-honking wallop to it. Produced by Robillard and with essentially him and his band backing Gordon for this session, this is a fun album that's thoroughly grounded in older styles. But at the same time, it's also informed with a strong sense of humor, and the performances have a contemporary sensibility, especially evident on the sing-talk vocal efforts "You Said She Wouldn't," "But Officer" and the title track. Gordon's tenor sax tone is as big as you could possibly ask for, invested with all the honking style hallmarks of greats like Gene Ammons, King Curtis, Joe Houston, and Junior Walker. Gordon's originals are every bit as strong as any of the obscure jazz classics he chooses to interpret on this debut outing, making the biggest impression here. Another retro sax album? Guess again. *—Cub Koda*

You Knock Me Out / Jan. 1, 2000 / Bullseye Blues ♦♦♦
When Charlie Parker and other beboppers were demonstrating how complex and intellectual saxophone playing could be, the honkers favored a much more accessible, groove-oriented approach. Gordon "Sax Gordon" Beadle's funky, grits-and-gravy style of tenor sax playing is right out of the honker school, and his very extroverted *You Knock Me Out* is a throwback to the days when Willis Jackson, Big Jay McNeely, Arnett Cobb, Doc Sausage, and others weren't afraid to play the you-know-what out of their horns. Indeed, hard-blowing instrumentals like "Crawling Home," "Lorenzo Leaps In," and "Speed Rack" (all of them Gordon originals) sound like they could have been written in the late '40s or early '50s. Red Tyler's "Lonely for You," with its dusky, evocative, "Harlem Nocturne"-ish mood, conjures up thoughts of an era of burlesque shows, Mike Hammer novels, and film-noir thrillers starring Veronica Lake and Alan Ladd. Though Gordon loves the honker era, the saxman/singer occasionally detours into '60s soul. "90 MPH" (one of the tunes he sings on), for instance, and "BY-YA" wouldn't have been out of place on a Stax release in the '60s; the latter, in fact, has a Booker T-ish appeal thanks to Tom West's organ playing. No, this jazz/R&B/blues effort isn't innovative, and yes, Gordon plays his share of clichés, but he plays them with a lot of heart and passion, making *You Know Me Out* quite rewarding if you're a lover of the tenor saxophone's honker school. *—Alex Henderson*

Gov't Mule

f. 1994

Group / Southern Rock, Hard Rock, Blues-Rock

The leaders of Gov't Mule, Warren Haynes and Allen Woody, should be well-known to Allman Brothers fans for their stint with Southern rock's most famous native sons. In 1989, Haynes became the second replacement for Duane Allman, providing a good foil for Gregg Allman and Dickey Betts on guitar and vocals; Woody filled out the Allman sound on bass. Five years after their debut, the duo joined drummer Matt Abts in the side project Gov't Mule, a band in which the Allman Brothers' influence is apparent but complicated with the psychedelic, bluesy power-trio feel of Cream. Gov't Mule debuted in 1995 with a self-titled album on Capricorn Records, followed by the stellar concert date *Live at Roseland Ballroom*. The studio follow-up *Dose* appeared in early 1998; another concert set, *Live ... With a Little Help from Our Friends*, followed a year later, with the complete show later appearing as a four-disc limited edition set. A new studio effort, *Life Before Insanity*, appeared in early 2000. A vital member of the band was lost, however, on August 26, 2000, when Allen Woody was found dead in a hotel room in New York City. The band had been preparing to record its next album, and after a time, Gov't Mule finally decided to carry on with the project, this time with guest bassists ranging from Flea to Bootsy Collins. The two-volume *Deep End* series for ATO Records resulted. Phish bassist Mike Gordon also got involved in the project, filming the recording of the albums for a planned documentary. In mid-September 2001, the group hit the road for a six-week tour in support of *Deep End, Vol. 1*; Oteil Burbridge filled in as bassist for most of the dates. *—John Bush*

● **Gov't Mule** / Oct. 1995 / Relativity ♦♦♦♦♦
Gov't Mule's self-titled debut is a scorching set of heavy blues-rockers. Although they have some difficulty coming up with memorable original material, the band is loose, funky, gritty, and real. They have enough burning licks to make the record a worthwhile listen for guitar fanatics. *—David Jehnzen*

Live at Roseland Ballroom / Oct. 22, 1996 / Foundation ♦♦♦♦
The consummate power trio of the '90s, Gov't Mule drew on influences from Mountain and Cream to the Jimi Hendrix Experience. This, the band's second album, was recorded live in concert with no overdubs, and it rocks hard. Warren Haynes and Allen Woody pull their experiences from several years with the Allman Brothers Band into the mix and turn out one impressive record. Highlights include the rock radio track "Mule" and "Kind of Bird," co-written by Dickey Betts of the Allmans, a song that was still in the Allmans' set list at the end of the '90s. *—Michael B. Smith*

Dose / Feb. 24, 1998 / Capricorn ♦♦♦♦
Gov't Mule's sound is a throwback to the '70s heyday of Southern rock, and their style is peppered with references to the best of the Allmans, with a liberal dose of early ZZ Top thrown in for good measure. Their second album shows no signs of a sophomore slump, featuring playing and songwriting every bit as strong as their debut outing. Warren Haynes' guitar work, if anything, is even more adventurous this time around, particularly effective on the opener "Blind Man in the Dark," "Thelonius Beck," and "Birth of the Mule." *—Cub Koda*

Live . . . With a Little Help from Our Friends / Mar. 23, 1999 / Capricorn ♦♦♦
Gov't Mule is almost single-handedly bringing back the spirit of the '60s and '70s power trios, the same kind of rock & roll magic that made Jimi Hendrix and Cream such musical icons. With this two-CD set, the Mule once again broke the rules by recording both their second release and their fourth record live in concert. But hey, that was OK for Warren Haynes, Matt Abts, and Allen Woody. This show was recorded on New Year's Eve, 1998, at the Roxy in Atlanta, GA, and documents the band in peak form, from the power-charged vocals and lead guitar of Warren Haynes to Abts' freight-train drumming and Woody's thunder-driven bass. On any given night, Gov't Mule alone would rock your socks off, but on this magical evening, the band was joined by some real brothers of the road—Allman Brothers, Rolling Stones, Eric Clapton, etc. sideman Chuck Leavell was there, along with Parliment's Bernie Worrell, former Black Crowes guitarist Marc Ford, Aquarium Rescue Unit's Jimmy Herring, Randall Bramblett, newly

appointed Allman Brothers bandmember Derek Trucks, and Yonrico Scott, the drummer from the Derek Trucks Band. Talk about a stage full of talent. The set kicks off with a pair of Mule originals, "Thorazine Shuffle" and "Dolhineus," before counting down the New Year clock and launching into an unexpected, but amazing, rendition of Black Sabbath's "War Pigs." Next comes a guitar-rocking take on Steve Marriott's "30 Days in the Hole" followed by Paul Rogers' "Mr. Big," featuring Marc Ford on guitar, followed by the blues-laced "Look Over Yonder," with some ultra-fine piano work from Leavell. Haynes and the boys keep up the momentum by bringing out Worrell and Trucks, in addition to Leavell, to perform the Haynes-penned Allman Brothers favorite, "Soulshine." Disc one closes with a hard-rocking "Mule," featuring Worrell again on organ, and incorporating a segment of Van Morrison's "I've Been Working." Dave Mason's "Sad and Deep as You" is given the Mule treatment to begin disc two, with Leavell's keyboards and Bramblett's sax enhancing the sound just that much more, and Herring and Worrell sit in on Haynes' "Devil Likes It Slow." Next comes yet another surprise for 1999, a dramatic reading of Neil Young's "Cortez the Killer," leading up to the closing all-star jam of "Afro Blue." "Live" clocks in at about two and a half hours, so there's no doubt you are getting much more bang for your buck, but it's not the quantity of the music that is important here, it's the quality, and believe you me, friends, you won't find more quality rock & roll and blues anywhere. [*Live with a Little Help from Our Friends* was also released as a limited-edition four-disc set, including video footage.] *—Michael B. Smith*

Life Before Insanity / Feb. 15, 2000 / Polygram ♦♦♦♦

Hot on the heels of the previous summer's collector's edition re-release of *Live... With a Little Help from Our Friends*—which chronicled the band's unprecedented New Year's Eve 1998 performance in Atlanta, GA, in a two-disc set released in March 1999, only to be reissued in its full-length, uncut four-disc glory later that year—the Mule recorded what by all accounts seemed to be their most creative and intelligent studio album to date. Produced by Michael Barbiero (Blues Traveler, Guns n' Roses), *Life Before Insanity* includes several songs that fans had been hearing in concert for well over a year, including the haunting title track and "Wandering Child," a powerful tune that had opened many Gov't Mule shows with its distinctive bassline, oddball time signature, and powerful dynamics. "No Need to Suffer" is another Warren Haynes-penned gem. It was a regular on the Mule set list for a while, along with "Lay Your Burden Down," which sounds quite a bit different here than it did live. Both versions are great, but on the CD, Haynes shares vocals with the plenary Ben Harper, making this one a real treat. Other special guests on the album are former Allman Brothers bandmate Johnny Neel, who plays the keyboards with bucket loads of soul and finesse, and Hook Herrera, a master of the harmonica. Both "Tastes Like Wine" and "In My Life" (a Haynes original, not the Lennon-McCartney song) are highly effective ballads, and "Fallen Down" blends influences from early Traffic with Mule originality to create a song that is destined for radio, filled with magnetic hook lines such as "Amazing grace is such a lonely place to heroes like you and me." The first single from the album was "Bad Little Doggie," a rocker heavily reminiscent of early ZZ Top. All 11 of the tracks are good. Actually, there are 12 if you include the "hidden" track, "If I Had Possession Over Judgement Day," a blues-rocker on which Haynes sings through some sort of megaphone-sounding device. *—Michael B. Smith*

The Deep End, Vol. 1 / Oct. 23, 2001 / ATO ♦♦♦♦♦

With the death of bassist Allen Woody, the surviving members of Gov't Mule faced that familiar question of how to carry on. Their answer is this sprawling two-disc set, on which a cavalcade of bassists and other visitors fly through the Mule tracks, each fitting into the groove in his own way. Drummer Matt Abts is especially adept at accommodating these guests, shifting from a medium tempo plod behind the clean-picked lines and world-weary vocals of Jack Bruce on "Fool's Moon" to a four-beat slam-out, reminiscent of "Dance to the Music," to accommodate former Sly Stone side monster Larry Graham during "Life on the Outside." And on "Same Price" he hammers fills behind Who alumnus John Entwistle with an energy that recalls Kenny Jones, if not quite Keith Moon, while Warren Haynes approximates Pete Townshend's harmony-driven style. With the band's rugged sound providing common reference, the style of each bassist proves easy to discern. Those who play inside the groove make their presence known through stealthy insinuation, like Flea on a catlike prowl through "Down and Out in New York City." On "Tear Me Down," Bootsy Collins follows a different tack, by flitting against the band's heavy tread with nimble lines that dance in and out of wah-wah effects, thumb-slap funk, and sly interactions with former P-Funk colleague Bernie Worrell's Minimoog. Allen Woody himself makes a posthumous appearance, on a previously unreleased cover of Grand Funk Railroad's "Sin's a Good Man's Brother." Here, the band stretches into a comfortable, loose, Hendrix-like feel, as all three members jam with intuitive interaction and raw passion; no other performance here feels quite so natural. Disc two features four live tracks, three of them marked by impeccable contributions from keyboard journeyman Chuck Leavell, including some classic duo improvising with Phish's Page McConnell before the beat kicks in on "Jesus Just Left Chicago." The last, "Soulshine," is a spirited solo guitar and vocal benediction by Haynes, not only a farewell of sorts for Woody, but a promise that the band's story is far from over. *—Robert L. Doerschuk*

Jon Dee Graham

Guitar, Lap Steel Guitar, Vocals / Roots Rock, Americana

Best known for his stint as a member of the acclaimed '80s roots-rock band the True Believers, singer/guitarist Jon Dee Graham was also a longtime fixture of the renowned Austin, TX music scene. Raised on a ranch located near the Texas-Mexico border, he picked up the guitar at age 12, years later dropping out of law school at the University of Texas to join the Austin punk band the Skunks. The group went on to open for the likes of the Clash and the Ramones, but in 1979 Graham—frustrated by his minimal input into their creative direction—left the Skunks to back blues singer Lou Ann Barton, followed during the early '80s as leader of the new wave units Five Spot and the Lift. He joined the True Believers in 1984, and although the group quickly emerged as a major critical favorite they were dropped by EMI in the wake of their self-titled 1986 debut, disbanding soon after.

Although Graham's gifts as a composer blossomed during his stint in the True Believers, he chose not to pursue a solo career in the wake of the band's collapse, instead relocating from Austin to Los Angeles and collaborating with X frontman John Doe on his solo debut *Meet John Doe*. Subsequently working with everyone from Michelle Shocked to Patty Smyth, Graham earned a reputation as a much sought-after sideman and writer before leaving the West Coast in 1995 to tour Europe with blues-rocker Calvin Russell. Upon returning to Austin the next year, he was by now so disenchanted with the music industry that he accepted a construction job; singer Kelly Willis ultimately lured Graham back to performing, however, and in 1997 he also began work on his long-awaited solo debut *Escape from Monster Island*. *Summerland* followed in 1999. *—Jason Ankeny*

Escape from Monster Island / Jun. 10, 1997 / Freedom ♦♦♦♦

Jon Dee Graham has a distinct, gruff voice delivering country/folk visions of undeniable vision and effect. This eloquent troubadour belies a Texas punk background as guitarists for the Skunks and then True Believers. Following this, stint in L.A. led Graham to work with members of X, Michelle Shocked, Simon Bonney and more. Distilling these varied experiences, Graham suggests "A dog may bark out in the night/The sound of the clock by the bed marking time/A door may slam, a dish may beak/I don't give a damn, some songs I can take." Graham has many sounds—from Texas blues to noncommercial rock—giving back a forlorn and abandoned beauty. The songbook on this stark album is direct, human and replete in effective metaphor. A variety of guitars (dobro, acoustic, electric and ghost steel) are complemented by piano and B-3 organ on this release. *—Thomas Schulte*

● **Summerland** / Mar. 23, 1999 / New West ♦♦♦♦

Former member of Austin cult band, True Believers, Graham's second album of gentle Americana features guest appearances by Patty Griffin on the minimalist "Look Up" and Bruce Hughes (ex-Poi Dog Pondering, Ugly Americans) on the darker, rockist "Black Box." Graham brings his unique, throaty voice to *Summerland*, which has everything from the gentlest melody ("Butterfly Wing") to intricate, instrumental fretwork ("Number 3") and even a spike of Latino music ("At the Dance"), all set to a beat provided by his crack band of Austin musicians. *—Denise Sullivan*

Hooray for the Moon / Jan. 15, 2002 / New West ♦♦♦

Austin-based roots rock singer/songwriter Jon Dee Graham continues his explorations of gritty Southwestern characters and love long gone on his album *Hooray for the Moon*. Assisted by guitarist Mike Hardwick, bassist Mark Andes, and legendary drummer Jim Keltner, Graham's throaty growl effectively recounts dark stories of busted desperadoes almost like a Texan Tom Waits. The similarity is most evident on Waits' "Way Down in the Hole," but carries through the disturbing "Laredo (Small Dark Something)" and the sweetly eerie "Restraining Order Song." The whole album isn't all creepy, as the stumbling Mexican love song "Volver" demonstrates, and the album's closer, "Tamale House #1," recounts an optimistic trip to a breakfast diner. Guests on the album include Mike Campbell (of the Heartbreakers), Davey Faragher (Camper Van Beethoven, Cracker, John Hiatt), and Austin Tejano favorite Little Joe, making for a full, well-rounded sound and carrying Graham's message well. *—Zac Johnson*

Porter Grainger

Piano / Vaudeville, Piano Blues, Songster

Very little is known about pianist Porter Grainger despite the fact that he appeared on many records in the '20s, mostly backing blues and vaudeville singers. Not considered that great a pianist, Grainger's main fame during his lifetime was as a composer for musical shows. He was playing music professionally at least as early as 1916 and in the '20s wrote for several shows. Grainger was Bessie Smith's accompanist in the 1928 production *Mississippi Days* and recorded with her in addition to Gladys Bryant, Ethel Finnie, Dolly Ross, Clint Jones, Ada Brown, Buddy Christian's Four Cry-Babies, and the Harmony Hounds, among others. Grainger's own two sessions as a leader found him backing either the Three Jazz Songsters or the Jubilee Singers, so there is precious little of him on record. After the close of the '20s, Porter Grainger slipped permanently into obscurity; even his birth and death dates are not known. A 1996 RST CD has many of Grainger's main recordings. *—Scott Yanow*

● **1923–1929** / 1995 / RST ♦♦

Porter Grainger was an obscure pianist from the '20s whose biggest claim to fame was that at one point he accompanied Bessie Smith. This CD from the Austrian RST label reissues nearly every recording that he ever appeared on, but unfortunately Grainger does not take a full solo on any of them. He backs a variety of mostly indifferent blues singers (Gladys Bryant, Ethel Finnie, Dolly Ross, the yodelling Clint Jones, and Ada Brown) and is buried behind such vocal groups as the Harmony Hounds, the Jubilee Singers, the Three Jazz Songsters, and the Four Cry-Babies. In general, the music is pretty mediocre and Porter Grainger's role is fairly minor, making this a well-packaged but ultimately rather frivolous CD. *—Scott Yanow*

Blind Roosevelt Graves

Vocals, Guitar / Prewar Gospel Blues, Prewar Country Blues

b. Rose Hill, MS

Blind Roosevelt Graves was a Mississippi guitarist and singer who mixed secular and sacred material and cut some entertaining, celebratory party tunes as well as reverential spirituals in the '20s and '30s. He played with pianists Will Ezell and Cooney Vaughn, and clarinetist Baby Jay. Graves was also a member of the Mississippi Jook Band, along with his brother—singer and tambourine player Uaroy Graves—and Vaughn.

Very few biographical details of Blind Roosevelt Graves' life are known. He and his brother Uaroy began playing juke joints in the Mississippi Delta in the early '20s. In 1929, the two brothers cut a number of sides for the Paramount and American Record Companies, which all appeared under Blind Roosevelt's name. They would continue to record until 1936. In the mid-'30s, the pair formed the Mississippi Jook Band with pianist Cooney Vaughn. The band recorded for the American Record Company in the mid- and late '30s.

After leaving behind these handful of recordings, Graves disappeared in the early '40s. It is not known where he settled, nor is his death date known. *—Ron Wynn & Stephen Thomas Erlewine*

- **Complete Recorded Works (1929–1936)** / 1929-1936 / Document ✦✦✦✦✦

The Document collection *Complete Recorded Works (1929-1936)* includes all 21 sides recorded by Blind Roosevelt Graves as a solo act, before he formed the Mississippi Jook Band in 1936. Many classic performances are featured, including "I Shall Not Be Moved," "Telephone to Glory," "Take Your Burden to the Lord," and "Guitar Boogie," most of them performed with help from Graves' brother, Uaroy. And since this is the only compilation available covering Graves, interested parties will be able to overlook the long running time and poor fidelity to own so much good music. *—Thom Owens*

Henry Gray

b. Jan. 19, 1925, Kenner, LA

Vocals, Arranger, Piano / Piano Blues, Electric Chicago Blues

Henry Gray was among the Chicago blues piano elite during the '50s. Unlike most of his contemporaries there, he was from Louisiana rather than Mississippi—and since 1968, he's been living there once again, a stalwart on the swamp blues circuit.

Gray rolled into Chicago in 1946 after fighting for his country during World War II in the Philippines. The formidable Big Maceo Merriweather was a primary influence on Gray's two-fisted playing. He procured steady gigs with Little Hudson's Red Devil Trio and guitarist Morris Pejoe before moving into extensive work as a session musician behind Jimmy Reed, Little Walter, Bo Diddley, Jimmy Rogers, Billy Boy Arnold, and Pejoe. In 1956, he joined the combo of the great Howlin' Wolf, digging in for a dozen-year run.

The pianist retreated to his home base outside Baton Rouge after leaving Wolf's employ. In 1988, he returned to Chicago long enough to cut his debut domestic album, *Lucky Man*, for Blind Pig Records. Guitarist Steve Freund produced and played on the set, an alluring combination of Windy City blues and bayou boogie. *—Bill Dahl*

- **Lucky Man** / 1988 / Blind Pig ✦✦✦✦

Renowned as a piano-rippling sideman on the '50s Chicago scene, Henry Gray returned to his native Louisiana in 1968 before anyone recorded him too prolifically as a leader. This album at least partially makes up for the oversight; backed by a solid Chicago combo, Gray alternates his own stuff with classics by Big Maceo Merriweather, Little Walter, and Jimmy Reed, his ruminative voice and rumbling ivories prowess nicely spotlighted. *—Bill Dahl*

Louisiana Swamp Blues, Vol. 2 / 1990 / Wolf ✦✦✦

Don't Start That Stuff / May 2, 2000 / Last Call ✦✦✦

Plays Chicago Blues / Feb. 27, 2001 / HMG ✦✦

Gray's a competent bluesman, if not a very inventive one. Because he's done session time with Bo Diddley and Howlin' Wolf, among others, this tribute to Southside Chicago blues rings of authenticity. And because he's been around, his voice infuses these songs with just enough grime and grit. But his backing band here is mediocre, and there's no way around the fact that most of the songs have been done better many times before. *—Michael Gallucci*

Cal Green

b. Jun. 22, 1937, Dayton, TX

Guitar / Modern Electric Blues

Few blues guitarists can boast the varied resumé of Texas native Cal Green. From blues to doo wop to jazz, Green has played 'em all—and done each idiom proud in the process.

Green's idol as a teenager was Lone Star wonder Clarence "Gatemouth" Brown. So pervasive was Gate's sway that Green and his ninth-grade pal Roy Gaines used to stage mock guitar battles imitating their idols (Gaines was a T-Bone Walker disciple) at various Houston bars. Cal didn't have to leave the house to find worthy competition; his older brother Clarence was also an accomplished picker who cut a load of killer instrumentals (notably 1962's "Red Light") for small Lone Star diskeries.

Cal Green played on RPM Records releases by Quinton Kimble and pianist Connie McBooker, but his main claim to fame is as the guitarist for Hank Ballard & the Midnighters, who roared through Houston in 1954 looking to replace their just-drafted axeman Arthur Porter, scooped up teenaged Green, and went on their way.

Green received plenty of solo space during his Midnighters stint. His ringing guitar provided a sturdy hook for the group's rocker "Don't Change Your Pretty Ways" and figured prominently on "Tore Up Over You" (later revived in blistering fashion by rockabilly giant Sleepy LaBeef) and "Open Up the Back Door." The Midnighters' label, Cincinnati-based Federal Records, thought enough of Green's slashing Texas licks to cut a couple of 45s on him in 1958: the double-sided instrumental "The Big Push"/"Green's Blues" and a pair of vocals, "I Can Hear My Baby Calling"/"The Search Is All Over."

A 1959 marijuana bust sent Green to a Texas slammer for 21 months, but he briefly rejoined the Midnighters in 1962. After that, jazz became Green's music of choice. He gigged with organist Jack McDuff and then singer Lou Rawls, eventually settling in L.A.

An acclaimed but tough-to-find 1988 album for Double Trouble, *White Pearl*, showed conclusively that Cal Green still knows his way around the blues on guitar. *—Bill Dahl*

- **White Pearl** / 1988 / Double Trouble ✦✦✦✦

After years as a sideman for Texas blues musicians and a session man for Los Angeleno jazz-pop musicians, guitarist Cal Green finally had the opportunity to record a solo album in 1988. Fortunately, the resulting record, *White Pearl*, is closer to his Texas roots than his jazz-pop aspirations. There are still some slick surfaces scattered throughout the album, but almost all of the record is nothing but the blues, giving Green chance to flaunt his chops. His voice isn't particularly strong, but his tasteful playing makes up for any vocal weakness and his stylish, sophisticated playing alone is reason for blues guitar nuts to check out this record. *—Thom Owens*

Clarence Green

b. 1937, Houston, TX, **d.** Mar. 13, 1997, Houston, TX

Vocals, Guitar / Modern Electric Texas Blues, Soul-Blues, Funk

Though not one of the best known of the modern Texas blues guitarists, Clarence Green is regarded by his peers as one of the best. Green (not to be confused with the late Clarence "Candy" Green, a Texas blues pianist) did session work for Duke Records in the '60s with Junior Parker, Bobby "Blue" Bland, and others, and performed with stars from Fats Domino to Johnny Nash. His own recordings have mostly been for small Houston labels. As Marcel Vos from Double Trouble Records wrote, "The Clarence Green of today plays a brand of Texas blues that is mixed with soul, jazz, and funk, not unlike the music of fellow Texans such as Roy Gaines, Cornell Dupree, and of course, his brother Cal Green." *—Jim O'Neal*

- **Green's Blues** / 1991 / Collectables ✦✦✦✦✦

A CD reissue of Texas blues, R&B, and pop, it's all very danceable and very enjoyable. The recordings are from 1958 to 1965. *—Niles J. Frantz*

Lillian "Lil" Green

b. Dec. 22, 1919, Mississippi, **d.** Apr. 14, 1954, Chicago, IL

Vocals / Acoustic Chicago Blues

Like so many Chicago blues artists, Lil Green first learned her craft in the church and country jukes down in Mississippi. After moving to Chicago in the '30s, she teamed up with Chicago mainstay Big Bill Broonzy and they worked the club circuit together. Her composition "Romance in the Dark" was a 1940 Bluebird hit and in 1941 she followed it with a best selling version of fellow Mississippi Joe McCoy's minor key blues novelty "Why Don't You Do Right?" By then she had outgrown Big Bill and the tavern scene and moved east to work as a rhythm and blues band vocalist.

For the next ten years she enjoyed a successful career touring theaters and clubs and recording for RCA, Aladdin and Atlantic, all major R&B labels. When she died in Chicago in 1954 she was only 35 years old.

Her experiences parallelled those of her male contemporaries and she made it bigger than most. From Southern jukes to Chicago clubs and on to the Apollo Theater, she participated in the major blues institutions of her time during the golden age of blues history. She was no stranger to trouble. According to R.H. Harris, the leader of the legendary gospel Soul Stirrers, she served time in prison because of her involvement in a juke-joint killing. He also remembered that she sang religious songs beautifully. Her former partner, Big Bill, remembered her in his autobiography as a deeply religious woman who neither smoked nor drank and as a warm-hearted friend.

Today, however, few people remember her or her fine work though they may be familiar with Peggy Lee's cover of her big hit, "Why Don't You Do Right?" We can only wonder why she has been overlooked while more obscure male guitar players with lesser output have received substantially more critical attention. Whatever the case, during her brief career, she proved to be one of the best blues vocalists of her time and her contemporary African-American audience appreciated her art. She deserves her place in history and today's listener would do well to listen to her music. *—Barry Lee Pearson*

- **1940–1942** / Mar. 6, 1995 / Blues Collection ✦✦✦✦

Blues Collection's *1940-1942* is an excellent collection featuring everything Lil Green cut during those two years. While Rosetta's *Chicago 1940-1947* is a more comprehensive collection, it's difficult to find and never been available on disc. Consequently, this disc is the best available compilation, even if it could have cast its net a little wider. *—Thom Owens*

Complete Recorded Works (1946–1951) / Oct. 14, 1998 / Document ✦✦✦✦

Peter Green (Peter Greenbaum)

b. Oct. 29, 1946, Bethnal Green, London

Vocals, Songwriter, Guitar / British Blues, Blues-Rock, Album Rock, Contemporary Blues, Modern Electric Blues

His career riddled by drug abuse and paranoia, Peter Green is still regarded by some fans as the greatest white blues guitarist ever, Eric Clapton notwithstanding. As he grew up in London's working-class East End, Green's early musical influences were Hank B. Marvin of the Shadows, Muddy Waters, B.B. King, Freddie King, and traditional Jewish music. Calling himself Peter Green by age 15, he played bass before being invited in 1966 by keyboardist Peter Bardens to play lead in the Peter B's, whose drummer was a lanky chap named Mick Fleetwood. The 19-year-old Green was with Bardens just three months before joining John Mayall's Bluesbreakers, whose rapidly shifting personnel included bassist John McVie and drummer Aynsley Dunbar. A keen fan of Clapton, Green badgered Mayall to give him a chance when the Bluesbreakers' guitarist split for an indefinite vacation in Greece. Green sounded great and, as Mayall recalls, was not amused when Clapton returned after a handful of gigs, and Green was out. When Clapton left the band for good six months later to form Cream, Mayall cajoled Green back. Fans were openly hostile because Green was not God, although they appreciated his replacement in time.

Producer Mike Vernon was aghast when the Bluesbreakers showed up without Clapton to record the album *A Hard Road* in late 1966, but was won over by Green's playing. On many tracks you'd be hard-pressed to tell it wasn't Clapton playing. With an eerie Green instrumental called "The Supernatural" he demonstrated the beginning of his trademark fluid, haunting style so reminiscent of B.B. King. When Green left Mayall in 1967, he took McVie and Fleetwood to found Peter Green's Fleetwood Mac. Jeremy Spencer and Danny Kirwan shortly afterward gave Fleetwood Mac an unusual three-guitar front line. Green was at his peak for the albums *Mr. Wonderful, English Rose, Then Play On*, and a live *Boston Tea Party* record. His instrumental "Albatross" was the band's first British number one single and "Black Magic Woman" was later a huge hit for Carlos Santana. But Green had been experimenting with acid and his behavior became increasingly irrational, especially after he disappeared for three days of rampant drug use in Munich. He became very religious, appearing on-stage wearing crucifixes and flowing robes. His bandmates resisted Green's suggestion to donate most of their money to charity, and he left in mid-1970 after writing a harrowing biographical tune called "The Green Manalishi."

After a bitter, rambling solo album called *The End of the Game*, Green saddened fans when he hung up his guitar except for helping the Mac complete a tour when Spencer suddenly joined the Children of God in Los Angeles and quit the band. Green's chaotic odyssey of almost a decade included rumors that he was a gravedigger, a bartender in Cornwall, a hospital orderly, and a member of an Israeli commune. When an accountant sent him an unwanted royalty check, Green confronted his tormentor with a gun, although it was unloaded. Green went to jail briefly before being transferred to an asylum. Green emerged in the late '70s and early '80s with albums *In the Skies*, *Little Dreamer*, *White Sky*, and *Kolors*, featuring at times Bardens, Robin Trower drummer Reg Isidore, and Fairport Convention drummer Dave Mattacks. He reprised the *Then Play On* Mac standard "Rattlesnake Shake" on Fleetwood's solo 1981 album *The Visitor*. British author Martin Celmins wrote Green's biography in 1995. Psychologically troubled, on medication, and hardly playing the guitar for most of the '90s, the reclusive Green resumed sporadic recording in the second half of the decade. He surfaces unexpectedly from time to time, most prominently Jan. 12, 1998 when Fleetwood Mac was inducted into the Rock and Roll Hall of Fame. In a rare, perfect moment, Green jammed with fellow inductee Santana on "Black Magic Woman." *—Mark Allan*

The End of the Game / 1970 / Reprise ✦

The directionless jamming on *The End of the Game*, the first solo release by Peter Green, is just what you'd expect from someone as psychologically messed up as he was when he cut it. He still plays wicked guitar, and sounds much like Jimi Hendrix in spots, but without Hendrix's vision. In fact, there's no coherent vision at all on this record. None of the musicians could have enjoyed themselves in spite of the opportunity to play with Green. It's drivel, from an immensely talented guitarist. Sad. *—Mark Allan*

In the Skies / 1979 / EMI ✦✦✦✦

After almost a decade of personal, drug-addled hell since his 1970 debut *The End of the Game*, Peter Green begins his comeback with *In the Skies*, and a title tune that sounds downright hopeful compared to where he left off. Although Green shares lead guitar work with Snowy White, it's clear from his fluid technique and haunting tone that he can still play. "A Fool No More" is the kind of slow blues Green excels at. Robin Trower drummer Reg Isidore gives way on one track to Godfrey MacLean, who played on *The End of the Game*. Green dips even farther back into his past, courtesy of keyboards by Peter Bardens, who gave him his first professional music job in 1966 in a band with Mick Fleetwood. Green's singing, never a particular strength, is not a weakness here. Five of the nine songs are instrumentals, continuing a longtime Green tradition. It's an unambitious but solid and welcome return by a guitarist who in his prime rivaled Eric Clapton. If that seems far-fetched, listen to *A Hard Road* by John Mayall's Bluebreakers or *Then Play On* by Fleetwood Mac. *—Mark Allan*

Little Dreamer / 1980 / PVK ✦✦✦

When Peter Green issued *Little Dreamer* in 1980, it was the second straight year he had released an album after a nine-year gap. Fairport Convention drummer Dave Mattacks must have wondered what he had gotten himself into because the opener, "Loser Two Times," is almost as close to disco as the Rolling Stones got with "Miss You." Green continues in a funky vein with "Mama Don't You Cry," as if shaking off the cobwebs and actually trying to pay attention to the current scene. He goes right back to his roots on the album's third tune with "Born Under a Bad Sign" and stays with blues derivatives the rest of the way. The album-ending title track sounds like a seven-minute version of the dreamy Green tune "Albatross," a hit for Fleetwood Mac in the '60s. Sounding more confident than on his comeback album, he seems more like the Greeny of old, although the move toward funk didn't really suit him. *—Mark Allan*

White Sky / 1981 / Headline ✦✦

After 1979 and 1980 albums by Peter Green were by turns bluesy and funky, *White Sky* from 1981 emphasizes rock. Maybe this is because all the songs are written by his older brother Mike Green, who sings on the title track. Mike's material doesn't quite work for Peter, who sounds ill at ease singing "Born on the Wild Side." And they could not in subsequent years get away with lyrics like "I'm your Indian lover and you're my squaw" from "Indian Lover." Drummer Reg Isidore of the Robin Trower band continues his collaboration with Green. After the preceding two albums were produced by Peter Vernon-Kell, Peter Green produced this one with Geoff Robinson. For the second straight album, he ends with a long, dreamy instrumental. *—Mark Allan*

Kolors / 1984 / Headline ✦✦✦

Kolors, a 1984 release by Peter Green, is not a bad record. Peter seems more at ease with material by his older brother Mike Green than on *White Sky* three years before. Dave Mattacks of Fairport Convention and Reg Isidore of the Robin Trower band share the drumming. Peter plays with more passion than in a long time. "Big Bad Feeling" showcases some great slide guitar and hearkens back to Peter's glory days with Fleetwood Mac. "Bandit," another in a long line of dreamy Green instrumentals, features pan pipes! But, unlike Peter's great Mac tunes, Mike's songs are sometimes pedestrian—after exploring "Indian Lover" on *White Sky*, he offers "Black Woman" here. "Black Magic Woman" it ain't. The album's effectiveness is damaged by a long, pointless "Funky Jam" to close the record, as if they came up short of material. *—Mark Allan*

● **Green and Guitar: The Best of Peter Green 1977–1981** / 1996 / Music Club ✦✦✦✦✦

This is a reasonably comprehensive collection, 78 minutes of music at mid-price, drawn from *In the Skies*, *Little Dreamer*, *Blue Guitar*, *White Sky*, and *Legend*, the first two albums having most of the best material here. Green's guitar playing is as impressive as ever, and his singing is nothing to ignore, a sweet, gently soulful rasp that recalls his one-time rival Eric Clapton at his best behind the microphone. There's just a bit of fall-off in quality between tracks like "Apostle" and "Little Dreamer," and later stuff like "Last Train from San Antone" when they're heard side by side. And a lot of this doesn't seem as strong today as it did in the late '70s, when Green was one of the last exponents of British blues still working in that genre and getting heard. But the sound is good, and the price is right. *—Bruce Eder*

Peter Green Splinter Group / 1997 / Snapper ✦✦✦

Peter Green tentatively returned to performing and recording in 1996, and *The Peter Green Splinter Group* is the first fruits of that comeback. The very fact that Green is performing again is encouraging, but the album sadly falls short of high expectations. A collection of blues covers, the record is filled with standards like "Going Down" and "Dark End of the Street," delivered professionally and without much flair. Green himself plays competently, but there are only a handful of times where his playing is unexpected and inspired. That might seem like a disappointment, but it's reassuring to have *any* flashes of brilliance, and they suggest that he could record a full-fledged return to form if given some time. *—Thom Owens*

The Robert Johnson Songbook / May 19, 1998 / Artisan ✦✦

The Robert Johnson Songbook is Peter Green's first recording made entirely of covers of the music written by the King of the Delta Blues. Unfortunately, though pleasant, *The Robert Johnson Songbook* lacks the warmth and soulfulness of its successor—*Hot Foot Powder*. *The Robert Johnson Songbook* features Green's Splinter Group, plus a guest appearance by Paul Rodgers. *—Tim Griggs*

A Night at the Marquee / Feb. 16, 1999 / Cleopatra ✦✦✦

A Night at the Marquee captures the Peter Green/Jeremy Spencer-era Mac at London's Marquee Club in the late '60s. The set list is split nearly evenly in half between originals from the group's debut, *Peter Green's Fleetwood Mac*, and classic blues covers. *—Steve Huey*

Soho Sessions / Mar. 23, 1999 / Snapper ✦✦✦

Recorded live at Ronnie Scott's Jazz Club in Soho, London, this two-disc set captures much of the essence of Green with the Splinter Group, his backing outfit for the last several years. And it's an interesting mix of material they come out with, from blues covers, a set of Robert Johnson material, as well as a trawl through the old Fleetwood Mac songbook—which might well be the big draw here. However, welcome as it is to have Green back as a regular performer, he's not the man he once was, and it's notable the guitar solos aren't defined—you can never tell who's playing, as colleague Nigel Watson has his tone and style down perfectly. In many ways, the most satisfying segment comes with six Robert Johnson tracks, which arrive without Green baggage or expectation, and really do satisfy, while the addition of the Street Angels, a gospel group, on vocals, strengthens the sound, which already has plenty of backbone. "The Supernatural," once one of Green's most incisive instrumentals, seems to have lost its bite—but that's true of all the old material. "Green Manalishi" was heavy as lead when it originally appeared, and now it's weightless, while the subtleties of "Albatross" have vanished, and "Black Magic Woman" seems oddly formless. This isn't to say it's a bad album by any means. It's perhaps unfortunate that Green has to deal with his own history. There are moments when the old genius shines, but they're few and far between. He's lived the blues, but his ability to transform that into music has mostly vanished. Satisfying if you take it on its own terms and don't expect the god-like playing that once defined Peter Green, the *Soho Session* is a British blues outfit with taste, chops, and occasional transcendent moments. *—Chris Nickson*

Destiny Road / Jul. 27, 1999 / Artisan ✦✦

Peter Green's return to recording hasn't been consistent, by any means, but there have been flashes of his old brilliance peeking through here and there, and he's never less than a good blues guitarist and singer, buoyed up by Nigel Watson and the other members of the Splinter Group, and with some interesting material to work with and search through. On *Destiny Road*, however, it all seems to have fallen apart. There's little in the performances—whether they're singing or playing—to make you think this is a man even halfway stumbling through a comeback, and much of the material is lackluster at best: Steve Winwood's "There's a River" doesn't approach the blues in any shape or form, and in these hands it has all the attraction of a lifeless mass. But there's no energy anywhere here, no sense of purpose or drive. In short, it's the album to make you wonder if Green's lost it all again, and to question the value of his coming back at all. This shouldn't have been released at all; it does neither the legend nor the man any justice. *—Chris Nickson*

Hot Foot Powder / May 2, 2000 / Artisan ✦✦✦

Hot Foot Powder is Peter Green's second album made up entirely of covers of the music by the legendary Delta bluesman Robert Johnson. In fact, with this album and its predecessor, *The Robert Johnson Songbook*, Green has recorded every song that Robert Johnson is known to have composed and recorded. Where Johnson often played and sang like a man whose life depended on it, Green plays and sings like a man whose next beer depends on it, surprisingly with very nice results. His performance on the title track is marvelously lazy and laid-back throughout this bluesy album, which also features Green's band, the Splinter Group, including Nigel Watson. Dr. John, Buddy Guy, Otis Rush, Hubert Sumlin, and Joe Louis Walker all make guest appearances on the album, along with Honey Boy Edwards, who knew and performed with Robert Johnson. The only slight drawback to this album are the few vocal performances of Nigel Watson, who is, perhaps, technically a better vocalist than Peter Green; however, his voice lacks Green's soulful weariness. *Hot Foot Powder*'s packaging, designed by 9th Planet, is both a creative and fun complement to the music within. *—Tim Griggs*

The Peter Green Collection / May 8, 2001 / Fuel 2000 ✦✦✦✦

Time Traders / Oct. 9, 2001 / Spitfire ♦♦♦
Green's sixth album since his out-of-nowhere but much welcome mid-'90s comeback shows the further development of his second version of the Splinter Group and showcases the songwriting of bandmembers Nigel Watson (a collaborator of Green's since the early '70s) and Roger Cotton. A new, more sublime take of Fleetwood Mac's spacy, psychedelic jam instrumental "Underway" welcomes former Green and David Gilmour sideman Snowy White back to the fold. Green sounds nowhere near his vocal or guitar-playing peak (somewhere around 1969), but it's good to see him diligently plugging away, making some fine modern blues music. *—John Duffy*

Rudy Greene

Piano, Vocals / Jump Blues, R&B, Electric Texas Blues
He was born Rudolph Spencer Greene and is often listed on liner notes as Rudy Green. Although neither a prolific nor famous blues artist, he is an artist who is often listed on liner notes, period. These albums are usually compilations of certain types of blues, early rock, or R&B with a focus on the rowdy, for this is the type of record that Greene apparently excelled at. Compilations that claim to be "stomping," "screaming and frantic," "jumping and jiving," or contain just plain "too much rocking" all have tracks by this artist, whose most famous songs include the hilarious "I Want a Bowlegged Woman" and the surreal "Juicy Fruit."

The latter track alone shows up on a handful of different early rock and regional label compilations, complete with the lyric "I got a car so long I park it in the air." Greene's work inhabits that netherworld somewhere between blues and rock, and he is even sometimes considered rockabilly, most likely because his earliest sides came out of Nashville. He was a disciple of the great blues guitarist T-Bone Walker and the only known photo of Greene reveals him picking with the guitar behind his head, a stunt for which his idol was well-known. The similarity to Walker extends well beyond visual hoopla, as many of the recorded Greene guitar solos feature the same sort of razor-sharp tone and liquid sense of melody.

Greene started out as a blues guitarist and singer, cutting several sides for that city's Bullet company in 1949. He did two sessions as a leader for the Chance label a few years later and also performed and recorded as a sideman behind singer Bobby Prince in 1953. In 1955, the same year he was holding down a regular gig at the Windy City's Club 34, Greene recorded for that city's Club 51 records as Rudy Greene & the Four Buddies. This was actually a combination of Greene and a separate vocal quartet consisting of five singers Ularsee Minor, Jimmy Hawkins, Irving Hunter, William Bryant, and Dickie Umbra. Fellow bluesmen Prince Cooper and Eddie Chamblee provided additional accompaniment on piano and saxophone, respectively, for this ensemble that hopefully counted time better than it did its membership. Greene sings solo in a style that has been compared to Roy Brown on one side from these sessions, the intense "Highway No. 1."

Perhaps inspired to hit the highway himself, Greene headed for a warmer climate and his own so-called 15 minutes of fame in 1956. Working out of the Tampa club scene, he was presented with the opportunity to record for the Ember label in New York City. His first record from this new contract was "Juicy Fruit," a superb effort that was infectious enough to be a regional hit. It could have also gone national had the label not become obsessed with a different release, "Walkin' With Mr. Lee," by Lee Allen. Showering its limited promotional abilities on this record, the company soon forgot how mouthwatering Greene's record had been. The same kind of promotional neglect killed his follow-up for the label and Greene faded from sight. *—Eugene Chadbourne*

Big John Greer

Vocals, Sax (Tenor), Saxophone / East Coast Blues
Never attaining the same glistening level of fame that fellow New York sax blasters Sam "The Man" Taylor and King Curtis enjoyed, Big John Greer nevertheless blew strong and sang long on a terrific series of waxings for RCA Victor and its Groove subsidiary from 1949 to 1955.

Greer was a childhood pal of future King Records producer Henry Glover. The pair attended high school together in Hot Springs and progressed to Alabama A&M College. Glover moved up quickly, playing trumpet and arranging for popular bandleader Lucky Millinder by 1948; when Millinder saxist Bull Moose Jackson split the aggregation to promote his blossoming solo career, Glover called his pal Big John Greer to fill Moose's chair. Greer's first record date as a leader was for Bob Shad's fledgling Sittin' in With label, but the great majority of his discography lies in Victor's vaults.

Initially recording as a singer/saxist with Millinder's unit for RCA, Greer stayed put when Millinder defected to King in 1950. That worked out nicely for Greer, who blew scorching tenor sax behind King stars Wynonie Harris (on "Mr. Blues Is Coming to Town" and "Bloodshot Eyes") and Bull Moose Jackson (on the incredibly raunchy "Nosey Joe"). Greer enjoyed his biggest hit as a vocalist in 1952 with the tasty blues ballad "Got You On My Mind" for RCA. The Howard Biggs-Joe Thomas composition attracted covers over the years from a mighty disparate lot, notably the Big Three Trio, Cookie & the Cupcakes, and Jerry Lee Lewis.

Greer's RCA and (from 1954 on) Groove platters were of uncommonly high standards, even for the polished New York scene. But no more hits ensued ("Bottle It Up and Go" and "Come Back Maybellene" certainly deserved a wider audience) for the powerful saxist. Glover brought him over to King in 1955, but a year there didn't slow his slide. Booze was apparently taking its toll on Greer's employment prospects; by 1957, he was back in Hot Springs, through as anything but a local attraction. He died at age 48, forgotten by all but the most dedicated R&B fans. *—Bill Dahl*

● **Rockin' With Big John** / 1992 / Bear Family ♦♦♦♦♦
Three discs' worth of an R&B saxist with only one legit R&B hit to his everlasting credit? Yep, and this 92-track examination of Greer's 1949-1955 stay at RCA Victor virtually never grows stale, either, thanks to the torrid jump blues tempos Greer often favored. "Got You on My Mind," and the often-covered blues ballad that proved Greer's lone hit, is here, as are rocking renditions of "Bottle It Up and Go," "Come Back Maybellene," and "Clambake Boogie." Guest vocalists include the Du Droppers, Annisteen Allen, and Damita Jo. Typically exhaustive liner notes and discographical info in the Bear Family tradition. *—Bill Dahl*

Grey Ghost (Roosevelt Thomas Williams)

b. Dec/ 7, 1903, Bastrop, TX, **d.** Jul. 17, 1996
Group / Texas Blues
Sparse and poorly recorded sessions are unfortunately the basis of Grey Ghost's (born Roosevelt Thomas Williams) fame. An exciting, if erratic, Texas barrelhouse pianist who was active since the '20s, Grey Ghost enjoyed a slight career boost in the '90s. Other than older fans who'd seen him playing around Austin and hardcore collectors, few people knew anything about the Ghost until the LP *Grey Ghost* surfaced on Catfish. A reissue of 1965 field recordings, its horrendous recording quality obscured the often captivating rhythms and his spirited vocals. But after its appearance, the Ghost was featured at several festivals, and was heard on a "Bluestage" show for National Public Radio in 1994. *—Ron Wynn*

● **Grey Ghost** / Oct. 30, 1992 / Spindletop ♦♦♦♦
Although he had played Austin and throughout the Southwest and nation since the '20s, much of the blues hardcore was unaware of Grey Ghost. Despite some rambling sections and others where rhythmic organization isn't a strong point, there's plenty of vintage boogie and good-natured barrelhouse playing and singing on this set. He wasn't among the greatest in the genre, but certainly belonged in the group close to the top. *—Ron Wynn*

Big Mike Griffin

b. Lawton, OK
Vocals, Guitar / Modern Electric Blues
Nashville's aptly named Big Mike Griffin (6'10", 350 lbs.) is a no-holds-barred blues guitarist new to the '90s blues scene. Griffin grew up in Lawton, OK, and regularly traveled 125 miles as a teen to hear blues in Dallas and Fort Worth clubs. Griffin was influenced by the second generation of blues artists, like Albert King, Mike Bloomfield, Albert Collins and the Paul Butterfield Blues Band. After the local economy turned sour, he left for Nashville. Initially, he did session guitar work for country artists and played anywhere he could, eventually building his own Unknown Blues Band.

After releasing a self-produced album that sold well in Nashville, the band signed with Malaco/Waldoxy Records in 1992. They had already earned a reputation beyond Nashville's city limits, playing at such prestigious festivals as the W.C. Handy Blues Festival in Memphis and the King Biscuit Blues Festival in Arkansas. The band toured incessantly and developed East and West Coast followings before recording *Gimme What I Got Comin'* in 1993, which was a hit among blues fans and DJs. Griffin played a month-long tour of Europe that year with labelmates Denise LaSalle, Little Milton, and Artie "Blues Boy" White. Griffin's unique, economical guitar style can also be heard on White's *Different Shades of Blue* album and James Peterson's *Don't Let the Devil Ride*. His three albums for Malaco include *Back on the Streets Again* (1992), *Gimme What I Got Comin'* (1993), and *Sittin' Here With Nothing* (1995). All are outstanding efforts that incorporate Griffin's gift for humorous storytelling and blend elements of jazz, funk, and swamp rock into his arrangements. *—Richard Skelly*

● **Back on the Streets Again** / Jun. 24, 1992 / Waldoxy ♦♦♦♦
Back on the Streets Again is perhaps the definitive Big Mike Griffin album, a record that showcases his knack for idiosyncratic guitar, soulful vocals and skewed humor. Most of the album consists of originals, with a few great covers—"Driving Wheel," "I'd Rather Go Blind"—thrown in for good measure. Throughout it all, he spits out terse, biting solos and invests true passion into his playing. It's a fine debut illustrating that Griffin is in a different class from the average modern bluesman. *—Thom Owens*

Gimme What I Got Comin' / Aug. 15, 1993 / Waldoxy ♦♦♦

Sittin' Here With Nothing / 1995 / Waldoxy ♦♦♦
Throughout *Sittin Here With Nothing*, Mike Griffin demonstrates his considerable skill as a lead blues guitarist. While his songwriting abilities don't quite match his instrumental prowess, the two Little Milton cuts here positively burn. *—Stephen Thomas Erlewine*

Grinderswitch

f. 1972, **db.** 1982
Group / Heavy Metal, Southern Rock, Hard Rock, Blues-Rock
Grinderswitch was a white blues-rock band that never rose above being a second-tier Capricorn Records act, not remotely as popular as the Allman Brothers or the Marshall Tucker Band. But Dru Lombar (vocals, guitar, slide guitar), Larry Howard (guitar), Stephen Miller (keyboards), Joe Dan Petty (bass), and Rick Burnett (drums) built a loyal following in the tens of thousands playing music that was influenced by British blues outfits like John Mayall's Bluesbreakers, Cream, and T.S. (Tony) McPhee's Groundhogs, but also the real article, especially Albert King and Booker T. & the MG's—Lombar sounded more Black than any white rock singer you've ever heard. They could have been a more soulful and exciting competitor to Canned Heat, but they weren't lucky enough to appear in hit festival movies or get the right single out at the proper time. Working in the commercial shadow of better-known acts, they counted as fans members of the Marshall Tucker Band and a lot of other musicians who felt they deserved a break. The group failed to emerge as much more than a top regional act and an opener for the Allmans and Charlie Daniels, among others, despite recording seven album between 1972 and 1982, first for Capricorn and later for Atlantic. *—Bruce Eder*

Honest to Goodness / 1974 / One Way ♦♦♦
Grinderswitch's debut album starts off well enough with the Dickey Betts-driven "Kiss the Blues Goodbye," which makes for a riveting introduction. Nothing else here really matches its tightness or excitement, and the songwriting isn't up to the standard that the

group would reach over the next couple of years. There's decent playing throughout, but apart from the opener, "Homebound" is the only track off the original album that begins to demonstrate Grinderswitch's potential, Dru Lombar's soulful voice finally finding a vehicle through which he can express himself properly. That, and a live bonus track ("You're So Fine"), are more representative of this band than most of the rest of this early effort. —*Bruce Eder*

Macon Tracks / 1975 / Capricorn ✦✦✦

Pullin' Together / 1977 / Capricorn ✦✦✦✦

Redwing / 1977 / Atco ✦✦✦✦

● **Live Tracks** / 1994 / One Way ✦✦✦✦✦
Southern rock never got any better than you hear it here, unless maybe it was in the hands of the Allman Brothers on a *really* good night. Fortunately for Grinderswitch fans and the rest of us, leader Dru Lombar saved a ton of live radio broadcast tapes of the group from a ten-year period. These are what comprise *Live Tracks*, filling in the only real gap in the group's output, the lack of a concert album. The selection includes a couple of very strong originals by Lombar and Howard, but the real delights are found in their covers of standards by Freddie King ("Hideaway"), Albert King ("You're Gonna Miss Me When I'm Gone"), Elmore James ("Pickin' the Blues"), and Chuck Willis ("Stoop Down Baby"). The sounds are smooth and soaring, a mix of Southern boogie and electric blues at their very best (this is the way one *wanted* Derek & the Dominos to sound in concert). Practically every cut here runs ten minutes or more, but the listener hardly knows it, because there's not a wasted note. A must-own disc, even for non-fans. —*Bruce Eder*

Unfinished Business / New South ✦✦✦✦
Grinderswitch was one of the most soulful bands that rocked the South, and indeed the rest of the world, during the '70s, highlighting Dru Lombar's powerful vocals and guitar work, Stephen Miller on keyboards, Larry Howard on guitar, Rick Burnett on drums, and the late Joe Dan Petty on bass. In 1977, the band found themselves in the studio working on their second album for the Atco/Rabbit label. This following the huge success of *Redwing*, and three less successful releases on Capricorn Records. Just as they got the album ready for release, they were shelved in favor of the latest trend in music, disco. It took 23 years for this fine album to finally be released in its entirety for the very first time. The record was produced by Paul Hornsby, perhaps the best-known producer ever to come out of the "Southern rock" scene of the '70s, and recorded and mixed by Sam Whiteside. The Muscle Shoals Horns are featured guests, as is the timeless Bonnie Bramlett, whose solo work and recordings with her former husband, Delaney, are the stuff of music history. "How Come It Is" is a straight-up rocker that opens the album, backed by a tight horn section and laced with an adequate dose of B-3 organ from Stephen Miller, who also wrote the tune. "Moving on Back to You," a soul-stirring R&B number, is power packed, and Larry Howard's "If the World Was My Guitar," is absolutely haunting in its beauty and spirit. When the band covers Albert King's "You're Gonna Miss Me," it is so hot you can shut your eyes, feel the heat, and see the burning embers smoldering. "That's What You Get for Loving Me" has the Otis Redding vibe down to a T, and Lombar once again sings at his soulful best. This is a great album, filled with soul, blues, rock, gospel, and even a little '60s pop, as in the band's rollicking cover of the Drifters' "I Count the Tears," a track that manages to combine elements of Southern rock with a definite early-'60s radio hit sound. "Dr. Hector's Traveling Show," which inspired the name of Dru Lombar's band, Dr. Hector & the Groove Injectors, is a fun-filled rocker that is highlighted by Lombar's red-hot slide guitar and catchy lyrics. This is an incredible documentation of one of the best bands to come out of the South since the Allman Brothers Band, and a welcomed addition to any collection. —*Michael Smith*

The Griswolds
f. 1959, Toledo, OH
Group / Modern Electric Blues
Toledo, Ohio-based brothers Art and Roman Griswold began playing blues together in 1959. In 1997, they released *All the Way Down*, their third studio album and the only one widely available to date, for the London-based JSP Records. On the recording, Art Griswold plays guitar and sings, while Roman contributes vocals and Hammond B-3 organ.

Both Art and Roman grew up surrounded by the sounds of bent guitar strings and wailing harmonicas. Art got his first guitar at age 17 after a motorcycle wreck laid him up for a few months. He moved to Little Rock, AR, and began sitting in with people like Big Moose Walker and others. After moving to Toledo, OH, he became the guitarist for Little Walter Mitchell and honed his craft at a variety of Toledo blues clubs.

Both brothers began their musical education with gospel music, listening to the radio and ordering the latest recordings by Elmore James, Muddy Waters, and others. By 1959, Art was joined in Toledo by his older brother Roman, who had completed a hitch in the armed forces, and quickly made his mark as a harmonica player. Roman hooked up with Art's band and the Griswolds landed a job at the club Hines Farm, where they had the opportunity to polish their chops backing up touring musicians like Jimmy Ricks, vocalist Little Esther Phillips, Freddie King, and Jimmy McCracklin. Finally, by 1965, Art Griswold opened his own tavern and made his own band the house band, playing six days a week. At this point, Roman began to pick up keyboards, since the lengthy jam sessions were taking their toll on him.

The Griswolds first entered the recording studio in the mid-'60s for the Fortune label in Detroit, where they recorded singles including "Pretty Mama" and "What the Judge Man Did to Me." Their singles found some airplay on R&B-oriented radio stations, and they began to tour regionally in Detroit, Houston, Memphis, and New Orleans.

The Griswolds continued to record (mostly singles) for small labels through the '70s disco boom, but by the '80s, they recorded and released their first full-length album, *Two Aces and a Jack*, with Toledo blues singer Big Jack Reynolds; the resulting airplay for the release brought them the chance to jam with Lee Atwater at a fundraiser for President

Reagan.

In 1990, the band, by this point paragons of the Toledo blues scene, recorded a live album, *Full Time Blues*, for the Highball label. Also in the early '90s, they released a studio album, *The Reel Deal*, for the same label. Saxophonist Rick "Big Daddy Cool" Schefdore joined the band in 1991, and he brought a wealth of experience to the group. He wrote two of the songs on *All the Way Down* and produced the band's first widely distributed album. *Cockeyed World* followed in early 2001. —*Richard Skelly*

All the Way Down / Feb. 25, 1997 / JSP ✦✦✦

● **Cockeyed World** / Feb. 13, 2001 / Blue Suit ✦✦✦

The Groundhogs
f. 1963
Group / British Psychedelia, Album Rock, Heavy Metal, Prog-Rock/Art Rock, Hard Rock, Blues-Rock
The Groundhogs were not British blues at their most creative; nor were they British blues at their most generic. They were emblematic of some of the genre's most visible strengths and weaknesses. They were prone to jam too long on basic riffs, they couldn't hold a candle to American blues singers in terms of vocal presence, and their songwriting wasn't so hot. On the other hand, they did sometimes stretch the form in unexpected ways, usually at the hands of their creative force, guitarist/songwriter/vocalist T.S. (Tony) McPhee. For a while they were also extremely popular in Britain, landing three albums in that country's Top Ten in the early '70s.

The Groundhogs' roots actually stretch back to the mid-'60s, when McPhee helped form the group, named after a John Lee Hooker song (the band was also known briefly as John Lee's Groundhogs). In fact, the Groundhogs would back Hooker himself on some of the blues singer's mid-'60s British shows, and also back him on record on an obscure LP. They also recorded a few very obscure singles with a much more prominent R&B/soul influence than their later work.

In 1966, the Groundhogs evolved into Herbal Mixture, which (as if you couldn't guess from the name) had more of a psychedelic flavor than a blues one. Their sole single, "Machines," would actually appear on psychedelic rarity compilations decades later. The Groundhogs/Herbal Mixture singles, along with some unreleased material, has been compiled on a reissue CD on Distortions.

After Herbal Mixture folded, McPhee had a stint with the John Dummer Blues Band before reforming the Groundhogs in the late '60s at the instigation of United Artists A&R man Andrew Lauder. Initially a quartet (bassist Pete Cruickshank also remained from the original Groundhogs lineup), they'd stripped down to a trio by the time of their commercial breakthrough, *Thank Christ for the Bomb*, which made the U.K. Top Ten in 1970. The Groundhogs' power-trio setup, as well as McPhee's vaguely Jack Bruce-like vocals, bore a passing resemblance to the sound pioneered by Cream. They were blunter and less inventive than Cream, but often strained against the limitations of conventional 12-bar blues with twisting riffs and unexpected grinding chord changes. McPhee's lyrics, particularly on *Thank Christ for the Bomb*, were murky, sullen anti-establishment statements that were often difficult to decipher, both in meaning and actual content. They played it straighter on the less sophisticated follow-up, *Split*, which succumbed to some of the period's blues-hard-rock indulgences, putting riffs and flash over substance.

McPhee was always at the very least an impressive guitarist, and a very versatile one, accomplished in electric, acoustic, and slide styles. *Who Will Save the World? The Mighty Groundhogs!* (1972), their last Top Ten entry, saw McPhee straying further from blues territory into somewhat progressive realms, even adding some mellotron and harmonium (though the results were not wholly unsuccessful). The Groundhogs never became well-known in the U.S., where somewhat similar groups like Ten Years After were much bigger. Although McPhee and the band have meant little in commercial or critical terms in their native country since the early '70s, they've remained active as a touring and recording unit since then, playing to a small following in the U.K. and Europe. —*Richie Unterberger*

Scratching the Surface / 1968 / BGO ✦✦✦

The Groundhogs With John Lee Hooker and John Mayall / 1968 / Cleve ✦✦✦

Blues Obituary / 1969 / BGO ✦✦✦

● **Thank Christ for the Bomb** / 1970 / BGO ✦✦✦✦✦
Their most popular album, and probably their most representative, although *Who Will Save the World?* may be more imaginative. McPhee's guitar playing is impressive, and the songs, if not terribly compelling, at least take some lyrical and instrumental chances, building off of a blues-rock base instead of being a slave to it. McPhee seems to be struggling with some very ambitious concepts here, but lacks the clarity and vision to fashion a truly out-of-the-ordinary statement. —*Richie Unterberger*

Split / 1971 / BGO ✦✦✦
As the Groundhogs' best example of their gritty blues-rock fire and unique form of guitar-driven music, *Split* reveals more about Tony McPhee's character, perseverance, and pure love for performing this style of blues than any other album. Based around the misunderstanding and mystery of schizophrenia, *Split* takes a raw, bottom-heavy recipe of spirited, spunky guitar riffs (some of the best that McPhee has ever played) and attaches them to some well-maintained and intelligently written songs. The first four tracks are simply titled "Part One" to "Part Four" and instantly enter *Split*'s eccentric, almost bizarre conceptual realm, but it's with "Cherry Red" that the album's full blues flavor begins to seep through, continuing into enigmatic but equally entertaining tracks like "A Year in the Life" and the mighty finale, entitled "Groundhog." Aside from McPhee's singing, there's a noticeable amount of candor in Peter Cruickshank's baggy, unbound percussion, which comes across as aimless and beautifully messy in order to complement the blues-grungy feel of the album. Murky, fuzzy, and wisely esoteric, *Split* harbors quite a bit of energy across its eight tracks, taking into consideration that so much atmosphere and spaciousness is conjured up by only three main instruments. This album, along with

1972's *Who Will Save the World?*, are regarded as two of the strongest efforts from the Groundhogs, but *Split* instills a little bit more of McPhee's vocal passion and dishes out slightly stronger portions of his guitar playing to emphasize the album's theme. *—Mike DeGagne*

Who Will Save the World? / 1972 / BGO ✦✦✦✦

McPhee took the unusual step of adding progressive rock elements on this album, especially in his use of mellotron and harmonium. Blues-rock and progressive rock is not exactly a fashionable combination among critics these days, but McPhee at least deserved credit for trying something a little bit different instead of endlessly recycling the blues-rock clichés he'd mastered. Lyrically, he reached back to the socially conscious (if not terribly clear) musings on war, peace, and philosophy that had preoccupied him on the *Thank Christ for the Bomb* album. It wasn't gripping enough to add up to something notable, and the band were still prone to wander off into headache-inducing extended riffs, as on the closing track, "The Grey Maze." *—Richie Unterberger*

Hogwash / 1972 / BGO ✦✦

Hogwash falls somewhere in between the Groundhogs' raw, blues-meets-electric rock sound of the late '60s and early '70s, and the less enthusiastic material that followed. It initiates more of a fundamental prog rock sound, with Tony McPhee's guitar work (along with a smattering of keyboard bits) taking on some well-maintained aggression. The album is the first for the former Egg drummer Clive Brooks, replacing Ken Pustlenik who left after 1972's *Who Will Save the World* album, while bass player Peter Cruickshank dishes out some of the group's better bottom-heavy riffs. But, even with a hearty progressive foundation in place, the material from *Hogwash* has a hard time competing with 1970's *Thank Christ for the Bomb* or the conceptual *Split* album, which came out a year later. "Earth Shanty" and "S'one Song" aren't overwhelming, but the defined British blues sound coming from McPhee's guitar playing on "I Love Miss Ogyny" makes up for them. "You Had a Lesson"'s energy comes from the erratic time signatures, while the one minute and 25 seconds of "The Ringmaster" is caught up in a psychedelic, space-rock ride. "3744 James Road" is pure Groundhogs, rumbling along with a slightly tainted blues chug, and accompanied by an unrefined vocal pounce. The band's inattentiveness begins to show up on "Sad Is the Hunter," "Mr. Hooker, Sir John," and infrequently throughout the albums last few tracks, with the genuine spunk and organic feel of the instruments losing their ruggedness. While *Hogwash* isn't their most solid album through and through, it has more fruitful moments than ineffective ones, and it still stands as the Groundhogs' last worthy release. 1974's *Solid* and both releases from 1976, *Crosscut Saw* and *Black Diamond*, show the band's evident dispersal from their original sound. *—Mike DeGagne*

The Groundhogs Best 1969–72 / 1974 / One Way ✦✦✦

Crosscut Saw / 1976 / BGO ✦✦✦

Groundhog Night . . . Groundhog Live / 1994 / Gopaco ✦✦

Anyone who feels a big gap in their life not having Cream around to perform and record will love *Groundhog Night*. But for anyone else, this double CD is problematic, capturing as it does McPhee's latter-day, re-formed Groundhogs live in concert in the '90s. The sound is very heavy, and heavily electric, with amplification more suited to late-'60s/early-'70s arena rock than mid-'60s blues-rock. Thus, the covers of standards like Muddy Waters' "Still a Fool," "No More Doggin'," and "I Want You to Love Me," and Willie Dixon's "Shake For Me" won't be to every taste, although McPhee's own established showcases, such as "Split Pts. 1 and 2" and "Thank Christ for the Bomb," fare reasonably well, and we even get a pleasing, restrained run through of "Groundhog Blues." There's lots of feedback and sustain, and it seems like McPhee and company try to turn "Still a Fool" into something akin to Cream's version of "Spoonful"—this isn't entirely successful, unless one is very much a fan of that brand of psychedelic or white electric blues. *—Bruce Eder*

The Best of the Groundhogs / Oct. 12, 1999 / EMI ✦✦✦✦

If you're in a band, you can either go with the flow the music takes or plant your feet and refuse to be moved. The Groundhogs, under the leadership of Tony McPhee, one of England's best guitarists, did the former. McPhee was a bluesman through and through, and the Groundhogs started life as a blues trio, but fairly quickly the music took a rock turn and suddenly the Groundhogs had a sizable following. After the cranked-out heavy blues-rock of *Blues Obituary*, they found their voice and came to notice with the very political *Thank Christ for the Bomb*, represented here by three tracks ("Strange Town," "Rich Man, Poor Man," "Eccentric Man") which show that while McPhee's writing might have been blues-based, he'd moved well beyond the three-chord, 12-bar format into something that used the band well, leaving room for his guitar solos but offering real substance in the ambitious songs. So it was a surprise when he pulled back from that for the riff-o-rama of *Split*, although it became their most successful album by far with its tale of schizophrenia. Certainly it's conspicuous here, with five tracks, including "Cherry Red," an inspiration to a generation of nascent electric guitarists. However, they definitely lost the plot with *Who Will Save the World?*, which took them too far from their base and into the more cerebral world of prog rock; listen to "Earth Is Not Room Enough" to get an idea of what was going on there. It simply doesn't work for them, and they'd head back to blues—where they were decidedly more comfortable—in the future; in fact, the version of "Amazing Grace" seems to indicate they knew they'd gone too far from home. If you want to understand the minor phenomenon that was the Groundhogs in the U.K. at the start of the '70s but don't want to splash out for *Thank Christ* or *Split*, this is the place to start. *—Chris Nickson*

Live at Leeds '71 / Feb. 5, 2002 / EMI ✦✦✦

3744 James Road: The HTD Anthology / Aug. 6, 2002 / Castle ✦✦✦✦

Guitar Johnny & the Rhythm Rockers

f. Boston, MA

Group / Modern Electric Blues, Rock & Roll, R&B

Guitar Johnny & the Rhythm Rockers was a group more famous for who was in their ranks than the scant bit of recorded music they made. Formed in Boston in the late '70s, they were led by guitarist-singer John Nicholas, who would later spend several years working in Asleep at the Wheel. The bassist was Sarah Brown, now noted as perhaps the most in-demand session bass player in the blues and roots music field and a songwriter of considerable note. The drummer was Fran Christina, who would move on to Roomful of Blues and eventually the Fabulous Thunderbirds in their hit making days. Blowing tenor was Mark "Kaz" Kazanoff, later going on to making a name for himself on the Austin, TX, music scene. The rhythm guitarist was none other than Ronnie Earl (Horvath), who later went on to a stint with Roomful before forming his own instrumental outfit, Ronnie Earl and the Broadcasters. Strictly a local phenomena in the Boston area, the group only left behind a four song 45 rpm EP on the now defunct Baron label that featured a couple of Nicholas originals and a vocal from Sarah Brown. They would all soon move on to bigger and better things. *—Cub Koda*

● **Guitar Johnny & Rhythm Rockers** / 1992 / New Rose ✦✦✦

Guitar Pete (Pete Brasino)

Guitar / Modern Electric Blues

Pete Brasino has been playing his rock & roll-flavored brand of blues ever since he was in high school. He began to teach himself to play guitar as a 16-year-old and within six months he had become so proficient with the instrument that his classmates dubbed him Guitar Pete—the nickname that would become his performing name. Another significant leftover from those early days is his playing style. Because he never had a guitar instructor, the left-handed musician never learned how to string the guitar the way a southpaw traditionally would. Instead, he plays upside down and backwards, holding the guitar lefty but using right-handed fingerings. Brasino's early heavy metal albums, released under the name Guitar Pete's Axe Attack, were not commercial successes, but they caught the attention of high-profile music industry professionals and eventually led to a 1994 recording deal for Brasino's band, Snakeyed Sue. The band's first record was produced by Steve Thompson and Michael Barbiro, producers whose resumés included work with Blues Traveler, Guns N' Roses, and Aretha Franklin. Snakeyed Sue dissolved shortly after the album's release, but four years later, Guitar Pete returned with a solo effort *Burning Bridges* that provided a showcase for his powerhouse blues sound. *—Evan Cater*

● **Burning Bridges** / Oct. 6, 1998 / Tangible ✦✦✦

Burning Bridges is a pretty apt title for Guitar Pete's incendiary solo debut. The artist keeps his namesake instrument blazing throughout the record, which essentially amounts to 43 minutes of gloriously shameless showboating. Pete is not a particularly talented vocalist; his booming, throaty bass is well-suited to the blues, but it would hardly earn him a recording deal on its own. On some tracks, he seems to give up entirely on the idea of singing, resorting instead to shouting the words rhythmically. Two of the album's best tracks ("J.B. Shuffle" and "Chillin'") are instrumental tunes that allow the guitar to wail for itself in a smoldering tizzy of dexterous showmanship. The album's sound is remarkably three dimensional for a three-piece band (Guitar Pete is joined by Anthony Bernardo on drums and Marc B. Gilman on bass guitar) playing a series of more or less run-of-the-mill Chicago-style blues songs. That's because Pete's fretwork is so dense and multifaceted, letting more than a little '70s jam band influence to crash his ostensibly traditional blues party. This is particularly true in his explosive take on the familiar blues-rock tune "Mustang Sally" and in the smoky rhythm and blues number "Do You Hear the Rain." *Burning Bridges* is not a brilliant album; it has no pretensions to greatness. It is simply straightforward showmanship and as such it's a pleasure. *—Evan Cater*

Guitar Shorty (David Kearney)

b. Sep. 8, 1939, Houston, TX

Vocals, Guitar / Modern Electric Blues, Soul-Blues

When he's not turning somersaults, doing backwards flips, and standing on his head—all while playing, of course—Guitar Shorty is prone to cutting loose with savagely slashing licks on his instrument. Live, he's simply amazing—and after some lean years, his recent albums for Black Top and Evidence have proven that all that energy translates vividly onto tape.

Born David Kearney on September 8, 1939, in Houston, TX, he started playing guitar at an early age. His early influences included fellow blues guitar slingers B.B. King, Guitar Slim, T-Bone Walker, and Earl Hooker. By the time he was 17, David Kearney was already gigging steadily in Tampa, FL. One night, he was perched on the bandstand when he learned that the mysterious "Guitar Shorty" advertised on the club's marquee was none other than he! His penchant for stage gymnastics was inspired by the flamboyant Guitar Slim, whose wild antics are legendary. In 1957, Shorty cut his debut single, "You Don't Treat Me Right," for Chicago's Cobra Records under Willie Dixon's astute direction. Three superb 45s in 1959 for tiny Pull Records in Los Angeles (notably "Hard Life"), rounded out Shorty's discography for quite a while.

During the '60s, he married Jimi Hendrix's stepsister and lived in Seattle, where the rock guitar god caught Shorty's act (and presumably learned a thing or two about inciting a throng) whenever he came off the road. Shorty's career had its share of ups and downs—once he was reduced to competing on Chuck Barris' zany *The Gong Show*, where he copped first prize for delivering "They Call Me Guitar Shorty" while balanced on his noggin.

Los Angeles had long since reclaimed Shorty by the time things started to blossom anew with the 1991 album *My Way or the Highway* for the British JSP logo (with guitarist Otis Grand in support). From there, Black Top signed Shorty; 1993's dazzling *Topsy Turvy* 1995's *Get Wise to Yourself* and 1998's *Roll Over, Baby* have been the head-over-heels results so far. In 2001 the appropriately titled *Get Wild* was released on the Evidence label, proving that Guitar Shorty has no intentions of slowing down; he remains a master showman and lively blues guitarist. —*Bill Dahl & Al Campbell*

My Way or the Highway / 1991 / JSP ✦✦✦✦

Until he joined forces with British guitarist Otis Grand's band and waxed this very credible comeback set, David "Guitar Shorty" Kearney's legacy was largely limited to a solitary single for Cobra and a handful of great but legendarily obscure followups for Los Angeles-based Pull Records during the late '50s. The acrobatic guitarist informed everyone he was alive and lively with this one, exhibiting his Guitar Slim roots on "Down Thru the Years" and slashing with a vengeance on "No Educated Woman" and the title cut (but shouldn't it have read "or the highway?"). —*Bill Dahl*

Topsy Turvy / 1993 / Black Top ✦✦✦✦✦

More impressive than Shorty's British venture thanks to superior production values and a better handle on his past (there's a stellar remake of "Hard Life"), *Topsy Turvy* made it clear that Guitar Shorty was back to stay stateside. Black Top assembled a fine New Orleans combo for the majority of the album, as Shorty proved that his act translates beautifully to record minus the crowd-pleasing acrobatic antics. —*Bill Dahl*

Get Wise to Yourself / 1995 / Black Top ✦✦✦

This gem of a disc shows Guitar Shorty (David Kearney) off on one of the highlights of his too-limited recorded efforts. He is one of the most flamboyant guitar players you will ever have the chance to see. His stage act was inspired by Guitar Slim, and he in turn inspired and influenced his stepbrother-in-law, a fellow by the name of Jimi Hendrix. This disc is filled with his searing blues guitar work. The only exception is the bouncy Mark "Kaz" Kazanoff tune "A Fool Who Wants to Stay," though Kazanoff is an associate producer of this disc (maybe that says enough). The rest will give you more than your fill of Shorty's inflammatory and slashing style of guitar licks, the very tight horn section arranged by Kazanoff augmenting him, and the solid musicians who are in the band that backs him. The best way to experience Shorty is live, but this is one of his best recorded efforts with fine production and a good clean sound that shows his abilities off in the best light. But if you get a chance, don't miss his show. Although he is now moving up in years, he still makes sure you get a good show, because he is a showman as well as being one hell of a guitar player. —*Bob Gottlieb*

Billie Jean Blues / Aug. 27, 1996 / Collectables ✦✦✦

Blues Is All Right / Aug. 27, 1996 / Collectables ✦✦✦

● **Roll Over, Baby** / Aug. 11, 1998 / Black Top ✦✦✦✦✦

William Kearney aka Guitar Shorty keeps it lean, mean and direct on this outing. Recorded in New Orleans, this session features his regular road band, abetted by Mark "Kaz" Kazanoff and some top N.O. players like Buckwheat Zydeco bassist Lee Allen Zeno. Shorty penned seven of the 12 tunes aboard, and the mix on this album runs from Texas shuffles ("Sugar Wugar," "I'm Going Back to Houston"), low down blues ("I Wonder Who's Sleeping in My Bed," "You're a Troublemaker," "Me and You Last Night") to New Orleans rock & roll ("I Want to Report a Crime," "Hard Time Woman," "The Porkchop Song" and the title track) and funk ("Don't Mess With My Woman," "Let's Get Close"), plus a heartfelt tribute to Hendrix on an extended workout on "Hey Joe." A wide and varied session that showcases the guitarist's wide-ranging chops and skills. —*Cub Koda*

I Go Wild / Oct. 23, 2001 / Evidence ✦✦✦

In his sixth decade of playing the blues, Guitar Shorty returns with the duly claimed *I Go Wild*. These 13 cuts cover gritty soul/blues the way Shorty would play 'em on any given Saturday night in any number of blues joints around the world. Shorty has not mellowed with age. One of the strong points of *I Go Wild* is Shorty's ability to translate the exhilaration and acrobatics (literally) of his live show into the studio. The showmanship of Shorty's mentor, Guitar Slim, and student, Jimi Hendrix, is evident. Needless to say, the 13 cuts provide matching passion and rambunctiousness. Jim Pugh's Hammond B-3 organ adds an extra dimension to the proceedings. —*Al Campbell*

Guitar Slim (Eddie Jones)

b. Dec. 10, 1926, Greenwood, MS, d. Feb. 7, 1959, New York, NY
Vocals, Guitar / New Orleans Blues, New Orleans R&B

No '50s blues guitarist even came close to equalling the flamboyant Guitar Slim in the showmanship department. Armed with an estimated 350 feet of cord between his axe and his amp, Slim would confidently stride on-stage wearing a garishly hued suit of red, blue, or green—with his hair usually dyed to match! It's rare to find a blues guitarist hailing from Texas or Louisiana who doesn't cite Slim as one of his principal influences; Buddy Guy, Earl King, Guitar Shorty, Albert Collins, Chick Willis, and plenty more have enthusiastically testified to Slim's enduring sway.

Born Eddie Jones in Mississippi, Slim didn't have long to make such an indelible impression. He turned up in New Orleans in 1950, influenced by the atomic guitar energy of Clarence "Gatemouth" Brown. But Slim's ringing, distorted guitar tone and gospel-enriched vocal style were his alone. He debuted on wax in 1951 with a mediocre session for Imperial that barely hinted at what would soon follow. A 1952 date for Bullet produced the impassioned "Feelin' Sad," later covered by Ray Charles (who would arrange and play piano on Slim's breakthrough hit the next year).

With the emergence of the stunning "The Things That I Used to Do" on Art Rupe's Specialty logo, Slim's star rocketed to blazing ascendancy nationwide. Combining a swampy ambience with a churchy arrangement, the New Orleans-cut track was a monster hit, pacing the R&B charts for an amazing 14 weeks in 1954. Strangely, although he waxed several stunning follow-ups for Specialty in the same tortured vein—"The Story of My Life," "Something to Remember You By," "Sufferin' Mind"—as well as the blistering rockers "Well I Done Got Over It," "Letter to My Girlfriend," and "Quicksand," Slim never charted again.

The guitar wizard switched over to Atlantic Records in 1956. Gradually, his waxings became tamer, though "It Hurts to Love Someone" and "If I Should Lose You" summoned up the old fire. But Slim's lifestyle was as wild as his guitar work. Excessive drinking and life in the fast lane took its inevitable toll over the years, and he died in 1959 at age 32. Only in recent years has his monumental influence on the blues lexicon begun to be fully recognized and appreciated.

Incidentally, one of his sons bills himself as Guitar Slim Jr. around the New Orleans circuit, his repertoire heavily peppered with his dad's material. —*Bill Dahl*

The Things That I Used to Do / 1964 / Specialty ✦✦

Great stuff, but irreparably changed by organ and guitar overdubs in an ill-advised attempt to update the classic New Orleans sound. —*Bill Dahl*

Battle of the Blues / 1987 / Ace ✦✦✦

Atco Sessions / Jul. 1988 / Atlantic ✦✦✦

Sometimes a bit subdued compared to his bone-chilling output for Specialty, these 1956-1958 sides for Atco still possess considerable charm, especially the tough "It Hurts to Love Someone" and "If I Should Lose You," which conjure up the same hellfire and brimstone intensity as Slim's earlier work. —*Bill Dahl*

★ **Sufferin' Mind** / 1991 / Specialty ✦✦✦✦✦

His guitar fraught with manic high-end distortion and his vocals fried over church-fired intensity, Eddie "Guitar Slim" Jones influenced a boatload of disciples while enjoying the rewards that came with his 1954 R&B chart-topper "The Things That I Used to Do." This 26-song survey of Slim's seminal 1953-1955 Specialty catalog rates with the best New Orleans blues ever cut—besides the often-imitated but never-duplicated smash, his "Story of My Life," "Sufferin' Mind," and "Something to Remember You By" are overwhelming in their ringing back-alley fury. Slim could rock, too: "Well I Done Got Over It," "Quicksand," "Certainly All," and the raucous introduction "Guitar Slim" drive with blistering power (saxist Joe Tillman was a worthy foil for the flamboyant guitarist in the solo department). —*Bill Dahl*

Guitar Slim Jr. (Rodney Armstrong)

b. 1951, New Orleans, LA
Vocals, Guitar / New Orleans Blues

Despite the fact that his first album earned a Grammy nomination, Guitar Slim Jr., remains a somewhat shadowy figure to the blues public. The son of Eddie "Guitar Slim" Jones, his real name is Rodney Armstrong. According to New Orleans historian Jeff Hannusch's notes on Slim's 1988 album, he "has been a fixture on the Black New Orleans club circuit for the better part of 20 years...[but] doesn't get to play the posher uptown clubs." His Orleans album featured mostly covers of his father's inspirational blues, which he was loath to play earlier in life, but Slim is also known for his extensive soul repertoire. —*Jim O'Neal*

● **Story of My Life** / 1988 / Orleans ✦✦✦✦✦

Contemporary blues, blues-rock, and soul comes from the son of the late blues/R&B legend. With mostly credible covers of his father's tunes, it was a Grammy nominee. —*Niles J. Frantz*

Nothing Nice / Jul. 30, 1996 / Warehouse Creek ✦✦✦

Arthur Gunter

b. May 23, 1926, Nashville, TN, d. Mar. 16, 1976, Port Huron, MI
Guitar, Vocals / Electric Blues, Louisiana Blues

As a recording artist for the Excello label in the early '50s, singer Arthur Gunter scored the imprint's first national hit with "Baby, Let's Play House." Born in Nashville, Gunter was a regular at the record shop owned by Excello chief Ernie Young and the association led to his short-lived recording career. In fact, possibly the most interesting thing about Gunter's recorded output is that Elvis Presley cut a version of "...Let's Play House" early in his career. All of Gunter's work could easily fit on a double CD and a 1995 set issued by Excello does much to compile the bulk of his recorded output. —*Steve Kurutz*

● **Baby Let's Play House: The Best of Arthur Gunter** / 1995 / AVI-Excello ✦✦✦✦

His lone Excello album is here in its entirety along with five very interesting solo demos, some stray 45s and one alternate take. As complete a package on this artist as you'll ever need. —*AMG*

Buddy Guy

b. Jul. 30, 1936, Lettsworth, LA
Vocals, Leader, Guitar (Electric), Guitar / Modern Electric Chicago Blues, Electric Chicago Blues, Chicago Blues, Electric Blues

He's Chicago's blues king today, ruling his domain just as his idol and mentor Muddy Waters did before him. Yet there was a time, and not all that long ago either, when Buddy Guy couldn't even negotiate a decent record deal. Times sure have changed for the better—Guy's first three albums for Silvertone in the '90s all earned Grammys. Eric Clapton unabashedly calls Buddy Guy his favorite blues axeman, and so do a great many adoring fans worldwide.

High-energy guitar histrionics and boundless on-stage energy have always been Guy's trademarks, along with a tortured vocal style that's nearly as distinctive as his incendiary rapid-fire fretwork. He's come a long way from his beginnings on the '50s Baton Rouge blues scene—at his first gigs with bandleader "Big Poppa" John Tilley, the young guitarist had to chug a stomach-jolting concoction of Dr. Tichenor's antiseptic and wine to ward off an advanced case of stage fright. But by the time he joined harpist Raful Neal's band, Guy had conquered his nervousness.

Guy journeyed to Chicago in 1957, ready to take the town by storm. But times were tough initially, until he turned up the juice as a showman (much as another of his early idols, Guitar Slim, had back home). It didn't take long after that for the new kid in town to establish himself. He hung with the city's blues elite: Freddy King, Muddy Waters, Otis

Rush, and Magic Sam, who introduced Buddy Guy to Cobra Records boss Eli Toscano. Two searing 1958 singles for Cobra's Artistic subsidiary were the result: "This Is the End" and "Try to Quit You Baby" exhibited more than a trace of B.B. King influence, while "You Sure Can't Do" was an unabashed homage to Guitar Slim. Willie Dixon produced the sides.

When Cobra folded, Guy wisely followed Rush over to Chess. With the issue of his first Chess single in 1960, Guy was no longer aurally indebted to anybody. "First Time I Met the Blues" and its follow-up, "Broken Hearted Blues," were fiery, tortured slow blues brilliantly showcasing Guy's whammy-bar-enriched guitar and shrieking, hellhound-on-his-trail vocals.

Although he's often complained that Leonard Chess wouldn't allow him to turn up his guitar loud enough, the claim doesn't wash: Guy's 1960-1967 Chess catalog remains his most satisfying body of work. A shuffling "Let Me Love You Baby," the impassioned down-beat items "Ten Years Ago," "Stone Crazy," "My Time After Awhile," and "Leave My Girl Alone," and a bouncy "No Lie" rate with the hottest blues waxings of the '60s. While at Chess, Guy worked long and hard as a session guitarist, getting his licks in on sides by Waters, Howlin' Wolf, Little Walter, Sonny Boy Williamson, and Koko Taylor (on her hit "Wang Dang Doodle").

Upon leaving Chess in 1967, Guy pacted with Vanguard. His first LP for the firm, *A Man and the Blues*, followed in the same immaculate vein as his Chess work and contained the rocking "Mary Had a Little Lamb," but *This Is Buddy Guy* and *Hold That Plane!* proved somewhat less consistent. Guy and harpist Junior Wells had long palled around Chicago (Guy supplied the guitar work on Wells' seminal 1965 Delmark set *Hoodoo Man Blues*, initially billed as "Friendly Chap" because of his Chess contract); they recorded together for Blue Thumb in 1969 as *Buddy and the Juniors* (pianist Junior Mance being the other Junior) and Atlantic in 1970 (sessions co-produced by Eric Clapton and Tom Dowd) and 1972 for the solid album *Buddy Guy & Junior Wells Play the Blues*. Buddy and Junior toured together throughout the '70s, their playful repartee immortalized on *Drinkin' TNT 'n' Smokin' Dynamite*, a live set cut at the 1974 Montreux Jazz Festival.

Guy's reputation among rock guitar gods such as Eric Clapton, Jimi Hendrix, and Stevie Ray Vaughan was unsurpassed, but prior to his Grammy-winning 1991 Silvertone disc *Damn Right, I've Got the Blues*, he amazingly hadn't issued a domestic album in a decade. That's when the Buddy Guy bandwagon really picked up steam—he began selling out auditoriums and turning up on network television (David Letterman, Jay Leno, etc.). *Feels Like Rain*, his 1993 encore, was a huge letdown artistically, unless one enjoys the twisted concept of having one of the world's top bluesmen duet with country hat act Travis Tritt and hopelessly overwrought rock singer Paul Rodgers. By comparison, 1994's *Slippin' In*, produced by Eddie Kramer, was a major step back in the right direction, with no hideous duets and a preponderance of genuine blues excursions. *Last Time Around: Live at Legends* followed in 1998.

A Buddy Guy concert can sometimes be a frustrating experience. He'll be in the middle of something downright hair-raising, only to break it off abruptly in mid-song, or he'll ignore his own massive songbook in order to offer imitations of Clapton, Vaughan, and Hendrix. But Guy, whose club remains the most successful blues joint in Chicago (you'll likely find him sitting at the bar whenever he's in town), is without a doubt the Windy City's reigning blues artist—and he rules benevolently. —*Bill Dahl*

Crazy Music / 1965 / Chess ♦♦♦

With the Blues / 1965 / Chess ♦♦♦

I Left My Blues in San Francisco / 1967 / Chess ♦♦♦♦♦
Guy's last Chess album finds him shifting gears to keep up with the scene. His turns on "Keep It to Yourself," "Crazy Love," "When My Left Eye Jumps," "Leave My Girl Alone," and "I Suffer With the Blues" are some examples of this mercurial guitarist at his explosive best. The rest of the album is filled with groovy, soul-styled workouts; some of them succeed and some sound a bit dated, but overall this is one of Buddy's stronger efforts. —*Cub Koda*

A Man and the Blues / 1968 / Vanguard ♦♦♦♦
The guitarist's first album away from Chess—and to be truthful, it sounds as though it could have been cut at 2120 S. Michigan, with Guy's deliciously understated guitar work and a tight combo anchored by three saxes and pianist Otis Spann laying down tough grooves on the vicious "Mary Had a Little Lamb," "I Can't Quit the Blues," and an exultant cover of Mercy Dee's "One Room Country Shack." —*Bill Dahl*

Blues Today / 1968 / Vanguard ♦♦♦

This Is Buddy Guy / 1968 / Vanguard ♦♦♦

Buddy and the Juniors / 1970 / MCA ♦♦
Strange, off-the-cuff set originally issued on Blue Thumb pairing Buddy Guy and Junior Wells with jazz pianist Junior Mance and no rhythm section. Guy plays acoustic guitar, Wells plays amplified harp, and the hoary setlist includes "Hoochie Coochie Man," "Five Long Years," and "Rock Me Mama." —*Bill Dahl*

In the Beginning (1958/64) / 1971 / Drive ♦
Bootleg-quality LP of Guy's early work. —*Bill Dahl*

Buddy Guy & Junior Wells Play the Blues / 1972 / Rhino ♦♦♦
Considering the troubled background of this album (Eric Clapton, Ahmet Ertegun, and Tom Dowd only ended up with eight tracks at a series of 1970 sessions in Miami; two years later, the J. Geils Band was brought in to cut two additional songs to round out the long-delayed LP for 1972 release), the results were pretty impressive. Guy contributes dazzling lead axe to their revival of "T-Bone Shuffle"; Wells provides a sparkling remake of Sonny Boy Williamson's "My Baby She Left Me," and Guy is entirely credible in a grinding Otis Redding mode on the Southern soul stomper "A Man of Many Words." —*Bill Dahl*

Hold That Plane / 1972 / Vanguard ♦♦
Lackluster set comprised of only seven lengthy workouts, including Guy's renditions of "I'm Ready," "Watermelon Man," and Sugar Pie DeSanto's "Hello San Francisco." Jazzman Junior Mance is pianist for the somewhat underwhelming album. —*Bill Dahl*

I Was Walking Through the Woods / 1974 / MCA/Chess ♦♦♦♦♦
This slim yet potent sampler of Guy's excellent early-'60s work for Chess will no doubt please newcomers looking for a bargain introduction to the blues guitarist/vocalist's prime sides. With his guitar tapped for maximum intensity, spiky and tremolo-heavy, and those vocals all pathos-rich screams and in-the-pocket bravado, Guy especially hits bedrock on the blues-personified narrative "The First Time I Met the Blues" and the perennial "My Time After a While"; from lean combo cuts to horn-rich swingers, the remaining tracks never stray too far from this high-quality mark. And ensuring a fine ride throughout, regal blues veterans like Junior Wells, Otis Spann, and Fred Below help provide the tasty accompaniment. A solid shot from one of Chicago blues' second-generation stars. —*Stephen Cook*

Live in Montreux / Jul. 9, 1977 / Evidence ♦♦♦
No blues tandem in recent memory has given more alternately brilliant and infuriating performances as the duo of Junior Wells and Buddy Guy. They can inspire or anger, stimulate or disgust, amaze or bore. They were in a great groove during the selections recorded at this concert for Isabel. They have been recently reissued with two bonus cuts as part of Evidence's huge cache of blues material. Wells' often rambling, sometimes disjointed and unorganized vocals were not only focused on this occasion but delivered with verve, direction, and intensity. Guy stayed in the background, but when summoned, played with less flair and more power, dispensing with distortion and feedback gimmicks and providing neat fills, slashing lines, and meaty riffs. Fine Wells/Guy material that is close, if not completely equal to, their best. —*Ron Wynn*

Pleading the Blues / Oct. 1979 / Evidence ♦♦♦♦♦
Recorded on Halloween night in 1979, this pairs up Wells and Guy in a fashion that hasn't been heard since *Hoodoo Man Blues*, their first, and best collaboration. Solid backing by The Philip Guy band (Buddy's brother) makes this album a rare treat. —*Cub Koda*

Stone Crazy! / 1981 / Alligator ♦♦♦
Buddy Guy mostly indulges his histrionic side throughout this high-energy set, first issued in France and soon picked up for domestic consumption by Alligator. It's a particularly attractive proposition for rock-oriented fans, who will no doubt dig Guy's non-stop incendiary, no-holds-barred guitar attack and informal arrangements. Purists may want to look elsewhere. —*Bill Dahl*

DJ Play My Blues / 1982 / JSP ♦

Drinkin' TNT 'n' Smokin' Dynamite / 1982 / Blind Pig ♦♦♦
Cut at the 1974 Montreux Jazz Festival with Stones bassist Bill Wyman anchoring the rhythm section, the set captures some of the ribald musical repartee that customarily distinguished the pairing of Buddy Guy and Junior Wells, though they certainly break no new ground as they roll through their signature songs. —*Bill Dahl*

Buddy Guy / 1983 / Chess ♦♦♦♦
This early roundup of guitarist/singer Buddy Guy's prime Chess cuts makes for the perfect introductory disc: It's full of gems and going for a bargain rate. Taken from his 1960-1967 tenure with the Chicago label, the 12 tracks find Guy bursting with manic energy, wielding those Guitar Slim-inspired licks and high-toned, hellfire vocals throughout. From classics like "Broken Hearted Blues" (his first Chess single) to the Little Milton-tinged horns-and-blues swinger "Hard but It's Fair," Guy effortlessly keeps up the charged mood while delivering the manna for such future blues prats as Robert Plant and Eric Clapton. Full throttle or after hours, Guy makes it all indelible. —*Stephen Cook*

The Original Blues Brothers Live / 1983 / Magnum ♦♦♦

Chess Masters / 1987 / Chess ♦♦♦♦♦
This anthology's value has been supplanted by the more intelligently sequenced, mastered and annotated two-disc *Complete Studio Recordings* issued in 1992. It's also out of print. —*Ron Wynn*

Complete DJ Play My Blues Session / 1987 / JSP ♦

Breaking Out / 1988 / JSP ♦

Alone & Acoustic / 1991 / Alligator ♦♦♦
The classic pairing of Buddy Guy and Junior Wells has been captured many times on vinyl, cassette, and disc over the years, but rarely with such intimacy and subtle, restrained energy as on this wonderful collection. Buddy Guy plays mostly 12-string guitar, and Junior laces his signature lines through the songs, engaging Guy in the kind of musical dialogue that only old friends can have. This is acoustic street-corner blues at its best, performed with incredible expressiveness, ease, and joy. One gets the feeling these two are just sitting down for a friendly jam session on a Saturday afternoon, and when things get loose, their laughter flows almost as freely as the music. Guy really shines on some of these tracks, his guitar lines fast, smooth, percussive, and seemingly effortless. Wells, always tasteful, plays counterpoint to Guy in the classic style and sings with honesty and conviction. What resulted is some absolutely fantastic music. —*David Lavin*

Damn Right, I've Got the Blues / 1991 / Silvertone ♦♦♦♦♦
Grammy-winning comeback set that brought Guy back to prominence after a long studio hiatus. Too many clichéd cover choices—"Five Long Years," "Mustang Sally," "Black Night," "There Is Something on Your Mind"—to earn unreserved recommendation, but Guy's frenetic guitar histrionics ably cut through the superstar-heavy proceedings (Eric Clapton, Jeff Beck, and Mark Knopfler all turn up) on the snarling title cut and a handful of others. —*Bill Dahl*

My Time After Awhile / 1992 / Vanguard ♦♦♦♦♦
My Time After Awhile is the best selection from Guy's Vanguard catalog. —*Bill Dahl*

The Complete Chess Studio Sessions / 1992 / MCA/Chess ✦✦✦✦
Here's everything that fleet-fingered Buddy Guy waxed for Chess from 1960 to 1966, including numerous unissued-at-the-time masters, offering the most in-depth peek at his formative years imaginable. Stone Chicago blues classics ("Ten Years Ago," "My Time After Awhile," "Let Me Love You Baby," "Stone Crazy"), rockin' oddities ("American Bandstand," "$100 Bill," "Slop Around"), even a cut that features guitarist Lacy Gibson's vocal rather than Guy's ("My Love Is Real")—some 47 sizzling songs in all. —*Bill Dahl*

★ **The Very Best of Buddy Guy** / 1992 / Rhino ✦✦✦✦✦
Credible attempt to digitally summarize Guy's entire pre-Silvertone career on a single 18-song disc. Encompasses the guitarist's 1957 demo "The Way You Been Treating Me," two killer Cobras, four of his hottest Chess sides, a couple notable Vanguards, a pair of alluring Atlantics, and three tremendously unsubtle 1981 items from Guy's days with the British JSP label. —*Bill Dahl*

Feels Like Rain / 1993 / Silvertone ✦✦✦
On Buddy Guy's second Silvertone release, he continues the practice of guest appearances begun on *Damn Right, I've Got the Blues*. In this case, the notables include Paul Rodgers, Travis Tritt, and John Mayall. The finest combination comes when Bonnie Raitt joins Guy on John Hiatt's "Feels Like Rain." Raitt's gritty vocals and sweet slide guitar add a pleasing nuance to the bittersweet track, and it is ultimately the high point of the record. Certain critics and blues purists have derided Guy's search for mainstream success as evidenced by his penchant for guest appearances and non-traditional blues forms, but Guy sounds fantastic in these unconventional situations (witness his burning version of the Moody Blues' "I Go Crazy"). Guy's vocals, often underappreciated, really sell this song. As for his guitar playing, it is slightly below his usually high standards. He often sounds sloppy and unfocused, an extremely noticeable exception being his explosive solo on the John Mayall duet "I Could Cry," but his singing, especially on the soulful "Feels Like Rain," is full of character. Guy's backing band is top-notch, particularly bassist Greg Rzab, who plays both more actively and more melodically than most bassists working in the blues idiom. Guy has recorded better blues in his career, but on Feels Like Rain he shows that he is comfortable in more mainstream situations as well. The blues on this record often just sound flat for some reason, like Guy and his band are just going through the motions. But on uptempo R&B tracks such as the Paul Rodgers duet "Some Kind of Wonderful" or Guy's pairing with Travis Tritt on "Change in the Weather," the bluesman sounds excited and fresh. It must be mentioned that the production is a bit on the thin side throughout, and many of the tracks simply do not pack enough punch. Despite this, the album is quite strong. *Feels Like Rain* is not the place to look for Guy the legendary blues guitarist, but, taken for what it is, it is extremely entertaining. —*Daniel Gioffre*

Slippin' In / 1994 / Silvertone ✦✦✦✦
Whereas on 1993's *Feels Like Rain* Buddy Guy flirted with pop and R&B material, on *Slippin' In*, released one year later, he firmly reasserts his bluesness. From the very first track on, Guy lets his incomparable guitar loose. Throughout the album, he even experiments with Hendrix-esque effects on his guitar (perhaps at the prodding of producer/engineer Eddie Kramer), but the results never seem kitschy or gimmicky. Accompanied on half of the tracks by ex-Stevie Ray Vaughan associates Tommy Shannon and Chris Layton, the groove is deep and swinging. It makes you realize how much of Vaughan's signature sound lay in his rhythm section. There are only two original Guy compositions on *Slippin' In*, but since he has always been better as an interpreter than a writer, this is a non-complaint. Playing a superb foil to the leader is none other than Johnnie Johnson, whose solo on "7-11" simply takes over the track. The difference in sound quality between this album and *Feels Like Rain* is astounding. Whereas on *Feels Like Rain* the sound was often thin and unimpressive, über-engineer Kramer has created an ideal sonic space here for Guy's music. Some may feel that the individual instruments are too distinct, but for those who feel that the development of multi-tracking and other advances in recording technology are good things will not be disappointed. Also absent from *Slippin' In* is the rotating all-star casts of notables that appeared both on *Damn Right, I've Got the Blues* and *Feels Like Rain*. This is encouraging, because an artist of Guy's stature and caliber does not need celebrity appearances to make his records worth investigating, a fact which he proves masterfully on this album. —*Daniel Gioffre*

Southern Blues 1957–63 / 1994 / Paula ✦✦✦
Kind of a thrown-together hodgepodge, but still a worthwhile add to your CD collection. Guy's four indispensable 1958 sides for Cobra are here (along with alternates of "This Is the End" and the Guitar Slim-influenced "You Sure Can't Do"), while Guy provides crackling lead guitar on four 1963 outings by singer Jesse Fortune (notably the minor-key rhumba "Too Many Cooks"). Finally, there are two demos that Guy cut at a Baton Rouge radio station back in 1957—or they're supposed to be here, anyway: the crudely engaging "The Way You Been Treatin' Me" is definitely Buddy Guy, but "I Hope You Come Back Home" isn't (no guesses from this corner on exactly who it may be, either). —*Bill Dahl*

Live: The Real Deal / Apr. 1996 / Silvertone ✦✦✦✦
As close as Buddy Guy's ever likely to come to recapturing the long-lost Chess sound. Cut live at his popular Chicago nightspot, Buddy Guy's Legends, with guitarist G.E. Smith's horn-leavened Saturday Night Live Band and pianist Johnnie Johnson in lush support, Guy revisits his roots on sumptuous readings of "I've Got My Eyes on You," "Ain't That Lovin' You," "My Time After Awhile," and "First Time I Met the Blues." No outrageous rock-based solos or Cream/Hendrix/Stevie Ray homages; this is the Buddy Guy album that purists have salivated for the last quarter century or so. —*Bill Dahl*

☆ **Buddy's Blues (Chess 50th Anniversary Collection)** / Apr. 8, 1997 / MCA/Chess ✦✦✦✦✦
As part of MCA's Chess Records 50th Anniversary series, this sweats his multi-disc retrospective, *The Complete Chess Studio Recordings*, down to a scintillating 15-track package and comes up with a bare-bones winner. There's loads of great guitar on classics like "First Time I Met The Blues," "Let Me Love You Baby," "Pretty Baby," "My Time After Awhile," "Stone Crazy," and Buddy's voice is at its whiplash exuberant best. Unexpected bonuses pop up in the comp's kickoff track, a full-length version of "Worried Mind," that's issued here without the overdubbed applause and crowd noises that accompanied its original release on the *Folk Festival of The Blues* album highlighting Muddy Waters and other blues greats. Also noteworthy is Junior Wells' appearance on chromatic harp on "Ten Years Ago," and Guy's stellar guitar behind Lacy Gibson's vocal on a Buddy Guy original, "My Love Is Real." And special note must also be made of the spacious stereo mixes used on this compilation, making these 30-year-old-plus tracks shine like diamonds coming off the laser beam. We also experience all the stylistic turns toward a kinship with the burgeoning soul and rock scenes that Buddy would make toward the end of his Chess tenure, along with the smoking slow burners that are his trademark, some of which clock in at four to six minutes here. With his very best tracks compiled on one disc and with beautiful transfers of them to enhance the listening experience, this should be one of your very first stops in absorbing the sides that made Buddy's reputation among blues fans and guitar aficionados the world over. —*Cub Koda*

As Good as It Gets / Mar. 10, 1998 / Vanguard ✦✦✦

Heavy Love / Jun. 2, 1998 / Silvertone ✦✦✦
Apparently, Buddy Guy subscribes to the theory "If you can't beat 'em, join 'em." Losing commercial ground to the blonde young guns of Johnny Lang and Kenny Wayne Shepherd, Guy hired their producer David Z and set out to record an album of loud, frenzied blues-rock. Purists will cringe at the unabashed commercial concessions Guy makes on *Heavy Love*—sure, he covers "Midnight Train," but it's a duet with Jonny Lang, which complements the funkified "I Just Wanna Make Love to You," psychedelicized licks, and ZZ Top cover ("I Need You Tonight"). Nevertheless, *Heavy Love* works well when compared to the modern electric blues of the post-Stevie Ray Vaughan era, especially since Guy once again contributes some scorching solos. Granted, his playing may veer too close to rock for some tastes, but anyone wanting an uninhibited, hard-rocking Buddy Guy record won't be disappointed with *Heavy Love*. —*Stephen Thomas Erlewine*

Last Time Around—Live at Legends / Nov. 10, 1998 / Jive ✦✦✦
Last Time Around—Live at Legends is a fitting farewell to the late great Junior Wells and his partnership, friendship, and kinship with Buddy Guy that lasted decades. The album is a historic release in many ways. It reunites two blues legends who began their unique association in the '50s. The album was recorded live in March 1993 at Buddy Guy's world-famous Chicago blues mecca Legends, and it's an acoustic document of many classic songs that made both Wells and Guy legends in their own right, such as "She's Alright" and "I've Been There," along with other classic blues standards such as "Hoochie Coochie Man" and "Key to the Highway," all delivered with a looseness and power that define both Guy and Wells. It also marks the last time the two ever played together. —*Matthew Greenwald*

Buddy's Baddest: The Best of Buddy Guy / Jun. 15, 1999 / Silvertone ✦✦✦
Buddy Guy revitalized his career when he signed with Silvertone Records in the early '90s. His first album for the label, *Damn Right, I've Got the Blues*, was a smash success, earning critical acclaim, awards, and sales hand over fist. Prior to that record, he was a legend only among blues fans; afterward, he was a star. Although it was a bit too rock-oriented and slick for purists, *Damn Right* was a terrific album, setting the pace not only for Guy but for modern electric blues in the '90s. As the decade wore on, Guy continued to make albums for Silvertone, some of them a little complacent, others quite excellent. *Buddy's Baddest: The Best of Buddy Guy* attempts to summarize those years in 14 songs, including three previously unreleased cuts. Not surprisingly, the compilers favor the Guy of *Damn Right*, featuring four songs from the record and three from its soundalike sequel, *Feels Like Rain*. Only two tracks from *Slippin' In*, his hardest blues record for the label, made the cut, while the fine live album *Live: The Real Deal* and the misguided *Heavy Love* are represented by a track apiece. In other words, a lot of good stuff remains on the original albums, which is doubly unfortunate since the three unreleased cuts are all throwaways. By relying so heavily on two records, *Buddy's Baddest* doesn't wind up being an accurate portrait of Guy's Silvertone recordings. That doesn't mean it's a bad listen, since the first ten songs are all very good and quite entertaining. However, anyone who has *Damn Right* but wants to dig deeper into Guy's Silvertone albums may prefer to pick up *Feels Like Rain*, which offers more of the same crossover Chicago blues, or *Slippin' In*, which is the real deal. —*Stephen Thomas Erlewine*

The Complete JSP Recordings: 1979–1982 / Mar. 21, 2000 / JSP ✦✦✦
The Complete JSP Recordings: 1979-1982 is a budget-priced three-disc set that contains *Live at the Checkerboard Lounge*, *DJ Play My Blues* and *Breaking Out*. These are not among Buddy Guy's greatest albums—some, in fact, are among his low points, though *Live at the Checkerboard Lounge* isn't bad—but completists that want all of his records may find this useful, since it offers three albums in a slipcase box at a reduced price. —*Stephen Thomas Erlewine*

Every Day I Have the Blues / Apr. 4, 2000 / Cleopatra ✦✦
A fair-to-middling-quality tape of Buddy and Junior doing a typical set in the mid-'70s. The lineup of Jack Meyers (bass), Fred Below (drums), and Donald Hankins (baritone sax) is nigh perfect, and always in the pocket, and hearing Buddy do "Satisfaction" is one of the more surreal experiences on this album. If this were even of soundboard quality, it might be an enjoyable experience; but the horribly muffled vocals and

frequent blasts of distortion, combined with mistitled and miscredited tunes (I'm sure that James Brown will be surprised to learn that Buddy and Junior wrote "Out of Sight") and a lack of hard recording dates and information, make this one strictly for completists. —*Cub Koda*

Buddy Guy & Junior Wells / Apr. 11, 2000 / Castle ◆◆◆

A real hodgepodge of tracks pulled from varying sources. The Buddy Guy material is a combination of club date leftovers (two versions of "We're Ready"), his sides for Artistic, and a stray Delmark performance thrown in while Junior's sides are a combination of his early States material, some Delmark work with Guy, some Chief and Profile sides from the early '60s, and a stray Vanguard track. Not essential stuff, but not really bad, either. —*Cub Koda*

Sweet Tea / May 15, 2001 / Jive ◆◆◆◆

Apparently somebody took the criticisms of Buddy Guy's late-'90s Silvertone recordings to heart. They were alternately criticized for being too similar to *Damn Right I Got the Blues* or, as 1998's *Heavy Love*, too blatant in its bid for a crossover rock audience. So, after a bit of a break, Guy returned in 2001 with *Sweet Tea*, an utter anomaly in his catalog. Recorded at the studio of the same name in deep Mississippi, this is a bold attempt to make a raw, pure blues album—little reliance on familiar covers or bands, no crossover material, lots of extended jamming and spare production. That's not to say that it's without its gimmicks. In a sense, the very idea behind this record is a little gimmicky—let's get Buddy back to the basics—even if it's a welcome one, but that's not the problem. The problem is that the production is a bit too self-conscious in its stylized authenticity. There's too much separation, too much echo, a strangely hollow center—it may sound rougher than nearly all contemporary blues albums, but it doesn't sound gritty, which it should. Despite this, *Sweet Tea* is still a welcome addition to Buddy Guy's catalog because, even with its affected production, it basically works. Playing in such an unrestricted setting loosens Buddy up even a tiny bit, but allows him to act his age without embarrassment (check the chilling acoustic opener, "Done Got Old"). This may not showcase the showman of the artist live, the way *Damn Right* did, but it does something equally noteworthy—it illustrates that the master bluesman still can sound vital and can still surprise. —*Stephen Thomas Erlewine*

20th Century Masters—The Millennium Collection: The Best of Buddy Guy / Nov. 20, 2001 / MCA ◆◆◆

Phil Guy

b. Apr. 28, 1940, Lettsworth, LA

Guitar / Chicago Blues, Modern Electric Blues

No, Phil Guy's never going to eclipse his older brother Buddy's status as a blues superstar. And in reality, Phil's funky brand of blues has yet to be captured correctly for posterity. But he remains an active attraction on the Chicago circuit, following in his sibling's footsteps and patiently waiting for his own star to rise. Like his sibling, Phil Guy played with harpist Raful Neal (for a decade) before leaving the Baton Rouge scene for Chicago in 1969. There he played with his brother's high-energy organization as well as behind harpist Junior Wells (Phil handles guitar duties with Sammy Lawhorn on Wells' underrated mid-'70s Delmark album, *On Tap*). Phil Guy has cut albums of his own for JSP; they've generally been lacking in originality if not spirit. —*Bill Dahl*

● **Bad Luck Boy** / 1983 / JSP ◆◆◆◆

Phil Guy never was able to establish an identity separate from his older brother Buddy, but as his debut album *Bad Luck Boy* shows, he didn't really try, either. Guy's stock-in-trade is Chicago blues, and while he doesn't perform with much imagination, he's hardly incompetent, either. The problem may be that he's simply competent, unwilling to shake things up even a tiny bit, but competency can be entertaining as well. That's the case on *Bad Luck Boy*. Guy never really got better than he did here, as he's supported by a number of Chicago veterans and he turns out a likeable, albeit predictable, set of Chicago blues, balancing covers with originals. There's not necessarily much passion here, but it's well-done music, and it illustrates that Guy can deliver the goods on occasion. —*Thom Owens*

It's a Real Mutha Fucka / 1985 / JSP ◆◆

Weak, cover-heavy album by Buddy's little brother. —*Bill Dahl*

Tough Guy / 1989 / Red Lightnin' ◆◆◆

Tina Nu / 1989 / JSP ◆◆

This set offers conclusive proof as to why Buddy's little brother may never shed his long-standing journeyman status—weak covers, done not particularly persuasively, with a mediocre band. —*Bill Dahl*

All Star Chicago Blues Session / Oct. 31, 1994 / JSP ◆◆◆

Breaking Out on Top / Sep. 5, 1995 / JSP ◆◆◆

Say What You Mean / Feb. 8, 2000 / JSP ◆◆◆

Travis Haddix

b. Nov. 26, 1938, Walnut, MS
Vocals, Guitar / Modern Electric Blues, R&B

Blues guitarist Travis Haddix was born on November 26, 1938. A native of Walnut, MS, Haddix was inspired in his early years by B.B. King's broadcasts on WDIA out of Memphis. In the Cleveland area, where he has lived since 1959, Haddix developed into a fine modern bluesman and songwriter with an original and soulful touch. While he had been developing his chops in front of rowdy audiences at juke joints and blues festivals throughout the '70s, he didn't begin his recording career in earnest until he signed with the Ichiban label in 1988. His stylish and poppy albums *Wrong Side Out* (1988), *Winners Never Quit* (1991), and *What I Know Right Now* (1992), were, incredibly, released while Haddix continued his job as a postal worker in Ohio.

As his popularity continued to grow, he began traveling to Europe several times a year and won numerous blues awards in both Europe and the States. Haddix resumed recording in 1994 with *Big Ole Goodun'* and also began to develop his interest in other areas of the entertainment business including the formation of his own publishing company and his own record label Wann-Sonn Records. In 2002, Haddix even became an author, releasing *Caught in the Middle*, a book of his musical memoirs. A quote Travis Haddix uses to close out many of his performances sums up his positive philosophical attitude: "I am the best that I can be, and since no one else can be me, there's none better." —*Jim O'Neal & Al Campbell*

Wrong Side Out / 1988 / Ichiban ♦♦♦
Impressive debut for this Cleveland-based vocalist. —*Bill Dahl*

● **Winners Never Quit** / 1991 / Ichiban ♦♦♦♦♦
Travis Haddix perfected his blend of Southern soul and contemporary blues on his second album, *Winners Never Quit*. While the production may be a little too clean for some tastes, Haddix has hit upon a winning formula, one that has a bit of grit and a bit of polish and just enough soul to keep things interesting. Chances are you won't mistake this for a Stax or Chess production, but there's enough passion and heart within Haddix as he balances gutsy blues interludes with kicking soul progressions to make this a thoroughly appealing record. —*Thom Owens*

What I Know Right Now / 1992 / Ichiban ♦♦♦♦♦
The prolific songwriter Travis Haddix leads a Clark Kent existence—he records modern electric blues for Ichiban Records in Atlanta but lives in Bedford, OH (outside of Cleveland), where he's been a postal worker for decades. This CD features Haddix's trademark songs that feature catchy titles and double entendre, risque lyrics that are more humorous than obscene. "No, No, No" explores the negative vibes associated with the word. A vocal chameleon, he goes a top notch Bobby "Blue" Bland growl on "Getting by with a Lie," a slow blues accented by a spine tingling guitar. He's even more Bland-ish on the slow, winding "Strange," while the infectious, loping "Through with Love" has lilt and charm. A typically solid Haddix album. —*Andrew Hamilton*

I Got a Sure Thing / 1993 / Ichiban ♦♦♦♦
Trevor Haddix continues to release quality music filled with innuendos and humor in a vocal style reminiscent of Bobby Bland. "I Got a Sure Thing," originally done by Ollie & the Nightingales, gets a smoldering update, while on "A Day Late and a Dollar Short," Haddix's vocal is as gritty and gutbucket as the painful lyrics. Upbeat blues gets represented by "Funny Bone" and "Expletive List," and "Caught in the Middle" is a good rolling blues number featuring a sultry guitar. Haddix wrote nine of the ten top-quality songs. —*Andrew Hamilton*

Big Ole Goodun' / 1994 / Ichiban ♦♦♦

American Roots: Blues / Apr. 2, 2002 / Ichiban ♦♦♦

Larry Hamilton

Bass / New Orleans Blues, R&B

Crescent City blues and R&B vocalist Larry Hamilton had a revelatory experience at age five when he first heard the Mardi Gras beats of Shriners bands. He took up drums, but his grandmother arranged for him to take piano lessons. He began singing at age 9 and wrote his first lyrics when he was 12. By the time he was 15, he began singing professionally with David Batiste and the Gladiators. His influences include Ray Charles, Nat "King" Cole, Sam Cooke, Big Joe Turner and Otis Redding. Hamilton sang with the Gladiators from 1965 until the mid-'70s, but also toured with Curtis Mayfield, Betty Swan, Jimmy Hughes, Jackie Wilson, Percy Sledge, Little Johnny Taylor, David Ruffin, Major Lance, Z.Z. Hill and Al Green. As a songwriter, Hamilton composed "Get on Your Job" for Etta James, "Feel Like Dynamite" for King Floyd, "She's Taking My Part" for Irma Thomas, and "The Feeling" for Albert King. He has also written tunes for Jean Knight, Wayne Cochran, and Johnny Adams.

At a recording session in the late '70s, Hamilton met producer/songwriter and impresario Allen Toussaint. He joined Toussaint's group and did some touring with him. The two remained close friends, and in 1996, Toussaint signed Hamilton to record for his own NYNO (New York/New Orleans) Records label. Hamilton has one album, *Larry Hamilton* (1997), out on the label. Although many of the songs on Hamilton's debut are Toussaint compositions, future recordings will likely showcase more of Hamilton's original material. —*Richard Skelly*

● **Larry Hamilton** / Apr. 8, 1997 / NYNO ♦♦♦♦
Larry Hamilton's music is R&B in its smooth incarnation, going along the path blazed by the likes of Lou Rawls; it isn't the grit-infused R&B of Bobby Evans and Terry King, or the Holmes Brothers. He has the benefit of being produced by Allen Toussaint and singing in front of the Sea-Saint House Band, a superb aggregation of New Orleans musicians. They seem to flow as one, providing exactly what is needed to highlight the lead instrument—that is, Larry Hamilton's rich, powerful voice—and let it take the spotlight. A powerful first effort on NYNO Records for Larry Hamilton. —*Bob Gottlieb*

Clay Hammond

b. Jun. 21, 1936, Roseback, TX
Vocals / Retro-Soul, R&B, Soul

Hammond may be best remembered as the author of Little Johnny Taylor's huge soul hit, "Part Time Love." He was also a decent Sam Cooke-style soul singer in his own right, however, who recorded for various labels in the '60s. His most well-known efforts from that time are the four singles he did for Kent between 1966-1969. These mixed Southern soul, gospel, and blues styles, yet also had a somewhat lighter and poppier production aura than much Southern soul, perhaps because they were recorded in Los Angeles. All eight songs from these 45s, as well as eight others that were recorded but not released in the '60s, appear on the Ace CD *Southern Soul Brothers*, which also includes ten tracks recorded for Kent around the same time by fellow soul vocalist Z.Z. Hill. Hammond recorded sporadic singles and albums for various labels after the '60s, in addition to singing in the lineups of groups such as the Drifters and the Rivingtons on the oldies circuit. —*Richie Unterberger*

Streets Will Love You / 1988 / Ichiban ♦♦♦

● **Southern Soul Brothers** / Aug. 29, 2000 / Kent ♦♦♦♦♦
Hammond has 16 of the 26 tracks on this split-artist compilation, which also includes ten songs recorded by Z.Z. Hill for the same label (Kent) during the same era (the mid- to late '60s). Hammond's 16 cuts include both sides of all four of his 1966-1969 Kent singles, as well as four from the same period that did not surface until a 1988 LP, and four more from the same time that were previously unissued until this CD. He was a minor but a worthy Southern soul-style vocalist who sounded much like a gentler Sam Cooke, writing all of his material on this disc. On his Kent sides (he had previously recorded for other labels), he adeptly crossed soul with shades of blues and gospel, although the arrangements were not as lugubrious and brassy as much soul actually produced in the South was. Occasionally he used pop-style production to good effect, as on the 1966 single "You Brought It All on Yourself," with its swinging, slightly jazz horn lines. Interestingly, his 1968 B-side "Do Right Woman" is not the famous Chips Moman/Dan Penn song, but a different song (albeit with some similarities to the more famous one), recorded at Moman's studio, no less. The eight songs that were not released in the '60s are good by outtakes standard. "Togetherness" has something of the ballad feel of Cooke's "A Change Is Gonna Come," while "My Sweet Baby Is Coming Home," with only an electric debut as backup, anticipates the sound of fellow Cooke acolyte Ted Hawkins. The ten songs that follow from Hill, incidentally, are average period soul that also have some stronger blues elements than many recordings from the genre, combining a few of Hill's 1966-1969 singles with four previously unissued numbers. —*Richie Unterberger*

John Hammond Jr.

b. Nov. 13, 1942, New York, NY
Slide Guitar, Vocals, Harmonica, Guitar / Folk Revival, Contemporary Blues, Blues-Rock, R&B

With a career that now spans in excess of three decades, John Hammond is one of handful of White blues musicians who was on the scene at the beginning of the first blues renaissance of the mid-'60s. That revival, brought on by renewed interest in folk music around the U.S., brought about career boosts for many of the same classic blues players, including Mississippi John Hurt, Rev. Gary Davis, and Skip James. Some critics have described Hammond as a white Robert Johnson, and Hammond does justice to classic blues by combining powerful guitar and harmonica playing with expressive vocals and a dignified stage presence. Within the first decade of his career as a performer, Hammond began crafting a niche for himself that is completely his own: the solo guitar man, harmonica slung in a rack around his neck, reinterpreting classic blues songs from the '30s, '40s, and '50s. Yet, as several of his mid-'90s recordings for the Pointblank label demonstrate, he's also a capable bandleader who plays wonderful electric guitar. This guitar playing and ensemble work can be heard on *Found True Love* and *Got Love If You Want It*, both for the Pointblank/Virgin label.

Born November 13, 1942, in New York City, the son of the famous Columbia Records talent scout, John Hammond Sr., what most people don't know is that young Hammond didn't grow up with his father. His parents split when he was young, and he would see his father several times a year. He first began playing guitar while attending a private high school, and he was particularly fascinated with slide guitar technique. He saw his idol, Jimmy Reed, perform at New York's Apollo Theatre, and he's never been the same since.

After attending Antioch College in Ohio on a scholarship for a year, he left to pursue a career as a blues musician. By 1962, with the folk revival starting to heat up, Hammond had attracted a following in the coffeehouse circuit, performing in the tradition of the classic country blues singers he loved so much. By the time he was just 20 years old, he had been interviewed for the *New York Times* before one of his East Coast festival performances, and he was a certified national act.

When Hammond was living in the Village in 1966, a young Jimi Hendrix came through town, looking for work. Hammond offered to put a band together for the guitarist, and got the group work at the Cafe Au Go Go. By that point, the coffeehouses were falling out of favor and instead the bars and electric guitars were coming in with folk-rock. Hendrix was approached there by Chas Chandler, who took him to England to record. Hammond recalls telling the young Hendrix to take Chandler up on his offer. "The next time I saw him, about a year later, he was a big star in Europe," Hammond recalled in a 1990 interview. In the late '60s and early '70s, Hammond continued his work with electric blues ensembles, recording with people like Band guitarist Robbie Robertson (and other members of the Band when they were still known as Levon and the Hawks), Duane Allman, Dr. John, harmonica wiz Charlie Musselwhite, Michael Bloomfield and David Bromberg.

As with Dr. John and other blues musicians who've recorded more than two dozen albums, there are many great recordings that provide a good introduction to the man's body of work. His self-titled debut for the Vanguard label has now been reissued on compact disc by the company's new owners, the Welk Music Group, and other good recordings to check out (on vinyl and/or compact disc) include *I Can Tell* (recorded with Bill Wyman from the Rolling Stones), *Southern Fried* (1968), *Sourcepoint* (1970, Columbia), and his most recent string of early- and mid-'90s albums for Pointblank/Virgin Records, *Got Love If You Want It*, *Trouble No More* (both produced by J.J. Cale), and *Found True Love*.

He didn't know it when he was 20, and he may not realize it now, but Hammond deserves special commendation for keeping many of the classic blues songs alive. When fans see Hammond perform them, as Dr. John has observed many times with his music and the music of others, the fans often want to go back further, and find out who did the original versions of the songs Hammond now plays.

Although he's a multi-dimensional artist, one thing Hammond has never professed to be is a songwriter. In the early years of his career, it was more important to him that he bring the art form to a wider audience by performing classic–in some cases forgotten–songs. Now, more than 30 years later, Hammond continues to do this, touring all over the U.S., Canada and Europe from his base in northern New Jersey. Anything can happen at a John Hammond concert, and he selects tunes from his vast repertoire like buckets of water from a well.

Whether it's with a band or by himself, Hammond can do it all. Seeing him perform live, one still gets the sense that some of the best is still to come from this energetic bluesman. *—Richard Skelly*

John Hammond / 1962 / Vanguard ◆◆◆

Big City Blues / 1964 / Vanguard ◆◆◆◆
Hammond's second effort was one of the first electric white blues recordings, and one of the very first that could be said to be blues-rock. Covering a variety of Chess Records classics and electrifying some older tunes, the playing, featuring Hammond, Billy Butler, and Jimmy Spruill on electric guitar, is first-rate. But Hammond's vocals are overly mannered and overwrought, and although he would improve, these flaws would keep him from rising to the top rank of white bluesmen. *—Richie Unterberger*

Country Blues / 1964 / Vanguard ◆◆◆◆
Although Hammond had already recorded electric material, he went back to a solo acoustic format for his fourth album, accompanying himself on guitar and harmonica on faithful interpretations of standards by Robert Johnson, Blind Willie McTell, John Lee Hooker, Sleepy John Estes, Jimmy Reed, Willie Dixon, and Bo Diddley. If it sounds a bit unimaginative and routine today, one has to remember that the general listening audience was much less aware of these artists and songs in the mid-'60s. Hammond did a commendable job of rendering them here, with fine guitar work and vocals that were a considerable improvement over his earliest efforts. *—Richie Unterberger*

So Many Roads / 1965 / Vanguard ◆◆◆◆
So Many Roads is Hammond's most notable mid-'60s Vanguard album, due not so much to Hammond's own singing and playing (though he's up to the task) as the yet-to-be-famous backing musicians. Three future members of the Band–Robbie Robertson, Garth Hudson, and Levon Helm–are among the supporting cast, along with Charlie Musselwhite on harmonica, and Mike Bloomfield also contributes. It's one of the first fully realized blues-rock albums, although it's not in the same league as the best efforts of the era by the likes of the Paul Butterfield Blues Band or John Mayall's Bluesbreakers. In part that's because the repertoire is so heavy on familiar Chicago blues classics by the likes of Willie Dixon, Bo Diddley, and Muddy Waters; in part that's because the interpretations are so reverent and close to the originals in arrangement; and in part it's also because Hammond's blues vocals were only OK. Revisionist critics thus tend to downgrade the record a notch. But in the context of its time–when songs like "Down in the Bottom," "Long Distance Call," "Big Boss Man" and "You Can't Judge a Book By the Cover" were not as well known as they would become–it was a punchy, well-done set of electric blues with a rock touch. *—Richie Unterberger*

I Can Tell / 1967 / Atlantic ◆◆◆◆
I Can Tell boasts an all-star backing band of rock & roll stars, featuring everyone from Bill Wyman to Robbie Robertson. Hammond leads the band through a set of Chicago blues standards, reaching deep into the catalogs of Willie Dixon, Elmore James, Howlin' Wolf, and many others. Although the performances can occasionally sound too studied, the album is by and large an unadulterated delight–the affection Hammond and his band have for the material is quite clear. The CD reissue includes four cuts from his 1970 album, *Southern Fried*, which feature Duane Allman on slide guitar. *—Thom Owens*

Sooner or Later / 1968 / Water ◆◆◆
Like several of Hammond's early albums, this 1968 effort would ultimately sound less impressive than it did at the time, simply because the original versions of the ten songs Hammond covered would become much more accessible. The material selected did testify to his good taste, but also stuck to the tried-and-true, including classics like "Dust My Broom," "Crosscut Saw," Sonny Boy Williamson's "Nine Below Zero" and "Don't Start Me Talking," and Howlin' Wolf's "How Many More Years." The title track, a slow Jimmy Mc-Cracklin piano tune, is about the least-familiar number on a program that's essentially revamped classic and still rather recent electric (and largely Chicago) blues classics with a very slightly more rock- and soul-oriented groove. Still, it's a lean and respectably hard-hitting electric blues set, comfortably integrating piano and (on occasion) Willie Bridges' saxes into the arrangements. *—Richie Unterberger*

John Hammond Solo / 1976 / Vanguard ◆◆◆

Footwork / 1978 / Vanguard ◆◆◆
A blues purist, John Hammond came to prominence in the mid-'60s and recorded for the prestigious Vanguard label, earning himself the title of "the white Robert Johnson" with his authentic National Steel guitar, voice, and harmonica blues. Highly praised in the blues and folk worlds, Hammond led a career spanning four decades with outstanding dedication to the purity of the blues. The Band served as rhythm section on some of his albums, but solo is arguably the best way to hear him–with no discredit to Robbie Robertson and company. It's just that Hammond is that kind of artist. *Footwork* was recorded in isolation by Hammond alone in 1978. The album is haunting in its pragmatic recording; every nuance of his gravelly voice and subtle inflection of the guitar and harmonica reverberate with an intimacy that had defined Delta blues. Such an ethic had become increasingly rare in the commercial world of watered-down or over-produced blues music of the time. Of the few artists working in authentic blues and folk, John Hammond is extraordinary, duly praised and loved by artists from the Rolling Stones to Bert Jansch. *—Skip Jansen*

Hot Tracks / 1979 / Vanguard ◆◆◆◆
In September of 1979, John Hammond went into Vanguard Records' 23rd Street Studio in New York with the Nighthawks–Jimmy Thackery, guitar; Mark Wenner, harmonica; Jan Zukowski, bass; Pete Ragusa, drums–and cut this record, one of his best (and which might've sold better with maybe some better cover art). The sounds are alternately hot and soulful on the ten-song collection, featuring covers of songs by Little Walter ("You Better Watch Yourself," "Last Night"), Chuck Berry ("Nadine"), Jimmy Reed ("Caress Me Baby," one of Hammond's slowest, most seductive numbers), and Robert Johnson ("Sweet Home Chicago"). Highlights include a stunningly beautiful rendition of Howlin' Wolf's "Who's Been Talkin'," a wailing reconsideration of John Lee Hooker's "Sugar Mama" with a really searing guitar break, a very powerful version of "Howlin' for My Darling," and even the best cover of Dixon's "Pretty Thing" this side of Bo Diddley himself, where Hammond and company manage to be raunchy and smooth at the same time. Nothing's going to make anyone forget Walter, Wolf, or Willie, but this isn't a bad way to spend 40 minutes, especially given the really crunchy guitar sound achieved by Jeff Zaraya and the uncredited producer. A real diamond in the rough, and one of Hammond's best albums. *—Bruce Eder*

Mileage / 1980 / Rounder ◆◆◆

Frogs for Snakes / 1982 / Rounder ◆◆◆

Nobody But You / 1988 / Flying Fish ◆◆◆
Hammond usually performs solo, but here he is backed by a five-piece band, including pianist Gene Taylor. It's good to hear him in this context. All the numbers are blues classics or standards written by John Lee Hooker, Muddy Waters, Arthur Crudup, Little Walter, and B.B. Fuller. *—Michael G. Nastos*

● **The Best of John Hammond** / 1989 / Vanguard ◆◆◆◆◆
Vanguard's *The Best of John Hammond* is an excellent collection that features 22 highlights from his early albums, balancing acoustic and electric material, including "My Babe," "Milk Cow Calf's Blues," "Big Boss Man," "See That My Grave Is Kept Clean," "Stones in My Passway," "Key to the Highway" and "Who Do You Love," among others. While his first albums hold up quite well as individual records, this collection does a good job of summarizing his strengths, making it a nice introduction to Hammond's peak years. *—Thom Owens*

Got Love If You Want It / 1992 / Charisma ◆◆◆
In many ways, *Got Love If You Want It* is standard-issue John Hammond Jr. The album is filled with covers by great bluesmen like Son House and Slim Harpo, as well as rock & rollers like Chuck Berry. The difference is ability–Hammond is a professional and is able to pull off convincing performances of these warhorses. Backed by Little Charlie and the Nightcats–who have rarely sounded better, incidentally–Hammond tears through these songs with passion, which makes even the oldest songs sound rather fresh. *—Thom Owens*

Live / Jan. 15, 1992 / Rounder ◆◆◆◆
John Hammond has dealt with issues of authenticity and origin, both musical and personal, and moved beyond them. This 18-song session, recorded live in 1983 and later

reissued on CD, may have been his definitive session. It was certainly a masterpiece, with Hammond doing confident, thoroughly distinctive versions of signature Delta and Chicago blues classics by Robert Johnson, Muddy Waters, Willie Dixon, Son House and others. While "Dust My Broom," "Drop Down Mama," "Wang Dang Doodle" and all the rest have certainly been done to death, Hammond's spirited vocals, riveting guitar work on acoustic or bottleneck and his overall charismatic performances made them seem like fresh discoveries. —*Ron Wynn*

Trouble No More / Jan. 25, 1994 / Pointblank ✦✦✦
John Hammond Jr. made the leap to the Virgin blues division Pointblank with *Got Love If You Want It* in 1992, but he truly made an artistic comeback with its follow-up, *Trouble No More*, an excellent collection split between solo acoustic numbers and storming electric blues. For the electric numbers, he's supported by Little Charlie & the Nightcats, who give Hammond a surprisingly gritty and flexible support. But the heart of the album is in the acoustic cuts, where he proves that he has absorbed the Delta blues completely. These are among his finest acoustic work, and they're what makes *Trouble No More* such an impressive effort. —*Thom Owens*

Found True Love / Jan. 23, 1996 / Virgin ✦✦✦
Found True Love offers the usual highly proficient replication of classic electric and acoustic blues one has come to expect from John Hammond. Although he can more than hold his own on both guitar and harp, he often prefers to collaborate with other bluesmen on recordings; here, he shares the spotlight even more than usual. Hammond blows harp on only five cuts and plays guitar on only four, leaving most of the fretwork to co-producer Duke Robillard (who brings along his regular rhythm section) and letting Charlie Musselwhite handle harp on a couple of tunes. Still, it is Hammond's alluring, leathery vocals that distinguish the recording. Hammond is an interpreter, not an originator, and on *Found True Love* he covers two each by Little Walter and Howlin' Wolf, and one each by Jimmy Reed, Leroy Carr, Blind Willie McTell, Baby Boy Warren, Lonnie Johnson, Little Brother Montgomery, Cousin Joe, and Sleepy John Estes. —*Steve Hoffman*

Long as I Have You / Apr. 21, 1998 / Virgin ✦✦✦✦
John Hammond's latest album marks a major departure in one respect—for the first time in anyone's memory, he sings, but plays nothing on one of his records, while Little Charlie & the Nightcats, led by guitarist Charlie Baty, handle the guitars and everything else. The difference is very subtle, the playing maybe a little less flashy than Hammond's already restrained work—think of how good Muddy Waters sounded on the early-'60s records where he sang and didn't play. And that comparison is an apt one—even more than 35 years after he started, Hammond inevitably ends up sounding like its 1961 and he's working at Chess studios in Chicago, cutting songs between Muddy Waters sessions. Harpist Rick Estrin also contributes a smooth and eminently enjoyable original amid a brace of covers of blues standards. There is not a weak number here, and this band is a kick to listen to, sounding more naturally authentic than anybody in the '90s has a right to (Baty's quiet pyrotechnics on "Lookin' for Trouble" would make this record worth owning, even if Hammond's singing and the rest of the songs weren't as good as they are). And the songs include numbers by Howlin' Wolf, Eddie Taylor, Little Walter, Sonny Boy Williamson, and Willie Dixon. And as a bonus, we get Hammond playing and singing on three unplugged acoustic tracks, accompanied by a washboard, where he shows off his still-formidable country blues sound, whetting the appetite for more like this. —*Bruce Eder*

Best of the Vanguard Years / Feb. 22, 2000 / Vanguard ✦✦✦✦✦
In lieu of a boxed set, the Welk Music Group (which owns the Vanguard Records library) has produced this rock-solid 23-track overview of Hammond's early recordings for Vanguard, covering highlights of the years 1963 through 1967 and his return to the label from 1976 through 1979. The tracks aren't in strict chronological order but are juxtaposed on a more general basis, and you can hear him gain confidence and maturity as this compilation chronologically moves on, from the rough-edged enthusiasm of the opener "32-20 Blues," to the closing "Guitar King." Six of the tracks are from the *So Many Roads* album that featured Mike Bloomfield, Charlie Musselwhite, and members of the Band in the lineup. The producers did more than remaster all of this material in 20-bit sound (though they did do that, too)—they also raided the vaults and found a pair of unissued songs, "Ask Me Nice" and "Hellhound Blues," that they've issued here. Cut with a small, uncredited backing band, "Ask Me Nice" could have fit in easily on either *Big City Blues* or *So Many Roads*, though it's more likely associated with the former, while "Hellhound Blues" is an ominous all-acoustic number, very different in character and texture. The resulting 75 minutes of music is the best (and best sounding) overview of his work for the label, and if you're going to add some John Hammond to the collection, this is a real good place to start. —*Cub Koda & Bruce Eder*

Wicked Grin / Mar. 13, 2001 / Virgin ✦✦✦✦
After 35 years into a career that spans 35 albums recorded for seven labels, you'd think John Hammond might get a little complacent. Thankfully the opposite is true, as 2001's *Wicked Grin* is the artist's most daring musical departure and arguably greatest achievement to date. Mining the rich Tom Waits catalog for 12 of its 13 tracks (the closing is a traditional gospel tune) and bringing Waits himself along as producer has resulted in a stunning collection that stands as one of the best in Hammond's bulging catalog. Never a songwriter, the singer/guitarist/harmonica bluesman has maintained a knack for picking top-notch material from the rich blues tradition without resorting to the hoary, overcovered classics of the genre. It's that quality that transforms these tunes into Hammond songs, regardless of their origin. His history of working with exceptional session musicians is also legendary, and this album's band, which features Doug Sahm sideman Augie Meyers on keyboards, harmonica wiz Charlie Musselwhite, longtime Waits associate Larry Taylor on bass, and Waits himself poking around on various songs, is perfect for the spooky, swampy feel he effortlessly conjures here. Choosing from a wide variety of

Waits' material, Hammond infuses these unusual tracks with a bluesman's spirit and a crackling energy that practically reinvents the songs, instilling them with an ominous, rhythmic swampy feel. The producer contributes two new tracks ("2:19" and "Fannin' Street," the latter is the album's only acoustic cut) that maintain the creepy but upbeat voodoo spirit that trickles and twists throughout. Hammond sings with a renewed spirit, adding a smoother but no less intense edge than Waits' typical rusty razor blade soaked whisky growl. With his dusky croon and idiosyncratic delivery, Hammond tears into this material with relish, spitting out the often offbeat, stream of consciousness lyrics as if he wrote them himself. Only the slow, ambling blues of "Murder in the Red Barn" would comfortably slot into Hammond's existing oeuvre; the remainder push the bluesman into previously uncharted territory with results that reveal fascinating layers of his own interpretive abilities. An experiment whose success will hopefully yield another volume, this partnership of John Hammond and Tom Waits brings out the best in both artists' substantial talents. —*Hal Horowitz*

W.C. Handy

b. Nov. 16, 1873, Muscle Shoals, AL, d. Mar. 28, 1958
Bandleader, Songwriter, Piano / Early American Blues
W.C. Handy, the "Father of the Blues," brought the music of rural Southern blacks into the mainstream by copyrighting old songs and writing new songs, spurring the blues into the mainstream of popular music during the 1910s and '20s. He was also a highly trained veteran of the music world who led all manner of groups: string quartets, brass bands, and a touring minstrel show group.

William Christopher Handy was born in Florence, AL, in 1873. His early years were spent living in a log cabin built by his grandfather, a local minister (as was his father). Handy was musical from an early age, and took lessons on the cornet from a local barbershop. After graduating from school near the top of his class, he began working as a teacher in Birmingham in 1893, but quit soon after (due to low wages) and began working at a factory job.

He also founded a string quartet, named the Lauzetta Quartet, and traveled with the band to perform at the World's Fair in Chicago. Though he also toured with the group, Handy was soon teaching again in his home state, this time at the Huntsville Normal School (later to become Alabama A&M). By 1896, he'd hit the road yet again, a three-year hitch playing cornet with the minstrel show Mahara's Minstrels that saw him appearing as far west as Oklahoma and as far south as Cuba. Around the turn of the century, Handy returned to Huntsville Normal and served as its band director from 1900 to 1902. After another short tour with Mahara's Minstrels (this time playing the Northwest), W.C. Handy moved to Clarksdale and became the director of a black band, the Colored Knights of Pythias, which played before both black and white audiences. Handy spent six years based in Clarksdale, where his previous brushes with blues music were intensified by time spent in the nominal home of the blues. Once, in 1903, while waiting for a train in the town of Tutwiler, he heard a musician playing his guitar with a knife and singing about a local spot where two railroads crossed; he later called it "the weirdest music I'd ever heard," but the song stuck in his head and he later copyrighted a song along the same theme, the famous "Yellow Dog Blues."

By 1909, Handy had moved to Memphis, where he published his first song, "Mr. Crump," that same year. Local political heavyweight Edward H. "Boss" Crump was running for mayor that year, and though the candidate was by no means a music fan, an orchestra led by Handy was hired for entertainment, and the song—actually including some serious criticisms of Crump himself—became famous around the city. Three years later, with different lyrics provided by George Norton, it became "The Memphis Blues," though Handy unwisely sold the copyright for 100 dollars. He soon set up his own publishing company (Pace & Handy Music Co., with Harry Pace) in the heart of Memphis' burgeoning entertainment district on Beale Street. In 1914, he published his most famous piece (and one of the most-recorded songs of all time), "The St. Louis Blues," as well as "Yellow Dog Blues." Two years later came "Beale Street Blues," and in September of 1917 Handy's Orchestra of Memphis (a 12-piece band) recorded several sides for Columbia in New York.

In 1918, Handy moved the entire operation to New York, where Handy Brothers Music Company, Inc. set up on another famous entertainment avenue, Broadway. Though he never produced another hit to rank with his compositions of the mid-'10s, the timing was fortuitous; in August of 1920, Mamie Smith recorded Perry Bradford's "Crazy Blues," not just an unlikely hit but a commercial explosion that made the blues as big a phenomenon as ragtime had been during the early '10s. Handy eventually copyrighted over 150 songs of secular and religious material, and Handy's Orchestra continued to record material, for Paramount and OKeh. In 1926, he wrote *Blues: An Anthology*, which not only compiled sheet music for the most famous blues songs but also attempted to explain their origins. Handy began to lose his vision during the late '20s, but worked steadily during the '30s, publishing *Negro Authors and Composers of the United States* in 1935, *W.C. Handy's Collection of Negro Spirituals* in 1938, and *Unsung Americans Sung* in 1944. He also authored an autobiography, *Father of the Blues*, in 1941. By 1943, however, his vision had completely failed after a serious fall. In 1954, he married for the second time (his first wife, Elizabeth, had died in 1937) and in 1958, Nat King Cole starred in the biopic *St. Louis Blues*. W.C. Handy had already died of pneumonia in March of that year. His legacy is not just a function of his copyrights; Memphis named a park on Beale Street after him, and the W.C. Handy Blues Awards is the premier awards ceremony for blues music. —*John Bush*

W.C. Handy's Memphis Blues Band / Sep. 21, 1917–May 1923 / Memphis Archives ✦✦✦
● **Father of the Blues** / 1923-1962 / DRG ✦✦✦✦
In addition to the nine performances of Handy songs included on this Blues Foundation of Memphis-produced document, there is also a wealth of interview excerpts from 1950 to 1955. The music is wide-ranging, from a 1923 instrumental "Memphis Blues" cut by Handy's Orchestra up to a 1962 Louis Armstrong remote. Also included is a 1934 aircheck vocal take of the aforementioned "Memphis Blues" sung by Mae West with the Duke

Ellington Orchestra, as well as the 1929 film soundtrack to Bessie Smith's *St. Louis Blues*. —*Jason Ankeny*

Pat Hare

b. Dec. 20, 1930, Cherry Valley, AR, **d.** Sep. 26, 1980, St. Paul, MN
Vocals, Guitar / Electric Memphis Blues
If highly distorted guitar played with a ton of aggression and just barely suppressed violence is your idea of great blues, then Pat Hare's your man. Born with the improbable name of Auburn Hare (one of those biographical oddities that even the most fanciful blues historian couldn't make up in a million years), he worked the '50s Memphis circuit, establishing his rep as a top-notch player with a scorching tone only rivaled by Howlin' Wolf's guitarist, Willie Johnson. Our first recorded glimpse of him occurs when he showed up at Sam Phillips' Memphis Recording Service sometime in 1953 to play on James Cotton's debut session for the Sun label. His aggressive, biting guitar work on both sides of that oft-anthologized single—"Cotton Crop Blues" and "Hold Me in Your Arms"—featured a guitar sound so overdriven that with the historical distance of several decades, it now sounds like a direct line to the coarse, distorted tones favored by modern rock players. But what is now easily attainable by 16-year-old kids on modern day effects pedals just by stomping on a switch, Hare was accomplishing with his fingers and turning the volume knob on his Sears & Roebuck cereal-box-sized amp all the way to the right until the speaker was screaming.

After working with Cotton and numerous others around the Memphis area, Hare moved North to Chicago and by the late '50s was a regular member of the Muddy Waters band, appearing on the legendary *Live at Newport, 1960* album. By all accounts Pat was a quiet, introspective man when sober, but once he started drinking the emotional tables turned in the opposite direction. After moving to Minneapolis in the '60s to work with fellow Waters bandmate Mojo Buford, Hare was convicted of murder after a domestic dispute, spending the rest of his life behind bars. In one of the great ironies of the blues, one of the unissued tracks Pat Hare left behind in the Sun vaults was an original composition entitled, "I'm Gonna Murder My Baby." —*Cub Koda*

Harlem Hamfats

f. 1936, Chicago, IL, **db.** 1939
Group / East Coast Blues, Acoustic Chicago Blues, Dirty Blues
The Harlem Hamfats were a crack studio band formed in 1936 by black talent scout Mayo "Ink" Williams. Its main function was backing jazz and blues singers such as Johnny Temple, Rosetta Howard, and Frankie "Half Pint" Jackson for Decca Records. The Hamfats' side career began when its first record "Oh Red" became a hit. Despite its name, none of the band's members came from Harlem, and none were hamfats, a disparaging term referring to indifferent musicians. Brothers Joe (guitar, vocals) and Charlie McCoy (guitar, mandolin) were blues players from Mississippi; leader Herb Morand (trumpet, vocals), Odell Rand (clarinet), and John Lindsay (bass) were from New Orleans; Horace Malcolm (piano) and drummers Pearlis Williams and Freddie Flynn were from Chicago. This territorial disparity created a sound which blended various blues styles with New Orleans, Dixieland, and swing jazz. The band's high-spirited playing and excellent musicianship compensated for what some critics have called lack of improvisational skill. The Hamfats' music has been somewhat neglected over the years. The vocalists tended to be derivative of other popular singers of the day such as Louis Armstrong, Fats Waller, and various blues singers. The lyrical content of their songs often revolved around subjects like drinking and sex, leading some to dismiss them as a lightweight novelty act. Although it is not seen as an innovative group, The Harlem Hamfats' riff-based style was influential to Louis Jordan, early Muddy Waters, and what would eventually become rhythm and blues and rock & roll. —*Jim Powers*

Hot Chicago Jazz, Blues and Jive: 1936–1937 / Oct. 2, 1936-Oct. 6, 1937 / Folklyric ♦♦♦♦
Hot Chicago Jazz, Blues and Jive: 1936-1937 collects 17 tracks the Harlem Hamfats recorded in those two years, featuring the band on their own, as well as accompanists. Most of these performances are quite good, and many of them have never been released on LP before, yet the presence of the sidemen tracks makes this more of interest to collectors than the curious. —*Thom Owens*

● **Harlem Hamfats (1936–1939)** / Oct. 1936-Sep. 1939 / Document ♦♦♦♦♦
Document's *Harlem Hamfats (1936-1939)* is an excellent 20-track collection that contains many of the group's greatest singles, thereby offering a nearly ideal summation of their career. —*Thom Owens*

Keep It Swinging Round and Round / Dec. 1936-Sep. 1939 / Blues Document ♦♦♦

Harlem Hamfats, Vol. 1 / Nov. 4, 1994 / Document ♦♦♦♦

Harlem Hamfats, Vol. 2 / Nov. 4, 1994 / Document ♦♦♦♦

Harlem Hamfats, Vol. 3 / Nov. 4, 1994 / Document ♦♦♦♦

Harlem Hamfats, Vol. 4 / Nov. 4, 1994 / Document ♦♦♦♦

James Harman

b. Jun. 8, 1946, Anniston, AL
Vocals, Harmonica / Modern Electric Blues
James Harman is a California-based blues singer, harmonica player, songwriter, and bandleader with an agenda that definitely distances him from the rest of the pack. A veteran of the blues roadhouse circuit, he has led various combinations of the James Harman Band over the years, most featuring top-notch talent (like guitarists Hollywood Fats and Kid Ramos) to match his own. With roots in the deepest of blues harmonica sources (Little Walter, Walter Horton, Sonny Boy Williamson), Harman scores consistently both live and on record. His most recent recorded efforts show a genuine flair for writing original material (always more important to Harman than just regurgitating his record collection), all of it laced with a generous dollop of wisecracking good humor. Always willing to stretch the boundaries and conceptions of what a good bar band should be capable of, Harman combines rich traditons and beatnik craziness for a blend that's mighty hard to resist.—*Cub Koda*

Those Dangerous Gentlemen / 1987 / Rhino ♦♦♦

Extra Napkins / 1988 / Cannonball ♦♦♦
Originally released on Rivera Records in 1988, this is the first of a projected series of compact discs chronicling the recording sessions that went into the making of James Harman's first fully formed studio endeavor. Harman approached the entire recording as if each song was a single, using whatever personnel were right for the song—his regular band on some tunes, horns and other guest artists on others. This initial volume in the set collects the 12 songs that appeared on the original album, which laid the groundwork for Harman's later recorded efforts. As some 53 tunes were recorded in that fertile two-year period between 1985 and the album's final lineup here, this batch is apparently just the tip of iceberg. —*Cub Koda*

Live in '85, Vol. 1 / 1990 / Rivera ♦♦♦
Consisting of tapes recorded live over two nights in March of 1985 at the Belly Up Tavern in Soldano Beach, California, this captures Harman and one of his best bands in full cry, warts and all. Kicking off with a James Brown-announcer-on-acid introduction from fellow harp maestro John "Juke" Logan, Harman and the boys kick hard and heavy through half a dozen of his better known numbers, including an earlier and electric version of "Goatman Holler." The guitar interplay between Hollywood Fats and Kid Ramos is textbook in its accuracy and passion, and the rock-steady rhythm section of Stephen Hodges on drums and William Campbell keeps things totally in groove territory every beat of the way. In this live setting, things get brought down and stretched out, but never unnecessarily so, and even the almost nine-minute shuffle "You're Gone" is worth every second the boys put into it. Although nowhere as wiseass or beatnik-cool as his current persona, Harman nonetheless blows with chops galore, and his vocals (and asides to the crowd between songs) here seem to come with their own built-in smirk. Worth more than a listen or two just for the late Hollywood Fats' stellar solo work and the rarity of being a live album that actually rocks without having to rely on shop-worn cover material. Certainly one of Harman's best efforts and very deserving of a much wider hearing. —*Cub Koda*

● **Do Not Disturb** / 1991 / Black Top ♦♦♦♦♦
James Harman's *Do Not Disturb* is a first-rate blues album, one that captures all the different sides of postwar blues. At its core, *Do Not Disturb* is Chicago blues, but Harman touches on swing, jump, and Texas roadhouse blues, banging out gritty, greasy harp licks with intensity. His band is up to the challenge of keeping up with him—they tear through the uniformly excellent songs with abandon. *Do Not Disturb* establishes Harman as one of the most exciting blues traditionalists of the '90s. —*Thom Owens*

Two Sides to Every Story / Jun. 1, 1993 / Black Top ♦♦♦♦

Cards on the Table / May 28, 1994 / Black Top ♦♦♦

Black & White / 1995 / Black Top ♦♦

Takin' Chances / Sep. 8, 1998 / Cannonball ♦♦♦♦♦
James Harman is incapable of making a bad album. Here, as in any of his previous releases, his vocals and harmonica playing are prominently featured. His writing is better than average, and he portrays the common themes of the blues in a collection of songs about gambling and love. His full, Southern gospel-inflected vocals are always a treat to listen to, and he plays electrified harp in the Little Walter style with the best of them. As always, his choice of sidemen, especially guitar players, is first-class. They embody the sound of jump blues from the late '40s and Chicago in the '50s and add considerable spark to the album. On three cuts, Harman plays some very tasty acoustic harmonica, à la Sonny Boy Williamson, which show his mastery of the instrument even without the excitement which amplification adds. It's good to see James Harman keeping the flame of postwar urban blues burning so brightly. —*Sigmund Finman*

Mo' Na'Kins, Please! / Apr. 25, 2000 / Cannonball ♦♦♦
When Harman recorded the now legendary *Extra Napkins* session for the Rivera label, he recorded some 53 tracks before making the final cut. Now for this second volume, he's gone back and culled 14 more from the vaults from those sessions. With players like Kid Ramos, Hollywood Fats, and Junior Watson in various lineups, the collection is no set of leftovers—far from it. Harman approached each tune separately, with specific arrangements and instrumentation in mind, and the care and time show in the end result. A set of unissued material well worth getting out there. —*Cub Koda*

Harmonica Fats (Harvey Blackston)

b. Sep. 8, 1927, McDade, LA, **d.** Jan. 3, 2000
Vocals, Harmonica / Contemporary Blues, Modern Electric Blues
Harmonica Fats was actually Harvey Blackston, a former Louisianan who learned the blues growing up on his grandfather's farm; his longtime partner, Bernie Pearl, a native Angeleno learned the blues from the musicians who frequented the fabled Ash Grove (a folk and blues club run by Pearl's brother Ed), including Lightnin' Hopkins and Mance Lipscomb.

In the early '50s, Fats took up harmonica as self-prescribed therapy while recuperating from an auto accident. Once confident, he formed a band, playing clubs around Los Angeles, and was known then as "Heavy Juice." Just as carefully, he perfected his songwriting, scoring on the R&B charts in 1961 with the self-penned single "Tore Up." After changing his name to Harmonica Fats, this success led to work as a studio musician, playing dates with performers as diverse as Bill Cosby, Ringo Starr, and Lou Rawls. He even did a stint as a traveling solo musician, seeking gigs as he drove in a station wagon around the country.

Pearl, through the Ash Grove, backed artists Big Mama Thornton, Bukka White, Mississippi Fred McDowell, Freddie King, and more. In the late '60s, '80s, and early '90s, he was a blues DJ, not only entertaining but educating with the knowledge he acquired during the Ash Grove days. Perhaps his best-known accomplishment was founding one of the West Coast's top blues events, the Long Beach Blues Festival, and he was the promoter of the Big Time Blues Festival, also held in Long Beach.

The Bernie Pearl Blues Band originated in 1984, with Robert Lucas on harmonica. Fats replaced Lucas in 1986. Fats' witty songs and on-stage magnetism is captured on *Live at Cafe Lido*, an album originally intended as a demo. The high demand for that album led Fats and Pearl to form Bee Bump Records, with its first release being *I Had to Get Nasty*. Pearl convinced Fats to work as an acoustic duo, releasing *Two Heads Are Better* in 1995. The following year, they released *Blow, Fat Daddy, Blow!*, dedicated to the memory of Fats' wife and civil rights activist Johnnie Tillman. *—Char Ham*

Live at Cafe Lido / 1990 / Pearl Til-Blac Prod ✦✦✦✦
Despite the muddiness in the recording, Fats punches it in with 320 pounds of high-energy, gut-wrenching blues. Listen to Fats' harmonica as he leads the band's rhythm section on "Boogie All the Way." Guesting on the Ray Charles hit "Georgia On My Mind," Papa John Creach wails a romantic treatment coupled with Hollis Gilmore's soulful sax. It's little wonder "Tore Up" was such a big hit for Fats—he roars life into the Hank Ballard penning. You can feel the fans filled with heightened vibes in "Harmonica Fats Blows," making one wish he or she were dancing along with Fats. However, on the finale, Robert Johnson would cringe if he heard the vocals on "Walkin' Blues." *—Char Ham*

● **I Had to Get Nasty** / 1991 / Bee Bump ✦✦✦✦✦
Fats is backed up by the Bernie Pearl Blues Band on this mostly electric effort, though hints of Fats' country origins stick out. On the fast-tempo numbers, Fats' driving, in-your-face energy comes out full bore, and on these songs the wit and humor of his lyrics stand out best. Pearl's attempt at lead vocals on Lightnin' Hopkins' "Automobile Blues" would have been better left off to allow Fats to expand his showman capabilties. *—Char Ham*

Two Heads Are Better / 1995 / Bee Bump ✦✦✦
Fats and Pearl change settings by turning acoustic, but if the album were mixed with more balance between the harmonica and guitar, it would more fittingly show their partnership. Perhaps Fats' greatest asset is the wit and humor in his songwriting, well illustrated in "Just Like Richard Nixon," a rollicking ode to the pre-Presidential days of Nixon interplayed with Fats' dilemma of being constantly hounded by girls. Funnier is "Blabbermouth Man," a supposed confessional about a tongue-wagging, testesterone-laced gossiper. Fats can sing about mundane aspects of life and turn them into curiosities, whether it be the virtues of soul food (what else but "Soul Food"?) or how making small wages isn't enough to post bail to spring the boss out of jail in "Everyday's a Working Day for Me." The downside is that the album lacks consistently high-quality material, such as "Vampire Blues," which is dosed with overt corniness. *—Char Ham*

Blow, Fat Daddy, Blow! / Mar. 19, 1996 / Bee Bump ✦✦✦✦✦
On their third album, the duo of Harmonica Fats and Bernie Pearl turn in a typically engaging set of acoustic blues. All of the songs on *Blow, Fat Daddy, Blow!* are originals, and it is to the duo's credit that they manage to sound respectful to tradition without being enslaved to it. Certainly, the quality of the material fluctuates somewhat—not every song cuts as deep as the rootsy "Why Should I Holler?" or the powerful "Blues Kaddish"—but the interaction between the two musicians is stellar. Pearl's guitar playing is subtly impressive and Harmonica Fats simply wails, making the set worthwhile for fans of good-humored, stripped-down blues. *—Thom Owens*

Harmonica Slim (Travis L. Blaylock)

b. Dec. 21, 1934, Douglassville, TX
Vocals, Harmonica / Soul-Blues, West Coast Blues
Over the history of the blues, there's been at least three different people plying their wares as Harmonica Slim, with one of them being far better known as Slim Harpo. But *this* Harmonica Slim was born Travis L. Blaylock down in Texas. He picked up the instrument around the age of 12 and was soon working as part of the Sunny South Gospel Singers gospel group, broadcasting over radio station KCMC in his hometown of Texarkana from the mid-'40s on. By 1949, he moved to Los Angeles, ingratiating himself into the burgeoning blues community, working package shows with Lowell Fulson and the like. He first recorded as a sideman on a group of dates in the mid-'50s for West Coast labels like Aladdin, Spry, and Vita. After spending most of the '60s working dates with Percy Mayfield, Harmonica Fats, B.B. King, T-Bone Walker and others, Slim finally got to record a full album under his own name for the Bluestime label in 1969. *—Cub Koda*

● **Back Bottom Blues** / Oct. 1995 / Trix ✦✦✦✦✦

Give Me My Shotgun / Sep. 23, 1997 / Fedora ✦✦✦

Cold Tacos and Warm Beer / Jun. 6, 2000 / Fedora ✦✦✦
Cold Tacos and Warm Beer is the first recorded collaboration from blues veterans Harmonica Slim and guitarist Hosea Levy. This duo has consistently played for a number of years together, mainly in their hometown of Fresno, California, at open-air rent parties featuring friends and family. The spark from these impromptu sessions combined with their natural passion to play is what makes this Fedora release what Slim describes as "blues real and true to life." *—Al Campbell*

The Harmonizing Four

f. Richmond, VA
Group / Traditional Gospel, Southern Gospel, Black Gospel
One of the top gospel quartets of the postwar era, the Harmonizing Four was also a relative anomaly of the period; as their contemporaries raced to modernize their sound, rejecting the traditional jubilee style in favor of the intensity of the burgeoning "hard gospel" movement, the Four remained true to their roots, focusing instead on the spirituals and hymns of a time gone by. For all of their renown, little is known about the group's formative years—their leader and manager, Joseph "Gospel Joe" Williams, forbade any of the members to agree to interviews unless they were paid in advance, and as a result the anecdotal information that does exist is sketchy and incomplete. Records have indicated that the Four made their formal debut at a grammar school in their native Richmond, VA, on October 27, 1927; founding members included Thomas "Goat" Johnson and Levi Handly, with Williams signing on in 1933 and Lonnie Smith—the father of jazz pianist Lonnie Liston Smith—joining four years later.

The Harmonizing Four made their recorded debut on Decca in 1943; in all likelihood they came to the label at the behest of Sister Rosetta Tharpe, whom they frequently backed both on record and in concert. After World War II, they landed on the tiny Coleman label; included in the roster during much of this period was Tommy Ellison, later of the Chosen Gospel Singers. A brief tenure on Gotham followed, and after 1952, the Harmonizing Four cut only one record, a single for the Religious Recordings label, prior to arriving at Vee-Jay in 1957. There, the group—Williams, Smith, Thomas Johnson and Jimmy Jones—finally began earning the fame long due them, honing their close harmony style to mellow perfection; Jones, in particular, earned renown as perhaps the greatest basso in gospel history, his canyon-deep voice distinguishing hits like "Motherless Child." After leaving Vee-Jay during the early '60s, the Harmonizing Four recorded for Nashboro, slowly easing into retirement in the years that followed. *—Jason Ankeny*

The Harmonizing Four / 1959 / Vee-Jay ✦✦✦✦✦
A collection of this close harmony quartet's singles circa 1957-1959. *—Opal Louis Nations*

Singing Is Our Life / 1965 / Buddah/Vee-Jay ✦✦✦✦✦
The group's last really great album. *—Opal Louis Nations*

★ **Gospel in My Soul** / 1974 / Chameleon ✦✦✦✦✦

Think of God / 1974 / Vee-Jay ✦✦✦✦
More strong material from 1958-1959 sessions. *—Opal Louis Nations*

Harmonizing Four/God Will Take Care of You / Apr. 1993 / Vee-Jay ✦✦✦✦✦
More beautiful hymn-like renditions from 1958-1959 sessions. *—Opal Louis Nations*

I Shall Not Be Moved / Sep. 1, 1995 / Charly ✦✦✦✦✦
Essential '50s Vee-Jay cuts, some with gospel's premier basso, Jimmy Jones. *—Opal Louis Nations*

1950–1955 / Dec. 7, 1995 / Heritage ✦✦✦✦
The quartet's most devout and touching Gotham sides. *—Opal Louis Nations*

Working for the Lord / 1996 / Jewel ✦✦✦✦
One of the finer, later collections by this seminal group. *—Opal Louis Nations*

When Day Is Done: The Very Best of the Harmonizing 4 / Mar. 3, 1998 / Collectables ✦✦✦✦
The best of the Vee-Jay sides featuring Ellis Johnson and Gospel Joe Williams. *—Opal Louis Nations*

God Will Take Care of You/Think of God / Jul. 10, 2001 / Collectables ✦✦✦✦

That Old Time Religion/Spirituals That Will Live Forever! / Jul. 10, 2001 / Collectables ✦✦✦✦

The Best of the Harmonizing Four / Capitol ✦✦✦
Featured is the bass voice of Ellis Johnson or the legendary Jimmy Jones. *—Opal Louis Nations*

Slim Harpo (James Moore)

b. Jan. 11, 1924, Lobdell, LA, **d.** Jan. 31, 1970, Baton Rouge, LA
Vocals, Leader, Harmonica, Guitar / Juke Joint Blues, Blues Revival, Swamp Blues, Louisiana Blues, Electric Blues, Electric Harmonica Blues
In the large stable of blues talent that Crowley, LA, producer Jay Miller recorded for the Nashville-based Excello label, no one enjoyed more mainstream success than Slim Harpo. Just a shade behind Lightnin' Slim in local popularity, Harpo played both guitar and neck-rack harmonica in a more down-home approximation of Jimmy Reed, with a few discernible, and distinctive, differences. Harpo's music was certainly more laid-back than Reed's, if such a notion was possible. But the rhythm was insistent and, overall, Harpo was more adaptable than Reed or most other bluesmen. His material not only made the national charts, but also proved to be quite adaptable for white artists on both sides of the Atlantic, including the Rolling Stones, Yardbirds, Kinks, Dave Edmunds with Love Sculpture, Van Morrison with Them, Sun rockabilly singer Warren Smith, Hank Williams Jr., and the Fabulous Thunderbirds.

A people-pleasing club entertainer, he certainly wasn't above working rock & roll rhythms into his music, along with hard-stressed, country & western vocal inflections. Several of his best tunes were co-written with his wife Lovelle and show a fine hand for song construction, appearing to have arrived at the studio pretty well formed. His harmonica playing was driving and straightforward, full of surprising melody, while his vocals were perhaps best described by writer Peter Guralnick as "if a black country & western singer or a white rhythm & blues singer were attempting to impersonate a member of the opposite genre." And here perhaps was Harpo's true genius, and what has allowed his music to have a wider currency. By the time his first single became a Southern jukebox favorite, his songs were being adapted and played by white musicians left and right. Here was good-time Saturday-night blues that could be sung by elements of the Caucasian persuasion with a straight face. Nothing resembling the emotional investment of a Howlin' Wolf or a Muddy Waters was required; it all came natural and easy, and its influence has stood the test of time.

He was born James Moore just outside of Baton Rouge, LA. After his parents died, he dropped out of school to work every juke joint, street corner, picnic, and house rent party that came his way. By this time he had acquired the alias of Harmonica Slim, which he used until his first record was released. It was fellow bluesman Lightnin' Slim who first steered him to local recordman J.D. Miller. The producer used him as an accompanist to Hopkins on a half-dozen sides before recording him on his own. When it came time to release his first single ("I'm a King Bee"), Miller informed him that there was another

Harmonica Slim recording on the West Coast, and a new name was needed before the record could come out. Moore's wife took the slang word for harmonica, added an "o" to the end of it, and a new stage name was the result, one that would stay with Slim Harpo the rest of his career.

Harpo's first record became a double-sided R&B hit, spawning numerous follow-ups on the "King Bee" theme, but even bigger was "Rainin' in My Heart," which made the Billboard Top 40 pop charts in the summer of 1961. It was another perfect distillation of Harpo's across-the-board appeal, and was immediately adapted by country, Cajun, and rock & roll musicians; anybody could play it and sound good doing it. In the wake of the Rolling Stones covering "I'm a King Bee" on their first album, Slim had the biggest hit of his career in 1966 with "Baby, Scratch My Back." Harpo described it "as an attempt at rock & roll for me," and its appearance in Billboard's Top 20 pop charts prompted the dance-oriented follow-ups "Tip on In" and "Te-Ni-Nee-Ni-Nu," both R&B charters. For the first time in his career, Harpo appeared in such far-flung locales as Los Angeles and New York City. Flush with success, he contacted Lightnin' Slim, who was now residing outside of Detroit, MI. The two reunited and formed a band, touring together as a sort of blues mini-package to appreciative white rock audiences until the end of the decade. The new year beckoned with a tour of Europe (his first ever) all firmed up, and a recording session scheduled when he arrived in London. Unexplainably, Harpo—who had never been plagued with any ailments stronger than a common cold—suddenly succumbed to a heart attack on January 31, 1970. *—Cub Koda*

Rainin' in My Heart / 1961 / Excello ✦✦✦✦✦

The original 12-song Excello album with the addition of six extra tracks, all of which were originally issued as singles only. With the exception of "Dream Girl," "My Home Is a Prison," and "What a Dream," everything on here also appears on the AVI double disc collection. *—AMG*

Sings Raining in My Heart / 1961 / Hip-O ✦✦✦✦✦

This was Excello's first album on Slim Harpo and still the one to beat. Besides the title track in all of its original mono and heavily echoed glory, we're treated to the double whammy of "I'm a King Bee" and its original single flip side, "I Got Love If You Want It," along with certified swamp-blues killers like "Buzz Me Babe," "My Home Is a Prison," "Blues Hangover," "Don't Start Crying Now" and "Dream Girl." "My Little Queen Bee (Got a Brand New King)," "Late Last Night" and "Tip On In, Part 2" are the three bonus CD tracks appended to the original track lineup, making this an excellent first purchase and a darn good backup even if you already have a Slim Harpo best-of in the pile.*—AMG*

I'm a King Bee / 1989 / Flyright ✦✦✦✦✦

Very generous (24 songs) collection emphasizing the laconic harpist's early (1957-1964) Excello output. The British import boasts the required "I'm a King Bee," "I Got Love If You Want It," and "Rainin' in My Heart," but also the more obscure and previously unissued (including Slim's take on John Lee Hooker's "Boogie Chillun"). *—Bill Dahl*

☆ **Scratch My Back: The Best of Slim Harpo** / 1989 / Rhino ✦✦✦✦✦

All the hits, including the original "I'm a King Bee," "Baby, Scratch My Back," "I Got Love If You Want It," "Shake Your Hips," "Rainin' in My Heart," "Tip on In," and "Strange Love." A best-of that really is, with top-flight sound as a bonus. *—Cub Koda*

Shake Your Hips / 1995 / Ace ✦✦✦✦✦

The second installment in Ace's overview of Harpo's swamp blues career, spanning 1962-1966 and including all four of the harpist's rare 1962 sides for Imperial (cut during a brief rift with his producer J.D. Miller). More rarities and unissued gems, including a few tracks that exhibit slight soul tendencies (a genre that Harpo took to surprisingly well). *—Bill Dahl*

Hip Shakin': The Excello Collection / 1995 / Excello ✦✦✦✦✦

A shapely two-disc retrospective, *Hip Shakin'* is the definitive Slim Harpo package. Collecting up all of his hits ("I'm A King Bee," "Got Love If You Want It," "Baby, Scratch My Back") along with other defining moments from his stay with the label, this 44 track compilation also includes three live recordings from a 1961 fraternity dance. *—AMG*

Tip on In / 1996 / Ace ✦✦✦

During the last few years of the '60s (which, as it turned out, were the last few years of his life), Harpo's records took a turn for the slightly more commercial, although they retained a great deal of continuity with his early work. This has 25 tracks recorded between 1967 and 1969, and while it's not quite as good as his prime stuff, it's pretty respectable, retaining his trademark vibrato-laden guitar, relaxed nasal vocals, and shaky harmonica. At this point he had terminated his relationship with longtime producer Jay Miller; rock and soul influences, and even occasional brass and lyrical references to the counterculture, update his sound slightly. But only slightly—although he milks his "Baby Don't You Scratch My Back" riff over and over, the groove is so consistently solid that it makes for listening that's more comfortably dependable than unduly repetitious. Highlighted by the modest R&B hits "Tip on In" and "Te-Ni-Nee-Ni-Nu," as well as one of his best originals, "I'm Gonna Keep What I've Got." *—Richie Unterberger*

The Scratch: Rare & Unissued / Feb. 1996 / Excello ✦✦✦✦✦

A 25-track single-disc compilation loaded with previously unissued sides and alternate takes (the title track is an interesting variant of his hit, "Baby, Scratch My Back"), making it the perfect companion volume to *Hip Shakin'*. This also has the added bonus of more (and even wilder) live recordings from the infamous 1961 frat party dance in Alabama. Dodgy sound on the live sides, but performances too great to leave in the can either way. *—AMG*

Sting It Then! / 1997 / Ace ✦✦✦✦✦

This CD is one of the most flukey and important live-blues documents you can find, rating right up there with B.B. King's *Live at the Regal* and the live Piano Red material from 1955. Recorded off the P.A. system at a 1961 show at the Sage Armory in Mobile, Alabama, it captures Slim Harpo in his only live concert document. Harpo's vocals are a little pushed back in the resulting recording, but his harmonica is caught really well (check out the playing and the clarity on the slow blues "You Know I Love You"), as are the guitars of Rudolph Richard and James Johnson, Willie "Tomcat" Parker's sax, and Sammy K. Brown's drums. Luckily, there's not much audience noise, so what we get is a close-up look at how the blues legend sounded on stage, doing classics like "I'm a King Bee," "Got Love if You Wants It," "Rainin' in My Heart" (his then-current hit), and songs like "Big Boss Man" and "Boogie Chillun," made famous by others. If the sound were slightly better, this would rate even higher, but any real fan should own this. Note that 11 of the 20 tracks have appeared previously in the United States, spread among two Slim Harpo compilations devoted to his work. *—Bruce Eder*

★ **The Best of Slim Harpo** / Nov. 4, 1997 / Hip-O ✦✦✦✦✦

There have been many Slim Harpo best-of's available over the years, some frustratingly incomplete. This one gets all the chart hits together with several of the obscure singles like "Wonderin' and Worryin'," "Strange Love," "One More Day" and "You'll Be Sorry One Day," along with album tracks like "Snoopin' Around" and "Blues Hangover." Transfers are clean and exemplary, and this makes as good an introduction into his music as any currently available. *—Cub Koda*

Corey Harris

b. Feb. 21, 1969, Denver, CO

Slide Guitar, Vocals, Guitar / Modern Electric Blues, Modern Acoustic Blues, Modern Delta Blues

Corey Harris has earned substantial critical acclaim as one of the few contemporary bluesmen able to channel the raw, direct emotion of acoustic Delta blues without coming off as an authenticity-obsessed historian. Although he *is* well versed in the early history of blues guitar, he's no well-mannered preservationist, mixing a considerable variety of influences—from New Orleans to the Caribbean to Africa—into his richly expressive music. In doing so, he's managed to appeal to a wide spectrum of blues fans, from staunch traditionalists to more contemporary sensibilities.

Corey Harris was born in Denver, CO, on February 21, 1969, and began playing guitar at age 12, when he fell in love with his mother's Lightnin' Hopkins records. He played in a rock & roll band in high school, as well as the marching band, and developed his singing abilities in church. Through Bates College in Maine (where he majored in anthropology), Harris traveled to Cameroon to study African linguistics, and returned there on a post-graduate fellowship; during his time there, he soaked up as much African music as possible, entranced by its complex polyrhythms. After returning to the U.S., Harris taught English and French in Napoleonville, LA, and during his spare time he played the clubs, coffeehouses, and street corners of nearby New Orleans. His local reputation eventually earned him a deal with Alligator, one of the pre-eminent blues labels in the South. In 1995, Alligator released Harris' debut album *Between Midnight and Day*, a one-man, one-guitar affair that illustrated his mastery of numerous variations on the Delta blues style. The record won rave reviews and even some mainstream media attention, marking Harris as an exciting new presence on the blues scene; it also earned him an opening slot on tour with ex-10,000 Maniacs singer Natalie Merchant.

Harris followed it up with *Fish Ain't Bitin'* in 1997, a record that began to expand his style by adding a New Orleans-style brass section on several tracks, while emphasizing his own original compositions to a much greater degree. The next year, Harris was invited to participate in the Billy Bragg/Wilco collaboration *Mermaid Avenue*, which set a selection of unfinished Woody Guthrie songs to music; Harris played guitar and contributed bluesy backup vocals to several tunes. In 1999, Harris released what most critics called his strongest work to date, *Greens from the Garden*; hailed as a landmark in some quarters, the record delved deeper into New Orleans funk and R&B, while recasting its covers in surprising but effective new contexts (even reggae and hip-hop). The result was a kaleidoscope of black musical styles that earned Harris even more widespread attention than his debut. Veteran pianist Henry Butler appeared on the record, and for the follow-up, Harris recorded an entire album in tandem with Butler; issued in 2000, *Vu-Du Menz* updated several different strains of early jazz and blues. Harris subsequently left Alligator for Rounder, and debuted for his new label in 2002 with *Downhome Sophisticate*, a typically eclectic outing that explored his African influences and added Latin music to his seemingly endless sonic palette. *—Steve Huey*

Between Midnight and Day / Nov. 1995 / Alligator ✦✦✦

An astonishingly good record, covering a multitude of Delta-based styles and songs from Charley Patton to Muddy Waters, as well as a few originals. It's just Harris and his acoustic guitar, some dazzling finger work and a voice that's about as good as you're going to hear from anyone doing blues and still walking around at the end of the 20th century. The material alternately surges and broods, and once in a while does both at the same time, and it's all worth hearing. *—Bruce Eder*

Fish Ain't Bitin' / Mar. 25, 1997 / Alligator ✦✦✦✦

Corey Harris' second outing for Alligator shows that he's no one-album flash in the pan, with this sophomore effort moving his modern-day acoustic Delta blues vision into even broader territory with delightful results. While his debut effort illustrated Harris' absolute mastery of older Delta styles, both instrumentally and vocally, *Fish Ain't Bitin'* charts new terrain using that first album as a stylistic building block. The big news here is that over half of the 17 songs are from Corey's own pen and compositions like "High Fever Blues" (heard here in two versions), "5-0 Blues," "Berry Owen Blues," and "If You Leave Me" show that he's more than adept in wedding contemporary influences to his down-home country sound. Adding to that are his takes on Son House's "Preaching Blues," Memphis Minnie's "Bumble Bee Blues," Big Maceo's "Worried Life Blues" and Blind Lemon Jefferson's "Jack O'Diamonds," all of them rendered in the proper spirit and context and all of them sounding nothing like the originals—a tough feat to pull off, but one that Harris does with consummate ease, imbuing these warhorses with the stamp of his personality. Several tracks also feature a trombone and tuba or string bass working in tandem with Corey's

National steel-bodied guitar, making a Mississippi-New Orleans musical connection that sounds perfectly natural. No sophomore jinx here, as Corey Harris has turned in one great little album that examines the music's past while looking forward to the future for more input. *—Cub Koda*

● **Greens from the Garden** / Mar. 23, 1999 / Alligator ✦✦✦✦✦
Greens from the Garden is nothing short of a *tour de force* for Corey Harris. Progressing from the solo acoustic blues of *Between Midnight and Day* and the stripped Dixie influence of *Fish Ain't Bitin'*, Harris' third album was a mixture of 20th century Americana that hits home runs in every genre in which it comes to bat. The diversity of styles in *Greens from the Garden* is reminiscent of Ry Cooder's *Paradise and Lunch*, in which the musician's personality is the glue holding all the styles together. Harris commits himself to the spirit of the songs here; despite his versatility, he never comes off as a *dilettante*, rather than a devoted *auteur*. Harris' New Orleans roots are deepened and widened, with affecting forays into French-sung Cajun waltz, "Pas Parlez") and several funk excursions worthy of the Nevilles and the Meters "Wild West," "Honeysuckle"). Most startling, is how well Harris' modern lyrical outlook fuses with 20th-century traditional styles; by trusting in the integrity of the music, he's able to steer the listener toward the spiritual sides of topical arguments in "Basehead" and "Lynch Blues," without once resorting to preaching or heavy-handedness. *Greens from the Garden's* covers are just as satisfying, with a delta reworking of "Diddy Wah Diddy" (a song that's also on Cooder's *Paradise and Lunch*) and a reggae restructuring of "Just a Closer Walk With Thee." Billy Bragg guests on "Teabag Blues," a Woody Guthrie lyric for which Harris wrote music—a by-product of Bragg's and Wilco's *Mermaid Avenue* sessions on which Harris guested. A tremendous journey that redefines the rules of revivalism. *—Paul Pearson*

Vu-Du Menz / Apr. 4, 2000 / Alligator ✦✦✦✦✦
This collaboration is the first full-length release from like-minded bluesmen guitarist Corey Harris and pianist Henry Butler. Although they had previously played together on live dates, the only other time they appear on CD is on Harris' *Greens From the Garden*. These 15 tracks cover more ground than the mere term "blues" implies. The duo recalls not only the best of traditional piano/guitar music of the '20s and '30s, but also New Orleans soul, barrelhouse, ragtime, and Delta blues. To their credit, Harris and Butler have the ability to bring these traditions into a modern context while retaining the soul that some modern blues recordings lack. Not only are duet settings heard but a few solo spots are featured. The playing is phenomenal, which shouldn't overshadow the emotional vocal performances, including the a cappella gospel on "Why Don't You Live So God Can Use You?" that closes out this highly recommended disc. *—Al Campbell*

Downhome Sophisticate / May 7, 2002 / Rounder ✦✦✦✦✦
Few artists reflect the breadth of black music as vividly as Corey Harris, who performs at the peak of his strength throughout *Downhome Sophisticate*. The overall feel is rural, with plenty of slide guitar slithering over raw, live rhythms. The hooks have a timeless feel, as on "Keep Your Lamp Trimmed and Burning," with its rootsy gospel vocal motif and an implied handclap beat over a "My Sharona" hook. But Harris nods as well toward acoustic folk-blues, softened and broadened on the solo track "Capitaine" by an almost John Redbourne feel (which owes a lot in itself to Son House). Instrumental tracks evoke images nearly as clearly as those with words; the jump boogie bounce of "BB" paints a picture of a Southern roadhouse on a Saturday night. But when Harris adds lyrics they enhance this eloquence, as on "Fire," whose references to Babylon, bloodshed, and perditional flames project an ominous, apocalyptic power. It's an easy leap for Harris from folklore to urgent urban settings; his depiction of a police car as a fearsome, prowling Biblical beast makes "Santoro" especially disturbing. The fact that Harris also borrows from Mexican and Latino traditions, especially on "Sista Rose" and the sensuous "Black Maria," makes the point that African-American culture, the center of Western pop, abuts multiple styles and is able to draw from each with equal ease. In the end, the title says it all: This is music both primitive and elusive, easy to absorb and more difficult to play than it seems. *—Robert L. Doerschuk*

Peppermint Harris (Harrison D. Nelson Jr.)

b. Jul. 17, 1925, Texarkana, TX, **d.** Mar. 19, 1999, Elizabeth, NJ
Vocals, Guitar / Jump Blues, West Coast Blues
The contemporary blues boom resuscitated the career of many a veteran blues artist who had been silent for ages. Take guitarist Peppermint Harris, who in 1951 topped the R&B charts with his classic booze ode "I Got Loaded." Nobody expected a new Peppermint Harris CD in 1995, but Home Cooking producer Roy C. Ames coaxed one out of old Pep for Collectables nonetheless. *Texas on My Mind* may not be as enthralling as Harris' early-'50s output, but it was nice to have him back in circulation.

By the time he was in his early twenties, Harrison Nelson Jr. was lucky enough to have found a mentor and friend on the Houston blues front: Lightnin' Hopkins took an interest in the young man's musical development. When Harris was deemed ready, Lightnin' accompanied him to Houston's Gold Star Records. Nothing came of that jaunt, but Harris eventually recorded his debut 78 for the company in 1948 (as Peppermint Nelson).

Bob Shad's Sittin' in With label was the vehicle that supplied Harris' early work to the masses—especially his first major hit, "Raining in My Heart," in 1950. These weren't exactly formal sessions—legend has it one took place in a Houston bordello! Nor was Shad too cognizant of Pep's surname—when he couldn't recall it, he simply renamed our man Harris.

Harris moved over to Eddie Mesner's Aladdin Records in 1951, cutting far tighter sides for the firm in Los Angeles (often with the ubiquitous Maxwell Davis serving as bandleader and saxist). After "I Got Loaded" lit up the charts in 1951, Harris indulged in one booze ode after another: "Have Another Drink and Talk to Me," "Right Back on It," "Three Sheets in the Wind." But try as they might, the bottle let Harris down as a lyrical launching pad after that.

He drifted from Money and Cash to RCA's short-lived subsidiary "X" and Don Robey's Duke logo (where he allegedly penned "As the Years Go Passing By" for Fenton Robinson) after that, but it wasn't until a long-lasting association with Stan Lewis' Shreveport, LA-based Jewel Records commenced in 1965 that Harris landed for longer than a solitary single.

Later, Harris worked various day jobs around Houston, including one at a record pressing plant, before moving to Sacramento, CA, and then to New Jersey to be with his daughter. He died in New Jersey in 1999, at the age of 73. *—Bill Dahl*

Peppermint Harris / 1962 / Time ✦✦✦
Nice early-'50s Texas R&B. *—Bill Dahl*

Sittin' in With / 1979 / Mainstream ✦✦✦✦
Here are 15 well-chosen 1950-1951 masters from Bob Shad's Sittin' in With label by Houston bluesman Peppermint Harris, including his hit "Rainin' in My Heart." Rowdy little bands behind the powerful singer sometimes included Goree Carter on guitar. *—Bill Dahl*

● **I Got Loaded** / 1987 / Route 66 ✦✦✦✦✦
Harris hit his full stride after signing with Aladdin Records in 1951 and moving his recording base to Los Angeles. Under saxist Maxwell Davis' direction, Harris waxed his smash "I Got Loaded" and a few more potent rounds after that ("Three Sheets in the Wind," "Have Another Drink and Talk to Me"). Unfortunately not yet available on CD, these sides comprise Pep's chief claim to fame. *—Bill Dahl*

Being Black Twice / 1991 / Collectables ✦✦✦
A curious collection of late-'50s and early-'60s recorded titles with unissued mid-'70s sides to pad things out. Oddly enough, Pep sounds the same despite the intervening years; his pleasing baritone rumbles through a set of his originals and standards like "Cherry Red" and "Key to the Highway." Collections of Harris' best are not exactly plentiful, but this one isn't the place to start; seek out his Aladdin sides instead. *—Cub Koda*

Texas on My Mind / Dec. 1995 / Collectables ✦✦✦
From the late '40s through the early '60s, Peppermint Harris recorded for a variety of labels to moderate success. Although he had a few records in the '70s, he was basically retired until 1995, when he recorded *Texas on My Mind* at the age of 72. Although the songs on the album are quite good (most of the numbers are originals), Harris' abilities had dwindled; with his limited voice and guitar skills, he simply didn't have the power to captivate an audience. *—Thom Owens*

Penthouse in the Ghetto / Oct. 21, 1997 / M.I.L. Multimedia ✦✦✦
Penthouse in the Ghetto features 20 tracks from Texas bluesman Peppermint Harris, including some of his famed "blues drinking songs." *—Steve Huey*

Lonesome as I Can Be: The Jewel Recordings / Oct. 9, 2001 / West Side ✦✦✦✦✦

Sam Harris

Guitar / Country Blues, String Bands, Acoustic Texas Blues, Ragtime
Not to be confused with Broadway performers, Motown singers, or football tacklers of the same name, Sam Harris was an early country blues rhythm guitarist who followed bassist partner Marco Washington into the ranks of the Dallas String Band, an innovative black string band that was a big part of the Texas blues scene of the late '20s. Harris' background was about as blues-drenched as one could get, including a stint with the early combos of Sonny Boy Williamson (John Lee Williamson).

Yet the Dallas String Band was hardly a straight blues band, playing a wide variety of ragtime and pop material and featuring a dual mandolin lineup on just under a dozen sides cut for Columbia, as well as an even larger and more unusual instrumentation including violin, trumpet, and clarinet, that never made it into the recording studio. The third founding member of the band was Coley Jones, a bluesman who started out playing guitar in minstrel shows before switching to mandolin. Blind Lemon Jefferson was said to have sat in with the band from time to time, and Jones later replaced Harris with none other than the legendary T-Bone Walker, either the nephew or stepson of playing partner Washington, depending on who is telling the tale. The group concocted several original numbers that have lived on through a variety of cover versions, including the lively "Dallas Blues," a fingerpicking feature for Stefan Grossman, and others: the corny "Hokum Blues" and the lovely "Chasin' Rainbows," which was covered by Robert Crumb's Cheap Suit Serenaders. *—Eugene Chadbourne*

Shakey Jake Harris (James Harris)

b. Apr. 12, 1921, Earle, AR, **d.** Mar. 2, 1990, Forrest City, AR
Vocals, Harmonica / Electric Chicago Blues, Harmonica Blues
Jake Harris knew how to shake a pair of dice in order to roll a lucrative winner. He also realized early on that his nephew, guitarist Magic Sam, was a winner as a bluesman. Harris may have not been a technical wizard on his chosen instrument, but his vocals and harp style were proficient enough to result in a reasonably successful career (both with Sam and without).

Born James Harris, the Arkansas native moved to Chicago at age seven. Admiring the style of Sonny Boy Williamson, Harris gradually learned the rudiments of the harp but didn't try his hand at entertaining professionally until 1955. Harris made his bow on vinyl in 1958 for the newly formed Artistic subsidiary of Eli Toscano's West Side-based Cobra Records. His only Artistic 45, "Call Me If You Need Me"/"Roll Your Moneymaker," was produced by Willie Dixon and featured Sam and Syl Johnson on guitars.

The uncompromising Chicago mainstream sound of that 45 contrasted starkly with Jake Harris' next studio project. Prestige's Bluesville subsidiary paired him with a pair of jazzmen—guitarist Bill Jennings and organist Jack McDuff—in 1960 for a full album, *Good Times* (the unlikely hybrid of styles working better than one might expect). The harpist encored later that year with *Mouth Harp Blues*, this time with a quartet including Chicagoan Jimmie Lee Robinson on guitar and a New York rhythm section (both of his Bluesville LPs were waxed in New Jersey).

Jake Harris and Magic Sam remained running partners for much of the '60s. They shared bandstands at fabled West Side haunts such as Sylvio's—where he was captured on tape in 1966 singing "Sawed Off Shotgun" and "Dirty Work Goin' On" (now available on a Black Top disc by Sam)—and Big Bill Hill's Copacabana before Harris moved to Los Angeles in the late '60s. He recorded for World Pacific and briefly owned his own nightclub and record label before returning to Arkansas (where he died in 1990). *—Bill Dahl*

Good Times / 1960 / Bluesville/Original Blues Classics ♦♦♦
Chicago harpist Shakey Jake Harris journeyed all the way to New Jersey to make his debut album in 1960. It was a huge stylistic departure for Harris—he was paired with jazz mainstays Brother Jack McDuff on simmering Hammond organ and blues-tinged guitarist Bill Jennings. The trio located some succulent common ground even without a drummer, Harris keeping his mouth organ phrasing succinct and laying out when his more accomplished session mates catch fire. *—Bill Dahl*

● **Mouth Harp Blues** / 1962 / Bluesville/Original Blues Classics ♦♦♦♦
When Harris returned to New Jersey later that same year to wax his Bluesville encore, he brought along fellow Chicagoan Jimmie Lee Robinson as his guitarist. A full rhythm section was used this time (New York cats all), but the overall approach was quite a bit closer to what he was used to hearing on Chicago's West side. *—Bill Dahl*

The Devil's Harmonica / 1972 / Polydor ♦♦♦♦

William Harris

b. Glendora, MS
Vocals / Prewar Country Blues
Virtually nothing is known about bluesman William Harris; as a result of the rhythmic intricacy of the guitar work in evidence on the nine songs which comprise his recorded legacy, historians have placed him as a product of the Mississippi Delta, although the geographic references scattered among his music also suggest an Alabama background.

Birmingham, AL was certainly the location of his first recording session, cut on July 18, 1927; accounts suggest that at the time Harris was a performer with F.S. Wolcott's Rabbit Foot Minstrels. Theories that he traveled the medicine show circuit are lent further credence by his second recording date, which occured over a three-day period in October 1928 in Richmond, IN; among the tracks cut by Harris was "Kansas City Blues," previously recorded by Jim Jackson, another medicine-show entertainer. Additionally, two other staples of the circuit, Frank Stokes and Papa Charlie Jackson, previously recorded "Take Me Back," updated by Harris as "Hot Time Blues." In all likelihood, these are mysteries that will never be solved—his trail ends after this final session. *—Jason Ankeny*

● **Complete Recorded Works (1927–1929)** / 1991 / Document ♦♦♦
Two early singer/guitarists have their entire output reissued on this typically definitive release by the European Document label. Actually, William Harris had originally recorded 14 selections but five were unable to be located for this CD; one would later be rediscovered and reissued on a sampler. With the exception of "I'm Leavin' Town," Harris is heard performing solo and, despite his obscurity, he was a fine second-level blues and folk song performer. Among his better numbers (dating from 1927-1928) are "Kansas City Blues," "Early Mornin' Blues" and "Hot Time Blues." Buddy Boy Hawkins' 12 solos from 1927-1929 find him performing in a similar vein and at a slightly higher level. His "Voice Throwin' Blues" (which over "Hesitatin' Blues" finds Hawkins having a call and response between two of his voices, including one allegedly being a ventriloquist's dummy) is a bit odd. Other selections include "Jailhouse Fire Blues," "Raggin' the Blues," "A Rag Blues" and "Snatch It and Grab It." Both Harris and Hawkins deserved more opportunities to record but at least these formerly rare recordings (which are in pretty good shape, except for Harris' "Electric Chair Blues") keep them from being totally lost to history. *—Scott Yanow*

Wynonie Harris

b. Aug. 24, 1915, Omaha, NE, **d.** Jun. 14, 1969, Los Angeles, CA
Vocals, Leader, Drums / Jump Blues, R&B
No blues shouter embodied the rollicking good times that he sang of quite like raucous shouter Wynonie Harris. "Mr. Blues," as he was not-so-humbly known, joyously related risque tales of sex, booze, and endless parties in his trademark raspy voice over some of the jumpingest horn-powered combos of the postwar era.

Those wanton ways eventually caught up with Harris, but not before he scored a raft of R&B smashes from 1946 to 1952. Harris was already a seasoned dancer, drummer, and singer when he left Omaha for L.A. in 1940 (his main influences being Big Joe Turner and Jimmy Rushing). He found plenty of work singing and appearing as an emcee on Central Avenue, the bustling nightlife strip of the Black community there. Wynonie Harris' reputation was spreading fast—he was appearing in Chicago at the Rhumboogie Club in 1944 when bandleader Lucky Millinder hired him as his band's new singer. With Millinder's orchestra in brassy support, Harris made his debut on shellac by boisterously delivering "Who Threw the Whiskey in the Well" that same year for Decca. By the time it hit in mid-1945, Harris was long gone from Millinder's organization and back in L.A.

The shouter debuted on wax under his own name in July of 1945 at an L.A. date for Philo with backing from drummer Johnny Otis, saxist Teddy Edwards, and trumpeter Howard McGhee. A month later, he signed on with Apollo Records, an association that provided him with two huge hits in 1946: "Wynonie's Blues" (with saxist Illinois Jacquet's combo) and "Playful Baby." Harris' own waxings were squarely in the emerging jump blues style then sweeping the West Coast. After scattered dates for Hamp-Tone, Bullet, and Aladdin (where he dueled it out with his idol Big Joe on a two-sided "Battle of the Blues"), Harris joined the star-studded roster of Cincinnati's King Records in 1947. There his sales really soared.

Few records made a stronger seismic impact than Harris' 1948 chart-topper "Good Rockin' Tonight." Ironically, Harris shooed away its composer, Roy Brown, when he first tried to hand it to the singer; only when Brown's original version took off did Wynonie cover the romping number. With Hal "Cornbread" Singer on wailing tenor sax and a rocking, socking backbeat, the record provided an easily followed blueprint for the imminent rise of rock & roll a few years later (and gave Elvis Presley something to place on the A side of his second Sun single).

After that, Harris was rarely absent from the R&B charts for the next four years, his offerings growing more boldly suggestive all the time. "Grandma Plays the Numbers," "All She Wants to Do Is Rock," "I Want My Fanny Brown," "Sittin' on It All the Time," "I Like My Baby's Pudding," "Good Morning Judge," "Bloodshot Eyes" (a country tune that was first released on King by Hank Penny), and "Lovin' Machine" were only a portion of the ribald hits Harris scored into 1952 (13 in all)—and then his personal hit parade stopped dead. It certainly wasn't Harris' fault—his King output rocked as hard as ever under Henry Glover's supervision—but changing tastes among fickle consumers that accelerated Wynonie Harris' sobering fall from favor.

Sides for Atco in 1956, King in 1957, and Roulette in 1960 only hinted at the raunchy glory of a short few years earlier. The touring slowed accordingly. In 1963, his chaffeur-driven Cadillacs and lavish New York home a distant memory, Harris moved back to L.A., scraping up low-paying local gigs whenever he could. Chess gave him a three-song session in 1964, but sat on the promising results. Throat cancer silenced him for good in 1969, ending the life of a bigger-than-life R&B pioneer whose ego matched his tremendous talent. *—Bill Dahl*

☆ **Good Rocking Tonight** / 1990 / King ♦♦♦♦♦
Equally splendid compilation of the raspy shouter's King label output from the British Charly logo. Contains 20 sides, including a few essentials that Rhino didn't bother with: a roaring "Rock Mr. Blues" that grants Harris vocal group backing; the lascivious rocker "I Want My Fanny Brown" and "Lollipop Mama," and a celebratory "Mr. Blues Is Coming to Town." Harris and King always used inexorably swinging bands—saxists include Red Prysock, David Van Dyke (who duel it out on the amazing "Quiet Whiskey"), Big John Greer, Hal Singer, and Tom Archia. *—Bill Dahl*

Women, Whiskey & Fish Tails / 1993 / Ace ♦♦♦♦
Ace's *Women, Whiskey & Fish Tails* spotlights some of the famous blues-shouter's latter-day work (1952-1957) for independent R&B label King. Now joined by Ace's '50s-centric Harris survey, *Lovin' Machine*, this 21-track disc takes the somewhat more obscure path through the catalog, substituting the still-electric likes of "Greyhound" and "Drinkin' Sherry Wine" for chart hit "Bloodshot Eyes" and the classic alcoholism narrative "Drinkin' Blues." Far from just an artist in repose, though, Harris is in top form for most of it, especially on the gospel-infused "The Deacon Don't Like It" and collection standout "Shake That Thing." The Ace titles are best left to listeners looking for a second roundup, while newcomers probably will want to first check out survey discs on Rhino or the chronologically minded Classics label for more of Harris' essential early hits and sides ("Good Rockin' Tonight"). *—Stephen Cook*

★ **Bloodshot Eyes: The Best of Wynonie Harris** / 1993 / Rhino ♦♦♦♦♦
Wynonie Harris was a hard-living, rousing R&B shouter who made some of the most sexually explicit songs in modern popular music history. Harris didn't leave much to the imagination, but he also possessed a booming voice with wonderful tone and range and the comedic skill to execute these tunes without becoming raunchy. There are many hilarious cuts on this 18-track anthology, among them "I Like My Baby's Pudding," "Grandma Plays the Numbers," and "Good Morning Judge." Harris roars, struts and wails over equally feverish arrangements and earns a draw with Joe Turner on "Battle of the Blues." These songs give a good portrait of a delightful, often spectacular vocalist who could be both provocative and compelling. *—Ron Wynn*

Everybody Boogie! / 1996 / Delmark ♦♦♦♦
This is one marvelous collection of 1945 recordings made for Apollo Records with Harris' powerhouse vocals backed by jump blues bands led by jazz greats Illinois Jacquet, Oscar Pettiford, and Jack McVea. No real honking and bar walking going on here; quite the opposite, as the Pettiford tunes have bop lines creeping in throughout. But Harris seems oblivious to it all as tracks like "Time to Change Your Town," "Here Come the Blues," "Stuff You Gotta Watch," and "Somebody Changed the Lock on My Door" are on an equal par for sheer bravado and intensity with the best of his later work for King. A welcome compilation. *—Cub Koda*

1944–1945 / Nov. 19, 1996 / Classics ♦♦♦♦
Blues shouter Wynonie Harris made his biggest impact while on the King label between 1948-1952. Alongside contemporary jump blues singer Roy Brown, Harris helped lay the foundations of rock & roll at the Cincinnati-based company, scoring such smashes as "Good Rockin' Tonight" (a Brown composition), "Bloodshot Eyes," and "All She Wants to Do Is Rock." Although Harris' beginnings were less auspicious, his talent was certainly in full view from the start; this first of three Classics discs makes the case with 22 of the finest slices of early R&B from the mid-'40s. In addition to such early hits as "Playful Baby" and "Wynonie's Blues," the mix contains lower-profile gems like the bop-infused "Everybody's Boogie" and the sonorous "Papa Tree Top." Harris' first recordings with bandleader Lucky Millinder, "Hurry, Hurry" and "Who Threw the Whiskey in the Well," are also included. And besides Millinder, the collection features the likes of Illinois Jacquet, a young Charles Mingus, and a combo comprised of drummer Johnny Otis, trumpeter Howard McGhee, and tenor saxophonist Teddy Edwards. A perfect disc for fans wanting to dig deeper into the Harris catalog. *—Stephen Cook*

1945–1947 / Nov. 3, 1998 / Classics ♦♦♦♦♦
The second Classics CD to feature blues singer Wynonie Harris' recordings as a leader finds him in the period right before he signed with the King label. The five four-song sessions on this disc (all quite jazz oriented) were cut for Hamp-Tone, Bullet, and Aladdin. First, Harris (who sounds quite enthusiastic in every setting) sings three numbers (including a two-part "Hey! Ba-Ba-Re-Bop") with a combo taken from the Lionel Hampton big band. The Bullet date was quite rare. Recorded in Nashville, it finds Harris backed by local players including Sun Ra in his first recording. Ra's piano is well featured throughout, including

on "Dig This Boogie." Harris is also heard with a Leonard Feather-organized band that includes trumpeter Joe Newman, altoist Tab Smith, and tenor saxophonist Allen Eager ("Mr. Blues Jumped the Rabbit" is the best-known selection), with an obscure backup band in New York (including for "Ghost of a Chance," an odd departure with a vocal group) and sharing the spotlight with Big Joe Turner on three numbers (including a slightly disorganized two-part "Battle of the Blues"). Throughout, Wynonie Harris sounds like he was ready for stardom. Recommended. *—Scott Yanow*

1947–1949 / Feb. 6, 2001 / Classics ✦✦✦✦✦
The third in the Classics label's series of the recordings of Wynonie Harris traces the blues/early R&B singer's career from just before the recording strike of 1948 up until the end of 1949. The seven sessions (all originally recorded for King) are not as well-known as Harris' earlier material, but they definitely have their moments of interest. Harris is typically exuberant throughout, and the highlights include "Wynonie's Boogie," "Good Morning Mr. Blues," "Crazy Love," "Good Rockin' Tonight" (a major hit), "Grandma Plays the Numbers," "Drinkin' Wine Spo-Dee-O-Dee," and "All She Wants to Do Is Rock." Heard from in the impressive backup groups are trumpeters "Hot Lips" Page, Jesse Drakes, Cat Anderson, and Joe Morris, along with tenors Hal Singer, Tom Archia, and Johnny Griffin. Highly recommended, as are the first two Harris Classics CDs. Fun music. *—Scott Yanow*

Rockin' the Blues / May 8, 2001 / Proper ✦✦✦✦
This four-disc set from Proper could qualify as the best Wynonie Harris collection going. Sporting a 52-page booklet with detailed biographical and discography information—not to mention the bargain price tag—*Rockin' the Blues* contains all of Harris' sides from 1944-1950. Just some of the many highlights include his first recordings with the Lucky Millinder band ("Who Threw the Whiskey in the Well"), picaresque confessionals like "Drinking By Myself," and the unexpected pop side "Ghost of a Chance." Of course, such cornerstone moments as his duet with Big Joe Turner on "Battle of the Blues" and early King hits like "Good Rockin' Tonight" and "All She Wants to Do Is Rock" are here as well. Sure, it would have been nice if just one more disc was thrown in to cover early-'50s standouts like "Bloodshot Eyes," but with this much bounty already on hand, who's complaining? And adding to the consistently top-notch Harris vocals, there's plenty of fine instrumental highlights from the likes of Howard McGhee, Dexter Gordon, Teddy Edwards, Arnett Cobb, Joe Wilder, "Hot Lips" Page, Bill Doggett, Elmo Hope, Charles Mingus, and many other jump blues and jazz notables (Sun Ra even shows up for four cuts taped in Nashville). A stellar example of how all retrospectives should be presented. *—Stephen Cook*

Lovin' Machine / May 7, 2002 / Ace ✦✦✦✦✦
This is a companion disc to Ace's earlier compilation, *Women, Whiskey & Fish Tails*, and likewise hones in on his '50s output for King Records, the 26 tracks hailing from 1951-1957. Though the early part of that stretch found him continuing to land some R&B smashes with "Lovin' Machine" and his cover of Hank Penny's "Bloodshot Eyes" (both included on the disc), generally it marked the point at which he began his absence from the charts. Actually there's not much difference between this body of work and his salad days, other than the lack of many obvious hits from the git-go like "Good Rockin' Tonight." Harris' problem was that his brand of jump blues-cum-R&B had itself passed its peak, though he continued to be one of its best practitioners. This isn't recommended for those who just want one or two Harris anthologies; his most well-known sides from the late '40s, like "Good Rockin' Tonight," are not represented, and Rhino's *Bloodshot Eyes* best-of collection takes a chronologically wider and more selective view of his top work. Also, to be honest, Harris worked the same approaches over and over, and it's too much at once if mid-20th century jump blues/R&B isn't your main dish. All that said, it's a good roundup of sides that aren't as frequently anthologized (for the most part) as his biggest hits, and Harris does delve into some ballads and mild detours into the mambo ("Good Mambo Tonight," a bandwagon-hopping takeoff from "Good Rockin' Tonight") and weird funereal, near-spiritual blues ("Song of the Bayou"). The version of "Rot Gut" was previously unissued, and it's actually one of the better items, its hangover tale fitting well into the singer's usual persona. Note also that the final track, "All Night Long," is actually a 1952 single by the vocal group the Royals, with Harris singing the middle eight. *—Richie Unterberger*

Wilbert Harrison

b. Jan. 5, 1929, Charlotte, NC, **d.** Oct. 26, 1994, Spencer, NC
Vocals, Drums, Piano, Guitar / Rock & Roll, R&B, Soul
Perceived by casual oldies fans as a two-hit wonder (his 1959 chart-topper "Kansas City" and a heartwarming "Let's Work Together" a full decade later), Wilbert Harrison actually left behind a varied body of work that blended an intriguing melange of musical idioms into something quite distinctive.

Country and gospel strains filtered into Wilbert Harrison's consciousness as a youth in North Carolina. When he got out of the Navy in Miami around 1950, he began performing in a calypso-based style. Miami entrepreneur Henry Stone signed Harrison to his Rockin' logo in 1953; his debut single, "This Woman of Mine," utilized the very same melody as his later reading of "Kansas City" (the first rendition of the Jerry Leiber/Mike Stoller composition by pianist Little Willie Littlefield came out in 1952, doubtless making an impression). Its flip, a country-tinged "Letter Edged in Black," exhibited Harrison's eclectic mindset.

After moving to Newark, NJ, Harrison wandered by the headquarters of Savoy Records one fortuitous day and was snapped up by producer Fred Mendelsohn. Harrison recorded several sessions for Savoy, beginning with a catchy cover of Terry Fell's country tune "Don't Drop It." Top New York sessioneers—arranger Leroy Kirkland, saxist Buddy Lucas and guitarists Mickey Baker and Kenny Burrell—backed Harrison on his 1954-1956 Savoy output, but hits weren't forthcoming.

That changed instantly when Harrison waxed his driving "Kansas City" for Harlem entrepreneur Bobby Robinson in 1959. With a barbed-wire guitar solo by Wild Jimmy Spruill igniting Harrison's no-frills piano and clenched vocal, "Kansas City" paced both the R&B and pop charts soon after its issue on Fury Records (not bad for a $40 session). Only one minor problem: Harrison was still technically under contract to Savoy (though label head Herman Lubinsky had literally run him out of his office some years earlier!), leading to all sorts of legal wrangles that finally went Robinson's way. Momentum for any Fury follow-ups had been fatally blunted in the interim, despite fine attempts with "Cheatin' Baby," the sequel "Goodbye Kansas City," and the original "Let's Stick Together."

Harrison bounced from Neptune to Doc to Constellation to Port to Vest with little in the way of tangible rewards before unexpectedly making a comeback in 1969 with his infectious "Let's Work Together" for Juggy Murray's Sue imprint. The two-part single proved a popular cover item—Canned Heat revived it shortly thereafter, and Brian Ferry chimed in with his treatment later on. Alas, it was an isolated happenstance—apart from "My Heart Is Yours," a bottom-end chart entry on SSS International in 1971, no more hits were in Wilbert's future. But Harrison soldiered on, sometimes as a one-man band, for years to come. *—Bill Dahl*

Let's Work Together / 1969 / Sue ✦✦✦
Quickie album supervised by Juggy Murray to cash in on the unexpected success of Harrison's "Let's Work Together," but not a bad effort all the same. Harrison brings his unique vocal delivery to oldies such as "Blue Monday," "Stagger Lee," "Louie Louie," and "Stand by Me," imparting his own personal stamp to each. This LP deserves digital reissue somewhere down the line. *—Bill Dahl*

Small Labels / 1986 / Krazy Kat ✦✦✦✦
Vinyl survey of Harrison's forays away from the famous indie diskeries, both before and after he hit with "Kansas City." Weirdly, his 1953 effort "This Woman of Mine" uses the same melody as "Kansas City," some six years prior to his hitting big with it. Harrison was liable to try anything to land a hit—he brands himself a "Calypso Man," tries a hillbilly tack on "Letter Edged in Black," and offers a salute to the 1964 "New York World's Fair"—all in that distinctive slurred voice of his. *—Bill Dahl*

Listen to My Song / 1987 / Savoy ✦✦✦✦
Harrison's first label association of any endurance commenced when he signed with Herman Lubinsky's Savoy logo in 1954 for a two-year stretch. Top New York sessioneers like guitarists Mickey Baker and Kenny Burrell and saxists Buddy Lucas and Budd Johnson help out on these 16 Savoy tracks (still unavailable on CD). He liked that C&W; Terry Fell's "Don't Drop It" is a tremendously catchy hillbilly tune given an R&B flavor by the young singer. *—Bill Dahl*

Greatest Classic R&B Hits / 1989 / Grudge ✦✦✦✦✦
This is the only available CD for Harrison's late-'60s material, long after his 1959 classic "Kansas City." *—Bill Dahl*

● **Kansas City** / 1992 / Collectables ✦✦✦✦✦
Finally, paydirt! Harrison smashed the charts in 1959 with his massive hit "Kansas City" for Bobby Robinson's Fury logo. Here we have 22 fine sides from the Fury hookup, some in stereo and many with Wild Jimmy Spruill on lead guitar. "Cheatin' Baby," "C.C. Rider," "1960," and the inevitable sequel "Goodbye Kansas City" are prime examples of Harrison's slightly off-kilter approach to his craft, while this infectious "Let's Stick Together" developed into the more worldly "Let's Work Together" toward the end of the decade. *—Bill Dahl*

Kansas City: His Legendary Golden Classics / 1994 / Collectables ✦✦✦

Alvin Youngblood Hart

b. Mar. 2, 1963, Oakland, CA
Slide Guitar, Guitar / Contemporary Blues, Blues-Rock
Guitarist, singer and songwriter Alvin Youngblood Hart is continuing in the path laid down by acoustic blues practitioners like Taj Mahal, Guy Davis and other '90s blues revivalists, but his roots go back much further than that, to the classic stylings of Bukka White, Charley Patton, Leadbelly and Blind Willie McTell.

Born in Oakland, CA, Hart accompanied his parents on summer trips to his grandparents' home in the hills of northern MS, and it was there that his passion for acoustic blues was first sparked. On visits to his grandmother's house, he saw people as they lived in the 19th century, without the luxuries of indoor plumbing or phones, and often saw horse-drawn wagons in place of cars. Although there was not a lot of music around the hills of Carrollton, MS, where his grandmother lived, his uncle sparked his interest by playing guitar and telling him stories about Charley Patton. His grandmother also played blues piano, furthering his knowledge and interest.

Despite the trips back to his roots, Hart cites recordings by Jimi Hendrix and the Rolling Stones with helping him along in his blues guitar studies. His father worked as a salesman for General Electric, so the Hart family moved a lot. He adopted the nickname "Alvin" from the harmonica-playing frontman for the TV cartoon group the Chipmunks. His parents had a good record collection, and he began playing guitar in his early teens, studying the recordings of Jimmy Reed, B.B. King and Jimmy Witherspoon.

After his parents settled in Schaumburg, IL, he began frequenting Maxwell Street in nearby Chicago. He eventually became known to the regular musicians there as "Youngblood." After attending a nearby community college, Hart's family moved again, to southern California. After becoming fed up with the politics of the local blues club scene there, he began finding his own voice, independent of any groups, playing acoustic blues by himself.

After signing up with the Coast Guard in 1986, he was stationed on a riverboat in Natchez, MS. There, he furthered his blues education by playing in local bars on his off-duty hours. After finishing his seven years in the Coast Guard in Berkeley, he befriended Joe Louis Walker, who invited Hart to open some of his shows in the area. His first big break came about in February 1995 while opening for Taj Mahal at an Oakland jazz club. Mahal's longtime road manager invited Hart to Grateful Dead guitarist Bob Weir's studio for an impromptu jam session.

Hart was signed to a management contract and recorded a demo that caught the ears of some executives at the OKeh subsidiary of Epic Records. OKeh was at one time the home of many of Hart's long-gone musical heroes, artists like Blind Boy Fuller, Brownie McGhee and Lonnie Johnson. In the summer of 1996, Hart was tapped for the Further Festival, which continued the spirit of the Grateful Dead after the death of guitarist/bandleader Jerry Garcia in the summer of 1995. Hart found himself exposed to a huge new audience while sandwiched between acts like Bruce Hornsby, Hot Tuna and Los Lobos on the Further Festival tour.

His brilliant 1996 debut, *Big Mama's Door*, for the OKeh division of Epic Records, received widespread critical acclaim and got his career as an international touring artist off the ground. He offers up blues-tinged covers of well-known folk songs like "When the Boys Were On the Western Plain" and "Gallows Pole." He also covers traditional classic blues tunes like "Hillbilly Willie's Blues" from Blind Willie McTell and "Pony Blues" from Charley Patton.

Based on the strength of his major-label debut and his live shows, Hart received five nominations at the 1997 W.C. Handy Blues Awards, tying him with Luther Allison. Hart was nominated for Best New Artist, Best Acoustic Artist, and Best Traditional Blues Artist, and Hart's album was nominated for both Acoustic Album of the Year and Traditional Album of the Year. Hart's follow-up album, *Territory* (1998), didn't win quite as much acclaim yet still garnered a substantial amount of attention for its diversity. On his third album, *Start With the Soul* (2000), he again took a different approach, this time focusing on a blues-rock sound. The guitarist returned two years later with his fourth album, *Down in the Alley* (2002). *—Richard Skelly*

● **Big Mama's Door** / Apr. 1996 / OKeh/550 Music ✦✦✦✦✦

The debut recording of 33-year-old Hart is extraordinarily simple and simply extraordinary. Except for three cuts on which he's joined by Taj Mahal, *Big Mama's Door* is just Hart on acoustic guitar and vocals, and he's not doing anything fancy—just playing prewar-style blues, mostly in a percussive Delta manner, recorded live to two-track. Yet he succeeds so well in blending technique and feeling, structure and spontaneity, tradition and freshness that he produces a minor gem of a blues record, evocative of the blues masters of the '20s and '30s. He covers Leadbelly, Blind Willie McTell, Charley Patton, and the Mississippi Sheiks and does originals that replicate older blues idioms, not just in the notes but in the nuances, and in the personal commitment he brings to the material. *—Steve Hoffman*

Territory / Jun. 23, 1998 / Hannibal ✦✦✦

Hart is so determined to display his stylistic dexterity that he winds up wandering all over the map: country swing, blues, reggae, gutbucket rock. Each selection is worthy, although a more consistent thematic thread would make the album more listenable. *—Tim Sheridan*

Start With the Soul / Apr. 25, 2000 / Rykodisc ✦✦✦

Guitarist Alvin Youngblood Hart dedicates his third release *Start With the Soul* to, among others, the late Thin Lizzy leader Phil Lynott. This isn't just lip service, as you can immediately hear when the opening roar of "Fightin' Hard" comes blaring through. Hart doesn't go out of his way to appeal only to blues followers. He has the natural ability to fuse twangy country, Hendrix, funk, and reggae into his Delta blues style without regard to genres. *Start With the Soul* is unlike other releases from artists who at the beginning of their career display an acoustic Delta approach only to end up incorporating a very commercial soul sound for the sake of reaching a wider audience or receiving minuscule radio airplay. The choice of cover versions is revealing; Chuck Berry's "Back to Memphis," Cornelius Brothers and Sister Rose's 1971 hit "Treat Her Like a Lady," and the Sonics' mid-'60s garage rocker "The Hustler" lose none of the vigor of the originals. Credit should be given to the legendary Memphis producer Jim Dickinson for capturing the gritty sound critical to this kind of undertaking. It will be interesting to see where Hart goes with future releases. *—Al Campbell*

Down in the Alley / Jul. 9, 2002 / Memhphis International ✦✦✦✦

Hart does a 180 after the husky, power trio/space/R&B/rock of 2000's *Start With the Soul* by spinning out a dozen blues covers in a solo acoustic setting. On his fourth album (for his fourth label), the contemporary bluesman sounds inspired and refreshed as he accompanies himself on acoustic six-string guitar, banjo, and mandolin. The production is from Memphis cult hero Jim Dickinson, who doesn't have a chance to do much other than provide inspiration in this sparse setting. Hart runs down fairly obscure tunes from Son House, Charley Patton, Leadbelly, Skip James, and Sleepy John Estes, infusing them with a jolt of energy while staying true to their original versions and invigorating them with inspired interpretations. Hart's voice is magnificent throughout—yowling, moaning, doleful, yet proud as he pays tribute to the Delta and country blues masters. Even the well-worn traditional "Motherless Child" sounds fresh in this context. Eschewing the diverse—some claim overly diverse—approach of his previous few releases, Hart sticks to basics here. He keeps the tone spare, naked, and dry, which best fits the somber mood, especially on his high-lonesome banjo interpretation of Odetta's "Chilly Winds." Recorded in just three days, this return to the artist's country blues roots is at turns harrowing, haunting, and uplifting, just like the originals. Those who found the Thin Lizzy-edged rock attack of his last release too far removed from Hart's earlier rootsy approach will rejoice in this unvarnished, stripped-down, deep blues release. *—Hal Horowitz*

Buddy Boy Hawkins (Walter Hawkins)

Vocals, Guitar / Acoustic Blues, Country Blues

The scant discography of Walter "Buddy Boy" Hawkins reveals one of the most distinctive country blues performers of the prewar era, a gifted vocalist whose taste for slow, dirge-like songs was ideally suited to his intricate guitar work. Almost nothing is known about the singer; various attempts to determine his date and place of birth have resulted in countless chronological and geographical inconsistencies, although the consenus places him as a product of either Alabama or the northern Delta region. Between 1927 and 1929, Hawkins recorded a dozen tracks for the Paramount, many of them portraits of trains and life on the railroad (another possible piece of the puzzle); in any case, these sessions are the only surviving document of his music, and his subsequent activities remain a mystery. *—Jason Ankeny*

● **Buddy B Hawkins and His Buddies** / 1968 / Yazoo ✦✦✦✦✦

This is somewhat deceptive packaging, as Hawkins only has half of the selections and the "buddies" have the other half. But since the buddies include Texas Alexander, their contributions are worth close scrutiny. Hawkins' fine vocals and distinctive guitar are still dominant, though. *—Ron Wynn*

Ernie Hawkins

b. 1947, Pittsburgh, PA

Guitar / Piedmont Blues, Delta Blues, Modern Acoustic Blues, Ragtime, Blues Gospel

Guitarist Ernie Hawkins was Pittsburgh's best-kept blues secret until the late '90s when he resumed his solo career as a Piedmont blues player. Like his contemporaries Stefan Grossman, Roy Book Binder, and Jorma Kaukonen, Hawkins studied with Reverend Gary Davis in the '60s and boasts a revivalist repertoire that runs the gamut of Delta blues, country blues, ragtime, and gospel. Hawkins two "comeback" acoustic blues albums, *Blues Advice* and *Bluesified*, proved him to be a remarkable interpreter of the music of Davis, Blind Willie McTell, and Skip James.

Born in Pittsburgh in 1947, Hawkins picked up the guitar and banjo as a teenager, initially playing bluegrass and country music before delving into the prewar blues of McTell, Mississippi John Hurt, and Blind Blake, among others. In 1965, Hawkins moved to New York City, where he spent a year learning ragtime guitar from Reverend Gary Davis. Hawkins spent the next decade in college and graduate school, but he remained active in music, eventually encountering and playing with bluesmen such as Mance Lipscomb, Robert Pete Williams, Fred McDowell, and Robert "Nyles" Jones, aka Guitar Gabriel. In 1978, Hawkins put aside his psychology career and became a full-time musician.

After recording *Ragtime Signatures* in 1980, Hawkins moved to Austin, TX, where he worked solo and also with electric blues and rockabilly bands. He returned to Pittsburgh in the mid-'80s and for the next ten years filled the lead guitar slot with local R&B act Gary Belloma and the Blues Bombers. 1996's *Blues Advice* signaled Hawkins' welcome return to the ragtime blues vein and it foreshadowed some of the traditional gospel directions Hawkins took on *Bluesified*, his 2000 release. Hawkins' reputation as one of the leading Gary Davis practitioners earned him a spot on the Andy Cohen-produced compilation *Gary Davis Style—A Tribute to Reverend Gary Davis*, as well as a recording session with Maria Muldaur for her acoustic blues album, *Richland Woman Blues*. *—Ken Chang*

● **Bluesified** / 2000 / Say Mo' ✦✦✦

Despite the title, *Bluesified* is as much a gospel album as a blues album, and it shows Ernie Hawkins taking a step closer to the masterful level of blues-and-spirituals versatility set by his two main influences, Reverend Gary Davis and Blind Willie McTell. As he did on his previous two solo albums, Hawkins pays considerable homage the Davis canon here, with achingly good results on "I Belong to the Band" (sung by guest vocalist Maria Muldaur) and a 12-string rendition of "Crucifixion" into which Hawkins also weaves the melody of "Jesus Gonna Make Up My Dying Bed." But whereas 1996's *Blues Advice* presented Hawkins in more of a revivalist mode, *Bluesified* has him stretching out, experimenting with musical roots ranging from prewar jazz to country to African folk songs. In the end, Hawkins still puts on a formidable ragtime guitar clinic—but he's obviously got a lot on his mind besides the blues. *—Ken Chang*

Blues Advice / Aug. 15, 2000 / Say Mo' ✦✦

Ernie Hawkins' long-awaited sophomore album (following 1980's *Ragtime Signatures*), *Blues Advice* is a gem of an acoustic guitar showcase that hones in on the styles of Skip James, Blind Blake, and Reverend Gary Davis. (Released in 1996, the album was meant to commemorate the centennial year of Davis' birth.) Hawkins' guitar is the most compelling voice here; five of the songs are solo finger-style instrumentals, including a strong reading of Davis' "Cocaine" plus three Davis-arranged tunes that have never been recorded before—all of which amounts to a stash of buried treasure for Piedmont blues aficionados. Hawkins' singing, meanwhile, comes across as a bit thin, and he sometimes struggles with his range and dynamics. Nonetheless, *Blues Advice* makes for a satisfying listen thanks to Hawkins' subtle guitar wizardry and his ambitious approach in tackling so many traditional techniques. *—Ken Chang*

Roy Hawkins

Vocals, Piano / West Coast Blues, Piano Blues, R&B

Not only was Roy Hawkins dogged by bad luck during his career (at the height of his popularity, the pianist lost the use of an arm in a car wreck), he couldn't even cash in after the fact. When B.B. King blasted up the charts in 1970 with Roy Hawkins' classic "The Thrill Is Gone," the tune was mistakenly credited to the wrong composers on early pressings.

Little is known of Hawkins' early days. Producer Bob Geddins discovered Hawkins playing in an Oakland, CA, nightspot and supervised his first 78s for Cavatone and Downtown in 1948. Modern Records picked up the rights to several Downtown masters before signing Hawkins to a contract in 1949. Two major R&B hits resulted: 1950's "Why Do Things Happen to Me" and "Thrill Is Gone" the following year. Hawkins recorded for the Bihari brothers' Modern and RPM imprints into 1954. After that, a handful of 45s for Rhythm and Kent were all that was heard of the Bay Area pianist on vinyl. He's rumored to have died in 1973. *—Bill Dahl*

Highway 59 / 1984 / Ace ✦✦✦✦

Early-'50s rarities from the vaults of the Bihari brothers' Modern label, with a good amount of unissued masters recommending this 16-song LP (no CD equivalent yet).

Hawkins' cool California blues piano blends well with the tasty little combos Modern provided; of special interest are the title cut and "Would You," a pair of 1952 gems that feature T-Bone Walker's incomparable guitar work. *—Bill Dahl*

● **The Thrill Is Gone** / Aug. 29, 2000 / Ace ✦✦✦✦✦
Here are 24 of Hawkins' 1949-1952 Modern sides, mostly taken from singles that came out during those years. Even by the standards of the Modern roster, Hawkins is a fairly forgotten figure—although he was, according to the liner notes, briefly the label's biggest moneymaker. As with all of Modern's early-'50s recordings, this has a dependable urban, slightly jazzy West Coast groove, very accomplished and not as variable as one might like over the course of a couple dozen numbers. Hawkins was a good piano player and a sufficient easygoing, slightly foggy-textured vocalist, capable of both rapid jump shuffles and morose ballads. "Gloom and Misery All Around" and "I Don't Know Just What to Do" were entirely typical sentiments of his slower tunes. His band featured an excellent underrated guitarist, Ulysses James, whose burning tone shines when it's given a little space to strut, as on "Wine Drinkin' Woman." His Modern output was most notable for the self-pitying ballad "Why Do Everything Happen to Me," a number three hit later covered by B.B. King and James Brown, and, more memorably, the original version of "The Thrill Is Gone," which became B.B. King's biggest hit a couple of decades later. The original renditions of both are on this CD, and the gloomy "The Thrill Is Gone," far more piano-based and small band-scaled in its arrangement than King's classic cover, in particular outclasses anything else in Hawkins' discography. Otherwise, Hawkins is not among the first West Coast blues stars of the era, or even among the first such artists on the Modern roster, one should hear, though if you've a jones for that style, this reliably delivers the goods. *—Richie Unterberger*

Screamin' Jay Hawkins

b. Jul. 18, 1929, Cleveland, OH, **d.** Feb. 12, 2000, Paris, France
Vocals, Piano / Jump Blues, Rock & Roll, R&B

Screamin' Jay Hawkins was the most outrageous performer extant during rock's dawn. Prone to emerging out of coffins onstage, a flaming skull named Henry his constant companion, Screamin' Jay was an insanely theatrical figure long before it was even remotely acceptable.

Hawkins' life story is almost as bizarre as his onstage shtick. Originally inspired by the booming baritone of Paul Robeson, Hawkins was unable to break through as an opera singer. His boxing prowess was every bit as lethal as his vocal cords; many of his most hilarious tales revolve around Jay beating the hell out of a musical rival!

Hawkins caught his first musical break in 1951 as pianist/valet to veteran jazz guitarist Tiny Grimes. He debuted on wax for Gotham the following year with "Why Did You Waste My Time," backed by Grimes and his Rockin' Highlanders (they donned kilts and tam-o'-shanters on stage). Singles for Timely ("Baptize Me in Wine") and Mercury's Wing subsidiary (1955's otherworldly "[She Put The] Wamee [On Me]," a harbinger of things to come) preceded Hawkins' immortal 1956 rendering of "I Put a Spell on You" for Columbia's OKeh imprint.

Hawkins originally envisioned the tune as a refined ballad. After he and his New York session aces (notably guitarist Mickey Baker and saxist Sam "The Man" Taylor) had imbibed to the point of no return, Hawkins screamed, grunted, and gurgled his way through the tune with utter drunken abandon. A resultant success despite the protests of uptight suits-in-power, "Spell" became Screamin' Jay's biggest seller ("Little Demon," its rocking flip, is a minor classic itself).

Hawkins cut several amazing 1957-1958 follow-ups in the same crazed vein—"Hong Kong," a surreal "Yellow Coat," the Jerry Leiber/Mike Stoller-penned "Alligator Wine"—but none of them clicked the way "Spell" had. DJ Alan Freed convinced Screamin' Jay that popping out of a coffin might be a show-stopping gimmick by handing him a $300 bonus (long after Freed's demise, Screamin' Jay Hawkins was still benefiting from his crass brainstorm).

Hawkins' next truly inspired waxing came in 1969 when he was contracted to Philips Records (where he made two albums). His gross "Constipation Blues" wouldn't garner much airplay, but remained an integral part of his legacy for quite a while.

The cinema was a beneficiary of Screamin' Jay's larger-than-life persona in later years. His featured roles in *Mystery Train* and *A Rage in Harlem* made Hawkins a familiar visage to youngsters who never even heard "I Put a Spell on You." He died February 12, 2000, following surgery to treat an aneurysm; Hawkins was 70. *—Bill Dahl*

I Put a Spell on You / 1957 / Collectables ✦✦✦
This is a straight-up—no bonus tracks—reissue of Screamin' Jay's landmark Epic album from the '50s. His wild-ass reinventions of old, staid standards like "I Love Paris," "Deep Purple," and "You Made Me Love You (I Didn't Want To Do It)" must be heard to be believed, but for surrealism at it best, check out "Take Me Back to My Boots and Saddle" and a dead straight reading of "Swing Low, Sweet Chariot" in the middle of all of it. The perfect opening shot from this one-of-a-kind artist. *—Cub Koda*

What That Is! / 1969 / Philips ✦✦✦
Screamin' Jay Hawkins never made an album that wasn't wildly uneven in performance quality, songs, production, arrangements, and musicianship. This one is no less erratic; sometimes Hawkins' inspired lunacy makes its mark, and other times it falls woefully short. But it's fun hearing him keep trying. *—Ron Wynn*

Frenzy / 1982 / Edsel ✦✦✦✦
Screamin' Jay Hawkins was a truly demented R&B shouter, as evidenced by the classic "I Put a Spell on You." It wasn't long before his camp schtick overshadowed his musical abilities, but for a brief while he had a certain warped genius. Most of these tracks were recorded for OKeh, and the 14-track compilation *Frenzy* contains most of the best of these recordings. Nothing ever quite touched "I Put a Spell on You," but the songs that came the closest are here. *Frenzy* may not be a comprehensive collection, but for anyone who wants more of the sound that made "I Put a Spell on You" a hit, this will sufice. *—Stephen Thomas Erlewine*

Real Life / 1983 / Charly ✦✦✦
An uneven batch of R&B and blues tracks from Screamin' Jay Hawkins cut in the mid-'80s. Hawkins never had that great a voice to begin with, and years of shouting and hollering have affected it even more. But you've got to admire his spirit and personality, which are the strong points of this session. *—Ron Wynn*

Live & Crazy / 1989 / Evidence ✦✦
While Screamin' Jay Hawkins can't really shout with the force or volume of the past and doesn't have the energy to keep a whole set moving briskly, he gets off enough good one-liners to make things a bit interesting. His band plays routine blues shuffles, workouts, R&B covers and Hawkins originals such as "The Whammy," "Constipation Blues" and of course "I Put a Spell on You." While nearly an hour of this eventually becomes tedious, Hawkins' fans will still enjoy it, and others can satisfy themselves with the occasional nuggets. *—Ron Wynn*

● **Voodoo Jive: The Best of Screamin' Jay Hawkins** / Feb. 1990 / Rhino ✦✦✦✦✦
Some maintain that Hawkins was a one-hit fluke and a one-dimensional performer with a limited singing voice and no other discernible skills. Others insist that Hawkins was a decent R&B and blues singer and an excellent entertainer and personality whose real talents were overshadowed by the success of "I Put a Spell on You." This anthology doesn't convincingly answer the argument, but it does collect 17 Hawkins singles from OKeh, Enrica, and Philips, including all of his major hits. The high (or low) point is perhaps 1969's "Constipation Blues." *—Ron Wynn*

Cow Fingers & Mosquito Pie / 1991 / Epic ✦✦✦✦✦
Magically weird 19-song collection of the bizarre shouter's mid-'50s OKeh/Epic output, when he was at the height of his strange and terrifying vocal powers. In addition to the prerequisite "I Put a Spell on You" and the surreal rockers "Yellow Coat," "Hong Kong," "Alligator Wine," and "Little Demon," there's the amusing "There's Something Wrong With You," a previously unissued "You Ain't Foolin' Me," and a deranged takeoff on the cowboy ditty "Take Me Back to My Boots and Saddle" (and what Jay does to the formerly stately "I Love Paris" and "Orange Colored Sky" is truly indescribable!). *—Bill Dahl*

Spellbound! 1955–74 / 1991 / Bear Family ✦✦✦
Bear Family's *Spellbound! 1955-74* is a double-disc set that captures highlights from Screamin' Jay Hawkins' recordings for Wing, Decca, Philips, and RCA. It's not quite the bargain it seems. Half of the 48 tracks were already issued on two Philips albums, which were combined on one Edsel CD. Furthermore, most of these songs date from the '60s, with only a handful coming from Hawkins' '50s peak. Strangely, of those songs, not one of them is the original "I Put a Spell on You," which makes this hardly the definitive overview that it should be. Instead of focusing on the best of Screamin' Jay Hawkins' best material, it has the campy, silly stuff from the '60s, which will try the patience of anyone outside devoted fans—and those devoted fans will prefer more complete compilations than this strangely scattershot effort from Bear Family. There are some good moments here, but overall, it has to rank as a disappointment. *—Stephen Thomas Erlewine*

Stone Crazy / 1993 / Rhino ✦✦✦
Stone Crazy is a latter-day album from Screamin' Jay Hawkins, recorded with his touring band the Chickenhawks. Musically, the album sounds surprisingly good, since the Chickenhawks are a tight little backing band, but Hawkins' schtick gets a little tiresome after a while, and there aren't many great songs on the album. Only the tribute to the *Twin Peaks* vixen "Sherilyn Fenn" really hits home, but dedicated fans will be pleased that the record does have sporadic fits of energetic playing. *—Stephen Thomas Erlewine*

Portrait of a Man / Feb. 14, 1995 / Edsel ✦✦✦
Portrait of a Man is a collection of rarities and obscurities from a man whose very career was filled with arcania. Of course, it contains the original version of "I Put a Spell on You," but what Screamin' Jay Hawkins collection doesn't? The main point of the disc is rarities that aren't anywhere else, whether it's a remake of "I Put a Spell on You" or his freak English hit "Heart Attack and Vine." There are more interesting things here than the average Screamin' album, which is both good ("Mountain Jive") and bad ("Armpit No. 6"). Either way, it's one of the handful of Hawkins compilations that aren't strict hits collections but are worth hearing. *—Stephen Thomas Erlewine*

Somethin' Funny Goin On / Apr. 16, 1995 / Bizarre/Straight ✦✦✦
Former Beat Farmer guitarist Buddy Blue sits in with Screamin' Jay Hawkins' on *Somethin' Funny Goin' On*. It's a fairly predictable set, with the traditional Screamin' antics and spooky blues, without any real standouts. There aren't any dogs on the album, either—it's just a mediocre record, one that fails to capture the wildness of Screamin' Jay and to deliver any memorable songs. *—Stephen Thomas Erlewine*

At Last / Mar. 10, 1998 / Last Call ✦✦
At Last is a collection of all-new material from Screamin' Jay Hawkins, featuring 12 of his originals and a suitably deranged cover of "I Shot the Sheriff." *—Steve Huey*

Ted Hawkins

b. Oct. 28, 1936, Biloxi, MS, **d.** Jan. 1, 1995, Los Angeles, CA
Vocals, Guitar / Contemporary Blues, Singer/Songwriter, Modern Acoustic Blues, Soul-Blues, Soul

Overseas, he was a genuine hero, performing to thousands. But on his L.A. hometurf, sand-blown Venice Beach served as Ted Hawkins' makeshift stage. He'd deliver his magnificent melange of soul, blues, folk, gospel, and a touch of country all by his lonesome, with only an acoustic guitar for company. Passersby would pause to marvel at Hawkins' melismatic vocals, dropping a few coins or a greenback into his tip jar on the way by.

That was the way Ted Hawkins kept body and soul together until 1994, when DGC/ Geffen Records issued *The Next Hundred Years*, his breakthrough album. Suddenly, Hawkins was poised on the precipice of stardom. And then, just after Christmas that same year, in a bout of cruel irony, he died of a stroke.

Ted Hawkins' existence was no day in the park. Born into abject poverty in Mississippi, an abused and illiterate child, Hawkins was sent to reform school when he was 12 years old. He encountered his first musical inspiration there from New Orleans pianist Professor Longhair, whose visit to the school moved the lad to perform in a talent show. But it wasn't enough to keep him out of trouble. At age 15, he stole a leather jacket and spent three years at Mississippi's infamous state penitentiary at Parchman Farm.

Roaming from Chicago to Philadelphia to Buffalo after his release, Hawkins left the frigid weather behind in 1966, purchasing a one-way ticket to L.A. Suddenly, music beckoned; he bought a guitar and set out to locate the ex-manager of Sam Cooke (one of his idols). No such luck, but he did manage to cut his debut 45, the soul-steeped "Baby"/"Whole Lot of Women," for Money Records. When he learned no royalties were forthcoming from its sales, Hawkins despaired of ever making a living at his music and took to playing on the streets.

Fortunately, producer Bruce Bromberg was interested in Hawkins' welfare, recording his delightfully original material in 1971 both with guitarist Phillip Walker's band ("Sweet Baby" was issued as a single on the Joliet label) and in a solo acoustic format (with Ted's wife Elizabeth occasionally adding harmonies). The producer lost touch with Hawkins for a while after recording him, Hawkins falling afoul of the law once again. In 1982, those tapes finally emerged on Rounder as *Watch Your Step*, and Hawkins began to receive some acclaim (*Rolling Stone* gave it a five-star review). Bromberg corralled him again for the 1986 encore album *Happy Hour*, which contained the touching "Cold & Bitter Tears."

At the behest of a British deejay, Hawkins moved to England in 1986 and was treated like a star for four years, performing in Great Britain, Ireland, France, even Japan. But when he came home, he was faced with the same old situation. Once again, he set up his tip jar on the beach, donned the black leather glove he wore on his fretting hand, and played for passersby—until DGC ever so briefly propelled him into the major leagues.

Ted Hawkins was a unique talent, unclassifiable and eminently soulful. For a year or so, he was even a star in his own country. *Love You Most of All: More Songs from Venice Beach* was issued posthumously in 1998. *—Bill Dahl*

Watch Your Step / 1982 / Rounder ♦♦♦
Guitarist/vocalist Ted Hawkins was an instant sensation when this session was originally released in 1982. At a time when slick, heavily produced urban contemporary material was establishing its domination on the R&B scene, Hawkins' hard-edged, rough, cutting voice, plus his crisp acoustic guitar accompaniment and country blues roots, seemed both dated and extremely fresh. This 15-track CD includes four numbers with Hawkins backed by Phillip Walker and his band, and others ranging from the humorous "Who Got My Natural Comb?" to the poignant "If You Love Me" and two versions of the title track. He also teamed with his wife Elizabeth on "Don't Lose Your Cool" and "I Gave It All I Had" for moving duets. *—Ron Wynn*

Happy Hour / 1986 / Rounder ♦♦♦♦♦
Guitarist/vocalist Ted Hawkins' second Rounder record enhanced his reputation. *Happy Hour* features Hawkins' memorable compositions, plus a wonderful version of Curtis Mayfield's "Gypsy Woman." Hawkins' vocals were even more gritty and striking, as was his acoustic guitar backing and chording. He teamed with his wife Elizabeth on "Don't Make Me Explain It," "My Last Goodbye," and "California Song," and with guitarist Night Train Clemons on "Gypsy Woman" and "You Pushed My Head Away." Hawkins blended soul and urban blues stylings with country and rural blues inflections and rhythms, making another first-rate release. *—Ron Wynn*

On the Boardwalk / 1986 / Unamerican ♦♦♦

The Next Hundred Years / Mar. 29, 1994 / Geffen ♦♦♦
The former L.A. street musician's major label breakthrough was in a great many ways a far weaker outing than what came before, largely due to a plodding band unwisely inserted behind Hawkins that tends to distract rather than enhance his impassioned vocals and rich acoustic guitar strumming. Mostly originals ("There Stands the Glass" returns, as does "Ladder of Success") that would have sounded so much better in an intimate solo context. *—Bill Dahl*

The Kershaw Sessions: Live at the BBC / 1995 / Varese Sarabande ♦♦♦
The material on *The Kershaw Sessions: Live at the BBC* was recorded for disc jockey Andy Kershaw's BBC radio show between 1986 and 1989. It captures Ted Hawkins in an intimate, unvarnished setting that strips his music down to its purest essentials, making it an intriguing listen for fans who want more of Hawkins' bare-bones street-troubadour sound. Only a little over half the songs are Hawkins compositions; the high percentage of covers and the minimalist production give *The Kershaw Sessions* a vibe similar to *Songs From Venice Beach*. This is the way many British listeners were introduced to Hawkins' music, and it makes an excellent listen for American devotees as well. *—Steve Huey*

Songs from Venice Beach / Oct. 1995 / Evidence ♦♦♦♦
Blending every form of roots music imaginable into his own singular soulful stew, the incomparable Ted Hawkins stuck mostly to R&B covers on this splendid 1985 solo outing—songs by Sam Cooke (his idol), Jerry Butler, Bobby "Blue" Bland, the Temptations, and Garnet Mimms receive gorgeous readings by the acoustic guitarist. But even though he only contributed one original, the touching "Ladder of Success," to the set, Hawkins wasn't content to remain in one genre—his commanding revival of Webb Pierce's hillbilly weeper "There Stands the Glass" ranks with the disc's very best moments (of which there are many). *—Bill Dahl*

● **The Ted Hawkins Story: Suffer No More** / Jan. 13, 1998 / Rhino ♦♦♦♦♦
Taken individually, Hawkins' albums didn't measure up to his critical reputation, due to uneven material, occasionally inappropriate production, and overreliance upon covers. More than most best-ofs, this 20-song compilation is a revelation of sorts. By focusing on his best moments, it's much easier to make a convincing case for Hawkins as a major, if erratic, roots-music performer who sounded like a coarsened, acoustic-oriented Sam Cooke. The set goes all the way back to both sides of his rare (and good) 1966 soul single on the Money label and highlights the best originals from the '70s and '80s sessions released on Rounder, wisely selecting sparsely from his cover-dominated albums of the mid-'80s. The songs from his major-label finale *The Next Hundred Years* can veer toward production slickness, but there's a pleasing bonus in three acoustic, previously unreleased cuts from the early '90s. It's an intelligently selected, well-rounded disc, presenting several sides of this idiosyncratic artist: composer, folky interpreter of material by Sam Cooke and Brook Benton, and country-tinged soul artist. *—Richie Unterberger*

The Final Tour / Jan. 13, 1998 / Evidence ♦♦♦♦♦
Ted Hawkins' story is one of the most interesting—and tragic—in the history of R&B. Who'd have thought that a fifty-something street singer who performed '60s-type soul in Venice Beach, CA. would have signed with Geffen's DGC label after decades of obscurity? That's exactly what happened, but tragically, a 58-year-old Hawkins died from a diabetes-related stroke just when things were really looking up for him. Recorded live at three 1994 concerts and released in 1998, *The Final Tour* shows how great Hawkins was sounding during the last months of his life. Nothing slick or elaborate happens on this album—it's just the charismatic Hawkins and his acoustic guitar, drawing on Sam Cooke's influence but always sounding like his own man. Those familiar with Hawkins' Rounder output will be familiar with heartfelt originals like "Bad Dog," "Bring It on Home, Daddy" and "Revenge of Scorpio," all of which demonstrate that he was as superb a composer as he was a singer. Hawkins is equally captivating on interpretations of Brook Benton's "I Got What I Wanted" and "All I Have to Offer You Is Me," a hit for country great Charley Pride that easily lends itself to Hawkins' brand of acoustic R&B. Soul lovers who haven't experienced the joys of Hawkins' music should make a point of obtaining this magnificent album. *—Alex Henderson*

Love You Most of All: More Songs from Venice Beach / Sep. 29, 1998 / Evidence ♦♦♦
Ted Hawkins always resisted being called a blues singer, and a look at his repertoire shows why. While Hawkins' strong but weather-beaten voice could communicate sorrow and heartbreak as few others could, he could also summon up a joyous fire that's a wonder to behold, and he could work this magic with practically any song he chose to perform, from Sam Cooke's "Bring It on Home to Me" to John Denver's "Take Me Home, Country Roads." Both of those songs appear on *Love You Most of All: More Songs from Venice Beach*, which (as the title suggests) features 13 songs from the same 1985 bare-bones guitar and voice sessions that produced Hawkins' *Songs from Venice Beach*, and, like the earlier album, it consists primarily of tunes Hawkins sang while busking for change along the Venice, CA, boardwalk. "Take Me Home, Country Roads" features a striking, hypnotic coda, in which Hawkins chants "so glad I'm a country boy/so glad I'm a country boy" until he's taken Denver's song to a soulful place no one (except possibly Toots Hibbert) could have imagined it going, and Hawkins manages a similar alchemy with such chestnuts as "Green Green Grass of Home," "Your Cheatin' Heart," and even "North to Alaska," as well as more likely Sam Cooke and Otis Redding covers. On this disc's best moments, Hawkins stands beside Arthur Alexander as one of the great unacknowledged links between country and R&B. Unfortunately, the best of the material from these sessions was used on the first album, and the five originals recorded in 1990 that close out the album simply aren't on a par with such Hawkins compositions as "Strange Conversation," "Sorry You're Sick," or "The Good and the Bad." But he never sound less than committed on any of the 18 tunes of *Love You Most of All*, and anyone who has encountered the heart-tugging power of Ted Hawkins' voice knows he never gave a bad performance in front of a microphone—and this disc preserves more than a few great ones. *—Mark Deming*

The Unstoppable Ted Hawkins / Feb. 27, 2001 / Catfish ♦♦♦
Ted Hawkins had been accepted more warmly in England in the late '80s than he had been in his native America. To his countrymen, he was a has-been soul singer, ex-junkie, and ex-con who'd never made it and was now a busker on the Venice Beach boardwalk. What America wouldn't get until his major label debut in 1994 was something the Brits seemed to grasp instinctively—Ted Hawkins was one of the great soul singers, a very decent writer, but an interpreter of other peoples' material blessed with a perfect insight to bring things to life. And he proves that here, on what was meant to be just a soundboard cassette recording. From Sam Cooke to Brook Benton, even the maudlin "Please Come to Boston" takes on a magic and depth in his voice, while something as innocuous of "Zip Pe Dee Doo Dah" positively brims over with spirit. His guitar work was never more than rudimentary, strumming an open chord, his left hand gloved to protect it, but it did the perfect job of framing that magnificent voice, which, as this album shows, was best heard live, where he could open up and let his dramatic tendencies take over without ever going overboard. His own writing coexists well with the better-known work, "Bring It on Home Daddy" a good juxtaposition to "Your Cheating Heart." But genre never mattered—it was about whether the song worked, be it something as wonderful as his take on Otis Redding's "Dock of the Bay" or John Denver's "Country Roads," his set closer. Saying it's all good can cheapen things. But in the case of Ted Hawkins, it really *was* all good. *—Chris Nickson*

Nowhere to Run / Oct. 9, 2001 / Catfish

Clifford Hayes

Violin / Prewar Country Blues, Jazz Blues, Classic Jazz, Jug Band
A shadowy figure in jazz and blues history, Clifford Hayes was a violinist, but was more significant as a leader of recording sessions. He recorded with Sara Martin (1924), and often teamed up with banjoist Cal Smith in early jug bands including the Old Southern

Jug Band, Clifford's Louisville Jug Band, the well-known Dixieland Jug Blowers (1926-1927), and Hayes' Louisville Stompers (1927-1929). One of the Dixieland Jug Blowers' sessions featured the great clarinetist Johnny Dodds, while pianist Earl Hines was a surprise star with the otherwise primitive Louisville Stompers (a jug-less group with a front line of Hayes' violin and Hense Grundy's trombone). Clifford Hayes' last recordings were in 1931, and all of his sessions (plus those of some other jug bands) are available on four RST CDs. —*Scott Yanow*

Dixieland Jug Blowers / 1991 / Yazoo ✦✦✦✦
Jug band material in the hokum and country blues variety. This one goes about as far to the margin as any jug band ever journeyed, thanks to Clifford Hayes' violin and Earl McDonald's jug. —*Ron Wynn*

Clifford Hayes & the Louisville Jug Bands, Vol. 1 / 1994 / RST ✦✦✦✦
The first of four volumes from the Austrian RST label that reissue the complete output from several historic jug bands from Louisville features violinist Clifford Hayes in several contexts. In 1924 he led the first jug band on record, backing blues singer Sara Martin on some exuberant performances that overcame the primitive recording quality. In addition this CD has Hayes leading The Old Southern Jug Band, Clifford's Louisville Jug Band and The Dixieland Jug Blowers; all of the groups greatly benefit from the exciting playing of Earl McDonald on jug. The CD is rounded out by four selections from Whistler's Jug Band. Historic and generally enjoyable music, it's recommended to '20s collectors. —*Scott Yanow*

● **Clifford Hayes & the Louisville Jug Bands, Vol. 2** / 1994 / RST ✦✦✦✦✦
The second of four CDs in a very valuable series from the Austrian RST label has 12 selections from the Dixieland Jug Blowers (a very spirited sextet with violinist Clifford Hayes, the colorful jug blowing of Earl McDonald, and on six numbers, clarinetist Johnny Dodds as a guest), eight from Earl McDonald's Original Louisville Jug Band, and four by Whistler's Jug Band (their leader, Buford Threlkeld, doubles on guitar and nose whistle). The monologue on the former group's "House Rent Rag" is quite memorable and humorous. Of the four CDs this is the most essential one, for it finds these historic groups in their prime. —*Scott Yanow*

Clifford Hayes & the Louisville Jug Bands, Vol. 3 / 1994 / RST ✦✦✦✦
The third of four CDs from the Austrian RST label has the final ten selections from the Dixieland Jug Blowers along with 14 by Clifford Hayes' Louisville Stompers. Although the former no longer had the powerful jug playing of Earl McDonald, the mysterious H. Clifford was a good substitute and the three-horn septet (which features two guest vocalists) certainly had plenty of spirit. The Louisville Stompers is essentially a stripped-down jugless version of the Jug Blowers, a jazz-oriented quartet comprised of violinist Clifford Hayes, trombonist Hense Grundy, pianist Johnny Gatewood and the impressive guitarist Cal Smith who makes "Blue Guitar Stomp" a classic. The final seven Stompers performances are a bit surprising for the pianist is the great Earl Hines who has a few short solos although mostly in a supporting role. All four of the CDs are easily recommended to collectors of the era for on a whole they contain the complete output of these unusual groups. —*Scott Yanow*

Clifford Hayes & the Louisville Jug Bands, Vol. 4 / 1994 / RST ✦✦✦✦
The fourth and final CD in this brief but important series from the Austrian RST label features jug bands in a variety of roles. There are the three last performances by Clifford Hayes' Louisville Stompers (the two versions of "You're Ticklin' Me" have Earl Hines on piano while "You Gonna Need My Help" features the classic blues singer Sippie Wallace), The Kentucky Jazz Babies (a quartet with violinist Clifford Hayes and trumpeter Jimmy Strange) does a good job on two numbers and Phillips' Louisville Jug Band (an odd quartet with Hooks Tifford on C-melody sax and Charles "Cane" Adams playing what is called "walking cane flute") performs eight songs. In addition Whistler and His Jug Band play two primitive numbers while violinist Clifford Hayes backs the minstrel singer Kid Coley and reunites with the great jug player Earl McDonald behind the vocals of country pioneer Jimmie Rodgers, Ben Ferguson and John Harris. An interesting set, to say the least, all four CDs in this series are recommended to fans of the era. —*Scott Yanow*

Frog Hop / Jun. 23, 1998 / Frog ✦✦✦✦

Louisville Stomp / Jun. 23, 1998 / Frog ✦✦✦✦

Nap Hayes
Guitar / Prewar Country Blues, String Bands
In February of 1928, guitarist Napoleon "Nap" Hayes and mandolinist Matthew Prater, two black musicians from Vicksburg, MS, recorded four instrumental tunes in Memphis. The tunes—"Somethin' Doin'," "Easy Winner," "Nothin' Doin'," and "Prater Blues"—showcase the clean musicianship of both players, with Hayes' guitar providing a steady rhythmic accompaniment for the skillful mandolin lead. The performances, while comprising only a small body of recorded work, reveal a unique and carefully stylized repertoire, fusing elements of string band, ragtime, and blues forms: the first two sides directly borrow themes and phrasings from Scott Joplin rags, "Something Doing" and "The Entertainer," respectively. Little biographical information is known regarding Hayes and Prater, who recorded as the Johnson Boys and the Blue Boys. The duo also recorded two numbers with popular bluesman Lonnie Johnson on violin, but those sides were not issued (they have only become available in recent years). The four duet recordings of Nap Hayes and Matthew Prater are collected on Document's *String Bands (1926-1929)*. —*Burgin Mathews*

Warren Haynes
Slide Guitar, Vocals, Guitar / Blues-Rock
You wouldn't know it from listening to Warren Haynes' work with Gov't Mule or the Allman Brothers Band, but there was a time when he didn't play guitar. He says, "I didn't

get my first guitar until I was 12. My oldest brother had an acoustic guitar and I would bang around on it and try to play." But guitar wasn't even his first love—it was singing. Around the time he was eight or nine, Haynes' two older brothers began turning him on to soul music. He would sit in his room, singing Smokey Robinson, Diana Ross, Otis Redding, and Wilson Pickett. He became fascinated with sounds of Motown and Memphis. "All I cared about was the singer. The really strong singers really knocked me out. Levi Stubbs of the Four Tops still is one of my favorite voices of all time. And I always liked B.B. King even before I liked the blues. His voice was the main thing."

Guitar didn't escape Haynes' attention for long, however: He would soon turn on to rock & roll. "I really liked Eric Clapton. He was the first guitar hero I had. I liked really heavy Cream stuff. I liked all the Derek & the Dominos stuff." Haynes' brothers used his admiration of Clapton to expand his musical horizons to take in the blues masters. They would tell him to check out Howlin' Wolf because Clapton played on it. Interviews with Haynes' favorite guitarists led him to other blues players, and the scope of his guitar playing grew accordingly.

Soon Haynes found himself performing at private gigs and pool parties. When he was about 14, he started hanging around a local pizza parlor that had been converted into a nightclub. About six months later, word got out that Haynes played guitar. The regulars wondered what this kid could do, so they offered to let him on stage.

It wasn't long before Haynes was playing in a band called Ricochet that developed a good regional following. One day, Haynes got a call from David Allan Coe, and it was a major break for the 20-year-old Haynes. He played with Coe from 1980 to 1984 (traveling all over the States and Europe) and played on nine of Coe's albums. Haynes also met Dickey Betts and Gregg Allman through Coe, and when Coe's band opened for the Allman Brothers at the Fox Theater in Atlanta, Betts sat in. Four years later, Haynes moved to Nashville to do session work, but the Allman connection was still there. Betts was doing some demos in Nashville and called someone to put together a group of background singers. As fate would have it, Haynes was one of them. Later, he called Haynes and invited him down to work on some songs. Those songs turned into Betts' solo album, *Pattern Disruptive*.

At the same time, Allman decided to record "Just Before the Bullets Fly," which Haynes co-wrote, as the title track to his 1988 album. It's no wonder that when the Allman Brothers re-formed for their reunion tour in 1989, Haynes got a call to join. That tour turned into two studio albums and two Grammy nominations for Best Instrumental Rock Performance (in 1990 for "True Gravity" and 1991 for "Kind of Bird," both of which were co-written by Haynes and Betts) and then a live album in 1992 *An Evening with the Allman Brothers Band*. Haynes' songwriting, singing, and playing helped make *Seven Turns*, *Shades of Two Worlds*, and *An Evening With the Allman Brothers Band* the Brothers' most critically acclaimed albums in years. Many critics give Haynes credit for putting the fire back in the Allman Brothers Band.

Haynes also took time out to release his first solo album, *Tales of Ordinary Madness*. The album featured the piano work of Chuck Leavell. Leavell also played on the album, joining another former Allman Brother, Johnny Neel, and Funkadelic's Bernie Worrell on keyboards. Marc Quinones, percussionist in the current Brothers lineup, also helped out.

After dropping out of the Allman Brothers Band in 1997 to pursue his side project (Gov't Mule) on a full-time basis, Haynes, along with bassist Allen Woody and drummer Matt Abts, released their third album in 1998, *Dose*, as a follow-up to their highly successful 1996 debut album and the 1996 recording *Live at Roseland Ballroom*. Gov't Mule has forged on following Woody's death in August 2000, and Haynes has also rejoined the Allman Brothers Band.—*Michael B. Smith*

● **Tales of Ordinary Madness** / 1993 / Megaforce ✦✦✦✦
Produced by Chuck Leavell, Warren Haynes' first solo album is a refreshing change of pace from his work with the latter-day incarnation of the Allman Brothers Band. Although the feel of this album is undeniably classic rock, with much of Free's bluesy swagger, it is also vaguely reminiscent of '80s rock at times (check out the Mr. Big-esque verse to "Fire in the Kitchen"). The focus on *Tales of Ordinary Madness* is clearly on Haynes' songwriting chops. For the most part, the songs on this record are tight and concise, focusing on immediate riffs, gritty vocals, and cool arrangements to sell them. This, however, is not to suggest that Haynes has stopped tearing it up with his guitar, and he amply demonstrates why he is one of the most lauded straight-ahead rock lead guitarists of the '90s. The various bands that backup Haynes are all quite good, and notables Bernie Worrell and producer Leavell both make guest appearances on keyboards. Standout tracks include the midtempo "Tattoos and Cigarettes," which is a great showcase for Haynes' under appreciated vocal talents. The smoky "Blue Radio" is also notable for the artist's emotive singing. In fact, the most exceptional thing about *Tales of Ordinary Madness* is his vocal performance, the overall impact of which stays with the listener far longer than any particular song or hook. There are some slow moments on this record, but it is great party music, and fans of Haynes' work with the Allman Brothers Band would surely be interested in this recording. —*Daniel Gioffre*

Patrick Hazell
Vocals, Drums, Piano, Harmonica / Modern Electric Blues
Patrick Hazell is a white one-man band (piano, neck rack harmonica, and drums) from Washington, IA. But skin color and point of origin hardly matter, as Hazell sounds like a complete throwback to the recordings of the late '40s and early '50s. His rhythmic drive is superlative while his sound and style are highly reminiscent of Memphis one-man-band star Joe Hill Louis. His raspy harp and vocals (sung into the same distorted microphone he plays through) are fortified with strong material, an unrelenting beat, and sensational ambience, as he ekes out a piece of blues turf that hasn't been occupied in a very long time. In the current white-boy blues community—where seemingly every street corner has five people on it with shades, pleated pants, and beat-up Stratocasters in hand—Patrick Hazell stands out as something very unique and cool. —*Cub Koda*

Back Country Shuffle / 1978 / Blue Rhythm ✦✦

Patrick Hazell / 1980 / Blue Rhythm ✦✦✦

After Hours / 1981 / Blue Rhythm ✦✦✦

● **Blues on the Run** / 1995 / Blue Rhythm ✦✦✦✦✦

Hazell's opus has all the portents of an album you'll find yourself still listening to ten years from now, both for its content and its sheer uniqueness. The title track is five minutes of nasty modal shouting and honking while the opener, "Here I Go Again," answers the question, "What would it have sounded like if Joe Hill Louis had cut a rock & roll record at Sun?" Hazell sounds his best when interpreting his own material, but even his take on a time-worn favorite like "Wang Dang Doodle" is well worth the listen. That he manages to pull off his one-man-band turn without the use of overdubbing makes the performances on this album all the more amazing. —*Cub Koda*

Blue Blood / 1996 / Blue Rhythm ✦✦✦✦

Hazell jettisons part of his one-man-band approach for his second album and, despite the loss of autonomy, loses none of the raw feel that has made his previous recordings so enjoyable. Enlisting fellow Iowa blues heads C-Boy James and Chris McCurdy to keep rudimentary time on drums and assorted lo-fi percussion throughout, Hazell turns in a multitude of great original performances on this disc. All 14 selections are written by him, and that same gritty vocal/Joe Hill Louis overamplified harmonica/boogie piano style that made his debut album so much fun is taken even further here. The opening track, "Here We Go Again" is an update of the first album's "Here I Go Again," recasting its lyrics this time toward the bar patron. There's a real ambient feel on several tracks, with the whole thing sounding like an old Trumpet 78 recorded at a deserted VFW hall, most notably on "Movin' Time," the minor-key "Walkin' on a Tightrope," the solo piano instrumental "Easy Time Blues," "Time Goes by So Quickly" and the set closer, "Avenue Called the Blues." That trademark one-man band feel of Hazell's comes to the fore on "All Mixed Up" and "Hot Cakes," while new territory is mined on the atmospheric "Unspoken Words," a drifting minor-key instrumental that almost veers into jazz territory. A superb harpist and an even better piano man (check out his work on "Washington Boogie" and the aforementioned "Easy Time Blues"), Hazell flexes his muscles beyond the novelty of one-man-band territory on this one, and the results are very fine, indeed. —*Cub Koda*

Prairie Songs / 1996 / Blue Rhythm ✦✦

Patrick Hazell has taken the prairieland as his subject of focus for this album. All of the lyrics from the album are well focused on the subject, never straying far off course. The music that colors the intriguing lyrics ranges from blues to American folk, with a new age/world feel in the depth and breadth of the melodies. Patrick Hazell reaches into a huge bag of captivating keyboard and harmonica phrases to piece together some charismatic melodies. His lyrical style works well with his cowboy-esque vocals. It's as though Hazell has climbed onto a horse and is playing the part of the singing prairie cowboy. Instead of the usual guitar, Hazell has inserted keyboard and outstanding harmonica riffs to complete the aural portrait. Patrick Hazell performed and recorded all of the instruments and vocals on the album between 1992 and 1996. Some of the instruments used were a 1916 Hazelton Brothers grand piano, a Yamaha DX-7 II FD keyboard, Hohner harmonicas, a Zube Tube, rattles, kettle drum, darbukka, snare and conga drums, as well as sleigh bells and cowbells. One of the key highlights from the album is "Home on the Range," which was penned by Dr. Brewster Higley in his one-room cabin in the prairieland. Hazell's interpretation takes this melodic classic to an all new level by instrumentally expanding on the original expertly. He also adds an intensity to the lyrical content with a powerful vocal presence. At a bit less than ten minutes, this song makes the acquisition of the album a guaranteed pleasure. —*Larry Belanger*

Dream Catcher / 1996 / Blue Rhythm ✦✦✦

For *Dream Catcher*, Patrick Hazell focuses on lyrics with a mystical dream quality. Most of the songs cling to the message of allure and tend to pique one's curiosity. But the best of the pieces have a Wolfman Jack-esque gritty quality. "The Ghost House" is an excellent example of when Patrick Hazell shines brightest. A blues essence is at the root of the melody, with sharp accentuating harmonica riffs coloring the piece vibrantly and Hazell's gritty vocal presentation complete the portrait. His weakest pieces melodically are his poetic compositions of which a majority of the songs fall under. "Come Dance With Me," "The Gravel Road," and "Where Can I Turn To" are some of the pieces which have a strong poetic character. The instrumental accents in these pieces are inserted for soundtrack effect and can be appreciated in that context only. While these songs make it hard to pigeonhole Hazell into one genre, they appear to be where he wants to focus his creative outlet. So having been linked to the jazz and blues genre does not satisfy Hazell, and he looks to expand to a more progressive and unrestricted style of songwriting. It works on a few of his pieces, but most fall into the uncommercial realm of music marketing—in other words, they fall short of reaching the pop music scene by quite a distance. Attractive to the minor music market, possibly, but even that may be of a speculative nature. Hazell has broken from tradition and wanders in a musical world few dare to explore. His presentations have strength, if not melodically, certainly his emotional strength is in the contents. If one is searching for something unique and complex, *Dream Catcher* may just be what one has been dreaming about. —*Larry Belanger*

Patrick Hazell With the Mothers Blue Band, 1975–1980 / 1996 / Blue Rhythm ✦✦✦✦

Patrick Hazell started the Mother Blues Band in 1968. Although the songs on the album were recorded between 1975 and 1980, the majority have the feel of the late '60s and early '70s. This was an era when blues and rock were blended together by a great number of bands. One band that made a great impression from this style music was the group the Yardbirds, which gave Eric Clapton, Jeff Beck, and Jimmy Page their first experience within the style. The Mother Blues Band has much of the same qualities which listeners sought out in that era, a tight soulful root blues essence. "Back on the Road Again," recorded in 1980, kicks off the album. A tight arrangement is at the core

of this piece. The multiple percussion accents lend the quick tempo an excellent quality. The overall groove is in a '60s rock & roll vein with a contagious presentation by a tight group of musicians. "Late Again Tonight," recorded in 1975, is the earliest tune on the album. The band presents a very tight performance and a high quality sound for their first experience. There are many great influences which can be heard throughout the composition, but the overall piece has an original charm. The guitar work, both rhythm and the lead solo, is a key element to the overall excellence of the presentation. "Late Again Tonight" is more rock than blues, but also displays how the two genres were used to create truly contagious music. "Late Again Tonight" is guaranteed to be a favorite from the album because of the infectious melody one will be unable to shake. Those who want to experience music from an era when musicians put their heart and soul into a performance are sure to enjoy this album. *Patrick Hazell With the Mother Blues Band* has captured a timeless sound which will live on in the hearts of many. If the blues fan acquires one album in the near future it should certainly be this entertaining album. —*Larry Belanger*

Sound Tracks / 1997 / Blue Rhythm ✦✦✦

For the double disc *Sound Tracks*, Patrick Hazell has focused on an improvisational jazz format. Armed with his neck harmonica holder and a grand piano, Hazell treats the listener to two hours of captivating music on a 22-track, all-original compilation. The 1916 Hazelton Brothers grand piano that Hazell uses is specially tuned to match the tuning of his Hohner Marine Band harmonicas. Hazell plays both instruments with an intense passion, which assists him in accomplishing his mission of presenting hearty original textured compositions. While "Reflections in Blue" features a rootsy improvisational jazz quality with expertly crafted piano riffs and steady harmonica played with emotional strength, "Bluesintegration" has a piano sound in a Thelonius Monk vein and a harmonica sound with a unique improvisational essence not unlike Walter Holden. Other songs from the album explore a jazz style with a more prominent blues presence, adding variety and a bit of spice to the contents. The second disc from the compilation appears more focused on the roots blues style, unlike the first disc with its stronger jazz focus. The songs with strong blues elements include "Bohemian Blues," which features intense, steady-rolling bass and melodic high piano phrases, and "Reeding the Blues," with its hearty roots blues quality in the piano parts and its harmonica riffs—running the entire spectrum from the high to low range and played with lungs of steel. These are some of the meatier presentations, but all of the compositions from the album are certainly hearty enough to please the improvisational jazz and blues lover. Exploring an area that few have tapped, Patrick Hazell has expertly put together an entertaining and infectious package in this double-disc presentation of improvisations on piano and harmonica. —*Larry Belanger*

Vicksburg / 2000 / Blue Rhythm ✦✦

On *Vicksburg*'s first disc, The Battlefield at Night, Patrick Hazell explores some unique musical territories. Some fall into the category of chanting, with almost a spiritual feel to them. One of the longer pieces is found on track 13, which contains some impressive and captivating chanting by Hazell. If one is searching for some great harmonica, then track seven on the first disc comes highly recommended because of the excellent Dixie-style phrases. None of the tracks from the album are titled and some appear to continue with hardly a break between them. The concept of the album is to commemorate the siege at Vicksburg during the Civil War. Hazell uses only instruments from the era—the harmonica, which was becoming popular at the time, as well as instruments like the bugle, marching drum, and flute. He also weaves in melodies with his original compositions which are from the Civil War era. Hazell recommends that the listener not listen to these recordings through headphones, as there are a number of cannon blasts which are not pleasing when presented through headphones. The second disc, The Battlefield at Dawn, has similar characteristics as the first disc but with far less chanting. The first song on the disc has the most melodic charisma displayed by Hazell's harmonica skills. The rest of the songs have more of a soundtrack essence, along with some that have a strong mystical flavor. As with all of Hazell's compilations, one should be ready to experience something unique when listening to *Vicksburg*. The question may arise as to whether Hazell's music is genius or merely eccentric; either way, Hazell's music is an exhilarating and original adventure. —*Larry Belanger*

Edward Hazelton

Harmonica / Country Blues, Field Recordings

Hazelton is mostly known to blues collectors as the harmonica player who split an album with the more renowned Eddie "One-String" Jones. Both Hazelton and Jones were discovered by Frederick Usher Jr. and Richard Barlow in Los Angeles' skid row in 1960; both were recorded, and both performed for a private gathering, before vanishing again into obscurity. Hazelton isn't nearly as interesting as Jones, who fashioned a diddley bow-type instrument out of a two-by-four to play some slide guitar-like blues on a steel wire. The Hazelton tracks, though, also offer a window into unrefined country blues styles that were hard to locate by 1960. —*Richie Unterberger*

Jeff Healey

b. Mar. 25, 1966, Toronto, Ontario, Canada

Vocals, Guitar / Blues-Rock, Modern Electric Blues

What makes Jeff Healey different from other blues-rockers is also what keeps some listeners from accepting him as anything other than a novelty—the fact that the blind guitarist plays his Fender Stratocaster on his lap, not standing up. With the guitar in his lap, Healey can make unique bends and hammer-ons, making his licks different and more elastic than most of the competition. Unfortunately, his material leans toward standard AOR blues-rock which rarely lets him cut loose, but when he does, his instrumental prowess can be shocking.

Healey lost his sight at the age of one, after developing eye cancer. He began playing guitar when he was three years old and began performing with his band Blues Direction at the age of 17. Healey formed the Jeff Healey Trio in 1985, adding bassist Joe Rockman and drummer Tom Stephen. The trio released one single on their own Forte record label, which led to a contract with Arista Records. The Jeff Healey Trio released their debut album, *See the Light*, in 1988 and the guitarist immediately developed a devoted following in blues-rock circles. Featuring the hit single "Angel Eyes," the record went platinum in the U.S. While the Jeff Healey Trio's subsequent records have been popular, none have been as successful as the debut. *—Stephen Thomas Erlewine*

See the Light / 1988 / Arista ♦♦♦♦
Jeff Healey's debut album *See the Light* may be similar to Stevie Ray Vaughan's high-octane blues-rock, but in blues and blues-rock, it's often the little things that count, such as guitar styles, and there's no denying that Healey has a distinctive style. Healey plays his Stratocaster flat on his lap, allowing him to perform unusually long stretches that give his otherwise fairly predictable music real heart and unpredictability. Throughout the album, his guitar work keeps things interesting, even on slow ballads like "Angel Eyes" (one of two John Hiatt songs, by the way, along with the ripping "Confidence Man"). That's what keeps *See the Light* interesting, and it's what makes it an intriguing, promising debut. Unfortunately, Healey has never quite fulfilled that promise, but it's still exciting to hear the first flowerings of his talent. *—Thom Owens*

Hell to Pay / 1990 / Arista ♦♦♦
A solid follow-up to Healey's impressive debut, *Hell to Pay* features some of the guitarist's hottest playing to date. *—Stephen Thomas Erlewine*

Feel This / Aug. 1992 / Arista ♦♦♦♦
Third time up for sightless guitar wunderkind Jeff Healey and gang; *Feel This* offers the power trio's meatiest and most satisfying outing. JHB's brand of roadhouse rock can be somewhat bland on disc; here the group captures much more of its trademark live intensity than in the past. The unobtrusive addition of keyboards adds a more expansive dimension to several tracks. Boogie fans will want to check out the ZZ Top-like "Cruel Little Number"; blues-rockers will come away satisfied with the likes of "House That Love Built." Hip-hop connoisseurs, on the other hand, will likely want to avoid JHB's rap spoof on "If You Can't Feel Anything Else." *—Roch Parisien*

Cover to Cover / Jun. 13, 1995 / Arista ♦♦
Jeff Healey's collection of cover songs is fitfully entertaining, but his choice of material is predictable and when he does take a chance, such as on Stealer's Wheel's "Stuck in the Middle With You," he spends too much time trying to make it fit into his trademark stomping blues-rock style. *—Stephen Thomas Erlewine*

● **The Master Hits: Jeff Healey Band** / Jul. 27, 1999 / Arista ♦♦♦♦
Arista celebrated its 30th anniversary by releasing *The Heritage Series*, spotlighting the most popular artists on the label. The Jeff Healey installment in *The Heritage Series* is pretty much a straight hits collection, featuring highlights from his stint at the label. While he was at Arista, he achieved the peak of his popularity with such radio hits as "Confidence Man," "Angel Eyes," "See the Light," "I Think I Love You Too Much," and "While My Guitar Gently Weeps." All those songs are here, along with some highlights from his albums, providing a nice retrospective of his time with Arista. *—Stephen Thomas Erlewine*

Johnny Heartsman

b. Feb. 9, 1937, San Fernando, CA, **d.** Dec. 27, 1996, Sacramento, CA
Vocals, Keyboards, Arranger, Guitar, Flute, Bass / Modern Electric Blues, Soul-Blues, Funk
Shaven-headed Johnny Heartsman did so many musical things so well that he's impossible to pigeonhole. His low-moaning lead guitar work greatly distinguished myriad Bay Area blues recordings during the '50s and '60s, and still he played his axe with delicious dexterity and dynamics into the '90s. But Heartsman was just as likely to cut loose on organ or blow a titillating solo on flute (perhaps the unlikeliest blues instrument imaginable). He possessed a mellow, richly burnished voice to boot.

Through one of his principal influences, guitarist Lafayette "Thing" Thomas, a teenaged Heartsman hooked up with Bay Area producer Bob Geddins. Heartsman played bass on Jimmy Wilson's 1953 rendition of "Tin Pan Alley," handling guitar or piano at other Geddins-supervised dates. He cut his own two-part instrumental, the "Honky Tonk"-inspired "Johnny's House Party," for Ray Dobard's Music City imprint and watched it become a national R&B hit in 1957.

The early '60s brought a lot more session work—Heartsman played on Tiny Powell's "My Time After Awhile" (soon covered by Buddy Guy) and Al King's remake of Lowell Fulson's "Reconsider Baby." By then, Heartsman's imaginative twiddling of the volume knob with his finger to produce an eerie moan had become his guitaristic trademark.

Stints in show bands, jazzy cocktail lounge gigs, and a stand as soul singer Joe Simon's trusty organist came prior to the inauguration of Heartsman's edifying back-to-the-blues campaign. In 1991, Dick Shurman produced Heartsman's most satisfying set to date for Alligator, *The Touch*. He remained a versatile performer until his death in December of 1996. *—Bill Dahl*

Sacramento / 1987 / Crosscut ♦♦♦

Music of My Heart / 1989 / Cat 'n Hat ♦♦♦
Solid LP that catches up with all of Heartsman's varied musical interests: blues, jazz, R&B, and all points in between. "Goose Grease" is a humorous Heartsman vocal outing, while powerful singer Frankie Lee guests on a remake of "My Time After Awhile" and harpist Curtis Salgado takes over behind the mike on "My First Mind." *—Bill Dahl*

● **The Touch** / 1991 / Alligator ♦♦♦♦♦
Few electric bluesman have been more versatile than Johnny Heartsman, and that versatility is impossible miss on *The Touch*. Recorded when Heartsman was 54, this unpredictable CD finds the singer incorporating soul and funk as well as rock and jazz and playing guitar, bass guitar, keyboards and flute. Heartsman (who shouldn't be confused with the late jazz singer Johnny Hartman) gets into a soul-minded groove on "Got To Find My Baby" and "You're So Fine," while "Attitude," "Walkin' Blues" and "Paint My Mailbox Blue" favor a hard-swinging blues/jazz approach à la Jimmy Witherspoon. Those jazz-influenced selections make it sound like Heartsman is backed by a soul-jazz organ combo, but in fact, there is no organist on this CD—rather, Heartsman uses his keyboards to emulate a Jimmy Smith/Jack McDuff type of Hammond B-3 sound. Meanwhile, instrumentals like the moody "Tongue" and the funk-drenched "Oops" illustrate his mastery of the flute—an unlikely instrument for a bluesman, to be sure. But then, certain jazz improvisers have demonstrated how funky the flute can sound—most notably, Herbie Mann, Rahsaan Roland Kirk and Hubert Laws—and similarly, the flute sounds like a very natural, logical blues instrument in Heartsman's risk-taking hands. Superb from start to finish, *The Touch* makes one wish that the late Californian had done a lot more recording as a leader. *—Alex Henderson*

Made in Germany / Jul. 31, 1995 / Inakustik ♦♦♦♦♦
It would be wrong to say that Johnny Heartsman died young, although he died at a *relatively* young age—Heartsman was 59 when the blues world lost him on December 27, 1996. You can certainly call his death premature, and you can say that he was at the height of his creative powers during the last years of his life. Recorded live at Vitischanze—a club in Osnabrück, Germany—in 1993, this album is a thoroughly rewarding document of the bluesman's late period. Heartsman's voice is in fine shape throughout his diverse set, and he is as confident on the guitar as he is on organ and flute. Although *Made in Germany* is a blues CD first and foremost, it's a blues CD that underscores his appreciation of jazz and soul. Heartsman's inspired performances of Junior Parker's "I Don't Want No Woman" and Albert Collins' "Cold Cold Feeling" are pure electric urban blues, but on the standard "Flip, Flop & Fly," the Californian reminds listeners how nicely he could handle jazz-influenced jump blues. Meanwhile, elements of soul, jazz, and blues come together on an instrumental version of Bill Withers' "Ain't No Sunshine," which gives Heartsman a chance to stretch out on flute. Very few bluesmen have been known for their flute playing, but in Heartsman's funky hands, the flute sounded perfectly logical as a blues instrument. *Made in Germany* makes one wish that he had recorded a lot more live albums during his career. *—Alex Henderson*

Still Shinin' / Jan. 1, 2000 / Have Mercy ♦♦♦

Lucille Hegamin

b. Nov. 29, 1894, Macon, GA, **d.** Mar. 1, 1970, New York, NY
Vocals / Classic Female Blues
A classic blues singer from the '20s, Lucille Hegamin survived long enough to be recorded again in the '60s. She sang in a church choir and locally before touring at age 15 with the Leonard Harper Revue. She was married to pianist Bill Hegamin from 1914-1923. After performing in Seattle for a long period, Hegamin became one of the first blues singers to record, cutting "Jazz Me Blues" and "Everybody's Blues" in Nov. 1920, shortly after moving to New York. She toured with her Blue Flame Syncopators and later on led the Dixie Daisies. In addition to performing at clubs, Hegamin appeared in several Broadway shows in the '20s. She worked with Doc Hyder's Southernaires later in the decade and performed at Atlantic City in 1933-1934 but eventually left music, becoming a nurse in 1938. In the '60s she emerged, appearing at a few charity benefits before retiring from music again. In all, Lucille Hegamin recorded 68 selections during 1920-1926 and two songs in 1932, appeared on part of a 1961 Bluesville LP (resulting in four titles) and recorded three additional cuts on a 1962 Spivey album. *—Scott Yanow*

● **Complete Recorded Works, Vol. 1 (1920–1922)** / Feb. 15, 1996 / Document ♦♦♦♦
One of the first of the classic female blues singers to record, Lucille Hegamin's material was mostly drawn from the world of vaudeville rather than actually being blues. A talented singer who was reasonably versatile, Hegamin's entire output in the '20s has been reissued on three Document CDs. The initial volume covers her first 17 months on records. Highlights include "The Jazz Me Blues" (from November, 1920), "Arkansas Blues," "Wang Wang Blues," "Wabash Blues" and two versions of a future standard that Hegamin first introduced, "He May Be Your Man but He Comes to See Me Sometimes." A special bonus is a pair of instrumentals ("Strut Miss Lizzie" and "Sweet Mama, Papa's Getting Mad") from May, 1921. In most cases, Hegamin is backed by her Blue Flame Syncopators, a combo of mostly obscure players that includes her husband Bill Hegamin on piano, Ralph Escudero on tuba and drummer Kaiser Marshall, along with four horns. Historic music that is still quite listenable; the recording quality is mostly quite good for the very early period. *—Scott Yanow*

Complete Recorded Works, Vol. 2 (1922–1923) / Mar. 5, 1996 / Document ♦♦♦♦
Lucille Hegamin was one of the finest singers on records during the first half of the '20s. Her strong voice and easy-to-take delivery resulted in her having a large recorded output in the period. The second of three Document CDs that has all of her recordings prior to 1960 features Hegamin backed by several unidentified bands (mostly the Dixie Daisies but also her Blue Flame Syncopators, her Bang-Up Six from Georgia and Sam Wooding's Society Entertainers) or just the piano of J. Russell Robinson or Cyril J. Fullerton. The recording quality is not bad for the time and the highlights among the 25 songs include "I've Got What It Takes but It Breaks My Heart to Give It Away," "Beale St. Mama," "Aggravatin' Papa," her third version of "He May Be Your Man but He Comes to See Me Sometimes," "Down Hearted Blues," "Saint Louis Gal," and "Dina." This series should be of strong interest to vintage classic blues collectors even though Hegamin was never technically a blues singer. *—Scott Yanow*

Complete Recorded Works, Vol. 3 (1923–1932) / Apr. 9, 1996 / Document ♦♦♦♦
The third, and final, Lucille Hegamin Document CD features her during 1923-1926 along

with two titles from 1932; Hegamin would not appear on records again until 1960. It is surprising that she did not pop up on records during the latter half of the '20s for she was quite active performing in shows and Hegamin's easy way with pop tunes of the period could have made her a strong seller. Her 1923-1926 records usually feature her backed by an unidentified combo called the Dixie Daisies, other than two duets with pianist J. Russell Robinson and a couple of 1926 selections ("Nobody But My Baby Is Getting' My Love" and "Senorita Mine") with Clarence Williams' group. Although the personnel is long lost, Hegamin's backup musicians are generally quite good, both in reading their parts and in jamming short solos. The singer is in heard in fine form on such numbers as "Rampart St. Blues," "If You Don't Give Me What I Want I'm Gonna Get It Somewhere Else," "Hard Hearted Hannah," "Alabama Bound," "Dinah," and "Poor Papa." The two selections from 1932 ("Shake Your Cans" and "Totem Pole") are lesser numbers (taken as duets with pianist Irving Williams) but show that Lucille Hegamin was still in prime form at the time. Recommended. —*Scott Yanow*

Alternate Takes & Remaining Titles / May 2, 1998 / Document ✦✦✦

Jessie Mae Hemphill

b. 1934, Senatobia, MS
Vocals, Guitar / Delta Blues
A Mississippi singer/guitarist, Jessie Mae Hemphill weaves strong Delta traditions into her idiosyncratic style. Hemphill comes from a musical background—reportedly, her grandfather was recorded in the fields by Alan Lomax in the '40s. Jessie Mae learned how to play guitar as a child by watching her relatives perform. Throughout the '60s and '70s, she sang with various Mississippi bar bands. In the early '80s, she decided to pursue a solo career.
Hemphill began playing solo dates, supporting herself only with an acoustic guitar and percussion. In 1981, she released her debut album, *She-Wolf*, on the European record label, Vogue. In 1987, her first American record, *Feelin' Good*, was released. In 1987 and 1988, she won the W.C. Handy Award for best traditional female blues artist. Hemphill abandoned a recording career after the late '80s, but she continued to perform into the '90s. Sadly, she suffered a stroke in 1994 that left her partially paralyzed and unable to play music; as of 2000, she was confined to a wheelchair and living in Senatobia, MS.
—*Cub Koda & Stephen Thomas Erlewine*

She-Wolf / 1981 / High Water ✦✦✦
This compact disc reissue gathers up all the original tracks from Jessie Mae's 1980 debut album for the French Vogue label along with four remixed bonus tracks, all seeing their first domestic release. Recorded by folklorist Dr. David Evans (who also contributes second guitar on 13 of the 15 tracks here) in various locales around Memphis and Mississippi, the music stays down-home and primal throughout. There's a strong sense of rhythm that permeates this record, whether it comes from the fife and drum-derived percussion work of Calvin Jackson and Joe Hicks or simply Jessie Mae's own foot-operated tambourine driving the beat home. Highlights include "Jessie's Boogie" and "Standing In My Doorway Crying" (both sides of her first 45 single, underwritten by the National Endowment for the Arts), "Honey Bee," "Boogie Side of the Road," "Crawdad Hole," "Lovin' In the Moonlight," "Married Man Blues" and the title track. The blues, real and raw. —*Cub Koda*

● **Feelin' Good** / 1987 / High Water ✦✦✦✦✦
Feelin' Good was the first album Jessie Mae Hemphill released in the United States and it differs from its predecessor *She-Wolf* in that it captures her at her rawest. Half of the record features her supported only by a rhythm guitar and drums, while the other half has Hemphill wailing away at her guitar and percussion simultaneously. The result is hypnotic, mesmerizing record that successfully updates Delta blues, making the covers sound as fresh as the originals. —*Thom Owens*

Duke Henderson

d. 1972, Los Angeles, CA
Vocals / West Coast Blues
For a guy with as voluminous a discography as Los Angeles shouter Duke Henderson, one would think someone might possess concrete biographical information about the guy. No such luck.
Henderson got his start as a recording artist with Apollo Records, a New York firm that sent a rep to Los Angeles in 1945 with the intention of recording blues. Tenor saxist Jack McVea recommended Henderson, who ended up cutting three Apollo dates that year with backing from some of L.A.'s finest sessioneers: saxists Wild Bill Moore, Lucky Thompson, and McVea, guitarist Gene Phillips, bassists Shifty Henry and Charlie Mingus, and drummers Lee Young and Rabon Tarrant.
Swinging as they were, Henderson's Apollo platters failed to sell in sufficient quantities to extend his contract. Thus began a label-hopping odyssey from Globe to Down Beat/Swing Time to Specialty to Modern to Imperial and finally to Flair, where he exhibited a knowledge of then-current sexual trends with his "Hey Mr. Kinsey" (issued as by Big Duke in 1953). Later, Henderson renounced his wicked blues-shouting past, sending the L.A. sanctified set as Brother Henderson, a minister and gospel DJ broadcasting for a time over XERB (the same powerful south-of-the-border frequency that Wolfman Jack dominated). —*Bill Dahl*

● **Get Your Kicks** / 1994 / Delmark ✦✦✦✦✦
Blues shouter Henderson was quite a popular jump blues shouter on the postwar L.A. scene. His 1945 output for Apollo, collected here, rates with his best; backed by top-drawer sidemen including saxists Lucky Thompson, Wild Bill Moore, and Jack McVea and guitarist Gene Phillips, Henderson's pipes convey the proper party spirit on these 20 swinging sides. —*Bill Dahl*

Mike Henderson

b. Jul. 7, 1951, Yazoo City, MS
Slide Guitar, Vocals, Songwriter, Guitar / Contemporary Country, Blues-Rock
Guitarist, singer and songwriter Mike Henderson carved a niche for himself as a session guitarist over the years in the Nashville studio scene before he began recording under his own name with his own blues band, the Bluebloods. He began playing mandolin and moved from Missouri to Nashville. Trained as a mandolin player and flat-top guitarist, he soon found work in the Nashville studio scene as a slide guitarist.
Henderson's albums on the Dead Reckoning label include *Edge of Night* (1994), *First Blood* (1996) and *Oakland Blues* (1998). Henderson uses a stellar lineup of supporting musicians on *First Blood*—Reese Wynans, Glenn Worf, and John Gardner—making it one of the best (and unfortunately most overlooked) releases of 1996. Collectively, these musicians have recorded and performed with John Hiatt, Emmylou Harris, Kevin Welch, Stevie Ray Vaughan, Mark Knopfler, Lonnie Mack, Aaron Neville, Larry Carlton, Johnny Cash, Al Kooper, Tracy Nelson, Rory Block, Sonny Burgess, and Delbert McClinton.
The band got some radio attention on its second release for their song, "Pay Bo Diddley," a song that addressed the inequities in U.S. record royalty laws. Not surprisingly, *First Blood* was recorded in the studio in Nashville over two days, with almost all the songs being recorded on the first take with no overdubs. The band lends their own spin to classic blues material like Sonny Boy Williamson's "So Sad to Be Lonesome," J.B. Hutto's "Hip Shakin'" and Hound Dog Taylor's "Give Me Back My Wig." —*Richard Skelly*

Country Music Made Me Do It / Mar. 15, 1994 / RCA ✦✦✦✦
This is pure roadhouse honky tonk, stoked with bent notes, twisted humor and a couple of tough, bittersweet ballads. —*Michael McCall*

Edge of Night / 1996 / Dead Reckoning ✦✦✦
Long one of Nashville's best-kept secrets, Mike Henderson's solo debut is all over the roots music map, flirting with Delta blues to honky-tonk to gospel; opening with "I Wouldn't Lay My Guitar Down," which sports a riff ripped from the pages of the Chuck Berry songbook, *Edge of Night* is a showcase for Henderson's blistering guitar work and soulful voice, and what the record lacks in innovation it makes up for in immediacy. —*Jason Ankeny*

First Blood / 1996 / Dead Reckoning ✦✦✦✦
First Blood harks back to the glory days of the '60s blues-rock boom—Mike Henderson and the Bluebloods' gritty sound is far from original, but years on the Nashville bar band circuit have honed their skills to a razor-sharp point, and the record is refreshingly raw and direct, distinguished by rock-solid musicianship. —*Jason Ankeny*

● **Thicker Than Water** / Jan. 12, 1999 / Dead Reckoning ✦✦✦✦✦
Nashville homeboy Mike Henderson belies his roadhouse roots with this crystalline studio blues record, singing, weirdly, as much like Ben Folds as he does like Stevie Ray Vaughan. This is a jubilant, no-nonsense toe-tapping album, staffed by Henderson's ever-present entourage of excellent musicians, including keyboardist John Jarvis and Dead Reckoning label co-captain Glenn Worf on bass. A longtime mandolin and flatpick guitar player, Henderson gets Jarvis into the Jerry Lee Lewis spirit with a demon-calling "Keep What You Got" and the house-rockin' "Scared of that Child." As he does on his previous and underrated album *First Blood*, Mike honors his idols Sonny Boy Williamson and Howlin' Wolf on the conga-thick "Mister Downchild" and classic downhome "My Country Sugar Mamma." In addition to fine guitar covers, Mike contributes a particularly clear vocal style with plenty of simultaneous character from both the blues and true-blue country music, which he began to cultivate in his early road days with the Snakes. A fine, versatile record for a good mood. —*Becky Byrkit*

Rosa Henderson

b. 1898, Henderson, KY, d. 1981, New York, NY
Vocals / Classic Female Blues, Classic Jazz
One of the early classic blues singers, Rosa Henderson (no relation to Fletcher or Horace Henderson) first began singing professionally in 1913 with her uncle's carnival troupe. She was based in Texas until 1918 when she married Slim Henderson and began touring with the Mason Henderson Show. She primarily spent the '20s performing in musical comedies in New York. Henderson, who began recording in 1923, sometimes used such pseudonyms as Flora Dale, Mamie Harris, Rosa Green, Sarah Johnson, Sally Ritz, Bessie Williams, Josephine Thomas and Gladys White on her records! In the late '20s she started gradually dropping out of the music scene although she continued performing now and then into the mid-'30s. Henderson worked outside of music (including in a New York department store), but re-emerging as a singer for charity benefits as late as the '60s. Rosa Henderson recorded 92 selections in all, including 88 during 1923-1927 and two apiece in 1928 and 1931; among her sidemen were Fletcher Henderson, Coleman Hawkins, Thomas Morris, Joe Smith, Cliff Jackson, Rex Stewart, Louis Metcalf, Fats Waller, and (on six numbers) James P. Johnson. —*Scott Yanow*

Complete Recorded Works, Vol. 1 (1923) / Nov. 30, 1995 / Document ✦✦✦✦
All of classic blues singer Rosa Henderson's recordings are available on four CDs from the Austrian Document label. The first volume mostly has Henderson accompanied by pianist Fletcher Henderson (no relation) with one number apiece with sidemen from Henderson's early band and the Virginians. The young tenor Coleman Hawkins pops up on "It Won't Be Long Now," while cornetist Thomas Morris and pianist Louis Hooper help out on two numbers. None of the 22 songs on this CD became hits but quite a few are memorable, including "I Ain't No Man's Slave," "So Long to You and the Blues," "He May Be Your Dog But He's Wearing My Collar," and "Got the World in a Jug, the Stopper's in My Hand." —*Scott Yanow*

Complete Recorded Works, Vol. 2 (1924) / Nov. 30, 1995 / Document ✦✦✦✦
The second of four Document CDs that reissue all of the recordings of the classic blues singer Rosa Henderson mostly has the vocalist accompanied by the unrelated pianist

Fletcher Henderson and his sidemen (including cornetist Joe Smith, altoist Don Redman, and tenor saxophonist Coleman Hawkins) or by the Choc Choo Jazzers, a small group with pianist Cliff Jackson. Best among the 23 selections are "I'm a Good Gal But I'm a Thousan' Miles From Home," "West Indies Blues," "My Papa Doesn't Two-Time No Time," "Strut Yo' Puddy," and "Somebody's Doing What You Wouldn't Do." Although she would eventually slip into obscurity, Rosa Henderson was one of the better blues singers of the period. *—Scott Yanow*

● **Complete Recorded Works, Vol. 3 (1924–1926)** / Nov. 30, 1995 / Document ✦✦✦✦✦
The strongest of the four Document CDs that reissue the entire output of '20s classic blues singer Rosa Henderson, this set matches the spirited vocalist with the Choo Choo Jazzers, the Kansas City Five, or a trio known as the Three Jolly Miners or the Three Hot Eskimos, including such sidemen as cornetists/trumpeters Rex Stewart, Louis Metcalf, and Bubber Miley plus pianist Cliff Jackson. Among the more memorable selections are "Hard-Hearted Hannah," "Don't Advertise Your Man," "Nobody Knows the Way I Feel 'Dis Mornin'," "Get It Fixed," and "What's the Matter Now." The latter number is one of two in which Henderson is backed by pianist Fats Waller. This is the Rosa Henderson CD to get. *—Scott Yanow*

Complete Recorded Works, Vol. 4 (1926–1931) / Nov. 30, 1995 / Document ✦✦✦✦
The fourth and final CD in Document's Rosa Henderson series finishes off her recording career with nine numbers from 1926, a dozen from 1927, and two from 1931. Most notable are six numbers in which Rosa Henderson is accompanied by the great stride pianist James P. Johnson (including "Black Snake Moan" and "Can't Be Bothered With No Sheik"). Other selections have her assisted by the Three Hot Eskimos, the Four Black Diamonds, pianist Cliff Jackson, and cornetist Louis Metcalf. A perfectly done reissue series paying tribute to a talented if forgotten classic blues singer of the '20s. *—Scott Yanow*

Jimi Hendrix

b. Nov. 27, 1942, Seattle, WA, **d.** Sep. 18, 1970, London, England

Vocals, Leader, Guitar (Electric), Songwriter, Guitar / Album Rock, Acid Rock, Psychedelic, Hard Rock, Blues-Rock, Psychedelic Soul

In his brief four-year reign as a superstar, Jimi Hendrix expanded the vocabulary of the electric rock guitar more than anyone before or since. Hendrix was a master at coaxing all manner of unforeseen sonics from his instrument, often with innovative amplification experiments that produced astral-quality feedback and roaring distortion. His frequent hurricane blasts of noise and dazzling showmanship—he could and would play behind his back and with his teeth and set his guitar on fire—has sometimes obscured his considerable gifts as a songwriter, singer, and master of a gamut of blues, R&B, and rock styles.

When Hendrix became an international superstar in 1967, it seemed as if he'd dropped out of a Martian spaceship, but in fact he'd served his apprenticeship the long, mundane way in numerous R&B acts on the chitlin circuit. During the early and mid-'60s, he worked with such R&B/soul greats as Little Richard, the Isley Brothers, and King Curtis as a backup guitarist. Occasionally he recorded as a session man (the Isley Brothers' 1964 single "Testify" is the only one of these early tracks that offers even a glimpse of his future genius). But the stars didn't appreciate his show-stealing showmanship, and Hendrix was straight-jacketed by sideman roles that didn't allow him to develop as a soloist. The logical step was for Hendrix to go out on his own, which he did in New York in the mid-'60s, playing with various musicians in local clubs, and joining white blues-rock singer John Hammond Jr.'s band for a while.

It was in a New York club that Hendrix was spotted by Animals bassist Chas Chandler. The first lineup of the Animals was about to split, and Chandler, looking to move into management, convinced Hendrix to move to London and record as a solo act in England. There a group was built around Jimi, also featuring Mitch Mitchell on drums and Noel Redding on bass, that was dubbed the Jimi Hendrix Experience. The trio became stars with astonishing speed in the U.K., where "Hey Joe," "Purple Haze," and "The Wind Cries Mary" all made the Top Ten in the first half of 1967. These tracks were also featured on their debut album, *Are You Experienced*, a psychedelic meisterwerk that became a huge hit in the U.S. after Hendrix created a sensation at the Monterey Pop Festival in June of 1967.

Are You Experienced was an astonishing debut, particularly from a young R&B veteran who had rarely sung, and apparently never written his own material, before the Experience formed. What caught most people's attention at first was his virtuosic guitar playing, which employed an arsenal of devices, including wah-wah pedals, buzzing feedback solos, crunching distorted riffs, and lightning, liquid runs up and down the scales. But Hendrix was also a first-rate songwriter, melding cosmic imagery with some surprisingly pop-savvy hooks and tender sentiments. He was also an excellent blues interpreter and passionate, engaging singer (although his gruff, throaty vocal pipes were not nearly as great assets as his instrumental skills). *Are You Experienced* was psychedelia at its most eclectic, synthesizing mod pop, soul, R&B, Dylan, and the electric guitar innovations of British pioneers like Jeff Beck, Pete Townshend, and Eric Clapton.

Amazingly, Hendrix would only record three fully conceived studio albums in his lifetime. *Axis: Bold as Love* and the double-LP *Electric Ladyland* were more diffuse and experimental than *Are You Experienced*. On *Electric Ladyland* in particular, Hendrix pioneered the use of the studio itself as a recording instrument, manipulating electronics and devising overdub techniques (with the help of engineer Eddie Kramer in particular) to plot uncharted sonic territory. Not that these albums were perfect, as impressive as they were; the instrumental breaks could meander, and Hendrix's songwriting was occasionally half-baked, never matching the consistency of *Are You Experienced* (although he exercised greater creative control over the later albums).

The final two years of Hendrix's life were turbulent ones musically, financially, and personally. He was embroiled in enough complicated management and record company disputes (some dating from ill-advised contracts he'd signed before the Experience formed) to keep the lawyers busy for years. He disbanded the Experience in 1969, forming the Band of Gypsys with drummer Buddy Miles and bassist Billy Cox to pursue funkier directions. He closed Woodstock with a sprawling, shaky set, redeemed by his famous machine-gun interpretation of "The Star Spangled Banner." The rhythm section of Mitchell and Redding were underrated keys to Jimi's best work, and the Band of Gypsies ultimately couldn't measure up to the same standard, although Hendrix did record an erratic live album with them. In early 1970, the Experience re-formed again—and disbanded again shortly afterward. At the same time, Hendrix felt torn in many directions by various fellow musicians, record-company expectations, and management pressures, all of whom had their own ideas of what Hendrix should be doing. Coming up on two years after *Electric Ladyland*, a new studio album had yet to appear, although Hendrix was recording constantly during the period.

While outside parties did contribute to bogging down Hendrix's studio work, it also seems likely that Jimi himself was partly responsible for the stalemate, unable to form a permanent lineup of musicians, unable to decide what musical direction to pursue, unable to bring himself to complete another album despite jamming endlessly. A few months into 1970, Mitchell—Hendrix's most valuable musical collaborator—came back into the fold, replacing Miles in the drum chair, although Cox stayed in place. It was this trio that toured the world during Hendrix's final months.

It's extremely difficult to separate the facts of Hendrix's life from rumors and speculation. Everyone who knew him well, or claimed to know him well, has different versions of his state of mind in 1970. Critics have variously mused that he was going to go into jazz, that he was going to get deeper into the blues, that he was going to continue doing what he was doing, or that he was too confused to know what he was doing at all. The same confusion holds true for his death: contradictory versions of his final days have been given by his closest acquaintances of the time. He'd been working intermittently on a new album, tentatively titled *First Ray of the New Rising Sun*, when he died in London on September 18, 1970, from drug-related complications.

Hendrix recorded a massive amount of unreleased studio material during his lifetime. Much of this (as well as entire live concerts) was issued posthumously; several of the live concerts were excellent, but the studio tapes have been the focus of enormous controversy for over 20 years. These initially came out in haphazard drabs and drubs (the first, *The Cry of Love*, was easily the most outstanding of the lot). In the mid-'70s, producer Alan Douglas took control of these projects, posthumously overdubbing many of Hendrix's tapes with additional parts by studio musicians. In the eyes of many Hendrix fans, this was sacrilege, destroying the integrity of the work of a musician known to exercise meticulous care over the final production of his studio recordings. Even as late as 1995, Douglas was having ex-Knack drummer Bruce Gary record new parts for the typically misbegotten compilation *Voodoo Soup*. After a lengthy legal dispute, the rights to Hendrix's estate, including all of his recordings, returned to Al Hendrix, the guitarist's father, in July of 1995.

With the help of Jimi's stepsister Janie, Al set up Experience Hendrix to begin to get Jimi's legacy in order. They began by hiring John McDermott and Jimi's original engineer, Eddie Kramer to oversee the remastering process. They were able to find all the original master tapes, which had never been used for previous CD releases, and in April of 1997, Hendrix's first three albums were reissued with drastically improved sound. Accompanying those reissues was a posthumous compilation album (based on Jimi's handwritten track listings) called *First Rays of the New Rising Sun*, made up of tracks from the *Cry of Love*, *Rainbow Bridge*, and *War Heroes*.

Later in 1997, another compilation called *South Saturn Delta* showed up, collecting more tracks from posthumous LPs like *Crash Landing*, *War Heroes*, and *Rainbow Bridge* (without the terrible '70s overdubs), along with a handful of never-before-heard material that Chas Chandler had withheld from Alan Douglas for all those years.

More archival material followed; *Radio One* was basically expanded to the two-disc *BBC Sessions* (released in 1998), and 1999 saw the release of the full show from Woodstock as well as additional concert recordings from the Band of Gypsys shows entitled *Live at the Fillmore East*. 2000 saw the release of the *Jimi Hendrix Experience* four-disc box set, which compiled remaining tracks from *In the West*, *Crash Landing*, and *Rainbow Bridge* along with more rarities and alternates from the Chandler cache.

The family also launched Dagger Records, essentially an authorized bootleg label to supply harcore Hendrix fans with material that would be of limited commercial appeal. Dagger Records has released several live concerts (of shows in Oakland, Ottawa and Clark University in Massachusetts) and a collection of studio jams and demos called *Morning Symphony Ideas*. *—Richie Unterberger & Sean Westergaard*

★ **Are You Experienced** / 1967 / MCA ✦✦✦✦✦
One of the most stunning debuts in rock history, and one of the definitive albums of the psychedelic era. On *Are You Experienced* Hendrix synthesized various elements of the cutting edge of 1967 rock into music that sounded both futuristic and rooted in the best traditions of rock, blues, pop, and soul. It was his mind-boggling guitar work, of course, that got most of the ink, building upon the experiments of British innovators like Jeff Beck and Pete Townshend to chart new sonic territories in feedback, distortion, and sheer volume. It wouldn't have meant much, however, without his excellent material, whether psychedelic frenzy ("Foxy Lady," "Manic Depression," "Purple Haze"), instrumental freak-out jams ("Third Stone from the Sun"), blues ("Red House," "Hey Joe"), or tender, poetic compositions ("The Wind Cries Mary") that demonstrated the breadth of his songwriting talents. Not to be underestimated were the contributions of drummer Mitch Mitchell and bassist Noel Redding, who gave the music a rhythmic pulse that fused parts of rock and improvised jazz. Many of these songs are among Hendrix's very finest; it may be true that he would continue to develop at a rapid pace throughout the rest of his brief career, but he would never surpass his first album in terms of consistently high quality. The British and American versions of the album differed substantially when they were initially released in 1967; MCA's 17-song CD reissue from 1993 does everyone a favor by gathering all of the material from the two records in one place, adding a few B-sides from early singles as well. *—Richie Unterberger*

☆ **Axis: Bold as Love** / 1967 / MCA ✦✦✦✦✦
When the Experience recorded their second album, they were in the process of solidfying their international stardom. That meant access to more studio time and more sophisi-

cated technology, but not, alas, a great deal of time to write the material. That may be why *Axis* isn't quite as much of a *tour de force* as *Are You Exerienced*, but it's nevertheless another major effort, showing Hendrix continuing to grow, particularly in his increasing mastery of the studio and more sophisticated lyrics. Soul and R&B influences are more prominent here than on his debut, though psychedelic experimentalism ran rampant (to great effect) on "If 6 Was 9." "Spanish Castle Magic," "Up from the Skies," "You Got Me Floatin'," and "Castles Made of Sand" all had funky grooves that gave the spiraling guitars and crunchy rhythm section a much-needed buoyancy. The best song, though, might have been the mellowest: "Little Wing" was Hendrix at his most delicate, and perhaps his most personal. *—Richie Unterberger*

☆ **Electric Ladyland** / Oct. 1968 / MCA ♦♦♦♦♦
With *Electric Ladyland*, Hendrix took psychedelic experimentation as far as he could within the original Experience trio format. That meant pushing the barriers of late-'60s studio technology as far as they could bend, particularly with regard to multi-tracking and effects that could only be achieved through certain treatments and manipulation of the tape itself. It also meant greater freedom and looseness in the playing and the songwriting, which could be both a plus and a drawback, as the compositions became both less constricted and less concise. Not all of the material here is top-of-the-line, but certainly much of this is Hendrix at his best: the dreamy wah-wah guitars of "Rainy Day, Dream Away" were only matched by the dreaminess of the lyrics, and "Have You Ever Been (To Electric Ladyland)" and "Gypsy Eyes" were also standouts. "1983 ... (A Merman I Should Turn to Be)" and "Voodoo Chile" were lengthy cuts dominated by jam-like instrumental passages; "Crosstown Traffic" and a cover of Dylan's "All Along the Watchtower," by contrast, were two of his catchiest and most pop-friendly tunes. "Voodoo Chile," "Voodoo Child (Slight Return)," and a cover of Earl King's "Come On" are three of his most determined forays into the blues, albeit the blues as fed through a nearly avant-garde filter. Originally released as a double album, the CD reissue fits the entire recording onto one 75-minute disc. *—Richie Unterberger*

Smash Hits / Jul. 1969 / MCA ♦♦♦♦♦
One of the first hits compilations assembled of Hendrix's catalog, *Smash Hits* remains one of the best, since it keeps its focus narrow and never tries to extend its reach. Basically, this album contains the songs everybody knows from Hendrix, drawing heavily from *Are You Experienced*, plus adding the non-LP "Red House," "51st Anniversary," and "Highway Chile." Those non-LP selections may still make this worth seeking out, even if they've appeared on subsequent hits collections, but the main strength of *Smash Hits* is that it contains the best-known, big-name songs in one place. Maybe not enough to make the collection essential, but still enough to make it a representative, accurate, sampler. *—Stephen Thomas Erlewine*

Band of Gypsys / 1970 / Capitol ♦♦♦♦♦
Band of Gypsys was the only live recording authorized by Jimi Hendrix before his death. It was recorded and released in order to get Hendrix out from under a contractual obligation that had been hanging over his head for a couple years. Helping him out were longtime friends Billy Cox on bass and Buddy Miles on the drums because the Experience had broken up in June of 1969, following a show in Denver. These new surroundings pushed Hendrix to new creative heights. Along with this new rhythm section, Hendrix took these shows as an opportunity to showcase much of the new material he had been working on. The music was a seamless melding of rock, funk, and R&B, and tunes like "Message to Love" and "Power to Love" showed a new lyrical direction as well. His absolute mastery of his guitar and effects is even more amazing considering that this was the first time he used the Fuzz Face, wah-wah pedal, Univibe, *and* Octavia pedals on stage together. The guitar tones he gets on "Who Knows" and "Power to Love" are powerful and intense, but nowhere is his absolute control more evident than on "Machine Gun," where Hendrix conjures bombs, guns, and other sounds of war from his guitar, all within the context of a coherent musical statement. Two Buddy Miles compositions are also included, but the show belongs to Jimi all the way. *Band of Gypsys* is not only an important part of the Hendrix legacy, but one of the greatest live albums ever. *—Sean Westergaard*

The Cry of Love / 1971 / Reprise ♦♦♦♦
This was the first of the posthumous releases in the Hendrix catalog and probably the best from the Alan Douglas years, as it collected most of the studio tracks that were either completed or very near completion before Hendrix died. Some of these tunes, like "Angel" and "Ezy Rider," have become well-known pieces in the Hendrix canon, but they sit alongside lesser-known gems like "Night Bird Flying" and the Dylanesque "My Friend." *The Cry of Love* as an album has been rendered as a footnote, since the Hendrix estate has recompiled, to Hendrix' specifications, *First Rays of the New Rising Sun*. This (originally) double-album set contains not only the entire *Cry of Love* LP, but the best studio tracks from *Rainbow Bridge*, *War Heroes*, and *Crash Landing*, presented in drastically improved sound. *—Sean Westergaard*

Jimi Plays Monterey / 1986 / Reprise ♦♦♦♦♦
Hendrix's show at the 1967 Monterey Pop Festival was the performance that broke him in the United States. While half of this was previously available as one side of an LP that also featured a side of live Otis Redding from the same event, this has his whole performances. Jimi and the Experience were in fine, lean, fiery form on this nine-song set, which showcased the most well-known tunes from the *Are You Experienced* album and covers of "Killing Floor," "Like a Rolling Stone," "Rock Me Baby," and "Wild Thing." *—Richie Unterberger*

Live at Winterland / 1987 / Rykodisc ♦♦♦♦♦
Jimi Hendrix's sonic assaults and attacks hypnotized, frightened, and amazed audiences in the late '60s. His studio recordings helped him attain his reputation, but his live works validated it. That's the case on the 13 songs from a 1968 Winterland concert that made their way onto CD in 1987. Whether he was doing short, biting songs like "Fire" or stretching out for sprawling blues statements like "Red House" and "Killing Floor," Jimi Hendrix turned the guitar into a battering ram, forcing everyone to notice and making every solo and note a memorable one. *—Ron Wynn*

Radio One / 1989 / Rykodisc ♦♦♦♦♦
Here are 17 songs from 1967 BBC broadcasts, when the Experience had yet to burn out from the wheel of constant touring, management hassles, and internal strife. They're in good, enthusiastic form as they run through early gems like "Hey Joe," "Foxy Lady," "Fire," and "Stone Free," the lack of studio polish giving these versions a loose feel. The Experience studio albums are still considerably superior to this set, but it's certainly worth acquiring by any serious Hendrix fan, not least because it has several covers that didn't make it onto the three proper Experience LPs. Several of these ("Hoochie Koochie Man," "Killing Floor," "Catfish Blues") reveal his sometimes overlooked affinity for Chicago-style electric blues; there are also a couple of surprises ("Hound Dog" and "Day Tripper"). With good sound, it's a solid addition to the Hendrix library, demonsrating his versatility in various rock, soul, and blues styles. *—Richie Unterberger*

Stages / 1991 / Reprise ♦♦♦
What more could a Hendrix fanatic searching for the ultimate live Jimi experience ask for? The 1991 box set *Stages* contains a total of four CDs, each containing one full concert from the years 1967 (in Stockholm), 1968 (Paris), 1969 (San Diego), and 1970 (recorded in Atlanta just two months before his death). Many Hendrix fans already owned bootlegged copies of these concerts, but this was the first time that they were released officially, in crystal clear sound and with informative liner notes. The four discs are an obviously interesting musical journey, showing the rapid musical transformation of Hendrix from showman to serious virtuoso. And although there is a bit of overlap on the discs ("Purple Haze" rears its head on all four), the versions of the repeated songs are strikingly different. Disc one (Stockholm 1967) features the Jimi Hendrix Experience in their formative stage, and contains the only official release of the Experience's raw cover of the Beatles' "Sgt. Pepper's Lonely Hearts Club Band." This disc is the shortest of the four (barely over 30 minutes in length), containing no-nonsense (and almost 100 percent jam-less) versions of such standards as "Fire" and "Burning of the Midnight Lamp." The second disc (Paris 1968) shows the group starting to stretch out musically (near nine-minute cover versions of both Muddy Waters' "Catfish Blues" and Curtis Knight's "Drivin' South" are the proof), and includes an absolutely gorgeous version of the electric ballad "Little Wing." Disc three (San Diego 1969) catches the Experience on one of their final tours with original bassist Noel Redding. The group is dedicated to jamming, combining a red-hot version of their "Spanish Castle Magic" with an explosive cover of Cream's "Sunshine of Your Love." Also included is a long take of "Voodoo Child (Slight Return)," which ends the show on a highly energetic and inspired note. By the final disc (Atlanta 1970), Hendrix had assembled the Band of Gypsys, with Hendrix's army buddy Billy Cox replacing the ousted Noel Redding on bass (with Mitch Mitchell still behind the drums). Jimi had completely shunned his early concert gimmickry (lighting his guitar on fire, etc.), and by 1970 was making a conscious attempt at forcing his audience to listen to the music, without any distractions. This disc has three songs that were not released while Hendrix was alive ("Lover Man," "Straight Ahead," and "Room Full of Mirrors"), intended for his never really completed *First Rays of the New Rising Sun* album. You'll also be treated to a rare live version of "Stone Free," with its tempo sped up a notch. Admittedly, *Stages* may be too much to take for the new Jimi fan, but for diehards, it simply can't be beat. *—Greg Prato*

The Ultimate Experience / Apr. 27, 1993 / MCA ♦♦♦♦♦
As a single-disc compilation, *The Ultimate Experience* is hard to beat. Drawing from all of the original Jimi Hendrix Experience albums, the 20-track collection hits all of the major highpoints—"Purple Haze," "All Along the Watchtower," "Little Wing," "Red House," "The Wind Cries Mary," "Highway Chile," "Angel"—and gives an accurate impression of why Hendrix was so revolutionary and influential. All three of Hendrix's completed studio albums are mandatory listening, but *The Ultimate Experience* is a terrific introduction to the guitarist. *—Thom Owens*

Blues / Apr. 26, 1994 / MCA ♦♦♦♦
While Hendrix remains most famous for his hard rock and psychedelic innovations, more than a third of his recordings were blues-oriented. This CD contains 11 blues originals and covers, eight of which were previously unreleased. Recorded between 1966 and 1970, they feature the master guitarist stretching the boundaries of electric blues in both live and studio settings. Besides several Hendrix blues-based originals, it includes covers of Albert King and Muddy Waters classics, as well as a 1967 acoustic version of his composition "Hear My Train A-Comin'." *—Richie Unterberger*

Jimi Hendrix: Woodstock / Aug. 2, 1994 / MCA ♦♦♦
Like most products issued from the Jimi Hendrix archive in the '90s, several separate releases featuring identical recordings of this one performance have been issued. 1994's *Jimi Hendrix: Woodstock* on MCA is the first formal packaging of this most famous of rock shows. Other, more collectable discs followed, often with much more extensive track lists. The Woodstock show that these discs commemorate was supposed to be a headline performance for Hendrix and his band, but after many delays and a fan exodus, the guitarist ended up playing to only a fraction of listeners a full day after the event was scheduled to end. The first performance with new backing outfit Hendrix's Gypsy Sun & Rainbows, this expanded outfit is often difficult to hear over Hendrix and his guitar on this recording. Although very significant, this isn't one of Hendrix's best recorded performances. Relatively pedestrian versions of hits like "Purple Haze" and "Fire" are included. The redefinition of "The Star Spangled Banner" is still considered one of the most chilling rock performances ever, and funky jams like "Hear My Train a Comin'" are also very

impressive. Fans might want to consider later releases of this performance that include more material, but one way or another, all devoted scholars of the greatest musician to ever plug in a Stratocaster should own at least one packaging of this performance. —*Vincent Jeffries*

Jimi By Himself: The Home Recordings / 1995 / Berkshire Studio ♦♦♦

This CD is only available (quite legitimately) with the hardback comic/graphic biography *Voodoo Child: The Illustrated Legend of Jimi Hendrix.* Be warned that if you're primarily (or only) interested in this half-hour disc of previously unreleased material, it only comes at a high price ($35 or so). If you want to take the plunge, you'll find the music—recorded unaccompanied by Hendrix in New York around April of 1968—quite worthwhile. The guitar is electric, but this is basically *Hendrix Unplugged*, with much quieter, reflective, and personal versions of songs that would get the full-on electric treatment on *Electric Ladyland* and other albums. "1983," "Gypsy Eyes," "Voodoo Chile," and "Angel" are particularly fascinating to experience in this context, as we hear Jimi tentatively working out (and sometimes fumbling through) skeletal versions of these compositions, with some different lyrics appearing on occasion. What this lacks in typical Hendrix firepower, it makes up for in poetic delicacy. In some respects, these performances bring us closer to the tender heart of his work than the famous official versions of these classics. —*Richie Unterberger*

Voodoo Soup / Apr. 1995 / MCA ♦♦♦

Voodoo Soup was supposed to be the outtake album that got it right. Instead, it was another in a line of botched attempts to recreate Jimi Hendrix's unfinished final studio album. For most fans, the re-recorded drum tracks by the drummer of the Knack was the most unforgivable sin, yet the album is also poorly sequenced and lacks several important tracks. The sound is polished to a disturbingly bright sheen, while the cover art is garishly retro. —*Stephen Thomas Erlewine*

First Rays of the New Rising Sun / Apr. 22, 1997 / MCA ♦♦♦♦

Because Hendrix's death in September 1970 occurred before his work on these tunes was completed, the questions still abound as to what Hendrix's ultimate vision for this double album would have been. Minus the worthless—though well-intentioned—overdubs and remix manipulation that occurred when this material was issued piecemeal over the years on *The Cry of Love, War Heroes, Rainbow Bridge,* and the disappointing *Voodoo Soup,* this collection finally gets listeners back to the master tapes residing in the Electric Lady vaults. This gets the listener as close to what Hendrix had in mind as possible (as subject to change as these versions obviously were) and also places the tunes in their original context as an album. Because this collection utilizes mixes that Hendrix and engineer Eddie Kramer were working on at the time, the tracks perhaps lack the sonic wallop of the first three Experience albums but have much more to offer than the stripped-away and re-dubbed versions that have been on the market. If one views *First Rays of the New Rising Sun* as an almost completed work in progress, then it becomes obvious that Hendrix was heading into a new direction and sound, one rife with funk and rhythm & blues as a bedrock foundation. The psychedelic workouts got more jamlike and experimental, and the ballads got prettier and even more dreamlike in their background soundscapes. What he would have eventually come up with and released as his next musical statement is anyone's guess, but this gets you as close to that answer—and that vision—as you're ever likely to get. —*Cub Koda*

South Saturn Delta / Oct. 7, 1997 / MCA ♦♦♦

Shortly after the Hendrix family reacquired the rights to Jimi's catalog, they signed a long-term deal with MCA Records and pulled many of the compilations of unreleased material and rarities off the shelves, with the intent of re-releasing the material in better collections. *First Rays of the New Rising Sun,* an attempt at assembling Hendrix's uncompleted last album, was the first release from Experience Hendrix, and it was followed months later by *South Saturn Delta,* a collection of rarities—all but one of the 15 tracks were never officially released in the U.S.—that spans his entire career. Its intent is to capture the full range of Hendrix's music through an alternate history, and it works pretty well. Among the highlights are tracks from the *War Heroes* and *Rainbow Bridge* albums ("Look Over Yonder," "Tax Free," "Midnight," "Pali Gap," "Bleeding Heart"), "Sweet Angel" (an early version of "Angel"), an instrumental "Little Wing," a solo take on "Midnight Lightning," and a studio version of "Message to the Universe (Message to Love)." There are also alternate mixes of "All Along the Watchtower," "Power of Soul," "Drifter's Escape," "South Saturn Delta," and "The Stars That Play With Laughing Sam's Dice." It's an intelligently sequenced, listenable collection of some of the very best outtakes and rarities from Hendrix, and is another sign that Experience Hendrix's restoration of Jimi's catalog will be smart, stylish, and logical. —*Stephen Thomas Erlewine*

BBC Sessions / Jun. 2, 1998 / MCA ♦♦♦♦

These are the recordings that Jimi Hendrix made for BBC radio in the late '60s. As such, they're loose, informal, and off-the-top-of-his-head improvisational fun. These versions of the hits "Foxy Lady," "Fire," two versions of "Purple Haze," and "Hey Joe" stay surprisingly close to the studio versions, but the tone of Hendrix's guitar on these is positively blistering and worth the price of admission alone. There's also a lot of blues on this two-disc collection, and Hendrix's versions of "Hoochie Coochie Man" (with Alexis Korner on slide guitar), "Catfish Blues," "Killing Floor," and "Hear My Train A-Comin'" find him in excellent form. But perhaps the best example of how loosely conceived these sessions were are the oddball covers that Hendrix tackles, including Stevie Wonder's "I Was Made to Love Her" (featuring Wonder on drums), Dylan's "Can You Please Crawl out Your Window?," the Beatles' "Day Tripper" and, in recognition of his immediate competition, Cream's "Sunshine of Your Love." No lo-fi bootleg tapes here (everything's from the original masters and gone over by Eddie Kramer), the music and

sound are class-A all the way, making a worthwhile addition to anyone's Hendrix collection. —*Cub Koda*

● ### Experience Hendrix: The Best of Jimi Hendrix / Nov. 3, 1998 / MCA ♦♦♦♦♦

Experience Hendrix: The Best of Jimi Hendrix is a terrific 20-track collection that features all of Hendrix's most essential material, from "Purple Haze" and "Hey Joe" to "All Along the Watchtower" and "Star Spangled Banner." There are a few fine moments missing, but everything a casual fan needs is here, making it a great introduction to the ground-breaking guitarist. —*Stephen Thomas Erlewine*

Live at the Fillmore East / Feb. 23, 1999 / MCA ♦♦♦♦

A series of performances from the *Band of Gypsys* concerts finally gets the deluxe treatment from MCA and Experience Hendrix, as tapes from both first and second shows are brought together, correctly identified (1986's *Band of Gypsys 2* actually featured three tracks that weren't by the band at all) in one deluxe two-disc set. This newly expanded edition contains the only live versions of "Earth Blues," "Auld Lang Syne," "Stepping Stone," and "Burning Desire"; Hendrix tunes specifically worked up for the performance that rarely surfaced again like "Izabella," "Power of Soul," and "Who Knows"; newly re-mastered versions of "Stop" and "Hear My Train A-Comin'" (both originally presented on *Band of Gypsys 2* in horrendous sound) and classic performances of "Stone Free," "Changes," "Voodoo Child (Slight Return)," and "Wild Thing." Equally as revelatory is one of the two alternate versions included of "Machine Gun," every bit as stunning as the better-known version. Though this new edition hardly makes all previous incarnations obsolete, it presents the man at his most challenged and brilliant. —*Cub Koda*

Live at Woodstock / Jul. 6, 1999 / MCA ♦♦♦

In August 1994, MCA Records released *Jimi Hendrix: Woodstock,* a single-disc collection of highlights from Hendrix's legendary closing set at Woodstock. Less than a year later, Al Hendrix won the rights to his son's recordings, and his company, Experience Hendrix, began reissuing definitive masters of Jimi's catalog. In the summer of 1999, Experience Hendrix rolled out *Live at Woodstock,* which features the entire set over the course of two discs. Hearing Hendrix's complete concert isn't as revelatory as you'd think, since it just emphasizes that he overcompensated for his under-rehearsed band by jamming. And does he ever jam—almost everything clocks in at over five minutes, with a couple weighing in at over ten minutes. Naturally, this will hardly be seen as a detriment by legions of Hendrix fans, and that's who this set is for. Listening to all of *Live at Woodstock* takes dedication and an active interest in the subtleties of Jimi's playing. He had disbanded the Experience only eight weeks before and was teamed with players who wanted to follow him, no matter where he went. Unfortunately, the lack of rehearsal meant that they were often striving to keep up with him; in turn, Hendrix runs wild, spinning off dizzying solos that are as fascinating as they are frustrating. Taken individually, these performances are usually enthralling, but *Live at Woodstock* will exhaust the average listener. Which is not to say it isn't a worthwhile experience. As a historical document, it is interesting and revealing, and Hendrix historians undoubtedly will find several of these performances necessary. But this not an essential addition to the average fan's library, simply because Hendrix blew minds at Woodstock through excess, not focus. —*Stephen Thomas Erlewine*

The Jimi Hendrix Experience / Sep. 12, 2000 / MCA ♦♦♦♦

The Hendrix family continues its reissue campaign with the release of *The Jimi Hendrix Experience,* a lavish four-disc box set that should be a boon to Hendrix collectors everywhere. With a beautiful 80-page booklet, and purporting to have 46 unreleased tracks, further inspection actually reveals less than meets the eye, at least for collectors. The problem is that real collectors have already heard most of this material, and not only through bootleg sources. Many of the previously unreleased tracks are just *new mixes* of live tracks that were issued as part of *Stages, Live at Monterey,* and *Lifelines.* Also included is a new mix of the "Gloria" single. While the sound quality is somewhat better (handled by the expert Eddie Kramer), the new mixes do not differ substantially from the earlier versions. With the inclusion of virtually all of *In the West,* and a few quality tracks from *Rainbow Bridge* and *Crash Landing* (without the wretched mid-'70s overdubs), *The Jimi Hendrix Experience* almost seems like a shelf-clearing exercise, taking care of the leftover tracks that fans have been clamoring for *en masse.* The real highlights of the set are the early studio outtakes, presumably from the cache that Chas Chandler withheld from Alan Douglas for so many years. Interestingly, one of the most enjoyable aspects of these studio outtakes is the control room banter that takes place. There isn't a ton of it, but there are some highly enjoyable moments. At the end of "Purple Haze," Hendrix starts to giggle and throws in "Mary Had a Little Lamb." The version of "Third Stone from the Sun" has Chandler and Hendrix's recording of the spoken bits used on the song, tacked on to the beginning. It's great to hear Hendrix cracking up throughout their interstellar conversation. Another moment subtly hints at the frictions that were to end up dissolving the Chandler-Hendrix partnership. After seven minutes of take 21 of "Bold as Love," Hendrix is heard to say, "Let's try it one more time, alright?" to which Chas Chandler dejectedly replies "Oooohh." The book itself is wonderful; all tracks are fully documented and annotated, with lots of photos, many previously unpublished. There are also recording studio log sheets, newspaper articles, poster/flyers, and Hendrix's handwritten lyrics reproduced. All in all, *The Jimi Hendrix Experience* is a fine addendum to the Hendrix legacy, but not the place to start; this is a set for someone who already has the studio albums and can't get enough of his genius. The disappointment a hardcore collector might feel at having heard most of this material already should be outweighed by the beautiful, warm sound achieved by Eddie Kramer and the general high quality of the package. —*Sean Westergaard*

Voodoo Child: The Jimi Hendrix Collection / May 8, 2001 / MCA ♦♦♦

Wading through the repackagings of Jimi Hendrix musical legacy is a daunting task which has not been made any easier in the digital age. This double-CD set features a disc of "studio" and "live" performances including several alternate and hard-to-find recordings of familiar classics. While nearly impossible to include everyone's favorites, this collection is a superior primer for those seeking a thumbnail sketch of Hendrix in both a studio and concert environment. Disc one cuts a chronological path through nearly 70 minutes of peak moments from Hendrix studio recordings as the leader of the Jimi Hendrix Experience and the Band of Gypsys. The sound is impeccable and the song selection hits most of the highlights. Conspicuously absent are vital contributions such as "If 6 Was 9," "Manic Depression," and "Can You See Me." In their stead are alternate versions of "Highway Chile," "All Along the Watchtower," "Stone Free," and "Spanish Castle Magic"—all of which are available elsewhere. The rare 45 featuring the Band of Gypsys on "Isabella" and "Stepping Stone" is a nice inclusion for collectors. Disc two highlights Hendrix concert performances, including several generation-defining moments—such as the reinvention of the electric guitar during "Wild Thing" at the Monterey Pop Festival as well as his inimitable "Star Spangled Banner" solo from the Woodstock Music and Arts Fair. Other highlights include a couple of oft-overlooked later-era pieces featuring the *Band of Gypsys.* "Red House" from the New York Pop Festival and the previously unissued—on CD at least—"Foxey Lady" from Maui, HI, are both stellar performances from July of 1970. All in all, *Voodoo Child: The Jimi Hendrix Collection* is a great touchstone for anyone wishing to begin a Jimi Hendrix experience. *—Lindsay Planer*

Clarence "Frogman" Henry

b. Mar. 19, 1937, Algiers, LA

Vocals, Trombone, Songwriter, Piano / New Orleans R&B, R&B

He could sing like a girl, and he could sing like a frog. That latter trademark croak, utilized to the max on his 1956 debut smash "Ain't Got No Home," earned good-natured Clarence Henry his nickname and jump-started a rewarding career that endures to this day around the Crescent City.

Naturally, Fats Domino and Professor Longhair were young Clarence Henry's main influences while growing up in the Big Easy. He played piano and trombone with Bobby Mitchell & the Toppers from 1952 to 1955 before catching on with saxist Eddie Smith's band. Henry improvised the basic idea behind "Ain't Got No Home" on the bandstand one morning in the wee hours; when the crowd responded favorably, he honed it into something unique. Paul Gayten (New Orleans A&R man for Chess Records) concurred, hustling Henry into Cosimo Matassa's studio in September of 1956. Local DJ Poppa Stoppa laid the "Frogman" handle on the youngster when he spun the 45 (issued on the Chess subsidiary Argo), and it stuck.

Despite some fine follow-ups—"It Won't Be Long," "I'm in Love," the inevitable sequel "I Found a Home"—Frog sank back into the marsh sales-wise until 1960, when Allen Toussaint's updated arrangement melded beautifully with a country-tinged Bobby Charles composition called "(I Don't Know Why) But I Do." Henry's rendition of the tune proved a huge pop smash in early 1961, as did a Domino-tinged "You Always Hurt the One You Love" later that year.

Frogman continued to record a variety of New Orleans-styled old standards and catchy originals for Argo (Chess assembled a Henry album that boasted what may be the worst cover art in the history of rock & roll), even recording at one point with Nashville saxist Boots Randolph and pianist Floyd Cramer. But the hits dried up for good after 1961. Henry opened 18 concerts for the Beatles across the U.S. and Canada in 1964, but his main source of income came from the Bourbon Street strip, where he played for 19 years. You'll likely find him joyously reviving his classics at the New Orleans Jazz & Heritage Festival every year come spring—and his croak remains as deep and melodious as ever. *—Bill Dahl*

● **Ain't Got No Home: The Best of Clarence "Frogman" Henry** / 1994 / MCA/Chess ♦♦♦♦♦
The New Orleans R&B singer with the joyous frog's croak in his voice is served well by this 18-song collection of his 1956-1964 output for the Chess subsidiary Argo Records. It begins with his definitive "Ain't Got No Home," and follows with his vicious Crescent City rockers "Troubles, Troubles," "It Won't Be Long," and "I'm in Love," and visits his comeback hits "But I Do" and "You Always Hurt the One You Love." *—Bill Dahl*

But I Do / 1994 / Charly ♦♦♦♦♦
Here are 20 Argo waxings by the roly-poly pianist—much duplication with the easier-to-locate MCA disc as far as the hits go, though the inclusion of the sequel "I Found a Home" and the lesser-known rockers "Steady Date," "Oh Why," and "Live It Right" certainly make this one worth looking for. *—Bill Dahl*

I Like That Alligator Baby / May 11, 1999 / Edsel ♦♦♦

Chuck Higgins

b. Apr. 17, 1924, Gary, IN

Vocals, Sax (Tenor) / Brown-Eyed Soul, R&B

Saxophonist Chuck Higgins earned R&B fame for his composition "Pachuko Hop," which remains a perennial favorite among Latino fans, but didn't gain enough general R&B acclaim to chart in the early '50s. Higgins also played trombone and trumpet. He moved from his native Gary to Los Angeles in 1940 as a teen. Higgins played trumpet in his high school band and later attended the Los Angeles Conservatory. While there, Higgins started a band with pianist Frank Dunn and saxophonist Johnny Parker, among others.

Higgins later became the band's saxophonist and wrote "Pachuko Hop." Its furious pace, roaring sax solo, and raw sound, plus the inclusion of the term "Pachuko," which was slang for a Mexican-American dressed in baggy pants with a key chain, made the song a '50s anthem for area Latinos. The B-side, "Motorhead Baby," was later the inspiration for Frank Zappa sideman James "Motorhead" Sherwood and the heavy metal band Motorhead. Higgins played dates in Los Angeles with everyone from Charlie Parker to The Orioles and his band at one point included Johnny "Guitar" Watson. Although none of Higgins' many singles for Aladdin, Caddy, Lucky, Specialty, or Dootone ever earned national acclaim, he was an extremely popular regional attraction through the '50s and into the early '60s, when he retired from performing to become a music teacher at local high schools and a college. A comeback faltered in the mid-'70s, when Higgins tried to update his sound by going disco. He returned to honking R&B in the late '70s and toured England in the mid-'80s, while performing once more in Los Angeles clubs. *—Ron Wynn*

● **Pachuko Hop** / 1956 / Specialty ♦♦♦♦♦
Raucous R&B tenor saxist Higgins, a longtime L.A. favorite, honks and blows like a wildman on these 20 sides, dating from 1954-1956. Much of Higgins' work for the Specialty and Money logos laid unissued before this collection came out. His band included guitarist Jimmy Nolen (later a James Brown mainstay), pianist H.B. Barnum, and Chuck's brother Fred (as Daddy Cleanhead) handling vocals. *—Bill Dahl*

The Highway Q.C.'s

f. 1945, Chicago, IL

Group / Traditional Gospel, Southern Gospel, Black Gospel

Not only among the top gospel groups of the postwar era, the Highway Q.C.'s were also the launching pad for such major secular pop stars as Lou Rawls, Johnnie Taylor and the immortal Sam Cooke. The group was formed in 1945 at Chicago's Highway Baptist Church by a number of teenagers that included Cooke, Creadell Copeland and two pairs of brothers, Marvin & Charles Jones and Curtis & Lee Richardson. Cooke exited in 1951 to join the ranks of hometown heroes the Soul Stirrers; his replacement was Rawls, himself an alumnus of another young Windy City group, the Holy Wonders. In time all of the Wonders' other members—Spencer Taylor, James Walker and Chris Flowers among them—would join the Highway Q.C.'s as well. Rawls remained for just two years, leaving at that time to join the Los Angeles-based Chosen Gospel Singers; his substitute was Johnnie Taylor, previously of the Kansas City group the Melody Kings. The group made their debut on the Vee-Jay label in 1955; in 1956 Spencer Taylor joined, and a year later Johnnie Taylor (no relation) quit to join the Soul Stirrers, ironically enough filling the gap created by the exit of Sam Cooke. Spencer Taylor remained the Highway Q.C.'s leader throughout the decades which followed, continuing to helm the group into the '90s. *—Jason Ankeny*

Spencer Taylor & the Highway Q.C.'s / 1959 / Vee-Jay ♦♦♦♦♦
Soul-stirring group, has some tracks led by Johnnie Taylor. *—Opal Louis Nations*

★ **Jesus Is Waiting** / 1960 / Vee-Jay ♦♦♦♦♦
The Highway Q.C.'s were considered gospel's greatest farm team, the place where aspiring quartet lead singers would hone their skills before joining a group on the A list. But that doesn't mean the group made inferior music; the songs on *Jesus Is Waiting*, a single-disc collection combining two albums they cut in the mid-'50s and early '60s, can stand with any issued by the better-name ensembles. A youthful Johnnie Taylor soars, whoops, and moans through songs done from 1955-1957, while Spencer Taylor comes on with equal might and ferocity on the later material. They may not have had the reputations or kept their members as long, but at times the Highway Q.C.'s made music that resounded with as much fury as anyone on the gospel trail. *—Ron Wynn*

The Lord Is Sweet / 1965 / Peacock ♦♦♦
Best of the group's late-'60s sides. Includes "Changes at the End" and "Rock Me." *—Opal Louis Nations*

The Best of the Highway Q.C.'s / 1990 / Chameleon ♦♦♦♦♦
A respectable collection for the group that acted as a feeder for The Soul Stirrers and other first-echelon groups. Prior editions included Johnnie Taylor and the unrecorded Sam Cooke and O.V. Wright. *—Ron Wynn*

Count Your Blessings / Sep. 1, 1995 / Charly ♦♦♦♦
Essential Vee-Jay tracks with and without Johnnie Taylor. *—Opal Louis Nations*

Nearer My God: The Very Best of the Highway Q.C.'s / Mar. 3, 1998 / Collectables ♦♦♦♦
The best of the Vee-Jay sides featuring Johnnie and Spencer Taylor. *—Opal Louis Nations*

The Highway Q.C.'s/Jesus Is Waiting / Jul. 31, 2001 / Collectables ♦♦♦♦♦

Bertha "Chippie" Hill

b. Mar. 15, 1905, Charleston, SC, **d.** May 7, 1950, New York, NY

Vocals, Accordion / Classic Female Blues

One of the better classic blues singers of the '20s (and much less vaudeville-oriented than many of her contemporaries), Chippie Hill was one of the few singers of her generation to make a full-fledged comeback in the '40s. One of 16 children, she started working in 1916 as a dancer before she became better known as a singer. She toured with Ma Rainey's Rabbit Foot Minstrels and then was a solo performer on vaudeville for a long period. Hill settled in Chicago in 1925 and recorded regularly for a few years. After working steadily in the Chicago area until 1930 (including touring with Lovie Austin), she eventually left music to raise seven children. Hill occasionally sang during the next 15 years (including with Jimmie Noone) but mostly worked outside of music. She was rediscovered by writer Rudi Blesh in 1946, working in a bakery. Appearances on Blesh's "This Is Jazz" radio series resulted in her coming back to the music scene, performing at the Village Vanguard and Jimmy Ryan's, and even appearing at Carnegie Hall in 1948 with Kid Ory. She sang at the Paris Jazz Festival, worked with Art Hodes in Chicago and was back in prime form in 1950 when she was run over by a car and killed. Chippie Hill, who introduced Richard M. Jones' "Trouble in Mind" in 1926, recorded 23 titles during 1925-1929 with such sidemen as Jones, Louis Armstrong, Shirley Clay, Georgia Tom Dorsey, Tampa Red, and Punch Miller. She also recorded nine selections on two dates in 1946 with Lee Collins, Lovie Austin, Baby Dodds, and Montana Taylor. *—Scott Yanow*

● **Complete Works, Vol. 1 (1925–1929)** / May 20, 1997 / Document ♦♦♦♦

Blind Joe Hill

b. 1941, Pennsylvania, **d.** Nov. 17, 1999, Los Angeles, CA

Vocals, Harmonica, Guitar / Electric Chicago Blues

A good one-man band performer in the tradition of Joe Hill Louis and Dr. Ross, Blind Joe Hill accompanied his craggy vocals with guitar, bass and drums. He was among the last in the tradition, and that adds some value to his recordings, despite a derivative playing style and erratic compositional skills. *—Ron Wynn*

- **Boogie in the Dark** / Jan. 1978 / Barrelhouse ♦♦♦♦♦

Opinions vary regarding the quality of Blind Joe Hill's one-man band recordings. He certainly wasn't the greatest in the genre, but he was a creditable exponent. There's nothing especially exciting here, but it was done with sincerity and energy. *—Ron Wynn*

Jessie Hill

b. Dec. 9, 1932, New Orleans, LA, **d.** Sep. 17, 1996, New Orleans, LA

Vocals / New Orleans R&B, R&B

Loose and wild, Jessie Hill cut a New Orleans party classic with his crazed "Ooh Poo Pah Doo." The two-sided single, a 1960 Allen Toussaint production on Minit, has Hill shouting the nearly unintelligible lyrics over a strong Crescent City groove, while the flip is an instrumental featuring saxist David Lastie. Hill cut several more boisterous outings with Toussaint at the helm before heading to the West Coast, where he made a disappointing album for Blue Thumb in 1970. *—Bill Dahl*

- **Golden Classics** / 1989 / Collectables ♦♦♦♦♦

Good-time New Orleans R&B from the early '60s, produced by prolific pianist Allen Toussaint. *—Bill Dahl*

King Solomon Hill (Joe Holmes)

b. 1897, McComb, MS, **d.** 1949, Sibley, LA

Vocals, Guitar / Juke Joint Blues, Delta Blues, Country Blues

One of the more fascinating footnotes in blues history, King Solomon Hill's scant recorded legacy suggests a singer and guitarist of considerable originality and primitive force. Born Joe Holmes circa 1897 in McComb, MS, he first attracted attention in the Lousiana area, becoming a constant at parties and juke joints; most certainly a self-taught guitarist, he is rumored to have roamed the Delta and Panhandle regions playing alongside Sam Collins, Ramblin' Thomas, Oscar "Lone Wolf" Woods, and possibly Blind Lemon Jefferson. Hill signed to the Paramount label in 1932, soon traveling to Grafton, WI, to record the six tracks—two of them alternate takes—which comprise his known discography; songs like the eerie "Gone Dead Train" and "Down on Bended Knee" feature apocalyptic, seemingly alien vocals certainly unique to their time and place, accompanied by a raw guitar sound distinguished by irregular rhythms and notes said to be stretched out by a cow bone. After this lone session, Hill returned to the juke joint circuit, eventually vanishing from sight; reputedly a heavy drinker, he died of a massive brain hemorrhage in Sibley, LA in 1949. *—Jason Ankeny*

Michael Hill

b. 1952, New York, NY

Vocals, Guitar / Contemporary Blues, Modern Electric Blues

Michael Hill, a Bronx-raised guitarist, singer, and songwriter, took his earliest inspiration from the sounds of Jimi Hendrix. His other songwriting influences include socially conscious artists like Marvin Gaye, Bob Marley and Curtis Mayfield.

Hill has recorded two albums for Alligator Records of Chicago, *Have Mercy!* (1996) and *Bloodlines* (1994), which both contain extensive social commentary. Both releases have gotten good reviews from critics and sold respectably, yet he's still considered too "heavy" for some U.S. festivals and clubs. Despite this, Hill has made tours of clubs and festivals around Germany, France, Scandinavia, Austria, England, Italy, Brazil, and Australia. The 45-year-old Hill argues that his political songs follow the true blues tradition, which includes sounding off on societal problems. Blues songs of the '20s and '30s by Leadbelly, Mance Lipscomb, and other classic blues artists often dealt head on with society's ills. Hill sees himself as following this tradition. Songs like "Falling Through the Cracks," "Bluestime in America," "Why We Play the Blues," "Evil in the Air," and "Presumed Innocent" reveal another side of life to today's fans of blues music, most of whom are middle class, suburban, and white.

Hill, based in Brooklyn, NY, since 1988, was born in the Bronx in 1952. The Bronx that Hill remembers was a working-class community with families who looked after one another's kids. Hill comes from a close-knit family, and his brother Kevin began playing bass with him when he formed his first band in 1973.

After seeing Jimi Hendrix play on five occasions around New York City, including at the Woodstock Festival, Hill knew what he wanted to do with the rest of his life. He began playing guitar in 1970, and was soon playing out in rock and soul bands by 1972. He took cues from guitar players including B.B. King, Buddy Guy, Albert King, and Carlos Santana, and his style is a comfortable mesh of all these, plus his own touch. Reading the books of Toni Morrison, James Baldwin, and other black novelists, Hill began writing songs that spoke about socially relevant subjects as well as more traditional blues topics.

By the mid-'70s, Hill was working as a sideman or session player with the likes of Little Richard, Archie Bell, Harry Belafonte, and Carla Thomas. In the mid-'80s, working with Living Colour's Vernon Reid, he helped establish the Black Rock Coalition, a New York City-based group of black rock & roll bands, craftspersons, and artists. He caught the attention of Alligator Records in 1993, and in 1994, the label released *Bloodlines*, which was hailed by some critics as the best debut blues album of the year.

Hill's range on his Steinberger guitar is awe-inspiring, and he'll often follow up a slow blues ballad with a fiery blues-rock shuffle that shows off his rock influences, people like Jeff Beck, Hendrix, and Santana. Backed by a trio known as the Blues Mob, which consists of keyboards, bass, and drums, Hill's live shows are an artful blend of originals and a few interpretive covers.

Combine great guitar playing with a strong voice and thinking man's lyrics, and you've got all the ingredients for major blues stardom, and Michael Hill's Blues Mob are helping the idiom continue its evolution. They returned in 1998 with *New York State of Blues*. *—Richard Skelly*

Bloodlines / 1994 / Alligator ♦♦♦

If it's possible to label anything "new," Michael Hill's Blues Mob are taking a "new" approach to the blues. Hill and his associates incorporate numerous musical influences and elements into contemporary material with a blues feel and sound. Hill's slashing slide guitar mixes rock, funk and reggae as well as blues inflections, and is consistently creative and engaging. The group's compositions feature lyrics which discuss issues and ideas as much as romantic situations and dilemmas, and Hill's vocals aren't pleading, but defiant, triumphant and aggressive. If you're seeking standard fare, this isn't your cup of tea, but those interested in music that expands the blues vocabulary and range will find Michael Hill's Blues Mob the ticket. *—Ron Wynn*

- **Have Mercy!** / 1996 / Alligator ♦♦♦♦

Michael Hill's primary attribute is his ambition. Where many contemporary bluesmen are content to turn out standard shuffles and boogies, he wants to bring it all together—Hendrix blues-rock, Chicago blues, soul-blues, jazz and reggae. It's a difficult task, so it isn't entirely surprising that he and his band, the Blues Mob, don't quite achieve his dreams on his second album, *Have Mercy!* What is surprising is how close they come. When Hill and the Blues Mob have everything working right, their music is a heady fusion with real passion and heart. These moments—including "Women Make the World Go Round," "Africa Is Her Name" and a reworking of "Stagolee"—are powerful enough to make the failed fusions forgivable, and they suggest that Hill could develop into a distinctive talent in his own right. *—Thom Owens*

New York State of the Blues / Jun. 23, 1998 / Alligator ♦♦♦♦

Michael Hill's third album for Alligator keeps the focus of his music squarely in urban territory. Hill's Hendrix-laden grooves and almost-heavy-metal guitar playing may be off-putting to some purists, but he combines and melds his source point with excellence and passion throughout. This time he splits with the blues in two spots, to contribute cover versions of the Temptations' "Papa Was a Rolling Stone" and Stevie Wonder's "Living for the City" as demonstrating part of the group's "roots." But he also plays adventurous slide guitar on "A Case of the Blues" and the group contributes some nice bluesy vocal harmonies to "Soul Doin' Time." Hill's lyrics, as always, address contemporary social concerns (nicely done on the title track and "Anytime, Anywhere," as well as on "This Is My Job"), but most interesting is his take on young blues players coming up by the carload in "Young Folk's Blues." His most accessible record to date. *—Cub Koda*

Larger Than Life / Aug. 21, 2001 / Singular ♦♦♦

Larger Than Life is every bit as good if not better than Hill's first three albums on Alligator, opening with a powerful blast of a cappella harmony. Equally as strong is Hill's slide playing throughout, with additional guitar support from Living Colour's Vernon Reid. The songs are divided into four categories: Love & Lust, Tales from the Hood, Shuffling Into Commitment, and At the End of the Day. Hill—always the storyteller—again champions the cause of the downtrodden and wrongly accused. "Monticello Nights" details Thomas Jefferson's affair with slave Sally Hemmings—now that's taking on a contentious topic. Hills' voice has the familiar comfort of an old friend, creative guitar licks abound, and—best of all—the songs stay with ya. *—Ann Wickstrom*

Z.Z. Hill (Arzell Hill)

b. Sep. 30, 1935, Naples, TX, **d.** Apr. 27, 1984, Dallas, TX

Vocals / Retro-Soul, Modern Electric Blues, Soul-Blues

Texas-born singer Z.Z. Hill managed to resuscitate both his own semi-flagging career and the entire genre at large when he signed on at Jackson, Mississippi's Malaco Records in 1980 and began growling his way through some of the most uncompromising blues to be unleashed on black radio stations in many a moon.

His impressive 1982 Malaco album *Down Home Blues* remained on *Billboard*'s soul album charts for nearly two years, an extraordinary run for such a blatantly bluesy LP. His songs "Down Home Blues" and "Somebody Else Is Steppin' In" have graduated into the ranks of legitimate blues standards (and there haven't been many of those come along over the last couple of decades).

Arzell Hill started out singing gospel with a quintet called the Spiritual Five, but the output of B.B. King, Bobby "Blue" Bland, and especially Sam Cooke made a more indelible mark on his approach. He began gigging around Dallas, fashioning his distinctive initials after those of B.B. King. When his older brother Matt Hill (a budding record producer with his own label, M.H.) invited Z.Z. to go west to southern California, the young singer did.

His debut single on M.H., the gutsy shuffle "You Were Wrong" (recorded in an L.A. garage studio), showed up on the pop chart for a week in 1964. With such a relatively successful showing his first time out, Hill's fine subsequent singles for the Bihari brothers' Kent logo should have been even bigger. But "I Need Someone (To Love Me)," "Happiness Is All I Need," and a raft of other deserving Kent 45s (many produced and arranged by Maxwell Davis) went nowhere commercially for the singer.

Excellent singles for Atlantic, Mankind, and Hill (another imprint operated by brother Matt, who served as Z.Z.'s producer for much of his career) preceded a 1972 hookup with United Artists that resulted in three albums and six R&B chart singles over the next couple of years. From there, Z.Z. moved on to Columbia, where his 1977 single "Love Is So Good When You're Stealing It" became his biggest-selling hit of all.

Hill's vocal grit was never more effective than on his blues-soaked Malaco output. From 1980 until 1984, when he died suddenly of a heart attack, Z.Z. bravely led a personal back-to-the-blues campaign that doubtless helped to fuel the current contemporary blues boom. It's a shame he couldn't stick around to see it blossom. *—Bill Dahl*

Lot of Soul / 1969 / Kent ♦♦♦

Brand New Z.Z. Hill / 1971 / Mankind ♦♦♦

This is a '70s Swamp Dogg-produced concept album. *—Richard Pack*

Dues Paid in Full / 1972 / Kent ♦♦♦

Z.Z. Hill's second album for Kent, *Dues Paid in Full*, collects a number of singles that he recorded for the label between 1964 and 1965. Hill pretty much played in a straight Texas style during these days, turning out a series of stinging high-octane singles during those two years. Granted, there wasn't much in the way of originality, but there were strong signs of individuality, which makes *Dues Paid in Full* worth investigation for both Hill fans and anyone with a fondness for electric Texas blues. *—Thom Owens*

The Best Thing That's Happened to Me / 1972 / United Artists ✦✦✦

Keep on Loving You / 1975 / United Artists ✦✦✦
Soul material predominates here. *—Bill Dahl*

Let's Make a Deal / 1978 / Columbia ✦✦✦
One of the most commercial of Hill's albums, this disco-tinged release included the minor hits "This Time They Told the Truth" and "Love Is So Good When You're Stealing It." *—Richie Unterberger*

The Mark of Z.Z. Hill / 1979 / Columbia ✦✦✦
Hill's second and final Columbia LP was essentially a continuation of the first. On both, Hill sounds like a journeyman Southern soul singer embellished with period disco/mainstream R&B production, which neither added to the quality of the music nor made it unlistenable. *—Richie Unterberger*

Z.Z. Hill / 1981 / Malaco ✦✦✦✦
The initial step in Hill's amazing rebirth as a contemporary blues star, courtesy of Jackson, Mississippi's Malaco Records and producers Tommy Couch and Wolf Stephenson. The vicious blues outings "Bump and Grind" and "Blue Monday" were the first salvos fired by Hill at the blues market, though much of the set—"Please Don't Make Me (Do Something Bad to You)," "I'm So Lonesome I Could Cry"—was solidly in the Southern soul vein. *—Bill Dahl*

The Rhythm & The Blues / 1982 / Malaco ✦✦✦✦
Led by Hill's second immediate standard—the Denise LaSalle-penned "Someone Else Is Steppin' In"—Hill's third Malaco album was another consistent effort, if not quite the blockbuster that his previous effort was. Hill again dipped into the Little Johnny Taylor songbook for a humorous slow blues, "Open House at My House," while relying on talented songwriters George Jackson and Frank Johnson for most of his tailor-made material. *—Bill Dahl*

☆ **Down Home** / 1982 / Malaco ✦✦✦✦✦
One of the very few classic blues albums of the '80s. Hill revitalized the genre among African-American listeners with his "Down Home Blues," which earned instant standard status. But the entire album is tremendously consistent, with the percolating R&B workouts "Givin' It Up for Your Love" and "Right Arm for Your Love" contrasting with an intimate "Cheatin' in the Next Room" and the straight-ahead blues "Everybody Knows About My Good Thing" and "When It Rains It Pours." *—Bill Dahl*

I'm a Blues Man / 1983 / Malaco ✦✦✦✦
Fueled by more impressive material from the pens of Jackson, Johnson, and LaSalle, Hill was in an amazing groove during the years prior to his untimely demise, and the crack Malaco house band was certainly up to the task. Just like the title track ably demonstrated, Z.Z. Hill had indeed rechristened himself as a blues man of the first order. *—Bill Dahl*

Bluesmaster / 1984 / Malaco ✦✦✦
Issued the year he died, *Bluesmaster* boasted more competent soul-blues hybrids by the man who reenergized the blues idiom with his trademark growl. LaSalle's "You're Ruining My Bad Reputation," "Friday Is My Day" (written by legendary Malaco promo man Dave Clark), and a nice reading of Paul Kelly's slinky "Personally" rate with the standouts. *—Bill Dahl*

★ **In Memorium (1935–1984)** / 1985 / Malaco ✦✦✦✦✦
Most of the highlights of Hill's glorious blues-singing stint at Malaco, although the individual albums possess more than their share of worthwhile moments that aren't here. But with hallowed titles like "Down Home Blues," "Someone Else Is Slippin' In," and "Everybody Knows About My Good Thing," this stunning collection neatly summarizes Hill's heartwarming rise to blues power. *—Bill Dahl*

Whoever Is Thrilling You / 1986 / Stateside ✦✦✦

The Best of Z.Z. Hill / 1987 / Malaco ✦✦✦✦✦
While it isn't flawless like the similar *In Memorium (1935-1984),* Malaco's *The Best of Z.Z. Hill* is a solid ten-track sampler of Hill's contemporary blues recordings for the label. The other collection is more comprehensive, but this offers the bare basics, making it a nice, concise introduction. *—Thom Owens*

Greatest Hits / 1990 / Malaco ✦✦✦✦✦
When he died in 1984 at the relatively young age of 48, Z.Z. Hill went down in history as a great blues singer. But he was also an excellent soul singer, and this 1990 CD reminds us that he had as much to do with earthy, gospel-drenched southern soul as he did with B.B. King-influenced electric blues. Focusing on Hill's Malaco output, *Greatest Hits* contains some inspired 12-bar numbers (including "Open House at My House," "Shade Tree Mechanic" and Denise LaSalle's "Someone Else Is Steppin' In"), but is just as heavy in its R&B content. "Right Arm for Your Love," "Get a Little, Give a Little" and "Cheatin' In the Next Room" serve as fine examples of his unpretentious approach to Stax-influenced soul. And, of course, the CD boasts what became Hill's signature song, the infectious "Down Home Blues." For those who haven't experienced the impressive material Hill was delivering during the last years of his life, this CD would be the appropriate starting point. *—Alex Henderson*

The Down Home Soul of Z.Z. Hill / 1992 / Kent ✦✦✦✦✦
Before Hill made his sensational '80s comeback as a blues growler, he sang a slightly sweeter brand of West Coast soul during the mid-'60s at Kent. Under saxist Maxwell Davis' supervision, Hill waxed a series of magnificent R&B ballads—"Happiness Is All I

Need," "I Need Someone (To Love Me)"—that should have hit but inexplicably didn't. Gathered on one 22-track import disc, they sound terrific in retrospect. *—Bill Dahl*

The Complete Hill/UA Recordings / Mar. 19, 1996 / Capitol ✦✦✦✦
The gritty singer made three albums for United Artists (mostly under his brother Matt's supervision) from 1972 to 1975, and they were an idiomatically mixed bag. All three LPs are housed in their entirety on this two-disc set, its selections ranging from the deep soul sincerity of "I've Got to Get You Back" and "Your Love Makes Me Feel Good" and the country-soul hybrids "You're Killing Me (Slowly But Surely)" and "Country Love" to the funky Lamont Dozier-produced "I Created a Monster" and an Allen Toussaint-supervised "I Keep on Lovin' You." *—Bill Dahl*

Love is So Good When You're Stealing It / Mar. 26, 1996 / Ichiban ✦✦✦
Much of Hill's 1978-1979 output for Columbia was laced with disco rhythms, but there were also plenty of soulful throwbacks to the sort of intense testifying that Hill did best: the surging midtempo "That's All That's Left," and a string-enriched "This Time They Told the Truth," an insistent "Need You By My Side," and the smoldering title tale of cheating in the wee hours that hit big for him. Ichiban has cobbled together both of Hill's Columbia LPs, the first being infinitely superior to the brutally formulaic disco-dominated encore. *—Bill Dahl*

This Time They Told the Truth: The Columbia Years / Feb. 17, 1998 / Columbia ✦✦✦✦
The best of Hill's late-'70s stay at Columbia Records, *This Time They Told the Truth* might be a bit of a shock to listeners not familiar with the period, for Hill's always smooth vocals are embellished with a very disco-fied production, not always disturbing, but definitely obtrusive in several places. The songs themselves are quite good (distilled from 1978's *Let's Make a Deal* and 1979's *The Mark of Z.Z. Hill*), including "Stop by and Love Me Sometime," "A Message to the Ladies" and the title track. *—John Bush*

Let's Make a Deal/The Mark of Z.Z. Hill / Apr. 10, 2001 / West Side ✦✦✦

The Hoax
f. 1991, db. 1999
Group / British Blues, Blues-Rock
British blues-rock group the Hoax consisted of Jon Amor on guitar, Hugh Coltman on vocals and harmonica, Jess Davey on guitar, Robin Davey on bass and Dave Raeburn on drums. The members were all young students of the blues and had played together since they were in their teens; songwriting and arrangements were worked out together by all five members. The Hoax began to attract attention while on tour with the Smokin' Joe Kubek Band around England, and Code Blue Records label chief Mike Vernon signed them to a deal. Vernon, a veteran producer who had worked with John Mayall, Eric Clapton, Ten Years After, Savoy Brown, and David Bowie, was impressed by the maturity in the band's playing. Critics in England were also impressed with the band's prowess and heaped praise on the Hoax, comparing them to the Yardbirds, John Mayall's Bluesbreakers, and the Rolling Stones. Their debut album, *Sound Like This*, was released in 1995 on the Code Blue/Atlantic label (although Code Blue was later jettisoned by Atlantic), and the recording is a good reflection of their live shows. On it, the band pays tribute to its influences, such as Albert Collins, Albert King, the Fabulous Thunderbirds, Robben Ford, and Stevie Ray Vaughan. *—Richard Skelly*

● **Sound Like This** / 1995 / Code Blue ✦✦✦✦

The Hodges Brothers
f. Memphis, TN
Group / R&B, Soul
Hi Records producer Willie Mitchell constructed his vaunted house rhythm section around three talented Hodges brothers during the late '60s: guitarist Mabon (nicknamed "Teenie"), bassist Leroy, and organist Charles. With drummer Howard Grimes (and on some of Al Green's sides, MG's trapsman Al Jackson Jr.) rounding out the lineup, this skin-tight Memphis quartet laid down surging, simmering grooves behind the entire Hi stable during the label's '70s heyday: Green, Ann Peebles, Otis Clay, Syl Johnson, and Mitchell himself, to name but a few. Mitchell had patiently molded the unit from when the Hodges brothers were in their teens (Grimes was a bit older, having worked as a sideman over at rival Stax during the early '60s).

As the succinctly monickered Hi rhythm section, they remain a cohesive unit, providing luxurious backing on Syl Johnson's wonderful 1994 comeback set for Delmark, *Back in the Game*. Meanwhile, the Hodges Brothers released a 1994 disc called "Perfect Gentlemen" on the tiny Velvet Recordings of America logo that also featured a fourth brother—Fred—on keys and veteran soul singer Percy Wiggins on several tracks. *—Bill Dahl*

● **Watermelon Hangin' on the Vine** / 1990 / Arhoolie ✦✦✦

Rob Hoeke
b. Jan. 9, 1943, New York, NY, d. Nov. 9, 1999, Krommenie, the Netherlands
Piano / Blues-Rock
A good boogie-woogie-styled pianist, Hoeke led the Rob Hoeke Rhythm and Blues Group in the mid-'60s, which had some success in Holland, although they were unknown elsewhere. Hoeke's outfit was probably the most accomplished of the numerous Dutch acts that tried to play blues-rock during the period (such as Cuby & the Blizzards). This was due in large measure to Hoeke's skill as an instrumentalist, and a sense that he had actually familiarized himself with the idiom for a few years, as opposed to some of the sloppier Dutch bands, which seemed to have leaped into R&B after hearing one Rolling Stones hit. Hoeke was also a good singer, with a pinched, hurt phrasing that was less affected than most '60s Continental rock singers performing in English.

Like most blues-rock groups of the time, Dutch or otherwise, Hoeke's band was most interesting when they brought a pop/R&B sensibility to their original material. They did this best on the sullen 1966 single "When People Talk"/"Rain, Snow, Misery," both sides of which have been reissued on compilations of '60s Dutch beat music. Their 1967 album

Save Our Souls, by contrast, was more focused on straight blues than one might have expected, with a few instrumentals showcasing Hoeke's boogie chops. —*Richie Unterberger*

● **Save Our Souls** / 1967 / Philips ✦✦✦✦
This doesn't quite measure up to the forceful, moody, defiant R&B of their 1966 singles, Hoeke using the LP format to indulge himself in a few piano-dominated instrumentals that stick to straight blues. It's just an OK album, with occasional more satisfying tracks in a scruffy R&B/rock style more akin to the Animals, Them, or early Stones, like "Drinking on My Bed" and "Let's Get Out of Here." —*Richie Unterberger*

Free and Easy / 1980 / Universe ✦✦✦

Rob Hoeke & the Real Boogie Woogie / 1987 / Down South ✦✦✦

Silas Hogan

b. Sep. 15, 1911, Westover, LA, d. Jan. 9, 1994, Scotlandville, LA
Vocals, Guitar / Swamp Blues, Louisiana Blues
In the collection of local Louisiana blues stars that made their mark on phonograph records bearing the Excello imprint under the aegis of Crowley producer Jay Miller, Silas Hogan was a local phenom who finally had a chance to record at a time when the commercial appeal of his sound was waning in the national marketplace. Hogan recorded for Excello from 1962 to early 1965, seeing the last of his single releases issued late that year.

Sometime in the late '20s Silas learned the basics of the guitar from his two uncles, Robert and Frank Murphy, who later went on to influence the idiosyncratic style of Robert Pete Williams. Learning his trade by playing assorted house parties and picnics in the local vicinity, by the late '30s Hogan was working regularly with guitarist Willie B. Thomas and fiddler Butch Cage, making the local juke-joint circuit his new found home.

A move to the Baton Rouge area in the early '50s brought changes to his music. Armed with a Fender electric guitar and amp, Hogan formed his first electric combo—the Rhythm Ramblers—becoming one of the top drawing cards on the Louisiana juke-joint circuit. In 1962, at the ripe old age of 51, Hogan was introduced by Slim Harpo to producer Jay Miller and his recording career finally began in earnest. The recordings he produced in the Crowley studio were solid, no-frills performances that mirrored the many variants of the "sound of the swamp."

After a few singles, Hogan's recording career came to an abrupt halt when Miller clashed with the new owners in 1966, ending the flow of Crowley product on the label. No longer an Excello recording artist, Hogan disbanded his group, going back to his day job at the Exxon refinery near Baton Rogue. The chance to record came around again in the '70s, with Hogan cutting sides for labels like Arhoolie and Blue Horizon while remaining active on the Southern blues festival circuit for pretty much the rest of the decade. With as little fanfare as his Excello singles were greeted in the marketplace, Silas Hogan quietly passed away in January of 1994. —*AMG*

So Long Blues / 1995 / Ace ✦✦✦

● **Trouble: The Best of the Excello Masters** / 1995 / AVI-Excello ✦✦✦✦✦
This 26-track single-disc retrospective may not have every last alternate take extant on it, but you'll never need a better compilation mirroring Hogan's stay at the label. "Trouble at Home Blues," "I'm Gonna Quit You Pretty Baby" and "Here They Are Again" are just about as low down as Louisiana swamp blues gets and Jay Miller's studio sorcery is clearly on hand. —*AMG*

The Godfather / Oct. 12, 1999 / Wolf ✦✦✦
This 1988 session in Baton Rogue finds Hogan surrounded by a band that includes his son Sam on both drums and guitar, unobtrusive guitar support from producer Julian Piper and Bruce Lamb, and effective harmonica from Oscar "Harpo" Davis. As Hogan blasts through a stack of old Excello tunes by Lightnin' Slim, as well as re-cuts of his own material, he's guest starred by the appearance of Arthur "Guitar" Kelley, who sings and plays on the last four tracks. This is a nice, understated session with two tracks cut in 1990 that proves that the "Excello sound" was still alive and well headed into the '90s. —*Cub Koda*

Willie "Smokey" Hogg

b. Jan. 27, 1914, Westconnie, TX, d. May 1, 1960, McKinney, TX
Vocals, Piano, Guitar / Electric Blues, R&B, Texas Blues
Smokey Hogg was a rural bluesman navigating a postwar era infatuated with R&B, but he got along quite nicely nonetheless, scoring a pair of major R&B hits in 1948 and 1950 and cutting a thick catalog for a slew of labels (including Exclusive, Modern, Bullet, Macy's, Sittin' in With, Imperial, Mercury, Recorded in Hollywood, Specialty, Fidelity, Combo, Federal, and Showtime).

During the early '30s, Hogg, who was influenced by Big Bill Broonzy and Peetie Wheatstraw, worked with slide guitarist Black Ace at dances around Greenville, TX. Hogg first recorded for Decca in 1937, but it was an isolated occurrence—he didn't make it back into a studio for a decade. Once he hit his stride, though, Hogg didn't look back. Both his chart hits—1948's "Long Tall Mama" and 1950's "Little School Girl"—were issued on Modern, but his rough-hewn sound seldom changed a whole lot no matter what L.A. logo he was appearing on. Hogg's last few sides were cut in 1958 for Lee Rupe's Ebb label.

Smokey's cousin John Hogg also played the blues, recording for Mercury in 1951. —*Bill Dahl*

Sittin' in With / 1949-1950 / Mainstream ✦✦✦✦✦
A compilation of 14 tracks Willie Smokey Hogg recorded for the Sittin' in With label between 1949 and 1950, this record doesn't offer any of his big hits, but it's an enjoyable slice of postwar Texas blues. —*Thom Owens*

Sings / 1961 / Crown ✦✦✦✦✦
Smokey Hogg was a fine guitarist and good vocalist, better at midtempo and slower material than uptempo numbers. These are some of his best early-'60s cuts; the sound quality is good, but not exceptional. —*Ron Wynn*

Smokey Hogg / 1962 / Time ✦✦✦
Early-'50s Texas blues. —*Bill Dahl*

Original Folk Blues / 1965 / United ✦✦✦✦✦
Some of Hogg's best early-'50s sides for Modern are here. —*Bill Dahl*

Sings the Blues / 1973 / Ember ✦✦✦

John Lee Hooker, Lightnin' Hopkins / 1973 / Specialty ✦✦✦

U Better Watch That Jive / 1974 / Specialty ✦✦✦

Going Back Home / 1984 / Krazy Kat ✦✦✦

● **Angels in Harlem** / 1992 / Specialty ✦✦✦✦✦
Angels in Harlem is a wonderful compilation of Smokey Hogg's early-'50s recordings for Specialty Records, containing 22 tracks, including "I Want a Roller," "Nobody Treats Me Right," "Evil Mind Blues," "I Ain't Gonna Put You Down," "Born on the 13th" and "Good Mornin' Baby." —*Thom Owens*

Penitentiary Blues / Feb. 28, 1995 / Collectables ✦✦✦✦

Deep Ellum Rambler / Mar. 13, 2001 / Ace ✦✦✦✦
This comprehensive retrospective of Hogg's 1947-1951 work for Modern Records gathers 27 tracks, including the Top Ten R&B hits "Little School Girl" (a Sonny Boy Williamson composition) and "Long Tall Mama," as well as ten previously unissued cuts. If only in hindsight, Hogg at this juncture can be seen to be a link between rural blues and citified R&B, using some accompanying musicians and some electric guitar, but not always going whole-hog into a full-band sound. His phrasing, too, is still grounded in country blues, but pushed toward more modern forms by some heavily rhythmic backing and barrelhouse piano. It's on the ragged side (pleasantly so) as just-post-World War II blues-cum-R&B goes, the arrangements sometimes giving the impression of being crafted on the spot, though Hogg's vocals are relaxed and authoritative. Sometimes it feels like a link between a Texas bluesman like Lightnin' Hopkins and the West Coast R&B of the late '40s and early '50s; the Modern label, of course, was at the forefront of the Western R&B/blues crossover mix. It's rather similar-sounding in one dose, as most single-artist compilations of material from this time on the Modern label are. Yet it's not as homogenous as some such anthologies are, in large degree because of Hogg's likable vocal persona. Almost everything was written by Hogg except, oddly enough, those two big hits, "Little School Girl" and "Long Tall Mama." —*Richie Unterberger*

Dave Hole

b. Mar. 30, 1948, Heswall, Cheshire, England
Slide Guitar, Vocals, Guitar / Slide Guitar Blues, Modern Electric Blues
Australian slide guitarist Dave Hole is noted for his energetic, high-volume rock & roll/blues music and unusual playing style. Though left-handed, Hole plays guitar right-handed and developed a technique to compensate for a finger injury in which he places his fingers over the top of the neck. He also uses a pick for a slide and utilizes finger-picking when playing normally.

Born on March 30, 1948, in England, but raised from age four in Perth, Australia, Hole became interested in blues guitar around age six after hearing a schoolmate's Muddy Waters album. He received his first guitar at age 12, but became discouraged trying to learn it by himself (teachers were in short supply in isolated Perth) and abandoned it until he was 16. This time, he began picking up riffs and techniques from records. Primary influences include Eric Clapton, Jimi Hendrix, Robert Johnson, Elmore James, and Mississippi Fred McDowell. Hole became a professional in 1972 when working with a band in London. Returning to Perth in 1974, he began his long stint touring the western Australian club circuit, playing 20 years in remote towns before making *Short Fuse Blues*, an album he financed, produced, and recorded with his band Short Fuse in three days in 1990. He then hawked the album during club performances and on a whim, sent a copy to *Guitar Player* magazine in the U.S. The editor listened to it, liked it, wrote a praise-filled article hailing him as the newest guitar wizard and comparing him to such greats as Stevie Ray Vaughan and Albert King. He then helped Hole land a distribution deal with Alligator Records and released *Working Overtime* (1993), *Steel on Steel* (1995), *Under the Spell* (1999), and *Outside Looking In* (2001). With each new release, Dave Hole continues to build a respectable following in the U.S. and European blues scene that grows stronger every year. —*Sandra Brennan & Al Campbell*

Short Fuse Blues / 1992 / Alligator ✦✦✦
Dave Hole's American debut album is a stunning display of slide guitar pyrotechnics. Hole runs through a dizzying array of licks and solos, pulling out a variety of different tones and textures from his guitar. He can play it straight and greasy or spooky, tough and gritty or subtle and melodic—his technique is quite impressive. Although the songs themselves are occasionally weak, *Short Fuse Blues* is essentially a guitar record, so the songs don't matter as much as the playing. And the playing is superb throughout *Short Fuse Blues*. —*Thom Owens*

● **Working Overtime** / 1993 / Alligator ✦✦✦✦
Hole's second disc features nine original compositions and covers of Muddy Waters and Big Bill Broonzy, rendered in a vocal and guitar style somewhat similar to Johnny Winter's best blues work but with an edge of youthful vigor. "Biting slide guitar work" is an understatement. Hole can also play the thoughtful Roy Buchanan card on the likes of "Berwick Road." —*Roch Parisien*

Steel on Steel / 1995 / Alligator ✦✦✦
With his third album, *Steel on Steel*, Dave Hole turns in another set of ready-made originals and covers, all highlighted by his sizzling slide guitar work. —*Stephen Thomas Erlewine*

Ticket to Chicago / Feb. 11, 1997 / Alligator ✦✦✦✦
Slide guitarist Dave Hole kicks up a fun ruckus on *Ticket to Chicago*, his fourth album

for Alligator Records. This native of Perth (Australia), the Chicago blues label's first overseas signing, realizes for the first time his dream of playing with Chicago blues musicians—bassist Johnny B. Gayden (Albert Collins), pianist Tony Z (Larry McCray, Buddy Guy), and drummer Ray "Killer" Allison (Buddy Guy), along with (on several tracks) a horn section and harmonica (courtesy of Billy Branch). The opening "Out of Here" serves as the starter's pistol—Hole and company play too fast, too loud, and sound too rowdy on just about every one of these 14 songs (13 Hole originals and William Harris' "Bullfrog Blues," here dedicated by Hole to late blues-rock guitarist Rory Gallagher). In other words, *Ticket to Chicago* is a wonderfully high-spirited blues album, the kind to listen to when you're in the mood to go out and raise some hell but you're either too tired, too broke, or too ripped up to actually go out and do it. —*Chris Slawecki*

Under the Spell / Apr. 20, 1999 / Alligator ♦♦♦

With *Under the Spell*, Australian guitarist Dave Hole and his veteran backup band manage to lasso in all of the energy from their live concerts, while under the roof of a usually antiseptic recording studio environment. All but three of the 12 tracks were written by Hole and rank among his best work to date. Rocking through "Demolition Man" and delivering a sweet soul-blues ballad with "Don't Say Goodbye," Hole once again expresses his musical diversity with a flair. He manages to remain a true original while still feeding off of his major influences—people like the Rolling Stones, Muddy Waters, the Animals, Howlin' Wolf, and Muddy Waters. "Holding Pattern" rocks with a Stevie Ray Vaughan feel, and Hole's passionate vocals are a real treat on his cover of John Lee Hooker's "Run With Me." "More Love, Less Attitude" is an infectious groove that begs to be heard time and time again, and Hole simply smokes on the electric slide—there are no two ways about it. *Under the Spell* combines excellent acoustic foundations, topped with blistering slide work and power-soaked vocals, to provide one of the finest blues albums of the year. The CD should be required listening for all fans and students of the slide guitar, as well as connoisseurs of the blues in general. —*Michael B. Smith*

Outside Looking In / Jun. 5, 2001 / Alligator ♦♦♦♦

Slide-slinging hotshot Dave Hole doesn't stray far from the basics on his sixth album for Alligator, which ought to please his established fans just fine. After all, he's not striving to bring new depth to high-energy blues-rock; he's happy to just keep the fire burning by whipping off biting, energetic riffs that slash and sting with the nimbleness of Duane Allman and the uncut fury of Elmore James, two of his most obvious influences. Although the majority of the album is self-penned, it's easy to hear strains of Rory Gallagher and Johnny Winter in Hole's attack. A few acoustic tracks—like the languid "Nobody," where the singer sounds a bit like Leon Redbone, and "Get a Job"—ease the sonic aggressiveness, but not for long. Hole's songwriting won't win him any comparisons to Willie Dixon, but who's going to argue when he plows through a simplistic Bo Diddley beat on "Insomniac" with pile-driving force and a vocal similarity to Eric Clapton, evoking Slowhand's "Willie and the Hand Jive." Even on ballads, like the beautifully languorous "Out of My Reach," Hole tosses in a flame-throwing solo reminiscent of David Lindley's work with Jackson Browne. Covers of B.B. King's "You Move Me So" and Jimmy McCracklin's "He Knows the Rules" become frameworks for Hole's fiery pyrotechnics. He's not changing the world, but with *Outside Looking In*, Dave Hole's just making it a little jumpier. Sure to enliven any party, this is fuel-injected high-quality house-rockin' music that'll blow the roof off any shindig. —*Hal Horowitz*

Billie Holiday (Eleanora Fagan Gough)

b. Apr. 7, 1915, Philadelphia, PA, d. Jul. 17, 1959, New York, NY
Vocals / Vocal Jazz, Traditional Pop, Swing, Ballads, Classic Female Blues, Torch Songs, Standards

The first popular jazz singer to move audiences with the intense, personal feeling of classic blues, Billie Holiday changed the art of American pop vocals forever. Almost fifty years after her death, it's difficult to believe that prior to her emergence, jazz and pop singers were tied to the Tin Pan Alley tradition and rarely personalized their songs; only blues singers like Bessie Smith and Ma Rainey actually gave the impression they had lived through what they were singing. Billie Holiday's highly stylized reading of this blues tradition revolutionized traditional pop, ripping the decades-long tradition of song plugging in two by refusing to compromise her artistry for either the song or the band. She made clear her debts to Bessie Smith and Louis Armstrong (in her autobiography she admitted, "I always wanted Bessie's big sound and Pops' feeling"), but in truth her style was virtually her own, quite a shock in an age of interchangeable crooners and band singers.

With her spirit shining through on every recording, Holiday's technical expertise also excelled in comparison to the great majority of her contemporaries. Often bored by the tired old Tin Pan Alley songs she was forced to record early in her career, Holiday fooled around with the beat and the melody, phrasing behind the beat and often rejuvenating the standard melody with harmonies borrowed from her favorite horn players, Armstrong and Lester Young. (She often said she tried to sing like a horn.) Her notorious private life—a series of abusive relationships, substance addictions, and periods of depression—undoubtedly assisted her legendary status, but Holiday's best performances ("Lover Man," "Don't Explain," "Strange Fruit," her own composition "God Bless the Child") remain among the most sensitive and accomplished vocal performances ever recorded. More than technical ability, more than purity of voice, what made Billie Holiday one of the best vocalists of the century—easily the equal of Ella Fitzgerald or Frank Sinatra—was her relentlessly individualist temperament, a quality that colored every one of her endlessly nuanced performances.

Billie Holiday's chaotic life reportedly began in Baltimore on April 7, 1915 (a few reports say 1912), when she was born Eleanora Fagan Gough. Her father, Clarence Holiday, was a teenaged jazz guitarist and banjo player later to play in Fletcher Henderson's Orchestra. He never married her mother, Sadie Fagan, and left while his daughter was still a baby. (She would later run into him in New York, and though she contracted many guitarists for her sessions before his death in 1937, she always avoided using him.) Holiday's

mother was also a young teenager at the time, and whether because of inexperience or neglect, often left her daughter with uncaring relatives. Holiday was sentenced to Catholic reform school at the age of ten, reportedly after she admitted being raped.

Though sentenced to stay until she became an adult, a family friend helped get her released after just two years. With her mother, she moved in 1927, first to New Jersey and soon after to Brooklyn.

In New York, Holiday helped her mother with domestic work, but soon began moonlighting as a prostitute for the additional income. According to the weighty Billie Holiday legend (which gained additional credence after her notoriously apocryphal autobiography *Lady Sings the Blues*), her big singing break came in 1933 when a laughable dancing audition at a speakeasy prompted her accompanist to ask her if she could sing. In fact, Holiday was most likely singing at clubs all over New York City as early as 1930-1931. Whatever the true story, she first gained some publicity in early 1933, when record producer John Hammond—only three years older than Holiday herself, and just at the beginning of a legendary career—wrote her up in a column for Melody Maker and brought Benny Goodman to one of her performances. After recording a demo at Columbia Studios, Holiday joined a small group led by Goodman to make her commercial debut on November 27, 1933, with "Your Mother's Son-In-Law."

Though she didn't return to the studio for over a year, Billie Holiday spent 1934 moving up the rungs of the competitive New York bar scene. By early 1935, she made her debut at the Apollo Theater and appeared in a one-reeler film with Duke Ellington. During the last half of 1935, Holiday finally entered the studio again and recorded a total of four sessions. With a pick-up band supervised by pianist Teddy Wilson, she recorded a series of obscure, forgettable songs straight from the gutters of Tin Pan Alley—in other words, the only songs available to an obscure black band during the mid-'30s. (During the swing era, music publishers kept the best songs strictly in the hands of society orchestras and popular white singers.) Despite the poor song quality, Holiday and various groups (including trumpeter Roy Eldridge, alto Johnny Hodges, and tenors Ben Webster and Chu Berry) energized flat songs like "What a Little Moonlight Can Do," "Twenty-Four Hours a Day" and "If You Were Mine" (to say nothing of "Eeny Meeny Miney Mo" and "Yankee Doodle Never Went to Town"). The great combo playing and Holiday's increasingly assured vocals made them quite popular on Columbia's discount subsidiaries Brunswick and Vocalion.

During 1936, Holiday toured with groups led by Jimmie Lunceford and Fletcher Henderson, then returned to New York for several more sessions. In late January 1937, she recorded several numbers with a small group culled from one of Hammond's new discoveries, Count Basie's Orchestra. Tenor Lester Young, who'd briefly known Billie several years earlier, and trumpeter Buck Clayton were to become especially attached to Holiday. The three did much of their best recorded work together during the late '30s, and Holiday herself bestowed the nickname "Pres" on Young, while he dubbed her "Lady Day" for her elegance. By the spring of 1937, she began touring with Basie as the female complement to his male singer, Jimmy Rushing. The association lasted less than a year, however. Though officially she was fired from the band for being temperamental and unreliable, shadowy influences higher up in the publishing world reportedly commanded the action after she refused to begin singing '20s female blues standards.

At least temporarily, the move actually benefited Holiday—less than a month after leaving Basie, she was hired by Artie Shaw's popular band. She began singing with the group in 1938, one of the first instances of a black female appearing with a white group. Despite the continuing support of the entire band, however, show promoters and radio sponsors soon began objecting to Holiday—based on her unorthodox singing style almost as much as her race. After a series of escalating indignities, Holiday quit the band in disgust. Yet again, her judgment proved valuable; the added freedom allowed her to take a gig at a hip new club named Café Society, the first popular nightspot with an inter-racial audience. There, Billie Holiday learned the song that would catapult her career to a new level: "Strange Fruit."

The standard, written by Café Society regular Lewis Allen and forever tied to Holiday, is an anguished reprisal of the intense racism still persistent in the South. Though Holiday initially expressed doubts about adding such a bald, uncompromising song to her repertoire, she pulled it off thanks largely to her powers of nuance and subtlety. "Strange Fruit" soon became the highlight of her performances. Though John Hammond refused to record it (not for its politics but for its overly pungent imagery), he allowed Holiday a bit of leverage to record for Commodore, the label owned by jazz record-store owner Milt Gabler. Once released, "Strange Fruit" was banned by many radio outlets, though the growing jukebox industry (and the inclusion of the excellent "Fine and Mellow" on the flip) made it a rather large, though controversial, hit. She continued recording for Columbia labels until 1942, and hit big again with her most famous composition, 1941's "God Bless the Child." Gabler, who also worked A&R for Decca, signed her to the label in 1944 to record "Lover Man," a song written especially for her and her third big hit. Neatly side-stepping the musician's union ban that afflicted her former label, Holiday soon became a priority at Decca, earning the right to top-quality material and lavish string sections for her sessions. She continued recording scattered sessions for Decca during the rest of the '40s, and recorded several of her best-loved songs including Bessie Smith's "'Tain't Nobody's Business If I Do," "Them There Eyes," and "Crazy He Calls Me."

Though her artistry was at its peak, Billie Holiday's emotional life began a turbulent period during the mid-'40s. Already heavily into alcohol and marijuana, she began smoking opium early in the decade with her first husband, Johnnie Monroe. The marriage didn't last, but hot on its heels came a second marriage to trumpeter Joe Guy and a move to heroin. Despite her triumphant concert at New York's Town Hall and a small film role—as a maid (!)—with Louis Armstrong in 1947's *New Orleans*, she lost a good deal of money running her own orchestra with Joe Guy. Her mother's death soon after affected her deeply, and in 1947 she was arrested for possession of heroin and sentenced to eight months in prison.

Unfortunately, Holiday's troubles only continued after her release. The drug charge made it impossible for her to get a cabaret card, so nightclub performances were out of the question. Plagued by various celebrity hawks from all portions of the underworld (jazz, drugs, song publishing, etc.), she soldiered on for Decca until 1950. Two years later, she began recording for jazz entrepreneur Norman Granz, owner of the excellent labels Clef, Norgran, and by 1956, Verve. The recordings returned her to the small-group intimacy of her Columbia work, and reunited her with Ben Webster as well as other top-flight musicians such as Oscar Peterson, Harry "Sweets" Edison, and Charlie Shavers. Though the ravages of a hard life were beginning to take their toll on her voice, many of Holiday's mid-'50s recordings are just as intense and beautiful as her classic work.

During 1954, Holiday toured Europe to great acclaim, and her 1956 autobiography brought her even more fame (or notoriety). She made her last great appearance in 1957, on the CBS television special *The Sound of Jazz*, with Webster, Lester Young, and Coleman Hawkins providing a close backing. One year later, the *Lady in Satin* LP clothed her naked, increasingly hoarse voice with the overwrought strings of Ray Ellis. During her final year, she made two more appearances in Europe before collapsing in May 1959 of heart and liver disease. Still procuring heroin while on her death bed, Holiday was arrested for possession in her private room and died on July 17, her system completely unable to fight both withdrawal and heart disease at the same time. Her cult of influence spread quickly after her death and gave her more fame than she'd enjoyed in life. The 1972 biopic *Lady Sings the Blues* featured Diana Ross struggling to overcome the conflicting myths of Holiday's life, but the film also illuminated her tragic life and introduced many future fans. By the digital age, virtually all of Holiday's recorded material had been reissued: by Columbia (nine volumes of *The Quintessential Billie Holiday*), Decca (*The Complete Decca Recordings*), and Verve (*The Complete Billie Holiday on Verve 1945-1959*). —*John Bush*

☆ **The Quintessential Billie Holiday, Vol. 1 (1933–1935)** / Nov. 27, 1933-Dec. 3, 1935 / Columbia ◆◆◆◆◆
After years of reissuing Billie Holiday's recordings in piecemeal fashion, Columbia finally got it right with this nine-CD *Quintessential* series. All of Lady Day's 1933-1942 studio recordings (although without the alternate takes) receive the treatment they deserve in this program. *Vol. 1* has Holiday's first two tentative performances from 1933 along with her initial recordings with Teddy Wilson's all-star bands. High points include "I Wished on the Moon," "What a Little Moonlight Can Do," "Miss Brown to You," and "Twenty-Four Hours a Day." —*Scott Yanow*

☆ **The Quintessential Billie Holiday, Vol. 2 (1936)** / Jan. 30, 1936-Oct. 21, 1936 / Columbia ◆◆◆◆◆
The second of nine volumes in this essential series (all are highly recommended) continues the complete reissue of Billie Holiday's early recordings (although the alternate takes are bypassed). This set is highlighted by "I Cried for You" (which has a classic alto solo from Johnny Hodges), "Billie's Blues" (from Holiday's first session as a leader), "A Fine Romance," and "Easy to Love." Holiday's backup crew includes such greats as pianist Teddy Wilson, baritonist Harry Carney, trumpeters Jonah Jones and Bunny Berigan, and clarinetist Artie Shaw. There's lots of great small-group swing. —*Scott Yanow*

☆ **The Quintessential Billie Holiday, Vol. 3 (1936–1937)** / Oct. 28, 1936-Feb. 18, 1937 / Columbia ◆◆◆◆◆
The third of nine CDs that document all of Billie Holiday's studio recordings of 1933-1942 for Columbia has classic versions of "Pennies From Heaven," "I Can't Give You Anything but Love" (on which she shows the influence of Louis Armstrong), and "My Last Affair," along with Lady Day's first meeting on record with tenor saxophonist Lester Young. Their initial encounter resulted in four songs, including "This Year's Kisses" and "I Must Have That Man." All nine volumes in this admirable series (if only the alternate takes had been included) are highly recommended. —*Scott Yanow*

☆ **The Quintessential Billie Holiday, Vol. 4 (1937)** / Mar. 31, 1937-Jun. 15, 1937 / Columbia ◆◆◆◆◆
The fourth of nine CDs in this essential series of Billie Holiday's studio recordings of 1933-1942 features the great tenor Lester Young on eight of the 16 performances. Pres and Lady Day make a perfect match on "I'll Get By" (although altoist Johnny Hodges steals the honors on that song), "Mean to Me," "Easy Living," "Me, Myself and I," and "A Sailboat in the Moonlight." Other strong selections without Young include "Moanin' Low," "Let's Call the Whole Thing Off," and "Where Is the Sun?" It's highly recommended, along with all of the other CDs in this perfectly done Billie Holiday reissue program. —*Scott Yanow*

☆ **The Quintessential Billie Holiday, Vol. 5 (1937–1938)** / Jun. 15, 1937-Jan. 27, 1938 / Columbia ◆◆◆◆◆
The fifth of nine CDs in the complete reissue of Billie Holiday's early recordings (sans alternate takes), this great set has 18 selections, all but four featuring tenor saxophonist Lester Young and trumpeter Buck Clayton. Among the classics are "Getting Some Fun Out of Life," "Trav'lin' All Alone," "He's Funny That Way," "My Man," "When You're Smiling" (on which Pres takes a perfect solo), "If Dreams Come True," and "Now They Call It Swing." All nine volumes in this series are highly recommended, but if one can only acquire a single entry, this is the one. —*Scott Yanow*

☆ **The Quintessential Billie Holiday, Vol. 6 (1938)** / May 11, 1938-Nov. 9, 1938 / Columbia ◆◆◆◆◆
The sixth of nine CDs in this very worthy series traces Billie Holiday's recording career throughout much of 1938. Although not containing as many true classics as *Vol. 5*, most of these 18 selections are quite enjoyable, particularly "You Go to My Head," "Having Myself a Time," "The Very Thought of You," and "They Say." All of the sets in this reissue program are recommended, featuring Lady Day when she was youthful and still optimistic about life. —*Scott Yanow*

The Quintessential Billie Holiday, Vol. 7 (1938–1939) / Nov. 28, 1938-Jul. 5, 1939 / Columbia/Legacy ◆◆◆◆◆
By 1939 when the bulk of these 17 selections were recorded, Billie Holiday was dominating her own recordings, allocating less space for her sidemen to solo. This was not really a bad thing since Lady Day's voice was getting stronger each year. On the seventh of

nine CD volumes that reissue all of Holiday's 1933-1942 Columbia recordings (other than the alternate takes which have been bypassed), Holiday sounds at her best on "More than You Know, Sugar" (featuring a superb Benny Carter alto solo), "Long Gone Blues" and "Some Other Spring." It's recommended along with all of the other entries in the *Quintessential* series. —*Scott Yanow*

The Complete Commodore Recordings / Apr. 20, 1939-Apr. 8, 1944 / GRP ◆◆◆
Billie Holiday recorded on four occasions for the Commodore label: once in 1939 (a date that resulted in "Fine and Mellow" and "Strange Fruit") and three sessions in 1944 (dates highlighted by "I Cover the Waterfront," "I'm Yours," "He's Funny That Way," "Billie's Blues," and "On the Sunny Side of the Street"). While the former session has Lady Day joined by a background octet that includes trumpeter Frankie Newton, the Eddie Heywood Sextet forms the nucleus of the later dates. This two-CD set has all 18 selections and no less than 27 alternate takes. Since the great majority of the performances are ballads, and with the exception of pianist Heywood, there are very few instrumental solos, there are no significant differences between the versions. Therefore, this set (as opposed to a single CD of the master takes), even though it is well-conceived, is strictly for completists. —*Scott Yanow*

★ **The Commodore Master Takes** / Apr. 20, 1939-Apr. 8, 1944 / GRP ◆◆◆◆◆
If you're a completist who insists on having everything that Billie Holiday recorded, *The Complete Commodore Recordings* is required listening. But for the more casual listener, it's best to pass on that two-CD set and stick with *The Commodore Master Takes*. While *The Complete Commodore Recordings* contains all of the alternate takes that Holiday recorded for Commodore in 1939 and 1944, this collection only concerns itself with the master takes (which total 16). Holiday never singed an exclusive contract with Commodore—she only freelanced for the label, and the ultra-influential jazz singer spent a lot more time recording for Columbia in the '30s and early '40s, and for Decca from 1944-1950. But her Commodore output was first-rate, and Lady Day excels whether she's joined by trumpeter Frankie Newton's octet at a 1939 session or by pianist Eddie Heywood's orchestra at three sessions in 1944. The CD gets off to an impressive start with the controversial "Strange Fruit," a bone-chilling account of lynching in the Deep South that ended up being released on Commodore because Columbia was afraid to touch it. Holiday is also quite expressive on performances that range from "Fine and Mellow," "I Got a Right to Sing the Blues" and "Yesterdays" in 1939 to "My Old Flame," "Billie's Blues," "I'll Be Seeing You," and "He's Funny That Way" in 1944. For those with even a casual interest in Holiday's legacy, this superb CD is essential listening. —*Alex Henderson*

☆ **The Quintessential Billie Holiday, Vol. 8 (1939–1940)** / Jul. 5, 1939-Sep. 12, 1940 / Columbia/Legacy ◆◆◆◆◆
The eighth of nine volumes that feature all of the master takes from Billie Holiday's Columbia recordings of 1933-1942 is one of the better sets, although all nine CDs are recommended. High points include "Them There Eyes," "Swing, Brother, Swing," "The Man I Love," "Ghost of Yesterday," "Body and Soul," "Falling in Love Again," and "I Hear Music." Among the variety of all-stars backing her, tenor saxophonist Lester Young makes his presence known on eight of the 18 numbers. —*Scott Yanow*

Control Booth Series, Vol. 1: 1940–1941 / Sep. 12, 1940-Mar. 21, 1941 / Jazz Unlimited ◆◆◆
Strictly for completists, this Storyville CD has 25 performances but just ten separate songs; 15 are alternate takes. Slightly more complete than an Affinity box set that covered the 1940 selections, this release surprisingly leaves out one version of "Loveless Love." The music, particularly the originally released versions, is excellent; Lady Day is in fine form, and there are some solos from trumpeter Roy Eldridge, Benny Carter (on clarinet), tenorman Georgie Auld, pianist Teddy Wilson and (on the final session) tenor saxophonist Lester Young. Among the tunes are "I Hear Music," "St. Louis Blues," "Let's Do It" and "Romance in the Dark." Most collectors would be satisfied with just having the regular versions, but one can appreciate slight differences in each rendition, particularly from the soloists. —*Scott Yanow*

The Quintessential Billie Holiday, Vol. 9 (1940–1942) / Oct. 15, 1940-Feb. 10, 1942 / Columbia/Legacy ◆◆◆◆◆
The final volume in this nine-CD series contains all of Billie Holiday's recordings from her final 16 months with the label. Highlights include "St. Louis Blues," "Loveless Love," "Let's Do It," "All of Me" (arguably the greatest version ever of this veteran standard), "Am I Blue," "Gloomy Sunday" and "God Bless the Child." All 153 of Lady Day's Columbia recordings (even the occasional weak item) are well worth hearing and savoring. —*Scott Yanow*

Control Booth Series, Vol. 2 / Mar. 21, 1941-Feb. 10, 1942 / Jazz Unlimited ◆◆◆
This Jazz Unlimited CD (available through Storyville) features multiple takes of Billie Holiday during the last four sessions from her early prime years. Strangely enough, three of the takes, including two masters, are not included on this otherwise complete set. Holiday is heard on such numbers as "All of Me," "God Bless the Child," "Am I Blue," "Gloomy Sunday" and a swinging arrangement of "It's a Sin to Tell a Lie"; other than short spots for trumpeter Emmett Berry and pianist Teddy Wilson (in addition to tenorman Lester Young on "All of Me"), the focus is entirely on Lady Day's voice. The many versions (which include eight that were previously unissued) should greatly interest collectors, but the missing renditions are quite unfortunate. —*Scott Yanow*

Billie's Blues / Jan. 12, 1942-Jan. 5, 1954 / Blue Note ◆◆◆◆◆
Most of this excellent CD features one of Billie Holiday's finest concert recordings of the '50s. Recorded in Europe before an admiring audience, this enjoyable set finds Lady Day performing seven of her standards with her trio and joining in for jam session versions of "Billie's Blues" and "Lover Come Back to Me" with an all-star group starring clarinetist Buddy DeFranco, vibraphonist Red Norvo and guitarist Jimmy Raney. These

performances (which find Holiday in stronger voice than on her studio recordings of the period) have also been included in Verve's massive CD box set. This program concludes with Holiday's four rare sides for Aladdin in 1951 (between her Decca and Verve periods) which are highlighted by two blues and "Detour Ahead," and her 1942 studio recording of "Trav'lin' Light" with Paul Whiteman's Orchestra. *—Scott Yanow*

Fine & Mellow / Jan. 18, 1944-Apr. 15, 1959 / Collectables ♦♦♦

This CD contains 20 selections featuring Billie Holiday in a variety of live performances covering a 15-year period. Starting with two songs in 1944 in which she was backed by the Esquire All-Stars and continuing through TV appearances and club dates, one can hear the gradual aging and decline of Lady Day's voice which definitely took a turn for the worse between 1955-1956. And yet oddly enough the last five numbers, which were performed April 15, 1959 (making them Holiday's final recordings), actually find her sounding stronger than she had in a few years, perhaps in a final gasp of energy. Of great historical value, this set has plenty of strong moments to justify its acquisition. *—Scott Yanow*

☆ **The Complete Decca Recordings** / Oct. 4, 1944-Mar. 8, 1950 / GRP ♦♦♦♦♦

Billie Holiday is heard at her absolute best on this attractive two-CD set. During her period on Decca, Lady Day was accompanied by strings (for the first time), large studio orchestras, and even background vocalists, so jazz solos from her sidemen are few. But her voice was at its strongest during the '40s (even with her personal problems) and to hear all 50 of her Decca performances (including alternate takes and even some studio chatter) is a real joy. Among the high points of this essential set are her original versions of "Lover Man" (Holiday's biggest selling record), "Don't Explain," "Good Morning Heartache," "'Tain't Nobody's Business if I Do," "Now or Never," "Crazy He Calls Me," and remakes of "Them There Eyes" and "God Bless the Child." *—Scott Yanow*

☆ **The Complete Billie Holiday on Verve 1945–1959** / Feb. 12, 1945-Mar. 1, 1959 / Verve ♦♦♦♦♦

This is a rather incredible collection: ten CDs enclosed in a tight black box that includes every one of the recordings Verve owns of Billie Holiday, not only the many studio recordings of 1952-1957 (which feature Lady Day joined by such jazz all-stars as trumpeters Charlie Shavers and Harry "Sweets" Edison, altoist Benny Carter, and the tenors of Flip Phillips, Paul Quinichette and Ben Webster). Also included are prime performances at Jazz at the Philharmonic concerts in 1945-1947, an enjoyable European gig from 1954, her "comeback" Carnegie Hall concert of 1956, Holiday's rather sad final studio album from 1959, and even lengthy tapes from two informal rehearsals. It's a perfect purchase for the true Billie Holiday fanatic. *—Scott Yanow*

Verve Jazz Masters 47: Sings Standards / Feb. 12, 1945-Mar. 1959 / Verve ♦♦♦

Of Verve's countless number of Billie Holiday samplers, this one—which is actually a second helping from the *Jazz Masters* series—is as good as any of them artistically. Like many of its cousins on the shelves, this one takes in the whole cross-section of Holiday's recordings for Norman Granz from an exuberant 1945 JATP concert all the way to her last poignant sessions with the Ray Ellis string orchestra in 1959. Unlike them, this one does not contain songs with which Billie is inextricably tied, but all of the well-worn standards are given the inimitable Holiday stamp, often in league with many of Granz's legendary soloists. Of course, this is the most troubling period for Holiday scholars, for her voice was going downhill fast in the '50s, yet one has to admit that her Verve recordings often pack an emotional wallop that eclipse most of the earlier ones. A few random highlights: the JATP "All of Me" and "Body and Soul" from the mid-'40s, with Holiday in fresh voice and a whole bunch of star horns wailing in tangled contrapuntal splendor underneath; and a "When It's Sleepy Time Down South" from the Ray Ellis sessions where the combination of Holiday's broken-down voice and exquisite phrasing will break your heart. Verve's thorough discographical entries, here and in the entire Jazz Masters series, are exemplary for what is, after all, an inexpensive sampler for newcomers to jazz. *—Richard S. Ginell*

Lady in Autumn: The Best of the Verve Years / Apr. 1946-Mar. 1959 / Verve ♦♦♦♦♦

There are many jazz lovers, even dedicated ones, who cannot afford to part with the $150 or so that the ten-disc *Complete Billie Holiday on Verve* commands, so this two-disc distillation will do very nicely as a detailed summary of her troubled, soulful Verve period. Set out in chronological order with a mighty overreaching sweep, this mini-box covers virtually the entire period, with a generous helping of the JATP events of the '40s, jumping a few years into the jazz all-star backings of the '50s and the 1956 Carnegie Hall concert, and closing with her heartbreakingly ravaged final sessions with Ray Ellis' string orchestra. Along the way, several Holiday landmark tunes like "Don't Explain," "God Bless the Child," "Lover Man," "Fine and Mellow," and "He's Funny That Way" are revisited and reinterpreted from a bitter, lifeworn perspective. But not all is stark tragedy, for life-affirming tracks like the 1957 "Stars Fell On Alabama" and "Gee Baby, Ain't I Good to You" add some balance to the picture. For very sensitive listeners, 128 minutes of Lady Day in her twilight years may well be all they'll need. *—Richard S. Ginell*

Billie Holiday at Storyville / Oct. 29, 1951-1953 / 1201 Music ♦♦♦

Billie Holiday is in generally good form for this club appearance. On most of the selections she is accompanied by the Carl Drinkard Trio but six others find her joined by Buster Harding's Trio; the great tenor Stan Getz sits in on three of these numbers, making one wish that he and Lady Day had collaborated more extensively. This set of standards (most of which had been recorded previously by Holiday) are not up to the quality of her Decca output but are enjoyable nevertheless. *—Scott Yanow*

The Billie Holiday Songbook / 1952-1958 / Verve ♦♦♦

Excellent play on the songbook trend, with Holiday doing her own material. *—Ron Wynn*

Lady Sings the Blues / 1954-1956 / Verve ♦♦♦

Immaculate 1954 and 1956 recordings with an all-star lineup and smashing Holiday cuts. One of her last great dates. *—Ron Wynn*

All or Nothing at All / 1955 / Verve ♦♦♦♦♦

This two-disc set features some of Billie Holiday's top Verve performances from the mid-'50s. Over the course of 28 cuts, she runs the emotional gamut from summery optimism ("Love Is Here to Stay") to pathos-rich musings ("Ill Wind"). Befitting her perennial after-hours mood while at the label, the majority of songs here feature Holiday in a low-down mood of the highest order: her versions of "Moonlight in Vermont" and "A Foggy Day" are classics of the jazz vocal tradition. And the supporting cast isn't bad either, what with the likes of Harry Eddison, Barney Kessel, Ben Webster, and Jimmy Rowles tagging along. A gem. *—Stephen Cook*

Songs for Distingué Lovers / Jun. 6, 1956-Jun. 7, 1956 / Verve ♦♦♦

During the six days and four sessions covered by this 1997 CD (which in its original form consisted of six songs), Billie Holiday recorded 18 titles; a dozen of the best are here, although "Comes Love" is unaccountably missing. This were the last series of extensive small-group recordings that Lady Day would make in the studios. Although her voice was largely shot at this point, she puts so much feeling into some of the lyrics that one can often overlook her dark sound. The all-star band (trumpeter Harry "Sweets" Edison, tenor saxophonist Ben Webster, pianist Jimmy Rowles, guitarist Barney Kessel, bassist Red Mitchell, and Alvin Stoller or Larry Bunker on drums) is a major asset, and there are plenty of short solos for Edison, Webster and Kessel. Holiday does her best on such numbers as "A Foggy Day," "One for My Baby," "Just One of Those Things" and "I Wished on the Moon," and there are plenty of haunting moments, even if one could tell (even at the time) that the end was probably drawing near for the singer. The music is still well worth having, although completists will prefer a collection with all 18 songs, while beginners should sample Holiday's Columbia and Decca output first. *—Scott Yanow*

Lady in Satin / Feb. 19, 1958-Feb. 21, 1958 / Columbia ♦♦♦♦♦

This is the most controversial of all Billie Holiday records. Lady Day herself said that this session (which finds her accompanied by Ray Ellis' string orchestra) was her personal favorite, and many listeners have found her emotional versions of such songs as "I'm a Fool to Want You," "You Don't Know What Love Is," "Glad to Be Unhappy" and particularly "You've Changed" to be quite touching. But Holiday's voice was essentially gone by 1958, and although not yet 43, she could have passed for 73. Ellis' arrangements do not help, veering close to Muzak; most of this record is very difficult to listen to. Late in life, Billie Holiday expressed the pain of life so effectively that her croaking voice had become almost unbearable to hear. The 1997 CD reissue adds two alternate takes of "I'm a Fool to Want You," part of which were used for the original released rendition, plus the stereo version of "The End of a Love Affair" (only previously released in mono) and examples of Lady Day rehearsing the latter song, including a long unaccompanied stretch. There is certainly a wide range of opinion as to the value of this set. *—Scott Yanow*

Stay With Me / 1959 / Verve ♦♦♦♦♦

A 1991 reissue from late in Billie Holiday's career. She was fading, but hadn't lost the dramatic quality in her delivery, nor her ability to project and tell a shattering story. She's backed by trumpeter Charlie Shavers, pianist Oscar Peterson, guitarist Herb Ellis, bassist Ray Brown, and drummer Ed Shaughnessy. The CD reissue has three bonus cuts. *—Ron Wynn*

V-Disc Recordings: A Musical Contribution By America's Best for Our Armed Forces Overseas / Jun. 16, 1998 / Collectors' Choice Music ♦♦♦♦

Billie Holiday's reputation as a jazz singer is such that any newly unearthed recordings are historically valuable. Her performances of nine songs for the '40s-era V-Disc program presented here could do with more annotation (for example, when did they take place exactly?), or even any at all, and one wishes they ran longer than 30 minutes. Also, some of them sound suspiciously like previously released recordings. But Holiday nevertheless is wonderful on some of her familiar tunes, notably a medley (or is it just an odd edit?) of "Do Nothin' Till You Hear From Me" and "I'll Get By" recorded live before a large, enthusiastic audience. Distributor Collectors' Choice Music notes in its catalog that Holiday is accompanied by the Louis Armstrong Orchestra on "Don't Explain," though this is not claimed on the disc itself. Actually, Armstrong introduces her and she is then backed by a solo piano. But Armstrong is clearly also present on "Do You Know What It Means to Miss New Orleans"—he duets with her. Both tracks appear to come from a promotional show for their 1947 film *New Orleans*. Holiday's other backing units are accomplished. Wonder who they are. For a price under ten dollars, the album is a reasonable value for the money. *— William Ruhlmann*

Greatest Hits / Nov. 17, 1998 / Columbia/Legacy ♦♦♦

There's something scandalous about the fact that this 13-song CD is, as of spring 2000, the only upgrade to date of Columbia Records' holdings on Billie Holiday. It's good as far as it goes, as part of Sony Music's 20-bit remastering of the highlights of its jazz catalog, but it makes one wonder how long listeners have to wait for the nine volumes of *The Quintessential Billie Holiday* to be upgraded for sound. These tracks were all recorded between July 2, 1935, and August 7, 1941; originally cut for Brunswick, Vocalion, and OKeh and now owned by Columbia, they represent highlights from her association with producer John Hammond. They feature Holiday working with Teddy Wilson, Benny Goodman, Johnny Hodges, Roy Eldridge, and Ben Webster on the earliest tracks; an early hook-up with Artie Shaw; samples of her collaborations with Lester Young and Buck Clayton; the rest of the core of the Count Basie Orchestra working as Billie Holiday and Her Orchestra; and her renditions of "God Bless the Child," "Solitude," "Gloomy Sunday," and "Body and Soul" from the early '40s. It's fascinating to hear the sampling of material featured here and the gradual darkening of Holiday's voice over the six years covered by this collection. There are gaps, of course, and it's interesting that the notes, apart from saying precious little of substance about the music or the recordings, never explain what is not here or why ("Strange Fruit," for example). This 13-song sampler is a decent overview of some highlights of her early work, with ample room for the soloists in her band, and a fine body of blues-influenced swing. Now if Sony would only go back and redo the rest of her catalogs. *—Bruce Eder*

1945–1948 / May 4, 1999 / Classics ♦♦♦♦♦
Trading in the loose combo swing of her Columbia recordings for some sophisticated charts by Sy Oliver and Gordon Jenkins, Billie Holiday cut some of her best sides while at Decca during the latter half of the '40s. And even though Decca's own two-disc *Complete Recordings* set is highly recommended, this single volume still offers a fine overview for those not quite ready to fully commit. The absence of "God Bless the Child" notwithstanding, the mix covers most of Lady Day's Decca highlights, including "Deep Song," "Big Stuff," "Porgy," and her own "Don't Explain." There's also some quality duet work with Louis Armstrong and fine contributions from clarinetist Edmond Hall, trumpeter Billy Butterfield, and guitarist Mundell Lowe. A fine and generous sampling of Holiday at her peak. *—Stephen Cook*

★ **Lady Day: The Best of Billie Holiday** / Sep. 28, 2001 / Columbia/Legacy ♦♦♦♦♦
Forget for a moment that *The Best of Lady Day: The Best of Billie Holiday* was tied into the release of the superb box set *Lady Day: The Complete Billie Holiday on Columbia*, thereby offering a bit of advertisement to the full-fledged set. That doesn't matter—even if there was never a box set, this would have been a welcome addition to Billie Holiday's catalog, since it's the first concise, yet comprehensive, introduction to her groundbreaking, perhaps greatest, recordings. Over the course of two discs, nearly all of her finest moments for Columbia are chronicled (along with a handful of rarities to entice the curious to the big box), providing a welcome summary for serious listeners on a budget. Prior to this release, the Columbia recordings were available either individually, as part of the *Quintessential* series, or on haphazard single-disc collections. This provides a logical, thorough overview of her acknowledged peak at Columbia (meaning that there's nothing from *Lady in Satin*) and that may be enough for serious listeners who don't have the money or inclination to delve into the full box. *—Stephen Thomas Erlewine*

☆ **Lady Day: The Complete Billie Holiday on Columbia (1933–1944)** / Oct. 2001 / Columbia/Legacy ♦♦♦♦♦
When Sony/Columbia began its ambitious Legacy reissue project, those who followed their jazz titles knew it was only a question of time before the massive Billie Holiday catalog under their ownership would see the light in its entirety. The question was how? Years before there was a host of box sets devoted to her material, but the sound on those left something to be desired. Would they remaster the material in two- or three-disc sets with additional notes? Would it be one disc at a time? Would the material be issued as budget or midline material or at full price? The last item could be ruled out based on the label's aggressive and very thorough packages of single discs by Charles Mingus, Miles Davis, Duke Ellington, and others. As for the box set issues, how could one successfully package this material with all of the foreign issues in a way that made sense? Again, there were fine precedents in the box set packages of the Miles Davis and Louis Armstrong packages, which are impeccably remastered, designed, and presented—six Grammy's worth.

The answer lies in this lavishly designed ten-CD package that looks on the outside like a 78 album sleeve with a tucked book of notes, track annotations, and rare photographs, and a deck of wondrously remastered CDs that are sequenced in such a way that the entire Columbia story is told in a way that not only makes sense, but is compelling in its revelations of Holiday's development as a vocalist and an interpreter of songs from 1933. The story begins with her first two recordings for the label with Benny Goodman in November and December of 1933, moves to two years later when she recorded another session, and ends some 43 sessions later in 1944 with her own band that starred Roy Eldridge, Barney Bigard, Art Tatum, Oscar Pettiford, and Sidney Catlett. These include a pair of V-disc recordings from that year. In all, this set contains 230 tracks. There are 153 masters recorded for Columbia and its subsidiaries, like Brunswick, Vocalion, OKeh, and Harmony. Thirty-five of these tracks have never before been issued in the United States, and those masters are included here beginning on CD seven and continuing throughout to the end of disc ten.

Musically, it is inarguable that these 11 years were the high point of Ms. Holiday's career, the stunning recordings she did with her own band that featured some of the greatest legends in jazz as well as those recorded with Teddy Wilson, Benny Goodman, Benny Carter, Count Basie, Eddie Heywood, and even one with Duke Ellington's band in 1935 ("Saddest Tale") from Ellington's *Symphony in Black* recording session. Musicians like Hot Lips Page, Don Byas, Kenny Clarke, Ben Webster, Lester Young, Charlie Shavers, Freddie Greene, Jo Jones, Cozy Cole, Chu Berry, Henry "Red" Allen, Bud Freeman, Milt Hinton, Buck Clayton, Johnny Hodges, and literally dozens of others contribute to the development of the Holiday legend.

What may appear confusing at the outset makes great sense as the set progresses. The first six discs are master takes recorded either with her orchestra or the other groups mentioned. Disc seven begins laying out the alternate takes and airchecks and personnel crisscrosses all over the set. While this might be irritating to some listeners, it serves a twofold purpose: one is that the integrity of the American masters is preserved, and the second is that the alternates and check-ins can be heard in a sequence that makes sense historically and aesthetically. Since these too are laid out chronologically as alternates, it's a pleasure to listen to them rather than wading through five or six or even two takes of the same song laid back to back. It's also on the alternates, far from the masters, that we get a different perspective on process and development, not only in terms of Holiday's singing, but also the different accents added or deleted from the orchestral accompaniment. Lastly, being able to go back and forth in these takes, we get to witness the sharp juxtaposition of her development as a singer from the raw, early bluesy material influenced deeply by Bessie Smith to the master songstress who could nuance a maximum emotion from just a few notes, smoothly and without a trace of edginess.

The unissued masters are a cipher. Literally, it is confounding that these recordings were previously unavailable here in that they mark her reunion with Benny Goodman or other fine sessions with Basie or her vocal collaborations with Johnny Mercer in 1939. In many ways the purchase of the set is worth it for discs nine and ten alone, as well as the killer packaging.

Lastly, it would be shameful not to make mention of the truly amazing liner notes by the esteemed Gary Giddins. He needs no more accolades, but his writing here paints a far bigger portrait of Ms. Holiday's contribution and her era than any previously published. It's a biographical essay written with a critic's eye and holds no punches where Ms. Holiday's particular strengths and limitations lie, and he voices his own surprise at hearing certain things on the set he was previously unfamiliar with. This is a new standard in what liner notes for these kinds of projects should aim for: humanizing a legend and cultural myth and making the contribution stand out somehow as something that exists almost in spite of whatever the human being's life was like.

There is also a fine cultural and socio-historical essay by Professor Farah Griffin from Columbia University. Her approach is Holiday's influence trans-aesthetically, her influence upon other singers, writers, painters, and photographers. It's a provocative read and is not written in the dread academy's attempt at communicable language. Griffin writes with heart and directness of purpose. There are tough arguments made here, but she makes them with grace and she makes them plainly. Finally, producer Michael Brooks provides—along with an introductory essay—a track-by-track analysis with all the data a jazz historian or musicologist could ever want, including matrix numbers.

This set finally puts Ms. Holiday's massive contribution to 20th century art in fitting perspective. There are untold hours to spend listening here for the fanatic or the foundling. The package is worthy of your coffee table instead of a book of photographs of who knows what, and the wealth of knowledge it provides about the history of jazz is literally incalculable. *—Thom Jurek*

Body and Soul / Mar. 12, 2002 / Verve ♦♦♦
This session comes from close to the end of the line (1959) in the erstwhile swinging company of Barney Kessel on guitar, Ben Webster on tenor, and naysayers will be quick to point out that "Lady Day" wasn't in peak form here. But Billie Holiday with some of the platinum chipped off the pipes is still *way* better than a bunch of finger-snappin' wannabes any day. Her interpretations of the title cut, "Let's Call the Whole Thing Off," and "Darn That Dream" hold you in the palm of her hand with their gentle swing and the band support here is never less than stellar. This Mobile Fidelity reissue (also available as an audiophile vinyl pressing) features in-the-control-room sound that makes this session sound even cozier. The Lady sings and swings. [The 2002 reissue features three different versions of "Comes Love."] *—Cub Koda*

A Musical Romance / Jul. 23, 2002 / Columbia/Legacy ♦♦♦♦
A Musical Romance gathers some of the most romantic songs Billie Holiday recorded with Lester Young, including "The Man I Love," "Time on My Hands (You in My Arms)," "I Must Have That Man," and "Who Wants Love?" Essentially a collection of some of the love songs featured on the excellent *Lady Day: The Complete Billie Holiday on Columbia (1933–1944)* box set, *A Musical Romance* offers a more focused—and, arguably, easily digested—way to explore the romantic side of her music. Though much of her work dealt with love won and lost, her collaborations with Young are especially lively and alluring, "He's Funny That Way," "A Sailboat in the Moonlight," and "Back in Your Own Backyard" chief among them. A charming and concise collection, *A Fine Romance* presents some of the very best moments from Holiday and Young's time together. *—Heather Phares*

Blue Billie / Jul. 23, 2002 / Columbia/Legacy ♦♦♦♦
Blue Billie collects some of the legendary songstress' best-known ballads and blues-inflected songs, including "Gloomy Sunday," "Billie's Blues," "Am I Blue?," and "God Bless the Child." Culled from the *Lady Day: The Complete Billie Holiday on Columbia* box set, this compilation offers a more focused—and, arguably, manageable—look at the way Holiday brought her own personal experiences to her work. "Long Gone Blues," "Why Was I Born?," "Moanin' Low," and the other tracks here are beautifully painful and painfully beautiful expressions of Holiday's talent. A casual or new fan looking to explore the brooding side of her work would be wise to investigate *Blue Billie*. *—Heather Phares*

Lady Day Swings / Jul. 23, 2002 / Columbia/Legacy ♦♦♦♦
Lady Day Swings collects some of the legendary songstress' best-known swing performances, including "What a Little Midnight Can Do," "Nice Work If You Can Get It," "Them There Eyes," and "I've Got My Love to Keep Me Warm." Culled from the *Lady Day: The Complete Billie Holiday on Columbia* box set, this compilation offers a more focused—and, arguably, easily digested—way to explore how Holiday brought her own personal experiences to her work. "Miss Brown to You," "A Fine Romance," and the other tracks here showcase the playfully alluring side of her work. A casual or new fan looking to explore the lively, charming aspects of Holiday's work would be wise to investigate *Lady Day Swings*. *—Heather Phares*

Tony Hollins

b. 1900, Clarksdale, MS, **d.** 1959, Chicago, IL
Vocals, Guitar / Acoustic Blues
Cited as a major influence by no less than John Lee Hooker, Delta blues singer/guitarist Tony Hollins was born in Clarksdale, MS, around the turn of the century. Few details are known of Hollins' life; he cut his first recordings for OKeh in 1941, with his fluid, insis-

tent performance of "Crawlin' King Snake" serving as the blueprint for Hooker's own later rendition. His "Traveling Man Blues" was also later appropriated by Hooker for his "When My Wife Quit Me"; clearly admired by his peers, Hollins never caught on as a popular favorite, and after another session in 1951, he gradually drifted out of music, focusing instead on his day job as a barber. He died in Chicago in 1959. —*Jason Ankeny*

The Holmes Brothers

f. 1980, New York, NY
Group / Retro-Soul, Modern Electric Blues, Soul-Blues
The Holmes Brothers' unique synthesis of gospel-inflected blues harmonies, accompanied by good drumming and rhythm-based guitar playing, gives them a down-home rural feeling that no other touring blues group can duplicate.

Brothers Sherman and Wendell Holmes, along with drummer Popsy Dixon (the falsetto voice), are the group's core members, although they occasionally tour with extra musicians. All three harmonize well together. The Holmes Brothers are so versatile, they're booked solid every summer at folk, blues, gospel and jazz festivals, as they play a style of music that is a gumbo of church tunes, blues and soul. Although people like Bo Diddley and especially Jimmy Reed were early influences on Wendell and Sherman, gospel music also played an important role in their respective upbringings.

Although they'd been performing in Harlem for years, the Holmes Brothers—originally from Christchurch, VA—have only recently become international blues touring stars. Thanks to a fair deal at Rounder Records, the group has released three recordings for that label, beginning with a 1990 release, *In the Spirit*. When this album made waves and got them off and running on the festival and club circuit around the U.S. and Europe, they followed it up two years later with *Where It's At* (1991), *Soul Street* (1993), and *Promised Land* (1997). The group's career has been aided by the interest of people like Peter Gabriel, who recruited them for his WOMAD (world music) festivals in England and who also recorded them in a gospel context on the album *Jubilation*, for his Real World subsidiary of Virgin Records in 1992. Joan Osborne was also a supporter of the group. Early in her career Osborne befriended the Holmes Brothers and eventually took them on tour as her backing band when she opened for Bob Dylan in 1997. She produced the group's first release on Alligator Records *Speaking in Tongues* in 2001. —*Richard Skelly & Al Campbell*

In the Spirit / 1990 / Rounder ✦✦✦✦✦
The Holmes Brothers' voices are too potent, their harmonies too smashing and their love of vintage sounds too immense for them to be content with producer-dominated, softer urban contemporary sounds. This set included some riveting gospel tunes like "None But The Righteous" and "Up Above My Head," plus a credible (if a little lengthy) version of "When Something Is Wrong With My Baby" and the tighter, hard-hitting tunes "Please Don't Hurt Me," "Ask Me No Questions" and "The Final Round." If straight-ahead, rousing shared leads and booming harmonies interest you, The Holmes Brothers do it the way they used to throughout the South in the '60s and '70s. —*Ron Wynn*

Where It's At / 1991 / Rounder ✦✦✦✦
Their second release contained 11 more wonderful tunes that easily moved from surging R&B to rousing blues with an occasional venture into gospel or country. They covered "Drown In My Own Tears" and "High Heel Sneakers" and had the requisite qualities for each one down pat, as well as "Never Let Me Go," "The Love You Save," and "I Saw The Light." But their own numbers, like "I've Been A Loser" and the title track, were even better, displaying a contemporary sensibility and classic style and sound. —*Ron Wynn*

Jubilation / 1992 / Real World ✦✦✦
Jubilation is a revealing, wonderful collection of the Holmes Brothers' distinctive soul. The brothers tie together a seemingly disconnected array of styles—everything from straightforward blues, R&B, and gospel to worldbeat and country—and come up with a cohesive whole. Even when the group delves into soukous or works with a Chinese flautist, it manages to retain the pure qualities of American blues and R&B. —*Thom Owens*

Soul Street / 1993 / Rounder ✦✦✦✦✦
This album continued The Holmes Brothers' tradition of doing tremendous covers ("You're Gonna Make Me Cry," "Down In Virginia" and "Fannie Mae"), authentic originals ("I Won't Hurt You Anymore," "Dashboard Bar") and adding gospel ("Walk In The Light") and honky-tonk ("There Goes My Everything") into their blend. There's little to criticize about The Holmes Brothers; their sound, vocals and harmonies aren't laid-back or restrained, and everything they sing is done with exuberance and integrity. It may not be commercially viable, but it's musically sound. —*Ron Wynn*

Promised Land / 1997 / Rounder ✦✦✦✦
The Holmes Brothers have honed their blend of rock, blues, gospel and soul to perfection on this, their fifth release. Whether it's Popsy Dixon's stunning interpretation of Tom Waits' "Train Song," the soul stirring harmonies on the gospel standard "I Surrender All," or an original, gritty guitar workout like "Start Stoppin'," there is simply not a bad song on this album. The Holmes Brothers continue to defy all classifications, except one: damn good music. —*Steve McMullen*

Speaking in Tongues / Jan. 30, 2001 / Alligator ✦✦✦✦✦
The sixth album by New York's Holmes Brothers is another all-spirituals set—though not in the traditional sense of the word. Produced by pop singer Joan Osborne (before she was a superstar, Osborne woodshedded with the Brothers and developed a fine rootsy singing style of her own), who was there in the Manhattan trenches with the band, this set goes a long, long way to capturing raw, excruciating grooves. With the a trio of singers as soulful as any group Memphis or Motown ever produced, the Holmes Brothers take it to the gut each and every time. This set opens with Ben Harper's "Homeless Child," and let's just say after the deep, grease-fire funk the vocalizing creates, Harper should never play it again. This song now *belongs* to the Holmes Brothers. Sherman Holmes' groove on his "Speaking in Tongues" borrows a piece of a Rick James bassline and builds an entire

gospel-funk number on top of it. This might not be the song you'd hear in church, but you should—you might actually go. With a six-voice chorus kicking the refrain through every single barrier between spirituality and carnality, weight is lent to the notion that this Jesus that Sherman sings of is a flesh-and-blood Jesus, inspiring devotion and reverence in the everyday world. Osborne is able to accomplish what no other producer who has worked with this band has been able to do: She leaves their sound alone. Its rough edges, knotty corners, and rough-hewn grace are all displayed without reservation or apology. This is the band's barroom sound enhanced with a trio of female voices who, if anything, make it more raucous, more slippery, and somehow nastier, even though this is sanctified music. It's body music that seeks to transcend the body. Thank God it hasn't yet.

Their Memphis soul-styled reading of Sister Rosetta Tharpe's "Can't No Grave Hold My Body Down" is revelatory. Taking her already deep blues and chunking it up with Wendell's wah-wahed guitar, and with Rob Arthur doubling on rhythm loops and funky organ, the thing threatens to lift right off the ground. Only the Precious Three anchor the tune's body to its heart and keep it earthbound. And besides the Holmes' originals, another definitive reading of Harper's "I Want to Be Ready," and Bob Dylan's "Man of Peace," their radical reworking of Gamble and Huff's classic disco-gospel tune "Love Train" is confounding in its essentialism. It takes the harmony of the original tune and uses it to drop the melody out; it's replaced with a different shuffling rhythm and a Curtis Mayfield-styled chorus. With the Holmes Brothers, the song becomes an anthem of a different kind. Only Wendell, Sherman, and Popsy Dixon could take secular material and redeem it without stretching the truth. If anything, they inject truth directly into the meaning of a song that merely implies it. And they do so with such openness and beauty, without judgment or musical one-upmanship, that their courteous grace is apparent everywhere.

This is the finest of the Holmes Brothers' recordings to make the street. It will be too bad if critics fault them for using Osborne as a producer, when she was uniquely qualified to bring their vision to the public. She's done a fine job, and one can only hope some of her fans will take notice of the greatest soul/gospel/blues/funk group on the planet. Awesome. —*Thom Jurek*

● **Righteous! The Essential Collection** / Jul. 16, 2002 / Rounder ✦✦✦✦✦
Andy Breslau described the Holmes Brothers' music as "gospel-infused doo wop funk," which pretty much captures the spirit and synthesis of their style. Combining old R&B, soul, and gospel, brothers Sherman and Wendell Holmes along with Popsy Dixon create a rich sound filled with lovely harmony. The intensity of the group's studio performances evokes a live feel, offering an inkling of what their performances at Lynch's in Manhattan must have sounded like during the '80s. *Righteous!* collects almost 75 minutes of material from the group's four Rounder albums, beginning with *In the Spirit* in 1990 and ending with *Promised Land* in 1997. The album kicks off with a bit of electric blues topped with a healthy dose of soul on "Got Myself Together," a song that jumps out of the gate at a gallop and holds to a steady gait for five minutes. Gospel-drenched pieces like "Promised Land," complete with electric guitar, will have non-believers singing along, while classics like "There Goes My Everything" combine classic soul with a touch of country. One also wouldn't want to miss the Holmes Brothers' takes on Tom Waits' "Train Song" and the Beatles' "And I Love Her." Breslau's liner notes, which travel back to the Holmes Brothers' residency at Lynch's, are both edifying and fun to read. While all of the albums the Holmes Brothers recorded for Rounder are worthy efforts, *Righteous!* offers a solid introduction to anyone who has missed out on their wonderful music. —*Ronnie D. Lankford Jr.*

Rick Holmstrom

b. May 30, 1965, Fairbanks, AK
Guitar / Contemporary Blues
Take a clean-cut boy-next-door type, stick a guitar in his hands, and place him in an environment of smoky, dimly lit bars surrounded by a bunch of blues sages. If you think it's fiction, you don't know Rick Holmstrom, who has been working with some of the best of the Los Angeles blues scene.

His father was a disc jockey in Alaska and baptized Holmstrom with music by bringing home records of Chuck Berry, Muddy Waters, the Ventures, and Buddy Holly. After moving to Southern California to attend school in 1985, he joined a garage-type blues band which rekindled his musical flame. Holmstrom began seeking live blues at places like the Pioneer Club, Babe & Ricky's, and the Pure Pleasure Club, which became his training ground through hanging out with greats such as Smokey Wilson and Junior Watson.

From 1985 to 1988, Holmstrom played and toured with harmonica guru William Clarke. During part of this period, Holmstrom spent a year as a rhythm guitarist only. Befriended by a former Delta bluesman, harpist Johnny Dyer, the duo recorded two earth-shaking albums for Black Top, 1994's *Listen Up!*, followed by *Shake It!* in 1995. When Alex Schultz gave his notice to Rod Piazza & the Mighty Flyers, Holmstrom was the obvious choice, as he worked with Rod on numerous occasions. Urged by Hammond Scott of Black Top Records, Holmstrom recorded *Lookout!* in 1996, an all-instrumental album that garnered airplay on blues and rock radio, sounding like hard-boiled blues instead of a clichéd blues-rock conglomeration. Holmstrom brought a much-needed blaze of fire to the Flyers, whose 1997 Tone Cool album, *Tough and Tender*, proves Rod and his group the hottest band on the circuit. The Holmstrom solo effort *Gonna Get Wild* followed in the spring of 2000. —*Char Ham*

Lookout! / 1996 / Black Top ✦✦✦✦
If you ever wanted to know where the spirit of the late Earl Hooker went, it's in the capable hands of young Rick Holstrom. All instrumental albums are a rarity in blues, but Holmstrom's inventive ideas are top notch, making each track stand mightily on its own. Perhaps better known for his excellent backing work behind harmonica ace Johnny Dyer (six of the tracks here are culled from Dyer's two Black Top releases), Rick steps to the plate on the debut release and connects with a home run. A real treat is "Rub It," a

stripped down barn burner with just drums and rub board in support of Holmstrom's blazing guitar work. *—Cub Koda*

● **Gonna Get Wild** / Mar. 21, 2000 / Tone-Cool ♦♦♦♦♦
Los Angeles axeman Rick Holstrom, best known for his work with Rod Piazza & the Mighty Flyers, delivers an album full of diversity on this, his first Tone-Cool release. The 13 songs included on *Gonna Get Wild* play out like a catalog of guitar stylings, running from the uptempo blues of "I'd Hate to See You Cry" to the sounds of swing and early rock & roll. Holstrom is able to pull off the different styles with ease and finesse, playing in rich, clean tones without overdoing it on the distortion. That's one reason why his songs have the uncanny ability to sound both retro and modern simultaneously.

On "Phlazzbo," Holstrom turns up the Latin rhythm, while "Have You Seen My Girl" delves into the New Orleans flavorings of zydeco. On "Lovin' Ways," a variation on the theme delivered by Jay McShann's "Hootie Blues," Holstrom swings to beat the band. "Lost in the Shuffle" is a fine swing-shuffle, with some excellent sax and a foot-tapping beat.

Rick brings in some top of the line guests on the album, including the aforementioned Rod and Honey Piazza, and the Mighty Flyers rhythm section including Bill Stuve (bass) and Steve Mugalian (drums), Jeff Turmes (ex-James Hartman Band), Andy Kaulkin (piano), Junior Watson, Johnny Dyer, Juke Logan (organ), Kad Kadison (tenor sax), Chris Hunter, Bobby Horton, Teddy Morgan, Henry Carvajal, Curtis Cunningham, and Steve Marsh (tenor sax). In an interesting new move, Holstrom steps up to the mike to sing lead vocals on eight of the tracks for the first time, and he sounds great. It kind of makes you wonder why he hasn't taken to the mike before.

The most refreshing quality about Rick Holstrom is the fact that he delivers music with technical savvy and traditional stylings, without sacrificing originality and pure adventure. And his knack for creating a melody line is unparalleled, and his open attitude toward varied musical genres paint a clear image of greatness in Holstom's immediate future. *—Michael Smith*

Hydraulic Groove / Jul. 16, 2002 / Tone-Cool ♦♦♦

Scott Holt

b. Jun. 26, 1966, Lawrenceburg, TN
Bass, Guitar / Blues-Rock, Modern Electric Blues
Blues guitarist and longtime Buddy Guy sideman Scott Holt was born June 26, 1966, in Lawrenceburg, TN; he did not begin learning guitar until the age of 20, but proved a quick study, seeking his earliest inspiration in the music of Jimi Hendrix and Stevie Ray Vaughan. Ultimately, Holt's chief influence was Buddy Guy, whom he first met after a show in 1987; the two collaborated infrequently in the months to follow, and in the autumn of 1989, Holt was invited to join Guy's band. Three years later, he formed his own group, the Scott Holt Band, to hone his chops during Guy's breaks from the road; in 1998 he cut his first headlining album, *Messing With the Kid*, followed a year later by *Dark of the Night. Angels in Exile* appeared in spring 2001. *—Jason Ankeny*

● **Dark of the Night** / Aug. 24, 1999 / Lightyear ♦♦♦
Give Scott Holt credit for trying to breathe life into the modern electric blues with his second album, *Dark of the Night.* He is clearly indebted to tradition—he spent over a decade as a sideman for Buddy Guy, and he performs not only with his band but with Stevie Ray Vaughan's Double Trouble and the Jimi Hendrix Experience as backing bands—but he never mimics his predecessors, even if he's covering "Crosstown Traffic." His guitar is lively and vibrant, projecting more of synthesis of various styles rather than duplication. Holt also chooses some unusual songs, opening the album with Prince's "Five Women" and the Clash's "Train in Vain (Stand By Me)." All of these departures from the norm are quite welcome, as is Holt's strong musicianship, but the record is occasionally bogged down by his strained, bluesy vocalizing, which unfortunately comes to the forefront on such interesting choices as "Train in Vain." Even with this weakness, however, the record has a considerable amount of life and style—enough to make it a satisfying step forward from Holt. *—Stephen Thomas Erlewine*

Angels in Exile / May 8, 2001 / Spitfire ♦♦
Longtime Buddy Guy sideman Scott Holt certainly doesn't suffer from a lack of talent. He's got the voice, the chops, and the look to be the next "great white hope" of the blues world. What Holt lacks is direction. This album is full of bristling guitar work and strong vocal stylings. What's missing is a sense of identity. Holt rips through a selection of house-rockers and choice cover songs without ever letting the listener know what exactly should separate Holt from the packs of wannabes in his wake. Most of the songs are penned by Scott with a few notable exceptions, including a cover of Dylan's "Blind Willie McTell." There maybe is the problem. That particular song has been done to death in recent years. Holt's first album was more adventurous. The standout song on that collection was probably the Clash's "Train in Vain." That sort of musical adventurousness promised strong things from this performer. This album, alas, doesn't deliver on that promise. All is not lost, however. Holt's voice is strong, and listeners will probably find themselves humming the title track some hours later. Hopefully, his next record will put his talents to better use. *—Rob Ferrier*

Earl Hooker

b. 1929, Clarksdale, MS, **d.** Apr. 21, 1970, Chicago, IL
Slide Guitar, Vocals, Guitar / Slide Guitar Blues, Delta Blues, Electric Chicago Blues
If there was a more immaculate slide guitarist residing in Chicago during the '50s and '60s than Earl Hooker, his name has yet to surface. Boasting a fretboard touch so smooth and clean that every note rang as clear and precise as a bell, Hooker was an endlessly inventive axeman who would likely have been a star had his modest vocal abilities matched his instrumental prowess and had he not been dogged by tuberculosis (it killed him at age 41).

Born in the Mississippi Delta, Hooker arrived in Chicago as a child. There he was influenced by another slide wizard, veteran Robert Nighthawk. But Hooker never remained still for long. He ran away from home at age 13, journeying to Mississippi. After another stint in Chicago, he rambled back to the Delta again, playing with Ike Turner and Sonny Boy Williamson. Hooker made his first recordings in 1952 and 1953 for Rockin', King, and Sun. At the latter, he recorded some terrific sides with pianist Pinetop Perkins (Sam Phillips inexplicably sat on Hooker's blazing rendition of "The Hucklebuck").

Back in Chicago again, Hooker's dazzling dexterity was intermittently showcased on singles for Argo, C.J., and Bea & Baby during the mid- to late '50s before he joined forces with producer Mel London (owner of the Chief and Age logos) in 1959. For the next four years, he recorded both as sideman and leader for the producer, backing Junior Wells, Lillian Offitt, Ricky Allen, and A.C. Reed and cutting his own sizzling instrumentals ("Blue Guitar," "Blues in D-Natural"). He also contributed pungent slide work to Muddy Waters' Chess waxing "You Shook Me." Opportunities to record grew sparse after Age folded; Hooker made some tantalizing sides for Sauk City, WI-based Cuca Records from 1964 to 1968 (several featuring steel guitar virtuoso Freddie Roulette).

Hooker's amazing prowess (he even managed to make the dreaded wah-wah pedal a viable blues tool) finally drew increased attention during the late '60s. He cut LPs for Arhoolie, ABC-BluesWay, and Blue Thumb that didn't equal what he'd done at Age, but they did serve to introduce Hooker to an audience outside Chicago and wherever his frequent travels deposited him. But tuberculosis halted his wandering ways permanently in 1970. *—Bill Dahl*

Two Bugs and a Roach / 1966 / Arhoolie ♦♦♦♦♦
This compact disc reissue of Earl Hooker's debut Arhoolie adds some tracks to the original lineup, making for a much more varied package. In addition to the contents of *Two Bugs and a Roach* (itself a varied lot, with vocals from Hooker, Andrew Odom, and Carey Bell in between the instrumentals, all cut in 1968), there are two tracks from stray sessions in late 1968 and July, 1969, along with four very early sides probably recorded in Memphis in the company of Pinetop Perkins, Willie Nix, and an unknown bass player. Of these, "Guitar Rag" is the least together, hampered by a bass player who can't find the changes, but "I'm Going Down the Line" and "Earl's Boogie Woogie" are both top-notch uptempo boogies full of fleet-fingered soloing. "Sweet Black Angel" was the A-side of a stray single from the early '50s and appears to be from another session, although it's an excellent example of Hooker playing in the Robert Nighthawk style. All in all, one of the must-haves in this artist's very small discography. *—Cub Koda*

Sweet Black Angel / 1970 / One Way ♦♦♦
Ike Turner co-produced this set with Blue Thumb Records boss Bob Krasnow. It's a wide-ranging collection, as its oddly generic song titles ("Country and Western," "Shuffle," "Funky Blues") would eloquently indicate. *—Bill Dahl*

There's a Fungus Amung Us / 1972 / M.I.L. Multimedia ♦♦♦

Do You Remember the Great Earl Hooker / 1973 / BluesWay ♦♦♦

Hooker n' Steve / 1975 / Arhoolie ♦♦♦

Two Bugs & a Roach/Hooker 'n' Steve / 1976 / Arhoolie ♦♦♦♦♦

Leading Brand / 1978 / Red Lightnin' ♦♦♦♦♦
Hooker's best early-'60s instrumentals for Mel London, along with a few sides that feature his guitar by Ricky Allen, Lillian Offitt, etc. Also featured are several equally memorable workouts by guitarist Jody Williams. *—Bill Dahl*

Blue Guitar / 1981 / Paula ♦♦♦♦♦
The slide guitar wizard's immaculate fretwork was never captured more imaginatively than during his early-'60s stay with Mel London's Age/Chief labels. 21 fascinating tracks from that period include Hooker's savage instrumentals "Blue Guitar," "Off the Hook," "The Leading Brand," "Blues in D Natural," and "How Long Can This Go On," along with tracks by A.C. Reed, Lillian Offitt, and Harold Tidwell that cast Hooker as a standout sideman. *—Bill Dahl*

Play Your Guitar Mr. Hooker / 1985 / Black Top ♦♦♦
1964-1967 output by the guitarist that was largely done for the tiny Cuca logo of Sauk City, WI. The normally tight-lipped Hooker proves that he could sing on this romping version of "Swear to Tell the Truth," while A.C. Reed, Little Tommy, Frank Clark, and Muddy Waters Jr. help out behind the mike elsewhere. A pair of live cuts from 1968 find Hooker stretching out in amazing fashion. *—Bill Dahl*

Moon Is Rising / Aug. 18, 1998 / Arhoolie ♦♦♦
The first eight tracks of this 79-minute compilation of late-'60s material originally appeared on Arhoolie's *Hooker n' Steve* LP; a couple of others showed up on Arhoolie's *His First & Last Recordings,* while the four remaining cuts were previously unreleased. Hooker didn't have long to live when these were laid down in 1968 and (for the most part) 1969, but he's in real good form on guitar, although he only takes an occasional vocal (other band members help out on other tracks, and some are instrumental). Indications are from the liner notes that the sessions were run on a no-frills budget, but it's very respectable '60s Chicago electric blues with a shade of funky soul and a hot live feel, and Hooker's guitar has an upfront bite and presence. Actually, the instrumentals are highlights, particularly "Hooker n' Steve" with its smoking guitar-organ duets. *—Richie Unterberger*

● **Simply the Best: Earl Hooker Collection** / May 18, 1999 / MCA ♦♦♦♦♦
Focusing on Earl Hooker's output as a leader as well as his work backing such dynamos as Muddy Waters, John Lee Hooker (his second cousin), Andrew "Big Voice" Odom, and Sonny Terry & Brownie McGhee, this CD spans 1956-1969 and paints an impressive picture of the distinctive guitarist. Most of the tunes from Hooker's own sessions are infectious, groove-oriented instrumentals like the funky "Frog Hop" from 1956, the twangy "Tanya" from 1962, and the playful "Hookin'" from 1969. Hooker's vocal on "You Got to Lose" points to the fact that while he wasn't a fantastic singer (he was a fantastic guitarist and an OK singer), his vocals did have a certain charm. Of course, Hooker backed quite a few first-class singers, and on this compilation they range from

Muddy Waters on "You Shook Me" (a 1962 gem that was covered by Led Zeppelin in 1969) and John Lee Hooker on "Messin' Around With the Blues" (1962) and "If You Miss 'Im…I Got 'Im" (1969) to Charles Brown on "Drifting Blues" (1969). Brown was a very different type of singer from Waters and John Lee Hooker, both of whom were, like Earl Hooker, Mississippi natives who started out playing acoustic country blues in the Deep South before heading north and going electric. The smoother Brown, however, was a jazz singer as well as a blues and R&B singer. But Hooker fits perfectly with the jazz/blues environment of "Drifting Blues," which finds him playing alongside soul-jazz saxman Red Holloway. Boasting comprehensive liner notes and excellent digital remastering, *Simply the Best* is a collection that blues lovers should go out of their way to obtain. *—Alex Henderson*

John Lee Hooker

b. Aug. 17, 1920, Clarksdale, MS, **d.** Jun. 21, 2001, Los Altos, CA

Vocals, Leader, Songwriter, Guitar / Detroit Blues, Blues Revival, Delta Blues, Country Blues, Electric Delta Blues, Acoustic Blues, Electric Blues

He was beloved worldwide as the king of the endless boogie, a genuine blues superstar whose droning, hypnotic one-chord grooves were at once both ultra-primitive and timeless. But John Lee Hooker recorded in a great many more styles than that over a career that stretched back more than half a century.

The Hook was a Mississippi native who became the top gent on the Detroit blues circuit in the years following World War II. The seeds for his eerily mournful guitar sound were planted by his stepfather, Will Moore, while Hooker was in his teens. Hooker had been singing spirituals before that, but the blues took hold and simply wouldn't let go. Overnight visitors left their mark on the youth, too—legends like Blind Lemon Jefferson, Charley Patton, and Blind Blake, who all knew Moore.

Hooker heard Memphis calling while he was still in his teens, but he couldn't gain much of a foothold there. So he relocated to Cincinnati for a seven-year stretch before making the big move to the Motor City in 1943. Jobs were plentiful, but Hooker drifted away from day gigs in favor of playing his unique free-form brand of blues. A burgeoning club scene along Hastings Street didn't hurt his chances any.

In 1948, the aspiring bluesman hooked up with entrepreneur Bernie Besman, who helped him hammer out his solo debut sides, "Sally Mae" and its seminal flip, "Boogie Chillen." This was blues as primitive as anything then on the market; Hooker's dark, ruminative vocals were backed only by his own ringing, heavily amplified guitar and insistently pounding foot. Their efforts were quickly rewarded. Los Angeles-based Modern Records issued the sides and "Boogie Chillen"—a colorful, unique travelogue of Detroit's blues scene—made an improbable jaunt to the very peak of the R&B charts.

Modern released several more major hits by the Boogie Man after that: "Hobo Blues" and its raw-as-an-open wound flip, "Hoogie Boogie"; "Crawling King Snake Blues" (all three 1949 smashes), and the unusual 1951 chart-topper "I'm in the Mood," where Hooker overdubbed his voice three times in a crude early attempt at multi-tracking.

But Hooker never, ever let something as meaningless as a contract stop him for making recordings for other labels. His early catalog is stretched across a roadmap of diskeries so complex that it's nearly impossible to fully comprehend (a vast array of recording aliases don't make things any easier).

Along with Modern, Hooker recorded for King (as the geographically challenged Texas Slim), Regent (as Delta John, a far more accurate handle), Savoy (as the wonderfully surreal Birmingham Sam and his Magic Guitar), Danceland (as the downright delicious Little Pork Chops), Staff (as Johnny Williams), Sensation (for whom he scored a national hit in 1950 with "Huckle Up, Baby"), Gotham, Regal, Swing Time, Federal, Gone (as John Lee Booker), Chess, Acorn (as the Boogie Man), Chance, DeLuxe (as Johnny Lee), JVB, Chart, and Specialty before finally settling down at Vee-Jay in 1955 under his own name. Hooker became the point man for the growing Detroit blues scene during this incredibly prolific period, recruiting guitarist Eddie Kirkland as his frequent duet partner while still recording for Modern.

Once tied in with Vee-Jay, the rough-and-tumble sound of Hooker's solo and duet waxings was adapted to a band format. Hooker had recorded with various combos along the way before, but never with sidemen as versatile and sympathetic as guitarist Eddie Taylor and harpist Jimmy Reed, who backed him at his initial Vee-Jay date that produced "Time Is Marching" and the superfluous sequel "Mambo Chillun."

Taylor stuck around for a 1956 session that elicited two genuine Hooker classics, "Baby Lee" and "Dimples," and he was still deftly anchoring the rhythm section (Hooker's sense of timing was his and his alone, demanding big-eared sidemen) when the Boogie Man finally made it back to the R&B charts in 1958 with "I Love You Honey."

Vee-Jay presented Hooker in quite an array of settings during the early '60s. His grinding, tough blues "No Shoes" proved a surprisingly sizable hit in 1960, while the storming "Boom Boom," his top seller for the firm in 1962 (it even cracked the pop airwaves), was an infectious R&B dance number benefiting from the reported presence of some of Motown's house musicians. But there were also acoustic outings aimed squarely at the blossoming folk-blues crowd, as well as some attempts at up-to-date R&B that featured highly intrusive female background vocals (allegedly by the Vandellas) and utterly unyielding structures that hemmed Hooker in unmercifully.

British blues bands such as the Animals and Yardbirds idolized Hooker during the early '60s; Eric Burdon's boys cut a credible 1964 cover of "Boom Boom" that outsold Hooker's original on the American pop charts. Hooker visited Europe in 1962 under the auspices of the first American Folk Blues Festival, leaving behind the popular waxings "Let's Make It" and "Shake It Baby" for foreign consumption.

Back home, Hooker cranked out gems for Vee-Jay through 1964 ("Big Legs, Tight Skirt," one of his last offerings on the logo, was also one of his best), before undergoing another extended round of label-hopping (except this time, he was waxing whole LPs instead of scattered 78s). Verve-Folkways, Impulse!, Chess, and BluesWay all enticed him into recording for them in 1965-1966 alone! His reputation among hip rock cognoscenti in the states and abroad was growing exponentially, especially after he teamed up with blues-rockers Canned Heat for the massively selling album *Hooker 'n Heat* in 1970.

Eventually, though, the endless boogie formula grew incredibly stagnant. Much of Hooker's '70s output found him laying back while plodding rock-rooted rhythm sections assumed much of the work load. A cameo in the 1980 movie *The Blues Brothers* was welcome, if far too short.

But Hooker wasn't through—not by a long shot. With the expert help of slide guitarist extraordinaire/producer Roy Rogers, the Hook waxed *The Healer*, an album that marked the first of his guest star-loaded albums (Carlos Santana, Bonnie Raitt, and Robert Cray were among the luminaries to cameo on the disc, which picked up a Grammy).

Major labels were just beginning to take notice of the growing demand for blues records, and Pointblank snapped Hooker up, releasing *Mr. Lucky* (this time teaming Hooker with everyone from Albert Collins and John Hammond to Van Morrison and Keith Richards). Once again, Hooker was resting on his laurels by allowing his guests to wrest much of the spotlight away from him on his own album, but by then, he'd earned it. Another Pointblank set, *Boom Boom*, soon followed.

Happily, Hooker enjoyed the good life throughout the '90s. He spent much of his time in semi-retirement, splitting his relaxation time between several houses acquired up and down the California coast. When the right offer came along, though, he took it, including an amusing TV commercial for Pepsi. He also kept recording, releasing such star-studded efforts as 1995's *Chill Out* and 1997's *Don't Look Back*. All this helped him retain his status as a living legend, and he remained an American musical icon—and his stature wasn't diminished upon his death from natural causes on June 21, 2001. *—Bill Dahl*

House of the Blues / 1960 / MCA/Chess ♦♦♦♦

Verbatim CD reissue of a 1959 Chess album that collected 1951-1954 efforts by the Hook. Some important titles here: an ominous "Leave My Wife Alone," and the stark "Sugar Mama" and "Ramblin' by Myself," and with Eddie Kirkland on second guitar, "Louise" and "High Priced Woman." *—Bill Dahl*

I'm John Lee Hooker / 1960 / Collectables ♦♦♦♦♦

Winding through the literally hundreds of titles in John Lee Hooker's catalog is a daunting task for even the most seasoned and learned blues connoisseur. This is especially true when considering Hooker recorded under more than a dozen aliases for as many labels during the late '40s, '50s, and early '60s. *I'm John Lee Hooker* was first issued in 1959 during his tenure with Vee-Jay and is "the Hook" in his element as well as prime. Although many of these titles were initially cut for Los Angeles-based Modern Records in the early '50s, the recordings heard here are said to best reflect Hooker's often-emulated straight-ahead primitive Detroit and Chicago blues styles. The sessions comprising the original 12-track album—as well as the four bonus tracks on the 1998 Charly CD reissue—are taken from six sessions spread over the course of four years (1955-1959). Hooker works both solo—accompanied only by his own percussive guitar and the solid backbeat of his foot rhythmically pulsating against plywood—as well as in several different small-combo settings. Unlike the diluted, pop-oriented blues that first came to prominence in the wake of the British Invasion of the early to mid-'60s, the music on this album is infinitely more authentic in presentation.

As the track list indicates, *I'm John Lee Hooker* includes many of his best-known and loved works. From right out of the gate comes the guttural ramble-tamble of "Dimples" in its best-known form. Indeed it can be directly traced to—and is likewise acknowledged by—notable purveyors of Brit rock such as Eric Burdon—who incorporated it into the earliest incarnation of the Animals, the Spencer Davis Group, as well as the decidedly more roots-influenced Duane Allman. Another of Hooker's widely covered signature tunes featured on this volume is "Boogie Chillen." This rendering is arguably the most recognizable in the plethora of versions that have seemingly appeared on every Hooker-related compilation available. Additionally, this version was prominently featured in *The Blues Brothers* movie as well as countless other films and adverts. Likewise, a seminal solo "Crawlin' King Snake" is included here. The tune became not only a staple of Hooker's, it was also prominently included on the Doors' *L.A. Woman* album and covered by notable bluesmen Albert King, B.B. King, and Big Joe Williams, whose version predates this one by several decades. *I'm John Lee Hooker* is one of the great blues collections of the post-World War II era. Time has, if anything, only reinforced the significance of the album. It belongs in every blues enthusiast's collection without reservation. *—Lindsay Planer*

Travelin' / 1960 / Collectables ♦♦♦♦♦

That's My Story / 1960 / Riverside ♦♦♦♦♦

Hooker's earliest Riverside albums presented him playing solo acoustic guitar, in a conscious effort to direct his work to listeners outside the R&B audience. Opinions differ on the matter, but this outing is more interesting than his solo acoustic Riverside records, due to the presence of a supporting rhythm section on most of the tracks. The liner notes (in the fashion of the day) are almost apologetic about this, emphasizing that it's not to create R&B rhythms, but "to free Hooker from the burden of carrying the full rhythm load." To make matters more palatable for the purists, maybe that's why a couple of jazz players were chosen for the job (bassist Sam Jones and drummer Louis Hayes, who formed the rhythm section for Cannonball Adderley at the time). What's important is not how pure the music is, but that it's a decent album, striking a good midpoint between his acoustic and electric sound. *—Richie Unterberger*

The Country Blues of John Lee Hooker / Jan. 1960 / Riverside/Original Blues Classics ♦♦♦

Hooker was still churning out R&B-influenced electric blues with a rhythm section for Vee-Jay when he recorded this, his first album packaged for the folk/traditional blues market. He plays nothing but acoustic guitar, and seems to have selected a repertoire with old-school country blues in mind. It's unimpressive only within the context of Hooker's body of work; in comparison with other solo outings, the guitar sounds thin, and the approach restrained. *—Richie Unterberger*

John Lee Hooker Sings the Blues / 1961 / King ♦♦♦♦♦

☆ **John Lee Hooker Plays and Sings the Blues** / 1961 / MCA/Chess ♦♦♦♦♦
A 1961 Chess album restored to digital print by MCA that's filled with 1951-1952 gems from the Hook's heyday. Chess originally bought "Mad Man Blues" and "Hey Boogie" from the Gone label; the rest first came out on Chess during Hooker's frenzied early days of recording, when his platters turned up on nearly every R&B indie label existent at the time. *—Bill Dahl*

The Folk Lore of John Lee Hooker / 1961 / Collectables ♦♦♦

Don't Turn Me from Your Door: John Lee Hooker Sings His Blues / 1963 / Atco ♦♦♦
Don't Turn Me from Your Door comprises a set of 1953 sessions that were originally released in 1963 and later in 1972, under the title *Detroit Special*. Despite its twisted historical background, this is fine, first-rate Hooker. A few tracks feature the support of guitarist/vocalist Eddie Kirkland, a few others, an unnamed bassist, but this is pretty much pure John Lee Hooker—just him and a guitar, running through a set of spare, haunting blues that include such tracks as "Blue Monday" and "Stuttering Blues." There are none of his best-known tracks on the album, but it's one of his most consistent original records. *—Thom Owens*

Burning Hell / 1964 / Riverside/Original Blues Classics ♦♦♦
In April 1959, Hooker recorded a couple of solo acoustic albums for Riverside that were his first efforts geared toward the folk/acoustic blues audience, rather than the commercial R&B one. One of these albums (*The Country Blues of John Lee Hooker*) was issued at the time; the other, *Burning Hell*, wasn't issued until 1964, and then only in England (in 1992, it finally came out in the U.S. on CD). This is very similar to *Country Blues*, mixing originals with covers of tunes by Muddy Waters, Howlin' Wolf, Lightnin' Hopkins, and Big Bill Broonzy. To my ears it has a slight edge—the singing and performances sound a little more committed. But anyone who likes one LP will like the other, though neither ranks among the best of Hooker's one-man recordings. *—Richie Unterberger*

The Big Soul of John Lee Hooker / 1964 / Collectables ♦♦♦

John Lee Hooker at Newport / 1964 / Vee-Jay ♦♦♦♦♦
Arguably his finest live date, this was John Lee Hooker minus the self-congratulatory mugging now an almost mandatory part of his sets. Instead, there's just lean, straight, defiant Hooker vocals and minimal, but effective backing. *—Ron Wynn*

Is He the World's Greatest Blues Singer? / 1965 / Collectables ♦♦♦
From the vaults of Vee-Jay records come an avalanche of classic John Lee Hooker reissues, featuring original art work, running order, and a budget price from the Collectables label. With the amount of Hooker material available on the market, some of it of dubious quality, you can't go wrong with these reissues. *Is He the World's Greatest Blues Singer?* was released in 1965 and acts as a greatest-hits package from that time period, combining 12 tracks of both acoustic and electric classics like "Crawlin' Kingsnake," "Boom Boom," and live versions of "Maudie," "the Mighty Fire," and "Talk That Talk Baby." Any of the Hooker Vee-Jay reissues are recommended. *—Al Campbell*

It Serves You Right to Suffer / Jun. 1966 / BGO ♦♦♦
Given Hooker's unpredictable timing and piss-poor track record recording with bands, this 1965 one-off session for the jazz label Impulse! would be a recipe for disaster. But with Panama Francis on drums, Milt Hinton on bass, and Barry Galbraith on second guitar, the result is some of the best John Lee Hooker material with a band that you're likely to come across. The other musicians stay in the pocket, never overplaying or trying to get Hooker to make chord changes he has no intention of making. This record should be played for every artist who records with Hooker nowadays, as it's a textbook example of how exactly to back the old master. The most surreal moment occurs when William Wells blows some totally cool trombone on Hooker's version of Berry Gordy's "Money." If you run across this one in a pile of 500 other John Lee Hooker CDs, grab it; it's one of the good ones. *—Cub Koda*

The Real Folk Blues / 1966 / MCA/Chess ♦♦♦♦
Listeners wanting to find a comprehensive collection of Hooker's work may not find it here, but they certainly won't be disappointed once the needle hits the grooves on this solid 1966 Chess release by the blues master. Featuring nine Hooker originals, the set is a fetching mix of raucously fun uptempo cuts ("Let's Go Out Tonight") and starkly slow classics ("Stella Mae"). And in between, one can sample classics like "I'm in the Mood" and the incredible ballad closer, "The Waterfront." *—Stephen Cook*

Live at Cafe Au Go-Go / 1967 / BGO ♦♦♦
A decent if somewhat low-key electric set, recorded in August of 1966. One of his better live bands, featuring support from Otis Spann and other members of Muddy Waters' group. The eight songs include Hooker standbys like "One Bourbon, One Scotch and One Beer" and "I'll Never Get Out of These Blues Alive." *—Richie Unterberger*

Live at Cafe Au Go-Go (And Soledad Prison) / 1967 / MCA ♦♦♦
This reissue contains the entirety of Hooker's 1967 *Cafe Au Go-Go* set, and adds five bonus tracks from his 1972 album, *Live at Soledad Prison*. Luther Tucker is one of the guitarists for the *Soledad* portion, which has a somewhat more electric, rock-oriented sound than the *Au Go-Go* material. The disc only has five of the seven cuts from the original *Soledad* album, but that's OK, as the two missing items featured John Lee Hooker Jr., on lead vocals, rather than Hooker himself. *—Richie Unterberger*

Urban Blues / 1967 / MCA ♦♦♦
The Boogie Man's 1967 ABC-BluesWay album in its entirety, with three bonus numbers from a couple of years later added on the end. Hooker's Chicago sidemen (including Eddie Taylor, Wayne Bennett, and Louis Myers) deftly handle Hooker's eccentricities on "Mr. Lucky," and the harrowing "The Motor City Is Burning," and a sprightly remake of "Boom Boom." *—Bill Dahl*

Simply the Truth / 1969 / One Way ♦♦♦
Overseen by noted jazz producer Bob Thiele, this session had Hooker backed by some of his fullest arrangements to date, with noted session drummer Pretty Purdie and keyboards in addition to supplementary guitar and bass. The slightly modernized sound was ultimately neither here nor there, the center remaining Hooker's voice and lyrics. His words nodded toward contemporary concerns with "I Don't Wanna Go to Vietnam" and "Mini Skirts," but the songs were mostly consistent with his usual approaches. Another of his many characteristically solid efforts, although it's not one of his more interesting albums. *—Richie Unterberger*

That's Where It's At! / 1969 / Stax ♦♦♦
A characteristic solo outing with moody compositions and that doomy one-electric-guitar-and-stomping-foot ambience. One of his sparer and more menacing post-'50s outings, highlighted by "Two White Horses" and a seven-minute "Feel So Bad," which features extended verbal sparring with an unidentified male partner. *—Richie Unterberger*

Get Back Home / Nov. 30, 1969 / Evidence ♦♦♦♦
John Lee Hooker's greatness lies in his ability to perform the same songs the same way yet somehow sound different and memorable in the process. He operates at maximum efficiency in minimal surroundings with little production or assistance. That was the case on a 1969 session for Black and Blue; it was just Hooker and his guitar moaning, wailing, and narrating on 10 tracks which included familiar ditties "Boogie Chillen," "Love Affair," "Big Boss Lady," and "Cold Chills." Evidence has now not only reissued these 10 but has added another six bonus cuts, bringing the CD total to 16. If you have ever heard any Hooker, you will not be surprised or stunned by these renditions; you will simply enjoy hearing him rework them one more time, finding a new word, phrase, line, or riff to inject. *—Ron Wynn*

Endless Boogie / 1971 / BGO ♦♦
A 1971 album with Hooker surrounded—in some cases, swamped—by various rock musicians on long, meandering jams that seem to be more showcases for the soloists than for the star of the show. Although Hooker has always had trouble finding bands that could keep up with his idiosyncratic timing, it's not an impossible task, and the musicians on board for this session just seem to be endlessly riffing rather than providing a sympathetic framework for John Lee to work his magic. By the time this session reaches the end, Hooker is far in the background, just letting the band blow, grabbing the paycheck, and scarcely involved. There are lots of JLH albums in the bin; pass this one by. *—Cub Koda*

Boogie Chillen / 1972 / Fantasy ♦♦♦♦♦
Recorded live in November 1962 in San Francisco, this dates from the period in which Hooker often presented himself as a sort of blues/folksinger for the coffeehouse crowd, toning down his volume and aggressiveness somewhat. There's something of a muted "unplugged" feel to these solo performances (though an electric guitar *is* used). It's not ineffective, though not among his best work; it's the kind of Hooker you might want to put on past midnight, just before going to sleep. Hooker's never been bashful about recycling songs, and "Boogie Chillun" appears here in one of its many versions, as does "Dimples" (retitled as "I Like to See You Walk"). He also tackles the rock/soul standard "Money," changing the title to "I Need Some Money," for which he also somehow gets awarded the songwriting credit on the sleeve. *—Richie Unterberger*

Free Beer & Chicken / 1974 / BGO ♦♦

Alone / 1976 / Tomato ♦♦♦
Because he's so loose and improvisatory—and because he loves to twist the 12-bar format into so many different shapes and sizes—John Lee Hooker can present a major challenge to sidemen. More than a few times, Hooker has done without sidemen altogether and gone it alone with thrilling results. That's exactly what happens on *Alone*, an outstanding two-CD set containing live performances at New York's Hunter College from 1976. Not having to concern himself with the needs of a drummer or a bassist, the singer/guitarist is especially introspective and doesn't hesitate to let loose and improvise on such familiar tunes as "Boogie Chillen," "Boom Boom" and "One Bourbon, One Scotch, One Beer." Hooker enjoys improvisation as much as a jazz musician, and on these magnificent recordings, he is at his most uninhibited and takes one liberty after another. *—Alex Henderson*

The Cream / Oct. 1978 / Tomato ♦♦
Joined by a full band that includes two other guitarists (John Garcia Jr. on lead and Ron Thompson on rhythm), John Lee Hooker is passionately rockin' on this live date (recorded at the Keystone in Palo Alto, CA in 1997). Hooker has always been known for taking quite a few liberties with his material, something that could easily throw some musicians off. Without a doubt, Hooker keeps a sideman on his toes—and he presents even more of a challenge on stage because there are no second and third takes. But this is a band that, although not in a class with Canned Heat, obviously understands (and even thrives on) his sense of spontaneity, and rises to the occasion on such familiar gems as "One Room Country Shack," "When My First Wife Left Me" and "Tupelo," as well as the invigorating "Boogie On" (one of the many variations of "Boogie Chillen" Hooker has provided over the years). Hooker doesn't do as much improvising as he did when playing unaccompanied at New York's Hunter College the previous year, but he never ceases to be confidently soulful. Although not quite essential, *The Cream* is an engaging CD that definitely has a lot going for it. *—Alex Henderson*

Detroit Blues 1950–1951 / 1986 / Collectables ♦♦♦

Detroit Blues / 1987 / Flyright ♦♦♦
Interesting collection of old 78s that Hooker recorded under various pseudonyms (Johnny Williams, John Lee) in 1950. Along with the original version of "House Rent Boogie" and

five others that ended up on the Philadelphia Gotham label, we have the bonus of a half dozen tracks by Hooker sideman Eddie Burns and Detroit bluesman Baby Boy Warren's first single. The sound is rough in the extreme, but the music's great. *—Cub Koda*

Jealous / May 1987 / Virgin ♦♦♦
While *Jealous* is propelled by the scarily spare stomp of Hook's guitar, it has few standout moments. Instead, it is a consistent record, with few highs or lows—it's a standard contemporary blues album, without many peaks or valleys. *Jealous* may be a grittier record than its successor, *The Healer*, but it tends to fade into the background, making it one of his more undistinguished albums. *—Thom Owens*

Sings the Blues: That's My Story / 1988 / Riverside/Original Blues Classics ♦♦♦♦
An acoustic date cut on February 9, 1960, this finds Hooker in top-notch form, running through a dozen performances in his instantly identifiable style. Except for three solo turns, Hooker is ably backed by bassist Sam Jones and drummer Louis Hayes, both wisely following John Lee's idiosyncratic timing and changes. All the tunes are stretched out to comfortable lengths, and his interpretations of then-R&B hits like "Money" and Rosco Gordon's "No More Doggin'" are so vastly reworked that they sound like totally original compositions. A good choice to pick up if you run across a copy. *—Cub Koda*

The Healer / 1989 / Chameleon ♦♦
The Healer was a major comeback for John Lee Hooker. Featuring a wide array of guest stars, including Bonnie Raitt, Keith Richards, Johnnie Johnson, and Los Lobos, *The Healer* captured widespread media attention because of all the superstar musicians involved in its production. Unfortunately, that long guest list is what makes the album a fairly unengaging listen. Certainly there are moments were it clicks, but that's usually when the music doesn't greatly expand on his stripped-down boogie. The other moments are professional, but not exciting. It's a pleasant listen, but never quite an engaging one. *—Thom Owens*

40th Anniversary Album / 1989 / DCC ♦♦♦
Fourteen rarities from the seemingly bottomless 1948-1952 stash of Detroit producer Bernie Besman, joined by a 1961 stereo "Blues for Abraham Lincoln" that's painfully out-of-tune. Includes "Boogie Chillen" and an alternate version of "I'm in the Mood." *—Bill Dahl*

The Hook: 20 Years of Hits / 1989 / Chameleon ♦♦♦
John Lee Hooker's excellent Vee-Jay material of the '50s and '60s has been reissued time and time again, both in the U.S. and in Europe. *The Hook* is a 16-song CD that Chameleon released in 1989 for its Vee-Jay Hall of Fame series. As was the case with other Chameleon reissues of Vee-Jay material, *The Hook's* liner notes are inadequate—neither personnel nor recording dates are listed. But the disc's sound quality and content are nothing to complain about. Many of his essential Vee-Jay recordings are here (including "Boom Boom," "Whiskey and Women," "Dimples," "Crawling Kingsnake," and one of his many remakes of "Boogie Chillen"), along with rare versions of "House Rent Boogie," "Nightmare," and "Big Legs, Tight Skirt." Because hits and rarities are combined, *The Hook* isn't really a best-of collection—and, in fact, Chameleon also reissued a CD titled *The Best of John Lee Hooker*. *—Alex Henderson*

Boogie Awhile / 1990 / Krazy Kat ♦♦♦♦♦
This was originally issued as a 31-track, double LP full of Hooker's earliest and rarest sides, almost all of it taken from goodly hacked-up acetates and 78 pressings. The compact disc deletes 11 of the most chewed up and attempts to clean up the rest with varying results. But this is one time when audiophile concerns don't count for much because this is quite simply Hooker at his earliest, his rarest and his very best. *—Cub Koda*

Detroit Lion / 1990 / Demon ♦♦♦
Demon's *The Detroit Lion* is a fine 15-track collection of material John Lee Hooker recorded for Modern Records between 1948 and 1952. By no means complete, the collection concentrates on songs that are off the beaten path. Sure, there's "Boogie Chillen" and "I'm in the Mood," but such singles as "Sally Mae," "Hobo Blues," "Hoogie Blues" and "Crawling King Snake Blues" are passed by in favor of "Hey's, The House Rent Boogie," "Baby How Can You Do It?," "Four Women in My Life," "This Is 19 and 52 Blues," and "Blues for Abraham Lincoln." The result is a disc that's aimed more at the fanatic and collector than the casual fan, and while these recordings are available on more comprehensive collections, this is still a nice way to acquire some of this material. *—Stephen Thomas Erlewine*

Mr. Lucky / 1991 / Pointblank ♦♦♦
His latest for Virgin's blues division, contains some entertaining material. It's not a classic, but it's not half-bad either. *—Ron Wynn*

The Best of John Lee Hooker / 1991 / JCI ♦♦♦♦♦
This was hardly the first collection titled *The Best of John Lee Hooker*, and it certainly wouldn't be the last. JCI released this particular CD in 1990 as part of its Masters of the Blues series, and the collection shows just how poorly executed the series was. The liner notes are embarrassing—neither personnel nor recording dates are listed, and there is no mention of the labels the material was recorded for (which included Vee-Jay and Chess). JCI does both CD buyers and Hooker a disservice by not being more informative. The label does offer a generous helping of material. A total of 18 songs are provided, including celebrated versions of "Boom Boom," "Whiskey and Women," and "Baby Lee." The digital remastering isn't terrible, but it could have been better. Consumers would do better to look for a best-of that isn't so carelessly assembled. *—Alex Henderson*

☆ **The Ultimate Collection (1948–1990)** / 1991 / Rhino ♦♦♦♦♦
Rhino's double-disc 1991 set *The Ultimate Collection* falls just short of the promise of its title, losing its focus toward the end of the set. That said, it comes close enough to satisfy, particularly because John Lee Hooker had such a long, convoluted discography, recording for a number of different labels over many decades. This gets the core of his legacy—the early, minimalist boogie, the gritty late-'50s sides, all the way through to the superstar-studded recordings of the late '80s. If the desire to be comprehensive hurts the collection somewhat—good though they may be, the '80s recordings really are for those that love all of Hooker's music, and the disc would have been better off if it was simply two discs of '40s through '70s—this nevertheless gets all the classics ("Boogie Chillen," "Crawlin' King Snake," "Boom Boom," "One Bourbon, One Scotch, One Beer," among them) while giving an idea of the scope of Hook's career, making it a great introduction. *—Stephen Thomas Erlewine*

More Real Folk Blues: The Missing Album / Sep. 10, 1991 / MCA/Chess ♦♦♦
Produced by Ralph Bass in 1966 but not issued by Chess at the time, *More Real Folk Blues* was unearthed by MCA only a few years back. It's no masterpiece, but certainly deserved release in its day—backed by Burns and a Chicago rhythm section that copes as well as can be expected with Hooker's singular sense of timing, the Boogie Man answers Sir Mack Rice with his "Mustang Sally & Gto" and keeps things way lowdown on several other cuts. *—Bill Dahl*

Hooker 'n Heat / Oct. 28, 1991 / EMI America ♦♦♦
Probably no other white blues band took John Lee Hooker's boogie rhythms and made a career out of it as much as Canned Heat. It was certainly inevitable that the two forces would unite for a joint recording project and this double CD package (recorded in 1970 and originally a double album) is the delightful result. Canned Heat certainly knew what they were going after, as Hooker brandishes a mean guitar tone that hadn't surfaced since his early Detroit recordings. Surprisingly, Canned Heat hangs back a bit as over half the material are riveting solo recordings, with the full band only coming in as support on the second half. Compare this with most of his '70s recordings for BluesWay (now MCA) and you'll quickly realize that these sides contain some of his most cohesive work with a band, ever. *—Cub Koda*

The Best of John Lee Hooker 1965–1974 / 1992 / MCA ♦♦♦
MCA's *The Best of John Lee Hooker* has a misleading title. All of the 16 selections are taken from his recordings for ABC, which were made at the end of the '60s and beginning of the '70s. During this time, his producers were experimenting with his sound, adding contemporary sonic touches like funk rhythms and wah-wah pedals. Needless to say, this sound didn't sit particularly well with Hooker's lean, haunting blues. However, these songs do take the best material from generally poor albums—anyone who wants to sample his ABC material should turn here first and they'll realize that they don't need to explore much further. *—Thom Owens*

Graveyard Blues / 1992 / Specialty ♦♦♦♦
At the beginning of his career, Hooker's sides were leased to several different labels. This 20-song anthology of material from the late '40s and early '50s was originally released on the Sensation and Specialty labels; while the track listings indicate a timespan of 1948-1950, the liner notes say that much of it was recorded in 1954. Doesn't anyone proofread these things? Anyway, this was mostly recorded solo, and boasts his characteristic spooky electric minimalist boogie sound. *The Legendary Modern Recordings*, covering the same era, is a better place to start for this kind of thing due to its stronger content. If you want more of the same, though, this (and Capitol's *Alternative Boogie*) is the next stop. *—Richie Unterberger*

Boom Boom / Nov. 17, 1992 / Pointblank ♦♦
Another guest-heavy collection. *—Bill Dahl*

Everybody's Blues / 1993 / Specialty ♦♦♦
John Lee Hooker reissues abound, as might be expected of a singer and guitarist who's recorded hundreds of songs for countless labels since the late '40s. What makes the 20 tracks on *Everybody's Blues* different from the mountain of other Hooker material available is the fact that seven of them are newly issued, and most were done in the studio with Hooker wailing and accompanying himself on guitar minus any backing chorus or production armada. Even the cuts with a supporting combo are animated and loose, with the vocal trademarks that are now established Hooker cliches sounding fresh and genuine. *—Ron Wynn*

1965 London Sessions / 1993 / Sequel ♦♦♦
Considering how these dates were done—first, Hooker was backed by a British band, Tony McPhee and the Groundhogs; later horns were overdubbed for American consumption—the results aren't too shabby at all. *—Bill Dahl*

John Lee Hooker on Vee-Jay, 1955–1958 / Jul. 1993 / Vee-Jay ♦♦♦♦♦
Some of Hooker's finest recordings with a band were also some of his first recordings with a band. The unpredictable guitarist seemed to mesh well with guitarist Eddie Taylor, harpist Jimmy Reed, and the rest of the sidemen he was given on his 1955-1958 Vee-Jay output. Includes the classic "Baby Lee" and "Dimples," along with 20 more that crackle with electricity. *—Bill Dahl*

☆ **The Legendary Modern Recordings 1948–1954** / 1994 / Virgin ♦♦♦♦♦
From the beginning of his career, Hooker recorded prolifically, sometimes for several labels at once, sometimes under a number of pseudonyms. That makes his discography a bit difficult for the collector to sort out, but if you want just one document of his early years, this is the anthology of choice, containing 24 sides from 1948 to 1954 that were issued on the Modern label. These, more than any other, are the recordings that did the most to establish the Hooker protoype—the overamplified electric guitar, the moody boogies, the stomping foot rhythms, performed without a rhythm section (some sides feature accompaniment by Eddie Kirkland on second guitar). Contains his two most massive early hits, "Boogie Chillen" and "I'm in the Mood," as well as his oft-covered "Crawling Kingsnake."

This one can get a bit similar-sounding over the course of two dozen tracks, but little other postwar electric blues can match the stark power here. *—Richie Unterberger*

☆ **The Early Years** / 1994 / Tomato ♦♦♦♦♦

Hooker's voluminous output for Vee-Jay Records is scattered across numerous compilations. This double CD contains 31 songs spanning the mid-'50s to the mid-'60s, and is probably the most extensive and satisfying retrospective of his Vee-Jay work (at least domestically). That's not to say it's perfectly assembled; Tomato, as usual, declines to include trimmings like songwriter credits, although Pete Welding's liner notes do (unlike most Tomato releases) provide dates and discuss the sessions in some detail. Hooker's Vee-Jay material was in most ways the most commercially minded of his early efforts, often employing a rhythm section and R&B-influenced arrangements, and occasionally using horns. It's sometimes been said that this approach diluted Hooker's strengths, but one listen to this collection refutes that notion soundly. This is by and large prime Hooker, with some of his best (and best-selling) songs, like "Boom Boom," "Dimples," "I'm So Excited," and "One Bourbon, One Scotch, One Beer." Hooker may have sometimes sounded a bit ill at ease with a band, but he usually worked with backing musicians very well. Non-purists will find these tracks to be some of his most accessible and dynamic performances. *—Richie Unterberger*

Chill Out / 1995 / Pointblank ♦♦

Chill Out isn't the superstar blowout of John Lee Hooker's late-'80s albums, yet it retains that flavor. Featuring some extended soloing from Carlos Santana, *Chill Out* is filled with long blues workouts, all captured in pristine, state-of-the-art technology. Nothing on the disc captures the raw vitality of Hooker's prime material—it's all relaxed blues-rock jams. The clean, sterile production doesn't help the basically directionless music. Certainly nothing on *Chill Out* is outright bad; in fact, most of it is pleasant, yet few of the songs on the album warrant repeated listens. *—Stephen Thomas Erlewine*

EP Collection . . . Plus / 1995 / See for Miles ♦♦♦

★ **The Very Best of John Lee Hooker** / Apr. 25, 1995 / Rhino ♦♦♦♦♦

This 16-track collection sweats down Rhino's two-disc anthology to a lean, mean and essential single disc. Here are the earliest recordings that established Hooker as a major blues artist—"Boogie Chillen," "Hobo Blues," "I'm In the Mood," "Crawlin' Kingsnake," and "Huckle Up Baby"—and they sound better here than on most other collections, reverberating with a clarity that belies their age. The rest of the set follows Hooker's move toward working with bands not always in step with his erratic timing, but still producing classic blues on favorites like "Dimples" and "Boom Boom." If you're going to own only one Hooker collection, add this one to the shopping basket. *—Cub Koda*

Alternative Boogie: Early Studio Recordings 1948–1952 / Oct. 24, 1995 / Capitol ♦♦♦♦♦

A whopping three CDs, and 56 songs, from Hooker's early sessions that were unreleased at the time, although they were available for a while in the early '70s on some United Artists LPs. Like his more widely-known material of the period, it mostly features Hooker unaccompanied, though he's aided by piano and second guitarists on a few tracks. Some of these are alternates of songs that were released in different versions, or embryonic renditions of compositions that evolved into somewhat different shapes. Especially interesting are early versions of his big hit "I'm in the Mood for Love." It's too much at once, though, and too unvarying in approach, for anyone but Hooker specialists. General fans are advised to stick with *The Legendary Modern Recordings*, which has 24 more renowned, and somewhat more accomplished, tracks from the same era. It's certainly a well-done package, though, containing a 38-page insert with detailed liner notes and session information. *—Richie Unterberger*

The Best of Hooker 'n Heat / 1996 / EMI ♦♦♦

These ten songs were originally released as part of a 1971 album (on Liberty 35002); this reissue, despite the lack of historical liner notes, isn't exactly short value, clocking in at 56 minutes. Canned Heat gets top billing, but really it's Hooker's show, as he sings all the tracks and takes all the songwriting credits for the material, which includes remakes of classics like "Dimples," "Boogie Chillen," "Burning Hell," and "Bottle Up and Go." With Hooker fronting a White blues-rock-boogie group, this doesn't offer the optimum circumstances to hear the man. But it's not bad either, Canned Heat playing with spirit and relative economy, although the 11-minute "Boogie Chillen" is excessive. *—Richie Unterberger*

Alone: The First Concert / May 21, 1996 / Blues Alliance ♦♦♦

Reissued by Concord's Blues Alliance label in 1996, this single CD boasts everything on Disc One of Tomato's two-CD set *Alone*, including heartfelt performances of "Boogie Chillen," "Boom Boom," "I'll Never Get Out of This Room Alive," and "One Bourbon, One Scotch, One Beer." The Tomato package contains two sets from Hooker's Hunter College engagement in 1996, whereas this CD focuses only on the first one. The format is just Hooker and his electric guitar, and in this intimate setting, the blues veteran has plenty of room to stretch out, improvise and say what needs to be said. Of course, those who already own the Tomato set don't need this reissue, which contains insightful liner notes by blues critic Kent Cooper. But because the Tomato set is out of print, it would be easier to find this disc and its companion CD *Alone: The Second Concert*. Either way, you're treated to some compelling blues. *—Alex Henderson*

Don't Look Back / Mar. 4, 1997 / Pointblank ♦♦♦

With new John Lee Hooker songs, new versions of old Hooker songs, four duets with and a new song by Van Morrison, *Don't Look Back* continues the venerable bluesman's string of excellent albums in his '90s renaissance. Produced by Morrison, it also celebrates the 25th anniversary of their first recording together, as Van guested on Hooker's seminal *Never Get Out of These Blues Alive* in 1972. *Don't Look Back* hits the ground running with a rowdy, thumpin' remake of "Dimples" with Los Lobos; "Spellbound" pounds out more of Hooker's stylistic trademark—throbbing, raw, hard-driving boogie. The Morrison tracks include the ruminative title cut and his haunting "The Healing Game." Hooker also gives Hendrix's classic blues "Red House" his own rough-hewn, distinctive treatment. *—Chris Slawecki*

Alone: The Second Concert / Apr. 29, 1997 / Blues Alliance ♦♦♦♦♦

Not just the boogie, but some *serious* blues too. This 1976 concert recording caught Hooker up close, giving both voice and guitar a lot of force. A candidate for best John Lee Hooker live album, complete with Hooker standards like "Boogie Chillen," "Hobo Blues" and "Crawling King Snake" (which comes equipped with a phantom harmonica player), it suffers only from being on the short side at forty-four minutes or so, dropping the listener into a silent void just as things are getting *really* warmed up. *—Steven McDonald*

His Best Chess Sides (Chess 50th Anniversary Collection) / Jun. 17, 1997 / Chess ♦♦♦

Hooker, as anyone with a decent-sized blues collection knows, recorded for a virtual parade of labels early in his career, including Chess, although his stays with the company were fairly brief. Hooker's best early recordings, most would agree, were issued on Modern and Vee-Jay, not Chess. Still, if the only Hooker extant was his Chess sides, his greatness would be readily apparent. Approached not as a best-of but simply as one of many Hooker compilations, this 15-song disc is fine, leaving heavily on early-'50s material (the source for eleven of the songs). This is typical of his early work in its stress on his great guitar work, walking rhythms, and drumless arrangements (most of it is played solo). It's good stuff, even if much of it is derivative of things he recorded elsewhere, and the mike plainly catches him coughing on "Bluebird." The solo on "Leave My Wife Alone" is almost avant-garde in conception, a series of plucked runs up and down the scale with little relation to convention, even by blues standards. Closing the set are four much more modern-sounding cuts from the mid-'60s, comprising the "I'm in the Mood"/"Let's Go Out Tonight" single and a couple of cuts from the *Real Folk Blues* LP (including his standard "One Bourbon, One Scotch and One Beer"). *—Richie Unterberger*

The Complete 50's Chess Recordings / Jan. 13, 1998 / Chess ♦♦♦

Hooker bounced around between label affiliations like crazy in the '50s, recording under almost as many fake names as he did labels during that decade. His two lasting record company hookups occurred with Chess in the early '50s and Vee-Jay later on in the decade. All of Hooker's Chess masters from that decade (he would later record in the '60s for them as well) are here on this two-disc, 31-track collection. Unlike other Chess artists, Hooker did little of his recording in Chicago, preferring to work out of his Detroit home base, where he continued to record for other labels under a variety of pseudonyms. His 1951 Chicago session excepted, the rest of the tracks emanate from Detroit sessions that also saw issuance on the local Gone, H-Q and Fortune labels. This is early John Lee at his solo-guitar, foot-stomping best, featuring boogies and introspective, slow blues that rival his best work. Some of the Detroit tracks reveal inbred distortion that can't be overcome even with modern day noise reduction techniques, but don't let that deter you from sampling some of the best John Lee Hooker available on compact disc for a second. *—Cub Koda*

The Best of Friends / Oct. 20, 1998 / Virgin ♦♦♦

John Lee Hooker's recordings for Virgin/Point Blank may have varied in quality, but never in formula. Once *The Healer* earned reams of praise and, more importantly, solid sales upon its 1989 release, it was pretty much set in stone that every future Hooker album would be painstakingly constructed and boast a plethora of superstar cameos. The guest stars were designed to bring in a larger audience, who would hopefully be impressed enough to stick around for Hooker's solid stuff, which was usually better than the attention-grabbing, star-studded tracks. Of course, the names are what sold, and Virgin did not overlook that fact, choosing to assemble a collection of highlights titled *The Best of Friends* in 1998. The title refers to the superstar duets, and while this very well may be the best of those cuts—well, almost all of the duets are here, including both the sublime ("I Cover the Waterfront," with Van Morrison) and the mediocre—this stuff still isn't as good as Hooker's solo recordings from this era. Which means this disc is primarily for listeners who like to think they like Hooker, but they really just want to hear Eric Clapton wail away. *—Stephen Thomas Erlewine*

The Best of John Lee Hooker / Jan. 18, 1999 / Music Club ♦♦♦

The Best of John Lee Hooker: 20th Century Masters—The Millennium Collection / Apr. 20, 1999 / MCA ♦♦♦

Like any record company worth their salt, MCA knows a good gimmick when they see it, and when the millennium came around... well, the *20th Century Masters—The Millennium Collection* wasn't too far behind. Supposedly, the millennium is a momentous occasion, but it's hard to feel that way when it's used as another excuse to turn out a budget-line series. But apart from the presumptuous title, *20th Century Masters—The Millennium Collection* turns out to be a very good budget-line series. True, it's impossible for any of these brief collections to be definitive, but they're nevertheless solid samplers that don't feature a bad song in the bunch. For example, take John Lee Hooker's *20th Century* volume—it's an irresistible 12-song summary of his MCA and Chess years. There may be a couple of noteworthy songs missing, but many of his best-known songs for the label are here, including "One Bourbon, One Scotch, One Beer," "I'm in the Mood," "I'm Bad Like Jesse James," "Sugar Mama," "Ground Hog Blues," "It's My Own Fault," and "It Serves You Right to Suffer." Serious fans will want something more extensive, but this is an excellent introduction for neophytes and a great sampler for casual fans, considering its length and price. That doesn't erase the ridiculousness of the series title, but the silliness is excusable when the music and the collections are good. *—Stephen Thomas Erlewine*

Definitive Collection / Apr. 25, 2000 / Metro ♦♦♦♦♦

No, it's not the definitive collection, covering just Hooker's time with Vee-Jay from the mid-'50s to the mid-'60s. In fact, it's not even the definitive collection of the Vee-Jay years, although with 24 tracks, it's pretty long for a single-disc retrospective of that phase. Hooker's Vee-Jay catalog is pretty well traveled, and this isn't the lengthiest survey of it. But because Hooker's Vee-Jay period was very good, this CD is very good, with its couple dozen slices of the label and era that produced his best full-band recordings (and the ones that are most approachable for R&B/rock listeners). As would happen with any 24-song Vee-Jay anthology, not everyone will think these are the best 24 tracks that could have been selected: "Maudie" and "One Bourbon, One Scotch, One Beer" are the most notable absentees. However, it does have some of his most familiar recordings—"Dimples," "Boom Boom," "I'm Mad Again" (covered by the Animals), the underrated "Don't Look Back" (covered by Them), the original version of "It Serves You Right to Suffer" (here titled "It Serves Me Right to Suffer"), and his Vee-Jay versions of "Boogie Chillen," "I'm in the Mood," and "Crawlin' Kingsnake." —*Richie Unterberger*

The Unknown John Lee Hooker: 1949 Recordings / May 16, 2000 / Flyright ✦✦✦
In 1949, Hooker played for a private gathering in the Detroit dining room of cartoonist, animator, and music fan Gene Deitch. Deitch had the foresight to record the performance on a portable machine. That acoustic performance—together with four tracks made a few days later in another casual gathering of music fans—was retrieved from Deitch's archives 50 years later for this hour-long, 20-cut CD. Hooker at this time had only just become a recording artist, and with the exception of four early 1949 sides done for Elmer Barbee, *The Unknown John Lee Hooker* represents the only known acoustic recordings by Hooker prior to the late '50s. Deitch and his friends asked Hooker to play older and more traditional songs, resulting in a set that included a greater concentration of country blues, spirituals, and folk tunes than Hooker was doing in his commercial recordings of the time. "Two White Horses," "Trouble in Mind," "John Henry," and "Jack O' Diamonds" are all here, for instance. Still, it's really not too far removed from what he was doing in the studio, given the inimitable Hooker stamp by his trademark omnipresent foot stomps and idiosyncratic rhythms. As both singer and guitarist Hooker, in this informal setting, sounds just as committed and inspired as he was on his studio dates; "Trouble in Mind," for instance, has guitar work as distinctive (and, at times, irregularly patterned and dissonant) as anything he did in the period. Nevertheless, this is primarily of historical interest, particularly as Hooker did do a wealth of similar folk/blues crossover sessions in the late '50s and early '60s that were captured in much better fidelity. The sound on this disc is listenable and certainly OK given the conditions of 1949 home recordings, but still a little hissy and muffled. This means that studio acoustic albums such as 1959's *The Country Blues of John Lee Hooker* are more highly recommended. —*Richie Unterberger*

On Campus / Jun. 20, 2000 / Collectables ✦✦✦
John Lee Hooker's Vee-Jay 1964 album *On Campus* is titled to sound like a live recording but it isn't. As part of the Collectables Vee-Jay reissue campaign, these 12 tracks originally tried to capitalize on Hooker's emergence on the coffeehouse/college tours he was involved in at the time. This is an electric album that contains excellent material from Hooker, even though the occasional background singers get in the way, attempting to modernize his gritty blues with a smoother soul sound. All of the Vee-Jay reissues of John Lee Hooker material are worth having and are budget priced as a bonus. —*Al Campbell*

Detroit: 1948–1949 / Jul. 18, 2000 / Savoy Jazz ✦✦✦✦
Acoustic or electric, alone or with a few friends, John Lee Hooker is always interesting. He has the gift to take the typical three-chord blues song and boil it down to its essence, relying on two, and sometimes no more than one, chord. *Detroit 1948-1949* captures him early in his career, delivering 16 songs on solo guitar (both acoustic and electric) and four with a raucous band. Savoy purchased the recordings—perhaps illegally since Hooker was under contract elsewhere—and never got around to issuing more than a few of them. It is funny to hear Hooker refer to himself in several places as "Slim," part of his effort to throw the record labels off the trail of his multiple commitments. These recordings reveal a bluesman that had already found his voice on numbers like "Landing Blues" and "Shady Grove Blues." This second number features the less than cheerful lyric, "Well they tell you the graveyard, is a low down dirty place/they take you way down to the graveyard, lord they throw dirt in your face." These lyrics are delivered in his characteristically uneven lines and punctuated by his idiosyncratic guitar playing. Also of special note are the four tracks featuring Hooker playing acoustic guitar, with energetic cuts like "Boogie Awhile" showing that his style remained intact plugged or unplugged. All of these songs are credited to Hooker and include no less than five songs with the word "boogie" in the title. While his voice lacks its noted resonance on these early recordings, it is nonetheless distinct. The detailed liner notes attempt to unravel just when these songs were recorded and under what circumstances. This makes for entertaining reading, but the important thing is the recording itself. It'll be a blessing to Hooker fans that these recordings are now available for everybody to enjoy. —*Ronnie Lankford Jr.*

The Complete 1964 Recordings / Aug. 1, 2000 / RPM ✦✦✦
John Lee Hooker's early band recordings tend to be among the more overlooked items in his catalog, and the 21 tracks here are among the least known of those group outings. This album is neatly divided in half between a spring 1964 session in Chicago with unknown players and a November 1964 session in London with the Groundhogs—the same band that would achieve considerable fame in the U.K. as a blues-rock act in the early '70s. These can't be considered his best early tracks to feature group backing, or his best '60s material, but the tracks are pretty good and well-played. The Chicago sessions are notable for the first appearance of one of his better-known songs, "It Serves You Right to Suffer" (although it was at this point called "It Serves Me Right to Suffer"). He and his accompanists get into a good swinging R&B groove on "Big Legs Tight Skirt," "Flowers on the Hour," and "Your Baby Ain't Sweet Like Mine," the last of which is explicitly derived from the Little Walter record "My Baby's Sweeter" (penned by Willie Dixon). The Groundhogs tracks

are just a bit less worthy and more subdued. But it must be said that the band plays well, and certainly as well as the accompanists he used in Chicago, in contrast to legends that have circulated as to how British musicians of the time who backed visiting American bluesmen weren't up to the task. These Groundhogs-backed Hooker tracks, by the way, appeared on Verve Folkways under the title...*And Seven Nights*. —*Richie Unterberger*

Boogie Chillen: 1948–1949 / Nov. 14, 2000 / EPM Musique ✦✦✦

House Rent Boogie / Apr. 10, 2001 / Ace ✦✦✦
There were already quite a few CDs' worth of early Hooker sides from the late '40s and early '50s on the market—such as *The Legendary Modern Recordings 1948-1954*, the three-CD *Alternate Boogie: Early Studio Recordings, 1948-1952*, and *Graveyard Blues*—prior to the 2001 appearance of this collection. So, is there a point to unearthing yet more tracks from his first years as a recording artist? Yes, actually, although this grab bag of early cuts, together with half a dozen previously unissued alternate versions, is not as solid or essential a pickup as *The Legendary Modern Recordings 1948-1954*. There may be no one alive who could ascertain exactly which of these tracks were never reissued prior to this release, or never reissued on CD prior to this release. Basically, however, it's known that several of these cuts (previously released or not) make their first appearance on compact disc here, and on the whole it's devoted to his lesser-known early Modern sides. Hooker was a very consistent artist even at the outset, and the trademarks that make his early recordings so appealing—the stomping foot, haunted vocals, and spidery guitar work—are all in force here. Particularly fine is the stomping title cut (an alternate take). Particularly unusual are the previously unissued take of "I'm in the Mood," which has a harmonica overdub, and the presence of sax, piano, and drums on a few numbers; the 1955 singles "Hug and Squeeze" and "I'm Ready" are very good full-band R&B arrangements. Eddie Kirkland (billed as "Little" Eddie Kirkland) appears on second guitar and vocals on a couple of tracks. —*Richie Unterberger*

Boogie Chillen / Jul. 10, 2001 / Indigo ✦✦✦
This 20-track compilation is taken solely from 1948-1949 sessions, an era that has been drawn from repeatedly for Hooker anthologies. If anyone ever assembles a comprehensive Hooker discography that delineates not only his original releases, but where and when these have been reissued, he or she deserves a government grant or something, because it's not so easy to determine where or if some of these have not appeared on reissues or CD elsewhere. It does, however, yield a sizable scoop of material from Hooker's most primeval phase, the first half devoted to recordings he issued under his own name, including the well-known "Boogie Chillen" and "Crawlin' King Snake." It's the final ten tracks that might be more of a draw for collectors, since it features songs he cut under the pseudonyms Delta John, Birmingham Sam, and Texas Slim. All of those songs are recognizably early Hooker, with their irregular meters, foot-stompin' beats, and intense bursts of citified Delta blues notes. Whether because these were cut under assumed names or due to other reasons, occasionally it seems like these were opportunities to ramble afield into rather far-out territory for urban blues of the era. "Goin' Mad Blues," originally credited to Birmingham Sam, has a compelling almost rock boogie rhythm and violently strident guitar riffs, while Texas Slim vented a darker side of the Hooker persona, as indicated in titles like "Nightmare Blues," "Devil's Jump," and "I'm Gonna Kill That Woman." By all means, there are more coherent overviews of John Lee Hooker's early recordings, but this has its rewards for those who want to dig deeply into the period. —*Richie Unterberger*

John Lee Hooker Is Hip: Greatest Hits / Jul. 31, 2001 / Music Club ✦✦✦✦
There have been few modern musicians who can embody the inherent contradictions of the blues as well as John Lee Hooker. Primitive and complicated, simple and complex, joyous and devastating, Hooker is never one or the other—he is always both. This collection of blues standards finds Hooker at the top of his game, announcing happily "This Is Hip" on one track and singing of the simple sexualized glory of a woman with "Big Legs, Tight Skirt" two tracks later. The collection is dominated by his highly stylized, uptempo boogies, and when Hooker chimes in with "It Serves Me Right to Suffer" near the end of the collection, he makes his suffering sound well worth it. —*Nate Cavalieri*

The Man, the Legend / Sep. 25, 2001 / Collectables ✦✦✦✦

Blue on Blues / Jan. 29, 2002 / Fuel 2000 ✦✦✦
In the liner notes, Bill Dahl points out that in many ways, John Lee Hooker and Lightnin' Hopkins were anachronisms. The acoustic country blues that they had grown up with was old hat by the late '40s. Still, both players built a repetition on idiosyncratic styles that had more in common with the old Delta than Muddy Waters. The half-dozen solo tracks by Hopkins originated from a 1969 session and the results are splendid. Old standbys like "Katie Mae" fit snugly between lovely gems like "I Hate I Got Married" and "Jailhouse Blues." There's something so strange about a Hopkins session when it works, a certain rough poetry in the way his lazy vocals and irregular guitar lines fall into place. Hooker kicks off his sides with a solo version of "Sally Mae" before being joined by piano, bass, and drums for a seven-minute take on "Rock With Me." While Hooker is in pretty good shape for this '70s session, the remaining tracks all run between six and nine minutes. This is a bit long for one-chord songs, and fails to match the intensity of the Hopkins material. While the Hooker material may not be the best introduction to his work, *Blue on Blues* does provide a good side by side comparison of two distinct, high-energy stylists. —*Ronnie D. Lankford Jr.*

The Real Folk Blues/More Real Folk Blues / Mar. 12, 2002 / MCA/Chess ✦✦✦✦
Of all the Chess albums in the *Real Folk Blues* series, the ones by John Lee Hooker might be most valued by hardened blues collectors. That's not so much because of the music—actually the *Real Folk Blues* albums by some other artists, like Howlin' Wolf, are better—but rather because, unlike the other records in the series, it was not simply a collection of various sessions that had often been previously issued. Hooker's *The Real Folk Blues* and

More Real Folk Blues, in contrast, were actually taken from a May 1966 session specifically recorded to produce the albums (which are both combined onto one CD with this reissue). Hooker was backed by a good electric band (though he goes it alone on "The Waterfront"), including his longtime friend Eddie Burns on guitar, Lafayette Leake on keyboards, and Fred Below on drums (the bassist's name has been forgotten). Only *The Real Folk Blues* was issued at the time, and it's the better of the two albums, particularly since it features the original version of one of his most famous tunes, "One Bourbon, One Scotch, One Beer." Hooker was noted for not being the easiest guy to put into an electric band situation, and the session is not his tightest, nor is the material (including a remake of his old hit "I'm in the Mood") his best or most diverse (even by his own self-cannibalizing standards). Still, it's reasonably good electric Hooker, a bit looser than Chess' usual standards, but pretty full-bodied and organized for a Hooker session. *More Real Folk Blues*, though recorded at the same session and intended to be released in the '60s, was not first issued until 1991. Not quite as strong as *The Real Folk Blues*, it's still OK, and notable for the raucous "Mustang Sally & GTO" and the inclusion of some social commentary in "This Land Is Nobody's Land." —*Richie Unterberger*

Live at Newport / Apr. 2, 2002 / Vanguard ✦✦✦
Live at Newport is an addition to the already huge pile of archival John Lee Hooker releases (one that will surely continue to grow as licenses to Hooker's myriad recordings for different labels exchange hands). What differentiates this release from many of the others is that it focuses on a pair of acoustic performances from the bluesman, a rarity in the Hooker catalog. In the early '60s, at the height of the "folk scare," Hooker stepped in front of crowds—at clubs, coffeehouses, and festivals—with his acoustic guitar. *Live at Newport* is split between two performances at the Newport Folk Festival—a solo shot from 1960 and a set (or set highlights?) with upright bassist Bill Lee from 1963. The former is stunning for its clarity, reveling in a warmth that can only be attained from placing a microphone in the vicinity of a man with an acoustic guitar, turning the levels way up, and absorbing everything: the scratch of the pick on the strings, the echo of the performer's foot as it taps on the platform, the bristle of buttons as they graze the back of the guitar, the intake of breath. The first cuts on the disc are exquisitely rendered, with a great sense of dynamics inherent in Hooker's patented free blues style. The sound quality of the latter tracks leaves much to be desired, with Hooker's guitar often getting lost in the ambience of the room or the muffled thump of Lee's bass. Still, there is some wonderfully intimate playing as Hooker simultaneously leads and plays off of Lee's parts. —*Jesse Jarnow*

Live at Sugar Hill, Vol. 2 / Aug. 20, 2002 / Fantasy ✦✦✦

Hoosegow

f. 1995

Group / Blues-Rock, Modern Electric Blues
Guitarist Elliott Sharp is most known for experimental outings that are characteristic of the late-20th century "downtown" New York scene, but he has also expressed a deep love for the blues. Even so, Hoosegow—which features Sharp on guitars and Queen Esther on vocals—will surprise much of his audience. Queen Esther and Sharp wrote all but one of the songs on their debut *Mighty*, which is rooted in the classic Chicago electric blues sound, although there is no instrumentation except for Sharp's guitars and Esther's vocals. Sharp proves himself to be quite the virtuoso on stinging blues guitar, and Esther a capable (though not thrilling) singer. The material is more restless and impressionistic than much contemporary blues, refusing to fall into good-timey cliches. It's just off-kilter enough to confuse traditional blues fans, and may be too traditional and accessible for Sharp's usual constituency. On top of that, it's being marketed by an alternative rock label, which means it could well fall between the cracks. That would be unfortunate, as it's a more interesting release than the usual contemporary blues fare, though hardly brilliant. —*Richie Unterberger*

● **Mighty** / 1996 / Homestead ✦✦✦
Sharp may not have much street cred (or even name recognition) among the listeners who usually buy blues records, but there's no denying his impressive skills in the idiom. The songs, too, are interestingly offbeat, being more absorbed with a sort of spiritual, questing attitude than the more mundane clichés of much modern blues. Queen Esther, however, is no more than an average vocalist, sounding as if she may be more at home with jazz than blues. —*Richie Unterberger*

Lightnin' Hopkins (Sam Hopkins)

b. Mar. 15, 1912, Centerville, TX, d. Jan. 30, 1982, Houston, TX

Vocals, Songwriter, Piano, Guitar, Organ / Blues Revival, Acoustic Texas Blues, Electric Texas Blues, Electric Blues, Texas Blues
Sam Hopkins was a Texas country bluesman of the highest caliber whose career began in the '20s and stretched all the way into the '80s. Along the way, Hopkins watched the genre change remarkably, but he never appreciably altered his mournful Lone Star sound, which translated onto both acoustic and electric guitar. Hopkins' nimble dexterity made intricate boogie riffs seem easy, and his fascinating penchant for improvising lyrics to fit whatever situation might arise made him a beloved blues troubadour.

Hopkins' brothers John Henry and Joel were also talented bluesmen, but it was Sam who became a star. In 1920, he met the legendary Blind Lemon Jefferson at a social function, and even got a chance to play with him. Later, Hopkins served as Jefferson's guide. In his teens, Hopkins began working with another prewar great, singer Texas Alexander, who was his cousin. A mid-'30s stretch in Houston's County Prison Farm for the young guitarist interrupted their partnership for a time, but when he was freed, Hopkins hooked back up with the older bluesman.

The pair was dishing out their lowdown brand of blues in Houston's Third Ward in 1946 when talent scout Lola Anne Cullum came across them. She had already engineered a pact with Los Angeles-based Aladdin Records for another of her charges, pianist Amos

Milburn, and Cullum saw the same sort of opportunity within Hopkins' dusty country blues. Alexander wasn't part of the deal; instead, Cullum paired Hopkins with pianist Wilson "Thunder" Smith, sensibly rechristened the guitarist Lightnin', and presto! Hopkins was very soon an Aladdin recording artist.

"Katie May," cut on November 9, 1946, in L.A. with Smith lending a hand on the 88s, was Lightnin' Hopkins' first regional seller of note. He recorded prolifically for Aladdin in both L.A. and Houston into 1948, scoring a national R&B hit for the firm with his "Shotgun Blues." "Short Haired Woman," "Abilene," and "Big Mama Jump," among many Aladdin gems, were evocative Texas blues rooted in an earlier era.

A load of other labels recorded the wily Hopkins after that, both in a solo context and with a small rhythm section—Modern/RPM (his uncompromising "Tim Moore's Farm" was an R&B hit in 1949), Gold Star (where he hit with "T-Model Blues" that same year), Sittin' in With ("Give Me Central 209" and "Coffee Blues" were national chart entries in 1952) and its Jax subsidiary, the major labels Mercury and Decca, and in 1954, a remarkable batch of sides for Herald where Hopkins played blistering electric guitar on a series of blasting rockers ("Lightnin's Boogie," "Lightnin's Special," the amazing "Hopkins' Sky Hop") in front of drummer Ben Turner and bassist Donald Cooks (who must have had bleeding fingers, so torrid were some of the tempos).

But Hopkins' style was apparently too rustic and old-fashioned for the new generation of rock & roll enthusiasts (they should have checked out "Hopkins' Sky Hop"). He was back on the Houston scene by 1959, largely forgotten. Fortunately, folklorist Mack McCormick rediscovered the guitarist, who was dusted off and presented as a folk-blues artist—a role that Hopkins was born to play. Pioneering musicologist Sam Charters produced Hopkins in a solo context for Folkways Records that same year, cutting an entire LP in Hopkins' tiny apartment (on a borrowed guitar). The results helped introduced his music to an entirely new audience.

Lightnin' Hopkins went from gigging at back-alley gin joints to starring at collegiate coffeehouses, appearing on TV programs and touring Europe to boot. His once-flagging recording career went right through the roof, with albums for World Pacific, Vee-Jay, Bluesville, Bobby Robinson's Fire label (where he cut his classic "Mojo Hand" in 1960), Candid, Arhoolie, Prestige, Verve, and in 1965, the first of several LPs for Stan Lewis' Shreveport-based Jewel logo.

Hopkins generally demanded full payment before he'd deign to sit down and record, and seldom indulged a producer's desire for more than one take of any song. His singular sense of country time befuddled more than a few unseasoned musicians; from the '60s on, his solo work is usually preferable to band-backed material.

Filmmaker Les Blank captured the Texas troubadour's informal lifestyle most vividly in his acclaimed 1967 documentary, *The Blues Accordin' to Lightnin' Hopkins*. As one of the last great country bluesmen, Hopkins was a fascinating figure who bridged the gap between rural and urban styles. —*Bill Dahl*

Blues Train / 1951 / Mainstream ✦✦✦✦
Classic sides from Hopkins' 1950-1951 stint with Bobby Shad's Sittin' in With logo. The disc's 15 selections include two of his biggest hits, "Hello Central" and "Coffee Blues." —*Bill Dahl*

☆ **Lightnin' Hopkins** / Jan. 16, 1959 / Smithsonian/Folkways ✦✦✦✦✦
Originally released as *The Roots of Lightnin' Hopkins*, Smithsonian/Folkways' *Lightnin' Hopkins* was recorded in 1959. Upon its initial release, it was a pivotal part of the blues revival and helped re-spark interest in Hopkins. Before it was recorded, the bluesman had disappeared from sight; after a great deal of searching, Sam Charters found Hopkins in a rented one-room apartment in Houston. Persuading Lightnin' with a bottle of gin, Charters convinced Hopkins to record ten songs in that room, using only one microphone. The resulting record was one of the greatest albums in Hopkins' catalog, a skeletal record that is absolutely naked in its loneliness and haunting in its despair. These unvarnished performances arguably capture the essence of Lightnin' Hopkins better than any of his other recordings, and it is certainly one of the landmarks of the late-'50s/early-'60s blues revival. —*Thom Owens*

Country Blues / 1960 / Tradition ✦✦✦
While Hopkins in his prime could crank out as many albums as there were days in the week (and sometimes more), some dates were more inspired than others and this casual recording is happily one of those times. In 1959, armed with nothing more than a single microphone mono tape recorder, folklorist Mack McCormick recorded Hopkins in an informal setting in hopes of catching some rough-edged performances that he felt were lacking from the bluesman's then-recent studio efforts. That he succeeded mightily is evidenced in this 15-song collection, almost casual in the way Lightnin' tosses off themes, lyrics, and emotion in a most cavalier fashion. Even with a thorough Sonic Solution No Noise process cleansing, these tapes still contain vocal and instrument distortion in spots where Hopkins got too close to the microphone. But none of it matters in the end, for here is Lightnin' truly in his element, playing for his friends and his own enjoyment, minus the comercial overlay of the times or the imposed "folk blues" posturing of his later acoustic recordings. Not the place to start, but a real good place to visit along the way. —*Cub Koda*

Strikes Again / Dec. 1960 / Collectables ✦✦✦

Lightnin' / 1961 / Prestige/Original Blues Classics ✦✦✦
Recorded for Prestige's Bluesville subsidiary in 1960 and reissued on CD for Fantasy's Original Blues Classics (OBC) series in 1990, *Lightnin'* is among the rewarding acoustic dates Lightnin' Hopkins delivered in the early '60s. The session has an informal, relaxed quality, and this approach serves a 48-year-old Hopkins impressively well on both originals like "Thinkin' 'Bout an Old Friend" and the familiar "Katie Mae" and enjoyable interpretations of Sonny Terry & Brownie McGhee's "Back to New Orleans" and Arthur "Big Boy" Crudup's "Mean Old Frisco." Hopkins' only accompaniment consists of bassist Leonard Gaskin and drummer Belton Evans, both of whom play in an understated fashion and do their part to make this intimate setting successful. From the remorseful "Come Back Baby" to more lighthearted, fun numbers like "You Better Watch Yourself" and

"Automobile Blues," *Lightnin'* is a lot like being in a small club with Hopkins as he shares his experiences, insights, and humor with you. —*Alex Henderson*

Last Night Blues / 1961 / Bluesville/Original Blues Classics ✦✦✦

How Many More Years I Got / 1962 / Fantasy ✦✦✦

Though he had been performing since the '20s, Texas bluesman Lightnin' Hopkins was a fresh face to the majority of the young folk audiences of the '60s. On the verge of drifting into obscurity, the singer had been rediscovered by enthusiast Mack McCormick and promoted to college crowds as a singer/guitarist in the folk-blues mold. What followed was a series of albums cut both solo and with session musicians for a variety of labels. *How Many More Years I Got* was one of the earliest. The players here are extremely loose, betraying a casual interest in the task at hand. They sound like a group of borrowed session men, but were in fact a small combo familiar both with each other and Hopkins himself. Bassist Donald Cooks, pianist Buster Pickens, drummer "Spider" Kilpatrick, and Hopkins' harp-playing cousin, Billy Bizor, all played on a number of the guitarist's dates during the early '60s. Hopkins was apparently reluctant to do second takes, however, and these recordings show it. The singer leads the group with his relaxed lines and Kilpatrick follows, further defining the tempo with the light, stiff patter of his drums. Bizor occasionally plays the role of catalyst, though his moans, hollers, and vocal/harmonica dialogues do little to increase the interest of his partners. Things pick up slightly during the album's second half, though even then the performances hardly approach the level of Hopkins' solo sides from the period, let alone his best work. —*Nathan Bush*

Mojo Hand / 1962 / Collectables ✦✦✦✦✦

This album, recorded for Fire Records, is especially interesting because it casts Hopkins in a more R&B-flavored environment. This obvious effort to get a hit makes for some excellent blues; moody and powerful performances play throughout. There's even a charming novelty Christmas blues, "Santa." —*Tim Sheridan*

Lightnin' Sam Hopkins & Spider Kilpatrick / Aug. 1962 / Arhoolie ✦✦✦✦

This recording is one of the best attempts to combine the eccentric blues structures of Houston's Lightnin' Hopkins with some kind of band backup. As blues idioms became more urbanized, the country bluesmen who were used to performing alone or in small acoustic combinations often experimented with recording with full bands, sometimes resulting in performances of such a lost nature that neither a compass nor a seeing-eye dog would be sufficient to get the group back on the same chord at the same time. The duets with drummer Spider Kilpatrick seemed a revelation at the time, as finally here was a musician who could follow Hopkins wherever he went, plus one providing a snappier beat that the guitarist could hang phrases of a bit more aggressive nature than usual on. These duets, of which two are included here, lose nothing of their brilliance with repeated listenings, and, of course, part of the endeavor's success is the absence of a bass player. A bassist actually does show up for four of the trio tracks, but these were instances where Hopkins took advantage of the group sound to play in a little bit different manner, and although these blues have a more set and normal blues structure, at least by Hopkins' standard, they work quite well and are recorded with quite a lot of impact. The bass is a bit low in the mix, probably intentionally. Something in the bridge of Hopkins' guitar makes one of his strings buzz like a sitar on these tracks, which might not have been intentional but certainly is a great effect. A bit of piano doodling and two beautifully intense guitar solos fill out the package. —*Eugene Chadbourne*

Blues in My Bottle / 1963 / Bluesville/Original Blues Classics ✦✦✦

Smokes Like Lightnin' / 1963 / Bluesville/Original Blues Classics ✦✦✦

Goin' Away / 1963 / Bluesville/Original Blues Classics ✦✦✦

For the 1963 album *Goin' Away*, Lightnin' Hopkins was backed by a spare rhythm section—bassist Leonard Gaskin and drummer Herb Lovelle—who managed to follow his ramshackle, instinctual sense of rhythm quite dexterously, giving Hopkins' skeletal guitar playing some muscle. Still, the spotlight remains Hopkins, who is in fine form here. There are no real classics here, but everything is solid, particularly "Stranger Here" and "You Better Stop Her," making it worth investigation by serious fans of Hopkins' classic material. —*Stephen Thomas Erlewine*

Hopkins Brothers: Lightnin', Joel, & John Henry / Feb. 1964 / Arhoolie ✦✦✦

A once-in-a-lifetime meeting of the three Hopkins brothers in Waxahatchie, TX, in 1964 produced this marvelous brace of field recordings. The oldest brother was considered the best songster in the family, and certainly his performances here are throwbacks to a more archaic style, although he's an amazingly energetic performer. Middle brother Joel is the crudest of the three, surprising since he's the one of the three who spent the most time around mentor Blind Lemon Jefferson. These are loose, conversational recordings made with a single microphone. They capture three brothers enjoying each other's company immensely. —*Cub Koda*

Swarthmore Concert / Apr. 1964 / Bluesville/Original Blues Classics ✦✦✦✦

A Lightnin' solo concert from his college kiddie-folk period (1964), this languished unissued in Fantasy Records' vaults until its release in the early '90s. That's a shame, because this concert captures Lightnin' at his beguiling best, spinning tales and blues magic with every track. His introductions are half the show, making even shopworn staples like "Baby Please Don't Go" and "My Babe" sound fresh. His guitar work is astounding, pulling off inventive leads while maintaining a constant boogie rhythm that makes other instruments superfluous. If you want a disc that clearly showcases Lightnin' Hopkins at his enchanting best, start your collection with this one; it's a charmer. —*Cub Koda*

Blue Lightnin' / 1965 / Jewel ✦✦✦

After a slew of albums aimed primarily at the folk-blues audience that resuscitated his flagging career during the early '60s, Hopkins attempted to regain his original fan base with these unpretentious 1965 sessions for Stan Lewis' Jewel logo. Pretty convincingly, too, with

the two-part "Move on Out" and a down-in-the-alley "Back Door Friend" among the standouts. Elmore Nixon, another Houston mainstay, plays piano on several cuts. —*Bill Dahl*

Hootin' the Blues / 1965 / Prestige/Original Blues Classics ✦✦✦

The most important part of Lightnin' Hopkins' career was spent in juke joints in Houston, but during the early '60s, he also became a star along the folk circuit, playing clubs that catered mostly to college students eager to hear authentic acoustic blues. Several of those shows were recorded over the years to capitalize, and while the albums don't have the same importance as Hopkins' classic blues sides of the '40s and '50s, they do show another side of the man, and one he seemed to take to very naturally. *Hootin' The Blues* is one of Hopkins' better folk club concerts, capturing him in an intense performance on acoustic guitar, rapping (in the sense of talking) about the blues and what it means as he introduces some powerful songs: "Blues Is a Feeling," "In the Evenin'," and "Meet Me in the Bottom," among others. The best moment, though, is his reinvention of Ray Charles' "What'd I Say" as an acoustic guitar number (trust me, it works), which displays the kind of fingering that must've made a young Eric Clapton want to sit down and cry. —*Bruce Eder*

Soul Blues / 1966 / Prestige/Original Blues Classics ✦✦✦

Live! At the 1966 Berkeley Blues Festival / 1966 / Arhoolie ✦✦✦

Recorded live on KAL radio in Berkeley, CA on April 15, 1966, this presents roughly equal shares of material from Lightnin' Hopkins, Mance Lipscomb, and Clifton Chenier, performing at the 1966 Berkeley Blues Festival. The sound is not state-of-the-art, but decent considering the vintage. The material is not going to surprise anyone familiar with the artists, which is good news if you're in love with their music and want typical excerpts of their sets, but bad news if you think you might have enough of them and you're considering whether to investigate further. Francis Clay plays drums as the sole other musician on Lightn' Hopkins' portion which, with its electric guitar, has a nice, mild electric R&B-rock feel. Half of this CD was previously available on Arhoolie LP 1030, but 11 of the 23 songs on the CD were previously unreleased, including two of Hopkins' seven contributions. —*Richie Unterberger*

Lightnin'! / 1967 / Arhoolie ✦✦✦✦

Lightnin'! is a fine introduction to Hopkins' electric blues material, and features performances of "Mojo Hand," "Rock Me Baby" and "Hold Up Your Head." —*Jason Ankeny*

In New York / 1970 / Candid ✦✦✦

This solo CD features the classic bluesman Lightnin' Hopkins on eight unaccompanied solos, not only singing and playing guitar but taking some rare solos on piano (including on "Lightnin's Piano Boogie"). Hopkins recorded a lot of albums in the '60s and all are quite listenable even if most are not essential; he did tend to ramble at times! This Candid release is one of his better sets of the period, highlighted by "Take It Easy," "Mighty Crazy," and "Mister Charlie." —*Scott Yanow*

Early Recordings, Vol. 2 / Nov. 1971 / Arhoolie ✦✦✦✦

The Arhoolie collection of recordings done for the Texas Gold Star label continued with a particularly well-assembled collection in which a few interesting variations in recording and backup musicians contribute to a sense of variety often missing from albums by this artist. There are also some vocal performances here that are among Hopkins' best committed to vinyl, such as the intense "Untrue Blues." These recordings are all very typical of the Hopkins approach in that many songs were probably improvised on the spot, or at least whipped up around a framework or some kind of skeletal idea. Hopkins has quite a strange attention span, sometimes approaching a song with strong concentration until he is halfway through, then becoming casual and letting things drift off completely. Aspects like this, and his way of improvising instrumental breaks in which the chord structure or tempo can be transformed at whim, make this a kind of blues that is challenging not only for the listener but for the performer as well. —*Eugene Chadbourne*

Legacy of the Blues, Vol. 12 / 1973 / GNP Crescendo ✦✦✦

Sam Charters produced this session, featuring Lightnin' and a three-piece band following him as best they can. Lightnin' is playing an acoustic with an electric pickup on it through an amplifier, and even throws in a bit of slide guitar on the chaotic opener, "Please Help Poor Me" and "The Hearse Is Backed Up to the Door." But ultimately the rhythm section isn't all that great a fit, and Lightnin' sounds distracted at times. Not essential, but it does have its moments. —*Cub Koda*

Double Blues / Jul. 1973 / Fantasy ✦✦✦✦

Lightnin' Hopkins' plaintive, soft-rolling blues style is exemplified on "Let's Go Sit on the Lawn," "Just a Wristwatch on My Arm," "I'm a Crawling Black Snake," Willie Dixon's "My Babe," and others. Accompanied only by himself on guitar (and oh what a guitar he plays), Leonard Gaskin (bass), and Herb Lovelle (drums), Hopkins' seductive, intricate guitar picks and strums will dance around in your head long after this CD has played. His voice, which sounds like it's aged in Camels and Jim Beam, conveys his heartfelt sagas to the fullest. A prolific songwriter, Hopkins wrote every song except the Dixon tune. —*Andrew Hamilton*

Early Recordings, Vol. 1 / 1975 / Arhoolie ✦✦✦

This is one of several collections put together from 78s recorded by Houston's Lightnin' Hopkins during the second half of the '40s. During this time he was a regular visitor at several studios with a regular jukebox market for his creations, and these are a really fine example of blues songs that are more like instant poetry that were concocted at the spur of the moment rather than slick, formalized, individualized song "hits." Much of the body of this blues artist's song catalog kind of runs together into a long odyssey, delivered in a rubato medium feel, sometimes locking into a steady beat but often hovering somewhere behind and ahead. As if performing an endless series of card tricks with only three cards, he comes up with variation after variation on the basic 12-bar form and a series of blues riffs that he has ready to fit any and all occasions. Listeners may not be able to tell one track from the next, but Hopkins' feel on guitar and charismatic, lilting voice has proven to be a winner with blues fans decade after decade. The ever adventuresome Hopkins cut some tracks on organ during this period, and these are parceled out among the collections. Although the resulting "Organ Boogie" certainly provides some variety, the songs with the guitar are of much more lasting music value, the organ numbers mostly of interest as an oddity. —*Eugene Chadbourne*

Po' Lightnin' / 1988 / Arhoolie ✦✦✦
On these recordings cut between 1961 and 1969, Hopkins exhibits the full scope of his music, picking up his electric guitar for a raw rendition of "Ice Storm Blues," sitting at the piano for a compelling version of "Jesus Will You Come By Here" and moving to the organ for an ethereal "My Baby's Gone." —*Jason Ankeny*

Lightnin' Hopkins, 1946–1960 / 1989 / DA Music ✦✦✦
21 songs from, as the title indicates, 1946 to 1960, mostly Lightnin' solo on guitar, although there are occasional additional instruments. This rather scattershot anthology isn't the best way to collect Hopkins. On the other hand, if you're not concerned with building a comprehensive discography, it's not a bad pickup, including an hour of decent music. —*Richie Unterberger*

The Herald Recordings, Vol. 2 / 1989 / Collectables ✦✦✦✦
Hopkins left a ton of tapes behind at New York-based Herald Records—enough to support this second volume of 1954 gems. —*Bill Dahl*

Nothin' But the Blues: Golden Classics Pt. 4 / 1989 / Collectables ✦✦✦✦✦
An interesting collection of stray Lightnin' sides from 1959 and 1960. On some, he's playing alone and acoustic, on others he's playing electric with a small band, even turning in chaotic instrumentals like "Guitar Lightnin,'" "Shake Yourself," and "Talk of the Town." Most of these are studio tracks, but there's some live stuff on here as well, most notably "Big Car Blues," the by-now-familiar version which shows up on a lot of other Hopkins anthologies. The most interesting track here is "Shaggy Dog," featuring a rhythm section that follow him every step of the way with a trombone player playing right along—and it all works! For a hodgepodge of leftovers, there's a lot of great Lightnin' on here. —*Cub Koda*

Texas Blues / 1990 / Arhoolie ✦✦✦
Recorded between 1961 and 1969, *Texas Blues* gets to the essence of Lightnin' Hopkins' music, delivering a fine sampling of his guitar work as well as the superior sense of humor which sends cuts like "Bald Headed Woman" and "Meet You at the Chicken Shack" over the top. —*Jason Ankeny*

Drinkin' in the Blues: Golden Classics, Pt. 1 / Mar. 12, 1990 / Collectables ✦✦✦✦
Almost 70 minutes of Lightnin' Hopkins, some live (no date or location listed) and some studio, but all pretty well indispensable for any fan, from the first words of the extraordinary opening monologue ("Big Black Cadillac Blues") on. He's playing acoustic live, and this sounds like one of his coffeehouse gigs along the folk circuit from the early '60s, except that the quality is better than on many of those shows, with a close sound on the guitar—the studio stuff is electric, natch. —*Bruce Eder*

☆ **The Complete Aladdin Recordings** / 1991 / Aladdin/EMI ✦✦✦✦✦
This is where it all began for the Houston troubadour: 43 solo sides, as evocative and stark as any he ever did, from 1946-1948. The first 13 sides find the guitarist in tandem with pianist Wilson "Thunder" Smith (who handles the vocals on a few tracks), but after that, old Lightnin' Hopkins went the solo route. "Katie May," "Short Haired Woman," "Abilene," "Shotgun"—all these and more rate with his seminal performances. —*Bill Dahl*

The Complete Prestige/Bluesville Recordings / 1991 / Prestige/Bluesville ✦✦✦✦✦
This is a seven-CD box set that repackages all 11 LPs that Lightnin' Hopkins recorded for Bluesville and Prestige during the first half of the '60s: *Last Night Blues, Lightnin', Blues in My Bottle, Walkin' This Road By Myself, Lightnin' and Co., Smokes Like Lightning, Hootin' the Blues, Goin' Away, Down Home Blues, Soul Blues,* and *My Life in the Blues.* The very prolific Hopkins (who was never loyal to any one label) also recorded for Candid, Arhoolie, Fire, and Vee-Jay during the period! The bulk of *My Life in the Blues* is actually a lengthy and rather historic interview that Samuel Charters conducted with Hopkins. A special bonus of the set is 13 often exciting tracks from a previously unissued concert at the Swarthmore College Folk Festival. The music throughout the box covers quite a variety of moods and subject matter (with Hopkins being unaccompanied on 34 of the tracks) and definitively sums up the veteran bluesman's later period. —*Scott Yanow*

Gold Star Sessions, Vol. 1 / 1991 / Arhoolie ✦✦✦✦✦
The first of two discs devoted to Hopkins' extensive recording activities during the late '40s for Bill Quinn's Gold Star logo. —*Bill Dahl*

Gold Star Sessions, Vol. 2 / 1991 / Arhoolie ✦✦✦✦✦
More wonderfully sparse ruminations by the Texas blues troubadour for Quinn's Gold Star label. Hopkins was amazingly prolific during his first few years of recording, and nearly everything he did back then has great artistic merit. —*Bill Dahl*

The Lost Texas Tapes, Vol. 1 / Oct. 22, 1991 / Collectables ✦✦✦
First in a series of five albums, cut at informal studio and live sessions in Houston, by Sam "Lightnin'" Hopkins with producer Aubrey Mayhew. Most of these sides, which were never intended for commercial release, and never before appeared anywhere, add immeasurably to the body of Hopkins' work, capturing as they do some of Hopkins' best solo electric blues playing at a time when he was more active doing acoustic "folk blues." —*Bruce Eder*

The Lost Texas Tapes, Vol. 2 / Oct. 22, 1991 / Collectables ✦✦✦
Clocking in at just over 23 minutes, this CD is on the short side, containing seven songs recorded on this particular day in an informal studio session. At his best here for about half of the the disc, Hopkins is in great form, coaxing several voices out of his single electric guitar while holding a beat very nicely. "Gonna Move Off This Street" is the best track here, but "Help Yourself (Christmastime)" is a close second—the solo guitar is captured close and crunchy. It's all very solid, despite the brevity of the proceedings. —*Bruce Eder*

The Lost Texas Tapes, Vol. 3 / Oct. 22, 1991 / Collectables ✦✦✦
The material here is among the best of Hopkins' later recording career, a good rival to his return to blues on Jewel after years of catering to acoustic folk audiences—recorded before a live audience, he plays his electric guitar down and dirty, getting it to "talk" in some surprisingly crisp and articulate tones. Most of the material ("I Heard My Baby Crying," "My Baby Laid Out All Night," "Rock Me Late At Night," etc.) is extended to four or five minutes or more, and it's all in duophonic stereo, with voice on one channel and guitar on the other, which makes it really cool for anyone who just wants to concentrate on the playing. —*Bruce Eder*

The Lost Texas Tapes, Vol. 4 / Oct. 22, 1991 / Collectables ✦✦✦

The Lost Texas Tapes, Vol. 5 / Oct. 22, 1991 / Collectables ✦✦
Billed as "Lightnin' Hopkins & Friends," and this is the least engaging of this series of five volumes, partly because of its brevity (26 minutes), and because Hopkins, according to producer Aubrey Mayhew, was drinking on the night that the live material here was recorded, and spent long stretches staring at the floor. But when he played "Back In My Mother's Arms," the sound was as hot as ever. He only does two solo live numbers, and the rest is studio stuff, supported by singer Curley Lee, who joins him variously on "Goodnight Irene," "One Meat Ball," and "Sorrow to My Heart," and is also represented—as is folksinger Irish O'Malley—on separate featured numbers. The sources and quality of the recordings vary from song to song, with some disc source material in evidence. —*Bruce Eder*

Sittin' in With / 1992 / Mainstream ✦✦✦✦
The second installment of Sittin' in With masters, some with bassist Donald Cooks and drummer Connie Kroll providing rock-solid support (L.C. Williams takes over as vocalist for two cuts). Supple boogies and dusty rural blues, all woven expertly by the Texas guitarist. —*Bill Dahl*

Live 1971 / 1992 / Diablo ✦✦✦
Two albums—released as separate CDs in 1992—taken from a two show performance in 1971 from an unknown source are combined onto one disc in this 1999 re-release. No information on where the recording took place or who the bass player and drummer accompanying Hopkins are, either. The recording source is obviously a p.a. board tape with strange volume fluctuations, microphone poppings and occasional feedback, oddly mixed in stereo and heavy on the bass. Audio disclaimers aside, this recording would be a welcome addition to anyone's collection as Hopkins is in rare form, telling incomprehensible jokes as he charms the pants off his audience while playing and singing his heart out. Unfortunately as the first set comes to a close, the bass player's tuning goes woefully flat and he plays several tunes in the wrong key and just can't get back in tune to save his life for the rest of the set. Finally exasperated, Lightnin' proceeds to tune him up right in the middle of a song and unable to stand it any longer, finally bitches him and the drummer out after a wobbly version of "Baby Please Don't Go" ('You're killin' me, all of ya'), launching into another chaotic instrumental and even more sloppy, out-of-tune playing. While there's a wealth of interesting and musically worthwhile performances on this package, you'll have to ignore about a third of the ones on here to get to the good stuff. —*Cub Koda*

It's a Sin to Be Rich / 1993 / Verve ✦
It's a sin that these sloppy, uninspired 1972 tapes ever saw the light of day. Hopkins and his cohorts (including John Lee Hooker, who also should have known better) stumble and bumble their way through some of the most disposable performances the guitarist ever knocked off. —*Bill Dahl*

Houston Bound / 1993 / Relic ✦✦✦✦
Thirteen of the last sides he cut for his former R&B audience. Under Bobby Robinson's tutelage, Hopkins' 1960 Fire sides rank with his finest—especially his boogie-based "Mojo Hand," a title he subsequently remade early and often. —*Bill Dahl*

Coffee House Blues: Charly Blues Masterworks, Vol. 33 / 1993 / Charly ✦✦✦
This brings together some early-'60s sides that Hopkins recorded for the Chicago-based Vee-Jay label, although all of them were recorded in his native Houston. Lightnin's spoken introduction sets up the hilarious "Big Car Blues," part of five live tracks aboard, before setting up eight heavily reverbed studio tracks from Bill Quinn's Gold Star Studios. The final two are full-band tracks produced by drummer King Ivory Lee Semiens with Lightnin' playing electric, the band following his erratic timing as best as they can. While the material on here is classic Lightnin', the sound is dodgy throughout, the live tracks pulled from vinyl and distorting out in several spots. If you can find the live material on another compilation and can audition it before buying, pass this one by. —*Cub Koda*

☆ **Mojo Hand: The Anthology** / May 18, 1993 / Rhino ✦✦✦✦✦
As with its John Lee Hooker two-disc set, Rhino offers a very pleasant way to begin serious appreciation of Hopkins' humongous recorded legacy with this 41-track anthology. His Aladdin, Gold Star, RPM, Sittin' in With, and Mercury output are all liberally sampled on disc one, and there are a half dozen of those electrifying 1954 Herald sides that verged on rock & roll. Disc two is a less exciting affair, those '60s folk-blues and later efforts usually paling in comparison to seminal early efforts. Still, for a cogent overview of the guitarist's daunting discography, this is the place to start. —*Bill Dahl*

The Herald Material 1954 / Aug. 30, 1994 / Collectables ♦♦♦♦♦
Lightnin' Hopkins in a heavily amplified mode (especially for 1954!) and tearing it up with some of the wildest licks of his long and storied career! It's hard to fathom a more torrid tempo than the one he employs for "Hopkins' Sky Hop," and "Flash Lightnin'," "Lightnin's Boogie," and "Lightnin' Stomp" aren't far behind. Alas, Hopkins' Herald waxings didn't sell particularly well—though they're downright astonishing in retrospect. *—Bill Dahl*

Blues Hoot / 1996 / DCC ♦♦♦
Lightnin' Hopkins is the star of this live recording, made at an August 1961 concert at the Ash Grove in Hollywood featuring Hopkins, Sonny Terry and Brownie McGhee (with Big Joe Williams sitting in on three numbers). It isn't remotely unique, joining a long list of club recordings by all three, although the original LP (on the Davon and Horizon labels) was obscure enough that collectors may welcome this CD. The sound is excellent, and the original master tape has yielded one extra Terry/McGhee track ("Po' Boy") and one extra Hopkins/Terry/McGhee song ("Early Morning Blues") from the same show—the producers have also added on two more songs ("I'm A Stranger Here," "Trouble In Mind") from an L.A. Troubador show by Terry and McGhee, bringing the running time up to 60 minutes. The sound is excellent, the performances are spirited enough, and the addition of the ominous "Early Morning Blues" shifts the record more toward blues than the folk/hootenanny orientation of the released Hopkins/Terry/McGhee tracks. "Blues For the Lowlands" is the best of the Terry/McGhee tracks, beautifully showcasing their harmonica/guitar interplay. It is difficult to say, however, anything distinguishes this set from the other folk club recordings that Hopkins, Terry and McGhee left behind on other labels. *—Bruce Eder*

Jake Head Boogie / Feb. 12, 1999 / Ace ♦♦♦♦♦
In the late '40s and early '50s, Hopkins recorded for Houston record producer Bill Quinn, the results appearing on several labels (including Quinn's own Gold Star company). In 1951, Quinn sold unreleased Hopkins masters to Modern, which issued some on its RPM subsidiary. This 31-track disc has all 14 of the Hopkins sides that came out on RPM, plus a bunch of other tracks from the same batch of Modern-by-way-of-Quinn masters; most were not available on CD outside of Japan before this release and were indeed usually hard to find anywhere. The sounds are what you'd expect from Hopkins if you've heard more widely circulated stuff from this period: Texas blues caught between the rural and electric era, done country style and performed solo, but usually played on a harshly amplified electric guitar that adds to the power. The title track especially has some of Hopkins' most effective guitar, getting into some really crunching and raunchy chords in the breaks. "Bad Luck and Trouble," "Beggin' You to Stay," "Mistreater Blues," "War News Blues," "Lonesome Dog Blues," "Everyday I Have the Blues"—it's not always the most optimistic fare, although it's delivered with casual good cheer. Collectors should note that some of these sound different from the actual Modern singles, which added a lot of reverb echo; Ace decided whenever possible to use the original acetates, which had only the natural echo of the room in which Lightnin' recorded. *—Richie Unterberger*

Straight Blues / Jul. 13, 1999 / Bluesville/Original Blues Classics ♦♦♦
A grab bag of early '60s Hopkins, four of the songs recorded solo in a Houston studio in July 1961, two recorded with bass and drums in New York in May 1964, and the other six recorded live as a solo in New York in December 1964. These were originally released on the following Prestige/Bluesville LPs: the 1961 cuts on *Walkin' this Road by Myself*, the two New York band songs on *Down Home Blues*, and the live New York tracks on *My Life in the Blues*. For a while this compilation was only available on CD as part of the seven-CD boxed set *The Complete Prestige/Bluesville Recordings*; in 1999, it was issued as a separate CD. So those on the lookout for this will probably be either gap-fillers, or listeners who are rather indiscriminate about which Hopkins releases to pluck from his large discography. The music itself is OK. Hopkins plays good country blues on the 1961 numbers, particularly on "Baby Don't You Tear My Clothes" and his interpretation of "Good Morning Little School Girl." The two 1964 band efforts are pretty good spare electric blues, whether "I Like to Boogie" or the more unusual "Get It Straight," which gets rather close to country music in its rhythms and guitar work. The half-dozen live New York songs are typical Hopkins performances, incorporating both narrative folky tunes with spoken introductions, and livelier boogies. *—Richie Unterberger*

Remaining Titles: 1950–1961, Vol. 1 / Oct. 12, 1999 / Document ♦♦♦

Lightnin' Boogie / May 16, 2000 / Catfish ♦♦♦
A 22-track collection of Lightnin's earliest sides, recorded between 1946 and 1949. Starting off with a two-song session with pianist Thunder Smith from 1946, the next 11 tracks are solo work from 1947 and 1948, although by this time Lightnin' was playing electric. In the midst of all these solo tracks, Thunder Smith takes over the vocal on "Can't Do Like You Used To," a raw boogie with Hopkins on backup guitar. Although the tracks are not in chronological order, the collection holds together quite well, showing off Lightnin's early sound and how little it changed with the intervening years. Texas blues at its best. *—Cub Koda*

Remember Me: The Complete Herald Singles / May 16, 2000 / Ember ♦♦♦
Sam Lightnin' Hopkins originally recorded the 26 tracks that make up *Remember Me* in April 1954 for the Herald label. It contains over 74 minutes of Hopkins on electric guitar accompanied by bassist Donald Cooks, drummer Ben "Gene" Turner, and a vocal track with Hopkins "protégée" (or girlfriend) Ruth Ames. This combination of Texas boogie and slow blues material has been previously issued with the exception of "Walking and Drinking" and "God Made Man." The songs don't always come across as complete, leaving Lightnin' to improvise a few of them. Thankfully he was the type of bluesman that had the second-nature experience to provide an enjoyable outcome. Generally the sound quality on this disc from the London-based label Ember is typically very good but be prepared for the odd drop out. *—Al Campbell*

★ **Blues Masters: The Very Best of Lightnin' Hopkins** / Aug. 15, 2000 / Rhino ♦♦♦♦♦
Pruning 16 tracks from Hopkins' extensive catalog for a best-of meant that some hard choices had to be made. The ones Rhino came up with won't satisfy everyone, but the label did take the correct road by sticking exclusively to the earliest part of his career, 1947-1961. Perhaps the decision will offend some fans who feel that his '60s and '70s work should be represented, but two things should be acknowledged. First, Hopkins, as is the case with most artists, did his most interesting recordings in the earlier part of his career. Second, as is the case with many blues artists, he did not vary his approach substantially throughout the decades. So what you have is a good assortment of his first 15 years on disc, taken from about ten labels, including both originals and covers, and placing the singer/guitarist in various instrumental contexts: with a full electric band (Sonny Terry is on a couple of 1961 cuts), as a solo guitarist, or accompanied by nothing more than a bass or additional guitarist. It's a good deal for those who want only one Hopkins disc, and for those who want a best-of that's more extensive, there's Rhino's own two-disc anthology, *Mojo Hand*. *—Richie Unterberger*

1946–1947: Complete First Recordings, Vol. 1 / Oct. 17, 2000 / EPM Musique ♦♦♦

From the Vaults of Everest / Feb. 13, 2001 / Collectables ♦♦♦

Fishing Clothes: The Jewel Recordings 1965–1969 / Apr. 10, 2001 / West Side ♦♦♦

Lightnin' and the Blues: The Herald Sessions / Apr. 17, 2001 / Buddha ♦♦♦

Best of Lightning Hopkins / Sep. 1, 2001 / Arhoolie ♦♦♦♦
While it's probably impossible to fully pin down a best-of from a man who constantly reinvented his own songs, it's only fitting that Arhoolie release this, since Lightnin' Hopkins (or Lightning Hopkins, as he's called here) was the inspiration for Chris Strachwitz to start his label. And while ten of the cuts are culled from Hopkins' Arhoolie recordings, Strachwitz has dug deeper, going back to the bluesman's seminal cuts for the Texas-based Gold Star label in the late '40s, making this a fine career cross-section. Hopkins was the link between the old and the new Texas blues, a man who'd played with the great Blind Lemon Jefferson before going on to influence a generation after his rediscovery in Houston in the late '50s. And while older solo pieces like "Whiskey Blues" and "Grosebeck Blues" seemingly have their roots in the '20s, Hopkins is equally comfortable with a band, as on the riotous "Bald Headed Woman." However, the later material seems geared for his new white audience, unlike the earlier raw juke-joint pieces. But Hopkins was a master improviser (much like Bukka White) who could change a lyric on a whim to put across what was on his mind—meaning there was rarely a definitive performance of any song, however high a standard he maintained. But there was also a strain of protest, whether on "Tim Moore's Farm" or the later "Please Settle in Vietnam," that kept his work topical. And, as an interesting aside, "Zolo Go" might be the very first recorded piece of modern zydeco, with Hopkins on organ attempting what his cousin, Clifton Chenier, would later do so successfully. *—Chris Nickson*

Blues / Jul. 9, 2002 / Collectables ♦♦♦
An album's title can do one of several things: describe the mood, the style, or the subject of the music. While one might be tempted to interpret a title like *Blues* in a general sense, it's meant, in this instance, in the most literal sense. Every song on this collection by Lightnin' Hopkins has the word "blues" in the title. There's "G-String Blues," "Blues for My Cookie," and "Sick Feelin' Blues." As with much of Hopkins' music, there are moments of brilliance, and there are non-distinct lapses. There's a down-and-dirty, lo-fi take on "Santa Fe Blues" and a soulful, live version of "Stool Pigeon Blues." "Mama got mad at Pop/'cause he didn't bring no coffee home," kicks off a bouncy, "Coffee House Blues," while Sonny Boy Williamson adds his harmonica to "Drinkin' in the Blues." There are moments, as with "Big Black Cadillac Blues," where Hopkins seems more interested in talking than singing, and the odd mixture of songs—solo, acoustic and full-band—seems abrupt at times. *Blues*' eclectic nature, however, does provide a good snapshot of Hopkins' multi-faceted approach to the saddest of musical genres. Blues fans, guitar players, and anyone curious about the endless possibilities of using "blues" in a song's title, will want to pick up a copy. *—Ronnie D. Lankford Jr.*

Big Walter Horton

b. Apr. 6, 1917, Horn Lake, MS, **d.** Dec. 8, 1981, Chicago, IL
Vocals, Harmonica / Juke Joint Blues, Harmonica Blues, Electric Memphis Blues, Electric Chicago Blues, Electric Harmonica Blues

Big Walter Horton, sometimes known as Shakey Walter Horton, is one of the most influential blues harmonica players of all time, and a particular pioneer in the field of amplified harmonica. He isn't as widely known as his fellow Chicago blues pioneers Little Walter or Sonny Boy Williamson, due mostly to the fact that, as a rather shy, quiet individual, he never had much taste for leading his own bands or recording sessions. But his style was utterly distinctive, marked by an enormous, hornlike tone, virtuosic single-note lines, fluid phrasing, and an expansive sense of space. Horton's amplified harp work graced sides by Muddy Waters, Jimmy Rogers, Otis Rush, Johnny Shines, Tampa Red, and many others; he was frequently cited as an inspiration by younger players, and most accounts of his life mention a testimonial from legendary bassist/songwriter Willie Dixon, who once called Horton "the best harmonica player I ever heard."

Walter Horton was born April 6, 1917, in Horn Lake, MS, near Memphis. He began teaching himself to play the harmonica—a gift from his father—at age five, and moved with his mother to Memphis not long after, where he played in Handy Park (near the famed Beale Street) for tips. During his preteen years in the late '20s, he played—and likely recorded at least a couple of sides—with the Memphis Jug Band (as Shakey Walter); he also learned more about his craft from Will Shade, the Jug Band's main harmonica player, and Hammie Nixon, a cohort of Sleepy John Estes. Horton played wherever he could during the Depression—dances, parties, juke joints, street corners—and teamed up with the likes of Robert Johnson, Johnny Shines, Homesick James, and David "Honeyboy" Edwards, among others; he also worked as a sideman in several touring blues bands, including those of Ma Rainey and Big Joe Williams, and spent his first brief period in Chicago. In 1939, he backed guitarist Charlie "Little Buddy" Doyle on some sessions for Columbia. Around the same time (according to Horton himself), he began to experiment with amplifying his harmonica, which if accurate may have made him the first to do so.

However, Horton largely dropped out of music for much of the '40s, working a variety of odd jobs to make ends meet (although he reportedly gave pointers to both Little Walter and Sonny Boy Williamson during this era). He returned to active duty in 1948, playing with the young B.B. King; the following year, he hooked up with bandleader Eddie Taylor. He recorded several sides for Sam Phillips in 1951, which were leased to Modern/RPM and credited to Mumbles (a nickname that particularly rankled Horton). The following year he recorded with longtime friend Johnny Shines, and was invited to settle permanently in Chicago by Eddie Taylor. In early 1953, not long after arriving, Horton got a chance to record with Muddy Waters, since regular harpman Junior Wells had been drafted into military service. Horton wound up joining Waters' band for most of the year, playing on cuts like "Forty Days and Forty Nights" and "Mad Love (I Want You to Love Me)." However, he was fired by year's end for breaking band commitments—either due to excessive drinking or playing too many side gigs, depending on the account.

By that point, however, Horton had established himself as a session man at Chess Records. He also returned to Memphis in 1953 to record several more sides for Sam Phillips' Sun label, along with guitarist Jimmy DeBerry; their single "Easy" ranks as one of the all-time classic harmonica instrumentals, and a Horton signature tune. Horton subsequently returned to Chicago, where he continued his session work for Chess (including several more with Waters) and recorded his own Chess singles under the auspices of producer Willie Dixon. He also cut sides for Cobra, States ("Hard Hearted Woman"), and Jewel during the '50s (again, mostly with Dixon producing), and turned in some of his greatest performances on Chicago blues classics like Jimmy Rogers' "Walking By Myself," Otis Rush's "I Can't Quit You Baby," and Johnny Shines' "Evening Sun."

In 1964, Horton recorded his first full-length album, *The Soul of Blues Harmonica*, for Chess subsidiary Argo; it was produced by Dixon and featured Buddy Guy as a sideman, though it didn't completely capture what Horton could do. Two years later, Horton contributed several cuts to Vanguard's classic compilation *Chicago/The Blues/Today!, Vol. 3*, which did much to establish his name on a blues circuit that was thriving anew thanks to an infusion of interest from white audiences; it also showcased his pupil Charlie Musselwhite. In addition to his own recordings, the '60s found Horton working often in Jimmy Rogers' band, and performing and recording with the likes of Johnny Shines, J.B. Hutto, Johnny Young, Big Mama Thornton, Koko Taylor, Robert Nighthawk, Sunnyland Slim, and the original version of Fleetwood Mac. Toward the end of the decade, he took on more pupils, most notably Peter "Madcat" Ruth and Carey Bell, the latter of whom recorded with his mentor on the 1973 Alligator LP *Big Walter Horton With Carey Bell*. Horton also became a regular on Willie Dixon's Blues All Stars package tours, which made their way through America and Europe over the '60s and '70s.

Despite the considerable acclaim he enjoyed from his peers, Horton never became a recording star on his own; he simply lacked the temperament to keep a band together for very long, preferring the sideman work where his shyness was less of a drawback. That, coupled with his often heavy drinking, meant that money was often scarce, and Horton kept working steadily whenever possible. After his 1973 album with Bell, he became a mainstay on the festival circuit, and often played at the open-air market on Chicago's legendary Maxwell Street, along with many other bluesmen. In 1977, he joined Johnny Winter and Muddy Waters on Winter's album *I'm Ready*, and during the same period recorded some material for Blind Pig, which later found release as the albums *Fine Cuts* and *Can't Keep Lovin' You*. Horton appeared in the Maxwell Street scene in the 1980 film *The Blues Brothers*, accompanying John Lee Hooker. He died of heart failure on December 8, 1981, and was inducted into the Blues Hall of Fame the following year. *—Steve Huey*

The Soul of Blues Harmonica / Jan. 13, 1964 / MCA/Chess ♦♦♦
Big Walter's first album and with an all star cast—Buddy Guy (guitar), Jack Myers (bass), Willie Dixon (vocals), and Willie Smith (drums). Although not definitive, this album is worth seeking out for Horton fans. It features Walter in a variety of musical styles, including a good rendition of "Hard Hearted Woman" and a wild version of "La Cucaracha" *—Michael Erlewine*

Southern Comfort / 1969 / Sire ♦♦

Offer You Can't Refuse [1 Side] / 1972 / Red Lightnin' ♦♦♦
An album released on the Red Lightnin' label in 1972 consisting of one side of Big Walter Horton and the other side with very early Paul Butterfield (1963). The Horton side consists of eight tracks of Horton with guitarist Robert Nighthawk (no bass or drums). Nighthawk is playing pure backup here, very little else. It is not clear when these were recorded. Perhaps not classic Walter, but any Big Walter is worth a listen. There are three instrumentals that make for good listening, including a version of "Easy" (not up to the original Walter recording). The instrumental "West Side Blues" has some interesting Walter harp licks that I have not heard elsewhere. The other five cuts are Walter singing. Of these, there is a great version of "Louise" and Walter singing "Tin Pan Alley" which never fails to raise the hair on the back of my neck. If you can find this album, it is good to have. *—Michael Erlewine*

Live at the El Mocambo / 1973 / Red Lightnin' ♦
Recorded at the El Mocambo Club in Toronto on July 25, 1973, this is not vintage Horton. *—Michael Erlewine*

Big Walter Horton With Carey Bell / Jan. 1973 / Alligator ♦♦♦♦
The teacher/pupil angle might be a bit unwieldy here—Bell was already a formidable harpist in his own right by 1972, when Horton made this album—but there's no denying that a stylistic bond existed between the two. A highly showcase for the often recalcitrant harp master, and only his second domestic set as a leader. *—Bill Dahl*

Fine Cuts / Apr. 1979 / Blind Pig ♦♦♦♦♦
Horton was tragically underrecorded as a bandleader; this album certainly attests to his talents in that regard, whether romping through a joyous "Everybody's Fishin'" or elegantly exmaining the tonal possibilities of the Duke Ellington chestnut "Don't Get Around Much Anymore." John Nicholas provides sympathetic backing on both guitar and piano, and Kaz Kazanoff is the stellar saxman. *—Bill Dahl*

Little Boy Blue / 1980 / JSP ♦♦♦
A 1980 live recording in Boston. Working with a pickup band consisting of Ronnie Earl on guitar, Mudcat Ward on bass, and Ola Dixon on drums, Horton catches fire and quite simply blows his heart out. The album features some of Horton's best late-period playing. *—Cub Koda*

Harmonica Blues Kings / May 1987 / Delmark ♦♦♦♦♦
This is very early amplified Walter, recorded in the fall of 1954 for the Black-owned United/States labels. On four of the cuts, Big Walter is playing backup harp and solos for singer Tommy Brown; the other two cuts represent Big Walter's first Chicago record under his own name. Includes the definitive recording of the classic Walter tune "Hard Hearted Woman." Reissued on compact disc by Delmark in 2000. *—Michael Erlewine*

Mouth Harp Maestro / 1988 / Ace ♦♦♦♦♦
Long before he arrived in Chicago, Horton was knocking 'em dead with his amplified harmonica wizardry in Memphis. Sam Phillips produced the classic sides that comprise much of this album in 1951, when Horton was billed as "Mumbles." Sizzling backup by guitarists Joe Hill Louis and Calvin Newborn urged the introverted harp giant on to dazzling heights on his earliest sides as a leader. *—Bill Dahl*

Can't Keep Lovin' You / 1989 / Blind Pig ♦♦♦
Probably from the mid-'70s, this is later Horton, with John Nicholas on guitar and Ron Levy on piano. The album features a variety of material, including a good version of "Hard Hearted Woman." Not vintage, but worth a listen. *—Michael Erlewine*

Memphis Recordings 1951 / 1991 / Kent ♦♦♦♦♦
These are the Modern/Cobra masters—17 cuts from the sessions Walter did with Sam Phillips in 1951, including several alternate takes. This is mostly great acoustic harp, but it does contain the songs "Have a Good Time," and "Need My Baby" with Walter playing amplified harp—and great songs and solos these are! Worth finding. *—Michael Erlewine*

Well All Right, Vol. 4: Ann Arbor Blues & Jazz Festival / Apr. 16, 1996 / Schoolkids ♦♦♦
Recorded at the 1973 Ann Arbor Blues and Jazz Festival, this set is for the serious collector/historian only—it has excellent, informative liner notes but the sound quality is less than perfect. The King Biscuit Boys are all Mississippi Delta blues veterans who never really made it big but were local fixtures in the region from doing the King Biscuit radio show. Houston Stackhouse mentored Robert Nighthawk but made few recordings of his own. Joe Willie Wilkins was a sideman on many of Sonny Boy Williamson's early recordings. The music is programmatic rough and tumble electric Delta blues played by veterans of the Delta juke joints. These guys had played together forever. Its enjoyable music played by a good backup band lacking a star to backup. Big Walter Horton is backed up by a group of local Ann Arbor neophytes (guitarist John Nicholas, bassist Sarah Brown and drummer Fran Christina) who became veterans of the Texas blues scene, recording and playing with Asleep at the Wheel, Stevie Ray Vaughn, the Fabulous Thunderbirds, and Marcia Ball, to name a few. Walter isn't really in top form but on his worst day he was still an amazing technical and musical harp virtuoso. There is enough octave jumping and beautifully controlled note-bending here to reaffirm his place in the upper pantheon of harp wizards. He never rushes, goes for quality not quantity, and teaches a course in restraint and soul. Big Walter's vocals take some getting used to and many prefer him as an accompanist. Try his six masterpieces backing up Johnny Shines on *Johnny Shines and Robert Lockwood* on Paula. *—Jim Coffin*

Hot Shot Love (Coy Love)

d. Jun. 4, 1980
Vocals, Harmonica / Memphis Blues, Harmonica Blues
Coy "Hot Shot" Love was a renaissance man, of a kind, in blues: sign-painter, street denizen, and a magician with a harmonica, who liked to adorn his leather jacket and his bicycle, and other personal items with messages regarding his outlook on life. He lived on Gayoso Street in Memphis, an itinerant musician and sometime sign-painter who got his one moment of glory in the recording studio on January 8, 1954, when he entered Sam Phillips' Sun Studios to record "Wolf Call Boogie" b/w "Harmonica Jam," backed by Mose Vinson at the piano, Pat Hare on guitar, Kenneth Banks on bass, and Houston Stokes on the drums. The A-side, of which an outtake exists, is practically a monologue with musical accompaniment, set at a tavern and filled with insults directed at a bartender and wry observations on life and love. The B-side is a duet between Love and Pat Hare, with the former getting the better of the guitar player, vocally and blowing some Sonny Terry-style harp, in a mismatched competition. Love never cut another single for Sun—accounts suggest he was juggling relationships with as many as seven women at once, indicating that he had better things to do than go into the recording studio—but "Wolf Call Boogie" is one of the most anthologized of all Sun blues tracks, appearing on numerous compilations from Rhino, Rounder, Charly, and Bear Family, and is regarded, at least in its freewheeling style and raunchy subject matter, as a step forward on the road from country blues to rock & roll. Love survived for decades after his one claim to recorded music legend, and died in a car accident in Interstate 55. *—Bruce Eder*

Houndog

Group / Modern Electric Blues
Houndog is the duo of Mike Halby, who has played with Canned Heat and John Mayall's Bluesbreakers, and David Hidalgo, of Los Lobos. Their self-titled 1999 debut album, recorded in Halby's home studio, is not so much swamp-blues as murk-blues. The basic,

at times lo-fi production and gutbucket songs give this a foggy mystery, akin to another of Hidalgo's side projects, the Latin Playboys. Halby has a voice so low it sometimes sounds like a 45 rpm single playing at 33 rpm, and his convincingly throaty style can recall, though it does not imitate, vintage Chess greats like Muddy and the Wolf. This is probably too arty for some straight blues fans, but Houndog succeeds at twisting electric blues into some interesting new directions while maintaining a lot of grit and funk. *—Richie Unterberger*

● **Houndog** / Mar. 2, 1999 / Columbia/Legacy ♦♦♦♦
With *Houndog*, Mike Halby and David Hidalgo have managed a feat that's rare in the dying days of the 20th century: an album that convincingly captures the spontaneous and earthy feel of vintage downhome blues, without sounding forced or cliched. It can be hard to decipher Halby's deep, mumbly vocals—sometimes it sounds like he's not just singing swamp blues, but literally singing from the bottom of a swamp—but, fortunately, lyrics are printed on the sleeve. Although the backbone of the arrangements are sparse lo-fi drums and sleepy, smoky guitar and bass licks, Hidalgo adds touches of violin, accordion, and lap steel to make the already interesting textures deeper. All songs are original, save "I'll Change My Style" (taken from Junior Parker). A quality and quirky afterhours blues album. *—Richie Unterberger*

Son House (Eddie James House Jr.)

b. Mar. 21, 1902, Riverton, MS, **d.** Oct. 19, 1988, Detroit, MI
Slide Guitar, Vocals, Songwriter, Guitar / Slide Guitar Blues, Field Recordings, Prewar Blues, Work Songs, Blues Revival, Delta Blues, Acoustic Blues

Son House's place, not only in the history of Delta blues, but in the overall history of the music, is a very high one indeed. He was a major innovator of the Delta style, along with his playing partners Charley Patton and Willie Brown. Few listening experiences in the blues are as intense as hearing one of Son House's original '30s recordings for the Paramount label. Entombed in a hailstorm of surface noise and scratches, one can still be awestruck by the emotional fervor House puts into his singing and slide playing. Little wonder then, that the man became more than just an influence on some White English kid with a big amp; he was the main source of inspiration to both Muddy Waters and Robert Johnson, and it doesn't get much more pivotal than *that*. Even after his rediscovery in the mid-'60s, House was such a potent musical force that what would have been a normally genteel performance by any other bluesmen in a "folk" setting, turned into a night in the nastiest juke joint you could imagine, scaring the daylights out of young White enthusiasts expecting something far more prosaic and comfortable. Not out of Son House, no sir. When the man hit the downbeat on his National steel bodied guitar and you saw his eyes disappear into the back of his head, you *knew* you were going to hear some blues. And when he wasn't shouting the blues, he was singing spirituals, a cappella. Right up to the end, no bluesman was torn between the sacred and the profane more than Son House.

He was born Eddie James House Jr., on March 21, 1902, in Riverton, MS. By the age of 15, he was preaching the gospel in various Baptist churches as the family seemingly wandered from one plantation to the next. He didn't even bother picking up a guitar until he turned 25; to quote House, "I didn't like no guitar when I first heard it; oh gee, I couldn't stand a guy playin' a guitar. I didn't like *none* of it." But if his ambivalence to the instrument was obvious, even more obvious was the simple fact that Son hated plantation labor even more and had developed a taste for corn whiskey. After drunkenly launching into a blues at a house frolic in Lyon, MS, one night and picking up some coin for doing it, the die seemed to be cast; Son House may have been a preacher, but he was part of the blues world now.

If the romantic notion that the blues life is said to be a life full of trouble is true, then Son found a barrel of it one night at another house frolic in Lyon. He shot a man dead that night and was immediately sentenced to imprisonment at Parchman Farm. He ended up only serving two years of his sentence, with his parents both lobbying hard for his release, claiming self defense. Upon his release—after a Clarksdale judge told him never to set foot in town again—he started a new life in the Delta as a full-time man of the blues. After hitchhiking and hoboing the rails, he made it down to Lula, MS, and ran into the most legendary character the blues had to offer at that point, the one and only Charley Patton. The two men couldn't have been less similar in disposition, stature, and musical and performance outlook if they had purposely planned it that way. Patton was described as a funny, loudmouthed little guy, who was a noisy, passionate showman, using every trick in the book to win over a crowd. The tall and skinny House was by nature a gloomy man, with a saturnine disposition who still felt extremely guilt-ridden about playing the blues and working in juke joints. Yet when he ripped into one, Son imbued it with so much raw feeling that the performance *became* the show itself, sans gimmicks.

The two of them argued and bickered constantly, and the only thing these two men seemed to have in common was a penchant for imbibing whatever alcoholic potable came their way. Though House would later refer in interviews to Patton as a "jerk" and other unprintables, it was Patton's success as a bluesman—both live and especially on record—that got Son's foot in the door as a recording artist. He followed Patton up to Grafton, WI, and recorded a handful of sides for the Paramount label. These records today (selling scant few copies in their time, and the few that did surviving a life of huge steel needles, even bigger scratches and generally lousy care) are some of the most highly prized collector's items of Delta blues recordings, much tougher to find than, say, a Robert Johnson or even a Charley Patton 78. Paramount used a pressing compound for their 78 singles that was so noisy and inferior sounding, that should someone actually come across a clean copy of any of Son's original recordings, it's a pretty safe bet that the listener would still be greeted with a blizzard of surface noise once the needle made contact with the disc.

But audio concerns aside, the absolutely demonic performances House laid down on these three two-part 78s ("My Black Mama," "Preachin' the Blues," and "Dry Spell Blues," with an unreleased test acetate of "Walkin' Blues" showing up decades later) cut through the hisses and pops like a brick through a stained glass window.

It was those recordings that led Alan Lomax to his door in 1941 to record him for the Library of Congress. Lomax was cutting acetates on a "portable" recording machine weighing over 300 pounds. Son was still playing (actually at the peak of his powers, some would say), but had backed off of it a bit since Charley Patton died in 1934. House did some tunes solo, as Lomax asked him to do, but also cut a session backed by a rocking little string band. As the band laid down long and loose (some tracks went on for over six minutes) versions of their favorite numbers, all that was missing was the guitars being plugged in and a drummer's back beat and you were getting a glimpse of the future of the music.

But just as House had gone a full decade without recording, this time after the Lomax recordings, he just as quickly disappeared, moving to Rochester, NY. When folk blues researchers finally found him in 1964, he was cheerfully exclaiming that he hadn't touched a guitar in years. One of the researchers, a young guitarist named Alan Wilson (later of the blues-rock group Canned Heat) literally sat down and retaught Son House how to play like Son House. Once the old master was up to speed, the festival and coffeehouse circuit became his oyster. He recorded again, the recordings becoming an important introduction to his music and for some, a lot easier to take than those old Paramount 78s from a strict audio standpoint. In 1965, he played Carnegie Hall and four years later found himself the subject of an eponymously titled film documentary, all of this another world removed from Clarksdale, MS, indeed. Everywhere he played, he was besieged by young fans, asking him about Robert Johnson, Charley Patton, and others. For young white blues fans, these were merely exotic names from the past, heard only to them on old, highly prized recordings; for Son House they were flesh and blood contemporaries, not just some names on a record label. Hailed as the greatest living Delta singer still actively performing, nobody dared call himself the King of the Blues as long as Son House was around.

He fell into ill health by the early '70s; what was later diagnosed as both Alzheimer's and Parkinson's disease first affected his memory and his ability to recall songs on stage and later, his hands, which shook so bad he finally had to give up the guitar and eventually live performing altogether by 1976. He lived quietly in Detroit, MI, for another 12 years, passing away on October 19, 1988. His induction into the Blues Foundation's Hall of Fame in 1980 was no less than his due. Son House *was* the blues. *—Cub Koda*

☆ **The Legendary Son House: Father of the Folk Blues** / 1965 / Columbia ♦♦♦♦♦
This was the first such presentation of a Delta blues musician done by Columbia, which seemed like a pretty hip label at the time, since they had both Bob Dylan and Paul Revere & the Raiders. The man's picture on the front is mesmerizing, in a word; the white shirt, black string tie, and silver steel guitar just adding to the excitement. Perhaps this album picture was the first glimpse many young listeners had of such a style of guitar. It was decades before Dire Straits appropriated the image. Revisionist critical thinking has it that the older recordings by Son House can't match the music created during his '30s sessions for Paramount. Here, of course, we have the music as sports syndrome, an area where the elderly are always going to fail in someone's eyes. So much of music enjoyment, however, is a subjective reaction that so often involves many other factors, among them time and place. The sound of the metal slide quietly hovering over the strings can bring to mind only one thing in the mind of a westerner: an angry rattlesnake. And the way many listeners' jaws dropped upon hearing music such as this for the first time may not be quite as intense as a hiker's facial expression upon encountering such a creature, but it is close enough.

There is a second blues legend appearing here as well. Guitarist and harmonica player Al Wilson was a founding member of Canned Heat, and a musician so good at what he did that he became a sterling example of the possibility that young white blues fans could actually learn to play this music really well, with intensity. The original pressing contains nine tracks, each of them gems. The length some of the tracks are allowed to go to is really wonderful. One of them is more than nine minutes long. Producers of country blues material in the 21st century would probably frown on such a thing because they are guilty of helping water the genre down over the years. The inevitable repackaging of material from these recording sessions in the '90s contained alternate takes, a decision that picks open arguments about whether the old man's playing at that time really warranted hearing every take, or, in fact, whether such documentation is really even that important in a genre such as blues. However one feels about such controversial subjects, it definitely seems like producer John Hammond picked the right tracks the first time out. *—Eugene Chadbourne*

At Home: Complete 1969 / 1969 / Document ♦♦♦♦
Document's *At Home: Complete 1969 Recorded Works* is a fascinating look at Son House in an intimate setting, and serious fans will find it necessary, but many of these performances aren't as strong as similar sets he recorded in the '60s. In other words, it's one for the completist. *—Thom Owens*

☆ **Complete Recorded Works of Son House & the Great Delta Blues Singers** / 1990 / Document ♦♦♦♦♦
Son House & the Great Delta Blues Singers isn't entirely devoted to Son House—there are cuts by several other musicians, including Willie Brown, Garfield Akers, Rube Lacy and Joe Calicott—but this disc, which contains a complete 1930 session, is the best place to get his earliest songs ("My Black Mama," "Preachin' the Blues," "Dry Spell Blues"), which are among his masterworks. *—Thom Owens*

★ **Delta Blues** / 1991 / Biograph ♦♦♦♦♦
In 1941 and 1942 folklorist Alan Lomax recorded these sides on House on a pair of field trips with a bulky, 300-pound acetate cutting machine for the Library of Congress. House was in peak form and the sides Lomax recorded are absolutely revelatory. The 1941 session finds him in the company of a driving little string band combo with the legendary Willie Brown (the man mentioned in Robert Johnson's "Crossroads") on second guitar. The effect of hearing Son House in this context is fairly astounding. The 1942 batch is solo recordings and equally as riveting. While there are other versions of these sides available in import form, the sound on this Biograph release features the best sound restoration. *—Cub Koda*

☆ **Masters of the Delta Blues: The Friends of Charlie Patton** / 1991 / Yazoo ♦♦♦♦♦
If you've only heard Son House's 1965 rediscovery recordings for Columbia (or his excellent 1941-1942 Library of Congress sessions), boy, are you in for a shock. This various-artists compilation collects up House's original 1930 recordings for the Paramount label, some of the rarest and hardest to find 78s in blues history. Recorded in Grafton, WI, House sounds positively demonic on the six issued titles (all of them two-part numbers, each being a separate take, rather than a single performance spread over both sides of a single) and with the inclusion of a previously unissued test acetate of "Walking Blues," this is the most complete document of his first recordings that has survived on this important Delta bluesman. The original Paramount 78s were always considered of inferior pressing quality even back in the days when turntables were called Victrolas and the hailstorm of surface noise on these sides seems by and large resistant to all forms of modern noise reduction devices employed here. But House's performances here cut through the crackles, pops, and hisses like slicing up a cold stick of butter with a soldering iron. Absolutely indispensable. *—Cub Koda*

Father of the Delta Blues: The Complete 1965 Sessions / 1992 / Columbia/Legacy ♦♦♦♦♦
After being rediscovered by the folk-blues community in the early '60s, Son House rose to the occasion and recorded this magnificent set of performances. Allowed to stretch out past the shorter running time of the original 78s, House turns in wonderful, steaming performances of some of his best-known material. On some tracks, House is supplemented by folk-blues researcher/musician Alan Wilson, who would later become a member of the blues-rock group Canned Heat and here plays some nice second guitar and harmonica on several cuts. This two-disc set features alternate takes, some unissued material and some studio chatter from producer John Hammond Sr., that ocassionally hints at the chaotic nature inherent to some of these '60s "rediscovery" sessions. While not as overpowering as his earlier work (what could be?), all of these sides are so power packed with sheer emotional involvement from House, they're an indispensable part of his canonade.*—Cub Koda*

Legendary 1969 Rochester Sessions / 1992 / Document ♦♦♦♦♦
Recorded at his home in September of 1969 by blues enthusiast Steve Lobb, Son House turns in one of the most vital and compelling performances available from his late career comeback. While the 1965 Columbia Records sessions require explanations about his age and extended retirement, there is no excuse necessary for the contents of this CD. Opening with the 20-minute long "Son's Blues," he radiates explosive power, his voice surging and his guitar strings snapping against the fretboard in a slow, fiery performance. The tension and sustained strength of this one piece makes this CD far more valuable as a specimen of Son's best work than any of the CBS material—this is the perfect companion to his inimitable Alan Lomax and Paramount recordings of the '30s and early '40s. Nothing else here quite matches the opening track, although Son still seems in far better form than he did on some of his better-known comeback recordings. *—Bruce Eder*

Delta Blues and Spirituals / Oct. 1995 / Capitol ♦♦♦♦♦
Recorded live for an enthusiastic audience at London's 100 Club on June 30 and July 14 of 1970 during House's final European tour, *Delta Blues and Spirituals* is a great last look at a true blues legend. Though Son House would live another 18 years after this recording, he would only perform for five more, and by most accounts he was only a shadow of his former self relatively shortly after this collection's release. Thus, *Delta Blues and Spirituals* remains one of the last vibrant documents of one of the most essential fathers of Delta blues at the top of his game. Though it's probably not a great place to start as an introduction, as it only includes eight songs, avid fans will no doubt enjoy House's two lengthy monologues and the excellent 30-page booklet included. The material itself is truly first-rate—four blues and four spirituals are represented, making fine examples of House's impassioned blues hollering. House is joined by Canned Heat's Alan Wilson on harmonica on "Between Midnight and Day" and "I Want to Go Home on the Morning Train," making this collection some of Wilson's last recorded work, as he would die a month and a half later. Overall, the disc makes for a compelling listen from start to finish, and definitely serves as more than just an impressive historical footnote. *—Matt Fink*

● **Original Delta Blues** / Jun. 30, 1998 / Columbia/Legacy ♦♦♦♦♦
Columbia/Legacy's *The Original Delta Blues* is a fine distillation of the label's double-disc set *Father of the Delta Blues*, containing 16 highlights from that comprehensive overview of his '60s rediscovery recordings. Curious listeners who are intimidated by the size of the previous set are advised to pick up this terrific sampler instead. *—Stephen Thomas Erlewine*

Preachin' the Blues / Apr. 18, 2000 / Catfish ♦♦♦♦♦
Here's the ultimate Son House collection. It contains all of his Paramount recordings. Decent transfers of these normally battered beyond belief masters make for easier listening than normal, followed by the legendary John Lomax Library of Congress recordings from 1941 and 1942, including the unissued test pressing of "Walkin' Blues." This is Son at his most intense and finer Delta blues recordings next to Charlie Patton and Robert Johnson would be very hard to find. Worth it just to hear "Walkin' Blues" alone with Willie Brown and Charlie Patton whooping it up in the background, true juke-joint music at its best. File under essential. *—Cub Koda*

Live at the Gaslight Cave NYC 1965 / Nov. 14, 2000 / Document ♦♦♦

Bee Houston (Edward Wilson Houston)

b. Apr. 19, 1938, San Antonio, TX, **d.** Mar. 19, 1991, Los Angeles, CA
Vocals, Guitar / Texas Blues
Guitarist/vocalist Edward Wilson "Bee" Houston's an exciting performer whose style blends elements of Texas shuffle blues and Southern gospel-tinged soul. Houston played in a high school drum and bugle corps as a youngster in San Antonio, and played in the backing bands of Little Willie John, Junior Parker, Bobby "Blue" Bland and others in the late '50s and early '60s. After a two-year army stint, Houston moved to the West Coast. He toured and recorded frequently with Big Mama Thornton in the '60s, and also accompanied several visiting blues players during West Coast visits. Houston recorded for Arhoolie in the '60s and '70s, and also made several festival appearances and club dates. *—Ron Wynn*

● **Bee Houston: His Guitar & Band** / 1981 / Arhoolie ♦♦♦♦
While not an instrumental giant, Bee Houston made many delightful and very explosive recordings. He seldom did covers, and this collection has several enjoyable originals. *—Ron Wynn*

Hustler / Nov. 18, 1997 / Arhoolie ♦♦♦♦
Long before soul and R&B rolled down different paths, they were comfortable cohabitants. Artists like the self-satisfied and energetic Bee Houston contain such elements. Houston can treat his guitar like a T-Bone Walker as quick as he can be a B.B. King. This exhorting and emphasizing vocalist was found suitable as a backing musician for Little Willie John, Junior Parker, Little Johnny Taylor and Bobby "Blue" Bland. His guitar work is not about flash, but brash support for soul shouting. Familiar with Big Mama Thornton's "Ball and Chain"? Well, Houston backed Big Mama on her classic 1968 recording of that song and Thornton shows up here singing on "Woke Up This Morning." This is a reissue of Bee's only previously issued album (also on Arhoolie) and another previously unissued album. Bee proves himself to be a consummate showman, stellar guitar stylist and creator of a superb, original songbook of blues-and-soul material. *—Thomas Schulte*

Joe Houston

b. 1927, Austin, TX
Vocals, Sax (Tenor) / Jump Blues, Rock & Roll, R&B
Joe Houston is a honking R&B saxman of wallpaper-peeling potency who recorded for virtually every major independent R&B label in Los Angeles during the '50s. When the jump blues tradition faded, he segued right into rock & roll, even cutting budget "twist" and "surf" albums for Crown that didn't sound very different from what he was doing a decade before.

Houston played around Houston (Texas, that is) with the bands of Amos Milburn and Joe Turner during the late '40s. It was Turner who got the young saxist his first deal with Freedom Records in 1949. Houston found his way to the West Coast in 1952 and commenced recording for labels big and small: Modern, RPM, Lucky, Imperial, Dootone, Recorded in Hollywood, Cash, and Money (as well as the considerably better-financed Mercury, where he scored his only national R&B hit, "Worry, Worry, Worry," in 1952).

Houston's formula was simple and savagely direct—he'd honk and wail as hard as he could, from any conceivable position: on his knees, lying on his back, walking the bar, etc. His output for the Bihari brothers' Crown label (where he was billed "Wild Man of the Tenor Sax") is positively exhilarating: "All Night Long," "Blow Joe Blow," and "Joe's Gone" are herculean examples of single-minded sax blasting.

Houston remains active musically, emphasizing his blues vocal talent more than he used to. *—Bill Dahl*

Rockin' at the Drive in / 1984 / Ace ♦♦♦♦♦
Fourteen characteristic sax-driven R&B tunes, most instrumental, from the '50s. There's no duplication with the Specialty *Cornbread and Cabbage Greens* CD, except for the well-known "All Night Long," so it's worth finding if you want more than one Houston collection. *—Richie Unterberger*

Cornbread and Cabbage Greens / Oct. 29, 1992 / Specialty ♦♦♦♦♦
Los Angeles was a mecca for honking, wailing R&B tenor saxmen during the '50s, and Joe Houston was one of the wildest in town. Twenty-six blasting workouts from the early to mid-'50s mark this CD as the best digital indication of Houston's sax-sational wailing now available (pretty much the only vintage one on the shelves, in fact). "All Night Long," "Celebrity Club Drag," and "Rockin' and Boppin'" are among the highlights, taken from the archives of John Dolphin's Recorded in Hollywood and Cash labels. *—Bill Dahl*

The Blues & Nothin' Else / 1996 / Shattered ♦♦♦♦
Of all the honkers who worked the table tops out on the West Coast, one of the very best was "Big" Joe Houston. Able to jump from big band to small combo blues and R&B with consummate ease, Houston was one of the first to test the waters of the newly emerging style that would become known as rock & roll. Cutting one brilliant single after another for a variety of labels—and seeing his early work among the first to be anthologized on myriad budget-label albums—Houston was the California version of the tenor men who honked and walked the bars in the Big Apple, often outdoing his New York contemporaries with sides of fervent blasting that could not be denied. Fortunately for us, that fervent blasting is alive and well and beating right alongside Houston's big heart on this, his first new album in a good number of years. The most notable fact is that Joe is singing on everything, relegating his tenor work to no more than a couple of choruses on each tune, framing it in proper perspective as another soloist in the very rockin' band that backs him here. The really good news is that Houston's voice is every bit as rough hewn as his sax playing, making you wonder why it took this long to get it properly documented on record. The final track lets you know that the man still has it and really isn't rationing *anything*; the set closer, "Full of Misery," is eight minutes and 25 seconds of Joe making a rarely heard appearance on alto sax, playing the blues all by his lonesome, and making it sound oh so sweet. *—Cub Koda*

● **Blows Crazy** / Oct. 17, 2000 / Ace ♦♦♦♦♦
Joe Houston's discography in the '50s was a mess to work out, as he recorded for more than a dozen labels, and sometimes did the same songs under different titles. Without access to all of those records—and probably very few people on the planet have heard all of them—it's impossible to determine whether any given '50s compilation, such as this

one, is the "best." However, considering that this has 24 recordings from the early '50s to the early '60s that were done for (or licensed by) Modern, and that it has his best and most definitive honk blaster ("All Night Long"), this makes a pretty fair bid for that choice. In addition to Houston's very first single (1951's "Blow Joe Blow"), it also contains several of his '50s Modern/RPM 45s; a few songs recorded for twist and surf albums for Crown in the early '60s; and half a dozen previously unissued alternate takes of Modern singles (although, oddly, the original takes of most of these are not included). As in the case of many vintage uptempo R&B/blues albums that are mostly instrumental, you couldn't say this is the most varied listening experience, though a few jazzy accents (including vibes and organ) are thrown in on the more subdued later sessions. It's better for nonstop car cruising and, given today's gas prices, who can afford to do that for the length of this CD? But as relentless rompin' stompin' sax-driven R&B verging on rock & roll's birth goes, it's one of the better single-artist comps around, never lacking in energy. *—Richie Unterberger*

Frank Hovington

b. Jan. 9, 1919, Reading, PA, **d.** Jun. 21, 1982, Felton, DE

Vocals, Ukulele, Guitar, Banjo / Piedmont Blues, Country Blues

A tremendous country blues musician who was singing vividly and playing with flair well after the genre's heyday, Franklin "Frank" Hovington started on ukulele and banjo as a child. He teamed with Willliam Walker in the late '30s and '40s playing at house parties and dances in Frederica, PA. Hovington moved to Washington, D.C., in the late '40s, and backed such groups as Stewart Dixon's Golden Stars and Ernest Ewin's Jubilee Four. He also worked with Billy Stewart's band. Hovington moved to Delaware in 1967, then was recorded by Flyright in 1975. His 1975 LP was a masterpiece, and alerted many in the blues community to his abilities. *—Ron Wynn*

● **Lonesome Road Blues** / 1975 / Rounder ♦♦♦♦♦

By the time Frank Hovington got a chance to record, the folk/blues boom had passed and there was almost no interest in country blues except among academics. But that didn't stop him from making a definitive album, which compared favorably to the genre's classics done in a different era. It's a textbook case of the right stuff at the wrong time. *—Ron Wynn*

Gone With the Wind / Oct. 31, 2000 / Flyright ♦♦♦

Howard & the White Boys

f. 1988

Group / Modern Electric Blues

During the '90s, Howard & the White Boys became one of Chicago's favorite local blues bands before slowly expanding their reach beyond the Windy City. The band formed in 1988 while most of the members–Dan Bellini (guitar/harmonica), Howard McCullum (vocals/bass), Steve Asma (guitar), Jim Christopulos (drums)–were studying at Northern Illinois University in Dekalb. The band's first break came when they opened for B.B. King. Later, they would perform alongside numerous other blues superstars such as Koko Taylor, Albert King, Junior Wells, Luther Allison, and Bo Diddley. In 1994, Howard & the White Boys released their first recording, *Strung Out on the Blues*, which the Los Angeles-based Mighty Tiger Records released and which featured mostly songs written by the band.

Around this same time, Howard & the White Boys began appearing regularly at Buddy Guy's Legends, a popular blues club in Chicago. The exposure broadened the band's audience, and before long, Guy embarked on a Midwestern tour with Howard & the White Boys as his opening act. All of the touring began to take a toll on Asma, who left the band to concentrate on academic pursuits. Another guitarist, Rocco Calipari, replaced Asma, and the band began touring extensively throughout the States (later touring Europe). Mighty Tiger released the band's second album in 1997, *Guess Who's Coming To Dinner?* The album attracted the Philadelphia label Evidence, who signed Howard & the White Boys to a four-album deal and released *The Big $core* (1999). During this same year, Calipari left the band to spend time with his family. In his place came another guitarist, Giles Corey. Yet he too left the band, and in July 2001, Calipari returned. *—Jason Birchmeier*

● **Strung Out on the Blues** / 1995 / Mighty Tiger ♦♦♦

Here are 14 high energy blues tracks played by Howard McCullum (vocalist/bassist), Dan Bellini (guitarist and harmonica player), Jim Christopulos (drummer), and guitarist Steve Asma. "She Can Cook" contains all the elements of good blues, humor, good playing, heartfelt singing, realistic lyrics about a woman who's not a beauty queen, or a whole host of other things, but can cook. Some songs, like "Nightmare Man," are as much country as blues. However, they never stray far from genuine blues, as is evident with "Baby's Painting the Town," "Turn on Your Love Light," "Black Cat," and two piledrivers: "Strung Out on the Blues," and "The Blues Are Killing Me." Bellini displays his mouth harp skills on "I'm Gonna Hate Myself in the Morning," and a guitarist plays some saucy riffs on "Let Me Be Your Slave." They give Jimmy Reed's "I Got My Mojo Working" a steroid injection, Bellini's harmonica drives the classic at a frantic pace. The sound is mediocre, but Howard & the White Boys' enthusiasm helps to buffer the primitive recording. *—Andrew Hamilton*

Guess Who's Coming to Dinner? / 1997 / Mighty Tiger ♦♦♦

Features good tunes that get marred by a drab, mono-sounding mix. Instrument separation isn't pronounced, let alone Howard's vocal, giving the tracks a muddy sound. "Bad Attitude's" chugging beat gives it legs, while some tasty guitar licks accent "What Can I Do," a blues ballad. Both "One Good Woman," and "Tight Pants" have commercial potential, each with memorable beats and conversational lyrics. They pay homage to Muddy Waters with "Call Muddy," and get high marks for the emulation, but the title track "Guess Who's Coming to Dinner," treads a well-worn path, lyrically and musically. A top-flight producer would do wonders for this group. *—Andrew Hamilton*

The Big $core / Mar. 16, 1999 / Evidence ♦♦♦

As their name implies, Howard & the White Boys play urban blues for wine spritzer-drinking yuppies, heavy on the palatable soul beats and party-atmosphere lyrics and long on the fuzztone guitar solos. Deep blues this isn't, but well played it certainly is as tunes like "Leave the Lights On," "Judge," "It's All You," "I Need Some Cash," and "The Last Time" shows a band that's tight and swinging in its command of modern grooves. Buddy Guy makes a guest appearance on a tepid cover of Sam & Dave's "I Thank You," taking the wind out of an otherwise enjoyable little blues album for the dancing crowd. *—Cub Koda*

Camille Howard

b. Mar. 29, 1914, Galveston, TX, **d.** Mar. 10, 1993, Los Angeles, CA

Vocals, Piano / Jump Blues, West Coast Blues, R&B

Piano-tinkling chanteuses were quite the rage during the war years. But Camille Howard's two-fisted thundering boogie style, much like her Los Angeles contemporary, Hadda Brooks, was undoubtedly the equivalent of any 88s ace, male or female.

Howard was part of the great migration from Texas to the West Coast. She was installed as pianist with drummer Roy Milton & the Solid Senders sometime during World War II, playing on all their early hits for Art Rupe's Juke Box and Specialty labels (notably the groundbreaking "R.M. Blues" in 1945).

Sensing her potential following the success of Milton's 1947 hit "Thrill Me" (with Howard's vocal), Rupe began recording her as a featured artist at the end of the year. Legend has it that Howard's biggest hit, the roaring instrumental "X-Temporaneous Boogie," was improvised at the tail end of her first date as a leader (its flip, the torch ballad "You Don't Love Me," was a hit in its own right).

Howard's vocal abilities were pretty potent too. Her "Fiesta in Old Mexico" was a hit in 1949, while "Money Blues," credited to Camille Howard & Her Boyfriends, registered strong coin in 1951. Howard cranked out storming boogies and sultry ballads for Specialty through 1953, then jumped from Federal to Vee-Jay before landing in Los Angeles for good. Howard's strong religious ties put a stop to her secular music career long ago. *—Bill Dahl*

● **Rock Me Daddy, Vol. 1** / 1993 / Specialty ♦♦♦♦♦

This 25-song reissue of her 1947-1952 Specialty material, about half previously unreleased, includes "You Don't Love Me" and "Money Blues," but not the chart items "Fiesta in Old Mexico" and "X-Temporaneous Boogie." Perhaps too suave and refined for the R&B/rock era, and as comfortable with jazzy ballads as boogies, Howard was nonetheless an important, and nowadays overlooked, star of the transitional era between jump blues and R&B. *—Richie Unterberger*

X-Temporaneous Boogie, Vol. 2 / Feb. 13, 1996 / Specialty ♦♦♦♦♦

Twenty of these 25 sides, recorded for Specialty between 1947 and 1952, were previously unissued. But there's no difference in quality between these and the better-known ones presented on volume one; the label's decision on what to release was based more on marketing strategies than the level of the performances. Divided between instrumentals and pop-influenced vocal numbers, Howard again proves herself the master of boogie and jump blues piano styles, sometimes slowing things down into a jazzier mode. In addition to the storehouse of vault material, this compilation also includes a couple of late-'40s Top Ten R&B hits, "Thrill Me" and "X-Temporaneous Boogie." *—Richie Unterberger*

Rosetta Howard

b. 1914, Chicago, IL, **d.** 1974

Vocals / East Coast Blues, Swing, Classic Female Blues

Rosetta Howard is sometimes thought of as a classic blues singer but she actually came up during a slightly later era. Not much is known about her life. Howard began singing professionally in 1932 and she worked in Chicago and later on New York throughout the '30s with the Harlem Hamfats and individually with Herb Morand and Odell Rand. During 1937-1939 and 1947, she recorded 40 selections, proving herself to be a versatile singer able to bridge the gap between classic blues and swing. Her 1937-1938 recordings were with the Harlem Hamfats and were reissued on two Document CDs. A CD put out by the Austrian RST label has all of her later recordings. The two 1939 dates are a session with the Harlem Blues Serenaders (which includes Charlie Shavers, Buster Bailey and Lil Armstrong) and one with a quintet that features Henry "Red" Allen and Barney Bigard.

Howard performed with a variety of mostly obscure musicians in Chicago during 1940-1946 (other than clarinetist Jimmie Noone) and then in 1947 was featured on 12 interesting recordings with Chicago blues stars of the period, including the Big Three (with bassist Willie Dixon) and guitarist Big Bill Broonzy. But although she sounds quite at home in this "modern" setting, the records did not sell (some were not issued at the time) and Rosetta Howard never recorded again. She worked in the '50s in the religious field with Thomas Dorsey at the Pilgrim Baptist Church in Chicago and slipped away into obscurity. Fortunately all of her recordings are currently available. *—Scott Yanow*

● **Complete Recorded Works 1939-1947** / 1994 / RST ♦♦♦♦

Rosetta Howard, a potential "classic blues" singer, was probably born ten years too late, being far too young to be active in the '20s when she might have made a bigger impact. Howard did record with the Harlem Hamfats in the late '30s and her five sessions as a leader are included on this CD from the Austrian RST label. Howard, who had an appealing if not overly memorable voice, is backed by jazz stars during two dates from 1939 (including either Charlie Shavers or Red Allen on trumpet and Barney Bigard or Buster Bailey on clarinet). Otherwise she is heard in 1947 performing with such blues players as the Big Three Trio (which included bassist Willie Dixon) and Big Bill Broonzy. This is a set that pre-rock blues collectors in particular will want to pick up. *—Scott Yanow*

Peg Leg Howell (Joshua Barnes Howell)

b. Mar. 5, 1888, Eatonton, GA, **d.** Aug. 11, 1966, Atlanta, GA

Guitar, Vocals / Country Blues, Acoustic Blues, Piedmont Blues

One of the first recorded products of the Atlanta blues community of the prewar era, Peg Leg Howell bridged the gap between the early country blues sound and the 12-bar stylings to follow, with his guitar work evolving over time to include fingerpicking and slide techniques. Born Joshua Barnes Howell in Eatonton, GA, on March 5, 1888, he was a self-taught guitarist who acquired his nickname after a 1916 run-in with an irate brother-in-law, which ended in a shotgun wound to the leg and, ultimately, amputation.

Unable to continue working as a farmhand, he migrated to Atlanta, where he began pursuing music full-time; in addition to playing street corners for passing change, Howell supplemented his income by bootlegging liquor, an offense which led to a one-year prison sentence in 1925. Soon after his release, he signed to Columbia; his first session for the label yielded the menacing "New Prison Blues," a song he'd learned while serving time.

Having amassed a huge repertory of songs over the years, Howell recorded prolifically over the following months, his work ranging from traditional ballads ("Skin Game Blues") to dance numbers (the minor hit "Beaver Slide Rag") to even jazz ("New Jelly Roll Blues"); while some of his sides comprised solo performances, others featured the backing of his street group, the Gang (guitarist Henry Williams and fiddler Eddie Anthony). Columbia pulled the plug in 1929, at which time Howell returned to playing Atlanta's famed Decatur Street district; Williams was himself imprisoned not long after, and following Anthony's 1934 death, Howell gradually disappeared from the area blues circuit. He spent the next several decades clouded in obscurity, with diabetes claiming his other leg in 1952. Howell was 75 when the Testament label sought him out in 1963 to record his first new material in over 40 years; he died in Atlanta on August 11, 1966. *—Jason Ankeny*

- ● **Peg Leg Howell & Eddie, Vol. 1** / Sep. 6, 2000 / Document ♦♦♦

Peg Leg Howell & Eddie, Vol. 2 / Sep. 6, 2000 / Document ♦♦♦

Howlin' Wolf (Chester Arthur Burnett)

b. Jun. 10, 1910, West Point, MS, **d.** Jan. 10, 1976, Hines, IL

Vocals, Leader, Harmonica, Guitar / Electric Chicago Blues, Chicago Blues, Electric Memphis Blues

In the history of the blues, there has never been anyone quite like the Howlin' Wolf. Six foot three and close to 300 pounds in his salad days, the Wolf was the primal force of the music spun out to its ultimate conclusion. A Robert Johnson may have possessed more lyrical insight, a Muddy Waters more dignity, and a B.B. King certainly more technical expertise, but no one could match him for the singular ability to rock the house down to the foundation while simultaneously scaring its patrons out of its wits.

He was born in West Point, MS, and named after the 21st President of the United States (Chester Arthur). His father was a farmer and Wolf took to it as well until his 18th birthday, when a chance meeting with Delta blues legend Charley Patton changed his life forever. Though he never came close to learning the subtleties of Patton's complex guitar technique, two of the major components of Wolf's style (Patton's inimitable growl of a voice and his propensity for entertaining) were learned first hand from the Delta blues master. The main source of Wolf's hard-driving, rhythmic style on harmonica came when Aleck "Rice" Miller (Sonny Boy Williamson) married his half-sister Mary and taught him the rudiments of the instrument. He first started playing in the early '30s as a strict Patton imitator, while others recall him at decade's end rocking the juke joints with a neck-rack harmonica and one of the first electric guitars anyone had ever seen. After a four-year stretch in the Army, he settled down as a farmer and weekend player in West Memphis, AR, and it was here that Wolf's career in music began in earnest.

By 1948, he had established himself within the community as a radio personality. As a means of advertising his own local appearances, Wolf had a 15-minute radio show on KWEM in West Memphis, interspersing his down-home blues with farm reports and like-minded advertising that he sold himself. But a change in Wolf's sound that would alter everything that came after was soon in coming because when listeners tuned in for Wolf's show, the sound was up-to-the-minute electric. Wolf had put his first band together, featuring the explosive guitar work of Willie Johnson, whose aggressive style not only perfectly suited Wolf's sound but aurally extended and amplified the violence and nastiness of it as well. In any discussion of Wolf's early success both live, over the airwaves, and on record, the importance of Willie Johnson cannot be overestimated.

Wolf finally started recording in 1951, when he caught the ear of Sam Phillips, who first heard him on his morning radio show. The music Wolf made in the Memphis Recording Service studio was full of passion and zest and Phillips simultaneously leased the results to the Bihari Brothers in Los Angeles and Leonard Chess in Chicago. Suddenly, Howlin' Wolf had two hits at the same time on the R&B charts with two record companies claiming to have him exclusively under contract. Chess finally won him over and as Wolf would proudly relate years later, "I had a 4,000 dollar car and 3,900 dollars in my pocket. I'm the onliest one drove out of the South like a gentleman." It was the winter of 1953 and Chicago would be his new home.

When Wolf entered the Chess studios the next year, the violent aggression of the Memphis sides was being replaced with a Chicago backbeat and, with very little fanfare, a new member in the band. Hubert Sumlin proved himself to be the Wolf's longest-running musical associate. He first appears as a rhythm guitarist on a 1954 session, and within a few years' time his style had fully matured to take over the role of lead guitarist in the band by early 1958. In what can only be described as an "angular attack," Sumlin played almost no chords behind Wolf, sometimes soloing right through his vocals, featuring wild skitterings up and down the fingerboard and biting single notes. If Willie Johnson was Wolf's second voice in his early recording career, then Hubert Sumlin would pick up the gauntlet and run with it right to the end of the howler's life.

By 1956, Wolf was in the R&B charts again, racking up hits with "Evil" and "Smokestack Lightnin'." He remained a top attraction both on the Chicago circuit and on the road. His records, while seldom showing up on the national charts, were still selling in decent numbers down South. But by 1960, Wolf was teamed up with Chess staff writer Willie Dixon, and for the next five years he would record almost nothing but songs written by Dixon. The magic combination of Wolf's voice, Sumlin's guitar, and Dixon's tunes sold a lot of records and brought the 50-year-old bluesman roaring into the next decade with a considerable flourish. The mid-'60s saw him touring Europe regularly with "Smokestack Lightnin'" becoming a hit in England some eight years after its American release. Certainly any list of Wolf's greatest sides would have to include "I Ain't Superstitious," "The Red Rooster," "Shake for Me," "Back Door Man," "Spoonful," and "Wang Dang Doodle," Dixon compositions all. While almost all of them would eventually become Chicago blues standards, their greatest cache occurred when rock bands the world over started mining the Chess catalog for all it was worth. One of these bands was the Rolling Stones, whose cover of "The Red Rooster" became a number-one record in England. At the height of the British Invasion, the Stones came to America in 1965 for an appearance on ABC-TV's rock music show, *Shindig*. Their main stipulation for appearing on the program was that Howlin' Wolf would be their special guest. With the Stones sitting worshipfully at his feet, the Wolf performed a storming version of "How Many More Years," being seen on his network-TV debut by an audience of a few million. Wolf never forgot the respect the Stones paid him, and he spoke of them highly right up to his final days.

Dixon and Wolf parted company by 1964 and Wolf was back in the studio doing his own songs. One of the classics to emerge from this period was "Killing Floor," featuring a modern backbeat and a incredibly catchy guitar riff from Sumlin. Catchy enough for Led Zeppelin to appropriate it for one of their early albums, cheerfully crediting it to themselves in much the same manner as they had done with numerous other blues standards. By the end of the decade, Wolf's material was being recorded by artists including the Doors, the Electric Flag, the Blues Project, Cream, and Jeff Beck. The result of all these covers brought Wolf the belated acclaim of a young, white audience. Chess' response to this was to bring him into the studio for a "psychedelic" album, truly the most dreadful of his career. His last big payday came when Chess sent him over to England in 1970 to capitalize on the then-current trend of *London Session* albums, recording with Eric Clapton on lead guitar and other British superstars. Wolf's health was not the best, but the session was miles above the earlier, ill-advised attempt to update Wolf's sound for a younger audience.

As the '70s moved on, the end of the trail started coming closer. By now Wolf was a very sick man; he had survived numerous heart attacks and was suffering kidney damage from an automobile accident that sent him flying through the car's windshield. His bandleader Eddie Shaw firmly rationed Wolf to a meager half-dozen songs per set. Occasionally some of the old fire would come blazing forth from some untapped wellspring, and his final live and studio recordings show that he could still tear the house apart when the spirit moved him. He entered the Veterans Administration Hospital in 1976 to be operated on, but never survived it, finally passing away on January 10th of that year.

But his passing did not go unrecognized. A life-size statue of him was erected shortly after in a Chicago park. Eddie Shaw kept his memory and music alive by keeping his band, the Wolf Gang, together for several years afterward. A child-education center in Chicago was named in his honor and in 1980 he was elected to the Blues Foundation Hall of Fame. In 1991, he was inducted into the Rock and Roll Hall of Fame. A couple of years later, his face was on a United States postage stamp. Live performance footage of him exists in the CD-ROM computer format. Howlin' Wolf is now a permanent part of American history. *—Cub Koda*

Howlin' Wolf / 1962 / Chess ♦♦♦♦♦

The Rockin' Chair Album / 1962 / Vogue ♦♦♦♦

Howlin' Wolf's second album brings together some of the blues great's best singles from the late '50s and early '60s. Also available as a fine two-fer with his debut, *Moanin' in the Moonlight*, the so-called *Rockin' Chair Album* represents the cream of Wolf's Chicago blues work. Those tracks afforded classic status are many, including "Spoonful," "The Red Rooster," "Wang Dang Doodle," "Back Door Man," "Shake for Me," and "Who's Been Talking?" Also featuring the fine work of Chess house producer and bassist Willie Dixon and guitarist Hubert Sumlin, *Rockin' Chair* qualifies as one of pinnacles of early electric blues, and is an essential album for any quality blues collection. *—Stephen Cook*

Live in Europe 1964 / 1964 / Sundown ♦♦♦

Of the myriad circulating live Wolf albums of dubious fidelity and legality, this is the best of the bunch, both from an audio standpoint and the pronouncement in the booklet that royalties were indeed being paid to Wolf's widow. This is Wolf's portion of the show as part of the traveling American Folk Blues entourage, the first festival type presentation of the whole blues spectrum to invade Europe. This 1964 tour is the one that brought the real thing to locales where he had previously been only a name on a phonograph record, and the romantic notions projected into the sound that record gave off. With somewhat subdued but nonetheless solid support from right hand man Hubert Sumlin on lead guitar, Sunnyland Slim on piano, Willie Dixon on upright bass, and Clifton James on drums, Wolf runs through a 45-minute set loaded with classics and presented with a positively genial charm. The lack of Wolf's regular rhythm section (although Dixon played bass on many of the records from this period) lends a different flavor to these versions. Many of the selections seem mistitled here ("Tell Me What I've Done" is "I Didn't Mean to Hurt Your Feelings," "Shake for Me" is "Shake It for Me," "May I Have a Talk With You" is "Love Me," etc.), but as this November 6th performance in Bremen, Germany, unfolds, it becomes apparent that the odd titles come from Wolf's introductions. Everything is stretched to a nice, comfortable length here, as Wolf sets both mood and pace, with no tune clocking in at anything less than four minutes and "Goin' Down Slow" and "Forty-Four" reaching the six- and seven-minute mark. Even though the drums and Sumlin's guitar are perhaps muted in the mix more than they should be, the overall sound shows just how well these blues veterans worked together. Just how essential this performance is to a Wolf collection would be in debate, but once you're under the spell, you want to hear it all, and this is a fine addition for someone who's in it for the long haul. *—Cub Koda*

The Real Folk Blues / 1966 / MCA/Chess ♦♦♦♦♦

This was originally released by Chess in 1966 to capitalize on the then-current folk music boom. The music, however—a collection of Wolf singles from 1956 to 1966—is full-blown electric featuring a nice sampling of Wolf originals with a smattering of Willie Dixon tunes. Some of the man's best middle period work is aboard here; "Killing Floor," "Louise," the hair-raisingly somber "Natchez Burning," and Wolf's version of the old standard "Sitting on Top of the World," which would become his set closer in later years. The

Mobile Fidelity version sounds as sonically sharp as anything you've ever heard on this artist and its heftier price tag is somewhat justified by the inclusion of two bonus cuts. But those on a budget who just want the music minus the high-minded audiophile concerns will be happy to note that this is also available as a Chess budget reissue. —*Cub Koda*

Live in Cambridge, 1966 / 1966 / New Rose ♦
These are some absolutely horrible sounding live recordings of a club date with Wolf and his band laying it down so tough and brutal that it almost negates this disc's woeful audio deficiencies. With Wolf, Hubert and Eddie Shaw getting a high octane kick in the pants from drummer Sam Lay, this thing rocks harder than most live blues albums have a right to. While it's a pity that it sounds so awful from a technical standpoint, it's even more amazing that it exists at all. Sumlin's playing on the slow blues "Tell Me What I've Done" is seven minutes of the wildest you'll ever hear out of him and the takes on "Dust My Broom" and "300 Pounds of Joy" are no less explosive. For diehards, true believers and completists who have to have it all. —*Cub Koda*

More Real Folk Blues / 1967 / MCA/Chess ♦♦♦♦♦
This companion volume to the *Real Folk Blues* album was issued in 1967 (after the Wolf had appeared on network television with the Rolling Stones, alluded to in the original liner notes) and couldn't be more dissimilar in content to the first one if you had planned it that way. Whereas the previous volume highlighted middle period Wolf, this one goes all the way back to his earliest Chess sessions, many of which sound like leftover Memphis sides. The chaotic opener, "Just My Kind," sets a familiar Wolf theme to a "Rollin' & Tumblin'" format played at breakneck speed and what the track lacks in fidelity is more than made up in sheer energy. For a classic example of Wolf's ensemble Chicago sound, it's pretty tough to beat "I Have a Little Girl" where the various members of his band seem to be all soloing simultaneously—not unlike a Dixieland band—right through Wolf's vocals. For downright scary, the demonic sounding "I'll Be Around" is an absolute must-hear. Wolf's harp solo on this slow blues is one of his best and the vocal that frames it sounds like the microphone is going to explode at any second. As soul singer Christine Ohlman commented upon hearing this track for the first time, "Boy, I'd sure hate to be the woman he's singing that one to." —*Cub Koda*

The Super Super Blues Band / 1968 / MCA ♦♦
Featuring Bo Diddley stubbing his toe on a wah-wah pedal, Wolf and Muddy clearly ill at ease trying to sing songs they don't know and a super annoying female chorus giving out banshee shrieks approximately every 45 seconds, this is one very chaotic, untogether super session to try and wade through. —*Cub Koda*

The London Howlin' Wolf Sessions / 1971 / MCA/Chess ♦♦
For the casual blues fan with a scant knowledge of the Wolf, this 1971 pairing, with Eric Clapton, Bill Wyman and Charlie Watts from the Rolling Stones, Ringo Starr and other British superstars, appears on the surface to be one hell of a super session. But those lofty notions are quickly dispelled once you slip this disc into the player and hit play. While it's nowhere near as awful as some blues purists make it out to be, the disparity of energy levels between the Wolf and his U.K. acolytes is not only palpable but downright depressing. Wolf was a very sick man at this juncture and Norman Dayron's non-production idea of just doing remakes of earlier Chess classics is wrongheaded in the extreme. The rehearsal snippet of Wolf trying to teach the band how to play Willie Dixon's "Little Red Rooster" shows just how far off the mark the whole concept of this rock superstar melange truly is. Even Eric Clapton, who usually welcomes *any* chance to play with one of his idols, has criticized this album repeatedly in interviews, which speaks volumes in and of itself. The rest of the leftover tracks are collected up on the 1974 hodgepodge *London Revisited*, later repackaged for compact disc consumption as *Muddy & the Wolf*. Avoid both of these turkeys like the plague they are. —*Cub Koda*

Live & Cookin' at Alice's Revisited / 1972 / Chess ♦♦♦
A CD reissue of Wolf's 1972 live album with the addition of two stellar bonus cuts. The first one, "Big House," first showed up on a hodgepodge Wolf bootleg album from the '70s. Its non-appearance on the original abum is somewhat of a mystery since it's arguably one of the best performances here. Set at a medium tempo, Wolf stretches out comfortably for over seven minutes, singing certain verses he likes two or three times as the band locks in with deadly authority. Certainly any list of great Howlin' Wolf vocal performances would have to include this one. The second bonus track, "Mr. Airplane Man," is Wolf working his one-riff-fits-all voodoo for all it's worth. You can tell from note one of his vocal entrance that the pilot light of inspiration is fully lit and the ensuing performance is the Wolf at his howlin' best. Also of special note are the wild and woolly takes on "I Had a Dream," "I Didn't Know," and Muddy Waters' "Mean Mistreater." There are mistakes galore out of the band and some PA system feedback here and there, both of which only add to the charm of it all. A great document of Wolf toward the end, still capable of bringing the heat and rocking the house down to the last brick. —*Cub Koda*

The Back Door Wolf / 1973 / Chess ♦♦♦
This, Wolf's last hurrah, is his final studio album. Cut with his regular working band, the Wolf Gang, everything here works well, despite Detroit Junior's annoying use of harpsichord on several tracks. Highlights include Eddie Shaw's "Coon on the Moon," Wolf's own "Moving" and "Stop Using Me," and both takes of "Speak Now Woman." Not the place to start a Wolf collection by any means, but a great place to end up. —*Cub Koda*

Change My Way / 1975 / Chess ♦♦♦
Originally compiled and issued in 1975 as a vinyl album in the original Chess Blues Masters Series, this 19-tracker is some of Wolf's best middle-period (1959-1963) material. Surprisingly, many of the tracks were cut in stereo and their appearance on compact disc does much to enhance their sonic ambience. Although some of this material surfaces on the three-disc Howlin' Wolf box set ("I Ain't Superstitious," "Just Like I Treat You"), this single disc stands mightily on its own. If you really want to hear Hubert Sumlin rip up the fretboard, this an excellent place to start. —*Cub Koda*

Ridin' in the Moonlight / 1982 / Ace ♦♦♦♦
Having moved from his home in Mississippi to Arkansas and eventually West Memphis, Howlin' Wolf recorded his first sides for Sam Phillips at the Memphis Recording Service between 1951-1953. These important recordings show that Wolf's gruff, Delta-fashioned and piledriving blues style was already intact before he hooked up with Chess for a successful stretch that would continue into the '60s. Featuring the fractured and menacing guitar work of Willie Johnson (equally celebrated axe man Hubert Sumlin would eventually supplant Johnson as the featured guitarist on Wolf's Chicago sides), the pumping piano of Ike Turner, and the ragged-but-right drumming of Willie Steel, the 16 tracks included on this Ace collection are alternate takes of some of the Memphis material originally released by Modern Records. While most of the master takes can be heard on Flair/Virgin's *Howlin' Wolf Rides Again*, the tracks on *Ridin' in the Moonlight* are certainly worthwhile, especially for collectors. With his permanently hoarse pipes and sour harmonica in the forefront, Wolf leads the band on highlights like the tittle track, "Chocolate Drop," "Keep What You Got," "Drivin' This Highway," and "Passing by Blues." A highly enjoyable release; newcomers, though, are advised to check out one of Wolf's Chess collections or the Flair album first. —*Stephen Cook*

★ **Howlin' Wolf/Moanin' in the Moonlight** / 1986 / MCA/Chess ♦♦♦♦♦
Howlin' Wolf's first and second Chess albums are essential listening of the highest order. They were compiled—as were all early blues albums—from various single sessions (not necessarily a bad thing, either), and blues fans will probably debate endlessly about which of the two albums is the perfect introduction to his music. But this CD reissue renders all arguments moot, as both album appear on one disc, making this a true best buy. Wolf's debut opus—curiously tacked on here *after* his second album—features all of his early hits ("How Many More Years," "Moanin' at Midnight," "Smokestack Lightning," "Forty Four," "Evil," and "I Asked for Water [She Gave Me Gasoline]"), and is a pretty potent collection in its own right. But it is the follow-up (always referred to as "the rocking chair album" because of Don Bronstein's distinctive cover art) where the equally potent teaming of Willie Dixon and Wolf produced one Chicago blues classic ("Spoonful," "The Red Rooster," "Back Door Man," "Wang Dang Doodle") after another. It's also with this marvelous batch of sides that one can clearly hear lead guitarist Hubert Sumlin coming into his own as a blues picking legend. The number of blues acolytes, both black and white, who wore the grooves down to mush learning the songs and guitar licks off these two albums would fill a book all by itself. If you have to narrow it down to just one Howlin' Wolf purchase for the collection, this would be the one to have and undoubtedly the place to start. This and *The Best of Muddy Waters* are the essential building blocks of any Chicago blues collection. And seldom does the music come with this much personality and brute force. —*Cub Koda*

☆ **Cadillac Daddy: Memphis Recordings, 1952** / 1989 / Rounder ♦♦♦♦♦
You can't possibly fault the material aboard this 12-song collection of Howlin' Wolf's Memphis recordings cut for Sam Phillips. The title track features some truly frightening guitar work from Willie Johnson, and all the material here is loaded with feral energy and a sense that it could fall apart at any second. It's totally intuitive music, with Wolf seemingly making it all up as he went along, which Sam Phillips had the patience to capture as it all went down. These are some of the great moments in blues history, but this part of Wolf's career is better documented on the two Bear Family volumes of the same material and the Flair/Virgin single disc of Memphis and West Memphis recordings. —*Cub Koda*

Memphis Days: Definitive Edition, Vol. 1 / 1989 / Bear Family ♦♦♦♦♦
These are Wolf's earliest and rarest sides recorded at the Sun studios, as raw and explosive as blues records come. Much of this was issued on various European albums during the '70s, always transferred off of muffled-sounding copy tapes. These 21 tracks (all but two of them off the master tapes) feature the amp-on-11 guitar work of Willie Johnson and the cave-man drumming of Willie Steel; they're loose and somewhat chaotic, with Wolf sounding utterly demonic. The real bonus on this volume is the first time inclusion of both sides of the only known acetate of Wolf's first session at Sam Phillips' 706 Union Avenue studio from 1951. With only Johnson and Steele in support (no bass, no piano), these early versions of "How Many More Years" and "Baby Ride with Me (Riding in the Moonlight)" are Wolf at his most primitive. —*Cub Koda*

The Memphis Days: Definitive Edition, Vol. 2 / 1990 / Bear Family ♦♦♦♦♦
The second volume in this series collects up all the known Memphis recordings that were either issued or originally offered to Chess. As such, it stands as a marvelous collection of Wolf's early 78s for that label. But what truly puts it over is the added bonus of a newly discovered acetate featuring several unissued versions of "How Many More Years" and "Baby Ride With Me (Riding in the Moonlight)." Much of this volume is pulled from discs, but the overall sound is good and the performances make it yet another must-have. —*Cub Koda*

☆ **The Chess Box** / 1991 / MCA/Chess ♦♦♦♦♦
This three-CD box set currently rates as the best—and most digestible—overview of Wolf's career. Disc one starts with the Memphis sides that eventually brought him to the label, including hits like "How Many More Years," but also compiling unissued sides that had previously only been available on vinyl bootlegs of dubious origin and fidelity. The disc finishes with an excellent cross section of early Chicago sessions including classic Wolf tracks like "Evil," "Forty Four," "I'll Be Around," and "Who Will Be Next." Disc two picks it up from there guiding us from mid- to late-'50s barnburners like "The Natchez Burnin'" and "I Better Go Now" to the bulk of the Willie Dixon classics. The final disc runs out the last of the Dixon sessions into mid-'60s classics like "Killing Floor" taking us

to a nice selection of his final recordings. A really nice bonus on this box set is the inclusion on the first two discs of snippets from a 1968 Howlin' Wolf interview and two performances of Wolf playing solo acoustic. If you've heard the sound of the Wolf, here's where you go to get a lot of it in one place. Definitely *not* the place to start (unless you have money to burn), but maybe just the perfect place to end up. *—Cub Koda*

☆ **Howlin' Wolf Rides Again** / 1993 / Flair ✦✦✦✦✦
While both Bear Family sets deal with a largely unissued wealth of material, this collection is devoted in the main to all the Memphis recordings from 1951 and 1952 that saw the light of day on a number of Los Angeles-based labels owned by the Bihari Brothers, being issued and reissued and reissued again on a plethora of $1.98 budget albums. Featuring recordings done in Sam Phillips' Memphis Recording Service and surreptitious sessions recorded by a young Ike Turner in makeshift studios, these 18 sides are the missing piece of the puzzle in absorbing Wolf's early pre-Chess period. It also helps that this just happens to be some of the nastiest sounding blues ever recorded. With no tracks being duplicated from the two Bear Family *Memphis Days* volumes, and sonics far surpassing all previous issues of this material (every last one of them horribly marred by an annoying 60-cycle hum), this is an essential part of any Wolf collection. Alternate-take freaks will revel in the inclusion of two extra takes of "Riding in the Moonlight" from an earlier and different session than the issued version also included. While not *quite* as essential as his first two Chess albums (and if you were making a judgement call on just passionate performances alone, even *that* would be debatable), this is definitely the next stop along the way in absorbing the raw genius of Howlin' Wolf. *—Cub Koda*

☆ **Ain't Gonna Be Your Dog** / 1994 / MCA/Chess ✦✦✦✦✦
This double-disc set features 42 rare and unissued performances, effectively cleaning out the Chess vaults of all but alternate takes of alternate takes. But these are no bottom-of-the-barrel scrapings here, quite the opposite. The first 14 tunes collect up the remainder of his Memphis recordings for Sam Phillips while the rest does the bootleggers one better, compiling masters that were previously only available on bad-sounding '70s vinyl albums. There's another snippet from his 1968 interview along with four more acoustic numbers from that same session (done, it turns out, as a promotional piece of sorts to preview his "soon-to-be-released psychedelic album," which Wolf always dismissed as "birds**t"), sadly the only time Chess ever tried to record him as a solo artist. A wonderful companion piece to any other Wolf collection you might own. *—Cub Koda*

Rockin' the Blues / 1996 / Collectables ✦✦✦
Collectables could probably do a better job of selling this nine-song CD if they'd indicate somewhere on the outside that it's a live performance from Germany in 1964. That puts it about seven years nearer to Wolf's prime than Chess' official live album (*At Alice's Revisited*) and makes this 1996 release an indispensable part of any serious blues or classic rock collection. Wolf and his band—Hubert Sumlin, guitar, Sunnyland Slim, piano, and Clifton James, drums (no credit for the bass player, but he's there)—open by easing into a loose-limbed instrumental jam. Wolf starts to build up a head of steam on "All My Life," but it isn't until "Howlin' for My Darlin'" that they hit their stride, picking up speed and tension as that voice cuts across the stage, rasping and moaning in a musical mating call—there are enough wrong notes to notice, but enough intensity not to care. "Dust My Broom" must have been something to see on stage, because it sure sounds from the tape like there's a lot of motion going on, and not just from James' jackhammer drumming. The recording of "Going Down Slow" is the best of several live versions left behind by Wolf; his savage-sounding, spoken-sung performance is a wonder to behold, and it's on performances like this that one can hear what Jimi Hendrix learned from listening to Hubert Sumlin. And just when it seems this disc couldn't get any better, along comes "Shake It for Me," a stage blowout that's sort of Wolf's answer to Muddy's "Got My Mojo Workin'." The 48 minutes of material here is some of best live Howlin' Wolf available, and forms a superb companion to his official Chess live releases while covering completely different material. The sound is exceptionally good, far superior to such recent live Wolf releases as the 1966 Massachusetts show. Only Collectables can say why they don't tell people it's a live recording, but it is out there and worth at least twice as much as they're asking. *—Bruce Eder*

★ **His Best (Chess 50th Anniversary Collection)** / Apr. 8, 1997 / MCA/Chess ✦✦✦✦✦
With the exception of a vinyl compilation issued in the early '80s (*His Greatest Sides, Volume 1*), there's never really ever been a single-disc Howlin' Wolf best-of package available. That all changes with this entry in MCA-Chess' *50th Anniversary* series, a 20-track retrospective that serves as the perfect introduction to the man and his music, some of the very best the blues has to offer. While some naysayers will always decry the exclusion—or inclusion—of any given number of tracks on any artists' best-of compilation, it's pretty hard to fault what's been collected here. Starting with the two-sided smash that brought him from Memphis to Chicago ("Moanin' at Midnight" b/w "How Many More Years"), this compilation hits all the high points and essential tracks, illustrating how his music developed into the mid-'60s. 11 of the 20 tunes on here are either written or co-written by Willie Dixon, and Wolf's original takes on "Back Door Man," "Spoonful," "The Red Rooster," "Wang Dang Doodle," and "I Ain't Superstitious" are truly the definitive ones, a place where personality and material symbiotically become as one. Even if you have already have this material, diehard Wolf fans—and audiophiles in particular—will want to investigate this package as the master transfers used here are absolutely stunning, with stereo mixes of "Killing Floor," "Built for Comfort," "Hidden Charms" (with the full-length Hubert Sumlin guitar solo), "Shake for Me," and the long version of "Going Down Slow" being particular standouts. This is a set so essential that it should on everyone's Top Ten first purchases in building the perfect blues collection. While Wolf's music will take you to many places (both musically and spiritually), here's where you start to absorb it all. *—Cub Koda*

☆ **His Best, Vol. 2** / Jul. 27, 1999 / MCA/Chess ✦✦✦✦✦
Where Chess' two-volume Muddy Waters' anthology *His Best* was divided according to chronological guidelines, the Howlin' Wolf series of the same name follows a different pattern. *His Best, Vol. 1* contained all of the Wolf's best-known songs—as if the label never planned a sequel. Consequently, when it came time to assemble *Vol. 2*, they had two major items ("The Natchez Burnin'," "Down in the Bottom") that didn't make the first cut, a take of "The Red Rooster" with dialogue, plus a host of songs familiar to Wolf fans, but not casual blues fans. Since Chester Burnett was one of the greatest bluesmen in history, these second-tier songs aren't castoffs—they're forgotten or unappreciated classics. They might not be as monumental as the songs on *His Best, Vol. 1*, yet they're great songs, making *His Best, Vol. 2* an excellent complement to its essential predecessor. *—Stephen Thomas Erlewine*

Smokestack Lightnin': Live in Germany 1964 / Nov. 13, 2001 / TKO Collectors ✦✦✦
This is a reissue of the November 6, 1964, Bremen concert that was previously available as *Live in Europe 1964* on the Sundown label, with the same incorrect title references. What is first-rate is the sound, which is head-and-shoulders above most of the Howlin' Wolf live recordings of this period, undoubtedly because the show was part of the American Folk-Blues tour, large chunks of which were recorded professionally, and also the performance, which comes from a time when Wolf was still in very robust health. It's been said that if Muddy Waters had been born in Africa, he would have been a king; this show, which Chess Records could only wish they'd recorded, is a reminder that if Howlin' Wolf had been born in Africa, he'd have been a witch doctor or shaman; he's spellbinding in his performance, and the band backing him (a kind of star combo itself, with Willie Dixon and Sunnyland Slim playing alongside Hubert Sumlin) is tight, if a little restrained. And to top it off, it's mid-priced. *—Bruce Eder*

☆ **The Real Folk Blues/More Real Folk Blues** / Mar. 12, 2002 / MCA/Chess ✦✦✦✦✦
The *Real Folk Blues* series on Chess wasn't really folk, but titled that way, perhaps to gain the attention of young white listeners who had started to get turned on to the blues during the '60s folk revival. And the Howlin' Wolf volumes in the series were not particularly more folk-oriented than his other Chess recordings, but more or less arbitrary selections of tracks that he'd done from the mid-'50s to the mid-'60s. It's thus also arbitrary to do a two-fer reissue of his *The Real Folk Blues* and *More Real Folk Blues*, combined here onto a single disc. That doesn't mean, though, that this isn't very good and sometimes great electric blues music. *The Real Folk Blues*, with tracks from 1956 to 1965, is by far the more modern of the pair in arrangements, and has a good share of classics: "Killing Floor," "Sittin' on Top of the World," "Built for Comfort," "Tail Dragger," and "Three Hundred Pounds of Joy." There were some lesser-known cuts on that record as well, never less than good and sometimes very good, like the blues-folk staple "Louise" and the driving "Poor Boy," as well as a couple brassy 1965 recordings with both Hubert Sumlin and Buddy Guy on guitars. *More Real Folk Blues*, in contrast, consists entirely of 1953-1955 recordings, which are considerably more lo-fi and not as stuffed with high-class memorable material. Yet these are fine raw '50s electric blues, and occasionally superb, as on the well-known "No Place to Go" and the propulsive "Just My Kind." You might already have some or many of the 24 tracks if you have a bunch of other Howlin' Wolf collections. But a lot of these, particularly from *More Real Folk Blues*, don't show up on the standard best-of anthologies, so more likely than not if you only have one or two Howlin' Wolf anthologies and want more, this is a pretty good one to get. *—Richie Unterberger*

Walk That Walk / Peavine/Chess ✦✦✦
Subtitled "Wolfman at the Chess Studio, 1957-59," this documents at least one complete alternate take of eight titles along with a plethora of breakdowns, false starts, and studio chitchat from Leonard Chess, Wolf, and some of the sidemen on the various dates. Actually, the "Chess studio" appellation is somewhat misleading, as the majority of these sides were either cut at Sheldon or Universal, two of Chicago's best equipped and busiest studios, where the Chess brothers did much of their early recording. The real joy, of course, is hearing how all these classic tracks came together in the studio, most of them shaped into finished form by the watchful eye and ear of label owner Leonard Chess. Chess always knew what he was looking for in a great blues performance, and the opening track, "I've Been Abused," sets the tone for this collection of wonderful fly-on-the-wall recordings. "I'm Leaving You" shows Chess working with Hubert Sumlin to nail a proper intro while getting the best out of Wolf and the rest of the band to get a finished take. "Howlin' for My Baby" is the furthest afield from the released version, as Wolf completely ignores Willie Dixon's lyrics and melody line for "Howlin' for My Darlin'," coming up with his own lyrics and tune to the riff. As Leonard Chess finally gets the drummer to lock in on a groove, he next goes after Wolf to get him back on course with middling results out of the cantankerous bluesman. "Nature" features studio chat between Wolf and one of the session players as he gets plenty steamed over the course of seven failed attempts at the song. "Moaning for My Baby" more or less comes off without a hitch, while the previously unissued instrumental "Wolf in the Mood" prompts Wolf into another altercation with Chess over the title. More nasty talk occurs on "Mr. Airplane Man" where Chess admonishes Wolf for screwing up the lyrics on the first take ("Uh Wolf, an airplane man flies, he don't sail! If he's an airplane man, he's got to fly. A boat man sails.") before starting up another attempt at the tune. The closer for this collection is the original run through of "I Better Go Now," which is followed by the first attempt to get it down on tape, a great raw moment of pure feeling. Although the practice of serving up alternate takes is a somewhat suspect one and listening to songs fall apart at a moment's notice while producer and artist cuss each other out—and it does get pretty raunchy at times—is not for everybody, hardcore Wolf (and Chess) fans will want to go the extra mile to seek this out to add to the collection anyway. Comes with a complete lyric sheet that also documents the studio chatter as well. *—Cub Koda*

Johnny Hoy

b. Connecticut

Vocals, Harmonica / Blues-Rock, Modern Electric Blues

Harmonica player, stonemason, and former commercial fisherman Johnny Hoy had good reason to call his band the Bluefish. The group, based in Martha's Vineyard, are all fishing fanatics, and they decided that the basic fighting characteristics of the typical bluefish suited the personalities of everyone in the band at the time.

Hoy was born in Connecticut and raised in New England and southern California. Unlike a lot of more straight-ahead blues harp player/singers, he has an eclectic set of musical and songwriting influences. They include Tom Waits, James Cotton, Ellen McIlvaine, and Muddy Waters. Waters frequented a club called the Shaboo Inn in Willimantic, CT, in the '70s, and Hoy was there at every show, jaws hanging agape at the sheer musical wizardry of the band of Chicago blues veterans.

Hoy and the Bluefish play a wide range of American roots music, not just Chicago blues, and this is reflected on their two albums for the Boston-based Tone-Cool Records. Hoy describes his band as a house-rockin' ensemble that enjoys playing clubs as much as it does theaters. Hoy and the Bluefish sneak zydeco music, some early rock & roll, some jump/swing blues, New Orleans funk, and rockabilly into their live shows.

The band cut their collective musical teeth in the greater Boston area, playing numerous functions on Martha's Vineyard, where Hoy has lived for the last two decades. On several occasions, they played private parties for President Clinton and other Democratic party leaders.

The band's two releases on Tone-Cool have titles that are both clever references to bluefishing jargon, *Trolling the Hootchy* (1995) and *You Gonna Lose Your Head* (1996). Their raw, garage band sounds are sure to delight fans of roadhouse blues and blues-rock for years to come. —*Richard Skelly*

Trolling the Hootchy / 1995 / Tone-Cool ✦✦✦✦

The official blues party band of Martha's Vineyard steps up to the plate with this debut disc featuring 13 tunes from the band's voluminous set list, including four originals from the pen of bandleader/harmonica man Johnny Hoy. Johnny's wife Barbara plays a rock-solid, nuthin'-fancy bass that drives the rhythm section, even with no less than three different players occupying the drum stool during the recording of this session. Jeremy Berlin's boogie piano is exceptionally fine, and he just may be the secret weapon on this album. Co-producer Danny Kortchmar contributes great guitar on six tracks, while Buck Shank provides a twangier approach on "Little Upsetter," "Johnny McEldoo," "Young and Restless," "Hidden Charms" and a duet between the Hoys on Willie Dixon's "Howlin' for My Darling." The originals stand up nicely against the set staples, and the singing is fresh and invigorating (particularly compelling is Hoy's chromatic turn on "Tennessee Waltz"), making this one potent party album. —*Cub Koda*

● **You Gonna Lose Your Head** / 1996 / Tone-Cool ✦✦✦✦✦

The Hoys (singer/songwriter/harmonica ace Johnny and his rock-solid bass-playing partner, Barbara Puciul Hoy) get way more adventurous on their second album with a brace of fresh tunes and finely picked covers. Johnny wrote nine of the 14 tracks on here and demonstrates a big jump forward in the songwriting department with "Beer Bellied Man," "Red Door" and "Made for One Another," heading the band into new waters this time around. Great covers of Lazy Lester's "You Better Listen," John Lee "Sonny Boy" Williamson's "Mellow Chick Swing" and Muddy Waters' "Just to Be With You" are worthy additions to the track lineup. While Jeremy Berlin's fine piano is still aboard, but the infusion of new blood in the ranks (Slim Bob Berosh on guitar for five tracks and Tauras Biskis kicking the drums around steadily) makes this second effort far more fun and interesting than the debut disc, showing that here's a band in it for the long haul. The party just keeps getting better. —*Cub Koda*

Walk the Plank / Apr. 7, 1998 / Tone-Cool ✦✦✦✦

This is one of those bands whose roots are in blues, but they have moved and taken the music in many wonderful new directions. They take the blues base and mix it with country and honky tonk as on "Just Another Wheel," and the band shows they are aware of the prominent influence of southwestern Louisiana with a little Cajun two-stepping in "Opelousas Sostan." One of the main draws of this disc is that the players seem to be enjoying what they do. The solos are kept short and everyone seems to get their chance to step up to the mic and shine. They do shine as their playing and the overall sound is a good step up from the ordinary. —*Bob Gottlieb*

Joe "Guitar" Hughes

b. 1938, Houston, TX

Vocals, Guitar / Electric Texas Blues, Modern Electric Texas Blues

Houston was home base to a remarkable cadre of red-hot blues guitarists during the '50s. Joe Hughes may not be known as widely as his peers Albert Collins and Johnny Copeland, but he's a solid journeyman with a growing discography. Another of his Houston neighbors, Johnny "Guitar" Watson, lit a performing fire in Hughes when he was 14.

Lone Star stalwarts T-Bone Walker and Clarence "Gatemouth" Brown also exerted their influence on Hughes' playing. His path crossed Copeland's circa 1953 when the two shared vocal and guitar duties in a combo called the Dukes of Rhythm. Hughes served as bandleader at a local blues joint known as Shady's Playhouse from 1958 through 1963, cutting a few scattered singles of his own in his spare time ("I Can't Go on This Way," "Ants in My Pants," "Shoe Shy"). In 1963, Hughes hit the road with the Upsetters, switching to the employ of Bobby "Blue" Bland in 1965 (he also recorded behind the singer for Duke) and Al "TNT" Braggs from 1967 to 1969.

A long dry spell followed, but Hughes finally came back to the spotlight with a fine set for Black Top in 1989 with *If You Want to See These Blues* (by that time, he'd inserted a "Guitar" as his middle name, much like his old pal Watson). Hughes' then released *Texas Guitar Slinger*, (1996, Bullseye Blues), *Down & Depressed: Dangerous* (1997, Munich), and *Stuff Like That* (2001, Blues Express), which contain slashing blends of blues and soul

with the ocassional tightly arranged horn section and, most importantly, enough axe to fulfill Hughes' adopted nickname. —*Bill Dahl & Al Campbell*

Texas Guitar Master Craftsman / 1988 / Double Trouble ✦✦✦

Craftsman / 1988 / Double Trouble ✦✦✦

● **If You Want to See These Blues** / 1989 / Black Top ✦✦✦✦✦

This contemporary of Albert Collins and Johnny Copeland only recently began accruing his own share of immortality—and it really started with this fine album, recorded in both New Orleans and Houston. Hughes' clean, crisp guitar work and hearty vocals may not be quite as distinctive as those of his Houston pals, but he's an authentic Texas blues guitarist all the way. —*Bill Dahl*

Texas Guitar Slinger / Mar. 1996 / Bullseye Blues ✦✦✦✦

The versatile Hughes at times slips a little soul influence into his Lone Star blues conception on this satisfying album. He stakes his undeniable claim as a "Texas Guitar Slinger" on one of the set's best songs, a gent who deserves enshrinement right alongside Johnny Copeland and Albert Collins. No argument there—he was there when they all got started. —*Bill Dahl*

Stuff Like That / Aug. 28, 2001 / Blues Express ✦✦✦✦

This journeyman Texas soul bluesman steps out from his usual role as a sideman for Bobby "Blue" Bland, the Upsetters, and others to deliver an excellent blues album, taking on the main guitar and vocal duties. Other than a skillful version of "When a Man Loves a Woman," this is all original material from Hughes. The album of top-notch Telecaster blues concludes with an interview track. —*Tom Schulte*

Humble Pie

f. 1968, Essex, England, db. 1975

Group / Album Rock, Boogie Rock, British Blues, Arena Rock, Hard Rock, Blues-Rock

A showcase for former Small Faces frontman Steve Marriott and onetime Herd guitar virtuoso Peter Frampton, the hard rock outfit Humble Pie formed in Essex, England in 1969. Also featuring ex-Spooky Tooth bassist Greg Ridley along with drummer Jerry Shirley, the fledgling group spent the first several months of its existence locked away in Marriott's Essex cottage, maintaining a relentless practice schedule. Signed to the Immediate label, Humble Pie soon issued their debut single "Natural Born Boogie," which hit the British Top Ten and paved the way for the group's premiere LP, *As Safe as Yesterday Is*.

After touring the U.S. in support of 1969's *Town and Country*, Humble Pie returned home only to discover that Immediate had declared bankruptcy. The band recruited a new manager, Dee Anthony, who helped land them a new deal with A&M; behind closed doors, Anthony encouraged Marriott to direct the group towards a harder-edged, grittier sound far removed from the acoustic melodies favored by Frampton. As Marriott's raw blues shouting began to dominate subsequent LPs like 1970's eponymous effort and 1971's *Rock On*, Frampton's role in the band he co-founded gradually diminished; finally, after a highly charged U.S. tour which yielded 1971's commercial breakthrough *Performance—Rockin' the Fillmore*, Frampton exited Humble Pie to embark on a solo career.

After enlisting former Colosseum guitarist Dave "Clem" Clempson to fill the void, Humble Pie grew even heavier for 1972's *Smokin'*, their most successful album to date. However, while 1973's ambitious double studio/live set *Eat It* fell just shy of the Top Ten, its 1974 follow-up *Thunderbox* failed to crack the Top 40. After 1975's *Street Rats* reached only number 100 before disappearing from the charts, Humble Pie disbanded; while Shirley formed Natural Gas with Badfinger alum Joey Molland, and Clempson and Ridley teamed with Cozy Powell in Strange Brew, Marriott led Steve Marriott's All-Stars before joining a reunited Small Faces in 1977.

In 1980, Marriott and Shirley re-formed Humble Pie with bassist Anthony Jones and ex-Jeff Beck Group vocalist Bobby Tench. After a pair of LPs, 1980's *On to Victory* and the following year's *Go for the Throat*, the group mounted a troubled tour of America: After one injury-related interruption brought on when Marriott mangled his hand in a hotel door, the schedule was again derailed when the frontman fell victim to an ulcer. Soon, Humble Pie again dissolved; while Shirley joined Fastway, Marriott went into seclusion. At the dawn of the '90s, he and Frampton made tentative plans to begin working together once more, but on April 20, 1991, Marriott died in the fire that destroyed his 16th century Arkesden cottage. He was 44 years old. —*Jason Ankeny*

As Safe as Yesterday Is / Apr. 1969 / Immediate ✦✦✦✦

Humble Pie, known as boogie hammerheads, at least once achieved American popularity in the mid-'70s. Its origins were quite different, however, and its debut album, *As Safe as Yesterday Is*, is a visionary blend of hard blues, crushing rock, pastoral folk, and postmod pop. It would be even more impressive if the group had written songs to support its sound, but it seemed to have overlooked that element of the equation. Still, there's no denying that the sound of the band isn't just good, it's quite engaging, as the band bring disparate elements together, letting them bump up against each other, forming a wildly rich blend of hippie folk and deeply sexy blues. Musically, this set a template for a lot of bands that followed later—Led Zeppelin seemed to directly lift parts of this, and Paul Weller would later rely heavily on this for his '90s comeback—and it's very intriguing, even rewarding, on that level. But it falls short of a genuine classic, even with its originality and influence, because the songwriting is rarely more than a structure for the playing and the album often sounds more like a period piece than an album that defined its times. —*Stephen Thomas Erlewine*

Town and Country / Aug. 1969 / Columbia ✦✦✦✦

Anyone who thinks of Humble Pie solely in terms of their latter-day boogie rock will be greatly surprised with this, the band's second release, for it is almost entirely acoustic. There is a gently rocking cover of Buddy Holly's "Heartbeat," and a couple of electrified Steve Marriott numbers, but the overall feel is definitely more of the country than the town or city. "The Sad Bag of Shaky Jake" is a typical Marriott country ditty, similar to those he would include almost as a token on each of the subsequent studio albums, and "Every Mother's Son" is structured as a folk tale. On "The Light of Love," Marriott even plays sitar. Peter Frampton's contributions here foreshadow the acoustic-based music he would make as a solo artist a few years later. As a whole, this is a crisp, cleanly recorded, attractive-sounding album, totally atypical of the Humble Pie catalog, but well worth a listen. —*Jim Newsom*

Humble Pie / 1970 / A&M ♦♦♦
Alternating hard-driving blues-rockers with country-folk numbers, *Humble Pie* neatly showcases the two sides of this band's personality on their first release for a major American label and third album overall. All of the elements are in place for the sound that would reach its studio peak with the next release, *Rock On*, and culminate with the classic *Live at the Fillmore* album. "Earth and Water Song" provides a blueprint for the acoustic guitar-based sound Peter Frampton would ride to multi-platinum success as a solo artist later in the decade. "One Eyed Trouser-Snake Rumba" and "Red Light Mama, Red Hot!" show the hard-rocking direction in which Steve Marriott would move the band after Frampton's departure the following year. —*Jim Newsom*

Rock On / 1971 / A&M ♦♦♦♦
On this, their second album, Humble Pie proved that they were not the "minor league Rolling Stones" as people often described them. Led by the soulful Steve Marriott, the Pie was a great *band* in every sense of the word. Although Peter Frampton elevated himself to superstar status in just a few years, this album proves what an excellent lead guitarist he was. The record has an undeniable live feel to it, due in part to Glyn Johns' humble yet precise recording, framing the group as if they were a boogie version of the Band. When all of these elements come together on songs such as "Sour Grain" and "Stone Cold Fever," it's an unbeatable combination. —*Matthew Greenwald*

Performance—Rockin' the Fillmore / 1971 / A&M ♦♦♦
Recorded while Peter Frampton was still in the band, *Performance—Rockin' the Fillmore* captures an early performance by Humble Pie where Steve Marriott's lyricism and ideas where balanced by Frampton's searing lead guitar. This is hardly as engaging as *As Safe as Yesterday Is*, which had studiocraft along with songcraft, but as a document of a band at a pivotal point in their existence, this is valuable and at times insightful. —*Stephen Thomas Erlewine*

Smokin' / 1972 / A&M ♦♦♦♦
After a couple of years of relentless touring, Humble Pie capitalized on their loyal U.S. following to capture the market with this, their third album. Although lead guitarist Peter Frampton was replaced by Clem Clempson—an excellent player—the band remained essentially the same. Led by singer/guitarist Steve Marriott's soulful wail, the group enjoyed a huge hit from this record, "30 Days in the Hole"—the track which defined the Pie's not-so-subtle appeal. The rest of the record is equally funky and intriguing. Stephen Stills guests on "Road Runner 'G' Jam," playing some nasty Hammond organ fills. In the end though, the group defined themselves as the undisputed leaders of the boogie movement in the early '70s, as a *band*. —*Matthew Greenwald*

Eat It / 1973 / A&M ♦♦♦
Although the quality of the material is decidedly uneven, the double album *Eat It* is the last Humble Pie record to capture the rough and tumble spirit of their heyday. Nevertheless, all of side four—which was recorded live in Glasgow—is worthless. —*Stephen Thomas Erlewine*

Thunderbox / 1974 / A&M ♦♦
With *Thunderbox*, it's clear that most of the inspiration has left Humble Pie, as the band turns in a set of by-the-numbers boogie. —*Stephen Thomas Erlewine*

Street Rats / 1975 / A&M ♦♦
Even more undistinguished than *Thunderbox*, the limp blues-rock of *Street Rats* illustrates why Humble Pie threw in the towel after the release of this record. —*Stephen Thomas Erlewine*

On to Victory / 1980 / Atco ♦♦
Five years after breaking up Humble Pie, Steve Marriott formed a new version of the band—featuring drummer Jerry Shirley, guitarist Bobby Tench, and bassist Anthony Jones—and recorded *On to Victory*. Unfortunately, *On to Victory* picks up exactly where *Street Rats* left off—it's a rote set of competent but faceless blues boogie —*Stephen Thomas Erlewine*

Go for the Throat / 1981 / Atco ♦
Peaking at number 60, the resurrected Humble Pie's first album *On to Victory* was surprisingly successful, allowing the group to have another chance to record an album. The ensuing record, *Go for the Throat*, was nearly identical to *On to Victory*, as the band ran through a set of bland, arena-ready blues-rock. The only difference was that the songs weren't as good as the last album, and those weren't very good to begin with. —*Stephen Thomas Erlewine*

● Classics, Vol. 14 / 1987 / A&M ♦♦♦♦♦
Released in 1987, during the thick of the *Classics* series, this compilation winds up being one of the most successful of its brethren, containing almost all of Humble Pie's greatest hits, including "I Don't Need No Doctor," "Hot 'n' Nasty," "Shine On," "30 Days in the Hole," and "C'mon Everybody." This isn't a strict hits compilation, yet it summarizes the band's strengths better than most of its ilk and winds up being an effective introduction to the band. —*Stephen Thomas Erlewine*

Hot 'n' Nasty—The Anthology / Jun. 7, 1994 / A&M ♦♦♦♦
Hot 'n' Nasty takes 31 tracks and spreads them across two discs, competently representing Humble Pie's blues boogie sound through the span of nine albums. Not only does this set compile the most worthy material from the band, but it also demonstrates how their

sound changed slightly as the '70s progressed. The first 11 tracks are taken from the band's first three albums, with the rare but worthwhile single "Big Black Dog" sandwiched in between. "Natural Born Woman," along with the brown-dirt gruffness of both "Buttermilk Boy" and "I'll Go Alone," are the best examples of Humble Pie in their early stages, while their self-titled album from a year later hands over the shaky "One-Eyed Trouser-Snake Rumba" and the rolly-polly enthusiasm of "Red Light Mama, Red Hot." Out of all the earlier material, 1971's *Rock On* was the weakest, although "Stone Cold Fever" and a shortened version of Muddy Waters' "Rollin' Stone" appears here as a couple of wise selections. Humble Pie's best song, the overly energetic "I Don't Need No Doctor" from the *Rockin' the Fillmore* album is an obvious and welcomed insertion, with "Four Day Creep" and "I'm Ready" rounding out that album's input. Peter Frampton departed after the *Fillmore* release, and 1972's *Smokin'* introduced his replacement with Dave "Clem" Clempson. "Hot 'n' Nasty," "You're So Good for Me," and the nine-minute "I Wonder" are all taken from *Smokin'*, which became their most successful album, gaining a number six spot on the album charts. The last eight cuts speak for Humble Pie's most disappointing albums, as the band somehow lost their homespun grittiness and their talent for producing abrasive, gut-heavy rock & roll. Only "Ninety-Nine Pounds" and "Road Hog" seem to carve any interest, with the latter coming from rather dismal *Street Rats* album, the group's last before they were reformed in 1981 by Steve Marriott and Jerry Shirley. An informative ramble through the band's career is also included in the form of a 20-page booklet, along with photos and detailed credits of each track. While a box-set may prove heartier, *Hot 'n' Nasty* provides a just-right assembly of Humble Pie's most essential morsels. —*Mike DeGagne*

King Biscuit Flower Hour: In Concert / Feb. 27, 1996 / King Biscuit ♦♦♦
Recorded on May 6, 1973, at San Francisco's Winterland Theater, *King Biscuit Flower Hour: In Concert* presents the post-Peter Frampton era of Humble Pie, featuring guitarist Dave Clempson backing what was by then Steve Marriott's vehicle. Marriott is in full cry on this recording, delivering his soulful, ingratiatingly over-the-top take on R&B-based hard rock with plenty of spirit; he even sings the between-song audience banter. In concert, Humble Pie displayed a ferocity that was sometimes missing from their studio albums, and *King Biscuit Flower Hour* not only captures that quality perfectly, it also does so arguably better than any other live album in the group's discography. —*Steve Huey*

The Scrubbers Session / May 5, 1997 / Archive ♦♦♦
The Scrubbers Session is a collection of unreleased material that Humble Pie and Steve Marriott recorded in the mid-'70s, as the group reached the end of the line. The music on the disc was initially planned as another Humble Pie album, yet it metamorphosized into a Marriott solo project over the course of recording. As a result, the record is substantially more interesting than many latter-day Humble Pie records, which were hampered by formulaic writing, yet the material is a little too unfocused to appeal to anyone but hardcore fans. Still, for those fans, *The Scrubbers Sessions* is essential, since it showcases Marriott breaking free from the limitations of Humble Pie and revitalizing himself artistically. —*Stephen Thomas Erlewine*

Running With the Pack / Oct. 12, 1999 / Pilot ♦♦♦
When singer Peter Frampton left Humble Pie in 1971 and became a full-time solo artist, it was a major blow for the British band, but not a fatal one. Some of Humble Pie's post-Frampton LPs were uneven, but some were solid. Assembled in 1999, this British release takes a generally enjoyable, 65-minute look at singer Steve Marriott's post-Frampton work with the British outfit. *Running With the Pack* contains four live performances (all of them from a December 1973 show in Philadelphia) and ten early-'70s studio recordings—and there is a major difference between the two. Taking the stage in Philly, Humble Pie gets into a heavy, guitar-powered hard rock/boogie groove on "Stone Cold Fever," "C'mon Everybody," "I Don't Need No Doctor," and "Four Day Creep" (which gives the impression that Marriott had been paying a lot of attention to Robert Plant's singing with Led Zeppelin). Much of the studio material, meanwhile, takes a funky, soul-drenched approach to rock—sort of Ike & Tina Turner meets Janis Joplin meets Otis Redding meets Rare Earth. And Marriott sounds like he is enjoying his soul obsession tremendously on Brown's "Think" as well as original material like "Snakes & Ladders," "Charlene," and "Midnight of My Life." But as John Hellier points out in his liner notes, the other members of Humble Pie didn't share Marriott's enthusiasm for this blue-eyed soul direction—and the result was a return to the heavier, guitar-powered hard rock/boogie mindset that one hears on the Philadelphia performances. All things considered, *Running With the Pack* paints an attractive, if imperfect, picture of Humble Pie's post-Frampton work. —*Alex Henderson*

● Natural Born Bugie: The Immediate Anthology / 2000 / Castle ♦♦♦♦♦
Steve Marriott left the Small Faces behind because he wanted to boogie. He no longer wanted to deal with the precious minutia and English whimsy that proved to be the Small Faces' greatest legacy; he wanted to adopt American blues, rock, and folk for his own—a character trait not unique to Marriott, since not only his peers felt the same way, but also generations of British rockers who would decide to leave England behind for American roots music whenever they wanted to prove their authenticity. Humble Pie would later sink into heavy, obvious grandiosity, shooting for the cheap seats (and succeeding) in American stadiums, but the band's initial albums were fascinating amalgams of rustic folk, blues, and heavy rock with a slight progressive tinge, all underpinned by an earnest student's love for a form he doesn't quite intuitively understand. These were the records that Marriott made while Peter Frampton was still in the band, and the ex-Herd member proved to be pivotal to the group's success, since the group had two solid songwriters who fed off each other's energies. Not that they were perfect—far from it, actually, since they were both too earnest and too eager to delve into directionless jams—but the end result was fascinating, as Castle's excellent double-disc anthology *Natural Born Bugie* proves.

Spanning two discs, this contains everything Humble Pie recorded for Immediate, including the band's debut single, _As Safe as Yesterday Is_, and _Town and Country_, plus no less than nine unreleased tracks and two songs only available on a German CD. This set makes a convincing argument that the group had a lot to offer in its early years, when country blues and folk were as prominent as driving bloozy boogie. So, there might not be any radio hits here, but this collection is often effective (and, at its worst, interesting) and easily the best way to hear the band at its peak. —_Stephen Thomas Erlewine_

BBC Sessions: Natural Born Boogie / Feb. 29, 2000 / Fuel 2000 ♦♦
For collectors only. Humble Pie's disappointing entry into the generally classy BBC series clocks in at an anemic 36 minutes and features slapdash, often incorrect track documentation (at least three tunes are credited to the wrong songwriters) as well as below par mono sound, which seems to be transferred from vinyl. Nine of the ten tunes are studio reproductions of existing album cuts and add little to the original versions. The majority were recorded before 1971 and feature Peter Frampton, but none of the performances are revelatory. An alternate version of the rare "The Big Black Dog" single, previously available only on the definitive double anthology _Hot 'n' Nasty_, is a worthy addition, but an album-closing live "I Don't Need No Doctor," seemingly recorded by a hand-held microphone in the middle of a field, sets a new low for fidelity on a non-bootleg release and pales in comparison to the classic _Performance—Rockin' the Fillmore_ version. Steve Marriott is in sturdy, soulful, high strutting voice throughout, but only diehard fans will find anything of interest here, and even they will be frustrated by this shoddily assembled, inconsequential addition to the catalog of a once impressive band. —_Hal Horowitz_

20th Century Masters—The Millennium Collection: The Best of Humble Pie / Oct. 10, 2000 / Interscope ♦♦♦♦
20th Century Masters—The Millennium Collection may not be the perfect Humble Pie collection, but it's perfectly serviceable for most casual fans, since it does contain such staples as "Natural Born Woman," "Stone Cold Fever," "Shine On," "Hot 'n' Nasty," and "I Don't Need No Doctor" among its 12 tracks. _The Best of Humble Pie_ might remain a better, tighter listen, but this covers much of the same ground and has a more appetizing front cover, which makes it a good choice for budget-minded curious listeners. —_Stephen Thomas Erlewine_

Helen Humes

b. Jun. 23, 1913, Louisville, KY, **d.** Sep. 9, 1981, Santa Monica, CA
Vocals / Vocal Jazz, Piedmont Blues, Prewar Country Blues, Jump Blues, Swing, Classic Female Blues, Ballads
Helen Humes was a versatile singer equally skilled on blues, swing standards, and ballads. Her cheerful style was always a joy to hear. As a child, she played piano and organ in church, and made her first recordings (ten blues songs in 1927) when she was only 13 and 14. In the '30s, she worked with Stuff Smith and Al Sears, recording with Harry James in 1937-1938. In 1938, Humes joined Count Basie's Orchestra for three years. Since Jimmy Rushing specialized in blues, Helen Humes mostly got stuck singing pop ballads, but she did a fine job.
After freelancing in New York (1941-1943) and touring with Clarence Love (1943-1944), Humes moved to Los Angeles. She began to record as a leader and had a hit in "Be-Baba-Leba:" her 1950 original "Million Dollar Secret" is a classic. Humes sometimes performed with Jazz at the Philharmonic, but was mostly a single in the '50s. She recorded three superb albums for Contemporary during 1959-1961, and had tours with Red Norvo. She moved to Australia in 1964, returning to the U.S. in 1967 to take care of her ailing mother. Humes was out of the music business for several years, but made a full comeback in 1973, and stayed busy up until her death. Throughout her career, Helen Humes recorded for such labels as Savoy, Aladdin, Mercury, Decca, Dootone, Contemporary, Classic Jazz, Black & Blue, Black Lion, Jazzology, Columbia, and Muse. —_Scott Yanow_

1927–1945 / Apr. 30, 1927-1945 / Classics ♦♦♦♦♦
When she was just 13 and 14 years old, Helen Humes made her recording debut, cutting ten risqué, double entendre-filled blues, naughty tunes that she later claimed to understand at the time. Until the release of this Classics CD in 1996, those numbers (which have backup in various settings by either De Loise Searcy or J.C. Johnson on piano and Lonnie Johnson or the guitar duo team of Sylvester Weaver and Walter Beasley) had never been reissued on the same set before. Humes sounds fairly mature on the enjoyable blues sides. Her next session as a leader would not take place until 15 years later, when she was 28 and a veteran of Count Basie's Orchestra. The singer is heard here with groups in 1942 and 1944-1945, performing three numbers with altoist Pete Brown's sextet (a band including trumpeter Dizzy Gillespie, who unfortunately does not solo), Leonard Feather's Hip-tet (which has some rare solos from trumpeter Bobby Stark) and Bill Doggett's spirited octet. The latter date is highlighted by classic renditions of "He May Be Your Man" and "Be-Baba-Leba." Highly recommended. —_Scott Yanow_

Her Best Recordings: 1927–1947 / Nov. 26, 1927-Dec. 31, 1947 / Best of Jazz ♦♦
Her Best Recordings: 1927-1947 presents a representative selection of vocalist Helen Humes' work with groups led by Harry James, Pete Brown, Buck Clayton, and Count Basie. It includes the youthful voice of Humes delivering swing tunes including "Jubilee," as well as blues numbers like "Jet Propelled Papa," the R&B jump number penned by Humes called "Be-Baba-Leba," and such pop classics as "My Heart Belongs to Daddy" and "Moonlight Serenade." The compilation has varying sound quality that's dependent upon the era's technology, but it is, overall, an excellent collection offering a worthwhile listen to an important voice of the swing era. —_Joslyn Layne_

E-Baba-Le-Ba / Nov. 20, 1944-Nov. 20, 1950 / Savoy ♦♦♦♦
Subtitled "The Rhythm and Blues Years," this highly enjoyable LP features the underrated and always cheerful singer Helen Humes in 1944 for four songs with Leonard Feather's Hip-tet (swing-oriented tunes that have been reissued on a Classics CD) and in 1950 with

bands led by altoist Marshall Royal, drummer Roy Milton (a live date), and tenor great Dexter Gordon. Humes had a flexible style that could sound quite credible on blues, ballads, swing, and early R&B. Among the many superior numbers heard from the 1950 dates are "This Love of Mine," "He May Be Yours," "E-Baba-Le-Ba," and "Helen's Advice." Hopefully, all of this music will be reissued on CD. —_Scott Yanow_

1947 / Aug. 1947-1948 / Trip ♦♦♦♦
The three sessions on this '70s Trip LP were originally cut for Mercury but have not yet been reissued on CD by Polygram. That is a pity, for the dozen selections feature Helen Humes in prime form, backed by the type of groups that accompanied Billie Holiday a decade earlier. Trumpeter Buck Clayton, tenor saxophonist John Hardee and (on one session) pianist Teddy Wilson all make their presence known, but Humes is the main star. Able to sing anything from lowdown blues to ballads and swinging stomps with equal skill, Humes is particularly memorable on "Jet Propelled Papa," "They Raided the Joint," "Flippity Flop Flop," and "Married Man Blues." Although it will be difficult to find, this album is worth tracking down. —_Scott Yanow_

Tain't Nobody's Biz-Ness If I Do / Jan. 5, 1959-Feb. 10, 1959 / Contemporary/OJC ♦♦♦♦♦
Helen Humes had not recorded as a leader in seven years when she made the first of three albums for Contemporary, all of which have been reissued on CD in the OJC series. Humes, 45 at the time, was at the peak of her powers, although she never really made a bad record. Accompanied by Benny Carter (on trumpet), trombonist Frank Rosolino, tenor saxophonist Teddy Edwards, pianist Andrew Previn, bassist Leroy Vinnegar and either Shelly Manne or Mel Lewis on drums, the singer is typically enthusiastic, exuberant and highly appealing on such numbers as "You Can Depend on Me," "When I Grow Too Old to Dream," and "'Tain't Nobody's Biz-ness If I Do." She even sings credible versions of "Bill Bailey" and "When the Saints Go Marching In" on this easily recommended CD. —_Scott Yanow_

★ **Songs I Like to Sing!** / Sep. 6, 1960-Sep. 8, 1960 / Contemporary/OJC ♦♦♦♦♦
One of the high points of Helen Humes' career, this Contemporary set (reissued on CD) features superior songs, superb backup, and very suitable and swinging arrangements by Marty Paich. Humes' versions of "If I Could Be With You," "You're Driving Me Crazy," and "Million Dollar Secret," in particular, are definitive. On four songs, she is backed by tenor great Ben Webster, a rhythm section, and a string quartet; the other numbers find her joined by a 14-piece band that includes Webster and Teddy Edwards on tenors along with altoist Art Pepper. This classic release is essential and shows just how appealing a singer Helen Humes could be. —_Scott Yanow_

Swingin' With Humes / Jul. 27, 1961-Jul. 29, 1961 / Contemporary/OJC ♦♦♦♦
The third of Helen Humes' three memorable Contemporary releases, all of which are out on CD, features the distinctive singer on a dozen standards that she had missed documenting thus far. With fine backup work by trumpeter Joe Gordon, tenor saxophonist Teddy Edwards, pianist Wynton Kelly, guitarist Al Viola, bassist Leroy Vinnegar, and drummer Frank Butler, Humes is in top form on such tunes as "When Day Is Done," "There'll Be Some Changes Made," "Pennies from Heaven," and "The Very Thought of You." One of her better albums. —_Scott Yanow_

Let the Good Times Roll / Aug. 1, 1973 / Classic Jazz ♦♦♦♦
Helen Humes had been retired for several years (and off record since 1961) when she began her comeback with this set. Recorded for the French Black & Blue label and made available domestically on a Classic Jazz LP, the album mostly features the veteran swing singer doing remakes, some of which top her earlier versions. Louis Jordan's "They Raided the Joint" is an exciting opener and is matched by "That Old Feeling," "Ooo Baba Leba," "He May Be Your Man," and Humes' classic "A Million Dollar Secret." Particularly strong assets in her notable backup group are tenorman Arnett Cobb, guitarists Al Casey and Clarence "Gatemouth" Brown, pianist Jay McShann and organist Milt Buckner. Wonderful music that deserves to be made widely available. —_Scott Yanow_

Sneakin' Around / Mar. 16, 1974 / Classic Jazz ♦♦♦♦
Helen Humes did both bawdy, double entendre-laden blues and R&B, and more sophisticated, jazz-tinged numbers during her career. This set, done with Gerald Badini, Gerald Wiggins, Major Holley, and Ed Thigpen, had a little of both, and was spiced up by Humes, singing with equal parts sass and grace. It was originally done for the Black and Blue label and was recently on CD. —_Ron Wynn_

On the Sunny Side of the Street / Jul. 2, 1974 / Black Lion ♦♦♦♦
Several major jazz personalities are heard on this Black Lion reissue CD, recorded live at the 1974 Montreux Jazz Festival. The fine singer Helen Humes sticks to standards and blues while accompanied by either Earl Hines or Jay McShann on piano, tenor saxophonist Buddy Tate, bassist Jimmy Woode and drummer Ed Thigpen. Although Hines and McShann are not the ideal accompanists, Humes fares quite well, winning the audience over with her enthusiasm and sincerity. —_Scott Yanow_

Helen Humes / Sep. 1974 / Audiophile ♦♦♦♦
This lesser-known Helen Humes album features the veteran singer in an intimate setting with pianist Connie Berry, guitarist Charlie Howard, and bassist Al Autry. Because she primarily sticks to ballads on the set (including "Wrap Your Troubles In Dreams," "Embraceable You," "A Hundred Years From Today," and a wonderful version of "More Than You Know"), this date lacks the excitement of her best albums. However, Helen Humes fans are well aware that she never made an indifferent or uninteresting record and will want this obscure effort too. —_Scott Yanow_

Talk of the Town / Feb. 18, 1975 / Columbia ♦♦♦♦
Two years into her return from a six-year retirement, Helen Humes was at the height of her fame when she reunited with producer John Hammond to make her lone Columbia

album. Joined by Buddy Tate (doubling on tenor and clarinet), guitarist George Benson (a Hammond discovery a decade earlier), pianist Ellis Larkins, bassist Major Holley and drummer Oliver Jackson, Humes is in fine form for a fairly typical mixture of blues, standards and ballads. She sounds particularly inspired during "He May Be Your Man," "Every Now and Then," "If I Could Be With You" and "Deed I Do." —*Scott Yanow*

Helen Humes and the Muse All Stars / Oct. 5, 1979+Oct. 8, 1979 / Muse ♦♦♦♦♦

Helen Humes' return to an active singing career was one of the happier events in jazz of the late '70s. Able to give great feeling and sensitivity to ballads but also a superb low-down blues singer, Humes flourished musically during her last years. On this excellent release (the CD reissue adds two alternate takes to the original program), Humes matches wits with altoist/singer Eddie "Cleanhead" Vinson on "I'm Gonna Move to the Outskirts of Town" and is in top form throughout. Tenors Arnett Cobb and Buddy Tate (along with a fine rhythm section led by pianist Gerald Wiggins) don't hurt either. An enthusiastic "Loud Talking Woman" and "My Old Flame" are highpoints. —*Scott Yanow*

Helen / Jun. 17, 1980+Jun. 19, 1980 / Muse ♦♦♦♦♦

Helen Humes was one of the most appealing jazz singers of the late '30s, and of the late '70s. Her comeback in her last few years was a welcome event, and all of her recordings for Muse are recommended. This one finds her backed by a veteran sextet including tenorman Buddy Tate, trumpeter Joe Wilder and pianist Norman Simmons. Her versions of "There'll Be Some Changes Made," "Easy Living" and "Draggin' My Heart Around" are particularly memorable. —*Scott Yanow*

Mark Hummel

b. Dec. 15, 1955, New Haven, CT

Vocals, Harp, Harmonica / Electric Harmonica Blues, Blues-Rock, Modern Electric Chicago Blues

Harmonica player, songwriter and singer Mark Hummel is a practitioner of the West Coast blues style, which typically includes elements of jazz and swing. A seasoned bandleader, Hummel is finally beginning to achieve wider recognition through nearly constant touring. Hummel was born in New Haven, CT, but raised in Los Angeles, CA. He became fascinated with the blues-rock of Cream, Jimi Hendrix, Big Brother & the Holding Company and the Rolling Stones. After seeing songwriter credits on the albums, he began to dig further back into those bands' blues roots.

He began playing harmonica in his teens in order to be different from the huge pack of guitar players in his high school. Hummel studied the styles of the Chicago-based players, including James Cotton, Sonny Boy Williamson, Big Walter "Shakey" Horton, and Little Walter Jacobs. Hummel moved to Berkeley, CA, in 1972 and played with local bluesmen there, including Boogie Jake, Cool Papa, Johnny Waters, and Sonny Lane. After graduating from high school, he hitchhiked around the country for three years, making stops in New Orleans, Boston, and Chicago to learn from those cities' top players.

In 1980, he formed the Blues Survivors, who have since performed at numerous blues festivals around the U.S., including the Chicago Blues Festival and the San Francisco Blues Festival.

Hummel has released a number of self-produced albums around his Oakland, CA home, including *Playing in Your Town* (1985, Rockinitis Records), *Up & Jumpin'* (with Canadian guitarist Sue Foley, 1989-1990), and *Hard Lovin' 1990s* (1992, Double Trouble Records). His widely available albums include *Feel Like Rockin'* (1994, Flying Fish Records), *Married to the Blues* (1995, Flying Fish), and most recently, *Heart of Chicago* (1997, Tone-Cool/Rounder), an album recorded in Chicago on which Hummel is accompanied by some veteran Chicago sidemen, including drummer Willie "Big Eyes" Smith, guitarist Dave Myers and producer/guitarist Steve Freund.

Considered one of the top harmonica players in the U.S., Hummel has also judged and played in the Hohner Harmonica World Championships, held in Germany; he issued *Low Down to Uptown* in 1998. *Golden State Blues* was next, released on new label Electro-Fi with support from Hummel's usual backing band, the Blues Survivors. —*Richard Skelly*

Hard Loving 1990s / 1992 / Double Trouble ♦♦♦♦

Harmonica Party / 1993 / Double Trouble ♦♦♦

Feel Like Rockin' / 1994 / Flying Fish ♦♦♦

● **Married to the Blues** / Oct. 1995 / Flying Fish ♦♦♦♦

Married to the Blues is one of Mark Hummel's finest releases, since it gives him ample opportunity to showcase his greasy, overdriven harmonica. The songs themselves aren't particularly distinctive, but they are good vehicles for him to strut his stuff, and that alone makes it a thoroughly enjoyable record. —*Thom Owens*

Heart of Chicago / Jan. 14, 1997 / Tone-Cool ♦♦♦

This collection of harmonica workouts gets rather tedious after a short while. Only devoted fans of harmonica blues will be able to stomach the onslaught of honking, as well as Hummel's thin voice, which is not suited to the task at hand. —*Tim Sheridan*

Low Down to Uptown / Jul. 14, 1998 / Tone-Cool ♦♦♦♦

Mark Hummel's James Cotton-inspired tone and ear for penning a solid tune come to the fore on his second disc on the Tone-Cool imprint. With Junior Watson's all-over-the-map style of guitar aboard on the majority of tracks here, the guest shots include Charles Brown (a fine reading of Duke Ellington's "In a Sentimental Mood"), David Maxwell on two tracks, and duets with Brenda Boykin on "Tain't What You Say" and Billie Holiday on "Now or Never." To say this album is stylistically diverse would be stating it mildly. The musical glue that holds it all together is Hummel's awesome talents on the harmonica and a band that never ceases to surprise with each genre switch of the track. Be it jazz, soul or straight-ahead blues, Hummel and company deliver the goods on this one. —*Cub Koda*

Alberta Hunter

b. Apr. 1, 1895, Memphis, TN, d. Oct. 17, 1984, Roosevelt, NY

Vocals / Standards, Classic Female Blues, Jazz Blues

An early blues vocalist in the '20s, a sophisticated supper-club singer in the '30s, and a survivor in the '80s, Alberta Hunter had quite a career. Hunter actually debuted in clubs as a singer as early as 1912, starting out in Chicago.

She made her first recording in 1921; wrote "Down Hearted Blues" (which became Bessie Smith's first hit); and used such sidemen on her recordings in the '20s as Fletcher Henderson, Eubie Blake, Fats Waller, Louis Armstrong, and Sidney Bechet. She starred in *Showboat* with Paul Robeson at the London Palladium (1928-1929), worked in Paris, and recorded straight ballads with John Jackson's orchestra. After returning to the U.S., Hunter worked for the USO during World War II and the Korean War, singing overseas. She retired in 1956 to become a nurse (she was 61 at the time), and continued in that field (other than a 1961 recording) until she was forced to retire, in 1977, when it was believed she was 65; actually, Hunter was 82, remarkably.

She then made a startling comeback in jazz, singing regularly at the Cookery in New York until she was 89, writing the music for the 1978 film *Remember My Name*, and recording for Columbia. After the '20s, Alberta Hunter recorded on an infrequent basis, but her dates from 1935, 1939, 1940, and 1950 have been mostly reissued by Stash; her Bluesville album (1961) is out in the OJC series; and her Columbia sets are still available. —*Scott Yanow*

Songs We Taught Your Mother / Aug. 16, 1961 / Bluesville/Original Blues Classics ♦♦♦

Although Alberta Hunter, who had briefly come out of retirement, gets first billing on this CD reissue, in reality she shares the spotlight with two other veterans of the '20s: Lucille Hegamin and Victoria Spivey. Each of the singers is featured on four songs apiece while backed by such top players as clarinetist Buster Bailey, trombonist J.C. Higginbottham, and Cliff Jackson or Willie "The Lion" Smith on piano. Hunter is in superior form on such numbers as "You Gotta Reap Just What You Sow" and "I Got a Mind to Ramble," although she would soon be out of music for another 15 years, continuing her work as a nurse. Hegamin (who had not recorded since 1932) was having a brief last hurrah, despite sounding good, and Spivey, reviving her "Black Snake Blues," would soon be launching her own Spivey label. This is a historic and enjoyable set recommended to both classic jazz and blues collectors. —*Scott Yanow*

Chicago: The Living Legends / Aug. 16, 1961 / Riverside ♦♦♦

This CD reissue is notable for two main reasons. It finds Alberta Hunter (who had retired from music in 1954 to become a nurse and who in the interim had only recorded once, two weeks earlier) in peak form on such numbers as "St. Louis Blues," "Downhearted Blues," and "You Better Change." In addition, it was pianist Lovie Austin's first recording in a couple decades; she was nearly 74 at the time and working as pianist at a Chicago dancing school. Austin's "Blues Serenaders" (a quintet also including trombonist Jimmy Archey, clarinetist Darnell Howard, bassist Pops Foster and drummer Jasper Taylor) has some concise solo space on the vocal pieces and takes three numbers (including Austin's "Gallion Stomp") as instrumentals. A well-conceived and historic set. —*Scott Yanow*

Remember My Name / 1977 / Columbia ♦♦♦♦

Although the cover on this album makes it look as if this is a soundtrack album (the singer had written several songs for the film "Remember My Name"), this is actually an important studio set. Alberta Hunter, a veteran of the '20s who was 82 at the time, was at the beginning of a remarkable comeback after having been out of music for 20 years (working as a nurse). The singer is absolutely delightful and often saucy on such numbers as "You Reap Just What You Sow," "I've Got a Mind to Ramble," "My Castle's Rockin'," and "Downhearted Blues," making this her definitive late-period album. In addition to Hunter and a fine rhythm section (pianist Gerald Cook, guitarist Wally Richardson, bassist Al Hall, and either Connie Kay or Jackie Williams on drums), three veteran horn players (trumpeter Doc Cheatham, trombonist Vic Dickenson, and tenor man Budd Johnson) help out with short solos. Highly recommended. —*Scott Yanow*

Amtrak Blues / 1978 / Columbia ♦♦♦

Alberta Hunter's second recording since launching her remarkable comeback (she was 83 when this album was cut) finds the veteran blues singer (a survivor of the '20s) still in surprisingly strong form and full of spirit. Such songs as "Darktown Strutters' Ball," "My Handy Man," "Old Fashioned Love," and "I've Got a Mind to Ramble" are given fine treatment by Hunter who is joined by the Gerald Cook quartet, trombonist Vic Dickenson, trumpeter Doc Cheatham, and tenor man Frank Wess on various tracks. —*Scott Yanow*

The Glory of Alberta Hunter / 1981 / Columbia ♦♦♦♦♦

Alberta Hunter's comeback after 20 years off the music scene was quite inspiring. She was (along with Sippie Wallace) virtually the only classic blues singer of the '20s still active during part of the '80s, and her four Columbia albums (of which this was the third) are surprisingly strong. With able backing by the Gerald Cook quartet, trumpeter Doc Cheatham, trombonist Vic Dickenson and tenor saxophonist Budd Johnson, Alberta Hunter sings some standards (including "Some of these Days," "The Glory of Love," and "I Cried for You"), a few religious hymns ("Ezekiel Saw the Wheel" and "Give Me That Old Time Religion"), the Yiddish tune "Ich Hob Dich Tzufil Lieba" and her own "Alberta's Blues" and "The Love I Have for You." —*Scott Yanow*

The Legendary Alberta Hunter: '34 London Sessions / 1981 / DRG ♦♦

This handsome album is a bit of an oddity. Alberta Hunter, famous as a jazz-oriented blues singer in the '20s, reinvented herself as a sophisticated stage singer in London. Her 11 recordings with Jack Jackson's society dance orchestra in 1934 are very straight, outside of jazz and somewhat dated today. Whether it be "Two Cigarettes in the Dark," "Miss Otis Regrets," or "Two Little Flies on a Lump of Sugar," Hunter interprets the romantic ballads like a cabaret singer. So, although this reissue was perfectly done (with extensive liner notes), there is little here to interest blues listeners. *—Scott Yanow*

Classic Alberta Hunter: The Thirties / 1981 / Stash ♦♦♦♦
After returning to the United States from England in 1935, Alberta Hunter continued working as a jazz-oriented singer in the U.S. although she maintained a lower profile than in the '20s. She just had three recording sessions during 1935-1940 (all of the music is included on this valuable LP) and eight numbers in 1950 (two of which are here) prior to retiring from music in the mid-'50s to become a nurse. Among the highlights of these 15 selections by the timeless singer are "You Can't Tell the Difference After Dark," a remake of "Downhearted Blues," "Someday, Sweetheart," and "The Castle's Rockin'." In the backup groups on some numbers are trumpeter Charlie Shavers, clarinetist Buster Bailey, and either Lil Armstrong or Eddie Heywood on piano, among others. Recommended. *—Scott Yanow*

Look for the Silver Lining / 1982 / Columbia ♦♦♦♦
Classic blues singer Alberta Hunter's final recording (made when she was 87, two years before her death) is as powerful as her previous three Columbia albums. The legendary delightful singer puts plenty of feeling into "Look for the Silver Lining," "He's Funny That Way," "Somebody Loves Me," and four of her originals. As was true of each of her final sets, Hunter is joined by the Gerald Cook quartet and several veteran horn players (trumpeters Doc Cheatham and Jonah Jones, trombonist Vic Dickenson, and tenor man Budd Johnson), all of whom sound quite happy to be supporting the ancient yet ageless singer. *—Scott Yanow*

The Twenties / 1988 / Stash ♦♦♦♦♦
This LP gives listeners a strong sampling of singer Alberta Hunter's work in the '20s. The 14 selections find her joined by such major jazz names as pianists Fletcher Henderson and Eubie Blake, cornetist Louis Armstrong, soprano saxophonist Sidney Bechet, and Fats Waller (on organ). Although best known during the era as a classic blues singer, Hunter was always flexible and able to sing a wide variety of material. The best way to acquire all of her '20s recordings is through her Document CDs, but this LP sampler is excellent, with the highlights including "Down Hearted Blues" (her composition which Bessie Smith would make into a big hit in 1923), "Nobody Knows the Way I Feel Dis Morning," "If You Can't Hold the Man You Love," and "I'm Going to See My Ma." *—Scott Yanow*

● **Young Alberta Hunter: The Twenties** / 1992 / Vintage Jazz Classics ♦♦♦♦♦
1921-1940. 23 classic tracks, both small and large backup bands (Fletcher Henderson). Good sound. *—Michael Erlewine*

Complete Recorded Works, Vol. 1 (1921-1923) / Feb. 15, 1996 / Document ♦♦♦
The first volume in Document's *Complete Recorded Works* series of Alberta Hunter compilations includes her earliest recordings from the '20s. Along with a 1922 version of her own song, "Downhearted Blues," which became a hit in the hands of Bessie Smith, the disc includes the classic performances "You Gotta Reap What You Sow" and "Chirpin' the Blues," plus sides recorded with help from some outstanding sidemen: Fletcher Henderson, Eubie Blake, and Don Redman, among others. For less-dedicated listeners, the long running time and poor fidelity will be hard to digest. The serious blues listener will find all these factors to be positive, but casual listeners will find that the collection is of marginal interest for those very reasons. *—Thom Owens*

Complete Recorded Works, Vol. 2 (1923–24) / Mar. 5, 1996 / Document ♦♦♦

Complete Recorded Works, Vol. 3 (1924–27) / Apr. 9, 1996 / Document ♦♦♦

Complete Recorded Works, Vol. 4 (1927–46) / Apr. 9, 1996 / Document ♦♦♦

Alternate Takes (1921–1924) / Sep. 23, 1997 / Document ♦♦♦

Ivory Joe Hunter

b. Oct. 10, 1914, Kirbyville, TX, **d.** Nov. 8, 1974, Memphis, TN
Vocals, Songwriter, Piano / West Coast Blues, Piano Blues, R&B
Bespectacled and velvet-smooth in the vocal department, pianist Ivory Joe Hunter appeared too much mild-mannered to be a rock & roller. But when the rebellious music first crashed the American consciousness in the mid-'50s, there was Ivory Joe, deftly delivering his blues ballad "Since I Met You Baby" right alongside the wildest pioneers of the era.

Hunter was already a grizzled R&B vet by that time who had first heard his voice on a 1933 Library of Congress cylinder recording made in Texas (where he grew up). An accomplished tunesmith, he played around the Gulf Coast region, hosting his own radio program for a time in Beaumont before migrating to California in 1942. It was a wise move since Hunter—whose real name was Ivory Joe, incidentally (perhaps his folks were psychic!)—found plenty of work pounding out blues and ballads in wartime California. He started his own label, Ivory Records, to press up his "Blues at Sunrise" (with Johnny Moore's Three Blazers backing him), and it became a national hit when leased to Leon Rene's Exclusive imprint in 1945. Another Hunter enterprise, Pacific Records, hosted a major hit in 1948 when the pianist's "Pretty Mama Blues" topped the R&B charts for three weeks.

At whatever logo Hunter paused from the mid-'40s through the late '50s, his platters sold like hotcakes. For Cincinnati-based King in 1948-1949, he hit with "Don't Fall in Love With Me," "What Did You Do to Me," "Waiting in Vain," and "Guess Who." At MGM, then new to the record biz, he cut his immortal "I Almost Lost My Mind" (another R&B chart-topper in 1950), "I Need You So" (later covered by Elvis), and "It's a Sin." Signing with Atlantic in 1954, he hit big with "Since I Met You Baby" in 1956 and the two-sided smash "Empty Arms"/"Love's a Hurting Game" in 1957.

Hunter's fondness for country music reared its head in 1958. Upon switching to Dot Records, he scored his last pop hit with a cover of Bill Anderson's "City Lights." Hunter's Dot encores went nowhere; neither did typically mellow outings for Vee-Jay, Smash, Capitol, and Veep. Epic went so far as to recruit a simmering Memphis band (including organist Isaac Hayes, trumpeter Gene "Bowlegs" Miller, and saxist Charles Chalmers) for an LP titled *The Return of Ivory Joe Hunter* that hoped to revitalize his career, but it wasn't meant to be. The album's cover photo—a closeup of Hunter's grinning face with a cigarette dangling from his lips—seems grimly ironic in the face of his death from lung cancer only a few years later. *—Bill Dahl*

Ivory Joe Hunter / 1957 / Atlantic ♦♦♦♦♦
His hitmaking peak. *—Bill Dahl*

Sings the Old and the New / 1958 / Atlantic ♦♦♦
More fine '50s sides. *—Bill Dahl*

16 of His Greatest Hits / 1958 / King ♦♦♦
Other than ruining his 1949 smash "Guess Who" entirely with hideous stereo overdubs, King has done pretty well by the pianist on this collection of his postwar output for the Cincinnati firm. Hunter was primarily in a sentimental blues ballad bag back then, some of his hits displaying a tinge of country influence. Sound quality is OK if not superlative. *—Bill Dahl*

The Return of Ivory Joe Hunter / 1971 / Epic ♦♦♦
A commendable attempt to update Ivory Joe Hunter's sound for early-'70s consumption, with an all-star Memphis aggregation that included Isaac Hayes on organ, saxist Charlie Chalmers, and a sax section lifted from the Hi studios. The ploy worked reasonably well, producing updated remakes of Hunter's hits and tasty versions of Don Covay's "I'm Coming Down With the Blues" and Chuck Willis' "What Am I Living For." *—Bill Dahl*

7th Street Boogie / 1980 / Route 66 ♦♦♦♦♦
These are wonderful mid-'40s and early-'50s sides from an extremely versatile vocalist and sorely neglected composer and pianist. Ivory Joe Hunter could sing everything from blues to soul to gospel to country magnificently; this is predominantly blues and R&B fare. *—Ron Wynn*

● **Since I Met You Baby: The Best of Ivory Joe Hunter** / Oct. 19, 1994 / Razor & Tie ♦♦♦♦♦
Bespectacled pianist Ivory Joe Hunter's crooning blues balladry made him a hot commodity from the late '40s through the late '50s, but he could rock reasonably convincingly hard too. He does both on this wonderful survey of his 1949-1958 MGM and Atlantic sides—"I Need You So," "I Almost Lost My Mind," and the title item are sophisticated and mellow, while "Rockin' Chair Boogie," "Love Is a Hurting Game," and "Shooty Booty" find the pianist in decidedly unsentimental moods. *—Bill Dahl*

Ivory Joe Hunter/Sings the Old & the New / Jul. 27, 1999 / Collectables ♦♦♦♦
Don't let the 28 tracks fool you; Collectables doesn't attempt a thorough overview of Ivory Joe Hunter's five-decade recording career, which spanned from the '30s to the '70s. These 28 tracks chronicle the Texas-born purveyor of West Coast blues' '50s stint with Atlantic Records. For some artists it can be done, but trying to cover Hunter's output in less than 30 songs is as impossible as covering a king-size mattress with a twin-size sheet. Hunter preceded dinosaurs like Frank Sinatra, Nat King Cole, the Andrews Sisters, Vic Damone, and the Isley Brothers. This disc features Hunter's two late-'50s Atlantic albums, the period of "Since I Lost My Baby (I Almost Lost My Mind)," the hit that made Hunter the oldest performer on the rock circuit. He matches that velvety offering with other smoothies. Ivory Joe Hunter was a stylish blues crooner who influenced countless singers with his low-key approach. *—Andrew Hamilton*

Jumping at the Dew Drop / Dec. 14, 1999 / Route 66 ♦♦♦
A European import slab of vinyl offering an overview of Hunter's 1947-1952 pre-Atlantic days. Emphasis on jump entries ("Are You Hep?," "She's a Killer," "We're Gonna Boogie," "Old Man's Boogie") is a welcome change-of-pace from Hunter's better-known propensity for velvety blues ballads. *—Bill Dahl*

Blues, Ballads & Rock 'n' Roll / 2000 / Ace ♦♦♦♦♦
All 28 of these tracks are from Hunter's 1955-59 stint with Atlantic Records, the period which saw him find his greatest pop success. Since Hunter's career was so lengthy, it inevitably omits enough material so that it could not be considered his best-of; "I Almost Lost My Mind," for instance, is not here. On the other hand, his biggest hit, "Since I Met You Baby," is on the CD, as are his big R&B charters "A Tear Fell," "It May Sound Silly," "Empty Arms," "Love's a Hurting Game," and "Yes I Want You." Though Hunter just about qualified as a rock & roll artist during this time, he was in fact smoother than just about any other black '50s rock & roll singer, and indeed smoother than most '50s R&B artists. At times this sounds a bit like Nat King Cole going rock & roll, and there's a prominent country tinge to some of his ballads, "Since I Met You Baby" being the pre-eminent example. As the title of this disc signifies, he was a versatile cat, trying out jump blues, smoochers, fairly straightforward rock & roll ("Shooty Booty"), and novelties ("I Got to Learn to Mambo"). That, in some ways, makes this a more engaging listen than the average single-artist '50s R&B comp, though at the same time it doesn't reach the energetic peaks scaled by many other major performers of the era. Listen to a doo wop- and pop-inflected cut like "I Want Somebody," and you get an idea of why Hunter was such a big influence on Elvis Presley. His Atlantic output did suffer slightly, though, from some obvious attempts to duplicate the formula of "Since I Met You Baby." [This U.K. import is not available for sale in North America.] *—Richie Unterberger*

1945–1947 / Mar. 5, 2002 / Classics ♦♦♦

1947 / May 7, 2002 / Classics ♦♦♦

Long John Hunter

b. 1931, Louisiana
Vocals, Guitar / Electric Texas Blues, Modern Electric Texas Blues
For much too long, the legend of Long John Hunter has largely been a local one, limited to the bordertown region between El Paso, Texas and Juarez, Mexico. That's where the guitarist reigned for 13 years (beginning in 1957) at Juarez's infamous Lobby Bar. Its

riotous, often brawling clientele included locals, cowboys, soldiers from nearby Fort Bliss, frat boys, and every sort of troublemaking tourist in between. Hunter kept 'em all entertained with his outrageous showmanship and slashing guitar riffs.

The Louisiana native got a late start on his musical career. When he was 22 and toiling away in a Beaumont, TX, box factory, he attended a B.B. King show and was instantly transfixed. The next day, he bought a guitar. A year later, he was starring at the same bar that B.B. had headlined.

Hunter's 1954 debut single for Don Robey's Houston-based Duke label, "She Used to Be My Woman"/"Crazy Baby," preceded his move to El Paso in 1957. Along the way, Phillip Walker and Lonnie Brooks both picked up on his licks. But Hunter's recording output was slim—a few hot but obscure singles waxed from 1961 to 1963 for the tiny Yucca logo out of Alamogordo, NM (standouts include "El Paso Rock," "Midnight Stroll," and "Border Town Blues"). Perhaps he was just too busy—he held court at the Lobby seven nights a week from sundown to sunup.

Fortunately, Hunter's reputation is finally outgrowing the Lone Star state. His 1992 set for the now-shuttered Spindletop imprint, *Ride With Me*, got the ball rolling. Now, his 1996 disc for Alligator, *Border Town Legend*, should expose this Texas blues great to a far wider (if not wilder) audience than ever before. *—Bill Dahl*

Texas Border Town Blues / 1988 / Double Trouble ♦♦♦

Ride With Me / 1992 / Spindletop ♦♦♦♦

Hunter's third album for Alligator finds him in tip-top form, sounding like a man half his age (62 at the time) and brandishing a nasty guitar tone that supposedly died out with '50s one-track mono recording. Everything on here is kept in a nice Texas roadhouse framework, with plenty of air moving behind Long John from a fine combo that includes Derek O'Brien on guitar and Sarah Brown on bass. For his end of it, Hunter sounds positively involved on tunes like "Irene," "Crazy Love," the rockin' "Bad Feet," the uptempo "Dream About the Devil," a fun duet with T.D. Bell on "West Texas Homecoming," and the title track. With his songwriting hand clearly defined on all ten tunes here, Hunter has made his most realized album to date, showing him still in sharp command of his prestigious powers. *—Cub Koda*

Smooth Magic / Dec. 20, 1994 / Double Trouble ♦♦♦♦

Border Town Legend / Jan. 30, 1996 / Alligator ♦♦♦♦♦

For many years Long John Hunter played in clubs without much attention, but that time sweating it out in roadhouses has paid off. During that time, he developed a gutsy, forceful technique that was fully evident on his belated 1992 debut, *Ride With Me*. Although his second album, *Border Town Legend*, is a slicker, more accessible effort, Hunter hasn't lost any of his spicy, distinctive flavor. Working with a horn section, he still manages to make himself the most powerful element on the record—both his guitar playing and his heated vocals ensure that. Furthermore, Hunter's songwriting is growing stronger. Out of the nine songs he has written or co-written for the album, he has contributed some first-rate tunes that might not stretch beyond generic conventions, but still are mighty fine. *—Stephen Thomas Erlewine*

Swinging from the Rafters / Sep. 2, 1997 / Alligator ♦♦♦♦♦

Long John's second album for the Alligator imprint is even more potent than his first, *Texas Border Legend*. This time around, Hunter's sly, drawling vocals and stinging clusters of guitar are well to the fore, keeping the spotlight firmly in place on this Texas guitar legend. The record was cut in Austin and Abilene, Texas, and as such boasts Lone Star talent like Derek O'Brien, who plays rhythm guitar on this disc and solos on "I Don't Care" and "V-8 Ford." Mark "Kaz" Kazanoff blows saxophone on eight tunes and harmonica on "Locksmith Man." For his part, Hunter contributes 10 of the 14 tunes, co-writing with various members of his Walking Catfish Band or his co-producers, Tary Owens and John Foose. Long John's no-holds-barred approach literally screams Texas blues, letting you know you're listening to an originator, not an imitator. *—Cub Koda*

• **Ooh Wee Pretty Baby!** / Nov. 2, 1999 / Norton ♦♦♦♦♦

Mississippi John Hurt

b. Jul. 3, 1893, Teoc, MS, **d.** Nov. 2, 1966, Grenada, MS

Vocals, Songwriter, Harmonica, Guitar / Field Recordings, Prewar Blues, Blues Revival, Country Blues, Acoustic Blues

No blues singer ever presented a more gentle, genial image than Mississippi John Hurt. A guitarist with an extraordinarily lyrical and refined fingerpicking style, he also sang with a warmth unique in the field of blues, and the gospel influence in his music gave it a depth and reflective quality unusual in the field. Coupled with the sheer gratitude and amazement that he felt over having found a mass audience so late in life, and playing concerts in front of thousands of people—for fees that seemed astronomical to a man who had always made music a sideline to his life as a farm laborer—these qualities make Hurt's recordings into a very special listening experience.

John Hurt grew up in the Mississippi hill country town of Avalon, population under 100, north of Greenwood, near Grenada. He began playing guitar in 1903, and within a few years was performing at parties, doing ragtime repertory rather than blues. As a farm hand, he lived in relative isolation, and it was only in 1916, when he went to work briefly for the railroad, that he got to broaden his horizons and his repertory beyond Avalon. In the early '20s he teamed up with white fiddle player Willie Narmour, playing square dances.

Hurt was spotted by a scout for OKeh Records who passed through Avalon in 1927, who was supposed to record Narmour, and signed to record after a quick audition. Of the eight sides that Hurt recorded in Memphis in February of 1928, only two were ever released, but he was still asked to record in New York late in 1928.

Hurt's dexterity as a guitarist, coupled with his plainspoken nature, were his apparent undoing, at least as a popular blues artist, at the time. His playing was too soft and articulate, and his voice too plain to be taken up in a mass setting, such as a dance—rather, his music was best heard in small, intimate gatherings. In that sense, he was one of the earliest blues musicians to rely completely on the medium of recorded music as a vehicle for mass success—where the records of Furry Lewis or Blind Blake were mere distillations of music that they (presumably) did much better on stage, in John Hurt's case the records were good representations of what he did best. Additionally, Hurt never regarded himself as a blues singer, preferring to let his relatively weak voice speak for itself with none of the gimmicks that he might've used, especially in the studio, to compensate. And he had no real signature tune with which he could be identified, in the way that Furry Lewis has "Kassie Jones" or "John Henry."

Not that Hurt didn't have some great numbers in his songbag: "Frankie," "Louis Collins," "Avalon Blues," "Candy Man Blues," "Big Leg Blues," and "Stack O' Lee Blues," were all brilliant and unusual as blues, in their own way, and highly influential on subsequent generations of musicians. They didn't sell in large numbers at the time, however, and as Hurt never set much store on a musical career, he was content to make his living as a hired hand in Avalon, living on a farm and playing for friends whenever the occasion arose.

Mississippi John Hurt might've lived and died in obscurity, if it hadn't been for the folk music revival of the late '50s and early '60s. A new generation of listeners and scholars suddenly expressed a deep interest in the music of America's hinterlands, not only in listening to it but finding and preserving it. A scholar named Tom Hoskins discovered that Mississippi John Hurt, who hadn't been heard from musically in over 35 years, was alive and living in Avalon, MS, and sought him out, following the trail laid down in Hurt's song "Avalon Blues." Their meeting was a fateful one—Hurt was in his seventies, and weary from a lifetime of backbreaking labor for pitifully small amounts of money, but his musical ability was intact, and he bore no ill-will against anyone who wanted to hear his music.

A series of concerts was arranged, including an appearance at the Newport Folk Festival, where he was greeted as a living legend. This opened up a new world to Hurt, who was grateful to find thousands, or even tens of thousands of people too young to have even been born when he made his only records up to that time, eager to listen to anything he had to sing or say. A tour of American universities followed, and a series of recordings, first in a relatively informal, non-commercial setting intended to capture him in his most comfortable and natural surroundings, and later under the auspices of Vanguard Records, with folksinger Patrick Sky producing.

It was 1965, and Mississippi John Hurt had found a mass audience for his songs 35 years late. He took the opportunity, playing concerts and making new records of old songs as well as material he'd never before laid down—whether he eventually put down more than a portion of his true repertory will probably never be clear, but Hurt did leave a major legacy of his and other peoples' songs, in a style that barely skipped a beat from his late-'20s OKeh sides.

As with many people to whom success comes late in life, certain aspects of the success were hard for him to absorb in stride—the money was more than he'd ever hoped to see, even if it wasn't much by the standards of a major pop star; $1000 concert fees were something he'd never even pondered having to deal with. What he did most easily was sing and play—Vanguard got out a new album, *Today!* in 1966, from his first sessions for the label. Additionally, the tape of a concert that Hurt played at Oberlin College in April of 1965 was released under the title *The Best of Mississippi John Hurt*—the 21-song live album was just that, even if it wasn't made up of previously released work (more typical of a "best-of" album), a perfect record of a beautiful performance in which the man did old and new songs in the peak of his form. Hurt got in one more full album, *The Immortal Mississippi John Hurt*, released posthumously, but even better was the record assembled from his final sessions, *Last Sessions*, also issued after his death—these songs broke new lyrical ground, and showed Hurt's voice and guitar to be as strong as ever, just months before his death.

Mississippi John Hurt left behind a legacy unique in the annals of the blues, and not just in terms of music. A humble, hard-working man who never sought fame or fortune from his music, and who conducted his life in an honest and honorable manner, he also avoided the troubles that afflicted the lives of many of his more tragic fellow musicians. He was a pure musician, playing for himself and the smallest possible number of listeners, developing his guitar technique and singing style to please nobody but himself—and he suddenly found himself with a huge following, precisely because of his unique style. Unlike contemporaries such as Skip James, he felt no bitterness over his late-in-life mass success, and as a result continued to please and win over new listeners with his recordings until virtually the last weeks of his life. Nothing he ever recorded was less than inspired, and most of it was superb. *—Bruce Eder*

Avalon Blues / Apr. 1963 / Rounder ♦♦♦♦♦

This is the first in a multiple-volume series devoted to the Piedmont recordings Hurt made upon his rediscovery in the early '60s. They capture him with his playing and singing still intact, untouched by the world around him, a world that had changed so much since he initially recorded back in the '20s. Many of his best-known tunes are here—"Candy Man Blues," "Salty Dog," "Spike Driver Blues," "Louis Collins," "Spanish Fandango," and the title track—and although Hurt was to re-record them for other labels, these versions are as fine as any. There's really no one else in the blues with the gentle wistfulness of John Hurt, and this collection makes a wonderful addition to anyone's blues or folk music collection. *—Cub Koda*

Worried Blues / Apr. 1963 / Rounder ♦♦♦♦♦

This second of two sessions devoted to Mississippi John Hurt's first recordings followed the same pattern as its predecessor. Hurt did mostly blues, with an occasional spiritual number like "Oh Mary Don't You Weep." He sang in a fragile, yet powerful manner, backing his vocals on acoustic guitar in an equally simple, gentle manner with lines and riffs that often surpassed passages with far more intricate voicings. These two CDs restored into public circulation very valuable recordings. *—Ron Wynn*

Memorial Anthology / Dec. 1964 / Genes ♦♦♦♦♦

Mississippi John Hurt's mid-'60s performances were usually distinctive and sometimes staggering. His guitar work was crisp, attractive and frequently brilliant, although his vocals were the real hook. Hurt's narratives, storytelling ability, and general communicative powers were at their peak on this two-CD set, which languished in a vault for nearly 30 years. Hurt covers such traditional numbers as "C.C. Rider" and "Staggerlee" with vigor, plays several originals, sometimes shifts to gospel, and does everything in an unassuming way that nevertheless grabs your attention. The set's treasure is a 31-minute interview with Pete Seeger in which Hurt lays bare his life, times and personality, doing so in the same steady, casual, gripping fashion that underscored his singing and playing. *—Ron Wynn*

The Best of Mississippi John Hurt / 1965 / Vanguard ✦✦✦✦✦
Contrary to what its title would make one believe, this record is not a collection of previously available recordings by Mississippi John Hurt—rather, it is a complete concert from Oberlin College on April 15, 1965. Regardless, the title is justified, as the concert features Hurt in excellent form doing most of his best known classic songs from the '20s as well as newer compositions. *—Bruce Eder*

Today! / 1966 / Vanguard ✦✦✦✦
Today! is Mississippi John Hurt's first and finest studio release since his "rediscovery" on his Avalon farm by folklorist Tom Hoskins in 1963. Eclipsed possibly only by his earlier *1928 Sessions*, this album shows a more mature Hurt picking his way through standards and originals after the Depression years and Hurt's fall into obscurity before the folk revival of the '60s. It shows, however, that all that the great bluesman has lost is years; his voice retains its characteristic Buddha-esque warmth and it is still difficult to believe that there is just one man playing on the seemingly effortless guitar work. The music on the album comes from a variety of different influences, from the fun and poppy "Hot Time in Old Town Tonight" and "Coffee Blues," to the bluesy standards "Candy Man" (Hurt's most famous song) and "Spike Driver's Blues" to the soulful spirituals "Louis Collins" and "Beulah Land." Hurt's tranquil guitar work—mixing country, Scottish folk, and Delta blues—strings all of the songs along the same simple and elegant thread. Hurt himself never could explain his guitar playing, as he used to say, "I just make it sound like I think it ought to." Regardless, that sound, along with a mellow and heartfelt voice, wizened here by decades, combine to make *Today!* an unforgettable whole. A truly essential album of the folk revival, unrivaled in its beauty and warmth. *—David Freedlander*

The Immortal / 1967 / Vanguard ✦✦✦✦✦
One of the best albums of country blues ever recorded. The fingerpicking is delicate, the vocals mellow and sweet. Many tunes that remain associated with Hurt are included here in versions that rival his legendary recordings from the late '20s. "Richland Woman Blues," "Stagolee," "The Chicken," and "Since I've Laid My Burden Down" sound as fresh as ever in these '60s versions. This album leaves little doubt as to why Hurt was so beloved after his rediscovery. *—Brian Beatty*

The Mississippi John Hurt / 1968 / Vanguard ✦✦✦
These '60s recordings are consistent with the spirit of Hurt's early work. *—Mark A. Humphrey*

Last Sessions / 1972 / Vanguard ✦✦✦✦✦
Recorded in New York during February and July of 1966, the 17 songs on this collection represent Mississippi John Hurt's final studio efforts. It is astonishing that this man, in the final months of his life, could do 17 songs that were the equal of anything he had done at his first sessions 45 years earlier, his playing (supported on some tracks with producer Patrick Sky on second guitar) as alluringly complex as ever and his voice still in top form. Hurt is brilliant throughout, his voice overpowering in its mixture of warmth, gentleness, and power, and in addition to the expected crop of standards and originals, he covers songs by Bukka White ("Poor Boy, Long Ways from Home") and Leadbelly ("Goodnight Irene")—all of it is worthwhile, with some tracks, such as "Let the Mermaids Flirt with Me" especially haunting. *—Bruce Eder*

1928 Sessions / 1988 / Yazoo ✦✦✦✦✦
The 13 original 1928 recordings of Hurt. Justifiably legendary, with gentle grace and power on these understated vocal and fingerpicking masterpieces. These are the ones to hear, although all Hurt is worth listening to. *—Michael Erlewine*

The Greatest Songsters: Complete Works (1927–1929) / 1990 / Document ✦✦✦✦✦
You can get a lot of arguments started about which Mississippi blues musician is the best, so let's just say that this is first-rate Mississippi John Hurt material and leave it at that. *—Ron Wynn*

Satisfying Blues / Apr. 24, 1995 / Collectables ✦✦✦

★ **Avalon Blues: The Complete 1928 OKeh Recordings** / Oct. 8, 1996 / Columbia/Legacy ✦✦✦✦✦
Hurt's latter day recordings after his rediscovery have somewhat obscured the importance of these debut sides, the ones that made his rediscovery an idea initially worth pursuing. They are the collector's items that made his rep in the first place and stand as some of the most poetic and beautiful of all country blues recordings. Hurt's playing is sheer musical perfection, with a keen sense of chord melody structure to make his bouncy, rhythmic execution of it sound both elegant and driving. Mississippi John's voice—he was 36 at the time of these recordings—was already a warm and friendly one, imbued with the laid-back wistfulness that would earmark his rediscovery recordings half a lifetime later. His best known songs—his adaptions of "Frankie (& Johnny)" and "Stack O' Lee," "Avalon Blues," "Nobody's Dirty Business," "Candy Man Blues"—are all accounted for in their original incarnations here and the NoNoiser remastering on this collection is superb. Mississippi John Hurt would go on to re-record this material for other labels in the '60s with fine results, but these are the originals and the ones that much of his justifiable reputation rests on. *—Cub Koda*

Legend / Oct. 7, 1997 / Rounder ✦✦✦
These 14 songs were recorded in 1963 and 1964; material from these sessions appeared briefly on Canada's Rebel label, as well as Piedmont. The mood is late-night informal, although there's little, if anything, in the Hurt catalog that could *not* be called informal. Hurt's originals are dotted with standards like "See See Rider," "Do Lord Remember Me," "Casey Jones'," and a seven-minute "Stack-O-Lee." It's not as forceful, perhaps, as his best-known recordings, and some of the songs are duplicated on other releases, but the sound quality (despite the destruction of the master tape) is OK, and Hurt fans will almost certainly find it to their liking. *—Richie Unterberger*

Rediscovered / Aug. 11, 1998 / Vanguard ✦✦✦✦
Featuring over 75 minutes and 23 tracks, *Rediscovered* compiles tracks off Hurt's four Vanguard releases—*Today!*, *The Immortal Mississippi John Hurt*, *Last Sessions*, and *The Best of Mississippi John Hurt*. The tracks selected are truly first-rate and give a fine cross-section of Hurt's gently rolling country blues, including many of his better-known tracks such as "It Ain't Nobody's Business" and "Avalon, My Home Town," as well as a few spirituals and a handful of live tracks. These recordings are some of the last Hurt would make before his death, and are fine evidence of just how good he still was up until his last days. *—Matt Fink*

The Complete Studio Recordings / Oct. 31, 2000 / Vanguard ✦✦✦✦✦

Live / Apr. 2, 2002 / Vanguard ✦✦✦✦
Mississippi John Hurt's vocal and guitar style are always easy on the ears. Unlike a number of Delta stylists with their high-pitched voices and slashing slide guitars, Hurt's approach to country blues is immediately accessible. Recorded (for the most part) at Oberlin College in 1965, *Live* captures Hurt a couple of years after his rediscovery and one year before his death. He kicks off with several spirituals, including "I Shall Not Be Moved" and "Nearer My God to Thee." As Billy Altman points out in the liner notes, religious material was often excluded from studio recordings because no one believed it marketable. The remainder of *Live* consists of folk-blues, from "Salty Dog Blues" to "Coffee Blues" to "Ain't Nobody's Business." Hurt's finger-style guitar reminds one of Elizabeth Cotton and has more in common with the Piedmont players in general than those of his Mississippi home. Perhaps this connection helps explain why Hurt, who is considered primarily a bluesman, covered so many traditional folk songs. Indeed, the inclusion of songs like "C.C. Rider" also connects him to that other great straddler of folk and blues, Leadbelly. The last three tracks—"Hop Joint," "Trouble, I've Had It All My Days," and "Spike Driver Blues"—originate from the Newport Folk Festival in 1965 and fit in well with the other material. Fans will thank their Maker that Tom Hoskins traveled to Mississippi in 1963 to find out if Hurt was still among the living. Otherwise, excellent recordings like *Live* would've never been made. *—Ronnie D. Lankford Jr.*

J.B. Hutto

b. Apr. 26, 1926, Blackville, SC, **d.** Jun. 12, 1983, Harvey, IL
Slide Guitar, Vocals, Guitar / Slide Guitar Blues, Electric Chicago Blues

Joseph Benjamin Hutto—along with Hound Dog Taylor—was one of the last great slide guitar disciples of Elmore James to make it into the modern age. J. B. Hutto's huge voice, largely incomprehensible diction and slash-and-burn playing was Chicago blues with a fierce, raw edge all its own. He entered the world of music back home in Augusta, GA, singing in the family oriented group the Golden Crowns Gospel Singers. He came north to Chicago in the mid-'40s, teaching himself guitar and eventually landing his first paying job as a member of Johnny Ferguson & His Twisters.

His recording career started in 1954 with two sessions for the Chance label supported by his original combo the Hawks (featuring George Mayweather on harmonica, Porkchop Hines on washboard traps and Joe Custom on rhythm guitar), resulting in six of the nine songs recorded being issued as singles to scant acclaim.

After breaking up the original band, Hutto worked outside of music for a good decade, part of it spent sweeping out a funeral parlor! He resurfaced around 1964 with a stripped down, two guitars-drums-no bass trio version of the Hawks, working regularly at Turner's Blue Lounge and recording blistering new sides for the first time in as many years. From there, he never looked back and once again became a full-time bluesman.

For the next 12 years, Hutto gigged and recorded with various groups of musicians—always billed as the Hawks—working with electric bass players for the first time and recording for small labels, both here and overseas. After fellow slide man Hound Dog Taylor's death in 1976, J.B. "inherited" his backup band, the Houserockers. Although never formally recorded in a studio, this short-lived collaboration of Hutto with guitarist Brewer Phillips and drummer Ted Harvey produced live shows that would musically careen in a single performance from smolderingly intense to utter chaos. Within a year, Hutto would be lured to Boston where he put together a mixed group of "New Hawks," recording and touring America and Europe right up until his death in the mid-'80s. Hutto was an incredibly dynamic live performer, dressed in hot pink suits with headgear ranging from a shriner's fez to a high-plains drifter's hat, snaking through the crowd and dancing on tabletops with his 50-foot guitar cord stretched to the max. And this good-time approach to the music held sway on his recordings as well, giving a loose, barroom feel to almost all of them, regardless of who was backing him. *—Cub Koda*

● **Hawk Squat!** / 1968 / Delmark ✦✦✦✦✦
The raw-as-an-open-wound Chicago slide guitarist outdid himself throughout an outrageously raucous album (most of it waxed in 1966) anchored by an impossible-to-ignore "Hip-Shakin'," the blaring title cut, and savage renditions of "20% Alcohol" and "Notoriety Woman." Sunnyland Slim augments Hutto's Hawks on organ, rather than his customary piano. *—Bill Dahl*

Slidewinder / 1973 / Delmark ✦✦✦
Disappointing Delmark encore from 1972 suffers from Bombay Carter's frequently out-of-tune electric bass and a comparatively uninspired song selection. *—Bill Dahl*

Slideslinger / Apr. 1, 1982 / Evidence ✦✦✦
While he was not in top shape during the early '80s, J.B. Hutto could still bend strings,

churn out whiplash chords, and offer exuberant shouts, which he did on this 1982 set, reissued on a 1992 CD with two bonus cuts. He did not always hit every note on the fretboard or maintain his vocal depth, but his spirit never flagged. Hutto's jagged lines, energized vocals, and inspiring presence made his originals standouts, while his covers of Little Walter Jacobs' "Tell Me Mama" and Elmore James' "Look At The Yonder Wall" resonated with the quality that only a genuine blues survivor could provide. The backing band of guitarist Steve Coveney, bassist Kenny Krumbholz, and drummer Leroy Pina gave Hutto good support, wisely yielding him the spotlight, where he belongs. —*Ron Wynn*

Slippin' & Slidin' / 1983 / Varrick ◆◆◆

Much smoother production by Scott Billington than was normal for Hutto's scathing output, but not alarmingly so. With pianist Ron Levy and the Roomful of Blues horn section augmenting Hutto's New Hawks, the slide guitarist did himself proud on covers of Fenton Robinson's "Somebody Loan Me a Dime" and Junior Parker's "Pretty Baby," alongside a passel of his own distinctive compositions. —*Bill Dahl*

And the Houserockers Live 1977 / 1991 / Wolf ◆◆◆

Culled from a couple of nights in a Boston jazz club and recorded on a cassette deck with two microphones, this stunning document of Hutto with Hound Dog Taylor's band in support gives new meaning to the phrase "raw'n'steamy." Although the trio is fleshed out at this point by the addition of a fairly obtrusive bass player (Mark Harris) and a guest piano man on a couple of tracks, the sheet metal tone of Phillips' and Hutto's twin Telecaster attack cuts through the murkiest of mixes and Ted Harvey swings mightily. —*Cub Koda*

Masters of Modern Blues / 1995 / Testament ◆◆◆◆

1966 was a banner year for Hutto and his Hawks—in addition to laying down the lion's share of his killer Delmark album, the slide master also waxed a similarly incendiary set for Pete Welding's Testament logo. Vicious versions of "Pet Cream Man," "Lulubelle's Here," and "Bluebird" are but a few of its charms, with Big Walter Horton's unmistakable harp winding through the proceedings. —*Bill Dahl*

Rock With Me Tonight / Jul. 13, 1999 / Bullseye Blues & Jazz ◆◆◆

This 1999 reissue of Hutto's final album on Varrick captures him in rare form, even more surprising and courageous in light of the fact that he was to die of cancer only a few months after these sessions. It finds Hutto with the last edition of his regular road band (Brian Besesi on guitar, Kenny Krumbholz on bass, and Leroy Pina on drums) with sit-ins from Ron Levy and the Roomful of Blues reed section on selected cuts, taking his brand of Chicago tavern blues once step further. Tunes like "Soul Lover" and "Black's Ball" show Hutto stretching out beyond the usual boogies and slow blues, while his takes of Junior Parker's "Pretty Baby," Fenton Robinson's "Somebody Loan Me a Dime," and Howlin' Wolf's "I'm Leaving You" are all stamped with the signature Hutto touch. This reissue also brings to light two previously unreleased tracks recorded at the same session, the whole package showing that Hutto was a bluesman to the end. —*Cub Koda*

Roy Hytower

b. Coffeeville, AL
Guitar / Modern Electric Blues, Soul-Blues

Well-regarded as a blues guitarist and soulful singer around Chicago, Roy Hytower has carved out an equally impressive niche as an actor in various Windy City musical productions. Among his starring roles: portraying Muddy Waters and Otis Redding.

After picking up some experience singing around Mobile, AL, Hytower came to Chicago in 1962, replacing Mighty Joe Young as rhythm guitarist for Otis Rush. Often adopting a soul-slanted sound, Hytower cut 45s for Avin, Expo, Brainstorm, and Mercury's Blue Rock subsidiary (where he sang the fine "I'm in Your Corner" and "Undertaker" in 1969). Hytower's 1988 album *Root Doctor* (with his band, Motif) was issued on Diamond Gem Records. He still performs locally. —*Bill Dahl*

● **Root Doctor** / 1988 / Urgent! ◆◆◆

Hytower is a very competent blues guitarist, but you'll find too little proof of that on this synthesizer-heavy set, cut with his band, Motif. Earthier production values would have greatly benefitted the stop-time title cut, and blues content elsewhere is only intermittent and overly derivative. —*Bill Dahl*

Bertha Idaho

Vocals / Classic Female Blues, Dirty Blues

The recording career of classic blues singer Bertha Idaho could not possibly be compared to the ample potato crop of her namesake state. Indeed, she cut only four songs in 1928 and 1929 with song titles that, if arranged correctly, tell a story right out of a film noir.

First, the stage is set "Down on Pennsylvania Avenue." Then, right to the action: "You've Got the Right Eye, But You're Peeping at the Wrong Keyhole" and "Move It on Out of Here," only to wind up with the ghoulish subject of "Graveyard Love," another piece of essential listening for social advocates who propose that rap, punk, and heavy metal artists have introduced objectionable concepts into pop music.

In the late '20s, it was songwriters such as Tom Delaney who were cooking up this type of material, in his case perhaps to get even with society for years spent in run-down orphanages. He encouraged Idaho to set new lows for a prostitute's price of services "Down on Pennsylvania Avenue": "Now if you want good lovin' and want it cheap, just drop around about the middle of the week./When the broad is broke and can't pay rent, get good lovin' boys, for 15 cents." Delaney fed material of this ilk to his main collaborator, singer Ethel Waters, as well as the likes of Idaho, Alberta Hunter, and Bessie Smith.

The pair of recording sessions that make up the entire Idaho discography represent in their skimpiness a logical explanation for why the name represents a mere hiccup in blues history when listed alongside the likes of Waters, Hunter, or any of the classic blues gals named Smith. It was probably this very level of deep obscurity, as well as the weird-sounding name, that inspired John Fahey to include Idaho in one of his greatest works of written historical fiction, the liner notes to his *Blind Joe Death* project. The impact of creative forces such as Idaho, whose musical statements continue to circulate slowly through reissues almost like ghosts haunting a house, is a classic element of the so-called positive existentialist outlook. But that might not explain in full why Fahey chose this particular singer as a subject for his tribute, plucked out of an apparently endless cast of obscure blues and old-time music characters. Possessing a "location" nickname or surname is in itself hardly rare in blues, a genre with so many of these types of monikers that AAA "triptych" planners sometimes find themselves staring idly at the blues section in record stores, mentally planning driving itineraries from Georgia Tom to Mississippi Fred McDowell to Bertha Idaho. —*Eugene Chadbourne*

Jabo (Donald Glenn)

b. Texas

Vocals / Zydeco

The self-proclaimed "Texas Prince of Zydeco," Jabo was among the Houston area's most prominent contemporary performers. Born Donald Glenn, he drew early influence from Clifton Chenier and Buckwheat Zydeco, basing his sound as much in the blues as in zydeco proper; in 1990, Jabo issued his debut LP, *Texas Prince of Zydeco.* —*Jason Ankeny*

● **Texas Prince of Zydeco** / 1990 / Maison de Soul ✦✦✦✦

Jabo is Donald Glenn, a bluesman whose affection for zydeco music inspired him to fuse the two on *Texas Prince of Zydeco.* Since the music is Lone Star State-oriented rather than from New Orleans, the resulting hybrid is intriguingly odd; saxophonist Leon Childs appears on every cut, and Glenn's own accordion sounds bluesy even on the most manic zydeco number. An inventive, worthwhile release. —*Jason Ankeny*

Bo Weavil Jackson

Guitar / Prewar Gospel Blues, Piedmont Blues, Prewar Country Blues

Despite the presence of many well-documented country blues performers with rich, elaborate recording catalogs, blues fans have always searched the nooks and crannies for shadowy characters who appear out of nowhere and then vanish off the face of the Earth, leaving behind a dozen sides, maybe less. It could be a bit of an insane compulsion researching a Bo Weavil Jackson, who could have been a man named Sam Butler, or was it James Butler? Sometimes a listener confronted with a recording by such an artist begins to wonder if a player such as this was actually superior to others who acquired much more fame. It certainly seems like it, when one listens to Jackson's fingers shimmying across the strings on the recordings he did during several sessions in Chicago in 1926. These recordings, done apparently just weeks apart, are mostly blues numbers, but also include several traditional gospel songs as well as an arrangement of "When the Saints Go Marching In." Jackson was clearly an original.

A record salesman of the time named Harry Charles recalls the bluesman as basically being a bum out on the street, playing for nickels when these sessions were done. Charles said the man behind the Bo Weavil Jackson sides was named James. But when Jackson cut some sides for a competing record label, Vocalion, he used the name Sam Butler, which is more commonly how he is identified and tends also to be the name under which his original songs with colorful titles such as "Some Scream High Yellow" and "You Can't Keep No Brown" are copyrighted. The Paramount label promoted the Bo Weavil man as having "come down from the Carolinas," but it has been widely believed that this artist is actually from Birmingham, AL, based on references to the area in his lyrics as well as the fact that this is where the talent scouts apparently found him.

If this was an example of the kind of musicians playing on the streets for spare change in Birmingham, then the situation has deteriorated over the years, to be sure. Jackson was a really brilliant, unusual guitarist who got around on the fingerboard faster than most country bluesmen. Some of his slow blues material actually brings to mind the acoustic blues recordings of Jimi Hendrix, of which Jackson can be considered a foreshadowing. Some of his recordings have been published in notation and tablature in various country and slide blues instruction books, allowing for more detailed study of his style. —*Eugene Chadbourne*

● **Complete Recordings in Chronological Order** / 1973 / Matchbox ✦✦✦✦

Sure, it is kind of a dry title for an album, but the effect it has on country blues fans is a bit like holding up a "free beer" sign in the lobby of a sorority. With many of these tracks previously available only on compilations, if at all, this pressing became something of a classic, its baker's dozen of Bo Weavil Jackson acquiring the shimmer of golden eggs. Supposedly this is the entire recording output of this man, all done within one month in Chicago circa the mid-'20s. The bluesman represents an attractive combination of elements one might associate with other, more well-known and prolifically recorded acoustic bluesmen. He plays slide, but not exclusively. All his playing is done with a touch so delicate it sounds like his fingers are dancing on the strings. This picking style sometimes sounds a bit like the ragtime-influenced 12-string bluesman Blind Willie McTell. Other tracks sound a bit like Blind Lemon Jefferson, perhaps more for the amount of original surface noise than musical similarities, although there are some, such as the rapid, wordy vocal lines and the intense rhythmic pace. The slide playing in the low register of the guitar has a wonderfully chunky sound. One unusual touch is the version of "When the Saints Go Marching In," part of his repertoire along with several traditional gospel numbers and a brace of blues numbers, some of them slightly on the raunchy side. This is a good one for blues fans to keep a watchful eye for, since pressings were limited and snatched up fast. —*Eugene Chadbourne*

Bull Moose Jackson (Benjamin Joseph Jackson)

b. Apr. 22, 1919, Cleveland, OH, **d.** Jul. 31, 1989, Cleveland, OH

Vocals, Saxophone / Dirty Blues, Jump Blues, R&B

Allegedly, Benjamin Jackson resembled a bull moose. At least, that's what a few wags in Lucky Millinder's band thought—and the colorful moniker stuck. Up until then, he was Benjamin Jackson, but it was as Bull Moose that he lit up the R&B charts repeatedly during the late '40s and early '50s. Jackson had a split musical personality—he sang "I Love You, Yes I Do" and "All My Love Belongs to You" like a pop crooner, then switched gears to belt out the double entendre naughties "I Want a Bowlegged Woman" and "Big Ten Inch Woman" with total abandon. Record buyers loved both sides of the Moose.

Jackson was a childhood violinist prior to taking up the sax. He proved accomplished on the latter, blowing jazz in a variety of situations before latching on with Millinder's outfit in 1944 as both singer and saxist. His first 78 under his own name for Syd Nathan's fledgling Queen logo was "I Know Who Threw the Whiskey in the Well," an answer to a popular Millinder tune from the year before that became a smash in its own right. Jackson dubbed his combo the Buffalo Bearcats due to his frequent gigs at a Buffalo nitery.

Moose hit big for Nathan's King diskery in 1947 with "I Love You, Yes I Do"; in 1948 with "Sneaky Pete," "All My Love Belongs to You," "I Want a Bowlegged Woman," "I Can't Go On Without You," and two more; and in 1949 with "Little Girl, Don't Cry" and "Why Don't You Haul Off and Love Me" (the latter a cover of Wayne Raney's hillbilly hit, a popular cross-fertilizing practice at King). He also made an appearance in the 1948 film *Boarding House Blues* with Millinder's band.

Some of Jackson's hilariously risqué stuff—"Big Ten Inch Record" and the astonishingly raunchy "Nosey Joe" (penned by the young but obviously streetwise Jerry Leiber and Mike Stoller), both from 1952—were probably too suggestive to merit airplay, but they're stellar examples of jump blues at its craziest.

Jackson stayed at King into 1955. Six years later, he briefly reentered the charts by remaking "I Love You, Yes I Do" for 7 Arts, but it was an isolated occurrence (catering kept the bills paid during the lean years in Washington, D.C.). There was a belated outbreak of *Moosemania!* in 1985 when his LP of that name emerged in conjunction with a Pittsburgh band called the Flashcats, but Moose's heartwarming comeback was short—lung cancer felled him in 1989. —*Bill Dahl*

Big Fat Mamas Are Back in Style Again / 1980 / Route 66 ✦✦✦✦

This fine collection includes a wide variety of prime Bull Moose Jackson cuts, covering the bandleader's most fruitful years between 1945-1956. Included are everything from jump blues numbers like his first 78 release, "I Know Who Threw the Whiskey (In the Well)," and the King hit "Sneaky Pete" to later rock & roll tunes like "Watch My Signals" and "I Wanna Hug Ya, Kiss Ya, Squeeze Ya." There are also prime examples of Jackson's salacious way with double entendres in "Nosey Joe" and "Miss Lucy." And lest anyone think Jackson only went in for raucous material, there's also the fine crooner's ballad "Let Your Conscience Be Your Guide" and the smoothly swinging instrumental "Bootsie"; these cuts additionally show off Jackson's fine pipes and tenor saxophone chops, as well as his top-notch band the Buffalo Bearcats. Unlike his many hits-filled collections on King ("Big Ten Inch Record," "I Want a Bowlegged Woman"), this Jackson compilation has more breadth, including both hits and more obscure gems. A fine purchase for fans of both Bull Moose Jackson and jump blues. —*Stephen Cook*

Sings His All-Time Hits / 1988 / King ✦✦✦✦

● **Badman Jackson That's Me** / 1991 / Charly ✦✦✦✦✦

The best representation of saxist Jackson's jump blues activities for King Records during the late '40s and early '50s. The Moose was a smooth ballad crooner, too, but you'll find none of his mellow stuff on this 22-tracker—just horn-leavened blasters, often with hilariously risqué lyrics. "Big Ten Inch Record" (here in two takes), "I Want a Bowlegged Woman," the country-rooted "Why Don't You Haul Off and Love Me," and most of all the Leiber & Stoller-penned sleaze-o "Nosey Joe" are party records guaranteed to excite any gathering! —*Bill Dahl*

Final Recordings / 1992 / Bogus ✦✦

This attempt to recreate jump blues style succeeds intermittently. —*Bill Dahl*

Greatest Hits: My Big Ten Inch / 1994 / King ✦✦✦

Jackson's run of hits for the King label came between 1947-1952. He was one of a handful of top-notch jump blues bandleaders who helped plant the roots of rock & roll, laying down some nicely salacious tracks and fiery saxophone solos along the way. This King *Greatest Hits* package, though, provides only a very small taste of Jackson's varied and exciting output—*Greatest Travesty* is really more apropos. In lieu of all Jackson's hits and a healthy dose of some other standout cuts, the label has included only four chart toppers (the title track, "Sneaky Pete," "I Can't Go On Without You," "Why Don't You Haul Off and Love Me") and a few filler cuts. Fans in search of a good overview of Jackson's career should check out Charly's 22-track *Badman Jackson That's Me* collection and steer clear of this flimsy release. *—Stephen Cook*

Cordell Jackson

b. Jul. 15, 1923, Memphis, TN

Guitar, Vocals / Modern Electric Blues

Born in 1923, Cordell Jackson, "Guitar Granny," started performing in the '30s with her father's band, the Pontiac Ridge Runners. She founded her own Moon Records, the oldest continuously operating label in Memphis, in 1956, to release her own recordings as well as those of other Memphis-based rock & roll artists. Although Moon Records didn't see a lot of activity in the intervening years, when she devoted her attentions more to selling houses, the label still existed. She would act as engineer, arranger and producer, using her living room as a studio. She started Moon Records to issue her "Beboppers Christmas" and "Rock and Roll Christmas" and then began releasing 45 rpm singles by other musicians. In 1980, she brought the label back to release an anthology of Moon Records recordings and began to record her own songs again.

Guitarist Jackson began writing and recording her own songs in the late '40s. She started performing at age 12 with her father's band and later played on the radio in Tupelo, Miss. During World War II, she moved to Memphis and began doubling on bass as well. The singles she released on Moon Records were mostly rockabilly and instrumental boogie recordings, and Allen Page was among the artists whose careers she tried to boost.

Although she spent much of her career selling real estate and running the label part-time, trying to promote the careers of other musicians, in the mid-'80s Jackson again moved her own career into the limelight, performing at music conventions and nightclubs. In 1986, she performed at New York's Lone Star Cafe and got a response that stunned her. She went back to the club again in 1988.

Although she doesn't hit the clubs all that often, Jackson still performs around Memphis and occasionally goes on forays around the country, playing where ever she's asked to. In 1983, Jackson released the instrumental, "Knockin' 60," the same song she later performed on a commercial for Budweiser beer, in which she appears with ex-Stray Cat guitarist Brian Setzer. Jackson, a Southern Baptist who doesn't let her religious beliefs interfere with her music, has two sons and 11 grandchildren.

Spurred by the notoriety the beer commercial gave her career, Jackson appeared in 1991 on the TV programs *Arsenio Hall, Late Night With David Letterman, Nashville Now,* and *Entertainment Tonight.* She said, "If I want to wang dang rock 'n' roll at 69 years old all dressed up in an antebellum dress, it ain't nobody's business but mine."

Compact disc reissues of much of Jackson's early material should be available in the coming years, either on her own Moon Records label or through a deal with another company. *—Richard Skelly*

- **Live in Chicago** / Jun. 24, 1997 / Bug House ✦✦✦

George Jackson

b. 1936, Greenville, MS

Songwriter, Guitar / Memphis Soul, Soul-Blues, R&B, Soul

Songwriter George Jackson wrote or co-wrote hits for Clarence Carter (the gold single "Too Weak to Fight"), Wilson Pickett ("A Man and a Half"), Bob Seger ("Old Time Rock and Roll," "Trying to Live My Life Without You"), Candi Staton ("I'd Rather Be an Old Man's Sweetheart (Than a Young Man's Fool)," "I'm Just a Prisoner [Of Your Good Lovin'"]), Z.Z. Hill ("Down Home Blues"), and the Osmonds (the million-selling "One Bad Apple" and "Double Lovin'"). He also several recorded Southern soul-flavored singles, charting with "That's How Much You Mean to Me" (number 48 R&B, summer 1970 on Fame) and "Aretha, Sing One for Me" (number 38 R&B, spring 1972 on Hi).

Born in 1936 in Greenville, MS, Jackson started recording for Ike Turner's Prann label in 1963 after introducing himself to Turner when the entertainer played a concert in Greenville. The single "Nobody Wants to Cha Cha With Me" b/w "Who Was That Guy" was recorded at Cosimo Matassa's New Orleans studio. Traveling to Memphis, Jackson was turned down by Stax Records, but while there he met Louis Williams and they started a vocal group called the Ovations. Recording for Goldwax Records, their single "It's So Wonderful to Be in Love" made it to number 22 R&B on Billboard's charts in spring 1965. While with Goldwax, Jackson wrote for the other artists on the label: "Coming Back to Me Baby" for James Carr and "Old Friend" and "He's Too Old" for Spencer Wiggens. He and songwriter Dan Greer recorded the Goldwax single "Good Times" b/w "You Didn't Know It but You Had Me." The group broke up and Jackson got a solo deal with Decca Records under the pseudonym Bart Jackson, releasing "Wonderful Dream" b/w "Dancing Man" in 1968.

At the suggestion of producer Billy Sherrill, Jackson journeyed to Muscle Shoals, AL, to work at producer Rick Hall's Fame Recording Studio where he became a staff songwriter and wrote hits for artists on the Fame label: Clarence Carter's million-selling single "Too Weak to Fight" (number three R&B, summer 1968) and Candi Staton's "I'd Rather Be an Old Man's Sweetheart (Than a Young Man's Fool)" (number nine R&B, summer 1969) and "I'm Just a Prisoner (Of Your Good Lovin')" (number 13 R&B, early 1970).

MGM Records act the Osmonds visited the hit factory that was Fame Recording Studios and Jackson submitted a song to them that he originally wrote for the Jackson 5. "One Bad Apple" went gold, hitting number six R&B, and parked at number one pop for five weeks in early 1971. "One Bad Apple" was also the opening theme to their self-titled 1972-1974 ABC-TV Saturday morning cartoon series. Because of the success, Jackson was allowed to record some singles for MGM.

Bob Seger recorded Jackson's song "Old Time Rock and Roll" from his five-million selling LP, *Stranger in Town*, which included "Still the Same" (number four pop, summer 1978) and "Trying to Live My Life Without You" (number five pop, fall 1981) from the three-million selling LP *Nine Tonight* (number three pop, spring 1981).

During the mid-'80s, Jackson joined Jackson, MS-based Malaco Records as a staff songwriter penning hits for Johnny Taylor, Bobby "Blue" Bland, Latimore, Denise LaSalle, and Z.Z. Hill. Jackson's own album *Heart to Heart Collect* was released by Hep Me Records in 1991.

George Jackson's songs are on found on numerous compilations and CD reissues by the aforementioned artists as well as on *Conversations* by Gregory Oquin, *The Ultimate Collection* [1998] by Smokey Robinson, *Greatest Hits, Vol. 2* by Alabama, *Still Trapped* by Denise LaSalle, *Honest Lullaby* by Joan Baez, *Strugglin' Lady* by Little Milton, *From the Heart* by Johnny Adams, *Wolf Tracks* by Walter Washington, and *Hello Laila* by Laila. *—Ed Hogan*

- **Sweet Down Home Delta Blues** / 1985 / Amblin' ✦✦✦

George Jackson's album *Sweet Down Home Delta Blues* is a straight-ahead collection of Delta blues. Considering that he's been a house writer for Malaco Records, where he specialized in merging contemporary blues with soul, that comes as a little bit of a surprise. Unfortunately, he doesn't do the Delta as well as he does soul-blues, and *Sweet Down Home Delta Blues* suffers from predictability and perfunctory performances. Occasionally, the music comes to life, either through inspired playing or a solid song, but that only serves to remind the listeners of what this could have been. *—Thom Owens*

Jim Jackson

b. 1890, Hernando, MS, **d.** 1937, Hernando, MS

Vocals, Keyboards, Guitar / Prewar Country Blues, Acoustic Memphis Blues

Coming from the rich medicine-show tradition of the Memphis area, Jim Jackson veered toward a more pronounced blues feel than most of his songster and jug band contemporaries. Born in Hernando, MS, in 1890, Jackson took an interest in music early on, learning the rudiments of guitar from his father. By the age of 15, he was already steadily employed in local medicine shows and by his twenties was working the country frolic and juke joint circuit, usually in the company of Gus Cannon and Robert Wilkins. After joining up with the Silas Green Minstrel Show, he settled in Memphis, working clubs with Furry Lewis, Cannon, and Will Shade. The entire decade known as the "roaring Twenties" found him regularly working with his Memphis cronies, finally recording his best known tune, "Kansas City Blues" (one of the great classics of the idiom), and a batch of other classics by the end of the decade. He also appeared in one of the early talkies, Hallelujah!, in 1929. While Jackson's best work may seem a bit quaint by modern standards, he was a major influence on Chicago bluesman J.B. Lenoir and his "Kansas City Blues" was a regular fixture of Robert Nighthawk's set list.*—Cub Koda*

- **Kansas City Blues** / 1980 / Agram ✦✦✦✦✦

Kansas City Blues collects 16 tracks Jim Jackson recorded between 1927 and 1929. This music is country music that has strong ties to minstrel and medicine show music, and may sound dated to some listeners. Nevertheless, the title track is one of the first great blues singles, and that alone makes the collection necessary listening for serious blues fans, even if Document's three-volume set will be of greater interest to historians. The curious will be better served by this concise compilation. *—Thom Owens*

Complete Recorded Works, Vol. 1 (1927–1928) / 1992 / Document ✦✦✦✦✦

Whew—any collection that opens up with both sides of "Jim Jackson's Kansas City Blues" in its original October 1927 recording (predating RCA's recording of the same number by Jackson by three months) is asking for trouble, because how do you follow up the best double-sided solo blues single this side of Furry Lewis' "Casey Jones, Pts. 1 & 2"? Well, you put on a 1928 rendition of "He's In the Jailhouse Now" that's as soulful as any ever done, and a version of "Old Dog Blue" from January 1928 that could be the earliest blues incarnation of what later became the Bo Diddley beat. And somewhere in there you throw in Jackson's subsequent version of "Kansas City Blues" (the earlier one is better). And the stuff gets better from there on one of the finest solo artist compilations in the Document line, mostly with good sound, too. In contrast to Furry Lewis and almost any other blues great you'd care to name, Jackson's playing on the guitar was pretty basic (check out "Mobile-Central Blues," a great, bitter topical song about the blues, that benefits from his repetitive playing), but the success of his work is proof that a smooth style matters more than technical skill, if the voice and the words are there. His playing fit his expressive voice, not too obtrusive, and gave his voice just the little bit of accompaniment it needed, even embellishing the beat (as on "Old Dog Blue") when required. The sound is generally good, and it's hard to complain about the notes being a little sketchy, given the relatively little hard information known about Jackson. Seventy minutes of pure, sweet golden acoustic blues, highlighted—with Document's usual thoroughness—by two different takes each of "I Heard the Voice of a Pork Chop," "Policy Blues," and "The Morning She Was Gone." *—Bruce Eder*

Complete Recorded Works, Vol. 2 (1928–1930) / 1992 / Document ✦✦✦✦✦

John Jackson

b. Feb. 25, 1924, Woodville, VA, **d.** Jan. 20, 2002, Fairfax Station, VA

Vocals, Guitar, Banjo / Piedmont Blues, Country Blues, Folk-Blues

For much of his life, John Jackson played for country house parties in Virginia, or around the house for his own amusement. Then in the '60s he encountered the folk revival, becoming the Washington, D.C. area's best-loved blues artist. Undoubtedly one of the finest of traditional Piedmont guitarists, Jackson exemplifies the songster tradition at its best. His eclectic repertoire embraced the music of his guitar heroes Willie Walker (who once visited his father's house), Blind Boy Fuller, and—most notably—Blind Blake. Besides the blues, rags, and dance tunes associated with these masters, Jackson played ballads, country songs, and what he termed old folk songs," such as "The Midnight Special." His confident fingerpicking, down-home Virginia accent, and contagious good humor marked his performances, live or on record, as something special. A world-class storyteller and party-thrower as well as a National Heritage Award-winning musician, Jackson recorded a half-dozen albums and toured the world as often as he wanted to. He died of liver cancer on January 20, 2002. *—Barry Lee Pearson*

Blues and Country Dance Tunes from Virginia / 1965 / Arhoolie ✦✦✦✦✦
John Jackson was an excellent country blues musician whose repertoire also included reels, mountain music, and folk tunes. This was an outstanding collection of vintage material done in what was about as contemporary a fashion as you could get in that genre in the mid-'60s. *—Ron Wynn*

John Jackson, Vol. 2 / 1968 / Arhoolie ✦✦✦✦
This is a country blues artist who, while retaining all the personality and intensity of others in the genre, also displays more than the usual amount of versatility. He can play a deep blues with as much power as John Lee Hooker, but then will turn around and come up with a old-time banjo instrumental with roots in both white and black music. He flatpicks and fingerpicks with the guitar in traditional position; he also turns the guitar over on his lap and plays it dobro style with a knife, definitely a hardcore old-timey blues move. The recordings made by Jackson in his prime tend to be done like this one, on portable equipment. The listener will get the impression that all one has to do is sit Jackson down, get the instrument cases open, and turn on the recorder and masterpieces will start popping out, and that isn't far from the truth. Some of the best stuff here includes the Blind Blake cover, "Police Dog Blues," and the touching "Death of Blind Boy Fuller." *—Eugene Chadbourne*

● **Don't Let Your Deal Go Down** / 1970 / Arhoolie ✦✦✦✦✦
This covers 26 tracks running over 70 minutes, recorded by John Jackson between 1965 and 1969 and featuring the rural blues legend at the very top of his form on vocals, guitar, and even banjo on one instrumental ("If Hattie Wants to Lu, Let Her Lu Like a Man"). Jackson's repertory here includes standards like "John Henry" (in one of the most exciting versions ever done, with some killer slide) and "Muleskinner Blues," established parts of other bluesmen's repertories (Blind Boy Fuller's "Rattlesnakin' Daddy," Blind Arthur Blake's "Police Dog Blues," and "Early Morning Blues"), as well as originals, such as the dazzling acoustic pyrotechnic displays on "John's Rag," "Graveyard Blues," and "Knife Blues" (the latter a slide guitar showcase worth the price of the disc by itself), and adaptations of popular songs ("Blind Blake's Rag," which borrows at one point from "Has Anybody Seen My Gal"). Good as his playing is, Jackson's singing is also to be admired, as his baritone voice surges with a quiet power and forcefulness, and a rich tone—"Boats Up the River," a children's song adapted from various traditional sources, is probably the vocal standout on this collection. The fidelity is excellent, these being modern recordings, and overall this CD is the best single overview of John Jackson's music, its value enhanced by the presence of detailed notes that have been updated to the '90s. It's records like this that humble lots of young white bluesmen. *—Bruce Eder*

Step It Up & Go / 1979 / Rounder ✦✦✦✦
Virginia ragtime, blues, and hillbilly from this amiable singer/guitarist. *—Mark A. Humphrey*

Country Blues & Ditties / May 18, 1999 / Arhoolie ✦✦✦
These 25 songs were recorded by Chris Strachwitz in April 1965, December 1967, and the fall of 1969, when Jackson was in his early to mid-forties. It's a pleasant set including interpretations of well-known classics like "Diddy Wah Diddy," "Matchbox Blues," "Just a Closer Walk With Thee" and "He's in the Jailhouse Now." He goes for more unexpected tunes with "I'll Step Aside," an Ernest Tubb hit, and "Lay Down My Old Guitar," probably learned from the Delmore Brothers; this is one of many examples of how Black and White rural music isn't as far apart as some have proclaimed. Without meaning any disrespect at all to the performer, this isn't the kind of recording to get you jumping up and down in excitement; it's relaxed acoustic blues, the kind you'd be happy to hear played at picnics or at a neighbor's home. Jackson's guitar picking is very good, and shown to best effect on the instrumental "John's Guitar Boogie." *—Richie Unterberger*

Front Porch Blues / May 25, 1999 / Alligator ✦✦✦
Just as the title says: a wonderful brace of simple country blues done in Jackson's warm Piedmont style. At age 75, his fingers are still nimble as he displays on a jazzy "Just Because" and his vocals still resonate nicely. Audiophile note: This album is nicely recorded and sounds like Jackson is performing about two inches from your face. A warm and engaging batch of performances not to be missed. *—Cub Koda*

"Jump" Jackson

Drums / Jump Blues
Started out in New Orleans, wound up in Chicago. The subject could be the blues backbeat, or it could be the life of Armand "Jump" Jackson. Or it could be both, since the two are almost one and the same. That fat, greasy sock rhythm that was heard on many of the blues records made in Chicago in the late '40s and '50s was created by the one and only Jump Jackson, sometimes while he was booking a tour in his head for one of his bands. In the late '40s, Jackson worked as a bandleader on sessions for labels such as Columbia, Specialty, and Aristocrat; his band backed up vocalists such as St. Louis Jimmy, Roosevelt Sykes, Sunnyland Slim, and Leonard "Baby Doo" Caston. He also drummed on at least a dozen classic urban blues albums, with leaders ranging from the most famous such as John Lee Hooker to the obscure but great Robert Nighthawk.

As well as performing, Jackson was indeed a certified booking agent. His taste for controlling as much of the business as possible spread to his recording career. In 1959 he founded La Salle Records and began putting out his own sessions as well as sides by Eddie Boyd, Eddy Clearwater, Little Mack Simmons, and his old playing partner pianist Slim. Performer Clearwater even got his name from Jackson, who came up with the stage name as a reaction to his friend Eddy Harrington's fondness for blues giant Muddy Waters. The blues audience was ready for clear water as well as muddy, since the change in names was just what this artist apparently needed for his career to start taking off.

In 1962, Jackson was chosen as the drummer for the first American Folk Blues Festival tour of Europe, although by then he could feel the cold wind of progress blowing on his neck, even among all the other breezes in the Windy City. The swing-era style of blues drumming he had pioneered was slowly being taken over by a newer kind of hard-edged backbeat, as practiced by blues drummer Fred Below, for example. *—Eugene Chadbourne*

Lee Jackson

b. Aug. 18, 1921, Jackson, MS, **d.** Jul. 1, 1979, Chicago, IL
Bass, Guitar / Chicago Blues
This Chicago blues artist was a driving force in the rhythm sections that recorded on many of the finest sides cut in the '70s, such as the intense *Master of Modern Blues* album by Johnny Shines on the Testament label. Although a fine guitarist in his own right, Jackson mostly recorded in the bass role, a part that although vitally functional in the music almost always guarantees anonymity on the part of the individual. But although largely unknown by name, the playing style of Jackson is vastly influential. Many young blues and rock players who got into roots music in the '80s cut their teeth on these records, the bassists copping so many of Jackson's licks that one might think the country chestnut about "goin' to" "Jackson" was about them.

The man's work on guitar is featured on the *Big Boss Men* collection of Willie Dixon and Jimmy Reed on the Indigo label, and he handled both instruments on his collaborations with the wonderful J.B. Hutto, also documented on several top-notch Delmark albums. One unfortunate and definitely final development that places him amongst an elite but distressingly large group of bluesmen was the fact that he was murdered, although the details of Jackson's slaying are not widely known. He is often confused with other musicians who share his admittedly common name, although the listener should definitely not believe in the existence of a single musical superhero if one man who could play blues with Sunnyland Slim, bass with the progressive rock group the Nice, and country picking with Lacy Gibson. *—Eugene Chadbourne*

● **Lonely Girl** / 1974 / ABC ✦✦✦

Little Willie Jackson

Sax (Baritone), Sax (Alto) / Jump Blues, Swing, Urban Blues, R&B
As a bandmember, saxophonist Little Willie Jackson most often played swing jazz, but on the sides he issued under his own name, he played the Los Angeles jazz/jump blues hybrid that was so important to the birth of R&B in the late '40s. The blind Jackson played with pianist Joe Liggins in the Creole Serenaders in San Diego in the mid-'30s. By the end of the '30s both he and Liggins had moved to Los Angeles, and in the mid-'40s they formed the Honeydrippers. The band had a number one R&B hit with "The Honeydripper" in 1945 that is viewed as one of the stepping stones to R&B and rock & roll, although Liggins is the name that history has associated with the record. Jackson sometimes sang with the Honeydrippers, as heard on the 1946 Exclusive single "Walkin'."

In 1947 Modern Records got the Honeydrippers minus Liggins to record for them, with Little Willie Jackson acting as singer and bandleader in addition to playing sax. At the end of the year he recorded a couple dozen sides for the label, which was stockpiling masters in the face of an imminent recording ban. This resulted in a half-dozen singles being issued on Modern in 1947 and 1948, and like much of the company's output in its early days, it straddled the line between the swing and jump blues eras, with a hefty dose of boogie.

Of the numerous Modern artists who plumbed that style during the era, Jackson was closer to jazz (and further removed from blues) than most, taking much of his repertoire from songs first performed in the early '30s and earlier. "I Ain't Got Nobody," "Muddy Water," "St. Louis Blues," and "There'll Be Some Changes Made" were all recorded (and sometimes left unreleased for more than 50 years), sometimes in a style not too far removed from Cab Calloway. Still, some of the songs had a more modern, boogying bluesy vibe, like the instrumentals "Jackson's Boogie" and "Watts Local." "Black and Blue," also recorded by Louis Armstrong, has some claim to be a racial commentary of sorts, as it was allegedly written for a Broadway show of the same name under instructions from gangster Dutch Shultz to write a song about the perils of being black.

Jackson made his last solo recording, "Who Put the Lights Out," with pianist Christine Chatman on Personality in the mid-'50s. He played on an album by Joe Liggins & the Honeydrippers in 1962, and also did an LP with Liggins at the end of the '60s for Johnny Otis' Spectrum label. He was still playing as late as 1983, when he participated in a Legends of the Rhythm & Blues show in Los Angeles. *—Richie Unterberger*

● **Jazz Me Blues** / Jul. 11, 2000 / Ace ✦✦✦✦✦
This is a comprehensive anthology of Jackson's late-'40s Modern sessions: both sides of six 1947-1948 singles, plus a dozen previously unreleased cuts (including some alternate takes). It's another in what is apparently a never-ending series of Ace compilations showcasing early Modern artists pivotal to the transition between swing jazz and jump blues, even if they (like Jackson) are virtually forgotten half a century later. Unlike some, perhaps most, of such Modern artists, Jackson might be more accurately classified as a jazz musician than a blues/R&B one. Boogie instrumentals are mixed with vocal outings in the Louis Armstrong/Cab Calloway mold, often favoring jazz and pop songs that, even by 1948, were on the verge of passing out of fashion. Jackson was a pleasantly passable singer with a slightly lower-than-normal register, though no great shakes. The recordings are more notable for the playing of the Honeydrippers, who, of course, are more known for their work on more famous records by Joe Liggins. The best numbers on the disc are those that are the bluesiest and loosest, such as the instrumentals "Jackson's Boogie" and "Watts Local," or "The Peanut Vendor" with its Mardi Gras-type rhythms. "Black and Blue" has some (muted) racial commentary in its doleful lyrics about the problems of being black, though these are subtle enough that it can almost be missed on casual hearing, and certainly too subtle to qualify this as an out-and-out protest song. The sound is very good considering the age of the source recordings. *—Richie Unterberger*

Mahalia Jackson

b. Oct. 16, 1911, New Orleans, LA, **d.** Jan. 27, 1972, Evergreen Park, IL
Vocals / Spirituals, Traditional Gospel, Black Gospel
General critical consensus holds Mahalia Jackson as the greatest gospel singer ever to live; a major crossover success whose popularity extended across racial divides, she was

gospel's first superstar, and even decades after her death remains for many listeners a defining symbol of the music's transcendent power. With her singularly expressive contralto, Jackson continues to inspire the generations of vocalists which follow in her wake; among the first spiritual perfomers to introduce elements of blues into her music, she infused gospel with a sensuality and freedom it had never before experienced, and her artistry rewrote the rules forever. Born in one of the poorest sections of New Orleans on October 16, 1911, Jackson made her debut in the children's choir of the Plymouth Rock Baptist Church at the age of four, and within a few years was a prominent member of the Mt. Moriah Baptist's junior choir. Raised next door to a sanctified church, she was heavily influenced by their brand of gospel, with its reliance on drums and percussion over piano; another major inspiration was the blues of Bessie Smith and Ma Rainey.

By the time she reached her mid-teens, then, Jackson's unique vocal style was fully formed, combining the full-throated tones and propulsive rhythms of the sanctified church and the deep expressiveness of the blues with the note-bending phrasing of her Baptist upbringing. After quitting school during the eighth grade, Jackson relocated to Chicago in 1927, where she worked as a maid and laundress; within months of her arrival, she was singing leads with the choir at the Greater Salem Baptist Church, where she joined the three sons of her pastor in their group the Johnson Brothers. Although other small choir groups had cut records in the past, the Johnson Brothers might have been the first professional gospel unit ever; the first organized group to play the Chicago church circuit, they even produced a series of self-written musical dramas in which Jackson assumed the lead role. Her provocative performing style—influenced by the Southern sanctified style of keeping time with the body and distinguished by jerks and steps for physical emphasis—enraged many of the more conservative Northern preachers, but few could deny her fierce talent.

After the members of the Johnson Brothers went their separate ways during the mid-'30s, Jackson began her solo career accompanied by pianist Evelyn Gay, who herself later went on to major fame as one half of gospel's Gay Sisters. During the week, Jackson also went to beauty school, and soon opened her own salon. As her reputation as a singer grew throughout the Midwest, in 1937 she made her first recordings for Decca, becoming the first gospel artist signed to the label; curiously, none of the tracks she recorded during her May 21 session was by Thomas A. Dorsey, the legendary composer for whom she began working as a song demonstrator around that same time. (He even wrote "Peace in the Valley" with her in mind.) While her Decca single "God's Gonna Separate the Wheat from the Tares" sold only modestly, prompting a lengthy studio hiatus, Jackson's career continued on the upswing—she soon began peforming live in cities as far away as Buffalo, New Orleans and Birmingham, becoming famous in churches throughout the country for not only her inimitable voice but also her flirtatious stage presence and spiritual intensity.

Jackson did not record again until 1946, signing with Apollo Records; although her relations with the label were often strained, the work she produced during her eight-year stay on their roster was frequently brilliant. While her first Apollo recordings, including "I Want to Rest" and "He Knows My Heart," fared poorly—so much so, in fact, that the label almost dropped her—producer Art Freeman insisted Jackson record W. Herbert Brewster's "Move on Up a Little Higher"; released in early 1948, the single became the best-selling gospel record of all time, selling in such great quantities that stores could not even meet the demand. Virtually overnight, Jackson became a superstar; beginning in 1950, she became a regular guest on journalist Studs Terkel's Chicago television series, and among white intellectuals and jazz critics, she acquired a major cult following based in large part on her eerie similarities to Bessie Smith. In 1952, her recording of "I Can Put My Trust in Jesus" even won a prize from the French Academy, resulting in a successful tour of Europe—her rendition of "Silent Night" even became one of the all-time best-selling records in Norway's history.

Jackson's success soon reached such dramatic proportions that in 1954 she began hosting her own weekly radio series on CBS, the first program of its kind to broadcast the pure, sanctified gospel style over national airwaves. The show surrounded her with a supporting cast which included not only pianist Mildred Falls and organist Ralph Jones, but also a white quartet led by musical director Jack Halloran; although her performances with Halloran's group moved Jackson far away from traditional gospel towards an odd hybrid which crossed the line into barbershop quartet singing, they proved extremely popular with white audiences, and her transformation into a true crossover star was complete. Also in 1954 she signed to Columbia, scoring a Top 40 hit with the single "Rusty Old Halo," and two years later made her debut on *The Ed Sullivan Show*. However, with Jackson's success came the inevitable backlash—purists decried her music's turn towards more pop-friendly production, and as her fame soared, so did her asking price, so much so that by the late '50s virtually no black churches could afford to pay her performance fee.

A triumphant appearance at the 1958 Newport Jazz Festival solidified Jackson's standing among critics, but her records continued moving her further away from her core audience—when an LP with Percy Faith became a smash, Columbia insisted on more recordings with orchestras and choirs; she even cut a rendition of "Guardian Angels" backed by comic Harpo Marx. In 1959, she appeared in the film *Imitation of Life*, and two years later sang at John F. Kennedy's presidential inauguration. During the '60s, Jackson was also a confidante and supporter of Dr. Martin Luther King Jr., and at his funeral sang his last request, "Precious Lord"; throughout the decade she was a force in the civil rights movement, but after 1968, with King and the brothers Kennedy all assassinated, she retired from the political front. At much the same time Jackson went through a messy and very public divorce, prompting a series of heart attacks and the rapid loss of over a hundred pounds; in her last years, however, she recaptured much of her former glory, concluding her career with a farewell concert in Germany in 1971. She died January 27, 1972. *—Jason Ankeny*

Bless This House / 1956 / Columbia ✦✦✦✦✦

Bless This House was released in 1956 and features Mahalia Jackson and the Falls-Jones Ensemble. This LP is a favorite of the gospel purists who feel alienated by Jackson's collaborations with pop artists like Percy Faith and Harpo Marx. The songs on *Bless This House* feature great supporting performances by pianist Mildred Falls and organist Ralph Jones. Highlights include a jazzy, swinging "Let the Church Roll On," a dark, bluesy "Trouble With the Word," and energetic versions of "Down By the Riverside" and "It Don't Cost Very Much." *Bless This House* includes some of Jackson's most serious offerings and reflects the influence of blues singers Bessie Smith and Ma Rainey on her vocal style. A great introduction to Jackson's joyous, religious music and a good beginning for new listeners. *—JT Griffith*

Live at Newport 1958 / Jan. 1958 / Columbia ✦✦✦✦✦

Stunning live performances from the 1958 Newport Jazz Festival. *—Opal Louis Nations*

The Power & The Glory / 1960 / Columbia ✦✦✦

With orchestra conducted by Percy Faith, Jackson sings 12 of her favorite hymns, including "Onward Christian Soldiers," "Just as I Am" and "Rock of Ages," among others. Though the accompaniment is not what listeners would expect from a Mahalia Jackson album, Faith is for the most part sympathetic. *—John Bush*

Silent Night (Songs for Christmas) / 1962 / Columbia ✦✦✦✦✦

Whether or not you like sacred music, one cannot help but be moved by the power and passion with which Mahalia Jackson sings "Sweet Little Jesus Boy" and the spiritual "Go Tell it on the Mountain." Her rendition of "Silent Night, Holy Night" is simply inspirational. *—Dennis MacDonald*

Greatest Hits / 1963 / Columbia ✦✦✦✦

Although it's a little skimpy, *Greatest Hits* is a good, basic collection of Mahalia Jackson's best, featuring ten undisputed classics, including "Nobody Knows the Trouble I've Seen," "That's the Way He's Done for Me," "How I Got Over," "The Upper Room" and "Walk in Jerusalem." There are more comprehensive collections on the market, but novices on a strict budget will find this quite useful. *—Stephen Thomas Erlewine*

In the Upper Room / 1965 / 601 ✦✦✦✦✦

Supported by Mildred Falls, the Southern Harmonaires and the Melody Echoes (the two vocal groups are on different tracks), Mahalia Jackson turns in a typically rousing effort with *In the Upper Room*. All of the songs are classic spirituals and sacred songs, and while this was recorded a little later in her career, Jackson nonetheless sings with an incendiary passion that rivals her classic '40s recordings. Anyone looking to round out a Mahalia Jackson collection should look here, as *In the Upper Room* is one of her finest latter-day efforts. *—Leo Stanley*

In Concert Easter Sunday, 1967 / Jul. 17, 1967 / Columbia ✦✦✦

Jackson's Easter performance at New York's Lincoln Center for the Performing Arts on March 26, 1967, was her first big concert since being afflicted with heart problems three years before that. Any discomfort or loss of form would be hard to detect in this strong performance, at which she was accompanied by piano, organ, guitar, and drums. For the most part it sticks to slow- to midtempo numbers, the shouter "Come on Children, Let's Sing" being the notable exception. The 2001 CD reissue on Columbia/Legacy adds four previously unreleased bonus tracks from the same concert, of which the jubilant "Elijah Rock," with a prominent organ and a melody similar to Little Willie John's "Fever," is a highlight. *—Richie Unterberger*

A Mighty Fortress / 1968 / Columbia/Legacy ✦✦✦✦

Included are ten tracks of Mahalia Jackson's genius, originally recorded in 1968 and reissued on CD 20 years later. Aside from the title track, Jackson also sings "It Is Well With My Soul," "Power in the Blood," "Sweet Hour of Prayer," and "Be Still My Soul." *—John Bush*

The World's Greatest Gospel Singer / May 4, 1975 / Columbia ✦✦✦✦✦

One of Mahalia's early Columbia albums, this brings the singer together with the Fall-Jones Ensemble. Kicking off with the autobiographical "I'm Going to Live the Life I Sing About in My Song," the set also includes stirring renditions of "Jesus Met the Woman at the Well," "I Will Move on Up a Little Higher," "Didn't It Rain," "Keep Your Hand on the Plow," "Walk Over God's Heaven," and even a spirited take on the old warhorse "When the Saints Go Marching In." One of her best. *—Cub Koda*

Sings America's Favorite Hymns / 1977 / Columbia ✦✦✦

Another cross-section of Jackson's '50s and '60s work. *—Kip Lornell*

Amazing Grace / 1989 / Sony Special Products ✦✦✦✦✦

A nice sampling of Jackson's later recordings. *—Kip Lornell*

★ **Gospels, Spirituals & Hymns** / 1991 / Columbia/Legacy ✦✦✦✦✦

Although it's missing some of her classic performances, the double-disc set *Gospels, Spirituals & Hymns* is nonetheless an excellent introduction to Mahalia Jackson, arguably the greatest gospel singer of all time. The box set features 36 performances she recorded for Columbia between 1954 and 1969, offering a comprehensive, but by no means exhaustive, introduction to Jackson and her most popular work. *—Leo Stanley*

☆ **Mahalia Jackson, Vol. 2** / Jul. 28, 1992 / Columbia/Legacy ✦✦✦✦✦

With its excellent sound, solid compiling work, and lengthy liner notes, the second 2-CD box set of Mahalia Jackson's Columbia recordings is just as essential as the first, *Gospels, Spirituals & Hymns*. *—AMG*

Go Tell It on the Mountain / 1993 / Arrival ✦✦✦

This disc features 10 of the original Apollo tracks by the great Mahalia Jackson. In addition to the title track, the disc also includes "Nobody Knows," "Just As I Am," and "Amazing Grace." If you like gospel music, this is the real thing! *—Jim Worbois*

The Apollo Sessions 1946–1951 / 1994 / Pair ✦✦✦✦

Her best sides with vocal group backing and simple rhythm accompaniment. *—Opal Louis Nations*

☆ **Live at Newport** / 1994 / Columbia/Legacy ✦✦✦✦✦

Live at Newport is a wonderful reissue of the *Newport 1958* album, containing all 15 songs that were on the original record. Jackson was at the peak of her career, and she gave a stunning performance at this show, lifting such songs as "He's Got the Whole World In His Hands," "Lord's Prayer," "Evening Prayer," "I'm on My Way," "Walk Over God's Heaven," and "His Eye is on the Sparrow" to glorious heights. It's not only one of the great live gospel albums, it's simply one of the great gospel albums. *—Leo Stanley*

The Best of Mahalia Jackson / 1995 / Columbia/Legacy ✦✦✦✦✦

The Best of Mahalia Jackson is a 16-track collection featuring many of Jackson's very best recordings—"God Put a Rainbow in the Sky," "He's Got the Whole World in His Hands," "Walk in Jerusalem," "God is So Good (To Me)," "Just a Little While to Stay Here"—thereby offering a long overdue single-disc introduction to one of the greatest gospel singers in history. *—Stephen Thomas Erlewine*

The Apollo Sessions, Vol. 2 / 1995 / Pair ✦✦✦

More of her finest work with piano/organ and quartet backgrounds. *—Opal Louis Nations*

★ **16 Most Requested Songs** / Aug. 20, 1996 / Columbia/Legacy ✦✦✦✦✦

If you're looking for something a little less comprehensive and pricey than one of the Mahalia Jackson box sets, this is the best single-disc compilation of her Columbia recordings, spanning the years 1954-1967 in 66 1/2 minutes. It features some amazing performances, including an April 1961 take of "How I Got Over" recorded live in Sweden, a few selections from the 1958 Newport Jazz Festival, and several tracks featuring Billy Preston on organ, among them the seven-minute 1963 version of "In The Upper Room." Jackson is uniformly excellent, and this sampler gives a good sense of the different approaches she took to her music during the Columbia years. Start here, and go on to the more extensive collections. *—William Ruhlmann*

For Collectors Only / Nov. 5, 1996 / Collectables ✦✦✦✦

Indispensable Apollo sides, early '50s (two-CD set). *—Opal Louis Nations*

Queen of Gospel / May 20, 1997 / Music Club ✦✦✦

These 16 tracks recorded for Bess Berman's Apollo Records from 1947 to 1954 mark the debut recordings of Mahalia Jackson, and the first gospel records to reach a mass audience. The single release from her second session in September of 1947, "Move On Up a Little Higher," was the first gospel record to sell over a million copies, eventually doubling that figure and making her a household name. Never had anyone heard gospel sung quite like this. Simplicity was at the root of her presentation and her eventual success: put Mahalia in the company of her lifelong accompanist, pianist Mildred Falls, and surround her with little more than an organ sustaining chords, an occasional drummer or jazz guitarist and—on even rarer occasions—a vocal group. This kept the focus on Jackson's incredible vocal range and interpretive skills, coming up with sides like "His Eye Is on the Sparrow," "Poor Pilgrim of Sorrow," and her versions of "Silent Night" and "Amazing Grace," which were drenched in gospel fervor and vocal majesty. Mahalia generally preferred to hear her voice unencumbered by backing choirs and such, but superb vocal backing from the Southern Harmonaires—later to record secularly for Apollo as the Larks—is present on "He's My Light," "In the Upper Room, Pt. 1" and "Said He Would," while the Melody Echoes sound equally wonderful behind her on "Up In Jerusalem" and "Beautiful Tomorrow." Although she would go on to make more successful and better-produced records when she later moved to Columbia in 1954, she made no greater music than these first recordings for Apollo. And here are 16 of the very best. *—Cub Koda*

In My Home over There / Oct. 20, 1998 / MCA ✦✦✦✦✦

The second release on MCA's 1998 Peacock Gospel Classics imprint was these early recordings by Mahalia Jackson. Taken off the best-condition surviving 78s, the sound quality shows a few scratches along the way, but the music's worth every bump and scuffle attached to it. Her treatment of her own "In the Upper Room, Pt. 1" is a beauty to hear and to kick the set off. Unfortunately, we only get to hear the first half of it, and as this was originally issued as a two part single, the non-appearance of side two and the rest of the song, especially in light of what could be accomplished with modern editing tools to reconnect the two parts, is perhaps the only bummer connected with this package. Mahalia's involvement on tracks like "Dig a Little Deeper" is as heavy and as involved as you could possibly ask any performer to be, impassioned and flowing with every note she puts across. There's a wit, verve, sass and a total soul connectedness that pours into the rocking "Get Away Jordan," "It Is No Secret," an almost bluesy "There's Not a Friend Like Jesus," "Do You Know Him," an amazing "Amazing Grace," "Nobody Knows," "Run All the Way" and the title track that are impossible to ignore. Mahalia Jackson made many extraordinary recordings during her wonderful career; add these to the essential list. *—Cub Koda*

How I Got Over: The Apollo Records Sessions / Oct. 27, 1998 / West Side ✦✦✦

With three discs featuring a total of 63 tracks, this is Jackson's complete output for the Apollo label from 1946 to 1954. These are the recordings that brought Mahalia to a national audience right up to her breakthrough with Columbia Records and the ones that literally made gospel recording history. Highlights anywhere the laser beam falls on any of these three discs in the set, but her performances of "Go Tell It on the Mountain," "His Eye Is on the Sparrow," "In the Upper Room, Pts. 1 & 2," "Move on Up a Little Higher," "What Could I Do," "Ever Me," "I'm Going to Tell God," "Dig a Little Deeper," and "Walk With Me," "In My Home Over There," "Just Over the Hill, Pts. 1 & 2," and "Walking in Jerusalem," are too perfect for words and should simply be in everyone's gospel collection as some of the best the genre has to offer. Marvelous transfers of the original master tapes plus great notes by AMG contributor Opal Louis Nations are just extra icing on the cake to this essential addition to anyone's collection. *—Cub Koda*

Sunday Morning Prayer Meeting With Mahalia / Jun. 26, 2001 / Columbia/Legacy ✦✦✦✦

While this compilation has 14 performances from 1956-1965, there's no indication that it was intended as a best-of, and indeed no indication as to exactly what theme upon which it might be centered. There are live performances and studio performances, and half of the cuts were previously unreleased. Some have full bands and backup vocals (jazz drummer Shelly Manne is even on some tracks); some only have keyboard accompaniment. It's good, yes, but curious, since it doesn't serve the needs of the general consumer looking for a best-of-type anthology, or totally serve the hardcore collector, since there's just the half that's been unavailable before. So perhaps the ultimate purpose is to get some more mileage out of the Jackson catalog. If none of those prickly concerns are an issue, the music's solid enough, and the previously unissued cuts are not of a radically different standard than the ones which were released. The full-band arrangements, such as "Down By the River" and "That's All Right," pack the most punch. *—Richie Unterberger*

20 Greatest Hits / Pentagon ✦✦✦✦✦

Fine selection of her early Apollo sides circa 1948-1953. *—Opal Louis Nations*

Melvin "Lil' Son" Jackson

b. Aug. 16, 1915, Tyler, TX, **d.** May 30, 1976, Dallas, TX

Vocals, Guitar / Acoustic Texas Blues, Blues Revival

Lil' Son Jackson was a stylistic throwback from the moment he first turned up during the immediate postwar era. He was a Texas country bluesman of the highest order whose rustic approach appealed wholeheartedly to the early-'50s blues marketplace.

Melvin Jackson's dad loved blues, while his mother played gospel guitar. Their son's initial experience came with a spiritual aggregation called the Blue Eagle Four. A mechanic by trade, he served in the Army during World War II before giving the idea of being a professional blues musician a shot.

In 1946, he shipped off a demo to Bill Quinn, who owned a Houston diskery called Gold Star Records. Quinn was suitably impressed, inking Jackson and enjoying a national R&B hit, "Freedom Train Blues," in 1948 for his modest investment. It would prove Jackson's only national hit, although his 1950-1954 output for Imperial Records must have sold consistently, judging from how many sides the L.A. firm issued by the Texas guitarist.

Jackson's best Imperial work was recorded solo. Later attempts to squeeze his style into a small band format (his idea, apparently) tended to emphasize his timing eccentricities. His "Rockin' and Rollin'," cut in December of 1950, became better-known through a raft of subsequent covers as "Rock Me Baby." He gave up the blues during the mid-'50s after an auto wreck, resuming work as a mechanic. Arhoolie Records boss Chris Strachwitz convinced Jackson to cut an album in 1960, but his comeback proved fleeting. *—Bill Dahl*

● **Lil' Son Jackson** / Mar. 1962 / Arhoolie ✦✦✦✦✦

Arhoolie's *Lil' Son Jackson* is a good colleciton of material Jackson recorded for the label in the early '60s, during the height of the blues revival. In many ways, these recordings are better than his original '40s sessions, since they capture him in a clean, well-recorded setting performing his best songs quite powerfully. The result is a minor gem and an excellent country blues record. *—Leo Stanley*

Blues Come to Texas / 1981 / Arhoolie ✦✦✦✦✦

Melvin "Lil' Son" Jackson could present stunning, poignant, ironic or gripping stories, and his vocals were ideal for the slow-paced, dramatic storytelling mode. Jackson scored several regional and jukebox hits in the '50s with his stories of woe, fame, misfortune, tribulation and perseverance. These were consistent themes emerging throughout the 20 cuts on this CD reissue from a 1960 session. It includes three unreleased cuts and a song ("Johnnie Mae") from another album. Jackson wrote (or adapted) all of the songs, and this disc is a fine portrait of an often overlooked but significant Texas blues performer. *—Ron Wynn*

Complete Imperial Recordings / 1995 / Capitol ✦✦✦

Two-disc, 55-track compilation of material from the first half of the '50s. This is blues in the transition from the country to the city, and indeed, much of the first disc lacks a rhythm section, although electric guitar is present. Jackson actually sounds considerably more comfortable when working in a Lightnin' Hopkins mode. In fact, the sides with full accompaniment sometimes sound like the *band* is uncomfortable with band arrangements. On some sides, the drummer seems to have his mind on another session; others boast tentative saxophone that borders on the haphazard. Jackson's subdued, countrified approach actually sounded a bit anachronistic even when these cuts were laid down, though the sloppiness does suit the atypical "Drinkin' Wine Spo-Dee-O-Dee" knockoff "Get High Everybody." At any rate, it's acceptable but somewhat journeyman stuff with a lack of variation that gets tiresome over the course of several dozen tracks, although some of the band-less sides, like "Thrill Me Baby" (with dreamy slide guitar licks) and "Movin' to the Country," hit a very good groove. *—Richie Unterberger*

Papa Charlie Jackson (Charlie Carter)

b. 1885, New Orleans, LA, **d.** 1938?, Chicago, IL

Vocals, Ukulele, Guitar, Banjo / Prewar Country Blues, Country Blues

Papa Charlie Jackson was the first bluesman to record, beginning in 1924 with the Paramount label, playing a hybrid banjo-guitar (six strings tuned like a guitar but with a banjo body that gave it a lighter resonance) and ukelele. And apart from his records and their recording dates, little else is known for sure about this pioneering blues performer, other than his probable city of birth, New Orleans—even his death in Chicago during 1938 is more probable than established fact.

Jackson spent his teen years as a singer/performer in minstrel and medicine shows, picking up a repertory of bawdy but entertaining songs that would serve him well for decades. He is known to have busked around Chicago in the early '20s, playing for tips on Maxwell Street, as well as the city's West Side clubs beginning in 1924. In August of that year, Jackson made his first record, "Papa's Lawdy Lawdy Blues" and "Airy Man Blues," for a Paramount label. He followed this up a month later with "Salt Lake City Blues" and "Salty Dog Blues," which became one of his signature tunes—he later re-recorded this number as a member of Freddie Keppard's Jazz Cardinals, also for the Paramount label, a common practice in those days as the notion of contracts and exclusivity was almost unknown in blues recording. Jackson made his first duet records in 1925, "Mister Man, Pts. 1 and 2," with singer Ida Cox, again for Paramount, and later cut duets with Ma Rainey and future Oscar-winning actress Hattie McDaniel.

He was already regarded as one of the Paramount label's more successful recording artists, and all but a handful of his recordings were done for Paramount over the next decade. Jackson had a wide diversity of material and voices in which he recorded—"Good Doing Papa Blues" and "Jungle Man Blues" presented Jackson as a ladies' man in playful settings, while "Ma and Pa Poorhouse Blues," cut in a duet with Ma Rainey, was a far more serious song, dealing with poverty and its attendant miseries. "Don't Break Down," by contrast, was a seductive love song with pop elements, while "Baby Please Loan Me Your Heart"—with its exquisite banjo strumming—is a sweetly romantic piece that could've come out of vaudeville. Whether he was strumming or fingerpicking, his music was always of interest for its structure, content, and execution.

Jackson reached a musical peak of sorts in September of 1929 when he got to record with his longtime idol, Blind (Arthur) Blake, often known as the King of Ragtime Guitar during this period. "Papa Charlie and Blind Blake Talk About It" parts one and two are among the most unusual sides of the late '20s, containing elements of blues jam session, hokum recording, and ragtime, containing enough humor to make it the '20s rival of tracks such as Bo Diddley's "Say Man" as well. More is the pity that better sources haven't survived for both sides, but what is here is beyond price—there may not be a dozen guitar records in any genre that are more important or more fascinating.

Jackson switched to guitar on some of his late '20s recordings, and occasionally played the ukelele as well, although he was back to using the five-string hybrid in 1934, when he cut his final sessions. For reasons that nobody has ever established, he parted company with Paramount after 1930, and never recorded for the label again, even though Paramount lasted another two years before going under amid the hardships of the Great Depression. His last sides for the label, "You Got That Wrong" and "Self Experience," were highly personal songs dealing with romance and an apparent brush with the law, after which he disappeared from recording for four years. Jackson continued performing, however, and he returned to the recording studio again in November of 1934 for sessions on the OKeh label, including three songs cut with his friend Big Bill Broonzy, which were never issued. Jackson was an important influence on Broonzy, who outlived his mentor by 20 years.

Papa Charlie Jackson remains a shadowy figure, considered a highly influential figure in the blues, though not quite a major blues figure, apart from the fact that he was the first male singer/guitarist who played the blues to get to record. His recordings are all eminently listenable, although most are not blues, but fall into such related areas as ragtime and hokum. *—Bruce Eder*

● **Fat Mouth** / 1970 / Yazoo ♦♦♦♦♦
Yazoo's *Fat Mouth* is the best overview of Papa Charlie Jackson's best recordings, offering 14 tracks he recorded between 1924 and 1927. While a few important songs didn't make it to this set, most of his very best did, and for many listeners this concise compilation is a preferable alternative to the exhaustive multi-volume Document series. *—Thom Owens*

Papa Charlie Jackson / 1972 / Biograph ♦♦♦♦♦
Jackson's mid-'20s material blended topical fare with hokum hilarity and blues laments, and Jackson's four and six-string banjo accompaniment was among country blues' most striking. His guitar work wasn't bad either. *—Ron Wynn*

Complete Recorded Works, Vol. 1 (1924–1926) / 1991 / Document ♦♦♦♦♦
The first 27 of Papa Charlie Jackson's recorded works is, on about ten counts, one of the most important blues documents you can find, dating all the way back to August of 1924, before there was even electrical recording or a true definition to "blues." Indeed, the popular highlight is a dance number called "Shake That Thing," which fairly overwhelmed a lot of Jackson's truer blues records with its beat. The opening number, "Papa's Lawdy Lawdy Blues," shows a kind of formative blues, with it and its B-side "Airy Man (aka "Hairy Man") Blues" closer in spirit to comic novelty numbers. The hybrid banjo-guitar that Jackson played was an absolute necessity on these and his other early records, for it was more audible than any guitar of the era would have been, and serves to keep a beat as well as provide full accompaniment. "Salt Lake City Blues" is closer to our modern definition of blues, a romantic lament that's as honest and cheerful as it is sexist. Jackson's first version of "Salty Dog Blues" is here, along with what is probably the earliest reference to Chicago's outdoor blues Mecca in "Maxwell Street Blues," dating from September of 1925. Other topical references to the future blues capital city can be heard in "Jackson's Blues," dealing with a local politician, and also worth checking out in that regard is "Mama Don't Allow It," telling of a country girl's descent into prostitution after coming to the big city. Also here is one of the earliest known source records for Willie Dixon's composition "Spoonful," tentitled "All I Want Is a Spoonful" (though anyone only familiar with the versions by Cream won't really recognize it), and a primordial incarnation of "I'm Alabama Bound" (later immortalized by Leadbelly). The audio quality is amazingly good throughout this disc (the only big exceptions, unfortunately, being the two duets with Ida Cox and the two takes of "Texas Blues," which are really in rough shape), and the sessionography and annotation are reasonably thorough, given how little we actually know about Jackson. *—Bruce Eder*

Complete Recorded Works, Vol. 2 (1926–1928) / 1991 / Document ♦♦♦
Featuring 26 of Papa Charlie Jackson's recordings dating between February 1926 and September 1928, and an extraordinary volume this is. Now firmly ensconced in the electrical recording era, the sound on these records brings out the rich texture of Jackson's banjo playing, and his singing is thoroughly enjoyable, as he runs through thinly veiled topical songs ("Judge Cliff Davis Blues"), playful romantic pieces ("Butter and Egg Man Blues"), bouncy rags ("Look Out Papa Don't Tear Your Pants"), and more ambitious remakes of his early songs, most notably an outtake of "Salty Dog," cut with Freddie Keppard's Jazz Cardinals (with New Orleans jazz great Johnny Dodds on clarinet). The two-part "Up the Way Bound," dating from the spring of 1926, isn't quite as well recorded as some of the rest, featuring Jackson on guitar, but his vocal performance carries the song well enough—unfortunately, the second half of this piece, from side two of the original Paramount release, is neither as well recorded nor as well preserved as the first half. There's lots of little slice-of-black-urban-life material here worth noting as well, including Jackson's homage to the numbers racket, "Four Eleven Forty Four." Jackson's vocal skills are vividly displayed in his extraordinarily impassioned singing on "Bad Luck Woman Blues," one of his finest performances. We also get his first version of "Skoodle-Um-Skoo," an upbeat dance number reminiscent of his earlier "Shake That Thing," awhich he recut some seven years later—this record also demonstrates better than almost any other side the full measure of advantage that the banjo had over the guitar in those days of blues recording, with a solo that fairly leaps out at the listener. *—Bruce Eder*

Complete Recorded Works, Vol. 3 (1928–1934) / 1991 / Document ♦♦♦
Papa Charlie Jackson's last 25 recordings, dating from September of 1928 through November of 1934, and doing more proper blues here than on either previous volume. By the time of the release of the material here, Jackson was one of the most seasoned of studio bluesmen, with nearly half a decade recording experience behind him—his vocal presence on all of these records is extraordinary, and he knows how to get the most out of his instrument, guitar or banjo. "Ma and Pa Poorhouse Blues" and "Big Feeling Blues," both duets with Ma Rainey, present him at his most mature and naturally expressive vocally, in sharp contrast to the almost perfunctory vocals on volume one of this set. The Hattie McDaniels duets, two halves of "Dentist Chair Blues," are also extremely worthwhile as far more than novelty numbers. In addition to some priceless topical songs, such as "You Got That Wrong," there are some notable re-recordings here, including a killer 1934 remake of Jackson's earlier hit "Skoodle-Um-Skoo" (which by then had entered the repertory of Big Bill Broonzy, who was taught guitar by Jackson), and his last follow-up to "Shake That Thing," "What's That Thing She's Shakin'." The delightfully risqué-sounding "You Put It in, I'll Take It Out" closes this collection. The only drawback to any of this is that, despite the fact that it consists of material recorded much later than anything on volumes one or two, the sound quality on this disc is far lower, with lots of distracting surface noise on many of the sources used for individual songs—the most disappointing of these are the two sides that Jackson cut with Blind (Arthur) Blake, who was very much an influence on Jackson; two of the greatest blues/ragtime guitarists and songsters of the early blues era together on record, and the scratchiness is nearly maddening. Only the four final 1934 sides really come up to the level one would wish on this stuff. *—Bruce Eder*

Colin James (Colin Munn)

b. Aug. 17, 1964, Regina, Saskatchewan, Canada
Vocals, Mandolin, Guitar / Contemporary Blues, Modern Electric Blues
This Canadian guitarist, singer and songwriter is Canada's answer to the U.S.'s Chris Duarte or Kenny Wayne Shepherd. Colin Munn grew up in Saskatchewan, listening to folk and blues. After learning the pennywhistle and mandolin, he quit school and worked with a succession of bands, among them, the Hoo Doo Men.

When he was 19 years old, he moved to Vancouver and joined the Night Shades. About two years later, performing under his changed name, Colin James, he was lucky enough to be noticed by the folks at Virgin Records, who signed him. James' 1988 self-titled debut was the fastest-selling album in Canadian history, and he followed that in 1990 with *Sudden Stop*, and *Colin James and the Little Big Band* in 1993. In 1995, James switched over to Warner Music Canada, and released *Bad Habits*. On *Bad Habits*, James is teamed with some good company: Bobby King and Terry Evans, Mavis Staples, guitarist Waddy Wachtel, Lenny Kravitz, and former Stevie Ray Vaughan and Double Trouble keyboardist Reese Wynans.

All of James' albums are well-recorded affairs. The only problem is, he doesn't tour the U.S. very much, and spends most of his time in Canada. In 1998, he toured with Steve Winwood, Little Feat, and Keith Richards; *Colin James and the Little Big Band II* followed a year later. *—Richard Skelly*

Colin James / 1988 / Virgin ♦♦♦♦
Although it's a little short on originality—at times you could swear Stevie Ray Vaughan showed him exactly what to play—Colin James' eponymous debut is an impressive collection of high-octane Blues-rock that, at its best, explodes with the intensity of a keg of dynamite. James' forte is his speedy, accomplished guitar playing, which is breathtaking at times, and that's enough to excuse the occasionally awkward originals and predictable covers that pepper the album. After all, good guitarists—even ones that borrow heavily from old masters—aren't all that easy to find, and sometimes you have to accept their flaws in order to embrace them. *—Thom Owens*

Sudden Stop / Oct. 1990 / Virgin ♦♦♦
A solid, stylistically varied followup by this Canadian guitarist. *—David Szatmary*

Colin James and the Little Big Band / 1993 / Virgin ♦♦♦
A tasty hybrid of rock & roll, jive, and blues, James' eponymous recording—a collection of standards from the late '40s-early '50s recorded live from the floor—takes a swingin' jump approach with horns and organ given equal billing to smooth, hollow-body guitar tones. Highlights: the finger-snapping, fedora-over-one-eye cool of "Evening" and a bopping, knockout version of "Train Kept A-Rollin'." *—Roch Parisien*

● **Bad Habits** / 1995 / Elektra ✦✦✦✦

Canadian blues guitarist Colin James turns in a fine set of both original and cover material. Paring back the sound of his previous effort to the basic guitar, bass and drums, James uses horns and keyboards to color and accentuate certain tracks rather than overwhelm. He works his blues magic on such covers as Robert Johnson's "Walkin' Blues" and Jerry Williams' "Standing on the Edge of Love" while proving his own songwriting capabilities on cuts like "Freedom" and "Better Days." A great return to form. —*James Chrispell*

Colin James and the Little Big Band II / 1998 / Elektra ✦✦✦

While the late '90s may be remembered as the era of the swing revival movement, Colin James was one of the first artists to rediscover this popular musical style of yesteryear. Although James started out first and foremost as a blues guitarist, he'd been a lover of swing since he was a teen, deciding to ditch his blues-rock for 1993's *Colin James and the Little Big Band*. The switch proved to be the right move back home, where the album was a double-platinum smash. But since the swing revival was a few years off in the early '90s, James returned to blues-rock with 1995's *Bad Habits*, before this release signaled a return to swing. Included are covers of such legends as Cab Calloway ("C'mon With the C'mon"), Ray Charles ("Mary Ann"), and Willie Dixon (You Know My Love), plus other highlights ("Jumpin' from 6 to 6," "I'll See It Through," etc). And fans of James' earlier work will be happy to learn that he hasn't given up blues entirely, especially after hearing the tracks "Let's Shout" and "Tin Pan Alley." —*Greg Prato*

National Steel / Jun. 30, 1998 / WEA International ✦✦✦

Elmore James

b. Jan. 27, 1918, Richland, MS, d. May 24, 1963, Chicago, IL
Slide Guitar, Vocals, Guitar (Electric), Songwriter, Guitar / Slide Guitar Blues, Electric Chicago Blues, Electric Blues

No two ways about it, the most influential slide guitarist of the postwar period was Elmore James, hands down. Although his early demise from heart failure kept him from enjoying the fruits of the '60s blues revival as his contemporaries Muddy Waters and Howlin' Wolf did, James left a wide influential trail behind him. And that influence continues to the present time—in approach, attitude and tone—in just about every guitar player who puts a slide on his finger and wails the blues. As a guitarist, he wrote the book, his slide style influencing the likes of Hound Dog Taylor, Joe Carter, his cousin Homesick James, and J.B. Hutto, while his seldom-heard single-string work had an equally profound effect on B.B. King and Chuck Berry. His signature lick—an electric updating of Robert Johnson's "I Believe I'll Dust My Broom" and one that Elmore recorded in infinite variations from day one to his last session—is so much a part of the essential blues fabric of guitar licks that no one attempting to play slide guitar can do it without being compared to Elmore James. Others may have had more technique—Robert Nighthawk and Earl Hooker immediately come to mind—but Elmore had the sound and all the feeling.

A radio repairman by trade, Elmore reworked his guitar amplifiers in his spare time, getting them to produce raw, distorted sounds that wouldn't resurface until the advent of heavy rock amplification in the late '60s. This amp on 11 approach was hot-wired to one of the strongest emotional approaches to the blues ever recorded. There is never a time when you're listening to one of his records that you feel—no matter how familiar the structure—that he's phoning it in just to grab a quick session check. Elmore James always gave it everything he had, everything he could emotionally invest in a number. This commitment of spirit is something that shows up time and again when listening to multiple takes from his session masters. The sheer repetitiveness of the recording process would dim almost anyone's creative fires, but Elmore always seemed to give it 100 percent every time the red light went on. Few blues singers had a voice that could compete with James'; it was loud, forceful, prone to "catch" or break up in the high registers, almost sounding on the verge of hysteria at certain moments. Evidently the times back in the mid-'30s when Elmore had first-hand absorption of Robert Johnson as a playing companion had deep influence on him, not only in his choice of material, but also in his presentation of it.

Backing the twin torrents of Elmore's guitar and voice was one of the greatest—and earliest—Chicago blues bands. Named after James' big hit, the Broomdusters featured Little Johnny Jones on piano, J.T. Brown on tenor sax, and Elmore's cousin Homesick James on rhythm guitar. This talented nucleus was often augmented by a second saxophone on occasion while the drumming stool changed frequently. But this was the band that could go toe to toe in a battle of the blues against the bands of Muddy Waters or Howlin' Wolf and always hold their own, if not walk with the show. Utilizing a stomping beat, Elmore's slashing guitar, Jones' two-fisted piano delivery, Homesick's rudimentary boogie bass rhythm, and Brown's braying nanny-goat sax leads, the Broomdusters were as loud and powerful and popular as any blues band the Windy City had to offer.

But as urban as their sound was, it all had roots in Elmore's hometown of Canton, MS. He was born in Richland, MS, on January 27, 1918, the illegitimate son of Leola Brooks and later given the surname of his stepfather, Joe Willie James. He adapted to music at an early age, learning to play bottleneck on a homemade instrument fashioned out of a broom handle and a lard can. By the age of 14, he was already a weekend musician, working the various country suppers and juke joints in the area under the names "Cleanhead" or Joe Willie James. Although he confined himself to a home base area around Belzoni, he would join up and work with traveling players coming through like Robert Johnson, Howlin' Wolf, and Sonny Boy Williamson. By the late '30s he had formed his first band and was working the Southern state area with Sonny Boy until the Second World War broke out, spending three years stationed with the Navy in Guam. When he was discharged, he picked off where he left off, moving for a while to Memphis, working in clubs with Eddie Taylor and his cousin Homesick James. Elmore was also one of the first "guest stars" on the popular *King Biscuit Time* radio show on KFFA in Helena, AR, also doing stints on the *Talaho Syrup* show on Yazoo City's WAZF and the *Hadacol* show on KWEM in West Memphis.

Nervous and unsure of his abilities as a recording artist, Elmore was surreptitiously recorded by Lillian McMurray of Trumpet Records at the tail end of a Sonny Boy session doing his now signature tune, "Dust My Broom." The legend has it that James didn't even

stay around long enough to hear the playback, much less record a second side. Mrs. McMurray stuck a local singer (Bo Bo Thomas) on the flip side and the record became the surprise R&B hit of 1951, making the Top Ten and conversely making a recording star out of Elmore. With a few months left on his Trumpet contract, Elmore was recorded by the Bihari brothers for their Modern label subsidiaries, Flair and Meteor, but the results were left in the can until James' contract ran out. In the meantime, Elmore had moved to Chicago and cut a quick session for Chess, which resulted in one single being issued and just as quickly yanked off the market as the Biharis swooped in to protect their investment. This period of activity found Elmore assembling the nucleus of his great band the Broomdusters and several fine recordings were issued over the next few years on a plethora of Bihari-owned labels with several of them charting and most all of them becoming certified blues classics.

By this time James had established a beachhead in the clubs of Chicago as one of the most popular live acts and regularly broadcasting over WPOA under the aegis of disc jockey Big Bill Hill. In 1957, with his contract with the Biharis at an end, he recorded several successful sides for Mel London's Chief label, all of them later being issued on the larger Vee-Jay label. His health—always in a fragile state due to a recurring heart condition—would send him back home to Jackson, MS, where he temporarily set aside his playing for work as a disc jockey or radio repairman. He came back to Chicago to record a session for Chess, then just as quickly broke contract to sign with Bobby Robinson's Fire label, producing the classic "The Sky Is Crying" and numerous others. Running afoul with the Chicago musician's union, he returned back to Mississippi, doing sessions in New York and New Orleans waiting for Big Bill Hill to sort things out. In August of 1963, Elmore returned to Chicago, ready to resume his on-again off-again playing career—his records were still being regularly issued and reissued on a variety of labels—when he suffered his final heart attack. His wake was attended by over 400 blues luminaries before his body was sent back to Mississippi. He was elected to the Blues Foundation's Hall of Fame in 1980 and was later elected to the Rock & Roll Hall of Fame as a seminal influence. Elmore James may not have lived to reap the rewards of the blues revival, but his music and influence continues to resonate. —*Cub Koda*

Whose Muddy Shoes / 1969 / MCA/Chess ✦✦✦✦✦

Elmore had recorded a session for Chess in 1953 before settling down with the Bihari brothers and again in 1960, shortly before starting his final recordings for Bobby Robinson's Fire, Fury and Enjoy labels. This collects up all of them on CD with the bonus addition of an alternate take of "The Sun Is Shining," which can be interpreted as a precursor to his later hit "The Sky Is Crying." The earlier sides from 1953 lack his inimitable slide, but the 1960 session produced classics like "Talk to Me Baby," "Madison Blues" and a powerful reading of T-Bone Walker's "Stormy Monday." These tracks of Elmore working with the Chess production team are delightfully fleshed out with a half dozen gems by the highly underrated John Brim, some of which include stellar harp work by Little Walter ("Rattlesnake," "Be Careful"—on which Walter stops playing in several spots to become an ad-lib backup vocalist—and "You Got Me") as well as the original version of "Ice Cream Man," better known to rock fans from Van Halen's cover version of it from their debut album. —*Cub Koda*

The Original Meteor & Flair Sides / 1984 / Ace ✦✦✦✦✦

The best of James' early-'50s sides with stunning slide and driving band support. At the top of his form, this is a perfect introduction to his music. —*Cub Koda*

Let's Cut It: The Very Best of Elmore James / 1986 / Flair ✦✦✦✦

Let's Cut It: The Very Best of Elmore James rounds up 18 tracks from his Modern, Flair and Meteor recordings. These are generally considered to be some James' greatest recordings, and there's no denying that there are incendiary performances throughout the record that more than prove James' legendary status is deserved. A few alternate takes are thrown in that are more noteworthy for collectors than general listeners. Then again, fans who only want one disc of Elmore will be best served by Rhino's *The Sky Is Crying*, which selects highlights from all of his many labels. This, in turn, is for fans who want to dig a little deeper than that set, since this contains the best of one of his best periods. —*Stephen Thomas Erlewine*

Elmore James, John Brim, Floyd Jones / 1986 / Vogue ✦✦✦

Both the artwork and the first two-thirds of this 20-track CD partially overlap the Chess Records release on Elmore James and John Brim. The last six songs are by Floyd Jones and include his classic "Dark Road" and "You Can't Live Long," cut on December 29, 1951, and September 17, 1952. All of the tracks feature Little Walter on harmonica, and the four 1951 songs also feature Jimmy Rogers. The sound is OK, and in the absence of any official Floyd Jones release from Chess, this is worth tracking down. —*Bruce Eder*

The Rollin' & Tumblin': The Best of Elmore James / 1992 / Relic ✦✦✦✦✦

Although the Capricorn box set does a great job of rounding at least one take of everything James cut for Bobby Robinson's Fire and Enjoy labels, if you want (or need) to sweat it down to bare essentials, this is the one to grab out of the blues bin and take home. The remastering by Little Walter Devenne on this single disc is exemplary and for late period Elmore, this truly is the best of the best. —*Cub Koda*

☆ **King of the Slide Guitar** / 1992 / Capricorn ✦✦✦✦✦

Elmore's last great recordings occurred in the '60s when he was signed by New York producer/label-owner Bobby Robinson. Unlike many of his contemporaries, James seemingly got *better* as the years went by and while none of the sides feature a slide guitar anywhere near as nasty as his early Modern and Flair recordings, he's still obviously giving it all on each and every side. These recordings are the ones most commonly issued on James and have surfaced on so many different compilations—all with varying levels of sound quality—that it would be futile to list them all here. Fortunately, to make things easier we have this two-disc 50-song box set rounding up at least one extant take of everything Elmore recorded with Robinson at the helm. While some of the material are recuts of his best known tunes ("Dust My Broom" resurfaces here in two versions from two different sessions and the version of "It Hurts Me Too" included here—it was originally cut for Chief in the late '50s—became a posthumous hit for him), the majority of it breaks new ground and stands as some of Elmore's most emotion-laden work. Nice essays in the booklet make up for the disgusting art work that adorns the box. —*Cub Koda*

Dust My Broom: The Best of Elmore James, Vol. 2 / 1992 / Relic ◆◆◆◆
A second Relic volume of classics from the Fire/Fury/Enjoy vaults that picks up where the company's first one left off. Even if you already own Capricorn's definitive two-disc collection of his Bobby Robinson-produced sides, you're missing one gem here: "Poor Little Angel Child," which features the robust vocal talent of harpist Sam Myers. Great sound quality throughout, with many stereo items. —*Bill Dahl*

☆ The Classic Recordings / 1993 / Flair ◆◆◆◆◆
After James hit the national charts with his Trumpet recording of "Dust My Broom," he came to record for the Bihari Brothers, first for their Meteor subsidiary, then later for their Flair and Modern labels. This multi-disc retrospective rounds up every existing master James recorded for the Biharis, plus his backup work behind bandmembers Little Johnny Jones and J.T. Brown. James' guitar tone is distorted and overamped to the extreme; *this* is the sound that changed the face of slide guitar forever, influencing everyone from Hound Dog Taylor to J.B. Hutto to George Thorogood and everybody in between. The intensity of James' vocals are nothing short of riveting and the material collected here (along with breakdowns, studio chat, etc.) is simply the best of James' early-'50s sides and a box set well worth saving up for.—*Cub Koda*

★ The Sky Is Crying: The History of Elmore James / Apr. 6, 1993 / Rhino ◆◆◆◆◆
With the confusing plethora of Elmore James discs out on the market, this is truly the place to start, featuring the best of his work culled from several labels. Highlights include James' original recording of "Dust My Broom," "It Hurts Me Too," "T.V. Mama" (with Elmore backing Big Joe Turner), and the title track, one of the best slow blues ever created. Slide guitar doesn't get much better than this, making this particular compilation not only a perfect introduction to Elmore's music, but an essential piece for any blues collection. —*Cub Koda*

The Best of Elmore James: The Early Years / 1995 / Ace ◆◆◆
This breaks down Elmore's Modern recordings into a single-disc retrospective and a damn fine one it is, too. This compiles the A and B sides of every single recorded for the Bihari brothers, with the original Trumpet recording of "Dust My Broom" standing in the place of "1839 Blues." If you really want to hear Elmore at his wildest and most unfettered and don't want to wade through a pile of alternate takes to get to it, we heartily suggest adding this one to the collection. Import. —*Cub Koda*

The Complete Fire & Enjoy Recordings / Sep. 1, 1995 / Collectables ◆◆◆
This three-disc set mirrors Capricorn's double box set of the same material. The Collectables set offers more alternate takes and stray vocals from Sammy Myers and an unidentified female vocalist, recorded at the same sessions, with Elmore contributing guitar, many of the tracks in true stereo. But the liner-note information is scant, and the lack of a proper booklet makes this set an also-ran compared to the more sensibly ordered and far better annotated Capricorn set, garish box graphics and all. Further points are docked for the inclusion of two tracks that certainly aren't Bobby Robinson recordings, the first version of "Make My Dreams Come True" and "I Can't Stop Lovin' You." —*Cub Koda*

Blues Masters: The Very Best of Elmore James / Mar. 14, 2000 / Rhino ◆◆◆◆◆
A good 16-song compilation, but a puzzling one. It essentially duplicates *The Sky Is Crying: The History of Elmore James*, but must be judged as slightly inferior, as that other compilation has 21 tracks. The puzzle is that *The Sky Is Crying*, like *The Very Best Of*, is also on Rhino, and was still in print when this compilation was released in 2000. True, this does have a couple of songs not on *The Sky Is Crying* ("Wild About You Baby" and "Coming Home"), and presents the tracks in chronological order, whereas *The Sky Is Crying* does not. Are these reasons to merit a second compilation in the same label's catalog? One would think not. However, if you could care less about such fine distinctions, this is as good a James anthology as any. And the expected classics are here, including "Shake Your Money Maker," "The Sky Is Crying," "Dust My Broom," "Madison Blues," "It Hurts Me Too," and "The Sun Is Shining." —*Richie Unterberger*

Shake Your Money Maker: The Best of the Fire Sessions / Mar. 6, 2001 / Buddha ◆◆◆◆◆
An intensely powerful singer and guitarist, Elmore James did not start his recording career until he was 33, and he only lived to be 45, but he made a very strong impact during his dozen years on records. Some of his finest work was cut for the Fire label during 1959-1961, roughly half of which is included on this single CD. Other than a final outburst of selections during February 1963, these were James' last studio sessions, and he is heard at the peak of his powers throughout. Among the best-known performances are the hit "Shake Your Money Maker," "The Sky Is Crying," and a remake of his famous "Dust My Broom," but all 16 selections are full of passion and fire. This is an essential acquisition for blues collectors, at least until a more complete James on Fire reissue comes out. —*Scott Yanow*

The Sky Is Crying: Classic Blues Collected / Sep. 11, 2001 / Music Club ◆◆◆◆◆

Shake Your Money Maker / Jul. 9, 2002 / Collectables ◆◆◆
Collectables' 2002 release *Shake Your Money Maker* relies heavily on familiar Fire-era material—"Dust My Broom," "It Hurts Me Too," "The Sky Is Crying," etc.—sprinkled with some enjoyable oddities along the way. Overall, it's an entertaining comp and it has enough of the key Elmore material that it will satisfy a lot of casual fans, but there are other, more thorough compilations on the market that serve as better introductions and overviews. However, the oddities on here do make it worth hearing for dedicated collectors. —*Stephen Thomas Erlewine*

Etta James (Jamesetta Hawkins)
b. Jan. 25, 1938, Los Angeles, CA
Vocals / Soul-Blues, R&B, Soul

Few R&B singers have endured tragic travails on the monumental level that Etta James has and remain on earth to talk about it. The lady's no shrinking violet; her autobiography, *Rage to Survive*, describes her past (including numerous drug addictions) in sordid detail.

But her personal problems have seldom affected her singing. James has hung in there from the age of R&B and doo wop in the mid-'50s through soul's late-'60s heyday and right up to today (where her 1994 disc *Mystery Lady* paid loving jazz-based tribute to one of her idols, Billie Holiday). Etta James' voice has deepened over the years, coarsened more than a little, but still conveys remarkable passion and pain.

Jamesetta Hawkins was a child gospel prodigy, singing in her Los Angeles Baptist church choir (and over the radio) when she was only five years old under the tutelage of Professor James Earle Hines. She moved to San Francisco in 1950, soon teaming with two other girls to form a singing group. When she was 14, bandleader Johnny Otis gave the trio an audition. He particularly dug their answer song to Hank Ballard & the Midnighters' "Work With Me Annie."

Against her mother's wishes, the young singer embarked for L.A. to record "Roll With Me Henry" with the Otis band and vocalist Richard Berry in 1954 for Modern Records. Otis inverted her first name to devise her stage handle and dubbed her vocal group the Peaches (also Etta's nickname). "Roll With Me Henry," renamed "The Wallflower" when some radio programmers objected to the original title's connotations, topped the R&B charts in 1955.

The Peaches dropped from the tree shortly thereafter, but Etta James kept on singing for Modern throughout much of the decade (often under the supervision of saxist Maxwell Davis). "Good Rockin' Daddy" also did quite well for her later in 1955, but deserving follow-ups such as "W-O-M-A-N" and "Tough Lover" (the latter a torrid rocker cut in New Orleans with Lee Allen on sax) failed to catch on.

James landed at Chicago's Chess Records in 1960, signing with their Argo subsidiary. Immediately, her recording career kicked into high gear; not only did a pair of duets with her then-boyfriend (Moonglows lead singer Harvey Fuqua) chart, her own sides (beginning with the tortured ballad "All I Could Do Was Cry") chased each other up the R&B lists as well. Leonard Chess viewed James as a classy ballad singer with pop crossover potential, backing her with lush violin orchestrations for 1961's luscious "At Last" and "Trust in Me." But James' rougher side wasn't forsaken—the gospel-charged "Something's Got a Hold on Me" in 1962, a kinetic 1963 live LP (*Etta James Rocks the House*) cut at Nashville's New Era Club and a blues-soaked 1966 duet with childhood pal Sugar Pie DeSanto, "In the Basement," ensured that.

Although Chess hosted its own killer house band, James traveled to Rick Hall's Fame studios in Muscle Shoals in 1967 and emerged with one of her all-time classics. "Tell Mama" was a searing slice of upbeat southern soul that contrasted markedly with another standout from the same sessions, the spine-chilling ballad "I'd Rather Go Blind." Despite the death of Leonard Chess, Etta James remained at the label into 1975, experimenting toward the end with a more rock-based approach.

There were some mighty lean years, both personally and professionally, for Miss Peaches. But she got back on track recording-wise in 1988 with a set for Island, *Seven Year Itch*, that reaffirmed her southern soul mastery. Her last few albums have been a varied lot—1990's *Sticking to My Guns* was contemporary in the extreme; 1992's Jerry Wexler-produced *The Right Time* for Elektra was slickly soulful, and her most recent outings have explored jazz directions. In 1998, she also issued a holiday album, *Etta James Christmas*. She was inducted into the Blues Hall of Fame in 2001.

In concert, Etta James is a sassy, no-holds-barred performer whose suggestive stage antics sometimes border on the obscene. She's paid her dues many times over as an R&B and soul pioneer; long may she continue to shock the uninitiated. —*Bill Dahl*

The Second Time Around / 1961 / MCA/Chess ◆◆◆◆
Etta James' second album isn't what you pull off the shelf when you want to hear her belt some soul. Like her debut, it found Chess presenting her as more or less a pop singer, using orchestration arranged and conducted by Riley Hampton, and mostly tackling popular standards of the '40s. If you're not a purist, this approach won't bother you in the least; James sings with gusto, proving that she could more than hold her own in this idiom as well. R&B isn't entirely neglected either, with the rousing "Seven Day Fool" (co-written by Berry Gordy Jr.) a standout; "Don't Cry Baby" and "Fool That I Am" were R&B hits that made a mild impression on the pop charts as well. —*Richie Unterberger*

★ At Last! / 1961 / MCA/Chess ◆◆◆◆◆
After spending a few years in limbo after scoring her first R&B hits "Dance With Me, Henry" and "Good Rocking Daddy," Etta James returned to the spotlight in 1960 with her first Chess release, *At Last!* James made both the R&B and pop charts with the album's title cut, "All I Could Do Was Cry," and "Trust in Me." What makes *At Last!* a great album is not only the solid hits it contains, but also the strong variety of material throughout. James expertly handles jazz standards like "Stormy Weather" and "A Sunday Kind of Love," as well as Willie Dixon's blues classic "I Just Want to Make Love to You." James demonstrates her keen facility on the title track in particular, as she easily moves from powerful blues shouting to more subtle, airy phrasing; her Ruth Brown-inspired, bad-girl growl only adds to the intensity. James would go on to even greater success with later hits like "Tell Mama," but on *At Last!* one hears the singer at her peak in a swinging and varied program of blues, R&B, and jazz standards. —*Stephen Cook*

Sings for Lovers / 1962 / Cadet ◆◆◆
Smooth and mellow. —*Bill Dahl*

Etta James Sings / 1962 / United ◆◆◆
A collection of her '50s hits, it includes "Roll with Me, Henry" (the answer song to Hank Ballard's "Work With Me Annie"). Out of print. —*George Bedard*

☆ **Etta James Rocks the House** / 1964 / MCA/Chess ✦✦✦✦✦
Simply one of the greatest live blues albums ever captured on tape. Cut in 1963 at the New Era Club in Nashville, the set finds Etta James in stellar shape as she forcefully delivers her own "Something's Got a Hold on Me" and "Seven Day Fool" interspersed with a diet of sizzling covers ("What'd I Say," "Sweet Little Angel," "Money," "Ooh Poo Pah Doo"). The CD incarnation adds three more great titles, including an impassioned reprise of her "All I Could Do Is Cry." Guitarist David T. Walker is outstanding whenever he solos. —*Bill Dahl*

Call My Name / 1966 / Cadet ✦✦✦✦
Still unavailable digitally, James' 1966 LP is dynamite Chicago soul, with the vaunted Chess house band in uplifting support. Among the many standouts are "I'm So Glad (I Found Love in You)," "It Must Be Your Love," and "Don't Pick Me for Your Fool." —*Bill Dahl*

Tell Mama / 1968 / MCA/Chess ✦✦✦✦✦
Leonard Chess dispatched Etta James to Muscle Shoals in 1967, and the move paid off with one of her best and most soul-searing Cadet albums. Produced by Rick Hall, the resultant album boasted a relentlessly driving title cut, the moving soul ballad "I'd Rather Go Blind," and sizzling covers of Otis Redding's "Security" and Jimmy Hughes' "Don't Lose Your Good Thing," and a pair of fine Don Covay copyrights. The skin-tight session aces at Fame Studios really did themselves proud behind Miss Peaches. —*Bill Dahl*

Losers Weepers / 1971 / Cadet ✦✦✦
Another vinyl-only LP from her Chess stint produced by Ralph Bass that traverses a wide range of material. Chess saxist Gene "Daddy G" Barge penned "I Think It's You," but his presence is matched by that of Duke Ellington ("I Got It Bad and That Ain't Good") and J. Fred Coots ("For All We Know") in the composers' credits. —*Bill Dahl*

Come a Little Closer / 1974 / Chess ✦✦✦
James was fighting serious substance-abuse problems when this record was recorded, commuting to the sessions from a rehab center. It was a triumph simply to complete the record at all. But although James' life may have been in rough shape outside of the studio, she delivered a fairly strong set that fused forceful '70s soul arrangements with some rock (Randy Newman and John Kay both contribute compositions), jazz, and New Orleans R&B. Some of the material's routine, but there are some very strong cuts here, like a rousing "Sookie Sookie," and "Out on the Street Again," with its slightly sinister funk groove. "Feeling Uneasy," in fact, counts as one of the unsung highlights of her career, with a wrenching, near-wordless scat-moan vocal over a suitably languorous, melancholy blues-jazz arrangement. The CD reissue adds a couple of interesting bonus tracks: the 1975 single "Lovin' Arms," a good rootsy ballad, and a single edit of one of the tracks from the album, "Out on the Street Again." —*Richie Unterberger*

Deep in the Night / 1978 / Bullseye Blues ✦✦✦✦
Originally released on Warners Brothers to scant acclaim in 1978, this Jerry Wexler-produced masterpiece finds James in astounding voice with a batch of great material to apply her massive interpretive powers to. The band, including the cream of the late-'70s Los Angeles session hot-shots (Cornell Dupree, Jeff Porcaro, Chuck Rainey, Plas Johnson, Jim Horn), lays it down soulful and simple and the result is a modern-day R&B classic. Highlights abound throughout, but special attention must be turned to James' takes on "Only Women Bleed" and the Eagles' "Take It to the Limit." —*Cub Koda*

Early Show, Vol. 1: Blues in the Night / 1986 / Fantasy ✦✦✦
Recorded live at Marla's Memory Lane Supper Club in Los Angeles, this 1986 date finds Etta James in front of a superb combo fronted by Eddie "Cleanhead" Vinson, with Red Holloway, Jack McDuff, and Shuggie Otis providing the supple and swinging backdrop. Vinson is featured on "Kidney Stew," "When My Baby Left Me," and "Railroad Porter Blues" before the turning the stage over to Etta, who provides a blistering "Something's Got a Hold on Me" and a sultry three-song medley of "At Last," "Trust Me," and "Sunday Kind of Love." The two stars duet on Percy Mayfield's "Please Send Me Someone to Love" before Etta closes the show with strong readings of "Lover Man" and "Misty." The small crowd's enthusiastic response makes this a show you wish you were there for; this disc is the next best thing to it. —*Cub Koda*

Late Show, Vol. 2: Live at Maria's Memory Lane Supper Club / 1986 / Fantasy ✦✦✦

R&B Dynamite / 1987 / Flair ✦✦✦✦✦
The singer in her precocious formative years, headed by her 1955 R&B smash "Roll With Me Henry" (aka "The Wallflower"). James' follow-ups included the driving "Good Rockin' Daddy," a bluesy "W-O-M-A-N," and the New Orleans raveup "Tough Lover," which found her backed by the gang at Cosimo's (notably saxman Lee Allen). Even though her tenure at Modern Records only produced a handful of hits, these 22 cuts are delightful artifacts of the belter's earliest days. The CD was reissued, with identical (though slightly resequenced) tracks and liner notes, as *Hickory Dickory Dock* on Ace. —*Bill Dahl*

The Sweetest Peaches: The Chess Years / 1988 / Chess ✦✦✦✦✦
A good 20-track survey of her Chess work on this double LP. All but two of the songs, however, are now available on the much more extensive CD *The Essential Etta James*, making this collection redundant. —*Richie Unterberger*

The Right Time / 1992 / Elektra ✦✦
Myriad big names came together for the making of this album. Jerry Wexler produced it, sidemen include Steve Cropper and Lucky Peterson—but the final product is a disappointment. It's just too slickly rendered to come close to the knockout punch of her vintage Chess material. —*Bill Dahl*

How Strong Is a Woman: The Island Sessions / 1993 / 4th & Broadway ✦✦✦
How Strong Is a Woman collects the highlights from Etta James' late-'80s and early-'90s

stint at Island Records. Although she didn't record any new classics while she was at the label, she demonstrated time and time again that she hadn't lost much of her vocal power and that she remained vital 40 years after she began recording. *How Strong Is a Woman* offers positive proof of that and is a good sampling of her work for Island. —*Thom Owens*

☆ **The Essential Etta James** / Jun. 8, 1993 / MCA/Chess ✦✦✦✦✦
Here are 44 tracks summarizing the long and brilliant Chess tenure of Miss Peaches, opening with her 1960 smash "All I Could Do Was Cry," and encompassing her torchy, fully orchestrated ballads "At Last," "My Dearest Darling," and "Trust in Me," and continuing on through her 1962 gospel rocker "Something's Got a Hold on Me," the Chicago soul standouts "I Prefer You" and "842-3089," and her 1967 Muscle Shoals-cut smash "Tell Mama." A few of the '70s sides that conclude the two-disc set seem makeweight when compared to what preceded them, but most of the essentials are aboard. —*Bill Dahl*

Something's Got a Hold / 1994 / Charly ✦✦✦
It's not that the contents of this 20-song disc aren't terrific; until the last four songs, anyway, they are. After all, this is Etta James' Chess legacy we're talking about here. But compared to MCA's superior-sounding (and annotated) anthologies, this disc falls a bit flat. —*Bill Dahl*

Live from San Francisco / 1994 / On the Spot ✦✦✦✦✦
Commercially, the '70s weren't nearly as kind to Etta James as the '50s and '60s had been. The sleekness that characterized Northern "uptown" soul and disco didn't appeal to the big-voiced belter, who stuck to her guns and continued to embrace the type of gritty, hard-hitting Southern soul and down-home blues that had earned her so devoted a following. Though absent from Black radio playlists, she had no problem attracting enthusiastic live audiences. At 41, James sounds like she's very much in her prime on this live recording from 1981. Whether tearing into an Otis Redding medley, her hit "Tell Mama" or Chicago blues staples like Willie Dixon's "I Just Want to Make Love to You" and Jimmy Reed's "Baby, What You Want Me to Do," the earthy singer clearly excels by sticking with what she does best. One of the CD's most pleasant surprises is a version of the Eagles' "Take It to the Limit," which works remarkably well in an R&B setting. —*Alex Henderson*

Mystery Lady: Songs of Billie Holiday / Mar. 1, 1994 / Private Music ✦✦✦
The popular Etta James usually performs raunchy single entendre blues so this surprisingly subtle outing is a real change of pace. She sounds quite laidback on a set of ballads associated with Billie Holiday and utilizes a jazz rhythm section led by pianist Cedar Walton plus three horn players including the great Red Holloway on tenor and alto. James makes no attempts at exploring uptempo material or scatting, sticking to soulful interpretations of the classic ballads. Despite the lack of variety in tempos, the music is quite satisfying. —*Scott Yanow*

These Foolish Things / 1995 / MCA/Chess ✦✦✦✦
James has long been a masterful blues balladeer—a talent spotlighted throughout the course of this 14-song collection. Some tracks are cushioned by string-enriched arrangements, others—notably 1965's passionate "Only Time Will Tell"—are melodic Chicago soul. Four tracks are previously unreleased, including her reading of Billie Holiday's "Lover Man." —*Bill Dahl*

★ **Her Best** / 1997 / Chess ✦✦✦✦✦
While several best-ofs from Etta's Chess period have been available over the years—with the two-disc, 44-track *Essential Etta James* at the top of the list in giving the big picture—this 20-track collection sweats *that* bigger picture down to bare essentials. For those wishing to finally sample Etta's classic period at Chess without opening the wallet for box set-anthology expense, this single-disc retrospective will fill the bill quite nicely. Featuring 20 of the tracks that appear on the double-disc *Essential* anthology without anything literally essential left off, this scintillating little disc now officially becomes the one-stop, first-time purchase in connecting with the emotional greatness inherent in Etta's siren song. There's plenty more after this to discover, but *this* is absolutely where you start. —*Cub Koda*

Love's Been Rough on Me / Apr. 29, 1997 / Private Music ✦✦✦
Love's Been Rough on Me is a terrific latter-day album from Etta James, capturing her at the peak of her powers. James' voice has diminished only slightly over the course of her career, and she knows how to make such warhorses as "I've Been Loving You Too Long" sound fresh. She also invests contemporary music, including John Berry's contemporary country hit "If I Had Any Pride Left at All," with real soul. The result is a record that delivers the real goods with grace and style. —*Leo Stanley*

Hickory Dickory Dock / Apr. 21, 1998 / Ace ✦✦✦✦✦
The music and liner notes are identical to the previous *R&B Dynamite* reissue, except that the tracks have been slightly resequenced, and a couple of songs bear different titles ("Number One" has been changed to "My One and Only," "How Big a Fool" to "Call Me a Fool"). —*Bill Dahl*

Life, Love & the Blues / Jun. 30, 1998 / Private Music ✦✦✦
This outing is slick, funky and thoroughly commercial. The queen of rhythm and blues does an admirable job of keeping her head above water, but this package of covers comes off more like the work of a tight lounge band than the work of a blues master. —*Tim Sheridan*

The Best of Etta James: 20th Century Masters—The Millennium Collection / Apr. 6, 1999 / MCA ✦✦✦
Like any record company worth their salt, MCA knows a good gimmick when they see it, and when the millennium came around…well, the *20th Century Masters—The Millennium Collection* wasn't too far behind. Supposedly, the millennium is a momentous occasion, but it's hard to feel that way when it's used as another excuse to turn out a budget-line series. But apart from the presumptuous title, *20th Century Masters—The*

Millennium Collection turns out to be a very good budget-line series. True, it's impossible for any of these brief collections to be definitive, but they're nevertheless solid samplers that don't feature a bad song in the bunch. For example, take Etta James' *20th Century* volume—it's an irresistible 11-song summary of her Chess years. There may be a couple of noteworthy songs missing, but many of her best-known songs for the label are here, including "At Last," "Something's Got a Hold on Me," "All I Could Do Was Cry," "Stop the Wedding," "Pushover," "Don't Cry Baby," "Trust in Me," "Tell Mama," "Almost Persuaded," and "I'd Rather Go Blind." Serious fans will want something more extensive, but this is an excellent introduction for neophytes and a great sampler for casual fans, considering its length and price. That doesn't erase the ridiculousness of the series title, but the silliness is excusable when the music and the collections are good. *—Stephen Thomas Erlewine*

The Heart of a Woman / Jun. 29, 1999 / Private Music ♦♦♦

There's no denying that Etta James is a powerhouse, one of the finest blues singers of the 20th century. Perhaps that's what makes her latter-day records so frustrating: The talent is still apparent and abundant, but the albums themselves are unsatisfying. All the ingredients are in the right place, but something went slightly awry during the execution. After all, *Heart of a Woman* is a great idea for an album. James chose 11 love songs from her favorite female singers—Billie Holiday, Dinah Washington, Sarah Vaughn, and Carmen McRae—augmenting the album with a new version of her signature song, "At Last." She has recorded several of these songs before (including Alice Cooper's "Only Women Bleed," which inexplicably became a standard for both her and McRae), but the difference with *Heart of a Woman* is the context. Here, they're put in a smooth jazz setting, masterminded by James, who has producer credit. No matter how well she sings the songs here—and she still possesses an exceptionally strong voice, robust and filled with passion—the well-scrubbed, glossy surfaces on the record keeps it from being engaging. It's not bad listening, it just never has the emotional impact James intended it to have. At times, it's hard not to wish that she worked with a producer who brought her back to the organic sound of her classic '50s and '60s sessions, but James has been pursuing this smoothed-out style for a decade now. It's clear that this is what she wants to do. She still sounds good, and that means her latter-day albums are listenable—but they don't resonate like the best of her records. *—Stephen Thomas Erlewine*

☆ **The Chess Box** / Jun. 27, 2000 / Chess ♦♦♦♦♦

Etta James is one of the towering figures of the blues, the foremost female blues vocalist of the second half of the 20th century, and the foundation of her legacy is her recordings for Chess Records in the '60s. Despite her reputation and enduring popularity, Etta didn't receive a box set retrospective between 1988 and 1990, the time when Chess was honoring such heavyweights as Chuck Berry, Muddy Waters, Howlin' Wolf, Bo Diddley, and Willie Dixon with multi-disc retrospectives. They eased away from box sets during the '90s, only issuing a comprehensive double-disc Little Walter set early in the decade, but they finally returned to the sets in 2000 with a long-overdue *Chess Box* for Etta James. Like before, when they assembled terrific sets on Berry and Waters, they got it right. Collectors may find a favorite side missing, but the great majority of her best work for Argo, Cadet, and Chess is here. Although there are a handful of unreleased tracks, the point behind this set is to provide a thorough overview of the most pivotal years in James' career, and on that level, it succeeds tremendously. Like many career-spanning sets, it does dip slightly in quality on the last disc, but not enough to make this anything less than an essential addition to a thorough blues library, since even on the lesser material, she sounds terrific. As a matter of fact, it's rather astonishing how strong all these recordings are, from her terrific vocals to the songs themselves. It's a shame it didn't come out with the first round of *Chess Box*es, but it was worth the wait. *—Stephen Thomas Erlewine*

Matriarch of the Blues / Dec. 12, 2000 / Private Music ♦♦♦

Having long ago established herself among the royalty of modern blues, Queen Etta seems rather content to sit back on her throne and her laurels and coast through a collection of classic and contemporary compositions. Unfortunately, her descendant band appears equally happy to sit back with her instead of working to shoot up the standards with another round of youthful vitality. The album opens with a rendition of Bob Dylan's "Gotta Serve Somebody" which serves more as a sleepy suggestion than a blues-injected imperative. While Al Green's "Rhymes" sounds very much like the Reverend, Etta's version of "Try a Little Tenderness" does phrase the slow dance in some subtly new directions. The real difference shows up about midway through when the Matriarch takes on the Glitter Twins with a raunchy slink through "Miss You" whose draggier pace and intermittent woofs gives the song that much more sex appeal. Otis Redding's "Hawg for Ya" slops with similar raunch. Ms. James does change things up with an educated and edifying stripped "Let's Straighten It Out" which builds musically as Etta lays down lessons of love and the woman's heart. Another exciting change is the funkification of John Fogerty's "Born on the Bayou," which strains the Clearwater through JB's "Hot Pants." After a gentle shout and sway through Brother Ray Charles' "Come Back Baby," the Queen retakes her throne while taking back her royal pet "Hound Dog" from the King with a swampy rendition of the Lieber and Stoller classic that appears to be more born on the bayou than that track. *—Matthew Robinson*

Tell Mama: The Complete Muscle Shoals Sessions / Apr. 24, 2001 / MCA/Chess ♦♦♦♦♦

As the title suggests, this is the definitive edition of Etta James' *Tell Mama* long-player. For this single-disc release the original album is augmented with five previously unissued tracks—documented during James' four Muscle Shoals sessions circa 1967-1968. The question of why a rural Alabama town became a conduit for some of the most memorable and instantly identifiable grooves may still be up for debate. The evidence exists in droves and *At Last* could certainly be considered exhibit A. These sessions feature the same impact that would redirect several first ladies of soul. Notable among them are Dusty Springfield's *Dusty in Memphis*, Aretha Franklin's *I Never Loved a Man (The Way I Love You)*, and to somewhat lesser acclaim, Jackie DeShannon's *Jackie*. *At Last* showcases some of the unique and admittedly darker qualities of what might best be described as R&B noir. "I'd Rather Go Blind," "Steal Away," "I'm Gonna Take What He's Got" all exemplify the essence of the blues—making the best of a bad situation. The flip side of the somber subject matter is the satisfying conviction in the music—which is where the remastering becomes particularly noticeable. No longer does the brass section sound alternately muffled or harsh as it has on previous releases. Likewise, the churning Hammond B-3 organ swells with rich textures. Perhaps the most sonically evident improvements are the subtle ones, such as the supple fretwork on "Sweet Dreams," "I'd Rather Go Blind," and the jazzy percussive shuffle of "The Same Rope"—which provided blue-eyed soul maven Van Morrison with the inspiration for the groove featured on his own "Sweet Dreams." *—Lindsay Planer*

Blue Gardenia / Aug. 21, 2001 / Private Music ♦♦♦

The legendary blues singer indeed lives up to the silly cliché about being able to sing the phone book and make it sound rich, meaningful, and soulful. Still, it's always exciting to hear her tackle materials she's missed before. Here she shifts gears impressively into the intimate jazz club mode, performing beautifully arranged takes on a wide variety of standards (from "Come Rain or Come Shine" to "Cry Me a River") under the direction of producer John Snyder and arranger/pianist Cedar Walton. Those two gathered a handful of great jazz players and recorded the initial tracks without James, who had a touch of the flu. A few months later she had recovered and did the amazing vocal sessions which truly sound live and in synch with the music. Beginning with the redemptive theme of "This Bitter Earth," each song allows her to explore both tenderness and guttural emotions, even a little irony on clever twists like "He's Funny That Way." There are also perfectly placed spotlights for the featured musicians. "This Bitter Earth" and "He's Funny That Way" feature a thoughtful improvisation by Walton, while Duke Ellington's "In My Solitude" has a passionate interlude by tenor saxophonist Red Holloway. Most of the vocals are textured over a bed of simmering brass, adding to the old school big band flavor that creates the atmosphere for the project. It's certainly common for great artists to thank their parents for various influences, but James goes one step further on the title track, allowing her mom to sing the tune; mom is no match for her daughter, but it's still a unique touch that adds emotional dimension to an already emotionally rich affair. *—Jonathan Widran*

Burnin' Down the House: Live at the House of Blues / May 7, 2002 / Private Music ♦♦♦♦

Playing *Burnin' Down the House* right after you have listened to some of Etta James' early recordings is quite revealing. The veteran soul/blues singer was only 16 when, in 1954, she made her first recordings for Modern Records; she was 63 when this excellent live album was recorded at the House of Blues in West Hollywood, CA, in December 2001—and it is obvious that vocally, she didn't lose anything along the way. Backed by a tight and rock-solid band, James demonstrates that her big, full voice lost none of its richness between 1954 and 2001. The Los Angeles native sounds as vital as ever, and she has no problem going that extra mile on gutsy performances of "Something's Got a Hold on Me," "I'd Rather Go Blind," "At Last," and other hits. For the most part, this is a soul concert; however, James makes a triumphant detour into electric urban blues on "I Just Want to Make Love to You" (one of the many Willie Dixon gems that Muddy Waters recorded for Chess in the '50s) and B.B. King's "Rock Me, Baby." The veteran singer pleasantly surprises us with some unlikely medleys; "I Just Want to Make Love to You" is successfully combined with Steppenwolf's "Born to Be Wild," and even more intriguing is her ability to unite the standard "My Funny Valentine" with two of Al Green's '70s hits ("Love and Happiness" and "Take Me to the River"). Some longtime fans may be disappointed to learn that she doesn't perform either "Tell Mama" or "Roll With Me Henry," aka "The Wallflower"; regardless, *Burnin' Down the House* is an exciting and powerful document of James at 63. *—Alex Henderson*

Sadie James

Vocals / Classic Female Blues, Dirty Blues

When it comes to the blues genre, the surname "James" brings to mind reverb-drenched electric slide guitars, and the Elmore James' tale of brooms being dusted. Or, the blues fan might immediately think of the sweet country blues artist, Skip James, his intricate and gentle fingerpicking and eerie falsetto vocals that were imitated by rock groups such as Cream and Canned Heat. The slight recording career of Sadie James consists of only two songs cut for Victor in 1927; and although these numbers have been reissued several times, she remains an ultra-obscure artist, not one whose name is likely to come up when blues fans are playing the "James game." This situation is possibly shameful, as it means an essential bit of philosophy, the answer to one of life's great questions is going unheard and undiscovered, mainly "What Makes a Bow-Legged Woman Crazy?" Actually, when the full title of this song is printed it makes even more sense: "What Makes a Bow-Legged Woman Crazy About Her Knock-Kneed Man."

James was one of dozens of female blues singers who cut songs in this period with lyrics ranging from slightly to incredibly nasty, accompanied usually by a pianist and sometimes a clarinet, trumpet, or banjo. For every classic female blues artist who became a big cheese, such as Bessie Smith or Alberta Hunter, there were many others such as James who only recorded a couple of numbers before dropping off the face of the earth. Tracks cut by these singers, including Edna Johnson, Alura Mack, and Coletha Simpson, among others, have been compiled on collections such as *Blue Girls, Vol. 1: 1924-1930* on the Document label. *—Eugene Chadbourne*

Skip James (Nehemiah Curtis James)

b. Jun. 21, 1902, Bentonia, MS, **d.** Oct. 3, 1969, Philadelphia, PA

Vocals, Kazoo, Songwriter, Piano, Guitar, Organ / Blues Revival, Delta Blues, Prewar Country Blues, Country Blues

Among the earliest and most influential Delta bluesmen to record, Skip James was the best known proponent of the so-called Bentonia school of blues players, a genre strain invested with as much fanciful scholarly "research" as any. Coupling an oddball guitar tuning set against eerie, falsetto vocals, James' early recordings could make the hair stand up on the back of your neck. Even more surprising was when blues scholars rediscovered him in the '60s and found his singing and playing skills intact. Influencing everyone from a young Robert Johnson (Skip's "Devil Got My Woman" became the basis of Johnson's "Hellhound on My Trail") to Eric Clapton (who recorded James' "I'm So Glad" on the first Cream album), Skip James' music, while from a commonly shared regional tradition, remains infused with his own unique personal spirit. —*Cub Koda*

She Lyin' / 1964 / Genes ✦✦✦✦✦

By the time James had been rediscovered in the '60s, he was still capable of playing entrancing, dynamic music, but was much less consistent and not as striking a vocalist. It was a testimony to his greatness that he still managed to make compelling records, and he was among the best storytellers and dramatic singers in the traditional realm. This mid-'60s CD features songs James recorded for the Adelphi label in 1964 that were never issued. It's hard to understand why this wasn't issued at the time it was recorded; it's just as solid as the albums James recorded for Columbia during the same period. —*Ron Wynn*

Today! / 1964 / Vanguard ✦✦✦✦

The 12 sides that comprise *Today!* are among the best James would record after his rediscovery in the '60s. His playing may be a bit less intricate than that captured on his legendary 78s from the '30s, but his unique falsetto sounds no less troubled or haunting than before on this album's definitive performances of "Hard Times Killing Floor Blues," "Special Rider Blues," and one of James' few later compositions, "Washington D.C. Hospital Center Blues." Additionally, modern recording techniques offer a better aural rendering of James' unique guitar fingerpicking and piano playing, making this album an easier listen than the dim, scratchy albums of 78 transfers available under various titles. This is a must-have collection for all acoustic blues and James fans, as well as a fine introduction for curious listeners unfamiliar with the blues' most uncompromising, spooked visions. —*Brian Beatty*

Greatest of the Delta Blues Singers / 1964 / Biograph ✦✦✦✦✦

Shortly after his triumphant resurrection at the 1964 Newport Folk Festival, Skip James returned to the recording studio for the first time in over three decades to cut the 12 sides which comprise the superb *Greatest of the Delta Blues Singers*, a career-capping overview which reprises some of the songs from his 1931 Paramount sessions and introduces a half-dozen new compositions as well. Although his guitar skills have lost a step in the intervening years, the passage of time has only made James' vocals that much more expressive; his new material is especially devastating, in particular "Sick Bed Blues" and "Washington D.C. Hospital Center Blues," both detailing the fight with cancer that eventually led to his death. —*Jason Ankeny*

☆ Skip James Today! / 1965 / Vanguard ✦✦✦✦✦

As quiet as it was kept then, Skip James might have made the best music of anyone who resurfaced during the mid-'60s "rediscovery" era for Mississippi country blues types. Certainly, there weren't many albums made during that time as good as this one; wonderful vocals, superb guitar and a couple of tunes with tasty piano make this essential. —*Ron Wynn*

Devil Got My Woman / 1968 / Vanguard ✦✦✦

Skip James made his original reputation with 17 recordings that he cut during February 1931 when he was 28. Although fluent on both the guitar and (to a lesser extent) the piano, James was most notable for his storytelling lyrics, his haunting high-pitched voice and his distinctive interpretations of the Delta blues. James was rediscovered 33 years after his early recordings, in time to appear at the 1964 Newport Folk Festival. He was quite active during 1964-1966, making the music on this solo CD (his last record) three years before his death in 1969. One can easily hear the influence that Skip James' music had on the then flourishing folk music movement and he still sang his country blues with great intensity. —*Scott Yanow*

Complete 1931 Session / 1986 / Yazoo ✦✦✦✦✦

Skip James estimated that he recorded 26 sides for the Paramount label in 1931, but no one has ever turned up more than the 18 songs on this disc in any form. This was the first comprehensive collection of James' early music, showcasing his piano playing as well as his skills with a guitar, and was essential listening in the '80s. However, the collection was only partly successful on a technical level. Paramount had been notorious for using the poorest and cheapest materials in its pressings and later junked its masters. Based on surviving production 78s, the quality of this release therefore left a lot to be desired even from a historical point of view. Yazoo later upgraded and retitled the collection when better sources and transferring techniques became available (see *The Complete Early Recordings of Skip James*). —*Bruce Eder*

Complete Recorded Works (1931) / 1990 / Document ✦✦✦✦✦

Document's *Complete Recorded Works (1931)* collects the 18 Skip James performances known to exist from his Paramount recordings of 1931, including career highlights like "Hard Time Killin' Floor Blues," "I'm So Glad," and "Devil Got My Woman." Though it's been supplanted by compilations with better notes and emphasis on archival sound quality (including Yazoo's *Complete Early Recordings*), it's still an excellent collection of performances by one of the best blues artists of all time. —*Thom Owens*

★ The Complete Early Recordings of Skip James / 1994 / Yazoo ✦✦✦✦✦

The Complete Early Recordings CD showcases a true guitar virtuoso who was no slouch on the piano either. His break on "Illinois Blues" is almost off-putting in the nonchalance with which he twists the notes around, and "How Long 'Buck'" features him giving forth some funky piano in an almost playful manner. This is a remastered edition of an earlier Yazoo collection, and features the same 18 songs that appeared on Document's *Complete Recorded Works*, but the sound quality is still a problem at times. High-quality sources for "What Am I to Do Blues," "4 O'Clock Blues," and several other of the numbers here are simply not known to exist, but these are the best-known editions of the songs until better 78 discs happen to turn up (if ever). Regardless of the surface noise, it is a delight listening to James' rippling guitar run on "4 O'Clock Blues" or his piano improvising (and improvising the percussion by pounding away with his feet) on "20-20 Blues." And his fiercely intense original rendition of "I'm So Glad" makes the repopularized version by Eric Clapton and Cream from the '60s seem like easygoing pop. Actually, James' vocals tend to suffer under the weight of the surface defects far more than his playing—the source discs distort on high-volume passages, which mostly occurs with his singing rather than his playing. Therefore, fans of blues guitar or piano need have no hesitation in picking this disc up. *The Complete Early Recordings* ought to be heard by anyone who claims an interest in the blues. —*Bruce Eder*

Live: Boston, 1964 / Jun. 2, 1994 / Document ✦✦✦

These recordings, made in coffee houses during the folk boom and James' comeback after 30 years of obscurity, find him still in remarkable control of his talents. His guitar and piano playing are agile and sensitive and his high tenor still sends a shiver down the spine. The sound is very good (save for the occasional drop out), but more importantly the performances are first rate, and with a little imagination you can put yourself right there in the room with this enormous talent. —*Tim Sheridan*

Blues from the Delta / Aug. 11, 1998 / Vanguard ✦✦✦✦

Drawing 18 tracks from Skip James' rediscovery recordings made on Vanguard Records—*Today!* and *Devil Got My Woman*, plus two previously unreleased tracks—*Blues From the Delta* is over 75 minutes of the best tracks James ever recorded. Where the definitive cuts of many of these songs haven't been preserved by modern technology without considerable flaws, these tracks, recorded in 1966 and 1968 (respectively), are clear and crisp, highlighting James' tremendous talents. Though it had been 35 years since James first recording sessions, he still possessed his spooky melodic sense, his distinctive guitar and piano playing, and the eerie falsetto that made his original recordings so sought after. These might not be the most historically relevant versions of James' quintessential works, but they are by no means inferior, and on the whole, are much easier to listen to. —*Matt Fink*

Complete Bloomington Indiana Concert, Vol. 1 (3/30/68) / Oct. 12, 1999 / Document ✦✦✦

This is part one of a concert recorded March 30, 1968, in Bloomington, IN, spotlighting one of the most influential Delta blues artists, Skip James, at the end of his career. It's eerie and heartbreaking to listen to what essentially amounts to a retrospective by a man who would pass away only seven months following this performance. James covered all the bases on this occasion from the spirituals "God is Real" and "Look at the People (Got to Go to Judgement)" to '60s originals "Lorenzo Blues," "Sickbed Blues," and "Washington D.C. Hospital Center Blues." James also played his familiar classics from the '30s, "Devil Got My Woman" and "I'm So Glad." It is to the credit of Document Records that they included James' spoken introductions to these songs, allowing the listener to gain further insight into the mind and heart of one of the preeminent acoustic blues performers of the 20th century. —*Al Campbell*

Complete Bloomington Indiana Concert, Vol. 2 (3/30/68) / Oct. 12, 1999 / Document ✦✦✦

Steve James

b. Jul. 15, 1950, New York, NY [Manhattan]

AMG Contributor, Slide Guitar, Vocals, Mandolin, Guitar / Contemporary Blues

A native of New York City (born 1950), James got into the blues via his father's guitar (at age 13) and phonograph (thanks to his father's 78s by Leadbelly and Josh White). He was primarily self-taught, although he received tutelage from veterans such as Furry Lewis, Sam McGee and Lum Guffin, after moving to Tennessee in the early '70s. He also trained in luthiery at Gurian Guitars (1970-1971) and was a DJ at WEVL in Memphis. In 1977 he settled in San Antonio, where he played solo and sometimes with R&B sax legend Clifford Scott. After moving to Austin he signed with Antone's Records in 1991. In addition to his solo CDs like 1993's *Two Track Mind*, 1996's *Art and Grit* and 2000's *Boom Chang*, he has backed blues singers Gary Primich and Angela Strehli on record, as well as singer-songwriter James McMurtry and others. He also served as a contributing editor to *Acoustic Guitar* magazine. —*Dan Forte*

Two Track Mind / 1993 / Discovery ✦✦✦

A rarity in today's field of acoustic blues pickers; a guitarist with encyclopedic knowledge who never sounds academic. James embraces a wide scope of fingerpicking styles—Piedmont school ragtime, hokum ("Huggin' and Chalkin'"), country (Sam McGee is the source of two tunes here), and slide (his showstopping take on Sylvester Weaver's "Guitar Rag") with super technique, humor, and a relaxed ease that borders on cockiness. Only one original here, but that situation was to be rectified on Steve's follow-up. —*Dan Forte*

● American Primitive / 1994 / Antone's ✦✦✦✦✦

Utilizing a jug band of fellow Austinites Danny Barnes (tenor guitar and banjo) and Mark Rubin (stand-up bass and Sousaphone—both of the Bad Livers) and harpist Gary Primich on some tracks, James sounds more mature here, evidenced by six originals (the John Hurt-esque "Talco Girl" is particularly nice) and one collaboration with bassist/

songwriter Sarah Brown ("My Last Good Car") and effective rather than affected vocals. Stellar guitar throughout, with an added treat: James' blues mandolin on "Midnight Blues." *—Dan Forte*

Art & Grit / Sep. 9, 1996 / Discovery ✦✦✦✦✦
James' first album was a solo effort; his second added a small combo. *Art and Grit*, his third, is a virtual celebration of acoustic string instruments. The Austin "jug band" of *American Primitive*—James, Danny Barnes, Mark Rubin, and Gary Primich—reunites on three cuts and forms the nucleus of three others. Guitar virtuoso Rob Brozman and Asleep at the Wheel's Cindy Cashdollar make guest appearances, and all told there are no fewer than eleven different instrument lineups on the disc, with guitars of many types (standard, slide, Hawaiian, and tenor), banjos (6- and 4-string), and mandolins presented solo and in various combinations. Most memorable cuts are James' delightfully archaic banjo rendition of the century-old "Buddy Bolden's Blues" and the joyfully clanging triple guitar attack on "Downbound Train" (an obscure Chuck Berry album cut, based on an old temperance song). Recording quality is exceptionally vivid, capturing the distinctive timbre of each instrument and making *Art and Grit* an old-timey blues lovers' delight. *—Steve Hoffman*

Not for Highway Use: Austin Sessions 1988–1995 / Jan. 1, 2000 / Settlement ✦✦✦

Boom Chang / Jun. 6, 2000 / Burnside ✦✦✦✦
Boom Chang is guitarist Steve James' fourth release overall but his debut for Burnside Records. This acoustic roots and blues disc features guest appearances from bassist Mark Rubin of the Bad Livers (playing tuba!), Alvin Youngblood Hart on guitar and mandolin, Cindy Cashdollar on Hawaiian guitar and Dobro, and harp master Gary Primich. The mood on these 14 tracks is raw and fun from James' rewriting of Stack Lee's "Blues to Country Fool" originally by Delta bluesman Bo Carter to the jugband workout on the original "Saturday Night in Jail." *—Al Campbell*

Frankie "Half-Pint" Jaxon

b. Feb. 3, 1895, Montgomery, AL, **d.** Los Angeles, CA
Vocals / East Coast Blues, Jive, Swing, Vaudeville Blues
Frankie "Half Pint" Jaxon was an eccentric singer and a mysterious figure who disappeared after the mid-'40s. Called "Half Pint" due to being 5'2", Jaxon (who was an orphan) grew up in Kansas City. At 15 he began singing in variety shows and at clubs. He toured with a theatrical troupe in Texas and Oklahoma, forming with Miss Gallie De Gaston a song and dance team that did well in vaudeville during 1912-1924. When he was 21, Jaxon began working regularly in Atlantic City (usually the Paradise Café) in the summer and the Sunset Café in Chicago in the winter. An expert at staging shows, Half Pint helped Bessie Smith and Ethel Waters (among others) put on their productions. Jaxon, who also worked as a female impersonator, a pianist-singer and a saxophonist, was mostly in Chicago during 1927-1941, a period when he made many recordings. In 1930 he formed the Quarts of Joy and he often appeared on the radio in the '30s. Jaxon used his best-known composition "Fan It" (which would later be recorded by Woody Herman) as a trademark song. Although still popular, Jaxon dropped out of music altogether in 1941, working for the government in Washington, D.C. In 1944 he moved to Los Angeles and largely disappeared, never to be heard from again by the musical world. Half Pint Jaxon's recordings as a leader (which date from 1926-1940) include such sidemen as washboardist Jasper Taylor, pianist Georgia Tom Dorsey, banjoist Ikey Robinson, cornetist Punch Miller, the Harlem Hamfats (1937-1938), clarinetist Barney Bigard, pianist Lil Armstrong, and trumpeter Henry "Red" Allen. *—Scott Yanow*

Frankie "Half-Pint" Jaxon (1927–1940) / Oct. 1, 1992 / Story of the Blues ✦✦✦✦
Frankie "Half-Pint" Jaxon definitely occupied his own musical niche. An eccentric singer who also worked as a female impersonator, Jaxon's music straddled the boundaries between jazz, blues and hokum. This 1992 CD sampling of his recordings (19 performances from a 13-year period) mostly consist of leftover tracks overlooked by other reissue programs although the Document series has since reissued the complete Half-Pint Jaxon. This version of "Operation Blues" was previously unissued, and four other numbers are taken from test pressings. The recording quality varies quite a bit from session to session, as does the personnel. Jaxon is heard backed by pianist Blanche Smith Watson, with a big band in 1933, and joined by such notable players as banjoist Ikey Robinson, pianist Georgia Tom Dorsey, cornetist Punch Miller and pianist Lil Armstrong, among many others. Some of the double entendre songs are either obvious or silly, and Jaxon's occasional decision to play the part of a foolish woman may not be to everyone's taste, but there is some good music here. Among the selections are "Corinne Blues," "You Got to Wet It," "Chocolate to the Bone," "Spank It" and "When a Woman Gets the Blues." *—Scott Yanow*

● **Complete Recorded Works, Vol. 1: 1926–1929** / Sep. 1, 1994 / Document ✦✦✦✦

Complete Recorded Works, Vol. 2: 1929–1937 / Sep. 1, 1994 / Document ✦✦✦

Complete Recorded Works, Vol. 3 / Sep. 1, 1994 / Document ✦✦✦

Blind Lemon Jefferson

b. Sep. 1893, Couchman, TX, **d.** Dec. 1929, Chicago, IL
Vocals, Guitar / Prewar Gospel Blues, Field Recordings, Country Blues, Acoustic Texas Blues
Country blues guitarist and vocalist Blind Lemon Jefferson is indisputably one of the main figures in country blues. He was of the highest in many regards, being one of the founders of Texas blues (along with Texas Alexander), one of the most influential country bluesmen of all time, one of the most popular bluesmen of the '20s, and the first truly commercially successful male blues performer. Up until Jefferson's achievements, the only real successful blues recordings were by women performers, including Bessie Smith and Ida Cox, who usually sang songs written by others and accompanied by a band. With Jefferson came a blues artist who was solo, self-accompanied, and performing a great deal of original material in addition to the more familiar repertoire of folk standards and shouts. These originals include his most well-known songs: "Matchbox Blues," "See That My Grave Is Kept Clean," and "Black Snake Moan." In all, Blind Lemon Jefferson recorded almost 100 songs in just a few years, making his mark on not only the bluesmen of the time (including Leadbelly and Lightnin' Hopkins) but also on music fans in the years to come. The legacy of Jefferson's unique and powerful sound did not fade with the passing decades.

Many specifics on the life of Blind Lemon Jefferson are not available, but general information on the man and his career can be traced somewhat through recordings, a few public records, and the memories of those who knew him. Although his birth has long been placed in July of 1897, research almost a century later uncovered a census record that listed his birth in September of 1893. Despite the uncertainty surrounding his birth date, a few things are certain: Jefferson was born on a farm in Couchman, TX, outside of Wortham, and, blind from the time of birth, he grew up as one of seven children. Around 1912, he began playing guitar and singing at picnics and parties in his home area. His musical influences included not only the singing of the cotton pickers and local guitar players but also the guitarists among the area's Mexican workers who often incorporated flamenco patterns in their playing. These influences eventually led to Jefferson's unique style of complex phrases and intricate, yet fast, finger work. Within a couple of years, Jefferson widened his performing radius to include Groesbeck, Buffalo, Waco, and other surrounding towns. Sometime around 1915, Jefferson also began playing in Dallas and, by 1917, was a resident of the city. He was most often found playing in the Deep Ellum area of Dallas where he eventually met another bluesman who would one day be famous, Leadbelly. Although Leadbelly was the senior bluesman of the two, it is generally recognized that Jefferson was the better guitarist. Leadbelly was so impressed with Blind Lemon Jefferson, in fact, that he would later record songs in tribute to Jefferson's ability, including the song, "Blind Lemon's Blues." The two men even played together for a short while, sometime before Leadbelly's first prison sentence.

From the late teens into the early '20s, Blind Lemon Jefferson traveled and performed his passionate brand of blues, hitting (at the very least) the Mississippi Delta and Memphis regions, although it is likely that his travels took him further. In 1922 or 1923 he married a woman named Roberta with whom he would have children, including a boy, in the mid-'20s. It was in 1925 that a Texas talent scout finally made a demo recording of Jefferson and sent it to Mayo Williams at Paramount Records in Chicago. Jefferson was soon (circa 12/25 and 1/26) brought to Chicago to record for the first time. The results were two gospel songs: "I Want to Be Like Jesus in My Heart" and "All I Want Is That Pure Religion," both of which were released under the pseudonym Deacon L.J. Bates. Two months later, Jefferson began recording blues 78s under his own name, but that initial session wasn't the last time Jefferson recorded under a pseudonym. In 1927, "He Arose From the Dead" and "Where Shall I Be?" were released under the names Deacon L.J. Bates and Elder J.C. Brown for the Paramount and Herwin labels, respectively. Jefferson recorded over 90 songs total in less than four years' time. Almost all of his recordings were for the Paramount label, with the exception of his two-day session for OKeh, which took place in Atlanta in March of 1927. This session resulted in the second version of "That Black Snake Moan," (11/26) this time entitled "Black Snake Moan," as well as the first recording of another song that became one of Jefferson's most famous originals, "Matchbox Blues," which he recorded again for Paramount just one month later. Jefferson's records did well immediately, making him one of the best-selling race recording artists of the time. This is surprising considering his decidedly noncommercial sound; his high, eerie voice (often described as having a "lonesome" sound), the desperate (and sometimes suggestive) nature of his lyrics, and his often-complex guitar work all combined into a particularly raw and hard-hitting blues.

In addition to his frequent recording sessions in Chicago throughout the late '20s, Blind Lemon Jefferson still performed in Texas and traveled around the South. He played Chicago rent parties, performed at St. Louis' Booker T. Washington Theater, and even worked some with Son House collaborator Rev. Rubin Lacy while in Mississippi. In late September of 1929, Jefferson went to Paramount's studios in Richmond, IN, for a fruitful session that included two songs—"Bed Springs Blues" and "Yo Yo Blues"—that were also issued on the Broadway label. Jefferson was back in Chicago in December of 1929 when, sadly, he was found dead following a particularly cold snowstorm. There are several stories regarding his death: It has been said that he got lost in the storm after leaving a friend's party at a late hour, or that he was abandoned by his chauffeur, or was killed in a car accident, while yet another version claims Jefferson had a heart attack and froze in the snow. Regardless, the influential bluesman was still in his thirties when he died, and no death certificate was issued, so the date of his passing is only known to be toward the end of December. Pianist and labelmate Will Ezell escorted Jefferson's body back to Wortham, TX, where Blind Lemon Jefferson was laid to rest, purportedly on New Year's Day, 1930. Unfortunately for the author of the pleading "See That My Grave Is Kept Clean," the grave itself went unmarked. This was finally remedied in 1967 when a metal Texas Historical Marker was placed on the approximate spot. By the '90s, however, Jefferson's grave was discovered to be in disrepair. A fundraiser was organized and, thanks to the efforts and donations of blues fans around the world, a granite headstone was finally placed upon Jefferson's grave, inscribed with his lyric, "Lord, it's one kind favor I'll ask of you. See that my grave is kept clean." It was also discovered during the preparation of the headstone that there is no support for the date widely believed to be that of Jefferson's birth—July 1897 (which even appeared on the original grave marker)—while the census documents in the State Archives listed Lemon Jefferson's birth to be in September of 1893. Thus, the new date was put on the gravestone.

Blind Lemon Jefferson was to Texas blues what Charley Patton was to Mississippi blues. His performances had a direct influence upon such legendary Texas musicians as Lightnin' Hopkins, T-Bone Walker, and Leadbelly, while his recordings helped bring his influence to an even larger audience. In the decades since, Jefferson's songs have been covered by countless musicians including Bob Dylan, John Hammond Jr., and Kelly Joe Phelps, to name just a few. The late '50s and early '60s brought the reissue of some of Jefferson's recordings on the Riverside and Milestone labels, sparking a renewal of widespread public interest in the bluesman. As a result, Blind Lemon Jefferson Clubs were opened in California and New York during the '60s, and the rock band Jefferson

Airplane reputedly chose their name after the great bluesman. A good single album compiling selections of Jefferson's music remains the Yazoo label's appropriately titled *King of the Country Blues*, which was eventually remastered for CD release. For completists, the Document label has since issued his entire recorded works in a four-volume CD series. In 1980, Blind Lemon Jefferson was inducted into the Blues Foundation's Hall of Fame. *—Joslyn Layne*

Blind Lemon Jefferson / Mar. 1961 / Milestone ♦♦♦♦♦
Solid collection (73 minutes' worth) of some of Lemon's best. "Jack O'Diamond Blues," "Match Box Blues," and "That Black Snake Moan" are all on board, and with the Sonic Solutions System employed on the audio restoration end, the result is about the best these surviving 60-year-old 78s have ever sounded. *—Cub Koda*

★ **King of the Country Blues** / 1985 / Yazoo ♦♦♦♦♦
King of the Country Blues compiles 28 of Blind Lemon Jefferson's finest songs, all presented in the original '20s versions. It is the finest introduction to the guitarist—as well as the most effective, concise retrospective—ever assembled. *—Thom Owens*

Complete Recorded Works, Vol. 1-4 / 1991 / Document ♦♦♦
Document's four-part series covering the complete late-'20s recordings of Blind Lemon Jefferson—each available as separate volumes—is an invaluable purchase for dedicated fans or academics. For less-interested listeners, the long running time, exacting chronological sequencing, poor fidelity (all cuts are transferred from original acetates and 78s), and number of performances will be hard to digest. *—Thom Owens*

Complete Recorded Works, Vol. 3 (1928) / 1991 / Document ♦♦♦♦♦
The third volume in Document's *Complete Recorded Works* series of Blind Lemon Jefferson collections features 21 songs, all recorded during 1928. Though the period included one stone-cold classic ("See That My Grave Is Kept Clean") and a few intriguing novelties ("Balky Mule Blues," "Piney Woods Money Mama"), most blues fans won't need to hear these tracks. *Complete Recorded Works, Vol. 3 (1928)* remains an interesting curiosity for completists and academics, exactingly sequenced but not as listenable as the more popular collections available. *—Thom Owens*

Complete Recorded Works, Vol. 4 (1929) / 1991 / Document ♦♦♦
Document's *Complete Recorded Works, Vol. 4 (1929)* is the final volume in a series of Blind Lemon Jefferson collections, reissuing the last 23 tracks he recorded before his tragic death in December. Despite a raft of great performances (including "Long Distance Moan" and "Black Snake Moan No. 2"), the lengthy running time and poor fidelity make it of only marginal interest to the great majority of blues fans. *—Thom Owens*

Moanin' All Over / Apr. 1996 / Tradition ♦♦♦
This ten-track, 26 1/2-minute mid-priced disc is a reissue of the Olympic Records LP *Blind Lemon Jefferson* (7134), and contains recordings originally made for Paramount Records in the '20s, among them "The Black Snake Moan." Despite sonic cleansing, the tracks are still primitive sounding, but Jefferson's distinctive singing and guitar playing can still be appreciated. For neophytes, this short, low-cost album provides a good curtain-raiser to Jefferson's work. *—William Ruhlmann*

The Best of Blind Lemon Jefferson / Oct. 10, 2000 / Yazoo ♦♦♦♦
Blind Lemon Jefferson's life contains a great deal of mystery. The date of his birth is uncertain, and the cause of his death—heart failure? freezing during a blizzard?—is unknown. What is known is that he left behind a number of blues recordings on which he accompanied himself on guitar. His expressive vocals and guitar work shine on well-worn classics like "Match Box Blues" or on unfamiliar songs like "Black Horse Blues." Preserving the fidelity of these recordings has been made difficult by poorly pressed records as well as the condition of the rare 78s. This is evident on "'Lectric Chair Blues" and "Prison Cell Blues," where surface noise cuts into the clarity of the lyrics. Still, both of these songs are effectively edgy because of their subject matter, with "'Lectric Chair Blues" being particularly chilling. Despite difficulties with fidelity, the majority of the vocals and guitar work are easy to discern and enjoy. The laid-back, relaxed quality of songs like "Bed Spring Blues" and "See That My Grave Is Kept Clean" are unpretentious and disarming. Jefferson also covers the unusual "He Arose From the Dead" and "I Want to Be Like Jesus in My Heart," two religious blues pieces (one can only hope that neither were recorded in the same session with "Bed Spring Blues"). Blake's guitar work covers a number of styles including boogie runs on "Rabbit Foot Blues" and slide on "Jack O' Diamond Blues." The liner notes cover what little is know about Jefferson and offer a good discussion of his vocal and guitar styles. With *The Best of Blind Lemon Jefferson*, Yazoo has done a fine job of preserving Jefferson's music and of documenting the early history of blues recordings. *—Ronnie D. Lankford Jr.*

The Jelly Roll Kings

Group / Contemporary Blues

The Jelly Roll Kings are a trio of state-of-the-art Mississippi Delta bluesmen who play their music raw and unvarnished, complete with lilting rhythms, dreamily atmospheric keyboards, dance-shuffle drums, and soul-drenched vocals. Led by guitarist Big Jack Johnson, the band includes two veterans of the Delta juke-joint scene—Frank Frost on keyboards and harmonica, and Sam Carr, the son of legendary blues musician Robert Nighthawk, on drums. Johnson, the group's guitarist, chief songwriter and lead vocalist, is the youngest of the three.

Carr began dancing at his father's gigs when he was eight and later took up drums. Harmonica player and keyboardist Frank Frost's background includes playing guitar for Sonny Boy Williamson II, recording in Nashville with Elvis Presley guitarist Scotty Moore, and releasing his own album on the Appaloosa label, *Frank Frost With Freddie and the Screamers*, in 1992. Frost also recorded an album for the British Charly label, *Frank Frost, Jelly Roll King: Charly Blues Masterworks Vol. 36.* . *—Richard Skelly*

● **Rockin' the Juke Joint Down** / 1979 / Earwig ♦♦♦♦
Michael Frank inaugurated his Earwig imprint with this 1979 album reteaming Frost, Johnson, and Carr in all their glory. Frank was mesmerized by the trio's almost telepathic musical interplay, a trait captured vividly by the album itself. This trio's repertoire was varied—the no-holds-barred "Slop Jar Blues" is offset by the bubbly instrumental "Sunshine Twist." Frost and Johnson share vocal duties. *—Bill Dahl*

Off Yonder Wall / Feb. 11, 1997 / Fat Possum ♦♦♦♦
The Jelly Roll Kings have recorded one album for the Fat Possum/Capricorn label, 1997's *Off Yonder Wall*. Produced by author/impresario Robert Palmer, the album does a superb job of capturing the complex interplay between Johnson, Carr, and Frost. The recording is suitably raw and stripped down, with a remarkable live club sound to it. The trio puts a fresh spin on old familiar blues standards like "That's Alright Mama" and "Baby Please Don't Go," while their originals remain true to the spirit of '90s-era Delta juke-joint blues. The result is one of the most unique-sounding albums of the year. *—Richard Skelly*

Johnny Jenkins

b. 1939, Macon, GA

Guitar / R&B

Guitarist, singer, and songwriter Johnny Jenkins may have had a long pause between records, but his heart, ears and mind were always close to blues music. Jenkins never wanted to be a professional musician, and always worked day jobs, including digging wells, logging and mechanic work. Jenkins' style is at times reminiscent of Elmore James, and at other times, one can hear echoes of Jimi Hendrix in Jenkins' guitar playing—probably because Jenkins was a seminal influence on Hendrix.

Jenkins, born in Macon, GA, in 1939, grew up in a rural area called Swift Creek. He listened to a battery-powered radio and first heard the sounds of blues and classic R&B, artists like Bill Doggett, Bull Moose Jackson, and others. Jenkins built his first guitar out of a cigar box and rubber bands when he was nine, and began playing at a gas station for tips. He played it left-handed and upside down, and this practice continued after his older sister bought him a real guitar a couple of years later.

Capricorn Records founder Phil Walden first heard Jenkins on a local radio talent show in 1959. Walden began to book Jenkins' band, the Pinetoppers, which included Otis Redding on lead vocals. Redding got his first big break in 1962 when he drove Jenkins to the Stax Studios in Memphis to record a follow-up to Jenkins' regional hit, "Love Twist." The producer encouraged the young Redding to take a turn at singing in the studio, and he recorded "These Arms of Mine" with some extra studio time. Redding's career began to take off and Jenkins was asked to become part of his band, but Jenkins refused, ironically because of his fear of airline travel.

Following Redding's untimely demise in an airplane crash, Jenkins stayed close to home, playing regionally and working day jobs to support his family. His unorthodox guitar style left lasting marks on the young, impressionable Jimi Hendrix, who came out to see Jenkins play while visiting relatives in the Macon area. Later, in 1969, Jenkins and Hendrix teamed up to play together at The Scene, a club owned by Steve Paul in New York. In 1970, Walden put Jenkins into the studio with several members of the Allman Brothers Band to record his debut album, *Ton-Ton Macoute!*, one of the fledgling Capricorn label's first releases. Although *Ton-Ton Macoute!* was released to high critical praise, the then-small label had other priorities to deal with, including the newly successful Allman Brothers.

In 1996, Capricorn founder Walden convinced Jenkins to record a "comeback" album, *Blessed Blues*. He's backed by a stellar cast of musicians, including Chuck Leavell on keyboards and Muscle Shoals percussionist Mickey Buckins. Capricorn also reissued Jenkins' now-legendary *Ton-Ton Macoute!* on compact disc in 1997. *—Richard Skelly*

● **Ton-Ton Macoute!** / 1970 / Capricorn ♦♦♦♦♦
What a fine bowl of Southern gumbo this Johnny Jenkins disc is. Aided and abetted by the likes of Duane Allman (this started as an Allman solo disc, but when he formed the Allman Brothers Band, Jenkins put his vocals over the tracks best suited), Dickey Betts, and those great guys from Muscle Shoals, Jenkins cooks on such cuts as "Down Along the Covell" from the pen of Bob Dylan, and Muddy Waters' "Rollin' Stone." But it is Dr. John's "I Walk on Guilded Splinters" which shines here and is the one which folks will recognize as the basis for Beck's hit "Loser." On the slippery "Blind Bats & Swamp Rats" you can almost feel the heat and humidity rolling out of the bayou. This reissue also includes the mighty fine bonus cuts "I Don't Want No Woman" and "My Love Will Never Die." Great Southern funk n' roll for the discerning listener. It even includes educational linear notes which tell the tale behind each cut. *—James Chrispell*

Blessed Blues / Aug. 13, 1996 / Capricorn ♦♦♦♦
Johnny Jenkins—a local legend around Macon, GA—released his second album, *Blessed Blues*, 26 years after releasing *Ton-Ton Macoute!* Featuring a selection of new songs, classic covers, and a new version of his 1962 hit "Miss Thing" (also known as "Love Twist"), *Blessed Blues* gives a good idea why Jenkins is revered in his home state. His playing is swampy, dirty, and impassioned—it is soaked in the sounds of the deep south. *Blessed Blues* doesn't clean up his sound at all, preferring to showcase Jenkins in all of his gritty glory. On the whole, it isn't quite as searing as *Ton-Ton Macoute!*—after all, that featured support by Duane Allman—but *Blessed Blues* proves that good things are worth waiting for. *—Thom Owens*

Beau Jocque (Andrus Espre)

b. Nov. 1, 1952, Duralde, LA, **d.** Sep. 10, 1999, Kinder, LA

Vocals, Accordion / Zydeco, Creole

Easily the biggest zydeco star of the '90s, Beau Jocque heralded the rise of the genre's new, urbanized style; infusing his high-octane sound with elements of rock, soul, hip-hop and even reggae, he bridged the gap between traditional Creole culture and contemporary music to create a funky, bass-heavy hybrid calculated for maximum mainstream appeal. Born Andrus Espre in Duralde, LA, in 1952, Jocque spent his early adult years working as an electrician, but in 1987 he suffered a serious back injury which left him paralyzed from the waist down for over a year; during his recovery period he picked up his father's Cajun accordion, but always bored by traditional zydeco, he set about updating the music more to his own contemporary tastes. Jocque and his wife Michelle then spent the next five years painstakingly researching zydeco clubs, discovering which kinds of songs earned the greatest response from patrons; at the same time he absorbed the music of Boozoo Chavis, drawn by his propulsive rhythms.

Finally, in 1991, he formed the Zydeco Hi-Rollers; the band was an immediate smash in the New Orleans circuit, drawing huge audiences—many of them new to the Creole dancehall scene—captivated by their hard-edged rhythms and Jocque's primal, cavernous vocals. A friendly rivalry with Chavis also increased his notoriety, and in 1993, the Hi-Rollers debuted with *Beau Jocque Boogie*, one of the best-selling zydeco records of all time. *Pick Up on This!* followed in 1994, and a year later they released the explosive live effort *Git It, Beau Jocque!*, which featured the hit "Give Him Cornbread." *Gonna Take You Downtown* appeared in 1996, followed two years later by *Check It Out, Lock It In, Crank It Up!* Beau Jocque died of a heart attack on September 10, 1999; the concert album *Give Him Cornbread, Live!* arrived nearly a year later. *—Jason Ankeny*

Beau Jocque Boogie / 1993 / Rounder ✦✦✦
Beau Jocque and the Zydeco Hi-Rollers represent the genre's new school; hip-hop and rap are an element of their style, as well as blues and R&B. Beau Jocque's music has the requisite kick and edge, with his vocals and non-stop excitement spilling out through such songs as "Richard's Club" and "Beau Jocque Boogie." Where he may raise eyebrows is his embrace of sampling technology alongside standard instrumentation. Jocque also speaks fluent French and covers some traditional songs, but puts more emphasis on his own music. This debut disc includes nine originals out of 14 numbers, with Jocque providing arrangements of classic tunes like "Oh Bye Moreau" and "Chere Allien" and establishing this band as prime challengers for honors as the top zydeco ensemble in the '90s. *—Ron Wynn*

Beau Jocque & the Zydeco Hi-Rollers / 1993 / Rounder ✦✦✦

My Name is Beau Jocque / 1994 / Paula ✦✦✦✦

● **Pick Up on This!** / Mar. 30, 1994 / Rounder ✦✦✦✦✦
Beau Jocque's first album for Rounder Records, *Pick Up on This!*, is arguably his best effort to date. The key is in the groove—there might not be much variety on the album, but he keeps the zesty zydeco rhythms pumping throughout. Jocque isn't the only one who shines, however. Every member of the band keeps things cooking, doing their best to ensure that *Pick Up on This!* is a first-rate party album. And that's exactly what it is. *—Thom Owens*

Git It, Beau Jocque! / 1995 / Rounder ✦✦✦

Nursery Rhyme / Nov. 28, 1995 / Beau Jocque ✦✦

Gonna Take You Downtown / 1996 / Rounder ✦✦✦✦✦
A stunning album of songs from all over the board. Beau Jocque here incorporates songs of his own making alongside those of other zydeco legends Clifton Chenier and Boozoo Chavis. To top it off, he throws in a couple from zydeco outsiders War and Bob Dylan, reformatted to force a dance. One of the main highlights of the album (and all Jocque albums, really) is the interplay between the more frantic Steve Charlot vocals and Jocque's slower, rougher returns. Jocque is always faster and a little more party-ready than Chenier, and this album displays that nicely. There are still some slightly easier-going pieces ("It's So Easy When You're Breezin'"). The things that set Jocque's band apart from other zydeco mainstays are the infusions of rock and funk, usually more or less missing from the genre. Stutter guitar and organ backings are no surprise in his music. If nothing else, pick it up for a cover of "Knockin' on Heaven's Door" that's more heartfelt than anything Guns N' Roses could ever muster. *—Adam Greenberg*

Check It Out, Lock It In, Crank It Up / Aug. 18, 1998 / Rounder ✦✦✦✦✦
Beau Jocque's fifth album for the Rounder imprint is a wide and varied effort showing musical growth and a depth previously unexplored on his previous outings. The High Rollers can still crank it out with a vengeance on tunes like "Come Go With Me" and "Like a Pot of Neckbones," and Bo's ear for a great cover like "Tequila," "Tighten Up," and "Keep a Knockin'" is just as well informed as ever. But musical surprises abound at every turn on this disc with the snaky slow blues "Going to the Country," the soul ballad "What You Gonna Do?," and a hip-hop mix of "Slide and Dip It" being particular standouts. *—Cub Koda*

Give Him Cornbread, Live! / Aug. 8, 2000 / Rounder ✦✦✦

The Best of Beau Jocque & The Zydeco Hi-Rollers / Aug. 14, 2001 / Rounder ✦✦✦✦

Johnny Nocturne Band

Group / Jump Blues, Modern Electric Blues, New Jack Swing
The Johnny Nocturne Band, led by saxophonist John Firmin, plays a mixture of instrumental jump blues and jazz covers from the '40s and '50s. Jazz and blues vocalist Brenda Boykin helps out on the band's first two albums for Bullseye Blues, *Wailin' Daddy* and *Shake 'Em Up*. The latter was recorded live in the studio with no overdubs and was produced by Firmin and David Luke. *Million Dollar Secret* followed in 1999. *—John Bush*

Wailin' Daddy / 1992 / Bullseye Blues ✦✦✦✦
A solid recreation of the jump blues genre from a modern perspective. *—Bill Dahl*

Shake 'Em Up / 1994 / Bullseye Blues ✦✦✦✦
Led by accomplished tenor saxman John Firmin, the Johnny Nocturne Band plays near-flawless renditions of '40s-era jump blues and swing. Featuring vocals by Brenda Boykin, *Shake 'Em Up* is a collection of bues and swing tunes recorded live in the studio. The eight-piece band blows through classics such as "Fool's Blues" and "I Ain't Got Nothin' But the Blues" while reproducing the feel and sound of a much larger orchestra, much of this due to the clever horn arrangements and robust playing of the four-piece horn section. *—Steve Kurutz*

● **Wild and Cool** / Mar. 10, 1998 / Bullseye Blues ✦✦✦✦
With a solid four-horn frontline that reads and solo in the fine old-time tradition of the territory bands of yore, the Johnny Nocturne Band come to the plate with their third album full of jazz heavily laced with blues. Leader and saxophonist John Firmin keeps his troops swinging throughout this 11-song set, working like a fine, precise machine regardless of the musical setting. Swing, bop, and blues with strong attachments to melody are the signposts here, and the playing on Bobby Troup's "Lemon Twist," "Tu ma qui te (Hey! Joli Blon)," "After the Lights Go Down Low" and "Don't Get Around Much Anymore" are among the numerous highlights. *—Cub Koda*

Million Dollar Secret / Oct. 26, 1999 / Bullseye Blues ✦✦✦✦
Saxophonist John Firmin's Johnny Nocturne Band has long been riding the top of the heap in the retro-swing sweepstakes, doing it better and longer than anybody. However, the band got a major kick in the pants with the addition of vocalist supremo Kim Nalley. A grade-A throwback to Ivey Washington, Dinah Washington, and Helen Humes, Nalley seductively purrs these tunes to life, giving a great band a great vocalist to front them. There's lots of retro swing out there, but this is the stuff that not only sounds right, but actually cooks the way this music is supposed to. Great, simply great. *—Cub Koda*

Alfred "Snuff" Johnson

b. Aug. 10, 1913, Cedar Creek, TX, **d.** Jan. 18, 2000
Vocals / Acoustic Texas Blues, Blues Gospel
Texas country bluesman Alfred "Snuff" Johnson played guitar since the '20s, but didn't perform "professionally" for another 60 years, and wasn't recorded until 1994. Johnson was born in Cedar Creek, TX, to parents Frank and Pearl Lee Johnson, who were sharecroppers. His father often played the fiddle with his uncle, Will Johnson, a guitarist. Both had an effect on the young Johnson, who watched and listened intently. Eventually, he was allowed to pick up his uncle's guitar. It was also around this time—around the age of 12—that he began using snuff and earned his nickname. His uncle threw country balls regularly, which featured slow dancing, folk blues and country tunes. The music heard at these influenced Snuff's repertoire, as did seeing Mance Lipscomb perform a few times.

Snuff's relaxed style includes a steady thumb-strummed bassline that reflects Lipscomb's influence. Johnson began playing his "black cowboy blues" at house parties and balls, but also played guitar in church. He settled in Austin after being discharged from the army in 1945 and remained there, working in construction, at a service station and, finally, as a piano mover. He played out (although not for pay) during the '50s and '60s, and in the mid-'70s met an auto mechanic who happened to be working on a Gibson guitar. Snuff picked it up and played it a bit, starting a friendship with the man. The mechanic was a music fan, Charles Devitalis, who went on to serve as informal advisor to Snuff, who couldn't read or write. After retiring in 1976, Snuff focused on his family (he has 13 children from three marriages) and the church. His material includes recompositions of old blues standards such as "Good Morning Blues" and "post-gospel, camp meeting era" religious songs, including hymns like "Going Back to Jesus" and "Old Time Religion." Johnson first performed professional shows in the late '80s, when he was invited to perform at Austin's Continental Club and Antone's. He turned down an Austin producer's recording offer in the early '90s, and shortly after was invited by Alan Govenar to play at the Dallas Museum of Art. The following year, Govenar brought Snuff back to Dallas to record, resulting in the 1994 Documentary Arts release *Black Cowboy Blues and Church Songs*. *—Joslyn Layne*

● **Black Cowboy Blues and Church Songs** / Nov. 17, 1999 / Documentary Arts ✦✦✦✦
Black Cowboy Blues and Church Songs is a mixture of songs from both named categories as performed by Alfred "Snuff" Johnson, a Texas bluesman who had been playing for around 70 years at the time of this recording. Accompanying himself with acoustic guitar, Johnson sings no-nonsense recompositions of "Good Morning Blues," "Getting Ready to Go," "Motherless Children," and more in his thick-throated, rich voice. An interesting smattering of unexpected sharps and minors get thrown into the guitar picking, but this can be chalked up more to choice and Johnson's relaxed style (that has, by the way, a Mance Lipscomb-influence of a thumb-strummed bassline) than to lack of ability, as Johnson also pulls off some mean guitar work on other songs, including "Hobo Blues" and "Blue Steel 44." Overall, it's good, low-key, acoustic country blues from a bluesman who, sadly, went unrecorded until the '90s. *—Joslyn Layne*

Big Jack Johnson

b. Jul. 30, 1940, Lambert, MS
Vocals, Guitar / Juke Joint Blues, Country Blues, Electric Delta Blues
Contemporary Mississippi blues doesn't get any nastier than in Big Jack Johnson's capable hands. The ex-oil truck driver's axe cuts like a rusty machete, his rough-hewn vocals a siren call to Delta passion. But he's a surprisingly versatile songwriter; *Daddy, When Is Mama Comin Home?*, his ambitious 1990 set for Earwig, found him tackling issues as varied as AIDS, wife abuse, and Chinese blues musicians in front of slick, horn-leavened arrangements!

Big Jack Johnson was a chip off the old block musically. His dad was a local musician playing both blues and country ditties at local functions; by the time he was 13 years old, Johnson was sitting in on guitar with his dad's band. At age 18, Johnson was following B.B. King's electrified lead. His big break came when he sat in with bluesmen Frank Frost and Sam Carr at the Savoy Theatre in Clarksdale. The symmetry between the trio was such that they were seldom apart for the next 15 years, recording for Phillips International and Jewel with Frost, the bandleader.

Chicago blues aficionado Michael Frank was so mesmerized by the trio's intensity when he heard them playing in 1975 at Johnson's Mississippi bar, the Black Fox, that

Frank Frost eventually formed Earwig just to capture their steamy repertoire. That album, *Rockin' the Juke Joint Down*, came out in 1979 (as by the Jelly Roll Kings) and marked Johnson's first recordings as a singer.

Johnson's subsequent 1987 album for Earwig, *The Oil Man*, still ranks as his most intense and moving, sporting a hair-raising rendition of "Catfish Blues." The '90s were good to Big Jack Johnson. In addition to *Daddy, When Is Mama Comin Home?*, he released a live record and two studio albums—1996's *We Got to Stop This Killin'* and 1998's *All the Way Back.* He also appeared in the acclaimed film documentary *Deep Blues* and on its resulting soundtrack, returning in 2000 with *Roots Stew.* —*Bill Dahl*

● **The Oil Man** / 1987 / Earwig ✦✦✦✦
With his barbed-wire guitar work and hearty vocal on a marathon rendition of "Catfish Blues," Johnson hauls the time-honored Delta tradition into contemporary blues. The entire album is an eminently solid, doggedly down-home affair, though nothing else quite measures up to the powerhouse attack of that one vicious workout. —*Bill Dahl*

Daddy, When Is Mama Comin' Home? / 1991 / Earwig ✦✦✦
The precise opposite of the Mississippi guitarist's previous Earwig release. This one's slick, horn-leavened, and full of down-home ruminations on everything from AIDS and spousal abuse to Chinese blues musicians. Too weird for some purists, but definitely engaging in its singular approach. —*Bill Dahl*

We Got to Stop This Killin' / Jun. 18, 1996 / M.C. ✦✦✦✦✦
Since many modern blues musicians are loath to break away from the norm, Big Jack Johnson can come as a shock. Johnson is determined to keep the blues a vital, living form, so he doesn't simply spit out the old standards again—he writes new songs about modern times, whether it's social commentary or love songs. Not only are his subjects fresh, but he makes sure that his music is fresh too, bringing funk and soul influences to his electrified Delta blues. In short, it fulfills the promise of *Daddy, When Is Mama Coming Home?* by keeping its ambition and adding the grit of *The Oil Man.* —*Thom Owens*

Live in Chicago / Dec. 24, 1997 / Earwig ✦✦✦✦
Mississippi bluesman Johnson comes North to play in Chicago and the results are indeed satisfying. Taken from two different shows at two different venues (Hothouse and Buddy Guy's Legends) over a period of two years (1994 and 1995), Johnson is ably backed by Aaron Burton's band with Lester "Mad Dog" Davenport contributing some nice harp on the set from the Legends show. Johnson keeps the set lists jumping, from straight-ahead blues ("Sweet Sixteen," "Black Rooster," "Fightin' Woman," Z.Z. Hill's "The Blues Is Alright") to Mississippi-juke-joint dance numbers (Hank Ballard's "The Twist," "Night Train") and even the stray "hillbilly blues" number like "Pistol Packin' Mama" and Ivory Joe Hunter's "Since I Met You Baby." Sound is dodgy in spots, but Johnson's palpable energy comes through just fine. —*Cub Koda*

All the Way Back / Mar. 31, 1998 / M.C. ✦✦✦✦
For *All the Way Back*, Big Jack Johnson decided to tame the instinct for social commentary and concentrate on what his audience loves—hard-hitting, electrified Delta blues. The result is a monster of a record, filled with great songs and unbridled, earth-shaking playing from Johnson. The key to his music is that he knows how to write a great song, one that adheres to blues traditions without being a slave to them. The funk and soul flourishes he brings to the blues don't compromise the form, but bring it into fresh new territory; that's what makes *All the Way Back* a terrific listen. —*Thom Owens*

Roots Stew / Apr. 11, 2000 / M.C. ✦✦✦✦
Johnson's third album for M.C. is his strongest outing to date, with more than its share of interesting little wrinkles. With the exception of one tune, Johnson penned everything on here, all of them sturdy juke-joint-styled blues that spotlight his trebly accented guitar work and husky vocals. But the real surprises are his acoustic tracks, where he plays driving mandolin in emulation of Yank Rachell, especially on his heartfelt tribute "So Long Frank Frost." Another off-the-wall delight is his eerily evocative instrumental take of "Since I Met You Baby" played on electric lap steel. A very strong effort, and one well worth picking up. —*Cub Koda*

The Memphis Barbecue Sessions / Feb. 26, 2002 / M.C. ✦✦✦✦
This album is a joy indeed—a journey inside the blues and down the Mississippi Delta. Johnson's always been an expressive singer, and in such a stripped-down setting his voice becomes more important than ever on classics like "Smokestack Lightning" and "My Babe." His guitar work offers the ideal backdrop, too, never fancy, but juke-joint friendly, serviceable, and offering a strong beat. Bringing in former Fabulous Thunderbirds frontman Kim Wilson to play harmonica proves to be an inspired move—he and Johnson conjure up a blues duo from the '50s, and when legendary pianist Pinetop Perkins sits in on a couple of numbers things really smoke. The Johnson originals on the album sit comfortably next to the classic covers, and the gutbucket style assures plenty of musical muscle, with Johnson and Wilson constantly pushing each other further. Where drums do come in, on three of the 13 tracks, they might as well not be there, they're so low in the mix and offer so little—they're certainly not missed anywhere else. On the evidence here, Johnson is every bit as comfortable on his own as he is with the backing of a band, and the more intimate, live setting (the disc was recorded in two days) brings out some subtleties in his singing and playing styles that get lost in a group setting. An enjoyable and even important modern blues record. —*Chris Nickson*

Blind Willie Johnson

b. 1902, Marlin, TX, **d.** 1947, Beaumont, TX
Slide Guitar, Vocals, Guitar / Slide Guitar Blues, Prewar Gospel Blues, Blues Gospel, Acoustic Texas Blues, Texas Blues
Seminal gospel-blues artist Blind Willie Johnson is regarded as one of the greatest bottleneck slide guitarists. Yet the Texas street-corner evangelist is known as much for the

his powerful and fervent gruff voice as he is for his ability as a guitarist. He most often sang in a rough, bass voice (only occasionally delivering in his natural tenor) with a volume meant to be heard over the sounds of the streets. Johnson recorded a total of 30 songs during a three-year period and many of these became classics of the gospel-blues, including "Jesus Make Up My Dying Bed," "God Don't Never Change," and his most famous, "Dark Was the Night—Cold Was the Ground."

It is generally agreed that Johnson was born in a small town just South of Waco near Temple, TX, around 1902. His mother died while he was still a baby, and his father eventually remarried. When Johnson was about seven years old, his father and stepmother fought and the stepmother threw lye water, apparently at the father, but the lye got in Willie Johnson's eyes, blinding him. As he got older, Johnson began earning money by playing his guitar, one of the few avenues left to a blind man to earn a living. Instead of a bottleneck, Johnson actually played slide with a pocketknife. Over the years, Johnson played guitar most often in an open D tuning, picking single-note melodies, while using his slide and strumming a bass line with his thumb. He was, however, known to play in a different tuning and without the slide on a few rare occasions. Regardless of his excellent blues technique and sound, Johnson didn't want to be a bluesman, for he was a passionate believer in the *Bible*. So, he began singing the gospel and interpreting Negro spirituals. He became a Baptist preacher and brought his sermons and music to the streets of the surrounding cities. While performing in Dallas, he met a woman named Angeline and the two married in 1927. Angeline added 19th century hymns to Johnson's repertoire, and the two performed around the Dallas and Waco areas.

On December 3, 1927, Columbia Records brought Blind Willie Johnson into the studio where he recorded six songs that became some of his most enduring recordings: a song about Samson and Delilah called "If I Had My Way," "Mother's Children Have a Hard Time" (often understood as "motherless children"), "It's Nobody's Fault but Mine," "Jesus Make up My Dying Bed," "I Know His Blood Can Make Me Whole," and Johnson's single most-acclaimed song, "Dark Was the Night—Cold Was the Ground," which is about the crucifixion of Christ. But after this session, Johnson didn't return to the studio for an entire year. The second visit (which took place on December 5, 1928) found him accompanied by his wife, Angeline, who provided backing vocals. The two recorded four songs, including "I'm Gonna Run to the City of Refuge" and "Lord, I Just Can't Keep from Cryin'." Songs from these first two sessions were also issued on the Vocalion label. Several months later, Willie and Angeline Johnson met Elder Dave Ross and went with him to New Orleans where Blind Willie Johnson recorded ten songs for Columbia. From this December 1929 session came a few more of his best-known songs, including "God Don't Never Change," "Let Your Light Shine on Me," and "You'll Need Somebody on Your Bond."

Although Blind Willie Johnson was one of Columbia's best-selling race recording artists, he only recorded for them one more time—in April 1930—after which he never heard from them again. This final session took place in Atlanta, GA (again, Johnson was accompanied by Angeline who actually sang lead on a few numbers this time), and consisted of ten songs, including "Can't Nobody Hide From God," "John the Revelator," and the slightly altered "You're Gonna Need Somebody on Your Bond." These last two songs were issued on one record that was withdrawn shortly after its release. Despite the fact that Johnson did not record after 1930, he continued to perform on the Texas streets during the '30s and '40s. Unfortunately, in 1947, the Johnsons' home burned to the ground. He caught pneumonia shortly thereafter and died in the ashes of his former home approximately one week after it was destroyed. Purportedly, Angeline Johnson went on to work as a nurse during the '50s.

Over the years, many artists have covered the gospel songs made famous by Blind Willie Johnson, including Bob Dylan, Eric Clapton, and Ry Cooder ("Dark Was the Night" inspired Cooder's score for the movie *Paris, Texas*). Johnson's song "If I Had My Way" was even revived as a popular hit during the '60s when it was covered by the contemporary folk band Peter, Paul & Mary. Several excellent collections of Blind Willie Johnson's music exist, including *Dark Was the Night* (on Sony) and *Praise God, I'm Satisfied* (on Yazoo). Johnson's music also appears on many compilations of country blues and slide guitar. —*Joslyn Layne*

Praise God I'm Satisfied / 1989 / Yazoo ✦✦✦✦✦
Yazoo's *Praise God I'm Satisfied* is an excellent collection of 14 tracks Blind Willie Johnson recorded in the '30s, including such numbers as "Jesus Make Up My Dying Bed," "Praise God I'm Satisfied," "Rain Don't Fall on Me" and "Jesus Is Coming Soon." These are excellent, haunting recordings, boasting some stellar guitar work, but everything that's on this disc and its companion, *Sweeter as the Years Go By*, is included on Columbia/Legacy's *The Complete Recordings of Blind Willie Johnson*, which makes this unnecessary for any serious listener. —*Stephen Thomas Erlewine*

Sweeter as the Years Go By / 1990 / Yazoo ✦✦✦✦✦
Blind Willie Johnson was perhaps the finest singing evangelist of all time. While the 16 tracks on this CD aren't as striking as those on the seminal *Praise God I'm Satisfied*, they're still invigorating and a vital part of his legacy. Johnson played acoustic rather than slide on several cuts, and didn't take flamboyant solos or add slashing counterpoint. But he demonstrated a skillful use of repetition and outstanding rhythmic and melodic skills. Johnson teamed with Willie B. Harris on several songs, and her rough, cutting voice proved an ideal match with his equally ragged sound. —*Ron Wynn*

☆ **The Complete Blind Willie Johnson** / Apr. 27, 1993 / Columbia/Legacy ✦✦✦✦✦
If you've never heard Blind Willie Johnson, you are in for one of the great, bone-chilling treats in music. Johnson played slide guitar, and sang in a rasping, false bass that could freeze the blood. But no bluesman was he; this was gospel music of the highest order, full of emotion and heartfelt commitment. Of all the guitar-playing evangelists, Blind Willie Johnson may have been the very best. Though not related by bloodlines to Robert Johnson, comparisons in emotional commitment from both men cannot be helped. This two-CD anthology collects everything known to exist, and that's a lot of stark, harrowing emotional commitment no matter how you slice it. Not for the faint of heart, but hey, the good stuff never is. —*Cub Koda*

★ **Dark Was the Night** / Jun. 30, 1998 / Columbia/Legacy ✦✦✦✦✦

Even in the blues, a style capable of wrenching unexplainable emotions from its audience, Blind Willie Johnson has few equals. With a voice capable of alternating effortlessly between sublime, trembling tenor and the sound of pure gravel, and unparalleled skill with the bottleneck (and knife), Johnson recorded 30 sides for Columbia (1927-1930) that stand as a high watermark for both country blues and raw gospel. Given the fact that his entire output has been issued by both Yazoo and Columbia, it's difficult to imagine opting for this single disc. Anyone looking for more material will be forced to purchase sets with redundant selections. Still, if you are only seeking one collection, you cannot go wrong with *Dark Was the Night*. Included are both "God Moves on the Water" and "Dark Was the Night, Cold Was the Ground," which are both utterly necessary, along with the classics "Praise God I'm Satisfied," "Jesus Make Up My Dying Bed," "John the Revelator," and 11 others. "God Moves" is a slide masterpiece in which Johnson's guitar interjections and responses become as captivating as his voice and a tale of the Titanic sinking at the will of God. "Dark Was the Night" is an otherworldly performance of gorgeously spun slide lines and Johnson's wordless moaning, aimed straight at the heart. Everything else on hand is nothing less than emotionally rich, consummately executed, and spiritually charged blues at its very best. —*Nathan Bush*

Buddy Johnson (Woodrow Wilson Johnson)

b. Jan. 10, 1915, Darlington, SC, d. Feb. 9, 1977, New York, NY

Leader, Arranger, Songwriter, Piano / New York Blues, Jump Blues, Swing, Rock & Roll, Big Band, R&B

With his sister Ella seductively serving for decades as his primary vocalist, pianist Buddy Johnson led a large jump blues band that enjoyed tremendous success during the '40s and '50s. The suave bandleader spotlighted a series of talented singers, including balladeers Arthur Prysock, Nolan Lewis, and Floyd Ryland, but it was Ella's understated delivery (beautifully spotlighted on the sumptuous ballad "Since I Fell for You") and Buddy's crisply danceable "Walk-Em Rhythm" that made the aggregation so successful for so long.

Buddy began taking piano lessons at age four. Although he specialized professionally in tasty R&B, classical music remained one of his passions. In 1939, Buddy Johnson waxed his first 78 for Decca, "Stop Pretending (So Hep You See)." Shortly thereafter, Ella joined her older brother; her delicious vocal on "Please Mr. Johnson" translated into long-term employment.

Buddy had assembled a nine-piece orchestra by 1941 and visited the R&B charts often for Decca during wartime with "Let's Beat Out Some Love," "Baby Don't You Cry," the chart-topping "When My Man Comes Home," and "That's the Stuff You Gotta Watch." Ella cut her beloved rendering of "Since I Fell for You" in 1945, a year after Buddy waxed his jiving gem "Fine Brown Frame."

In addition to their frequent jaunts on the R&B hit parade, the Johnson organization barnstormed the country to sellout crowds throughout the '40s. Buddy moved over to Mercury Records in 1953 and scored more smashes with Ella's "Hittin' on Me" and "I'm Just Your Fool," the latter a 1954 standout that was later purloined by Chicago harpist Little Walter.

Rock & roll eventually halted Buddy Johnson's momentum, but his band (tenor saxophonist Purvis Henson was a constant presence in the reed section) kept recording for Mercury through 1958, switched to Roulette the next year, and bowed out with a solitary session for Hy Weiss' Old Town label in 1964.

Singer Lenny Welch ensured the immortality of "Since I Fell for You" when his velvety rendition of the Johnson-penned ballad reached the uppermost reaches of the pop charts in 1963. It was a perfect match of song and singer; Welch's smooth, assured delivery would have fit in snugly with the Johnson band during its heyday a couple of decades earlier. —*Bill Dahl*

Wails / 1957 / Mercury ✦✦✦

This is first-rate music, but is really vintage instrumental R&B with swing foundation. Johnson was a tremendous, energetic pianist who had some hit records with his sister, vocalist Ella Johnson, and also had some sessions produced by Quincy Jones. He is a different player from the veteran jazz saxophonist Budd Johnson. —*Ron Wynn*

● **Go Ahead and Rock and Roll** / 1958 / Collectables ✦✦✦✦

Buddy Johnson was one of the top R&B bandleaders and composers in the '50s, as well as being an above-average vocalist. This is prototype '50s material, an era when swing-derived R&B was being mixed with country and gospel and rock was emerging from the stew. The songs are either raw, stirring uptempo tunes or steamy ballads, and they're done at a powerhouse pace. Johnson, like most great R&B acts, was a singles artist, but the songs featured here are good at worst and often magical despite clearly being from another era. —*Ron Wynn*

Buddy and Ella Johnson 1953–1964 / 1992 / Bear Family ✦✦✦✦✦

Four discs (104 tracks in all) that exhaustively document the Mercury, Roulette, and Old Town output of big-band veteran Buddy Johnson, whose eternally swinging outfit was seductively fronted by his sister Ella (along with several interchangeable male crooners). Buddy's band wasn't as big as it once was during his Mercury tenure (tenor saxman Purvis Henson was at the core of the blazing horn section), but the tightly arranged New York-style sizzle remained. —*Bill Dahl*

1939–1942 / 1996 / Classics ✦✦✦✦

Pianist Buddy Johnson is best-known for leading a swinging R&B-oriented big band in the late '40s and '50s that, with his sister Ella Johnson as the main star, introduced "Since I Fell for You." On this CD from the European Classics label, Johnson's first 24 numbers recorded as a leader are reissued and most of the tracks were formerly quite rare. At the time Buddy Johnson was an Earl Hines-influenced pianist who was searching for his own sound. A few numbers feature vocals by the so-so Mack Sisters and various band-members including the leader himself but it is the songs with Ella Johnson (particularly

"Please, Mister Johnson" and "It's the Gold") that stand out. During the two-year period covered by this CD, Buddy Johnson's band grew from a septet to a nonet but the glory years were still in the future. —*Scott Yanow*

Walk 'Em: Decca Sessions / Jul. 2, 1996 / Ace ✦✦✦✦✦

A fine 24-track distillation of Johnson's lengthy career for Decca, during which he and his musicians served as a key link between Harlem big bands, jump blues, and R&B. Spanning 1941 to 1952, the focus is on the bluesier and/or more uptempo sides credited to either Buddy or sister Ella, as well as tracks with Johnson associations cut by Arthur Prysock and Harold "Geezil" Minerve. Several of the Johnson clan's most celebrated performances are here: "Walk 'Em" (a sort of signature tune for Buddy), Ella's original version of "Since I Fell for You," Ella's huge R&B hits "That's the Stuff You Gotta Watch" and "When My Man Comes Home," and Buddy's 1949 Top 20 pop hit, "Did You See Jackie Robinson Hit That Ball?" (surely one of the greatest baseball/pop novelties ever). Some of the raunchy sax breaks are signposts for a style that would become prevalent in R&B and early rock & roll; the gritty instrumental "Shake 'Em Up," for instance, anticipates the sound of Bill Doggett's "Honky Tonk" by four years. —*Richie Unterberger*

1942–1947 / Jan. 11, 2000 / Classics ✦✦✦

1942-1947 is the second volume chronicling Buddy Johnson's piano-led jump blues with his orchestra. An enjoyable listen, it offers a good sampling of the different vocalists Johnson worked with, including Chester Boone, James Lewis, Warren Evans, and—happily—seven tunes featuring the warm vocals of his sister Ella Johnson. "Let's Beat Out Some Love" and "Fine Brown Frame" are some of the only covers amidst Johnson-penned numbers such as "South Main," "Walk 'Em," and his biggest hit with Ella, "Since I Fell for You." —*Joslyn Layne*

1947–1949 / Sep. 12, 2000 / Classics ✦✦✦✦

The Buddy Johnson Orchestra was one of the few big bands that were able to stay together during the second half of the '40s. They did that by featuring the vocals of Ella Johnson and Arthur Prysock, leaning towards R&B at times and hinting at (but not outright playing) bebop. This CD has the music from Johnson's last three sessions of 1947 and his three 1949 dates; the 1948 recording strike caused a gap. There were no major soloists in the band, but the musicianship was high, the vocalists (heard along with Buddy Johnson himself on all but four numbers) were excellent and there was plenty of spirit. —*Scott Yanow*

Walk 'Em Rhythm Band 1940/1950 / Aug. 7, 2001 / EPM Musique ✦✦✦✦

Dink Johnson

b. Oct. 28, 1892, Biloxi, MS, d. Nov. 29, 1954, Portland, OR

Drums, Piano, Clarinet / New Orleans Jazz, Classic Jazz, Piano Blues, Modern Electric Blues

Dink Johnson was nothing if not versatile, as one can judge from the three instruments that he played. Johnson started out working in New Orleans as a pianist in Storyville. He traveled to Los Angeles where he was a member of Bill Johnson's Creole Band in 1913, as a drummer. Johnson freelanced, played drums during Jelly Roll Morton's stay in California and in 1922 recorded with Kid Ory's band (Spikes' Seven Pods of Pepper), on clarinet! Johnson spent much of his career in California, leading the Five Hounds of Jazz (later renamed the Los Angeles Six) and then mostly working as a solo pianist. Although he ran his own restaurant in Los Angeles, he remained active as a player into the late '40s. Johnson was much better-known locally than he was nationally, performing in an early style that fell between stride and ragtime. Dink Johnson recorded fairly extensively (mostly as a pianist) for American Music during 1946-1947, Euphonic (1948) and Nola (1950). —*Scott Yanow*

● **Piano Players** / Aug. 11, 1994 / American Music ✦✦✦

Ella Johnson

b. Jun. 22, 1923, Darlington, SC

Vocals / East Coast Blues, Jump Blues, Ballads, Classic Female Blues, R&B

Ella Johnson made her mark as the vocalist with Buddy Johnson's big band during the '40s and '50s, and it is in that context she really shines. Her later solo sides for Mercury are pale imitations of her work with the band.

Although many of Ella's hits are uptempo (e.g., "I Don't Want Nobody"), it is on ballads and torchy blues that she really brings it together. In fact, her earliest work for Decca during the mid-'40s (much of which is not yet reissued) is uncannily good. At her best, Ella sounds like a pouty, vulnerable, and very sexy young girl. Like so much of her life, it was no affectation. The comparison to Billie Holiday is inevitable, but Ella is her own singer. —*Hank Davis*

● **Swing Me** / 1956 / Verve ✦✦✦✦✦

It's good to get these 20 tracks, most previously available only as singles, back into circulation; hopefully, they'll enable Johnson to be "discovered" once more. —*Ron Wynn*

Say Ella / 1983 / Jukebox ✦✦✦✦✦

Juke Box Lil's *Say Ella* contains 16 songs Ella Johnson recorded with her brother Buddy's big band for Decca and Mercury between 1942 and 1957. In other words, these 16 songs are among her very best recordings, containing such classics as "I Don't Care Who Knows," "You Got to Walk That Chalk Line," "Somehow, Somewhere," "'Til My Baby Comes Back," "That's How I Feel About You," "One More Time," and "Mush Mouth." In other words, it's an excellent single-disc introduction to one of the finest female R&B vocalists of her era. —*Thom Owens*

Ernie Johnson

b. Winnsboro, LA

Bass / Retro-Soul, Soul-Blues

Ernie Johnson continues in the soul-blues singing path forged by artists like Bobby "Blue" Bland, Z.Z. Hill, Little Milton and R.L. Griffin. Born in Winnsboro, LA, Johnson didn't begin singing professionally until after moving to Dallas. His vocal influences included Nat King Cole, Dee Clark, Clyde McPhatter, Jackie Wilson, and especially Bobby "Blue" Bland; he recalled that hearing Bland sing "Further on Up the Road" was a revelatory experience. Johnson had a chance to open for Miss Lavelle White and Guitar James in Mexia, Texas, and stole the show. At that point, he quit his day job with the Dallas parks department and formed a band, the Soul Blenders. He recorded his first single, "Lovin You" b/w "Cold Cold Heart," for Fats Washington's Movin' Records in 1968. Johnson recorded other singles before his first album for Ronn Records, *Just in Time*.

Johnson has played the blues festivals in San Francisco and Monterey, and his first compact disc, *It's Party Time*, was released on the Louisiana-based Paula Records label in 1993. Johnson financed and produced the album himself, and wrote all the songs except for his rendition of Otis Redding's "Dreams to Remember." In 1995, Malaco Records released another album, *In the Mood*; *Hot and Steamy* followed three years later. Although he doesn't tour that widely, Johnson does get around on the blues festival circuit. *—Richard Skelly*

● **It's Party Time** / 1993 / Paula ♦♦♦♦
Although he doesn't show much imagination anywhere on the disc, Ernie Johnson's debut album, *It's Party Time*, is a fine collection of contemporary soul-blues. Most of the record is devoted to originals, which are solid numbers in the classic Chicago and Stax traditions, even if they're not particularly memorable. They do give Johnson an opportunity to spill his guts out vocally, and he proves to be a good vocalist in the tradition of Bobby Bland, Little Milton and Z.Z. Hill, even if he doesn't quite reach their heights. He is good enough, however, to make *It's Party Time* an enjoyable record for fans of that style. *—Thom Owens*

In the Mood / Oct. 3, 1995 / Waldoxy ♦♦♦

Hot & Steamy / May 5, 1998 / Waldoxy ♦♦♦

Squeeze It / Aug. 28, 2001 / Phat Sound ♦♦♦

Herman E. Johnson

b. Louisiana, **d.** Feb. 2, 1975, Scotlandville, LA
Vocals / Louisiana Blues, Acoustic Louisiana Blues, Blues Revival
Another of the many performers briefly illuminated by the spotlight of the folk-blues revival of the '60s, Louisiana-born country bluesman Herman E. Johnson was the product of a highly religious family environment, a background which heavily informed the spiritual imagery which was a hallmark of his later work as a performer. His early adult years were spent in a fruitless search for steady work which led him from the country to the city and back again; he picked up the guitar around 1927 as a respite from jobs ranging from picking cotton to pouring concrete to working at a scrap metal yard. Eventually, Johnson landed work at the Esso refinery in Baton Rouge, where he worked for 15 years before being unexpectly fired; scrambling to find work—an experience memorably recalled in his song "Depression Blues"—he finally was hired as a janitor at Southern University in nearby Scotlandville. He held the same job at the time of his lone recording session, cut in Baton Rouge by Dr. Harry Oster in 1961; after suffering a stroke in 1970, Johnson went into retirement, and died on February 2, 1975. *—Jason Ankeny*

● **Louisiana Country Blues** / 1981 / Arhoolie ♦♦♦

Jimmy Johnson

b. Nov. 25, 1928, Holly Springs, MS
Vocals, Keyboards, Harmonica, Guitar / Electric Chicago Blues, Modern Electric Blues, Soul-Blues
Chicago guitarist Jimmy Johnson didn't release his first full domestic album until he was 50 years old. He's determinedly made up for lost time ever since, establishing himself as one of the Windy City's premier blues artists with a twisting, unpredictable guitar style and a soaring, soul-dripping vocal delivery that stand out from the pack.

Born into a musical family (younger brother Syl Johnson's credentials as a soul star are all in order, while sibling Mack Thompson was Magic Sam's first-call bassist), Jimmy Thompson moved to Chicago with his family in 1950. But his guitar playing remained a hobby for years—he toiled as a welder while Syl blazed a trail on the local blues circuit. Finally, in 1959, Jimmy Thompson started gigging with harpist Slim Willis around the West side. Somewhere down the line, he changed his surname to Johnson (thus keeping pace with Syl).

Since there was more cash to be realized playing R&B during the '60s, Jimmy Johnson concentrated on that end of the stylistic spectrum for a while. He led polished house bands on the South and West sides behind Otis Clay, Denise LaSalle, and Garland Green, cutting an occasional instrumental 45 on the side. Johnson found his way back to the blues in 1974 as Jimmy Dawkins' rhythm guitarist. He toured Japan behind Otis Rush in 1975 (the journey that produced Rush's album *So Many Roads—Live in Concert*).

With the 1978 release of four stunning sides on Alligator's first batch of *Living Chicago Blues* anthologies and the issue of *Johnson's Whacks*, his first full domestic set on Delmark the next year, Jimmy Johnson's star began ascending rapidly. *North/South*, the guitarist's 1982 Delmark follow-up, and the 1983 release of *Bar Room Preacher* by Alligator continued to propel Johnson into the first rank of Chicago bluesdom. Then tragedy struck: On December 2, 1988, Johnson was driving his band's van when it swerved off the road in downstate Indiana, killing bassist Larry Exum and keyboardist St. James Bryant.

Understandably, Johnson, himself injured in the wreck, wasn't too interested in furthering his career for a time after the tragedy. But he's back in harness now, cutting a solid set for Verve in 1994, *I'm a Jockey*, that spotlights his blues-soul synthesis most effectively. *Every Road Ends*, recorded in France and released on Ruf, followed in 1999. A collaboration with his brother Syl appeared in the summer of 2002, the cleverly titled *Two Johnsons Are Better Than One*." *—Bill Dahl*

Jimmy Johnson & Luther Johnson / 1977 / MCM ♦♦

Tobacco Road / 1978 / MCM ♦♦

Johnson's Whacks / 1979 / Delmark ♦♦♦♦
Uncommon wit runs through the lyrics of this varied set, certainly one of the more intriguing Chicago blues albums of the late '70s. Johnson's high-pitched vocals are particularly soulful on the impassioned "I Need Some Easy Money" and "Ashes in My Ashtray," while "The Twelve Bar Blues" and "Poor Boy's Dream" are upbeat entries that don't sound as comfortable for the guitarist. Johnson gets away with a honky-tonk reprise of Ernest Tubb's country classic "Drivin' Nails in My Coffin," but his rehash of Dave Brubeck's "Take Five" should have stayed on the bandstand. *—Bill Dahl*

North/South / 1982 / Delmark ♦♦♦
Another lyrically challenging effort from Johnson (unfortunately not on CD yet), though some of the most daring musical aspects of his previous efforts have been smoothed off (for better or worse). Bassist Larry Exum was a bedrock of funky grooves for the guitarist's band. *—Bill Dahl*

● **Bar Room Preacher** / 1983 / Alligator ♦♦♦♦♦
Unlike his Delmark sets, almost everything on this set (first issued in France on Black & Blue) is a cover (only the observant "Heap See" boasts original lyrics). Still, *Bar Room Preacher* stands as the Chicago guitarist's most satisfying and consistent album, as he deals out gorgeous, shimmering versions of "Little By Little," "Cold, Cold Feeling," and "You Don't Know What Love Is" tailored to his soaring vocals and twisting guitar riffs (ominous minor keys often play a role in his rearrangements). *—Bill Dahl*

I'm a Jockey / 1995 / Verve ♦♦♦♦
It shouldn't have taken Johnson a full decade to find his way back into a studio, but such are the injustices of the record business. The wait was worth it, though—backed by his touring trio of the timeframe, Johnson mixes blues and soul, originals (a heartfelt "Black & White Wall" and the soaring ballad "My Ring") and covers (his takes on McKinley Mitchell's "End of a Rainbow" and Wilson Pickett's "Engine Number 9" hit home), in decidedly solid contemporary form. *—Bill Dahl*

Every Road Ends / Aug. 10, 1999 / Ruf ♦♦♦

Ma Bea's Rock / Sep. 4, 2001 / Storyville ♦♦♦♦

Livin' the Life / Sep. 3, 2002 / Black & Blue ♦♦♦

Johnnie Johnson

b. Jul. 8, 1924, Fairmont, WV
Piano / Piano Blues, Rock & Roll, R&B
Legendary piano player Johnnie Johnson isn't exactly a household name, even among followers of blues music. That's because for 28 years, he worked as a sideman to one of rock & roll's most prominent performers, Chuck Berry. Berry joined Johnson's band, the Sir John Trio, on New Year's Eve, 1953, and afterward, Berry took over as the group's songwriter and frontman/guitar player. On the strength of a recommendation from Muddy Waters and an audition, Berry got a deal with Chess Records. Johnson's rhythmic piano playing was a key element in all of Berry's hit singles, a good number of which Johnson arranged. The pair's successful partnership lasted a lot longer than most rock & roll partnerships last these days.

Johnson was born July 8, 1924, in Fairmont, WV, and he began playing piano at age five, thanks to his mother, who provided the funds to purchase one and encouraged the young Johnson's interest. His parents had a good collection of 78-rpm records, including items by Bessie Smith and Ethel Waters. In his teens, he listened to the radio broadcasts of big bands, and taught himself based on what he heard from the likes of Art Tatum, Earl "Fatha" Hines, and Meade "Lux" Lewis. Johnson's goal in all of this listening and playing in his teenage years was to come up with his own distinctive style. His own somewhat ailing career got a shot in the arm with the Chuck Berry concert film, *Hail! Hail! Rock 'n' Roll*, and by his involvement in Keith Richards' solo release with Richards' band, the X-Pensive Winos.

In a 1995 interview, Johnson explains his abilities with piano as his mother did, a gift from God. "I can hear something and keep it in my mind until such point as I can get to a piano, and then I'll play it… that is a gift, the ability to do that."

Johnson's albums under his own name include *Blue Hand Johnnie* for the St. Louis-based Pulsar label in 1988; *Johnnie B. Bad* in 1991 for the Elektra American Explorer label; *That'll Work* in 1993 for the same label, and most recently, *Johnnie Be Back* for the New Jersey-based Music Masters label in 1995. All four are winners, and all are available on compact disc. *—Richard Skelly*

● **Blue Hand Johnnie** / 1987 / Evidence ♦♦♦♦♦
Johnnie Johnson's rolling, barrelling licks are as enticing as ever on this reissued Evidence CD, but there are some other things that are not so grand. These include barely tolerable vocalists Barbara Carr and Stacy Johnson, whose enthusiasm is commendable, but whose vocals often get in the way. Johnson's covers of Fats Washington's "O.J. Blues" and "Black Nights" are great, as are his versions of "Honky Tonk" and "See See Rider." But he falters on "Baby, What You Want Me To," in part because he does not convey either the original's loping stride or laconic quality, and also because it is not the kind of peppy arrangement and backbeat suited to his style. A decent effort that might have been a superior one with a couple of added touches. *—Ron Wynn*

Rockin' Eighty Eights / Apr. 1990 / Modern Blues ♦♦♦♦♦
Three underrated pianists, Clayton Love, Johnnie Johnson, and Jimmy Vaughn, typify the St. Louis Blues piano tradition on this solid sender. *—Bill Dahl*

Johnnie B. Bad / 1992 / Elektra/Nonesuch ♦♦♦♦♦
Keith Richards, Eric Clapton, and various NRBQ members guest on this pianist's inconsistent major-label debut. *—Bill Dahl*

That'll Work / 1993 / Elektra/Nonesuch ♦♦
With *That'll Work*, the Kentucky Headhunters made their blues-rock roots explicit by working with legendary pianist Johnnie Johnson, which is both for better and worse. They certainly can work a heavy, bluesy groove with dexterity, but they lack the gonzo charm

they had on their debut, *Pickin' On Nashville*—there simply isn't the sense of careening fun, nor is there the reckless fusions that resulted in such an invigorating listen. What's left is enjoyable and competent, but not particularly special. —*Thom Owens*

Complete Recorded Works Volumes 1-3 / 1995 / Document ♦♦♦♦♦

Johnnie Be Back / Oct. 1995 / Music Masters ♦♦♦

L.V. Johnson

b. 1946, Chicago, IL, **d.** Nov. 22, 1994, Chicago, IL

Vocals, Guitar / Retro-Soul, Chicago Blues, Soul-Blues

A mournful, often gripping singer and a good guitarist, Chicago performer L.V. Johnson actually did better as a writer than a lead artist. His songs "Are You Serious" and "True Love Is Hard to Find" were big hits for Tyrone Davis, while "Country Love" did moderately well for Bobby "Blue" Bland, and "Give Your Baby a Standing Ovation" was among the Dells' finest soul performances. Johnson played with Davis before going on his own in the '80s. The nephew of Elmore James, Johnson learned guitar from B.B. King. Besides working with Davis, Johnson was a staff guitarist at Stax, playing on sessions for the Bar-Kays, Johnnie Taylor, and the Soul Children. He recorded for ICA, Phono, and Ichiban, although his sound and approach to soul were far too deep for the Urban marketplace. Johnson was also part-owner of a steakhouse and nightclub in Chicago. —*Ron Wynn*

● **Cold & Mean** / 1991 / Ichiban ♦♦♦♦

From Clarence Carter to Curtis Mayfield, the Atlanta-based Ichiban Records has been a safe haven for soul veterans the majors lost interest in. In the late '80s and '90s, one of Ichiban's brightest lights was L.V. Johnson, who joined the label with the outstanding *Cold & Mean*. Instead of aiming for the urban contemporary market, the gruff, big-voiced soul shouter excels with an unapologetically '70s-sounding approach. Combining a silky production style with hard-edged, gospel-influenced vocals, gems like "It's So Cold and Mean (The Drug Scene)," "It's Not My Time," and "Make You Mine" sound like they could have been recorded 15 years earlier. Another high point is "One In a Million You," originally recorded by Larry Graham in 1980. On these confident, soaring performances, the R&B veteran lets us know that he's still at the height of his powers. —*Alex Henderson*

I Got the Touch / 1991 / Ichiban ♦♦♦

I Got the Touch found L.V. Johnson making a few concessions to urban contemporary tastes, but only a few. Despite some new jack moves here and there, this CD leaves no doubt that classic soul is where his heart lies. While the title song is a new jack-oriented number with a pedestrian cameo by rapper Styles, silky medium-tempo songs like "Are You Serious," "Take a Little Time to Know Her," and "I Am Missing You" could have easily been recorded in 1972. Tina Turner fans will be surprised by "What Do You Mean Love Ain't Got Nothing To Do With It," a clever response to her 1984 smash "What's Love Got To Do With It." Though it falls short of the excellence of *Cold and Mean*, *Touch* definitely has a lot going for it. —*Alex Henderson*

Unclassified / 1992 / Ichiban ♦♦♦

After going for a few urban contemporary touches on *I Got the Touch*, L.V. Johnson returns to a consistently soul-oriented approach on his third Ichiban release *Unclassified*. Stronger than its predecessor and every bit as impressive as *Cold and Mean*, *Unclassified* sounds like an album the deep-voiced singer wanted very much to make. Recalling the smooth Northern soul coming out of Chicago, Detroit, and Philadelphia in the '70s, slow- and medium-tempo gems like "Voodoo Woman," "Four Walls," and "Whatever Happened" are retro in the best sense of the word. For fans of classic '70s soul, this heartfelt CD is something to savor. —*Alex Henderson*

Larry Johnson

b. May 15, 1938, Atlanta, GA

Vocals, Bass / Modern Acoustic Blues, Modern Electric Blues

Among the postwar generation of blues artists, Larry Johnson—from Riceville, GA—is one of the most devoted to pure Delta and Texas styles of the '20s. He was born on May 15, 1938, in Atlanta, GA. His father was a preacher and his son would often travel with him from town to town. In this environment, Johnson was exposed to early blues records and he especially loved those of Blind Boy Fuller. It was Fuller's records that made Johnson pick up a guitar. After a stint in the Navy from 1955 to 1959, Johnson moved to New York and befriended Brownie and Sticks McGhee and began playing on records by Big Joe Williams, Harry Atkins, and Alec Seward, aka Guitar Slim. It was Seward who introduced Johnson to his future mentor, Rev. Gary Davis. He released his first single, "Catfish Blues"/"So Sweet," in 1962 and appeared on numerous live dates with Davis. By 1970, Johnson began releasing albums on small labels, including a date with John Hammond called *Fast & Funky* reissued on CD as *Midnight Hour Blues*. After years of living from gig to gig, Johnson retreated from the grind of the road. He still played occasionally, but only on his own terms. He did, however, manage to release two albums, *Johnson! Where Did You Get That Sound?* in 1983 and *Basin Free* with Nat Riddles in 1984. By the '90s, Johnson began receiving better offers for live performances, especially in Europe. While abroad, he recorded *Railroad Man* released in 1990 on JSP and *Blues for Harlem* in 1999 on the Armadillo label. Two years later, Johnson collaborated with National slide guitar extraordinaire Brian Kramer and his band the Couch Lizards, resulting in the relaxed, yet mainly uptempo, *Two Gun Green* on Armadillo. Johnson's excellent fingerpicking and acoustic blues remain timeless. —*Richard Meyer & Al Campbell*

Presenting the Country Blues / 1970 / Blue Horizon ♦♦♦♦

Country Blues / 1974 / Biograph ♦♦♦

● **Fast & Funky** / 1974 / Blue Goose ♦♦♦♦♦

A great collection of old-time blues, it includes "Picked Poor Robin Clean," "Charley Stone," and "Two White Horses." —*Richard Meyer*

Railroad Man / 1990 / JSP ♦♦♦

Midnight Hour Blues / 1995 / Biograph ♦♦♦

Saturday Night Blues / Oct. 3, 1995 / Biograph ♦♦♦♦

Two Gun Green / Jun. 11, 2002 / Armadillo ♦♦♦♦

Blues for Harlem / Jun. 11, 2002 / Armadillo ♦♦♦♦

Lil Johnson

Vocals / Classic Female Blues, Piano Blues, Chicago Blues

Lil Johnson made use of one thing that always sells in music, everytime: sex. She eventually toned down her lyrics somewhat, since record company censorship was beginning to plague her as well as shifting public taste. Nonetheless, she recorded quite a few sides between the late '20s, when she first appeared in the recording studios, and 1937, when she performed on her last-known songs. Like many pianists and singers from this period, her recordings fell into a state of copyright limbo in which just about anyone capable of sequencing a series of tracks was able to release her songs on anthologies relating to the blues and boogie-woogie piano. There was a particular interest in Johnson's case among producers of collections such as *Copulatin' Blues*, a title that apparently seems appealing enough to be used for several different collections by unrelated labels. Song titles such as "You'll Never Miss Your Jelly Till Your Jelly Roller Is Gone" reveal how appropriate her material is to such collections, although she never really made up her mind which direction she wanted to go into with the food-equals-sex metaphors; at one point switching from jelly rolls to peanuts—"Get 'Em from the Peanut Man," the listener is advised—and eventually settling on something that is actually healthy, cabbage. "Anybody Want to Buy My Cabbage?" Johnson asks on this side, one of several of her records in which the solid feel of the rhythm and the peskiness of the blues improvisations make up for relatively uninspired lyrics. —*Eugene Chadbourne*

● **1936–1937 "Hottest Gal in Town"** / Sep. 1, 1991 / Story of the Blues ♦♦♦♦♦

Although this fine singer represents a link in the classic chain of recordings by the "Classic Blues Singers," she is actually a few steps closer to the down-home blues essence than many of her peers. Here Johnson applies an earthy, conversational style employing frequent and effective use of vibrato to material ranging from risqué ensemble ragtime to vaudeville hokum. Big Bill Broonzy and Black Bob add their legendary talents to this entertaining set. —*Larry Hoffman*

Complete Works in Chronological Order, Vol. 1 (1929–1936) / Feb. 15, 1995 / Document ♦♦♦♦♦

All of the recordings by the good-time blues singer Lil Johnson have been reissued on three Document CDs. Virtually nothing is known about Johnson outside of the recordings that she made. *Vol. 1* starts off with five numbers from 1929, in which she is backed by either Montana Taylor or Charles Avery on piano (with Tampa Red sitting in on "House Rent Scuffle"). Otherwise all of this music is from 1935-1936, with Johnson usually accompanied by pianist Black Bob and various bassists, plus, on two numbers, guitarist Big Bill Broonzy. Her best-known number, "Get 'Em from the Peanut Man (Hot Nuts)," is here (in three different versions), along with such other rollicking tunes as "Anybody Want to Buy My Cabbage," "If You Can Dish It (I Can Take It)," "Press My Button (Ring My Bell)," and "Sam the Hot Dog Man." Fun music. —*Scott Yanow*

Complete Works in Chronological Order, Vol. 2 (1936–1937) / Feb. 15, 1995 / Document ♦♦♦♦

The good-time blues and hokum singer Lil Johnson sounds typically exuberant and full of double entendres on the 24 selections heard on this second of three CDs of her complete work. Accompanied by combos that sometimes include clarinetist Arnett Nelson, Lee Collins or Alfred Bell on trumpet, usually pianist Black Bob, Bill Settles or John Lindsay on bass, and occasional guest guitarist Big Bill Broonzy, along with other unknown musicians, Johnson sometimes goes a bit over the line in her sexual innuendoes, which is why the two versions of "My Baby (Squeeze Me Again)" were never released previously. The music may overall be limited in subject matter and chord structures, but it is consistently fun and spirited. —*Scott Yanow*

Complete Works in Chronological Order, Vol. 3 (1937) / Feb. 15, 1995 / Document ♦♦♦♦

This CD has the final 20 recordings by the good-time hokum/blues singer Lil Johnson, including eight performances that were previously unreleased. It seems strange, considering how much she recorded, that virtually nothing is known about her. Backed by a variety of partly unknown combos (with Black Bob, Aletha Robinson, or Blind John Davis mostly on piano), Johnson digs into such risqué numbers as "You Stole My Cherry," "Take Your Hand Off It," and "Snake in the Grass." Her very last recording, "Buck Naked Blues," was released for the first time on this CD, and it is taken from a private acetate that might have been from the early '40s. Wrapping up this CD are four numbers (two previously unreleased) by the equally unknown Barrel House Annie, whose identity has never been established but whose style is complementary to Lil Johnson's. Vintage blues collectors will want this enjoyable music. —*Scott Yanow*

Lonnie Johnson (Alonzo Johnson)

b. Feb. 8, 1899, New Orleans, LA, **d.** Jun. 16, 1970, Toronto, Ontario, Canada

Vocals, Violin, Guitar, Guitar (Acoustic) / Blues Revival, Piedmont Blues, Prewar Country Blues, Country Blues, Jazz Blues, Classic Jazz, Acoustic Blues, St. Louis Blues

Blues guitar simply would not have developed in the manner that it did if not for the prolific brilliance of Lonnie Johnson. He was there to help define the instrument's future within the genre and the genre's future itself at the very beginning, his melodic conception so far advanced from most of his prewar peers as to inhabit a plane all his own. For more than 40 years, Johnson played blues, jazz, and ballads his way; he was a true blues originator whose influence hung heavy on a host of subsequent blues immortals.

Johnson's extreme versatility doubtless stemmed in great part from growing up in the musically diverse Crescent City. Violin caught his ear initially, but he eventually made the guitar his passion, developing a style so fluid and inexorably melodic that instrumental backing seemed superfluous. He signed up with OKeh Records in 1925 and commenced to recording at an astonishing pace—between 1925 and 1932, he cut an estimated 130 waxings. The red-hot duets he recorded with white jazz guitarist Eddie Lang (masquerading as Blind Willie Dunn) in 1928-1929 were utterly groundbreaking in their ceaseless invention. Johnson also recorded pioneering jazz efforts in 1927 with no less than Louis Armstrong's Hot Five and Duke Ellington's orchestra.

After enduring the Depression and moving to Chicago, Johnson came back to recording life with Bluebird for a five-year stint beginning in 1939. Under the ubiquitous Lester Melrose's supervision, Johnson picked up right where he left off, selling quite a few copies of "He's a Jelly Roll Baker" for old Nipper. Johnson went with Cincinnati-based King Records in 1947 and promptly enjoyed one of the biggest hits of his uncommonly long career with the mellow ballad "Tomorrow Night," which topped the R&B charts for seven weeks in 1948. More hits followed posthaste: "Pleasing You (As Long as I Live)," "So Tired," and "Confused."

Time seemed to have passed Johnson by during the late '50s. He was toiling as a hotel janitor in Philadelphia when banjo player Elmer Snowden alerted Chris Albertson to his whereabouts. That rekindled a major comeback, Johnson cutting a series of albums for Prestige's Bluesville subsidary during the early '60s and venturing to Europe under the auspices of Horst Lippmann and Fritz Rau's American Folk Blues Festival banner in 1963. Finally, in 1969, Johnson was hit by a car in Toronto and died a year later from the effects of the accident.

Johnson's influence was massive, touching everyone from Robert Johnson, whose seminal approach bore strong resemblance to that of his older namesake, to Elvis Presley and Jerry Lee Lewis, who each paid heartfelt tribute with versions of "Tomorrow Night" while at Sun. —*Bill Dahl*

Blues By Lonnie Johnson / Mar. 8, 1960 / Bluesville/Original Blues Classics ✦✦✦✦
After four years off records and in obscurity, Lonnie Johnson launched his final comeback with this release, which has been reissued on CD. Teamed with tenor saxophonist Hal Singer, pianist Claude Hopkins, bassist Wendell Marshall, and drummer Bobby Donaldson, Johnson sings and plays guitar on a variety of blues, showing that the layoff (he was working at the time as a janitor) had not hurt his abilities in the slightest. —*Scott Yanow*

★ **Blues & Ballads** / Apr. 5, 1960 / Bluesville/Original Blues Classics ✦✦✦✦✦
This combination works quite well. Guitarist/singer Lonnie Johnson was just starting a successful comeback, and here he is teamed up with acoustic rhythm guitarist Elmer Snowden (who had not recorded since 1934) and bassist Wendell Marshall. Johnson sings smooth blues and sentimental ballads with equal skill, and both guitarists have opportunities to display their complementary but distinctive styles. This CD reissue is easily recommended, as is its more instrumental counterpart, *Blues, Ballads, and Jumpin' Jazz, Vol. 2.* —*Scott Yanow*

Blues, Ballads, and Jumpin' Jazz, Vol. 2 / Apr. 5, 1960 / Bluesville/Original Blues Classics ✦✦✦✦
When producer Chris Albertson brought Lonnie Johnson and guitarist Elmer Snowden into a studio for this album on April 9, 1960, both musicians hadn't recorded in a number of years. Indeed, Snowden hadn't seen the inside of a studio in 26 years, but you'd never know it by the fleet-fingered work he employs on the opening "Lester Leaps In," where he rips off one hot chorus after another. Johnson plays a dark-toned electric while Snowden plays acoustic, with Wendell Marshall rounding things out on bass. Given Johnson's reputation as a closet jazzer, it's remarkable that he merely comps rhythm behind Snowden's leads on "C-Jam Blues" and "On the Sunny Side of the Street." Johnson handles all the vocals, turning in an especially strong turn on the second take of "Stormy Weather." Lots of studio chatter make this disc of previously unissued material a real joy to listen to, a loose and relaxed session with loads of great playing and singing to recommend it. —*Cub Koda*

Losing Game / Dec. 28, 1960 / Bluesville/Original Blues Classics ✦✦✦✦
Johnson recorded prolifically for Prestige's Bluesville during his early-'60s comeback; this 1960 set is a typically gorgeous solo outing that ranges from torchy standards of the Tin Pan Alley species ("What a Difference a Day Makes," "Summertime") to bluesier pursuits of his own creation. —*Bill Dahl*

Idle Hours / Jul. 13, 1961 / Bluesville/Original Blues Classics ✦✦✦✦
Johnson and Victoria Spivey had known one another for decades (they duetted on the ribald "Toothache Blues" way back in 1928), so it's no surprise that their musical repartee on 1961's *Idle Hours* seems so natural and playful. Spivey guests on three tracks (including the title number) and plays piano on her one solo entry. Johnson does the majority of the disc without her, benefitting from pianistic accompaniment by Cliff Jackson. —*Bill Dahl*

Another Night to Cry / Apr. 6, 1962 / Bluesville/Original Blues Classics ✦✦✦
Lonnie Johnson, a talented vocalist and guitarist who chose to spend much of his life playing blues (although in the '20s he recorded with some of the top jazz stars), had his fifth recording for Prestige/Bluesville (a solo set) reissued on this CD. "Blues After Hours" is an instrumental that shows off his jazz roots and many of the 11 songs (all of which are Johnson originals) have spots for his guitar. Since there is only around 34 minutes on this set (which could have been combined on one CD with the music from another LP) and none of the individual songs even reach four minutes, this is not one of the more essential Lonnie Johnson releases but it does have its strong moments. —*Scott Yanow*

Stompin' at the Penny / Nov. 1965 / Columbia/Legacy ✦✦
This set (reissued on CD) is a bit unusual, for it features bluesman Lonnie Johnson with a Canadian Dixieland band, McHarg's Metro Stompers. In addition to including a few Johnson vocals, he takes credible solos on some trad jazz standards, including "China Boy." Six of the 13 numbers do not have the guitarist, putting the focus on the fine

Dixieland band, which includes cornetist Charlie Gall, and clarinetist Eric Neilson in addition to the leader on bass. The original LP only sold 1,000 copies, so this reissue brings back music heard by very few at the time; this was Lonnie Johnson's last regular recording, although he did cut a series of numbers for Smithsonian in 1967. —*Scott Yanow*

The Complete Folkways Recordings / 1967 / Smithsonian/Folkways ✦✦✦✦
An even two dozen solo performances from late in the legendary guitarist's amazing career (1967), but chock full of stellar moments all the same. Artists of Johnson's versatility were rare even then—he brings a multitude of shadings to "My Mother's Eyes" and "How Deep Is the Ocean," then delivers a saucy "Juice Headed Baby" with the same stunning complexity. —*Bill Dahl*

Tomorrow Night / 1976 / Gusto ✦✦✦✦
Here's a two-LP collection just begging for digital reissue. Its 22 sides from Johnson's King stay include the immortal blues ballad "Tomorrow Night," and his definitive renditions of "Careless Love" and "Jelly Roll Baker," and the lightly jumping "Trouble Ain't Nothin' But the Blues"—none of which grace Charly's CD compilation by the late blues great. —*Bill Dahl*

Mr. Johnson Blues / 197 / Mamush ✦✦✦
Fourteen cuts from the late '20s to early '30s, with Eddie Lang, Victoria Spivey, Texas Alexander, Mooch Richardson, Katherine Baker, and Violet Green. Highlights include "Uncle Ned Don't Use Your Head" and "Winnie the Wailer." —*Barry Lee Pearson*

The Originator of Modern Guitar Blues / 1980 / Blues Boy ✦✦✦✦✦
Later Lonnie Johnson, demonstrating his proficiency on everything from pop to blues and R&B. It's excellently remastered, sequenced and presented, covering '40s and '50s cuts. —*Ron Wynn*

Blues Roots, Vol. 8 (Swingin' With Lonnie) / Oct. 16, 1983 / Storyville ✦✦✦
Backed by pianist Otis Spann, singer/guitarist Lonnie Johnson performs blues and ballads on this well-rounded set. Included are such numbers as his old hit "Tomorrow Night," "See See Rider," "Jelly Jelly," and a lone instrumental, "Swingin' With Lonnie." An above-average outing by the veteran bluesman. —*Scott Yanow*

★ **Steppin' on the Blues** / 1990 / Columbia/Legacy ✦✦✦✦✦
Groundbreaking guitar work of dazzling complexity that never fails to amaze—and this stuff was cut in the '20s! Lonnie Johnson's astonishingly fluid guitar work was massively influential (Robert Johnson, for one, was greatly swayed by his waxings), and his no-nonsense vocals (frequently laced with threats of violence—"Got the Blues for Murder Only" and "She's Making Whoopee in Hell Tonight" are prime examples on this 19-cut collection) are scarcely less impressive. Johnson's torrid guitar duets with jazzman Eddie Lang retain their sense of legend over seven decades after they were cut. —*Bill Dahl*

Me and My Crazy Self / 1991 / Charly ✦✦✦✦✦
With a firm emphasis on the less schmaltzy side of Johnson's 1947-1952 stint at Cincinnati's King Records, this 20-tracker finds the blues pioneer coming into the age of electric blues and R&B quite adroitly. His dignified vocal style similarly weathered the ensuing decades nicely—"You Can't Buy Love," "Friendless Blues," and the title track are bittersweet outings sporting multiple levels of subtlety. —*Bill Dahl*

Complete Recorded Works (1925–1932), Vol. 1: 1925-1926 / 1991 / Document ✦✦✦✦✦

Complete 1937 to June 1947 Recordings, Vol. 2: 22 May 1940 to 13 February 1942 / 1991 / Document ✦✦✦✦
This CD completes Lonnie Johnson's prewar recordings with 23 titles (including four previously unreleased numbers from a club date) from the 1940-1942 period. Johnson is mostly heard in trios with such sidemen as pianists Lil Hardin Armstrong and Blind John Davis, and bassist Andrew Harris. There is only one instrumental ("Secret Emotions") but Johnson's guitar gets its spots along the way. Highlights include "Somebody's Got to Go," "Rambler's Blues," "The Devil's Woman," and "He's a Jelly-Roll Baker." —*Scott Yanow*

Complete Recorded Works (1925–1932), Vol. 2: 1926-1927 / 1991 / Document ✦✦✦✦
Lonnie Johnson came into his own during the period of time covered by this CD. A brilliant blues-oriented guitarist, Johnson is heard on such instrumentals as "To Do This, You Got to Know How," "I Done Tole You," "Steppin' on the Blues," "Four Hands Are Better Than Two," and "Woke Up With the Blues in My Fingers." He is also heard backing blues singers Helen Humes (who was 13 at the time), Joe Brown, and Raymond Boyd and singing his own variety of low-down blues. Recommended. —*Scott Yanow*

Complete Recorded Works (1925–1932), Vol. 3: 1927-1928 / 1991 / Document ✦✦✦✦
The third of seven CDs that have all of guitarist/singer Lonnie Johnson's recordings of 1925-1932 is notable for including nine instrumentals among the 25 selections, including "6/88 Glide," "Playing With the Strings," "It's Hot-Let It Alone," and "Stompin' 'Em Along Slow." Johnson is assisted on various tracks (including vocal blues numbers) by pianists Porter Grainger, John Erby, De Loise Searcy, and Jimmy Blythe. Other highlights include "St. Louis Cyclone Blues," "When a Man Is Treated Like a Dog," "Sweet Potato Blues," and the two-part "Kansas City Blues." Classic blues. —*Scott Yanow*

Complete Recorded Works (1925–1932), Vol. 4: 1928–1929 / 1991 / Document ✦✦✦✦✦
The period of time covered in the fourth of seven Lonnie Johnson Document CDs found the guitarist/singer being well-featured as a leader in many settings. He is heard on three two-part double entendre performances with singer Victoria Spivey ("New Black Snake Blues," "Toothache Blues," and "Furniture Man Blues"); on five guitar duets with the great Eddie Lang (during which Lang was billed as Blind Willie Dunn); in a vocal duet with Spencer Williams; on the two-part "It Feels So Good" with Lang, King Oliver, and Hoagy Carmichael; as part of Blind Willie Dunn's Gin Bottle Four; and as a solo blues performer. Everything works. Considering that this is a strictly chronological release, the music

is consistently rewarding, making this one of the key Lonnie Johnson CDs to pick up. *—Scott Yanow*

Complete Recorded Works (1925–1932), Vol. 6: 1930–1931 / 1991 / Document ♦♦♦♦
The music on this CD, the sixth of seven Document discs that trace Lonnie Johnson's recording career during the 1925-1932 period, alternates between blues and hokum. Johnson performs good-time vocal duets with Spencer Williams (such as "Keep It to Yourself" and "The Bull Frog and the Toad") and Clara Smith (an excellent four-song session from 1930 including "What Makes You Act Like That" and "Don't Wear It Out"), plus a variety of solo numbers. Other highlights include the two-part "I Got the Best Jelly Roll in Town," "I Have to Do My Time," and "Let All Married Women Alone." *—Scott Yanow*

Complete Recorded Works (1925–1932), Vol. 7: 1931–1932 / 1991 / Document ♦♦♦♦
Lonnie Johnson, who had played both creative blues and advanced jazz in the '20s, was sticking exclusively to blues (with some good-time hokum) by 1931. These 21 performances ended his classic period with OKeh before Johnson disappeared from records for five years. All of the selections are solo vocal/guitar numbers with the exception of three cuts, where he switches to piano and one duet with pianist Fred Longshaw. Johnson is in excellent form on such numbers as "Low Down St. Louis Blues," "Hell Is a Name for Sinners," "Best Jockey in Town," "She's Dangerous With the Thing," and "Racketeers Blues." True blues collectors will want all seven Lonnie Johnson CDs in this valuable series. *—Scott Yanow*

Complete 1937 to June 1947 Recordings, Vol. 1: 8 November 1937 to 22 May 1940 / 1992 / Document ♦♦♦♦
Lonnie Johnson was off records for five years during 1932-1937, working in Cleveland with Putney Dandridge, appearing on the radio, and working outside of music. In 1937, he moved to Chicago, where he returned to full-time music and began recording regularly for the Decca label. Three Document CDs cover his work of 1937-1947. This CD features Johnson as a solo blues performer (showcasing his guitar on instrumental versions of "Swing Out Rhythm" and "Got the Blues for the West End") and singing such numbers as "Flood Water Blues," "Devil's Got the Blues," and "Blue Ghost Blues." Some numbers have Johnson joined by either Roosevelt Sykes or Joshua Altheimer on piano along with a few unknown musicians. Rarely reissued, these performances are consistently excellent. *—Scott Yanow*

Complete 1937 to June 1947 Recordings, Vol. 3: 14 December 1944 to 2 June 1947 / 1992 / Document ♦♦♦♦
Among the most obscure recordings from Lonnie Johnson's career, the 23 selections on this CD were cut after the recording strike of 1942-1944 ended and just prior to the blues singer/guitarist joining the King label. Johnson is heard in trios (usually including pianist Blind John Davis) plus on two numbers on which he backs the singing of Karl Jones. The music is (as was true throughout his career) consistently enjoyable with strong musicianship and a gentler side of the blues than was usually performed by Johnson's country blues counterparts. Well worth exploring. *—Scott Yanow*

Complete Recorded Works (1925–1932), Vol. 5: 1929–1930 / 1992 / Document ♦♦♦♦♦
Lonnie Johnson straddled the boundaries between blues and jazz during the 1927-1930 period before deciding to stick to the former. This 22-song collection features five guitar duets with Eddie Lang (including "Bull Frog Moan" and "Hot Fingers"), vocal duets with Spencer Williams (including "It Feels So Good Parts 3 and 4" and "Once or Twice"), Victoria Spivey (the two-part "You Done Lost Your Good Thing Now") and Clarence Williams ("Wipe It Off"), and such blues numbers as "From Now on Make Your Whoopee at Home," "She's Making Whoopee in Hell Tonight," and "Another Woman Booked Out and Bound to Go." Lonnie Johnson at his best. *—Scott Yanow*

He's a Jelly Roll Baker / Sep. 1992 / Bluebird/RCA ♦♦♦♦♦
This 20-song collection covers '30s and '40s material in which Johnson primarily performs blues tunes, doing salty, sassy, mournful and suggestive numbers in a distinctive, memorable fashion. His vocals on "Rambler's Blues," "In Love Again," the title cut and several others are framed by brilliant, creative playing and excellent support from such pianists as Blind John Davis, Lil Hardin Armstrong, and Joshua Altheimer. This is tight, intuitive music in which Johnson set the tone and dominated the songs. If you're unaware of Lonnie Johnson's brilliant blues material, here's an excellent introduction. *—Ron Wynn*

Playing With the Strings / Nov. 22, 1994 / JSP ♦♦♦

The Unsung Blues Legend: The Living Room Sessions / 2000 / Music Magnet Media ♦♦♦
This one-of-a-kind CD, a never-before-released solo performance by Lonnie Johnson, features the bluesman five years before his death, playing guitar and singing in the living room of painter and friend Bernie Strassberg in 1965. The raw recording quality and solo guitar-and-voice format recall the classic delta blues recordings of Robert Johnson (no relation). The ultra-informal setting also brings to mind Lenny Breau's *Cabin Fever*, on which the acoustic 7-string master was recorded in an isolated log cabin. While there's a deeply traditional blues feeling to Lonnie Johnson's performances, many of the songs he performs come from the jazz canon: "I'm Confessin'," "I Can't Give You Anything But Love," Kurt Weill's "September Song," Duke Ellington's "Solitude," Hoagy Carmichael's "Rockin' Chair," and Gershwin's "Summertime." But there's also plenty of straight blues, in particular Johnson's own "New Orleans Blues" and Bessie Smith's "Back Water Blues." Johnson's singing voice is remarkably versatile—effortless and earthy on the blues, yet sophisticated enough to handle the tricky melodies of Ellington and Weill. Johnson goes for long stretches without a break, stringing together as many as seven songs back-to-back; a few are barely more than a minute long. But he stretches out for over five minutes on his own "There's Been Some Changes Made," and he pulls off a seven-minute *tour de force* on W.C. Handy's "St. Louis Blues." Throughout, Johnson displays an all-out mastery of the guitar, playing deft call-and-response licks in the manner of Nat King Cole, subtle chord-melody passages à la Eddie Lang, and screaming blues outbursts that nearly suggest Jimi Hendrix. One is struck by Johnson's stylistic breadth and depth and his contributions to a whole range of 20th century genres. *—David R. Adler*

Luther "Guitar Junior" Johnson

b. Jul. 15, 1939, Itta Bena, MS
Vocals, Guitar / Electric Blues, Modern Electric Chicago Blues
Of the three blues guitarists answering to the name of Luther Johnson, this West Side-styled veteran is probably the best known. Adding to the general confusion surrounding the triumvirate: like Luther "Georgia Boy" Johnson, "Guitar Junior" spent a lengthy stint in the top-seeded band of Muddy Waters (1972-1979).

Gospel and blues intersected in young Luther Johnson's life while he was still in Mississippi. But after he moved to Chicago in the mid-'50s, blues was his main passion, working with Ray Scott and Tall Milton Shelton before taking over the latter's combo in 1962. Magic Sam was a major stylistic inspiration to Johnson during the mid-'60s (Johnson spent a couple of years in Sam's band). The West Side approach remains integral to Johnson's sound today, even though he moved to the Boston area during the early '80s.

Johnson's 1976 debut album, *Luther's Blues*, was cut during a European tour with Muddy Waters. By 1980, he was on his own, recording with the Nighthawks as well as four tracks on Alligator's second series of *Living Chicago Blues* anthologies. With his own band, the Magic Rockers, and the Roomful of Blues horn section, Johnson released *Doin' the Sugar Too* on Rooster Blues in 1984. Since 1990, Johnson has been signed to Ron Levy's Bullseye Blues logo; his three albums for the firm have been sizzling, soul-tinged blues (with a strong West Side flavor often slicing through). *—Bill Dahl*

Luther's Blues / Nov. 1, 1976 / Evidence ♦♦♦
The confidence that ex-Muddy Waters sideman Luther "Guitar Junior" Johnson exudes on his contemporary albums wasn't quite there in abundance yet when the French Black & Blue imprint produced this album in 1976 with the rest of his Waters bandmates in tow. A few too many hoary covers ("Sweet Home Chicago," "Mother-In-Law Blues") also grate. But as his first solo album, it's an important chapter in his development. *—Bill Dahl*

Doin' the Sugar Too / 1984 / Rooster Blues ♦♦♦
A step in the right direction—much better production, savvier song selection, including a few snappy originals, and the five-piece Roomful of Blues horn section in staunch support. The guitarist's Magic Rockers include keyboardist Ron Levy, who would go on to produce Johnson's Bullseye Blues output. Bullseye Blues reissued *Doin' the Sugar Too* on CD in 1997. *—Bill Dahl*

I Want to Groove With You / 1990 / Bullseye Blues ♦♦♦♦♦
Now this is more like it. Johnson and his New England-based Magic Rockers sizzle the hide off the genre with tough West Side-styled grooves redolent of Johnson's Chicago upbringing but up-to-the-minute in their execution. With this set, Johnson fully came into his own as a recording artist. *—Bill Dahl*

It's Good to Me / 1992 / Bullseye Blues ♦♦♦♦
Another barn-burner mixing the guitarist's West Side roots with soul and blues shadings to present some of the fieriest contemporary blues on the market. Saxist Gordon Beadle and keyboardist Joe Krown distinguish themselves behind Johnson. *—Bill Dahl*

Country Sugar Papa / Mar. 30, 1994 / Bullseye Blues ♦♦♦♦
Johnson's third and final album for producer Ron Levy's Bullseye Blues diskery is every bit as spellbinding as the prior pair. Whether fronting his latest batch of Magic Rockers or going it alone, Johnson is totally convincing. *—Bill Dahl*

● **Slammin' on the West Side** / Apr. 1996 / Telarc ♦♦♦♦♦
Lousy album title, great album. Johnson hasn't been based out of Chicago in years, but that sound remains at the heart of his approach—even when he's recording in Louisiana with a funky New Orleans rhythm section (bassist George Porter Jr. and drummer Herman Ernest). Jump blues in the form of Buddy Johnson's "A Pretty Girl (A Cadillac and Some Money)," the Magic Sam tribute "Hard Times (Have Surely Come)," the solo acoustic "Get Up and Go," a soul-slanted "Every Woman Needs to Be Loved"—Johnson smokes 'em all. *—Bill Dahl*

Got to Find a Way / Sep. 29, 1998 / Telarc ♦♦♦
The appeal of the blues is its earthiness, simplicity, honesty and the humanity of its purveyors. *Got to Find a Way* has all of these; plus, it's a rockin' good time from beginning to end. Anchored by five originals and several classic blues songs, this disc finds Luther "Guitar Junior" Johnson and his band, the Magic Rockers, dishing out the real thing. In fact, it's so real that when the rhythm guitarist hits the wrong chord toward the end of "Home Alone," the mistake is left in rather than being doctored with a retake or studio magic. Lynwood Cooke's saxophone and Johnson's own guitar versatility help *Got to Find a Way* stake its claim in the crowded field of modern blues recordings. In addition, this is an enhanced CD featuring video of Johnson performing acoustically. *—Jim Newsom*

Live at the Rynborn / Mar. 3, 1999 / M.C. ♦♦♦♦
This was recorded with Johnson's regular New England working band, blowing the roof off the hotel he was living at in 1995. Released on a dime sized local label, it kicked enough noise to be picked for a more national release by M.C. Records in 1999. The new reissue still reflects the same crude editing between songs in a sloppy attempt to give the illusion of that "these all came from the same set" nonsense that plagued the original, and the back to back to back to back pile-up of slow blues at the end does hamper the momentum a bit. But it's Luther Johnson, doing what he (and Magic Slim) do best: rocking a crowd down to the bricks while keeping the real blues alive. *—Cub Koda*

Talkin' About Soul / Feb. 27, 2001 / Telarc ♦♦♦♦

Luther "Houserocker" Johnson

b. Atlanta, GA

Vocals, Guitar / Modern Electric Blues

The latest Luther Johnson to add his name to the blues directory is an adept singer/guitarist who is a current favorite on the Atlanta blues scene. Proficient in various shadings of the electric blues idiom, Johnson has recently extended his repertoire from covers of blues standards to his own material, performed with the same '50s/'60s flavor.

Johnson taught himself how to play guitar when he was a teenager in Atlanta by listening to records. Soon, he began playing guitar in pickup bands, which gave him the opportunity to support such touring musicians as Johnny Winter. After several years playing in bar bands, Johnson formed his own group, the Houserockers.

The Houserockers played bars and clubs around Georgia for several years, eventually landing a record contract with Ichiban in 1989. The next year Johnson released his debut album, *Takin' a Bite Outta the Blues*. Two years later, his second record, *Houserockin' Daddy*, appeared. Luther "Houserocker" Johnson continued to tour the U.S. throughout the '90s. —*Jim O'Neal & Stephen Thomas Erlewine*

Takin' a Bite Outta the Blues / 1990 / Ichiban ✦✦✦

Luther "Houserocker" Johnson isn't a huge name in the blues market, although he did enjoy a small following in Atlanta when he recorded *Takin' a Bite Outta the Blues* for Ichiban in April 1990. That album didn't bring him fame, though it did give blues enthusiasts outside of Atlanta (where Ichiban was based) the chance to hear him. Not fantastic but likable and sincere, *Takin' a Bite Outta the Blues* left no doubt that Johnson (who should not be confused with fellow bluesman Luther "Guitar Junior" Johnson) was very much a disciple of the late Chicago blues icon Jimmy Reed. The influence of Reed is impossible to miss on familiar classics like Ray Charles' "What'd I Say," B.B. King's "Rock Me, Baby," and a number of songs that Reed wrote ("Hush, Hush," "Where Can My Baby Be") or defined (Willie Dixon's "Pretty Thing"). Several years after its 1990 release, *Takin' a Bite Outta the Blues* went out of print; however, half of the songs on the album were reissued on Ichiban's 1998 collection, *Retrospectives*. —*Alex Henderson*

● **Houserockin' Daddy** / 1991 / Wild Dog ✦✦✦✦✦

Johnson is a traditional electric bluesman (now living and working in the Atlanta area) who was heavily influenced by Jimmy Reed. The album includes covers of Jimmy Reed, Lightnin' Slim, Howlin' Wolf, and Guitar Slim tunes. It's simple, driving, to the point, streamlined, no-frills blues. —*Niles J. Frantz*

Retrospectives / Jun. 30, 1998 / Ichiban ✦✦✦✦

American Roots: Blues / Jun. 4, 2002 / Ichiban ✦✦✦

Luther Snake Boy Johnson

b. Aug. 30, 1934, Davisboro, GA, d. Mar. 18, 1976

Vocals, Guitar / Electric Chicago Blues, Electric Blues

The confusing plethora of artists working under the name of Luther (nickname here) Johnson can leave even those with a decent knowledge of blues in a major state of confusion. But in this biographical entry, we concern ourselves with the life and times of Luther "Georgia Boy/Snake Boy" Johnson who, to make matters even *more* confusing, also worked and recorded under the names Little Luther and Luther King.

He was born in 1934 in Davisboro, GA, which explains at least one of his nicknames, but it turns out his real name wasn't even Luther, but Lucius. One of ten children working on a farm, he started playing at the tender age of seven. He soon ran away from home and was placed in a reform school by 1947. A three-year stint in the Army followed. Upon his military discharge, he picked guitar as a member of the Milwaukee Supreme Angels gospel group, working the local church circuit. But the blues bug hit and he soon had his own little blues trio together, eventually settling in Chicago by the early '60s. He played for a while with Elmore James and was a regular fixture in the Muddy Waters band by the mid-'60s. He recorded as Little Luther for Chess in the mid-'60s ("The Twirl," available on the Ace anthology, *Houserockin' Blues*, listed in the compilation section) and by 1970 was relocated to Boston, MA, working as a solo artist. The next five years found him working steadily on the college and blues festival circuit before cancer overtook him on March 18, 1976, at a mere 41 years of age. —*Cub Koda*

Come on Home / 1969 / Douglas ✦✦✦

The Muddy Waters Blues Band / Dec. 1969 / Douglas ✦✦

Born in Georgia / 1972 / Black & Blue ✦✦✦

Chicken Shack / 1974 / Muse ✦✦✦✦✦

● **Lonesome in My Bedroom** / Dec. 18, 1975 / Evidence ✦✦✦✦✦

This was Johnson's final album before his death in 1976, and it was originally cut for Black & Blue (now reissued with three bonus tracks). While various tracks reflect the influence of Muddy Waters, Jimmy Reed and John Lee Hooker, Johnson's own inimitable vocals, raspy lines and tart guitar eventually create his own aura. He is nicely backed by drummer Fred Below, bassist Dave Myers, guitar burner Lonnie Brooks and the solid rhythm work of Hubert Sumlin. This was a fine session for a good, occasionally outstanding blues artist. —*Ron Wynn*

On the Road Again / 1976 / Evidence ✦✦✦

On the Road Again, an early-'70s outing, shows Johnson in fine form, assisted by a tough backing band. Cut in France. —*Bill Dahl*

Get Down to the Nitty Gritty / 1976 / New Rose ✦✦✦

Culled from a radio broadcast made for a Rochester, NY, radio station in 1976, *Get Down to the Nitty Gritty* is a nifty set of hard-edged Chicago blues. Luther Johnson pays homage to his mentor and employer, Muddy Waters, throughout the album, playing classics like "Hoochie Coochie Man" and originals in the same vein. Although the sound quality of the recording is poor—there are dropouts and tape hiss all over the place—the performance is stellar. Johnson sings with passion and his guitar solos are blistering. *Get Down*

to the Nitty Gritty is a rough gem that is worthwhile to any fan of Johnson or Muddy Waters. —*Thom Owens*

Margaret Johnson

Vocals, Piano / Prewar Blues, Classic Female Blues, Classic Jazz

Although lumped together with many female classic blues singers from the '20s, Margaret Johnson's career was a bit more diverse, including her recording output. She was one of the few female vocalists of her era that made records with a strong country blues influence, particularly the collaborations involving the harmonica-and-guitar team of Bobby Leecan and Robert Cooksey. Of course, she also took part in sessions typical of this era, which combined blues singing with extremely strong New Orleans jazz combos, cutting tracks with masterful players such as Sidney Bechet, Louis Armstrong, and Clarence Williams. Both she and pianist/composer Williams secretly took part in sessions by banjoist Buddy Christian's band the Jazz Rippers, Williams taking no credit at all, and Johnson hiding out under the pseudonym of Margaret Carter. Many of the blues numbers originating from this period indulged in cleverness for its own sake, sometimes with more than a dash of smut; but there is no denying the potential philosophical impact of Johnson's better recordings, titles often overlooked as consumers flock to the tried-and-true "Dead Drunk Blues." Some of her other recordings include "Who'll Chop Your Suey (When I'm Gone)" (from the same genre of song that contains the classic country number "Who'll Take the Garbage Out When I'm Gone?"), "Folks in New York City Ain't Like Folks Down South" (a cousin to the Buck Owens number "I Wouldn't Live in New York City if They Gave Me the Whole Damn Town"), and "When a 'Gator Holler, Folks Say It's a Sign of Rain" (a song unique enough to inhabit a class of its own).

The Document label holds a pretty full deck when it comes to her '20s recordings, offering a set of her complete works as well as a separate collection of the material with Leecan and Cooksey, released under their name. As is true of much of the classic blues material from the '20s and '30s, Johnson's recordings have also been folded into more than a dozen compilations originating in almost as many different countries. Another difference between Johnson and the colleagues featured on these recordings was that she didn't drop off the music scene once the public taste for classic blues momentarily dwindled. In the '30s, she concentrated on the piano, becoming an in-demand accompanist in an era when female instrumentalists were strongly discouraged, and recording on a variety of tracks by the sublime jazz vocalist Billie Holiday. Her tenure with "Lady Day" coincides with that of one of Holiday's favorite playing partners, tenor saxophonist Lester Young, meaning that Johnson can be heard to good effect on the collection *Lady Day and Prez*, among others. One type of blues that has nothing to do with this artist is *Butterscotch Blues*, one of the book titles by Afro-American novelist Margaret Johnson-Hodge, who shares the blues artist's name, but no family ties. —*Eugene Chadbourne*

● **Complete Recorded Works (1923–27)** / May 14, 1996 / Document ✦✦✦✦✦

Mary Johnson

b. 1900, Eden Station, MS

Vocals, Accordion / Piano Blues, Classic Female Blues

Blues singer Mary Johnson was born Mary Williams in Mississippi's Yazoo City in 1905. Ten years later, she moved with her mother to St. Louis, where she eventually worked with many of the area's artists. She was married to bluesman Lonnie Johnson from 1925 to 1932. She also recorded with bottleneck guitar great Tampa Red, with Judson Brown, an obscure barrelhouse pianist, and with the duo of pianist Henry Brown and trombonist Ike Rodgers. In the '50s, Mary Johnson abandoned the blues for religion. —*Joslyn Layne*

● **Complete Works in Chronological Order (1929–1936)** / Feb. 15, 1995 / Document ✦✦✦✦

The complete output of Mary Johnson is on this single CD. The wife of blues guitarist/singer Lonnie Johnson during 1925-1932 (a period when she had six children!), Mary Johnson was a fine lowdown blues singer herself. She recorded 14 selections during 1929-1930, two in 1932, four in 1934, and two final numbers in 1936. She was accompanied by either Henry Brown, Judson Brown, Roosevelt Sykes, or Peetie Wheatstraw on piano, and some selections add trombonist Ike Rodgers, guitarist Tampa Red, violinist Artie Mosby, or guitarist Kokomo Arnold. None of the 22 songs became hits, but they do show off Johnson's haunting voice and expressive style. Recommended to serious blues collectors. —*Scott Yanow*

Pete Johnson

b. Mar. 25, 1904, Kansas City, MO, d. Mar. 23, 1967, Buffalo, NY

Piano / Jazz Blues, Boogie-Woogie

Pete Johnson was one of the three great boogie-woogie pianists (along with Albert Ammons and Meade "Lux" Lewis) whose sudden prominence in the late '30s helped make the style very popular. Originally a drummer, Johnson switched to piano in 1922. He was part of the Kansas City scene in the '20s and '30s, often accompanying singer Big Joe Turner. Producer John Hammond discovered him in 1936 and got him to play at the Famous Door in New York. After taking part in Hammond's 1938 Spirituals to Swing Carnegie Hall concert in 1938, Johnson started recording regularly and appeared on an occasional basis with Ammons and Lewis as the Boogie Woogie Trio. He also backed Turner on some classic records. Johnson recorded often in the '40s and spent much of 1947-1949 based in Los Angeles. He moved to Buffalo in 1950 and, other than an appearance at the 1958 Newport Jazz Festival, he was in obscurity for much of the decade. A stroke later in 1958 left him partly paralyzed. Johnson made one final appearance at John Hammond's January 1967 Spirituals to Swing concert, playing the right hand on a version of "Roll 'Em Pete" two months before his death. —*Scott Yanow*

● **1938–1939** / Dec. 30, 1938-Dec. 19, 1939 / Classics ♦♦♦♦♦
This superlative CD reissue features boogie-woogie pianist Pete Johnson on two classic numbers with singer Big Joe Turner (the original versions of "Goin' Away Blues" and "Roll 'Em Pete"), with inspiring trumpeter Harry James ("Boo Woo" and "Home James"), with his Boogie Woogie Boys (a sextet that includes Turner and trumpeter Hot Lips Page), interacting with fellow pianists Albert Ammons and Meade "Lux" Lewis (joining Big Joe on "Café Society Rag"), and on a pair of trio numbers. However, it is Johnson's ten unaccompanied piano solos (mostly released previously by Solo Art) that are the rarest and most notable. Taken as a whole, this is Pete Johnson's definitive release, showing that he was much more than just a one-dimensional (although powerful) boogie-woogie specialist. *—Scott Yanow*

Radio Broadcasts Film Soundtracks Alternate Takes (1939–1947) / Jan. 31, 1939-1947 / Document ♦♦♦
This Pete Johnson CD collects a number of rare recordings from radio airchecks, film soundtracks, radio transcription discs, and unissued alternate takes, featuring the pianist in a variety of settings; the fidelity is surprisingly good on most tracks. His inventive "Bus Robinson Blues," and the lively boogie woogie "Dive Bomber" are piano solos; he's heard with occasional partner Albert Ammons in a revival of their "Boogie Woogie Prayer," as well as an untitled duet and two rehearsals. Johnson accompanies singers Lena Horne and blues great Big Joe Turner, and also with small groups that include Hot Lips Page on trumpet and either Budd Johsnon or Ben Webster on tenor sax. Johnson sits in with Benny Goodman & His Orchestra for "Roll 'Em" (not the Mary Lou Williams piece with the identical name). Several tracks are taken from the soundtrack to the film *Boogie Woogie Dream*, and unfortunately include dialogue, though it is mercifully brief. A nice touch is the inclusion of the various radio announcers; the introduction to a 1940 broadcast is a hilarious parody of the often pompous classical announcers, though long time *Metropolitan Opera* radio host Milton Cross plays along with the insulting script denouncing boogie woogie as he introduces Johnson and Ammons' "Boogie Woogie Prayer." Detailed liner notes by Konrad Nowakowski, the vintage photographs, and fairly detailed discography add to the value of this recommended CD. *—Ken Dryden*

The Boogie Woogie Boys / Feb. 1939-Jan. 1953 / Document ♦♦♦♦♦

King of Boogie / Apr. 16, 1939-May 8, 1941 / Milan ♦♦♦♦♦
Seventeen songs, each one more surprising and satisfying than the last in its textures, shadings, and rhythms, cut by Johnson between April 1939 and May 1941, both solo and as part of a trio with Abe Bolar and Ulysses Livingston, as well as with a band featuring Hot Lips Page on the trumpet, Don Byas and Don Stoval on alto and tenor saxes (playing some glorious solos), and John Collins on guitar. Assuming that the sources for these performances are as claimed, the sound restoration is extraordinary—one gets the feeling of sitting right up next to Johnson's piano, and even the rhythm guitar on the cuts where it appears comes through with stunning clarity. Tracks include 14 Johnson-credited originals and covers of a handful of pieces including Leroy Carr's "How Long, How Long." Even given the questions surrounding the sources for this material—the notes claim they were from concerts in France that would have happened, in some instances, under the German occupation of the country—there's still no reason not to grab this extraordinary boogie-woogie piano workout, most of it solo and all of it (except for the moody ballad "Pete's Blues No. 2") hot. *—Bruce Eder*

1939–1941 / Dec. 19, 1939-Jun. 17, 1941 / Classics ♦♦♦

Master of Blues and Boogie Woogie, Vol. 3 / Dec. 19, 1939-Apr. 1949 / Oldie Blues ♦♦♦
This Dutch LP features pianist Pete Johnson in four different settings spanning a decade of time. Six titles are trio and solo numbers taken from his 1939 Blue Note dates (bassist Abe Bolar is mistakenly listed as playing drums). Much rarer are three songs from a 1946 quintet set with organist Bill Gooden and guitarist Jimmy Shirley, and three songs with a rollicking R&B-ish sextet in 1949. But overall, collectors will prefer to get these performances in complete versions with their original sessions. Good music, but this LP is not essential. *—Scott Yanow*

Boogie Woogie Mood (1940–1944) / Nov. 11, 1940-Feb. 17, 1944 / MCA ♦♦♦
This 1980 LP was quite valuable when it was released, although it has been largely superseded by later CDs. Pianist Pete Johnson is heard jamming with a Kansas City band on "627 Stomp," taking four numbers with a trio (including "Death Ray Boogie" and "Just For You"), and on eight unaccompanied piano solos. The emphasis, as usual, is on boogie-woogie although Johnson could also play very credible swing and blues. *—Scott Yanow*

1944–1946 / Feb. 17, 1944-Jan. 31, 1946 / Classics ♦♦♦♦♦
The third "complete" Pete Johnson CD put out by the European Classics label features the great boogie-woogie pianist in three different settings. There are eight formerly rare piano solos from 1944 that cover a variety of moods, five selections with a hot Kansas City octet which includes trumpeter Hot Lips Page, tenorman Budd Johnson and two vocals from the young Etta Jones, and eight intriguing numbers in which Johnson is gradually joined by an additional musician on each track. "Page Mr. Trumpet" is an exciting outing for Hot Lips, and the other top players include clarinetist Albert Nicholas, trombonist J.C. Higginbotham and tenorman Ben Webster. A particularly exciting release. *—Scott Yanow*

Pete's Blues / Jan. 2, 1946-Jan. 26, 1946 / Savoy ♦♦♦♦
This very enjoyable Pete Johnson disc finds the great boogie-woogie pianist in the company of some of the very best swing-era soloists. Something of an informal concept album, the first of the two 1946 sessions here works as a Johnson housewarming party cum jam session, with soloists being added for each successive number. Before the guests show up, though, Johnson demonstrates his fine solo keyboard touch on the slow boogie number "Pete's Lonesome Blues." After cuts marking the arrival of drummer J.C. Heard and later a bassist and guitarist, the session begins to really blossom as front-line soloists individually come aboard over the course of four tracks: clarinetist Albert Nicholas, trumpeter Hot Lips Page, tenor great Ben Webster, and trombonist J.C. Higginbotham all turn in choice solos over some medium-tempo blues. The jam session finally comes to a close with the full-band swinger "Pete's Housewarming." Rounding the record out are four more informal numbers featuring Johnson, Page again on trumpet, trombonist Clyde Bernhardt, and tenor saxophonist Budd Johnson. Joining the band for two cuts is a very young Etta Jones on vocals. A tightly swinging set with an after-hours feel, *Pete's Blues* spotlights the innovative pianist in one of the era's more underrated trad recordings. *—Stephen Cook*

Central Avenue Boogie / Apr. 18, 1947-Nov. 29, 1947 / Delmark ♦♦♦
Boogie-woogie pianist Pete Johnson is in excellent form on these selections but this complete reissue of his Apollo recordings does not have much meat. Johnson only cut eight sides for the label so three alternate takes are included plus two titles (and an alternate) from pianist Arnold Wiley's only Apollo session. The results are enjoyable (particularly Johnson's versions of "Margie" and "Swanee River") although few surprises or real high-points occur. *—Scott Yanow*

1947–1949 / Apr. 18, 1947-Apr. 1949 / Classics ♦♦♦
This is the fourth Classics installment chronicling 21 final key recordings of boogie-woogie pianist Pete Johnson. *1947-1949* found Johnson leading three different quartets (the second with Al McKibbon on bass and J.C. Heard on drums) for the Apollo, Modern, and French Jazz Selection labels, while the final session features a sextet on six tracks, blistering through the excellent "Rocket 88 Boogie, Parts 1 and 2" for the Down Beat/Swingtime label. These sessions have a common thread in the predominate use of guitar from Charles Norris, Carl Lynch, Johnny Rogers, and Herman Mitchell thoroughly featured alongside Johnson's piano throughout. Soon after these sessions Johnson left his West Coast home for Buffalo where he essentially retired, showing up occasionally at the odd live appearance or on other musicians' sessions. *—Al Campbell*

St. Louis Parties of July 20 & August 1, 1954 / Jul. 30, 1954-Aug. 1, 1954 / Document ♦♦♦
The unusual music featured on this CD was recorded at a pair of private parties held in St. Louis in the summer of 1954. The great boogie-woogie pianist Pete Johnson is featured playing blues, swing tunes, and standards. Sometimes the guests are a bit noisy in spots, but at other times they were obviously paying close attention to his playing. Throughout these performances, Johnson shows that he was more than just a boogie-woogie specialist, digging into such songs as "Perdido," "12th Street Rag," "Stardust," and "Honeysuckle Rose," striding away. Two numbers find him joined by as many as three other pianists (all playing the same piano): he backs Bill Atkinson's singing on two cuts, Tom Harris sings "K.C. Blues," and on "Harris Propelled," Johnson plays drums behind Harris' piano playing. In addition he is on a very rare vocal on "How Long How Long." Because the recording quality is not impeccable and there is some crowd noise in spots, this is not an essential release, but fans of Pete Johnson and his style of piano playing will find these performances to be of great interest. *—Scott Yanow*

Robert Johnson

b. May 8, 1911, Hazlehurst, MS, **d.** Aug. 16, 1938, Greenwood, MS
Slide Guitar, Vocals, Songwriter, Guitar, Guitar (Acoustic) / Slide Guitar Blues, Prewar Blues, Delta Blues, Prewar Country Blues

If the blues has a truly mythic figure, one whose story hangs over the music the way a Charlie Parker does over jazz or a Hank Williams does over country, it's Robert Johnson, certainly the most celebrated figure in the history of the blues. Of course, his legend is immensely fortified by the fact that Johnson also left behind a small legacy of recordings that are considered the emotional apex of the music itself. These recordings have not only entered the realm of blues standards ("Love in Vain," "Crossroads," "Sweet Home Chicago," "Stop Breaking Down"), but have been adapted by rock & roll artists as diverse as the Rolling Stones, Steve Miller, Led Zeppelin, and Eric Clapton. While there are historical naysayers who would be more comfortable downplaying his skills and achievements (most of whom have never made a convincing case as where the source of his apocalyptic visions emanates from), Robert Johnson remains a potent force to be reckoned with. As a singer, a composer, and a guitarist of considerable skills, he produced some of the genre's best music and the ultimate blues legend to deal with. Doomed, haunted, driven by demons, a tormented genius dead at an early age, all of these add up to making him a character of mythology who—if he hadn't actually existed—would have to be created by some biographer's overactive romantic imagination.

The legend of his life—which by now, even folks who don't know *anything* about the blues can cite to you chapter and verse—goes something like this: Robert Johnson was a young black man living on a plantation in rural Mississippi. Branded with a burning desire to become great blues musician, he was instructed to take his guitar to a crossroad near Dockery's plantation at midnight. There he was met by a large black man (the Devil), who took the guitar from Johnson, tuned it, and handed it back to him. Within less than a year's time, in exchange for his everlasting soul, Robert Johnson became the king of the Delta blues singers, able to play, sing, and create the greatest blues anyone had ever heard.

As success came with live performances and phonograph recordings, Johnson remained tormented, constantly haunted by nightmares of hellhounds on his trail, his pain and mental anguish finding release only in the writing and performing of his music. Just as he was to be brought to Carnegie Hall to perform in John Hammond's first Spirituals to Swing concert, the news had come from Mississippi: Robert Johnson was dead, poisoned by a jealous girlfriend while playing a juke joint. Those who were there swear he was last seen alive foaming at the mouth, crawling around on all fours, hissing and snapping at onlookers like a mad dog. His dying words (either spoken or written on a piece of scrap paper) were, "I pray that my redeemer will come and take me from my grave." He was buried in a pine box in an unmarked grave, his deal with the Devil at an end.

Of course, Johnson's influences in the real world were far more disparate than the legend suggests, no matter how many times it's been retold or embellished. As a teenage plantation worker, Johnson fooled with a harmonica a little bit, but seemingly had no major musical skills to speak of. Every attempt to sit in with local titans of the stature of Son House, Charley Patton, Willie Brown, and others brought howls of derision from the older bluesmen. Son House: "We'd all play for the Saturday night balls, and there'd be this little boy hanging around. That was Robert Johnson. He blew a harmonica then, and he was pretty good at that, but he wanted to play a guitar. He'd sit at our feet and play during the breaks and such another racket you'd never heard." He married young and left Robinsonville, wandering the Delta and using Hazelhurst as base, determined to become a full-time professional musician after his first wife died during childbirth. Johnson returned to Robinsonville a few years later, and when he encountered House and Willie Brown at a juke joint in Banks, MS, according to House, "When he finished all our mouths were standing open. I said, 'Well, ain't that fast! He's gone now!'" To a man, there was only one explanation as how Johnson had gotten *that* good, *that* fast; he had sold his soul to the Devil.

But Johnson's skills were acquired in a far more conventional manner, born more of a concentrated Christian work ethic than a Faustian bargain with old Scratch. He idolized the Delta recording star Lonnie Johnson—sometimes introducing himself to newcomers as "Robert Lonnie, one of the Johnson brothers"—and the music of Scrapper Blackwell, Skip James, and Kokomo Arnold were all inspirational elements from which he drew his unique style. His slide style certainly came from hours of watching local stars like Charley Patton and Son House, among others. Perhaps the biggest influence, however, came from an unrecorded bluesman named Ike Zinneman. We'll never really know what Zinneman's music sounded like (we do know from various reports that he liked to practice late at night in the local graveyard, sitting on tombstones while he strummed away) or how much of his personal muse he imparted to Johnson, if any. What *is* known is that after a year or so under Zinneman's tutelage, Johnson returned with an encyclopedic knowledge of his instrument, an ability to sing and play in a multiplicity of styles and a very carefully worked-out approach to song construction, keeping his original lyrics with him in a personal digest.

As an itinerant musician, playing at country suppers as well as on the street, his audience demanded someone who could play and sing everything from blues pieces to the pop and hillbilly tunes of the day. Johnson's talents could cover all of that and more. His most enduring contribution, the boogie bass line played on the bottom strings of the guitar (adapted from piano players), has become part and parcel of the sound most people associate with down-home blues. It is a sound so very much of a part of the music's fabric that the listener cannot imagine the styles of Jimmy Reed, Elmore James, Eddie Taylor, Lightnin' Slim, Hound Dog Taylor, or a hundred lesser lights existing without that essential component part. As his playing partner Johnny Shines put it, "Some of the things that Robert did with the guitar affected the way everybody played. He'd do rundowns and turnbacks. He'd do repeats. None of this was being done. In the early '30s, boogie on the guitar was rare, something to be heard. Because of Robert, people learned to complement theirselves, carrying their own bass as their own lead with this one instrument." While his music can certainly be put in context as part of a definable tradition, what he did with it and where he took it was another matter entirely.

Although Robert Johnson never recorded near as much as Lonnie Johnson, Charley Patton, or Blind Lemon Jefferson, he certainly traveled more than all of them put together. After his first recordings came out and "Terraplane Blues" became his signature tune (a so-called "race" record selling over three or four thousand copies back in the early to mid-'30s was considered a hit), Johnson hit the road, playing anywhere and everywhere he could. Instilled with a seemingly unquenchable desire to experience new places and things, his wandering nature took him up and down the Delta and as far afield as St. Louis, Chicago, and Detroit (where he performed over the radio on the *Elder Moten Hour*), places Son House and Charley Patton had only seen in the movies, if that. But the end came at a Saturday-night dance at a juke joint in Three Forks, MS, in August of 1938. Playing with Honeyboy Edwards and Sonny Boy Williamson (Rice Miller), Johnson was given a jug of moonshine whiskey laced with either poison or lye, presumably by the husband of a woman the singer had made advances toward. He continued playing into the night until he was too sick to continue, then brought back to a boarding house in Greenwood, some 15 miles away. He lay sick for several days, successfully sweating the poison out of his system, but caught pneumonia as a result and died on August 16th. The legend was just beginning.

In 1961, Columbia Records released *King of the Delta Blues Singers*, the first compilation of Johnson's music and one of the earliest collections of pure country blues. Rife with liner notes full of romantic speculation, little in the way of hard information, and a painting standing for a picture, this for years was the world's sole introduction, to the music and the legend, doing much to promote both. A second volume—collecting up the other master takes and issuing a few of the alternates—was released in the '70s, giving fans a first-hand listen to music that had been only circulated through bootleg tapes and albums or cover versions by English rock stars. Finally in 1990—after years of litigation—a complete two-CD box set was released with every scrap of Johnson material known to exist plus the holy grail of the blues: the publishing of the only two known photographs of the man himself. Columbia's parent company, Sony, was hoping that sales would maybe hit 20,000. The box set went on to sell over a million units, the first blues recordings ever to do so.

In the intervening years since the release of the box set, Johnson's name and likeness has become a cottage growth merchandising industry. Posters, postcards, T-shirts, guitar picks, strings, straps, and polishing cloths—all bearing either his likeness or signature (taken from his second marriage certificate)—have become available, making him the ultimate blues commodity with his image being reproduced for profit far more than any contemporary bluesman, dead or alive. Although the man himself (and his contemporaries) could never have imagined it in a million years, the music and the legend both live on. —*Cub Koda*

☆ **King of the Delta Blues Singers** / 1961 / Columbia/Legacy ✦✦✦✦
Reading about the power inherent in Robert Johnson's music is one thing, but actually *experiencing* it is another matter entirely. The official 1998 edition of the original 1961 album was certainly worth the wait, remastered off the best-quality original 78s available, of far superior quality to any of the source materials used on even the 1991 box set. Johnson's guitar takes on a fullness never heard on previous reissues, and except for a nagging hiss in spots on "Terraplane Blues" (the equalization on this disc is extreme to even sport some minute turntable rumble in the low end), this really brings his music alive. If there is such a thing as a greatest-hits package available on Johnson, this landmark album, which jump-started the whole '60s blues revival, would certainly be the one. The majority of Johnson's best-known tunes, the ones that made the legend, are all aboard: "Crossroads," "Walkin' Blues," "Me & the Devil Blues," "Come on in My Kitchen," and the apocalyptic visions contained in "Hellhound on My Trail" are the blues at its finest, the lyrics sheer poetry. And making its first appearance anywhere is a newly discovered (in 1998) alternate take of "Traveling Riverside Blues" that's appended to the original 16-track lineup. If you are starting your blues collection from the ground up, be sure to make this your very first purchase. —*Cub Koda*

☆ **King of the Delta Blues Singers, Vol. 2** / 1970 / Columbia/Legacy ✦✦✦✦
A wonderful follow-up to the first compilation (*King of the Delta Blues Singers*) of Robert Johnson's small library of recorded work. This album boasts the first album appearance of "Love in Vain," as well as a number of other blues classics penned by the artist. "Sweet Home Chicago," "I Believe I'll Dust My Broom," "They're Red Hot," and "Malted Milk" are all present (and all covered by a multitude of artists—the Blues Brothers, Elmore James, the Red Hot Chili Peppers, and Eric Clapton, respectively). As is generally the practice with Robert Johnson albums, a painting stands in for the cover (there are only two known photographs of the artist in the first place, and every other album released uses one of them). The music is certainly impeccable—the self-accompanying bass line boogie was one of Johnson's greatest contributions to the blues, and it's displayed in all its beauty here. To top this, there's the beauty of his melodic work, and the interplay with his semi-gruff voice that help to make his songs memorable. He is the true legend of the blues, and anyone with even the slightest curiosity in that genre or rock needs to own both this album and its predecessor, or else the box set released in 1990 that covers both of them. —*Adam Greenberg*

☆ **The Complete Recordings** / 1990 / Columbia/Legacy ✦✦✦✦✦
A double-disc box set containing everything Robert Johnson ever recorded, *The Complete Recordings* is essential listening, but it is also slightly problematic. The problems aren't in the music itself, of course, which is stunning and the fidelity of the recordings is the best it ever has been or ever will be. Instead, it's in the track sequencing. As the title implies, *The Complete Recordings* contains all of Johnson's recorded material, including a generous selection of alternate takes. All of the alternates are sequenced directly after the master, which can make listening to the album a little intimidating and tedious for novices. Certainly, the alternates can be programmed out with a CD player, but the set would have been more palatable if the alternate takes were presented on a separate disc. Nevertheless, this is a minor complaint—Robert Johnson's music retains its power no matter what context it is presented in. He, without question, deserves this kind of deluxe box-set treatment. —*Stephen Thomas Erlewine*

King of the Electric Blues Singers / 1996 / [Bootleg] ✦✦
One can either view this bootleg, lo-fi six-song cassette as a multi-track experiment gone terribly wrong, the ultimate bad taste commercialization and bastardization of Johnson's music, or a practical joke of the highest order, take your pick. The accompanying "press release" (everything on this homemade "package'" has been Xeroxed again and again) claims that in the early '70s an executive at Columbia Records requisitioned the Johnson masters from the company vaults, then surreptitiously booked a session with a blues-rock band signed to the label overdubbing themselves on top of them. The idea (supposedly) was to make Johnson more accessible to rock audiences by doing a "Buddy Holly" on him (modern-day backings dubbed onto solo tapes). The end result would then be marketed via album (hence the goofy title) and singles, getting further mileage out of the slim Johnson catalog. However, as the six songs clearly prove, the band doing the overdubbing were no match for Johnson's irregular time and chord changes, and the whole project was abandoned after the one session. While the players (highly amplified and very distorted lead guitar, bass, and drums) lock in here and there—"Sweet Home Chicago" and "Walkin' Blues" are the best-*played* examples of what they were attempting to do—they frequently stumble and lose the beat, lay in wait for the next change to come, or just merely blast away, seemingly oblivious to what is happening on the original recording. While most blues fans will find this whole experiment blues heresy of the highest order (the audio equivalent of painting a headband on the Mona Lisa, not to mention the trashiest, cash-grabbing corruption of Robert's art imaginable), those with a nose for the perverse, the odd, and the just plain weird will want to hear this cheezoid collection at least *once*. —*Cub Koda*

★ **King of the Delta Blues** / Oct. 7, 1997 / Columbia/Legacy ✦✦✦✦✦
This 16-track single-disc compilation gathers up the best-known tracks from the two original volumes of *King of the Delta Blues Singers* for a nice entry-level collection of Robert's best. Utilizing the latest in remastering technology, these recordings have never sounded quite this clear and full-bodied before, and the difference between this and the first pressing of the *Complete Recordings* box set is quite noticeable. While sweating down Johnson's best to a 16-track selection is an arbitrary choice at best, it's hard to fault the selection here. It's also a focused set that isn't hampered by the inclusion of the more collector-oriented alternate takes that bog down much of the box set's listenability. —*Cub Koda*

Tommy Johnson

b. 1896, Terry, MS, **d.** Nov. 1, 1956, Crystal Springs, MS

Vocals, Kazoo, Guitar / Prewar Blues, Delta Blues, Prewar Country Blues, Country Blues, Acoustic Blues

Next to Son House and Charley Patton, no one was more important to the development of pre-Robert Johnson Delta blues than Tommy Johnson. Armed with a powerful voice that could go from a growl to an eerie falsetto range and a guitar style that had all of the early figures and licks of the Delta style clearly delineated, Johnson only recorded for two years—from 1928 to 1930—but left behind a body of work that's hard to ignore.

The legend of Tommy Johnson is even harder to ignore. The stories about his live performances—where he would play the guitar behind his neck in emulation of Charley Patton's showboating while hollering the blues at a full-throated level for hours without a break—are part of it. So is his uncontrolled womanizing and alcoholism, both of which constantly got him in trouble. Johnson's addiction to spirits was so pronounced that he was often seen drinking Sterno-denatured alcohol used for artificial heat—or shoe polish strained through bread for the kick each could offer when whiskey wasn't affordable or available in dry counties throughout the South. Then there's the crossroads story. Yes, years before the deal with the Devil at a deserted Delta crossroad was being used as an explanation of the other-worldly abilities of young Robert Johnson, the story was being told repeatedly about Tommy, often by the man himself to reinforce his abilities to doubting audiences.

Then there's the music. His "Cool Water Blues" got amped up in the '50s by one of his early admirers, Howlin' Wolf, and became "I Asked for Water (She Brought Me Gasoline)." Another signature piece, his "Maggie Campbell," came with a chord progression that was used for infinite variations by blues players dating all the way back to his contemporary Charley Patton through Robert Nighthawk. Two of his best-known numbers have survived into modern times; "Big Road Blues" is probably best known to contemporary blues fans from adaptions by Floyd Jones and others, while his "Canned Heat Blues"—a bone-chilling account of his complete addiction to alcohol and his slavish attempts to score it by whatever means necessary—was the tune that gave a California blues-rock band their name. After awhile, all of the above starts adding up, no matter how you slice it. Tommy Johnson was one tough hombre, and a real piece of work.

He was born in 1896 in Hinds County, MS, on the George Miller plantation. Once the family moved to Crystal Springs in 1910, Tommy picked up the guitar, learning from his older brother, LeDell. By age 16, Johnson had run away from home to become a "professional" musician, largely supporting himself by playing on the street for tips. By the late teens-early '20s, Tommy was frequently playing in the company of rising local stars Charley Patton, Dick Bankston, and Willie Brown, their collective ouevre planting seed, later becoming the first greening of the Mississippi Delta blues. Johnson spent most of the '20s drinking, womanizing, gambling, and playing in the company of Rube Lacy, Charlie McCoy, Son Spand, Walter Vincent, and Ishman Bracey when the money got low and apparently, only when the mood struck him. By all acounts, Tommy felt no particular drive to relentlessly promote himself and—while he played music for pay until the very end of his life—he certainly wasn't as serious about his career as he was about his drinking. He cut his first records for the Victor (later RCA Victor, now BMG) label at sessions held in Memphis, TN, in 1928. Johnson's first releases hit the area hard, inspiring a raft of up and comers that reads like the proverbial who's who list; you could easily count Howlin' Wolf, Robert Nighthawk, Houston Stackhouse, Floyd Jones, Boogie Bill Webb, K.C. Douglas, Johnnie "Geechie" Temple, and Otis Spann among his many disciples.

He cut one more stack of great records for the Paramount label in 1930, largely through the maneuvering of fellow drinking buddy Charley Patton. Then the slow descent into alcoholism started taking its toll, the one too many nights of Sterno and shoe polish buzzes reducing his once prodigious talents to small, sporadic flickerings of former genius. He worked on a medicine show with Ishman Bracey in the '30s, but mostly seemed to be a mainstay of the juke and small party dance circuit the rest of his days. He was playing just such a local house party in November of 1956 when he suffered a fatal heart attack and went out in probably the exact fashion he wanted to. Whether the story about the deal with the Devil at the crossroads was something he truly believed or just something Johnson said to drum up local interest in himself, it seems odd that you'll find him buried at the Warm Springs Methodist Church Cemetery in Crystal Springs. Maybe he mellowed out toward the end, maybe he found God. Some things about the blues you'll never know, no matter how many computers you hook up to it. *—Cub Koda*

★ **Complete Recorded Works (1928–1929)** / 1990 / Document ♦♦♦♦♦

An essential Tommy Johnson collection, Document's *Complete Recorded Works (1928-1929)* features 17 songs from the Delta blues pioneer, including two alternative takes and a pair of previously unissued songs known respectively as "Morning Prayer Blues" and "Boogaloosa Blues." Culled from the great Delta musician's recording sessions in Memphis and Grafton, WI, from February 1928 to December 1929, this collection shines a light on all of Johnson's known output during his most active recording years. As with most music taken straight from original 78s, the sound quality varies between tracks; all in all, the pops and static aren't too distracting here. The music is well worth seeking out as the writing, guitar playing, and singing are all exceptional. Johnson's voice, one of the distinctive early Delta blues voices along with Son House and Charley Patton, changes from a deep rumble to a woeful falsetto while his guitar playing is characteristic of the early Delta style. With the exception of a few of the tracks from an August 1928 session, other players accompany Johnson on the tracks. Highlights include the well-known material such as "Cool Drink of Water Blues" and "Canned Heat Blues," as well as scratchy lesser-known gems from his later sessions. The tracks "Ridin' Horse" and "Alcohol and Jake Blues" were taken from what is believed to be the only remaining copy of the 78 they were originally released on. These two songs had not been released on CD prior to this collection. On the two versions of "Black Mare Blues" included, Johnson is joined by the New Orleans Nehi Boys, featuring Kid Ernest Marshall on clarinet and Charley Taylor on piano. The CD includes informative notes by Paul Oliver, personnel lineups for each session, along with issue numbers for the original releases. This is highly recommended for those who have never heard Johnson's music and equally recommended for those who have. *—Jeff Schwachter*

Tommy Johnson (1928–1930) / 1998 / Wolf ♦♦♦♦♦

Austria-based Wolf Records has done a masterful job on this 12-song collection (missing only two of Johnson's works, which have never turned up), much of it surprisingly clean and crisp. Most of the best sounding material here has already appeared on RCA/BMG's *Canned Heat Blues* compilation, which seems to be headed out-of-print at this writing. "Cool Drink of Water Blues" and "Canned Heat Blues" are by far the best known of Johnson's works, but they've got a lot of worthy pieces surrounding them. "Big Road Blues" is a fine showcase for Johnson's and Charlie McCoy's paired guitars, playing two complex, interwoven figures. And "Bye Bye Blues" and "Maggie Campbell Blues" show off his unique vocal qualities, not the dark heaviness typical of bluesmen at the time, but a more flexible, lighter toned, more relaxed instrument that, coupled with his and McCoy's guitars, made his music as "busy" as it was beautiful. The songs featuring only Johnson's guitar are no less intriguing, if only for his ability to get a lot of sound from some surprisingly simple strumming and picking. The later songs, "I Wonder To Myself," "Slidin' Delta," "Lonesome Home Blues," and "Black Mare Blues," leave something to be desired in terms of sound, but at least they're represented here. *—Bruce Eder*

Wallace Johnson

b. 1937, Louisiana

Vocals / New Orleans R&B, Modern Electric Blues, Soul-Blues

Vocalist Wallace Johnson last sang around New Orleans clubs more than 20 years ago. But it's only recently that his singing has been recorded and made available to a larger public outside of New Orleans, thanks to New Orleans-based pianist/songwriter/arranger/producer Allen Toussaint. Best described as a soul-blues singer, Johnson's album, *Whoever's Thrilling You*, was the debut for Toussaint's NYNO (New York/New Orleans) label, released in 1996.

Born on a plantation in 1937, Johnson got married and joined the Army at age 17. He first performed in public during his term in the Army in the mid-'50s, and after singing around Thibodaux, LA, in the early '60s, he recorded four singles for AFO Records in 1962, a label Harold Battiste, Toussaint, Dr. John, and other New Orleans-based musicians founded. With a wife and a growing family, Johnson reached a crossroads of sorts, and decided to put his singing career on the back burner for a number of years. But fortunately for us, Toussaint stayed in touch with Johnson and recorded eight more singles with him between 1965 and 1972 at Toussaint's home studios.

Between 1972 and 1992, Johnson put show business aside, working as a longshoreman and running a music club, Mr. J's, in Thibodaux for a number of years. Johnson stayed in touch with Toussaint, though, and would go an visit the producer from time to time.

After being urged to go back on-stage and sing by his fiancée, and bassist Alonzo Johnson (Rockin' Dopsie), he sang in public once again in April 1993 at the New Orleans French Quarter Festival. Since then, Johnson has been making regular appearances in Crescent City clubs and in late 1995, he returned to Toussaint's studios to record his first full-length album.

The release of *Whoever's Thrilling You* in the spring of 1996 coincided with his performance at the 1996 New Orleans Jazz and Heritage Festival. Toussaint wrote nine of the album's 12 songs specifically with Johnson in mind. On the album, Johnson sings songs with a wide variety of tempos. His gospel-influenced, soul-drenched vocals are unique, powerful and moving. *—Richard Skelly*

● **Whoever's Thrilling You** / May 7, 1996 / NYNO ♦♦♦

Andrew "Jr. Boy" Jones

Guitar / Modern Electric Blues, Soul-Blues, Modern Electric Texas Blues

Guitarist, songwriter and singer Andrew "Jr. Boy" Jones began working professionally at age 16 with Freddie King's backing band, the Thunderbirds. He got his first guitar from his uncle, jazz musician Adolphus Sneed. Jones cites an eclectic array of influences: Freddie King, Cornell Dupree and Larry Carlton. For many years, he's backed various Dallas-area vocalists on guitar, but in the mid-'90s, he came into his own as a vocalist with an album for JSP Records, *I Need Time* (1997), which showcases his crafty songwriting, great guitar playing, and powerful singing.

In 1967, Jones joined Dallas-area vocalist Bobby Patterson's outfit, the Mustangs. Through most of the '70s, Jones backed various artists, including Patterson, Johnnie Taylor and Charlie Robertson. In late 1987, he went to California and joined the Silent Partners with bassist Russell Jackson and drummer Tony Coleman, the latter of whom is best known for his work with B.B. King's orchestra. Jones recorded with Bay Area piano player and singer Katie Webster on her critically praised Alligator Records album, *Swamp Boogie Queen*.

Jones met harmonica player Charlie Musselwhite at a Sonny Rhodes recording session, and Musselwhite persuaded him to stay in California and join his band. Jones played guitar on Musselwhite's three late-'80s/early-'90s albums for Alligator Records (*Ace of Harps*, *In My Time*, and *Signature*). He also had the chance to do some extensive world touring with the harmonica master.

Jones left Musselwhite's band amicably in the mid-'90s, returning to Dallas to accompany Dallas-area blues singers like R.L. Griffin, Hal Harris and the Lowlifers, and others. He issued *Watch What You Say* in 1998. *—Richard Skelly*

I Need Time / Feb. 25, 1997 / Bullseye Blues ♦♦♦

● **Watch What You Say** / Jun. 9, 1998 / Bullseye Blues ♦♦♦♦

On his second full album (he shows up on some JSP multi-artists blues compilations), Junior Boy brings his brand of Texas blues to 13 tunes firmly in a contemporary mode. Jones' guitar is highly influenced by Freddie King, but every once in a while you'll catch a strain of Albert Collins or Johnny Copeland popping in as well. Nine of the 13 tunes aboard come from Jones' pen, while bandmembers Tommy Hill and Ronnie Bramhall contribute one tune apiece. Nice covers of King Curtis' "Soul Serenade" and Junior Wells' "Little by Little" complete the package. Jones' vocals are less than thrilling, but a load of solid playing and well-thought-out arrangements wedded to well-above-average material makes this album worth a listen for fans of modern blues. —*Cub Koda*

Casey Jones

b. Jul. 26, 1939, Nitta Yuma, MS
Drums / Electric Chicago Blues, Modern Electric Chicago Blues
Long recognized as one of the Chicago circuit's premier drummers, charismatic Casey Jones has moved out in front of his band over the last decade instead of hiding behind his kit. Casey discovered that beating his way through the world was fun while drilling with his high school marching band back in Greenville. He moved to Chicago in 1956. Before the end of the year, he was drumming professionally with an outfit called Otis Luke & the Rhythm Bombers (for a whopping five bucks a night). One auspicious 1959 night, Jones was forced to sing live for the first time when the pianist leading his band was tossed in jail. He found screaming like Little Richard was pretty enjoyable too. Early-'60s session work behind Earl Hooker, A.C. Reed, McKinley Mitchell, and Muddy Waters (1962's "You Need Love") kept Jones busy, as did playing on the South and West sides with the likes of Otis Rush and Freddy King. His profile rose markedly in 1978 when he slid into the drum chair with Albert Collins' hand-picked combo, the Icebreakers. His impeccable timekeeping powered the band for six-and-a-half years, and he played on Collins' first six Alligator albums (notably *Ice Pickin'* and the 1985 summit meeting *Showdown!* with Robert Cray and Johnny Copeland).

Casey Jones held down Sunday nights at Chicago's popular Kingston Mines nightclub for nearly a decade—a period during which his own discography grew steadily. Released in 1987, *Solid Blue* for Rooster Blues preceded the formation of his own label, Airwax Records (source of 1993's *The Crowd Pleaser* and *[I-94] On My Way to Chicago* in 1995). —*Bill Dahl*

Solid Blue / 1987 / Rooster Blues ✦✦✦✦
One of the Chicago drummer's best solo outings, still not yet available on CD. Eight originals, all of them well-done (especially the chunky "Mr. Blues" and a rocking "Hip Hip Hooray"). Jones' vocals are enthusiastic and his backing is expert—sidemen include harpist Billy Branch, guitarist Maurice Vaughn, and bassist Johnny B. Gayden (the latter Jones' former cohort in Albert Collins' band, the Icebreakers). —*Bill Dahl*

Crowd Pleaser / 1993 / Airwax ✦✦✦✦
A very enjoyable collection of new and recent (three songs, including "Tribute to the Boogie Men" and "Mr. Blues," stem from "Solid Blue") numbers on Jones' own Airwax logo. Of course, he handles his own timekeeping throughout. —*Bill Dahl*

● **(I-94) On My Way to Chicago** / 1995 / Airwax ✦✦✦✦✦
As good a place to begin your Casey Jones collection as any, since his vocals remain strong and his songwriting is as pleasing as ever. The title cut, "I Know I Got a Good Woman," and the sinuous "She Treats Me Right" all make highly favorable impressions. —*Bill Dahl*

Curtis Jones

b. Aug. 18, 1906, Naples, TX, **d.** Sep. 11, 1971, Munich, Germany
Vocals, Piano / Piano Blues, Electric Chicago Blues
The origins of the blues standard "Tin Pan Alley" can be traced directly back to pianist Curtis Jones, who also enjoyed considerable success in 1937 with his "Lonesome Bedroom Blues" for Vocalion (a song inspired by a breakup with his wife).

Jones started out on guitar but switched to the 88s after moving to Dallas. He arrived in Chicago in 1936 and recorded for Vocalion, Bluebird, and OKeh from 1937 to 1941. But the war ended his recording career until 1953, when powerful deejay Al Benson issued a one-off single by Jones, "Wrong Blues"/"Cool Playing Blues," on his Parrot label with L.C. McKinley on guitar. In 1960, Jones waxed his debut album, *Trouble Blues*, for Prestige's Bluesville subsidiary with a classy crew of New York session aces and Chicagoan Johnny "Big Moose" Walker on guitar. By then, his audience was shifting drastically, as he became a fixture on the Chicago folk circuit. His next LP, *Lonesome Bedroom Blues*, was a 1962 solo affair for Delmark offering definitive renditions of the title cut and "Tin Pan Alley." Jones left Chicago permanently in January of 1962, settling in Europe and extensively touring the continent until his 1971 death. —*Bill Dahl*

● **Trouble Blues** / 1960 / Bluesville/Original Blues Classics ✦✦✦✦✦
The taciturn pianist in the company of a fine New York rhythm section and Johnny "Big Moose" Walker (but on guitar, not piano) made for a winning combination on this 1960 album. Jones delivers his downbeat "Suicide Blues," "Low Down Worried Blues," "Lonesome Bedroom Blues"... well, you get the picture. Jones wasn't exactly an upbeat kind of guy. The compilers did unearth a bonus for the CD version: Jones' treatment of "Pinetop Boogie." —*Bill Dahl*

Lonesome Bedroom Blues / 1962 / Delmark ✦✦✦✦
Jones, solo and at the top of his powers on piano and vocally, on a set produced by Bob Koester. The pianist was an exceptional lyricist, evidenced by his classic "Tin Pan Alley" and several lesser-known numbers on this album. —*Bill Dahl*

Now Resident in Europe / 1968 / Blue Horizon ✦✦✦

Complete Works, Vol. 1 (September 1937–May 1938) / Feb. 15, 1995 / Document ✦✦✦

Complete Works, Vol. 2 (June 1938–June 1939) / Feb. 15, 1995 / Document ✦✦✦

Complete Works, Vol. 3 (June 1939–September 1940) / Feb. 15, 1995 / Document ✦✦✦

Complete Works, Vol. 4 (January 1941–May 1953) / Feb. 15, 1995 / Document ✦✦✦

Eddie "One String" Jones

b. Dec. 10, 1926
Guitar / Slide Guitar Blues, Acoustic Blues
In most blues reference books, the name Eddie Jones refers to the given handle of the New Orleans guitarist better known as "Guitar Slim." But this time, we take pause to relate what little information exists on another Eddie Jones, this one a street musician situated in Los Angeles' Skid Row.

Eddie "One String" Jones was, by no stretch of the imagination, a professional musician. Nor, like his more famous namesake, was he even a guitar player. Had it not been for his chance discovery by folklorist and ethnic musicologist Frederick A. Usher in February of 1960, it's a pretty safe bet that no recorded document of him would probably exist.

Usher was in Los Angeles' Skid Row section on business with an associate when he was accosted by two panhandlers. One of those two men (Jones) was holding a rough cut two-by-four plank, a homemade one-stringed instrument of the crudest construction. After a bit of cajoling from Usher, Jones reached into his pocket and fished out the other two working tools he used to make music with the board, a half pint whiskey bottle to slide with and a carefully whittled stick to bang the single string with in place of a guitar pick. The sound was raw, jangly, and chaotic, as far removed from normal slide or bottleneck techniques as Usher (or anyone else) had ever heard. This was evidently a direct tie to the African instrument known as the "diddleybow"; but Jones' technique with the stick gave the music an otherworldly edge, multiple tones to be derived from a single note, and a total departure from what most folklorists had previously known about the instrument.

Sensing that Jones was a modern-day link to an African art form long since dissipated, Usher was bowled over and ran back home as fast as he could to grab his portable tape recorder. After hooking up to a nearby store's electricity in a deserted back alley, Usher made the first recordings of Eddie "One String" Jones. But Jones' lifestyle as a homeless person made all attempts by Usher to mainstream him into folk music circles a virtual impossibility. "One String" was most secretive about his technique, the origin of the instrument, even his given name, which—it turns out—could have been Eddie Jones or Jessie Marshall. After scheduling two more informal recording sessions (one of which appears to be a no-show) and a chance to play for a group of Usher's friends in Hollywood, Jones slipped back into obscurity and has eluded all modern-day blues detective work to even try and append his bio with a date of his death. If there's a romantic, mystery figure in blues history, Eddie "One String" Jones would certainly be at the top of the list. —*Cub Koda*

● **One String Blues** / 1993 / Gazell ✦✦✦✦✦
Jones shares this 15-track compilation with harmonica street player Edward Hazelton, another one of Frederick Usher's elusive Skid Row discoveries, who contributes a half dozen sides featuring a stripped-down Sonny Terry style. The first nine tracks by Jones are primitive in the extreme, untouched by any commercial considerations whatsoever. His instrument—described on the front cover as "a home-made African derived Zither-Monochord"—delivers tones that border on somewhere between keening, rhythmic, and downright eerie. Even repeated listening to any of the early Delta blues slide greats will not prepare you for the sound on this recording, which is trebly, bordering on metallic. Blues as folklore, but a whole lot of fun to explore as well. —*Cub Koda*

Floyd Jones

b. Jul. 21, 1917, Marianna, AR, **d.** Dec. 19, 1989, Chicago, IL
Vocals, Songwriter, Guitar / Acoustic Chicago Blues, Electric Chicago Blues
His sound characteristically dark and gloomy, guitarist Floyd Jones contributed a handful of genuine classics to the Chicago blues idiom during the late '40s and early '50s, notably the foreboding "Dark Road" and "Hard Times."

Born in Arkansas, Jones grew up in the blues-fertile Mississippi Delta (where he picked up the guitar in his teens). He came to Chicago in the mid-'40s, working for tips on Maxwell Street with his cousin Moody Jones and Baby Face Leroy Foster and playing local clubs on a regular basis. Floyd was right there when the postwar Chicago blues movement first took flight, recording with harpist Snooky Pryor for Marvel in 1947; pianist Sunnyland Slim for Tempo Tone the next year (where he cut "Hard Times"), JOB and Chess in 1952-1953, and Vee-Jay in 1955 (where he weighed in with a typically downcast "Ain't Times Hard").

Jones remained active on the Chicago scene until shortly before his 1989 death, although electric bass had long since replaced the guitar as his main axe. He participated in Earwig Records' *Old Friends* sessions in 1979, sharing a studio with longtime cohorts Sunnyland Slim, Honeyboy Edwards, Big Walter Horton, and Kansas City Red. —*Bill Dahl*

● **Masters of Modern Blues** / 1994 / Testament ✦✦✦✦✦
Eight priceless 1966 tracks by tragically underrecorded guitarist Floyd Jones are paired for this CD with eight more by sessionmate Eddie Taylor. Produced in both cases by Testament boss Pete Welding with Big Walter Horton on harp, pianist Otis Spann, and drummer Fred Below lending their collective hands, Jones recreates his dour, uncompromising "Dark Road," "Hard Times," and "Stockyard Blues" with an early-'50s sense of purpose. —*Bill Dahl*

Masters of Modern Blues, Vol. 3 / 1994 / Testament ✦✦✦✦✦
Don't be put off by the murky sound on this one, because it features Jones, guitarist Eddie Taylor, harmonica wizard Big Walter Horton, pianist Otis Spann, and drummer Fred Below playing their hearts out. —*Cub Koda*

JW-Jones

b. 1981
Guitar / Jump Blues, West Coast Blues
What could a teenager possibly know about the blues? Traditionally the blues are about years of hard living and paying a hard price for it, and about serious lovin' and serious loss. Parodies, which frequently are based on kernels of truth, tell us that a bluesman worth the name must know about women, whiskey, and jail, and not necessarily in that order. But all these assumptions and kernels of truth fly right out the window when it

comes to the youthful Canadian blues guitarist known as JW-Jones (and yes, the hyphen is in the right place). Born in Ottawa, he wasn't yet 20 years old when he triumphed in a hometown competition known as the Blues Guitar Riff-Off in 1999. Jones built on his early success, and with a band he had pulled together the previous year of musicians who were about as young as he was or younger, the guitarist and his JW-Jones Blues Band set out to record an album. He debuted with *Defibrillatin'* in 2000. The CD features some numbers that were recorded at home, some that were laid down in a studio as demos, as well as a couple of live numbers. While some critics groused a tiny bit about the quality of the release's sound, they quickly followed the complaint with superlatives for Jones' talent. His band is comprised of "Southside" Steve Marriner, the champion in 1999 of the Blues Harp Blow-Off in Ottawa, on harmonica; Pierre Chretien on organ and piano; drummer Steve Hiscox, and upright bass player Nathan Morris. Jones penned seven of the debut album's tracks. Chretien wrote one song, as did Marriner.

Before turning to the guitar, Jones was initially interested in the drums. A change of heart brought him to the guitar after he found himself intently listening to and watching an Ottawa guitarist named Tony D. The guitarist's moves so impressed Jones that he hammered questions at Tony D after his shows. The working musician took the time to answer the teenager's questions, provide tips, and recommend a list of recordings. The switch to guitar from drums was cemented when Jones' grandparents gave him an electric guitar in late 1996. Keyboardist Chretien is credited with bringing a jazz influence to Jones' and the band's sound. Jones met Marriner through the Johnny Russell Band when both played with the outfit. In 2001, the Maple Blues Awards honored *Defibrillatin'* with a nomination. The following year, the Maple Blues Awards listed Jones as a nominee for New Artist of the Year and named Marriner as a finalist for Harp Player of the Year. He followed those achievements up with 2002's *Bogart's Bounce*, featuring help from Fabulous Thunderbirds Kim Wilson and Gene Taylor. *—Linda Seida*

- **Defibrillatin'** / Sep. 5, 2000 / Orchard ♦♦♦

Like Jimmy Witherspoon, T-Bone Walker, and Dave Specter, JW-Jones is the sort of person who likes a lot of jazz in his blues. *Defibrillatin'*, the Canadian guitarist/singer's debut album, doesn't cater to bop snobs—Jones doesn't spend all of his time trying to show you how fast he can play John Coltrane's "Giant Steps" or Sonny Rollins' "Oleo," but he does sound like the sort of bluesman who has spent a lot of time listening to guys like Jimmy Smith and Jimmy McGriff (not to mention T-Bone Walker). And he plays the sort of jump blues and blues-jazz that comes naturally when you like to blow and improvise; Jones' fondness for jazz comes through on the vocal numbers as well as the instrumentals. The closest that Jones gets to bop on this CD is "Dizzy Spells," an instrumental that was obviously named after trumpeter Dizzy Gillespie. Although likable, the vocal numbers point to the fact that Jones is more of a guitarist than a singer—in fact, he didn't start singing until he was advised that doing so would increase his commercial appeal. *Defibrillatin'* isn't earth-shattering, but it's a decent, if derivative, debut. And to his credit, Jones handles most of the writing himself instead of inundating listeners with overdone blues standards. *—Alex Henderson*

Bogart's Bounce / Jun. 18, 2002 / Northern Blues ♦♦

Some records are good but never develop the kind of critical mass to stand out from the pack. *Bogart's Bounce* is like that, with JW-Jones airing his admiration for Stevie Ray and the Fabulous Thunderbirds (plus a couple of touches of soul), but never really making any kind of lasting impression. There's nothing wrong with the record at all—everyone can play well, and the guests, including Kim Wilson, add their textures, but it simply never takes off. While he might be a pleasure live, where the sweat pours and the adrenaline flows, on disc he simply becomes, well, ho hum. "You Forgot to Come Back," with the vocal from Roxanne Potvin, lends some variety, but it's a bit of a lone beacon. This label has put out some remarkably good blues albums; unfortunately, this isn't one of them. *—Chris Nickson*

Little Johnny Jones

b. Nov. 1, 1924, Jackson, MS, **d.** Nov. 19, 1964, Chicago, IL

Vocals, Arranger, Piano, Harmonica / Piano Blues, Electric Chicago Blues, Chicago Blues

In 40 short years on earth, Johnny Jones established himself as one of the greatest piano players ever to inhabit the Chicago blues scene. Best known for his rock-solid accompaniment to slide guitarist Elmore James both in the studio and as an on-stage member of James' Broomdusters, "Little Johnny" also waxed a handful of terrific sides as a leader. Jones arrived in Chicago from Mississippi in 1946 well-versed on the 88s. Influenced greatly by pianist Big Maceo Merriweather, Jones followed him into Tampa Red's band in 1947 after Maceo suffered a stroke. Johnny Jones' talents were soon in demand as a sideman—in addition to rolling the ivories behind Tampa Red for RCA Victor from 1949 to 1953, he backed Muddy Waters on his 1949 classic "Screamin' and Cryin'" and later appeared on sides by Howlin' Wolf.

But it's Elmore James that he'll forever be associated with; the indispensable pianist played on James' halcyon 1952-1956 Chicago sessions for the Bihari brothers' Meteor, Flair, and Modern logos, as well as dates for Checker, Chief, and Fire. The Broomdusters (rounded out by saxist J.T. Brown and drummer Odie Payne Jr.) held down a regular berth at the West Side blues club Sylvio's for five years.

When he got the chance to sit behind a microphone, Jones' insinuating vocal delivery was equally enthralling. Muddy Waters, Jimmy Rogers, and Leroy Foster backed Jones on his 1949 Aristocrat label classic "Big Town Playboy" (later revived by Eddie Taylor, another unsung Chicago hero), while Elmore James and saxist J.T. Brown were on hand for Jones' 1953 Flair coupling "I May Be Wrong"/"Sweet Little Woman" (the latter a wonderfully risqué "dozens" number). The rocking "Hoy Hoy," his last commercial single, was done in 1953 for Atlantic and also featured James and his group in support. Jones continued to work in the clubs (with Wolf, Sonny Boy Williamson, Syl Johnson, Billy Boy Arnold, and Magic Sam, among others) prior to his 1964 death of lung cancer.

Ironically, Jones was reportedly the first cousin of another Chicago piano great, Otis Spann. *—Bill Dahl*

- **Live in Chicago With Billy Boy Arnold** / 1979 / Alligator ♦♦♦♦♦

Thank heaven Norman Dayron had the presence of mind to capture these sides by Chicago pianist Johnny Jones when he played at the Fickle Pickle in 1963—as little as remains on tape of his talents as a singer, we're eternally indebted to Dayron's actions. Jones' insinuating vocals and bedrock 88s are abetted by harpist Billy Boy Arnold on these performances, and that's it—he had no rhythm section to fall back on. *—Bill Dahl*

Little Sonny Jones (Johnny Jones)

b. Apr. 15, 1931, New Orleans, LA, **d.** Dec. 17, 1989, New Orleans, LA

Vocals / New Orleans Blues

When Black Top reissued Little Sonny Jones' 1975 album *New Orleans R&B Gems* recently, even some true blues fans probably shook their heads and wondered, "Who?" But rest assured: folks in the Crescent City recall Jones with great affection. He was born there and he died there, making some fine music in between.

Born Johnny Jones, the singer picked up his enduring nickname from his pal Fats Domino when they were both playing at the Hideaway Club in the ninth ward during the late '40s. Domino hit it big, but Jones' vinyl fortunes weren't as lucky: a 1953 single on Specialty ("Do You Really Love Me"/"Is Everything Allright") preceded a four-song session for Imperial the next year under Dave Bartholomew's direction (songs included "I Got Fooled" and "Winehead Baby"). All three 45s stiffed, but Fats kept him employed as a warm-up act until 1961.

After seven years back home singing with the band of brothers David and Melvin Lastie, Jones retired until his 1975 album (first issued on Black Magic Records overseas). The set accurately recreated the Crescent City R&B sound of the '50s, thanks to Little Sonny Jones' rich singing and the efforts of veterans Dave "Fat Man" Williams on piano and vocals, saxists Clarence Ford and David Lastie, guitarist Justin Adams, bassist Frank Fields, and drummer Robert French.

Jones came out to play the annual Jazz & Heritage Festival until his 1989 death of heart failure. *—Bill Dahl*

- **New Orleans R&B Gems** / 1995 / Black Top ♦♦♦♦♦

Little known outside his Crescent City homebase, singer Little Sonny Jones' pipes deserved wider acclaim. Thanks to the efforts of Black Top, who recently reissued this collection on CD, maybe he'll finally receive a little posthumously. Though cut in 1975, the set sounds as though it was done a couple of decades earlier. Pianist Dave "Fat Man" Williams (who handles a few vocals as well), saxists Clarence Ford and David Lastie, and guitarist Justin Adams were all vets of that bygone era, and their love for the genre shines through every infectious track. *—Bill Dahl*

Maggie Jones (Fae Barnes)

b. 1900, Hillsboro, TX

Vocals / Classic Female Blues

Maggie Jones, "The Texas Nightingale," was born Fae Barnes in Texas around 1900. She first showed up in New York in 1922 and joined the black vaudeville circuit on the TOBA. By 1926 she was in Clarence Muse's company and was singing in the Hall Johnson choir. Maggie Jones was part of the touring company of the show *Blackbirds of 1928*, in which she appeared with Bill Robinson. Ultimately she returned to Texas and appeared in her own revue in Fort Worth—she is also known to have run her own clothing store. After 1934 she was not heard from again.

Maggie Jones made her debut on one of the last issued Black Swan records in July of 1923. She also appeared on Pathe and Paramount, but the lion's share of her 38 issued titles came out on Columbia in its 14000-D "race" series. Jones was a good blues singer, and accompanied on her records by a wide range of interesting performers including Louis Armstrong, Fletcher Henderson, trombonist Charlie Green, banjoist Elmer Snowden, and pianist Lemuel Fowler. Maggie Jones made her last record on October 3, 1926. *—Uncle Dave Lewis*

- **Complete Recorded Works, Vol. 1 (1923–1925)** / Aug. 1, 1995 / Document ♦♦♦♦

Collecting up all of Maggie Jones' earliest recordings from August 1923 to April 1925, this 24-track compilation features her in a variety of settings. Starting out with simple piano accompaniment from Don Redman or Fletcher Henderson, her later sides in the set find her working with fuller combos counting up at various times contributions from Louis Armstrong and guitarists Sam Clark and Roy Smeck. Taken from rarer-than-rare original 78s in fairly battered shape, two of the tracks have skips in them that no amount of noise reduction can fix. A seasoned theater performer, Jones had a classic blues style that wears well. Here's where her story begins. *—Cub Koda*

Complete Recorded Works, Vol. 2 (May 1925–June 1926)/Gladys Bentley (1928–1929) / Aug. 1, 1995 / Document ♦♦♦

Two different blues-oriented vaudeville singers are featured on this CD, which is the follow-up to *Vol. 1*. Jones had a strong voice and is heard on the first 16 selections, backed by some Fletcher Henderson sidemen (including cornetist Joe Smith), the St. Louis Rhythm Kings, clarinetist Bob Fuller, trumpeter Louis Metcalf, and pianist Clarence Williams, among others. In addition, this CD has all eight recordings by singer-pianist Gladys Bentley, a male impersonator whose style is a bit of an acquired taste; guitarist Eddie Lang is fortunately on four of the numbers. This well-done release is not essential but has its moments of interest. *—Scott Yanow*

Paul "Wine" Jones

Vocals, Guitar / Modern Electric Blues, Electric Delta Blues

Like Big Jack Johnson, Sam Carr, and his other labelmates at Fat Possum/Capricorn, guitarist, singer, and songwriter Paul "Wine" Jones grew up with blues all around him. He learned to play guitar at his father's feet at age four, taking his earliest inspiration from his father's playing. Jones' brother, Casey, is the in-demand Chicago blues drummer who's backed Albert Collins, Koko Taylor, and dozens of others. Jones played music as an avocation for many years, working farming jobs until 1971, when he became a professional welder in Belzoni, MS. He's been based in Belzoni ever since.

In 1995 and 1996, as part of Fat Possum's Mississippi Juke Joint Caravan, he had the opportunity to perform for the first time outside of Mississippi. His 1995 debut for the Fat Possum/Capricorn label, *Mule*, is deeply rooted in the rural juke-joint tradition of the Delta, and his style is totally original, a combination of synchronized guitar and vocal phrasings and electric country blues. He's joined on the album by drummer Sam Carr and guitarist Big Jack Johnson. *Mule* was produced by blues scholar/impresario Robert Palmer, author of the book *Deep Blues*. *Pucker Up Buttercup* followed in 1999. *—Richard Skelly*

● **Mule** / 1995 / Fat Possum ♦♦♦
Like many artists on the Fat Possum label, Paul "Wine" Jones was discovered by rock critic Robert Palmer. A professional welder, Jones released his first album, *Mule*, in 1995, although the record is much rawer than most '90s blues record. Gritty and greasy, *Mule* is driven by Jones' simple, pounding guitar rhythms, which are occasionally embellished by guitarists Big Jack "The Oil Man" Johnson and Kenny Brown, who play on two tracks each. *—Stephen Thomas Erlewine*

Pucker Up Buttercup / Jul. 13, 1999 / Fat Possum ♦♦♦
Like most releases on Fat Possum (including his first effort, *Mule*), Paul Jones' second album, *Pucker Up Buttercup*, boasts a raw, careening sound and enthusiastically gritty performances that make it an easy album to enjoy. The problem is, there's not much there—the songs are merely vehicles for the performances. That results in a record that is enjoyable while it's playing, but ultimately a little unmemorable. *—Stephen Thomas Erlewine*

Tutu Jones (John Jones Jr.)

b. Sep. 9, 1966, Dallas, TX
Vocals, Guitar / Modern Electric Blues, Soul-Blues
The son of Dallas-based R&B guitarist John Jones, Tutu Jones was truly a product of his environment—growing up in a house frequently populated by guests including Freddie King, Little Joe Blue and Ernie Johnson, his own future as a bluesman was never in doubt.

Born John Jones Jr., on September 9, 1966, he became a professional drummer while still a teen, backing his uncles Curly "Barefoot" Miller and L.C. Clark before moving on to work with the likes of Z.Z. Hill and R.L. Burnside. At the same time, however, Jones was also honing his guitar and songwriting skills, and eventually began fronting bands of his own; he cut his solo debut *I'm for Real* in 1994, followed by *Blue Texas Soul* in 1996. Two years later, he released *Staying Power*. *—Jason Ankeny*

I'm for Real / Jul. 29, 1994 / JSP ♦♦♦

Blue Texas Soul / 1996 / Bullseye Blues ♦♦♦
This Dallas-based guitarist/singer has an impressive resumé, having served as a sideman drummer and guitarist and a warm-up singer for a number of Texas-based blues and soul men like Z.Z. Hill and Little Joe Blue, and having grown up with the blues (his dad and two uncles were active on the local Dallas scene). But on the basis of this and his prior CD (*I'm For Real* on JSP), he has yet to forge his own distinctive sound. His guitar solos, which rely on heavily plucked, long sustained notes, tend toward monotony over the 45 minutes length of the disc, although fans of contemporary blues guitar will be impressed by their muscular quality. *—Steve Hoffman*

● **Staying Power** / May 5, 1998 / Bullseye Blues ♦♦♦♦
Jones' second album is even more powerful and better formatted than his successful and enticing debut, *Blue Texas Soul*. Once again producing and writing all the songs, Jones' talents are in abundance on this disc: from the slow blues of "The Milkman Game" to the soulful strut of "Can't Leave Your Love Alone" (which features his wife Sheila White Jones on background vocals), to the jazzy instrumental work on "After Midnight." Utilizing the same band that backed him so well on his debut disc, certain tracks also include the Memphis Horns providing stellar musical punctuation on soul-driven tracks like "Be Good to Your Lady" and "You Shatter My Heart." No sophomore slump here; this is one very well-thought-out and well-executed record. *—Cub Koda*

Janis Joplin

b. Jan. 19, 1943, Port Arthur, TX, **d.** Oct. 4, 1970, Los Angeles, CA
Vocals / Album Rock, Hard Rock, Blues-Rock
The greatest white female rock singer of the '60s, Janis Joplin was also a great blues singer, making her material her own with her wailing, raspy, supercharged emotional delivery. First rising to stardom as the frontwoman for San Francisco psychedelic band Big Brother & the Holding Company, she left the group in the late '60s for a brief and uneven (though commercially successful) career as a solo artist. Although she wasn't always supplied with the best material or most sympathetic musicians, her best recordings, with both Big Brother and on her own, are some of the most exciting performances of her era. She also did much to redefine the role of women in rock with her assertive, sexually forthright persona and raunchy, electrifying on-stage presence.

Joplin was raised in the small town of Port Arthur, TX, and much of her subsequent personal difficulties and unhappiness has been attributed to her inability to fit in with the expectations of the conservative community. She'd been singing blues and folk music since her teens, playing on occasion in the mid-'60s with future Jefferson Airplane guitarist Jorma Kaukonen. There are a few live pre-Big Brother recordings (not issued until after her death), reflecting the inspiration of early blues singers like Bessie Smith, that demonstrate she was well on her way to developing a personal style before hooking up with the band. She had already been to California before moving there permanently in 1966, when she joined a struggling early San Francisco psychedelic group, Big Brother & the Holding Company.

Big Brother's story is told in more detail in their own entry. Although their loose, occasionally sloppy brand of bluesy psychedelia had some charm, there can be no doubt that Joplin—who initially didn't even sing lead on all of the material—was primarily responsible for lifting them out of the ranks of the ordinary. She made them a hit at the 1967 Monterey Pop Festival, where her stunning version of "Ball and Chain" (perhaps her very best performance) was captured on film. After a debut on the Mainstream label, Big Brother signed a management deal with Albert Grossman, and moved on to Columbia. Their second album, *Cheap Thrills*, topped the charts in 1968, but Joplin left the band shortly afterwards, enticed by the prospects of stardom as a solo act.

Joplin's first album, *I Got Dem Ol' Kozmic Blues Again Mama!*, was recorded with the Kozmic Blues Band, a unit that included horns, and retained just one of the musicians that had played with her in Big Brother (guitarist Sam Andrew). Although it was a hit, it wasn't her best work; the new band, though more polished musically, were not nearly as sympathetic accompanists as Big Brother, purveying a soul-rock groove that could sound forced. That's not to say it was totally unsuccessful, boasting one of her signature tunes in "Try (Just a Little Bit Harder)."

For years, Joplin's life had been a roller coaster of drug addiction, alcoholism, and volatile personal relationships, documented in several biographies. Musically, however, things were on the upswing shortly before her death, as she assembled a better, more versatile backing outfit, the Full Tilt Boogie Band, for her final album, *Pearl* (ably produced by Paul Rothschild). Joplin was sometimes criticized for screeching at the expense of subtlety, but *Pearl* was solid evidence of her growth as a mature, diverse stylist who could handle blues, soul, and folk-rock. "Mercedes Benz," "Get It While You Can," and Kris Kristofferson's "Me and Bobby McGee" are some of her very best tracks. Tragically, she died before the album's release, overdosing on heroin in a Hollywood hotel in October 1970. "Me and Bobby McGee" became a posthumous number one single in 1971, and thus the song with which she is most frequently identified. *—Richie Unterberger*

I Got Dem Ol' Kozmic Blues Again Mama! / 1969 / Columbia/Legacy ♦♦♦
Joplin's solo debut was a letdown at the time of release, suffering in comparison with Big Brother's *Cheap Thrills* from the previous year, and shifting her style toward soul-rock in a way that disappointed some fans. Removed from that context, it sounds better today, though it's still flawed. Fronting the short-lived Kozmic Blues Band, the arrangements are horn heavy and the material soulful and bluesy. The band sounds a little stiff, though, and although Joplin's singing is good, she would sound more electrifying on various live versions of some of the songs that have come out over the years. The shortage of quality original compositions—indeed, there are only eight tracks total on the album—didn't help either, and the cover selections were erratic, particularly the Bee Gees' "To Love Somebody." On the other hand, "Try" is one of her best soul outings, and the reading of Rodgers-Hart's "Little Girl Blue" is inspired. The 1999 CD reissue adds three bonus tracks: a cover of Bob Dylan's "Dear Landlord" from the *Kozmic Blues* sessions that was first heard on the *Janis* box set and previously unreleased versions of "Summertime" and "Piece of My Heart" from the Woodstock Festival. "Summertime" is OK, but this "Piece of My Heart" really pales next to the Big Brother interpretation. *—Richie Unterberger*

☆ **Pearl** / Feb. 1971 / Columbia/Legacy ♦♦♦♦♦
Joplin's second masterpiece (after *Cheap Thrills*), *Pearl* was designed as a showcase for her powerhouse vocals, stripping down the arrangements that had often previously cluttered her music or threatened to drown her out. Thanks also to a more consistent set of songs, the results are magnificent—given room to breathe, Joplin's trademark rasp conveys an aching, desperate passion on funked-up, bluesy rockers, ballads both dramatic and tender, and her signature song, the posthumous number one hit "Me and Bobby McGee." The unfinished "Buried Alive in the Blues" features no Joplin vocals—she was scheduled to record them on the day after she was found dead. Its incompleteness mirrors Joplin's career; *Pearl*'s power leaves the listener to wonder what else Joplin could have accomplished, but few artists could ask for a better final statement. The 1999 CD reissue adds four previously unreleased live July 1970 recordings: "Tell Mama," "Little Girl Blue," "Try," and "Cry Baby." *—Steve Huey*

In Concert / May 1972 / Columbia ♦♦♦
About half of this two-record set features Janis Joplin with Big Brother & the Holding Company in 1968, performing songs like "Down on Me" and "Piece of My Heart." The rest, recorded in 1970, finds her with her backup group, Full Tilt Boogie, mostly performing songs from *I Got Dem Ol' Kozmic Blues Again Mama!* Joplin puts herself out on-stage, both in terms of singing until her voice is raw and describing her life to her audiences. Parts of this album are moving, parts are heartbreaking, and the rest is just great rock & roll. *—William Ruhlmann*

● **Janis Joplin's Greatest Hits** / Jul. 1973 / Columbia/Legacy ♦♦♦♦♦
A solid, if skimpy, ten-track best-of that gathers the most important songs from Joplin's solo career, as well as her stint with Big Brother & the Holding Company. The compilation *18 Essential Songs* offers a wider selection, but does not include the original version of "Me and Bobby McGee," which makes *Greatest Hits* the better purchase for those who only want one Janis Joplin disc, even if it isn't definitive. The 1999 CD reissue adds two bonus tracks, "Maybe" and "Mercedes Benz." *—Steve Huey*

Farewell Song / 1983 / Columbia ♦♦♦
A ragtag collection of odds and ends, live and studio, from both the Big Brother and solo era. The best cuts are on the *Janis* box in different versions, but serious fans will find some interesting items here, especially the *Cheap Thrills*-era outtakes and live performances; "Misery 'N," "Farewell Song," and "Catch Me Daddy" were easily good enough to have qualified for inclusion on that album. *—Richie Unterberger*

Janis / Nov. 23, 1993 / Columbia/Legacy ♦♦♦♦♦
This three-CD box set is the most thorough and valuable retrospective of Janis Joplin's career. Besides including all of her most essential recordings with and without Big Brother & the Holding Company, this 49-song package features quite a few enticing rarities; 18 of the tracks were previously unissued. These include a 1962 home recording of the Joplin original "What Good Can Drinkin' Do," which marked the first time her singing was

captured on tape, a pair of acoustic blues tunes from 1965 with backup guitar by future Jefferson Airplane star Jorma Kaukonen, an acoustic demo of "Me and Bobby McGee," a 1970 birthday song for John Lennon, and live performances from her appearance on "The Ed Sullivan Show" in 1969. The real showstopper is the previously unissued, eight-minute version of "Ball and Chain" from Big Brother's first set at the 1967 Monterey Pop Festival (the cut on the *Monterey Pop* box set is from their second set). The more forgettable tracks from her solo albums are wisely excised, as are the Big Brother songs which did not feature her vocals. This is the rare multi-disc set of a major artist that manages to cover all the official milestones and present a bounty of worthwhile rarities at the same time. *—Richie Unterberger*

18 Essential Songs / Jan. 24, 1995 / Columbia/Legacy ✦✦✦✦✦
18 Essential Songs is a one-disc distillation of the triple-disc *Janis* box set. Running 70 minutes, it is a more extensive best-of than the ten-track 1973 *Janis Joplin's Greatest Hits* album. But it is denied "first pick" status because, unlike that album, it does not contain the hit version of Joplin's only number one single, "Me and Bobby McGee." (It does, however, contain an alternate demo version of that song.) *—William Ruhlmann*

Box of Pearls: The Janis Joplin Collection / Aug. 31, 1999 / Columbia/Legacy ✦✦✦✦✦
A limited-edition five-CD box set comprising both albums that Joplin made with Big Brother & the Holding Company (*Cheap Thrills* and *Big Brother & the Holding Company*), both of her solo albums (*I Got Dem Ol' Kozmic Blues Again Mama!* and *Pearl*), and a bonus EP with five previously unreleased recordings. Each of these four albums includes previously unreleased bonus tracks, and each is available separately with the same material. The tracks on the bonus EP aren't available anywhere else, and if you're devoted enough to consider laying out for this deluxe box, you're probably *most* interested in what's on that fifth disc. There are a couple of *Cheap Thrills* outtakes, "It's a Deal" and "Crazy Once You Know How," with a garage-y feel and some typically scorching, uninhibited Big Brother lead guitar; it can be seen why they may not have been deemed strong enough for the album, but they're pretty cool to have. The live versions of "Maybe" (April 1969) and "Raise Your Hand" (October 1969) are OK, but not essential; of greater curiosity is the raw live charge through "Bo Diddley" (also October 1969). Note that this box does *not* include a good deal of material that has shown up on the *Janis* box, the *Janis* movie soundtrack, *In Concert*, and *Farewell Song*, so it's not a complete collection of Joplin's recordings. *—Richie Unterberger*

Love, Janis / May 8, 2001 / Columbia/Legacy ✦✦
Since this is a companion CD to the off-Broadway stage musical *Love, Janis*, it alternates classic tracks from her Big Brother & the Holding Company and solo albums with spoken excerpts from letters to her family (read by Catherine Curtin, not by Joplin herself). No album that contains "Piece of My Heart," "Summertime," "Ball & Chain," "Me and Bobby McGee," and "Get It While You Can" can be dismissed with the absolute lowest rating. But really, this is *not* an advisable way to hear these songs, either as an introduction or a best-of. If it's the music you care about, all of the material is easily available on the Big Brother and Joplin solo albums (except for the 1962 performance of "What Good Can Drinkin' Do," which is on the *Janis* box set). If you want to read the letters, you can buy the book *Love, Janis*, written by her sister, Laura Joplin. If you live in the right place, you can even see the play. This jumble of well-traveled tunes is just an attempt to wring more mileage out of the Joplin back catalog. *—Richie Unterberger*

Charley Jordan

b. 1890, Mabelville, AR, **d.** Nov. 15, 1954, St. Louis, MO
Vocals, Guitar / Prewar Country Blues, Acoustic Memphis Blues, Acoustic Blues, St. Louis Blues
A fine St. Louis guitarist and vocalist, Charley Jordan teamed with many blues luminaries for some fine recordings in the '20s, '30s, and '40s. After traveling throughout the Southeast as a hobo in the '30s, Jordan settled in St. Louis. He played with Memphis Minnie, Roosevelt Sykes, Casey Bill Weldon, Peetie Wheatstraw, and many others. Jordan overcame a permanent spine injury he suffered during a shooting incident in 1928. He recorded for Vocalion and Decca in the '30s, and also doubled as a talent scout for both labels. Jordan worked often with Big Joe Williams in the late '30s and the '40s. *—Ron Wynn*

• **Charley Jordan Vol. 1, 1930–31** / 1992 / Document ✦✦✦✦✦
A fine St. Louis singer and guitarist, this was the first volume of songs Charley Jordan did in the early '30s. He could be very humorous or cuttingly poignant, and there are examples in both veins on this anthology. The sound quality ranges from good to awful. *—Ron Wynn*

Charley Jordan Vol. 2, 1931–34 / 1992 / Document ✦✦✦
As good as the Charley Jordan material here is, the real find of this disc is Hi Henry Brown's recording of "Titanic Blues" and its guitar duet between Brown and Jordan. As a piece of belated topical blues, it is an extraordinary song, but the exciting interplay between two guitars really makes the record and, coupled with Brown's rough-hewn voice, makes it a track to own—the additional Brown/Jordan tracks "Preacher Blues" and "Nut Factory Blues" constitute a good bonus. This volume of Charley Jordan's material covers the period from his brief stay at Victor Records (four sides cut in September of 1931) to his first session with a full band on Decca Records in the summer of 1934. The four Victor sides (which were cut in Chicago) have a peculiar, authentic "live" ambience that, coupled with their good fidelity, makes them especially vibrant; Peetie Wheatstraw's piano accompaniment has a certain distance and echo that evokes a true club atmosphere. Jordan's subsequent Vocalion sides give much greater prominence to the guitar and Wheatstraw's piano isn't nearly as vivid. As a solo player, Jordan was more laidback, but he still manages to impress as a virtuoso. The four Decca sides are the best recordings here on a technical level—"It Ain't Clean" is amazingly crisp—but two of them, "Lost Airship Blues" (what a title, and what a phallic image) and "Rolling Moon Blues," are particularly notable for the presence of a full band, complete with sax and violin. Their sound is completely different (although Jordan still makes himself felt on guitar) from Jordan's earlier output, but both find him able to work well in this more sophisticated idiom. The overall audio quality is good, apart from the barely listenable "Brown Skin Angel"—a few sides, like "Hell Bound Boy Blues" and the wonderful "Rolling Moon Blues," are a little noisy, but that's par for the course. *—Bruce Eder*

Charley Jordan Vol. 3, 1935–37 / 1992 / Document ✦✦✦
This volume is somewhat less compelling than the other two in the series, if only because even the producers themselves acknowledge that eight of the 23 songs here, credited to "The Two Charlies," probably don't feature the St. Louis-based Charley Jordan at all, but another artist of the same name, while four others, credited to Leroy Henderson, *may* feature Jordan. On other songs, Jordan sings duets with Verdi Lee and Mary Harris (possibly also Verdi Lee working under a pseudonym), and those are great tracks, to be recommended without reservation, except perhaps for the fact that the guitar is a bit muted on these numbers, compared with Jordan's solo stuff. "Signifying at You" is a great piece of female-sung blues, raw, angry, defiant and funny. The Two Charlies tracks, featuring a Charley Jordan working with a guitarist/singer named Charlie Manson, are fine acoustic blues, all good songs (especially "Don't Put Your Dirty Hands On Me") and even better guitar duets, including the surprisingly dissonant "Pork Chop Blues," but they sound much more like Atlanta blues than St. Louis material—their inclusion here adds nothing to the St. Louis Charley Jordan's reputation, but they make an enjoyable interlude. *—Bruce Eder*

Louis Jordan

b. Jul. 8, 1908, Brinkley, AR, **d.** Feb. 4, 1975, Los Angeles, CA
Vocals, Sax (Alto), Saxophone, Leader / East Coast Blues, Jump Blues, Swing, Urban Blues
Effervescent saxophonist Louis Jordan was one of the chief architects and prime progenitors of the R&B idiom. His pioneering use of jumping shuffle rhythms in a small combo context was copied far and wide during the '40s.

Jordan's sensational hit-laden run with Decca Records contained a raft of seminal performances, featuring inevitably infectious backing by his band, the Tympany Five, and Jordan's own searing alto sax and street corner jive-loaded sense of humor. Jordan was one of the first Black entertainers to sell appreciably in the pop sector; his Decca duet mates included Bing Crosby, Louis Armstrong, and Ella Fitzgerald.

The son of a musician, Jordan spent time as a youth with the Rabbit Foot Minstrels and majored in music later on at Arkansas Baptist College. After moving with his family to Philadelphia in 1932, Jordan hooked up with pianist Clarence Williams. He joined the orchestra of drummer Chick Webb in 1936 and remained there until 1938. Having polished up his singing abilities with Webb's outfit, Jordan was ready to strike out on his own.

The saxist's first 78 for Decca in 1938, "Honey in the Bee Ball," billed his combo as the Elks Rendezvous Band (after the Harlem nightspot where he frequently played). From 1939 on, though, Jordan fronted the Tympany Five, a sturdy little aggregation often expanding over quintet status that featured some well-known musicians over the years: pianists Wild Bill Davis and Bill Doggett, guitarists Carl Hogan and Bill Jennings, bassist Dallas Bartley, and drummer Chris Columbus all passed through the ranks.

From 1942 to 1951, Jordan scored an astonishing 57 R&B chart hits (all on Decca), beginning with the humorous blues "I'm Gonna Leave You on the Outskirts of Town" and finishing with "Weak Minded Blues." In between, he drew up what amounted to an easily followed blueprint for the development of R&B (and for that matter, rock & roll—the accessibly swinging shuffles of Bill Haley & the Comets were directly descended from Jordan; Haley often pointed to his Decca labelmate as profoundly influencing his approach).

"G.I. Jive," "Caldonia," "Buzz Me," "Choo Choo Ch' Boogie," "Ain't That Just Like a Woman," "Ain't Nobody Here but Us Chickens," "Boogie Woogie Blue Plate," "Beans and Cornbread," "Saturday Night Fish Fry," and "Blue Light Boogie"—every one of those classics topped the R&B lists, and there were plenty more that did precisely the same thing. Black audiences coast-to-coast were breathlessly jitterbugging to Jordan's jumping jive (and one suspects, more than a few whites kicked up their heels to those same platters as well).

The saxist was particularly popular during World War II. He recorded prolifically for the Armed Forces Radio Service and the V-Disc program. Jordan's massive popularity also translated onto the silver screen—he filmed a series of wonderful short musicals during the late '40s that were decidedly short on plot but long on visual versions of his hits (*Caldonia*, *Reet Petite & Gone*, *Look Out Sister*, and *Beware*, along with countless soundies) that give us an enlightening peek at just what made him such a beloved entertainer. Jordan also cameoed in a big-budget Hollywood wartime musical, *Follow the Boys*.

A brief attempt at fronting a big band in 1951 proved an ill-fated venture, but it didn't dim his ebullience. In 1952, tongue firmly planted in cheek, he offered himself as a candidate for the highest office in the land on the amusing Decca outing "Jordan for President."

Even though his singles were still eminently solid, they weren't selling like they used to by 1954. So after an incredible run of more than a decade-and-a-half, Jordan moved over to the Mesner brothers' Los Angeles-based Aladdin logo at the start of the year. Alas, time had passed the great pioneer by—"Dad Gum Ya Hide Boy," "Messy Bessy," "If I Had Any Sense," and the rest of his Aladdin output sounds great in retrospect, but it wasn't what young R&B fans were searching for at the time. In 1955, he switched to RCA's short-lived "X" imprint, where he tried to remain up-to-date by issuing "Rock 'n Roll Call."

A blistering Quincy Jones-arranged date for Mercury in 1956 deftly updated Jordan's classics for the rock & roll crowd, with hellfire renditions of "Let the Good Times Roll," "Salt Pork, West Virginia," and "Beware" benefiting from the blasting lead guitar of Mickey Baker and Sam "The Man" Taylor's muscular tenor sax. There was even time to indulge in a little torrid jazz at Mercury; "The JAMF," from a 1957 LP called *Man, We're Wailin'*, was a sizzling indication of what a fine saxist Jordan was.

Ray Charles had long cited Jordan as a primary influence (he lovingly covered Jordan's "Don't Let the Sun Catch You Crying" and "Early in the Morning"), and paid him back by signing Jordan to the Genius' Tangerine label. Once again, the fickle public largely ignored his worthwhile 1962-1964 offerings.

Lounge gigs still offered the saxman a steady income, though, and he adjusted his on-stage playlist accordingly. A 1973 album for the French Black & Blue logo found Jordan covering Mac Davis' "I Believe in Music" (can't get much loungier than that!). A heart attack silenced this visionary in 1975, but not before he acted as the bridge between the big-band era and the rise of R&B.

His profile continues to rise posthumously, in large part due to the recent acclaimed Broadway musical *Five Guys Named Moe*, based on Jordan's bubbly, romping repertoire and charismatic persona. —*Bill Dahl*

At the Swing Cat's Ball / Jan. 15, 1937-Nov. 1937 / JSP ✦✦✦✦
This very interesting collector's CD features altoist/singer Louis Jordan at the beginning of his career, tracing his progress until right before he hit it big. Jordan is heard in 1937 taking three almost unrecognizable ballad vocals with Chick Webb's Orchestra, backing singer Rodney Sturgis on three tunes, performing two selections from late 1938 with his Elks Rendezvous Band (including a hot instrumental, "Honey In the Bee Ball") and jamming a dozen numbers from his two sessions in 1939 with his recently formed Tympany Five. Of the latter, highlights include "Flat Face," "At the Swing Cat's Ball," and "Honeysuckle Rose." Louis Jordan fans will really want this British CD if they do not already have the Classics release 1934-1940. —*Scott Yanow*

☆ **Let the Good Times Roll: The Complete Decca Recordings 1938–54** / 1938-1954 / Bear Family ✦✦✦✦✦
The price of this multi-disc import box set is indeed a hefty one, but it contains every track the pioneering saxman waxed for Decca—the multitude of hits that inexorably influenced the future of R&B and eventually rock & roll. Bear Family's attention to detail in its presentation is always immaculate, and the sound quality follows suit. —*Bill Dahl*

1940–1941 / Mar. 13, 1940+Nov. 15, 1941 / Classics ✦✦✦✦✦
The second in the Classics label's CD series that reissues all of Louis Jordan's early recordings features the masterful entertainer with his Tympany Five in the period that directly preceded his great commercial successes. Although most of these 26 selections (including "Somebody Done Hoodooed the Hoodoo Man," "After School Swing Session," "Saxa-Woogie," and "De Laff's On You") are quite obscure, the playing by the group is quite infectious and enjoyable. Singers Daisy Winchester and Mabel Robinson are heard on the Mar. 13, 1940, session for a song apiece, but otherwise, the focus is on Jordan and his fine band, which features tenor saxophonist Kenneth Hollon and several trumpeters, including (on one date) Freddy Webster. Recommended to listeners who want to hear more Louis Jordan than just his hit records. —*Scott Yanow*

1941–1943 / Nov. 15, 1941-Nov. 1943 / Classics ✦✦✦✦✦
During the era covered by this Classics CD (the third in their "complete" Louis Jordan series), Jordan and his Tympany Five became major successes. Among the 24 selections are such hits as "Knock Me a Kiss," "I'm Gonna Move to the Outskirts of Town," "Five Guys Named Moe," and "Is You Is or Is You Ain't My Baby." In addition to the regular Decca recordings, the set includes four numbers originally rejected, plus six Jordan V-Disc performances. Louis Jordan's music (featuring his alto and vocals, plus hot backup work from trumpeter Eddie Roane and a swinging rhythm section) acted as a bridge between small-group swing and early R&B. Highly recommended. —*Scott Yanow*

Five Guys Named Moe: Original Decca Recordings, Vol. 2 / Jul. 21, 1942-May 8, 1952 / Decca ✦✦✦✦
Another 18 of the saxist's Decca label classics (although "Five Guys Named Moe" turns up again, in deference to the hit Broadway production). "Is You Is or Is You Ain't (My Baby)," "Jack, You're Dead," "Texas and Pacific," "Boogie Woogie Blue Plate," and "G.I. Jive" are high on the list of gems this time, along with his persuasive 1952 campaign "Jordan for President." —*Bill Dahl*

The Just Say Moe!: Mo' of the Best of Louis Jordan / Jul. 21, 1942-Nov. 6, 1973 / Rhino ✦✦✦✦
A nice across-the-board compilation spanning his Decca, Aladdin, RCA, Mercury, and Tangerine label stints. The Decca standouts include "Don't Worry 'Bout That Mule" and the often-covered "Ain't That Just like a Woman," while his Mercury output includes "Big Bess" and "Cat Scratchin'." Could have done without the live "I Believe in Music" at the end, though—that isn't the way we want to remember this wonderful performer. —*Bill Dahl*

Five Guys Named Moe / Aug. 1943-1946 / Decca ✦✦✦✦✦
Included on this CD are 27 formerly rare performances by altoist/singer Louis Jordan and his famous Tympany Five. Consisting of radio appearances, plus specially recorded V-discs, the release has quite a few songs not otherwise recorded by Jordan, along with different versions of "Five Guys Named Moe," "Outskirts of Town" and "Caldonia." A special bonus is hearing clarinetist Barney Bigard jam "Rose Room" with the band. The front cover of the CD proclaims "The Father of Rock n' Roll," and in ways that is true, although ironically the rise of rock in the mid-'50s knocked Louis Jordan permanently off the pop charts. Recommended. —*Scott Yanow*

1943–1945 / Nov. 22, 1943-Jul. 12, 1945 / Classics ✦✦✦✦✦
Although Louis Jordan's greatest hits are continually reissued, this Classics CD (the fourth in the series) gives listeners an opportunity to hear many of his lesser-known recordings, quite a few of which sound as if they could have been hits too. Jordan, a fine R&Bish altoist who was an underrated singer and a brilliant comedic talent who knew a good line when he heard one (there are many memorable ones throughout this program), is heard in peak form. The 23 performances are Decca sides (including five not originally released), some V-Discs and the privately recorded "Louis' Oldsmbile Song."

Bing Crosby sings duets with Jordan on "My Baby Said Yes" and "Your Socks Don't Match," there are two major hits ("G.I. Jive" and "Caldonia") and among the sidemen are the fine trumpeter Eddie Roane, the forgotten but talented pianist Tommy Thomas, trumpeter Idrees Sulieman (on the January 19, 1945, session) and (for the final two songs) pianist Wild Bill Davis. Other highlights include "You Can't Get That No More," "I Like 'Em Fat Like That," "Deacon Jones," and "They Raided the House." Highly recommended. —*Scott Yanow*

1944–1945 / 1944-1945 / Circle ✦✦✦✦
This interesting album features altoist/vocalist Louis Jordan and three versions of his Tympany Five during 1944–1945, when he was reaching the peak of his popularity. With such sidemen as either Eddie Roane, Idrees Sulieman, or Aaron Izenhall on trumpet and (on a few numbers) pianist Wild Bill Davis, Jordan and his group are heard recording radio transcriptions for World Broadcasting. Other than "G.I. Jive," the music emphasizes lesser-known tunes and contains plenty of fine solos from Jordan, including the surprisingly advanced "Re-Bop." —*Scott Yanow*

1945–1946 / Jul. 16, 1945-Oct. 10, 1946 / Classics ✦✦✦✦✦
Louis Jordan was at the top of his fame when the 23 recordings reissued on this Classics CD were cut. The influential altoist/singer/entertainer during this era led a version of his Tympany Five that also featured trumpeter Aaron Izenhall, Josh Jackson on tenor and pianist Wild Bill Davis (years before he switched to organ). Among the hits included on the set are "Beware," "Don't Let The Sun Catch You Crying," "Choo-Choo Ch'Boogie," "Ain't Nobody Here But Us Chickens," "Let the Good Times Roll," and "Jack You're Dead," but even the lesser-known tracks are entertaining. In addition, a couple of unlikely duets with Ella Fitzgerald ("Stone Cold Dead in the Market" and "Petootie Pie") are quite fun. Recommended to listeners not satisfied with owning only Louis Jordan's hits. —*Scott Yanow*

One Guy Named Louis / Jan. 1954-Apr. 1954 / Blue Note ✦✦✦
It is a strange fact that as rock & roll began to catch on, one of the artists who helped influence its birth was dropping rapidly in popularity. Singer/altoist Louis Jordan, who had had dozens of hits with his Tympany Five while on Decca, recorded 21 songs for Aladdin in 1954 (all of which are included on this CD) and none of them sold well. The strange part is that there is nothing wrong with the music. It compares quite well artistically with his earlier performances; it was just out of style. That fact should not trouble latter-day Jordan fans, for the formerly rare music on this set is witty, swinging and eternally hip. —*Scott Yanow*

Rock 'n Roll Call / Mar. 18, 1955-Apr. 17, 1956 / RCA ✦✦✦
Louis Jordan's string of hits ended in 1952, but he was still in his musical prime throughout the '50s, even though he was no longer on the charts. During 1955-1956, he cut three record sessions for the RCA subsidiaries Vik and X, which resulted in the dozen numbers on this 1993 CD. Due to its brevity (just over 29 minutes), this release was sold as a budget item by RCA. Few of Jordan's fans have probably heard these rarities. The altoist/singer/entertainer was doing his best to adjust to the times, performing early rock & roll, a couple of ballads (including "Whatever Lola Wants"), and novelties. The recordings, which sold poorly, do have their moments. On two of the three sessions, Jordan's septet is greatly expanded, but he is always the star throughout. Among the better numbers are "Slow, Smooth and Easy," "Chicken Back," "Hard Head," and "Texas Stew." Not essential, but Louis Jordan fans who wonder what happened to their hero will want to hear these obscurities. —*Scott Yanow*

Rock 'N' Roll / Oct. 22, 1956-Aug. 28, 1957 / Verve ✦✦✦
This 21-track French import that contains the best of Jordan's 1956-1957 stay at Mercury. Here are the rockin' remakes of his timeless hits, cut with a New York mob including Sam "The Man" Taylor on tenor sax and guitarist Mickey Baker, as well as fresh nuggets like "Big Bess," "Cat Scratchin'," and "Rock Doc." The JAMF" is a scorching jazz showcase for Jordan's alto, and he does a nice easy-swinging job on "Got My Mojo Working." —*Bill Dahl*

No Moe!—Greatest Hits / Oct. 22, 1956-Aug. 1957 / Verve ✦✦✦
With the exception of four numbers taken from a 1957 set in which he heads a quintet co-starring organist Jackie Davis, this CD consists of a dozen songs taken from a 1956 date already reissued (with additional material) on the previously issued CD *Rock 'N' Roll*. Louis Jordan, who had not had a new hit since 1951 (and unfortunately none were in the future) is mostly heard remaking his earlier triumphs such as "Saturday Night Fish Fry," "Ain't Nobody Here but Us Chickens" and "Choo Choo Ch'Boogie." The music is spirited but the earlier CD is the better purchase. —*Scott Yanow*

Louis Jordan & Chris Barber / Dec. 1962-Dec. 1974 / Black Lion ✦✦✦
It seems strange that by 1962, altoist/singer Louis Jordan was thought of as a has-been, for he was actually still in his prime. However, Jordan had run out of new hits and seemed very much passé to some listeners. Most of this CD reissue features Jordan sounding quite exuberant and creative on a 1962 set with trombonist Chris Barber's flexible Dixieland band. The nine selections include four remakes (including "Choo Choo Ch'Boogie" and "Is You Is or Is You Ain't My Baby"), a few newer songs, and bright renditions of "Sister Kate" and "Indiana"; Jordan, Barber, trumpeter Pat Halcox and clarinetist Ian Wheeler form a potent frontline. Also on the CD are five selections taken from unrelated Barber sessions, including three Duke Ellington songs. Recommended to fans of Dixieland, small-group swing and Louis Jordan. —*Scott Yanow*

I Believe in Music / Nov. 6, 1973 / Black & Blue ✦✦✦
Louis Jordan's final recording (he died 15 months later) has been reissued on this CD, along with six previously unreleased selections. Although Jordan had not been a hit-maker in around 20 years and had been somewhat neglected during the decade before the set, he was still in his musical prime both vocally and instrumentally. The altoist is teamed with tenorman Irv Cox and a rhythm section led by pianist Duke Burrell. There are a few remakes of past hits (including "Caldonia," "Is You Is or Is You Ain't My Baby,"

"Saturday Night Fish Fry," and "I'm Gonna Move to the Outskirts of Town"), along with newer jump material. Jordan is in good form and high spirits throughout this date. Recommended. — *Scott Yanow*

★ **The Best of Louis Jordan** / 1977 / MCA ✦✦✦✦✦
This is a best-of CD collection that actually lives up to its name. Virtually all of Louis Jordan's hits, which musically bridged the gap between small-group swing, R&B, and rock & roll, are on this single CD, including "Choo Choo Ch'Boogie," "Let the Good Times Roll," "Ain't Nobody Here but Us Chickens," "Saturday Night Fish Fry," "Caldonia," "Five Guys Named Moe," and "Don't Let the Sun Catch You Crying." Serious collectors will want to explore a more complete series, particularly the one put out by Classics, but for a single acquisition, this is the Louis Jordan set to get. Jordan's very likable and good-humored vocals and his hot alto, as well as the playing of the Tympany Five, belong in everyone's music collection. — *Scott Yanow*

Look Out Sister / 1983 / Krazy Kat ✦✦✦
Louis Jordan checks into a sanitarium for a rest, then dreams himself out West to a dude ranch in this all-Black 1948 musical. Like all of Jordan's low-budget features, there's plenty of hot music by the alto saxman. — *Bill Dahl*

Complete Recordings 1938–1941 / 1992 / Affinity ✦✦✦✦
Just what it says—two discs' worth of Jordan's earliest Decca work, filled with jivey novelties and lusty sax work by the leader of the Tympany Five. Ends with a couple of his earliest hits, "Knock Me a Kiss" and "I'm Gonna Move to the Outskirts of Town." Forty-nine tracks in all. — *Bill Dahl*

V-Disc Recordings / Oct. 20, 1998 / Collectors' Choice Music ✦✦✦✦
On seven occasions between 1943 and 1945, Louis Jordan & His Tympany Five were featured on V-Disc releases. Most of the material comes from radio transcriptions of the Armed Forces Radio Show broadcasts, although some result from studio recordings made by Jordan intended for release as a V-Disc. These are especially welcome since they represent the only studio recording Jordan and his group ever made of some of these tunes. During this 1943-1945 period, Jordan was at the top of his form, combining his special blend of musicianship and showmanship as he and the Five romp through a play list of uptempo numbers for the benefit of the men in the armed services during World War II. Included on the program are Jordan compositions that have become classics, such as "Is You Is or Is You Ain't My Baby?" Longtime Tympany Five trumpet player Eddie Roane gets a lot of exposure. His fabulous lead on "I Like 'Em Fat Like That" and the give and take with Jordan on "I've Found a New Baby" are two of the album's highlights. Wild Bill Davis shows up to play the piano on "Bahama Joe" and "Nobody But Me." This is an album that simply bursts with joy in a treasure of jazz and blues as only Jordan could provide. Kudos to Collectors' Choice for gathering up this material and releasing it on a CD, even though there are barely 30 minutes of music. — *Dave Nathan*

Jump Jive!: The Very Best of Louis Jordan / Jan. 18, 1999 / Music Club ✦✦✦✦

☆ **Let the Good Times Roll: Anthology 1938–1953** / Feb. 23, 1999 / MCA ✦✦✦✦✦
Overlooking Bear Family's comprehensive nine-disc box, this double-CD set is the best reissue ever on Louis Jordan, and the first truly comprehensive domestic release on Jordan's work to feature state-of-the-art sound. There are holes—only a relative handful of the tracks that Jordan and the Tympany Five recorded in 1939 and 1940 are included, although those that are here represent most of the best of them—but not huge ones, and every major Jordan track from 15 years of work is present. The quality of the digital transfers is as alluring than the selection, the mastering so clean, that it sounds 20 years newer than one could ever expect any of it to, based on their actual ages. The 1941 vintage "Pan Pan" and "Saxa-Woogie" place the band practically in the listener's lap, with solos on clarinet, tenor sax, etc., that have smooth, rippling textures and barely a trace of the noise one should expect from early '40s tracks bumped to digital—and the fidelity of these, and "Boogie Woogie Came to Town," "Rusty Dusty Blues," etc., all run circles around any earlier reissues. Similarly, the drums, high-hat, trumpet, sax, and ensemble singing on "Five Guys Named Moe" are crisp enough to pass for modern re-records, except they're not. Indeed, until you get to "Ration Blues," from 1943, there aren't many overt hints of the compression inherent masters of this vintage, and that's the exception—"G.I. Jive" and "Caldonia," cut one and two years later, have the kind of sound textures one more expects out of audiophile releases. Disc two opens with "Ain't That Just Like a Woman," a perfect blueprint in style and execution (check out Carl Hogan's guitar intro) for the sound that Chuck Berry popularized ten years later. Of the later material, only "Run Joe" sounds a little less distinct than the rest. "Life Is So Peculiar" features Louis Armstrong, as vocalist with Jordan, in a beguilingly funny duet from 1951. By that time, Jordan's formula for success was past its prime, and he and Decca records were looking for new approaches— "Teardrops from My Eyes" wasn't it, adding an obtrusive organ played by Wild Bill Davis to the mix. The later incarnation of Jordan's band on these tracks is a more restrained and sophisticated big-band unit, without much of the wild jump-blues feel of the '40s

Tympany Five—a 19-year-old Oliver Nelson can be heard on alto sax, incidentally—but occasionally they capture the feel of the old band, as on "Fat Sam from Birmingham." This version of the band and the way they're recorded are still superior to the incarnations of Jordan's group that turn up on his later recordings for Aladdin and Mercury. — *Bruce Eder*

20th Century Masters—The Millennium Collection: The Best of Louis Jordan / Sep. 14, 1999 / MCA ✦✦✦
A very fun but very short (37 minutes) sampling of Louis Jordan hits recorded for Decca between 1942 ("Five Guys Named Moe") and 1953 ("I Want You to Be My Baby"). Designed as more of an introduction, *20th Century Masters* includes such Jordan staples as "Caldonia" and "Saturday Night Fish Fry." This brief compilation may be a good place to start, but it'll leave you wanting more. — *Joslyn Layne*

Saturday Night Fish Fry: The Original Greatest Hits / Apr. 18, 2000 / Jasmine ✦✦✦✦
Subtitled *The Original and Greatest Hits*, this 24-track package is exactly that, a really great one stop for those of you wanting to get into the music of this jump blues pioneer. With biggies aboard like "Caldonia Boogie," "Is You Is or Is You Ain't My Baby," "Let the Good Times Roll," "Choo Choo Ch'Boogie," and "Five Guys Named Moe," this makes a perfect starting point for any Louis Jordan collection you might want to amass. Excellent transfers and well-written liners by Arthur Braine make this a collection well worth hunting down. — *Cub Koda*

1947–1949 / Jan. 9, 2001 / Classics ✦✦✦✦✦
Louis Jordan was at the height of his fame during the period covered by this *Classics* CD. His last session from 1947 is here along with the music recorded during his first five recording dates of 1949. Among the hits are "Safe, Sane and Single," "Beans and Corn Bread," "School Days," and the two-part "Saturday Night Fish Fry." Jordan's Tympany Five had grown to seven pieces by late 1947 and expanded to nine in 1949; among his sidemen were trumpeter Aaron Izenhall, Eddie Johnson, or Josh Jackson on tenor and pianist (and future organist) Bill Doggett. In addition to such favorites as "Don't Burn the Candle at Both Ends," the catchy "Cole Slaw," and "Hungry Man," there are two songs ("Baby, It's Cold Outside" and "Don't Cry, Cry Baby") in which Jordan shares the vocals with Ella Fitzgerald. Highly enjoyable music. — *Scott Yanow*

Juicy Lucy

f. 1969, United Kingdom, **db.** 1972
Group / Blues-Rock

Saucy blues-rockers Juicy Lucy formed in 1969 from the ashes of cult-favorite garage band the Misunderstood, reuniting vocalist Ray Owen, steel guitarist Glenn "Ross" Campbell and keyboardist Chris Mercer; with the additions of guitarist Neil Hubbard, bassist Keith Ellis and drummer Pete Dobson, the group immediately notched a U.K. Top 20 hit with their reading of the Bo Diddley perennial "Who Do You Love," with their self-titled debut LP falling just shy of the Top 40. Ex-Zoot Money singer Paul Williams, guitarist Mick Moody, and drummer Rod Coombes replaced Owen (who exited for a solo career), Hubbard and Dobson for 1970's *Lie Back and Enjoy It*, with bassist Jim Leverton assuming Ellis' duties for the follow-up, 1971's *Get a Whiff a This*. The constant turnover clearly took its toll on the group both creatively and commercially, with co-founders Campbell and Mercer both exiting prior to the fourth Juicy Lucy album, 1972's *Pieces*, which was recorded by a makeshift lineup of Williams, Moody, keyboardist Jean Roussel, and the former Blodwyn Pig rhythm section of bassist Andy Pyle and drummer Ron Berg. Juicy Lucy finally disbanded shortly thereafter. — *Jason Ankeny*

● **Juicy Lucy/Lie Back and Enjoy It** / Nov. 1995 / BGO ✦✦✦✦
Beat Goes On combined Juicy Lucy's first two albums—*Juicy Lucy* and *Lie Back and Enjoy It*—on one CD in 1995. Since the band didn't have much sustained momentum in their career, this is essentially a best-of collection. All their best moments arrive on the debut, particularly their heavy cover of Bo Diddley's "Who Do You Love." The horribly named *Lie Back and Enjoy It* follows the same pattern as the debut, as the group churns out heavy blooze-boogie, but without as much conviction. For hardcore fans, this doesn't really matter—it's just nice to get these two albums on one disc—but if you're not a devotee of late-'60s/early-'70s hard rock and heavy blues, this isn't going to change your mind. — *Stephen Thomas Erlewine*

Lie Back and Enjoy It/Get a Whiff a This / 1997 / One Way ✦✦✦
One Way combined Juicy Lucy's second and third albums—*Lie Back and Enjoy It* and *Get a Whiff a This*—on one CD in 1997. Both albums have terrible titles (some could argue that the latter is even revolting) and both are musically similar, containing standard-issue heavy blooze-rock. By the time the band recorded *Get a Whiff*, several original members had departed, and their sound had become turgid and predictable, with none of the forward momentum that propelled their first album to popularity. However, hardcore fans will still like this disc, since it combines two albums that have long been out of print on one compact disc. — *Stephen Thomas Erlewine*

Ernie K-Doe (Ernest Kador Jr.)

b. Feb. 22, 1936, New Orleans, LA, d. Jul. 5, 2001, New Orleans, LA

Vocals, Songwriter / New Orleans R&B, R&B

Ernie K-Doe scored one of the biggest hits (possibly *the* biggest) in the history of New Orleans R&B with "Mother-in-Law," a humorous lament that struck a chord with listeners of all stripes on its way to the top of both the pop and R&B charts in 1961. The song proved to be K-Doe's only major success, despite several more minor hits that were equally infectious, yet he remained one of New Orleans' most inimitable personalities. Born Ernest Kador Jr. in New Orleans in 1936, he began singing at age seven in the Baptist church where his father served as minister. During his teen years, Kador performed with local gospel groups like the Golden Chain Jubilee Singers and the Zion Travelers, when he was influenced chiefly by the Five Blind Boys of Mississippi. He entered and won talent competitions and became more interested in secular R&B and blues, and at 17, he moved to Chicago with his mother and began performing at local clubs. Thanks to connections he made there, he got the chance to sing with the Flamingos and Moonglows, as well as the Four Blazes, a gig that earned him his first recording session in late 1953 for United.

Kador returned to New Orleans in 1954 and honed his flamboyant stage act at numerous local hangouts (including the famed Dew Drop Inn), both solo and as part of the vocal group the Blue Diamonds. The Blue Diamonds cut a couple of sides for Savoy in 1954, and the following year, Kador (still billed under his real name) recorded his first solo single, "Do Baby Do," for Specialty. In 1957, he recorded a few more sides for Ember, as both Ernie Kado and Ernie K-Doe. Finally, in 1959, he caught on with the newly formed Minit label and hooked up with producer/songwriter/pianist/arranger/future legend Allen Toussaint. His first Minit single, "Make You Love Me," flopped, but the follow-up "Hello My Lover" was a substantial regional hit, selling nearly 100,000 copies. K-Doe struck gold with 1961's "Mother-in-Law," a Toussaint-penned tune on which K-Doe traded choruses with bass vocalist Benny Spellman. That, coupled with the playful cynicism of the lyrics, made for a rollicking good time in the best New Orleans R&B tradition, and K-Doe was rewarded with a number one record on both the pop and R&B charts. He toured the country and landed a few more follow-up hits—"Te-Ta-Te-Ta-Ta," "I Cried My Last Tear," "A Certain Girl" (later covered by the Yardbirds), "Popeye Joe"—but none approached the phenomenon of "Mother-in-Law," and were more popular on the R&B scene.

Minit soon went under, and K-Doe followed Toussaint to the Instant label, but two 1964 singles failed to revive K-Doe's chart fortunes, partly because the early prime of New Orleans R&B was fading as Motown gained prominence. Over the remainder of the '60s, K-Doe recorded for Peacock and Duke, landing two very minor R&B chart entries in 1967 with "Later for Tomorrow" and "Until the Real Thing Comes Along" on the latter label.

However, he had a difficult time adapting his loose, playful style to the R&B trends of the day. He reunited with Toussaint for a brief period in the early '70s, to no avail, and drifted into a long period of alcoholism. Fortunately, K-Doe was able to reclaim some of his popularity around New Orleans when he began hosting a radio program in 1982, earning an audience with his wild antics and blatant self-promotion. In 1994, K-Doe opened his own club, the Mother-In-Law Lounge, in New Orleans, and frequently performed there in the years to come, occasionally returning to the studio as well. He was inducted into the city's Music Hall of Fame in 1995 and generally acknowledged for his contributions up until his death from kidney and liver failure on July 5, 2001. —*Steve Huey*

The Building Is Shakin' & the Walls Are Tremblin' / Apr. 20, 1999 / Aim ✦✦✦

Produced by Milton Battiste in the mid-'90s, this baker's dozen of cuts (really 12 songs; tracks 12 and 13 are the same title) attests to the fact that Ernie K-Doe was about more than just his million-seller "Mother-In-Law." The songs are R&B, blues, contemporary soul, and reggae ("Only 11 Roses.") Highlights include a duet with Lisa Lee on "When Something Is Wrong With My Baby," a remake of Jimmy Reed's "Baby What You Want Me to Do," parts one and two of "Your Wish Is My Command," and two uptempo numbers ensconced in rhythm & blues: "A Certain Girl" and "Hello My Lover." —*Andrew Hamilton*

● **Absolutely the Best** / Oct. 30, 2001 / Fuel 2000 ✦✦✦✦✦

Leading off with his 1961 smash "Mother-in-Law," *Absolutely the Best* cycles through 18 tracks of Ernie K-Doe's best material recorded for Minit and Duke during the '60s. Aside from "Mother-in-Law," K-Doe wasn't much of a hitmaker, though a few of his follow-ups were even better than the original, paced by the irresistible "A Certain Girl." Another rare chart hit, "I Cried My Last Tear," descends into bathos, but *Absolutely the Best* is a great wrap-up of one of New Orleans' most enjoyable, distinctive singers. —*John Bush*

A Real Mother-In-Law for Ya: The Allen Toussaint Sessions / Jun. 26, 2002 / West Side ✦✦✦✦✦

Since his big hit was "Mother-In-Law," a funny song that could easily be perceived as a novelty, Ernie K-Doe is often dismissed when it comes to the top rank of New Orleans R&B singers. That's an inaccurate assessment, as West Side's delightful 2002 compilation

A Real Mother-In-Law for Ya: The Allen Toussaint Sessions 1959-63 proves. Part of the reason, of course, is that these are the Toussaint sessions, and Allen Toussaint is the king of late-'50s and '60s New Orleans R&B, not only writing classics like "Mother-In-Law" but producing sessions that had precisely the right combination of rolling rhythms, horns, mellow funk, pianos, and warm vocals, from the friendly, skilled Ernie K-Doe. He didn't have as rich a selection of material as, say, Fats Domino or Lee Dorsey, but he was at the top tier of the second tier, as this compulsively listenable 29-track collection proves. This is nearly all top-shelf material—from hits like "A Certain Girl" and "I've Cried My Last Tear" (the A and B, respectively, of one of the greatest R&B singles of the early '60s), to lesser-known material like Toussaint's "Hello My Lover" or the rollicking "Wanted $10,000 Reward." After hearing this collection, it's hard not to think of Ernie K-Doe as one of the great New Orleans R&B artists of his time, and it's hard to imagine a serious New Orleans collection without this disc. —*Stephen Thomas Erlewine*

Candye Kane

Vocals / Blues-Rock, Modern Electric Blues

A former stripper and men's magazine model who also did the occasional X-rated video shoot back in the '80s, Candye Kane would be the blues version of the Andrea True Connection, but for one vitally important fact: This woman can really sing! An updated version of Bessie Smith with a wicked sense of humor and a gleefully omnisexual persona, Candye Kane and her backup band the Swingin' Armadillos aren't just a novelty act, but a sassy, smart, and always-entertaining mix of sex, showbiz, and swing.

Los Angeles-native Kane started her musical career with 1994's *Home Cookin'*, but really hit her stride with 1995's *Knockout* and, especially, 1997's excellent *Diva la Grande*. The short-lived swing revival led to a major-label deal for 1998's *Swango*, but that cocktail-influenced swing record didn't give her jump blues brassiness its due, and when Sire gave Kane her walking papers, she settled in the far more hospitable environs of Rounder, which released the much improved *The Toughest Girl Alive* in 2000. —*Stewart Mason*

Home Cookin' / 1994 / Antone's ✦✦✦✦

After releasing her own cassette (the partially live *Burlesque Swing*—the best introduction to Candye's unique talents), this stew may be a case of too many cooks. And despite a star-studded cast—including two Paladins and one member of Los Lobos (who are also listed among the six producers—not counting Kane), R&B guitar great Roy Gaines, Blaster Dave Alvin, Fab T-Bird Kim Wilson—the result is neither fish nor fowl. The hardcore blues numbers—"Big Mama Candye's Blues" and "Don't Blame It on Me" (a duet with Wilson)—are fairly standard fare, and her ribald side is virtually absent, but the conjunto "She Wore a Red Carnation" and country two-step "Dance Hall Girls" show Candye's singing and songwriting to their best advantage. (Her Antone's follow-up, 1995's *Knockout*, is far from a "blues album"—with country and rock material penned by Dylan, Jack Tempchin, Rickie Lee Jones, Van Dyke Parks, and Lowell George—but features better vocal performances by Candye and production by Val Garay.) —*Dan Forte*

Knockout / Sep. 1995 / Antone's ✦✦✦

Diva la Grande / May 27, 1997 / Discovery ✦✦✦✦

Former sex industry worker Candye Kane's third album is her breakthrough, the record where she finally perfected her blend of jump blues, rockabilly, and big-band swing, combined with her brassy, gleefully omnisexual persona and big-as-life voice. Besides the obvious personal anthems like "You Need a Great Big Woman," "Gifted in the Ways of Love," and, of course, "All You Can Eat (And You Can Eat It All Night Long)," Kane does more than credible versions of classics ranging from "I Got a Feelin'" to a Cajun-ized version of Lee Hazlewood's "These Boots Are Made for Walkin'." Producer Dave Alvin and Kane's longtime backing band, the Swingin' Armadillos, set Kane's alternately booming and flirty voice in swinging settings that emphasize her vocal strengths while minimizing the occasional flatness that marred Kane's first couple of albums. More importantly, while jump blues in the '90s is by definition a stylized genre, there's nothing overly cute or retro about *Diva la Grande*. This is a fun, sexy, rocking good time. —*Stewart Mason*

Swango / Aug. 18, 1998 / Sire ✦✦✦

Candye Kane's sole major-label release, 1998's *Swango*, isn't one of her best albums. Producer Mike Vernon (who had run the famous U.K. blues-rock label Blue Horizon in the '60s) uses the then-current swing revival to reduce the more authentic jump blues elements of Kane's earlier records. The result is a kind of hipsterrific cocktail-nation cloyingness that makes Kane seem like a novelty act. Kane is singing better than ever, especially on the opening statement of intent, "200 Pounds of Fun," and a terrific version of the standard "Dream a Little Dream of Me," and her songwriting is growing increasingly sharper as well. The title track's a particular gem. (Longtime fans will be disappointed to find, however, that this is by far Kane's least-bawdy record.) So really, the fault comes down to the stiff arrangements and inappropriate production; look past those and *Swango* is an appealing, entertaining record. It may take a few listens to get to that point, however. —*Stewart Mason*

● **The Toughest Girl Alive** / Jun. 6, 2000 / Rounder ♦♦♦♦
Candye Kane is a big-voiced blues singer with a twist. Though they are mostly credited as originals, the tunes are familiar from other blues, R&B, and jump blues compositions. The differences lie in Kane's lyrics and in her enthusiasm in singing them. The former adult film star stakes out a pan-sexual stance that she expounds lustily. Jack Tempchin's "Who Do You Love?" finds her endorsing homosexuality, a ménage à trois, and prostitution, and assuring her listeners that God does, too. Her own "(Hey Mister!) She Was My Baby Last Night" portrays an unexpected combination in a romantic triangle. In "For Your Love," Kane lists a series of sexual fantasy characters ranging from "a dominatrix with a whip up above" to "a White House intern." And "Let's Commit Adultery" states its position in its title. The backing band, which occasionally features Dave Alvin and Marcia Ball, is excellent, but the distinctive element in the mix is Kane's lusty persona. —*William Ruhlmann*

Fred Kaplan

b. Apr. 23, 1954, Los Angeles, CA
Piano, Producer / Blues-Rock, Electric Blues
Kaplan's place in blues history is best known as a member of the immortal Hollywood Fats Band, but even more so, he belongs on the pedestal of Angeleno blues pioneers.

He was drawn to the ivories at age three, and performed his first recital when he was seven. While working for his father's furniture store, one of his father's customers sold him discarded records at a nickel a piece from his juke box servicing business. Records like T-Bone Walker, Big Joe Turner, Bo Diddley, Chuck Berry, and Little Richard opened new frontiers and wetted Kaplan's appetite to learn more.

To meet blues greats, Kaplan swept floors at the Golden Bear and during his time off, hung around the Ash Grove, meeting Buddy Guy, Muddy Waters, and the like. But Kaplan's most profound experience came from befriending Lloyd Glenn. One of Kaplan's favorite memories was playing some unreleased tapes to Art Tatum to Glenn. Glenn got up and played all the material, verbatim, then continued with a personal jazz set.

Through Al Blake, Kaplan met Fats, playing first as the Headhunters, which then evolved into the Hollywood Fats Band. They recorded one self-titled album, later retitled *Rock This House* when reissued on Blacktop and broke up in the early '80s. Sadly, the band nearly reformed but ended with Fat's abrupt death in 1986.

During the dry years, Kaplan worked occasional gigs, some which included prominent figures like William Clarke. In 1997, Kim Wilson of the Fabulous Thunderbirds formed Blue Collar Music, devoted to recording and promoting stylists steeped in early blues. Kaplan was tapped as vice president and recorded his solo, *Signifyin'*, then supported Blake's Blue Collar debut of *Mr. Blake's Blues*. —*Char Ham*

● **Signifyin'** / Nov. 25, 1997 / Blue Collar ♦♦♦
What's puzzling is why it's taken years for Kaplan to release a solo challenge. After all, he is a member of the Hollywood Fats Band, and has supported some of the cream of the crop of the Southern California blues scene—James Harman, William Clarke, Junior Watson, and Robert Lucas. Could it be he shies away from front-stage glory, and instead uses his hands to speak on the ivories? Even with the generous solo space granted on this release, he remains humble and prefers to praise his mentor, Lloyd Glenn and the Almighty. No meat byproducts and cereal fillers here—great rib-stickin', back-to-basics piano blues are featured here. —*Char Ham*

Bruce Katz

b. Aug. 19, 1952
Piano, Organ / New Orleans R&B, Hard Bop
Rarely does a musician display brilliant dexterity, coupled with sparks of creativity, equally in both blues and jazz. One such rare bird is Bruce Katz, who not only meets these characteristics, but excels in his understanding of the genres and unleashes the strongest assets of each.

Best known as a member of Ronnie Earl & the Broadcasters, Katz took up music at age five when he outperformed his sister at the classical pieces she was assigned for piano lessons. Discovering classic jazz and a Bessie Smith record planted the seeds of a passion for jazz and blues.

In the early '80s his first major supporting gig was Big Mama Thornton; he then worked and toured with Barrence Whitfield and the Savages, Bo Diddley, Chuck Berry, Jimmy Witherspoon, Johnny Adams, and Tiger Okoshi. Burned out from life on the road, he enrolled at New England Conservatory, earning a master's degree in jazz. Five months after graduation, he met Ronnie Earl, who hired Katz.

During the nearly five-year stint with Earl, Katz performed on six CDs, and also co-wrote songs with Earl, some of which were "The Colour of Love," "Ice Cream Man," and "Hippology." In 1992, Katz debuted his first solo album *Crescent Crawl*, then the following year, released *Transformation*. Just before the release of *Mississippi Moan*, Katz left the Broadcasters to concentrate on a solo career. In addition to performing, Katz teaches piano and taught the first ever in-depth blues course at Berklee College. His album roster includes 1993's *Transformation* and 1997's *Mississippi Moan*. *Three Feet to the Ground* followed in mid-2000. —*Char Ham*

Crescent Crawl / 1992 / AudioQuest ♦♦♦♦
After many years as a side man, Bruce Katz stepped out on his own in 1992 to record *Crescent Crawl*. Although it is an all-instrumental album, Katz is the "frontman" on this recording, taking the spotlight—and most deservedly so—on both piano and Hammond B-3 organ. *Crescent Crawl* blurs the line between blues and jazz (the utilization of an upright bass assists in this effort). The title tune has—as you would expect—has a New Orleans groove. "Contrition" appeared on Ronnie Earl's *Still River* a few years later when Katz was a member of Earl's band, although this version is a bit more understated. Both "Contrition" and "BK's Broiler" feature Katz on the B-3. "Buzz Cut" is essentially a swing tune, but one with a funky feel thanks to guitarist Kevin Barry's rhythmic backing. Billy Preston's "Will It Go Round in Circles" is superb. Katz closes with a harmonically complex solo piano version of "Just a Closer Walk With Thee," a tune he also included in every live gig in the early '90s. This disc is about loose definitions of blues and jazz, strong grooves, and, first and foremost, improvisation—Just check out the Irish jig that suddenly dances from Bob Malach's sax on "One Way Ticket"! —*Ann Wickstrom*

Transformation / Nov. 6, 1993-Nov. 7, 1993 / AudioQuest ♦♦♦
The follow-up to the Bruce Katz Band debut CD *Crescent Crawl*, *Transformation* is more of the same great instrumental blues/jazz, although a bit harder to get your arms around. Consisting of all originals, Katz plays piano on seven of the tracks and Hammond B-3 organ on the other three. It has more of an avant-garde approach than its predecessor, *Crescent Crawl*, and its successor, *Mississippi Moan*. It has everything from a stride shuffle ("Larry the Spinning Poodle") to New Orleans grooves ("But Now I See") to deep jazzy blues ("The Sweeper" and "Deep Pockets"). "Deep Pockets" was later recorded by Ronnie Earl & the Broadcasters, of which Katz was a member. —*Ann Wickstrom*

Mississippi Moan / Oct. 7, 1997 / AudioQuest ♦♦♦♦
The music on this CD is comprised mostly of instrumentals, with Bruce Katz sticking primarily to piano, performing just a few numbers on the organ, the instrument for which he is best known. Katz's style ranges from Albert Ammons and Jimmy Smith to the flash of Jerry Lee Lewis. The selections include straight blues, a few stomps, some solo boogie-woogie, a couple of more advanced jazz tunes, and vocals by Mighty Sam McClain on "Hanging on the Cross" and "I'm Gonna Love You." Due to its variety and strong jazz content, this release (which also features guitarist Julien Kasper and Tom Hall on tenor and baritone) is easily recommended to both blues and jazz collectors. —*Scott Yanow*

● **Three Feet Off the Ground** / Aug. 15, 2000 / AudioQuest ♦♦♦♦
It has been said that instrumentalist Bruce Katz has one foot in jazz and the other foot in the blues, but those aren't the only styles that interest the organist/pianist; rock, soul, and gospel are also part of what he does. All of those influences assert themselves on *Three Feet Off the Ground*, which tends to be more aggressive and rockin' than the album that preceded it, 1997's *Mississippi Moan*. "Wrecking Ball" and "Beef Jerky" (which brings to mind Lee Morgan's "The Sidewinder") are definitely among the more forceful things Katz has recorded, and his guitarist Julien Kasper sounds equally uninhibited. Although Katz is a talented acoustic pianist with a healthy appreciation of Albert Ammons, his piano playing takes a back seat to the organ this time. Katz's Hammond B-3 dominates the CD, and one is reminded how appealing he is on the instrument. As an organist, Katz has a gritty, earthy sound that is somewhere between Jimmy Smith and Stax hero Booker T. Jones (of Booker T. & the MG's fame). *Three Feet Off the Ground* is a release that blues, jazz, and rock fans alike will want to hear. —*Alex Henderson*

Big Kat Kaylor

Piano, Vocals / Blues-Rock, Soul-Blues
Michael "Big Kat" Kaylor is a singer/songwriter/piano player who hails from Nashville, TN. This would normally tie him into that city's musical scene, which automatically brands any new artist as the next hat hunk wannabe. But Kaylor's music is as far removed from cookie-cutter country or other genre paint-by-numbers approaches. Kaylor works in a definite modern rhythm & blues groove, taking time-honored soul and R&B modes and infusing them with lyrics that can be sometimes introspective and often slyly humorous. His voice carries with it a world-weary conviction, giving his lyrics great weight and space within the song's context. The Kingsport, TN, native took to music as a youngster, learning to sing and play keyboards at an early age. Although country was the steady genre diet in his parents' household, Mike's tastes ran to blues, soul, and Elvis, with James Brown also mixed in as a formative influence.

He moved to Nashville in 1985 not to pursue a musical career, but merely to take on a job as a real estate appraiser. Aside from forming a weekend band with bassist Robert Stapleton (Mike "Big Kat" Kaylor and the Blue Lines) and pitching some gospel tunes he had written around Music City, Kaylor's musical profile was decidedly low. It really wasn't until he met up with the staff at Step One Records and offered them a tape of his music that things started rolling towards his debut album, released in 1996. Kaylor's music draws from a number of styles and, as such, makes for a wonderful melting pot of American music to savor. As he puts it, "There's lots of R&B players in Nashville. It's a music town. I think the industry is open to what I'm doing, and I think it's the right time for me to be doing this." —*Cub Koda*

● **Scattered** / 1996 / Step One ♦♦♦♦
Nashville boogie piano man and songwriter Mike "Big Kat" Kaylor makes a big splash with the 11 tracks on this, his debut album. Connected to mainstream country only by mutual geographical locale, Kaylor is a bona fide soul man more than a piano-pounding wildman, his well-worn voice imparting a wistfulness to his lyrics that really brings these songs to life. Producer and multi-instrumentalist (seven different listings in the booklet) Robert Stapleton is also co-writer or lone writer of eight of the 11 tunes on here, and through the miracle of overdubbing often functions as the complete band on several tracks. The title track is based on a phrase used by waitresses at the Waffle House chain of Southern restaurants, connecting a mental state to directions for preparing hash browns. But this good-humored wordplay is tempered with the dark-hued lyricism of "Hard to Take It Alone," "Still a Man," and "Set Me Down Easy." But the varied writing on here works well with Kaylor at the center of it all, and his jazzy "Bar Room Blues," with its bittersweet lyrics and changes, is as powerful as anything on here. Not exactly blues, soul, jazz, rhythm & blues or adult contemporary, but a rather heady mixture of all of it, Mike Kaylor has come up with a very original-sounding debut outing here. File under impressive. —*Cub Koda*

Keb' Mo' (Kevin Moore)

b. Oct. 3, 1951, Los Angeles, CA

Slide Guitar, Vocals, Guitar / Contemporary Blues, Modern Acoustic Blues

Keb' Mo' draws heavily on the old-fashioned country blues style of Robert Johnson, but keeps his sound contemporary with touches of soul and folksy storytelling. He writes much of his own material and has applied his acoustic, electric, and slide guitar skills to jazz and rock-oriented bands in the past as well.

Born Kevin Moore in Los Angeles to parents of Southern descent, he was exposed to gospel music at a young age. At 21, Moore joined an R&B band later hired for a tour by Papa John Creach and played on three of Creach's albums. Opening for jazz and rock artists such as the Mahavishnu Orchestra, Jefferson Starship, and Loggins & Messina helped broaden Moore's horizons and musical abilities.

Moore cut an R&B-based solo album, *Rainmaker*, in 1980 for Casablanca, which promptly folded. In 1983, he joined Monk Higgins' band as a guitarist and met a number of blues musicians who collectively increased his understanding of the music. He subsequently joined a vocal group called the Rose Brothers and gigged around L.A. In 1990, Moore portrayed a Delta bluesman in a local play called *Rabbit Foot* and later played Robert Johnson in a docudrama called *Can't You Hear the Wind Howl?* He released his self-titled debut album as Keb' Mo' in 1994, featuring two Robert Johnson covers, 11 songs written or co-written by Moore, and his guitar and banjo work. Keb' Mo' performed a well-received set at the 1995 Newport Folk Festival. Keb' Mo's second album, *Just Like You*, was equally well-received. *Slow Down* followed in 1998 and *Door* was issued two years later. *—Steve Huey*

● **Keb' Mo'** / Jun. 3, 1994 / OKeh/550/Epic ✦✦✦✦

Keb' Mo's self-titled debut is an edgy, ambitious collection of gritty country blues. Keb' Mo' pushes into new directions, trying to incorporate some of the sensibilites of the slacker revolution without losing touch of the tradition that makes the blues the breathing, vital art form it is. His attempts aren't always successful, but his gutsy guitar playing and impassioned vocals, as well as his surprisingly accomplished songwriting, make *Keb' Mo'* a debut to cherish. *—Thom Owens*

Just Like You / Jun. 18, 1996 / OKeh/550/Epic ✦✦✦

On his second album, Keb' Mo' begins to expand the borders of his Delta blues by recording with a full band on a couple of tracks and attempting more expansive, rock-based song structures. The attempts aren't entirely successful and it's ironic that he decided to try rock-oriented material after he received such praise for his traditionalist debut. Still, there are a few songs on the album that rank with the best on his first album, which suggests that *Just Like You* is merely a sophomore slump. *—Thom Owens*

Slow Down / Aug. 25, 1998 / OKeh/550/Epic ✦✦✦

At the beginning of his career, Keb' Mo' appeared to be a clever update of the acoustic bluesman, one that managed to recall country blues but offer a contemporary spin on tradition—sort of like a '90s version of Taj Mahal. With each new album, however, it became clear that authenticity was not a concept that troubled Keb' Mo'. He was more concerned with offering a nice, smooth bluesy pop that was perfect for the House of Blues, not for seedy roadhouse. That's not necessarily a bad thing—it's just the kind of thing that would irritate blues purists who may have placed hope in him in the first place. *Slow Down*, Mo's third album, will nevertheless be the kind of album that will please listeners who like laid-back, polished blues, not gritty Chicago or Delta blues. Approaching *Slow Down* with this knowledge is helpful, since it isn't a bad album—it's well-constructed and professionally performed, emphasizing Keb' Mo's ability to craft good, slick blues-rock. If you like that sound—the sound of post-Robert Cray blues, with no trace of Stevie Ray Vaughan pyrotechnics—*Slow Down* may be just your pace. *—Stephen Thomas Erlewine*

The Door / Oct. 10, 2000 / OKeh/550/Epic ✦✦✦

Keb' Mo''s self-titled first album, from its Robert Johnson covers to its appearance on a resuscitated OKeh Records, seemed to suggest the arrival of a Delta blues traditionalist, even though the former Kevin Moore was really a Los Angeles native who had kicked around the music business for years playing various styles of music. The follow-up, *Just Like You*, was therefore a disappointment to blues purists, since it clearly used folk-blues as a basis to create adult contemporary pop in the Bonnie Raitt mold. But to the music industry, that was just fine, since it fostered the hope that here was an artist (finally!) who could find a way to make the blues—consistently revered but commercially dicey—pay, and Keb' Mo' won a Best Contemporary Blues Album Grammy for his effort. *Slow Down* (1998) brought him a second Grammy and got even higher in the charts. *The Door* is more of the same. Keb' Mo''s slightly gritty voice and fingerpicking are the focus of the music, but he does not hesitate to add mainstream pop elements, beginning with writing partners who include Bobby McFerrin and Melissa Manchester, and continuing with a backup band that features such session aces as keyboard player Greg Phillinganes and drummer Jim Keltner. This is music that is folkish and bluesy rather than being actual folk-blues. Just in case anyone hasn't gotten the point yet, Keb' Mo' begins the album's sole cover, Elmore James' "It Hurts Me Too," in authentic folk-blues style, after which the arrangement lurches into a heavily percussive, anything-but-traditional direction. It's fair warning that the singer/guitarist is interested in tradition only as a jumping-off point. Maybe that's what "contemporary blues" is. *—William Ruhlmann*

Big Wide Grin / Jun. 5, 2001 / Sony Wonder ✦✦✦

The rise in the number of titles in the children's music category around the turn of the century was accompanied by a shift in the approach to such recordings. As baby boomers, who remain loyal record buyers, have become parents, the artists who appeal to them have turned to children's music, but it often seems as though the records are still being made for the boomers, not their children. Though the recordings often concern the subjects of childhood and parenting, it is often hard to imagine a child actually enjoying the music. Such is the case with the Keb' Mo' children's album, *Big Wide Grin*, which is better regarded as a regular Keb' Mo' album on the theme of family rather than an album for children. The singer covers a number of pop evergreens from the late '60s and '70s—the O'Jays' "Love Train," Bill Withers' "Grandma's Hands," the Winstons' "Color Him Father," Sly and the Family Stone's "Family Affair," Joni Mitchell's "Big Yellow Taxi," and Stevie Wonder's "Isn't She Lovely"—and he reaches back even further for the swing-era standard "The Flat Foot Floogie" and "America the Beautiful." All of these are likely to be familiar to parents of a certain age, and most have something to do with family issues, but only a couple are likely to appeal to children. This is not to say that, to be a children's album, a record must be filled with singalongs for the preschool set. But albums like this belong to a recent subset of the children's market that should perhaps be labeled "parents' music." In the case of Keb' Mo', the recording serves to ease him even more in the direction of being a folk-pop interpreter, an approach he has embraced increasingly since initially coming across as a new-style folk-blues singer. *—William Ruhlmann*

Jack Kelly

d. 1960

Drums / Jug Band, Prewar Country Blues, Acoustic Memphis Blues

Singer/guitarist Jack Kelly was the frontman of the South Memphis Jug Band, a popular string band whose music owed a heavy debt to the blues as well as minstrel songs, vaudeville numbers, reels, and rags. Little is known of the hoarse-voiced Kelly's origins; he led the group in tandem with fiddler Will Batts, and they made their first recordings in 1933, followed in 1939 by a second and final session. Although the South Memphis Jug Band's lineup changed frequently, Kelly remained a constant, leading the group in various incarnations until as late as the mid-'50s; he died in Memphis in 1960. *—Jason Ankeny*

● **Complete Recorded Works (1933–1939)** / 1990 / Document ✦✦✦✦✦

Document's *Complete Recorded Works (1933-1939)* is an exhaustive overview of Jack Kelly's career. However, for all but completists and academics, the disc is a mixed blessing due to its exacting chronological sequencing, poor fidelity (all cuts are transferred from original acetates and 78s), and sheer number of performances. Casual fans are better off with a less comprehensive package. *—Thom Owens*

Jo Ann Kelly

b. Jan. 5, 1944, London, England, **d.** Oct. 21, 1990

Vocals, Guitar / British Blues, Country-Rock

The rock era saw a few white female singers, like Janis Joplin, show they could sing the blues. But one who could outshine them all—Jo Ann Kelly—seemed to slip through the cracks, mostly because she favored the acoustic, Delta style rather than rocking out with a heavy band behind her. But with a huge voice, and a strong guitar style influenced by Memphis Minnie and Charley Patton, she was the queen.

Born January 5, 1944, Kelly and her older brother Dave were both taken by the blues, and born at the right time to take advantage of a young British blues scene in the early '60s. By 1964 she was playing in clubs, including the Star in Croydon, and had made her first limited-edition record with future Groundhogs guitarist Tony McPhee. She expanded to play folk and blues clubs all over Britain, generally solo, but occasionally with other artists, bringing together artists like Bessie Smith and Sister Rosetta Tharpe into her own music.

After the first National Blues Federation Convention in 1968, her career seemed ready to take flight. She began playing the more lucrative college circuit, followed by her well-received debut album in 1969. At the second National Blues Convention, she jammed with Canned Heat, who invited her to join them on a permanent basis. She declined, not wanting to be a part of a band—and made the same decision when Johnny Winter offered to help her. Throughout the '70s, Kelly continued to work and record solo, while also gigging for fun in bands run by friends, outfits like Tramp and Chilli Willi—essentially pub rock, as the scene was called, and in 1979 she helped found the Blues Band, along with brother Dave, and original Fleetwood Mac bassist Bob Brunning. The band backed her on an ambitious show she staged during the early '80s, Ladies and the Blues, in which she paid tribute to her female heros.

In 1988, Kelly began to suffer pain. A brain tumor was diagnosed and removed, and she seemed to have recovered, even touring again in 1990 with her brother before collapsing and dying on October 21. Posthumously, she's become a revered blues figure, one who helped clear the path for artists like Bonnie Raitt and Rory Block. But more than a figurehead, her recorded material—and unreleased sides have appeared often since her death—show that Kelly truly was a remarkable blueswoman. *—Chris Nickson*

● **Jo Ann Kelly** / 1969 / BGO ✦✦✦✦✦

Same Thing on Their Minds / 1969 / Sunset ✦✦✦

Fahey, Kelly, Mann, Miller, Seidler / 1972 / Blue Goose ✦✦✦

Do It / 1976 / Red Rag ✦✦

It's Whoopie / 1978 / Columbia ✦✦✦✦

Just Restless / 1984 / Appaloosa ✦✦

Key to the Highway / Feb. 12, 1999 / Mooncrest ✦✦✦✦

People have begun to discover just how good a blueswoman the late Jo Ann Kelly was. That's led to a trawling through the vaults, which have turned up albums like this, of obscure compilation and unreleased cuts. *Key to the Highway* covers what's arguably her most prolific period, as her star was ascending and was at its critical height (although it should be noted that the 1974 end date in the title is very elastic—there are six cuts from 1975, and two conversation pieces from 1988). While all too often material has remained unreleased for a good reason, everything here is prime. Kelly's definition of blues is definitely loose, including Hank Williams' "You Win Again," with some strong piano from Bob Hall, and even Marvin Gaye's "Can I Get a Witness" and Rufus Thomas' "Walking the Dog." However, in her hands, blues is exactly what they are. While generally accompanied, the stunning a cappella "Levee Camp Holler" shows the power she had, enough to put her up there with the top rank, and where her fretwork shows through, as on "I Can't Be Satisfied," she was a superb guitar player, with a slide technique to make Bonnie Raitt envious. The audio here might not be the best, somewhat crackly and aged, but in many ways that simply adds to the authentic patina of blues. She shows that you don't have to be male and African-American to have the blues. And a record like this simply increases her legacy. —*Chris Nickson*

Talkin' Low: Rare Unissued Recordings 1966–1988 / Mar. 21, 2000 / Mooncrest ◆◆◆
Tramp 1974: Rare & Unissued Recordings, Vol. 3 / May 22, 2001 / Mooncrest ◆◆
The subtitle, "Rare and Unissued Records, Vol. 3," is not the most promising indicator of value for an archive compilation by a minor artist. This isn't garbage, but unless you're a dedicated fan of the artist or an absolute maniac for British blues, you'd be hard-pressed to get excited over its arrival. Half of this is taken from studio sessions in 1974, with musicians including (brief) original Fleetwood Mac bassist Bob Brunning. Brunning also plays on the live tracks, also from the spring of 1974, the lineup including a couple more British blues-rock vets in drummer Keef Hartley and ex-Fleetwood Mac guitarist Danny Kirwan (his last-known live performance, according to the liner notes). Kelly had an adequate low bluesy voice without anything in the way of raising the hairs on the back of your neck, and the studio tracks are adequate blues songs dipped in early-'70s rock, soul, and funk influences. The fidelity is not quite stellar on the live stuff, but it's OK, with Kelly concentrating more on straight blues numbers like "Baby What You Want Me to Do," "You Don't Love Me Baby," and "You Got to Move." It's sufficient as far as pub bands or support-bill acts go, but Kelly lacked the musical personality or power to take it to any higher level than that. —*Richie Unterberger*

Vance Kelly

b. Jan. 24, 1954, Chicago, IL
Guitar / Chicago Blues, Modern Electric Chicago Blues
Already a Chicago blues institution for over a quarter century, Vance Kelly finally began raising his international profile during the mid-'90s. Born January 24, 1954, he began making waves on the South Side club circuit while still a teenager, performing both as a solo artist and as a sideman; over time he developed a ringing guitar sound, and a 1987-1990 tenure as a member of A.C. Reed's Sparkplugs also profoundly influenced his supple vocal style. A favorite among his peers, Kelly and his Backstreet Blues Band still failed to attract record company attention prior to 1992, when he signed with Wolf; his acclaimed debut *Call Me* appeared in 1994, followed a year later by *Joyriding in the Subway*. He resurfaced in 2000 with *Beautiful Creature*. —*Jason Ankeny*

Call Me / Jul. 29, 1994 / Wolf ◆◆◆
● **Joyriding in the Subway** / 1995 / Wolf ◆◆◆◆
On his second album *Joyriding in the Subway*, Vance Kelly pushes into new directions, blending funk and soul into traditional Chicago blues. Armed with a sturdy set of originals and covers, Kelly storms through the album, spitting out hot solos and singing with an abandon. His band provides supple support, giving him the freedom to branch into new areas with both his guitar and voice. The production may be a little too pristine for some tatstes, but there's no arguing that Kelly provides enough grit on his own. —*Thom Owens*

Hands Off! / Jun. 18, 1998 / Wolf ◆◆◆
What Three Old Ladies Can Do / May 16, 2000 / Wolf ◆◆◆

Tiny Kennedy (Jesse Kennedy Jr.)

b. Dec. 20, 1925, Chattanooga, TN
Vocals / East Coast Blues, Jump Blues
Tiny Kennedy was anything but diminutive, either in stature or vocal range. "Big and fat" was how Trumpet Records boss Lillian McMurry vividly described him, and she should know: Trumpet recorded the shouter in 1951 and again in 1952.
The vocalist, born Jesse Kennedy Jr., had recorded with the great Kansas City pianist Jay McShann for Capitol in 1949 prior to joining Tiny Bradshaw's jumping band as one of its featured front men. After a session with Elmore James in 1951 didn't result in anything releasable, McMurry sent Kennedy up to Sam Phillips' fledgling Memphis Recording Service in September of 1952. Musicians on the session, which produced the fine "Strange Kind of Feelin'," "Early in the Mornin', Baby" (with overdubbed crowing by "Elmer, the Disc Jockey Rooster"), and "Blues Disease," included guitarist Calvin Newborn and saxist Richard Sanders. After a 1955 date for RCA's Groove subsidiary, Kennedy disappeared permanently from the R&B scene. —*Bill Dahl*

● **Strange Kind of Feeling** / 1993 / Trumpet ◆◆◆◆◆
Three of the unsung heroes on Lillian McMurry's Trumpet label fill this anthology with their early-'50s work. Kennedy's sides were cut in Memphis under Sam Phillips' supervision in 1952. "Strange Kind of Feelin'" and "Blues Disease" rate with the best things the rotund shouter waxed. —*Bill Dahl*

Chris Kenner

b. Dec. 25, 1929, Kenner, LA, **d.** Jan. 25, 1976, New Orleans, LA
Vocals / New Orleans R&B, R&B
Kenner wrote a number of enduring New Orleans R&B classics, although subsequent cover versions eclipsed all but "I Like It Like That," his Grammy-nominated greatest hit in 1961. Kenner co-wrote "Sick and Tired" with Fats Domino and charted with it in 1957 on Imperial, but Domino's version blew it out of the water. Signing with Joe Babashak's Instant label, Kenner's "I Like It Like That," "Land of 1000 Dances," and "Something You Got" sported Allen Toussaint's rolling piano behind Kenner's raw vocals. —*Bill Dahl*

● **I Like It Like That: Golden Classics** / 1987 / Collectables ◆◆◆◆◆
Vocalist Kenner's early-'60s sides for Instant, with Allen Toussaint laying down rolling piano behind him, represent New Orleans R&B at its most infectious. —*Bill Dahl*

Willie Kent

b. Sep. 24, 1936, Sunflower County, MS
Vocals, Bass / Modern Electric Blues, Modern Electric Chicago Blues
Bassist Willie Kent and his band, the Gents, are among the last of a dying breed around Chicago: a combo that intuitively knows the meaning of ensemble playing, rather than functioning as a generic backdrop for endless guitar solos. The Mississippi-born Kent has been laying down bedrock bass lines for decades, and his uncommonly powerful vocals make him even more of a standout.
Kent hit Chicago during the '50s, weaned on Muddy Waters, John Lee Hooker, and Robert Nighthawk. He apprenticed long and hard on the West Side, playing with the Hudson brothers, Ralph & the Red Tops, Eddie Taylor, Little Walter, Fenton Robinson, and plenty more before folks started taking notice of his bandleading skills. A 1987 heart bypass operation forced him to abandon his day job as a truck driver; from then on, music has been his full-time vocation. Two outstanding albums for Delmark, 1991's *Ain't It Nice* (with a guest vocal by frequent cohort Bonnie Lee), 1994's *Too Hurt to Cry*, and 1996's *Long Way to Ol' Miss* have solidified Kent's reputation. —*Bill Dahl*

● **Ain't It Nice** / 1991 / Delmark ◆◆◆◆
West Side bassist Kent and his Gents serve up Chicago blues the way it was meant to be played (but too often isn't nowadays): with tight ensemble passages that greatly enhance the power of Kent's gruff vocals. His first album for Delmark beautifully typifies his groove-heavy approach; whether digging into a slow grinding blues or an upbeat soul-inflected item, he and his comrades keep their business together. —*Bill Dahl*

Too Hurt to Cry / 1994 / Delmark ◆◆◆
There's little newness anyone should expect to hear on a contemporary blues record. The only thing that makes them valuable is if the performer has their own notion of the blues and can state it in a distinctive manner. Willie Kent certainly can; his mournful, often powerful vocals are frequently memorable, even when he's mining the reliable formula of heartache and anguish. If his compositions aren't lyrically transcendent, Kent's rendering of the words elevates them. You never tire of hearing him sing, and he makes you feel and believe his messages, even as his backing band plugs in familiar progressions and lines behind him. Indeed, it's only when Kent covers someone else's music that things become less interesting. —*Ron Wynn*

Live in Chicago at BluesFest / Jul. 29, 1994 / Wolf ◆◆◆
The King of Chicago's West Side Blues . . . / 1996 / Wolf ◆◆◆
Long Way to Ol' Miss / Nov. 26, 1996 / Delmark ◆◆◆
Everybody Needs Somebody / May 12, 1998 / Wolf ◆◆◆
Make Room for the Blues / Sep. 22, 1998 / Delmark ◆◆◆◆
Blues bassist Willie Kent has strong, supple bottom lines that have supported all the best groups, but he's led his own band as well. This is his fourth Delmark date, and Kent heartily asserts himself as a singer, with a tone like Johnny Adams with a rougher edge. His equally excellent band features lead guitarists Bill Flynn and Jake Dawson alternating tracks, with rhythm guitarist Willie Davis, pianist Kenny Barker, and drummer James Carter. Baritone saxophonist/arranger Willie Henderson from the old Tyrone Davis band leads a three-piece horn section on three tracks. This 13-song program—ten written by Kent—comprises mostly classic 12-bar, IV-V-I blues changes. A hard-swinging "3-6-9," with Dawson's swift guitar and Barker's boogie piano, supports a bitch session for Kent. He is fairly believable on the B.B. King-styled "Address in the Street." Albert King's style is more prevalent on a long, loping eight-minute title track with horns, and the more R&B-ish "I'm Hooked," again with Flynn doing a Memphis soul style of interpreting. Flynn can also play tasty Elmore James-type slide as on the easy, lowdown "I Had a Dream." Most fun is the typical Chicago blues "Do You Love Me?," which jumps and jives with all the flavor and depth you expect from the real thing. The deepest emotion is in the slower numbers. "I Know Where You've Been" is patient, deliberate, and cocksure, while "Teach Me How to Lie" is a down-home contradiction that perfectly exemplifies what everyone has to/doesn't do in this convoluted society. Unquestionably a great modern blues document, and one of the best CDs of 1998. —*Michael G. Nastos*

Junior Kimbrough (David Kimbrough)

b. Jul. 28, 1930, Hudsonville, MS, **d.** Jan. 17, 1998
Vocals, Guitar / Modern Delta Blues, Electric Country Blues, Electric Delta Blues
Cited as a prime early influence by rockabilly pioneer Charlie Feathers, Mississippi Delta bluesman Junior Kimbrough's modal, hypnotic blues vision remained a regional sensation for most of his career. He finally transcended the confines of his region in the early '90s, when he appeared in the 1991 movie *Deep Blues* and on its Anxious/Atlantic soundtrack, leading to his own debut for Fat Possum Records, *All Night Long*.
Junior Kimbrough was born and raised in Hudsonville, MS, where he learned how to play guitar by listening to records by Delta bluesmen. In 1968, he cut his first single, "Tramp," for the local Philwood label. For the next two decades, Kimbrough didn't have the opportunity to record frequently—he recorded a single, "Keep Your Hands Off Her," for High Water and his "All Night Long" was available on the various artists compilation *National Downhome Festival, Vol. 2*, released on Southland Records.
During the '70s and '80s, Kimbrough played juke joints throughout Mississippi, which is where music journalist Robert Palmer discovered him in the late '80s. Palmer featured Kimbrough in his documentary film *Deep Blues*. The exposure in the movie led to a national record contract for Kimbrough—he signed with Fat Possum and released his first full-length album, *All Night Long*, in 1992. The record was critically acclaimed by both blues and mainstream publications, as was *Deep Blues* and its accompanying soundtrack. All of the media attention led to performances outside of the Delta, including a few shows in England. After the flurry of activity in 1992, Junior Kimbrough returned to playing juke joints in the Delta, recording occasionally—he released his second album, *Sad Days, Lonely Nights*, in 1993. *Most Things Haven't Worked Out* followed in 1997, and a year

later Kimbrough returned with *God Knows I Tried.* He died of a heart attack on January 17, 1998. —*Bill Dahl & Stephen Thomas Erlewine*

All Night Long / 1992 / Fat Possum ✦✦✦✦✦

A beautifully packaged edition of Junior Kimbrough's first album, recorded live in the converted church that replaced Kimbrough's original wooden shack juke joint. The lineup is Kimbrough on vocals and guitar, Garry Burnside on bass, and Kenny Malone on drums (it's a family business around this area, and you'll find Burnsides and Malones all over Fat Possum's releases). *All Night Long* is a big, scruffy racket of an electric blues album, and it's fantastic material, a mix of charging, biting rhythms, intense slow blues, hollerin', stompin' and moanin'. The lack of studio polish is a big plus here—producer Robert Palmer was absolutely right to give this to us flubs and all—and the energy is wonderful. A great electric blues portrait that's getting widespread attention at last—and deserves it all. —*Steven McDonald*

Sad Days, Lonely Nights / 1993 / Fat Possum ✦✦

If *All Night Long* was a great electric blues portrait, this sophomore release, given more widespread distribution via Fat Possum's deal with Capricorn, is an extension of the portrait, but with a lot more grit and grind thrown in, given a darker, deeper sound by a change in location (still Kimbrough's joint, but a different building). The vocals are further back, buried in the thick, heavy electric mix—some of this music here is Southern electric blues sounding about the way it might when the apocalypse is just around the corner. Forget the fancy stuff, the polished edges, the studio touches—there are no second takes, no overdubs, no last chances. It's terrifyingly compelling at times. Junior Kimbrough plays the blues with a raw edge, and it's brilliant, dark and mesmerizing—and it's on CD, with nothing buried, nothing hidden, and nothing safe, all the sharp edges intact. —*Steven McDonald*

Most Things Haven't Worked Out / Mar. 25, 1997 / Fat Possum ✦✦✦

While this album lacks the revelatory impact of Kimbrough's debut, *All Night Long,* or a hair-raising number like that release's "You Better Run," it is akin to his debut in both its packaging and its production values. With three of the tracks recorded directly from Junior Kimbrough's Juke Joint, the sound here is absolutely raw; aside from the ugly drum tone in "Everywhere I Go," it's a perfect evocation of live performance. Indeed, half the fascination in Kimbrough's works are the strange harmonics, "off" notes, and just sheer noise that gives a murky depth to his repetitive looping around a song's tonic note. Even the lyrics are often buried beneath layers of blues grunge, but it hardly matters—the whole album qualifies as a liminal, half-waking Mississippi dream. Highlights include the hypnotic "I'm in Love," and the stomping "Burn in Hell," which Kimbrough introduces by ribbing a bandmate: "If I die before you, I go before you, I'm gonna be there to open the door—come on in, brother!" With less than a year left to live, Kimbrough could still laugh at eternity. —*Paul Collins*

Do the Rump / Aug. 12, 1997 / HMG ✦✦✦

God Knows I Tried / Aug. 25, 1998 / Fat Possum ✦✦✦

Meet Me in the City / Sep. 21, 1999 / Fat Possum ✦✦

At its best, *Meet Me in the City* seems like a postmortem rarities tribute to a blues great who never got his proper due. At its worst, the record is cashing in on a Kimbrough recording that just happens to be lying around. The first four songs, home recordings from 1992, are so horribly noisy and hazy sounding that it's difficult to hear Kimbrough's down-home modern offbeat Delta blues and his rough, weathered vocals. Still, the tracks present an intimate and relaxed look at the elder bluesman—they are chilling, ghost-like, and off-the-cuff. The last four songs, from 1996 and 1993, respectively, are of better sonic quality, without distracting echo and distorted microphones. The riffs and beat of "Junior's Place" are directly descended from the tried "Good Morning Little Schoolgirl." It's too bad that the album didn't contain more selections from the 1993 Sunflower Blues Festival: here, Kimbrough incorporates the boogie stomp of John Lee Hooker into the irregular frequency of his own romp, and as a result, the record closes on an upbeat and fresh note. Since Kimbrough is on the level next to blues pioneers Son House and Tommy Johnson, it's hard to dismiss the importance of any record blessed with his mastery. Still, with several studio albums to choose from (the first coming in 1992), it's not like the music on *Meet Me in the City* is as rare as the music on House's *Delta Blues,* which is the only lasting aural document from his early and most illustrative days. The absence of any liner notes, captivating photos, or essays makes the record lean toward the cash-in-on-death direction. What all this means is that *Meet Me in the City* is exclusively for those already in love with Kimbrough's dissonant blues guitar style. —*Bob Gendron*

● **You Better Run: The Essential Junior Kimbrough** / Jul. 9, 2002 / Fat Possum ✦✦✦✦✦

Gathering the best of his all-too-brief recording career, *You Better Run: The Essential Junior Kimbrough* includes most of his best-known songs, including "Done Got Old," "Meet Me in the City," "You Better Run," and "All Night Long." The collection does a good job of representing each of Kimbrough's albums, ranging from the rough-and-ready sound of *All Night Long*; *Sad Days, Lonely Nights'* dark, swampy feel (exemplified here by the title track and "Old Black Mattie"); the dense sonics of *Most Things Haven't Worked Out's* title track; and the gritty, uncompromising edge to *God Knows I Tried's* "Tramp." For anyone unsure where to dive into Kimbrough's catalog, *You Better Run* offers the ideal starting point. —*Heather Phares*

King Curtis (Curtis Ousley)

b. Feb. 7, 1934, Fort Worth, TX, d. Aug. 14, 1971, New York, NY

Sax (Tenor) / Southern Soul, East Coast Blues, Soul-Jazz, Instrumental Rock, R&B

King Curtis was the last of the great R&B tenor sax giants. He came to prominence in the mid-'50s as a session musician in New York, recording, at one time or another, for most East Coast R&B labels. A long association with Atlantic/Atco began in 1958, especially on

recordings by the Coasters. He recorded singles for many small labels in the '50s—his own Atco sessions (1958-1959), then Prestige/New Jazz and Prestige/TruSound for jazz and R&B albums (1960-1961). Curtis also had a number one R&B single with "Soul Twist" on Enjoy Records (1962). He was signed by Capitol (1963-1964), where he cut mostly singles, including "Soul Serenade." Returning to Atlantic in 1965, he remained there for the rest of his life. He had solid R&B single success with "Memphis Soul Stew" and "Ode to Billie Joe" (1967). Beginning in 1967, Curtis started to take a more active studio role at Atlantic, leading and contracting sessions for other artists, producing with Jerry Wexler, and later on his own. He also became the leader of Aretha Franklin's backing unit, the Kingpins. He compiled several albums of singles during this period. All aspects of his career were in full swing at the time he was murdered in 1971. —*Bob Porter*

Have Tenor Sax, Will Blow / 1959 / Atco ✦✦✦

This is one fun dance record, right from the opening bars of "Midnight Ramble," a piece that sounds like a cross-breeding of "Bo Diddley," with both the sax and the lead guitar having fun with the central riff, and "Yakety Sax." Not everything here is as delightful, hypnotically frenetic as that Curtis Ousley semi-original, but most of the album is done with an infectious sense of humor, and even the predictable numbers here, like "Linda," with its tango tempo, is eminently listenable, if not exactly breaking any new horizons in R&B. Other tracks, like "Jaywalk" and "Lil Brother," are slightly more adventurous; and the band has a lot of fun with "Peter Gunn." The final two numbers, "Birth of the Blues" and "Chili," don't quite fit in with the rest of the record, both utilizing orchestral accompaniment in lieu of the band. —*Bruce Eder*

The New Scene of King Curtis / Apr. 21, 1960 / Prestige/New Jazz/OJC ✦✦✦✦

At first glance, this would appear to be a CD reissue well worth picking up. R&B tenor saxophonist King Curtis is heard in a rare jazz outing, holding his own with cornetist Nat Adderley (in prime form), pianist Wynton Kelly, bassist Paul Chambers, and drummer Oliver Jackson on four originals and "Willow Weep for Me." But the single-CD *Soul Meeting* not only contains this entire session, but another related six-song set as well. Only get this particular release if it is found at a budget price. —*Scott Yanow*

Soul Meeting / Apr. 21, 1960+Sep. 18, 1960 / Prestige ✦✦✦✦✦

King Curtis, an influential and greatly in-demand R&B tenorman, made relatively few jazz dates in his career. This CD has two of the best, complete albums originally called *The New Scene of King Curtis* and *Soul Meeting*; the former is also available as a separate CD but should be skipped in favor of this one. Curtis teams up with the passionate cornetist Nat Adderley, pianist Wynton Kelly, either Paul Chambers or Sam Jones on bass, and Oliver Jackson or Belton Evans on drums. The music is blues-based bop, with seven basic Curtis originals and four standards. Highly recommended, this set serves as proof that King Curtis could have been a viable jazz player. —*Scott Yanow*

Old Gold / Sep. 19, 1961 / Tru ✦✦✦

King Curtis with Jack McDuff on the Hammond organ, Billy Butler and Eric Gale on guitar. Funky renditions of standards like "Honky Tonk" and "Fever." —*Michael Erlewine*

Country Soul / 1962 / Capitol ✦✦

This album of country standards was intended to be King Curtis' answer to Ray Charles' *Modern Sounds in Country and Western Music.* It never sold remotely as well as Charles' album, primarily because of Curtis' more perfunctory singing and some unwise choices of music to cover—"Night Train to Memphis," "Raunchy" (which *is* an instrumental), and "I'm Movin' On" work as R&B instrumentals, with the latter benefiting from some sizzling interplay between the guitars, the trumpets, and Curtis' sax. But "High Noon" and "Home On the Range" are a lot less convincing, conceptually as well as in execution. There are a few surprises, however, such as a version of "Your Cheatin' Heart" that tries desperately to transform itself into "Stand By Me." —*Bruce Eder*

Soul Serenade / 1964 / Capitol ✦✦✦✦✦

Curtis' second Capitol album is a triumph on every level. The tragedy is that, apart from the hit title track, almost nothing off of this superb album was heard by the public—most of the singles he was doing were very different from this material. The album featured Curtis' covers of songs like the Bill Doggett co-authored "Honky Tonk," and Chuck Berry's "Memphis," the hottest, most soulful version of the Champs' old hit "Tequila" ever recorded, and Herbie Hancock's "Watermelon Man," as well as a re-recording of his hit "Soul Twist," and a version of his "Night Train," a big hit for Jimmy Forrest. Maybe the biggest surprise here is the cover of the blues standard "Hide Away," written by Curtis' old friend Freddie King. Sharing the spotlight with Curtis' sax throughout this record is Cornell Dupree on lead guitar, adding just the right accompaniment variously as a lead and rhythm instrument—the two make the oft-heard cover of "Hide Away" by John Mayall and Eric Clapton sound like a poor demo. There's not a wrong or wasted note. —*Bruce Eder*

Plays Hits Made By Sam Cooke / Mar. 9, 1965+Mar. 11, 1965 / Capitol ✦✦✦✦

This is about the only Sam Cooke tribute record—other than individual songs cut by Otis Redding—that one could imagine Cooke himself not only would have approved of fully, but might have enjoyed himself, had it been recorded under other circumstances. One could even visualize him dancing to the versions of "Shake," which does have a few echoes of "Night Train" in it, or "Twistin' the Night Away" or "Good Times." Curtis had known and worked with Cooke, and the singer's shooting death late in 1964 affected the saxophonist deeply, as it did millions of people. This album was the result, a dozen covers that blow away most any other Sam Cooke tribute album (including the still highly collectible Supremes' *We Remember Sam Cooke*). —*Bruce Eder*

Blues at Montreux / 1971 / Atlantic ✦✦✦

This live set from the 1971 Montreux Jazz Festival was co-led by tenor saxophonist King Curtis (who tragically would be killed three months later) and veteran blues pianist/vocalist Champion Jack Dupree. With guitarist Cornell Dupree (in excellent form), bassist

Jerry Jemmott, and drummer Oliver Jackson laying down the foundation, Curtis and Dupree find a great deal of common musical ground. Dupree has quite a few witty vocals (particularly the near-classic "Junker's Blues") while taking choruses of irregular length that keep his sidemen continually guessing. Curtis' distinctive tenor is also heard from, making one truly regret that this was his final recording. *—Scott Yanow*

Live at Fillmore West / Feb. 5, 1971-Feb. 7, 1971 / Koch ♦♦♦♦♦
Recorded in front of an enthusiastic audience and released just one week before Curtis' murder in 1971, *Live at Fillmore West* is a brilliant confirmation of the saxophonist's place in popular music. Backed up by Atlantic's top session men, as well as Billy Preston and the Memphis Horns, Curtis rips through some of the biggest hits of the day, transforming them into showcases for his soulful playing and the group's outstanding rhythmic interplay. Beautiful renditions of "A Whiter Shade of Pale" and "I Stand Accused" are highlights, but it's full-throttle rockers like "Changes" and "Memphis Soul Stew" that comprise the heart of the album. Curtis occasionally gets lost in the mix, but it doesn't matter; with so much great music going on, you probably won't notice. *—Jim Smith*

Didn't He Play / 1988 / Red Lightnin' ♦♦
Drawn from Curtis' peak during the late '50s and '60s, this collection, while diverse, is shaky at best. It contains none of his most familiar soul and R&B hits (although an early run-through of "Memphis Soul Stew" is included), and is a prime example of how record producers of the era (in this case, Atlantic Records co-founder Herb Abramson) would surround great players like Curtis with sub-par singers, session men and material. As a result, Curtis' excellent sax playing wound up sharing grooves with a one-note, 20-second guitar solo on "Soul Groove Part II," or cutting songs like Jimmy Breedlove's "Don't Be Cruel" rehash "Jealous Fool"—hardly material fit for King. *—Jason Ankeny*

Trouble in Mind / Jul. 1988 / Tru-Sound ♦♦♦
This CD reissue brings back a very unusual King Curtis set. Rather than playing R&B-ish tenor as usual, Curtis switches to alto, plays effective guitar on a few numbers, and sings most of the tunes. Joined by guitarists Al Casey, and Mac Pierce, pianist Paul Griffin, bassist Jimmy Lewis, drummer Belton Evans and three female vocalists, Curtis sticks mostly to veteran blues songs (including "Nobody Knows You When You're Down and Out," "Bad Bad Whiskey," and "Ain't Nobody's Business") and lets the band stretch out on the eight-minute "Deep Fry." A fun (if temporary) departure in King Curtis' career. *—Scott Yanow*

Blow Man, Blow! / 1992 / Bear Family ♦♦♦♦♦
These 71 songs spread among three CDs cover King Curtis' tenure at Capitol from 1962 until 1965. This wasn't the most productive period in Curtis' career, but it was his first chance to make records on more than a piecemeal basis under his own name; the result is a dazzling array of sounds and songs. Hidden among the country covers and abortive early sides on disc one is a lot of gold, most notably "Slow Drag" and the previously unreleased "New Dance," which features some killer guitar; the early unissued material is superb, including the Curtis original "Frisky," a slow version of "Alexander's Ragtime Band," the beguiling "Sukiyaki," and a gorgeous bossa nova called "Amorosa." (Many of these tracks feature guitarist Cornell Dupree, who was to figure in Curtis' most successful records for Capitol.) Disc two is where things start to cook: from "More Soul" on through to the previously unreleased "Hung Over," there's not a note of filler on the disc, which encompasses all of the *Soul Serenade* album as well as a brace of unreleased songs and some very fine singles, including a dazzling cover of the Acker Bilk standard "Stranger on the Shore," and a soulful recomposition of Jackie Gleason's "Melancholy Serenade." Disc three comprises material ranging from reinterpretations of pop standards like "Moon River" and "The Girl from Ipanema" through a dozen covers of Sam Cooke songs, all worthwhile. *—Bruce Eder*

Soul Twist and Other Golden Classics With King Curtis / 1992 / Collectables ♦♦♦♦♦
Here's an interesting set of singles featuring the great tenor saxophonist recording for various Bobby Robinson imprints. His big hit "Soul Twist" (this is the stereo remix, lacking a bit in bite from the original 45) is the centerpiece, but Curtis also sits in with Les Cooper on "Wiggle Wobble" (again the stereo mix, but sounding just fine), and tracks with Choker Campbell, Noble Watts, Curley Hammer, and Willis Jackson demonstrate what an adaptable musical giant the man truly was. Transfers vary from track to track, and again, like most early Collectables packages, there are no liner notes to speak of, but the music will have you dancing across the room. *—Cub Koda*

● **Instant Soul: The Legendary King Curtis** / Oct. 19, 1994 / Razor & Tie ♦♦♦♦♦
Nice overview of Curtis' solo career, beginning with the breakthrough success of "Soul Twist" and "Soul Serenade" and moving through his later recordings for Atlantic. It's interesting to hear Curtis in both the Memphis and Muscle Shoals settings and how he adapts his horn to different grooves along the way. A solid collection of this artist's best, although points get shaved off for the inclusion of a later recut version of "Wiggle Wobble," rather than the original by Les Cooper on which Curtis blew so magnificently. *—Cub Koda*

Piping Hot: The Complete Enjoy Sessions / Sep. 5, 1995 / Relic ♦♦♦♦
King Curtis never officially "joined" Bobby Robinson's Enjoy label. Rather, he came aboard only provisionally, willing to cut a couple of sides and see if they hit, and once they did, he would sign. Robinson ran the session for "Soul Twist" and got Curtis to feature the guitar, the organ, and the piano alternating with his sax—the record became Curtis' first hit, and an album followed, but Curtis never signed to Enjoy, choosing to go with Capitol Records instead in May 1962. The 15 songs here were all that came of his early 1962 association with Robinson, bold numbers mostly featuring very prominent guitar (played by Billy Butler and Joe Richardson) and organ (by Ernie Hayes)—check out "What'd I Say, Pts. 1- 2"—and even a harmonica solo by the King himself on "Harmonica Twist," along with the expected sax breaks. Robinson's big discovery was that Curtis blew all the way through his previous records, rather than using his band for contrast. The sound is excellent, and the notes, though a little sketchy, tell us a lot about how these records, among Curtis' best (certainly superior to the country & western venture Capitol threw him into), were made. *—Bruce Eder*

The Best of King Curtis / 1996 / Capitol ♦♦♦♦♦
Best of King Curtis collects the bulk of King Curtis' singles for Capitol, plus selected album tracks. Although he didn't have many hits while on Capitol—only "Soul Serenade" hit the charts—this collection demonstrates the depths of Curtis' talents, showcasing his stabs at jazz and blues in addition to his trademark R&B. *Instant Soul* remains a stronger introduction, but for fans who want to dig a little deeper, *The Best of King Curtis* is an excellent purchase. *—Stephen Thomas Erlewine*

Hot Sax, Cool Licks / 2000 / Ace ♦♦♦
Here's a complete summary of Curtis' sessions as a soloist for Atlantic in the late '50s. It includes not only the tracks he cut under his own name for both the 45 and long-playing formats, but also five previously unissued songs, and three hits he played on as a session man (the Coasters' "Yakety Yak" and "That Is Rock & Roll," and Chuck Willis' "What Am I Living For?"). Curtis' playing on these is very good, cementing his standing as perhaps the finest rock saxophonist of the time. It also shows more versatility than he was able to convey with the famous trademark stuttering style that was heard on solos such as the one he played for the Coasters' "Yakety Yak." What keeps this from being that great a CD, though, is the failing common to many instrumental rock collections: The songs are not terribly strong *or* varied. Many of these are pretty basic R&B-rock crossover workouts (sometimes with a calypso beat), though they do benefit from support by noted sidemen, including guitarists Jimmy Spruill, Mickey Baker, and Al Casey; drummer Panama Francis; and tenor saxophonist Noble Watts. The 1958 single "Castle Rock" is the best track, with a jazzy beat, hot Casey solos, and drum solos on the order of Cozy Cole's "Topsy II." Curtis does get a chance to stretch into relatively straight jazz occasionally (as on the previously unissued "Splankin'"). The 1958 single "You Made Me Love You (I Didn't Want to Do It)" makes its first appearance on a reissue here, though as a jazz ballad with female vocals that seem to be backgrounds missing a lead, it's one of his worst records. [This U.K. import is not available for sale in North America.] *—Richie Unterberger*

Have Tenor Sax, Will Blow/Live at Small's Paradise / Jun. 20, 2000 / Collectables ♦♦♦♦
This Collectables reissue combines two King Curtis albums originally released on Atco. *Have Tenor Sax, Will Blow* is from 1959 and *Live at Small's Paradise* from 1966. This is fun soul instrumental music of its time but occasionally generic, highlighted by the two separate versions of the "Peter Gunn Theme." *—Al Campbell*

King Ernest (Ernest Baker)

b. May 30, 1939, Natchez, MS, **d.** Mar. 4, 2000
Vocals / Soul-Blues

Vocalist King Ernest came up singing in the lively Chicago blues club scene of the '50s and '60s, sharing stages with the likes of Tyrone Davis, Syl Johnson and Little Milton Campbell.

Born and raised in Natchez, MS, he learned basic blues from his father, a sharecropper who used to play guitar at local juke joints. After a year at Southern University in Baton Rouge, he moved to Chicago, where he found his inspiration in clubs that hosted the likes of Muddy Waters and Chester Burnett, better known as Howlin' Wolf. His first professional shows in Chicago were with guitarist Byther Smith. Later, he discovered the soul-blues stylings of singers like Syl Johnson and Tyrone Davis. These singers made a bigger impact on his own singing style, and he established a reputation in Chicago's club scene in the early '60s as Good Rockin' Ernie.

In 1964, Baker left Chicago for New York City, where a new band he formed there gave him the nickname "King" for his wild dancing antics on stage. In 1965, Baker recorded his first single, "I Feel Alright" b/w "I'm So Tired," for the Old Town label, and enjoyed modest success through the '60s on the East Coast's R&B club circuit until returning to Chicago in 1967. He remained in Chicago for another ten years, recording a number of singles for Chicago labels, including Sonic, Barry, and his own Blue Soul Records. But recognition on a national level still eluded Baker, who moved to Los Angeles in 1980. After a record deal he had there failed to come to fruition, he dropped out and took a job with the L.A. County Sheriff's Department, doing most of his singing in church as a member of the Crenshaw Christian Center Choir.

After retiring from his day job, he began playing shows again at L.A. nightclubs, and his powerful vocals and still-energetic stage persona quickly attracted a small legion of dedicated fans to his club shows. After being discovered by promoter and producer Randy Chortkoff, he began touring up and down the California coast and into Canada.

His debut album for Evidence Records, *King of Hearts*, released in 1997, helped to expand his audience from a regional following in New York, Chicago and Los Angeles to an international following. On his recording, Baker offers up his interpretations of songs by Charlie Musselwhite, Hound Dog Taylor, Junior Parker, and Harold Burrage. He also tackles "Better Days," a track co-written by guitarist Jimmy Rip and vocalist Mick Jagger of the Rolling Stones. Appropriately, Rip accompanies King Ernest on this track on the album. *Blues Got Soul* followed three years later. It would unfortunately be his last recording. King Ernest was killed in an automobile accident on March 4, 2000. *—Richard Skelly*

● **King of Hearts** / Jan. 21, 1997 / Evidence ♦♦♦♦
The title is descriptive of why Ernest deserves a royal title, as his punchy vocals are blues laden with a splash of soul. Also, the title serves as the central theme of the material which runs the gamut of emotions ranging from heartbreak ("Tell Me the Reason," "Better Days," and "Cryin' for My Baby"), doubt ("I'm Not the One"), preference to escape life's problems ("Black Bag Blues"), disgust ("I Resign"), jealousy ("In the Dark"), desire ("Sadie"), and remorse ("Forgive Me"). Ernest's musicians are proven blue(s) bloods, some

of them being Paul Bryant (Robert Lucas), "Jimmy Rip" (Mick Jagger), and Lester Butler. Jagger's contribution, "Better Days," was originally slated for one of Jagger's solo albums, but then rightfully deeded to Ernest's pipes. Other well-chosen royal subjects come from songwriters/artists Junior Parker, Charlie Musselwhite, and Hound Dog Taylor. Hats go off to producer Randy Chortkoff, whose bold moves to record Ernest rightfully grants him the throne that's been denied him for far too long. *—Char Ham*

Blues Got Soul / Sep. 26, 2000 / Epitaph ♦♦♦
Tragically, singer King "Ernest" Baker only got to hear the final mixes of this album, *Blues Got Soul*, before he was killed in an automobile accident a few days later. Ernest was a fiery vocalist in the soul/blues vain of Little Milton or Bobby "Blue" Bland, incorporating a mixture of gospel and gritty funk inspiration. While Ernest had been performing off and on throughout his life, he decided after retiring from his job with the Los Angeles County Sheriff's Department to continue pursuing music. It's a shame that his career ended just as he was making promising steps forward. Highlights include the Ernest originals "Suffer and Stay," "Fallin' Down on My Face With the Blues," and the haunting Tom Waits-penned "House Where Nobody Lives." *—Al Campbell*

Albert King (Albert Nelson)

b. Apr. 25, 1923, Indianola, MS, **d.** Dec. 21, 1992, Memphis, TN
Vocals, Guitar (Electric), Guitar / Modern Electric Blues, Soul-Blues, R&B, Urban Blues
Albert King was truly a "King of the Blues," although he didn't hold that title (B.B. does). Along with B.B. and Freddie King, Albert King is one of the major influences on blues and rock guitar players. Without him, modern guitar music would not sound as it does—his style has influenced both black and white blues players from Otis Rush and Robert Cray to Eric Clapton and Stevie Ray Vaughan. It's important to note that while almost all modern blues guitarists seldom play for long without falling into a B.B. King guitar cliché, Albert King never did—he had his own style and unique tone from the beginning.

Albert King played guitar left-handed, without re-stringing the guitar from the right-handed setup; this "upside-down" playing accounted for his difference in tone, since he pulled down on the same strings that most players push up on when bending the blues notes. King's massive tone and totally unique way of squeezing bends out of a guitar string had a major impact. Many young white guitarists—especially rock & rollers—have been influenced by King's playing, and many players who emulate his style may never have heard of Albert King, let alone heard his music. His style is immediately distinguishable from all other blues guitarists, and he was one of the most important blues guitarists to ever pick up the electric guitar.

Born in Indianola, MS, but raised in Forrest City, AR, Albert King (born Albert Nelson) taught himself how to play guitar when he was a child, building his own instrument out of a cigar box. At first, he played with gospel groups—most notably the Harmony Kings—but after hearing Blind Lemon Jefferson, Lonnie Johnson, and several other blues musicians, he solely played the blues. In 1950, he met MC Reeder, who owned the T-99 nightclub in Osceola, AR. King moved to Osceola shortly afterward, joining the T-99's house band, the In the Groove Boys. The band played several local Arkansas gigs besides the T-99, including several shows for a local radio station.

After enjoying success in the Arkansas area, King moved to Gary, IN, in 1953, where he joined a band that also featured Jimmy Reed and John Brim. Both Reed and Brim were guitarists, which forced King to play drums in the group. At this time, he adopted the name Albert King, which he assumed after B.B. King's "Three O'Clock Blues" became a huge hit. Albert met Willie Dixon shortly after moving to Gary, and the bassist/songwriter helped the guitarist set up an audition at Parrot Records. King passed the audition and cut his first session late in 1953. Five songs were recorded during the session and only one single, "Be On Your Merry Way"/"Bad Luck Blues," was released; the other tracks appeared on various compilations over the next four decades. Although it sold respectably, the single didn't gather enough attention to earn him another session with Parrot. In early 1954, King returned to Osceola and re-joined the In the Groove Boys; he stayed in Arkansas for the next two years.

In 1956, Albert moved to St. Louis, where he initially sat in with local bands. By the fall of 1956, King was headlining several clubs in the area. King continued to play the St. Louis circuit, honing his style. During these years, he began playing his signature Gibson Flying V, which he named Lucy. By 1958, Albert was quite popular in St. Louis, which led to a contract with the fledgling Bobbin Records in the summer of 1959. On his first Bobbin recordings, King recorded with a pianist and a small horn section, which made the music sound closer to jump blues than Delta or Chicago blues. Nevertheless, his guitar was taking a center stage and it was clear that he had developed a unique, forceful sound. King's records for Bobbin sold well in the St. Louis area, enough so that King Records leased the "Don't Throw Your Love on Me So Strong" single from the smaller label. When the single was released nationally late in 1961, it became a hit, reaching number 14 on the R&B charts. King Records continued to lease more material from Bobbin—including a full album, *The Big Blues*, which was released in 1963—but nothing else approached the initial success of "Don't Throw Your Love on Me So Strong." Bobbin also leased material to Chess, which appeared in the late '60s.

Albert King left Bobbin in late 1962 and recorded one session for King Records in the spring of 1963, which were much more pop-oriented than his previous work; the singles issued from the session failed to sell. Within a year, he cut four songs for the local St. Louis independent label Coun-Tree, which was run by a jazz singer named Leo Gooden. Though these singles didn't appear in many cities—St. Louis, Chicago, and Kansas City were the only three to register sales—they foreshadowed his coming work with Stax Records. Furthermore, they were very popular within St. Louis, so much so that Gooden resented King's success and pushed him off the label.

Following his stint at Coun-Tree, Albert King signed with Stax Records in 1966. Albert's records for Stax would bring him stardom, both within blues and rock circles. All of his '60s Stax sides were recorded with the label's house band, Booker T. & the MG's, which gave his blues a sleek, soulful sound. That soul underpinning gave King crossover appeal, as evidenced by his R&B chart hits—"Laundromat Blues" (1966) and "Cross Cut Saw" (1967) both went Top 40, while "Born Under a Bad Sign" (1967) charted in the Top 50. Furthermore, King's style was appropriated by several rock & roll players, most notably Jimi Hendrix and Eric Clapton, who copied Albert's "Personal Manager" guitar solo on the Cream song, "Strange Brew." Albert King's first album for Stax, 1967's *Born Under a Bad Sign*, was a collection of his singles for the label and became one of the most popular and influential blues albums of the late '60s. Beginning in 1968, Albert King was playing not only to blues audiences, but also to crowds of young rock & rollers. He frequently played at the Fillmore West in San Francisco and he even recorded an album, *Live Wire/Blues Power*, at the hall in the summer of 1968.

Early in 1969, King recorded *Years Gone By*, his first true studio album. Later that year, he recorded a tribute album to Elvis Presley (*King Does the King's Things*) and a jam session with Steve Cropper and Pops Staples (*Jammed Together*), in addition to performing a concert with the St. Louis Symphony Orchestra. For the next few years, Albert toured America and Europe, returning to the studio in 1971, to record the *Lovejoy* album. In 1972, he recorded *I'll Play the Blues for You*, which featured accompaniment from the Bar-Kays, the Memphis Horns, and the Movement. The album was rooted in the blues, but featured distinctively modern soul and funk overtones.

By the mid-'70s, Stax was suffering major financial problems, so King left the label for Utopia, a small subsidiary of RCA Records. Albert released two albums on Utopia, which featured some concessions to the constraints of commercial soul productions. Although he had a few hits at Utopia, his time there was essentially a transitional period, where he discovered that it was better to follow a straight blues direction and abandon contemporary soul crossovers. King's subtle shift in style was evident on his first albums for Tomato Records, the label he signed with in 1978. Albert stayed at Tomato for several years, switching to Fantasy in 1983, releasing two albums for the label.

In the mid-'80s, Albert King announced his retirement, but it was short-lived—Albert continued to regularly play concerts and festivals throughout America and Europe for the rest of the decade. King continued to perform until his sudden death in 1992, when he suffered a fatal heart attack on December 21. The loss to the blues was a major one—although many guitarists have tried, no one can replace King's distinctive, trailblazing style. Albert King is a tough act to follow. *—Daniel Erlewine & Stephen Thomas Erlewine*

The Big Blues / 1963 / King ♦♦♦♦♦
Searing early-'60s sides. *—Bill Dahl*

Travelin' to California / 1967 / Polydor ♦♦♦♦

☆ **Born Under a Bad Sign** / 1967 / Stax ♦♦♦♦♦
Albert King recorded a lot in the early '60s, including some classic sides, but they never quite hit the mark. They never gained a large audience, nor did they really capture the ferocity of his single-string leads. Then, he signed with Stax in 1966, and recorded a number of sessions with the house band Booker T. & the MG's, and everything just clicked. The MG's gave King supple Southern support, providing an excellent contrast to his tightly wound lead guitar, allowing to him to unleash a torrent of blistering guitar runs that were profoundly influential, not just in blues but in rock & roll (witness Eric Clapton's unabashed copping of King throughout Cream's *Disraeli Gears*). Initially, these sessions were just released as singles, but they were soon compiled as King's Stax debut, *Born Under a Bad Sign*. Certainly, the concentration of singles gives the album a consistency—these were songs devised to get attention—but, years later, it's astounding how strong this catalog of songs is: "Born Under a Bad Sign," "Crosscut Saw," "Oh Pretty Woman," "The Hunter," "Personal Manager," "Laundromat Blues" form the very foundation of Albert King's musical identity and legacy. Few blues albums are this on a cut-by-cut level; the songs are exceptional, and the performances are rich, from King's dynamic playing to the Southern funk of the MG's. It was immediately influential at the time and, over the years, it has only grown in stature as one of the very greatest electric blues albums of all time. *—Stephen Thomas Erlewine*

Live Wire/Blues Power / 1968 / Stax ♦♦♦♦♦
Live Wire/Blues Power is one of Albert King's definitive albums. Recorded live at the Fillmore Auditorium in 1968, the guitarist is at the top of his form throughout the record—his solos are intense and piercing. The band is fine, but ultimately it's King's show—he makes Herbie Hancock's "Watermelon Man" dirty and funky and wrings out all the emotion from "Blues at Sunrise." *—Thom Owens*

Years Gone By / 1969 / Stax ♦♦♦♦♦
King cranked out this solid, if typical, album for the Stax label after the success of *Born Under a Bad Sign*. With Booker T. drummer Al Jackson producing, the set includes such staples as "You Threw Your Love on Me Too Strong," "Wrapped Up in Love Again," and a powerful version of Howlin' Wolf's "Killing Floor." For fans of King's guitar work, the inclusion of the instrumental workouts on "You Don't Love Me" and "Drowning on Dry Land" are a special bonus. Not an essential Albert King album, but one of his good ones. *—Cub Koda*

Jammed Together / 1969 / Stax ♦♦♦

★ **King of the Blues Guitar** / 1969 / Atlantic ♦♦♦♦♦
Atlantic's original vinyl edition of this was comprised of Albert's Stax singles—a few from *Born Under a Bad Sign*, along with "Cold Feet," "I Love Lucy" (two of King's patented monologues), and the beautiful "You're Gonna Need Me." Great stuff. Even greater, though, is the CD reissue, which includes those singles (which didn't appear on any other LPs) and *all* of *Born Under a Bad Sign*. Need more be said? *—Dan Forte*

Blues for Elvis: Albert King Does the King's Things / 1970 / Stax ♦♦♦
Originally titled *King Does the King's Thing*, here's Albert King adding his own touch to a batch of Elvis Presley tunes. Because King's style is so irreducible, the concept actually works, as he fills this album with his traditional, high-voltage guitar work and strong vocals. That isn't surprising, since four of the nine tunes on here originally started as R&B hits covered by Presley, including an instrumental version of Smiley Lewis' "One Night."

No matter what the original sources may be, though, this is a strong showing in King's catalog. —*Cub Koda*

The Lost Session / 1971 / Stax ✦✦

Lost Session is an interesting historical curiosity, but it is rather unsuccessful musically. John Mayall produced the record and he tried to move Albert King toward jazz. First of all, King's style isn't quite suited for jazz—he's too direct and forceful. Furthermore, the songs are simply skeletons—their only function is to let the band solo. And there are a couple of good solos, all of them from King. But ultimately, it's a forgettable exercise that should have been left in the vault. —*Thom Owens*

Lovejoy / 1971 / Stax ✦✦✦

This 1970 studio effort teamed up Albert with producer Don Nix, who supplied the majority of the original material here. Kicking off with a typical reading of the Stones' "Honky Tonk Woman" and including Taj Mahal's "She Caught the Katy and Left Me a Mule to Ride," the session is split between a Hollywood date with Jesse Ed Davis, Jim Keltner, and Duck Dunn in the band and one at Muscle Shoals with Roger Hawkins, David Hood, and Barry Beckett in the lineup. Although all of this is well-produced, there's hardly any fireworks out of Albert or any of the players aboard, making this an unessential addition for any but Albert King completists. —*Cub Koda*

I'll Play the Blues for You / 1972 / Stax ✦✦✦✦

It's not as if Albert King hadn't tasted success in his first decade and a half as a performer, but his late-'60s/early-'70s recordings for Stax did win him a substantially larger audience. During those years, the label began earning significant clout amongst rock fans through events like Otis Redding's appearance at the Monterey International Pop Festival and a seemingly endless string of classic singles. When King signed to the label in 1966, he was immediately paired with the Stax session team Booker T. & the MG's. The results were impressive: "Crosscut Saw," "Laundromat Blues," and the singles collection *Born Under a Bad Sign* were all hits. Though 1972's *I'll Play the Blues for You* followed a slightly different formula, the combination of King, members of the legendary Bar-Kays, the Isaac Hayes Movement, and the sparkling Memphis Horns was hardly a risky endeavor. The result was a trim, funk-infused blues sound that provided ample space for King's oft-imitated guitar playing. King has always been more impressive as a soloist than a singer, and some of his vocal performances on *I'll Play the Blues for You* lack the intensity one might hope for. As usual, he more than compensates with a series of exquisite six-string workouts. The title track and "Breaking Up Somebody's Home" both stretch past seven minutes, while "I'll Be Doggone" and "Don't Burn Down the Bridge" (where King coaxes a crowd to "take it to the bridge," James Brown-style) break the five-minute barrier. Riding strutting lines by bassist James Alexander, King runs the gamut from tough, muscular playing to impassioned cries on his instrument, making *I'll Play the Blues for You* one of a handful of his great Stax sets. —*Nathan Bush*

Blues at Sunset / 1973 / Stax ✦✦✦

I Wanna Get Funky / 1974 / Stax ✦✦✦

Another very solid, early-'70s outing. —*Bill Dahl*

Montreux Festival / 1974 / Stax ✦✦✦

Albert / 1976 / Rhino ✦✦

Gilded by strings and horns, keyboards and flutes, and driven by a propulsive disco beat, *Albert* is about as slick as Albert King ever got, but he manages to turn in a few strong performances on the album. On the whole, the songs aren't particularly distinctive, and the instrumental support is way too anonymous, but hardcore Albert fans may find a couple solos, a couple of phrases worth hearing beneath all the heavy-handed production and thumping beats. —*Thom Owens*

Truckload of Lovin' / 1976 / Rhino ✦✦✦

The best of King's mid-'70s, slightly disco-fied period. —*Bill Dahl*

King Albert / 1977 / Charly ✦✦

Rebounding slightly from the nadir of *Albert*, Albert King delivered *King Albert*, a record that at least sticks to the tough, soul-inflected blues that made his reputation. Granted, the sound of the album is entirely too polished, but there is genuine grit in the performances and some strong songs, such as "You Upset Me Baby" and "Good Time Charlie," on the record. That may be enough for some hardcore fans to give a listen, but they should be forewarned that even those inspired moments aren't enough to make *King Albert* a worthwhile release. —*Thom Owens*

The Pinch / 1977 / Stax ✦✦✦

One of King's more soul-oriented efforts, from sessions recorded in 1973 and 1974. It's been retitled as *The Blues Don't Change* for its CD reissue. —*Richie Unterberger*

New Orleans Heat / 1978 / Rhino ✦✦

Allen Toussaint is one of the greatest R&B producers ever to grace New Orleans, but his touch as a blues producer is shaky at best. This attempt to update King's early classics is a snooze. —*Bill Dahl*

Chronicle (With Little Milton) / 1979 / Stax ✦✦✦

This compilation has a leftover feel; the liner notes provide no sources and dates, admitting only that these are "Stax recordings, some never before available on LP." If you're a big fan of one or both of the artists involved, though, it's not bad, with a quality that's generally consistent with their fully baked Stax-era albums, though the King half of the program is somewhat superior to the Milton tracks. —*Richie Unterberger*

Albert Live / 1979 / Charly ✦✦✦

Albert King Live was in some ways the finest live blues album King ever made, although it wasn't as successful as the recordings he made at the Fillmore West. But it featured numerous spectacular solos, with King showing his complete guitar technique. Rhino's recent CD reissue unfortunately opted to trim the superb, lengthy cut, "Jam in A-Flat,"

which featured blistering solos by King, Rory Gallagher, and Louisiana Red. That dubious decision doesn't negate the CD's value, but certainly casts a pall over it, particularly since they retained Robert Palmer's exhaustive original notes and convey the impression that you're getting the total session intact. Still, King's versions of "Stormy Monday," "Kansas City," "Watermelon Man" and "I'll Play the Blues for You" are marvelous, as are "Matchbox Holds My Clothes," "As the Years Go Passing By," and "Don't Burn Down the Bridges." —*Ron Wynn*

San Francisco '83 / 1983 / Fantasy ✦✦✦

Early-'80s studio LP, reissued in its entirety on CD under the title *Crosscut Saw: Albert King in San Francisco*. As that reissue adds two extra previously unreleased tracks, it's the recommended alternative to the original vinyl edition. —*Richie Unterberger*

In San Francisco-Crosscut Saw / Mar. 1983 / Stax ✦✦✦

A reissue of King's 1983 album *San Francisco '83* (a studio album, not a live one), with the addition of two previously unreleased cuts. His first new release in five years, it wasn't one of King's better records. But it did represent a return to a basic five-piece sound, an improvement upon his over-produced outings of the late '70s. —*Richie Unterberger*

I'm in a Phone Booth, Baby / 1984 / Stax ✦✦✦

King's most recent studio album shows he is still tough. —*Bill Dahl*

The Best of Albert King, Vol. 1 / 1986 / Stax ✦✦✦✦✦

"The best of Albert King"? More like the best material that he happened to record for Stax between 1968 and 1973. Even that's debatable, the 13 tracks including covers such as "Honky Tonk Woman," "Sky Is Crying," and "Hound Dog." It does present a reasonable cross-section of his soul-inflected work of the period, drawing from over a half-dozen LPs and a couple of singles, though you might be as well or better off with his more focused individual titles. And for the true "best of Albert King," Rhino's *Ultimate Collection* remains the hands-down winner. —*Richie Unterberger*

Blues at Sunrise: Live at Montreux / 1988 / Stax ✦✦✦

Recorded at Albert King's appearance at the 1973 Montreux Jazz Festival, *Blues at Sunrise: Live at Montreux* is a typically engaging live record from the guitarist. King is in good form and the set list is a little unpredictable, featuring standards like "Blues at Sunrise" and "I'll Play the Blues for You" as well as lesser-known items like "Little Brother (Make a Way)" and "Don't Burn Down the Bridge." —*Thom Owens*

Let's Have a Natural Ball / 1989 / Modern Blues ✦✦✦✦✦

Great compilation of King's Bobbin sides of the late '50s and early '60s. —*Bill Dahl*

Door to Door / 1990 / MCA/Chess ✦✦✦

Half of *Door to Door* is devoted to early-'60s King, the other half to Otis Rush Chess efforts of the same era. —*Bill Dahl*

Wednesday Night in San Francisco: Recorded Live at the Fillmore Auditorium / 1990 / Stax ✦✦✦

Wednesday Night in San Francisco: Recorded Live at the Fillmore Auditorium was recorded in June of 1968—it's culled from the very same dates as *Live Wire/Blues Power*. It's slightly weaker than *Live Wire*, which isn't surprising since it consists of outtakes. Nevertheless, Albert King is in fine form throughout the record, throwing out stinging solos with passion. It's a necessary purchase for any King fan. —*Thom Owens*

Thursday Night in San Francisco: Recorded Live at the Fillmore Auditorium / 1990 / Stax ✦✦✦

Recorded live in San Francisco in 1968, here's Albert King pretty much at the top of his game, blasting out tons of great guitar and singing his heart to an appreciative crowd of young hippies. With a tight four-piece road band backing him, King fires up his Flying V and slams down hard on material like Freddie King's "San-Ho-Zay," "You Upset Me Baby," "Call It Stormy Monday," "Crosscut Saw," and "Drifting Blues." This is one of two volumes from the same Fillmore stand and both are absolutely essential to any Albert King collection; in many ways, they're the perfect introduction to this blues giant. —*Cub Koda*

The Blues Don't Change / 1992 / Stax ✦✦✦

Previously titled *The Pinch* when it was issued on LP in 1977, this material was actually recorded in 1973 and 1974. These are some of King's most soul-oriented sessions, with contributions from the Memphis Horns and a couple of the MG's. Blues-oriented fans may find this one of his lesser efforts, putting less emphasis on King's guitar work than usual, and more on the vocals and arrangements. This approach has its merits, though, as it's one of the more relaxed items in the King catalog, with none of the occasional excess that creeped into his blues guitar solos. —*Richie Unterberger*

☆ **The Ultimate Collection** / 1993 / Rhino ✦✦✦✦✦

Rhino's 1993 double-disc set *The Ultimate Collection* remains the greatest of all Albert King collection, gathering the best of his recordings. True, the collection is tilted toward his Stax recordings, somewhat shortchanging his '50s and early-'60s recordings, but it is also true that the late-'60s/early-'70s recordings are the cornerstone of King's legacy, the ones that showcase his stinging guitar at its blistering best. By acknowledging as much the set *gains* credibility, it doesn't lose it, and while an artist with a career as long as King's will certainly have some great cuts left off of a two-disc, 38-song collection, but this truly does contain his very best work, particularly in regards to showcasing his influence as a guitarist. If you're looking for a succinct introduction, turn to *Born Under a Bad Sign*, one of the greatest blues albums and one that captures the full scope of his skills as well as this double-disc set, but if you want something a little more comprehensive, containing the great moments that aren't on that album, this is what to get. After all, it doesn't just contain all but one song from that album, it's one of the great blues collections. —*Stephen Thomas Erlewine*

Funky London / 1994 / Stax ✦✦✦

Albert King cut his teeth on the blues circuits of Arkansas and St. Louis, developing his style in a number of electric outfits. His recording career was, at least initially, erratic, though the quality of the sides he cut for the Parrot, King, and Coun-Tree imprints certainly was not. It wasn't until King signed to Stax in 1966, however, and the guitarist's electric blues fused with the muscular bass, funky guitars, and sparkling horns of the label's outstanding session players, that he found his first home. King stayed with the label for eight years, leaving only when Stax was entering its financial decline. *Funky London* manages to dig up a few from the period that nearly got away, compiling three 45 sides and six unreleased tracks. The singles include a pair of instrumentals (a cover of James Brown's "Cold Sweat" and "Funky London," a dispensable, uptempo 12-bar workout) and one vocal ("Can't You See What You're Doing to Me"). By the nature of the material, those songs and the six that follow lack the cohesiveness of an album, though the quality of the music ultimately prevails. Downshifting for "Lonesome," the combo is steeped in the blues. After a false start ("What's the matter with y'all!?" asks King), the band begins again, King's crying guitar lines joined by keyboard commentary, smoky threads of wah-wah guitar and an exquisite horn arrangement. "Sweet Fingers" is an excellent example of funky blues ensemble playing and "Driving Wheel" a fine interpretation of the Roosevelt Sykes tune. Perhaps most important is the fact that the majority of the music here maintains the standards established on King's official Stax releases, making this a desirable set. *—Nathan Bush*

Tomato Years / 1994 / Rhino ✦✦✦
Albert King enjoyed an erratic but memorable reign at Tomato in the '70s. The label aimed to continue the success King had enjoyed at Stax mixing blues backing and vocals with pop/soul arrangements and lyrics. He recorded six LPs for Tomato; this anthology culls 14 cuts from his Tomato releases, among them the slashing numbers "Blues At Sunrise" and "I'm Gonna Call You Soon As The Sun Goes Down," which vividly illustrated King's guitar prowess. Others, like "Truckload Of Lovin'" and "We All Wanna Boogie," show how he skillfully crammed moments of inspiration into formulaic outings. *—Ron Wynn*

Hard Bargain / Feb. 1996 / Stax ✦✦✦
A collection of B-sides, alternate takes, and previously unissued outtakes from King's Stax prime (1966-1972), some instrumental. It's not as good as King's best Stax material, but it's not far behind, often benefiting from house players like Booker T. & the MG's, Isaac Hayes, and the Bar-Kays. *—Richie Unterberger*

The Very Best of Albert King / Apr. 20, 1999 / Rhino ✦✦✦✦✦
There have been many compilations of Albert King's classic Stax recordings over the years, including the wonderful double-disc set *The Ultimate Collection*, but Rhino's *The Very Best of Albert King* is perhaps the best for curious listeners, since it offers 16 classics on one disc. There may be a few favorites missing, from "The Hunter" to "The Phone Booth," but the disc does a wonderful job of summarizing the classic Stax years while adding some highlights from his latter-day recordings for Tomato. In the end, what matters is that the bare basics—"Let's Have a Natural Ball," "C.O.D.," "Laundromat Blues," "Oh Pretty Woman," "Crosscut Saw," "Born Under a Bad Sign," "Personal Manager," "Blues Power"—are all here, making this ideal for neophytes on a tight budget. (Of course, *Born Under a Bad Sign* remains an excellent introduction on its own terms, as well.) *—Stephen Thomas Erlewine*

In Session / Aug. 17, 1999 / Stax ✦✦✦✦✦
Recorded in December 1983, *In Session* captures an in-concert jam between Albert King and Stevie Ray Vaughan, who had become the hot blues guitarist of the year thanks to his debut *Texas Flood*, as well as his work on David Bowie's hit *Let's Dance*. Vaughan may have been the new news, but King was not suffering, either. He had a world-class supporting band and was playing as well as he ever had. In other words, the stage was set for a fiery, exciting concert and that's exactly what they delivered. Vaughan was clearly influenced by King—there are King licks all over his first two recorded efforts, and it was an influence that stayed with him to the end—and he was unafraid to go toe-to-toe with his idol. King must have been impressed, since *In Session* never devolves into a mere cutting contest. Instead, each musicians spurs the other to greater heights. For aficionados of either guitarist, that means the album isn't just worth a listen—it means that it's a record that sounds as exciting on each subsequent listen as does the first time through. *—Stephen Thomas Erlewine*

Guitar Man: An Essential Collection / Jul. 17, 2001 / Fuel 2000 ✦✦✦
A veritable electric blues legend, any Albert King record presents equal parts of heartache and euphoria, melancholy and exuberance. These combinations make up the essence of the American blues tradition, and over the course of his life, Albert King solidified a place in that tradition alongside the likes of blues guitar greats B.B. King and Freddie King. Listening to the leadoff "Cadillac Assembly Line" from *Guitar Man: An Essential Collection*, it is immediately apparent that Albert King's legacy is characterized by the unique ability to meld his tasteful electric guitar licks with the roots of contemporary funk and R&B. When the record ends with the funk-infused "I Got the Blues," Albert King has clearly separated himself from the pack of electric blues heroes with innovative twists on standard blues formulas and a soulful strut that will be impossible to reproduce. *—Nate Cavalieri*

I Get Evil: Classic Blues Collected / Sep. 11, 2001 / Music Club ✦✦✦

More Big Blues of Albert King / Nov. 13, 2001 / Ace ✦✦✦✦
All of King's recordings for the Bobbin label are on this 22-track disc, including everything from his 1959-1963 singles for the label and previously unissued alternate takes of "Why Are You So Mean to Me," "The Time Has Come," and the previously unissued "Blues at Sunrise." While these are decent journeyman urban blues/R&B, they're not up to the level of his subsequent recordings for Stax. Albert King just sounds too much like the records another King—B.B. King, that is—was making during the same era. There are similar horn arrangements and alternation of stinging guitar with smooth, confident vocal phrasing. It's a tribute to Albert King's abilities, in a way, that it *does* sound confident, and not the work of an imitator, despite the similarities. Some more variety to largely self-penned songs would have made his Bobbin era stand out more too. It does feature his sole big R&B hit from his stint with the label, "Don't Throw Your Love on Me So Strong," a showcase for his mean, lean guitar licks that increases the drama with changing drum tempos. Of the other songs, the standout is "Ooo-Ee Baby," in which King really draws out the vibrato in a slow blues with earthy tension, sounding more spontaneous than he did on many of his other Bobbin singles. The production's more basic than that of his Stax sides, but is hardly raw, with a jazzy lilt to the horns in particular. Rock fans will recognize "I Get Evil" as essentially the same song as "Don't Lie to Me," which the Rolling Stones covered (and whose composition was erroneously credited to Mick Jagger and Keith Richards when it appeared on the Stones' *Metamorphosis*). *—Richie Unterberger*

B.B. King (Riley B. King)

b. Sep. 16, 1925, Indianola, MS
Vocals, Leader, Guitar (Electric), Songwriter, Guitar / Modern Electric Blues, Soul-Blues, Memphis Blues, R&B

Universally hailed as the reigning king of the blues, the legendary B.B. King is without a doubt the single most important electric guitarist of the last half century. A contemporary blues guitar solo without at least a couple of recognizable King-inspired bent notes is all but unimaginable, and he remains a supremely confident singer capable of wringing every nuance from any lyric (and he's tried his hand at many an unlikely song—anybody recall his version of "Love Me Tender"?).

Yet B.B. King remains an intrinsically humble superstar, an utterly accessible icon who welcomes visitors into his dressing room with self-effacing graciousness. Between 1951 and 1985, King notched an amazing 74 entries on *Billboard*'s R&B charts, and he was one of the few full-fledged blues artists to score a major pop hit when his 1970 smash "The Thrill Is Gone" crossed over to mainstream success (engendering memorable appearances on *The Ed Sullivan Show* and *American Bandstand*!).

The seeds of King's enduring talent were sown deep in the blues-rich Mississippi Delta. That's where Riley B. King was sired—in Itta Bena, to be exact. By no means was his childhood easy. Young Riley was shuttled between his mother's home and his grandmother's residence. The youth put in long days working as a sharecropper and devoutly sang the Lord's praises at church before moving to Indianola—another town located in the very heart of the Delta—in 1943.

Country and gospel music left an indelible impression on King's musical mindset as he matured, along with the styles of blues greats T-Bone Walker and Lonnie Johnson and jazz geniuses Charlie Christian and Django Reinhardt. In 1946, B.B. King set off for Memphis to look up his cousin, rough-edged country blues guitarist Bukka White. For ten invaluable months, White taught his eager young relative the finer points of playing blues guitar. After returning briefly to Indianola and the sharecropper's eternal struggle with his wife Martha, King arrived in Memphis once again in late 1948. This time, he stuck around for a while.

King was soon broadcasting his music live via Memphis radio station WDIA, a frequency that had only recently switched to a pioneering all-Black format. Local club owners preferred that their attractions also held down radio gigs so they could plug their nightly appearances on the air. When WDIA deejay Maurice "Hot Rod" Hulbert exited his airshift, King took over his record-spinning duties. At first tagged "The Peptikon Boy" (an alcohol-loaded elixir that rivaled Hadacol) when WDIA put him on the air, King's on-air handle became the "Beale Street Blues Boy," later shortened to Blues Boy and then a far snappier B.B.

King had a four-star breakthrough year in 1949. He cut his first four tracks for Jim Bulleit's Bullet Records (including a number entitled "Miss Martha King" after his wife), then signed a contract with the Bihari brothers' Los Angeles-based RPM Records. King cut a plethora of sides in Memphis over the next couple of years for RPM, many of them produced by a relative newcomer named Sam Phillips (whose Sun Records was still a distant dream at that point in time). Phillips was independently producing sides for both the Biharis and Chess; his stable also included Howlin' Wolf, Rosco Gordon, and fellow WDIA personality Rufus Thomas.

The Biharis also recorded some of King's early output themselves, erecting portable recording equipment wherever they could locate a suitable facility. King's first national R&B chart-topper in 1951, "Three O'Clock Blues" (previously waxed by Lowell Fulson), was cut at a Memphis YMCA. King's Memphis running partners included vocalist Bobby "Blue" Bland, drummer Earl Forest, and ballad-singing pianist Johnny Ace. When King hit the road to promote "Three O'Clock Blues," he handed the group, known as the Beale Streeters, over to Ace.

It was during this era that King first named his beloved guitar "Lucille." Seems that while he was playing a joint in a little Arkansas town called Twist, fisticuffs broke out between two jealous suitors over a lady. The brawlers knocked over a kerosene-filled garbage pail that was heating the place, setting the room ablaze. In the frantic scramble to escape the flames, King left his guitar inside. He foolishly ran back in to retrieve it, dodging the flames and almost losing his life. When the smoke had cleared, King learned that the lady who had inspired such violent passion was named Lucille. Plenty of Lucilles have passed through his hands since; Gibson has even marketed a B.B.-approved guitar model under the name.

The '50s saw King establish himself as a perennially formidable hitmaking force in the R&B field. Recording mostly in L.A. (the WDIA airshift became impossible to maintain by 1953 due to King's endless touring) for RPM and its successor Kent, King scored 20 chart items during that musically tumultuous decade, including such memorable efforts as "You Know I Love You" (1952); "Woke Up This Morning" and "Please Love Me" (1953); "When My Heart Beats like a Hammer," "Whole Lotta' Love," and "You Upset Me Baby" (1954); "Every Day I Have the Blues" (another Fulson remake), the dreamy blues ballad "Sneakin' Around," and "Ten Long Years" (1955); "Bad Luck," "Sweet Little Angel," and a Platters-like "On My Word of Honor" (1956); and "Please Accept My Love" (first cut by Jimmy Wilson) in 1958. King's guitar attack grew more aggressive and pointed as the decade progressed, influencing a legion of up-and-coming axemen across the nation.

In 1960, King's impassioned two-sided revival of Joe Turner's "Sweet Sixteen" became another mammoth seller, and his "Got a Right to Love My Baby" and "Partin' Time" weren't far behind. But Kent couldn't hang onto a star like King forever (and he may have been tired of watching his new LPs consigned directly into the 99-cent bins on the Biharis' cheapo Crown logo). King moved over to ABC-Paramount Records in 1962, following the lead of Lloyd Price, Ray Charles, and before long, Fats Domino.

In November of 1964, the guitarist cut his seminal *Live at the Regal* album at the fabled Chicago theater and excitement virtually leaping out of the grooves. That same year, he enjoyed a minor hit with "How Blue Can You Get," one of his many signature tunes. 1966's "Don't Answer the Door" and "Paying the Cost to Be the Boss" two years later were Top Ten R&B entries, and the socially charged and funk-tinged "Why I Sing the Blues" just missed achieving the same status in 1969.

Across-the-board stardom finally arrived in 1969 for the deserving guitarist, when he crashed the mainstream consciousness in a big way with a stately, violin-drenched minor-key treatment of Roy Hawkins' "The Thrill Is Gone" that was quite a departure from the concise horn-powered backing King had customarily employed. At last, pop audiences were convinced that they should get to know King better: Not only was the track a number three R&B smash, it vaulted to the upper reaches of the pop lists as well.

King was one of a precious few bluesmen to score hits consistently during the '70s, and for good reason: He wasn't afraid to experiment with the idiom. In 1973, he ventured to Philadelphia to record a pair of huge sellers, "To Know You Is to Love You" and "I Like to Live the Love," with the same silky rhythm section that powered the hits of the Spinners and the O'Jays. In 1976, he teamed up with his old cohort Bland to wax some well-received duets. And in 1978, he joined forces with the jazzy Crusaders to make the gloriously funky "Never Make Your Move Too Soon" and an inspiring "When It All Comes Down." Occasionally, the daring deviations veered off-course—*Love Me Tender*, an album that attempted to harness the Nashville country sound, was an artistic disaster.

Although his concerts have long been as consistently satisfying as anyone's now working in the field (and he remains a road warrior of remarkable resiliency who used to gig an average of 300 nights a year), King has tempered his studio activities somewhat. Still, his 1993 MCA disc *Blues Summit* was a return to form, as King duetted with his peers (John Lee Hooker, Etta James, Fulson, Koko Taylor) on a program of standards. Other notable releases include 1999's *Let the Good Times Roll: The Music of Louis Jordan* and 2000's *Riding with the Kings*, a collaboration with Eric Clapton.

King's immediately recognizable guitar style, utilizing a trademark trill that approximates the bottleneck sound shown him by cousin Bukka White all those decades ago, has long set him apart from his contemporaries. Add his patented pleading vocal style and you have the most influential and innovative bluesman of the postwar period. There can be little doubt that B.B. King will reign as the genre's undisputed king (and goodwill ambassador) for as long as he lives. *—Bill Dahl*

Singin' the Blues / 1956 / Crown ✦✦✦✦✦

Absolutely seminal material; his classic hits. *—Bill Dahl*

Sing Spirituals / 1960 / Diablo ✦✦✦

The Blues / 1960 / Crown ✦✦✦✦✦

More invaluable sides. *—Bill Dahl*

B.B. King Wails / 1960 / Crown ✦✦✦

The Great B.B. King (B. B. King and His Orchestra) / 1960 / Crown ✦✦✦

This collection of singles (1954-1961) includes R&B hits "Sweet Sixteen," "Someday Baby" and "Sneaking Around." *—George Bedard*

My Kind of Blues / 1961 / EMI-Capitol Special Markets ✦✦✦

According to his biographer, Charles Sawyer, this is King's personal favorite among his recordings. Unlike most of his albums from this period (which are mostly collections of singles), this was recorded in one session and takes him out of his usual big-band setting, using only bass, drums, and piano for accompaniment. The result is a masterpiece: a sparse, uncluttered sound with nothing to mask King's beautiful guitar and voice. "You Done Lost Your Good Thing Now" (its unaccompanied guitar intro is a pure distillation of his style), "Mr. Pawn Broker," "Someday Baby" (R&B Top Ten, 1961), "Walkin' Dr. Bill," and a great version of "Drivin' Wheel" are highlights. *—George Bedard*

King of the Blues / Jul. 1961 / Crown ✦✦✦✦

Included are R&B hits from 1960—among them, "I've Got a Right to Love My Baby" and "Good Man Gone Bad." *—George Bedard*

I Love You So / 1962 / Crown ✦✦✦

More vintage King from the '50s, its highlights include "The Woman I Love," "We Can't Make It," and "I've Got Papers on You Baby." *—George Bedard*

Mr. Blues / 1963 / ABC ✦✦✦✦✦

Has some very nice moments. *—Bill Dahl*

★ **Live at the Regal** / 1964 / ABC/MCA ✦✦✦✦✦

B.B. King is not only a timeless singer and guitarist, he's also a natural-born entertainer, and on *Live at the Regal* the listener is treated to an exhibition of all three of his talents. Over percolating horn hits and rolling shuffles, King treats an enthusiastic audience (at some points, they shriek after he delivers each line) to a collection of some of his greatest hits. The backing band is razor-sharp, picking up the leader's cues with almost telepathic accuracy. King's voice is rarely in this fine of form, shifting effortlessly between his falsetto and his regular range, hitting the microphone hard for gritty emphasis and backing off in moments of almost intimate tenderness. Nowhere is this more evident than at the climax of "How Blue Can You Get," where the Chicago venue threatens to explode at King's prompting. Of course, the master's guitar is all over this record, and his playing here is among the best in his long career. Displaying a jazz sensibility, King's lines are sophisticated without losing their grit. More than anything else, *Live at the Regal* is a textbook example of how to set up a live performance. Talking to the crowd, setting up the tunes with a vignette, King is the consummate entertainer. *Live at the Regal* is an absolutely necessary acquisition for fans of B.B. King or blues music in general. A high point, perhaps even the high point, for uptown blues. *—Daniel Gioffre*

Blues Is King / 1967 / MCA ✦✦✦✦

Blues on Top of Blues / 1968 / BGO ✦✦✦✦✦

This isn't his most well-known stuff, but it's a very solid late-'60s set. Featuring brassy arrangements by Johnny Pate (who also worked with many prominent Chicago soul acts during the '60s), it presents King's sound at its fullest without sacrificing any of his grit or sophisticated swing. No famous classics here, but the material is very strong throughout. *—Richie Unterberger*

Lucille / 1968 / BGO ✦✦✦✦

A decent but short (nine songs) late-'60s set, with somewhat sparser production than he'd employ with the beefier arrangements of the "Thrill Is Gone" era. Brass and stinging guitar plays a part on all of the songs, leading off with the eight-minute title track, a spoken narrative about his famous guitar. *—Richie Unterberger*

His Best: The Electric B.B. King / 1968 / BluesWay ✦✦✦

Although this collection has "Don't Answer the Door," "Paying the Cost to Be the Boss" and a nice live re-cut of "Sweet Sixteen" to highly recommend it, this 1968 issue is hardly King's best, and the "electric" part of the title makes it sound like there's an acoustic B.B. King album lurking around somewhere that you and I somehow missed in the last 40 years. To be sure, these are rock-solid performances all recorded between 1965 to 1968, just as King's music was getting slicker and more urban. But this was one of the albums that helped introduce B.B. to a more modern audience (it's gone on to sell over a million copies in 30 years' time), heading straight to the timeline of "The Thrill Is Gone" putting him on the map worldwide. This 1998 CD reissue also includes three bonus tracks, studio versions of "Waitin' on You" and "Night Life," plus "Messy But Good" from the motion picture soundtrack *For the Love of Ivy*. Not his best, certainly *electric*, and ultimately, a good one to add to the collection after you've gotten about five or six others first. *—Cub Koda*

Completely Well / 1969 / MCA ✦✦✦✦

This was B.B.'s breakthrough album in 1969, which finally got him the long-deserved acclaim that was no less than his due. It contained his signature number, "The Thrill Is Gone," and eight other tunes, six of them emanating from B.B.'s pen, usually in a co-writing situation. Hardliners point to the horn charts and the overdubbed strings as the beginning of the end of B.B.'s old style that so identifiably earmarked his early sides for the Bihari brothers and his later tracks for ABC, but this is truly the album that made the world sit up and take notice of B.B. King. The plus points include loose arrangements and a small combo behind him that never dwarfs the proceedings or gets in the way. B.B., for his part, sounds like he's having a ball, playing and singing at peak power. This is certainly not the place to start your B.B. King collection, but it's a nice stop along the way before you finish it. *—Cub Koda*

Anthology of the Blues: B.B. King / 1969 / Kent ✦✦✦✦✦

Some of King's very first records are included—some possibly unreleased, as they don't appear on the singles chart included in his biography. Although kind of crude compared to the later stuff, these are still some fine spirited recordings—a fascinating look at his young developing style. *—George Bedard*

Live & Well / 1969 / BGO ✦✦✦

Although *Live & Well* wasn't a landmark album in the sense of *Live at the Regal*, it was a significant commercial breakthrough for King, as it was the first of his LPs to enter the Top 100. That may have been because recognition from rock stars such as Eric Clapton had finally boosted his exposure to the White pop audience, but it was a worthy recording on its own merits, divided evenly between live and studio material. King's always recorded well as a live act, and it's the concert tracks that shine brightest, although the studio ones (cut with assistance from studio musicians like Al Kooper and Hugh McCracken) aren't bad. *—Richie Unterberger*

Back in the Alley / 1970 / MCA ✦✦✦✦

Indianola Mississippi Seeds / 1970 / BGO ✦✦✦✦

B.B. King hasn't made many better pop-flavored albums than this. Besides making Leon Russell's "Hummingbird" sound like his own composition, King showed that you can put the blues into any situation and make it work. Carole King was one of several pop luminaries who did more than just hang on for the ride. *—Ron Wynn*

In London / 1971 / BGO ✦✦

The plodding rhythms laid down by a coterie of British rock stars for this set make one long for King's road-tested regular band. But it was the fashion in 1971 to dispatch American blues legends to London to record mediocre LPs with alleged rock royalty (the lineup here includes Ringo Starr, Peter Green, Alexis Korner, and Klaus Voorman. *—Bill Dahl*

☆ **Live in Cook County Jail** / 1971 / MCA ✦✦✦✦✦

B.B. King has cut a lot of albums since the success of *Live at the Regal*. And, like the live shows they document, none of them are any less than solid and professional, hallmarks of King's work aesthetic. But every so often B.B. truly catches fire; his playing and singing comes up an extra notch or two, and the result is a live album with some real sparks to it. *Live in Cook County Jail* is one of those great concerts that the record company was smart enough to be there to capture, documenting B.B. firing on all cylinders in front of an audience that's just damn happy for him to be there. Possibly the best live version of "The Thrill Is Gone" of all its many incarnations, and rock-solid renditions of classics like "Everyday I Have the Blues," "How Blue Can You Get?," "Sweet Sixteen," and a great medley of "3 O'Clock Blues" and "Darlin' You Know I Love You." *Live at the Regal* is still the champ of King's live output, but many say this runs a close second, and they just may be right. —*Cub Koda*

L.A. Midnight / 1972 / ABC ✦✦✦
This release comes straight from B.B. King's commercial peak (that is, prior to the unprecedented Top Ten success of *Riding With the King* in 2000), and it is a perplexing LP where greatness and aimlessness lie side by side. Using a freely eclectic mix of sidemen from Los Angeles, King strides to some sterling performances in certain tracks. The King is at his sly peak on "I Got Some Help I Don't Need," uproariously humorous and hurt at the same time, with crazy wah-wah filigrees laced within, and "Can't You Hear Me Talking To You" is also tight and right. One of his best recordings of "Sweet Sixteen" leads off Side Two, where the lyric is updated to suit the times ("I just got back from Vietnam, baby/And you know I'm a long, long way from New Orleans") and band, singer and his guitar rise to an emotional crescendo down the stretch. Yet "(I Believe) I've Been Blue Too Long" falters on a clumsy riff and can't get going, and the rest of the album is frittered away with directionless blues jamming. Guitarists Jesse Ed Davis and Joe Walsh join King on the two longest jams ("Midnight," "Lucille's Granny") yet they don't really mesh that well. Get this one secondhand for the outstanding disciplined stuff and don't sweat the rest; as per the nature of the beast, some jams don't yield pay dirt. —*Richard Ginell*

Guess Who / 1972 / MCA ✦✦✦
When B.B. King is cajoled into covering the Lovin' Spoonful's "Summer in the City," you know material's in dangerously short supply. It's the lead number on this rather undistinguished album, cut with most of his road band of the time. One staple of his live show, the sentimental blues ballad "Guess Who," came from this set. —*Bill Dahl*

To Know You Is to Love You / 1973 / MCA ✦✦✦
The combination of King and the well-oiled Philly rhythm section that powered hits by the O'Jays, Spinners, and Stylistics proved a surprisingly adroit one. Two huge hits came from this album, the Stevie Wonder/Syreeta Wright-penned title track and "I Like to Live the Love," both of them intriguing updates of King's tried-and-true style. —*Bill Dahl*

The Best of B.B. King / 1973 / MCA ✦✦✦✦
True, this 1973 vintage best-of album covers a ridiculously slim wedge of time in the blues king's long career. Yet this period was quite significant, for it marks the crest of B.B. King's initial entry into the pop music mass market—and this album surfs succinctly, if not comprehensively, over the high points of his turn-of-the-decade winning streak. There's a potent slice of King's triumphant *Live at Cook County*—one of his sassiest "How Blue Can You Get?" on records—the huge hit "The Thrill Is Gone" extracts from his surprisingly pleasing early excursions into pop/rock territory on *In London* and *Indianola Mississippi Seeds*, and plenty of flavorful electric blues ("Sweet Sixteen," "Why I Sing the Blues") at full length. There are some quirks—"Caldonia" is shortened because one of the unnamed participants on the session demanded the cut, and the "compatible stereo/quad" sound on the LP has some details drastically mixed down when it's played back in ordinary stereo. Most curious of all is the last track, where King plunks out "Nobody Loves Me but My Mother" on a tack piano and then his closing words are converted into a weird, gradually slowed-down, echotized electronic blur that settles into a creepy locked-end groove. —*Richard Ginell*

Together for the First Time . . . Live / 1974 / MCA ✦✦✦
Although the duo of Bobby "Blue" Bland and B.B. King was one of the most popular touring acts of the '70s and '80s, their first duet album—appropriately titled *Together for the First Time . . . Live*—doesn't quite live up to expectations. Both musicians are in fine form, but rarely do any sparks fly. Occasionally, King turns out a good solo and Bland sings with passion, but usually the vibe of the record is too relaxed to be truly engaging. It's a pleasant record, just not the essential listening that it should have been. —*Thom Owens*

King Size / 1977 / ABC ✦✦✦
The '70s and '80s may be scattered with routine B.B. King albums, but rumors to the contrary, this is not one of them. Despite the occasional pop string and/or brass backings and mostly relaxed vocal delivery by King, the Memphis and L.A. studio bands kick hard—aided and abetted by some conga players—and the material is often superior. The record even hits a hot streak on side two with three excellent tracks in a row—a very funky "Got My Mojo Workin'" with a bumpy clavinet going full-tilt underneath King's easygoing vocal, "Walkin' in the Sun," with a nicely relaxed funky beat offsetting the strings, and "Mother Fuyer" may be the best one of all, with its humorous lyrics and driving beat. "Don't Lie to Me" opens the album on a nice, rolling groove that King rides real easy, and the medley of "I Just Want to Make Love to You/Your Lovin' Turns Me On" has the smokin' guest R&B tenor of Jimmy Forrest juicing up the solo break. Not much guitar here, but King does erupt now and then with some good signature breaks. —*Richard Ginell*

Midnight Believer / 1978 / MCA ✦✦✦
Another collaboration that worked a lot better than one might have expected. King and the Crusaders blended in a marginally funky, contemporary style for the buoyant "Never Make Your Move Too Soon" and an uplifting "When It All Comes Down." —*Bill Dahl*

Take It Home / 1979 / MCA ✦✦
This 1979 effort finds B.B. interpreting a number of pop-blues tunes, many of them co-written by Will Jennings and co-producer Joe Sample, with King co-writing two of the songs aboard. Even with a large, contemporary backdrop (including a seven-piece horn section and female backup singers), there's still plenty of room for B.B.'s stinging guitar and stentorian vocals in the mix. Highlights include the gospel-tinged "Better Not Look Down," "Same Old Story (Same Old Song)," "Happy Birthday Blues," "The Beginning of

the End" and the title track. As one of B.B.'s more pop-oriented offerings, this succeeds admirably. —*Cub Koda*

Live "Now Appearing" at Ole Miss / 1980 / MCA ✦✦
Surely the worst, most lethargic live album that King ever made. Rumor has long had it that after-the-fact enhancements were added to the live tapes to make them more palatable—if so, it didn't work! —*Bill Dahl*

There Must Be a Better World Somewhere / 1981 / MCA ✦✦✦
During his decade recording for MCA, B.B. King was generally teamed with overblown accompaniment rather than his regular (and perfectly complementary) traveling band. This CD finds the masterful vocalist/guitarist joined by a more logical backup group than usual (with altoist Hank Crawford, tenor saxophonist David "Fathead" Newman and baritonist Ronnie Cuber in the tentet). The two most basic selections ("There Must Be a Better World Somewhere" and "The Victim") are easily the most successful while the other four are funky, more R&B-oriented and overly commercial; it sounds like B.B. was consciously trying for a hit record. Despite some fine solos by Newman and Crawford, this session was rather erratic, brief (under 36 minutes) and far from essential. —*Scott Yanow*

Great Moments With B.B. King / 1981 / MCA ✦✦✦✦
Very solid 23-track package culled from some of King's best mid- to late-'60s ABC-Paramount and BluesWay LPs. Some of the best cuts stem from a sizzling live album; "Gambler's Blues," "Waitin' on You," and a stunning "Night Life" find his reverb level rising to the boiling point. A brassy "That's Wrong Little Mama," "Dance with Me," and "Heartbreaker" exhibit concise consecutive right hooks, and his rousing smash "Paying the Cost to Be the Boss" is also on board. —*Bill Dahl*

Love Me Tender / 1982 / MCA ✦
B.B. King's extremely ill-advised foray into mushy Nashville cornpone. Hearing him croon the title track in front of an array of Music Row's most generic pickers is enough to drive one screaming into his or her record collection for a surefire antidote: some '50s King on RPM! Ahh . . . —*Bill Dahl*

Memphis Masters / 1982 / Ace ✦✦✦✦✦
Only the absence of substantial or even minimal recording information keeps this from being a showcase release. The songs, culled from early-'50s sessions, are formative King material and should be closely studied by the hordes who only know King from over-arranged major-label LPs and *Tonight Show* appearances. —*Ron Wynn*

Blues 'n' Jazz / Aug. 1983 / MCA ✦✦✦
Swinging session that plays to King's strengths. —*Bill Dahl*

Completely Live & Well / 1986 / Charly ✦✦✦✦✦
Here's much of the material that helped B.B. King make his move into the hearts and minds of mainstream America. Whether you think that was ultimately good or bad, it's still necessary to hear it. —*Ron Wynn*

Six Silver Strings / 1988 / MCA ✦✦
For a recording fervently hyped as a special occasion—B.B. King's 50th album and all that—this one is surprisingly patchy in concept and erratic in execution. Five of the tracks are Miami sessions prosaically produced by longtime King cohort Dave Crawford, who also co-wrote most of them with Luther Dixon. The routine pop/rock backing tracks produce an often apathetic response from King; even Dixon's "Big Boss Man" is depressingly routine. Oddly enough, the only numbers that have any grit are the three co-produced by filmmaker John Landis (of the Blues Brothers notoriety) and Ira Newborn from the soundtrack to the former's film *Into the Night*. Indeed, Newborn's "My Lucille," the ultimate apotheosis to King's beloved guitar, is an underrated signature classic—even Lucille herself gets a lot of space to sing out—and "In the Midnight Hour" also strikes fire. Buy it for "My Lucille," if you don't mind the filler and the fact that the album offers appallingly short weight at just under 34 minutes. —*Richard Ginell*

Do the Boogie! B.B. King's Early '50s Classics / 1988 / Flair ✦✦✦✦✦
20 killer tracks from B.B. King's '50s heyday, including quite a few alternate takes and a few tough-to-locate items ("Bye Bye Baby," "Dark Is the Night," "Jump with You Baby"). Many of the titles are familiar ones—"Woke Up This Morning," "Every Day (I Have the Blues)," "Please Love Me," "Whole Lotta Love"—but often as not, compiler Ray Topping unearthed contrasting versions from the same sessions that shed new, fascinating light on King's studio techniques. —*Bill Dahl*

King of Blues: 1989 / Nov. 14, 1988 / MCA ✦✦

Live at the Apollo / Nov. 1990 / GRP ✦✦✦
There are both good and bad points to this CD. Of the latter, the Phillip Morris "Super Band" is confined to background work with—other than a few spots for Plas Johnson's tenor—no soloists being heard from. As an ensemble, the all-star orchestra performs well, but is essentially anonymous. Also, despite the backing, B.B. King does not attempt to play jazz, a wasted opportunity. But, switching to the good points, *Live at the Apollo* is an excellent example of a strong B.B. King live performance. Somehow he always makes his combination of blues and familiar hits sound fresh. With a liberal amount of space set aside for his guitar solos, B.B. is in top form throughout the well-paced set, which is far superior to most of his overproduced studio sessions for MCA. Even if the big band is mostly irrelevant, this CD is recommended for B.B. King's singing and playing. —*Scott Yanow*

Spotlight on Lucille / 1991 / Flair ✦✦✦✦
From the contemporary-looking cover, this would appear to be recently recorded material. But wait—these are all '50s/early-'60s instrumentals from the Modern/Kent vaults, spotlighting B.B. King's pristine lead guitar in an often jazzier mode than he usually adopted in the studio. His workout on Louis Jordan's "Just like a Woman" is a *tour de force*

that's been reissued often, but much of the compilation is rare stuff that gives Lucille her full due. *—Bill Dahl*

The Fabulous B.B. King / 1991 / Flair ✦✦

The Best of B.B. King, Vol. 1, also on Flair, has 20 tracks from the same era covered by this collection, which only has 12. So you should really stick with the other Flair compilation, even if it's a bit more expensive. Which doesn't mean that this CD is bad; the 12 songs, all from the early and mid-'50s, include some of his most famous early classics, such as "Three O'Clock Blues," "Everyday I Have the Blues," and "Sweet Little Angel." *—Richie Unterberger*

☆ **The Best of B.B. King, Vol. 1** / 1991 / Ace ✦✦✦✦✦

A 20-track hits compilation that should have been a great deal better than it is. The disc embarrassingly uses an inferior remake of King's classic "Whole Lotta Love" instead of the original, while drums and electric bass have been clumsily overdubbed on the original takes of "You Upset Me Baby," "Every Day," and "Please Love Me," absolutely ruining them. What a shame, since two-thirds of the collection is just fine. *—Bill Dahl*

Live at San Quentin / Jun. 1991 / MCA ✦✦

B.B. King's pleas to the literally captive audience for a round of applause for the guards watching over the prisoners on his first live album in nearly a decade is almost laughable. Unlike Johnny Cash's smirking irony on his album recorded at the same facility in 1969, where you can sense Cash's disdain for the captors is just as strong as the inmates', King seems to be totally oblivious to the fact that these are prisoners being held against their will. And that's the problem with this competent, if unremarkable, record: King is merely going through the motions. He could just as well be playing to a blue-blooded audience under the stars at some shed in the Midwest. *—Michael Gallucci*

Why I Sing the Blues / 1992 / MCA ✦✦✦

MCA Special Products' *Why I Sing the Blues* collects ten highlights from his late-'60s and early-'70s recordings for ABC, which were later acquired by MCA. Considering that this is a budget-priced compilation, and therefore limited in its scope, this isn't a bad sampler at all, containing the hit version of "The Thrill Is Gone," plus good takes of "Hummingbird," "How Blue Can You Get?" and "Sweet Sixteen," along with such oddities as "Chains and Things," which features Carole King on piano. Certainly, it's not enough to make it of interest to hardcore collectors, who will likely own all of this, nor is it a comprehensive collection by any means; but it's still a fun sampler considering its price. *—Stephen Thomas Erlewine*

There Is Always One More Time / 1992 / MCA ✦✦✦

Most of B.B. King's studio albums of the '80s and '90s tend to de-emphasize his guitar playing and consist largely of forgettable originals and obvious attempts at pop hits. However, this CD (which was cut in the studios) is on a higher level and is quite rewarding. Most of the tunes were co-written by pianist Joe Sample and Will Jennings and the majority are quite catchy and memorable. Certainly it is easy to sing along with the refrains of "I'm Moving On," "Back In L.A," and "Roll, Roll, Roll." B.B. usually overdubbed his guitar to play along with his vocals (somehow the interplay does not sound spontaneous), but it does not detract from the final results. The intelligent and philosophical lyrics fit King's style very well and his voice is very much in prime form. Well worth acquiring. *—Scott Yanow*

☆ **Singin' the Blues/The Blues** / 1992 / Flair ✦✦✦✦✦

Two great original Crown albums from the '50s appear on one import CD, including most of King's Top Ten R&B hits from the period: "3 O'Clock Blues," "Please Love Me," "You Upset Me Baby," "You Know I Love You," "Woke Up This Morning," and "Sweet Little Angel," plus one of his best, "Crying Won't Help You." This is the stuff that was so hugely influential to other blues guitarists and singers in its original recorded version. Here is lots of the real early, gritty stuff: "That Ain't the Way to Do It," "When My Heart Beats Like a Hammer," "Don't You Want a Man Like Me?" The guitar intro to "Early in the Morning" is one of the finest examples of King in a jazzy mode. Great guitar! *—George Bedard*

Heart & Soul / 1992 / Pointblank ✦✦✦

The Biharis harbored dreams of crossing the rich-voiced King over into the pop market during the '50s, trying him out on some of the dreariest ballads imaginable. Many of those limp outings turn up on this collection—hearing the king of the blues croon "On My Word of Honour" and "My Heart Belongs to You" like a refugee from the Platters ain't a good time by any means! Fortunately, not everything is so dire: "Story from My Heart and Soul," "Lonely and Blue," and the delicious "Sneakin' Around" sport a more edifying mix of blues and balladry. *—Bill Dahl*

King of the Blues / 1992 / MCA ✦✦✦✦✦

No way can a mere four discs cover every facet of the blues king's amazing recording career, but MCA makes a valiant stab at it. The first two discs, as expected, are immaculate: opening with his Bullet Records debut ("Miss Martha King"), the box continues with a handful of pivotal RPM/Kent masters before digging into his '60s ABC-Paramount material ("I'm Gonna Sit in 'Til You Give In" and "My Baby's Comin' Home" are little-recalled gems). The hits—"The Thrill Is Gone," "Why I Sing the Blues," "To Know You Is to Love You"—are all here, and if much of the fourth disc is pretty disposable, it only mirrors King's own winding down in the studio. *—Bill Dahl*

Blues Summit / 1993 / MCA ✦✦✦

On this release, King comes close to equaling his past triumphs on small independent labels in the '50s and '60s. He's ditched the pseudo-hip production fodder and cut a 12-song set matching him with blues peers. His duets with Buddy Guy, John Lee Hooker, and Albert Collins are especially worthy, while the songs with Koko Taylor, Ruth Brown, and Irma Thomas have some good-natured banter and exchanges, as well as tasty vocals. The master gives willing pupils Joe Louis Walker and Robert Cray valuable lessons on their collaborations. There's also a medley in which King invokes the spirit of his chitlin circuit days, taking the vocal spotlight while his Orchestra roars along underneath. *—Ron Wynn*

My Sweet Little Angel / Oct. 5, 1993 / Flair ✦✦✦✦

Another 21-track anthology chock full of alternate takes and previously unreleased masters from B.B. King's '50s stint at RPM/Kent. A wild cross-section of material—signature items like "Sweet Little Angel" and "Please Accept My Love," an off-the-wall reading of Tony Bennett's "In the Middle of an Island," and best of all, a torrid jazzy instrumental called "String Bean" that finds King pulling some astounding guitar tricks out of a seemingly bottomless bag. *—Bill Dahl*

☆ **Early Blues Boy Years, Vol. 1: 1949–51** / 1995 / Opal ✦✦✦✦✦

MCA has anthologized B.B. King's ABC-Paramount years with *King of the Blues*, and Flair/Virgin has issued some of his '50s work for the Bihari brothers' various labels (Modern, Kent etc.). In the absence of a boxed set devoted to those '50s sides, however, this disc and its companion volumes from the Barcelona-based Opal label are the best you're likely to do in assembling the best of B.B. King's work from that era. The sound is OK, and the sessionography is pretty fair, though a proper boxed set would probably be more thorough. *—Bruce Eder*

Early Blues Boy Years, Vol. 2: 1952–54 / 1995 / Opal ✦✦✦✦✦

This 20-song collection continues B.B. King's mid-'50s history on the Bihari brothers' various labels (Modern, Kent etc.), including his "big band" work, including "When My Heart Beats Like a Hammer," "Woke Up This Morning," and "I Love You." There's lots of fiery guitar on this volume, opening with "You Upset Me Baby" and "Blind Love." The material is all first rate, from rollicking rave-ups like "Boogie Woogie Woman" to moody, mournful blues numbers like "Past Day." Unlike the first volume, however, there are no musician or session credits included, partly because they may not exist for much of his work during this period. The sound is quite good through, with lots of bite to the brass and a sense that his guitar and voice could be in the same room with you. Many of these cuts have been issued by Flair/Virgin, but this is still the best comprehensive collection. *—Bruce Eder*

How Blue Can You Get / Jul. 14, 1995 / Prime Cuts ✦✦✦

How Blue Can You Get is a real hodgepodge of very early B.B. 78s, live air shots, and later studio tracks with a big band. It's interesting to hear King's style evolve from the cruder RPM sides cut in Memphis and Los Angeles to his later sides after success had come his way. Loads of great guitar and great singing, and although some of the transfers are more than a little scratchy, the music's just fine. As budget sets go, this one's a keeper. *—Cub Koda*

How Blue Can You Get?: Classic Live Performances 1964 to 1994 / Jun. 18, 1996 / MCA ✦✦✦

The double-disc collection *How Blue Can You Get: Classic Live 1964 to 1994* covers 30 years of B.B. King's remarkably popular and groundbreaking career, picking out choice live performances from a variety of sources. King has always been acknowledged as one of the most electrifing blues guitarists, as well as one of the best all-around entertainers that the genre has to offer, so it stands to reason that the compilation is filled with terrific music. And it certainly is—from his astonishing performance at the Regal to recent performances in Japan, B.B. shines throughout the set. Despite all of the fine music this has to offer, it doesn't capture the spark of one of his live shows, where he interacts brilliantly with the audience; you still have to pick up *Live At the Regal* to experience that. Even though *How Blue Can You Get* lacks the kinetic energy of a live concert, there's enough prime material to make it an essential addition to any B.B. King fan's library. *—Thom Owens*

Deuces Wild / Nov. 4, 1997 / MCA ✦✦✦

This is B.B.'s celebrity duet album, and a straight-ahead blues album this is not. But long-time fans who are aware of King's genre-stretching capabilities will find much to savor here. Kicking off with B.B. playing some beautiful fills and solo work behind Van Morrison on "If You Love Me," the superstars start lining up to jam with the King, with Tracy Chapman ("The Thrill Is Gone"), Eric Clapton (a funkified "Rock Me Baby"), the Rolling Stones ("Paying the Cost to Be the Boss," with a fine harp solo from Mick Jagger), Willie Nelson (his "Nightlife," long a standard in B.B.'s set list), Bonnie Raitt ("Baby I Love You") and Marty Stuart ("Confessin' the Blues") all turning in fine efforts. The only clinker aboard here is an ill-advised attempt to make a rap record with Heavy D, the execrable "Keep It Coming." *—Cub Koda*

King Biscuit Flower Hour Presents B.B. King / Apr. 28, 1998 / King Biscuit ✦✦

B.B. King's *King Biscuit Flower Hour* captures the legendary blues guitarist in concert in the '80s. The presence of George Benson on "I Got Some Help I Don't Need" and "Just a Little Love," and Johnny & Edgar Winter on "Goin' Down Slow," suggests that the concert was more special than it actually was. In reality, it was simply an average concert with B.B. running through average material; the only classics were "How Blue Can You Get" and "The Thrill Is Gone." The performances are competent, but not inspired, making the disc really of interest to hardcore B.B. collectors, especially since there's a lot of better live B.B. on the market. *—Stephen Thomas Erlewine*

Greatest Hits / Aug. 25, 1998 / MCA ✦✦✦

There's more than one B.B. King best-of out on the racks, but this 1998 issue updates his latest chart achievements and puts it together in a modern, 16-track package for both the novice and casual modern blues listener. Kicking off with a pair of tunes from the influential *Live at the Regal* album ("Sweet Little Angel," "Everyday I Have the Blues"), the set moves through mid- to late-'60s breakthrough hits like "How Blue Can You Get?," "Paying the Cost to Be the Boss," "Why I Sing the Blues," "Don't Answer the Door" and his signature tune, "The Thrill Is Gone." The pop-blues fusions King experimented with in the '70s and '80s show up on "To Know You Is to Love You," "I Like to Live the Love" and "Hummingbird." The modern-day end of things is represented by duets with Robert Cray on "Playin' With My Friends" and rock group U2 on "When Love Comes to Town." Although missing all of his early-'50s hits, this is a good buy for the casual fan coming to his music for the first time and for longtime aficionados looking for a quick-fix update. *—Cub Koda*

Blues on the Bayou / Oct. 20, 1998 / MCA ♦♦♦
King made his debut as producer with this album released in October, 1998. He employs the most basic of ideas for this project: record an album of B.B. King tunes, with B.B. King's regular road band, under B.B. King's supervision. Keeping it loose, relaxed and focused, B.B. cut this album in four days down at a secluded studio in Louisiana and came up with one of his strongest modern day albums in many years. No duets, no special guests, just King and his road warrior band, playing *his* songs with *him* producing the results—no overdubs, just simple, no nonsense blues done like he would do them onstage. The result is a no-frills, straight-ahead session that shows that B.B. might be have been 73 at the time of this date, but still had plenty of gas left in the tank. Tracks like "I'll Survive," and the jumping "Shake It Up and Go," "Darlin' What Happened," the minor keyed "Blues Boy Tune," and the instrumental "Blues We Like," and the closing "If That's It, I Quit" show him stretching out in a way he has seldom done in a studio environment and the result is one of his best albums in recent memory. *—Cub Koda*

RPM Hits 1951–1957 / Feb. 26, 1999 / Ace ♦♦♦♦♦
This is a first-rate summary of the cream of the first few years of B.B. King's career, the 26 songs all taken from 1951-57 singles on the RPM label. Though relatively few of these have survived down the years to become famous standards or oldies, they were incredibly successful in their time; 18 of them were R&B hits, and another couple scraped into the bottom of the pop charts. "Three O'Clock Blues" and "Sweet Little Angel" are a couple of King's most famous tunes, but there are plenty of other ballads and shuffles here that made their mark in their day, like "You Know I Love You," "Woke Up This Morning" (how's that for titling a hit after one of the most overused blues clichés), "Please Hurry Home," and "You Upset Me Baby." These are quite fully produced R&B arrangements for the era, with roadhouse piano and fat horns rounding out the punch. King's stinging guitar and vocals, both less prone to drawn-out phrasing than his crossover soul-blues work of the '60s and '70s, are at the forefront. It's true these tracks have been around the block a few times on other reissues, but these have been remastered, often from newly discovered masters, to yield a quality of sound you won't always find on reissues of '50s blues and R&B. [This U.K. import is not available for sale in North America.] *—Richie Unterberger*

Best of B.B. King: 20th Century Masters / Mar. 23, 1999 / MCA ♦♦♦
Like any record company worth their salt, MCA knows a good gimmick when they see it, and when the millennium came around...well, the *20th Century Masters—The Millennium Collection* wasn't too far behind. Supposedly, the millennium is a momentous occasion, but it's hard to feel that way when it's used as another excuse to turn out a budget-line series. But apart from the presumptuous title, *20th Century Masters—The Millennium Collection* turns out to be a very good budget-line series. True, it's impossible for any of these brief collections to be definitive, but they're nevertheless solid samplers that don't feature a bad song in the bunch. For example, take B.B. King's *20th Century* volume—it's an irresistible ten-song summary of his MCA recordings. There may be a couple of noteworthy songs missing, but many of his best-known songs for the label are here, including "The Thrill Is Gone," "Ain't Nobody Home," "Let the Good Times Roll," "Don't Answer the Door," "Sweet Sixteen" and "Paying the Cost to Be the Boss." Serious fans will want something more extensive, but this is an excellent introduction for neophytes and a great sampler for casual fans, considering its length and price. That doesn't erase the ridiculousness of the series title, but the silliness is excusable when the music and the collections are good. *—Stephen Thomas Erlewine*

Live in Japan / May 18, 1999 / MCA ♦♦♦♦
It took 28 years, but in 1999, *Live in Japan* finally became available in the U.S. Recorded at Sankei Hall in Tokyo on March 4 and 7, 1971, *Live in Japan* was originally released as a two-LP set in Japan. At the time, King's superb *Live at Cook County Jail* was a respectable seller for ABC, and the label also planned to release *B.B. King in London*—so ABC felt that because a fair amount of live King albums were coming out in the U.S., it was best to release the Sankei Hall recording only in Japan. But many of King's American fans wanted it anyway, and collectors went out of their way to find imported copies of the double LP. Parts of *Live in Japan* did come out on various U.S. releases, but it was not released in its entirety in the U.S. until this 1999 reissue. Backed by many of the same players heard on *Live at Cook County Jail*, King is in excellent form on spirited, gutsy performances of "The Thrill Is Gone" and "Sweet Sixteen" as well as Sonny Boy Williamson's "Eyesight to the Blind," Leon Russell's "Hummingbird," and Peter Chatman's "Every Day I Have the Blues." The instrumentals "Japanese Boogie" and "Jamming at Sankei Hall" give the band a chance to let loose and improvise, and "Lucille" (King's name for his guitar) gets in some passionate, inspired solos. Although *Live at the Regal* or *Live at Cook Country Jail* are King's most essential live albums, *Live in Japan* is a fine CD that his fans will definitely want. *—Alex Henderson*

Let the Good Times Roll: The Music of Louis Jordan / Oct. 5, 1999 / MCA ♦♦♦♦
Even if B.B. King is the King of the Blues, some might find it strange that he chose to record *Let the Good Times Roll*, a tribute album to Louis Jordan, the King of Jump Blues. King's work was never as boisterous or enthusiastic as Jordan's, but his debt is apparent from the first cut of the album. King may have never done straight jump blues, but his sophisticated urban blues—complete with horn sections and an emphasis on vocals—shows as much jump influence as it does Delta. *Let the Good Times Roll* brings that home with a quiet, seductive insistence. Backed by a stellar band—featuring Dr. John on piano, drummer Earl Palmer, alto saxophonist Hank Crawford, and tenor saxophonist Dave "Fathead" Newman, among others—B.B. King sounds loose and natural. There are stars in the band, but this is hardly a bloated all-star effort, since the focus in on delivering no-nonsense performances. Strangely enough, King doesn't play that much guitar on the album, concentrating on his vocals and letting the band interact. When he does solo, it's as elegant and tasteful as always, but the focal point is always the songs. Since he's such a fine guitarist, B.B.'s singing often goes underappreciated, but here it's at the forefront, and he shines. His phrasing is impeccable, and he always captures the spirit of the songs, either through humor or heart. Of course, that's a skill that Jordan had, as well, and realizing that sheds new light on B.B.'s music. Much of his celebrated skills as a showman and a performer indirectly came from Jordan, as did elements of his musical style. Never has that been as clear as it is on *Let the Good Times Roll*. *—Stephen Thomas Erlewine*

Makin' Love Is Good for You / Apr. 25, 2000 / MCA ♦♦♦
Over the years, the music world has seen its share of over-70 singers who kept performing even though they didn't have much of a voice left: Peggy Lee and Frank Sinatra are among the names that come to mind. But when B.B. King entered his seventies, the veteran blues singer/guitarist could still belt it out with confidence, and he does exactly that on *Makin' Love Is Good for You*, which was recorded when King was 74. Although this blues/soul effort won't go down in history as one of his all-time classics, it's a respectable CD that finds his voice continuing to hold up well. King's charisma remains, and he has no problem getting his points across on 12-bar blues numbers like "Ain't Nobody Like My Baby," "I Got to Leave This Woman," and Willie Dixon's "Don't Go No Farther," as well as soul offerings such as the title song and an interpretation of Barbara George's 1961 hit "I Know." Because King has such a huge catalog, one could spend a fortune trying to acquire every title that he has out on CD. So unless you you're a serious collector and have a large budget, it's best to stick to his more essential recordings; and *Makin' Love Is Good for You*, although decent and respectable, isn't essential and isn't as interesting as 1999's *Let the Good Times Roll: The Music of Louis Jordan*. Nonetheless, it can be an enjoyable addition to your blues library if you're among King's diehard fans. *—Alex Henderson*

☆ **The Best of the Kent Singles 1958–1971** / Jun. 26, 2000 / Ace ♦♦♦♦♦
This isn't as straightforward an anthology as you might suppose from the title. Yes, it has King singles released on Kent between 1958 and 1971. King, however, left Kent in 1962, after which the label continued putting out singles from the tracks he had done with the company; often, these singles charted. Therefore, all of the material on this CD is from the late '50s and early '60s—not that this is a drawback. Furthermore, some of the singles were produced by altering the original recordings with newly dubbed instrumentation. Ace has made some judgment calls and, in many instances, used the original undubbed versions, although in the case of "Worry, Worry," the overdubbed single version *is* used. As for the different versions that were omitted due to these judgment calls, Ace promised, upon the 2000 release of this compilation, that all missing sides would eventually be issued on other Ace CDs. Having gotten all that straight, this is a good collection of King's late-'50s, early-'60s material. It includes some of his signature tunes, like "Why Does Everything Happen to Me," "Rock Me Baby," and "Sweet Sixteen, Pts. 1 & 2," not to mention his crunchy version of "Eyesight to the Blind," the Sonny Boy Williamson song whose lyrics were later adapted by the Who in *Tommy*. King's arrangements were getting jazzier by this time, often employing horns, although they were still somewhat rawer than the ones that would bring him crossover success by the late '60s. It may be unpopular to note that this, like many King compilations, isn't the most diverse listen, and 25 songs at once might be more than enough. At the same time, for King fans, of which there are many, it probably *isn't* enough. *—Richie Unterberger*

☆ **Anthology** / Nov. 7, 2000 / MCA ♦♦♦♦♦
MCA's double-disc set *Anthology* is a bit of a blessing, actually, a welcome entry to B.B. King's extensive catalog, since the last half of his career has not been anthologized often (it was most notably on the box set *The King of Blues*). Once King's career entered the '70s, he never lost his way, but his recordings became uneven. The situation didn't improve in the '80s or '90s, either—he was always reliable, but the records could either be too slick or uninspired or just solid journeyman efforts. *Anthology* does a terrific job of consolidating the years between 1963 and 1998, his time at ABC and MCA, respectively. Smartly, the compilers lean heavily on the '60s and early-'70s material, with only a handful of tracks from 1980-1998. There are certainly some terrific tracks missing, but by concentrating on his great recordings of the mid-'60s, plus the work that just followed it, they wind up with not just a very enjoyable compilation, but one that's a testament to B.B.'s talents as a guitarist, vocalist, stylist, and showman. This, in conjunction with a compilation of early Flair recordings and *Live at the Regal*, provide a better history of the great bluesman's career than his box set. *—Stephen Thomas Erlewine*

Here & There: The Uncollected B.B. King / Aug. 28, 2001 / Hip-O ♦♦
Ever since John Lee Hooker's *The Healer*, the record industry favored teaming up veteran artists with hot-shot contemporary artists, or at least pairing that veteran with another veteran of equal stature. Of course, duet albums were not rare prior to that—B.B. King, for example, often recorded with Bobby "Blue" Bland, and teaming hot acts has been standard since the beginning of the business—but the calculated superstar duets albums proliferated, along with tribute albums, and reliable artists like B.B. King started to appear on tons of albums. Hip-O's 2001 compilation *Here & There: The Uncollected B.B. King* gathers up 11 of these performances (several, it should be noted, are for records now owned by Universal), and while this is hardly complete (although it does

have a couple of items for collectors—the previously unreleased "Yes Man" and the unavailable-in-the-States "All You Ever Give Me is the Blues," both from a Vernon Ried and Jon Tiven-produced session; they're the best things here, by the way, the hardest-driving cuts here), it is enough to let you know that these performances aren't worth seeking out. B.B. is professional as always and he turns in professional, deliberately classy performances that are fine, but just not that interesting. It will fill in some holes in a B.B. King collection, but those kinds of fans who collect the best of B.B. will sleep easy without this in their collections. *—Stephen Thomas Erlewine*

A Christmas Celebration of Hope / Nov. 6, 2001 / MCA ♦♦♦
It took B.B. King a long time to get around to his first Christmas album, which didn't appear until about half a century into his recording career. It's an adequate, good-humored reprisal of various holiday chestnuts, among them some material with blues/R&B origins, like "Merry Christmas Baby." King wrote just one new song for the album, the instrumental "Christmas Love," though he did originally record another of the tracks, "Christmas Celebration," back in 1960. Wisely he plays "Auld Lang Syne" as a funky instrumental instead of vocalizing the singalong lyrics. In addition to periodic bursts of King's trademark guitar, there is plenty of brass and organ in the peppy arrangements. The Nashville String Machine adds its strings to just three tracks, which cuts down on over-produced excess (which is only a problem on "Please Come Home for Christmas"). It's hardly the first King you'll pull off your shelf, and not the first R&B Christmas album you'll turn to either, but you could do worse in the holiday season. *—Richie Unterberger*

☆ **The Vintage Years** / 2002 / Ace ♦♦♦♦♦
This impressive, impeccably packaged four-CD box set focuses solely on B.B. King's '50s and '60s recordings for the Modern family of labels. That was a period that basically encompassed the vast majority of his work prior to 1962, though he did a few non-Modern sides before signing with ABC Paramount in early 1962 and did a few other sides for Modern in the mid-'60s. So this is basically a box-set overview of King's early career, one that saw him score many R&B hits and build a career as a blues legend, even as the blues were falling out of fashion in favor of rock and soul. As many tracks as there are here—106 in all, four of them previously unreleased—this isn't a catchall roundup of everything the prolific King did for the label. Additional material shows up on more specialized retrospectives, like Ace's own *The Modern Recordings, 1950-1951.* King's output during this period might be more consistent than it is varied, but both King fans and committed blues enthusiasts in general will be mighty happy with this set, presenting the considerable bulk of his significant Modern sides with intelligence. Each individual CD focuses on a theme of sort. Disc one, "The Great B.B.," concentrates on the hits and most familiar tunes, like "Sweet Little Angel," "Every Day I Have the Blues," "Sweet Sixteen," "Downhearted (How Blue Can You Get?)," "Rock Me Baby," "3 O'Clock Blues," and "Did You Ever Love a Woman." The disc titled "Memphis Blues'n'Boogie" is pretty self-explanatory and perhaps the least exciting of the CDs, as it's the most samey-sounding. The disc "Take a Swing With Me" is devoted to King's mild stylistic tours into soul, gospel, doo wop, and rock & roll, though it's usually a case of King absorbing such influences into blues than trying something too different. The final CD, "King of the Blues," puts the spotlight on his later recordings for the label, in which his sound was maturing into something more urbanely soulful, though "Fishin' After Me" (aka "Catfish Blues") sounds like a Howlin' Wolf track with a typically smooth B.B. King vocal dubbed onto it. There are a lot of good tracks here that even those with relatively large B.B. King collections might not be too intimate with, and even the more generic ones virtually always maintain a high level of professionalism and passion. A major bonus is the 76-page booklet, with detailed essays on King's early career, the Modern label, King's early road tours, an interview with early King producer Sam Phillips, and a thorough B.B. King/Modern discography. *—Richie Unterberger*

Classic Masters / Jan. 29, 2002 / Capitol ♦♦♦♦♦
BB King's edition of *Classic Masters* concentrates on his RPM recordings from the first half of the '50s, adding two cuts from his stint at Kent in the early '60s. At 12 tracks, this isn't particularly extensive, nor is the track selection very imagination, but it nevertheless is very strong all the same, containing such staples as "Three O'Clock Blues," "You Upset Me Baby," "Every Day I Have the Blues," "Sweet Little Angel" and "Peace of Mind," all in clean remastered sound. While there are some collections from the '90s that present this material in a more comprehensive form, few American collections are as sharp and concise concerning his early material as this, making this a good choice for those on a budget or those looking for a streamlined introduction to BB's early years. *—Stephen Thomas Erlewine*

The Modern Recordings, 1950–1951 / Apr. 23, 2002 / Ace ♦♦♦
Be aware straightaway that this is a release for the very serious B.B. King fan, certainly not the general one, and perhaps not even one who wants a good number of albums by the guitarist in the house. This two-CD, 33-track retrospective of his earliest recordings for Modern is more for the scholar and completist. It includes not only his singles from the era (among them "3 O'Clock Blues"), but also alternate takes and outtakes, some of which have been released on other reissues over the years, eight of which are issued here for the first time. The biggest strike against it, for the casual listener, is that it's sequenced so that the multiple versions of the same song are bunched together, so that you'll often hear the same tune twice or three times in a row. For the intense blues and King admirer, though, that could be considered an advantage, allowing close inspection of his early studio work. It's certainly a valid approach for those who want microscopic close-ups of an artist's oeuvre, and Ace handles it well, with detailed liners that in part go into collector arcania like the numbering of Modern releases and grid charts of early session details. Getting back to the music—which is, nominally, why listeners bother with such stuff in the first place—it's good early electric blues/R&B crossover, though King had a way to go before reaching his peak. There are some burning sides here, like "Fine Lookin' Woman," "Shake It Up and Go," "B.B. Boogie," and "That Ain't the Way to Do It," as well as more routine, smoother blends. As for the alternates, they really don't differ enormously from the takes initially approved for release, though careful listeners will detect some variations in tempo and phrasing. There are some harsh surface noises carried over from the sources used for mastering on occasional cuts, but generally the fidelity is as good as can be. *—Richie Unterberger*

Bobby King

b. Nov. 4, 1943, South Carolina, **d.** Chicago, IL
Vocals / R&B, Soul
The duo of soul singers Bobby King and Terry Evans first teamed on the Los Angeles club circuit of the early '70s; both also enjoyed prolific session careers, and in 1974 lent their distinctive harmonies to Ry Cooder's *Paradise and Lunch*, the first in a series of collaborations with the acclaimed guitarist. Sessions with artists including Boz Scaggs, John Fogerty, and Bob Dylan followed and in 1988, King and Evans cut their first headlining effort, *Live and Let Live!*; *Rhythm, Blues, Soul & Grooves* followed two years later. *—Jason Ankeny*

● **Live and Let Live!** / 1988 / Rounder ♦♦♦♦♦
While much contemporary R&B and soul offers more production than quality, the duo of Bobby King and Terry Evans demonstrated on this 1988 set that they could bring '60s passion to a '80s recording session. The duo's shared leads, rousing singing and inspiring qualities turned such numbers as "Seeing is Believing," "Saturday Night," and the title track into exciting, smashing treatments. Although their version of "Dark End of the Street" may run a bit long at seven minutes plus, they don't do anything to ruin that number's legacy of memorable renditions. *—Ron Wynn*

Rhythm, Blues, Soul & Grooves / 1990 / Rounder ♦♦♦
The duo of Bobby King and Terry Evans followed their well-received 1988 duet session with a solid second outing, this time taking over the production chores as well as performing. The ten tracks included anguished love tunes, uptempo dance cuts, and moving ballads, with the accent on their own material as they split writing duties and penned nine of the cuts. With Evans' huge, resonant bass voice often booming and soaring, King's striking falsetto tenor contrasted it with vigor. Sadly, this sound had little chance for getting any exposure at urban contemporary radio, but those who love great singing should savor it. *—Ron Wynn*

Chris Thomas King (Chris Thomas)

b. Oct. 14, 1964, Baton Rouge, LA
Vocals, Guitar, Producer, Arranger / Modern Electric Blues, Modern Acoustic Blues, Hip-Hop, Blues-Rock, Soul
Initially known for his audacious fusion of blues and hip-hop, Chris Thomas King reached a whole new audience with the Coen Brothers film *O Brother, Where Art Thou?*, not only appearing on the award-winning soundtrack but playing a prominent supporting character as well. Despite the much-celebrated, down-to-earth rootsiness of *O Brother*'s music, King had previously been a determined progressive, hoping to reinvigorate the blues as a living African American art with a more contemporary approach and adamantly refusing to treat it as a museum piece whose "authentic" forms needed careful preservation. King eventually modified that approach to a certain degree, attempting to create a more explicit link between blues tradition and the general musical present.

Chris Thomas King (born Chris Thomas on October 14, 1964, Baton Rouge, LA) is the son of respected Louisiana bluesman and club owner Tabby Thomas and thus was surrounded by music from a very young age. He began playing trumpet in sixth grade and learned guitar shortly thereafter, soaking up as much as he could by hanging out at his father's club. Even so, the young Thomas was still affected more by rock (especially Jimi Hendrix), soul, and early rap music; he didn't really settle on the blues until his late teenage years when he accompanied his father on a tour of Europe and found the audiences much larger and more enthusiastic than he'd ever experienced at home. Upon his return to the States, Thomas (as he was still known) recorded a demo tape that landed him a deal with Arhoolie Records. He played all the instruments on his debut album, *The Beginning*, which appeared in 1986. Thomas supported the record with tour dates in Europe and Texas, and afterwards he relocated to Austin, where he spent the next four years expanding his musical horizons and honing a more contemporary sound.

During that period, Thomas caught on with the Hightone label, for whom he debuted in 1990 with the critically acclaimed *Cry of the Prophets*. Afterward, Thomas proposed a follow-up project fusing blues guitar with hip-hop beats, rapped lyrics, and DJ scratching. However, parent company Warner—which distributed Thomas through its Sire imprint—declined to release the material, having just been burned by the controversy over Ice-T's rap-metal band Body Count. Meanwhile, Hightone wanted Thomas to continue in a more traditional vein and had him re-enter the studio to work on another record; after cutting some material, Thomas abandoned the project due to lack of interest. Over his objections, Hightone eventually released those tracks as *Simple* in 1993 and despite the unfinished nature of the material, Thomas again received good reviews.

Thomas took his rap-influenced material to Sony, which wasn't sure what to make of it and declined to release it. Frustrated, Thomas moved to London in hopes of finding a more receptive record company; when that didn't happen, he traveled to Copenhagen in 1991 and met a couple of Danish musicians who extensively worked on the project with him. Eventually, British producer John Porter (who worked on Buddy Guy's acclaimed comeback *Damn Right, I've Got the Blues*) heard the tapes and helped set up a deal with RCA/BMG subsidiary Private Music. Thomas returned to the States after a three-year absence, completing the record in Los Angeles. *21st Century Blues…From da 'Hood* was finally released in early 1995 and was predictably met with considerable controversy;

some reviews were highly complimentary, but many festival and club promoters refused to book Thomas at all. He did find success on the concert circuit in Europe and upon his return to the U.S., he began billing himself as Chris Thomas King.

King debuted his new moniker on a self-titled album for Scotti Brothers in 1997, delving deeply into the funky, gritty sound of Memphis soul. The follow-up, *Red Mud*, appeared on Black Top in 1998 and found King returning to the roots of the blues with mostly acoustic, folk-blues-flavored material. By this time, King was regularly playing around Louisiana, often backed by a bassist and DJ. This setup provided the foundation for his next record, 2000's *Me, My Guitar and the Blues*, which combined most of King's previous interests—electric and acoustic blues, funky soul, New Orleans R&B, and hip-hop—into a more integrated whole.

In late 2000 came King's breakthrough. For their Deep South retelling of Homer's *Odyssey O Brother, Where Art Thou?*, the Coen Brothers cast King in the prominent supporting role of real-life Delta bluesman Tommy Johnson, who claimed to have sold his soul to the devil at the crossroads even before a similar legend spread about Robert Johnson. King also recorded an eerie version of Skip James' "Hard Time Killing Floor Blues" for the soundtrack, which became an unexpected multi-platinum sensation over the course of 2001 and won a surprise Grammy for Album of the Year. King also appeared on *Down from the Mountain: O Brother, Where Art Thou?*, a live album featuring many of the *O Brother* artists. All the exposure helped raise King's profile considerably and although he didn't completely stick to a more traditional approach for his next project, it was clear that his recent immersion in early blues was having an impact on his music. Released in 2001, *The Legend of Tommy Johnson Act 1: Genesis 1900's-1990's* was the beginning of a sweeping historical overview in which King hoped to cover as many different blues styles as possible for the benefit of his new-found audience. —*Steve Huey*

The Beginning / May 1986 / Arhoolie ✦✦✦✦

King's debut album was released in 1986 when he was still billed as Chris Thomas. It's quality modern blues that sounds cognizant of contemporary trends without being forced. Largely written by King, the songs are reasonably satisfying electric blues that admit some influences from modern blues-rock players, particularly Jimi Hendrix, as well as a bit of funk and rock in the rhythm. At the same time he ground out some down-home gutbucket boogie blues that would be at home in a Southern roadhouse, like "Soon This Morning" and "Take Yo Time," and Chuck Berry-type songwriting with "Mary Jane." The rhythm section can sound a little flat and under-recorded, but at least underproduction serves this sort of music better than overproduction does. The record was reissued on CD, billed to Chris Thomas King under the new title *It's a Cold Ass World—The Beginning*, on Arhoolie in 2001, with new historical liner notes. —*Richie Unterberger*

● **Cry of the Prophets** / 1990 / Sire ✦✦✦✦✦

Thomas whipped up a fine debut, full of gospel urgency ("Dance to the Music") and hard rock bite. —*John Floyd*

Simple / 1993 / Hightone ✦✦✦

Chris Thomas King / Aug. 29, 1997 / Scotti Bros. ✦✦✦

Red Mud / Sep. 15, 1998 / Black Top ✦✦✦

The son of Louisiana bluesman Tabby Thomas makes an acoustic with real bite to it on this outing. Daddy Tabby joins him for a remake of "Hoodoo Party" and "Bus Station Blues," but for the rest of the album, it's mostly Chris working out on various resonator dobro guitars and harmonica. Besides nine of his originals on this 14-tracker, he boldly takes on a pair of Robert Johnson tunes ("Rambling on My Mind" and "Come on in My Kitchen") and Son House's "Death Letter Blues" in the midst of contemporary offerings like the urban "Alive" and the poppish "Wanna Die With a Smile on My Face." There's just as much of a folk vibe to this session as there is a blues one, and the blend works well for Thomas' all-encompassing style. —*Cub Koda*

Me, My Guitar and the Blues / May 16, 2000 / Blind Pig ✦✦✦

On *Me, My Guitar and the Blues*, Chris Thomas King ventures out into eclectic musical territories. King sings and plays all the instruments on his first disc for the Blind Pig label. Recorded in New Orleans, this release retains some of those Crescent City funk influences while "Superstitious Blues," "Gambling Woman," and Robert Johnsons' "Stones in My Passway" are gritty acoustic delta blues. However, the majority of this release finds King reaching for a broader more popular approach that will likely turn off blues purists. "Born Under a Bad Sign" injects hip-hop into this blues classic, "You Are My Heaven" is comparable to the soul sound of Robert Cray, while the synth laden "Stay Just As You Are" would be the obvious pick for crossover radio play specifically going after a more mainstream pop audience. —*Al Campbell*

It's a Cold Ass World: The Beginning / Aug. 14, 2001 / Arhoolie ✦✦✦✦

This is a CD reissue of King's debut album, released in 1986 as simply *The Beginning*, when he was still billed as Chris Thomas. It's quality modern blues that sounds cognizant of contemporary trends without being forced. Largely written by King, the songs are reasonably satisfying electric blues that admit some influences from modern blues-rock players, particularly Jimi Hendrix, as well as a bit of funk and rock in the rhythm. At the same time, he grounds out some down-home gutbucket boogie blues that would be at home in a Southern roadhouse, like "Soon This Morning" and "Take Yo Time," and Chuck Berry-type songwriting with "Mary Jane." The rhythm section can sound a little flat and under-recorded, but at least underproduction serves this sort of music better than overproduction does. —*Richie Unterberger*

The Legend of Tommy Johnson, Act 1: Genesis 1900's–1990's / Oct. 9, 2001 / Valley ✦✦✦

Inspired by his screen debut as Delta bluesman Tommy Johnson in *O Brother, Where Art Thou?*, Chris Thomas King takes a whirlwind tour through 80 years of blues history on this unique concept album. He begins a cappella, with a song written on the movie set but not used in the soundtrack, proceeds through several pared-down period covers (Tommy Johnson's "Canned Heat Blues" and Blind Willie Johnson's "Trouble Will Soon Be Over") and originals written and played in a similar mode, and then plugs into the postwar Chicago era and kicks up a full band for the closing tracks. Before his casting in *O Brother*, King specialized in a rap-blues hybrid rather than in prewar country blues, and there are many other revivalists who play in this style with more authority then he shows on, for instance, the slide piece "Flooded in the Delta" (inspired by the movie's climactic flood scene). He fares much better on "Watermelon Man," an entertaining yarn built over a Bukka White-style one-chord groove, and on electric rockers like "Do Fries Go With That Shake?" and "Red Shoes." Throughout the album, King proves himself a soulful singer and versatile multi-instrumentalist, more interested in melody than in the soloing calisthenics heard in so much contemporary blues. —*Jeffrey Pepper Rodgers*

Earl King (Earl Johnson)

b. Feb. 7, 1934, New Orleans, LA

Vocals, Guitar / New Orleans R&B, New Orleans Blues, R&B

Unilaterally respected around his Crescent City homebase as both a performer and a songwriter, guitarist Earl King has been a prime New Orleans R&B force for more than four decades—and he shows no signs of slowing down.

Born Earl Johnson, the youngster considered the platters of Texas guitarists T-Bone Walker and Clarence "Gatemouth" Brown almost as fascinating as the live performances of local luminaries Smiley Lewis and Tuts Washington. King met his major influence and mentor, Guitar Slim, at the Club Tiajuana, one of King's favorite haunts (along with the Dew Drop, of course), the two becoming fast friends. Still billed as Earl Johnson, the guitarist debuted on wax in 1953 on Savoy with "Have You Gone Crazy" (with pal Huey "Piano" Smith making the first of many memorable supporting appearances on his platters).

Johnson became Earl King upon signing with Specialty the next year (label head Art Rupe intended to name him King Earl, but the typesetter reversed the names!). "A Mother's Love," Earl's first Specialty offering, was an especially accurate Guitar Slim homage produced by Johnny Vincent, who would soon launch his own label, Ace Records, with King one of his principal artists. King's first Ace single, the seminal two-chord south Louisiana blues "Those Lonely, Lonely Nights," proved a national R&B hit (despite a soundalike cover by Johnny "Guitar" Watson). Smith's rolling piano undoubtedly helped make the track a hit.

King remained with Ace through the rest of the decade, waxing an unbroken string of great New Orleans R&B sides with the unparalleled house band at Cosimo's studio. But he moved over to Imperial to work with producer Dave Bartholomew in 1960, cutting the classic "Come On" (also known as "Let The Good Times Roll") and 1961's humorous "Trick Bag" and managing a second chart item in 1962 with "Always a First Time." King wrote standout tunes for Fats Domino, Professor Longhair, and Lee Dorsey during the '60s.

Although a potential 1963 pact with Motown was scuttled at the last instant, King admirably rode out the rough spots during the late '60s and '70s. Since signing with Black Top, his performing career has been rejuvenated; 1990's *Sexual Telepathy* and *Hard River to Cross* three years later were both superlative albums. —*Bill Dahl*

Street Parade / 1981 / Charly ✦✦✦

Funky 1972 tracks that should have fueled a comeback for the Crescent City mainstay but didn't (a lease deal with Atlantic fell through). Allen Toussaint was apparently in charge of the sessions, which produced updates of "Mama and Papa" and "A Mother's Love" as well as a bevy of fresh nuggets (notably the fanciful "Medieval Days," later revived by King on Black Top), and the two-part title item. —*Bill Dahl*

Trick Bag / 1983 / EMI ✦✦✦✦✦

Here's an extremely hard-to-find French LP that remains the only place where King's wonderful early-'60s Imperial Records catalog was gathered in one place (a handful grace EMI's two-disc Dave Bartholomew set; he produced them). Earl changed his sound to fit the funkier Crescent City sound of the time on the two-part "Come On," and the humorous "Trick Bag" and "Mama and Papa," and a passionate "You're More to Me than Gold." —*Bill Dahl*

Glazed / 1988 / Black Top ✦✦✦

The coupling of funky Crescent City guitarist Earl King with the East Coast-based Roomful of Blues wasn't exactly made in heaven (the band excels at jump blues; at second-line beats, they're fairly clueless), but it did mark the beginning of King's heartwarming comeback as a recording artist. King's songwriting skills were certainly in fine shape: "It All Went Down the Drain," "Iron Cupid," and "Love Rent" were typically well-observed originals. —*Bill Dahl*

Sexual Telepathy / 1990 / Black Top ✦✦✦✦✦

Reunited with a more sympathetic New Orleans rhythm section (bassist George Porter Jr., and drummer Kenny Blevins) and a funkier horn section, King excelled handsomely on this uncommonly strong outing. As we've come to expect from him, he brought a sheaf of new originals to the sessions, from a saucy "Sexual Telepathy" to a heartwarming "Happy Little Nobody's Waggy Tail Dog." Remakes of his "Always a First Time" and "A Weary Silent Night" were welcome inclusions (especially since we can't easily lay our hands on the originals!). —*Bill Dahl*

Hard River to Cross / 1993 / Black Top ✦✦✦✦✦

The quirky guitarist with the endlessly wavy hair made it two winners in a row with this one. Snooks Eaglin guests on guitar for three tracks (including the hilarious "Big Foot" and a joyous "No City Like New Orleans," while Porter and drummer Herman Ernest III lay down scintillating grooves behind King's ringing axe and wise vocals. —*Bill Dahl*

Those Lonely, Lonely Nights / 1993 / P-Vine ✦✦✦✦✦
Why must New Orleans guitarist Earl King's '50s material be so difficult to locate on CD? This expensive Japanese import does the job handily, if you can find it—all eight of King's Guitar Slim-influenced Specialty sides (including "A Mother's Love" and its rocking flip, "I'm Your Best Bet Baby") and 17 of his terrific efforts for Ace, notably the hit title track, the equally moving "My Love Is Strong," and the jumping "Everybody's Carried Away," "Little Girl," and "I'll Take You Back Home." *—Bill Dahl*

New Orleans Street Talkin' / Mar. 18, 1997 / Black Top ✦✦✦

● **Earl's Pearls** / May 5, 1998 / West Side ✦✦✦✦✦
This top-notch collection brings together 25 tracks from King's 1955-1960 tenure with Ace Records in Jackson, Mississippi. Classic '50s New Orleans music doesn't come much finer than this, and Earl's contributions to the genre are plentiful on this disc, starting with his big hit, the original "Those Lonely, Lonely Nights." A real treat is hearing Huey "Piano" Smith soloing with complete abandon on tracks like "Nobody Cares," "Little Girl," "I'll Take You Back Home" and "Baby You Can Get Your Gun." Earl's guitar playing is equally fine and his Guitar Slim-derived style is well to the fore on "My Love Is Strong" and "I'm Packing Up." Although King's discography encompasses many labels and sessions, this is a great place to start absorbing this Crescent City genius. *—Cub Koda*

King of New Orleans / Apr. 17, 2001 / Varese Sarabande ✦✦✦

Eddie King (Edward Lewis Davis Milton)

b. Apr. 1, 1938, Alabama
Guitar / Electric Chicago Blues, Modern Electric Blues
For a blues musician to change his surname to King to get attention may seem a bit on the ludicrous side, kind of like an actor or actress changing his or her name to Barrymore. But this is just what guitarist Eddie Milton did when he transformed himself into Eddie King, becoming in the process the least well-known of the blues guitar King dynasty; despite his tireless efforts as a sideman with many blues greats, as well as a career as a bandleader during the later part of his life. He was born Edward Lewis Davis Milton in Alabama, eventually gravitating toward the busy blues scene of Chicago's South and West Side in the late '50s and '60s. His earliest musical influences were his parents, including a father who apparently played country blues guitar in the John Lee Hooker style. His mother was also a blues and gospel singer.

As a youngster, he was too young to get into blues clubs, but learned guitar by smushing his face up against the windows, watching the guitarists in action, memorizing the patterns and runs he saw on the fret board, then finally sprinting home to see if he could remember any of it. Milton's musical peers were players from the second generation of Windy City bluesmen who came up on the sounds of artists such as Muddy Waters, Howlin' Wolf, and Little Walter. Some of these associates, such as Luther Allison, Magic Sam, Junior Wells, and Freddie King, became fairly big on the international blues scene; while others, such as the wonderful Eddie C. Campbell or Milton, became better known as typical examples of high-quality blues artists that were basically laboring in obscurity.

A fairly short fellow, he learned to get around the taller and sometimes somewhat better guitar competition by learning to be a showman. "Little Eddie" was actually his first stage name, obviously leading to confusion with the rhythm & blues artist Little Milton. When he began picking in a style heavily influenced by B.B. King, Little Eddie King became first a nickname only used by friends, but evolved into a stage name as well. Another diminutive bluesman, Little Mac Simmons, gave him his first big break, although the reason for the hiring might have had more to do with not wanting to have any taller sidemen on-stage than his musical ability. Eddie King's first recordings were with bassist and songwriter Willie Dixon, leading to a second guitar position on several Sonny Boy Williamson sides in 1960.

The next major period in his career was as lead guitarist with Koko Taylor. He was with this fiery blues singer for more than two decades. In 1969, he and bassist Bob Stroger formed Eddie King & the Kingsmen, a group that worked together off and on for the next 15 years, at first overlapping with the Taylor stint. From the early '80s onward, he has been based out of Peoria, IL. Into his sixties, he still was playing with the energy of a young man. His first solo record finally came out while others his age were busy concentrating on collecting their senior citizen's benefits, the well-received but obscure *Another Cow's Dead* on a small label co-owned by a belly dancer. This album won a W.C. Handy Award for best comeback album of the year.

Besides his exciting guitar work, King is also known as a superior soul shouter, again in a style modeled after the singing of B.B. King. He still presents a mixed bag from blues history, ranging from modern urban blues to the type of country blues he grew up with. He has also ventured into the Southern soul genre, and will mix up the material of a given gig based on what the audience is responding best to. Young players such as bassist Jamie Jenkins, drummer Kevin Gray, and Doug Daniels doubling on sax and keyboards have been regular members of his combos. As a bandleader, King demonstrated that he may be a late bloomer as a songwriter, but that in blues it is never too late to come up with good material, including the hilarious tune "Kitty Kat." The Swamp Bees is the name of his own group since the '90s, and this outfit has swarmed onto stages at blues venues nationally and internationally. *—Eugene Chadbourne*

● **Another Cow's Dead** / Apr. 8, 1997 / Roesch ✦✦✦✦
King's recorded output is slight bordering on criminal, so these 12 tracks from the West Side Chicago bluesman are a welcome addition to his scant discography indeed. King sports a strong, gospel-tinged voice and a nasty, thick-toned guitar style that never grates, and both are well served here. Featuring the Blues Brothers-plus horn section of Birch "Slide" Johnson, Alan Rubin, and "Blue" Lou Marini, abetted by Ronnie Cuber on baritone saxophone, the originals veer between soul and straight blues with "Kitty Kat," "Walk Right on In," "How Long Are You Going to Be Gone," "Pocketful of Blues, "Never Loved a Woman," and the set closer "Hey Mr. Bluesman." The covers mine the same genre turf with Luther Ingram's "If Lovin' Is Wrong," Albert King's "Angel of Mercy," Eddy Giles' "Losin' Boy," and Elmore James' "Yonders Wall" being notable highlights. This album just makes you want to hear more from this highly overlooked artist. *—Cub Koda*

Freddie King

b. Sep. 3, 1934, Gilmer, TX, **d.** Dec. 28, 1976, Dallas, TX
Vocals, Leader, Guitar (Electric), Guitar / R&B, Electric Texas Blues, Modern Electric Blues
Guitarist Freddie King rode to fame in the early '60s with a spate of catchy instrumentals which became instant bandstand fodder for fellow bluesmen and white rock bands alike. Employing a more down-home (thumb and finger picks) approach to the B.B. King single-string style of playing, King enjoyed success on a variety of different record labels. Furthermore, he was one of the first bluesmen to employ a racially integrated group on-stage behind him. Influenced by Eddie Taylor, Jimmy Rogers, and Robert Jr. Lockwood, King went on to influence the likes of Eric Clapton, Mick Taylor, Stevie Ray Vaughan, and Lonnie Mack, among many others.

Freddie King (who was originally billed as "Freddy" early in his career) was born and raised in Gilmer, TX, where he learned how to play guitar as a child; his mother and uncle taught him the instrument. Initially, King played rural acoustic blues, in the vein of Lightnin' Hopkins. By the time he was a teenager, he had grown to love the rough, electrified sounds of Chicago blues. In 1950, when he was 16 years old, his family moved to Chicago, where he began frequenting local blues clubs, listening to musicians like Muddy Waters, Jimmy Rogers, Robert Jr. Lockwood, Little Walter, and Eddie Taylor. Soon, the young guitarist formed his own band, the Every Hour Blues Boys, and was performing himself.

In the mid-'50s, King began playing on sessions for Parrott and Chess Records, as well as playing with Earlee Payton's Blues Cats and the Little Sonny Cooper Band. Freddie King didn't cut his own record until 1957, when he recorded "Country Boy" for the small independent label El-Bee. The single failed to gain much attention.

Three years later, King signed with Federal Records, a subsidiary of King Records, and recorded his first single for the label, "You've Got to Love Her With a Feeling," in August of 1960. The single appeared the following month and became a minor hit, scraping the bottom of the pop charts in early 1961. "You've Got to Love Her With Feeling" was followed by "Hide Away," the song that would become Freddie King's signature tune and most influential recording. "Hide Away" was adapted by King and Magic Sam from a Hound Dog Taylor instrumental and named after one of the most popular bars in Chicago. The single was released as the B-side of "I Love the Woman" (his singles featured a vocal A-side and an instrumental B-side) in the fall of 1961 and it became a major hit, reaching number five on the R&B charts and number 29 on the pop charts. Throughout the '60s, "Hide Away" was one of the necessary songs blues and rock & roll bar bands across America and England had to play during their gigs.

King's first album, *Freddy King Sings*, appeared in 1961, and it was followed later that year by *Let's Hide Away and Dance Away With Freddy King: Strictly Instrumental.* Throughout 1961, he turned out a series of instrumentals—including "San-Ho-Zay," "The Stumble," and "I'm Tore Down"—which became blues classics; everyone from Magic Sam and Stevie Ray Vaughan to Dave Edmunds and Peter Green covered King's material. "Lonesome Whistle Blues," "San-Ho-Zay," and "I'm Tore Down" all became Top Ten R&B hits that year.

Freddie King continued to record for King Records until 1968, with a second instrumental album (*Freddy King Gives You a Bonanza of Instrumentals*) appearing in 1965, although none of his singles became hits. Nevertheless, his influence was heard throughout blues and rock guitarists throughout the '60s—Eric Clapton made "Hide Away" his showcase number in 1965. King signed with Atlantic/Cotillion in late 1968, releasing *Freddie King Is a Blues Masters* the following year and *My Feeling for the Blues* in 1970; both collections were produced by King Curtis. After their release, Freddie King and Atlantic/Cotillion parted ways.

King landed a new record contract with Leon Russell's Shelter Records early in 1970. King recorded three albums for Shelter in the early '70s, all of which sold well. In addition to respectable sales, his concerts were also quite popular with both blues and rock audiences. In 1974, he signed a contract with RSO Records—which was also Eric Clapton's record label—and he released *Burglar*, which was produced and recorded with Clapton. Following the release of *Burglar*, King toured America, Europe, and Australia. In 1975, he released his second RSO album, *Larger Than Life.*

Throughout 1976, Freddie King toured America, even though his health was beginning to decline. On December 29, 1976, King died of heart failure. Although his passing was premature—he was only 42 years old—Freddie King's influence could still be heard in blues and rock guitarists decades after his death. *—Stephen Thomas Erlewine & Cub Koda*

Let's Hide Away and Dance Away With Freddy King / 1961 / King ✦✦✦✦✦
Powerful blues-guitarist Freddie King appears in strong '70s concert footage from an outdoor festival sponsored by Leon Russell. King's tight band backs him with solid contemporary grooves, and Freddie's in typically fine form. *—Bill Dahl*

Bossa Nova & Blues / 1962 / King ✦✦✦

Boy Girl Boy / 1962 / King ✦✦✦

Freddie King Goes Surfin' / 1963 / King ✦✦

A Bonanza of Instrumentals / 1963 / ✦✦✦✦

Vocals & Instrumentals: 24 Great Songs / 1966 / King ✦

Freddie King Is a Blues Master / 1969 / Atlantic ✦✦✦
This solid set emphasizes King's vocals. *—Bill Dahl*

Hide Away / 1969 / Starday ✦✦✦✦

My Feeling for the Blues / 1970 / Atlantic ✦✦✦
Another vocal heavy set. *—Bill Dahl*

Texas Cannonball / 1972 / Shelter ♦♦♦
Similar to his first Shelter outing (*Getting Ready*), but with more of a rock feel. That's due as much to the material as the production. Besides covering tunes by Jimmy Rogers, Howlin' Wolf, and Elmore James, King tackles compositions by Leon Russell and, more unexpectedly, Bill Withers, Isaac Hayes-David Porter, and John Fogerty (whose "Lodi" is reworked into "Lowdown in Lodi"). King's own pen remained virtually in retirement, as he wrote only one of the album's tracks. Reissued in its entirety on *King of the Blues*. *—Richie Unterberger*

Woman Across the River / 1973 / Shelter ♦♦♦
King's last Shelter album was his most elaborately produced, with occasional string arrangements and female backups vocals, although these didn't really detract from the net result. Boasting perhaps heavier rock elements than his other Shelter efforts, it was characteristically divided between blues standards (by the likes of Willie Dixon and Elmore James), Leon Russell tunes, and more R&B/soul-inclined material by the likes of Ray Charles and Percy Mayfield. It's been reissued, along with his other Shelter albums, on the *King of the Blues* anthology. *—Richie Unterberger*

Burglar / 1974 / BGO ♦♦♦♦
Produced in part by Mike Vernon, who worked on *The Legendary Christine Perfect Album*, this is an entertaining and concise package of ten songs performed by the late Freddie King and a slew of guests. Opening with Gonzalez Chandler's "Pack It Up," featuring the Gonzalez Horn Section, the youthful legend was only 40 years of age when he cut this career LP two years before his death. Though no songs went up the charts like his Top Five hit in 1961, "Hide Away," *Burglar* is one of those gems that journeymen can put together in their sleep. Tom Dowd produced "Sugar Sweet" at Criteria Studios in Miami, FL, featuring Jamie Oldaker on drums, Carl Radle on bass, and guitarists Eric Clapton and George Terry, which, of course, makes this album highly collectable in the Clapton circles. The sound doesn't deviate much from the rest of the disc's Mike Vernon production work; it is pure Freddy King, like on the final track, E. King's "Come On (Let the Good Times Roll)," where his guitar bursts through the horns and party atmosphere, creating a fusion of the pure blues found on "Sugar Sweet" and the rock that fans of Grand Funk grooved to when he opened for that group and was immortalized in their 1973 number one hit "We're an American Band" a year after this record's release. Sylistically, Freddie King is from the same school as Buddy Guy, two men instrumental in bringing this art form to a mass audience. King stretches those sounds with great fervor on the Hayes/Porter number "I Had a Dream," containing the strength Mark Farner said the blues artist displayed in concert, which could snap a guitar neck. The voice of Freddie King is what drives J.J. Cale's "I Got the Same Old Blues," the horns and the guitar battling between verses and uniting to ooze under the guitarist's vocal expression. Rhythm guitarist Bob Tench, producer Mike Vernon, bassist DeLisle Harper, drummer Steve Ferrone, and pianist Roy Davies all co-wrote "Texas Flyer" with Freddie King, a prime example of the modern blues this artist was developing. With Brian Auger and Pete Wingfield contributing to the title track, Jerry Ragovoy's "She's a Burglar," this project stands as a solid representation of an important musician which is as enjoyable as it is historic. *—Joe Viglione*

Just Pickin' / 1989 / Modern Blues ♦♦♦♦
Both of Freddy's all-instrumental albums for the King label (*Let's Hide Away and Dance Away With Freddy King* and *Freddy King Gives You a Bonanza of Instrumentals*) on one compact disc. "Hide Away," "The Stumble" and "San-Ho-Zay" are the numbers that made King's rep and influenced guitarists on both sides of the Atlantic. *—Cub Koda*

Freddy King Sings / 1989 / Modern Blues ♦♦♦♦♦
Great stuff from this influential Texas Bluesman—the haunting "Lonesome Whistle Blues," "I'm Tore Down," and other classics. From the B.B. King school, but with his own searing style of singing and playing, it's a must for fans of modern blues. *—George Bedard*

★ **Hide Away: The Best of Freddy King** / 1993 / Rhino ♦♦♦♦♦
Although not always placed in the upper echelon of blues performers alongside the other Kings (B.B. and Albert), Freddie King was a dynamo. He was both a powerhouse, imaginative guitarist and a glorious, soulful vocalist who could belt out come-ons, shout with gusto or wail in anguish. His instrumentals were also catchy, usually simply structured but vigorous and vividly articulated. This tremendous 20-cut sampler includes familiar hits like "Going Down" and the title cut, plus the shattering "Have You Ever Loved a Woman" and the poignant "Lonesome Whistle Blues." The tracks are exquisitely remastered and intelligently sequenced, and the notes are informative and thorough without being academic or fawning. *—Ron Wynn*

King of the Blues / 1995 / EMI/Shelter ♦♦♦
Double-CD compilation that includes all three of the albums King recorded for Leon Russell's Shelter label in the early '70s, as well as some other cuts (half a dozen of which were previously unissued) recorded around the same period. King's vocal and guitar-playing skills remained intact when he joined Shelter, but these recordings aren't among his best. That's partially because he was playing with rock-oriented sidemen, and partially because the material—divided between covers of blues standards, contemporary rock and soul items, and songs written by Leon Russell—wasn't especially exciting or sympathetic. Most crucial was the near-total absence of material from the pen of King himself. Although this set isn't bad, when you want to turn to classic King, you'll go elsewhere, particularly to the sides he recorded for the King label in the '60s. *—Richie Unterberger*

Getting Ready / 1996 / Shelter ♦♦♦
The first of King's three albums for Leon Russell's Shelter label set the tone for his work for the company: competent electric blues with a prominent rock/soul influence. King sings and plays well, but neither the sidemen nor the material challenge him to scale significant heights. Part of the problem is that Freddie himself wrote none of the songs, which are divided between Chicago blues standards and material supplied by Leon Russell and Don Nix. The entire album is included on the compilation *King of the Blues*. *—Richie Unterberger*

Live at the Electric Ballroom, 1974 / Feb. 20, 1996 / Black Top ♦♦♦
An Atlanta concert that wasn't issued for two decades. Archival releases of this sort tend to be for collectors only, but this is a cut above the standard. The sound is very good, the band is pretty tight, and King solos with fire and sings with conviction, sticking mostly to covers of warhorses like "Dust My Broom," "Key to the Highway," and "Sweet Home Chicago." It's a better deal, in fact, than his studio albums for Shelter in the early '70s, boasting a far more suitable, no-frills small combo approach. As a neat bonus, it also contains two solo acoustic performances recorded at a Dallas radio station in the '70s. *—Richie Unterberger*

The Best of the Shelter Years / Jun. 20, 2000 / The Right Stuff ♦♦♦♦
King's Shelter years were covered in toto on the 1995 double-CD *King of the Blues*, which had everything from all three of his Shelter albums and then some. Although all of the 18 songs on this single-disc anthology were on *King of the Blues*, this is a more manageable survey of the same era. Not an era, it should be said, that was King's best, with more ordinary material and less canny production than was used on his best earlier work. It does, however, have some of the better cuts from his '70s recordings, such as "Going Down," "Lowdown in Lodi," the string-drenched Leon Russell tune "Help Me Through the Day," the brassy instrumental "Guitar Boogie," and covers of chestnuts like "Reconsider Baby," "I'd Rather Be Blind," and "Please Send Me Someone to Love." *—Richie Unterberger*

☆ **Ultimate Collection** / Apr. 10, 2001 / Hip-O ♦♦♦♦♦
Hip-O's *Ultimate Collection* is one of the first truly comprehensive overviews of Freddie King's career, starting with his seminal recordings for Federal and running all the way to his final recordings for RSO in the mid-'70s. This is a mixed blessing. On one hand, it's nice to have a disc that tells the whole story, but the shifting production values and performance aesthetics make for slightly uneven listening. Throughout it all, though, King's playing shines and it's clear that even if his material and approach wavered toward the '70s, there was plenty to enjoy within his musicianship. Nevertheless, this is a place to go when you want to dig a little deeper, when you want a map of his entire career; if you want to delve in, head toward Rhino's collection of his Federal/King sides. *—Stephen Thomas Erlewine*

☆ **The Very Best of Freddy King, Vol. 1** / Jan. 22, 2002 / Collectables ♦♦♦♦♦
The phrase "very best of" in an album title usually indicates a highly selective collection of an artist's career highlights. By that standard, in one sense Collectables Records' *The Very Best of Freddy King, Vol. 1* should be called something else; a more accurate description of the contents would be "The Complete Freddy King on Federal Records, Vol. 1." That's because this is the first of three discs that present every recording King made for the King Records subsidiary Federal in chronological order. This disc traces King's Federal stint from his first recording session on August 26, 1960, to the following July. But in another sense, *The Very Best of Freddy King* is an apt title. King enjoyed all of his singles chart success during 1961, scoring six entries on the R&B charts and five on the pop charts, and all of those tracks are included here, from "You've Got to Love Her With a Feeling" to "Christmas Tears." King's biggest hit was the instrumental "Hide Away," which hit the pop Top 40 and the R&B Top Five and gained even more recognition when it was remade by John Mayall and Eric Clapton on the Bluesbreakers album. Perhaps King's best-known song was the B-side of "You've Got to Love Her With a Feeling," "Have You Ever Loved a Woman," which Clapton remade on the celebrated Derek & the Dominos album *Layla*, and of course King's version is included here. Indeed, it is difficult at this juncture to listen to almost any King recording and not be reminded of his chief disciple, Clapton. But that only means this collection is an essential addition to the basic library of blues fans. *—William Ruhlmann*

The Very Best of Freddy King, Vol. 2 / Jan. 22, 2002 / Collectables ♦♦♦♦
The phrase "very best of" in an album title usually indicates a highly selective collection of an artist's career highlights. By that standard, Collectables Records' *The Very Best of Freddy King, Vol. 2* should be called something else; a more accurate description of the contents would be "The Complete Freddy King on Federal Records, Vol. 2." That's because this is the second of three discs that present every recording King made for the King Records subsidiary Federal in chronological order. It picks up at the end of a July 25, 1961, session and continues through November 29, 1962. King enjoyed considerable chart success throughout 1961, but the hits stopped coming after that. This album finds him trying different approaches to meet the marketplace. "Sittin' on the Boondock," cut January 10, 1962, betrays the influence of Lee Dorsey's fall 1961 hit "Ya Ya"; there are four duets with Federal labelmate Lula Reed and even one song, "Your Love Keeps A-Working on Me," sung by Reed alone; and there are numbers with titles that use the words bossa nova and twist (and even one called "The Bossa Nova Watusi Twist") in an attempt to cash in on fads. It was all unavailing and, happily, on his November 1962 sessions King finally returned to more of a straight blues approach. Blues fans will respond most strongly to the final seven tracks on the album, which display his undiminished authority as a blues guitarist. While not nearly as impressive a set as the first volume in the series, this one still has enough good blues playing to make it worth adding to one's blues collection. *—William Ruhlmann*

The Very Best of Freddy King, Vol. 3 / Jan. 22, 2002 / Collectables ♦♦♦
This is the third and final volume compiling all of the material Freddie King recorded for the King/Federal label. It picks up at a session on November 29, 1962, and continues until his last recordings for the imprint on September 14, 1966. A full two years separated

the final two dates, but his style remained similar even though a young, completely unidentifiable Lonnie Mack was added on second guitar for his last Federal studio recordings. While there are a handful of cheesy tunes aimed at the teen market ("Surf Monkey" and "Monkey Donkey" reflect an odd simian theme, with the latter describing a pseudo dance not far removed from the twist), King basically sticks to the tough Texas blues and R&B that was his forte. By this time, he had thankfully abandoned the schlocky bossa nova and twist music that marred *Vol. 2* of this three-disc history. On even the least successful tracks, such as the surf instrumental "Fish Fare," King's guitar still stings, providing relief from the by the numbers backing and song structure. None of these 27 tracks nibbled at the singles charts or are even historically influential, yet their obscurity makes them a gold mine for King fans who want to dig deeper into his catalog. There are also some diamonds in the rough here, like the stabbing slow blues of "You've Got Me Licked," a powerful song in the "Have You Ever Loved a Woman" style with King providing a cutting-edge solo. The remastered sound is excellent, providing transparency to King's voice and especially guitar that adds clarity to the bluesman's already legendary skills. Nimble remote fingers will certainly help the experience, but this is a most welcome compilation, although obviously not the place for newcomers to start their Freddie King collections. *—Hal Horowitz*

Little Jimmy King (Manuel Gales)

b. Dec. 4, 1968, Memphis, TN

Vocals, Guitar / Modern Electric Blues, Memphis Blues

Memphis-based left-handed guitar player Little Jimmy King is certainly one of the most exciting of the new crop of blues players to emerge on the scene in the '90s. King was born December 4, 1968, as Manuel Gales but renamed himself for his two favorite guitar heroes, Jimi Hendrix and Albert King. He got started as a rock & roller, but by the mid-'80s had switched to blues. By 1988, he had left the Memphis blues scene to go on the road with his hero as part of Albert King's band. The late Albert King called Little Jimmy his grandson, and the late Stevie Ray Vaughan also had high praise for the young guitarist. In a moment King will never forget, Vaughan told him: "Play on, brother, you've got it. Don't stop playing for nobody."

King's self-titled debut was released in 1991 on the Rounder Bullseye Blues label, and he followed it up in 1994 with *Something Inside of Me*, on which he's accompanied by former Double Trouble bassist Tommy Shannon and drummer Chris "Whipper" Layton. King can also be heard playing guitar on Ann Peebles' *Full Time Love* and Otis Clay's *I'll Treat You Right* and *On My Way Home*. King's 1995 record with his two guitar playing brothers, Eric Gales and Eugene Gales, *Left Hand Brand* was released by the House of Blues label in 1995. While the brothers often play gigs together, so far it is the only album they have made. In 1997 King released his third record for Bullseye Blues, the Willie Mitchell-produced *Soldier for the Blues*.

Little Jimmy King's live shows, as documented on 2001's *Live at Monterey*, like his three highly praised studio recordings for Bullseye Blues, are full of fire and fury, passionate guitar playing within the context of his band, the Memphis Soul Survivors, great vocals and clever songs. When you realize how young this guy is, you know why he's being called "the future of blues guitar." King is taking the idiom to a whole new generation of younger fans and he's also a key link in the music's required, ongoing evolution. *—Richard Skelly*

- **Little Jimmy King & the Memphis Soul Survivors** / 1991 / Bullseye Blues ♦♦♦♦♦

Hailing from the Jimi Hendrix and Stevie Ray Vaughan school of blues-rock, Little Jimmy King turns in a promising eponymous debut. Though he leans a little too heavily toward rock & roll for some tastes—at his rootsiest, he sounds like Albert King—there's no denying his skill. King runs through a number of rollicking uptempo tracks, shuffles, R&B grinders, smoldering slow blues and even funk in the form of a cover of Sly Stone's "Sex Machine." Though his songwriting isn't quite up to par, his conviction carries him through the weakest moments and he shows signs of developing into a more distinctive songwriter. On the whole, it's an exciting, promising debut. *—Thom Owens*

Something Inside of Me / Mar. 30, 1994 / Bullseye Blues ♦♦♦

Little Jimmy King's second Bullseye/Rounder session matches the slashing guitarist with the rhythm section that once backed Stevie Ray Vaughan. King soars on these 11 cuts; while he lacks Vaughan's speed and is more a straight blues technician, he plays with more imagination and drive than on his debut. He contributes six originals and does a competent job of reworking material by Elmore James, Albert King, and even Phil Collins. While there's nothing here startling or surprising, King effectively teams with Chris Layton and Tommy Shannon, and producer/organist Ron Levy crafts an entertaining program of contemporary blues-rock with vintage sensibilities and overtones. *—Ron Wynn*

Soldier for the Blues / Jun. 24, 1997 / Bullseye Blues ♦♦♦

Little Jimmy King's third album finds him in the well-placed hands of Memphis producing and arranging legend Willie Mitchell. With Mitchell's publishing branch supplying six of the 12 selections here, there's a much more pronounced soul/blues feeling to this album than his two previous efforts, spelled out in a most contemporary manner on the confessional opening track, "Living In the Danger Zone" and "We'll Be Together Again." As always, Little Jimmy tips his hat to his mentor, the late Albert King with every note he hits on his Flying V, squeezing strings over several frets to get those classic Albert microtonal bends on tracks like "I Don't Need Nobody That Don't Need Me," "Drawers" and the title track. This is a thoroughly contemporary blues album that could—and should—expand King's audience beyond the usual blues circles. *—Cub Koda*

Live at Monterey / Feb. 26, 2002 / Bullseye Blues & Jazz ♦♦♦

Saunders King

b. Mar. 13, 1909, Staple, LA, **d.** Aug. 31, 2000, Oakland, CA

Vocals / Jump Blues, West Coast Blues

Pioneering R&B guitarist Saunders King had his first hit in 1942 with "S.K. Blues." King was a preacher's son who sang gospel in his father's church in Oakland. He learned piano, banjo and ukulele. In 1938 he began playing guitar and wound up singing with the Southern Harmony Four for an NBC radio station in San Francisco. He soon developed his passion for blues and "S.K. Blues" was an enormous hit. It also features one of the earliest examples of electric blues guitar, the style for which T-Bone Walker would soon be famous. King recorded for the Aladdin, Modern, and Rhythm labels. He may have made a greater impact in the burgeoning West Coast blues scene of the '40s but was saddled with numerous personal problems including the suicide of his wife in 1942, a serious wound from a .45-caliber pistol fired by his landlord in 1946, and his serving time at San Quentin prison for heroin possession. King retired from music in 1961 and dedicated time to the church. In 1979, he briefly came out of retirement to play on his son-in-law Carlos Santana's *Oneness* album. By 1999 he had suffered a stroke that partially paralyzed him. He passed away on August 31, 2000, at his Oakland home. He was 91. *—Al Campbell*

- **First King of the Blues** / 1988 / Ace ♦♦♦

Cool Blues, Jumps & Shuffles / Nov. 15, 2002 / Ace ♦♦♦♦

Shirley King

b. Oct. 26, 1949, West Memphis, AR

Vocals / Modern Electric Chicago Blues

The daughter of the legendary B.B. King, vocalist Shirley King carried on the family tradition to become a favorite among Chicago's North Side blues club denizens. Born October 26, 1949, in West Memphis, AR, she pursued a career as an exotic dancer before turning to the blues in 1991; a year later she and harpist Chicago Beau recorded her debut LP, *Jump Through My Keyhole*, a showcase for her husky wail. *—Jason Ankeny*

Jump Through My Keyhole / 1992 / GBW ♦♦♦

- **Daughter of the Blues** / 1999 / Diva ♦♦♦

The Kinsey Report

f. 1984, Gary, IN

Group / Modern Electric Chicago Blues, Modern Electric Blues

This family band consists of Donald Kinsey (vocal, guitar), Ralph "Woody" Kinsey (drums), Kenneth Kinsey (bass), and Ronald Kinsey (guitar). Solidly based in the blues as a result of lifelong training in the Big Daddy Kinsey household, the Kinsey scions are also versed in a broad range of music. The older brothers Donald and Ralph had an early blues-rock trio (White Lightnin') in the mid-'70s, long before they regrouped as the Kinsey Report in 1984 and began to launch new excursions into rock. Donald also recorded and toured with Albert King and with Bob Marley, and the influence of those giants (as well as that of Big Daddy Kinsey, naturally) shows through in the music of the Kinsey Report. The band expertly covers all the bases from Chicago blues through reggae, rock, funk, and soul, and their recordings are also distinguished by the songwriting talents and self-contained production approach of the Kinseys. *—Jim O'Neal*

- **Edge of the City** / 1987 / Alligator ♦♦♦♦

The Kinsey Report's debut album, *Edge of the City*, crackles with excitement, illustrating that it is possible to unite electric Chicago blues with rock and funk. There's a kinetic energy to the group's interaction that carries the group over occasionally undistinguished songwriting. Instead of sounding forced, the fusions are organic and unpredictable, resulting in some truly compelling music. The Kinsey Report never quite captured that thrilling balance of power ever again, but it's fortunate that they got the mix right at least once. *—Thom Owens*

Midnight Drive / 1989 / Alligator ♦♦♦

With *Midnight Drive*, the Kinsey Report attempts to expand the sonic palette of blues by adding elements of funk and hard rock. Although there are some interesting moments—primarily in the skillful solos—the music often falls flat and the songwriting isn't distinctive. The band's attempts at diversity are admirable, but ultimately unsuccessful. *—Thom Owens*

Powerhouse / 1991 / Pointblank ♦♦♦

This hard-rock album is spiced (lightly) with blues. *—Niles J. Frantz*

Crossing Bridges / May 4, 1993 / Capitol ♦♦

Crossing Bridges is a disappointing set of rock meanderings. *—Bill Dahl*

Smoke and Steel / Sep. 15, 1998 / Alligator ♦♦♦

With a strong, rock-drenched approach to their brand of blues, the Kinsey Report comes roaring back with their third full length album for the Alligator imprint. The band has matured and, if nothing else, acquits themselves in a thoroughly professional manner like the old-school gospel/blues/R&B veterans they truly are. While the whole thing pulsates and rocks with an almost bludgeoning intensity at times, Donald's blistering guitar is equal parts roadhouse funk and rock volume blues infused with lots of Johnny Winter and Jimi Hendrix with the Kinsey family twist put to it. Brothers Kenny and Ralph hold the bass-drums groove down tight, tight, tight, while guest guitars, keyboards and Lester Davenport on harmonica show up along the way to spice things up. Highlights include the minor-key reggae groove of "This Old City," and the funk flavors on "When the Church Burned Down" and "Can't See the Hook," the soul ballad "Loved Ones," the low-down mean country romp of John Fogerty's "Rattlesnake Highway" and "Down In the Dungeon," and the slow blues workout on "Code of the Streets." Strong, strong songwriting (Billy Gibbons of ZZ Top co-wrote one of the tunes here) and a varied approach throughout makes this a modern blues album that holds up to repeated listenings. —*Cub Koda*

Big Daddy Kinsey (Lester Kinsey)

b. Mar. 18, 1927, Pleasant Grove, MS, d. Apr. 3, 2001, Gary, IN
Vocals, Harmonica, Guitar / Chicago Blues, Modern Electric Blues, Electric Delta Blues
Long before Lester "Big Daddy" Kinsey and his clan hit the international blues circuit, he established himself as the modern-day blues patriarch of Gary, IN, and as the Steeltown's answer to Muddy Waters. A slide guitarist and harp blower with roots in both the Mississippi Delta and postwar Chicago styles, Kinsey worked with local bands only long enough for his sons to mature into top-flight musicians, and since 1984 (when Big Daddy recorded his debut album, *Bad Situation*) the family act has become one of the hottest attractions in contemporary blues. Big Daddy's material ranged from deep blues in the Muddy Waters vein to hard-rocking blues with touches of funk and even reggae, courtesy of sons Donald and Ralph (who venture even further afield in their own outings as The Kinsey Report). In the early '90s Kinsey released one of the most successful albums of his career, *I Am the Blues* which featured contributions from Buddy Guy, James Cotton, Sugar Blue, and Pinetop Perkins. On April 3, 2001, he succombed to prostate cancer, dying at the age of 74. —*Jim O'Neal*

Bad Situation / 1985 / Rooster Blues ♦♦♦
Crisp, funky and modern, *Bad Situation* shows Big Daddy and the band in fine form. —*Bill Dahl*

● **Can't Let Go** / 1990 / Blind Pig ♦♦♦♦♦
When the Kinsey Report signed on to back their father for *Can't Let Go*, the group was at their peak, so it would have made commercial sense for the boys to move their direction. Fortunately, they went the other way, choosing to stick to Chicago blues. The Kinseys don't play it straight, however, they rock it hard, which energizes Big Daddy and makes *Can't Let Go* a thoroughly enjoyable collection of hard-rocking contemporary Chicago blues. —*Thom Owens*

I Am the Blues / Jan. 1993 / Verve ♦♦
On this disappointingly pompous set, Kinsey seems to want to occupy Muddy Waters' shoes, even recruiting his old band here; it didn't work! —*Bill Dahl*

Ramblin' Man / Dec. 12, 1995 / Polygram ♦♦♦

Eddie Kirkland

b. Aug. 16, 1928, Jamaica
Vocals, Harmonica, Guitar / Electric Blues, Modern Electric Blues, Soul-Blues
How many Jamaican-born bluesmen have recorded with John Lee Hooker and toured with Otis Redding? It's a safe bet there's only one: Eddie Kirkland, who's engaged in some astonishing onstage acrobatics over the decades (like standing on his head while playing guitar on TV's *Don Kirshner's Rock Concert*).

But you won't find any ersatz reggae grooves cluttering Kirkland's work. He was brought up around Dothan, AL, before heading north to Detroit in 1943. There he hooked up with Hooker five years later, recording with him for several firms as well as under his own name for RPM in 1952, King in 1953, and Fortune in 1959. Tru-Sound Records, a Prestige subsidiary, invited Kirkland to Englewood Cliffs, NJ, in 1961-1962 to wax his first album, *It's the Blues Man!* The polished R&B band of saxist King Curtis crashed head on into Kirkland's intense vocals, raucous guitar and harmonica throughout the exciting set.

Exiting the Motor City for Macon, GA, in 1962, Kirkland signed on with Otis Redding as a sideman and show opener not long thereafter. Redding introduced Kirkland to Stax/Volt co-owner Jim Stewart, who flipped over Eddie's primal dance workout "The Hawg." It was issued on Volt in 1963, billed to Eddie Kirk. By the dawn of the '70s, Kirkland was recording for Pete Lowry's Trix label; he also waxed several CDs for Deluge in the '90s. —*Bill Dahl*

It's the Blues Man! / 1961 / Tru-Sound ♦♦♦♦♦
Wildman guitarist/harpist Kirkland brought his notoriously rough-hewn attack to this vicious 1962 album for Tru-Sound, joined by a very accomplished combo led by saxman extarordinaire King Curtis and including guitarist Bill Doggett. As the crew honed in on common stylistic ground, the energy levels soared sky-high, Kirkland roaring "Man of Stone," "Train Done Gone," and "I Tried" with ferocious fervor. —*Bill Dahl*

Have Mercy / 1988 / Evidence ♦♦♦
Kirkland's roaring guitar and garbled, gospel-tinged vocals are pretty much submerged in the mix here, a hodge podge of standard blues readymades and hyperactive funk-blues workouts. —*Cub Koda*

● **Three Shades of the Blues** / 198 / Relic ♦♦♦♦♦
Kirkland's eight sides on this compilation are as hard-driving and intense as you could possibly ask for. It also includes four sides each from B.B. King-disciple Mr. Bo and the Ohio Untouchables, with dazzling guitar work from Robert Ward on the latter. —*Cub Koda*

All Around the World / 1992 / Deluge ♦♦
All Around the World is a comparatively lackluster set. —*AMG*

Some Like It Raw / Sep. 1993 / Deluge ♦♦♦
Recorded live at a blues bar in Vancouver, British Columbia, this finds Kirkland in typical latter day form, full of buzzy guitar, garbled vocals, and loads of intensity. Alternating between original material (most of it in a soul-funk vein) and blues classics (few of which bear much likeness to their original counterparts), Kirkland gets solid support from the young, white backing band here and the recording quality is quite good. —*Cub Koda*

The Devil and Other Blues Demons / Apr. 16, 1995 / Trix ♦♦♦
Eddie Kirkland has long straddled the fence between bluesy soul and soulful blues. He was at a low point when he recorded for Trix in 1973, but this session recharged him musically, if not sales-wise. It is great to have it available again; whether Kirkland is doing

silly numbers, offering taut blues licks or giving examples of his philosophy, he finds creative ways to utilize the standard 12-bar scheme. —*Ron Wynn*

Where You Get Your Sugar / Nov. 7, 1995 / Deluge ♦♦♦
Kirkland remains an amazingly raucous entertainer whose freeform sense of blues convention remains elusive to capture on records; perhaps he's best experienced live. This album's no exception—fiery at times, meandering and frustrating at others. To his credit, Kirkland's no moldy fig, mixing thoroughly contemporary rhythms and unusual chord changes into his rowdy musical stew. —*Bill Dahl*

Lonely Street / Nov. 18, 1997 / Telarc ♦♦♦
Jamaican-born bluesman Kirkland has always stretched the boundaries of his music and on this outing moves further into contemporary waters. Guest stars abound on this album, and Kirkland's idiosyncratic guitar work is answered and abetted by appearances from Tab Benoit, Sonny Landreth, Kenny Neal, Cub Koda, Christine Ohlman, and G.E. Smith, as well as driving work from drummer Jaimoe and organist Richard Bell. The material is all over the road, but particularly noteworthy as highlights are Kirkland's take on Elmore James' "Done Somebody Wrong," "Snake In the Grass," "Nightgirl," and the title track. —*AMG*

The Complete Trix Recordings / Oct. 26, 1999 / 32 Jazz ♦♦♦
This two-CD set contains *Front and Center* and *The Devil and Other Blues Demons* reissues. Both recordings date back to the early '70s. *Front and Center* finds Kirkland mining country blues. During Kirkland's Detroit tenure he worked and toured with John Lee Hooker. The Hooker influence is detectable on "When I First Started Hoboing" and, of course, "Eddie's Boogie Chillen." Except for a couple backing musicians on "Have You Seen That Lonesome Train," Kirkland presents a solo performance on guitar and vocals. Often playing slide guitar and finding extra space for a soulful vocal delivery, *Front and Center* is the dynamic Kirkland's most personal project. His energy potential comes through on *The Devil and Other Blues Demons*. Here Kirkland, backed by a full band, turns spirited on the proto-funk tracks. There is still the detectable Hooker influence. Vocally, one hears more of another former employer, Otis Redding. Together on *The Complete Trix Recordings*, these selections show the two sides of the "Energy Man": one side deeply rooted in the Delta traditions and another side burning hot with early R&B vitality. —*Tom Schulte*

Bob Kirkpatrick

b. Jan. 1, 1934, Haynesville, LA
Guitar, Vocals / Texas Blues, Modern Electric Blues
Dallas-based guitarist, singer, and songwriter Bob Kirkpatrick may not be a household name, but he's been quietly building an audience for the last 30 years in clubs around Texas, Mississippi and Louisiana. Although he hadn't recorded in 23 years prior to 1996's *Going Back to Texas*, Kirkpatrick has long been a regional star in the Texas triangle, but since he has always made family his first priority, his recording/blues career fell somewhere down the ladder.

Kirkpatrick, born in 1934 in Haynesville, TX, became interested in music at age six, starting out on piano and switching to guitar. Kirkpatrick worked with Ivory Joe Hunter while attending school at Grambling, doing some road dates, but it wasn't until he saw B.B. King in 1958 that he became a true convert to the blues. When Kirkpatrick's doctors recommended that he take some time off from school after an illness, Kirkpatrick went to Dallas and played in clubs while holding down several different day jobs over the years.

In 1968, he was offered the chance to go on the road as a substitute guitarist for Bobby "Blue" Bland's regular guitarist, but Kirkpatrick chose to stay home with his young children. Kirkpatrick's brother was involved with the Newport Folk Festival and was able to book him several times, beginning in 1970. In 1973, he recorded *Feeling The Blues* for Moses Asch's Folkways Records (now marketed through the Smithsonian Institution). Kirkpatrick stayed in Dallas, raising his children and playing at the Elks Lodge in south Dallas on weekends for 16 years. After retiring in 1986, Kirkpatrick was urged to get back on the bandstand at area blues clubs by a friend who owned a club. Since the mid-'80s, he has been writing new songs and playing regionally again. Collectors may want to look around vinyl shops for his Folkways album, but easier to find is his 1996 JSP album *Going Back To Texas*, which shows B.B. King's influence on his vocals and guitar playing. Four years later, Kirkpatrick released *Drive Across Texas.* —*Richard Skelly*

Feeling the Blues / 1973 / Smithsonian/Folkways ♦♦♦

● **Going Back to Texas** / May 7, 1996 / JSP ♦♦♦♦
Bob Kirkpatrick's comeback album *Going Back to Texas* is a charming record. Kirkpatrick has a classy, jazzy guitar style and he leads his band through a set of originals and covers, putting an attractive, swinging spin on the music. Even if a couple tracks fall flat, *Going Back to Texas* is an engaging album of swinging Texas blues. —*Thom Owens*

Drive Across Texas / Aug. 1, 2000 / Red Lightnin' ♦♦♦

Danny Kirwan

b. May 13, 1950
Vocals, Guitar / Blues-Rock
Guitarist/singer Danny Kirwan was a member of Fleetwood Mac, helping to bridge their early blues-rock phase to their eventual conventional pop/rock approach, from the late '60s through the early '70s (just prior to the arrival of Stevie Nicks and Lindsey Buckingham). Born Daniel David Kirwan in South London on May 13, 1950, Kirwan was spotted by Fleetwood Mac members Peter Green and Mick Fleetwood at the age of 18 fronting a local group called Boilerhouse. Green took the young guitarist under his wing, attempting to help Kirwan find other musicians to play with (that were up to his caliber), but when none where found, he was invited to join Green in Fleetwood Mac in August of 1968. Although Kirwan's presence helped inspire the band to issue such classic releases as 1969's *Then Play On*, 1970's *Kiln House*, 1971's *Future Games*, and 1972's *Bare Trees*,

his fellow bandmembers quickly saw the dark side of the young musician, who was alcoholic and prone to mood swings.

The situation began to put a strain on the group, and after one specific incident while on tour in 1972 (which Kirwan smashed his guitar prior to a show and refused to play onstage), the 22-year-old guitarist was handed his walking papers. Kirwan then embarked on a solo career, issuing such obscure releases as 1975's *Second Chapter* (which saw the guitarist joined by ex-Chicken Shack members Andy Sylvester and Paul Raymond), 1976's *Midnight in San Juan*, and 1979's *Hello There Big Boy!*, before the once promising musician seemingly fell off the face of the earth. Rumors persisted throughout the '90s that Kirwan was by this time homeless and down on his luck, which he in fact confirmed himself in an interview with a London newspaper in 1993. But by the dawn of the 21st century, it appeared as though Kirwan had put his life back on track somewhat, while a 15-track compilation of his solo work, *Ram Jam City*, was issued in May of 2000. — *Greg Prato*

● **Second Chapter** / 1975 / DJM ✦✦✦✦

The first solo album from Fleetwood Mac singer/songwriter Daniel David Kirwan has the future producer for Human League and Buzzcocks Martin Rushent utilizing those skills here, as well as engineering. The sound is crystal clear, and a feather in the cap for Rushent as well as Kirwan. It starts off with an uncharacteristic "Ram Jam City," which has more Lindsey Buckingham sounds than one would expect, especially since the two guitarists come from two different musical worlds. "Odds and Ends" is more lighthearted, the kind of music Paul McCartney toyed with on *The White Album's* "Rocky Raccoon." What *Second Chapter* immediately sets forth is the importance of Kirwan as a pop artist, and how, despite Fleetwood Mac's success after he left, his sounds could still have been beneficial to that supergroup. "Hot Summers Day" is a fine example of that, a beautiful song that could offset Buckingham's gritty ramblings. It would have made a nice counterpoint as Stevie Nicks complemented Christine McVie's tunes with her adventures, bringing an important change of pace to that popular band's overplayed hits. Arguably, the one flaw in the latter-day Fleetwood Mac is Buckingham's presence going unchecked. Play "Mary Jane" off this album next to Lindsey Buckingham's material all over the *Tusk* double set to get a good idea of what Fleetwood Mac lost when Danny Kirwan left. The jacket looks like a dusty old family-album style book holding Kirwan's *Second Chapter*. And the music reflects that old-world feel in titles like "Skip a Dee Doo" and "Falling in Love With You." Three of the best songs on this excellent outing are "Love Can Always Bring You Happiness," the title track, "Second Chapter," and a sleepy and beautiful number called "Silver Streams." (Gee, wonder if Stevie Nicks nicked the title for "Silver Spring"?) Kirwan's tune is haunting as well with its lilting "all you need is love to show you the way from here" chorus. As on a follow-up album, he tends to sound a little like the group America, the vocals with that same America tone and warmth. They very well could have covered "Silver Stream" or "Cascades," the album's final track. This material was crafted right in the middle of America's run of hits, and maybe they should have replaced Dan Peek with Dan D. Kirwan? The artist's three solo discs cut in the '70s make for a very pleasant and thought-provoking listening experience, and that this collection is so good only shows he kicked his departure from the big band off with a vengeance. — *Joe Viglione*

Midnight in San Juan / 1976 / DJM ✦✦✦

Hello There Big Boy! / 1979 / DJM ✦✦✦✦

This is not just a tremendous album by Danny Kirwan, this is an extraordinary set of recordings that makes one wonder "what if?" What if Fleetwood Mac had talents like Peter Green, Jeremy Spencer, Danny Kirwan, Dave Walker, and Bob Welch come back to the fold for different projects? This is light pop on a mission, and it is perfectly produced by, of all people, Clifford Davis (though one should consider Kirwan's excellent production work on *The Legendary Christine Perfect Album* and wonder if the manager wasn't just putting his name on Kirwan's creative ideas). There's no denying that each tune here, from "End Up Crying" (which sounds like the soft rock Fleetwood Mac) to the final track, "Summer Days and Summer Nights," is superior pop music — intricate guitar lines, a double-barrel keyboard approach by John Cook and Kevin Kitchen which is just lovely, and sterling vocals by Kirwan. "Only You" could be a reworking of the Moody Blues' "Story in Your Eyes," but "California" is totally original and unique, both songs dynamite performances of their respective styles. "California" is more accessible than some of the popular versions of Fleetwood Mac, and given Bob Welch's success with *French Kiss* two years before the release of *Hello There Big Boy!*, it is surprising this was not embraced by both Top 40 and FM radio. "Spaceman" continues the smooth '70s pop that "California" introduced the listener to, the guitars more eerie, harking back to the *Bare Trees* period of Fleetwood Mac seven years earlier (which had so much of Kirwan's identity all over it). There was life before Stevie Nicks and Lindsey Buckingham, and this cohesive work is proof of that; covering Randy Edelman's "You" is actually quite clever, the exiles of Mac having reputations more as singer/songwriters than as interpreters. This may be Danny Kirwan produced by Clifford Davis, the man who put the fake Fleetwood Mac on stage, but it is no fluke and it is no fake. *Hello There Big Boy!* is a great album from the singer/guitarist who, according to Mick Fleetwood's book *My Twenty Five Years in Fleetwood Mac*, "went beserk…smashed his head against the wall…(and)…was fired." Sounds like genius, and it is here on this recording for all to see — and hear. A truly great comeback that sadly got lost in the shuffle of life. — *Joe Viglione*

Danny Kirwan / 1981 / DJM ✦✦✦✦

On his follow-up to 1975's *Second Chapter*, his first solo disc after being such an important element of Fleetwood Mac, Danny Kirwan gives fans another taste of *Bare Trees* with the lovely song "Castaway," which ends the album, and the instrumental "Rolling Hills," which could be a sequel to the sublime "Sunny Side of Heaven," a treat both when Fleetwood Mac performed it live and when it appeared on *Bare Trees*. Kirwan's person-

ality shines on those tracks, and this album is chock-full of quality material — there isn't a bad track on it musically. Where followers of this artist might have a problem is that it seems to be a conscious effort to go off in the commercial direction taken by the folk band America, of all people. Both tracks which open side one and two, "I Can Tell" and "Misty River" respectively, would have perfectly fit in America's "Sister Golden Hair," "Don't Cross the River," and "Ventura Highway" set list. This is decidedly different music from the slick pop of 1979's *Hello There Big Boy!*, which retained only pianist John Cook from these sessions. That episode had him sounding more like his ex-Fleetwood Mac mate Bob Welch, no surprise since Welch actually charted in 1977 with his *Bare Trees* track "Sentimental Lady." "Life Machine" on this disc actually sounds like a Bob Welch track, and it is too bad the two artists didn't join forces at this point in time. The strange one here is a reggae version of "Let It Be," which, in its brashness, becomes a nice turning point for the disc, showing real personality. Too many artists cover the Beatles note for note while Kirwan gives the world ten new originals and a creative reworking of a classic hit by "the Fab Four." This album was titled *Danny Kirwan in North America*, while the British release took its name from the other instrumental track, a synthesized journey called "Midnight in San Juan." "Angel's Delight" and "Windy Autumn Day" sound like Fleetwood Mac meets the band America, a very saleable commodity if you think about it, the Beatles-style ending to "Windy Autumn Day" driving the point home. Dick James Records really should have gotten more solidly behind this artist — there's no doubt the talent for Top 40 success here was enormous. — *Joe Viglione*

Ram Jam City / May 16, 2000 / Mooncrest ✦✦✦

Cub Koda

b. Oct. 1, 1948, Detroit, MI, **d.** Jul. 1, 2000

AMG Contributor, Liner Notes, Vocals, Harmonica, Guitar / Detroit Rock, Retro-Rock, Rockabilly, Blues-Rock, Electric Chicago Blues, Rock & Roll

Best known as the leader of Brownsville Station and composer of their hit, "Smokin' in the Boys Room," Cub Koda proved that his roots went far deeper, both before the band's formation, during its days in the sun, and long after its demise. His high school band, the Del-Tinos, was dipping into blues and rockabilly as far back as 1963 — not only pre-Butterfield, but pre-Beatles. Similarly, he recorded legendary home tapes during his off-hours from Brownsville, before the rockabilly revival had uttered its first hiccup, and later teamed with Hound Dog Taylor's former rhythm section, the Houserockers, to play the blues in the '80s. Along the way he cranked out a monthly column ("The Vinyl Junkie") and recorded a series of albums that kept roots music of all kinds alive without ever treating it like a museum piece.

Originally a drummer at age five, Koda switched over to guitar when he formed his first band, the Del-Tinos, a teenage garage combo equally influenced by rock & roll, blues, and rockabilly. The group cut their first single — Roy Orbison's "Go Go Go" — in the fall of 1963, and released two more 45s independently before they disbanded in 1966. By this time, Koda had become so immersed in the blues, that the last Del-Tinos' single had the trio doing Muddy Waters' "I Got My Mojo Workin'" on one side and Robert Johnson's "Ramblin' on My Mind" on the other.

After a couple of bands in the late '60s that largely went unrecorded, Koda formed Brownsville Station in early 1969. After playing local Midwest gigs and releasing a handful of singles, the band released their first album in 1970. But it wasn't until "Smokin' in the Boys Room" that Brownsville had a genuine hit. Released as a single in the fall of 1973, "Smokin'" climbed all the way to number three, eventually selling over two million copies.

But Koda began to back away from the group's loud, overdriven rock sound — at least in private. He purchased a multi-track tape recorder and started producing one-man-band tapes, where he overdubbed all the instruments and vocals. For the next several years, Koda made home recordings of rockabilly, blues, R&B, country, jazz, and early rock & roll — the exact opposite of Brownsville's heavy rock stance; the rockabilly tapes were eventually released as *That's What I Like About the South*, in the early '80s, with other tracks showing up on compilations as late as 1993.

When Brownsville disbanded in 1979, Cub began writing a column called "The Vinyl Junkie" for *Goldmine* magazine, later published in *DISCoveries*. Through the column's success, Koda established himself as an expert record collector and critic — eventually, Cub would compile and write liner notes for a number of projects, including three volumes in Rhino's acclaimed *Blues Masters* series.

In 1980, Koda worked with Hound Dog Taylor's backing band, the Houserockers. Over the next 15 years, Koda, guitarist Brewer Phillips, and drummer Ted Harvey performed and recorded together, with their first album, *It's the Blues*, appearing in 1981 and the latest, *The Joint Was Rockin'*, being released in 1996.

Throughout the '80s and '90s, Koda continued to divide his time equally between touring, recording, and writing. 1993 saw the twin release of *Smokin' in the Boy's Room: The Best of Brownsville Station* on Rhino and *Welcome to My Job*, a retrospective of his non-Brownsville material on Blue Wave, followed a year later by *Abba Dabba Dabba: A Bananza of Hits* on Schoolkids' Records.

During the second half of the '90s, Koda increased his presence as a writer, in addition to staying musically active. In addition to editing the *All Music Guide to Blues*, he wrote and edited *Blues for Dummies*. He also continued writing liner notes, contributing work to retrospectives of the Trashmen, Jimmy Reed, J.B. Hutto, the Kingsmen, and the Miller Sisters, among others. He also supervised the 1996 release of *The Joint Was Rockin'*, a live album of Cub with the Houserockers in the early '80s, plus a 1998 Norton reissue of recordings he made with the Del-Tinos.

Cub wasn't just an archivist during this time. In 1997, he released *Box Lunch* on J-Bird Records, his first collection of new material since *Abba Dabba Dabba*. *Box Lunch* was a solo, all-acoustic album unlike anything he had recorded in the past. Koda returned to hard-driving, loud rock & roll with 2000's *Noise Monkeys*, an album he recorded live with a reunited Points in 1999. Released in the spring, *Noise Monkeys* was receiving strong reviews, including a positive notice by Robert Christgau in the *Village*

Voice, when tragedy struck. Koda had been sick for a while, but he was slowly recovering. In the spring, he was put on kidney dialysis, and he was recovering, but then he suddenly took sick during the evening of June 30, 2000. He died early in the morning on July 1, 2000, at the age of 51. Considering that he was sick, perhaps it shouldn't have been a surprise that he succumbed to his illness, but Cub kept working and rocking until the end—he was writing and recording music in the last week of his life. He never lost his love for music and he always shared that love anyway he could, whether it was as a musician, journalist, DJ, or friend. As he said, he was "somewhere between a cult figure and rock & roll legend" and to anyone who knew him, that was the gospel truth. *—Stephen Thomas Erlewine*

Cub Koda & the Points / 1980 / Fan Club ♦♦♦♦
Koda's first solo album after Brownsville Station. Highlights include "Jail Bait" and "Welcome to My Job." *—Stephen Thomas Erlewine*

It's the Blues / 1981 / Fan Club ♦♦♦
The addition of bass and special guests Left Hand Frank and Lefty Dizz only distract from the chemistry between Cub and the Houserockers (even more obvious on their belated live follow-up), but this is a strong session, with the ex-stadium boogie boy sounding totally at home with these blues veterans. His vocal duet with Brewer Phillips on J.B. Lenoir's "Talk to Your Daughter" is a joy, and thankfully not every note is perfectly in place—or in the case of Brewer's guitar, in tune. Added treats: Koda's big-toned harp on "Rockin' This Joint Tonight" and humorous dialog with Frank on "Dirty Duck Blues." *—Dan Forte*

Cub Digs Chuck / 1989 / Garageland ♦♦♦
Koda's tribute album to Chuck Berry, featuring blistering versions of "Johnny B. Goode," "Maybellene," and others. *—Stephen Thomas Erlewine*

Cub Digs Bo / 1991 / Garageland ♦♦♦♦
Koda's tribute album to Bo Diddley, including powerhouse renditions of "Mumblin' Guitar," "Roadrunner," and "Background to a Music." *—Stephen Thomas Erlewine*

Live at B.L.U.E.S. 1982 / 1991 / Wolf ♦♦♦♦♦
What's wrong with this picture? The sawed-off bespectacled singer/guitarist from Brownsville Station fronting the late Hound Dog Taylor's ex-rhythm section, the Houserockers—blasphemy, you say? Get a life. Koda smokes like he's: 1) out to dispel any doubts about his legitimacy, and 2) having the time of his life. Opening with Howlin' Wolf's "Highway 49" (a rather tall order), the Cubmaster grabs the Chicago crowd by its collective neck and shakes it into submission. His guitar trade-offs with Brewer Phillips (no bass in this band) are a delight, and by "You Can't Sit Down" drummer Ted Harvey is blowing his police whistle—signalling that things be rockin'! Eddie Clearwater sits in on one tune, and Koda tips his hat to the guitarist with a stellar rendition of Eddie's "Hillbilly Blues." This is worthy of wider release, not to mention an encore. *—Dan Forte*

● **Welcome to My Job: The Cub Koda Collection 1963–93** / 1993 / Blue Wave ♦♦♦♦♦
Covering everything from his pre-Brownsville Station days to two brand-new songs, *Welcome to My Job* is the definitive collection of Cub Koda's versatile solo career. *—Stephen Thomas Erlewine*

Abba Dabba Dabba: A Bananza of Hits / Jul. 19, 1994 / Schoolkids ♦♦♦♦♦
Cub Koda's first album for Schoolkids' Records is his wildest, funniest, and simply best album in years. *—Stephen Thomas Erlewine*

The Joint Was Rockin' / 1996 / Deluge ♦♦♦♦
The Joint Was Rockin' is a raw, rowdy and deliriously fun record capturing Cub Koda live with the Houserockers in the early '80s. The Houserockers bash away like they were supporting Hound Dog Taylor and Cub proves that he can play the blues with true passion and feeling. More than anything, however, *The Joint Was Rockin'* is a bracing jolt of energy and fun that's just as good as *Live at B.L.U.E.S. 1982*, his previous live set with the Houserockers. *—Stephen Thomas Erlewine*

Box Lunch / 1997 / J-Bird ♦♦♦♦
Cub Koda tried a lot of different things in his long career, but he never made anything close to *Box Lunch*. It's not just that the album consists of nothing but acoustic material; he had never been this open with his emotions. There are a few rockers—"Double Barrel Hell" is menacing and "Gimme Trash" is a tongue-in-cheek kitsch celebration—but the heart of the record is in the ballads, whether it's the nostalgic "We Were Crazy Back Then," the yearning "Runaway Heart," or the lovely "How Could Life Turn Out This Way," which evokes the spirit of Hank Williams. Cub was rarely this naked with his feelings and the results are frequently moving. And, to cap it all off, he throws out "Susan Hayward's Diary," a charming fingerpicked instrumental. Moments like this made you hope that it wouldn't be the last acoustic album Cub would make—*Box Lunch* is so good, you wish there were seconds. *—Stephen Thomas Erlewine*

Noise Monkeys / Mar. 2000 / J-Bird ♦♦♦♦♦
Arriving on the heels of the introspective, acoustic *Box Lunch*, *Noise Monkeys*—Cub Koda's reunion album with the Points, his first band after the demise of Brownsville Station—may come as a bit of a surprise. Make no mistake about it, the title of the record tells you what this album is all about: This is loud, dumb, fun, hard-driving rock & roll, the kind that sounds like it was cut by a bunch of noise monkeys. Some fans may have forgotten that Koda could rock hard when he wanted to, and that's what he did with the Points on *Noise Monkeys*. The bulk of the album was recorded live in the studio in one day in June 1999; the final two songs were recorded live in concert the following day. Not surprisingly, the album is a bracing, immediate, and above all, loud record, filled with guitars, guitars, and guitars. He hadn't rocked this hard or this intensely since the first Points album. But this record is a better one on many levels, due to the fact that the bandmembers had matured as musicians. They knock off these songs in one take and sound totally convincing and energetic. But don't think that this is sophisticated music—this is dumb rock & roll, and proudly so—and it's all the better for it. Koda and the Points pound away, sounding stronger and better at the turn of the millennium than they did at the turn of the '70s. Sure, some of the songs are silly, but that's the point. The end result is a satisfying hard rock album with humor and character—something like that doesn't come along every day. *—Stephen Thomas Erlewine*

Koerner, Ray & Glover

f. 1962, Minneapolis, MN

Group / Blues Revival, Acoustic Blues, Folk-Blues

In today's climate of a blues band seemingly on every corner with "the next Stevie Ray Vaughan" being touted every other minute, it's hard to imagine a time when being a white blues singer was considered kind of a novelty. But in those heady times of the early '60s and the folk and blues revival, that's *exactly* how it was. But into this milieu came three young men who knew it, understood it, and could play and sing it; their names were Koerner, Ray, and Glover. They were folkies, to be sure, but the three of them did a lot—both together and separately—to bring the blues to a white audience and in many ways, set certain things in place that have become standards of the Caucasian presentation of the music over the years.

The three of them were college students attending the University of Minnesota, immediately drawn together by their common interests in the music and by the close-knit folk community that existed back then. As was their wont, they all decided to append their names with colorful nicknames; there was "Spider" John Koerner, the Jesse Fuller and Big Joe Williams of the group, Dave "Snaker" Ray, a 12-string playing Leadbelly aficionado, and Tony "Little Sun" Glover on harmonica, holding up the Sonny Terry end of things. This simple little act of reinvention resonates up to the present day, with myriad white practitioners throwing their mundane appellations out the window to recast themselves as something along the lines of Juke Joint Slim and the Boogie Blues Blasters.

They worked in various configurations within the trio unit, often doing solo turns and duets, but seldom all three of them together. Their breakthrough album, *Blues, Rags & Hollers*, released in 1963, sent out a clarion call that this music was just as accessible to White listeners—and especially players—as singing and strumming several choruses of "Aunt Rhody." While recording two excellent follow-ups for Elektra, both Koerner and Ray released equally fine solo albums. Tony Glover, for his part, put together one of the very first instructional books on how to play blues harmonica (*Blues Harp*) around this time, and its excellence and conciseness still make it the how-to book of choice for all aspiring harmonica players. Both Koerner and Ray still maintain an active performing schedule and every so often, the three of them get back together for a one-off concert. *—Cub Koda*

● **Blues Rags & Hollers** / 1963 / Red House ♦♦♦♦♦
Red House's reissue of *Blues Rags & Hollers*, the first album from Koerner, Ray & Glover, follows through on the folk and country blues leanings of the blues revival. The result is a strong, catchy album that nevertheless sounds closer to folkies than the typical British blues record. *—Thom Owens*

Lots More Blues, Rags & Hollers / 1964 / Red House ♦♦♦♦
John Koerner, Dave Ray and Tony Glover, who emerged from the same University of Minneapolis music scene that produced Bob Dylan, were the best white folk-blues group of their day. This reissue of one of their influential mid-'60s albums—which sounds at times like a cross between the Kingston Trio and Sonny Boy Williamson—provides ample evidence of that. Koerner and Ray were first-rate guitarists, Glover could play harmonica like nobody's business and they all sang with style, enthusiasm, and a dash of humor. Plus, they had great material, some from blues giants like Leadbelly and Memphis Minnie, but much of it original. Three cheers to the folks who put together this reissue so well. The 21 remastered tracks include all of the original album, plus five songs from the same sessions that got bumped from the LP due to the format's space limitations. The liner notes feature all the original commentary from critic Paul Nelson and an extensive new essay by Tony Glover. *—Jeff Burger*

Return of Koerner, Ray & Glover / 1966 / Red House ♦♦♦♦
The last in a series of three reissues of classic, folk-blues albums from Koerner, Ray & Glover, this beautifully remastered 1965 collection is filled with the humor, rhythm, soulful vocals and top-notch material that made the outfit such a standout. Among the best of the 15 tracks: a reading of Leadbelly's "Titanic," about how boxer Jack Johnson narrowly avoided being on its doomed voyage; Koerner's irresistibly rhythmic "The Boys Was Shootin' It Out Last Night" and Glover's "Don't Let Your Right Hand Know What Your Left Hand Do," in which—to quote the liner notes—"Tony kicks the bass harp through some places you've never heard." If you like this kind of music, it's a safe bet that you'll love this album. *—Jeff Burger*

Good Old Koerner, Ray & Glover / 1972 / Mill City ♦♦♦

Al Kooper

b. Feb. 5, 1944, Brooklyn, NY

Vocals, Keyboards, Guitar, Organ / Folk-Rock, Psychedelic, Singer/Songwriter, Blues-Rock, Rock & Roll

Al Kooper, by rights, should be regarded as one of the giants of '60s rock, not far behind the likes of Bob Dylan and Paul Simon in importance. In addition to co-writing one classic mid-'60s pop/rock song, "This Diamond Ring" (though it was written as an R&B number), he was a very audible session man on some of the most important records of mid-decade, including Bob Dylan's "Like a Rolling Stone." Kooper also joined and led, and then lost two major groups, the Blues Project and Blood, Sweat & Tears. He played on two classic blues-rock albums in conjunction with his friend Mike Bloomfield. As a producer at Columbia, he signed the British Invasion act the Zombies just in time for them to complete the best LP in their entire history; still later, Kooper discovered Lynyrd

Skynyrd and produced their best work. Instead, in terms of public recognition, Kooper has been relegated to second-rank status, somewhere midway between John Mayall and Steve Winwood. Apart from the fact that he's made, and continues to make, great music, it's the public's loss that he's not better respected outside the ranks of his fellow musicians.

Kooper was born in Brooklyn, New York, in 1944, the son of Sam and Natalie Kooper. As a boy, he enjoyed singing along to the Bessie Smith records that his father played, and they provided his introduction to blues and, by extension, gospel, R&B, and soul, all of the sounds that would form the basis for his own music. Equally important, he revealed himself a natural musician—one day he sat down in front of a piano and started playing one of the then-current hits of the early '50s, with no prior training or experience. He learned on his own, and also took up the guitar. Kooper's main interest during the '50s lay in gospel music. When rock & roll broke, Kooper was drawn to the vocal side of the new music, forming a doo-wop outfit that sang on street corners in his neighborhood in the late '50s. He turned professional in 1959, joining the lineup of the Royal Teens ("Short Shorts," "Believe Me") as a guitarist. By the early '60s, he'd begun writing songs, and among his early efforts was "I Must Be Seeing Things," which was a hit for Gene Pitney.

Kooper's biggest hit as a songwriter came in late 1964, with a song that he co-authored with Bob Brass and Irwin Levine called "This Diamond Ring"—they'd written it with the Drifters in mind, but the legendary R&B group passed, and it ended up in the hands of Liberty Records producer Snuff Garrett. He made it the first song to be cut by a new group called Gary Lewis & the Playboys. The record entered the charts late in 1964 and spent the early weeks of 1965 in the number one spot. The recording, although not to Kooper's liking compared to what he'd visualized for the Drifters, started a string of almost unbelievably fortuitous events in his life and career. In those days, he was trying to make a big part of his living as a session guitarist, and when a friend, producer Tom Wilson, invited him to observe at a Bob Dylan recording session that spring, he brought his instrument along with him in the hope that something might happen. When they needed a second keyboard player for the organ on "Like a Rolling Stone," Kooper bluffed his way to the spot. Dylan loved the part that Kooper improvised and boosted it in the mix.

Kooper later played as part of the band that backed Dylan when he introduced electric music to the Newport Folk Festival in 1965, and was on the *Blonde on Blonde* album as well. That same year, Kooper was invited by Wilson to sit in on keyboards for an audition tape by a newly formed New York blues-rock outfit called the Blues Project, and was asked to join the group. He eventually became one of the lead singers, and three massively important and critically acclaimed albums coincided with his yearlong stay. By the time he'd exited the Blues Project, Kooper was ready to start a band with a jazz and R&B sound that he had in mind—one with a serious horn section—and the result was Blood, Sweat & Tears. Signed to Columbia Records in late 1967, they cut a debut album that was made up almost entirely of Al Kooper songs, and which set the music pages and their authors afire with enthusiasm—*The Child Is Father to the Man*, as their debut record was titled, was one of the most important and daring albums of the '60s, as essential as any long-player ever cut by the Beatles or the Rolling Stones.

Unfortunately, Blood, Sweat & Tears generated more press than sales—although that debut album did ride the low reaches of the charts for almost a year—and tensions within the group and pressure from the record company, which wanted a more commercial sound that would sell more records, led to Kooper's exit from the band. Now out of his second successful group in two years, Kooper returned to playing sessions and turned up on records by Jimi Hendrix, the Who, and the Rolling Stones ("You Can't Always Get What You Want"). He also got a job at Columbia Records—a runner-up prize for having been forced out of Blood, Sweat & Tears (which, by then, was making a fortune for the label with a retooled sound and lineup)—as a producer. He engineered a concert recording by Simon & Garfunkel that could have been their first official live album. More important was a pair of albums that Kooper cut with his longtime friend, guitarist Michael Bloomfield. Those records, *Super Session*, cut with Stephen Stills, and *The Live Adventures of Mike Bloomfield and Al Kooper*, were among Columbia's best-selling LPs of the period; they were the kind of albums that, coupled with *The Child Is Father to the Man*, helped put Columbia Records on the cutting edge of popular music.

Kooper's other major contribution during his tenure at Columbia was signing the Zombies, a British Invasion-era band that hadn't charted a single in two years, for one album. The group seemed to be on their last legs and were, in fact, about to break up, but Columbia got one classic album (*Odessey & Oracle*) and a monster hit single ("Time of the Season") from the deal. The least prominent of Kooper's projects during this era, ironically enough, was his solo album *I Stand Alone*, on which he cut new versions of songs he'd written or been associated with over the previous decade. He spread himself too thin in making the record, and the album failed to sell in serious numbers. A follow-up record, *Kooper Session*, was similarly ignored despite the presence of blues guitar prodigy Shuggie Otis, but Kooper remained one of the most successful names in rock music.

During the early '70s, Kooper had his own label, Sounds of the South, set up through MCA—his big discovery was Lynyrd Skynyrd. He produced their first three albums, whose sales eventually numbered in the millions. Kooper also produced records by the Tubes, B.B. King, Nils Lofgren, and Joe Ely, among many others, during the '70s, and he found time during that decade to write what remains the best book ever written about rock & roll from an insider's perspective, *Backstage Passes*. Kooper's recording activity slackened off in the '80s, although he performed with Dylan, Tom Petty, and Joe Walsh, and did some soundtrack work in television and films. During the '90s, after a more-than-20-year hiatus, he returned to recording his own sound with *Rekooperation*, an instrumental album released by the Music Masters label, a company much more closely associated with jazz and classical than rock.

Equally important were a handful of live gigs by principal members of the original Blood, Sweat & Tears, their first shows in 25 years. These performances led to a series of birthday shows at New York's Bottom Line in 1994, which yielded the double-CD concert recording *Soul of a Man*. Kooper covered most of his own music history with the key members of the original Blood, Sweat & Tears and the definitive Blues Project lineup (who had gotten back together every so often, beginning in the early '70s). Kooper pulled together a unified sound, built around soul, jazz, and gospel influences, despite the varied personnel involved, in his most accomplished solo project ever. Anyone counting the records on which Al Kooper has played a key role—as songwriter, singer, keyboardman, guitarist, or producer—would come up with tens of millions of albums and singles sold, and a lot of radio airtime. His career recalls that of Steve Winwood in some respects, though he's never had a solo hit. Even today, however, Kooper remains a formidable performing talent, and one of the most inspired and intelligent people in rock music. *—Bruce Eder*

I Stand Alone / 1969 / Columbia ✦✦✦

Al Kooper's first solo effort following his split from Blood, Sweat & Tears finds him mining the same vein of musical gold he had with that band, only this time he didn't have to worry about group democracy getting in the way of his creativity. Covering a wide and varied field of musical tastes, Kooper added various sound effects to the mix, with sometimes comical results. This didn't detract from the music, though, as Kooper went from covering "Blue Moon of Kentucky" to "One" (from Harry Nilsson) to Gamble & Huff's "Hey, Western Union Man," carefully injecting originals along the way. A fine testament from a creative eccentric. *—James Chrispell*

You Never Know Who Your Friends Are / 1969 / Columbia ✦✦

Live Adventures of Al Kooper & Mike Bloomfield / 1969 / Edsel ✦✦✦

One of the seminal live albums of the late '60s, *Live Adventures of Al Kooper & Mike Bloomfield* was a natural, organic offshoot of the hugely successful *Super Session* album from 1968, which contained performances by both of these groundbreaking musicians, as well as Stephen Stills. The idea of musical spontaneity both in live performance and in the recording studio had reached a certain apex in 1968, and spontaneous excursions by musicians such as Jimi Hendrix, Steve Winwood, and the Southern California musical covenant that eventually became Crosby, Stills, Nash & Young, as well as a host of others, were indeed a sign of the times. But it was the union of Bloomfield and Kooper that can truly claim an origination of the phenomenon, and this album takes it to another level entirely. Utilizing a fine and tight rhythm section of John Kahn and Skip Prokop, the two musicians duel and embrace each other on such cuts as the accurately named "Her Holy Modal Highness" and a great, revamped rock/soul re-working of Paul Simon's "Feelin' Groovy," which is buttressed by a guest studio vocal overdub by the author himself. The album's high point may be Bloomfield's rendering of Albert King's epic "Don't Throw Your Love on Me So Strong," which may indeed also be one of his finest career recordings. Like the *Super Session* album, history repeated itself, as Bloomfield's chronic insomnia caught up with him by the morning of the second night of the two-night gig, rendering him unavailable. Kooper enlisted the help of Steve Miller and a practically unknown Carlos Santana (himself a Bloomfield devotee) for several tracks, particularly a loose and free version of "Dear Mr. Fantasy," which sort of embodies the whole affair and era. Undoubtedly a necessity from the period, the record has been remastered for CD, and the results are truly glorious, and do this legendary album justice. *—Matthew Greenwald*

Easy Does It / 1970 / Columbia ✦✦✦

New York City (You're a Woman) / 1971 / Columbia ✦✦✦✦✦

This is the fourth solo album from rock and roll wunderkind Al Kooper. He congregates two very distinct bands—one in London and the other in Los Angeles—to accompany some of his most emotive compositions to date. This is ironic when considering the title track is a paean to the Big Apple. The U.K. aggregate consists of musicians from Hookfoot, including Herbie Flowers (bass), Caleb Quay (guitar), and Roger Pope (drums). The band were fresh from several collaborations with Elton John, most notably his third studio effort *Tumbleweed Connection*. The LA sessions included legends such as Carol Kaye (bass), Paul Humphries (drums) and Louis Shelton (guitar). Also to Kooper's credit is his own talents as a multi-instrumentalist—best exemplified on the title track, which is in essence performed by a trio since Kooper handles all the guitars and keyboards. His nimble piano work recalls the same contributions that he made to Blood, Sweat & Tears' rendering of Tim Buckley's "Morning Glory." (Incidentally, an alternate version of the track "New York City (You're a Woman)"—with significantly less mellotron in the mix—is available on the best-of compilation *Al's Big Deal/Unclaimed Freight*.) "John the Baptist (Holy John)" could easily be mistaken for a long-lost composition from the Band—right down to the Rick Danko-esque vocals. The upbeat number is similar to a pepped-up version of "Katie's Been Gone" or even "The Rumor." Although Kooper credits the Fab Four as his inspiration to "Going Quietly Mad," from the nasal-sounding lead electric guitar to the highly introspective lyrics, it has many of the characteristics of an early Joe Walsh composition such as "Turn to Stone." As he had done on the title track, Kooper tastefully incorporates a string section without coming off as pretentious or sonically overbearing. Another song not to be missed is the cover of Elton John's "Come Down in Time." This version blends both backing bands as Herbie Flowers reprises his timeless bass lines from the original, while Kooper and the LA all-stars provide the remainder of the instrumental. *—Lindsay Planer*

Naked Songs / 1973 / Columbia ✦✦✦✦

Much more soulful and blues-influenced than previous efforts, *Naked Songs* finds Al Kooper reflecting the influences he'd soaked up by working with the Atlanta Rhythm Section, who appear on the record, and Lynyrd Skynyrd. Kooper covers John Prine's "Sam Stone" to chilling effect, and his take on the blues "As the Years Go Passing By" is worth the price alone. *Naked Songs* finds Al Kooper baring his soul to his audience, and it works. *—James Chrispell*

Al's Big Deal (Unclaimed Freight) / 1975 / Columbia ✦✦✦✦

As an anthology, the humorously titled *Al's Big Deal/Unclaimed Freight* captures the stylistic essence of what has made Al Kooper such a vital addition to rock & roll. Although somewhat superseded in the digital domain by *Rare + Well Done: The Greatest & Most Obscure Recordings*, this title was available almost two decades prior to that 2001 two-CD set. This collection delves into Kooper's solo canon as well as his ensemble work with the *Child Is Father to the Man* version of Blood, Sweat & Tears. There is also a healthy sampling of his super sessions and collaborations with such luminaries as Michael Bloomfield, Stephen Stills, Shuggie Otis, and even Bob Dylan. The material is split into the self-explanatory subheadings of "The Songs" and "The Jams." The former incorporates shorter and more focused standout performances such as "I Can't Quit Her" and "I Love You More Than You'll Ever Know" from BS&T. There are highlights from Kooper's solo discs as well. These include "Brand New Day" and the haunting cover of John Prine's "Sam Stone," as well as the respective title tracks from the LPs *I Stand Alone* and *New York City (You're a Woman)*. Incidentally, the latter track is available here in a remixed form exclusive to this package. "The Jams" reveal the amazing instrumental prowess that Kooper brings to his collaborative efforts. As a musician, his ability to interact and improvise are no more evident than on "Albert's Shuffle" and "Season of the Witch" from the definitive *Super Session* album. However, at the center is Kooper's uncanny ability to support guitarists Stills and Bloomfield. In essence, he aurally corrals their sinuous and soulful fretwork with his tastefully pervasive organ leads. The 1989 CD pressing of *Al's Big Deal/Unclaimed Freight* omitted the tracks "Without Her," "My Days Are Numbered," and "So Much Love" and added "The Heart Is a Lonely Hunter"—which was concurrently not available on CD elsewhere. *—Lindsay Planer*

Act Like Nothing's Wrong / 1976 / One Way ♦♦♦

Kooper's sixth solo release opens daringly enough, with his own funky version of "This Diamond Ring," which he transforms completely from its Drifters-inspired origins. Most of the album is in a mid-'70s soul-funk vein, with Tower of Power turning up elsewhere and Kooper trying (with considerable success) to sound soulful on songs like "She Don't Ever Lose Her Groove" and "I Forgot to Be Your Lover." The playing throughout is excellent, with guitars by Kooper himself (who also plays sitar, Mellotron, organ, and synthesizer) as well as Little Beaver and Reggie Young, with Joe Walsh sitting in on one song, and horn arrangements by Kooper and veteran soundtrack composer Dominic Frontiere. The real centerpiece is the epic-length "Hollywood Vampire," which can't quite sustain its seven-minute length. The funkier numbers work, but some of the rest, like "In My Own Sweet Way," don't come off so well. This is two-thirds of a pretty fair album, and only lacks consistency. *—Bruce Eder*

Rekooperation / 1994 / Music Masters ♦♦♦♦

The best of all of Al Kooper's studio albums, *Rekooperation* is a mostly instrumental album, on which the artist (playing organ and piano, and occasional guitar) and a band including Jimmy Vivino, Harvey Brooks, and Fred Walcott, among others, roar and pound their way through a baker's dozen of R&B, rock & roll, and soul classics. Everything from chestnuts like "Soul Twist," "Honky Tonk," "Johnny B. Goode," "Clean Up Woman," and "Don't Be Cruel" to originals such as "Downtime" and "Alvino Johnson's Shuffle," without a notable gap in quality between them, are included—and the one vocal number, "I Wanna Little Girl," contains one of the finest singing performances that Kooper has ever turned in on record (but is also played so well, that it would work as an instrumental too). In many ways, this recording is a distant cousin to Blood, Sweat & Tears' *Child Is Father to the Man*, and was his first attempt at leading a band since that 1968 venture, which was sort of fitting since it led to *Soul of a Man*, Kooper's live-in-concert career retrospective album, the next time out. *—Bruce Eder*

Soul of a Man: Al Kooper Live / 1995 / Music Masters ♦♦♦♦

A gift from heaven is the only adequate way of describing this superb double-CD set, which comes in a slipcase with a neat little booklet. It is the definitive Al Kooper solo project, and a career reconsideration and retrospective, but it's also damn close to definitive as a document of the Blues Project and the original Blood, Sweat & Tears as well. At three February 1994 gigs at New York's Bottom Line, Kooper got together the original members of both bands (with BS&T billed as "Child Is Father to the Man") and his own Rekooperators, including John Simon and Harvey Brooks, with John Sebastian sitting in on harmonica, to perform new versions of 33 years' worth of repertory. The eerie thing is that it sounds like Kooper didn't skip a beat between the last shows of any of those bands and these gigs—his voice is better than ever, and the performance on "I Can't Quit Her" (a song he introduces by saying he hates playing it "except with these guys"—the original BS&T) and the rest of the '60s repertory has all of the energy one could wish for, and more precision than the group might have achieved in 1968 (and certainly better sound). There are some new arrangements on numbers like "My Days Are Numbered," which features a soaring trumpet duel between Randy Brecker and Lew Soloff, and some hot guitar by Jimmy Vivino—all of which only adds to the original. And "I'll Love You More than You'll Ever Know" features such an intense performance by Kooper, that by itself it's worth the price of the double CD. The Blues Project pick up where they left off in 1967, doing hard, crunchy renditions of Muddy Waters songs ("Two Trains Runnin'") and classic originals, including a glorious nine-minute "Flute Thing." The Rekooperators, led by Mike Bloomfield disciple Jimmy Vivino, do glowing performances of Bloomfield-Kooper repertory such as "Albert's Shuffle" and "Season of the Witch," and Kooper-related numbers like "You Can't Always Get What You Want" (part of a surging medley with "Season of the Witch"), and the Ronnie VanZant number "Made in the Shade" (featuring Kooper on blues mandolin). The Uptown Horns and backup soul singers Sheryl Marshall and Catherine Russell fill in the sound on various songs, on what must have been three extraordinary nights. For some reason, Steve Katz refused to allow his guitar to appear on the release, so his part has been wiped and replaced by Jimmy Vivino and other guest players on both the Blues Project and Child Is Father to the Man tracks, but that seems to be the only major sweetening done in the studio. The beautiful part of this set, beyond the superb performances and the excellent sound quality, is that the music has been treated with respect in the packaging—the heavily annotated booklet even lists each soloist on every number, in the manner of proper jazz releases. *—Bruce Eder*

● **Rare + Well Done: The Greatest & Most Obscure Recordings** / Sep. 18, 2001 / Columbia ♦♦♦♦

Using an uncommon format, this two-CD set is divided into a rarities disc and a kind of best-of disc. It features primarily solo material, but also throws in some cuts from his group projects with Blood, Sweat, & Tears, the Blues Project, and '60s collaborations/jam sessions with Mike Bloomfield and Stephen Stills. As either a rarities compilation or a best-of collection, this anthology has its shortcomings. Those who want the rare stuff may already have much of the best-of disc; the interest of those who want the best-of section might not extend to rarities; and either way, one will have to pay for two discs, which might be more material than desired. The rare component is quite erratic, and his material from after the early '70s on that disc is far inferior to the tracks from 1964-1972. Some goodies are unearthed, like his 1964 "Somethin' Goin' On" gospel/blues demo, his quirky 1965 solo single "New York's My Home (Razz-A-Ma-Tazz)" (aka "The Street Song"), a 1971 live version of "Baby Please Don't Go," and a 1970 cover of Bob Dylan's "Went to See the Gypsy," which Kooper had in mind as an arrangement for Dylan's own version. Yet these are outweighed by tracks of more later vintage that offset his intact knack for gospel/pop/blues/jazz-rock songwriting with inappropriately heartless modern keyboards, drums, and production. The well-done section avoids that problem by taking all but three of its selections from the 1966-1971 era, including such highlights as the Blues Project's "Flute Thing," Blood, Sweat, & Tears' "I Love You More Than You'll Ever Know," and the title cut of his *I Stand Alone* album. It also has some tracks that even those fairly familiar with Kooper might have overlooked, like 1969's "Bury My Body" (with Shuggie Otis on guitar). *—Jimmy James*

Alexis Korner

b. Apr. 19, 1928, Paris, France, **d.** Jan. 1, 1984, London, England

Vocals, Guitar / Blues Revival, British Blues, Blues-Rock, Electric Blues

Without Alexis Korner, there still might have been a British blues scene in the early '60s, but chances are that it would have been very different from the one that spawned the Rolling Stones, nurtured the early talents of Eric Clapton and made it possible for figures such as John Mayall to reach an audience. Born of mixed Turkish/Greek/Austrian descent, Alexis Korner spent the first decade of his life in France, Switzerland, and North Africa, and arrived in London in May of 1940, just in time for the German blitz, during which Korner discovered American blues. One of the most vivid memories of his teen years was listening to a record of bluesman Jimmy Yancey during a German air raid. "From then on," he recalled in an interview, "all I wanted to do was play the blues."

After the war, Korner started playing piano and then guitar, and in 1947 he tried playing electric blues, but didn't like the sound of the pick-ups that were then in use, and returned to acoustic playing. In 1949 he joined Chris Barber's Jazz Band and in 1952 he became part of the much larger Ken Colyer Jazz Group, which had merged with Barber's band. Among those that Korner crossed paths with during this era was Cyril Davies, a guitarist and harmonica player. The two found their interests in American blues completely complementary, and in 1954 they began making the rounds of the jazz clubs as an electric blues duo. They started the London Blues and Barrelhouse Club, where, in addition to their own performances, Korner and Davies brought visiting American bluesmen to listen and play. Very soon they were attracting blues enthusiasts from all over England.

Korner and Davies made their first record in 1957, and in early 1962, they formed Blues Incorporated, a "supergroup" (for its time) consisting of the best players on the early-'60s British blues scene. Korner (guitar, vocals), Davies (harmonica, vocals), Ken Scott (piano), and Dick Heckstall-Smith (saxophone) formed the core, with a revolving membership featuring Charlie Watts or Graham Burbridge on drums, Spike Heatley or Jack Bruce on bass, and a rotating coterie of guest vocalists including Long John Baldry, Ronnie Jones, and Art Wood (older brother of Ron Wood). Most London jazz clubs were closed to them, so in March of 1962 they opened their own club, which quickly began attracting large crowds of young enthusiasts, among them Mick Jagger, Keith Richards, and Brian Jones, all of whom participated at some point with the group's performances—others included Ian Stewart, Steve Marriott, Paul Jones, and Manfred Mann. In May of 1962, Blues Incorporated was invited to a regular residency at London's Marquee Club, where the crowds grew even bigger and more enthusiastic. John Mayall later credited Blues Incorporated with giving him the inspiration to form his own Bluesbreakers group.

Record producers began to take notice, and in June of 1962 producer Jack Good arranged to record a live performance by the band. The resulting record, *R&B from the Marquee*, the first full-length album ever made by a British blues band, was released in November of 1962. The album consisted of largely of American standards, especially Willie Dixon numbers, rounded out with a few originals. At virtually the same time that Blues Incorporated's debut was going into stores, Cyril Davies left the group over Korner's decision to add horns to their sound. Korner soldiered on, but the explosion of British rock in 1963, and the wave of blues-based rock bands that followed, including the Rolling Stones, the Animals, and the Yardbirds undercut any chance he had for commercial success. His more studied brand of blues was left stranded in a commercial backwater—there were still regular gigs and recordings, but no chart hits, and not much recognition. While his one-time acolytes the Rolling Stones and Cream made the front pages of music magazines all over the world, Korner was relegated to the blues pages of England's music papers, and, though not yet 40, to the role of "elder statesman."

For a time, Korner hosted *Five O'Clock Club*, a children's television show that introduced a whole new generation of British youth to American blues and jazz. He also wrote about blues for the music papers, and was a detractor of the flashy, psychedelic and commercialized blues rock of the late '60s, which he resented for its focus on extended solos and its fixation on Chicago blues. He continued recording as well, cutting a never-completed album with future Led Zeppelin vocalist Robert Plant in early 1968. Korner's performing career in England was limited, but he could always play to large audiences in Europe, especially in Scandinavia, and there were always new Korner records coming out. It was while touring Scandinavia that he first hooked up with vocalist Peter Thorup, who became Korner's collaborator over the next several years in the band New Church.

After his dismissal from the Rolling Stones, Brian Jones considered joining New Church; Korner, however, rejected the idea, because he didn't want his new band to be caught up in any controversy. In 1972, he became peripherally involved in the breakup of another band, inheriting the services of Boz Burrell, Mel Collins, and Ian Wallace when they quit King Crimson.

It was during the '70s that Korner had his only major hit, as leader (with Peter Thorup) of the 25-member big band ensemble CCS. Their version of Led Zeppelin's "Whole Lotta Love" charted in England, and led to a tour and television appearances. In response, Korner released *Bootleg Him!*, a retrospective compiled from tapes in his personal collection, including recordings with Robert Plant, Mick Jagger, and Charlie Watts. Korner played on the "supersession" album *B.B. King in London*, and cut his own, similar album, *Get Off My Cloud*, with Keith Richards, Peter Frampton, Nicky Hopkins, and members of Joe Cocker's Grease Band. When Mick Taylor left the Rolling Stones in 1975, Korner was mentioned as a possible replacement, but the spot eventually went to Ron Wood. In 1978, for Korner's 50th birthday, an all-star concert was held featuring Eric Clapton, Paul Jones, Chris Farlowe, and Zoot Money, which was later released as a video.

In 1981, Korner formed the last and greatest "supergroup" of his career, Rocket 88, featuring himself on guitar, Jack Bruce on upright bass, Ian Stewart on piano, and Charlie Watts on drums, backed by trombonists and saxmen, and one or two additional keyboard players. They toured Europe and recorded several gigs, the highlights of which were included on a self-titled album released by Atlantic Records. In contrast to the many blues-rock fusion records with which Korner had been associated, *Rocket 88* mixed blues with boogie-woogie jazz, the group's repertory consisting largely of songs written by W.C. Handy and Pete Johnson.

After a well-received appearance at the Cambridge Folk Festival in the early '80s, there were rumors afterward that he intended to become more active musically, but his health was in decline by this time. A chain smoker all of his life, Korner died of lung cancer at the beginning of 1984. —*Bruce Eder*

R&B from the Marquee / 1962 / Ace of Clubs ✦✦✦✦✦
Alexis Korner's Blues Incorporated's early, raw, unpretentious British take on American blues. The album shows a multitude of influences, from rural, country blues to the electric sounds of Chess Records, Sleepy John Estes to Willie Dixon and Muddy Waters. Note that the British Decca CD from the late '80s has four bonus tracks not on the original album, but the American Mobile Fidelity CD reissue from 1996 has yet another previously unreleased bonus track, a cover of Willie Dixon's "Built for Comfort," that Decca missed on its CD. —*Bruce Eder*

At the Cavern / 1964 / Oriole ✦✦✦
The group is still called Blues Incorporated, but without Cyril Davies or Long John Baldry, who were present on the first record. Recording at Liverpool's Cavern Club was more a gimmick than anything else, and the music is not as well made or exciting as the group's first album. This record shows Korner's more big-band type blues work, favoring horns. A good album, but not one that was going to make much noise amid the work of the Rolling Stones, the Animals, the Yardbirds et al. —*Bruce Eder*

Red Hot from Alex / 1964 / Transatlantic ✦✦
Blues Incorporated / 1964 / Polydor ✦✦✦
Sky High / 1966 / Spot ✦✦✦
I Wonder Who / 1967 / BGO ✦✦
Recorded in a mere two sessions, this had the potential to be a decent, if hardly innovative, effort. At this point, Korner's group was in one its most stripped-down phases, featuring just Alexis on guitar, Danny Thompson on bass, and Terry Cox on drums. Very shortly after this disc, Thompson and Cox would form the rhythm section of Pentangle, so these cuts are somewhat akin to hearing the bare bones of Pentangle in a much more blues/jazz-based context. The musical backing is not the problem, nor is the material, divided between Korner originals and blues standards by the likes of Jimmy Smith, Percy Mayfield, Ma Rainey, and Jelly Roll Morton. The problem is that Korner elected to sing these himself in his gruff, scraggly croak. It's not like listening to Dylan or Buffy Sainte-Marie, who take some getting used to, but have considerable, idiosyncratic talent—Korner simply cannot, objectively speaking, sing. (His butchering of Herbie Hancock's "Watermelon Man" has to be heard to be believed.) And that makes this album downright difficult to bear, despite the fine, spare musical arrangements (the instrumental cover of Jimmy Smith's "Chicken Shack Back Home" is a major standout in this context). If Korner had the wisdom to employ even a minor-league British bluesman like, say, Duffy Power (who guested with him occasionally during this time) as his singer for these sessions, the results would have been immeasurably better. —*Richie Unterberger*

New Generation of Blues / 1968 / BGO ✦✦✦
A basically competent, though hardly enthralling, effort from the British bluesman that alternates between minimal, acoustic-flavored production and fuller arrangements with jazzy touches of flute and upright bass. Korner wrote about half of the material, leaving the rest of the space open for R&B/blues covers and adaptations of traditional standards. "The Same for You" has a strange, ever-so-slight psychedelic influence, with its swirling flute, fake fadeout, and odd anti-establishment lyrics. Korner's voice is (and always would be) a tuneless bark, but it sounds better here than it did on the first album to prominently feature his vocals (*I Wonder Who*, 1967). As such, this album is one of the best representations of Korner as a frontman. —*Richie Unterberger*

Bootleg Him! / 1972 / Castle ✦✦✦✦✦
The best of all the Korner anthologies, boasting unreleased tapes and a lot of interesting one-off recordings from the various nooks and crannies of his career. —*Bruce Eder*

Get Off My Cloud / 1975 / See for Miles ✦✦✦
The lineup makes this album virtually an offshoot of Korner's participation on *B.B. King in London* from four years earlier, including Steve Marriott, Peter Frampton etc., with

Keith Richards making a guest appearance. Songs include the Rolling Stones title hit, and a cover of the Doors' "The Wasp (Texas Radio)." Nothing to make anyone forget the originals, nor is the new material terribly memorable, but everyone sounds like they're having fun here. —*Bruce Eder*

Rocket 88 / 1981 / Atlantic ✦✦✦✦✦
This was the best record Korner had made since 1962, and featured a core membership of former acolytes—Charlie Watts, Jack Bruce, and Ian Stewart. The sound is as much jazz as blues-influenced, it was all cut live on tour of Europe, and nobody involved ever sounded better, happier, or more relaxed. Not yet released on CD, and worth its weight in gold on vinyl, this was both Korner's and Stewart's final efforts. —*Bruce Eder*

● **The Alexis Korner Collection** / 1988 / Castle ✦✦✦✦✦
Castle's *Alexis Korner Collection* is a good single-disc collection that does a nice job of summarizing Korner and his various supporting bands throughout his career. Along the way, most of his popular songs and a healthy selection of his best material are showcased, making this an excellent introduction to his prodigious body of work. —*Thom Owens*

Live in Paris / 1988 / Magnum ✦✦✦
Korner working acoustically in the company of another guitarist (who plays electric) and bassist in Paris in 1993. The crowd is largely folkie restrained as Korner delivers a laidback performance of standards like "Blue Monday," "Key to the Highway," "Sweet Home Chicago," "I Got My Mojo Working," and "Working in the Coalmine" with several of his originals fleshing things out. The recording quality is good and Korner and company turn in an enjoyable—and very British—set of blues and R&B in the grand old tradition. —*Cub Koda*

1961–1972 / Jul. 30, 1996 / Castle ✦✦✦✦

Smokin' Joe Kubek

b. Nov. 30, 1956, Grove City, PA

Vocals, Guitar / Modern Electric Texas Blues, Electric Texas Blues
Another young Texas axeman from the old school, Smokin' Joe Kubek issued his band's debut disc in 1991 on Bullseye Blues, *Steppin' Out Texas Style*. Kubek was already playing his smokin' guitar on the Lone State chitlin circuit at age 14, supporting such musicians as Freddie King. Soon, he formed his own band and began playing a number of bars across Dallas. In the '80s, he met guitarist/vocalist Bnois King, a native of Monroe, LA, and the duo formed the first edition of the Smokin' Joe Kubek Band. The Smokin' Joe Kubek Band began playing the rest of the southwest in the late '80s. In 1991, they signed to Bullseye Blues, releasing their debut *Steppin' Out Texas Style* the same year. Following its release, the band launched their first national tour. For the rest of the '90s, the Smokin' Joe Kubek Band toured the United States and toured frequently and issued records like 1993's *Texas Cadillac*, 1996's *Got My Mind Back*, and 2000's *Bite Me!* —*Bill Dahl & Stephen Thomas Erlewine*

● **Steppin' Out Texas Style** / 1991 / Bullseye Blues ✦✦✦✦✦
Smokin' Joe Kubek's debut album is a delight. Kubek leads his band through a set of smoking hot Texas and Memphis blues, delivered with passion—they can play this music with precision, but they choose to be looser and more fun than most traditionalists. Kubek's a skillful guitarist and Bnois King, his vocalist and rhythm guitarist, can play nearly as well and their duels are the high watermark of an already wonderful album. —*Thom Owens*

Chain Smokin' Texas Style / 1992 / Bullseye Blues ✦✦✦
Smokin' Joe Kubek is pure Texas blues—he's a forceful guitarist and his band rocks with a loose, greasy vibe. What makes the album so much fun is the combination of solid material and piledriving performances—it may follow a tradition, but it manages to be unpredictable. —*Thom Owens*

Texas Cadillac / 1993 / Bullseye Blues ✦✦✦✦✦
Smokin' Joe Kubek's third Rounder album juggles blues-rock originals with faithful, exuberant covers of Jimmy Reed, Willie Dixon, Muddy Waters and Little Walter Jacobs, among others. Kubek is a good, sometimes captivating guitarist and entertaining singer, if not the greatest pure vocalist, and the band rips through the 11 cuts in a relaxed, yet passionate fashion. But it's hard for any longtime blues fan to get excited over hearing another version of "Little Red Rooster" or "Mean Old World"; it's impossible to reinvent Delta, urban, Texas or West Coast blues. The solution is probably to make the best music you can and hope you hook those willing to listen to contemporary blues rather than spurn it for the originals. —*Ron Wynn*

Keep Comin' Back / 1995 / Bullseye Blues ✦✦✦

Got My Mind Back / 1996 / Bullseye Blues ✦✦✦✦
There is no need for guest musicians when Smokin' Joe Kubek is around, for the explosive guitarist completely fills up the ensembles with distortions worthy of acid rock. Kubek is a fairly well-rounded player who occasionally leaves space and during at least two songs ("All the Love There Is" and "She's It") on this CD creates some surprising tones on his instrument (sounding like a keyboard on the former and playing '70s-style wahwah notes during the latter). With B'nois King contributing smooth but emotional vocals and bassist Paul Jenkins and drummer Mark Hays supporting Kubek, this is a tight group that probably puts on a killer live show. —*Scott Yanow*

Take Your Best Shot / Apr. 7, 1998 / Bullseye Blues ✦✦✦✦
Smokin' Joe Kubek is a powerful and often quite intense guitarist who creates a wide variety of unusual sounds and makes expert use of distortion on the rockish side of the blues. He has long teamed up with the passionate yet laid-back vocalist Bnois King (who also plays rhythm guitar) and the combination works well; the two musicians often sound as if they are the same person. Most of the selections on this CD (their sixth for Bullseye

in seven years) are played by their basic two-guitar quartet with extra percussion and two background vocalists added to a pair of songs apiece, along with guest appearances by Jimmy Thackery and Little Milton. Fans of Stevie Ray Vaughan and blues guitarists who are touched by Jimi Hendrix will want this enjoyable set. —*Scott Yanow*

Bite Me! / Apr. 4, 2000 / Bullseye Blues ♦♦♦
Guitarist Smokin' Joe Kubek and his partner, singer/guitarist Bnois King, were signed to Bullseye Blues just after the bubble burst on the crossover appeal of electric Texas blues, with the breakup of the Fabulous Thunderbirds and the death of Stevie Ray Vaughan in 1990. While the label may have hoped they would fill those shoes, Kubek and King have never, in seven albums, really made much of a move to the mainstream, remaining content to turn out faithful re-creations of Texas-style blues. On their first few albums, they recorded a lot of covers, while their most recent efforts have consisted entirely of band originals, which is also the case on *Bite Me!* But the musical structures are so familiar that the songwriting credits are only nominal; Kubek and King are more about playing than writing. They work in the occasional novelty, such as the "talkbox" Kubek sucks on in the opening track, "If You Know What I'm Sayin'," but King makes the players' fidelity clear in the lyrics—"you know what the blues is about." They do, and they perform it as well here as they ever have. —*William Ruhlmann*

Lady Bianca (Bianca Thornton)

b. Aug. 8, 1953, Kansas City, MO
Vocals / Modern Electric Blues

While primarily a blues vocalist, Lady Bianca first earned notice as a session singer on a wide range of projects including recordings from Van Morrison, Frank Zappa, and Merle Haggard. Born Bianca Thornton in Kansas City, MO, on August 8, 1953, she was influenced by gospel as a child and studied at the San Francisco Conservatory of Music before lending her contralto to the role of Billie Holiday in an acclaimed production of Jon Hendrick's *Evolution of the Blues*; in the early '80s, she appeared on Morrison LPs including *Beautiful Vision* and *Inarticulate Speech of the Heart*, and also backed blues legends like John Lee Hooker and Willie Dixon. In the late '80s, Lady Bianca teamed with songwriter Stanley Lippitt, an alliance yielding a number of tracks that grabbed the attention of Joe Louis Walker and in turn resulted in a record deal; she made her solo debut in 1995 with *Best Kept Secret*. Her long-awaited follow-up appeared six years later on Rooster Blues. —*Jason Ankeny*

Best Kept Secret / Oct. 1995 / Telarc ♦♦♦

● **Rollin'** / Jun. 12, 2001 / Rooster Blues ♦♦♦♦
It's been six years since Lady Bianca released her debut album, and if her sophomore effort makes one thing clear, it's that she needs to spend less time doing whatever else it is she does with her life and start making more albums. Her rich, chesty voice shifts effortlessly between a clear, classically trained contralto and a soulful growl, and she can burn her way through a slow blues better than just about anyone alive. The songs on *Rollin'* veer stylistically between straight-up blues and rocking R&B, and lyrically between "My man is sexy" ("Lookin' at My Man," "Easy Lovin'") and "Keep your hands off my man" ("Keep My Baby Outta Your Eyes," "You Slept With My Man Last Night"). Her backing band delivers a sound that has all the supple groove of Memphis and all the muscle of Kansas City, and the combination of that band with her voice is incendiary. Highlights include the quietly menacing "You Slept With My Man Last Night" and the celebratory "Easy Loving." Highly recommended. —*Rick Anderson*

Ernie Lancaster

Guitar / Blues-Rock, Modern Electric Blues, R&B, Contemporary Blues
Electric blues guitarist Ernie Lancaster played on albums by numerous artists throughout the '80s and '90s and released a solo album, *Ernestly*, in 1991. More than anything, Lancaster is perhaps best known as Root Boy Slim's guitarist in the Sex Change Band. He also played guitar for such artists as Ace Moreland, Kenny Neal, Lucky Peterson, Noble Watts, and Rev. Billy C. Wirtz. His solo album, *Ernestly*, featured the guitarist leading a small band through ten entirely instrumental songs that he had written. Over the course of the album, Lancaster veers from instrumental blues-rock to jazz-pop, and soul-jazz. —*Jason Birchmeier*

● **Ernestly** / 1991 / Ichiban ♦♦♦
After playing as a sideman on albums by artists ranging from artists ranging from bluesmen Lucky Peterson and Kenny Neal to soul singer Rufus Thomas, Ernie Lancaster took center stage with the entirely instrumental *Ernestly*. Ranging from instrumental blues-rock to jazz-pop and soul-jazz, this little-known, underproduced CD has a bar band quality and avoids slickness. Much of the time, *Ernestly* makes you feel like you're in an off-the-beaten-path (but certainly enjoyable) roadhouse in Kansas City, Milwaukee, or upstate New York. Next to Lancaster's guitar solos, one of the main reasons to hear this album is the fact that Peterson is prominently featured. Although Peterson is a fine blues singer, he doesn't do any singing at all on *Ernestly*. Rather, Peterson is heard as an instrumentalist and concentrates mainly on the electric Hammond B-3 organ. As an organist, Peterson draws heavily on the influence of soul-jazz heroes like Jack McDuff and the seminal Jimmy Smith. Although not stunning, *Ernestly* provides some gritty and unpretentious fun. —*Alex Henderson*

Sonny Landreth

b. Feb. 1, 1951, Caton, MS
Slide Guitar, Vocals, Guitar, Dobro / Swamp Blues, Louisiana Blues, Southern Rock, Modern Electric Blues
Southwest Louisiana-based guitarist, songwriter, and singer Sonny Landreth is a musician's musician. The blues slide guitar playing found on his two Zoo Entertainment releases, *Outward Bound* (1992) and *South of I-10* (1995) is distinctive and unlike anything else you've ever heard. His unorthodox guitar style comes from the manner in which he simultaneously plays slide and makes fingering movements on the fret board. Landreth, who has an easygoing personality, can play it all, like any good recording-session musician. His distinctive guitar playing can be heard on recordings by John Hiatt, Leslie West and Mountain, and other rock & rollers.

Landreth was born February 1, 1951, in Canton, MS, and his family lived in Jackson,

MS, for a few years before settling in Lafayette, LA. Landreth, who still lives in southwest Louisiana, began playing guitar after a long tenure with the trumpet. His earliest inspiration came from Scotty Moore, the guitarist from Elvis Presley's band, but as time went on, he learned from the recordings of musicians and groups like Chet Atkins and the Ventures. As a teen, Landreth began playing out with his friends in their parents' houses. "They would ping-pong us from one house to another, and though we were all awful at first, as time went on we got pretty good. It's an evolutionary process, just like songwriting is," Landreth explained in an interview on his 44th birthday in 1995. After his first professional gig with accordionist Clifton Chenier in the '70s (where he was the only White guy in the Red Beans and Rice Revue for awhile), Landreth struck out on his own, but not before he recorded two albums for the Blues Unlimited label out of Crowley, LA, *Blues Attack* in 1981 and *Way Down in Louisiana* in 1985. If anyone is living proof of the need to press on in spite of obstacles, it is Landreth.

The second of those two albums got him noticed by some record executives in Nashville, which in turn led to his recording and touring work with John Hiatt. That led to still more work with John Mayall, who recorded Landreth's radio-ready "Congo Square." More recently, he's worked with New Orleans bandleader and pianist Allen Toussaint (who guests on several tracks on *South of I-10*, as does Dire Straits guitarist Mark Knopfler).

On Landreth's brilliant albums for Zoo, the lyrics draw the listener in to the sights, sounds, smells and heat of southwest Louisiana, and a strong sense of place is evident in many of Landreth's songs. Although his style is completely his own and his singing is more than adequate, Landreth admits that writers like William Faulkner have had a big influence on his lyric writing. The fact that it's taken so long for academics at American universities to recognize the great body of poetry that blues is concerns Landreth as well. Robert Johnson is Landreth's big hero when it comes to guitar playing. "When I finally discovered Robert Johnson, it all came together for me," Landreth said, noting that he also closely studied the recordings of Skip James, Mississippi John Hurt, and Charley Patton. —*Richard Skelly*

Outward Bound / 1992 / Zoo ♦♦
Sonny Landreth is the Louisiana-based slide-guitar master known for his work with John Hiatt and B.C.'s Sue Medley (both make backup vocal appearances here). Like fellow ace Ry Cooder, Landreth's playing sizzles and slashes on his debut solo outing *Outward Bound* without idle wanking. There's lots of space where what isn't played is just as important as what is. "Back to Bayou Teche" echoes the performer's early days backing some of Louisiana's best known Cajun musicians; aboriginal rhythms grace "Sacred Ground"; commercial pop meets Southern boogie on "New Landlord"; Landreth borrows a lick or two from buddy Hiatt for "Common-Law Love." —*Roch Parisien*

Down in Louisiana / Mar. 23, 1993 / Acadia ♦♦♦
This is music from the Saturday night dances in Louisiana; the hot and sweaty have a good time dancing, drinking, and looking at all the people. Do not look for the Royal Albert Hall production on this CD, as on his stunning *South of I-10* with its myriad "guest artists." The feel for this music is shown by someone who grew up with it. Listen to the respect and feeling he gives to Clifton Chenier's "If I Ever Get Lucky." Try to keep your body and feet from bouncing to the beat of "Sugar Cane" or "Little Linda." Doesn't your eye start to look around for a dance partner, even though you're in your living room? There is solid playing throughout this CD even though the sound is a bit thin at times and the big-name guests are nowhere to be found. It is a solid effort that spans the musical boundaries of all of Louisiana. Cajun, zydeco, blues, and country are all blended together so they are no longer confining, but a homogenous mix. A solid effort. —*Bob Gottlieb*

South of I-10 / 1995 / Praxis/Zoo ♦♦♦♦♦
Sonny Landreth's screaming slide guitar plows right into you and carries you along on its feral journey. This CD opens going for your guts and never quits, though at times its touch is more caressing than careening, as in "Cajun Waltz." This CD got a lot of airplay yet never got tiresome, the true test of good music. A wide variety of slide guitar styles, backed by an extremely tight rhythm section and various other New Orleans musicians adds to the pleasure of the album. This music combines the best of zydeco, New Orleans R&B, Cajun, and rock & roll into one mood-elevating experience. Listen to "Mojo Boogie" next to "C'est Chaud," then go on to "Shootin' for the Moon"; there is no letdown, but there is great variety. A must-buy. —*Bob Gottlieb*

Blues Attack / 1996 / AVI ♦♦

Crazy Cajun Recordings / Jun. 22, 1999 / Edsel ♦♦♦♦

● **Prodigal Son: The Collection** / Feb. 8, 2000 / Music Club ♦♦♦♦
This 15-track compilation brings together slide guitar master Sonny Landreth's earliest known recordings. The bulk of these sides were recorded in a single session in 1973 (when Landreth was 22), while the remaining tracks were cut in 1977. It's a youthful Landreth, playing more Southern than distinctly Louisianian, but this still holds some of

the secrets of his signature style. A fascinating glimpse into this slide genius' beginnings. —*Cub Koda*

Levee Town / Oct. 17, 2000 / Sugar Hill ✦✦✦✦
This is slide guitar wizard, Sonny Landreth's most ambitious work and true to form it comes with no glossy fanfare (even the packaging is sepia tint) just straight-ahead well-crafted songs played with his usual intelligent, heartfelt playing. Like the photos, that are easily passed over due to the quiet subtly of the sepia tones, the intricacy of his guitar work can easily be overshadowed by the flash that is inherent in the slide guitar. He takes the time here to do a number of acoustic songs and show that there is more to him than the loud flash, and that there is a guitarist who knows how to play without noise to disguise mistakes. Give a listen to "Love and Glory," in which he is helped out by Jennifer Warnes and Herb Pederson doing background vocals, Errol Verret on accordion, and some stunning fiddle work by Michael Doucet. He wrote all the songs except "Angeline," which he co-wrote with Will Jennings, and his sophistication as a storyteller is becoming more fully developed. This is a disc that shows his true maturity as a songwriter. He has a tight band working with him, and he employs his friends who help out to best advantage. There is plenty of straight-ahead high-voltage zydeco here, and there is also that quieter more introspective song that serves as a peek inside the man. A well-realized and balanced piece of work that truly reflects his zydeco/Louisiana roots. —*Bob Gottlieb*

Jonny Lang (Jon Gordon Langseth)
b. Jan. 29, 1981, Fargo, ND
Vocals, Guitar / Blues-Rock, Modern Electric Blues
Modern blues in the '90s had a weird phenomenon of teenage blues guitarists rocketing to popularity with their first album. The entire trend culminated with Jonny Lang, a guitarist from Fargo, ND, who released his solo debut album *Lie to Me* when he was 15. At the age of 12, he attended a show by the Bad Medicine Blues Band and began playing with the group. Several months later he had become the leader, and the newly renamed Kid Jonny Lang & the Big Bang relocated from Fargo to Minneapolis and released their debut album, *Smokin*, in 1995. The LP became a regional hit, leading to a major-label bidding war and culminating in Lang's signing to A&M Records in 1996. Early in 1997, his major-label debut, *Lie to Me*, was released to mixed reviews; *Wander This World* followed late the next year. —*Stephen Thomas Erlewine*

Smokin / 1995 / Oarfin ✦✦
Lie to Me / Jan. 28, 1997 / A&M ✦✦✦
Like his peers Kenny Wayne Shepherd and Chris Duarte, Jonny Lang is a technically gifted blues guitarist, capable of spitting out accomplished licks and riffs at an astonishingly rapid rate. That doesn't necessarily mean the album has much emotional weight—Lang can deliver the style, but not the substance, simply because he still needs to grow as a musician. Lang does boast an impressive array of licks and instrumental technique, but he needs something more to make *Lie to Me* a substantive record. —*Stephen Thomas Erlewine*

● **Wander This World** / Oct. 20, 1998 / A&M ✦✦✦✦
When reviewers heard a teenage Jonny Lang's debut album of 1997, *Lie to Me*, many of them commented on how mature the blues singer/guitarist sounded for his age. Similarly, Lang's second album, *Wander This World*, often sounds like it could have been the work of a man of 30. With David Z (known for his work with Prince) producing, the Midwesterner delivers an exciting sophomore effort that has as much to do with soul, funk and rock as it does with actual blues. Far from a purist, Lang takes an approach that is best described as Albert Collins, B.B. King, and Luther Allison by way of Otis Redding, Stax Records and Eric Clapton. While "Angel of Mercy" and the moody "Cherry Red Wine" demonstrate his mastery of the 12-bar format, most of the other selections aren't actual 12-bar blues, but rather Southern-style soul, funk or rock with a wealth of blues feeling. Lovers of '60s Memphis soul should appreciate "Walking Away" and "Second Guessing," while "The Levee" and "Still Raining'" have more of a rock orientation. The haunting title song finds Lang singing a little *too* convincingly about loneliness—even though Lang didn't actually write the lyrics, hearing an adolescent sounding so world-weary and isolated is rather disconcerting. There's nothing even remotely bubblegum about this excellent CD, which proves that Lang's supporters had every right to be enthusiastic. —*Alex Henderson*

Denise LaSalle (Denise Craig)
b. Jul. 16, 1939, LeFlore County, MS
Vocals / Northern Soul, Black Gospel, Soul-Blues
Unlike so many other blues vocalists who just re-interpret material given to them by songwriters, Denise LaSalle is a seriously talented songwriter. Although her soul blues style has strong urban contemporary overtones at times, it's best to think of LaSalle as a modern-day Bessie Smith, because that's really what she is. She writes funny songs full of sassy attitude and it's an attitude she carries with her on stage. Off stage, LaSalle accommodates all autograph seekers and gladly obliges journalists and radio disc jockeys.

The Jackson, TN-based LaSalle was raised in Belzoni, MS (also home to Joe Willie "Pinetop" Perkins some years earlier), but she got started singing in local churches around Leflore County. She was born July 16, 1939, as Denise Craig. Growing up, she listened to the Grand Ole Opry radio broadcasts and then in Belzoni, lived across the street from a juke joint. LaSalle's early influences, from the jukeboxes around Belzoni and over the radio, included Ruth Brown, Dinah Washington, and LaVern Baker. LaSalle moved north to Chicago when she was in her early twenties and would attend shows at the Regal Theatre, always returning home to write songs. She got to know blues musicians and began giving her songs to them, until one day a Chess Records executive stopped by at Mixer's Lounge, where LaSalle was working as a bar maid. He listened to one of her songs and took it down to Chess Records, and the company later signed her as a vocalist, but never recorded her. Two years later, LaSalle recorded and produced her own record with

the help of Billy "The Kid" Anderson, the Chess executive who'd originally shown an interest in her. After the record made some waves on local radio, Chess stepped in and purchased the master and took it to Europe. Meanwhile, LaSalle continued writing songs and sitting in with blues musicians around the Chicago clubs.

LaSalle's first big hit came about in 1971 when her "Trapped By a Thing Called Love" broke on the radio in Chicago and then Detroit. That record was for the Westbound label and then she signed with ABC Records in 1975, cutting three albums in three years until the label was sold to MCA. After MCA dropped her because of the label's "difficulty in promoting black acts" at that time, she continued performing as much as she could in Chicago and Memphis. In 1980, a Malaco executive called to ask her to write a song for Z.Z. Hill. A positive relationship with the company was quickly developed, which resulted in LaSalle recording 11 discs for the label, including *Lady in the Street* (1983), *Right Place, Right Time* (1984), *Love Talkin'* (1985), *Hittin' Where It Hurts* (1989), *Still Trapped* (1990), *Still Bad* (1994), and *Smokin' in Bed* (1997). While her Malaco sides are probably her most important recordings, other than the original of her early-'70s hit "Trapped," she still releases excellent gospel crossover material, including *This Real Woman* (2000) and *There's No Separation* (2001) on Ordena Records —*Richard Skelly & Al Campbell*

Trapped By a Thing Called Love / 1972 / Westbound ✦✦✦✦✦
Kicking off her Westbound stay with a gem, Denise LaSalle gave the world a new take on Southern soul with this late-nite entrée of Stax-y grooves and tales of love on the rocks. *Trapped By a Thing Called Love* and her two other Westbound LPs (*On the Loose* and *Here I Am Again*) set the pace for other Dixie divas like Millie Jackson and Betty Wright, thanks to the finely gauged originals and heavy dose of swagger they contained. The symphonic soul charts of both Gene "Bowlegs" Miller and Hi Records arranger Willie Mitchell (Al Green, O.V. Wright) are on display, too, and the fare ranges from a few choice covers (Barbara Lynn's "You'll Miss a Good Thing") to now-canonized R&B sides like the LaSalle-penned title track. Once available on vinyl and as a two-fer disc that also included *On the Loose*, *Trapped By a Thing Called Love* is lost in the vaults once again and awaiting a re-release makeover befitting its classic status. —*Stephen Cook*

● **On the Loose** / 1973 / Westbound ✦✦✦✦✦
This follow-up to LaSalle's breakthrough album, *Trapped by a Thing Called Love*, carries on with another solid round of Southern-fried blues and soul. Atop arranger Bowlegs Miller's groove-centric charts, LaSalle particularly shines on her own "Man Size Job," Bill Withers' "Lean on Me," and the Civil Rights anthem "There Ain't Enough Hate Around (To Make Me Turn Around)." Mostly, though, LaSalle evokes early influences like Ruth Brown and such contemporaries as Millie Jackson and Betty Wright while plying her gospel-infused, blues-grit way through fine cheatin' songs like "Breaking up Somebody's Home" and "Your Man & Your Best Friend." But, lest one thinks it's all about codependency and dissipation, she rebounds on the album closer, "I'm Over You," confidently stepping out on her own amidst a stunning backdrop of funky smooth strings. With a whole lot of blues and soul—plus a dash of country for good measure—LaSalle delivers a gem from her early-'70s stay at the Westbound label. —*Stephen Cook*

Here I Am Again / 1975 / Westbound ✦✦✦✦✦
Nearly eclipsing her fine *On the Loose* release from a few years before, Denise LaSalle cut this follow-up in 1974, once again utilizing Gene "Bowlegs" Miller's top-notch charts and the backing of the Memphis Horns and Muscle Shoals. The third and last of her Westbound albums, *Here I Am Again* also features several fine songs from LaSalle's pen, many of which show her very original take on the Southern soul sounds of Memphis' Stax and Hi records; Miller complements this bluesy base with sage doses of electric piano and strings on the ballads and plenty of in-the-pocket organ, horn, and guitar work for the funkier cuts. LaSalle, of course, displays both power and suppleness throughout, whether bouncing atop a cool-breeze groove ("Stay With Me Awhile"), digging into a bit of shuffle-bump salaciousness ("I Wanna Do What's on Your Mind"), or hitting the vocal heights on a rootsy ballad ("Don't Nobody Live Here")—even the Barry White sound-alike, "Here I Am Again," finds its own legs under her guidance. Another fine album from LaSalle's stellar yet brief stay at Westbound. —*Stephen Cook*

Second Breath / 1976 / ABC ✦✦✦
The Bitch Is Bad / 1977 / ABC ✦✦✦
Like fellow Southern soul diva Millie Jackson, Denise LaSalle can often transform inane material into something worthwhile. On *The Bitch Is Bad*, she makes it easy to overlook the plodding disco arrangement for "Move Your Body" or overwrought synth squiggles on "A Love Magician" with solidly soulful vocal performances. Even a cheap imitation of Marvin Gaye's "Let's Get It On"—titled "Fool Me Good" here—survives thanks to her smoldering delivery. The predominantly lightweight arrangements, though, ultimately diffuse the impact of LaSalle's voice. It's not that the songs are a wash, or that LaSalle should be excluded from musical exploration; it's more that we don't get to hear her at her best, as on the 1972 Stax-inspired *On the Loose* or the recent return-to-form outings for the Malaco label. Whether it was the ABC Records' skewed career-reviving strategy or her own lapse in taste (remember Jackson's disastrous *Just a Lil' Bit Country?*), LaSalle's attempt to jump on the disco/light soul bandwagon in the late '70s didn't work. A consolation, though, certainly must be the *The Bitch Is Bad*'s over-the-top album cover—clad in a black silk night dress, LaSalle stands poolside atop a fake lionskin rug whilst being fondled by a bathing stud. It's a must for any kitsch album cover collection, but the music within unfortunately does not make this indulgent tableau icing on the cake, or represent the best LaSalle can offer. —*Stephen Cook*

Unwrapped / 1979 / MCA ✦✦✦
Classy, sassy soul from Denise LaSalle, who peaked with "Trapped By a Thing Called Love." The Memphis Horns embellish the rhythm section and give the recording a warm sound. Denise testifies on the Newcomers' "Too Little in Common to Be Lovers," taking you straight to Soulsville, USA. Side two has only two selections: Rod Stewart's "Do Ya

Think I'm Sexy" and the scrumptious 14-minute, 52-second medley of Bettye Swann's "Make Me Yours," Jackie Moore's "Precious, Precious," and LaSalle's "Trapped By a Thing Called Love." —*Andrew Hamilton*

Right Place, Right Time / 1984 / Malaco ✦✦✦
The title cut came close to getting Denise LaSalle a little attention beyond the standard Southern boundaries. The rest of the album is her familiar litany of terse, crusty dialogues, country and blues-tinged wailers, and hard-hitting soul tunes. At times, LaSalle and others of her generation seem like illogical warriors, fighting to keep alive a sound that's long since faded as a viable commercial proposition. But as long as she keeps making records and putting her heart and soul into them, they deserve a listen by fans of the genre. —*Ron Wynn*

Love Talkin' / 1985 / Malaco ✦✦✦
As with all her Malaco albums, Denise LaSalle mixes things up nicely, going from hard-hitting, trash-talking tunes to heartfelt ballads, bluesy numbers, and country/soul wailers. She's had a string of regionally successful releases since joining Malaco in the '80s, but has never been able to break the embargo on Southern soul. She's been around too long to change at this point, and really shouldn't anyway. Her albums are reliable and enjoyable, even if they're a throwback. —*Ron Wynn*

Lady in the Street / 1986 / Malaco ✦✦✦
The title track was among LaSalle's best Malaco tunes, a stomping, urgently sung, sassy bit that walked the line between confrontation, invitation, and remorse. The other tunes weren't quite as inspired, but were equally well performed. Few performers have ever staked out an area and remained loyal to it like LaSalle, who's been doing country blues soul since the early '70s and seldom strayed from the path, despite numerous trends and changes on the black music scene. Some would call that suicidal; others would say it's commendable. —*Ron Wynn*

Rain and Fire / 1986 / Malaco ✦✦
Denise LaSalle has drawn some fire at times for her frank, no-holds-barred dialogues and album cuts. She also has remained loyal to vintage soul and blues/country-tinged songs that will never get urban contemporary airplay and attention because they're thoroughly Southern in style, sound, and production values. Thus, each Malaco album is almost doomed from the beginning, other than as a regional proposition. That said, here's another one right in that same vein, and it's as fine as all the rest in what it does. —*Ron Wynn*

It's Lying Time Again / 1987 / Malaco ✦✦✦
Denise LaSalle's Malaco albums have all been fine productions, usually featuring some sassy love songs, heartfelt bluesy ballads, and one or two numbers complete with spoken interludes in which the woman tells off the man. Unfortunately, none of them have matched her Westbound or ABC/MCA releases, mainly because soul no longer gets the same kind of widespread airplay outside the South. LaSalle has the kind of rough, tough yet vulnerable sound ideal for these songs, and her delivery has as much country and blues influence as soul and gospel. Her style and Malaco's productions may be dated, but they're the kind of vintage sound that anyone who grew up in the '50s and '60s will always revere. —*Ron Wynn*

Hittin' Where It Hurts / 1988 / Malaco ✦✦✦✦
When high-tech urban contemporary sounds became R&B's norm in the '80s, the small, Jackson, MS-based Malaco Records continued to specialize in traditional, Southern-style soul music. One of Malaco's best sellers has been Denise LaSalle, a big-voiced soul shouter with a gospel-influenced delivery along the lines of Millie Jackson, Betty Wright, and Laura Lee. One of LaSalle's strongest Malaco releases, *Hittin' Where It Hurts* was recorded in 1988, but often sounds like it could have been recorded in 1967. LaSalle sounds as inspired as ever on such gritty, horn-laden fare as "If You Can't Do Me Right," "Eee Tee," and the bluesy "Caught in Your Own Mess," all of which recall the splendor of Stax Records. Many soul veterans have gone unrecorded in the '80s and '90s, but thankfully, LaSalle isn't one of them. —*Alex Henderson*

Still Trapped / 1990 / Malaco ✦✦✦✦
Still Trapped found Denise LaSalle entering the '90s without having changed her approach very much since the '70s. Rejecting slick, technology-driven urban contemporary music, the gritty singer continued to excel by pretty much sticking with the type of Southern-style soul and blues Stax Records was recording 20 and 25 years earlier. LaSalle had long since disappeared from black radio playlists, but still commanded a loyal following (especially in the Deep South). A welcome addition to her catalog, *Still Trapped* is state-of-the-art LaSalle—earthy, humorous and sassy as hell. From an inspired cover of Al Green's "Love and Happiness" to such hard-edged LaSalle originals as "Chain Letter," "Drop That Zero," and "Wild Thing (All Night Long)," this CD makes listeners grateful that LaSalle has remained true to herself. —*Alex Henderson*

On the Loose/Trapped By a Thing Called Love / 1992 / Westbound ✦✦✦✦✦
This British import contains much of her best work, including "Trapped By a Thing Called Love," "Now Run and Tell That," and "A Man Sized Job." —*John Lowe*

Still Bad / Dec. 6, 1994 / Malaco ✦✦✦✦
Still Bad demonstrated that at 54, Denise LaSalle was still very much on top of her game. As its title indicates, the veteran soul and blues singer hadn't mellowed with age—those who love to hear LaSalle taking a sassy, in-your-face approach won't be disappointed by trash-talking numbers like "1-900-GET-SOME," "Right Side of the Wrong Bed," or "The Bitch Is Bad." But true to form, LaSalle has no problem turning around and showing a more sensitive side of herself on "Child of the Ghetto," an inspiring, poignant ballad describing a poor woman's determination to improve her life. LaSalle's Malaco output of the '80s and '90s was quite consistent, and with *Still Bad*, the singer once again excels by sticking with what she does best. —*Alex Henderson*

Smokin' in Bed / Mar. 4, 1997 / Malaco ✦✦✦✦
Another hot one from the first lady of raunchy Southern soul. Bright, sparkling Southern horns accent many cuts, including "Juke Joint Woman," an uptempo saga about a barfly. The blues never sounded better than on "Blues Party Tonight," which features B.B. King-inspired guitar licks on top of a laid-back groove, or "Dirty Old Woman," a dated-sounding jump number. At times her sexual tales sound contrived, but she excels on the Southern-fried ballads and midtempo smokers that dominate the latter half of the album—"Goin' Through Changes," "Never Been Touched Like This," and "Why Am I Missing You" are pure LaSalle. —*Andrew Hamilton*

God's Got My Back / Jun. 22, 1999 / Angel in the Midst ✦✦✦✦
Denise LaSalle's 1999 album *God's Got My Back* focuses on the vocalist's spiritual side and includes tracks like "Tell Him What You Want," "His Mighty Love," and "God Don't Make No Mistakes." LaSalle's bluesy delivery adds another layer of emotion to these uplifting songs. —*Heather Phares*

Last Chance Jug Band

f. 1989, Memphis, TN
Group / Modern Acoustic Blues, Jug Band
Headed by musicologist David Evans, The Last Chance Jug Band is a modern-day incarnation of the jug bands that existed in the Memphis area during the '20s and '30s, namely The Memphis Jug Band led by Will Shade and Cannon's Jug Stompers headed up by Gus Cannon. The band consists of Evans (vocals, guitar, kazoo), Jobie Kilzer (harmonica and jug), Dick Raichelson (piano), Tom Janzen (drums), and Richard Graham (one-string bass, washboard, jug, percussion).
Formed in 1989 in Memphis, the band released its debut album *Shake That Thing* (the title cut originally recorded by Papa Charlie Jackson) in 1997. In an attempt to modernize the sound for contemporary audiences, the group chose to use electric instruments (keyboards and amplified guitar) and add drums. The album is made up of mostly traditional material along with three originals (two by Evans and one by Raichelson). There is a very entertaining version of the historic W.C. Handy tune "Mister Crump," also known as the "Memphis Blues" and a positively inspiring version of the spiritual "Time is Winding Up," a traditional song that Evans learned from New Orleans street singer Babe Stovall. —*Keith Brown*

● **Shake That Thing** / Sep. 23, 1997 / Inside Sounds ✦✦✦✦

Booker T. Laury

b. Sep. 2, 1914, Memphis, TN, **d.** Sep. 23, 1995, Memphis, TN
Piano / Memphis Blues, Black Gospel, Boogie-Woogie
Booker T. Laury grew up with Memphis Slim and the two are good friends. Consequently, his piano style has much of the same barrelhouse sound as Slim's. Laury has stayed in Memphis, however, playing in the same clubs his entire life. Although some foreign albums were released, he had no domestic full-length. Therefore, Bullseye Blues released *Nothin' but the Blues*, with Laury's voice and piano the only instruments on the record. —*John Bush*

● **Nothin' but the Blues** / 1993 / Bullseye Blues ✦✦✦✦
A veteran of the old Beale Street scene and once a partner of the legendary Memphis Slim, Laury never got his shot at fame and fortune, or even the opportunity to cut a record. Now, approaching his 80th birthday, Laury finally made his debut and shows on this rollicking, highly delightful CD that his boisterous voice and piano skills remain in good shape. Every number is an original, as Laury opens the session with some uncensored remembrances about old Southern sanitary habits. From there, you get terse, spirited singing, powerful left- and right-hand piano lines, and a percussive, pounding attack that features octave-jumping forays and furious phrasing. One record can't correct a lifetime of being unfairly overlooked, but it can go a long way. —*Ron Wynn*

Live / Jul. 29, 1994 / Wolf ✦✦✦

Sammy Lawhorn

b. Jul. 12, 1935, Little Rock, AR, **d.** Apr. 29, 1990, Chicago, IL
Guitar / Chicago Blues
As a teenager, guitarist Sammy Lawhorn worked as a King Biscuit Boy for Sonny Boy Williamson and learned slide guitar from Houston Stackhouse. After a stint in the service, Lawhorn returned to Arkansas and played and/or recorded with Willie C. Cobbs, the Five Royals, Eddie Boyd, and Roy Brown. He moved to Chicago in the early '60s and became part of the house band at Theresa's, one of Chicago's main blues clubs. He worked on and off with Muddy Waters for about ten years and toured with that band. Lawhorn became best known as the resident guitarist at Theresa's club, where he played behind just about any great blues artist you could name. He was especially drawn to slide and Hawaiian-style guitar, and became well-known for his use of the tremolo bar. He is considered as one of finest examples of postwar style Chicago blues guitar, and can be heard on recordings of Muddy Waters, Big Mama Thornton, Otis Spann, Junior Wells, John Lee Hooker, Eddie Boyd, and many others. —*Michael Erlewine*

Johnny Laws

b. Jul. 12, 1943, Chicago, IL
Vocals / Chicago Blues
While a fixture of Chicago's South Side blues community since the mid-'60s, singer/guitarist Johnny Laws long remained unknown outside of his native Windy City, and did not make his debut recordings for another three decades. In 1943, he garnered considerable local attention as a result of his aching falsetto voice, in addition to a vast and eclectic repertoire of songs; still, Laws remained little more than a cult favorite until the release of his 1995 Wolf label debut *My Little Girl* finally made his music available to a wider audience. *Blues Burnin' in My Soul* followed in 1999. —*Jason Ankeny*

● **My Little Girl** / 1995 / Wolf ♦♦♦

Blues Burnin' in My Soul / Aug. 10, 1999 / Electro-fi ♦♦♦

Sam Lay

b. Mar. 20, 1935, Birmingham, AL

Vocals, Drums / Electric Chicago Blues, Blues-Rock

Sam Lay was born March 20, 1935, in Birmingham, AL, and began his career as a drummer in Cleveland in 1954, working with the Moon Dog Combo. In 1957 he joined the Original Thunderbirds and stayed with that group until 1959, when he left for Chicago to work with the legendary Little Walter.

Lay began to work with Howlin' Wolf in 1960 and spent the next six years with that group. He and bassist Jerome Arnold were hired away from Wolf's band by Paul Butterfield in 1966 and became part of the Paul Butterfield Blues Band, recording that classic first album. Lay toured with Butterfield until he accidentally shot himself.

Lay backed Bob Dylan at the historic 1965 Newport Folk Festival, when Dylan first introduced electric rock to the folk crowd. He went on to record with Dylan on *Highway 61 Revisited*. He can be heard on more than 40 classic Chess blues recordings, and his famous double-shuffle is the envy of every would-be blues drummer. In 1969, Lay played drums for the Muddy Waters *Fathers and Sons* album, now a classic. He also was the original drummer for the James Cotton Blues Band.

Later in 1969, he also worked with the Siegel-Schwall Band. He went on to form the Sam Lay Blues Revival Band, which has involved many players over the years including Jimmy Rogers, George "Wild Child" Butler, Eddie Taylor, and others.

Sam Lay was inducted into the Blues Hall of Fame in 1992 and received a nomination for a W.C. Handy award. He formed the Sam Lay Blues Band and had recordings on Appaloosa Records (*Shuffle Master*, *Live*) and on Alligator with the Siegel-Schwall Band, with whom he often plays. The 1996 release *Stone Blues* was followed four years later by *Rush Hour Blues*. *Live on Beale Street* also followed in fall 2000. *—Michael Erlewine*

Sam Lay in Bluesland / 1968 / Blue Thumb ♦♦

● **Shuffle Master** / 1992 / Appaloosa ♦♦♦♦

Shuffle Master finds Sam Lay in fine form, turning in a propulsive, energetic collection of Chicago blues. There are no revelations here, just Chicago blues played as it should be played, which makes the disc a worthwhile listen. *—Thom Owens*

Stone Blues / 1996 / Evidence ♦♦♦

Chicago blues drummer Sam Lay's credentials speak for themselves. At various times his patented shuffle beat has been heard on classic discs by Howlin' Wolf, the initial version of the Butterfield Blues Band, Bob Dylan (when he first went electric), James Cotton, Muddy Waters, and the list goes on. This session, recorded in 1994, dosen't rival any of those past achievements. However, *Stone Blues* does have its classic moments, including "Red White and Blues" with burning harp provided by Billy Farlow, "Walkin' Thru the Park" with Lay doing a vocal imitation of Muddy Waters that is dead on, and the Bo Diddley shuffle of "I Got Wise." No big suprises here, just a consistently great performance. *—Al Campbell*

Live / Jan. 22, 1996 / Appaloosa ♦♦♦

Rush Hour Blues / Jan. 25, 2000 / Telarc ♦♦♦

Live on Beale Street / Oct. 17, 2000 / Blue Moon ♦♦♦

Lazy Lester (Leslie Johnson)

b. Jun. 20, 1933, Torras, LA

Washboard, Vocals, Percussion, Harmonica, Guitar / Swamp Blues, Harmonica Blues, Electric Harmonica Blues

His colorful sobriquet (supplied by prolific south Louisiana producer J.D. Miller) to the contrary, harpist Lazy Lester swears he never was all that lethargic. But he seldom was in much of a hurry either, although the relentless pace of his Excello Records swamp blues classics "I'm a Lover Not a Fighter" and "I Hear You Knockin'" might contradict that statement too. His entrée into playing professionally arrived quite by accident: While riding on a bus sometime in the mid-'50s, he met guitarist Lightnin' Slim, who was searching fruitlessly for an AWOL harpist. The two's styles meshed seamlessly, and Lester became Slim's harpist of choice. In 1956, Lester stepped out front at Miller's Crowley, LA, studios for the first time. During an extended stint at Excello that stretched into 1965, he waxed such gems as "Sugar Coated Love," "If You Think I've Lost You," and "The Same Thing Could Happen to You." Lester proved invaluable as an imaginative sideman for Miller, utilizing everything from cardboard boxes and claves to whacking on newspapers in order to locate the correct percussive sound for the producer's output. Lester gave up playing for almost two decades (and didn't particularly miss it, either) before inaugurating a comeback that included a nice 1988 album for Alligator, *Harp & Soul*. *—Bill Dahl*

☆ **True Blues** / 1967 / Excello ♦♦♦♦♦

His original album collects the best of the early Excello sides. Includes "Sugar Coated Love," "I Hear You Knockin'," and "I'm a Lover, Not a Fighter." *—Cub Koda*

Lester's Stomp / 1987 / Flyright ♦♦♦♦♦

These primitive and rocking '50s sides came from an overlooked harmonica genius who epitomized the ragged-but-right ethic of producer Jay Miller. *—John Floyd*

Poor Boy Blues / 1987 / Flyright ♦♦♦

After two decades away from the music scene, Lazy Lester has been making up for lost time with a spate of recordings. Why was he away from the music all that time? According to Lazy Lester, he just did not feel like playing. The guitarist turned harmonica player from Baton Rouge, LA, made a name for himself playing with Lightnin' Slim. Lazy Lester called his style of playing swamp blues. It's a lot like the blues of Chicago, but steamier, like the country from where it originates. Leslie Johnson's moniker of Lazy Lester was given to him by record producer Jay Miller, who noted the lackadaisical attitude of the harpist. Lazy Lester, sounding like a meditation master, says that he is never in a hurry because it is easier on the system. But when he plays the harmonica, he sounds anything but laid-back. Since his comeback in 1988, Lester has been fronting his own bands in live concerts and on recordings, and he has proved to be anything but lazy in his recording schedule since his return to performing the blues. His high-energy, soulful harmonica growls out the blues with passion and authority. His recordings *All Over You* and *Blues Stop Knockin'* won accolades from the critics. His release *Poor Boy Blues* may be his best CD. Featured are some of the artist's best-known tunes, such as "The Same Thing Could Happen to You" and the title cut, "Poor Boy Blues." He reaches back in time for a reprise of his classic "I Hear You Knockin'." "You Got Me Where You Want Me" drives hard, "Sugar Coated Love" still has its edge, and "Sad Sad City" is the blues personified. Lazy Lester is a living legend. This recording shows why. *—Rose of Sharon Witmer*

Lazy Lester Rides Again / Jul. 1987 / King Snake ♦♦♦

Harp & Soul / 1988 / Alligator ♦♦♦♦

After a lengthy hiatus from the music business, Lester was in the midst of his comeback when he waxed this album for Alligator. The overall sound is redolent of those Louisiana swamp-blues classics, but with a cannily updated contemporary edge that works well. *—Bill Dahl*

Rides Again / 1988 / Sunjay ♦♦♦♦♦

His original rediscovery album pairs him with English blues musicians, with surprisingly great results. *—Cub Koda*

Lazy Lester / 1989 / Flyright ♦♦♦♦

Alternate takes and unissued titles from the cache of producer J.D. Miller, whose tiny Crowley, LA, studio was the prime site for recording swamp blues during the '50s and '60s. A fine companion to AVI's essential Lester compilation. *—Bill Dahl*

★ **I Hear You Knockin'! The Excello Singles** / Nov. 29, 1994 / Excello ♦♦♦♦♦

Southern Louisiana swamp blues doesn't get more infectious or atmospheric than in the hands of Lazy Lester, whose late-'50s/early-'60s catalog for Excello Records (produced by the legendary J.D. Miller) is splendidly summarized with the 30 sides here. Lester's insistent harp and laconic vocals shine brightly on the rollicking "I'm a Lover, Not a Fighter," "Sugar Coated Love," "I Hear You Knockin'," and "If You Think I've Lost You," serving to help define the genre's timeless appeal. *—Bill Dahl*

All Over You / Oct. 6, 1998 / Antone's ♦♦♦♦

The last time Lester released an album was 1988's *Harp & Soul* on Alligator, an uneven affair. This 1999 effort for Antone's is a vast improvement with producer Derek O'Brien providing linchpin guitar support and fronting a band that includes stellar contributions from Mike Buck on drums and Sarah Brown on bass. Although the intervening years have added a bit of rust to Lester's vocal chops, the added graininess just enhances the performances of old chestnuts like "Strange Things Happening," "If You Think I've Lost You," "Irene," "I'm a Lover, Not a Fighter," "I Need Money," and "The Sun Is Shining." The classic Excello is called on for most of the album but the big surprise comes with two solo performances by Lester, singing and playing guitar on Lightnin' Slim's "Nothing but the Devil" and Lonesome Sundown's "My Home Is a Prison." His most cohesive album since his first for Excello. *—Cub Koda*

Blues Stop Knockin' / Aug. 21, 2001 / Antone's ♦♦♦

Not the most nimble harp player on the blues block, Lazy Lester nonetheless connects when he's backed by a sympathetic band, as he is on this recording, his first in three years. Aided immensely by guitarists Jimmie Vaughan and Derek O'Brien (who also produces) on all but one track, the 70-year-old Lester returns to his swampy Excello label past on this sturdy release. Although it was recorded in Texas, Lester effortlessly evokes his Louisiana roots in a set predominantly consisting of covers that feature his moody harmonica and deep, bluesy sound. With muscular songs and a band that knows its way around a muddy groove, Lester is in fine, low-key form throughout. Far from energetic, as his moniker implies, he sounds remarkably inspired throughout. When he hits his mark on the slow blues of "Sad City Blues" (featuring guests Sue Foley, Sarah Brown, and Gene Taylor) or connects on the Jimmy Reed-ish "Miss You Like the Devil," his quivering voice and unamplified harp evoke the sound of those great '60s songs he turned into models of the genre. He even resembles Muddy Waters on "Go Ahead," gradually unwinding on a slow shuffle. Re-recording some of his old favorites, like the self-referential "They Call Me Lazy," is a questionable move for many elder musicians hoping to regain a lost spark, but these versions maintain the slow, laconic, if not quite lazy atmospheric vibe that made his classic stuff so influential. Not a great blues album, but a surprisingly good one and better than most would have expected from one of the blues' fringe figures in his waning years. *—Hal Horowitz*

Leadbelly (Huddie William Ledbetter)

b. Jan. 20, 1888, Mooringsport, LA, **d.** Dec. 6, 1949, New York, NY

Composer, Vocals, Accordion, Piano, Guitar / Field Recordings, Folksongs, Folk Revival, Folk-Blues, Country Blues, Acoustic Blues, Songster

Leadbelly was the first blues musician to achieve fame among white audiences. For this reason alone, and more for the sheer novelty of his career as an ex-convict-turned-singer than for any recognition of his abilities, he was the first bluesman to be treated as a major media figure in the mainstream press.

Huddie Ledbetter was born on January 20, 1888, not far from the Texas border. He remained in school until he was 12 or 13 and could read and write, and was a precocious child, serious and ambitious beyond his years. Ledbetter was surrounded by a multitude of influences growing out of the post-slavery/post-Reconstruction era of the late-19th century, including blues, spirituals, and minstrel songs. By the time he was 14, he was known for his ability with the guitar and his way with a song. He played before audiences on most Saturday nights, at parties and square dances in the area around Mooringsport, LA, but before he was far into his teens, he was attracted to the red-light district in Shreveport. Apart from the women, however, the district's main attraction to the teenager was its music. He was married by the first decade of the 20th century, but the relationship and the marriage didn't last. The music, however, did, with an important new wrinkle—Ledbetter switched from the six-string to the 12-string guitar, a pivotal decision in the development of his own career. He was already performing songs of his own and adapting others during the 1890s, and his abilities in this area grew with his experience. He first picked up a song known as "Irene" sometime in the first decade of the 20th century and as "Goodnight Irene" it became one of Leadbelly's best-known songs.

Sometime around 1915 he made the acquaintance of Blind Lemon Jefferson, from whom he learned slide guitar. Despite some months of working together, Ledbetter was left behind by Jefferson, a result of his inability to stay clear of the law. Finally, in 1917, he was arrested for shooting a man and sentenced by the state of Texas to 30 years in prison. On the Shaw State Prison Farm, Leadbelly's talents served him just as well as they had outside. His singing and guitar playing made him one of the more popular prisoners. He was ultimately released in 1925 after he played for the visiting Texas governor, Pat Neff, requesting a pardon. The pardon was signed by Neff on virtually his last day in office.

Leadbelly, as he was now known professionally, tried working regular jobs for the remainder of the '20s, but was never able to stay far from the rambling life that had led him into trouble back in the previous decade. Finally, in 1930, he was arrested and convicted in Louisiana of assault with intent to commit murder, and sentenced to 30 years in the Louisiana State Penitentiary at Angola, a prison farm with a reputation as bad as, or worse, than the Texas prison from which he'd been released.

And it was there, in 1933, that he first met John Lomax, an ambitious researcher for the Library of Congress, who was traveling through the South with his son Alan, collecting blues and any other authentic American music that they could find. Leadbelly's reputation within the prison was well-known, and it was inevitable that he would meet the Lomaxes. They found in Leadbelly a talent and a resource beyond anything they could have hoped for—the man was not only a gifted player who exuded a musical charisma that transcended the prison setting, but he was a veritable human jukebox, in the range of songs that he knew. Leadbelly dazzled the Lomaxes with his singing, playing, songwriting, and Lomax recognized in his new discovery a talent that was very different from the makers of the commercial "race" records of the period. Leadbelly's style and repertory were unaffected by the currents running through commercial blues and country music, but a talent that was worth trying to develop commercially, into a valid and successful brand of Black American folk music.

Leadbelly was released in 1934 with help from John Lomax, and began an extended relationship with him and his son, serving as driver and valet while making recordings and preparing plans for concerts. It was Lomax's intention to make Leadbelly and—as his manager and "discoverer"—himself into stars. On the positive side, this resulted in Lomax trying to get Leadbelly to record virtually every song he knew, an impossible task given the sheer range of music to which he'd been exposed since the 1890s, but one that resulted in dozens upon dozens of sides for the Library of Congress, cut on Lomax's relatively crude "portable" recording unit, and later many attempts at commercial recording as well.

On the negative side, however, it resulted in a terrible exploitation of Leadbelly, who appeared in photos and on stage in striped prison uniforms, and whose violent past was emphasized along with his musical abilities. The result was a flurry of publicity that brought Leadbelly some exposure in the white community, but also made him give one the impression of a captured savage. It would have been demeaning for any man, but was especially so for Leadbelly, and ultimately not terribly profitable for Lomax. The copyrights that he signed his name to as Leadbelly's songwriting "collaborator" ultimately proved to be worth a small fortune, but at the time, he quickly discovered that sensationalistic press didn't necessarily translate into large paying audiences.

Moreover, Leadbelly quickly grew beyond Lomax's ability to control him, and later rebelled at their relationship. Lomax found out as early as 1935, following Leadbelly's first commercial recording sessions for the American Record Company, that Leadbelly's brand of blues was of virtually no interest to black audiences, who had already moved to more modern sounds. Ironically, the ARC sides contain some of Leadbelly's best music; brought into a real recording studio for the first time, he took to the new environment like a natural, his voice booming larger than life and his guitar captured more crisply than ever before.

Leadbelly moved to New York City, and subsequently split with Lomax, although they remained close. It was in New York that Leadbelly came to find some success, reaching a small, but dedicated, following of white listeners, mostly consisting of folk song enthusiasts and members of the city's uniquely Bohemian intelligentsia. Leadbelly did some sessions for Musicraft, and also for Bluebird label, but his major activities during the early '40s were with Moe Asch, the founder of Folkways Records.

Leadbelly's music at any phase of his career was startling, but his sound also evolved, a process made all the more vivid by the many different versions of his songs that he recorded across his career. By the early '40s, he even began to develop a consciousness that prefigured the topical songwriters of the early '60s. This was all pretty strong stuff to do in the middle of World War II. And, yet, Leadbelly also did whole programs and concerts devoted to songs intended specifically to entertain children; those recordings were among the most successful of the huge body of his work that Moe Asch recorded.

Leadbelly never gave up the hope that he might become a star in the music world, and recognized enough that was special in his life story that he even tried to interest Hollywood in signing him up. That didn't work, although a visit to California did result in a short-lived contract with Capitol Records in 1944, yielding a dozen sides.

Soon after this period, however, he began developing the health problems that would ultimately kill him. Leadbelly continued working into 1949, but it was too early for the folk revival boom that would have embraced him. He played his last concert at the University of Texas on June 15th of that year. The recording of that concert is very poignant—as he leaves the stage, he promises to come back, vowing to get well now that he has a new doctor. Instead, he was hospitalized a month later, and died in New York on December 6, 1949. Two years later, his one-time protégés, the Weavers, had a million-selling hit with their recording of "Goodnight Irene," starting the whole folk song revival—and six years later, England's Lonnie Donegan had a hit with a version of "Rock Island Line," a song that Leadbelly adapted and brought to modern audiences.

Leadbelly's place in blues history is a peculiar one; unassailable as a source for much of the country blues repertory as it has been passed down to us, and a major contributor to the folk music revival of the '50s, but virtually nonexistent in terms of his effect upon the commercial blues market in his own lifetime or since. *—Bruce Eder*

Convict Blues / 1935 / Aldabra ♦♦♦♦♦

Convict Blues collects a number of recordings he made for the American Record Corporation in 1935, which were, for the most part, never released. These 16 tracks are straight blues songs, delivered with passion. While it's not as essential as his Folkways or Library of Congress recordings, there's a wealth of terrific music here. *—Thom Owens*

Congress Blues / 194? / Aldabra ♦♦♦♦♦

Congress Blues collects a batch of folk songs that Leadbelly recorded in the early '40s. There is wonderful music here, to be sure, but it is available on better collections from Folkways and Rounder. *—Thom Owens*

Includes Legendary Performances Never Before Released / Mar. 21, 1952 / Everest ♦♦♦♦♦

While one should always be suspicious about how "legendary" material can be that was originally withheld from circulation, there's little that Leadbelly did that isn't worth hearing. That holds true here. *—Ron Wynn*

Leadbelly / 1962 / Columbia ♦♦♦♦

Taken as a whole, the recording career of Leadbelly provides ample evidence that he wasn't just a bluesman. Indeed, some of his most famous numbers, such as "Goodnight, Irene," are not blues at all. Blues numbers developed into only a part of his repertoire, and listeners whose interest is primarily blues may want to keep an eye cocked for this set. This album collects the artist's first commercial recordings, done in the mid-'30s, after he had sung himself out of a jail sentence for the second time in his life, or so the story goes. Blues numbers dominate completely, and there is a strong influence from Blind Lemon Jefferson, certainly not a bad thing in itself. One of the best songs is even kind of a tribute, entitled "Blind Lemon," although most tributes don't go into such detail about the subject's personal problems. Leadbelly's later recordings were bold and brash, the work of a professional entertainer with spirit and emotion to spare. In contrast, these recordings reveal a touch of microphone nervousness which complements the intensity of the material perfectly. Performances on both the six- and 12-string guitars are included. The folklore collecting brothers Alan and John Lomax manage to get themselves listed as songwriters on many of the tracks. *—Eugene Chadbourne*

☆ **Library of Congress Recordings** / 1966 / Elektra ♦♦♦♦♦

These powerful performances date from 1939-1943 when Ledbetter had moved to New York City after his years in prison. He was a fluid performer and his command of his trademark 12-string guitar is evident. Recorded by John and Alan Lomax, these sessions include "BollWeevil," "The Titanic," "Tight Like That," and "Henry Ford Blues." *—Richard Meyer*

Good Mornin' Blues (1936-1940) / 1969 / Indigo ♦♦♦♦♦

Wonderful mid-'30s and early-'40s material from Leadbelly, including some of his finest and most colorful blues tunes and good folk numbers as well. *—Ron Wynn*

Negro Folk Songs for Young People / 1989 / Smithsonian/Folkways ♦♦♦

Leadbelly's repertoire for children did not differ all that much from what he played for general audiences, as this compilation makes clear, although he did stress songs that were easy to sing along with. He had faith that kids could appreciate numbers that were a little more sophisticated than the usual nursery rhyme-type schemes—an approach from which many other children's music performers could learn. "Rock Island Line," "Boll Weevil," "Swing Low, Sweet Chariot" and "John Henry" are among the better-known selections here, although they don't overshadow less standard tunes like "We're in the Same Boat, Brother." The material from this album has been reissued as part of the Smithsonian Folkways CD *Sings for Children*, a recommended alternative to the original LP, as it more than doubles the length of the album with other kid-friendly performances that Moe Asch recorded by Leadbelly in the '40s. *—Richie Unterberger*

Huddie Ledbetter's Best / May 17, 1989 / BGO ♦♦♦♦

When this tasty slice of vinyl first came out, record consumers no doubt saw it on display alongside a new album by the Beatles, and guess which got the most attention? As years pass by, the pale yellows of the front cover seem to glow with a positively symbolic golden hue. Whatever microphones were used in this Hollywood studio grab the sound of his 12-string guitar, tuned down a step or two for the memorable "Grasshoppers in My Pillow." Special mention should be made of the boogie-woogie guitar solo on this number: a great musical moment. The artist had been performing professionally for close to a decade at this point, having rhapsodized his way out of jail for the second time. There are also several tracks featuring piano, with which the performer fails to establish the same kind of close relationship he has with his guitars. Technique certainly has something to do with that; on the keyboard, he is stuck having to play a few of the same licks over and over. Having a zitherist accompanying on most of the pieces sounds weirder than it is. In fact, it hardly sounds at all, since Paul Mason Howard is quite far back in the mix. The dozen tracks present a perfect blend of material, Leadbelly crossing back and forth between blues and folk material like a juggler. He succeeds in bringing aspects of each music into the other, driving a folk anthem along with a near boogie beat or giving a blues lyric the pathos of a mountain ballad. *—Eugene Chadbourne*

Sings Folk Songs / 1990 / Smithsonian/Folkways ♦♦♦♦♦

Leadbelly was a consummate song stylist; not necessarily a blues artist, although he certainly could deliver the blues with earnestness and authority. His forte was taking all types of songs, whether they were simple, filled with chilling metaphors, funny stories, or tragic events, and making them unforgettable personal anthems. That's what he does on all 15 cuts on *Leadbelly Sings Folk Songs*, teaming with such fellow greats as Woody Guthrie, Cisco Houston, and Sonny Terry. Leadbelly made many great albums with Folkways; this was certainly among them. *—Ron Wynn*

Sings Folk Songs / 1990 / Smithsonian/Folkways ♦♦♦♦♦
Included are '40s Folkways recordings with Woody Guthrie, Cisco Houston, and Sonny Terry. *—Mark A. Humphrey*

Alabama Bound / 1990 / RCA ♦♦♦♦♦
Sixteen of the sides that Leadbelly cut for Victor's Bluebird label in the summer of 1940, many backed by the Golden Gate Singers. The mix of blues with a gospel chorus doesn't always work, although "Pick a Bale of Cotton," "Rock Island Line," and "Midnight Special" are appealing, and there are Leadbelly solo covers of "Roberta," "Easy Rider," "New York City," etc. *—Bruce Eder*

☆ **Gwine Dig a Hole to Put the Devil In** / 1991 / Rounder ♦♦♦♦♦
An excellent sampling of material from Leadbelly's early Library of Congress sessions, including versions of some of the first songs he ever learned, "Green Corn" and "Po' Howard," his song to Governor Neff that helped secure his release from a Texas prison in 1925, his first recorded version of "If It Wasn't for Dickie" (later transformed into "Kisses Sweeter than Wine")—the master of which is, alas, somewhat damaged—and "C.C. Rider." *—Bruce Eder*

★ **King of the 12-String Guitar** / 1991 / Columbia/Legacy ♦♦♦♦♦
Although Huddie Ledbetter had recorded for the Library of Congress while still in jail in 1933, this CD contains some of the music from his earliest commercial recording date, only five months after getting out of prison for the second (and final) time. The majority of the material (other than the first four numbers) consists of alternate takes and previously unissued performances, although some of the numbers were formerly out on LPs by Folkways or Biograph. The music (ranging from blues to folk music) is highly recommended both to veteran collectors (who otherwise probably do not have most of these cuts) and to those just discovering the legendary and unique musician. Forty-six at the time, Leadbelly's powerful voice and his work on 12-string guitar are consistently memorable. *—Scott Yanow*

Let It Shine on Me / 1991 / Rounder ♦♦♦♦♦
The third volume of Leadbelly's incredible Library of Congress sessions includes several searing spiritual numbers, among them "Down in the Valley to Pray," "Must I Be Carried to the Sky," "Run Sinners" and "You Must Have That Religion, Hallaloo." The CD begins with an informative interview/performance segment that features Leadbelly answering questions about his life and stylistic influences, then demonstrating techniques and recounting the origins of particular songs. The disc also contains an interesting renditions of "When I Was a Cowboy" and the topical tunes "Mr. Hitler," "The Scottsboro Boys," and "The Roosevelt Song." Leadbelly's mournful, moving and authoritative vocals, plus his sometimes surging, sometimes reflective guitar playing, were never more moving, or appealing than during the Library of Congress sessions. *—Ron Wynn*

☆ **Midnight Special** / 1991 / Rounder ♦♦♦♦♦
In early July of 1933, Alan and John Lomax visited Angola Penitentiary in Louisiana with the intention of recording the music of the inmates who lived there. That day, Huddie Ledbetter, aka Leadbelly, cut his first recorded version of what became known as "Goodnight Irene" and 11 other songs, opening a career that would keep his name alive more than a half-century after his death, carried far beyond the boundaries of Louisiana and the United States. Those sides are not on this CD but the sides that he cut on their next visit, a year later, are here. The runs, fills, fingerpicking, and strumming heard on this disc are at a virtuoso level to match the work of just about any bluesman playing in 1934. On "Ella Speed," which clocks in at nearly six minutes, Leadbelly doesn't even keep a particularly quick tempo, yet he generates a range of sound suggesting that more than his lone guitar is accompanying him. "Red River" is just as startling, with Leadbelly shouting out the lyrics like a field holler as his guitar chimes and surges, alternating the lyrical and sweet with the emphatic and powerful. There are a number of classics-to-be on this disc, including the title track, "Irene," "Take a Whiff on Me," and "Roberta," making this an essential piece of Leadbelly's output. The CD transfer is clean enough to pull out some of the ambient sound behind the performance, giving a vague sense of the space and place. There were earlier blues recordings, to be sure, and Leadbelly recorded hundreds of songs in the 15 years that followed, but the impact of these early recordings cannot be underestimated. *—Bruce Eder*

Leadbelly ("Irene Goodnight") / 1992 / Blues Encore ♦♦♦♦♦
This represents a solid two years of Leadbelly's recordings for Capitol, Folkways, and Disc. With the exception of four tracks with Bunk Johnson (available on an American Music CD), this is his complete output from this important period, with sessions recorded in Hollywood, San Francisco, and New York City. The typical eclectic mix of blues, children's songs, folk tunes, and field hollers makes this a nice cross-section of the man's best work. Part of a multi-volume set, this also makes a nice stand-alone collection. *—Cub Koda*

Leadbelly's Last Sessions / 1994 / Smithsonian/Folkways ♦♦♦
Four CDs containing the best part of Leadbelly's only recordings on magnetic recording tape, which allowed him to stretch his songs to their usual length for the first time on record. The clarity of the recording, the presence of the between-song comments, and the selection of material makes this a seminal part of any serious collection. *—Bruce Eder*

Complete Studio Recordings, Vols. 4–5 / 1994 / Document ♦♦♦♦
These two European bootlegs cover a lot of material available elsewhere on legitimate American releases, but between them, they also contain the complete Leadbelly Capitol recording sessions of 1944, which have never surfaced on CD. The quality is superb, and the material is unique as the last commercial sides that Leadbelly ever cut. *—Bruce Eder*

Kisses Sweeter Than Wine / 1994 / Omega ♦♦♦♦♦
This is actually a Weavers double CD, and if you buy it for the Leadbelly material, make sure that it has the third bonus disc with his stuff on it inside. A dozen songs cut by Leadbelly for Musicraft in 1947—not mentioned in any discography—and forgotten for the next 46 years, all found on tapes in the label owner's garage when he moved to Florida. The singing is good, the material is unique, and it includes his last recording of "If It Wasn't for Dickie," the Irish folk song Leadbelly taught the Weavers that they turned into "Kisses Sweeter than Wine." *—Bruce Eder*

Pickup on This / Mar. 30, 1994 / Rounder ♦♦♦♦♦
Like the other volumes that came before it, *Pickup on This* is full of wonderful music and interviews from Leadbelly's Library of Congress recordings. *—AMG*

The Titanic, Vol. 4 / Mar. 30, 1994 / Rounder ♦♦♦♦♦
Part of the Lomax collection of Leadbelly recordings, this set focuses on Library of Congress recordings made between 1939 and 1943, after the singer had exiled himself from the South and moved to New York City. It's the singer's usual cornucopia of blues, work songs, spirituals, children's tunes and topical songs. The centerpiece is the title track, a nearly five-minute-long monologue about heavyweight champion Jack Johnson trying to board the doomed ship and his reaction upon hearing of its eventual end. The sound is grainy and scratchy, but far superior to other issues of this same material, and a solid addition to anyone's American folk music or blues collection. *—Cub Koda*

Nobody Knows the Trouble I've Seen, Vol. 5 / Mar. 30, 1994 / Rounder ♦♦♦♦
Lead Belly recorded a prodigious amount of music for Folkways, Stinson, and the Library of Congress between the time of his release from Angola State Prison in 1934 to his death from Lou Gehrig's disease in 1949. While anyone unfamiliar with the rougher edges of earlier folk recordings will prefer the recordings he made in the '40s for Folkway, hardcore fans prefer the energy of the Library of Congress recordings. These latter fans argue that these recordings come closer to capturing the "true" Lead Belly before he polished his sound for urban audiences. The tracks on *Nobody Knows the Trouble I've Seen* were recorded between 1939 and 1943, and the sound quality reminds one more of field recordings than a studio effort. While Lead Belly's enunciation of the lyrics isn't always clear, he performs well-worn pieces like "Rock Island Line" with an urgency—an edge—that would be absent from later renditions. It's also interesting how this song and pieces like "Little John Henry" are performed a cappella and interspaced with dialogue. While popular fare from Tin Pan Alley occasionally showed up in Lead Belly's repertoire, these work, spiritual, and other folk songs clearly have older origins, thus offering a glimpse at "uncontaminated" traditional music. The quality of this set is also highlighted by the inclusion of a great deal of material unavailable on other collections. *—Ronnie D. Lankford Jr.*

Golden Classics: Pt. 2 (Defense Blues) / May 12, 1994 / Collectables ♦♦♦
Rather thin at ten songs, of indeterminate origin, but the material is all very strong, including "Defense Blues," "Jim Crow," and a short version of "Midnight Special." *—Bruce Eder*

Bourgeois Blues: Golden Classics, Pt. 1 / Aug. 30, 1994 / Collectables ♦♦♦
Thirteen songs, mostly from the early '40s (though there are no credits or sessionography), featuring a wide range of Leadbelly's repertory, from topical to traditional, and with the singer playing accordion in addition to his usual guitar. *—Bruce Eder*

Complete Works, Vol. 4 / Sep. 1, 1994 / Document ♦♦♦
Covering Leadbelly's recordings from May through October 1944, this volume of his complete recorded works brings together 29 tracks recorded in New York and Hollywood and originally issued on the Stinson, Asch, Folkways, and Capitol labels. Highlights include "Easy Rider," "Jim Crow Blues," "Julianna Johnson," "Ella Speed," "Rock Island Line," "Goodnight Irene," and a rare outing on piano on "The Eagle Rocks." *—Cub Koda*

Party Songs/Sings & Plays / 1995 / Collectables ♦♦♦

Memorial, Vols. 3 & 4 / 1995 / Collectables ♦♦♦

Go Down Old Hannah / 1995 / Rounder ♦♦♦
Another entry in Rounder's look at the Lomax recordings made between 1939 and 1943. This batch is slanted toward the spiritual side of Leadbelly's song list, with strong versions of "Prayer," "Swing Low Sweet Chariot," "Stand Your Test in Judgment," "Old Time Religion," and "Amazing Grace" being particular standouts. The transfers here are a bit cleaner than other volumes in the series, although a bit fusty in spots. *—Cub Koda*

Memorial, Vol. 1–2 / Feb. 28, 1995 / Collectables ♦♦

Goodnight Irene / 1996 / Tradition ♦♦♦
The date of these recordings is unclear, and the sleeve is not of much help. The liner notes identify them as being taped in 1943 and 1944, while the back cover confidently refers to a 1939 date [though it seems much more likely that they were made in the '40s]. At any rate, these are very good performances, with Leadbelly in fine voice. Most are performed solo on his 12-string guitar, although Sonny Terry and Josh White make cameos on one track each. "Goodnight Irene," "New Orleans" (essentially the same song as "House of the Rising Sun"), "John Hardy," and "When I Was a Cowboy" are all among the most famous tunes that he helped to popularize. But at a mere 28 minutes, this is pretty short on running time. *—Richie Unterberger*

Masters of the Country Blues / 1996 / Biograph ♦♦♦
This representative pair of folk-blues talent spread over two discs crystallizes succinctly the early direction of the blues tradition. Leadbelly, aka Huddie Ledbetter, and Blind Willie McTell were recorded in 1935 and 1940, respectively. Each performer represents a primitive, folk-blues form with a semi-narrative, almost storytelling delivery on top of a

bright melody. As principle sources, Leadbelly and McTell on these vintage, historical recordings exude the blues that spawned numerous, lesser imitators. While not as well-known as Leadbelly, McTell had the more prolific commercial career. His music comes across as the most diverse, from his instrumental rendition of "Amazing Grace" to the lively "Kill-It-Kid Rag." Each disk in the *Masters of the Country Blues* series comes with descriptive and historical liner notes. *—Thomas Schulte*

Leadbelly in Concert / 1996 / Magnum ✦✦✦✦✦

Leadbelly's final concert from June 15, 1949, reissued on CD at last. The sound is very clean, the fidelity excellent, and the recording indispensable. *—Bruce Eder*

Where Did You Sleep Last Night: Lead Belly Legacy, Vol. 1 / Feb. 20, 1996 / Smithsonian/Folkways ✦✦✦✦✦

The bulk of the best performances by Leadbelly—whose influence on the folk revival of the '50s and '60s cannot be overstated—were recorded during the '40s for Folkways Records founder Moses Asch. Inferior copies and re-recordings of these tunes have appeared over the years, but the original masters have sat in the vaults of Folkways. The three-volume *Lead Belly Legacy* collection shows what we've been missing: The compilers dug out the best-available versions of Leadbelly's finest songs and carefully transferred them from the original acetate masters. As the liner notes promise, "these recordings can again be heard the way they sounded in the early '40s, for in the original masters you can still hear the ringing of the guitar and thumping of the bass." This 34-song first volume is a must for anyone interested in the roots of American folk. It opens with "Irene," which (as "Goodnight Irene") became a national hit for the Weavers less than a year after Leadbelly died while on welfare; it includes many more of his most-famous tunes, among them "Rock Island Line," "Cotton Fields," and "Good Morning Blues." *—Jeff Burger*

In the Shadow of the Gallows Pole / Apr. 1996 / Tradition ✦✦✦

There seems to be some kind of unwritten rule against giving exact session dates on most Tradition CD reissues, although at least one of the tracks comes from 1939. The sleeve does note that the material "is digitally remastered directly from rare, mint condition 78s contained in Leadbelly's first full album, *Negro Sinful Songs*, and from 78s released on the Stinson label." There's some interest in the variety of instrumentation—Leadbelly uses not only his 12-string guitar, but also piano and button accordion (the last of which is used to unusual effect on the version of "John Hardy"). "The Bourgeois Blues" is also a bit unusual in that its lyric derives not from folk traditions, but from an incident in Washington, D.C., in 1935 in which Leadbelly encountered segregation. This couldn't be recommended as one of his more essential releases, however, particularly as the running time is a mere 28 minutes. *—Richie Unterberger*

Bourgeois Blues: Lead Belly Legacy, Vol. 2 / Mar. 18, 1997 / Smithsonian/Folkways ✦✦✦✦✦

Volume two in a three-volume series of the recordings Leadbelly made for Folkways founder Moses Asch is as indispensable as the first. The 28 songs have been beautifully remastered, and the liner notes—including a 1946 tribute by Woody Guthrie—are extensive and revealing. This second CD focuses mostly on best-available versions of songs that first appeared on Folkways' *Easy Rider: Leadbelly's Legacy, Vol. 4* and *Midnight Special*. Among the standout tracks: Leadbelly's own "Bourgeois Blues" and such folk standards as "Careless Love," "John Henry," and "Midnight Special." *—Jeff Burger*

Shout On: Lead Belly Legacy, Vol. 3 / Mar. 17, 1998 / Smithsonian/Folkways ✦✦✦✦

Although the original Leadbelly LP bearing this name (Folkways 31030) was drawn from October 1948 sessions, the CD reissue adds 17 tracks, some recorded as early as 1941, and so should be now considered an anthology of '40s work. This does not rate among the best Leadbelly collections: due to illness, his guitar skills had diminished by the 1948 sessions that comprise much of the disc, and there are better versions of some of the songs elsewhere. It's still plenty worthwhile, though, particularly when Leadbelly is boosted by Sonny Terry's vocal and harmonica on several numbers, including Leroy Carr's blues "How Long, How Long." The CD is divided into thematic sections that, other than the 1948 recordings, feature three patriotic tunes about U.S. efforts in World War II; five numbers recorded with Woody Guthrie and Cisco Houston in 1946, including the perennial favorite "Midnight Special"; and seven children-oriented selections. *—Richie Unterberger*

Sings for Children / Mar. 23, 1999 / Smithsonian/Folkways ✦✦✦✦✦

A dozen of these 28 songs were first issued on the 1960 Folkways album *Negro Folk Songs for Young People*. But this is not so much a CD expansion of that album as a lengthy compilation of children-friendly performances from the '40s that uses *Negro Folk Songs for Young People* as its core. The additional tracks were recorded by Moe Asch of Folkways in 1941-1948, and include five of the six songs released on the 1941 album *Play Parties in Song and Dance as Sung By Lead Belly*, and a previously unreleased radio broadcast of "Take this Hammer." While many of these are simple tunes that can easily be picked up by young kids for singing along to, like "Skip to My Lou" and "Blue-Tailed Fly (Jimmy Crack Corn)," a bunch of these are classic folk songs of equal appeal to all age groups. Some of them are particularly identified with Leadbelly's interpretations, such as "Rock Island Line," "John Henry," "Cotton Fields," "Midnight Special," "Pick a Bale of Cotton," and "Take this Hammer"; other familiar standards like "Swing Low, Sweet Chariot" and "Sally Walker" are also aboard. As the liner notes explain, Leadbelly didn't limit the repertoire of his performances for children solely to simple tunes, also putting in blues and folk songs that you wouldn't think of as kids' tunes, like "Good Morning Blues." The result is a disc that is simply a good Leadbelly album, whether listened to by kids or others. *—Richie Unterberger*

Bridging Lead Belly / Oct. 26, 1999 / Rounder ✦✦✦

Bridging Lead Belly connects two Leadbelly recording sessions. The first is 12 tracks recorded for the BBC in 1938. The final five selections come from a 1946 live recording. Leadbelly is a master of the acoustic country blues. We hear this on the yodeling of "I'm Goin' Mother" that he shares the same roots with another rural tradition, that of the "singing cowboy." Beside such melancholy ballads, there are hearty tracks full of pep such as "Boll Weevil" and "(Baby) Take a Whiff on Me." The live recording is from a house party. A real gem in this section is "Frankie and Albert." Here Leadbelly elaborates to great length on the relationship. He does this—to the point where it becomes part soap opera and part social drama—of these two mythical figures of the blues. *—Tom Schulte*

My Last Go Round / Dec. 1, 1999 / Recall ✦✦✦

Presenting 40 songs in all, *My Last Go Round* is a good compilation focusing on Leadbelly's blues tunes. Disc one consists of solo tracks recorded in early 1935, including "CC Rider," both parts of "Death Letter Blues," "Ox Drivin' Blues," and "Yellow Jacket." The sound quality is decent—only slightly fuzzy, with mild distortion. Disc two spans the next five years and includes signature Leadbelly tunes such as "Good Morning Blues," "Rock Island Line," and "Goodnight, Irene," plus a few curiosities like a recording of "Midnight Special" with the Golden Gate Quartet (recorded by John Lomax in 1940) and Leadbelly playing piano (!) on "Eagle Rock Rag." *—Joslyn Layne*

Leadbelly, Vol. 1: 1934–1935 / Sep. 7, 2000 / Document ✦✦✦✦

Leadbelly, Vol. 2: 1935 / Sep. 7, 2000 / Document ✦✦✦✦

Leadbelly, Vol. 3: 1935 / Sep. 7, 2000 / Document ✦✦✦✦

Leadbelly, Vol. 4: 1935–1938 / Sep. 7, 2000 / Document ✦✦✦✦

Leadbelly, Vol. 5: 1938–1942 / Sep. 7, 2000 / Document ✦✦✦✦

Absolutely the Best / Oct. 3, 2000 / Fuel 2000 ✦✦✦✦

Leadbelly stands like a cornerstone in modern folk music. He showed that folk songs didn't have to be 300 years old and originate from the British Isles; instead they could be born out of American experience. *Absolutely the Best* offers a number of Leadbelly classics including "Roberta," "Midnight Special," and "In New Orleans (House of the Rising Sun." There is a wonderful version of "The Bourgeois Blues," filled with cutting social commentary, and a haunting version of "Where Did You Sleep Last Night." There is a simple, affecting version of "Goodnight Irene" and two versions of the outlaw ballad "John Hardy." Most of the cuts feature no more than the singer and his guitar, allowing Leadbelly's powerful voice to stand front and center. "How Long" receives a fuller arrangement with Sonny Terry's harmonica giving it a down and dirty blues feel. This disc will be educational for those who have only heard Creedence Clearwater Revival's version of "Midnight Special" or Led Zeppelin's "Gallows Pole." The difference is that Leadbelly could approach "Midnight Special" with sincerity, having spent a number of years in prison himself for murder. While there is nothing to complain about concerning this collection, it is irritating to find, on the song credits, Alan Lomax's name taking co-credit on songs like "The Bourgeois Blues." Lomax was an excellent field recorder, and he deserves praise for helping Leadbelly in a number of ways, but his helping hand came with a price. Leadbelly is an American original, and one has to know him to know American folk music. *Absolutely the Best* offers a good place for the listener to begin the acquaintance. *—Ronnie Lankford Jr.*

Chuck Leavell

b. Apr. 28, 1952, Birmingham, AL

Keyboards, Piano / Blues-Rock

In the who's who of rock & roll, Chuck Leavell is a very big someone. His piano and keyboard playing has graced the albums and/or stages of the Rolling Stones, Eric Clapton, the Allman Brothers Band, the Black Crowes, George Harrison, Blues Traveler, the Marshall Tucker Band, Hank Williams Jr., and a long list of others.

Leavell was born in Birmingham, AL, on April 28, 1952. At age 13 he formed his first band, the Misfitz, playing both organ and guitar. While still in high school, he played on his first local recording sessions. At 15, Leavell moved to Muscle Shoals, AL, and spent the next two years in and out of the world famous studios there. His recordings during that time included an appearance on Freddy North's "Don't Take Her, She's All I've Got." He then left for Macon, GA, and became connected with the newly formed Capricorn Records, joining Alex Taylor's band for *With Friends & Neighbors* (Taylor is the brother of singer James Taylor). After a year and a half, Leavell went on the road with Dr. John, spending six months observing and soaking up all he could.

Leavell was recruited by the Allman Brothers Band in 1972, shortly after the death of Duane Allman. He was just 20 years old. His first Allman Brothers Band record was the Billboard chart-topper *Brothers and Sisters*, yielding the hits "Ramblin' Man" and "Jessica." He remained with the band for four years; after its 1976 breakup, he formed Sea Level (pun intended) with Jimmy Nalls and former Allmans Jai Johanny Johanson and Lamar Williams. They recorded four albums that were embraced by fans and critics alike, and they toured extensively for five years. *The Best of Sea Level* was released in 1978. Leavell's career has been bringing him to new heights ever since, including album contributions and immense tours with the Rolling Stones (he's often referred to as the "sixth Rolling Stone") as well as numerous other accomplishments, the extent of which can really only be appreciated by a study of his discography. His first solo piano CD, *Forever Blue*, was released in 2001. It went hand in hand with his book, *Forever Green: The History and Hope of the American Forest*. The book is a result of Leavell's passion for forestry and conservation, which began developing in the late '80s. He and his wife, Rose Lane White, developed her family's ranch near Macon, GA, into a tree farm they named Charlane Plantation. When Leavell isn't in the studio or on the road, he can be found there with his family, horses, and the bird dogs he trains for field trials and quail hunting. *—Ann Wickstrom*

What's in That Bag? / Oct. 6, 1998 / Capricorn ✦✦✦

In blues-rock circles, Chuck Leavell was famed for his work with the Allman Brothers and the Rolling Stones, but he never cut a solo album to showcase his talents. When he began his solo career in 1998, he made an odd choice—he decided to record a Christmas album, *What's in That Bag?* Even though it isn't a choice many other musicians may have made, the resulting album is quite charming. His backing group of studio musicians, including the Muscle Shoals Horns and vocalist Lisa Fischer, is first-rate, and the album has a warm feel which suits the carols just right. Leavell throws in a couple of originals (including the great "Hey Santa") and newly written tunes to balance such standards as "Merry Christmas Baby," "Greensleeves," "Away in a Manger," "We Three Kings," "Joy to the World," and "God Rest Ye Merry Gentlemen." It all makes for a pleasing, bluesy holiday album that happens to also confirm Leavell's great talents as a keyboardist. *—Stephen Thomas Erlewine*

● **Forever Blue: Solo Piano** / May 29, 2001 / Terminus ♦♦♦♦♦
It's a long way from "Jumpin' Jack Flash" to the solo piano music of *Forever Blue*, but that only goes to further validate Chuck Leavell's stylistic versatility. The highly sought-after piano man extraordinaire boasts a massive discography varied enough to include the Rolling Stones, the Allman Brothers Band, Aretha Franklin, and Hank Williams Jr. *Forever Blue* was released in conjunction with Leavell's book, *Forever Green*, an informative work that addresses his other passion—forestry—which he avidly pursues on his tree farm in central Georgia. Seven of the ten songs on *Forever Blue* are originals; some are stripped-down versions of tunes Leavell recorded with his band, Sea Level, in the '70s ("A Lotta Colada" and "Song for Amy," a bouncing, Vince Guaraldi-style tune he wrote while watching his daughter at play when she was a toddler). Leavell's playing is creative and original, yet remains strongly connected to bluesy, Southern roots. A New Orleans feel is often present, particularly on "Walk a Little Closer." He comes down hard on the keys on the gospel standard "Higher Ground," but also gives a valuable lesson in dynamics when he quickly shifts to a gentle, feather-light touch, demonstrating that the distance between forceful emphasis and nimble delicacy can be just a few seconds. Leavell included his take on "Ashokan Farewell," a Jay Ungar song popularized when it was used in the PBS TV documentary *The Civil War*. Although the song has been recorded more than 30 times, Leavell is one of only a handful of artists who took a gamble on it and made it his, following his own musical trail rather than treating the song as a precious entity not to be tampered with. Even listeners intimately familiar with the tune will be taken to some new territory. The same goes for "Georgia," one of the bluesiest versions of the song you're ever likely to hear. Leavell gets totally inside a tune and goes where the music leads him, yet you get the sense he knows where it's going to lead him. In his hands, some old familiar songs sound as fresh as they did the first time they landed on human ears. Chuck Leavell has loads of chops and plays straight from the heart, resulting in music that is magnificently accomplished and sensitively executed. It's also highly accessible and deeply moving in a simple, straightforward manner. For example, "Comin' Home" was written during the last few days of a tour with the Stones. Leavell was looking forward to returning home to the peace and quiet of the Georgia countryside, and you can literally feel the anticipation he built into this song. A vision of him walking down a long, tree-lined driveway comes to mind. It's not easy to get a full sound on piano, but Leavell does it on *Forever Blue*, with fat chords on top and nice rhythmic bass lines that are used to cover bass and tenor sounds. Superb, fluid fingering produces beautiful flowing and cascading runs, nice trills, and showy licks, all while covering several octaves of the scale in just a few measures. He utilizes the pedals for some great dramatic stops and employs both a linear and a circular way of playing. He runs through the chord progressions several times, but they aren't obviously recycled since they are often phrased differently. Best of all, every note in Leavell's playing has a purpose. This CD would go perfectly with a pitcher of lemonade on the front porch on a hot summer day. It is as down-home and genuine as the man himself—and that's saying a whole lot. *—Ann Wickstrom*

Led Zeppelin

f. Jul. 1968, England, **db.** Dec. 1980, London, England
Group / Album Rock, British Blues, British Metal, Arena Rock, Heavy Metal, Hard Rock, Blues-Rock

Led Zeppelin was the definitive heavy metal band. It wasn't just their crushingly loud interpretation of the blues—it was how they incorporated mythology, mysticism, and a variety of other genres (most notably world music and British folk)—into their sound. Led Zeppelin had mystique. They rarely gave interviews, since the music press detested the band. Consequently, the only connection the audience had with the band was through the records and the concerts. More than any other band, Led Zeppelin established the concept of album-oriented rock, refusing to release popular songs from their albums as singles. In doing so, they established the dominant format for heavy metal, as well as the genre's actual sound.

Led Zeppelin formed out of the ashes of the Yardbirds. Jimmy Page had joined the band in its final days, playing a pivotal role on their final album, 1967's *Little Games*, which also featured string arrangements from John Paul Jones. During 1967, the Yardbirds were fairly inactive. While the Yardbirds decided their future, Page returned to session work in 1967. In the spring of 1968, he played on Jones' arrangement of Donovan's "Hurdy Gurdy Man." During the sessions, Jones requested to be part of any future project Page would develop. Page would have to assemble a band sooner than he had planned. In the summer of 1968, the Yardbirds' Keith Relf and James McCarty left the band, leaving Page and bassist Chris Dreja with the rights to the name, as well as the obligation of fulfilling an upcoming fall tour. Page set out to find a replacement vocalist and drummer. Initially, he wanted to enlist singer Terry Reid and Procol Harum's drummer B.J. Wilson, but neither musician was able to join the group. Reid suggested that Page contact Robert Plant, who was singing with a band called Hobbstweedle.

After hearing him sing, Page asked Plant to join the band in August of 1968, the same month Chris Dreja dropped out of the new project. Following Dreja's departure, John Paul Jones joined the group as its bassist. Plant recommended that Page hire John Bonham, the drummer for Plant's old band, the Band of Joy. Bonham had to be persuaded to join the group, as he was being courted by other artists who offered the drummer considerably more money. By September, Bonham agreed to join the band. Performing under the name the New Yardbirds, the band fulfilled the Yardbirds' previously booked engagements in late September 1968. The following month, they recorded their debut album in just under 30 hours. Also in October, the group switched their name to Led Zeppelin. The band secured a contract with Atlantic Records in the United States before the end of the year. Early in 1969, Led Zeppelin set out on their first American tour, which helped set the stage for the January release of their eponymous debut album. Two months after its release, *Led Zeppelin* had climbed into the U.S. Top Ten. Throughout 1969, the band toured relentlessly, playing dates in America and England. While they were on the road, they recorded their second album, *Led Zeppelin II*, which was released in October of 1969.

Like its predecessor, *Led Zeppelin II* was an immediate hit, topping the American charts two months after its release and spending seven weeks at number one. The album helped establish Led Zeppelin as an international concert attraction, and for the next year, the group continued to tour relentlessly. Led Zeppelin's sound began to deepen with *Led Zeppelin III*. Released in October of 1970, the album featured an overt British folk influence. The group's infatuation with folk and mythology would reach a fruition on the group's untitled fourth album, which was released in November of 1971. *Led Zeppelin IV* was the band's most musically diverse effort to date, featuring everything from the crunching rock of "Black Dog" to the folk of "The Battle of Evermore," as well as "Stairway to Heaven," which found the bridge between the two genres. "Stairway to Heaven" was an immediate radio hit, eventually becoming the most played song in the history of album-oriented radio; the song was never released as a single. Despite the fact that the album never reached number one in America, *Led Zeppelin IV* was their biggest album ever, selling well over 16 million copies over the next two and a half decades.

Led Zeppelin did tour to support both *Led Zeppelin III* and *Led Zeppelin IV*, but they played fewer shows than they did on their previous tours. Instead, they concentrated on only playing larger venues. After completing their 1972 tour, the band retreated from the spotlight and recorded their fifth album. Released in the spring of 1973, *Houses of the Holy* continued the band's musical experimentation, featuring touches of funk and reggae among their trademark rock and folk.The success of *Houses of the Holy* set the stage for a record-breaking American tour. Throughout their 1973 tour, Led Zeppelin broke box-office records—most of which were previously held by the Beatles—across America. The group's concert at Madison Square Garden in July was filmed for use in the feature film *The Song Remains the Same*, which was released three years later. After their 1973 tour, Led Zeppelin spent a quiet year during 1974, releasing no new material and performing no concerts. They did, however, establish their own record label, Swan Song, which released all of Led Zeppelin's subsequent albums, as well as records by Dave Edmunds, Bad Company, the Pretty Things, and several others. *Physical Graffiti*, a double album released in February of 1975, was the band's first release on Swan Song. The album was an immediate success, topping the charts in both America and England. Led Zeppelin launched a large American tour in 1975 but it came to a halt when Robert Plant and his wife suffered a serious car crash while vacationing in Greece. The tour was cancelled and Plant spent the rest of the year recuperating from the accident.

Led Zeppelin returned to action in the spring of 1976 with *Presence*. Although the album debuted at number one in both America and England, the reviews for the album were lukewarm, as was the reception to the live concert film *The Song Remains the Same*, which appeared in the fall of 1976. The band finally returned to tour America in the Spring of 1977. A couple of months into the tour, Plant's six-year-old son Karac died of a stomach infection. Led Zeppelin immediately cancelled the tour and offered no word whether or not it would be rescheduled, causing widespread speculation about the band's future. For a while, it did appear that Led Zeppelin was finished. Robert Plant spent the latter half of 1977 and the better part of 1978 in seclusion. The group didn't begin work on a new album until late in the summer of 1978, when they began recording at ABBA's Polar studios in Sweden. A year later, the band played a short European tour, performing in Switzerland, Germany, Holland, Belgium, and Austria. In August of 1979, Led Zeppelin played two large concerts at Knebworth; the shows would be their last English performances.

In Through the Out Door, the band's much-delayed eighth studio album, was finally released in September of 1979. The album entered the charts at number one in both America and England. In May of 1980, Led Zeppelin embarked on their final European tour. In September, Led Zeppelin began rehearsing at Jimmy Page's house in preparation for an American tour. On September 25, John Bonham was found dead in his bed—following an all-day drinking binge, he had passed out and choked on his own vomit. In December of 1980, Led Zeppelin announced they were disbanding, since they could not continue without Bonham.

Following the breakup, the remaining members all began solo careers. John Paul Jones returned to producing and arranging, finally releasing his solo debut *Zooma* in 1999. After recording the soundtrack for *Death Wish II*, Jimmy Page compiled the Zeppelin outtakes collection, *Coda*, which was released at the end of 1982. That same year, Robert Plant began a solo career with the *Pictures at Eleven* album. In 1984, Plant and Page briefly reunited in the all-star oldies band the Honeydrippers. After recording one EP with the Honeydrippers, Plant returned to his solo career and Page formed the Firm with former Bad Company singer Paul Rogers. In 1985, Led Zeppelin reunited to play Live Aid, sparking off a flurry of reunion rumors; the reunion never materialized. In 1988, the band re-formed to play Atlantic's 25th anniversary concert. During 1989, Page remastered the band's catalog for release on the 1990 box set, *Led Zeppelin*. The four-disc set became the biggest selling multi-disc box set of all time, which was followed up three years later by another box set, the mammoth ten-disc set *The Complete Studio Recordings*.

In 1994, Jimmy Page and Robert Plant reunited to record a segment for *MTV Unplugged*, which was released as *Unledded* in the fall of 1994. Although the album went platinum, the sales were disappointing considering the anticipation of a Zeppelin reunion. The following year, Page and Plant embarked on a successful international tour, which eventually led to an all new studio recording in 1998—the Steve Albini-produced *Walking Into Clarksdale*. Surprisingly, the album was met with a cool reception by the record-buying public, as Page and Plant ended their union shortly thereafter, once again going their separate ways (Page would go on to tour with the Black Crowes, while Plant would resume his solo career). Further Zeppelin compilation releases saw the light of day in the late-'90s, including 1997's stellar double-disc *BBC Sessions*, plus Zep's first true best-of collections—1999's *Early Days: The Best of Vol. 1* and 2000's *Latter Days: The Best of Vol. 2*. *—Stephen Thomas Erlewine & Greg Prato*

☆ **Led Zeppelin** / Jan. 12, 1969 / Atlantic ♦♦♦♦♦

Led Zeppelin had a fully formed, distinctive sound from the outset, as their eponymous debut illustrates. Taking the heavy, distorted electric blues of Jimi Hendrix, Jeff Beck, and Cream to an extreme, Zeppelin created a majestic, powerful brand of guitar rock constructed around simple, memorable riffs and lumbering rhythms. But the key to the group's attack was subtlety: It wasn't just an onslaught of guitar noise, it was shaded and textured, filled with alternating dynamics and tempos. As *Led Zeppelin* proves, the group was capable of such multi-layered music from the start. Although the extended psychedelic blues of "Dazed and Confused," "You Shook Me," and "I Can't Quit You Baby" often gather the most attention, the remainder of the album is a better indication of what would come later. "Babe I'm Gonna Leave You" shifts from folky verses to pummeling choruses; "Good Times Bad Times" and "How Many More Times" have groovy, bluesy shuffles; "Your Time Is Gonna Come" is an anthemic hard rocker; "Black Mountain Side" is pure English folk; and "Communication Breakdown" is a frenzied rocker with a nearly punkish attack. Although the album isn't as varied as some of their later efforts, it nevertheless marked a significant turning point in the evolution of hard rock and heavy metal. *—Stephen Thomas Erlewine*

☆ **Led Zeppelin II** / Oct. 22, 1969 / Atlantic ♦♦♦♦♦

Recorded quickly during Led Zeppelin's first American tours, *Led Zeppelin II* provided the blueprint for all the heavy metal bands that followed it. Since the group could only enter the studio for brief amounts of time, most of the songs that compose *II* are reworked blues and rock & roll standards that the band were performing onstage at the time. Not only did the short amount of time result in a lack of original material, it made the sound more direct. Jimmy Page still provided layers of guitar overdubs, but the overall sound of the album is heavy and hard, brutal and direct. "Whole Lotta Love," "The Lemon Song," and "Bring It on Home" are all based on classic blues songs—only, the riffs are simpler and louder and each song has an extended section for instrumental solos. Of the remaining six songs, two sport light acoustic touches ("Thank You," "Ramble On"), but the other four are straight-ahead heavy rock that follow the formula of the revamped blues songs. While *Led Zeppelin II* doesn't have the eclecticism of the group's debut, it's arguably more influential. After all, nearly every one of the hundreds of Zeppelin imitators used this record, with its lack of dynamics and its pummeling riffs, as a blueprint. *—Stephen Thomas Erlewine*

☆ **Led Zeppelin III** / Oct. 5, 1970 / Atlantic ♦♦♦♦♦

On their first two albums, Led Zeppelin unleashed a relentless barrage of heavy blues and rockabilly riffs, but *Led Zeppelin III* provided the band with the necessary room to grow musically. While there are still a handful of metallic rockers, *III* is built on a folky, acoustic foundation which gives the music extra depth. And even the rockers aren't as straightforward as before: The galloping "Immigrant Song" is powered by Plant's banshee wail, "Celebration Day" turns blues-rock inside out with a warped slide guitar riff, and "Out on the Tiles" lumbers along with a tricky, multi-part riff. Nevertheless, the heart of the album lies on the second side, when the band delve deeply into English folk. "Gallows Pole" updates a traditional tune with a menacing flair, and "Bron-Y-Aur Stomp" is an infectious acoustic romp, while "That's the Way" and "Tangerine" are shimmering songs with graceful country flourishes. The band haven't left the blues behind, but the twisted bottleneck blues of "Hats Off to (Roy) Harper" actually outstrips the epic "Since I've Been Loving You," which is the only time Zeppelin sound a bit set in their ways. *—Stephen Thomas Erlewine*

★ **Led Zeppelin IV** / Nov. 8, 1971 / Atlantic ♦♦♦♦♦

Encompassing heavy metal, folk, pure rock & roll, and blues, Led Zeppelin's untitled fourth album is a monolithic record, defining not only Led Zeppelin but the sound and style of '70s hard rock. Expanding on the breakthroughs of *III*, Zeppelin fuse their majestic hard rock with a mystical, rural English folk that gives the record an epic scope. Even at its most basic—the muscular, traditionalist "Rock & Roll"—the album has a grand sense of drama, which is only deepened by Plant's burgeoning obsession with mythology, religion, and the occult. Plant's mysticism comes to a head on the eerie folk ballad "The Ballad of Evermore," a mandolin-driven song with haunting vocals from Sandy Denny, and on the epic "Stairway to Heaven." Of all of Zeppelin's songs, "Stairway to Heaven" is the most famous, and not unjustly. Building from a simple fingerpicked acoustic guitar to a storming torrent of guitar riffs and solos, it encapsulates the entire album in one song. Which, of course, isn't discounting the rest of the album. "Going to California" is the group's best folk song, and the rockers are endlessly inventive, whether it's the complex, multi-layered "Black Dog," the pounding hippie satire "Misty Mountain Hop," or the funky riffs of "Four Sticks." But the closer, "When the Levee Breaks," is the one song truly equal to "Stairway," helping give *IV* the feeling of an epic. An apocalyptic slice of urban blues, "When the Levee Breaks" is as forceful and frightening as Zeppelin ever got, and its seismic rhythms and layered dynamics illustrate why none of their imitators could ever equal them. *—Stephen Thomas Erlewine*

☆ **Houses of the Holy** / Mar. 28, 1973 / Atlantic ♦♦♦♦♦

Houses of the Holy follows the same basic pattern as *Led Zeppelin IV*, but the approach is looser and more relaxed. Jimmy Page's riffs rely on ringing, folky hooks as much as they do on thundering blues-rock, giving the album a lighter, more open atmosphere. While the pseudo-reggae of "D'Yer Mak'er" and the affectionate James Brown send-up "The Crunge" suggest that the band were searching for material, they actually contribute to the musical diversity of the album. "The Rain Song" is one of Zep's finest moments, featuring a soaring string arrangement and a gentle, aching melody. "The Ocean" is just as good, starting with a heavy, funky guitar groove before slamming into an a cappella section and ending with a swinging, doo-wop-flavored rave-up. With the exception of the rampaging opening number, "The Song Remains the Same," the rest of *Houses of the Holy* is fairly straightforward, ranging from the foreboding "No Quarter" and the strutting hard rock of "Dancing Days" to the epic folk/metal fusion "Over the Hills and Far Away." Throughout the record, the band's playing is excellent, making the eclecticism of Page and Plant's songwriting sound coherent and natural. *—Stephen Thomas Erlewine*

☆ **Physical Graffiti** / Feb. 24, 1975 / Swan Song ♦♦♦♦♦

Led Zeppelin returned from a nearly two-year hiatus in 1975 with *Physical Graffiti*, a sprawling, ambitious double album. Zeppelin treats many of the songs on *Physical Graffiti* as forays into individual styles, only occasionally synthesizing sounds, notably on the tense, Eastern-influenced "Kashmir." With John Paul Jones' galloping keyboard, "Trampled Underfoot" ranks as their funkiest metallic grind, while "Houses of the Holy" is as effervescent as pre-Beatles pop and "Down By the Seaside" is the closest they've come to country. Even the heavier blues—the 11-minute "In My Time of Dying," the tightly wound "Custard Pie," and the monstrous epic "The Rover"—are subtly shaded, even if they're thunderously loud. Most of these heavy rockers are isolated on the first album, with the second half of *Physical Graffiti* sounding a little like a scrap-heap of experiments, jams, acoustic workouts, and neo-covers. This may not be as consistent as the first platter, but its quirks are entirely welcome, not just because they encompass the mean, decadent "Sick Again," but the heartbreaking "Ten Years Gone" and the utterly charming acoustic rock & roll of "Boogie With Stu" and "Black Country Woman." Yes, some of this could be labeled as filler, but like any great double album, its appeal lies in its great sprawl, since it captures elements of the band's personality rarely showcased elsewhere—and even at its worst, *Physical Graffiti* towers above its hard rock peers of the mid-'70s. *—Stephen Thomas Erlewine*

Presence / 1976 / Swan Song ♦♦♦

Presence scales back the size of *Physical Graffiti* to a single album, but it retains the grandiose scope of that double record. If anything, *Presence* has more majestic epics than its predecessor, opening with the surging, ten-minute "Achilles Last Stand" and closing with the meandering, nearly ten-minute "Tea for One." In between, Zeppelin add the lumbering blues workout "Nobody's Fault but Mine" and the terse, menacing "For Your Life," which is the best song on the album. These four tracks take up the bulk of the album, leaving three lighthearted throwaways to alleviate the foreboding atmosphere—and pretensions—of the epics. If all of the throwaways were as focused and funny as those on *Physical Graffiti* or *Houses of the Holy*, Zeppelin would have had another classic on their hands. However, the Crescent City love letter of "Royal Orleans" sags in the middle, and the ersatz rockabilly of "Candy Store Rock" doesn't muster up the loose, funky swagger of "Hots on for Nowhere," which it *should* in order to work. The three throwaways are also scattered haphazardly throughout the album, making it seem more ponderous than it actually is, and the result is the weakest album Zeppelin had yet recorded. *—Stephen Thomas Erlewine*

The Song Remains the Same / 1976 / Swan Song ♦♦

Led Zeppelin's initial popularity was based as much on their concerts as their albums, so it's strange that the group's only official live album is such an uninspired, boring affair. Released in conjunction with the pseudo-documentary film of the same name, *The Song Remains the Same* reproduces the very things that made Zeppelin concerts legendary—lengthy solos, intertwining interplay between Page and Plant, and ridiculously long songs ("Dazed and Confused" is nearly an entire half hour)—but the group's performance is not intoxicating, it's long-winded. As scores of bootlegs prove, Led Zeppelin could produce magic with the same formula, but *The Song Remains the Same* is excruciatingly dull. *—Stephen Thomas Erlewine*

In Through the Out Door / 1979 / Swan Song ♦♦♦

Somewhere between *Presence* and *In Through the Out Door*, disco, punk, and new wave had overtaken rock & roll, and Led Zeppelin chose to tentatively embrace these pop revolutions, adding synthesizers to the mix and emphasizing John Bonham's inherent way with a groove. The album's opening number, "In the Evening," with its stomping rhythms and heavy, staggered riffs, suggests that the band haven't deviated from their course, but by the time the rolling shuffle of "South Bound Suarez" kicks into gear, it's apparent that they've regained their sense of humor. After "South Bound Suarez," the group try a variety of styles, whether it's an overdriven homage to Bakersfield County called "Hot Dog," the layered, Latin-tinged percussion and pianos of "Fool in the Rain," or the slickly seductive ballad "All My Love." "Carouselambra," a lurching, self-consciously ambitious synth-driven number, and the slow blues "I'm Gonna Crawl" aren't quite as impressive as the rest of the album, but the record was a graceful way to close to their career, even if it wasn't intended as the final chapter. *—Stephen Thomas Erlewine*

Coda / 1982 / Swan Song ♦♦♦

An odds-and-sods collection assembled after John Bonham's death, *Coda* is predictably a hit-or-miss affair. The best material comes from later in their career, including the ringing folk stomp of "Poor Tom," the jacked-up '50s rock & roll of "Ozone Baby," and their response to punk rock, the savage "Wearing and Tearing." The rest of the album—sadly including the Bonham showcase "Bonzo's Montreux"—is average, despite the presence of some stellar playing, especially on the early blues-rock blitzkrieg "I Can't Quit You Baby" and "We're Gonna Groove." *—Stephen Thomas Erlewine*

Led Zeppelin [Box Set] / Sep. 1990 / Swan Song ♦♦♦

Led Zeppelin's primary method of artistic expression was their albums. Although they had a handful of hit singles and selected album tracks were played endlessly on the radio, the true range of their music is only evident on the original albums, which were carefully sequenced and assembled. Consequently, the notion of a Led Zeppelin anthology is a bit strange—their records worked as individual pieces. Nevertheless, the four-disc box set *Led Zeppelin* includes most of their best and most famous material. Jimmy Page determined the set's running order, taking the songs out of their familiar contexts and placing them in a new, occasionally jarring, sequence, providing new insights to the band's music that dedicated fans will appreciate. *Led Zeppelin* is the only album in their catalog to include the classic B-side "Hey Hey What Can I Do," as well as their unreleased version of Robert Johnson's "Travelling Riverside Blues" and a live medley of Page's "White Summer/Black Mountain Side." Most fans will find these three tracks essential, but will balk at the price, especially since all of Zeppelin's albums have been re-mastered since the original release of the box set. While the box contains a wealth of brilliant music, all of it is better heard in its original incarnation. *—Stephen Thomas Erlewine*

Led Zeppelin Remasters / Feb. 21, 1992 / Swan Song ♦♦♦
A collection of most of Zeppelin's best-known tracks, this double-disc set only gives a slight idea of what the band accomplished in its career; stick with the original albums instead. *—Stephen Thomas Erlewine*

Led Zeppelin [Box Set 2] / Mar. 19, 1993 / Swan Song ♦♦♦
Rounding up all of the studio tracks that didn't appear on the first box (as well as the pleasant, but unremarkable, "Baby Come on Home"), *Boxed Set 2* is the perfect way to complete a Led Zeppelin library begun with the first box set. *—Stephen Thomas Erlewine*

Complete Studio Recordings / Sep. 24, 1993 / Swan Song ♦♦♦
Collecting all of Led Zeppelin's groundbreaking studio albums (as well as a reworked *Coda*) in one unattractive box, *The Complete Studio Recordings* is only necessary for hardcore fans wishing to replace their old records. Although the artwork inside the package is lavish, the box features no new material or remastering, making it completely irrelevant for those who already own the first two box sets. The music here is brilliant, but it's available in better, more attractive, and less expensive packages. *—Stephen Thomas Erlewine*

BBC Sessions / Nov. 11, 1997 / Atlantic ♦♦♦♦♦
Led Zeppelin's BBC sessions were among the most popular bootleg items of the rock & roll era, appearing on myriad illegal records and CDs. They were all the more popular because of the lack of official Led Zeppelin live albums, especially since *The Song Remains the Same* failed to capture the essence of the band. For anyone that hadn't heard the recordings, the mystique of Zeppelin's BBC Sessions was somewhat mystifying, but the official 1997 release of the double-disc *BBC Sessions* offered revelations for any fan who hadn't yet heard this music. While some collectors will be dismayed by the slight trimming on the "Whole Lotta Love Medley," almost all of the group's sessions are included here, and they prove why live Zeppelin was the stuff of legend. The 1969 sessions, recorded shortly after the release of the first album, are fiery and dynamic, outstripping the studio record for sheer power. Early versions of "You Shook Me," "Communication Breakdown," "What Is & What Should Never Be" and "Whole Lotta Love" hit harder than their recorded counterparts, while covers of Sleepy John Estes' "The Girl I Love She Got Long Black Wavy Hair," Robert Johnson's "Travelling Riverside Blues" and Eddie Cochran's "Something Else" are welcome additions to the Zeppelin catalog, confirming their folk, blues and rockabilly roots as well as their sense of vision. Zeppelin's grand vision comes into sharper relief on the second disc, which is comprised of their 1971 sessions. They still have their primal energy, but they're more adventurous, branching out into folk, twisted psychedelia, and weird blues-funk. Certainly, *BBC Sessions* is the kind of album that will only appeal to fans, but anyone who's ever doubted Zeppelin's power or vision will be set straight with this record. *—Stephen Thomas Erlewine*

Early Days: The Best of Led Zeppelin, Vol. 1 / Nov. 23, 1999 / Atlantic ♦♦♦♦
As legend has it, Led Zeppelin never played the singles game. That's not entirely true—"Whole Lotta Love" was a gold-selling, Top Five single, while "Immigrant Song," "Black Dog," and "D'yer Mak'er" all went Top 20. But since their reputation was built in part through album-rock radio, and since they never released "Stairway to Heaven" as a single, the impression that they were above hits and singles grew and grew. Zeppelin fostered it by refusing to issue compilations for years, forcing every fan to become familiar with the group on an album-by-album basis. Things began to change a bit in 1990, when Jimmy Page assembled the four-disc *Led Zeppelin* box, the group's first official compilation; it eventually opened the door for the 1999 release of *Early Days: The Best of Led Zeppelin, Vol. 1. Early Days* focuses on the first four Zeppelin albums, taking four songs from the first, just two apiece from the second and third, and the entire first side of *IV*, along with "When the Levee Breaks." And for the diehards, a video clip of Zeppelin performing "Communication Breakdown" on an English TV show is thrown onto the enhanced CD portion of the disc. It's basically the album longtime Zeppelin fans thought would never be released: a straight-up greatest-hits album. At one point, this may have been seen as sacrilege among devotees, but at this point, it's hard to imagine who would care about *Early Days* one way or another. Apart from the handful of casual fans who just want the radio staples on one disc—while not caring that other classics are absent—there really is no audience for this, since it doesn't recontextualize the catalog like the box sets. It's still pretty entertaining, yet *Early Days* feels unnecessary. Yet that cover photo is priceless. *—Stephen Thomas Erlewine*

Latter Days: The Best of Led Zeppelin, Vol. 2 / Mar. 21, 2000 / Atlantic ♦♦♦♦
Latter Days—The Best of Led Zeppelin, Vol. 2 offers ten highlights from *Houses of the Holy, Physical Graffiti, Presence*, and *In Through the Out Door*. While all fans can argue about missing album tracks—some may choose "The Rover" and "Over the Hills and Far Away" for should-have-beens, while others take "Custard Pie," "For Your Life" and "Hots on for Nowhere"—the only true staples missing are "Dancing Days" and the exquisite faux-Brazilian "Fool in the Rain." Thus, this is a pretty fine compilation for casual fans, the kind who only want the songs they hear on the radio all the time (such as "The Song Remains the Same," "No Quarter," "Trampled Underfoot," "Kashmir," "In the Evening"). Of course, any true Zeppelin enthusiast will want the full albums, but as a sampler of their last four records, *Latter Days* is just fine. *—Stephen Thomas Erlewine*

Rosie Ledet (Mary Roszela Bellard)

b. Oct. 25, 1971, Louisiana
Vocals / Zydeco

Accordionist, singer, and songwriter Mary Roszela Bellard, "Rosie" Ledet (pronounced led-dett), was raised on rock & roll music. During her teenage years in southwest Louisiana, she listened to classic rock & roll radio stations in nearby Eunice; her favorite groups included Santana and Z.Z. Top.

Like so many other French kids raised in rural southwest Louisiana, she paid no particular attention to all the zydeco music that was around her in her formative years; even though her parents had tried to raise her with a healthy respect for zydeco music, the music held little appeal for her as a kid. But one day, after attending a zydeco dance when she was 16, hearing Boozoo Chavis, and meeting Morris Ledet—who would later become her husband— she was smitten.

She married Morris, the bassist in her band, when she was 17, and while he was on the road touring regionally with a group he led, she stayed home and took care of her ailing mother-in-law. It was during this period of several years that Ledet worked on her accordion playing, honing her skills. At first, she would play along to the recordings of Boozoo Chavis and John Delafose. She began to learn songs intuitively, by ear, and one day surprised her husband by playing a complete Delafose song. Her husband encouraged young Rosie to continue in her efforts, and within a matter of months, she had recorded a demo of her own songs and secured a record deal with Maison de Soul, a zydeco label in nearby Ville Platte.

In a very short time, the prolific songwriter released three albums of her own material, with a backing band that included her husband and father-in-law on bass and rub board, respectively. Ledet's albums include *Sweet Brown Sugar* (1994), *Zydeco Sensation* (1997) and *It's a Groove Thing!* (2000), all for the Maison de Soul label of the Flat Town Music Co. in Ville Platte. All of Ledet's albums showcase superb songs, strong vocals and adequate accordion playing. She and her band began performing in 1994 throughout the Texas-Louisiana triangle, and gradually began to spread their touring base to include the rest of the U.S. Ledet and band have been on several European tours as well. *—Richard Skelly*

● **Sweet Brown Sugar** / 1994 / Maison de Soul ♦♦♦♦
Since there aren't many female zydeco singers, the very existence of Rosie Ledet would be noteworthy. Fortunately, her debut album, *Sweet Brown Sugar*, shows that there's a reason to be interested in her outside of sheer novelty. Ledet proves herself to be a strong songwriter and energetic accordionist on *Sweet Brown Sugar*. Her voice may be a little too restrained for some tastes, but she makes up for that with her propulsive, infectious instrumental work. Also, her songs suggest that she could develop into a distinctive lyrical voice in her own right. All in all, it's a fine debut. *—Thom Owens*

Zesty Zydeco / 1995 / Maison de Soul ♦♦
Floyd Soileau's Ville Platte, Louisiana-based Maison de Soul label has been cranking out a lot of fair-to-middling zydeco in recent years, and *Zesty Zydeco* is another effort that fails to rise from the pack. That's too bad, because as one of few female zydeco singers, Rosie Ledet has potential to stand out. There are two terrific songs on this disc: "Casino Nights" (a catchy little tune in which she warns her man that he'll lose her love as well as his money if he keeps going out to play the slot machines instead of staying home with her) and "I'm Gonna Take Care of Your Dog" (a deliciously sexy song about a "pussycat" who threatens to steal another woman's "dog" that keeps coming into her yard). More than any other music in America, zydeco remains a family affair, and her band consists mostly of other Ledets. Zydeco is a simple music form—that's part of its charm—but the same pentatonic ostinatos played over and over on the accordion become monotonous over the length of this CD. *—Steve Hoffman*

Zydeco Sensation / 1997 / Maison de Soul ♦♦♦
Rosie Ledet's playing is solid, and her singing is soulful, if untrained. But what she brings to this music is not your bayou-variety heat. "Roll It Over" and "My Joy Box" churn insistently while Ledet purrs and moans. "Sweetheart Style" shows that she can also be a tad more subtle, though for the most part the thrust (sorry) of *Zydeco Sensation* is sex. This is a good thing. The chugging rhythms work well with her choice of lyrics. The sound is sparse, and a tad underproduced, though this doesn't detract from this memorable music whatsoever. *—Brian Briscoe*

I'm a Woman / 1999 / Maison de Soul ♦♦♦

It's a Groove Thing! / Jun. 6, 2000 / Maison de Soul ♦♦♦

Show Me Something / Aug. 7, 2001 / Maison de Soul ♦♦♦♦
The growth from her earliest albums is wonderful for this sensuous singer; no longer are her albums held back by the repetitious beats that used to ensnare her early discs. Most importantly, she is using that wonderful, husky voice that is her natural and best asset to wrap around her insightful lyrics, which reflect a woman's point of view. She is one of the few female zydeco performers who is worth the price of admission. She does sound her best on the slower tempo of "Days Gone By," where she can work with the full expressiveness of her voice. She always seems to sing with a heartfelt integrity in her voice. She started performing in about 1995, when in one night she went to her first zydeco dance to hear Boozoo Chavis and fell in love with both the music and her to-be husband, Morris. Morris had his own band and played the accordion, which she learned by watching him and practicing when he was off at work. She showed him what she could do one day and eventually began leading the band; he is the bass player. She writes most

of her own songs, which is a rarity for most zydeco performers, no matter their gender. When she cranks up "Zydeco for a Living," that voice of hers sets the temperature soaring. There is room here to grow, but this is a very solid effort by someone who you'd better keep your eye on. *—Bob Gottlieb*

Bonnie Lee

b. Jun. 11, 1931, Bunkie, LA

Vocals / Chicago Blues, Soul-Blues

Although she's been singing on the Chicago scene since the '60s, Bonnie Lee is mostly renowned for one song: the midtempo grinder "I'm Good," which has become her trademark (she's cut it several times, including a solid version on bassist Willie Kent's 1992 Delmark set *Ain't It Nice*; and Johnny Winter covered it on his Alligator LP *Third Degree*). *—Bill Dahl*

● **Sweetheart of the Blues** / 1995 / Delmark ♦♦♦♦♦

Bonnie Lee cut her first full-length album, *Sweetheart of the Blues*, in 1995, nearly 30 years after she established herself as a staple of the Chicago scene. During those years, she sang constantly, and it's clear from the first note that this album is the work of a seasoned pro. Lee pretty much sticks to standards like "Baby, What You Want Me to Do," "Walking Blues," and "That's All Right," but that's all right, because it gives her the opportunity to wail. And wail she does, proving she's a fine soul-blues vocalist, capable of great things. She doesn't reach greatness here, but *Sweetheart of the Blues* is a classy set of Chicago blues. It's just too bad that it took her so long to cut the record.*—Stephen Thomas Erlewine*

Bryan Lee

b. 1945, Wisconsin

Guitar, Producer, Vocals / Modern Electric Blues

A longtime staple of New Orleans' famed Bourbon Street club circuit, blues guitarist Bryan Lee was born in Wisconsin in 1945; inspired by B.B. King, Albert King and others, his Midwest upbringing also resulted in a distinctively Chicago-styled sound which his long stay in the South did little to erase. Billed variously as "The Braille Blues Daddy" and "The Blind Blues Daddy," Lee first surfaced in New Orleans in 1983, quickly becoming a favorite of tourists in the city's French Quarter and regularly playing live at least six nights a week; he made his solo debut in 1991 with *The Blues Is...*, followed in 1993 by *Memphis Bound*. After 1995's *Heat Seeking Missile*, Lee issued 1997's *Live at the Old Absinthe House Bar: Friday Night*, an ideal souvenir for the many patrons of his club dates. *Crawfish Lady* followed in the spring of 2000, and *Six String Therapy* in fall 2002. *—Jason Ankeny*

● **The Blues Is...** / 1991 / Justin Time ♦♦♦♦

Bryan Lee's debut album *Blues Is...* is a solid collection of greasy New Orleans blues. While he may not always have great original songs, Lee can conjure the sound of the swamp with his big, bluesy guitar, and that's enough to make this an entertaining listen, especially for fans of Crescent City blues. *—Thom Owens*

Memphis Bound / 1993 / Justin Time ♦♦♦♦

Braille Blues Daddy / Feb. 21, 1995 / Justin Time ♦♦♦

Heat Seeking Missile / Oct. 1995 / Justin Time ♦♦♦

Live at the Old Absinthe House Bar: Friday Night / Nov. 4, 1997 / Justin Time ♦♦♦

From the beginning of the opening cut, "Think," and throughout the entire show on this live CD, blues guitarist-singer Bryan Lee puts on an explosive performance full of fire and passion. Lee talks enthusiastically to the audience, giving them the background to many of the songs before shouting out his vocals, but it his intense guitar flights that are most impressive. Lee welcomes his young friends and fellow guitarists Kenny Wayne Shepherd and Frank Marino as guests on a few numbers. If anything, their participation make the music even more fiery. With the assistance of a fine background group that includes both organist Marc Adams and John Banks on keyboards, this CD certainly does not lack in spirit, power or intensity. *—Scott Yanow*

Crawfish Lady / Apr. 18, 2000 / Justin Time ♦♦♦♦

Crawfish Lady is the seventh release for the Justin Time label from Bryan Lee. This New Orleans blues guitarist manages to combine his Crescent City influences with Memphis soul and Chicago and Texas blues. Lee's guitar abilities bring to mind the spirits of Elmore James, Albert King, and Albert Collins. The appearances of Ward Smith and Jody Golick on tenor sax, Barney Floyd on trumpet, and longtime bandmember Marc Adams on organ add fiery flavor to this musical gumbo. *—Al Campbell*

Frankie Lee

b. Apr. 29, 1941, Mart, TX

Vocals / Modern Electric Blues, Soul-Blues, R&B, Soul

Vocalist Frankie Lee has always been an engaging and energetic live performer, though his recorded output is still very small, given the number of years he's been around and how legendary his live shows have become. If Denise LaSalle is a modern day Bessie Smith, than Lee is a '90s Otis Redding. One of Lee's live-show trademarks (like the late Albert Collins' guitar walks) is the point in the show in which he leaves his mic on stage and walks out into his audience, be it a festival of 10,000 people or a small club of 50. Lee's motto is, "whether it's one or 1,000, me and my band are gonna put on a show."

Lee was born April 29, 1941, in rural Mart, TX. His early influences included Sam Cooke, but before that, he sang in church groups. He recalled in several interviews that his grandmother made him sing, never realizing he'd end up singing blues, not gospel. He began recording in 1963 with Don Robey's Duke/Peacock label out of Houston. He recorded three singles that attracted regional attention: "Full Time Lover," "Taxi Blues" and "Hello, Mr. Blues." While he and Sonny Rhodes were living in Austin, Lee was heard by Ike Turner. That night, Turner invited him to join the Ike & Tina Turner road show. He was off with them the next day, gaining invaluable performing experience.

After returning from the road trips with their revue, Lee settled in Houston and had the chance to work with the people he admired, including Big Mama Thornton, Bobby "Blue" Bland, Clarence "Gatemouth" Brown, Ted Taylor, Junior Parker, O.V. Wright, James "Thunderbird" Davis, and Joe Hinton. Don Robey heard Lee in a Houston nightclub and offered him the chance to record. Later, Lee began working with guitarist Albert Collins, and the two became good friends, finally leaving Texas together in 1965 for California.

Lee sang with Collins' band for the next six years. By 1971, Lee was in Los Angeles, working with his cousin Johnny "Guitar" Watson. (Watson passed away at age 61 on May 17, 1996.) He recorded for Elka Records, with Watson producing. In 1973, Lee moved north to the San Francisco Bay area, and in the late '70s, he recruited a young guitarist, Robert Cray, to play in his backup band. Finally Lee landed a contract with Hightone Records, a then developing label, and recorded his debut album, *The Ladies and the Babies* in 1984.

After successful performances with Sonny Rhodes at the Chicago Blues Festival, Lee moved to New Jersey in 1986, where he quickly established a following at clubs and festivals throughout the northeast. Lee was signed to record for the Flying Fish label in 1992, and *Sooner or Later*, with Doug Newby and the Virginia-based Bluzblasters, was the result. Lee's *Going Back Home* is on the San Francisco-based Blind Pig label. The album was actually recorded back in the mid-'80s, but wasn't released until 1994.

Oddly enough, during the mid-'90s, Lee's live clubs shows were as energetic as ever, and he'd lost none of his enthusiasm for performing, despite the fact that he was in his mid-fifties. He's got a whole lot of talent and energy left, so there will be more recordings from this exciting vocalist and showman in the future. Records worth owning include *The Ladies and the Babies* and *Going Back Home*. Any of his singles for the Peacock or Elka labels, such as "Full Time Lover" b/w "Don't Make Me Cry," are collector's items, and should be snatched up without hesitation. *—Richard Skelly*

● **The Ladies and the Babies** / 1984 / Hightone ♦♦♦♦

Frankie Lee's debut album, *The Ladies and the Babies*, was one of the first contemporary blues albums to successfully negotiate the territory between post-Bobby Bland blues and southern soul. As one of the first albums on Hightone Records, the album helped set the stage for the numerous records and artists that teetered between soul and blues. To Lee's immense credit, he achieved this balance quite skillfully, thanks to solid songs, tight arrangements and powerful vocalists. He followed the record with several others quite like it, but none matched the energy or quality of *The Ladies and the Babies*. *—Thom Owens*

Going Back Home / 1994 / Blind Pig ♦♦♦

Here I Go Again / 1999 / Blues Express ♦♦♦♦

Lovie Lee (Eddie Lee Watson)

b. Mar. 17, 1909, Chattanooga, TN, **d.** May 23, 1997, Chicago, IL

Piano / Contemporary Blues, Modern Electric Blues

Best known as Muddy Waters' final piano accompanist, the sadly under-recognized Lovie Lee was a longtime staple of the Chicago club circuit. Born Eddie Lee Watson in Chattanooga, TN, on March 17, 1909, he worked during the day as a factory woodworker, honing his skills each night in the Chicago blues clubs from the '50s onward; the adoptive father of harpist Carey Bell, he acquired an impressive local reputation over time, but was little known outside of the Midwest in spite of his association with Waters during the legend's final years. In 1984 and 1989, Lee recorded much of the material which later comprised his 1992 release *Good Candy*, which was rounded out by latter-day efforts cut with Bell; his lone solo release, it too garnered little notice. Lee died May 23, 1997. *—Jason Ankeny*

● **Good Candy** / 1992 / Earwig ♦♦♦

Bobby Leecan

Guitar / Country Blues, Vaudeville Blues

From Fats Waller and "yo' feet's too big" to country blues and you're "standin' at the crossroads" wasn't really such a great distance, at least if one was to judge from some of the characters who were part of the inner workings of the engine. Journeyman guitarist Bobby Leecan played in a country blues duo with harmonica player Robert Cooksey, the two East Coast bluesmen hardly playing the style straight out of the book (or the non-book). There was more than just a trace of ragtime influence, and even some subversive swing jazz influence. From the mid-'20s to the early '30s, these sorts of pseudo country blues players were just as much a part of the fledgling big city recording scene as the jazz players, and were often encouraged to mingle. Sometimes sessions involved interesting combinations completely out of serendipity, because players who were coming and going happened to run into each other and hit it off. The recordings Waller made playing the organ are cherished by his fans, and Leecan is the guitarist on a batch of these numbers that were recorded in 1927. The combo at this session was organized by cornetist and bandleader Thomas Morris, and also featured drummer Eddie King and the flamboyant trombonist Jimmy Archey. The guitarist was also a member of Waller's Six Hot Babies, also with Morris as well as Joe Nanton on trombone and the interesting pianist Nat Shillkret. Leecan's harmonica partner, Cooksey, was based out of New York, and was unique in his clean approach to the harp. This does not mean he washed the insides of the instrument out—you're not supposed to—but that he favored a clear tone without utilizing many sound effects, more similar to Larry Adler than Sonny Boy Williamson. Leecan and Cooksey teamed up for the first time in 1926 to cut sides for Victor, their recording output inhabiting a borderland between blues, vaudeville, and jazz.

Leecan had a fine and subtle single-string style with clear tone and much flexibility in his picking, and also recorded as banjoist, vocalist, and huffing into the occasional kazoo. Most blues anthropologists think the duo was based out of Philadelphia. The harmonica player also had a short recording collaboration with another guitarist named Alfred Martin, and some unfortunate confusion was created by sloppy reissue projects that credit these Martin recordings to Leecan. As a result, some of the written analysis of Leecan's guitar style is corrupted by descriptions of Martin. Leecan recorded on his own for Bluebird in the early '30s, including the fast moving "Apaloosa Blues." The *Times Ain't What They Used to Be* compilations on Yazoo feature demanding tracks by Bobby Leecan

& His Need More Band. One of the more unusual items from Leecan's career was his recording of a series of the traditional "Cornfield Hollers" for the anthology of *Negro Blues and Hollers*. These performances, once and for all, stress the rootsy rural background of this musician, who was just as comfortable in urban, sophisticated hot jazz settings. *—Eugene Chadbourne*

- **Complete Works in Chronological Order, Vol. 1 (1924–27)** / Feb. 15, 1995 / Document ♦♦♦♦

Complete Works in Chronological Order, Vol. 2 (1927–28) / Feb. 15, 1995 / Document ♦♦♦

Left Hand Frank (Frank Craig)

b. Oct. 5, 1935, Greenville, MS, **d.** Jan. 14, 1992, Los Angeles, CA

Vocals, Guitar / Modern Electric Chicago Blues, Electric Chicago Blues

Southpaw guitarist Frank Craig (like many of his peers, he played an axe strung for a right-hander, strapping it on upside down) never really transcended his reputation as a trusty sideman instead of a leader—and that was just fine with him. But he stepped into the spotlight long enough to sing four fine tunes for Alligator's *Living Chicago Blues* anthologies in 1978.

Craig was already conversant with the guitar when he moved to Chicago at age 14. Too young to play inside the Club Zanzibar (where Muddy Waters, Little Walter, and Wolf held forth), Frank and his teenaged pals, guitarist Eddie King and bassist Willie Black, played outside the joint for tips instead. Legit gigs with harpist Willie Cobbs, guitarist James Scott Jr., Jimmy Dawkins, Junior Wells, Good Rockin' Charles, Jimmy Rogers, and Hound Dog Taylor kept Frank increasingly active on the Chicago circuit from the mid-'50s to the late '70s. He moved to Los Angeles not too long after the Alligator session, eventually hanging up his guitar altogether due to health problems. *—Bill Dahl*

- **Live at the Knickerbocker Cafe** / 1992 / New Rose ♦♦♦♦

Live at the Knickerbocker Cafe was recorded in the late '70s, toward the end of Left Hand Frank's unheralded career. For much of his life, he worked as a sideman, never officially releasing a studio album as a leader. This album (originally released on the French MCM label) is the only addition to a meager discography, but it demonstrates just how much he had to offer. Left Hand Frank didn't shake up the Chicago blues tradition, choosing to celebrate it instead, and the result is a kinetic, entertaining set of greasy blues. There are a few unexpected flourishes, such as the reverb detour "Surfin' with Frank," that keep things interesting, and the end result is cool little Chicago blues gem from a guitarist that was sadly under-recorded. *—Thom Owens*

The Legendary Blues Band

f. 1980, Chicago, IL

Group / Electric Chicago Blues, Modern Electric Chicago Blues

The Legendary Blues Band includes Calvin Jones (b.1926, Greenwood, MS; bass, violin), Willie Smith (b.1935, Helena, AR; drum), and various others on vocals, guitar, harmonica, piano. When the Muddy Waters band quit the master en masse in 1980, most of the sidemen stuck together and formed their own group. The Legendary Blues Band, as they were named, included Pinetop Perkins, Jerry Portnoy, Willie Smith, and Calvin Jones throughout its early years. Short-term member Louis Myers, another Muddy Waters' alumnus, appeared as guitarist on the band's first album (Rounder, 1981). The band has since changed personnel with some regularity, and while its lineup has become progressively less "legendary" in name or historic associations, its music has remained solid and true to the mainstream Chicago style. In a later configuration, they even made the *Billboard* charts. Recent albums have featured guitarist Billy Flynn and harmonicist Madison Slim. The rhythm section of Jones and Smith has anchored the unit throughout the changes, never failing to deliver the Chicago blues with aplomb. *—Jim O'Neal*

Life of Ease / 1981 / Rounder ♦♦♦

Acceptable journeyman classic-style Chicago blues, mixing originals by harmonica player Jerry Portnoy with covers of oldies by Little Richard, Leroy Carr, Jimmy Reed, and the like. *—Richie Unterberger*

- **Red Hot 'n' Blue** / 1983 / Rounder ♦♦♦♦♦

For their second album, the Legendary Blues Band—featuring members of Muddy Waters backing band, including Pinetop Perkins, Peter Ward, Calvin Jones, Jerry Portnoy, and Willie Smith—nearly captured the big, powerful sound of Muddy at his peak. Perkins and Jones don't have the same presence as Waters, but they're fine vocalists in their own right, and the band itself has the same intoxicating rush that made such latter-day Muddy efforts as *Hard Again* so enjoyable. And that means that *Red Hot 'n' Blue* is as close to Waters as you're going to get without Muddy himself—and that means it's one of the better Chicago blues records of its era.*—Stephen Thomas Erlewine*

Woke Up With the Blues / 1989 / Ichiban ♦♦♦

Keepin' the Blues Alive / 1990 / Ichiban ♦♦♦♦♦

Only bassist Calvin Jones and drummer Willie Smith remain from Muddy Waters' old crew, but guitarist John Duich helps keep the traditional Chicago sound in place. *—Bill Dahl*

U B da Judge / 1991 / Ichiban ♦♦

When *U B da Judge* was released in 1991, the Legendary Blues Band's lineup still included former Muddy Waters sidemen Willie Smith (drums, vocals) and Calvin Smith (bass, vocals), as well as harp player Madison Slim, keyboardist Willie O'Shawny, and guitarists Billy Flynn and Tony O. *U B da Judge* isn't a great album by any means, though it has a few decent cuts, including the originals "Watch Your Enemies" and "I Can't Trust You, Man" and a cover of Jimmy Reed's "Don't Say That No More." The CD may have been recorded in Atlanta, but the band's sound is unmistakably Chicago. Completists and diehard collectors may want this so-so CD, but for beginners, the Legendary Blues Band's Rounder albums with Pinetop Perkins would be a much better investment. *—Alex Henderson*

Prime Time Blues / 1992 / Ichiban ♦♦

Money Talks / 1993 / Wild Dog ♦♦♦

All of a sudden, on their 1993's *Money Talks*, drummer Willie Smith has become a very credible singer. *—Bill Dahl*

Leiber & Stoller

Group / Brill Building Pop, Rock & Roll, R&B

A complete biography of the lives of Jerry Leiber and Mike Stoller and their contribution to rock & roll could easily take up an entire book. Very simply, Leiber & Stoller are two of the most important songwriters of the early days of rock & roll. Although they had penned songs for R&B artists such as Jimmy Witherspoon, Floyd Dixon, and Charles Brown in the early '50s, Leiber & Stoller more or less exploded onto the rock scene in 1953 by writing "Hound Dog" for Big Mama Thornton (later to be covered by Elvis). From that point on, the duo composed and produced a string of hits that include some of the most instantly recognizable songs in rock history. They were also pushing the art of rock songwriting (and record production) into, at the time, uncharted territory. As is noted by critic Greg Shaw in the *Rolling Stone Illustrated History of Rock and Roll*: "They were the true architects of pop/rock... Their signal achievement was the marriage of rhythm & blues in its most primal form to the pop tradition."

Few songwriters of this era had the Midas touch as did Leiber & Stoller. A partial list of their credits include "Riot in Cell Block No. 9" (1953), "Love Me" (1956), "Charlie Brown" (1959), "Stand By Me" (1961), "On Broadway" (1963), and numerous songs for Elvis, including songs for the films *Jailhouse Rock* and *King Creole*. Along with wedding R&B with the pop tradition, Leiber & Stoller also introduced string arrangements to R&B records (the Drifters featuring Ben E. King's "There Goes My Baby"), and by doing so created the foundation for a new era of soul music production that would come on the heels of the fading doo wop style. Among the many artists and writers they influenced, few were more important than Phil Spector, who cut his teeth learning production techniques from them while they painstakingly assembled the great early Drifters tracks.

In 1964, Leiber & Stoller started their own record label, Red Bird, devoted to girl groups. Wisely, they also hired the talented songwriting duo of Ellie Greenwich and Jeff Barry, who were at their peak powers, composing some of the most lasting songs of the albeit brief heyday of girl group music, including the Shangri-Las' "Leader of the Pack" and the Dixie Cups' "Chapel of Love." Leiber & Stoller, however, became disinterested in the business side of Red Bird and sold the label two years later, just as the girl group sound was on the wane. So, too, were the hit-making days of Leiber & Stoller on the wane. They continued to write songs, mostly for the Coasters, but they no longer dominated the pop and R&B charts the way they once did. Still, they survived, taking on the august role of rock & roll elder statesmen, eventually landing a spot in the Rock and Roll Hall of Fame in 1987. Later, their songs were the basis of a successful Broadway musical entitled *Smokey Joe's Cafe*, which revived interest in their great body of work, and also brought the music of Jerry Leiber and Mike Stoller to a whole new audience. Not bad for a couple of guys who, in the words of Mike Stoller, never wanted to write rock & roll songs, just good R&B. *—John Dougan*

- **Leiber & Stoller Present the Spark Records Story** / Aug. 14, 2001 / Ace ♦♦♦♦

Before becoming fully established as national hit songwriters and producers with the Coasters, Elvis Presley, and others in the late '50s, Jerry Leiber and Mike Stoller were two of the five partners in Los Angeles R&B indie label Spark. This collects 30 of the mid-'50s sides issued by the company, many of which were written and produced by Leiber & Stoller. In fact, this comprises the majority of Spark's output; it put out only 22 singles in all. Only three of these songs will be well-known: the Robins' classic comic R&B/rock numbers "Riot in Cell Block No. 9" and "Smokey Joe's Cafe," and Willy & Ruth's "Love Me," the original version of a song covered with considerable success by Presley in 1956. Just because the rest is damned obscure, however, doesn't mean it isn't worth checking out. Indeed, although Leiber & Stoller's talents had yet to blossom, this is a couple cuts above the norm for a mid-'50s R&B compilation. That's mostly because there's so much more humorous verve on this stuff than there was on much R&B and early rock that was immediately forgotten. The half-dozen cuts by the Robins (who, of course, evolved into the Coasters) are still the highlights, but there are exuberant jump blues and R&B novelties by the likes of the Honey Bears, Big Boy Groves & Band, and the Sly Fox (a raw bluesy cat by Spark's standards, or anyone's standards). Some routine ballads and straight R&B tunes are interwoven as well, but this is still recommended to both fans of Leiber & Stoller, and to R&B specialists looking for something that offers pleasure as well as scholarly insight. Blues harmonica player Garland the Great's "Strike a Match" was previously unreleased, and marks the first-ever appearance of this Leiber-Stoller composition. *—Richie Unterberger*

Keri Leigh

b. Apr. 21, 1969, Birmingham, AL

Vocals, Drums, Percussion, Harmonica, Guitar, Bass / Modern Electric Blues

Vocalist, songwriter, record-producer, journalist, and author Keri Leigh is one of these multi-talented, accomplished individuals that the blues music world can't seem to get enough of. And the fact that she's barely 30 years old insures that she'll be around, pursuing her number one passion—singing the blues—for a long time.

Her latest album, *Arrival* (1995), for the Jackson, MS-based Malaco Records label, isn't with her usual backing band, the Blue Devils, but it was recorded at Muscle Shoals Studios (which Malaco owns), and Leigh and her husband acted as co-producers of the record.

Leigh moved to Austin from her native Oklahoma with her guitarist/husband Mark Lyon, in 1990. Fortunately, they were welcomed for the most part with open arms by the Austin blues community, and certainly by Clifford Antone, owner of Antone's (blues nightclub), who booked them into his place every week for about a year. Within a year of so of her moving to Austin, she began work on her first book, *Stevie Ray: Soul to Soul*, (Taylor Books, Dallas), a passionate account of the ups and downs of the late guitarist's all-too-short life. Leigh first met Vaughan when she interviewed him in 1986, and after several interviews, they became friends. In May 1990, they began work on what was to be his autobiography, but in August of that year, Vaughan was killed in a helicopter accident in Wisconsin.

Leigh's recordings all have a Joplin-esque quality to them, and one way to describe her singing style is as a Janis Joplin for the '90s; in fact, some critics have described her as the greatest voice to come out of Texas since Joplin.

Leigh has used her background as a radio and newspaper journalist to get publicity for the Blue Devils, and a glance at her overflowing press-clips folder shows what a hustler she is. But Leigh and her band work as hard as any of the other touring blues musicians around the U.S., and they spend upwards of 150 nights a year on the road. Leigh's husband Lyon is one of the most naturally gifted slide guitarists you'll ever hear, and the ease with which he handles the instrument makes it look deceptively simple. In fact, good blues guitar is very difficult to play, but Lyon has all the moves down pat.

Leigh and her Blue Devils have two releases out on Amazing Records (a now-defunct label), *No Beginner* (1993) and *Blue Devil Blues*, their debut (1991), in addition to their latest Malaco album. *Arrival*, consisting of one-half originals and one-half cover tunes, is certainly the most accessible of her recordings. Leigh and her group have many more good years ahead of them; wherever they go, their affable ways earn them new friends and fans in the blues world. They also have a knack for making new blues converts out of rock & rollers. *—Richard Skelly*

Blue Devil Blues / 1991 / Amazing ♦♦♦

Keri Leigh's debut album isn't much more than standard Texas blues, but her passion for the music shines through every song, and that is what makes it a worthwhile listen. Leigh and guitarist Mark Lyon lead the band through eight covers and three fairly average originals, but they deliver the material with conviction, especially when they attack nuggets like Son House's "Preachin' Blues." Leigh's forceful, raspy voice sounds terrific and Lyon is a good guitarist, but the album is hampered by its predictability. *—Thom Owens*

● **No Beginner** / Jun. 8, 1993 / Amazing ♦♦♦♦

Keri Leigh's second album, *No Beginner*, is a more distinguished effort than her debut. Leigh and her guitarist/husband Lyon stake out a territory between Texas blues and blues-rock, much like their predecessors Stevie Ray Vaughan, Janis Joplin and ZZ Top. Leigh's music doesn't have as many rock & roll overtones, but she and her band, the Blue Devils, play with a fiery rock energy and that energy comes across more clearly here than on their debut. *—Thom Owens*

Arrival / 1995 / Waldoxy/Malaco ♦♦♦♦

Keri Leigh is a superior vocalist who is heard at her best during her Waldoxy release singing conventional electric blues where her expressive skills (and her ability to come up with interesting lyrics) can really be heard. She wrote the words to six of the dozen selections but her two strongest performances are actually on the witty and boisterous "Use What You Got" and Koko Taylor's "Voodoo Woman" where she struts her stuff. Also worth hearing are a couple of acoustic country blues numbers although Leigh's occasional departures into Aretha Franklin-influenced R&B are throwaways. But with Mark Lyon's versatile guitar solos and fine four-piece horn section offering her strong support, Keri Leigh's release is a well-paced set and an easily recommended release. *—Scott Yanow*

Kim Lembo

Vocals / Soul-Blues, Contemporary Blues

Along with her band Blue Heat, blues vocalist Kim Lembo recorded several albums for Blue Wave beginning in 1994. The Syracuse, NY-based vocalist worked with multi-instrumentalist/producer Mark Doyle for her debut album, which she named after her band. Two years later, she again worked with Doyle for her follow-up, *Mama Lion*. During this time in the mid-'90s, Lembo built a sizable following in New York state, where she continued to perform on a regular basis and win much acclaim. By the time Blue Wave released her third album, *Ready to Ride* (1999), she'd built quite a following. This growing audience resulted in an opportunity to perform a series of shows in Paris during January 2000 at the Chesterfield Cafe. These shows were later compiled on the *Paris Burning* album released later that year. *—Jason Birchmeier*

Blue Heat / 1994 / Blue Wave ♦♦♦

Mama Lion / May 7, 1996 / Blue Wave ♦♦♦♦

● **Ready to Ride** / Mar. 2, 1999 / Blue Wave ♦♦♦♦♦

Kim Lembo is a real-deal blues-beltin' house mama, and her third full-length album for Blue Wave finds her in top form. Although she writes and contributes "Sunday Morning" to the ten songs collected here, Ms. Lembo's strong suit is interpreting, and her pick of the litter on this outing includes takes on Otis Rush's "Keep On Lovin' Me Baby" (originally issued on her *Steamers* promo sampler), Keith Sykes' "Love to Ride," Tampa Red's "Love Crazy," a medley of "It's Love Baby" and Son Seals' "Four Full Seasons of Love," and Tom Cosgrove's "Outside Love." As usual, there's loads of top-notch playing aboard from her band Blue Heat, featuring Mark Doyle on guitar, with guest shots along the way from Scott Ebner on organ, Paul "Big Daddy" LaRonde on bass, Mark Tiffault on drums, Pete McMahon on harp, and Kim Simmonds on dobro. Stellar versions of "Stop," "Mean Old Daddy," "Ain't No Love In the Heart of the City" and a tribute to the late Lester Butler in his "Goin' to the Church" complete this top-notch session. *—Cub Koda*

Paris Burning: Live at the Chesterfield Cafe / Sep. 19, 2000 / Blue Wave ♦♦♦

J.B. Lenoir

b. May 5, 1929, Monticello, MS, **d.** Apr. 29, 1967, Urbana, IL

Vocals, Guitar / Electric Chicago Blues, Chicago Blues

Newcomers to his considerable legacy could be forgiven for questioning J.B. Lenoir's gender upon first hearing his rocking waxings. Lenoir's exceptionally high-pitched vocal range is a fooler, but it only adds to the singular appeal of his music. His politically charged "Eisenhower Blues" allegedly caused all sorts of nasty repercussions upon its 1954 emergence on Al Benson's Parrot logo (it was quickly pulled off the shelves and replaced with Lenoir's less controversially titled "Tax Paying Blues").

J.B. (that was his entire legal handle) fell under the spell of Blind Lemon Jefferson as a wee lad, thanks to his guitar-wielding dad. Lightnin' Hopkins and Arthur "Big Boy" Crudup were also cited as early influences. Lenoir spent time in New Orleans before arriving in Chicago in the late '40s. Boogie grooves were integral to Lenoir's infectious routine from the get-go, although his first single for Chess in 1951, "Korea Blues," was another slice of topical commentary. From late 1951 to 1953, he waxed several dates for Joe Brown's JOB logo in the company of pianist Sunnyland Slim, drummer Alfred Wallace, and on the romping "The Mojo," saxist J.T. Brown.

Lenoir waxed his most enduring piece, the infectious (and often-covered) "Mama Talk to Your Daughter," in 1954 for Al Benson's Parrot label. Lenoir's 1954-1955 Parrot output and 1955-1958 Checker catalog contained a raft of terrific performances, including a humorously defiant "Don't Touch My Head" (detailing his brand-new process hairdo) and "Natural Man." Lenoir's sound was unique: saxes (usually Alex Atkins and Ernest Cotton) wailed in unison behind Lenoir's boogie-driven rhythm guitar as drummer Al Galvin pounded out a rudimentary backbeat everywhere but where it customarily lays. Somehow, it all fit together.

Scattered singles for Shad in 1958 and Vee-Jay two years later kept Lenoir's name in the public eye. His music was growing substantially by the time he hooked up with USA Records in 1963 (witness the 45's billing: J.B. Lenoir & his African Hunch Rhythm). Even more unusual were the two acoustic albums he cut for German blues promoter Horst Lippmann in 1965 and 1966. *Alabama Blues* and *Down in Mississippi* were done in Chicago under Willie Dixon's supervision, Lenoir now free to elaborate on whatever troubled his mind ("Alabama March," "Vietnam Blues," "Shot on James Meredith").

Little did Lenoir know his time was quickly running out. By the time of his 1967 death, the guitarist had moved to downstate Champaign—and that's where he died, probably as a delayed result of an auto accident he was involved in three weeks prior to his actual death. *—Bill Dahl*

Natural Man / 1968 / MCA/Chess ♦♦♦♦♦

This collection of J.B.'s mid-'50s tenure at the label—originally issued in the '70s—duplicates two songs from the Parrot collection (a label which Chess later acquired), but the rest of it is more than worth the effort to seek out. The rocking "Don't Touch My Head," the topical "Eisenehower Blues" and the sexually ambiguous, chaotic and cool title track are but a few of the magical highlights aboard. Either this or the Parrot sides will do in a pinch, but I can't imagine being without either one. *—Cub Koda*

Crusade / 1970 / Polydor ♦♦♦♦♦

J.B. Lenoir / 1974 / Chess ♦♦♦

Chess Blues Master Series / 1976 / Chess ♦♦♦♦♦

Aside from many fans not being able to properly pronounce his name, J.B. Lenoir also suffered from being severely underrated. He was both a first-rate uptempo vocalist and outstanding interpreter and composer. This double-LP anthology has long since disappeared from general circulation, but should be ardently pursued, as it contains definitive Lenoir cuts from Chess, Parrot and Checker recorded in the '50s. *—Ron Wynn*

Mojo Boogie / 1980 / Flyright ♦♦♦

J.B. Lenoir made some marvelous recordings for the JOB label in the early '50s, often working with pianist Sunnyland Slim and saxophonist J.T. Brown. They're available on this reissue. *—Ron Wynn*

Down in Mississippi / 1980 / L&R ♦♦♦

Recorded in September 1966, shortly before his death the following spring, this session was Lenoir's most effective fusion of acoustic blues, African percussion, and contemporary, topical songwriting. "Round and Round," "Voodoo Music," and "Feelin' Good" bring the African influence to the fore, while J.B. addresses tough issues like Vietnam and discrimination more directly than any other bluesman of the time on cuts like "Down In Mississippi," "Shot on Meredith," and "Vietnam Blues." Supervised by Willie Dixon, this recording also featured top Chicago blues drummer Fred Below. *—Richie Unterberger*

Chess Masters / 1984 / Chess ♦♦♦

★ **The Parrot Sessions, 1954–55: Vintage Chicago Blues** / 1989 / Relic ♦♦♦♦♦

Lenoir's sound really got locked in during this period, using twin saxes, himself on boogie rhythm guitar (with an occasional minimal solo), revolving piano, and bass stools and Al Gavin—certainly the strangest of all Chicago drummers—constantly turning the beat around. This is Lenoir at his creative and performing best, including his best-known songs "Mama Talk to Your Daughter" (with the famous "one note for 12 bars" guitar solo), "Eisenhower Blues," and "Give Me One More Shot," where Gavin starts out the tune on the wrong beat, gets on the right beat by mistake, then "corrects" himself! Lyrics as metaphorically powerful as any in the blues against grooves alternating between low-down slow ones and Lenoir's patented boogie. *—Cub Koda*

His JOB Recordings 1951–1954 / 1991 / Paula ♦♦♦♦♦

These are Lenoir's earliest sides in a very stripped down setting compared to the Parrot and Chess sides. Over half of the 14 sides feature Lenoir on guitar with only Sunnyland Slim on piano and Alfred Wallace on drums in support, with J.T. Brown on tenor sax aboard for the next session. They all suffer from a curiously muffled sound, but early delights like "The Mojo (Boogie)" and "Let's Roll" make all audio points mute. This CD also includes seven tracks fronted by Sunnyland Slim recorded the same day with Lenoir in a supporting role. *—Cub Koda*

Vietnam Blues: The Complete L&R Recording / 1995 / Evidence ♦♦♦♦♦

Greatly admired among his peers during his short life, and highly acclaimed by blues aficionados, J.B. Lenoir was a singular blues artist and a prolific songwriter. The Evidence Records release of *Vietnam Blues* combines J.B. Lenoir's final two albums before his death in 1967, *Alabama Blues* (1965) and *Down in Mississippi* (1966). Willie Dixon produced the sessions for L&R Records and lends backup vocals to a few of the tracks. The acoustic sound (no bass, occasional drums) notes a shift back to the primary elements of prewar blues. These recordings aren't nostalgic endeavors, however, but ensure that the songs get the best listening environment possible. The enigmatic Lenoir called the style he was developing during these sessions, "African Hunch," and it's apparent that he was bursting with creativity, dedicated equally to both the words and music. Early Lenoir compositions such as "I Feel So Good" and "Mojo Boogie" are resurrected, but Lenoir's new material, with its finger on the pulse of the mid-'60s, are startling rich and haunting at times. Civil rights, racism, lynching, and the Vietnam War, among other relevant issues are encapsulated with an originality and poignancy that's hard to find in other blues during the time. Lenoir's singing comes off as a high-pitched near-squeal, and his multi-dimensional guitar playing shows the influence of Lightnin' Hopkins' and other southern blues guitarists. Characteristically, Lenoir's guitar playing interweaves pensive eerie open chords with deft muting and rhythmic displays. Drummer Freddie Below, whose shuffling beats really accent the sound of Lenoir's acoustic guitar, enhances the sound on every song he contributes to, such as "Mojo Boogie," "Talk to Your Daughter," and the grooving "I Want to Go." As a storyteller, songwriter, musician, and performer, J.B. Lenoir was a giant and he gave something back to the blues to help it grow and keep going. You'll thank Evidence Records for reissuing these unique and brilliant little masterpieces. —*Jeff Schwachter*

Mojo Boogie: An Essential Collection / Feb. 26, 2002 / Fuel 2000 ✦✦✦

Ron Levy (Reuvin Zev ben Yehoshua Ha Levi)

b. May 29, 1951, Cambridge, MA
Organ (Hammond), Piano, Organ / Modern Electric Blues, Soul-Jazz, Jazz Blues
Organist/pianist Ron Levy has devoted most of his career to keeping the flame of funky, bluesy soul-jazz alive. Born Reuvin Zev ben Yehoshua Ha Levi in 1959 in Cambridge, MA, Levy played clarinet as a child but switched to piano after seeing Ray Charles at age 13. When he encountered the music of Jimmy Smith, Billy Preston, and Booker T. & the MG's, he fell in love with the Hammond B-3 and made the switch.

Levy began working the Boston blues club scene as a teenager, and was hired by Albert King in 1971, before even graduating from high school. He spent a year and a half with King, and then joined B.B. King's backing band, where he remained for the next seven years. He also began working with the Rhythm Rockers in 1976, an association that lasted four years, and then became a member of Roomful of Blues from 1983-1987. It was during that time that Levy recorded his first session as a leader, 1985's *Ron Levy's Wild Kingdom* for the Black Top label. *Safari in New Orleans* followed in 1988, after which Levy moved to the Bullseye Blues label, where he eventually became an in-house producer (an area where he's garnered seven Grammy nominations). His albums for Bullseye Blues include 1992's *B-3 Blues and Grooves* and 1996's *Zim Zam Zoom: Acid Blues on B-3*. 1998's *Greaze Is What's Good* (recorded for Cannonball) featured an all-star roster of guests, including Freddie Hubbard, Melvin Sparks, David T. Walker, Steve Turre, Idris Muhammad, and Preston Shannon. Since 1988 Levy hasn't released anything under his own name, but continues to tour regularly and collaborate with and produce artists like Jimmy King, Karl Denison, and Charles Earland. —*Steve Huey*

Ron Levy's Wild Kingdom / Sep. 1985 / Black Top ✦✦✦
Ten tunes with an all-star cast including Ronnie Earl (guitar), Kim Wilson (harmonica), Greg Piccolo (sax), Wayne Bennett (guitar), and other excellent players. Plenty of fine guitar, keyboards, harmonica, and uptempo blues music. —*Michael Erlewine*

Safari to New Orleans / 1988 / Black Top ✦✦
Ron Levy's piano playing shines throughout *Safari to New Orleans*, but he fails to come up with enough strong songs to make the album memorable. —*Thom Owens*

● **B-3 Blues and Grooves** / 1992 / Bullseye Blues ✦✦✦✦
Ron Levy is one of the finest young masters of the Hammond B-3. Here are 11 soul-satisfying cuts that feature Levy's funky keyboard playing—many written by Levy himself. Those who look for B-3 jams in the soul-jazz vein that are as funky as can be will not be disappointed. This is a great CD to own. —*Michael Erlewine*

Zim Zam Zoom: Acid Blues on B-3 / Mar. 19, 1996 / Bullseye Blues ✦✦✦✦
If you like blues and funky soul-jazz (with just a twist of the future), this is an album to enjoy. Hammond B-3 artist Ron Levy gathers some of the greatest groove players of all time for this steam session, including Melvin Sparks on guitar and the great Idris Muhammad on drums. Call it retro or acid-jazz if you want, but groove lover Levy never stops playing that funky soul-jazz long enough to look back. This album carries the groove tradition on, maintaining that integrity. Produced by Bob Porter. —*Michael Erlewine*

Greaze Is What's Good / Mar. 10, 1998 / Cannonball ✦✦✦
On *Greaze Is What's Good*, Ron Levy is joined by trumpeter Freddie Hubbard, guitarists Melvin Sparks and David T. Walker, drummer Idris Muhammad, and trombonist Steve Turre, plus Memphis blues guitarist Preston Shannon, for a solid set of grooving, bluesy soul-jazz. —*Steve Huey*

Furry Lewis (Walter Lewis)

b. Greenwood, MS, **d.** Sep. 14, 1981, Memphis, TN
Vocals, Harmonica, Guitar / Blues Revival, Piedmont Blues, Acoustic Memphis Blues, Acoustic Blues
Furry Lewis was the only blues singer of the '20s to achieve major media attention in the '60s and '70s. One of the most recorded of Memphis-based guitarists of the late '20s, Lewis' subsequent fame 40 years later was based largely on the strength of those early sides. One of the very best blues storytellers, and an extremely nimble-fingered guitarist

right into his seventies, he was equally adept at blues and ragtime, and made the most out of an understated, rather than an overtly flamboyant style.

Walter Lewis was born in Greenwood, MS, sometime between 1893 and 1900—the exact year is in dispute, as Lewis altered this more than once. The Lewis family moved to Memphis when he was seven years old, and Lewis made his home there for the remainder of his life. He got the name "Furry" while still a boy, bestowed on him by other children. Lewis built his first guitar when he was still a child from scraps he found around the family's home. Lewis' only admitted mentor was a local guitarist whom he knew as "Blind Joe," who may have come from Arkansas, a denizen of Memphis' Brinkley Street, where the family resided. The middle-aged Blind Joe was Lewis' source for the songs "Casey Jones" and "John Henry," among other traditional numbers. The loss of a leg in a railroad accident in 1917 doesn't seem to have slowed his life or career down—in fact, it hastened his entry into professional music, because he assumed that there was no gainful employment open to crippled, uneducated blacks in Memphis. Lewis' real musical start took place on Beale Street in the late teens, where he began his career. He picked up bottleneck playing early on, and tried to learn the harmonica but never quite got the hang of it. Lewis started playing traveling medicine shows, and it was in this setting that he began showing off an uncommonly flashy visual style, including playing the guitar behind his head.

Lewis' recording career began in April 1927, with a trip to Chicago with fellow guitarist Landers Walton to record for the Vocalion label, which resulted in five songs, also featuring mandolin player Charles Jackson on three of the numbers. The songs proved that Lewis was a natural in the recording studio, playing to the microphone as easily as he did to audiences in person, but they were not, strictly speaking, representative of Lewis' usual sound, because they featured two backup musicians. In October of 1927 Lewis was back in Chicago to cut six more songs, this time with nothing but his voice and his own guitar. Lewis seldom played with anyone else, partly because of his loose bar structures, which made it very difficult for anyone to follow him. The interplay of his voice and guitar, on record and in person, made him a very effective showman in both venues. Lewis' records, however, did not sell well, and he never developed more than a cult following in and around Memphis. A few of his records, however, lingered in the memory far beyond their relatively modest sales, most notably "John Henry" and "Kassie Jones, Pts. 1-2," arguably one of the great blues recordings of the '20s.

Lewis gave up music as a profession during the mid-'30s, when the Depression reduced the market for country blues. He never made a living from his music—fortunately, he found work as a municipal laborer in Memphis during the '20s, and continued in this capacity right into the '60s. His brand of acoustic country blues was hopelessly out-of-style in Memphis during the postwar years, and Lewis didn't even try to revive his recording or professional performing career. In the intervening years, he played for friends and relatives, living in obscurity and reasonably satisfied. At the end of the '50s, however, folksong/blues scholar Sam Charters discovered Lewis and persuaded him to resume his music career. In the interim, all of the blues stars who'd made their careers in Memphis during the '30s had passed on or retired, and Lewis was a living repository of styles and songs that, otherwise, were scarcely within living memory of most Americans.

Lewis returned to the studio under Charters' direction and cut two albums for the Prestige/Bluesville labels in 1961. These showed Lewis in excellent form, his voice as good as ever and his technique on the guitar still dazzling. Audiences—initially hardcore blues and folk enthusiasts, and later more casual listeners—were delighted, fascinated, charmed, and deeply moved by what they heard. Gradually, as the '60s and the ensuing blues boom wore on, Lewis emerged as one of the favorite rediscovered stars of the '30s, playing festivals, appearing on talk shows, and being interviewed. He proved to be a skilled public figure, regaling audiences with stories of his life that were both funny and poignantly revealing, claiming certain achievements (such as being the inventor of bottleneck guitar) in dubious manner, and delighting the public. After his retirement from working for the city of Memphis, he also taught in an antipoverty program in the city.

Furry Lewis became a blues celebrity during the '70s, following a profile in *Playboy* magazine and appearances on *The Tonight Show*, and managed a few film and television appearances, including one as himself in the Burt Reynolds action/comedy *W.W. and the Dixie Dance Kings*. By this time, he had several new recordings to his credit, and if the material wasn't as vital as the sides he'd cut at the end of the '20s, it was still valid and exceptionally fine blues, and paid him some money for his efforts. Lewis died in 1981 a beloved figure and a recognized giant in the world of blues. His music continued to sell well, attracting new listeners many years later. —*Bruce Eder*

☆ **Complete Recorded Works (1927-1929)** / 1927-1929 / Document ✦✦✦✦✦
This release supplants both the Yazoo *In His Prime* and the Wolf Records 1990 *Complete Works* collections released earlier. This time *everything* that Lewis recorded for Victor and Vocalion during those extraordinary two years of work during the '20s has been gathered together, including both parts of "Kassie Jones." The sound has been improved as well, and the notes are decent if, as is usual with Document, unexceptional. But this is one instance where Document's release of the complete works of an artist are preferable to Yazoo's picking and choosing. —*Bruce Eder*

Furry Lewis Blues / 1959 / Smithsonian/Folkways ✦✦✦

Back on My Feet Again / Apr. 1961 / Prestige/Bluesville ✦✦✦
An April 1961 session of traditional material such as "Shake 'Em on Down," "John Henry," "Roberta," and "St. Louis Blues." The album has been combined with another 1961 LP, *Done Changed My Mind*, for the CD reissue compilation *Shake 'Em on Down*. —*Richie Unterberger*

Done Changed My Mind / May 1961 / Prestige/Bluesville ✦✦✦
A May 1961 session of traditional material along the lines of "Casey Jones" and "Frankie and Johnnie." It's been combined with a similar 1961 LP, *Back on My Feet Again*, onto one disc for the CD reissue compilation *Shake 'Em on Down*. —*Richie Unterberger*

On the Road Again / 1970 / Genes ✦✦✦
This 1969 recording captures a relaxed blues session of Furry Lewis, Bukka White, and

Gus Cannon that is full of warmth and gentle humor. These unwound acoustic tunes are sung and played neither for dancing to nor for damning you, but instead capture a mood akin to early evening song swapping among these old-time gentlemen of country-folk blues. The elder of the group, Cannon (of Cannon's Jug Stompers), sings two tunes here—"Lela," and "Goin' Back (to Memphis, TN)"—while his uniquely tuned banjo accompanies him on a few more. White's playing is Mississippi Delta slide all over his National guitar, and his voice is a gruff box that straightens just a little for the kind teasing in "Give Me an Old Lady." The majority of the tracks come from Lewis, whose fuzz-edged voice delivers in a close, familiar manner that comes off as an unassuming performance for a couple of friends. *On the Road Again* is an endearing bit of kicking back by some seminal bluesmen. *—Joslyn Layne*

☆ **Shake 'Em on Down** / 1972 / Fantasy ✦✦✦✦✦
A 20-song single CD reissue of Lewis' first modern commercial recordings, done for two Prestige/Bluesville albums (*Back on My Feet Again, Done Changed My Mind*) in April and May of 1961 at Sun Studios in Memphis. Lewis is in brilliant form throughout, his fingers nearly as fast and his voice as rich as they were 30-odd years earlier. The disc includes the definitive version of "John Henry" (not just Lewis' definitive version—*the* definitive version), one of the greatest vocal performances ever put on record and a guitar workout so dazzling that you'd swear there was more than one guy playing. What's more, with the extended running time available on tape (Lewis' sessions in the '20s having been captured on 78 rpm discs with limited running times), he really stretched out here and obviously loves doing it. The slight reverb in the studio also gives Lewis a larger-than-life stature on this recording. *—Bruce Eder*

Fourth & Beale / 1975 / Lucky Seven ✦✦✦
Recorded in Memphis on March 5, 1969, with Lewis in bed—essentially an impromptu concert for the microphone and whoever happened to be there—these nine tracks show Lewis to fairly good advantage. They're more laidback than his work at the other end of the decade for Prestige/Bluesville, with Lewis playing more slowly and singing more roughly than those earlier sessions. His slide work is still stingingly effective, however, and his voice still highly expressive, and he knows how to put over a song even at this late date, playing with an almost hypnotic intensity—the songs include new renditions of "John Henry" and "Casey Jones," as well as "When the Saints Go Marching In" and W.C. Handy's "St. Louis Blues." *—Bruce Eder*

★ **In His Prime (1927–1928)** / 1988 / Yazoo ✦✦✦✦✦
The best overview of Lewis' classic late-'20s sides, containing 14 songs from the period (though not "John Henry"), all of which are crisply remastered, showing off both his superb guitar playing and his brilliantly expressive singing (the vocal performance on "Falling Down Blues" alone is worth the price of the disc) to excellent advantage. A seminal part of any blues collection, as well as any collection of Lewis' material. *—Bruce Eder*

Canned Heat Blues: Masters of Memphis Blues / 1992 / BMG ✦✦✦
This 21-song three-artist collection (with Tommy Johnson and Ishmon Bracey) is a good introduction to Lewis' work (or that of the others) for those unwilling to spring for $15 for one of the Yazoo or Wolf releases. The mastering quality is generally excellent, and the eight Lewis songs on hand include both parts of "Kassie Jones," though not "John Henry." It's a beginning, and anyone who likes this sampling can go to the more serious collections. It's apparently out-of-print at this writing, but relatively easy to find. *—Bruce Eder*

Blues Magician / Feb. 9, 1999 / Lucky Seven ✦✦✦
Recorded in Lewis' apartment in the summer of 1969, this record is an honest and unusual glimpse at the blues great. While the disc begins a little too ragged, Lewis rises to the occasion with great versions of "Lay My Burden Down" and "Furry's Rag," accompanying himself on guitar. While the inclusion of some cryptic between-song chat is unwise, the informal charm of intimate setting is nicely captured. *—Tim Sheridan*

Take Your Time / 2000 / Genes ✦✦✦
Memphis bluesman Furry Lewis was pushing 80 (depending on which of the various dates of birth you go by) when this recording was made in October 1969. Lewis, coaxed out of retirement after a career as a sanitation worker (he gave up music during the Depression), had spent the '60s as the toast of the folk-blues revival circuit, and his playing with avid student Lee Baker Jr., had by this time coalesced into a true duo. Even with Lewis' penchant for randomly inserting and removing bars from his chord progressions and equally wild vocal flights, Baker's accompaniment keeps up. The duo takes on Lewis standards like the signature tune "Natural Born Eastman" (aka "Kassie Jones") and "Take Your Time," as well as versions of the old-time standards Lewis loved to reworked in his gruff, yet powerfully effective voice; "Let Me Call You Sweetheart" and "See That My Grave Is Kept Clean," as well as the Southern gospel tune "Glory Hallelujah." An intimate studio recording that still retains the boisterous atmosphere of a front-porch jam. *—John Duffy*

Johnie Lewis

b. Oct. 8, 1908, Eufaula, AL
Vocals, Guitar / Country Blues
Johnie Lewis was a decent, if unexceptional, singer and guitarist in the Southern rural style, particularly accomplished at playing slide. Though he was born in Alabama and grew into adulthood in Georgia, Lewis spent most of his life in Chicago, moving the city in the '30s. A painter by profession, Lewis only pursued music as an avocation, but through one of his painting jobs, he came to the notice of a filmmaker doing a documentary about Chicago blues. His appearance in that film lead to recording sessions for Arhoolie in the early '70s. *—Richie Unterberger*

● **Alabama Slide Guitar** / 1970 / Arhoolie ✦✦✦
Eighteen songs recorded by Lewis in 1970 and 1971. If Lewis were one of the few practitioners of the Southern country blues slide guitar, this would be an important document. But the fact is that because there are so many similar performers in the style who recorded more prolifically and with greater imagination, it's just a solid journeyman entry in the field. Lewis does have an affable storytelling manner to his songwriting, and gets in some nifty laidback slide licks; a couple of the more ambitious tunes were inspired by Dr. Martin Luther King Jr. *—Richie Unterberger*

Meade "Lux" Lewis

b. Sep. 4, 1905, Chicago, IL, **d.** Jun. 7, 1964, Minneapolis, MN
Piano / Boogie-Woogie, Piano Blues
One of the three great boogie-woogie pianists (along with Albert Ammons and Pete Johnson) whose appearance at John Hammond's 1938 Spirituals to Swing concert helped start the boogie-woogie craze, Meade "Lux" Lewis was a powerful if somewhat limited player. He played regularly in Chicago in the late '20s and his one solo record of the time, "Honky Tonk Train Blues" (1927), was considered a classic. However, other than a few sides backing little-known blues singers, Lewis gained little extra work and slipped into obscurity.

John Hammond heard Lewis' record in 1935 and, after a search, found Lewis washing cars for a living in Chicago. Soon, Lewis was back on records and after the 1938, concert he was able to work steadily, sometimes in duets or trios with Ammons and Johnson. He became the first jazz pianist to double on celeste (starting in 1936) and was featured on that instrument on a Blue Note quartet date with Edmond Hall and Charlie Christian; he also played harpsichord on a few records in 1941. After the boogie-woogie craze ended, Lewis continued working in Chicago and California, recording as late as 1962, although by then he was pretty much forgotten. Lewis led sessions through the years that have come out on MCA, Victor, Blue Note, Solo Art, Euphonic, Stinson, Atlantic, Storyville, Verve, Tops, ABC-Paramount, Riverside, and Philips. *—Scott Yanow*

1927–1939 / Dec. 1927-Jan. 6, 1939 / Classics ✦✦✦

1939–1941 / Jan. 6, 1939-Apr. 9, 1941 / Classics ✦✦✦

☆ **The Complete Blue Note Recordings** / Jan. 6, 1939-Aug. 22, 1944 / Mosaic ✦✦✦✦✦
Mosaic's *Complete Blue Note Recordings* contains all of the recordings Meade "Lux" Lewis made for the label between 1939 and 1944, making it the definitive statement on the influential boogie-woogie pianist. *—Leo Stanley*

Meade Lux Lewis (1939–1954) / Feb. 1939-Sep. 25, 1954 / Story of the Blues ✦✦✦✦✦
This CD reissue collects together solo, duet and trio sides by the great boogie-woogie pianist Meade "Lux" Lewis, many of which do not duplicate other readily available collections. Most of the first nine selections surprisingly feature Lewis playing blues with a light stride rather than a boogie bassline. Two titles from 1944 are more typical of what the public expected, while the final three numbers (from 1953-1954) are a bit subpar, sloppy if spirited honky tonk music played on a poor piano. This CD is a gap filler for completists but otherwise not too essential. *—Scott Yanow*

1941–1944 / Apr. 9, 1941-Aug. 22, 1944 / Classics ✦✦✦

Meade Lux Lewis / Aug. 18, 1944 / Stinson ✦✦✦
Vintage boogie-woogie and blues from a piano master. Lewis ranked alongside Albert Ammons, Pete Johnson, and Jimmy Yancey as boogie-woogie's finest, and he shows why on this reissued collection featuring Lewis' solos from the mid-'40s. *—Ron Wynn*

Tidal Boogie / 1954 / Tradition ✦✦✦✦✦
The running time on these ten tracks, recorded in 1954 by Lewis with bassist Red Callender and an unknown electric guitarist, is a paltry 27 minutes, but they're 27 delightful minutes. Lewis' work is captured in between his 1952 Atlantic sessions and his 1957 Verve recordings, playing an easy, rollicking set that includes "Basin Street Blues," "Darktown Strutters' Ball," "Birth of the Blues," and the title track. Ironically, the unnamed guitarist almost dominates "Birth of the Blues" and "Tidal Boogie," and it's a shame his name hasn't been preserved or recorded, but Lewis gets to shine on this number as well. The audio restoration by Seth Winner puts the piano practically against the ear of the listener, so that one can actually feel the action of the keys, and the bass and guitar are a match. *—Bruce Eder*

Cat House Piano / Jun. 28, 1954-Jan. 16, 1955 / Verve ✦✦✦
This single CD from 1998 has all of the music from boogie-woogie pianist Meade "Lux" Lewis' two Verve LPs of 1954-1955. The earlier date is a set of duets with drummer Louie Bellson, while the later session finds Lewis accompanied by bassist Red Callender and drummer Jo Jones. The packaging is perfect, and with 76 and a half minutes of playing, the amount of music is generous. The only problem is that there is a definite sameness to the 14 selections (which mostly clock in between four and seven minutes), the majority of which are medium-tempo blues romps. None of the melodies (all Lewis originals) are at all memorable. The romping momentum of the music overall is difficult to resist, but it is advisable to listen to this set in small doses. *—Scott Yanow*

● **The Blues Piano Artistry of Meade Lux Lewis** / Nov. 1, 1961 / Riverside/Original Blues Classics ✦✦✦✦✦
Boogie-woogie pianist Meade "Lux" Lewis' next-to-last record was his first recording in five years and his final opportunity to stretch out unaccompanied. This solo Riverside set (reissued by OJC on CD) as usual finds Lewis generally sticking to the blues (with "You Were Meant for Me" and "Fate" being exceptions), mostly performing originals. On a few of the songs Lewis switches effectively to celeste. It apparently only took Meade "Lux" Lewis two hours to record the full set and the results are quite spontaneous yet well organized, a fine all-around portrait of the veteran pianist in his later period. *—Scott Yanow*

Barrel House Piano / 1992 / Jasmine ✦✦✦
Meade "Lux" Lewis was recorded in spurts during his musical career. This record features Lewis on a metallic-sounding honky tonk piano, accompanied by an unidentified guitarist and bassist. This gives the album a very dated sound that makes it less desirable

than if he had recorded the same tracks on a normal piano. Boogie-woogie aficionados will find desirable material such as Lewis' revival of his "Six Wheel Chaser," tho once popular but now nearly forgotten standards "Jada" and "Darktown Strutters' Ball," and enjoyable versions of "Bugle Call Rag" and "St. Louis Blues." *Barrel House Piano* was reissued as an LP by Everest and in 1992 as a Jasmine release under the same title. —*Ken Dryden*

Alternate Takes Live Performances Soundies / 1997 / Document ✦✦✦

Noah Lewis

b. Sep. 3, 1895, Henning, TN, **d.** Feb. 7, 1961, Ripley, TN

Harmonica, Vocals / Prewar Country Blues, Acoustic Memphis Blues, Jug Band

A key figure on the Memphis jug band circuit of the '20s, singer and harpist Noah Lewis was born September 3, 1895, in Henning, TN. Upon relocating to Memphis, he teamed with Gus Cannon, becoming an essential component of Cannon's Jug Stompers; the group made their debut recordings for the Paramount label in 1927, with several more sessions to follow prior to their final date in late 1930. On a series of sides cut in the first week of October 1929, Lewis made his debut as a name artist, cutting three blistering harmonica solos as well as "Going to Germany," which spotlighted his plaintive vocal style. Later recording with Yank Rachell and John Estes, as the Depression wore on Lewis slipped into obscurity, living a life of extreme poverty; his death on February 7, 1961 was a result of gangrene brought on by frostbite. —*Jason Ankeny*

Smiley Lewis (Overton Lemons)

b. Jul. 5, 1913, DeQuincey, LA, **d.** Oct. 7, 1966, New Orleans, LA

Vocals, Piano, Guitar / New Orleans R&B, New Orleans Blues, Piano Blues, R&B

Dave Bartholomew has often been quoted to the effect that Smiley Lewis was a "bad luck singer," because he never sold more than 100,000 copies of his Imperial singles. In retrospect, Lewis was a lucky man in many respects—he enjoyed stellar support from New Orleans' ace sessioneers at Cosimo's, benefited from top-flight material and production (by Bartholomew), and left behind a legacy of marvelous Crescent City R&B. We're lucky he was there, that's for sure.

Born with the unwieldy handle of Overton Lemons, Lewis hit the Big Easy in his midteens, armed with a big, booming voice and some guitar skills. He played clubs in the French Quarter, often with pianist Tuts Washington (and sometimes billed as "Smiling" Lewis). By 1947, his following was strong enough to merit a session for DeLuxe Records, which issued his debut 78, "Here Comes Smiley." Nothing happened with that platter, but when Lewis signed with Imperial in 1950 (debuting with "Tee-Nah-Nah") things began to move.

As the New Orleans R&B sound developed rapidly during the early '50s, so did Lewis, as he rocked ever harder on "Lillie Mae," "Ain't Gonna Do It," and "Big Mamou." He scored his first national hit in 1952 with "The Bells Are Ringing," but enjoyed his biggest sales in 1955 with the exultant "I Hear You Knocking" (its immortal piano solo courtesy of Huey Smith). Here's where that alleged bad luck rears its head—pop chanteuse Gale Storm swiped his thunder for any pop crossover possibilities with her ludicrous whitewashed cover of the plaintive ballad.

But Storm wouldn't dare come near its roaring flip, the Joe Turnerish rocker "Bumpity Bump," or some of Smiley Lewis' other classic mid-'50s jumpers ("Down the Road," "Lost Weekend," "Real Gone Lover," "She's Got Me Hook, Line and Sinker," "Rootin' and Tootin'"). In front of the Crescent City's hottest players (saxists Lee Allen, Clarence Hall, and Herb Hardesty usually worked his dates), Lewis roared like a lion.

Strangely, Fats Domino fared better with some of Smiley Lewis' tunes than Lewis did ("Blue Monday" in particular). Similarly, Elvis Presley cleaned up the naughty "One Night" and hit big with it, but Lewis' original had already done well in 1956 (as had his melodic "Please Listen to Me"). His blistering "Shame, Shame, Shame" found its way onto the soundtrack of the steamy Hollywood potboiler *Baby Doll* in 1957 but failed to find entry to the R&B charts.

After a long and at least semi-profitable run at Imperial, Lewis moved over to OKeh in 1961 for one single, stopped at Dot in 1964 just long enough to make a solitary 45 (produced by Nashville DJ Bill "Hoss" Allen) and bowed out with an Allen Toussaint-produced remake of "The Bells Are Ringing" for Loma in 1965. By then, stomach cancer was eating the once-stout singer up. He died in the autumn of 1966, all but forgotten outside his New Orleans home base.

The ensuing decades have rectified that miscarriage of justice, however. Smiley Lewis' place as one of the greatest New Orleans R&B artists of the '50s is certainly assured. —*Bill Dahl*

I Hear You Knocking / 1961 / EMI ✦✦✦✦✦

★ **The Best of Smiley Lewis** / Nov. 3, 1992 / Capitol ✦✦✦✦✦

Smiley Lewis made several fabulous singles, had a booming, terrific voice, and received the same great backing and support that defined the city's R&B sound. But Lewis' records seldom made it outside New Orleans, even though they were frequently brilliant. This great 24-track anthology contains the four that did make it to the charts, among them the signature song "I Hear You Knocking." It shows Lewis doing first-rate novelty tracks, ballads, weepers, uptempo wailers, and blues, and making wonderful recordings. The set also includes a thorough discography and good notes and is superbly mastered. It's magnificent, exuberant R&B, and deserved a much better national fate than it enjoyed. —*Ron Wynn*

Shame, Shame, Shame / 1993 / Bear Family ✦✦✦✦✦

Exhaustive, multi-disc set comprising everything recorded by this New Orleans singer. With the songwriting talents of Dave Bartholomew aboard, utilizing the sound of the legendary J&M Studios, and the best Crescent City musicians available, this is truly New Orleans music at its very best. —*Cub Koda*

Jimmy Liggins

b. Oct. 14, 1922, Newby, OK, **d.** Jul. 18, 1983, Durham, NC

Vocals, Guitar / Jump Blues, R&B

Another of the jump blues specialists whose romping output can be pinpointed as a direct precursor of rock & roll, guitarist Jimmy Liggins was a far more aggressive bandleader than his older brother Joe, right down to the names of their respective combos (Joe led the polished Honeydrippers; Jimmy proudly fronted the Drops of Joy).

Inspired by the success of his brother (Jimmy toiled as Joe's chauffeur for a year), the ex-pugilist jumped into the recording field in 1947 on Art Rupe's Specialty logo. His "Tear Drop Blues" pierced the R&B Top Ten the next year, while "Careful Love" and "Don't Put Me Down" hit for him in 1949. But it's Liggins' rough-and-ready rockers—"Cadillac Boogie," "Saturday Night Boogie Woogie Man," and the loopy one-chord workout "Drunk" (his last smash in 1953)—that mark Liggins as one of rock's forefathers. His roaring sax section at Specialty was populated by first-rate reedmen such as Harold Land, Charlie "Little Jazz" Ferguson, and the omnipresent Maxwell Davis.

Liggins left Specialty in 1954, stopping off at Aladdin long enough to wax the classic-to-be "I Ain't Drunk" (much later covered by Albert Collins) before fading from the scene. —*Bill Dahl*

● **Jimmy Liggins and His Drops of Joy** / 1989 / Specialty ✦✦✦✦✦

The music of Jimmy Liggins differs greatly from his elder brother Joe's in many respects. Whereas Joe was a more schooled musician, Jimmy was harder, brasher and altogether from the rougher and cruder side of the street. This 25-track collection brings together all the notable tracks Jimmy recorded for Art Rupe's Specialty label between 1947 and 1954. The music Liggins made during his stay at the label produced several R&B hits, most notably the jump-blues perennial "Drunk" (complete with crudely overdubbed lead vocal) and the proto-rock & roll classic "Cadillac Boogie," which in turn provided the basis for Jackie Brenston's "Rocket 88." —*Cub Koda*

Rough Weather Blues, Vol. 2 / 1992 / Specialty ✦✦✦✦✦

Twenty-five more Specialty cookers, including an undubbed version of "Drunk," plenty of horn-leavened jump blues outings, and several unissued artifacts (including a rare example of the Drops of Joy getting jazzy on "Now's the Time"). —*Bill Dahl*

Joe Liggins

b. Jul. 9, 1915, Guthrie, OK, **d.** Aug. 1, 1987, Lynwood, CA

Vocals, Piano / Jump Blues, R&B

Pianist Joe Liggins and his band, the Honeydrippers, tore up the R&B charts during the late '40s and early '50s with their polished brand of polite R&B. Liggins scored massive hits with "The Honeydripper" in 1945 and "Pink Champagne" five years later, posting a great many more solid sellers in between.

Born in Oklahoma, Liggins moved to San Diego in 1932. He moved to Los Angeles in 1939 and played with various outfits, including Sammy Franklin's California Rhythm Rascals. When Franklin took an unwise pass on recording Liggins' infectious "The Honeydripper," the bespectacled pianist assembled his own band and waxed the tune for Leon Rene's Exclusive logo. The upshot: an R&B chart-topper. Nine more hits followed on Exclusive over the next three years, including the schmaltzy "Got a Right to Cry," the often-covered "Tanya" (Chicago guitarist Earl Hooker waxed a delicious version), and "Roll 'Em."

In 1950, Joe joined his brother Jimmy at Specialty Records. More hits immediately followed: "Rag Mop," the number one R&B smash "Pink Champagne," "Little Joe's Boogie," and "Frankie Lee." During this period, the Honeydrippers prominently featured saxists Little Willie Jackson and James Jackson Jr. Liggins stuck around Specialty into 1954, later turning up with solitary singles on Mercury and Aladdin. But time had passed Liggins by, at least right then; later, his sophisticated approach later came back into fashion, and he led a little big band until his death. —*Bill Dahl*

Joe & Jimmy Liggins / 1976 / Sonet ✦✦✦

Early vinyl reissue import. —*Bill Dahl*

★ **Joe Liggins & the Honeydrippers** / 1989 / Specialty ✦✦✦✦✦

Pianist Joe Liggins presented a fairly sophisticated brand of swinging jump blues to jitterbuggers during the early '50s, when his irresistible "Pink Champagne" scaled the R&B charts. Twenty-five of his very best 1950-1954 Specialty sides grace this collection, including a tasty remake of "The Honeydripper," "Rhythm in the Barnyard," and the syncopated "Going Back to New Orleans" (recently revived by Dr. John). —*Bill Dahl*

Dripper's Boogie, Vol. 2 / 1992 / Specialty ✦✦✦✦✦

An encore helping of 20 rarities by Joe Liggins from Specialty, dotted with unissued discoveries (including two versions of "Little Joe's Boogie" and "Hey, Betty Martin") from 1950-1954. —*Bill Dahl*

1944–1946 / May 7, 2002 / Classics ✦✦✦✦

Papa George Lightfoot

b. Mar. 2, 1924, Natchez, MS, **d.** Nov. 28, 1971, Natchez, MS

Vocals, Harmonica / Electric Blues, Electric Harmonica Blues

Thanks to a handful of terrific '50s sides, the name of Papa Lightfoot was spoken in hushed and reverent tones by '60s blues aficionados. Then, producer Steve LaVere tracked down the elusive harp master in Natchez, cutting an album for Vault in 1969 that announced to the world that Lightfoot was still wailing like a wildman on the mouth organ. Alas, his comeback was short-lived; he died in 1971 of respiratory failure and cardiac arrest.

Sessions for Peacock in 1949 (unissued), Sultan in 1950, and Aladdin in 1952 preceded an amazing 1954 date for Imperial in New Orleans that produced Lightfoot's "Mean Old Train," "Wine Women Whiskey" (comprising his lone single for the firm) and an astonishing "When the Saints Go Marching In." Lightfoot's habit of singing through his harp microphone further coarsened his already rough-hewn vocals, while his harp playing was simply shot through with endless invention. Singles for Savoy in 1955 and Excello the next year (the latter billed him as "Ole Sonny Boy") closed out Lightfoot's '50s recording activities, setting the stage for his regrettably brief comeback in 1969. *—Bill Dahl*

Natchez Trace / 1969 / Vault ♦♦♦♦♦
Mississippi vocalist and harmonica player Papa George Lightfoot made a fine recording in 1969 for Vault, a rare full-length LP. It got limited distribution and disappeared shortly afterward. This is a reissue, and it's vital material. *—Ron Wynn*

Rural Blues, Vol. 2 / 1969 / Liberty ♦♦♦

● **Goin' Back to the Nachez Trace** / 1995 / Ace ♦♦♦♦♦
Until producer Steve LaVere redicovered him in 1969, harp giant Papa Lightfoot was revered for a mere handful of '50s sides. This album for Vault served as his comeback announcement, a gloriously down-in-the-alley affair cut at then-fledgling Malaco studios in Jackson, MS. Six bonus tracks, including three minutes of spoken monologue, have been added to the import CD reissue, enhancing an already fine album. *—Bill Dahl*

Lightnin' Slim (Otis Hicks)

b. Mar. 13, 1913, St. Louis, MO, **d.** Jul. 24, 1974, Detroit, MI
Vocals, Guitar / Swamp Blues, Louisiana Blues
The acknowledged kingpin of the Louisiana school of blues, Lightnin' Slim's style was built on his grainy but expressive vocals and rudimentary guitar work, with usually nothing more than a harmonica and a drummer in support. It was down-home country blues edged two steps further into the mainstream; first by virtue of Lightnin's electric guitar, and secondly by the sound of the local Crowley musicians who backed him being bathed in simmering, pulsating tape echo. As the first great star of producer J.D. Miller's blues talent stable, the formula was a successful one, scoring him regional hits that were issued on the Nashville-based Excello label for over a decade, with one of them, "Rooster Blues," making the national R&B charts in 1959.

Combining the country ambience of a Lightnin' Hopkins with the plodding insistence of a Muddy Waters, Slim's music remained uniquely his own, the perfect blues raconteur, even when reshaping other's material to his dark, somber style. He also possessed one of the truly great voices of the blues; unadorned and unaffected, making the world-weariness of a Sonny Boy Williamson sound like the second coming of Good Time Charlie by comparison. His exhortation to "blow your harmonica, son" has become one of the great, mournful catchphrases of the blues, and even on his most rockin' numbers, there's a sense that you are listening less to an uptempo offering than a slow blues just being played faster. Lightnin' always sounded like bad luck just moved into his home approximately an hour after his mother-in-law did.

He was born with the unglamorous handle of Otis Hicks in St. Louis, MO, on March 13, 1913. After 13 years of living on a farm outside of the city, the Hicks family moved to Louisiana, first settling in St. Francisville. Young Otis took to the guitar early, first shown the rudiments by his father, then later by his older brother, Layfield. Given his recorded output, it's highly doubtful that either his father or brother knew how to play in any key other than E natural, as Lightnin' used the same patterns over and over on his recordings, only changing keys when he used a capo or had his guitar de-tuned a full step.

But the rudiments were all he needed, and by the late '30s/early '40s he was a mainstay of the local picnic/country supper circuit around St. Francisville. In 1946, he moved to Baton Rouge, playing on weekends in local ghetto bars, and started to make a name for himself on the local circuit, first working as a member of Big Poppa's band, then on his own.

The '50s dawned with harmonica player Schoolboy Cleve in tow, working club dates and broadcasting over the radio together. It was local disc jockey Ray "Diggy Do" Meaders who then persuaded Miller to record him. He recorded for 12 years as an Excello artist, starting out originally on Miller's Feature label. As the late '60s found Lightnin' Slim working and living in Detroit, a second career blossomed as European blues audiences brought him over to tour, and he also started working the American festival and hippie ballroom circuit with Slim Harpo as a double act. When Harpo died unexpectedly in 1970, Lightnin' went on alone, recording sporadically, while performing as part of the American Blues Legends tour until his death in 1974. Lazy, rolling, and insistent, Lightnin' Slim is Louisiana blues at its finest. *—Cub Koda*

The Early Years / 1976 / Flyright ♦♦♦♦♦
There is some duplication here with *Bell Ringer*, although there are also some numbers done even earlier than those. *—Ron Wynn*

Bell Ringer / 1987 / Excello ♦♦♦♦♦
Superb early Slim Excello material. He never sang with more clarity or conviction, nor did his harmonica or guitar playing ever sound more electrifying than on these songs, many of which were popular singles. Other than Rice Miller's (Sonny Boy Williamson) definitive anthem, Slim's rendition of "Don't Start Me To Talking" was the finest. *—Ron Wynn*

★ **Rooster Blues** / 1987 / Hip-O ♦♦♦♦♦
When people talk about Louisiana swamp blues, *this* is what they're talking about. Excello Records' first foray into albums came with this wonderful collection of singles by Lightnin' Slim largely issued around the success of the title track, an R&B hit in 1960. "Long Leanie Mama," "My Starter Won't Work," "It's Mighty Crazy," "Hoo-Doo Blues," "Tom Cat Blues," "Lightnin' Troubles," "G.I. Slim," and "Feelin' Awful Blues" are all certified swamp blues classics and about as lowdown as the genre can get possibly get. With Lazy Lester on harmonica for the majority of the tracks here, the stripped-down approach to Slim's brand of blues casts these sides in a decidedly front-porch ambience with the added pulsating tape echo and oddball percussive effects just making everything on here sound even more doom-laden. "Lightnin's Blues," the John Lee Hooker-inspired "Just Made Twenty One" and "Sugar Plum," the A-side and both sides of his first and third singles for Excello, are the three bonus CD tracks appended to the original track lineup on this 1998 CD reissue. An essential blues purchase. *—AMG*

☆ **Rollin' Stone** / 1991 / Flyright ♦♦♦♦♦
With all six sides from Slim's earliest singles for the Feature label, plus excellent alternate takes of his best-known Excello numbers, this album is the perfect place to start. (Import) *—Cub Koda*

King of the Swamp Blues 1954–61 / 1992 / Flyright ♦♦♦♦♦
Lightnin' Slim true believers will want to take the extra time to search for this one. It's a 20-track collection that brings together a rash of alternate takes, previously unissued sides, studio warm-ups, and the like, all recorded by producer Jay Miller between 1954 and 1961. This is no bottom-of-the-barrel scrapings; Slim's outtakes can sometimes be better than some of the later sides released on Excello. Listeners are treated to an unreleased track from what is believed to be Slim's audition for Miller, a bare-bones reading of Jimmy Rogers' "That's All Right." One of the few examples of Slim recording without a supporting harmonica, the starkness of his guitar and vocal against the rudimentary drums of disc jockey Ray "Diggy Do" Meaders makes this the track that fans of the low-down will enthusiastically embrace. Another unreleased song from the same tape is an original, "Love Me for Myself," which features Lightnin's guitar front and center doing rare fills in the upper register between vocal lines. Several more sides emanate from these first sessions in 1954, including a wobbly tape reel alternate of his first record, "Bad Luck," and Slim in support of harmonica ace Wild Bill Phillips. Phillips' amplified harp tone is huge and distorted on the rocking "Paper in My Shoe" and Slim encores the same supporting role behind Schoolboy Cleve on three tracks. Five alternate takes illustrate how Miller and the artists shaped material for release in his Crowley, LA, studio, but mavens of unreleased material will revel in the studio warm-up of "Don't Mistreat Me" where Slim breaks a guitar string in mid-song and starts cussing out his guitar. Certainly not the place to start with this artist, but an interesting addition to his recorded legacy that hard-core fans will definitely want to pick up. *—Cub Koda*

Hoodoo Blues / 1994 / CSI ♦♦♦
One of many mysterious Classic Sound Inc. blues releases, with no indication of whence the material originated. The sound is decent but nothing special, and some of the balances are haywire (some guitars pushed too far into the mix etc.), but the CD is a mess. The songs include "Rooster Blues" (with an awkward brass section somewhere in the background), "G.I. Blues," "Crazy About You Baby," "My Babe," "Things I Used to Do," "That's All Right," and "Lightning's Bad Luck" (which reappears, in what seems to be the very same cut, as "Bad Luck Blues," seven songs later), all licensed from a British outfit called Prestige Records. The material sounds like it was done much later than Slim's classic Excello sides, leading one to believe that it originated during the British phase of his career, when he was playing to audiences overseas—it could have been a busted "London Sessions"-style collection. For all of its sloppiness, this is a decent budget-priced disc, and a nice appendix to the important part of Slim's career, for all of its mystery—but it's a pity it isn't a live concert, like the Muddy Waters and Howlin' Wolf CSI releases. *—Bruce Eder*

I'm Evil / 1995 / Excello ♦♦♦♦♦
A goldmine of 27 '50s and '60s obscurities from one of the lonesomest bayou blues greats ever. Filled with alternate takes and outright unissued efforts, *I'm Evil* reverberates with lowdown treatises that cut to the heart and soul of the swamp. "Bad Luck," "Mean Ol' Lonesome Train," and "Rock Me Mama" are pure, unadulterated Louisiana blues of the highest order. *—Bill Dahl*

Nothing But the Devil / 1996 / Ace ♦♦♦♦♦
This 24-song collection undoubtedly overlaps with some of the U.S.-issued Excello material—including the same alternate takes of "Rooster Blues" and "It's Mighty Crazy"—but there's just enough that they don't share to make this worth a look, if not a purchase, by owners of the U.S. material. The sound, as is usual with Ace, is excellent, and the stuff is worthy of inclusion with the best of Slim's work. Among the best tracks here are two outtakes unique to this set at this time, "I'm Leavin' You Baby," on which Slim steps over into Howlin' Wolf territory ("Moanin' at Midnight," etc.), and "Sweet Little Woman," where he crosses swords with Sonny Boy Williamson II. *—Bruce Eder*

Winter Time Blues / May 1998 / Ace ♦♦♦♦♦

The Best of Lightnin' Slim / Jul. 27, 1999 / Hip-O ♦♦♦♦
Whether the 16 tracks collected here represent Slim's absolute best is open to debate. Here are 16 performances issued on ten different singles during his heyday at Excello, covering a time frame from of 1956 to 1962. What this package *does* do is provide a nice addition to Slim's *Rooster Blues* record, with only three of the tunes from that album duplicated here. Tracks like "Bad Luck and Trouble," "I'm a Rollin' Stone," "Nothin' but the Devil," and "Cool Down Baby" catch Lightnin' in peak form, and the later tracks like "Winter Time Blues" and "I'm Evil" rock with a heavier guitar intensity. Once you get hooked into Lightnin' Slim, you're going to want it all, and here's a great little stop along the way. *—Cub Koda*

Lil' Ed & the Blues Imperials

f. 1975, Chicago, IL
Group / Modern Electric Chicago Blues, Modern Electric Blues
Lil' Ed & the Blues Imperials are among the premier party bands to have come out of Chicago during the '80s. Often compared to Elmore James and Hound Dog Taylor, fiery, flamboyant slide guitarist Lil' Ed Williams and his group play dedicated, rough-edged and hard-rocking dance music and have established an international reputation. A native of Chicago, Williams was first inspired by his uncle, renowned slide guitarist J.B. Hutto, with whom he studied as a young teen. Hutto not only taught him slide, but also introduced Williams to bass and drums. Williams' half-brother, James Young, was also a student of Hutto, and later became the bassist for the Blues Imperials.

The brothers co-founded their group in the early '70s and went professional in 1975, playing at Big Duke's Blue Flame on the West Side. The gig earned them a whopping six bucks, which the group members split evenly. In those early years, Williams worked days at a car wash while Young drove a school bus. Despite their humble start, Williams and the Blues Imperials kept performing at night and by the early '80s had developed a substantial regional following. Signing to Alligator in the mid-'80s, they released their debut album, *Roughhousin'*, in 1986 and found themselves receiving national attention. They began playing urban clubs and festivals all over the country and eventually toured Canada, Europe, and Japan.

They released their second album, *Chicken, Gravy & Biscuits*, in 1989, and the success continued as the Blues Imperials began appearing with such artists as Koko Taylor and Elvin Bishop during the Alligator Records 20th anniversary tour. They released their third album *What You See is What You Get* in 1992. If Ed, half-brother Pookie Young, and the latest members of the revamped Blues Imperials never did much to modernize their blues or develop a new sound, that was just fine with the band's followers ("Ed Heads," no less), to whom the raucous, rocking slide guitar heritage of Hutto, Hound Dog Taylor, and Elmore James is blues nirvana. Following their third album, the group went on hiatus for a few years during which Lil' Ed Williams released two albums on Earwig, 1996's *Keep On Walking* with Dave Weld and 1998's *Who's Been Talking* with Willie Kent. In 1999 the band reconvened and released *Get Wild*. They followed it up with *Heads Up*, their fifth Alligator record. *—Jim O'Neal & Sandra Brennan*

Roughhousin' / 1986 / Alligator ✦✦✦
Wild & greasy blues at its best, a two-song session for an anthology turned into an all-night, live-in-the-studio jam. Sounds like it was great fun. *—Niles J. Frantz*

● **Chicken, Gravy & Biscuits** / 1989 / Alligator ✦✦✦✦✦
Wild, raw, rough-edged Chicago slide guitar blues, this is jumpin', partyin' music in the tradition of Hound Dog Taylor and J.B. Hutto (Lil' Ed's uncle). Recorded live in the studio with no overdubs, it includes nine original compositions plus covers of Hutto and Albert Collins' tunes. *—Niles J. Frantz*

What You See is What You Get / 1992 / Alligator ✦✦✦
This group fits the bill for listeners who enjoy hard-driving good-time electric blues. Lil' Ed Williams only has an average voice but his slashing guitar works well with rhythm guitarist Mike Garrett and the rest of the quintet (which includes Eddie McKinley on tenor) is well rehearsed and spirited. The result is an above average set of rockish blues that, although not terribly distinctive, is sure to satisfy. *—Scott Yanow*

Get Wild / Jul. 13, 1999 / Alligator ✦✦✦✦
After disbanding his group to take time off to clean up his life, Lil' Ed reforms the Blues Imperials for this 1999 entry, his first for Alligator since *What You See Is What You Get*. The good news is that the time off has totally reinvigorated Ed's playing, singing and songwriting, ultimately turning in a great batch of originals infused with blistering raw energy. The only non-originals out of the 14 tracks assembled here are nice takes on "Too Late" and "Pet Cream Man," both tunes written by Ed's uncle and principal inspiration, the late J.B. Hutto. Call this a comeback album if you must, but if great, raw Chicago blues is your thing, consider this one great album, period. *—Cub Koda*

Heads Up / Jul. 9, 2002 / Alligator ✦✦
Sometimes the bloodlines show up and at other times they explode with a fanfare that shows itself to the world. Lil' Ed Williams traces his heritage back to his uncle, one of the Chicago blues legends, slide guitar master J.B. Hutto. He was tutored by his uncle, and the West Side Chicago blues scene that nurtured him, and readily gives J.B. much of the credit for his prowess. He captures some of that same raw street energy that was his uncle's trademark on many of the tracks on this, his fifth Alligator release. Listen to "The Creeper" to get an idea of the savage fury that he can channel through his slide guitar work. This disc manifests that feel for the blues that can't be taught, but must be both lived and seen from the inside. His vocals have that same intuitive feel that is visible in his guitar playing. He has a grit and soul that put a real bite into his vocals. He wrote 11 of the 13 songs here, and there are a few that have the potential to become standards in the field. He is a throwback to the raucous raw sound of the early electric Chicago blues, and yet his songs and feel are every bit a part of today's world. He is strongly backed by his band, which is solidly anchored by his half-brother, Pookie, on the bass. This is a dose of your good-time party blues served up as raw as you can stand it with his stinging guitar and tumultuous vocals. Don't miss it. *—Bob Gottlieb*

Li'l Ronnie & the Grand Dukes

Group / Blues Revival, Modern Electric Blues, R&B, Rockabilly Revival, Swamp Blues
Rooted in swampy '50s R&B, greasy rockabilly, and various shades of the blues spectrum, Li'l Ronnie & the Grand Dukes are true believers in the American musical tradition. The band was led by veteran harpist Ronnie Owens, who had been in the blues revival scene since his teens, backing up blues legends such as John Lee Hooker, Taj Mahal, and John Mayall on his way to earning a Hohner harmonica endorsement, before fronting his own bands in 1979. Eventually recruiting Bobby Olive on drums, Craig Schneider on bass, Mike Dutton on guitar, Steve Utt on piano/organ, and Terry Hummer on saxophone, the Grand Dukes lineup was intact. Their first release, 1999's *Too Fast for Conditions*, was a hit among the blues revivalists, just as 2000's *Young and Evil* drew similarly favorable reviews. *—Matt Fink*

Too Fast for Conditions / May 11, 1999 / Planetary ✦✦✦

● **Young and Evil** / May 8, 2001 / Planetary ✦✦✦✦
An accomplished and entertaining set of traditional electric blues, Li'l Ronnie & the Grand Dukes translate reverence into impassioned performance. Joined by guitarist Anson Funderburgh, Ronnie Owens deftly leads his band through a roll call of blues genre exercises, from the loosely rocking Texas blues of "Leavin' Here Tonight" to a jump blues cover of Amos Milburn's "Chicken Shack Boogie" and a slow burning rendition of George Smith's "Early One Monday Morning." Owens more than holds his own on the seven originals here, as well, with big swinging blues shouters, tight soul grooves, and jazzy instrumentals all sharing time. As Owens is a soulful vocalist and standout harpist, he does well to allow his backing band to share the spotlight in his powerhouse performances. Sure, it's all been done before, but this kind of enthusiasm and authenticity makes for an addition that should be welcome in any blues collection. *—Matt Fink*

Charley Lincoln (Charlie Hicks)

b. Mar. 11, 1900, Lithonia, GA, **d.** Sep. 28, 1963, Cairo, GA
Vocals, Guitar / Piedmont Blues, Prewar Country Blues, Country Blues
Aliases and pseudonyms aside, Charlie Hicks, aka Charley, or Charlie Lincoln, was an above-average country blues vocalist. He teamed often with either his brother Robert Hicks, aka Barbecue Bob, or with Peg-Leg Howell. His guitar voicings and style were influenced by Curley Weaver, but Hicks was a colorful singer and flashy player. Weaver's mother Savannah taught Lincoln the guitar as a teenager. Lincoln recorded with his brother for Columbia from 1927-1930; he continued playing with him into the '50s, though his performance and playing schedule was highly irregular. A murder conviction ended his career in 1955; he was in prison until his death in 1963. *—Ron Wynn*

● **Complete Recorded Works (1927–1939)** / 1984 / Document ✦✦✦
Document's *Complete Recorded Works (1927-1930)* is an exhaustive overview of Charley Lincoln's career. The exacting chronological sequencing, poor fidelity (all cuts are transferred from original acetates and 78s), and number of performances will appeal more to the serious blues listener, but casual listeners will find that the collection is of marginal interest for those very reasons. *—Thom Owens*

Hip Linkchain (Willie Richard)

b. Nov. 10, 1936, Jackson, MS, **d.** Feb. 13, 1989, Chicago, IL
Vocals, Guitar / Electric Chicago Blues
Cancer struck guitarist Hip Linkchain down before he could shed his status as a Chicago blues journeyman. With a fine album on the Dutch Black Magic logo, *Airbusters*, to his credit shortly before he died, Linkchain might have managed to move up a rung or two in the city's blues pecking order had he lived longer.

Born Willie Richard in Mississippi, his odd stage name stemmed from being dubbed "Hipstick" as a lad. (White residents of the area gave his seven-foot-tall dad the name Linkchain because he wore logging chains around his neck). Dad and older brother Jesse both played the blues, and Hip followed in their footsteps. He heard Elmore James, Little Milton, and Sonny Boy Williamson while living in the Delta before relocating to Chicago during the early '50s.

Linkchain made inroads on the competitive Chicago circuit during the '50s and '60s, playing with harpists Dusty Brown, Willie Foster, and Lester Davenport. His own band, the Chicago Twisters, was fronted by a very young Tyrone Davis in 1959. Linkchain cut a handful of very obscure 45s for the tiny Lola and Sanns logos prior to the emergence of his debut domestic album for Teardrop Records, *Change My Blues*, circa 1981. *—Bill Dahl*

Change My Blues / Jun. 1983 / Teardrop ✦✦
Anemic album by journeyman Chicago blues guitarist Linkchain that didn't come close to capturing his stinging sound. *—Bill Dahl*

● **Airbusters** / 1993 / Evidence ✦✦✦✦
Linkchain was a solid, no frills bluesman and this album (his last before his death in 1989) showcases him at his best. Loads of great original material, with the added bonus of top notch playing from Chicago's finest blues players. Standout tracks include "Blow Wind Blow," "I'll Overcome," and "Take Out Your False Teeth." *—Cub Koda*

I Am on My Way / 1996 / MCM ✦✦✦

Mance Lipscomb

b. Apr. 9, 1895, Navasota, TX, **d.** Jan. 30, 1976, Navasota, TX
Vocals, Violin, Guitar / Songster, Country Blues
Like Leadbelly and Mississippi John Hurt, the designation as strictly a blues singer dwarfs the musical breadth of Mance Lipscomb. Born on April 9, 1895, in Navasota, Texas, Lipscomb was a sharecropper/tenant farmer all his life who didn't record until 1960, "songster" fits what Lipscomb did best. A proud, yet unboastful man, Lipscomb would point out that he was an educated musician, his ability to play everything from classic blues, ballads, pop songs to spirituals in a multitude of styles and keys being his particular mark of originality. He appeared at numerous blues and folk festivals throughout the sixties, released several albums on Arhoolie and even one for a major label, Reprise, in 1970, *Trouble in Mind*. Four years later, Lipscomb retired from the festival circuit and passed away on January 30, 1976, in his hometown of Navasota, Texas. He was 81. With a wide-ranging repertoire of over 90 songs, Lipscomb may have gotten a belated start in recording, but left a remarkable legacy to be enjoyed. *—Cub Koda & Al Campbell*

★ **Texas Sharecropper & Songster** / 1960 / Arhoolie ✦✦✦✦✦
Arhoolie's *Texas Sharecropper & Songster* is a recording made in 1960, during the blues revival. Prior to the blues revival, Lipscomb was an unknown, and his discovery was one of the positive by-products of the revival. He was a great country blues man, and this is perhaps his greatest effort, capturing him running through a number of traditional songs. Most of the songs are augmented by his jackknife slide guitar, and all feature his raw, haunted vocals, which make these classic songs sound timeless. *—Thom Owens*

Texas Songster, Vol. 2 / 1964 / Arhoolie ✦✦✦✦
The material on this album was re-released on compact disc in the '90s, with outtakes and whatnot bumping the song catch up to 20 songs. This original vinyl pressing features a baker's dozen tracks, all recorded one spring when the charming Mance Lipscomb was out in California doing the folk revival circuit. Like most of his albums, this one is a good example of his versatility. Just when a listener thinks they have the man's style mentally pigeonholed, then along comes something else quite surprising. It is instructive to hear his "Spanish Flang Dang" in comparison with Elizabeth Cotten. Both are talented finger-pickers, and both are relying on memory to reconstruct a hit instrumental record from the early '30s. The variations are fascinating. The blues material here is also strong, rang-

ing from the tough "Cocaine Done Killed Me Baby" to the light-hearted "Boogie in A." Producer Chris Strachwitz did a great job with the sound, and it is the type of acoustic guitar tone that really sounds better in analog. —*Eugene Chadbourne*

Mance Lipscomb: Texas Songster, Vol. 2 (You Got to Reap What You Sow) / 1964 / Arhoolie ✦✦✦✦

Mance Lipscomb was a great songster, someone who knew hundreds of songs and could deliver any and all of them in different but effective ways. He sang blues, spirituals, old folk numbers, and his own tunes. Lipscomb had few rivals when it came to telling stories, setting up situations, creating characters, and depicting incidents. This 24-song reissued disc from 1964 puts Lipscomb in a perfect context, ripping through various songs and talking about everything from drugs to domestic conflict and police worries to spiritual concerns. —*Ron Wynn*

Texas Blues Guitar / 1994 / Arhoolie ✦✦✦

A 15-cut disc issued in conjunction with the song transcription book *Mance Lipscomb: Texas Blues Guitar*, this is a fine introduction to the Texas bluesman's work, and includes acoustic performances of "Ain't It Hard," "Motherless Children" and "You Got to Reap What You Sow." —*Jason Ankeny*

Captain, Captain: The Texas Songster / Apr. 21, 1998 / Arhoolie ✦✦✦

Eight of these 24 tracks come from an April 1966 session and were originally released on LP (on Arhoolie); the other 17 are previously unissued, five of them sourced from April 1966, the rest from 1960. It's entirely typical of Lipscomb's output: versatile, relaxed, and samey-sounding acoustic blues with some prominent ragtime and folk influences. The 1960 material doesn't boast fidelity as strong as the 1966 takes (though it's certainly adequate), and has more of a down-home flavor; the 1966 tracks sound more innocuous and front-porch-relaxed by contrast. —*Richie Unterberger*

Texas Songster, Vol. 4: Live! At the Cabale / Sep. 21, 1999 / Arhoolie ✦✦✦

All but three of these 21 tracks were previously unreleased; all but two of them recorded live at the Cabale in Berkeley in 1964 (the other two were done live in Sacramento in 1972). Lipscomb made many albums, and it was a wise decision on compiler Chris Strachwitz's part to focus on songs that were not available on previous CDs by the singer. Repertoire aside, this is very much of a piece with the "songster" style Lipscomb projects on other recordings: good-natured acoustic tunes that draw from boogie, ragtime, and folk, with a warm vocal delivery and accomplished guitar picking. Some of the songs, in fact, will be pretty familiar to most blues fans, if not always duplicated by Lipscomb on other CDs: "Meet Me in the Bottom," "Trouble in Mind," "Key to the Highway," "Rock Me Mama," and "Baby Don't You Lay It on Me" (which sounds close to the folk standard "Baby Let Me Follow You Down"). One of the tracks, incidentally, is largely a 12-minute spoken story, "Early Days Back Home." —*Richie Unterberger*

Texas Country Blues / Aug. 27, 2002 / Arhoolie ✦✦✦

Virginia Liston

b. 1890, d. Jun. 1932, St. Louis, MO
Vocals / Classic Female Blues, Classic Jazz

Virginia Liston was one of the blues singers whose career was spent primarily in Black vaudeville. She is said to have gotten her start in show business around 1912 in Washington, D.C. In 1920 she married entertainer Sam Gray and toured with him as part of a husband-and-wife team called Liston & Liston. They divorced in 1925. In the early '20s Liston came in contact with Clarence Williams, who recorded with her for OKeh for the first time in September, 1923. Thirty-six issued sides for OKeh and Vocalion came out under Virginia Liston's name through the summer of 1926, the most famous being a pairing that united Liston with Clarence Williams' Blue Five, then including Louis Armstrong and Sidney Bechet.

Virginia Liston remarried and retired from show business in 1929, afterward settling in St. Louis to work in the church. Three years later she was dead. —*Uncle Dave Lewis*

● **Virginia Liston, Vol. 1: 1923–1924** / Sep. 7, 2000 / Document ✦✦✦✦

An obscure but talented classic blues singer, Virginia Liston recorded 36 selections during 1923-1926. The first 23 are on this Document CD. Although Liston did not have any hits, many of her recordings are memorable. *Vol. 1* is highlighted by "You Thought I Was Blind but Now I See," "You Can Have It (I Don't Want It)," "Early in the Morning," and "You've Got the Right Keyhole." The latter two songs have Liston joined by Clarence Williams' Blue Five, which at the time included cornetist Louis Armstrong, Sidney Bechet (on clarinet and soprano), and trombonist Charles Irvis. All of the other selections have Williams on piano (usually solo) except for "Jail House Blues," which has a guitarist who might possibly be Bechet (in his only recording on the instrument). As usual, Document does an excellent job of reissuing obscure recordings complete and in chronological order. Collectors of '20s classic blues will want this set and its follow-up, *Vol. 2.* —*Scott Yanow*

Virginia Liston, Vol. 2: 1924–1926 / Sep. 7, 2000 / Document ✦✦✦✦

Virginia Liston recorded 36 selections during 1923-1926, and the final 13 begin this interesting CD from Document's "complete" series of classic blues recordings. The backup groups are just adequate (mostly with Clarence Williams on piano), but such memorable tunes as "Papa De Da Da," "Make Me a Pallet," "Titanic Blues," and "You Can Dip Your Bread in My Gravy, But You Can't Have None of My Chops" are given excellent treatments, finishing off Virginia Liston's career. Also on the CD are the only ten recordings of Lavinia Turner, a vaudevillian singer who only recorded during 1921-1922. Although backed by bands on the majority of the tunes, this talented (if very obscure) singer is heard at her best accompanied by pianist James P. Johnson on two selections from November 1921. A fine acquisition for classic blues vocal fans. —*Scott Yanow*

Little Buster (Edward Forehand)

b. Sep. 28, 1942, Hereford, NC
Vocals, Guitar / Modern Electric Blues, Soul-Blues, Soul

Anyone lucky enough to stumble across Little Buster's 1995 debut album for Bullseye Blues might well have been asking themselves, "Where's this guy been all this time?" The answer: For the last three decades or so, the blind guitarist had been serving up his soulful brand of blues around his adopted home of Long Island, NY, with his band, the Soul Brothers.

Edward "Little Buster" Forehand was born on September 28, 1942, in Hereford, NC. He left the North Carolina School for the Deaf and Blind when he was 16 years old, moving to New York and breaking into the local R&B scene almost immediately. Buster recorded sparingly during the '60s, waxing the Doc Pomus-penned "Young Boy Blues" for Jubilee in 1967. But the world-at-large remained ignorant of Buster's impressive command of the soul and blues lexicons until 1995, when *Right on Time!* blew onto the contemporary scene like an unexpected breath of fresh air. *Looking for a Home* followed in 1997. While his recorded output has unfortunately been sparse, Buster continues to tour consistently playing clubs and festivals throughout the world. —*Bill Dahl & Al Campbell*

● **Right on Time** / 1995 / Bullseye Blues ✦✦✦✦✦

Literally from out of nowhere did this remarkable debut album arise by blind guitarist Little Buster and his combo (he's no stranger to the studio, though, with a handful of late-'60s 45s to his credit). Mixing blues and soul traditions with melismatic passion, Buster was responsible for one of 1995's best albums—debut or otherwise. —*Bill Dahl*

Looking for a Home / Feb. 25, 1997 / Sequel ✦✦✦

Work Your Show / 2000 / Fedora ✦✦✦✦

Little Charlie & the Nightcats

f. 1976, San Francisco, CA
Group / Modern Electric Chicago Blues, Modern Electric Blues

One of the hardest-working barroom blues bands on the West Coast, Little Charlie & the Nightcats started out in the mid-'70s, began recording around a decade later, and just kept on going strong. The two constants over the Nightcats' long history were co-founders Little Charlie Baty (guitar) and Rick Estrin (harmonica, lead vocals). Baty's biting licks were the perfect complement to Estrin's devil-may-care swagger and wryly humorous, storytelling lyrics, and that combo was enough to maintain a decades-long career as a popular live act all across the blues circuit. The band's music relies chiefly on electric urban blues of the Chicago variety, but mixes in bits of many other compatible styles, including early rock & roll, soul, surf, swing, jump blues, and Western swing.

Charlie Baty was attending UC-Berkeley and studying mathematics when he formed Little Charlie & the Nightcats with Rick Estrin in 1976. Initially, both of them were harmonica players and singers, but Baty happened to play guitar as well, and he made the switch permanently when Estrin established himself as the stronger of the two. Joined by bassist Jay Peterson and drummer Dobie Strange, the band moved to Sacramento and made a living playing the local blues clubs. Eventually, they sent a demo tape to the prominent blues label Alligator, and despite the unsolicited nature of their submission, Alligator immediately signed them after catching their live act. After just over a decade in existence, Little Charlie & the Nightcats issued their debut album, *All the Way Crazy*, in 1987. The record helped establish them on the blues festival and club circuits, and they began touring the country extensively, playing a number of international venues as well. Follow-ups *Disturbing the Peace* (1988) and *The Big Break* (1989) consolidated their status, and the gigs poured in.

In 1990, the group had their first personnel change; Peterson departed and was replaced by Brad Lee Sexton, who debuted on the 1991 concert set *Captured Live*. 1993's *Night Vision* featured "My Next Ex-Wife," a witty blues-rocker that won Estrin a W.C. Handy Award for Song of the Year, highlighting his steadily growing reputation for songwriting prowess. Estrin's material was soon being covered by artists like Koko Taylor and Robert Cray. Sexton left in 1994, and Ronnie James Weber joined up as the band's third bassist, debuting the following year on *Straight Up!* Original drummer Dobie Strange left in 1996 after 20 years with the group, and his spot was taken by June Core. Core debuted on 1998's *Shadow of the Blues*, and that year the group also backed John Hammond Jr., on his album *Long as I Have You*. Little Charlie & the Nightcats returned in 2002 with a new album, *That's Big*, and a new rhythm section, bassist Frankie Randall and drummer Joey Ventittelli. —*Steve Huey*

All the Way Crazy / 1987 / Alligator ✦✦✦

This 1987 outing found the band in fine form with its usual mix of strong originals and choice covers. Estrin's harp work on "Poor Tarzan" shows him to be a blower of chops equal to shining guitar whiz Charlie Baty's mercurial flights. Baty, as usual, struts vintage approved tones and blows hotter than a flamethrower on "Suicide Blues," and sprays Magic Sam licks all over Bobby Guitar's "When Girls Do It." Another solid entry in this band's discography. —*Cub Koda*

Disturbing the Peace / 1988 / Alligator ✦✦✦✦✦

This 1988 outing is another seamless part of the thread that is this eclectic West Coast band, brimming with equal parts good humor and sensational playing. Charlie Baty tears into his guitar on the opener, "That's My Girl," and keeps the heat up throughout this set, turning in jazzy work on "My Money's Green," rockabilly licks galore on "She's Talking," and getting quite bluesy on the slow one, "V-8 Ford." Rick Estrin contributes explosive harp work on "Nervous," "I Ain't Lyin'," and "Don't Boss Me," plus vocals full of sly charm on every track along the line. If you like these guys, add this one to the shopping cart if you haven't already. —*Cub Koda*

The Big Break / 1989 / Alligator ✦✦✦

Here is another raucous, rollicking release. —*Niles J. Frantz*

Captured Live / 1991 / Alligator ✦✦✦

This enjoyable live set captures the group's manic energy. —*Niles J. Frantz*

Night Vision / 1993 / Alligator ♦♦♦

Unlike their previous efforts (where it sounded like the band pulled the van up to the studio, unloaded their gear, and played a set and split before someone hollered out for last call), this one sounds more like a real album. With Joe Louis Walker producing, the boys explore new twists on their wide-ranging bag of tricks. The band's humor is found in abundance on sleazy blues items like "I'll Never Do That No More" and the soul rocker opener "My Next Ex-Wife," while the boys truly get down to business on the rockabilly-tinged "Backfire" and the smokin' shuffle "Can't Keep It Up." Augmenting their basic lineup are guest appearances by Walker and a host of others in support, making this their most musical sounding album yet. *—Cub Koda*

Straight Up! / 1995 / Alligator ♦♦

Straight Up! is a typically rollicking, humorous collection of updated Chicago blues from Little Charlie & the Nightcats. As with any of the of the band's albums, the quality of the material is slightly uneven, but the band's good-natured energy makes those shortcomings somewhat forgivable, especially if you are already a fan. *—Stephen Thomas Erlewine*

● **Deluxe Edition** / Oct. 28, 1997 / Alligator ♦♦♦♦♦

Deluxe Edition is a wonderful 15-track collection that compiles all of the highlights from his first six albums for Alligator Records. Although a few of Little Charlie & the Nightcats' albums hold up as individual works, they've all been a little uneven, which means the appearance of this best-of collection is all the more welcome. Not only will it satisfy the needs of the curious, but fans who just want the cream of the crop will be thrilled with this record. *—Thom Owens*

Shadow of the Blues / Oct. 13, 1998 / Alligator ♦♦♦♦

Little Charlie & The Nightcats' seventh album for Alligator found the group at the top of their respective game, a combination of sharp songwriting combined with the expert playing of a group that has spent years on the road honing their craft. Rick Estrin's sleazy used-car-salesman-as-blues-singer persona comes shining through on his originals "Never Trust a Woman," "New Old Lady," and "Big and Fat," while Charlie Baty's guitar mastery is brought to the fore on the dazzling instrumental "Percolatin'." The title track is a great minor-key slow late-night piece, full of atmosphere and sporting great chromatic harp work from Estrin and a jazzy break from Baty. Down-home award winner goes to the only cover on board, Big Boy Spires' "Murmur Low" which also features Estrin in the rare role of second guitarist. As always, the rhythm section of Ronnie James Weber on bass and June Core on drums provides swinging support throughout and the addition on certain tracks of Jimmy Pugh on piano and organ is a most welcome addition. The result is another solid album of modern-day blues served up by one of the genre's best working bands. *—Cub Koda*

That's Big / Mar. 12, 2002 / Alligator ♦♦♦♦

Although founders Little Charlie Baty and harpist/singer/songwriter Rick Estrin welcome two new cats on bass and drums, little else has changed on Little Charlie & the Nightcats' eighth studio effort, again on Alligator, the only label for which they have recorded. While that could be a problem for some outfits, the music here is so perfectly conceived, well-written, and performed with cracking musicianship that only the grouchiest blues purist will complain they aren't breaking much new ground. Estrin's slimy, woman-distrusting, often comical delivery on his compositions—such as "Desperate Man," "Livin' Good," and a duet with the equally non-PC West Coast singer/harp player James Harman trading quips on the title track—make for a lighthearted listening experience. But clearly these guys can also play; Baty and guest guitarist Rusty Zinn's dueling hollow-body guitars on "Bluto's Back" and Estrin's chromatic harp solo on "Coastin' Hank" (two of the disc's three instrumentals) prove that the group's chops are as finely tuned as their ability to cut up and add a dose of levity to the usually ultra-serious blues. The occasional use of horns on four tracks injects a jazzy R&B sensibility to the proceedings and fills out the sound. Zinn's vocal on "It Better Get Better" also takes the focus off Estrin, whose schtick starts to wear thin by the 12th track—the album's lone cover—a version of "Steady Rollin' Man," credited to Sonny Boy Williamson, who wrote these particular lyrics, not Robert Johnson. The group's roots in Louis Jordan's swinging jump blues are showcased in "Money Must Think I'm Dead" and even new drummer Joey Ventittelli gets a songwriting credit on the Chicago blues of the album's kickoff track, "Real Love," which features some lip-shredding, overdriven, electrified harp from Estrin. Established fans will rejoice in this exceptional release that treads water in all the right ways, and newcomers can start here to appreciate Little Charlie & the Nightcats' charming, unorthodox yet dedicated approach to the blues. *—Hal Horowitz*

Little Feat

f. 1969, Los Angeles, CA

Group / Album Rock, Boogie Rock, Southern Rock, Hard Rock, Blues-Rock, Rock & Roll

Though they had all the trappings of a southern-fried blues band, Little Feat were hardly conventional. Led by songwriter/guitarist Lowell George, Little Feat was a wildly eclectic band, bringing together strains of blues, R&B, country and rock & roll. The group was exceptionally gifted technically and their polished professionalism sat well with the slick sounds coming out of southern California during the '70s. However, Little Feat were hardly slick—they had a surreal sensibility, as evidenced by George's idiosyncratic songwriting, which helped the band earn a cult following among critics and musicians. Though the band earned some success on album-oriented radio, the group was derailed after George's death in 1979. Little Feat re-formed in the late '80s, and while they were playing as well as ever, they lacked the skewed sensibility that made them cult favorites. Nevertheless, their albums and tours were successful, especially among American blues-rock fans.

However, Little Feat wasn't conceived as straight-ahead blues-rock group. Its founding members, Lowell George (vocals, guitar, slide guitar) and Roy Estrada (bass), were veterans of Frank Zappa's Mothers of Invention. George had a long musical career before joining the Mothers. As a child, he and his brother Hampton performed a harmonica duet on television's *Ted Mack's Original Amateur Hour.* During high school, he learned how to play flute, which led to him appearing as an oboist and baritone saxophonist on several Frank Sinatra recording sessions. He formed the folk-rock group the Factory with drummer Richard Hayward in 1965. Before disbanding, the Factory made some recordings for Uni Records, but the tapes sat unreleased until the '90s. Following the group's demise, George joined the Mothers of Invention where he met Estrada. Zappa convinced George to form his own band after hearing "Willin'," but the guitarist was reluctant to begin a band until he participated in a brief Standells reunion.

George and Estrada formed Little Feat in 1969 with Hayward and keyboardist Bill Payne. Neither its eponymous first album (1971) nor 1972's *Sailin' Shoes* were commercial successes, despite strong reviews. As a result, the group temporarily disbanded, with Estrada leaving music to become a computer programmer. When the group reconvened later in 1972, he was replaced by New Orleans musician Kenny Gradney. In its second incarnation, Little Feat also featured guitarist Paul Barrere and percussionist Sam Clayton, who gave the music a funkier feeling, as demonstrated by 1973's *Dixie Chicken.* The band toured heavily behind the record, building a strong following in the South and on the East Coast. Nevertheless, the group remained centered in Los Angeles, since the members did a lot of session work on the side.

Though the band was earning a cult following, several members of the group were growing frustrated by George's erratic behavior and increasing drug use. Following 1974's *Feats Don't Fail Me Now,* Barrere and Payne became the band's primary songwriters and they were primarily responsible for the jazzy fusions of 1975's *The Last Record Album.* Little Feat continued in that direction on *Time Loves a Hero* (1977), the double-live album *Waiting for Columbus* (1978), and *Down on the Farm* (1979). Frustrated with the band's increasingly improvisational and jazzy nature, George recorded a solo album, *Thanks I'll Eat It Here,* which was released in 1979. Following its release, George announced that Little Feat had broken up, and he embarked on a solo tour. Partway through the tour, he died of an apparent heart attack. *Down on the Farm* was released after his death, as was the rarities collection, *Hoy-Hoy!* (1981).

After spending seven years as sidemen, Payne, Barrere, Hayward, Gradney, and Clayton re-formed Little Feat in 1988, adding vocalist/guitarist Craig Fuller and guitarist Fred Tackett. The heavily anticipated *Let It Roll* was released in 1988 to mixed reviews, but it went gold. The group's subsequent reunion albums—*Representing the Mambo* (1989), *Shake Me Up* (1991), and *Ain't Head Enough Fun* (1995)—each sold progressively less, but the band remained a popular concert attraction. On the latter album, the band traded the strongly Lowell George-esque voice of Fuller for female singer Shaun Murphy; this lineup went on to release *Under the Radar* in 1998 and *Chinese Work Songs* in 2000. *—Stephen Thomas Erlewine*

☆ **Little Feat** / 1971 / Warner Brothers ♦♦♦♦♦

It sold poorly (around 11,000 copies) and the band never cut anything like it again, but Little Feat's eponymous debut isn't just one of their finest records, it's one of the great lost rock & roll albums. Even dedicated fans tend to overlook the album, largely because it's the polar opposite of the subtly intricate, funky rhythm & roll that made their reputation during the mid-'70s. *Little Feat* is a raw, hard-driving, funny and affectionate celebration of American weirdness, equal parts garage rock, roadhouse blues, post-Zappa bizarreness, post-Parsons country-rock, and slightly bent folk storytelling. Since it's grounded in roots rock, it feels familiar enough, but the vision of chief songwriter/guitarist/vocalist Lowell George is wholly unique and slightly off-center. He sees everything with a gently surreal sense of humor that remains affectionate, whether it's on an ode to a "Truck Stop Girl," the weary trucker's anthem "Willin'," or the goofy character sketch of the crusty old salt "Crazy Captain Gunboat Willie." That affection is balanced by gutsy slices of Americana like the careening travelogue "Strawberry Flats," the darkly humorous "Hamburger Midnight" and a jaw-dropping Howlin' Wolf medley guest-starring Ry Cooder, plus keyboardist Bill Payne's terrific opener, "Snakes on Everything." The songwriting itself is remarkable enough, but the band is its equal—they're as loose, vibrant and alive as the Stones at their best. In most respects, this album has more in common with George's earlier band the Factory than the rest of the Little Feat catalog, but there's a deftness in the writing and performance that distinguishes it from either band's work, which makes it all the more remarkable. It's a pity that more people haven't heard the record, but that just means that anyone who owns it feels like they're in on a secret only they and a handful of others know. *—Stephen Thomas Erlewine*

☆ **Sailin' Shoes** / 1972 / Warner Brothers ♦♦♦♦♦

Little Feat's debut may have been a great album but it sold so poorly, they had to either broaden their audience or, in all likelihood, they'd be dropped from Warner. So, *Sailin' Shoes* is a consciously different record from its predecessor—less raw and bluesy, blessed with a varied production and catchier songs. That still doesn't make it a pop record, since Little Feat, particularly in its first incarnation, was simply too idiosyncratic, earthy and strange for that. It is, however, an utterly thrilling, individual blend of pop, rock, blues and country, due in no small part to a stellar set of songs from Lowell George. If anything, his quirks are all the more apparent here than they were on the debut, since Ted Templeman's production lends each song its own character, plus his pen was getting sharper. George truly finds his voice on this record, with each of his contributions sparkling with off-kilter humor, friendly surreal imagery and humanity, and he demonstrates he can authoritatively write anything from full-throttle rock & roll ("Teenage Nervous Breakdown"), sweet ballads ("Trouble," a sublimely reworked "Willin'"), skewered folk ("Sailin' Shoes"), paranoid rock ("Cold, Cold, Cold") and blues ("A Apolitical Blues") and, yes, even hooky mainstream rock ("Easy to Slip," which should have been the hit the band intended it to be). That's not to discount the contributions of the other members, particularly Bill Payne and Richie Hayward's "Tripe Face Boogie," which is justifiably one of the band's standards, but the thing that truly stuns on *Sailin' Shoes* is George's songwriting and how the band brings it to a full, colorful life. Nobody could master the twists and turns within George's songs better than Little Feat, and both the songwriter and his band are in prime form here. *—Stephen Thomas Erlewine*

★ **Dixie Chicken** / 1973 / Warner Brothers ♦♦♦♦♦

Following Roy Estrada's departure during the supporting tour for *Sailin' Shoes*, Lowell George became infatuated with New Orleans R&B and mellow jamming, all of which came to a head on their third album, 1973's *Dixie Chicken*. Although George is firmly in charge—he dominates the record, writing or co-writing seven of the 10 songs—this is the point where Little Feat found its signature sound as a band, and no album they would cut from this point on was too different from this seductive, laid-back, funky record. But no album would be quite as good, either, since *Dixie Chicken* still had much of the charming lyrical eccentricities of the first two albums, plus what is arguably George's best-ever set of songs. Partially due to the New Orleans infatuation, the album holds together better than *Sailin' Shoes* and George takes full advantage of the band's increased musical palette, writing songs that sound easy but are quite sophisticated, such as the rolling "Two Trains," the gorgeous, shimmering "Juliette," the deeply soulful and funny "Fat Man in the Bathtub" and the country-funk of the title track, which was covered nearly as frequently as "Willin'." In addition to "Walkin' All Night," a loose bluesy jam by Barrere and Bill Payne, the band also hauls out two covers which fit George's vibe perfectly: Allen Toussaint's slow burner "On Your Way Down" and "Fool Yourself," which was written by Fred Tackett, who later joined a reunited Feat in the '80s. It all adds up to a nearly irresistible record, filled with great songwriting, sultry grooves, and virtuosic performances that never are flashy. Little Feat, along with many jam bands that followed, tried to top this album, but they never managed to make a record this understated, appealing and fine. *—Stephen Thomas Erlewine*

Feats Don't Fail Me Now / 1974 / Warner Brothers ♦♦♦♦

If *Dixie Chicken* represented a pinnacle of Lowell George as a songwriter and band leader, its sequel *Feats Don't Fail Me Now* is the pinnacle of Little Feat as a group, showcasing each member at their finest. Not coincidentally, it's the moment where George begins to recede from the spotlight, leaving the band as a true democracy. These observations are only clear in hindsight, since if *Feats Don't Fail Me Now* is just taken as a record, it's nothing more than a damn good rock & roll record. That's not meant as a dismissal, either, since it's hard to make a rock & roll record as seemingly effortless and infectious as this. Though it effectively builds on the Southern-fried funkiness of *Dixie Chicken*, it's hardly as mellow as that record—there's a lot of grit, tougher rhythms, lots of guitar and organ. It's as supple as *Chicken*, though, which means that it's the sound of a touring band at their peak. As it happens, the band is on the top of their writing game as well, with Bill Payne contributing the rollicking "Oh Atlanta" and Paul Barrere turning in one of his best songs, the jazzy funk of "Skin it Back." Each has a co-writing credit with George—Payne on the unreleased *Little Feat*-era nugget "The Fan" and Barrere (plus Fred Martin) on the infectious title track—who also has a couple of classics with "Rock and Roll Doctor" and the great "Spanish Moon." *Feats* peters out toward the end, as the group delves into a 10-minute medley of two *Sailin' Shoes* songs, but that doesn't hurt one of the best albums Little Feat ever cut. It's so good, the group used it as the template for the rest of their career. *—Stephen Thomas Erlewine*

The Last Record Album / 1975 / Warner Brothers ♦♦♦

The title of *The Last Record Album* isn't literally accurate, but it cuts a lot closer than the band intended, for this is really is the last album of the group's classic era. Starting with this album, leader Lowell George fades into the woodwork, and while the remainder of the group tries valiantly to keep the band afloat, the timing of friction was wrong and the amount of tension was too great. Musically, the group attempts to make *Feats Don't Fail Me Now, Pt. 2*, but the production from George is curiously flat, and, truth be told, the group just isn't inspired enough to make a satisfying album. For a very short album—only eight songs—too many of the cuts fall flat. Those that succeed, however, are quite good, particularly Paul Barrere and Bill Payne's gently propulsive "All That You Dream," Lowell George's beautiful "Long Distance Love," and the sublime "Mercenary Territory." Even these songs don't have the spark or character they would have had on the more organic *Feats*, due to George's exceedingly mellow So-Cal production, which is pleasant but doesn't provide Little Feat with enough room to breathe. There are enough signs of Little Feat's true character on *The Last Record Album*—the three previously mentioned songs are essential for any Feat fan—to make it fairly enjoyable, but it's clear that the band is beginning to run out of steam. [The CD reissue of *The Last Record Album* includes two bonus tracks, "Don't Bogart That Joint" and "A Apolitical Blues," that were originally included on the 1978 live album *Waiting for Columbus*. They were pulled from the CD reissue of that album due to time restrictions, and appeared here instead.] *—Stephen Thomas Erlewine*

Time Loves a Hero / 1977 / Warner Brothers ♦♦♦

When Little Feat headed into the studio to record *Time Loves a Hero*, tensions between the band members—more specifically, Lowell George and the rest of the band—were at a peak. George had not only succumbed to various addictions, but he was growing restless with the group's fondness for extending their jams into territory strikingly reminiscent of jazz fusion. The rest of the group brought in Ted Templeman, who previously worked on their debut and produced *Sailin' Shoes*, to mediate the sessions. George wasn't thrilled with that, but that's probably not the only reason why his presence isn't large on this release—all signs point to his frustration with the band, and he wasn't in great health, so he just didn't contribute to the record. He wrote one song, the pleasant but comparatively faceless "Rocket in My Pocket," and collaborated with Paul Barrere on "Keepin' Up With the Joneses." Barrere was responsible for the only bright moments on the album, the ingratiatingly silly "Old Folks' Boogie" and, along with Bill Payne and Ken Gradney, the funky singalong title track. Elsewhere, Barrere and Payne come up dry, turning out generic pieces that are well-played but not as memorable as comparable Doobie Brothers' cuts from the same time. Then there's "Day at the Dog Races," a lengthy fusion jam that Templeman and everyone in the band loved—except for George, who, according to Bud Scoppa's liner notes in *Hotcakes & Outtakes*, disparagingly compared it to Weather Report. He was right—no matter how well Feat play on this track, it comes across as self-serving indulgence, and the clearest sign on this muddled album that they had indeed lost the plot. *—Stephen Thomas Erlewine*

Waiting for Columbus / 1978 / Warner Brothers ♦♦♦♦♦

Little Feat was one of the legendary live bands of the '70s, showered with praise by not only their small, fiercely dedicated cult of fans, but such fellow musicians as Bonnie Raitt, Robert Palmer, and Jimmy Page. Given all that acclaim, it only made sense for the group to cut a live album. Unfortunately, they waited until 1977, when the group had entered its decline, but as the double-album *Waiting for Columbus* proves, Little Feat in its decline was still pretty great. Certainly, the group is far more inspired on stage than they were in the studio after 1975—just compare "All That You Dream," "Oh Atlanta," "Old Folks' Boogie," "Time Loves a Hero," and "Mercenary Territory" here to the cuts on *The Last Record Album* and *Time Loves a Hero*. The versions on *Waiting* are full-bodied and fully realized, putting the studio cuts to shame. Early classics like "Fat Man in the Bathtub" and "Tripe Face Boogie" aren't as revelatory, but it's still a pleasure to hear a great band run through their best songs, stretching them out and finding new quirks within them. If there are any flaws with *Waiting for Columbus*, it's that the Feat do a little bit too much stretching, veering toward excessive jamming on occasion—and that mildly fuzzy focus is really the only way you'd be able to tell that this is a great live band recorded slightly after their prime. Even so, there's much to savor on *Waiting for Columbus*, one of the great live albums of its era, thanks to rich performances that prove Little Feat were one of the great live bands of their time. *—Stephen Thomas Erlewine*

Down on the Farm / 1979 / Warner Brothers ♦♦

As Little Feat were working on their seventh studio album, Lowell George was just marginally part of the group, spending much of his time completing his solo album, *Thanks I'll Eat It Here*. While he was touring in support of the record, he suffered a massive heart attack and died, leaving behind an uncompleted record with Little Feat. After mourning, the band regrouped and patched together *Down on the Farm*, the last album of the Lowell-led era. Since George was preoccupied during the recording, it's not surprising that he only makes himself heard on occasion on the album. It's also not surprising that the group was suffering, not just from the loss of a colleague, but from a lack of direction. They were drifting on *Time Loves a Hero*, after all, and while this is musically a little more straightforward than that fusion-flavored affair, it still is fairly uninspired. The surfaces are very slick, as should be expected with late-'70s Californian rock, which again doesn't let the group breathe, but the real problem is that the material is just not terribly memorable. Given the circumstances surrounding the completion of *Down on the Farm*, it's fairly easy to forgive the band this misstep, but it doesn't make the album any less disheartening. *—Stephen Thomas Erlewine*

Hoy-Hoy! / 1981 / Warner Brothers ♦♦♦♦♦

Perhaps realizing that *Down on the Farm* wasn't the proper swan song for Little Feat, the group persuaded Warner Brothers to release a compilation of rarities and overlooked tracks as a swan song and farewell to fans. Filled with live performances, obscurities, album tracks, and a new song apiece from Bill Payne and Paul Barrere, *Hoy Hoy* is a bit scattered, a bit incoherent, a little bewildering, and wholly delightful—a perfect summation of a group filled with quirks, character, and funk, traits which were as much a blessing as they were a curse. *Hoy Hoy* is one of those rare albums that may be designed for diehards—who else really needs radio performances, early recordings from before the band was signed, and outtakes, especially if they're surrounded by early album tracks?—but still is a great introduction for novices. That doesn't mean it's as good as such masterpieces as *Sailin' Shoes*, *Dixie Chicken*, or *Waiting for Columbus*, but it does capture the group's careening, freewheeling spirit, humor, and musical versatility, arguably better than any single album. That's one of the nice things compilations like this can do—they can summarize what a band was all about in a way a straight studio album couldn't. So, that's why it may be a good gateway into the band for novices, even though it's missing such essentials as "Willin'" and "Fat Man in the Bathtub," but it's truly for the dedicated, who will not only love the rarities (and these live cuts are hotter, on whole, than *Columbus*) but will savor the context. *—Stephen Thomas Erlewine*

Let It Roll / Jul. 1988 / Warner Brothers ♦♦♦

When Little Feat reunited in 1988, they were embraced by some dedicated fans, but were spurned by nearly an equal number of cultists. That's because to certain diehards, Little Feat belonged to Lowell George and, without him, the group doesn't exist. While it is true that George was the main songwriter and visionary during the early years of the group, he had pulled away from the group in the last half of the '70s and only had a marginal impact on their final three albums of the '70s. Also, throughout their career, the band contributed significantly, co-writing songs with George, writing their own tunes and, of course, shaping the band's sound with their musicianship. Although George was gone, they still had the desire to perform, so it was understandable that they wanted to reunite, with Craig Fuller taking George's place. What's surprising about *Let It Roll* is not just that it works, but that it works smashingly. It sounds as if the group picked up after *The Last Record Album*, deciding to return to the sound of *Feats Don't Fail Me Now*. True, the songwriting might not have the idiosyncratic genius of George, but it's strong, catchy and memorable, from the fine singles "Hate to Lose Your Lovin'" and "Let it Roll" to album tracks. More importantly, the band sounds lively and playful—Little Feat hasn't sounded this good in the studio since *Feats*, so it's easy to see why the members wanted to regroup. Yes, George is missed—it's hard not to miss such a gifted songwriter and musician—but *Let It Roll* isn't disrespectful of his memory, it keeps his music alive, which is the greatest compliment it can be paid. *—Stephen Thomas Erlewine*

Representing the Mambo / 1989 / Warner Brothers ✦✦
Having demonstrated on *Let It Roll* that they could produce an effective Little Feat soundalike record, the reconstituted band should have stopped while they were ahead. This follow-up shows a decline in songwriting, making the absence of Lowell George unmistakably apparent. *—William Ruhlmann*

Shake Me Up / Sep. 24, 1991 / Morgan Creek ✦✦
With this pedestrian third reunion album, Little Feat should have lost the right to use its noble name. Little of the band's original spark remained. *—William Ruhlmann*

● **As Time Goes By: The Very Best of Little Feat** / Feb. 10, 1994 / Warner Brothers ✦✦✦✦✦
As Time Goes By: The Very Best of Little Feat is an extraordinary collection that contains almost every essential Little Feat song from their '70s heyday with Lowell George, plus the two hits ("Let It Roll," "Hate to Lose Your Lovin'") from their late-'80s comeback. Most of the band's albums are worth hearing, but this is a great introduction for the curious and—since it features "Dixie Chicken," "Willin'," "Two Trains," "Fat Man in the Bathtub," "Sailin' Shoes," "Oh Atlanta" and "All That You Dream" in one place—it's a great summation of the group's achievements, and George's songwriting talent in particular. Unfortunately, *As Time Goes By* has only been released by the British division of Warner Brothers, but it's worth tracking down.*—Stephen Thomas Erlewine*

Ain't Had Enough Fun / Apr. 25, 1995 / Zoo ✦✦✦
The members of the group that has the legal right to call itself "Little Feat" perhaps are to be complimented for their realization, after three albums, that having Craig Fuller imitate the voice of the band's deceased founder, Lowell George, was ethically suspect. Or maybe they didn't realize; this album's liner notes say only that "mister fuller decided that the road life was not for him." In any case, the surviving "featsters" have cast against type, recruiting one Shaun Murphy, who can't imitate George but certainly can imitate longtime Feat booster Bonnie Raitt. The addition of a female voice allows for greater variety in lyric writing and some entertaining call-and-response singing, however, and more important, it begins to free the group from the ghost of Lowell George. The featsters locate themselves more than ever in the mythology of New Orleans, alternating second-line rhythms with John Lee Hooker boogie. One may still wish they had found another name to distinguish themselves from George's group, but *Ain't Had Enough Fun* is a worthy addition to their catalog on its own terms. *—William Ruhlmann*

Live from Neon Park / Jun. 18, 1996 / Zoo ✦✦✦
Live from Neon Park is an exhaustive double-disc live set recorded on the tour supporting *Ain't Had Enough Fun*, the first Little Feat album that featured vocalist Shaun Murphy. The double-disc features all of the band's best-known material, from "Dixie Chicken" to "Let It Roll." The Feat have always been one of the best live rootsy rock bands, so they naturally give inspired performances, even if they occasionally sound like they've performed these songs one too many times. Still, dedicated Little Feat fans will find this to be an entertaining memento of the latter-day edition of the band. *—Thom Owens*

Under the Radar / Jun. 16, 1998 / CMC International ✦✦✦
Little Feat's first album for CMC International, *Under the Radar*, finds the group's new lineup fully assimilated, with Shaun Murphy sharing many of the lead vocals with mainstays Paul Barrere and Bill Payne. While the record is not as instantly accessible and spontaneous as the last record with Murphy, *Ain't Had Enough Fun*, there is a confidence that permeates every cut. Feat's slightly trippy Southern-fried music has made an amazing leap into the '90s, and *Under the Radar* continues their rebirth. Tracks such as Barrere's "Home Ground" and "Loco-Motives" are good-time funky rockers, driven by Barrere's excellent slide guitar. Payne's title cut and "Eden's Wall" have a slightly dark hopefulness that has become a big part of the band's style. The final cut, "Calling the Children Home," is one of the group's greatest records, closing the album out in joyous New Orleans style. *—Matt Greenwald*

Chinese Work Songs / Jun. 20, 2000 / CMC International ✦✦✦
Some fans of Little Feat's classic '70s recordings argue that the band should have lost the right to use that name when Lowell George died in 1979; as they see it, the band heard on 2000's *Chinese Work Songs* isn't really Little Feat. If this band can get away with calling itself Little Feat, the argument goes, why shouldn't Bob Weir assemble a band without the late Jerry Garcia and call it the Grateful Dead? You have no doubt heard those arguments, and while it's true that Little Feat recorded its best work in the '70s, the lineup heard on *Chinese Work Songs* isn't half bad. In its 2000 incarnation, Little Feat's lineup ranges from '70s members Bill Payne (keyboards), Richie Hayward (drums), Paul Barrere (guitar), Kenny Gradney (bass), and Sam Clayton (percussion) to more recent additions like guitarist Fred Tackett and female singer Shaun Murphy. The addition of Murphy in the '90s proved to be a plus for the band, and her whiskey-voiced, Bonnie Raitt-influenced belting is a definite asset on this CD. *Chinese Work Songs* isn't in a class with 1973's *Dixie Chicken* or 1974's *Feats Don't Fail Me Now*, but it's a decent, if uneven, outing, and the 2000 lineup is faithful to the band's roots rock-Southern rock history on original material as well as covers of Bob Dylan's "It Takes a Lot to Laugh, It Takes a Train to Cry," the Band's "Rag Mama Rag," the Hooters' "Gimme a Stone," and Phish's "Sample in a Jar." Although not essential and not recommended to casual listeners—who would be better off with a collection of Little Feat's '70s recordings for Warner Brothers—diehard Feat fans will find that *Chinese Work Songs*, despite its imperfections, is enjoyable more often than not. *—Alex Henderson*

Hotcakes & Outtakes: 30 Years of Little Feat / Sep. 19, 2000 / Rhino/Warner Archives ✦✦✦✦✦
Rhino's four-disc box set *Hotcakes & Outtakes* treats all of Little Feat's incarnations with equal respect. This even-handed approach has advantages, even if Lowell George dominates the proceedings. How could he not? He was a musician of immense talents, shaping the band's core sound while building an impressive body of songs. This set reveals that the rest of the band, while not writers of George's ilk, still wrote their share of great songs and, best of all, their fusion of funk, blues, country, rock and jazz still sounded lively, even when they reunited a decade after his death. Yes, it was missing his unique brilliance and vision, yet the reunited Feat still carried the torch well, which this set proves. Still, the best thing about the box is the fourth disc, devoted to "Studio Artifacts," all dating from George's heyday with the band. Actually, it goes a little further than that, beginning with cuts from George and Roy Estrada's mid-'60s band the Factory and pre-Warner Bros recordings, plus a generous selection of outtakes and demos, including selections from George's solo album, *Thanks I'll Eat It Here*. It's a treasure trove for any Little Feat fan, filled with amazing cuts like the barn-storming "Rat Faced Dog"—tracks so good, it's hard to believe they haven't been released before. The fourth disc is reason for any devoted fan to pick up this set, but is this worthwhile for the curious? Well, yes, since this offers a great summary of their fascinating career, even if it duplicates some songs at the expense of album tracks like "A Apolitical Blues" which really should be here. Even with that flaw, *Hotcakes & Outtakes* performs its job well, proving that Little Feat is an American rock & roll band like no other. *—Stephen Thomas Erlewine*

Waiting for Columbus [Expanded] / Apr. 2, 2002 / Rhino ✦✦✦✦✦
Little Feat's lone official live album was chopped up for its initial CD release, with two tracks lopped off so it could fit on a single disc (they showed up, inexplicably, as bonus tracks on the CD issue of *The Last Record Album*). After years of neglect, the album was finally restored in 2002, except "restored" might not be the right word for it. It was rethought and expanded, with the original album now spilling over onto a second disc (which is where the encore is), which is fleshed out with seven previously unissued outtakes, plus three songs initially released on *Hoy-Hoy*. It's a lovely package, with copious notes from Bud Scoppa and lots of photos, great remastered sound, and generous bonus tracks. It's as well done as could be expected, but be forewarned—none of the unreleased material is as good as what made the record, tending to be a little slack and emphasizing their encroaching fascination with fusion. That's really not that big of a deal, of course, since collectors will buy this no matter what, and they'll be happy with this lavish, loving package. *—Stephen Thomas Erlewine*

Raw Tomatos, Vol. 1 / Jun. 18, 2002 / Hot Tomato ✦✦✦✦
This is what Little Feat fans have been waiting years for: a series dedicated to live and rare recordings. Problem is, there are two kinds of Little Feat fans—those who love the band unconditionally, soaking up recordings made in the '80s and '90s as easily as those from the '70s, and those who love the band, but only when Lowell George is around. The first group will treasure *Raw Tomatos, Vol. 1*, along with its companion, *Ripe Tomatos, Vol. 1*, while the latter will grudgingly accept both volumes, since the Lowell recordings are spread among the two double-disc sets. It's hard not to think they'd have a point, since each volume flows identically, with about half-a-disc of vintage George material, before leading to a disc-and-a-half of post-reunion recordings. If this were one volume, sequenced this way, it'd be easy to accept and cherish anything you've been given, since there has been no archival Little Feat release prior to this. Simultaneous releases, sequenced similarly, however, make you wonder why all the George-era recordings were on one stellar disc, and the rest put to another series. Even if you're a fan wondering this, you will purchase it anyway, because the George material is so good—a spare, funky "Crack in Your Door" with great piano by Bill Payne; a demo of "Trouble"; a nasty "Apolitical Blues"; an addictive lo-fi demo of "Fat Man in the Bathtub" with different lyrics; Bonnie Raitt singing on "Sailin' Shoes"; and a wonderful throwaway "Ass for Days," which runs less than a minute. The rest of the material is uniformly good, sometimes delightfully so ("Those Feat'll Steer Ya Wrong Sometimes," a gritty version of "Strawberry Flats"), but never surprising, like the best of their '70s recordings. This is all very good music, but the George stuff is genius—and while you grab genius where you can, it's hard not to wish it was distilled for those that just wanted to hear that, instead of everything else. *—Stephen Thomas Erlewine*

Ripe Tomatos, Vol. 1 / Jun. 18, 2002 / Hot Tomato ✦✦✦✦
The companion volume to Hot Tomato/RedEye's *Raw Tomatos, Vol. 1*, *Ripe Tomatos, Vol. 1* contains a robust selection of live Little Feat rarities from throughout their career—both with Lowell George and their years without him. Like its predecessor, it suffers from its all-inclusiveness; many Feat fans love it all, but there are a select group, just as passionate, that only love George. By treating both groups as the same, these discs suffer. They flow well, in and of themselves, but once the George material runs out halfway through the first disc, it's hard not to wish that each era was given its own volume. That said, the music here, like the music on its companion piece, is uniformly excellent, illustrating exactly why the band has always been considered live titans. But, as before, the transcendent material is with George—not just because he was a genius songwriter and guitarist, but because the band was grittier, earthier, funkier back then. There's nothing here as revelatory as the demos on *Raw Tomatos*, but live versions of "Teenage Nervous Breakdown," "Cold Cold Cold," "Dixie Chicken," "Hamburger Midnight," and "Apolitical Blues" (featuring Lowell saying "Howlin' Wolf invented rock & roll"), are priceless. So, you take what you can get, when you can get it; even if you wish you were getting more, there's no way you'd part with what you have. *—Stephen Thomas Erlewine*

Little Mike & the Tornadoes

f. 1990, New York, NY

Group / Modern Electric Blues, Contemporary Blues, Blues-Rock

Harmonica player and keyboardist Mike Markowitz, born in Queens, NY, and raised in New York City's burgeoning '80s blues club scene, has made his mark in the blues world through a lot of hard touring and a bit of good old fashioned New York salesmanship, or "chutzpah."

Born November 23, 1955, Markowitz cites his earliest influences as John Lee Hooker, Muddy Waters and Little Walter Jacobs. In 1978, he formed his first blues band and began playing the blues bars around lower Manhattan, but his reputation began to grow when he began backing up legendary musicians like pianist Pinetop Perkins, Hubert Sumlin and Jimmy Rogers when they came to New York or New Jersey to perform. Markowitz's passion for blues, as a fan and as a performer, is legendary, and he carried it over into the producer's chair in 1988, when he recorded albums for Perkins and later for Sumlin.

In 1990, Little Mike and the Tornadoes got their own recording contract with Blind Pig, a San Francisco-based label, and his output has been quite prolific since then. The group's first album, *Heart Attack*, includes guest performances by Perkins, Paul Butterfield and Sumlin. Two years later, he recorded *Payday*, also for Blind Pig, before recording his debut for Flying Fish Records (a label that has since been acquired by Rounder Records), *Flynn's Place*.

Markowitz is an extremely hard working, level-headed blues musician who will no doubt surface again and again on records, whether for Rounder or for some other label. All three of Markowitz's albums are available on compact disc, and worth seeking out. *—Richard Skelly*

● **Heart Attack** / 1990 / Blind Pig ✦✦✦✦✦

On this competent White-guy bar-band sort-of blues, four cuts feature Paul Butterfield on harp (believed to be his last recordings). Other guests are Ronnie Earl, Pinetop Perkins, Big Daddy Kinsey, and Hubert Sumlin. *—Niles J. Frantz*

Payday / 1992 / Blind Pig ✦✦✦

Little Mike & the Tornadoes don't alter their musical approach on *Payday* at all, but they don't need to—they deliver driving Chicago blues with no frills and lots and lots of passion. The group doesn't just churn out the same old covers, either—they tear through a set of 12 originals that are written in the style of classic '50s and '60s blues. Occasionally their songwriting falters, but never their performances. Every song is delivered with conviction, and Little Mike positively wails on both the piano and harp. *—Thom Owens*

Flynn's Place / 1995 / Flying Fish ✦✦✦

Flynn's Place is another excellent collection of piledriving, good-time blues and boogie from Little Mike & the Tornadoes, featuring a fine selection of originals and smoking solos. *—Thom Owens*

Hot Shot / Jan. 20, 1998 / Wild Dog ✦✦✦

Although not a blues band in the truest sense of the word, consider this their "roots music" album. Frontman Little Mike Markowitz turns in a batch of original tunes that more than tip their collective and stylistic hat to Willie Dixon, Muddy Waters, Louis Prima and James Cotton. The band goes through its workmanlike paces and that same blue-collar approach applies to the lyrical themes on these songs, full of tried and true formulaic stories about sex, the road and bad whiskey and women. It's a shame that the blues can sometimes be reduced down to a pile of clichés but at least the musical side of the equation works. *—Cub Koda*

Little Milton (James Milton Campbell)

b. Sep. 7, 1934, Inverness, MS

Vocals, Leader, Guitar / Retro-Soul, Electric Blues, Modern Electric Blues, Soul-Blues, R&B

He may not be a household name, but die-hard blues fans know Little Milton as a superb all-around electric bluesman—a soulful singer, an evocative guitarist, an accomplished songwriter, and a skillful bandleader. He's often compared to the legendary B.B. King—as well as Bobby "Blue" Bland—for the way his signature style combines soul, blues, and R&B, a mixture that helped make him one of the biggest-selling bluesmen of the '60s (even if he's not as well-remembered as King). As time progressed, his music grew more and more orchestrated, with strings and horns galore. He maintained a steadily active recording career all the way from his 1953 debut on Sam Phillips' legendary Sun label, with his stunning longevity including notable stints at Chess (where he found his greatest commercial success), Stax, and Malaco.

James Milton Campbell was born September 7, 1934, in the small Delta town of Inverness, MS, and grew up in Greenville. (He would later legally drop the "James" after learning of a half-brother with the same name.) His father Big Milton, a farmer, was a local blues musician, and Milton also grew up listening to the Grand Ole Opry radio program.

At age 12, he began playing the guitar and saved up money from odd jobs to buy his own instrument from a mail-order catalog. By 15, he was performing for pay in local clubs and bars, influenced chiefly by T-Bone Walker but also by proto-rock & roll jump blues shouters. He made a substantial impression on other area musicians, even getting a chance to back Sonny Boy Williamson II, and caught the attention of R&B great Ike Turner, who was doubling as a talent scout for Sam Phillips at Sun. Turner introduced the still-teenaged Little Milton to Phillips, who signed him to a contract in 1953. With Turner's band backing him, Milton's Sun sides tried a little bit of everything—he hadn't developed a signature style as of yet, but he did have a boundless youthful energy that made these early recordings some of his most exciting and rewarding. Unfortunately, none of them were hits, and Milton's association with Sun was over by the end of 1954. He set about forming his own band, which waxed one single for the small Meteor label in 1957, before picking up and moving to St. Louis in 1958.

In St. Louis, Milton befriended DJ Bob Lyons, who helped him record a demo in a bid to land a deal on Mercury. The label passed, and the two set up their own label, christened Bobbin. Little Milton's Bobbin singles finally started to attract some more widespread attention, particularly "I'm a Lonely Man," which sold 60,000 copies despite being the very first release on a small label. As head of A&R, Milton brought artists like Albert King and Fontella Bass into the Bobbin fold, and with such a high roster caliber, the label soon struck a distribution arrangement with the legendary Chess Records. Milton himself switched over to the Chess subsidiary Checker in 1961, and it was there that he would settle on his trademark soul-inflected, B.B. King-influenced style. Initially a moderate success, Milton had his big breakthrough with 1965's "We're Gonna Make It," which hit number one on the R&B charts thanks to its resonance with the civil rights movement. "We're Gonna Make It" kicked off a successful string of R&B chart singles that occasionally reached the Top Ten, highlighted by "Who's Cheating Who?," "Grits Ain't Groceries," "If Walls Could Talk," "Baby I Love You," and "Feel So Bad," among others.

The death of Leonard Chess in 1969 threw his label into disarray, and Little Milton eventually left Checker in 1971 and signed with the Memphis-based soul label Stax (also the home of his former protégé Albert King). At Stax, Milton began expanding his studio sound, adding bigger horn and string sections and spotlighting his soulful vocals more than traditional blues. Further hits followed in songs like "Annie Mae's Cafe," "Little Bluebird," "That's What Love Will Make You Do," and "Walkin' the Back Streets and Cryin'," but generally not with the same magnitude of old. Stax went bankrupt in 1975, upon which point Little Milton moved to the TK/Glades label, which was better known for its funk and disco acts. His recordings there were full-blown crossover affairs, which made "Friend of Mine" a minor success, but that label soon went out of business as well.

Milton spent some time in limbo; he recorded one album for MCA in 1983 called *Age Ain't Nothin' But a Number*, and the following year found a home with Malaco, which sustained the careers of quite a few old-school Southern soul and blues artists. During his tenure at Malaco, Milton debuted the song that would become his latter-day anthem, the bar band staple "The Blues Is Alright," which was also widely popular with European blues fans. Milton recorded frequently and steadily for Malaco, issuing 13 albums under their aegis by the end of the millennium. In 1988, he won the W.C. Handy Award for Blues Entertainer of the Year, and was also inducted into the Blues Hall of Fame. *—Steve Huey*

We're Gonna Make It / 1965 / Chess ✦✦✦✦✦

Sings Big Blues / 1968 / Chess ✦✦✦

This is one of the hottest collective blues albums of the '60s. *—Bill Dahl*

If Walls Could Talk / 1970 / MCA/Chess ✦✦✦✦✦

On *If Walls Could Talk* Little Milton continues to fuse blues with soul—if anything, the album leans toward soul more than blues. Supported by a band with a thick, wailing horn section, Little Milton sings and plays with power. Though there a couple of wonderful solos, the focus of the record is on the songs, which all sound terrific, thanks to Milton's compassionate vocals. *—Thom Owens*

Grits Ain't Groceries / Jan. 1970 / Stax ✦✦✦

Grits Ain't Groceries is another set of soul and R&B songs from the blues guitarist Little Milton, highlighted by the scorching title track. *—Thom Owens*

Greatest Hits / 1972 / MCA/Chess ✦✦✦

Greatest Hits offers a good sampling of Little Milton's singles for Chess Records in the '60s, including the hits "We're Gonna Make It" and "If Walls Could Talk." It may be a little brief, but there are no bad songs on the record at all and it's an excellent introduction to the guitarist's talents. *—Thom Owens*

Waiting for Little Milton / 1973 / Stax ✦✦✦

Although Little Milton's Stax recordings aren't as blues-oriented as his classic Chess and Checker recordings, there are still plenty of things to recommend about them. Primarily, they're of interest because they focus on his soulful vocals and those vocals shine on *Waiting for Little Milton*. On the whole, the album is a little uneven—the songs aren't always first-rate and the production is a little too smooth—but the performances make it worthwhile for most dedicated fans. *—Thom Owens*

What It Is / 1973 / Stax ✦✦✦

What It Is captures Little Milton at the 1973 Montreux Blues and Jazz Festival, where the guitarist was in fine form. Throughout the concert, Milton sings and solos with flair, making it more than just another live album from the guitarist and turning it into something special. *—Thom Owens*

Blues 'N' Soul / 1974 / Stax ✦✦✦

Having already recorded for both Sun and Chess Records, two of the most historically significant labels in the history of blues and rock, Little Milton signed to Stax in the early '70s, adding yet another heavyweight to his catalog. On *Blues 'N' Soul*, he is joined by many of the same musicians that backed him on his Stax studio debut, *Waiting for Little Milton*, including drummer Willie Hall, guitarist Bobby Manuel, bassist Willie Murphy, and pianist Lester Snell. An impassioned singer, Milton's early-'70s output indeed began to walk the fine line between the blues and soul of the album title, a fact accentuated by the sparkling touches of the Memphis Horns. Although there are only two originals in the set, the singer's interpretations of songs popularized by Charlie Rich ("Behind Closed Doors"), Linda Ronstadt ("You're No Good") and Freddie King ("Woman Across the River") are just as convincing. Milton's own "Sweet Woman of Mine" captures the combo in an uptempo mode, simultaneously tough and swinging. "Tain't Nobody's Business If I Do" is a *tour de force* of soul-blues that paces itself exquisitely across six and a half minutes, and "Hard Luck Blues" concludes the set with a hard funk groove. Throughout the album, the arranging skills of James Mitchell demonstrate how strings can be incorporated into a hard blues setting. Though they provide ample color to these productions, they do little to dilute the essential nature of the music. Excluding the singles collection *Walking the Back Streets, Blues 'N' Soul* may very well be Milton's best set for Stax. *—Nathan Bush*

Montreux Festival / 1974 / Stax ✦✦✦

Tin Pan Alley / 1975 / Stax ✦✦✦✦✦
Most of the guitarist's best soul/blues Stax sides of the '70s with plenty of his crisp guitar. —*Bill Dahl*

Friend of Mine / 1976 / Collectables ✦✦✦

Chess Blues Master Series / 1976 / Chess ✦✦✦✦✦
Little Milton hit his creative and playing stride at Chess, at least in terms of blues. "Grits Ain't Groceries," "We're Gonna Make It," and many other gems were available on this LP anthology. It's no longer available except in used record stores, but is still worth pursuing. —*Ron Wynn*

Walkin' the Back Streets / 1981 / Stax ✦✦✦✦
Little Milton made his last batch of great studio recordings for the legendary Stax label during the early '70s, releasing the studio sets *Waiting for Little Milton* and *Blues 'N' Soul*, live outings like *What It Is*, and a clutch of excellent 45s. *Walking the Back Streets*, released years after his stint with the label had ended, gathers cuts that didn't appear on the full-length albums. For his backing band, Stax provided linchpins from their typically excellent pool of session players. These included guitarists Michael Toles and Bobby Manuel, drummer Willie Hall, keyboard player Lester Snell, and, of course, the Memphis Horns. Though Milton failed to offer a great deal of fresh material during the period, this was hardly a problem, as the singer has always been an exceptional interpreter of the blues in general. Most of the songs selected here are excellent vehicles for displaying both his vocal and guitar prowess. The title track, a slice of smoldering blues driven by exquisite musicianship, still stands out. Not many instrumentalists are capable of deferring to a frontman and displaying ample chops at the same time, the way Manuel, Toles, and Snell are here. The mix enhances this fact perfectly: the rhythm guitarists split between left and right channels, Snell in between but set back in the spectrum, and Milton himself slicing away up front. The band slip into smoky blues funk on the excellent "Somebody's Tears," while "Open the Door to Your Heart," "Letter Full of Tears," and "Bet You I'll Win" all capture the singer in a soulful mood. An excellent set. —*Nathan Bush*

Raise a Little Sand / 1982 / Red Lightnin' ✦✦✦
Raise a Little Sand collects Little Milton's recordings for Sun and Bobbin Records, which rank as his rawest, most exciting work. Although the quality of this package isn't quite as good as it could have been—the sound and the presentation could have been more carefully considered—this is top-notch, essential music that should be heard in any form. —*Thom Owens*

The Blues Is Alright / Dec. 1982 / Evidence ✦✦
The Blues Is Alright leans toward the blues more than his late-'70s and early-'80s collections. However, the quality of Milton's performance isn't quite up to par, making the collection a bit of a disappointment. —*Thom Owens*

Age Ain't Nothin' but a Number / 1983 / Mobile Fidelity ✦✦✦
Little Milton Campbell made an excellent modern blues/soul album for MCA in the early '80s that languished due to inadequate promotional efforts. The failure of *Age Ain't Nothin' but a Number* convinced him to move to Malaco. Mobile Fidelity's recent remastered CD reissue of this underrated session provides a perfect sonic framework for Milton's taut, tantalizing and nicely executed guitar, soulful, often biting vocals, and solid arrangements and songs. The title cut was a mild hit, one of the last times Milton reached the R&B charts, while other numbers such as "Why Are You So Hard to Please," "Don't Leave Me," and "Living on The Dark Side of Love" were as expertly crafted as any of his best Chess dates. —*Ron Wynn*

Playing for Keeps / 1984 / Malaco ✦✦✦
Playing for Keeps is one of Little Milton's best latter-day albums, featuring a smooth, but not too slick production, impassioned vocals, and a generally strong set of songs, highlighted by "The Blues Is Alright." —*Thom Owens*

Greatest Sides / 1984 / MCA/Chess ✦✦✦✦✦
Greatest Sides contains a few of Little Milton's best cuts—including "We're Gonna Make It"—but the packaging isn't very good and the songs are presented haphazardly. There might be some good music on *Greatest Sides*, but there are far better compilations to purchase. —*Thom Owens*

We're Gonna Make It/Little Milton Sings Big Blues / 1986 / MCA/Chess ✦✦✦✦✦
This CD of two of Little Milton's classic, early-'60s titles for the Checker label, *We're Gonna Make It* and *Sings Big Blues*, features a nice variety of blues material and some stellar arrangements. Towering above it all, though, is Milton's powerful voice: a solid combination of gospel intensity and fluid phrasing that sprang from Roy Brown, moved through B.B. King, and found its way to both Bobby "Blue" Bland and Milton, among others. The program features one of Milton's biggest hits "Were Gonna Make It" and other uptempo, blues-soul hybrids, like "Who's Cheating Who?" and "Can't Hold Back the Tears" (all benefiting from Milton's fine, sinewy guitar lines). On more traditional, yet vibrant blues cuts, Milton shows off his tremendous vocal control, seamlessly alternating between soft, earnest tones and guttural shouts on "Blind Man" and expertly blending jazz and blues phrasing on "I'm Gonna Move to the Outskirts of Town." Rounding out the set are some fine blues and soul covers, including B.B. King's "Sweet Sixteen," Lowell Fulson's "Reconsider Baby," James Brown's "Please, Please, Please," and Milton's reconfiguration of Guitar Slim's "Well I Done Got Over It" ("Ain't No Big Deal on You"). Everything is held together nicely by some of the most tasteful and tight arrangements you'll hear on a blues album, compliments of Phil Wright and tenor saxophonist James Carter. This two album CD is a great bargain when in print and a worthwhile purchase even if you already have one of Milton's career retrospectives from Chess. —*Stephen Cook*

Movin' to the Country / 1987 / Malaco ✦✦✦

Annie Mae's Cafe / 1987 / Malaco ✦✦✦
Annie Mae's Cafe is one of the strongest albums Little Milton recorded for Malaco. Milton's solos are crisp and stinging throughout the album and his vocals are impassioned. Because he's in top form, he can save the lesser material and that's what makes the album so consistent. —*Thom Owens*

I Will Survive / 1988 / Malaco ✦✦✦

Back to Back / 1988 / Malaco ✦✦✦✦
From a soul standpoint, *Back to Back* was the strongest album that Little Milton recorded for Malaco in the '80s. Though the CD contains a few noteworthy 12-bar numbers (including "Penitentiary Blues" and "It's Hard to Explain"), R&B is dominant. Those who fancy '70s-type soul shouldn't miss Milton's passionate, confessional storytelling on such treasures as "(I Had) Too Much Heaven Last Night," "Caught in the Act (Of Gettin' It On)," and the heartbreaking "I Was Tryin' Not Break Down." The gruff, big-voiced singer/guitarist even breathes some life into "Wind Beneath My Wings," a corny pop ballad that was unbearably insipid in Bette Midler's hands but is easier to take when Milton gets a hold of it. —*Alex Henderson*

Too Much Pain / 1990 / Malaco ✦✦✦
Though not essential and not as strong as *Back to Back*, *Too Much Pain* was a welcome addition to Milton's catalog. Milton never claimed to be a purist, and the album illustrates his effectiveness as both a bluesman and a soul shouter. Highlights of this likable date range from the smooth '70s-ish uptown soul of "The Woman I Love" (which wouldn't have been inappropriate on a Harold Melvin & the Bluenotes album) to "So Much Pain," "Count the Days" and Denise LaSalle's amusing "Your Wife Is Cheating on Us." If you're into clever double entendres, get into "Runway," a Stax-ish soul gem that finds Milton equating a cheating lover with an airport runway in that everyone is landing on her. —*Alex Henderson*

☆ **Sun Masters** / 1990 / Rounder ✦✦✦✦✦
While he was at Sun, Little Milton tried a variety of different sounds and styles—sounding like everybody from Elmore James and B.B. King to Fats Domino—which was all tied together by his raw, manic lead guitar. *The Sun Masters* collects many of Milton's absolute finest moments—he never again sounded quite as wild or reckless, either vocally or instrumentally, as he did here. —*Thom Owens*

Strugglin' Lady / 1992 / Malaco ✦✦✦
OK contemporary blues-soul set. —*Bill Dahl*

Me for You, You for Me: The Glades Masters / Aug. 5, 1993 / Collectables ✦✦✦

I'm a Gambler / 1994 / Malaco ✦✦✦✦
Malaco releases usually mix straight blues with a slicker variety of R&B aimed at "urban contemporary" radio airplay, but *I'm a Gambler* has a very high blues content. Milton sings with vigor, like he was feeling at the top of his game when he recorded this CD—and no wonder, since the material is quite strong. Highlights include the humorous "Casino Blues," the cocky "Like a Rooster on a Hen," and the bayou swamp rocker "Polk Salad Annie" (which Little Milton really makes his own). —*Steve Hoffman*

Welcome to the Club: The Essential Chess Recordings / 1994 / MCA/Chess ✦✦✦✦✦

Greatest Hits / Sep. 5, 1995 / Malaco ✦✦✦
For fans of Little Milton's Chess, Checker, and Sun sides, his '80s records for Malaco aren't particularly attractive, since they are slicker and more polished. Nevertheless, he cut several first-rate songs for the label, songs that showcase his considerable guitar and vocal talents, and the majority of those songs are collected on *Greatest Hits*. It's a solid introduction to the latter part of Milton's career. —*Thom Owens*

Cheatin' Habit / 1996 / Malaco ✦✦✦
Having found a suitable home at Malaco, the leading label of the '80s and '90s for Southern soul-blues, Little Milton has settled into a prolific recording schedule; this is his already his tenth CD for the label (eleventh, if you count a greatest hits compilation). It contains ingredients to satisfy his core audience but is not one of his best. The songs are mostly the cheatin' or leavin' variety (he's cheating or she's cheating, he's leaving or she's leaving). The guitar fills and horn parts are quite formulaic. —*Steve Hoffman*

★ **Greatest Hits (Chess 50th Anniversary Collection)** / Jun. 17, 1997 / MCA/Chess ✦✦✦✦✦
Milton Campbell was a blues chameleon in his early recording career for Sun and Bobbin, changing styles seemingly with every record he made. But he found his groove—a Bobby Bland-style R&B with a bluesy edge to it—when he came to Chess Records in 1963. These 16 tracks collect the highlights of his six-year tenure at the label, featuring the hits "We're Gonna Make It," "Who's Cheating Who?" and "If Walls Could Talk." The majority of the sides feature strong horn charts courtesy of Oliver Sain and Gene Barge, the core of Milton's sound during this period. The stylistic connection of Milton to Bland is no more stronger evidenced than on his cover of "Blind Man," but equal mention in the soulful department must go to the heart-wrenching ballad "Let Me Down Easy" and "Poor Man's Song," one of two songs collected here that Campbell had a hand in writing. Interesting updates of Little Willie John's "All Around the World" ("Grits Ain't Groceries"), Chuck Willis's "I Feel So Bad" and Rosco Gordon's "Just a Little Bit" complete the package. As part of MCA's Chess 50th anniversary series, this sweats the two-disc *Welcome to the Club: The Essential Chess Recordings* down to a perfect introductory package to this sometimes misunderstood (is he blues? soul? R&B?) artist. —*Cub Koda*

Count the Days / Sep. 23, 1997 / 601 ✦✦✦✦

For Real / May 26, 1998 / Malaco ✦✦✦
For Real is another strong soul/blues cocktail served up by Little Milton, although it runs a bit heavy in the ballad department. Granted, Milton is plenty versatile enough to adopt the sentimental croon required to cover "To Love Somebody" and "A Rainy Night in Georgia," but it's really at his best when he's tearing into the blues with a guitar in his

hands. Two slow blues numbers steal the show here: "Blues for Mr. C," which is a straightforward 12-bar burner, and "If That's What You Wanna Do," which rides a slicker, urban groove in the circa-'70s Albert King tradition. (These two songs are the only originals on the entire album.) The more upbeat R&B material on *For Real* generally hits its mark, albeit with a thick coat of production polish that could have used some thinning out. Not exactly the cream of the crop of his work on Malaco, but this album gets the job done. *—Ken Chang*

Welcome to Little Milton / Aug. 7, 1999 / Malaco ✦✦
Here's Milton's superstar album, finding the R&B legend dueting with the likes of Lucinda Williams, Keb' Mo', Peter Wolf, Dave Alvin, Delbert McClinton, Gov't Mule, G. Love & Special Sauce, and Susan Tedeschi. By far the most interesting track is John Sinclair's recitation of Mother Earth preceding the duet between Milton and Tedeschi of it. While this collection of celebrity duets has its moments, one would definitely want to look elsewhere to start their Little Milton collections. *—Cub Koda*

Reality / 199 / Malaco ✦✦✦
Some blues enthusiasts would have us believe that Little Milton's heavily arranged Malaco dates have paled in comparison to his Sun, Chess and Stax output, but in fact, they've been consistent and generally quite enjoyable. The thing is that they have as much to do with soul and R&B as they do with actual 12-bar blues, and if you're a blues purist who isn't comfortable with the idea of Milton recording a lot of songs that would have been appropriate for the O'Jays or the Dramatics in the '70s, it's best to pass on *Reality*. However, if you hold blues and '70s soul in equally high regard, you should find the CD appealing. Milton shows how gutsy a bluesman he can be on 12-bar songs like "A Right to Sing the Blues" and "I'm Jealous of Her Husband," but he's equally convincing on the '70s-type soul of "I Want My Baby Back," "I've Got to Remember," and Bobby Womack's "That's the Way I Feel About It." Milton never claimed to be a purist, and *Reality* points to the fact that he is anything but. *—Alex Henderson*

★ **Anthology 1953–1961** / Jul. 23, 2002 / Varese Sarabande ✦✦✦✦✦
Little Milton's 1953-1954 Sun sessions, and his 1958-1961 stay at Bobbin Records, comprised virtually everything he recorded in his early career prior to joining Chess. This collection doesn't gather every last bit he did for Sun and Bobbin, and doesn't have anything from his two mid-'50s singles for Meteor. But it's still the best compilation of his pre-Chess material ever done, the 27 songs split almost in half between his Sun and Bobbin output. The dozen Sun sides include both sides of his three singles for the label, along with half a dozen outtakes. These are good, sturdy early blues-R&B crossover cuts, the only substantial criticism being that the singer's still in the process of finding his own voice, at times sounding derivative of B.B. King, Fats Domino, Guitar Slim, and even (on "If You Love Me") Elmore James. These do often showcase Little Milton's rawest and most exciting guitar work. The Bobbin sides (mostly from singles, though there's an outtake and an alternate take) are expectedly more refined and mature, with a B.B. King-like brassy shuffle on his very first outing for the label, "That Will Never Do." There's a little identity-shuffling too, even if Milton's getting closer to his brand of blues-soul, with "I'm a Lonely Man" sounding a little like a cross between Howlin' Wolf and Bobby "Blue" Bland and "Hey Girl!" indebted to Ray Charles. At times he seems to be groping for something a little more mainstream, whether it's a jazzy ballad like "Strange Dreams," the near-jazz of "My Baby Pleases Me," the doo wop of "Cross My Heart," or the upbeat rock & roll of "I'm in Love." Usually, though, the Bobbin sides are fine mixes of '50s electric blues with sharp, jazzy brass and urbane R&B influences in the singer's songwriting. *—Richie Unterberger*

Little Richard (Richard Wayne Penniman)

b. Dec. 5, 1935, Macon, GA
Vocals, Piano / New Orleans R&B, Rock & Roll, R&B
One of the original rock & roll greats, Little Richard merged the fire of gospel with New Orleans R&B, pounding the piano and wailing with gleeful abandon. While numerous other R&B greats of the early '50s had been moving in a similar direction, none of them matched the sheer electricity of Richard's vocals. With his bullet-speed deliveries, ecstatic trills, and the overjoyed force of personality in his singing, he was crucial in upping the voltage from high-powered R&B into the similar, yet different, guise of rock & roll. Although he was only a hitmaker for a couple of years or so, his influence upon both the soul and British Invasion stars of the '60s was vast, and his early hits remain core classics of the rock repertoire.

Heavily steeped in gospel music while growing up in Georgia, when Little Richard began recording in the early '50s he played unexceptional jump blues/R&B that owed a lot to his early inspirations Billy Wright and Roy Brown. In 1955, at Lloyd Price's suggestion, Richard sent a demo tape to Specialty Records, who were impressed enough to sign him and arrange a session for him in New Orleans. That session, however, didn't get off the ground until Richard began fooling around with a slightly obscene ditty during a break. With slightly cleaned-up lyrics, "Tutti Frutti" was the record that gave birth to Little Richard as we know him—the gleeful "woo!"s, the furious piano playing, the sax-driven, pedal-to-the-metal rhythm section. It was also his first hit, although, ridiculous as it now seems, Pat Boone's cover version outdid Richard's on the hit parade.

Pat Boone would also try to cover Richard's next hit, "Long Tall Sally," but by that time it was evident that audiences black and white much preferred the real deal. In 1956 and 1957, Richard reeled off a string of classic hits—"Long Tall Sally," "Slippin' and "Slidin'," "Jenny, Jenny," "Keep a Knockin'," "Good Golly, Miss Molly," "The Girl Can't Help It"—that remain the foundation of his fame. While Richard's inimitable mania was the key to his best records, he also owed a lot of his success to the gutsy playing of ace New Orleans session players like Lee Allen (tenor sax), Alvin Tyler (baritone sax), and especially Earl Palmer (drummer), who usually accompanied the singer in both New Orleans and Los Angeles studios. Richard's unforgettable appearances in early rock & roll movies, especially *The Girl Can't Help It*, also did a lot to spread the rock & roll gospel to the masses.

Little Richard was at the height of his commercial and artistic powers when he suddenly quit the business during an Australian tour in late 1957, enrolling in a Bible college in Alabama shortly after returning to the States. Richard had actually been feeling the call of religion for a while before his announcement, but it was nonetheless a shock to both his fans and the music industry. Specialty drew on unreleased sessions for a few more hard-rocking singles in the late '50s, but Richard virtually vanished from the public eye for a few years. When he did return to recording, it was as a gospel singer, cutting a few little-heard sacred sides for End, Mercury, and Atlantic in the early '60s.

By 1962, though, Richard had returned to rock & roll, touring Britain to an enthusiastic reception. Among the groups that supported him on those jaunts were the Rolling Stones and the Beatles, whose vocals (Paul McCartney's especially) took a lot of inspiration from Richard's. In 1964, the Beatles cut a knockout version of "Long Tall Sally," with McCartney on lead, that may have even outdone the original. It's been speculated that the success of the Beatles, and other British Invaders who idolized Richard, finally prompted the singer into making a full-scale comeback as an unapologetic rock & roller. Hooking up with Specialty once again, he had a small hit in 1964 with "Bama Lama Bama Loo." These and other sides were respectable efforts in the mold of his classic '50s sides, but tastes had changed too much for Little Richard to climb the charts again. He spent the rest of the '60s in a continual unsuccessful comeback, recording for Vee-Jay (accompanied on some sides by Jimi Hendrix, who was briefly in Richard's band), OKeh, and Modern (for whom he even tried recording in Memphis with Stax session musicians).

It was the rock & roll revival of the late '60s and early '70s, though, that really saved Richard's career, enabling him to play on the nostalgia circuit with great success (though he had a small hit, "Freedom Blues," in 1970). He had always been a flamboyant performer, brandishing a six-inch pompadour and mascara, and constant entertaining appearances on television talk shows seemed to ensure his continuing success as a living legend. Yet by the late '70s, he'd returned to the church again. Somewhat predictably, he eased back into rock and show business by the mid-'80s. Since then, he's maintained his profile with a role in *Down and Out in Beverly Hills* (the movie's soundtrack also returned him to the charts, this time with "Great Gosh A-Mighty") and guest appearances on soundtracks, compilations, and children's rock records. At this point it's safe to assume that he never will get that much-hungered-for comeback hit, but he remains one of rock & roll's most colorful icons, still capable of turning on the charm and charisma in his infrequent appearances in the limelight. *—Richie Unterberger*

Here's Little Richard / Mar. 1957 / Specialty ✦✦✦✦✦
Little Richard's debut album wasn't released until more than a year after he first broke through nationally with "Tutti Frutti" in early 1956. By the time Specialty Records got around to introducing him to LP buyers, Little Richard had already scored six Top 40 pop hits. This album didn't contain all of them, but it did contain "Tutti Frutti," "Long Tall Sally," "Slippin' and Slidin' (Peepin' and Hidin')," "Rip It Up," "Ready Teddy," "Jenny, Jenny," and "Miss Ann," all of which had made the pop charts and been in the R&B Top Ten. ("True, Fine Mama," also included, would chart as the B-side of "Ooh! My Soul" a year later.) Thus, *Here's Little Richard* was more of a compilation than just a debut album, a consistent collection containing many of Little Richard's classic recordings. It was also his highest charting and probably best-selling effort. *—William Ruhlmann*

Little Richard / 1958 / Specialty ✦✦✦✦✦
Like his debut album, *Here's Little Richard*, Little Richard's self-titled second album was, in essence, a compilation record rather than a newly recorded LP. Among its 12 selections were nine songs that had been chart singles between 1956 and 1958, including "Keep A-Knockin'" and "Good Golly, Miss Molly," which had hit the pop Top Ten, and "Lucille," which had topped the R&B charts. Other former singles were "Heeby-Jeebies," "The Girl Can't Help it," "Send Me Some Lovin'" (all three R&B Top Tens), "Ooh! My Soul" (Little Richard's final Top 40 pop hit), "All Around the World," and "Baby Face." Little Richard's spectacular two-year run of hits was over by mid-1958, with the singer having renounced rock & roll as of October 1957, but *Little Richard* gathers together a generous helping of his most remarkable work. *—William Ruhlmann*

The Fabulous Little Richard / 1959 / Specialty ✦✦✦
With Little Richard having long since given up pop music for religion, Specialty Records released as his third album a collection of tracks recorded mostly at his first session in 1955 (with a few 1956 and 1957 recordings as well). Richard handles these R&B songs well, but, with the exception of the medley "Kansas City/Hey-Hey-Hey-Hey" (later copied note for note by The Beatles), the songs and performances do not match his incendiary hits of the period. *—William Ruhlmann*

Grooviest 17 Original Hits! / 1959 / Specialty ✦✦✦✦✦
Despite its trendy title, *Grooviest 17 Original Hits!* was the most complete collection of Little Richard's hits yet released. By this point, Little Richard had re-recorded his hits for Vee-Jay, Modern, and OKeh, and Specialty seems to have wanted an album with the word "original" in the title, emphasizing that they possessed the actual hit versions. Taking the 12 tracks from 1963's *His Greatest Hits*, the company added five more tracks, among them "Ready Teddy," "Miss Ann," and "Ooh! My Soul," chart records they had skipped the first time around. "The Girl Can't Help It" still didn't appear on a Little Richard hits collection, but *Grooviest 17 Original Hits!* was the single-disc Little Richard hits collection to own for a long time to come. *—William Ruhlmann*

The Explosive Little Richard / 1967 / OKeh ✦✦✦
In 1966, OKeh Records took its turn at trying to revive the recording career of Little Richard. In the fall of that year, they put him in a studio in Hollywood with his former Specialty Records associate Larry Williams producing, and the two cut this album of rock & roll ravers, which was released in January 1967. Little Richard is as frantic as ever, notably on the lead-off track, "I Don't Want to Discuss It," later a showstopper for Delaney & Bonnie, but rock music trends were far removed from his style of rocking abandon by 1967, and this album went unnoticed. OKeh recorded Little Richard doing his hits that

January and released the results several months later as *Little Richard's Greatest Hits Recorded Live*, but that was the end of this comeback. [*The Explosive Little Richard!* originally was released by OKeh Records in January 1967 as OKeh 14117. It has been reissued several times by Epic Records, most recently in 1986 as Epic 40390.] *—William Ruhlmann*

The Rill Thing / 1971 / Reprise ♦♦♦
The Rill Thing represented Little Richard's most serious attempt at a comeback since his '50s heyday. "Freedom Blues," Richard's debut Reprise single, released in April 1970, was a mid-chart hit, his first in five years. "Greenwood Mississippi," released as a single concurrently with the album, also charted. Richard adopted a Cajun/country-rock approach (even covering "Lovesick Blues"), with a heavy beat and twangy guitar backing up his rough, forceful vocals. Despite the indulgence of the rambling ten-minute instrumental title track, the LP was a convincing update on his early work. But it did not propel Little Richard back to the top of the charts. *—William Ruhlmann*

Essential / 1985 / Specialty ♦♦♦♦♦
Speciality's *Essential* lives up to its billing, featuring 20 of Little Richard's finest recordings for the label. Not only are all the hits here, but there's some terrific lesser-known tunes and cult favorites slipped on at the end of the record, making this yet another great compilation of Richard's Specialty material. It proves that it would be nearly impossible to release a bad compilation of these recordings. *—Stephen Thomas Erlewine*

☆ **18 Greatest Hits** / 1985 / Rhino ♦♦♦♦♦
18 Greatest Hits is the definitive single-disc collection of Little Richard's Specialty singles, especially for listeners who only want the hits. Every one of Richard's biggest hits—"Tutti Frutti," "Long Tall Sally," "Slippin' and Slidin'," "Rip It Up," "Ready Teddy," "The Girl Can't Help It," "Lucille," "Send Me Some Lovin'," "Keep a-Knockin'," "Good Golly Miss Molly"—are here, plus singles like "Heeby-Jeebies," "She's Got It," "Ooh! My Soul," "Miss Ann," "Kansas City/Hey Hey Hey," and "Bama Lama Bama Loo" that were bigger hits on the R&B charts than the pop charts. All of the singles are presented in chronological order, and the disc simply rips it up from beginning to end. It's a definitive collection. *—Stephen Thomas Erlewine*

The Specialty Box Set / 1989 / Specialty ♦♦♦♦♦
Dig it—a collection of all 73 songs that Little Richard cut for Specialty Records from 1955 through 1959, including early working versions of hits including "Long Tall Sally" and "Slippin' and Slidin'," may seem like overkill to the casual listener, but if you're thinking of buying this three-CD box, chances are you're not a casual listener. And if you're not thinking about it, then you should be. This set covers only four years in Little Richard's career, but manages to sum up virtually everything you need to know about him (his earlier sides, available on Bear Family, are an interesting appendix, but of his later stuff, only the early- and mid-'60s material, with Jimi Hendrix on guitar, hold any significance, mostly as a curiosity). Not only does the music make you want to get up and dance, but the notes—spread out on a lavishly illustrated booklet and the individual jewel boxes—tell the whole story of Specialty Records and the people behind it, including Art Rupe, Bumps Blackwell, Dave Bartholomew, and, of course, Richard Penniman himself. The session information alone could keep owners busy for a week. The sound is nothing less than breathtaking, loud and raunchy but razor sharp, and the price of this set—about $42 retail—makes it competitive with other Little Richard single-disc sets as well as more attractive than the price of boxes devoted to Elvis Presley and Chuck Berry. The only complaint—why couldn't the producers list the songs on the individual jewel boxes? *—Bruce Eder*

The Specialty Box Set / 1989 / Ace ♦♦♦♦
For the hardcore Little Richard fan—the kind that has to hear every recording the architect of rock & roll ever made—there's little question that Ace's *Specialty Box Set* is the motherlode. Spanning six discs and over a hundred tracks, this is for serious listeners. Since Specialty's condensed, three-disc version of this set also included numerous working versions, alternate takes and commercials, it was also targeted for dedicated listeners, but this set—which is twice as large—is for fans who love to immerse themselves in minute details and unfinished takes. For those listeners, this set is certainly worth the money, since it is lavishly produced and boasts every single thing Little Richard recorded at the label. But most fans—including most serious listeners—will be satisfied with the more concise, but nevertheless comprehensive, three-disc set on Specialty. *—Stephen Thomas Erlewine*

The Formative Years 1951–53 / Jul. 1989 / Bear Family ♦♦♦♦
Early Richard, pre-"Tutti Frutti." *—Cub Koda*

Good Golly! / 1991 / Fantasy ♦♦♦
Absolutely flawless ten-song budget collection of Richard's best. All the original Specialty recordings of "Tutti Frutti," "Long Tall Sally," "Slippin' and Slidin'," "Lucille," "Keep a Knockin'," "Rip It Up," "Ready Teddy," "Jenny Jenny," "The Girl Can't Help It," and "Good Golly Miss Molly." If you need a quick fix of Richard's absolute best, grab this one, you can't possibly go wrong here. *—Cub Koda*

★ **The Georgia Peach** / Aug. 5, 1991 / Specialty ♦♦♦♦♦
Perhaps the greatest of Little Richard's greatest hits compilations, the 25-track *Georgia Peach* features all of his biggest hits in chronological order, as well as terrific singles that never were as big as "Tutti Frutti" and "Good Golly Miss Molly." On top of the sublime song selection and sound, the liner notes by compiler Billy Vera are splendid and insightful. *—Stephen Thomas Erlewine*

Greatest Hits Recorded Live / 1994 / Epic ♦♦♦
By January 25, 1967, when he cut this live album, Little Richard had re-recorded his original Specialty Records hits for Vee-Jay and for Modern Records. Now, he was signed to OKeh, and before a live audience at "Club OKeh" in Hollywood, he laid them down once again—"Tutti Frutti," "Long Tall Sally," and ten others—fronting a band led by his old Specialty Records compatriot Larry Williams. It's an exciting set before an enthusiastic audience, and as long as you keep in mind that these are not the original recordings, a good buy. [Originally released in July 1967 on OKeh Records as OKeh 14121, *Greatest Hits Recorded Live* has been reissued by Epic Records several times, most recently in 1986 as Epic 40389.] *—William Ruhlmann*

Shag on Down By the Union Hall / Feb. 13, 1996 / Specialty ♦♦♦♦♦
For those who want more classic Little Richard than a greatest-hits collection but aren't devoted enough to spring for the expensive box sets, this is an excellent anthology of 24 of his best lesser-known tracks. Most of it dates from his classic era at Specialty (1955-1957), with alternate takes of a lot of his hits and some decent B-sides; there are also a few songs that he cut for the label during his 1964 comeback, including the minor hit "Bama Lama Bama Loo." *—Richie Unterberger*

God Is Real / Jun. 15, 1999 / MCA ♦♦
These are Richard's gospel recordings made for the Coral label in 1959. Titles include "Every Time I Feeel The Spirit," "Does Jesus Care," "I'm Tramping," "Milky White Way," "Just a Closer Walk With Thee," and "Jesus Walked This Lonesome Valley." An interesting chapter in this giant's recorded career. *—Cub Koda*

The Best of the Vee-Jay Years, Vol. 1 / Oct. 17, 2000 / Collectables ♦♦♦

The Best of the Vee-Jay Years, Vol. 2 / Oct. 17, 2000 / Collectables ♦♦♦
Little Richard recorded for the Vee-Jay label in the early '60s, after his historic stint with Specialty Records and the restored rock & roll vigor that followed his sudden religious conversion. While at Vee-Jay, Richard re-recorded some of his classic mid-'50s tracks (in this case "Rip It Up," "Jenny Jenny," "The Girl Can't Help It," "Tutti Frutti," and "Good Golly Miss Molly"), trying to recapture the natural initial hysteria. While a toned-down Little Richard is still worth hearing, the record-buying public was duped into believing these Vee-Jay sides were the original Specialty versions, only to be greatly disappointed after getting the record home. While Richard's wild whoops and furious piano still come through, especially on the neglected newer material, it goes without saying that the Vee-Jay reissues should only be investigated after obtaining the Specialty sides. *—Al Campbell*

Talking 'Bout Soul / Feb. 1, 2001 / RPM ♦♦♦
In the mid-'60s, Little Richard was attempting, with little commercial success, to jump back into the rock and R&B frontlines with recordings on various labels. *Talking 'Bout Soul* collects 28 songs that he cut for Vee-Jay in 1964 and 1965, which (especially during the latter part of that span) were poorly exposed as Vee-Jay headed toward bankruptcy. Little Richard had just recently emerged from his layoff of several years from the rock & roll scene, and was still a strong and exciting vocalist; after all, he was still only in his early thirties. His problems, both as far as sales and the quality of his records, had more to due with unremarkable material and production. There was also a sense that his style just wasn't as adaptable to the soul era as that of a rough contemporary such as, say, James Brown. These sides are fair, but not often better than fair, soul-rockers that sometimes move into more contemporary R&B bags, such as the classy, agonized ballad "I Don't Know What You Got," written by Don Covay, or Alvin Tyler's New Orleans-flavored "Crossover." Little Richard wrote some reasonable if generic originals for Vee-Jay, too, but his repertoire was way too heavy on remakes of old '50s rock songs, whether his own or others like "Whole Lotta Shaking Going On" and "Money Honey." The production is tinnier than it should be, and the arrangements and playing sound more rushed than they should, too. Jimi Hendrix plays on a few of these sides, incidentally, although it's not made clear in the liner notes exactly which tracks are graced by his appearance. *—Richie Unterberger*

Little Sonny (Aaron Willis)

b. Oct. 6, 1932, Greensboro, AL

Vocals, Harmonica / Electric Harmonica Blues, Electric Blues

The Stax empire wasn't exactly renowned for its legion of blues harpists, but Little Sonny found the Memphis firm quite an agreeable home during the early '70s (he even appeared in the label's grandiose concert film, *Wattstax*, albeit very briefly).

Little Sonny, whose birth name is Aaron Willis, is a product of Detroit's blues scene. He moved to the Motor City in 1953 after growing up on his dad's farm in Alabama (his mom gave him his nickname). When Little Sonny wasn't working local haunts with John Lee Hooker, Eddie Burns, Eddie Kirkland, Baby Boy Warren, or Washboard Willie (who gave him his first paying gig), he was snapping photos of the patrons for half a buck a snap.

Sonny Boy Williamson rambled through town in 1955 and gave Willis some valuable pointers. In 1958, Sonny made his blues recording debut, cutting for both Duke ("I Gotta Find My Baby") and local entrepreneur Joe Von Battle, who leased Little Sonny's "Love Shock" to Nashville's Excello imprint.

The harpist acquired a two-track tape machine and took matters into his own hands during the early '60s, helming his tiny Speedway label. He leased "The Creeper" and "Latin Soul" to Detroit's Revilot Records (his labelmates included Darrell Banks and George Clinton's Parliament) in 1966. That set the stage for his joining Stax's Enterprise label in 1970; his first album was the largely instrumental *New King of the Blues Harmonica*—a rather brash boast for a relative unknown!

Two more Enterprise sets that more effectively featured Little Sonny's vocal talents soon followed: *Black & Blue* and 1973's *Hard Goin' Up*, the latter distinguished by the Bettye Crutcher-penned "It's Hard Going Up (But Twice as Hard Coming Down)" and a variety of other soul-inflected tracks.

Not much was heard of the harpist in recent years until the British Sequel imprint released *Sonny Side Up* in 1995. His backing crew included keyboardist Rudy Robinson and guitarist Aaron Willis Jr., (his son), both of whom graced *Hard Goin' Up* more than two decades before. *—Bill Dahl*

• **New King of Blues Harmonica** / 1970 / Stax ♦♦♦♦♦
New King of Blues Harmonica, the first album recorded by Little Sonny, finds the harpist living up to his name, turning out a hard-driving collection of Chicago blues. At times, he's a little too hung up on sounding like Sonny Boy Williamson, but for the most part, this is thoroughly enjoyable, high-octane Chicago blues. However, the presence of an organ on most of the record may be a little distracting for purists. *—Thom Owens*

Hard Goin' Up / 1973 / Enterprise ♦♦♦
Because he hasn't promoted himself aggressively enough, Little Sonny isn't nearly as well known in either blues or R&B circles as he should be. But make no mistake, Sonny is a first-class electric bluesman who's also a pearl of a soul singer. And he excels in both areas on *Hard Goin' Up*, which Fantasy reissued on CD in the U.S. in 1997. "You Made Me Strong," "It's Hard Going Up (But Twice as Hard Coming Down)" and "You Can Be Replaced" illustrate his mastery of the 12-bar form, while "You're Spreading Yourself a Little Too Thin" and "Do It Right Now" are invigorating examples of the type of horn-driven, sock-it-to-'em soul music Sonny embraced with such conviction. The punchy "My Woman Is Good to Me" was a minor hit, and *Hard* made it to number 42 on Billboard's R&B albums chart. It's possible that had it not been for the problems Stax was having with CBS at the time, the album would have enjoyed a lot more exposure. At any rate, *Hard Goin' Up* is one of Sonny's finest accomplishments. *—Alex Henderson*

New King of Blues Harmonica/Hard Goin' Up / 1990 / Ace ♦♦♦♦♦
A import coupling of the harpist's first and third LPs for Stax's Enterprise subsidiary and the best spot to inaugurate a Little Sonny CD collection. 1970's *New King* is mostly instrumental and places Sonny in a funky, contemporary setting; 1973's *Hard Goin' Up* was his best album for the firm, benefitting from excellent material spotlighting his vocal talents in a soul-slanted format. Stax offers *New King* by itself as a domestic CD. *—Bill Dahl*

Black & Blue / 1992 / Stax ♦♦♦♦
Originally released on Stax's short-lived Enterprise label, this finds Detroit harp man Aaron "Little Sonny" Willis backed by Memphis players working in an early-'70s blues-rock groove. The Bar-Kays provide the horn blasts, and although it would be a sin for Memphis players to overplay on anything, nothing here really catches fire; the whole session stays in low gear throughout. *—Cub Koda*

Sonny Side Up / 1995 / Glynn ♦♦♦
It's unequivocally nice to have Little Sonny back in harness after a long recording hiatus, but the harpist's comeback offering suffers from backing that feels too mechanical to really do his supple harp justice. A little more earthiness would have suited the project much better. *—Bill Dahl*

Ann Arbor Blues & Jazz Festival, Vol. 2: Blues With a Feeling / 1995 / Schoolkids ♦♦♦
One of a series of compilations from John Sinclair's stash of tapes from the Ann Arbor fests, this 1972 performance caught Little Sonny at his funk-tinged finest. He pleased the youthful throng with a few of his own numbers—"The Creeper Returns," "They Want Money"—and harp standards first done by Little Walter and Jimmy Reed. *—Bill Dahl*

Blues With a Feeling / 1996 / Sequel ♦♦♦

Little Walter (Marion Walter Jacobs)

b. May 1, 1930, Marksville, LA, **d.** Feb. 15, 1968, Chicago, IL
Vocals, Leader, Accordion, Songwriter, Harmonica / Harmonica Blues, Electric Chicago Blues, Chicago Blues, Electric Harmonica Blues

Who was the king of all postwar blues harpists, Chicago division or otherwise? Why, the virtuosic Little Walter, without a solitary doubt. The fiery harmonica wizard took the humble mouth organ in dazzling amplified directions that were unimaginable prior to his ascendancy. His daring instrumental innovations were so fresh, startling, and ahead of their time that they sometimes sported a jazz sensibility, soaring and swooping in front of snarling guitars and swinging rhythms perfectly suited to Walter's pioneering flights of fancy.

Marion Walter Jacobs was by most accounts an unruly but vastly talented youth who abandoned his rural Louisiana home for the bright lights of New Orleans at age 12. Walter gradually journeyed north from there, pausing in Helena (where he hung out with the wizened Sonny Boy Williamson), Memphis, and St. Louis before arriving in Chicago in 1946.

The thriving Maxwell Street strip offered a spot for the still-teenaged phenom to hawk his wares. He fell in with local royalty—Tampa Red and Big Bill Broonzy—and debuted on wax that same year for the tiny Ora-Nelle logo ("I Just Keep Loving Her") in the company of Jimmy Rogers and guitarist Othum Brown. Walter joined forces with Muddy Waters in 1948; the resulting stylistic tremors of that coupling are still being felt today. Along with Rogers and Baby Face Leroy Foster, this super-confident young aggregation became informally known as the Headhunters. They would saunter into South Side clubs, mount the stage, and proceed to calmly "cut the heads" of whomever was booked there that evening.

By 1950, Walter was firmly entrenched as Waters' studio harpist at Chess as well (long after Walter had split the Muddy Waters band, Leonard Chess insisted on his participation on waxings—why split up an unbeatable combination?). That's how Walter came to record his breakthrough 1952 R&B chart-topper "Juke"—the romping instrumental was laid down at the tail end of a Waters session. Suddenly Walter was a star on his own, combining his stunning talents with those of the Aces (guitarists Louis and David Myers and drummer Fred Below) and advancing the conception of blues harmonica another few light years with every session he made for Checker Records.

From 1952 to 1958, Walter notched 14 Top Ten R&B hits, including "Sad Hours," "Mean Old World," "Tell Me Mama," "Off the Wall," "Blues With a Feeling," "You're So Fine," a threatening "You Better Watch Yourself," the mournful "Last Night," and a rocking "My Babe" that was Willie Dixon's secularized treatment of the traditional gospel lament "This Train." Throughout his Checker tenure, Walter alternated spine-chilling instrumentals with gritty vocals (he's always been underrated in that department; he wasn't Muddy Waters or the Wolf, but who was?).

Walter utilized the chromatic harp in ways never before envisioned (check out his 1956 free-form instrumental "Teenage Beat," with Robert Jr. Lockwood and Luther Tucker manning the guitars, for proof positive). 1959's determined "Everything Gonna Be Alright" was Walter's last trip to the hit lists; Chicago blues had faded to a commercial nonentity by then unless your name was Jimmy Reed.

Tragically, the '60s saw the harp genius slide steadily into an alcohol-hastened state of unreliability, his once-handsome face becoming a roadmap of scars. In 1964, he toured Great Britain with the Rolling Stones, who clearly had their priorities in order, but his once-prodigious skills were faltering badly. That sad fact was never more obvious than on 1967's disastrous summit meeting of Waters, Bo Diddley, and Walter for Chess as the Super Blues Band; there was nothing super whatsoever about Walter's lame remakes of "My Babe" and "You Don't Love Me."

Walter's eternally vicious temper led to his violent undoing in 1968. He was involved in a street fight (apparently on the losing end, judging from the outcome) and died from the incident's after-effects at age 37. His influence remains inescapable to this day—it's unlikely that a blues harpist exists on the face of this earth who doesn't worship Little Walter. *—Bill Dahl*

☆ **The Best** / 1958 / MCA/Chess ♦♦♦♦♦
If there's a blues harmonica player alive today who *doesn't* have this landmark album in their collection, they're either lying or had their copy stolen by another harmonica player. This 12-song collection is the one that every harmonica player across the board cut his teeth on. All the hits are here: "My Babe," "Blues With a Feeling," "You Better Watch Yourself," "Off the Wall," "Mean Old World," and the instrumental that catapulted him from the sideman chair in Muddy Waters' band to the top of the R&B charts in 1952, "Juke." Walter's influence to this very day is so pervasive over the landscape of the instrument that this collection of singles is truly one of the all-time greatest blues harmonica albums, one of the all-time greatest Chicago blues albums, and one of the first ten albums you should purchase if you're building your blues collection from the ground floor up. *—Cub Koda*

Hate to See You Go / 1969 / MCA/Chess ♦♦♦♦♦
Many blues fans identify this album by the scar on its front cover, and this doesn't mean that their copy got damaged lying around in the used-record pile. A larger than life black-and-white photograph of Little Walter fills the front cover with a visual impact that just cannot be matched in the petite world of compact discs. A jewel case would also be too much protection against the scar in the middle of Little Walter's forehead. Biographical information on this artist no doubt provides the explanation of where this scar came from, and it can be assumed he did not earn it with bad harmonica playing. This album was part of a reissue series that Chess launched in the early '70s, irritating most blues fans despite the quality of the grim graphic design with its superior black-and-white photography, of which the scar shot was only one example. The problem was that too much of the Chess material had been out of print for too long, and the new generations of blues fans were hardly satisfied by the stingy serving of tracks the producers served up, even if it came wrapped in film noir trappings. The series miscalculated what the public actually wanted out of record companies in terms of reissue material, which would be lavish double-album sets loaded with information and sold at a discount. This trend would begin quickly after Chess had already started its black-and-white series of single albums; the company quickly rendered them all obsolete by rushing out its own series of double-record sets.

Take a good look at the song titles on this record, that is, if one can still see them. The text was printed in a small white typeface on top of a black background, and the printing over the years suffered from a kind of disappearing effect. The album consists of a combination of songs that were huge hits for this artist, such as "Mellow Down Easy," "Roller Coaster," and "Nobody But You," combined with other performances that the producers thought were especially worthwhile. It is a well-sequenced effort, mastered powerfully, but the songs might as well have been chosen at random. None of the dozens of previously unreleased Little Walter tracks the label had lying around were touched for this project; all of the material here had already seen the light of day and proved its appeal with the blues public. That Little Walter is a brilliant harmonica player and a real innovator in terms of both the amplified sound of the small harp and the use of the chromatic version in blues and R&B is a well-established fact of American musical history. The relationship he had with his fellow players hasn't gotten as much attention, but as one enjoys these tracks, it is easy to feel the strength of Little Walter as a bandleader. He comes up with inventive devices within the familiar blues structures and is, in fact, one of the music's most ingenious arrangers of the electric blues combo sound. Like the airlines are fond of saying, consumers have a lot of choices when it comes to Little Walter material. The window-seat view of the scar might be an acquired taste, but musically this is a smooth ride all the way. *—Eugene Chadbourne*

Blue and Lonesome / 1970 / Le Roi du Blues ♦♦♦♦♦
Previously unreleased or outtake material can be dreck, true, but sometimes it is just the opposite case. Part of what can be exciting is the sense of a particular artist's world expanding as listeners get to hear brand new examples of the artist's genius. In the case of Little Walter, the Chicago blues harmonica ace, many blues fans felt that they had already heard everything this artist had done—and probably many times to boot—when these French albums were originally released. Hearing a whole bunch of new tracks was a thrill, and in this case one that can be repeated, since the power of these tracks does not come from their previously unheard status alone. All are first-rate performances, and many are purely great. Why some of these tracks would have languished on a shelf is a bit of a mystery, but perhaps not if one considers some of the boorish comments made about musicians such as this by their slave lords, the brothers Leonard and Marshall Chess. Little Walter is one of those players who one of the brothers once described as only "primitive" or "rudimentary." He is actually a great figure in American music, some think

one of the most important Chicago blues artists, but why expect someone who almost became a millionaire off his music to know that? When leading his own sessions, his approach effortlessly combined the country and Delta blues legacy of his old boss, Muddy Waters, with the influence of modern jazz, swing, and R&B music. The combination gives his blues recordings a real punch, his choice of harmonica sound often helping to define which of the possible influences will have the strongest effect on a track's groove.

He has two completely distinctive harp approaches. When playing the standard harmonica through amplification, his sound is instantly recognizable, and it is one of those musical presences that can knock one over with one note, like Jimi Hendrix or John Coltrane to name a few others in his league. His choice of weapon for the jazzier numbers is always the chromatic harmonica, and he surely helped set the standard for new approaches to instrumentals spotlighting this appealing instrument. Every arrangement here demonstrates that at least somebody was thinking about coming up with unique arrangements and new grooves and, from the sound of the interesting (and sometimes mildly obscene) studio patter that has been preserved and edited between the tracks, Little Walter was one of the hands-on dudes. He always seems to have a sense of the perfect tempo for a tune, sometimes using the rhythm itself to unseat expectations, such as the version of "Going Down Slow," a blues warhorse renewed brilliantly here by using a slightly faster shuffle. There is also fine lead guitar playing from Robert Jr. Lockwood, a player who was strongly influenced by Little Walter's direction and continued combining many of the same styles throughout his career. Pianists Henry Gray and Otis Spann also provide excellent playing. The rhythm sections often feature drummer Fred Below, above all others in timekeeping skills in this music, as well as other familiar names from the Chicago scene. Much of this music was eventually released in other collections by Chess itself; there is good reason to believe the original company did not authorize this release, and that the French company's mere possession of the tapes was the work of a light-fingered Louis. No information is provided about composers. *—Eugene Chadbourne*

That Southern Feeling / 1970 / Le Roi du Blues ✦✦✦✦✦
Chicago blues fans will know him simply as Little Walter—no surname necessary. He is not only one of the great blues harmonica players, he was a bandleader of considerable talent and something of a recording studio genius, despite the pressure of his bosses, Leonard and Marshall Chess. Neither man seemed to really understand the value of what he or anybody else on their label was doing. A good example of this is the fact that there were three albums' worth of Little Walter material the Chess label had left lying around through the '60s and into the '70s, when a French record producer apparently saw fit to smuggle some of these pancakes of tapes out of the label's archives, possibly in a secret compartment in the lining of his beret. Blues fans went crazy over these releases when they came out, as the tracks represented a treasure trove of first-class Chicago blues material involving many major players from the scene. Hardly weak or incomplete performances, these are examples of superb, grooving blues playing in which a series of alternate takes evolve and deepen interplay, rather than simple presentations of hapless musicians trying something over due to a perceived fudge-up. The French editors were nonetheless kind to the listeners by spreading these alternate versions of songs out throughout the series rather than lumping them together and risking boredom. When the Chess brothers sold out to parent company MCA, the coming of the CD era led to producers scrounging around label vaults and finally liberating much of this material via so-called legitimate release. Whether the estate of Little Walter got any more money from the MCA productions than from these French releases is an interesting question, but at least he probably couldn't have gotten less.

Subsequent Chess sets from the '90s contain everything really worth owning from the unreleased backlog, yet the bootleg status of the French series is not to suggest that these records suffer from shoddy production or bad sound quality. Indeed, these recordings shame a lot of the over-produced blues recordings from the decades that followed in terms of sound quality and band mix, and that isn't even mentioning the subject of the actual blues playing. Little Walter grew up from the hard-edged Delta blues roots of his former boss Muddy Waters, who appears on some of these tracks along with several other brilliant bluesmen such as Buddy Guy and Robert Jr. Lockwood. But he also has his own distinctive jazzy, swinging approach, featuring sparkling chromatic harmonica solos and a rhythm section backup of the sort most bandleaders would die for. Harmonica buddies will really like these instrumentals, tossed off with the determination and fortitude of a mountain climber and given titles such as "Last Boogie" and "Fast Boogie," as if they were student etudes. Which, let's face it, they ought to be. And with "killer" going in and out of style as an expression of greatness, "Dead Presidents" is a blues track good enough to earn the distinction of being called an "assassination." It is one of two recordings from 1963 in which the size of the band fattens, boasting two keyboardists, the three-in-one guitar attack of Buddy Guy, and soulful drummer Al Duncan. Unusual items include two tracks on which the harmonica player is featured as a sideman, backing up the doo wop group the Coronets. The blending of the R&B, doo wop, and blues scenes in the Chicago studios is fascinating indeed, the study of which is most enjoyable when it involves listening to material such as this. No information is provided on composers for the songs. *—Eugene Chadbourne*

Chess Blues Masters Series / May 1977 / Chess ✦✦✦✦✦
These singles by harmonica magician and vocal ace Marion "Little Walter" Jacobs are among the cornerstones of Chicago blues. They've also been reissued ad infinitum for years, and are now available in a better mastered and annotated two-disc set, *The Essential Little Walter*. *—Ron Wynn*

Boss Blues Harmonica / 1986 / Chess ✦✦✦✦
The high rating is for the music. Served in a portion as generous as one could typically fit over four slabs of vinyl, these vintage recordings of Chicago blues cannot be denied. "Juke," "Flying Saucer," "Boom Boom, Out Go the Lights"—these are all out and out classics of urban blues, delivered with zest and zeal by an artist who matched flawless and flamboyant harmonica technique and a devastating amplified sound with a vocal style that was mischievous to the point of irritating Rumpelstiltskin. His musical company here is the cream of the crop, killer players all. The interplay between guitars and harmonica is fantastic by itself, while the antics of the rhythm section are a subject for extensive study as well. As a bandleader, Little Walter was an inventive character, meaning that each track has something fresh about its arrangement, often just a little touch or sometimes an entire groove that with that magic combination of familiarity and surprise. There isn't a bum track on this collection, which is why it didn't matter that the tracks on the third and fourth sides of the collection were shuffled like a deck of cards for the '80s version of this two-fer repackage, about which the following competition can be launched: Which of the two-record set covers used for the *Boss Blues Harmonica* sets is uglier? Is it the '70s version, in which a heavy soaking of toilet-bowl blue coloring fails to hide the fact that almost the entire back cover is taken up with a drawing of a drum set? Or was it the '80s set, featuring a crude drawing of someone who doesn't look at all like Little Walter, standing in front of a bar in what looks like the middle of a vacant field. The earlier set didn't bother to provide a clear listing of session men and discographical information. *—Eugene Chadbourne*

The Blues World of Little Walter / 1988 / Delmark ✦✦✦✦✦
If you really want to hear what Little Walter sounded like in his pre-amplified days and early stages of development with the Muddy Waters band, this is the one to get. The title is a bit of a misnomer as Walter is featured more as a sideman to Baby Face Leroy, Muddy Waters and others on early Parkway, Regal and Savoy sides, but it's clear that Walter at this stage of the game should have been paying royalties to both Sonny Boys and Walter Horton in particular. One of the high points features explosive slide work from Waters on a pre-Chess version of "Rollin' & Tumblin'," as crude as a version as you'll ever hear and certainly not to be missed. Although many of these sides have appeared on other compilations (usually taped up off of old scratchy 78s), this one features superior sound taken from the original lacquer masters. *—Cub Koda*

☆ **The Best of Little Walter** / 1988 / Chess ✦✦✦✦✦
If there's a blues harmonica player alive today who *doesn't* have a copy of this landmark album in their collection, they're either lying or had their copy of it stolen by another harmonica player. This 12-song collection is the one that every harmonica player across the board cut their teeth on. All the hits are here: "My Babe," "Blues With a Feeling," "You Better Watch Yourself," "Off the Wall," "Mean Old World" and the instrumental that catapulted him from the sideman chair in Muddy Waters' band to the top of the R&B charts in 1952, "Juke." Walter's influence to this very day is so pervasive over the landscape of the instrument that this collection of singles is truly: 1) one of the all-time greatest blues harmonica albums, 2) one of the all-time greatest Chicago blues albums, and 3) one of the first ten albums you should purchase if you're building your blues collection from the ground floor up. *—Cub Koda*

☆ **The Best of Little Walter, Vol. 2** / 1989 / MCA/Chess ✦✦✦✦✦
This ten-song budget compilation continues the overview of Walter's enormous output for the Chess label. For rock fans, the most familiar track on here is the original version of "Boom Boom (Out Go the Lights)." But there's more where that came from, including the smoking uptempo "It Ain't Right," the blistering instrumental "Boogie," and the soulful strut of "I Don't Play." Another bonus is the inclusion of an early Muddy Waters instrumental featuring Walter on acoustic harp, "Evans' Shuffle." A great, cost effective way to add some more Walter to the collection. *—Cub Koda*

☆ **The Chess Years 1952–1963** / 1992 / Charly ✦✦✦✦✦
Damn near everything (*Blues With a Feeling* popped any semblance of absolute completion) that the Chicago harp genius ever waxed for Chess (95 sides in all), spread over four generously programmed discs. Particularly revealing are the lengthy snippets of studio chatter on the final rarities disc—Sonny Boy had nothing on Walter when it came to verbally sparring in the studio with Leonard Chess! *—Bill Dahl*

☆ **The Essential** / Jun. 8, 1993 / MCA/Chess ✦✦✦✦✦
In many ways, this supplants the original single disc, *Best of Little Walter*, and appends it with 35 more classics of Chicago blues harp genius, although one track from the original 12-song lineup is (perhaps purposely) left off. If you want to start your Walter collection with a nice generous helping of his best, this one runs the entire gamut of his solo career, from the classic 1952 instrumental "Juke" up to the Willie Dixon-penned "Dead Presidents." 46 tracks, one dynamite booklet, nice remastering, a great value for the cash outlay involved and best of all, an album title that truly delivers the goods. *—Cub Koda*

Blues Masters / 1994 / Tomato ✦✦
These live performances have been circulating around bootleg channels under a plethora of titles on vinyl and cassette for over a decade and a half. The Otis Rush cuts fare OK, although the sound quality is pretty awful and will generally make any decent stereo playback system sound like there's a pile of blankets draped over the speakers. The Walter cuts are another matter entirely. On one of its earlier vinyl bootleg incarnations, these tracks were purported to be recorded live at Pepper's Lounge in Chicago sometime in the late '60s. If they were, it must have been amateur night. The backing band heard here behind Walter are a bunch of rhythmically challenged ham-fisted hacks who sound like every blues lover's worst nightmare; buzzing obtrusive bass lines, clumsy, lumbering drums that sound like the guy's building a house, and a lead guitar that sounds like he's plugged into a 100-watt kazoo. As for Walter himself, he's in the absolute worst recorded form ever documented. His harp playing is raggedy and short-winded (to be fair, by this time he *was* trying to blow with one collapsed lung) and he forgets lyrics left and right, letting out frustrated yelps as he keeps losing his place midsong, breaking time constantly. *—Cub Koda*

Blues With a Feeling / Oct. 24, 1995 / MCA/Chess ♦♦♦♦♦
A 40-song double CD of material that didn't appear on *The Essential Little Walter.* Much of this is pretty rare, having only appeared on long unavailable singles or hard-to-get import LPs; almost a dozen, in fact, had not previously been officially released anywhere. Its appeal isn't limited to collectors, though. Anyone who likes a Little Walter greatest-hits anthology will like this almost as much, including as it does some excellent performances ("Flying Saucer," "Teenage Beat," "Who," "Crazy for My Baby," "Thunderbird") that don't appear on *The Essential Little Walter.* The dozen or so alternate takes get closer to specialist territory, but even so they're worth hearing even if you're not a fanatic, sometimes varying substantially from the official versions. *—Richie Unterberger*

Confessin' the Blues / Nov. 19, 1996 / MCA/Chess ♦♦♦♦
This release is a little confusing, coming out as it does more than a year after the release of MCA-Chess' Little Walter rarities collection *Blues With a Feeling*, and two years after the double CD anthology set that contains most of the best parts of this collection. Still, for those who can't afford either of those pricey sets, this disc, coupled with the two best-of volumes, and the other Walter compilations, fills in some holes that are well worth filling. Made up of songs cut between 1953 and 1959—none of which had ever appeared on LP before the original 1974 release of this collection—the selection features Walter in his prime, playing alongside Robert Jr. Lockwood and Louis Myers or Luther Tucker on guitar (with Muddy Waters present, on slide, on one indispensable track, "Rock Bottom"), mostly Willie Dixon on bass, and Fred Below on the drums, with Lafayette Leake or Otis Spann on piano. His harp work was never than first rate during the era covered by this collection, and there are some top flight instrumentals featured, but the material (check out "Crazy Legs," with its dazzling interplay between Walter on harp and Louis and Dave Myers on guitars) here also features some of Walter's best singing, including the romantic "One More Chance With You," the quietly raunchy "Temperature," and "Confessin' the Blues." The sound, as is usual on these MCA-Chess reissues, is superb, although certain tracks, such as "I Got to Go," seem slightly compressed. *—Bruce Eder*

★ **His Best (Chess 50th Anniversary Collection)** / Jun. 17, 1997 / MCA/Chess ♦♦♦♦♦
As MCA reconfigures their Chess catalog, this 20-track single-disc compilation now takes the place of their original 12-track *Best of Little Walter* collection, a landmark blues album which had remained in print for over three decades. This collections reprises ten of those seminal tracks (leaving off the echoey "Blue Light" and "You Better Watch Yourself," the latter being available on the two-disc anthology *The Essential Little Walter*) and brings ten others cherry-picked from the catalog to the mix. If you've never experienced the innovative instrumental genius of Little Walter, classics like "Juke," "Off the Wall," "Mean Old World," "Sad Hours," "Blues With a Feeling," "My Babe," "Boom Out Goes the Light," "Last Night," "Mellow Down Easy" and "Roller Coaster" (written by Bo Diddley, who also guests on guitar) will come as a major revelation. These are the recordings that changed the sound and style of blues harmonica forever, and everyone who came after him was as influenced by him as jazz saxophonists were by Charlie Parker. Everyone who fancies themselves a blues harmonica player should have this one in their collection as an textbook instructional tool, while the rest of us can just bask in the glow of his genius. Essential first purchase doesn't even begin to describe it. *—Cub Koda*

Live in the Windy City / Feb. 15, 2000 / Columbia River ♦
This is a rehash of a very bad CD on the Tomato label entitled *Blues Masters.* It consists of extremely lo-fi recordings of Otis Rush and Little Walter performing *separately* with two entirely different backing groups. Purportedly recorded at the Chicago Blues Festival in 1967, the Otis Rush four-song set sounds more like a club recording than an outdoor festival date, but because the sound is so muffled and grainy, it's a tough call. There's only one real blues in the mix: the disc's opener, "It's Hard for Me to Believe, Baby." Otis then whips off two James Brown numbers, "May Be the Last Time" and "I Feel Good," before laying down the jazzy instrumental "Jambo" (here creatively titled "Otis' Blues"). The real heartbreakers come with the four Little Walter tracks. Not only is Walter at the end of the line, attempting to blow harp with a collapsed lung, but he's saddled with the lousiest, no-time-keeping bunch of hippie blues players imaginable. Walter's time gets all over the place on "You're So Fine" (here stupidly retitled "Lovin' You All the Time"), and his version of "Goin' Down Slow" is such a painful portrait of what his life had become that it'll tear your heart out. But he gamely blows with whatever he's got left on "Walter's Blues" and "Watermelon Man" (here retitled "Blue Mood"). For completists only. *—Cub Koda*

Blue Midnight / Le Roi du Blues ♦♦♦♦♦
It's hard to determine the worth of Le Roi du Blues Little Walter rarity compilations these days. Not only has much of the material been reissued on CD; it's sometimes hard to determine what's been reissued elsewhere and what hasn't, given the minimal differences between some of these alternate takes. It's reasonably certain that *Blue Midnight*, the third and final volume of the series, had the rarest material of the lot, and the most songs that remained unused on Chess' CD compilations. The material is good, but not as impressive as the previous two Le Roi du Blues' volumes (*Blue and Lonesome* and *Southern Feeling*), drawing more from his '60s recordings than the other installments. *—Richie Unterberger*

Little Willie John

b. Nov. 15, 1937, Cullendale, AR, **d.** May 26, 1968, Walla Walla, WA
Vocals / R&B, Soul
He's never received the accolades given to the likes of Sam Cooke, Clyde McPhatter, and James Brown, but Little Willie John ranks as one of R&B's most influential performers. His muscular high timbre and enormous technical and emotional range belied his young age (his first hit came when he was 18), but his mid-'50s work for Syd Nathan's King label would play a great part in the way soul music would sound. Everyone from Cooke, McPhatter, and Brown to Jackie Wilson, B.B. King, and Al Green has acknowledged his debt to this most overlooked of rock and soul pioneers. His debut recording, a smoking version of Titus Turner's "All Around the World" from 1955, set the pattern for a remarkable string of hits: "Need Your Love So Bad," "Suffering with the Blues," "Fever," "Let Them Talk," and his last, "Sleep," from 1961. His version of "Fever" was copied note for note by Peggy Lee and Elvis Presley, both of whom had bigger hits with it; John's version, however, remains definitive. His second hit, "Need Your Love So Bad," contains one of the most intimate, tear-jerking vocals ever caught on tape.

John had a volatile temper, fueled by a taste for liquor and an insecurity regarding his slight height (five feet, four inches). He was known to pack a gun and knife; in 1964, he stabbed a man and was sent to the Washington State Penitentiary, where he died of pneumonia in 1968. James Brown recorded a tribute album to John that year, and his material has been recorded by scores of artists from the Beatles to Fleetwood Mac to the Blasters. Nevertheless, Little Willie John remains a stranger to most listeners and has never received the respect his talent deserves.

Little Willie John was one of the first artists featured in Rhino's King reissues series. *Fever* was issued late in 1993, and the single-disc, 20-track anthology included such John releases as "Need Your Love So Bad," "Suffering With the Blues," and the title cut. *—John Floyd*

Talk to Me / 1959 / Sing ♦♦♦♦♦
The reissue of John's second King album includes the title hit, "Person to Person," and the exquisite "There Is Someone in This World for Me." *—John Floyd*

Mister Little Willie John / 1960 / King ♦♦♦♦♦
His third King long-player is one of the '50s finest albums. "You're a Sweetheart" is an R&B landmark. *—John Floyd*

Sure Things / 1961 / King ♦♦♦
Another vintage reissue, it features his gorgeous reading of Billy Eckstine's "A Cottage for Sale" and the original version of "I'm Shakin'," which The Blasters covered on their debut. *—John Floyd*

● **Fever: The Best of Little Willie John** / Nov. 16, 1993 / Rhino ♦♦♦♦♦
Little Willie John had a commanding delivery, remarkable projection and a charismatic sound that was both instantly recognizable and unforgettable. His magical singles are all contained on this superb 20-track anthology, arguably the best single-disc set of John material available. It includes his best-known song, "Fever" (Peggy Lee's cover version became a huge smash), plus such marvelous numbers such as "Home at Last," "Heartbreak (It's Hurtin' Me)" and "You Hurt Me." While John was a dynamic heartache wailer, he could also do excellent dance/novelty and double entendre tunes such as "Let's Rock While the Rockin's Good" and "Leave My Kitten Alone." This anthology demonstrates why he's still held in such high regard throughout the world of R&B and soul. *—Ron Wynn*

Greatest Hits / Jan. 1, 1996 / King ♦♦♦♦
This brief CD cuts to the chase of Little Willie John, the legendary diminutive soul singer who left us much too soon. The songs "Fever," "All Around the World," "I Need Your Love So Bad," "Talk to Me, Talk to Me," "Let Them Talk," and "Sleep," are as compelling now as when they were first released. Sam Cooke, among others, borrowed from Little Willie John's delivery. Pain was his game; every note bursts on your heart like a giant teardrop. His voice, filled with ache and anguish, never fails to make you feel the abject hurt expressed from the depths of a troubled, but gifted soul. *—Andrew Hamilton*

The Very Best of Little Willie John / Oct. 9, 2001 / Collectables ♦♦♦♦
Collectables' *The Very Best of Little Willie John* gathers most of the influential R&B singer's definitive tracks, including "Fever," "Talk to Me, Talk to Me," "Leave My Kitten Alone," "All Around the World," "I'm Shakin'," and "Let Them Talk." Very nearly as good as Rhino's *Fever: The Very Best of Little Willie John*, this collection is a solid introduction to John's powerful voice and eclectic singles. *—Heather Phares*

The Early King Sessions / Jun. 11, 2002 / Ace ♦♦♦♦
A career-spanning best-of compilation will be a satisfactory helping of Little Willie John for most listeners. But for devoted fans of the singer, and indeed of '50s R&B in general, this more specialized anthology is useful, gathering both sides of all 12 of his first singles, all originally issued in 1955-1957. The only really well-known songs here are the original version of "Fever," "All Around the World" (adapted by Little Milton into "Grits Ain't Groceries," his '60s soul hit), and "Need Your Love So Bad," and they are the best tunes on this collection. John's vocals are uniformly rich and moving, but the material is just too similar to place it in the same league as recordings during the same era by, say, Ray Charles. Still, these are sides in which you can hear R&B, blues, rock & roll, and bits of pop (particularly in "Fever" and its sound-alike follow-up, "My Nerves") coming together in a form that hints at early soul, on songs that were more apt to dip into minor keys than much other R&B of the time. Hardcore completists will note that the version of "I'm Sticking With You Baby" is actually a different take that eventually showed up on an LP, and not the one from the original 45. *—Richie Unterberger*

Little Willie Littlefield

b. Sep. 16, 1931, El Campo, TX
Vocals, Piano / Jump Blues, West Coast Blues, Boogie-Woogie, Piano Blues, R&B
Before he was 21 years old, Texas-born pianist Little Willie Littlefield had etched an all-time classic into the blues lexicon. Only trouble was, his original 1952 waxing of "Kansas City" (here titled "K.C. Loving") didn't sell sufficiently to show up on the charts (thus leaving the door open for Wilbert Harrison to invade the airwaves with the ubiquitous Jerry Leiber/Mike Stoller composition seven years later).

Influenced by Albert Ammons, Charles Brown, and Amos Milburn, Little Willie was already a veteran of the R&B recording wars by the time he waxed "K.C. Loving," having made his debut 78 in 1948 for Houston-based Eddie's Records while still in his teens. After a few sides for Eddie's and Freedom, he moved over to the Bihari brothers' Los Angeles-headquartered Modern logo in 1949. There he immediately hit paydirt with two major R&B hits, "It's Midnight" and "Farewell" (he added another chart entry, "I've Been Lost," in 1951).

Littlefield proved a sensation upon moving to L.A. during his Modern tenure, playing at area clubs and touring with a band that included saxist Maxwell Davis. At Littlefield's first L.A. session for King's Federal subsidiary in 1952, he cut "K.C. Loving" (with Davis on sax), but neither it nor several fine Federal follow-ups returned the boogie piano specialist to the charts.

Other than a few 1957-1958 singles for Oakland's Rhythm logo, little was heard from Little Willie Littlefield until the late '70s, when he began to mount a comeback at various festivals and on the European circuit. While overseas, he met a Dutch woman, married her, and settled in the Netherlands, where he remains active musically. *—Bill Dahl*

Jump With Little Willie Littlefield / 1949-1957 / Ace ✦✦✦✦

It's Midnight / 1979 / Route 66 ✦✦✦✦✦

Although it may be a little hard to find, *It's Midnight* is a valuable collection that contains the highlights from Little Willie Littlefield's recordings for Modern and Federal between 1949 and 1957. These recordings capture Littlefield at his best, rocking through a number of jump blues, R&B and blues songs, including "K.C. Loving," "It's Midnight," "Farewell," and "I've Been Lost." It's an excellent collection that should be reissued on compact disc. *—Thom Owens*

Going Back to Kay Cee / Feb. 7, 1995 / Ace ✦✦✦✦✦

Littlefield's stint with Federal was brief (1952-1954), and not nearly as commercially successful as his time with Modern prior to that. Nonetheless he did a good amount of recording in that period, from which 19 tracks emerged to form this CD retrospective of his Federal years. It, together with Ace's slightly more extensive overview of Littlefield's Modern era, *Kat on the Keys*, forms a satisfying document of his most productive years. The Modern stuff is a little more well-known, and though it's a close call as to which disc is better (not that you can't get both), the nod might go to *Going Back to Kay Cee* by a whisker, if only for the inclusion of Littlefield's most famous recording, the 1953 single "K.C. Lovin'." This is the original model for the song that would be adapted into Wilbert Harrison's number one hit "Kansas City" and become a rock standard. Of course Federal wanted to milk that cow as much as it could, which is why a take of "K.C. Lovin'" was overdubbed with rockier instrumentation and retitled "Kansas City" on a 1959 single. That "Kansas City" single (which is actually not at all bad) is here too, along with a few "Kansas City" soundalikes. Actually, however, this is a pretty strong and (for the early-'50s piano blues genre) a fairly diverse set, including a couple of vocal duets with Little Esther and one with Lil Greenwood; some effectively brooding, but not dragging, blues such as "Blood Is Redder Than Wine"; and the strikingly unusual "(Please Don't Go) O-O-O-Oh," where Littlefield adopts an effective and unique gargling vocal style. Littlefield's vocals are wise and aged beyond his years, and his piano playing is fine throughout; the instrumental showcase for his boogie "Jim Wilson's Boogie" is superb. *—Richie Unterberger*

● **Kat on the Keys** / Nov. 23, 1999 / Ace ✦✦✦✦✦

This is a 25-song compilation drawn from Littlefield's output for Modern between 1949 and 1952, including the sole hit he scored for that label, "It's Midnight (No Place to Go)." Littlefield is somewhat more obscure than many other artists mining a similar blues/R&B crossover field in Los Angeles studios in the early '50s, such as Charles Brown, Amos Milburn, and Floyd Dixon. On the basis of the music here, Littlefield deserves to be in the same echelon as the aforementioned performers. He was a fine pianist who was skilled in the boogie-woogie style and tempered for the times with a modern R&B influence. His use of triplets, according to the liner notes, influenced Fats Domino. He was also more versatile than some piano bluesmen of the era, and was comfortable with slow and melancholy-tinged ballads as well as jumping uptempo R&B tunes (the boasting "I Like It" is a standout). His singing was more easygoing than distinctive, but still had a relaxed charm. Many of the sides here were cut with some of the Los Angeles studio musicians—horn player Maxwell Davis, guitarist Johnny Moore, and others—that were instrumental in setting the paces for the jazzy, urbane R&B music of the early '50s in L.A. The sound is very good, and is mastered from the original acetate lacquers, with only occasional (and slight) surface noise peeping through. The disc includes five previously unissued cuts (three of which are alternate takes). A second volume of Littlefield's Modern sides was in the works from Ace as of the 1999 issue of this collection. *—Richie Unterberger*

Johnny Littlejohn (John Funchess)

b. Apr. 16, 1931, Lake, MS, **d.** Feb. 1, 1994, Chicago, IL

Vocals, Guitar / Electric Chicago Blues

Johnny Littlejohn's stunning mastery of the slide guitar somehow never launched him into the major leagues of bluesdom. Only on a handful of occasions was the Chicago veteran's vicious bottleneck attack captured effectively on wax, but anyone who experienced one of his late-night sessions as a special musical guest on the Windy City circuit will never forget the crashing passion in his delivery.

Delta-bred John Funchess first heard the blues just before he reached his teens at a fish fry where a friend of his father's named Henry Martin was playing guitar. He left home in 1946, pausing in Jackson, MS, Arkansas, and Rochester, NY, before winding up in Gary, IN. In 1951, he began inching his way into the Gary blues scene, his Elmore James-influenced slide style making him a favorite around Chicago's south suburbs in addition to steel mill-fired Gary.

Littlejohn waited an unconscionably long time to wax his debut singles for Margaret (his trademark treatment of Brook Benton's "Kiddio"), T-D-S, and Weis in 1968. But before the year was out, Littlejohn had also cut his debut album, *Chicago Blues Stars*, for Chris Strachwitz's Arhoolie logo. It was a magnificent debut, the guitarist blasting out a savage Chicago/Delta hybrid rooted in the early '50s rather than its actual timeframe.

Unfortunately, a four-song 1969 Chess date remained in the can. After that, another long dry spell preceded Littlejohn's 1985 album *So-Called Friends* for Rooster Blues, an ambitious but not altogether convincing collaboration between the guitarist and a humongous horn section that sometimes grew to eight pieces. The guitarist had been in poor health for some time prior to his 1994 passing. *—Bill Dahl*

● **Chicago Blues Stars** / 1969 / Arhoolie ✦✦✦✦✦

This November 14, 1968, session was recorded in Chicago, co-produced by Chris Strachwitz of Arhoolie Records and Willie Dixon. It's decent, though journeyman, '60s electric Chicago blues augmented by a couple of tenor saxes. Littlejohn has a pleasant voice and is a skilled guitarist, but does not have the fire or individuality that leaps from some of the musicians to whom one might compare him. Those might include figures like Buddy Guy, say, or Elmore James' more fully produced sides, or on something like "Catfish Blues," the Muddy Waters approach. Littlejohn did write most of the dozen tunes, interspersed with covers of songs by James, Dixon, Brook Benton (a refreshingly unusual choice for a mainstream '60s Chicago bluesman), and J.B. Lenoir. *—Richie Unterberger*

Funky from Chicago / Sep. 1974 / BluesWay ✦✦✦

So-Called Friends / 1985 / Rooster Blues ✦✦✦

Surrounding Littlejohn with a huge horn section probably wasn't the greatest idea in retrospect; the booming brass detracts at times from his pungent slide work, rather than enhancing it. But hearty renditions of his signature "Chips Flying Everywhere," and a sturdy "She's Too Much," and several songs written by bassist Aron Burton recommend the vinyl-only LP nonetheless. *—Bill Dahl*

Johnny Littlejohn's Blues Party / May 1991 / Wolf ✦✦✦

When Your Best Friends Turn Their Back on You / 1993 / JSP ✦✦✦

Dream / 1995 / Storyville ✦✦✦

Recorded live on the West Side of Chicago in 1976, this disc is an excellent document of Littlejohn's live show. What his husky, passionate vocal delivery lacks in grace, it makes up in honesty. And his guitar and slide playing are both strong. Much of the disc focuses on slow blues weepers, with the exception of a few jump tunes, like Littlejohn's own "Kiddeo." A smoky, deep-blue piece of work. *—Tim Sheridan*

Slidin' Home / Aug. 18, 2001 / Arhoolie ✦✦✦✦✦

Slidin' Home is a reissue of the November 14, 1968 session originally released as *Chicago Blues Stars* in 1969. *—Richie Unterberger*

Paula Lockheart

Vocals / Contemporary Blues, Jazz Blues

Paula Lockheart is a talented and interesting vocalist, songwriter, and interpreter of classic blues and jazz. Her influences include Bessie Smith, Dinah Washington, Alberta Hunter, and Joe Williams. Paula's recordings generally feature topflight musicians backing her sexy, stylized, understated vocal mannerisms in a variety of settings from solo guitar accompaniment to horn-driven big band in full swing. She has performed regularly in and around New York City, along with festival appearances and tours of the U.S., Canada, and Europe. Paula has performed and recorded with, among others, John Hammond, David Bromberg, and Dr. John. She was nominated for a W. C. Handy Blues Award in 1982 and a New York City Music Award in 1986. *—Niles J. Frantz*

Paula Lockheart With Peter Ecklund & Friends / 1977 / Flying Fish ✦✦✦

This is a strong debut album. *—AMG*

It Ain't the End of the World / 1979 / Flying Fish ✦✦✦

This expressive singer uses a mixture of blues and rock. *—AMG*

● **The Incomplete** / 1980 / Flying Fish ✦✦✦✦

This best-of collection features cuts from her other three Flying Fish releases and is the most effective showcase of her versatility and consistent quality. *—Niles J. Frantz*

Voo-It / 1987 / Flying Fish ✦✦✦

Robert Jr. Lockwood

b. Mar. 27, 1915, Turkey Scratch, AR

Vocals, Arranger, Harmonica, Guitar / Delta Blues, Prewar Country Blues, Electric Delta Blues, Acoustic Blues, Chicago Blues

Robert Jr. Lockwood learned his blues first-hand from an unimpeachable source: the immortal Robert Johnson. Lockwood can still conjure up the bone-chilling Johnson sound whenever he so desires, but he's never been one to linger in the past for long—which accounts for the jazzy swing he often brings to the licks he plays on his 12-string electric guitar.

Now in his mid-eighties, Lockwood is one of the last living links to the glorious Johnson legacy. When Lockwood's mother became romantically involved with the charismatic rambler in Helena, AR, the quiet teenager suddenly gained a role model and a close friend—so close that Lockwood considered himself Johnson's stepson. Robert Jr. learned how to play guitar very quickly with Johnson's expert help, assimilating Johnson's technique inside and out.

Following Johnson's tragic murder in 1938, Lockwood embarked on his own intriguing musical journey. He was among the first bluesmen to score an electric guitar in 1938 and eventually made his way to Chicago, where he cut four seminal tracks for Bluebird. Jazz elements steadily crept into Lockwood's dazzling fretwork, although his role as Sonny Boy Williamson's musical partner on the fabled KFFA *King Biscuit Time* radio broadcasts during the early '40s out of Helena, AR, probably didn't emphasize that side of his dexterity all that much.

Settling in Chicago in 1950, Lockwood swiftly gained a reputation as a versatile in-demand studio sideman, recording behind harp genius Little Walter, piano masters Sunnyland Slim and Eddie Boyd, and plenty more. Solo recording opportunities were scarce, though Lockwood did cut fine singles for Mercury in 1951 ("I'm Gonna Dig Myself a Hole" and a very early "Dust My Broom") and JOB in 1955 ("Sweet Woman from Maine"/"Aw Aw Baby").

Lockwood's best modern work as a leader was done for Pete Lowry's Trix label, including some startling workouts on the 12-string axe that he daringly added to his arsenal in 1965. He later joined forces with fellow Johnson disciple Johnny Shines for two eclectic early-'80s Rounder albums. Intent on satisfying his own instincts first and foremost, the sometimes taciturn Lockwood is a priceless connection between past and present. *—Bill Dahl*

Steady Rollin' Man / Aug. 12, 1970-Aug. 1970 / Delmark ♦♦♦
Sophisticated, mellow set cut in 1970 that occasionally gets a little too laidback. Lockwood's complex lead guitar work and aged-in-the-wood vocals are a delight, but guitarist Louis Myers asserts himself as soloist more than he should have in such a situation, making one yearn for more Robert Jr. riffs. *—Bill Dahl*

Contrasts / 1974 / Trix ♦♦♦♦♦
Robert Jr. Lockwood has never been a conventional musician or blues artist. This was one of a pair of spectacular albums done for Trix in the '70s. Johnson's version of "Driving Wheel" maintains the spirit of Roosevelt Sykes' familiar rendition, but has his own compelling twists. Otherwise, the session featured Lockwood songs, and he demonstrated the probing, animated qualities that made him a legend and a survivor. *—Ron Wynn*

Blues Live in Japan / 1975 / Advent ♦♦♦
Recorded in concert at Tokyo's Yubin Chokin Hall on November 27th and 28th, 1974, this teams Lockwood with the Aces (Louis Myers on guitar and harmonica, brother Dave on bass and Fred Below on drums), who backed him so splendidly on Delmark's *Steady Rollin' Man* album. Kicking off with "Sweet Home Chicago," the interplay between Lockwood and Myers is both empathetic and respectful of each other's space. A jazzy "Going Down Slow" and a Robert Johnson-style "Worried Life Blues" are next, setting the stage for Louis Myers' slide work on "Anna Lee" and Mercy Dee's "One Room Country Shack." Lockwood returns center stage on a great version of "Stormy Monday" and his own "Feel All Right Again" before mixing it up with the Aces on "Honky Tonk." The album closes with great versions of "Mean Black Spider" and the encore, "Little and Low," on which Myers blows harp with great passion. The response from the Japanese crowd is so overwhelming that you actually feel the musicians being swept away by it all (the usually taciturn Lockwood even acknowledges this before the encore in his usual phlegmatic way), a sure sign of emotions running rampant and one great live session as a result of it. *—Cub Koda*

Does 12 / 1977 / Trix ♦♦♦♦
The liner notes kick off with the claim that this blues guitarist is different than many others because he, unlike them, "is into musical evolution." The proof would be in the pudding, as just about everything involving this session has something to do with pushing at boundaries, not playing the blues in the same old way. To start, he focuses on the 12-string guitar, which—lovely as it is—has been as popular in blues as the zither, with the exception of a few stray 12-bangers in the hands of players such as Blind Willie McTell. Anyone who has ever tried to play a blues-style "bend" on a 12-string will understand why. If that isn't enough, Lockwood assembles a band that is able to bring jazz and rhythm & blues influences in, giving the music an ultra-expansive feel. The presence of a Robert Johnson cover followed by one by soul-bop saxophonist Gene Ammons pretty much sums it up. The leader does some sharp playing and, although his sidekicks aren't quite on his level, they certainly don't do anything to seriously hinder the music. Lockwood continued bouncing back and forth between this style of playing and the more traditional, but may not have nailed it all so perfectly again as he did on this date. *—Eugene Chadbourne*

Hangin' On / 1979 / Rounder ♦♦♦
Two of the principal keepers of the Robert Johnson flame joined forces for a Rounder LP that's stunning in its non-conformity to what purists might like to hear from the two veterans. Jazz and swing influences invest much of the LP, the pair sharing vocal and guitar duties. *—Bill Dahl*

Mr. Blues Is Back to Stay / 1980 / Rounder ♦♦♦
Another pairing of the venerable Delta blues vets, and it's even less traditional than their previous outing. Utilizing a jazz-steeped two-piece sax section, Lockwood swings with impugnity. Shines had recently suffered a serious stroke that left him unable to play guitar, so his contributions are limited to vocals only. *—Bill Dahl*

● **Plays Robert and Robert** / Nov. 28, 1982 / Evidence ♦♦♦♦♦
Lockwood in a beautifully recorded solo context (cut in France in 1982 for Black & Blue), doing what he does best—his own songs and those of his legendary mentor, Robert Johnson. Purists may quiver at Lockwood's use of the 12-string guitar as his primary axe, but he long ago made the instrument his own blues tool of choice, and he handles its nuances expertly. *—Bill Dahl*

Robert Lockwood / 1991 / Paula ♦♦♦♦♦
All 20 of these tracks were recorded for JOB in the early '50s, but only half feature Lockwood; the others are Johnny Shines solo sides. The title is a bit misleading; the Lockwood tracks, recorded in 1951 and 1955, mix genuine Lockwood solo performances with sides on which he supported Sunnyland Slim and Alfred Wallace. It's decent sparse, early Chicago blues, though not as good as the preceding Shines tracks on the disc. *—Richie Unterberger*

I Got to Find Me a Woman / Mar. 17, 1998 / Verve ♦♦♦♦♦
These 14 tracks, cut in 1996 when Lockwood was 81 years old, are among the most accessible music that he has ever laid down. Had this record—with its mix of spare, raw solos and duets juxtaposed with full band pieces that thunder quietly or roar loud and clear—come out in the late '60s, it might have been as big and important a record as anything cut by Muddy Waters (maybe more, since Waters didn't get to make albums as strong and straightforward as this until the '70s). Lockwood's playing (accompanied by B.B. King on two tracks) on six- or 12-string, electric or acoustic, is bold yet articulate. His singing is unrivaled, recalling Waters at his late-career peak in expressiveness if not power. The band backing him up really rocks, especially Richard Smith's electric bass, which anchors the rhythm section. Most of the tracks are Lockwood originals, juxtaposed with new interpretations of songs by Robert Johnson, Roosevelt Sykes, Leroy Carr, et al., but his numbers don't suffer at all from the presence of those classics. *—Bruce Eder*

Complete Trix Recordings / Feb. 23, 1999 / 32 Jazz ♦♦♦
A two-CD re-release of some of Lockwood's works recorded in the early to mid-'70s. The first CD is the bluesier of the two, while the second has more R&B romps. Lockwood's fine guitar and vocals are showcased throughout this collection. The *Complete Trix Recordings* features 25 tracks, including "Little Boy Blue" and several Robert Johnson tunes. This stuff is fun, but only in small dosages. *—Tim Griggs*

Just the Blues / Jul. 13, 1999 / Bullseye Blues & Jazz ♦♦♦
This brings together all the Lockwood-fronted tracks from his two Rounder albums with Johnny Shines. Lockwood shines on a brace of originals that range from jazzy to bluesy to proto-funk ("Here It Is, Brother") as well as tackling everything from Larry Darnell's swinging "For You My Love" to Leroy Carr's "Mean Mistreater." Featuring Lockwood in duo settings with Shines and with a full band of Cleveland regulars, this is a nice sampling of one of the blues' most exploratory musicians. *—Cub Koda*

Delta Crossroads / 2000 / Telarc ♦♦♦♦
For *Delta Crossroads*, Robert Jr. Lockwood, a former student of Robert Johnson, returns to his Delta blues roots. This 16-track album features Lockwood with only his 12-string acoustic guitar. It is rather strange hearing old Delta blues sung by one of its originals on a modern recording. All of the notes from the guitar are clear. Plus, his voice isn't scuffed up by the scratches and pop of the vinyl recording. Lockwood plays a mix of Robert Johnson tunes, a few of his own, and some blues standards including "C.C. Rider." With its high production quality and Lockwood's unique and possibly near-extinct style of singing, *Delta Crossroads* is a strong testament to the endurance of a Delta blues original. *—Curtis Zimmermann*

Cripple Clarence Lofton (Albert Clemens)

b. Mar. 28, 1887, Kingsport, TN, **d.** Jan. 9, 1957, Chicago, IL
Vocals, Piano / Piano Blues, Boogie-Woogie
Cripple Clarence Lofton is one of those colorful names that adorned many an album collection of early boogie-woogie piano 78s in the early days of the '60s folk-blues revival. An early practitioner of the form, along with his fellow contemporaries Cow Cow Davenport, Meade "Lux" Lewis, Pinetop Smith, and Jimmy Yancey, Lofton was one of the originators who spread the word in Chicago in the early '20s.

The physically challenged nicknamed he used—seen by modern audiences as a tad exploitative, to say the least—was a bit of a ringer. Although he suffered a birth defect in his leg that made him walk with a pronounced limp, it certainly didn't stop him from becoming an excellent tap dancer, his original ticket into show business. He quickly developed a stage act that consisted of pounding out the boogie-woogie on the piano while standing up, dancing, whistling, and vocalizing while—as one old bluesman put it—"carrying on a lotta racket." Lofton's technique—or lack of it—stemmed more from a tent show background and those listening to his earliest and most energetic recordings will quickly attest that hitting every note or making every chord change precisely were not exactly high priorities with him. But this wild, high energy act got the young showman noticed quickly and by the early '30s, he was so much a fixture of Chicago night life firmament that he had his own Windy City nightclub, the oddly named Big Apple. Lofton remained on the scene, cutting sides for the Gennett, Vocalion, Solo Art, Riverside, Session and Pax labels into the '40s. When the boogie-woogie craze cooled off and eventually died down in the late '40s, Lofton went into early retirement, staying around Chicago until his death in 1957 from a blood clot in the brain. *—Cub Koda*

Honky-Tonk and Boogie-Woogie Piano / 1954 / Riverside ♦♦♦

Cripple Clarence Lofton / Jul. 14, 1954 / Riverside ♦♦♦

Cripple Lofton & Walter Davis / 1971 / Yazoo ♦♦♦♦♦
Marvelous blues piano and singing from Cripple Clarence Lofton, and nearly as fine an effort from Walter Davis. *—Ron Wynn*

● **Complete Recorded Works, Vol. 1 (1935–1939)** / 1991 / RST ♦♦♦♦♦
Some of Lofton's best, with the selections "Strut That Thing," "Monkey Man Blues," and "Pitchin' Boogie" being particular standouts. (Import) *—Cub Koda*

Complete Recorded Works, Vol. 2 (1939–1943) / Jan. 10, 1991 / Document ♦♦♦
Complete Works, Vol. 2 (1939-1943) continues Document's exhaustive overview of Cripple Clarence Lofton's recordings. As with the other installments, the disc features some classic performances, long running time, exacting chronological sequencing, and poor fidelity (all cuts are transferred from original acetates and 78s). The serious blues listener will find all these factors to be positive, but enthusiasts and casual listeners will find that the collection is of marginal interest. *—Thom Owens*

John "Juke" Logan

Vocals, Keyboards, Harmonica / Electric Harmonica Blues, Modern Electric Blues
Although John "Juke" Logan is not yet a household name, you've probably heard his harmonica without knowing it. His harp has appeared on television in the themes of *Home Improvement* and *Roseanne*, on the big screen with *Crossroads* and *La Bamba*, and even in commercials for Jack-in-the-Box and Cherry Coke. Yet beneath the studio musician lies a composer whose talents have been exposed by John Mayall, with "Fanning the Flames," and harp player Gary Primach with "The Sound of Money Talkin'" and "Hustler."

Among Logan's early breaks were working as a road musician with Dobie Gray and a four-year stint with Leon Russell, including Russell's New Grass Revival. In the late '80s, he worked with ex-Blaster Dave Alvin and his Allnighters Band. Through his association with Ry Cooder on the soundtracks for *Streets of Fire* and *Crossroads*, Logan moved into the studio world. Around Los Angeles, he has shared the airwaves with co-host Ellen Bloom on their weekly radio show, *The Friday Night Blues Revue*. After years of studio work, Logan released *The Chill* in 1995 and *Juke Rhythm* in 1998, both reflecting his love for the blues. A live album followed in 1999, *Live as It Gets. —Char Ham*

● **The Chill** / 1995 / Razor & Tie ✦✦✦✦

Juke Rhythm / Jun. 22, 1999 / Mocombo ✦✦✦✦
Again, Logan stretches the genre far beyond its musical boundaries, both as exploring hip hop territory in "Da Blues Hip Hop," and the album's theme as blues as cultural diversity. Thoughtful creative juices water the appetite with issues ranging from analyzing the conflicts in Washington, D.C., to redefining the adage "look before you leap." Ever the witty lyricist, he weaves jazz idioms in "Dancing on the Edge of a Razorblade." *—Char Ham*

Live as It Gets / Jul. 13, 1999 / Mocombo ✦✦✦
This live recording was done at one of their many gigs at B.B. King's in Universal City-walk in California, but a listener could almost swear it was recorded on high-end equipment in the coziness of his or her Uncle Frank's living room. These gentlemen, known for their solo work, dissipate fears of swollen egos from such super ventures. With the exception of one standard, all selections come from either artist's pen and although not originally written for a duo setting, they seem tailor-made for such an arrangement. If the listener thinks at the end that he or she has accidently hit the "repeat" mode on the CD remote box when hearing strains of the first song, it's a prank by two kids at heart. *—Char Ham*

Lonesome Sundown (Cornelius Green)

b. Dec. 12, 1928, Donaldsville, LA, d. Apr. 23, 1995, Gonzales, LA
Vocals, Guitar / Swamp Blues, Louisiana Blues
Unlike many of his swamp blues brethren, the evocatively monickered Lonesome Sundown (the name was an inspired gift from producer J.D. Miller) wasn't a Jimmy Reed disciple. Sundown's somber brand of blues was more in keeping with the gruff sound of Muddy Waters. The guitarist was one of the most powerful members of Miller's south Louisiana stable, responsible for several seminal swamp standards on Excello Records.

The former Cornelius Green first seriously placed his hands on a guitar in 1950, Waters and Hooker providing early inspiration. Zydeco pioneer Clifton Chenier hired the guitarist as one of his two axemen (Phillip Walker being the other) in 1955. A demo tape was enough proof for Miller—he began producing him in 1956, leasing the freshly renamed Sundown's "Leave My Money Alone" to Excello.

There were plenty more where that one came from. Over the next eight years, Sundown's lowdown Excello output included "My Home Is a Prison," "I'm a Mojo Man," "I Stood By," "I'm a Samplin' Man," and a host of memorable swamp classics preceded his 1965 retirement from the blues business to devote his life to the church. It was 1977 before Sundown could be coaxed back into a studio to cut a blues LP; *Been Gone Too Long*, co-produced by Bruce Bromberg and Dennis Walker for the Joliet imprint, was an excellent comeback entry but did disappointing sales (even after being reissued on Alligator). Scattered live performances were about all that was heard of the swamp blues master after that. *—Bill Dahl*

Lonesome Lonely Blues / 1970 / Excello ✦✦✦

Been Gone Too Long / 1977 / Hightone ✦✦✦
The Louisiana blues vet's 1977 comeback album was a well-done affair, capturing some of the flavor of his '50s material (but with a modern edge). Producers Bruce Bromberg and Dennis Walker (who doubled on bass) recruited guitarist Phillip Walker, a longtime Sundown cohort, to handle some of the fret load, and the predominantly original songlist was worthy of Sundown's lowdown sound. *—Bill Dahl*

Lonesome Sundown / 1990 / Flyright ✦✦✦✦
Twenty-one sides for producer J.D. Miller's Crowley, LA vaults, dominated by alternate takes of the guitarist's best-known sides and some otherwise unreleased numbers. Backing musicians include keyboardist Katie Webster, harpist Lazy Lester, and drummer Warren Storm. Tough stuff! *—Bill Dahl*

● **I'm a Mojo Man: The Best of the Excello Singles** / 1995 / Ace ✦✦✦✦✦
One of the swamp blues stalwarts in south Louisiana producer J.D. Miller's stable receives the deluxe treatment with a 24-song anthology spanning his 1956-1964 Excello tenure. Sundown's sparse, nasty sound was influenced by Muddy Waters as much as the prevailing bayou beat, giving an extra discernible tang to his "Leave My Money Alone," "My Home Is My Prison," and the title cut. *—Bill Dahl*

Clarence Lonnie

Piano / Piano Blues
Although one of the earliest pianists to record in the newly energized postwar electric blues style, this artist apparently did not follow the great harmonica player and bandleader Sonny Boy Williamson to Chicago, and the prolific recording activity that was waiting there. He appears only on the very early tracks by the blues harp man, originally broadcast over the *King Biscuit Flour Hour*. At this stage of the game, the presence of a piano in a blues combo was something new, having been heard since the '20s as a solo instrument or accompanying female classic blues singers. Lonnie dropped out of sight after leaving the Williamson band, never developing the powerful style of later players such as Otis Spann. *—Eugene Chadbourne*

Big Joe Louis & His Blues Kings

Group / Blues Revival
Playing and writing electric blues in the mold of the classic '50s Chess Records prototype, Big Joe Louis and his crew suffer the same mixed blessing common to many White (and some British) blues bands. Their command of their instruments and genuine love of the music is offset by mediocre if energetic vocals (from guitarist/singer Louis) and a revivalist mindset that recreates with precision, but lacks original vision. They get credit for writing most of the material on their 1996 CD, *Big Sixteen*, and executing it with assured competence, though they fall into the huge category of bands that could produce a high old time seen live, but aren't anything special on disc. *—Richie Unterberger*

● **Big Sixteen** / 1996 / Ace ✦✦✦✦
Fair modern white blues, distinguished from the bar-band norm by arrangements which consciously echo vintage Chess Records, down to the standup bass and Little George Sueref's able approximations of Little Walter's harmonica style. *—Richie Unterberger*

Big Joe Louis & His Blues Kings/The Stars in the Sky / Jun. 26, 2002 / Ace ✦✦✦✦

Joe Hill Louis (Lester Hill)

b. Sep. 23, 1921, Raines, TN, d. Aug. 5, 1957, Memphis, TN
Vocals, Drums, Harmonica, Guitar / Electric Memphis Blues
Joe Hill Louis created quite a racket as a popular one-man blues band around Memphis during the '50s. If not for his tragic premature demise, his name would surely be more widely revered.

Lester (or Leslie) Hill ran away from home at age 14, living instead with a well-heeled Memphis family. A fight with another youth that was won by young Hill earned him the "Joe Louis" appellation. Harp came first for the multi-instrumentalist; by the late '40s, his one-man musical attack was a popular attraction in Handy Park and on WDIA, the groundbreaking Memphis radio station where he hosted a 15-minute program billed as *The Pepticon Boy*.

Also known as the Be-Bop Boy, Louis made his recording debut in 1949 for Columbia, but the remainder of his output was issued on R&B indies large and small: Phillips (Sam Phillips' first extremely short-lived logo), Modern, Sun, Checker, Meteor, Big Town (where he cut the blistering "Hydramatic Woman," a tune he'd cut previously for Sun in 1953 with Walter Horton on harp, but Phillips never released it), and House of Sound. Louis was only 35 when he died of tetanus, contracted when a deep gash on his thumb became infected. *—Bill Dahl*

The One Band Band / Sep. 1972 / Muskadine ✦✦✦

● **The Be-Bop Boy With Walter Horton and Mose Vinson** / 1992 / Bear Family ✦✦✦✦✦
Raw, chaotic, one-man band blues of the highest order. Highlights include the original version of "Tiger Man," and Louis' scorching lead guitar work on "She Treats Me Mean and Evil." Compiling virtually all the recordings he made for Sam Phillips in Memphis in the early '50s, this CD also features astonishing harmonica work from Big Walter Horton on several tracks. (Import) *—Cub Koda*

Boogie in the Park / Jun. 12, 2001 / Ace ✦✦✦✦
Everything that Joe Hill Louis recorded for Modern and Meteor in the early '50s is on this 28-track compilation. That includes singles, scattered cuts that would first show up on numerous anthologies on different labels years after they were recorded, and a previously unissued alternate take of "At the Woodchopper's Ball (Jack Pot)." Virtually all of Louis' Sam Phillips-produced sides are here, and there's even an extensive interview with Phillips in the liner notes. Most of the Phillips material is one-man blues, stuff that in its way reflects the transition from country blues to electric blues and rock & roll. Perhaps it's heretical to say so, but some of this might have been better served by a full band. Louis was a sturdy, engagingly good-natured singer and decent electric guitarist and harmonica player, capable of dishing out some good instrumental boogies once in a while as well. But the rhythm, supplied by hi-hat and bass drum, is perfunctory in both its texture and power. In fact, one of the Phillips-overseen songs (Sonny Boy Williamson's "Eyesight to the Blind") does add piano and drums, and some of the 1953 Meteor tracks got bass and drum overdubs. At any rate, it's decent early electric Memphis blues and the one-man multi-instrumentalist approach does set it off from the pack a bit, although the songs are more limited in musical range and adventurousness than those of the best Memphis bluesmen who followed in the next few years. *—Richie Unterberger*

Louisiana Red (Iverson Minter)

b. Mar. 23, 1936, Vicksburg, MS
Vocals, Harmonica, Guitar / Modern Electric Blues, Acoustic Blues, Slide Guitar Blues
Louisiana Red (born Iverson Minter) is a flamboyant guitarist, harmonica player, and vocalist. He lost his parents early in life through multiple tragedies; his mother died of pneumonia a week after his birth, and his father was lynched by the Ku Klux Klan when he was five. Red began recording for Chess in 1949, then joined the army. After his discharge, he played with John Lee Hooker in Detroit for almost two years in the late '50s. He maintained a busy recording and performing schedule through the '90s and into the 2000s, having done sessions for Chess, Checker, Atlas, Glover, Roulette, L&R, and Tomato among others. *—Ron Wynn*

● **Lowdown Back Porch Blues** / 1963 / Collectables ✦✦✦✦✦
Recorded in New York with Tommy Tucker, *Lowdown Back Porch Blues* is Louisiana Red's first album and, in many ways, it's his best. Supported by a bare-bones rhythm section, Red plays a number of traditional tunes and originals. His guitar is nearly as powerful and overwhelming as his vocals, making this a truly compelling listen. *—Thom Owens*

Louisiana Red Sings the Blues / 1972 / Atlantic ✦✦✦

Sweet Blood Call / 1975 / Blue Labor ✦✦✦✦✦
At the time this album was recorded, the particularly intense blues artist Louisiana Red

was a protégé of the Blue Labor/Labor recording empire, which was actually two guys, Kent Cooper and jazz arranger and composer Heiner Stadler. Cooper's involvement with Red led, as in many cases of blues producers and their clients, to co-authorship on some of the songs recorded. Cooper and Stadler regarded Red as an artist cut from the same cloth as John Lee Hooker or Lightnin' Hopkins, and of the same quality—meaning an intense, mood-setter of a bluesman with a sizzling improvisatory style. They were certainly accurate in their appraisal of his talent, and their interest in recording Red led to several classic blues albums. The fine studio sound they got on these solo recordings makes for a superior album, and it was the first Red would record unencumbered by a combo backing him up. Every nuance of his playing is captured, and he is definitely the type of blues player who thrives on solo work. He rarely sticks to a formula bar structure and likes to stretch out his licks as if casting out a line for fish, but he isn't a player who just stays on one chord like Hooker often did. One of Red's original blues, in which he describes how his wife died of cancer, has got to set some kind of a record for misery described in a blues song, meaning it is the saddest of the sad. *—Eugene Chadbourne*

Midnight Rambler / 1982 / Rhino ♦♦♦

At times harrowing, this is one of Red's more intense efforts. *—Bill Dahl*

Always Played the Blues / Oct. 31, 1994 / JSP ♦♦♦♦

The Best of Louisiana Red / 1995 / Evidence ♦♦♦♦♦

Assembled from tapes recorded in New York City with producer Herb Abramson between 1965 and 1973, *The Best of Louisiana Red* is an ideal introduction to one of the blues' most unique and memorable characters. Never a musical innovator, Red's true gift was instead to absorb the lessons of contemporary greats like Muddy Waters and Elmore James, employing their lyrical and instrumental motifs as a means to forge his own evocative style; James' slide guitar, in particular, haunts cuts like "The Story of Louisiana Red," "Where Is My Friend," and "Freight Train to Ride." Red's lyrics, on the other hand, are startlingly original, his surreal narratives unprecedented in the blues canon; the amazing "Red's Dream" details a journey to the UN to outline a plan to solve the Cuban missile crisis, while its follow-up, "Red's New Dream," portrays its hero as the first blues singer in outer space. *—Jason Ankeny*

Walked All Night Long / Apr. 29, 1997 / Blues Alliance ♦♦♦♦

Walked All Night Long marked the first recorded pairing of blues guitarists Louisiana Red and Lefty Dizz in 1976. Most of the tracks are originals, with the exception of the traditional "Ever Heard a Churchbell Sound" and Slim Harpo's "King Bee." The intensity here is not for the faint of heart, evident on tracks like "Bring Me My Machine Gun," "Stole From Me" (featuring blazing harmonica from Red), "Too Poor to Die," and "Cold White Sheet." The later features piano backup from Kyril Bromley who also appears on two other tracks. If you're a fan of hard-hitting gritty slide guitar with raw emotion, *Walked All Night Long* is a treasure you should search for from the Blues Alliance label. *—Al Campbell*

Blues Spectrum of Louisiana Red / Apr. 7, 1998 / JSP ♦♦♦

Millennium Blues / May 11, 1999 / Earwig ♦♦♦♦♦

It's an event when Iverson Minter, aka Louisiana Red, puts out a recording, but even rarer a date that has Willie "Big Eyes" Smith, an exceptional blues drummer, wailin' on the harmonica! Add bassist Willie Kent, keyboardist Alan Batts, drummer Dave Jefferson, and second guitarist Brian Bisesi for an excellent blues crew. In the middle is Red's gruff vocals and simple, loping guitar, the catalyst for the fireworks on this authentic roots and contemporary Chicago-style blues CD. These are mostly personal songs, reflecting the tragedy and sorrow of Red's childhood, and the injustice of the current world we live in. The first piece, "Red's Vision," speaks of the President's impeachment, churches burning, and memories of Muddy Waters and Lightnin' Hopkins. "That Detroit Thing" recalls his time in the Motor City. "Arlene Blues" asks "what kinda gal are you?" Then you have good-time tunes like "Let Me Be Your Electrician" so "I can turn your power on." There are three instrumentals, the easygoing swing of "Red's Jazz Groove" the "Killin' Floor"-like "Texas Jump," and the Muddy Waters ramblin' rock of the title track. In the middle of the program is an acoustic guitar and vocals-only autobiographical section, with songs about being in an orphanage, a story about old squeeze "Leechie Geddens," and the tale of running away and being "Home in a Rock." These are more in the Leadbelly to Mississippi Fred McDowell bag, and an intriguing change of pace. Red sounds good, the band sounds good, Smith is a surprisingly good harmonica player, and there's no reason why blues fans everywhere won't get next to this CD by a man who intimately knows the blues from a deep, personal perspective, and is not shy about telling you how he feels. Highly recommended. *—Michael G. Nastos*

Live in Montreux / Apr. 15, 2000 / Labor ♦♦♦♦

Recorded live in Switzerland in 1975, here's Louisiana Red performing solo to a wildly appreciative audience. Armed with nothing more than his slide guitar and a voice that consumes most of the space in the mix, Red lays down a set of originals and old standards like Sam Cooke's "Bring It on Home to Me" with equal flair. This is a very inspired performance and one of Red's best albums to date. Highly recommended. *—Cub Koda*

Driftin' / May 22, 2001 / Earwig ♦♦♦♦

Louisiana Red is a versatile performer capable of playing standard electric blues, interacting with his guitar à la Muddy Waters ("Hard Hard Time" is a good example), paying tribute to both B.B. King and Lightnin' Hopkins, or singing a religious hymn ("He Will See You Through"). Whether playing solo or performing as part of a fine blues quintet that includes Willie "Big Eyes" Smith on harmonica, Louisiana Red shows on this CD that he is one of the more significant blues stylists of the early-21st century, performing in each setting and idiom with equal sincerity and skill. Well worth exploring. *—Scott Yanow*

A Different Shade of Red: The Woodstock Sessions / May 7, 2002 / Severn ♦♦♦♦

This raw, extremely eclectic, and quirky disc works on many levels, and the natural energy of Louisiana Red comes through with the high emotion this performer brings to each session. His highly unpredictable guitar playing never fails the song, and in fact adds additional layers by being outside the anticipated (listen to "Where's My Friends?"). His singing is strong and does not always follow what you are expecting. A cut that contains some beautiful vocal work is "Sleep Little Robert." This disc was recorded in Woodstock, NY, at the studio of Levon Helm (the Band). Red is backed by a strong contingent of the musicians who inhabit this celebrated town, including Helm, handling the drums with his usual funk and drive. There is some stellar work by Garth Hudson on organ and sax, David Maxwell on piano and organ, and guitarists Jimmy Vivino and Brian Bisesi on the majority of the cuts. There are also a couple of cuts where Red gets to show off his acoustic chops; of particular note is "Laundromat Blues," where his work on the acoustic slide guitar just makes one step back and listen. Most of the disc is in the electric mode, however, and he takes off time and time again with scorching electric slide guitar work punctuating his tough vocal delivery. He was born Iverson Minter in 1932, and that is why you will see that name accompanying all the songs that he wrote on the disc (everything except "Laundromat Blues"). This is a disc filled with great surprises and deserves a good hard listen, as there is some outstanding work here. *—Bob Gottlieb*

Eugene Lounge

Drums / Chicago Blues

According to blues drummers, there are only so many basic feels within this genre, one of the main ones being the shuffle, or the "shuffle off to Buffalo" as a disgruntled percussionist who had had a bit too much shuffling for one night described it. Although not as well-known as some master blues timekeepers such as Fred Below, Odie Payne, or Al Duncan, Chicago drummer Eugene Lounge is an undisputed master of the shuffle feel whose stock in trade is rising all the time due to interesting new reissues that highlight his playing. For example, the *Harp and Soul* collection on the Fuel 2000 label presents Lounge as part of an incredible band fronted by Louis Myers, best-known as Buddy Guy's rhythm guitarist, but also a killer harmonica player.

His recording band also featured Willie Dixon on double bass and the dual guitar power of Syl Johnson and Dave Myers. It was for all purposes the normal backup band for Junior Wells, who had left to work with Chicago blues godfather Muddy Waters. Never mind that one of this group's rare tracks is misspelled as "Just Whaling," when the real preoccupation of Chicago's bluesmen in the mid-'50s would have been *wailing*, perhaps whoever took care of the liner notes thought this was a live track from a festival in Newfoundland or something. Despite the presence of big names such as Wells and Sonny Boy Williamson, many reviewers have found the time to point out the incredible shuffling of Lounge as a high point of the set. One writer mentioning "the genius drumming" goes on to assert that Lounge "was every bit the equal of Fred Below," which if the discussion was about army generals would be like a comparison with Alexander the Great.

The Myers brothers and Below are of course even better known under the collective name of the Aces, considered to be one of the best of the Chicago blues rhythm sections. Lounge is one of the few players from outside this tight circle who can be considered technically to have been a member of the Aces, as well. Among many other pleasant tasks, this led to serving as a backup unit for players such as Wells and the rambunctious guitarist Otis Rush in the mid- to late '50s.

When working with Wells, this band also sometimes featured the amazing guitarist Earl Hooker. During this period, a variety of singles was cut for small labels such as Profile, Abco, Chief, and USA. The Lounge tenure in the Aces took place during a re-shuffling in sidemen experienced by the mighty Little Walter band. For several years, this harp man and vocalist had enjoyed a string of hits and one of the most popular bands on the scene, the grooving rhythms supremely benefited by the presence of the Myers brothers and Below, or the classic lineup of the Aces.

When the Myers brothers decided to call it quits with Little Walter, drummer Below stayed put for a bit longer. During this interim period, the Myers brothers chose Lounge as one of the only drummers worthy of sitting on what had been Below's drum chair, and that doesn't mean the floor. For a year or two, this lineup worked clubs under the name of the Aces, meaning Lounge was technically a member, the brilliance of his shuffling underscoring the technique in technical. Lounge mostly seems to be a presence on '50s blues recordings, however.

Later productions done for Delmark and other labels going for the silver lining in the blues revival cloud feature other drummers such as Below, Payne, or the underrated Billy Warren, leading to speculation that the Lounge must have closed for good, the shuffling stopped, without much information available as to the why. Cyberspace research on the whereabouts of Lounge unfortunately produces only reports on a lounge in Eugene, OR, that has been fined for liquor violations—not even close, and no shuffle. *—Eugene Chadbourne*

Love Sculpture

f. 1966, Cardiff, Wales, **db.** 1970

Group / Prog-Rock/Art Rock, Blues-Rock

A British blues-rock band of the late '60s that, despite being very good, would normally be relegated to footnote status if it were not for the fact that the lead guitarist of this trio was the soon-to-be-famous Dave Edmunds. Like many similar bands of the times, Love Sculpture was really a showpiece for Edmunds' guitar-playing talents (which on the first LP are considerable), and little else. The covers are well-chosen, slightly revved-up, but mostly reverent versions of blues classics. They had a fluke hit in 1968 with a cover of the classical piece "Sabre Dance," rearranged for guitar. After two LPs, Love Sculpture split up in 1970. Edmunds went on to solo success ("I Hear You Knockin'") and a long, sometimes contentious relationship with ex-Brinsley Schwarz bassist Nick Lowe, which culminated in the great band Rockpile. Still, Love Sculpture, though slightly dated, is a hoot to hear. And Edmunds, full of youthful bravado and dazzling technique, certainly knows his way up and down a fretboard. —*John Dougan*

Blues Helping / 1968 / EMI ✦✦✦✦✦
As hyperkinetic blues albums by White English kids go, this is a good one. Dave Edmunds, armed only with a 1959 Gibson 335 and a 100-watt Marshall stack, cranks through these recognizable blues covers (with one original instrumental) with reckless abandon and gobs of technique. Backup support is handled by bassist John Williams and drummer Congo Jones, who do their best to keep up and provide a rhythmic foundation for Edmunds to wail over. Edmunds also handled nearly all the vocals, and as blues singers go, he's merely serviceable, but what makes this album worthwhile is the revved-up guitar playing, especially when Edmunds shreds both Freddie King's "The Stumble" and Willie Dixon's "Wang Dang Doodle." —*John Dougan*

Forms & Feelings / 1969 / Parrot ✦✦✦
Forms & Feelings essentially replicates the high-voltage attack of *Blues Helping*, only with a notable lack of energy and an eye on the charts. It's no coincidence that the group chose to revamp L'Arlésienne's "Farandole," given that "Sabre Dance" was the only thing that distinguished Love Sculpture from the legions of British blues bands. But this time around, "Farandole" and all of *Forms & Feelings* sounded tired and redundant, with only a fraction of the passion that made the debut worthwhile. —*Stephen Thomas Erlewine*

● **Single's A's & B's** / 1980 / Harvest ✦✦✦✦✦
With 20 tracks Edmunds issued with Love Sculpture and Rockpile in the late '60s and early '70s, this import collection is certainly the best retrospective of his early years, if you can find it. Edmunds' image is that of a roots-rocker, and you'll find a lot of that here, ranging from the huge 1970 hit "I Hear You Knocking" to pedestrian oldies covers. Actually, though, he wasn't at all settled on this identity at the time, also cutting some psychedelia, folk-rock, and primitive art rock. The magnificent Love Sculpture version of Khachaturian's "Sabre Dance," featuring faster-than-light riffs by Edmunds, was a British Top Ten hit; "Farandole" was an unsuccessful attempt to do the same for Bizet. Cuts like "Seagull," Tim Rose's oft-covered "Morning Dew," "In the Land of the Few," and the Moody Blues-like "River to Another Day" are uncharacteristically wistful reflections of late-'60s hippie rock. The album also includes the rare 1967 single by Edmunds' pre-Love Sculpture band, the Human Beans. —*Richie Unterberger*

Billy "Red" Love

b. Mississippi
Vocals, Piano / Electric Memphis Blues
There is not a whole lot of tangible information to convey about pianist Billy "Red" Love, who signed to record for fledgling producer Sam Phillips in 1951. Phillips passed off an early Love performance, "Juiced," to Chess as the latest effort by Jackie Brenston (then red-hot as a result of "Rocket 88").

Love's own debut record, "Drop Top," came out on Chess and reportedly did fairly well regionally, but after a 1952 Chess encore, "My Teddy Bear Baby," Chess dropped him. He stuck around Sun through 1954, working sessions behind Rufus Thomas and Willie Nix and recording a wealth of unissued sides of his own.

Love left plenty of jumping blues behind in the Sun vaults—enough to fill half an LP on Charly that he shared with Little Junior Parker. Love's rocking "Gee I Wish," one of those long-delayed masters, has been revived by guitarist Duke Robillard. Love left Memphis in 1955 for parts unknown. —*Bill Dahl*

Clayton Love

b. Nov. 15, 1927, Mattson, MS
Vocals, Piano / Electric Memphis Blues, Electric Blues, R&B
Pianist Clayton Love was a prominent member of Ike Turner's Kings of Rhythm during the mid-'50s, making some of his finest platters with the legendary band. But Love made his first vinyl appearance on Lillian McMurry's Jackson, MS-based Trumpet Records in 1951 with his own jump band, the Shufflers.

The combo was a fixture around Vicksburg, where Love was attending Alcorn A&M as a pre-med student. Love's cousin, Natchez bandleader Earl Reed, had recorded for Trumpet and recommended his young relative to McMurry. Love's 1951 debut, "Susie"/"Shufflin' With Love," exhibited infectious enthusiasm if not a great deal of polish. From there, Love moved over to Aladdin in 1952 (with saxist Raymond Hill's band backing him), Modern (with Turner on guitar) in 1954, and in 1957, Love fronted and played the 88s with Turner and the Kings of Rhythm on their Federal platters "Do You Mean It," "She Made My Blood Run Cold," and "The Big Question."

Turner had nothing to do with Love's pair of 1958 singles for St. Louis-based Bobbin Records; bassist Roosevelt Marks led the backing band for the clever coupling "Limited Love"/"Unlimited Love." Long settled in the Gateway City, Love made an album for Modern Blues Recordings in 1991 with fellow ivories aces Johnnie Johnson and Jimmy Vaughn, *Rockin' Eighty-Eights*. —*Bill Dahl*

● **Blues Come Home** / Oct. 24, 1995 / Monad ✦✦✦

Willie Love

b. Nov. 4, 1906, Duncan, MS, d. Aug. 19, 1953, Jackson, MS
Vocals, Piano / Piano Blues, Boogie-Woogie
Harpist Rice Miller, known to his legion of fans across the Delta as Sonny Boy Williamson, first encountered pianist Willie Love in Greenville, MS, in 1942. The talented pair played regularly on Nelson Street, the main drag of the Black section of Greenville, musically intertwining with remarkable empathy. And it was Williamson who brought Love into the fold at Trumpet Records (the label responsible for Love's entire recorded legacy as a leader).

Love was deeply influenced by Leroy Carr and equally conversant on boogies and down-in-the-alley blues. He played piano on several of Sonny Boy Williamson's Trumpet

sessions, but Love didn't utilize his pal on any of his own 1951-1953 dates for the Jackson, MS, firm. Love's debut, "Take It Easy, Baby," was a rollicking boogie outing, and he followed it up with the equally sturdy "Everybody's Fishing," "Vanity Dresser Boogie," and "Nelson Street Blues." Love's last session in April of 1953 found him backed by a White bassist and drummer—certainly a rarity for the era. Four months later, Love, who had long suffered from alcoholism, was dead. —*Bill Dahl*

Trumpet Masters, Vol. 1: Lonesome World Blues / Nov. 25, 1991 / Collectables ✦✦✦✦✦
Willie Love played exciting, if sometimes unorganized piano and sang in an equally unpredictable and galvanizing fashion. This is how Mississippi juke joints sounded during the early '50s (they're not that different now). —*Ron Wynn*

● **Clownin' With the World** / 1993 / Alligator ✦✦✦✦✦
Instead of assembling a single disc highlighting this Delta piano great, Alligator has spread pianist Willie Love's Trumpet catalog over three marvelous anthologies drawn from the early-'50s archives of Lillian McMurry's Trumpet Records. After eight terrific sides by Sonny Boy, Love pounds out "Take It Easy, Baby," "Little Car Blues," "Feed My Body to the Fishes," and five more, conjuring up a steamy Delta juke joint ambience. —*Bill Dahl*

Delta Blues: 1951 / 1993 / Alligator ✦✦✦
Six more classic 1951 performances by Love from Trumpet's vaults, including the romping "Everybody's Fishing," "My Own Boogie," and "Vanity Dresser Boogie." The pianist shares this disc with country bluesmen Luther Huff and the omnipresent Big Joe Williams; both turned in some inspired work for Lillian McMurry's logo. —*Bill Dahl*

Greenville Smokin' / Mar. 28, 2000 / Mimosa ✦✦✦✦
Willie Love spent most of his short career working around Mississippi as part of Sonny Boy Williamson's King Biscuit Entertainers, but he also recorded as a solo artist for Trumpet Records in Jackson, MS. This 18-track set brings together all of his extant recordings for the label, some featuring Elmore James, a young Little Milton, and Joe Willie Wilkins on guitar. Hard barrelhouse piano and Love's laconic vocals frame classics like "V-8 Ford," "Feed My Body to the Fishes," and the bouncy "Everybody's Fishing." A bluesman who deserves a wider listen. —*Cub Koda*

Shout Brother Shout / Oldie Blues ✦✦✦✦
A more varied mix of musical styles than on the first two anthologies (everything from Wally Mercer's rocking R&B to Beverly White's schmaltzy lounge sounds). Love leads three more solid sides from 1953: the title item, "Way Back," and "Willie Mae." —*Bill Dahl*

Lobby Loyde

Guitar / Aussie Rock, Album Rock, Prog-Rock/Art Rock, Hard Rock, Blues-Rock
Australia's first guitar hero, Lobby Loyde helped shape the sound of classic local bands such as Billy Thorpe and the Aztecs and Rose Tattoo, as well as have a successful solo career.

In 1963, then known as Barry Lyde, he joined the Stilettos, a Shadows-inspired outfit, and by 1964, had joined the R&B band the Impacts. A name change to the Purple Hearts saw their career take off and the band solidified a reputation as one of Australia's best R&B bands. Barry Lyde changed his name to Lobby Loyde in 1967 and joined the Wild Cherries, whom he transformed into an experimental psychedelic group. He left the Wild Cherries at the end of 1968 and joined Billy Thorpe and the Aztecs. Loyde's guitar work helped Billy Thorpe to become the leader of Australia's rock scene during the early '70s.

Loyde left the Aztecs in October 1970 and released the classic solo album *Plays With George Guitar* in September 1971. He formed a backing band called the Wild Cherries, comprised of Teddy Toi on bass and Johnny Dick on drums, which lasted until February 1972. He then formed a new band, Coloured Balls, which broke up at the end of 1974. He then released a solo single, "Do You Believe in Magic?"/"Love Lost on Dream Tides," in December 1975.

Loyde issued his second solo album, *Obsecration*, in May 1976, another impressive collection of heavy rock guitar work. He moved to the U.K. where Virgin showed interest in releasing the album, but with England in the throes of punk music, a deal was never sealed. He returned to Australia in 1979 and formed a new lineup with Gil Matthews (drums), Gavin Carroll (bass), and Mándu, known as Southern Electric. They recorded the album *Live with Dubs*, later released in October 1980.

In 1979, Loyde contributed the track "John's Song" to the various artists disc *Australian Guitar Album* and then joined Rose Tattoo as a bass player. They recorded an album in Los Angeles that was never released, nonetheless Loyde toured with the band from October 1979 to September 1980. Loyde then turned his attention to producing other bands, working with the Sunnyboys, Machinations, X, and Painters and Dockers. In 1990 he played bass in a short-lived band called Dirt, and in 1997 he formed a new band called Fish Tree Mother. —*Brendan Swift*

● **Lobby Loyde and the Coloured Balls** / 1997 / Fable ✦✦✦✦

Robert Lucas

b. Jul. 25, 1962, Long Beach, CA
Slide Guitar, Vocals, Harmonica / Contemporary Blues, Modern Electric Blues
West Coast vocalist, guitarist and songwriter Robert Lucas has been forging a path for himself in the blues world since his much-hailed 1990 self-produced debut cassette, *Across the River*. Lucas, based in Long Beach, California, records for the Audioquest label out of San Clemente.

Lucas was born into a middle-class family in Long Beach and was 14 or 15 when he started getting seriously into blues-rock. He had started to play guitar then, inspired by Jimi Hendrix, but gave up on it, concluding his hands were too small. He started playing harmonica instead, listening to recordings by John Mayall and the Bluesbreakers before going back to source material, including the recordings of Little Walter Jacobs, Sonny Boy Williamson, George "Harmonica" Smith, Snooky Pryor and James Cotton.

Lucas began playing the National steel guitar at 17 when a co-worker at the Long

Beach Arena sold him the instrument. Lucas hooked up with guitarist Bernie Pearl and began taking lessons from him. After joining Pearl's band as a harmonica player, he got to play behind the likes of Big Joe Turner, George Smith, Pee Wee Creighton, Lowell Fulson, Eddie "Cleanhead" Vinson, Percy Mayfield, and other West Coast bluesmen. He carefully honed his singing and playing, with Pearl's band and on his own, for several years before forming Luke and the Locomotives in 1986.

Lucas' career as a national touring act was launched when his *Across the River* tape got a rave review in a Los Angeles newspaper. As a result, one of the Audioquest warehouse workers came to see him at a Los Angeles sushi bar. The employee called the company president, who came to hear Lucas that same night.

Lucas is a multi-talented harmonica player, guitarist, singer and songwriter who can do it all: on one recording for Audioquest, *Usin' Man Blues*, he plays solo, and on another, *Luke and the Locomotives*, he performs with his band. The sound on all of his albums is raw and gritty, with just a few originals on each album. Classic blues fare like Sonny Boy Williamson's "Good Morning Little Schoolgirl" and John Lee Hooker's "Meet Me In the Bottom" are given new life with Lucas' talented hands and vocal chops.

Lucas pays homage to traditional blues but has carefully crafted his own singing and slide guitar style. These talents are on ample display on his albums for Audioquest. His albums include *Luke and the Locomotives*, *Usin' Man Blues*, *Built for Comfort*, *Layaway*, and *Completely Blue*, all recorded since 1990. —*Richard Skelly*

Usin' Man Blues / Jul. 1990 / AudioQuest ♦♦♦♦♦
Credible acoustic blues with admirable humor. —*Bill Dahl*

Luke and the Locomotives / 1991 / AudioQuest ♦♦♦
Crying out the pains and joys of the blues is not just an act for this band—it genuinely bleeds through. Don't believe it? Look at the back liner note endorsements by Willie Dixon and Robert Jr. Lockwood. Even more brilliant is Lucas' songwriting, poking fun at himself in "Big Man's Mambo," and offering the advantages of having a large frame to the ladies. His moaning harmonica effectively plays into the subject of growing old with its aches and pains in "Shed a Tear," and is equally as effective in "I'm So Tired." —*Char Ham*

Built for Comfort / 1992 / AudioQuest ♦♦♦
Another laudable set. —*Bill Dahl*

Layaway / 1994 / AudioQuest ♦♦♦

● **Completely Blue** / May 5, 1997 / AudioQuest ♦♦♦♦♦
Right from the bongo drum intro on the first number, it's apparent that this album veers in a different direction for Lucas. Add the eerie organ sounds and the jazzy guitar licks, and this album has great musical depth. Even his songwriting expands topic-wise, whether warning his one night stand the consequences of telling all to his wife, or society's lack of common sense while suffering economic woes, even giving a little snippet of commentary on the O.J. Simpson case. There's some magnificent and expansive keyboard work by Fred Kaplan, both on piano and B-3 organ. Along with co-writer/ guitarist David Melton, Lucas' "Two for Nothing" is a nice Stax-sounding duet. Joining Melton on guitar duties is former Mighty Flyer Alex Schultz, who can flesh out equally well on rhythm as well as burn on solos. Rounding out and heading for home, Lucas ends with an acoustic interpretation of Hendrix's "Voodoo Chile," which presents how Robert Johnson might have performed it had he lived into the latter half of the 20th century. —*Char Ham*

Bill Lupkin

b. 1947, Fort Wayne, IN
Harmonica, Vocals / Modern Electric Blues
Chicago blues singer/harpist Bill Lupkin was born in Fort Wayne, IN, in 1947; first exposed to the music of key influences like Muddy Waters, Chuck Berry, Bo Diddley and Jimmy Reed by his older brother, he began playing the drums at 17, moving to harmonica two years later. Upon relocating to the Windy City in 1968, Lupkin joined the Aces, followed by a lengthy stint backing Jimmy Rogers; he continued playing the local circuit in the years to follow, eventually forming his own backing band, the Chicago Blues Coalition, which for a time included teen guitar phenom Lil' Frank Krakowski. Lupkin's debut album *Live at the Hot Spot* appeared on Blue Loon in late 1999. —*Jason Ankeny*

● **Live at the Hot Spot** / Jan. 25, 2000 / Blue Loon ♦♦♦

Joe Lutcher

b. Lake Charles, LA
Sax (Alto), Vocals / New Orleans R&B, Jump Blues, Boogie-Woogie, R&B
Alto saxophonist and vocalist Joe Lutcher had R&B hits in the late '40s with "Shuffle Woogie" (for Capitol in 1948), "The Rockin' Boogie" (for Specialty in 1948), and "Mardi Gras" (for Modern in 1949). While he was a competent vocalist, his true forte was the sax. His repertoire mixed instrumentals with vocal numbers, employing an approach that generally fell within the Los Angeles jump blues-R&B style of the late '40s and early '50s, although he often added New Orleans accents and sometimes went into a straighter big-band jazz mode. He's not nearly as well known, though, as his sister Nellie Lutcher, who was a more successful hitmaker as a vocalist.

Lutcher was born in Lake Charles, LA, moving to Los Angeles in the early '40s, following his sister (who had moved there in the mid-'30s). He played sax with the Nat King Cole Trio for a time before forming his own band and signing to Specialty in 1947. After some success with both Specialty and Capitol (where Nellie Lutcher recorded), he joined Modern in 1949. Modern encouraged him to add New Orleans spice to his recordings, and one of those tracks, "Mardi Gras," was an R&B Top 20 hit, preceding the more famous version of the song by Professor Longhair.

Lutcher did some subsequent records for Peacock, London, and Masters Music, but left R&B for gospel music, forming the gospel label Jordan Records. It's been written that he was influential in advising Little Richard to leave rock & roll for religious studies in the late '50s. —*Richie Unterberger*

● **Jumpin' at the Mardi Gras** / May 2, 2000 / Ace ♦♦♦
This is quite a comprehensive collection (25 tracks) for a relatively minor early R&B performer. However, it shouldn't be considered a best-of as it only covers his stint with Modern in the late '40s and early '50s, not including any of his Capitol and Specialty material, and thus omitting the R&B hits "Shuffle Woogie" and "The Rockin' Boogie" (although "Mardi Gras" *is* here). In fact, only nine of the numbers (both sides of four 1949-1950 singles, plus a song that didn't come out until a 1983 Ace compilation) were previously released; the remaining two-thirds are previously unissued outtakes and alternates. Like many of the musicians recording in L.A. in the late '40s (including many of the ones doing Modern sessions), Lutcher was at the pivot in the transition between jazz, jump blues, and R&B that was vital to the birth of rock & roll. As such pioneering saxophonists go, Lutcher was a little more traditional than most, at times sounding like a link between older New Orleans jazz and R&B. On other sides, such as the 1949 single "Ojai," he's closer to the big band mood of Dizzy Gillespie or even Benny Goodman than he is to R&B and pre-rock & roll. What history will most remember his Modern stint for, however, are the cuts with a Mardi Gras influence (particularly in the rhythms), which stand as some of the first tracks ever recorded to bear an identifiably New Orleans R&B stamp. "Mardi Gras" itself, which was done before Professor Longhair's more famous version, is certainly the most galvanizing of those. Otherwise the disc is an energetic but somewhat samey-sounding hybrid of jump R&B, jazz, and the occasional New Orleans flavor, encompassing vocals (including two songs with an unidentified female vocalist) and instrumentals. —*Richie Unterberger*

Barbara Lynn (Barbara Lynn Ozen)

b. Jan. 16, 1942, Beaumont, TX
Vocals, Guitar / Northern Soul, New Orleans R&B, Blues-Rock, R&B, Soul
Singer/guitarist Barbara Lynn was a rare commodity during her heyday. Not only was she a female instrumentalist (one of the very first to hit the charts), but she also played left-handed—quite well at that—and even wrote some of her own material. Lynn's music often straddled the line between blues and Southern R&B, and since much of her early work—including the number one R&B hit "You'll Lose a Good Thing"—was recorded in New Orleans, it bore the sonic imprint of the Crescent City. Lynn was born Barbara Lynn Ozen in Beaumont, TX, on January 16, 1942; she played the piano as a child before switching to guitar, inspired by Elvis Presley. In junior high, Lynn formed her own band, Bobbie Lynn and the Idols; at this point, her musical role models veered between bluesmen (Guitar Slim, Jimmy Reed) and female pop singers (Brenda Lee, Connie Francis). After winning a few talent shows and playing some teen dances, the still-underage Lynn started working the local clubs and juke joints, risking getting kicked out of school if she had been discovered. Singer Joe Barry caught her live act and recommended her to his friend, producer/impresario Huey P. Meaux, aka the Crazy Cajun.

With her parents' consent, Meaux brought Lynn to New Orleans to record at the legendary Cosimo's studio. Lynn cut a few singles for the Jamie label with the understanding that if none hit, she was to attend college instead of pursuing music right off the bat. In 1962, her self-penned ballad "You'll Lose a Good Thing" became a national hit, reaching the pop Top Ten and climbing all the way to number one on the R&B charts. Her first album (of the same name) was also released that year, featuring ten of her originals among its 12 tracks. Lynn continued to record for Jamie up through 1965, producing follow-up R&B hits like "You're Gonna Need Me" and "Oh Baby (We Got a Good Thing Goin')," the latter of which was recorded by the Rolling Stones in 1965. In 1966, Lynn switched over to Meaux's Tribe label and cut "You Left the Water Running," which became something of an R&B standard and was covered by the likes of Otis Redding. In 1967, she signed with Atlantic and had another R&B hit with "This Is the Thanks I Get" early the following year; she also issued another album, *Here Is Barbara Lynn*, in 1968. Lynn scored one last hit for Atlantic in 1972's "(Until Then) I'll Suffer," but by this point, she had several children to worry about raising; dissatisfied with her promotion anyway, she wound up effectively retiring from the music business for most of the '70s and '80s, though she did play the occasional low-key tour.

Lynn returned to music in the mid-'80s, touring Japan for the first time in 1984; she later cut a live album there, called *You Don't Have to Go*, which was eventually issued in the States by Ichiban. Lynn had managed to retain a cult following among connoisseurs of American soul and blues in several different pockets of the world, and toured internationally during the early '90s. In 1994, Bullseye Blues issued her first full-fledged studio album in over two decades, *So Good*; *Until Then I'll Suffer* followed in 1996. Lynn later caught on with the respected blues label Antone's, and in 2000 she cut *Hot Night Tonight*, which featured a couple of raps by her son Bachelor Wise. —*Steve Huey*

You'll Lose a Good Thing / 1962 / Jamie ♦♦♦♦♦
Barbara Lynn Ozen's smoky voice and fine guitar playing was one of the better blends of soul vocals and blues embellishment. Huey P. Meaux produced this early-'60s record, which featured the classic title track. Other Lynn numbers, like "I'll Suffer," were equally outstanding; Lynn was sometimes tough and confrontational, and tender, inviting or anguished at other times. Meaux didn't clutter the works with unnecessary firepower; his arrangements and charts were just enough to augment Lynn's sturdy vocals. Lynn also wrote ten of the 12 songs. —*Ron Wynn*

So Good / 1993 / Bullseye Blues ♦♦
It's been a long time since Lynn has made a satisfying album, although she's given it a shot a few times. While this isn't flawless, it's a step in the right direction. The material isn't merely remakes or soul covers, but also includes a good version of Babyface's "I Love You Babe." Of course, Lynn couldn't desert classic soul, and she gives solid treatments to her own hit "This Is The Thanks I Get" and Tyrone Davis' "Can I Change My Mind." The familiar guitar riffs buttress her vocals, which still sound authoritative, even if the range and luster aren't quite as arresting. —*Ron Wynn*

The Best of Barbara Lynn: The Atlantic Years / Nov. 22, 1994 / Ichiban ✦✦✦
This 20-track collection gathers most of Lynn's output for Atlantic between 1968 and 1973, including most of her 1968 *Here Is Barbara Lynn* album and several non-LP singles. Commercially, Lynn's stay at Atlantic was not fruitful, yielding only a couple moderate R&B hits, the self-penned "This Is the Thanks I Get" and "Until Then, I'll Suffer" (both included). Artistically, this is fairly solid period soul, but a bit faceless. It seems as though Atlantic tried to fit Lynn into current soul trends; many of the 1968 tracks are quite derivative of Motown, and many of the later sides take a Memphis/Muscle Shoals approach. Those are fine influences, of course, but Lynn's strengths were her original songwriting and bluesy Southern phrasing. The most outstanding tracks are from her first Atlantic single, "This Is the Thanks I Get" and "Ring Telephone Ring," when much of her original relaxed Texas/New Orleans R&B style was still in evidence. The version of "You'll Lose a Good Thing" here, incidentally, is a remake, not the original 1962 hit. *—Richie Unterberger*

Until Then I'll Suffer / Jul. 16, 1996 / ITP ✦✦✦

● **You'll Lose a Good Thing** / 1997 / Bear Family ✦✦✦✦✦
Single-disc, 28-track compilation of her best early sides from 1962-1965, including a half-dozen previously unreleased cuts. Although the material is a bit uneven, it's worthy, idiosyncratic stuff with a bluesier, swampier feel than most any other soul being made during the time. New Orleans-styled horns, bluesy organ, and some gutsy guitar licks usually decorate the arrangements, while Lynn puts the tunes across with an assured reserve. The prize obscurity here is the original version of "Oh Baby (We Got a Good Thing Goin')" (which Lynn wrote), covered by the Rolling Stones in 1965, though it must be said that the Stones' more assertive, guitar-driven version outclasses Lynn's less forceful presentation. The documentation is unusually incomplete by Bear Family standards—there's no indication, for instance, of when the unreleased material was recorded. But at any rate, it's good overlooked soul, usually upbeat, sometimes with a downcast feel that verges on the morose, as on "Dedicate the Blues to Me" and "Ring Telephone Ring." Another oddity is "Can't Buy My Love," on which it sounds like producer Huey Meaux was trying to replicate the organ-colored polka-rock he'd just crafted for the Sir Douglas Quintet. *—Richie Unterberger*

Promises / Nov. 1, 1997 / Bear Family ✦✦✦✦✦

Movin' on a Groove: Live in Concert / 2000 / Goldmine/Soul Supply ✦✦✦
Lefty guitarists are rare; a left-handed woman guitarist who sings is even rarer, but that's what you get with Barbara Lynn. This live set includes her biggest hit, "You'll Lose a Good Thing," and the notable "Until Then I Suffer." Lynn remakes William Bell's "Trying to Love Two," but really shines on the soulful Maurice & Mac cut "You Left the Water Running"—there are two versions: the on-stage performance, and a gritty rehearsal take. Cock-a-doodling horns introduce "We Got a Good Thing Going (Oh Baby)," and keeps you awake throughout the song; the Motown-ish "Take Your Love and Run," finds Lynn's female accompaniment doing a Vandellas imitation; the title track is a sweet Southern shuffler, à la Betty Wright. Lynn didn't record many live sets and hasn't exactly painted the globe in appearances, particularly north of the Mason-Dixon Line in the States, so this is a good introduction to the talented Ms. Lynn. *—Andrew Hamilton*

Hot Night Tonight / Aug. 22, 2000 / Antone's ✦✦✦
Barbara Lynn returned to performing in the mid-'80s after a family-related layoff of a decade and a half, but her musical approach has remained that of an early '60s R&B artist. On *Hot Night Tonight* she turns in a set of bluesy shuffles, including a couple of '60s Stax covers—"Never Found a Man" and "When Something's Wrong" (aka the Sam and Dave hit "When Something Is Wrong With My Baby")—and some new originals, all prominently featuring her voice and guitar. The only nod to contemporary music is the inclusion of two versions of "You're the Man" featuring Lynn's son Bachelor Wise, who raps. Elsewhere, working with a sympathetic backup band, she smolders through romantic sentiments that range from the regretful "I Let a Good Man Go" to the assertive "Don't Hit Me No More." "It's Been So Long" is an impressive solo performance, just Lynn accompanying herself on guitar, while "Lynn's Blues" is a tasty near-instrumental with only one vocal chorus. Recorded for Antone's Records, *Hot Night Tonight* sounds like a club set in a locale not unlike Antone's itself. *—William Ruhlmann*

Trudy Lynn

b. Houston, TX
Vocals / Retro-Soul, Electric Blues, Modern Electric Blues, Soul-Blues
Lynn was raised in Houston and continues to use the city as her home base. She began her career in the late '60s as a Stax-styled R&B singer opening shows for Ike & Tina Turner and others passing through town. She began recording in late '80s for the Georgia-based British Ichiban label, cutting a fine mix of Southern soul and Delta blues albums produced by Buzz Amato. Lynn currently appears on several blues festival bills, primarily abroad. *—Bil Carpenter*

Sings the Blues / 1989 / Ichiban ✦✦✦✦
This, the bluesiest of her records, includes the nine-minute title track plus covers of Aretha's "Dr. Feelgood" and Big Mama Thorton's "Ball & Chain." *—Niles J. Frantz*

Come to Mama / 1990 / Ichiban ✦✦✦✦
Although Trudy Lynn is far from a big name in the music world, her live appearances and good-to-excellent Ichiban output have earned her a small following on the blues circuit. However, it would be wrong to think of the brassy, big-voiced Lynn as strictly as a blues singer when she devotes so much time to the blues. In fact, you'll find more R&B than outright blues on her second Ichiban album, *Come to Mama*. "Fish Girl Blues" is the only actual 12-bar blues on the CD; the other selections are pure R&B. Lynn's R&B isn't high-tech urban contemporary, but rather recalls the organic soul music of the '60s and '70s. "When You Took Your Love From Me" and "Right Back In the Water" take us back to the type of rough-and-tumble soul that Memphis and Muscle Shoals were known for in the '60s, while "Making Love to Me" has a '70s-type flavor. Lynn isn't one to hold back emotionally; like Koko Taylor and Etta James, she screams, shouts, testifies and gets her points across in a highly convincing way. *—Alex Henderson*

The Woman in Me / 1991 / Ichiban ✦✦✦
There are more dance grooves and bluesy one-chord vamps here, but it's still real nice and truly soulful. *—Niles J. Frantz*

● **I'll Run Your Hurt Away** / 1993 / Ichiban ✦✦✦✦✦
Lynn adroitly treads her familiar territory, on the fence separating gutbucket and contemporary blues, on what seems to be her most pleasing album yet. Opening with the spirited juke blues of "Loose Lips," ashe easily moves into some soul balladry on "Try to Leave Me." The album climaxes on the salacious double entendre barrelhouse blues of "Instant Breakfast," a song sure to not only become one of Lynn's signature songs over the next few years, but also a frequent cover for other adventurous singers. Picking an obscure Ruby Johnson classic from *Stax: The Complete Singles (1959-1968)*, Lynn gives a somewhat shrill, though enjoyable, work-out of the belting ballad, though Johnson's is still the superior version. The album ends with an ode to Otis Redding with bluesy renditions of his ballads "Lover's Prayer" and "Pain in My Heart." *—Bil Carpenter*

24 Hour Woman / 1994 / Ichiban ✦✦✦

First Lady of Soul / 1995 / Ichiban ✦✦✦

Retrospectives / Jun. 30, 1998 / Ichiban ✦✦✦✦
Part of the blues-oriented *Retrospectives* series that Ichiban launched in 1998, this 12-song CD unites six previously unreleased tracks with six songs Trudy Lynn recorded after signing with the label in 1989. A retrospective that paints an accurate picture of Lynn's Ichiban output would have to fluctuate between electric urban blues and gutsy soul, which is exactly what the album does. Ichiban's choices aren't bad at all—"Whole Lotta Leave Me Alones" and the full-of-attitude "Trudy Sings the Blues" show how convincing a blues singer she can be, while "8 Days on the Road" is pure Southern R&B in the '60s Memphis/Muscle Shoals tradition. Bobby Womack's "Woman's Got to Have It," however, has a sleeker '70s type of feel. The new material ranges from live versions of Muddy Waters' "Got My Mojo Workin'" and Aretha Franklin's "Dr. Feelgood" to "Chilly Wind" (a rare example of Lynn embracing acoustic rural blues). For those who've never experienced the pleasures of Lynn's gutbucket belting, *Retospectives* would be the logical starting point. *—Alex Henderson*

U Don't Know What Time It Is / Oct. 19, 1999 / Ruf ✦✦✦
The exciting Southern-brand singer's first CD since the fall of Ichiban Records, where she cut sassy, R-rated Southern soul with energy, is a bit of a letdown to those familiar with her previous output. Trudy Lynn's pipes are in good shape and the material, including three Robert Johnson songs, is strong; it's just not what her fans are accustomed to and will take a few spins to register. The opening cut, "Shake, Rattle N' Roll" (no, not that one), is fiery and Lynn's hoarse delivery is man-provoking, but those explicit double entendres are missing. Lucky Peterson plays a multitude of instruments, but really gets your attention when he's messing with a big, old B-3 organ. Bernard Allison and Butch Bonner are on time every time on guitars, and James Robertson's understated drumming never misses a beat. But the magic that made her every man's dream is missing. There isn't a bad performance and everything rates between a C and B-minus, but the Ichiban stuff rated from B to A-plus. Whether you're a Trudy Lynn adorer or not, *U Don't Know What Time It Is* is worth having for the masterful performances. Just don't expect the down-low and dirty, salacious Trudy Lynn whom listeners have come to love. This is Trudy Lynn without the frills and the racy lyrics. Some picks: "Time Is Running Out" (a strong ballad) and "I Should Have Known" (good old-fashioned down-home blues). *—Andrew Hamilton*

American Roots: Blues / Jul. 9, 2002 / Ichiban ✦✦✦
Get ready for an exciting blues/Southern soul experience by the underrated Trudy Lynn, a singer who knows only one way to record—all out. Lynn's enthralling, full-throated deliveries are like the mail—on time. She captures the essence of a song, personalizes it, and then makes special deliveries straight to your heart. This features too many good songs to list, but try "I've Been Thinkin'," "Loose Lips," and "2 Girls for the Price of One" for starters. Like any Trudy Lynn album, this one is excellent. *—Andrew Hamilton*

Lynyrd Skynyrd

f. 1965, Jacksonville, FL
Group / Album Rock, Boogie Rock, Arena Rock, Southern Rock, Hard Rock, Blues-Rock
Lynyrd Skynyrd was the definitive Southern rock band, fusing the overdriven power of blues-rock with a rebellious, Southern image and a hard rock swagger. Skynyrd never relied on the jazzy improvisations of the Allman Brothers. Instead, they were a hard-living, hard-driving rock & roll band—they may have jammed endlessly on stage, but their music remained firmly entrenched in blues, rock, and country. For many, Lynyrd Skynyrd's redneck image tended to obscure the songwriting skills of its leader, Ronnie VanZant. Throughout the band's early records, VanZant demonstrated a knack for lyrical detail and a down-to-earth honesty that had more in common with country than rock & roll. During the height of Skynyrd's popularity in the mid-'70s, however, VanZant's talents were overshadowed by the group's gritty, greasy blues-rock. Sadly, it wasn't until he was killed in a tragic plane crash in 1977 along with two other band members that many listeners began to realize his talents. Skynyrd split up after the plane crash, but they reunited a decade later, becoming a popular concert act during the early '90s.

While in high school in Jacksonville, FL, Ronnie VanZant (vocals), Allen Collins (guitar), and Gary Rossington (guitar) formed My Backyard. Within a few months, the group added bassist Leon Wilkeson and keyboardist Billy Powell, and changed their name to Lynyrd Skynyrd, a mocking tribute to their gym teacher Leonard Skinner, who was notorious for punishing students with long hair. With drummer Bob Burns, Lynyrd Skynyrd began playing throughout the South. For the first few years, the group had little success, but producer Al Kooper signed the band to MCA after seeing them play at an Atlanta club called Funocchio's in 1972. Kooper produced the group's 1973 debut, *Pronounced Leh-Nerd Skin-Nerd*, which was recorded after former Strawberry Alarm Clock guitarist Ed King joined the band. The group became notorious for their triple guitar attack, which was showcased on "Free Bird," a tribute to the recently deceased Duane Allman. "Free Bird" earned Lynyrd Skynyrd their first national exposure and it became one of the staples of album-rock radio, still receiving airplay nearly 25 years after its release.

"Free Bird" and an opening slot on the Who's 1973 *Quadrophenia* tour gave Lynyrd Skynyrd a devoted following, which helped its second album, 1974's *Second Helping*, become its breakthrough hit. Featuring the hit single "Sweet Home Alabama"—a response to Neil Young's "Southern Man"—*Second Helping* reached number 12 and went multi-platinum. At the end of the year, Artimus Pyle replaced drummer Burns, and King left the band shortly afterward. The new sextet released *Nuthin' Fancy* in 1975, and it became the band's first Top Ten hit. The record was followed by the Tom Dowd-produced *Gimme Back My Bullets* in 1976, which failed to match the success of its two predecessors. However, the band retained its following through its constant touring, which was documented on the double-live album *One More from the Road*. Released in late 1976, the album featured the band's new guitarist Steve Gaines and a trio of female backup singers, and it became Skynyrd's second Top Ten album.

Lynyrd Skynyrd released its sixth album, *Street Survivors*, on October 17, 1977. Three days later, a privately chartered plane carrying the band between shows in Greenville, SC, and Baton Rouge, LA, crashed outside of Gillsburg, MS. Ronnie VanZant, Steve Gaines, and his sister Cassie, one of the group's backing vocalists, died in the crash; the remaining members were injured. (The cause of the crash was either fuel shortage or a fault with the plane's mechanics.) The cover for *Street Survivors* had pictured the band surrounded in flames; after the crash, the cover was changed. In the wake of the tragedy, the album became one of the band's biggest hits. Lynyrd Skynyrd broke up after the crash, releasing a collection of early demos called *Skynyrd's First and...Last* in 1978; it had been scheduled for release before the crash. The double-album compilation *Gold and Platinum* was released in 1980.

Later in 1980, Rossington and Collins formed a new band which featured four surviving members. Two years later, Pyle formed the Artimus Pyle Band. Collins suffered a car crash in 1986, which killed his girlfriend and left him paralyzed; four years later, he died of respiratory failure. In 1987, Rossington, Powell, King, and Wilkeson reunited Lynyrd Skynyrd, adding vocalist Johnny VanZant and guitarist Randall Hall. The band embarked on a reunion tour, which was captured on the 1988 double-live album, *Southern By the Grace of God/Lynyrd Skynyrd Tribute Tour—1987*. The re-formed Skynyrd began recording in 1991, and for the remainder of the decade, the band toured frequently, putting out albums occasionally. The reunited Skynyrd frequently switched drummers, but it had little effect on their sound.

During the '90s, Lynyrd Skynyrd were made honorary colonels in the Alabama State Militia, due to their classic-rock staple "Sweet Home Alabama." During the mid-'90s, VanZant, Rossington, Wilkeson, and Powell regrouped by adding two Southern rock veterans to Skynyrd's guitar stable: former Blackfoot frontman Rick Medlocke and ex-Outlaw Hughie Thomasson. With ex-Damn Yankee Michael Cartellone bringing stability to the drum chair, the reconstituted band signed to CMC International for the 1997 album *Twenty*. This lineup went on to release *Lyve from Steeltown* in 1998, followed a year later by *Edge of Forever*. The seasonal effort *Christmas Time Again* was released in fall 2000. —*Stephen Thomas Erlewine*

☆ **Pronounced Leh-Nerd Skin-Nerd** / Sep. 1973 / MCA ✦✦✦✦✦
The Allman Brothers came first, but Lynyrd Skynyrd epitomized Southern rock. The Allmans were exceptionally gifted musicians, as much bluesmen as rockers. Skynyrd was nothing but rockers, and they were Southern rockers to the bone. This didn't just mean that they were rednecks, but that they brought it all together—the blues, country, garage rock, Southern poetry—in a way that sounded more like the South than even the Allmans. And a large portion of that derives from their hard, lean edge, which was nowhere more apparent than on their debut album, *Pronounced Leh-Nerd Skin-Nerd*. Produced by Al Kooper, there are few records that sound this raw and uncompromising, especially records by debut bands. Then again, few bands sound this confident and fully formed with their first record. Perhaps the record is stronger because it's only eight songs, so there isn't a wasted moment, but that doesn't discount the sheer strength of each song. Consider the opening juxtaposition of the rollicking "I Ain't the One" with the heartbreaking "Tuesday's Gone." Two songs couldn't be more opposed, yet Skynyrd sounds equally convincing on both. If that's all the record did, it would still be fondly regarded, but it wouldn't have been influential. The genius of Skynyrd is that it unselfconsciously blended album-oriented hard rock, blues, country, and garage rock, turning it all into a distinctive sound that sounds familiar but thoroughly unique. On top of that, there's the highly individual voice of Ronnie VanZant, a songwriter that isn't afraid to be nakedly sentimental, spin tales of the South, or to twist macho conventions with humor. And, lest we forget, while he does this, the band rocks like a mother*****. It's the birth of a great band who birthed an entire genre with this album. —*Stephen Thomas Erlewine*

☆ **Second Helping** / Apr. 1974 / MCA ✦✦✦✦✦
Lynyrd Skynyrd wrote the book on Southern rock with their first album, so it only made sense that they followed it for their second album, aptly titled *Second Helping*. Sticking with producer Al Kooper (who, after all, discovered them), the group turned out a record that replicated all the strengths of the original, but was a little tighter and a little more professional. But it also revealed that the band, under the direction of songwriter Ronnie VanZant, was developing a truly original voice. Of course, the band had already developed their own musical voice, but it was enhanced considerably by VanZant's writing, which was at turns plainly poetic, surprisingly clever, and always revealing. Though *Second Helping* isn't as hard a rock record as *Pronounced*, it is the songs that make the record. "Sweet Home Alabama" became ubiquitous, yet it's rivaled by such terrific songs

as the snide, punkish "Workin' for MCA," the Southern groove "Don't Ask Me No Questions," the affecting "The Ballad of Curtis Loew," and "The Needle and the Spoon," a drug tale as affecting as their rival Neil Young's "Needle and the Damage Done," but much harder rocking. This is the part of Skynyrd that most people forget—they were a great band, but they were indelible because that was married to great writing. And nowhere was that more evident than on *Second Helping*. —*Stephen Thomas Erlewine*

Gimme Back My Bullets / Feb. 1976 / MCA ✦✦✦
Lynyrd Skynyrd begins to show signs of wear on their third album, *Gimme Back My Bullets*. The band had switched producers, hiring Tom Dowd, the producer that served Atlantic's roster so well during the label's heyday. Unfortunately, he wasn't perfectly suited for Skynyrd, at least at this point in their history. The group had toured regularly since the release of their debut and it showed, not just in their performance, but in the songwriting of Ronnie VanZant, who had been so consistent through their first three albums. Not to say that he was spent—the title track was defiant as "All I Can Do Is Write About It" was affecting, while "Searching" was a good ballad and "Double Trouble" was a good rocker. These songs, however, were surrounded by songs that leaned to the dull side of generic (unlike those on *Nuthin' Fancy*) and Dowd's production didn't inject energy into the group's performances. This doesn't mean *Gimme Back My Bullets* is a bad record, since the group was still in fairly good shape and they had some fine songs, but coming after three dynamite albums, it was undoubtedly a disappointment—so much so that it still sounds like a disappointment years later, even though it's one of only a handful of records by the original band. —*Stephen Thomas Erlewine*

One More from the Road / Sep. 1976 / MCA ✦✦✦
Double live albums were commonplace during the '70s, even for bands that weren't particularly good in concert. As a travelin' band, Lynyrd Skynyrd made their fame and fortune by being good in concert, so it made sense that they released a double-live, entitled *One More from the Road*, in 1976, months after the release of their fourth album, *Gimme Back My Bullets*. That might have been rather quick for a live album—only three years separated this record from the group's debut—but it was enthusiastically embraced, entering the Top Ten (it would become one of their best-selling albums, as well). It's easy to see why it was welcomed since this album demonstrates what a phenomenal catalog of songs they accumulated. *Street Survivors*, which appeared the following year, added "That Smell" and "You Got That Right" to the canon, but this pretty much has everything else, sometimes extended into jams as long as the Allmans on this record, but always much rawer, nearly dangerous. That catalog, as much as the strong performances, makes *One More From the Road* worth hearing. Heard here, on one record, the consistency of Skynyrd's work falls into relief, and they not only clearly tower above their peers based on what's here, the cover of "T for Texas" illustrates that they're carrying on the Southern tradition, not starting a new one. Like most live albums, this is not necessarily essential, but if you're a fan, it's damn hard to take this album off after it starts. —*Stephen Thomas Erlewine*

Street Survivors / Oct. 1977 / MCA ✦✦✦✦✦
Street Survivors appeared in stores just days before Lynyrd Skynyrd's touring plane crashed, tragically killing many members of the band, including lead singer and songwriter Ronnie VanZant. Consequently, it's hard to see *Street Survivors* outside of the tragedy, especially since the best-known song here, "That Smell," reeks of death and foreboding. If the band had lived, however, *Street Survivors* would have been seen as an unqualified triumph, a record that firmly re-established Skynyrd's status as the great Southern rock band. As it stands, it's a triumph tinged with a hint of sadness, sadness that's projected onto it from listeners aware of what happened to the band after recording. Viewed as merely a record, it's a hell of an album. The band springs back to life with the addition of guitarist Steve Gaines, and VanZant used the time off the road to write a strong set of songs, highlighted by "That Smell," "You Got That Right," and the relentless boogie "I Know a Little." It's tighter than any record since *Second Helping* and as raw as *Nuthin' Fancy*. If the original band was fated to leave after this record, at least they left with a record that serves as a testament to Skynyrd's unique greatness. —*Stephen Thomas Erlewine*

★ **Gold & Platinum** / Dec. 1979 / MCA ✦✦✦✦✦
Gold and Platinum was compiled by Gary Rossington and Allen Collins, the two surviving members of Lynyrd Skynyrd, after the band's tragic plane crash of 1977. Though many years have elapsed since its 1979 release, the double-record set remains the best, most concise compilation of the ground-breaking southern rock band. Over the course of two albums, all of Skynyrd's hits—"Sweet Home Alabama," "Free Bird," "Saturday Night Special," "What's Your Name," "You Got That Right"—are featured, as well as essential album tracks like "That Smell," "Down South Jukin'," "Gimme Three Steps," "I Know A Little," and "Tuesday's Gone." Some great songs like "Working for MCA" are missing, and the four-disc box set may be more comprehensive, but it's hard to imagine a better, more concise greatest hits collection than *Gold and Platinum*. —*Stephen Thomas Erlewine*

Skynyrd's Innyrds / Apr. 1989 / MCA ✦✦✦
Skynyrd's Innyrds—Their Greatest Hits comes close to being a solid single-disc overview of the Southern rockers' biggest hits, but it falls short in a number of important ways. Most notably, "Free Bird" is not in either its studio or live incarnations; it's presented as an outtake, something that will only be of interest to hardcore Skynyrd fans, just like the outtake of "Double Trouble." Also, several major songs—"Down South Jukin'," "You Got That Right," "Whiskey Rock-a-Roller," "Simple Man," "Tuesday's Gone," "I Know a Little"—are missing, with album cuts in their place. That said, it has most of the big hits—"Sweet Home Alabama," "Gimme Three Steps," "Saturday Night Special," "What's Your Name," "That Smell," plus "Workin' for MCA" and "Call Me the Breeze," which were not on *Gold & Platinum*—which is enough to make it a good sampler, even

if it doesn't provide as complete an introduction as *Gold & Platinum*. —*Stephen Thomas Erlewine*

Lynyrd Skynyrd 1991 / Jun. 11, 1991 / Atlantic ✦✦

The 1987 reunion tour proved to be quite successful, so the reunited Lynyrd Skynyrd decided to record a full-fledged new record. Though it's hard not to miss the songwriting of Ronnie VanZant, this is still a strong band, capable of turning out convincing rockers and ballads. There may not be many songs that distinguish themselves beyond something generic, but the group is passionate and tight, making this reunion seem necessary, not a cash-in. This still isn't an essential release, even for the devoted, but it is enjoyable. —*Stephen Thomas Erlewine*

Lynyrd Skynyrd [Box Set] / Nov. 12, 1991 / MCA ✦✦✦✦✦

It was only fitting that the ultimate Southern rock institution Lynyrd Skynyrd—certainly one of the more tragic stories in rock & roll history—should be one of the first bands to benefit from a comprehensive box set. Following the format of the highly successful Led Zeppelin box set, this three-disc, 47-song anthology provides a near-perfect career retrospective, complete with a carefully researched booklet with meticulous historical essays and rare photos for the new and rabid fan alike. The latter will probably be most interested in disc one, which features a number of early demos dating back as early as 1970 and not featured in prior collections, as well as an embryonic demo of "Freebird" minus its extended-jam coda. The nine-minute version from the band's milestone debut, *Pronounced...* is also featured here, of course, as is most of the material from the group's next album, *Second Helping*, generally regarded as their career peak. Disc two alone could serve as a greatest-hits set, as classic after classic is rattled off in mind-blowing succession. And even when the creative fires finally begin to wane somewhat as the set approaches the *Nuthin' Fancy* and *Gimme Back My Bullets* material (recorded at a time when the band was plagued by overwork and escalating drug abuse), the set wisely offers alternate versions and live renditions to keep things interesting. The first half of disc three alternates never-before-heard concert performances with other, equally inspired live versions. Its second half is dominated by the unintentional swan song *Street Survivors*. Released only three days before the fateful plane crash, the album saw a re-energized Skynyrd achieving a new level of maturity, power, and purpose. Although most box sets tend to be a bit too much for the casual fan to swallow, this one feels just right. —*Ed Rivadavia*

Twenty / Apr. 29, 1997 / CMC International ✦✦

As the title says, *Twenty* is the 20th album from Lynyrd Skynyrd, but perhaps a more relevant yardstick is that it is the fifth record the group has released since reuniting in the late '80s. Prior to recording *Twenty*, the group added two new members—ex-Blackfoot Rick Medlocke and former Outlaw Hughie Thomasson—making the group a virtual Southern rock supergroup, and that's part of the problem. There are too many egos involved to make the album truly captivating—especially since the songwriting is usually undistinguished—but occasionally, the star power gels and results in some hot rock & roll. In other words, specialists and aficionados will find plenty of stuff to enjoy here, but most casual fans will think that it's all been said before. —*Stephen Thomas Erlewine*

The Essential Lynyrd Skynyrd / Aug. 25, 1998 / MCA ✦✦✦

Putting together the definitive Lynyrd Skynyrd retrospective would be a daunting prospect to all but the most callous of critics who still deny the group their place at the table of rock & roll heroes and innovators. This two-disc, 25-track (!!) anthology makes the perfect introductory set to this Southern rock institution and one great career overview for longtime fans. All the hits like "Sweet Home Alabama," "Gimme Three Steps," "Saturday Night Special," and "That Smell" are aboard, along with "What's Your Name," "Workin' for MCA," "I Know a Little" and "Free Bird" in both live and original studio versions. Other highlights include great album tracks like "The Ballad of Curtis Loew," "Call Me the Breeze" and "You Got That Right," an acoustic version of "All I Can Do Is Write About It," and early demo versions of "Four Walls of Raiford" and "Comin' Home." If you're planning on only making one Lynyrd Skynyrd entry into your collection, this is certainly the one to get. —*Cub Koda*

Skynyrd's First: Complete Muscle Shoals / Nov. 17, 1998 / MCA ✦✦✦✦✦

This may be the greatest unissued first album ever to surface from a major band. The story behind the 78 minutes of music on this CD, cut two years before their official debut album, could fill a chapter of a book. Cut primarily during late June and late July of 1971, with a quintet of 1972-vintage tracks added, they constitute the group's complete studio recordings from the period when they were still trying to get signed and were playing lots of small-time local gigs for barely enough money to live on. Seven of the songs were released on the 1978 album *Skynyrd's First and... Last*, and three others appear on the 1991 boxed set, while "Comin' Home" turned up on *The Essential Lynyrd Skynyrd* earlier that same year, but this is the first time this potent body of work has been assembled properly, in one place. And, additionally, one previously unissued track justifies the price of this disc by itself—the original demo version of "Free Bird," on which the soaring harmonies, Billy Powell's beautiful piano, and the Collins-Rossington guitar duo plays with startling fire and lyricism. Several of the tracks do contain overdubs laid on in the mid-'70s (mostly Ed King's bass and some guitar, and even a Mellotron on "White Dove"—it would be great to hear that song without the electronic string section), but this is still the band at its most raw and unaffected, in terms of what the core members are playing. Ronnie VanZant's singing was not only powerful, but beautiful at this stage of his career, and the group's playing—especially the Rossington-Collins double lead guitar attack—is filled with a fresh spirit of experimentation and adventure that makes these tracks essential listening for anyone who has ever enjoyed this band's work. Evidently, the material and related demos scared the crap out of most record company executives when it was shown around in 1971-1972, and it's easy to see why—the sound is fierce, the songs not only boldly played but boldly written as well (even the Rick Medlocke-written and sung "The Seasons" is a killer piece of semi-acoustic country-rock), and running anywhere from five to ten minutes; anyway, most record company executives being inherently cowardly, or stupid, or both, it's easy to see them running from the room over these sounds. Anyone who owns any of the group's releases should add this magnificent, lost chapter in their history. —*Bruce Eder*

Edge of Forever / Aug. 10, 1999 / CMC International ✦✦✦

From the opening sound of a rattlesnake rattle, it is obvious that the newer members of Lynyrd Skynyrd are stepping out of the shadows and into the limelight where they belong. After all, Rick Medlocke, the "rattlesnake rocker" was himself a powerful frontman for his band Blackfoot in the '70s, while Hughie Thomasson performed the same duties for the Outlaws. On *Edge of Forever*, both Medlocke and Thomasson are heard with their individually unique guitar sounds. Unfortunately, they are still held back from performing any lead vocals, a chore either man could easily carry off. The opening song, "Workin'" assaults the senses with a massive guitar attack that hooks the listener from the outset. Johnny VanZant's vocals are as close to his late brother Ronnie VanZant as they have ever been, and on the next song, "Full Moon Night," the swampy rock sound contains some definite early-Skynyrd influence, but also has hints of both the Blackfoot and Outlaws sounds. "Preacher Man" rocks with a refreshingly different sound; it no longer sounds like the boys are trying to imitate the *Street Survivors* record. The rowdiness that surrounds Southern rock comes to a head on "Mean Streets," with Gary Rossington, Thomasson, and Medlocke smoking across the fretboards in true rebel fashion. Next up is "Tomorrow's Goodbye," a ballad that can only be called modern country. The song is the highlight of the album, with VanZant singing about saving the planet, and there is even a mention of brother Ronnie in the lyric, accented with one of Rossington's "freebird" guitar notes that comes out of left field straight to your heart. The title track is a millennium song that returns to the old Skynyrd sound, while "Gone Fishin'" is one of the record's weaker moments. "Fishin'" is more filler than killer. Actually, the next song, "Through It All" is a bit weak as well, when compared to the rest of the album. "Money Back Guarantee" has some excellent piano work from Billy Powell, and "Get It While the Gettin's Good" is a very nice rocker, which leads into the power ballad "Rough Around the Edges," another of the better tracks here. "FLA" closes the set, a boogie-woogie rocker that makes a fitting closer for an overall good rock & roll record. While there are those who feel that Lynyrd Skynyrd died with the plane crash of 1977, one listen to *Edge of Forever* proves that their legacy is alive and well in 1999, and Lynyrd Skynyrd has more than a few good ideas left in their collective head. —*Michael B. Smith*

Solo Flytes / Oct. 12, 1999 / MCA ✦✦✦

Lynyrd Skynyrd wisely disbanded after the tragic 1977 plane crash that killed its leader, Ronnie VanZant. The band later reunited, another wise move, but at that point in time, the members needed time to grieve and move on by pursuing other projects. And that's exactly what they did. Guitarists Gary Rossington and Allen Collins formed the Rossington-Collins Band, which featured various other Skynyrd members. A little while later, drummer Artimus Pyle formed his own band. Both groups were active in the early '80s, with Collins releasing his own album in 1983, but tragedy struck again in 1986 when Collins suffered a car accident that left him paralyzed. Rossington carried on briefly, before reforming Skynyrd. Highlights from these three post-Skynyrd bands, plus a solo cut by Steve Gaines, the guitarist who joined Skynyrd for the *Street Survivors* album, are compiled on 1999's *Solo Flytes*, a 17-track collection that tells everything that needs to be told about this period in the band's history. Neither the Rossington-Collins Band (which dominates this disc with 11 songs), the Artimus Pyle Band, nor the Allen Collins Band made any classics, but they were entertaining Southern rock outfits. By and large, the music on *Solo Flytes* is generic material in the best sense—meaning that it typifies its genre—but it suffers from songwriting that is not only weaker than Ronnie VanZant's, but not as good as that of .38 Special, the most popular Southern rock band of the early '80s. That said, dedicated fans of Lynyrd Skynyrd will likely find this interesting and, by and large, pretty enjoyable. It fills in some gaps nicely, pulling the best songs from records that were well-done but uneven. —*Stephen Thomas Erlewine*

All Time Greatest Hits / Mar. 14, 2000 / MCA ✦✦✦✦

Lynyrd Skynyrd's 2000 compilation *All Time Greatest Hits* suffers from the same ailments that plague many compilations of its time, but there is one problem in particular that hurts it: instead of offering all of the "all time greatest hits" on one disc, the compilers pulled their punches, overlooking a few big songs while occasionally substituting live or acoustic versions for the original studio versions. That means that this is a Skynyrd compilation without the famed original recording of "Free Bird"—a live version is here instead. It doesn't really matter that it's a good version, taken from 1976's *One More from the Road*, or that the live version actually charted in the Top 40; nor does it matter that "All I Can Do Is Write About It" is a good acoustic version originally released on the eponymous 1991 box set, because this is a collection made for a general audience. It should, therefore, have the versions that a general audience knows best. Apart from that, and the usual nitpicking over songs which should have been included ("Workin' for MCA," "Don't Ask Me No Questions," etc.), this remains a solid collection, containing most of the Skynyrd material that a casual follower could want. If the double-album *Silver & Gold* remains the greater compilation, that's because it captures the essence of the band better. This includes most of the best-known songs on one disc, and that's noteworthy in its own right; it may even be preferable for some listeners. —*Stephen Thomas Erlewine*

Skynyrd Collectybles / Nov. 21, 2000 / MCA ✦✦✦✦

Skynyrd Collectybles is a set for the devoted, a collection of rarities from Lynyrd Skynyrd's prime period—namely, when Ronnie VanZant led the band. The great thing about this is that it doesn't play as something *just* for the devoted—it's quite enjoyable for anyone who's a fan of Skynyrd's classic work. This does have some historically significant material, namely the inclusion of the early, pre-Skynyrd "Shade Tree Recordings," cut between 1968 and 1970, and the "Quinvy Recordings" from 1970. There are also outtakes from *Second Helping* and *Street Survivors*, and a full album's worth of live material recorded either at the Fox Theater in 1976 or on WMC-FM in 1973. Nothing is particularly revelatory, even the early recording of "Free Bird," but it's all of high quality and anything that adds to classic Skynyrd's body of work is welcome indeed. — *Stephen Thomas Erlewine*

One More from the Road [Deluxe Edition] / Sep. 11, 2001 / MCA ✦✦✦✦
Few concert albums defined their genre more aptly than *One More from the Road.* If Southern rock was about integrity fuelled by pride, then Lynyrd Skynyrd was definitely in the right place at the right time—two days after the American Bicentennial in Atlanta, GA. This deluxe edition commemorates the album's 25th anniversary by augmenting the original 14-track release with ten additional performances taken from the July 7-9, 1976, shows at the fabulous Fox Theater. By the time that Lynyrd Skynyrd hit the road to support *Gimmie Back My Bullets*, their fan base had mushroomed out of their distinctly Southeastern home turf. With the support of national FM radio coverage as well as open-

ing slots on tours with the Who, Skynyrd brought it all back home to the place they were discovered (by Al Kooper, who signed the band to his Sounds of the South subsidiary record label in 1971). Live Lynyrd Skynyrd performances circa the *Gimmie Back My Bullets* tour contained a sampling from each of their long-players, as well as some kick-ass covers—such as "T for Texas" and "Crossroads"—in addition to "Travellin' Man," a new composition worked up specifically for this tour. Indicating some degree of performance alteration for these shows and the subsequent recordings is the inclusion of a perfunctory "Tuesday's Gone"—which was done at the beset of the set's producer, Tom Dowd. His uncanny and legendary instincts pay off, as the strength and conviction of that performance places the track literally as well as figuratively at the center of this release. One of the most notable and distinguishing improvements unique to this edition of *One More from the Road* is all-encompassing sound, which was remastered top to bottom from the original 16-track tapes. As revealed in the 28-page full-color liner-notes essay, these tapes had to undergo a series of processes to physically stabilize the tape long enough to be transferred into the digital domain. The results are astounding, making this deluxe edition more or less a final statement. — *Lindsay Planer*

Willie Mabon

b. Oct. 24, 1925, Hollywood, TN, **d.** Apr. 19, 1985, Paris, France
Vocals, Piano / Piano Blues, R&B, Chicago Blues

The sly, insinuating vocals and chunky piano style of Willie Mabon won the heart of many an R&B fan during the early '50s. His salty Chess waxings "I Don't Know," "I'm Mad," and "Poison Ivy" established the pianist as a genuine Chicago blues force, but he faded as a R&B hitmaker at the dawn of rock & roll.

Mabon was already well-grounded in blues tradition from his Memphis upbringing when he hit Chicago in 1942. Schooled in jazz as well as blues, Mabon found the latter his ticket to stardom. His first sides were a 1949 78 for Apollo as Big Willie and some 1950 outings for Aristocrat and Chess with guitarist Earl Dranes as the Blues Rockers.

But Mabon's asking price for a night's work rose dramatically when his 1952 debut release on powerful Windy City deejay Al Benson's Parrot logo, "I Don't Know," topped the R&B charts for eight weeks after being sold to Chess. From then on, Mabon was a Chess artist, returning to the top R&B slot the next year with the ominous "I'm Mad" and cracking the Top Ten anew with the Mel London-penned "Poison Ivy" in 1954. Throughout his Chess tenure, piano and sax were consistently to the fore rather than guitar and harp, emphasizing Mabon's cool R&B approach. Mabon's original version of Willie Dixon's hoodoo-driven "The Seventh Son" bombed in 1955, as did the remainder of his fine Chess catalog.

Mabon never regained his momentum after leaving Chess. He stopped at Federal in 1957, Mad in 1960, Formal in 1962 (where he stirred up some local sales with his leering "Got to Have Some"), and USA in 1963-1964. Mabon sat out much of the late '60s but came back strong after moving to Paris in 1972, recording and touring Europe prolifically until his death. —*Bill Dahl*

Chicago 63 / 1974 / America ♦♦♦♦♦
Stylish piano and vocals ranging from clever to cranky to anguished. Willie Mabon is seldom powerful, but can convey more shadings and nuances than many blues vocalists or singers in several other genres as well. —*Ron Wynn*

The Seventh Son [LP] / 1981 / Crown Prince ♦♦♦♦♦
Eighteen sensational Chess sides from 1952-1956 collected on import vinyl, quite a few of which unfortunately don't appear on the Charly CD: "Wow I Feel So Good," "Would You Baby," "Say Man" (not the Bo Diddley routine), "Cruisin'," and "Late Again," for starters. —*Bill Dahl*

Original USA Recordings / 1981 / Flyright ♦♦♦
More Mabon sides, these from 1963-1964 and the USA label, that haven't made it to the digital domain yet (at least domestically). The USA stuff wasn't as consistent as his early Chess work, but there are some nice moments—the salacious "Just Got Some," a chunky "I'm the Fixer" and Willie's mouth organ workout "Harmonica Special." —*Bill Dahl*

Blue Roots, Vol. 16 / 1982 / Chess ♦♦♦♦♦
While it may be a little difficult to track down, *Willie Mabon: Blue Roots, Vol. 16* is a solid overview of the pianist's greatest sides for Chess Records. Augmented by a couple of pleasant, but ultimately inconsequential, unreleased cuts, the collection is a good way to acquire the original versions of his big Chess hits until Chess gets around to reissuing these on CD. —*Thom Owens*

● Seventh Son [CD] / 1993 / Charly ♦♦♦♦♦
Since MCA hasn't gotten around to this insinuating character's splendid Chess catalog as yet, we'll have to opt for a 16-song import that encompasses his three major hits "I Don't Know" (here in alternate take form, for whatever reason), and the Mel London-penned "Poison Ivy." Mabon's urban R&B approach was something of a departure for the Delta-rooted blues prevalent at Chess at the time, but his laconic vocals on "The Seventh Son," "Knock on Wood," and "Got to Have It" made him a star (albeit briefly). —*Bill Dahl*

Chicago Blues Session! / 1995 / Evidence ♦♦♦
Chicago Blues Session! features a session pianist Willie Mabon cut on Independence Day 1979 with guitarist Hubert Sumlin, guitarist Eddie Taylor, bassist Aron Burton and drummer Casey Jones. The album was originally released on the German L&R label, mainly because American labels were shunning the blues. That could be the only reason this album wasn't released at the time, since it's a nice, straight-ahead Chicago blues record. There are several Mabon originals, all of them strong and memorable, plus several Willie Dixon tracks and a Howlin' Wolf cut. This Howlin' Wolf song is one of a handful of tributes to Chicago blues legends—the others are to Jimmy Reed and Willie Dixon—but the true tribute is the spirit and passion the group puts into their music. That's what makes the album a worthwhile listen for serious fans of Chicago blues. —*Thom Owens*

Alura Mack

Vocals / Classic Female Blues, Dirty Blues

The grisly "Beef Blood Blues" is about as far out as a classic blues singer of the late '20s ever got, and it is one of the things that makes the recording career of Alura Mack so alluring. Another is the interesting range of outlooks she offered in her catalog of songs, from bragging about being "Loose Like That" to claiming "I Ain't Puttin' Out Nothin' Blues." It can be assumed that the former ditty is not about the condition of a wing nut, while the latter is probably not the anthem of a forest ranger who has decided to go on strike. Sexual subjects were the required menu for this style of female blues singers, whose recordings during this era featured lyrics ranging from slightly to incredibly nasty, accompanied usually by a pianist and sometimes a clarinet, trumpet, or banjo. Mack often worked in conjunction with bluesman Tommie Bradley.

It was an era in recording history when the popular records of the day rivaled the filth of rap artists who would come along some seven decades later. For every female classic blues artist who became a big star, such as Bessie Smith or Alberta Hunter, there were many others with varying careers of which Mack falls somewhere between the fairly successful and complete shadows (the latter includes Sadie James, who only recorded a couple of numbers before dropping off the face of the earth). Tracks cut by these singers, including Edna Johnson, Mack, James, and Coletha Simpson, among others, have been compiled on collections such as *Blue Girls, Vol. 1: 1924-1930* on the Document label. Material by Mack tends to dominate these sets, with one collection featuring a dozen of her tracks, while other artists featured performing on only one or two. As if desiring to experience the taste of deeper obscurity, but probably just wanting to make some extra money without violating a preexisting contract, Mack also recorded for the Superior label in the late '20s under the name of Clara Andrews. Other Mack records include "I'm Busy, You Can't Come In." —*Eugene Chadbourne*

Lonnie Mack (Lonnie McIntosh)

b. Jul. 18, 1941, Harrison, IN
Vocals, Leader, Guitar / Instrumental Rock, Modern Electric Blues, Rock & Roll, R&B

When Lonnie Mack sings the blues, country strains are sure to infiltrate. Conversely, if he digs into a humping rockabilly groove, strong signs of deep-down blues influence are bound to invade. Par for the course for any musician who cites both Bobby Bland and George Jones as pervasive influences.

Fact is, Lonnie Mack's lightning-fast, vibrato-enriched, whammy bar-hammered guitar style has influenced many a picker too—including Stevie Ray Vaughan, who idolized Mack's early singles for Fraternity and later co-produced and played on Mack's 1985 comeback LP for Alligator, *Strike like Lightning.*

Growing up in rural Indiana not far from Cincinnati, Lonnie McIntosh was exposed to a heady combination of R&B and hillbilly. In 1958, he bought the seventh Gibson Flying V guitar ever manufactured and played the roadhouse circuit around Indiana, Ohio, and Kentucky. Mack has steadfastly cited another local legend, guitarist Robert Ward, as the man whose watery-sounding Magnatone amplifier inspired his own use of the same brand.

Session work ensued during the early '60s behind Hank Ballard, Freddy King, and James Brown for Cincy's principal label, Syd Nathan's King Records. At the tail end of a 1963 date for another local diskery, Fraternity Records, Mack stepped out front to cut a searing instrumental treatment of Chuck Berry's "Memphis." Fraternity put the number out, and it leaped all the way up to the Top Five on *Billboard*'s pop charts!

Its hit follow-up, the frantic "Wham!," was even more amazing from a guitaristic perspective with Mack's lickety-split whammy-bar-fired playing driven like a locomotive by a hard-charging horn section. Mack's vocal skills were equally potent; R&B stations began to play his soul ballad "Where There's a Will" until they discovered Mack was of the Caucasian persuasion, then dropped it like a hot potato (its flip, a sizzling vocal remake of Jimmy Reed's "Baby, What's Wrong," was a minor pop hit in late 1963).

Mack waxed a load of killer material for Fraternity during the mid-'60s, much of it not seeing the light of day until later on. A deal with Elektra Records inspired by a 1968 *Rolling Stone* article profiling Mack should have led to major stardom, but his three Elektra albums were less consistent than the Fraternity material. (Elektra also reissued his only Fraternity LP, the seminal *The Wham of That Memphis Man.*) Mack cameoed on the Doors' *Morrison Hotel* album, contributing a guitar solo to "Roadhouse Blues," and worked for a while as a member of Elektra's A&R team.

Disgusted with the record business, Lonnie Mack retreated back to Indiana for a while, eventually signing with Capitol and waxing a couple of obscure country-based albums. Finally, at Vaughan's behest, Mack abandoned his Indiana comfort zone for hipper Austin, TX, and began to reassert himself nationally. Vaughan masterminded the stunning *Strike like Lightning* in 1985; later that year, Mack co-starred with Alligator labelmates Albert Collins and Roy Buchanan at Carnegie Hall (a concert marketed on home video as *Further on Down the Road*).

Mack's Alligator encore, *Second Sight*, was a disappointment for those who idolized Mack's playing—it was more of a singer/songwriter project. He temporarily left Alligator in 1988 for major-label prestige at Epic, but *Roadhouses and Dancehalls* was too diverse to easily classify and died a quick death. Mack's most recent album from 1990, *Live! Attack of the Killer V*, was captured on tape at a suburban Chicago venue called FitzGerald's and once again showed why Lonnie Mack is venerated by anyone who's even remotely into savage guitar playing. —*Bill Dahl*

☆ **The Wham of That Memphis Man** / 1964 / Alligator ✦✦✦✦✦
This is a vinyl reissue of Mack's first album for Fraternity in 1964, the one thousands of guitarists cut their teeth on. Muddy Waters once sang, "The blues had a baby and they named the baby rock & roll." This is the album that proves it. Instrumental versions of R&B hits ("Memphis," "Susie Q," "The Bounce") rebound against heartfelt soul numbers ("Farther Down the Road," "Why?") right next to dazzling fretboard blues romps both slow and fast ("Wham!," "Down and Out"). Mack sings his rear end off, the band—with saxes and Hammond organ and pumping soul bass—is right in there and Mack's vibrato-drenched guitar stings, wounds, and amazes. It remains his defining moment. —*Cub Koda*

Glad I'm in the Band / 1969 / Elektra ✦✦✦
With the exception of his comeback album for Alligator, *Strike Like Lightning*, nothing Mack has done since leaving Fraternity Records has come close to the wham-fisted brilliance of those seminal sides. This LP isn't bad at all, though—besides passable remakes of "Memphis" and "Why," Mack attacks Frankie Ford's "Roberta," Ted Taylor's "Stay Away from My Baby," and Little Willie John's "Let Them Talk" with a slightly rockier edge than his previous stuff. R&B vet Maxwell Davis did the horn charts. —*Bill Dahl*

Whatever's Right / 1969 / Elektra ✦✦✦
With a passel of familiar faces in the cast (ex-James Brown bassist Tim Drummond, pianist Denny "Dumpy" Rice, harpist Rusty York), the reclusive Mack rocks up some memorable dusties his way—the Falcons' "I Found a Love," and Bobby "Blue" Bland's "Share Your Love with Me," Little Walter's "My Babe," and Jimmy Reed's chestnut "Baby What You Want Me to Do," along with his own "Gotta Be an Answer." —*Bill Dahl*

For Collectors Only / 1970 / Elektra ✦✦✦✦✦
For Collectors Only is reissue of Mack's sole Fraternity LP. —*Bill Dahl*

Memphis Sounds of Lonnie Mack / 1974 / Trip ✦✦✦✦✦
Memphis Sounds of Lonnie Mack is a fine collection of rarities recorded for the Fraternity label. —*Bill Dahl*

Home at Last / 1977 / One Way ✦✦
The bearded guitar wonder in a mainstream country setting that largely doesn't do him justice. —*Bill Dahl*

Lonnie Mack With Pismo / 1977 / One Way ✦✦
Country-rock (mostly) from the versatile and unpredictable master picker. Pismo's members included bassist Tim Drummond and keyboardist Stan Szelest (frequent Mack cohorts), while Troy Seals, Graham Nash, and David Lindley contributed to the product as well. The unabashed rockers "Lucy" and "Rock and Roll like We Used To" have some life in them, but some of this stuff is dreary. —*Bill Dahl*

Strike Like Lightning / 1985 / Alligator ✦✦✦✦
Co-produced by Stevie Ray Vaughn, this was Lonnie's ticket back to the show after a few years on the sidelines. To say it was an inspired date would be putting it mildly. With his batteries recharged, Mack was in peak form, playing and singing better than ever. A major highlight is an inspired duet between Stevie and Lonnie on "Wham (Double Whammy)," going toe to toe for several exciting choruses. —*Cub Koda*

Second Sight / 1987 / Alligator ✦✦✦
After the sizzle of *Strike Like Lightning*, this mellow set was a major disappointment. Yes, Mack is an exceptional vocalist, but the pop crossover ambience exploited here came at the expense of his unequalled guitar work—not a fair trade at all. —*Bill Dahl*

Road Houses & Dance Halls / 1988 / Epic ✦✦
The folks at Columbia had no idea how to market Mack, so this fairly undistinguished album died a quick and practically unnoticed death. —*Bill Dahl*

Attack of the Killer V: Live / 1990 / Alligator ✦✦✦
Cut in front of an appreciative throng at FitzGerald's in suburban Chicago, Mack cuts loose the way he so often does in concert, sticking almost exclusively to his Alligator-era tunes ("Satisfy Suzie," "Cincinnati Jail," the tortured soul ballad "Stop") and never looking too far backwards. —*Bill Dahl*

Lonnie on the Move / 1992 / Ace ✦✦✦✦✦
These 19 Flying V-soaked sides pack the same punch and hail from the same mid-'60s timeframe as Mack's seminal LP *Wham of That Memphis Man*. He unleashes his vibrato-drenched axe on the torrid "Soul Express," "Lonnie on the Move," "Florence of Arabia," and an astonishing instrumental version of "Stand by Me" that'll send aspiring guitarists' jaws crashing to the floor. For a change of pace, "Men at Play" mines a jazzy walking groove to equally satisfying ends. —*Bill Dahl*

★ **Memphis Wham!** / Jul. 27, 1999 / Ace ✦✦✦✦✦
At first glance, this might seem like nothing more than a retread of the classic *The Wham of That Memphis Man*, as the disc includes all 14 songs from that album. This is a quality upgrade/supplement to that record, though, adding 11 more tracks of 1963-1967 vintage from both rare singles and previously unreleased outtakes. This is hardly filler that only collectors will care about; it's good stuff, sometimes ace stuff, that's almost all on the same level of *The Wham*. "Oh, I Apologize," a cover of an obscure Barrett Strong track, is white soul singing on par with Mack's best vocal efforts, while "Cry, Cry, Cry" is a great instrumental version of a Bobby "Blue" Bland number; both of these cuts, unbelievably, were not released prior to this CD. The singles "Say Something Nice to Me" and "Save Your Money" (from 1964 and 1967) are more filet of white soul, and "Tension Pts. 1 & 2" (a 1966 single) another cool roadhouse instrumental. Some of the rare add-ons are less

essential than others (like the instrumental reading of the Beatles' "From Me to You"), but taken together it's certainly the best Mack collection, enhanced by Bill Millar's informative liner notes. By the way, in one of those inexplicable occurrences bound to cause collectors to run around in circles, the song titled "Farther on Down the Road" on *The Wham of That Memphis Man* recording is here titled "Farther on Up the Road" and listed as previously unreleased, although in fact it seems to be the same track as the one given a different title on the LP. (To cause further confusion, Mack definitely sings the lyric "Farther on up the road," not "Farther on down the road," as it was originally titled.) —*Richie Unterberger*

From Nashville to Memphis / Jul. 31, 2001 / Ace ✦✦✦
As the third and final volume of the trilogy of Ace compilations covering Lonnie Mack's '60s Fraternity recordings, this at a glance looks like a mop-up of the bottom of the can. If that's so, though, it's quite an enjoyable mop-up, albeit with an erratic streak in both the quality and form of the material. About half of this is previously unreleased, including some alternate takes of officially released sides. Some of the 1963-1967 singles are really fine, like the instrumental "Nashville," which has mean blues-rock licks on par with anything Mack's done—meaning that they're on par with *anyone's* blues-rock licks. Otherwise there are some honky-tonk twist instrumentals; some quite fine blue-eyed soul vocals with horns, like "She Don't Come Here Anymore" and "Crying Over You"; and a genuine hit (low-charting, admittedly, at number 78), "Honky Tonk '65." It gets wackier: a rather cool instrumental adaptation of "I Left My Heart in San Francisco," mixing lounge horns with biting guitar riffs; a mix of surf reverb and soundtrack theme on "When I'm Alone"; and straight country music on "Are You Guilty?" There are also rare singles by Beau Dollar & the Coins, Denny "Dumpy" Rice, the Charmaines, and Max Falcon on which Mack played, as well as a mono version of his big hit, "Memphis." Some of this CD is so-so, but the high points ensure that it won't disappoint Mack lovers. —*Richie Unterberger*

Still on the Move / Jun. 11, 2002 / Ace ✦✦✦✦
Still on the Move is a somewhat revised and expanded version of the 1992 Ace CD compilation *Lonnie on the Move*, which was itself a slightly revised reissue of a mid-'70s double-LP compilation album of '60s Fraternity recordings. It's "somewhat revised" because it actually eliminates two tracks from *Lonnie on the Move*, "Soul Express" and "Jam and Butter." That's because those are actually different titles for the same recording, and also because that recording appears under its proper name, "The Freeze," on another Mack anthology on Ace, *Memphis Wham!. Still on the Move* also adds a bunch of tracks that haven't been included on reissue comps before, among them sides from rare mid-'60s Fraternity singles and five previously unreleased alternate takes. Determining what previously appeared where is a complicated enough exercise to make you wish, actually, that you didn't even know about those other compilations. What's important is that, when combined with the other two Mack Ace CD anthologies, *From Nashville to Memphis* and *Memphis Wham!*, *Still on the Move* provides all the '60s Mack Fraternity recordings you could possibly want. What's more important is that this is very good rock-R&B-country-soul, not quite as good as his best '60s Fraternity stuff (as heard on the *Memphis Wham!* comp), but not far off that mark. His idiosyncratic vibrato guitar is consistently excellent, and the material (whether instrumental or vocal) is frankly much more varied and interesting than those of many other artists from the time who were working the same territory. "Wildwood Flower" sounds like a more even-tempered Link Wray, "Snow on the Mountain" is a first-class overlooked blue-eyed soul cooker from 1967, and the overdone "Money" gets a very cool minor-keyed interpretation. His singing is good enough to make you wish that he'd sung more often, and indeed some cuts, like "I Found a Love," sound suspiciously like they were meant to have lead vocals but never got overdubbed with them, as they have full backup vocal choruses. On the other hand, instrumental workouts like "Stand By Me" bring a fresh interpretation to such standards that wouldn't have been possible if they'd included vocals. —*Richie Unterberger*

Doug MacLeod

b. Apr. 21, 1946, New York, NY
Vocals, Guitar / Contemporary Blues, Acoustic Blues, Modern Electric Blues
Unlike some other bluesmen now leading their own bands, guitarist and singer/songwriter Doug MacLeod spent many years as an apprentice before forming his own band. MacLeod has worked as a sideman for many different artists from the Los Angeles-area blues scene, including Big Joe Turner, Charles Brown, Pee Wee Crayton, Eddie "Cleanhead" Vinson, and George "Harmonica" Smith. MacLeod was born in New York on April 21, 1946, and his parents moved to St. Louis shortly after his birth. He spent his teen years frequenting the blues clubs there, learning from people like Albert King, Little Milton, and Ike and Tina Turner. He took up the bass in his teens and played around St. Louis with local bands before enlisting in the Navy. MacLeod was stationed in Norfolk, VA, and spent his off-duty time playing in blues bars. He eventually settled in Los Angeles, accompanying many other blues performers before forming his own band. His songs have been recorded by Albert King, Albert Collins, and Son Seals. MacLeod's 1984 album, *No Road Back Home*, was nominated for a W.C. Handy Award in 1984 and has since been reissued on compact disc on the Hightone label. MacLeod has widely available albums on Audioquest—*Come to Find* (1994), *You Can't Take My Blues* (1996), *Unmarked Road* (1997), and *Whose Truth, Whose Lies?* (2000). His first Audioquest disc features guest appearances by harmonica players Carey Bell and fiddle player Heather Hardy, while the second has a guest appearance by harp player George "Harmonica" Smith. MacLeod has also recorded for a variety of independent labels, including such albums as *Woman in the Street*, *54th and Vermont*, and *Ain't the Blues Evil*. 2002 saw the release of MacLeod's *A Little Sin*, recorded in July of that year with producer/frequent collaborator Joe Harley. —*Richard Skelly & Al Campbell*

No Road Back Home / 1984 / Hightone ♦♦♦♦♦

Ain't the Blues Evil / 1991 / Volt ♦♦

MacLeod and his band continue in a storytelling jazz-tinged blues bag, whether in "Just Like a Minstrel," where he bemoans the trials and tribulations of road life (eating cold hot dogs and sleeping in dirty hotel rooms) or in "One Fool Lookin' for Another," recalling troubles with women. Hammond B-3 and military drum rolls underlie "Placquemine," telling of a man who trails a lover from place to place, only to find her using him as a stepping stone toward a Hollywood career. Fellow George Smith alumna Rod Piazza accompanies and blows an ultra-cool solo on "(I Think You're) Steppin' Out on Me." "SRV (For Stevie Ray)," is an inspirational instrumental which is both a tribute and a thank you to the great Mr. Vaughan. *—Char Ham*

Come to Find / 1994 / AudioQuest ♦♦♦

The sparseness of the arrangements make this album admirable and draw even more attention to the music both overall and in its subtleties. It showcases brilliantly Bill Stuve's upright bass work, and for Jimi Bott, how unusually placed but effective drumbeats prove him a blues drummer deserving greater recognition. "Since I Left St. Louis" has MacLeod reflecting on his early adult years of fast life, women, and drinking, and the lessons painfully learned from those experiences. The title track is a realization that making the most out of life is better than a life of abuse, whether it be child abuse, substance abuse, or any other kind. Always a master on the harmonica, Charlie Musselwhite blows on Willie Dixon's "Bring It on Home" and the MacLeod-penned "Lost Something This Morning." A great example of Piedmont-style blues is illustrated in "Old Virginia Stomp," dedicated to mentor Ernest Banks. Backup singers Black Cherry round the album out with the uplifting gospel feel of "Ain't No Grave," which tells of the triumph of the afterlife over death. *—Char Ham*

You Can't Take My Blues / 1996 / AudioQuest ♦♦♦♦

Doug MacLeod displays several sides of his artistry on this AudioQuest CD. His music ranges from solo folk numbers in the idiom of Leadbelly (but covering different subjects) to country blues with a trio, a few romps with the wailing harmonica of Carey Bell and two collaborations with the country fiddle of Heather Hardy. MacLeod's appealing voice is easy to understand, his lyrics are thoughtful and fresh (even when covering universal subjects) and his melodic guitar playing is versatile. MacLeod's well-conceived set should appeal to collectors of acoustic blues and folk music. *—Scott Yanow*

● **Unmarked Road** / Oct. 7, 1997 / AudioQuest ♦♦♦♦♦

Doug MacLeod's dark singing and sparse guitar playing are a throwback to the country blues artists of the '30s, although his lyrics have more modern sensibilities. Much of this superior CD is haunting and mildly disturbing, giving one the feeling that there is a great deal beneath the surface. It is the type of blues-folk recording worth experiencing several times, in contrast to those of recent times that express more obvious sentiments. Bassist Jeff Turmes is on just seven of the dozen songs (five of which also include drummer Stefe Mugalian); three of the remaining tunes are duets by MacLeod with percussionist Oliver Brown, and the two others are unaccompanied solo performances. Although the leader's guitar playing is impressive, it is his distinctive and very sincere voice on his dozen originals that sticks in one's mind. *—Scott Yanow*

Whose Truth, Whose Lies? / Jul. 11, 2000 / AudioQuest ♦♦♦♦♦

In 2000, you would have been hard-pressed to find a more lowdown blues-oriented recording than singer/guitarist Doug MacLeod's *Whose Truth, Whose Lies?*, which should appeal to anyone who likes his/her blues dark, shadowy, and moody. This isn't a CD that tries to win you over with slickness; whether MacLeod is going electric or acoustic, he obviously identifies with the simplicity and honesty that characterized the country blues artists of the '30s and '40s. Not that *Whose Truth, Whose Lies?* sounds like a recording from that time. MacLeod's lyrics obviously aren't pre-World War II lyrics, and he has been influenced by soul, rock, and folk as well as country and urban blues. Not everything on this superb album adheres to a 12-bar format, and some of the tunes fall into the folk category. But even when he is getting into a folk or R&B groove, MacLeod can always be counted on to provide a wealth of blues feeling. *Whose Truth, Whose Lies?* may not be the work of a purist, but it is certainly compelling. *—Alex Henderson*

Madcat & Kane

f. Ann Arbor, MI

Group / Contemporary Blues, Contemporary Folk, Folk-Blues

Peter "Madcat" Ruth (harmonica) and Shari Kane (guitar, vocals) are a folk-blues duo based in Ann Arbor, MI. Ruth's multi-note style appears on tracks with the Southern rock group Blackfoot among others while Kane's slide work is a descendant of her mentor and leading inspiration, the legendary Johnny Shines. *Key to the Highway* has been released on Schoolkids' Records. *—John Bush*

● **Key to the Highway** / 1992 / Schoolkids ♦♦♦

Blues-lite, perfect for campfire sing-a-longs (though Madcat Ruth's harp chops are undeniably impressive). *—Bill Dahl*

Up Against the Wall / 1999 / Hit ♦♦♦

Madcat & Kane's second album finds them exploring traditional themes but with far more emphasis on original material than on their debut album. Guest appearances from Ann Rabson, slide man Kevin Maul and vocalist Claudia Schmidt pepper up certain tracks, but in the main it's Peter and Shari's show here, and the spotlight stays on their estimable talents. Kane is every bit the equal of a Rory Block, both vocally and instrumentally, while Ruth's harmonica tone is wide and pervasive throughout and sometimes other-worldly sounding on certain tracks. Standout tracks include "Rosalie," "Did You Save Me a Taste?," "You Used to Call Me Mama," "Darkness" and a country-styled version of Hop Wilson's "Black Cat Bone." *—Cub Koda*

Magic Sam (Samuel Maghett)

b. Feb. 14, 1937, Grenada, MS, **d.** Dec. 1, 1969, Chicago, IL

Vocals, Leader, Guitar / Modern Electric Chicago Blues, Electric Chicago Blues

No blues guitarist better represented the adventurous modern sound of Chicago's West Side more proudly than Sam Maghett. He died tragically young (at age 32 of a heart attack), right when he was on the brink of climbing the ladder to legitimate stardom—but Magic Sam left behind a thick legacy of bone-cutting blues that remains eminently influential around his old stomping grounds to this day.

Mississippi Delta-born Sam Maghett (one of his childhood pals was towering guitarist Morris Holt, who received his Magic Slim handle from Sam). In 1950, Sam arrived in Chicago, picking up a few blues guitar pointers from his new neighbor, Syl Johnson (whose brother Mack Thompson served as Sam's loyal bassist for much of his professional career). Harpist Shakey Jake Harris, sometimes referred to as the guitarist's uncle, encouraged Sam's blues progress and gigged with him later on, when both were West Side institutions.

Sam's tremolo-rich staccato fingerpicking was an entirely fresh phenomenon when he premiered it on Eli Toscano's Cobra label in 1957. Prior to his Cobra date, the guitarist had been gigging as Good Rocking Sam, but Toscano wanted to change his nickname to something old-timey like Sad Sam or Singing Sam. No dice, said the newly christened Magic Sam (apparently Mack Thompson's brainstorm).

His Cobra debut single, "All Your Love," was an immediate local sensation; its unusual structure would be recycled time and again by Sam throughout his tragically truncated career. Sam's Cobra encores "Everything Gonna Be Alright" and "Easy Baby" borrowed much the same melody but were no less powerful; the emerging West Side sound was now officially committed to vinyl. Not everything Sam cut utilized the tune; "21 Days in Jail" was a pseudo-rockabilly smoker with hellacious lead guitar from Sam and thundering slap bass from the ubiquitous Willie Dixon. Sam also backed Shakey Jake Harris on his lone 45 for Cobra's Artistic subsidiary, "Call Me If You Need Me."

After Cobra folded, Sam didn't follow labelmates Otis Rush and Magic Slim over to Chess. Instead, after enduring an unpleasant Army experience that apparently landed him in jail for desertion, Sam opted to go with Mel London's Chief logo in 1960. His raw-boned West Side adaptation of Fats Domino's mournful "Every Night About This Time" was the unalloyed highlight of his stay at Chief; some other Chief offerings were less compelling.

Gigs on the West Side remained plentiful for the charismatic guitarist, but recording opportunities proved sparse until 1966, when Sam made a 45 for Crash Records. "Out of Bad Luck" brought back that trademark melody again, but it remained as shattering as ever. Another notable 1966 side, the plaintive "That's Why I'm Crying," wound up on Delmark's *Sweet Home Chicago* anthology, along with Sam's stunning clippity-clop boogie instrumental "Riding High" (aided by the muscular tenor sax of Eddie Shaw).

Delmark Records was the conduit for Magic Sam's two seminal albums, 1967's *West Side Soul* and the following year's *Black Magic*. Both LPs showcased the entire breadth of Sam's West side attack: the first ranged from the soul-laced "That's All I Need" and a searing "I Feel So Good" to the blistering instrumental "Lookin' Good" and definitive remakes of "Mama Talk to Your Daughter" and "Sweet Home Chicago," while *Black Magic* benefitted from Shaw's jabbing, raspy sax as Sam blasted through the funky "You Belong to Me," an impassioned "What Have I Done Wrong," and a personalized treatment of Freddy King's "San-Ho-Zay."

Sam's reputation was growing exponentially. He wowed an overflow throng at the 1969 Ann Arbor Blues Festival, and Stax was reportedly primed to sign him when his Delmark commitment was over. However, heart problems were fast taking their toll on Sam's health. On the first morning of December of 1969, he complained of heartburn, collapsed, and died.

Even now, more than a quarter century after his passing, Magic Sam remains the king of West Side blues. That's unlikely to change as long as the sub-genre is alive and kicking. *—Bill Dahl*

Magic Touch / 1966 / Black Top ♦♦♦♦

Another rare glimpse at Magic Sam hard at work, this time at another fabled West Side haunt, Sylvio's, in 1966. No saxes this time, but uncle Shakey Jake was around for a few guest shots, while bassist Mack Thompson and drummer Odie Payne provide supple backing as Sam launches into another terrific set of numbers that for the most part he never recorded in the studio—songs by Freddy King, Albert Collins, James Robins, Junior Parker, and Jimmy McCracklin that briliiantly suited his soaring pipes and singular guitar style. *—Bill Dahl*

★ **West Side Soul** / 1967 / Delmark ♦♦♦♦♦

To call *West Side Soul* one of the great blues albums, one of the key albums (if not *the* key album) of modern electric blues is all true, but it tends to diminish and academicize Magic Sam's debut album. This is the inevitable side effect of time, when an album that is decades old enters the history books, but this isn't an album that should be preserved in amber, seen only as an important record. Because this is a record that is exploding with life, a record with so much energy, it doesn't sound old. Of course, part of the reason it sounds so modern, is because this is the template for most modern blues, whether it comes from Chicago or elsewhere. Magic Sam may not have been the first to blend uptown soul and urban blues, but he was the first to capture not just the passion of soul, but also its subtle elegance, while retaining the firepower of an after-hours blues joint. Listen to how the album begins, with "That's All I Need," a swinging tune that has as much in common with Curtis Mayfield as it does Muddy Waters, but it doesn't sound like either—it's a synthesis masterminded by Magic Sam, rolling along on the magnificent delayed cadence of his guitar and powered by his impassioned vocals. *West Side Soul* would be remarkable if it only had this kind of soul-blues, but it also is filled with blistering, charged electric blues, fueled by wild playing by Sam and Mighty Joe Young—not just on the solos, either, but in the rhythm (witness how "I Feel So Good (I Wanna Boogie)" feels *unhinged* as it barrels along). Similarly, Sam's vocals are sensitive or forceful, depending on what the song calls for. Some of these elements might have been heard before, but never in a setting so bristling with energy and inventiveness; it doesn't sound like it was recorded in a studio, it sounds like the best night in a packed club. But it's more than that, because there's a diversity in the sound here, an originality so fearless, he not only makes "Sweet Home Chicago" his own (no version before or since is as definitive as this), he creates the soul-injected, high voltage modern blues sound that everybody has emulated and nobody has topped in the years since. And, again, that makes it sound like a history lesson, but it's not. This music is alive, vibrant and vital—nothing sounds as tortured as "I Need You So Bad," no boogie is as infectious as "Mama, Mama Talk To Your Daughter," no blues as haunting as "All of Your Love." No matter what year you listen to it, you'll never hear a better, more exciting record that year. *—Stephen Thomas Erlewine*

Black Magic / 1968 / Delmark ✦✦✦✦✦

This album's color cover photo is an action shot, showing Magic Sam in the process of choking and bending his strings, a good hike up the fretboard. It isn't clear exactly what he is playing from the picture, although that certainly didn't stop dozens of pimply hippie guitar players from trying to figure it out. In the meantime, the record goes on and the first soloist out of the gate is Eddie Shaw, playing tenor sax. He is blowing over the top of an R&B riff that, although not out of the syntax of Chicago blues, would also have been quite fitting on a Wilson Pickett record. It is unfortunate that Magic Sam's recording career came to such an abrupt end, as he was one of the best artists working in the musical area between the urban blues tradition and newly developing soul music forms. This fusion was on the minds of many blues artists during the late '60s, and not just because it was aesthetically conceivable. It was also a matter of commerce, as audiences—particularly black audiences—didn't want to hear any blues that sounded too much like something their parents might have listened to. The harmonica player Junior Wells was another one who decided to get a bit of James Brown into his act, not always with great results. What listeners have here, on the other hand, is frankly delicious, the results of the surplus of talent Magic Sam possessed, a triple threat as a guitarist, singer, and songwriter. Yet with all this talent, the label should also get some credit. This period of the Delmark discography set a high standard for blues recordings, the sound quality and tight interplay among the musicians every bit the equal of the classic jazz recordings on labels such as Blue Note and Prestige. There is nothing fancy about the production, and no gimmicks. It is just a great band, allowed to play the music exactly the way it wanted to. The musicians have obviously worked together a great deal and either had these arrangements down cold from live gigs or had plenty of time to get things tight. This doesn't mean that the music doesn't breathe, as there are plenty of little touches such as drum fills and turnarounds that show the presence of musicians thinking on their feet. The passage of time also increases the musical value of this music, as the eventual popularity of commercial projects such as the Blues Brothers has only served to dilute the power of urban blues. Labels big and small have forsaken this type of honest and straightforward production, preferring to try concocting a higher level of funkiness through extravagent over-production, boring superstar guest appearances, and insipid studio practices such as prerecorded rhythm tracks and dipstick guitar solos punched in a note at the time. Forget all this jive and check out a track such as "You Belong to Me," where the guitarist cuts loose with a restrained solo that sometimes dances ahead of the beat like a country fiddler while the band pumps away on a superb riff. The players here, including the fine guitarist Mighty Joe Young, pianist Lafayette Leake, and a muscular rhythm section, are the best of the best. No information is provided on the songwriting, so the assumption is that these tunes are all originals by Magic Sam. None are too obviously adopted from standards, but the opening "I Just Want a Little Bit" was much copied by other blues artists. "I Have the Same Old Blues" has a medium, loping blues tempo that swings so perfectly it should be used as an instruction course for lame blues bar bands. *—Eugene Chadbourne*

Magic Rocker / 1980 / Flyright ✦✦✦✦✦

Otis Rush & Magic Sam / 1980 / Flyright ✦✦✦✦✦

A pair of blues giants, each given ample room. While you can find better Rush and Sam, that's no slam on what's here. What you're getting are excellent songs that didn't make it onto the first reissue of Magic Sam/Shakey Jake material, plus powerhouse Rush that didn't make *Groaning the Blues*. In other words, this isn't exactly fodder. *—Ron Wynn*

Live at Ann Arbor & In Chicago / Jul. 1982 / Delmark ✦✦✦

While the sound quality leaves something to be desired, fans of electric Chicago blues should hear Magic Sam live. Recorded at two separate locations, the Alex Club in Chicago in 1963 and 1964 and the Ann Arbor Blues and Jazz Festival in 1969, this disc captures the raw energy not only of the musicians, but the crowds' tremendous response to them. Sam is in his natural environment at the Alex Club with an interchanging quintet, including electric pianist Tyrone Carter and tenor saxophonists Eddie Shaw and A.C. Reed, playing in front of a rowdy audience, ready to party. The Ann Arbor performance, on the other hand, finds him playing with a stripped down trio at an outdoor festival to a mainly white hippie crowd; performer and audience are somewhat unfamiliar with each other. This doesn't stop Sam's trio from blazing through their set and once again igniting the crowd. It should be noted that the energy level of the audience and band was exceptionally tense after Sam arrived late to the festival site without a drummer. Sam Lay was called upon at the last minute to fill the drum seat, as Charlie Musselwhite's band filled in for them while they set up. Ignore the rotten sound quality, this is raw blues power and provides a priceless document of Sam Maghett's vital showmanship. *—Al Campbell*

The Late Great Magic Sam / 1984 / Evidence ✦✦✦

The ten 1963-1964 sides that make up the majority of this set have sort of fallen through the historical cracks over the years. They didn't deserve such shoddy treatment—Sam didn't record "Back Door Friend" or "Hi-Heel Sneakers" anywhere else, and he's in top shape throughout. Two live tracks at the set's close from 1969 don't add much to the overall package. *—Bill Dahl*

The Magic Sam Legacy / 1989 / Delmark ✦✦✦✦

Alternate takes and unissued surprises from the *West Side Soul* and *Black Magic* sessions, along with a couple of welcome 1966 sides ("I Feel So Good" and "Lookin' Good") that didn't see the light of day when they were recorded. Sam's versions of Jimmy Rogers' "Walkin' By Myself" and "That Ain't It" are important additions to his immortal legacy. *—Bill Dahl*

Easy Baby / 1990 / Charly ✦✦✦

Here are all the issued recordings Magic Sam made between his debut on Cobra in 1957 all the way up to just before signing with Delmark and releasing the epochal *West Side Soul* album. In addition to Cobra masterpieces like "All Your Love" and the title track, it also includes "Magic Rocker" and "Love Me This Way" (both not originally issued as singles) from the same sessions. The set also includes both sides of the Shakey Jake single he contributed the lead guitar on, his four later singles for Chief, and his stray 1966 single for Crash. Although Sam tended to repeat certain themes again and again, here's a nice chunk of the records that helped make his legend. *—Cub Koda*

Live at the Alex Club / 1990 / Delmark ✦✦✦✦

For the first half of this frequently amazing disc, Magic Sam plays for his West Side homefolks at the Alex Club. The time is 1963-1964, he's backed by saxists A.C. Reed and Eddie Shaw and his longtime bassist, Mack Thompson, and he's blasting the hits of the day with a joyous abandon. A little over six years later, Sam wowed the Ann Arbor Blues Festival with a sensational trio set just as inordinately powerful in its own way. Sound quality is rough on both artifacts, but no matter. *—Bill Dahl*

☆ **1957–1966** / 1991 / Paula ✦✦✦✦✦

Never mind Otis Rush and Buddy Guy—this is the bedrock document of Chicago's West Side blues guitar movement. Ten seminal numbers that constitute Sam's complete Cobra stash (notably "All Your Love," "Easy Baby," and the rockabilly tinged "21 Days in Jail"), another pair by his harp-blowing uncle Shakey Jake, five numbers from 1960 that first appeared on Mel London's Chief logo (a tortured cover of Fats Domino's "Every Night About This Time" is the killer), and a couple of solid 1966 outings that reinforce Sam's standing as the king of the West Side prior to his untimely demise. *—Bill Dahl*

Give Me Time / 1991 / Delmark ✦✦✦

We now adjourn to Sam's West Side living room, where he's holding court in 1968 with only a few friends and family members on hand. Some of the tunes are familiar—"That's All I Need," "You Belong to Me"—but there are other originals only available here, and the super-intimate atmosphere brings out the intimate side of the late guitarist. *—Bill Dahl*

☆ **The Essential Magic Sam: The Cobra and Chief Recordings 1957–1961** / Feb. 27, 2001 / Fuel 2000 ✦✦✦✦✦

Fuel 2000's *Essential Magic Sam: The Cobra and Chief Recordings 1957-1961* is the latest, best-sounding repackaging of this material. If you already have this material elsewhere in your collection (and given the number of times it's come out in various incarnations, you very well may), you don't need to replace your previous disc, but if you're looking for the best available collection of this seminal material, turn here. *—Stephen Thomas Erlewine*

With a Feeling 57–67: The Cobra, Chief & Crash Recordings / Mar. 13, 2001 / West Side ✦✦✦✦✦

Magic Slim (Morris Holt)

b. Aug. 7, 1937, Grenada, MS

Vocals, Leader, Guitar / Electric Chicago Blues, Modern Electric Blues

Magic Slim & the Teardrops proudly uphold the tradition of what a Chicago blues *band* should sound like. Their emphasis on ensemble playing and a humongous repertoire that allegedly ranges upwards of a few hundred songs give the towering guitarist's live performances an endearing off-the-cuff quality: you never know what obscurity he'll pull out of his oversized hat next.

Born Morris Holt on August 7, 1937, the Mississippi native was forced to give up playing the piano when he lost his little finger in a cotton gin mishap. Boyhood pal Magic Sam bestowed his magical moniker on the budding guitarist (and times change as Slim's no longer slim). Holt first came to Chicago in 1955, but found that breaking into the competitive local blues circuit was a tough proposition. Although he managed to secure a steady gig for a while with Robert Perkins' band (Mr. Pitiful & the Teardrops), Slim wasn't good enough to progress into the upper ranks of Chicago bluesdom.

So he retreated to Mississippi for a spell to hone his chops. When he returned to Chicago in 1965 (with brothers Nick and Lee Baby as his new rhythm section), Slim's detractors were quickly forced to change their tune. Utilizing the Teardrops name and holding onto his Magic Slim handle, the big man cut a couple of 45s for Ja-Wes and established himself as a formidable force on the South side. His guitar work dripped vibrato-enriched nastiness and his roaring vocals were as gruff and uncompromising as anyone's on the scene.

All of a sudden, the recording floodgates opened up for the Teardrops in 1979 after they cut four tunes for Alligator's *Living Chicago Blues* anthology series. Since then, a series of nails-tough albums for Rooster Blues, Alligator, and a slew for the Austrian Wolf logo have fattened Slim's discography considerably. The Teardrops weathered a potentially devastating change when longtime second guitarist John Primer cut his own major-label debut for Code Blue, but with Slim and bass-wielding brother Nick Holt still on board, it's doubtful the quartet's overall sound will change dramatically in Primer's absence. In 1996, Slim signed with Blind Pig and has cut some of the most-celebrated albums of his career, including *Scufflin'* in 1996, *Black Tornado* in 1998, *Snakebite* in 2000, and *Blue Magic* in 2002. *—Bill Dahl & Al Campbell*

Highway Is My Home / Nov. 19, 1978 / Evidence ✦✦✦

Magic Slim's style is a full-speed-ahead, hard-edged, ragged one, with a deep, sometimes sloppy vocal approach and an equally cutting guitar approach. It is not pretty, flashy, pop-oriented, or even particularly appealing, but it is genuine. The stripped-down Slim sound was mostly on target throughout the 10 tracks (one bonus cut) on this late-'70s date originally recorded for Black and Blue. This Evidence CD features Slim being assertive, as close to romantic as he can get, and otherwise powering straight-ahead. Only on Elmore James' "The Sky Is Crying" does he sound overwhelmed, more by the song's litany (Albert King's equally transcendent version also looms in the background). Otherwise, blues for the non-crossover set. —*Ron Wynn*

Live at the Zoo Bar / 1980 / Candy Apple ♦♦
The towering guitarist and his Teardrops were only hinting at their future greatness when they cut this live set at the Zoo Bar in Nebraska. —*Bill Dahl*

● **Grand Slam** / 1982 / Rooster Blues ♦♦♦♦♦
This raw-boned LP captures Slim's unpretentious house-rocking sound about as well as any studio set possibly could. Among its highlights: the hard-shuffling "Early Every Morning," and a surreal "Scuffling," and Slim's tribute to his late pal Magic Sam, "She Belongs to Me." —*Bill Dahl*

Raw Magic / Jun. 1983 / Alligator ♦♦♦
A more consistent studio collection that first came out over in France and translated well to domestic consumption. Only seven titles, including Slim's lusty "Mama Talk to Your Daughter," and a crowd-pleasing "Mustang Sally," and three tunes of the quartet's own making (which is rather rare with this cover-heavy combo). —*Bill Dahl*

TV Dinner Blues / Oct. 1984 / Blue Dog ♦♦♦

Live at B.L.U.E.S. / 1987 / B.L.U.E.S. R&B ♦♦♦♦
Captured at Chicago's intimate B.L.U.E.S. nightclub, this is surely one of the best live sets the quartet ever committed to tape. The vinyl time constraints limited the program to eight songs, but apart from a marathon "Mother Fuyer," and they're not his usual standards—Chuck Willis' grinding "Keep a Drivin'," a resigned "Poor Man But a Good Man," and Slim's own "Help Yourself." —*Bill Dahl*

Gravel Road / 1990 / Blind Pig ♦♦♦
Another solid Slim set with an additional emphasis on the considerable contributions of second guitarist John Primer, who handles vocals on three cuts (including covers of Otis Redding's "Hard to Handle" and Eugene Church's "Pretty Girls Everywhere"). This was a particularly potent edition of Teardrops, pounding through Slim's own title cut and "Please Don't Waste My Time" and Albert King's shuffling "Cold Women With Warm Hearts" with barroom bravado. —*Bill Dahl*

Chicago Blues Session, Vol. 10 / May 20, 1994 / Wolf ♦♦♦
From three separate sessions held in Chicago in 1986, 1987, and 1989, this captures Slim and the Teardrops at the top of their game. The bulk of this disc emanates from a 1986 session held at the radio station WRDE, catching the combo raw and wild on nice readings of "Mama Talk to Your Daughter," "Bad Avenue," "Gambler," and "Ain't That Nice." These tracks are simply loaded with stinging guitar from Slim and John Primer and it's Primer contributing the lead vocals on "Think" and "She Moves Me." A hot session that's pretty representative of their down-home sound. —*Cub Koda*

Scufflin' / 1996 / Blind Pig ♦♦♦

Black Tornado / May 19, 1998 / Blind Pig ♦♦♦♦
Magic Slim has released a pile of albums, all of them true to his group's house-rocking credo. The idea this time around was to hook him up with producer Dick Shurman and get Slim to record tunes he hadn't committed to wax yet. With a tight version of the Teardrops aboard (the ubiquitous Nick Holt on bass and vocals, Michael Dotson on rhythm, Allen Kirk on drums with Slim's son Shawn Holt making a guest appearance on "Young Man's Blues"), Slim turns in a solid effort here. But perhaps the biggest change this time around is the inclusion of four original tunes from Slim, big news for a combo that many consider to be the ultimate blues cover band. Counting Nick Holt's "Playin' With My Mind" and Shawn Holt's "Young Man's Blues," the original material is up to the 50 percent mark, making this their most adventuresome outing to date. —*Cub Koda*

44 Blues / Feb. 15, 2000 / Wolf ♦♦♦
Taken from two nights of performances at a club in Zugabe, Vienna, this is a typical set from Chicago's favorite down-home combo. John Primer handles the vocals on the opener, "Big Fat Woman," and Bonnie Lee comes up to belt out her signature tune, "I'm Good," but by and large it's Magic Slim's show—a set full of greasy small-club blues played by a master. Decent sound quality for this type of affair, too. —*Cub Koda*

Snakebite / Mar. 21, 2000 / Blind Pig ♦♦♦♦♦
Snakebite is the best and most cohesive Magic Slim album to date, where all the things he does best come together in one place. Expertly produced by Dick Shurman, this spotlights all the groove that makes Slim a bandstand favorite, with none of the rough edges that mar his other studio or live efforts. The songs are top-notch (seven of the 11 tunes here are Slim originals), and this version of the Teardrops—Nick Holt on bass, Allen Kirk on drums, and Michael Dotson on second guitar—lay a greasy pocket down behind their leader that fits perfectly. Slim's vocals are spot-on, and his guitar work is his most focused yet. A truly inspired session, this is the perfect introduction to Magic Slim. —*Cub Koda*

Blue Magic / Jul. 9, 2002 / Blind Pig ♦♦♦♦

Taj Mahal (Henry St. Clair Fredericks)
. . . .
b. May 17, 1942, New York, NY
Slide Guitar, Vocals, Piano, Harmonica, Guitar, Bass, Banjo / Contemporary Blues, Folk-Blues, Electric Country Blues, Modern Acoustic Blues
One of the most prominent figures in late-20th century blues, singer/multi-instrumentalist Taj Mahal played an enormous role in revitalizing and preserving traditional acoustic blues. Not content to stay within that realm, Mahal soon broadened his approach, taking

a musicologist's interest in a multitude of folk and roots music from around the world—reggae and other Caribbean folk, jazz, gospel, R&B, zydeco, various West African styles, Latin, even Hawaiian. The African-derived heritage of most of those forms allowed Mahal to explore his own ethnicity from a global perspective and to present the blues as part of a wider musical context. Yet while he dabbled in many different genres, he never strayed too far from his laid-back country blues foundation. Blues purists naturally didn't have much use for Mahal's music and according to some of his other detractors, his multi-ethnic fusions sometimes came off as indulgent, or overly self-conscious and academic. Still, Mahal's concept seemed somewhat vindicated in the '90s, when a cadre of young bluesmen began to follow his lead—both acoustic revivalists (Keb' Mo', Guy Davis) and eclectic bohemians (Corey Harris, Alvin Youngblood Hart).

Taj Mahal was born Henry St. Clair Fredericks in New York on May 17, 1942. His parents—his father a jazz pianist/composer/arranger of Jamaican descent, his mother a schoolteacher from South Carolina who sang gospel—moved to Springfield, MA, when he was quite young and while growing up there, he often listened to music from around the world on his father's short-wave radio. He particularly loved the blues—both acoustic and electric—and early rock & rollers like Chuck Berry and Bo Diddley. While studying agriculture and animal husbandry at the University of Massachusetts, he adopted the musical alias Taj Mahal (an idea that came to him in a dream) and formed Taj Mahal & the Elektras, which played around the area during the early '60s. After graduating, Mahal moved to Los Angeles in 1964 and, after making his name on the local folk-blues scene, formed the Rising Sons with guitarist Ry Cooder. The group signed to Columbia and released one single, but the label didn't quite know what to make of their forward-looking blend of Americana, which anticipated a number of roots rock fusions that would take shape in the next few years; as such, the album they recorded sat on the shelves, unreleased until 1992.

Frustrated, Mahal left the group and wound up staying with Columbia as a solo artist. His self-titled debut was released in early 1968 and its stripped-down approach to vintage blues sounds made it unlike virtually anything else on the blues scene at the time. It came to be regarded as a classic of the '60s blues revival, as did its follow-up, *The Natch'l Blues*. The half-electric, half-acoustic double-LP set *Giant Step* followed in 1969 and taken together, those three records built Mahal's reputation as an authentic yet unique modern-day bluesman, gaining wide exposure and leading to collaborations or tours with a wide variety of prominent rockers and bluesmen. During the early '70s, Mahal's musical adventurousness began to take hold; 1971's *Happy Just to Be Like I Am* heralded his fascination with Caribbean rhythms and the following year's double-live set, *The Real Thing*, added a New Orleans-flavored tuba section to several tunes. In 1973, Mahal branched out into movie soundtrack work with his compositions for *Sounder* and the following year he recorded his most reggae-heavy outing, *Mo' Roots*.

Mahal continued to record for Columbia through 1976, upon which point he switched to Warner Bros.; he recorded three albums for that label, all in 1977 (including a soundtrack for the film *Brothers*). Changing musical climates, however, were decreasing interest in Mahal's work and he spent much of the '80s off record, eventually moving to Hawaii to immerse himself in another musical tradition. Mahal returned in 1987 with *Taj*, an album issued by Gramavision that explored this new interest; the following year, he inaugurated a string of successful, well-received children's albums with *Shake Sugaree*. The next few years brought a variety of side projects, including a musical score for the lost Langston Hughes/Zora Neale Hurston play *Mule Bone* that earned Mahal a Grammy nomination in 1991. The same year marked Mahal's full-fledged return to regular recording and touring, kicked off with the first of a series of well-received albums on the Private Music label, *Like Never Before*. Follow-ups, such as *Dancing the Blues* (1993) and *Phantom Blues* (1996), drifted into more rock, pop, and R&B-flavored territory; in 1997, Mahal won a Grammy for *Señor Blues*. Meanwhile, he undertook a number of small-label side projects that constituted some of his most ambitious forays into world music. 1995's *Mumtaz Mahal* teamed him with classical Indian musicians; 1998's *Sacred Island* was recorded with his new Hula Blues Band, exploring Hawaiian music in greater depth; 1999's *Kulanjan* was a duo performance with Malian kora player Toumani Diabate. —*Steve Huey*

☆ **The Natch'l Blues** / 1968 / Columbia/Legacy ♦♦♦♦♦
Taj Mahal's second album, recorded in the spring and fall of 1968, opens with more stripped-down Delta-style blues in the manner of his debut, but adds a little more amplification (partly courtesy of Al Kooper on organ) before moving into wholly bigger sound on numbers like "She Caught the Katy and Left Me a Mule to Ride" and "The Cuckoo"—the latter, in particular, features crunchy electric and acoustic guitars and Gary Gilmore playing his bass almost like a lead instrument, like a bluesman's answer to John Entwistle. Most notable, however, may be the two original closing numbers, "You Don't Miss Your Water ('Til Your Well Runs Dry)" and "Ain't That a Lot of Love," which offer Taj Mahal working in the realm of soul and treading onto Otis Redding territory. This is particularly notable on "You Don't Miss Your Water," which achieves the intensity of a gospel performance and comes complete with a Stax/Volt-style horn arrangement by Jesse Ed Davis that sounds more like the real thing than the real thing. "Ain't That a Lot of Love," by contrast, is driven by a hard electric guitar sound and a relentless bass part that sounds like a more urgent version of the bass line from the Spencer Davis Group's "Gimme Some Lovin'." The fall 2000 CD reissue includes a trio of bonus tracks: a faster-paced rendition of "The Cuckoo" with a more prominent lead guitar, the slow electric lament "New Stranger Blues" featuring some good mandolin-style playing on the guitar, and the rocking instrumental "Things Are Gonna Work Out Fine," which is a killer showcase for Davis' lead electric guitar and Taj Mahal's virtuosity on the harmonica. —*Bruce Eder*

☆ **Taj Mahal** / 1968 / Columbia/Legacy ♦♦♦♦♦
Taj Mahal's debut album was a startling statement in its time and has held up remarkably well. Recorded in August of 1967, it was as hard and exciting a mix of old and new blues sounds as surfaced on record in a year when even a lot of veteran blues artists (mostly at the insistence of their record labels) started turning toward psychedelia. The

guitar virtuosity, embodied in Taj Mahal's slide work (which had the subtlety of a classical performance), Jesse Ed Davis' lead playing, and rhythm work by Ry Cooder and Bill Boatman, is of the neatly stripped-down variety that was alien to most records aiming for popular appeal, and the singer himself approached the music with a startling mix of authenticity and youthful enthusiasm. The whole record is a strange and compelling amalgam of stylistic and technical achievements—filled with blues influences of the '30s and '40s, but also making use of stereo sound separation and the best recording technology. The result was numbers like Sleepy John Estes' "Diving Duck Blues," with textures resembling the mix on the early Cream albums, while "The Celebrated Walkin' Blues" (even with Cooder's animated mandolin weaving its spell on one side of the stereo mix) has the sound of a late '40s Chess release by Muddy Waters. Blind Willie McTell ("Statesboro Blues") and Robert Johnson ("Dust My Broom") are also represented, in what had to be one of the most quietly, defiantly iconoclastic records of 1968. —*Bruce Eder*

Giant Step / 1969 / Columbia ✦✦✦
Giant Step/De Old Folks at Home is a two-record set that features one album of Delta blues that was recorded with a full electric band and one album of solo acoustic blues. The electric record is the better collection, but only by a small margin—the acoustic record suffers from poor production that prevents a listener from completely connecting with Taj Mahal's blues. Nevertheless, there are terrific moments on both records and, on the whole, it is one of his finest albums. —*Thom Owens*

Happy Just to Be Like I Am / 1971 / Columbia ✦✦✦✦
With *Happy Just to Be Like I Am*, Taj Mahal offers another (possibly his most effective) course in roots music, this time dabbling in Caribbean rhythms in addition to his more-or-less standard take on acoustic country blues. While his good intentions and craftsmanlike execution can't be denied, one hopes the listener will eventually decide to seek out the inspirations for these recordings. —*AMG*

Recycling the Blues & Other Related Stuff / 1972 / Columbia ✦✦✦
The title *Recycling the Blues & Other Related Stuff* certainly sums up the album quite well—that's exactly what Taj Mahal has been doing for several years by this point. The first side features laidback in-the-studio work with some nice gospel-inflected backup from the Pointer Sisters. The second (and preferable) side offers a good look at Mahal's stage show. —*AMG*

The Real Thing / 1972 / Columbia/Legacy ✦✦✦
The Real Thing is double-live album featuring a new batch of songs as well as some old favorites augmented by, oddly enough, a four-piece tuba section. The change in arrangements may be a point of curiosity, but in the end, the album is bogged down by directionless jamming. —*AMG*

Ooh So Good 'N' Blues / 1973 / Columbia ✦✦✦
Ooh So Good 'N' Blues, takes a more straight-ahead approach that, with the exception of the the jazzy misstep titled "Teacup's Jazzy Blues Tune," keeps the experimentation down to a minimum. As a result, this is one of his most consistently enjoyable and even albums. —*AMG*

Sounder / 1973 / Columbia ✦✦
On his first film score, *Sounder*, Taj Mahal mixes a handful of originals with fragmented sound effects and incidental passages. Certainly not an easy listen, this is one of his more indulgent studies. —*AMG*

Mo' Roots / Apr. 1974 / Columbia ✦✦✦
Mo' Roots finds Mahal stepping away from the blues, choosing instead to focus on reggae. While he can often be faulted for his all-too-academic approach, with *Mo' Roots* he turns in an album that truly expresses his appreciation and connection with the music. —*AMG*

Music Keeps Me Together / 1975 / Columbia ✦✦

Satisfied 'N Tickled Too / 1976 / Columbia ✦✦

Anthology, Vol. 1 (1966–1975) / 1976 / Columbia ✦✦✦✦✦
Taj Mahal's often-indulgent experimentations have flawed most of his albums to different degrees; *The Taj Mahal Anthology, Vol. 1* rights these self-inflicted wrongs by compiling a coherent look at his early career (1966-1976). Though this collection is currently out-of-print, it provides the best introduction to his easygoing take on the blues. —*AMG*

Music Fuh Ya (Music Para Tu) / 1977 / Warner Brothers ✦✦✦
Though an expectedly eclectic mix of blues, calypso, Caribbean music, and bits of reggae, disco, and other pop forms, *Music Fuh Ya (Musica Para Tu)* was not one of Mahal's more inspired outings. No one could criticize Mahal for lack of ambition in his efforts to integrate more styles into the folk-blues blend at the core of his music. But the surfeit of instrumentation, particularly the steel drums, were sometimes distractions more than enhancements, resulting in a forced, slick party atmosphere to cuts like "You Got It." Something like a cover of the blues-folk classic "Freight Train" plays much more to Mahal's strengths, but the trimmings of jazzy sax and steel drums aren't necessary when Taj alone could do a more convincing version. On "Baby, You're My Destiny," he gets more into the ingratiating Leon Redbone old-time/ragtime mood, and "The Four Mills Brothers," a nod to old jazz-pop vocal bands, works better than most cuts. He uses reggae (on "Honey Babe") and disco (on "Curry") rhythms to lesser effect, though. —*Richie Unterberger*

Evolution (The Most Recent) / 1977 / Warner Brothers ✦✦✦
Contrary to the intimations of the title, *Evolution (The Most Recent)* was a predictable continuation of the pleasing but sleepy groove that Mahal had fallen into by the mid-'70s, heavy on the Caribbean accents. The use of an almost disco-ish backing on "Sing a Happy Song" put him close to the sound coming out of Miami studios in the '70s, though that's not a form for which he was well suited. Mahal made a diverse record, true. There was a

venture into something approaching straight soul on "Lowdown Showdown," and "The Most Recent (Evolution) of Muthafusticus Modernusticus," in addition to giving space for lengthy jazzy brass solos, was a pretty solid bid for the record title least likely to be announced in full by an FM DJ in 1978. For all his flirtations with Caribbean rhythms, the songs that put those in the background and let his blues and R&B inclinations come to the fore were superior. He does quite a credible Howlin' Wolf imitation on "The Big Blues," while "Southbound with the Hammer Down" is a pretty reasonable facsimile of Dr. John. Mahal would have been wiser to sound like himself, though, and by this time his best qualities seemed in danger of drowning in a Caribbean sunset. —*Richie Unterberger*

Brothers / 1977 / Warner Brothers ✦✦
Brothers was the soundtrack to a seldom-viewed film of the same name, based on experiences of African-American activists George Jackson and Angela Davis (though different names were used by the movie's characters). Like many soundtracks, it was a side project (his last studio album had come out less than two months before) that few would expect to be on the same levels as his usual catalog. The songs are in the mode that Mahal was usually immersed in during the mid-'70s: bluesy, low-key tunes with a lot of Caribbean influence, particularly in the steel drums. The songs are pleasant but not especially ear-catching, exuding a languorous but streetwise feel. The most sensuous traits of Taj's voice come to the fore on "Brother's Doin' Times," one of the bluesiest and hence more satisfying tracks. Soundtracks often give artists license to dig into styles with which they're not usually associated, and Mahal did so here with the percussive chant "Free the Brothers." Less impressively, the instrumental passages dominating other tracks are unremarkable sweet background music with echoes of jazz fusion. —*Richie Unterberger*

The Best of Taj Mahal, Vol. 1 / 1981 / Columbia ✦✦✦✦✦
Best of Taj Mahal provides a concise career overview with a broader scope than *Anthology, Vol. 1*. —*AMG*

Live & Direct / 1987 / LaserLight ✦✦✦
While the disco vibe on some of these tunes is a bit cheesy, there are several outstanding performances by Taj and his International Rhythm Band. Indeed, "Little Brown Dog" catches Taj in one of his transcendental live moments when he gets so down in the groove you never want him to stop. —*Tim Sheridan*

Shake Sugaree / Sep. 1988 / Music for Little People ✦✦✦
Shake Sugaree is a wonderful children's album. Taj Mahal leads kids through a musical journey, taking them through the Caribbean, Africa, and the Deep South, telling stories and singing songs all the while. Some of the tracks feature a choir composed of his own children, and every song and story is not only entertaining, but educational as well. Simply a delightful record. —*Thom Owens*

Peace Is the World Smiling / 1989 / Music for Little People ✦✦✦
Peace Is the World Smiling is a sweet, good-natured project by Taj Mahal, Pete Seeger, Holly Near, Sweet Honey in the Rock, and many others that is directed toward world peace. Some of the tracks are bland, but it is hard to criticize the musician's intentions. Besides, there a handful of very nice songs on the album. —*Thom Owens*

Like Never Before / Oct. 1991 / Private Music ✦✦✦
After a string of children's albums and other side projects, Taj Mahal returns to his roots with *Like Never Before*—an eclectic assortment of styles featuring traditional covers and a new batch of originals. —*AMG*

Mule Bone / Nov. 1, 1991 / Gramavision ✦✦✦
Taj Mahal won a Grammy nomination with this music from the Broadway production of the Hurston/Hughes play. —*Mark A. Humphrey*

Taj's Blues / Jun. 16, 1992 / Columbia/Legacy ✦✦✦✦
Taj's Blues is an entertainingly diverse record, featuring a variety of blues and roots-music styles, all fused together into a distinctive sound of its own. Half of the album is played on acoustic, the other with an electric band (which includes guitarists Ry Cooder and Jesse Ed Davis on a handful of tracks), which gives a pretty good impression of the range of Mahal's talents. It's a good collection, featuring many of his best performances for Columbia, including "Statesboro Blues" and "Leaving Trunk," as well as the unreleased "East Bay Woman." —*Thom Owens*

Dancing the Blues / 1993 / Private Music ✦✦✦
Taj Mahal has always been a more inclusive, eclectic musician than even some admirers understand; his work was never simply or totally blues, even though that strain was at the center and seldom far from anything he performed either. That's the case with this newest collection, a 12-song set that includes splendid covers of Muddy Waters and Howlin' Wolf tunes, but also equally respectful, striking renditions of soul standards such as "Mockingbird," with special guest Etta James, and "That's How Strong My Love Is." There are also strong Mahal originals like "Blues Ain't Nothin'" and "Strut," with Mahal singing and playing in his wry, delicate, yet forceful way. —*Ron Wynn*

World Music / Jun. 1, 1993 / Columbia ✦✦✦

Mumtaz Mahal / May 16, 1995 / Waterlily Acoustics ✦✦✦
Taj Mahal is joined by Indian master musicians N. Ravikiran and V.M. Bhatt on a selection of tunes that ultimately owe more to obvious blues clichés than they do to cross-cultural collaboration. Perhaps that's because nearly half of the album's selections—including Robert Johnson's "Come on in My Kitchen," "Mary Don't You Weep," and "Johnny Too Bad"—have long been staples of Taj Mahal's concert catalog. This isn't to say that the set doesn't have any moments of inspired improvisation and nuanced playing; there are a few instances of brilliance. But that seems a terrible waste of the talent gathered, unless the listener is looking for nothing more than an unlikely blues workout. —*Brian Beatty*

Live at Ronnie Scott's, London / Jan. 23, 1996 / DRG ♦♦♦
Recorded in 1988 at the famous Ronnie Scott's Club, Mahal is backed by keyboardist Wayne Henderson, bassist Ward Allen, singer Carey Williams, drummer Ozzie Williams and percussionist Kester Smith. *—Jason Ankeny*

Phantom Blues / Feb. 27, 1996 / Private Music ♦♦♦
An eclectic bluesman would seem to be a contradiction in terms, but Taj Mahal, who has moved through the worlds of folk, rock, and pop to reach his present categorization, fits the description, and here he takes several pop and R&B oldies that came from blues roots—"Ooh Poo Pah Doo," "Lonely Avenue," "What Am I Living For?," "Let the Four Winds Blow"—and returns them to those roots. He also calls in such guest stars as Eric Clapton and Bonnie Raitt, who have more than a nodding acquaintance with the blues, to assist him. The result is progressive blues hybrid that treats the music not as a source, but as a destination. *—William Ruhlmann*

An Evening of Acoustic Music / Oct. 29, 1996 / Ruf ♦♦♦♦♦
If you've ever caught Taj live solo, this recording, cut during an appearance in Germany, is what you've been waiting for. His sublime performances of "Satisfied and Tickled Too" and "Candy Man" are out of this world. While the inclusion of tuba on a few tracks does prove somewhat annoying, for the most part this is an excellent example of what makes Taj a treasure. *—Tim Sheridan*

Señor Blues / Jun. 17, 1997 / Private Music ♦♦♦♦
Señor Blues is one of Taj Mahal's best latter-day albums, a rollicking journey through classic blues styles performed with contemporary energy and flair. There's everything from country blues to jazzy uptown blues on *Señor Blues*, and Taj hits all of areas in between, including R&B and soul. Stylistically, it's similar to most of his albums, but he's rarely been as effortlessly fun and infectious as he is here. *—Thom Owens*

Shakin' a Tailfeather / Oct. 28, 1997 / Rhino ♦♦♦
This melange of early rock and pop hits like "Rockin' Robin" and traditional songs like "Shortnin' Bread" suffers from an overabundance of sincerity. There's just a bit too much trying to get across a message and too little just having fun. That's a serious problem for a disc aimed at kids. *—Ross Boissoneau*

Sacred Island / Apr. 7, 1998 / Private Music ♦♦♦
Taj Mahal experienced something of a renaissance in the '90s, turning out a series of surprisingly strong records for Private Music. Since the albums were a success, it gave him the opportunity to make *Sacred Island*, a collection of Hawaiian music and Hawaiian-flavored blues. Even though there are a couple of weak moments, it works better than you might think, since Taj Mahal has never been a blues purist. As a result, it's an interesting detour that longtime fans will find fascinating. *—Stephen Thomas Erlewine*

In Progress & In Motion (1965–1998) / Oct. 13, 1998 / Columbia/Legacy ♦♦♦♦♦
For being a nearly omnipresent figure, Taj Mahal has never quite gotten the respect he's deserved. At the beginning of his career, he earned a significant amount of attention, but as the years passed, he had woven himself into the fabric of blues culture so well that his presence was taken for granted. That is why the 1998 release of *In Progress & In Motion 1965-1998* was so welcome. Spanning three discs and over three decades, the box set accurately summarizes Mahal's career and makes a convincing case for his talents as a roots synthesist. Dedicated fans may notice a favorite or two missing, but they'll be pleased by the 15 unreleased tracks, including two songs intended for his debut album. There are a number of other rarities for the dedicated here, including several unheard live cuts, material from his early group the Rising Sons, and his entire contribution to the Rolling Stones' legendary *Rock & Roll Circus*. Even with this plethora of rarities, *In Progress & In Motion* is primarily for fans who want a solid, comprehensive summary of Mahal's achievements without delving into the particular records, especially since it chooses its songs judiciously, concentrating on his groundbreaking late-'60s/early-'70s work. Indeed, much of his post-Columbia/CBS recordings are quickly recounted on the third disc, but that isn't a problem—the first two discs show how Mahal created his own sound; the third shows how he maintained it. By balancing the music this way, Mahal and his partner, Lawrence Cohn, have created a representative, enlightening retrospective that is appealing to casual and hardcore fans alike. *—Stephen Thomas Erlewine*

Blue Light Boogie / Apr. 27, 1999 / Private Music ♦♦♦
Blue Light Boogie is a compilation drawn from Taj Mahal's work for the Private Music label during the '90s, specifically the albums *Like Never Before* (1991) and *Dancing the Blues* (1993); there's also an ample and varied helping of covers ranging from traditional, rural blues to rock & roll. It's sort of an odd tactic for a compilation, given that *The Best of the Private Years*, released a year later, doesn't duplicate any of this material; as a result, that supposedly balanced introduction ends up skewed away from *Blue Light Boogie*'s sources, not featuring *any* songs from *Like Never Before*. Still, even if all of this is a ham-handed way for a record company to handle an artist's discography, *Blue Light Boogie* is overall a pretty decent sampler and an entertaining listen. Just don't expect an introduction to Mahal's '90s recordings that has any sense of completeness. *—Steve Huey*

Kulanjan / Aug. 3, 1999 / Hannibal ♦♦♦♦
This informal collaboration between veteran American bluesman Mahal and Malian kora (it's a 21-stringed lute-like instrument) master Toumani Diabate was recorded in an Athens, GA, studio with a sextet of West African string instrumentalists and vocalists. It sounds like a half a world away, with the two mixed cultures merging to create traditional blues based on non-traditional musical values. Mahal's gruff, weary voice is soothed by the Malian crew's sweet tones; conversely, the leaders' picking styles sound as if they were harvested from the same land. Natural, unpretentious, and occasionally sensual, *Kulanjan* is classy world music without the stuffy undertones. *—Michael Gallucci*

● **The Best of Taj Mahal** / 2000 / Columbia/Legacy ♦♦♦♦♦
Columbia/Legacy's 2000 collection *The Best of Taj Mahal* is a first-rate overview of Taj Mahal's classic late-'60s/early-'70s work for Columbia. Spanning 17 tracks, including a previously unreleased cut "Sweet Mama Janisse" from 1970, this hits many of the key points from the records he released between 1967 and 1974, including "Statesboro Blues," "Leaving Trunk," "She Caught the Katy and Left Me a Mule to Ride," and "Fishin Blues." Although his albums were constructed and worked as actual albums, this does an excellent job of summarizing these thematic affairs and functions as a nice introduction to Mahal's music. *—Stephen Thomas Erlewine*

Best of the Private Years / Apr. 18, 2000 / Private Music ♦♦♦♦♦
A rockin' good time is guaranteed for all who listen to some of these blistering blues numbers from the legendary singer's best work of the last decade, but the real reward is the depth that goes beyond just the hearty partying. "Blues Ain't Nothin'" is classic bar band rock-blues all the way, with Mahal texturing his raspy voice over his flurrying harmonica and the guitar fire of Johnny Lee Schell and John Porter. "Here in the Dark" captures the more melancholy aspects of Mahal's blues leanings, with his vocals itching for relief over a simmering horn section and the crisp, distorted lines of Eric Clapton. This sort of typical bluesmaking is balanced beautifully by folksy, New Orleans-styled gems like Hank Williams' "Mind Your Own Business" and the aggressive blues meets bebop energy of the Horace Silver tune "Señor Blues." Then its back to the jamming on "Ooh Poo Pah Doo." Mahal has a rich history, and this collection is living proof that a good bluesman gets better with age. *—Jonathan Widran*

Shoutin' in Key: Taj Mahal & the Phantom Blues Band Live / Jun. 20, 2000 / Hannibal ♦♦♦
Recorded at the Mint in Los Angeles in November 1998, *Shouting in Key* showcases Taj Mahal in a live and electric set with the Phantom Blues Band. Starting off the proceedings with a lazy version of Bill Doggett's classic instrumental "Honky Tonk," the band proceeds to glide through the jazzy Latin-tinged instrumental "Sentidos Dulce," the "Give Me Some Lovin" takeoff "Ain't That a Lot of Love," and the B-3 ballad "Woulda Coulda Shoulda." The eclectic pace for the remainder of the set incorporates folk, soul, and reggae, proving Taj Mahal and his band can achieve the combination effortlessly and sound like they had a good time doing it. *—Al Campbell*

Sing a Happy Song: The Warner Bros. Recordings / Aug. 23, 2001 / Rhino Handmade ♦♦♦
Mahal's stint with Warner Bros. was not among his most artistically productive, documenting an era in which he become preoccupied with fusing his brand of blues with Caribbean rhythms and steel drums. This double-CD set contains the entirety of three 1976-1978 LPs for the label, in addition to some unreleased material. Those three LPs—1976's *Music Fuh Ya (Musica Para Tu)*, 1977's *Evolution (The Most Recent)*, and the soundtrack to the little-known film *Brothers*—form most of what's on this compilation. There's a sameness to Mahal's easygoing blues-on-the-beach approach, and a sometimes irritating reliance on Caribbean steel drums for color, that wears down the listener's attention span in such a large dose. The highlights, though not that high, tend to be the times he cuts the Caribbean arrangements down to emphasize more of his blues roots ("Freight Train," "The Big Blues"), or at least go in some unexpected directions (the Dr. John-like "Southbound With the Hammer Down," the Mills Brothers' tribute "The Four Mills Brothers," the good-timey jazz strut "Honey Babe"). For many inclined to check this out, the chief attractions will be the unreleased material, comprising seven live songs from a February 1977 show. It's well-recorded, repeating only two songs that are found as studio versions elsewhere on the set (both from *Music Fuh Ya (Musica Para Tu)*), but is no more exciting than (and similar to) everything else here. *—Richie Unterberger*

Sidney Maiden

b. 1923, Mansfield, LA
Harmonica / Piedmont Blues, West Coast Blues, Harmonica Blues
Born in Mansfield, LA, in 1923, singer and harmonica blower Sidney Maiden made his mark on the blues with the classic "Eclipse of the Sun." In the '40s, Maiden moved to California where he first met guitarist K.C. Douglas. They bonded immediately since they both had a purist attitude towards rural blues and didn't compromise that style of playing once they left the south. They played clubs on the West Coast, and recorded "Eclipse of the Sun" in 1948 for the Down Town label ran by Bob Geddins. It would be the first and only hit for Maiden. Four years later a session was recorded for Imperial with the Blues Blowers (including Douglas), followed in 1953 by "Hurry Hurry Baby" for the Flash label. In 1961 Maiden participated in a recording session, set up by Arhoolie Records boss Chris Strachwitz, reuniting him with Douglas for *Trouble an' Blues* released on Bluesville. Since then Maiden has performed sporadically in the Fresno area in both solo and group situations. *—Al Campbell*

● **Trouble an' Blues** / 1994 / Bluesville/Original Blues Classics ♦♦♦

Harvey Mandel

b. Mar. 11, 1945, Detroit, MI
Guitar / Psychedelic, Blues-Rock, Modern Electric Blues, Rock & Roll
In the mold of Jeff Beck, Carlos Santana, and Mike Bloomfield, Mandel is an extremely creative rock guitarist with heavy blues and jazz influences. And like those guitarists, his vocal abilities are basically nonexistent, though Mandel, unlike some similar musicians, has always known this, and concentrated on recordings that are entirely instrumental, or feature other singers. A minor figure most known for auditioning unsuccessfully for the Rolling Stones, he recorded some intriguing (though erratic) work on his own that anticipated some of the better elements of jazz-rock fusion, showcasing his concise chops, his command of a multitude of tone pedal controls, and an eclecticism that found him working with string orchestras and country steel guitar wizards. Mandel got his first toehold

in the fertile Chicago white blues-rock scene of the mid-'60s (which cultivated talents like Paul Butterfield, Mike Bloomfield, and Steve Miller), and made his first recordings as the lead guitarist for harmonica virtuoso Charlie Musselwhite. Enticed to go solo by Blue Cheer producer Abe Kesh, Harvey cut a couple of nearly wholly instrumental albums for Philips in the late '60s that were underground FM radio favorites, establishing him as one of the most versatile young American guitar lions. He gained his most recognition, though, not as a solo artist, but as a lead guitarist for Canned Heat in 1969 and 1970, replacing Henry Vestine and appearing with the band at Woodstock. Shortly afterward, he signed up for a stint in John Mayall's band, just after the British bluesman had relocated to California. Mandel unwisely decided to use a vocalist for his third and least successful Philips album. After his term with Mayall (on *USA Union* and *Back to the Roots*) had run its course, he resumed his solo career, and also formed Pure Food & Drug Act with violinist Don "Sugarcane" Harris (from the '50s R&B duo Don & Dewey), which made several albums.

In the mid-'70s, when the Rolling Stones were looking for a replacement for Mick Taylor, Mandel auditioned for a spot in the group; although he lost to Ron Wood, his guitar does appear on two cuts on the Stones' 1976 album, *Black & Blue*. Recording intermittently since then as a solo artist and a sessionman, his influence on the contemporary scene is felt via the two-handed fretboard tapping technique that he introduced on his 1973 album *Shangrenede*, later employed by Eddie Van Halen, Stanley Jordan, and Steve Vai. *—Richie Unterberger*

Cristo Redentor / 1968 / EG ✦✦✦
Mandel's debut remains his best early work, introducing an accomplished blues-rock guitarist capable of producing smooth, fluid lines and a variety of tasteful distortion and buzzing via an assortment of tone pedals and customized amplifiers. He augmented his flash with an adventurous appetite for orchestrated, quasi-classical strings (especially in the eerie symphonic title cut), jazz-blues-rock fusion in the mold of The Electric Flag (as on "Before Six"), and even a bit of country in the presence of top steel guitarist Pete Drake. Available in its entirety on the reissue compilation *The Mercury Years*. *—Richie Unterberger*

Righteous / 1969 / Philips ✦✦✦
Not as consistent as his debut, due to the presence of a few pedestrian blues-rock numbers. The better tracks, though, show Mandel continuing to expand his horizons with imagination, particularly on the cuts with string and horn arrangements by noted jazz arranger Shorty Rogers. Harvey's workout on Nat Adderley's "Jazz Samba" is probably his best solo performance, and an obvious touchstone for the Latin-rock hybrid of Carlos Santana (whose own debut came out the same year); on the other side of the coin, "Boo-Bee-Doo" is one of his sharpest and snazziest straight blues-rockers. Available in its entirety on the reissue compilation *The Mercury Years*. *—Richie Unterberger*

Games Guitars Play / 1970 / Philips ✦✦
Feeling that he needed a singer to compete commercially, Mandel decided to abandon his instrumental format, taking on multi-instrumentalist Russell Dashiel as lead vocalist for a good share of the tracks. Alas, Dashiel was a mediocre singer who typified some of the lesser White blues-rock stylings of the period, and the material (with a higher percentage of blues and soul covers) was not up to the level of Mandel's first two efforts, although Harvey's playing remained accomplished and imaginative (as is evident on the original instrumental "Ridin' High" and the cover of Horace Silver's "Señor Blues"). Available in its entirety on the reissue compilation *The Mercury Years*. *—Richie Unterberger*

Baby Batter / 1971 / BGO ✦✦✦✦✦
Fiery, jazz-influenced, blues-based rock by a former Canned Heat guitarist. *—David Szatmary*

The Snake / 1972 / BGO ✦✦✦
Mandel's fifth album, like Jeff Beck's best '70s efforts, add bluesy, jazzy shadings to a rock base. But *The Snake* is more firmly entrenched in blues-rock than, say, *Blow by Blow*. Harvey's playing (occasionally augmented by violinist Don "Sugarcane" Harris) is always impressive, but the compositions (all but one instrumental) aren't gripping, and meander too much. It's not as good as Mandel's late-'60s recordings for Philips, but it's still one of the better early rock-based fusion recordings. *—Richie Unterberger*

Twist City / 1994 / Western Front ✦✦
Although he took blues guitar to uncharted sonic territory in the late '60s with Charlie Musselwhite and on his own solo discs, this '90s return to 12-bar roots was a bit like forcing Mandel to play handcuffed—he seems constrained by the standard-fare repertoire. Mark Skyer's affected, generic vocals and the title track's trite lyrics don't help. *—Dan Forte*

Snakes & Stripes / 1995 / Clarity ✦✦✦
Back to a more varied approach—encompassing Latin, funk, jazz-rock, and even country ("Country Rose")—with nice results. Nine instrumentals and only two vocals (reprising Canned Heat's "Future Blues" and Pure Food & Drug Act's "My Soul's on Fire"), handled by Lori Davidson, on this live-in-the-studio audiofile set. Mandel's nod to B.B. King on "Mashed Potato Twist" is worth the price of admission. *—Dan Forte*

• **The Mercury Years** / Oct. 24, 1995 / Mercury ✦✦✦✦✦
Double-CD reissue repackages the entire contents of his first three LPs (1968's *Cristo Redentor*, 1969's *Righteous*, 1970's *Games Guitars Play*) in their original track sequence, with extensive, informative liner notes. It could be that a more selective, single-disc distillation of the best Mercury material that weeded out the more generic blues-rock tunes would have been more effective. Still, it's a good retrospective of the early work of a somewhat overlooked '60s guitar hero, who helped lay the groundwork for the better elements of fusion and Latin-rock cross-fertilization. *—Richie Unterberger*

Baby Batter/The Snake / Dec. 12, 1995 / Western Front ✦✦✦✦✦
Mandel shares more similarities with Jeff Beck than he's probably willing to admit: both are stunning virtuoso guitarists who can't write consistently first-rate material or sing. Mandel's fifth album, *The Snake*, like Beck's best '70s efforts, adds bluesy, jazzy shadings to a rock base, but is more firmly entrenched in blues-rock than, say, *Blow by Blow*. Harvey's playing (occasionally augmented by violinist Don "Sugarcane" Harris) is always impressive, but the compositions (all but one instrumental) aren't gripping, and, like much of the genre, meander too much. It's not as good as Mandel's late-'60s recordings for Philips, but it's still one of the better early rock-based fusion recordings. This two-fer reissue adds his 1971 LP *Baby Batter*. *—Richie Unterberger*

Bob Margolin

b. May 9, 1949, Boston, MA
Guitar / Modern Electric Chicago Blues
With each new album, guitarist, singer and songwriter "Steady Rollin'" Bob Margolin continues to expand the boundaries of modern blues. Margolin, a sideman for Muddy Waters from 1973 to 1980, was born on May 9, 1949, and raised in Brookline, Massachusetts, became enamored with the recordings of Chuck Berry while still in high school and began playing out a few years later while attending Boston University in the early '70s.

Working with a variety of Boston area blues bands and one he called the Boston Blues Band, he elected to pursue music full-time. In 1973, he joined Waters on the road and in the studio for seven years, playing festivals and clubs around the U.S., Canada and Europe with the legendary bluesman, who died in 1983. Highlights of his career with Waters' band included the taping for *The Last Waltz* on Thanksgiving Day, 1976, and performing at the White House for Jimmy Carter in August, 1978.

In 1980, two years after getting his nickname from a Boston DJ, Margolin began leading a band under his own name and did so for nine years before recording his first album for Tom Principato's Powerhouse label. He later recorded a second album for Powerhouse, but both are now out of print. He continued touring before getting his second big break in 1993, signing up with Bruce Iglauer's Alligator label, which by then had grown by leaps and bounds and had secured stable worldwide distribution. Margolin's albums for Alligator are superb recordings that advance the traditional boundaries of the music: *Down in the Alley* (1993), *My Blues & My Guitar* (1995), and *Up & In* (1997). Each one is a delightful mix of familiar blues covers and Margolin's idiosyncratic, insight-filled, and sometimes funny original songs. *Hold Me to It* followed in 1999. *—Richard Skelly & Al Campbell*

The Old School / 1988 / Powerhouse ✦✦✦
The title says it all—*The Old School* adheres to postwar Chicago blues, with a couple of Delta or New Orleans tracks thrown in for good measure. To his credit, Bob Margolin does delve deep into the catalogs of Robert Johnson, Willie Dixon, Muddy Waters, and Percy Mayfield, among others, digging out songs that haven't been covered as frequently as others. His originals—which are in the style of his idols, naturally—can't help but pale next to the classics he's chosen, but they are competent genre exercises. Margolin, on the whole, isn't a particularly remarkable player—he doesn't have a gripping voice or a distinctive slide guitar technique—but he is passionate about this music, and it shows. And that means *The Old School* is entertaining while it's on, but it doesn't leave much of a lasting impression. *—Thom Owens*

• **Chicago Blues** / 1990 / Ichiban ✦✦✦✦✦
Best known for his association with Muddy Waters in the '70s, Steady Rollin' Bob Margolin is reunited with three other former Waters' sidemen on this inspired solo effort: pianist Pinetop Perkins, bassist Calvin "Fuzzy" Jones, and drummer Willie "Big Eyes" Smith. The title sums it up—the album may have been recorded in various parts of the South, but the style is pure, unadulterated Chicago blues. A number of gutsy originals are included (most notably, "She and the Devil" and "Born in the Wrong Time") along with such time-honored Muddy Waters classics as "Mean Disposition," "She's So Pretty," and "Rollin' and Tumblin'." As enjoyable as the band recordings are, the most inspired offering is the unaccompanied solo number "Born in the Wrong Time." On this under-produced, demo-quality recording, Margolin rants and raves about life in the early '90s and says some gut-level things that desperately needed to be said. *—Alex Henderson*

Down in the Alley / 1993 / Alligator ✦✦✦
On *Down in the Alley*, his first album for Alligator Records, Steady Rollin' Bob Margolin doesn't quite follow though on the success of its predecessor *Chicago Blues*, yet that's only a relative scale. Margolin is one of a handful of musicians to keep classic Chicago blues alive in the '90s, both through covers and original material. His association with Muddy Waters is, if anything, overhyped by journalists and Alligator alike, but it has to be said that he does Muddy proud with down-and-dirty recordings like this. Margolin's guitar has true muscle, and there's genuine grit to the recording, unlike many contemporary Chicago blues albums. For some tastes, the album may be a little predictable since he never breaks from the tradition, but anyone looking for a straight-ahead slice of electric blues like Chess used to make them should be pleased with *Down in the Alley*. *—Stephen Thomas Erlewine*

My Blues & My Guitar / Nov. 1995 / Alligator ✦✦✦✦✦
Steady Rollin' Bob Margolin really comes into his own with *My Blues & My Guitar*, his second album for Alligator Records. He still pays homage to his mentor, Muddy Waters, not only through covers but simply through his driving musical style. He blends the familiar ("Rip It Up," "Going Home," "The Same Thing") with unpredictable ("See Me in the Evening," "Drip Drop," "Peace of Mind") in his choice of covers, and he has written a set of originals that are sturdy and memorable. Furthermore, he has loosened up a little bit, bringing some jazzy flourishes to his solos and nuance to his vocals. The result is one of his strongest albums, one that is exciting upon the first listen and rewarding upon repeated plays. *—Thom Owens*

Up & In / Apr. 29, 1997 / Alligator ✦✦✦✦
Former Muddy Waters sideman and current *Blues Revue* magazine columnist Bob Margolin brings his encyclopedic knowledge of blues and chops galore with him on this,

his third album for Alligator. Ten of the 14 selections are penned by Margolin, with selected covers of material from Bobby Charles, Grady Jackson, Snooky Pryor and Gladys Knight and the Pips rounding out the mix. This time around Margolin stretches his musical boundaries into new directions, adding to his already wide range of blues subgenres. The title track is a solid homage to Chuck Berry, while Grady Jackson's "Coffee Break" is the kind of atmospheric, sax-driven track that would have fit perfectly on any Aladdin blues-after-hours 10-inch album. "Imagination" gets a true soul workout, as does "The Window," with its funky lead fills. His guitar tone can sometimes get positively trashy and as distorted as any old blues 78 you've ever heard, as on "Alien's Blues" and "Blues For Bartenders" while the cleaner side of his playing comes up for air on "'Bout Out," "Not What You Said Last Night," and the jazzy "Long Ago and Far Away." Margolin turns in a dead-on Muddy Waters slide guitar impression in a duet turn with former Waters' piano man Pinetop Perkins on "She and the Devil" while turning in fine slide work on "Goin' Back Out on the Road" and "Why Are People Like That?" As a vocalist, Margolin is still in the passable category; he sings in tune, but seldom displays the kind of passion that earmarks the best of his guitar work. Still, this is his best solo turn to date, with solid playing from guests Kaz Kazanoff, Dave Maxwell and a host of others. *—Cub Koda*

Hold Me to It / Sep. 7, 1999 / Blind Pig ♦♦♦

Bob Margolin continues to pay homage to Muddy Waters with each record he cuts and this debut for Blind Pig is no exception. His slide playing is Waters to a tee while his songwriting chops stay firmly in the mold of what Waters himself would come up with, albeit less inspired. Margolin's band is a three-piece knockoff of the old Waters band with Tad Waleters blowing harp in the Little Walter tradition while drummer Wes Johnson supplies a solid Chicago beat, no frills or overplaying out of any of them. If you like your Chicago blues served up '50s style without a lot of technical niceties, this album's right up your alley. *—Cub Koda*

Johnny Mars

b. Dec. 7, 1942, Laurens, SC

Vocals, Harmonica / Harmonica Blues, Modern Electric Blues

Songwriter, harmonica player and singer Johnny Mars was raised in a sharecropping family. He was given his first harmonica at age nine. His family lived in various places around the South, including North Carolina, Georgia and Florida.

When Mars' mother died in 1958, the older family members settled in Florida, while Johnny and his younger brother went to live in New Paltz, NY. After he graduated from high school, he played club shows around New York and recorded with his band Burning Bush for Mercury Records.

In the mid-'60s, Mars moved to San Francisco, where he met Dan Kennedy and formed the Johnny Mars Band, playing clubs and festivals in northern California, as well as shows for rock promoter/impresario/producer Bill Graham.

However, Mars could not seem to expand his audience much in San Francisco. After hearing about the greener pastures across the pond from his friend Rick Estrin of Little Charlie and the Nightcats, he toured England in 1972. There, he recorded a couple of albums, eventually moving to West London in 1978. Working with producer Ray Fenwick, who also worked with Spencer Davis and Ian Gillan, Mars met with success on the much praised album, *Life on Mars.*

In 1991, Mars became a featured soloist with the British New Wave pop group Bananarama. The group used him on their singles "Preacher Man," "Megalomaniac," and "Long Train Running," and he appeared in the group's video of "Preacher Man." Through the '90s, Mars retained his strong European fan base, and he enjoys particularly strong followings in Ireland, Scotland and Scandinavia. Critics there have called him "the Jimi Hendrix of the harmonica." Over the years, Mars has shared bills with Hendrix (before he was well-known) and Magic Sam.

In 1992, after a long absence from the Bay Area blues scene, owing to his new foothold in England and the rest of Europe, Mars was invited to play at the San Francisco Blues Festival. Mars' 1994 U.S. release for MM&K Recordings, *Stateside with Johnny Mars*, features brilliant, original, topical compositions and superb, unique harmonica playing, unfettered by the standard Chicago blues conventions. *—Richard Skelly*

Blues from Mars / 1972 / Polydor ♦♦♦

● **Oakland Boogie** / 1976 / Big Bear ♦♦♦♦

Johnny Mars found his stride on his second album, *Oakland Boogie.* Recorded in London with producer Ray Fenwick, the album is a powerful collection of hard-edged blues rockers, highlighted by Mars' searing vocals and impassioned, slurred harmonica. *—Thom Owens*

Mighty Mars / 1980 / JSP ♦♦

Originally released in 1980, this JSP reissue of *Mighty Mars* features the blues harmonica of Johnny Mars in a rock setting that rarely works. Mars is a ferocious harmonica player full of raw emotion, but unfortunately this material doesn't come close to matching Mars' intensity. Recorded in London with members of the pub-rock scene, versions of "Mellow Down Easy," "Rocket 88," "Your Cash Ain't Nothing but Trash," and "I'll Go Crazy" sound forced and unnecessary. It's regrettable Mars didn't give up the idea of mixing rock and blues and create a record that would defy genres. *—Al Campbell*

Life on Mars / 1984 / BGO ♦♦♦

King of the Blues Harp / Oct. 31, 1994 / JSP ♦♦♦♦

Stateside / Nov. 17, 1999 / MM&K ♦♦♦

Martin, Bogan & the Armstrongs

f. Virginia

Group / Acoustic Blues

Only violinist, storyteller, and philosopher Howard Armstrong remains to tell of the exploits of this remarkable African-American string band. Virginia-born guitar and mandolin blues artist Carl Martin died in 1979, and guitarist Ted Bogan passed away a few years ago. But in their prime, Martin, Bogan, and Armstrong enjoyed multiple incarnations, first (in the '30s) as The Four Keys, The Tennessee Chocolate Drops, and the Wandering Troubadours. They played individually and collectively throughout the mid-South on radio, with medicine shows, and at country jukes before eventually making it to Chicago in the late '30s and '40s, where they made records but mostly supported themselves by what Armstrong calls "pulling doors." This meant going into different cafes and taverns and playing for tips if they weren't thrown out. Playing various ethnic neighborhoods, the group took advantage of Armstrong's gift with languages and learned to sing in a variety of tongues. Best described as an acoustic string band (violin, guitar, mandolin, bass), the group played blues, jazz, pop, country, and various non-English favorites. As skilled musicians eager to earn tips by playing whatever their audiences wanted, they built a necessarily large repertoire.

After years of separation the group reunited as Martin, Bogan, & Armstrong in the early '70s and enjoyed substantial blues revival acclaim. After Carl Martin died, Bogan and Armstrong continued. When I worked with them in 1986, Bogan and Armstrong were still the greatest living exponents of the African-American string band style, equally at home playing blues, swing, jazz, ragtime, or older Black string band material. Armstrong, who speaks seven languages and is a painter and a sculptor, was a National Heritage Award winner in 1990. What made their music so wonderful, besides its energy and flawless presentation and their personable good humor, was their ability to remind us that good music transcends classifications and a skilled artist can draw from many streams. *—Barry Lee Pearson*

● **Martin, Bogan & the Armstrongs** / 1974 / Flying Fish ♦♦♦♦♦

When this ensemble first burst onto the traditional acoustic music scene in the '70s, the effect was like some kind of revelation, and many new possibilities seemed imminent. Looking over the unfortunately too-small collected discography of the band, it now seems clear that this first effort was the biggest winner of all, and the full potential of the ensemble was never really exploited on recordings. Perhaps the band only gave off the illusion of a vast repertoire and couldn't deliver in the studio, or maybe it was the handling by the record companies. At one point, Flying Fish turned the band over to Steve Goodman for genius production, and the results, although enjoyable, hardly have the impact of this album. There were four members in total, with father and son Howard and Tom Armstrong eventually honing the precision on the band's name by altering it to Martin, Bogan & the Armstrongs. The senior members of this project were all veterans of the string band scene from the the '30s and '40s, thus setting them several giant steps ahead of many of the young revival bands of the '70s. More important, this was a rare black string band, but one that seemed comfortable tossing in mountain music, country & western, or even a Hawaiian number. In the latter department, "You'll Never Find Another Kanaka Like Me" remains one of this group's favorite songs among its fans. Much of the repertoire also came from black music traditions, but it was a blend that one only heard from the most versatile artists: blues, swing jazz, and jive that bordered on rock & roll. The fiddle, mandolin, and guitar soloing are excellent throughout. Musically, this is the band's most solidly enjoyable set, and adding to the perfection is the packaging, including a good historical essay as well as three delightful cartoons by the elder Armstrong. No information is given about the composers of the titles, however. A few are traditional, but many come from the Tin Pan Alley mill of publishers who are still out watching for every penny they are owed, so the oversight is surprising. In the '90s, the label created a CD re-release that combined most of this album with the Goodman-produced material, but unfortunately left off some good tracks. *—Eugene Chadbourne*

That Old Gang of Mine/Martin, Bogan & the Armstrongs / Sep. 13, 1993 / Flying Fish ♦♦♦

This title must have been something of a labor of love for label owner Bruce Kaplan, who had brought these artists over to his Flying Fish label when he left his management and production position at Rounder. He hired folk artist and songwriter Steve Goodman to produce a remarkable American string band that had roots in the hills of Tennessee in the '30s yet was able to cover just about any type of music from swing jazz to country blues. An argument might be made that Goodman proceeded to water down the lemonade, adding session players such as Hugh MacDonald to some tracks as well as his own guitar picking. On the other hand, the loss of hearing in both ears would be a prerequisite to any complaints about the presence of mandolin picker Jethro Burns; he's a master and hearing him combined with fiddler Howard Armstrong's bebop leanings and Carl Martin's deeply contrasting mandolin style is definitely one of the highlights of this album. "Jamaica Farewell" is an unusual cut, combining Ted Bogan with guest Howard Levy, overdubbing himself on vibes and harmonica a few years before he went on play with banjoist Béla Fleck. Too bad they didn't pick a different tune to work out on, as they both seem constrained by this one. Levy also plays piano on "Nagging Woman Blues," providing Martin with a chance to do a blues vocal, once again a nice track but not really typical of what the band shines at. "Sheik of Araby" is the best example of that here, displaying both the swing and fun aspects and the flashy picking, and to nobody's surprise it features the basic group unadorned by guests. The smart way to get this material is to grab the CD version, complete with original cover artwork, which also includes the totality of the group's first self-titled Flying Fish album. Thus, one gets a full program featuring this band at its best along with the mixed results of Goodman's attempt at musical expansion. [The 1993 re-release also includes their full-length eponymous album tacked onto the second half of the disc, adding nine more songs] *—Eugene Chadbourne*

Barnyard Dance / 199 / Rounder ♦♦♦

This group attracted lots of attention when it made its first nationally distributed recordings in the early '70s. Also known as Martin, Bogan & the Armstrongs, it was certainly an outfit that had been around the block. Three members of the group were original core members of the Four Keys String Band, which was first formed in West Virginia in 1931.

In a folk music revival world dominated by fortified genres, the all-encompassing repertoire this group had built up playing square dances, churches, picnics, weddings, and bars included a range of material that could turn the average folk traditions workshop into an exorcism. Violinist Howard Armstrong represented both a typical and completely untypical traditional string band artist. Like many players in this genre, he hailed from the South and started playing music at an early age. Unlike others, he spoke seven languages, including Mandarin Chinese, and freely tossed in Charlie Parker licks whether playing a swing number such as "Lady Be Good" or the old-time "Knox County Stomp." Carl Martin and Ted Bogan brought in solid country blues and ragtime influences, while sibling L.C. Armstrong held it all together with rhythm guitar and bass. The brew should definitely appeal to fans of the Jim Kweskin Jug Band, Dan Hicks & His Hot Licks, or any good-timey form of string music played with versatility. This was a production of Bruce Kaplan when he was still involved with the Rounder label; he would soon leave this too-prissy outfit and start up his own Flying Fish imprint, recording several more projects with Carl Martin and the rest of these characters in the process. *—Eugene Chadbourne*

Carl Martin

b. Apr. 1, 1906, Big Stone Gap, VA, **d.** May 10, 1979, Pontiac, MI

Conga, Percussion, Guitar / East Coast Blues, Piedmont Blues, Songster, Vaudeville Blues

Carl Martin was born near Big Stone Gap, VA, on April 1, 1906. His main instrument was mandolin but he also mastered the guitar, and according to those who saw him perform, could play anything with strings. Martin not only performed solo, but also spent much of his career in a trio featuring Ted Bogan (guitar) and Howard Armstrong (violin). The trio enjoyed a career that spanned five decades and was known under several different monikers, including the Four Keys, the Tennessee Chocolate Drops, and the Wandering Troubadours. Martin, Bogan, and Armstrong initially traveled all over the south entertaining at medicine shows, county fairs, and on the radio. When they couldn't get an actual paying gig, they would play for tips in local taverns. In the late '30s, they followed the great migration to Chicago where they would eventually go their separate ways, occasionally playing together. In the ensuing years, Martin would benefit greatly from playing for the diverse ethnic crowds spread out over countless neighborhoods in Chicago, developing a repertoire of blues, jazz, pop, country, and even non-English songs. Following years of playing solo, Martin, Bogan, and Armstrong reunited in the early '70s and played the folk and blues festival circuit all over the country. Luckily, a few discs remain in print that trace Martin's long career from the '30s to his final sessions before he passed away in Pontiac, MI, on May 10, 1979. *—Al Campbell*

● **Complete Works, Vol. 1** / May 1, 1995 / Document ♦♦♦

Roberta Martin

b. Feb. 12, 1907, Helena, AR, **d.** Jan. 18, 1969, Chicago, IL

Vocals, Piano / Traditional Gospel, Black Gospel

This talented pianist started a quartet with Theodore Frye in the '30s. This aggregation gradually evolved into The Roberta Martin Singers by the '50s. It is now known that she copied the piano style of blind pianist Arizona Dranes, who also influenced The Ward Singers. Martin's singers sang loudly and dramatically. She also wasn't concerned about a harmonious sound; when one member of the group was leading a song, whether male or female, you could easily identify the backing voices. This lack of synchronicity made the group's urgent sound a unique and welcome change amid the repetitive quartets of the time. Robert Anderson was one of Martin's principal singers. She herself was referred to as The Helen Hayes of the Gospel World. She died in 1969. *—Bil Carpenter*

Old Ship of Zion / 1973 / Kenwood ♦♦♦♦♦

Prime Apollo sides from the late '40s/early '50s with fine leads from Roberta, Bessie Folk, Eugene Smith and Norsalus McKissick. *—Opal Louis Nations*

● **The Best of the Roberta Martin Singers** / 1979 / Savoy ♦♦♦♦♦

Most of Martin's best early work from the late '40s through the '50s is out of print, but this is a nice introduction to this dynamic singer and group leader. *—Kip Lornell*

Sallie Martin

b. Nov. 20, 1895, Pittfield, GA, **d.** Jun. 18, 1988, Chicago, IL

Vocals / Traditional Gospel, Black Gospel

Proclaimed "The Mother of Gospel" by the National Convention of Gospel Choirs and Choruses, Sallie Martin is widely credited with introducing spiritual music to the masses; while her rough, unmodulated voice lacked the finesse of many of the singers in her wake, she was an artist who nevertheless commanded absolute respect from both her audiences and peers, and her innovations forever altered not only the music but also the business behind it. Martin was born November 20, 1895, in Pittfield, GA; after quitting school during the eighth grade, she moved to Atlanta, where she began a succession of jobs including babysitting, cleaning houses and washing clothes. In 1916 she joined the Fire Baptized Holiness Church, relishing the spontaneity and spirit of the Sanctified singing she encountered there. During the 1920s, Martin, her husband and their son relocated to Chicago; following the couple's 1929 divorce, she began working at a nearby hospital, in her off hours continuing to pursue her interest in gospel.

Through the grapevine, Martin had heard about Thomas A. Dorsey, a onetime blues pianist whose original gospel songs were electrifying the Chicago church circuit. Through a mutual friend, she arranged to audition for Dorsey; despite serious misgivings—her style was thoroughly unrefined, complete with whooping, groaning and a great deal of physical movement (the latter a hallmark of the Pentecostal church), and to top it off, she couldn't even read music—he eventually agreed to let her come aboard, and in early 1932 Martin made her debut with his group at the Ebenezer Baptist Church. A year passed before she was awarded her first solo, and for all of her lack of polish, Martin nevertheless instantly connected with audiences; over time Dorsey became increasingly aware of her value not only as a performer but also as an entrepreneur, as she took over his music store and within a few months was turning a tidy profit. Their relationship was often adversarial, but quickly it was apparent that neither could succeed without the other.

As gospel choruses instructed to sing Dorsey's songs began appearing throughout the Chicago area, Martin traveled to Cleveland in 1933 to organize a chorus there as well; in the years to follow, she helped set up similar groups throughout the South and Midwest, and also joined Dorsey in organzing the annual National Convention of Gospel Choirs and Choruses, serving as its first vice president until the time of her death. In 1940, however, relations between Martin and Dorsey reached their breaking point, and she went solo, teaming with a young pianist named Ruth Jones—later to rocket to fame under the name Dinah Washington—and began touring the country, traveling a gospel circuit which her earlier journeys had helped establish. That same year, Martin and gospel composer Kenneth Morris joined forces with finanical backer Rev. Clarence H. Cobb to found Martin and Morris, Inc., a publishing company which in a few years was the biggest of its kind in the United States.

Martin's touring collaboration with the volatile Jones was short-lived, and she next began performing with the gifted pianist and arranger Roberta Martin (no relation). Again the partnership did not last, and she next formed her own ensemble, the Sallie Martin Singers; believed to be the first female group in gospel history, they existed until the mid-'50s. Despite her national renown, Martin never enjoyed the same kind of success on record earned by many of her contemporaries; she did score a few hits, however, among them "Just a Closer Walk With Thee" and "He'll Wash You Whiter Than Snow," performed with Professor Alex Bradford. An active supporter of Dr. Martin Luther King Jr., her involvement in the civil rights movement led to an invitation to attend the 1960 celebration marking the independence of Nigeria; Martin's visit inspired her to donate to the Nigerian Health Program, resulting in a state office building named in her honor. An astute businesswoman and tireless supporter of charitable causes, she died in Chicago on June 18, 1988. *—Jason Ankeny*

★ **Throw Out the Lifeline** / 1993 / Specialty ♦♦♦♦♦

The most instrumentation these tracks ever had was an organ, a piano and an occasional drum. Originally issued on Specialty Records in the 1950-1953 period, these 29 tracks are Black congregational styled numbers, 23 of them previously unissued. These sides also include six selections where Brother Joe May joined the singers. Most of the rest finds Sallie and Cora Martin trading leads. A fine example of Sallie's powers shows up on "Ain't That Good News." *—Bil Carpenter*

Precious Lord / Jul. 1993 / Vee-Jay ♦♦♦♦♦

Sallie Martin disbanded her famous singing group in the '50s when her daughter Cora told her she didn't want to do any more tours. She briefly resurrected two new editions in the early '60s and cut two albums for Vee-Jay before disbanding them again. Although the 23 songs on this single-disc reissue aren't as glorious or memorable as the group's Specialty recordings, they are still valuable, both to hear Martin's rough but effective leads and harmonizing with new vocalists, and also because the resignation and mournful quality in Martin's singing during the 1963 sessions were an indication that she'd had enough of the performance/recording/touring grind. *—Ron Wynn*

Sara Martin

b. May 18, 1884, Louisville, KY, **d.** May 24, 1955, Louisville, KY

Choir, Chorus, Vocals / Piedmont Blues, Prewar Country Blues, Classic Female Blues

Known in her heyday as "the blues sensation of the West," the big-voiced Sara Martin was one of the best of the classic female blues singers of the '20s.

Martin began her career as a vaudeville performer, switching to blues singing in the early '20s. In 1922, she began recording for OKeh Records, cutting a number of bawdy blues like "Mean Tight Mama." She continued recording until 1928. During this time, Martin became a popular performer on the southern Theater Owners' Booking Association circuits, eventually playing theaters and clubs on the east coast as well.

In the early '30s, Sara Martin retired from blues singing and settled in her hometown of Louisville, KY. While she was in Louisville, she ran a nursing home and occasionally sang gospel in church. Sara Martin died after suffering a stroke in 1955. *—Cub Koda & Stephen Thomas Erlewine*

● **1922–1928** / 1922-1928 / Best of Blues ♦♦♦♦

Sara Martin was already 38 and a veteran performer by the time she made her first recording on October 17, 1922. During the next six years she would record steadily, often being accompanied by pianist Clarence Williams (who sometimes used her musically as a substitute for his wife, Eva Taylor). Martin was able to sing both blues and vaudeville-type songs quite credibly. This first of four Document CDs that reissue all of her recordings (other than some oddities that have been reissued in other series) has 24 fine examples of Martin's singing. She is heard either accompanied by Williams' rather basic piano, having four vocal duets with Williams or Eva Taylor (usually also being joined by Thomas Morris' cornet) or on three songs being backed by W.C. Handy's Orchestra. Martin covers a wide variety of material including her hit "Sugar Blues" (which was her very first recording), "Keeps on A-Rainin'," "Joe Turner Blues," "Original Blues," "If You Don't Like It, Leave," "Nobody in Town Can Bake a Sweet Jelly Roll Like Mine" and "Hesitation Blues." Since most of these recordings (some of which are a bit worn out technical-wise although quite listenable) were formerly quite rare, blues collectors will certainly love this series. *—Scott Yanow*

Complete Recorded Works, Vol. 1: 1922–1923 / Feb. 15, 1996 / Document ♦♦♦♦

Recommended for completists only, Document's *Complete Recorded Works, Vol. 1: 1922-1923* offers a complete overview of Sara Martin's first recordings. Though there are some solid performances here, the long running time, chronological sequencing, and poor fidelity will send casual listeners in search of something more consistently listenable. *—Thom Owens*

Complete Recorded Works, Vol. 2: 1923–1924 / Mar. 5, 1996 / Document ♦♦♦♦

Based on the music that Sara Martin recorded at the beginning of her career (and released on *Vol. 1* of this four-CD series), she was primarily a superior vaudevillian performer. However, *Vol. 2* shows that Martin was actually an even better blues singer. In general, the material that she recorded had improved by mid-1923, as had her singing, and there are many gems among the 23 songs included on this disc. Martin is accompanied on the first seven selections by pianist Clarence Williams, is joined on four numbers by small groups led by Williams (and including cornetist Tom Morris and soprano saxophonist Sidney Bechet), is backed by pianist Porter Grainger on six songs and then, most intriguingly, performs duets with Sylvester Weaver (heard on two numbers apiece on guitar and banjo). Other than the band numbers, the focus throughout is mostly exclusively on the singer who is heard in prime form on such tunes as "New Orleans Hop Scop Blues," "Mistreated Mama Blues," "Slow Down Sweet Papa, Mama's Catching Up with You" and "Everybody's Got the Blues." Formerly rare music that is both historical and quite strong for the period. *—Scott Yanow*

Complete Recorded Works, Vol. 3: 1924–1925 / Apr. 9, 1996 / Document ♦♦♦♦
The third of four Document CDs that reissue all of the classic blues singer Sara Martin recordings (except for a few numbers with famous musicians that have been reissued elsewhere) has the bulk of her 1924-25 performances. Martin is heard in several different settings: duets with guitarist Sylvester Weaver, small group dates with Clarence Williams, duets with Williams or pianist Lemuel Fowler and backing by a violin-guitar-banjo trio. Sara Martin's voice and emotional range grew gradually throughout the '20s and such numbers as "Got to Leave My Home Blues," "Some Blues," "I'd Rather Be Blue Than Green," "I Can Always Tell When a Man Is Treatin' Me Cool" and "Mournful Blues" are among the finest recordings of her career. *—Scott Yanow*

Complete Recorded Works, Vol. 4: 1925–1928 / Apr. 9, 1996 / Document ♦♦♦♦
It is ironic that so many classic female blues singers recorded a ton of material between 1921 and 1924 and, when the recording techniques had advanced greatly and the musicianship of their accompaniments had vastly improved, the vocalists had much less opportunity to be documented. Sara Martin recorded three CDs worth of material during 1922-1925, and then just 23 tunes during the three years covered by this CD. Martin was at her best during the latter period but she only had three recording sessions in 1926, one in 1927 and three in 1928 before her recording career came to an end. She was accompanied by many impressive players during this era including several groups led by Clarence Williams (which had such musicians as King Oliver, Charlie Irvis, Bubber Miley and Benny Waters), Richard M. Jones' Jazz Wizards, the piano of Eddie Heywood on two duets and three numbers with Harry's Happy Four, a hot quartet consisting of Harry Cooper and Louis Metcalf on cornets, pianist Earres Prince and banjoist Bernard Addison. The diverse material is highlighted by "What More Can a Monkey Woman Do," a hot version of "Yes, Sir, That's My Baby," a rare vocal version of "The Last Time" (recorded two years later by Louis Armstrong's Savoy Ballroom Five), "What's the Matter Now," "Late Last Night," "Cushion Foot Stomp" and "Death Sting Me Blues." Vintage blues completists will want all four of the Sara Martin CDs but others who just want a sampling of her best work are advised to get *Vol. 4* and *Vol. 3* first. *—Scott Yanow*

The Famous Moanin' Mama: 1922–1927 / Oct. 2, 2001 / Challenge ♦♦♦♦
For Sara Martin's most obsessive fans, the four exhaustive volumes of *The Complete Recorded Works* that Document assembled in 1996 was a blessing. But not everyone who listens to classic female blues is a completist or a hardcore historian. And for those who have only a casual interest in the singer's legacy, *The Famous Moanin' Mama: 1922-1927* would be a more logical choice. This Dutch release contains 22 captivating examples of Martin's work and, as its title indicates, spans 1922-1927. Many of the tracks are essential, including "What More Can a Monkey Woman Do?," "Brother Ben," the sassy "Take Your Black Bottom Outside," and Martin's 1922 performance of the standard "'Tain't Nobody's Business if I Do." Although some of the material contains elements of country blues, Martin was essentially an urban blues artist. Urban blues, of course, didn't start with Muddy Waters and Willie Dixon in Chicago; classic blues, which was heavily influenced by New Orleans and Chicago jazz, often had a big-city outlook. While a country bluesman of the '20s or '30s could be happy with nothing more than an acoustic guitar, classic blues women like Bessie Smith, Ma Rainey, Victoria Spivey, and Martin had a strong appreciation of jazz's sophistication and worked with major jazz improvisers. The material on this 67-minute CD finds Martin being backed by such pre-bop jazz heavyweights as Fats Waller and Sidney Bechet. The latter is heard on soprano sax in 1923, which is 37 years before John Coltrane did so much to popularize that instrument with his 1960 recording of "My Favorite Things." Is *The Famous Moanin' Mama: 1922-1927* the last word on Martin's '20s output? No. But for the casual listener, it would be a fine starting point. *—Alex Henderson*

Allison Mathis

Vocals, Slide Guitar / Country Blues, Folk-Blues
Allison Mathis is an unusual name for a country blues artist, perhaps sounding more like the wayward bluegrass picking daughter of a '50s lounge singer. Nonetheless, Mathis was at least one of the stage names of an obscure Georgia country blues performer in the early '40s when various archivists from the Library of Congress were scouting the South looking for blues-bloods to record. Sometimes the performer in question is identified as Alison Mathis, the spelling indicating that perhaps the scholarly blues attitude toward the number of consonants in this artist's name might be "What the L!" Anderson Mathis is also the same artist and an account of an early '40s Fort Valley State College Folk Festival where Mathis was recorded by ethnomusicologist John Work suggests that this might be the most accurate version of the artists' name of them all. Anderson Mathis is also the birth name of Georgia rapper Bubba Sparxxx, creating a coincidental but apparently not genealogical link in American black music history from the peach state. Anderson or Allison Mathis of the '40s was indeed a fine slide guitarist, coaxing heartfelt blues licks and sometimes even a shimmering rainbow of tones from the guitar in a style that has been compared to Fred McMullen or Curley Weaver. Much praise has been poured on the Mathis version of "Bottle Up and Go," as he apparently created a recognizably different variation of this country blues and folk anthem, also often titled "Step It Up and Go." The Mathis knack for personalizing material has also been compared to the sometimes eccentric recordings of later bluesman Lightnin' Sam Hopkins, but in this performer's case the motivation was obviously to convince fly-by-night record labels that he had new material, which he actually didn't. The recording career of Mathis is nowhere near as prolific as Hopkins and as a result, the reasons or motivations behind some of his arrangements are quite mysterious and listeners can only speculate as to what sources and influences could have been. Most of the existing evidence of Mathis seems to be linked to trips up the road to the aforementioned festival in the '40s. He was a prize winner and a repeat invite for the first two years of the event, to which folk music nuts such as Alan Lomax flocked. This area of Georgia reeled from the resurgence of interest in a type of music that had once taken place casually on street corners throughout the state; by the '40s, the main attraction of this area was now a type of chopped barbecued pork smothered with vinegar. Mathis sometimes played with the fine harmonica player Jesse Stroller, definitely a good choice for walking blues and in the mid-'40s was also appearing at festival events as a guitar accompanist to other acts. "Mama You Goin' to Quit Me" is the moving track most often chosen as an example of Mathis' slide guitar artistry, as some of the improvised passages are simply sublime. This performance was reissued by the Library of Congress on a collection entitled *Red River Blues* released on the Travelin' Man label, but shows up on other compilations as well. *—Eugene Chadbourne*

James Mathus & His Knock-Down Society

Group / Retro Swing, Delta Blues, Swamp Blues, Modern Delta Blues
Along with his work in the Squirrel Nut Zippers, singer/songwriter/multi-instrumentalist Jim Mathus pursued projects outside of the group, appearing on collaborator Andrew Bird's albums *Thrills* and *Bowl Of Fire*. In 1997 Mathus, the Zippers' bassist Stu Cole, producer Mike Napolitano and pianist Greg Bell formed the Knockdown Society and released *Play Songs For Rosetta*, a collection of bluesman Charley Patton's songs that benefitted his daughter Rosetta and her family. His music took another turn in late 2001 with the release of *National Antiseptic*, this time offering tribute to the electric juke-joint swamp rock of the deep South. *—Heather Phares*

● **Play Songs for Rosetta** / Oct. 7, 1997 / Mammoth ♦♦♦♦♦
Mathus, one of the masterminds behind the Squirrel Nut Zippers, here cuts it Clarksdale style for the sake of bluesman Charley Patton's daughter, Rosetta. Not surprisingly, Rosetta doesn't see a dime from the sale of Patton's music, and Mathus saw an opportunity to give back. Give back to the music? Well, yes, but also to Rosetta herself, who helped raise Mathus from knee-pants. And the result is a righteous paella of roots music: rattling Delta style, jug band and parlor jazz with Dixieland and country blues to boot. It's all so fresh and lively you may wonder how you lived your life without it. Dig the winking ragtime cover of Leadbelly's "Keep Your Hand's Off Her" or the country scrawl of Mathus' "Turkey Buzzard in a Pork Pie Hat." *—Tim Sheridan*

National Antiseptic / Oct. 16, 2001 / Mammoth ♦♦♦
Former Squirrel Nut Zippers frontman James Mathus has worn many hats during his career. From the Zippers' goofy post-vaudeville hot jazz to his own solo experiments with Delta blues, he has been a tough guy to pin down, and *National Antiseptic* is no exception. On this 2001 release, James Mathus & His Knockdown Society churn out dirty and gritty swamp blues with an authentic fervor that similar artists like the Jon Spencer Blues Explosion and White Stripes have also toyed with. Drums are pushed into the red on almost every track, eclipsed only by Mathus' crunched-out electric guitar and his loose juke joint murmurs and howls. Like other successful white blues interpreters (Koerner, Ray & Glover in the '60s and G. Love & Special Sauce in the '90s come to mind), Mathus seems to draw from a well that has eluded Jonny Lang and Kenny Wayne Shepherd. This may be because Lang, Shepherd, and their contemporaries are recalling Eric Clapton and Stevie Ray Vaughan in their tributes, while Mathus & His Knockdown Society seem to have stacks of old Charley Patton and Lightnin' Hopkins 78s in their briefcase full of blues. Whatever the reasons, these guys certainly play an authentic brand of roots music, sounding as if most of the record could have come out on Fat Possum records alongside T-Model Ford and R.L. Burnside's recent recordings. Bar-room stomps like "Innit for the Money" and "Stranger" stand out as highlights, recalling not only early electric blues records, but a little stride piano and honkin' R&B saxophone as well. Those expecting a continuation of Mathus' work from any of his previous incarnations may be disappointed, but anyone who appreciates a good, loose, gritty blast through some time-honored musical styles will be warmly delighted. *—Zac Johnson*

David Maxwell

b. Mar. 10, 1950, Waltham, MA
Piano / Modern Electric Blues
Pianist David Maxwell has been a part of the Boston blues scene as a sideman since the late '60s, but has only in the '90s begun leading his own band and recording under his own name.

Maxwell took some of his early stylistic cues from the likes of Spann, Sunnyland Slim and Pinetop Perkins, also listening to the recordings of Big Maceo, Ray Charles and Memphis Slim. He became friendly with Muddy Waters' longtime piano player, Otis Spann, in the late '60s.

Maxwell went on to back many great players over the years, including Freddie King, whom he worked with for two years in the early '70s; Bonnie Raitt, whom he worked with in 1974 and '75, while she was still based in Boston; and James Cotton from 1977 to 1979. He toured Europe and Japan with Otis Rush in the '90s, and has performed over the years with dozens of others, including John Lee Hooker, Jimmy Rogers, Paul Oscher, Hubert Sumlin, Bob Margolin, John Primer and Ronnie Earl. He has joined many of these same people on their studio efforts, including Cotton for his 1997 Grammy-winning *Deep in the Blues.* Maxwell also can be heard on the soundtrack to the movie *Fried Green Tomatoes* with longtime Boston musicians Ronnie Earl and Peter Wolf.

Maxwell's debut record for Tone-Cool, *Maximum Blues Piano,* is a collection of instrumental tunes that showcase many of the Boston scene's veteran players: Ronnie Earl and Duke Levine on guitars, Kaz Kazanoff and Gordon Beadle on saxophones, drummer Marty Richards and bassist Marty Ballou. Echoes of all of his influences can be heard throughout the tracks, including Pete Johnson on "Down at P.J.'s Place," and Otis Spann on "Deep Into It." *—Richard Skelly*

● **Maximum Blues Piano** / 1997 / Tone-Cool ✦✦✦✦✦
Maxwell's solo debut has been a long time in coming, but it been worth the wait, as he neatly sidesteps the curse of the non-vocalist bandleader. Bringing in Darrell Nulisch for one vocal ("Heart Attack") only distracts from this fine instrumental showcase for David's prodigious abilities. Maxwell literally sparkles on the gospel-ish sanctified shout of "Sister Laura Lee," the New Orleans strut of "Breakdown on the Bayou," the boogie-woogie classic "Honky Tonk Train" and "Manhattan Max," trading licks throughout with guest stars Ronnie Earl, Duke Levine and saxman supreme Mark "Kaz" Kazanoff, basically the cream of the New England blues mafia. The fact that Maxwell has learned his slow blues lessons well is exhibited on the Pete Johnson tribute, "Down at P.J.'s Place," "Deep Into It" and a seven-minute-plus rendition of Avery Parrish's "After Hours." This is more than just an impressive debut; this is a record of great playing and uncommon musical depth. *—Cub Koda*

Brother Joe May

b. Nov. 9, 1912, Macon, Mississippi, **d.** Jul. 14, 1972
Vocals / Traditional Gospel, Black Gospel
Dubbed "The Thunderbolt of the Middle West" by his mentor, the legendary Willie Mae Ford Smith, Brother Joe May was arguably the greatest male soloist in the history of gospel music; a tenor whose dramatic sense of showmanship was surpassed only by his unparalleled command of vocal dynamics and projection, he possessed a voice of unimaginable range and power, moving from a whisper to a scream without the slightest suggestion of effort. May was born in Macon, Mississippi on November 9, 1912; raised in the Church of God denomination—where all men are called "Brother," hence his stage name—he began singing at the age of nine, later joining the Little Church Out on the Hills' senior choir. His subsequent tenure as a soloist with the Church of God Quartet solidified his strong reputation throughout the Southern gospel circuit.

After graduating high school, May worked as a day laborer in Macon before he and his family relocated to East St. Louis, Illinois in 1941, at which time he hired on at a chemical plant. In the St. Louis area he became a protégé of the pioneering Smith, and with her aid honed his sense of phrasing, modeling his own vocal acrobatics on hers; their connection was so strong that May even copied her theatrical performing style. Smith was also the director of the Soloists' Bureau of songwriter Thomas A. Dorsey's National Convention of Gospel Choirs and Choruses, at whose conventions May began to build a name for himself throughout the country; during one such convention in Los Angeles in 1949, he came to the attention of Specialty Records talent scout J.W. Alexander, and upon signing to the label cut his first session later that same year, scoring a major hit with his debut release "Search Me Lord."

May's initial success allowed him to quit his day job by 1950, and he began touring the nation, often performing alongside the likes of the Soul Stirrers and the Pilgrim Travelers. With his titanic voice and commanding stage presence, he was often called "the male Mahalia Jackson," a comparison suggested even by Jackson herself. However, despite his popularity—both "Search Me Lord" and 1950's "Do You Know Him?" were estimated to have sold over one million copies each, making him Specialty's best-selling artist of the period—May never crossed over to white audiences, the ultimate measure of commerical success at that time. Despite acknowledging Bessie Smith as a major early influence, May also refused to pursue a career as a secular blues singer, and his adamant rejection of all musical traditions but gospel likely played a role in his exit from Specialty in 1958.

Now a free agent, May quickly signed with the Nashboro label, where he also began recording many of his own original compositions. As a result of the Nashville-based company's regional focus, the majority of his subsequent live appearances were scheduled across the Deep South, where his fame continued to grow enormously in the years to follow. An extended stretch of the early '60s also found May starring in the musical *Black Nativity* in the company of Marion Williams, and after playing Broadway the production toured the U.S. and Europe. After its run was completed, May returned to the South, where his health began to slowly fail; regardless, he maintained his strenuous touring pace, keeping his declining condition a secret even from family members. Finally, while en route to a performance in Thomasville, Georgia, May suffered a massive stroke and died on July 14, 1972, at the age of 60. *—Jason Ankeny*

☆ **Thank You Lord for One More Day** / 1967 / Specialty ✦✦✦✦✦
Thank You Lord for One More Day is a wonderful collection of Brother Joe May's Specialty sides, highlighted by collaborations with Sister Wynona Carr and the Pilgrim Travelers. *—Leo Stanley*

Brother Joe May Story / 1972 / ✦✦✦

Search Me, Lord / 1974 / Specialty ✦✦✦✦✦
Authoritative gospel and energized vocals with support from the Pilgrim Travelers and the Sallie Martin Singers. *—Ron Wynn*

★ **In Loving Memory . . .** / 1974 / Specialty ✦✦✦✦✦
In Loving Memory of Brother Joe May is a collection of May's finest shouts and duets on Specialty, supported on some cuts by the Pilgrim Travelers, the Sallie Martin Singers, or a live audience. *—Ron Wynn*

Thunderbolt of the Middle West / 1974 / Specialty ✦✦✦
Brother Joe May was the male counterpart to Mahalia Jackson, a full-voiced tenor of amazing range and power. Although he recorded prolifically for the Nashboro label for the bulk of his career, this 27-track collection brings together his earliest recordings for the Specialty label. Although many of these tracks feature him working with the Sallie Martin Singers, Sister Wynona Carr, the Pilgrim Travelers, and his daughter Annette May, the real star of the show is Brother Joe, whose voice simply soars no matter what the surroundings. *—Cub Koda*

Brother Joe May Live, 1952–1955 / 1994 / Specialty ✦✦✦✦✦
Brother Joe May earned his "Thunderbolt of the Midwest" nickname with incandescent, riveting vocals that could blow a roof off or reduce listeners to tears, often at the same time. The 16 tracks on this CD were done live, usually at services or during church performances, and they frequently paired him with the Sallie Martin Singers. While they and Prof. J. Earle Hines are fine, May is in another dimension. His flamboyant, dynamic voice shudders, roars, rises, moans and flails, and he fortifies the songs with commentary that's nearly as inspiring. Even devout atheists will be impressed by the power of Brother Joe May. *—Ron Wynn*

The Best of Brother Joe May / Jan. 31, 1995 / Nashboro ✦✦✦✦
The last great recordings by the legendary "Thunderbolt of the Midwest." Nashboro material. *—Opal Louis Nations*

Mark May

Guitar, Vocals / Modern Electric Blues
Music was a part of Mark May's life from an early age. A brother had worked with Pure Prairie League's Craig Fuller, and his mom was drawn to the strains of country and bluegrass. A native of Ohio, the blues guitarist began learning to play the instrument when he was five years old, and during his teen years he became involved with several bands. By the time he'd turned 16, he had played the first of what would become many professional gigs. Upon relocating to Houston during the early '80s, May continued to perform professionally with a variety of country outfits. He went on to work with rock groups, but his heart always was with the blues. Thanks to a friend, he discovered an affinity for Albert Collins' brand of the blues. He soon pulled together his own blues-rock group. The band included saxophonist Eric Dimmer, drummer Danny Goza, and singer and bass player "Fretless" Dan Cooper. Dimmer left the group to work with Clarence "Gatemouth" Brown, and singer and harpist Dave Nevling came aboard. May and the Agitators, his Houston-based band, headed into the studio and made their demo, *You Can Call on the Blues.*

Before a month had passed, Icehouse/Priority Records executive Johnny Philips was ready to sign May and the Agitators. After the record company issued a CD titled *Call on the Blues*, the band's lineup shifted. Guitarist Billy Wells and drummer Greg Grubbs stepped in to take over for Goza and Nevling. Icehouse issued May's sophomore effort, *Telephone Road Houston, Texas,* in 1997. The CD features contributions from the Agitators' former saxophonist, Dimmer, as well as Alan Haynes, Larry McCray, and the Memphis Horns. Two years later, May was dubbed Houston Press Musician of the Year. Previously, he had been named a nominee in the city's Best Guitar Contest. The band's lineup evolved into May on vocals and guitar, drummer Clyde Dempsey, and Kirk McKim on guitar and vocals, while Cooper remained on bass. *—Linda Seida*

Call on the Blues / Sep. 26, 1995 / Icehouse ✦✦✦

● **Telephone Road Houston, Texas** / Nov. 18, 1997 / Icehouse ✦✦✦✦
Blues-rock with a distinct Texas edge is Mark May's thing. His playing recalls various Texas legends like Johnny Winter and Albert Collins, while always skirting the rock speed-demon side of the musical equation. This outing finds him surrounded by his regular rhythm section of Dan Cooper on bass, Travis Doyle on organ and Greg Grubbs on drums. May shares guitar soloing duties throughout the album with Alan Haynes ("Don't Give Up"), Billy Wells ("Mercury Blues") and Larry McCray (an impassioned Albert Collins duel on their mentor's "The Lights Are On, But Nobody's Home"), producing fireworks with every trill and bent note. Also noteworthy are several tracks featuring the Memphis Horns, who shine brightly on "Icehouse Special" and the soul ballad "Took Me By Surprise." When May keeps his playing roped in and restrained, the musical results are well worth a second listen. *—Cub Koda*

John Mayall

b. Nov. 29, 1933, Macclesfield, Cheshire, England
Vocals, Ukulele, Tambourine, Leader, Keyboards, Harpsichord, Harmonium, Piano, Harmonica, Guitar, Organ / Blues Revival, British Blues, Electric Harmonica Blues, Blues-Rock
The elder statesman of British blues, it is Mayall's lot to be more renowned as a bandleader and mentor than as a performer in his own right. Throughout the '60s, his band, the Bluesbreakers, acted as a finishing school for the leading British blues-rock musicians of the era. Guitarists Eric Clapton, Peter Green, and Mick Taylor joined his band in a remarkable succession in the mid-'60s, honing their chops with Mayall before going on to join Cream, Fleetwood Mac, and the Rolling Stones, respectively. John McVie and Mick Fleetwood, Jack Bruce, Aynsley Dunbar, Dick Heckstall-Smith, Andy Fraser (of Free), John Almond, and Jon Mark also played and recorded with Mayall for varying lengths of times in the '60s.

Mayall's personnel has tended to overshadow his own considerable abilities. Only an adequate singer, the multi-instrumentalist was adept in bringing out the best in his younger charges (Mayall himself was in his thirties by the time the Bluesbreakers began to make a name for themselves). Doing his best to provide a context in which they could play Chicago-style electric blues, Mayall was never complacent, writing most of his own material (which ranged from good to humdrum), revamping his lineup with unnerving regularity, and constantly experimenting within his basic blues format. Some of these experiments (with jazz-rock and an album on which he played all the instruments except drums) were forgettable; others, like his foray into acoustic music in the late '60s, were quite successful. Mayall's output has caught some flak from critics for paling next to the real African-American deal, but much of his vintage work—if weeded out selectively—is quite strong, especially his legendary 1966 LP with Eric Clapton, which both launched Clapton into stardom and kick-started the blues boom into full gear in England.

When Clapton joined the Bluesbreakers in 1965, Mayall had already been recording for a year, and been performing professionally long before that. Originally based in Manchester, Mayall moved to London in 1963 on the advice of British blues godfather Alexis Korner, who thought a living could be made playing the blues in the bigger city. Tracing a path through his various lineups of the '60s is a daunting task. At least 15 different editions of the Bluesbreakers were in existence from January 1963 through mid-1970. Some notable musicians (like guitarist Davy Graham, Mick Fleetwood, and Jack Bruce) passed through for little more than a cup of coffee; Mayall's longest-running employee, bassist John McVie, lasted about four years. The Bluesbreakers, like Fairport Convention or the Fall, was more a concept than an ongoing core. Mayall, too, had the reputation of being a difficult and demanding employer, willing to give musicians their walking papers as his music evolved, although he also imparted invaluable schooling to them while the associations lasted.

Mayall recorded his debut single in early 1964; he made his first album, a live affair, near the end of the year. At this point the Bluesbreakers had a more pronounced R&B influence than would be exhibited on their most famous recordings, somewhat in the mold of younger combos like the Animals and Rolling Stones. Quite respectable it was too, but the Bluesbreakers would take a turn for the purer with the recruitment of Eric Clapton in the spring of 1965. Clapton had left the Yardbirds in order to play straight blues, and the Bluesbreakers allowed him that freedom (or stuck to well-defined restrictions, depending upon your viewpoint). Clapton began to inspire reverent acclaim as one of Britain's top virtuosos, as reflected in the famous "Clapton is God" graffiti that appeared in London in the mid-'60s.

In professional terms, though, 1965 wasn't the best of times for the group, which had been dropped by Decca. Clapton even left the group for a few months for an odd trip to Greece, leaving Mayall to straggle on with various fill-ins, including Peter Green. Clapton did return in late 1965, around the time an excellent blues-rock single, "I'm Your Witchdoctor" (with searing sustain-laden guitar riffs), was issued on Immediate. By early 1966, the band were back on Decca, and recorded their landmark *Bluesbreakers* LP. This was the album that, with its clean, loud, authoritative licks, firmly established Clapton as a guitar hero, on both reverent covers of tunes by the likes of Otis Rush and Freddie King, and decent originals by Mayall himself. The record was also an unexpected commercial success, making the Top Ten in Britain. From that point on, in fact, Mayall became one of the first rock musicians to depend primarily upon the LP market; he recorded plenty of singles throughout the '60s, but none of them came close to becoming a hit.

Clapton left the Bluesbreakers in mid-1966 to form Cream with Jack Bruce, who had played with Mayall briefly in late 1965. Mayall turned quickly to Peter Green, who managed the difficult feat of stepping into Clapton's shoes and gaining respect as a player of roughly equal imagination and virtuosity, although his style was quite distinctly his own. Green recorded one LP with Mayall, *A Hard Road*, and several singles, sometimes writing material and taking some respectable lead vocals. Green's talents, like those of Clapton, were too large to be confined by sideman status, and in mid-1967 he left to form a successful band of his own, Fleetwood Mac.

Mayall then enlisted 19-year-old Mick Taylor; remarkably, despite the consecutive departures of two star guitarists, Mayall maintained a high level of popularity. The late '60s were also a time of considerable experimentation for the Bluesbreakers, which moved into a form of blues-jazz-rock fusion with the addition of a horn section, and then a retreat into mellower, acoustic-oriented music. Mick Taylor, the last of the famous triumvirate of Mayall-bred guitar heroes, left in mid-1969 to join the Rolling Stones. Yet in a way Mayall was thriving more than ever, as the U.S. market, which had been barely aware of him in the Clapton era, was beginning to open up for his music. In fact, at the end of the '60s, Mayall moved to Los Angeles. 1969's *The Turning Point*, a live, all-acoustic affair, was a commercial and artistic high point.

In America at least, Mayall continued to be pretty popular in the early '70s. His band was no more stable than ever; at various points some American musicians flitted in and out of the Bluesbreakers, including Harvey Mandel, Canned Heat bassist Larry Taylor, and Don "Sugarcane" Harris. Although he's released numerous albums since and remained a prodigiously busy and reasonably popular live act, his post-1970 output generally hasn't matched the quality of his '60s work. Following collaborations with an unholy number of guest celebrities, in the early '80s he reteamed with a couple of his more renowned vets, John McVie and Mick Taylor, for a tour. It's the '60s albums that you want, though there's little doubt that Mayall has over the past decades done a great deal to popularize the blues all over the globe, whether or not the music has meant much on record. *—Richie Unterberger*

John Mayall Plays John Mayall / Mar. 26, 1965 / Decca ✦✦✦
Recorded live at the British club Klooks Kleek in late 1964 before Clapton joined (Roger Dean plays lead guitar), this is a fine set of early British R&B with a more pronounced rock feel (akin to the Rolling Stones) than Mayall's other '60s work. Mayall wrote all but one of the songs on this overlooked but driving, highly enjoyable LP that is recommended to connoisseurs of early British blues-rock. *—Richie Unterberger*

★ **Bluesbreakers With Eric Clapton** / Jul. 1966 / Deram ✦✦✦✦✦
Bluesbreakers With Eric Clapton was Eric Clapton's first fully realized album as a blues guitarist—more than that, it was a seminal blues album of the '60s, perhaps the best British blues album ever cut, and the best LP ever recorded by John Mayall's Bluesbreakers. Standing midway between Clapton's stint with the Yardbirds and the formation of Cream, this album featured the new guitar hero on a series of stripped-down blues standards, Mayall pieces, and one Mayall/Clapton composition, all of which had him stretching out in the idiom for the first time in the studio. This album was the culmination of a very successful year of playing with John Mayall, a fully realized blues creation, featuring sounds very close to the group's stage performances, and with no compromises. Credit has to go to producer Mike Vernon for the purity and simplicity of the record; most British producers of that era wouldn't have been able to get it recorded this way, much

less released. One can hear the very direct influence of Buddy Guy and a handful of other American bluesmen in the playing. And lest anyone forget the rest of the quartet: future pop-rock superstar John McVie and drummer Hughie Flint provide a rock-hard rhythm section, and Mayall's organ playing, vocalizing, and second guitar are all of a piece with Clapton's work. His guitar naturally dominates most of this record, and he can also be heard taking his first lead vocal, but McVie and Flint are just as intense and give the tracks an extra level of steel-strung tension and power, none of which have diminished across four decades. In 1998, Polygram Records issued a remastered version of this album on CD, featuring both the stereo and mono mixes of the original tracks and new notes. *—Bruce Eder*

A Hard Road / Feb. 17, 1967 / Deram ✦✦✦✦
Eric Clapton is usually thought of as Mayall's most important righthand man, but the case could also be made for his successor, Peter Green. The future Fleetwood Mac founder leaves a strong stamp on his only album with the Bluesbreakers, singing a few tracks and writing a couple, including the devastating instrumental "Supernatural." Green's use of thick sustain on this track clearly pointed the way to his use of this feature on Fleetwood Mac's hits "Albatross" and "Black Magic Woman," as well as providing a blueprint for Carlos Santana's style. Mayall acquits himself fairly well on this mostly original set (with occasional guest horns), though some of the material is fairly mundane. Highlights include the uncharacteristically rambunctious "Leaping Christine" and the cover of Freddie King's "Someday After a While (You'll Be Sorry)." *—Richie Unterberger*

John Mayall's Bluesbreakers With Paul Butterfield / Apr. 1967 / Decca ✦✦
A summit meeting of the leading U.S. and U.K. blues-rock bandleaders of their time resulted in this four-song seven-inch EP, which, like most such projects, didn't add up to the sum of its parts. By either man's standards, it's routine, if unobjectionable. Mayall takes a much stronger role than Butterfield; "Riding on the L&N" is about the best cut on a disc that also has a version of Junior Wells' "Little By Little" and one Mayall original, "Eagle Eye." Personnel is not listed on this rarity; one could reasonably assume from the date of release that it features the Peter Green version of the Bluesbreakers, but rock reference books are in conflict as to whether Mick Fleetwood and/or Peter Green appear on the disc or not. *—Richie Unterberger*

Crusade / Sep. 1, 1967 / London ✦✦✦✦✦
The final album of an (unintentional) trilogy, *Crusade* is most notable for the appearance of a very young, pre-Rolling Stones Mick Taylor on lead guitar. Taylor's performance is indeed the highlight, just as Eric Clapton and Peter Green's playing was on the previous album. The centerpiece of the album is a beautiful instrumental by Taylor titled "Snowy Wood," which, while wholly original, seems to combine both Green and Clapton's influence with great style and sensibility. The rest of the record, while very enjoyable, is standard blues-rock fare of the day, but somewhat behind the then-progressive flavor of the period 1967. Mayall, while being one of the great bandleaders of London, simply wasn't really the frontman that the group needed so desperately, especially then. Nevertheless, *Crusade* is important listening for Mick Taylor aficionados. *—Matthew Greenwald*

The Blues Alone / Nov. 1967 / Deram ✦✦✦
The Blues Alone was the first Mayall "solo" album (without the Bluesbreakers). Mayall played and overdubbed all instruments except drums, which were handled by Bluesbreaker Keef Hartley. The album also tried to serve notice that, despite his band being a spawning ground for several British stars by now, the real star of the group was its leader. But it didn't quite prove that, since Mayall, while certainly competent on harmonica, keyboards, and guitars, doesn't display the flair of an Eric Clapton or Peter Green, and the overdubbing, as is so often the case, robs the recording of any real sense of interplay. *—William Ruhlmann*

Blues From Laurel Canyon / 1968 / Deram ✦✦✦✦✦
Mayall's first post-Bluesbreakers album saw the man returning to his roots after the jazz/blues fusion that was *Bare Wires*. *Blues From Laurel Canyon* is a blues album, through and through. Testimony to this is the fact that there's a guitar solo only 50 seconds into the opening track. Indeed, Mayall dispersed the entire brass section for *Blues From Laurel Canyon*, and instead chose the solid but relatively limited backing of Mick Taylor (guitar), Colin Allen (drums), and Steve Thompson (bass). Instantly, it is apparent that John Mayall hasn't lost his touch with the blues. "Vacation," the album's opener, reminds one exactly why this artist is so celebrated for his songwriting ability. The staggering Mick Taylor (here still in his teens) truly proves his worth as a blues guitarist, while Stephen Thompson (also in his late teens) works superbly with one of the genre's most interesting drummers, Colin Allen. *Blues From Laurel Canyon* is as unerring as *Bluesbreakers With Eric Clapton*, and equally as musically interesting. Not only is this one of the finest John Mayall albums, it is also a highlight in the blues genus. *—Ben Davies*

Bare Wires / Jun. 21, 1968 / Deram ✦✦✦
Bare Wires was the first Bluesbreakers album of new studio material since *A Hard Road*, released 16 months before. In that time, the band had turned over entirely, expanding to become a septet. Mayall's musical conception had also expanded—the album began with a 23-minute "Bare Wires Suite," which included more jazz influences than usual and featured introspective lyrics. In retrospect, all of this is a bit indulgent, but at the time it helped Mayall out of what had come to seem a blues straitjacket (although he would eventually return to a strict blues approach). It isn't surprising that he dropped the "Bluesbreakers" name after this release. (The album was Mayall's most successful ever in the U.K., hitting number three.) *—William Ruhlmann*

Looking Back / Aug. 1969 / Deram ✦✦✦
Reasonably interesting collection of non-LP singles from 1964 to 1968, featuring almost all of the notable musicians that passed through the Bluesbreakers throughout the decade. "Sitting in the Rain" (with Peter Green) showcases fine fingerpicking, the haunt-

ing "Jenny" is one of Mayall's best originals, and "Stormy Monday" is one of the few cuts from 1966 that briefly featured both Eric Clapton and Jack Bruce. The rest is largely passably pleasant and doesn't rank among Mayall's finest work. —*Richie Unterberger*

Empty Rooms / 1969 / Polydor ✦✦✦

This was John Mayall's studio-recorded followup to the live *The Turning Point*, featuring the same drumless quartet of himself, guitarist Jon Mark, reed player Johnny Almond, and bassist Steve Thompson. Mayall was at a commercial and critical peak with this folk-jazz approach; the album's lead-off track, "Don't Waste My Time," had become his sole singles chart entry prior to the LP's release, and although his former label, London, confused matters by releasing the two-year-old *Diary of a Band* [Volume 1] in the U.S. just before this new album appeared in early 1970, the new crop of fans he'd found with *The Turning Point* stuck with him on this gentle, reflective release. *Empty Rooms* hit number 33 in the U.S.; in the U.K. it got to number 9. —*William Ruhlmann*

The Turning Point / 1969 / BGO ✦✦✦✦✦

Recorded just after Mick Taylor departed for the Stones, Mayall eliminated drums entirely on this live recording. With mostly acoustic guitars and John Almond on flutes and sax, Mayall and his band, as his typically overblown liner notes state, "explore seldom-used areas within the framework of low volume music." But it does work. The all-original material is flowing and melodic, with long jazzy grooves that don't lose sight of their bluesy underpinnings. Lyrically, Mayall stretches out a bit into social comment on "The Laws Must Change" on this fine, meditative mood album. —*Richie Unterberger*

USA Union / 1970 / Polydor ✦✦

John Mayall's *Turning Point* band—Jon Mark, Johnny Almond, and Steve Thompson—broke up in June 1970 after a European tour. Mayall then assembled his first all-American band and recorded this album in July. It had more drive than the previous outfit, and Mayall turned to environmentalism on the leadoff track, "Nature's Disappearing." But much of his low-volume, reflective approach remained on an album that was still more of a jazz-pop outing than the blues sessions of his early career. *USA Union* had the highest U.S. chart peak of his career, hitting number 22. But in the U.K., where its title confirmed Mayall's U.S. leanings, the album showed a big dropoff from his usual sales. —*William Ruhlmann*

Back to the Roots / 1971 / Polydor ✦✦✦

For this double-LP, recorded in November 1970, John Mayall gathered together prominent musicians who had played in his bands during the past several years, including Don "Sugarcane" Harris, Eric Clapton, Johnny Almond, Harvey Mandel, Keef Hartley, and Mick Taylor. Mayall's compositions aren't all that impressive, but the sidemen frequently shine, especially Clapton. *Back To The Roots* hit number 52 in the U.S. and number 31 in the U.K., where it was Mayall's final album to reach the charts. It was reissued in altered form under the title *Archives To Eighties* in 1988. —*William Ruhlmann*

Thru the Years / 1971 / Deram ✦✦✦✦✦

A grab bag of rare tracks from the '60s, some of which stand among Mayall's finest. His debut 1964 single "Crawling Up a Hill" is one of his best originals; this comp also includes a couple of 1964-1965 flipsides that were never otherwise issued in the U.S. The eight songs featuring Peter Green include some top-notch material that outpaces much of the only album recorded by the Green lineup (*A Hard Road*), particularly the Green originals "Missing You" and "Out of Reach," a great B-side with devastating, icy guitar lines and downbeat lyrics that ranks as one of the great lost blues-rock cuts of the '60s. The set is filled out with a few songs from the Mick Taylor era, the highlight being the vicious instrumental "Knockers Step Forward." Look for the CD reissue and not the early-'70s double U.S. album of the same name, which includes a lot of superfluous material and omits the three 1964-1965 songs from British 45s. —*Richie Unterberger*

Memories / Dec. 1971 / Polydor ✦✦✦

Having gone *Back to the Roots*, John Mayall returned to his forward-looking musical explorations with 1971's *Memories*, the true followup to *USA Union*, on which he retained bassist Larry Taylor, replaced Harvey Mandel with guitarist Jerry McGee of The Ventures, and dropped Don "Sugarcane" Harris, for an unusually small trio session. Actually, he was still looking back on a set of autobiographical lyrics about growing up, starting with the title track, and including "Grandad," and "Back from Korea." (Forced to compete with the simultaneous release of the London Records compilation *Thru the Years*, *Memories* managed to reach only number 179 in the U.S. charts.) —*William Ruhlmann*

Ten Years Are Gone / 1973 / Polydor ✦✦✦

Mayall returned to the studio in 1973 for this double album. The ten years Mayall had in mind, of course, were the previous ten, which had seen him start as a local musician in Manchester, England, and emerge a decade, almost two dozen albums, and nearly as many lineups later with an evolved jazz-blues style and an international following. The album allows the ensemble considerable room to solo on Mayall's typically simple, blues-based song structures, and the approach is perhaps excessively casual. The second LP is a live date recorded at the Academy of Music in New York, and here things stretch out even more: "Harmonica Free Form" clocks in at 12 minutes and "Dark of the Night" runs 17:41. —*William Ruhlmann*

Latest Edition / 1974 / Polydor ✦✦✦

The title makes a virtue of necessity, as John Mayall introduces another all-new lineup (actually, bassist Larry Taylor is returning from an older edition). Two guitarists, Hightide Harris and Randy Resnick, lead the band in more of an uptempo R&B style than has been used in much of Mayall's music during the past several years, starting with the timely "Gasoline Blues" (1974 was the year of the gas lines, remember?) and going on to "Troubled Times" (which advises impeaching President Nixon). Still, this was a lackluster set, which is only appropriate since it was Mayall's swan song with Polydor, and the album became his first to miss the charts in the U.S. since 1967. —*William Ruhlmann*

Primal Solos / 1977 / Deram ✦✦

Fuzzy live tapes from 1966 and 1968 of dubious quality, in both sonics and performance. Side one has Clapton on lead and Bruce on bass on familiar Chicago blues standards by the likes of John Lee Hooker, Willie Dixon, and Sonny Boy Williamson. Side two is from a couple of 1968 gigs with Mick Taylor, with three lengthy tracks that have little to recommend them. For fanatics only. —*Richie Unterberger*

Last of the British Blues / 1978 / One Way ✦✦✦

This was the last of the six albums John Mayall originally made for Blue Thumb/ABC Records between 1975 and 1978, about which he has said, "ABC released six of my albums as a tax write-off. A week after they were released you couldn't find them in any store." It's a live album on which Mayall fronts a quartet consisting of guitarist James Quill Smith (who sings lead on several songs), bassist Steve Thompson, and drummer Soko Richardson. The approach is rock-oriented, and the set list includes such Bluesbreakers favorites as Mose Allison's "Parchman Farm" and Freddie King's "Hideaway" (taken at a frantic tempo), along with the usual complement of generic Mayall originals, among them, a remake of "The Bear" from *Blues From Laurel Canyon*. —*William Ruhlmann*

Behind the Iron Curtain / 1985 / GNP Crescendo ✦✦

On his first new album in four years (and first new U.S. release in seven years), John Mayall reclaims the "Bluesbreakers" name for the first time in 18 years to highlight a quintet featuring two lead guitarists, Coco Montoya and Walter Trout, along with a rhythm section of Bobby Haynes (bass) and Joe Yuele (drums). The album was recorded in concert in Hungary in June, 1985, and takes a fairly bluesy approach with lots of space for the guitarists to shine, a format similar to that of The Bluesbreakers lineups of 1965-1968. Sound quality is only fair, and this is not an inspired performance, but Mayall has latched onto a cohesive unit here, and the results are encouraging for the future. —*William Ruhlmann*

Chicago Line / Aug. 1988 / Island ✦✦

John Mayall's first new studio album to be released in the U.S. in more than a decade shows that his current crop of Bluesbreakers—Coco Montoya, Walter Trout, Bobby Haynes, and Joe Yuele—who have been together longer than any previous outfit, play like a seasoned blues band, sparking each other (especially guitarists Montoya and Trout), and never falling into complacency. Mayall presides over the music without dominating it, which makes The Bluesbreakers more of a group than they've been since the '60s. —*William Ruhlmann*

Crocodile Walk / 1990 / ✦✦

Pretty fair, if hardly revelatory, compilation of 1965-1967 BBC sessions with Mayall's best lineups, variously featuring Roger Dean, Eric Clapton, and Peter Green on guitar. A few of the songs ("Cheating Woman," "Nowhere To Run," "Bye Bye Bird") were never recorded officially by Mayall during this period. Clapton actually doesn't shine particularly brightly on the few tracks that feature his playing, but the fidelity is good and the material pretty strong. The three closing tracks, recorded live with Mick Taylor in 1968, are a waste: lousy sound, tedious jamming. —*Richie Unterberger*

A Sense of Place / Mar. 1990 / Island ✦✦✦

A Sense of Place represents Mayall's full-fledged return to major-label record-making, with all the good and bad things that implies, from a high-profile producer, R.S. Field, to the introduction of such cover material as Wilbert Harrison's "Let's Work Together" and J.J. Cale's "Sensitive Kind." Field uses a spare production style, light on atmosphere and heavy, as is the current fashion, on unusual percussion. This makes for an identifiable sound, to be sure, but you can't help thinking that it isn't what The Bluesbreakers sound like on a good night in a small club. The result, as intended, was Mayall's first chart appearance in 15 years, but as a commercial comeback, the record ultimately failed. —*William Ruhlmann*

London Blues (1964-1969) / Oct. 20, 1992 / Deram ✦✦✦✦✦

Featuring 40 tracks over two discs, *London Blues* is an excellent collection of most of the best moments from Mayall and the Bluesbreakers' early recordings, a time when Eric Clapton, Peter Green, and Mick Taylor all passed through the band. —*Stephen Thomas Erlewine*

Room to Move (1969-1974) / Oct. 20, 1992 / Polydor ✦✦✦✦✦

The majority of Mayall and the Bluesbreakers' best material from the early '70s is collected on this 29-track, double-disc set. Although Clapton appears on a couple of songs, the playing on *Room to Move* isn't as universally breathtaking as it is on *London Blues*, but the collection is thoroughly listenable, and it does feature many fine musicians. —*Stephen Thomas Erlewine*

Wake Up Call / Apr. 6, 1993 / Silvertone ✦✦✦

Fuelled by Coco Montoya's searing but economical string-slashing, drummer Joe Yuele, and bassist Rick Cortes, John Mayall has managed to keep a stable core of Bluesbreakers together in recent years. Mayall rarely does the same album twice, and *Wake Up Call* finds him returning to a basic, physical sound after 1990's more progressive/highly produced *A Sense of Place*. The harp whiz has rarely flirted with the pop charts over the decades, a track record that will likely handicap the title track—a potential hit featuring guest vocalist Mavis Staples and some take-charge riffing from former mate Mick Taylor. For pure guitar joy though, Montoya turns the trick all on his own with barnburners "Loaded Dice" and "Nature's Disappearing." —*Roch Parisien*

Spinning Coin / 1995 / Silvertone ✦✦✦

Somehow the grandfather of British blues still had the fire in his belly to record a strong album almost 40 years after he began his storied career. Buddy Whittington acquits himself well as the latest in a long line of hotshot guitarists for this multi-instrumentalist, who still does his best work on harmonica. He still admires long-dead bluesman J.B. Lenoir, including "Voodoo Music" here. A lot of credit for this strong outing goes to R.S. Field, lyricist and sometime producer for Webb Wilder. "Long Story Short" would pass for a Wilder tune were it not for Mayall's distinctive voice. *—Mark Allan*

Blues for the Lost Days / Apr. 15, 1997 / Jive ♦♦♦

Blues for the Lost boasts an intriguing concept, as it captures John Mayall reminiscing about all the friends, family, heroes, lovers and places he has loved and lost over the years. The album is startling in its unvarnished autobiographical approach, but the concept doesn't work nearly as well as it should. Most of Mayall's songs meander into mawkish nostalgia, and the laidback, cool blues never makes such sentiments compelling. Lead guitarist Buddy Whittington contributes a few good solos, but most of the record is sadly unengaging. *—Thom Owens*

As It All Began: The Best of John Mayall & the Bluesbreakers 1964–1969 / Jan. 27, 1998 / Polydor ♦♦♦♦♦

As It All Began: The Best of John Mayall & the Bluesbreakers 1964-1969 is an excellent 20-track retrospective, capturing Mayall's band at their peak. The Bluesbreakers went through several different lineups during those four years, with musicians the caliber of Eric Clapton, Mick Taylor, Paul Butterfield, Mick Fleetwood, John McVie, and Peter Green floating through the group. Hardcore fans of any of those musicians, or of British blues, will naturally want to familiarize themselves with the original albums, but *As It All Began* is a fine sampler for the casual fan, featuring such staples as "Lonely Years," "Bernard Jenkins," "All Your Love," "Parchman Farm," "Double Trouble," "The Death of J.B. Lenoir," and "Miss James." Even at 20 tracks, there are a number of fine moments missing from this collection, but *As It All Began* remains the best available single-disc overview of the Bluesbreakers' prime period. *—Stephen Thomas Erlewine*

Drivin' On: The ABC Years (1975–1982) / Sep. 22, 1998 / MCA ♦♦♦♦

This two-disc, 32-track compilation brings together highlights from Mayall's output for ABC Records in the '70s, pulling from the albums *New Year, New Band, New Company*; *Notice to Appear*; *Lots of People*; *A Banquet of Blues*; *A Hard Core Package*; and *Last of the British Blues*. These cherry-picked tracks do a nice job of highlighting Mayall's estimable writing skills as well. Highlights include "Seven Days Too Long," "Old Time Blues," "You Can't Put Me Down," "Sitting on the Outside," "My Train Time," and the title track. As a special bonus, there's the second-disc inclusion of four live tracks from a 1982 Bluesbreaker reunion gig, featuring John McVie back at his original post on bass and Mick Taylor on lead guitar providing the fireworks. *—Cub Koda*

Silver Tones: The Best of John Mayall & the Bluesbreakers / Nov. 10, 1998 / Jive ♦♦♦

Padlock on the Blues / Jun. 1, 1999 / Cleopatra ♦♦♦

John Mayall's career may be distinguished but it's also been checkered, as he's swung from a celebrated talent scout to a journeyman bandleader. At times, he's in fashion, at others he's not. The late '90s was one of the times when he wasn't in fashion. Because of this, he was one of the first artists that Cleopatra signed when they began to move into high-profile new releases. *Padlock on Blues*, his first effort for the label and his first album in four years, finds Mayall pulling out all the stops, contributing 11 new tunes and lining up an impressive array of guest stars, including John Lee Hooker, Coco Montoya and Ernie Watts. All the extra effort has resulted in a solid record—but one that's not all that notably different from his Silvertone releases of the early '90s. The main difference is that the production isn't as impeccably clean as it was on the Silvertone albums. That doesn't mean it's grittier since, after all, he's still attempting the same sort of modern electric blues. Still, his performances have enough weight to be enjoyable, even if the songwriting is a little spotty. And, in that sense, it isn't all that different from any latter-day Mayall record—it's the kind of album that will generally please the faithful, no matter what the faults are. However, it may also frustrate them, since it is no better nor no worse—simply no different—than any record he's released since the beginning of the '80s. *—Stephen Thomas Erlewine*

The Masters / Jan. 18, 2000 / Spitfire ♦♦

Like its companion CD of sorts, *Live at the Marquee 1969*, this two-disc set is taken from the soundtrack of a rarely seen documentary of John Mayall and his band playing and rehearsing circa mid-1969, *The Turning Point*. And like *Live at the Marquee 1969*, it suffers from mediocre, bootleg-like fidelity. It does have a slight edge on that other release in that its material differs more from what is found on the official 1969 album *The Turning Point*. Disc one of *The Masters* is taken from three separate performances in England in June 1969, and suffers from the same disadvantage of *Live at the Marquee 1969* in a crucial respect: all of the songs are available, in far superior fidelity and similar arrangements, on the expanded CD reissue of *The Turning Point*. It might be a tad more interesting, though, in that these performances are a little earlier than the June 30, 1969, set featured on *Live at the Marquee 1969*, and just a mite less polished. Disc two, though less satisfying from a purely musical point of view, has more archival interest in that it combines tapes of rehearsals by the musicians who played on *The Turning Point* with interviews done for the film documentary. (There's also a none-too-impressive live version of "Parchman Farm" from May 1969 by the Bluesbreakers lineup, including Mick Taylor on lead guitar, that just preceded the one formed for *The Turning Point*.) Again, the sound is only on the threshold of listenability, and the songs (including brief bits inspired by "Greensleeves" and Bill Haley) more workouts of ideas than complete numbers. Mayall and one-time Bluesbreakers like Eric Clapton, Colin Allen, Peter Green, and John McVie offer occasionally interesting comments in the spoken interview segments, but even these are often afflicted by poor, mumbly sound (including points at which the voices contend with what sound like overhead airplanes!). *—Richie Unterberger*

Live at the Marquee 1969 / Jan. 18, 2000 / Spitfire ♦♦

This set was recorded at a June 30, 1969, performance at London's famous Marquee club. At that time, Mayall had just formed and started gigging with the drumless band that would play on what was (other than the Bluesbreakers' sole album with Eric Clapton) probably his most popular recording, *The Turning Point*. The set happened to be recorded because Mayall and his band were being filmed for a documentary, also called *The Turning Point*, which though released in the early '70s has rarely been shown. So far, all sounds good as far as signs indicating that this CD might be an interesting relic for Mayall fans. It's not, though, primarily because the sound is pretty crummy, on the order of an average live bootleg of the era. Actually, the instruments come through with fair (though not good) clarity, but the vocals are tinny, distant, and often indistinct. What's more, all seven of the these tracks (including two versions of "California") are available, with virtually the same arrangements and immensely superior sound, on the expanded CD version of the official album *The Turning Point*, recorded a mere two weeks later. Unless you're dying to hear the brief bit of "Sunshine of Your Love" that crops up in "So Hard to Share," there's no reason to pick this up when *The Turning Point* essentially captures the same band and the same set at the same moment in time, but with much better sound. *—Richie Unterberger*

Along for the Ride / May 8, 2001 / Red Ink ♦♦♦

By the time this was released in 2001, John Mayall was more known for the people who played in his seminal British band, the Bluesbreakers rather than his own accomplishments. The success of 1999's *Padlock on the Blues* afforded Mayall the opportunity to fulfill his dreams and gather an all-star lineup of blues and rock luminaries. "A World of Hurt" and "That's Why I Love You So" both typify the good but not great groove that permeates *Along for the Ride*. Better tracks "Yo Yo Man" and "Early in the Morning" are easygoing blues that feature the great rhythm section of John McVie and Mick Fleetwood. Fellow Fleetwood Mac and Bluesbreaker alum, the reclusive Peter Green plays acoustic slide guitar on "Yo Yo Man." "So Many Roads" has Mayall dueting with Otis Rush, and it soon becomes a contest on who sounds more disgruntled. The playful "Testify" features vocals and subtle guitar lines from blues phenom Shannon Curfman. This ends on the strong note. The powerful and wry "She Don't Play By the Rules" has Mayall with arguably the strongest and most subtle band with Mick Taylor on lead guitar and Andy Fairweather Low on acoustic guitar. *Along for the Ride* is produced, engineered, and mixed by David Z. Despite the camaraderie, a lot of the hooks here don't stick, and fans of Mayall and superstar sessions will get the most from this effort. *—Jason Elias*

Archive / Jun. 12, 2001 / Rialto ♦♦♦

Archive brings together a total of nine live performances by British blues rocker John Mayall. Several of the inclusions clock over ten minutes in length as Mayall often leads his band off on some unexpected tangents. This is the most captivating aspect of *Archive*, certainly more captivating than the at times frustrating sound quality and the album's somewhat haphazardly assembled feel. Mayall fans should find this a nice addition to their collection, though it's by no means essential or definitive—it's mostly something for fanatical completists to seek out. Plus, it's not exactly readily available, giving you yet another reason to look elsewhere first. *—Jason Birchmeier*

The Turning Point [Bonus Tracks 2001] / Oct. 30, 2001 / Polydor ♦♦♦♦♦

Recorded just after Mick Taylor departed for the Rolling Stones, Mayall eliminated drums entirely on this live recording. With mostly acoustic guitars and John Almond on flutes and sax, Mayall and his band, as his typically overblown liner notes state, "explore seldom-used areas within the framework of low-volume music." But it does work. The all-original material is flowing and melodic, with long, jazzy grooves that don't lose sight of their bluesy underpinnings. Lyrically, Mayall stretches out a bit into social comment on "The Laws Must Change" on this fine, meditative mood album. The 2001 CD reissue is a definite upgrade, though perhaps not enough to make you rush out and buy a new copy, in its addition of three previously unreleased bonus tracks from the same performance. Those are all respectable songs that fit in well with the rest of the set, particularly "Sleeping by Her Side" with its catchy and dreamy flute line, and the brisk "Don't Waste My Time," which has a nearly country & western feel. The newly added historical liner notes are another plus. *—Richie Unterberger*

Percy Mayfield

b. Aug. 12, 1920, Minden, LA, **d.** Aug. 11, 1984, Los Angeles, CA

Vocals, Songwriter, Piano / Urban Blues, West Coast Blues, Piano Blues, R&B, Soul

A masterful songwriter whose touching blues ballad "Please Send Me Someone to Love," a multi-layered universal lament, was a number one R&B hit in 1950, Percy Mayfield had the world by the tail until a horrific 1952 auto wreck left him facially disfigured. That didn't stop the poet laureate of the blues from writing in prolific fashion, though. As Ray Charles' favorite scribe during the '60s, he handed the Genius such gems as "Hit the Road Jack" and "At the Club."

Like so many of his postwar LA contemporaries, Mayfield got his musical start in Texas but moved to the coast during the war. Surmising that Jimmy Witherspoon might like to perform a tune he'd penned called "Two Years of Torture," Mayfield targeted Supreme Records as a possible buyer for his song. But the bosses at Supreme liked his own gentle reading so much that they insisted he wax it himself in 1947 with an all-star band that included saxist Maxwell Davis, guitarist Chuck Norris, and pianist Willard McDaniel.

Art Rupe's Specialty logo signed Mayfield in 1950 and he scored a solid string of R&B smashes over the next couple of years. "Please Send Me Someone to Love" and its equally potent flip "Strange Things Happening" were followed in the charts by "Lost Love," "What a Fool I Was," "Prayin' for Your Return," "Cry Baby," and "Big Question," cementing Mayfield's reputation as a blues balladeer of the highest order. Davis handled sax duties on most of Mayfield's Specialty sides as well. Mayfield's lyrics were usually as insightfully downbeat as his tempos; he was a true master at expressing his innermost feelings, laced with vulnerability and pathos (his "Life Is Suicide" and "The River's Invitation" are two prime examples).

Even though his touring was drastically curtailed after the accident, Mayfield hung in there as a Specialty artist through 1954, switching to Chess in 1955-1956 and Imperial in 1959. Charles proved thankful enough for Mayfield's songwriting genius to sign him to his Tangerine logo in 1962; over the next five years, the singer waxed a series of inexorably classy outings, many with Brother Ray's band (notably "My Jug and I" in 1964 and "Give Me Time to Explain" the next year).

It's a rare veteran blues artist indeed who hasn't taken a whack at one or more Mayfield copyrights. Mayfield himself persisted into the '70s, scoring minor chart items for RCA and Atlantic while performing on a limited basis until his 1984 death. *—Bill Dahl*

My Jug and I / 1962 / Tangerine ✦✦✦✦✦

Mayfield's gentle vocal delivery and the big, brassy sound of Ray Charles' orchestra were a match made in heaven. Mayfield brought some first-class material to this party (which begs for CD reissue): "My Jug and I," "Stranger in My Own Home Town" (later covered by Elvis Presley), the untypically jumping "Give Me Time to Explain," and a handful of Specialty remakes. *—Bill Dahl*

Bought Blues / 1969 / Tangerine ✦✦✦✦

Another elegant, beautifully arranged collection fraught with brilliant, sometimes heartbreaking material: "Ha Ha in the Daytime," "We Both Must Cry," "My Bottle Is My Companion." *—Bill Dahl*

★ **Poet of the Blues** / 1990 / Specialty ✦✦✦✦✦

The insightful songwriting skills of this West Coaster were matched by his wry, plaintive vocal delivery (Mayfield was usually his own best interpreter). The 25 sides here date from his hit-laden 1950-1954 stay at Art Rupe's Specialty logo and include his univesal lament "Please Send Me Someone to Love," and the resolutely downbeat "Strange Things Happening" and "Lost Love," and an ironic "The River's Invitation." Saxman Maxwell Davis led the horn-powered combos providing sympathetic support behind Mayfield. *—Bill Dahl*

Percy Mayfield Live / 1992 / Winner ✦✦✦

Although the first-ever release of live Mayfield material is culled from performances between 1981 and 1983, the twilight of the singer's blues career, he remains in fine, laidback voice throughout. The selections draw on all periods of his three decades as a songwriter, and include "Please Send Me Someone to Love," "The River's Invitation," and "Don't Start Lying to Me." Founding Paul Butterfield Blues Band pianist Mark Naftalin backs Mayfield throughout the collection; he also served as the set's producer. *—Jason Ankeny*

For Collectors Only / Apr. 6, 1992 / Specialty ✦✦✦

As the title suggests, this gives a deeper look at Mayfield's early career. Alternate takes and unissued material are included. *—Hank Davis*

Memory Pain / Sep. 17, 1992 / Specialty ✦✦✦✦✦

Ranging from major hits to alternate takes and rarities, this CD (released in 1992) illustrates the prolific nature of Percy Mayfield's Specialty Records output during the '50s. Though not everything on *Memory Pain* is essential, the collection of early R&B and 12-bar blues is consistently satisfying. The best known song here is the number one hit of 1950, "Please Send Me Someone to Love," and many listeners will also be familiar with such gems as "Strange Things Happening" and the title song. A singer who was flexible as well as charismatic, Mayfield is as convincing on a rare version of the mournful, jazz-tinged "Nightless Lovers" as he is on 12-bar numbers like "My Blues" and "The Big Question." The CD ends on an interesting note with a demo of "Hit the Road Jack" (which became a major hit for Ray Charles). Highly recommended. *—Alex Henderson*

Palmer McAbee

Harmonica / Country Blues

Palmer McAbee was an early American master of the harmonica, including but not limited to that instrument's grandiose capability to imitate the sounds of trains. While many a harmonica player has attempted to create the sound of a choo-choo pulling into the station, few have done it with as much imagination and fervor as McAbee, who created effects both realistic and surrealistic sometimes by blowing over the top of the harp. His vintage recording efforts have been reissued on a selection of anthologies devoted to country blues and more specifically the harmonica. The *Train 45* collection on Rounder presents a view limited to the railroad tracks, assembling a selection of recordings that either imitate trains, tell train stories, or both. Listeners who feel this might be a bit too much train lore to choo-choo should not despair, the harmonica player's aptly titled "McAbee's Railroad Piece" is also available on other blues compilations.

"This artist may be white" is a somewhat typical example of the information, or rather lack of information, available about McAbee. In terms of early-American folk music, particularly anything at all related to blues, any uncertainty over the race of the artist can be considered a compliment. Obviously not everyone agrees, as a summary of a New World anthology of traditional Southern instrumental styles indicates there is "one track by Palmer McAbee, the rest of the artists are white." Can one conduct racial profiling from a person's harmonica playing? Obviously not. Anyone attempting to make a judgment one way or another would be seriously hampered by the Indigo release *Devil in the Woodpile: Blues Harmonica 1926-1940*, in which two songs credited to McAbee are actually performances by George "Bullet" Williams. McAbee hailed from Alabama, although his recordings were made in Atlanta, GA. His race obviously would have made a great difference in either state, but harmonica players seem more interested in discussing the man's control and various effects than the color of his skin, the consensus being only a few players, such as Noah Lewis or Freeman Stowers, have approached his mastery. In some ways McAbee is equally known for what he leaves out than what he puts in: "The same great chug, without all the falsetto nonsense" is how one "harmaniac" described a McAbee cut in one intense harmonica chat room exchange. The year of 1928 was when he cut his famous recordings for Victor, but is often given out as the year of his birth. This would make his appearance on anthologies from the '20s and '30s something of a neat trick, since he plays much better harmonica than somebody's four-year-old cousin or ten-year-old son. *—Eugene Chadbourne*

Jerry "Boogie" McCain

b. Jun. 18, 1930, Gadsden, AL

Vocals, Drums, Trumpet, Songwriter, Harmonica, Guitar / Swamp Blues, Harmonica Blues, Electric Harmonica Blues, Modern Electric Blues

Not only is Alabama-born Jerry McCain a terrific amplified harpist, he's also one of the funniest songwriters working the genre and has been for more than four decades, as anyone who's dug his out-of-control '50s Excello rockers "My Next Door Neighbor" and "Trying to Please" will gladly testify. McCain was born on June 18, 1930, in Gadsden, AL. As a youngster, Little Walter was McCain's main man on harp, an instrument McCain began playing at age five. Walter passed through Gadsden one fateful night in 1953 with his Aces, offering encouragement and a chance to jam at a local nightspot. That same year, "Boogie" McCain made his vinyl debut for Lillian McMurray's Trumpet label in Jackson, MS, with "East of the Sun"/"Wine-O-Wine" and his brother, Walter McCain, playing drums on the sides. McCain's 1954 Trumpet encore, "Stay Out of Automobiles"/"Love to Make Up," was solid Southern blues, but barely hinted at the galvanic energy of his subsequent output.

Jerry McCain signed with Ernie Young's Nashville-based Excello logo in 1955, cutting "That's What They Want" with his usual sidekick Christopher Collins on guitar. "Run, Uncle John! Run," "Trying to Please," the torrid "My Next Door Neighbor" (a prior homemade demo version of the track that surfaced much later was even crazier), and "The Jig's Up" ranked with McCain's best 1955-1957 Excello efforts.

The harpist is probably best-known for his two-sided 1960 gem for Rex Records, "She's Tough"/"Steady." The Fabulous Thunderbirds later appropriated the insinuating midtempo A-side, while McCain's harp chops were strikingly showcased on the flip. McCain waxed three 45s for OKeh in Nashville in 1962, utilizing Music Row mainstays Floyd Cramer, Grady Martin, and Boots Randolph as his backup for "Red Top" and "Jet Stream." A series of 1965-1968 sides for Stan Lewis' Shreveport-based Jewel Records included a tailor-made tribute to the company, "728 Texas (Where the Action Is)" (Jewel's address).

After too many years spent in relative obscurity, McCain rejuvenated his fortunes in 1989 by signing with Ichiban Records and releasing *Blues 'n' Stuff*, followed three years later by *Struttin' My Stuff* and *Love Desperado*. In 2000, McCain released an all-star album *This Stuff Just Kills Me* for the Jericho label featuring Johnnie Johnson, John Primer, Anson Funderburgh, Jimmie Vaughan, along with the Double Trouble rhythm section of Tommy Shannon and Chris Layton. McCain resurfaced on Ichiban in 2002 with the release of *American Roots: Blues*. *—Bill Dahl and Al Campbell*

Choo Choo Rock / 1981 / White Label ✦✦✦✦✦

These demo recordings for Excello (ca. 1956) are wild and raucous, featuring overamplified guitars, crashing drums, and bizarre lyrics. What a rock & roll album by Little Walter might have sounded like. *—Cub Koda*

Blues 'n' Stuff / 1989 / Ichiban ✦✦✦

There's nothing aboard this OK outing that would suggest how amazing McCain's early work for Trumpet, Excello, and Rex was. *—Bill Dahl*

Strange Kind of Feelin' / 1990 / Alligator ✦✦✦

These are McCain's earliest sides, cut in 1953 and 1954 for Lillian McMurray's Trumpet label in Jackson, Mississippi. Both sides of his two Trumpet 78s plus the addition of three previously unissued tracks make up his total output for the label, so the collection is filled out with five tracks by Tiny Kennedy plus two by pianist Clayton Love. Although longtime axeman Christopher Collins is well to the fore on these tracks, McCain's harp is somewhat under-recorded, giving a lopsided effect to the music. But minor gems like "Stay Out of Automobiles," "Fall Guy," "Middle of the Night" and "Crazy 'Bout That Mess" are all sign pointers to the Excello material and make this a collection well worth seeking out. *—Cub Koda*

Love Desperado / 1992 / Ichiban ✦✦✦

The Alabama harpist's contemporary releases for Ichiban are certainly competent, but that insane energy level that marked his Excello output of the '50s is ancient history—and so too, for the most part, is the gleeful irreverence that made his early sides such a delight. *—Bill Dahl*

Struttin' My Stuff / Jun. 1, 1992 / Ichiban ✦✦✦

Alabaman Jerry McCain is a veteran of the blues and in fact recorded for the Trumpet label in Jackson, MS, at the same time as Elmore James and Sonny Boy Williamson. As one would expect, his harp work is both traditional and solid. Although original, his instrumental style bears resemblance to the work of past masters—the Sonny Boys and the Walters—while his original lyrics reflect modern life. This is a fine set of funky, urban blues—a standout from the Ichiban catalogue. *—Larry Hoffman*

I've Got the Blues All over Me / 1993 / Wild Dog ✦✦✦

● **That's What They Want: The Best of Jerry McCain** / 1995 / Excello ✦✦✦✦✦

McCain has always marched to the beat of a different drummer and the proof of it is right here, 23 recordings that define the place where the blues and rock & roll meet at the end of a dark alley. The first 12 tracks are McCain's complete singles output for Excello Records, the sides upon which most of his reputation rests. From the cold-hearted bravado of the the title track to the rocking insanity of "Trying To Please," this music is as special as it comes. The following 11 tracks come from homemade demo tapes circa 1955 that were cut in Jerry's living room with a single mike, one track home tape recorder. Featuring grinding, massively distorted guitars, crashing drums and lyrical texts concerning themselves with going crazy to rock & roll, rock & roll as salvation ("Rock & Roll Ball," "Geronimo's Rock"), or going crazy from outside worldly pressures ("Bell In My Heart," "My Next Door Neighbors"), these masterpieces answer the musical question: what would a rock & roll album by Little Walter have sounded like? *—AMG*

Retrospectives / Jun. 30, 1998 / Ichiban ♦♦♦
When Jerry McCain re-emerged on Ichiban in 1989 after many years of not doing nearly enough recording, followers of the Alabama native were delighted to see him back in the studio again. This 1998 CD (which spans 1989-1993) points to the fact that while his Ichiban output may not have been in a class with his great Excello recordings of the '50s, he could still blow a mean harp and make us laugh with his funny, insightful storytelling. "Brand New Mojo" and "Spoiled Rotten to the Bone" are excellent examples of how witty he can be, and on "Sue Somebody," he takes an amusing jab at Americans who file frivolous lawsuits. Many of the selections have an urban blues outlook, although "Lucy Pearl," "Strut Your Stuff" and "I've Got the Blues All Over Me" are pure Louisiana-style swamp blues. Close your eyes while listening to these tunes, and it's easy to pretend you're in the steamy Louisiana bayous. Although not quite essential, *Retrospectives* paints an enjoyable picture of McCain as he sounded when he was in his late fifties and early sixties. *—Alex Henderson*

Good Stuff! / May 18, 1999 / Varese Sarabande ♦♦♦♦♦
McCain's career didn't quit with his Excello sides of the '50s. He went on to cut his most remembered singles ("She's Tough" and "Steady") for the Rex label and kept cutting a steady stream of obscure but inspired 45s and a stray album for labels like Jewel, OKeh, Continental, Gas, Esco, Bad, and Royal American. Sixteen of the best sides are compiled on this one with "What About You" and "Rough Stuff" emanating from the same groove-filled session that produced "She's Tough" and "Steady." "Ting-Tang-Tagalu," "Welfare Cadillac Blues," and the soulful "I'll Come Running Back for More" are all highlights, but the closer "Pussycat A-Go-Go," issued as the Shindigs and supposedly featuring Sam the Sham and the Pharoahs as the backing group, may be the blues at both its hippest and most surreal. Like the title says, good stuff. *—Cub Koda*

This Stuff Just Kills Me / Jun. 13, 2000 / Jericho ♦♦♦♦
Produced by Mike Vernon and recorded in Memphis, Austin, and Chicago in May of 1999 with an all-star cast, this catches McCain in peak form. With the Stevie Ray Vaughan & Double Trouble rhythm section of Chris Layton and Tommy Shannon anchoring things down, the guitar work is ably handled by Anson Funderburgh, Derek O'Brien, and John Primer with several guest appearances from Jimmie Vaughan sprinkled throughout the set. Add Johnnie Johnson guesting on four tracks and match it all up with some solid, humorous songwriting and you have one of McCain's most consistent efforts in years. A winner all the way. *—Cub Koda*

Absolutely the Best: Complete Jewel Singles 1965–1972 / Feb. 6, 2001 / Fuel 2000 ♦♦♦♦

American Roots: Blues / Jul. 30, 2002 / Ichiban ♦♦♦

Cash McCall (Morris Dollison Jr.)

b. Jan. 28, 1941, New Madrid, MO
Vocals, Guitar / Modern Electric Blues
Guitarist Cash McCall has segued from gospel to soul to blues over a distinguished career spanning more than three decades. Born Morris Dollison Jr., he found that the best way to exit his rural existence was to enlist in the Army. After completing his hitch, he relocated in Chicago (where his family lived for a time when he was a child). Gospel was Dollison's initial passion—he sang with the Gospel Songbirds (he also played guitar with the group, recording with them for Excello in 1964 with fellow future R&B hitmaker Otis Clay singing lead) and the Pilgrim Jubilee Singers.

He waxed his first secular single, the two-part workout "Earth Worm," for One-derful Records' M-Pac! subsidiary in 1963 as Maurice Dollison. In 1966, he made a demo of a soul number called "When You Wake Up" that he had penned with producer Monk Higgins. He was doubtless shocked to learn of its subsequent release on the Thomas label, billed to one Cash McCall! The tune proved a national R&B hit, sending the newly christened McCall on the road with Dick Clark's Caravan of Stars (others on the bill: Lou Christie and Mitch Ryder).

Similarly tasty R&B follow-ups for Thomas and Checker failed to hit the same commercial heights. McCall was a valuable session guitarist and composer at Chess, learning the business end of his trade from Chess in-house legend Willie Dixon. McCall's blues leanings grew more prominent during the next decade. He cut an LP for Paula in 1973 called *Omega Man* before relocating to L.A. in 1976. In 1983 McCall released his first solo record in ten years, *No More Doggin,'* and followed it up with Cash Up Front in 1987. McCall's ties to Willie Dixon remained strong, he co-produced Dixon's Grammy-winning *Hidden Charms* in 1988 and worked as a sideman with Dixon's band, the All-Stars. McCall has since toured frequently as a solo blues artist and has often appeared on stage with the Chicago Rythym and Blues Kings, who were formerly known as the Mellow Fellows, backed singer Big Twist, and performed in the Chicago Blues Review. *—Bill Dahl*

No More Doggin' / 1983 / Evidence ♦♦♦
While he rightfully earned his share of renown on the Chicago soul scene of the '60s as a writer/producer/singer/sideman, guitarist McCall has re-invented himself as a blues-man in recent years. This 1983 outing blends both genres on a predominantly original set (the lone cover is an update of Rosco Gordon's "No More Doggin'"). *—Bill Dahl*

● **Cash Up Front** / 1987 / Stony Plain ♦♦♦♦♦
An excellent, varied blues and R&B album, it has ten original compositions. Top-notch session musicians give this the sheen of studio perfection rather than bar-band rawness. Yet McCall can still get down in the alley, as he does on the cheatin' story "Girlfriend, Women, and Wife." *—Niles J. Frantz*

Mighty Sam McClain

b. 1941, Monroe, LA
Vocals / Retro-Soul, Modern Electric Blues, Soul-Blues
Vocalist Mighty Sam McClain is a specialist in Southern soul-blues, one of the original masters from the '60s, when the music enjoyed its peak popularity. He carries on the tradition of vocalists like Bobby "Blue" Bland, Solomon Burke, Otis Clay, James Carr and Otis Redding. His excellent '90s recordings are now widely available, but that wasn't always the case.

Like so many other soul-blues vocalists, McClain began singing gospel in his mother's choir when he was five. At 13, owing to disagreements with his stepfather, he left home and lived with grandparents for a while before hooking up with Little Melvin Underwood. He worked with Underwood first as a valet and later as a featured vocalist in his road show.

His inspirations included Little Willie John, Clyde McPhatter of the Drifters, B.B. King, and Bobby "Blue" Bland. McClain recalled seeing Bland at the city auditorium in Monroe, LA as a revelatory moment. Years later, McClain would open for Bland at Tipitina's, a blues club in New Orleans. To this day, he considers Bland's nod of approval a high point of his career.

While working at the 506 Club in Pensacola, Fla., in the mid-'60s, he was introduced to producer and DJ Don Schroeder. Working with Schroeder, he recorded Patsy Cline's hit "Sweet Dreams." After this, several other visits to Muscle Shoals Studios in Alabama yielded singles like "Fannie Mae" and "In the Same Old Way." McClain continued to create an ever-broadening audience for his singing via his engagements at the 506 Club and later at the Apollo Theatre in Harlem. He recorded a single for Malaco and two singles for Atlantic in 1971 before falling off the music scene for awhile.

For the next 15 years or so, McClain took menial day jobs, living in Nashville and New Orleans. The Neville Brothers and others from the Crescent City scene have been credited with helping him revive his career as a singer. McClain met Mason Ruffner's drummer Kerry Brown, and the two put a band together. Shortly after, they recorded a single for Carlo Ditta's Orleans label, and McClain's recording and performing career was rejuvenated. After recording with Hubert Sumlin on *Hubert Sumlin's Blues Party* for the Black Top label in 1987, McClain began to re-establish his former reputation as a great soul-blues singer, touring with Sumlin and his entourage. By the late '80s, McClain had moved from Houston to Boston. For most of the '90s, he lived in Boston and southern New Hampshire.

McClain didn't record his first studio album under his own name until he was 50, through his Boston drummer Lorne Entress, who made a connection with the California-based Audioquest label.

McClain's Audioquest albums include *Give It Up to Love* (1992), *Keep on Movin'* (1995), and *Sledgehammer Soul and Down Home Blues* (1996), the last nominated for a W.C. Handy Award. All received rave reviews from the critics, and for the first time in his life, he's in control of his own song publishing rights. Most of the songs on all three albums utilize a full horn section, and on top of this ride McClain's deep, powerful vocals, oftentimes in self-penned songs. (*Give It Up to Love* has since been re-released (1997) on the JVC label.) *Blues for the Soul* (2000) was issued on Sundazed and *Sweet Dreams* followed on Telarc in 2001.

Since the late '80s, McClain's career has been on the upswing again, as he's put together some great backing bands and carved a niche for himself in Europe. McClain also continued to tour the U.S., Europe and Canada. *—Richard Skelly*

Live in Japan / 1988 / Orleans ♦♦♦
A sophisticated bluesman in the tradition of Bobby "Blue" Bland or Joe Williams, Mighty Sam McClain had not recorded in some 13 years when he cut a demo of song called "Pray" in 1984. The demo attracted the attention of a Japanese promoter, who subsequently coordinated the Japanese tour from which this live album, recorded in Tokyo, is culled. Despite the presence of ace session guitarist Wayne Bennett, McClain's backing band is sub-standard and lifeless; few moments generate any heat. *—Jason Ankeny*

Give It Up to Love / Nov. 1992 / AudioQuest ♦♦♦♦
McClain sings soul with incredible power—he knows when to pull the punches and when to cool it down. "Give It Up to Love," the title track, acknowledges his gospel roots; he performs it as a vocal prayer to God asking for wisdom, love, and strength. Bruce Katz's contributions on B-3 Hammond organ expands McClain's sound, particularly on the "Green Onions"-influenced "What You Want Me to Do." The sparsely effective arrangement on "Here I Go Falling in Love Again" brings McClain up front as he cries of being a soul stripped to the bare bones. Kevin Barry's funky bass blows while McClain declares himself as a child of God in "Child of the Mighty Mighty." *—Char Ham*

Keep on Movin' / 1995 / AudioQuest ♦♦♦
McClain pours out his soul, but this album lacks the power evidenced on *Give It Up to Love.* The problem lies not with McClain, but with some of his supporting musicians. The closest cohesion exists between McClain and the musician on the title track, while "Who Made You Cry" has McClain sounding sympathetic and helpful to someone's plight, expertly complemented by Kevin Barry on guitar. However, the horn section extenuates the problems by cluttering up the arrangements and detracting from McClain's performance, while the Hammond B-3 lacks a nimble, crisp feel, and at times sounds buried in the mix. *—Char Ham*

Sledgehammer Soul and Down Home Blues / 1996 / AudioQuest ♦♦♦♦
The title of this CD couldn't be more descriptive of its contents, for it illustrates that Mighty Sam McClain is indeed a master of sledgehammer soul and down-home electric blues. Influenced by Bobby "Blue" Bland but nonetheless his own person, the Louisiana native is a charismatic singer who is as convincing on blues gems like "Where You Been So Long," "They Call Me Mighty," and the haunting "When the Hurt Is Over" (the perfect marriage of Bland and John Lee Hooker) as he is on such Southern soul treasures as "Trying to Find Myself" and "Things Ain't What They Used to Be." When it comes to R&B,

McClain's approach is essentially Southern and very '60s-influenced—the sleekness that characterized so much of the soul-pop of Detroit, Philadelphia and Chicago isn't an influence on this fine album, and he shows no awareness whatsoever of mid-'90s trends in urban contemporary music. But McClain (who is joined by a solid band that includes horns, electric Hammond organ and a rhythm section) does surprise us by embracing reggae on the uplifting "Pray." This is definitely a CD to savor. *—Alex Henderson*

Journey / Mar. 24, 1998 / AudioQuest ♦♦♦
Singing praises to God and sharing his love for others despite having faced tragedy and setbacks in his past, McClain is rather reminiscent of the Biblical character, Job (who despite losing everything, still praised God, and then was blessed with twice as much wealth and a bigger family than before). McClain's life journey has often been rocky; he has faced rejection by his family, survived substance abuse, and been ignored by the music industry despite his hard-working attempts to gain attention. But turning to God, he remained faithful and is now blessed with a critically acclaimed career and a loving family. This album shares all of this, and his honest, retrospective outlook wins hands down. Take a look at "No More Tears," twhere he takes the familiar line of "walking the backstreets," translating it to his life experiences—feeling frustrated, moving from place to place without seeing his situation improve. This honesty transcends to the supporting musicians, who give from-the-bottom-of-the-heart solos without sounding mushy, from bassist Tim Ingles' funky jazz feel on "I'm Yours," to Bruce Katz thumping the ivories or the B-3. *—Char Ham*

Joy & Pain / Jul. 28, 1998 / Ruf ♦♦♦
This live recording of McClain from a 1997 tour in Germany demonstrates how clearly interconnected the blues, soul, and gospel are. Songs express his love for people, life, and the Almighty, making the message simple yet mountain moving. The title simply states what his voice carries—joy and pain. *—Char Ham*

Soul Survivor: The Best of Mighty Sam McClain / Jun. 8, 1999 / AudioQuest ♦♦♦♦
Good overview of McClain's four AudioQuest releases, along with two previously unreleased tracks. "Keep on Movin'" should have been included, as its catchy arrangements are ideal bumper music for a late night TV talk show. *—Char Ham*

Blues for the Soul / Jun. 27, 2000 / Telarc ♦♦♦

● **Papa True Love: The Amy Sessions** / Jul. 18, 2000 / Sundazed ♦♦♦♦
This compilation of the singer's prime '60s work has both sides of his eight 1966-1968 Amy singles, as well as "Nothing but the Truth" from Bell's LP *Bell's Cellar of Soul Vol. 2* and a previously unreleased 1966 cover of Don Gibson's "A Stranger to Me." Mighty Sam was a good '60s Southern soul singer, but not a great one; the kinds of people who collect this sort of stuff can go back and forth as to whether he was a top-of-the-second-division artist or the best of a journeyman class. Often he sounded like a somewhat bluesier Otis Redding, more apt to break into growly rasps, though not as inclined in that direction as, say, James Brown was. "Sweet Dreams (Of You)" in particular seems like a conscious emulation of the kind of success Otis Redding was having in 1965-1966 with wrenching ballads like "I've Been Loving You Too Long." He did benefit from a few Spooner Oldham-Dan Penn compositions but didn't get the sort of classic material that might have made him more than a cult favorite. All that taken into consideration, this remains a fairly solid platter of little-known soul music, the vocalist shining brightest on midtempo tunes that have him pleading a case without getting too sentimental. The production's pretty good as well, with frequent stinging blues-soul guitar licks and eerie organ of the kind made famous on Percy Sledge's "When a Man Loves a Woman." *—Richie Unterberger*

Sweet Dreams / 2001 / Telarc ♦♦♦♦

Tommy McClennan

b. Apr. 8, 1908, Yazoo City, MS, **d.** c. 1958, Chicago, IL
Vocals, Guitar / Delta Blues, Prewar Country Blues, Soul-Blues, Prewar Blues
A gravel-throated back-country blues growler from the Mississippi Delta, McClennan was part of the last wave of down-home blues guitarists to record for the major labels in Chicago. His rawboned 1939-1942 Bluebird recordings were no-frills excursions into the blues bottoms. He left a powerful legacy that included "Bottle It Up and Go," "Cross Cut Saw Blues," "Deep Blue Sea Blues" (aka "Catfish Blues"), and others whose lasting power has been evidenced through the repertoires and re-recordings of other artists. Admirers of McClennan's blues would do well to check out the 1941-1942 Bluebird sessions of Robert Petway, a McClennan associate who performed in a similar but somewhat more lyrical vein. McClennan never recorded again and reportedly died destitute in Chicago; blues researchers have yet to even trace the date or circumstances of his death. *—Jim O'Neal*

☆ **Travelin' Highway Man** / 1939-1942 / Travelin' Man ♦♦♦♦♦
Travelin' Highway Man is an excellent, 20-track overview of recordings Tommy McClennan made between 1939 and 1942, offering many of his greatest recordings—"Bottle It Up and Go," "Whiskey Head Woman," "My Baby's Gone," "It's Hard to Be Lonesome," "New Shake 'Em on Down"—as well as a thorough biography, making this a cornerstone of any comprehensive Delta blues collection. However, its usefulness has been diminished, since RCA's double-disc set *Bluebird Recordings 1939-1942* offers everything that *Travelin' Highway Man* has in better fidelity; it also has twice the music. *—Thom Owens*

★ **Bluebird Recordings 1939–1942** / Apr. 29, 1997 / Bluebird/RCA ♦♦♦♦♦
McClennan's hoarse, shouted vocals, spoken vaudeville asides and scrappy guitar work make for a pretty irresistible combination, especially in light of the simple fact that most blues fans have never been exposed to his music in large doses. This double disc rounds up every known extant side recorded for Bluebird between 1939 to 1942, when the label dropped him for problems with alcohol. The music on here comes from five sessions and is uniformly excellent, if a bit samey. But it is blues at its most intense and unfettered, and tracks like "Bottle It Up and Go," "You Can Mistreat Me Here," "Baby Please Don't Tell On Me," "New Shake 'Em on Down," and "Baby Don't You Want to Go?" (the latter his adaption of "Sweet Home Chicago") are full of energy and verses worth requoting. This set is one of the true hidden treasures of the "Bluebird" period in blues history and, as such, deserves a much, much wider hearing. *—Cub Koda*

Guitar King 1939–1942 / May 27, 1997 / EPM Musique ♦♦♦♦

1939–1940 Whiskey Head Woman, Vol. 1 / Jul. 2, 2002 / Document ♦♦♦

Cross Cut Saw Blues, Vol. 2 1940–1942 / Aug. 6, 2002 / Document ♦♦♦

Delbert McClinton

b. Nov. 4, 1940, Lubbock, TX
Vocals, Harmonica / Americana, Country-Rock, Blues-Rock, Modern Electric Blues
The venerable Delbert McClinton is a legend among Texas roots music aficionados, not only for his amazing longevity, but for his ability to combine country, blues, soul, and rock & roll as if there were no distinctions between any of them in the best time-honored Texas tradition. A formidable harmonica player long before he recorded as a singer, McClinton's career began in the late '50s, yet it took him nearly two decades to evolve into a bona fide solo artist. A critics' darling and favorite of his peers, McClinton never really became a household name, but his resurgence in the '90s helped him earn more widespread respect from both the public at large and the Grammy committee.

Delbert McClinton was born in Lubbock, TX, on November 4, 1940, and grew up in Fort Worth. Discovering the blues in his teenage years, McClinton quickly became an accomplished harmonica player and found plenty of work on the local club scene, where musicians often made their living by playing completely different styles of music on different nights of the week. His most prominent early gig was with the Straitjackets, the house band at a blues/R&B club; it gave McClinton the opportunity to play harp behind blues legends like Howlin' Wolf, Jimmy Reed, Sonny Boy Williamson II, and Bobby "Blue" Bland. In 1960, McClinton's cover of Williamson's "Wake Up Baby" made him the first white artist to have a record played on the local blues station KNOK. McClinton's harmonica was prominently featured on Fort Worth native Bruce Channel's 1962 number one smash "Hey! Baby"; brought along for Channel's tour of England, McClinton wound up giving harp lessons to a young John Lennon. Upon returning to the States, McClinton founded a group called the Rondells (sometimes listed as the Ron-Dels), which had a minor chart single in 1965 with "If You Really Want Me to, I'll Go." Although the Rondells recorded for several different labels, wider success eluded them and McClinton spent much of the '60s making the rounds of the Texas club and roadhouse circuit, where his reputation kept growing steadily.

In 1972, McClinton moved to Los Angeles, where he teamed up with Fort Worth singer/songwriter Glen Clark as Delbert & Glen. Signed to the small Atlantic affiliate Clean Records, Delbert & Glen recorded two albums in a mostly country-rock vein, 1972's *Delbert & Glen* and 1973's *Subject to Change.* Neither sold well and McClinton returned to Texas in 1974, where he was able to land a solo deal with ABC on the strength of his emerging songwriting talent. His first solo album, *Victim of Life's Circumstances*, was released in 1975; although he was marketed as part of the emerging progressive country movement, McClinton's music was too indebted to blues and R&B to neatly fit that tag. *Genuine Cowhide* (1976) and *Love Rustler* (1977) followed to highly positive reviews, if not much commercial attention, and other artists started to mine McClinton's catalog for material; in 1978, Emmylou Harris took his "Two More Bottles of Wine" all the way to the top of the country charts. A switch to Capricorn produced two albums, 1978's *Second Wind* and 1979's *Keeper of the Flame*; the former featured his original version of "B Movie Boxcar Blues," later a part of the Blues Brothers repertoire. When Capricorn folded, he moved to the Muscle Shoals Sound imprint and his 1980 label debut, *The Jealous Kind*, gave him his first Top 40 single in "Givin' It Up for Your Love," which hit on both the pop and country charts.

Unfortunately, Muscle Shoals Sound folded not long after McClinton's follow-up, 1981's *Plain From the Heart*, and he subsequently took a long hiatus from recording, concentrating instead on live performances. His next prominent appearance was an acclaimed vocal turn on guitarist Roy Buchanan's 1986 album *Dancing on the Edge*; that guest appearance helped land him a deal with Alligator. In 1989, McClinton issued the comeback album *Live From Austin*, which earned him his first Grammy nomination (for Best Contemporary Blues Album). He signed with Curb in 1990, debuting that year with *I'm With You*, and moved to Nashville, where he soon became a much sought-after songwriter (often in tandem with new partner Gary Nicholson) in the contemporary country field. Over the next few years, McClinton placed material with stars like Wynonna, Vince Gill, Lee Roy Parnell, and Martina McBride, among others. His biggest break, though, came when he was tapped for a duet with Bonnie Raitt on 1991's *Luck of the Draw*, the follow-up to her much-lauded comeback *Nick of Time.* The result, "Good Man, Good Woman," brought McClinton his first Grammy for Best Rock Vocal, Duo or Group, which suddenly raised his profile tenfold. He capitalized with 1992's *Never Been Rocked Enough*, which featured not only his duet with Raitt, but also guest appearances from Tom Petty and Melissa Etheridge, and his biggest hit single since 1980, "Every Time I Roll the Dice." Later that year, he hit the country charts with another duet, this time with Tanya Tucker on "Tell Me About It." The song later appeared on McClinton's next album, 1993's simply titled *Delbert McClinton.*

Despite enjoying the greatest commercial success of his career, McClinton's relationship with Curb was beginning to sour. His next two albums were released to comparatively little attention and he finally extricated himself from his contract to sign with Rising Tide, a small label associated with Universal. 1997's *One of the Fortunate Few* was designed to restore McClinton to his early-'90s stature, featuring an array of guest stars, including Vince Gill, Patty Loveless, Lyle Lovett, Pam Tillis, B.B. King, John Prine, and Mavis Staples. It was still definitely McClinton's show, however, and as such it received mostly complimentary reviews; it also sold more than 250,000 copies before Rising Tide went belly-up. McClinton next returned in 2001 on the Austin, TX-based New West imprint with another acclaimed effort, *Nothing Personal.* It proved to be one of the most popular recordings of his career, gaining substantial airplay on Americana radio and ending up one of the year's biggest hits on *Billboard's* blues chart; it also won him another Grammy for Best Contemporary Blues Album. —*Steve Huey*

Delbert & Glen / 1972 / Clean ✦✦✦

Subject to Change / 1973 / Clean ✦✦✦

Victim of Life's Circumstances / 1975 / Raven ✦✦✦

Genuine Cowhide / 1976 / ABC ✦✦✦✦

Love Rustler / 1977 / ABC ✦✦✦

As a vocalist, McClinton is an often-captivating purveyor of country/R&B. Although he had been in the business since the early '60s, he had recorded only a handful of albums. *Love Rustler* is his third for ABC. While 1976's *Genuine Cowhide* was spirited and inspired enough for McClinton to take on the standard "Let the Good Times Roll" as well as work from Big Joe Turner and James Brown, this is often a more cautious project. Despite the good mix of country and R&B, the title track has silly lyrics like, "A saw a woman's picture/On a warning sign." The untrusting "Under Suspicion" has McClinton playing the role of the cuckold to good effect, as he's the victim of a "hit and run love affair." Laura Lee's "As Long As I Got You" is turned into a country & western offering with hokey background singers to boot. The southern disco of Tony Joe White's "Hold on to Your Hiney" comes off more fatuous than fun despite McClinton's good vocal. While the offhanded take on warhorses like "In the Jailhouse Now" and "Ain't No More Cane" aren't going to win any converts, one song just might. On *Love Rustler*, McClinton earns high marks by doing a remake of Bobby "Blue" Bland's "Turn on Your Love Light." Normally not an easy artist to cover, the track is revved up, and with a subdued vocal and a wild country guitar on the bridge, McClinton nearly walks away with it. Unfortunately, most of *Love Rustler* shows McClinton's promise but not his true skills and strengths. —*Jason Elias*

Second Wind / 1978 / Mercury ✦✦✦✦

The textbook loved yet underrated artist, *Second Wind* is Delbert McClinton's fourth album and first for Capricorn. Throughout the '70s, McClinton attained a cult following with ABC albums like *Genuine Cowhide* and *Love Rustler*. While the efforts no doubt had their moments, often McClinton was depicted as too dense because the production was often undistinguished. Not so on *Second Wind*. Throughout this effort, McClinton hits all of the right notes as the mix of country, R&B, and boogie are seamlessly melded into a near subgenre. Perhaps more than any other effort, *Second Wind*, produced by Johnny Sandlin, displays McClinton as a multi-layered singer because his rough edges and intelligence were shown to great effect. The wry "B Movie Boxcar Blues" has McClinton riding thumb back home to see his true love, all the while having "relations" with every woman who picked him up. Although his originals here are good to great, what makes *Second Wind* so striking is his command on the covers. Jesse Winchester's "Isn't That So" is brimming with McClinton's confidence as he sang each line like he wrote it himself. The blues classic "Spoonful" is given great nervous energy and has smooth backing vocals. Johnny Cash's "Big River" is changed to an off-time shuffle with McClinton playing harmonica and putting his indelible style on the track. *Second Wind* has expert and stylish backing from esteemed Muscle Shoals players and the equally famous horn section. The album closes with McClinton's own "Lovinest Man," which has great horn riffs and an understated vocal. *Second Wind* offers no filler and is one McClinton's best efforts. —*Jason Elias*

Keeper of the Flame / 1979 / Mercury ✦✦

Slowly but surely, Delbert McClinton was earning more fans with his polished fusion of country, soul, and blues. 1978's album, *Second Wind*, his first album for Phil Walden's Capricorn, introduced him to a new audience. Deciding to strike while the iron was hot, McClinton followed up *Second Wind* with this 1979 release. Reunited with producer Johnny Sandlin, *Keeper of the Flame* revisits some of the sonic values of its predecessor. Bassist Willie Weeks and drummer Andy Newmark are the rhythm section throughout. That idea would have worked, but the confidence isn't as strong here, and neither is the material. The first track is "Plain Old Makin' Love," which adds disco-styled flourishes to the mix for better or worse. The sly "Shot From the Saddle" has him doing the effortless soul that typified McClinton's best late-'70s work. Despite McClinton and Sandlin's best intentions, the magic is hard to come by on *Keeper of the Flame*. "Two More Bottles of Wine" and "I Received a Letter," both McClinton originals, are well performed—good but not great. The covers make or break this effort. The best of the lot is a revved up version of Chuck Berry's "I'm Talking About You." Unlike McClinton albums of the time, most of *Keeper of the Flame* was recorded at the Record Plant in Los Angeles. Despite the songs, this turned out to be too cautious and over produced for some of McClinton's fans. —*Jason Elias*

The Jealous Kind / 1980 / Capitol ✦✦

This is McClinton's first release for Capitol and its related label, MSS (Muscle Shoals Sound). The fact that McClinton would be again doing sessions in Muscle Shoals was no doubt heartening for his fans. The album before this, *Keeper of the Flame* did some of its tracks at Record Plant in Los Angeles, and it often lacked the gritty appeal of his best work. Barry Beckett and the Muscle Shoals Rhythm Section produced this. McClinton's band for the effort is lauded Muscle Shoals players like Jimmy Johnson, David Hood, and Roger Hawkins. The biggest hit here, the confident and polished "Giving It Up for Your Love," has McClinton at his commercial best, aided by Bonnie Bramlett's backing vocals. Sidestepping some of the radio ready concerns of a few of the tracks, the rousing "Going Back to Louisiana" and the prime country/rock of "Baby Ruth" seems to bring out the best of the artist and producers. Everything doesn't work well here, however. McClinton recasts Al Green's 1974 classic "Take Me to the River" into a country boogie, and it diminishes the song's potent sexual energy. McClinton quickly rebounds with a wry cover of the Temptations "Shaky Ground," which ranks with McClinton's best work. The last

track, the ingratiating "My Sweet Baby," ends the album on the right note. Despite the enjoyable tracks here, the waste cuts drag the effort down and make *The Jealous Kind* not as good as it could have been. —*Jason Elias*

Plain from the Heart / 1981 / Capitol ✦✦✦

While '80s *The Jealous Kind* did do well commercially, peaking at number 34 on the pop charts, it had a few sloppy moments. Unlike this album's predecessor, McClinton's vocals are surer throughout, and the production is more suited to his voice. Like *The Jealous Kind*, *Plain from the Heart* is produced by Barry Beckett and the Muscle Shoals Rhythm Section. This set starts off with three originals, "Be Good to Yourself," "A Fool in Love," and "Heartbreak Radio," that have his personality saving the derivative lyrics and arrangements. Since McClinton was writing few originals, this effort had to rely on his prowess at doing covers. His take on Otis Redding's "I've Got Dreams to Remember" is serviceable, but doesn't dig deep enough to get the song's inherent painful core. After the misfires of the popular remakes and newer material, the album gains momentum when it begins to find work that got McClinton enthused. The great and understated "I Want to Thank You Baby" and "Sandy Beaches" finds him thoroughly engaged on his new originals. The final tracks are great, inspired takes on standards, "I Feel So Bad" and "Rooster Blues," both of which McClinton makes sound like his own. While *Plain From The Heart* didn't do enough business to keep the MSS label afloat; it shows the production team getting more comfortable with McClinton, and he does turn in some good performances here. —*Jason Elias*

Honky Tonkin' / 1989 / Alligator ✦✦✦

The Best of Delbert McClinton / 1989 / Curb ✦✦✦✦✦

It's only 11 tracks, but *The Best of Delbert McClinton* contains nearly everything you need to know about how the eclectic blues/country/soul performer sounds, even if it doesn't have every good song he recorded. Nevertheless, it has the best moments from his early '70s records, and is a terrific introduction to his work. —*Thom Owens*

Live from Austin / 1989 / Alligator ✦✦✦✦

I'm With You / 1990 / Curb ✦✦✦

This is another solid release from the road-tested, fan-approved vocalist. At the time of this release, McClinton hadn't done a studio effort since 1981's somewhat disappointing *Plain From The Heart*. The gift of *I'm With You* is that McClinton makes it sound like he had been away for ten days rather then almost ten years. "That's The Way I Feel" is an effortless country blues bop with great, punchy Memphis by way of Tower Of Power styled horns. Unlike many artists, McClinton wasn't stingy with a good track and Jimmy Hall shows up on the old-fashioned "Got You On My Mind" and offers great harmony. Although *I'm With You* has McClinton is good voice and spirits, the tracks tend to run together and the results don't click during the first listen. The album standout, "The Real Thing" has McClinton put through the ringer in a good way by a conquest as he bellows the title and the lyrics with glee. The last track "My Love Is Burnin'" has McClinton extending the album's horny nature with another great vocal. *I'm With You* was co-produced by McClinton and Muscle Shoals stalwart, Barry Beckett. Rather than trying to replicate McClinton's late 70's sound, *I'm With You* has subtle touches of the newer commercial and polished country of the time mixed with the soul McClinton is known for. Although many fans may think they've heard this all before and better, this has a way of impressing with repeated plays. —*Jason Elias*

Never Been Rocked Enough / 1992 / Curb ✦✦✦

One of those influential "musician's musician" types, vocalist/harp-player Delbert McClinton was able to call on the likes of Bonnie Raitt, Tom Petty and Melissa Etheridge for support on *Never Been Rocked Enough*. The results cover the whole checkerboard while remaining vintage McClinton: his harp wails on "Everytime I Roll the Dice"; "Can I Change My Mind" flirts with Motown soul; "Blues as Blues Can Get" defines the confessional blues ballad; "I Used to Worry" and the title track chug into Band/Little Feat territory. The disc also includes the performer's Grammy winning duet with Bonnie Raitt, "Good Man, Good Woman." —*Roch Parisien*

Delbert McClinton / Jul. 13, 1993 / Curb ✦✦✦✦

Classics, Vol. 1: The Jealous Kind / 1994 / Curb ✦✦✦✦

Classics, Vol. 1: The Jealous Kind is a ten-track, budget-priced collection that features a good cross-section of highlights from McClinton's Curb and Capitol recordings, including "Shotgun Rider," "I Can't Quit You," "Going Back to Louisiana," "Take Me to the River" and "My Sweet Baby." —*Stephen Thomas Erlewine*

Classics, Vol. 2: Plain from the Heart / 1994 / Curb ✦✦✦✦

Classics, Vol. 2: Plain from the Heart is a ten-track budget-priced collection that features a good cross-section of highlights from McClinton's Curb and Capitol recordings, including "Be Good to Yourself," "A Fool in Love," "I've Got Dreams to Remember," "In the Midnight Hour," "Sandy Beaches," "Lipstick Traces (On a Cigarette)" and "I Feel So Bad." —*Stephen Thomas Erlewine*

Let the Good Times Roll / 1995 / MCA Special Products ✦✦

Great Songs: Come Together / 1995 / Curb ✦✦

One of the Fortunate Few / Oct. 7, 1997 / Rising Tide ✦✦✦

Like the first track says, Delbert McClinton is like an old weakness, comin' on strong. McClinton's music is a hybrid of rock, country and blues, though that's much too analytical for this roadhouse. Sung and played thoughout with sass and a knowing grin, this is music that speaks to everyone. And for once the guest artists add just the right amount, neither dominating nor lessening the proceedings. —*Ross Boissoneau*

Crazy Cajun Recordings / Feb. 18, 1999 / Edsel ✦✦✦

- **The Ultimate Collection** / Jun. 1, 1999 / Hip-O ✦✦✦✦✦
Hip-O's *The Ultimate Collection* comes very close to fulfilling the promise of its title. Over the course of 18 tracks, the compilation traces the evolution of Delbert McClinton's career, concentrating on his recordings for ABC, Capricorn, Capitol and Rising Tide, while hitting almost all of the major highlights. True, there may be a personal favorite or two missing for hardcore fans, but there is no better introduction to this acclaimed Texas musician than this. —*Stephen Thomas Erlewine*

Don't Let Go: The Collection / Mar. 28, 2000 / Music Club ✦✦✦✦

Genuine Rhythm & the Blues / Mar. 28, 2000 / Hip-O ✦✦✦
Far from a comprehensive overview of Delbert McClinton's four decade career, this is an enjoyable yet relatively brief disc focusing entirely on covers of classic R&B material. Compiled from the rugged Texas singer's four early solo albums recorded from 1974 through 1979, it shines a light onto McClinton's varied influences as well as being a consistently enjoyable listen.

A cursory scan of the song titles initially indicates there's not much exciting here. Many of these classics such as Bobby "Blue" Bland's "Turn on Your Lovelight," Fats Domino's "Blue Monday," and Don Covay's "Have Mercy" are well known through either their original versions or numerous renditions throughout the years. Upon closer listen though McClinton's approach to them is effortlessly soulful, and some of his arrangements—in particular transforming Willie Dixon's "Spoonful" from a wailing Chicago blues to a swampy soul stirrer—are refreshingly unique. McClinton's sand- and honey-inflected vocals flow easily, and his sharp band including horns, female backing vocals and tight ensemble playing, wrap themselves around the songs with loose precision.

The songs of Elvis Presley, Jimmie Rodgers, Chuck Berry, Johnny Ace, Big Joe Turner, The Clovers and Bo Diddley all become McClinton tunes as he latches onto their varied genres and transforms them into rollicking R&B. The anthology shares only one selection with the excellent *Ultimate Collection*, but even though it's cobbled together from albums recorded over five years, McClinton's cohesive style bonds these tracks into a surprisingly unified whole. Thoughtful and informative liner notes explain the source material, and the lack of individual personnel listings, as well as the album's relative brevity, prove to be minor shortcomings. —*Hal Horowitz*

Nothing Personal / Mar. 6, 2001 / New West ✦✦✦✦
McClinton's first outing for the independent Austin label New West, *Nothing Personal* features more of the Texan harp player's loose blend of rock, blues, and honky tonk. He penned all the cuts here, sometimes in tandem with producer Gary Nicholson and Benmont Tench of Tom Petty and the Heartbreakers fame (Tench also sits in on keyboards for a few cuts). The lyrical concerns take in the usual stories of love and its travails, which McClinton consistently phrases in his own rough-hewn yet sweet way. He also contributes some of his ace harmonica work to several of the tracks. The selections feature McClinton's standard variety, ranging from bar room rockers like "Squeeze Me" and the vintage country side "Birmingham Tonight" to the south-of-the-border ballad "When Rita Leaves." Another fine release from one of Texas' best. —*Stephen Cook*

Bobby McClure

b. Apr. 21, 1942, Chicago, IL, **d.** Nov. 13, 1992, Los Angeles, CA
Vocals / Chicago Soul, Northern Soul, R&B, Soul
Soul singer Bobby McClure was born on April 21, 1942, in Chicago, IL. By the time of his second birthday, his family had relocated to St. Louis, and by the age of nine, McClure had begun singing in church. His fine tenor voice quickly caught the attention of others, as he sang with several of the area's best-known gospel groups, including the Soul Stirrers, which Sam Cooke was singing lead with at the time. It wasn't long though until McClure tried his hand at singing other musical styles, including R&B and doo wop, honing his talents with such outfits as Bobby and the Vocals, drummer Big Daddy Jenkins' band, and singing in renowned bandleader Oliver Sain's outfit. McClure also took a pair of up-and-coming artists under his wing, Little Milton and Fontella Bass, who would both go on to successful music careers (McClure and Bass would eventually record a duet together in 1965, "Don't Mess Up a Good Thing," which was a U.S. Top 40 hit). During the '60s, McClure had relocated back to Chicago, where he worked with both Otis Clay and Little Milton, before moving to St. Louis, where he duetted with Shirley Brown and recording a few singles for the Memphis-based Hi label. Although McClure would record a few singles during the '80s, for the most part, he turned his back on music, working as a corrections officer in an Illinois penitentiary. But he couldn't stay out of music for long, as he moved to Los Angeles to play with others and record. But McClure's career was cut short on November 13, 1992, when he died at the age of 50 from a stroke following a brain aneurysm. —*Greg Prato*

- **Hi Records Presents Bobby Mcclure & Willie Clayton** / 1992 / Hi ✦✦✦

Charlie McCoy

b. May 26, 1909, Jackson, MS, **d.** Jul. 26, 1950, Chicago, IL
Vocals, Guitar (Electric), Mandolin, Guitar / Delta Blues, Prewar Country Blues
In the company of his older brother Joe, the versatile Charlie McCoy ranked among the great blues accompanists of his era, his nimble, sensitive guitar work enriching recordings from performers including Tommy Johnson and Ishmon Bracey. Born May 26, 1909, in Jackson, Mississippi, the self-taught McCoy was recording regularly by the late 1920s, often alongside Walter Vincson; he also sat in with the Mississippi Sheiks, Rubin Lacy, Son Spand and the many other Delta bluesmen who passed through the Jackson area in the years to follow, occasionally appearing on not only guitar but also mandolin (the latter most notably on his mid-'30s sessions backing sister-in-law Memphis Minnie). With his pleasantly high tenor voice, McCoy could well have become a star in his own right, but he seemed to prefer remaining in the background; among his scattered solo sessions is the first known recorded rendition of the song which eventually became "Sweet Home Chicago." Between 1936 and 1939, he also cut a number of sessions with his groups Papa

Charlie's Boys and the Harlem Hamfats, the latter also featuring his brother. The war cut short McCoy's career, and he made no more recordings after 1942, dying in Chicago on July 26, 1950. —*Jason Ankeny*

- **Complete Recorded Works (1928–1932)** / 1992 / Document ✦✦✦✦✦
An excellent 24-track collection, including "Times Ain't What They Used to Be," "Your Valves Need Grinding," and "It's Hot like That." —*Cub Koda*

Kansas Joe McCoy

b. May 11, 1905, Jackson, MS, **d.** Jan. 28, 1950, Chicago, IL
Guitar / Prewar Country Blues, Acoustic Chicago Blues, Acoustic Memphis Blues
Alongside his younger brother Charlie, Joe McCoy is enshrined among the greatest sidemen in blues history, his spartan slide style most notably preserved on the landmark recordings of his wife Memphis Minnie. Born in May 11, 1905, in Jackson, MS, he was primarily known as Kansas Joe McCoy, but his laundry list of aliases includes appearances as the Hillbilly Plowboy, Mud Dauber Joe, Hamfoot Ham, the Georgia Pine Boy and Hallelujah Joe. A self-taught player, he relocated to Memphis during the mid-'20s, joining Jed Davenport's Beale Street Jug Band and meeting Memphis Minnie. McCoy later became her husband, and during their six-year marriage accompanied her on such country blues classics as "Bumble Bee" and "When the Levee Breaks"; the couple migrated to Chicago in 1930, where—in the company of notables like Big Bill Broonzy and Tampa Red—they helped modernize the country blues sound to fit more comfortably into their new urban surroundings. With his eloquent, inventive guitar work and deep vocals, McCoy could well have risen to stardom in his own right, but he appeared to prefer his sideman role, and after his divorce from Minnie he and sibling Charlie formed the Harlem Hamfats, recording regularly between 1936 and 1939. Upon the group's demise, he founded Big Joe and His Washboard Band, which evolved into Big Joe and His Rhythm during the mid-'40s. McCoy died on January 28, 1950. —*Jason Ankeny*

- **The Best of Kansas Joe, Vol. 1, 1929–1935** / 1982 / Earl Archives Blues Documents ✦✦✦

Robert McCoy

b. Mar. 31, 1910, Aliceville, Al
Piano / Piano Blues
Alabama bluesman Robert McCoy was far from a big name in the blues world; the obscure singer/barrelhouse pianist only recorded sporadically, and many blues enthusiasts have never even heard of him. Nonetheless, he was a deserving and likable artist along the lines of Leroy Carr. McCoy was born in the small town of Aliceville, AL, in 1908 but moved to Birmingham when he was only a baby and ended up spending the rest of his life there. McCoy, whose parents had been tenant farmers, had two older brothers who were both interested in barrelhouse piano. Johnny and Willie McCoy, the Alabaman's brothers, did a lot to encourage his interest in barrelhouse playing, and in the '20s, he was greatly influenced by the well-known Leroy Carr. By the late '20s, McCoy was being hired to perform at dances and in African-American jook joints around Birmingham. McCoy's first recordings as a leader came in the '30s, a decade that found him working with Jaybird Coleman and Guitar Slim as well as James Sherell, aka Peanut the Kidnapper. But McCoy had a hard time earning a living as a singer/musician, and he ended up paying his bills and supporting his family with non-musical "day gigs" (including construction work). However, he continued to sing and play the piano on the side in the '40s and '50s. It wasn't until the early '60s that the Birmingham resident returned to professional recording.

In 1961, McCoy came to the attention of Patrick Cather, an aspiring blues producer who also lived in Birmingham. Cather was only a teenager (he was 40 years younger than McCoy), but he knew that he wanted to start a label and produce blues records—and Birmingham saxophonist Frank Adams felt that McCoy would be a good person for him to work with. At the time, Birmingham was still extremely segregated, and racist hate groups like the Ku Klux Klan were quite willing to resort to violence to combat racial integration and the civil rights movement. But Cather (who is white and gay) had no use for racism or segregationist Jim Crow laws (the Southern U.S.'s version of the apartheid laws that once plagued South Africa) and quickly became good friends with McCoy (an African-American). In 1962, Cather produced McCoy's first full-length LP, *Barrellhouse Blues*, which was released on Cather's own Vulcan Records. About 400 copies were pressed. The following year, Cather produced McCoy's sophomore album, *Blues and Boogie Classics*, also released on Vulcan; that rare, little-known LP only sold about 100 copies. Both albums found McCoy (who did his share of songwriting) accompanying himself on acoustic piano. After *Blues and Boogie Classics*, McCoy didn't record any more albums, although he did record a few informal duets with drummer Clarence Curry in the mid-'60s (none of which were released commercially until 2002). McCoy hoped to do some more work with Cather, but, sadly, Cather's demons often got the best of him in the '60s and '70s—the producer was plagued by severe depression, and he turned to drugs and alcohol in an attempt to cope. In 1978, Cather was hospitalized for substance abuse; after conquering his addiction and getting sober, he was sad to learn that McCoy had died in 1977.

In 1983, McCoy (who was in his late sixties when he died) was posthumously inducted into the Alabama Jazz Hall of Fame, and in, 1991, Cather was also inducted (partly because of his desire to document McCoy). The late singer/pianist wasn't really a jazz artist, but his barrelhouse piano playing did contain jazz elements. In 2002, Chicago's independent Delmark label reissued the little-known recordings that Cather had produced for McCoy in 1962 and 1963 on a CD titled *Bye Bye Baby*. Delmark president Bob Koester hired Cather to write the liner notes, and seven bonus tracks were added (including some crudely done recordings from 1958 and the previously unreleased mid-'60s duets with drummer Curry). —*Alex Henderson*

Barrelhouse Blues and Jook Piano / Nov. 1963 / Vulcan ✦✦✦

- **Bye Bye Baby** / May 28, 2002 / Delmark ✦✦✦

Jimmy McCracklin

b. Aug. 13, 1921, St. Louis, MO

Vocals, Leader, Piano / West Coast Blues, Piano Blues, Soul-Blues, R&B

A full half-century from when he started out in the blues business, Jimmy McCracklin is still touring, recording, and acting like a much younger man. In fact, he vehemently disputes this commonly accepted birthdate—but since he began recording back in 1945, it seems reasonable.

McCracklin grew up in Missouri, his main influence on piano being Walter Davis (little Jimmy's dad introduced him to the veteran pianist). McCracklin was also a promising pugilist, but the blues eventually emerged victorious. After a stint in the Navy during World War II, he bid St. Louis adieu and moved to the West Coast, making his recorded debut for the Globe logo with "Miss Mattie Left Me" in 1945. On that platter, J.D. Nicholson played piano; most of McCracklin's output found him handling his own 88s.

McCracklin recorded for a daunting array of tiny labels in Los Angeles and Oakland prior to touching down with Modern in 1949-50, Swing Time the next year, and Peacock in 1952-1954. Early in his recording career, McCracklin had Robert Kelton on guitar, but by 1951, Lafayette "Thing" Thomas was installed as the searing guitarist with McCracklin's Blues Blasters and remained invaluable to the pianist into the early '60s.

By 1954, the pianist was back with the Bihari brothers' Modern logo and really coming into his own with a sax-driven sound. "Couldn't Be a Dream" was hilariously surreal, McCracklin detailing his night out with a woman sent straight from hell, while a 1955 session found him doubling credibly on harp.

A series of sessions for Bay Area producer Bob Geddins' Irma label in 1956 (many of which later turned up on Imperial) preceded McCracklin's long-awaited first major hit. Seldom had he written a simpler song than "The Walk," a rudimentary dance number with a good groove that Checker Records put on the market in 1958. It went Top Ten on both the R&B and pop charts, and McCracklin was suddenly rubbing elbows with Dick Clark on network TV.

The nomadic pianist left Chess after a few more 45s, pausing at Mercury (where he cut a torrid "Georgia Slop" in 1959, later revived by Big Al Downing) before returning to the hit parade with the tough R&B workout "Just Got to Know" in 1961 for Art-Tone Records. A similar follow-up, "Shame, Shame, Shame," also did well for him the next year. Those sides eventually resurfaced on Imperial, where he hit twice in 1965 with "Every Night, Every Day" (later covered by Magic Sam) and the uncompromising "Think" and with "My Answer" in 1966.

McCracklin's songwriting skills shouldn't be overlooked as an integral factor in his enduring success. He penned the funky "Tramp" for guitarist Lowell Fulson and watched the old pal take it to the rarified end of the R&B lists in 1967, only to be eclipsed by a sassy duet cover by Stax stalwarts Otis Redding and Carla Thomas a scant few months later. Ever the survivor, McCracklin made a string of LPs for Imperial, even covering "These Boots Are Made for Walkin'" in 1966, and segued into the soul era totally painlessly.

Latter-day discs for Bullseye Blues proved that McCracklin still packed a knockout punch from behind his piano—no matter what his birth certificate says. —*Bill Dahl*

Twist With / 1961 / Crown ◆◆◆◆

Undoubtedly it was a mite difficult to twist to jump blues records from the mid-'50s, but this budget LP at least gave McCracklin's Modern catalog renewed life in the Crown catalog. Some of his best '50s rockers: the hilarious "Couldn't Be a Dream," "You Don't Seem to Understand," "Reelin' and Rockin'," "I'm Gonna Tell Your Mother." Overdue for CD reissue!! —*Bill Dahl*

Jimmy McCracklin Sings / 1961 / Chess ◆◆◆◆◆

Great late-'50s rocking R&B. —*Bill Dahl*

I Just Gotta Know / 1961 / Imperial ◆◆◆◆◆

It's always a "Shame, Shame, Shame" (to quote one of this LP's best numbers) when a 35-year-old slab of vinyl must be cited as what may be an artist's finest collection—but since no one has yet touched McCracklin's massive '60s Imperial catalog for CD reissue, here you go! Contains his definitive soul-tinged ballad "Just Got to Know," the Amos Milburn-derived jump-blues "Club Savoy," and several more late-'50s rockers that Imperial acquired from various small concerns after he began to hit with regularity. —*Bill Dahl*

My Rockin' Soul / 1963 / United ◆◆◆

Every Night, Every Day / 1965 / Imperial ◆◆◆◆

Another vintage LP by the ex-boxer that's well worth the search. Along with the hit title track, there's a remake of "The Walk," and his sturdy "Looking for a Woman," and an energetic "Let's Do It All." —*Bill Dahl*

Think / 1965 / Imperial ◆◆◆◆

There's a ton of great McCracklin material patiently awaiting reissue—this LP boasts the infectious title item, a sinuous "Steppin' Up in Class," and a driving "My Best Friend," for starters. —*Bill Dahl*

New Soul of Jimmy McCracklin / 1966 / Imperial ◆◆◆

On *New Soul of Jimmy McCracklin*, McCracklin has a more modern feel. —*Bill Dahl*

My Answer / 1966 / Imperial ◆◆◆◆◆

Conveniently enough, Imperial slapped together what amounts to a greatest-hits set here, and it serves as the best introduction to the pianist's '60s catalog. Contains "Just Got to Know," "Every Night, Every Day," "Think," "Steppin' Up in Class," and the title item—every one of them occupying an intriguing island midway between blues and soul. —*Bill Dahl*

Let's Get Together / 1968 / Minit ◆◆◆

Soul all the way. —*Bill Dahl*

Stinger Man / 1969 / Minit ◆◆◆

All-soul LP. —*Bill Dahl*

High on the Blues / 1971 / Stax ◆◆◆

Given that this was co-produced by Al Jackson (of Booker T. & the MG's) and Willie Mitchell (of Hi Records), and adds embellishment by the Memphis Horns, it's unsurprising that this is very much a soul-blues record. It's a workmanlike effort with an early-'70s Stax period feel, including remakes of two of his past R&B singles, "Think" and "Just Got to Know." The CD reissue adds a couple of previously unreleased bonus tracks. —*Richie Unterberger*

Yesterday Is Gone / 1972 / Stax ◆◆◆

Rockin' Man / 1978 / Route 66 ◆◆◆◆◆

Early R&B sides from the '50s. —*Bill Dahl*

And His Bluesblasters / 1981 / Ace ◆◆◆◆◆

My Story / 1991 / Bullseye Blues ◆◆◆◆◆

Pianist Jimmy McCracklin returned to form with 1991's *My Story*, his first effort for Bullseye Blues. Nine of the 12 songs on the album are brand new originals, all of which prove that McCracklin's talent for turning out well-crafted, memorable blues and R&B songs has not faded. Just as importantly, his chops are fluent, and he's arguably playing better than ever. Much of the album was recorded in New Orleans with a wonderful studio band, featuring drummer Herman Ernest and guitarists John Mooney and Wayne Bennett; among the highlights of these sessions are a pair of duets with Irma Thomas. A handful of cuts were made in Oakland, with Pee Wee Ellis leading a horn section. While the sessions don't quite have the same mood, both are stellar showcases for the revitalized McCracklin, and, as *My Story* illustrates, it's just nice to have him back. —*Thom Owens*

Jimmy McCracklin: The Mercury Recordings / 1992 / Bear Family ◆◆◆◆

McCracklin's liaison with Mercury was relatively brief, from late 1958 to the fall of 1960, and Bear Family has only managed to locate 13 songs for this CD. But it's a rewarding chapter in the pianist's endlessly nomadic recording career, featuring his original dance tunes "Georgia Slop" and "Let's Do It (The Chicken Scratch)," a New Orleans-cut cover of Johnny Cash's "Folsom Prison Blues," and some smoothly arranged (by Clyde Otis, Brook Benton's collaborator) pop/R&B outings that suggest Mercury had big plans for McCracklin that never quite panned out. —*Bill Dahl*

Taste of the Blues / 1994 / Bullseye Blues ◆◆◆

Now these are the sort of cameos that make a contemporary blues disc work! Lowell Fulson, Larry Davis, Smokey Wilson, Barbara Lynn, and Johnny Otis all guested on McCracklin's most recent album for Bullseye Blues, making it clear that the pianist is no museum piece with their swinging grooves and sharp solos. —*Bill Dahl*

● **The Walk: Jimmy McCracklin at His Best** / 1997 / Razor & Tie ◆◆◆◆◆

McCracklin has always been one of those artists whose currency always ran higher in the black blues community than it has in the subsequent years of white historical revision. But decent career retrospectives of McCracklin—who had sides issued on almost a dozen labels in as many years—on compact disc are somewhere between few and far between and non-existent. But this 20-track single-disc compilation goes a long way toward rectifying that situation. Containing his biggest hits (the title track, the original versions of "The Georgia Slop" and "Get Back"—later hits for Big Al Downing and Roy Head, respectively) along with the best of his Art-Tone and Imperial sides ("Just Got to Know" and "Every Night, Every Day," now both staples of the Chicago blues repertoire after being covered in the early '60s by Magic Sam), this makes a perfect introduction to his style as well as a powerful testament to his superb songwriting skills. —*Cub Koda*

Modern Recordings 1948–1950 / Jul. 27, 1999 / Ace ◆◆◆

Although McCracklin had already been recording for a few years, his association with Modern marked his first reasonably long tenure with an established label. This 25-track disc covers his first stay with the company, covering a half dozen singles, three songs that first showed up on the 1981 Ace album *And His Blues Blasters*, and ten demos, outtakes, and alternate takes that were previously unissued. It's solid small-combo West Coast jump blues, sometimes embellished by the tenor saxophone of Maxwell Davis. It's more interesting on the speedy, jumpy numbers, although McCracklin was competent at setting an after-hours vibe on the slower ones. The drums-piano-guitar trio, especially guitarist Robert Kelton, gets into a real frenetic groove on the 1948 instrumental "Blues Blasters' Shuffle"; "Hamburger Joint" is a silly novelty whose spoken repartee verges on sleaziness. In a more serious mood are two previously unissued McCracklin solo piano demos, "Mistreating Me" and "Bad Health Blues." —*Richie Unterberger*

Roots of Rhythm & Blues / Roots ◆◆◆◆

The country of origin of this disc remains murky, but its 18 McCracklin tracks, from his 1957-1958 layover at Chess (there was a belated 1962 date as well), are in dire need of domestic reissue—so until that happens, this one (shared with Paul Gayten) will just have to do. McCracklin's smash dance tune "The Walk" is here, along with the amusing playlet "He Knows the Rules" (immaculate axe by Lafayette "Thing" Thomas), a jumping "Everybody Rock," and another workout that didn't fare as well, "The Wobble." —*Bill Dahl*

Blast 'em Dead! / Ace ◆◆◆◆

McCracklin's vast catalog is perhaps more fully appreciated overseas than in his home. British Ace assembled 18 of the piano-pounder's Duke waxings for this searing LP, which features frequent interjections from guitarist Lafayette Thomas. Jumping stuff! —*Bill Dahl*

Larry McCray

b. Apr. 5, 1960, Magnolia, AR

Vocals, Guitar / Modern Electric Blues, R&B

If contemporary blues has a longterm future as we boldly venture into the 21st century, it's very likely that guitarist Larry McCray will play a recurring role in its ongoing development. His first two albums, *Ambition* and *Delta Hurricane*, signal both a strong commitment to the tradition and the vision to usher the genre in exciting new directions.

McCray's first influence on guitar was none other than his sister, Clara, who toured regionally around Arkansas with her own combo, the Rockets. Clara never got to record her Freddie King-styled blues for posterity—but her little brother has at least partially made up for that omission. Larry followed Clara up to Saginaw, MI, in 1972. She turned him on to the joys of the three Kings (B.B., Freddie, and Albert), Albert Collins, and Magic Sam, and Larry added superheated rock licks (à la Jimi Hendrix and the Allman Brothers) to his arsenal as he began playing the local circuit with his brothers Carl on bass and Steve on drums.

Working on General Motors' assembly line occupied a great deal of Larry McCray's time after he finished high school. But he eventually found enough free hours to put together *Ambition*, his 1991 debut album for Pointblank, in a Detroit friend's basement studio. The stunning set was a convincing hybrid of blues, rock, and soul, McCray combining the interrelated idioms in sizzling fashion. Suddenly, the stocky young guitarist was touring with label-mate Albert Collins. His 1993 Pointblank encore, *Delta Hurricane*, was a slicker affair produced by veteran British blues maven Mike Vernon that McCray much prefers to his homemade debut. He followed *Delta Hurricane* with *Climbin' Up* in 1995 and *Meet Me At the Lake* in 1996. *Born to Play the Blues* appeared in 1998. *Believe It* was followed in early 2001. —*Bill Dahl*

● **Ambition** / 1991 / Charisma ✦✦✦✦✦
Burly Larry McCray crashed the consciousness of the blues world with his stunning debut album, comprised of equal parts blues, soul, and rock. Guitar fanatics will no doubt wax rhapsodic about McCray's blazing pyrotechnics on "Nobody Never Hurt Nobody With the Blues," but it's the mellower R&B material buried toward the end of the CD—"Secret Lover," "Me and My Baby"—that best displays the warmth of the young bluesman's voice. Tab him for 21st century blues stardom! —*Bill Dahl*

Delta Hurricane / 1993 / Pointblank ✦✦✦✦
Blues guitarist and vocalist Larry McCray's second Pointblank CD gets off to a dreary start with the title track, a tune with neither interesting lyrics nor a good arrangement. But after that flop fades, the remaining 10 cuts are almost as powerful as the material on his critically acclaimed debut. McCray has the kind of tough, down-in-the-dirt voice you can neither fake nor acquire. His guitar work is equally authentic; there aren't any flashy phrases or flamboyant riffs, just pile-driving lines, barreling statements and energetic support for his vocals. There aren't many better contemporary blues albums being made by major labels; McCray is the real deal. —*Ron Wynn*

Meet Me at the Lake / 1996 / Atomic Theory ✦✦✦
A good-time workout with the Bluegills backing up McCray. The record grew out of a friendship between McCray and Bluegills leader Charlie Walmsley, and while the result isn't the most stunning blues disc on the market, it's quite enjoyable and good-natured. There's also some nice lead guitar work to recommend it. —*Steven McDonald*

Born to Play the Blues / Jun. 30, 1998 / House of Blues ✦✦✦✦
After a brief detour with the Bluegills' duet album *Meet Me at the Lake*, Larry McCray returned to form with the storming *Born to Play the Blues*. Since his 1991 debut *Ambition*, McCray has been hailed as one of the great contemporary bluesmen of the '90s, and this record reminds us why. It isn't that he offers any innovations or surprises—it's that he is a pure, no-nonsense bluesman, delivering solid guitar lines and soulful vocals. McCray also gets credit for not sticking with tried-and-true material, choosing to write his own songs and try out several tunes from Dave Steen and taking a stab at a Warren Hayes cover. Throughout it all, he plays and sings with passion and heart, confirming his position as one of the finest contemporary bluesmen around. —*Stephen Thomas Erlewine*

Believe It / Feb. 13, 2001 / Magnolia ✦✦✦✦
Magnolia, AR, native Larry McCray is not always mentioned when the subject of hot blues guitarists arises. That sort of oversight borders on criminal neglect. *Believe It* is just the sort of showcase that will make McCray's chops stick in the minds of blues fans. He's the complete package: a stirring vocalist blessed with a formidable guitar technique who can also help himself out as a songwriter (co-writing with brother/drummer Steve). Cue up the track "Love Gone Bad" and sit back for a guitar/vocal *tour de force*. McCray evokes a dirty guitar sound to die for and backs it up with a fierce vocal effort that would send any audience into a fit. The way in which McCray brings together the elements of this number is a specific clue as to the general excellence of *Believe It*. McCray folds blues, rock, and soul into a visceral, exciting sound that gives the lie to a lot of the blues pretenders out there nowadays. Anyone who takes a spin through this disc will, indeed, believe it by the time they're finished. This record burns with the sort of intensity and blues savvy that makes the genre something special, in the hands of the right artist. —*Philip Van Vleck*

Floyd McDaniel

b. Jul. 21, 1915, Athens, AL, **d.** Jul. 23, 1995, Chicago, IL
Guitar / Jazz Blues, Modern Electric Blues, Jump Blues
Known for blues-drenched jazz and jazz-drenched blues, Floyd McDaniel was a part of the Chicago scene for most of his 80 years. The singer/guitarist was born in Athens, AL, but spent much of his life in the Windy City, which he moved to when he was 15 in 1930.

As a teenager, McDaniel played and sang the blues on the streets of Chicago, and in 1933, he joined a washboard band called the Rhythm Rascals. In the early '40s, McDaniel learned to play the electric guitar and joined the Four Blazes, a jump blues combo that later became the Five Blazes and recorded for Aristocrat in 1947 and United Artists in 1952-1953. The Blazes went through their share of personnel changes; some of the artists McDaniel played with in the group included bassist Thomas Braden and pianist Ernie Harper. After the Blazes drifted apart in the late '50s, McDaniel was involved in a variety of activities, including operating a tavern on Chicago's South Side in the '50s and '60s and playing with a version of the Ink Spots in the '70s. In the '80s, McDaniel joined forces with Dave Clark, a veteran tenor saxophonist who ended up joining McDaniel's final group, the Blues Swingers. McDaniel, who recorded for Delmark in the '90s, died in Chicago on July 23, 1995—only two days after his 80th birthday. —*Alex Henderson*

● **Let Your Hair Down** / 1994 / Delmark ✦✦✦
Floyd McDaniel was 78 when, in 1994, he recorded *Let Your Hair Down!* for the Chicago-based Delmark. Through the years, the singer/guitarist had been the type of artist who had one foot in pre-bebop jazz and one in urban blues—and that approach continues to serve him nicely on this CD. McDaniel's credentials as a jump blues shouter are illustrated by inspired versions of Louis Jordan's "Caldonia," T-Bone Walker's "Blue Mood" and Roy Milton's "R.M. Blues," while his talents as a jazz singer are evident on Duke Ellington's "It Don't Mean That Thing" and Billie Holiday's "God Bless The Child." On this album, McDaniel leads a cohesive, swinging octet known as the Blues Swingers, which consists of a hard-swinging rhythm section and four horn players, including trumpeter Mike McLaughlin, tenor saxophonist Dave Clark, alto saxophonist Paul Mundy and baritone saxophonist/clarinetist Martin "Van" Kelly. *Let Your Hair Down!* would be among McDaniel's last recordings; the veteran artist died the following year. —*Alex Henderson*

West Side Baby (Live in Europe) / 1997 / Delmark ✦✦✦
Recorded in May of 1994—just months before McDaniel's death—this gritty European date finds the singer/guitarist joined by Dave Specter and the Bluebirds. —*Jason Ankeny*

Mississippi Fred McDowell

b. Jan. 12, 1904, Rossville, TN, **d.** Jul. 3, 1972, Memphis, TN
Slide Guitar, Vocals, Guitar / Blues Revival, Delta Blues
When Mississippi Fred McDowell proclaimed on one of his last albums, "I do not play no rock'n'roll," it was less a boast by an aging musician swept aside by the big beat than a mere statement of fact. As a stylist and purveyor of the original Delta blues, he was superb; equal parts Charley Patton and Son House coming to the fore through his roughed-up vocals and slashing bottleneck style of guitar playing. McDowell *knew* he was the real deal and while others were diluting and updating their sound to keep pace with the changing times and audiences, Mississippi Fred stood out from the rest of the pack simply by not changing his style one iota. Though he scorned the amplified rock sound with a passion matched by few country bluesmen, he certainly had no qualms about passing any of his musical secrets along to his young, White acolytes, prompting several of them—including a young Bonnie Raitt—to develop slide guitar techniques of their own. Although generally lumped in with other blues "rediscoveries" from the '60s, the most amazing thing about him was that this rich repository of Delta blues had never recorded in the '20s or early '30s, didn't get "discovered" until 1959, and didn't become a full-time professional musician until the mid-'60s.

He was born in 1904 in Rossville, TN, and was playing the guitar by the age of 14 with a slide hollowed out of a steer bone. His parents died when Fred was a youngster and the wandering life of a traveling musician soon took hold. The 1920s saw him playing for tips on the street around Memphis, TN, the hoboing life eventually setting him down in Como, MS, where he lived the rest of his life. There McDowell split his time between farming and keeping up with his music by playing weekends for various fish fries, picnics, and house parties in the immediate area. This pattern stayed largely unchanged for the next 30 years until he was discovered in 1959 by folklorist Alan Lomax. Lomax was the first to record this semi-professional bluesman, the results of which were released as part of an American folk music series on the Atlantic label. McDowell, for his part, was happy to have some sounds on records, but continued on with his farming and playing for tips outside of Stuckey's candy store in Como for spare change. It wasn't until Chris Strachwitz—folk-blues enthusiast and owner of the fledgling Arhoolie label—came searching for McDowell to record him that the bluesman's fortunes began to change dramatically.

Two albums, *Fred McDowell, Volume 1 and Volume 2*, were released on Arhoolie in the mid-'60s, and the shock waves were felt throughout the folk-blues community. Here was a bluesman with a repertoire of uncommon depth, putting it over with great emotional force and to top it all off, had seemingly slipped through the cracks of late-'20s/early-'30s field recordings. No scratchy, highly prized 78s on Paramount or Vocalion to use as a yardstick to measure his current worth, no romantic stories about him disappearing into the Delta for decades at a time to become a professional gambler or a preacher. No, Mississippi Fred McDowell had been in his adopted home state, farming and playing all along, and the world coming to his doorstep seemed to ruffle him no more than the little boy down the street delivering the local newspaper.

The success of the Arhoolie recordings suddenly found McDowell very much in demand on the folk and festival circuit, where his quiet good natured performances left many a fan utterly spellbound. Working everything from the Newport Folk Festival to coffeehouse dates to becoming a member of the American Folk Blues Festival in Europe, McDowell suddenly had more listings in his resumé in a couple of years than he had in the previous three decades combined. He was also well-documented on film, with appearances in *The Blues Maker* (1968), his own documentary *Fred McDowell* (1969) and *Roots of American Music: Country and Urban Music* (1970) being among them. By the end of the decade, he was signed to do a one-off album for Capitol Records (the aforementioned *I Do Not Play No Rock'n'Roll*) and his tunes were being mainstreamed into the blues-rock firmament by artists like Bonnie Raitt (who recorded several of his tunes, including notable versions of "Write Me a Few Lines" and "Kokomo") and the Rolling Stones, who included a very authentic version of his classic "You Got to Move" on their *Sticky Fingers* album. Unfortunately, this career largess didn't last much longer, as McDowell was diagnosed with cancer while performing dates into 1971. His playing days suddenly behind him, he lingered for a few months into July of 1972, finally succumbing to the disease at age 68. And right to the end, the man remained true to his word; he *didn't* play any rock & roll, just the straight, natural blues. —*Cub Koda*

★ **Mississippi Delta Blues** / Aug. 1964 / Arhoolie ✦✦✦✦✦
Arhoolie's *Mississippi Delta Blues* is one of the definitive Mississippi Fred McDowell albums. Culled from two sessions, recorded in 1964 and 1965 respectively, this blues revival-era recording finds McDowell at his very best, performing powerful versions of traditional Delta blues songs, as well as a handful of originals. McDowell recorded many fine albums, but this is arguably his best. *—Thom Owens*

My Home Is in the Delta / Sep. 1964 / Testament ✦✦✦✦✦
Mississippi Fred McDowell's home may have been in the Delta, but his music belonged to the world. This is heartfelt, raw, glorious country blues, delivered without an ounce of pretension or nostalgia. *—Ron Wynn*

Mississippi Blues / Dec. 1965 / Black Lion ✦✦✦
"Mississippi" Fred McDowell played simple, haunting blues with vivid, demonstrative passion and power. He wasn't a great guitarist, but his voicings and backings were always memorable, while his singing never lacked intensity or conviction or failed to hold interest. This 1965 set contains mostly McDowell compositions, with the exception of the set's final number, a nearly seven-minute exposition of Big Bill Broonzy's "Louise." Assisted only at times by his wife Annie, Fred McDowell makes every song entertaining, whether they're humorous, poignant, reflective, or bemused. *—Ron Wynn*

Long Way from Home / 1966 / Milestone/Original Blues Classics ✦✦✦
Good no-frills set of acoustic solo blues on bottleneck guitar. The accent is on traditional material, including "Milk Cow Blues," "John Henry," "Big Fat Mama," and the title track. *—Richie Unterberger*

Fred McDowell / 1966 / Flyright ✦✦✦

Amazing Grace / 1966 / Testament ✦✦✦✦✦
The connection between rural blues and spiritual music is sometimes overlooked. This 1966 recording, featuring McDowell, his guitar, and the Hunter's Chapel Singers of Como, Mississippi (including his wife Annie Mae), is one of the best illustrations of how closely the styles can be linked. McDowell and company perform what the record subtitle calls "Mississippi Delta spirituals" on this stark and moving set, which includes a version of one of his signature tunes, "You Got to Move." The CD reissue adds three previously unreleased tracks. *—Richie Unterberger*

Mississippi Delta Blues, Vol. 2 / 1966 / Arhoolie ✦✦✦✦✦
Amongst the giants of the Delta blues genre, Mississippi Fred McDowell might not be the absolute greatest genius or the most intense. In some ways that really count, however, he created some of the most consistently engaging albums of this kind of music, performing with great power during the period when microphones were being put in front of him. While not totally forsaking the pure and simple nature of this music's structural gambits, he played with plenty of variation and a good supply of song subjects, tempos, and moods. When he is as well-recorded as is the case here, the sound of his acoustic guitar is unforgettable. One of his favorite tricks is alternating between the singing slide guitar anthems and a simple percussive strumming patter. "You Got to Move" is an absolute classic, heard here in all its glory, and Mick Jagger can eat his heart out. This is one of those albums that can be slid forward gently when the subject of owning one, and only one, album of blues music comes up. *—Eugene Chadbourne*

Mississippi Fred McDowell & His Blues Boys / 1969 / Arhoolie ✦✦✦

I Do Not Play No Rock 'n' Roll / 1969 / Capitol ✦✦✦✦✦
Blues purists were disappointed to hear McDowell pick up an electric guitar for the first time on this LP, as well as work with a young, white rhythm section. To the rest of the listeners, this session sounds pretty good, McDowell's vocals, guitar playing, and integrity coming through just as strongly as it had on his acoustic work. The title track, and the rap that opens it up, is a mini-classic in its own right—if McDowell does not play no rock & roll, as he claims, he certainly keeps a beat pretty well. The album, as well as a second one cut at the same sessions (released on the Just Sunshine label) and some previously unreleased tracks, was released as an expanded double CD by Capitol in 1995. *—Richie Unterberger*

Going Down South / 1970 / Polydor ✦✦✦

Mississippi Fred McDowell & Furry Lewis: When I Lay My Burden Down / 1970 / Biograph ✦✦

Mississippi Fred McDowell in London / 1970 / Sire ✦✦✦

Mississippi Fred McDowell / 1971 / Rounder ✦✦✦✦
Tracks drawn from a 1962 recording of McDowell playing in his Como, MS, house. The recordings were initially made purely as a document of a performer and a style, but eventually found their way to record and, finally, to compact disc. Somewhat raw, though the sound is actually very good, the recordings caught McDowell at his best, playing just for his own satisfaction. *—Steven McDonald*

Live in New York / 1971 / Oblivion ✦✦✦✦
His motto was "I do not play no rock & roll," and Mississippi Fred McDowell proceeds to play the "straight and natural blues" throughout this live engagement in New York City. When introducing "Shake 'Em on Down," which opens the set, he adds the qualification, "but it kinda sounds like it." Good point. "Shake 'Em on Down" and "Baby Please Don't Go," which concludes it, really do *rock* even if they don't quite qualify as rock & roll. As McDowell adds, before launching into the sad tale of "John Henry," "Blues is a feeling, and I really feel what I'm playing." Clearly, labels didn't mean much to the Delta bluesman, although he does draw a distinction between the blues and spirituals (pronounced "specials" in his deep Southern accent) prior to performing "Mercy." Blues, he notes, come from what he knows, whereas spirituals come from the heart. Honest and forthright to a fault, McDowell confesses that he hadn't been intending to play "You Got to Move" (popularized by the Rolling Stones on *Sticky Fingers*), because he's tired of it. But if it's what the audience wants, he'll be happy to give it to them. And that he does, gracing the enthusiastic crowd with a laid-back but far from perfunctory reading. McDowell certainly took his obligation to his fans seriously, and this entire performance is a fine example of that ethos (it certainly didn't take much coaxing on their part to get him to play one more song, the aforementioned barnburner "Baby Please Don't Go"). *—Kathleen C. Fennessy*

Somebody Keeps Callin' Me / 1977 / Antilles ✦✦✦
This recording was released first on the Antilles label. It was a few years after the death of Mississippi Fred McDowell, and the new label was attempting to establish a reputation for class and sophisticated artistry. The superb black-and-white photograph of McDowell on the front cover buys lots of both; he was a great blues artist who functioned not as an eerie ghost of former glories but performed with gusto within the possibilities of what was available to him as a blues artist on the American music scene. Hands down, he was the best promoted bluesman in the history of the genre. During the height of the creative music uproar of the late '60s, Capitol records took out full-page advertisements in all the hip rock publications indicating that all one had to do was write back in order to receive a brand new, free Mississippi Fred McDowell album. The proportion of cheapskates being turned onto blues climbed mightily in this year, obviously. What they heard was McDowell playing electric guitar, with a rock rhythm section. This is also what is featured on this session, originally recorded in Jackson, MS, and "mixed" in NY by Michael Cuscuna, perhaps better known as a producer of jazz records. In fact, these tracks come from the same recording session as the Capitol giveaway, which was entitled "I Do Not Play No Rock and Roll." The title alone might have been the reason the company felt it had to give away copies, considering the dominant rock climate at that time. There is nothing that wrong with the music, since McDowell is such a great player and singer and has such a wonderful repertoire of songs. The problem is just that, in the end, he makes much better music alone with an acoustic guitar. This is not to join the ranks of folks who tossed rotten fruit at Bob Dylan for going electric at the Newport Folk Festival and so forth. It is not a case of electric versus acoustic, it is totally a musical judgment. Alone, McDowell is the master of his own universe. On his Mount Olympus, there are musical gods who are more than just effective. There is his low-end bass note work, played with and without the slide. His tone in the low end can be galvanizing. There is his pace and timing in introducing and repeating the slide guitar riffs on the high strings. There is his sense of rhythm, which is perfect. Introduce electric bass and a drum set, and it is elephants on the ballet floor. And they are not executing pirouettes. Since there was absolutely no tradition of using electric bass and a drum set in Delta blues, players such as Jerry Puckett on bass and Durin Lancaster on drums have no one to even imitate. A good eccentric drummer who forced McDowell to react would have been interesting, but here we just have someone trying to be tasteful and not get in the way, and it adds nothing to the music. Puckett is in an even more problematic situation, playing bass in a music that doesn't really need the reinforcement in the bottom end. He ends up getting in the way of McDowell's own bass concept. Puckett's own career doesn't suggest any reason to think he would have been able to add much to a session like this; he worked with more cosmopolitan blues artists such as Bobby "Blue" Bland, and always as a guitarist, not a bassist. Sure, most guitarists that play blues and rock probably think they could play bass with an old blues guy who sometimes stays on one chord, but that doesn't mean they can. This album is good, and still steps above the efforts of blues imitators, but fans of McDowell will inevitably want his recordings without the rock rhythm section. *—Eugene Chadbourne*

Mississippi Fred McDowell and Johnny Woods / 1977 / Rounder ✦✦✦✦
Although this label has over-produced many a blues session, this particular project saw the light of the day in a rougher, more honest form than might be the norm for Rounder. It originally popped up on vinyl in the mid-'70s, several years after Mississippi Fred McDowell had died. In the '90s, the material was re-released on compact disc on Philo as well as the original label. The continued interest in this recording is not difficult to understand. It certainly is exactly what it was presented as: a casual and off-the-cuff get-together between two old friends, recorded down in their neighborhood, and not the result of some nervous and sloppily organized trip to the big city recording studio. McDowell made his best music solo, but this is a chance to hear him making sparks fly with another musician. Johnny Woods is no virtuoso harp player, but he comes up with many nice touches and the instrument itself does not get in the way of McDowell's approach, which is more than one can say for other recordings in which drummers and bassists get stuck in the door. McDowell seems to have relied on a few too many tried and true numbers for this recording, trotting out both "Smokestack Lightning" and "John Henry" as well as "Red Cross Store," a number he recorded several times. This sets it apart from superior recordings by the artist in which he came up with a surprising amount of varied material, but the intensity and stretched-out nature of some of these performances makes up for it. *—Eugene Chadbourne*

☆ **You Gotta Move** / Nov. 30, 1993 / Arhoolie ✦✦✦✦✦
You Gotta Move is an excellent 19-track compilation of McDowell's best-known work, spotlighting his Mississippi Delta slide guitar virtuosity, as well as his superior songwriting skills; perhaps most familiar to many listeners is the title track, which inspired a Rolling Stones cover version on the group's classic *Sticky Fingers* album. *—Jason Ankeny*

This Ain't No Rock 'n' Roll / 1995 / Arhoolie ✦✦✦✦
Adding ten bonus tracks to the original release, 1995's *This Ain't No Rock 'n' Roll* is an impressive, extensive collection of the later work of Mississippi Fred McDowell. Though he uses a backup band consisting of second guitar, bass, and drums, the majority of the tracks simply feature McDowell unaccompanied, showing off his masterful bottleneck guitar skills. The material here documents a rather transitional period for the artist, as he was using electric instruments and expanding his repertoire to include some traditional

songs which he was rediscovering. To be sure, a good deal of the material is of traditional origin, with "Levee Camp Blues," "When the Saints Go Marching In," and "Dankin's Farm." Covering over 75 minutes and 18 tracks, this is a pretty complete picture of where McDowell was in the late '60s. *—Matt Fink*

Live at the Mayfair Hotel / 1995 / Onyx Classix ♦♦♦♦♦
Running 64 minutes, this compact disc gives us the complete contents of two British Red Lightnin' LPs, and McDowell's complete 1969 show from London's Mayfair Hotel. He is completely in his element here, scratching out dazzling licks on his hollow-body electric guitar, which is turned up loud enough to crunch and grind as he strums and sting real loud when he picks, but not so loud as to distort or overwhelm his singing. The highlights, which could really be the entire album, include "61 Highway," "Shake 'Em on Down," Willie Dixon's "My Babe," Mance Lipscombe's "Evil Hearted Woman," and McDowell's own "Kokomo Blues." Renowned British blueswoman Jo Ann Kelly sits in on one song, "When I Lay My Burden Down," which builds in intensity almost hypnotically, on what may be the best single CD in McDowell's output, and certainly his best concert release. *—Bruce Eder*

I Do Not Play No Rock 'N' Roll: Complete Sessions / Oct. 24, 1995 / Capitol ♦♦♦♦♦
A reissue of his popular 1969 electric album, expanded into a double CD with the addition of other material recorded at the same sessions (most of which was issued on an LP on the Just Sunshine label). It makes more sense to pick this up rather than the original vinyl album, as it rounds up all the material recorded at the *I Do Not Play No Rock 'N' Roll* sessions in November 1969, and adds lengthy liner notes. *—Richie Unterberger*

Steakbone Slide Guitar / Apr. 1996 / Rykodisc/Tradition ♦♦♦
Ten songs recorded by McDowell when he was appearing in England during the mid-'60s, and originally released on the Transatlantic album *In London, Vol. 2* and the Archive of Folk Music album *Mississippi Fred McDowell.* He performs these numbers, including "You Got to Move," "Levee Camp Blues," "I Heard Somebody Call," "Fred's Worried Life Blues," and "The Train I Ride," with a good deal of forcefulness and tension, although the repertory is hardly unique. The cleaning up of the sources has done a lot of good, although there is some evidence on certain tracks that vinyl sources were used for some of this. *—Bruce Eder*

First Recordings: The Alan Lomax Portait Series / Sep. 9, 1997 / Rounder ♦♦♦♦♦
In September, 1959, these 14 seminal tracks were recorded by Alan Lomax. Traversing the South with a bulky reel-to-reel tape recorder, this part of his field trip documents the very first recordings (and subsequent "discovery" in folk circles) of McDowell. The recordings were captured outdoors on a front porch, and even though Lomax was recording him at a semi-professional speed on his tape deck (7 1/2 inches per second as opposed to the then-standard 15 ips), seldom did McDowell's subsequent recordings capture this much ambience. Loose and informal, these sides showcase Fred solo and working in tandem with guitarist Miles Pratcher ("I'm Going Down the River," "Shake 'Em on Down," "You're Gonna Be Sorry"), the utterly surreal tissue-paper-and-comb work of Fanny Davis and—at various times—his wife Annie Mae ("Keep Your Lamps Trimmed and Burning"), James Shorty ("I Want Jesus to Walk With Me"), Sidney Carter and Rose Hemphill ("When the Train Come Along") on background vocals. As an added bonus for fans and historians alike, ten of the 14 tracks are previously unissued and include some of the best sides Fred ever recorded. *—Cub Koda*

Levee Camp Blues / Feb. 3, 1998 / Testament ♦♦♦
When Mississippi Fred McDowell recorded these sides in March of 1968, producer Pete Welding encouraged McDowell to recall the earliest material he had learned when he first started playing. The result is a selection of tunes that simply don't show up on his other recordings, both stylistically and because of their previously unreleased status. Highlights include "Let Me Lay Down In Your Cool Iron Bed," "My Baby Don't Treat Me Like Humankind," "Jim Steam Killed Lula," "Will Me Your Gold Watch and Chain," "Dark Clouds A-Rising" and "Pea Vine Special." Also included are two previously unissued tracks recorded in 1966 before the bulk of this session. *—Cub Koda*

Shake 'Em on Down / Jul. 1, 1999 / Charly ♦♦♦
Recorded live in New York City in November of 1971, this captures McDowell accompanied by Tom Pomposello on bass guitar. McDowell is in top form, blasting out electric versions of "John Henry," "Baby, Please Don't Go," and the title track. It sounds as if Pomposello is playing second guitar on some tracks rather than bass, but his playing never intrudes, and he actually provides a nice second slide part on "Shake 'Em On Down." A nice document of Fred in concert at the peak of his rediscovery. *—Cub Koda*

Live at the Gaslight / Oct. 24, 2000 / Live Archive ♦♦♦♦
Recorded on November 5, 1971, *Live at the Gaslight* stands as the final recording of Delta blues legend Mississippi Fred McDowell. The bottleneck guitarist was in his seventies when this album was cut, but his voice and playing show no signs of age and his passion and conviction seem to have strengthened with the years. At this point in McDowell's career he had shifted to playing electric slide guitar, and during this Gaslight performance he was also supported by sparse bass playing from Tom Pomposello. Accompanying McDowell's gruff voice, the guitar often seems to finish the singer's sentences for him; it's like listening to an old married couple. The setting is very intimate, allowing for friendly interaction with the audience and warm reactions to McDowell's occasional introductions and commentary. Throughout the two-disc set there is a real sense of inspiration as if the singer was releasing this music from his soul for the first time. One of the first things McDowell admits is that he "don't play no rock & roll," but the raw power of even his soundcheck nearly contradicts that statement. While there are slight distractions on the first disc (an out-of-tune rendition of "When the Saints Go Marchin' In," a confusing track-listing error on the back cover), there are certainly points of interest including the plaintive cry of "Baby Please Don't Go" and the righteous crunch of "You Got to Move." While the first CD has a few minor trouble spots, disc two really shines. The soulful moan of "Goin' to the River" blasts into the fiery punch of "Shake 'Em on Down," openly disputing his proclamation that he doesn't play rock & roll. The reverential conviction of "Good Mornin' Little Schoolgirl" precedes the last two songs, both inspirational numbers in true blues style: "Don't Mistreat Nobody" instructs his audience to be kind to their fellow man, and "Get Right Church" is almost a duet with his familiar bottleneck slide, chillingly foretelling his upcoming journey "home." *Live at the Gaslight* is a bright example of the raw power of Delta bottleneck blues by one of the genre's masters, and is not to be missed. *—Zac Johnson*

The Best of Mississippi Fred McDowell / Oct. 23, 2001 / Arhoolie ♦♦♦♦♦
Mississippi Fred McDowell lays down Delta blues as though time pretty much stood still. Discovered by Alan Lomax in the late '50s, his career as an authentic bluesman took off in the '60s, thanks to Arhoolie. *The Best of Mississippi Fred McDowell* showcases the singer's gritty vocals and slide guitar on some of his best '60s work. The power of "Fred's Worried Life Blues" and "Write Me a Few of Your Lines" resonates deep in the bones, while forceful versions of "Good Morning Little School Girl" and "You Gotta Move" strip away a hundred rip-offs. These cuts also feature McDowell's instrument of choice, the acoustic guitar. While resistant to new currents, he nonetheless plugged in on occasion. Earth-shaking electric cuts like "Levee Camp Blues" and "Meet Me Down in Froggy Bottom" rumble and hum. Even with a band, though, McDowell reminds one more of Lightnin' Hopkins than Muddy Waters. He remains rooted in the Delta. When he delivers a bit of blues, like "My Baby," he reaches deep and finds something elemental. McDowell opens two live cuts by saying "I don't play no rock & roll stuff," and then offers fine takes on "Shake 'Em on Down" and "Louise." *The Best of Mississippi Fred McDowell* serves up a taste of the Delta, honest and true, and impresses as a fine introduction to a great bluesman. *—Ronnie D. Lankford Jr.*

I Do Not Play No Rock 'N' Roll [Bonus Tracks] / Oct. 30, 2001 / Fuel 2000 ♦♦♦♦♦
This reissue of the original Capitol landmark from 1969 adds five tracks totaling 20 minutes to the playing time, yet falls short of the 1995 Capitol re-release *The Complete Sessions*, which tacked on ten tunes. Interestingly, three of these additional songs that close this 2001 reissued disc—"You Got to Move," "The Train I Ride," and "You Ain't Gonna Worry My Life Anymore"—weren't included in those ten and don't feature the bass and drums that were an integral part for most of the session. Regardless, the performance is classic and retains all of its spiky edginess. Even though blues purists griped because it was the first recording where the previously acoustic McDowell played electric guitar, his lines are so stark, spare, and jagged that the fullness and volume the instrument provides works perfectly with his hardcore Delta approach. McDowell is in wonderful voice and exuberant spirits throughout, spinning lively stories on the nine-minute "Everybody's Down on Me," where he doesn't start playing guitar or singing until four minutes into the track. The raconteur expresses, as well as explains, the album's title on the opening version of Big Joe Williams' "Baby Please Don't Go," the session's only cover. The rhythm section that caused such commotion on the album's initial release remains ensconced in the background, and the drummer's contributions are so subtle as to be almost inaudible. This keeps the focus on McDowell, whose guitar work is stunning, complex, and emotionally moving. He spins quicksilver slide runs that echo and answer his sung lines like he's been plugged in all his life. Smoother and less abrasive than some of the Fat Possum artists that first appeared in the '90s, McDowell nonetheless exudes frightening power when he hits his stride on the jagged "61 Highway" and his version of "The Train I Ride," complete with chugging chords and "Mystery Train" verses. A perfect place to learn about Mississippi Fred McDowell since it includes both "Kokomo Me Baby" and "You Got to Move," two of his most popular tracks. *I Do Not Play No Rock 'N' Roll* is an essential part of any Delta blues lover's collection. This 2001 reissue (with short but informative new liner notes from Bill Dahl) returns the folk/blues classic to the shelves, putting it back in print, hopefully for good. *—Hal Horowitz*

Rev. F.W. McGee (Ford Washington McGee)

b. Oct. 5, 1890, Winchester, TN, **d.** 1971

Drums / Country Gospel, Country Blues

Expertly blending lively congregational singing with powerful preaching, the Reverend F.W. McGee was among the most popular country gospel performers of the pre-Depression era. Born Ford Washington McGee in Winchester, Tennessee on October 5, 1890, he was raised primarily in Hillsboro, Texas; married at the age of 20, within a year he began a career as a teacher, soon after relocating to Oklahoma. Previously a pastor in a Methodist church, McGee converted to Charles H. Mason's Memphis-based Church of God in Christ in 1918, in part attracted to their more energetic singing style. By 1920 he had largely abandoned teaching to pursue preaching full-time, and through his revival meetings became a crucial figure in the GOGIC's encroachment into Kansas and Iowa. He later built a congregation in Oklahoma City with the assistance of the noted sanctified singer/pianist Arizona Dranes; by 1925, McGee had also established the first of two tents in the Chicago area.

When Dranes made her first recordings for OKeh in 1926, she recruited McGee and his Jubilee Singers to back her up; in early 1927, he made his headlining debut—albeit mistakenly labeled "Rev. F.N. McGee"—with "Lion of the Tribe of Judah." He next appeared on Victor a few months later, recording four more titles; among them were "Jonah in the Belly of the Whale" and "With His Stripes We Are Healed," which coupled together on a 78 reportedly sold over 100,000 copies. Another Victor session followed before the end of year, yielding the hit "Babylon Is Falling Down"; McGee's popularity as a recording artist also greatly increased the size of his congregation, and by 1928 he had outgrown his tents and built his own Chicago church. His later recording sessions focused primarily on preaching, with musical backing almost incidental; a July 16, 1930, New York City studio date was McGee's last, although he remained active in the GOGIC throughout the decades to follow. He died in 1971. —*Jason Ankeny*

• **Complete Recorded Works, Vol. 1: 1927–1929** / 1992 / Document ✦✦✦✦
Highlighted by "Jonah in the Belly of the Whale" and "With His Stripes We Are Healed," which together combined for one of the biggest "race records" of its time, the first volume in this retrospective of the career of Rev. F.W. McGee assembles some of the finest gospel sides of the prewar era. Opening with "Lion of the Tribe of Judah," McGee's lone recording for OKeh and a prime example of the sanctified tradition, the disc also includes "The Crooked Made Straight" and "Rock of Ages," both of which are fascinating attempts to combine congregrational singing with impassioned preaching. —*Jason Ankeny*

Complete Recorded Works, Vol. 2: 1929–1930 / 1992 / Document ✦✦✦✦
With the second volume in the series, Rev. F.W. McGee's gospel style turns almost exclusively to straight-ahead preaching, with only minimal musical backing. It's not that much of a stretch to suggest that this kind of gospel is a kind of early precursor to rap—the rhythms and patterns of McGee's preaching are highly musical, and his wordplay on sides like "Women's Clothes (You Can't Hide)" and "Testifyin' Meeting" is lyrical and imaginative. While these sermonizing records are by no means the place for new listeners to begin, for historians they offer fascinating insight into another of the many facets of the prewar gospel sound. —*Jason Ankeny*

Brownie McGhee (Walter McGhee)

b. Nov. 30, 1915, Knoxville, TN, **d.** Feb. 23, 1996, Oakland, CA

Vocals, Kazoo, Piano, Guitar / Blues Revival, East Coast Blues, Piedmont Blues, Prewar Country Blues, Country Blues, Folk-Blues

Brownie McGhee's death in 1996 represents an enormous and irreplaceable loss to the blues field. Although he had been semi-retired and suffering from stomach cancer, the guitarist was still the leading Piedmont-style bluesman on the planet, venerated worldwide for his prolific activities both on his own and with his longtime partner, the blind harpist Sonny Terry.

Together, McGhee and Terry worked for decades in an acoustic folk-blues bag, singing ancient ditties like "John Henry" and "Pick a Bale of Cotton" for appreciative audiences worldwide. But McGhee was capable of a great deal more. Throughout the immediate postwar era, he cut electric blues and R&B on the New York scene, even enjoying a huge R&B hit in 1948 with "My Fault" for Savoy (Hal "Cornbread" Singer handled tenor sax duties on the 78).

Walter Brown McGhee grew up in Kingsport, TN. He contracted polio at the age of four, which left him with a serious limp and plenty of time away from school to practice the guitar chords that he'd learned from his father, Duff McGhee. Brownie's younger brother, Granville McGhee, was also a talented guitarist who later hit big with the romping "Drinkin' Wine Spo-Dee-O-Dee"; he earned his nickname, "Stick," by pushing his crippled sibling around in a small cart propelled by a stick.

A 1937 operation sponsored by the March of Dimes restored most of McGhee's mobility. Off he went as soon as he recovered, traveling and playing throughout the Southeast. His jaunts brought him into contact with washboard player George "Oh Red" (or "Bull City Red") Washington in 1940, who in turn introduced McGhee to talent scout J.B. Long. Long got him a recording contract with OKeh/Columbia in 1940; his debut session in Chicago produced a dozen tracks over two days.

Long's principal blues artist, Blind Boy Fuller, died in 1941, precipitating OKeh to issue some of McGhee's early efforts under the sobriquet of Blind Boy Fuller No. 2. McGhee cut a moving tribute song, "Death of Blind Boy Fuller," shortly after the passing. McGhee's third marathon session for OKeh in 1941 paired him for the first time on shellac with whooping harpist Terry for "Workingman's Blues."

The pair resettled in New York in 1942. They quickly got connected with the city's burgeoning folk music circuit, working with Woody Guthrie, Pete Seeger, and Leadbelly. After the end of World War II, McGhee began to record most prolifically, both with and without Terry, for myriad R&B labels: Savoy (where he cut "Robbie Doby Boogie" in 1948 and "New Baseball Boogie" the next year), Alert, London, Derby, Sittin' in With and its Jax subsidiary in 1952, Jackson, Bobby Robinson's Red Robin logo (1953), Dot, and Harlem, before crossing over to the folk audience during the late '50s with Terry at his side. One of McGhee's last dates for Savoy in 1958 produced the remarkably contemporary "Living with the Blues," with Roy Gaines and Carl Lynch blasting away on lead guitars and a sound light years removed from the staid folk world.

McGhee and Terry were among the first blues artists to tour Europe during the '50s, and they ventured overseas often after that. Their plethora of late-'50s/early-'60s albums for Folkways, Choice, World Pacific, Bluesville, and Fantasy presented the duo in acoustic folk trappings only, their Piedmont-style musical interplay a constant (if gradually more predictable) delight.

McGhee didn't limit his talents to concert settings. He appeared on Broadway for three years in a production of playwright Tennessee Williams' *Cat on a Hot Tin Roof* in 1955 and later put in a stint in the Langston Hughes play *Simply Heaven*. Films (*Angel Heart*, *Buck and the Preacher*) and an episode of the TV sitcom *Family Ties* also benefited from his dignified presence.

The wheels finally came off the partnership of McGhee and Terry during the mid-'70s. Toward the end, they preferred not to share a stage with one another (Terry would play with another guitarist, then McGhee would do a solo), let alone communicate. One of McGhee's final concert appearances came at the 1995 Chicago Blues Festival; his voice was a tad less robust than usual, but no less moving, and his rich, full-bodied acoustic guitar work cut through the cool evening air with alacrity. His like won't pass this way again. —*Bill Dahl*

Back Country Blues / Nov. 1958 / Savoy ✦✦✦✦✦
Brownie McGhee's solo material had a certain charm and compelling quality missing from his collaborations with Terry. For whatever reason, he tended to try more things alone and vary his approach, sound and delivery. This is first-rate country and topical material, delivered without the forced humor that eventually made his dates with Terry more camp than substance. —*Ron Wynn*

Traditional Blues, Vol. 2 / Feb. 1961 / Smithsonian/Folkways ✦✦✦

Brownie's Blues / 1962 / Bluesville/Original Blues Classics ✦✦✦
Brownie's Blues was originally released by Bluesville Records in 1962. Supported by his longtime accompanist Sonny Terry, as well as second guitarist Benny Foster, Brownie turns in a nicely understated record that's distinguished by surprisingly harmonically complex and jazzy guitar work. Among the highlights are versions of "Killin' Floor," "Trouble in Mind" and "Every Day I Have the Blues," as well as the boogying "Jump, Little Children" and "I Don't Know the Reason." —*Thom Owens*

I Couldn't Believe My Eyes / 1973 / BGO ✦✦✦

Midnight Special / 1978 / Fantasy ✦✦✦

Facts of Life / 1985 / Blue Rock'it ✦✦✦

California Blues / 1990 / Fantasy ✦✦✦

Hometown Blues / 1990 / Mainstream ✦✦✦✦
Plenty of delightful interplay between McGhee and Terry recommends these 18 1948-1951 sides for producer Bobby Shad for his Sittin' in With label, but they predate the duo's later folk period by a longshot. Back then, they were still aiming their output solely at the R&B crowd—meaning "Man Ain't Nothin' But a Fool," "Bad Blood," "The Woman Is Killing Me," and "Dissatisfied Woman" are straight-ahead, uncompromising New York-style blues. —*Bill Dahl*

★ **The Folkways Years (1945–1959)** / 1991 / Smithsonian/Folkways ✦✦✦✦✦
Folkways Years (1945-1959) is a wonderful 17-track compilation of Brownie McGhee's Folkways recordings. During this time, McGhee became a staple on the blues-folk revival circuit, and accordingly these recordings find the Piedmont bluesman playing in a folk style, which he excelled at. Many of the most powerful tracks are straight from the rural Piedmont tradition, but the folkier material shows what a rich musician he was. It's an excellent sampler, one that demonstrates the depth and breadth of his Folkways recordings. —*Thom Owens*

☆ **The Complete Brownie McGhee** / 1994 / Columbia/Legacy ✦✦✦✦✦
Well, complete as far as his prewar country blues waxings for OKeh sans Sonny Terry (except for one or two where the whooping harpist provided accompaniment). McGhee was working firmly in the Piedmont tradition by 1940, when he signed with OKeh and began cutting the 47 enlightening sides here, which represent some of the purest country blues he ever committed to posterity. —*Bill Dahl*

Climbin' Up / 1995 / Savoy ✦✦✦✦
Nice collection of 1952-1955 sides with an urban blues twist by McGhee, with Terry's contributions limited to harmonica only and guitarists Stick McGhee and Mickey Baker checking in over the course of the dozen entries. McGhee was a world-class electric bluesman, too—a fact that frequently gets lost in the folk-slanted duo material he cut with longtime partner Terry. —*Bill Dahl*

Not Guilty Blues / Mar. 12, 1996 / Magnum Collectors ✦✦✦✦
Here's an 18-track collection of McGhee's earliest recordings, all of it emanating from sessions held in 1940 and the following year. Brownie's recordings as Blind Boy Fuller No. 2 are here, as well as the first recordings pairing him with longtime future partner Sonny Terry. His work with washboard player Oh Red (aka "Bull City Red") and the mysterious Jordan Webb playing harmonica is every bit as effective, though, and tracks like "Picking My Tomatoes" and "Born For Bad Luck" get this set off to a wonderful start; the musical quotient stays high all, the way to the end. Everything is pulled off of old, beat-up 78s, and the quality is up and down on every track, but this as fine an early Brownie McGhee set as you'll come across. —*Cub Koda*

Blues Is Truth / May 21, 1996 / Blues Alliance ✦✦✦✦
Brownie McGhee was 60 when *Blues Is Truth* (reissued on CD by Concord's Blues Alliance label in 1996) was recorded in White Plains, NY, in 1976, and the veteran bluesman was still a powerful, authoritative singer. Although not quite in a class with McGhee's magnificent work with Sonny Terry in the '50s and '60s, *Truth* is a consistently appealing date that unites him with such solid players as guitarist Louisana Red (who's also an excellent singer, though he doesn't sing here), harmonica player Sugar Blue and pianist Sammy Price. McGhee is in fine form on everything from the lonely desperation of "Rainy Day" to the upbeat, party-time atmosphere of "Walk On" and sibling Sticks McGhee's familiar "Wine Sporty Orty." The band is quite cohesive, and McGhee never sounds less than inspired. —*Alex Henderson*

A Long Way from Home / Mar. 24, 1998 / MCA ✦✦✦✦
Music from Brownie and Sonny's latter period, circa March and September of 1969. This combines two albums (*A Long Way from Home* and *I Couldn't Believe My Eyes*, both cut in two days) recorded for ABC-BluesWay, with the inclusion of a stray unreleased track, "Beggin' You," from the second session in September. The personnel stays basically the same for both sessions with excellent rhythm section support from drummer Panama Francis and bassist Jimmy Bond, while the September session also includes Earl Hooker on guitar. Solid, relaxed, rockin' grooves are the hallmarks here with both artists in fine form. —*Cub Koda*

New York Blues 1946–1948 / Feb. 15, 2000 / EPM Musique ✦✦✦✦
Invited to Washington, D.C., by Paul Robeson to appear at a civil-rights defense concert along with Leadbelly, Brownie McGhee and Sonny Terry came up north in 1942 and eventually settled in New York where they played all manner of hootenannies and loft parties around Greenwich Village with other big names in the growing folk boom: Leadbelly, Big Bill Broonzy, Woody Guthrie, and Pete Seeger. *New York Blues 1946-1948* in-

cludes 22 tracks recorded for the labels Alert, Disc, and Savoy during McGhee's first few years there, with celebrated sidemen like Sonny Terry (on six tracks), his brother Sticks McGhee, Champion Jack Dupree, Baby Dodds, Pops Foster, and others. The music emphasizes not his Village folk-revival style but a bluesy urban R&B for songs like "Sportin' Life Blues," "Big Legged Woman," "Worried Life Blues," "Drinkin' Wine Spo-Dee-O-Dee," and "My Fault." Though the sound quality is inferior, these are great performances. *—John Bush*

The Last Great Blues Hero / Oct. 24, 2000 / Music Club ♦♦♦

These dozen songs were recorded in a six-hour session on May 6, 1995. Intended to promote a tour of Australia and New Zealand, it ended up being Brownie McGhee's last recording date. Already ill with stomach cancer, the tour never took place, and the singer died the following year. Not issued until 2000, this turns out to be a surprisingly vital performance from a man nearly 80 years old who may not have been in the best health. That's the good news. On the other hand, it offers no surprises, as McGhee reprises familiar folk-blues crossover standards like "John Henry," "Rock Island Line," "Pick a Bale of Cotton," "Key to the Highway," "Walk on," and a song from his brother, Sticks McGhee, "Drinking Wine." The band accompaniment is (unlike as is often the case on such occasions) appropriately low-key and sympathetic, adding some additional harmonica and guitar, but not rocking out too hard. A pleasantly likable session, but not exciting or essential, *Last Great Blues Hero* finds McGhee sounding about the same as he'd always sounded for the last several decades of his life. Even if you're a devoted McGhee fan, you'll probably concede that more important versions of most of these tunes exist elsewhere, whether by McGhee or other singers; indeed, the liner notes observe that the newest song here, "Rainy Day," was first recorded in 1961. *—Richie Unterberger*

Sticks McGhee (Granville McGhee)

b. Mar. 23, 1917, Kingsport, TN, **d.** Aug. 15, 1961, New York, NY

Vocals, Guitar / R&B, Jump Blues

He may have not been as prolific or celebrated as his brother Brownie, but guitarist Stick McGhee cut some great boozy blues and R&B from 1947 to 1960—including the immortal "Drinkin' Wine Spo-Dee-O-Dee" (a tune that Jerry Lee Lewis, for one, picked up on early in life and has revived often since).

Young Granville McGhee earned his nickname by pushing his polio-stricken older brother Brownie through the streets of Kingsport, TN, on a cart that he propelled with a stick. McGhee was inspired to pen "Drinkin' Wine" while in Army bootcamp during World War II; it was apparently a ribald military chant that the McGhees cleaned up for public consumption later on. Stick McGhee's first recorded version of the tune for J. Mayo Williams' Harlem logo made little impression in 1947, but a rollicking 1949 remake for Atlantic (as Stick McGhee & his Buddies) proved a massive R&B hit (brother Brownie chiming in on guitar and harmony vocal). The tune has attracted countless covers over the years—everyone from Jerry Lee Lewis and Johnny Burnette to Wynonie Harris and Larry Dale has taken a sip from this particular wine flask.

After one more smash for Atlantic, 1951's "Tennessee Waltz Blues," McGhee moved along to Essex, King (where he waxed some more great booze numbers from 1953 to 1955—"Whiskey Women and Loaded Dice," "Head Happy with Wine," "Jungle Juice," "Six to Eight," "Double Crossin' Liquor"), Savoy, and Herald, where he made his last 45 in 1960 before lung cancer cut him down the following year. *—Bill Dahl*

● **Stick McGhee & His Spo-Dee-O-Dee Buddies** / 1953-1955 / Ace ♦♦♦♦♦

The British Ace label—long a prime source for quality compilations—has done Brownie's little brother proud, collecting his dozen 1953-1955 jump blues sides for the King logo, many of them detailing the effects of booze. Also aboard are four country blues-styled numbers by Ralph Willis, and four more by the pseudonymous Big Tom Collins (two of them feature Brownie McGhee's vocals, the other pair Champion Jack Dupree!). *—Bill Dahl*

Highway of Blues / 1959 / Deluxe ♦♦

Contains some of his fine '50s jump blues tracks for King. *—Bill Dahl*

New York Blues / Feb. 7, 1995 / Ace ♦♦♦♦

1947–1951 / Feb. 5, 2002 / Classics ♦♦♦

Rollee McGill

Saxophone, Vocals / Rock & Roll, R&B

Virtually nothing is known of the life and full career of this Philadelphia-based saxman and vocalist. What is known is that he cut some sizzling rhythm & blues between 1954 and 1965 (and maybe beyond, for all anyone can tell) and played one of the most famous and familiar breaks in the history of '50s rock & roll, the sax solo on the Silhouettes' 1958 smash "Get a Job"—this puts Rollee McGill right up there with Jimmy Wright and his work at Gee Records, Gone Records, and the like, and with Frankie Lymon & the Teenagers et al., as a star sideman, except that McGill also sang and cut sides on his own.

As a singer, he was similar to Johnny "Guitar" Watson, and he also wrote most of his own material. Yet this brilliant tenor sax player, commanding vocalist—who was as impressive on the ballads as the jump numbers—and prodigious composer only had one hit of his own, "There Goes That Train." Originally cut for Piney Records in Philadelphia, this record became a local hit and was picked up by Mercury Records for national distribution, and enjoyed a number ten R&B hit in the summer of 1955. And then nothing. McGill undoubtedly played lots of sessions, including the Silhouettes date that yielded "Get a Job," but he never charted another record nationally. He cut searing singles like "Rhythm Rockin' Blues" and slow blues numbers like "Come on In" (both originals), featuring players like Mercury resident pianist Ernie Freeman, that went unbought during the heyday of the R&B explosion of the mid-'50s, and later recorded ballads and jump numbers for the Kaiser, Junior, Chelsea, and Riff labels, into the mid-'60s, and apparently was working well into the '80s, playing locally and on various sessions by other artists.

In 1999, Bear Family Records of Germany finally gave long-delayed acknowledgment to this lost legend of the R&B by releasing a CD of his known recordings. A year later, on November 1, 2000, McGill died at the age of 68. *—Bruce Eder*

● **Rhythm Rockin' Blues** / Feb. 23, 1999 / Bear Family ♦♦♦

This is one hot CD, and it's everything that one would expect from the man who recorded (and spontaneously devised) the sax break on the Silhouettes' "Get a Job." There are ballads here, to be sure, and they're sung well enough by McGill, but his real forte is hard R&B and digressions into blues, which are brilliantly represented here. From his one chart hit, "There Goes That Train," cut in 1954, through a pair of 1965 sides, McGill's complete known output of his own sides is featured. One wishes there was session information available on who besides McGill was playing—one longs to know the name of the guitarist responsible for the hard, jangling solo on "I'll Forgive You Baby," or the names of the pianist and guitarist on the slow blues "Goin' Down South"—but otherwise, all of this material is prime R&B representing the dominant styles from the hot, rhythm-driven mid-'50s through the more lyrical, ballad-oriented mid-'60s. One track, "Cry for Happy," a piece of Oriental ersatz, was likely unfinished and is a bizarre digression, but most of the rest is fine listening in its own right. Some of the early '60s stuff does have a slightly retro feel—"Introduce Yourself" could just as easily have been cut five year earlier than it was, but the man's talent was sufficient to allow him to move with the times. *—Bruce Eder*

Ellen McIlwaine

b. Oct. 1, 1945, Nashville, TN

Slide Guitar, Vocals, Guitar / Contemporary Singer/Songwriter, Progressive Folk, Blues-Rock, Folk-Rock, Country-Folk

Guitarist, singer, and songwriter Ellen McIlwaine is a gutsy, spirited performer who plays and sings a fiery brand of blues like few other female blues singers. Why she's not more widely known is one of the mysteries of the record business, as she's been on the scene a long time.

Adopted and raised by missionaries, McIlwaine spent her first 15 years in Japan. She began playing piano at five and began singing in the church choir. She began listening to U.S. Armed Forces Radio in junior high school, becoming enamored with singers like Fats Domino, Ray Charles and Professor Longhair. McIlwaine returned to the U.S. with her parents when she was 17 and attended King College in Bristol, Tenn. and DeKalb College in Atlanta. She left college after two years and began her professional performing career in Atlanta in 1966.

Shortly after she began playing out professionally, folksinger Patrick Sky heard her and encouraged her to come to New York City. Sky's manager secured her some bookings at the Cafe Au Go Go in Greenwich Village, and there, she shared bills with Jimi Hendrix, John Lee Hooker and Howlin' Wolf. Richie Havens and Randy California taught her a few things about slide guitar, and she took it from there. She moved back to Atlanta and formed her first and only group, Fear Itself.

With that group, she pioneered what was then a novel concept: she was both the guitar-slinging bandleader and the group's lead vocalist. A year later, the all-male backup group went with her to New York to record their self-titled debut album for Dot Records.

McIlwaine's other recordings, which may be difficult to locate, include *Honky Tonk Angel* (1972) and *We the People* (1973), both for Polydor. In 1975, she recorded *The Real Ellen McIlwaine* for a Canadian label, Kot'Ai Kot. Her output since then has been somewhat sporadic, but her performances are just as spirited. More recent recordings include *Ellen McIlwaine* (1978) for United Artists; *Everybody Needs It* (1982) for the San Francisco-based Blind Pig label, and a 1988 release on Stony Plain, a Canadian label, *Looking for Trouble*. Fortunately, many of her old vinyl sides have been reissued on compact disc by Stony Plain.

After many years in Connecticut, McIlwaine relocated to Toronto, Ontario, in the late '80s. Fans can get information on her recordings and tour schedules from her website, www.ellenmcilwaine.com. *—Richard Skelly*

Honky Tonk Angel / 1972 / Polydor ♦♦♦

An album of songs by McIlwaine, Hendrix, Jack Bruce, Steve Winwood, Isaac Hayes, and Bobbie Gentry. A sweet date. One side is live, the other is a studio recording. *—Michael G. Nastos*

We the People / 1973 / Polydor ♦♦♦♦♦

The brilliant slide playing that inspired the respect of fellow guitarists John Lee Hooker, Johnny Winter, Jeff Healey, David Lindley, and others is obvious right off the top. In her unfettered scat singing is a hint of the fiery independence that scared off record company execs and radio playlisters alike. This is a strong sophomore effort in New York City by a sadly underexposed talent who settled in the Western Canadian city of Calgary after many nomadic years. As she would at other times in her long career, she offers her own distinctive cover of a song by sometimes collaborator Jack Bruce. Her own "All to You" finds her in a rare romantic mood, while the traditional "Farther Along" is a moving gospel number that might have pleased this powerful performer's missionary foster parents. *—Mark Allan*

The Real Ellen McIlwaine / 1975 / Kot'ai ♦♦♦♦♦

Her best. McIlwaine sings and plays slide guitar in a blues-rock vein and composes prolifically. This album also includes music by Stevie Wonder, Jack Bruce, John Lee Hooker, Booker T., and Tracy Nelson. Dedicated to Jimi Hendrix. *—Michael G. Nastos*

Ellen McIlwaine / 1978 / United Artists ♦♦♦

Everybody Needs It / 1982 / Blind Pig ♦♦♦

This early-'80s recording with Jack Bruce is dedicated to Professor Longhair and Tim Hardin. One half of the album features McIlwaine's own compositions. *—Michael G. Nastos*

Looking for Trouble / 1988 / Stony Plain ♦♦♦

Recorded for a small Western Canadian label, this release is an unusual but affecting blend of world beat and electronics, combined with the passionate performer's powerful playing and singing. Ever restless and experimental, she delves into Jamaica with a reggae-fied "Can't Find My Way Home." A spacy "All to You" revisits one of her most enduring melodies from the 1973 release *We the People*. Her masterful slide guitar playing isn't front and center as much as usual on her most rhythmic album to date. Dedicated, among other things, to the 12 steps to recovery, this album finds McIlwaine on the verge of moving to Canada in search of a new direction for her music and her life. *—Mark Allan*

Women in (E)motion / 1998 / Tradition & Moderne ♦♦♦

This live recording from Germany captures the essence of her stage show at the turning of the millennium. It's stark evidence of how increasingly rhythmic her work became through the years. She routinely incorporates reggae, funk, and other black styles into her distinctive, perhaps unique, sound that includes a fat, rich tone achieved by few guitarists of either gender. Covers of songs by one-time collaborator Jimi Hendrix, John Lee Hooker, Bo Diddley, and the Isley Brothers reveal some of her touchstones, although by this point she's evolved far beyond her blues roots. Her yodeling will put off some listeners. If you can get past that, you're in for a ride. *—Mark Allan*

Up from the Skies: The Polydor Years / Jul. 7, 1998 / Polygram ♦♦♦♦♦

Big Jay McNeely (Cecil James McNeely)

b. Apr. 29, 1927, Watts, CA

Sax (Tenor), Saxophone / Jazz Blues, Jump Blues, Soul-Jazz, West Coast Blues, R&B

His mighty tenor sax squawking and bleating with wild-eyed abandon, Big Jay McNeely blew up a torrid R&B tornado from every conceivable position—on his knees, on his back, being wheeled down the street on an auto mechanic's "creeper" like a modern-day pied piper. As one of the titans who made tenor sax the solo instrument of choice during rock's primordial era, Big Jay McNeely could peel the paper right off the walls with his sheets of squealing, honking horn riffs.

Cecil McNeely and his older brother Bob (who blew baritone sax lines with Jay in unison precision on some of Jay's hottest instrumentals) grew up in Los Angeles, where jazz reigned on Watts' bustling nightlife strip. Inspired by Illinois Jacquet and tutored by Jack McVea, McNeely struck up a friendship with Johnny Otis, co-owner of the popular Barrelhouse nitery. Ralph Bass, a friend of Otis, produced McNeely's debut date for Savoy Records in 1948 (Savoy boss Herman Lubinsky tagged the saxist Big Jay, in his eyes a more commercial name than Cecil). McNeely's raucous one-note honking on "The Deacon's Hop" gave him and Savoy an R&B chart-topper in 1949, and his follow-up, "Wild Wig," also hit big for the young saxist with the acrobatic stage presence.

From Savoy, McNeely moved to Exclusive in 1949, Imperial in 1950-1951, King's Federal subsidiary in 1952-1954 (where he cut some of his wildest waxings, including the mind-boggling "3-D"), and Vee-Jay in 1955. McNeely's live shows were the stuff that legends are made of—he electrified a sweaty throng of thousands packing L.A.'s Wrigley Field in 1949 by blowing his sax up through the stands and then from home plate to first base on his back! A fluorescently painted sax that glowed in the dark was another of his show-stopping gambits.

In 1958, McNeely cut his last hit in a considerably less frantic mode with singer Little Sonny Warner. The bluesy "There Is Something on Your Mind" was committed to tape in Seattle but came out on deejay Hunter Hancock's Swingin' imprint the next year. McNeely's original was a huge smash, but it was eclipsed the following year by New Orleans singer Bobby Marchan's dramatic R&B chart-topping version for Fire. Since then, it's been covered countless times, including a fine rendition by Conway Twitty!

Honking saxists had fallen from favor by the dawn of the '60s, so McNeely eventually became a mailman and joined Jehovah's Witnesses (no, that's not the name of a combo). Happily, his horn came back out of the closet during the early '80s. Today, McNeely records for his own little label and tours the country and overseas regularly. This deacon's still hopping! *—Bill Dahl*

Big Jay in 3-D / Aug. 26, 1952-Apr. 8, 1954 / King ♦♦♦♦

Tenor saxophonist Big Jay McNeely swings and honks his way through 12 classic Federal sides from 1952-1954. Joined by brother Robert on baritone, McNeely and his combo work a well-worn jump blues groove on gospel-imbued scorchers like "Hot Cinders" and "The Goof." Equally adept at torrid and moderate tempos, McNeely also shows off his Illinois Jacquet-inspired chops with a dizzying array of bleats, screeches, and guttural smears, even throwing in some svelte lines when appropriate. And while cuts like "Ice Water" presage the coming of rock & roll, classy swingers such as "Hardtack" offer a unique blend of R&B and jazz adorned with bongo accompaniment. And then there's "3-D," the centerpiece of the set and one of the most blistering of R&B instrumentals. Even amidst the almost pneumatic rhythm, McNeely masterfully wails above the band, not missing a beat during his irrepressible call-and-response workout with the other horn players. Whether blowing teenage brains out at L.A.'s Shrine Auditorium or with classic records like this, Big Jay McNeely always backed up the hysteria with loads of good music. *—Stephen Cook*

The Deacon Rides Again / 1952-1957 / Marconi ♦♦♦

Hot tenor licks, sweltering vocals from Jesse Belvin, and bluesy inflections courtesy of Mercy Dee. *—Ron Wynn*

Live at Birdland: 1957 / 1957 / Collectables ♦♦♦♦

An amazing artifact from 1957, when live recordings like this one didn't happen very often. A Seattle engineer with a spanking-new stereo tape recorder captured the contents of this disc while McNeely and his swinging combo were working out at a Seattle nightspot called the Birdland. He gets plenty of room to peel the paper from the gin joint's walls as he wails on "Flying Home," "How High the Moon," and "Let It Roll." *—Bill Dahl*

Swingin' / 1958-1960 / Collectables ♦♦♦♦

Gymnastic sax maniac's output for L.A. deejay Hunter Hancock's Swingin' logo during the late '50s and early '60s. Naturally, his smash "There Is Something on Your Mind" is front and center, alongside the oddly titled "Back...Shack...Track," "Psycho Serenade," and "Blue Couch Boogie." Little Sonny Warner is the vocalist on some sides. *—Bill Dahl*

From Harlem to Camden / Aug. 1983-Sep. 1983 / Ace ♦♦♦

An album of lusty, robust honking sax on standard R&B arrangements. *—Ron Wynn*

Meets the Penguins / Oct. 1983 / Ace ♦♦♦

This reissue of raucous, upbeat R&B cuts also includes the doo-wop harmony ensemble The Penguins. *—Ron Wynn*

● **Nervous** / 1995 / Saxophile ♦♦♦♦♦

A thorough 19-track examination of McNeely's early heyday, incorporating a live 1951 reprise of his signature "Deacon's Hop," and the King label classics "3-D," "Nervous Man Nervous," and "Texas Turkey," a handful of live 1957 efforts that include the crazed "Insect Ball," and McNeely's original hit version of the incendiary blues ballad "There Is Something on Your Mind" (with Little Sonny Warner handling the Ray Charles-influenced lead vocal). *—Bill Dahl*

Central Avenue Confidential / Aug. 15, 2000 / Atomic Theory ♦♦♦

1948–1950 / Oct. 2, 2001 / Classics ♦♦♦♦

Tony T.S. McPhee

b. Mar. 22, 1944

Vocals, Songwriter, Guitar / Psychedelic, Hard Rock, Blues-Rock

Tony McPhee was part of the first generation of young British blues disciples influenced by Cyril Davies and his band Blues Incorporated. A member of the same generation of young blues buffs as Mick Jagger, Keith Richards and Brian Jones, he never ascended to the heights achieved by the future Rolling Stones, but has recorded a small, highly significant body of blues-rock.

Originally a skiffle enthusiast, he received his first guitar as a Christmas present and formed his first band soon after, while still in school. He gravitated toward the blues during the early '60s, and soon discovered Cyril Davies. After seeing a few performances by Davies with Blues Incorporated at the Marquee Club in London during 1962, he became hopelessly hooked on blues and R&B, and decided to try and make it as a blues singer/guitarist.

McPhee's first group was the Dollarbills, a pop band featuring John Cruickshank on vocals, Pete Cruickshank on bass, and Dave Boorman on drums. He quickly steered toward blues, most notably the sound of John Lee Hooker, and with the addition of Bob Hall on piano, the group changed its name to the Groundhogs, in recognition of Hooker's "Ground Hog Blues."

The Groundhogs were a very solid blues/R&B outfit, playing soulful American R&B and raw American blues at venues such as Newcastle's Club A-Go-Go, and they subsequently became the backing band to Champion Jack Dupree at a series of gigs at the 100 Club. Finally, in July of 1964, the Groundhogs reached their zenith when they were chosen to back John Lee Hooker himself during his current British tour. Hooker later selected the group to back him on his next tour, and also sent an acetate recording of the group to executives at his label, Vee-Jay Records. That acetate, the hard-rocking, piano-and-harmonica-driven band original "Shake It" backed with a very powerful and persuasive cover of Little Son Jackson's "Rock Me Baby," was released on the Interphon label, a Vee-Jay subsidiary. It failed to reach the charts, but it did mark the group and McPhee's first American release.

Meanwhile, back in England, the group recorded a studio album with Hooker, somewhat misleadingly entitled *Live at the A-Go-Go Club, New York*. The group's fortunes seemed to improve in 1965 when producer Mike Vernon recorded three tracks, "Big Train Blues," "Can't Sit Down," and "Blue Guitar," but none saw any major release or success, and only "Blue Guitar" ever received much U.S. exposure, appearing on the '70s Sire Records collection *Anthology of British Blues*.

By the end of 1965, the British blues boom had expended itself, and soul was becoming the new sound of choice. McPhee had already shown a predilection for soul music in his writing, especially "Hallelujah," which the group cut with its newly added brass section in 1965. The Groundhogs transformed themselves into a soul band, and were persuaded to record a song called "I'll Never Fall in Love Again." As a first soul outing it was a promising beginning, despite a beat that was too reminiscent of Otis Redding's "Can't Turn You Loose"—the dissonant guitar in the break was a refreshing change that would never have made it out the door at Stax Records. The song failed to get much airplay or achieve a chart position, and its B-side, the upbeat, haunting McPhee original "Over You Baby" disappeared as well.

The Groundhogs split up soon after, and McPhee did session work for a time, as well as recording some blues sides on his own, under the auspices of producer Jimmy Page, that later turned up on various British blues anthologies released by Andrew Loog Oldham's Immediate Records label, backed up by Jo-Ann Kelly and fellow Groundhog Bob Hall. Unlike a lot of other blues enthusiasts from the early '60s, McPhee remained true to his roots, and was good enough to rate a berth as a sessionman on Champion Jack Dupree's 1966 Decca album *From New Orleans to Chicago*.

In August of 1966, McPhee and bassist Pete Cruickshank teamed up with drummer Mike Meekham to form Herbal Mixture, a Yardbirds-like outfit mixing psychedelic and blues sounds at a very high amperage. They were one of the more soulful and muscular psychedelic outfits, reflecting their R&B (as opposed to pop) roots, and even their spaciest material has a bluesy feel. "A Love That's Died" relies on fuzz-tone guitar, and would have made good competition for anything by the Yardbirds had anyone been given a chance to hear it. Their cover of "Over You Baby" is, if anything, superior to the Groundhogs' original, and deserved a better hearing than it got. Herbal Mixture had some success playing the Marquee and Middle Earth clubs in London, and were good enough to get a gig opening for the newly-formed Jeff Beck Group at the London Roundhouse. Their records, however, didn't sell, and at the end of 1967, following Meekham's departure, the band ceased to exist.

McPhee continued playing blues in his spare time, however, and passed through the John Dummer Blues Band during early 1968. His music had left an impression on at least one record company executive—in 1968, Andrew Lauder of United Artists' British operation offered McPhee the chance to record a complete album if he could put together a band. He formed a new Groundhogs, carrying over bassist Pete Cruickshank, and the album *Scratching the Surface* was duly recorded and released that year. Ironically, this incarnation of the Groundhogs, put together for the one album session, ended up lasting far beyond its origins—five additional albums, including his best-known long-player, *Me and the Devil*, were recorded through 1972, and the group has remained a viable unit, continuing to perform in England and the European continent (where there's always work for British blues bands) with McPhee as its leader. *—Bruce Eder*

• **Hooker & the Hogs** / 1965 / Indigo ♦♦♦♦♦
McPhee and the Groundhogs' most important musical legacy, this 1996 reissue has an unusual history. Tony McPhee and the Groundhogs first played with John Lee Hooker in June of 1964, when John Mayall's Bluesbreakers were unable to fulfill a commitment to back Hooker on the final week of his British tour. The Groundhogs were deputized on the spot and played their first show with him at the Twisted Wheel in Manchester. At the end of the week, Hooker told McPhee how much he liked working with his band and agreed to use the Groundhogs as his backing band on his next visit to England. Hooker was back in May and June of 1965, and not only used them as his band but recorded this album with the Groundhogs. The band was Tony McPhee on guitar, Pete Cruickshank on bass, Dave Boorman on drums, and Tom Parker on keyboards—some of the stuff here may have surfaced elsewhere, on the Interchord label (as *Don't Want Nobody*) with brass dubbed on, but this release consists of the undubbed recordings. The sound is raw, tight, and raunchy, some of the best band-backed recordings of Hooker's career. He's notoriously difficult to play support for because of the spontaneity of his work, but these guys keep up and then some, adding engaging flourishes and grace notes. Hooker is in excellent voice, and his material is as strong as any album in his output, rough, dark, and moody. The ominous, surging "Little Dreamer" is worth the price of admission all but itself. The 11 tracks with the Groundhogs are rounded out with four Hooker solo bonus tracks, which are even louder and more savage than the Groundhogs' stuff, though a little noisy (like that ever mattered with The Hook). *—Bruce Eder*

Me and the Devil / 1968 / Liberty ♦♦♦

I Asked for Water / 1969 / Liberty ♦♦♦

Same Thing on Their Minds / 1971 / Sunset ♦♦♦

Two Sides of Tony McPhee / 1973 / Castle ♦♦♦♦
Aptly titled, *Two Sides of Tony McPhee* not only explores McPhee's conceptions about love, relationships, religion, and aging, but the album is divided up musically, showcasing his talent as both a guitarist and a keyboard player. After displaying his keenness for composing a concept album with *Split*, a piece that he recorded with his band the Groundhogs based on the complexities of schizophrenia, McPhee decided to record an album that was more exclusive and personal. The result was *Two Sides of Tony McPhee*, with McPhee playing an acoustic and electric guitar for the first four tracks, then switching to three different synthesizers and an electric piano for side two, a lengthy spoken poem entitled "The Hunt." What results is an extremely entertaining and engrossing conceptual production that is equal to anything he's done with the Groundhogs. McPhee's writing is penetrating and resonant, unleashing his thoughts on the transcendence of life ("Three Times Seven"), the bitterness of failing relationships ("All My Money Alimony"), the pain of loss ("Morning Eyes"), and pure anger ("Don't Dog Me Bitch"), with each song accompanied by the guitar and nothing else. The second half of the album is comprised of "The Hunt," which is just as esoteric and sagacious as it is long and opens up with the ARP 2600 synthesizer mimicking an eerie, echoed howl of a dog in the distance. McPhee bellows and rants in a penetrating manner about the unethical nature of war and humankind's inhumanity throughout the ages, switching ever so smoothly to his abstract philosophies about the corruption of power and the mystery of fate, life, and death. Not only is his poetry forceful, but the overlapping of the electric piano and drum synthesizer shroud the piece with an ornate progressive ambience, adding a deeper sense of intrigue to his words and creating a rather bizarre electronic climate. The entire album is riveting, and *Two Sides of Tony McPhee* hinted at McPhee's fondness for progressive rock, an area in which he eventually led the Groundhogs into with their next few albums. Although this album has been eclipsed by what McPhee has accomplished with his band, its revelations about McPhee as a musician and a philosopher are quite gripping, and this is a must-hear for all Groundhog fans. *—Mike DeGagne*

Dealing with the Devil / 1991 / Sony ♦♦♦
A multi-artist compilation featuring two Tony McPhee numbers, "You Don't Love Me" and the John Lee Hooker-inspired "Ain't Gonna Cry No More," with the singer supported by Jo-Ann Kelly and Bob Hall. Out-of-print. *—Bruce Eder*

Herbal Mixture-Groundhogs / 1996 / Distortion ♦♦♦♦
First-rate blues and R&B-based rock gives way to psychedelic rock, heavy on the fuzztones and the soulful lead vocals. This could almost be a lost Yardbirds album, and anyone who digs the group's "Heart Full of Soul" period will love this. Three alternate versions of "A Love That's Died" may seem like overkill, but they're each played in completely different fashion, and they're all fascinating. *—Bruce Eder*

Slide, T.S., Slide / Mar. 19, 1996 / M.I.L. Multimedia ♦♦♦
Now this is more like it—Tony McPhee alone in his home studio with just his Yamaha FG180 on the first six tracks, doing whatever comes to mind. Mostly, as the title suggests, he plays some nimble slide guitar through some appropriately raspy-voiced renditions of "Reformed Man," "Mean Disposition," "Tell Me Baby," and the obviously autobiographical "Hooker & the Hogs." The other nine songs were cut solo by McPhee in concert during 1993, and he comes off even better there, his playing even more nimble and his singing far more expressive on songs like Son House's "Death Letter," Muddy Waters' "I Just Can't Be Satisfied," and Howlin' Wolf's "Down In the Bottom" and "No Place To Go," among others. The fidelity on the live stuff, cut with a Yamaha APX-6 in Vienna, is also excellent. *—Bruce Eder*

Me and The Devil/I Asked for Water / Aug. 25, 1998 / BGO ♦♦♦
These two compilations, paired up here on a double-CD set, were just among the many to come out in the late '60s dedicated to British blues. And every single one seemed to feature the remarkable Jo-Ann Kelly (simply one of the best blues singers of any time and place, who sadly, died in 1990) and Tony McPhee, who'd go on to greater fame and fortune and guitarist and leader of the Groundhogs. They were among the leading lights of the scene, and the ones who rose above (even if, ridiculously, Kelly didn't think her voice had matured). But the richness of the scene can be heard from the presence of artists like Andy Fernbach, Simon & Steve, and Dave Kelly, brother to Jo-Ann. John Lewis—who'd reemerge after the heady days of punk as Jona Lewie and score a couple of U.K. novelty hit singles—Brett Marvin and the Thunderbolts (best described as a jug band, one which, like Lewie, earned a pair of British hits), and those who vanished without trace, like Jim Pitts and Graham Hines. The very best of them channel the spirit of the Mississippi Delta in their singing and playing—to hear Kelly and McPhee together on "Oh Death" is a spiritual experience—but the first of the two CDs actually seems to have more depth about it, while the second is content to settle for throwaways like "Crazy With the Blues" or Lewis' "London's Got the Blues," which don't seem to do anyone any favors. The first disc, produced by Mike Batt (of Wombles fame) has more sonic depth, while McPhee's work behind the board on the second is thin—which is surprising, given the fact that some of the tracks, like "She's Gone" by the John Mayall-sounding Andy Fernbach Connexion, feature full electric bands. As snapshots of a time and place, these compilations are invaluable; they let us reflect on the fact that British blues isn't an oxymoron, and that, for a while at least, the quality approached that of Chicago, Memphis, or even Clarksdale. *—Chris Nickson*

Blind Willie McTell (William Samuel McTell)

b. May 5, 1901, Thomson, GA, **d.** Aug. 19, 1959, Milledgeville, GA
Vocals, Accordion, Harmonica, Guitar, Guitar (Acoustic) / East Coast Blues, Piedmont Blues, Prewar Country Blues, Country Blues, Acoustic Blues

Willie Samuel McTell was one of the blues' greatest guitarists, and also one of the finest singers ever to work in blues. A major figure with a local following in Atlanta from the 1920s onward, he recorded dozens of sides throughout the '30s under a multitude of names—all the better to juggle "exclusive" relationships with many different record labels at once—including Blind Willie, Blind Sammie, Hot Shot Willie, and Georgia Bill, as a backup musician to Ruth Mary Willis. And those may not have been all of his pseudonyms—we don't even know what he chose to call himself, although "Blind Willie" was his preferred choice among friends. Much of what we do know about him was learned only years after his death, from family members and acquaintances. His family name was, so far as we know, McTier or McTear, and the origins of the "McTell" name are unclear. What is clear is that he was born into a family filled with musicians—his mother and his father both played guitar, as did one of his uncles, and he was also related to Georgia Tom Dorsey, who later became the Reverend Thomas A. Dorsey.

McTell was born in Thomson, Georgia, near Augusta, and raised near Statesboro. Willie was probably born blind, although early in his life he could perceive light in one eye. His blindness never became a major impediment, however, and it was said that his sense of hearing and touch were extraordinary. His first instruments were the harmonica and the accordion, but as soon as he was big enough he took up the guitar and showed immediate aptitude on the new instrument. He played a standard six-string acoustic until the mid-'20s, and never entirely abandoned the instrument, but from the beginning of his recording career, he used a 12-string acoustic in the studio almost exclusively. Willie's technique on the 12-string instrument was unique. Unlike virtually every other bluesman who used one, he relied not on its resonances as a rhythm instrument, but, instead, displayed a nimble, elegant slide and fingerpicking style that made it sound like more than one guitar at any given moment. He studied at a number of schools for the blind, in Georgia, New York, and Michigan, during the early '20s, and probably picked up some formal musical knowledge. He worked medicine shows, carnivals, and other outdoor venues, and was a popular attraction, owing to his sheer dexterity and a nasal singing voice that could sound either pleasant or mournful, and incorporated some of the characteristics normally associated with White hillbilly singers.

Willie's recording career began in late 1927 with two sessions for Victor records, eight sides including "Statesboro Blues." McTell's earliest sides were superb examples of storytelling in music, coupled with dazzling guitar work. All of McTell's music showed extraordinary power, some of it delightfully raucous ragtime, other examples evoking darker, lonelier sides of the blues, all of it displaying astonishingly rich guitar work.

McTell worked under a variety of names, and with a multitude of partners, including his one-time wife Ruthy Kate Williams (who recorded with him under the name Ruby Glaze), and also Buddy Moss and Curley Weaver. McTell cut some of his best songs more than once in his career. Like many bluesmen, he recorded under different names simultaneously, and was even signed to Columbia and OKeh Records, two companies that ended up merged at the end of the '30s, at the same time under two names. His recording career never gave Willie quite as much success as he had hoped, partly due to the fact that some of his best work appeared during the depths of the Depression. He was uniquely popular in Atlanta, where he continued to live and work throughout most of his career, and, in fact, was the only blues guitarist of any note from the city to remain active in the city until well after World War II.

Willie was well known enough that Library of Congress archivist John Lomax felt compelled to record him in 1940, although during the war, like many other acoustic country bluesmen, his recording career came to a halt. Luckily for Willie and generations of listeners after him, however, there was a brief revival of interest in acoustic country blues after World War II that brought him back into the studio. Amazingly enough, the newly founded Atlantic Records—which was more noted for its recordings of jazz and R&B—took an interest in Willie and cut 15 songs with him in Atlanta during 1949. The one single released from these sessions, however, didn't sell, and most of those recordings remained unheard for more than 20 years after they were made. A year later, however, he was back in the studio, this time with his longtime partner Curley Weaver, cutting songs for the Regal label. None of these records sold especially well, however, and while Willie kept playing to anyone who would listen, the bitter realities of life had finally overtaken him, and he began drinking on a regular basis. He was rediscovered in 1956, just in time to get one more historic session down on tape. He left music soon after, to become a pastor of a local church, and he died of a brain hemorrhage in 1959, his passing so unnoticed at the time that certain reissues in the '70s referred to Willie as still being alive in the '60s.

Blind Willie McTell was one of the giants of the blues, as a guitarist and as a singer and recording artist. Hardly any of his work as passed down to us on record is less than first rate, and this makes most any collection of his music worthwhile. A studious and highly skilled musician whose skills transcended the blues, he was equally adept at ragtime, spirituals, story-songs, hillbilly numbers, and popular tunes, excelling in all of these genres. He could read and write music in braille, which gave him an edge on many of his sighted contemporaries, and was also a brilliant improvisor on the guitar, as is evident from his records. Willie always gave an excellent account of himself, even in his final years of performing and recording. *—Bruce Eder*

☆ **Atlanta Twelve String** / 1949 / Atlantic ✦✦✦✦✦

In 1949, a brief flurry of interest in old-time country blues resulted in this 15-song session by McTell for the newly formed Atlantic Records. Only two songs, "Kill It Kid" and "Broke Down Engine Blues," were ever issued on a failed single, and the session was forgotten until almost 20 years later. McTell is mostly solo here, vividly captured on acoustic 12-string (his sometime partner Curley Weaver may have been present on some tracks), and in excellent form. The playing and the repertory are representative of McTell as he was at this point in his career, a blues veteran rolling through his paces without skipping a beat and quietly electrifying the listener. Songs include "Dying Crapshooter's Blues," "The Razor Ball," and "Ain't I Grand to Live a Christian." *—Bruce Eder*

Last Session / 1960 / Yazoo ✦✦✦✦✦

This recording has a less-than-stellar reputation, principally because it was done so late in McTell's career, and it is true that he lacks some of the edge, especially in his singing, that he showed on his other postwar recordings. On the other hand, his 12-string playing is about as nimble as ever and a real treat. McTell cut these sides for record store owner Ed Rhodes, who had begun taping local bluesmen at his shop in Atlanta in the hope of releasing some of it—McTell took to the idea of recording only slowly, then turned up one night and played for the microphone and anyone who happened to be listening, finishing a pint of bourbon in the process—the result was a pricelessly intimate document, some of the words slurred here and there, but brilliantly expressive and stunningly played. No apologies are needed for "The Dyin' Crapshooter's Blues," "Don't Forget It," or "Salty Dog," however. McTell lived a few more years but never recorded again, which is a pity because based on this tape he still had a lot to show people. Rhodes never did anything with the tapes, and might've junked them if he hadn't remembered how important the McTell material was—they turned out to be the only tapes he saved, out of all he'd recorded. *—Bruce Eder*

Love Changin' Blues / 1968 / Biograph ✦✦✦

This is a nice collection of country blues material from the late '40s, even including a track by blues guitarist Jimmy Rogers, which is tacked onto the end of the second side because it was in the same series of master numbers as the Memphis Minnie session. Fans of Rogers, whose style of blues is quite different than the artists who are mainly featured here, may not even know that this track is lurking quietly in this collection, but the Rogers piece was later folded into other anthologies by this artist. Chances are good the sidemen on this track include Muddy Waters and Little Walter. Both McTell and Memphis Minnie were somewhat advanced guitarists whose playing style owed much to ragtime and swing jazz as well as blues. This gives their music a lighter feel than, for example, the Delta blues influence of Rogers and his partners. The McTell tracks were pretty much discoveries when they were first reissued here, and in some cases are new versions of songs he had recorded, the performances so different that some listeners may not even recognize the originals. He is accompanied by Curley Weaver, playing a regular six-string, while McTell cleanly picks and strums his 12-string, coming up with a sound that is at times similar to Leadbelly but involves much more variation in accompanying figures and seemingly more spontaneous decisions. The Minnie tracks come from Chicago, where this unusual blues artist did most of her recording, creating a legacy as one of the few proficient female blues guitarists. She has the backing of a small band and, although the bass and drums are not identified and verge on inaudible to boot, the pianist is the superb Sunnyland Slim. There are two different versions of her "Night Watchman Blues," and the completely different guitar solos should serve as an explanation of why alternate takes are sometimes fun to have. By compact disc standards, the amount of material here seems a bit on the slim side. *—Eugene Chadbourne*

The Early Years 1927–1933 / 1989 / Yazoo ✦✦✦

This is one of the few Yazoo records that cannot be recommended as a potential first choice, because it was done relatively early. The sound is OK, but the song selection—all made up of pre-World War II material, as usual for Yazoo—is rather paltry compared with McTell collections that have come out since. It's not a bad choice, just not as good as some others, and it does include a decent, if limited, cross-section of early material, including "Statesboro Blues." *—Bruce Eder*

☆ **Complete Recorded Works, Vol. 1 (1927–1931)** / 1990 / Document ✦✦✦✦✦

Of all the compilations of McTell's early work, this is probably the most rewarding, because it includes both his Victor songs (including "Statesboro Blues") and his Columbia sides (which have been issued separately by Columbia-Legacy), and RCA-BMG seems to be in no hurry to put any of the Victor material out as a comprehensive collection. The songs all have some noise—there are no "masters" to speak of on acoustic blues of this vintage—but none of it is overly obtrusive, and the orderly chronology is very illuminating. Subsequent volumes from Document are also worthwhile, but Sony-Legacy does have superior workmanship in dealing with much of the same material. *—Bruce Eder*

Complete Recorded Works, Vol. 2 (1931–1933) / 1990 / Document ✦✦✦✦✦

The second volume in Document's series opens with the first of two October 1931 sessions pairing Blind Willie McTell with the Atlanta street singer Ruth Willis; although her vocals remain the primary focus, these tracks contain some of McTell's most impressive instrumental work, with his playing deceptively simple and loose. Curley Weaver lends second guitar to a number of other performances, allowing McTell's 12-string to return to its proper position of prominence; also included are his early excursions into gospel, with performances of "Lord Have Mercy If You Please" and "Don't You See How This World Made a Change" distinguished by some devastating slide work. *—Jason Ankeny*

Complete Recorded Works, Vol. 3 (1933–1935) / 1990 / Document ✦✦✦✦✦

Blind Willie McTell's final prewar sessions are the subject of the third and last disc in Document's series. The set begins with a September 1933 session covering a wide range of stylistic ground, ranging from the songster staple "Honey Fare Thee Well" (covered here as "East St. Louis Blues") to Bumble Bee Slim's "B and O Blues"; most remarkable is "Bell Street Lightnin'," a gripping and vivid portrait of Depression-era life at its most tragic. The final dates, from April 1935, comprise McTell's material for Decca, recorded with wife Kate and guitarist Curley Weaver; assembled in large part of gospel material, they also include "Hillbilly Willie's Blues," an overt and hugely entertaining attempt to appeal to the Southern white listening audience. *—Jason Ankeny*

☆ **Pig 'n Whistle Red** / 1993 / Biograph ✦✦✦✦✦

This collection of 20 songs, cut by McTell with Curley Weaver on second guitar and sharing the vocals, was left out of many McTell biographical accounts until it resurfaced in 1993. Cut for Regal Records in 1950, it's a remarkable document, capturing McTell and Weaver in vivid modern sound, and includes remakes of McTell's 1933 "Talkin' to You Mama" and "Good Little Thing" as well as more recent material that the two had been doing, and even outtakes, showing very different interpretations of the 1920s pop standard "Pal of Mine" and the gospel number "Sending Up My Timber." The sheer diversity of material makes this an indispensable (as well as a delightful) recording, and except for some minor tape damage on "A to Z Blues" and one other cut, there are few technical flaws here. The playing is so sharp and crisp, and vocals so delicate in their textures, that this collection has to be considered essential to any serious blues collection. McTell and Weaver were a legendary duo in Atlanta from before World War II, and it is nothing less than a gift to have them still together and in excellent form on this postwar recording. *—Bruce Eder*

★ **The Definitive Blind Willie McTell** / 1994 / Columbia/Legacy ✦✦✦✦✦

This double-CD set is a little misleading. It is definitive, but only in terms of McTell's Columbia and OKeh sides—you won't find "Statesboro Blues" or his other earliest sides here, because they were done for Victor. But the material that is here is all worthwhile, and this is the best single source for McTell's work for those labels (done under a variety of names) from the mid-'30s, very nicely remastered and thoroughly annotated, although producer Lawrence Cohn concedes that even Sony Legacy was unable to locate sources on a handful of songs that McTell is known to have recorded. *—Bruce Eder*

Stomp Down Rider, 1927–1931 / 1995 / Collectables ✦✦✦

The Complete Victor Recordings 1927–1932 / Oct. 1995 / Victor ✦✦✦

Victor Recordings 1927–1934 / Jan. 30, 1996 / BMG ✦✦✦

Medicine Head

f. 1968, Stafford, England, **db.** 1976

Group / British Blues

Formed in Stafford, England in 1968, the British blues duo Medicine Head comprised vocalist/multi-instrumentalist John Fiddler and Peter Hope-Evans, who played the harmonica and Jew's harp. Upon their formation at art college, Medicine Head became a staple of the local club circuit, eventually recording a demo which found its way to influential BBC radio personality John Peel, who began championing the track "His Guiding Hand." Other DJs soon followed suit, and quickly the duo was on the brink of stardom.

With Peel's continued assistance, Medicine Head entered the studio to begin recording their 1970 debut LP *New Bottles Old Medicine*. Their focus shifted from basic blues to a more intricate sound for 1971's *Heavy on the Drum*, produced by former Yardbird Keith Relf; after scoring a surprise hit with the single "(And the) Pictures in the Sky," Hope-Evans left the group, and was replaced by Relf and drummer John Davies for 1972's *The Dark Side of the Moon*. Hope-Evans rejoined prior to 1973's *One & One Is One*, which launched the title track to the Top Three of the U.K. singles chart.

Now a five-piece also including guitarist Roger Saunders, onetime Family drummer Rob Townsend and bassist George Ford, Medicine Head notched two more hit singles, "Rising Sun" and "Slip and Slide," but 1974's *Thru' a Five* failed to chart, and the group began to disintegrate. Only Fiddler and Hope-Evans remained by the time of 1976's *Two Man Band*, and after one last single, "Me and Suzy Hit the Floor," Medicine Head officially disbanded. Fiddler later resurfaced in the British Lions, followed by a stint in Box of Frogs and finally a solo career, while Hope-Evans contributed to the Pete Townshend albums *Empty Glass* and *White City*. *—Jason Ankeny*

New Bottles Old Medicine / 1970 / Repertoire ✦✦✦

One of the most refreshing hits of the very early '70s was Medicine Head's "Pictures in the Sky," a song so subtly woven and effortlessly understated that it was almost difficult to actually hear it; rather, you absorbed it straight into your subconscious, then wandered round wondering what it was you were humming. That was the band's first hit single, and their first album, one should not be too shocked to discover, is basically cut from the same cloth. True, not every track is so superbly sublime; true, not every melody as deeply, darkly haunted. But two guys with a Jew's Harp, a handheld drum, a harmonica, and an acoustic guitar nevertheless make mountains move, and would probably have moved them even further if they'd recorded the hit in time for the album. Unfortunately, they didn't. The opening "When Night Falls" sets the scene instead, haunted harp and funereal pounding keeping time behind vocalist John Fiddler's lonesome, confessional lyric. There's a ghostly Dylan air to a lot of Medicine Head's early work, and this one shows you where it came from. Or maybe that honor should go to "Ooee Baby," which throws a muddy riff, a bluesy holler, and a driving rhythm into play and spins all expectations for the album upside down. Judas could not have turned out more shocking. Those moods continue through the album: one moment reflective, one moment boisterous, but always loose and laconic enough to remind you just what kind of arsenal was making all the noise. Like Mungo Jerry, the only other band of the era capable of making such a racket with the minimum of rock toys, Medicine Head's achievement isn't simply in writing and performing such memorable songs. It lies in making them sound so memorable as well, and *New Bottles* overflows with that magic. *—Dave Thompson*

Heavy on the Drum / 1971 / Dandelion ♦♦♦

Dark Side of the Moon / 1972 / Dandelion ♦♦♦

One & One Is One / 1973 / Polydor ♦♦♦
Riding on the back of two successive U.K. hit singles, the jerkily insistent "Rising Sun" and the quietly lazy "One and One Is One," Medicine Head's fourth album captures the duo expanding and electrifying with maniacal zeal. Without sacrificing the understated joys which were Medicine Head's traditional calling cards, *One & One Is One* is littered with unexpected flourishes and accents, bass and keyboards (courtesy of producer Tony Asheton) underpinning the sparseness with a warm, subtle flair: the traffic sounds which wrap up the opening "Out on the Street," the slinky bass line bleeding through "Another Lay," the jabbing guitar and squelching organ which propel "Rising Sun." Of course it's business as usual around these highlights. The skiffle/jug jollity of "How Does It Feel" could have slipped on or off any past Medicine Head album, while the gentle acoustics of "Morning Light" and "Instant Karma Kid" are potent reminders of Fiddler's songwriting genius at its most naked. But if Medicine Head once hid their lights beneath a bushel of eclectic solitude, *One & One Is One* is the sound of them inching into a wider world—and a weirder one. The closing "All the Fallen Teenangels" is archetypal Medicine Head. But it also has a reggae beat. And if that doesn't leave you feeling absolutely dislocated, nothing will. *—Dave Thompson*

● **New Bottles, Old Medicine . . . Plus** / 1995 / See for Miles ♦♦♦♦♦
See for Miles' reissue of Medicine Head's 1970 debut album *New Bottles, Old Medicine* is augmented by a couple of bonus tracks, but the record remains the group's best and bluesiest effort. Medicine Head was never one of the best British blues bands, but there are enough good moments on the record to make it of interest to collectors of that style. *—Thom Owens*

Live at the Marquee 1975 / May 29, 2001 / Angel Air ♦♦
Recorded near the end of their career, these performances feature Medicine Head in their two-man-band incarnation, with Peter Hope-Evans on vocals, harmonica, and Jew's harp, and John Fiddler on everything else, which included guitars, drums, and more harmonica. Fiddler's playing in particular is impressive for coaxing a lot of sound out of several instruments simultaneously, although it does mean that the drums move toward rudimentary thumping. It's good-natured bluesy, folky rock that sometimes explores a gently contemplative air, and sometimes goes into more standard blues-rock stomp. Fiddler gets a nice trembly sound from his guitar on the slower, folkier tunes. It's not as derivative as much British rock of the kind in the early to mid-'70s, and it's not all that interesting either, other than the aforementioned achievement of getting such a full sound from two musicians. The sound is alright, but a little hollow, which slides this further into the area of "essential for fans only." Those fans, though, will like the packaging, as the liner notes include a thorough band history and discography, even down to a complete (and surprisingly long) list of the sessions they did on Britain's Radio 1, replete with dates and song titles. As another bonus, there's a home demo of "Pictures in the Sky" with ex-Yardbirds singer Keith Relf on guitar. *—Richie Unterberger*

Best of Medicine Head / Nov. 6, 2001 / Music Club ♦♦♦♦

Meditation Singers

f. 1947, Detroit, MI
Group / Traditional Gospel, Black Gospel
While never achieving the national popularity of contemporaries like the Ward Singers or the Caravans, the Meditation Singers were indisputably the premier Detroit-based female gospel group of the '50s; the first Motor City act to reject a cappella vocal traditions in favor of instrumental backing, their ranks also produced a pair of secular pop stars in Della Reese and Laura Lee. Formed in 1947 as a product of Detroit's New Liberty Baptist Church's renowned Moments of Meditation choir, the Meditation Singers were primarily led by Earnestine Rundless, the wife of onetime Soul Stirrer E.A. Rundless. Created in response to calls from other churches seeking the Moments of Meditation to perform, the group was originally an octet, but their size made crosstown travel prohibitive; upon trimming down to a quartet, the Meditation Singers' original lineup comprised Rundless, Reese (who often assumed lead duties as well), alto Marie Waters (Reese's sister), and soprano Lillian Mitchell.

As the Meditations' notoriety quickly spread, they began performing throughout the Midwest, and in early 1953 cut their first session at a local record store. Reese left the group to pursue pop success soon after, and was replaced by Lee, Rundless' teenage daughter; unbeknownst to the Meditations, their record was then licensed to the Deluxe label, and in short time they were signed to Specialty. By the time of their next session in the spring of 1954, their studio lineup also included co-lead Carrie Williams, tenor Herbert Carson, and pianist Emory Radford; Williams remained with the group only briefly before returning to Detroit to operate a beauty salon, while Carson later enlisted with the Herman Stevens Singers, among others. Poor sales prompted Specialty to drop the Meditations, who then spent the middle years of the '50s concentrating on the road; by the end of the decade, however, they were working regularly with the legendary James Cleveland, and his involvement led Specialty to offer a new contract.

The Meditations' third Specialty session followed in mid-1959; however, the label soon exited the gospel business altogether, and a fourth session never materialized. Instead, the group signed to the Hob label, recording once more with Cleveland before he left their ranks. Over the course of the '60s, the Meditations appeared on a series of labels, among them SAR, Chess, Checker, Savoy and Jewel; they also toured constantly, in 1962 becoming one of the first gospel acts ever to play Las Vegas when they backed Reese during a performance at the Flamingo Casino. Their performance there even caught the attention of Frank Sinatra, who singled out Lee's potential for pop stardom; she remained with the group until 1965, at which time she moved into secular soul music and later scored a hit with "Women's Love Rights." The Meditations carried on in her absence, continuing to tour regularly until the early '80s. *—Jason Ankeny*

● **Good News** / 1992 / Specialty ♦♦♦♦♦

Change Is Gonna Come / Sep. 23, 1994 / Jewel ♦♦♦
Earnestine Rundless and the gals shake up the church. *—Opal Louis Nations*

Alright / Jewel ♦♦

Mellow Fellows

f. Chicago, IL
Group / Contemporary Blues, Modern Electric Chicago Blues, Modern Electric Blues
Now known as The Chicago Rhythm And Blues Kings, The Mellow Fellows held their personnel together after the 1990 death of singer Larry "Big Twist" Nolan. Saxist Terry Ogolini and guitarist Pete Special, co-founders of the group, recruited Twist's pal Martin Allbritton to front the band, and they cut the buoyant *Street Party* for Alligator in 1990 with part-time member Gene "Daddy G" Barge helping out on sax and vocals. When Special split, the band switched-to its current regal billing. *—Bill Dahl*

● **Street Party** / 1990 / Alligator ♦♦♦♦
Martin Allbritton, a melismatic and undeniably more powerful vocalist than the finesse-oriented Twist, proves an eminently worthy successor to the beloved big man on this highly enjoyable effort. Barge also pitches in with a few lead vocals as the group attacks a handful of joyous originals ("We'll Be Friends," "Street Party," "Broad Daylight") and storming R&B classics by Sam & Dave and Harold Burrage. *—Bill Dahl*

Memphis Jug Band

f. Memphis, TN
Group / Prewar Country Blues, Acoustic Memphis Blues, Jug Band
One of the definitive jug bands of the '20s and early '30s, this seminal group was comprised of Will Shade, Will Weldon, Hattie Hart, Charlie Polk, Walter Horton, and others, in various configurations.

Guitarist/harpist Will Shade formed the Memphis Jug Band in the Beale Street section of Memphis in the mid-'20s. A few years after their formation, Shade signed a contract with Victor Records in 1927. Over the next seven years, Shade and the Memphis Jug Band recorded nearly 60 songs for the record label. During this time, a number of musicians passed through the group, including Big Walter Horton, Furry Lewis, and Casey Bill Weldon. Throughout all of the various lineup incarnations, Shade provided direction for the group. The Memphis Jug Band played a freewheeling mixture of blues, ragtime, vaudeville, folk, and jazz, which was all delivered with good-time humor. That loose spirit kept the group and its records popular throughout the early '30s.

Although the group's popularity dipped sharply in the mid-'30s, Will Shade continued to lead the group in various incarnations until his death in 1966. *—Cub Koda & Stephen Thomas Erlewine*

★ **Memphis Jug Band** / 1990 / Yazoo ♦♦♦♦♦
This Yazoo label collection has been the definitive release of Memphis Jug Band recordings for decades. While it's a little hard to forgive them for leaving off five of the songs from the original double-LP release on this CD reissue (look at the cover: you'll see half of the "8" in "28 Songs" blacked out to make the cover read "23 Songs"!), who's to complain—it's great to have this collection available again. This sampling is a fine document of the raw and irreverent music made by this historic, fun-loving jug band. The included recordings span 1927 to 1934, and less than half of the songs are found on the 2001 *Best of the Memphis Jug Band.* Whichever one is picked, anybody who is a fan of early blues needs to own a Memphis Jug Band release. *—Joslyn Layne*

Complete Recorded Works, Vol. 1 (1927–1928) / 1990 / Document ♦♦♦♦♦
One of the greatest of all jug bands and possibly the most influential, the Memphis Jug Band recorded extensively from 1927-1930. All of its recordings (other than three sessions from 1934) have been reissued by the European Document label on three CDs. The original version of the group consisted of Will Shade on harmonica, guitar and/or vocals; Ben Ramey on kazoo; guitarist/signer Will Weldon; and Charlie Polk on jug. During the year-long period covered in this CD, the only significant personnel change was the addition of Vol Stevens on banjo-mandolin and guitar. The good-time music that they performed ranged from blues to pop numbers and even a couple waltzes. All three of the Document CDs are fairly equal in quality, with the second volume getting a slight edge. Among the highlights of *Vol. 1* are "Memphis Jug Blues," "I Packed My Suitcase, Started to the Train," "Kansas City Blues" (recorded just a few days after Jim Jackson's famous version), the heated "Beale Street Mess Around" and a previously unreleased "She Stays Out All Night Long." Fun music that still communicates to today's listeners. *—Scott Yanow*

☆ **Complete Recorded Works, Vol. 2 (1928–1929)** / 1990 / Document ✦✦✦✦

The Memphis Jug Band was quite popular from 1927-1930, particularly if one judges the group by its many recordings (which fill up three CDs in this series). The second volume has slightly better material than the other two CDs, but all are easily recommended. During 1928 and 1929 the Memphis Jug Band featured its leader Will Shade on guitar, harmonica and vocals, and guitarist Charlie Burse (guitarist Will Weldon and banjo-mandolist Vol Stevens from the first group departed by 1929). The band also included the highly expressive kazoo playing of Ben Ramey and Jab Jones' enthusiastic jug playing (an improvement on his predecessor Charlie Polk). Additionally, there are two selections included in which the band accompanies singer Minnie Wallace and there are a few guest musicians and singers on various tracks. Among the many high points of the spirited program are "She Stays Out All Night Long," "Lindberg Hop," "Stealin' Stealin'," "Jug Band Waltz," "The Old Folks Started It" and "Memphis Yo Yo Blues." An important if often overlooked genre of vintage American music. —*Scott Yanow*

☆ **Complete Recorded Works, Vol. 3 (1930)** / 1990 / Document ✦✦✦✦✦

The third of three Document CDs has all of the Memphis Jug Band's 1930 recordings. Despite the onset of the Depression, the influential band's good-time style was unchanged and actually had improved a bit during the past couple of years. Will Shade was still its leader and alternated between guitar, harmonica and vocals. The other original member was Ben Ramey on kazoo. During 1930, such players as mandolinist Charlie Burse, Hambone Lewis and Jab Jones on jug, singer Charlie Nickerson, Vol Stevens on banjo & mandolin and even guest vocalist/guitarist Memphis Minnie (on "Bumble Bee Blues" and "Meningitis Blues") passed through the band. Among the more memorable selections of their highly enjoyable CD are "Everybody's Talking About Sadie Green," "Cocaine Habit Blues," "Fourth Street Mess Around," "Going Back to Memphis," "Move that Thing" and "He's in the Jailhouse Now." —*Scott Yanow*

Complete Recorded Works (1932–1934) / 1990 / Document ✦✦✦

The Document collection *Complete Recorded Works (1932-1934)* is an exhaustive overview of the Memphis Jug Band's early-'30s records, including 16 sides recorded in 1934 and five tracks from the associated Picaninny Jug Band recorded in 1932. The emphasis on archival performances and exacting chronological sequencing can be off-putting for casual listeners, though serious blues enthusiasts will find much here to enjoy. —*Thom Owens*

State of Tennessee Blues / Nov. 21, 1995 / Memphis Archives ✦✦✦✦

State of Tennessee Blues offers 18 tracks from the miraculous Memphis Jug Band, all recorded between 1927 and 1929, during the first three years of the group's collective career. Though the band recorded a number of exuberant, jazz-oriented breakdowns, particularly during its post-Depression resurgence, *State of Tennessee Blues* tends typically toward its more plaintive, slow-dragging moments—dirge-like, whiskey-drenched, and gravelly, invested with the steady rocking rhythms of work and of sex, of the good-times dancing construed as a defense from the blues. The group's versatility remains evident throughout the collection, enhanced by the fine contributions of an ever-shifting membership of Memphis musicians. Perpetually at the helm is the arguably ingenious, multi-faceted Will Shade, joined at turns by Vol Stevens on mandolin, Charlie Burse or Will Weldon on guitar, and Jab Jones on jug; singer Jennie Clayton joins the number on the title track and on a couple of others, providing near-tortured vocals on "Bob Lee Junior Blues," which evolves in the end into a pounding instrumental take on "Careless Love." Though this collection lacks such "greatest hits" as "Stealin' Stealin'" or "K.C. Moan," Memphis Jug Band seems incapable of turning out a single dud, and the more obscure titles are richly entertaining and endlessly soulful. State of Tennessee Blues offers considerably good sound quality and no overlap with Yazoo's definitive *Memphis Jug Band* collection. Though the Yazoo album may provide the beginner's best introduction to the band, this compilation, released by the Memphis Archives label, is also a first-rate testament to one of the finest down-home outfits of its or any other era. —*Burgin Mathews*

The Memphis Jug Band Story: 1927–1934 / Apr. 11, 2000 / EPM Musique ✦✦✦✦

This 23-track set brings together all the early recordings by the Memphis Jug Band and various offshoot groups. On these sides is a large chunk of early Memphis music, well documented and beautifully transferred off the original 78s. Featuring guest shots from Memphis Minnie, Hattie Hart, and Minnie Wallace, this gathers up a portion of early blues history that seldom gets documented with such care. Well done. —*Cub Koda*

The Essential Memphis Jug Band / May 1, 2001 / Classic Blues ✦✦✦

The Best of the Memphis Jug Band / Jun. 12, 2001 / Yazoo ✦✦✦✦✦

The liner notes implicitly state that no other jug band surpassed the Memphis Jug Band in breadth and scope. They played all styles—blues, rags, and pop—and performed them better than their competitors. Since few listeners or reviewers are experts on jug bands, there is little use in arguing the point. All one need do is place *The Best of the Memphis Jug Band* in the disc player and listen. There are classics like "Cocaine Habit Blues" ("Hey, hey honey take a whiff on me") and the Jimmie Rodgers hit "He's in the Jailhouse Now." Utilizing banjo, guitar, harmonic, a jug, and a kazoo, Will Shade and a number of cohorts stick to a relaxed groove on catchy pieces like "She Stays Out All Night Long" and the bluesy "Meningitis Blues." Deadheads will also recognize old favorites like "On the Road Again" and "Stealin' Stealin'," leftover from the Grateful Dead's jug band days. The Memphis Jug Band plays with a tranquil surety, perfectly in sync with one another on songs like "State of Tennessee Blues." A helpful essay by Don Kent and Bengt Olsson reviews the history of the band, while the song notes list the individual players on each track (a non-existent piece of knowledge on many early recording sessions). The recording quality is also good. *The Best of the Memphis Jug Band* offers 70 minutes of first-rate

traditional music and is a fine introduction to the band. It's also a necessary addition to the music library of anyone who appreciates old-time music. —*Ronnie D. Lankford Jr.*

Memphis Minnie (Lizzie Douglas)

b. Jun. 3, 1897, Algiers, LA, d. Aug. 6, 1973, Memphis, TN

Vocals, Guitar, Banjo / Prewar Country Blues, Acoustic Chicago Blues, Acoustic Memphis Blues, Classic Female Blues, Acoustic Blues

Tracking down the ultimate woman blues guitar hero is problematic because woman blues singers seldom recorded as guitar players and woman guitar players (such as Rosetta Tharpe and Sister O.M. Terrell) were seldom recorded playing blues. Excluding contemporary artists, the most notable exception to this pattern was Memphis Minnie. The most popular and prolific blueswoman outside the vaudeville tradition, she earned the respect of critics, the support of record-buying fans, and the unqualified praise of the blues artists she worked with throughout her long career.

Despite her Southern roots and popularity, she was as much a Chicago blues artist as anyone in her day. Big Bill Broonzy recalls her beating both him and Tampa Red in a guitar contest and claims she was the best woman guitarist he had ever heard. Tough enough to endure in a hard business, she earned the respect of her peers with her solid musicianship and recorded good blues over four decades for Columbia, Vocalion, Bluebird, OKeh, Regal, Checker, and JOB. She also proved to have as good taste in musical husbands as music and sustained working marriages with guitarists Casey Bill Weldon, Joe McCoy, and Ernest Lawlers. Their guitar duets span the spectrum of African-American folk and popular music, including spirituals, comic dialogs, and old-time dance pieces, but Memphis Minnie's best work consisted of deep blues like "Moaning the Blues." More than a good woman blues guitarist and singer, Memphis Minnie holds her own against the best blues artists of her time, and her work has special resonance for today's aspiring guitarists. —*Barry Lee Pearson*

Blues Classics by Memphis Minnie / Oct. 1965 / Blues Classics ✦✦✦✦✦

This artist recorded more than 200 different sides between the late '20s and late '50s, not bad considering the hard row she had to hoe as one of the few female guitar pickers in the business, let alone a blues player. Despite the obvious presence of women as blues singers, even the commonly used name for a blues musician, "bluesman," defines a masculine gender. While it is considered all right for a woman to have a guitar draped around her neck while looking pretty on stage, the serious female guitar stranglers are few and far between, and can look up to Memphis Minnie as one of their goddesses. She is a great guitarist whose approach to blues is more along the lines of a the fluid versatility of Tampa Red, who she apparently bested in a musical cutting contest once, than the stark intensity of a John Lee Hooker or Muddy Waters. Her rhythmic chordal accompaniment has an accuracy in terms of tempo that is sweet and uncanny. This gives her music a swinging feeling that eludes many other blues artists completely. In fact, the amount of momentum achieved without ever really seeming to break a sweat is a marvel here, and could serve as valuable instruction to many an over-baked performer. Her vocal style is marvelously unforced, going through appealing stylistic changes as these tracks jump around between 1929 and 1942, including solos as well as small-band efforts including bass and the piano talents of Black Bob. She is a simply a classic blues artist, and anyone who doesn't believe it can look at this record as sheer evidence. After all, it is not only entitled *Blues Classics*, it is on the Blues Classics label and is even the first record ever released by this lovable outfit, whose thick and sturdy black-and-white packaging has survived the test of time in terms of both appeal and construction. —*Eugene Chadbourne*

I Ain't No Bad Gal / 1988 / Portrait ✦✦✦

Minnie was the toughest guitar-picking femme of bluesdom, with plugged-in 1941 performances that included "Me and My Chauffeur Blues." —*Mark A. Humphrey*

Complete Recorded Works, Vol. 1 (1929–1930) / 1991 / Document ✦✦✦✦✦

Complete Recorded Works, Vol. 2 (1930–1931) / 1991 / Document ✦✦✦✦✦

Document's *Complete Recorded Works, Vol. 2 (1930-1931)* reissues 23 sides from Memphis Minnie and Kansas Joe, including classics like "Memphis Minnie-Jitis Blues," "Frankie Jean (That Trottin' Fool)," and a version of "Bumble Bee." Still, the lengthy running time, poor sound quality, and all conspire to cut into the collection's casual listenability of this compilation. —*Thom Owens*

Complete Recorded Works, Vol. 3 (1931–1932) / 1991 / Document ✦✦✦

The third volume in Document's series picks up in early 1931, with the Depression era in full swing; although Memphis Minnie and Kansas Joe were still actively recording, very little of their material was actually seeing release. Ironically, these were some of the duo's finest sides to date, with Minnie's vocals and guitar work achieving new peaks of poignancy and intensity; with "Shake Mattie" and "My Wash Woman's Gone," she introduces her bottleneck style, while on "Let's Go to Town" she and Joe face off in a fiery instrumental duel. The latter half of the collection, recorded in New York, focuses on more traditional material; their rendition of the minstrel song "Fishin' Blues" is widely assumed to be the inspiration for subsequent versions by Son House, Bumble Bee Slim and many others. —*Jason Ankeny*

Complete Recorded Works, Vol. 4 (1933–1934) / 1991 / Document ✦✦✦

Although the title credits the material herein to Memphis Minnie and Kansas Joe, very few of the tracks which comprise this volume are actually collaborative efforts between the duo—by 1933 their personal and professional relationships were both on the rocks, with Minnie instead recording solo and Joe working with his guitarist brother Charlie. The Minnie solo sides which open the set are uniformly excellent, with the saucy "My Butcher Man" spotlighting her gifts as a lyricist and the Mississippi-styled "Too Late" underscoring her guitar prowess. By mid-1934, some measure of reconciliation had clearly been reached, as the couple was now performing together again; although their reunion was short-lived—and their subsequent break final—these last sides are also powerful, with the revealing "Moaning the Blues" capping their career in peak form. *—Jason Ankeny*

☆ **And Kansas Joe: 1929–1934** / 1991 / Document ✦✦✦✦✦
Minnie's earliest recordings with husband Kansas Joe McCoy. Includes "I Want That," "Bumble Bee," "Squat It," "I Don't Want That Junk Outta You," and the original version of "When the Levee Breaks," later covered by (and re-credited to) Led Zeppelin. *—Cub Koda*

Complete Recorded Works, Vol. 1 (1935) / 1991 / Document ✦✦✦✦✦
The first volume in Document's series of Memphis Minnie solo recordings collects the material she cut in Chicago over a period of six sessions between the first weeks of 1935 and Halloween of that same year. Her first sides following her personal and professional breakup with Kansas Joe McCoy, the material suggests a rebirth of sorts, marked by a new sense of experimentation—two tracks, "Let Me Ride" and "When the Saints Go Marching Home," are pure gospel, while "Ball and Chain Blues" is her first step into the band style prevalent at the end of the '30s. Among the other highlights are the tracks from her final Decca session, a solo date which spotlights her amazing guitar work. *—Jason Ankeny*

Complete Recorded Works, Vol. 2 (1935–1936) / 1991 / Document ✦✦✦
The second volume in Document's series of *Complete Recorded Works*, covering Memphis Minnie, includes a few classic performances, like "Ice Man (Come on Up)" and "New Orleans Stop Time" (the latter finding her co-billed with Bumble Bee Slim). Still, casual fans will find the disc a mixed blessing; the lengthy running time and poor fidelity will prompt many listeners to look elsewhere. *—Thom Owens*

Complete Recorded Works, Vol. 3 (1937) / 1991 / Document ✦✦✦
Volume three in Document's series continues where the previous collection left off, with Memphis Minnie still in the midst of her so-called "band period"; beginning here with a series of mid-1937 dates, her backing musicians include both a trumpeter and a pianist (presumably Black Bob Hudson), although their subtle performances allow Minnie to take full command of the material in ways her recent sessions had not. New Orleans clarinetist Arnett Nelson is on hand for the remaining sides, most of which were previously unissued. *—Jason Ankeny*

Complete Recorded Works, Vol. 4 (1938–1939) / 1991 / Document ✦✦✦
The fourth volume in the series opens with Memphis Minnie's lone 1938 studio date; backed by mandolinist (and former brother-in-law) Charlie McCoy, the session possesses elements of the classic string band sound, with sides like "I'd Rather See Him Dead" and "Good Biscuits" among the most sexually explicit in her catalog. The remaining material, all cut in February 1939, is comprised of guitar-duet accompaniments with Ernest "Little Son Joe" Lawlers, heralding the format consistent throughout the majority of Minnie's prewar recordings; indeed, as stellar performances of "Keep Your Big Mouth Closed" and "Low Down Man Blues" indicate, perhaps no other arrangement was more ideally suited to her unique style. *—Jason Ankeny*

Complete Recorded Works, Vol. 5 (1940–1941) / 1991 / Document ✦✦✦✦✦
The fifth and final volume in Document's series begins with a mid-1940 studio date, Memphis Minnie's first in over a year; recorded with Little Son Joe on second guitar, these simple, unaffected sides are among her strongest, with tracks like "Ma Rainey" (a tribute to the recently deceased blues great) and "Nothing in Rambling" brimming with confidence and inspiration. Her final prewar session, recorded late in 1941, closes out the set; performing on amplified guitar, Minnie's music adopts a relatively urbanized sound on tracks like the superb "I Am Sailin'" and "Don't Turn the Card," precipitating the Chicago blues of the postwar era. *—Jason Ankeny*

★ **Hoodoo Lady (1933–1937)** / Apr. 15, 1991 / Columbia/Legacy ✦✦✦✦✦
Memphis Minnie is a unique figure in blues history, a female country blues singer who emerged in the late 1920s when the field (at least on record) was exclusively filled by men. But, gender aside, she was one of the most talented blues singer-guitarists of the '30s and '40s. This CD reissue primarily dates from her period between her partnerships with Cousin Joe and Little Son Joe. Minnie is heard mostly playing her variations of goodtime urban blues (à la Bill Broonzy), an even 12 bars to a chorus but with the feeling and emotion of the country blues. Pianist Blind John Davis and Charlie McCoy's mandolin help out on some of the tracks of the accessible set which serves as a fine introduction to Memphis Minnie; five of its 20 selections were previously unreleased. *—Scott Yanow*

Early Rhythm & Blues from the Rare Regal Sessions: 1934–1942 / 1992 / Biograph ✦✦✦✦✦
You can't go wrong with Memphis Minnie at almost any point in her estimable career. During the '30s and early '40s, she made the adjustment to changing styles, but in the early '30s she *made* the style. The sound quality is pretty good throughout the set, although it's better on the later tunes. *—Ron Wynn*

Queen of the Blues / Oct. 7, 1997 / Columbia/Legacy ✦✦✦✦✦
Eighteen stellar selections recorded between 1929 and 1946 that clearly show what a potent musical force this woman truly was. Working with second and third husbands Kansas Joe McCoy and Ernest "Little Son Joe" Lawlars, this was a prime period for Minnie's creativity, going from the lowdown blues of "Has Anyone Seen My Man?" to the celebratory novelty of "Joe Louis Strut." Three of the tracks here ("Fashion Plate Daddy," "Killer Diller Blues" and "Please Don't Stop Him") are previously unissued, and the disc transfers are clean and sharp throughout. This perfect little primer set also includes the original version of "When the Levee Breaks," later recorded and partially credited to Led Zeppelin. *—Cub Koda*

Volume 1 (1944–1946) / Jun. 19, 1998 / Wolf ✦✦✦

Volume 2 (1946–1947) / Jun. 19, 1998 / Wolf ✦✦✦

Me & My Chauffeur Blues / Jun. 6, 2000 / Aim ✦✦✦✦
This Australian export brings together 18 classic recordings from the peaks of Minnie's career. Decent transfers of the rare 78s make this a better than average listening experience and what the liner notes leave out in recording dates and other information, it gives back with a good bio and a good understanding of the material. With classics aboard like "Bumble Bee," "Memphis Minnie-Jitis Blues," and the title track, it's hard to fault this one as a first purchase to investigate one of the grandest ladies of the blues. *—Cub Koda*

Travelling Blues / Aldabra ✦✦✦✦✦
Travelling Blues collects a number of sessions recorded with Kansas Joe McCoy, Memphis Minnie's second husband. Make no mistake about it—with her impassioned vocals, Memphis Minnie controls these recordings. Although most of these cuts are available on better collections, this album sounds fine and contains a wealth of terrific music. *—Thom Owens*

With Kansas Joe / Blues Classics ✦✦✦✦✦
When she was married to Kansas Joe McCoy, Memphis Minnie was making wailing blues, memorable laments and brilliant double entendre tunes. He in turn supplied her with excellent accompaniment and nice complementary vocals. These are simply marvelous songs. *—Ron Wynn*

The Memphis Pilgrims

f. Memphis, TN
Group / Roots Rock, Blues-Rock

The Memphis Pilgrims, led by guitarist, singer and songwriter Michael Falzarano, have one album out on the Brooklyn-based Relix Records label. Falzarano is a name familiar to followers of Hot Tuna guitarist Jorma Kaukonen; the two frequently perform together at coffeehouses and clubs around the U.S. and Europe. Falzarano's songs appear on the Hot Tuna albums *A Pair a Dice Found* and *Live at Sweetwater*. Falzarano has also written songs for several of Kaukonen's solo albums, including *Land of Heroes* and *Christmas*, both for the American Heritage label.

The group plays heavily blues-based melodic roots-rock. Members of the Memphis Pilgrims include guitarist Jimmy Eppard, bassist Steve Rust, drummer Harvey Sorgen and keyboardist/accordionist Adam Hurwitz. All have extensive backgrounds as sidemen and studio session musicians. Eppard, based in Woodstock, NY, has recorded with members of the Band, the New Bohemians, Pete Seeger and Orleans. Eppard is also an accomplished lap steel and slide guitar player. Bassist Rust has performed with jazz flutist Hubert Laws, Sam and Dave and jazz saxophonist Nick Brignola. Drummer/percussionist Sorgen has performed and recorded with Ahmad Jamal, Bill Frisell, NRBQ, David Torn and Jack DeJohnette. Keyboardist and accordionist Hurwitz has worked with the Band and Ronnie Hawkins, among others.

Their debut album, *Mecca*, blends elements of rockabilly, blues and soul music with the band's roots-rock base. *—Richard Skelly*

● **Mecca** / 1996 / Relix ✦✦✦

Memphis Slim (John Peter Chatman)

b. Sep. 3, 1915, Memphis, TN, **d.** Feb. 24, 1988, Paris, France
Vocals, Piano / Piano Blues, Acoustic Blues

An amazingly prolific artist who brought a brisk air of urban sophistication to his frequently stunning presentation, John "Peter" Chatman—better known as Memphis Slim—assuredly ranks with the greatest blues pianists of all time. He was smart enough to take Big Bill Broonzy's early advice about developing a style to call his own to heart, instead of imitating that of his idol, Roosevelt Sykes. Soon enough, other 88s pounders were copying Slim rather than the other way around; his thundering ivories attack set him apart from most of his contemporaries, while his deeply burnished voice possessed a commanding authority.

As befits his stage name, John "Peter" Chatman was born and raised in Memphis; a great place to commit to a career as a bluesman. Sometime in the late '30s, he resettled in Chicago and began recording as a leader in 1939 for OKeh, then switched over to Bluebird the next year. Around the same time, Slim joined forces with Broonzy, then the dominant force on the local blues scene. After serving as Broonzy's invaluable accompanist for a few years, Slim emerged as his own man in 1944.

After the close of World War II, Slim joined Hy-Tone Records, cutting eight tracks that were later picked up by King. Lee Egalnick's Miracle label reeled in the pianist in 1947; backed by his jumping band, the House Rockers (its members usually included saxists Alex Atkins and Ernest Cotton), Slim recorded his classic "Lend Me Your Love" and "Rockin' the House." The next year brought the landmark "Nobody Loves Me" (better known via subsequent covers by Lowell Fulson, Joe Williams, and B.B. King as "Everyday I Have the Blues") and the heartbroken "Messin' Around (With the Blues)."

The pianist kept on label hopping, moving from Miracle to Peacock to Premium (where he waxed the first version of his uncommonly wise down-tempo blues "Mother Earth") to Chess to Mercury before staying put at Chicago's United Records from 1952 to 1954. This was a particularly fertile period for the pianist; he recruited his first permanent guitarist, the estimable Matt "Guitar" Murphy, who added some serious fret fire to "The Come Back," "Sassy Mae," and "Memphis Slim U.S.A."

Before the decade was through, the pianist landed at Vee-Jay Records, where he cut definitive versions of his best-known songs with Murphy and a stellar combo in gorgeously sympathetic support (Murphy was nothing short of spectacular throughout).

Slim exhibited his perpetually independent mindset by leaving the country for good in 1962. A tour of Europe in partnership with bassist Willie Dixon a couple of years earlier had so intrigued the pianist that he permanently moved to Paris, where recording and touring possibilities seemed limitless and the veteran pianist was treated with the respect too often denied even African-American blues stars at home back then. He remained there until his 1988 death, enjoying his stature as expatriate blues royalty. *—Bill Dahl*

Memphis Slim at the Gate of the Horn / 1959 / Vee-Jay ♦♦♦♦♦

Only this disc's short length (34 minutes) qualifies as something worthy of complaint; otherwise, this is seminal blues piano, performed by a great player and singer, Memphis Slim. This 1959 session had everything: super piano solos, a strong lineup of horn players, clever, well-written and sung lyrics, and a seamless pace that kept things moving briskly from beginning to end. Other than Slim, instrumental honors go to guitarist Matt "Guitar" Murphy, a marvelous accompanist who was able to blend sophistication, technique, and earthiness into one dynamic package. Even at its bargain-basement length, *At the Gate of Horn* belongs in any blues fan's library. *—Ron Wynn*

Blue This Evening / Jul. 1960 / 1201 Music ♦♦♦

Another artifact from the same historic tour of England. These 19 numbers, many of them the storied standards that long comprised Slim's repertoire, feature backing by guitarist Alexis Korner and drummer Stan Greig (who may be involved in the other British CD above). The same criticism applies: they weren't Murphy and Stepney, and the difference grates. *—Bill Dahl*

Memphis Slim / 1961 / MCA/Chess ♦♦♦♦

A straight CD reissue of a vintage Chess LP, its contents dating back to the early '50s and most tracks originally issued on the Premium logo. Includes an early and very nice reading of "Mother Earth;" also sharp as a tack is "Rockin' the Pad." In an unusual move, Slim is joined by a smooth vocal group, the Vagabonds, for "Really Got the Blues." *—Bill Dahl*

Steady Rollin' Blues / 1961 / Bluesville/Original Blues Classics ♦♦♦

Like Slim's other Bluesville work, this is a characteristic and very consistent effort, though not what you would single out as the cream of his recorded work. He varies the program between originals and covers of standards like "Mean Mistreatin' Mama," "Rock Me Baby," and "Goin' Down Slow," providing a touch of unpredictability by switching from the piano to the organ on a few tracks. *—Richie Unterberger*

Memphis Slim: U.S.A. / 1961 / Candid ♦♦♦

Alone with My Friends / Apr. 25, 1961 / Battle/Original Blues Classics ♦♦♦

Memphis Slim devoted all but one of the ten songs on this April 1961 session to covers of some of his favorite songwriters. He's only accompanied by his own piano playing as he provides serviceable, laidback interpretations of numbers by Big Bill Broonzy, Blind Lemon Jefferson, Willie Dixon, Sonny Boy Williamson, and others, as well as his own "Sunnyland Train." Not the first or last place to check out Slim on record. *—Richie Unterberger*

Memphis Slim: U.S.A. / 1962 / Delmark ♦♦♦♦♦

Slim's classic United label sessions from 1954 comprise this exceptional document of the master pianists work, 19 of the some 30 tracks he waxed during four sessions, and very well produced considering the time frame. A 24 year old Matt "Guitar" Murphy contributes mightily, tenor saxophonists Neil Green and Jim Conley smoothly fill in the cracks, while bassist Henry Taylor and drummer Otho Allen keep thing nicely swinging along. As a blues pianist Slim is in a class by himself. His tinklings, jazzy affectations and distinct chordal punctuations are the mark of a true master. His singing is equally robust, occasionally wailin' but mostly in a storytellers mode. Many of the tunes are old warhorses; "Blues All Around My Head" has two takes, one with unedited studio banter, "Blue & Lonesome" with more squawking before the slow melody line, while "Wish Me Well" is a patient boogie if there is such a thing. Slim excells on loping, half shuffles with horn complement as "Sassy Mae," Two of a Kind" and the killer "Four Years of Torment." He plays celeste on another three, the hard swinging "Got to Find My Baby," and twelve bar "She's Alright" with second take. At their roughest on "Slim Was Just Kiddin'" they can't decide what to do, settling on "Shake, Rattle & Roll." The T-Bone Walker influence definitely comes out for Murphy's instrumental features on the easy going "Jive Time Bounce" and out-and-out "Backbone Boogie." The calypso informed "Banana Oil" is somewhat of an anomaly, but a delightful aside. This recording shows the complete prowess of Slim and his ability to lead a band. Murphy's spice makes it all that much tastier. A highly recommended CD and an important historical bookmark in the career of an enduring legend of blues piano. *—Michael G. Nastos*

Memphis Slim & Willie Dixon in Paris / 1962 / Battle ♦♦♦

Recorded live in Paris, this has the two blues legends accompanying each other (Slim on piano, Dixon on bass) and trading lead vocals, backed by drummer Phillipe Combelle. It's not a landmark event in either of the legends' distinguished recording careers, but it's a nice enough outing with a friendly, low-key tone. Slim recorded a lot of LPs in the early '60s, often as a solo pianist/vocalist, and this is frankly more lively than his norm for the era, if for nothing else than the fact that he's playing in a band. The Dixon-sung tracks are interesting inasmuch as he didn't record much during this period, though he's really adequate at best as a singer. When Slim sings, he sticks mostly to self-penned material; the Dixon-fronted cuts may stir some curiosity among blues fans due to the inclusion of some of Willie's more obscure compositions, like the novelty-tinged "African Hunch with a Boogie Beat." *—Richie Unterberger*

All Kinds of Blues / 1963 / Bluesville/Original Blues Classics ♦♦♦♦♦

This early-'60s date was the second—and one of the best—of Memphis Slim's many top-notch Bluesville recordings. Featuring Slim accompanying himself on the piano, *All Kinds of Blues* is a vintage set of mellow yet deep blues by one of the music's most urbane performers. Whether reveling in his considerable boogie-woogie chops ("Three-in-One-Boogie") or tossing off a wryly sexual romp ("Grinder Man Blues"), Slim always seems to be totally at ease and in command. And while newcomers are advised to start out with one of his early-'50s sets on Chess, this will be one collection no Memphis Slim fan will want to overlook. *—Stephen Cook*

The Real Folk Blues / 1966 / MCA/Chess ♦♦♦♦

One of the more unsung blues giants on Chess, pianist Memphis Slim plied an urbane form of barrelhouse blues a notch or two removed from the more raw stylings of, say, Muddy Waters and Howlin' Wolf. This edition of the label's bargain survey series, *Real Folk Blues*, features Slim in his prime from the early '50s. And while he would later cut many fine sessions alone at the piano, the 12 tracks here feature Slim backed by a variety of top combos. Smooth yet dusky, the mix includes such stellar party odes as "Having Fun" and lowdown gems like "Trouble Trouble." The perfect place to start your Memphis Slim collection. *—Stephen Cook*

Mother Earth / 1969 / One Way ♦♦♦

Excellent singing and rousing, sparkling barrelhouse, boogie-woogie and straight blues piano playing from a certified legend. Memphis Slim wasn't shy about making records, and they were seldom not worth hearing. This one didn't break the string of quality efforts. *—Ron Wynn*

Messin' Around With the Blues / 1970 / King ♦♦♦♦♦

He wasn't messing around with either his singing or playing here. Memphis Slim made dozens of albums; most were good, some were very good, and a handful were great. This was among the handful. *—Ron Wynn*

Bad Luck & Trouble / 1972 / CBS ♦♦♦

Here's a wonderful tribute to the bluesmen who inspired this great Memphis blues pianist and his sidemen, harp player Jazz Gillum and guitarist Arbee Stidham. As with Mississippi Fred McDowell's terrific 1969 album *I Do Not Play No Rock and Roll*, one of the best things about *Bad Luck and Troubles* is the heartfelt spoken intros. "Once upon a time, I was known as a carbon copy of Roosevelt Sykes," Slim says in a deep, slow drawl without a hint of self-consciousness. Allowing Gillum and Stidham such prominence on ten of the 26 tracks is a generous gesture that prevents this album from being even better, because neither is in the headliner's league. The relaxed 1961 New York City session among friends is at its best on the Leroy Carr classic "In the Evening" and Bill Big Broonzy's "I Feel So Good." Slim, whose real name was Peter Chatman, showcases his chops on rollicking solo piano instrumentals such as "Forty-Four Blues" and "Cow Cow Blues." The album is produced by well-known jazz critic Nat Hentoff. *—Mark Allan*

Baby Please Come Home / 1972 / Battle ♦♦♦

Recorded in Paris, France in November of 1962, this captures Slim and Dixon on one of their many European jaunts, this time working with drummer Phillipe Combelle to an appreciative crowd. The vocals are split fairly evenly between the two singers, and although several of the titles here are wrong (Dixon's "Do the Do" is spelled "Do De Do" and "Shame Pretty Girls" is actually "Pretty Girls"), it's a very enthusiastic set by this trio that moves right along, capped off with a slam-bang rendition of Slim's "All by Myself." A nice one. *—Cub Koda*

Old Times, New Times / 1972 / Barclay ♦♦♦♦

As the legend of the blues shouter goes, a big band would be churning away and from behind the bar would step the bartender, clad in an apron but lacking a microphone. His assured voice would soar over the full band, and something charismatic in his tone would make the entire room follow every word. This is a pretty good description of the kind of ambience Memphis Slim sets up when he plays and sings, whether he is working solo or fronting a group. This particularly nice set is of the heavy-duty meeting ilk, when blues giants of one sort or another are thrust together to supposedly make magic together. On one disc Slim gets together with fellow ivory tickler Roosevelt Sykes, and it is indeed sheer joy. These two are spirits of mirth, with more rhythmic feel than a paddy wagon full of drummers; their historic banter will be delightful to those who like their blues scrambled with tall tales. On some of the tunes they take turns with lead vocals, and their dual piano interplay is a blast. On the second disc Slim meets up with the Buddy Guy band while they are on tour with the Rolling Stones. As a result, the band is more warmed-up than usual, and the odd studio mix—in which Guy's normally fire-breathing guitar sounds like it is going straight into the board—even suits the musical adventures somehow. Slim's number on harpsichord is amusing. *—Eugene Chadbourne*

Soul Blues / 1973 / Ember ♦♦♦

This solid early-'70s collection includes tracks like "Let the Good Times Roll Creole," "True Love," "I'll Just Keep on Swinging with the Blues," and "It's Been Too Long." *—John Bush*

Legacy of the Blues, Vol. 7 / 1973 / GNP Crescendo ♦♦♦

Following discs showcasing the styles of blues greats Bukka White, Champion Jack Dupree, Big Joe Williams, and others, pianist Memphis Slim received his due on volume seven of GNP Crescendo's *Legacy of the Blues* series. Born and raised in Memphis, TN, Slim didn't record until moving to Chicago in 1940. The music that followed over the next 14 years (numerous sides as a leader and accompanist scattered across ten labels) helped define urban blues, giving a rural music form a big-city polish. This set gathers nine Slim-led small combo performances recorded for producer Clyde Otis. The disc opens with Slim revisiting one of his signature tunes, the excellent "Everyday I Got the Blues." Originally recorded in 1948 as "Nobody Loves Me," the song has since become a virtual blues standard, having been rendered by blues (B.B. King), rock (Fleetwood Mac), and jazz (Sarah Vaughan) artists alike. The material that follows ranges from uptempo numbers like "Let's Get With It," "Sally Mae," and "Broadway Blues" to the shuffle blues of "A Long Time Gone" and the slow swagger of "Gambler's Blues." Throughout the set, Slim is happy to lend the spotlight to his sidemen, working the 88s behind Eddie Chamblee's tenor solo on "I Am the Blues" and Billy Butler's guitar on "Ballin' the Jack." Even in these situations however, the pianist is dazzling and his commentary always worth paying attention to. *—Nathan Bush*

Raining the Blues / Jul. 1973 / Fantasy ♦♦♦

★ **Rockin' the Blues** / 1981 / Charly ♦♦♦♦♦
The most complete gathering of Slim's 1958-1959 Vee-Jay output available on disc (16 songs to the even dozen on the *Gate of Horn* domestic disc) and the best-sounding too. This is the crowning achievement in Memphis Slim's massive legacy—he delivers his classics one right after another, backed by his unparalleled combo that was anchored by Matt "Guitar" Murphy's startlingly fresh solos. Along with the standbys—"Messin' Around," "Mother Earth," "Wish Me Well"—there's the catchy instrumental "Steppin' Out," later covered by Eric Clapton; the romping "What's the Matter," and a blistering "Rockin' the House" where the band nearly sails right out of the studio! *—Bill Dahl*

Memphis Heat / 1981 / Polygram ♦♦
The combination of Memphis Slim and Canned Heat didn't generate much in the way of sparks when they were brought together for this set in 1974. And a five-strong edition of the Memphis Horns, brought in at some point to add a little punch to the proceedings, actually seem to get in the way. Safe to skip this one, with so much prime Slim available on CD. *—Bill Dahl*

I'll Just Keep on Singin' the Blues / 1981 / 32 Jazz ♦♦♦♦
Recorded in 1961 in Chicago just before pianist Memphis Slim was to embark on a European tour and take up permanent residence there. Backed by members of his exciting '50s band the House Rockers (including Matt "Guitar" Murphy), *I'll Just Keep on Singin' the Blues* is a lost masterpiece. Slim and his band are in great form on this set of originals that ooze gutbucket postwar Chicago blues. This forgotten gem was reissued in 2000 on the budget label 32 jazz. *—Al Campbell*

Together Again One More Time/Still Not Ready For... / 1990 / Antone's ♦♦♦
A modern-day reunion of the revered pianist and his favorite guitarist at Austin, TX-based Antone's nightclub, preserved for posterity. They sound mighty happy to see one another. *—Bill Dahl*

Life Is Like That / 1990 / Charly ♦♦♦♦♦
Some of Slim's earliest postwar sides for Miracle and King (1946-1949), and some of his best. He'd already assembled his little combo with saxists Alex Atkins and Ernest Cotton by that time (interchangeable bassists included Willie Dixon and Big Crawford; no drums necessary), and the classics were flowing: "Lend Me Your Love," "Nobody Loves Me" (adapted by Lowell Fulson as "Every Day I Have the Blues"), and the luxurious "Messin' Around With the Blues." *—Bill Dahl*

1960 London Sessions / 1993 / Sequel ♦♦♦
The pianist was quite an attraction when he first ventured overseas, and he received plenty of offers to record while he was there. The uncredited combo on these 15 rare tracks is too timid to give Slim what he needed out of a band, but his irrepressible power saves the show. *—Bill Dahl*

Aux Trois Mailletz: Jazz in Paris / 1993 / Verve ♦♦♦
Although this CD by pianist Memphis Slim and bassist Willie Dixon is marketed as a part of Verve's *Jazz in Paris* reissue series, it is, of course, a blues date, with a fair amount of boogie-woogie. The two veterans, who had worked together previously, are joined by drummer Phillipe Combelle during the two 1962 sessions recorded at Les Trois Mailletz, complete with a typically out of tune piano and a fair amount of noise from the audience at times. The pianist's gruff voice dominates a fair amount of the performances, although most of the songs are Dixon's. The bassist steals the show during the opener, "Rocking and Rolling the House," with a fine solo. In fact, the only standard not written by either man is a campy miniature take of Big Bill Broonzy's "All by Myself." Blues fans will want up to pick up this live recording by two legendary musicians. *—Ken Dryden*

Lonesome / 1994 / Drive Archive ♦♦♦♦
Sound quality isn't exactly superb here on this 1961 album first out on Strand, but the contents are. Another House Rockers album featuring Murphy, saxists John Calvin and Johnny Board, bassist Sam Chatmon, and drummer Billie Stepney flying high on "Let the Good Times Roll Creole" (likely the only time Slim and Bill Haley battled it out for bragging rights on a tune), the crackling title track, and a very oddly titled "What Is the Mare-Rack." Slim wouldn't make any more albums with this band (after all, they didn't relocate to Paris with him), making it all the more precious. *—Bill Dahl*

Live at the Hot Club / 1994 / Milan ♦♦
Recorded live in 1980 in Paris, this is not the Memphis Slim that you want for your collection, unless you're the type that has to have everything in a discography just because it's there. Slim is actually in decent enough form. The problems are that his only accompanist is a clunky drummer, and that the fidelity is fairly funky (although not truly grating). And with so many other Memphis Slim recordings available, this ranks pretty far down the list. *—Richie Unterberger*

Very Best of Memphis Slim: The Blues Is Everywhere / Jan. 5, 1998 / Collectables ♦♦♦
The Very Best of Memphis Slim: The Blues is Everywhere collects 12 songs Slim recorded in the mid-'60s, probably for King and Scepter Records. While there are some good performances on this disc, there are no liner notes explaining the origins of the tracks, and the sound is uneven. It's not a bad collection, especially for collectors searching for a few specific cuts, but novices would be better served by more comprehensive, thorough collections. *—Stephen Thomas Erlewine*

The Folkways Years: 1959–1973 / Feb. 22, 2000 / Smithsonian/Folkways ♦♦♦♦♦
These 21 tracks, selected from the recordings Memphis Slim did for Folkways, tend to be in solo piano or sparsely accompanied arrangements, as one would figure since Folkways was a traditionally oriented label. Still, it doesn't sound like a forced or awkward attempt to steer the pianist toward an outdated approach. It's just on the quiet and restrained side, and not different from numerous recordings Memphis Slim did for more commercially minded labels throughout his career. Although half of the material is just Slim alone at the piano (sometimes singing, sometimes not), it does actually show him in a variety of contexts. Willie Dixon accompanies him on bass on a few numbers; Jazz Gillum does the vocal and harmonica for "Key to the Highway" (which is actually a track on which Memphis Slim was the sideman, not the featured artist); Matt Murphy plays electric guitar on a few songs; Pete Seeger joins Memphis Slim and Dixon on "Midnight Special"; and there are actually drums by "Jump" Jackson on a couple of tunes. It's assured piano blues whatever the situation, not among his very best recordings, but certainly respectable. Unfortunately, the liner notes, quite detailed in most respects, do not give the dates of recordings for the individual tracks; from the sound of things, most of these date from 1959 and the early '60s, although the title indicates a timespan of 1959-1973. Three of the cuts were previously unreleased, including "Every Day I Have the Blues," the atypical organ instrumental "The Gimmick," and the piano instrumental "The Dirty Dozens." *—Richie Unterberger*

The Complete Recordings, Vol. 2: 1946–1948 / Feb. 6, 2001 / EPM Musique ♦♦♦♦♦
Memphis Slim's passionate voice and excellent pacing made his recordings some of the landmark moments in blues music. In fact, even more than Robert Johnson (whose brilliance was rediscovered years later), Slim had created a sound that was imitated by virtually every blues musician around during this period, surpassing even his own idols with his amazing grasp of the genre. These recordings represent a peak in his career, he was really starting to come into his own and his music was finding the mainstream blues audience in America. It was during this period where he recorded his three most influential songs, "Rockin' the House," "Lend Me Your Love," and the amazing "Nobody Loves Me (Everyday I Have the Blues)." It was the tortured genius of this last track that may forever be his legacy, as his pleasant bouncing piano playing betrayed the depressing tone of the lyrics. He would later go on to make more great music with Matt Murphy (including some incredible re-recordings of those three songs), but for the most part this is the point in his career that may be remembered as the most important. Any serious blues fan should try to add this to their collection, while anyone curious about classic blues should at least try to hear these songs, as they represent a creative high point for one of the genre's most important innovators. *—Bradley Torreano*

The Complete Recordings, Vol. 3: 1948–1950 / Mar. 5, 2002 / EPM Musique ♦♦♦♦

Memphis Willie B. (Willie Borum)

b. Nov. 4, 1911, Shelby County, TN
Vocals, Harmonica, Guitar / Acoustic Memphis Blues, Jug Band
Willie Borum, better known under his recording sobriquet of Memphis Willie B., was a mainstay of the Memphis blues and jug band circuit. Adept at both harmonica and guitar, Borum could add pep to any combination he worked in, as well as leaving a striking impression as a solo artist.

He was born in 1911 in Shelby County, TN. He took to the guitar early in his childhood, being principally taught by his father and Memphis medicine show star Jim Jackson. By his late teens, he was working with Jack Kelly's Jug Busters, working for tips on the street with the occasional house party and country supper rounding out his meager paycheck. This didn't last long, as Borum joined up with the Memphis Jug Band, one of two professional outfits in existence at that time. The group frequently worked what later became W.C. Handy Park in Memphis, their touring stretching all the way down to New Orleans during the Mardi Gras. Sometime in the '30s he learned to play harmonica, being taught by no less a master than Noah Lewis, the best harp blower in Memphis and mainstay of Gus Cannon's Jug Stompers. As his style began to move further away from a strict jug band approach, Willie B. began working on and off with various traveling Delta bluesmen, performing at various functions with Rice (Sonny Boy Williamson) Miller, Willie Brown, Garfield Akers, and Robert Johnson. He finally got to make some records in New York under his own name in 1934 for Vocalion, but quickly moved back into playing juke joints and gambling houses with Son Joe, Joe Hill Louis and Will Shade until around 1943, when he became a member of the U.S. Army.

It was a much different world he returned to and after a brief fling at trying to pick up where he left off, Borum soon cashed in his chips and started looking for a day job. That would have been the end of the story, except in 1961—with the folk and blues revival in full hootenanny steam—Borum was tracked down and recorded an absolutely marvelous session at the Sun studios for Prestige's Bluesville label. It turned into a little bit of a career upswing for the next few years; Willie B. started working the festival and coffeehouse circuit with old Memphis buddies Gus Cannon and Furry Lewis. But then just as quickly, he dropped out of the music scene and eventually out of sight altogether. The reports of his death in the early '70s still remain unconfirmed as of press time. *—Cub Koda*

Introducing Memphis Willie B. / 1961 / Bluesville/Original Blues Classics ♦♦

Hardworking Man Blues / Jun. 30, 1995 / Bluesville/Original Blues Classics ♦♦♦

● **Bluesville Years, Vol. 3** / 1995 / Prestige ♦♦♦♦♦
Beale Street Get-Down is the folksiest of the bunch, most of it recorded at the Sun studios in Memphis with country blues guitarists Furry Lewis and Memphis Willie B. (Borum) and pianist Memphis Slim all contributing to the fray. *—Cub Koda*

Big Maceo Merriweather (Major Merriweather)

b. Mar. 31, 1905, Atlanta, GA, **d.** Feb. 26, 1953, Chicago, IL
Vocals, Piano / Piano Blues, Chicago Blues
The thundering 88s of Big Maceo Merriweather helped pave the way for the great Chicago blues pianists of the '50s—men like Johnny Jones, Otis Spann, and Henry Gray. Unfortunately, Merriweather wouldn't be around to enjoy their innovations—he died a few years after suffering a debilitating stroke in 1946.

Major Merriweather was already a seasoned pianist when he arrived in Detroit in 1924. After working around the Motor City scene, he ventured to Chicago in 1941 to make his recording debut for producer Lester Melrose and RCA Victor's Bluebird subsidiary. His first day in the studio produced 14 tracks—six of his own and eight more as accompanist to renowned Chicago guitarist Tampa Red. One of his initial efforts, "Worried Life Blues," has passed into blues standard status (Chuck Berry was hip to it, covering it for Chess).

Merriweather remained Tampa Red's favorite pianistic accompanist after that, gigging extensively with him and Big Bill Broonzy on Chicago's South side. The pianist cut a series of terrific sessions as a leader for Bluebird in 1941-1942 and 1945 (the latter including his *tour de force*, "Chicago Breakdown") before the stroke paralyzed his right side. He tried to overcome it, cutting for Victor in 1947 with Eddie Boyd assuming piano duties and again for Specialty in 1949 with Johnny Jones, this time at the stool. His health fading steadily after that, Merriweather died in 1953. *—Bill Dahl*

☆ **Chicago Breakdown** / Oct. 1975 / Bluebird/RCA ✦✦✦✦✦

Chicago Breakdown is worth searching out since it contains seven extra songs that aren't on the similiar Arhoolie release *King of Chicago Blues Piano, Vol. 1-2*, including "It's All Up to You," "Why Should I Hang Around," "Come on Home," and "It's All Over Now." Mike Rowe's fascinating liner notes are utilized for both *Chicago Breakdown* and *King of Chicago Blues Piano* packages, so there's no clear-cut advantage in that department. *—Bill Dahl*

Volume One / 1976 / RCA ✦✦✦✦✦

Big Maceo / 1984 / RCA ✦✦✦✦✦

The King of Chicago Blues Piano, Vol. 1 / 1984 / Blues Classics ✦✦✦✦✦

Like Leroy Carr and Lonnie Johnson before him, Big Maceo Merriweather helped popularize an urbane rendition of the rough country blues sound. His fetching combination of grainy vocals and smoothly rolling piano split the screen between the gruff ways of the rural South and the sophisticated hum of northern cities like Chicago. And while seen as a predecessor to electric blues innovators like Muddy Waters, Maceo really deserves more attention as one of the best in a long line of acoustic-based blues performers. That's made clear on this fine collection, as he is heard reeling off 16 of his first sides with the great slide guitarist Tampa Red. Cut in Chicago between 1941-1942, tracks like the classic "Worried Life Blues" effortlessly move along thanks to Maceo and Red's smooth interplay; their intimate style even makes one forget about the drums and bass listed for some tracks. Sporting not only some of Carr's subtle phrasing, but a bit of Fats Waller's rambunctious vocal delivery and stride piano work as well, Maceo's keen mix of both down-home and uptown not only makes for great listening, but should help neutralize some of the provincial views of blues performers. A great collection. *—Stephen Cook*

The King of Chicago Blues Piano, Vol. 2 / 1984 / Arhoolie ✦✦✦✦✦

The Best of Big Maceo: The King of Chicago Blues Piano / 1992 / Arhoolie ✦✦✦✦✦

The title *The King of Chicago Blues Piano* is no joke—while never achieving the level of fame won by many of his contemporaries, Big Maceo was indeed a major force behind the development of the Windy City sound, and these '40s sides, cut in collaboration with guitarist Tampa Red, remain his most enduring legacy. Combining startling instrumental proficiency with a traditional blues sensibility, Maceo was also a powerful vocalist; despite recording just 28 sides—all but three of which are included here—he was still a pivotal figure, bridging the country blues of the 1920s with the urbanized electric sound of the '50s. Among the highlights: the instrumental closer "Chicago Breakdown," an instrumental tribute to his incredible prowess, and "Worried Life Blues," later covered by Chuck Berry. *—Jason Ankeny*

☆ **The King of Chicago Blues Piano, Vol. 1–2** / 1992 / Arhoolie ✦✦✦✦✦

A slightly truncated CD version of the RCA two-record set that first anthologized the thundering '40s RCA Bluebird sides of pianist Big Maceo (25 cuts on the CD, 32 on the vinyl). The CD opens with Maceo's immortal blues "Worried Life Blues," and closes with his instrumental *tour de force* "Chicago Breakdown," and boasts a great deal of blues piano magic in between. *—Bill Dahl*

Bluebird Recordings 1941–1942 / Jan. 30, 1996 / RCA ✦✦✦✦✦

Bluebird Recordings 1941-1942 contains all 16 tracks Big Maceo Merriweather recorded for the label during that year, including the classic "Worried Life Blues." Merriweather was one of the most influential barrelhouse blues pianists, and these Bluebird recordings form the core of his legacy. While these recordings are available in more thorough anthologies, this single disc remains an excellent introduction to his best work. *—Thom Owens*

★ **Victor/Bluebird Recordings 1945–1947** / Apr. 29, 1997 / Bluebird/RCA ✦✦✦✦✦

The recordings Big Maceo made in the two years covered by this set are some of the last he made for Bluebird before a stroke incapacitated him. In fact, the last four sides were recorded after his stroke, still able to vocalize sweetly, but with Eddie Boyd brought in to play piano on the date. As always, all of these sides feature the immaculate guitar work of Tampa Red and tracks like "Kid Man Blues," "Maceo's 32-20," and "Chicago Breakdown" show the two off to good effect. Excellent-sounding transfers make this a package well worth adding to the collection. *—Cub Koda*

The Meters

f. 1966, New Orleans, LA, **db.** 1977

Group / New Orleans R&B, R&B, Funk, Soul

The Meters defined New Orleans funk, not only on their own recordings, but also as the backing band for numerous artists, including many produced by Allen Toussaint. Where the funk of Sly Stone and James Brown was wild, careening, and determinedly urban, the Meters were down-home and earthy. Nearly all of their own recordings were instrumentals, putting the emphasis on the organic and complex rhythms. The syncopated, layered percussion intertwined with the gritty grooves of the guitar and organ, creating a distinctive sound that earned a small, devoted cult during the '70s, including musicians like Paul McCartney and Robert Palmer, both of whom used the group as a backing band for recording. Despite their reputation as an extraordinary live band, the Meters never broke into the mainstream, but their sound provided the basis for much of the funk and hip-hop of the '80s and '90s.

Throughout their career, the Meters were always led by Art Neville (keyboard, vocals), one of the leading figures of the New Orleans musical community. As a teenager in high school, he recorded the seminal "Mardi Gras Mambo" with his group, the Hawketts, for Chess Records. The exposure with the Hawketts led to solo contracts with Specialty and Instant, where he released a handful of singles that became regional hits in the early '60s. Around 1966, he formed Art Neville and the Sounds with his brothers Aaron and Charles (both vocals), guitarist Leo Nocentelli, drummer Joseph "Zigaboo" Modeliste and bassist George Porter Jr. The band grew out of informal jam sessions the musicians held in local New Orleans nightclubs. After spending a few months playing under the Sounds name, producer Allen Toussaint and Marshall Sehorn hired the group—without the vocalists—to be the house band for their label Sansu Enterprises.

As the house band for Sansu, the Meters played on records by Earl King, Lee Dorsey, Chris Kenner and Betty Harris, as well as Toussaint himself. They also performed and recorded on their own, releasing danceable instrumental singles on Josie Records. "Sophisticated Cissy" and "Cissy Strut" became Top Ten R&B hits in the spring of 1969, followed by the number 11 hits "Look-Ka Py Py" and "Chicken Strut" a year later. The Meters stayed at Josie until 1972, and during that entire time they reached the R&B Top 50 consistently, usually placing within the Top 40. In 1972, the group moved to Reprise Records, yet they didn't sever their ties with Sansu, electing to keep Toussaint as their producer and Sehorn as their manager. Ironically, the Meters didn't have nearly as many hit singles at Reprise, yet their profile remained remarkably high. If anything, the group became hipper, performing on records by Robert Palmer, Dr. John, Labelle, King Biscuit Boy and Paul McCartney. By the release of 1975's *Fire on the Bayou*, the Meters had a Top 40 hit with *Rejuvenation*'s "Hey Pocky A-Way" (1974), and they had gained a significant following among rock audience and critics. *Fire on the Bayou* received significant praise, and the group opened for the Rolling Stones on the British band's 1975 and 1976 tours.

During 1975, the Meters embarked on the Wild Tchoupitoulas project with Neville's uncle and cousin George and Amos Landry, two members of the Mardi Gras ceremonial black Indian tribe, the Wild Tchoupitoulas. The Meters, the Landrys and the Neville Brothers—Aaron, Charles, Art and Cyril—were all involved in the recording of the album, which received enthusiastic reviews upon its release in 1976. Cyril joined the Meters after the record's release. Despite all of the acclaim for *The Wild Tchoupitoulas*, its adventurous tendencies indicated that the group was feeling constrained by its signature sound. Such suspicions were confirmed the following year, when they separated from Toussaint and Sehorn, claiming they needed to take control of their artistic direction. Following the split, the Meters released *New Directions* in 1977, but shortly its appearance, Toussaint and Sehorn claimed the rights to the group's name. Instead of fighting, the band broke up, with Art and Cyril forming the Neville Brothers with Aaron and Charles, while the remaining trio became session musicians in New Orleans. Modeliste, in particular, became a well-known professional musician, touring with the New Barbarians in 1979 and moving to LA during the '80s.

The Meters reunited as a touring unit in 1990 with Russell Batiste taking over the drum duties from Modeliste. Four years later, Nocentelli left the band, allegedly because he and Art Neville disagreed whether the band should be paid for samples hip-hop groups took from their old records; he was replaced by Brian Stoltz, who had played with the Neville Brothers. The Meters continued to tour throughout the '90s. *—Stephen Thomas Erlewine*

The Meters / 1969 / Sundazed ✦✦✦

This seminal New Orleans funk group's debut album features the semi-hit "Cissy Strut" and its follow-up, "Sophisticated Sissy." This 1999 reissue also offers two previously unreleased bonus tracks, "The Look of Love" and "Soul Machine." Other highlights include "Here Comes the Meter Man," "Live Wire," and "Sehorn's Farm." *—Cub Koda*

Struttin' / 1970 / Sundazed ✦✦✦

As the third full-length album released by the Meters, *Struttin'* may not appear to be drastically different than its predecessors, at least not on the surface. After all, the title of the lead single "Chicken Strut" intentionally recalls their previous biggest "Cissy Strut," and it has the same basic Meters groove. And if the essential sound remains unchanged, that's because that organic, earthy funk is the Meters' signature. Other groups have tried to replicate it, but nobody ever played it better. Because of that, *Struttin'* is an enjoyable record, even if it never quite feels like anything more focused than a series of jam sessions; after all, that's what it was. This time around, however, the Meters did make a conscious decision to emphasize vocals, and not just with shout-alongs on the chorus ("Chicken Strut," "Same Old Thing"), but with Art Neville's leads on covers of Ty Hunter's soulful uptown shuffle "Darling, Darling, Darling," Jimmy Webb's groovy ballad "Wichita Lineman," and Lee Dorsey's "Ride Your Pony" (the Meters provided support on the original recording). This gives the album a bit more diversity than its predecessors, which is welcome, even for devotees of the group's admittedly addictive sound. But the real difference is how the band seems willing to expand their signature sound. "Hand Clapping Song" is a spare, syncopated breakdown without an obvious through-line, while "Joog" turns the group's groove inside out. These variations are entertaining—as entertaining as the vocals—and the songs that are solidly in the Meters tradition are also fun. The results are pretty terrific, though given the fact that *Struttin'* never really pulls itself into a coherent album, it may be the kind of first-rate record only aficionados of the band will need to seek out. *—Stephen Thomas Erlewine*

Look-Ka Py Py / 1970 / Rounder ✦✦✦✦

The Meters' great '60s singles anticipated the coming of funk. They made short, catchy tunes and scored occasional hits, particularly the single "Look-Ka Py Py," one of 12 outstanding tunes on this CD. These were the ultimate party/dance records, and they also showed the link between traditional African rhythms, New Orleans shuffle, second line sounds, soul and funk. Marvelous rhythm music at its hottest. *—Ron Wynn*

Cabbage Alley / 1972 / Sundazed ♦♦♦♦
Leaving Josie for Reprise did change the Meters, even if the change wasn't necessarily for the better. They became slicker, jammier, and, in the conventional sense, funkier, even if the grit seemed to start to dissipate. So, even if this is just the Meters' fourth album, *Cabbage Alley* does mark a sea-change in their outlook, bringing them fully into the '70s and finding them sacrificing feel for texture, even if that's a very subtle transition. Part of the problem is that the group doesn't really have any good songs to hang their sounds onto, but, if you're looking just for sounds and groove, *Cabbage Alley* doesn't disappoint. The Meters' overall feel might have gotten a little softer than necessary, but they still are a remarkably sympathetic, supple group and it's a pleasure to hear them play. Still, there's not much here outside of hearing them play, and while that's pretty great, it's hard not to wish that there were songs, even when they delve into smooth soul like "Birds" or when the group simply jams on midtempo grooves, that stood out from the pack. [Sundazed's 2000 reissue contains two bonus tracks—both parts of "Chug Chug Chug-A-Lug (Push and Shove)."] *—Stephen Thomas Erlewine*

Rejuvenation / 1974 / Sundazed ♦♦♦♦♦
The title is a tip-off, as is the garish, blaxploitation-chic photo on the cover—*Rejuvenation*, the Meters' second album for Reprise, should be seen as a bit of a new beginning for the quintessential New Orleans funk group. It's not a clean beginning, since they were pointing in this direction on *Cabbage Alley*, but this is where their glistening, clear production, crisp performances, rock influences, and hard-edged funk coalesce into a sound distinct from their Josie recordings—not better, just different. As such, this is the definitive Reprise album from the Meters, not just because the material is stronger (which admittedly is true), but because the performances are continually inspired and the production is professional but hits at a gut level, resulting in a first-class funk album. [Sundazed's 2000 reissue contains the single versions of "People Say" and "Hey Pocky A-Way" as bonus tracks.] *—Stephen Thomas Erlewine*

Cissy Strut / 1974 / Island ♦♦♦♦♦
The Meters made their anthemic funk cuts on Josie in the late '60s. The New Orleans crew backed Fats Domino, Lee Dorsey, and Aaron Neville before they started jamming on their own in the late '60s. Island issued this anthology of Josie material in the mid-'70s. It came out in the U.S. too. Rounder has since reissued some of this material. *—Ron Wynn*

Fire on the Bayou / 1975 / Sundazed ♦♦♦♦♦
The Meters' third album for Reprise, *Fire on the Bayou*, is their best record for the label for a variety of reasons, not least of which is the high quality of material throughout the record and a focus from the band that keeps the music simmering, even if it never quite reaches a boil. That's not a bad thing, because the music IS simmering, always hot and enticing, never lukewarm or too cool. There's not anything that comes out and grabs your throat, the way that "Hey Pocky A-Way" does, but there never seems to be a concession to mainstream funk, the way *Cabbage Alley* or *Rejuvenation* seemed to be. This just keeps things rolling, nice and smooth. There's not anything that separates itself from its partners—something that's unfortunately true of all of the Reprise albums—but the overall feel is better than the Meters' other Reprise albums, since it has more grit and presence than its compatriots. [Sundazed's 2000 reissue contains one bonus track, a "long version" of "Running Fast."] *—Stephen Thomas Erlewine*

The Best of the Meters / 1975 / Mardi Gras ♦♦♦
A good collection of this quintessential New Orleans funk group's best '70s singles for the Reprise label. Of course they did their finest cuts for Josie, but turned in some reasonably good work on Reprise in a more rock/funk direction. "Hey, Pocky A-Way" was probably the closest Reprise cut to matching the superb Josie singles. But these are the songs that got them gigs with the Rolling Stones and work with Paul McCartney and Robert Palmer, so they did have some value. *—Ron Wynn*

Trick Bag / 1976 / Sundazed ♦♦
This is, undeniably, where everything started to go pear-shaped for the Meters. Take the opening track, "Disco Is the Thing Today," a four-on-the-floor pumper that sounds nothing like the Meters and everything like BT Express. For the rest of the record the Meters and producer Allen Toussaint don't necessarily prove that sentiment true, but they do strive to sound as mainstream as possible, turning out slick ballads, frothy dance numbers, and pop-funk without spine. There are a couple of exceptions to the rule—"Mister Moon" is the one time when the glossy formula works and turns sultry, "(Doodle Loop) The World Is a Little Bit Under the Weather" nearly grooves, and their take on "Honky Tonk Women" has some real grit—but this is record is pretty much a dead end, and a pretty dispiriting one at that, best evidenced by the crushing disappointment that's their flat reading of Earl King's classic title track. *—Stephen Thomas Erlewine*

New Directions / 1977 / Sundazed ♦♦♦
The title of the Meters' final album is hopeful, and *New Directions* does indeed represent if not a new direction, at least a shift from the disco dead end of *Trick Bag*. From the second "No More Okey Doke" kicks off the record, it's clear that the Meters are gritty again, kicking out some really funky grooves—maybe not as dirty as their Josie recordings, maybe a little cleaned up, but still pretty funky. The slower numbers betray their era, but in a pleasing way, something that's also true of generic numbers like "My Name Up in Lights," which may have too much talk-box guitar, but still grooves effectively. That may not be a new direction, per se, but it is a welcome change-up after the dud *Trick Bag*. It wasn't enough to save the Meters and it's not really a lost treasure, but it's a far more dignified way to bow out. *—Stephen Thomas Erlewine*

Good Old Funky Music / 1990 / Rounder ♦♦♦
There are some good moments on this disc, culled from unissued material from the Meters' Josie heyday in the late '60s and early '70s, but there's too much filler. *—Bill Dahl*

The Original Funkmasters / 1992 / Instant ♦♦♦♦♦
An absolutely essential CD to own if you want the answer to the burning question "Where does funk come from?" In the very late '60s and early '70s, the mighty quartet of Art Neville (keyboards), Leo Nocentelli (guitar), George Porter Jr. (bass), and Joseph "Zigaboo" Modeliste (drums) delivered a groovy gumbo of funky soul that kept the New Orleans club scene so famous. Most of the tracks here were recorded by the Meters over a three-year period, when both the R&B and pop charts made room for them in their rosters (due to their early 1969 hit, "Sophisticated Cissy"). This 1992 compilation from Instant Records showcases the live energy of the band, with songs like "Funky Miracle" and "Live Wire," plus the late-night chill-out of "Ease Back" and the let's-close-up-for-the-night "Stormy," a beautiful and melancholy bit of R&B to catch your breath before the funkmasters take it away from you again. These songs are a little older and limited in recording technology (take note of the occasional extreme stereo separation), but in some ways this vintage sound makes *The Original Funkmasters* one of the best recordings to own, compared to the cleaner and flatter Neville Brothers albums that absorbed Meters members and continued making records for the next two decades. Fans of the more recent acid jazz movement or appreciators of hip-hop take note: This is the music that your favorite acts sample and imitate. This is tight, organic musicianship performed by actual musicians (not programmers or DJs), and the best that money can buy. So by all means do. *—Keir Langley*

Uptown Rulers: The Meters Live on the Queen Mary / 1992 / Rhino ♦♦♦♦♦

The Meters Jam / Mar. 1, 1992 / Rounder ♦♦
The 10 songs on this CD are a mixed bag, mainly because The Meters insisted on singing and simply weren't great vocalists. Their leads and harmonies on "Come Together" and "Bo Diddley," among others, were exuberant, but didn't add much to the proceedings. On the other hand, there haven't been many groups in any style that clicked any more smoothly and soulfully. Their inspired, funky playing almost overshadows the tepid vocals. *—Ron Wynn*

☆ **Funkify Your Life** / Feb. 28, 1995 / Rhino ♦♦♦♦♦
Two discs of the Meters is a lot to ask of most casual fans, yet for the devoted few, *Funkify Your Life* is essential. Featuring tracks from both their Josie and Warner years, the double-disc set captures some of the rawest New Orleans funk recorded in the Crescent City. *—Stephen Thomas Erlewine*

★ **The Very Best of the Meters** / Jun. 10, 1997 / Rhino ♦♦♦♦♦
In keeping with the drift of Rhino's *Very Best of* volumes, this 16-track disc provides a more concise, budget-minded retrospective for listeners who might not want a set that offers twice as much or more (in this case, Rhino's own two-disc *Funkify Your Life* anthology). That's not necessarily a criticism—funk grooves can get tiring over the course of two hours if you're not a rhythm fiend. Should you want to keep your Meters to the one-sitting level, this smartly chosen, well-annotated set is fine, including all of the cuts ("Cissy Strut," "Sophisticated Cissy," "Look-Ka Py Py," "Hey Pocky A-Way," "Fire on the Bayou") you'd expect to find on a greatest-hits set. *—Richie Unterberger*

Kickback / Feb. 2001 / Sundazed ♦♦♦
Not for one minute will you mistake this collection of unreleased recordings as a proper album. It isn't just the preponderance of covers, it's the subtle shifts in production and tone, lending a general unevenness to this record, even if it's culled just from 1975 and 1976 (meaning they're leftovers from *Fire on the Bayou* and *Trick Bag*). That doesn't mean it's a bad listen by any stretch, since even if *Kickback* is second-rate and leftover Meters, they're still an incredibly supple, engaging band that can take such bad choice of material like Neil Young's "Down by the River" and turn it into something listenable. Such cover choices as that, the Beatles' "Come Together," and Stephen Stills' "Love the One You're With" all sound intriguing, particularly to the record geek that's this album's core audience, but apart from the latter (and a fine, surprisingly hard-rocking alternate version of "Honky Tonk Women"), these kind of choices play better in theory than in actuality. The rest of the record may not have as distinctive a calling card, but they're better, finding the band laying back and doing what they do best, which is laying down a solid, irresistible groove. No, there's not much here that's essential, but it's fine second-tier stuff that will satisfy the dedicated. And, truth be told, second-tier Meters still sounds pretty good to the unconverted, too. *—Stephen Thomas Erlewine*

Anthology: Josie Years / Mar. 27, 2001 / Repertoire ♦♦♦♦♦
This two-disc import set includes the band's three early albums for the Josie label in sequence, plus a selection of outtakes from the same fertile period. Among the surprises is a heavy cover of the Beatles' "Come Together." The relentlessly syncopated backbeats and stuttering guitar lines have a way of sneaking up on the unaware listener, too—all the way to the dancefloor. This is seminal New Orleans funk in an affordable package that serves as a better introduction than Rhino's previous retrospectives (which include material from the band's Warner Brothers disco years). *—Brian Beatty*

Hazel Meyers

Vocals / Prewar Blues, Classic Female Blues
Hazel Meyers was a Black vaudeville artist in the 1920s who made records that were marketed as blues, and not an inconsiderable number of them. She made 41 titles in all between September, 1923 and August of 1924, primarily for Ajax, but also for Brunswick (issued on Vocalion), Pathe, Banner, Bell, and Emerson. Her last two sides were made for OKeh in June, 1926. She frequently worked with accompanists of outstanding quality, including Fletcher Henderson, Porter Grainger, Bubber Miley, Don Redman and even, on one occasion, Fats Waller.

About her career on stage, details are much more sketchy. She appeared in *Steppin' High*, a Harlem variety show for which Fletcher Henderson's Orchestra provided the music, and is known to have made other appearances in black vaudeville through 1930. Otherwise, nothing else is known about Hazel Meyers. —*Uncle Dave Lewis*

Complete Recorded Works, Vol. 1 (1923–24) / May 14, 1996 / Document ✦✦✦

Mickey & Sylvia

f. 1956, **db.** 1965
Group / Rock & Roll, R&B

Although this duo is primarily remembered as a one-hit act—for "Love Is Strange," which reached number 11 in 1957—they actually recorded quite a few exciting hybrids of R&B and rock & roll in the mid- and late '50s. Playing on countless '50s sessions for various labels (especially Atlantic and OKeh), Mickey Baker was one of the greatest guitar players of early rock & roll. With his partner (and former guitar student) Sylvia Robinson, he got to stretch out a bit from his usual role, with some trailblazing, piercing, lean, and bluesy leads. Vocally, Mickey & Sylvia had an engagingly playful, occasionally sly and sassy repartee that makes up in charm what it might lack in smoke and firepower. Their recordings were inconsistent, but at their best they offered a fetching blend of blues, Bo Diddley, calypso, and doo wop.

After "Love Is Strange," whose devastating licks inspired countless guitarists, the duo notched a couple more substantial R&B hits. But although they recorded as late as 1965, they never approached the Top 20 again. Mickey Baker recorded as a solo artist and enjoyed a fairly successful career as an expatriate sessionman in France. Sylvia Robinson unexpectedly re-emerged with the number three pre-disco hit "Pillow Talk" in 1973, and co-founded the pioneering rap label Sugar Hill in the late '70s. —*Richie Unterberger*

Love Is Strange / 1990 / Bear Family ✦✦✦
This two-CD, 60-song (!) set includes many alternate takes and a fair amount of previously unreleased material, spanning 1955 to 1964. A lot of the obscurities are in the close harmony, doo wop vein, and are disappointingly short on verbal sparring and scorching Baker guitar. Lovingly packaged, but everyone except hardcore specialists should stick with the RCA compilation. —*Richie Unterberger*

Love Is Strange & Other Hits / Mar. 1990 / RCA ✦✦✦✦✦
Unless you're a major R&B collector, it's likely you've never heard anything by this duo besides "Love Is Strange," their only major hit (and a great one). With 20 cuts from 1956–1960, this disc reissues the bulk of their most interesting work. "Love Is Strange" will remain their most memorable tune after you've heard this, but on the whole, this is way-above-average '50s R&B/rock. If you're hungering for more great solos like the ones in "Love Is Strange," you'll find some here, especially in "There Oughta Be a Law" and the instrumental "Shake It Up," although Baker's virtuosity doesn't dominate most of the songs. Some of these tunes are routine doo wop, but a little over half the material is pretty strong, ranging from the calypso-rock they're best remembered for to ballads to straight-ahead R&B shouters, with King Curtis on sax. —*Richie Unterberger*

The Willow Sessions / 1995 / Sequel ✦✦✦
Mickey & Sylvia are properly thought of as '50s rock & rollers, but they actually did a good deal of recording in the '60s, though without much notable commercial success. Most of this 19-track CD was recorded in the early '60s for their own label, Willow; only one song, "Baby You're So Fine," was a hit, making the R&B Top 30. The album doesn't have the fire of their best sides for RCA in the '50s, but it's not bad, usually purveying a groove similar to their early work, though tamer. Occasionally Mickey brandishes blues-rock chops to show that he can still cut deep with his axe, especially on "Darling (I Miss You So)" and the previously unissued instrumentals "Sylvia's Blues" and "Mickey's Blues." There are also a few curious (but fairly respectable) cuts dating from the late '60s that Sylvia recorded for the All Platinum label in a much more contemporary soul vein. —*Richie Unterberger*

● **Love Is Strange: A Golden Classics Edition** / Apr. 22, 1997 / Collectables ✦✦✦✦✦
Although the packaging and sound are a little below par, *Golden Classics Edition* contains 18 tracks from Mickey & Sylvia's prime period—not just "Love Is Strange," but a wealth of strong, lesser-known singles—making it a good overview of the underrated R&B duo. —*Stephen Thomas Erlewine*

The Mighty Clouds of Joy

f. 1959, Los Angeles, CA
Group / Traditional Gospel, Southern Gospel, Black Gospel

Contemporary gospel's preeminent group, the Mighty Clouds of Joy carried the torch for the traditional quartet vocal style throughout an era dominated by solo acts and choirs; pioneering a distinctively funky sound which over time gained grudging acceptance even among purists, they pushed spiritual music in new and unexpected directions, even scoring a major disco hit. The Mighty Clouds of Joy were formed in Los Angeles during the mid-'50s by schoolmates Joe Ligon and Johnny Martin; while still in their teens, the original group—which also included brothers Ermant and Elmer Franklin, Leon Polk and Richard Wallace—made their recorded debut in 1960 with "Steal Away to Jesus," cut for the Peacock label. Their debut LP *Family Circle* arrived a year later. In the years that followed, the Mighty Clouds earned a reputation among gospel's greatest showmen; one of the first groups to incorporate choreographed moves into their act, their nimble footwork and bright, color-coordinated outfits earned them the sobriquet "The Temptations of Gospel." More importantly, they were the first group to add bass, drums and keyboards to the standard quartet accompaniment of solo guitar, resulting in a sound which horrified traditionalists but appealed to younger listeners—so much so, in fact, that the Mighty Clouds became the first gospel act ever to appear on television's *Soul Train*, where they performed their disco smash "Mighty High." Their crossover success continued with opening slots for secular pop stars including Marvin Gaye, the Rolling Stones and Paul Simon, whom the group backed during a month-long stint at Madison Square Garden. While lineup changes plagued the Mighty Clouds throughout their career, they remained active

through the '90s; in addition to co-founders Ligon and Wallace, their latter-day incarnation also included Michael McCowin, Wilbert Williams, Johnny Valentine and Ron Staples. —*Jason Ankeny*

Family Circle / 1960 / Peacock ✦✦✦✦
Pyrotechnic performances by this sensational group. —*Opal Louis Nations*

A Bright Side / 1960 / MCA Special Products ✦✦✦
The Clouds at their peak. —*Opal Louis Nations*

The Mighty Clouds Live at the Music Hall / 1966 / Peacock ✦✦✦✦✦
More church wrecking. —*Opal Louis Nations*

Sing Live Zion Songs / 1968 / HOB ✦✦✦✦✦
Little Joe Ligon and the group live from Will Rogers Park circa 1958. —*Opal Louis Nations*

★ **The Best of the Mighty Clouds of Joy** / 1973 / MCA ✦✦✦✦✦
Best of the early Peacock material when the quartet was in their prime. —*Opal Louis Nations*

The Best of the Mighty Clouds of Joy, Vol. 2 / 1973 / MCA ✦✦✦✦

Live and Direct / 1977 / ABC ✦✦✦✦✦
Live & Direct is a wonderful, inspiring live recording from the Mighty Clouds of Joy. Although the group was past its peak when they recorded this in the late '70s, they nevertheless retained much of their vocal power, and their interplay is simply breathtaking at times. And, since it features all of their classic material, the album functions as a best-of sampler, and it's certainly not a bad way to become acquainted with this extraordinary group. —*Leo Stanley*

Mighty Clouds of Joy Live / 1990 / MCA ✦✦✦

Pray for Me / 1990 / Word ✦✦✦
Being recorded in 1990, the backing and sound of "Pray for Me" is of course a little tainted by late-'80s/early-'90s slickness. But compared to most soul and gospel from that time, this sounds more genuine and has aged less. As the concert goes on, or at least as it is presented on the record, that polish also wears off and the basic sweaty qualities of the Mighty Clouds of Joy take over. Most sweaty is probably the lead singer, and the interplay between his raw, almost vulgar voice and the slick choruses gives the songs an irresistible drive. On the B-side the concert turns partly into a sermon. The preaching gets a little boring the tenth time you listen to the album, like spoken parts of an album often do, but it does add to the gospel atmosphere. And while the talk about the vices of rock & roll feels a little conservative, you probably wouldn't be listening to gospel music if you can't stand that. At the same time it is slightly amusing, regarded how much the Mighty Clouds of Joy borrowed from secular music and how close to rock they come themselves when they are at their best. —*Lars Lovén*

Memory Lane: The Best of the Mighty Clouds of Joy / 1993 / Word ✦✦✦
Despite spanning from 1960 to 1993, *Memory Lane* is anything but an all-inclusive Mighty Clouds of Joy retrospective; while all ten of its performances are indeed stirring, the narrow scope of the set is hugely disappointing. Including neither "Mighty High" nor "Time," their disco-era R&B hits, the collection instead draws primarily from just a handful of LPs, with no less than four tracks apiece from the LPs *Cloudburst* and *Mighty Clouds Alive*; while *Memory Lane* does offer new listeners a decent idea of just what the Mighty Clouds are about, longtime fans hoping for an exhaustive career overview are looking in the wrong place. —*Jason Ankeny*

Glad About It / Oct. 24, 1995 / HOB ✦✦✦✦
Glad About It is a solid effort from the Mighty Clouds of Joy, featuring 12 gospel tracks, both familiar and relatively new. The group has cut better albums, but this is far from bad, and it boasts such fine moments as "There's No Friend Like Jesus," "His Blood for Me," "Have a Little Faith," "Over in Zion," "My Religion" and "Man Can't Get Satisfaction." —*Stephen Thomas Erlewine*

Faith, Mercy, Glory / Jan. 1, 1996 / King ✦✦✦✦✦
Great collection of recent vintage spiced with previously unissued material. —*Opal Louis Nations*

Glory Hallelujah / Jan. 2, 1996 / MCA Special Products ✦✦✦✦
Ace collection of some of this shouting group's best Peacock sides. —*Opal Louis Nations*

It Was You / Oct. 19, 1999 / CGI Platinum ✦✦✦
The Mighty Clouds of Joy soldier on into the next millennium, releasing *It Was You* in 1999. There aren't any real surprises on the album—by now, fans know what to expect from a Mighty Clouds of Joy record—but the group's members are consummate professionals, delivering committed performances on material of generally high quality. And sometimes, that's all you need to do. —*Steve Huey*

20th Century Masters—The Millennium Collection: The Best of the Mighty Clouds of Joy / Apr. 30, 2002 / MCA ✦✦✦
This discount-priced compilation is drawn from the Mighty Clouds of Joy's earliest recordings for Peacock Records, starting with their first session on September 28, 1960, and continuing up to August 1965. Although Universal also controls the ABC and Dunhill catalogs that contain the group's R&B hits of the '70s, this collection is restricted to their more traditional early material, on which the gravel-voiced Joe Ligon leads them through familiar hymns like "Amazing Grace" and "Nearer to Thee." "Family Circle" is the same song as what is known in country music as "Will the Circle Be Unbroken." "A Bright Side (Sermonette)" is a seven-and-a-half minute peroration by Ligon that amply demonstrates his preaching side. David Walker spells the leader on his composition "You'll Never Know," and "Nobody Can Turn Me Around" has high-pitched vocals reminiscent of the Impressions, but for the most part, the Mighty Clouds of Joy's music is dominated by Ligon's emotive, cavernous voice. This is a good sampler of the group's early work, but it

is not the collection you want to get if you're looking for big hits like "Mighty High." *—William Ruhlmann*

Amos Milburn

b. Apr. 1, 1927, Houston, TX, **d.** Jan. 3, 1980, Houston, TX

Vocals, Piano / Jump Blues, West Coast Blues, Piano Blues, R&B

Boogie piano master Amos Milburn was born in Houston, and he died there a short 52 years later. In between, he pounded out some of the most hellacious boogies of the postwar era, usually recording in Los Angeles for Aladdin Records and specializing in good-natured upbeat romps about booze and its effects (both positive and negative) that proved massive hits during the immediate pre-rock era.

The self-taught 88s ace made a name for himself as the "He-Man Martha Raye" around Houston before joining the Navy and seeing overseas battle action in World War II. When he came out of the service, Milburn played in various Lone Star niteries before meeting the woman whose efforts would catapult him to stardom.

Persistent manager Lola Anne Cullum reportedly barged into Aladdin boss Eddie Mesner's hospital room, toting a portable disc machine with Milburn's demo all cued up. The gambit worked—Amos Milburn signed with Aladdin in 1946. His first date included a thundering "Down the Road Apiece" that presaged the imminent rise of rock & roll. But Milburn was capable of subtler charms too, crooning mellow blues ballads in a Charles Brown-influenced style (the two would later become close friends, playing together frequently).

The first of Milburn's 19 Top Ten R&B smashes came in 1948 with his party classic "Chicken Shack Boogie," which paced the charts and anointed his band with a worthy name (the Aladdin Chickenshackers, natch). A velvet-smooth "Bewildered" displayed the cool after-hours side of Milburn's persona as it streaked up the charts later that year, but it was rollicking horn-driven material such as "Roomin' House Boogie" and "Sax Shack Boogie" that Milburn was renowned for. Milburn's rumbling 88s influenced a variety of famous artists, notably Fats Domino.

With the ascent of "Bad, Bad Whiskey" to the peak of the charts in 1950, Milburn embarked on a string of similarly boozy smashes: "Thinking and Drinking," "Let Me Go Home Whiskey," "One Scotch, One Bourbon, One Beer" (an inebriating round John Lee Hooker apparently enjoyed!), and "Good Good Whiskey" (his last hit in 1954). Alcoholism later brought the pianist down hard, giving these numbers a grimly ironic twist in retrospect. Milburn's national profile rated a series of appearances on the Willie Bryant-hosted mid-'50s TV program *Showtime at the Apollo* (where he gave out with a blistering "Down the Road Apiece").

Aladdin stuck with Milburn long after the hits ceased, dispatching him to New Orleans in 1956 to record with the vaunted studio crew at Cosimo's. There he recut "Chicken Shack Boogie" in a manner so torrid that it's impossible to believe it didn't hit (tenor saxist Lee Allen and drummer Charles "Hungry" Williams blast with atomic power as Milburn happily grunts along with his pounding boogie piano solo). In 1957, he left Aladdin for good.

Amos contributed a fine offering to the R&B Yuletide canon in 1960 with his swinging "Christmas (Comes but Once a Year)" for King. Berry Gordy gave Milburn a comeback forum in 1962, issuing an album on Motown predominated by remakes of his old hits that doesn't deserve its extreme rarity today (even Little Stevie Wonder pitched in on harp for the sessions).

Nothing could jump-start the pianist's fading career by then, though. His health deteriorated to the point where a string of strokes limited his mobility and his left leg was eventually amputated. Not too long after, one of the greatest pioneers in the history of R&B was dead. *—Bill Dahl*

Rockin' the Boogie / 1954 / Aladdin ♦♦♦♦♦

Just what it promises. *—Bill Dahl*

Let's Have a Party / 1957 / Score ♦♦♦♦♦

Milburn's Aladdin sides are perfect for any bash. *—Bill Dahl*

The Return of Blues Boss / Apr. 9, 1963 / Motown ♦♦♦

Milburn's sole LP for Motown was an interesting effort that updated his saucy rhythm & blues without compromising it. No need to look for the rare original vinyl; it's been reissued in its entirety on *The Motown Sessions, 1962-1964*, which adds several previously unreleased bonus tracks. *—Richie Unterberger*

☆ **The Complete Aladdin Recordings of Amos Milburn** / 1994 / Mosaic ♦♦♦♦♦

Seven discs tracing the entire 1946-1957 Aladdin Records legacy of jump blues pioneer Amos Milburn, whose rippling boogie-based piano talent and predilection of songs about booze made him a postwar R&B superstar. One hundred forty-five tracks in all (including plenty of unissued goodies) tab this as the ultimate collection for Milburn fans. He boogied like a champ at his first L.A. date for Aladdin with a thundering "Down the Road Apiece" and rocked equally hard a decade later down in New Orleans when he was recutting "Chicken Shack Boogie" with the crew at Cosimo's. Mosaic does their usual elegant presentational job on this R&B legend, not skimping on a thing. Fabulous box set. *—Bill Dahl*

★ **Best of Amos Milburn—Down the Road Apiece** / Jan. 11, 1994 / EMI America ♦♦♦♦♦

Pianist Amos Milburn mixed boogie-woogie with vocal energy and intensity to forge a style that was among early R&B's most exciting and appealing. Milburn's '40s and '50s singles were sometimes fiery and sometimes silly, ranging from drinking songs and celebratory uptempo numbers to stomping instrumentals and an occasional blues or love tune. This excellent 26-track anthology contains such classic Milburn anthems as "Chickenshack Boogie," "One Scotch, One Bourbon, One Beer," "Let's Have a Party," and "Bad, Bad Whiskey," as well as lesser-known but just as spirited romps. The mastering bolsters the sound, but doesn't deaden it, while Joseph Laredo's liner notes clearly and completely outline Milburn's musical and cultural/historical significance. *—Ron Wynn*

Blues, Barrelhouse & Boogie Woogie: 1946–1955 / 1996 / Capitol ♦♦♦♦♦

Here's a very reasonable compromise between the pricey Mosaic box and EMI's incomplete single-disc treatment of Milburn's Aladdin legacy: a three-disc, 66-song package that's heavy on boogies and blues and slightly deficient in the ballad department (to that end, his smash "Bewildered" was left off). Everything that is aboard is top-drawer, though—the booze odes, many a party rocker, and a plethora of the double entendre blues that Milburn reveled in during his early years. The absent 1956 remake of "Chicken Shack Boogie" is a humongous omission, though. *—Bill Dahl*

The Motown Sessions, 1962–1964 / Feb. 1996 / Motown ♦♦♦♦♦

Signed to Motown years after his peak as an R&B star, Milburn's association with the label turned out to be something of a non-event, producing only an obscure album and flop single. A commercial non-event, that is; Milburn's skills were still intact, resulting in some fine if somewhat uncharacteristic performances. This compilation reissues that album (*Return of the Blues Boss*) and adds seven unreleased tracks. Milburn may still have been singing blues/R&B, but he was with Motown, which meant that a fair amount of soul-pop flavor inevitably seeped through. You can hear it in the occasional female backup vocals, swinging brass arrangements, and even a brief harmonica solo by Stevie Wonder on "Chicken Shack Boogie"; the arrangement on "I'll Make It Up to You Somehow" wouldn't have been out of place on an early Mary Wells single. The results are pleasantly surprising, updating Milburn's sound (which would have been quite anachronistic in the early '60s) into the early soul era. The material is pretty strong, including both bluesy ballads and more uptempo numbers that don't totally smother his boogie-woogie roots. *—Richie Unterberger*

The Best of the Aladdin Recordings / Mar. 19, 1996 / Capitol ♦♦♦♦♦

Best of the Aladdin Recordings is quite similar to *Best of Amos Milburn—Down the Road Apiece*, which appeared two years before *The Aladdin Recordings*. All the key Milburn tracks are on both collections, and there isn't much difference between the minor cuts, which means either disc is essentially interchangeable and a good addition to a comprehensive R&B collection. *—Thom Owens*

Essential Recordings / Jan. 9, 2001 / Cleopatra ♦♦♦♦

"Bad, Bad Whiskey," "Baby, Baby All the Time," "One Scotch, One Bourbon, One Beer," and "Chicken Shack Boogie," the recordings that made Amos Milburn a blues legend, are as humorous as ever and crisp as frying bacon in CD format. You'll weep with the smooth blues singer on "Bewildered" and assimilate his pain on the slow piano blues quagmire "Evening Shadows Coming Down on Me." Classic drinking music by one of the classiest blues singers ever. *—Andrew Hamilton*

The Best Of Amos Milburn / Mar. 13, 2001 / EMI-Capitol Special Markets ♦♦♦♦

Bad Bad Whiskey: 1946–1950 / Sep. 4, 2001 / EPM Musique ♦♦♦♦

Lizzie Miles (Elizabeth Mary [née Landreaux] Pajaud)

b. Mar. 31, 1895, New Orleans, LA, **d.** Mar. 17, 1963, New Orleans, LA

Vocals / Classic Female Blues, Classic Jazz, New Orleans Jazz

Lizzie Miles was a fine classic blues singer from the 1920s who survived to have a full comeback in the '50s. She started out singing in New Orleans during 1909-1911 with such musicians as King Oliver, Kid Ory, and Bunk Johnson. Miles spent several years touring the South in minstrel shows and playing in theaters. She was in Chicago during 1918-1920 and then moved to New York in 1921, making her recording debut the following year.

Her recordings from the 1922-1930 period mostly used lesser-known players, but Louis Metcalf and King Oliver were on two songs apiece and she recorded a pair of duets with Jelly Roll Morton in 1929. Miles sang with A.J. Piron and Sam Wooding, toured Europe during 1924-1925, and was active in New York during 1926-1931. Illness knocked her out of action for a period, but by 1935, she was performing with Paul Barbarin, she sang with Fats Waller in 1938, and recorded a session in 1939. Lizzie Miles spent 1943-1949 outside of music, but in 1950 began a comeback, often performing with Bob Scobey or George Lewis during her final decade. *—Scott Yanow*

Moans and Blues / 1954 / Cook ♦♦♦♦

With Tony Almerico's Dixieland Band / 1954-1956 / Rondo ♦♦♦

After gaining her initial reputation in the 1920s, Lizzie Miles made a comeback in the '50s, when she often appeared with Bob Scobey's band. This particular LP is one of several she made for the Cook and Rondo labels late in her career, when her voice was fortunately still in good form. Joined by a spirited New Orleans band including trumpeter Tony Almerico, trombonist Jack Delaney and clarinetist Tony Costa, Miles mostly sticks to warhorses including "Some of These Days," "Bill Bailey," "Waitin' for the Robert E. Lee" and "Darktown Strutters' Ball." *—Scott Yanow*

● **Queen Mother of the Rue Royale** / 1955 / Cook ♦♦♦♦♦

An unjustly forgotten name in classic blues annals. Lizzie Miles was a great entertainer and versatile song stylist who could handle everything from vaudeville to classic blues to traditional New Orleans jazz. She had passed her prime by these recordings, but was still able to retain her grit and intensity while relying on experience rather than power. *—Ron Wynn*

Hot Songs My Mother Taught Me / 1955 / Cook ♦♦♦♦

This is one of the best of Lizzie Miles' '50s recordings (none of her solo dates have yet been reissued on CD). Eight of the 14 songs find her accompanied by pianist Red Camp; three add the banjo of Albert French; and three are with a Dixieland band headed by trumpeter Tony Almerico. The mostly intimate settings allow the still strong-voiced Miles to put lots of feeling not only into some typical standards, but such numbers as "Take Yo' Finger Off It," "A Cottage for Sale" and "Dyin' Rag." *—Scott Yanow*

Lizzie Miles / Apr. 7, 1994 / American Music ♦♦♦♦

A well-documented blues and vaudevillian singer in the 1920s, Lizzie Miles was off records after 1930 for over 20 years, except for eight selections cut on one day in 1939. This CD has her later "comeback" session, four songs cut for Rudi Blesh's Circle label in 1952. In addition, Miles is heard on an alternate take of "Basin Street Blues" from that day, nine previously unreleased performances from a month earlier, two unheard selections from the mid-'50s, and a pair of tunes (previously put out by the Dawn Club label) that find her performing live with the George Lewis band. In most cases, Miles is backed by a trio comprised of either Fred Neumann or Lester Santiago on piano, Frank Federico or Ernest McLean on guitar, and Joe Locacano or Richard McLean on bass. Her delivery of the standards (which include "Careless Love," "Ace in the Hole," "Some of These Days," "Someday Sweetheart" and "St. Louis Blues") is relaxed, swinging and full of joy; Miles comes across much more like a vintage jazz singer than a classic blues vocalist. The recording quality is generally quite good on these rarities. The mid-'50s numbers have her joined by a New Orleans sextet that includes cornetist Johnny Wiggs and clarinetist Raymond Burke, while the George Lewis group is supportive on the final two numbers. A perfect introduction to the infectious singing of Lizzie Miles. *—Scott Yanow*

Complete Recorded Works, Vol. 1 (1922–23) / Sep. 10, 1996 / Document ✦✦✦✦✦
Lizzie Miles is better-known than most of the classic blues singers of the '20s because she made a comeback in the '50s when she emerged still in prime form. Actually her earliest recordings are quite obscure, making this first of three Document CDs a valuable acquisition for vintage blues collectors. Miles' initial 22 recordings feature her during 1922-1923, mostly backed by unknown musicians in combos ranging from five to seven pieces on such numbers as "She Walked Right Up and Took My Man Away," "He May Be Your Man, But He Comes to See Me Sometimes," "Hot Lips," "The Yellow Dog Blues," "Aggravatin' Papa" and "You've Gotta Come and See Mama Every Night." Miles sounds quite comfortable both on vaudeville-type numbers and blues. The last three selections find her backed only by pianist Clarence Johnson, and on "Haitian Blues" she takes a kazoo solo that is surprisingly advanced for March 1923, a period of time when there were few horn solos on record. Recommended. *—Scott Yanow*

Complete Recorded Works, Vol. 2 (1923–28) / 1996 / Document ✦✦✦✦✦
The second of three CDs that reissue all of Lizzie Miles' recordings from the 1922-1939 period features the versatile singer in 1923 (being accompanied by either Clarence Johnson or J. Russell Robinson on piano), and during 1927-1928, after a successful period spent as a cabaret singer in Paris. For the latter recordings, Miles is assisted by Clarence Johnson, Louis Hooper or Porter Grainger on piano, cornetist Louis Metcalf on two fine numbers and the dated gaspipe clarinet of Bob Fuller on the final four selections (which include two versions of "A Good Man Is Hard to Find"). One of the finer singers of the '20s, Miles' delivery was quite accessible and one can always understand the words she sings. Highlights of this excellent set include "You're Always Messin' Round with My Man," "Cotton Belt Blues," "Lonesome Ghost Blues" and "If You Can't Control Your Man." Virtually all of the material on this 1996 CD was formerly very rare. *—Scott Yanow*

Complete Recorded Works, Vol. 3 (1928–39) / 1996 / Document ✦✦✦✦✦
The third of three Document Lizzie Miles CDs has some of the finest recordings of the singer's career, particularly on the first half of this disc. After three numbers with a trio not helped by the presence of clarinetist Bob Fuller, Miles performs two superior songs ("You're Such a Cruel Papa to Me" and "My Dif'rent Kind of Man") while joined by cornetist King Oliver, Albert Socarras (doubling on flute and alto) and pianist Clarence Williams. Miles fits right in with a hot combo led by the unknown Jasper Davis (probably a pseudonym) that includes cornetist Louis Metcalf, altoist Charlie Holmes and pianist Cliff Jackson. She is also featured on two songs in duet with the great pianist Jelly Roll Morton, three tunes with pianist Harvey Brooks (including "My Man O' War" and "Electrician Blues") and joined by the trio of pianist Porter Grainger, guitarist Teddy Bunn and bassist Pops Foster (highlighted by "Yellow Dog Gal Blues") in 1930. Nine years passed before Lizzie Miles had an opportunity to record again. At the age of 44 she sounds fine on seven numbers with the Melrose Stompers (a Chicago swing septet whose personnel is long lost) from 1939; the band is also heard taking "Mellow Rhythm" as an instrumental. Highly recommended, particularly for the 1928-30 recordings, this CD has Lizzie Miles' last recordings before she began her comeback in 1952. *—Scott Yanow*

Steve Miller

b. Oct. 5, 1943, Milwaukee, WI

Vocals, Keyboards, Songwriter, Guitar / Album Rock, Arena Rock, Pop/Rock, Psychedelic, Blues-Rock

Steve Miller's career has encompassed two distinct stages: one of the top San Francisco blues-rockers during the late '60s and early '70s, and one of the top-selling pop/rock acts of the mid- to late '70s and early '80s with hits like "The Joker," "Fly Like an Eagle," "Rock'n Me," and "Abracadabra."

Miller was turned on to music by his father, who worked as a pathologist but knew stars like Charles Mingus and Les Paul, whom he brought home as guests; Paul taught the young Miller some guitar chords and let him sit in on a session. Miller formed a blues band, the Marksmen Combo, at age 12 with friend Boz Scaggs; the two teamed up again at the University of Wisconsin in a group called the Ardells, later the Fabulous Night Trains. Miller moved to Chicago in 1964 to get involved in the local blues scene, teaming with Barry Goldberg for two years. He then moved to San Francisco and formed the first incarnation of the Steve Miller Blues Band, featuring guitarist James "Curly" Cooke, bassist Lonnie Turner, and drummer Tim Davis. The band built a local following through a series of free concerts and backed Chuck Berry in 1967 at a Fillmore date later released as a live album. Scaggs moved to San Francisco later that year and replaced Cooke in time to play the Monterey Pop Festival; it was the first of many personnel changes. Capitol signed the group as the Steve Miller Band following the festival.

The band flew to London to record *Children of the Future*, which was praised by critics and received some airplay on FM radio. It established Miller's early style as a blues-rocker influenced but not overpowered by psychedelia. The follow-up, *Sailor*, has been hailed as perhaps Miller's best early effort; it reached number 24 on the Billboard album charts and consolidated Miller's fan base. A series of high-quality albums with similar chart placements followed; while Miller remained a popular artist, pop radio failed to pick up on any of his material at this time, even though tracks like "Space Cowboy" and "Brave New World" had become FM rock staples. 1971's *Rock Love* broke Miller's streak with a weak band lineup and poor material, and Miller followed it with the spotty *Recall the Beginning: A Journey From Eden.* Things began to look even worse for Miller when he broke his neck in a car accident and subsequently developed hepatitis, which put him out of commission for most of 1972 and early 1973.

Miller spent his recuperation time reinventing himself as a blues-influenced pop-rocker, writing compact, melodic, catchy songs. This approach was introduced on his 1973 LP *The Joker* and was an instant success, with the album going platinum and the title track hitting number one on the pop charts. Now an established star, Miller elected to take three years off. He purchased a farm and built his own recording studio, at which he crafted the wildly successful albums *Fly Like an Eagle* and *Book of Dreams* at approximately the same time. *Fly Like an Eagle* was released in 1976 and eclipsed its predecessor in terms of quality and sales (over four million copies) in spite of the long downtime in between. It also gave Miller his second number one hit with "Rock'n Me," plus several other singles. *Book of Dreams* was almost as successful, selling over three million copies and producing several hits as well. All of the hits from Miller's first three pop-oriented albums were collected on *Greatest Hits 1974-1978*, which to date has sold over six million copies and remains a popular catalog item.

Miller again took some time off, not returning again until late 1981 with the disappointing *Circle of Love.* Just six months later, Miller rebounded with *Abracadabra*; the title track gave him his third number one single and proved to be his last major commercial success. None of his remaining '80s albums were consistent enough to be critically or commercially successful. A box set covering most of Miller's career was compiled by the artist himself in 1994. *—Steve Huey*

Children of the Future / 1968 / Capitol ✦✦✦✦✦
A psychedelic blues rock-out, 1968's *Children of the Future* marked Steve Miller's earliest attempt at the ascent that brought him supersonic superstardom. Recorded at Olympic Studios in London with storied producer Glyn Johns at the helm, the set played out as pure West Coast rock inflected with decade-of-love psychedelia but intriguingly cloaked in the misty pathos of the U.K. blues ethic. Though bandmate Boz Scaggs contributed a few songs, the bulk of the material was written by Miller while working as a janitor at a music studio in Texas earlier in the year. The best of his efforts resonate in a side one free-for-all that launches with the keys and swirls of the title track and segues smoothly through "Pushed Me Through It" and "In My First Mind," bound for the epic, hazy, lazy, organ-inflected "The Beauty of Time Is That It's Snowing," which ebbs and flows in ways that are continually surprising. The second half of the LP is cast in a different light—a clutch of songs that groove together but don't have the same sleepy flow. Though it has since attained classic status—Miller himself was still performing it eight years later—Scaggs' "Baby's Callin' Me Home" is a sparse, lightly instrumentalized piece of good old '60s San Francisco pop. His "Steppin' Stone," on the other hand, is a raucous, heavy-handed blues freakout with a low-riding bass and guitar breaks that angle out in all directions. And whether the title capitalized at all on the Monkees' similarly titled song, released a year earlier, is anybody's guess. *Children of the Future* was a brilliant debut. And while it is certainly a product of its era, it's still a vibrant reminder of just how the blues co-opted the mainstream to magnificent success. *—Amy Hanson*

Sailor / 1968 / Capitol ✦✦✦✦
Most definitely a part of the late-'60s West Coast psychedelic blues revolution that was becoming hipper than hip, Steve Miller was also always acutely aware of both the British psychedelic movement that was swirling in tandem and of where the future lay, and how that would evolve into something even more remarkable. The result of all those ideas, of course, came together on 1968's magnificent *Sailor* LP. Speaking to *Goldmine* magazine in 2002, Miller reiterated that he was always aware of forward thinking: "It's amazing what the breakthroughs are, and the quality is absolutely better and you don't have the digital/analog argument anymore about what sounds the best. It's all new. And now anybody in the world can do what I wanted to do so badly when I got my deal with Capitol Records and got to finally go into a recording studio." What was begun on *Children of the Future* is more fully realized on *Sailor*, most notably on the opening "Song for Our Ancestors," which begins with a foghorn and only gets stranger from there. Indeed, the song precognizes Pink Floyd's 1971 opus "Echoes" to such an extent that one wonders how much the latter enjoyed Miller's own wild ride. Elsewhere, the beautiful, slow "Dear Mary" positively shimmers in a haze of declared love, while the heavy drumbeats and rock riffing guitar of "Living in the U.S.A." are a powerful reminder that the Steve Miller Band, no matter what other paths they meandered down, could rock out with the best of them. And, of course, this is the LP that introduced many to the Johnny "Guitar" Watson classic "Gangster of Love," a song that would become almost wholly Miller's own, giving the fans an alter ego to caress long before "The Joker" arose to show his hand. Rounding out Miller's love of the blues is an excellent rendering of Jimmy Reed's "You're So Fine." At their blues-loving best, *Sailor* is a classic Miller recording and a must-have—especially for the more contemporary fan, where it becomes an initiation into a past of mythic proportion. *—Amy Hanson*

Your Saving Grace / 1969 / Capitol ✦✦✦
Your Saving Grace is a much more earthy collection of tunes when compared to the band's previous three long-players. While there are distinct psychedelic remnants of the Boz Scaggs (guitar/vocals) and Jim Peterman (keyboards) era, the addition of keyboardists Ben Sidran and Nicky Hopkins—which began on the Steve Miller Band's pre-

vious effort, *Brave New World*—adds a jazzier facet to this second incarnation of the group. Harking back to the band's blues roots, *Your Saving Grace* includes a couple of distinct blues originals—such as the uptempo and gospel-doused "Don't Let Nobody Turn You Around" and a somewhat uninspired arrangement of "Motherless Children," which sounds more synchronous with the *Sailor* or *Brave New World* albums. The funky "Little Girl," the elegantly pensive "Baby's House," and the title track—which is oddly programmed as the LP's final cut—are among the highlights of this disc. Once again, the production is handled by Glyn Johns, whose contributions here are more subdued, yet no less noticeable. This is especially true of Miller's crystalline slide guitar licks on Lonnie Turner's cryptically titled "The Last Wombat in Mecca." The same upfront clean sound holds true on the laid-back and bluesy "Feel So Glad"—which is punctuated by some inspired and unmistakable ivory tickling by studio wunderkind Nicky Hopkins. Although the album is not as thoroughly solid as earlier efforts, *Your Saving Grace* and the follow-up, *Number 5*, are definite bridges between the early trippy montages prevalent on *Children of the Future* and the direction that Miller would take on his much more successful mid-'70s discs. *—Lindsay Planer*

Brave New World / 1969 / Capitol ♦♦♦♦♦
Blasting out of stereo speakers in the summer of 1969, *Brave New World* was more fully realized, and rocked harder, than the Steve Miller Band's first two albums. From the opening storm of the uplifting title track to the final scorcher, "My Dark Hour," featuring Paul McCartney (credited as "Paul Ramon"), this recording was the strongest project before Miller's *Fly Like an Eagle* days. "Celebration Song" has a sliding bass line, while "LT's Midnight Dream" features Miller's slide guitar. "Can't You Hear Your Daddy's Heartbeat" sounds like it was lifted right off of Jimi Hendrix's *Are You Experienced*, and "Got Love 'Cause You Need It" also has a Hendrix-ian feel. "Kow Kow" is a wonderfully oblique song featuring Nicky Hopkins' distinctive piano style. Hopkins' piano coda on that song alone is worth the price of this album. "Space Cowboy," one of several songs co-written with Ben Sidran, defined one of Miller's many personas. "Seasons," another Sidran collaboration, is a beautifully atmospheric, slow-tempo piece. Steve Miller's guitar playing is the star of this album, blazing across the whole affair more prominently than on any other release in his lengthy career; many of the songs have a power trio feel. In addition to the fine guitar work, Miller's vocals are stronger here, and during this era in general, than they would be in his hitmaking days in the mid-'70s, when he was much more laid-back and overdubbed. Ever the borrower, adapter, and integrator, Steve Miller shapes the blues, psychedelia, sound effects, sweet multi-tracked vocal harmonies, and guitar-driven hard rock into one cohesive musical statement with this release. *—Jim Newsom*

Number 5 / 1970 / Capitol ♦♦♦♦
Released in the summer of 1970, *Number 5* was the fifth LP by the Steve Miller Band in just over two years. While it compares favorably to its immediate predecessor, *Your Saving Grace*, it is not quite up to the consistent excellence of the potent *Brave New World* from the previous summer. However, it does have a fair share of delights, especially the opening triumvirate of "Good Morning," "I Love You," and "Going to the Country." These selections, and all of side one, have a distinctly more rural feel than did previous recordings, due perhaps to the fact that the tracks were recorded in Nashville. Charlie McCoy contributes harmonica to several of these cuts, and Buddy Spicher plays fiddle on "Going to the Country," while Bobby Thompson adds banjo to "Tokin's." Side two is more uneven, with the leadoff midtempo rocker, "Going to Mexico," serving as a conclusion to the first side's thematic coherence, and the closing "Never Kill Another Man" a string-laden ballad. Sandwiched between them are three experimental-sounding pieces, seasoned with sound effects, buried vocals, and semi-political themes. Although it couldn't have been predicted at the time, *Number 5* represented the end of an era for Steve Miller and bandmates, and subsequent albums would sound nothing like this first batch of great recordings. *—Jim Newsom*

Rock Love / 1971 / Capitol ♦
What a disappointing surprise. A full year had elapsed since the release of *Number 5*, completing a string of excellent albums by the Steve Miller Band. The unsuspecting record buyer had every right to expect another quality product. What he got instead was this travesty of generic white-boy bluesisms, recorded live but sounding dead. In retrospect, the title track can be heard as a precursor to "The Joker," but there is no reason to own this album except to wonder if the Steve Miller Band was really this boring in concert, and if so, why it was documented. *—Jim Newsom*

Recall the Beginning: A Journey from Eden / 1972 / Capitol ♦♦♦

Anthology / 1972 / Capitol ♦♦♦♦♦
Released in 1972, *Anthology* provides a 16-track summary of the Steve Miller Band's first five albums, distilling their uneven space blues into a tight, effective collection of highlights. These songs are hardly as tuneful or effortlessly catchy as the songs on 1978's *Greatest Hits*—apart from "Living in the USA," "Space Cowboy," and "Going to Mexico," there's nothing particularly immediate here—but they're first-rate period pieces, capturing Miller's space blues at its most effectively spacey. *—Stephen Thomas Erlewine*

The Joker / 1973 / Capitol ♦♦♦
With *The Joker*, Steve Miller reached new heights of popularity and commercial success but sank to a level of musical and lyrical banality from which he would not soon recover. This is not to say this is a terrible album, but measured against his classic first five albums, *The Joker* is very disappointing. While the title track is a catchy piece of fluff that hit the number one spot on the singles charts, most of the tracks on this recording sound like filler. "Mary Lou" is a cover of an old Ronnie Hawkins' song; "Your Cash Ain't Nothin' but Trash" is a '50s doo wop song by the Clovers, and "Come on in My Kitchen" is the oft-recorded Robert Johnson blues song, credited here to Woody Payne (the same songwriting credit given by John Renbourn on his *Faro Annie* album a year earlier). Even the originals here are based on borrowed ideas. "Sugar Babe" and "Shu Ba Da Du Ma Ma Ma Ma" are pleasant diversions, but as the titles suggest, of very little substance. The album sounds at times like it was recorded in a cave, with the drums sounding like cardboard boxes. This recording reached number two on the album charts on the strength of the single, but for those familiar with Steve Miller's music from 1968-1970, *The Joker* was little more than trash. *—Jim Newsom*

Fly Like an Eagle / 1976 / Capitol ♦♦♦♦♦
Steve Miller had started to essay his classic sound with *The Joker*, but 1976's *Fly Like an Eagle* is where he took flight, creating his definitive slice of space blues. The key is focus, even on an album as stylishly, self-consciously trippy as this, since the focus brings about his strongest set of songs (both originals and covers), plus a detailed atmospheric production where everything fits. It still can sound fairly dated—those whooshing keyboards and cavernous echoes are certainly of their time—but its essence hasn't aged, as "Fly Like an Eagle" drifts like a cool breeze, while "Take the Money and Run" and "Rock'n Me" are fiendishly hooky, friendly rockers. The rest of the album may not be quite up to those standards, but there aren't any duds, either, as "Wild Mountain Honey" and "Mercury Blues" give this a comfortable backdrop, thanks to Miller's offhand, lazy charm. Though it may not quite transcend its time, it certainly is an album rock landmark of the mid-'70s and its best moments (namely, the aforementioned singles) are classics of the idiom. *—Stephen Thomas Erlewine*

Book of Dreams / 1977 / Capitol ♦♦♦♦
Unless the Black Crowes dress up in NASA drag or Garth Brooks takes his glam-industrial doppelganger Chris Gaines into Mothership terrain, Steve Miller should retain his monopoly on the "Space Cowboy" moniker for many years to come. And it is here, on this 1977 blockbuster, that Miller shored up his cosmic persona: From the winged horse on the album cover to a judicious smattering of synthesizers in the music, *Book of Dreams* bridged the gap between blues-rock and the indulgences of prog rock. Things do go awry when Renaissance Faire whimsy takes over clunkers like "Wish Upon a Star" and "Babes in the Wood," but luckily the balance of the record offers a satisfying blend of meaty blues and country riffs and tasteful atmospherics. The well-known suspects include "Swingtown," "Wintertime," and "Threshold," with relatively straightforward rock & boogie highlights coming by way of "True Fine Love," "Jet Airliner," and "Jungle Love." The non-hit cuts, "Sacrifice" and "My Own Space," do stand up to these FM favorites but fall short of making the album something the casual fan should consider with Miller's *Greatest Hits 1974-1978* in hand (that collection includes seven tracks off of *Book of Dreams*, plus all the hits from *The Joker* and *Fly Like an Eagle*). Still, this is a highlight of the '70s classic rock era and one of Miller's finest releases. *—Stephen Cook*

● **Greatest Hits 1974–1978** / 1978 / Capitol ♦♦♦♦♦
Greatest Hits 1974-1978 collects the majority of Steve Miller's biggest hits—"The Joker," "Take the Money and Run," "Rock'n Me," "Fly Like an Eagle," "Jet Airliner," "Jungle Love," "Swingtown"—and seven album tracks that received a fair amount of airplay on album rock radio. The collection only covers a total of three albums—*The Joker, Fly Like an Eagle, Book of Dreams*—with the latter two providing the bulk of the material. Because of this, "Living in the USA," one of Miller's biggest hits of the late '60s/early '70s, isn't included but it isn't missed, since all of his other hits of the '70s are included. The thoroughness of *Greatest Hits 1974-1978* makes it an excellent introduction to Miller and for many casual fans, it also means that they can contain their Steve Miller collection to one disc. *—Stephen Thomas Erlewine*

Circle of Love / 1981 / Capitol ♦♦♦
Divided in half, with one side of catchy pop tunes and one side devoted to a 16-minute space blues workout called "Macho City," the design of *Circle of Love* feels like a throwback to 1971, when people truly paid attention to the flow of an album. In 1981, it was a bit of anachronism, but its old-fashioned feel (and its tedious "Macho City") are saved by the mini-album of pop/rock that might not have produced any undeniable classics, but includes tuneful, well-crafted numbers that serve as worthy follow-ups to *Fly Like an Eagle* and *Book of Dreams*. *—Stephen Thomas Erlewine*

Abracadabra / 1982 / Capitol ♦♦♦
Steve Miller was always catchy and tuneful, but he never turned out an unabashed pop album until 1982's *Abracadabra*. This isn't just pop in construction, it's pop in attitude, filled with effervescent melodies and deeply silly lyrics, perhaps none more noteworthy than the immortal couplet "Abra-Abracadabra/I wanna reach out and grab ya." Those words graced the title track, which turned out to be one of his biggest hits, and if nothing else is quite as irresistibly goofy as that song, there still is a surplus of engagingly tuneful material, all dressed up in psuedo-new wave production so favored by AOR veterans in the early '80s. All of that may not make this one of Miller's definitive albums, especially in the view of hardcore space blues heads, but it's pretty damn irresistible for listeners who find "Abracadabra" one of the highlights of faux-new wave AOR. *—Stephen Thomas Erlewine*

Steve Miller Band: Live! / 1983 / Capitol ♦♦
Released in 1983 *Steve Miller Band: Live!* is culled from a concert, or several concerts, that SMB gave on the supporting tour for *Abracadabra*. They run through all the big hits—the most obscure this gets is "Mercury Blues," from their most popular album, *Fly Like an Eagle*—in performances that pretty much stick to the record. There's not much here that's different and, accordingly, there are zero revelations, but this is pleasant and enjoyable. There's no real reason to get the record, since it isn't even infused with much live energy, but once it's playing, it's easy to get sucked into the greatest-hits set list. (By the way, the town where SMB performed is not listed in the liners, but the crowd does give a hearty cheer for "Detroit City" in "Rock'n Me," so maybe that's where it was cut.) *—Stephen Thomas Erlewine*

Italian X Rays / 1984 / Capitol ✦✦

Living in the 20th Century / Dec. 15, 1987 / Capitol ✦✦

Born 2B Blue / 1988 / Capitol ✦✦✦
Disregard the fact that the "space" in Steve Miller's "space blues" was a large part of why he had his own distinctive musical identity, because if you're going into 1988's *Born 2B Blue* looking for a return to his trademark space blues, or even a revitalization of his roots, you'll be sorely disappointed. In fact, this isn't even a blues album—it's a jazz album, pitched halfway between soul-jazz and smooth jazz. He's able to draft such heavy-hitters as Phil Woods and Milt Jackson for guest spots, and his taste in material is quite nice, balancing the overly familiar ("Willow Weep for Me," "God Bless the Child") with relatively obscure R&B cuts ("Ya Ya," "Mary Ann") and selections that demonstrate that he's a genuine fan, such as Horace Silver's "Filthy McNasty." Now, does all this make *Born 2B Blue* a worthwhile genre exercise? Well, in a sense, it does, since Miller is passionate as he can be, turning in charmingly laid-back performances that may not be noteworthy, but are pleasant as can be. So, it winds up being something that's modestly impressive and enjoyable as it's playing, but no matter what its virtues are, it's more noteworthy for what it is than what it gives. *—Stephen Thomas Erlewine*

The Best of 1968–1973 / 1990 / Capitol ✦✦✦✦✦
The Best of 1968-1973 is a solid collection that features many of the highlights from Steve Miller's first five years of recording, including "The Joker," "Living in the U.S.A.," "Space Cowboy," and "Gangster of Love." This compilation isn't as consistently thrilling as *Greatest Hits 1974-1978*, which also features "The Joker," and it's not as sharply assembled as 1972's *Anthology*, but it remains an adequate overview of Miller's early records, especially for fans only familiar with *Greatest Hits*. *—Stephen Thomas Erlewine*

Wide River / Jun. 8, 1993 / Polydor ✦✦
Steve Miller returns to the bluesy pop/rock sound that made his career so successful with *Wide River*, a pleasant collection of new songs that will appeal greatly to fans of "The Joker," "Take the Money and Run," and "Rock n' Me." *—AMG*

Steve Miller Band / Jul. 26, 1994 / Capitol ✦✦✦✦✦
Close to definitive is the best way to describe the three-disc box *Steve Miller Band*. That, or missed opportunity. The set is divided pretty well, with the first disc being devoted to the early years, the second to the hitmaking era, and the third to the blues. Now, this isn't a hard-and-fast breakdown, since there's no one on God's green earth who would call "Abracadabra" a blues, but it's a pretty good template for a box. The problem is the execution, particularly as the box gets off the ground. The historical childhood recordings that kick off the first disc are interesting, but they're alienating for anyone outside of hardcore fans. Then, much of the early work is present in oddly edited versions, which aren't particularly welcome. Still, this does round up nearly all of the highlights from throughout Miller's career, which does make it valuable for fans who want a pretty exhaustive, but not definitive, compilation. Nevertheless, *Anthology* and *Greatest Hits*, especially, remain the best way to hear Miller at his peak. *—Stephen Thomas Erlewine*

Greatest Hits / Nov. 3, 1998 / Polygram International ✦✦✦✦✦
Save for the few hits that cropped up in the first half of the '80s, Steve Miller's prime covers the years 1974-1978. With blockbuster albums like *Fly Like an Eagle* and *Book of Dreams*, Miller dominated the FM airwaves in the mid-'70s and became a fixture of that decade's mammoth outdoor festival circuit. While not quite on par with earlier hits like "Jet Airliner," "The Joker," and "Rock'n Me," early-'80s singles like "Abracadabra," "Keeps Me Wondering Why," and "Heart Like a Wheel" managed to keep the "Space Cowboy" magic going. This 20-track hits collection includes all these sides plus other smashes like "Jungle Love," "Fly Like an Eagle," "Swingtown," and "Wild Mountain Honey." Supplanting the earlier *Greatest Hits 1974-1978* release, this expanded and updated hits package qualifies as the essential first-disc choice for newcomers. And save for a few duds like the pop reggae "Give It Up" and 1993's "Wide River" and "Cry, Cry, Cry," the album is solid from start to finish. *—Stephen Cook*

Greatest Hits / Dec. 28, 1999 / Eagle ✦✦✦✦✦
Released in 1998—as Steve Miller notes in the liner notes, the 30th Anniversary of his recording career—this 20-track Australia-only collection trumps all other existing Miller collections, including the classic standard-bearer, *Greatest Hits*, by chronicling SMB's hitmaking peak, from "The Joker" through "Abracadabra" to "Wide River." This does mean that the spacy blues of their earliest recordings are entirely ignored, but all the FM radio favorites are here, including many that aren't on that aforementioned collection, all in terrific sound and blessed with track-by-track commentary by Miller taken from an interview with John Tobler. It may cost a little bit more for non-Australian fans, but it's worth it. *—Stephen Thomas Erlewine*

Steve Miller Band: On Tour 1973–1976 / Jul. 9, 2002 / King Biscuit ✦✦✦
The two discs of *Steve Miller Band: On Tour 1973-1976* feature two Steve Miller Band concerts recorded in 1973 and 1976, respectively, by (and for eventual broadcast on) the infamous *King Biscuit Flower Hour*. The soundboard recordings are pristine, with each bandmember occupying an equal part of the spectrum. The 1973 incarnation, captured at Shady Grove in Washington, D.C., still holds some connection to the earlier, more blues-based years of the band. As such, the disc contains a good deal of blues-rock jamming, much of which is admirably tight, though it falls prey to some of the era's excesses. Also contained is an early version of "Fly Like an Eagle," which Miller road-tested in several versions before setting it to wax. Following extensive touring around that period, Miller took an extended hiatus from the road, during which time he recorded both *Fly Like an Eagle* and *Book of Dreams*, what would prove to be his two most successful albums. Following the recording of those albums, Miller took to the road again, with a new band featuring Gary Mallaber, Lonnie Turner, Norton Buffalo, David Denny, and Byron Allred. The music is different, too. The blues influence is still there, but the band is sleeker and more modern. They have Miller's catalog of soon-to-be-classics at their disposal, and make good use of them, including good renditions of "The Joker" and the revamped "Fly Like an Eagle." The band's sound, though perhaps even more grounded in the era than the 1973 band, is also more original, regardless of whether or not one enjoys what they are doing. *—Jesse Jarnow*

Roy Milton

b. Jul. 31, 1907, Wynnewood, OK, **d.** Sep. 18, 1983, Los Angeles, CA
Vocals, Leader, Drums / Jazz Blues, Jump Blues, West Coast Blues, R&B
As in-the-pocket drummer of his own jump blues combo, the Solid Senders, Roy Milton was in a perfect position to drive his outfit just as hard or soft as he so desired. With his stellar sense of swing, Milton did just that; his steady backbeat on his 1946 single for Art Rupe's fledgling Juke Box imprint, "R.M. Blues," helped steer it to the uppermost reaches of the R&B charts (his assured vocal didn't hurt either).

Milton spent his early years on an Indian reservation in Oklahoma (his maternal grandmother was a native American) before moving to Tulsa. He sang with Ernie Fields' territory band during the late '20s and began doubling on drums when the band's regular trapsman got arrested one fateful evening. In the mood to leave Fields in 1933, Milton wandered west to Los Angeles and formed the Solid Senders. 1945 was a big year for him—along with signing with Juke Box (soon to be renamed Specialty), the band filmed three soundies with singer June Richmond.

"R.M. Blues" was such a huge seller that it established Specialty as a viable concern for the long haul. Rupe knew a good thing when he saw it, recording Milton early and often through 1953. He was rewarded with 19 Top Ten R&B hits by the Solid Senders, including "Milton's Boogie," "True Blues," "Hop, Skip and Jump," "Information Blues," "Oh Babe" (a torrid cover of Louis Prima's jivey jump), and "Best Wishes." Milton's resident boogie piano specialist, Camille Howard, also sang on several Milton platters, including the 1947 hit "Thrill Me," concurrently building a solo career on Specialty.

After amassing a voluminous catalog as one of Specialty's early bedrocks, Milton moved on to Dootone, King (there he cut the delectable instrumental "Succotash"), and Warwick (where he eked out a minor R&B hit in 1961, "Red Light") with notably less commercial success. Sadly, even though he helped pioneer the postwar R&B medium, rock & roll had rendered Roy Milton an anachronism.

The drummer remained active nonetheless, thrilling the throng at the 1970 Monterey Jazz Festival as part of Johnny Otis' all-star troupe. It's a safe bet he was swinging until the very end. *—Bill Dahl*

The Great Roy Milton / 1963 / Specialty ✦✦✦

★ **Roy Milton & His Solid Senders** / Feb. 1978 / Specialty ✦✦✦✦✦
Certainly this is the place to go for Milton's most popular and influential material—a whopping 18 of the 25 cuts made the R&B Top Ten in the late '40s and early '50s. These include such classics as "R.M. Blues," "The Hucklebuck," and "Hop, Skip & Jump" (given a great rockabilly treatment in the '50s by the Collins Kids). All of the tracks are prime jump blues, Milton occasionally slowing down the boogies into ballads; one number ("Thrill Me") features fellow jump blues star Camille Howard on vocals. *—Richie Unterberger*

R.M. Blues / 1985 / Specialty ✦✦✦
Specialty's *R.M. Blues* is a fine collection that features 15 highlights from Roy Milton's jumping Specialty recordings. While his time at Specialty was unquestionably the finest period of his career, and there are some timeless performances here ("R.M. Blues," "Night and Day," "Wakin' Up Baby," "Milton's Boogie," "Information Blues"), these same recordings have appeared on better, more comprehensive CD reissues which are preferable to this LP edition. *—Thom Owens*

Groovy Blues, Vol. 2 / 1992 / Specialty ✦✦✦✦✦
The rarities and unissued material begin to pop up on *Vol. 2*, making it even more of a feast for collectors. Milton's Solid Senders, featuring pianist/singer Camille Howard, guitarist Johnny Rogers, and a crew of roaring saxmen, were one of the tightest and most respected on the Coast. *—Bill Dahl*

Blowin' With Roy / 1994 / Specialty ✦✦✦✦✦
The third and presumably final entry in Specialty's exhaustive Milton reissue series is by no means a makeweight affair. Even when the Solid Senders tackled Tin Pan Alley fare like "Along the Navajo Trail," "Coquette," and "When I Grow Too Old to Dream," they swung 'em. More late-'40s/early-'50s rarities and unissued items galore. *—Bill Dahl*

Rhythms and Blues from California 1945–1949 / Sep. 12, 2000 / EPM Musique ✦✦✦✦

Roy Milton Blues / Speed ✦✦✦
Exciting, stomping, vintage R&B by a great bandleader. *—Ron Wynn*

Mississippi Heat

f. 1992, Chicago, IL
Group / Contemporary Blues, Modern Electric Blues
A contemporary blues combo resurrecting the vintage Chicago sound of the '50s, Mississippi Heat was formed in the Windy City in 1992 by vocalist/drummer Robert Covington, harpist Pierre Lacocque, guitarists Billy Flynn and James Wheeler, and bassist Bob Stroger. While remaining a fixture of the local club circuit, the band's lineup remained in flux in the years to follow; Covington exited in 1993, and was replaced by vocalist Deitra Farr and drummer Allen Kirk in time to record their debut LP *Straight From the Heart*. *Learned the Hard Way* followed in 1994, with *Thunder in My Heart* appearing a year later; both Farr and Kirk exited in 1996, and in 1997 Mississippi Heat welcomed vocalists Mary Lane and Zora Young, pianist Barrelhouse Chuck and drummer Kenny Smith. *—Jason Ankeny*

Straight from the Heart / 1993 / Van der Linden ✦✦✦
Debut by this solid mainstream Chicago outfit, *Straight from the Heart* is harp and guitar dominated. —*Bill Dahl*

● **Learned the Hard Way** / 1994 / Van der Linden ✦✦✦✦
More impressive work by this newcomer group with a classic approach; veteran Deitra Farr is an exceptional vocalist. —*Bill Dahl*

Mississippi Sheiks

f. 1926, Jackson, MS, **db.** 193?
Group / String Bands, Prewar Country Blues, Country Blues, Acoustic Blues
The Mississippi Sheiks were one of the most popular string bands of the late '20s and early '30s. Formed in Jackson around 1926, the band blended country and blues fiddle music—both old-fashioned and risqué—and included guitarist Walter Vinson and fiddler Lonnie Chatmon, with frequent appearances by guitarists Bo Carter and Sam Chatmon, who were also busy with their own solo careers. The musicians were the sons of Ezell Chatmon, uncle of Charley Patton and leader of an area string band that was popular around the turn of the century. The Mississippi Sheiks (who took their name from the Rudolph Valentino movie *The Sheik*) began recording for OKeh in 1930 and had their first and biggest success with "Sitting on Top of the World," which was a crossover hit and multi-million seller. In fact, the song became a national standard and has been recorded by Howlin' Wolf, Ray Charles and many more. The Mississippi Sheiks' popularity peaked in the early '30s, and their final recording session happened in 1935 for the Bluebird label. By the end of their career, the prolific and influential string band had recorded well over 60 songs, including the successful "Stop and Listen." —*Joslyn Layne*

☆ **Mississippi Sheiks Complete Recorded Works, Vols. 1–4** / 1991 / Document ✦✦✦✦
There's absolutely no way you can go wrong with this superlative four-CD import set of this seminal blues band. Covers everything they ever recorded from 1930 to 1936. —*Cub Koda*

Complete Recorded Works, Vol. 1 (1930) / 1991 / Document ✦✦✦✦

Complete Recorded Works, Vol. 2 (1930–1931) / 1991 / Document ✦✦✦✦

Complete Recorded Works, Vol. 3 (1931–1934) / 1991 / Document ✦✦✦✦

Complete Recorded Works, Vol. 4 (1934–1935) / 1991 / Document ✦✦✦✦

★ **Stop and Listen** / 1992 / Yazoo ✦✦✦✦✦
Stop and Listen collects 20 tracks the Mississippi Sheiks recorded in the early '30s, gathering together most of their best-known material (including "Sitting on Top of the World," plus the previously unreleased "Livin' in a Strain." These records are of significant historical importance and this is the definitive compilation of this groundbreaking—and popular—string band. —*Thom Owens*

Mississippi Sheiks: The Essential / Aug. 6, 2002 / Classic Blues ✦✦✦✦

Mr. B (Mark Braun)

Piano / Boogie-Woogie, Piano Blues
A superior blues and boogie-woogie pianist, Mr. B, aka Mark Braun, has recorded several excellent sets that find him revitalizing the vintage style. He started playing piano when he was 15 and, although he had heard much of the pop and rock music of the era, when his father brought home a record by Jimmy Yancey, it convinced him of the musical path he should take. Braun was fortunate enough to visit Chicago on several occasions, seeing, talking to and drawing inspiration from Little Brother Montgomery, Blind John Davis and Sunnyland Slim. He also heard Boogie Woogie Red play at the Blind Pig club in Detroit every Monday night for 11 years. By the mid-'70s, Mr. B was playing with regional bands and gaining a strong reputation.

Because he chose to stay in Ann Arbor, Mr. B is not as well-known as he should be, but he has recorded excellent sets for Blind Pig: 1987's *Shining the Pearls* which features J.C. Heard and Marcus Belgrave and 1988's *Partners in Crime* which also features Heard. In 1991 he released *My Sunday Best* for Ann Arbor label Schoolkids and followed it up with a big band record, *Hallelujah Train* in 1994. This record also came out on Schoolkids and features Ann Arbor's stalwart big band the Bird of Paradise Orchestra. Mr. B can be found every year at the Ann Arbor Art Fair pounding out some boogie for the enthralled hordes of tourists or on the mound at Vet's Park pitching his amateur baseball team to another victory. —*Scott Yanow*

Shining the Pearls / May 1987 / Blind Pig ✦✦✦
Mr. B's *Shining the Pearls* has some fine moments, especially when the pianist sticks to the blues. However, the album suffers from somewhat meandering arrangements and the lack of a rhythm section to keep the whole thing in focus. —*Thom Owens*

Partners in Time / 1988 / Blind Pig ✦✦✦✦✦
Partners in Time is a typically tasteful set from Mr. B, featuring a selection of originals peppered with a couple of classic covers. The pianist shows that he's comfortable with the style by dropping allusions to other players, pulling it all together into an enjoyable boogie-woogie romp. —*Thom Owens*

My Sunday Best / 1991 / Schoolkids ✦✦✦✦
Mark Braun, aka Mr. B, is a throwback both to the Chicago blues pianists of the '50s and the boogie-woogie masters of the 1920s and '30s. On this live set (recorded in Ann Arbor, Michigan), Mr. B (who takes a couple of heartfelt vocals) is featured at the head of a trio that includes bassist Kurt Krahnke and several different drummers, including Roy Brooks on six of the dozen selections. With the exception of Brooks' "Blues for a Carpenter" (which features the composer on musical saw!), Blind John Davis' "When I Lost My Baby," "Roll 'Em Pete" and a couple of adaptations of traditional material (including "Swanee River Boogie"), the material is comprised of all Braun originals. This CD is easily recommended to blues, jazz and boogie-woogie collectors. —*Scott Yanow*

● **Hallelujah Train** / Sep. 3, 1994+Jan. 7, 1995 / Schoolkids ✦✦✦✦✦
Mr. B is a talented boogie-woogie pianist who on this CD teams up successfully with bassist Paul Keller's Bird of Paradise orchestra, a seven-year-old big band from Michigan. The arrangements smoothly integrate Mr. B into the orchestra and these enthusiastic live performances are often quite memorable. Although largely a "no-name" big band, the many soloists are consistently talented (with the standouts being Mark Hynes on tenor, altoist Scott Peterson and trumpeter Paul Finkbeiner) and the pianist is in consistently inspired form. Highlights include "Hallelujah Train," "Brauny," tributes to Little Brother Montgomery, Horace Silver and Eddie Palmieri, an exciting rendition of "Down the Road Apiece," "Air Mail Special" and a lengthy "B's Boogie Woogie." Highly recommended. —*Scott Yanow*

Bobby Mitchell

b. Aug. 16, 1935, Algiers, LA, **d.** Mar. 17, 1989, New Orleans, LA
Trumpet / New Orleans R&B, Piano Blues, Rock & Roll, R&B
Bobby Mitchell & the Toppers were part of the wave of New Orleans rock & rollers who followed in the wake of Fats Domino and Lloyd Price. Although the group had limited success (their best known song, "Try Rock 'n Roll," climbed into the R&B Top 20 nationally, and "I'm Gonna Be a Wheel Someday" was a smash in numerous localities without ever charting nationally) and broke up in 1954, Mitchell remained a popular figure in New Orleans R&B for 35 years.

Bobby Mitchell (Aug. 16, 1935-Mar. 17, 1989) was born in Algiers, Louisiana, the second oldest of what were eventually 17 children in a family that made its living fishing the Mississippi River—Mitchell himself contributed to the family's well-being by cutting and selling wood. When he was ten years old, Mitchell got a job after school making deliveries for a liquor store, and it was while hanging around the store that he started singing—he was good enough then that people gave him nickels and dimes for his performances.

Mitchell played football in school until an injury sidelined him permanently, after which he joined the school chorus. By the time he was done with school, the music teacher was giving him solos on numbers such as "Ol' Man River" and "You'll Never Walk Alone." At age 17, he was in his first singing group, the Louisiana Groovers. By that time, Mitchell was falling firmly under the influence of R&B, most especially the sound of Roy Brown.

Mitchell wrote his first original song, "One Friday Morning," a doo wop-style ballad, which he cut as a demo with help from a teacher with a tape recorder (still a relative rarity in 1952). That tape got auditioned at a local radio station, and this led to the formation of a backing group called the Toppers, consisting of Lloyd Bellaire (tenor), Joseph Butler (tenor), Willie Bridges (baritone), Frank Bocage (bass), and Gabriel Fleming (piano). Vocally, they were influenced by acts such as Clyde McPhatter and the Dominoes, although they also listened to the records of Roy Hamilton and Nat King Cole. One factor that prevented them from coming up with a firmer direction of their own at the time was their youth—Mitchell was barely 17 at the time.

Eventually, they hooked up with producer Dave Bartholomew, and at his urging they cut some demos for Imperial Records. The group did as asked, but at the time it seemed as though it wasn't going to work out too well. The six of them were walking eight miles each day to the studio to practice with Bartholomew, and in the end Imperial only wanted Mitchell, until the singer insisted that it was all of them or nothing. Bartholomew relented, and in the meantime, the group had its first original song, "Rack 'Em Back," written by Joe Butler in response to the clowning on those long walks.

This became the B-side of their debut single, while a Lloyd Bellaire original, "I'm Crying," was the A-side. Released in May of 1953, it didn't sell well, although it was a beginning—Mitchell's voice was powerful and extremely expressive but quirkily uneven in the beginning, which made recording him tricky; the Toppers' singing was smooth, and the backing, by Lee Allen on tenor sax, Earl Palmer on drums, and Red Taylor on baritone sax (with Bartholomew on trumpet), was as solid as any rock & roll cut in New Orleans during that era. On stage in those early days, however, the group's instrumental backing was Gabriel Fleming's piano.

"I'm Crying" sold well in places like Cincinnati and Houston, but Mitchell and his group were unable to appear there to push the record any further, largely because of their ages and the fact that they were still required to attend school. Additionally, they weren't able to play any nightclubs even locally because they were underage, so they played high school dances, parties, weddings, and events at places like the American Legion Hall. Their recording career continued with more sessions resulting in classics such as "4x11 equals 44," a rock tune built around a set of popular lottery numbers.

Mitchell had trouble juggling the requirements of a career with school, and the Toppers endured until early 1954, when they finally split up after a session that included two hot songs, the raucous "School Boy Blues," with its killer guitar intro by Justin Adams, and "Sister Lucy," the latter highlighted by a Lee Allen solo. "Sister Lucy" ended up as a the B-side of a local double-sided hit with Bellaire's "My Baby's Gone"; "Sister Lucy" pulled in white listeners, while Bellaire's song reached the Black stations and clubs.

The Toppers' breakup came about because of the military draft, which claimed the members as they turned 18. Lloyd Bellaire joined the Army, while Frank Bocage joined the Navy, and Joseph Butler and Willie Bridges joined the Air Force. They did cut one more session late in the year, but essentially ceased to exist in the spring of 1954. Ironically, just at that moment "My Baby's Gone" and "Sister Lucy" became local hits. Mitchell and the Toppers were suddenly in serious demand, and with Gabriel Fleming, he organized a new group called the King Toppers.

The local success of "My Baby's Gone" was never repeated nationally, and his next record, "Nothing Sweet As You"/"I Wish I Knew," failed to chart. Mitchell was inactive in the studio for 1955. He returned to recording early in 1956 with a song tailor-made for the period, "Try Rock 'n Roll," one of those tunes meant to exploit the now-popular music style and name. That record made it to number 14 on the Billboard R&B chart, although it did far better than that in certain cities, and Mitchell was now getting booked onto all-star shows as far away as New York and Los Angeles.

In 1957, Bartholomew received a song by a Cajun writer named Roy Hayes called "I'm Gonna Be a Wheel Someday," and gave it to Mitchell to record. It became a hit locally in

Philadelphia, New Orleans, and Kansas City, among other places, and got Mitchell a spot on *American Bandstand*. Mitchell also proved something of a surprise to promoters and deejays in those cities where he'd never played before, because they assumed, on the basis of that record, that he was white.

Mitchell's sporadic success on Imperial ended in 1958, as the label dropped most of its New Orleans acts except for Fats Domino. He continued performing and recording, now trying to support a wife and her three children by a previous marriage. He signed with a succession of smaller labels in the early '60s, along the way working with Dr. John. By the mid-'60s, the couple had eight children and Mitchell's career had stalled. He still played shows in Houston and Mobile, but his records weren't selling—he was back with Imperial Records very briefly, and then returned to Rip Records, where he'd previously cut a couple of singles. Those sides for Rip and Sho-Biz were among the finest songs that Mitchell ever recorded, but were largely unheard.

A heart attack in the early '60s brought an end to his career on the road. Mitchell continued performing in New Orleans, where he remained a music celebrity for the next 29 years, performing regularly and eventually finding new recognition. Toward the end of his life, he also saw the first money from his original Imperial recordings with the release of a reissue LP, *I'm Gonna Be a Wheel Someday*. Mitchell became one of New Orleans' most visible and forthcoming '50s veterans. He passed away in 1989 after years of worsening illnesses, including diabetes, kidney failure, and two further heart attacks.

Many of Mitchell's early recordings were influenced by the dominant musical personalities of his day, including Roy Brown, Roy Hamilton, and, especially, Fats Domino, which was understandable since he shared the same producer and was on the same label. His voice had a distinct quality all its own, however, which became recognizable once he became comfortable in the studio. The Toppers, who ceased working with Mitchell after mid-1954, were a somewhat unpredictable group musically, mostly owing to their ages, and their sound was consciously derivative of numerous vocal groups of the period, especially the early Drifters. With Bartholomew's top session men backing them up, however, their records were solid New Orleans R&B at its best, and many of the records are classics of the sound from that era, if not on a par with those of Fats Domino then certainly residing on the level just below his and Lloyd Price's. —*Bruce Eder*

● **I'm Gonna Be a Wheel Someday** / 1997 / Bear Family ◆◆◆◆
The only earthly reason for making this two-CD set an oversized box, as opposed to a small double jewel box, was so that the booklet could accommodate the notes and photos—but it adds nothing to the retail cost, and the booklet is pretty cool. The 47 tracks here cover Mitchell's entire recording career through 1964, on the Imperial, Sho-Biz, Ron, and Rip labels, all in surprisingly consistent sound given the age and varied sources of the recordings. The early tracks, Mitchell and the Toppers' first sessions from 1953, are a little crude, as was typical of R&B from this era—though the singing and playing overcome this inherent difficulty. By the time of their 1954 sessions, the group and their recordings are rather more sophisticated, and Mitchell's vocals are more confident as well. Disc two covers the second half of Mitchell's career with Imperial, including the classic "I'm Gonna Be a Wheel Someday." The four songs that Mitchell cut for Imperial on his brief return in 1962 show him working in an Arthur Alexander-type mode, doing slow romantic ballads extremely effectively. But the real jewels on Disc two are the songs Mitchell cut with Dr. John on the Sho-Biz and Ron labels, which include a raft of dazzling, soulful rockers. If anything, these rock harder than the Imperial sides, and Mitchell sounds more comfortable, with an arrangement, backing band, and tempos more suited to his strengths as a singer, stretching out and finally finding a voice and sound completely his own. Those tracks and some unreleased numbers deserved hit status, and why they failed, apart from the modest resources of the labels they were done for, is anyone's guess. The box concludes with Mitchell's answer song to his second biggest hit, "I Don't Want to Be a Wheel No More," and his towering 1963 single "Walking in Circles"—lushly scored for a full band and chorus, Mitchell's voice in these surroundings soars to majestic new heights of soulfulness. —*Bruce Eder*

You Always Hurt the One You Love / Mar. 18, 1997 / Bear Family ◆◆◆◆

McKinley Mitchell
b. Dec. 25, 1934, Jackson, MS, d. Jan. 18, 1986, Chicago Heights, IL
Vocals / Electric Blues, Soul-Blues, R&B, Soul
Blessed with an extraordinary set of soaring pipes, McKinley Mitchell waxed a series of superb Chicago soul platters during the '60s, later veering stylistically closer to contemporary blues in his last years of performing.

At age 16, Mitchell was already fronting a gospel group, the Hearts of Harmony, in Jackson. After spending time singing spirituals in Springfield, MS, and Philadelphia, Mitchell hit Chicago in 1958 and went secular. A rocking debut for the tiny Boxer label the next year preceded his signing with George Leaner's fledgling One-derful logo in 1961.

His first single for the firm, the gorgeous soul ballad "The Town I Live In," proved a national R&B hit and launched the imprint in high style. Mitchell's One-derful follow-ups, including the imaginative "A Bit of Soul," failed to equal the heights of his first single; neither did 45s for Chess (produced by Willie Dixon) and a variety of Dixon-owned labels.

Finally, in 1977, Mitchell returned to the R&B charts with "The End of the Rainbow," another beautiful R&B ballad, for Malaco's Chimneyville subsidiary. An eponymous LP for the label the next year stunningly showcased Mitchell's still-potent voice on a program that combined blues and soul material. A 1984 LP for Retta's, *I Won't Be Back for More*, was among the singer's last releases (by then, he was back living in Jackson). —*Bill Dahl*

Featuring 12 Great Songs / 1979 / P-Vine ◆◆◆◆
Until someone sorts out precisely who owns the masters originally on Chicago's One-derful label, we'll have to make do (if we can find it, of course) with this Japanese vinyl

collection of Mitchell's early-'60s R&B gems. Includes his haunting first hit, "The Town I Live In," and a clever "A Bit of Soul." —*Bill Dahl*

● **Complete Malaco Collection** / 1992 / Waldoxy ◆◆◆◆◆
The former Chicago soul singer found new life and a second chance at the brass ring at Malaco during the late '70s. The gent with the soaring pipes wrote the touching ballad "The End of the Rainbow" himself; seldom have singer and song matched any closer. —*Bill Dahl*

Prince Phillip Mitchell
b. 1945, Louisville, KY
Vocals, Piano, Percussion, Guitar / Soul-Blues, Disco, Soul
A veteran composer, vocalist, guitarist, and pianist, Prince Phillip Mitchell's roots are in vintage R&B, although he's better known for soul tunes. Mitchell sang with both The Premiers and The Checkmates in the late '50s and early '60s. He was also a dancer with The Bean Brothers in Los Angeles. Mitchell had hits recorded by Mel & Tim, Millie Jackson, Norman Connors, Joe Simon, and Candi Staton, but hasn't had as much luck on his own as a vocalist. His only moderate hit was "One On One" for Atlantic in 1978, and it only cracked the R&B Top 40. Mitchell has also recorded for Event and Ichiban. —*Ron Wynn*

Top of the Line / 1979 / Atlantic ◆◆◆
It didn't receive much attention upon its initial release, nor has it gained much of a following in the years since, but *Top of the Line* is a solid soul album. Its production is a little slick, but Prince Phillip Mitchell's vocals are in good form, making the mediocre songs on the record fairly enjoyable. —*Thom Owens*

● **Loner** / 1991 / Ichiban ◆◆◆
More often than not, Prince Phillip Mitchell was among R&B's behind-the-scenes people—his songs were recorded by well-known artists like Norman Connors and Joe Simon, although he was never huge as a solo artist. Nonetheless, he's a talented singer who has a small following, and that is who he catered to when, at 45, he recorded *Loner* for the Atlanta-based Ichiban label. Although this nine-song CD came out in 1991, it often sounds like it could have been recorded in the '70s. *Loner* isn't urban contemporary—it's '70s-style soul, and Mitchell doesn't try to be relevant to the urban scene of the early '90s. There are no hip-hop beats on *Loner*, no attempts to appeal to new jack swing aficionados or win over Bell Biv DeVoe fans. Instead, Mitchell (who produced the album and wrote all of the songs) sounds like someone who knows his audience—a Baby Boomer soul audience—and gives fans what they want on "Starting From Scratch," "Nothing Hurts Like Love," and other sleek yet gritty originals. Although this CD was recorded in three southern cities (Atlanta, Louisville, KY, and Muscle Shoals, AL), it certainly isn't without northern influences. *Loner* doesn't sound like an Otis Redding or Rufus Thomas album from the '60s; it has more in common with the albums that some Southern artists provided in the '70s—a time that found Southerners like Johnnie Taylor and Eddie Floyd being influenced by the sleeker Northern soul that was coming out of Philadelphia, Chicago, and Detroit. The seductive "Come to Bed," in fact, wouldn't have been out of place on one of Teddy Pendergrass' Philadelphia International albums of the late '70s. *Loner* falls short of superb, but it's sincere and enjoyable. —*Alex Henderson*

Monkey Joe (Jesse Coleman)
b. Mississippi
Vocals, Piano / Country Blues, Piano Blues
The amount of real information known about Jesse "Monkey Joe" Coleman, who recorded extensively in the '30s for Lester Melrose in Chicago and who was still playing clubs in the Windy City in the '60s and '70s, is astonishingly small. He was born sometime around or before 1906, probably in Mississippi, and seems to have played the juke joints in the area around Jackson in the early '30s, as well as New Orleans, where he cut his first session for RCA-Victor's Bluebird imprint in 1935, in tandem with Little Brother Montgomery. Coleman first used the "Monkey Joe" name sometime in the '30s.

He later turned up in Chicago as part of Lester Melrose's stable of bluesmen, and had his next session there in 1938 backed by guitarist Charlie McCoy and drummer Fred Williams. He seems to have worked variously under the names Jack Newman at Vocalion and George Jefferson elsewhere, as accompanist to singer Lulu Scott. He cut further sides for Melrose, including a group of sides on which he was billed as "Monkey Joe and His Music Grinders." He also recorded for the OKeh label.

Not much is known of Monkey Joe's exact activities between the '30s and the '60s, only that he was a fixture at the clubs in the Chicago area in the '60s and beyond. He is presumed to have died sometime after the early '70s. One album, *Crescent City Blues*, coupling him with Little Brother Montgomery, surfaced in the early '70s. —*Bruce Eder*

Complete Recorded Works, Vol. 1 (1935-39) / Mar. 5, 1996 / Document ◆◆◆◆
Jesse "Monkey Joe" Coleman's first 26 extant sides, two accompanying Lulu Scott but otherwise all him, including the singing. Coleman's voice is a kind of high tenor, very distinctive and expressive, while his piano style is lively and highly percussive—he loved to pound those ivories—lending itself to a very animated performing style. His New Orleans Bluebird sessions, accompanied by guitarist Walter Vincson, yielded four very outgoing numbers in which the piano and guitar compete very loudly and effectively for the listener's attention. The Illinois sessions from three years later have Coleman generally working in a much more restrained manner, achieving greater subtlety in his singing while his piano mixes quietly with Charlie McCoy's mandolin and guitar. Occasionally, however, he'd revert to his older sound on songs like "Hair Parted In the Middle," a wonderful rocking little number. The songs are generally first-rate, and it's a surprise that Coleman didn't find a bigger audience for his records. The Lulu Scott numbers fit together very well with Coleman's own stuff, since his piano playing (leading the accompaniment) is so similar to that on his own music, and he joins her on vocals for one number. Her

version of "Everybody Do the Shag" alone is almost worth the cost of the CD, and Coleman's "Taxes on My Pole" is one of the more comically suggestive blues numbers you're likely to hear. The sound quality is more than acceptable on the early numbers, with no overly poor sources—the later material, from 1938-1939, beginning with "Just Out of the Big House," which still sounds good, suffer from increasing noise, but one suspects these were the best copies available, and they're still acceptable. *—Bruce Eder*

● **Complete Recorded Works, Vol. 2 (1939–40)** / Apr. 9, 1996 / Document ♦♦♦♦

Little Brother Montgomery (Eurreal Montgomery)

b. Apr. 18, 1906, Kentwood, LA, **d.** Sep. 6, 1985, Champaign, IL

Vocals, Piano / Piano Blues

A notable influence to the likes of Sunnyland Slim and Otis Spann, pianist "Little Brother" Montgomery's lengthy career spanned both the earliest years of blues history and the electrified Chicago scene of the '50s.

By age 11, Montgomery had given up on attending school to instead play in Louisiana juke joints. He came to Chicago as early as 1926 and made his first 78s in 1930 for Paramount (the booty that day in Grafton, WI, included two of Montgomery's enduring signature items, "Vicksburg Blues" and "No Special Rider"). Bluebird recorded Montgomery more prolifically in 1935-36 in New Orleans.

In 1942, Little Brother Montgomery settled down to a life of steady club gigs in Chicago, his repertoire alternating between blues and traditional jazz (he played Carnegie Hall with Kid Ory's Dixieland band in 1949). Otis Rush benefitted from his sensitive accompaniment on several of his 1957-1958 Cobra dates, while Buddy Guy recruited him for similar duties when he nailed Montgomery's "First Time I Met the Blues" in a supercharged revival for Chess in 1960. That same year, Montgomery cut a fine album for Bluesville with guitarist Lafayette "Thing" Thomas that remains one of his most satisfying sets.

With his second wife, Janet Floberg, Montgomery formed his own little record company, FM, in 1969. The first 45 on the logo, fittingly enough, was a reprise of "Vicksburg Blues," with a vocal by Chicago chanteuse Jeanne Carroll (her daughter Karen is following in her footsteps around the Windy City). *—Bill Dahl*

Tasty Blues / 1960 / Prestige/Original Blues Classics ♦♦♦♦♦

Here's a very attractive example of a pianist with roots dug deep in prewar tradition updating his style just enough to sound contemporary for 1960. With a little help from bassist Julian Euell and Lafayette Thomas (better-known as Jimmy McCracklin's guitarist), Montgomery swoops through his seminal "Vicksburg Blues" and "No Special Rider" with enthusiasm and élan. *—Bill Dahl*

Little Brother Montgomery / 1961 / Decca ♦♦

● **Chicago: The Living Legends** / 1961 / Riverside/Original Blues Classics ♦♦♦♦♦

Chicago: The Living Legends was recorded live at the Birdhouse in Chicago. Much of the record is performed by Montgomery solo, although there's a handful of wonderful cuts that feature him with a small group of traditional jazz musicians. Most of the album is devoted to classic songs from the likes of Duke Ellington and Jelly Roll Morton, yet there are a couple of originals thrown in the mix as well. It's all distinguished by Montgomery's wonderful, laidback performances, which make this a little gem. *—Thom Owens*

Piano, Vocal, and Band Blues / Jul. 1962 / Riverside ♦♦♦

No Special Rider / 1968 / Genes/Adelphi ♦♦♦

Barrelhouse piano player Eurreal "Little Brother" Montgomery played boogie from the crowds as a touring, pre-teen performer. Also a vocalist, Montgomery began his half-century of recording in the Depression with such songs of loss as "Vicksburg Blues" and "No Special Rider." On these 1969 recordings, rich, full-throated Jeanne Carroll ("Penny Pinching Blues") appears on four of the 12 tracks. She carefully enunciates her way through a rendition of Ma Rainey's "You Gotta See Your Mama Every Night." The excellent blues vocalist and pianist Little Brother Montgomery, an influence to Willie Dixon, Otis Spann, and Skip James, here guides us from his home through the tradition of classic early, post-ragtime piano blues. *—Tom Schulte*

Goodbye Mister Blues / 1973-1976 / Delmark ♦♦♦

While Eurreal "Little Brother" Montgomery was among blues' greatest barrelhouse and boogie pianists, he was also well versed in traditional jazz. This disc's 13 cuts feature him working with The State Street Swingers, an early jazz unit, doing faithful recreations of such chestnuts as "South Rampart St. Parade," "Riverside Blues" and "Panama Rag." Montgomery's vocals were stately, yet exuberant, while his piano solos were loose and firmly in the spirit, showing the link between early jazz and blues. While the emphasis is more on interaction and ensemble playing than individual voices, players expertly maximized their solo time. This is a fine example of a vintage style. *—Ron Wynn*

At Home / 1990 / Earwig ♦♦♦

Very informally recorded for the most part in the latter days of the fabulous pianist's career, these tapes provide a glimpse at what Montgomery played to please himself (and wife Jan, of course). *—Bill Dahl*

☆ **Complete Recorded Works (1930–1936)** / 1992 / Document ♦♦♦♦♦

This single CD from the European Document label has all of Montgomery's 26 prewar recordings as a leader. Two solo numbers are from 1930, including "Vicksburg Blues"; there are a couple songs from 1931 and four duets with guitarist Walter Vincson from 1935. The remainder of this release features Montgomery during a marathon session on Oct. 16, 1936 that resulted in 18 solo selections. All the numbers except the final three on this CD have vocals by Montgomery, but the most rewarding selections are those three instrumentals. On "Farish Street Jive," "Crescent City Blues" and "Shreveport Farewell," Little Brother Montgomery shows just how talented a pianist he was, making one regret that he felt compelled to sing (in a likable but not particularly distinctive voice) on all of the other numbers. A very complete and historic set. *—Scott Yanow*

Complete Recorded Works (1930–1954) / Jun. 2, 1994 / Document ♦♦♦♦

Monte Montgomery

b. Birmingham, AL

Guitar / Modern Electric Blues, Modern Electric Texas Blues

As a leading voice on the music scene in Austin, TX, guitarist Monte Montgomery slowly gained national recognition for his amazing dexterity, fluid harmonics, percussive dynamics, and melodic sensibility. Montgomery won his fourth consecutive title as best acoustic guitarist at the 2001 Austin Music Awards at the SXSW Festival. Songs written by Montgomery in early 2001 followed suit from his previous releases, 1998's *1st and Repair* and 1999's *Mirror*, in that they all focus on storytelling, a quality he derived from listening to Guy Clark, Townes Van Zandt, and Bob Dylan. "Tug of War," a song written in 2001, was about the give and take in relationships. "All on Me" started as a slow ballad, then transformed into a guitar anthem. Montgomery continued to tour in 2001 with his quartet—bassist Lonnie Trevino, drummer Phil Bass, and percussionist Mike Urdy—performing songs loosely based on his experiences or gathered from his understanding of and observations of other people. Montgomery's sandy voice and rapid fingerpicking gained him comparisons to Mark Knopfler and Bruce Cockburn, but his true heritage lay in the tradition of Texas guitarists B.W. Stevenson, Shake Russell, and Guy Clark, whom he discovered in his youth.

National acclaim started to come his way after appearances on PBS music television shows, such as *Austin City Limits*, *CD Highway*, and *Texas Music Cafe*. His growing talents as a guitarist and songwriter came from the understanding of melody and rhythm he gained from hearing pop icons Lindsay Buckingham of Fleetwood Mac, Stevie Wonder, and the Neville Brothers. Montgomery's journey to guitar stardom started in the Hill Country hamlet near Fredericksburg, TX, where his mom (Maggie Montgomery, herself a folk-country singer and guitarist in Luckenbach, TX) let him strum her guitar while she fingered the chords. Montgomery lived out of the back of his mother's pickup for a while. He played for tips and paid a lot of dues early in his career.

He and his mother used to hang out at the Kerrville Folk Festival in Texas where they met a lot of songwriters. David Montgomery, his dad, factored into his development, too. Monte Montgomery was born in Birmingham, AL, where his father, a choir director, took him to church and introduced him to gospel singers. A lot of his apprenticeship during the '80s took place in San Antonio, where he honed his skills by performing cover songs in cafes and honky-tonks. He commuted to Austin to perform his original songs. Before long, he became a mainstay on the music scene there.

After signing with Heart Music to record his first two CDs, Montgomery began to rise in popularity. In 1998, Montgomery moved to Austin. The songs on his 2000 CD, *Mirror*, ranged from the flashy guitar style on "Hopin' That You'd Slow Down" to the beautiful lyricism of the ballad "Magnolia." Well into 2001, Montgomery brought both parental forces to bear in the rich harmonic interplay of his voice and his guitar. *—Robert Hicks*

1st and Repair / Jan. 27, 1998 / Heart Music ♦♦♦

● **Mirror** / Jun. 15, 1999 / Heart Music ♦♦♦♦

There are 11 tracks on *Mirror*, reflecting a wide range of styles and melody, each with its own charms and hooks. All of the songs were written by Monte Montgomery, proving that he is not only one of Texas' finest guitarists, he is also a top-notch songwriter. From the catchy pop of "Hopin' That You'd Slow Down" to the beautiful "Magnolia," and at all points in between, "Mirror" stands as one fine album. There are hints of Elvis Costello, Tom Petty, and, of course, Mark Knopfler, but Monte is far and away his own man when it comes to his music. There are subtle hints at influences, but he doesn't really sound like anyone you've ever heard before, and that is the primary draw here. That's what sucks you in, like a hyperactive Hoover. "I Know You By Heart" is a radio-ready pop tune if ever there was one, featuring a guest appearance from Arista recording artist and Grammy nominee Abra Moore; and "Tear Down the Wall" rocks with a Springsteen-meets-Joel vibe that will have you clamoring for a pen to join the Monte Montgomery fan club. One of the album's best tunes is a live version of Montgomery's borderline-reggae "When Will I," with Montgomery using his voice both to carry the melody and as a percussive instrument, spouting off words that often times sound like raps on a drum. The song was recorded live on the PBS stage of *Austin City Limits*, and the CD even features a video of the performance tailor made for your iMac or PC. Along with Phil Bass on drums and Chris Maresh on bass guitar, Monte Montgomery, who was voted best acoustic guitarist at the Austin Music Awards during 1998, 1999, and 2000, delivers an album that will continually find its way to the top of your stack of CDs. This is jaw-dropping guitar magic from a man who can get more different sounds out of his beaten-up 1989 Alvarez acoustic box than most players could get with five guitars and a rack full of effects. This is the cream, folks. Look for it to rise to the top soon. *—Michael B. Smith*

Wishing Well / Jul. 31, 2001 / Antone's ♦♦♦♦

Monte Montgomery takes the challenge of being a male soloist well, creating a great mix of vocals and instruments to form many different sounds in his latest collection of modern electric blues music. While from the beginning it appears that the album will fall into a repetitious sound, making every song sound alike, Montgomery quickly breaks from that pattern to really create a solid mix of music. While the subjects of his songs vary—from relationships in the first track, "Tug of War," to many others—what the songs do have in common is their masterful lyrics. Montgomery has the songwriting ability to tell a story fluidly, without the overuse of chorus lines and repetition. In an age of poor songwriting, it is refreshing to open the liner notes and see magical and lengthy poetry. Perhaps the best example, as well as the best track on the album, is "Erased," a slower song that sounds very similar to a middle-aged Bob Dylan. A hopeful song with a catchy sound, it really draws the listener in as well as highlights Montgomery's vast vocal talents. Of course, this album isn't all about the lyrics. "Bagpipe" is a wonderful instrumental piece that combines great acoustic and electric guitar playing with some catchy percussion sounds. It is a nice break in the record, giving the listener a break from Montgomery's voice, while at the same time showing off his and his bandmates' instrumental talents as they create a great bagpipe sound, without actually playing the instrument. A true highlight for this record. Montgomery ends the album on a high note, with a somewhat fast-paced and upbeat song, "Radio Girl." It is unlike the other tracks in that it has a jazzy sound, leaving the listener feeling good after the record completes. This comes after the marathon song, "All on Me," which combines unbelievable electric guitar with Montgomery's voice and a nice chorus background. On an album that mixes vocals with instruments so well, this is a perfect track, because it does both of those things so well, for over seven minutes. *—Shawn Nicholls*

Coco Montoya

b. 1951, Santa Monica, CA

Vocals, Guitar / Modern Electric Blues, Soul-Blues

Though he grew up as a drummer and was raised on rock & roll, Coco Montoya became an outstanding blues guitarist in the '90s after stints in the bands of Albert Collins and John Mayall. Montoya debuted as a leader in 1995 with the Blind Pig album *Gotta Mind to Travel* and garnered an award for Best New Blues Artist at the following year's W.C. Handy Awards ceremonies.

Born in Santa Monica, Montoya played drums for a local rock band that toured the region during the mid-'70s, playing in area clubs. Although he had recently been turned on to blues at an Albert King show, he was somewhat unprepared to sit in with another blues legend—"the Iceman" Albert Collins—when a bar-owner friend of Montoya invited the bluesman to play at his nightclub. Though his inexperience showed, the young drummer impressed Collins enough to hire him for a Pacific Northwest tour three months later. The tour soon ended, but the pair's affiliation remained for more than five years, while Montoya learned much about the handling of blues guitar from "the Master of the Telecaster."

By the early '80s, Coco Montoya was back in the small-time nightclub business, playing guitar with several regional bands. At one night's show, he realized that John Mayall was in the audience, so he dedicated a cover of "All Your Love" to the British blues maestro. The song prompted Mayall to hire Montoya as lead guitarist for a new version of the Bluesbreakers he had formed. Despite the enormous pressure of filling a spot once held by Eric Clapton and Peter Green, Montoya jumped at the opportunity.

His first album with the Bluesbreakers came in 1985. Mayall had not released an album in five years at that point and the Bluesbreakers had been dead for more than 15, but the live album *Behind the Iron Curtain* proved Mayall's viability thanks mostly to the fiery work of Montoya. The guitarist appeared on three studio albums with Mayall and the Bluesbreakers, but then struck out on his own by the mid-'90s. Signed to Blind Pig, Montoya released *Gotta Mind to Travel* in 1995 with help from Mayall and another former Bluesbreaker compatriot, rhythm guitarist Debbie Davies. After years of toil under Collins and Mayall, Montoya was finally in the spotlight and his award as Best New Blues Artist of 1996 proved quite ironic, given his years of experience. His second album, *Ya Think I'd Know Better*, was followed by 1997's *Just Let Go*. At that point, Montoya and Blind Pig parted company and he signed with Alligator Records. *Suspicion* was released in 2000, followed two years later by *Can't Look Back*, a disc that incorporated a definitive soul/R&B approach. *—John Bush & Al Campbell*

Gotta Mind to Travel / 1995 / Blind Pig ✦✦✦✦

Years of apprenticeship with Albert Collins and John Mayall paid off handsomely for Montoya on this debut effort. Even with help from some famous friends (Debbie Davies, Al Kooper, Richie Hayward [Little Feat], and both former employers), Montoya asserts himself as the focal point. Sadly, this was one of Collins' last studio appearances before his death, playing on the Lowell Fulson-penned "Talking Woman Blues" (commonly known as "Honey Hush"). Although Montoya showcases his massive guitar muscle, it is merely a fraction of the power of his live performances. *—Char Ham*

● **Ya Think I'd Know Better** / May 1996 / Blind Pig ✦✦✦✦

With his second album *Ya Think I'd Know Better*, Coco Montoya ditches the guest stars and opts for a menu of pure, unadulterated Montoya. The results are quite impressive, to say the least. For the moment, overlook his somewhat pedestrian vocals and just concentrate on his scintillating guitar work. It's no secret that Montoya cultivated a reputation as one of the finest guitarists of the '80s and '90s through his session work, but even those familiar with his gutsy, electrifying style will be taken aback by the stylistic variety and musical depth on *Ya Think I'd Know Better*. Montoya even pulls skunk-hot solos out of the most predictable blues-rockers, while his smoldering solos on slower numbers like "Dyin' Flu" are passionate and moving. Best of all, Coco puts down his electric for acoustic romps like the earthy "Hiding Place." In short, *Ya Think I'd Know Better* answers the question whether Coco Montoya is a vital bluesman for the '90s, and the answer is an emphatic "yes!" *—Thom Owens*

Just Let Go / Sep. 23, 1997 / Blind Pig ✦✦✦✦

Coco Montoya's often ferocious guitar is the main reason to acquire this 1997 release. His singing is expressive and reasonably effective, but it is the blazing guitar solos that make one wish that he would record a full set of instrumentals; "Cool Like Dat" is a real cooker. Montoya performs some soul, R&B, and even country-tinged music on the set but he is at his best on the blues, particularly the B.B. King-inspired "Do What You Want to Do." Although his backup band is fine, this interesting if not quite essential release is primarily a showcase for the passionate Montoya. Recommended in particular to fans of the rock side of the blues. *—Scott Yanow*

Suspicion / Jan. 25, 2000 / Alligator ✦✦✦

Montoya's first solo disc for Alligator finds the former Albert Collins sideman following in the doorsteps of his "godfather" with an album simply top-heavy with fiery guitar work and comfortable vocals. The production from Jim Gaines is as fat as any modern-day blues record has a right to be, and Montoya does not disappoint at any moment along the ride. He tips his hat to his old employer on Collins' "Get Your Business Straight," but the stronger tunes here come from Coco's own pen, like the closing "Nothing But Love." A strong and solid effort that also sounds great in the car when you're driving a little faster than the speed limit allows. *—Cub Koda*

Can't Look Back / Jun. 4, 2002 / Alligator ✦✦✦✦

Coco Montoya's second album for Alligator records finds the guitarist moving away from the sound of his mentor, Albert Collins—although there certainly are licks throughout the album clearly inspired by "the Iceman," particularly when the tempo slows down—and toward big rock productions. This album sounds huge: The rhythm section provides a gigantic foundation, sprawling from speaker to speaker, then the keyboards and backing vocals are added, with guitars pushed to the forefront. On top of that, Montoya is demonstrating a greater inclination to soul and R&B than ever before, choosing to cover Holland-Dozier-Holland (a terrific take on "Something About You"), along with other tuneful soul tunes, and writing it that vein as well. This suits him well, since not only his full-throated vocals feel at ease with these melodies, he's turning out tasteful, melodic solos that punctuate and further the tune, instead of just being virtuosic showcases. The production may still be too big for some tastes, but look beyond that and hear what Montoya is doing with the music, and it becomes clear this is a nice step forward. *—Stephen Thomas Erlewine*

John Mooney

b. Apr. 3, 1955, East Orange, NJ

Slide Guitar, Vocals, Guitar / Contemporary Blues, Ragtime

John Mooney is a slide guitarist, working primarily in a traditionalist Delta acoustic style. Originally hailing from Rochester, NY, Mooney learned his craft first hand from country blues legend Son House. Later in his career, he moved to New Orleans, switched to electric guitar and began enlivening his music with Second Line rhythms indigenous to the area.

Born in New Jersey but raised in Rochester, New York, John Mooney began playing guitar following a meeting with Son House, who also lived in Rochester. Mooney learned the basics of blues guitar from House and he returned the favor by supporting the guitarist during the mid-'70s. In 1976, Mooney relocated to New Orleans and within a year of his arrival, he landed a contract with Blind Pig. In 1977, he released his debut album, *Comin' Your Way*.

After performing straight acoustic Delta blues for several years, Mooney changed his musical direction in 1983, when he formed Bluesiana, a more eclectic—and electric—outfit. Throughout the '80s, he toured and recorded with Bluesiana, opening for the likes of Albert King, Bonnie Raitt, and Clarence "Gatemouth" Brown. After a few years of touring, Mooney was able to sign another record contract, releasing *Telephone King* on the Powerhouse label in 1991. His next records were one-offs on small labels: 1992's *Testimony* for Domino and 1995's *Travelin' On* on Crosscut. Mooney toured consistently at this time, building his fan base one blues club at a time. His hard work paid off when in 1996 he signed up with the House of Blues label and released his first nationally distributed record *Against the Wall*. This deal turned out to be a one-off as well but after releasing a live solo album for Ruf in 1997, Mooney returned to Blind Pig to release 2000's *Gone to Hell* and 2002's *All I Want*. Both albums are solid additions to Mooney's discography. *—Cub Koda & Stephen Thomas Erlewine*

Comin' Your Way / 1979 / Blind Pig ✦✦✦

This album features acoustic guitar and arresting vocals on high-energy blues. *—AMG*

Late Last Night / 1980 / Bullseye Blues ✦✦✦✦

Bluesman John Mooney has a very appealing tone in his slide guitar work, a relatively strong voice and, by varying moods, subject matter and grooves, he put together a particularly strong program for his Bullseye Blues debut. Influenced by both the country blues and country music, Mooney's guitar acts as both a contrasting and a complementary voice to his vocals, sometimes functioning in unison and other times as an equal partner in a musical "conversation." Enjoyable music. *—Scott Yanow*

Telephone Blues / Mar. 1984 / Powerhouse ✦✦✦

● **Telephone King** / 1991 / Blind Pig ✦✦✦✦✦

Contemporary blues musicians tend to sound more reverential than stirring, but not John Mooney. He's not doing tributes, he's having a party, and that's the spirit that makes this session both intriguing and enjoyable. *—Ron Wynn*

Testimony / 1992 / Domino ✦✦✦✦✦

Testimony captures the driving intensity of John Mooney's live shows. Recorded with a stellar supporting band—featuring drummer Johnny Vidacovich and the Meters' bassist George Porter Jr.—*Testimony* featuring seven covers (including cuts by Robert Johnson and Son House) and seven originals, which are easily among the best that Mooney has ever written. But the key to the record is the sound—not only is Mooney's guitar playing hot and greasy, but there's a tense fury to his vocals that brings the whole thing to a boil. *Testimony* is a gripping listen and one of the best albums Mooney ever recorded. *—Thom Owens*

Against the Wall / Apr. 1996 / House of Blues ✦✦✦✦✦

Mooney is one of a handful of younger blues players who has forged his own style, a jarring juxtaposition of angular Delta guitar and funky New Orleans backbeats. He explores the dark sides of those traditions in *Against the Wall*, a harrowing and stark work. Mooney's voice and guitar, both quivering, conjure up the image of a lost soul at a Delta crossroads at midnight; his shadowy bass-and-drum rhythm section evokes the ominous powers of voodoo. Standouts include "Sacred Ground," which opens the set, and "Somebody Been Missing Somebody (2 Long)," which closes it. On "Late on in the Evening," a mournful blues about a marital breakup, if the verse about his little boy begging him not to go doesn't get you, the stinging, Muddy Waters-style slide guitar break surely will. Very minimalist production throughout illustrates the principle that, in roots music, less equals more. *—Steve Hoffman*

Dealing With the Devil / Apr. 15, 1997 / Ruf ♦♦♦♦
Known for the passionate assault he commits upon his guitar when he plays, this disc is him playing acoustically by himself in a live setting, and he is every bit as alive and dynamic here as with a full band. Listen to his subtle playing and impeccable timing on "U Told Me," or the quiet control of "It Don't Mean a Doggone Thing." He never seems to put his slide down, and that is to his benefit, as his is some of the most inventive slide playing there is. Evidently he studied with and had as his mentor Sleepy John Estes. This edifies some of the playing and phrasing that at times has that slight familiar ring, but is a step or two removed from the master. This disc should not be missed. *—Bob Gottlieb*

Gone to Hell / Apr. 25, 2000 / Blind Pig ♦♦♦
This disc by John Mooney stretches his boundaries without compromising his music at all. He adds some New Orleans rhythm & blues/funk to the solid, deep Delta blues foundation on which his music is based. It works yet he doesn't seem quite comfortable with it all yet even though he wrote nine of the 13 songs (some of his strongest songs yet). Of course, he has enlisted some of the finest, such as Dr. John to plink the ivories, and some friendly familiar faces like Jeff Sarli on bass, to assist him in this endeavor. This is more a group-orientated effort and it is excellent in that respect, however, that means Mooney's guitar work is not as prominent in the mix and, thus, it requires more attention by the listener because he has not lost any of his ferocity at all. His guitar playing is some of the most savage and ferocious ever. A big plus on this disc is Mooney's singing because he is sounding more comfortable each time out and he has a voice perfectly matched in passion to the raw and fervid nature of his Delta-based material. Even his R&B is anchored in the mud of the mighty river that feeds the area. The blues are associated with the devil and passion and if you are dealing with the devil it is assumed you generally wind up down in Hell. What many people forget is that the same passion that can take you down to Hell can also raise you up to Heaven. The disc is titled *Gone to Hell*, and it is filled with the fierceness that takes you on the express train to whatever your destination. Where ever John Mooney is going he is riding that express with the type of dedication that is a force and fury that show a total dedication and must be reckoned with. A must for all interested in the blues and honest music that is played from the heart. *—Bob Gottlieb*

All I Want / Apr. 16, 2002 / Blind Pig ♦♦♦♦
One of the few blues guitarists to forge a unique style, John Mooney continues to refine his Delta blues/New Orleans second-line approach on this excellent follow-up to 2000's *Gone to Hell* comeback. Whether digging into the Delta on an acoustic version of Willie Brown's "Future Blues," or giving his funky slide a sizzling workout on the appropriately titled "Feel Like Hollerin'," Mooney attacks these songs with an electric ferocity that nearly slashes the speakers. His sparse backing rhythm section, including longtime bassist Jeff Sarli and especially percussionist Alfred "Uganda" Roberts, provides a solid bedrock for Mooney to blast off. Sticking predominantly with slide, which is his forte, Mooney can be light and playful, as on the finger-popping "Tell Me Who," or nearly demonic, like his cover of mentor Son House's "Son's Blues." When he howls "Lord have mercy on my wicked soul," he sounds like he means it and is not merely mouthing words sung countless times in the past. A respectable cover of Mississippi Fred McDowell's chestnut "You Got to Move" doesn't add much to either the original or even the Stones' version, but a rollicking ride through Professor Longhair's "Hey Little Girl" is alone worth the price of the album, as Mooney rips off lightning runs, slicing into the song with an incisive combination of lecherous, playful, and muscular riffs. Mooney tips the balance of his style here to the New Orleans licks that provide the album's most exhilarating moments. But between his acoustic Delta roots, gruff yet expressive voice, and blistering guitar work, this is a perfect example of a confident bluesman who has established his direction and is working at the peak of his powers. *—Hal Horowitz*

The Moonglows

f. 1951, Louisville, KY

Group / Doo Wop, R&B

Among the most seminal R&B and doo wop groups of all time, the Moonglows' lineup featured some of the genre's greatest pure singers. The original lineup from Louisville included Bobby Lester, Harvey Fuqua, Alexander Graves, and Prentiss Barnes, with guitarist Billy Johnson. They were originally called the Crazy Sounds, but were renamed by disc jockey Alan Freed as the Moonglows. The group also cut some recordings as the Moonlighters. Their first major hit was the number one R&B gem "Sincerely" for Chess in 1954, which reached number 20 on the pop charts. They enjoyed five more Top Ten R&B hits on Chess from 1955 to 1958, among them "Most of All," "We Go Together," "See Saw," and "Please Send Me Someone to Love," as well as "Ten Commandments of Love." Fuqua, the nephew of Charlie Fuqua of the Ink Spots, left in 1958. He recorded "Ten Commandments of Love" as Harvey & the Moonglows with Marvin Gaye, Reese Palmner, James Knowland, and Chester Simmons before founding his own label, Tri-Phi. Fuqua created and produced the Spinners in 1961 and wrote and produced for Motown until the early '70s. The Moonglows disbanded in the '60s, then reunited in 1972 with Fuqua, Lester, Graves, Doc Williams, and Chuck Lewis. They recorded for RCA and a reworked version of "Sincerely" eventually charted, but wasn't a major hit. *—Ron Wynn*

Their Greatest Hits / 1984 / Chess ♦♦♦♦♦
Before MCA issued the definitive two-CD anthology containing every significant Moonglows single, this mid-'80s anthology was a good sampler covering seminal material from the vocal group that championed "blow" harmony. The Moonglows' finest tracks—among them "Sincerely," "The Ten Commandments of Love," and "Twelve Months of the Year"—featured brilliant vocals from Bobby Lester or Harvey Fuqua. The sound was acceptable, and the annotation was brief but thorough. This is no longer in print, but the MCA collection eclipses it anyway. *—Ron Wynn*

On Stage / 1992 / Relic ♦♦♦
This is an offbeat release for Relic, which usually issues vintage doo wop material from the '50s. Instead, we have an undated body of live performances featuring Bobby Lewis, probably from the '70s. Lewis' widow provided the tape, which is his musical testament to the world. The sound is stereo and pretty modern, although it's not state-of-the-art by a long shot, a two-microphone recording that does catch the group in superb form—it's just not totally professional level, the applause cut off between numbers and the "mix," such as it is, fairly basic. The songs include "Sincerely," "Love Is a River," "Sea Saw," "When I'm With You," and "The Beating of My Heart," mostly sung in achingly beautiful fashion. It is a nice coda to the MCA remastered editions of the Moonglows' work. *—Bruce Eder*

Blue Velvet: The Ultimate Collection / Dec. 7, 1993 / Chess ♦♦♦♦♦
Few rivaled the Moonglows in musical sophistication, inventiveness or flair. They could sing gorgeous heartache ballads, rollicking uptempo rhythm tunes, creditable period-piece novelty numbers, wonderful pop covers or shattering originals. This two-disc set contains 44 outstanding numbers, with every major Moonglows anthem and several others that weren't big hits but deserved to be, such as "Penny Arcade" and "Love Is a River." This collection updates and expands the *Greatest Sides* single LP release briefly available when Sugar Hill had the Chess catalog in the '70s. It wisely restricts material to the era when they were at their best, the '50s, and includes an excellent booklet. *—Ron Wynn*

Encore of Golden Hits / Feb. 6, 1996 / Starr Digital ♦♦♦
Twenty tracks of vocal group excellence from the pioneers of blow harmony, a technique created by Harvey Fuqua involving the elongation of vowel sounds that contrasted the traditional doo, doo sound everybody else was doing. Like most '50s R&B groups, Pop acts covered the Moonglows unmercifully, their "Sincerely" a beautiful doo wop/pop ballad aced the R&B charts but stopped at number 20 on the Pop chart, while the McGuire Sisters' cover achieved gold status. Equally as exquisite "Most of All," featuring a great lead from Bobby Lester, was also covered, their original went to number five R&B, while Don Cornell's rehashing was a number 14 Pop hit. The "Ten Commandments of Love," their most identifiable song, recorded as Harvey & the Moonglows, became their second most popular recording reaching number nine R&B & number 22 Pop. Other classics include "In My Diary" (which Harvey recorded in the '60s on the Spinners); a slow, easy "Secret Love" (nothing like Billy Stewart's frantic '60s rendition); the wistful, innocent "We Go Together," the emulated "When I'm With You," and the out-of-character (for the Moonglows) "See Saw," it's straight R&B with no pop inclinations. The Moonglows: Harvey Fuqua, Bobby Lester, Prentiss Barnes, Alexander Walton, aka Pete Graves, and guitarist Billy Johnson should be in the Rock & Roll's Hall-of-Fame, as well as, the Flamingos and other pioneers. The only glaring omission "Shoo Doo Be Doo," recorded as the Moonlighters. There's also nothing by Harvey & the New Moonglows which featured Marvin Gaye. The best album never recorded by Motown: *The Temptations Sing the Moonglows*, Fuqua, a honcho at Motown, never cut an album with the Temptations doing songs by the Moonglows, and one can only wonder why, it would have been a nice theme recording. Imagine Melvin Franklin bassing on "Ten Commandments of Love," Eddie Kendricks' buttery falsetto on "Most of All," David Ruffin's rough tenor delivering "In My Diary," and Paul Williams' baritone on "Sincerely." *—Andrew Hamilton*

Rare a capella Recordings / Mar. 5, 1996 / Starr Digital ♦♦♦♦♦
A stone masterpiece! Arguably one of the best vocal performances ever captured on record. Absolutely stunning! The Moonglows lay down the 10 commandments of harmony, a cappella, on 16 heavenly tracks. No matter what genre of music you favor, you'll appreciate this astounding display of awesomely smooth, intricate harmony blends. You'll marvel at Prentiss Barnes' foggy bass, and Pete Graves' floating tenor—meshing with Bobby Lester's mellow second tenor, and Harvey Fuqua's smooth baritone. Every cut's a musical highlight piece, but kudos to "Most of All," "In My Diary," "When I'm With You," and "The Beating of My Heart." And special honors to the four well-done medleys: the "Lonely Medley," the "Diary Medley," the "Lovers Medley," and the "Needing You Medley." *—Andrew Hamilton*

● **Their Greatest Hits** / May 20, 1997 / MCA/Chess ♦♦♦♦♦
At 16 tracks, *Their Greatest Hits* isn't nearly as comprehensive as the two-CD *Blue Velvet*, which has 44 songs. But for someone who wants just the highlights, as opposed to just about everything, *Their Greatest Hits* is the better buy, including their most celebrated tunes ("Ten Commandments of Love," "Sincerely," "Blue Velvet"). The only selection not on *Blue Velvet* is a different take of "Over and Over Again," presented in its "fast version." It does not, however, include "Mama Loocie," which featured Marvin Gaye's first recorded lead vocal. *—Richie Unterberger*

20th Century Masters—The Millennium Collection: The Best of the Moonglows / Jul. 2, 2002 / MCA ♦♦♦♦♦
This 12-song collection is the almost the same as the 1997 anthology *Their Greatest Hits*, which has all 12 of these selections plus four additional tracks. For that reason, this slightly abridged version is slightly less preferable. Still, it does hone in on their most popular '50s Chess recordings, including the hits "Sincerely," "Most of All," "We Go Together," "When I'm With You," "See Saw," "Please Send Me Someone to Love," and "The Ten Commandments of Love." Although the packaging is on the budget side, it's a good representation of the very best of one of the era's finest R&B/doo wop vocal groups. *—Richie Unterberger*

Aaron Moore

b. Greenwood, MS

Vocals / Piano Blues, Chicago Blues

Chicago-based blues pianist, singer and songwriter Aaron Moore is locally famous, but still rather obscure on the national blues scene. Moore spent most of the last 40 years in Chicago, backing up a long list of musicians including Little Walter, Lonnie Brooks, Hound Dog Taylor, Howlin' Wolf, Muddy Waters and B.B. King. Born and raised in Greenwood, Mississippi, Moore was encouraged in his piano playing by his mother, who was a music teacher and church piano player; early on, he was influenced by Curtis Jones, and later Memphis Slim. Later on, after moving to Chicago, he learned from boogie-woogie paragon Roosevelt Sykes, and the two would often team up in blues clubs around Chicago. Moore worked for the city of Chicago for 36 years and played blues strictly on a freelance basis on weekends, backing up local bluesmen in club shows. After retiring from the Chicago Sanitation Department, Moore relocated to Milwaukee in 1990 and has been poised to make blues his full-time vocation in his retirement years. On *Hello World*, his 1996 Delmark release, Moore is accompanied by James Wheeler, guitar, Willie Black, bass and Huckleberry Hound, drums. *—Richard Skelly*

Hello World / Nov. 26, 1996 / Delmark ✦✦✦

● **Boot 'Em Up** / Jul. 27, 1999 / Delmark ✦✦✦✦

At 71, blues pianist/singer Moore is only up to his second CD, but it's a very good one. He's definitely reminiscent of his main influence, Roosevelt Sykes, just not as bawdy. Traces of Jay McShann also creep in here and there. Moore wrote all seventeen of these tracks, but you've heard them all under the guise of more familiar blues standards. The backup band is solid; guitarist James Wheeler is an expert at economical, sweet, tasty solos and fills, Bob Stroger knows the right bass lines to lay down, and drummer Willie "Big Eyes" Smith is a legend. When Moore gets on a roll, he stays there, as the majority of his tunes are easy shuffles with New Orleans flourishes. "I Thought Your Love Was True," "Bedroom Invitation," "Just Let Me Love You," "I Can't Stand to Be Alone," "You Came to Me in a Dream," and "Waiting on Your Love" could all be the same tune. "I Want My Baby Back" is a lighter boogie with sexual overtones, "Hind Part Boogie" much heavier and Sykes-like. "You Look So Good to Me" is in more of a Jimmy Reed style, while the title track is a jump 'n' shout fire breather, and "Faithful Love," just Moore playing and singing, is similar to "Sunny Side of the Street. Not much soloing here, but traces of his jazz influence... Count Basie, Teddy Wilson, and Earl Hines, come across as a compact approach that has no need for grandstanding. Slower ballads and shuffles as the 12 bar "My Love Is Out of Control" and "Made a Change in Your Love" shows Moore's tender side, but then he cranks it back us with "Real Throw Down," a true down-home blues perfect for your next party. Moore's style is getting to be a lost art, and while a bit more diversity could make this fine pianist a true blues star, there's absolutely nothing wrong with what he's doing here. Recommended. *—Michael G. Nastos*

Dorothy Moore

b. Oct. 13, 1946, Jackson, MS

Vocals / Soul-Blues, Disco, Soul

Dorothy Moore had two huge hits in 1976 for Malaco with "Misty Blue" and "Funny How Time Slips Away." "Misty Blue" was a number two R&B and number three pop single and a sizzling piece of heartache soul, while "Funny How Time Slips Away" wasn't as definitive a soul recasting of Willie Nelson's composition as Joe Hinton's version, but it did better on the charts, reaching number seven R&B. Moore continued on Malaco through the '80s, landing one more Top Ten R&B hit in 1977 with "I Believe You." She signed with the reactivated Volt label in the late '80s, and recorded two LPs for them. Her most recent was *Winner* in 1989. *—Ron Wynn*

Once Moore With Feeling / 1968 / Malaco ✦✦

Another good, if conservatively produced, arranged, and written, Southern soul and R&B set featuring Dorothy Moore. Her sound, sensibility, delivery, and approach are simple and down-to-earth, reflecting strong blues, gospel, and country roots, that Moore inevitably wouldn't appeal to a mass audience. Malaco tried a few things, sometimes casting her in the same territory as Denise LaSalle (hard-talking sister) and other times repeating the "Misty Blue" formula (heartache ballads). But otherwise they simply let Moore go in the studio and sing with zest, then marketed the results to a regional audience. *—Ron Wynn*

Definitely Dorothy / 1970 / Malaco ✦✦✦

Dorothy Moore had one huge crossover hit with the single "Misty Blue." That was ironically not the best or most soulful song she ever made, but it was the one that struck a chord with the pop and urban contemporary audience. Moore wisely didn't try to do anything different after it hit, and made several solid, straight soul and R&B albums for Malaco, like this one. There's nothing fancy, just animated, well-sung numbers produced and arranged in standard soul fashion. Moore's gospel-tinged vocals wouldn't have made the transition to smooth pop or urban contemporary anyhow, so she was smart not to attempt it. *—Ron Wynn*

● **Misty Blue** / May 1976 / Malaco ✦✦✦✦✦

A classic album of Southern soul. *—Bil Carpenter*

Dorothy Moore / Jul. 1977 / Malaco ✦✦

Pop/disco and country-styled soul ballads. *—Bil Carpenter*

I'm Givin' It Straight to You / 1986 / Rejoice ✦✦✦

Traditional styled gospel. *—Bil Carpenter*

Time Out for Me / 1988 / Volt ✦✦✦

Dorothy Moore left Malaco and tried her luck with the reactivated Volt label in the late '80s, evidently thinking that Fantasy might be able to get her more exposure outside the South. That didn't prove the case with her debut for the new Volt, partly because there wasn't the monster hit that could break the urban contemporary radio embargo against Southern product. It also had such an old-time soul quality that its appeal was limited from the start. That doesn't mean it wasn't well-sung, produced, and arranged, or that Moore didn't deserve to make the music she felt comfortable doing. It just made the whole project a long shot, and it never was able to beat the odds. *—Ron Wynn*

Winner / 1989 / Volt ✦✦

One-time gospel and later soul vocalist Dorothy Moore tried a comeback in the late '80s on the reactivated Volt label. This was her second album for them, and it was well produced, with the same heartache ballads, wailers, and uptempo soul songs she'd previously recorded for Malaco and on her previous Volt release. Unfortunately, the album sank like a stone. *—Ron Wynn*

Feel the Love / 1990 / Malaco ✦✦✦

Bluesy southern soul. *—Bruce Eder*

Stay Close to Home / 1992 / Malaco ✦✦✦

This is Southern soul 1970 style. Standouts include the bouncy title track and "Blues in the Night," a rocking number with heavy horn lines. Other notable tunes include the syrupy Memphis-styled ballads such as "A Woman Without Love," "It's Rainin' on My Side of the Bed" and the poppish anthem, "Till the End of Time." *—Bil Carpenter*

More of Moore / Apr. 1996 / Malaco ✦✦✦

Dorothy Moore sounds more Southern than she ever has on this late-career Malaco Records CD. The singer, who ascended the charts with "Misty Blue" way back when, now has a voice that has aged, husky and more than capable of delivering three-hearts-in-a-tangle sagas and mistreated woman dramas. Only the horns and backing singers (both splendid) keep one from classifying the ballads as deep soul; lovers of that style will find much to like with *More Moore*. Standouts include "Why Is Leaving You So Hard to Do," "Lie to Me," and "Stop What You're Doing to Me." It's shameful this type of music is absent on mainstream radio. *—Andrew Hamilton*

Misty Blue & Other Hits / Jun. 18, 1996 / Malaco ✦✦✦

Misty Blue & Other Hits contains all of Dorothy Moore's biggest hits and best-known songs, including "I Believe You," "Let the Music Play," and the title track. *—Thom Owens*

Greatest Hits / Oct. 16, 2001 / Varese Sarabande ✦✦✦✦

Gary Moore

b. Apr. 4, 1952, Belfast, Northern Ireland

Vocals, Guitar / Hard Rock, Blues-Rock, Guitar Virtuoso

One of rock's most underrated guitarists (both from a technical and compositional point of view), Gary Moore remains relatively unknown in the U.S., while his solo work has brought him substantial acclaim and commercial success in most other parts of the world—especially in Europe. Born on April 4, 1952, in Belfast, Ireland, Moore became interested in guitar during the '60s, upon discovering such blues-rock masters as Eric Clapton, Jimi Hendrix, and perhaps his biggest influence of all, Fleetwood Mac's Peter Green.

After relocating to Dublin later in the decade, Moore joined a local rock group called Skid Row, which featured a young singer by the name of Phil Lynott, who would soon after leave the group to double up on bass and form Thin Lizzy. Skid Row persevered however, eventually opening a show for Moore's hero, Peter Green/Fleetwood Mac, and making such an impression on the veteran group, that Green personally requested their manager help secure Skid Row a recording contract with CBS (in addition, Green sold Moore one of his most-used guitars, a maple 1959 Gibson Les Paul Standard, which would become Moore's primary instrument).

Skid Row would go on to issue several singles and albums (including 1970's *Skid* and 1971's *34 Hours*), and although the group mounted a few tours of Europe and the U.S., failed to obtain breakthrough commercial success, leading to Moore's exit from the group in 1972. Moore then formed his own outfit, the Gary Moore Band (along with members drummer Pearse Kelly and bassist John Curtis), for which the guitarist also served as vocalist. But after the trio's debut album, 1973's *Grinding Stone*, sunk without a trace, Moore hooked up once more with ex-bandmate Lynott in Thin Lizzy. Moore's initial tenure in Lizzy proved to be short-lived however, as his fiery playing was featured on only a handful of tracks. Moore then set his sights on studio work (appearing on Eddie Howell's 1975 release, *Gramophone Record*), before joining up with a prog-rock/fusion outfit, Colosseum II. But once more, Moore's tenure in his latest outfit was fleeting; he appeared on only three recordings (1976's *Strange New Flesh*, plus a pair in 1977, *Electric Savage* and *War Dance*), as Moore accepted an invitation by his old buddy Lynott to fill in for a Thin Lizzy U.S. tour, playing arenas opening for Queen.

1978 proved to be a busy year for Moore, as the guitarist appeared on three other artist's recordings—Andrew Lloyd Webber's *Variations*, Rod Argent's *Moving Home*, and Gary Boyle's *Electric Glide*. The same year, Moore issued his second solo release (almost five years after his solo debut), *Back on the Streets*, which spawned a surprise Top Ten U.K. hit in May of 1979, the bluesy ballad "Parisienne Walkways," and featured vocal contributions by Lynott. Moore joined forces with his Lizzy mates once more in 1979, appearing on arguably the finest studio album of their career, *Black Rose*, which proved to be a huge hit in the U.K. (for a fine example of Moore's exceptional guitar skills, check out the album's epic title track). But predictably, Moore ultimately exited the group once more (this time right in the middle of a U.S. tour), as a rift had developed between Moore and Lynott. Undeterred, Moore lent some guitar work to drummer Cozy Powell's solo release, *Over the Top*, in addition to forming a new outfit, G-Force, which would only remain together for a lone self-titled release in 1980.

During the early '80s, Moore united with former ELP guitarist/bassist/singer Greg Lake, appearing on a pair of Lake solo releases (1981's self-titled release and 1983's *Manoeuvres*), in addition to guesting on another Cozy Powell solo release, *Octopuss*. But it was also during the '80s that Moore finally got serious with his solo career—issuing such heavy metal-based works as 1982's *Corridors of Power*, 1983's *Victims of the Future*, 1984's *Dirty Fingers* and the in-concert set *We Want Moore!*, 1985's *Run for Cover*, 1987's *Wild Frontier*, plus 1989's *After the War*—establishing a large following in Europe, despite remaining virtually unknown Stateside. But the decade wasn't all rosy for Moore however—although he was able to patch up his friendship with Phil Lynott (appearing with Lizzy for several tracks on *Life/Live*, and teaming with Lynott for a pair of tracks in 1985, "Military Man" and "Out in the Fields," the latter a U.K. hit), years of hard living finally caught up with Lynott, leading to his passing in January of 1986. Moore would subsequently dedicate "Wild Frontier" to Lynott, and honored Thin Lizzy's former frontman on the track "Blood of Emeralds" (from *After the War*).

Fed up with the pressure to pen hit singles and tired of his metallic musical direction, Moore returned to his blues roots for 1990's *Still Got the Blues*, the most renowned and best-selling release of his career, as the album featured such special guests as Albert Collins, Albert King, and George Harrison. Moore continued in his newly rediscovered blues style on such subsequent releases as 1992's *After Hours* and 1993's *Blues Alive*, before forming the short-lived super group BBM, along with Cream's former rhythm section—bassist Jack Bruce and drummer Ginger Baker—which lasted for a single album, 1994's *Around the Next Dream*. Up next for Moore was a tribute album for Peter Green, 1995's *Blues for Greeny*, which saw him put his own personal stamp on 11 tracks either penned or performed at some point by Green. Moore experimented with different musical styles on his next two solo releases, 1997's *Dark Days in Paradise* and 1999's *A Different Beat*, before embracing the blues once more on his first release of the 21st century, 2001's *Back to the Blues*. Over the years, Gary Moore has been the subject of countless compilations, the best of the bunch being 1998's metal-oriented *Collection* and 2002's blues-based *Best of the Blues*, as well as *Out in the Fields: The Very Best of Gary Moore*, which was split 50/50 between his metal and blues excursions. Teaming with Skunk Anansie bassist Cass Lewis and Primal Fear drummer Darrin Mooney, Moore started work on much harder and alternative-influenced rock in the spring of 2002 and released the results as *Scar*. *—Greg Prato*

Grinding Stone / 1973 / Castle ✦✦✦

Grinding Stone is hard to place musically in Gary Moore's early, pretty varied career, but fits somewhere in between Colosseum II and Skid Row. In any case, as well as being his solo debut, it is one of Gary Moore's most overlooked albums. A description of the music could be something as seemingly self contradictory as experimental boogie rock, but on the album Moore explores a number of styles, from the title track's instrumental boogie rock to soulful vocals in "Sail Across the Mountain" and 17 minutes of guitar and keyboard excursions in the surprisingly funky "Spirit." In some ways *Grinding Stone* gives a taste of what would be heard from Colosseum II a few years later, but if the word fusion can be used here, it is not in the generic sense. The album is far from well held together though, and the quality of the songs vary wildly. It may not be an album for the casual metal fan, it is not representative for Moore and it is not his best album. But never again would Moore try such an eclectic mix, and the highly personal and mostly instrumental blues heard on *Grinding Stone* (for at the core, deep down, it is blues) is not only quite unique, but also far more interesting than the hit list blues he would play in the '90s, and more creative than most of the British blues rock heard in 1973. *—Lars Lovén*

G-Force / 1979 / Castle ✦✦✦

After cooperating with Phil Lynott on *Back on the Streets*, Gary Moore moved to L.A. and formed the group G-Force with Willie Dee, Tony Newton, and drummer Mark Nauseef. The group did not hold together much longer than it took to finish the first album, and on its re-release on CD, only Moore gets credit. But the album they left behind, also named *G-Force*, is clearly underrated. As expected, it does contain the elements that would later make Moore famous, like hard rock riffs and long instrumental solos. Looking for this, listen to "White Knuckles/Rockin' and Rollin'," which would stay in his repertoire for a long time. But the album also shows a side later hardly seen. "Hot Gossip" and "The Woman's in Love" are catchy pop tunes that, except for the guitars, have more in common with Elvis Costello than with Moore's coming albums, or with the weird boogie rock of *Grinding Stone*. These tracks could appeal to a pop audience if they would ever find them, which is unlikely. And surprisingly, these are two of the tracks written exclusively by Moore. Yes, one can suspect that some of the humor of the quirky choruses is unintentional, but the timing is perfect. But if underrated, the album still holds problems for the buyer. Except for the apparent difficulty of appealing to two different audiences, the album also contains a few tracks ranking among Moore's worst. So despite a number of great songs, *G-Force* is probably best bought by listeners who want to find a few unexpected gems. It may contain too few true Gary Moore songs for rock fans and too many guitar solos for pop fans. In 1990 the album was re-released on CD by Castle Communications. *—Lars Lovén*

Back on the Streets / 1979 / Grand Slamm ✦✦✦

1979 was a busy year for Irish guitarist Gary Moore, who after years of seemingly aimless wandering across the musical landscape (including a flirtation with jazz-rock fusion while fronting G-Force) simultaneously re-launched his long-dormant solo career and became a full-time member of Thin Lizzy. Moore had originally agreed to help his old partner in crime Phil Lynott only temporarily, while longtime Lizzy guitarist Brian Robertson recovered from a broken hand incurred in a barroom brawl. But due to Robbo's increasing unreliability, Moore was persuaded to stay on and record Lizzy's *Black Rose* album in exchange for Lynott's help in shaping his own solo effort, *Back on the Streets*. And a good trade it was, too, as with the exception of the title track's gutsy hard rock, Lynott's singing and songwriting contributions wound up providing the album with its most coherent and satisfying moments. These included the highly amusing "Fanatical Fascists," a mellow reworking of Lizzy's "Don't Believe a Word," a whimsical acoustic ballad called "Spanish Guitar," and the simply exquisite Moore *tour de force* "Parisienne Walkways." Unfortunately, these are rudely interrupted by a number of misplaced instrumental fusion workouts (no doubt G-Force leftovers) and a terribly saccharine ballad called "Song for Donna." Half winner, half dud, the album would at least serve notice of Moore's rebirth as a solo artist, and he would show marked improvement on his next album, *Corridors of Power*. *—Ed Rivadavia*

Corridors of Power / 1982 / Mirage ✦✦✦✦

This is the first of Irish guitar virtuoso Gary Moore's true heavy metal albums. Boasting a crisp, aggressive sound, *Corridors of Power* kicks off with the foot-stomping "Don't Take Me for a Loser," delivers the token power ballad in "Always Gonna Love You," and floors the gas pedal on "Rockin' Every Night." However, the album's climax has to be the epic "End of the World," with it's two-minute long guitar solo intro and vocals courtesy of Cream's Jack Bruce. *—Ed Rivadavia*

Victims of the Future / 1983 / Mirage ✦✦✦✦✦

Gary Moore might just be the greatest guitar hero America's never heard of, probably because only his recent blues recordings have benefited from proper distribution in these parts. In fact, Moore has worn so many hats during his near-30 year career that the words eclectic and unfocused immediately come to mind. *Victims of the Future* arrived in the middle of the most consistent phase of his career—that of a heavy metal guitar slinger. Between the epic cold war-inspired title track, and the massive riffing of "Murder in the Skies" (written about the Korean airliner shot own by Russian fighter jets), Moore assaults the listener with more guitar notes than appear in most careers. These are great songs though, and his powerful vocals are also very effective, especially on the hit ballad "Empty Rooms." None of Gary Moore's recordings are very easy to find in America, but make sure this is the first one you look for. *—Ed Rivadavia*

We Want Moore! / 1984 / Virgin ✦✦✦✦

This album is a jaw-dropping affair for anyone who believes that Eddie Van Halen is the ultimate guitar-shredding experience. Gary Moore's classic live album *We Want Moore!* is about as good as it gets. Drawing mainly from the Irish guitarist's previous two studio albums, every cut gets a shot in the arm from Moore's extended soloing, most notably the Yardbird's "Shapes of Things" at almost nine minutes. Recorded in places as distant as Tokyo, Glasgow and Detroit, the performances also benefit from the impressive vocal tag team between Moore and rhythm guitarist Neil Carter. *—Ed Rivadavia*

Run for Cover / 1985 / EMI ✦✦✦✦

Run for Cover took the heavy metal ingredients of Gary Moore's previous two albums and added a little pop refinement to the mix. Thankfully, this did not compromise the overall heaviness of the record, and Moore even achieves a successful remake of his classic ballad "Empty Rooms." Calling on his many friends to help in the studio, Moore obtains fantastic vocal performances from former Deep Purple bassist/vocalist Glenn Hughes on "Reach for the Sky" and "All Messed Up"; and former Thin Lizzy leader and childhood friend Philip Lynott on the dramatic "Military Man." The latter also trades vocals with Moore on the album's biggest single "Out in the Fields." Written about the religious turmoil in their native Ireland, it was actually Lynott's final recorded performance before his tragic death. It also presaged the musical and lyrical Irish themes which would dominate Moore's future work. *—Ed Rivadavia*

Wild Frontier / 1987 / Virgin ✦✦

This album attempted to repeat the pop-metal formula of Gary Moore's 1985 album, *Run for Cover*, but falls short for various reasons. First, the songwriting wasn't quite up to par and except for "Over the Hills and Far Away, the title track, and "The Loner"—a beautifully moody guitar instrumental, Moore seemed to be going through the motions. Second, and most fatal was the decision to use a drum machine throughout the album; a failed experiment which just plain sounds wrong. Still, this is hardly a bad record, just slightly disappointing. *—Ed Rivadavia*

After the War / 1989 / Virgin ✦✦✦

Gary Moore's 1989 release, *After the War* features a return to the metal guitar riffing of his '80s records ("Speak for Yourself" and "Running From The Storm"), while continuing to explore more conventional pop dynamics with mixed results—it works great on "Ready to Love." Also, after dedicating his last album to fallen childhood friend and musical partner in crime, Philip Lynott, Moore finally honored him in song with the moving "Blood of Emeralds." As it turned out, this would be Gary Moore's last hard rock album before becoming a "born-again" bluesman. *—Ed Rivadavia*

● **Still Got the Blues** / May 1990 / Charisma ✦✦✦✦✦

Relieved from the pressures of having to record a hit single, he cuts loose on some blues standards as well as some newer material. Moore plays better than ever, spitting out an endless stream of fiery licks that are both technically impressive and soulful. It's no wonder *Still Got the Blues* was his biggest hit. *—David Jehnzen*

After Hours / Mar. 10, 1992 / Charisma ✦✦✦✦✦

Not wanting to leave a good thing behind, Moore reprises *Still Got the Blues* on its follow-up, *After Hours*. While his playing is just as impressive, the album feels a little calculated. Nevertheless, Moore's gutsy, impassioned playing makes the similarity easy to ignore. *—David Jehnzen*

Blues Alive / Jul. 1, 1992 / Virgin ✦✦✦

Live at the Marquee Club / Jul. 1, 1992 / Castle ✦✦✦

This live album, recorded circa 1980 at London's Marquee Club is a mixed bag, featuring material from Gary Moore's 1979 solo album *Back on the Streets* and his band project G-Force. Most impressive perhaps is the incredible musicianship in this performance from Moore and drummer Tommy Aldridge. Besides rocking out with "Back on the Streets" and "Run to Your Mama," the band locks on a great groove for "She's Got You." But they reach an absolute peak with a beautiful rendition of Moore's first U.K. hit, the instrumental ballad "Parisienne Walkways." A melody so lovely that Moore plagiarized himself 12 years later, tweaking it only slightly to create his hit "Still Got The Blues." *—Ed Rivadavia*

Blues for Greeny / 1995 / Charisma ✦✦✦

Gary Moore's tribute to Fleetwood Mac guitarist Peter Green, *Blues for Greeny*, is more of a showcase for Moore's skills than Green's songwriting. After all, Green was more famous for his technique than his writing. Consequently, Moore uses Green's songs as a starting point, taking them into new territory with his own style. And Moore positively burns throughout *Blues for Greeny*, tearing off licks with ferocious intensity. If anything, the album proves that Moore is at his best when interpreting other people's material—it easily ranks as one of his finest albums. —*Stephen Thomas Erlewine*

Ballads & Blues, 1982–1994 / Mar. 21, 1995 / Charisma ✦✦
This ill-advised compilation rudely splices the early ballads from Gary Moore's "metal period" ("Empty Rooms," "Johnny Boy") with his better-known latter-day blues experiments ("Midnight Blues," "Story of the Blues"). Its mostly solid material notwithstanding, however, this record can only be described as a doomed marriage—the kind which could only have made sense to awful people like record company execs. Even worse, the record exposes the troubling similarity between 1979's "Parisienne Walkways" (co-written by Thin Lizzy main man Phil Lynott) and 1990's "Still Got the Blues" (Moore's biggest stateside success) in a blatant case of self-plagiarism. —*Ed Rivadavia*

● **Out in the Fields: The Very Best of Gary Moore** / Dec. 1, 1998 / Virgin ✦✦✦✦✦
Irish guitarist Gary Moore has built an entire career on stubborn self-recycling. Just when listeners think they have him pegged within a particular musical style (heavy metal guitar slinger, soft-hearted acoustic player, jazz fusion experimentalist, electric blues purist), the enduring six-string legend throws a curve ball and changes artistic direction—seemingly just to spite his critics. Because of this, his extensive recorded legacy as a solo artist has defied adequate encapsulation into greatest-hits packages, and in America, where his profile has never exceeded the status of a connoisseur's favorite, taking a first stab at discovering his work becomes an even more vexing task. *Out in the Fields: The Very Best of Gary Moore* doesn't solve this problem, but it does alleviate it somewhat by concentrating on Moore's best-known guise among the aforementioned connoisseur club—hard rock and heavy metal guitar shredder. Included here are the rare mainstream hits ("Out in the Fields," "Wild Frontier"), balls-out metal headbangers ("Run for Cover," "Military Man"), sublime ballads ("Parisienne Walkways," "Empty Rooms"), and later-day blues successes ("Cold Day in Hell," "Still Got the Blues"). In an imperfect world and a less-than-perfect career, this is about as spot-on as one can expect. —*Ed Rivadavia*

Back to the Blues / 2001 / CMC International ✦✦✦
Six years after his successful tribute to Peter Green, Gary Moore follows with another solid electric blues-rock effort that falls squarely in line with his similarly themed albums *Still Got the Blues*, *After Hours*, and *Blues Alive*. Although he adds brass on a rollicking version of B.B. King's "You Upset Me Baby," Moore predominantly sticks to the basics here, pounding out energetic and full-bodied blues-rock and leading a stripped-down trio with a journeyman's enthusiasm and his trademark thick, sustained guitar solos slashing through the proceedings. The majority of the tracks are originals, although even the best of them sound suspiciously like rewritten blues standards. "Cold Black Night" is little more than a speeded-up "Messin' With the Kid," and "Picture of the Moon" sounds awfully similar to Moore's own "Still Got the Blues." And whether the world needs yet another version of "Stormy Monday" or "I Ain't Got You" is debatable. But Moore pulls off even the most clichéd material with his phenomenal prowess; supple, identifiable vocals; and a guitar tone that effortlessly shifts from a Santana/Peter Green-styled hovering intensity to a slashing Stevie Ray Vaughan attack. While Moore isn't redefining the genre or even his own approach to it, he's adding his stamp to blues-rock with *Back to the Blues*. Consistently rugged, moving, and heartfelt, the album is a reminder that even without reinventing an established musical style, an artist can effectively work within its boundaries to produce a satisfying, if not quite fresh, interpretation relying solely on talent and passion. —*Hal Horowitz*

Best of the Blues / Feb. 19, 2002 / Virgin ✦✦✦✦
A handy and generous double-disc (one live, one studio) compilation of Gary Moore's four Virgin label blues albums is predominantly an excellent introduction to this showy hard rocker turned midlife third-generation bluesman. The 31 tracks liberally sample from his relatively short five-year association with Virgin (roughly 1990-1995) but ignore his excellent 2001 *Back to the Blues* release on Sanctuary. Still, there are more than enough hot licks here to prove that Moore could be a convincing blues musician if he decided to give up his more ostentatious shred rock profession and focus on blues full time. While purists may gripe as Moore tears off searing, high-voltage riffs on covers of tracks made popular by Johnny "Guitar" Watson, Otis Rush, and John Mayall as well as Freddie, B.B., and Albert King (the latter two along with Albert Collins turn up as guests on both discs), there's no denying the emotional ties the guitarist has to this material or his obvious vocal and instrumental talents. Unfortunately, *Blues for Greeny*, Moore's successful tribute to philosophical mentor Peter Green, is under-represented with only a handful of cuts, one of which ("Need Your Love So Bad") is presented in an edited single version. Otherwise, this is a well-selected but poorly annotated (bandmembers aren't even mentioned, nor are sources of the songs or when and where the live tracks were recorded) compilation that shows how a rugged rock star can transform into a respectable bluesman, albeit one who plays very loud. Gary Moore may not be a rootsy, down-home guitarist, but he's just as passionate about this music as anyone who recorded for Chess. If Moore can expose other generations to the blues as Cream and the Rolling Stones did before him, he has done his job well. —*Hal Horowitz*

Rev. James Moore

b. Detroit, MI
Vocals / Traditional Gospel, Contemporary Gospel, Black Gospel
Accorded entry into the gospel field thanks to a scholarship received at the 1974 Gospel Music Workshop of America, Rev. James Moore earned a record contract with Savoy that same year and began releasing albums. Born in Detroit, he made his first appearance at the front of church at the age of seven and was introduced to gospel matriarch Mattie

Moss Clark by a friend. With the help of Clark—and the tremendous influence of the Revs. James Cleveland and Richard White—Moore entered gospel music with 1974's *I Thank You Master*. He was also invited by Rev. Gerald Thompson to appear on his LP *I Can't Stop Now* that same year.

Rev. James Moore recorded infrequently during the '80s (for a variety of labels), but returned to Malaco/Savoy in 1988 for *Live: Rev. James Moore*. The album hit the Top Ten on the gospel charts, and earned Moore a Stellar Award for Best Male Solo Performance. He appeared on the debut album by the Mississippi Mass Choir in 1987, and enjoyed the LP's enormous success (over half a year at the top of the gospel charts, almost a dozen awards from GMWA and Dove); the choir returned the favor by appearing on one of his albums, 1991's *Live with the Mississippi Mass Choir*. It also went to number one, prompting live albums recorded in Moore's hometown of Detroit and Jackson State University during the mid-'90s. His 1994 album *I Will Trust in the Lord* earned Rev. Moore his first Grammy nomination. —*John Bush*

Live: Rev. James Moore / 1988 / Malaco ✦✦✦

Live with the Mississippi Mass Choir / 1991 / Malaco ✦✦✦

● **Live in Detroit** / 1993 / Malaco ✦✦✦✦
Live in Detroit is a ten-track album that captures the Rev. James Moore live in concert in the early '90s. Moore is in great form, adding life to the music when the going gets predictable, even on the overly familiar "He Was There All the Time." Occasionally, Moore gets carried away with preaching and testifying, letting the songs run on a little too long—"He's All I Need" clocks in at nearly 13 minutes—but it's easy to hear that this was captivating live, even if the kineticism is lessened on record. There are better Moore albums and better live Moore albums available, but once you get to listening to *Live in Detroit*, you're likely to get caught up in the infectious spirit of this usually rousing music. —*Thom Owens*

I Will Trust in the Lord / 1994 / Malaco ✦✦✦✦

Brothers & Sisters I Will Be Praying for You / Oct. 4, 1994 / A&M ✦✦✦✦

Live at Jackson State University / 1995 / Malaco ✦✦✦✦

It Ain't Over (Till God Says It's Over) / Aug. 5, 1997 / Malaco ✦✦✦

Solid Rock / Jul. 6, 1999 / 601 ✦✦✦
Solid Rock is a solid collection by Rev. James Moore, who utilizes his powerful voice to maximum effect. —*Steve Huey*

Johnny B. Moore

b. Jan. 24, 1950, Clarksdale, MS
Vocals, Guitar / Modern Electric Chicago Blues
Very few young Chicago bluesmen bring the depth and knowledge of tradition to the table that Johnny B. Moore does. His sound is a slightly contemporized version of what's been going down on the West side for decades, emblazoned with Moore's sparkling rhythmic lead guitar lines and growling vocals.

Moore first met the legendary Jimmy Reed in Clarksdale, when he was only eight years old. By the time he was 13 or so, Moore was sharing a bandstand or two with Reed up in Chicago. Letha Jones, widow of piano great Johnny Jones, took an interest in Moore's musical development, spinning stacks of blues wax for the budding guitarist.

Moore joined Koko Taylor's Blues Machine in 1975, touring and recording with the Chicago blues queen (on her 1978 LP for Alligator, *The Earthshaker*). He went out on his own around the turn of the '80s, waxing a fine 1987 album for B.L.U.E.S. R&B, *Hard Times*, that impressively spotlighted his versatility.

After some rough spots, Moore is now more visible than ever on the Chicago circuit, with two new albums (one for Austrian Wolf, the other, *Live at Blue Chicago*, for Delmark). In addition to playing as a leader, Moore is likely to turn up on local stages as a sideman behind everyone from Mary Lane and Karen Carroll to rock-solid bassist Willie Kent. If Johnny B. Moore isn't a star in the making, there's no justice in the blues world. —*Bill Dahl*

Lonesome Blues Chicago Blues Session, Vol. 5 / Jun. 15, 1993 / Wolf ✦✦✦

Live at Blue Chicago / 1996 / Delmark ✦✦✦✦

● **Johnny B. Moore** / Feb. 6, 1996 / Delmark ✦✦✦✦
Johnny B. Moore's eponymous effort for Delmark record is arguably his best record yet. There's nothing that different on the surface—it's still the same overdriven Chicago blues that is his trademark—but there's more passion and fire to his performances here, and that's enough to make the album worth a listen by hardcore Chicago blues fans. —*Thom Owens*

Troubled World / Apr. 29, 1997 / Delmark ✦✦✦

911 Blues / Jul. 1, 1997 / Wolf ✦✦✦

Los Angeles Blues: Complete Recordings 1949–1950 / Dec. 15, 1998 / West Side ✦✦✦✦

Acoustic Blue Chicago / Apr. 6, 1999 / Blue Chicago ✦✦✦
This home-styled live recording features Chicago veterans Johnny B. Moore and Willie Kent, plus guest spots for Lester Davenport and Bonnie Lee. —*Earl Simmons*

Born in Clarksdale Mississippi / Oct. 30, 2001 / Wolf ✦✦✦

Monette Moore

b. May 19, 1902, Gainesville, TX, **d.** Oct. 21, 1962, Garden Grove, CA
Vocals / Standards, Classic Female Blues
Monette Moore was always a bit obscure, even when recording prolifically in the '20s, but she was a surprisingly versatile blues and swing singer with a pleasing delivery of her own. Moore grew up in Kansas City and moved to New York in the early '20s. During that decade she worked in many cities (including Chicago, Dallas and Oklahoma City) and spent a period singing regularly with Charlie Johnson's Paradise Ten at Small's Paradise.

In addition to her own recordings, Moore recorded a few titles with Johnson from 1927-1928 (including "You Ain't the One" and "Don't You Leave Me Here").

Although the blues became less popular during the Depression, Moore worked fairly steadily in the '30s and '40s, including three years as Ethel Waters' understudy. Moore performed primarily in New York, Chicago (including with Zinky Cohn in 1937) and eventually Hollywood. After a return to New York during which time she worked with Sidney Bechet and Sammy Price, she permanently settled in Los Angeles in November 1942. Moore appeared regularly at L.A. area nightclubs, was featured in James P. Johnson's *Sugar Hill* show and also appeared in a few Hollywood films in small roles. She spent most of the '50s outside of music except on a part-time basis. During 1923-1927, Moore recorded 44 songs as a leader (plus three alternate takes and some under the pseudonym of Susie Smith); among her sidemen were Tommy Ladnier, Jimmy O'Bryant, Jimmy Blythe, Rex Stewart, Bubber Miley and Elmer Snowden. In addition Moore, cut two selections apiece in 1932 (duets with Fats Waller) and 1936 plus six from 1945-1947. Moore's last regular job was working with the Young Men of New Orleans in Disneyland from 1961-1962 before dying from a heart attack. —*Scott Yanow*

Complete Recorded Works, Vol. 1 (1923–1924) / Aug. 1, 1995 / Document ◆◆◆◆◆
● **Complete Recorded Works, Vol. 2 (1924–1932)** / Aug. 1, 1995 / Document ◆◆◆◆◆

Whistlin' Alex Moore

b. Nov. 22, 1899, Dallas, TX, d. Jan. 20, 1989, Dallas, TX
Vocals, Piano / Piano Blues
One of the last of the old-time Texas barrelhouse pianists, Alex Moore was an institution in Dallas, his lifelong home. A colorful entertainer with a poetic gift for rambling improvisations, Moore had one of the longest recording careers in blues history (his first sides for Columbia were made in 1929; his final session was in 1988). Yet it was hardly one of the most prolific, as there were usually lengthy gaps between sessions. The spontaneous, autobiographical nature of his latter-day recordings imbue his albums with a special charm.

Moore began performing in the early '20s, playing clubs and parties around his hometown of Dallas; he usually performed under the name Whistlin' Alex. In 1929, he recorded his first sessions, which were for Columbia Records. The sides didn't gain much attention and Moore didn't record again until 1937, when he made a few records for Decca. Between his first and second sessions, he continued to play clubs in Dallas. The time span between his second session in 1937 and his third was even longer than the time between his first and second—Moore didn't record again until 1951, when RPM/Kent had him cut several songs. Throughout the '40s and '50s, Moore performed in clubs throughout Dallas, occasionally venturing to other parts of Texas.

Alex Moore's national break coincided with the blues revival of the early '60s. Arhoolie Records signed the pianist in 1960, and those records helped make him a national name. For the rest of the '60s, he played clubs and festivals in America, as well as a handful of festival dates in Europe. Although he didn't make many records in the '70s and '80s, Moore continued to perform until his death in 1989. The year before his death, he recorded a final session for Rounder Records, which was released as the *Wiggle Tail* album. —*Jim O'Neal & Stephen Thomas Erlewine*

Wiggle Tail / 1988 / Rounder ◆◆◆
Wiggle Tail turned out to be Alex Moore's final recording, and while that makes it a little bittersweet, it's nice that he was able to sign out with such a lovely album. There's nothing new here, to be sure, just Texas blues, but the years have been kind to Moore—he's still able to play with grace and passion. These performances might not have the spark and excitement of his classic '50s recordings, but hearing an old master play the blues is always a welcome, revealing experience. —*Thom Owens*

● **From North Dallas to the East Side** / 1994 / Arhoolie ◆◆◆◆◆
Recorded over three separate dates spanning 1947 to 1969, *From North Dallas to the East Side* is an excellent overview of Moore's singular combination of boogie and barrelhouse; his wildly improvised lyrics are sometimes hilarious, sometimes grim, and always singular. —*Jason Ankeny*

● **Complete Recorded Works 1929–1951** / Jun. 2, 1994 / Document ◆◆◆◆
Complete Recorded Works (1929-1951) rounds up all of Whistlin' Alex Moore's early recordings for Columbia, Decca and RPM/Kent. The sound quality is a little rough, and since it spans several decades, the collection doesn't quite gel into a cohesive listening experience, but there's no denying that these rowdy barrelhouse blues are powerful and entertaining—they're worth the time of any serious piano blues fan.—*Stephen Thomas Erlewine*

Ice Pick Blues / Oct. 20, 1995 / Collectables ◆◆◆

Ace Moreland

b. Oklahoma
Harmonica, Guitar / Blues-Rock
Oklahoma-born blues/rock singer, guitarist, and harmonica player. Part Cherokee Indian, Ace Moreland has cut two rocking discs at Bob Greenlee's Florida studios. *Sizzlin' Hot*, issued on King Snake in 1990, featured Edgar Winter on alto sax, while *I'm a Damn Good Time*, Moreland's 1992 follow-up, was released on Ichiban. Following 1996's *Keepin' a Secret*, Moreland spent the remainder of the decade out of the studio, finally returning in mid-2000 with *Give It to Get It.* —*Bill Dahl*

● **Sizzlin' Hot** / 1990 / Ichiban ◆◆◆◆
Ace Moreland isn't a particularly distinctive guitarist or singer. He's content to turn out Southern-fried hard rock and heavy boogie without attempting to update the sound whatsoever. That's not necessarily a bad thing, since Moreland does this stuff fairly well. There isn't much spark or originality to his playing, but his debut *Sizzlin' Hot* is a reasonably appealing record that should satisfy fans of Southern blues-rock, at least initially. It may not leave many lasting impressions, but it sounds good while it's playing and suggests

that, with a little effort, Moreland could develop into a strong journeyman guitarist. —*Thom Owens*

I'm a Damn Good Time / 1992 / Ichiban ◆◆◆
A small Sanford, FL-based label that Ichiban distributed in the '90s, King Snake Records showed some promise in the blues-rock field with CDs by Smokehouse, the Backtrack Blues Band and Ernie Lancaster. One of the things that made King Snake's releases effective was their lack of pretense; many of them sounded like something you'd hear in an out-of-the-way (but very happening) dive on the outskirts of Kansas City or Tampa. Nothing fancy, but honest and real. Those words certainly describe *I'm a Damn Good Time*, an obscure blues-rock/roots-rock date by singer/guitarist/ harmonica player Ace Moreland. Although a bit uneven, this is a generally tasty slice of Americana. Whether he's taking the 12-bar approach on "The Blues Gonna Get Me," "Down to the Bottom" and "Can't Get Enough" or providing earthy roots-rock on "Just Like a Surfer" and the Rolling Stones-influenced "Your Love Is a Lie," you know that Moreland is coming from the heart. A few of the tunes are forgettable, but overall, *I'm a Damn Good Time* paints an appealing picture of the underexposed Moreland. —*Alex Henderson*

I'm a Jealous Man / 1993 / Wild Dog ◆◆◆
By the time Ace Moreland recorded his third album, *I'm a Jealous Man*, his Southern blues-rock had become a little bit staid and predictable. There still were good moments on the record, but there were no new twists on his horn-spiked contemporary blues. Moreland's problem is that he doesn't break tradition enough, preferring to stick with tried and tested. That can be good when he's digging out forgotten classics like B.B. King's "Sell My Monkey," but most of the original songs on the album are simply perfunctory and performed in a similar fashion. That may be enough for his cult, but they also may find it a little frustrating that he's stuck in a rut. —*Thom Owens*

Keepin' a Secret / Feb. 20, 1996 / King Snake ◆◆◆◆

Give It to Get It / Jun. 20, 2000 / Icehouse ◆◆◆

Jimmy Morello

Vocals / Modern Electric Blues
A powerful vocalist and super-quick drummer, Jimmy Morello began playing drums at age 11 and formed his first band at 13. His vocal style has been influenced by great blues shouters like Roy Brown, Big Joe Turner and Jimmy Rushing. His mother's record collection had an impact on him in his early years, vocal groups like the Platters, the Drifters, the Coasters, and others. He fell in love with blues music after attending a revue concert in 1971 with Ray Charles, T-Bone Walker and Jimmy Reed. Shortly after this, he befriended a Pittsburgh DJ who introduced him to Louisiana Red. Red took a shine to Morello's band, Cold Steel, and the two began working together regularly in Pittsburgh blues venues. After becoming a tight working unit, they hit the road, playing Washington, D.C., Philadelphia, Boston and other cities around the Northeast.

After Red left for Europe in 1980, Morello moved to Sacramento, California to join the Blue Flames. By 1989, Morello moved to Phoenix, Arizona, where he hooked up with the Rocket 88s, playing drums and singing with that band for four years. After leaving the Rocket 88s, Morello toured with former Muddy Waters guitarist "Steady Rollin'" Bob Margolin. Returning to Phoenix, he put together his own band, the Stingrayz, which featured his drum kit front and center, so he could sing and play drums simultaneously, much the same way Doyle Bramhall does.

Morello recorded two albums with Dallas-based guitarist Pat Boyack (with whom he had worked in the Rocket 88s) for Rounder's Bullseye Blues label. More road work followed those two mid-'90s releases, and finally in 1997, Morello got his own album, showcasing his own songs and singing, on the London-based JSP Records. Titled *Can't Be Denied*, it features Morello's kinetic drumming and powerful blues shouter-styled vocals. He dedicated the album to some of his mentors: Big Al Smith, Roy Brown, Big Joe Turner and William Clarke. —*Richard Skelly*

Can't Be Denied / Feb. 25, 1997 / JSP ◆◆◆

● **The Road I Travel** / Nov. 10, 1998 / JSP ◆◆◆◆◆
Here's a disc that will satisfy fans of postwar blues. Jimmy Morello and his hot band cook up a smorgasbord of blues delights covering different styles from the '40s and '50s, all with enthusiasm and authenticity. They pay homage to Roy Brown and Big Joe Turner's jump blues and Ike Turner's down-in-the-alley strolling blues, just to mention a couple. Each of the 12 songs (all originals) is strong, and everybody digs in. Morello loves to shout, and he's quite good. He does a credible imitation of Turner on one cut. Almost all of the lead guitar work is handled with aplomb by the talented Alex Schultz. He's one of the most tasteful guitarists around and is always a pleasure to listen to. The band is fleshed out on some cuts by the Almighty Horns, who fill out the sound and help create that tasty postwar ambience. A fine disc all-around. —*Sigmund Finman*

West Coast Redemption: The Jimmy Morello Story / Sep. 11, 2001 / JSP ◆◆◆

Mike Morgan

b. Nov. 30, 1959, Dallas, TX
Harmonica, Guitar / Modern Electric Texas Blues, Contemporary Blues, Harmonica Blues, Electric Harmonica Blues, Electric Texas Blues, Modern Electric Blues
A Texas blues band, with twangy guitarist Mike Morgan and vocalist/harpist Lee McBee prominently spotlighted, the Dallas quartet the Crawl is set squarely in the Lone Star blues tradition. Their 1990 debut for Black Top, *Raw & Ready*, was followed by the more polished *Mighty Fine Dancin'* the next year. Subsequent releases include 1994's *Ain't Worried No More*, 1996's *Looky Here!*, 1998's *The Road* and 1999's *I Like the Way You Work It.* —*Bill Dahl*

Raw & Ready / 1990 / Black Top ◆◆◆
Atmospheric but somewhat derivative contemporary Texas guitar blues. —*Bill Dahl*

● **Mighty Fine Dancin'** / 1991 / Black Top ✦✦✦✦✦
The production may be a little bit cleaner than on *Raw and Ready*, but the Mike Morgan Crawl have turned out a better record the second time around with *Mighty Fine Dancin'*. The key is in the musicianship, which is skilled and accomplished, making the record a classy blues showcase. Some tastes might prefer a looser, rawer atmosphere, but the strong playing and solid song selection make *Mighty Fine Dancin'* a mighty fine time. — *Thom Owens*

Full Moon over Dallas / 1992 / Black Top ✦✦✦✦✦
Full Moon over Dallas is a fun set of driving roadhouse blues and R&B, highlighted by Mike Morgan's piercing guitar and Lee McBee's hard-edged vocals. The set may be a little to predictable for some tastes—they rarely deviate from the standard Texas blues formula—but their songwriting is good and their sound is tight, even if it is a bit too polished. — *Thom Owens*

Ain't Worried No More / Mar. 30, 1994 / Black Top ✦✦✦

Let the Dogs Run / Aug. 2, 1994 / Black Top ✦✦✦

Looky Here! / Jun. 1996 / Black Top ✦✦✦✦
Longtime frontman and vocalist Lee McBee left Mike Morgan's the Crawl after the recording of *Let the Dogs Run*. Morgan chose to replace him not with another harpist but with Chris Whynaught, a powerful vocalist and saxophonist. His presence gives the band a stronger R&B edge, which revitalizes the group's Texas blues and makes *Looky Here* into their most enjoyable record in years. — *Thom Owens*

The Road / Mar. 10, 1998 / Black Top ✦✦✦✦
Morgan's seventh album for the Black Top imprint brings some new and welcome twists to the mix. First is the production chores being handled by label head Hammond Scott. Second is the return of harmonica ace/vocalist Lee McBee after a three-year hiatus from the lineup to pursue a solo career. The third notable feature is the abundance of fine original material. Rather than a set of bandstand ready-mades, you can tell some time and work went into the production of this album. McBee's harp work is as strident as ever, and Morgan's guitar still maintains its blazing Texas fury, but framing it with a horn section here and there, Riley Osbourne on piano and Hammond B-3 organ and Rhandy Simmons subbing on bass for six of the 11 tracks keeps this album from ever getting samey or predictable. Particularly noteworthy are "Bad Luck and Trouble," "You're Gonna Miss Me" and the title track. — *Cub Koda*

I Like the Way You Work It / May 11, 1999 / Black Top ✦✦✦
Over the course of the '90s, Mike Morgan & the Crawl built a solid following by releasing albums every bit as solid as *I Like the Way You Work It*. There's really no surprises on this, their sixth album, but that doesn't mean that it's a disappointment, either. True, there aren't any songs that are instant knockouts, but there aren't any outright losers, and the Crawl's performance is muscular and committed throughout the record. Morgan's stinging solos are still a treat and Lee McBee's vocal and harmonica work are only getting better with age. If these two were working with a set of truly stellar material, the results could have been remarkable. As it stands, *I Like the Way You Work It* simply has good generic songs. And while that may not be enough for it to transcend its generic roots, it's enough to make it a good listen. — *Stephen Thomas Erlewine*

Texas Man / Feb. 26, 2002 / Severn ✦✦✦

Teddy Morgan

b. Jul. 8, 1971, Minneapolis, MN
Vocals, Guitar / Modern Electric Blues
Minneapolis native Teddy Morgan began playing guitar in his early teen years. As a singer and songwriter, Morgan was first influenced by Bob Dylan, but after hearing an album by Lightnin' Hopkins, he decided to pursue a straight-ahead blues track instead. Although he paid attention to Dylan's blues as well as the Allman Brothers and Jimi Hendrix, Morgan wanted to play blues full-time; but, like so many other younger players, he is influenced almost as much by blues-rock as he is by classic blues players like Hopkins.
Morgan quit high school at 17 and the next year joined the Lamont Cranston Band, which led to the chance to record and tour with James Harman and R.J. Mischo. The Fabulous Thunderbirds' Kim Wilson heard Morgan playing guitar in a club and took Morgan under his wing, encouraging him to come to Austin to check out the blues club scene there. Clifford Antone, the owner of Austin's longest-running blues club, Antone's, flew Morgan down to Austin to perform, and Morgan soon became part of the talent roster at the Antone's label. When the Antone's label formed a partnership with Discovery Records, Morgan's recording career got a boost, as much of the Antone's back catalog was reissued. Morgan has two albums out on the Antone's/Discovery label: 1994's *Ridin' In Style*, with his band the Sevilles, and 1996's *Louisiana Rain*, which features Kim Wilson on harp, Derek O'Brien and Gurf Morlix on guitars, and "Blue" Gene Taylor on piano. His Hightone label debut *Lost Love & Highways* followed in 1999. — *Richard Skelly*

Ridin' in Style / 1994 / Discovery ✦✦✦✦

Teddy Morgan & The Sevilles / 1995 / Antone's ✦✦✦

● **Louisiana Rain** / Sep. 9, 1996 / Discovery ✦✦✦✦
Louisiana Rain is a delightfully eclectic romp that effectively showcases the full range of Teddy Morgan's talents. Although he is fluent in a number of different styles, Morgan is no mere blues encyclopedist—he has absorbed classic blues traditions and spiked them with a modern spirit and a sense of swing. Most of the album is devoted to country blues and jump blues, all of which are given a nice, laidback sense of swing which is utterly charming. — *Thom Owens*

Lost Love & Highways / Nov. 2, 1999 / Hightone ✦✦✦✦
This third album by roots rocker Teddy Morgan may not break a single square inch of new ground, musically or lyrically, but you won't care much about that once it starts to play. Backed mostly just by his own guitar plus bassist Jon Penner and drummer Chris Hunter, Morgan combines the twang of the Tennessee Three with the rock sensibility of Buddy Holly and a host of blues influences. The result is largely terrific, with the strongest tracks—rockers like "Bullet from a Gun," "Nothing to Go Back To," and the title cut—sounding as infectious as anything from Tom Petty and as earthy as anything from Steve Earle. But the ballads shine too, with the tender vocal on "One More Night" in particular revealing that there's more than one side to this artist. — *Jeff Burger*

Big Bill Morganfield

b. 1956, Chicago, Illinois
Guitar / Modern Electric Blues, Contemporary Blues
Many men try to fill their father's shoes when they join the family business. Few, however, must prove they are up to the task in front of an audience as large as the one that watched Big Bill Morganfield. Blues lovers the world over revere his late father, Muddy Waters.
Morganfield didn't take up the challenge until several years after his dad passed away in 1983. When he realized he wanted to delve into the world of blues as his father had, he purchased a guitar, intending to pay homage to the legendary Waters, whose real name was McKinley Morganfield. That tribute was six long years in coming, years that Morganfield spent teaching himself how to play the instrument. An evening spent playing at Center Stage in Atlanta with Lonnie Mack followed. The audience, which numbered 1000, went wild over the performance and set the novice musician's spirit afire.
He went on to establish a contemporary blues group, but abandoned the idea after several months. Dissatisfied with the music he was making, he pulled back from performing to further hone his skills. He concentrated on traditional blues and also learned how to write songs. During this time, Morganfield supported himself by teaching. He possesses degrees in English and communications, which he earned at Tuskegee University and Auburn University, respectively.
The years of dedication and hard work paid off handsomely. Morganfield's debut album, *Rising Son*, was released in 1999 to popular and critical acclaim. The magazine *Guitar Player* expressed their belief that Morganfield's album would have brought a smile to his father's face. The following year, the W.C. Handy Awards dubbed Waters' son the Best New Blues Artist.
Morganfield recorded *Rising Son* in Chicago, the site of many of Waters' recording sessions. Bob Margolin, Waters' guitarist, served as producer and also appeared on the album. Featured were several of Waters' bandmates, including: drummer Willie "Big Eyes" Smith, piano player Pinetop Perkins, and harmonica player Paul Oscher. Also in attendance was blues bassist Robert Stroger, an ex-member of Sunnyland Slim's band.
Ramblin' Man, Morganfield's second album, featured an appearance by Taj Mahal on two songs, which also featured Billy Branch on harmonica. Mahal also contributed his original composition "Strong Man Holler" to the album. One of Waters' songs, "You're Gonna Miss Me," was also included.
Morganfield grew up in Florida, where he resided with his grandmother, and later made his home in Atlanta. He performed in a tribute to his father staged at the Kennedy Center in Washington, D.C. He kept in his possession his father's guitars and a touring amp. — *Linda Seida*

Rising Son / Apr. 6, 1999 / Blind Pig ✦✦✦
He's got some of the biggest shoes to fill in the history of blues, but Muddy Waters' son, Big Bill Morganfield leads three of his father's former compatriots through a stirring set of blues standards and new tracks. Morganfield's slide guitar is an excellent addition to the proceedings. — *Earl Simmons*

● **Ramblin' Mind** / Feb. 13, 2001 / Blind Pig ✦✦✦✦
Due to some sly humor, a few jazz-oriented numbers (including "Mellow Chick Swing"), and the consistently strong material, this blues set is also recommended to fans of straight-ahead jazz. Ranging from a couple swinging pieces and some lowdown Muddy Waters-type blues to two strong appearances by Taj Mahal, this is a release that never lets up. Mr. B's piano solos are a major joy, the harmonica playing (by Bill Lupkin, Billy Branch, and Paul Oscher) is excellent, Morganfield's expressive vocals always hit their mark, and the music is quite enjoyable. Highly recommended. — *Scott Yanow*

Buddy Moss (Eugene Moss)

b. Jan. 16, 1914, Jewel, GA, d. Oct. 19, 1984, Atlanta, GA
Vocals, Harmonica, Guitar / East Coast Blues, Piedmont Blues, Prewar Country Blues, Country Blues
Eugene "Buddy" Moss was, in the estimation of many blues scholars, the most influential East Coast blues guitarist to record in the period between Blind Blake's final sessions in 1932 and Blind Boy Fuller's debut in 1935. A younger contemporary of Blind Willie McTell and Curley Weaver, Eugene "Buddy" Moss was part of a near-legendary coterie of Atlanta bluesmen, and one of the few of his era lucky enough to work into the blues revival of the '60s and '70s. A guitarist of uncommon skill and dexterity, he was a musical disciple of Blind Blake, and may well have served as an influence on Piedmont-style guitarist Blind Boy Fuller. Although his career was halted in 1935 by a six-year jail term, and then by the World War II, Moss lived long enough to be rediscovered in the '60s, when he revealed a talent undamaged by time or adversity.
Moss was one of 12 children born to a sharecropper in Jewel, a town in Warren County, Georgia, midway between Atlanta and Augusta. There is some disagreement about his date of birth, some sources indicating 1906 and many others of more recent vintage claiming 1914. He began teaching himself the harmonica at a very early age, and he played at local parties around Augusta, where the family moved when he was four and remained for the next 10 years. By 1928, he was busking around the streets of Atlanta. "Nobody was my influence," he told Robert Springer of his harmonica playing, in a 1975

interview. "I just kept hearing people, so I listen and I listen, and listen, and it finally come to me."

By the time he arrived in Atlanta, he was good enough to be noticed by Curley Weaver and Robert "Barbecue Bob" Hicks, who began working with the younger Moss. It was Weaver and Bob that got him his first recording date, at the age of 16, as a member of their group the Georgia Cotton Pickers, on December 7, 1930 at the Campbell Hotel in Atlanta, doing four songs for Columbia: "I'm on My Way Down Home," "Diddle-Da-Diddle," "She Looks So Good," and "She's Comin' Back Some Cold Rainy Day." The group that day consisted of Barbecue Bob and Curley Weaver on guitars and Moss on harmonica. Nothing more was heard from Buddy Moss on record until three years later. In January of 1933, however, he made his debut as a recording artist in his own right for the American Record Company in New York, accompanied by Fred McMullen and Curley Weaver, cutting three songs cut that first day, "Bye Bye Mama," "Daddy Don't Care," and "Red River Blues."

In the three years leading up to that date, he'd taught himself the guitar, at which he became so proficient that he was a genuine peer and rival to Weaver. He frequently played with Barbecue Bob, and after Bob died of pneumonia on October 21, 1931, he found a new partner and associate in Blind Willie McTell, performing with the Atlanta blues legend as local parties in the Atlanta area. By the time he started recording in 1933, Moss was so good as a player and singer, that all 11 songs that he cut during the four days of sessions were released, far more than saw the light of day from McMullen or Weaver at those same sessions.

In later years, Moss credited Barbecue Bob with being a major influence on his playing, which would be understandable given the time they spent together. Scholars also attribute Blind (Arthur) Blake as a major force in his development, with mannerisms and inflections that both share. It is also suggested by Alan Balfour and others that Moss may have been an influence on no less a figure than Blind Boy Fuller, although who influenced whom is anyone's guess—it is clear that Moss' first recordings display some inflections and nuances that Fuller didn't put down on record until some years later.

The January 1933 sessions also featured Moss returning to the mouth harp, as a member of the Georgia Browns—Moss, Weaver, McMullen, and singer Ruth Willis—for six songs done at the same sessions. But it was on the guitar that Moss would make his name over the next five years.

Moss' records were released simultaneously on various budget labels associated with ARC, and were so successful that in mid-September of 1933, he was back in New York along with Weaver and Blind Willie McTell. Moss cut another dozen songs for the company, this time accompanied by Curley Weaver, while he accompanied Weaver and McTell on their numbers.

These songs sold well enough, that he was back in New York in the summer of 1934, this time as a solo guitarist/singer, to do more than a dozen tracks. At this point, Moss' records were outselling those of big name colleagues Weaver and McTell, and were widely heard through the southern and border states. This body of recordings also best represents the bridge that Moss provided between Blind Blake and Blind Boy Fuller—his solo version of "Some Lonesome Day," and also "Dough Rollin' Papa," from 1934 advanced ideas in playing and singing that Blind Boy Fuller picked up and adapted to his own style, while one could listen to "Insane Blues" and pick up the lingering influence of Blind Blake.

By August of 1935, Moss saw his per-song fee doubled from $5 to $10 (in a period when many men were surviving on less than that per week), and when he wasn't recording, he was constantly playing around Atlanta alongside McTell and Weaver. When Moss returned to the studio in the summer of 1935, it was with a new partner, Josh White, working under his alias as "The Singing Christian." The two recorded a group of 15 songs in August of 1935, and it seemed like Moss was destined to outshine his one-time mentors Weaver and McTell, when personal and legal disaster struck.

In an incident that has never been fully recounted or explained, Moss was arrested, tried, and convicted in the murder of his wife and sentenced to a long prison term. The truth behind the crime, and validity of the subsequent conviction were further called into doubt by the efforts that began almost immediately to secure Moss' release, all to no avail until 1941, when a combination of his own good behavior as a prisoner, coupled with the entreaties of two outside sponsors willing to assure his compliance with parole helped get him out of jail. It was while working at Elon College under the parole agreement that he met a group of blues musicians that included Sonny Terry and Brownie McGhee.

In October of 1941, Moss, Terry, and McGhee went to New York to cut a group of sides for OKeh/Columbia, including 13 numbers by Moss featuring his two new colleagues. Only three of the songs were ever released, and then events conspired to cut short Moss' recording comeback. The entry of the United States into World War II in December of the same year forced the government to place a wartime priority on the shellac used in the making of 78-rpm discs—there was barely enough allocated to the recording industry to keep functioning, and record companies were forced to curtail recordings by all but the most commercially viable artists; a ban on recording work by the Musicians' Union declared soon after further restricted any chance for Moss to record; and the interest in acoustic country blues, even of the caliber that he played, seemed to be waning, further cutting back on record company interest.

Moss continued performing in the area around Richmond, VA and Durham, NC, during the mid-'40s, and with Curley Weaver in Atlanta during the early '50s, but music was no longer his profession or his living. He went to work on a tobacco farm, drove trucks, and worked as an elevator operator, among other jobs, over the next 20-odd years.

Although he still occasionally played in the area around Atlanta, Moss was largely forgotten. Despite the fact that reference sources even then referred to him as one of the most influential bluesmen of the '30s, he was overlooked by the blues revival. In a sense, he was cheated by the fact that his recording career had been so short—1933 to 1935—and had never recovered from the interruption in his work caused by his stretch in prison.

Fate stepped in, in the form of some unexpected coincidences. In 1964, he chanced to hear that his old partner Josh White was giving a concert at Emory University in Atlanta. Moss visited White backstage at the concert, and the white acolytes hanging around established legend White suddenly discovered a blues legend in their midst. He was persuaded to resume performing in a series of concerts before college audiences, most notably under the auspices of the Atlanta Folk Music Society and the Folklore Society of Greater Washington. He also had new recording sessions for the Columbia label in Nashville, but none of the material was ever issued.

A June 10, 1966 concert in Washington, D.C., was recorded and portions of it were later released on the Biograph label. Moss played the Newport Folk Festival in 1969, and appeared at such unusual venues as New York's Electric Circus during that same year. During the '70s, he played the John Henry Memorial Concert in West Virginia for two consecutive years, and the Atlanta Blues Festival and the Atlanta Grass Roots Music Festival in 1976.

Buddy Moss died in Atlanta in October of 1984, once again largely forgotten by the public. In the years since, his music was once again being heard courtesy of the Biograph label's reissue of the 1966 performance and the Austrian Document label, which has released virtually every side that he released between 1930 and 1941. As a result, his reputation has once again grown, although he is still not nearly as well known among blues enthusiasts as Blind Willie McTell or Blind Boy Fuller. *—Bruce Eder*

● **Buddy Moss 1933–1935** / 1933-1935 / Document ✦✦✦✦✦
Document's *Buddy Moss 1933-1935* does a nice job of collecting the highlights from the Piedmont bluesman's peak years, making it a solid single-disc introduction to the influential guitarist. *—Thom Owens*

Atlanta Blues Legend / 1967 / Biograph ✦✦✦✦✦
Recorded live on June 10, 1966 at a Washington, D.C. concert, this 11-song album (fleshed out to 18 numbers on CD with additional live tracks from elsewhere) was considered miraculous in its own time, and remains so. Moss' fingering was slowed only slightly from the ravages of time, and his voice had aged beautifully. He gets sympathetic harmonica accompaniment (some of it most impressive, especially on "Pushin' It") from Jeff Espina and occasional help (seemingly unneeded) from a second guitarist billed only as "J.J." Moss, who was then either 52 or 60 years old, rises to the occasion, turning in some dazzling acoustic guitar work (check out "Comin' Back"), very moving and expressive singing, and overall a performance that one can only guess is uncannily like the kind he would've done 30 years earlier. Included are fresh renditions of "Oh Lawdy Mama" and Moss' own, unique renditions of "I'm Sitting on Top of the World" and "Key to the Highway" (done as a guitar showcase that would put Eric Clapton and Duane Allman to shame, and referred to here as "I've Got to Keep to the Highway"). One of the most impressive, and maybe the best, of all '60s rediscovery records by any '30s blues star—64 minutes of pure golden blues. *—Bruce Eder*

Complete Recorded Works, Vols. 1–3 / 1992 / Document ✦✦✦✦✦
These three CDs contain all of Moss' recordings made between January 1933 and October 1941. The sound is generally good to excellent, and as for the material, it is just about the most sophisticated and beautifully played Atlanta blues of its period. From his very earliest sessions in January of 1933, Buddy Moss made his guitar sing almost like a human voice even *without* a slide, just strumming, and his own voice was one of the most expressive in the blues. And when he played slide . . . well, Atlanta blues didn't get any better than this, especially with Curley Weaver ("Prowling Woman" and "T.B.'s Killing Me," for the guitar duet, are worth the price of *Vol. I*) or Fred McMullen providing the second guitar part (and Blind Willie McTell's voice turning up every so often), or, a little later, Josh White playing with him. Among the more fascinating anomalies is "Daddy Don't Care" from *Volume I*, which anticipates Blind Boy Fuller's "You've Got Something There." But the real reason for getting these three discs—and all three are necessary—is to take in one of the genuine, deserving blues giants in history on 67 of the greatest sides ever laid down. *—Bruce Eder*

Rediscovery / Biograph ✦✦✦✦✦
The original vinyl version of this release is one of the few on this label that is a new recording and not dredged up out of old scratched 78s. The music came from a live concert in Washington, D.C., in the mid-'60s. It was almost a perfect live album, although consumers who were scared of damaging their eyes might not have realized how contemporary the material actually was. Something about this label's packaging just makes one expect recordings circa 1934, or having to squint at columns of type to figure out when they were done. Blues fans who were around at this time had the unique opportunity to contrast releases consisting of archival recordings with actual live performances by aging bluesmen, some of whom seemed like they had been taken out of a closet and dusted off for the occasion. Moss had had a typically hard-knock life by the time he was "rediscovered," getting by as a truckdriver or elevator operator with gigs on the side. When he is heard in concert here, he was hardly a participant in the so-called bigtime music business. He still played very well, was capable of expressing a great deal of emotion in subtle ways, and had a provocative repertoire of original numbers and slightly altered standards that he was capable of stretching out on. "Everyday Seems Like Sunday," credited as an original, and "I Got a Woman, Don't Mean Me No Good" are both longer than five minutes, and are killer blues tracks. When it came time to put this back out on CD, a pocket full of additional tracks were grafted onto the beginning of the program, apparently garnered from other live recordings around the same time. *—Eugene Chadbourne*

Mother Earth

f. Nashville, TN

Group / Blues-Rock, Contemporary Blues

The late-'60s/early-'70s blues-rock outfit Mother Earth was led by singer Tracy Nelson and issued several somewhat underappreciated releases during their time span. Nelson was originally from Madison, WI, and it was while attending the University of Wisconsin that the singer was discovered by producer Sam Charters and was eventually signed to a recording contract with the Prestige label. 1965 saw the release of Nelson's solo debut, the folk-based *Deep Are the Roots*, and when it didn't exactly burn up the charts, Nelson decided to relocate to San Francisco, with the hopes of forming a more conventional rock outfit. Shortly after arriving on the West Coast, Mother Earth was formed, which led to performances at the famed Fillmore West, opening for the likes of Janis Joplin, Jimi Hendrix, and Eric Burdon. After an appearance on the soundtrack to the 1968 motion picture *Revolution* (which also featured the Quicksilver Messenger Service and the Steve Miller Band), Mother Earth signed with Mercury Records and issued a steady stream of releases until the early '70s.

These albums included 1968's *Living With the Animals* 1969's *Tracy Nelson Country* and *Make a Joyful Noise*, 1970's *Satisfied*, 1971's *Bring Me Home*, 1972's *Tracy Nelson/Mother Earth*, and 1973's *Poor Man's Paradise*, before Nelson pursued a solo career. Subsequently, Nelson earned a Grammy nomination in 1974 for the track "After the Fire Is Gone" (a duet with Willie Nelson) and continued to issue solo albums until the early '80s, when she became disillusioned with the direction that popular music was going in (although she did sing backup for Neil Young for a spell in the mid-'80s, including appearing with Young at the mammoth Live Aid concert in 1985). Nelson returned to music in the '90s, beginning with 1993's *In the Here and Now*, continuing to issue solo recordings (and in 1998, earned another Grammy nomination for the release *Sing It!*, a collaboration with Marcia Ball and Irma Thomas). *—Greg Prato*

Living With the Animals / 1968 / Mercury ♦♦♦♦

Though Mother Earth is oft-remembered as a vehicle for Tracy Nelson, *Living With the Animals* is a true group effort, combining memorable vocal performances with tight R&B—derived playing. Side one is a showcase for Nelson's blues belting and piano, particularly on "Down So Low" and "Mother Earth." Not to be overlooked is the blues shuffle "I Did My Part" and R. P. St. John's sardonic "Living with the Animals." Side two pales somewhat but only in relative greatness. The horn section asserts itself on "Cry On" and "Goodnight Nelda Grebe," supporting two more stellar Nelson' vocals. "The Kingdom of Heaven Is Within You" is a fitting album closer. *Living with the Animals* deserves enshrinement on CD. *—J.P. Ollio*

Revolution / 1968 / United Artists ♦♦♦

Make a Joyful Noise / 1969 / Mercury ♦♦♦♦

Make a Joyful Noise neatly divides Mother Earth's inclinations into the City Side and the Country Side. The City Side is an R&B workout, powered by a robust horn section and the vocals of Rev. Ron Stallings. Tracy Nelson contributes a lusty cover of Little Willie John's "Need Your Love So Bad." The Country Side is more subdued, adorned by steel guitars and R. P. St. John's quavering vocals on "I'll Be Moving On" and the strange "I, the Fly." Tracy's version of Doug Sahm's "I Wanna be Your Mama Again" is definitive. *Make a Joyful Noise* remains an overlooked classic. *—J.P. Ollio*

Tracy Nelson Country / 1969 / Mercury ♦♦♦

● **Satisfied** / 1970 / Mercury ♦♦♦

By the time of *Satisfied*, Mother Earth had become pretty much a vehicle for Tracy Nelson plus backing band. There's just one original on this set, Nelson's "Andy Song," and the album sticks to a loose but R&B-focused groove, sometimes stretching the songs out in a fashion that probably would have been more tightly edited had such an approach not been in vogue in 1970. Nelson's vocals are consistently strong and stirring, and the material is commendably diverse, though overall it's just an OK album that could use a little more oomph. The white R&B vibe is tempered by strong streaks of gospel, New Orleans music, and even a bit of jazz, particularly on the smoother parts of "Groovy Way." *—Richie Unterberger*

Bring Me Home / 1971 / Reprise ♦♦♦

Tracy Nelson/Mother Earth / 1972 / Warner Brothers ♦♦♦

The very title of this LP indicated a vagueness as to whether Mother Earth were still a group, or a vehicle for Nelson's solo career. It's a solid, if laid-back, set of rock with strong country and soul flavorings, and a bit of gospel now and then. It sounds a little like Janis Joplin's final solo recordings, but more subdued, both vocally and instrumentally. The songs include three compositions by Louisiana swamp pop legend Bobby Charles and an early effort by John Hiatt, "Thinking of You." *—Richie Unterberger*

Poor Man's Paradise / 1973 / Acadia ♦♦

Matt "Guitar" Murphy

b. Dec. 29, 1927, Sunflower, MS

Vocals, Arranger, Guitar / Electric Chicago Blues, Modern Electric Blues

Probably best-known for playing behind the Blues Brothers (and appearing prominently in their 1980 hit movie), Matt "Guitar" Murphy deserves enshrinement in the blues-guitar hall of fame anyway. His jazz-tinged, stunningly advanced riffing behind Memphis Slim elevated the towering pianist's '50s output for United and Vee-Jay Records to new heights.

Guitar playing ran in the Murphy household (which moved from Mississippi to Memphis when Matt was a toddler). Matt and his brother Floyd both made a name for themselves on the early-'50s Memphis scene (that's Floyd on Little Junior Parker & the Blue Flames' 1953 Sun waxings of "Feelin' Good" and "Mystery Train"). Matt played with Howlin' Wolf as early as 1948 (harpist Little Junior Parker was also in the band at the time). Murphy added hot licks to early sides by Parker and Bobby "Blue" Bland for Modern before latching on with Memphis Slim's House Rockers in 1952. Normally, the veteran pianist eschewed guitarists altogether, but Murphy's talent was so prodigious that he made an exception.

Murphy's consistently exciting guitar work graced Slim's United waxings from 1952-1954 and his 1958-1959 platters for Vee-Jay. Another solid Memphis Slim LP for Strand in 1961 and dates with Chuck Berry, Otis Rush, Sonny Boy Williamson, Etta James, and the Vibrations at Chess preceded Murphy's memorable appearance on the 1963 American Folk Blues Festival tour of Europe (along with Slim, Sonny Boy Williamson, Muddy Waters, Lonnie Johnson, Big Joe Williams, Victoria Spivey, and Willie Dixon). On that pioneering tour (promoted by Lippmann and Rau), Murphy commanded the spotlight with a thrilling "Matt's Guitar Boogie" that showcased his ultra-clean rapid-fire picking.

Harpist James Cotton was the sweaty beneficiary of Murphy's prowess during much of the '70s. Murphy's crisp picking matched Cotton's high-energy blowing on the harpist's 1974 Buddah album *100% Cotton* (the guitarist penned a non-stop "Boogie Thing" for the set). From there, it was on to aiding and abetting John Belushi and Dan Aykroyd's antic mugging, both on stage and in *The Blues Brothers* flick (where he played Aretha Franklin's guitarist hubby, convinced to come out of retirement by the boys in black).

Murphy has toured as a bandleader in recent years, having recorded an album of his own in 1990, *Way Down South*, for Antone's (with brother Floyd on rhythm guitar). His repertoire encompasses blues, funk, jazz, R&B, and even a few of those Blues Brothers chestnuts (he usually carries someone in the entourage to sing 'em, Belushi-style). Murphy's latest disc, *The Blues Don't Bother Me!*, recently emerged on Roesch Records. *—Bill Dahl*

● **Way Down South** / 1990 / Discovery ♦♦♦♦♦

The dazzling guitarist has recorded very sparingly as a leader over the course of his long career, preferring the relative anonymity of sideman duties behind Memphis Slim, James Cotton, and the Blues Brothers. But he acquits himself most competently here, mixing blues, funk, R&B, and a little jazz into his sparkling fretwork. His brother Floyd Murphy, a Memphis blues guitar legend himself, is on hand for a family reunion. *—Bill Dahl*

Blues Don't Bother Me / Mar. 26, 1996 / Roesch ♦♦♦

Lucky Charm / Oct. 17, 2000 / Roesch ♦♦♦

Willie Murphy

Piano, Bass / Modern Electric Blues

A blues pianist and former leader of Willies and the Bees, Murphy has long been a fixture on the Minneapolis club scene. His album *Mr. Mature* conveys his style well. *—Dan Heilman*

● **Mister Mature** / 1988 / Atomic Theory ♦♦♦♦♦

Murphy uses a full band to good effect. *—Dan Heilman*

Piano Hits / Aug. 15, 1995 / Atomic Theory ♦♦♦

This album of covers, plus one original, shows off the considerable piano talents of Minneapolis troubadour Willie Murphy, which he has lent throughout his career to Bonnie Raitt and Isaac Hayes, among others. The instrumentation on *Piano Hits*, which consists only of a piano and Murphy's ragged voice, can be tiresome at times, but it is precisely his exhausted voice, a cross between Dr. John and a latter-day Bob Dylan, that keeps the songs exciting. He is almost as cocky and self-assured as Howlin' Wolf on the Wolf's "Riding In the Moonlight," and he lends a swinging feel to Robert Johnson's "Ramblin' on My Mind." Also to his credit is the lone original song on *Piano Hits*, the sentimental "Fairy Tale," which rides a touching melody line to its conclusion. *—Steve Kurutz*

Monkey in the Zoo / Jan. 14, 1997 / Atomic Theory ♦♦♦

Complete with a quote on the album jacket by Vladimir Lenin, this record seems more like a vehicle for Murphy's politics than a collection of songs. Whether he is discussing the ills of society or singing about the world community we should be living in, Murphy never stops preaching (even reciting a God-awful rap about time at one point). There are moments, such as the wonderfully arranged "Keep on Running," but for the most part the music collapses under the weight of the message. *—Steve Kurutz*

Hustlin' Man Blues / Oct. 27, 1998 / Atomic Theory ♦♦

Former Bonnie Raitt bandleader and producer (her first album) Willie Murphy sure likes to mug while he's playing and singing his brand of blues. This mugging can consist of outrageous shouting and yelled exhortations or be conversational in tone, but it's always there. While this approach is probably wonderful in the context of a club performance, it does little to extend his rep as a recording artist. It also doesn't help that Murphy has chosen to fill up this album with songs so overrecorded ("My Own Fault," "Built for Comfort," "Spoonful," "300 Pounds of Joy," "Reelin' & Rockin'") that you almost resent their presence on this disc, no matter how much Murphy's versions deviate from the originals. It takes Willie almost half the album to get around to putting an original song or two in the mix, and "What Daddy Wants (Momma Needs)" and the title track feature lyrics strewn with cliché after cliché and vocals so over-the-top and comical you wonder at times whether you're supposed to take any of this seriously. This won the Best Blues Album for 1998 award at the Minnesota Music Awards. But this is largely generic bar-band blues for the yuppie crowd, short on subtleties and long on yahoo-style entertainment. *—Cub Koda*

Bobby Murray

b. Jun. 9, 1953, Nagoya, Japan

Guitar / Modern Electric Blues

Longtime Etta James band guitarist Bobby Murray spent many years carefully honing his guitar-playing skills around the blues clubs of San Francisco and Oakland. In the '70s and '80s, he played backup for musicians like Sonny Rhodes and Frankie Lee before getting a big break in 1988 and joining up with James' Roots Band. Murray was born in 1953 in Nagoya, Japan, grew up in Tacoma, WA, and cites Albert Collins as one of his most important guitar influences. Murray and Robert Cray went to high school together, and upon their graduation, they booked Collins for the school's graduation party; the three became friends and later went on to appear in concert together often. Murray, who spent many years in apprenticeship, learned from some of the best the Bay Area had to offer, sharing stages with Charlie Musselwhite, Otis Rush, Jimmy Witherspoon, Taj Mahal and John Lee Hooker, among others. He can be heard on B.B. King's Grammy Award-winning album, *Blues Summit*, and he duets with former classmate Cray on King's "Playing With My Friends." Murray's style is fluid and rhythmic, and, freely admitting he's not one of the world's greatest singers, often has a singing guitarist with him. There's plenty of guitar wizardry from Murray on his debut album, *The Blues Is Now*, released in 1996 on the

New York-based Viceroots label, with guests including vocalist Frankie Lee and organist Jimmy Pugh. —*Richard Skelly*

● **The Blues is Now** / Feb. 13, 1996 / Viceroots ✦✦✦
Longtime sideman Bobby Murray shines on his solo debut album, *The Blues Is Now*. Murray wisely hired Freddie Hughes and Frankie Lee as vocalists, freeing him to concentrate on his guitar. And he's a fine guitarist, as he proves here, turning out jazzy, classy solos that separate him from the rest of the crowd. That's the key to *The Blues is Now*—Murray plays it cool where others play it hot, and that turns out to be rather refreshing. —*Thom Owens*

Waiting for Mr. Goodfingers.... / 1999 / No Cover Productions ✦✦✦

Charlie Musselwhite

b. Jan. 31, 1944, Kosciusko, MS
Vocals, Harmonica, Guitar / Harmonica Blues, Electric Harmonica Blues, Electric Chicago Blues, Modern Electric Blues

Harmonica wizard Norton Buffalo can recollect a leaner time when his record collection had been whittled down to only the bare essentials: *The Paul Butterfield Blues Band* and *Stand Back! Here Comes Charley Musselwhite's South Side Band*. Butterfield and Musselwhite will probably be forever linked as the two most interesting, arguably most important, products of the "White blues movement" of the mid- to late '60s–not only because they were near the forefront chronologically, but because they each stand out as being especially faithful to the style. Each certainly earned the respect of his legendary mentors. No less than the late Big Joe Williams said, "Charlie Musselwhite is one of the greatest living harp players of country blues. He is right up there with Sonny Boy Williams, and he's been my harp player ever since Sonny Boy got killed." —*Dan Forte*

★ **Stand Back! Here Comes Charley Musselwhite's Southside Band** / 1967 / Vanguard ✦✦✦✦✦
Vanguard may have spelled his name wrong (he prefers Charlie or Charles), but the word was out as soon as this solo debut was released: Here was a harpist every bit as authentic, as emotional, in some ways as adventuresome, as Paul Butterfield. Similarly leading a Chicago band with a veteran Black rhythm section (Fred Below on drums, Bob Anderson on bass) and rock-influenced soloists (keyboardist Barry Goldberg, guitarist Harvey Mandel), Musselwhite played with a depth that belied his age—only 22 when this was cut! His gruff vocals were considerably more affected than they would become later (clearer, more relaxed), but his renditions of "Help Me," "Early in the Morning," and his own "Strange Land" stand the test of time. He let his harmonica speak even more authoritatively on instrumentals like "39th and Indiana" (essentially "It Hurts Me Too" sans lyrics) and "Cha Cha the Blues," and his version of jazz arranger Duke Pearson's gospel-tinged "Cristo Redentor" has become his signature song—associated with Musselwhite probably more so than with trumpeter Donald Byrd, who originally recorded the song for Blue Note. Goldberg is in fine form (particularly on organ), but Mandel's snakey, stuttering style really stands out—notably on "Help Me," his quirky original "4 P.M.," and "Chicken Shack," where he truly makes you think your record is skipping. —*Dan Forte*

Stone Blues / 1968 / Vanguard ✦✦✦

Louisiana Fog / 1968 / Blues Legends ✦✦✦
The first disappointment in the Musselwhite catalog, this hodgepodge of material and sidemen still has some standouts, especially Little Richard's R&B ballad "Directly from My Heart"—which features the Ford brothers Pat and Robben, and Tim Kaihatsu and Clay Cotton (back in the lineup from the *Stone Blues* days). "Big Legged Woman" and "Takin' Care of Business" are respectable, but overall the album ranges from uneven to subpar. —*Dan Forte*

Blues from Chicago / 1968 / Cherry Red ✦✦✦

☆ **Tennessee Woman** / 1969 / Vanguard ✦✦✦✦✦
The addition of jazz pianist Skip Rose gave a new dimension to the ensemble sound, and provided a perfect foil to Charlie's own soloing–especially on the re-take of "Cristo Redentor," extended to 11 minutes, shifting to double-time in spots. Rose's instrumental, "A Nice Day for Something," is a welcome change of pace, and Musselwhite's "Blue Feeling Today" compares favorably to fine covers of Little Walter and Fenton Robinson tunes. —*Dan Forte*

Memphis Charlie / 1969 / Arhoolie ✦✦✦✦
The 14 performances on *Memphis Charlie* include some loose live sides and even a taste of slide guitar from Musselwhite. They're the work of a more mature artist than the brash kid on *Stand Back*. —*AMG*

Chicago Bues Star / 1969 / Blue Thumb ✦✦✦

Mylon / 1971 / Cotillion ✦✦✦

Takin' My Time / 1974 / Arhoolie ✦✦✦✦✦
Another highly talented and original ensemble—Rose still on piano, with the Ford brothers, Pat and Robben, on drums and guitar, respectively. Again, Rose contributes an original departure, the solo piano ballad "Two Little Girls"—and, as usual, it is to Charlie's credit that he welcomed such far-from-blues mood swings. Otherwise, the band's (especially Robben's) jazzier leanings were checked at the studio door, and Robben's guitar is mixed too low throughout. At this stage, Charlie was changing personnel too quickly to give any unit a second chance in the studio, which would have been especially interesting with this outfit. —*Dan Forte*

Goin' Back Down South / 1975 / Arhoolie ✦✦✦
Combining two leftovers from *Takin' My Time* with a much later session featuring Chicago pianist Lafayette Leake didn't do much for this LP's continuity, but it was nice to see the tracks see the light of day (especially Robben Ford's jazz instro "Blue Stu," a rare recorded example of him on alto sax). Ussel and Leake together proves a natural, espe-

cially on "On the Spot Boogie," with Musselwhite quoting Charlie Parker's "Now's the Time." Musselwhite's guitar playing makes its first appearance on vinyl here: the primitive country blues of "Taylor, Arkansas" and a nod to Earl Hooker's slide playing, "Blue Steel." —*Dan Forte*

Leave the Blues to Us / 1975 / Capitol ✦✦
Musselwhite's major-label debut was unfortunately a lackluster run-through. This isn't a bad album; it's just that there's nothing very special about it. His working band centered around Kaihatsu and Sevareid (again, from *Stone Blues*), with the addition of saxophonist Ray Arvizu, a honking tenor as opposed to Robben Ford's jazzy alto. Cameos by Barry Goldberg and Mike Bloomfield only add to an inexplicably cacophonous mix; Goldberg's organ on "Keys to the Highway" is especially obnoxious. Charlie's singing and harp playing are well and good, but this sounds surprisingly *low*-budget compared to his previous independent releases. —*Dan Forte*

Light of Your Shadow / 1977 / Sussex ✦✦✦

Times Gettin' Tougher Than Tough / 1978 / Crystal Clear ✦✦✦
Cutting an audiofile session direct-to-disc (meaning that each entire side of the LP is recording live in the studio, with the band literally pausing between tunes, then forging ahead), someone came up with the bright idea of teaming Charlie with a band that he (mostly) had never played with, including a three-piece horn section. Under normal circumstances (retakes, overdubs, mixing—Charlie's vocals should be louder) this could have been a killer; as it is, it's yet another interesting side of this complex bluesman. Horns and piano (Skip Rose returns) give "Help Me" a whole new wrinkle, and Mose Allison's "Nightclub" is channeled through "Got My Mojo Working." Interesting, yes; definitive, no. —*Dan Forte*

Harmonica According to Charlie / 1979 / Blind Pig ✦✦✦
Ostensibly an instructional blues harp album (with an exhaustive accompanying book penned by Charlie), this is emotional and listenable rather than academic. Charlie covers a wide range of blues styles (and harp positions), and ventures to the outer fringes of the genre for the instrumentals "Hard Times" (from Ray Charles' sax man David "Fathead" Newman) and his Latin original "Azul Para Amparo" (backed only by guitarist Sam Mitchell). The English studio band is sympathetic, especially pianist Bob Hall. —*Dan Forte*

Dynatones Live—Featuring Charlie Musselwhite / 1982 / War Bride ✦✦
After several years without a new record, this confusing item appeared—in hindsight, looking like a scam to launch Charlie's backup band into a career of its own. Musselwhite gets second billing, even though he sings five of the seven vocal tunes—the lone instrumental being a so-so version of his by-now signature piece "Cristo Redentor"—and the crowd that came to this live gig no doubt didn't see "Dynatones" on the marquee. Confusing. But around this itme that had become the norm in Charlie's recording career. —*Dan Forte*

Tell Me Where Have All the Good Times Gone? / 1984 / Blue Rock'it ✦✦✦✦
Drummer/label head Pat Ford reunited with Charlie and brought along brother Robben on guitar, producing this return to form. Charlie is up to the task in all departments—singing, playing (great tone), and especially songwriting (the title tune and "Seemed Like the Whole World Was Crying," and inspired by Muddy Waters' death)—but it had been a while since Robben had played lowdown blues (touring with Joni Mitchell, putting in countless hours in L.A. studios). Pianist Clay Cotton is in fine form, and it may have been wiser to give the guitar chair to Tim Kaihatsu, who by this time had seniority (in terms of hours on the bandstand with Musselwhite) over any of Charlie's alumni. The to-be-expected-by-now deviations this time out: Don & Dewey's "Stretchin' Out," an impressive chromatic harp rendering of "Exodus," and Charlie's solo guitar outing, "Baby-O." Easily Charlie's best-engineered album (nice job, Greg Goodwin). —*Dan Forte*

Memphis Tennessee / 1984 / Crosscut ✦✦✦✦✦
Though steel guitarist Freddie Roulette was pictured on *Tennessee Woman*, he did not play on the album; luckily he is given ample space here, and the combination of his eerie vocal-like sound, Jack Myers' solid but adventurous bass playing, and Skip Rose's jazz piano voicings made this edition of the Musselwhite band one of the most original blues outfits ever. Charlie is in fine form as well, on a rock-solid cover of Muddy's "Trouble No More," and a lyrical reading of "Willow Weep for Me," and his harp *tour de force* "Arkansas Boogie." —*Dan Forte*

Mellow-Dee / 1986 / Crosscut ✦✦
By this time Charlie was confident enough to include four acoustic guitar vehicles—one ("Baby Please Don't Go") with overdubbed harp, one ("I'll Get a Break") from his old pal Will Shade of the Memphis Jug Band. The ensemble numbers feature a German backup band with expatriate Jim Kahr on guitar. A more expansive workout (than the Chicago BlueStars' version) on "Coming Home Baby" is nice, and "Cristo Redentor" (Charlie's fourth recording of the song, this time subtitled "Slight Return") gets a beautiful piano-harp duet treatment. Unfortunately the proceedings are sabotaged by completely inappropriate engineering—mechanical-sounding drums, tons o' reverb, way too much high-end. Ouch! —*Dan Forte*

Ace of Harps! / 1990 / Alligator ✦✦✦
"This is the best band I've ever had," Musselwhite proclaims on the back of this LP; longtime fans would find that debatable. Rather than schooled on the Chess sounds that provided Charlie with his foundation, these guys play a Malaco strain of blues, and Tommy Hill is simply one of the busiest (read: obnoxious) drummers anywhere. A "Boogie Chillen" takeoff ("River Hip Mama") is surprisingly *not* just same-old, same-old, but for the most part the funkified blues contrasts sharply with the album's two most poignant numbers, the jazz standard "Yesterdays" (with Charlie on chromatic, borrowing from

trumpeter Clifford Brown's "strings" album) and "My Road Lies in Darkness"—just Charlie and his acoustic guitar. *—Dan Forte*

Signature / Oct. 1991 / Alligator ✦✦✦

Signature is a typically engaging release from Charlie Musselwhite. The harpist runs through a set of modern blues, complete with jazz and funk overtones—indeed, there are two straight jazz instrumentals, "Catwalk" and "What's New?," which showcase his astonishing technique. Not only is Musselwhite in fine form, his band is tight, soulful, and sympathetic, making *Signature* a worthwhile listen for most blues fans. *—Thom Owens*

In My Time / 1993 / Alligator ✦✦✦✦✦

Charlie Musselwhite takes four different approaches on this Alligator release. On two tracks, he turns to guitar, proving a competent instrumentalist and convincing singer in a vintage Delta style. He also does two gospel numbers backed by the legendary Blind Boys of Alabama, which are heartfelt, but not exactly triumphs. Musselwhite reveals his jazz influence on three tracks, making them entertaining harmonica workouts. But for blues fans, Musselwhite's biting licks and spiraling riffs are best featured on such numbers as "If I Should Have Bad Luck" and "Leaving Blues." Despite the diverse strains, Musselwhite retains credibility throughout while displaying the wide range of sources from which he's forged his distinctive style. *—Ron Wynn*

Blues Never Die / 1994 / Vanguard ✦✦✦✦

This may be an overview of Musselwhite's career (from the late '60s to the present—with some previously unreleased tracks, including the title cut), but it is not the best introduction to the artist. For that, his Vanguard '60s output is still recommended, along with the 1984 session on Blue Rock'it and Alligator's *In My Time*. *—Dan Forte*

Rough News / Apr. 8, 1997 / Virgin ✦✦✦

With much of the backing personnel returning from his outstanding 1993 Alligator release *In My Time*, a mediocre follow-up album would be unexpected. Yet something is missing from this Pointblank release, aside from the extensive liner notes. Charlie's voice is not as casual, his band not as loose, and the end result is an album that at times seems too formulaic. Undoubtedly Charlie still has a set of the best harp chops in the business, but the moments that rise to the top from this CD (such as the instrumental title track) are much less frequent than listeners spoiled by *In My Time* may care for. *—Jeff Crooke*

Curtain Call Cocktails / Oct. 27, 1998 / West Side ✦✦

Harpin' on a Riff: The Best of Charlie Musselwhite / 1999 / Music Club ✦✦✦✦✦

Music Club has done it again with this amazing retrospective of blues guitarist and harmonicat Charlie Musselwhite. The Mississippi-born, Memphis-raised, and Chicago-trained bluesman has issued so many strong recordings it's a wonder that this isn't a box set. But if you have to boil it down to a single disc for a budget price, this is the one to have without question. Contained within its 20 selections are tracks from his two '70s Arhoolie albums, *Takin' My Time* and *Goin' Back Down South*, from 1971 and 1974, respectively; *The Harmonica According to Charlie Musselwhite*, issued first on Kicking Mule and later on Blind Pig in 1978 and 1994, respectively; and finally from his Alligator albums, *Ace of Harps* (1990 and a Grammy winner), *Signature* (1992 and Grammy nominated), and *In My Time* (1994, also Grammy nominated). These tracks come from Musselwhite's most fertile years when he was playing with reckless abandon a style of music he learned playing with Big Joe Williams on Maxwell Street and Muddy Waters in the clubs of Chicago. Featured here are the title track, "Finger Lickin' Good," "When It Rains It Pours," "Revelation," "Hear Me Talkin'," "This Old Nightlife," "It's Getting Warm In Here," "Crazy for My Baby," and more than a dozen more. The pace is nonstop, and it shows Musselwhite's development and refinement of his signature style on the harp and on the guitar. This is a blues album that's guaranteed to raise the roof at a party before it burns the joint down and will satisfy any aficionado's ear for the best of Musselwhite. The only criticism might have been to include some of the '60s live stuff he did with Muddy Waters, but it's really a small complaint. This thing delivers the bluer-than-blue goods raw, immediate, and full of pathos. For the price, there isn't a better Musselwhite album available anywhere. *—Thom Jurek*

Continental Drifter / Apr. 20, 1999 / Virgin ✦✦✦

For over 30 years, Charlie Musselwhite has released consistent, if not classic, blues albums in the great Chicago tradition. An acknowledged master of the harmonica, Musselwhite's rough voice is also a recognizable aural trait and on *Continental Drifter* he uses both to evoke a world weariness. In the same way a bluesman might rootlessly travel from town to town, the swinging melodies of songs like "Edge of Mystery" and "No" seem to drift and amble musically. Though it's not one of his best efforts, the album—which also has Musselwhite dabbling with Tex-Mex on two tracks—is a solid offering. *—Steven Kurutz*

Best of the Vanguard Years / Feb. 22, 2000 / Vanguard ✦✦✦✦

This 20-track collection of Musselwhite's early days shows that even back then the man could blow effectively in a variety of settings. In addition to the groundbreaking recordings he made with his own group, this also includes Musselwhite backing John Hammond on two tracks and a duet with Walter Horton from the *Chicago, The Blues Today!* sessions—nice additions. Highlights include "Chicken Shack," "Cristo Redentor," "Cha Cha the Blues," and "I Don't Play." A nice introduction to this blues veteran. *—Cub Koda*

Up & Down the Highway Live: 1986 / May 16, 2000 / Indigo ✦✦✦✦

This is Charlie Musselwhite captured at what he does best: performing in front of an appreciative audience backed up by a couple of friends in a casual atmosphere. Musselwhite is joined by Bob Hall on piano and guitarist Dave Peabody on this acoustic recording from London's Indigo label. Musselwhite picked songs he grew up listening to and learned firsthand from blues legends he performed with on Chicago's South side, like Big Walter "Shakey" Horton ("Need My Baby") and Little Walter ("Everybody Need Somebody").

Musselwhite's voice and harp playing are in excellent form on these performances recorded in 1986 while touring through Europe. *Up and Down the Highway* is highly recommended. *—Al Campbell*

One Night In America / Feb. 26, 2002 / Telarc ✦✦✦✦

Charlie Musselwhite continues his prolific four-decade career jumping over to Telarc for his first album of the millennium after spending the '90s recording for Alligator and Virgin. A recap of his formative Memphis roots, Musselwhite receives substantial assistance from guests Robben Ford on guitar (Musselwhite provided Ford with his first gigs when the guitarist was in his late teens), Texas vocalist Kelly Willis, and guitarist/mandolin player Marty Stuart; the last two bring a rootsy, laid back country feel to the album that effectively fuses the swampy C&W, R&B, and blues of Memphis into a cohesive statement. Musselwhite blows unamplified harp on every track, but it's his weathered, understated vocals that infuse these songs with down-home charm. Covers from Jimmy Reed, Los Lobos (the album takes its title from their "One Time One Night"), Ivory Joe Hunter, and Kieran Kane flow beautifully into each other as the artist masterfully blurs the lines between genres. He tears into Johnny Cash's "Big River" like it was a Chicago blues classic and retells his own childhood in the affecting original "Blues Overtook Me." He and producer Randy Labbe generate a Creedence-styled swamp vibe on the opening "Trail of Tears," with both Willis and Christine Ohlman chiming in on gripping backing vocals that set the atmosphere. But the album resonates most effectively on the sparsest tracks. "Ain't It Time" exudes a resigned, almost gospel feel in its achingly slow groove, and "In Your Darkest Hour," another Musselwhite original, shimmers with just harp and T-Bone Wolk's spooky walking bass creating a foggy mood that envelopes the listener. Not just a fresh start at a new label, this album is a sentimental and sincere recap of Musselwhite's influences and a stirring listen throughout. *—Hal Horowitz*

Cambridge Blues / Big Beat ✦✦✦

Yet another intriguing setting: Musselwhite in an essentially acoustic trio format, backed by pianist Bob Hall and acoustic guitarist Dave Peabody, both from England, live at that country's Cambridge Folk Festival. The crowd's thunderous response says it all—a rare and satisfying night by three great blues players, each skilled in the art of supportive interplay. *—Dan Forte*

Dave Myers

b. Oct. 30, 1926, Byhalia, MS

Guitar, Bass / Chicago Blues

Celebrated among the principal architects of the classic Chicago blues sound, bassist Dave Myers was born October 30, 1926, in Byhalia, MS. He and guitarist brother Louis learned the blues from Lonnie Johnson, who lived in the family's basement. By his teens, Myers was a staple at local house rent parties alongside the likes of Sonny Boy Williamson, Robert Nighthawk, and Memphis Minnie. He and Louis relocated to Chicago in 1941, and four years later, the siblings formed the Little Boys, rechristened the Three Deuces with the addition of harpist Junior Wells.

The Windy City's first electric blues band, the group—which next settled on the moniker the Three Aces—quickly emerged as one of the most popular attractions on the local music scene, becoming a fixture at clubs, including the famed Checkerboard Lounge and Theresa's; greatly influenced by jazz, they honed an urbane, sophisticated approach well ahead of its time, with Myers' subtle, percussive rhythms earning him the nickname "Thumper." With the 1950 enlistment of drummer Fred Below, the quartet again changed its name, this time to the Four Aces; finally, to simplify matters once and for all, the group performed as simply the Aces. In 1952, Wells exited to join the Muddy Waters band, filling the vacancy created by the recent departure of harpist Little Walter Jacobs; ironically, Jacobs himself quickly signed the remaining Aces as his new backing unit, renaming the trio the Jukes. A series of seminal recordings followed—"Mean Old World," "Sad Hours," "Off the Wall," and "Tell Me Mama" among them—before Louis' 1954 exit resulted in the Jukes' gradual dissolution.

The first bluesman to adopt the electric bass, Dave Myers then became Chicago's premier session bassist throughout the '50s, appearing on sessions headlined by everyone from Otis Rush to Earl Hooker. In 1970, the Myers brothers and Below reunited under the Aces moniker in 1970 to tour Europe before once again going their separate ways. Dave later formed the New Aces with Fabulous Thunderbirds frontman Kim Wilson, guitarist Robert Jr. Lockwood (Louis' replacement in the Jukes), and drummer Kenny Smith. Though preferring sideman duties throughout his career, in 1998, Dave Myers finally headlined his first solo effort, the Black Top label release *You Can't Do That*. Despite the 2000 amputation of a leg due to complications from diabetes, Myers still performed regularly in the months to follow, making his final public appearance in February of 2001; he died September 3 of that year at the age of 74. *—Jason Ankeny*

● **You Can't Do That** / 1998 / Black Top ✦✦✦✦✦

Dave Myers helped make Chicago blues history as the leader of the Aces-Jukes, Little Walter's backup group during the harmonica genius' heyday in the '50s. While he's played both guitar and bass on a pile of classic blues recordings as a sideman over the intervening decades, this marks his first album as a featured artist. The wait was evidently worth it, as Myers is flanked by a top-notch band featuring Rusty Zinn on guitar and Kim Wilson on harmonica and simply turns in the best traditional blues record to be released in a long, long time. Myers' guitar style is thoroughly down-home and swinging (especially fine on the instrumental "Legs Up") and has taken on absolutely no modern accoutrements over the years; the band turns in well-formed and integrated performances that recall the Chess studio sessions of the '50s. Myers' singing voice isn't the strongest, but instead imparts a warm, good-natured blues feeling to it, heard to good effect on "Ting-A-Ling," the Little Walter tribute "Oh Baby," John Lee "Sonny Boy" Williamson's "Elevate Me, Mama" and "You Can't Love Me That Way." Dave also brings six originals to this 14-track outing, with the title track sounding like a lost Chicago classic from the

'50s. This one absolutely defies the odds; if you really can't go home again, then this one comes awful darn close. —*Cub Koda*

Louis Myers

b. Sep. 18, 1929, Byhalia, MS, **d.** Sep. 5, 1994, Chicago, IL

Vocals, Arranger, Harmonica, Guitar / Modern Electric Chicago Blues, Electric Chicago Blues

Though he was certainly capable of brilliantly fronting a band, remarkably versatile guitarist/harpist Louis Myers will forever be recognized first and foremost as a top-drawer sideman and founding member of the Aces—the band that backed harmonica wizard Little Walter on his immortal early Checker waxings.

Along with his older brother David—another charter member of the Aces—Louis left Mississippi for Chicago with his family in 1941. Fate saw the family move next door to blues great Lonnie Johnson, whose complex riffs caught young Louis' ear. Another Myers brother, harp-blowing Bob, hooked Louis up with guitarist Othum Brown for house party gigs. Myers also played with guitarist Arthur "Big Boy" Spires before teaming with his brother David on guitar and young harpist Junior Wells to form the first incarnation of the Aces (who were initially known as the Three Deuces). In 1950, drummer Fred Below came on board.

In effect, the Aces and Muddy Waters traded harpists in 1952, Wells leaving to play with Waters while Little Walter, just breaking nationally with his classic "Juke," moved into the front man role with the Aces. Myers and the Aces backed Walter on his seminal "Mean Old World," "Sad Hours," "Off the Wall," and "Tell Me Mama" and at New York's famous Apollo Theater before Louis left in 1954 (he and the Aces moonlighted on Wells' indispensable 1953-1954 output for States).

Plenty of sideman work awaited Myers—he played with Otis Rush, Earl Hooker, and many more. But his own recording career was practically non-existent; after a solitary 1956 single for Abco, "Just Whaling"/"Bluesy," that found Myers blowing harp in Walter-like style, it wasn't until 1968 that two Myers tracks turned up on Delmark.

The Aces reformed during the '70s and visited Europe often as a trusty rhythm section for touring acts. Myers cut a fine set for Advent in 1978, *I'm a Southern Man*, that showed just how effective he could be as a leader (in front of an L.A. band, no less). Myers was hampered by the effects of a stroke while recording his last album for Earwig, 1991's *Tell My Story Movin'*. He courageously completed the disc but was limited to playing harp only. His health soon took a turn for the worse, ending his distinguished musical career. —*Bill Dahl*

● **I'm a Southern Man** / 1978 / Testament ♦♦♦♦♦

Despite his vaunted reputation as a versatile standout on the Windy City circuit, Louis Myers seldom recorded as a leader. This is the best set he did as a front man; cut in 1978, it was ironically recorded in Hollywood. Fellow ex-Little Walter sideman Freddy Robinson shared guitar duties with Myers (who also played harp) on a well-produced set strong on

tradition but with one eye cocked toward contemporary developments (witness Myers' stylish diatribe on "Women's Lib"). —*Bill Dahl*

Walking the Blues / 1983 / JSP ♦♦♦

Tell My Story Movin' / 1992 / Earwig ♦♦♦

Since a serious stroke had largely robbed Myers of his revered ability to play guitar, this effort really isn't indicative of his vast talent. But you've got to give him points for courage—Myers summoned up the strength to play harp and sing on what would be his final release. A nice Chicago combo that included guitarists Steve Freund and John Primer undoubtedly put Myers' mind at ease. —*Bill Dahl*

Sam Myers

b. Mar. 19, 1936, Laurel, MS

Vocals, Drums, Harmonica / Electric Harmonica Blues, Soul-Blues

Sam Myers got a second chance at the brass ring, and he's happily made the most of it. As frontman for Anson Funderburgh & the Rockets, the legally blind Myers' booming voice and succinct harp work have enjoyed a higher profile recently than ever before. Although he was born and mostly raised in Mississippi, Myers got into the habit of coming up to visit Chicago as early as 1949 (where he learned from hearing Little Walter and James Cotton). Myers joined a band, King Mose & the Royal Rockers, after settling in Jackson, MS, in 1956. Myers' 1957 debut 45 for Johnny Vincent's Ace logo, "Sleeping in the Ground"/"My Love Is Here to Stay," featured backing by the Royal Rockers.

Myers played both drums and harp behind slide guitar great Elmore James at a 1961 session for Bobby Robinson's Fire label in New Orleans. Myers cut a standout single of his own for Robinson's other logo, Fury Records, the year before that coupled his appealing remake of Jimmy Reed's "You Don't Have to Go" with "Sad, Sad Lonesome Day."

Myers made some albums with a loosely knit group called the Mississippi Delta Blues Band for TJ during the early '80s before teaming up with young Texas guitar slinger Funderburgh. Their first collaboration for New Orleans-based Black Top Records, 1985's *My Love Is Here to Stay*, was followed by several more albums—*Sins, Rack 'Em Up, Tell Me What I Want to Hear*, 1995's *Live at the Grand Emporium*—each one confirming that this was one of the most enduring blues partnerships of the '90s. —*Bill Dahl*

● **My Love Is Here to Stay** / 1985 / Black Top ♦♦♦♦♦

Young Texas guitarist Anson Funderburgh and veteran harpist Sam Myers got along so well during the making of this fine set that they got their act together and took it on the road. Happily, it remains there, with Myers deftly fronting Funderburgh's Rockets. Myers' booming voice and rocking harp and Funderburgh's crisp, tradition-laden lead guitar mesh beautifully here—the disc features brash remakes of Myers' past triumphs "My Love Is Here to Stay" and "Poor Little Angel Child" and a host of fresh titles. —*Bill Dahl*

Down Home in Mississippi / TJ ♦♦♦

Mark Naftalin

b. Aug. 2, 1944, Minneapolis, MN
Vibraphone, Keyboards, Accordion, Piano, Guitar, Organ / Modern Electric Blues
Blues musician, composer and producer Mark Naftalin played keyboards with the original Paul Butterfield Blues Band from 1965 to 1968. Since then he has recorded with top blues players like John Lee Hooker, Otis Rush, Percy Mayfield, James Cotton, Michael Bloomfield, Lowell Fulson, Big Joe Turner, and dozens of others—a sideman on over 100 albums.

Naftalin is sought after for his elegant, understated keyboard accompaniment and tasty solos. Although first known as an organist, he has also recorded on piano, guitar, accordion, vibes, and various electric keyboards. In his solo concerts he plays mostly acoustic piano.

Born in Minneapolis, MN, in 1944, Naftalin moved to Chicago in 1961 and enrolled at the University of Chicago, where he jammed along on piano at many of the campus "twist parties," the rage at the time. It was at these parties that Naftalin had his first opportunity to play with harmonica player Paul Butterfield and guitarist Elvin Bishop, the nucleus of what was to become the Paul Butterfield Blues Band.

In 1964, Naftalin moved to New York City, where he spent a year at the Mannes College of Music, and it was there that he sat in with the Butterfield band during a recording session warmup song, playing the Hammond organ (for the first time!). Michael Bloomfield had recently joined the band. The group liked the organ sound (and his playing) and Naftalin went on to record eight of the 11 songs on the first Butterfield album that very day. Butterfield asked Naftalin to join the group during that first session.

In the late '60s, after the first four Butterfield albums, Naftalin went out on his own, settling in the San Francisco Bay area. There he put together the Mark Naftalin Rhythm & Blues Revue and has been active in blues and rock recording sessions, solo gigs and revue shows, and as a producer of concerts, festivals and radio shows. He also played with Michael Bloomfield as a duo and in a band (most often called Mike Bloomfield & Friends) from the late '60s through the mid-'70s, and hosted *Mark Naftalin's Blue Monday Party*, a weekly blues show (1979-1983) that featured over 60 blues artists and groups and was the scene of 86 live radio broadcasts and three TV specials.

More recently, Naftalin has produced the Marin County Blues Festival (1981 to the present) and has been the associate producer of the Monterey Jazz Festival's Blues Afternoon (1982-1991). His weekly radio show, *Mark Naftalin's Blues Power Hour* has been on the air almost continuously since 1979 on San Francisco's KALW-FM.

Naftalin co-founded the Blue Monday Foundation and, in 1988, started his own label, Winner Records, which has issued classic era recording by artists including Paul Butterfield and Percy Mayfield. He continued to perform, both solo and ensemble, in the Bay area and elsewhere, often with slide guitar virtuoso Ron Thompson, a longtime associate. —*Michael Erlewine*

Steve Nardella

b. Jun. 26, 1948, Providence, RI
Vocals, Harmonica, Guitar / Contemporary Blues, Blues-Rock, Rock & Roll
Strong, American roots-music performer, equally adept at rockabilly and low-down blues. His first known recording behind Detroit bluesman Bobo Jenkins on "Shake 'Em on Down" also featured the debut work of Austin, TX, mainstay Sarah Brown and Fran Christina of the Fabulous Thunderbirds. Formed local Boogie Brothers band with Brown, Christina and John Nicholas (Asleep at the Wheel, Guitar Johnny & the Guitar Rockers), backing every blues legend who came into their native Ann Arbor, appearing on Atlantic's 1972 Ann Arbor Blues & Jazz Festival behind Johnny Shines, and doing their own solo turn. After nucleus of band moved to Boston with Nicholas, Nardella formed the Silvertones with local guitar hot-shot George Bedard, recording one fine album for the Blind Pig label. Has continued on his own since then, expanding his musical genres beyond just straight blues forms and turning out some interesting music along the way. —*Cub Koda*

It's All Rock & Roll / 1979 / Blind Pig ♦♦♦
Extraordinary rock, R&B, and rockabilly influences all come out of Nardella's love for blues. As well as possessing a strong voice, Nardella is also an electrifying guitarist in the Chuck Berry mold. Nardella's a rare bird, with more talent than he can harvest. —*Michael G. Nastos*

● **Daddy Rollin' Stone** / 1993 / Schoolkids ♦♦♦♦
Well over a decade after he released his first album, the Detroit roots-rocker Steve Nardella recorded his second album, *Daddy Rollin' Stone*, for the fledgling Ann Arbor label Schoolkids Records. During that decade, Nardella kept busy, supporting a number of visiting bluesmen and playing many gigs on his own. That hard work paid off big time on *Daddy Rollin' Stone*. While the record doesn't quite capture the energy of Nardella's live shows, it nevertheless functions as a good showcase for his talents, proving that he's a consummate roots-rocker, capable of playing rockabilly and blues with equal flair. His voice isn't distinctive, but his guitar and passion are, and that's why *Daddy Rollin' Stone* is a modest triumph. —*Thom Owens*

Nathan & the Zydeco Cha Chas

f. 1988, St. Martinville, LA
Group / Swamp Pop, Zydeco
Nathan Williams is the leader of the Zydeco Cha Chas. His stylings on the piano accordion have made him one of the most-admired players in the zydeco scene, following in Clifton Chenier's and Buckwheat Zydeco's huge footsteps. Nathan Williams was the youngest of seven children and grew up in St. Martinville, LA. Times were hard for the Williams family and Nathan Williams lost his father when he was only seven years old.

Williams grew up admiring his uncle, Harry Hypolite, who is best-known for his guitar work with Clifton Chenier. Later in life, Williams moved to Lafayette to live with his older brother, Sid Williams, and his wife. He worked in Sid's grocery store and began practicing on the accordion and practiced in the bathroom because he didn't want anyone to hear him play. With the aid of one of his friends, Buckwheat Zydeco, and steady hard work, it was not long before he was playing for people. Just five years after graduating from high school, he was recording 45s on his brother's El Sid indie record label.

He got his lucky break when Buckwheat Zydeco left Rounder Records for Island Records, leaving Rounder in need of an accordion player to fill a slot on a project they had lined up. Buckwheat Zydeco suggested Nathan Williams for the spot and he auditioned and got the job. In the year 2000, Williams released his seventh album for Rounder Records, *Let's Go!* The Zydeco Cha Chas members include Dennis Paul Williams as guitarist, Allen "Cat Roy" Broussard on alto and tenor saxophones, Wayne Burns on bass, Mark Anthony Williams on rub board, and Gerard St. Julien Jr. on drums. Special guest artist on the 2000 release was tenor saxophonist Derek Huston and Scott Billington played harmonica and produced the album. With Nathan & the Zydeco Cha Chas, fame and fortune take a back seat to the music they play. They want to bring zydeco and traditional Louisiana Cajun music to the attention of mainstream music listeners. They believe that the energy and uptempo Louisiana music has been regionalized for far too long and is due for international and worldwide acclaim. As one listens to their music, it is easy to agree that the time has come for the world to be introduced to the best-kept secret in the music world. —*Larry Belanger*

Steady Rock / 1989 / Rounder ♦♦♦♦♦
Nathan Williams has emerged near the head of the class among contemporary zydeco artists. This release featured mostly zydeco-tinged versions of blues and R&B tracks, although the cuts "Zydeco Joe" and "Everything on the Floor" were closer in structure and arrangements to straight zydeco. But Williams' voice, flair and energy, coupled with his band's ability to keep the beat moving, helped him retain a sizable following among Louisiana music purists, yet also branch out and do material that could gain attention from less knowledgeable fans. It was fiery, enjoyable music, produced with a modern sensibility and performed in vintage fashion. —*Ron Wynn*

Your Mama Don't Know / Oct. 1991 / Rounder ♦♦♦
Nathan Williams continued his string of solid releases with this 1991 release. It included good pop and R&B tracks like "Outside People" and "Don't Burn No Bridges," plus vibrant traditional material such as "El Sid O's Zydeco Boogaloo" and "Mardi Gras Zydeco." Williams again sang with zest, drive and non-stop intensity, while the band showed once more why they're considered the tightest unit working in the genre. There weren't any surprises nor low points, just a consistently fine set spotlighting the best group in '90s zydeco. —*Ron Wynn*

● **Follow Me Chicken** / 1993 / Rounder ♦♦♦♦♦
A rich product of the Creole-American culture in Louisiana, singer/accordion player Nathan Williams and his band the Zydeco Cha Chas became one of the most popular zydeco dance bands of the late '80s and early to late '90s. *Follow Me Chicken* points to the fact that while Williams is very much an admirer of the great Clifton Chenier, he's also a fine artist in his own right. This CD is full of surprises—in addition to providing sweaty originals like "Hey Maman" and "Tout Partout Mon Passe," *Chicken* finds Williams interpreting bluesman Z.Z. Hill's "I Need Someone to Love Me" and translating Stevie Wonder's 1977 hit "Isn't She Lovely" into French Creole. Another high point of the risk-taking album is "Mama's Tired," which combines zydeco with both ska and '60s-type soul. And African influences are incorporated on "Zydeco Road" and "Zydeco Is Alright," both of which employ guest Kenyatta Simon on the djembe (a West African instrument). *Follow Me Chicken* is a disc that zydeco enthusiasts should make a point of obtaining. —*Alex Henderson*

Creole Crossroads / Oct. 3, 1995 / Rounder ♦♦♦
Michael Doucet teams up with Nathan Williams for a power-filled set that constantly blurs the line between what is Cajun and what is zydeco. The set list is a nice blend of

modern originals from both men (Williams' "Zydeco Hog" and Doucet's "La Nuit de Clifton Chenier") and traditional favorites like "Jolie Noir" and "I Want to Be Your Chauffeur," all of them suitably souped for the ocassion. A spirited session that makes you want to dance. *—Cub Koda*

I'm a Zydeco Hog: Live at the Rock 'N' Bowl, New Orleans / Aug. 5, 1997 / Rounder ♦♦♦

Let's Go / Feb. 8, 2000 / Rounder ♦♦♦♦
From "Let's Go," the first track on the album, be prepared to be rocked in the good old Louisiana fashion, because that's the way Nathan & the Zydeco Cha Chas do it. This song serves to showcase everybody in the band as they all have their own little solo, even the rub board player gets a chance to shine. If the search is for melodic tunes, this album certainly fits the bill. With 14 original tunes that have a familiar charm, it won't be long until one finds themselves singing along. It could also be the charismatic piano accordion playing from Nathan Williams that attracts many a listener. Or quite possibly it's the tight arrangements that fill the album that pull the listener's ear to the groove. Whatever it is that attracts the listener to Nathan & the Zydeco Cha Chas, it's common opinion that they have found the perfect formula that keeps the party going and going all night long. This album is a prime example of what Nathan & the Zydeco Cha Chas can do with playful lyrics and bouncing rhythms. They have captured the essence of vibrant and colorful Louisiana music at its finest, as one will find on "Zydeco Rumble" (which has been used on commercials for Louisiana tourism). The lyrics are provocative and entertaining, keeping the listener sitting on the edge of their seat with keen interest, as in the bluesy "Hard Times." This is far from being the typical Zydeco album, it is as original and fresh as one can hope to find within the genre. Nathan & the Zydeco Cha Chas have bestowed Cajun/zydeco fans with an extraordinary dance music album that will have everyone shouting, "Let's Go!" one more time. *—Larry Belanger*

Kenny Neal

b. Oct. 14, 1957, New Orleans, LA
Vocals, Piano, Harmonica, Guitar / Swamp Blues, Modern Electric Blues
The future of Baton Rouge swamp blues lies squarely in multi-instrumentalist Kenny Neal's capable hands—the second-generation southern Louisiana bluesman is entirely cognizant of the region's venerable blues tradition and imaginative enough to steer it in fresh directions, as his albums for Alligator confirm. His dad, harpist Raful Neal, was a Baton Rouge blues mainstay whose pals included Buddy Guy and Slim Harpo (the latter handed three-year-old Kenny an old harp one day as a toy, and that was it). At age 13, Neal was playing in his father's band, and he picked up a bass at 17 for Buddy Guy. In 1987, Neal cut his debut LP for Florida producer Bob Greenlee—a stunningly updated swamp feast initially marketed on King Snake Records as *Bio on the Bayou*. Alligator picked it up the following year, retitled it *Big News from Baton Rouge!!*, and young Neal was on his way. Neal's sizzling guitar work, sturdy harp, and gravelly, aged-beyond-his-years vocals have served him well ever since. *—Bill Dahl*

Big News from Baton Rouge!! / 1988 / Alligator ♦♦♦♦
The debut release for the second-generation bayou blues guitarist/harpist, whose gruff-before-their-time vocals retain their swamp sensibility while assuming a bright contemporary feel that tabs him as a leading contender for future blues stardom. [*Big News from Baton Rouge* was originally released in 1987 as *Bio on the Bayou* on King Snake Records.] *—Bill Dahl*

Devil Child / 1989 / Alligator ♦♦♦♦
Backed by a punchy horn section and sizzling rhythms, Neal didn't suffer from any sophomore jinx. Between Neal, his bass-playing co-producer Bob Greenlee, and drummer Jim Payne, there's some very crafty songwriting going on here—"Any Fool Will Do," "Bad Check," and "Can't Have Your Cake (And Eat It Too)" are among the standouts. *—Bill Dahl*

Walking on Fire / 1991 / Alligator ♦♦♦♦
Another in the remarkably consistent Alligator catalog of Kenny Neal that strikingly captures his contemporary Baton Rouge blues sound. He gets a little hot help from the Horny Horns—alto saxist Maceo Parker and trombonist Fred Wesley—who once filled a smiliar role behind the Godfather of Soul himself, James Brown. Two songs find Neal going the unplugged route, just as he had performed them in the Broadway musical *Mule Bone*. *—Bill Dahl*

Bayou Blood / 1992 / Alligator ♦♦♦♦♦
You really can't go wrong with any of the guitarist's fine Alligator albums, but this one sparkles as brightly as any, with memorable outings like "Right Train, Wrong Track," "That Knife Don't Cut No More," and the steamy title track. Neal's albums are invariably dominated by well-chosen originals—no small feat these days. *—Bill Dahl*

Hoodoo Moon / 1994 / Alligator ♦♦♦♦
Neal is one of the most impressive young blues artists on the scene today—a fact borne out by the contents of this collection. Ably backed by a band that includes his brother Noel on bass and keyboardist Lucky Peterson, Neal indulges in a couple of covers this time, but the majority of the disc is original and incendiary. *—Bill Dahl*

● **Deluxe Edition** / Oct. 28, 1997 / Alligator ♦♦♦♦♦
Deluxe Edition is a great compilation of 15 highlights from Kenny Neal's first five albums for Alligator Records. Neal's records were more consistent than those from some of his Alligator peers, but this best-of collection is welcome since it provides a nice introduction for the neophyte. And, since it isolates the cream of the crop on one record, it's also not a bad bet for serious fans who want all the good stuff in one place. *—Thom Owens*

Blues Fallin' Down Like Rain / Jun. 16, 1998 / Telarc ♦♦♦♦
After building an impressive catalog at Alligator, Kenny Neal switched to Telarc Blues with *Blues Fallin' Down Like Rain*. Some blues enthusiasts wondered if the Baton Rouge singer/guitarist would fare as well creatively at Telarc as he had at Alligator, but they needn't have worried, for this excellent CD is every bit as strong as his Alligator dates. Neal's foundation continued to be Louisiana swamp blues, with the occasional detour into Louisiana R&B. It doesn't get much swampier than "Strike While the Iron Is Hot" and the haunting "Shadow On the Moon." Neal turns his attention to Chicago blues on Jimmy Reed's hit "Big Boss Man" and the often recorded Willie Dixon classics "My Babe" and "I'm Ready," all of which he gives a Louisiana-style makeover. Never have these blues standards sounded more swampy than they do in Neal's hands. Meanwhile, he gets into a Louisiana R&B groove on "Someday" and brings a touch of funk to "Just a Matter of Time." *Blues Fallin' Down Like Rain* is an album that Neal should be proud of. *—Alex Henderson*

What You Got / Apr. 25, 2000 / Telarc ♦♦♦♦♦
This is Neal's third album for Telarc and it's definitely one of his best releases to date. He's long been known for his Louisiana blues groove, but this CD will force critics and fans to reassess their take on Neal's sound. Tracks like "Two Wrongs Don't Make a Right," "Little Brother (Make a Way)," "I'm the Man Your Mama Told You About," "Loving on Borrowed Time," and "Deja Vu" are robust numbers that variously evince Chicago and Memphis influences, while the title track is a gorgeous bit of soul music that showcases Neal's mature voice. In fact, one of the major highlights of this collection is Neal's vocal work. He has become an exceptional blues singer, with a powerful and wonderfully nuanced voice. Add his excellent lead guitar work and make note of the fact that he wrote, or co-authored, nine of the 12 songs on this disc. The guy has become a multiple-threat bluesman and this album, in demonstrating that, has to be seen as a pivotal point in Neal's discography. *—Philip Van Vleck*

One Step Closer / May 22, 2001 / Telarc ♦♦♦

Raful Neal

b. Jun. 6, 1936, Baton Rouge, LA
Vocals, Harmonica / Louisiana Blues, Modern Electric Blues
When he wasn't busy siring progeny (the Neal household produced ten kids, most of them seemingly now playing the blues), Raful Neal was staking his claim as one of the top harpists on the Baton Rouge blues front. Unfortunately, until recently, his discography didn't reflect that status—but albums for Alligator and Ichiban have righted that injustice.

Neal took up the harp at age 14, tutored by a local player named Ike Brown and influenced by Chicago mainstay Little Walter. Neal's first band, the Clouds, also included guitarist Buddy Guy. This was the band Little Walter heard while in Baton Rouge and invited them to move up to Chicago and fill in at the gigs Walter couldn't make. Guy jumped at the chance but Neal decided to stay in Louisiana and raise his family. The harpist debuted on vinyl in 1958 with a 45 for Don Robey's Houston-headquartered Peacock Records. But "Sunny Side of Love," fine though it was, didn't lead to an encore for Peacock or anywhere else until much later, when Neal turned up with 45s on Whit, La Louisianne, and Fantastic.

Neal's debut album, the aptly titled *Louisiana Legend*, first emerged on Bob Greenlee's King Snake Records and was picked up by Alligator in 1990. *I Been Mistreated*, Neal's equally swampy follow-up, was released on Ichiban the following year; sons Noel (on bass) and Raful Jr. (on guitar) pitched in to help their old man out. Since then Neal has spent his time touring around the world and in 1997 he contributed harp to a couple of tracks on Tab Benoit's *Live: Swampland Jam* record.*—Bill Dahl*

● **Louisiana Legend** / 1990 / Alligator ♦♦♦♦♦
Kenny Neal's dad Raful is a longtime Baton Rouge swamp blues stalwart whose own discography is way sparser than it should be. This album, first out on Bob Greenlee's King Snake logo, is an atmospheric indication of what the elder Neal can do with a harmonica, mixing covers ("Steal Away," "Honest I Do," "No Cuttin' Loose") with spicy originals. *—Bill Dahl*

I Been Mistreated / 1991 / Ichiban ♦♦♦♦
Neal wrote the majority of the sides on this satisfying disc himself. His supple band includes two sons, Raful Jr. on guitar and Noel on bass, and Lucky Peterson on keys. *—Bill Dahl*

Old Friends / May 26, 1998 / Club Louisianne ♦♦♦

Beaver Nelson

Vocals / Americana, Roots Rock, Singer/Songwriter, Country-Rock
Hailed as a prodigy by Rolling Stone at the tender age of 19, Beaver Nelson nevertheless had to trudge through a near decade's worth of the proverbial hard knocks of the music business and was well into his twenties before he was able to make any headway with his music. By the time he emerged for the first time on record in the late '90s, his music fully lived up to the early hype and established the singer/songwriter as one of the most promising writers of the entire decade.

As a teenager attending Christian youth camp, Beaver Nelson was introduced to the albums of Bob Dylan, Steve Earle, Lou Reed, Neil Young, Townes Van Zandt, and the Rolling Stones by one of his counselors, Will T. Massey, and it changed his life forever. Already playing guitar since the age of 14, he immediately began developing his songwriting chops. Soon he had put together two homemade cassettes of his songs, eventually selling 800 copies of each to school and camp friends. By 1989 and 1990, during his last couple of high school years, Houston native Nelson would occasionally drive into Austin to take part in open mic nights at singer/songwriter breeding ground Chicago House at the invitation of Massey.

Following graduation from school, he took a counselor position at his old youth camp and spent four months doing cowboy work in San Saba while playing open mic nights in Waco, San Antonio, and Austin. In 1991, Nelson moved to Austin to attend the University of Texas. Instead of tending to his classwork, he could more frequently be found playing around the city's music scene. He was soon offered a slot at a regular acoustic showcase that Loose Diamonds members Scrappy Jud Newcomb and Troy Campbell, two old pals from the Chicago House, were organizing at El Chino. At the club, Nelson forged friendships with local songwriters and musicians such as Kris McKay, Jo Carol Pierce, David Halley, and Rick Brotherton. His El Chino and Chicago House gigs eventually translated into regular spots opening for various friends at the Hole in the Wall, and he earned his own Wednesday night hosting gig at Chicago House. Work was coming his way so easily and regularly that Nelson quit college after a single semester to continue playing professionally.

Local veterans Brotherton and Don Harvey were soon offering to play in his band and help finance a six-song tape to shop to major labels. The demo landed him a publishing deal with an imprint of Warner-Chappel and provided him with enough money that he could live without a day job. The publishing company also brokered Nelson a development deal with Columbia Records, for whom he recorded an additional four songs to add to the original demo. The Columbia partnership was ill-fated from the start, however, and he lost his deal a month after the recording. Nelson's publisher quickly found him another deal with new label Lightstorm, a subsidiary of Sony, but with the stipulation that he first fire his Austin band and move to Los Angeles. He recruited bassist Tony Scalzo and drummer Joey Sheffield, who would eventually become two-thirds of Fastball, and they recorded a complete album in Memphis and Los Angeles. Lightstorm was dissatisfied with the recordings, however, only because they were looking for more of a grunge-driven album in line with the commercial trends of the times, and they ultimately rejected the record's release. Nelson continued to play around town with yet another band while the label had him contractually tied up, but most of his early luster had seemingly worn off.

Frustrated, slightly depressed, and musically confused, Nelson fired the band and returned to Austin and solo performances. Over the next couple years, he produced two more unreleased efforts and, echoing the Dylan-Guthrie symbiosis, attended Townes Van Zandt's 1997 funeral in Nashville, which inspired him to concentrate once again on songwriting instead of performing. By the end of the year, his composing confidence had returned to the point that he was ready to tackle both performing and recording again, and Nelson signed to independent local Freedom Records. With Scrappy Jud Newcomb producing, he released his official debut, *The Last Hurrah*, in 1998. The album found him reestablishing old musical ties, and it earned acclaim from publications such as No Depression and Mojo. His second effort, *Little Brother*, followed in 2000. *—Stanton Swihart*

Last Hurrah / Oct. 13, 1998 / Freedom ♦♦♦♦
In the same vein as Townes Van Zandt, Beaver Nelson is a songwriter with an interesting bent and a most individual way of looking at the world. Having survived the disappointment of several run-ins with Nashville, Nelson surfaces strong and without compromise. His music is very much about the pain of simply being alive, yet he injects a dose of humor into his view of things. Songs like "Landed In the Mud" and "One Car Collision" are typical. Lyrically, he shows a great deal of skill, and his wordplay flows fluidly into his music. "Too Much Moonlight" and "Things Get Shaky 'Round Midnight" are fine examples of his almost scholarly approach. A wise old soul who has lived many lifetimes, Nelson continues to forge ahead, charting new territory as a songwriter of distinction. More ragged troubadour than stage-crashing pop-star, Beaver Nelson is an original whose gruff façade becomes more and more attractive as the moonlight fades and the music takes over. *—Jana Pendragon*

● **Little Brother** / Feb. 2, 1999 / Black Dog ♦♦♦♦♦
If his debut, *Last Hurrah*, was more of a troubadour record for lonely midnight souls, *Little Brother* is Beaver Nelson's Friday night album. A raucous, rootsy club set, the album is peppered with Texas-style stompers, sweet-and-sour Nashville country, and beer-fueled two-step ballads, not to mention a quasi-funk ditty in "Fever Kept Me Up All Night" and some characteristically wonderful introspective singer/songwriter tunes. It may only be Nelson's second record, but the music is full of experience and hard knocks. Instead of making him embittered or cynical, however, the rough road that he has traveled only broadens and deepens his wry, complex observations into endlessly compelling songs. *Little Brother* certainly proves that early comparisons to heroes such as fellow Texans Townes Van Zandt and Steve Earle are deserved, but in a larger sense Nelson more closely recalls Bob Dylan. Neither a Dylan imitator nor a "next Dylan" acolyte, he nevertheless is an outstanding lyricist whose words carry the same type of heft and create a similar affect. Almost every line is dosed with both world-weary resignation and black humor, and Nelson self-deprecates all over the place in a manner that draws you in as much as it makes you cringe with self-recognition. The songs can seem very personal one moment, and yet, as with Dylan, there is the peculiar sense that Nelson is standing outside looking in, having lived and come to terms with his experiences already and so is at liberty to sing about them non-judgmentally and without the sort of emotional attachment that could blur their cold, knotty truths. That notion is enhanced even further because he delivers each of his songs in a been-there, done-that, wasn't-that-impressed vocal that makes any tune sound matter-of-fact even when the sentiment isn't necessarily so. It is a trick that few songwriters manage to master but a gift that Nelson has in spades. None of the intellectual considerations of his music, however, should obscure the fact that much of *Little Brother* simply rocks hard. Whether they are pounding like a bar band, the early '70s Rolling Stones, or with the power of hardened country combo (all of which they do expertly), his assembled band of Austin veterans bolsters the credibility of everything Nelson sings about. The music is so tough yet so full of moments where vulnerability is allowed to surface. There are plenty of hooks and beefy melodies throughout the album, but what you are ultimately left with is that lasting emotional resonance. It is mournful in a very tangible way, and when you are listening to the album it feels like you are losing something or letting go, and yet even loss can be festive, if it leads to something new. *—Stanton Swihart*

Undisturbed / Sep. 18, 2001 / Black Dog ♦♦♦
After two albums that favored rough-and-tumble roots rock, Beaver Nelson puts the emphasis on his singer/songwriter side for *Undisturbed*. The Austin-based musician has always demonstrated a keen ability to write emotionally weighty songs—"Little Brother Blues," from his previous album, *Little Brother*, being an excellent example—but he seems to have calmed down his rambunctious spirit some on this record. Opting for a generally quieter sound, Nelson reveals himself to be in a contemplative, questioning mood, as songs like "Did You Know?," "Where Are You?," and "What Is That to Me?" all bear out. This isn't to say that he has given up on doing raucous bar rockers. "Eleven Again," his ode to carefree youth, is a hell-raisin' tune, but it's more of the exception on this album than the rule. Another punchy rocker, however, is anything but adolescent; "God's Tears" finds Nelson proclaiming: "I feel a fire right between my ears/Science is a liar and those are God's tears." Although Nelson's writing is more introspective, he never comes off sounding overwrought. His rough, raspy vocals add the right mix of earnestness and wariness to his tunes. With the aid of his longtime guitarist/producer Scrappy Jud Newcomb, Nelson frames his songs in warm arrangements that favor acoustic guitars, pianos, and organs. Famed Faces keyboardist and current Austin resident Ian MacLagan contributes his Wurlitzer handiwork on several numbers. *Undisturbed* feels like a transitory piece, as Nelson sheds his twenty-something scruffiness for a more adult musical persona, and the disc offers an intriguing look into a rapidly maturing artist. *—Michael Berick*

Jimmy Nelson

b. Apr. 17, 1928, Philadelphia, PA
Vocals / R&B, Jump Blues
Heavy-voiced Jimmy Nelson was very briefly a star in 1951, when his downbeat "T-99 Blues" topped the R&B charts for Modern Records' RPM subsidiary. Strangely, he was unable to ever return back to hitdom, despite some very worthy follow-ups.

Though he was based out of Houston, Nelson did most of his early recording in California. After debuting on wax in 1948 with a single for Olliet, he cut his only smash, the aforementioned "T-99 Blues," at the Clef Club in Richmond, TX, in 1951, with backup from pianist Peter Rabbit's trio. (The exultant slow blues was covered by bandleader Tiny Bradshaw for King.)

From then on, Nelson did his studio work for RPM in L.A. with a cadre of the city's top session men: saxist Maxwell Davis, pianist Willard McDaniel, guitarist Chuck Norris, bassists Red Callender and Ted Brinson, and drummer Lee Young. For unknown reasons, the ominous "Meet Me with Your Black Dress On," "Second Hand Fool," "Sweetest Little Girl," and the rest failed to repeat for the singer.

Nelson made a single for Chess in Houston in 1955 (the typically laidback "Free and Easy Mind"), ventured next to Ray Dobard's Bay Area-based Music City diskery in 1957 to wax "The Wheel," and tried his luck with a variety of tiny Texas labels during the mid-'60s with no further success. At last report, Nelson was still active vocally. *—Bill Dahl*

● **Jimmy Mr T99 Nelson** / 1981 / Ace ♦♦♦♦♦
No CD exists containing Texas shouter Nelson's early-'50s output for Modern, but Ace did assemble a nice vinyl collection of his best material that'll have to suffice (if you can find it) until they get around to issuing it digitally. *—Bill Dahl*

Rockin' and Shoutin' the Blues / Jul. 27, 1999 / Bullseye Blues ♦♦♦♦
Earthy and proud, Jimmy "T99" Nelson's blues is a sax-backed, boastful, and commanding performance. His five-decade career brings him to this Bullseye release as one of the last great blues shouters. Rich Lataille and Doug James from Roomful of Blues with "Sax" Gordon Beadle provide the horns for this legendary vocalist in the tradition of Big Joe Turner. His foundation in proto-R&B jump blues makes the master of the small ensemble swing sound ripe for renewed success. Indeed, Turner mentored Nelson personally, making Nelson a living, direct connection back to these moving, vintage sounds.*—Tom Schulte*

Romeo Nelson (Iromeio Nelson)

Piano / Boogie-Woogie, Acoustic Chicago Blues
"Now Sister Fullbosom and Brother Lowdown" sings boogie-woogie pianist Romeo Nelson at the beginning of his song "Getting Dirty Just Shaking That Thing," setting the stage for a barrelhouse blues so raunchy that it might still raise eyebrows in the age of rap music. The song is one of a handful this artist recorded, a small supply of titles to be sure, but material so well liked, and so obviously accessible to copyright claim jumpers, that it has appeared on more than a dozen different piano anthologies.

Born Iromeio Nelson, the pianist stayed put in Chicago from the age of six, except for an interlude of about five years in East St. Louis beginning in 1915. Ironically, it was during this period that he learned the piano skills that he would use the rest of his life on the Chicago music scene. He got busy playing rent parties and clubs until the early '40s, but otherwise supported himself by gambling. In 1929, he recorded four titles for Vocalion, among them "Head Rag Hop," one of his most often anthologized numbers and even the subject of a three-minute color short created in 1970 by director Peter Turner. Blues piano fanatics tend to pick Nelson's recordings as some of the finest boogie-woogie showpieces on record. The music is multi-dimensional, involving great amounts of keyboard technique, an interesting harmonic imagination, and an obvious sense of humor. He often takes the works of his competitors on the piano, such as Pinetop Perkins, and plays them at greatly enhanced speed, an effect as overwhelming as it is comical. An interview conducted the '60s by the Jazz Institute of Chicago indicated that Nelson had retired from music, yet they might not have been talking to the right guy, since an alternate theory of the man's biography has him checking out for boogie-woogie heaven as early as 1940. *—Eugene Chadbourne*

Tracy Nelson

b. Dec. 27, 1947, Madison, WI
Vocals, Keyboards / Retro-Soul, Contemporary Blues, Folk-Blues, Country-Rock
A very versatile and talented vocalist, Tracy Nelson is better known for her role as lead singer of Mother Earth. The Nashville sextet had three albums in a country-rock vein make the charts in the late '60s and early '70s. But Nelson is just as capable in soul, R&B,

and blues, though she hasn't released many records in that style. Her albums for Flying Fish were more indicative of her eclecticism, but her R&B and blues roots are really evident on her 1993 release, *In The Here And Now,* and 1995's *I Feel So Good*—both on Rounder Records.

Born in California but raised in Madison, WI, Nelson began playing music when she was a student at the University of Wisconsin. Nelson began singing folk and blues at coffeehouses and R&B and rock & roll at parties with a covers band called the Fabulous Imitators. In 1964, she recorded an album for Prestige, *Deep Are the Roots*, which was produced by Sam Charters.

Two years after recording *Deep Are the Roots,* Nelson headed out to the West Coast, spending some time in Los Angeles before settling in San Francisco. After arriving in San Francisco, she formed Mother Earth in 1968, moving the group to Nashville the following year. The band stayed together for five years, recording several albums for Mercury Records, among a handful of other labels. Nelson left the band in the mid-'70s, embarking on a solo career that saw her release albums for a variety of labels, including Columbia, Atlantic, and Flying Fish.

Tracy Nelson continued to record and perform into the '90s. In 1993, she released *In the Here and Now,* her first album for Rounder Records and, not coincidentally, her first straight blues record since she began recording in the '60s. Nelson followed *In the Here and Now* with several acclaimed records of gritty blues-rock for Rounder. *—Ron Wynn & Stephen Thomas Erlewine*

Deep Are the Roots / 1965 / Prestige ♦♦♦
Nelson's debut album was very much in the traditional acoustic folk-blues style, without any of the rock influence that would enter her work when she joined Mother Earth. Vocally, Nelson (who also plays guitar and piano on the disc) took inspiration from early female blues singers Ma Rainey and Bessie Smith (both of whose songs are covered on the album), also interpreting some familiar early blues standards like "Candy Man" and "Baby Please Don't Go." Nelson's singing is already mature at this point, and the record isn't as dry as many other traditional folk albums from the '60s, since she uses other musicians on guitar, piano, and harmonica to fill out the sound, harmonica player Charlie Musselwhite being the most notable of these. Her version of "House of the Rising Sun" is pretty interesting, since it uses a melody totally different from the one played by the Animals and numerous folk musicians of the era. *—Richie Unterberger*

Tracy Nelson/Mother Earth / 1972 / Reprise ♦♦♦
The very title of this LP indicated a vagueness as to whether Mother Earth were still a group, or a vehicle for Nelson's solo career. It's a solid, if laid-back, set of rock with strong country and soul flavorings, and a bit of gospel now and then. It sounds a little like Janis Joplin's final solo recordings, but more subdued, both vocally and instrumentally. The songs include three compositions by Louisiana swamp pop legend Bobby Charles and an early effort by John Hiatt, "Thinking of You." *—Richie Unterberger*

Mother Earth / 1972 / Reprise ♦♦♦♦♦

Tracy Nelson / 1974 / Atlantic ♦♦♦

Sweet Soul Music / 1975 / One Way ♦♦♦♦

Time Is on My Side / 1976 / One Way ♦♦♦

Homemade Songs / 1978 / Flying Fish ♦♦♦
This album features gospel-tinged blues from this big-voiced, intense singer. *—AMG*

Come See About Me / 1980 / Flying Fish ♦♦
Her second Flying Fish album features R&B music. *—AMG*

In the Here & Now / Jun. 1, 1993 / Rounder ♦♦♦♦
Tracy Nelson has always brought a wealth of blues feeling to her work, but being bluesy doesn't necessarily mean that one is actually singing the blues—one can certainly bring the feeling of the blues to rock, R&B, reggae, country, bluegrass, zydeco, or jazz (all of which have been affected by the blues). In fact, Nelson has often showed listeners just how blues-minded rock, soul, or country can be. *In the Here and Now,* however, isn't just bluesy—it is blues-oriented, and this time, there are plenty of tracks that actually have 12 bars. Nelson, who was 45 when this album came out in 1993, really soars on passionate performances of "Motherless Child Blues" and "Go Down Sunshine" as well as Chicago blues gems like Elmore James' "It Hurts Me Too" and Willie Dixon's "Whatever I Am, You Made Me." And Nelson never sounded more confident than she does on "Please Send Me Someone to Love," which finds her performing a duet with veteran New Orleans soul great Irma Thomas. This Percy Mayfield classic, which was first recorded in 1950, is one of those standards that has been beaten to death over the years—as great as the song is, there is such a thing as overkill. But Nelson and Thomas manage to make the tune sound fresh and vital, which is impressive because their 1993 version was recorded 43 years after the original version. Nelson, in fact, was only two years old when Mayfield first recorded "Please Send Me Someone to Love." *In the Here and Now* is hardly the only Nelson CD that is worth owning, but it is safe to say that it is among the strongest albums that she provided in the '90s. *—Alex Henderson*

I Feel So Good / 1995 / Rounder ♦♦♦

Homemade Songs/Come See About Me / 1996 / Flying Fish ♦♦♦♦

Move On / Jul. 29, 1996 / Rounder ♦♦♦
The third album in Tracy Nelson's '90s comeback, *Move On* finds her sharing the microphone with the likes of Delbert McClinton, Phoebe Snow, Bonnie Raitt, and Maria Muldaur (the last three on "Ladies' Man"), singers with whom she shares a taste in bluesy rock with a country tinge. She is in typically fine voice on a set of songs more notable for the tasty playing on them than for their distinctiveness. The best among them is Nelson's own "Playin' It Safe" (one of her four compositions) which has a gospel feel to support the lyric's sage advice. Blues fans who caught up with Nelson on 1993's *In the Here and Now* or 1995's *I Feel So Good* may find this album, with its pop, rock, and R&B elements, a bit eclectic for their taste, but fans of Bonnie Raitt who long for her earlier, grittier music may find a new heroine. *—William Ruhlmann*

Tracy Nelson Country / Sep. 9, 1996 / Reprise Archives ♦♦♦♦
Originally released in 1969 with some of Music City's most royal musicians holding court, the ten original album tunes and three other remnants of a week-long recording session are included here. On Elvis Presley's rocker "That's All Right, Mama," Nelson sizzles, and on Boz Scaggs' almost vaudevillian "Now, You're Gone" blues she gives a Broadway-bound performance. On Chuck "The Sheik of the Blues" Willis' soft shuffle "You're Still My Baby," the harmonica and handclaps are so spirited it sounds as if the listener is in the midst of the session. The album's very best selections were the least known. The self-penned "Stay As Sweet As You Are" had a mellow Southern rock feeling with a distinctive country string refrain in the background. "Can't Go on Loving You" is sweetly plaintive, while the desperate "Wait, Wait, Wait" reveals a woman begging her man for one more chance. A woman trusting a man whom she's found to have cheated on her yet again provides the backdrop for Hank Williams' "You Win Again." With that in mind, Nelson becomes the victim as she makes this a midtempo '50-style R&B ballad with a keyboard workout that would make Fats Domino proud. To then say that Nelson wails her betrayal on the song would be putting it lightly. She lives it for four minutes and fifteen seconds. In fact, she lives all of these songs. That's how life must be in Tracy Nelson country. *—Bill Carpenter*

● **The Best of Tracy Nelson & Mother Earth** / Sep. 9, 1996 / Reprise Archives ♦♦♦♦♦
Janis Joplin may have gotten all of the fame and glory, but she was far from the only white female blues shouter to emerge from the San Francisco music scene of the mid-'60s; *The Best of Tracy Nelson/Mother Earth* is proof positive of that, providing an excellent introduction to one of the more sadly overlooked talents of her time and place. Despite any number of passing similarites to Joplin, Nelson sings with greater finesse; her style is more adaptable as well, capable of fitting comfortably into R&B, psychedelia and pop ballads, all the while remaining grounded in classic roots music traditions. Highlighted by her perennial "Down So Low"—subsequently recorded by everyone from Linda Ronstadt to Etta James—this 17-track compilation also spotlights performances spanning from a wrenching cover of Little Willie John's "Need Your Love So Bad" to contemporary material like Steve Young's "Seven Bridges Road" and John Hiatt's "Thinking of You," offering a comprehensive overview of her earliest and most enduring work. *—Jason Ankeny*

Ebony and Irony / Apr. 24, 2001 / Madacy ♦
On her 20th album Tracy Nelson has been nice enough to show you what might have been if Janis Joplin had lived but remained a horrible drunk. The liner notes tell the fascinating tale of why this remarkably bad record was rejected by record label after record label until the artist decided to do you the favor of releasing it herself. Gee thanks. If you love vibrato—and you better because every song is soaked with it—this is sure to appeal to you. If you're looking for something a cut above the gang that's appearing at your local Ramada Inn keep searching. *—Rob Ferrier*

The Neville Brothers

f. 1977, New Orleans, LA
Group / New Orleans R&B, R&B, Funk, Soul
Throughout their long careers as both solo performers and as members of the group that bore their family name, the Neville Brothers proudly carried the torch of their native New Orleans' rich R&B legacy. Although the four siblings—Arthur, Charles, Aaron, and Cyril—did not officially unite under the Neville Brothers aegis until 1977, all had crossed musical paths in the past, while also enjoying success with other unrelated projects: Eldest brother Art was the first to tackle a recording career, when in 1954 his high school band the Hawketts cut "Mardi Gras Mambo," a song that later became the annual carnival's unofficial anthem. Both Aaron and Charles later joined the Hawketts as well, and when Art joined the Navy in 1958, he handed Aaron the group's vocal reins.

Two years later, Aaron scored his first solo hit, "Over You"; in 1966, he notched a pop smash with the classic "Tell It Like It Is," a lush ballad showcasing his gossamer vocals. Art, meanwhile, returned from the service to begin his own solo career, and recorded a series of regional hits like "Cha Dooky Doo," "Zing Zing" and "Oo-Whee Baby." In 1967, he formed Art Neville and the Sounds, which included both Aaron and Charles as featured vocalists and quickly became a sensation on the local club circuit.

In 1968 producer Allen Toussaint hired the group as the house band for his Sansu Enterprises; minus Aaron and Charles, the Sounds evolved into a highly-regarded rhythm section which backed artists as diverse as Lee Dorsey, Robert Palmer and Labelle before eventually finding fame on their own as the Meters. Consequently, Aaron resumed his solo career, although with only sporadic success; as a result, he also worked as a dock hand. Charles, meanwhile, relocated to New York City, where his skills as a saxophonist led to tenures with a variety of jazz units; after returning to New Orleans, he was arrested for possession of marijuana and served a three-year sentence at the Angola Prison Farm. In 1975, the Meters backed the Wild Tchoupitoulas, a group led by the Nevilles' uncle, George "Big Chief Jolly" Landry. Both Aaron and Charles were enlisted for the session, as was youngest brother Cyril; when the Meters disbanded the following year, the four brothers backed the Tchoupitoulas on tour, and in 1977 they offically banded together as the Neville Brothers. Despite their gift for intricate four-part harmonies, their self-titled 1978 debut unsuccessfully cast the vocal quartet as a disco band, and following a dismal response they were dropped by their label, Capitol.

The Nevilles spent the following three years without a contract, but after signing with A&M, fan Bette Midler helped secure the services of producer Joel Dorn for 1981's superior *Fiyo on the Bayou*, which spotlighted Aaron's angelic tenor on standards like "Mona Lisa" and "The Ten Commandments of Love" along with renditions of "Iko Iko" and "Brother John." Despite widespread critical acclaim, the album sold poorly, and again the Nevilles were cut loose from their contract. After signing to the tiny Black Top label, they issued 1984's *Neville-ization*, an incendiary live set recorded at the Crescent City landmark Tipitina's which featured Duke Ellington's "Caravan" and Aaron's perennial "Tell It Like It Is" alongside the brothers' own "Africa" and "Fear, Hate, Envy, Jealousy."

After another concert album, 1987's *Live at Tipitina's*, the Nevilles signed with EMI and returned to the studio in 1987 with *Uptown*, which again met with commercial failure despite cameo appearances from Keith Richards, Jerry Garcia and Carlos Santana. In 1989, they re-signed to A&M and recruited the services of famed New Orleans producer Daniel Lanois; the atmospheric *Yellow Moon*, the group's finest hour, finally earned them success on the charts, thanks in part to the anthemic single "Sister Rosa." 1990's *Brother's Keeper* fared even better, no doubt spurred by Aaron's concurrent success with Linda Ronstadt on the smash duet "Don't Know Much."

In subsequent years, Aaron reignited his solo career while also remaining with his brothers; while the Nevilles retained their cult following with LPs like 1992's *Family Groove*, 1994's *Live on Planet Earth* and 1996's *Mitakuye Oyasin Oyasin/All My Relations*, Aaron scored a Top Ten hit in 1991 with the single "Everybody Plays the Fool," taken from the Ronstadt-produced *Warm Your Heart*. In 1993, he notched a minor hit with "Don't Take Away My Heaven" from the LP *The Grand Tour*; a year later, he found success with "I Fall to Pieces," a duet with country star Trisha Yearwood. In 1990, Charles also issued the jazz collection *Charles Neville and Diversity*.

In addition, a second generation of Nevilles also began making their mark on music; in 1988, Aaron's son Ivan, a member of Keith Richards' backing band the X-Pensive Winos, released his solo debut, *If My Ancestors Could See Me Now*. The Neville Brothers legacy continued in 1999 with *Valence Street*. —*Jason Ankeny*

Fiyo on the Bayou / Apr. 1981 / A&M ✦✦✦✦✦
A brilliant updating of the New Orleans R&B sound to include strains of Cajun, rock, and reggae on standards ranging from "Hey Pocky Way" to "The Ten Commandments of Love" and "Sitting in Limbo." —*William Ruhlmann*

Neville-ization / Jun. 1984 / Diablo ✦✦✦
It took Black Top Records two years to put this record out after the Neville Brothers recorded it live at Tipitina's in New Orleans in September, 1982, and one reason may be that it presents a mediocre, going-through-the-motions set. At their best, the Nevilles achieve a transcendent musical mixture, and even at the level of mere professionalism they're an impressive unit, but this just isn't the live album of which they are capable. —*William Ruhlmann*

★ **Treacherous: A History of the Neville Brothers** / 1986 / Rhino ✦✦✦✦✦
The music of the Neville Brothers was more a matter of rumor than documentation to most record buyers outside the New Orleans area until 1986, when Rhino Records finally gathered together their various solo and group records dating back 30 years and presented their story coherently on this two-disc set. Suddenly, it all makes sense, and the Nevilles' mixture of styles emerges as a singular American genre unto itself. This record is a revelation. —*William Ruhlmann*

Uptown / Mar. 1987 / EMI ✦✦
The Neville Brothers displayed their eclecticism on this lone EMI album. They played with some high class guest stars, including Branford Marsalis, Jerry Garcia, Ronnie Montrose, Carlos Santana, and Keith Richards. But despite these excellent musicians and the Nevilles' usual tight playing and exuberant collective vocals, once more, the album failed to either get them a huge hit or faithfully recreate the quality of their live shows. —*Ron Wynn*

Yellow Moon / 1989 / A&M ✦✦✦✦
The Neville Brothers made a bid for pop/rock stardom with this well-produced album for A&M, their first under a new pact with the label inked in the late '80s. It was certainly as solid as any they cut for A&M; the vocals were both nicely arranged and expertly performed, the arrangements were basically solid, and the selections were intelligently picked and sequenced. The album charted and remained there for many weeks, while the Nevilles toured and generated lots of interest. It didn't become a hit, but it did respectably and represents perhaps their finest overall pop LP. —*Ron Wynn*

Brother's Keeper / Jul. 1990 / A&M ✦✦✦
Why doesn't more R&B sound like this? Although hampered by a poor mix, *Brother's Keeper* is nevertheless a classic example of what makes the Neville Brothers so good— and so frustrating. Tracks like the booty-shaking funk of "Brother Jake" or the gospel-tinged "Steer Me Right" are full of soulful vocals and wonderful harmonies. Aaron Neville's timeless voice is displayed beautifully on "Fearless," where he is joined by Linda Ronstadt for one of the strongest tracks on the record. The Neville Brothers' ecumenical spirituality permeates every second of *Brother's Keeper*, making for a few awkward moments (like the head-scratching opener "Brother Blood," for example), but a few moments of true sublimity (as when Art Neville spits "Pro choice-no choice/We're sending our sons and daughters to their slaughter" on "Sons and Daughters"). The pop material on *Brother's Keeper* (such as Link Wray's "Fallin' Rain," works well, but other tracks, like "River of Life," seem forced. If the Neville Brothers showed a little discretion with regard to their lyrics and cut a couple tracks, they would have had a much stronger album, which in a way is as good a statement as one could make about their entire career. —*Daniel Gioffre*

Treacherous Too: A History of the Neville Brothers, Vol. 2 (1955–1987) / Feb. 1, 1991 / Rhino ✦✦✦✦✦
OK, there's no such thing as secondhand revelation, but the Neville Brothers had more than enough stray tracks from their decades of local music-making around New Orleans to justify this second, single-disc follow-up to Rhino's first Nevilles history. There's more of an emphasis on novelty material here, but once again you can hear the roots of the Nevilles' cross-genre appeal in pop, R&B, and soul music dating back to the '50s. Since most of these songs were recorded as singles, they have an immediate surface appeal, but

repeated listenings also bring out the sounds of the tight session bands (including members of the Meters) who backed the Nevilles up. Actually, it's only the five '80s tracks from just-OK albums like *Neville-ization* and *Uptown* that keep this collection from classic status, not the older stuff. —*William Ruhlmann*

Family Groove / May 5, 1992 / A&M ✦✦✦
New Orleans' favorite sons, the Neville Brothers, pool their talents again on this CD. *Family Groove* is a clever reference not only to the musical abilities of the four brothers, but to the shared interests and concerns of the brothers and their families. All the usual Neville elements are here: Charles Neville on the saxophone, Cyril Neville on the drums, Art Neville on piano, and the inimitable voice of Aaron Neville. Their message is the Neville gospel of social and political justice, as well as the importance of love and family. Hence, the family groove. In "Line of Fire," brother Art Neville speaks to the growing problem of drugs and guns claiming the lives of many young black men in the cities. Aaron's son, Jason Neville, makes an appearance with a rap tune lamenting the tragic plight of the homeless in the richest country in the world and the complacent America that looks the other way. The one-world outlook of the Nevilles is exemplified on the beautiful harmonies of "Let My People Go," as well as in their closing number, a traditional "Maori Chant." They sing their recognition that people all over the world want the same thing: freedom, peace, and love. This is vintage Neville Brothers philosophy delivered as always with the funky beat and unique Neville sound that has captivated fans all over the world. —*Rose of Sharon Witmer*

Live on Planet Earth / Apr. 19, 1994 / A&M ✦✦✦
Clearly, this is intended to be the definitive live document of a band that has always been defined by its live work. Clocking in at 71 minutes, the album was culled from a world tour. The rhythm section of drummer Willie Green and bassist Tony Hall keeps up a steady groove from song to song, and The Nevilles trade off lead and harmony vocals on original songs that range across their career and add everything from Bob Marley compositions to "Love the One You're With" and "Amazing Grace." They Neville-ize all comers, throwing them into the pot and coming out with a tasty gumbo. If there's anything missing, it's the small club atmosphere from which the Nevilles emerged: this is a wide-screen treatment of a music that gained impact from its intimacy but now seeks to form a global conga line. —*William Ruhlmann*

Mitakuye Oyasin Oyasin/All My Relations / May 14, 1996 / A&M ✦✦✦
The Neville Brothers have made a family affair of their first studio album in four years, writing much of the material themselves and co-producing the record with James Stroud. As a result, they are making less of an effort to secure a pop hit this time, even though they do throw in a little rap and a funky cover of Bill Withers' "Ain't No Sunshine." But part of the reason they tend to be more interesting live than on record is that, beyond being well-meaning, they haven't got much to say. Most of the songs here are homilies to brotherhood, responsibility, and environmentalism, set against tracks that evoke Brazilian music, mbaqanga, reggae, R&B, and soul and are heavy on percussion and horns. Occasionally, as on the respectable cover of the Grateful Dead's "Fire of the Mountain," with guest guitarist Bob Weir, or on Aaron Neville's typically ethereal "Saved By the Grace of Your Love," the music transcends both the message and the groove. But this is an album of small pleasures rather than the larger statement it seems intended to be. —*William Ruhlmann*

● **The Very Best of the Neville Brothers** / Jan. 14, 1997 / Rhino ✦✦✦✦✦
Sixteen-track compilation focusing almost exclusively on the period spanning the late '70s to the late '80s. A couple of Aaron Neville's big '60s hits ("Tell It Like It Is" and "Over You") are thrown in as well, as are a couple of cuts from the Wild Tchoupitoulas' 1976 album. Some may argue that the Nevilles' sprawling output is too difficult to condense into a single disc. On the other hand, given how often they're criticized for underachieving on record, this is a pretty suitable purchase for someone whose interest only runs deep enough for one anthology. —*Richie Unterberger*

Live at Tipitina's 1982 / Aug. 18, 1998 / Rhino ✦✦✦✦✦
This two-CD set gathers both previously released albums from the Neville Brothers' September 1982 gigs at local New Orleans hangout Tipitina's, 1984's *Neville-ization/Live at Tipitina's* and 1987's *Nevillization II/Live at Tipitina's*, and strives to roll them into one complete, concise work. The only problem is that although the albums were recorded similarly, they were eventually released under different circumstances: the second part was augmented with studio-sweetened instruments and audience noises, and at times the overdubs are glaringly, and intrusively, obvious. Still, the first half of *Live at Tipitina's* (the original *Neville-ization* one) remains one of the Crescent City's most representative documents—"Fever," "Tell It Like It Is" and "Fear, Hate, Envy, Jealousy" just plain sizzle— and one of the Neville Brothers' most revered volumes (as well as one of the best live albums of the '80s). Think of the sequel as an extended, if not totally successful, bonus disc. —*Michael Gallucci*

Valence Street / Feb. 16, 1999 / Columbia ✦✦✦✦
For their Columbia Records debut, the Neville Brothers returned to a classic production and songwriting style more typical of their early years than of their work of the '80s and '90s, and they named it after the street they grew up on to signal their renewed focus on local concerns. Gone was the wet, murky sound mix of Daniel Lanois, replaced by dry aural clarity and precise instrument placement in a production by the brothers themselves. While retaining the second-line funk rhythms of New Orleans, their music hewed much more to a traditional R&B/soul sound, with little dabbling in world music. The title track, written by Charles, was even an instrumental that wouldn't have sounded out of place on a Meters album, and you could also say that about "Real Funk," co-written by Art. Though the brothers traded off vocals and Cyril turned in an excellent performance on the soulful romantic ballad "Until We Meet Again," co-written by Charles, Aaron's

voice had long since become so identifiable beyond the group that his vocals on songs like "Little Piece of Heaven," the standard "If I Had a Hammer," and "Give Me a Reason," and even in occasional asides on other songs, tended to stick out the way Michael Jackson used to on Jackson's albums, rendering him, through no one's fault, a solo artist within a group and hurting the record's overall balance. *—William Ruhlmann*

Uptown Rulin': The Best Of / Aug. 24, 1999 / Interscope ◆◆◆◆

The Neville Brothers had always been critic's favorites, but never more so than during their tenure at A&M Records during the late '80s and early '90s. They released their first album, *Yellow Moon*, for the label in 1989, a few years after the acclaimed Rhino compilation *Treacherous: A History of the Neville Brothers* appeared on the shelves. *Treacherous* contained selections from all the Neville Brothers—not just group recordings but side-projects and solo cuts—and helped cement their reputation among record collectors and critics, which in turn set the stage for the enthusiastic reception of *Yellow Moon*. That enthusiasm failed to wane over the next few years, as each subsequent album was greeted by critics with open arms. The problem was, each record was pretty much the same. With producer Daniel Lanois, the Nevilles attempted to create grand, mythical albums, heavy with import and meaning. Lanois didn't abandon his trademark hazy, murkily mysterious production—a style that wasn't necessarily suited for the organic Nevilles, even if it did result in some evocative sonic hybrids. Consequently, each of the A&M albums functioned best as a series of moments, even if they were designed to work as individual albums (the prototype, *Yellow Moon*, unsurprisingly standing as the lone exception to the rule). That's why *Uptown Rulin': The Best Of* is a solid addition to their catalog. By collecting highlights from the A&M albums, it offers fans a good summary of these intriguing but mixed years. It isn't on the same level as *Treacherous* or its sequel, but it's a nice addendum to fans of that groundbreaking compilation. *—Stephen Thomas Erlewine*

Aaron Neville

b. Jan. 24, 1941, New Orleans, LA
Vocals / Pop-Soul, New Orleans R&B, Adult Contemporary, R&B, Soul

Although Neville is often compared to singer Sam Cooke in terms of sheer vocal refinement, he has a voice and style uniquely his own. Today he is well known as part of the New Orleans sound of the Neville Brothers. Yet, aside from the 1967 number one R&B hit "Tell It Like It Is," few have heard his incredible early solo recordings. Many of the first recordings of Aaron Neville, in the early and mid-'60s, were arranged, produced, and often written by the brilliant Allen Toussaint—another talent only now being really appreciated. Most of these sides were cut for the Minit (and later) Parlo labels. Songs like "She Took You for a Ride" and "You Think You're So Smart" on Parlo are masterpieces. While his more recent work, including that with Linda Ronstadt, makes for pleasant listening, it lacks the sheer persuasion of his early songs. Aaron has re-recorded his early work often, and it is important to hear the originals. The early sides of Aaron Neville are just waiting to be heard.

Aaron Neville has ventured more into other waters besides R&B. 1993's *The Grand Tour* included a remake of a George Jones song that got Neville a little country attention, and he announced plans in 1994 to do a complete country album. He was also one of several R&B artists who teamed with country stars for the *Rhythm, Country and Blues* session. Neville was paired with Trisha Yearwood, and the duo also performed together in a benefit concert for the LP held in Los Angeles in April 1994. The LP made history by debuting in the Top Ten on the pop, R&B, and country charts. *—Michael Erlewine & Ron Wynn*

Tell It Like It Is / 1967 / Collectables ◆◆◆◆

Eleven of Neville's best Parlo cuts, including those mentioned above, are included on one CD. His biggest solo smash from 1966, plus more songs in the same style. Sublime stuff. *—Bill Dahl*

● Tell It Like It Is: Golden Classics / 1989 / Collectables ◆◆◆◆◆

One of many collections covering Aaron Neville's superb early R&B and soul classics. The burly Neville, whose delicate, feathery voice stands in vivid contrast to his muscular body, made great heartache ballads, uptempo wailers, and brilliantly sung originals for tiny New Orleans labels, often not even getting widespread soul airplay. Now that's he's hot property, the domestic anthologies are coming out left and right. This one is as good as any other, although for my money the import labels have still done a better job on early Neville than the American companies. *—Ron Wynn*

Show Me the Way / Aug. 1989 / Charly ◆◆◆◆

Here are 22 of his early Minit recordings, many of them incredible. *—Michael Erlewine*

Greatest Hits / 1990 / Curb ◆◆◆

Early New Orleans soul from velvet-voiced Aaron Neville, including the smooth, aching "Tell It Like It Is" and the gutsy, declarative "Over You," a shuffling R&B number. The eight other selections, especially "Jail House," "Hard Nut to Crack," and "Since You're Gone," offers an insightful overview of the golden tenor whose vocal abilities get more amazing with time. *—Andrew Hamilton*

My Greatest Gift / 1991 / Rounder ◆◆◆

The songs that made Neville famous among soul and R&B fans were done years before he became a recognized star, for tiny Southern labels. The 12 tracks on this anthology were recorded in the late '60s, when Neville's soaring falsetto, emphatic delivery and gutwrenching treatments were locked out of the pop mainstream. Although this isn't the definitive version of "Tell It Like It Is," it's far from a throwaway. On "Love Letters," "Hercules," "Mojo Hannah," and "Where Is My Baby," Aaron Neville tackled the soul mountain and conquered it. *—Ron Wynn*

The Very Best of Aaron Neville / Jan. 11, 2000 / A&M ◆◆◆◆

In some ways, *The Very Best of Aaron Neville* is a very welcome addition to his catalog, since it's the first collection to touch on all areas of Neville's long career. However, it winds

up being a bit unsatisfying, not just because it only has one cut from the Neville Brothers, but because his New Orleans R&B and down-home soul just don't fit that well with his smooth, cleanly produced latter-day work. Then again, the compilers didn't spend too much time with the early recordings, since the collection contains only a handful of R&B nuggets (including, of course, "Tell It Like It Is," plus "Over You") before settling into the '80s and '90s albums. It's not a bad summary of those albums, actually, containing such hits as "Don't Know Much" and "Everybody Plays the Fool," plus a good cross-section of album tracks and lesser-known cuts, such as his version of "Stardust" with Rob Wasserman. As such, *The Very Best of Aaron Neville* is recommended primarily to fans of his later recordings. Listeners who prefer the early R&B work or the Neville Brothers should look to compilations of that material, since they won't be satiated by this disc. *—Stephen Thomas Erlewine*

● Ultimate Collection / Aug. 21, 2001 / Hip-O ◆◆◆◆◆

Although it not surprisingly shares a whopping nine tracks with 2000's *The Very Best of Aaron Neville*, 2001's *Ultimate Collection* cherry picks from a far wider range of years (1960-1997) than the A&M period which was used almost exclusively for the former anthology. As such, it's a considerably broader and ultimately a better representation of the Neville Brothers' famed muscular singer with the impossibly angelic falsetto voice. The compilation kicks off with the string-laden "To Make Me Who I Am," a sort of capsule of Neville's tough life, complete with a heartfelt spoken coda which would have made a perfect album closer, certainly better than "Tell It Like It Is," his first crossover hit from 1966. The track does make a good lead-in to "Don't Know Much," the singer's smash duet with Linda Ronstadt, though. From there the disc gradually shifts moods and years, smartly bunching most of the upbeat '60s selections (including some interesting obscurities like "Why Worry," the original B-side of "Tell It Like It Is") toward the middle. The collection also rescues a pair of gorgeous R&B covers ("Pledging My Love" and "For Your Precious Love") from an obscure 1985 Joel Dorn-produced EP, as well as "The 10 Commandments of Love," included in the difficult to find Neville Brothers' 1981 release, *Fiyo on the Bayou*. It smartly plays down the rest of their music which is easily available elsewhere, but does include Aaron's dramatic rendition of Sam Cooke's "A Change Is Gonna Come," one of his most stirring performances from *Yellow Moon*. Thankfully the album doesn't get bogged down in some of the slick and sappy concoctions Neville often gravitates to. While the rather forced rock & roll of Chuck Berry's "You Never Can Tell" doesn't quite fit the predominantly languorous mood, and the track list strangely omits Neville's version of George Jones' "The Grand Tour" or Skylark's "Wildflower"—both of which remain concert staples—this is a stunning and consistently enjoyable representation of one of the most distinctive and memorable voices in American music. *—Hal Horowitz*

20th Century Masters—The Millennium Collection: The Best of Aaron Neville / Jun. 18, 2002 / A&M ◆◆◆

With the release of *20th Century Masters—The Millennium Collection: The Best of Aaron Neville* in 2002, Universal Music Group had released three Aaron Neville compilations in three years, following 2000's *The Very Best of Aaron Neville* on A&M and 2001's *Ultimate Collection* on Hip-O. Consumers might well be confused, and even when explained, the distinctions are a bit fine. Neville has had a long career on many different labels, though he enjoyed some commercial success on A&M in the '90s. *Ultimate Collection*, released at a list price of about $18, is a 20-track compilation that, like all of Hip-O's similarly titled compilations, does not stint on licensing material from other labels to create a well-rounded look at the artist. *The Very Best of Aaron Neville*, listing at about $17 on release, contains 18 tracks, some of which are licensed from other labels, but focuses more on the A&M recordings. Nevertheless, it shares nine tracks with *Ultimate Collection*, and you've got to wonder if there isn't some competition between divisions at Universal to have such similar titles in the marketplace. The *20th Century Masters* compilation is easier to understand, since it is the discount-priced entry in the bunch, listing for about $12 and containing 12 tracks (eight of which are on *The Very Best Of*), only one of them, the 1966-1967 hit "Tell It Like It Is," licensed from outside. Otherwise, it is a reasonable sampling of the A&M years, which saw Neville back in the Top Ten with a revival of the Main Ingredient's "Everybody Plays the Fool" and achieving platinum sales with the albums *Warm Your Heart* and *The Grand Tour*. No one should mistake this for a true overview of Neville's career, but that you can get by spending the extra bucks to buy *Ultimate Collection*. *—William Ruhlmann*

Art Neville

b. Dec. 17, 1937, New Orleans, LA
Vocals, Keyboards, Piano, Organ / New Orleans R&B, Rock & Roll, R&B, Soul

New Orleans vocalist and keyboardist. As a founding member of the Meters and Neville Brothers, Neville helped immeasurably to shape the contemporary New Orleans funk sound. Neville's first band, The Hawketts, tasted local success in 1954 with the carnival perennial "Mardi Gras Mambo" on Chess. He cut some nice solo singles for Specialty during the late '50s, notably "Cha Dooky-Doo," as well as contributing two choruses of storming piano to Jerry Byrne's 1958 classic "Lights Out." "All These Things," a gentle ballad, also did well locally in 1962 on the Instant logo. He assembled the Meters in the mid-'60s and the instrumental quartet proved the Crescent City's answer to The MG's until their 1977 breakup. That's when Art and his siblings formed the Neville Brothers, and today they reign as the leading musical export from New Orleans. *—Bill Dahl*

Mardi Gras Rock & Roll / 1976 / Ace ◆◆◆

Art Neville cut some of this CD's most pertinent tracks right before serving in the Navy in the late '50s and never got the chance to properly promote the records that came out on Art Rupe's Specialty label. Perennial Mardi Gras favorite "Mardi Gras Mambo," which has reportedly sold more than a million copies over the years; "Cha Dooky Doo," a regional hit; and "What's Going On," a local favorite, are the main attractions. The rest have that same Cajun flavor, making it an essential for lovers of Big Easy music. *—Andrew Hamilton*

• **That Old Time Rock 'n' Roll** / 1992 / Specialty ✦✦✦✦✦
Twenty of his earliest solo sides, from the late '50s, a few of them previously unissued. A lot of this New Orleans R&B is derivative of Fats Domino and Lloyd Price, but the harder-rocking, funkier sides point to his more individual work of later decades. "Cha Dooky-Doo," "Arabian Love Call," and a previously unreleased duet with Larry Williams on "Rockin' Pneumonia and the Boogie-Woogie Flu" are typically fun and infectious New Orleans R&B novelties; "I'm a Fool to Care" gives us a taste of his soulful ballad singing. *—Richie Unterberger*

Hambone Willie Newbern

b. 1899, **d.** 1947

Vocals, Guitar / Prewar Country Blues, Songster

Little is known about blues songster Hambone Willie Newbern; a mere half-dozen sides comprise the sum of his recorded legacy, but among those six is the first-ever rendition of the immortal Delta classic "Roll and Tumble Blues." Reportedly born in 1899, he first began to make a name for himself in the Brownsville, TN, area, where he played country dances and fish fries in the company of Yank Rachell; later, on the Mississippi medicine show circuit, he mentored Sleepy John Estes (from whom most of the known information about Newbern originated). While in Atlanta in 1929, Newbern cut his lone session; in addition to "Roll and Tumble," which became an oft-covered standard, he recorded songs like "She Could Toodle-Oo" and "Hambone Willie's Dreamy-Eyed Woman's Blues," which suggest an old-fashioned rag influence. By all reports an extremely ill-tempered man, Newbern's behavior eventually led him to prison, where a brutal beating is said to have brought his life to an end around 1947. *—Jason Ankeny*

• **The Greatest Songsters: Complete Works (1927–1929)** / 1990 / Document ✦✦✦✦✦

Chubby Newsome

b. Detroit, MI

Vocals / New Orleans Blues, New Orleans R&B

A legendary blues belter, Chubby Newsome was born in Detroit but gravitated toward New Orleans, both for a style to embrace and for a home. Newsome was something of a legendary beauty whose most notable feature—aside from a very pretty face, lustrous hair, and a big voice—was enormous hips, which she learned to use to her advantage as a singer and performer on the vaudeville circuit in the '40s.

She arrived in New Orleans in 1948 and quickly began making a name for herself locally in venues such as the Dew Drop Inn, where she was spotted by bandleader Paul Gayten, who got her signed up to the Deluxe label and recorded her late that year. Newsome's debut was the appropriately titled "Hip Shakin' Mama," which became a number eight hit on the rhythm & blues charts in early 1949. Newsome released four more singles for Deluxe backed by Dave Bartholomew and his band, but none was remotely as successful as her debut, despite being excellent records and some of the most delightfully raunchy New Orleans-style rhythm & blues of their era. She subsequently left Deluxe and split with Gayten's band after marrying his resident male vocalist, Ken Gorman. The union lasted through only part of 1949 and when Newsome next surfaced, it was fronting her own band at the Dew Drop Inn. She recorded a brace of excellent sides for the Regal label during the years 1949-1951, none of which were particularly successful. During the mid-'50s, Newsome surfaced as a member of the Bluzettes, an all-female R&B vocal group whose members also included Alberta Adams. Her last known recording sessions took place in 1957. *—Bruce Eder*

Johnny Nicholas

Piano, Guitar / Contemporary Blues, Modern Electric Blues, Western Swing Revival

Although considered a Texas blues man, Johnny Nicholas actually honed his chops on around and about the Midwest, on the blues scenes of Providence, Detroit, and Chicago in the '60s. He was frontman for Ann Arbor's Boogie Brothers in the early '70s when this genre of music was as popular as could be in this music-loving college town. Then came the move to Texas, a state known for many styles of traditional music as well as blues. He dug right in, playing Cajun music with Link Davis and Western swing with the Grammy award winning Austin band Asleep at the Wheel. He also recorded with blues master Big Walter Horton in Chicago in 1977. In the next decade, he stepped down from the music business in order to raise a family. The couple opened a restaurant which did quite well, and Nicholas stayed away from the blues until the early '90s. He started out again slowly, bending the strings a little around home and on the festival circuit. Nicholas formed a group with some of his favorite musicians from San Antonio and Austin. In 1994, he cut the recording *Thrill on the Hill* for the Antone's label, followed by *Rockin' My Blues to Sleep: Texas/Louisiana Blues and Dance Hall Favorites* on Hilltop. *—Eugene Chadbourne*

• **Too Many Bad Habits** / 1978 / Blind Pig ✦✦✦✦
Rural and urban blues is played with the assistance of Walter Horton and Johnny Shines. *—AMG*

Thrill on the Hill / Oct. 18, 1994 / Antone's ✦✦✦

Rockin' My Blues to Sleep / Oct. 2, 2001 / Topcat ✦✦✦

Robert Nighthawk (Robert McCollum)

b. Nov. 30, 1909, Helena, AR, **d.** Nov. 5, 1967, Helena, AR

Slide Guitar, Vocals, Harmonica, Guitar / Slide Guitar Blues, Acoustic Chicago Blues, Electric Chicago Blues, Chicago Blues, St. Louis Blues

Of all the pivotal figures in blues history, certainly one of the most important was Robert Nighthawk. He bridged the gap between Delta and Chicago blues effortlessly, taking his slide cues from Tampa Red and stamping them with a Mississippi edge learned first hand from his cousin, Houston Stackhouse. Though he recorded from the '30s into the early '40s under a variety of names—Robert Lee McCoy, Rambling Bob, Peetie's Boy—he finally took his lasting sobriquet of Robert Nighthawk from the title of his first record, "Prowling Night Hawk." It should be noted that the huge lapses in the man's discography are direct results of his rambling nature, taciturnity, and seeming disinterest in making records. Once you got him into a studio, the results were almost always of a uniform excellence. But it might be two years or more between sessions.

Nighthawk never achieved the success of his more celebrated pupils, Muddy Waters and Earl Hooker, finding himself to be much happier to be working one nighters in taverns and the Maxwell Street open market on Sundays. He eventually left Chicago for his hometown of Helena, AR, where he briefly took over the *King Biscuit Radio Show* after Sonny Boy Williamson [II] died, while seemingly working every small juke joint that dotted the landscape until his death from congestive heart failure in 1967. Robert Nighthawk is not a name that regularly gets bandied about when discussing the all-time greats of the blues. But well it should, because his legacy was all-pervasive; his resonant voice and creamy smooth slide guitar playing (played in standard tuning, unusual for a bluesman) would influence players for generations to come and many of his songs would later become blues standards. *—Cub Koda*

Bricks in My Pillow / 1977 / Delmark ✦✦✦
This 14-song collection, consisting of tracks recorded on July 12, 1951, and October 25, 1952, completely transforms the landscape where Robert Nighthawk's music is concerned. Up to now, apart from seeking out his prewar, unamplified work as Robert Lee McCoy (or McCullum) on Bluebird or grabbing a few tracks from some Chess reissues, there hasn't been a lot of Robert Nighthawk in one place. Now there are 14 hard-rocking tracks, cut for United Records in Chicago and showing Nighthawk in his prime and loving it, playing a mean slide underneath some boldly provocative singing that could have given Muddy Waters a run for his money. The style is there, and the voice and the guitar are there, so why didn't Nighthawk hit it big? Based on this collection, his style with an electric guitar just wasn't as distinctive as Waters' playing; additionally, he just didn't have Waters' (or Chess songwriter Willie Dixon's) way with a catch phrase—there are some OK songs here ("Kansas City," "You Missed a Good Man," "Bricks in My Pillow"), but nothing as catchy or instantly memorable as "I Can't Be Satisfied," "Hoochie Coochie Man," or "Got My Mojo Working." A pair of instrumentals, "Nighthawk Boogie" and "U/S Boogie," both driven by Nighthawk's guitar and a romping piano, pretty much make this collection worthwhile and show the man in his peak form. Included on this collection are a pair of previously unissued tracks, an alternate take of "Seventy-Four," and a loud, crunchy, but, alas, unfinished version of "The Moon Is Rising." The sound is surprisingly clean and rich, especially given the 1951-1952 origins of the tapes. *—Bruce Eder*

Complete Recorded Works (1937–1940) / 1985 / Wolf ✦✦✦✦✦
For a glimpse into Nighthawk's earliest sides for the Victor label, this is the place to go. The sound—all of it taken off old 78s with little regard for modern noise reduction—is less than stellar, but the performances are nothing but. This includes the tune that gave his permanent nom de plume, "Prowling Night Hawk." *—Cub Koda*

★ **Live on Maxwell Street** / 1988 / Rounder ✦✦✦✦✦
Recorded by Norman Dayron live on the street (you can actually hear cars driving by!) in 1964 with just Robert Whitehead on drums and Johnny Young on rhythm guitar in support, Nighthawk's slide playing (and single-string soloing, for that matter) are nothing short of elegant and explosive. Highlights include "The Maxwell Street Medley," which combines his two big hits "Anna Lee" and "Sweet Black Angel"; a mind-altering 12-bar solo on "The Time Have Come," which proves that Nighthawk's lead playing was just as well developed as his slide work; and a couple of wild instrumentals with Carey Bell sitting in on harmonica. Nighthawk sounds cool as a cucumber, presiding over everything with an almost genial charm while laying the toughest sounds imaginable. One of the top three greatest live blues albums of all time. The 2000 CD reissue on Bullseye Blues & Jazz adds five previously unreleased bonus tracks, although Nighthawk doesn't have a lead vocal on any of these. "The Real McCoy" is an instrumental, Young sings on "Big World Blues" and "All I Want for Breakfast/Them Kind of People," Bell sings "I Got News for You," and J.B. Lenoir takes a guest lead vocal on "Mama Talk to Your Daughter" (though Peter Gurlanick's liner notes express doubt that the singer is actually Lenoir). *—Cub Koda*

Black Angel Blues / 1991 / Charly ✦✦✦

Masters of the Modern Blues / 1994 / Testament ✦✦✦✦

The Nighthawks

f. 1972, Washington, D.C.

Group / Blues-Rock, Bar Band, Modern Electric Blues

A hard-driving DC-based bar band with strong Chicago blues roots. Formed in 1972 by harpist and vocalist Mark Wenner and guitarist Jimmy Thackery, the band earned a reputation as a solid outfit through more than a decade of touring and recording projects with John Hammond and former members of Muddy Waters' band. Thackery left in 1986, but Wenner regrouped around longtime members Jan Zukowski on bass and Pete Ragusa on drums. *Trouble*, their 1991 release on Powerhouse, is a blend of blues, R&B, and rock influences, with a typically energetic sound born in thousands of one-night stands across the country. Subsequent efforts include 1993's live *Rock This House*, 1996's *Pain & Paradise* and 1999's *Still Wild*. *Citizenwayne*, their first studio album in four years, was issued in fall 2000. The following tour was documented for a live album, which eventually saw release in the spring of 2002 as *Live Tonight*. *—Bill Dahl*

Rock and Roll / 1972 / Aladdin ✦✦✦

• **Open All Nite** / 1976 / Adelphi ✦✦✦✦✦
When *Open All Nite* was first released on LP in 1976, the Nighthawks had only been together for four years—little did they know that they would still be together in the 21st century and would celebrate their 30th anniversary in 2002. Some young bands sound

like they still have some growing and developing to do, but the Nighthawks never sound the least bit undeveloped on *Open All Nite*. The blues-rockers always sound focused, and they know exactly what they're going for on gritty performances of "Nine Below Zero," Jimmy Reed's "Big Boss Man," and other Chicago blues staples. The Nighthawks were never innovative, but they were always sincere and honest, which is why they bring so much enthusiasm to these performances. Over the years, the Nighthawks have often been described as a "bar band"—and most of the time, it is meant as a compliment. In most cases, people who call the Nighthawks a "bar band" are celebrating their rawness and lack of pretense. In fact, *Open All Nite* and other Nighthawks albums of the '70s sound like a rebellion against slickness—the blues-rockers sound like they're downright proud of their raw, rugged, bare-bones approach, and they seem oblivious to the glossier sounds of the '70s. In that sense, one can see some parallels between *Open All Nite* and the punk bands that were starting to make their presence felt in 1976. The Nighthawks were never a punk band, but they did share punk's love of rawness and believed in keeping things simple, emotionally direct, and straightforward. This album, which Mobile Fidelity Sound Lab reissued on CD in the '90s, is a fine document of the Nighthawks' early period. —*Alex Henderson*

Jacks & Kings / 1977 / Genes ✦✦✦✦✦
Classic material and stirring playing. A must-find. —*Michael G. Nastos*

Side Pocket Shot / 1977 / Genes/Adelphi ✦✦✦
A studio album with The Rhythm King's Horns. Another solid album. —*Michael G. Nastos*

Live at the Psychedelly / Jan. 1977 / Genes ✦✦✦
The Nighthawks, at their heart, are a bar band in the best sense of the term—they're at their best in a live setting. *Live at the Psychedelly* captures them at their mid-'70s peak, running through standards ("Jail House Rock," "Hound Dog") and contemporary rockers ("Can't Get Next to You," "Whammer Jammer," "Tripe Face Boogie"), with fire and energy. The CD reissue includes four bonus tracks recorded at the El Mocambo. —*Thom Owens*

The Nighthawks / 1980 / Mercury ✦✦✦

Best of the Nighthawks / 1982 / Genes ✦✦✦

10 Years Live / 1982 / Varrick ✦✦✦✦
A highly recommended two-fer that celebrates their decade together. —*Michael G. Nastos*

Rock-N-Roll / 1983 / Varrick ✦✦✦

Jacks & Kings 'full House / 1983 / Adelphi ✦✦✦

Backtrack / 1988 / Varrick ✦✦✦

Live in Europe / 1990 / Varrick ✦✦✦

Hard Living / 1991 / Varrick ✦✦✦✦

Trouble / Jan. 1991 / Powerhouse ✦✦✦
Over the years, the Nighthawks have done their share of label-hopping. 1991 found them briefly recording for Powerhouse, a small Florida label that Ichiban was distributing at the time. *Trouble*, which the Nighthawks dedicated to Doc Pomus, was their only album for Powerhouse—and it is a solid blues-rock outing that sometimes detours into blue-eyed soul and early rock & roll. Whatever the style, the Nighthawks bring a lot of grit and enthusiasm to the material, which ranges from Leiber and Stoller's "The Chicken and the Hawk" to Bobby "Blue" Bland's "(I Wouldn't) Treat a Dog." The band also turns its attention to Sonny Terry & Brownie McGhee's "Ride and Roll," a song that blues lovers associate with the Piedmont, GA, school of Southern country blues. But in the Nighthawks' hands, "Ride and Roll" doesn't sound like Georgia blues—they give the tune an electric blues-rock makeover, and their version is closer to Chicago than Georgia. Another highlight of the album is Bob Dylan's "You Go Your Way"; the Nighthawks haven't recorded many songs by the folk-rock icon, but this one works well for them. On many of their albums, the DC residents have been totally self-contained; but on *Trouble*, they have a few guests. One of them is "Steady Rollin'" Bob Margolin, who recorded for Powerhouse as a solo artist in the early '90s. Margolin is best known for his years as Muddy Waters' guitarist, which makes him a perfect guest for the Nighthawks—both of them both worship anything having to do with Chess Records. *Trouble* falls short of essential, but even so, it is an enjoyable (if overlooked) footnote in the Nighthawks' history. —*Alex Henderson*

Rock This House / 1993 / Big Mo ✦✦✦
A live set of dependably accomplished bar-band contemporary blues with a slight rock edge. The set list won't win any prizes for originality, with covers of moldies by Muddy Waters, Jimmy Reed, Merle Travis, James Brown, Carl Perkins, and Otis Rush, and just one original tune. Yet it's executed quite competently, and the fidelity is good. —*Richie Unterberger*

Pain & Paradise / 1996 / Big Mo ✦✦✦
With harmonica player/singer Mark Wenner, bassist Jan Zukowski, and drummer/singer Pete Ragusa now well into their third decade together, the Nighthawks are a veteran blue-collar band that gets the job done, and *Pain & Paradise* is one of their better studio efforts. Guitar chores are now handled by relative newcomer Pete Kanaras, who replaced Danny Morris. The Nighthawks' reach never exceeds their grasp, and this album displays their excellent grasp of the Muddy Waters/Little Walter-style Chicago blues and bar-band rock & roll that lie at the core of their sound. They kick butt enough that you know you've been kicked, but not so much that it hurts, and they're even confident enough to ease up every now and then. —*Steve Hoffman*

Still Wild / Apr. 20, 1999 / Ruf ✦✦✦
When they were first formed in 1972 by vocalist Mark Wenner and guitarist Jimmy Thackery, the Nighthawks were unabashed blues-rockers, filtering the Chicago sound of

Muddy Waters and Howlin' Wolf through an East Coast bar band's sensibilities. Not much has really changed during the 27 years between their debut album and the release of 1999's *Still Wild*. The Nighthawks have branched out a little in the years following Thackery's late-'80s departure, the band mixing elements of classic R&B, roots rock, and country into their hard-hitting, crowd-pleasing performances. *Still Wild* furthers their gradual evolution into a powerful genre-jumping outfit, the band throwing out typical blues covers like Willie Dixon's "Tiger in Your Tank" and Muddy Waters' "Read Way Back" alongside raucous, country-flavored rave-ups like Charlie Rich's "Washed My Hands." The road-weary veterans in the Nighthawks romp through timeless R&B covers like the Marvin Gaye hit "That's The Way Love Is" and soulful originals "Guard My Heart" or the instrumental "Slow Dance" with as much energy and enthusiasm as any rock band half their collective ages. As long as Wenner's mouth harp is wailing and the rhythm section is jumping courtesy of longtime bassist Jan Zukowski and drummer Pete Ragusa, the Nighthawks are always going to deliver Grade "A" choice American music, and in this aspect, *Still Wild* does not disappoint. —*Rev. Keith A. Gordon*

Live Tonite! / Apr. 9, 2002 / Ruf ✦✦✦
In 2002, the Nighthawks celebrated their 30th anniversary. The Chicago-minded blues-rock outfit had not changed very much over the years; the Nighthawks of the early 2000s didn't sound much different from the Nighthawks of the early '70s. A collection of live performances from 2001, *Live Tonite!* makes no attempt to reinvent the blues-rock wheel—this CD is hardly a radical departure from what the Washington, D.C., band was doing 25 and 30 years earlier. But if the Nighthawks are predictable on *Live Tonite!*, they are predictably enjoyable. The gritty blues-rockers always sound inspired; that is true whether they are turning their attention to Howlin' Wolf's "Who'll Be the Next One" or Muddy Waters' "Still a Fool." And even though *Live Tonite!* is far from groundbreaking, at least the Nighthawks don't inundate listeners with overdone blues standards. A lot of Chicago-minded blues releases favor the repertory approach; they stick to standards that blues fans have heard time and time again. But the Nighthawks don't always choose the most obvious songs. Jimmy Reed's "Hush Hush" hasn't been beaten to death the way that "Big Boss Man" and "Baby What You Want Me to Do" have, and Waters' "Still a Fool" isn't the standard that "Got My Mojo Working" is. There is no law stating that every blues-rock CD that comes out has to be groundbreaking, but it is nice when blues-rockers do some digging and find deserving songs that their fans haven't heard 1,000 times. And not every song that the Nighthawks pick has some type of connection to Chicago or Chess Records; "Boogie Woogie Country Girl," for example, is a Doc Pomus classic. The Nighthawks bring a lot of grit and passion to that song and everything else on *Live Tonite!*, which is a pleasing way to celebrate the bar band's 30th anniversary. —*Alex Henderson*

Ollie Nightingale (Ollie Hoskins)

b. 1956, Batesville, TN, **d.** Oct. 26, 1977, Memphis, TN
Vocals / Electric Blues, Soul-Blues, Soul
Call him a blues singer if you prefer, but Ollie Nightingale will likely always be recalled most readily for the emotionally charged Memphis soul he cut from 1968 to 1970 as front man for Ollie & the Nightingales.

Like most great soul singers, Ollie Hoskins came straight out of church musically. He was the lead singer of the Dixie Nightingales, a Memphis spiritual aggregation, by 1958, when they made their vinyl debut on tiny Pepper Records. Influenced by gospel greats Kylo Turner and Ira Tucker, Hoskins hung in with the group as they moved to Nashboro in 1962 before signing with Stax's short-lived Chalice gospel logo.

Stax exec Al Bell convinced the group to go pop in 1968, though that sanctified spirit rings through melismatically on their R&B hits "I Got a Sure Thing," "You're Leaving Me," and "I've Got a Feeling." Hoskins went solo at the turn of the decade, billing himself as Ollie Nightingale and scoring a couple of R&B chart items ("It's a Sad Thing" and "May the Best Man Win") in 1971-1972. The Nightingales soldiered on, recruiting singer Tommy Tate to replace him in the studio.

Nightingale remained a popular blues and soul singer around Memphis. In 1993, he had a performing cameo in *The Firm*, a movie thriller starring Tom Cruise. Not long after, Nightingale began regularly releasing albums on Ecko Records. He made four in all for the label. The last, *Ollie Style*, was released after his death of complications resulting from untreated pneumonia. —*Bill Dahl*

● **I'll Drink Your Bathwater, Baby** / 1995 / Ecko ✦✦✦✦
After spending several years performing in local Memphis clubs, Ollie Nightingale was given the opportunity to return the recording studio to cut his first full-length solo album. The resulting record, *I'll Drink Your Bathwater, Baby*, may have had an ugly title, but the record itself was an excellent slice of contemporary soul-blues. Nightingale tears through the selection of originals and covers with true passion, elevating the average songs to something quite passionate and inspired. It's an excellent way to revive his recording career. —*Thom Owens*

Tell Me What You Want Me to Do / Jul. 30, 1996 / Ecko ✦✦✦

Make It Sweet / Sep. 23, 1997 / Ecko ✦✦✦

Ollie Style / Oct. 13, 1998 / Ecko ✦✦✦
The late Ollie Nightingale's recordings always capture one's attention, even when the material is mundane. *Ollie Style* contains some prime cuts, including bawdy blues tales like the eight-minute-plus "I'm Gonna Turn This Bed Over" and midtempo Southern soul beauties like "I'll Work for You," on which Nightingale sings "I'll work for you like a Georgia mule" to a lilting beat, accompanied by E. Nelson and Bertram Brown on background vocals. He gets things moving on "Booty Scoot," which appeared on a previous album but gets recycled and remixed for maximum effect here. *Ollie Style* is not without its humdrum moments—the pop/country ballads "That's What You Are to Me" and "I'm Going to See You Again Tonight" display Nightingale's range but detract from his

strengths, making him sound too smooth and pretty. The swaggering "I'm Good at What I Do," however, is right up his alley. Overall, a good effort, and a fine introduction to Nightingale's work. *—Andrew Hamilton*

The Best of Ollie Nightingale / Sep. 14, 1999 / Ecko ♦♦♦♦
This album of 14 of Ollie Nightingale's best Ecko recordings contains good songs like "Booty Scoot," and "I'm Ready to Party," which were ignored by the radio. Listeners will relish the real-life tales "I'm Gonna Turn This Bed Over," "Why I Sing the Blues," and a song about a woman so fine that Ollie sings "I'll Drink Your Bath Water Baby." He updates his Stax Records oldie "I Got a Sure Thing," and offers some splendid grinders and shuffler's like "You've Got a Booger Bear Under There" and "If You're Lucky Enough to Have a Good Woman," which is similar to Jerry Butler & the Impressions' "For Your Precious Love." *—Andrew Hamilton*

At His Best / Jul. 23, 2002 / Ecko ♦♦♦

Willie Nix

b. Aug. 6, 1922, Memphis, TN, **d.** Jul. 8, 1991, Leland, MS
Vocals, Drums, Guitar / Memphis Blues, Electric Memphis Blues, Chicago Blues
Willie Nix came out of the rural South with a great beat and a way with lyrics that made him something of a topical urban poet. Despite recordings for RPM and Sun, and then Chance in Chicago, he never advanced beyond the ranks of the also-rans in the quest for blues success, in either Memphis or Chicago; however, if anyone ever deserved to do better based on the evidence that's left behind, it was Willie Nix.

Born in Memphis, he first entered performing as a tap dancer at age 12, and as a teenager during the late '30s, he toured with the Rabbit Foot Minstrels Shows as a dancing comedian. He appeared in various variety venues during the early '40s, and performed on streets and parks around Memphis. In 1947, Nix appeared with Robert Jr. Lockwood, on a Little Rock, AR, radio station, and subsequently worked with Sonny Boy Williamson II, Willie Love and Joe Willie Wilkins as the Four Aces in Arkansas, Tennessee and Mississippi.

Nix joined B.B. King and Joe Hill Louis for appearances on Memphis radio, and worked with The Beale Streeters during the late '40s. He made his first records in Memphis for RPM in 1951, and cut sides for Chess Records' Checker offshoot in 1952. Sam Phillips signed him up as "the Memphis Blues Boy" for Sun in early 1953, as a singing drummer with a band, and he later cut sides for Art Sheridan's Chance label in Chicago. He worked with Elmore James, Sonny Boy Williamson, Johnny Shines, and Memphis Slim during the mid-'50s, but at the end of the decade was back in Memphis, and did a short stretch in prison late in the decade. Nix's health and abilities deteriorated during the '60s and '70s, and he hoboed around, performing occasionally, telling tall tales about his life and generally acting erratically.

Nix never saw any success as a recording artist, and never stayed with one label long enough to record anything resembling an album's worth of material. His work appears on various label compilations, however, and is distinctive for his driving beat and his extraordinary cleverness with lyrics, especially the Chance sides. *—Bruce Eder*

● **The Original Sun Singles, Vol. 1** / 1994 / Bear Family ♦♦♦♦♦
Nix's "Seems Like a Million Years" and his delightfully scatological "Baker Shop Boogie" appear on disc one of this four-CD set, and are seminal early Sun sides. *—Bruce Eder*

Chicago Blues: The Chance Story / 1997 / Charly ♦♦♦♦♦
A handful of Willie Nix cuts, with dazzling topical lyrics and a hard-driving, compelling beat, spark this two-CD set. *—Bruce Eder*

Hammie Nixon (Hammie Nickerson)

b. Jan. 22, 1908, Brownsville, TN, **d.** Aug. 17, 1984, Jackson, TN
Harmonica, Guitar / Harmonica Blues
Harmonica player Hammie Nixon was born on January 22, 1908, in Brownsville, TN. An orphan at a young age, he was raised by foster parents. He began his career as a professional harmonical player in the '20s, but also played the kazoo, guitar, and jug. He performed with Sleepy John Estes for more than 50 years, first recording with Estes in 1929 for the Victor label. He also recorded with Little Buddy Doyle, Lee Green, Charlie Pickett, and Son Bonds.

Nixon helped to pioneer the use of the harmonica as an accompaniment instrument with a band in the '20s. Previous to that time, it had been mostly a solo instrument. He played with many jug bands. After Estes died, Nixon played with the Beale Street Jug Band (also called the Memphis Beale Street Jug Band) from 1979 onward. Hammie Nixon died August 17, 1984. *—Michael Erlewine*

● **Tappin' That Thing** / 1984 / High Water ♦♦♦♦
Former Sleepy John Estes musical partner moves out on his own with this collection of solo recordings from the early '80s. Produced by David Evans for a small record company run out of the University of Memphis (High Water), these recordings find Nixon laying down vocals and working his magic on jug, kazoo and harmonica in more of a jug band setting. This compilation brings together both sides of a High Water single, an entire vinyl abum on the same label and the inclusion of three previously unissued tracks, all recorded between 1982 and 1984. That Nixon still had a lot of gas left in the tank is very evident from the energetic versions of "Sugar Mama," "It's a Good Place to Go," "Viola Lee Blues," "Bottle Up and Go," "Kansas City Blues" and the title track. The inclusion of drums on three tracks blasts the music further into the realm of an amplified session, but Nixon retains his country edges regardless of setting. *—Cub Koda*

Sugar Ray Norcia

Vocals, Harmonica / Modern Electric Blues, Electric Harmonica Blues, Soul-Blues
Harmonica player, lyricist and singer Sugar Ray Norcia has been leading his band, the Blue Tones, around New England since the late '70s. The band began to break nationally in the late '80s and early '90s with the release of their debut for the Rounder/ Varrick label, *Knockout*. While leading his own band and touring on a regional basis around the New England states, Norcia spent many years in apprenticeship as a sideman. This fact is evident on his recordings, as Norcia's singing is deep and heartfelt and his harmonica playing that of a seasoned blues club veteran.

Norcia first began playing blues harmonica in high school in his native Rhode Island. The Blue Tones were founded after Norcia moved to Providence, and they became a house band at a small club there. They further developed their skills while backing up visiting musicians like Walter "Shakey" Horton, Big Mama Thornton, Joe Turner, and Roosevelt Sykes in nearby Boston-area clubs. Beginning in the late '70s, the band worked exclusively with Ronnie Earl as its lead guitarist until he left to play with Roomful of Blues.

Norcia's music comes from an eclectic set of influences, and it probably shows most in his original tunes. He cites musicians like Nat King Cole, Joe Williams, Muddy Waters, and Bobby "Blue" Bland as important, but equally important to him are country music stylists like Ernest Tubb and George Jones.

With his quiet, cheerful, unassuming personality, Norcia is the kind of person people go to with their personal problems, and some of this (as well as his own life experience) provides fodder for his songs.

Norcia's recordings under his own name include the EPs *Sugar Ray and the Blue Tones* for Baron Records in 1979; *Ronnie Earl and the Broadcasters Featuring the Sensational Sugar Ray* in 1982 for Leopard Records, as well as his two Rounder releases, *Knockout* (1989) and *Don't Stand In My Way* (1991). Both *Knockout* and *Don't Stand In My Way* are stylistically diverse records showcasing a range of harmonica styles as well as blues styles, including urban Chicago, Texas shuffles, Memphis soul and R&B, as in a cover of Bobby Bland's "I'm Not Ashamed" on their debut, and Boston-area big guitar blues. The Blue Tones' *Don't Stand In My Way* served as the inaugural release for Rounder's then-new Bullseye Blues label. The Blue Tones also accompany Miki Honeycutt on her debut for the Rounder label, *Soul Deep.*

In 1991 Sugar Ray joined the legendary jump blues-based Roomful of Blues and became their lead vocalist. Roomful released three successful records during Norcia's tenure and toured incessantly. Norcia also kept busy outside of the band: he can be heard on a Bullseye Blues release by trombonist Porky Cohen, *Rhythm and Bones*, (1996) and on the album *Little Anthony and Sugar Ray: Take It From Me*, (1994), for the Tone-Cool subsidiary of Rounder. Sugar Ray left Roomful of Blues in 1998 and released *Sweet & Swingin'*, an eclectic record that featured songs by Hank Williams, Arthur Alexander, Big Walter Horton and an appearance by the Jordanaires. 1999 found Sugar Ray contributing to the Grammy-nominated album *Superharps*, a project that also included James Cotton, Billy Branch, and Charlie Musselwhite. Lately he has been keeping busy contributing harp on records by Pinetop Perkins, Doug James, and others as well as touring with the Sugar Ray Norcia Big Band.*—Richard Skelly*

● **Sweet & Swingin'** / Jun. 9, 1998 / Bullseye Blues ♦♦♦♦
After fronting Roomful of Blues for a half dozen years, Sugar Ray Norcia released this solo collection of tunes that range from bar-band favorites to material he claims he always wanted to record. Far from being just a retro blues album, Norcia digs deep and comes up with nice versions of Arthur Alexander's "You Better Move On" (one of two songs featuring the Jordanaires doing backups), Hank Williams' "My Sweet Love Ain't Around," Lonnie Johnson's "Tomorrow Night" and Jimmy Rogers' "Money, (Marbles and Chalk)." Blues lovers are rewarded with the more-to-form renditions of "Love, Life and Money," "It's a Low Down Dirty Shame," Big Walter Horton's "Need My Baby," and Pee Wee Crayton's "You Better Change Your Way of Loving." An odd collection of tunes and styles that somehow holds together nicely. *—Cub Koda*

North Mississippi Allstars

f. 1996
Group / Retro-Rock, American Trad Rock, Americana, Roots Rock, Alternative Pop/Rock, Blues-Rock
Moving into much rootsier territory than their former punk band DDT, brothers Luther (guitar, mandolin, vocals) and Cody Dickinson (drums, sampling) formed the North Mississippi Allstars in 1996 with bassist Chris Chew. The sons of longtime Memphis production staple Jim Dickinson were born in Fayette County, TN, and their family later moved to northern Mississippi, where the boys soaked up the country blues sound of the region from artists like Mississippi Fred McDowell and R.L. Burnside. That became the chief inspiration for the Allstars, but the group also mixes in a rock edge, an alternative aesthetic (comparable to outfits like the Jon Spencer Blues Explosion or G. Love and Special Sauce), and a trad-rock jam-band sensibility (think Phish, Widespread Panic, or even Medeski, Martin & Wood). After touring as an opening act for a variety of artists, thus honing their chops as a unit, the North Mississippi Allstars issued their debut album, *Shake Hands With Shorty*, in the spring of 2000. *—Steve Huey*

● **Shake Hands With Shorty** / May 9, 2000 / Tone-Cool ♦♦♦♦
Luther and Cody Dickinson (the sons of Memphis producer-musician Jim Dickinson) play guitar and drums like two true brothers on this debut outing. Exploring the world of Mississippi modal juke-joint music, the duo, with bassist Chris Chew, come up with the freshest style to hit roots music in decades. Their sound is a little bit of ZZ Top, a little bit Allman Brothers, some hip-hop beats and samples, a touch of Cream, and a little bit of Little Feat with the modern inflection of jam bands like Widespread Panic—sometimes happening all in the same song. Although the set list is as old-timey as it gets ("Shake 'Em on Down," "Drop Down Mama," "Drinkin' Muddy Water"), what they *do* to the material is anything but; just when you think you have them figured out, the beat, the sound, or the approach will change. Although the disc is loaded with guest artists ranging from fife player Othar Turner to the Tate Country Singers, it's ultimately the band's show, and the success of this album rests in their hands. Highly, highly recommended. *—Cub Koda*

51 Phantom / Oct. 9, 2001 / Uni/Tone ♦♦♦
The second outing from North Mississippi Allstars Luther and Cody Dickinson consolidates their growing strengths, both instrumental (read: fewer drum machines) and com-

positional (only two covers here, as opposed to the raft of Mississippi Fred McDowell/R.L. Burnside titles on 2000's *Shake Hands With Shorty*). Featuring guests like ancient fife player Othar Turner and Big Ass Truck's John C. Stubblefield, the band certainly smokes like they did on their debut, opening with an excellent driving rocker (the title track) that ends with Luther cooing just like Howlin' Wolf. The second song, "Snakes in My Bushes," is a dead-ringer for an age-old blues along the lines of "Stones in My Passway," though ironically it's also one of the few tracks with a drum machine. Yes, *51 Phantom* does lose in the comparison game to its excellent predecessor: the Dickinson brothers can't quite hold up an LP with their own songs, and a few of the guitar licks end up as recycled Led Zeppelin clichés. Still, North Mississippi Allstars make the blues sound just as energetic, raucous, and earthy as it's sounded in years. Added bonus: closing out with a raging, nearly demonic "Mud" (a quasi-cover of the Tin Pan Alley standard "Mississippi Mud"), a track verging on grindcore or rap-rock. —*John Bush*

Darrell Nulisch

b. Sep. 14, 1952, Dallas, TX

Vocals, Harmonica / Contemporary Blues, Electric Blues, Modern Electric Blues

Darrell Nulisch was born in Dallas, TX, in 1952. He grew up on soul singers like Otis Redding and Al Green, inspiring him to take up a similar path and work on his voice. He was a founding member of Anson Funderburgh's Rockets and sang with that group in the '80s, when he also did time in groups like Ronnie Earl's Broadcasters. He eventually left Texas and started a solo career in 1991, relocating to Boston and releasing albums that showcased his incredible blues-harmonica skills and his passionate voice. Even legendary soul singer James Cotton asked Nulisch to work with his touring band when Cotton lost his voice, giving Nulisch a chance to work with someone he admired. He continued his solo efforts into the next century, releasing the critically acclaimed *I Like It That Way* in the spring of 2000. —*Bradley Torreano*

● **Business as Usual** / 1991 / Black Top ✦✦✦✦

Darrell Nulisch burns throughout *Business as Usual*, but his band fails to give him the needed rhythmic support that would have made this album great. As it is, it's merely a good set of contemporary blues, made worthwhile by Nulisch's dynamic harp. —*Thom Owens*

Bluesoul / 1996 / Higher Plane ✦✦✦

Whole Truth / Aug. 11, 1998 / Severn ✦✦✦✦

This disc blurs the boundaries between soul music and the blues even further for this hot Texas singer, who was raised in the Dallas area listening to all that Texas has to offer. Now based in Boston, this singer runs the whole gamut of emotions with his experienced and well-traveled tenor voice. He has also put together a crack band that stays with the song wherever it goes. Be it deep-down Chicago-style blues as on "At-Cha-Mama-Nims," a harmonica-driven instrumental, which he penned with his long time bassist, Steve Gomes; or the fantastic cover of R.C. Hammond's "There Goes That Train," a slow Southern soul/blues cut that leads off this disc. Nulisch has served his time and his resumé is impressive, being the singer both for Ronnie Earl and the Broadcasters and for Anson Funderburg and the Rockets, as well as his own band Texas Heat. He is well-traveled, and his voice is expressive, capable of wringing out all the emotional angst that there is to be had in a song. His harp work is better than average and truly shines on "Like Reed." The album stays together very well until you come to the last cut, "Lyla Tov (Good Night)," a jazzy noodling that seems out of place. Also this disc gives notice that Jon Moeller, who handles the guitar work, is going to a force to be reckoned with in the future. Just give a listen to George "Harmonica" Smith's "Telephone Blues" and try to convince someone that this sizzling work won't be shining somewhere in the future. The band is good and does justice to the fine material picked out for your aural pleasure. —*Bob Gottlieb*

I Like It That Way / Apr. 11, 2000 / Severn ✦✦✦✦

As a vocalist for hire, Texas born Darrell Nulisch has worked with the likes of Otis Grand, Anson Funderburgh, James Cotton, and Ronnie Earl, lending his gritty honeyed voice to a variety of blues styles, however Nulisch's love for Southern R&B of the Bobby "Blue" Bland/O.V. Wright style is best experienced on his solo albums. On his fourth release, the soul-driven singer/songwriter and under-appreciated harp player dives in and doses out ten stunning tracks of pure rhythm & blues gold. The Stax horns and bubbling organ of the album's opening blast, a cover of Ann Peebles' "I'm Gonna Tear Your Playhouse Down" (the main protagonist is changed to female with reworked lyrics and an altered title of "You Tore My Playhouse Down") set the stage for this dynamic album. Nulisch's voice yearns and cries, backed by a full soul ensemble that gives the song plenty of breathing room. Like Robert Cray's similar approach on his late '90s releases, Nulisch keeps the predominantly midtempo tunes on a low boil, never overwhelming the material with excess clutter. He even downplays his own harmonica skills, relegating harp solos to only a few tracks. Covers of Otis Redding's "Trick or Treat," Otis Rush's "Mean Old World," B.B. King's "Worried Dream," and Junior Parker's "I Like Your Style" nestle comfortably next to Nulisch's, and longtime co-songwriter and bassist Steve Gomes', compositions. In fact, the pair's originals are often as strong as their classic covers. Not since the heyday of Hi Records in the late '60s has an artist so effectively conveyed the hurt, sorrow and pride that Darrell Nulisch embodies in every song here. He is one of the most expressive singers in his admittedly limited genre, and *I Like It That Way* is a sumptuous example of his striking talents. —*Hal Horowitz*

St. Louis Jimmy Oden

b. Jun. 26, 1903, Nashville, TN, **d.** Dec. 30, 1977, Chicago, IL
Vocals, Songwriter / Piano / Piano Blues, St. Louis Blues
Few blues songs have stood the test of Father Time as enduringly as "Goin' Down Slow." Its composer, St. Louis Jimmy Oden, endured rather impressively himself—he recorded during the early '30s and was still at it more than three decades later.

If not for a fortuitous move to St. Louis circa 1917, James Oden might have been known as Nashville Jimmy. He fell in with pianist Roosevelt Sykes on the 1920s Gateway City blues circuit (the two remained frequent musical partners through the ensuing decades). Oden enjoyed a fairly prolific recording career during the '30s and '40s, appearing on Champion, Bluebird (where he hit with "Goin' Down Slow" in 1941), Columbia, Bullet in 1947, Miracle, Aristocrat (there he cut "Florida Hurricane" in 1948 accompanied by pianist Sunnyland Slim and a young guitarist named Muddy Waters), Mercury, Savoy, and Apollo.

Scattered singles for Duke (with Sykes on piano) and Parrot (a 1955 remake of "Goin' Down Slow") set the stage for Oden's 1960 album debut for Prestige's Bluesville subsidiary (naturally, it included yet another reprise of "Goin' Down Slow"). Oden was backed by guitarist Jimmie Lee Robinson and a swinging New York rhythm section. As much a composer as a performer, Oden wrote "Soon Forgotten" and "Take the Bitter With the Sweet" for Muddy Waters. —*Bill Dahl*

Goin' Down Slow / Nov. 19, 1960 / Prestige/Original Blues Classics ◆◆◆◆◆
Oden offers ten of his own compositions on his first full-length album session, with low-key backing from a full band (Robert Banks' piano is especially prominent). He's a serviceable though not outstanding vocalist, and offers his tales with a sort of good-natured fatalism, the most celebrated number being the title track. While he was an outstanding songwriter, it may have been best that Oden's compositions are primarily known through the interpretations of others. On this recording at least, the arrangements could really benefit from less uniformity, the tempo rarely escaping a pace somewhere between slow and medium. —*Richie Unterberger*

1932–1948 / Jan. 1991 / Story of the Blues ◆◆◆◆◆
A solid sixteen-track import collection of Oden's earliest and best sides. —*Cub Koda*

● **Back on My Feet Again** / 1995 / Collectables ◆◆◆◆◆
Although little discographical info is offered in its liner notes, this collection presumably dates from the '30s and '40s. Oden's dignified, slightly dry vocal delivery rings true on these sides, which include a fine vintage rendition of his signature tune, "Going Down Slow." —*Bill Dahl*

Complete Works, Vol. 1 / May 1, 1995 / Document ◆◆◆

Complete Works, Vol. 2 / May 1, 1995 / Document ◆◆◆

St. Louis Jimmy Oden, Vol. 2: 1944–1955 / Document ◆◆◆◆
"Goin' Down Slow" is one of the true acknowledged classics of the blues, but very few fans have ever heard the original by St. Louis Jimmy Oden, the song's composer. The original is aboard here along with 23 other fine examples of this singer's catchy songwriting ability. Highlights include "Bad Condition," "Sittin' and Thinkin'," "So Nice and Kind" (featuring slide guitar courtesy of Muddy Waters), and a big-band remake of "Goin' Down Slow." A missing chapter in blues history. —*Cub Koda*

Andrew Odom

b. Dec. 15, 1936, Denham Springs, LA, **d.** Dec. 23, 1991, Chicago, IL
Vocals / Modern Electric Chicago Blues, Electric Chicago Blues, Soul-Blues
Eminently capable of serving up spot-on imitations of both Bobby "Blue" Bland and B.B. King, Andrew Odom was also a man of many interrelated nicknames: Big Voice, B.B., Little B.B., B.B. Junior. Perhaps his chameleonic talents held him back; Odom was a journeyman Chicago singer who recorded relatively sparingly.

Like the majority of his peers, Odom started out singing spirituals but fell in with Albert King and Johnny O'Neal on the St. Louis blues scene of the mid-'50s and began plying his trade there. He made an unobtrusive recording debut in 1961, singing "East St. Louis" with the band of one Little Aaron for the highly obscure Marlo imprint. He arrived in Chicago around 1960, hooking up with Earl Hooker as the slide guitar wizard's vocalist. A single for Nation Records in 1967 (as Andre Odom) preceded his debut album for ABC-BluesWay (cut in 1969, it remained in the can for quite a while before the label finally issued it).

A guest spot on Jimmy Dawkins' encore Delmark LP, *All for Business*, was a highlight of the '70s for the singer. He cut his own album for the French Isabel label in 1982 in the company of Magic Slim & the Teardrops (reissued by Evidence in 1993), but it was a 1992 set for Flying Fish, *Goin' to California* (co-produced by guitarist Steve Freund), that probably captured his considerable vocal charms the best.

Odom was a popular attraction on the Windy City circuit right up until the fateful night when he suffered a heart attack while driving from Buddy Guy's Legends to

another local blues mecca, the Checkerboard Lounge. He's been missed ever since. —*Bill Dahl*

Farther on the Road / 1969 / BluesWay ◆◆
Disappointing debut album by the Chicago singer with the mellifluous pipes. Even with Earl Hooker on lead guitar, the spark just wasn't there. —*Bill Dahl*

● **Goin' to California** / 1991 / Flying Fish ◆◆◆◆
Not long before he died, Odom made the album of his life with a combo called the Gold Tops, who provided precisely the right backing to properly spotlight his booming voice. A few overdone standards—"Rock Me Baby," "Woke Up This Morning," "Next Time You See Me"—intrude a bit, but Odom's own "Bad Feelin'," "Why Did You Leave Me," and "Come to Me" make impassioned amends. Steve Freund, best-known for his long stint with Sunnyland Slim, contributes stellar lead guitar. —*Bill Dahl*

Omar & the Howlers

f. Austin, TX
Group / Modern Electric Texas Blues, Electric Texas Blues, Blues-Rock
The European blues fans all adore Austin, TX-based guitarist and singer/songwriter Omar Kent Dykes. That's because he fits the stereotypical image many of them have of the American musician: he's tall, wears cowboy boots and has a deep voice with a Southern accent. However, Dykes does not carry a gun, and though he looks rough and tough, he's actually an incredibly peaceful and intelligent musician, and a veteran at working a crowd in a blues club or a festival. While Dykes still has a sizeable American audience owing to his albums for Columbia Records, he still spends a good portion of his touring year at festivals and clubs around Europe.

Omar Kent Dykes was born in 1950, in McComb, MS, the same town from which Bo Diddley hails. He first set foot into neighborhood juke joints at age 12 and after he'd been playing guitar for a while, he went back into the juke joint. After graduating from high school, Dykes lived in Hattiesburg and Jackson, MS, for a few years before relocating to Austin in 1976. He'd heard the blues scene in Texas was heating up. At that time, Stevie Ray Vaughan was still playing with Paul Ray & the Cobras.

By the early '80s, Omar & the Howlers had gained a solid reputation for their invigorating live shows. They also released two albums on independent labels, *Big Leg Beat* (1980), followed four years later by *I Told You So*. Among white blues musicians, Dykes is truly one of a kind, a fact Columbia Records recognized in the mid-'80s when they signed Omar & the Howlers. Unfortunately, it was a fleeting relationship at best. After releasing *Hard Times in the Land of Plenty* (1987) and *Wall of Pride* (1988) the band was dropped when the company was bought by Sony. While it was inconvenient, it didn't stop Dykes. His post-1990 output has been nothing short of extraordinary. Starting in 1991, Omar & the Howlers recorded three discs for Rounder/Bullseye Blues: *Live at Paradiso* (1991), followed by *Blues Bag* and *Courts of Lulu* (both in 1992). In 1995, they switched to the Austin, TX-based Watermelon Records and released *Muddy Springs Road* (1995), *World Wide Open* (1996), and *Southern Style* (1997). After 15 years of dealing with record contracts, Dykes needed a break from being tied down to one particular label for any length of time. Since then, he and the Howlers have released excellent discs on Discovery (*Monkey Land*) (1997) Black Top (*Swing Land*) (1999), and Blind Pig (*Big Delta*) (2002). —*Richard Skelly & Al Campbell*

Big Leg Beat / 1980 / Amazing ◆◆◆
Omar & the Howler's debut *Big Leg Beat* is an impressive piece of work. Omar Kent Dykes was an imposing, forceful vocalist from the start and the Howlers are a tough, exciting band, slamming through gritty Chicago blues with passion. Although they made better albums later in their career, *Big Leg Beat* remains an invigorating listen. —*Thom Owens*

● **I Told You So** / 1984 / Austin ◆◆◆◆◆
I Told You So is one of the finest records Omar & the Howlers ever released, filled with roaring, impassioned performances and a sharp set of material. —*Thom Owens*

Hard Times in the Land of Plenty / 1987 / Sony Special Products ◆◆◆◆◆
For their major-label debut, Omar & the Howlers were trimmed down to a trio, but that didn't decrease their power. If anything, the group sounds leaner and meaner. *Hard Times in the Land of Plenty* is one of their finest releases for this reason—it's a rough and tumble collection that is driven as much by fine original songwriting as it is by the band's edgy sound. —*Thom Owens*

Live at Paradiso / Sep. 1991 / Bullseye Blues ◆◆
For a band that usually sounds alive and vibrant on record, *Live at Paradiso* is a disappointingly sedate live album from Omar & the Howlers. Although there are a couple of fine moments scattered throughout the album, there's not enough to make the album a captivating listen. —*Thom Owens*

Courts of Lulu / 1992 / Bullseye Blues ◆◆◆
Omar & The Howlers' misadventures at the majors began when they trimmed the blues and padded the rock. Since returning to Rounder/Bullseye, they have smartly managed

to keep the balance, and that's the case on their latest. The 13 tracks alternate between boogie shuffles, swaggering wailers, and heartache testimonies, with Omar's flailing guitar and spiraling harmonica nicely backed by his trio and such assistants as organist Reese Wynans, vocalist Kris McKay and saxophonist John Mills. Plenty of blues and more than enough rock fervor. —*Ron Wynn*

Blues Bag / 1992 / Bullseye Blues ✦✦

This CD was the solo debut of vocalist-guitar Omar, the leader of Omar & the Howlers. Although his musicianship is strong (as is the harmonica playing of Fingers Taylor), it may take listeners a little while to get used to Omar's voice which is a mixture of Howlin' Wolf and disc jockey Wolfman Jack! The first nine songs on the CD are essentially duets between Omar and Taylor with the final six tracks adding electric bassist Bruce Jones and drummer Gene Brandon. Many of the songs are light-hearted and, despite a certain lack of variety, blues fans will find the set difficult to resist. —*Scott Yanow*

World Wide Open / 1996 / Watermelon ✦✦✦

Supported by a new batch of Howlers, Omar Dykes doesn't show any signs of wear and tear on *World Wide Open*. The band continues to turn out a gut-busting mixture of blues and dirty rock & roll, occasionally sounding like Howlin' Wolf, other times like the Stones or Creedence Clearwater Revival. As always, the quality of songs is slightly inconsistent but the band never sounds tired—they perform with as much energy, if not more, than they ever have. —*Thom Owens*

Southern Style / Feb. 4, 1997 / Watermelon ✦✦✦

Omar shakes up the Howlers' lineup yet again for *Southern Style*, yet the changes don't affect his sound much at all. Working with guitarist Stephen Bruton, bassist Paul Junior, drummer Steve Kilmer, percussionist Mark Hallman and organist Nick Connolly, Omar Dykes kicks out a set of swampy blues-rock that alternates between New Orleans grunge and tight Memphis grooves. Though the band sounds great, the lack of compelling material means *Southern Style* isn't appealing to anyone but specialists. —*Thom Owens*

Monkey Land / Feb. 11, 1997 / Discovery ✦✦✦

A solid effort, it benefits from its excellent label. —*David Szatmary*

Swing Land / Feb. 23, 1999 / Black Top ✦✦✦

One doesn't recall Omar & the Howlers as a straight-out jump blues combo, but it looks as if they're on the bandwagon with this CD. Omar Dykes has a squirrelly voice that falls between sandpaper gruff and churlish shouting, a cross twixt Dr. John and Howlin' Wolf. Help from the capable Howlers, big-time backup from saxophonists David "Fathead" Newman and Mark "Kaz" Kazanoff and harmonica whiz Gary Primich on three cuts gives Omar, who also plays guitar throughout, all the support and inspiration he needs. As much as the band does predictably jump and swing hard on the majority of these cuts, there's always a surprise. Obvious choices like "Hit the Road Jack," "Just Like a Woman," and the hardest swinger "So Mean to Me" come naturally. Taj Mahal's loping "Going up to the Country" is one that fits Omar's range perfectly, and he really cops "the Wolf" on "Yellow Coat." The most daring move is his singing the Oscar Brown Jr. lyrics to Nat Adderley's "Work Song" with the saxophonists trading licks nicely, or Charles Brown's lesser-known upbeat flag-waver "That's Your Daddy Yaddy-O." An instrumental version of the famous Albert Collins' number "Don't Lose Your Cool" really cooks, Omar and Derek O'Brien on electric six strings working out. And they do return to their straight blues base on the final two cuts, Primich standing up firmly and wailing on "One Room Country Shack," the band getting down right dirty and nasty on "Alligator Wine." "Swing Land" has lots of teeth and the bite to match. It's sincere, authentic, well played, and represents better than a lot of the phony swing bands copying songs and well-worn riffs. —*Michael G. Nastos*

Live at the Opera House Austin, Texas: August 30, 1987 / Mar. 21, 2000 / Phoenix Rising ✦✦✦

Omar Dykes tears it up big-time on this marvelous live outing. Pulling tunes largely from his then-current *Hard Times in the Land of Plenty* album, Dykes and his band deliver the goods with loads of panache and attitude for a hometown crowd hanging on every note. Dykes' voice is poised somewhere between Howlin' Wolf and Bob Seger, while his guitar style is a Texas version of John Fogerty's work with Creedence, but the sound he produces out of all this is totally unique. The disc is loaded with solid Dykes originals like "Mississippi Hoo Doo Man," "Same Old Grind," "Hard Times in the Land of Plenty," and a wild encore performance of Jerry McCain's "Rock 'n' Roll Ball." One great little package. —*Cub Koda*

The Screamin' Cat / Sep. 12, 2000 / Provogue ✦✦✦

Although no new ground is covered on *The Screamin Cat*, Austin-based Omar & the Howlers simply continue to forge ahead, creating another energetic blues and boogie disc. Luckily, the Howlers have never stuck to one style of blues; they aren't purists, which allows plenty of room for a hopped-up mixture of swamp blues, Memphis soul, roots rock, and whatever else it takes to get their audience moving. Their party ethics are personified on *The Screamin Cat* by songs like "Party Girl," "Steady Rock," "Snake Oil Doctor," and the title track. Lead guitarist Omar Dykes' gravelly Howlin' Wolf roar remains intact while Howler musical duties are shared by Bruce Jones on bass (three tracks); Rick Chilleri on drums (one track); Malcolm "Papa Mali" Welbourne on guitar, B-3, and bass; and B.E. "Frosty" Smith on drums, percussion, B-3, and Fender Rhodes. —*Al Campbell*

Big Delta / Feb. 12, 2002 / Blind Pig ✦✦✦✦

Now on his 14th release for approximately ten different labels, Texan Omar Dykes keeps the faith by re-recording some of his better tracks, and adding a few new covers. While it looks on paper to be treading water, this is really one of the band's strongest releases, since the material—which has often been inconsistent—is top-notch, and the new Howlers are a crack unit with impeccable chops. Omar attacks and rearranges these songs with the experience of having played them for years, in many cases making these versions

more definitive than the originals, an unusual occurrence when an artist revisits his own work. Whether taking "Muddy Springs Road" down to the swamp and saturating the tune with greasy acoustic slide guitar or rescuing the slow blues of "Life Without You" from obscurity while singing it with crying emotional intensity, this makes a case for Dykes as one of the most talented and least recognized contemporary bluesmen. There are a few missteps; the band's plodding version of Mountain's "Mississippi Queen" adds nothing to the original, other than proving how much Omar's voice sounds like Leslie West's, and the Bob Seger-isms of the simplistic rock & roller "Caveman Rock" seem forced and stilted. But it's great to hear terrific older tracks like "Bad Seed" and "Wall of Pride" redone with restraint and class. Dykes is in fine voice throughout, growling and howling with raspy delight, a combination of Howlin' Wolf and John Fogerty wading through the muddy southern river banks. Since as of 2002 there was no comprehensive, multi-label Omar collection available (and with the different imprints he recorded for, one does not seem likely), this fills the bill just fine as a greatest hits compilation. Those who want a taste of the deep, moody, growling blues-rock of Omar & the Howlers should start here. —*Hal Horowitz*

Paul Oscher

b. Apr. 5, 1950, Brooklyn, NY
Harmonica / Chicago Blues,,
Guitarist, singer, songwriter, pianist and harp player Paul Oscher has paid his dues, and then some. Those who have been following blues for a long time will remember Oscher from the late '60s as the white kid who played harmonica in the Muddy Waters Band. Blues caught the Brooklyn-raised Oscher's ears at age 12 and he began playing professionally at age 15, frequenting clubs like the Baby Grand, the 521 Club and the Seville Lounge. Oscher also made frequent trips to the Apollo Theater in the mid-'60s. On one trip, he met guitarist Muddy Waters, and a friendship between the two developed. Several years later, Waters' band was in New York and they needed a harmonica player; Oscher got the nod. Oscher joined Waters on stage for two numbers, "Baby Please Don't Go" and "Blow Wind Blow." Waters hired him. As a full member of Waters' band, he had the chance to rub shoulders with greats like Otis Spann, Sammy Lawhorn, and S.P. Leary. Oscher, the only white member of the band, performed with Waters through tours of the U.S., Europe and Canada. He also recorded with Waters' band at the Chess Studios in Chicago.

As one who was there at the height of the late-'60s blues renaissance, Oscher's harmonica playing influenced lots of other players who came to prominence after him. His sessionography is extensive, including albums with Johnny Copeland, Muddy Waters, Otis Spann, Luther Johnson, and Johnny Young.

Oscher's veteran skills on guitar and harmonica are showcased on his debut for the New York-based Vice Roots Records, a division of Viceroy Music. Oscher's *Knockin' on the Devil's Door*, a 1996 release, brought his music before a bigger audience. Provided he can back it up with the kind of touring required to support independent records, Oscher should find himself in demand again on the festival/club circuit around the U.S. and Europe. Oscher's debut for Viceroots was produced by a longtime admirer, Dave Peverett, from the blues-rock quartet Foghat. —*Richard Skelly*

The Deep Blues of Paul Oscher / 1996 / Blues Planet ✦✦✦

● **Knockin' on the Devil's Door** / Mar. 19, 1996 / Viceroots ✦✦✦✦

After years of being a sideman and gigging without recorded, Paul Oscher—a former harpist for Muddy Waters—made his first album, *Knockin' on the Devil's Door*, in 1996. Oscher stays true to his Chicago blues roots, but he wisely doesn't run through the same old standards again. Instead, he's written a set of impassioned originals, augmented by a couple of appropriate covers. Working with a talented supporting group—featuring harpist Steve Guyger, bassist Mudcat Ward, pianist David Maxwell, and drummer Big Eyes Smith—Oscher devotes himself to guitar, showing a flair for gritty riffs and solos. But the key to the record's success are his fully realized originals, which make the album an impressive, if much belated, debut. —*Thom Owens*

Living Legends / May 16, 2000 / Blues Leaf ✦✦✦

New York Really Has the Blues / Spivey ✦✦✦

The Oscher Chicago Breakdown Blues Band's *New York Really Has the Blues* was a bit of an all-star session organized by Paul Oscher, the former harpist for Muddy Waters. Assembling a great cast of musicians—including Victoria Spivey, Sugar Blue, Smokey Hogg, Ben Jackson, Robert Ross, and Sonny Boy Parker—Oscher leads the group through a number of Chicago standards. At times, there are a few too many cooks in the kitchen, but the record remains quite enjoyable. —*Thom Owens*

Johnny Otis (John Veliotes)

b. Dec. 28, 1921, Vallejo, CA
Vibraphone, Vocals, Leader, Drums, Piano / Jump Blues, West Coast Blues, R&B
Johnny Otis has modeled an amazing number of contrasting musical hats over a career spanning more than half a century. Bandleader, record producer, talent scout, label owner, nightclub impresario, disc jockey, TV variety show host, author, R&B pioneer, rock & roll star—Otis has answered to all those descriptions and quite a few more. Not bad for a Greek-American who loved jazz and R&B so fervently that he adopted the African-American culture as his own.

California-born John Veliotes changed his name to the blacker-sounding Otis when he was in his teens. Drums were his first passion—he spent time behind the traps with the Oakland-based orchestra of Count Otis Matthews and kept time for various Midwestern swing outfits before settling in Los Angeles during the mid-'40s and joining Harlan Leonard's Rockets, then resident at the Club Alabam.

It wasn't long before the Alabam's owner entreated Otis to assemble his own orchestra for house-band duties. The group's 1945 debut sides for Excelsior were solidly in the big-band jazz vein and included an arrangement of the moody "Harlem Nocturne" that sold well. Shouter Jimmy Rushing fronted the band for two tracks at the same date. Otis' rep as a drummer was growing; he backed both Wynonie Harris and Charles Brown (with Johnny Moore's Three Blazers) that same year.

The Otis outfit continued to record for Excelsior through 1947 (one date featured Big Jay McNeely on sax), but his influence on L.A.'s R&B scene soared exponentially when he and partner Bardu Ali opened the Barrelhouse Club in Watts. R&B replaced jazz in Otis' heart; he pared the big band down and discovered young talent such as the Robins, vocalists Mel Walker and Little Esther Phillips, and guitarist Pete Lewis that would serve him well in years to come.

Otis signed with Newark, NJ-based Savoy Records in 1949, and the R&B hits came in droves: "Double Crossing Blues," "Mistrustin' Blues," and "Cupid's Boogie" all hit number one that year (in all, Otis scored ten Top Ten smashes that year alone!); "Gee Baby," "Mambo Boogie," and "All Nite Long" lit the lamp in 1951, and "Sunset to Dawn" capped his amazing run in 1952 (vocals were shared by Esther, Walker, and other members of the group). By then, Otis had branched out to play vibes on many waxings.

In late 1951, Otis moved to Mercury, but apart from a Walker-led version of Floyd Dixon's "Call Operator 210," nothing found pronounced success with the public. A 1953-1955 contract with Don Robey's Peacock logo produced some nice jump-blues sides but no hits (though the Otis orchestra backed one of his many discoveries, Big Mama Thornton, on her chart-topping "Hound Dog," as well as a young Little Richard while at Peacock). Otis was a masterful talent scout; among his platinum-edged discoveries were Jackie Wilson, Little Willie John, Hank Ballard, and Etta James (he produced her debut smash "Roll with Me Henry").

In 1955, Otis took studio matters into his own hands, starting up his own label, Dig Records, to showcase his own work as well as his latest discoveries (including Arthur Lee Maye & the Crowns, Tony Allen, and Mel Williams). Rock & roll was at its zenith in 1957, when the multi-instrumentalist signed on with Capitol Records; billed as the Johnny Otis Show, he set the R&B and pop charts ablaze in 1958 with his shave-and-a-haircut beat, "Willie and the Hand Jive," taking the vocal himself (other singers then with the Otis Show included Mel Williams and the gargantuan Marie Adams & the Three Tons of Joy). During the late '50s, Otis hosted his own variety program on L.A. television, starring his entire troupe (and on one episode, Lionel Hampton), and did a guest shot in a 1958 movie, *Juke Box Rhythm*.

After cutting some great rock & roll for Capitol from 1957 to 1959 with only one hit to show for it, Otis dropped anchor at King Records in 1961-1962 (in addition to his own output, Otis' band also backed Johnny "Guitar" Watson on several sides). Later in the decade, Otis recorded some ribald material for Kent and watched as his young son Shuggie built an enviable reputation as a blues guitarist while recording for Columbia. Father and son cut an album together for Alligator in 1982, accurately entitled *The New Johnny Otis Show*. *—Bill Dahl*

Rock and Roll Hit Parade, Vol. 1 / 1957 / Dig ♦♦♦
Enjoyable sound-alike covers of popular mid-'50s R&B hits by Otis, singers Mel Williams and Arthur Lee Maye, and the Jayos. *—Bill Dahl*

The Johnny Otis Show / 1958 / Savoy ♦♦♦♦♦
Some of the R&B bandleader's earliest and best work (1945-1951) for Savoy. The cast includes singers Little Esther and Mel Walker, the Robins, and guitarist Pete Lewis. *—Bill Dahl*

Live at Monterey / 1971 / Epic ♦♦♦♦♦
An R&B oldies show with a difference, the artists represented the cream of the crop of jump blues, and in 1970, they were still in fine form. The disc stars Otis, Esther Phillips, Eddie Vinson, Joe Turner, Ivory Joe Hunter, Roy Milton, Roy Brown, Pee Wee Crayton, and Johnny's guitar wielding son, Shuggie. *—Bill Dahl*

New Johnny Otis Show / 1982 / Alligator ♦♦♦
This features recent recordings with Shuggie Otis. Nice, but non-essential. *—Mark A. Humphrey*

The Capitol Years / 1989 / Collectables ♦♦♦♦♦
Unfortunately now out-of-print, this set anthologizes Otis' late-'50s rise to rock & roll fame, thanks to his shave-and-a-haircut special "Willie and the Hand Jive." Like every other style of R&B Otis drifted into, he excelled at it—"Castin' My Spell," "Crazy Country Hop," "Willie Did the Cha Cha," and "Three Girls Named Molly" are catchy rockers. Otis had a terrific band—guitarist Jimmy Nolen (later James Brown's main axeman), pianist Ernie Freeman, drummer Earl Palmer, and a tight horn section (along with singers Marie Adams and Mel Williams) gave him all the help he could possibly need. *—Bill Dahl*

Let's Live It Up / 1991 / Charly ♦♦♦
Otis stopped off at King Records for a while during the early '60s, making clever 45s that no one paid much attention to. Twenty-two of them are here, including five by the late Johnny "Guitar" Watson (whose "In the Evenin'" is chillingly direct). It's a mixed bag—vocal group stuff, twist workouts, and the inevitable sequel "Hand Jive One More Time" (alas, nobody did). *—Bill Dahl*

Be Bop Baby Blues / 1991 / Night Train ♦♦♦
A bit skimpy at 14 songs, this disc casts Otis mostly in a bandleader role on late-'40s sides culled from the Excelsior, Supreme, and Swing Time labels. Vocalists fronting the Otis outfit include the extremely obscure Joe Swift, Earl Jackson, Clifford "Fat Man" Blivens, and Johnny Crawford. Swinging, horn-leavened jump blues all the way. *—Bill Dahl*

Creepin' With the Cats: The Legendary Dig Masters / 1991 / Ace ♦♦♦
Twenty-two tracks, almost half previously unreleased, from circa 1956-1957 that Otis recorded for his own short-lived Dig label. Not as vivacious as the sides he recorded for Capitol in the late '50s, this is spirited but generic jump blues/R&B, divided evenly between vocals and instrumentals. Occasional cuts like the silly novelty instrumental "Ali Baba's Boogie" stand out from the pack. The one commanding greatest interest is "Hey! Hey! Hey!," which served as the model for Little Richard's version, which in turned was covered by the Beatles in the mid-'60s (as "Kansas City"). *—Richie Unterberger*

Spirit of the Black Territory Bands / 1992 / Arhoolie ♦♦♦
This nostalgic throwback to the big-band jazz era is competent but hardly thrilling. *—Bill Dahl*

Too Late to Holler / 1994 / Night Train ♦♦♦♦
A more generous selection of late-'40s Swing Time and Excelsior sides, again featuring Swift (who dominates the compilation), Jackson, and Blivens in front of the powerful Otis orchestra. Very little duplication exists between the two discs. *—Bill Dahl*

★ **Original Johnny Otis Show, Vol. 1** / 1994 / Savoy ♦♦♦♦♦
Here are 27 of the Otis aggregation's best early sides for Savoy and Excelsior, including a slew of the group's early-'50s Little Esther and/or Mel Walker-fronted R&B smashes ("Mistrustin' Blues," "Cry Baby," "Sunset to Dawn"). Jimmy Rushing and the Robins also share vocal duties, as does Otis himself on a jumping "All Nite Long." This is one time when the bonus cuts are on the vinyl version—it contained 32 cuts appearing on a *Completer Disc* that Savoy Jazz reissued at the same time as this CD. The original artwork and liner notes have been reduced so much for the CD that they're unreadable (Pete Welding's essay deserves more respect). *—Bill Dahl*

Johnny Otis Rock 'N Roll Hit Parade / Oct. 17, 2000 / Ace ♦♦♦
Johnny Otis originally released a 12-song version of this CD in 1957 on his Dig label. That LP centered around the Jayos, a group assembled by Otis that at times included Richard Berry, Jesse Belvin, Mel Williams, Arthur "Lee" Maye (a future Major Leaguer), Harold Lewis, Sonny Moore, Tony Allen, and others. Nobody brought anything resembling an original song to these sessions; practically all the tunes are remakes or, in some instances, covers, and even the few that aren't sound like something you heard before by someone else. Ace tacked on 12 more tracks (most previously unreleased) for a more thorough perspective of Otis' late-'50s empire. The Jayos do hits by the El Dorados, the Platters, the Drifters, the Penquins, Hank Ballard and the Midnighters, and others, and did them well, but what else would you expect from a lineup of vocal harmony superstars? The Johnny Otis Orchestra pumps out three tracks, and there are tunes by some So Cal singers that are unknown to those outside the region. Jeannie Barnes does tunes made famous by Faye Adams and Ruth Brown; Mel Williams duets with Arthur Lee Maye on Gene and Eunice's "Ko Ko Mo, I Love You So"; Maye solos on Little Willie John's "Fever. Tracks by Prince Moreland, Harold Lewis and Mel Williams fill out the interesting compilation. If you just like the original versions of songs this CD won't interest you. But if enjoy good music, regardless of who came first, you'll find this to be a fine collection of '50s R&B/doo wop. *—Andrew Hamilton*

Watts Funky / 2001 / BGP ♦♦♦♦
Whether as an artist, mentor, and/or small-time record label entrepreneur, Johnny Otis was continuing to make some interesting R&B-based music in the late '60s and '70s, though little of it is familiar to anyone but devoted collectors. *Watts Funky* collects 20 tracks from the late '60s through the mid-'70s that he was involved with, though only about half are billed to either Johnny Otis or the Johnny Otis Show. It's erratic, eccentric, but generally refreshing soul-funk, reflecting the trends of the era, but more idiosyncratic than much of the stuff being put out via more high-profile outlets. Certainly the best track by a country mile is Shuggie Otis' "Strawberry Letter 23," a spaced-out soul ballad that owes a lot to contemporary hippie singer/songwriters as well, and was covered by the Brothers Johnson for a hit in 1977. Shuggie Otis fans will be excited by the inclusion of a couple of previously unreleased cuts from the same era, but actually those are much more ordinary, with "Miss Pretty" sounding a little like Sly Stone as sung by Van Morrison. It's very unlikely you'll have heard of anyone else but the Otises on the disc's artist list, except maybe Preston Love. But there's credible funk by Vera Hamilton on "But I Ain't No More (G.S.T.S.K.D.T.S)," and the Vibrettes sound like they should be singing backup for James Brown funk sides on "The Humpty Dump." There's some pretty humorous, sly late-'60s soul by the Johnny Otis Show on "Country Girl," and Otis himself comes through with some top-drawer jazzy James Brown-ish instrumental funk on "Jaws." *—Richie Unterberger*

Essential Recordings / Jan. 9, 2001 / Cleopatra ♦♦
Alternately a songwriter, performer, bandleader and talent scout, Johnny Otis was a pioneering figure in American R&B. As the 21st century dawned, however, his impressive catalog was largely in disarray. Too few titles were in print, and there seemed to be no single-disc compilation providing an accurate overview of his work. Though, by the title of this 2001 release from Cleopatra Records, it may have seemed like a remedy had arrived, but *Essential Recordings* did little to change the situation. This set misses far too many Otis classics and includes far too many lesser sides to warrant its title. The fact is that the task had been difficult from the outset: Otis recorded for a total of six labels, including his own Dig Records, during his first 14 years alone. The set does get off on the right foot, beginning with the most logical of introductory cuts, "Harlem Nocturne," Otis' big band masterpiece (and a sizable hit) recorded in 1945. Otis had clearly learned a great deal during his tenure with the Count Basie Orchestra, though he quickly struck out on his own, performing jump blues and R&B material. Fans of these styles may enjoy songs like "Low Down Dirty Dog Blues" and slow blues like "Bad Luck Shadow," though they will probably have little patience for crude numbers like "Country Girl" and "The Signifyin' Monkey." Culled from the 1968 *Cold Shot* set, the songs are notable only for the guitar playing of a young Shuggie Otis, Johnny's gifted son. Add to its many shortcomings an insufficient 33-minute playing time and you end up with a rather unessential offering. *—Nathan Bush*

Jack Owens

b. Nov. 17, 1904, Bentonia, MS, **d.** Feb. 9, 1997, Yazoo City, MS

Vocals, Guitar / Delta Blues, Country Blues

Like Skip James, Owens hails from Bentonia, MS. Owens is much less famous than James, but he's often compared to Skip due to his high, rich vocals and intricate guitar styles, which finds him using several tunings and occasional minor keys. His material, it must be noted, is not nearly as strong or tightly constructed as James', although it draws from some of the same sources. Noted folklorist and blues scholar David Evans made several recordings with Owens in the late '60s and early '70s. *—Richie Unterberger*

● **It Must Have Been the Devil** / 1971 / Testament ✦✦✦

Although this album is credited to Owens and Bud Spires, it's really Owens' show; Spires adds some harmonica accompaniment to Jack's playing and singing. Although David Evans (who produced these recordings) intimates that Owens is better than Skip James in his liner notes, it's really not that hard to figure out why James is better known; James' songs are simply better written, more gripping, and more memorable, and Owens tends to ramble pleasantly. If you're looking for the Bentonia sound, though, this is certainly a down-home, well-recorded representation, and has an advantage over those vintage James (or any vintage blues) sides in that the fidelity is much, much clearer. Recorded in 1970, the 1995 CD reissue adds five previously unreleased tracks. *—Richie Unterberger*

Jay Owens (Isaac Jerome Owens)

b. Sep. 6, 1947, Lake City, FL

Vocals / Modern Electric Blues, Soul-Blues

A top-notch sideman and songwriter, Jay Owens also enjoyed acclaim as a solo artist. Born Isaac Jerome Owens in Lake City, FL, on September 6, 1947, he learned to sing in the church where his mother presided as minister; at the age of 11, he received his first guitar, and began performing professionally while in high school. With his friend Johnny Kay, Owens went on to lead many of the most notable Tampa Bay/St. Petersburg-area backing bands of the '70s and '80s, among them the Barons, the Funk Bunch and the Dynamites; artists he supported included Stevie Wonder, Al Green, O.V. Wright, and Donny Hathaway. With more than 100 songs to his credit as well, Owens formed his own band during the late '80s; he made his solo debut in 1993 with *The Blues Soul of Jay Owens*, followed in 1995 by *Movin' On. —Jason Ankeny*

The Blues Soul of Jay Owens / 1993 / Atlantic ✦✦✦✦

● **Movin' On** / 1995 / Code Blue ✦✦✦✦✦

The production may be a little too clean and the playing may be a little too pat, but there's no denying that *Moving On* is the work of a fine blues craftsman. Jay Owens has written a set of strong songs in the soul-blues tradition, spiking his straight-ahead foundation with flourishes of funk and Chicago blues. Owens delivers his songs with passion, which make the weaker moments sound convincing, thereby elevating *Movin' On* to the status of his best latter-day effort. *—Thom Owens*

Horace Palm

Piano, Vocals / Chicago Blues, Doo Wop, R&B
If the Chicago music scene of the '40s and '50s was in the palm of anyone's hand, it might as well have been Horace Palm, a pianist and vocalist who seemed to be all over the place, from studio to bandstand and back again. Many listeners associate the Windy City simply with Muddy Waters and the blues, yet Palm and his cohorts were actually more representative of the city's musical direction. Palm played plenty of blues and R&B, but he also backed doo wop bands and played in many trios, aping the sound of Nat "King" Cole and his sophisticated balladacio. He was a mainstay of the Vee-Jay label's house band, playing on dozens of sessions in which arrangements were simply thrown together as the tape began to roll. These performances survive as great testaments to the inspiration of musicians when allowed to create outside of stiff, confining production processes.

Palm is not a man about which there are a series of raucous anecdotes. He also never made a recording as a leader, or asserted his personality in any way that left a mark, other than his superb accompaniment. Rumors of his reliability are completely backed up by his many recording credits, as well as his presence in certain key performing groups. The lion's share of his work seems to have taken place between the late '40s and mid-'50s. Around the end of the '40s, he was part of bassist Duke Groner's first trio, also featuring Emmett Spicer on guitar and one of many trios going for the Cole style. The trio recorded for Aristocrat in both 1947 and 1948 and was particularly known for Palm's ballad singing. Another of his frequent playing partners was Lefty Bates, with whom he formed a trio in 1952. Quinn Wilson was the bassist in this band, which played regularly through much of the decade, sometimes increased to a quartet with a horn player.

Clubs such as Duke Slater's Vincennes Lounge, the Shalimar, Trocadero Lounge, and Spruce's Duck Inn Lounge were the haunts of these types of combos. Another such dive that Palm took residence in was the Cotton Club, one of the rare clubs run by musicians. It was opened in 1953 by pianist Harold Youngblood, vibraphonist Bobby Payne, and drummer Tony Smith. Payne was the real owner, but had to be anonymous on the license because of a felony conviction. It is possible that some of the musicians had to be extra tough simply to fight off the efforts of local businessmen to take over the music scene. Some of these impresarios named their record companies after themselves, thus ensuring immortality on the blues scene.

There is no blues collection on earth without a few Chess sides on it, and Palm was front and center when Marshall and Leonard Chess took over the Aristocrat label. As Groner recalled to the Chicago Jazz Institute's oral history project, "That's when I made 'Dragging My Heart Around.' Horace Palm was the vocalist. Chess and two ladies picked out two tunes for us to do. One called 'Blue Bird of Happiness.' Chess made a remark to someone that before it was over, he was going to own every black musician out there, and put them on his label…"

But if Palm was "owned" by a label, it would have been Vee-Jay. By 1955, he was well established as part of this label's house band, a hard-working unit that included Bates, bassist Wilson, Paul Gusman on drums, saxophone players Red Holloway and Lucias Washington, and the brilliant drummer Vernell Fournier, who later became a key part of the Ahmad Jamal Trio. If horns were needed, there was McKinley "Mac" Easton on baritone and Harlen "Booby" Floyd on trombone, among others. Some of the quickie style arranging was done by the legendary Von Freeman, and of course nobody would forget the bandleader, Al Smith, despite his incredibly common name. Smith was nearly adored by musicians, because he got lots of gigs and they always paid well. Many of the musicians already mentioned worked regularly with Smith, as did tenor saxophonist Von Freeman and even Sun Ra.

During the '50s, the sharpie Smith had recording sessions sewed up at four different independent labels in Chicago. Working with Smith, Palm backed vocal groups such as the Flamingos, the Swans, and the Parrots, bringing to mind strange images of exotic birds flocking to nest on the branches of the musical Palm tree. Sometimes they would back a solo singer who didn't have a band of his/her own. In all cases, the group would toss together instrumental tracks whenever there was studio time left over. At the start of a typical session, the group would jam some instrumentals while producers prepared to cut sides with an R&B singer, such as Bobby Prince. As soon as Prince had made his final bow for the day, the studio doors would open and in would come legendary bluesman Tampa Red, ready to tape a few songs with just the rhythm section backing. Since he was under contract to someone else, these tracks came out under the name of the Jimmy Eager Trio.

Vee-Jay likes to boast that it was there well before Motown, but once the latter company came along, the public's interest in R&B began shifting toward the new soul music, a concept that put Palm in a pocket with a hole in it. The creation of a Vee-Jay reissue program now allows listeners an opportunity to revisit the Chicago music scene that kept Palm busy. *—Eugene Chadbourne*

Earl Palmer

b. Oct. 25, 1924, New Orleans, LA

Drums / New Orleans R&B, Bop, Rock & Roll, R&B
Earl Palmer was first-call drummer on the New Orleans R&B recording scene from 1950 to 1957. Talk about a supreme recommendation—in a city renowned for its second-line rhythms and syncopated grooves, Palmer was the man, playing on countless sessions by all the immortals: Little Richard, Fats Domino, Smiley Lewis, Dave Bartholomew, and too many more to list here.

Born to a mother who was a vaudevillian, little Earl Palmer was learning rhythmic patterns as a tap dancer at age four. Such contacts led him to be around drum kits on a regular basis, and it didn't take him long to master them. Bebop jazz was his first love, but R&B and blues paid the bills starting in 1947, when Palmer joined Bartholomew's band.

Palmer remained the king of the traps at Cosimo's fabled recording studio until 1957, when a Shirley & Lee session led to an A&R offer from Aladdin Records boss Eddie Mesner. Palmer found studio work just as plentiful in Los Angeles, making major inroads into the rock, jazz, and soundtrack fields as well as playing on countless R&B dates with his frequent compadres Rene Hall on guitar and saxist Plas Johnson. Occasionally, Palmer would record as a leader—the instrumental "Johnny's House Party" for Aladdin, a couple of early-'60s albums for Liberty.

But even the best session men grapple with a certain sense of anonymity. So the next time you pull out Little Richard's "Tutti Frutti," Smiley Lewis' "I Hear You Knockin'," Lloyd Price's "Lawdy Miss Clawdy," or Fats Domino's "The Fat Man," please keep in mind that it's Earl Palmer feverishly stoking that beat—with a saucy second-line sensibility that drove those songs in fresh, utterly innovative directions. *—Bill Dahl*

Drumsville / 1961 / Liberty ♦♦♦

Percolator Twist / 1962 / Liberty ♦♦♦
Strictly-by-the-book album of formulaic twist instrumentals that exhibits precious little of the imaginative rhythmic flair that had previously made Palmer such an in-demand New Orleans session drummer. *—Bill Dahl*

● **The World's Greatest Drummer, Ever!** / May 11, 1999 / Ace ♦♦♦♦
This 30-song selection of tracks on which Palmer played in the late '50s cannot, and does not purport to, tell the whole story of his career. After all, there's only one track apiece from his work with Little Richard and Fats Domino. What this various-artists compilation (only four tracks were actually released under Earl Palmer's name) does, however, is give a pretty good idea of Palmer's early rock & roll contributions via a few well-known hits, a lot of rarities, and a bunch of styles. While Fats Domino's "I'm Walkin'," Bobby Day's "Rockin' Robin," Ritchie Valens' "La Bamba," Thurston Harris' "Little Bitty Pretty One," and Eddie Cochran's "Somethin' Else" are here, most of this is pretty obscure R&B, catching that music's transition to rock. In addition to fairly little-heard sides by Lloyd Price, Richard Berry, and Shirley & Lee, there's hard R&B from Smiley Lewis ("Shame, Shame, Shame"), Amos Milburn, and Charles Brown; gravelly jump and jive from Roy Montrell; Etta James' rock & roll remake of "Dance with Me Henry" (*not* the same as her first and more famous version, "The Wallflower"); instrumental sax rock by Lee Allen; Big T Tyler's insane "King Kong"; Don & Dewey's great harmony romp "Koko"; the rockin' Top Five hit version of "In the Mood" by Ernie Fields; and minor-league rockabilly by Jesse James. The instrumentals cut under his own name are pretty generic stuff ("Johnny's House Party" is a "Honky Tonk" rip), but you'd be checking this out for the cuts graced by Palmer's session drums rather than his own sides anyway. *—Richie Unterberger*

The Paramount Singers

f. 1936, Austin, TX

Group / Traditional Gospel, Black Gospel
Although eclipsed in popularity by contemporaries including the Soul Stirrers and the Dixie Hummingbirds, the Paramount Singers were among the longest-lived gospel groups of the modern era, upholding the tradition of classic a cappella harmonizing for well over half a century. Assembled in Austin, Texas in 1936, the Paramounts initially consisted of two pairs of brothers, Geno and Kermit Terrell and Erman and A.C. Franklin, in addition to Herbert Sneed and Ben Williams. Sneed had been replaced by James Medlock—later of the Soul Stirrers—by the time they recorded for the Library of Congress in 1941; months later, however, the group's original incarnation came to an end when the Terrell brothers were drafted to fight in World War II, and upon receiving their respective discharges both siblings settled in the San Francisco area. There they reunited with Williams to form a new Paramounts lineup, also enlisting two other Austin natives, Sam Reece and Victor L. Medearis.

This new incarnation of the Paramount Singers' roster was in a seemingly constant state of flux, and in time Geno Terrell and Williams were the lone remaining original members; they were soon joined by new recruits Vance "Tiny" Powell, Archie Reynolds, E. Morris Kelley and, albeit briefly, Paul Foster, who also later rose to fame as a member of the Soul Stirrers. Foster's replacement was Joseph Dean, who signed on in 1948; three years later, Powell exited to join the Five Blind Boys of Mississippi, but soon returned to the Paramounts' fold. Despite recording for nationally distributed companies like Coral and Duke between the late '40s and mid-'50s, the Paramounts never earned the notoriety of many of their peers, largely because their day jobs and family ties kept their touring activity confined almost exclusively to the West Coast; Dean once even rejected an offer to join the famed Spirit of Memphis simply because of their hectic traveling schedule.

A 1955 session for Duke was the Paramounts' last commercial recording for close to four decades, but the group continued regularly performing throughout the years to follow. The lineup shifts continued—Powell again exited in 1963 to pursue a career singing the blues, although he continued to rehearse with the Paramounts until his 1973 death, while the 1979 death of co-founder Williams cost the group not only their bass singer but also their guitar accompaniment. Unable to find a compatible bass vocalist, Reynolds took over the bottom himself; when no suitable guitarist arose, the Paramounts, who had long included a number of a cappella numbers in their repertoire, simply began performing without any instrumental backing at all, and found that many audiences seemed to prefer their new style. In 1992, the Paramounts—now consisting of Reynolds and Dean in addition to relative newcomers Clyde Price, J.B. Williams, William Johnson, and the Rev. Odis Brown—issued *Work & Pray On*, their first new record in 37 years. *—Jason Ankeny*

Work & Pray On / 1992 / Arhoolie ♦♦♦♦

Work & Pray On is recorded by a latter-day incarnation of the Paramount Singers. Only two of the members of the sextet were part of the group in the '40s, yet the group still carried on with their classic sound, updated slightly with fresh arrangements. The album suffers from having a few too many undistinguished songs and running a little too long, but it remains an excellent example of how good classic gospel can be. *—Leo Stanley*

● **Paramount Singers** / ♦♦♦♦♦

Bobby Parker

b. Aug. 31, 1937, Lafayette, LA

Vocals, Guitar / Contemporary Blues

Guitarist, singer, and songwriter Bobby Parker is one of the most exciting performers in modern blues, and it's quite apparent he'll inherit the top blues spots left open by the unfortunate, early passings of people like Albert King, Johnny "Guitar" Watson and others. That's because Parker can do it all: He writes brilliant songs, he sings well, and he backs it all up with powerful, stinging guitar. But things weren't always so good for Parker, and much of his newfound success is the result of years of hard work and struggling around the bars in Washington, D.C., and Virginia.

He was born August 31, 1937, in Lafayette, LA, but raised in southern California after his family moved to Los Angeles when he was six. Going to school in Hollywood, the young Parker was bitten by the scenery, and decided he wanted to be in show business. At the Million Dollar Theatre, he saw big stage shows by Count Basie, Duke Ellington, Billy Eckstine, and Lionel Hampton. Although he had an early interest in jazz, the blues bit him when artists like T-Bone Walker, Lowell Fulson, Johnny "Guitar" Watson, and Pee Wee Crayton came to town.

He began playing in the late '50s as a guitarist with Otis Williams and the Charms after winning a talent contest sponsored by West Coast blues and R&B legend Johnny Otis. Later, he backed Bo Diddley, which included an appearance on *The Ed Sullivan Show* before joining the touring big band of Paul "Hucklebuck" Williams. He settled in Washington, D.C., in the '60s, dropping out of Williams' band and making a go of it on his own.

He is perhaps best known for his 1961 song, "Watch Your Step," a single for the V-Tone label that became a hit on British and U.S. R&B charts. Parker's song was later covered by several British blues groups, most prominent among them the Spencer Davis Group. And though Parker may not yet be a name as familiar to blues fans as say, Eric Clapton or B.B. King, he's been cited as a major musical influence by Davis, John Mayall, Robin Trower, Clapton, Jimmy Page, drummer Mick Fleetwood, John Lennon, and, most importantly, Carlos Santana. Parker's style has been described by his protégé Bobby Radcliff as Guitar Slim meets James Brown, and that's not that far off the mark. In the summer of 1994, Santana was so happy about Parker's comeback on the Black Top/Rounder label that he took him on the road for some arena shows on the East and West Coasts.

"Carlos likes to tell people that he saw me playing in Mexico City when he was a kid, and that inspired him to pick up the guitar," Parker explained in a recent interview. Santana pays homage to Parker on his *Havana Moon* album, on which he covers "Watch Your Step." Dr. Feelgood also covered the tune in the '70s.

Unlike so many other blues musicians, Parker was destined to be one of the major players on the blues circuit, provided his stellar output and rigorous touring schedules continue. Unlike so many other blues musicians, Parker's live shows are almost entirely his own songs. He does very few covers. "Unless the music of the day has some kind of substance to it, the blues always comes back," Parker says, adding, "I think Stevie Ray Vaughan had a lot to do with bringing the blues to white audiences, and Z.Z. Hill helped bring the black audience back to the blues."

Parker has two brilliant albums out on the Black Top label out of New Orleans (distributed by Rounder), *Shine Me Up* (1995) and *Bent Out of Shape* (1993). *—Richard Skelly*

● **Bent Out of Shape** / 1993 / Black Top ♦♦♦♦♦

The production on *Bent Out of Shape* may be a little too clean, but that can't distract from the fact that Bobby Parker's belated first album is a storming statement of purpose. His songwriting is sturdy and memorable, his singing impassioned and his guitar simply stings. He could have carried the album with just a little combo, but he's assembled a large, soulful backing band that gives the album soulful finesse. It would have been nice if the production was a little grittier, since Parker's performances are, but there's no denying his playing and songs elevate *Bent Out of Shape* to the status of one of the best blues records of the early '90s. *—Thom Owens*

Shine Me Up / 1995 / Black Top ♦♦♦♦

Guitarist Bobby Parker continued his '90s comeback with *Shine Me Up*, an album filled with fiery leads and gritty, soulful R&B-based material. *—Thom Owens*

Junior Parker (Herman Parker Jr.)

b. May 27, 1932, Clarksdale, MS, **d.** Nov. 18, 1971, Chicago, IL

Vocals, Leader, Harmonica / Electric Memphis Blues, Soul-Blues, R&B

His velvet-smooth vocal delivery to the contrary, Junior Parker was a product of the fertile postwar Memphis blues circuit whose wonderfully understated harp style was personally mentored by none other than regional icon Sonny Boy Williamson.

Herman Parker Jr. only traveled in the best blues circles from the outset. He learned his initial licks from Williamson and gigged with the mighty Howlin' Wolf while still in his teens. Like so many young blues artists, Little Junior (as he was known then) got his first recording opportunity from talent scout Ike Turner, who brought him to Modern Records for his debut session as a leader in 1952. It produced the lone single "You're My Angel," with Turner pounding the 88s and Matt "Guitar" Murphy deftly handling guitar duties.

Parker and his band, the Blue Flames (including Floyd Murphy, Matt's brother, on guitar), landed at Sun Records in 1953 and promptly scored a hit with their rollicking "Feelin' Good" (something of a Memphis response to John Lee Hooker's primitive boogies). Later that year, Little Junior cut a fiery "Love My Baby" and a laidback "Mystery Train" for Sun, thus contributing a pair of future rockabilly standards to the Sun publishing coffers (Hayden Thompson revived the former, Elvis Presley the latter).

Before 1953 was through, the polished Junior Parker had moved on to Don Robey's Duke imprint in Houston. It took a while for the harpist to regain his hitmaking momentum, but he scored big in 1957 with the smooth "Next Time You See Me," an accessible enough number to even garner some pop spins.

Criss-crossing the country as headliner with the Blues Consolidated package (his support act was labelmate Bobby "Blue" Bland), Parker developed a breathtaking brass-powered sound (usually the work of trumpeter/Duke-house-bandleader Joe Scott) that pushed his honeyed vocals and intermittent harp solos with exceptional power. Parker's updated remake of Roosevelt Sykes' "Driving Wheel" was a huge R&B hit in 1961, as was the surging "In the Dark" (the R&B dance workout "Annie Get Your Yo-Yo" followed suit the next year).

Parker was exceptionally versatile—whether delivering "Mother-In-Law Blues" and "Sweet Home Chicago" in faithful downhome fashion, courting the teenage market with "Barefoot Rock," or tastefully howling Harold Burrage's "Crying for My Baby" (another hit for him in 1965) in front of a punchy horn section, Parker was the consummate modern blues artist, with one foot planted in Southern blues and the other in uptown R&B.

Once Parker split from Robey's employ in 1966, though, his hitmaking fortunes declined. His 1966-1968 output for Mercury and its Blue Rock subsidiary deserved a better reception than it got, but toward the end, he was covering the Beatles ("Taxman" and "Lady Madonna," for God's sake!) for Capitol. A brain tumor tragically silenced Junior Parker's magic-carpet voice in late 1971 before he reached his 40th birthday. In 2001, he was inducted into the Blues Hall of Fame. *—Bill Dahl*

Blues Consolidated (Barefoot Rock & You Got Me) / May 1958 / Duke ♦♦♦♦♦

Half Parker, half Bland, all great '50s Texas blues and R&B. *—Bill Dahl*

Driving Wheel / 1962 / Duke ♦♦♦♦

Junior's emerging from his fin-tailed Cadillac on the front of this vintage LP, which contains all kinds of gems not on MCA's CD. For example: an irresistibly upbeat "How Long Can This Go On," the richly arranged blues ballads "I Need Love So Bad" and "Someone Somewhere," Junior's dance hit "Annie Get Your Yo Yo" (all done with Duke's brassy house band), and the New Orleans-cut "The Tables Have Turned" and "Foxy Devil." *—Bill Dahl*

Like It Is / 1967 / Mercury ♦♦♦

Blues with a smooth R&B tinge. *—Bill Dahl*

Baby Please / 1967 / Mercury ♦♦♦

Parker traveled back to his old Memphis stomping grounds to cut this quality set for Mercury under Bobby Robinson's supervision with a coterie of the city's hotter young R&B-oriented studio hands: guitarists Reggie Young and Tommy Cogbill, organist Bobby Emmons, and Willie Mitchell's horn section. "Just like a Fish," "Cracked Up Over You," and "Sometimes I Wonder" are among its smooth highlights. *—Bill Dahl*

The Best of Junior Parker / 1967 / Duke ♦♦♦♦♦

Solid hits package. *—Bill Dahl*

Blues Man / 1969 / Minit ♦♦♦

Soulful blues hybrid. *—Bill Dahl*

Honey-Drippin' Blues / 1969 / Blue Rock ♦♦♦♦

Junior Parker a Chicago soul singer? Yeah, on at least four cuts of this fine LP for Mercury's Blue Rock R&B subsidiary. "I'm So Satisfied" (penned by Cash McCall), "Ain't Gon' Be No Cutting Aloose" (later covered by James Cotton for Alligator), "You Can't Keep a Good Woman Down," and "Easy Lovin'" stem from a soulful 1969 date in the Windy City. Also aboard: considerably bluesier remakes of Lowell Fulson's "Reconsider Baby" and Percy Mayfield's "What a Fool I Was." *—Bill Dahl*

Sometime Tomorrow / 1973 / BluesWay ♦♦♦

Cobbled together from mostly unissued performances out of the Duke vaults, we have here a nice Parker LP anthology emphasizing his early- to mid-'60s soul-inflected sound. He whoops it up like Little Richard on the torrid "If You Can't Take It (You Sure Can't Make It)" (sensible, since Richard wrote it), and gives a warm reading to "Today I Sing the Blues" (generally associated with female singers, primarily Helen Humes amd Aretha Franklin). *—Bill Dahl*

The ABC Collection / 1976 / ABC ♦♦♦♦

Housed in something that looks vaguely like a square gray envelope that's guaranteed to wear out if you're not careful, this album is still one of the only places to locate many of Parker's best 1958-1966 Duke sides (unless you've got the 45s salted away somewhere). "Man or Mouse," "Dangerous Woman," the two-part "These Kind of Blues," and "I'll Forget About You" are prime vehicles for Parker's uncommonly smooth vocals and occasional harp blasts. *—Bill Dahl*

Mystery Train / 1990 / Rounder ♦♦♦♦♦
This excellent little compilation features at least one extant take of everything Junior and his original band, the Blue Flames, recorded at Sun Records between 1952 to 1954. His debut single for the label and his first hit, the classic "Feelin' Good" is aboard as well as the equally fine (but originally unissued) "Feelin' Bad." His leanings toward smoother Roy Brown stylings are evident with tracks like "Fussing and Fighting Blues" and "Sitting and Thinking," but the follow-up to his first Sun single, the original version of "Mystery Train" and two takes of the flip side, "Love My Baby," are the must-hears on this collection. Fleshing out Parker's meager output for Sun are essential early tracks from James Cotton. Cotton doesn't blow harp on any of these, but the sax-dominated "My Baby," and especially "Cotton Crop Blues" and "Hold Me in Your Arms" with Pat Hare on super-distorted blistering guitar are '50s Memphis blues at its apex. Hare himself also rounds out the compilation with two tracks, the prophetic "I'm Gonna Murder My Baby" (Hare did exactly that and spent the rest of his life behind bars as a result) and the previously unissued "Bonus Pay." Don't let the short running time of this CD stop you from picking this one up; the music is beyond excellent. *—Cub Koda*

★ **Junior's Blues: The Duke Recordings, Vol. 1** / 1992 / MCA ♦♦♦♦♦
After the non-success of "Mystery Train" on the R&B charts, Parker jumped contract and signed with Don Robey's Houston-based Duke Records. With his smooth vocal approach, Parker clearly envisioned himself as the next Roy or Charles Brown. But from the evidence of these early sides, it's clear that Robey wanted to piggyback off the success of the Sun sound. Tracks like "I Wanna Ramble" were virtual carbon copies of the "Feelin' Good" riff and Parker's recasting of old favorites like Robert Johnson's "Sweet Home Chicago," Roosevelt Sykes' "Driving Wheel," "Yonder's Wall," and "Mother-In-Law Blues," were all clearly in the down-home vein that Parker felt was too "old timey" for an up-to-date musician/vocalist of his caliber. His first big hit for the label, the horn-driven "Next Time You See Me" is here with others in the same vein, but this otherwise excellent collection is curiously missing "Pretty Baby," Parker's version of Howlin' Wolf's "Riding in the Moonlight," certainly one of his best. *—Cub Koda*

Mercury Recordings / Nov. 5, 1996 / Collectables ♦♦♦

Love Ain't Nothin But a Business Goin' On / Feb. 18, 1997 / Simitar ♦♦♦

Backtracking: The Duke Recordings, Vol. 2 / Jun. 16, 1998 / Duke/Peacock ♦♦♦
This second volume of Parker's best for the Duke label, while leaving off early classics like "I Wanna Ramble," and still delivers on a pile of great early and late tunes for the Houston-based label. Kicking off with the jump blues "Please Baby Blues" and the Howlin' Wolf-like "Can't Understand" from a 1953 session, the early sides vacillate between small rhythm sections with Pat Hare on guitar, to larger ensembles pointing toward Parker's musical future. The early sides reach their peak with the inclusion of "Pretty Baby," recorded in 1956, and Parker's version of Wolf's first single "Riding in the Moonlight." But in two years' time, Junior is recording more R&B-style material like "Barefoot Rock," "You're on My Mind," and culminating in "Annie Get Your YoYo" in 1961. "Get Away Blues" from 1965 and "Man or Mouse" from the following year complete the package. As always, Parker's smooth-as-silk voice and Sonny Boy-derived harp playing carry the day, making a strong case for him as a major mover and shaker on the blues scene during this period. *—Cub Koda*

I'm So Satisfied: The Complete Mercury & Blue Rock Recordings / Jul. 21, 1998 / Polygram ♦♦♦
This is not Junior Parker's best material, nor is it his best-known. That said, it's pretty good all the same. Parker was on Mercury, then their subsidiary Blue Rock, in the second half of the '60s, and throughout he recorded elegant but rollicking soul-blues—very similar to what he did at Duke, but a little smoother, with a little heavier accent on the blues and with material that wasn't quite as good. Despite all this, Junior reminded a consummate, elegant performer, backed by a professional band, and this is all very enjoyable, and certainly the first place to go after absorbing the Duke material. But it should be heard after the Duke material all the same. *—Stephen Thomas Erlewine*

Kenny Parker

Producer, Guitar, Mixing, Vocals / Modern Electric Blues
In the mid-'90s, Detroit blues guitarist and songwriter Kenny Parker released his debut album, *Raise the Dead,* for the London-based JSP Records. Parker's blues education began with the Beatles in the early '60s, but it wasn't long before he discovered the roots of their music. Parker grew up in Albion, MI, and began playing in his first band, the Esquires, at 14. He begin listening to Albert King and B.B. King in high school via the local record store, and he took his inspiration from them. He graduated from Eastern Michigan University in 1976 and took a job in a Cadillac factory while looking around for the right opportunities to play blues at night. He began working with a paragon of the Detroit scene, Mr. Bo (Louis Bo Collins), and later joined the Butler Twins.

While Parker toured Europe with the Butler Twins, JSP founder John Stedman heard him and decided to sign him up for his own recording. The Butler Twins accompany Parker on his debut recording, and he's also backed by harp master Darrell Nulisch, best known for his work with Anson Funderburgh and the Rockets. The Butler Twins and Nulisch contribute vocals on Parker's *Raise the Dead,* and since Parker doesn't consider himself a singer, his guitar playing takes center stage. *—Richard Skelly*

● **Raise the Dead** / Nov. 12, 1996 / JSP ♦♦♦

Robert Parker

b. Oct. 14, 1930, Crescent City, LA
Vocals, Saxophone / Pop-Soul, R&B, Soul
Parker's dance raver "Barefootin'" was one of the biggest hits to come out of New Orleans during the mid-'60s. Parker played sessions as a saxophonist back in 1949 with the legendary pianist Professor Longhair, and his 1959 solo debut for Ron, "All Night Long," was a scorching two-part instrumental. But Parker's under-utilized vocal talents suddenly emerged in 1966, when his highly infectious "Barefootin'" became a giant hit on tiny Nola. Only one other Parker single, "Tip Toe," charted the next year, but Parker remains a popular attraction in his hometown. *—Bill Dahl*

● **Barefootin'** / 1966 / Collectables ♦♦♦♦♦
Originally issued in 1987 on vinyl by England's Charly, this collection includes Parker's main claim to fame, the 1966 R&B and pop dance smash "Barefootin'"; its flip side, "Let's Go Baby (Where the Action Is)"; both sides of a 1969 single Parker cut for Silver Fox; and a number of '70s recordings the erstwhile sax player waxed for Sansu Enterprises. Much of the CD, including the title cut, is infectious New Orleans R&B of a high caliber, but other tracks find Parker attempting to cut mainstream funk and disco, usually with less-than-inspiring results. If possible, find the Charly release, because Collectables, in their typically shoddy manner, do not bother to provide songwriting credits, let alone track credits or liner notes. A good policy is to buy Collectables only if there is no other anthology of the same material issued anywhere else in the world, no matter what the price difference. *—Rob Bowman*

Michael Parrish

Clavinet / American Trad Rock, Country Blues
The country blues unit the Michael Parrish Band comprised singer/guitarist/keyboardist Parrish, guitarists Chris Hansen and Jonny Sheehan, bassist Joe Engravalle, and drummer Tommy Kaelin. A Bay Area native, Parrish travelled to Chicago to tenure as the pianist for blues vocalist B.B. Odum before, at the urging of producer and folklorist Tim Duffy, moving to North Carolina to contribute to a series of blues field recordings later released as Music Maker label's audiophile blues series.

After touring with the likes of Guitar Gabriel and Big Boy Henry, Parrish also appeared on seven tracks on the 1995 LP *A Living Past: The Music Maker Patron Sampler,* followed later that year by *Came So Far* and *Guitar Gabriel Vol. 1.* He and Duffy also teamed as a folk duo, the Puritans. After touring in support of *Automobility,* his 1995 debut solo effort (self-released on his Geographic Records label), Parrish returned to New York City, where he formed a band comprising former Other Half members Hansen and Engravalle, onetime Hatters drummer Kaelin, and occasional songwriter Sheehan; after issuing their 1997 disc *Beautiful Rocks,* the Michael Parrish Band played several dates on the HORDE tour. *—Jason Ankeny*

● **Beautiful Rocks** / 1997 / Geographic ♦♦♦
The Michael Parrish Band's debut, *Beautiful Rocks* minimizes the traditional blues flavor of Parrish's earlier work to adopt a rootsier, more rough-edged sensibility closer in spirit to the alternative country movement; tracks like "Bird Brain Daddy" and "Listen to This Jive" should also appeal to fans of Blues Traveler and other American trad rock acts. *—Jason Ankeny*

Christy's Big Secret / 1999 / Geographic ♦♦♦

Charley Patton

b. 1887, Edwards, MS, **d.** Apr. 28, 1934, Indianola, MS
Slide Guitar, Vocals, Leader, Guitar, Guitar (Acoustic) / Slide Guitar Blues, Prewar Gospel Blues, Prewar Blues, Delta Blues, Prewar Country Blues, Country Blues
If the Delta country blues has a convenient source point, it would probably be Charley Patton, its first great star. His hoarse, impassioned singing style, fluid guitar playing, and unrelenting beat made him the original King of the Delta Blues. Much more than your average itinerant musician, Patton was an acknowledged celebrity and a seminal influence on musicians throughout the Delta. Rather than bumming his way from town to town, Patton would be called up to play at plantation dances, juke joints, and the like. He'd pack them in like sardines everywhere he went, and the emotional sway he held over his audiences caused him to be tossed off of more than one plantation by the ownership, simply because workers would leave crops unattended to listen to him play any time he picked up a guitar. He epitomized the image of a '20s "sport" blues singer: rakish, raffish, easy to provoke, capable of downing massive quantities of food and liquor, a woman on each arm, with a flashy, expensive-looking guitar fitted with a strap and kept in a traveling case by his side, only to be opened up when there was money or good times involved. His records—especially his first and biggest hit, "Pony Blues"—could be heard on phonographs throughout the South. Although he was certainly not the first Delta bluesman to record, he quickly became one of the genre's most popular. By late-'20s Mississippi plantation standards, Charley Patton was a star, a genuine celebrity.

Although Patton was roughly five foot, five inches tall and only weighed a Spartan 135 pounds, his gravelly, high-energy singing style (even on ballads and gospel tunes it sounded this way) made him sound like a man twice his weight and half again his size. Sleepy John Estes claimed he was the loudest blues singer he ever heard and it was rumored that his voice was loud enough to carry outdoors at a dance up to 500 yards away without amplification. His vaudeville-style vocal asides—which on record give the effect of two people talking to each other—along with the sound of his whiskey- and cigarette-scarred voice would become major elements of the vocal style of one of his students, a young Howlin' Wolf. His guitar playing was no less impressive, fueled with a propulsive beat and a keen rhythmic sense that would later plant seeds in the boogie style of John Lee Hooker. Patton is generally regarded as one of the original architects of putting blues into a strong, syncopated rhythm, and his strident tone was achieved by tuning his guitar up a step and a half above standard pitch instead of using a capo. His compositional skills on the instrument are illustrated by his penchant for finding and utilizing several different themes as background accompaniment in a single song. His slide work—either played in his lap like a Hawaiian guitar and fretted with a pocket knife, or in the more conventional manner with a brass pipe for a bottleneck—was no less inspiring, finishing vocal phrases for him and influencing contemporaries like Son House and up-and-coming youngsters like Robert Johnson. He also popped his bass strings (a technique he developed some 40 years before funk bass players started doing the same thing), beat his guitar like a drum, and stomped his feet to reinforce certain beats or to create counter rhythms, all of which can be heard on various recordings. Rhythm and excitement were the bywords of his style.

The second, and equally important, part of Patton's legacy handed down to succeeding blues generations was his propensity for entertaining. One of the reasons for Charley Patton's enormous popularity in the South stems from his being a consummate barrelhouse entertainer. Most of the now-common guitar gymnastics modern audiences have come to associate with the likes of a Jimi Hendrix, in fact, originated with Patton. His ability to "entertain the peoples" and rock the house with a hell-raising ferociousness left an indelible impression on audiences and fellow bluesmen alike. His music embraced everything from blues, ballads, ragtime, to gospel. And so keen were Patton's abilities in setting mood and ambience, that he could bring a barrelhouse frolic to a complete stop by launching into an impromptu performance of nothing but religious-themed selections and still manage to hold his audience spellbound. Because he possessed the heart of a bluesman with the mindset of a vaudeville performer, hearing Patton for the first time can be a bit overwhelming; it's a lot to take in as the music, and performances can careen from emotionally intense to buffoonishly comic, sometimes within a single selection. It is all strongly rooted in '20s black dance music and even on the religious tunes in his repertoire, Patton fuels it all with a strong rhythmic pulse.

He first recorded in 1929 for the Paramount label and, within a year's time, he was not only the largest-selling blues artist but—in a whirlwind of recording activity—also the music's most prolific. Patton was also responsible for hooking up fellow players Willie Brown and Son House with their first chances to record. It is probably best to issue a blanket audio disclaimer of some kind when listening to Patton's total recorded legacy, some 60-odd tracks total, his final session done only a couple of months before his death in 1934. No one will never know what Patton's Paramount masters really sounded like. When the company went out of business, the metal masters were sold off as scrap, some of it used to line chicken coops. All that's left are the original 78s—rumored to have been made out of inferior pressing material commonly used to make bowling balls—and all of them are scratched and heavily played, making all attempts at sound retrieval by current noise-reduction processing a tall order indeed. That said, it is still music well worth seeking out and not just for its place in history. Patton's music gives us the first flowering of the Delta blues form, before it became homogenized with turnarounds and 12-bar restrictions, and few humans went at it so aggressively. *—Cub Koda*

★ **Founder of the Delta Blues** / 1969 / Yazoo ✦✦✦✦
A cornerstone of any blues collection, this is where you start. As compilations go, this originally started life as a double record set featuring all of Patton's best-known titles and sound wise was miles above all previous versions. Its compact disc incarnation here trims the tune list to 24 tracks, but all the seminal tracks are here: "Pony Blues," "High Water Everywhere," "Screamin' and Hollerin' the Blues," "A Spoonful Blues," "Shake It and Break It," and the wistful "Poor Me," recorded at his final session in 1934, a scant two months before he died. *—Cub Koda*

Complete Recorded Works, Vols. 1-3 / 1990 / Document ✦✦✦✦✦
This is a 61-track, three-CD set that encompasses a complete chronological run of Patton's recorded output. All of his solo sides are here, his duets with Bertha Lee and Henry Sims and his backup work behind both of them. All previous incarnations of this material don't sound near as good as they do on these three volumes, all of them given the full deluxe Cedarization noise reduction treatment from the Document folks. This is as nice as this stuff's probably ever gonna sound, thus justifying the usual hefty import price. *—Cub Koda*

☆ **King of the Delta Blues** / 1991 / Yazoo ✦✦✦✦
This excellent companion volume to *Founder of the Delta Blues* pulls together 23 more Patton tracks (including some alternate takes that were for years thought to be lost) to give a much more complete look at this amazing artist. It's interesting here to compare the tracks from his final session to his halcyon output from 1929. Highlights include "Mean Black Cat Blues," Patton's adaption of "Sitting on Top of the World" ("Some Summer Day") and both parts of "Prayer of Death," originally issued under the *nom de plume* of "Elder J.J. Hadley." The sound on this collection is vastly superior, from a noise-reduction standpoint, to its companion volume. *—Cub Koda*

Pony Blues: His 23 Greatest Songs / Feb. 9, 1999 / Wolf ✦✦✦✦
You could make a valid case that anything recorded by Charley Patton is seminal to the history of blues. These, however, are the secular pieces (in his final 1934 session he also recorded some religious titles) on which his reputation stands, and upon listening it's easy to understand why. He sang and played with total conviction, and so much of his repertoire has become standard over the years. Listen to "Pony Blues," for example, from his first session in 1929, and you can not only hear his haunting voice, but some superb guitar work, utterly individual and far ahead of anything else that was being recorded at the time. This was the real blues, earthy, rich, and resonant of the South (Patton's experiences around Dockery's Plantation), performed with a power no one else could equal until Robert Johnson. That first session, which yielded 14 sides, was perhaps his best, and eight of the titles here are drawn from it, including "Peavine Blues," which has become a Delta blues classic. But maybe the high point came from his second session in late 1929 and "High Water Everywhere," Patton's song about the 1927 Mississippi floods that decimated the Delta region. It's a masterpiece of tension and storytelling that says as much now as when it was originally recorded. The last five titles on the disc come from the final session Patton recorded in New York in 1934. He was ailing by then, soon to die, and the difference five years made is easy to tell. He sounds tired and weary of the world. But that didn't stop him from performing a classic "High Sheriff Blues," another indispensable piece of Patton blues. Even if the blues didn't start with Patton, he was certainly one of the first truly great recorded blues singer/guitarists—and the finest from the early days of the Delta blues. The sound quality might not be perfect, by any means, but the music stands. As an introduction to Charley Patton, this is unbeatable. *—Chris Nickson*

The Definitive Charley Patton / Mar. 13, 2001 / Catfish ✦✦✦✦✦
The digital remastering on this compilation is just as superior to any previous attempts to transcribe Patton's marginally recorded and preserved legacy as that of the Document discs. And as it is only slightly less thorough—the Document discs include extra takes on "Elder Green Blues," "Hammer Blues," and "Some of these Days I'll Be Gone"—this compilation seems the likely choice for anyone with an interest in prewar Delta blues. Both affordable and handsomely packaged, the three-disc box includes extensive liner notes written by blues historians Keith Briggs and Alex Van Der Tuuk, with reminiscences by Patton crony Son House. *—Travis Drageset*

☆ **Screamin' and Hollerin' the Blues: The Worlds of Charley Patton** / Oct. 23, 2001 / Revenant ✦✦✦✦
Perhaps the most sumptuous, nay incredible, box set package ever devised for a blues artist, this lavish production contains seven CDs that not only contain everything Patton recorded as a soloist, but a ton of peripheral tracks to which he contributed or was associated. Yes, this has all 54 known extant Patton performances (including four unissued alternate takes), but that is, quite literally, not the half of it. There are also cuts recorded by other acts at Patton's sessions, including Walter Hawkins, Edith North Johnson, Henry Sims, Willie Brown, Son House, Louise Johnson, the gospel quartet the Delta Big Four, and Bertha Lee. Some of these he played on; some of them he *might* have played on; and some of them he didn't play on, though he knew (or might have known, anyway) the musicians. There are even a couple of test recordings of Paramount talent scout H.C. Speir reading headlines, which takes even this sort of fanaticism to the extreme, but why not the whole nine yards, right? Then there's an entire disc of tracks by other blues artists, spanning 1924 to 1957 (though mostly weighted toward the early years of that period), spotlighting songs that were related to Patton's repertoire, or inspired in some way by songs in his discography. That CD includes some pretty big names, like Ma Rainey, Furry Lewis, Tommy Johnson, Howlin' Wolf, Son House, Joe Williams, and even the Staple Singers, though room's also made for unknowns, including one "Blues" by Unidentified Convict. And *then* there's an entire disc of interviews about Patton with Howlin' Wolf, Rev. Booker Miller, H.C. Speir, and Pops Staples; the Rev. Booker Miller portion is more entertaining than most such spoken recordings, as he occasionally plays some guitar himself to illustrate points. Patton's own tracks are consistently inspired Delta blues, though the sound quality inevitably varies widely, sometimes coming through quite clearly, at other times fighting a wall of static.

One's interest in the non-Patton selections, other than those on the solid CD of Patton-related tunes and Patton-inspired performers, might vary. Certainly the Son House 1930 recordings (including "Preachin' the Blues") are classic Delta blues songs in any setting, as are the far more obscure ones by Willie Brown. However, others, such as the ones by Edith North Johnson and the Delta Big Four, bear vaudevillian jazz and gospel influences that Delta blues fans might not take a shine to. The non-Patton tracks, too, sometimes suffer from unavoidably poor sound quality due to the extremely rough shape of the only surviving original copies. On top of all this, the packaging is extraordinary by any measure, and would take a lengthy review in itself to even cursorily summarize. Suffice it to say that if you're a serious Patton fan (and it's hard to imagine you'll get this if you're not), you're in for several hours of entertainment even when the CDs aren't in the stereo. The set is packaged like a vintage, full-sized photo album, in the manner "albums" of discs were assembled prior to the invention of the 33 1/3 RPM LP, with slots for each of the seven CDs. There are 128 pages of portfolio-sized liner notes, including essays on Patton and his records, transcriptions of all of the lyrics, stories behind most of the songs/tracks, a "thematic catalogue" of Patton's music, photos, reproductions of old advertisements for 78s, repros of the labels on the original 78s, even an interview with a noted bluesologist about collecting original releases from the artist. Thrown in is the complete 112-page book that John Fahey wrote about Patton in 1970 (an actual book, separate from the liner notes) as part of a series of monographs for Blues Paperbacks, and a reprint of the liner notes Bernard Klatzko wrote for the first Patton compilation, *The Immortal Charlie Patton.* Due to the expense and zealous completism of this release, most blues fans will be content to limit themselves to an intelligent single-CD compilation of Patton's work, such as Yazoo's *Founder of the Delta Blues.* If you have any serious hunger to go beyond that, though, and are wondering whether to splurge on this museum-quality piece—do it. It truly is the last word, and one of the most impressively packaged box sets in all of popular music. *—Richie Unterberger*

Odie Payne

b. Aug. 27, 1926, Chicago, IL, **d.** Mar. 1, 1989, Chicago, IL
Drums / Chicago Blues

Drummer Odie Payne was born in Chicago on August 27, 1926. Fascinated by music as a child, Payne listened to everything he could get his hands on—classical, pop, musicals, big band. Even as a teen he would sneak into clubs to watch and listen to what the drummers were doing. He studied music through high school and was drafted into the Army when his schoolwork fell off. After release from the military, Payne studied drums and graduated with high honors from the Roy C. Knapp School of Percussion. While playing with pianist Johnny Jones in 1949, Payne met Tampa Red and soon joined Red's band. They played and recorded together for several years. Payne states that he apprenticed himself to Red.

In 1952 Payne and pianist Johnny Jones became part of Elmore James' dance band the Broomdusters. Payne stayed with the band for three years, but recorded with James until 1959—recording some 31 singles. He became a highly sought-after studio musician and, in the later '50s, recorded on many essential recordings for the Cobra label, including artists like Otis Rush, Magic Sam, and Buddy Guy. Odie Payne developed the famous double-shuffle, later used by Fred Below and Sam Lay to great effect. Payne recorded for Chess including a number of classic Chuck Berry tunes like "Nadine" and "No Particular

Place to Go." He recorded with most of the great Chicago blues artists: Otis Rush, Sonny Boy Williamson, Muddy Waters, Jimmy Rogers, Eddie Taylor, Magic Sam, Yank Rachell, Sleepy John Estes, Little Brother Montgomery, Memphis Minnie, and many others.

Much watched and admired by other Chicago drummers, Payne was perhaps most famous for his trademark use of the cowbell, lightning-fast bass drum pedal, and extended cymbal and drum rolls. Odie Payne died March 1, 1989, in Chicago. Loved and respected by those who knew him, Payne served as a role model for many working musicians. *—Michael Erlewine*

Asie Payton

b. 1937, Washington County, Mississippi, **d.** May 19, 1997, Holly Ridge, Mississippi
Vocals, Guitar / Electric Country Blues, Electric Delta Blues
Though he was also a bluesman, most of Asie Payton's 60 years were spent as a farmer, driving a tractor on his land in Holly Ridge, MS. Living in a shotgun shack and working his fields took most of Payton's time, but he also wrote and performed blues originals, playing at places like the local grocery store, Junior Kimbrough's club, and Jimmy's Auto Care. Two of his club performances were recorded by Fat Possum records, with the intention of using them as demo tapes for a studio album. Payton's ties to his land were strong, however, and the label was unable to get him into the studio before he succumbed to a heart attack in 1997. Two years later, Fat Possum released the tapes as Payton's first and only album, *Worried*. *—Heather Phares*

● **Worried** / Jun. 15, 1999 / Fat Possum ♦♦♦♦
Asie Payton never released a record in his life, despite the best efforts of Fat Possum. The label spent nearly two years in the middle of the '90s trying to convince the Mississippi bluesman that he should record or gig outside of his home of Washington County. Eventually, the coaxed him into two recording sessions, one at their old studio, the other at Junior Kimbrough's club. This music was never released during Payton's lifetime, but it provides the basis for *Worried*, Fat Possum's posthumous 1999 release. For anybody who complains that modern electric blues sounds too clean and careful, *Worried* is the perfect antidote—this is gritty, dirty electric blues, sounding every bit as greasy as the classic recordings of the '50s and '60s. What's even more impressive is that the songs are rarely predictible blues standards—they're traditional songs (only "Can't Be Satisfied" and "Skinny Legs & All" are crossover favorites), given original, idiosyncratic arrangements by Payton. Usually, he's simply performing with drummer Sam Carr, but they're as raucous, loud and overpowering as a full band (as proven by the few tracks that are augmented by other musicians, which are no less chaotic than the stripped-back cuts). In an age when most blues albums sound canned, this is vibrant, exciting and real, reminiscent of the golden age of blues. And that's a pretty powerful last testament. *—Stephen Thomas Erlewine*

Just Do Me Right / Mar. 12, 2002 / Fat Possum ♦♦♦
This posthumous complement to Payton's only studio disc is something of a revelation. Not only does it confirm that he was a great blues and soul singer (just check out "Back to the Bridge," with its "In the Midnight Hour" riff, or the lazy groove of "I Got a Friend," with its percolating wah-wah guitar line), but it shows the man could play funk too—"1000 Years" roars out of the speakers straight to the dancefloor, powered by some unexpected horns, and "Need My Help" has all the power of a latter-day Hendrix song. All of that isn't to say he didn't play a lot of gutbucket acoustic blues, too; "Livin' in So Much Pain" is about as down-home as you can get. In many ways, there seemed to be no end to his passion for different styles of music. "Nobody But You" could almost have come out of the Stax studios circa 1965, while "Watch Yourself" is a barnburning R&B/early rock & roll track that kicks like a mule. While Payton's other album showed him to be a man of talent, this offers that talent to its full extent, drawn together from sessions recorded in studios and at the houses of friends. But instead of being a ragtag collection of odds and sods, the result is a soaring testimony to someone who was an unsung great in his lifetime. *—Chris Nickson*

Peg Leg Sam (Arthur Jackson)

b. Dec. 18, 1911, Jonesville, SC, **d.** Nov. 27, 1977, Jonesville, SC
Vocals, Harmonica / Prewar Country Blues, Country Blues, Vaudeville Blues
Peg Leg Sam was a performer to be treasured, a member of what may have been the last authentic traveling medicine show, a harmonica virtuoso, and an extraordinary entertainer. Born Arthur Jackson, he acquired his nickname after a hoboing accident in 1930.

His medicine show career began in 1938, and his repertoire—finally recorded only in the early '70s—reflected the rustic nature of the traveling show. "Peg" delivered comedy routines, bawdy toasts, and monologues; performed tricks with his harps (often playing two at once); and served up some juicy Piedmont blues (sometimes with a guitar accompanist, but most often by himself). Peg Leg Sam gave his last medicine-show performance in 1972 in North Carolina and was still in fine fettle when he started making the rounds of folk and blues festivals in his last years. *—Jim O'Neal*

● **Joshua** / 1975 / Tomato ♦♦♦♦♦
Originally released on the indie label Blue Labor in 1975, *Joshua* is the first record Peg Leg Sam ever recorded, and it certainly shows his roots as a medicine show performer. The music falls halfway between medicine show burlesque and straight country blues. Peg Leg Sam was a fine harmonica player and guitarist who captured the essence of the medicine show, even after that tradition had died. Louisiana Red, who accompanies Peg Leg on several tracks, doesn't quite get into the spirit and sounds uncomfortable with the material, which only shows that Sam was a master of a forgotten art. Nevertheless, to many blues fans, this music may sound more like a historical curiosity than a lost treasure. *—Thom Owens*

Peg Leg Sam With Louisiana Red / 1975 / Tomato ♦♦♦♦
Recorded shortly before his death, this album features Peg Leg Sam with Louisiana Red performing a set of old-timey, traditional blues—the kind of that was frequently heard at traveling medicine shows. Although it was recorded late in his career, the album captures the essence of Peg Leg Sam. *—Thom Owens*

Early in the Morning / May 21, 1996 / Blues Alliance ♦♦♦

Kickin' It / Oct. 10, 2000 / 32 Jazz ♦♦♦
Peg Leg Sam was not your typical country blues performer—he was in a class all his own. Born in 1911, he naturally embraced the country blues of his generation, while also maintaining the early medicine show roots he learned as a child. Sam's sometimes humorous and always impassioned monologues, combined with harp virtuosity (he sometimes played two of them at once), came from a life of dedicated showmanship built up after years of passing the hat for crowds of spectators. Since Sam was definitely underrecorded, he has gained status as one of those irreplaceable characters who fell through the cracks, making these sessions fortunate to have available. These tracks were originally released on the Trix label as *Medicine Show Man*, and are now available as *Kickin' It* on 32 Blues. Sam is accompanied separately on the disc by guitarists Baby Tate and Rufe Johnson, from two South Carolina sessions recorded in Spartanburg during 1970 and Jonesville two years later. *—Al Campbell*

Dan Penn (Daniel Pennington)

b. Nov. 16, 1941, Vernon, AL
Vocals / Americana, Roots Rock, Singer/Songwriter
Songwriter/producer Dan Penn has been a quiet force behind Southern soul music for over 30 years. Always moving just out of view of the limelight, Penn has produced and written hits for the Box Tops, Solomon Burke, Aretha Franklin and Ronnie Milsap, among others.

Originally from Vernon, Alabama, Penn began his career as a performer, leading several white R&B bands around the Muscle Shoals area. Achieving early success by selling a hit song to Conway Twitty ("Is a Bluebird Blue?"), the songwriter eventually moved to Memphis, joining producer Chips Moman at his American Studios. Together the two, along with Penn's writing partner, organist Spooner Oldham, wrote and/or produced several hits for the Box Tops, such as "The Letter" and "Cry Like a Baby," throughout the late '60s.

Penn eventually returned to Muscle Shoals during the period when Atlantic Records vice president Jerry Wexler was bringing acts like Aretha Franklin and Solomon Burke down from New York to record there. This led to Franklin cutting the Penn/Oldham composition "Do Right Woman," and for the next several years, Penn compositions such as "Dark End of the Street," "Woman Left Lonely," and "I'm Your Puppet" became soul classics and were recorded by such greats as James Carr, Janis Joplin, and Dionne Warwick, respectively.

Never really considered a performer, in 1994 Penn released the long-awaited follow-up to his 1973 solo album *Nobody's Fool*. This album contains Penn performances of songs that others are known for such as "I'm Your Puppet," as well as new material. *Moments from This Theater* followed in 1999. *—Steve Kurutz*

Nobody's Fool / 1973 / Bell ♦♦♦♦
Dan Penn has written many great soul songs—the problem is, he didn't keep any for this album. It's fine, as far as it goes, but it just doesn't go far enough, as you can tell when a cover of John Fogerty's "Lodi" becomes the most soulful thing here. To be fair, soul and country are cousins under the skin, and Penn does have his country touches, but the countrypolitan "I Hate You"—which sounds like Charlie Rich with a bad case of middle-of-the-roaditis—is just over the top, maudlin sentimentality. "Prayer for Peace" fares a little better, but in comparison to his classic compositions, it's hippie-dippy drivel that never gets to the core of emotions, the way Penn can at his very best (and the overblown backing vocals don't help either). And the spoken-word closer, "Skin," with its string accompaniment, is the kind of thing to make any soul fan cringe in sheer embarrassment. Even at its best, on the Philly-style "Raining in Memphis," this sounds geared more for the nightclub (or a Paul McCartney album outtake) than the gritty dancefloor. Not the man at the peak of his form. *Nobody's Fool* was reissued on CD by Repertoire in 1996. *—Chris Nickson*

● **Do Right Man** / 1994 / Warner Brothers ♦♦♦♦♦
If James Brown is Soul Brother Number One, you can make a very credible case for Dan Penn being number two. The Alabama native has had a hand in writing a fair number of classic soul songs, and here he commits his versions of them to tape for the first time, recording, of course, in Muscle Shoals, with their fabulous house band, and a horn section including former Memphis Horn member Wayne Jackson. It's a tall order Penn sets himself, offering himself up for comparison with greats like James Carr, Aretha Franklin, and James and Bobby Purify, who have sung his songs—and that's just the start of the list. However, he comes out very well, beginning with a quiet take on "The Dark End of the Street," coming across like a note to a secret lover, rather than a cry of pain. "It Tears Me Up" conveys the anguish, "You Left the Water Running" bounces in its pain, and "Do Right Woman, Do Right Man" is advice to a friend, instead of Aretha's extra freedom cry for equal rights. "I'm Your Puppet" becomes a sigh of resignation. Given tracks like that, the other songs will inevitably suffer by comparison, and, to be fair, "Memphis Women and Chicken" is little more than a throwaway. But even the lesser-known material from a craftsman-like Penn is head and shoulders above most of the competition, and "Zero Willpower," a song that he took 20 years to complete, has soul classic written all over it, as good as the greatest hits. Penn can't just write 'em, he can perform 'em too, in a manner as soulful as the greats, as this record shows. The man deserves to be an American musical icon. *—Chris Nickson*

Moments from This Theater / Sep. 14, 1999 / Proper ♦♦♦♦♦
After starting out in Muscle Shoals Alabama and then moving on to Memphis to work with Chips Moman at American Studios, Dan Penn proceeded to co-write and produce several '60s soul hits for artists like Solomon Burke, Aretha Franklin, James Carr, and

blue-eyed soul band the Box Tops. Some of the classics Penn and Memphis/Muscle Shoals' studio veteran Spooner Oldham wrote include "Cry Like a Baby," "Sweet Inspiration," "Do Right Woman, Do Right Man," "The Dark End of the Street," and "I'm Your Puppet." These and several other of their tunes are featured on *Moments from This Theater*, a collection of live duets taken from 1998 dates in Dublin, London, and South Petherton, Somerset. With Oldham laying down a tasty soul base on the Wurlitzer piano and Penn strumming easeful guitar chords and singing in his sweetly powerful way, the duo glide through 14 gospel-inflected, country-soul gems, eloquently touching on Southern living, loneliness, and the joys and trials of love. There's also a good dose of humor here in songs like "Lonely Women Make Good Lovers" and "Memphis Women and Chicken." An intimate and inspiring recording by two of the unsung giants of Southern soul. —*Stephen Cook*

Pinetop Perkins (Joe Willie Perkins)

b. Jul. 13, 1913, Belzoni, MS
Vocals, Piano, Guitar / Boogie-Woogie, Piano Blues, Chicago Blues
He admittedly wasn't the originator of the seminal piano piece "Pinetop's Boogie Woogie," but it's a safe bet that more people associate it nowadays with Pinetop Perkins than with the man who devised it in the first place, Clarence "Pinetop" Smith. Although it seems as though he's been around Chicago forever, the Mississippi native actually got a relatively late start on his path to Windy City immortality. It was only when Muddy Waters took him on to replace Otis Spann in 1969 that Perkins' rolling mastery of the ivories began to assume outsized proportions.

Perkins began his blues existence primarily as a guitarist, but a mid-'40s encounter with an outraged chorus girl toting a knife at a Helena, AR, nightspot left him with severed tendons in his left arm. That dashed his guitar aspirations, but Joe Willie Perkins came back strong from the injury, concentrating solely on piano from that point on. Perkins had traveled to Helena with Robert Nighthawk in 1943, playing with the elegant slide guitarist on Nighthawk's KFFA radio program. Perkins soon switched over to rival Sonny Boy Williamson's beloved *King Biscuit Time* radio show in Helena, where he remained for an extended period. Perkins accompanied Nighthawk on a 1950 session for the Chess brothers that produced "Jackson Town Gal," but Chicago couldn't hold him at the time.

Nighthawk disciple Earl Hooker recruited Perkins during the early '50s. They hit the road, pausing at Sam Phillips' studios in Memphis long enough for Perkins to wax his first version of "Pinetop's Boogie Woogie" in 1953. He settled in downstate Illinois for a spell, then relocated to Chicago. Music gradually was relegated to the back burner until Hooker coaxed him into working on an LP for Arhoolie in 1968. When Spann split from Muddy Waters, the stage was set for Pinetop Perkins' reemergence.

After more than a decade with the Man, Perkins and his bandmates left en masse to form the Legendary Blues Band. Their early Rounder albums (*Life of Ease, Red Hot 'n' Blue*) prominently spotlighted Perkins' rippling 88s and rich vocals. He had previously waxed an album for the French Black & Blue logo in 1976 and four fine cuts for Alligator's *Living Chicago Blues* anthologies in 1978. Finally, in 1988, he cut his first domestic album for Blind Pig, *After Hours*. Ever since then, Pinetop Perkins has made up for precious lost time in the studio. Discs for Antone's, Omega (*Portrait of a Delta Bluesman*, a solo outing that includes fascinating interview segments), Deluge, Earwig, and several other firms ensure that his boogie legacy won't be forgotten in the decades to come. —*Bill Dahl*

Boogie Woogie King / Nov. 1, 1976 / Evidence ◆◆◆

Although he did not have an album issued under his name as a leader until 1988, pianist Pinetop Perkins actually should have had one released in 1976, when he cut the eight tracks on this recently reissued Evidence CD for the Black and Blue label. They did not appear until 1992, which is a shame. Perkins' trademark boogie-woogie riffs, rumbling rhythms, left-hand lines, and spinning phrases were in fine form. His accompaniment and supporting phrases behind guitarist/vocalist Luther "Guitar Junior" Johnson are equally tasty and inviting. Johnson, as erratic a performer as any in contemporary blues, came ready to play and sing on this date. His vocals had plenty of grit, conviction, and energy, while his playing had no excesses and was delivered with zip and flair. —*Ron Wynn*

● **After Hours / 1988 / Blind Pig ◆◆◆◆◆**

Easy-grooving blues and boogie is backed by the competent New York City-based blues band Little Mike and the Tornadoes. Though Perkins followed Otis Spann as the piano player in Muddy Waters' band, these are the first domestically available recordings under his own name. —*Niles J. Frantz*

Pinetop's Boogie Woogie / 1992 / Discovery ◆◆◆◆

The maze of new and recent discs by this veteran Chicago piano man can be daunting, but rest assured that this is one of his best to date. Many of the songs are Perkins standbys—"Kidney Stew," "Caldonia," and of course, "Pinetop's Boogie Woogie"—but the backing here is so stellar (sidemen include harpists James Cotton and Kim Wilson, guitarists Matt "Guitar" Murphy, Jimmy Rogers, Hubert Sumlin, and Duke Robillard, and several driving rhythm sections)—that the project rises above most of Perkins' output. —*Bill Dahl*

On Top / Jan. 1992 / Deluge ◆◆◆

Solid entry in Perkins' ever-growing discography of contemporary CDs. —*Bill Dahl*

Portrait of a Delta Bluesman / 1993 / Vanguard ◆◆◆◆◆

Considerably more ambitious than just another Perkins set, this solo disc intersperses key songs from his storied history with interview segments that reveal much about the man himself, from his Delta beginnings to when he replaced Otis Spann in Muddy Waters' vaunted band. —*Bill Dahl*

With the Blue Ice Band / 1995 / Earwig ◆◆

The pianist is as charming and effervescent as ever on this live/studio outing—but he's often undermined by the presence of mediocre harpist Chicago Beau and an Icelandic

band that doesn't know the meaning of the words subtlety or taste. Rock-drenched guitar solos fly with abandon, destroying any semblance of Chicago-style ambience. —*Bill Dahl*

Live Top / 1995 / Deluge ◆◆◆

A very competent combo offers incendiary support behind the veteran Chicago pianist throughout the album, recorded live before an appreciative gathering. —*Bill Dahl*

Born in the Delta / May 27, 1997 / Telarc ◆◆◆

Pinetop Perkins was 83 when he recorded *Born in the Delta* in 1996. As a singer, Perkins still had plenty of soul and spirit and got his points across convincingly. And as a pianist, he still had sizable chops. In terms of material, Perkins tends to favor blues standards that have been done to death, including Jimmy Reed's "Baby, What You Want Me to Do?," Peter Chatman's "Everyday I Have the Blues," Leroy Carr's "How Long, How Long Blues," and Paul Gayton's "For You My Love." One could nitpick about the onetime Muddy Waters sideman so often choosing the obvious, but given how much fun he's clearly having at this session, it's hard to complain. Thankfully, Perkins gives himself sufficient solo space, and he has competent support in harmonica player Jerry Portnoy and electric guitarist Tony O. —*Alex Henderson*

Down in Mississippi / Jan. 13, 1998 / HMG ◆◆◆

Despite the romantic title, these are private recordings done in Pinetop's home in Chicago in 1996 and 1997. This album finds him in an unaccompanied solo setting, with the first six selections featuring him manning an electric piano while the other seven tracks put him behind a conventional acoustic model. Lots of boogies and shuffles here for Perkins to stretch out on, and he pays tribute to many of his early inspirations, like Sunnyland Slim, Leroy Carr, Eddie Boyd, and others. Highlights include "Kidney Stew," "Pinetop's Boogie Woogie," "Song for Sunnyland Slim," "Five Long Years," and the title track. If you want to hear a boogie-woogie master unencumbered by surrounding instruments in the band and laying it down with élan and pizzazz, this disc fills the bill nicely. —*Cub Koda*

Legends / Oct. 27, 1998 / Telarc ◆◆

A session that Pinetop Perkins co-led with one-time Howlin' Wolf sideman Hubert Sumlin, *Legends* should have been outstanding but is merely average. Singer/pianist Perkins (who was 84 when *Legends* was recorded in May 1998) and singer/guitarist Hubert Sumlin both had strong Chicago blues credentials going way back, and one greets *Legends* with very high expectations. But while *Legends* isn't a bad album, the sparks don't fly the way they should have. Embracing familiar electric blues classics like Willie Dixon's "I'm Your Hoochie Coochie Man," Jimmy Reed's "Shame, Shame, Shame," and B.B. King's "Rock Me, Baby," Perkins and Sumlin simmer without ever really igniting. And their accompaniment (which includes guitarist Doug Wainoris, harmonica player Annie Raines, bassist Rod Carey, and drummer Per Hanson) doesn't go that extra mile either. The CD sinks to its lowest point when Wainoris and Raines sing lead on Clarence "Gatemouth" Brown's "She Walks Right In"—while Wainoris is a competent singer, Raines has a terrible voice and makes listeners painfully aware of the fact that she should stick to harmonica playing. For the most part, however, *Legends* isn't disastrous—just mildly disappointing. This is a CD that only completists will want. —*Alex Henderson*

Live at 85 / Oct. 19, 1999 / Shanachie ◆◆◆

Back on Top / May 23, 2000 / Telarc ◆◆◆◆

Live at Antone's, Vol. 1 / Aug. 22, 2000 / Antone's ◆◆◆

Pinetop Perkins spent the bulk of his career playing in bands, and this 1995 live set, recorded at the 20th anniversary of Antone's in Austin, TX, the month he turned 82, is very much a band album. Perkins sings in a creaky, breathy voice and plays piano in his trademark barrelhouse style, but his accompaniment, consisting of regular bassist Calvin Jones and drummer Willie Smith, plus guests Kim Wilson on harmonica, Rusty Zinn on guitar, and Mark "Kaz" Kazanoff on tenor sax, makes the show a group effort in which the nominal sidemen get extensive solo time. Wilson especially makes his presence felt with long improvisations, though Kazanoff and Zinn are also heard from frequently. Perkins gets his share of playing time, too, particularly on the slow blues "I Almost Lost My Mind" and Jimmy Smith's "Chicken Shack," but anyone looking for a Perkins piano album should look elsewhere. On the other hand, if you want to hear a hot, Chicago-style blues band playing Muddy Waters favorites like "Got My Mojo Working" and "Hoochie Coochie Man," songs Perkins had occasion to familiarize himself with as a member of Waters' band, this excellent live album will fill the bill. —*William Ruhlmann*

Pinetop Is Just Top / Jun. 4, 2002 / Black & Blue ◆◆◆

Roy Perkins (Ernie Suarez)

b. 1932, Lafayette, LA
Piano / Swamp Pop, New Orleans R&B, Rock & Roll
Louisiana pianist Roy Perkins made some minor singles on small regional labels in the late '50s and early '60s that were very much in the style of the era's New Orleans rock & roll and R&B. Perkins was not actually from New Orleans, but from Lafayette in Cajun country some ways to the west, and his recordings sometimes had a touch of swamp pop as well. Perkins also was involved in some recordings by Bobby Page, Scatmin Patin, and Harry Simoneaux, musicians with whom he played in the Riff Raffs.

Perkins was born Ernie Suarez, and began playing R&B as a teenager in high school in the early '50s, when there were still very few White musicians playing the music. His name was changed to Roy Perkins by Mel Mallory of Mel-A-Dee Records, which released a single by Perkins and his band, "You're on My Mind." It was a number one hit in Lafayette and did well in New Orleans, and was covered by swamp pop singer Rod Bernard in 1959.

In the late '50s Perkins moved to the Ram label, which operated out of Shreveport, LA, and his "Drop Top" was leased by Mercury, but went nowhere. He moved from piano to bass in the Riff Raffs. He did another single for Dart, and continued to play with the Riff

Raffs until they broke up in 1962. Perkins wrote much of his material and was an amiable enough practitioner of New Orleans-styled rock, but frankly just a so-so talent whose compositions sounded sincere but formulaic. He never was a full-time musician; unlike a lot of fellows with his assets, he *did* keep his day job. But he did a few more singles after the Riff Raffs split, as well as an album, and played with swamp pop singer Johnnie Allan. He did a lot of unreleased tracks for Ram, and by combining a couple of his singles with that vault material and sessions he did with Scatman Patin, Bobby Page, and Harry Simoneaux, Ace was able to issue a 25-track retrospective of his work in the late '50s and early '60s. —*Richie Unterberger*

● **Roy "Boogie Boy" Perkins** / Apr. 16, 1996 / Ace ✦✦✦✦✦
It takes a bit of doing to make a 25-track Roy Perkins compilation, as he only recorded a few singles in the time frame this anthology covers (late '50s-early '60s). But Ace manages to do so with its characteristic archival diligence, fishing out a number of unreleased performances from the Ram vaults, and adding singles and sessions he did with Bobby Page, Scatman Patin, and Harry Simoneaux. Frankly, this is one of those situations where you wonder whether all that effort was justified. Perkins was just another Louisiana rock musician, playing and writing fair but derivative music that sounded like clock-eaters from New Orleans late-'50s rock sessions (although this was not done in New Orleans). Even if you only compare Perkins to fellow white Louisiana rockers, he's a long ways behind Frankie Ford and Bobby Charles. His boogie-triplet piano style is good, though not great, and his songs often in the good-natured Fats Domino mold, though the single "Drop Top" is more uptempo, with a "Bony Maronie"-like riff. On real slowies he gets closer to swamp popdom; "Am I the One" is a little like a swamp pop Ritchie Valens. Most of the material, apparently, comes from the Ram vaults whether it was released or unreleased at the time (the liner notes are not totally specific on details), but this does have his 1959 Dart single "True Love"/"Sweet Lilly." It does not, however, contain his regional hit "You're on My Mind," which was recorded for Mel-A-Dee. —*Richie Unterberger*

Bill Perry

b. Chester, NY

Vocals, Guitar / Contemporary Blues, Modern Electric Blues

Although guitarist, songwriter and singer Bill Perry may seem like a newcomer to the blues scene to some, he's actually put in a long apprenticeship with folk-rock singer Richie Havens. Perry was Havens' main guitarist for shows he performed with a band through the '80s.

Signed in 1995 to an unprecedented five-album deal with the Pointblank/Virgin label, Perry's a sharp songwriter, an adequate singer and a fiery guitar player. Perry's style could best be characterized as hard-driving blues for the '90s. Perry's song, "Fade to Blue" is covered by Havens on his recent album, *Cuts to the Chase*.

Perry was born in the upstate town of Chester, NY, and grew up in a music-filled household. His grandmother played organ in the church, but a young Perry was attracted to his father's Jimmy Smith albums, which featured guitarist Kenny Burrell. Perry began playing guitar at age six and played in his first talent show at 13. By high school, he led bands as vocalist and lead guitarist before graduation. After graduating, he lived in California and Colorado, all the while honing his distinctive guitar playing. He moved back to upstate New York and accompanied Havens on most of his shows with a band through the '80s. Perry toured with the Band's Garth Hudson and Levon Helm at the same time he was working with Havens, and all that traveling spurred him on to form his own band, and he did in the early '90s. He released his first album for Pointblank, *Love Scars* in 1996. He followed it up with the more polished *Greycourtlightning* in 1998. Neither album did much box office and Perry was let go by Pointblank. His next release was 1999's live album, *High Octane*, recorded at New York nightclub Manny's Car Wash. Perry then hooked up with indie blues label Blind Pig and issued *Fire It Up* in 2001. The album featured Conan O'Brien's bandleader Jimmy Vivino and offers proof of Bill Perry's still vital talent. —*Richard Skelly*

● **Love Scars** / Feb. 6, 1996 / Pointblank ✦✦✦✦✦
Love Scars is an impressive debut from Bill Perry, a singer-songwriter that fuses '70s folk with blues. Perry occasionally can sound too earnest—which could be expected from a former supporting musician for Richie Havens—but there's genuine skill and craft in his songs. His lyrics are strong and melodies are sturdy, and they're delivered with conviction, which makes up for the occasional awkward moments that should be expected from a debut record. Still, those little missteps are nowhere near enough to prevent *Love Scars* from being a promising debut. —*Thom Owens*

Greycourtlightning / Mar. 31, 1998 / Virgin ✦✦✦✦
On his second album, *Greycourtlightning*, Bill Perry stakes out new territory by delivering a tight, focused effort where the songs are fleshed out by other instruments as much as his guitar. Perry's songs follow blues conventions, but twist them slightly, making them sound fresh and exciting. Furthermore, his playing is filled with unexpected turns, as he throws in jazz, folk and rock flourishes to his blistering solos. With its selection of great songs and great playing, *Greycourtlightning* proves that Perry's debut, *Love Scars*, was no fluke. —*Thom Owens*

High Octane / 1999 / Car Wash ✦✦✦
This independent release captures Bill Perry live at one of New York's most authentic blues venues, Manny's Car Wash. His band is rocking and raw, pounding out five Perry originals, Elmore James' "Dust My Broom," Jane Feather's "How Blue Can You Get," and a Bo Diddley-style version of "Johnny B. Goode." One hears Jimi Hendrix's influence not only in Perry's high-octane guitar playing, but also in the inclusion of "All Along the Watchtower" and "Little Wing." Perry's voice and songs are very much in the classic blues-rock mold of the Allman Brothers and Stevie Ray Vaughan. There's even a hint here and there of early AC/DC. Nothing terribly original—just rock-solid electric blues in a whiskey-soaked live setting. —*David R. Adler*

Fire It Up / May 22, 2001 / Blind Pig ✦✦✦
Like Blind Pig labelmate Jimmy Thackery, New Yorker Bill Perry churns out a rugged blend of electric blues-rock and the occasional ballad, infused with authority, class, and dogged dedication to his craft. While he's not breaking any stylistic barriers, Perry and his band—led by *the Conan O'Brien Show*'s music director Jimmy Vivino (who also coproduced)—grind out a satisfying set of rough originals with a few obscure covers. As an adequate representation of his style, neither the songs nor Perry's gruffly serviceable vocals on his third studio album will shoot him into the blues-rock stratosphere. But *Fire It Up* is the souvenir you'll take home after experiencing his notoriously electrifying live act. This band, featuring legendary Johnny Winter/Son Seals/Albert Collins bassist Johnny B. Gayden, is a no-frills outfit that leaves plenty of room for Perry's muscular yet remarkably compact leads. The album's John Lee Hooker-styled opening boogie, "Itchin' for It," and the swampy following tune, "Clean Thing," are indicative of Perry's workmanlike approach. The album's closing solo acoustic slide on "Cheatin' Blues" shows he's been inspired by Johnny Winter's "Dallas," and is a vital indication of his talents. Perry displays his Freddie King side on the hyperactive double-time instrumental "G & L Jump." While *Fire It Up* likely won't end up as a blues-rock fan's most treasured possession, it's a sturdy, tough, unfussy work that offers proof of Bill Perry's guitar abilities without resorting to extraneous flourishes or frivolous grandstanding. —*Hal Horowitz*

James Peterson

b. Nov. 4, 1937, Russell County, AL

Vocals, Guitar / Modern Electric Blues, Soul-Blues

Florida-based guitarist, singer and songwriter James Peterson plays a gritty style of southern-fried blues that is at times reminiscent of Howlin' Wolf and other times more along the lines of Freddie King. He formed his first band while he was living in Buffalo, NY, and running Governor's Inn, House of Blues in the '60s. He and his band would backup the traveling musicians who came through, including blues legends like Muddy Waters, Howlin' Wolf, Big Joe Turner, Freddie King, Lowell Fulson, and Koko Taylor.

Peterson was born November 4, 1937, in Russell County, Alabama. Peterson was strongly influenced by gospel music in the rural area he grew up in, and he began singing in church as a child. Thanks to his father's jukejoint, he was exposed to blues at an early age, and later followed in his footsteps in upstate New York. After leaving home at age 14, he headed to Gary, IN, where he sang with his friend John Scott. While still a teen, he began playing guitar, entirely self-taught. Peterson cites musicians like Muddy Waters, Howlin' Wolf, Jimmy Reed, and B.B. King as his early role models. After moving to Buffalo, N.Y. in 1955, he continued playing with various area blues bands, and ten years later, he opened his own blues club.

In 1970, Peterson recorded his first album, *The Father, Son and the Blues* on the Perception/Today label. While he ran his blues club at night, he supplemented his income by running a used-car lot during the day. Peterson's debut album was produced and co-written with Willie Dixon, and it featured a then-five-year-old Lucky Peterson on keyboards. Peterson followed it up with *Tryin' to Keep the Blues Alive* a few years later. Peterson's other albums include *Rough and Ready* and *Too Many Knots* for the Kingsnake and Ichiban labels in 1988 and 1991, respectively.

The album that's put Peterson back on the road as a national touring act is his 1995 release, *Don't Let the Devil Ride* for the Jackson, Mississippi-based Waldoxy Records. A master showman who has learned from the best and knows how to work an audience, he's also a crafty songwriter endowed with a deep, gospel-drenched singing style. —*Richard Skelly*

● **Rough and Ready** / 1988 / Kingsnake ✦✦✦✦✦
A pleasant album of original compositions by this Alabama-born bluesman, it features James' son Lucky Peterson (Alligator recording artist) on guitar and keyboards. Reissued on CD by Ichiban in 1990. —*Niles J. Frantz*

Too Many Knots / 1991 / Ichiban ✦✦✦

Don't Let the Devil Ride / Mar. 21, 1995 / Waldoxy ✦✦✦

Preachin' the Blues / 1996 / Waldoxy ✦✦✦

Lucky Peterson

b. Dec. 13, 1964, Buffalo, NY

Vocals, Organ (Hammond), Drums, Piano, Guitar, Bass, Organ / Modern Electric Blues, Soul-Blues

Child-prodigy status is sometimes difficult to overcome upon reaching maturity. Not so for Lucky Peterson—he's far bigger (in more ways than one) on the contemporary blues circuit than he was at the precocious age of six, when he scored a national R&B hit with the Willie Dixon-produced "1-2-3-4."

Little Lucky Peterson was lucky to be born into a musical family. His dad, James Peterson, owned the Governor's Inn, a popular Buffalo, NY, blues nightclub that booked the biggies: Jimmy Reed, Muddy Waters, Bill Doggett. The latter's mighty Hammond B-3 organ fascinated the four-and-a-half-year-old lad, and soon Peterson was on his way under Dixon's tutelage. "1-2-3-4" got Peterson on *The Tonight Show* and *The Ed Sullivan Show*, but he didn't rest on his laurels—he was doubling on guitar at age eight, and at 17, he signed on as Little Milton's keyboardist for three years.

A three-year stint with Bobby "Blue" Bland preceded Peterson's solo career launch, which took off when he struck up a musical relationship with Florida-based producer Bob Greenlee. Two Greenlee-produced albums for Alligator, 1989's *Lucky Strikes!* and the following year's *Triple Play*, remain his finest recorded offerings. Extensive session work behind everyone from Etta James and Kenny Neal to Otis Rush also commenced during this period.

In 1992, Peterson's first Verve label album, *I'm Ready*, found him boldly mixing contemporary rock and soul into his simmering blues stew. More high-energy Verve sets followed, making it clear that Peterson's luck remains high (as does his father's, who's fashioned his own career as a bluesman with albums for Ichiban and Waldoxy). Lucky made his debut for new label Blue Thumb with a self-titled effort released in 1999. *Double Dealin'* followed in early 2001. —*Bill Dahl*

Ridin' / Mar. 1984 / Evidence ✦✦✦✦

As a child prodigy, keyboardist and organist Lucky Peterson's exploits were legendary. The stories grew even more widespread as he became a teen and stints with Little Milton and Bobby "Blue" Bland only added to his fame. But Peterson's records have not always justified or reaffirmed his reputation. That is not the case with the cuts on this 1984 set, recently reissued by Evidence. The spiraling solos, excellent bridges, turnbacks, pedal maneuvers, and soulful accompaniment are executed with a relaxed edge and confident precision. If you have wondered whether Lucky Peterson deserves the hype and major label bonanza, these songs are the real deal. —*Ron Wynn*

Lucky Strikes / 1989 / Alligator ✦✦✦✦

Peterson's real coming-out party as a mature blues triple threat: his guitar and keyboard skills are prodigious (though he's no longer a child prodigy), and his vocals on "Pounding of My Heart," "Can't Get No Loving on the Telephone," and "Heart Attack" (all written by producer/bassist Bob Greenlee) served notice that more than luck was involved in Peterson's adult rise to fame. —*Bill Dahl*

● **Triple Play** / 1990 / Alligator ✦✦✦✦

Even more impressive than his previous Alligator set, thanks to top-flight material like "Don't Cloud Up on Me," "Let the Chips Fall Where They May," and "Locked Out of Love," the fine house band at Greenlee's King Snake studios, and Peterson's own rapidly developing attack on two instruments. —*Bill Dahl*

I'm Ready / Aug. 1992 / Verve ✦✦✦

Lucky Peterson is a smooth operator, cool and always in control with a guitar tone reminiscent of the more restrained sides of Roy Buchanan or Carlos Santana. He's capable of lashing out, though, as the livewire showstopper "Don't Cloud Up on Me" ably proves. But this versatile musician is most distinctive with his Hammond organ and Wurlitzer electric piano sound, instruments that he's been playing professionally since the age of five. Check out the heady swirl of instrumental workout "Junk Yard" on this front although comparisons to Billy Preston will be inevitable. —*Roch Parisien*

Beyond Cool / 1994 / Verve ✦✦

Once Peterson arrived at Verve, his taste in material seemed to sail right out the window. This disc is confusingly unfocused (rock influences are as prominent as blues) and a far cry indeed from his fine Alligator sets of a precious few years before. —*Bill Dahl*

Lifetime / Mar. 5, 1996 / Verve ✦✦✦

Move / Feb. 10, 1998 / Polygram ✦✦✦

Call this Peterson's "back to my roots" blues album, but it finds him in more retro territory than his previous outings. There's a distinctive Albert King-Freddie King-Albert Collins almost-'70s feel to all the music here and the support of roots players like Johnny B. Gayden, Dennis Chambers and Butch Bonner makes this much more of a ensemble effort. Highlights include the storming "You're the One for Me," a great King-like solo on "Tin Pan Alley," an instrumental tribute to Albert Collins on "Pickin'" and oddball covers of the Isley Brothers' "It's Your Thing" and Prince's "Purple Rain." Peterson is stylistically all over the road on this disc but his versatility on both guitar and keyboards ultimately pays off in the end. —*Cub Koda*

Lucky Peterson / Oct. 5, 1999 / Polygram ✦✦✦

As a triple threat, guitarist/organist/singer Lucky Peterson is able to vary the usual repetitive patterns that a full-length album of blues music can fall into, and though the back cover of his self-titled 1999 album advises "File Under: BLUES," advice we would not dispute, a lot of different bases are covered on the album. "Shake," with the addition of the Late Night Horns, is a convincing remake of the Sam Cooke soul classic, Willie Nelson's "Funny How Time Slips Away" provides a country-style platform for a duet between Peterson and Joe Louis Walker, and the most surprising selection, Bobbie Gentry's "Ode To Billie Joe," turns out to be the outline for an extended instrumental organ solo. In between the stylistic changes of pace, however, there is still plenty of room for the updated Chicago blues in which Peterson specializes, notably on Ernie Isley's "Deal With It," Earl King's "Seduction," and Peterson's own self-descriptive "Tribute To Luther Allison." —*William Ruhlmann*

Double Dealin' / Mar. 13, 2001 / Blue Thumb ✦✦✦✦

As one of the most versatile players in blues, Lucky Peterson ranks among the best of the best. His first release for the Blue Thumb label, *Double Dealin'* showcases the artist on 12 great songs soaked in the sentiments and emotions that characterize the blues style. Peterson plays the lead guitar, the Hammond B-3, and sings his gut-wrenching blue notes with a great band that includes Johnny Lee Schell on rhythm guitar, Jon Cleary on keyboards, Reggie McBride on bass guitar, Tony Braunagel on drums, and Tamara Peterson on background vocals. The Texacali Horns back the personnel with exceptional clarity using a serious combination of brass techniques. Peterson's use of an emotionally direct style is also rapidly establishing him as a great storyteller. "When My Blood Runs Cold," "4 Little Boys," and "Remember the Day" are among the themes he deals with from an original perspective and are among the standouts of the hard blues intonations. This CD is reflective of the successful urban blues techniques used on his previous efforts in that it specifically captures the essence of both the "chitlin circuit" and the electric blues associated with the Chicago style without compromising the traditional aspects of the blues form. A welcome addition to any blues collection. —*Paula Edelstein*

Robert Petway

Vocals, Guitar / Country Blues

A well-respected country blues artist despite his limited output, Robert Petway was a blues guitarist who recorded eight sides for Bluebird Records in 1941 and followed those

up with eight more in 1942 (of which six were issued). Little biographical information is available on Petway, although it is known that he lived and played in Mississippi. The only surviving image of him shows him in overalls, holding a metal-bodied National resonator guitar. His song "Catfish Blues" gained some notoriety when it was recorded by Muddy Waters, who renamed it "Rollin' Stone," providing the inspiration years later for the name of the Rolling Stones rock band. —*Stacia Proefrock*

● **Catfish Blues: Mississippi Blues, Vol. 3 (1936–1942)** / Jul. 2, 2002 / Document ✦✦✦✦

Kelly Joe Phelps

b. Oct. 5, 1959, Sumner, WA

Slide Guitar, Vocals / Contemporary Blues

Portland, Oregon-based acoustic/slide guitar player and singer-songwriter Kelly Joe Phelps has been carving a growing niche for his music throughout the '90s and *Roll Away The Stone* (Rykodisc, 1997).

Phelps was raised in Washington and learned country and folk songs, as well as drums and piano, from his father. At first, he concentrated on free jazz and took his cues from musicians like Ornette Coleman, Miles Davis and John Coltrane before finding his true calling as a blues musician in the late '80s, when he began listening to acoustic blues masters like Fred McDowell and Robert Pete Williams. He began singing as well, and released his critically praised debut, *Lead Me On*, in 1995. Six original songs showcase Phelps' ability in the blues idiom, but he also tackles, and does justice to, traditional numbers like "Motherless Children" and "Fare Thee Well."

Phelps, as deft and creative an acoustic slide guitarist as you'll hear anywhere in the U.S., also made appearances on Greg Brown's album *Further In*, Tony Furtado's *Roll My Blues Away*, and Townes Van Zandt's *The Highway Kind*. In recent years, he's opened shows for B.B. King, Leo Kottke, Keb' Mo', Robben Ford, and Little Feat. He released his second album, *Roll Away the Stone*, in 1997, and followed it up with 1999's *Shine Eyed Mister Zen*. —*Richard Skelly*

Lead Me On / 1995 / Burnside ✦✦✦✦

This is the real deal—Phelps performs with the full authority and authenticity of the Delta bluest tradition without ever once sounding like a Folkways museum piece. There's nothing more to it than the 34-year-old's raspy, swamp-infused vocals, lapstyle acoustic guitar played using fingerpicking and slide, and self-accompanied stomp-box percussion. For the six originals and seven gospel and prewar blues selections on offer here, it's more than enough. File alongside the likes of Ben Harper and Keb' Mo'. —*Roch Parisien*

● **Roll Away the Stone** / Aug. 26, 1997 / Rykodisc ✦✦✦✦

If anything, *Roll Away the Stone* is an even better record than Kelly Joe Phelps' debut, *Lead Me On*. Phelps continues to grow as both a musician and songwriter, and his interpretations of classic blues songs show increased imagination. Although it's based in classic blues, this music doesn't sound ancient—it sounds vital and alive, like any great music should. —*Thom Owens*

Shine Eyed Mister Zen / Jul. 13, 1999 / Rykodisc ✦✦✦✦

Phelps' third album is an accomplished serving of country blues that combines the sweet and sour power of his guitar playing with the equally bittersweet charge of Phelps' wearied voice. *Shine Eyed Mister Zen* features a lot of singing, but most importantly it spotlights the singing of Phelps' slide guitar, which integrates a humid and natural style that invokes the mystery and religion that these mostly original songs lean toward. The dusty delta Phelps conjures here is at once familiar and nostalgic; it's to his credit that Phelps is able to add his own voice to the spiritual mix. A mystical and unaffected recording. —*Michael Gallucci*

Sky Like a Broken Clock / Jul. 10, 2001 / Rykodisc ✦✦✦

Recorded in a live studio setting with no overdubs, *Sky Like a Broken Clock* has a pure sound and the seamless flow that can only be achieved by a group of accomplished, and complementary, musicians. Producer George Howard, who also worked on Jess Klein's *Draw Them Near* and *Mojave* by the Willard Grant Conspiracy, has a knack for creating a warm, clean-sounding folk music, captured with an almost eerily crystalline feel. Known for his imaginative take on the country blues of artists like Skip James, Blind Lemon Jefferson, and Mississippi Fred McDowell, Phelps put together an album entirely of originals for this venture. The result is a set of low-key, abstract story-songs about voodoo, sin, and prostitution, with "Worn Out," the album's closer, having a lullaby-like quality. Phelps' guitar work on this album is fairly straightforward (unfortunately not featuring his signature acoustic slide), and is backed by Larry Taylor on string bass and Billy Conway on drums. —*Travis Drageset*

Beggar's Oil / Feb. 5, 2002 / Rykodisc ✦✦✦

Brewer Phillips

b. Nov. 16, 1924, Coila, MS

Vocals, Guitar / Juke Joint Blues, Electric Chicago Blues

Brewer Phillips is one of the more unique sidemen in Chicago blues history. His guitar playing combines the rhythmic sense of an Eddie Taylor (an early childhood friend and fishing buddy) with the stinging lead work of a Pat Hare. Born on a plantation in Coila, MS, he came under the early tutelage of Memphis Minnie and grew up with the legends of the blues all around him, seeing many of them perform firsthand. After leaving Mississippi, he moved to Memphis, becoming a professional musician and making his first recordings as a member of Bill Harvey's band, along with a session behind pianist Roosevelt Sykes that has yet to surface. Best known for his work as a member of the Houserockers (see Hound Dog Taylor entry), his backup work behind Taylor—a trio with no bass player—finds him alternating between the icepick-in-your-ear sheet-metal lead tones produced from his battered Telecaster to comping bass lines while simultaneously combining chords, all of it executed with a thumbpick and bare fingers. It's a sound totally rooted in the juke joint sounds of Phillips' Mississippi upbringing and there's simply no equal to it in the blues today. Since Taylor's death in 1976, he has recorded on his own and worked sporadically with J.B. Hutto, Lil Ed, Cub Koda, and others while remaining a largely shadowy figure in Chicago blues circles. *—AMG*

Whole Lotta Blues / 1982 / JSP ♦♦♦
Originally released on vinyl in 1982, this album captures Phillips with a rough-and-tumble band on a fairly inspired set of favorites. Ted Harvey's drumming provides a familiar rhythmic foundation, although the inclusion of an electric bass simply doesn't add anything to these tracks. Phillips' tone is distorted and trebly, as raw and unpolished as a modern-day blues recording could be without falling apart. The CD version features two bonus tracks, the closing instrumental, "Just Pickin'," and the low-down and funky "Cleo." This was re-released by JSP in 2000 as part of a three-disc "box set" (with separate albums by Lefty Dizz and Jimmy Dawkins) entitled *Bad Avenue*. *—Cub Koda*

• **Good Houserockin'** / 1995 / Wolf ♦♦♦♦
This combines various late-'70s and early-'80s recordings into one package. The first 11 tracks are from Phillips' 1982 solo album for the label, *Ingleside Blues*. The next six tracks were recorded live in 1977 in Vienna and Boston, featuring Brewer fronting J.B. Hutto and the Houserockers. The last two sides are unissued leftovers from the 1980 Cub Koda and the Houserockers' *It's the Blues!* album. Phillips' longtime playing partner, drummer Ted Harvey, is present on all 19 tracks and shares billing with him on this disc. Some of the recording quality (especially on the live Hutto tracks) is unbelievably crude and harsh sounding, making the overall sound of this disc very spotty and uneven. This collection is probably the most complete—though not necessarily the best—collection of Phillips' solo work. *—AMG*

Homebrew / Feb. 6, 1996 / Delmark ♦♦♦
It's amazing to think that Brewer Phillips would be 70-plus years old before releasing his U.S. debut album, but after a couple of years in virtual seclusion, Delmark coaxed him back into the studio for this fine set. Phillips' regular working band is aboard with pianist Aaron Moore handling the bulk of the vocals, Magic Sam's drummer, Robert "Huckleberry Hound" Wright, and Willie Black on bass providing simple but effective support. Phillips sings on the Jimmy Reed classic "You Don't Have to Go," "Looking for a Woman," and "Lunch Bucket Blues" and his single string work is highlighted on the instrumental title track. A simple, laid-back album with some surprising fireworks in all the unexpected places. *—Cub Koda*

Gene Phillips

b. Jul. 25, 1915, St. Louis, MO
Vocals, Guitar / Jump Blues, West Coast Blues, R&B
A West Coast session stalwart who appeared on myriad jump-blues waxings during the late '40s and early '50s, guitarist Gene Phillips faded from view even before the dawn of rock & roll. Any serious collector of the Bihari brothers' budget-priced Crown albums (you know, the ones with those ubiquitous cheesy cover illustrations by artist "Fazzio") should be intimately familiar with Phillips' LP—it's one of the best Crown acquisitions you can possibly make (especially since there's no CD equivalent yet).

The T-Bone Walker-influenced Phillips recorded extensively for the Biharis' Modern Imprint from 1947 through 1950. His often-ribald jump blues gems for the firm included "Big Legs," "Fatso," "Rock Bottom," "Hey Now," and a version of Big Bill Broonzy's witty standard "Just a Dream." Phillips' bandmates were among the royalty of the L.A. scene: trumpeter Jake Porter, saxists Marshall Royal, Maxwell Davis, and Jack McVea, and pianist Lloyd Glenn were frequently on hand. Phillips returned the favor in Porter's case, singing and playing on the trumpeter's 1947 dates for Imperial.

After a 78 of his own for Imperial in 1951 ("She's Fit 'n Fat 'n Fine"), Phillips bowed out of the recording wars as a leader with a solitary 1954 effort for Combo, "Fish Man," backed by McVea's band. *—Bill Dahl*

• **Swinging the Blues** / Apr. 4, 2000 / Ace ♦♦♦♦♦
This 25-song compilation doesn't contain exact recording dates, but it can be safely assumed that most or all of this was cut between 1947 and 1951; about half appeared on singles from that period, while some showed up on a 1963 Crown album (although they were obviously done much earlier), and others weren't released until Ace LP collections in the '80s. (There's also a previously unissued "Happy Birthday," cut for Modern's Jules Bihari's birthday.) Regardless of the specifics, it's early jump blues from the stage at which it was in transition from jazz to R&B, leaning in some cases closer to jazz than R&B. That may be why Phillips was pretty much a forgotten case by the mid-'50s. In any event, this remains decent, historically important early jump blues by an unheralded early pioneer of the electric guitar, as you can hear when he gets the chance to stretch out on numbers like "Slippin' & Slidin'" and "Gene Jumps the Blues." It's also notable for being some of the first material to bear the stamp of the Modern house sound, although musically it's a little more restrained and less bluesy than some of the Modern acts who would follow. Lyrically, though, Phillips was often quite ribald, as song titles like "Big Fat Mama," "Snuff Dripping Mama," "Fatso," and "Short Haired Ugly Woman" let you know before you even tear off the shrink-wrap. That kind of politically incorrect view of women hasn't aged wonderfully. You do wonder how Phillips and Modern thought they were going to get away with "Punkin' Head Woman," with lines sung to sound very much like "fuckin' head mama." The collection has surprisingly clear and vibrant sound quality, considering the age of the sources. *—Richie Unterberger*

Piano Red (William Lee Perryman)

b. Oct. 19, 1911, Hampton, GA, **d.** Jul. 25, 1985, Decatur, GA
Vocals, Piano / Piano Blues, Boogie-Woogie
Willie Perryman went by two nicknames during his lengthy career, both of them thoroughly apt. He was known as Piano Red because of his albino skin pigmentation for most of his performing life. But they called him Doctor Feelgood during the '60s, and that's precisely what his raucous, barrelhouse-styled vocals and piano were guaranteed to do: cure anyone's ills and make them feel good.

Like his older brother, Rufus Perryman, who performed and recorded as Speckled Red, Willie Perryman showed an aptitude for the 88s early in life. At age 12, he was banging on the ivories, influenced by Fats Waller but largely his own man. He rambled some with blues greats Barbecue Bob, Curley Weaver, and Blind Willie McTell during the '30s (and recording with the latter in 1936), but mostly worked as a solo artist.

In 1950, Red's big break arrived when he signed with RCA Victor. His debut Victor offering, the typically rowdy "Rockin' with Red," was a huge R&B hit, peaking at number five on *Billboard*'s charts. It's surfaced under a variety of guises since: Little Richard revived it as "She Knows How to Rock" in 1957 for Specialty, Jerry Lee Lewis aced it for Sun (unissued at the time), and pint-sized hillbilly dynamo Little Jimmy Dickens beat 'em both to the punch for Columbia.

"Red's Boogie," another pounding rocker from the pianist's first RCA date, also proved a huge smash, as did the rag-tinged "The Wrong Yo Yo" (later covered masterfully by Carl Perkins at Sun), "Just Right Bounce," and "Laying the Boogie" in 1951. Red became an Atlanta mainstay in the clubs and over the radio, recording prolifically for RCA through 1958 both there and in New York. There weren't any more hits, but that didn't stop the firm from producing a live LP by the pianist in 1956 at Atlanta's Magnolia Ballroom that throbbed with molten energy. Chet Atkins produced Red's final RCA date in Nashville in 1958, using Red's touring band for backup.

A 1959 single for Checker called "Get Up Mare" and eight tracks for the tiny Jax label preceded the rise of Red's new guise, Dr. Feelgood & the Interns, who debuted on Columbia's OKeh subsidiary in 1961 with a self-named rocker, "Doctor Feel-Good," that propelled the aging piano pounder into the pop charts for the first time. Its flipside, "Mister Moonlight" (penned and ostensibly sung by bandmember Roy Lee Johnson), found its way into the repertoire of the Beatles. A subsequent remake of "The Right String but the Wrong Yo-Yo" also hit for the good doctor in 1962. The Doc remained with OKeh through 1966, recording with veteran Nashville saxist Boots Randolph in his band on five occasions.

Red remained ensconced at Muhlenbrink's Saloon in Atlanta from 1969 through 1979, sandwiching in extensive European tours along the way. He was diagnosed with cancer in 1984 and died the following year. *—Bill Dahl*

Jump Man, Jump / 1956 / Groove ♦♦♦♦
Raucous barrelhouse blues and boogies with a hot R&B combo on these swinging sides. *—Bill Dahl*

Piano Red in Concert / 1956 / Groove ♦♦♦
On this pioneering live set cut at Atlanta's Magnolia Ballroom, the sound is surprisingly clean and Red rocks the house! *—Bill Dahl*

Doctor Feelgood / 1962 / Delmark ♦♦
Willie Perryman, younger brother of Rufus, aka Speckled Red, is your basic, deliberate barrelhouse and honky tonk pianist whose percussive approach, stride inferences, and two-chord signatures are prevalent throughout this solo set. His singing is a bit rough and raggedy, but nonetheless sweet and tuneful. Piano Red also wrote the bulk of these twelve two+ minute tracks. The majority of the tunes are half-time 4/4, such as "Coochi" (actually pronounced "coocha"), the similar "I Know You Care for Me," the quintessential rent party blues "We'll Have a Good Time Tonight," the fun take of the classic "Please Don't Talk About Me When I'm Gone," and the beat of "Barrelhouse Boogie," whose 50/50 measured and strident/non-swinging pace is typical of this whole set. The variations are a slower honky tonk-type line on the title track, the most straight boogie-woogie with slowed down segments on the instrumental "Boogie Time," a straight 12-bar take of Leroy Carr's "Low Down Dog Blues," and the pining "Let's Fall in Love," not the well-known standard, but Red's original. The rest are instrumentals, with an occasional yelp or whoop. A tonking "Jump, Man Jump," the simple song "Think She Ain't," and the joyous two-chord line of "Comin' On" all sound fine without lyrics. Red is one of those unsung heroes in the lexicon of older jazz and blues piano stylings. This is a good CD, and should be available at a discount price due to the limited length, just short of 32 minutes total. *—Michael G. Nastos*

Dr. Feelgood All Alone With His Piano / 1975 / Arhoolie ♦♦♦

Atlanta Bounce / 1992 / Arhoolie ♦♦♦
Two distinct timeframes are represented on this slightly schizophrenic disc. Much of it is comprised of latter-day barrelhouse and blues waxed by Arhoolie, but there's also a thrilling handful of raucous live items from a 1956 concert at Atlanta's Magnolia Ballroom that capture the albino 88s ace at his most enthralling. *—Bill Dahl*

Blues, Blues, Blues / 1992 / Black Lion ♦♦♦♦
Originally release in the mid-'70s on LP as *Ain't Gonna Be Your Lowdown Dog No More*, this 1992 CD covers parts of two sets from Piano Red's very successful Montreux concerts. Piano Red treats his huge Montreux audience to the same mixture of good time blues and boogie woogie as the visitors to Muhlenbrink's Saloon in the old Underground Atlanta, where he was a fixture for years. Highlights include "The Right String but The Wrong Yo-Yo," a medley of "Pinetop's Boogie" with "Red's Boogie," and the original record's title track. Twelve studio tracks recorded a few days after Piano Red's Montreux performances are an added bonus. *—Ken Dryden*

The Doctor Is In! / 1993 / Bear Family ♦♦♦♦♦
This four-CD set, containing 122 songs (23 of them previously unreleased) cut between 1950 and 1966 for RCA, Groove, OKeh, and Columbia is, literally, the best of Piano Red, and may be the best box in the entire Bear Family catalog. This is about as good as piano blues and R&B got, and also some of the best piano-based rock & roll you'll ever hear—rivaling *anything* that Jerry Lee Lewis or Little Richard ever cut—with barely a second-rate track. Even the multiple versions of his signature tune, "The Right String but the Wrong Yo-Yo," are welcomed, from its lean, mean piano-bass-drums original 1950 version,

to the live 1955 rendition and the broader 1961 remake (at the "Mr. Moonlight" session), because they're each different enough to justify their presence. And, yet, the most amazing thing about the 16 years covered on these four discs is the consistency of the music and performances—Red hardly changed at all until the early '60s, always giving his audience a good show whether he was making records or playing live. The second and third discs are arguably the best parts of the set, with Red at the peak of his prowess as a pianist and singer. He made the jump into rock & roll more easily than most bluesmen of his age, with the result that his music from this period is as solid as anything else he ever did. Still later, on the fourth disc, once he moves into a more produced, pop-oriented R&B sound, he holds up almost as well. The sound is excellent, the notes are thorough, and the $100 list price of this 122-song set makes it proportionately *more* attractive than any $15/15-song best-of on Red that might ever show up (and there *isn't* one). *—Bruce Eder*

Flaming Hurricane / Sep. 28, 1999 / West Side ♦♦♦

An 11 track album that's been sitting in the Ace (Jackson, MS, version) vaults since the '70s, this is classic Piano Red all the way. His good-time singing, rough and garbled though it may be, and his barrelhouse piano playing are both in fine form on this hitherto undocumented session. With a small rhythm section, the focus stays firmly on Red as he turns in re-cuts of "Dr. Feelgood," "The Right String, but the Wrong Yo-Yo," Joe Turner's "Shake, Rattle and Roll," "Corrina, Corrina," and a nice sampling of what must have been some set list favorites. The deepest blues on here is "Whiskey Man," aka "Ten Cent Shot," a splendid talking blues with nice, understated slide guitar from the unknown guitarist on this date. But in the main it's Red in high rockin' gear, a man who was truly ahead of his time. While not rivaling his early RCA sides, this session comes as a really nice surprise. *—Cub Koda*

● **Wildfire** / Matchbox ♦♦♦♦♦

Although it's hardly comprehensive, Matchbox's *Wildfire* is the best available single-volume sampler of Piano Red's music, containing 12 of his greatest numbers, including "Red's Boogie" and "Diggin' the Boogie." *—Thom Owens*

Rod Piazza

b. Dec. 18, 1947, Riverside, CA

Vocals, Harmonica / Electric Harmonica Blues, West Coast Blues, Modern Electric Blues

A California-based blues bandleader, harmonica player, and singer, Rod Piazza's stratospheric harmonica wailings owe a heavy debt to both Little Walter and George "Harmonica" Smith. Piazza began his professional career as a member of the Dirty Blues Band in the mid-'60s. The Dirty Blues Band recorded two albums for ABC/BluesWay—an eponymous debut in 1967 and 1968's *Stone Dirty*. Piazza left the band after the release of *Stone Dirty*, choosing to hit the road with his idol George "Harmonica" Smith instead.

Over the next decade and a half, Piazza and Smith performed together frequently under the name Bacon Fat; they also recorded the occasional album. In 1969, Bacon Fat released their eponymous debut album on Blue Horizon. While he was performing with Smith, Piazza released his own solo albums, the first of which—*Rod Piazza Blues Man*—appeared on LMI in 1973. The second, *Chicago Flying Saucer Band*, was released in 1979 on Gangster Records.

As Smith's health began to decline in the early '80s, Piazza assembled the Mighty Flyers—with his wife Honey Alexander on keyboards—which began playing clubs in 1980. Between 1981 and 1985, the Mighty Flyers released three albums: *Radioactive Material* (1981), *File Under Rock* (1984), and *From the Start to the Finish* (1985). During the early '80s, Piazza became a session musician, working with artists as diverse as Pee Wee Crayton and Michelle Shocked. In the mid-'80s, he began a full-fledged solo career, releasing *Harpburn* on Murray Brothers in 1986 and *So Glad to Have the Blues* in 1988.

Piazza and the Mighty Flyers signed a contract with Black Top Records in 1991; the label later re-released the group's albums on CD. Throughout the '90s, Piazza continued to record and perform with the Mighty Flyers, releasing the occasional solo album, like 1999's *Here and Now*. *Beyond the Source* appeared in 2001. *—Cub Koda & Stephen Thomas Erlewine*

Bluesman / 1973 / LMI ♦♦♦

Harpburn / 1986 / Black Top ♦♦♦

So Glad to Have the Blues / 1988 / Murray Bros ♦♦♦

Blues in the Dark / 1991 / Black Top ♦♦♦

A contemporary band, led by harmonica player/vocalist Piazza, has nice piano from Honey Alexander. *—Niles J. Frantz*

Alphabet Blues / 1992 / Black Top ♦♦♦♦

Another fine effort from Rod Piazza and the Mighty Flyers, *Alphabet Blues* alternates between first-rate slow blues and cooking uptempo boogies and shuffles, both of which showcase their versatile, many-sided talents. There are a few weak songs, but the album on the whole is quite entertaining. *—Thom Owens*

● **The Essential Collection** / 1992 / Hightone ♦♦♦♦

Compilation of fairly recent sides by the powerhouse West Coast harpist; like most of his work, it smokes! *—Bill Dahl*

Live at B.B. King's Blues Club / 1994 / Big Mo ♦♦♦

This harp master really turns out the discs; boogies and blues. *—Bill Dahl*

California Blues / Feb. 4, 1997 / Black Top ♦♦♦

Tough and Tender / Jul. 8, 1997 / Tone-Cool ♦♦♦

Tough and Tender was the first new studio for Piazza and the Mighty Flyers since 1992's *Alphabet Blues*. The kickoff track, "Power of the Blues," announces their triumphant return with a clarion call from Rod that "we've got the power of the blues." Piazza's harmonica is locked in sync with guitarist Rick "L.A. Holmes" Holmstrom's on the intro before Holmstrom whips off a slashing solo in the middle that recalls the phrasing of both T-Bone Walker and Pee Wee Crayton. Rod's solo on this opener is also textbook playing, full of taste, control and the deepest of tones. The title track is a new Piazza classic that illustrates the empathy between every player in the band with Honey Piazza's boogie-woogie piano soloing making an apt foil for Rod's chromatic harp work. "She Can't Say No" and "Sea of Fools" bring Jonny Viau and Allen Ortiz's horns to the party for New Orleans-style R&B and a blues rhumba. Piazza's harp is highlighted again on the instrumental "The Teaser." Other highlights include the loping West Coast swing of "Blues and Trouble," the jazzy instrumental "Under the Big Top," Honey's showcase on "Hang Ten Boogie," and the set-closing "Searching for a Fortune." This album clearly shows why Piazza and his band have been favorites on the blues circuit for quite some time and why that fan base shows no signs of getting smaller. *—Cub Koda*

Vintage Live: 1975 / Aug. 18, 1998 / Tone-Cool ♦♦♦♦

This medium to lo-fi live club recording (location and exact date unspecified) finds Piazza and a young, enthusiastic band playing it by the record collection as they mine their way through ten Chicago blues classics. With Hollywood Fats on guitar and former Canned Heat bassman Larry Taylor, the licks are suitably retro and blues-approved, as Piazza devotes over half the set to letter-perfect re-creations of Little Walter staples like "My Babe," "Oh Baby," "Key to the Highway," "Mellow Down Easy," "I Had My Fun," and "Mean Old World." Piazza extends the Walter approach to include likeminded versions of Muddy's "Standing Around Crying" and "Take a Walk With Me," Eddie Boyd's "Third Degree," and Howlin' Wolf's "Rocking Daddy." What sounds still sounds pretty impressive (if somewhat derivative) some 20 years later must have seemed absolutely revelatory at the time. *—Cub Koda*

Here and Now / Mar. 2, 1999 / Tone-Cool ♦♦♦♦

Here And Now is as about as near to perfect as a modern-day blues album should get. Rod Piazza and the Mighty Flyers shine collectively like a well-polished diamond on this outing, produced by Piazza and guitarist extraordinaire Rick Holmstrom. The production is real live-on-the-floor stuff, expertly put into nice, retro-flavored mixes that make the quintet sound enormous. Piazza blows powerful harp free of clichés (particularly potent on his showcase piece "Strat-O-Spheric") while writing or co-writing nine of the 11 tunes aboard here. Holmstrom's distorted Willie Johnson-like guitar sprays expert licks all over the place on top of the rock-solid support of string bassist Bill Stuve and drummer Steve Mugalian. But the real secret weapon on this album is Honey Piazza. Her piano work—always prominent in the mix—absolutely shines on "Brought Together By the Blues" and "First Love," two of the six tunes she co-wrote with husband Rod on here. Pushing himself and his band in new directions, this album makes a marvelous antidote to modern-day, paint-by-numbers cookie-cutter blues-rock fare. *—Cub Koda*

Beyond the Source / Jul. 17, 2001 / Tone-Cool ♦♦♦

Greg Piccolo

b. May 10, 1951, Westerly, RI

Vocals, Sax (Tenor) / Jump Blues, R&B

Former Roomful of Blues vocalist and sax man Greg Piccolo was born May 10, 1951, in Westerly, RI. At the age of 13 he was playing sax with a six-piece rock band, the *Rejects*. Two years later he joined Duke Robillard as a vocalist for the *Variations*, a British Invasion cover band. Piccolo rejoined Robillard in 1970 to create that first Roomful of Blues, inspired by the R&B band, the Buddy Johnson Orchestra. The group was further modified in 1971 and Piccolo began playing sax. The band worked up and down the Northeast gradually building up a national following. Robillard left the group in 1979 and was replaced by blues guitarist Ronnie Earl. By this time, Piccolo was the *de facto* leader. *Dressed Up to Get Messed Up* features a number of his compositions. The group stayed together until the early '90s when Piccolo went out on his own.

Piccolo has released two solo albums in the acid-jazz vein, *Heavy Juice* on Black Top Records (1990) and *Acid Blue* (1995) on Fantasy. Greg Piccolo lives in Rhode Island. In 2000 he released a solo album entitled *Homage*, which paid tribute to classic tenor players. *—Michael Erlewine*

● **Heavy Juice** / Sep. 13, 1990 / Black Top ♦♦♦♦♦

These stomping tenor sax instrumentals come from the jazz and R&B repertoire of the '40s and '50s. Many Roomful of Blues alumni, such as Duke Robillard (guitar) and Al Copley (piano), contribute. It doesn't rock any harder than this. *—Bob Porter*

Acid Blue / Jun. 1995 / Fantasy ♦♦♦♦

Red Lights / Jun. 3, 1997 / Fantasy ♦♦♦♦

Former Roomful of Blues saxophonist Greg Piccolo stretches his musical wings even further on this, his third solo outing since leaving the group in 1990. In addition to his brawny tenor sax wailings, Piccolo also plays lead guitar (in a crude, but effective style somewhat reminiscent of Roy Buchanan and Carlos Santana) and alto sax this time around, coaxing acid-jazz sounds out of the latter instrument. With his regular working combo Heavy Juice providing stellar support in a multiplicity of styles (Piccolo jumps from swing to bop to acid jazz to soul ballads and even a taste of rock & roll on this one) and 14 Karat Soul providing backup vocals on "Money" and the title track, *Red Lights* is Greg Piccolo's most musically ambitious album to date. *—Cub Koda*

Homage / Feb. 13, 2001 / Emit Doog Music ♦♦♦♦♦

Here's one modern tribute disc that's worth celebrating—a Greg Piccolo showcase where he covers tunes once done to a turn by husky-toned tenor sax growlers in the jazz and R&B arenas. Illinois Jacquet, Red Prysock, Gene Ammons, Eddie "Lockjaw" Davis, Ben Webster, Clifford Scott, and Joe Houston are the objects of Piccolo's veneration, and he can make you do a double-take at the accuracy and grit of his impressions. Lester Young is the ringer on the tribute list, in a category separate from the heavier-toned players listed above, yet Piccolo appropriately lightens his tone a bit while retaining the slurred majesty of the other tracks on "Lester Smooths It Out." This recording contains none of the usual genuflecting reverence that grips most tribute albums, for it has plenty of fire, spirit, and a sense of fun; dig, for example, Piccolo's R&B honking and ultrasonic squealing on Houston's "Blow Joe Blow" and the gospel-driven fervor on Prysock's "Handclappin'." The band (Reese Wynans on organ and piano, Marty Ballou on basses, Jeffrey Cashien on acoustic guitar, and Bobby Ruggiero on drums) easily swerves back and forth between jazz and R&B, generating some pretty tough swing along the way, and Piccolo gets in a few lead guitar licks. What's also unusual about this CD is that Piccolo tries to stay mostly within the time limits of 78 RPM discs and early LPs; no track runs over five minutes, and most are considerably shorter. There's something to be said for that practice; it enforces conciseness and reduces listener fatigue. *—Richard Ginell*

Dan Pickett

b. Aug. 31, 1907, Pike County, AL, **d.** Aug. 16, 1967, Boaz, AL

Vocals, Guitar / Piedmont Blues, Country Blues

Reissuers have unearthed little information about Dan Pickett: He appears to have come from Alabama, he played a nice slide guitar in a Southeastern blues style, and he did one recording session for the Philadelphia-based Gotham label in 1949. That session produced five singles, all of which have now been compiled along with four previously unreleased sides on a reissue album that purports to contain Pickett's entire recorded output—unless, of course, as some reviewers have speculated, Dan Pickett happens also to be Charlie Pickett, the Tennessee guitarist who recorded for Decca in 1937. As Tony Russell observed in *Juke Blues*, both Picketts recorded blues about lemon-squeezing, and Dan uses the name Charlie twice in the lyrics to "Decoration Day." 'Tis from such mystery and speculation that the minds of blues collectors do dissolve. *—Jim O'Neal*

● **1949 Country Blues** / 1990 / Collectables ♦♦♦♦♦

1949 Country Blues is an invaluable reissue of ten sides originally released on 78s during 1949, plus four previously unreleased songs. During the '60s, these sides were highly collectable, and earned the reputation of being among the finest country blues. That reputation wasn't misguided—he was truly unique among country bluesmen. Pickett had a distinctive rhythmic style and unique phrasing that makes his records compelling decades after his release. He made songs from the likes of Blind Boy Fuller ("Lemon Man," also known as "Let Me Squeeze Your Lemons") and Leroy Carr ("How Long") sound like his own. At times, the music on *1949 Country Blues* is simply astonishing. No serious blues collector should be without this disc. *—Thom Owens*

Pilgrim Jubilee Singers

f. Chicago, IL

Group / Black Gospel

Since the early '50s, the Pilgrim Jubilee Singers have used their hard, rockin' gospel music as a powerful means of testifying their faith, love, and charitable hope that humanity will find a way to bring itself closer to the kingdom of heaven. Over its long history, the group has undergone numerous personnel changes. The first incarnation originated in the '40s on the Mississippi Delta by Elgie and Theopholis Graham, but the most famous version of the Pilgrim Jubilees began in Chicago, 1952, when younger Graham brothers Clay and Cleve resurrected the group. Since then, these two have remained the group's spiritual and musical core.

While growing up in Mississippi, all four Graham brothers were trained to sing. It was Theopholis who left the first group to live in Chicago; the rest of his brothers followed in 1951, and all four briefly sang in the group. The Pilgrim Jubilees toured quite a bit (when not working their day jobs, which for the Graham brothers meant working in their separate barber shops), and this proved too much for the older brothers, who gradually dropped out. Shortly thereafter, Clay and Cleve invited baritone Major Roberson and lead singer Percy Clark (both from Mississippi) to join. They also took on guitarist Richard Crume and bassist Roosevelt English, and began recording; through the '50s, they released sides and albums for assorted labels, including Peacock, Chance, and Nashboro. Soon after signing to Peacock in 1960, the band gained national exposure with their label debut, "Stretch Out." Its success allowed the Pilgrim Jubilees to finally go professional. Crume eventually left the group to join the Soul Stirrers, but the other three remained together and carried on. *—Sandra Brennan*

Walk On / 1963 / Peacock ♦♦♦♦♦

Fine close harmony quartet with both talent and conviction. *—Opal Louis Nations*

The Old Ship of Zion / 1964 / Peacock ♦♦♦♦♦

This one includes "Pearly Gates" and "If You Don't Mind." *—Bil Carpenter*

Don't Let Him Down / 1974 / Peacock ♦♦♦♦

With the sound of a brief guitar intro, the tone of this classic recording kicks into hard-driving shout gospel. Having enjoyed a long history of quality recordings, this 1973 release from the Pilgrim Jubilees is no exception to their ability to capture ageless issues of perseverance and religious commitment. A generous balance between the group's two main lead singers, Clay Graham and his older brother Cleve Graham, give the listener a chance to hear both of these vocal legends at full throttle. The title cut "Don't Let Him Down" has become one of the Pilgrim Jubilees' trademark songs that is still part of their repertoire. Though this original version is merely a taste of what was to come on their 1979 live version recorded for Nashboro records, the power and fervor is defiantly present. This album represented a shift in recording technology, as well as the group's song selections. This album places a great emphasis on society and the injustices of life in America during the early '70s. Though messages of social reform was not a new concept for the group, the radical messages of selections such as "Trouble in the Street," "It Isn't Safe Anymore," and "A Great Tragedy" were definitely risky jabs at police brutality and other political and social issues. The trademark sound of Bobby McDougle's soulful guitar is present throughout, and his use of the new multi-tracking technology is effective in making a memorable album that is yet to enjoy reissue in its full original format. *—Minister Donnie Addison*

☆ **Back to Basics** / 1990 / Malaco ♦♦♦♦♦

Another solid effort recorded by this label, which helped to bring good Southern gospel music into the '90s. *—Kip Lornell*

Gospel Roots / 1990 / Malaco ♦♦♦♦♦

This dynamic album shows why the Pilgrim Jubilees have remained one of the most respected "hard" gospel groups for so many years. *—Kip Lornell*

★ **Walk On/The Old Ship of Zion** / 1992 / Mobile Fidelity ♦♦♦♦♦

Mobile Fidelity's *Walk On/The Old Ship of Zion* combines two Peacock albums—1963's *Walk On* and 1964's *The Old Ship of Zion*—on one compact disc. Both albums capture the Pilgrim Jubilee Singers at their peak, demonstrating that they were one of the greatest hard gospel quartets of their time. *—Leo Stanley*

Homecoming / May 23, 1995 / Nashboro ♦♦♦

Possibly the last significant sides by this major postwar quartet. *—Opal Louis Nations*

Pilgrim Travelers

f. 1931, Houston, TX, **db.** 1956

Group / Traditional Gospel, Black Gospel

The Specialty label's most prolific gospel act, the Pilgrim Travelers were among the most successful and influential groups of gospel's golden era; famed for their distinctive "walking rhythm" sound, they also earned renown for their riotous live perfomances and breathless showmanship. The Pilgrim Travelers were formed in Houston during the early '30s by Joe Johnson and Willie Davis; the latter relocated the group to Los Angeles in 1942, taking with him cousins Kylo Turner and Keith Barber. By mid-1945, their ranks included bass Raphael Taylor as well as J.W. Alexander, a light tenor and onetime semi-pro baseball player with Negro league teams including the Ethiopian Clowns and the New Orleans Crescent Stars; he soon assumed managerial control of the group as well.

Like other groups of the period, the Pilgrim Travelers consciously modeled their sound after the Soul Stirrers and the Golden Gates; although Turner was naturally a baritone, he sang in a note-bending falsetto style not far removed from pop crooning, while his co-lead Barber possessed a pure, sweet voice and a flamboyant stage presence. To give the Travelers an edge on the competition, Alexander pushed his partners to hone a tightly choreographed live show which over the years became increasingly frenetic, much to the delight of the many women attending their performances. In early 1947, the group made their first recordings, issuing singles on a handful of tiny L.A. labels; by the end of the year they signed to Specialty, at which time they brought on board a new baritone, Jesse Whitaker, to replace Davis.

After a handful of a cappella songs, the Travelers began recording their material with a microphone picking up the sound of their percussive foot-tapping; Specialty's early press for the group proclaimed "Something New—Walking Rhythm Spirituals," and the unique sound quickly caught on with consumers. In 1948, the group issued six singles; after just three the following year, in 1950 Specialty released no less than ten Pilgrim Travelers sides, all of them to strong sales (particularly "Jesus Met the Woman at the Well" and "Mother Bowed"). However, at the peak of their success, Barber was involved in a 1950 auto accident which left his voice ravaged; at the same time, the emergence of the Soul Stirrers' Sam Cooke made Turner's vocal style appear increasingly outdated, and seemingly overnight the group's fortunes began to wane.

In the years to follow, lineup changes plagued the Pilgrim Travelers as well—in 1954 Taylor was replaced by bass George McCurn, and by the middle of the decade both Turner and Barber had exited; by the time of their 1956 demise, the ensemble had recorded over 100 songs. A later incarnation of the group, dubbed simply the Travelers, included Lou Rawls, but was otherwise unremarkable. In 1959, Alexander teamed with Sam Cooke to found SAR Records; the new company attempted to relaunch Turner's career, but in the passing years the singer had succumbed to alcoholism, and he arrived in Los Angeles too drunk to enter the studio. He eventually returned to Texas, where he died a few years after his cousin Barber; Whitaker retired to his family farm in New Jersey, while Alexander remained a sought-after producer and manager. *—Jason Ankeny*

Lou Rawls & the Pilgrim Travelers / 1957 / Andex ♦♦♦♦

Lou's finest moments with the group at its best. *—Opal Louis Nations*

Lou Rawls & the Pilgrim Travelers / 1962 / Capitol ♦♦♦

Lou and the group singing Soul Stirrers songs and arrangements. *—Opal Louis Nations*

The Best of the Pilgrim Travelers, Vol. 1 / 1970 / Specialty ♦♦♦♦♦

Classic Travelers material, 1950-1954. *—Opal Louis Nations*

The Best of the Pilgrim Travelers, Vol. 2 / 1971 / Specialty ♦♦♦♦♦

More toe-tapping with leads Keith Barber and Kylo Turner. *—Opal Louis Nations*

Everytime I Feel the Spirit / 1971 / Chameleon ♦♦♦

Shake My Mother's Hand / 1972 / Specialty ♦♦♦

Close a cappella singing with that unmistakable walking-in-rhythm. *—Opal Louis Nations*

● **The Best of the Pilgrim Travelers, Vol. 1–2** / 1990 / Specialty ♦♦♦♦♦

Reissue of the quartet's two fine albums of the early '70s filled with great toe-tapping gospel. *—Opal Louis Nations*

Walking Rhythm / 1992 / Specialty ♦♦♦♦♦

Better Than That / 1994 / Specialty ♦♦♦

The Pilgrim Travelers were Specialty's most prolific group, recording more than any their other ensemble in any style. They were versatile enough to be sensational as an a cappella unit, and almost as magnificent with instrumental accompaniment. The 28 cuts from this most recent anthology shows them adjusting to instrumental support, as lead vocalists Kylo Turner and Keith Barber effectively duel and contrast against organs, keyboards, bass and drums. The collection also contains 13 previously unissued songs, most of them incredible unaccompanied performances. They may not have been Specialty's greatest gospel group, but the Pilgrim Travelers weren't far behind the Soul Stirrers. *—Ron Wynn*

Lonnie Pitchford

b. Oct. 8, 1955, Lexington, MS, **d.** Nov. 8, 1998

Vocals, Slide Guitar, Diddley Bow / Modern Delta Blues

Diddley bow player Lonnie Pitchford was an obscure Delta blues player until he was "discovered" by ethnomusicologist Worth Long. He began to attract crowds playing the music of Robert Johnson, songs like "Come on in My Kitchen" and "Terraplane Blues," on his one-stringed didley bow. Pitchford began playing Johnson's tunes after meeting guitarist Robert Jr. Lockwood at the World's Fair in Knoxville, Tennessee. Lockwood showed Pitchford some basic Johnson chord changes and arrangements, and for several years after that, Pitchford was accompanied by the late Alabama bluesman Johnny Shines, as well as Lockwood.

Pitchford began making his one-stringed diddley bows as a five-year-old, fashioning them mostly out of parts from old electric guitars. Also an accomplished six-string guitarist and piano player, Pitchford has forged his reputation as a skilled diddley bow player. His fascination with blues began as a child, when he heard blues and gospel on the radio. Raised in a musical family, Pitchford got his start playing house parties and learned a lot from his father and brothers, who also played blues guitar and piano.

Pitchford's festival resumé includes the Smithsonian Festival of American Folklife in Washington, D.C., and several major blues gatherings around the South. He was one of the youngest performers at the 1984 Downhome Blues Festival in Atlanta.

Pitchford's albums include *All Around Man* for Rooster Blues, a 1994 release, as well as several compilations, including *Mississippi Moan*, a 1988 release on the German L&R Records, *Roots of Rhythm and Blues: A Tribute to the Robert Johnson Era*, a 1992 Columbia Records release, and *Deep Blues* (1992), for Anxious Records.

Although he'd put in dynamic, spirited performances at the Smithsonian Festivals, Pitchford unfortunately didn't tour much because of his lack of recordings. He was able to make occasional road trips to Memphis and other cities where his music was appreciated. He divided his time between road trips to play blues and working as a carpenter. Pitchford was voted as one of *Living Blues* magazine's "top 40 under 40" new blues players to watch. Unfortunately, his life was cut short in 1998 at the age of 43. *—Richard Skelly*

● **All Around Man** / Oct. 11, 1994 / Rooster Blues ♦♦♦

Mississippi bluesman Lonnie Pitchford makes good on his claim with *All Around Man*. Voted as one of the 40 best under-40 blues musicians by *Living Blues* magazine, Pitchford was an accomplished pianist and rhythm, slide, and lead guitarist, as well as a master of the diddley bow, a one-stringed instrument he played since the age of five. Rearranging popular standards such as "See See Rider" and "If I Had Possession Over Judgement Day," Pitchford blends his own style with that of his idols, namely Robert Johnson and Elmore James. Containing a little bit of everything, the record see-saws between Pitchford fronting an electric band, playing unaccompanied guitar, and playing a moving rendition of "My Sunny" on acoustic piano. *All Around Man* is just that, a fine introduction to the various sides of Pitchford's muse. *—Steve Kurutz*

Shawn Pittman

b. Oklahoma City, OK

Vocals, Guitar / Contemporary Blues, Blues-Rock, Modern Electric Blues

With young, young Stevie Ray Vaughan-abees the latest way for the blues to reach a mainstream audiences (read: big bucks and Chinese rug success), even the smaller independents are grooming their own versions of this sub-subgenre for the next in promotion line, hoping lightning will strike again in *their* sales department. Shawn Pittman has been kicking up a lot of noise in his native Dallas for awhile, and producer/Cannonball Records owner Ron Levy decided to produce a full-length album after witnessing a live show packed with enthusiastic ladies.

Born in Oklahoma City to musical parents, Pittman started out on piano and drums, eventually turning to guitar and getting a Stratocaster after hearing—you guessed it—Stevie Ray Vaughan. But Pittman's guitar style, while heavily indebted to SRV, has more than one flavor to it and is of more substance than flash. His vocals also show more true feeling than most, eschewing sore-throated hollering as a way to supposedly show authenticity. As an up-and-comer, Shawn Pittman exhibits *much* promise. *—Cub Koda*

● **Burnin' Up** / Apr. 21, 1998 / Cannonball ♦♦♦♦

Pittman's debut opus for Cannonball shows a strong stylistic tip of the gaucho hat to the Vaughan brothers, SRV in particular. But there are actual sparks of originality in even the more pedestrian and derivative tracks on here. Pittman's vocals exhibit a maturity and assurance not usually heard on these types of records, and his songwriting—taking in seven of the 11 tracks aboard—are more than just paint-by-numbers compositions. Nice covers of Freddie King's "Night Stomp" and Hound Dog Taylor's "Gimme Back My Wig" make this a debut well worth investigating. *—Cub Koda*

Something's Gotta Give / Aug. 3, 1999 / Cannonball ♦♦♦♦

Pittman's second album shows no sophomore jinx as he tackles a stack of original tunes with energy galore. No speed burner or Stevie Ray Vaughan-abee, Pittman exhibits not only taste and tone, but a wide range of influences from Hound Dog Taylor to Eddie Taylor and an understanding of when to burn and when to lay back. His lyrics show a large development from his debut disc and tunes like "Make It Through," "Just a Game" and the title track display a depth you usually don't find on "young man blues" albums. Those looking for a new blues guitar hero who also exhibits taste and subtlety would do well to pick this one up. *—Cub Koda*

Full Circle / 2001 / Shawn Pittman Music ♦♦♦

Cousin Joe Pleasant

b. Dec. 20, 1907, Wallace, LA, **d.** Oct. 2, 1989, New Orleans, LA

Vocals, Piano, Guitar / New Orleans R&B, New Orleans Blues

Few blues legends have the presence of mind to write autobiographies. Fortunately, Pleasant Joseph did, spinning fascinating tales of a career in his 1987 tome *Cousin Joe: Blues from New Orleans* that spanned more than half a century.

Growing up in New Orleans, Pleasant began singing in church before crossing over to the blues. Guitar and ukulele were his first axes. He eventually prioritized the piano instead, playing Crescent City clubs and riverboats. He moved to New York in 1942, gaining entry into the city's thriving jazz scene (where he played with Dizzy Gillespie, Sidney Bechet, Charlie Parker, Billie Holiday, and a host of other luminaries).

He recorded for King, Gotham, Philo (in 1945), Savoy, and Decca along the way, doing well on the latter logo with "Box Car Shorty and Peter Blue" in 1947. After returning to New Orleans in 1948, he recorded for DeLuxe and cut a two-part "ABCs" for Imperial in 1954 as Smilin' Joe under Dave Bartholomew's supervision. But by then, his recording career had faded.

The pianist was booked on a 1964 *Blues and Gospel Train* tour of England, sharing stages with Muddy Waters, Otis Spann, Brownie McGhee and Sonny Terry, and Sister Rosetta Tharpe and appearing on BBC-TV with the all-star troupe. He cut a 1971 album for the French Black & Blue label, *Bad Luck Blues*, that paired him with guitarists Clarence "Gatemouth" Brown and Jimmy Dawkins and a Chicago rhythm section—hardly the ideal situation, but still a reasonably effective showcase for the ebullient entertainer (it was reissued in 1994 by Evidence). *—Bill Dahl*

● **Bad Luck Blues** / Nov. 1971 / Evidence ♦♦♦♦♦

The New Orleans pianist ventured overseas in 1971 and waxed this CD along the way with a mighty unlikely band: guitarists Clarence "Gatemouth" Brown and Jimmy Dawkins and a Chicago rhythm section (bassist Mack Thompson and drummer Ted Harvey). A lesser musician might have wilted with players so unfamiliar with his basic approach, but Pleasant's bubbly ebullience and the strength of his "Box Car Shorty," "Life Is a One Way Ticket," and "Railroad Porter Blues" saved the day. *—Bill Dahl*

Bluesman from New Orleans / 1974 / Big Bear ♦♦♦♦

Gospel Wailing / 1982 / Big Bear ♦♦♦

Poonanny

Producer / Retro-Soul, Modern Electric Blues

Bawdy, blues singing Joe Poonanny, aka the God Father of the chitlin circuit, came up in Birmingham, AL. His parents' house was across the street from a show bar, and he could look out his window and watch the drummer play, and aspired to do the same, especially after watching *The Gene Krupa Story*. He practiced daily and played his first professional gig at 17. He drummed around for years but wanted something more substantial, so in 1975 he worked behind the scenes operating nightclubs and managing bands, but quit in 1981 citing a dislike of the lifestyle. Always the clown, Poonanny built a reputation by singing risqué, double entendre blues tales in clubs and cabarets but didn't record until 1993 when Waldoxy Records released *Poonanny Be Still*! It became a hot item in the South and four more have followed: *The Grindin' Man*, *Ponyrider*, and *Brand New Cadillac*, and *That Baby Ain't Black Enough*. *—Andrew Hamilton*

● **Poonanny Be Still!** / 1993 / Waldoxy ♦♦♦♦

Birmingham, AL, resident Joe Poonanny had been a fixture on the Southern chitlin circuit for around 30 years when, in 1993, he finally recorded his debut album, *Poonanny Be Still*! for Malaco's Waldoxy label. Other labels had expressed interest in the blues/soul singer known for his raunchy humor, but allegedly, Poonanny was distrustful of record companies in general and couldn't be persuaded to record an album until Malaco's Tommy Couch Jr., came along. This fun, highly entertaining CD won't appeal to those who shy away from off-color humor—it isn't as explicit as a 2 Live Crew album, but it isn't exactly gospel either. Clarence Carter's "Strokin'," Latimore's "Let's Straighten It Out" and Denise LaSalle's "Steppin' Out" were perfect choices for Poonanny, whose album has as much to do with Southern R&B as it does with the blues. *Poonanny Be Still*! did especially well in the South—the people who bought this disc were the same people who were into soul-minded bluesmen like Bobby "Blue" Bland, Little Johnny Taylor and the late Z.Z. Hill and blues-friendly souls singers like Carter and LaSalle. With *Poonanny Be Still*!, national audiences finally got a chance to hear a talented singer who had gone unrecorded for too long. *—Alex Henderson*

The Grindin' Man / Nov. 22, 1994 / Waldoxy ♦♦♦♦

Joe Poonanny's a throwback, a modern day purveyor of the raunchy, bawdy recordings of the '40s and '50s that stereotyped R&B for years. "The Devil's music," as some elders called it, changed by the late '50s when R&B cleaned its image and began selling to the masses. "3 People Sleepin' In My Bed" and "Trashy Women" are the tamest selections; others, however, describe love and sex so descriptively they can only be played when kids aren't present. The titles, including "Meatman," "Out Grindin' the Grindin' Man," "Beat Your Meat," "I Ain't Beggin', I'm Buyin'," and "Rump Ringer," say it all. Producer Tommy Couch Jr., gets great performances from all involved. This is first-class party music; an excellent ice breaker for gatherings. *—Andrew Hamilton*

Ponyrider / Aug. 6, 1996 / Waldoxy ♦♦♦

Brand New Cadillac / Oct. 13, 1998 / Waldoxy ♦♦♦

That Baby Ain't Black Enough / Aug. 7, 2001 / Waldoxy ♦♦♦

Ana Popovic

b. May 13, 1976, Belgrade, Yugoslavia

Vocals, Guitar / Soul-Blues, Blues-Rock, Funk, Modern Electric Blues

Ana Popovic is a gritty, earthy blues-rocker who has been directly or indirectly influenced by artists like Koko Taylor, Etta James, Ruth Brown, Esther Phillips, and Tina Turner, but she isn't from Chicago, Memphis, New Orleans, or anywhere else in the United States. The singer/guitarist grew up in Yugoslavia, an unlikely place for someone to learn to sing and play the blues. But in fact, that was exactly where she became interested in American blues, rock, soul, funk, and jazz. Popovic was born in Belgrade, Yugoslavia, on May 13, 1976, when Eastern Europe was still dominated by oppressive communist regimes. As a teenager, she not only learned to sing blues and rock, she also learned to play guitar and was influenced by Elmore James' electric slide guitar techniques.

Popovic was in her late teens when in 1995 she formed her first band, Hush. By that time, the Iron Curtain was no more; communism had disappeared from the countries of Eastern Europe, and musicians in that part of the world were able to travel freely. Hush played countless shows in Yugoslavia and in 1998, traveled to Hungary and Greece for some gigs. In 1998, Hush recorded an album, titled *Hometown*, that didn't receive much exposure in the U.S., but was reviewed in various European publications. During 1999 an eventful year for Popovic; that year, she moved to the Netherlands, put together a new band (which was billed as the Ana Popovic Band), and signed with the German Ruf label as a solo artist. In October 2000, she visited the U.S. and recorded most of her debut solo album, *Hush!*, in Memphis before finishing the album in Utrecht, Holland. *Hush!* (which was named after her first band) points to the fact while Popovic is blues-oriented, she is not a blues purist and does not embrace a traditional 12-bar format all of the time.

Popovic, who sings with only a slight trace of an East European accent and is quite easy to understand, combines blues with rock, soul, funk, and jazz and she has no problem delivering a muscular blues-rock attack while being quite jazzy and moody when she wants to. *Hush!* was released by Ruf in January 2002 and made it to U.S. stores as an import. *—Alex Henderson*

● **Hush!** / Jan. 22, 2002 / Ruf ✦✦✦

While the U.S., Britain, and to a lesser extent Canada don't have a stranglehold on the blues, these countries account for the majority of music being produced in that genre. Therefore, when someone from a different nationality releases a strong album in the States, it usually makes news, at least in the rarefied blues universe. Born and raised in Yugoslavia, Ana Popovic would seem to have been brought up in an unusual area to soak in the deep soul, robust swamp rock, and husky R&B she reveals on her first album. But music is a universal language, and Popovic, along with noted blues-rock producer Jim Gaines, has delivered a rugged, confident, and eclectic debut that showcases the artist's many strengths (especially on slide guitar) in songs that shift from jazz ("I Won't Let You Down," "Minute 'Til Dawn") to deep funk (an innovative cover of Tom Waits' "Downtown") and soulful pop ("How Lonely Can a Woman Get?"). With a husky, sensuous voice similar to the Pretenders' Chrissie Hynde, she digs into these tunes with authority, even if English isn't her first language. A duet (guitar and vocal) with Bernard Allison on Johnny Copeland's "Bring Your Fine Self Home" is both sexy and gritty, as the two trade verses and riffs with obvious excitement and mutual respect. A raging version of Buddy Guy's "A Man of Many Words" (here titled "Girl of Many Words") rescues that song from obscurity as Popovic whips out a slimy version with rollicking horns that updates the tune while making it her own. Her originals don't push the limits of the genre, yet they are compressed slices of blues-rock that are excellent showcases for Popovic's tough vocals, wiry, Hendrix-styled leads, and robust stance. The self-penned "Hometown," a greasy, slinky trip down to New Orleans with hypnotic tribal drums, is but one of the album's gripping centerpieces. Recorded in Memphis and sounding like it, Popovic has captured the city's evocative, unvarnished R&B charm on this polished but far-from-slick album. A welcome shot of sex and showmanship in the blues world, Ana Popovic's American debut is a *tour de force* for this newcomer brimming with sass, brains, and talent. *—Hal Horowitz*

Jerry Portnoy

b. Nov. 25, 1943, Evanston, IL

Vocals, Harmonica / Harmonica Blues

Another ex-Muddy Waters employee, Jerry Portnoy's biting, flailing harmonica style rivals any within contemporary blues circles for fluency, range, or emotional range. His vocals are effective enough, especially when punctuated by his harp accompaniment and solos.

Portnoy began his professional musical career as part of Muddy Waters' backing band in the early '70s. Jerry replaced Mojo Buford in 1974 and he stayed with the band for six years. During his tenure with Waters, he appeared on the albums *I'm Ready*, *Muddy "Mississippi" Waters Live*, and *King Bee*. In 1980, Portnoy, bassist Calvin Jones, pianist Pinetop Perkins, and drummer Willie Smith all left Muddy to form the Legendary Blues Band.

Throughout the early '80s, Portnoy stayed with the Legendary Blues Band, recording the albums *Life of Ease* and *Red Hot & Blue*. In 1986, he left the band and he briefly retired. By the end of 1987, he had returned to the scene, founding the Broadcasters with Ronnie Earl. Two years later, he and Earl had a falling out, causing Jerry to leave the group.

Portnoy formed his own band, the Streamliners, in 1989. Two years later, the band released their debut, *Poison Kisses*, on Modern Blues Recordings. Between 1991 and 1993, Portnoy was part of Eric Clapton's All-Star Blues Band. After leaving Clapton's band in 1993, he played a number of concerts, releasing his second album, *Home Run Hitter*, in 1995. *Blues Harmonica Masterclass* appeared six years later. *—Ron Wynn & Stephen Thomas Erlewine*

● **Poison Kisses** / 1991 / Modern Blues ✦✦✦✦✦

Jerry Portnoy's debut album, *Poison Kisses*, is a fine set of rollicking Chicago blues. Portnoy is at his best when he is blowing away on the harp, and there's no exception to the rule here—the whole album can fall apart when he's simply singing, but when he's playing the harp, the music catches fire. Worthwhile for harmonica fans. *—Thom Owens*

Home Run Hitter / 1995 / Indigo ✦✦✦

Blues Harmonica Masterclass / Jun. 26, 2001 / Jerry Portnoy's ✦✦✦

Down in the Mood Room / Feb. 26, 2002 / TinyTown ✦✦✦✦

Harp master Jerry Portnoy give his blues a vintage swing on *Down in the Mood Room*, transporting listeners to the smoky jazz joints of a bygone era. This concept album is rewarding from start to finish, if you appreciate sultry jazz and blues played on the harp. Its classy retro tones will be a welcome change of pace for blues harp enthusiasts who like to mellow down easy. Producer Duke Robillard gives the album a wonderful vintage sound. Portnoy also proves he's no jazz slouch. On standards like "Lullaby of Birdland," "Canadian Sunset," "Sentimental Journey," and "Stormy Weather," his clarity of tone and sense of melody are remarkable, rivaling the original jazz harp impresario, Toots Thielemans. He doesn't just honk, he truly sings on this record. His harmonic and tonal gymnastics will amaze as well, as he jumps from a whisper to a wail in a single breath. The record's material is refreshingly diverse, while still common in theme. Beyond nostalgic ballads and blues, Portnoy cuts it up on a swinging rendition of Horace Silver's "Doodlin'" and several raucous originals. Highlights include his "Mood Room Boogie" and "Once Too Often." His noir-ish "Endless Road" is also a bona fide classic. Another nice surprise: Portnoy and Robillard's campy yet cool vocals are reminiscent of Cab Calloway. Robillard's reading of "You Rascal You" is priceless. This is jazz and blues in their pure form from two greats. *—William Meyer*

Powder Blues Band

f. 1978

Group / Contemporary Blues

Guitarist Tom Lavin, bassist Jack Lavin, and a keyboard player formed Powder Blues Band in 1978, later adding trumpeter Mark Hasselbach, drummer Duris Maxwell, and saxophonists Wayne Kozak, Gordie Bertram, and David Woodward. The group signed with Capitol, which released *Uncut* and *Powder Blues* in 1980. Other albums include *Thirsty Ears* (1981), *Party Line* (1982), *Red Hot/True Blue* (1983), *First Decade-Greatest Hits* (1990), and *Let's Get Loose* (1993). *—John Bush*

Uncut / 1980 / RCA ✦✦✦✦

These real-life Blues Brothers dependably deliver fun, danceable tunes in a classic jump blues groove. The Canadian West Coast band evokes Kansas City and Chicago. Tunes by Albert King and Wynonie Harris notwithstanding, the highlights here are "Doin' It Right," "Boppin' With the Blues," and "Hear That Guitar Ring"—all written by the band's likable guitarist, Tom Lavin. *—Mark Allan*

● **Powder Blues** / 1980 / Liberty ✦✦✦✦✦

Red Hot/True Blue / 1983 / Flying Fish ✦✦✦

First Decade/Greatest Hits / 1990 / Warner Brothers ✦✦✦✦

Hailing from Vancouver, this lively and entertaining blues outfit had little success on the charts, but their fiery brand of Chicago-style blues was enough to give them a Juno award in 1981 (Canada's version of the Grammy) and the W.C. Handy award in 1985 for Best Foreign Blues Band, presented in Memphis, TN. *First Decade/Greatest Hits* is a delectable 19-track hits package that contains all of the Powder Blues Band's most important tracks, including a handful from both 1980's *Uncut* album and 1981's *Thirsty Ears* release, with the former going double platinum, selling over 200,000 copies. Brothers Tom Lavin and Jack Lavin lead the way on guitar, sounding especially sharp on "Doin' It Right" and "Thirsty Ears," the band's biggest singles, all with the help of some highly intoxicating saxophone bits. Mixing the blues with some solid sounding rock & roll, tracks like "Hear That Guitar Ring," "Joyridin'," and "I'm on the Road Again" proved the band could integrate both styles effectively through Tom Lavin's wide-awake vocals and an even keel of piano, saxes, and trumpet. Best of all, the Powder Blues Band maintained a small-club sound without sounding amateurish, and this tasty bunch of tracks proved that their talents far exceeded their commercial accomplishments. *—Mike DeGagne*

Duffy Power

b. Sep. 9, 1941

Vocals, Harmonica / British Invasion, Blues-Rock

Power is a lost figure of the '60s who drifted into the inner circle of British blues after a middling career as a teen idol in the early '60s. He recorded one of the first Beatles covers (an early 1963 single of "I Saw Her Standing There") and never experienced acclaim as a commercial pop singer or blues vocalist. But he recorded some fine little-known blues-cum-R&B/rock sides in the '60s, some of which featured present and future members of the Graham Bond Organisation, Cream, and Pentangle. The pleasures of Power are subtle and not easily captured in print. His original material is strong, his arrangements imaginative, and his performance sincere; he's grounded in the blues, but doesn't fall into shopworn clichés, bringing a lot of himself and the innovations of British '60s rock into the picture. *—Richie Unterberger*

Mary Open the Door / 1986 / Rock Machine ✦✦✦✦✦

Blues Power / 1992 / See for Miles ✦✦✦✦

Most of the recordings on *Blues Power* were originally released on Power's self-titled album on the tiny U.K. Spark label in 1969. Duffy says in the liner notes of this reissue that the album was never intended for release, and that these sessions were acoustic demos for an LP that never got produced with the arrangements he had envisioned. That may be so, but it's still a worthy document of this underrated British bluesman at his most bare-boned and haunting. With just his guitar and harmonica, Power runs through both moody originals and covers of R&B/blues standards (with The Beatles' "Fixing a Hole" thrown in) that are rearranged and drastically stripped down. This reissue includes the 15 tracks from the 1969 release, a couple more from the same sessions that were issued on the extremely obscure *Firepoint* compilation album, and three from the mid-'60s (also included on the *Little Boy Blue* reissue) that also explore acoustic moods, forming a picture of Power's most intimate work. *—Richie Unterberger*

● **Little Boy Blue** / 1992 / Edsel ✦✦✦✦✦

His best recordings, as noteworthy for the players on the album as Power himself. Laid down sometime in the mid-'60s, Power (who sings and plays occasional guitar and harp) is backed by a rotating ensemble including, at various points, John McLaughlin and Jack Bruce (before they gained fame), as well as future Pentangle members Danny Thompson and Terry Cox. Neither as rock-oriented as the Stones nor as strictly revivalist as Alexis Korner (with whom Power played for a time), this is one of the best British blues recordings, cutting straight down the middle between gutbucket blues and soulful R&B. Divided equally between Power originals and R&B blues covers, the material and performances are spare, powerful, and as consistent as any '60s British blues album. Unfortunately, these sessions were unissued for several years, surfacing briefly under the title *Innovations* in 1970 on the British Transatlantic label. This reissue on another tiny British label is equally obscure, but should not be missed by fans of '60s British R&B. —*Richie Unterberger*

Just Say Blue / 1995 / Retro ✦✦✦✦
While not up to the level of the other vintage Power compilations available (*Little Boy Blue* and *Blues Power*), this is a worthwhile supplement to those CDs, featuring 21 tracks of rare and unreleased material cut by the singer from 1965 to 1971. The first half, focusing on his 1965-1967 output, is the more interesting portion by a considerable margin, as much for the jazz-blues-R&B fusion of the arrangements (featuring contributions from Jack Bruce, John McLaughlin, Ginger Baker, and Pentangle's Danny Thompson and Terry Cox) as Power's singing. The early-'70s songs that make up the remainder of the disc have a more pedestrian blues-rock feel, but there are some good, inspired moments, with cameos by Rod Argent, Thompson, Cox, and Alexis Korner. —*Richie Unterberger*

Sky Blues / May 27, 2002 / Hux ✦✦✦
For a guy who's never been too well-known or even managed to make a heck of a lot of records, Duffy Power made quite a few appearances on the BBC as far back as the late '50s. This 19-track compilation is actually only a fraction of those, but it's well assembled and satisfying, though it's unfortunate that a 1970 solo session and a 1967 one as leader of Duffy's Nucleus could not be cleared for inclusion. All but three songs come from the late '60s and early '70s, a time at which he was, to admit a begged-for pun, at full power. And even if its primary appeal is to fans of this fine, eclectic, cult blues-rock artist, it's of above-average interest as far as BBC compilations go, since it captures Power in some quite different settings. Five acoustic songs from a 1970 session have Power backed by British blues great Alexis Korner on guitar and serve as further evidence that Power was one of the U.K.'s finest folk-bluesmen, on both originals (including the otherwise unreleased "Halfway Blues") and covers of "That's All Right Mama" and Robert Johnson's "Hellhound." Six songs from a 1971 session are backed only by Mike Hall on keyboards, but are just as effective in their stark yet sensitive delivery. These include the exceptionally haunting jazz-blues Power original "The River," and oddities like "Baby Let's Play House" and a bluesy reworking of the Beatles' "I Saw Her Standing There" (which Power had covered on disc way back in 1963). The four 1973 tracks have a more standard, full-blues-rock band backing, and though not as outstanding as the other sessions, command decent respect. The CD's rounded out by three 1994 cuts on which he's backed only by acoustic guitar and Dick Heckstall-Smith's saxophone, and one rather rough-fidelity cut from a 1968 session, a cover of "Gin House Blues." Actually the sound on the 1970 session is mediocre (though listenable) too, but on the whole this is a good collection as both a listening experience and a document of facets of his work that weren't always readily available on official releases. —*Richie Unterberger*

Preacher Boy (Christopher Watkins)
b. 1968, Iowa City, IA
National Steel Guitar, Vocals / Country Blues, Modern Acoustic Blues
Christopher Watkins, a twenty-something rocker from the San Francisco Bay area, is turning a whole new generation of teenage and twenty-something alternative rock fans on to the eternal hipness of the blues. Watkins, who uses the stage name Preacher Boy, is backed on his club shows around the Bay area and other parts of the West Coast by his band, Natural Blues.

Watkins was born in Iowa City, but lived in Michigan, Kansas, Italy, and Washington before moving to San Francisco. At 16, his mom brought him a copy of Sam Charters' book *The Country Blues* from the library. Mrs. Watkins knew her son was becoming obsessed with a Howlin' Wolf record he'd found in the family record collection. After reading about country blues musicians in Charters' book, Watkins became fascinated with the styles of classic country blues players like Mississippi John Hurt, Son House, Bukka White, Robert Johnson, Blind Willie Johnson, and Mance Lipscomb.

Watkins played guitar in a number of bar bands for several years before forming Preacher Boy & the Natural Blues in 1992. The band soon found themselves sharing stages with touring acts like Counting Crows, Chris Isaak, Los Lobos, J.J. Cale, and others on their San Francisco tour stops.

The band's self-titled debut for Blind Pig Records of San Francisco may not have been an overwhelming critical success, but change, whether it's in jazz or blues, is never easy. The band has a fresh take on the blues, and they turned out to be a surprise hit of the 1995 San Francisco Blues Festival. Watkins who has a gruff, Tom Waits-like voice and jumpy, rhythmic guitar playing, shows an infectious energy and the band shows a maturity in the development of their style on their second album for Blind Pig, the 1996 release *Gutters and Pews*. On this album, the band successfully blends a range of Americana styles, including folk-blues, roots-rock, funk, gospel and early, blues-based jazz. In 1998, Preacher Boy relocated to the U.K., signed with Wah Tup, and released *Crow*. While opening for Eagle-Eye Cherry on tour promoting *Crow*, the two formed a songwriting partnership leading to Preacher Boy co-writing and playing on five tracks on Cherry's 2001 release *Living in the Present Future*. In 1999, Preacher Boy was back in the States recording the follow-up to *Crow*. *The Devil's Buttermilk* was released in 2000 on Manifesto and showed Preacher Boy further expanding his unique approach to the blues. Also in 2000, he contributed a version of "Old Boyfriends" to the Tom Waits' tribute, *New Coat of Paint: Songs of Tom Waits*—*Richard Skelly & Tim Sendra*

Preacher Boy & the Natural Blues / 1995 / Blind Pig ✦✦✦

Gutters and Pews / 1996 / Blind Pig ✦✦✦
This CD is a rocking session most notable for the strange voice of Preacher Boy, who makes Louis Armstrong sound like a tenor. Preacher Boy (listed as playing various

guitars, mandolin, bass guitar, mellotron, banjo, accordion, organ, piano, melodica, corn whiskey jug, tamborine, washboard, trumpet, wrench, and egg) is joined by a colorful and versatile group for a set of originals. Listeners who can get used to the leader's very raspy bullfrog voice (which dominates the music) will find this spirited program of rockish blues to have some moments of interest. —*Scott Yanow*

Crow / Mar. 7, 2000 / Orchard ✦✦✦

● **The Devil's Buttermilk** / Oct. 3, 2000 / Manifesto ✦✦✦

Elvis Presley
b. Jan. 8, 1935, Tupelo, MS, d. Aug. 16, 1977, Memphis, TN
Vocals, Guitar / Pop/Rock, Pop, Rockabilly, Rock & Roll
Elvis Presley may be the single most important figure in American 20th century popular music. Not necessarily the *best*, and certainly not the most consistent. But no one could argue that he was not the musician most responsible for popularizing rock & roll on an international level. Viewed in cold sales figures, his impact was phenomenal. Dozens upon dozens of international smashes from the mid-'50s to the mid-'70s, as well as the steady sales of his catalog and reissues since his death in 1977, may make him the single highest-selling performer in history.

More important from a music lover's perspective, however, are his remarkable artistic achievements. Presley was not the very first white man to sing rhythm & blues; Bill Haley predated him in that regard, and there may have been others as well. Elvis was certainly the first, however, to assertively fuse country and blues music into the style known as rockabilly. While rockabilly arrangements were the foundations of his first (and possibly best) recordings, Presley could not have become a mainstream superstar without a much more varied palette that also incorporated pop, gospel, and even some bits of bluegrass and operatic schmaltz here and there. His '50s recordings established the basic language of rock & roll; his explosive and sexual stage presence set standards for the music's visual image; his vocals were incredibly powerful and versatile.

Unfortunately, to much of the public, Elvis is more icon than artist. Innumerable bad Hollywood movies, increasingly caricatured records and mannerisms, and a personal life that became steadily more sheltered from real-world concerns (and steadily more bizarre) gave his story a somewhat mythic status. By the time of his death, he'd become more a symbol of gross Americana than of cultural innovation. The continued speculation about his incredible career has sustained interest in his life, and supported a large tourist/ entertainment industry, that may last indefinitely, even if the fascination is fueled more by his celebrity than his music.

Born to a poor Mississippi family in the heart of Depression, Elvis had moved to Memphis by his teens, where he absorbed the vibrant melting pot of Southern popular music in the form of blues, country, bluegrass, and gospel. After graduating from high school, he became a truck driver, rarely if ever singing in public. Some 1953 and 1954 demos, recorded at the emerging Sun label in Memphis primarily for Elvis' own pleasure, helped stir interest on the part of Sun owner Sam Phillips. In mid-1954, Phillips, looking for a white singer with a black feel, teamed Presley with guitarist Scotty Moore and bassist Bill Black. Almost by accident, apparently, the trio hit upon a version of an Arthur "Big Boy" Crudup blues tune, "That's All Right Mama," that became Elvis' first single.

Elvis' five Sun singles pioneered the blend of R&B and C&W that would characterize rockabilly music. For quite a few scholars, they remain not only Elvis' best singles, but the best rock & roll ever recorded. Claiming that Elvis made blues acceptable for the white market is not the whole picture; the singles usually teamed blues covers with country and pop ones, all made into rock & roll (at this point a term that barely existed) with the pulsing beat, slap-back echo, and Elvis' soaring, frenetic vocals. "That's All Right Mama," "Blue Moon of Kentucky," "Good Rockin' Tonight," "Baby Let's Play House," and "Mystery Train" remain core early rock classics.

The singles sold well in the Memphis area immediately, and by 1955 were starting to sell well to country audiences throughout the South. Presley, Moore, and Black hit the road with a stage show that grew ever wilder and more provocative, Elvis' swiveling hips causing enormous controversy. The move to all-out rock was hastened by the addition of drums. The last Sun single, "I Forgot to Remember Forget"/"Mystery Train," hit number one on the national country charts in late 1955. Presley was obviously a performer with superstar potential, attracting the interest of bigger labels and Colonel Tom Parker, who became Elvis' manager. In need of capital to expand the Sun label, Sam Phillips sold Presley's contract to RCA in late 1955 for $35,000—a bargain, when viewed in hindsight, but an astronomical sum at the time.

This is the point where musical historians start to diverge in opinion. For many, the whole of his subsequent work for RCA—encompassing over 20 years—was a steady letdown, never recapturing the pure, primal energy that was harnessed so effectively on the handful of Sun singles. Elvis, however, was not a purist. What he wanted, more than anything, was to be successful. To do that, his material needed more of a pop feel; in any case, he'd never exactly been one to disparage the mainstream, naming Dean Martin as one of his chief heroes from the get-go. At RCA, his rockabilly was leavened with enough pop flavor to make all of the charts, not just the country ones.

At the beginning, at least, the results were hardly any tamer than the Sun sessions. "Heartbreak Hotel," his first single, rose to number one and, aided by some national television appearances, helped make Elvis an instant superstar. "I Want You, I Need You, I Love You" was a number one follow-up; the double-sided monster "Hound Dog"/"Don't Be Cruel" was one of the bigest-selling singles the industry had ever experienced up to that point. Albums and EPs were also chart-toppers, not just in the U.S., but throughout the world. The 1956 RCA recordings, while a bit more sophisticated in production and a bit less rootsy in orientation than his previous work, were still often magnificent, rating among the best and most influential recordings of early rock & roll.

Elvis' (and Colonel Parker's) aspirations were too big to be limited to records and live appearances. By late 1956, his first Hollywood movie, *Love Me Tender*, had been released; other screen vehicles would follow in the next few years, *Jailhouse Rock* being the best. The hits continued unabated, several of them ("Jailhouse Rock," "All Shook Up," "Too Much") excellent, and often benefiting from the efforts of top early rock songwriter Otis

Blackwell, as well as the emerging team of Jerry Leiber-Mike Stoller. The Jordanaires added both pop and gospel elements with their smooth backup vocals.

Yet worrisome signs were creeping in. The Dean Martin influence began rearing his head in smoky, sentimental ballads such as "Loving You"; the vocal swoops became more exaggerated and stereotypical, although the overall quality of his output remained high. And although Moore and Black continued to back Elvis on his early RCA recordings, within a few years the musicians had gone their own ways.

Presley's recording and movie careers were interrupted by his induction into the Army in early 1958. There was enough material in the can to flood the charts throughout his two-year absence (during which he largely served in Germany). When he reentered civilian life in 1960, his popularity, remarkably, was at just as high a level as when he left.

One couldn't, unfortunately, say the same for the quality of his music, which was not just becoming more sedate, but was starting to either repeat itself, or opt for operatic ballads that didn't have a whole lot to do with rock. Elvis' rebellious, wild image had been tamed to a large degree as well, as he and Parker began designing a career built around Hollywood films. Shortly after leaving the Army, in fact, Presley gave up live performing altogether for nearly a decade to concentrate on movie-making. The films, in turn, would serve as vehicles to both promote his records and to generate maximum revenue with minimal effort. For the rest of the '60s, Presley ground out two or three movies a year that, while mostly profitable, had little going for them in the way of story, acting, or social value.

While there were some quality efforts on Presley's early '60s albums, his discography was soon dominated by forgettable soundtracks, mostly featuring material that was dispensable or downright ridiculous. In time he became largely disinterested in devoting much time to his craft in the studio. The soundtrack LPs themselves were sometimes filled out with outtakes that had been in the can for years (and these, sadly, were often the highlights of the albums). There were some good singles in the early '60s, like "Return to Sender"; once in a while there was even a flash of superb, tough rock, like "Little Sister," or "(Marie's the Name) His Latest Flame." But by 1963 or so there was little to get excited about, although he continued to sell in large quantities.

The era spanning, roughly, 1962-1967 has generated a school of Elvis apologists, eager to wrestle any kernel of quality that emerged from his recordings during this period. They also point out that Presley was assigned poor material, and assert that Colonel Parker was largely responsible for Presley's emasculation. True to a point, but on the other hand it could be claimed, with some validity, that Presley himself was doing little to rouse himself from his artistic stupor, letting Parker destroy his artistic credibility without much apparent protest, and holing up in his large mansion with a retinue of yes men who protected their benefactor from much day-to-day contact with a fast-changing world.

The Beatles, all big Elvis fans, displaced Presley as the biggest rock act in the world in 1964. What's more, they did so by writing their own material and playing their own instruments—something Elvis had never been capable of, or particularly aspired to. They, and the British and American groups the Beatles influenced, were not shy about expressing their opinions, experimenting musically, and taking the reins of their artistic direction into their own hands. The net effect was to make Elvis Presley, still churning out movies in Hollywood as psychedelia and soul music became the rage, seem irrelevant, even as he managed to squeeze out an obscure Dylan cover ("Tomorrow Is a Long Time") on a 1966 soundtrack album.

By 1967 and 1968, there were slight stirrings of an artistic reawakening by Elvis. Singles like "Guitar Man," "Big Boss Man," and "U.S. Male," though hardly classics, were at least genuine rock & roll that sounded better than much of what he'd been turning out for years. A 1968 television special gave Presley the opportunity he needed to reinvent himself as an all-out leather-coated rocker, still capable of magnetizing an audience, and eager to revisit his blues and country roots.

The 1968 album *Elvis in Memphis* was the first LP in nearly a decade in which Presley seemed cognizant of current trends, as he updated his sounds with contemporary compositions and touches of soul to create some reasonably gutsy late '60s pop/rock. This material, and 1969 hits like "Suspicious Minds" and "In the Ghetto," returned him to the top of the charts. Arguably, it's been overrated by critics, who were so glad to have him singing rock again that they weren't about to carp about the slickness of some of the production, or the mediocrity of some of the songwriting.

But Elvis' voice *did* sound good, and he returned to live performing in 1969, breaking in with weeks of shows in Las Vegas. This was followed by national tours that proved him to still be an excellent live entertainer, even if the exercises often reeked of show-biz extravaganza. (Elvis never did play outside of North America and Hawaii, possibly because Colonel Parker, it was later revealed, was an illegal alien who could have faced serious problems if he traveled abroad.) Hollywood was history, but studio and live albums were generated at a rapid pace, usually selling reasonably well, although Presley never had a Top Ten hit after 1972's "Burning Love."

Presley's '70s recordings, like most of his '60s work, are the focus of divergent critical opinion. Some declare them to be, when Elvis was on, the equal of anything he did, especially in terms of artistic diversity. It's true that the material was pretty eclectic, running from country to blues to all-out rock to gospel (Presley periodically recorded gospel-only releases, going all the way back to 1957). At the same time, his vocal mannerisms were often stilted, and the material—though not nearly as awful as that '60s soundtrack filler—sometimes substandard. Those who are not serious Elvis fans will usually find this late-period material to hold only a fraction of the interest of his '50s classics.

Elvis' final years have been the subject of a cottage industry of celebrity bios, tell-alls, and gossip screeds from those who knew him well, or (more likely) purported to know him well. Those activities are really beyond the scope of a mini-bio such as this, but it's enough to note that his behavior was becoming increasingly unstable. His weight fluctuated wildly; his marriage broke up; he became dependent upon a variety of prescription drugs. Worst of all, he became isolated from the outside world except for professional purposes (he continued to tour until the end), rarely venturing outside of his Graceland mansion in Memphis. Colonel Parker's financial decisions on behalf of his client have also come in for much criticism.

On August 16, 1977, Presley was found dead in Graceland. The cause of death remains a subject of widespread speculation, although it seems likely that drugs played a part. An immediate cult (if cult is the way to describe millions of people) sprang up around his legacy, kept alive by the hundreds of thousands of visitors that make the pilgrimage to Graceland annually. Elvis memorabilia, much of it kitsch, is another industry in his own right. Dozens if not hundreds make a comfortable living by impersonating the King in live performance. And then there are all those Elvis sightings, reported in tabloids on a seemingly weekly basis.

Although Presley had recorded a mammoth quantity of both released and unreleased material for RCA, the label didn't show much interest in repackaging it with the respect due such a pioneer. Haphazard collections of outtakes and live performances were far rarer than budget reissues and countless repackagings of the big hits. In the CD age, RCA finally began to treat the catalog with some of the reverence it deserved, at long last assembling a box set containing nearly all of the '50s recordings. Similar, although less exciting, box sets were documenting the '60s, the '70s, and his soundtrack recordings. And exploitative reissues of Elvis material continue to appear constantly, often baited with one or two rare outtakes or alternates to entice the completists (of which there are many). In death, as in life, Presley continues to be one of RCA's most consistent earners. Fortunately, with a little discretion, a good Elvis library can be built with little duplication, sticking largely to the most highly recommended selections below. *—Richie Unterberger*

★ **Elvis Presley** / Mar. 1956 / RCA ♦♦♦♦♦

Today it all seems so easy—RCA signs up the kid from Memphis, television gets interested at around the same time, and the rest is history. The circumstances surrounding the music on this album were neither simple nor promising, however, nor was there anything in the history of popular music up to that time to hint that Elvis Presley was going to be anything other than "Steve Sholes' folly." That was what rival record industry executives were already whispering about this latest talent acquisition by the head of RCA's country division (there were even whispers that Sholes had left Sam Phillips at Sun with a performer that he regarded as potentially bigger than Elvis, in one Carl Perkins). So a lot was unsettled and untried at the first of two groups of sessions that produced the songs on the Elvis Presley album—it wasn't even certain that there was any reason for a rock & roll artist to cut an album, because teenagers bought 45s, not LPs, and it was something of an inspiration on Sholes' part that he was thinking of an LP release on Elvis Presley from his first RCA recording session. The January 10, 1956, Nashville session where the first of Elvis' RCA sides were cut yielded one song, "Heartbreak Hotel," which seemed a potential single, but which no one thought would sell, and a few tracks that would be good enough for an album, if there were one. No one involved knew anything for sure about this music—Chet Atkins, the session guitarist who usually ran the RCA country sessions out of Nashville and often led whatever band was involved, mostly strummed along on rhythm guitar or sat on the sidelines, deferring to Elvis' established band of guitarist Scotty Moore (ironically, a huge Atkins fan) and bassist Bill Black. "Heartbreak Hotel" was released 17 days later, and for about a month it did nothing—then it began to move, and then Elvis Presley made his appearances on the Dorsey Brothers' show and Milton Berle, and had a number one pop single. The album Sholes wanted out of Elvis came from two groups of sessions in January and February, augmented by five previously unissued songs from the Sun library. This was as startling a debut record as any ever made, representing every side of Elvis' musical influences except gospel—rockabilly, blues, R&B, country, and pop were all here in an explosive and seductive combination. *Elvis Presley* became the first rock & roll album to reach the number one spot on the national charts, and RCA's first million dollar-earning pop album. For the 1999 remastering, the sound been upgraded numerous steps, so that one gets a much clearer impression of what Scotty Moore, Elvis, and Atkins are playing (and of the rhythm section of Bill Black and D.J. Fontana), and the bonus tracks show just how far Presley's sound evolved in the space of only two months—in addition to "Heartbreak Hotel" b/w "I Was the One," the extra songs include "Shake, Rattle & Roll" and "Lawdy, Miss Clawdy," rejects from the initial sessions for a projected second album are here, and so is "I Want You, I Need You, I Love You," recorded the month of the original album's release (the single's B-side was "My Baby Left Me," from the album), which shows Presley having developed into much more dramatic singer, more mature and far more controlled as an artist and technical performer. The notes are a little more sketchy than they need have been, but the quality of everything else—especially the sound—makes this an essential part of any collection. *—Bruce Eder*

☆ **Elvis** / Oct. 1956 / RCA ♦♦♦♦♦

Elvis Presley's second album was really his first to be conceived and cut as an album—his debut long-player, *Elvis Presley,* although a brilliant record, was assembled from busted singles attempts and a quintet of Sun Records outtakes. "Anyway You Want Me (That's How I Will Be)" and the classic "Love Me" display glimpses of sophistication and control as a singer on this album that would increasingly drive his singing in years to come. The rhythm numbers include three Little Richard songs that he performs extremely well, most notably "Long Tall Sally," indicating either a strong preference by Elvis or a dearth of acceptable material brought to the September 1956 sessions by Steve Sholes. The surprises on this album include "Paralyzed," one of the lesser known Otis Blackwell compositions, and Elvis' cover of Arthur "Big Boy" Crudup's "So Glad You're Mine" (cut at Elvis' late-January 1956 RCA sessions, but unused), which would have been among any artist's top output during this period. The 1999 remastering, in addition to significantly improved sound on the existing tracks, extends the CD by eight songs including "Hound Dog" and "Don't Be Cruel," the two sides of the biggest-selling single by anybody in 1956, which were cut at sessions overlapping the conception of this album, "Too Much" and "Playing for Keeps," which came from these sessions, and "Love Me Tender," which was cut at a session overlapping the making of this album. *—Bruce Eder*

★ **From Elvis in Memphis** / May 1969 / RCA ♦♦♦♦♦
After a 14-year absence from Memphis, Elvis Presley returned to cut what was certainly his greatest album (or, at least, a tie effort with his RCA debut LP from early 1956). The fact that *From Elvis in Memphis* came out as well as it did is something of a surprise, in retrospect—Presley had a backlog of songs he genuinely liked that he wanted to record and had heard some newer soul material that also attracted him, and none of it resembled the material that he'd been cutting since his last non-soundtrack album, six years earlier. And he'd just come off of the NBC television special which, although a lot of work, had led him to the realization that he could be as exciting and vital a performer in 1969 as he'd been a dozen years before. And for what was practically the last time, the singer cut his manager, Tom Parker, out of the equation, turning himself over to producer Chips Moman. The result was one of the greatest white soul albums (and one of the greatest soul albums) ever cut, with brief but considerable forays into country, pop, and blues as well. Presley sounds rejuvenated artistically throughout the dozen cuts off the original album, and he's supported by the best playing and backup singing of his entire recording history. The spring 2000 remastered edition matches the sound quality on the two-CD set *Suspicious Minds*, but restores the original album's classic cover and song order, with six bonus tracks cut at the same sessions but only released as singles at the time. This disc proves that he not only came back—he was *better* than he'd ever been as a singer or stylist—and is an essential part of any music collection. *—Bruce Eder*

☆ **Reconsider Baby** / 1985 / RCA ♦♦♦♦♦
A 12-song, budget-priced compilation of Elvis' most notable blues sides for the label. A good place to start digging Elvis' commitment to the music—always returning to it right up through the '70s like an old friend, whenever he needed a quick fix of the *real* thing—as he takes on everything from R&B slices like Tommy Tucker's "High Heel Sneakers" to Percy Mayfield's "Stranger in My Own Home Town." Major highlights on this collection are Elvis playing acoustic rhythm guitar and driving the band through a take of the Lowell Fulson title track, blistering versions of two Arthur "Big Boy" Crudup songs, an unreleased Sun recording of Lonnie Johnson's "Tomorrow Night," and the R-rated take of Smiley Lewis' "One Night (of Sin)." *—Cub Koda*

☆ **The Memphis Record** / 1987 / RCA ♦♦♦♦♦
The Memphis Record was RCA's first serious effort to assemble the highlights of what is usually called Elvis Presley's comeback, but which, arguably, could be considered the best album sessions of his career. For the first time since the middle to late '50s, he went into the studio without "Colonel" Tom Parker, his manager, in control of the repertoire, and cut songs because they were good and he liked them, without regard for whether Elvis' business half had an interest in the publishing. The result was one of the greatest white R&B albums ever done, filled from beginning to end with some of the best work of Elvis' career: "Suspicious Minds," "Kentucky Rain," and "In the Ghetto" became hit singles and speak for themselves, but "Any Day Now," "Stranger in My Home Town," "Long Black Limousine," and "Only the Strong Survive," among the other cuts here, are the equal of anything he ever recorded in musical excellence, excitement, and intensity. This material, some of which was originally divided up between two separate LPs, *From Elvis in Memphis* and *Back In Memphis*, has since been recompiled yet again on *Suspicious Minds* (1999), and that is the ultimate compilation of these songs, but this one is more than adequate for more casual fans who want a revelation or two (or three) in their listening. *—Bruce Eder*

☆ **The Complete Sun Sessions** / 1987 / RCA ♦♦♦♦♦
This is it, your perfect starting point to understanding how Elvis—as Howlin' Wolf so aptly put it—"made his *pull* from the blues." All the source points are there for the hearing; Arthur Crudup's "That's All Right (Mama)," Roy Brown's "Good Rockin' Tonight," Kokomo Arnold's "Milkcow Blues Boogie," Arthur Gunter's "Baby, Let's Play House," and Junior Parker's "Mystery Train." Modern-day listeners coming to these recordings for the first time will want to reclassify this music into a million subgenres, with all the hyphens firmly in place. But what we ultimately have here is a young Elvis Presley, mixing elements of blues, gospel, and hillbilly music together and getting ready to unleash its end result—rock & roll—on an unsuspecting world. *—Cub Koda*

☆ **The Million Dollar Quartet** / Feb. 1990 / RCA ♦♦♦♦♦
One of the most important things to remember about this album is it's really just three guys in a room shooting the breeze, goofing around, and stumbling through a few old songs they happen to remember. This wouldn't be the least bit interesting under most circumstances, but the three guys in question happen to be Elvis Presley, Jerry Lee Lewis, and Carl Perkins, which, as you might imagine, makes quite a difference. Perkins was doing a recording session at the Sun Records studio in Memphis on December 4, 1956, with Lewis playing piano on the date, when Elvis, in the midst of his first burst of fame and back in Memphis after a stretch of the road, stopped by to say hello. Elvis, Perkins, and Lewis began casually jamming—mostly on old gospel tunes they remembered from a shared Baptist upbringing—and Sam Phillips had the presence of mind to switch on the tape machine and record the proceedings. (A famous picture taken that day shows Johnny Cash with the group, but if he stuck around to sing a few tunes, he stayed far enough away from the mic to be absent on these recordings.) To call the performances casual taxes understatement, and if you were expecting the ultimate rockabilly moment from these guys, be aware it's about halfway through the session before rock & roll begins to rear its head, and even then it's obvious these guys can play "Farther Along" or "Down By the Riverside" off the top of their heads a lot more easily than "Brown Eyed Handsome Man" or "Too Much Monkey Business." But half the fun of this album is the playful casualness of the performances (and hearing three of rock's great legends in such non-legendary form). And their personalities certainly manifest themselves right off the bat: Elvis is effortlessly authoritative, and at once amused and perplexed by his sudden fame, while Lewis harmonizes like a wild man, determined to show he's the star of the show, and Perkins displays characteristic modesty, content to add churchy harmonies and the occasional signature guitar break. It's also fun to hear Elvis imitate Jackie Wilson imitating him, and Perkins marveling at the genius of Chuck Berry. Like I said, just three guys goofing off—but from these three guys, "goofing off" is really something to hear. *—Mark Deming*

☆ **The King of Rock 'n' Roll: The Complete 50's Masters** / Jun. 23, 1992 / RCA ♦♦♦♦♦
A casual Elvis fan wanting to assemble a decent overview of the King's '50s sides could probably sweat it down to the *Sun Sessions* CD and the first volume the *Top Ten Hits* compilation. But for those of you who take your '50s Presley seriously, *The King of Rock 'n' Roll—The Complete 50s Masters* is absolutely essential. For the hardcore Elvis fan, the booklet and CD graphics for this five-disc set provide incentive enough to justify its purchase. The liner notes by Presley expert Peter Guralnick are passionate, contagious in their enthusiasm, and filled with a real sense of history, time, and place. The treasure-trove of unpublished photos, session information and Elvis memorabilia accompanying the booklet text is no less inspiring. But it's the music (140 tracks in all) that's the real meat and potatoes of this set. Every studio track cut during the '50s—the seminal Sun sides, the early RCA hits, movie soundtracks, alternates, live performances, rarities (including both sides of the long-lost acetate he cut for his mother back in 1953)—it's all here in one gorgeous package. Soundwise, this box makes any of the previous issues of this material pale by comparison, the proper (non-reverbed) inclusion of the Sun masters being a particular treat. This is no mere rehash of what's been around a dozen times before—there's a lot of thought and care behind this package, and no serious fan of American rock & roll should consider a collection complete without it. *—Cub Koda*

☆ **From Nashville to Memphis: The Essential 60's Masters** / Sep. 28, 1993 / RCA ♦♦♦♦♦
Continues the tradition of first-quality sound remastering and packaging. Much of Elvis' '60s work is arguably not as essential as the '50s stuff, but this meticulous five-disc/130-track set makes an impressive case for the defense. A thick booklet contains riveting liner notes, full-color photos, complete discography and session listings; a sheet of RCA album cover stamps tops off the set. *—Roch Parisien*

Amazing Grace: His Greatest Sacred Songs / Oct. 25, 1994 / RCA ♦♦♦♦
Elvis recorded quite a bit of gospel over the course of his career, and this two-CD, 55-song set has the bulk of it. Most of this is drawn from his three gospel LPs (*His Hand in Mine*, 1960; *How Great Thou Art*, 1967; *He Touched Me*, 1972), as well as a 1957 EP. Presley was undoubtedly heavily influenced by gospel (at times he indicated regret at not having chosen to become a gospel singer), and this material has played pretty well with critics. Elvis sings with skill and reasonable commitment, and the backing musicians include such Elvis/Nashville standbys as Scotty Moore, Hank Garland, Floyd Cramer, Charlie McCoy, Pete Drake, the Jordanaires, and James Burton. At the same time, let's have a reality check here. Rock- and pop-oriented fans are going to find this two-and-a-half hour set tough going, unless they have a taste for spirituals as well. Things get a little more accessible when the tempos brighten, but often it's on the sedate side. For both collectors and listeners, highlights of the collection are five previously unreleased tracks from 1972. Recorded with only Charlie Hodges on piano and J.D. Sumner & the Stamps on backing vocals, they present Presley's gospel at its sparsest and most spontaneous. *—Richie Unterberger*

☆ **Walk a Mile in My Shoes: The Essential 70's Masters** / Oct. 10, 1995 / RCA ♦♦♦♦♦
In most conventional rock criticism, Elvis Presley's '70s records are considered his weakest, as they were recorded while he was falling deeper into drug addiction. However, as Dave Marsh argues in the liner notes of *Walk a Mile in My Shoes—The Essential 70's Masters*, the music on the five-CD box set is among the most personal and adventurous of Elvis' career, even if the individual albums don't always reflect that diversity. By cutting away all of the dross that accumulated over the decade and sequencing the songs in a logical, entertaining manner, *Walk a Mile in My Shoes* supports the argument. On the first two discs, all of the singles Presley released during the '70s are presented, and while there are a couple of weak numbers, the music stands as an impressive continuation of his artistic rebirth of the late '60s. *—Stephen Thomas Erlewine*

Elvis '56 / Mar. 5, 1996 / RCA ♦♦♦♦♦
Sure the music on here's great. How could it not be? It has 22 of his hottest tracks from his first year at RCA, including not only the hits "Heartbreak Hotel," "Hound Dog," "Don't Be Cruel," and "Too Much," but such noted early rockers as "My Baby Left Me," "Blue Suede Shoes," "Money Honey," and "So Glad You're Mine." From a collector's viewpoint, though, you have to wonder whether it was really necessary. The only previously unreleased item is a sparser earlier take of "Heartbreak Hotel." Everything else has been widely available (even on CD) for years, and it's a good bet that many of the Elvis fans who buy this already have virtually all of the contents on the *King of Rock 'n' Roll* box set. *—Richie Unterberger*

★ **Sunrise** / Feb. 9, 1999 / RCA ♦♦♦♦♦
Elvis Presley's legendary recordings for Sun Records had been reissued many times before *Sunrise* appeared in early 1999, most notably in the 1987 collection *The Complete Sun Recordings*. Despite its title, *The Complete Sun Recordings* was missing a few odds and ends, plus its sequencing on CD was a little didactic, resulting in a repetitive listen. Those flaws are corrected on the exceptional *Sunrise*, a generous 38-song double-disc set that contains all of Elvis' Sun recordings, including alternate takes and several previously unreleased live performances. The compilers wisely decided to devote the first disc to the original takes, dedicating the second to alternate takes: six live cuts from 1955 and four private demos from 1953 and 1954. This sequencing emphasizes the brilliance of this music. Not only is listening to all 19 masters in a row quite breathtaking, but the second disc winds up as a revelatory experience, since it offers a kind of alternate history by following Elvis' pre-professional recordings from his Sun sessions to early live performances.

As such, *Sunrise* is essential for the curious and the collector alike. *—Stephen Thomas Erlewine*

☆ **Suspicious Minds** / Apr. 13, 1999 / RCA ✦✦✦✦✦
Elvis Presley's comeback recordings from the late '60s are generally regarded as some of the finest music he ever made, not only because they proved he could still be exciting, but because they're musically diverse and emotionally rich. That was evident on *From Elvis in Memphis*, the first record released from his landmark sessions of 1968 and 1969, and latter-day compilations like *The Memphis Record* made clear how deep those recordings were. Twelve years after *The Memphis Record*, the double-disc set *Suspicious Minds* was released, and it stands as the definitive overview of these sessions. All of the familiar hits are here, of course, but for collectors, what makes this essential is that it not only contains all the master takes, but it provides nine alternate takes of classics such as "True Love Travels on a Gravel Road," "Kentucky Rain," "Suspicious Minds," "In the Ghetto," and "I'm Movin' On." None of these are particularly revelatory, but they are interesting enough to be the icing on the cake on an exceptional collection. Since they're more concise, *The Memphis Record* or *From Elvis in Memphis* remain better bets for some listeners, but all true aficionados or rock historians will need to add *Suspicious Minds* to their collections. *—Stephen Thomas Erlewine*

Peace in the Valley: The Complete Gospel Recordings / Sep. 12, 2000 / RCA ✦✦✦
An expanded three-disc collection that attempts to trump a 1994 double-disc set (*Amazing Grace: His Greatest Sacred Songs*) by offering virtually every single Elvis recording of a sacred song, *Peace in the Valley: The Complete Gospel Recordings* accomplishes the mission in its title, but at a hefty price that won't appeal to any but the most obsessive-compulsive fan. Obviously, it includes each track from his three gospel LPs—1960's *His Hand in Mine*, 1967's *How Great Thou Art*, and 1972's *He Touched Me*—plus scattered alternate takes that are previously unreleased. The third disc is padded out with an array of Elvis' sacred recordings that are easily available elsewhere, like the 13 gospel tracks on the raw *Million Dollar Quartet* session recorded at Sun in 1956, the "Gospel Medley" from his 1968 TV Special, and a version of "(There'll Be) Peace in the Valley" originally aired on Ed Sullivan's television show. Though there's no doubt that *Peace in the Valley: The Complete Gospel Recordings* is a complete set, most Elvis fans will gain little from owning it. *—John Bush*

Jimmy Preston

b. Aug. 18, 1913, Chester, PA
Saxophone, Drums / Jump Blues, R&B
Alto sax blower Jimmy Preston is another one of the legion of postwar R&B figures that can accurately be cited as a genuine forefather of rock & roll. His chief claim to fame: the blistering 1949 smash "Rock the Joint," which inspired a groundbreaking cover by Bill Haley & the Comets in 1952.

"Rock the Joint" wasn't Preston's first trip to the R&B Top Ten. Earlier in 1949, he'd hit with "Hucklebuck Daddy." Both were cut for Ivin Ballen's Philadelphia-based Gotham logo. The scorching sax breaks on "Rock the Joint" weren't Preston's doing, but tenor saxist Danny Turner's. Preston cut rather prolifically for Gotham through much of 1950 (including a session with jazzman Benny Golson on tenor sax) before switching to Derby Records and scoring his last hit, "Oh Babe" (with a vocal by Burnetta Evans). The 1950 date for the New York label was apparently his last. *—Bill Dahl*

Jimmy Preston / Oct. 22, 1991 / Collectables ✦✦✦✦
Jump-blues pioneer Preston, a solid alto saxist, with some of his 1949-1950 outings for Philadelphia's Gotham imprint. The titles tell it all: "Swingin' in the Groove," "Hang Out Tonight," "Estellina Bim Bam." *—Bill Dahl*

● **Rock the Joint, Vol. 2** / Oct. 22, 1991 / Collectables ✦✦✦✦✦
Saxman Preston waxed one of the first legitimately traceable rock & roll singles with his scorching jumper "Rock the Joint" for Philadelphia-based Gotham Records in 1949. It's here, along with his inexorably swinging "Hucklebuck Daddy," "Messin' With Preston," and "They Call Me the Champ." *—Bill Dahl*

1948–50 / Nov. 28, 1995 / Flyright ✦✦✦✦✦

Jimmy Preston, Vol. 1 / Dec. 25, 1999 / Krazy Kat ✦✦✦✦

Lloyd Price

b. Mar. 9, 1933, Kenner, LA
Vocals / New Orleans R&B, Rock & Roll, R&B
Not entirely content with being a '50s R&B star on the strength of his immortal New Orleans classic "Lawdy Miss Clawdy," singer Lloyd Price yearned for massive pop acceptance. He found it, too, with a storming rock & roll reading of the ancient blues "Stagger Lee" and the unabashedly pop-slanted "Personality" and "I'm Gonna Get Married," (the latter pair sounding far removed indeed from his Crescent City beginnings).

Growing up in Kenner, a suburb of New Orleans, Price was exposed to seminal sides by Louis Jordan, the Liggins brothers, Roy Milton, and Amos Milburn through the jukebox in his mother's little fish-fry joint. Lloyd and his younger brother Leo (who later cowrote Little Richard's "Send Me Some Lovin'") put together a band for local consumption while in their teens. Bandleader Dave Bartholomew was impressed enough to invite Specialty Records boss Art Rupe to see the young singer (this was apparently when Bartholomew was momentarily at odds with his longtime employers at rival Imperial).

At his very first Specialty date in 1952, Price sang his classic eight-bar blues "Lawdy Miss Clawdy" (its rolling piano intro courtesy of a moonlighting Fats Domino). It topped the R&B charts for an extended period, making Lloyd Price a legitimate star before he was old enough to vote. Four more Specialty smashes followed: "Oooh, Oooh, Oooh," "Restless Heart," "Tell Me Pretty Baby," "Ain't It a Shame"—before Price was drafted into the Army and deposited most unhappily in Korea.

When he finally managed to break free of the military, Lloyd Price formed his own label, KRC Records, with partners Harold Logan and Bill Boskent and got back down to business. "Just Because," a plaintive ballad Price first cut for KRC, held enough promise to merit national release on ABC-Paramount in 1957 (his ex-valet, Larry Williams, covered it on Price's former label, Specialty).

"Stagger Lee," Price's adaptation of the old Crescent City lament "Stack-A-Lee," topped both the R&B and pop lists in 1958. By now, his sound was taking on more of a cosmopolitan bent, with massive horn sections and prominent pop background singers. Dick Clark insisted on toning down the violence inherent to the song's storyline for the squeaky-clean *American Bandstand* audience, accounting for the two different versions of the song you're likely to encounter on various reissues.

After Lloyd Price hit with another solid rocker, "Where Were You (On Our Wedding Day)?," in 1959, the heavy brass-and-choir sound became his trademark at ABC-Paramount. "Personality," "I'm Gonna Get Married," and "Come Into My Heart" all shot up the pop and R&B lists in 1959, and "Lady Luck" and "Question" followed suit in 1960.

Always a canny businessman, Price left ABC-Paramount in 1962 to form another firm of his own with Logan. Double L Records debuted Wilson Pickett as a solo artist and broke Price's Vegas lounge-like reading of "Misty" in 1963. Later, he ran yet another diskery, Turntable Records (its 45s bore his photo, whether on his own sizable 1969 hit "Bad Conditions" or when the single was by Howard Tate!), and operated a glitzy New York nightspot by the same name.

But the music business turned sour for Price when his partner, Logan, was murdered in 1969. He got as far away from it all as he possibly could, moving to Africa and investing in nonmusical pursuits. Perfect example: he linked up with electric-haired Don King to promote Muhammad Ali bouts in Zaire (against George Foreman) and Manila (against Joe Frazier). He indulged in a few select oldies gigs (including an appearance on NBC-TV's *Midnight Special*), but overall, little was seen of Lloyd Price during the '70s.

Returning to America in the early '80s, he largely resisted performing until a 1993 European tour with Jerry Lee Lewis, Little Richard, and Gary U.S. Bonds convinced him there was still a market for his bouncy, upbeat oldies. Price's profile has been on the upswing ever since—he guested on a PBS-TV special with Huey Lewis & the News, and regularly turns up to headline the Jazz & Heritage Festival in his old hometown. *—Bill Dahl*

Mr. Personality / 1959 / ABC ✦✦✦
Recorded in absolutely breathtaking stereo that greatly enhances the brass-heavy arrangements, this LP is worth grabbing any time you run across it. Sure, Lloyd Price sounds offkey on the Tin Pan Alley chestnuts "I Only Have Eyes for You" and "Time After Time," but a forceful "I Want You to Know," the torchy "Dinner for One," and a rocking "Is It Really Love?" make up for the intrusions. *—Bill Dahl*

Lloyd Price: His Originals / 1959 / Specialty ✦✦✦✦✦
Subtitled "My 14 Favorites," this is a nice collection of his very first recordings for Art Rupe's Specialty label in the early '50s. His first hit, "Lawdy Miss Clawdy," is aboard, along with classics like "Mailman Blues," "Oh, Oh, Oh," and "Wish Your Picture Was You." These tracks were cut in New Orleans using the cream of that town's session players, and as such, the music swings with a verve that his later, brassier hits for ABC-Paramount lack, fine as they are. If you want to come in at the start of one of the longer and more varied careers in R&B music, this is the one to pick up. *—Cub Koda*

Mr. Personality Sings the Blues / 1960 / ABC ✦✦✦✦
Blues was no big stretch for the vocalist—his Crescent City output was solidly rooted in the idiom. On this LP, he does a fine job on Eddie Vinson's "Kidney Stew," and Paul Perryman's "Just to Hold My Hand," and his own blasting "I've Got the Blues and the Blues Got Me." *—Bill Dahl*

Sings the Million Sellers / 1961 / ABC ✦✦✦
Lloyd Price sang the hits of the immediate time frame on this long out-of-print album, doing particular justice to "Ain't That Just Like a Woman" (then a minor seller for Fats Domino), the Miracles' "Shop Around," the Midnighters' "The Hoochie Coochie Coo," and the Drifters' "I Count the Tears." Uptown soul arrangements by future Motown staffer Gil Askey give Price full-bodied support. *—Bill Dahl*

Greatest Hits / 1982 / MCA ✦✦✦✦✦
Price wasn't content with R&B fame; he yearned for pop acceptance too. He got plenty at ABC-Paramount from 1957 to 1960 (the time frame this 18-song retro addresses). Creating a brassy, accessible sound, Price hit huge with his rock & roll rendition of "Stagger Lee" (here in two versions—original and *American Bandstand*-sanitized) and went all the way pop with the undeniably catchy "Personality." Innovative arrangements and Price's earnest vocals greatly distinguish "Have You Ever Had the Blues?," "Lady Luck," "Three Little Pigs," and "Where Were You (On Our Wedding Day)," and there's a previously unissued "That's Love" to further up the ante. *—Bill Dahl*

Greatest Hits / 1990 / Curb ✦✦✦
Inadequately shallow peek at the New Orleans singer's biggest hits, largely the pop ones—"Personality," "Stagger Lee." Doesn't even make a tiny dent in Lloyd Price's vast catalog. *—Bill Dahl*

★ **Lawdy!** / Aug. 5, 1991 / Specialty ✦✦✦✦✦
Lloyd Price was a teenager when he scored his first hit, "Lawdy Miss Clawdy," for Art Rupe's young Specialty imprint. Backed by trumpeter/arranger Dave Bartholomew's band (featuring special guest Fats Domino on the 88s), Price's song soared to the top of the R&B charts, scoring Rupe his first crossover hit by racking up sales among both white and black audiences. Though Price's time with Specialty was cut short when he was drafted in 1953, he managed nearly 50 storming, pre-rock & roll sides for the label, 25 of which are gathered on *Lawdy*. Though nothing here was as big a hit as his debut, many of these songs easily could have come close were they selected over later Specialty smashes like "Ooh Ooh Ooh" or "Restless Heart." A shout singer with enough edge on his

voice to be convincing (even as a teenager), Price's early style was tailor-made for the 45 format. With little thought to pacing himself, the singer seems to approach each number as if it may be his last time at the microphone and, therefore, his last chance at a hit. Though that sense is exactly what makes the music so thrilling, it's also what makes these 25 sides difficult to digest *en masse.* That said, for "Lawdy Miss Clawdy" alone this set is worth it, and the high quality of nearly everything else on hand makes for a desirable package of the singer's early work. *—Nathan Bush*

Heavy Dreams, Vol. 2 / 1993 / Specialty ✦✦✦✦✦
No discernible artistic dropoff on Specialty's encore Price retrospective, distinguished by his classics "Oooh-Oooh-Oooh," "Tell Me Pretty Baby," "Ain't It a Shame?" (not Fats Domino's hit), "Country Boy Rock," and "Why" (he later recut the latter for ABC-Paramount). *—Bill Dahl*

★ **Greatest Hits: The Original ABC-Paramount Recordings** / 1994 / MCA ✦✦✦✦✦
Lloyd Price's recordings of ABC-Paramount were bigger, glossier than his recordings for Specialty, complete with female backing vocals, strings and pop production. This, of course, means that certain audiences don't consider them as real as his raw, gritty Specialty recordings, and if that's what you're looking for from Price, turn to their excellent *Lawdy!* compilation. But if you want to hear the second, hit-making half of Price's career, this is the collection to get, and it provides numerous pleasures. First among those, of course, is the phenomenal "Stagger Lee," a storming version of the classic folk ballad that brought the tale of a murdering outlaw into the pop charts, creating enormous controversy and producing an absurdly sanitized version (known as the Bandstand Version, since it was initially recorded for use on *American Bandstand*). Both versions of the song are here, both terrific (with the original version getting the obvious edge), along with other hits like the yearning "Just Because," the giddy stroll "Personality," the galloping "Where Were You (On Our Wedding Day)?" and a tamer re-recording of "Lawdy Miss Clawdy," along with 12 other sides that might not have been hits, but most are very enjoyable. True, this isn't gutsy R&B like the Specialty sides, but these were meant to be rock & roll hits, and they not only were, they're among the best of their kind from the late '50s. Essential music. *—Stephen Thomas Erlewine*

Lloyd Price Sings His Big Ten / Feb. 8, 1994 / Curb ✦✦✦✦✦
Like all standard Curb anthologies, this is too skimpy, numbering ten tracks. It does, however, include all of Price's major hits—"Stagger Lee," "Personality," "I'm Gonna Get Married," "Where Were You On Our Wedding Day," "Lady Luck." And in its favor, it also includes the most famous of his pre-ABC hits, "Lawdy Miss Clawdy." *—Richie Unterberger*

Lawdy Miss Clawdy / Aug. 1, 1995 / Ace ✦✦✦✦
This British import rounds up 16 of the sides Lloyd Price recorded for Specialty between 1952 and 1956 (digitally transferred from the original master and session tapes). The title track wasn't just his biggest hit for the L.A. label, but the first thing he ever recorded. For those who haven't heard it, "Lawdy Miss Clawdy," an original composition (covered by Elvis Presley a few years later), is more Fats Domino—who plays piano on it—than Little Richard or Chuck Berry, who tended to dance to the beat of a faster drummer. In other words, R&B with the accent more on the B (blues) than the R (rhythm). Price, who is sometimes referred to as "Mr. Personality" (after his 1959 hit "Personality") is a rough and ready vocalist on these early recordings. In place of polish and finesse, he offers grit, soul, and an infectious sense of fun as on vendor's lament "Frog Legs" or the call-and-response "What's the Matter Now." The collection also includes his second single, "Restless Heart," which is virtually a rewrite of the first (pleading tone, stride piano, and all). The other sides allow him to stretch his wings a little more, although "Lawdy Miss Clawdy" remains Price at his youthful best. Ray Topping provided the informative liner notes. *—Kathleen C. Fennessy*

20th Century Masters—The Millennium Collection: The Best of Lloyd Price / Jul. 2, 2002 / MCA ✦✦✦✦
As an overview of Price's ABC-Paramount years, this is markedly inferior to MCA's prior CD collection, *Greatest Hits: The Original ABC-Paramount Recordings.* That disc had 18 tracks; this one has just 12, all of which are also on *Greatest Hits: The Original ABC-Paramount Recordings.* Still, it does zero in on his most popular recordings for the label, at the time during which Price's pop crossover success peaked. The biggest hits are all here: "Stagger Lee," "Just Because," "Where Were You (On Our Wedding Day)," "I'm Gonna Get Married," "Personality," "Lady Luck," and "Question." It might not be as down-home New Orleans R&B as his earlier Specialty recordings, but it's good late-'50s rock & roll that comfortably integrates R&B and pop. Note that the version of "Lawdy Miss Clawdy" is not his original 1952 R&B hit (recorded for Specialty), but a late-'50s remake. *—Richie Unterberger*

Sammy Price

b. Oct. 6, 1908, Honey Grove, TX, **d.** Apr. 14, 1992, New York, NY
Piano / Jump Blues, Swing, Boogie-Woogie, Piano Blues
Sammy Price had a long and productive career as a flexible blues and boogie-woogie-based pianist. He studied piano in Dallas and was a singer and dancer with Alphonso Trent's band during 1927-1930. In 1929, he recorded one solitary side under the title of "Sammy Price and His Four Quarters." After a few years in Kansas City, he spent time in Chicago and Detroit. In 1938, Price became the house pianist for Decca in New York and appeared on many blues sides with such singers as Trixie Smith and Sister Rosetta Tharpe. He led his own band on records in the early '40s which included (on one memorable session) Lester Young. Price worked steadily on 52nd Street, in 1948 played at the Nice Festival with Mezz Mezzrow, spent time back in Texas, and then a decade with Red Allen; he was also heard on many rock & roll-type sessions in the '50s. In later years he recorded with Doc Cheatham. Sammy Price was active until near his death, 63 years after his recording debut. *—Scott Yanow*

1929–1941 / Sep. 29, 1929-Dec. 10, 1941 / Classics ✦✦✦✦✦
This single CD from the European Classics label collects all of pianist Sammy Price's postwar recordings as a leader. Despite its title, only two titles preceded the 1940-1941 period: "Blue Rhythm Stomp" by Price's Four Quarters in 1929, and "Nasty But Nice," which finds Price on the same day accompanying trombonist Bert Johnson. Otherwise, the music features Price's Texas Blusicians, New York-based septets and octets put together especially for recordings. The emphasis is on blues, with Price taking several vocals, but such notable guests as altoist Don Stovall, trumpeters Shad Collins and Emmett Berry, and (on four songs) tenor great Lester Young uplift the music. Recommended to small-group swing collectors. *—Scott Yanow*

Singin' With Sammy, Vol. 1 / May 18, 1938-Apr. 6, 1944 / Contact ✦✦✦
As a house pianist for the Decca label, Sammy Price recorded with quite a few vocalists during the period covered by this European LP. Many of the 14 selections on this LP are a bit rare. They find Price swinging with small groups behind such blues-oriented singers as Ollie Shepard (on a date including tenor saxophonist Chu Berry), Jimmie Gordon, Yack Taylor, Perline Ellison, Bea Booze, Christine Chatman, and Lem Johnson. In addition, Price has the chance to be in the spotlight and sing "Queen Street Blues." An interesting, if not essential collection. *—Scott Yanow*

Sammy Price and His Bluesicians—1944 / Mar. 1, 1944 / Circle ✦✦✦✦
This LP has all of the music that pianist Sammy Price and his sextet (which includes trumpeter Bill Coleman, tenor saxophonist Ike Quebec, altoist Joe Eldridge, the young bassist Oscar Pettiford and drummer Hal "Doc" West) recorded at a radio transcription session in 1944. As was often true of many of the Circle LPs from the mid-'80s, the set is programmed somewhat eccentrically, with some (but not all) of the incomplete and alternate takes issued on a different side of the LP than the other versions, making it difficult to trace the evolution of a performance. There are eight songs in all (mostly basic originals, plus "Sweet Lorraine" and "Honeysuckle Rose"); the eight master takes are joined by four full-length alternate versions, four incomplete takes and five false starts. But due to the very interesting players—Coleman and Quebec were in prime form during this era—swing collectors will want this release. *—Scott Yanow*

Sammy Price and Sidney Bechet in Paris / 1956 / Brunswick ✦✦✦✦✦
With Sidney Bechet (sop sax), Price's "Bluesicians" hit on old-time and good time standards—Bechet, as always, in good tune. *—Michael G. Nastos*

Rib Joint—Roots of Rock & Roll / Oct. 17, 1956-Mar. 24, 1959 / Savoy ✦✦✦✦✦
Here's a two-LP set that truly deserves immediate CD reissue. Price led a mighty New York R&B combo through three Savoy Records sessions in 1956-1957 that elicited some sizzling instrumentals: "Rib Joint" (here in two takes), "Back Room Rock," "Juke Joint," "Chicken Out," "Ain't No Strain" (sidemen included guitarist Mickey Baker and saxman King Curtis). A slightly more restrained 1959 date sans sax that comprises the second LP is no less joyful. *—Bill Dahl*

Blues and Boogies / Nov. 14, 1969 / Black & Blue ✦✦✦✦✦
Price is heard here on solo piano and vocal, playing eight Price originals and "See See Rider." It is good to hear him alone on this rare solo album, recorded in France. *—Michael G. Nastos*

Barrelhouse and Blues / Dec. 4, 1969 / Black Lion ✦✦✦✦
After being largely off records (at least as a leader) since 1961, pianist Sammy Price recorded four sets in Europe for Black & Blue and Black Lion before disappearing from records again until 1975. This CD reissues a surprisingly Dixieland-ish outing with a British sextet that includes trumpeter Keith Smith, trombonist Roy Williams, and clarinetist Sandy Brown. Since Price loved to play boogie-woogie and blues, there is a fair sampling of that music on the date (including "West End Boogie" and "Boogie Woogie Minuet"), and such Dixieland favorites as "Rosetta," "Keeping Out of Mischief Now," and "Royal Garden Blues." An exuberant, spirited set with all of the musicians playing in fine form. *—Scott Yanow*

Fire / May 1, 1975 / Black & Blue ✦✦✦
This LP by pianist Sammy Price (put out domestically by Classic Jazz) can easily be split into two parts. Seven songs pay tribute in their titles to France and showcase Price mostly playing blues in a trio with bassist Carl Pruitt and drummer J.C. Heard. The remaining four songs add a trio of veteran swing-era horn players (trumpeter Doc Cheatham, trombonist Gene "Mighty Flea" Conners, and altoist Ted Buckner) on three blues and the one non-Price standard, "Tain't Nobody's Business If I Do." Although the inclusion of the horns gives added interest to the date, there is a certain sameness to much of the material and a predictability to the enjoyable but unsurprising outcome. *—Scott Yanow*

Boogie & Jazz Classics / May 25, 1975 / Black & Blue ✦✦✦✦✦
Price, a delightful, romping pianist in the vintage barrelhouse and boogie-woogie genres, interpreted, reworked, and remade a series of traditional blues and jazz tunes on this fine 1975 release. Everything, from song selection to solos, is wonderful. *—Ron Wynn*

Copenhagen Boogie / Sep. 1, 1975 / Storyville ✦✦✦✦
Pianist Sammy Price's solo and trio work tended to emphasize the blues and boogie-woogie, so it was always fun to hear him playing jazz standards with a larger group. Although this LP has five blues-oriented pieces (including "St. Louis Blues"), it also finds Price taking an unaccompanied solo on "Begin the Beguine" and jamming "Honeysuckle Rose" and "Please Don't Talk About Me When You're Gone." On most of the songs, Price is joined by a four-horn sextet from Scandinavia that includes trombonist/leader Ole "Fessor" Lindgreen, trumpeter Finn Otto Hansen, and two fine reed players. The ensembles are consistently joyous; Price is still in prime form at this late date (he was 67), and the results are quite enjoyable. *—Scott Yanow*

Just Right / Nov. 2, 1977 / Black & Blue ♦♦♦
A sextet with George Kelly (sax) and Freddie Lonzo (trombone) plays two of Price's tunes, five standards (two by W.C. Handy), and one by trumpeter Johnny Lettman. *—Michael G. Nastos*

Sweet Substitute / Nov. 1, 1979 / Sackville ♦♦♦♦
71 years old at the time, pianist Sammy Price had been a working jazz, blues and boogie-woogie musician for over 50 years when he recorded this set of unaccompanied solos. Typecast as a blues musician (partly because that was his favorite music), Price here also performs a variety of swing standards including "It Don't Mean a Thing," "A Hundred Years From Today," "Don't Blame Me," and "Stormy Weather." He shows throughout the melodic, relaxed and bluesy date that he was a superior swing player. This LP is worth searching for. *—Scott Yanow*

Paradise Valley Duets / Feb. 26, 1988-Feb. 28, 1988 / Parkwood ♦♦♦♦
Veteran pianist Sammy Price, who was 79 at the time of this project (which might be his last recording), is heard performing a set of duets with three different Detroit-based musicians. There are three songs apiece with either the modern but flexible trumpeter Marcus Belgrave or George Benson (no relation to the guitarist) on alto or tenor; in both cases, Price performs two swing standards and an original blues. The second side of the small-label LP has five duets by Price with drummer J.C. Heard, including "Honeysuckle Rose," "After Hours," and a romping "Little Rock Getaway." Delightful music. *—Scott Yanow*

King of Boogie Woogie / 1995 / Storyville ♦♦♦
On this odd CD reissue, pianist Sammy Price seems intent on becoming the Muhammad Ali of jazz. He brags throughout the liner notes about how he is the king of boogie-woogie and might very well (based on his five vocals on the date) also be the king of the crooners. In reality, Price's piano playing on the basic material (lots of blues and a few standards) is fine, while his vocals are a novelty at best. With backup work from bassist Arvell Shaw and drummer Panama Francis, this is a decent but not particularly riveting set. *—Scott Yanow*

Sammy Price Story, 1940–1948 / 1999 / Jazz Archives ♦♦♦♦
A 20-track collection of early Sammy Price sides, both as a leader and as a sideman. Kicking off with a duo with drummer Big Sid Catlett, the set moves on to solo sides from 1945, trio sides from 1948, small group dates with his Texas Bluesicians, and finishing up with backup work behind Mezz Mezzrow and Sidney Bechet, Big Joe turner, Cousin Joe, Sister Rosetta Tharpe, and Marie Knight. If you love boogie-woogie piano played with a real flair, you came to the right place. *—Cub Koda*

Blues Boogie Woogie from Texas / Aug. 10, 1999 / EPM Musique ♦♦♦

1942–1945 / Feb. 15, 2000 / Classics ♦♦♦
A nice collection of Price's 1942-1945 recordings that spotlights this highly undervalued boogie pianist. Kicking off with four sides backing Mabel Robinson, the set also includes ten sides that Price's small groups cut for the Decca label, as well as ten piano solos recorded in New York but originally issued in France. A stray duo track with drummer Big Sid Catlett rounds out the collection. A hidden treasure. *—Cub Koda*

Sammy Price and the Blues Singers / Sep. 4, 2001 / Document ♦♦♦♦

● **And the Blues Singers** / Wolf ♦♦♦♦♦
When the Austrian Wolf logo decided to pay tribute to pianist Sammy Price's prolific legacy as both leader and sideman, they really did it up right. Ninety-four sides on four discs dating from 1929 to 1950 spotlight Price's rippling ivories behind a plethora of vocalists—Peetie Wheatstraw, Harmon Ray, Bea Booze, Johnny Temple, Monette Moore, Scat Man Bailey, and a great many more—as well as some very tasty instrumentals of his own. *—Bill Dahl*

Louis Prima

b. Dec. 7, 1911, New Orleans, LA, **d.** Aug. 24, 1978, New Orleans, LA
Vocals, Trumpet / Traditional Pop, Jump Blues, Swing, Dixieland, R&B
Louis Prima became very famous in the '50s with an infectious Las Vegas act co-starring his wife (singer Keely Smith) that mixed together R&B (particularly the honking tenor of Sam Butera), early rock & roll, comedy, and Dixieland. Always a colorful personality, Prima was leading a band in New Orleans when he was just 11.

In 1934, he began recording as a leader with a Dixieland-oriented unit and soon he was a major attraction on 52nd Street. His early records often featured George Brunies and Eddie Miller, and Pee Wee Russell was a regular member of his groups during 1935-1936. Prima, who composed "Sing, Sing, Sing" (which for a period was his theme song), recorded steadily through the swing era, had a big band in the '40s, and achieved hits with "Angelina" and "Robin Hood."

In 1954, he began having great success in his latter-day group (their recordings on Capitol were big sellers and still sound joyous today), emphasizing vocals and Butera's tenor, but he still took spirited trumpet solos. Although he eventually broke up with Keely Smith, Louis Prima (who voiced a character in Walt Disney's animated film *The Jungle Book* in 1966) remained a popular attraction into the '70s. *—Scott Yanow*

1934–1935, Vol. 1 / Sep. 27, 1934-Apr. 8, 1935 / TOM ♦♦♦♦
On the first of four Louis Prima LPs released by the collector's label titled The Old Masters (TOM), the popular musician is heard on his first 16 recordings. At the time Prima and fellow trumpeter-vocalist Wingy Manone were major entertainers on New York's 52nd Street. Unfortunately none of the records in this series give exact personnel and dates (discographies have to be consulted), but Prima's sidemen for the freewheeling performances (which are halfway between Dixieland and swing) are quite impressive, including trombonist George Brunies, clarinetist Sidney Arodin, tenor saxophonist Eddie Miller, and pianist Claude Thornhill. Highlights of the good-time performances include "Jamaica Shout," "'Long About Midnight," "Breakin' the Ice," and "Let's Have a Jubilee." *—Scott Yanow*

1934–1935 / 1934-1935 / Classics ♦♦♦

1934–1939 Broadcasts, Vol. 1 / 1934-1939 / Reflections ♦♦♦
Few jazz musicians had a wider range of tastes, or a broader based career, than Louis Prima. This first volume chronicling his live work from the '30s showcases that fact with performances from three different sources. The set kicks off with nine radio transcriptions of Prima working a one-off date with Joe Venuti's Orchestra in 1934, turning in nice readings of "I'm Confessin'," "Sleepy Time Down South," and "After You've Gone" (these songs mark the only time Prima worked with both Venuti and Red Norvo). Next up are the three tunes from Prima's film debut, *Swing It*, featuring Pee Wee Russell and Louis' New Orleans Gang. Louis Prima & His Jump Band close things out with an eight-song performance taken from a 1939 aircheck. Transfers range from decent to tinny, depending on the original source. All of this is sanctioned by the Prima estate, and comes with a booklet full of informative notes from Will Friedwald. *—Cub Koda*

1935–1936, Vol. 2 / Apr. 3, 1935-Nov. 30, 1935 / TOM ♦♦♦♦♦
The second of four Louis Prima LPs put out by the TOM (The Old Masters) label continues the chronological reissuance of the trumpeter-vocalist's earliest recordings. Personnel and exact dates are not given on the record (which looks like a bootleg) but it is worth noting that on all but the first two songs (which have Eddie Miller), Pee Wee Russell is the clarinetist. Prima, who is the main star, fortunately gave Russell plenty of solo space (the other players are lesser-known). Highlights include "Chinatown, My Chinatown," "Basin St. Blues," "I'm Shooting High," and "I've Got My Fingers Crossed," but in general all 16 selections are quite enjoyable and show that Louis Prima was an appealing entertainer from the start. *—Scott Yanow*

1935–1936 / 1935-1936 / Classics ♦♦♦
Here's Louis from his first flush of success at the Famous Door in New York City. Backed by his New Orleans gang, Prima's distinctive style was already emerging on material like "How'm I Doin'," "Plain Old Me," "Sweet Sue," "Lazy River," "Dinah," and the original version of "Sing, Sing, Sing." Although the backing is strictly New Orleans (and thus a long way stylistically from his later Capitol sides with Sam Butera & the Witnesses), most of the tunes boast the highly inventive clarinet work of Pee Wee Russell, and Prima's horn is well to the fore on these sides. One for hardcore Prima fans. *—Cub Koda*

1936, Vol. 3 / Feb. 28, 1936-Nov. 16, 1936 / TOM ♦♦♦♦♦
On the third of four Louis Prima albums on this obscure label (which has reissued all of the trumpeter-vocalist's earliest recordings but unfortunately does not provide recording dates or personnel), Louis Prima is heard with a septet on six numbers and with his short-lived big band on ten others. A constant force during the performances (and functioning as a co-star) is the unique clarinetist Pee Wee Russell, the only "name" player among the sidemen. Among the high points are "Dinah," "Alice Blue Gown," "Cross Patch," "Mr. Ghost Goes to Town," and the earliest version of Prima's most famous composition, "Sing, Sing, Sing" (from Feb. 28, 1936). All of these albums are highly recommended to swing collectors but will probably be difficult to find. *—Scott Yanow*

1937–1938, Vol. 4 / May 20, 1937-May 16, 1938 / TOM ♦♦♦♦
The fourth and final LP in the TOM label's Louis Prima series has 16 titles cut during a one-year period. With the departure of clarinetist Pee Wee Russell, Prima's sidemen (who include altoist George Moore, tenor saxophonist Joe Catalyne, clarinetist Meyer Weinberg, and pianist Frank Pinero) lack any recognizable names, but the swing/Dixieland music is quite consistent. Prima alternated ballads with stomps and his personable vocals and New Orleans-oriented trumpet keep the performances interesting. Best are "Fifty-Second Street," "Tin Roof Blues" (the lone instrumental), "Now They Call It Swing," and "Rosalie." *—Scott Yanow*

1940–1944 / 1940-1944 / Classics ♦♦♦
During 1940-1941, Louis Prima led a medium-size (ten-piece) combo, which by 1944 had expanded to a full big band. Although a popular figure during this era, Prima was not quite a star and his big band never really caught on. The 23 numbers on this good-natured CD include a couple instrumentals ("To You, Sweetheart, Aloha" and the swinging "Look Out"), novelties, vocal numbers for Lily Ann Carol, and the debut versions of "Robin Hood," "Angelina," and "Oh Marie" (which hints at Prima's '50s rendition). The leader is the main star throughout the historic release. *—Scott Yanow*

Plays Pretty for the People / Feb. 1944-Jan. 1947 / Savoy ♦♦♦♦
This CD contains a cross-section of Louis Prima's big band recordings of the mid-'40s. While Prima had a fine orchetra (which featured some vocals from Lily Ann Carol), the leader was essentially the whole show. A masterful entertainer who became popular during the swing era, Prima sang well and also played fine New Orleans trumpet. Not all of his humor has dated well but most of the 20 selections on this fine CD still can communicate to today's listeners. High points include "Robin Hood," "Angelina," "Brooklyn Boogie," and "Chinatown, My Chinatown." This is one of the few Louis Prima swing-era CDs currently available. *—Scott Yanow*

Versatile Mr. Prima: Trumpet, Vocal and Hits / Feb. 1944-May 1947 / Jasmine ♦♦♦♦
Subtitled "Trumpet, Vocal & Hits," this features two dozen of Prima's big-band sides recorded for the tiny Varsity, Hit, and Majestic labels in the '40s. Many of Prima's Italian novelties are here, including "Felicia No Capicia," "Josephina, Please No Leana on the Bell," "Baciagaloop (Makes Love on the Stoop)," "Oh! Marie," "Angelina," and "Please No Squeeza Da Banana." But the set also includes such Prima mainstays as "Just a Gigolo," "Robin Hood," and "A Sunday Kind of Love." Few early Prima collections give you a taste of the man's real talents, but this one does. *—Cub Koda*

Say It With a Slap / Jul. 24, 1947-May 27, 1949 / Buddah ♦♦♦

Beepin' & Boppin' / 1949-Apr. 19, 1954 / Hip-O ♦♦♦♦
Beepin' & Boppin' collects some of Louis Prima's finest recordings for Decca and Mercury between 1949 and 1954. Fun, energetic cuts like "Ai-Ai-Ai," "I Beeped When I Should

Have Bopped," and "Yes We Have No Bananas" spotlight Prima's distinctive singing and trumpet playing, and make up the mainstay of this upbeat collection. Guest vocalist Keely Smith joins in on the fun on several tracks. *—Heather Phares*

Angelina / 1950 / Viper's Nest ♦♦♦♦
Swing may have been dead by 1950 but one cannot tell that from this excellent CD which has three radio broadcasts from the Louis Prima big band. Prima, an exciting performer, shows his versatility on a diverse program and takes quite a few hot trumpet solos while his wife Keely Smith (just 22 at the time) is heard on some ballads. However it is the sound of Prima's excellent and hard-swinging orchestra that is the biggest revelation; it is a pity that the personnel is unknown. The repertoire ranges from swing (the driving "Boogie in the Bronx" is most notable) and a few Dixieland numbers to versions of Prima's hits (such as "Robin Hood" and "Angelina") and some standards. Taken from Prima's second of three periods (after he broke up his regular dixieland band of the '30s and a few years before he hit it big in Las Vegas), this set is quite definitive of his music of the time. *—Scott Yanow*

Breaking It Up! / Oct. 18, 1951-Feb. 18, 1953 / Columbia/Legacy ♦♦♦
In late 1951, Louis Prima was hot on the heels of a comeback success the year before with "Oh Babe!," and a record so big that it spawned numerous cover versions from everyone from Wynonie Harris and Lionel Hampton to Kay Starr and even a Spanish language version by Lalo Guerrero ("Chitas Patas Boogie" on Imperial and used in the movie *Zoot Suit* with Edward James Olmos). After three follow-ups went nowhere (one of which was the immortal "Zooma Zooma"), Prima came to Columbia Records and handed over to A&R chief Mitch Miller. And here was part of the problem. Prima's audience liked a cruder Louis and were used to records cut on shoestring budgets with production values that were as raw as the music they framed, while Miller's production was state-of-the-art squeaky-clean. Miller had Prima covering R&B hits of the day ("One Mint Julep") jump blues ("Oooh-Dahdilly-Dah" and one of the few tracks to feature Keely Smith on here), Latin-flavored tunes ("Chili Sauce"), novelty tunes like "Barnacle Bill the Sailor," "Boney Bones," and "It's Good As New (I Painted It Blue)," as well as his patented Italian shuffles like "Eleanor," "Basta," "Luigi," "The Bigger the Figure," and a bombastic version of "Oh Marie" (perhaps the only dud in this entire package), framed in the corniest *Sing Along With Mitch* arrangement imaginable and a million light-years away from his famous Capitol recording of the same tune. This entire combines all 14 sides of the seven singles issued on him, plus the addition of "Chop Suey, Chow Mein" along with the original 1958 cover art to Columbia's original issue of this material. Not his best, but an interesting one to add to the collection after you have most of everything else. *—Cub Koda*

Return of the Wildest / 1955 / Dot ♦♦♦
Just prior to signing with Capitol, trumpeter/singer/comedian Louis Prima, singer Keely Smith and tenor saxophonist Sam Butera (leading his Witnesses) recorded several dates for the Dot label. There are some moments of magic on this long out of print LP, but the overall results are not as explosive as they would be in the near future. Prima is featured on such numbers as "Come Back to Sorrento," "After You've Gone," and "Chinatown My Chinatown"; Keely Smith is in the spotlight on "For Sentimental Reasons"; Butera gets to honk a bit; and trombonist Lou Sino goes a little crazy on "South Rampart Street Parade." The only Prima-Smith duet ("Absent-Minded Lover") is a bit forgettable. An enjoyable if not essential outing. *—Scott Yanow*

★ **Capitol Collectors Series** / Apr. 19, 1956-Feb. 23, 1962 / Capitol ♦♦♦♦♦
What Louis Prima accomplished musically in the company of Sam Butera and the Witnesses and vocalist Keely Smith is in hard evidence on this excellent 26-track compilation. All the classics are aboard with excellent liner notes from Scott Shea and crisp transfers of the original masters ("Angelina-Zooma Zooma," "That Old Black Magic," "I've Got You Under My Skin," "Buona Sera"—which includes a great snippet of studio chatter kicking it off—"Oh Marie," and the obligatory "Just a Gigolo-I Ain't Got Nobody"). Although this duplicates several tracks with Rhino's *Zooma! Zooma!* compilation (now long out of print), with the addition of several singles and unissued tracks, this stands as the best single-disc collection available of Prima's tenure with Capitol Records. The perfect place to start your Louis Prima collection. *—Cub Koda*

Wild, Cool & Swingin / Apr. 19, 1956-Aug. 30, 1962 / Capitol ♦♦♦
Capitol dug through their archives and produced *Louis Prima: Wild, Cool & Swingin*, a continuation of their popular *Ultra Lounge* series. Prima's two-CD retrospective includes some of his finest work for the label, including "That Old Black Magic," "Oh Marie," "Jump, Jive & Wail," and "Angelina/ Zooma Zooma." The set also features vocals from Keely Smith for the total Prima experience. *—Heather Phares*

The Capitol Recordings / Apr. 19, 1956-Dec. 20, 1962 / Bear Family ♦♦♦♦♦
This excellent eight-disc Bear Family box celebrates Louis Prima's *Capitol Recordings* of the '50s and '60s. Since his wife and comedic foil Keely Smith and Sam Butera and the Witnesses (Prima's ace backing unit) both recorded as solo acts during this period, they're exhaustively represented by this box as well. The first three discs cover all of Prima's studio sides and starts up the live recordings with the 1962 Harrah's Club in Tahoe sides, while disc four covers all of the seminal live tracks from 1957 and 1958. Discs five and six are the complete Keely Smith solo recordings, while the last two round up all the sides by Sam Butera and the Witnesses. The truly amazing thing about the 199 (!!!) tracks collected here is how little of it is unissued material. Even if Prima cut some duds now and then, it's pretty wild that Capitol used up damn near every last thing the man ever committed to magnetic tape, such was the high quality of rockin' mayhem he was laying down. And rock it does, all of it infested with much good humor along with Prima's and Butera's other contribution to big-beat mania, the invention of the Vegas shuffle, a loping beat that could be sped up to almost double tempo on any given number. This effect—the solid core of Prima's rockin' groove—is best heard on tracks like "When You're Smiling/The Sheik of Araby," and the later version from the *Hey Boy! Hey Girl!* movie soundtrack of "Oh Marie" (stupendous in the scattin' and honkin' exchange between Prima and Butera), "Basin Street Blues/When It's Sleepy Time Down South," and, of course, "Just a Gigolo/I Ain't Got Nobody," the track that David Lee Roth brought to the charts in the '80s. The duets with Keely Smith ("I've Got You Under My Skin," "That Old Black Magic") and Sam Butera (Richard Berry's "Next Time") are here to savor as well and it's all very fine, indeed. After four discs of Prima's wild-ass genius, the next two of Smith with big-band backings from Nelson Riddle and Billy May will seem sedate by comparison, but they're '50s-style Capitol tracks with their own charm. Great tunes and arrangements, plus the inclusion of her duets with Frank Sinatra makes a nice bonus highlight. The final two discs of Sam Butera come much closer to Prima's rockin' slant on things, with rocked-up jazz classics and R&B tunes galore keeping the party goin' all night long. Needless to say, if you're a Louis Prima fan bordering on fanatic, this is the one to have. *—Cub Koda*

☆ **The Wildest!** / Jan. 1957 / DCC ♦♦♦♦♦
A veritable greatest-hits album, *The Wildest!* is the gem of Louis Prima's catalogue. None of his other efforts transcend its raunchy mix of demented gibberish, blaring sax, and explosive swing, which rocked as hard as anything released at the time. Almost all of Prima's signature songs are found here: "Just a Gigolo/I Ain't Got Nobody," "Oh Marie," "Jump, Jive & Wail," and "Buona Sera," to name a few. A plethora of greatest-hits packages (especially Capitol's *Collectors Series*) may offer wider song selection and greater value, but the reissue of Prima's masterpiece is a welcome event that's been a long time coming. *—Jim Smith*

The Call of the Wildest / Jul. 1957 / Capitol ♦♦♦♦♦
Louis Prima's second Capitol LP with Keely Smith, Sam Butera and the Witnesses is just as exciting as his first. The trumpeter-vocalist was a natural entertainer and comedian, and all of his skills are on evidence during this spirited program. The honking tenor of Sam Butera, Keely Smith's appealing voice and the mixture of Dixieland and R&B results in some remarkable and very accessible music. Highlights include the medley of "When You're Smiling" and "The Sheik of Araby," trombonist Red Blount's feature on "Blow, Red, Blow," "Pennies from Heaven," "The Birth of the Blues," and "When the Saints Go Marching In." What a band. *—Scott Yanow*

The Wildest Show at Tahoe / Jan. 1958 / Capitol ♦♦♦♦♦
This was the third straight classic album by trumpeter/singer Louis Prima with his wife-singer Keely Smith and the spirited R&B tenor saxophonist Sam Butera; it is as exciting as the first two. Recorded live in Lake Tahoe, the band romps through four medleys (including "On the Sunny Side of the Street/Exactly Like You" and "Don't Worry 'Bout Me/I'm in the Mood for Love"), Keely's feature on "A Foggy Day," Butera's showcase on "Come Back to Sorrento," and trombonist Red Blount's extroverted rendition of "How High the Moon." Toss in a few vocal duets and the results are quite memorable. All three of these Capitol records (which have thus far only been reissued on CD in samplers) are highly recommended for they document a unique group at the height of its power. *—Scott Yanow*

Zooma Zooma: The Best of Louis Prima / Jan. 1957-Feb. 1959 / Rhino ♦♦♦♦
This excellent sampler LP gives listeners some of the high points of Louis Prima's popular Capitol recordings. Although largely superceded by his CD in the Capitol Collectors series, this is an excellent all-round collection. The trumpeter-vocalist and singer Keely Smith are heard at their best on several medleys (particularly "I'm in the Mood for Love/Basin Street Blues," "Just a Gigolo/I Ain't Got Nobody," and "When You're Smiling/The Sheik of Araby") and their rendition of "That Old Black Magic" is classic. An ideal Las Vegas party band, Prima, Keely, and tenor saxophonist Sam Butera & the Witnesses were a perfect combination. *—Scott Yanow*

Hey Boy! Hey Girl! / 1959 / Capitol ♦♦♦
Louis Prima and Keely Smith were at the height of their fame when they starred in the Hollywood film *Hey Boy! Hey Girl!* This soundtrack album has ten numbers from the film including spots for Prima's trumpet on "Oh Marie" and "When the Saints Go Marching In," two numbers for Smith on which she is backed by the Nelson Riddle Orchestra, a feature for Sam Butera on "Fever," and several notable vocal duets by the stars (including "Lazy River" and two versions of the title cut). The music never quite cuts loose but does include some exciting moments. Louis Prima fans will want to search for this collector's item. *—Scott Yanow*

Louis and Keely! / 1960 / Jasmine ♦♦♦
Louis Prima and Keely Smith perform a dozen vocal duets on this enjoyable Dot recording. With spirited backup by tenor saxophonist Sam Butera and the Witnesses, Prima and Keely are heard in top form on such standards as "Night and Day," "Tea for Two," "I'm Confessin'," and "Bei Mir Bist Du Schon," although they do not quite reach the crazy heights of their best Capitol recordings. *—Scott Yanow*

Plays Pretty for the People / 1963-1964 / Jazz Band ♦♦♦
Although Louis Prima and Keely Smith had split up by the time of the two live performances that comprise this collector's LP, Prima (on vocals and occasional trumpet) was still in fine form. Teamed with a future wife (singer Gia Maione) and still using R&B tenor Sam Butera & the Witnesses (which featured the extroverted trombonist Little Red Blount), Prima mixes together his older hits (including "Buona Sera," "Robin Hood," and "Sing, Sing, Sing") with some Dixieland standards and more recent material. The recording quality is decent and, even with Smith's absence, Prima sounds quite happy to be performing. *—Scott Yanow*

Let's Fly With Mary Poppins / Feb. 3, 1998 / Disney ♦♦
The score of *Mary Poppins* was recorded by many singers and musicians after the movie's premiere in 1964, including Duke Ellington and John Coltrane ("Chim Chim Cheree").

Singer/trumpeter Louis Prima was one of the first, cutting versions of "A Spoonful of Sugar" and "Stay Awake" before executives from the Buena Vista label (owned by Disney) suggested he record enough additional material for a full album. The music was reissued on this 1998 CD but it is quite lightweight. The set is very brief (27 minutes), Prima only takes one trumpet solo (a rather weak statement on "The Perfect Nanny") and the ten numbers (two of which are performed twice, the second time in Italian) are essentially treated as novelties by Prima and his wife of the period Gia Maione. Only one number is longer than 2:41 and, although there is a cheerful warmth in the vocal interplay of Prima and Maione, the end results are rather pointless. "Supercalifragilisticexpialidocious" (especially the Italian version) is difficult to sit through. A historical curiosity but little more. *—Scott Yanow*

1940's Broadcasts With Keely Smith, Vol. 2 / Feb. 15, 2000 / Reflections ✦✦✦
The lost part of Prima's lengthy career involves the big-band sides he made for the Varsity, Hit, and Majestic labels between 1941 and 1947. These are also the first sides with Keely Smith in the fold (albeit as a straight big-band singer). These three airchecks catch Prima in his big-band mode, with plenty of early Italian novelties and many of the tunes that would stay in his repertoire for the rest of his career. The transfers are pretty decent and all the material is sanctioned by the Prima estate, making this another important chunk of the man's history finally coming to light. *—Cub Koda*

1950's & 60's Broadcasts, Vol. 3: Just a Gigolo / Feb. 15, 2000 / Reflections ✦✦✦
This volume of Prima's radio broadcasts is a mixed affair, with its share of high points amidst the dross. Kicking off with two tracks from a big-band broadcast, the set suddenly goes into Prima doing voice-overs for his Capitol sides (taken from the original vinyl here). A set from the Casbah Theater in Las Vegas with Sam Butera & the Witnesses makes up the bulk of the collection, with good versions of "Oh! Marie" and "Buona Sera," but there are way too many tunes spotlighting Gia Maione. A couple of stray bonus cuts are from the big-band era ("Brooklyn Boogie") and much later vintage ("It's Impossible"). Unfortunately, the sound quality varies wildly on this set, far more than on any other volume in the series. *—Cub Koda*

The EP Collection / Sep. 12, 2000 / See for Miles ✦✦✦✦

Plays Pretty for the People [Collector's Choice] / Jun. 12, 2001 / Collectors' Choice Music ✦✦✦✦

John Primer

b. Mar. 3, 1945, Camden, MS
Vocals, Guitar / Modern Electric Chicago Blues, Soul-Blues
By any yardstick, Chicago guitarist John Primer has paid his dues. Prior to making *The Real Deal* for Mike Vernon's Atlantic-distributed Code Blue label, Primer spent 13 years as the ever-reliable rhythm guitarist with Magic Slim & the Teardrops. Before that, he filled the same role behind Chicago immortals Muddy Waters and Willie Dixon.

All that grounding has paid off handsomely for Primer. His sound is rooted in the classic Windy City blues sound of decades past: rough-edged and uncompromising and satisfying in the extreme. He's one of the last real traditionalists in town.

By the time he came to Chicago in 1963, Primer was thoroughly familiar with the low-down sounds of Waters, Wolf, Jimmy Reed, B.B. and Albert King, and Elmore James. He fronted a West Side outfit for a while called the Maintainers, dishing out a mix of soul and blues, before joining the house band at the South side blues mecca Theresa's Lounge for what ended up a nine-year run. Elegant guitarist Sammy Lawhorn proved quite influential on Primer's maturing guitar approach during this period.

Always on the lookout for aspiring talent, Willie Dixon spirited him away for a 1979 gig in Mexico City. After a year or so as one of Dixon's All-Stars, Primer was recruited to join the last band of Muddy Waters, playing with the Chicago blues king until his 1983 death. Right after that, Primer joined forces with Magic Slim; their styles interlocked so seamlessly that their partnership seemed like an eternal bond.

But Primer deserved his own share of the spotlight. In 1993, Michael Frank's Chicago-based Earwig logo issued Primer's debut domestic disc, *Stuff You Got to Watch*. It was a glorious return to the classic '50s Chicago sound, powered by Primer's uncommonly concise guitar work and gruff, no-nonsense vocals. With the 1995 emergence of *The Real Deal*—produced by Vernon and featuring all-star backing by harpist Billy Branch, pianist David Maxwell, and bassist Johnny B. Gayden, Primer's star appeared ready to ascend. He soon transferred back to the Wolf label for sets such as 1997's *Cold Blooded Blues Man*, 1998's *Blues Behind Closed Doors*, and 2000's *It's a Blues Life*. *—Bill Dahl*

Poor Man Blues: Chicago Blues Session, Vol. 6 / 1991 / Wolf ✦✦✦✦✦
Poor Man Blues: Chicago Blues Session, Vol. 6 showcases the exceptional guitar skills of John Primer, who long served as a guitarist for Muddy Waters and Magic Slim. Primer falls somewhere between the two, turning out tough Chicago blues fueled by his biting slide guitar. His original songs aren't particularly interesting, but they function as good vehicles for exciting jams. In the end, Primer might not add anything new to Chicago blues, but he has a great time playing, and it sure is fun to listen to him play. *—Thom Owens*

Stuff You Got to Watch / 1993 / Earwig ✦✦✦✦
Chicago guitarist Primer's domestic debut album was doubtless an eye-opener for anyone not familiar with his searing slide work and sturdy vocal abilities. Apart from a very ill-advised cover of Glen Campbell's "Rhinestone Cowboy" (yuck!), the album resonates with mean, lowdown guitar work and fine ensemble backing. *—Bill Dahl*

● **The Real Deal** / 1995 / Atlantic ✦✦✦✦✦
Thought they didn't make traditional Chicago blues albums worthy of the name anymore? Guess again: Primer's major-label bow is an entirely satisfying affair produced by Mike Vernon that's long on intensity and devoid of pretension. Lots of originals; a handful of well-chosen covers, and a vicious band (pianist David Maxwell and harpist Billy Branch solo stunningly) help make the set go, while Primer grabs hold of the opportunity with a vise-like grip and makes believe it's the '50s all over again. *—Bill Dahl*

Cold Blooded Blues Man / Apr. 23, 1997 / Wolf ✦✦✦

Blues Behind Closed Doors / Jun. 18, 1998 / Wolf ✦✦✦

Easy Baby: Zoo Bar Collection, Vol. 6 / Feb. 9, 1999 / Wolf ✦✦✦

Knockin' at Your Door / Jun. 8, 1999 / Telarc ✦✦✦✦
John Primer's debut leaves a bit to be desired for fans of down-home blues. Although Primer sings and plays with extreme conviction, the problem is the backing band on this 12-song set. With the McCray brothers on guitar and drums, Matthew Skoller on harmonica, and Ken Saydak on piano, there's simply way too much busy playing for the group to sound like a well-meshed ensemble. Skoller's harp swamps everything in its path, and McCray's drumming is lumbering in spots. With a more sympathetic backing group, Primer has the makings of a great album in him somewhere. *—Cub Koda*

It's a Blues Life / Apr. 11, 2000 / Wolf ✦✦✦

Gary Primich

b. Apr. 20, 1958, Chicago, IL
Vocals, Harmonica / Electric Harmonica Blues, Modern Electric Blues
Don't let his intelligence, charm and self-effacing manner fool you: Gary Primich is one bad-ass harmonica player. And he's more than competent guitar player, too.

Primich was born April 20, 1958, in Chicago and raised in nearby Gary, IN. He learned harmonica from the masters at the Maxwell Street Market in nearby Chicago as a teen. By the early '80s, however, Primich became dissatisfied with the blues scene in Chicago, and in 1984, shortly after he earned his degree in radio and television from Indiana University, he moved to Austin, TX.

After landing a job at the University of Texas doing electrical work, he began to work as a sideman at Austin area clubs. In 1987, he ran into former Frank Zappa/Mothers of Invention drummer Jimmy Carl Black, who had also relocated to Austin, and the two formed a band, the Mannish Boys. Their debut album on the now-defunct Amazing Records label was called *A L'il Dab'll Do Ya*. Though Black left the band, Primich led the Mannish Boys through another album for Amazing, *Satellite Rock*. Both albums attracted sufficient attention to Primich that he was able to record under his own name for the Amazing label, and in 1991 he cut his self-titled debut for the label. He followed it up with *My Pleasure* in 1992. After Amazing Records folded, he was picked up by the Chicago-based Flying Fish label. Primich recorded two equally brilliant albums for Fish, and they include *Travelin' Mood* (1994) and *Mr. Freeze* (1995).

On his last two albums for Flying Fish (a label that has since been acquired by Rounder Records), Primich's talents as a songwriter really start to come through, but he was soon without a label again, although still nurturing his fan base through almost constant touring. By the new millennium, Primich did have a deal with the Texas Music Group. He issued powerfully sassy *Dog House Music* in Spring 2002. *—Richard Skelly*

Gary Primich / 1991 / Amazing ✦✦✦
Gary Primich's eponymous album is an uneven collection, hampered by a handful of rote, by-the-book tracks but its best moments are vibrant, eclectic and quite exciting. Unfortunately, the album gets off to a weak start, running through a bunch of uptempo blues-rockers. After those are through, Primich begins to open up his sound, diving deep into New Orleans R&B, as well as some jump blues and Latin-tinged rhythms. It's on these numbers that Primich reveals his talents as a vocalist and harpist, not on the conventional numbers. *—Thom Owens*

● **My Pleasure** / 1992 / Amazing ✦✦✦✦✦
My Pleasure is pretty much straight-up Chicago blues, delivered with authority by Gary Primich. Fellow harpist James Harman produced the record, and he tames Primich's more adventurous qualities. However, he does bring out the grease and grit of Primich's straightforward blues that was lacking on the previous record, which makes this a very enjoyable, if predictable, album. *—Thom Owens*

Hot Harp Blues / 1993 / Amazing ✦✦✦✦✦

Travelin' Mood / 1994 / Flying Fish ✦✦
A strong effort from harmonica ace Gary Primich, *Travelin' Mood* expands on the work he did with his previous band, the Mannish Boys. From the self-penned "House Rockin' Party" to a fine reading on Duke Ellington's "Caravan," Primich and company, which includes Shorty Lenoir on guitar, deliver an album that swings and sways with the best of them. And, unlike other virtuosos, Primich knows better than to let his harmonica playing run away with the album. Yet when he does let loose, as on the instrumental "The Poodle Bites," he shows an instinctive ability for melody and tone that other harp players would kill for. *—Steve Kurutz*

Mr. Freeze / 1995 / Flying Fish ✦✦✦✦
Although he had made solid, workmanlike albums in the past, *Mr. Freeze* is where all the cherries came up at once on Gary Primich's musical slot machine. While his harp playing was never in dispute, his vocals on this outing finally find their own style, sounding for the first time comfortable, assured, and totally in the pocket. Kicking off with the high-octane shuffle "Bad Poker Hand" featuring Mark Korpi's stylistic nod to Brewer Phillips, Primich contributes four of his own compositions to this 13-tracker while jumping on such stylistically diverse material as Gene Ammons' "Red Top" and Washboard Sam's "Easy Ridin' Mama," vaulting between subgenres with consummate ease. Other highlight tracks include a harp showcase on "You Came a Long Way from St. Louis" and the rumbling boogie of Mark Korpi's "Slap You Silly." Featuring guest turns from the aforementioned Korpi, bassist supreme Sarah Brown, Mark Rubin, Gene Taylor, and acoustic slide man Steve James along with Gary's regular working band, there's a wide variety of real good stuff to enjoy here. If you were to pick just one album to start absorbing this harp blower's eclectic genius, this one would make a perfect calling card. *—Cub Koda*

Company Man / 1997 / Black Top ✦✦✦✦
Primich's recording career has been indeed a work in progress, with his earliest efforts showing much promise with a workmanlike aura to them, with each new release heading into some mighty cool terrain, taking—as always—the path less traveled. And *Company Man* is certainly the most adventurous of his releases to date, taking his fine songwriting craft and huge harp tone in a multitude of directions. Needless to say, the highlights abound throughout, but most notable in passing are a pair of Smiley Lewis numbers, "Jail Bird" and "Hook, Line, and Sinker," with the former getting the jug-band romp of its life, the Big Walter-borrows-Little Walter's-band instrumental "Varmint," or the jazzy-as-hell "Ain't You Trouble." Or that eerie minor-key voodoo piece, "What's It Gonna Be," or the lowdown "Dry County Blues," which is probably the dirtiest *sounding* vocal Primich has ever laid down, pure gravel all the way. *—AMG*

Botheration / Mar. 23, 1999 / Black Top ✦✦✦

Dog House Music / Apr. 23, 2002 / Antone's ✦✦✦
Blues vocalist/harmonica player Gary Primich has crafted a righteously rollicking effort with "Dog House Music." He channels the ghosts of rockabilly and jump on the energetic opener, "Mr. Lucky," then launches into the expansive, good-time blues-rock of "Dog House" (which contains echoes of the Band's rocking Americana). On the slower side, Primich settles into the wrenching ballad "That's What Love Was Made For" like an old comfortable shoe, his heartworn pipes spilling all over the track. "Elizabeth Lee," one of the highlights here, is a searing, sinister blues-rocker that tears the doors off the roadhouse and features Primich's Elmore James-influenced singing and blistering harmonica leads. Gary Primich is a grand, vibrato-laden belter and this is top-notch modern blues that contains all the right echoes of the past. *—Erik Hage*

The Prisonaires

f. 1953, **db.** 1955
Group / R&B
The Prisonaires were just that, five African-American male singers who also happened to be inmates of the Tennessee State Penitentiary in Nashville, TN. Despite what normally would be considered circumstances too onerous to start a pop music career, the Prisonaires were celebrities, albeit briefly, after the recording of the one and only hit record, "Just Walkin' in the Rain," which Sam Phillips released on Sun in 1953—a song that three years later became a million seller for Johnnie Ray. The band was formed by lead singer Johnny Bragg, who had been a penitentiary inmate since the age of 17 after being convicted of six charges of rape. A singer since childhood, Bragg had joined a prison gospel quintet soon after his incarceration, but after a falling out, Bragg took two of its singers, Ed Thurman and William Stewart, each of whom were doing 99 years for murder, and hooked up with recent penitentiary arrivals John Drue (three years for larceny) and Marcel Sanders (one-to-five for involuntary manslaughter), and the Prisonaires were born.

They were discovered by radio producer Joe Calloway, who heard them singing while preparing a news broadcast from the prison. Calloway suggested to warden James Edwards that the group be allowed out to perform on the radio. Edwards, a liberal reform-minded warden who saw this as part of his strategy of rehabilitation, agreed. In the meantime, Bragg was busy selling songs to music publisher Red Wortham, who sent a tape of the Prisonaires radio performance to Jim Bulliet, a minority shareholder in Sun Records. Bulliet sent the tape to Sam Phillips, and despite his initial reservations (Phillips was not a huge fan of the group's Ink Spots-style close harmony crooning), arranged to have the groups transported under armed guard to Memphis to record. A few weeks later, "Just Walkin' in the Rain' was released and quickly sold 50,000 copies, a small success that was not without long-term ramifications. Peter Guralnick notes that "Just Walkin' in the Rain" was likely the record that captured the attention of a young Elvis Presley as he read about the studio, the label, and more importantly, Sam Phillips. The attendant publicity was more than had been predicted, and soon warden Edwards was allowing the group out on day passes to tour throughout the state of Tennessee. The band became favorites of the state's governor Frank Clement and frequently performed for assembled guests at the governor's mansion.

The group never had another hit, and within a year they were finished, the result of the rise of rock & roll and Phillips' preoccupation with a young singer from Tupelo, MS, named Presley. Most of the Prisonaires had no careers outside of the prison with the notable exception of Bragg, who, despite remaining in jail off and on until 1969, recorded some marginal R&B and country for small labels in Nashville. Bragg, the group's lone surviving member, remained in Nashville and could be heard singing on Sundays at his local church. *—John Dougan*

● **Just Walkin' in the Rain** / 1990 / Bear Family ✦✦✦✦✦
Although the Prisonaires are remembered for the song "Just Walkin in the Rain," this collection proves that they were a fine pop/gospel group. Johnny Bragg was a huge fan of the Ink Spots and their lead singer, Bill Kenny, and it's no wonder that much of the material on this disc has that smooth crooning style favored by pre-rock & roll vocal groups. This typically well-researched and documented Bear Family disc includes all of the Sun recordings and unreleased material, which shows the group attempting some hard-ass R&B (e.g., "Surleen" and "Rocking Horse") with mixed results. In terms of their overall output, it's the early stuff that's really compelling, as the Prisonaires proved that they could sing with the best of the vocal groups of the era. Nothing is as good as the title track, but that's a song for the ages, a beautiful piece of pop loneliness infused with near palpable heartbreak. Fans of this type of old-style harmony singing shouldn't pass this up. *—John Dougan*

Professor Longhair (Henry Roeland Byrd)

b. Dec. 19, 1918, Bogalusa, LA, **d.** Jan. 30, 1980, New Orleans, LA
Vocals, Leader, Arranger, Songwriter, Piano / New Orleans R&B, New Orleans Blues, Piano Blues
Justly worshipped over two decades after his death as a founding father of New Orleans R&B, Roy "Professor Longhair" Byrd was nevertheless so down and out at one point in his long career that he was reduced to sweeping the floors in a record shop that once could have moved his platters by the boxful.

That Fess made such a marvelous comeback testifies to the resiliency of this late legend, whose Latin-tinged rhumba-rocking piano style and croaking, yodeling vocals were as singular and spicy as the second-line beats that power his hometown's musical heartbeat. Byrd brought an irresistible Caribbean feel to his playing, full of rolling flourishes that every Crescent City ivories man had to learn inside out (Fats Domino, Huey Smith, and Allen Toussaint all paid homage early and often).

Roy Byrd grew up on the streets of the Big Easy, tap dancing for tips on Bourbon Street with his running partners. Local 88s aces Sullivan Rock, Kid Stormy Weather, and Tuts Washington all left their marks on the youngster, but Byrd brought his own conception to the stool. A natural-born card shark and gambler, Longhair began to take his playing seriously in 1948, earning a gig at the Caldonia Club. Owner Mike Tessitore bestowed Byrd with his professorial nickname (due to Byrd's shaggy coiffure).

Longhair debuted on wax in 1949, laying down four tracks (including the first version of his signature "Mardi Gras in New Orleans," complete with whistled intro) for the Dallas-based Star Talent label. His band was called the Shuffling Hungarians, for reasons lost to time! Union problems forced those sides off the market, but Longhair's next date for Mercury the same year was strictly on the up-and-up. It produced his first and only national R&B hit in 1950, the hilarious "Bald Head" (credited to Roy Byrd & His Blues Jumpers).

The pianist made great records for Atlantic in 1949, Federal in 1951, Wasco in 1952, and Atlantic again in 1953 (producing the immortal "Tipitina," a romping "In the Night," and the lyrically impenetrable boogie "Ball the Wall"). After recuperating from a minor stroke, Longhair came back on Lee Rupe's Ebb logo in 1957 with a storming "No Buts—No Maybes." He revived his "Go to the Mardi Gras" for Joe Ruffino's Ron imprint in 1959; this is the version that surfaces every year at Mardi Gras in New Orleans.

Other than the ambitiously arranged "Big Chief" in 1964 for Watch Records, the '60s held little charm for Longhair. He hit the skids, abandoning his piano playing until a booking at the fledgling 1971 Jazz & Heritage Festival put him on the comeback trail. He made a slew of albums in the last decade of his life, topped off by a terrific set for Alligator, *Crawfish Fiesta*.

Longhair triumphantly appeared on the PBS-TV concert series *Soundstage* (with Dr. John, Earl King, and the Meters), co-starred in the documentary *Piano Players Rarely Ever Play Together* (which became a memorial tribute when Longhair died in the middle of its filming; funeral footage was included), and saw a group of his admirers buy a local watering hole in 1977 and rechristen it Tipitina's after his famous song. He played there regularly when he wasn't on the road; it remains a thriving operation.

Longhair went to bed on January 30, 1980, and never woke up. A heart attack in the night stilled one of New Orleans' seminal R&B stars, but his music is played in his hometown so often and so reverently, you'd swear he was still around. *—Bill Dahl*

New Orleans Piano / 1972 / Atlantic ✦✦✦✦✦
All 16 of the Atlantic sides from 1949 and 1953 (including a handful of alternate takes) on one glorious disc. Longhair's work for the label was notoriously marvelous—this version of "Mardi Gras in New Orleans" reeks of revelry in the streets of the French Quarter; "She Walks Right In" and "Walk Your Blues Away" ride a bedrock boogie, and "In the Night" bounces atop a parade-beat shuffle groove and hard-charging saxes. *—Bill Dahl*

Rock 'n Roll Gumbo / 1977 / Dancing Cat ✦✦✦✦✦
Recorded in 1974, this album almost never saw the light of day. Fortunately, the master tapes were found and the album was released posthumously. Professor Longhair was a giant in the New Orleans music community, but had not recorded in over ten years when he was convinced to start playing again. From the opening riffs, one can understand the stature of Professor Longhair as a great pianist—he demonstrates that he is equally at home playing rhumba boogie, blues songs, and calypso. He plays New Orleans standards (many penned by himself), but what makes this recording a classic is the chance to hear him play with guitarist Clarence "Gatemouth" Brown. The interplay of these music veterans is mesmerizing. The piano playing is breathtaking, and has a percussive quality unlike any other player before or since. It is hard to believe that Professor Longhair languished in obscurity for so many years after hearing the jubilance of "Mardi Gras in New Orleans," a song that will have you tapping your feet and hands as if you were in the parade. This album is essential for fans of New Orleans music and those aspiring to be rock & roll pianists. *— Vik Iyengar*

Live on the Queen Mary / 1978 / One Way ✦✦✦✦✦
Ask what was Paul and Linda McCartney's *most* important contribution to music, and you just might get the answer—this album, which is also more exciting than anything Wings ever did. Professor Longhair's first live recording came about at a March 24, 1975, party hosted by the McCartneys aboard the Queen Mary in Long Beach, CA. It captures some of the excitement that Ahmet Ertegun and several lesser-known talent scouts found when they came upon Henry Roeland Byrd playing road houses around New Orleans in the late '40s. Highlights include the rollicking "Mess Around," and the standards "Stagger Lee," "Everyday I Have the Blues," "I'm Movin' On," and his hits "Mardi Gras in New Orleans" and "Tipitina." The lack of instrumental credits prevents one from praising the lead guitarist by name for his playing on "Everyday I Have the Blues" and "I'm Movin' On," but he and the rest of the band still do well backing this legend. *—Bruce Eder*

Crawfish Fiesta / 1980 / Alligator ✦✦✦✦✦
Probably the best of all the many albums Longhair waxed during his comeback (and likely the last). A tremendously tight combo featuring three horns and Dr. John on guitar delightfully back the Professor every step of the way as he recasts Solomon Burke's "Cry to Me" and Fats Domino's "Whole Lotta Loving" in his own indelible image and roars, yodels, and whistles out wonderful remakes of his own oldies "Big Chief" and "Bald Head." *—Bill Dahl*

Mardi Gras in New Orleans / 1981 / Nighthawk ◆◆◆◆◆

Plenty of rarities are featured on this valuable cross-section of the Professor's early releases. Both sides of the pianist's first two 78s for Star Talent Records are aboard, as well as sides he cut for Mercury, Federal ("Curly Haired Baby," "Gone So Long"), Wasco ("East St. Louis Baby"), Atlantic, and Ebb. —*Bill Dahl*

House Party New Orleans Style / 1987 / Rounder ◆◆◆

Boiling blues and trademark Afro-Latin and boogie-woogie riffs were the menu when Professor Longhair brought his Crescent City music show to Baton Rouge and Memphis in 1971 and 1972, respectively. The 15 numbers on this set matched the great pianist with an esteemed array of musicians that included outstanding guitarist Snooks Eaglin on both sessions, and fine rhythm sections as well. Eaglin's flashy, inventive solos were excellent contrasts to Longhair's rippling keyboard flurries and distinctive mix of yodels, yells, cries and shouts. —*Ron Wynn*

Mardi Gras in Baton / 1991 / Rhino ◆◆◆◆

Some of the earliest sides from Longhair's rediscovery period (1971-1972), featuring a lot of tunes inexorably associated with him through previous versions and a few ("Jambalaya," "Sick and Tired") that weren't. An added bonus is the magical presence of guitarist Snooks Eaglin, whose approach is every bit as singular as the Professor's was. —*Bill Dahl*

Rum & Coke / 1993 / Rhino ◆◆◆

★ **Fess: The Professor Longhair Anthology** / Nov. 16, 1993 / Rhino ◆◆◆◆◆

The rhumba-rocking rhythms of Roy "Professor Longhair" Byrd live on throughout Rhino's 40-track retrospective of the New Orleans icon's amazing legacy. Most of the seminal stuff arrives early on: "Bald Head," the rollicking ode Byrd cut for Mercury in 1950, is followed by a raft of classics from his 1949 and 1953 Atlantic dates ("Tipitina," "Ball the Wall," "Who's Been Fooling You"), the storming 1957 "No Buts—No Maybes" and "Baby Let Me Hold Your Hand" for Ebb, and his beloved "Go to the Mardi Gras" as waxed for Ron in 1959. The second disc is a hodge-podge of material from his '70s comeback, all of it wonderful in its own way but not as essential as the early work. —*Bill Dahl*

1949 / Jul. 10, 2001 / Classics ◆◆◆◆

Big Easy Stomp / Jan. 8, 2002 / Fuel 2000 ◆◆◆

Big Chief / Jun. 25, 2002 / Tomato ◆◆◆

Professor's Blues Revue

db. 1992

Group / Modern Electric Chicago Blues, Modern Electric Blues

"Professor" Eddie Lusk worked frequently as a session keyboardist during the '70s and '80s on the Chicago blues scene. His own revue showcased several singers over the years, notably Gloria Hardiman (featured on their "Meet Me With Your Black Drawers On" on Alligator's 1987 anthology, *The New Bluebloods*) and Karen Carroll, principal singer on the band's 1989 Delmark album, *Professor Strut*. Tragically, Lusk took his own life by plunging into the Chicago River. —*Bill Dahl*

● **Professor Strut** / 1989 / Delmark ◆◆◆

Eddie Lusk's only solo album is a blues revue, as he leads a variety of singers through several classic blues songs from all of the music's subgenres. The concept is good one, but the performance is decidedly uneven—several of the singers are mediocre and the fidelity on the release is poor. For those that want to sit through the rough spots, they'll find a handful of good solos, but not much more. —*Thom Owens*

Snooky Pryor (James Edward Pryor)

b. Sep. 15, 1921, Lambert, MS

Vocals, Drums, Harmonica / Harmonica Blues, Electric Chicago Blues, Chicago Blues

Only in the last few years has Snooky Pryor finally begun to receive full credit for the mammoth role he played in shaping the amplified Chicago blues harp sound during the postwar era. He's long claimed he was the first harpist to run his sound through a public-address system around the Windy City—and since nobody's around to refute the claim at this point, we'll have to accept it! He's still quite active musically, having cut potent discs for Austin, TX-based Antone's Records and other labels in recent years.

James Edward Pryor was playing harmonica at the age of eight in Mississippi. The two Sonny Boys were influential to Pryor's emerging style, as he played around the Delta. He hit Chicago for the first time in 1940, later serving in the Army at nearby Fort Sheridan. Playing his harp through powerful Army PA systems gave Pryor the idea to acquire his own portable rig once he left the service. Armed with a primitive amp, he dazzled the folks on Maxwell Street in late 1945 with his massively amplified harp.

Pryor made some groundbreaking 78s during the immediate postwar Chicago blues era. Teaming with guitarist Moody Jones, he waxed "Telephone Blues" and "Boogie" for Planet Records in 1948, encoring the next year with "Boogy Fool"/"Raisin' Sand" for JOB with Jones on bass and guitarist Baby Face Leroy Foster in support. Pryor made more more classic sides for JOB (1952-1953), Parrot (1953), and Vee-Jay ("Someone to Love Me"/"Judgment Day") in 1956, but commercial success never materialized. He wound down his blues-playing in the early '60s, finally chucking it all and moving to downstate Ullin, IL, in 1967.

For a long while, Pryor's whereabouts were unknown. But the 1987 Blind Pig album *Snooky*, produced by guitarist Steve Freund, announced to the world that the veteran harpist was alive and well, his chops still honed. A pair of solid discs for Antone's, *Too Cool to Move* and *In This Mess Up to My Chest*, were next, and other discs followed. Pryor stays just as busy as he cares to nowadays, still ensconced in Ullin (where life is good and the fishing is easy). —*Bill Dahl*

● **Snooky Pryor** / 1969 / Flyright ◆◆◆◆◆

These tracks from the JOB label, recorded from the early '50s to early '60s, include the classics "Boogie" and "Stockyard Blues" and the raucous, echo-laden stomp of "Boogie Twist." These are Pryor's finest moments on wax. —*Cub Koda*

Do It If You Want / 1973 / BluesWay ◆◆

Homesick James Williamson & Snooky Pryor / 1974 / Caroline ◆◆◆

Snooky & Moody / 1980 / Flyright ◆◆◆◆◆

The team of Snooky Pryor and Moody Jones doesn't have the same reputation as other tandems like Leroy Carr and Scrapper Blackwell or Tampa Red and Big Maceo Merriweather, but they certainly created several fine numbers themselves. This collection highlights several of them, showing that each musician was a capable performer and interpreter. —*Ron Wynn*

Snooky / 1987 / Blind Pig ◆◆◆◆

An outstanding comeback effort by Chicago harp pioneer Snooky Pryor, whose timeless sound meshed well with a Windy City trio led by producer/guitarist Steve Freund for this set. Mostly Pryor's own stuff—"Why You Want to Do Me Like That," "That's the Way to Do It," "Cheatin' and Lyin'"—with his fat-toned harp weathering the decades quite nicely. —*Bill Dahl*

Snooky Pryor / 1991 / Paula ◆◆◆◆◆

If anyone doubts the longevity and journeyman greatness of Snooky Pryor, this collection of sides should do much to quiet them. Starting with the 1947 Floyd Jones (the classic "Stockyard Blues") and Johnny Young sessions for Old Swingmaster with Snooky in support and running right from the early-'50s into the early-'60s sides for the JOB label with "Boogie Twist" (his Vee-Jay and Parrot sides are not here), this is ground-floor Chicago blues one step removed from Maxwell Street. Lots of unissued sides—all of them great—plus the inclusion of the instrumental "Boogie," which became the blueprint for Little Walter's hit "Juke." Pryor's finest moments on wax. —*Cub Koda*

Too Cool to Move / 1992 / Antone's ◆◆◆◆

Another excellent recent set from the veteran harpist, cut down in Austin with a mixture of Texans and Chicagoans in support: pianist Pinetop Perkins, guitarists Duke Robillard and Luther Tucker, and drummer Willie "Big Eyes" Smith. Pryor's made quite a substantial to his long-dormant discography in the last few years. —*Bill Dahl*

In This Mess Up to My Chest / 1994 / Antone's ◆◆◆◆

Pryor reaffirms his mastery of postwar blues harp over the course of this sturdy set, again done with the help of some fine Texas and Chicago players. Pryor's downhome vocals shine on the distinctive "Bury You in a Paper Sack" and "Stick Way Out Behind." —*Bill Dahl*

Mind Your Own Business / Jan. 14, 1997 / Discovery ◆◆◆

Good chunky barroom blues on this outing from a grand old harmonica player. Pryor saves the serious energy for his harp blowing, but he does just fine as a vocalist too, with a nicely aged and lived-in voice. Everybody on the record has a set place and knows their moves, and that's OK too. This is a good-times kind of album. —*Steven McDonald*

Shake My Hand / Feb. 9, 1999 / Blind Pig ◆◆◆◆

Veteran harp man Pryor (who claims to be the first to amplify his harmonica) was still capable of some potent blues when he released this album in early 1999. Kicking off with a solo version of Faye Adams' "Shake a Hand" (its lyrics reworked heavily into the title track) that owes a huge debt to idol Sonny Boy Williamson, Pryor settles into a comfortable groove with a tight little trio behind him consisting of Bob Stroger on bass, Billy Flynn on guitar, and Jimmy Tilman on drums. His version of Hank Ballard's "Annie Had a Baby" is so radically different that it almost qualifies as an original, while his covers of Al Dexter's "Pistol Packin' Mama" and Sleepy John Estes' "Someday Baby" stay closer to the originals. The rest of the set features Snooky's great originals, with the minor-keyed "Headed South," "In This Mess," "Jump for Joy," and a nice remake of his "Telephone Blues" being particular standouts. Simple, no-frills production makes this a modern-day blues album that delivers the wallop of the old singles. —*Cub Koda*

Country Blues / Dec. 25, 1999 / Sequel ◆◆◆

Pitch a Boogie Woogie If It Takes Me All Night Long / Jun. 26, 2002 / West Side ◆◆◆◆

Hand Me Down Blues / Relic ◆◆◆◆◆

A nice 16-track compilation of rare blues material from the Parrot label, this features both sides of Snooky's lone single for the label, "Crosstown Blues" and "I Want You For Myself." Also features obscure and unissued tracks by Little Willie Foster ("Four Day Jump"), Dusty Brown ("Yes She's Gone"), John Brim ("Gary Stomp"), Sunnyland Slim ("Devil Is A Busy Man"), early Albert King ("Little Boy Blue" and the title track), plus Henry Gray with four previously unissued sides, all of them sloppy and great. —*Cub Koda*

Ann Rabson

b. Apr. 12, 1945, New York, NY

Vocals, Piano / Piano Blues, Modern Acoustic Blues, Boogie-Woogie

"Music Makin' Mama" Ann Rabson played a considerable role in helping to revive acoustic blues in the post-Stevie Ray Vaughan era, both as a solo artist and with Saffire–the Uppity Blues Women, the group she co-founded in 1988. Although she's best known as a boogie-woogie pianist, Rabson worked primarily as a guitarist for the first two decades of her music career, and she boasts the rather unique ability to switch from Chicago barrelhouse piano-pounding to Piedmont fingerpicking at the drop of a hat. Rabson's rootsy approach also draws heavily from the styles of female blues singers of the prewar era, such as Lucille Bogan, Ida Cox, and Bessie Smith. Like her contemporaries Rory Block and Bonnie Raitt, Rabson ranks as an important modern blueswoman who has brought tremendous crossover appeal to the genre.

Born in New York City in 1945, Rabson grew up in Ohio and started tuning into blues and jazz at a very early age. She picked up guitar at 17, and within a year was playing solo gigs and honing a repertoire inspired by the likes of Memphis Minnie, Bessie Smith, Tampa Red, and Leroy Carr. In 1971, Rabson moved to Fredericksburg, VA, where she devoted the next seven years to playing music full-time. Though she eventually went back to working a day job (as a computer programmer), Rabson continued to perform and teach guitar lessons through the '80s. Incidentally, it was playing music part-time that allowed Rabson the chance to study piano–in particular, the boogie-woogie styles of Jimmy Yancey, Meade "Lux" Lewis, and Amos Milburn.

In 1984, Rabson and one of her guitar students, Gaye Adegbalola, formed Saffire and began performing together around Virginia; they later recruited bassist Earlene Lewis to join the group. By the late '80s, Rabson, Adegbalola, and Lewis had committed to Saffire full-time and were touring regionally. The trio signed with Alligator Records in 1989 (they were the first all-acoustic band to record for the label), and a year later their self-titled debut album became a critical and commercial success. Rabson's composition "Elevator Man" (from Saffire's follow-up album *Hot Flash*) was nominated for a W.C. Handy Award in 1992 for Song of the Year.

In addition to touring and recording with Saffire, Rabson has continued to work as a solo act and session player. After recording with a number of blues and folk musicians in the '90s (including Steve James, Deborah Coleman, and Ani DiFranco), Rabson finally released her first solo album in 1997. *Music Makin' Mama* showcased Rabson's talents in a variety of contexts–boogie-woogie, R&B, Piedmont blues, and ballads–and earned her three more Handy Award nominations in 1998. M.C. Records released Rabson's second solo album, *Struttin' My Stuff*, in September 2000 to critical acclaim. *–Ken Chang*

● **Music Makin' Mama** / Feb. 11, 1997 / Alligator ✦✦✦✦

Music Makin' Mama starts with a bang and ends with a boogie–the bang is Rabson's revved-up take on Huey "Piano" Smith's "Baby, Every Once in a While," and the boogie is a solo instrumental ode to two of her piano heroes, Jimmy Yancey and Meade "Lux" Lewis. Between these two end pieces, Rabson navigates through bluesy territory with her trademark gusto, digging up songs by Ray Charles, Big Bill Broonzy, Bessie Smith, and Cow Cow Davenport, while also throwing in a few originals for good measure. Not surprisingly, *Music Makin' Mama* will sound a fair bit rootsier than the typical Saffire–the Uppity Blues Women album; Rabson, after all, has long been the traditionalist torchbearer in the group, and her burning reverence for the dusty, old blues song certainly shines through here. While this is technically her debut solo album, Rabson has been playing some of these songs for decades, and there's nothing tentative about her playing here. The solo cuts in particular (Smith's "He's Got Me Goin'," Roosevelt Sykes' "Skin and Bones," and Rabson's "Blue Boogie") stand out for their simple charm and pinpoint delivery. On the ensemble numbers, Rabson gets a helping hand from an all-star backing band that includes saxman Greg Piccolo, violinist Mimi Rabson (Ann's sister), and Alligator labelmates John Cephas, Phil Wiggins, and Bob Margolin. In 1998, *Music Makin' Mama* was nominated for two W.C. Handy Awards (for Acoustic Blues Album of the Year and Traditional Blues Album of the Year). *–Ken Chang*

Struttin' My Stuff / Sep. 12, 2000 / M.C. ✦✦✦

Blues historian and founding member of Saffire–the Uppity Blues Women, Ann Rabson's second solo effort, *Struttin' My Stuff*, finds her doing just that. She is unaccompanied on the majority of these 16 tracks, effortlessly switching between piano on seven tracks, guitar on three (including her first recorded attempt using electric guitar), and three featuring the rhythm section of Richard Crooks on drums and Marty Ballou on acoustic bass. The music encompasses an emotional and dynamic display of vitality while her choice of cover versions instantly reveals where her heart lies: Amos Milburn's "Let Me Go Home, Whiskey," Chuck Berry's "School Days," and the New Orleans romp of Eddie Bo's "Check Mr. Popeye." *Struttin' My Stuff* is available on the American roots label M.C. Records. *–Al Campbell*

Yank Rachell (James Rachell)

b. Mar. 16, 1910, Brownsville, TN, **d.** Apr. 9, 1997, Indianapolis, IN

Vocals, Mandolin, Harmonica, Guitar / Prewar Country Blues, Country Blues, St. Louis Blues, Piedmont Blues, Jug Band

James "Yank" Rachell was the primary exponent of blues mandolin, although he also played guitar, violin, harp and sang expertly well. Born on a farm outside Brownsville, TN, Yank Rachell picked up the mandolin at the age of eight, mainly teaching himself; an early encounter with Hambone Willie Newbern early on helped him as well. Rachell began to work dances with singer and guitarist Sleepy John Estes in the early '20s. In early 1929, he co-formed the Three J's Jug Band with Estes and pianist Jab Jones. The Three J's Jug Band were an instant hit and managed to work the dances during the lucrative jug-band craze in Memphis and traveled often to Paducah, Kentucky. The group recorded 14 sides credited jointly to Estes and Rachell for Victor for 1929 and 1930.

After the record business was flattened by the depression, the Three J's broke up. Estes and harmonica player Hammie Nixon went on to Chicago to seek their fortune in the nightclubs, but Yank Rachell decided to try his hand at farming and also worked for the L&N Railroad. Ironically, it was Rachell who was next to record–during a stopover in New York Rachell teamed up with guitarist Dan Smith and laid down 25 titles for ARC in just three days, though only six of them were issued.

Shortly before the ARC date, Yank Rachell had discovered a kid harmonica player that he believed had real talent, John Lee "Sonny Boy" Williamson. They worked together at the Blue Flame Club in Jackson, Tennessee, starting in 1933. In 1934 Williamson went north to Chicago. With the success of Williamson's first Bluebird dates of 1937, Rachell decided to join Sonny Boy in Chicago for sessions in March and June of 1938. Yank Rachell also contributed four sides of his own to each session, and then 16 more in 1941 with Sonny Boy backing him up. Some of the 1941 tracks are among his best: "It Seem Like a Dream," "Biscuit Baking Woman," and "Peach Tree Blues" were all successes for both Rachell and Bluebird.

But in 1938, while working in St. Louis with Peetie Wheatstraw, Yank Rachell had married and started to raise a family. During the peak of his musical career, Rachell kept his day job and did not lead "the life," at least not the same one that claimed his friend Sonny Boy Williamson on June 1, 1948. After Williamson's murder, Rachell drifted away from music and relied solely on straight jobs to make his living, settling permanently in Indianapolis in 1958. His wife passed away in 1961, and afterward he began to resume performing. In 1962, Rachell was reunited with Nixon and Estes, and the three of them began tearing up the college and coffeehouse circuit, recording for Delmark as Yank Rachell's Tennessee Jug Busters. Estes died in 1977, and from that time Rachell worked mainly as a solo act. Yank Rachell was a longtime regular at the Slippery Noodle in Indianapolis, and recorded only sporadically in his last years. Nonetheless, he was working on a new album when he died at age 87. *–Uncle Dave Lewis*

Complete Recorded Works, Vol. 1 (1934–38) / 1934-1938 / Wolf ✦✦✦

Complete Recorded Works, Vol. 2 (1938–1941) / 1938-1941 / Wolf ✦✦✦✦✦

Mandolin Blues / 1986 / Delmark ✦✦✦✦

Yank Rachell has long been a legend in the blues world. One of the few blues mandolin players, Rachell recorded several notable sessions during 1929-1941 and then was off record for 22 years. After spending time outside of music, he was rediscovered and in 1963 he performed the music on this CD reissue. Rachell (who was in his fifties at the time), is in excellent voice throughout the date although it is his mandolin work that makes this set particularly special. He is reunited with two notable friends from the '30s (guitarist Sleepy John Estes and Hammie Nixon who is heard on harmonica and jug) and is assisted on some numbers by both Big Joe Williams and the up and coming Mike Bloomfield on guitars; several numbers find Rachell backed by three guitars. Yank Rachell would remain active until shortly before his death on April 9, 1997. This comeback set (which adds six previously unreleased tracks to the original ten-song program) is one of his definitive recordings and is a perfect showcase of the great bluesman's talents. *–Scott Yanow*

Blues Mandolin Man / 1986 / Blind Pig ✦✦✦

This contains fine material by one of the few great mandolin bluesmen. *–Barry Lee Pearson*

● **Chicago Style** / 1987 / Delmark ✦✦✦✦✦

While Yank Rachell was past his prime when he began recording for Delmark in the '60s, he was still an effective, often exciting vocalist and mandolin player. He seldom sounded more striking and enjoyable than on the nine cuts that comprised *Chicago Style*, recently reissued on CD. Rachell sang with a spirited mix of irony, anguish, dismay, and bemusement on such numbers as "Depression Blues," "Diving Duck," and "Going To St. Louis." *–Ron Wynn*

Bobby Radcliff

b. Sep. 22, 1951, Washington, D.C.

Vocals, Guitar / Modern Electric Blues, R&B

Although Bobby Radcliff has spent the last 25 years honing his craft in bars around his native Washington, D.C., and in New York City and Chicago, the 45-year-old guitarist, singer and songwriter is just now coming into his prime.

Born September 22, 1951, Radcliff grew up in Bethesda, MD, and had easy access to Washington, D.C., blues clubs, where he learned from people like Bobby Parker. Before graduating from high school, he'd already made several trips to Chicago to meet his idol, Magic Sam Maghett, owing to a small but growing blues club scene in Washington. Radcliff began playing when he was 12, and he started off taking classical guitar lessons. After his guitar teacher showed him some blues, he began buying every blues guitar album he could get his hands on.

In 1977, Radcliff moved to New York City and worked in a bookstore by day until 1987, when he realized he was making enough money playing in clubs to give up his day job. Since he hooked up his recording deal with Black Top Records, Radcliff has toured the U.S., Canada and Europe more than a dozen times, and his fiery guitar playing is always a festival crowd-pleaser.

Parker has four excellent albums out on the Black Top label that showcase his songwriting, guitar playing, and soulful singing. They include his debut, *Dresses Too Short* (1989), *Universal Blues* (1991), *There's a Cold Grave in Your Way* (1994), and *Live at the Rynborn.* Collectors will seek out his 1985 vinyl release, *Early in the Morning*, on the A-Okay label. *—Richard Skelly*

● **Dresses Too Short** / Oct. 1989 / Black Top ♦♦♦♦♦

Bobby Radcliff turns in a tight, tough update of Magic Sam-style Chicago blues with *Dresses Too Short.* The songs are either too familiar or a weak approximation of the genre, but the playing throughout is terrific—his guitar playing is alternately subtle and ferocious. Best of all is the handful of tracks cut with Ronnie Earl & the Broadcasters who spur Radcliff on to his best performances. *—Thom Owens*

Universal Blues / 1991 / Black Top ♦♦♦

Universal Blues is another successful reworking of Chicago blues from Bobby Radcliff. It's less flashy than the previous *Dresses Too Short*, but that's a plus—without all the pyrotechnics, Radcliff's guitar actually sounds more powerful and versatile, which makes the album quite entertaining. *—Thom Owens*

There's a Cold Grave in Your Way / 1994 / Black Top ♦♦♦♦♦

Live at the Rynborn / Apr. 15, 1997 / Black Top ♦♦♦

This raw, intense, honest performance was captured in November 1996 at the Rynborn Theatre in Antrim, NH. Radcliff's in-your-face style demonstrates his bravery, for this recording is not flawless (it is live, after all) and there are times where you find yourself saying "What was that?"—but that's what makes it so appealing. Radcliff is not an imitator but rather an interpreter, and he is an especially great admirer of the Chicago Westsiders, particularly Magic Sam. Although this CD is 90 percent standards (just one original), he manages to surprise even those listeners who thought they'd heard it all. Selections range from Bill Doggett's "Honky Tonk" to a well-disguised Kool & the Gang medley. Playing here with a trio, Radcliff rips off solo after solo throughout. He switches back and forth between lead and rhythm, shifting gears frequently when it comes to the rhythms themselves. He sings on several tunes but vocals are definitely not his strong suit. At it's worst, *Live at the Rynborn* is an interesting listening experience; at it's best it is a volatile and brash performance in a very cool way. It is not for the faint of heart, and that's what makes it a lot of fun. *—Ann Wickstrom*

The Radio Kings

f. 1991, Boston, MA

Group / Modern Electric Blues

A Boston-based traditional blues duo almost eerily reminiscent of the likeminded Fabulous Thunderbirds, the Radio Kings primarily comprised vocalist/harpist Brian Templeton and guitarist Michael Dinallo. Formed in 1991, the group debuted in 1994 with the Icehouse label release *It Ain't Easy*, a showcase for their clear affection for the gritty sound of giants including Howlin' Wolf, Little Walter, and Slim Harpo; *Live at B.B. King's* followed a year later, and in 1998, the Radio Kings returned with *Money Road.* *—Jason Ankeny*

It Ain't Easy / 1994 / Icehouse ♦♦♦

Live at B.B. King's / Oct. 10, 1995 / Priority ♦♦♦

● **Money Road** / Feb. 10, 1998 / Bullseye Blues ♦♦♦

If the Radio Kings sound more than a little bit like the Fabulous Thunderbirds, it's more than just the similar instrumentation. T-Bird drummer Fran Christina's brother Bob is the drummer in this band, and singer/harmonica man Brian Templeton sounds so much like Kim Wilson, both vocally and instrumentally, that you have to keep checking the personnel credits in the CD booklet. The final nail in the coffin is Michael Dinallo's expert Jimmie Vaughan imitations on guitar, however unintentional. That said, they nonetheless turn in a disc full of original material that would probably be more impressive if there was an equally original approach applied in presenting it. High spots of the material include "Money In My Pocket," "Virginia," the Lazy Lester soundalike "Disturb Me Baby," "Song of Love" and the title track. *—Cub Koda*

Ma Rainey (Gertrude Pridgett)

b. Apr. 26, 1886, Columbus, GA, **d.** Dec. 22, 1939, Columbus, GA

Vocals / Classic Female Blues, Classic Jazz, Jug Band, Acoustic Blues

Ma Rainey wasn't the first blues singer to make records, but by all rights she probably should have been. In an era when women were the marquee names in blues, Ma Rainey was once the most celebrated of all—the "Mother of the Blues" had been singing the music for more than 20 years before she made her recording debut (Paramount, 1923). With the advent of blues records, she became even more influential, immortalizing such songs as "See See Rider," "Bo-Weavil Blues," and "Ma Rainey's Black Bottom." Like the other classic blues divas, she had a repertoire of pop and minstrel songs as well as blues, but she maintained a heavier, tougher vocal delivery than the cabaret blues singers who followed. Ma Rainey's records featured her with jug bands, guitar duos, and bluesmen such as Tampa Red and Blind Blake, in addition to the more customary horns-and-piano jazz-band accompaniment (occasionally including such luminaries as Louis Armstrong, Kid Ory, and Fletcher Henderson).

Born and raised in Columbus, GA, Ma Rainey (born Gertrude Pridgett) began singing professionally when she was a teenager, performing with a number of minstrel and medicine shows. In 1904, she married William "Pa" Rainey and she changed her name to "Ma" Rainey. The couple performed as "Rainey and Rainey, Assassinators of the Blues" and toured throughout the south, performing with several minstrel shows, circuses, and tent shows. According to legend, she gave a young Bessie Smith vocal lessons during this time. By the early '20s, Ma Rainey had become a featured performer on the Theater Owners' Booking Association circuit.

In 1923, Ma Rainey signed a contract with Paramount Records. Although her recording career lasted only a mere six years—her final sessions were in 1928—she recorded over one hundred songs and many of them, including "C.C. Rider" and "Bo Weavil Blues," became genuine blues classics. During these sessions, she was supported by some of the most talented blues and jazz musicians of her era, including Louis Armstrong, Fletcher Henderson, Coleman Hawkins, Buster Bailey, and Lovie Austin.

Rainey's recordings and performances were extremely popular among black audiences, particularly in the South. After reaching the height of her popularity in the late '20s, Rainey's career faded away in the early '30s as female blues singing became less popular with the blues audience. She retired from performing in 1933, settling down in her hometown of Columbus. In 1939, Ma Rainey died of a heart attack. She left behind an immense recorded legacy, which continued to move and influence successive generations of blues, country, and rock & roll musicians. In 1983, Rainey was inducted into the Blues Foundation's Hall of Fame; seven years later, she was inducted to the Rock & Roll Hall of Fame. *—Jim O'Neal & Stephen Thomas Erlewine*

● **Ma Rainey's Black Bottom** / 1990 / Yazoo ♦♦♦♦♦

Appointed "Mother of the Blues" during her '20s heyday, singer Ma Rainey was one of the best of the many classic woman blues singers of the period. An inspiration to the "Empress of the Blues," Bessie Smith, Rainey was a Georgia native who was discovered in Chicago during the early '20s. While not the possessor of a voice as powerful as Smith had, Rainey still cut a slew of strong sides featuring a fine blend of country blues intensity and jazz band sophistication. This excellent Yazoo collection captures Rainey in her prime from 1924-1928. Backed by large combos and minimal guitar and piano tandems, Rainey shines on such highlights as "Booze and Blues," "Shave 'Em Dry," and "Lucky Rock Blues." Topped off with stellar contributions by blues and jazz luminaries like Don Redman, Coleman Hawkins, Kid Ory, and Georgia Tom Dorsey, *Ma Rainey's Black Bottom* makes for an excellent introduction to blues singer's small but potent catalog. *—Stephen Cook*

Ma Rainey / 1992 / Milestone ♦♦♦

Nobody could belt it out like Ma Rainey, and here's a great collection that showcases it. All of the lady's biggest hits ("See See Rider," "Jealous Hearted Blues," "Black Cat, Hoot Owl Blues," "Ma Rainey's Black Bottom") are here, and the sound is as good as one can expect from the old Paramount 78s, probably the worst-pressed discs of the '20s. Still, Ma's ebullient personality comes through the hisses and pops and scratches loud and clear. An essential blues buy for the collection. *—Cub Koda*

Complete Recorded Works: 1928 Sessions / Jun. 2, 1994 / Document ♦♦♦♦♦

Complete Recorded Works, Vol. 1 (1923–1924) / Jan. 2, 1998 / Document ♦♦♦♦

Complete Recorded Works, Vol. 2 (1924–1925) / Jan. 2, 1998 / Document ♦♦♦♦

Complete Recorded Works, Vol. 3 (1925–1926) / Jan. 2, 1998 / Document ♦♦♦♦

Complete Recorded Works, Vol. 4 (1926–1927) / Jan. 2, 1998 / Document ♦♦♦♦

1923–1928 / Oct. 27, 1998 / Giants of Jazz ♦♦♦

Bonnie Raitt

b. Nov. 8, 1949, Burbank, CA

Slide Guitar, Vocals, Guitar / Slide Guitar Blues, Album Rock, Pop/Rock, Adult Contemporary, Singer/Songwriter, Blues-Rock

Long a critic's darling, singer/guitarist Bonnie Raitt did not begin to win the comparable commercial success due her until the release of the aptly titled 1989 blockbuster *Nick of Time*; her tenth album, it rocketed her into the mainstream consciousness nearly two decades after she first committed her unique blend of blues, rock, and R&B to vinyl. Born in Burbank, CA, on November 8, 1949, she was the daughter of Broadway star John Raitt, best known for his starring performances in such smashes as *Carousel* and *Pajama Game.* After picking up the guitar at the age of 12, Raitt felt an immediate affinity for the blues, and although she went off to attend Radcliffe in 1967, within two years she had dropped out to begin playing the Boston folk and blues club circuit. Signing with noted blues manager Dick Waterman, she was soon performing alongside the likes of idols including Howlin' Wolf, Sippie Wallace, and Mississippi Fred McDowell, and in time earned such a strong reputation that she was signed to Warner Bros.

Debuting in 1971 with an eponymously titled effort, Raitt immediately emerged as a critical favorite, applauded not only for her soulful vocals and thoughtful song selection but also for her guitar prowess, turning heads as one of the few women to play bottleneck. Her 1972 follow-up, *Give It Up*, made better use of her eclectic tastes, featuring material by contemporaries like Jackson Browne and Eric Kaz, in addition to a number of R&B chestnuts and even three Raitt originals. *Takin' My Time*, released in 1973, was much acclaimed, and throughout the middle of the decade she released an LP annually, returning with *Streetlights* in 1974 and *Home Plate* a year later. With 1977's *Sweet Forgiveness*, Raitt scored her first significant pop airplay with her hit cover of the Del Shannon classic "Runaway"; its follow-up, 1979's *The Glow*, appeared around the same time as a massive all-star anti-nuclear concert at Madison Square Garden mounted by MUSE (Musicians United for Safe Energy), an organization she'd co-founded earlier.

Throughout her career, Raitt remained a committed activist, playing hundreds of benefit concerts and working tirelessly on behalf of the Rhythm and Blues Foundation. By the early '80s, however, her own career was in trouble—1982's *Green Light*, while greeted with the usual good reviews, again failed to break her to a wide audience, and while beginning work on the follow-up, Warners unceremoniously dropped her. By this time, Raitt was also battling drug and alcohol problems as well; she worked on a few tracks with Prince, but their schedules never aligned and the material went unreleased. Instead, she finally released the patchwork *Nine Lives* in 1986, her worst-selling effort since her debut. Many had written Raitt off when she teamed with producer Don Was and recorded *Nick of Time*; seemingly out of the blue, the LP won a handful of Grammys, including Album of the Year, and overnight she was a superstar. Released in 1991 *Luck of the Draw* was also a smash, yielding the hits "Something to Talk About" and "I Can't Make You Love Me." After 1994's *Longing in Their Hearts*, Raitt resurfaced in 1998 with *Fundamental*. *—Jason Ankeny*

Bonnie Raitt / 1971 / Warner Brothers ♦♦♦♦
The astounding thing about Bonnie Raitt's blues album isn't that it's the work of a preternaturally gifted blues woman, it's that Raitt doesn't choose to stick to the blues. She's decided to blend her love of classic folk blues with folk music, including new folk-rock tunes, along with a slight R&B, New Orleans, and jazz bent and a mellow Californian vibe. Surely, *Bonnie Raitt* is a record of its times, as much as Jackson Browne's first album is, but with this, she not only sketches out the blueprint for her future recordings, but for the roots music that would later be labeled as Americana. The reason that *Bonnie Raitt* works is that she is such a warm, subtle singer. She never oversells these songs, she lays back and sings them with heart and wonderfully textured reading. Her singing is complemented by her band, which is equally as warm, relaxed, and engaging. This is music that goes down so easy, it's only on the subsequent plays that you realize how fully realized and textured it is. A terrific debut that has only grown in stature since its release. *—Stephen Thomas Erlewine*

Give It Up / Sep. 1972 / Warner Brothers ♦♦♦♦♦
Bonnie Raitt may have switched producers for her second album *Give It Up*, hiring Michael Cuscuna, but she hasn't switched her style, sticking with the thoroughly engaging blend of folk, blues, R&B, and Californian soft rock. If anything, she's strengthened her formula here, making the divisions between the genres nearly indistinguishable. Take the title track, for instance. It opens with a bluesy acoustic guitar before kicking into a New Orleans brass band about halfway through—and the great thing about it is that Raitt makes the switch sound natural, even inevitable, never forced. And that's just the tip of the iceberg here, since *Give It Up* is filled with great songs, delivered in familiar, yet always surprising, ways by Raitt and her skilled band. For those who want to pigeonhole her as a white blues singer, she delivers the lovely "Nothing Seems to Matter," a gentle midtempo number that's as mellow as Linda Ronstadt and far more seductive. That's the key to *Give It Up*: Yes, Raitt can be earthy and sexy, but she balances it with an inviting sensuality that makes the record glow. It's all delivered in a fantastic set of originals and covers performed so naturally it's hard to tell them apart and roots music so thoroughly fused that it all sounds original, even when it's possible to spot the individual elements or influences. Raitt would go on to greater chart successes, but she not only had trouble topping this record, generations of singers, from Sheryl Crow to Shelby Lynne, have used this as a touchstone. One of the great Southern California records. *—Stephen Thomas Erlewine*

Takin' My Time / 1973 / Warner Brothers ♦♦♦♦
This album is an overlooked gem in the catalog of Bonnie Raitt. On *Takin' My Time*, she wears her influences proudly in an eclectic musical mix containing blues, jazz, folk, New Orleans R&B, and calypso. Although she did not write her own material for this album, she demonstrates an excellent ear for songs and chooses material from some of the best songwriters of the day. She is a great interpreter, and her renditions of Jackson Browne's "I Thought I Was a Child" and Randy Newman's "Guilty" from this album are the definitive versions of these songs. The highlights of this album are the romantic ballads "I Gave My Love a Candle" and "Cry Like a Rainstorm," where Raitt adds an emotional depth to the performance unusual for such a young woman. (Perhaps that's a result of her spending time with elder statesmen of the blues community such as Mississippi Fred McDowell and Sippie Wallace.) Although the faster-paced songs like the calypso "Wah She Go Do" seem a little out of place, the playful tune is welcome among an album filled with the heartache of the slower tunes. Despite being a relative newcomer, Raitt had already earned the respect of her mentors and her peers, as evidenced by the musical contributions of Taj Mahal, and Little Feat members Lowell George and Bill Payne on the album. This is the last consistent album she would make until her comeback in the mid-'80s. *—Vik Iyengar*

Streetlights / 1974 / Warner Brothers ♦♦♦♦
Bonnie Raitt had delivered three stellar albums, but chart success wasn't forthcoming, even if good reviews and a cult following were. So, she teamed with producer Jerry Ragovoy for *Streetlights* and attempted to make the crossover record that Warner so desperately wished she'd release. Over the years, the concessions that she made here—particularly the middle-of-the road arrangements (as opposed to the appealingly laid-back sounds of her previous records), the occasional use of strings, but also some of the song selections—have consigned *Streetlights* to noble failure status. There's no denying that's essentially what *Streetlights* is, but that makes it out to seem worse than it really is. It winds up paling to the wonderful ease and warm sensuality of her first three albums—she only occasionally hits that balance—but it's still undeniably pleasant, and there are moments here where she really pulls off some terrific work, including the opening cover of Joni Mitchell's "That Song About the Midway," a good version of John Prine's "Angel From Montgomery," and the much-touted take on Allen Toussaint's "What Is Success." It may be easy to lament the suppression of the laid-back sexiness and organic feel of Raitt's earlier records, but there's still enough here in that spirit to make this worthwhile. *—Stephen Thomas Erlewine*

Home Plate / 1975 / Warner Brothers ♦♦♦
Homeplate takes Bonnie Raitt even further down the path toward mainstream production than the unjustly maligned *Streetlights*, but, ironically, it works better than its predecessor. Perhaps that's because producer Paul A. Rothchild has helped Raitt craft a record that's unapologetically pitched at the mainstream, where *Streetlights* often seemed to be torn between two worlds. The great thing about that is, regardless of the production, the essentials of Raitt's music have not changed. It remains a wonderful hybrid of American music, built on a thoroughly impressive set of songs, all delivered with Raitt's warm, expertly shaded, and undeniably sexy singing. She's such an accomplished singer, she sells these songs through productions that are much slicker than those that graced her earlier records, plus with a supporting crew of studio musicians. This production will undoubtedly dismay listeners that just like the earthiness of *Give It Up*, but *Homeplate* is still a success because, even though the recording is glossier, Raitt and her music remain the same and, if you're looking for that, it's still irresistible. *—Stephen Thomas Erlewine*

Sweet Forgiveness / Apr. 1977 / Warner Brothers ♦♦
Since *Home Plate* brought Bonnie Raitt within shooting distance of the Top 40, thereby being the greatest chart success she yet attained, it made sense that she re-teamed with its producer Paul A. Rothchild for its follow-up, *Sweet Forgiveness*. Rothchild's modus operandi remains slickness, but he has backed away from his fondness for studio musicians, letting Raitt record the majority of the record with her touring band (who only were spotted occasionally throughout *Homeplate*). All this means is that the near-hit "Runaway" is almost a ringer, largely because it's a poor choice for Raitt's sweetly funky Californian rock that was obviously designed as a bid for a single, therefore it was slicked up more than the rest of the record (which remains slick, but not glossy). *Sweet Forgiveness* is actually looser than *Homeplate*, a little less constrained. Then why isn't it quite as successful, artistically? That comes down to a selection of songs that aren't quite as effective as those Raitt usually picks—and, in that sense, "Runaway" was a good indicator of the album. However, the selection of material isn't bad. If the tunes don't happen to form into a whole, it's still filled with great moments, from Earl Randall's opener "About to Make Me Leave Home" to Karla Bonoff's closer "Home." *Sweet Forgiveness* may not be one of Raitt's unqualified successes (despite its hit status), it's still a solid record, one that's hard to deny if you're already a Raitt fan. *—Stephen Thomas Erlewine*

The Glow / 1979 / Warner Brothers ♦♦♦

Green Light / 1982 / Warner Brothers ♦♦♦♦♦
Since 1975's *Homeplate*, Bonnie Raitt has veered closer to the mainstream than she has to the organic, sexy funk of her early-'70s records. This bothered many listeners, who chose to concentrate on the surface instead of the substance, but Raitt retained many of the same special qualities she demonstrated on those records into the '80s—namely, her excellent taste in material, fondness for blurring folk, blues, country, and rock, and her wonderfully subtle, always engaging, interpretations. *Green Lights* may suffer a bit from a production that clearly pegs it as a 1982 release, but strip away its production and it's yet another satisfying collection of roots-rockers and bluesy ballads from the always reliable Raitt. Producer Rob Fraboni's recording may be a little bit too mainstream, lacking the new wave spark of, say, Dave Edmunds' similar-sounding recordings of this era, but Raitt nevertheless rises above the limitations of the recording and delivers a tight, enjoyable collection of amiable mainstream rockers with just a hint of roots. This isn't nearly as sexy as even *Sweet Forgiveness*, and it doesn't have much grit, but it has spirit and is fun, and it's a nice, smooth ride for those that like the direction Raitt's going. *—Stephen Thomas Erlewine*

Nine Lives / 1986 / Warner Brothers ♦♦♦
Bonnie Raitt's ninth and final album for Warner Bros. Records was a star-crossed affair that began in 1983 in a session with producer Rob Fraboni, which was a typical Raitt mixture of different genres and songwriters, from Jerry Williams ("Excited") and Eric Kaz ("Angel") to reggae star Toots Hibbert ("True Love Is Hard to Find") in a style similar to her 1982 album *Green Light*. This record seems to have been rejected by Warner, but three years later Raitt returned to the studio with Bill Payne (Little Feat) and George Massenburgh and cut a group of commercial-sounding songs by the likes of Bryan Adams and Tom Snow. *Nine Lives* splits the difference between the two sessions, with four tracks rescued from 1983, and five added from 1986, plus the theme from a forgotten Farrah Fawcett movie ("Stand Up to the Night" from *Extremities*). The result is predictably scattered and strained, and it was Raitt's lowest-charting album since her debut. Not surprisingly, it was also the last straw in her relationship with Warner. *—William Ruhlmann*

● **Nick of Time** / Mar. 1989 / Capitol ♦♦♦♦♦
Prior to *Nick of Time*, Bonnie Raitt had been a reliable cult artist, delivering a string of solid records that were moderate successes and usually musically satisfying. From her 1971 debut through 1982's *Green Light*, she had a solid streak, but 1986's *Nine Lives* snapped it, falling far short of her usual potential. Therefore, it shouldn't have been a surprise when Raitt decided to craft its follow-up as a major comeback, collaborating with producer Don Was on *Nick of Time*. At the time, the pairing seemed a little odd, since he was primarily known for the weird hipster funk of Was (Not Was) and the B-52's quirky eponymous debut, but the match turned out to be inspired. Was used Raitt's classic early-'70s

records as a blueprint, choosing to update the sound with a smooth, professional production and a batch of excellent contemporary songs. In this context, Raitt flourishes; she never rocks too hard, but there is grit to her singing and playing, even when the surfaces are clean and inviting. And while she only has two original songs here, *Nick of Time* plays like autobiography, which is a testament to the power of the songs, performances and productions. It was a great comeback album that made for a great story, but the record never would have been a blockbuster success if it wasn't for the music, which is among the finest Raitt ever made. She must have realized this, since *Nick of Time* served as the blueprint for the majority of her '90s albums. *—Stephen Thomas Erlewine*

The Bonnie Raitt Collection / Jun. 28, 1990 / Warner Brothers ✦✦✦
Since Bonnie Raitt didn't score any big hits during her nine-album tenure at Warner Bros., compiling a best-of from those records is largely a matter of taste, and after Raitt's commercial breakthrough on Capitol with *Nick of Time* in 1989, Warners decided to trust her own taste in choosing songs for this compilation. The artist's input is usually considered a good thing, but in this case it has resulted in an idiosyncratic selection that fails to be representative or to cull the real highlights from Raitt's Warners catalog. Basically, that catalog breaks down into three sections—the first three solid albums, the second three good, but uneven albums, and the last three mediocre, compromised albums. Raitt has opted to try to find at least a couple of tracks from each album, which means she necessarily slights her best work in favor of her weakest. Even by choosing four tracks from *Give It Up*, she still misses "Been Too Long at the Fair," and by restricting herself to two tracks from *Takin My Time*, she misses "Cry Like a Rainstorm" and "I Gave My Love a Candle." On later albums, the problem is more about selection than quantity. Why "Sugar Mama" from *Home Plate* and not "Run Like a Thief" and "I'm Blowin' Away"? Why "(Goin') Wild for You Baby" from *The Glow* and not the Grammy-nominated "You're Gonna Get What's Coming"? Why "Willya Wontcha" from *Green Light* and not "Me and the Boys"? Even taking into account differences in taste, Raitt's choices run in the face of the preferences of fans and critics to the point that the album fails to make the case for her Warners recordings as true expressions of her talents, a case that could have been made decisively with a better selection. *—William Ruhlmann*

Luck of the Draw / Jun. 1991 / Capitol ✦✦✦✦✦
Nick of Time not only was an artistic comeback for Bonnie Raitt, it brought her largest audience yet, so there was no reason to mess with success for its sequel, *Luck of the Draw*. And sequel is the appropriate word, since *Luck of the Draw* is nothing if it isn't "Nick of Time, Part 2." True, there's a heavier reliance on original material this time around, but the sound and feel of the record is identical to its predecessor. There is one slight difference—several of the songs appear tailor-made for crossover success, where *Nick of Time* felt organic. Nevertheless, *Luck of the Draw* is an unqualified success, filled with strong songs—including the hits "Something to Talk About" and "I Can't Make You Love Me," plus the Delbert McClinton duet "Good Man, Good Woman"—appealing productions and just enough dirt to make old-school fans feel at home. *—Stephen Thomas Erlewine*

Longing in Their Hearts / Mar. 14, 1994 / Capitol ✦✦✦✦✦
On the follow-up to the follow-up (and another million-selling number one hit), Bonnie Raitt contributes more than her usual share of original songs, writing four songs herself and setting a lyric of her husband's to music for a fifth. Elsewhere, she draws on such strong writers as Richard Thompson and Paul Brady, all for a collection devoted to devotion. Song after song expresses passion, usually with happy results—this is not the album of a woman with the blues. Even when she's dressing down a parent in her own "Circle Dance," Raitt offers forgiveness and understanding. There, and in other songs, the object of her emotions rarely seems to be perfect, but she takes that in and loves him, anyway. Co-producer Don Was provides a detailed production in which single elements—an accordion, a harmony vocal by Levon Helm or David Crosby—effectively color arrangements and complement Raitt's always soulful singing. *—William Ruhlmann*

Road Tested / Nov. 7, 1995 / Digital Sound ✦✦✦✦✦
In a 24-year recording career, Bonnie Raitt had not previously released a live album, so this concert set was overdue. Coming off three multi-platinum studio albums, Raitt and Capitol pulled out all the stops, compiling a 22-track, double-disc package from dates recorded in July 1995 in Portland and Oakland. Raitt ranged over her career, reaching back to her early folk-blues days and forward to the pop/rock songs that finally made her a big star in the late '80s and early '90s. She also shared the spotlight with such guests as Bruce Hornsby, Ruth Brown, Charles Brown, Kim Wilson of the Fabulous Thunderbirds, Bryan Adams, and Jackson Browne. But that didn't keep an artist who has spent the bulk of her career pleasing live audiences rather than cutting hits from displaying her personal warmth along with her singing and playing skills. She also introduced half a dozen songs new to her repertoire, including a surprising cover of Talking Heads' "Burning Down the House" and a few that had potential to help promote the album as singles, including "Never Make Your Move Too Soon" and "Shake a Little." Inexplicably, Capitol (which probably wished the album had been a more reasonably priced single-disc) failed to bring the record home to consumers. The company's choice for a single was the anonymous Adams rocker "Rock Steady," done as a duet with him—apparently, they were confusing Raitt with Tina Turner. As a result, the album stopped at gold, spending less than six months in the charts. Despite that commercial disappointment, it will be for many Bonnie Raitt fans an example of her at her best that effectively bridges the two parts of her career, and also a good sampler for first-time listeners. *—William Ruhlmann*

Fundamental / Apr. 7, 1998 / Capitol ✦✦✦
Apparently in an attempt to find new sounds that would appeal to a new audience, Bonnie Raitt severed her ties with her comeback producer Don Was for *Fundamental*, hiring those masterminds of experimental adult pop, Mitchell Froom and Tchad Blake. Although Froom and Blake have worked with a number of singer-songwriters and roots musicians—including Elvis Costello, Suzanne Vega, Richard Thompson, Los Lobos and Crowded House—they often emphasize the production over the song, pouring on layers of effects and novelty instruments that tend to obscure the songs and performances. While they don't go overboard on *Fundamental*, like they did on Los Lobos' *Colossal Head*, they have pushed too much of their own style on Raitt. There are good songs scattered throughout the record, but it's hard to pick them out underneath the gauzy, murky production. Eventually, the album becomes a bit of a chore, since the sounds wear on the ears. That's too bad, because Raitt remains a vital artist—it's just that Froom and Blake haven't allowed her to rely on her talents here. *—Stephen Thomas Erlewine*

Silver Lining / Apr. 9, 2002 / Capitol ✦✦✦✦
With her road band laying the groundwork and with production responsibilities reverted primarily to her own hands, Raitt delivers varied and vivid performances throughout *Silver Lining*. Jon Cleary, an addition to the lineup, plays the pivotal role; his piano drives the steaming New Orleans groove on "Fool's Game," the posturing street funk of "Monkey Business," and the dusty blues tread on the acoustic-textured "No Gettin' Over You." The material, culled from American and African songwriters, along with a few Raitt originals, lends itself more to vocal interpretation than to straight-ahead blowing. Raitt's singing has never been more finely tuned, especially on the introspective title cut and on the final track, "Wounded Heart," a breathtaking duet recorded in one take with keyboardist Benmont Tench; after nailing it, Raitt reportedly fled the studio, moved to tears; any second attempt proved both undoable and unnecessary. On these performances Raitt exceeds her own standards for interpreting a lyric without compromise to her full-throated timbre. To balance these reflective moments, there are plenty of hotter ones; these also focus on the vocal, but with some exceptional guitar accompaniment as well, including Steve Cropper's licks on the low-key, Memphis-flavored "Time of Our Lives" and the greasy rhythms that push the band throughout "Gnawin' on It." Incendiary slide guitar work heats up parts of that track and several others, with another slide legend, Roy Rogers, joining in on the lascivious "Gnawin' on It." Still, *Silver Lining* is ultimately a showcase for exceptional singing and riveting backup work. It is also a likely milestone in Raitt's ongoing transition from blues guitar whiz to an artist of wider focus. The fires of her youth still blaze, though now they illuminate a more complex weave of techniques and a much greater depth of emotion. *—Robert L. Doerschuk*

Kid Ramos

b. Jan. 13, 1959, Fullerton, CA
Guitar / Modern Electric Blues, Contemporary Blues, Blues-Rock
Born on January 13, 1959, in Fullerton, CA, blues-rock guitarist David "Kid" Ramos inherited his love of music from his parents, who were both professional opera singers. When his father grew tired of life on the road, he settled down with his family, buying a gas station in Anaheim. One day, when Kid was eight, he bought his son an electric guitar and amplifier from a customer passing through. By his teenaged years, Ramos was playing friend's parties and nightclubs on a regular basis, joining harmonica expert James Harman's blues-based band in 1980 (all its members sported sharkskin suits), playing up and down California alongside such punk bands as X, Oingo Boingo, the Blasters, and the Plimsouls. Kid played with the Harman Band for most of the '80s, until his departure in 1988, and although he filled in as the guitarist for the outfit Roomful of Blues, decided to put his musical career on the back burner to focus on his home life and start a family (for the next seven years, Ramos was employed as a water delivery man).

Eventually though, his desire to play music returned and Ramos formed the Big Rhythm Combo with singer Lynwood Slim (issuing *The Big Rhythm Combo* in 1994), in addition to releasing his first-ever solo album, *Two Hands One Heart*, in 1995. The same year, Ramos was invited to join one of his favorite all-time bands, the Fabulous Thunderbirds, at the personal request of their singer, Kim Wilson. Ramos promptly accepted and he returned back to the road. In addition to his work with the T-Birds, Ramos has continued to issue solo albums on a regular basis, including 1999's self-titled sophomore effort, 2000's *West Coast House Party*, and 2001's *Greasy Kid's Stuff*. *—Greg Prato*

Two Hands One Heart / Oct. 1995 / Black Top ✦✦✦

Kid Ramos / Aug. 24, 1999 / Evidence ✦✦✦✦
With his second album (self-titled, as if it were his debut), Kid Ramos turns in a solid set of greasy roadhouse blues that hits harder than most contemporary blues albums from the '90s. Ramos not only knows how to select his material (all 15 songs are covers, but only "Three Hundred Pounds of Joy" is overly familiar) and can play all variations of blues, but he keeps the record loose and raw, never polishing the sound too much and letting the music breathe. The result is a thoroughly engaging, entertaining set that sucks you in with "Dead Love," keeps your interest through the extraordinary version of James Harman's "Walk-Around Telephone Blues" (the writer contributes harp here), and doesn't let go until the end. An appealing effort that establishes Ramos as a worthy artist in his own right even after years of winning audiences as a member of Roomful of Blues, the Red Devils, and the Fabulous Thunderbirds. *—Stephen Thomas Erlewine*

● **West Coast House Party** / Aug. 29, 2000 / Evidence ✦✦✦✦
The third release from The Fabulous Thunderbirds' muscular lead guitarist is less a solo album than a forum for the obviously well-connected Kid Ramos to host a congregation of some of the country's best swing-influenced talent as they blow through an hour of prime West Coast jump blues. Between the ever-present horns and a long list of lead vocalists, including Lynwood Slim, Duke Robillard, Big Sandy, the Thunderbirds' Kim Wilson, and ex-employer James Harman, trading off the spotlight, it's tough for Ramos to assert himself as a guitarist with a distinctive sound amongst the excitement of all the guest appearances. Interestingly, the star also invites like-minded guitarists such as Little Charlie Baty, Rusty Zinn, and one of the genre's founding fathers, Clarence "Gatemouth" Brown to his party, further diluting the effect of his own contributions. That minor complaint aside, this is a consistently exciting and joyously well-performed disc of upbeat jump blues, played with a one-take intensity that's contagious. The musicians sound like

they're having a blast and that infectious feeling translates to the music, as this gifted crew runs through relatively obscure covers of Amos Milburn, Ray Brown, and Dave Bartholomew tunes, along with a handful of originals that sound as if they were written in the '50s—the golden age of this swinging sound. "Real Gone Lover," featuring Kim Wilson's vocal and powerful harp, is the only track where the horns sit out and the sound is stripped down to a rugged trio, providing the listener a chance to hear Kid Ramos tear through a tune without regard to the tight charts that are this album's feature attraction. The extensive 12-page booklet not only offers detailed track information—a must with a project that includes so many different musicians and soloists on each tune—but provides a capsule history of jump blues, adding immensely to the enjoyment of the disc. Ultimately, you won't learn much more about Kid Ramos' substantial talents as anything but a terrific bandleader and the guy you'd want in charge of the guest list to your next shindig. But it's to his credit that he selflessly hands over the focus on his own release to his talented backing band and guest stars, culminating in a winning project, astonishingly free of egos from any of its participants. *—Hal Horowitz*

Greasy Kid's Stuff / Oct. 9, 2001 / Evidence ✦✦✦

For his fourth solo release, and third on the Evidence label, the Fabulous Thunderbirds' guitarist, Kid Ramos, once again calls in some high-profile blues friends for assistance. Instead of last album's guitarists and jump-blues horns, this time Ramos sticks with harpists/vocalists to provide the momentum on a set of relatively stripped-down, greasy blues. He's also the only guitarist on the sessions, which makes this a spotlight for his picking as well as his bandleading abilities. Harmonica aces Rick Estrin (Little Charlie & the Nightcats), Paul deLay, Lynwood Slim, Johnny Dyer, James Harman (who only plays on one of his three tracks and sings on the others), and Charlie Musselwhite, along with Rod Piazza, all contribute. The leadoff title cut, an instrumental that sounds like it was left over from his last horn-infused West Coast album, is the one exception. The sessions were cut in two days, which gives them a raw, not quite primal edge that adds to the gritty nature of the recording. Although the original intent was to perform exclusively covers, nearly all the harp-playing guests brought in their own original material. Just a handful of interpretations remain: Willie Dixon's "I Don't Care Who Knows"; an obscure Lightnin' Slim track, "Mean Ol' Lonesome Train"; an old uncredited Excello side, "Rich Man's Woman"; and Bobby "Blue" Bland's "Hold Me Tenderly." It sure sounds like this was one big part, as each guest plays with a relaxed gusto, whipping off harp lines with nonchalant intensity. Ramos' tough yet flexible guitar fills the holes and takes the lead just often enough so the listener knows whose album it is. Otherwise he's content to leave the majority of the spotlight to his high-profile guests, who turn in sterling performances. While few of their original tunes sound drastically different from standard blues fare, the ensemble playing and electrified atmosphere adds a palpable excitement to the tracks. The various vocals also infuse a diverse feel to the album, with Ramos' guitar and presence being the thread that holds it together. The closing "Harmonica Hangover" features Estrin and Musselwhite on what seems to be an improvised duet, with both harp men discussing the proceedings and other guests, as well as trading licks on an appropriately upbeat shuffle. It's a fitting finale to an album that works because of the loosely structured environment that Ramos provides, meshed with the remarkable talents of his talented contributors. *—Hal Horowitz*

Al Rapone (Al Lewis)

b. 1936, Lake Charles, LA

Vocals, Accordion / Contemporary Blues, Zydeco

The brother of zydeco's renowned Queen Ida, accordionist and guitarist Al Rapone was not only a driving force behind the success of his sister but also a noted solo performer. Born Al Lewis in Lake Charles, LA, in 1936, he first picked up the accordion at age 13, and following the family's relocation to California he was regularly performing live throughout the West Coast by the early '50s. Within a few years, Rapone also began playing guitar, quickly becoming a noted sideman on the San Francisco blues circuit, where he backed the likes of Big Mama Thornton, Clarence "Gatemouth" Brown, and Jimmy Reed; while in college, he studied composing, producing and arranging, and after graduation formed a group with his sister. However, as Queen Ida soon settled down to raise a family, Rapone assembled a new unit, the Bon Ton Zydeco Band, and over time forged a unique sound combing his distinctive guitar leads with zydeco accordion and country music rhythms. Ida began sitting in with the group during the mid-'70s, and as her career blossomed, the Bon Ton Zydeco Band mutated to become her permanent backing band; Rapone served not only as his sister's ace sideman but also as her producer and arranger, helming her 1982 Grammy-winner *Queen Ida and the Bon Ton Zydeco Band on Tour*, as well as composing one of her best-loved songs, "Frisco Zydeco." Soon afterwards, Rapone left the group to again pursue a solo career, enjoying his greatest success in Germany, where he recorded efforts including 1982's *Cajun Creole Music* and 1984's *C'Est La Vie*; upon returning Stateside, he settled in New Orleans, issuing *Zydeco to Go* in 1990. *—Jason Ankeny*

C'Est La Vie! / 1984 / L&R ✦✦✦

Zydeco to Go / Oct. 1990 / Blind Pig ✦✦✦✦

On his second album, *Zydeco to Go*, Al Rapone turns out an infectious, joyful record, filled with good spirits and great music. The album is firmly in the classic zydeco tradition, spiked with some blues, R&B and Cajun country, and Rapone shines on each of the tracks, as does his supple, sympathetic supporting band. His cousin, Roy L. Chantier, drops in to sing a couple of tracks, turning "Our Hearts Will Dance in Love Again" into a beautiful thing and making sure that "Good Ole Cajun Music" and "Yvette U.B. Dancin'" catch fire. Still, this is Rapone's show, and he keeps things cooking with his robust accordion and gleeful vocals. All in all, *Zydeco to Go* is a good-time record that delivers. *—Thom Owens*

● **Plays Tribute: A Tribute to Clifton Chenier** / May 6, 1997 / Atomic Theory ✦✦✦✦✦

It may be a salute to the master of zydeco, but Al Rapone's *A Tribute to Clifton Chenier* is a terrific testimonial to his own talents as well. Part of the reason the album works so well is that there isn't a weak song on the record—in fact, almost all of the 15 songs are acknowledged zydeco classics. These songs give Rapone a platform for his rambunctious, infectious accordion style. He plays these songs a little bluesier than Chenier, but it's great to hear them played in a different way, and the record itself is just a blast. *—Thom Owens*

Live at Dingwall's Dancehall / Sep. 3, 2002 / JSP ✦✦✦

Moses Rascoe

b. Jul. 27, 1917, Windsor, NC, **d.** Mar. 6, 1994, Lebanon, PA

Vocals, Guitar / Folk-Blues, Electric Blues

Moses Rascoe got his first guitar in North Carolina at the age of 13 and turned professional in Pennsylvania some 50-odd years later. In between, he traveled the roads as a day laborer and truck driver, playing guitar only for "a dollar or a drink," as he told Jack Roberts in *Living Blues*. But he'd picked up plenty of songs over the years, from old Brownie McGhee Piedmont blues to Jimmy Reed's '50s jukebox hits, and when he retired from trucking at the age of 65, he gave his music a shot. The local folk-music community took notice, as did blues and folk festivals from Chicago to Europe. Rascoe recorded his first album live at Godfrey Daniels, a Pennsylvania coffeehouse, in 1987. *—Jim O'Neal*

● **Blues** / 1987 / Flying Fish ✦✦✦✦✦

A former truck driver turned touring bluesman, Rascoe primarily covers other people's tunes and classic blues themes. There is much Jimmy Reed and "traditional" material. *—Niles J. Frantz*

Johnny Rawls

b. 1951, Hattiesburg, MS

Vocals / Contemporary Blues, Soul-Blues

Singer, songwriter, guitarist, arranger and producer Johnny Rawls draws on the '50s' and '60s' deep soul-blues tradition in his guitar playing, yet his lyrics and singing are completely '90s.

Rawls got his early musical education from his grandfather, John Paul Newson, a blind guitarist who played around the Hattiesburg area. Rawls began playing clarinet and saxophone in third grade, and by the time he was in his teens, the band instructor hired Rawls to play in his band. As a teen, Rawls had the opportunity to back singers like Joe Tex and Z.Z. Hill. He began playing guitar at age 12, learning as much as he could from players in other area blues bands. After leaving Mississippi for a year when he was 17, he returned, determined to form his own blues/soul ensemble. They found work backing up touring musicians and by the mid-'70s, Rawls joined O.V. Wright's band, working with Wright until his death in 1980. After Wright's death, the band continued to perform his music for 13 years as the O.V. Wright Band, opening shows for people like B.B. King, Little Milton Campbell and Bobby "Blue" Bland. In the mid-'80s, the O.V. Wright Band also toured with Little Johnny Taylor, Latimore, B.B. Coleman, Blues Boy Willie, and others, including Lynn White.

Working with guitarist L.C. Luckett, Rawls recorded 45 rpm singles for his own label, Touch Records, and continued working around the South, touring regionally with soul-blues singers. In 1994, Rawls and Luckett recorded their first album, *Can't Sleep at Night*, for the Rooster Blues label. In 1995, Rawls parted with Luckett to lead a new group and found a record company that was interested, the London-based JSP label. *Here We Go*, his debut for JSP Records, was recorded in 1996, he has followed it up with several releases since then.

Rawls carries on the soul-blues tradition of people like O.V. Wright, Otis Redding, and Z.Z. Hill in his singing style and guitar playing, but his arrangement, production and lyrics are steeped in the '90s techniques and subject matter. Rawls is a true soul-blues renaissance man and with any luck. *—Richard Skelly*

● **Here We Go** / Aug. 27, 1996 / JSP ✦✦✦✦

Johnny Rawls turns in an impressive debut with *Here We Go*. Although he doesn't do anything new to the soul-blues genre, the record is entertaining in the vein of Z.Z. Hill and latter-day Bobby Bland. Rawls has a powerful, soulful voice which can make mediocre material sound convincing. Unfortunately, there are a few too many half-hearted cuts here, but that doesn't prevent the album from being a promising debut. *—Thom Owens*

Louisiana Woman / Sep. 9, 1997 / JSP ✦✦✦

My Turn to Win / Feb. 9, 1999 / JSP ✦✦✦

Put Your Trust in Me / Jan. 30, 2001 / JSP ✦✦✦

Lucky Man / Apr. 1, 2002 / ✦✦✦

Dave Ray & Tony Glover

Vocals, Harmonica, Guitar / Contemporary Blues

Minnesota based singer/guitarist Dave "Snaker" Ray and harmonica player Tony "Little Sun" Glover recorded both solo, duet and trio efforts with guitarist/singer/songwriter "Spider" John Koerner throughout the early '60s. Among the first to successfully tackle the Delta blues form and do it well. *—AMG*

● **Ashes in My Whiskey** / 1990 / Rough Trade ✦✦✦

Ashes in My Whiskey is the first studio record Ray & Glover made since 1965 and it proves that even with the extended layoff, the duo remained vital. They play a set of 15 acoustic, traditional blues numbers that include a couple of startlingly successful originals, particularly the haunting "HIV Blues." But the key to the record's success is the sympathetic, natural interplay the guitarist and harpist have—their performances offer definitive proof that many bluesmen get better with age. *—Thom Owens*

Kenny "Blue" Ray

b. Jan. 11, 1950, Lodi, CA

Guitar / Modern Electric Blues

Guitarist Kenny "Blue" Ray has the kind of fat guitar overtones, complex chord changes and lightning-fast chops that tend to draw rock fans into the blues fold. Not unlike Stevie Ray Vaughan, Ray's playing owes almost as much to his rock influences as to his blues mentors.

Ray's resumé includes performances and recording sessions with William Clarke, Little Charlie and the Nightcats, Charlie Musselwhite, Smokey Wilson, and a bevy of other West Coast blues stylists.

Ray first became interested in music via his father, who played guitars, harmonica, fiddle, and piano. Seeing Elvis Presley perform on *The Ed Sullivan Show* was a turning point for him, and later that year, his father bought him a guitar. As a youngster, Ray would listen to disc jockey Wolfman Jack at night, listening to music by Jimmy Reed, Howlin' Wolf, and others. Ray often skipped school to play guitar with his friends. He made his amateur debut at a high school dance in the mid-'60s.

While in the Air Force, Ray was stationed in London from 1969 to 1972. There, he met Ferdnand Jones and began playing '60s-style soul and blues. After coming back to the U.S., Ray toured with the Paul Hermann Band until 1975, when he took a job as lead guitarist with Little Charlie and the Nightcats, then a regional northern California band.

In 1976, Ray left the Nightcats to head back to Los Angeles. There, he became part of the house band at a club run by guitarist and singer Smokey Wilson. Onstage at Wilson's Pioneer Club, Ray had the chance to back up legendary artists like Big Joe Turner, Pee Wee Crayton, Lowell Fulson and Big Mama Thornton. A few years later, Ray made his recording session debut with the likes of harmonica player William Clarke and vocalist Finis Tasby.

After moving to Austin, TX in 1980, Ray joined the Marcia Ball Band, touring with her for four years around the Texas Triangle. Ray can be heard on Ball's 1985 album for Rounder, *Soulful Dress*. He befriended guitarist Stevie Ray Vaughan and continued his career as a session man, recording with Ball, Mitch Woods, Charlie Musselwhite, Greg "Fingers" Taylor, Ron Thompson, and Tommy Castro, among dozens of others.

By 1990, Ray decided it was time to start leading his own band, and in 1994, he recorded *Fired Up!*, the first album for his own Blue Ray/Tone King label. Ray's releases helped broaden his touring base beyond central Texas and northern California. His other mid-'90s recordings include *Cadillac Tone* (1995), *Pull the Strings* (1996), and *Git It!* (1997), all for his own Blue Ray/Tone King label. Ray recorded *In All of My Life* (1997) for the London-based JSP Records. He was accompanied by John Firmin (tenor sax) of the Johnny Nocturne Band, as well as Rob Sudduth of Huey Lewis & the News on baritone and tenor saxes.

On record and on stages around the U.S., Ray's guitar playing reflects his smorgasbord of influences: Albert King, Stevie Ray Vaughan, Albert Collins, and Aaron "T-Bone" Walker. His vocals are powerful and soul-filled. Ray continues to tour around the U.S., Canada, and Europe. *—Richard Skelly*

Fired Up! / 1994 / Blue Ray ♦♦♦

● **In All of My Life** / May 6, 1997 / JSP ♦♦♦♦
Kenny Ray delivered on his promise with 1997's *In All of My Life*. Working with vocalist Jimmy Morello and a horn section, Ray has created an album that hits as hard as blues but swings like soul. He keeps things from becoming predictable by contributing some gutsy, idiosyncratic guitar work. Morello's vocals follow the same path, and the result is a wonderful blues record that honors traditions by not being beholden to them. *—Thom Owens.*

Keep the Mojo Workin' / 1999 / Tone King ♦♦♦
Never one to disappoint, this is another fine "real deal" blues album from the West Coast cat who wastes no notes and no time (neither yours nor his). Most of *Keep the Mojo Workin'* was recorded live, with just a few overdubbed solos, and was completed in just two sessions. You'll find instrumental tributes to Anson Funderburgh, Jimmie Vaughan, and Ray's late great boss, William Clarke. You also get some Billy Gibbons harmonics and early-'60s-style B.B. King/Duke Jethro sounds. Covers include Albert Collins' "Backstroke," Little Walter's "Mean Old World," Eddie Taylor's immortal 1955 hit "Bad Boy," Jimmy Reed's laconic shuffle "You Don't Have to Go," and the Elmore James classic "I Believe." In addition to some great West Coast, Texas, and Chicago blues guitar playing, Ray takes to the Hammond B-3 on four of the songs. This one also showcases Charlie Chavez on vocals and harp and Stan Powell on chromatic harp. *—Ann Wickstrom*

Bless My Axe / Jan. 1, 2000 / Tone King / ♦♦♦♦
There's no mistake why he's dubbed the "Tone King." He employs the often imitated West Coast sound, but stands out by incorporating a variety of colors and textures. Never restricted to the Wild West sound, he stretches out in "Cadillac Drive," paying homage to jazz great Wes Montgomery, and tackling the Stanley Turrentine classic "Sugar," peppering blue notes within its jazz base. Acknowledging a passion for transitional country-electric blues, he wisely chooses a lesser-known John Lee Hooker tune, "Maudie," and an original, "Mississippi 3 A.M." To truly enjoy his range, listen to "Tone Party," a cooker filled with single-note passages, each possessing a powerful punch. *—Char Ham*

Milton Rector

d. Apr. 4, 1994, Chicago, IL
Bass / Chicago Blues, R&B
The lazy, loping shuffle associated with bluesman Jimmy Reed was one of many grooves this important Chicago bassist was known for helping to create. Milton Rector could also play blues of a much more aggressive nature, as demonstrated on many fine '60s recordings by harmonica boss Sonny Boy Williamson. The bass line to the song "Help Me" is one of the most famous in blues, although whether it, or the very similar lick to "Green Onions," was the source seems to be a chicken-and-eggs debate. Like many of the Windy City's players from the prolific recording period of the '50s and '60s, the bassist was an eclectic performer who seemed to have as much interest in genre categories as a gangster has in abiding by the law. The great Chicago pianist Johnnie Johnson has recalled working in the late '40s in the Milton Rector Jazz Band, indicating both a jazz background and an obvious explanation for the swing feeling that is always present in his bass lines. Blues scholars who just can't be satisfied listening to the most famous artists can check Rector out in the company of J.B. Lenoir and Homesick James Williamson in a set of sessions that were apparently cut on the same day in the early '60s for the USA label. It was a case of "United We Delete" as well, since these recordings tend to show their smiling faces in cutout bins. Other action-packed recording sessions that are also dripping with obscurity were recordings produced by bandleader and man-about-town Al Smith, featuring leaders Morris Pejoe and Arthur "Big Boy" Spires. These recordings were cut in Smith's basement for the United and States labels, but have remained in reissue circulation, unlike the sides on the previously mentioned, patriotically named imprint. *—Eugene Chadbourne*

A.C. Reed

b. May 9, 1926, Wardell, MO
Vocals, Saxophone / Modern Electric Chicago Blues, Electric Chicago Blues, Soul-Blues
To hear tenor saxist A.C. Reed bemoan his fate on-stage, one might glean the impression that he truly detests his job. But it's a tongue-in-cheek complaint—Reed's raspy, gutbucket blowing and laid-back vocals bely any sense of boredom.

Sax-blowing blues bandleaders are scarce as hen's teeth in Chicago; other than Eddie Shaw, Reed's about all there is. Born in Missouri, young Aaron Corthen (whether he's related to blues legend Jimmy Reed remains hazy, but his laconic vocal drawl certainly mirrors his namesake) grew up in downstate Illinois. A big band fan, he loved the sound of Paul Bascomb's horn on an obscure Erskine Hawkins 78 he heard tracking on a tavern jukebox so much that he was inspired to pick up a sax himself.

Arriving in Chicago during the war years, he picked up steady gigs with Earl Hooker and Willie Mabon before the '40s were over. In 1956, he joined forces with ex-Ike Turner cohort Dennis "Long Man" Binder, gigging across the Southwest for an extended period. Reed became a valuable session player for producer Mel London's Age and Chief labels during the early '60s; in addition to playing on sides by Lillian Offitt, Ricky Allen, and Hooker, he cut a locally popular 1961 single of his own for Age, "This Little Voice."

More gems for Age—"Come on Home," "Mean Cop," "I Stay Mad"—followed. He cut 45s for USA in 1963 ("I'd Rather Fight Than Switch"), Cool ("My Baby Is Fine," a tune he's recut countless times since) and Nike ("Talkin' 'Bout My Friends") in 1966, and "Things I Want You to Do" in 1969 for TDS.

Reed joined Buddy Guy's band in 1967, visiting Africa with the mercurial guitarist in 1969 and, after harpist Junior Wells teamed with Guy, touring as opening act for the Rolling Stones in 1970. He left the employ of Guy and Wells for good in 1977, only to hook up with Alligator acts Son Seals and then the Master of the Telecaster, Albert Collins. Reed appeared on Collins' first five icy Alligator LPs, including the seminal *Ice Pickin'*.

During his tenure with Collins, Reed's solo career began to reignite, with four cuts on the second batch of Alligator's *Living Chicago Blues* anthologies in 1980 and two subsequent LPs of his own, 1982's *Take These Blues and Shove 'Em!* (on Ice Cube Records, a logo co-owned by Reed and drummer Casey Jones) and *I'm in the Wrong Business!* five years later for Alligator (with cameos by Bonnie Raitt and Stevie Ray Vaughan). Reed remains an active force on the Chicago circuit with his band, the Spark Plugs (get it? AC sparkplugs? Sure you do!). *—Bill Dahl*

Take These Blues and Shove 'Em / 1982 / Rooster Blues ♦♦♦
The first of the saxist's humorous diatribes detailing his tongue-in-cheek hatred of his life's calling. His argument doesn't hold water, though, since the LP is so refreshingly funky ("I Am Fed Up With This Music" remains a bandstand staple for him) and enjoyable. Drummer Casey Jones, Reed's longtime bandmate behind Albert Collins, coproduced with the sardonic horn man. *—Bill Dahl*

● **I'm in the Wrong Business** / 1987 / Alligator ♦♦♦♦♦
Solid, soulful blues, often with humorous, self-deprecating lyrics, comes from the well-respected vocalist, tenor player, composer, and veteran of the bands of Albert Collins, Buddy Guy, Magic Sam, and Son Seals. Reed has been called "the definitive Chicago blues sax player." This album features Reed's band, with guests Bonnie Raitt and Stevie Ray Vaughan. *—Niles J. Frantz*

Junk Food / Apr. 28, 1998 / Delmark ♦♦♦
Tenor saxophonist Reed was retired for a brief time while he wrote the songs for this recording, and then came back to live performing and touring. His band is a bit rough and a little out of control at times, as the backing guitars are sharp and out of tune. For the most part, though, things are together. There are two cuts from unearthed older sessions featuring the late Albert Collins, some neat horn charts, and cameos from singers Maurice John Vaughn, Sammy Fender, and Arthur Irby, which work to varying degrees. Reed's songs emphasize various social ills, some optimism, and a blues-chasing attitude that always feels good. Reed's signature funky blues crops up on the title track, a travelers anthem about Mickey D's, B.K., and similar places, during which he admits that he eventually "ate a foot long dog," knowing it wasn't good for him. That same funk forms the basis for "Give It Up," a reference to quit smoking with Vaughn chiming in about saying no to drugs, while "Fed Up" has Reed complaining about not getting paid one night after a gig. The Collins features include a slower-paced "Broke Music" (in reference to the blues being broke all the time) and the easy-swinging "I Got Mad," where a female abuser is chided in regards to an eventual Bobbitt incident. Collins' role is, for the most part, incidental. Reed praises Bill Clinton effusively as a saxophonist and leader on the John Lee Hooker-type boogie "The President Plays"; he uses a similar rhythm about "Two Women in a Pick-Up" headin' for New Orleans, and complements his "Big Woman" who went to Jenny Craig and who is "now... slim & fine" in a slinky, slow 12-bar, pure Chicago blues style. In a "Killin' Floor"-mode "Florine" has Reed adopting a Howlin' Wolf vocal stance. "Lonely Man" is a down-home blues, and the Fender goes soulful on an Albert King-flavored "You're Going to Miss Me." Irby sounds like he's straining to hit high notes on a version of the Doors' "Roadhouse Blues." In the final cut, "Last Time Around," Reed sounds seriously like he has had enough of the music business, given that the song centers around him quitting, harkening back to his previous CD *I'm in the Wrong Business*. If this is the musician's last recording, it's a good one, with his typical tenor swagger

present and accounted for; so typical of bar-walking R&B saxophonists of the '50s, it is compact yet on the edge. His singing is also solid and easily identifiable. The horn backing sounds great throughout, and Reed himself doesn't seem like he is done yet musically. Recommended. *—Michael G. Nastos*

Dalton Reed

b. Aug. 23, 1952, Cade, LA, **d.** Sep. 24, 1994, Minneapolis, MN

Vocals / Deep Soul

Dalton Reed attempted to keep the sweet sound of deep soul alive in the '90s. The Lafayette, LA, singer comes from a gospel background—a prerequisite for success in the genre—and cut his first single for his own little label in 1986.

When he was child, Dalton Reed sang gospel in church and played trumpet in his high school marching band. Reed fell in love with R&B and soul as a teenager, prompting him to join a few local bands. Soon, he formed his own group, Dalton Reed & the Musical Journey Band. In a short while, the band was playing bars and clubs throughout Louisiana, Alabama, and Texas.

Reed founded his own record label, Sweet Daddy Records, in 1986, releasing his debut single, "Givin' on in to Love," that same year. Within a few years after the formation of Sweet Daddy, Dalton and his brother Johnny Reed formed another independent label, Reed Brothers Records.

In 1990, Bullseye Blues signed Dalton Reed and the label released his debut album, *Louisiana Soul Man*, the following year. Three years later, his second album, *Willing & Able*, appeared. When he wasn't recording, Reed toured, playing concerts throughout America. *—Bill Dahl*

Louisiana Soul Man / Dec. 1991 / Bullseye Blues ♦♦♦

Dalton Reed's *Louisiana Soul Man* establishes the singer as an heir to the deep Southern soul of such artists as Otis Redding, Arthur Conley, and Percy Sledge. Despite the title, there's no hint of Cajun music or zydeco on the record—it's pure testifiying from start to finish. The new material is usually quite good, and it should be with songwriters like Doc Pomus, Dr. John, Dan Penn, and Delbert McClinton involved. *Louisiana Soul Man* is for anyone who believed that pure Southern soul died with Otis Redding. *—Thom Owens*

● **Willing & Able** / Mar. 30, 1994 / Bullseye Blues ♦♦♦♦♦

Dalton Reed is a classic gospel-based soul vocalist. There's nothing sophisticated in his approach, staid in his delivery, or polite and detached in his sound. He explodes, attacks, and rips through the 10 tracks on his second Bullseye blues LP, his voice full of animation and expressiveness. These songs are done in the vivid, overwrought manner considered too intense by the urban contemporary tastemakers; you won't hear trendy backgrounds or drum machines on these numbers. This is unapologetic soul from a vocalist who will never appeal to the crossover audience, but is making some of the better R&B in today's market. *—Ron Wynn*

Francine Reed

b. Jul. 11, 1947, Chicago, IL

Vocals / Soul-Blues, Contemporary Blues

Vocalist Francine Reed can't remember a time when she didn't sing. In her youth, the Chicago-born, Phoenix-raised song stylist sang in church and in grammar school. She began singing professionally with her family when she was five and continued into her teens. She got married young and had four children, whom she ended up raising alone. She worked a variety of day jobs and kept her singing career an avocation until 1985, when some friends introduced her to Lyle Lovett. Lovett was interested in finding a female vocalist for his new band and found his singer in Reed. She toured with Lovett for ten years as a member of Lovett's Large Band, and did several TV performances with the Texas singer/songwriter. While her association with Lovett continues, she has embarked on the kind of solo career she always wanted when working the day jobs to support her family.

Reed recorded two albums for the Atlanta-based Ichiban label in 1995 and 1996. Her amphitheater performances with Lovett must have surely had an effect on sales of these two records. Reed also got a few other nice breaks, including the chance to do some singing for TV commercials. Tom Cruise cranks her album up in a scene from the 1993 movie *The Firm.*

Reed's albums for Ichiban include *I Want You to Love Me* (1995) and *Can't Make It On My Own* (1996). The former features a duet with bandleader Lovett, while the latter includes a duet with Delbert McClinton. On both albums, Reed continues the tradition already set down by great women soul-blues vocalists like Carla Thomas, Irma Thomas and Etta James; she returned in 1999 with *Shades of Blue* on the Intersound label. In 2001, following the demise of Ichiban Records (which left her first two records out of print) and unavailable, Reed and longtime collaborator Marvin Taylor re-recorded some of her best material live in the studio and released the results as *I Got a Right!... To Some of My Best.* The record business being as unpredictable as it is, Ichiban was resurrected in 2002 and released *American Roots: Blues*, a compliation of her first two records.

Reed continues to tour with Lyle Lovett. *—Richard Skelly*

I Want You to Love Me / Apr. 25, 1995 / Ichiban ♦♦♦♦

By the time she released her debut album, Francine Reed had established herself as a fine blues singer through her work with Lyle Lovett. *I Want You to Love Me* proves that she can do it on her own. Lovett drops in for the opening cut, "Why I Don't Know," but this remains Reed's show, and she shows she knows what she's doing. She can sing sultry slow blues, belt out soul, and get down and dirty—in short, she can do it all. Furthermore, she has the songs to prove her talents, relying on classics from Jerry Butler and Muddy Waters, among others. The result is a thoroughly entertaining record from an accomplished artist. *—Thom Owens*

Can't Make It on My Own / 1996 / Ichiban ♦♦♦

Shades of Blue / Sep. 21, 1999 / Intersound ♦♦♦

I Got a Right!... To Some of My Best / Jul. 31, 2001 / CMO Productions ♦♦♦♦

There aren't many women who can sing the blues like this semi-legendary Atlanta-based belter, and as the title indicates, *I Got a Right!* compiles 13 audience favorites onto one CD. Since the out-of-print original recordings of most of these tunes were tied up in legal wrangling when Ichiban records went under, Reed and longtime collaborator Marvin Taylor simply took the band back into the studio and re-recorded the suckers, boasting proudly in the liner notes that most of these versions came on the first or second take. It's a smart approach that captures the fresh feel of Reed's raucous live shows, where songs like "Been There, Done That" and "One Monkey (Don't Stop No Show)" have earned her a Mae West-like reputation. Fan and friend Willie Nelson stops by for a duet on the lilting, New Orleans-style jazz of "The Night Life," and Reed finds a personal anthem of sorts in the brassy "Wild Women Don't Get the Blues." Her band is in top form here, with a sizzling horn section and smoking guitar solos from Taylor, but Reed is undoubtedly the star of this show, howling, wailing, and growling with every ounce of passion in her soul. If you're a blues fan and don't know Francine Reed, here's a wonderful chance to find out what you've been missing. *—Bret Love*

● **American Roots: Blues** / Apr. 23, 2002 / Ichiban ♦♦♦♦♦

Jimmy Reed

b. Sep. 6, 1925, Dunleith, MS, **d.** Aug. 29, 1976, Oakland, CA

Vocals, Leader, Songwriter, Harmonica, Guitar / Blues Revival, Electric Harmonica Blues, Electric Chicago Blues, R&B

There's simply no sound in the blues as easily digestible, accessible, instantly recognizable, and as easy to play and sing as the music of Jimmy Reed. His best-known songs—"Baby, What You Want Me to Do," "Bright Lights, Big City," "Honest I Do," "You Don't Have to Go," "Going to New York," "Ain't That Lovin' You Baby," and "Big Boss Man"—have become such an integral part of the standard blues repertoire, it's almost as if they have existed forever. Because his style was simple and easily imitated, his songs were accessible to just about everyone from high-school garage bands having a go at it, to Elvis Presley, Charlie Rich, Lou Rawls, Hank Williams Jr., and the Rolling Stones, making him—in the long run—perhaps the most influential bluesman of all. His bottom-string boogie rhythm guitar patterns (all furnished by boyhood friend and longtime musical partner Eddie Taylor), simple two-string turnarounds, country-ish harmonica solos (all played in a neck-rack attachment hung around his neck), and mush-mouthed vocals were probably the first exposure most white folks had to the blues. And his music—lazy, loping, and insistent and constantly built and reconstructed single after single on the same sturdy frame—was a formula that proved to be enormously successful and influential, both with middle-aged blacks and young white audiences for a good dozen years. Jimmy Reed records hit the R&B charts with amazing frequency and crossed over onto the pop charts on many occasions, a rare feat for an unreconstructed bluesman. This is all the more amazing simply because Reed's music was nothing special on the surface; he possessed absolutely no technical expertise on either of his chosen instruments and his vocals certainly lacked the fierce declamatory intensity of a Howlin' Wolf or a Muddy Waters. But it was *exactly* that lack of in-your-face musical confrontation that made Jimmy Reed a welcome addition to everybody's record collection back in the '50s and '60s. And for those aspiring musicians who wanted to give the blues a try, either vocally or instrumentally (no matter what skin color you were born with), perhaps Billy Vera said it best in his liner notes to a Reed greatest-hits anthology: "Yes, anybody with a range of more than six notes could sing Jimmy's tunes and play them the first day Mom and Dad brought home that first guitar from Sears & Roebuck. I guess Jimmy could be termed the '50s punk bluesman."

Reed was born on September 6, 1925, on a plantation in or around the small burg of Dunleith, MS. He stayed around the area until he was 15, learning the basic rudiments of harmonica and guitar from his buddy Eddie Taylor, who was then making a name for himself as a semi-pro musician, working country suppers and juke joints. Reed moved up to Chicago in 1943, but was quickly drafted into the Navy where he served for two years. After a quick trip back to Mississippi and marriage to his beloved wife Mary (known to blues fans as "Mama Reed"), he relocated to Gary, IN, and found work at an Armour Foods meat-packing plant while simultaneously breaking into the burgeoning blues scene around Gary and neighboring Chicago. The early '50s found him working as a sideman with John Brim's Gary Kings (that's Reed blowing harp on Brim's classic "Tough Times" and its instrumental flip side, "Gary Stomp") and playing on the street for tips with Willie Joe Duncan, a shadowy figure who played an amplified, homemade one-string instrument called a Unitar. After failing an audition with Chess Records (his later chart success would be a constant thorn in the side of the firm), Brim's drummer at the time—improbably enough, future blues guitar legend Albert King—brought him over to the newly formed Vee-Jay Records, where his first recordings were made. It was during this time that he was reunited and started playing again with Eddie Taylor, a musical partnership that would last off and on until Reed's death. Success was slow in coming, but when his third single, "You Don't Have to Go" backed with "Boogie in the Dark," made the number five slot on *Billboard*'s R&B charts, the hits pretty much kept on coming for the next decade.

But if selling more records than Muddy Waters, Howlin' Wolf, Elmore James, or Little Walter brought the rewards of fame to his doorstep, no one was more ill-equipped to handle them than Jimmy Reed. With signing his name for fans being the total sum of his literacy, combined with a back-breaking road schedule once he became a name attraction and his self-description as a "liquor glutter," Reed started to fall apart like a cheap suit almost immediately. His devious schemes to tend to his alcoholism—and the just plain aberrant behavior that came as a result of it—quickly made him the laughingstock of his show-business contemporaries. Those who shared the bill with him in top-of-the-line R&B venues like the Apollo Theater—where the story of him urinating on a star performer's dress in the wings has been repeated verbatim by more than one old-timer—still shake their heads and wonder how Reed could actually stand up straight and perform, much less hold the audience in the palm of his hand. Other stories of Reed being "arrested" and thrown into a Chicago drunk tank the night before a recording session also reverberate throughout the blues community to this day.

Little wonder then that when he was stricken with epilepsy in 1957, it went undiagnosed for an extended period of time, simply because he had experienced so many attacks of delirium tremens, better known as the "DTs." Eddie Taylor would relate how he sat directly in front of Reed in the studio, instructing him while the tune was being recorded exactly when to start to start singing, when to blow his harp, and when to do the turnarounds on his guitar. Jimmy Reed also appears, by all accounts, to have been unable to remember the lyrics to new songs—even ones he had composed himself—and Mama Reed would sit on a piano bench and whisper them into his ear, literally one line at a time. Blues fans who doubt this can clearly hear the proof on several of Jimmy's biggest hits, most notably "Big Boss Man" and "Bright Lights, Big City," where she steps into the fore and starts singing along with him in order to keep him on the beat.

But seemingly none of this mattered. While revisionist blues historians like to make a big deal about either the lack of variety of his work or how later recordings turned him into a mere parody of himself, the public just couldn't get enough of it. Jimmy Reed placed 11 songs on the *Billboard* Hot 100 pop charts and a total of 14 on the R&B charts, a figure that even a much more sophisticated artist like B.B. King couldn't top. To paraphrase the old saying, nobody liked Jimmy Reed but the people.

Reed's slow descent into the ravages of alcoholism and epilepsy roughly paralleled the decline of Vee-Jay Records, which went out of business at approximately the same time that his final 45 was released, "Don't Think I'm Through." His manager, Al Smith, quickly arranged a contract with the newly formed ABC-BluesWay label and a handful of albums were released into the '70s, all of them lacking the old charm, sounding as if they were cut on a musical assembly line. Jimmy did one last album, a horrible attempt to update his sound with funk beats and wah-wah pedals, before becoming a virtual recluse in his final years. He finally received proper medical attention for his epilepsy and quit drinking, but it was too late and he died trying to make a comeback on the blues festival circuit on August 29, 1976.

All of this is sad beyond belief, simply because there's so much joy in Jimmy Reed's music. And it's that joy that becomes self-evident every time you give one of his classic sides a spin. Although his bare-bones style influenced everyone from British Invasion combos to the entire school of Louisiana swamp-blues artists (Slim Harpo and Jimmy Anderson in particular), the simple indisputable fact remains that—like so many of the other originators in the genre—there was only one Jimmy Reed. *—Cub Koda*

I'm Jimmy Reed / 1959 / Collectables ♦♦♦♦♦
Reed's debut was a most auspicious event in blues history, as it introduced listeners to one of the most distinct voices in the music's storied legacy. Having already traveled from his Mississippi home to live in Chicago at the age of 15, and subsequently getting stationed in California with the Navy, Reed—with his wife Mary—moved to Gary, IN, in the late '40s to pursue a blues career. After working around Gary and Chicago, Reed signed to the independent Vee-Jay label after having been turned down by Chess Records. This 1952 debut was the first fruits of a decade-long relationship that would yield many Reed hits. Highlights include smashes like "Honest I Do," "You Don't Have to Go," "Ain't That Lovin' You Baby," and "You Got Me Dizzy." *—Stephen Cook*

Rockin' With Reed / 1959 / Collectables ♦♦♦♦♦
Reed's second Vee-Jay album was even more impressive than his debut for the independent label. Joined by long-time collaborator and guitarist Eddie Taylor, Reed polishes off such now classic cuts as "Going to New York," "Take Out Some Insurance," and "Down in Virginia." Reed's slyly sensuous voice and lithe guitar work are heard to fine effect over the course of the 12 stellar tracks here. In addition to Taylor, Reed also gets fine support from guitarists Albert King and John Littlejohn and drummer Earl Phillips. One of the best places for Reed newcomers to start their collection. *—Stephen Cook*

The Best of Jimmy Reed / 1961 / Vee-Jay ♦♦♦♦♦
Another tough-to-beat old album full of Reed's finest and most influential work. *—Bill Dahl*

☆ **Live at Carnegie Hall/The Best of Jimmy Reed** / Aug. 1961 / Vee-Jay ♦♦♦♦♦
This was originally issued as a vinyl double album by Vee-Jay in the early '60s. The first 12 tracks are not "live" at all (the disclaimer is in the liners) but instead are some nice middle-period studio tracks while the following dozen constitutes a "reissue" of the label's *Best of Jimmy Reed* album. Stereophiles will love this as the sound is Mobile Fidelity impeccable, even on the mono masters, while stereo masters of such classics as "Baby What You Want Me to Do" and "Big Boss Man" sound almost revelatory. Not the place to start (even with most of the hits aboard), but if you have to have some classic Jimmy Reed in clean stereo, this is the place to go. *—Cub Koda*

Just Jimmy Reed / 1962 / Collectables ♦♦♦
Strong Vee-Jay collection. *—Bill Dahl*

12 String Guitar Blues / 1963 / Collectables ♦♦♦♦♦
This release added yet another wrinkle to Jimmy Reed's mystique. Even most of his fans would concede that Reed's guitar skills were far short of virtuoso level. Yet, Jimmy Reed—not a celebrated 12-string guitar player like Leadbelly or any of the other renowned instrumentalists who came up in Leadbelly's wake—cut this acoustic 12-string instrumental album, which has become an enduring classic of the genre. Reed was as skilled at presenting his guitar work as he was as a singer, and his playing on *12 String Guitar Blues* is smooth, sinewy, lean, and lyrical, with a tight band behind him. Consisting of recognizable Reed originals and a couple of other blues standards thrown in, the music comes off very well, mixing electric guitar with acoustic 12-string and Reed's harmonica substituting for the vocal parts. The harmonica is on a separate track, making use of a natural sounding stereo separation that keeps the sound of the band—featuring Eddie Taylor and Lefty Bates on guitar, Marcus Johnson on bass, and Morris Wilkerson and Earl Phillips on drums—unified. The result is yet another classic album by Reed, and one of the more straightforward and accessible bodies of blues played on 12-string that one can find. This fall 2000 Collectables reissue, licensed through Rhino Records, features impeccable sound and recreates the original album art and jacket notes. *—Bruce Eder*

The Best of the Blues / 1963 / Collectables ♦♦♦♦♦

Boss Man of the Blues / 1964 / Vee-Jay ♦♦♦

Jimmy Reed at Soul City / 1964 / Collectables ♦♦♦

The Legend—The Man / 1965 / Collectables ♦♦♦♦♦
Jimmy Reed's *The Legend—The Man* was originally released in 1965 on Vee-Jay records and was reissued by Collectables in 2000. While it contains a number of classics, like "Baby What You Want Me to Do," "Big Boss Man," "Ain't That Lovin' You Baby," and "Bright Lights, Big City," what makes this reissue so compelling are the short interview sections with Reed at the start of each track. Conducted in 1964 by Vee-Jay A&R man Calvin Carter, we hear Reed discussing his career and trying to put it into chronological and often humorous perspective. This former cotton picker, junk man, butcher, and "shakeout man in the foundry working in 118 degree heat" went on to become a legend of modern blues. This is not only a perfect introduction anthology to his music, but a blues history lesson that anyone interested in Reed or the genre should find fascinating. *—Al Campbell*

Now Appearing / 1966 / Vee-Jay ♦♦♦

T'Aint No Big Thing / 1968 / Collectables ♦♦♦
Contains his classic rocker "Shame Shame" and plenty more. *—Bill Dahl*

Found Love / 1971 / Collectables ♦♦♦
Over the years the Collectables label has done an admirable job reissuing music with great sound quality and original packaging at a budget price. This is certainly the case with the reissue set of Jimmy Reed (and John Lee Hooker) Vee-Jay sides released in the summer of 2000. There isn't a bad track on *Found Love*. Not only are some of Reed's biggest hits included—"Baby What You Want Me To Do," "Big Boss Man," and "Hush Hush"—but the title track is particularly notable, as it contains a one note harp wail that proves to be vibrant, heartfelt, and timeless. The playing time is admittedly short at just over 30 minutes, but the quality of music and the budget price attached to this disc, makes for an undeniably attractive deal. *—Al Campbell*

The Blues Is My Business / May 1976 / Collectables ♦♦♦
Decent LP with several rarities. *—Bill Dahl*

The Best of Jimmy Reed / 1977 / GNP Crescendo ♦♦
Add this one to the pile of bad Jimmy Reed reissues currently glutting the compact disc bins. Like the others, there's certainly nothing wrong with the song lineup, a solid 20 track-assembly of Reed's best-known tunes. Also like the others, however, the transfers range from sloppy to downright indifferent. Although listed as "stereo" on the front, almost everything on here is in mono, the majority lifted off of very scratchy records with the entire intro of "Baby What You Want Me to Do" edited out for no earthly reason. Pass right by this one—even if it's offered at bargain prices—and grab the Rhino version instead. *—Cub Koda*

High & Lonesome / 1981 / Charly ♦♦♦♦♦
A great collection of Reed's earliest and rarest sides. *—Cub Koda*

Upside Your Head / 1985 / Charly ♦♦♦♦♦
The loping, laconic Jimmy Reed sound was never better than during his Vee-Jay years. This is a tremendous collection gathering 16 tunes from the mid-'50s to the mid-'60s. Since Vee-Jay is now issuing Reed titles themselves, you might want to save the import difference and get them, but if you ever see this, don't hesitate to get it either on disc or in vinyl. *—Ron Wynn*

Big Boss Blues / 1986 / Charly ♦♦♦♦♦
Although many "best of Jimmy Reed" compilations exist on the market (most with variable sound quality and maddening duplication), this import features all the influential hits and is the perfect place to start. *—Cub Koda*

Bright Lights, Big City / 1988 / Chameleon ♦♦♦
One of the many "best of Jimmy Reed" albums released over the years, *Bright Lights, Big City* is a 16-song CD that the independent Chameleon put out in 1988 for its *Vee-Jay Hall of Fame Series*. The liner notes are poor; exact recording dates and personnel are missing, and a brief summary only scratches the surface in describing Reed's accomplishments. But the sound quality isn't bad, and the material itself is nothing to complain about. Laidback hits like "Baby, What You Want Me to Do," "Big Boss Man," "Honest I Do," and "Shame, Shame, Shame" are included along with some enjoyable rarities, including the playful "Sugar, Sugar," the infectious "Don't Say Nothin'," and "Honey, Where You Goin'." These 16 songs certainly wouldn't be a bad introduction to Reed's legacy, but a bluesman of his magnitude deserves better than Chameleon's skimpy, inadequate liner notes. *—Alex Henderson*

Ride 'Em on Down / 1989 / Charly ♦♦♦♦♦
Reed shares this compilation with Eddie Taylor (with Reed in support on four tracks) and features a dozen tracks from Reed's early days. Good sound throughout (this has the most listenable disc transfer of Reed's first single "High & Lonesome") and the perfect companion piece to the above. *—Cub Koda*

Best of Jimmy Reed / 1990 / JCI ♦♦
More than a few best-of compilations by Jimmy Reed by have been released over the years. This particular release came out in 1990 as part of JCI's poorly assembled Masters of the Blues series, for which the small, L.A.-based label dug into the Chess or Vee-Jay vaults and released CDs by John Lee Hooker, Howlin' Wolf, Muddy Waters, Etta James and others. The packaging and liner notes on *The Best of Jimmy Reed* are embarassing—neither exact recording dates nor personnel are listed—although the selections are first

rate. From "Bright Lights, Big City" and "Big Boss Man" to "Pretty Thing," "Honest I Do" and "Baby, What You Want Me To Do," most of Reed's essential Vee-Jay hits are here. Everything on this 18-song CD illustrates just how charismatic and distinctive a blues-man Reed was, but sadly, the sound quality is far from ideal—digital remastering was never JCI's strong point. Between the sound and the packaging, JCI should have been ashamed. —*Alex Henderson*

Jimmy Reed / 1991 / Paula ✦✦✦
With so much attention paid to Jimmy's seminal Vee-Jay sides, it's hard to realize that he had a recording career that extended past the label's demise in the mid-'60s. But with manager Al Smith producing, Reed turned out a bushelbacket of albums for the ABC-Bluesway and Exodus labels, the best of which are collected here. These 21 tracks—recorded between 1966 and 1971—vary quite a bit from the original vinyl issues, which were edited and sometimes retitled for release. Not Reed at his best, but for a complete picture of the man and his music, you'll definitely want to add this one to the pile. —*Cub Koda*

☆ **Speak the Lyrics to Me, Mama Reed** / Jan. 1993 / Vee-Jay ✦✦✦✦✦
Although many *Best of Jimmy Reed* compilations exist on the market (most with variable sound quality and maddening duplication), this 25-tracker is currently the one to beat. Including all the influential hits and a few of the best rare ones ("You Upset My Mind" and the single version of "Little Rain," different than the take on his debut album), this features impeccable sound (except on the disc transfer of Reed's first single, "High & Lonesome") and is the perfect place to start. —*Cub Koda*

Is Back / Apr. 28, 1994 / Collectables ✦✦✦

Classic Recordings / 1995 / Tomato ✦✦✦✦✦
This three-CD, 55-song box is the most comprehensive domestic retrospective of Reed's career (a six-CD box is available on import). The material is fine and consistent, but this isn't the best deal for either the average fan or the completist. Reed is one of the most homogenous blues greats, and unless your interest is deep, three CDs at once will become monotonous; you're better off with one of the several fine single-disc compilations available. Also, this has no information whatsoever on release dates or session info, and inexplicably omits one of his two Top 40 hits, "Honest I Do" (covered by the Rolling Stones on their first album). —*Richie Unterberger*

Rockin' With Reed / Jan. 1, 1996 / Eclipse Music Group ✦✦
Don't confuse this cheap package with Reed's second album for Vee-Jay. Instead, this is a grab bag of a few very poorly transferred hits, some B-sides of hit singles, and a stray album cut or two. The hits all seem to come from electronic stereo sources, making them sound hollow and echoey when use of the original mono masters would have solved the audio mishap that's here. The title track sounds like it was taken from a *very* scratchy 78. The only bright spot is the inclusion of "Cold and Lonesome," a slow blues that seldom gets anthologized on Reed best-ofs. —*Cub Koda*

Honest I Do & Other Classics / Feb. 23, 1996 / Intercontinental ✦✦✦✦✦
It seems that after an artist has been around for so many years, record companies stop releasing the artist's proper albums and instead release an array of collections of the artist's songs with tags like "greatest hits," "the best of," or "and other hits" attached to the title. While this practice probably initially came into vogue because many artists only released songs as singles on 45s and the labels were compiling their songs to construct a long-player, there can only be so many collections of an artist's songs released before it starts to feel like greedy repackaging (seriously, there are countless Jerry Lee Lewis compilations with a few fine tracks scattered among throwaways and various takes of "Great Balls of Fire"). Ranking high among these endlessly repackaged artists is Jimmy Reed. *Honest I Do & Other Classics* is yet another compilation of the Mississippi bluesman's songs. However, whereas many greatest-hits packages really only consist of two hit songs and eight hard to find or not worth finding B-sides, *Honest I Do* sticks with the hits, offering such blues staples as "Baby What You Want Me to Do," "Bright Lights, Big City," the title track, and, of course, "Big Boss Man." Reed's wife can be heard singing on this last one, because by this point in his career the notoriously drunk bluesman couldn't remember the words on his own. (Reed was eventually diagnosed with epilepsy, which may actually have been as much to blame for his deterioration as his drinking.) While he is known for his simplistic, some would say overly so, style of songwriting, Reed is perhaps even more well known for his skill as a harmonica player, which is featured prominently on the tracks selected for this record. Like his songs in general, what makes Reed's harmonica work so great is that it isn't overdone; it's not stiffly utilitarian, but it's not overly flamboyant either, which is a balance that many modern players fail to achieve. Every one of Reed's songs is based around rhythms and chords that are so classic that it is impossible to think of the blues without thinking of them, even if you don't know them by name. Overall, *Honest I Do & Other Classics* is a fine introduction to Reed's catalog (and probably about all the Reed that most casual blues fans will ever need), though it doesn't really cover any ground that a dozen other compilations haven't already taken care of. —*Karen E. Graves*

Big Legged Woman / Aug. 27, 1996 / Collectables ✦✦✦

New Jimmy Reed Album/Soulin' / Apr. 8, 1997 / See for Miles ✦✦✦
See For Miles reissued two albums Jimmy Reed recorded in the late '60s, *New Jimmy Reed Album* and *Soulin'*, on a single CD in 1997. While both records have their moments, they are bogged down by a production that tries to move Reed into the blues-rock era. Consequently, the album is primarily of interest to completists, since even hardcore Reed fans may find the production disconcerting. —*Stephen Thomas Erlewine*

Big Boss Man/Down in Virginia / Apr. 8, 1997 / See for Miles ✦✦
Two of Reed's later Bluesway albums on one disc. Reed was in pretty sad shape by this time in his life and the monotonous approach to these songs (tunes constantly fade in and

out as if only this much of the performance was salvageable) gives these recordings a real assembly line quality that's most unsettling. Stick with his original Vee-Jay recordings for the best the man has to offer and pass this paint-by-numbers junk by. —*Cub Koda*

Lost in the Shuffle / Oct. 21, 1997 / 32 Jazz ✦✦✦✦
It's hard to screw up a Jimmy Reed anthology, and that's exactly why there are so many of them floating around. Generally, these compilations include most or all of Reed's Vee-Jay hits from the early '50s to the early '60s, and the ones packaged with a little more tender loving care (like *Lost in the Shuffle*) will undoubtedly point out that the drummer on Reed's 1953 hit "You Don't Have to Go" was none other than Albert King. 32 Jazz has a respectable track record when it comes to blues reissues, and the label doesn't disappoint here; producer Joel Dorn compiles all of Reed's familiar, often-covered hits ("Big Boss Man," "Bright Lights Big City," "Honest I Do," et al.) and recruits *Living Blues* writer Bill Dahl to pen some colorful liner notes. Purists may lament the absence of the quirky instrumental "Odds and Ends," but *Lost in the Shuffle* still ranks as a comprehensive overview of Reed's hit-making tenure with Vee-Jay. —*Ken Chang*

★ **Blues Masters: The Very Best of Jimmy Reed** / Mar. 14, 2000 / Rhino ✦✦✦✦✦
Over the years, many, many Jimmy Reed compilations have been released, including many repackagings of his classic Vee-Jay material. Sometimes, the compilations have been excellent—the 1993 disc *Speak the Lyrics to Me, Mama Reed* is a prime example—other times they've been shabby, and since many of them have featured the same basic songs, it's hard for novices to discern which are worthwhile and which aren't. Fortunately, Rhino's 2000 release *The Very Best of Jimmy Reed* provides first-timers with an ideal introductory package, while satisfying longtime fans by serving 17 of his very best sides for Vee-Jay. All of the classic songs are here—"Ain't That Lovin' You Baby," "You've Got Me Dizzy," "Honest I Do," "Take Out Some Insurance," "Going to New York," "Baby What You Want Me to Do," "Big Boss Man," and "Bright Lights, Big City"—along with such stellar, lesser-known items as his first Vee-Jay single "High and Lonesome," "Oh John," the eerie violin-laced "Odds and Ends," and its boogie-minded flip side "Ends and Odds." It's a well-rounded, compelling collection that proves Reed's music is always satisfying, even if it's all variations on a basic, three-chord boogie. Or, as Reed expert Cub Koda states in the liner notes, it's "nothin' fancy, but it sure hits the spot every single time." *The Very Best of Jimmy Reed* proves his statement true with 17 timeless tracks. This is an essential cornerstone of any blues collection. —*Stephen Thomas Erlewine*

EP Collection . . . Plus / May 2, 2000 / See for Miles ✦✦✦✦
Another winner in the See for Miles *EP Collection* series, this time devoted to the overseas issues of Jimmy Reed Vee-Jay sides. Culled from U.K., French, and Swedish extended-play records (45 singles with two or more songs on each side) issued in the '60s, this brings together 22 tracks culled off of six different EPs with four non-EP bonus tracks to beef things up. It's a combination of regulation hits ("You Don't Have to Go," "Ain't That Lovin' You Baby," "You Got Me Dizzy," "Honest I Do," "Baby What You Want Me to Do," and "Big Boss Man"), cool B-sides and album tracks ("Boogie in the Dark," "Can't Stand to See You Go," "A String to Your Heart," "I'm Gonna Get My Baby," "Caress Me Baby," "I Know It's a Sin," and "Take Out Some Insurance"), and off-the-wall later recordings that don't usually show up on these collections ("Cold and Lonesome," "I'm Gonna Help You," "Help Yourself," "Heading for a Fall," "A New Leaf," "I'm Going Upside Your Head"), making this a Jimmy Reed compilation that's a little off the beaten track and all the better for it. If you can put up with the duplication to whatever Jimmy Reed best-of you already have, then this is definitely worth adding to the collection. —*Cub Koda*

Big Boss Men / Jun. 25, 2001 / Indigo ✦
Jimmy Reed's four live 1972 tracks on this CD take up only half of this disc, the other half being comprised of live Willie Dixon numbers recorded in 1971 at the same venue (Liberty Hall in Houston). Out of respect to Reed's memory, perhaps even aficionados who think they need everything he's done might want to consider leaving it alone. The band—personnel unlisted, except for Johnny Winter, who plays guitar—is sloppy and untogether. Concise Chicago blues classics like "Big Boss Man," "You Don't Have to Go," and "Bright Lights, Big City" are stretched to an unseemly six-to-12-minute length with the sluggish, overlong arrangements. The recording quality is subpar. Worst of all, Reed himself is in poor form, mumbling or skipping lyrics, and not sounding at all in command of his own compositions. The six songs by Dixon on the CD, incidentally, are much better performance-wise, but also suffer from lackadaisical fidelity, and two of the songs credited to Dixon are really Winter performances, since he joins the players to take over the lead vocals and guitar. —*Richie Unterberger*

Big Boss Man / Nov. 27, 2001 / Collectables ✦✦✦✦✦
There is no denying that the classic Jimmy Reed sides cut for Vee-Jay Records are a must-have. Realistically though, as amazing as this material is, the Jimmy Reed *Big Boss Man [Box Set]* is for rabid Reed fanatics. While Collectables did an admirable job on this limited-edition ten-CD set, ten CDs of Reed can get repetitive. Most listeners will be happy with the single Rhino disc, *Blues Masters: The Very Best of Jimmy Reed*. If you want more material, Collectables has released the original Reed albums that make up the box set (original cover art and all) separately, some as two-fers. No matter what, its great to have such quality material from Jimmy Reed easily available. —*Al Campbell*

Lula Reed

Vocals / R&B

A longtime cohort of pianist/producer Sonny Thompson, singer Lula Reed recorded steadily for Cincinnati-based King Records during the mid-'50s after debuting on wax in 1951 to sing Thompson's original version of the moving ballad "I'll Drown in My Tears" (a 1956 smash for Ray Charles as "Drown in My Own Tears").

After serving as Thompson's vocalist at first, the attractive chanteuse was sufficiently established by 1952 to rate her own King releases. She was versatile, singing urban blues most of the time but switching to gospel for a 1954 session. Reed's strident 1954 waxing "Rock Love" was later revived by labelmate Little Willie John. She briefly moved to the Chess subsidiary Argo in 1958-1959 but returned to the fold in 1961 (as always, under Thompson's direction) on King's Federal imprint. While at Federal, she waxed a series of sassy duets with guitarist Freddie King in March of 1962. Another move—to Ray Charles' Tangerine logo in 1962-1963—soon followed. After that, her whereabouts are unknown. *—Bill Dahl*

● **Blue and Moody** / 1959 / King ✦✦✦✦✦
The longtime protegée of King Records house pianist/arranger/ producer Sonny Thompson possessed a sultry style well-suited to blues ballads in the urban vein and lighthearted upbeat fare—both of which reside on this reissue of her vintage King album. *—Bill Dahl*

Terry Reid

b. Nov. 13, 1949, Huntington, England
Vocals, Guitar / Folk-Rock, Hard Rock, Blues-Rock, Rock & Roll, Soul
A minor but interesting late-'60s British rock singer, Terry Reid could have been a lot more famous if he hadn't turned down the slot of lead singer for the New Yardbirds in 1968. That slot, of course, went to Robert Plant, and the New Yardbirds became Led Zeppelin. Unlike Plant, Reid was also a guitarist, and the opportunity to head his own group no doubt played a part in his decision to gun for a solo career. Leading a guitar/organ/drums power trio, he recorded a couple of respectable, though erratic, hard rock albums while still a teenager in the late '60s. Some bad breaks and creative stagnation combined to virtually bring his career to a halt, and he never cashed in on the momentum of his promising start.

A teen prodigy of sorts, Reid had turned professional at the age of 15 to join Peter Jay & the Jaywalkers. His first couple of singles as a headliner found him singing in a sort of poppy blue-eyed soul vein. But by the time of his 1968 debut *Bang, Bang You're Terry Reid*, produced by Mickie Most, he'd switched to more of a hard rock approach. Most was also handling Donovan and the Jeff Beck Group at the time, and similarities to both of those acts can be heard in Terry Reid's first two albums—proto-hard rock on the louder tunes, sweeter folk-rock on the mellow ones (Reid in fact covered a couple of Donovan compositions, although he wrote most of his own material). Reid's high voice was reminiscent of Robert Plant's, though not nearly as shrill, and his folky numbers especially are reminiscent of Led Zeppelin's most acoustic early cuts.

Reid, oddly, was considerably more well-known in the U.S. than the U.K. His first album, *very* oddly, was not even issued in Britain, although it made the American Top 200. Though he declined Jimmy Page's offer to join Led Zeppelin, he did influence history in a big way by recommending Plant and drummer John Bonham as suitable candidates, after Plant and Bonham's pre-Led Zep outfit (the Band of Joy) played support at one of Reid's early gigs. Reid felt confident enough in his solo prospects to also turn down an offer to join Deep Purple (Ian Gillan was recruited instead).

An opening spot on the Rolling Stones' famous 1969 tour of America seemed to augur even brighter prospects for the future, but this is precisely where Reid's career stalled, at the age of 20. First he became embroiled in litigation with Mickey Most, which curtailed his studio activities in the early '70s. After a couple of personnel changes, he disbanded his original trio, leading a group for a while that included David Lindley and ex-King Crimson drummer Michael Giles (this quartet, however, didn't release any records). He moved to California in 1971 and signed to Atlantic, but his long-delayed third album didn't appear until 1973. Reid would release albums for other labels in 1976 and 1979, but none of his '70s recordings were well-received, critically or commercially (though 1976's *Seed of Memory* did briefly chart). He's barely recorded since, though he did play some sessions, and *The Driver* appeared in 1991. *—Richie Unterberger*

Bang, Bang You're Terry Reid / 1968 / BGO ✦✦✦✦
Bang, Bang introduced a hard rocker whose eclecticism is both impressive and unnervingly inconsistent. The covers of "Season of the Witch" and "Summertime Blues" are overlong and dated, but the frenetic version of Cher's "Bang, Bang" is inspired, and the rendition of Gene Pitney's "Something's Gotten Hold of My Heart" shows his poppier roots. Over half of the material was penned by Reid, and while these compositions are sometimes generic late-'60s hard rockers, he also shows a facility for Donovon-esque folk-rock ("Sweater") and impressive soul-rock vocalizing ("When I Get Home"). Originally not released in the U.K., it's ironically only available now as a U.K. import. *—Richie Unterberger*

Move Over for Terry Reid / 1969 / Epic ✦✦✦

● **Terry Reid** / 1969 / BGO ✦✦✦✦✦
Reid's initial pair of albums are very similar, and it's really a toss-up as to which one is better. If either rates a slight edge, it would be *Terry Reid*, as it finds his songwriting skills slightly more developed. The Donovan influence is again apparent on the cover of the Scotsman's "Superlungs My Supergirl," and "Stay With Me Baby" is another well-done blue-eyed soul showcase. As a songwriter, Reid still had a way to go, sounding better on the gentler, folkier numbers than the all-out power trio numbers. Such unfulfilled promise was understandable to a degree, as Reid was not yet 20 when this was released; unfortunately, he would never significantly expand on the promise of his first two LPs. The CD reissue adds four bonus cuts from the two rare non-LP singles he recorded in 1967 and 1968, prior to the issue of *Bang, Bang You're Terry Reid*. *—Richie Unterberger*

River / 1973 / Atlantic ✦✦✦

Rogue Waves / 1979 / Capitol ✦✦
When this album came out, in the middle of the punk and disco booms, it seemed like a breath of fresh air, a stomping mix of heavy metal and soul, filled with engaging originals by Reid and spiced by heavy-handed but bracing versions of harmony-based numbers like "Baby I Love You," "Then I Kissed Her," "Walk Away Renee," and "All I Have to Do Is Dream." Today, they don't hold up so well, and the album seems a bit over-the-top, overdone, and excessive. Doug Rodrigues and Reid share guitar chores, and the best parts of their playing are the softest moments. The backing vocals by Denise Williams, Dyanne Chandler, and Maxine Willard are often ravishing, and Reid's singing is as powerful as ever—it all just seems a bit arch and artificial, perhaps because of the way-too-close bass and drum sound, and the too-heavy guitar; that works for blues, as Led Zeppelin proved most of the time, but it makes for some distinctly unsubtle R&B. *—Bruce Eder*

The Hand Don't Fit the Glove / 1985 / See for Miles ✦✦✦

Seed of Memory / Sep. 26, 1995 / Edsel ✦✦✦
Terry Reid moved to California in the mid-'70s, befriending a number of musicians from those parts and broadening his sound in the process. One result was this album, produced by Graham Nash and featuring David Lindley on acoustic and slide guitars. *Seed of Memory* isn't as heavy as his earlier work, and not remotely the bold, strident virtuoso rock production of his first LP—most of it, apart from the vaguely Led Zeppelin-ish "The Way You Walk," is fairly laid-back by Reid's standards. "Ooh Baby" tries for a kind of meld of funk and British blues. But several numbers, like "Brave Awakening," with its relaxed beat, high harmonies, and understated backing orchestration, or the ominous acoustic-textured "To Be Treated Rite," seem more like outtakes from Nash's *Songs for Beginners* or his subsequent albums, or one of Neil Young's mid-'70s albums, than they do like the work of one of England's most promising '60s bluesmen. The album ends on an ambitious but disjointed note, with the ambitious but not wholly successful "Fooling You," which makes extensive use of the saxophone. It all just might not be what fans look for in Reid's work, and lacks some of the excitement of his other albums. *—Bruce Eder*

Johnny Reno

b. Arkansas
Sax (Tenor), Sax (Baritone) / Retro-Soul, R&B
Best known as the frontman of the jump-blues revival unit the Sax Maniacs, tenor saxophonist Johnny Reno was also among the most prominent sidemen on the contemporary Texas blues circuit. A native of Arkansas, Reno first emerged during the late '70s as a member of Stevie Ray Vaughan's Triple Threat Revue; from 1980 to 1983, he also played with the Fort Worth-based Juke Jumpers. He led the Sax Maniacs for much of the decade, and alongside such like-minded groups as Roomful of Blues helped keep the horn-powered sound of traditional jump-blues alive during the modern era. At the tail end of the '80s, he formed the Johnny Reno Band, a more rock-influenced concern than his previous projects; after spending the early '90s touring with Chris Isaak, Reno then moved on to his next retro-styled band, the self-expanatory Lounge Kings. *—Jason Ankeny*

Born to Blow / 1983 / Black Top ✦✦✦✦
Johnny Reno & the Sax Maniacs is arguably the best release the saxophonist and his band have ever cut, a jumping, swinging set of blues and R&B in the style of classic '50s swing. *—Thom Owens*

Full Blown / 1985 / Rounder ✦✦✦

● **Johnny Reno & the Sax Maniacs** / 198 / Black Top ✦✦✦✦

Swinging & Singing / Sep. 1, 1998 / Menthol ✦✦✦

Blind Joe Reynolds (Joseph Sheppard)

b. 1900, Arkansas, **d.** Mar. 10, 1968, Monroe, LA
Guitar, Vocals / Country Blues, Prewar Blues
Blind Joe Reynolds was the *nom de disque* of a Louisiana street singer by the name of Joe Sheppard, who devised his false recording names primarily to keep one step ahead of the law. He was blinded in the mid-'20s during an altercation with another man who shot Reynolds in the face with a shotgun. Throughout his life, Reynolds was known throughout the South not only as a singer, but for his open disrespect for police and the legal system, his contempt for conventional morality, and his pursuit of trouble. His surviving recordings are characterized by Reynolds' shrieking, high-pitched vocals; his rolling, generous, and infectiously rhythmic slide work; and his lyrics, which tend to focus on unfaithful women.

Blind Joe Reynolds was discovered in the late '20s by Memphis record store owner H.C. Spier, who recommended Reynolds to Paramount (as he had Charley Patton). In November 1929, under the name Blind Joe Reynolds, he made two records, "Outside Woman Blues" b/w "Nehi Blues" (issued as Paramount 12927) and "Cold Woman Blues" b/w "99 Blues" (issued as Paramount 12983). Reynolds was one of the last "new" blues singers that Paramount took on and they didn't ask for him back. Nonetheless, Reynolds made another pair of records when the Victor truck stopped in Memphis a year later. On November 26, 1930, under the name Blind Willie Reynolds, he recorded "Married Man Blues" and "Third Street Woman Blues" (issued as Victor 23258). Two other titles made on this occasion, "Short Dress Blues" and "Goose Hill Woman Blues" were not issued by Victor and test copies have yet to be found. For some time, this was further complicated by the fact that no copies of Paramount 12983, though issued, seemed to be extant. These 1929 to 1930 records were the only ones made by Blind Joe Reynolds.

Afterward, Reynolds disappeared into history, but his legend and its many attendant anecdotes are recorded in Gayle Dean Wardlow's 1998 book *Chasin' That Devil Music*. In 1967, the English band Cream recorded "Outside Woman Blues" on the album *Disraeli Gears*; no doubt they would've been floored to learn that the song's original composer was not only still alive, but at that time still performing as a street musician in the American South. But Blind Joe Reynolds would die less than a year later, narrowly eluding the attention of blues revivalists and of booking agents who ran the large folk festivals. A new chapter of study on Reynolds was opened up with the discovery in 2001 of the missing Paramount issue, found by an Ohio music teacher in a Tennessee flea market. "Cold Woman Blues" from this disc was included on the 2001 Revenant release *Screamin' and Hollerin' the Blues*, devoted to the music of Charley Patton. Thereon,

Reynolds is included as a member of Patton's "circle," although he was based in Tennessee and not in the Mississippi Delta. Nor is Reynolds known to have been acquainted with Patton, although in a superficial sense there is enough similarity between the two to suggest some kind of stylistic, and hence personal, connection. *—David N. Lewis*

Eugene Rhodes

Vocals / Country Blues

If there is a more obscure country blues artist than this fellow, then he is probably locked up somewhere, as well, one hastens to add, because that was the situation when blues scholar Bruce Jackson first discovered Eugene Rhodes. He was doing a ten- to 25-year stretch at the Indiana State Prison, which was where a remarkable album was recorded of 15 songs and a little talking that was eventually released on a label even more obscure than the bluesman, if such a thing is possible. By the time Rhodes was discovered, he seemed like he was in his late fifties and apparently nervously disparaged "them old alley blues" that nobody wanted to hear anymore now that all the public wanted was jazz. His opinions as expressed to his recording producer do well in indicating his cultural isolation as a prisoner, because he was apparently unaware of the huge white audience for country blues that existed in the '60s, a time when an elderly black gent with a slide on his finger would be considered "cool," although it is unsure whether that judgment would extend all the way to the tough-looking prisoner pictured in grimy black and white on the cover of his album *Talkin' 'Bout My Time.*

In the '20s and '30s, Rhodes had traveled through the south as a one-man band, including a harmonica rack with a special mount on the side for a horn, a foot pedal powered drum, and of course, a guitar. He reportedly played in the Dallas area, where he claims to have met Blind Lemon Jefferson. He also crossed paths with Blind Boy Fuller in the Carolinas and Buddy Moss in Georgia, the effects of his traveling adventures turning into seasonings in which the spirits of musical influences are nimbly suggested in his own picking. Although the history of the blues contains several happy tales of prisoners set back out into the world based on their brilliant performances, the release of this artist's album had no such result. He also seems not to have left much of a trail after being released from prison, if he ever was. He is not the same Eugene Rhodes who was the "singing minister" behind the album *I Don't Need a Reason.* *—Eugene Chadbourne*

● **Talkin' About My Time** / Collector's Issue ✦✦✦✦

Difficult to find, this album sometimes passes for Folkways, a polite way of saying it was packaged as if someone was trying to prove the ease with which such a counterfeit could be created. Closer inspection of the logo in front reveals that it is a cheesy drawing of a Greek god type, not something that seems to have a whole lot in common with the plight of the artist featured. Blues music is full of legends of imprisoned pickers who were released on the strengths of their string-bending alone. But then there are the folks such as Eugene Rhodes, who apparently recorded this record during a prison sentence and was not only not instantly liberated due to its musical merits, but failed to make much of a name for himself when he finally did complete his ten to 25. A shame, because he is an individual stylist from a generation of wandering one-man band types, an area of country blues that sometimes crosses into sounds more associated with folk music. The true-to-life nature of this particular artist and the grit that shakes off the grooves as he jumps into "Blues Leaping from Texas," muses through "I Keep Wondering," slurps "Jelly Jelly," and inquires "Who Went out Back?" indicates this isn't Peter, Paul & Mary folk. "Fast Life" is another great track, and listening to the song while looking at the grim black-and-white photo of the artist on the front cover will create a nasty feeling in a listener's stomach. For whatever reason this fellow wound up in prison, his guitar playing and singing were excellent, delivered with an enthusiasm for music that is echoed in the bluesman's comments about his own favorite artists in the interesting but too short liner notes. *—Eugene Chadbourne*

Sonny Rhodes (Clarence Edward Smith)

b. Nov. 3, 1940, Smithville, TX

Vocals, Guitar (Steel), Guitar, Bass / Modern Electric Blues, Slide Guitar Blues

Blues guitarist, singer, and songwriter Sonny Rhodes is such a talented songwriter, so full of musical ideas, that he's destined to inherit the to seats left open by the untimely passing of blues greats like Albert King and Albert Collins.

Born November 3, 1940, in Smithville, TX, he was the sixth and last child of Le Roy and Julia Smith, who were sharecroppers. Rhodes began playing seriously when he was 12, although he got his first guitar when he was eight as a Christmas present. Rhodes began performing around Smithville and nearby Austin in the late '50s, while still in his teens. Rhodes listened to a lot of T-Bone Walker when he was young, and it shows in his playing today. Other guitarists he credits as being influences include Pee Wee Crayton and B.B. King. Rhodes' first band, Clarence Smith and the Daylighters, played the Austin area blues clubs before Rhodes decided to join the Navy after graduating from high school.

In the Navy, he moved west to California, where he worked for awhile as a radio man and closed-circuit Navy ship disc jockey, telling off-color jokes in between the country and blues records he would spin for the entertainment of the sailors.

Rhodes recorded a single for Domino Records in Austin, "I'll Never Let You Go When Something Is Wrong," in 1958, and also learned to play bass. He played bass behind Freddie King and his friend Albert Collins. After his stint in the Navy, Rhodes returned to California while in his mid-twenties, and lived in Fresno for a few years before hooking up a deal with Galaxy Records in Oakland. In 1966, he recorded a single, "I Don't Love You No More" b/w "All Night Long I Play the Blues." He recorded another single for Galaxy in 1967 and then in 1978, out of total frustration with the San Francisco Bay Area record companies, he recorded "Cigarette Blues" b/w "Bloodstone Beat" on his own label.

Rhodes toured Europe in 1976, and that opened a whole new European market to him, and he was recorded by several European labels, but without much success. His European recordings include *I Don't Want My Blues Colored Bright* and a live album, *In Europe.* In desperation again, Rhodes went into the studio again to record an album in 1985, *Just Blues*, on his own Rhodesway label.

Fortunately, things have been on track for Rhodes since the late '80s, when he began recording first for the Ichiban label and later for Kingsnake. His albums for Ichiban include *Disciple of the Blues* (1991) and *Living Too Close to the Edge* (1992).

More recently, Rhodes has gotten better distribution of his albums with the Sanford, Florida-based Kingsnake label. Aside from his self-produced 1985 release *Just Blues* (now available on compact disc through Evidence Music), his best albums include the ones he's recorded for Kingsnake, for these are the records that have gotten Rhodes and his various backup bands out on the road together throughout the U.S., Canada and Europe. They include *The Blues Is My Best Friend* and his 1996 release, *Out of Control.* On these albums we hear Rhodes, the fully developed songwriter, and not surprisingly, both releases drew high marks from blues critics. *—Richard Skelly*

Disciple of the Blues / 1991 / Ichiban ✦✦✦✦✦

This be-turbaned bluesman plays lap steel guitar. This is a good one, but he's got an even better one in him. *—Niles J. Frantz*

● **Livin' Too Close to the Edge** / 1992 / Ichiban ✦✦✦✦✦

Livin' Too Close to the Edge is an exciting, blistering set of contemporary blues, driven by Sonny Rhodes' innovative lap steel playing. *—Thom Owens*

The Blues Is My Best Friend / 1994 / King Snake ✦✦✦

Just Blues / 1995 / Evidence ✦✦✦

On *Just Blues*, Sonny Rhodes delivers danceable soul blues featuring punchy horns and strong vocals, but not nearly enough of his lap steel guitar playing. Rhodes' lap steel playing is grittiest on "Please Me." A number of covers are included: "The Things I Used to Do," "Strange Things Happening," and "It Hurts Me Too." You get the impression if this session would have been recorded live in front of an audience, the end results would have been much different. *Just Blues* is enjoyable, but non-essential. *—Al Campbell*

Won't Rain in California / Feb. 22, 1996 / EPM Musique ✦✦✦

Out of Control / Mar. 19, 1996 / King Snake ✦✦✦✦

I Don't Want My Blues Colored Bright / May 27, 1997 / Black Magic ✦✦✦

Born to Be Blue / Sep. 23, 1997 / Kingpin ✦✦✦

Blue Diamond / 1999 / Stony Plain ✦✦✦

This very unique lap steel player of the blues stretches out on this Canadian roots label's release. Those who have seen him will never forget his shows, where he goes out of his way to entertain an audience. From his bright red suit to his bejeweled turban, and the legendary smile that is absolutely radiant, to the good humor he displays on stage, add his prowess on his lap steel, and he is every bit the entertainer. This same warm and embracing energy is captured on this disc and given as a bonus to the listener. The lap steel is far more common in country music, but it is an instrument that he has adapted to the blues and he finds it gives him the musical expressions and tones he was looking for. He was born in Texas and the blues that he heard growing up, as played by T-Bone Walker, Freddie King, and Chuck Willis can still be heard in his music. This combined with his strong and imaginative songwriting—he wrote or co-wrote ten of the songs on this disc—and his expressive voice make for a very worthy disc, plus as a bonus there is an in-depth interview at the tail end of the disc. Take special note of the expression and intensity displayed in "Blues Walk." This man, born Clarence Edward Smith, has come a far piece of ground from his roots, yet his appreciation and hard work—he is on the road 250 days a year—has honed his sound to sheer enjoyment. He is a true diplomat of the blues. *—Bob Gottlieb*

Good Day to Sing & Play the Blues / Aug. 14, 2001 / Stony Plain ✦✦✦

Sonny Rhodes is a performer who believes in giving his all with every show, and when you see this turbaned performer in one of his bright suits you won't be disappointed. Although a strong effort, this disc suffers from some inconsistent material for him to let loose and really play the blues. He was born and raised in Texas, and you can hear that in his vibrant playing; however, he lived for years in the Bay Area and thus was exposed to and influenced by a wide variety of influences. His lap steel playing is sharp, gritty, and at times stinging to the bone. His vocals display his strong Texas upbringing; he played behind Albert Collins and Freddie King when he was younger, and these roots are exposed at their most basic in his phrasing. The material here (he wrote or co-wrote eight of the 13 cuts) is not weak—it is just not as strong and animated throughout as the session during which he recorded *Blue Diamond*, which was as sharp, cutting, and balanced a performance as watching a fine cutting horse work his magic on the poor hapless cow. The music here is good, but he set a benchmark for himself, and he doesn't quite reach up to it on this one (though for anyone else it would be considered a great effort). This is a showman you truly have to see live to appreciate. The consummate showman can play the blues. *—Bob Gottlieb*

Rev. D.C. Rice

b. 1888, Barbour County, AL, **d.** Mar. 1973

Vocals / Prewar Gospel Blues, Black Gospel

The sound of Reverend D.C. Rice is one part fiery preaching and two parts scratchy-but-sanctified singing. It is also heavily influenced by the 78s of Reverend J. M. Gates and most especially by those of Rev. F.W. McGee. Born and raised a Baptist's son in Barbour County, Alabama, Rice left his rural home in the late teens and moved to Chicago. There he joined Bishop Hill's Pentecostal congregation at the Church of the Living God.

Around 1920, following the death of Bishop Hill, Rice became the leader of a tiny Church of the Living God congregation; he was a strong preacher and soon found himself attracting a following. After hearing the recordings of the aforementioned preachers, he was inspired to make his own records and so went to Vocalion to meet with Jack Kapp. Kapp sent some folks to Rice's next Sunday gathering, but was unimpressed and refused to record Rice. But a few days later, Kapp had a sudden, inexplicable change of heart and called Rice in to record in exchange for $75 a side, but no royalties. On these sung sermons, Rice was typically accompanied by percussion, a trombone, piano, and bass. The ensuing discs, of which "I'm on the Battlefield of the Lord" (1929) is his best known, were distributed liberally throughout Chicago; by August 1928, he had ten singles out and was giving Sunday services on the radio.

He continued recording for Vocalion through 1930. He then twice tried to sign to Paramount, but got no contract and so moved to lead a church in Jackson, AL, for two years. He then began preaching at the Oak Street Holiness Church in Montgomery. Rice was appointed Bishop of the Apostolistic [sic] Overcoming Holy Church of God, for Alabama, Florida, and Georgia in 1941. Although he made other recordings after Vocalion, they have been lost. *—Sandra Brennan*

● **Complete Recorded Works in Chronological Order (1928–1930)** / 2000 / Document ♦♦♦♦♦
Complete Recorded Works (1928-1930) is an excellent disc that contains all 20 known preformances from the Rev. D.C. Rice, an impassioned country blues-gospel singer. These are some of the finest blues-gospel recordings of their era, and this is likely the best presentation they'll ever receive. *—Thom Owens*

Tommy Ridgley

b. Oct. 30, 1925, New Orleans, LA, **d.** Aug. 11, 1999
Vocals, Piano / New Orleans Blues, Modern Electric Blues, R&B, New Orleans R&B
Tommy Ridgley was on the Crescent City R&B scene when it first caught fire, and he remains a proud part of that same scene today. That's a lot of years behind a microphone, but Ridgley doesn't sound the slightest bit tired; his 1995 Black Top album *Since the Blues Began* rates with his liveliest outings to date.

Ridgley cut his debut sides back in 1949 for Imperial under Dave Bartholomew's direction. His "Shrewsbury Blues" and "Boogie Woogie Mama" failed to break outside of his hometown, though. Sessions for Decca in 1950 and Imperial in 1952 (where he waxed the wild "Looped") preceded four 1953-1955 sessions for Atlantic that included a blistering instrumental, "Jam Up," that sported no actual Ridgley involvement but sold relatively well under his name (incomparable tenor saxist Lee Allen was prominent).

New York's Herald Records was Ridgley's home during the late '50s. The consistently solid singer waxed "When I Meet My Girl" for the firm in 1957, encoring with a catchy "Baby Do-Liddle." From there, it was on to his hometown-based Ric logo, where he laid down the stunning stroll-tempoed "Let's Try and Talk It Over" and a bluesy "Should I Ever Love Again" in 1960. He recorded intermittently after leaving Ric in 1963, waxing a soulful "I'm Not the Same Person" in 1969 for Ronn.

Ridgley always remained a hometown favorite even when recording opportunities proved scarce. Happily, *Since the Blues Began* ranked with 1995's best albums, Ridgley sounding entirely contemporary but retaining his defining Crescent City R&B edge. *How Long* appeared in 1999. Not long afterward, Ridgley passed away, on August 11, 1999. *—Bill Dahl*

● **The New Orleans King of the Stroll** / 1988 / Rounder ♦♦♦♦♦
Tommy Ridgley was a solid R&B vocalist who was quite successful with novelty tunes and silly songs, but was also a good romantic balladeer. This 15-track collection mostly covers Ridgley material from 1960 to 1964 for the Ric label, and ranges from laments like "Please Hurry Home" and "I Love You Yes I Do" to such comic material and dance-based numbers as "Double Eyed Whammy" and "The Girl From Kooka Monga." Ridgley wasn't as booming or dynamic as some other Crescent City vocalists, but made several nice period pieces and soul tunes, several of which are included on this set. *—Ron Wynn*

She Turns Me On / 1992 / Modern Blues ♦♦♦
Competent contemporary effort that proved Ridgley's voice was still in excellent shape, albeit a less engaging outing overall than his subsequent Black Top release. *—Bill Dahl*

The Herald Recordings / Nov. 30, 1992 / Collectables ♦♦♦♦
There's some very nice late-'50s New Orleans R&B recommending this 17-track collection, along with a few superfluous instrumental backing tracks that could have safely been jettisoned altogether. Ridgley's stint at Herald included the sizzling "When I Meet My Girl," "Baby Do Little," and several more impressive rocking efforts, backed by the esteemed crew at Cosimo's Crescent City studio—saxist Lee Allen, etc. *—Bill Dahl*

Since the Blues Began / 1995 / Black Top ♦♦♦♦
The veteran New Orleans singer remains a contemporary force to be reckoned with. Guitarist Snooks Eaglin, bassist George Porter Jr., and saxist Kaz Kazanoff help Ridgley out on what's easily his finest contemporary release. There are a handful of remakes of his earlier triumphs, but for the most part, he is commendably living in the present, incorporating funk-tinged rhythms into his delectable musical gumbo. *—Bill Dahl*

How Long / Jun. 8, 1999 / Sound of New Orleans ♦♦♦

Bob Riedy

Piano / Piano Blues, Chicago Blues
Blues fans on Chicago's North Side couldn't avoid pianist Bob Riedy during the '70s. Tirelessly gigging with his own band and booking various clubs at the same time, Riedy helped pioneer the area's now-thriving blues circuit. Ironically, he's not around to enjoy it—he hasn't been sighted around the Windy City in years. *—Bill Dahl*

Just off Halsted / Mar. 1975 / Flying Fish ♦♦♦♦
As you might guess from the title, here are blues played by a band from the Windy City. *—AMG*

Lake Michigan Ain't No River / 1977 / Rounder ♦♦♦

● **Bob Riedy Blues Band** / 1977 / Rounder ♦♦♦♦♦
The Bob Riedy Blues Band is a reissue of the group's 1977 album *Lake Michigan Ain't No River,* a storming set featuring a cameo from famed harpist Carey Bell. While the album doesn't really offer any surprises, it's a fine collection of straight-ahead Chicago blues that may please fans of the genre. *—Thom Owens*

Paul Rishell

b. Jan. 17, 1950, Brooklyn, NY
Vocals, Guitar / Contemporary Blues
Boston-area blues guitarist and singer Paul Rishell specializes in the country blues, but in recent years, he's been proving his mettle on occasional gigs with an electric band as well. Rishell has been riding the wave of renewed interest in acoustic music in general, and he's taken his style of acoustic country blues to festivals and clubs around the U.S., often accompanied by his harmonica playing partner, Little Annie Raines. Before he ever entered the recording studio, Rishell spent many years studying his craft, and he's shared stages with good people: Son House, Johnny Shines, Howlin' Wolf, Sonny Terry and Brownie McGhee, Buddy Guy and Junior Wells, John Lee Hooker, and Bonnie Raitt. Rishell has a number of albums out on the Tone-Cool label, *Blues on a Holiday* (1990), *Swear to Tell the Truth* (1993), *I Want You to Know* (1996), and *Moving to the Country* (1999). *—Richard Skelly*

Blues on a Holiday / 1990 / Tone-Cool ♦♦♦♦♦
Blues on a Holiday is divided between full-band numbers and songs guitarist Paul Rishell performed on a solo guitar. Both sides are exciting, offering invigorating updates of Delta and Chicago blues. Although the solo numbers—which were all performed on a National Steel—are raw and exciting, the songs recorded with a full band give a good idea of the depths of Rishell's talent. It is on these songs that he really tears loose, demonstrating what a versatile guitarist he is. *—Thom Owens*

Swear to Tell the Truth / 1993 / Tone-Cool ♦♦♦
The tendency to be snide and cynical whenever encountering contemporary versions of vintage country blues is great, mainly because there is no way anyone singing Skip James or Son House tunes in the '90s could possibly best the originals. Paul Rishell's versions of their songs are neither faceless covers nor spectacular reworkings; they are merely Rishell's earnest attempt to communicate the music he loves. Sometimes it works and other times it doesn't, but it is never pretentious or solemn. The better tracks are the jumping version of Earl Hooker's "Do You Swear to Tell the Truth," with guitar by Ronnie Earl, and Rishell's own "I'm Gonna Jump and Shout." This is not Hall of Fame stuff, but it also should not be curtly dismissed or unfairly ridiculed. *—Ron Wynn*

● **I Want You to Know** / 1996 / Tone-Cool ♦♦♦♦♦
The team of guitarist Paul Rishell and Annie Raines on harmonica (both sing) is so appealing that their acoustic duets make the occasional guests (and electrification of the music) seem unnecessary although Ronnie Earl gets in a few good guitar solos. Five originals by the Rishell/Raines team fit right in with songs by the likes of Blind Boy Fuller, Bo Carter, Barbecue Bob, J.B. Lenoir, Otis Spann, Peg Leg Howell, and Big Bill Broonzy. A touching version of "I Shall Not Be Moved" is the set's highpoint but all of the 16 selections (which range from country blues and early folk music to later electric blues) are well worth hearing. Highly recommended roots music. *—Scott Yanow*

Moving to the Country / Aug. 10, 1999 / Tone-Cool ♦♦♦♦
This second treasure trove of country blues is a wonderful mixture of older, some known but mostly forgotten, gems that had been gathering dust, and five songs written by these two artists that fit right in with the earlier diamonds, making the whole disc a wonderful way to kick back and enjoy no matter where you are. This album owes a big part of its appeal to the stunning finger picked lines that Rishell seems to lay down so effortless as to appear common place, blended with the supportive and sensitive harp work of Raines. These two are not only sharing the rich traditions of these country blues, but they are ever widening the audience with their precision playing and empathetic treatment of the music. They bring this style of music to the forefront and make it a living and vital organism. The two have a wonderful chemistry that stems from the genuine love of this music, and the joy they so obviously share with each others playing. It is serious and yet at the same time joyous. It is the quiet joy of a couple that have been together so long, and shared so much, that they can just in a look communicate the whole world to their partner. On six of the cuts they have some other musicians playing with them, and rather than lose some of their intimacy due to the intrusion of others into the mix, they seem to gain. The other musicians have no trouble letting them go and do what they do, and they stay in the background and in a most supportive way fill out the sound, allowing Rishell and Raines to use their support to reach for a fuller sound. The joy and love of their music is the very solid foundation to this disc, and the stunning musical mastery of their instruments is the result of long hours of playing. Listen to Rishell's delivery of the vocal on "My Washerwoman's Gone." He has the intonation that is needed for this bawdy song, then pause long enough to listen to what he is playing on his guitar and how effortless it sounds. That is a sound they achieve by the consequence of both love and dedication to their craft. This is a gem on many levels. *—Bob Gottlieb*

Bob Roberts

Guitar / Country Blues
The existence of country blues artists more obscure than Bob Roberts is a fact in itself; to be more obscure than Roberts would imply not having left any sort of trace, whereas the mighty Roberts has "Persian Lamb Rag" and perhaps a few other recordings floating around, all done prior to the Second World War recording ban. "Persian Lamb Rag" is the best known, having made it onto the classic Yazoo anthology entitled *String Ragtime: To Do This You Gotta Know How,* but while biographical tidbits were provided on other fine artists on this collection such as Jim & Bob, the Genial Hawaiians, a gag order of sorts was apparently issued on Roberts, because there is nary a word about him, as if his track was actually not even on the collection.

Meanwhile, hosts of other performers of the same name lurk in the wings, threatening to erroneously increase the size of this one's contribution to the music scene. Bob Roberts is most often confused with the guitarist and songwriter who worked in the following decade and in the '60s as well with the likes of Elvis Presley and Annette Funicello. The country bluesman Roberts performed in the early '40s at folk festivals such as the Fort Valley State College Festival, from which this scrap of information appeared: "Bob Roberts might have been from out-of-state, for his residence was simply '523 Army Lot, Macon Street,' which could well have referred to nearby army camps like Fort Benning or Camp Wheeler, as (festival organizer) Edgar Clark had gone out of his way to invite wartime groups of soldiers to the festival." From the evidence on the Yazoo record, Roberts was an excellent player. *—Eugene Chadbourne*

Duke Robillard

b. Oct. 4, 1948, Woonsocket, RI

Vocals, Guitar / Contemporary Blues

Duke Robillard is one of the founding members of Roomful of Blues, as well as one of the guitarists that replaced Jimmie Vaughan in the Fabulous Thunderbirds in 1990. Between that time, Robillard pursued a solo career that found him exploring more musically adventurous territory than either Roomful of Blues or the T-Birds. On his solo recordings, the guitarist dips into blues, rockabilly, jazz, and rock & roll, creating a unique fusion of American roots musics.

In 1967, Duke Robillard formed Roomful of Blues in Westerly, Rhode Island. For the next decade, he led the band through numerous lineup changes before he decided that he had grown tired of the group. Robillard left the band in 1979, initially signing on as rockabilly singer Robert Gordon's lead guitarist. After his stint with Gordon, Robillard joined the Legendary Blues Band.

In 1981, the guitarist formed a new group, the Duke Robillard Band, which soon evolved into Duke Robillard & the Pleasure Kings. After a few years of touring the group landed a contract with Rounder Records, releasing their eponymous debut album in 1984. For the rest of the decade, Robillard & the Pleasure Kings toured America and released a series of albums on Rounder Records. Occasionally, the guitarist would release a jazz-oriented solo album.

In 1990, Robillard joined the Fabulous Thunderbirds. Even though he had become a member of the Austin group, the guitarist continued to record and tour as a solo artist, signing with the major label Point Blank/Virgin in 1994 for *Temptation. Duke's Blues* followed two years later, and after one more album for Virgin, 1997's *Dangerous Place*, Robillard signed to Shanachie for 1999's *New Blues for Modern Man. Conversations in Swing Guitar* followed later that year, and the prolific guitarist returned in mid-2000 with *Explorer. —Stephen Thomas Erlewine*

Too Hot to Handle / 1985 / Rounder ♦♦♦

With the Pleasure Kings. *—AMG*

Rockin' Blues / 1988 / Rounder ♦♦♦

Robillard, both a good blues guitarist and knowledgeable swing player, displays his rocking side on this 1988 date. There are flashier solos, more uptempo cuts, and an aggressive, frenetic quality that's missing on Robillard's jazz-oriented releases. *—Ron Wynn*

You Got Me / 1988 / Rounder ♦♦♦♦

Duke Robillard's sessions have alternated between jazzy, sophisticated, low-key ventures and bluesy, more energetic, rousing dates. This was on the robust side, matching Robillard's guitar and good-natured, celebratory vocals with the talents of a great guest corps that included Dr. John and Ron Levy on keyboards, guitarist Jimmie Vaughan, bassist Thomas Enright and drummer Tommy DeQuattro (the Pleasure Kings). These weren't always musical triumphs, but even the songs that didn't quite work were entertaining, while the more inspirational offerings like "You're the One I Adore" and "Don't Treat Me Like That" nicely balance tremendous instrumental support with energetic vocal performances. *—Ron Wynn*

Swing / Oct. 1988 / Rounder ♦♦♦

While he makes his fame and fortune cutting blues-rock, guitarist Duke Robillard periodically issues albums of stylish, restrained, subtly swinging jazzy material. This date included guest appearances from swing-influenced contemporary instrumentalists, such as tenor saxophonist Scott Hamilton and guitarist Chris Flory, who teams with Robillard on "Glide On" for some excellent twin guitar fireworks. Otherwise, it's Jim Kelly who matches licks with Robillard on "Jim Jam" and "What's Your Story, Morning Glory." It's relaxed, elegant music, with just enough grit to keep things interesting. *—Ron Wynn*

Duke Robillard & the Pleasure Kings / 1989 / Rounder ♦♦♦

Featuring fine T-Bone Walker-influenced guitar and vocals from the leader, these trio recordings mostly contain original compositions. This is good for what it is, but it seems to lack the punch that larger instrumentation might provide. *—Bob Porter*

Turn It Around / 1990 / Rounder ♦♦♦

Guitarist Duke Robillard emphasized the rocking blues and barrelhouse side of his musical personality on this 1991 session that highlighted what was then his band. Vocalist Susan Forrest provided a lusty, sensual quality while bassist Scott Appelrough and drummer Doug Hinman laid down sparse rhythmic backgrounds. Robillard provided the lead guitar presence and energy, adding more flashy chords, riffs, licks and driving solos than on his more restrained jazz-based material. It was an effective session, though Forrest's vocals weren't always as hard-hitting as the material demanded. But Robillard and his mates provided instrumental cover when Forrest didn't quite hit the mark, and were even more on target when she did. *—Ron Wynn*

● **After Hours Swing Session** / May 1990 / Rounder ♦♦♦♦♦

While guitarist Duke Robillard has won widespread popularity for his facility with rocking blues and barrelhouse numbers, he also loves understated, quietly swinging jazz fare. He got a chance to demonstrate his proficiency in this style on this intimate combo session. The eight songs featured on the CD include brisk workouts as well as light-hearted numbers that showcase Robillard's decent, if not great, voice, along with his fluid, tasty fills and crisp, clean acoustic and electric guitar solos. Here's another side of Duke Robillard, one that deserves equal billing with the flashy, burning one. *—Ron Wynn*

Temptation / 1994 / Pointblank ♦♦♦♦

It may not offer anything new, but *Temptation* is a solid album from Duke Robillard. Supported by drummer Jeffery McAllister and bassist Marty Ballou, he runs through a set of nine originals and two covers, playing with typical taste and class. Robillard's blues doesn't really burn with intensity; rather, it simmers with style. That means this *Temptation* is slyly seductive, and while there are a few missteps along the way, it's still a successful seduction. *—Thom Owens*

Duke's Blues / Jan. 23, 1996 / Pointblank ♦♦♦

With *Duke's Blues*, guitarist Duke Robillard pays tribute to his blues idols, such as Albert Collins, T-Bone Walker, Guitar Slim, and Lowell Fulsom. As expected, it's an affectionate and professional tribute. Robillard works with an augmented blues combo, featuring a second guitarist, piano, and a small horn section. The band runs through the material precisely and efficiently. Although there's plenty of fine musicianship throughout *Duke's Blues*, it's the kind of record to admire, not love—it's expertly executed, but it never catches fire. *—Thom Owens*

Dangerous Place / Jun. 3, 1997 / Virgin ♦♦♦♦

Duke Robillard's place in blues history seems secure—the founder of Roomful of Blues, a stint in the Fabulous Thunderbirds, and a veteran of sessions with such venerable bluesmen as Snooky Pryor, Jimmy Witherspoon, John Hammond and Pinetop Perkins, R&B queen Ruth Brown, the king of Kansas City swing Jay McShann, and rock legend Bob Dylan—and in this *Dangerous Place*, the writer, arranger, producer, singer, guitarist and leader of the Duke Robillard Band presents a total *tour de force* of all the different dimensions of that deceptively simple music known as "the blues": the brass-stoked swing of "Had To Be Your Man"; the straight-from-the-gut Chicago harp-and-guitar moan of "No Time"; the heartbreak of "All Over But the Paying"; the wry joviality of "I May Be Ugly (But I Sure Know How to Cook)"; the ruminative "Can't Remember to Forget" (courtesy of the pen of former Eric Clapton and Muddy Waters harpmeister Jerry Portnoy); and the slinky and silky set-ending instrumental "Black Negligee." The Duke's electric guitar solo in the sexy, sassy "Ain't Nothing Like You (Where I Come From)," typical of this entire album, is an absolute model of sheer style and sly wit. *—Chris Slawecki*

Plays Jazz: The Rounder Years / Oct. 21, 1997 / Bullseye Blues ♦♦♦

This disc is the companion to *Plays Blues*, another anthology of tracks recorded for Rounder's Bullseye Blues subsidiary. Of the two discs, this one is definitely the most fun. That's mainly because when Duke Robillard says "jazz" he means it more in the Louis Jordan sense than the Duke Jordan sense. The uptempo numbers are that sort of jump blues, proto-R&B-type thing that Joe Jackson went for on his *Jumpin' Jive* album—you keep expecting to hear Cab Calloway chime in on the choruses. "Shivers," "Sweet Georgia Brown," and "Shufflin' With Some Barbeque" are the best examples of Duke's affectionate retroactivity; he throws off elegant and speedy guitar runs with giddy abandon, and his band positively cooks. The cool urbanity of a song like "I'll Never Be the Same" calls for a bit more voice than Duke has to offer, but to his credit, he doesn't try to gussy it up; that makes him honest, not fun to listen to. *—Rick Anderson*

Plays Blues: The Rounder Years / Oct. 21, 1997 / Bullseye Blues ♦♦♦

The title is bound to confuse (and possibly annoy) some blues purists. Except for a handful of straight blues numbers—including one of the most heartfelt T-Bone Walker tributes ever in "Duke's Mood"—*Plays Blues: The Rounder Years* is mostly a rock-oriented anthology drawn from the post-Roomful of Blues but pre-Fabulous Thunderbirds stage of Robillard's career. No bonus tracks or previously unissued takes—just reissued material culled from four albums released on Rounder between 1983 and 1991. (Note that Robillard's "Rounder Years" also produced some fantastic swing music, but you won't find any of it here since it's been allocated to the sister compilation *Plays Jazz: The Rounder Years*.) The '80s were an interesting decade for Robillard, as he took on a more stripped-down, roots rock (but still bluesy) approach with his trio, the Pleasure Kings, and then headed into that contemporary blues-rock zone often associated with the Fabulous Thunderbirds and Stevie Ray Vaughan. For Robillard, it wasn't always an ideal fit, but he obviously had fun doing it; you can sense his playful swagger on power-chord rockers such as "You Got Me" and "If This Is Love." Still, it's the "simpler" blues format that seems to really unleash the fire in Robillard's guitar playing, the best example being the marathon 12-bar shuffle "I Think You Know" (which also happens to be the first blues tune Robillard ever wrote). Overall, *Plays Blues: The Rounder Years* isn't a bad start, but if you're after the real thing, check out *Duke's Blues*, which Robillard specifically recorded as a tribute to his blues heroes. *—Ken Chang*

Stretchin' Out / Sep. 29, 1998 / Stony Plain ♦♦♦♦♦

The night was November 26, 1995; the club, Richard's on Richards in Vancouver; and the lineup with Robillard was Marty Ballou on bass, Marty Richards on drums, and "Sax" Gordon Beadle on tenor and baritone sax. They were touring with Jimmy Witherspoon and this album captures the set before they brought "Spoon" to the stage. It was taped for the Canadian Broadcasting Corporation's *Saturday Night Blues* program with host Holger Petersen. Seven of the nine songs on *Stretchin' Out* also appear on 1996's *Duke's Blues*. That one is truly a gem but for fans who don't have it yet, one might recommend this recording instead. "Too Hot to Handle" and "That's My Life" are the only tracks that aren't on *Duke's Blues*. If you DO have *Duke's Blues, Stretchin' Out* is still well worth the purchase because of the great extended jams and shoot-from-the-hip guitar licks you won't find anywhere else. Duke sings a few bars on Albert Collins' "Dyin' Flu" with no mic. You have to strain to hear him over the inevitable amplifier hums and crowd support of a live recording (one fan yells "Duke it out!"), but that's what makes it so cool and compelling. In addition to "Dyin' Flu," "Gee I Wish" is a highlight. Robillard swings his way through a solo nearly as long as the song itself. This recording features plenty of his trademark Gibson jangle and ring, and a healthy dose of jump and swing tunes where the boys were definitely cookin'. *Stretchin' Out* leaves you wishing you had been in the club during this recording. Two thumbs WAY up! *—Ann Wickstrom*

New Blues for Modern Man / Apr. 20, 1999 / Shanachie ♦♦♦
Duke Robillard's 1999 album, *New Blues for Modern Man*, displays the singer/guitarist's skill at integrating all styles of blues, rock and soul into his own unique sound. This set of originals ranges from Gulf Coast blues to New Orleans party rock to Chicago shuffles to soulful ballads. His debut for Shanachie Records, *New Blues for Modern Man* displays the goods that keep Robillard sounding fresh and vital. *—Heather Phares*

Conversations in Swing Guitar / Oct. 26, 1999 / Stony Plain ♦♦♦♦
This is a not very challenging, but thoroughly charming, summit meeting between a blues guitar master and a jazz guitar legend. Taking four classic swing tunes ("Just Squeeze Me," "Avalon," Stuffy," and, inevitably, "Flyin' Home"), two Robillard originals, and a jointly composed slow blues, and helped out by bassist Marty Ballou and drummer Marty Richards, Duke Robillard and Herb Ellis deliver a 48-minute swing guitar master class. Ellis comes from jazz and Robillard from the blues, so their approaches are just distinct enough to keep things interesting; although both play with a clean, fat jazz tone and no one ever really hauls off and shreds, Robillard tends towards bent notes and funky chordal things while Ellis thinks a bit more in terms of long lines and florid ornamentation. Every so often you might find yourself wishing that the edges were just a bit rougher, but both of these guys are clearly having a great old time, and you will too. *—Rick Anderson*

Explorer / Jun. 13, 2000 / Shanachie ♦♦♦
No matter what musical turn singer/guitarist Duke Robillard chooses to incorporate, it is always steeped in the blues. *Explorer* is his second release on the Shanachie label and integrates jazz ("You Mean Everything to Me" and "Jumpin With Duke"), horn-laden soul ("Male Magnet," "Just Between Me and You"), New Orleans-style rhumba ("Sayin Don't Make It So"), and even Celtic overtones ("Lonesome Old Town"). *Explorer* lives up to its title and finds Robillard and his band providing another eclectic blues/roots set in the process. *—Al Campbell*

Living With the Blues / May 21, 2002 / Stony Plain ♦♦♦♦
Best known as the founder of Roomful of Blues and for his short stint with the Fabulous Thunderbirds (replacing Jimmie Vaughan), Duke Robillard had only released two blues albums between 1996 and 2002. Although he was awarded the W.C. Handy Best Blues Guitarist award for 2000 and 2001 and his tireless road work always included plenty of stinging solos, Robillard left the jazz and worldbeat tangents behind for this welcome return to his first love. Those who have followed Robillard's career know that he's never been tied to one style, and *Living With the Blues* highlights his eclectic talents. Robillard crackles on everything here, from the straight-ahead Chicago approach of Willie Dixon by way of Muddy Waters' "I Live the Life I Love" to the Roomful-styled hard swing of the obscure Willie Egans' "I'm Mad About You Baby" to the acoustic treatment of Tampa Red's "Hard Road" and the jump blues of his own "Sleepin' on It" (reprised from the Roomful years). He turns the Brownie McGhee title track into a tough Chicago shuffle, featuring the rollicking tenor sax of old Roomful alumnus Doug James, and closes with a bluesy rhumba-styled version of B.B. King's "Long Gone Baby." He also adds tough spunk to Little Milton's "If Walls Could Talk," throwing in one of the disc's greasiest solos along the way. Through it all, Robillard is obviously having a blast, whipping out tight guitar solos with white-hot precision and snazzy arrangements that never overwhelm the band or the song. The horns that dominate the album return Robillard to the Roomful sound that he clearly loves and, even though his gruff vocals are still an acquired taste, his singing is filled with such enthusiasm that you can forgive its technical shortcomings. There's a real sense of joy that infuses every track here, making it perfect for established Duke Robillard fans or newcomers who want to get a taste of the man's substantial talents. *—Hal Horowitz*

Rev. Cleophus Robinson

b. Mar. 18, 1932, Canton, MS
Vocals / Traditional Gospel, Southern Gospel, Black Gospel
While never achieving the commercial success of many of his contemporaries, the Rev. Cleophus Robinson was a prominent figure on the gospel circuit throughout the better part of the postwar era, perhaps best known for hosting a coast-to-coast gospel television series which ran for a quarter century. Born March 18, 1932, in Canton, MS, according to family legend Robinson suddenly sang his first gospel song, "Who Will Be Able to Stand?," at the age of three; from that point on, he sang regularly while working in the cotton fields, influenced in great measure by his mother Lillie, a gospel shouter in the tradition of Mahalia Jackson whose own vocal prowess was renowned throughout the region. As a teen, Robinson gave his first solo recitals at St. John's Church of Canton; in 1948 he moved to Chicago, where he performed in a variety of area churches and appeared with the Roberta Martin Singers alongside Jackson herself.

Through Evelyn Gay of the Gay Sisters, Robinson was introduced to Miracle Records chief Lee Egalnick, and in September 1949 he went into the studio to make his debut recordings. Credited as Bro. Cleophus Robinson, he issued the single "Now Lord"; sales were unimpressive, and he soon relocated to Memphis, where he moved in with his uncle, the Reverend L.A. Hamblin (who in 1968 recorded the sermon "When God Walks Out of the Field" for the Jewel label). After finishing high school, Robinson began his own weekly radio show, *The Voice of the Soul*, and began regularly appearing with famous gospel artists as they passed through town, among them Brother Joe May, who became something of a mentor to the young singer. During the same period he began collaborating with pianist Napoleon Brown, who played with Robinson both on record and at live dates for the next several decades.

In 1953, Robinson signed to the Houston-based Peacock Records, soon issuing the single "In the Sweet By and By"; he released several more efforts for the label, none of them hugely successful, before deciding to pursue a career as an actor. After enrolling as a drama major at Leymole College, he frequently found himself called away from his studies to promote his records; his grades suffered, and after a year he returned to music full-time. By 1956, Robinson's gospel career was in a rut, and he had yet to score a hit record; that all changed upon the release of "Pray for Me," a duet recorded with his sister Josephine James. A year later, he moved to St. Louis to accept a position with the Bethlehem Missionary Baptist Church, resulting in an erratic recording schedule which ended with the 1962 release of the LP *Pray for Me*. Throughout the decade, Robinson also hosted his *Hour of Faith* weekly radio program; beginning in 1964, he also starred in his own gospel TV program.

In 1962, Robinson signed to Battle Records, a subsidiary of Riverside, and there recorded a number of tracks backed by the Gospel Chimes before returning to Peacock in 1964. His first release after going back to the label, "Solemn Prayer," was that rare sermon record which became a major seller. Later that same year, he moved to Savoy, scoring another hit a year later with "How Sweet It Is to Be Loved by God"; by the end of 1965, he had again returned to Peacock, where his music adopted a bluesier flavor. After touring Europe, Robinson made yet another label change in 1969, this time jumping to Nashboro; there he scored his biggest hit ever with "Wrapped Up, Tied Up, Tangled Up," a crossover hit with white audiences as well. It led to a return engagement with Savoy in the '70s, and in 1975 he appeared at the Montreux Jazz Festival in Switzerland. Robinson's pace slowed in the years to follow, although in 1980 he sang at the White House and in 1986 notched another hit with "Save a Seat for Me." *—Jason Ankeny*

Rev. Cleophus Robinson With Jessy Dixon & the Gospel Chimes / 1962 / Battle ♦♦♦♦♦
Robinson fronting a gospel quartet—some rare and great moments. *—Opal Louis Nations*

God's Sons and Daughters / 1965 / Peacock ♦♦♦♦♦
Striking renditions with great organ and guitar accompaniment. *—Opal Louis Nations*

● **Someone to Care (The Battle Sessions)** / 1994 / Specialty ♦♦♦♦♦
If anything could be considered a sleeper among the most recent Fantasy Legends of Gospel line, that might be the CD featuring Rev. Cleophus Robinson. The Reverend cut several songs for Riverside's subsidiary Battle label, which didn't last very long. After more than 30 years, these songs are again available, and its fire and fury might surprise those looking for sedate, reverential praise tracks. Rev. Robinson was a shouter and wailer, although he could also do mournful, moving ballads. But the uptempo stompers are the cuts to savor among the 28, with Rev. Robinson's rippling voice getting more and more hypnotic as it goes up the ladder. *—Ron Wynn*

Wrapped Up, Tied Up, Tangled Up / Jun. 20, 1995 / Nashboro ♦♦♦♦
All his best-selling and best-sounding sides from his stay on the Nashboro label during the '70s. *—Opal Louis Nations*

What You Need / Nov. 14, 1995 / Malaco ♦♦♦

Live in St. Louis / Sep. 30, 1997 / Malaco ♦♦♦♦

I Shall Know Him / Mar. 9, 1999 / MCA ♦♦♦♦
A multi-talent, Robinson's so-called "gospel-jazz" style reached its apex with a batch of recordings for the Peacock and the Nashboro labels in the late '60s. This 10-track compilation features music from that period including his big hit from 1969, "Wrapped Up, Tied Up, Tangled Up" and "Pray for Me." Other highlights include "Elijah Rock," "Sweet Home," "Uncloudy Day," "Because He Lives," "There's Only One Bridge," and "I Shall Know Him." *—Cub Koda*

Elzadie Robinson

Vocals / Classic Female Blues
'20s blues vocalist Elzadie Robinson hailed from Shreveport, LA, but remained in Chicago, after going there to record. Her recordings span 1926-1929, and during that time she worked with several pianists including Bob Call, and her regular accompanist and fellow Shreveport native, Will Ezell. Elzadie Robinson chiefly recorded for the Paramount label, but also cut several sides for Broadway under the alias Bernice Drake. *—Joslyn Layne*

● **Complete Works, Vol. 1** / Jul. 12, 1994 / Document ♦♦♦♦
Elzadie Robinson was never too famous. One of many female classic blues singers in the '20s who had opportunities to record, Robinson recorded 34 songs from 1926-1929; all of those titles plus five alternate takes are included on a pair of Document CDs. *Vol. 1* has the first 22 performances, counting four alternates). In most cases, the singer is backed by pianist Will Ezell. Two numbers apiece have either pianist Bob Call or guitarist Johnny St. Cyr in Ezell's place. In addition, there are two selections in 1926 with such players as either B.T. Wingfield or Shirley Clay on cornet, Tiny Parham or Richard M. Jones on piano, and a couple other players. In 1928, for two versions apiece of "Pay Day Daddy Blues" and "Elzadie's Policy Blues," Robinson is joined by clarinetist Johnny Dodds, guitarist Blind Blake, and either pianist Jimmy Blythe or Jimmy Bertrand on xylophone. Elzadie Robinson had an effective voice, although she was not on the same level as the giants of the era; the recording quality of some of these titles (particularly the alternates and earlier titles) is streaky. The best numbers are "Humming Blues," "Houston Bound," "Tick Tock Blues," "The Santa Claus Crave," "St. Louis Cyclone Blues," and the selections with Dodds. Not essential music, but this set should greatly interest vintage blues collectors. *—Scott Yanow*

Complete Works, Vol. 2 / Jul. 12, 1994 / Document ♦♦♦♦
The final 17 selections (including a previously unreleased alternate take) from the obscure Elzadie Robinson's recording career are on this excellent Document CD. Robinson

was a second-level blues singer whose voice seemed to get stronger with time; he is accompanied by pianist Tiny Parham on two numbers and Will Ezell for the other 15. On such selections as "Wicked Daddy," "It's Too Late Now," "Unsatisfied Blues," "Cheatin' Daddy," and "Ain't Got Nobody," Robinson shows that her work should be re-evaluated, for she is quite effective. This CD is rounded off by six alternate versions of songs recorded by the even lesser-known vocalist Lottie Beaman in 1924. Beaman is joined by either the Pruitt Twins (banjoist Milas Pruitt and guitarist Miles Pruitt) or pianist Jimmy Blythe and (on one number) banjoist Papa Charlie Jackson. While Beaman fares well, the reason to acquire this CD is the long-forgotten Elzadie Robinson. *—Scott Yanow*

Fenton Robinson

b. Sep. 23, 1935, Minter City, MS, **d.** Nov. 25, 1997

Vocals, Guitar / Modern Electric Chicago Blues, Texas Blues, Soul-Blues

His Japanese fans reverently dubbed Fenton Robinson "the mellow blues genius" because of his ultra-smooth vocals and jazz-inflected guitar work. But beneath the obvious subtlety resides a spark of constant regeneration—Robinson tirelessly strives to invent something fresh and vital whenever he's near a bandstand.

The soft-spoken Mississippi native got his career going in Memphis, where he'd moved at age 16. First, Rosco Gordon used him on a 1956 session for Duke that produced "Keep on Doggin'." The next year, Fenton made his own debut as a leader for the Bihari brothers' Meteor label with his first reading of "Tennessee Woman." His band, the Dukes, included mentor Charles McGowan on guitar; T-Bone Walker and B.B. King were Robinson's idols.

In 1957, Fenton also teamed up with bassist Larry Davis at the Flamingo Club in Little Rock. Bobby "Blue" Bland caught the pair there and recommended them to his boss, Duke Records prexy Don Robey. Both men made waxings for Duke in 1958, Robinson playing on Davis' classic "Texas Flood" and making his own statement with "Mississippi Steamboat." Robinson cut the original version of the often-covered Peppermint Harris-penned slow blues "As the Years Go Passing By" for Duke in 1959 with New Orleans prodigy James Booker on piano. The same date also produced a terrific "Tennessee Woman" and a marvelous blues ballad, "You've Got to Pass This Way Again."

Fenton moved to Chicago in 1962, playing South Side clubs with Junior Wells, Sonny Boy Williamson, and Otis Rush and laying down the swinging "Say You're Leavin'" for USA in 1966. But it was his stunning slow blues "Somebody (Loan Me a Dime)," cut in 1967 for Palos, that insured his blues immortality. Boz Scaggs liked it so much that he covered it for his 1969 debut LP. Unfortunately, he initially also claimed he wrote the tune; much litigation followed.

John Richbourg's Sound Stage 7/Seventy 7 labels, it's safe to say, didn't really have a clue as to what Fenton Robinson's music was all about. The guitarist's 1970 Nashville waxings for the firm were mostly horrific—Robinson wasn't even invited to play his own guitar on the majority of the horribly unsubtle rock-slanted sides. His musical mindset was growing steadily jazzier by then, not rockier.

Robinson fared a great deal better at his next substantial stop: Chicago's Alligator Records. His 1974 album *Somebody Loan Me a Dime* remains the absolute benchmark of his career, spotlighting his rich, satisfying vocals and free-spirited, understated guitar work in front of a rock-solid horn-driven band. By comparison, 1977's *I Hear Some Blues Downstairs* was a trifle disappointing despite its playful title track and a driving T-Bone tribute, "Tell Me What's the Reason."

Alligator issued *Nightflight*, another challenging set, in 1984, then backed off the guitarist. His most recent disc, 1989's *Special Road*, first came out on the Dutch Black Magic logo and was reissued by Evidence Music not long ago. Robinson passed away on November 25, 1997, at the age of 62 due to complications from brain cancer. *—Bill Dahl*

Monday Morning Boogie & Blues / 1972 / 77 ✦✦

Too rock-oriented. *—Bill Dahl*

★ **Somebody Loan Me a Dime** / 1974 / Alligator ✦✦✦✦✦

One of the most subtly satisfying electric blues albums of the '70s. Robinson never did quite fit the "Genuine Houserocking Music" image of Alligator Records—his deep, rich baritone sounds more like a magic carpet than a piece of barbed wire, and he speaks in jazz-inflected tongues, full of complex surprises. The title track hits with amazing power, as do the chugging "The Getaway," a hard-swinging "You Say You're Leaving," and the minor-key "You Don't Know What Love Is." In every case, Robinson had recorded them before, but thanks to Bruce Iglauer's superb production, a terrific band, and Robinson's musicianship, these versions reign supreme. *—Bill Dahl*

I Hear Some Blues Downstairs / 1977 / Alligator ✦✦✦

A disappointment in its inconsistency following such a mammoth triumph as his previous set, yet not without its mellow delights. The title track is untypically playful; Robinson's revisiting of the mournful "As the Years Go Passing By" is a moving journey, and his T-Bone Walker tribute "Tell Me What's the Reason" swings deftly. On the other hand, a superfluous remake of Rosco Gordon's "Just a Little Bit" goes nowhere, and nobody really needed another "Killing Floor." *—Bill Dahl*

Getaway / 197 / 77 ✦✦✦

More rock-slanted '70s stuff. *—Bill Dahl*

Blues in Progress / 1984 / Black Magic ✦✦✦

Smooth and jazzy. *—Bill Dahl*

Nightflight / 1984 / Alligator ✦✦✦

For the most part, another easygoing trip to the mellower side of contemporary blues, Robinson's jazzy tone and buttery vocals applied to a couple of his '50s-era numbers ("Crazy Crazy Lovin'" and "Schoolboy") along with some intriguing new iteams and Lowell Fulson's mournful "Sinner's Prayer." Tasty backing helps too. *—Bill Dahl*

Special Road / Apr. 1989 / Evidence ✦✦✦

Fenton Robinson is among the second-line blues musicians who have come close but never made it over the hump. He has certainly got the guitar goods, and his vocals are often memorable and anguished. Unfortunately, the 13 songs he did on this 1989 date were mostly good but nowhere as intense as he has delivered on other occasions. Neither is the instrumental work on this Evidence CD; his solos are firmly articulated, often elaborately constructed and paced, but they lack impact. Too many times Robinson falls just short of turning in a triumphant or exciting number, either through a less than emphatic vocal or a mundane solo. This is not necessarily a bad session, just a disappointing one. *—Ron Wynn*

Mellow Fellow / 1993 / Charly ✦✦

Clearly, the folks at Sound Stage 7 Records had no idea what Fenton Robinson was all about during his 1970-1971 stay there. Hell, they even took the guitar out of his hands altogether at one dreadful session reproduced on this 19-track retrospective in its entirety, entrusting the lead work instead to some pitiful rock players better left anonymous. The last few sides are much better—"Little Turch" actually sounds like Robinson, his elegant guitar work back up front where it belongs. *—Bill Dahl*

Freddy Robinson

b. Feb. 24, 1939, Memphis, TN

Guitar / Northern Soul, Contemporary Blues, Jazz Blues

Blues fans know him as one of harp genius Little Walter's studio accompanists during the latter portion of his tenure at Chess. Jazz aficionados are aware of him for the albums he did for World Pacific. Freddy Robinson has been one versatile guitarist across the decades. Robinson played both bass and guitar behind Walter at Chess circa 1959-1960. His own recording career commenced in 1962 with a jazz-laced instrumental pairing, "The Buzzard"/"The Hawk," for King's short-lived Queen subsidiary. He gave singing a try in 1966, cutting "Go-Go Girl" for Checker (with Barbara Acklin and Mamie Galore helping out as background vocalists). By 1968, he was recording with pianist Monk Higgins and the Blossoms (Darlene Love's vocal group) in Los Angeles for Cobblestone.

Blues fans may find the material Robinson cut for *At the Drive In* in 1972 noteworthy; "At the Drive-In" and "Bluesology" are in-the-alley blues efforts that hark back to the guitarist's early days in Chicago. Robinson later recorded for Al Bell's ICA logo. *—Bill Dahl*

The Coming Atlantis / Apr. 1970 / Pacific Jazz ✦✦✦

Freddy Robinson's debut album *Coming Atlantis* is plagued by some late-'60s clichés—hippie lyrics, spacy instrumental interludes, and some blues-rock flourishes—but there are some strong blues songs and soloing from Robinson that make it worth a listen. *—Thom Owens*

● **At the Drive In** / 1972 / Enterprise ✦✦✦✦

It's rather hard to get a handle on this phase of Robinson's career—there's some reasonably lowdown blues with the guitarist speaking the lyrics as much as singing them here, but he was mainly a jazz musician by then. *—Bill Dahl*

Off the Cuff / Mar. 1974 / Enterprise ✦✦

Ikey Robinson

b. Jul. 28, 1904, Dublin, VA, **d.** Oct. 25, 1990, Chicago, IL

Vocals, Guitar, Banjo / Classic Jazz

Ikey Robinson was an excellent banjoist and singer who was versatile enough to record both jazz and blues from the late '20s into the late '30s. Unfortunately, he spent long periods off records after the swing era, leading to him being less known than he should be. After working locally, Robinson moved to Chicago in 1926, playing and recording with Jelly Roll Morton, Clarence Williams, and (most importantly) Jabbo Smith during 1928-1929. He led his own recording sessions in 1929, 1931, 1933, and 1935 (all have been reissued on a CD from the Austrian label RST). Robinson played with Wilbur Sweatman, Noble Sissle, Carroll Dickerson, and Erskine Tate in the '30s, recorded with Clarence Williams, and led small groups from the '40s on. In the early '60s he was with Franz Jackson, and in the '70s (when he was rediscovered) he had an opportunity to tour Europe and be reunited with Jabbo Smith. *—Scott Yanow*

● **"Banjo" Ikey Robinson** / Jan. 4, 1929-May 19, 1937 / RST ✦✦✦✦✦

It would not be an understatement to call this CD definitive of Ikey Robinson's work since it includes every selection (except for two songs that have Half Pint Jaxon vocals) ever led by the banjoist/vocalist. The diversity is impressive, for Robinson is heard (on "Got Butter on It" and "Ready Hokum") with a hot group featuring cornetist Jabbo Smith singing the blues, performing with the Hokum Trio and the Pods of Pepper (both good-time bands), backing singer Charlie Slocum, and heading his own Windy City Five (a fine swing group) in 1935; he even plays clarinet on one song. This consistently enjoyable Austrian import is well worth searching for. *—Scott Yanow*

Jimmie Lee Robinson

b. Apr. 30, 1931, Chicago, IL

Guitar / Chicago Blues, Electric Chicago Blues, Modern Electric Chicago Blues

Unlike many of his Chicago blues contemporaries, Jimmie Lee Robinson wasn't a Mississippi Delta émigré. The guitarist was born and raised right in the Windy City—not far from Maxwell Street, the fabled open-air market on the near West Side where the blues veritably teemed during the '40s and '50s.

Robinson learned his lessons well. He formed a partnership with guitarist Freddie King in 1952 for four years (they met outside the local welfare office), later doing sideman work with Elmore James and Little Walter and cutting sessions on guitar and bass behind Little Walter, Eddie Taylor, Shakey Jake, and St. Louis Jimmy Oden. Robinson cut three singles for the tiny Bandera label circa 1959-1960; the haunting "All My Life" packed enough power to be heard over in England, where John Mayall faithfully covered it. Another Bandera standout, "Lonely Traveller," was revived as the title track for Robinson's 1994 Delmark comeback album.

Europe enjoyed a glimpse of Robinson when he hit the continent as part of Horst Lippmann and Fritz Rau's 1965 American Folk Blues Festival alongside John Lee Hooker,

Buddy Guy, and Big Mama Thornton. After that, his mother died, and times grew tough. Robinson worked as a cabbie and security guard for the Board of Education for a quarter century or so until the members of the Ice Cream Men—a young local band with an overriding passion for '50s blues—convinced Robinson that he was much too young to be retired. His comeback was documented by his first full length record, *Lonely Traveller* being released on Delmark in 1994. In the mid-'90s he released *Guns, Gangs, and Drugs* on his own Amina label.

The beginning of 1998 found Robinson back in the studio working on a set of mostly original songs that became his second album, *Remember Me*, which was released in 2000 on the APO label. At the end of 1998 Robinson began what ended up to be a 91-day fast to protest the tearing down of the historic Maxwell Street area. He was a member of Maxwell Street Historic Preservation Coalition and wrote their theme song, the "Maxwell Street Tear Down Blues" but decided a more direct action needed to be taken. The fast brought attention to the cause, including a front-page story in the New York Times, but ultimately the area was almost completely demolished so that the University of Chicago campus could expand. In 1999 Robinson recorded *All My Life*, which was released in 2001. —*Bill Dahl*

● **Lonely Traveller** / 1994 / Delmark ✦✦✦✦
Jimmie Lee Robinson doesn't do everything in the standard 12-bar blues form; sometimes he half-sings, half-talks through songs, or varies the tempo, breaks up the rhythms and paces the performances in an unusual manner. His solos also aren't the usual piercing or flashy phrases and riffs, but sometimes more decorative or sparse underneath the words. His diverse style and unpredictable vocal manner make this one of the more striking modern blues outings in quite some time, despite the fact that he's neither a great vocalist nor a spectacular instrumentalist. But he's written much of the material, and those songs that he covers, such as Lightnin' Hopkins' "Can't Be Successful" or Big Bill Broonzy's "Key to the Highway," are certainly not reflective of their original creators. —*Ron Wynn*

Remember Me / May 2, 2000 / APO ✦✦✦

All My Life / Jun. 12, 2001 / APO ✦✦✦

Tad Robinson

b. Jun. 24, 1956, New York, NY
Vocals, Harmonica / Electric Blues, Soul-Blues
Tad Robinson would have fit in snugly with the blue-eyed soul singers of the '60s. His vocals virtually reeking of soul, he's capable of delving into a straight-ahead Little Walter shuffle or delivering a vintage O.V. Wright R&B ballad. Add his songwriting skills and exceptional harp technique and you have quite the total package.

Robinson grew up in New York City on a nutritious diet of Stax, Motown, and Top 40, digging everyone from Otis Redding and Arthur Alexander to Eric Burdon and Joe Cocker. He matriculated at Indiana University's school of music in 1980, fronting a solid little combo on the side called the Hesitation Blues Band that made it up to Chicago now and then (where he soon relocated).

Long respected locally, his reputation outside the city limits soared when he took over as vocalist with Dave Specter & the Bluebirds. Their 1994 Delmark disc, *Blueplicity*, was an inspiring marriage of Robinson's soaring vocals and Specter's tasty, jazz-laced guitar and featured the striking Robinson-penned originals "What's Your Angle," "Dose of Reality," and "On the Outside Looking In."

Delmark granted Tad Robinson his own album later that year. *Ode to Infinity* escorted him ever further into soul territory (guests on the set included Mighty Flyers guitarist Alex Schultz, the mystical Robert Ward, and Specter). Now living once more in Indiana, Robinson still makes it into Chicago on a regular basis (but never frequently enough for his followers). —*Bill Dahl*

● **One to Infinity** / 1994 / Delmark ✦✦✦✦
Harpist Robinson displays his multi-faceted talents, exploring a multitude of shades of blues and soul. The backing on each song neatly fits the piece—guitarist Robert Ward briefly turns up as a sideman as Robinson proves he's one of the top young vocalists on the contemporary circuit. —*Bill Dahl*

Last Go Round / Sep. 22, 1998 / Delmark ✦✦✦

Rockin' Sidney (Sidney Semien)

b. Apr. 9, 1938, Lebeau, LA, **d.** Feb. 25, 1998
Vocals, Accordion, Harmonica, Guitar, Organ / Swamp Blues, Zydeco
With his 1985 novelty smash "My Toot Toot," Rockin' Sidney scored zydeco's first true international hit. Born Sidney Semien on April 9, 1938, in Lebeau, LA, he began playing harmonica and guitar professionally while in his teens, and made his first R&B-styled recordings on the Fame and Jin imprints during the late '50s; his first regional hit, "No Good Woman," appeared in 1962. Between the mid-'60s and the late '70s, Sidney cut well over 50 singles for the Louisiana-based Goldband label, working in a variety of contemporary blues, soul, and R&B modes; none proved successful, however, and upon learning the accordion he began playing zydeco.

He issued his first true zydeco record, *Give Me a Good Time Woman*, on the Maison de Soul label in 1982; two years later he cut *My Zydeco Shoes Got the Zydeco Blues*, which included the track "My Toot Toot." Although Sidney himself was reportedly unhappy with the song, it became a local jukebox hit, and soon regional radio stations began playing it regularly; in time, the single became a grassroots smash, selling well over a million copies on its way to charting in the U.S. and the U.K. and even winning a Grammy Award. While Sidney never again reached the same commercial peaks, he remained one of zydeco's most notable artists, setting up his own label, Bally Hoo, and touring regularly until his death on February 25, 1998. —*Jason Ankeny*

● **My Toot Toot** / 1986 / Ace ✦✦✦✦✦
Rockin' Sidney had the biggest zydeco release of all time—"My Toot Toot"—and it has enjoyed many subsequent covers. Some of this release is unfortunately unacceptable, as it includes updated covers of the time, but he rises above it most of the time. —*Jeff Hannusch*

My Toot Toot / 1987 / Maison de Soul ✦✦✦

Live With the Blues / 1988 / JSP ✦✦✦

Zydeco Is Fun / Jul. 2, 1996 / Maison de Soul ✦✦✦

Judy Roderick

b. 1942, Elkhart, IN, **d.** Jan. 28, 1992, Grantsdale, MT
Vocals, Guitar / Folk-Blues, Singer/Songwriter, Blues Revival
One of the finest white folk/blues singers of the early to mid-'60s, Judy Roderick developed a loyal following, fostered by her concert and club appearances at the best known venues on the East Coast—the Second Fret (Philly), Club 47 (Cambridge), and Cafe Au Go Go (New York City). Her album releases on Columbia and Vanguard Records were critically acclaimed. By 1966, Roderick had begun to write music in collaboration with lyricist Bill Ashford and signed with Atlantic/Atco records in 1970, for whom she recorded one album of original material, *Nevada Jukebox*, with her band, 60,000,000 Buffalo.

Judy attended the University of Colorado, and worked at the available music rooms in Boulder and Denver, including the Attic, where she crossed paths with fellow working musicians Judy Collins and David Crosby, among others. She moved to New York City and signed with Columbia Records in 1963, recording two albums, only one of which was released. *Ain't Nothin' But the Blues* was an eclectic mix of traditional acoustic folk tunes and large arrangements of blues tunes. This album includes early contributions on harmonica by John Hammond. The second album was considered by Roderick to be an artistic debacle, and led to her leaving the label. It remains unreleased.

Judy was quickly signed by Vanguard Records, were she recorded the stunning *Woman Blue* in 1965. She was featured on one volume of the Newport Folk Festival recordings released by the label. She spent the next several years sharing venues with Eric Anderson, Vince Martin, Fred Neil, Tim Hardin, the Youngbloods, and others. In 1969, she returned to Colorado, signed with Atlantic, formed 60,000,000 Buffalo, and in 1971 recorded the seminal rock album *Nevada Jukebox* with producer Bill Szymczyk. The band broke up the next year.

Judy spent her last years in Montana. "Floods of South Dakota," co-written with Bill Ashford, was recorded by Tim and Mollie O'Brien on their album *Remember Me*. Their performance of the song received a Grammy nomination. Roderick's last recordings were on a privately released cassette and featured Mac Rebennack on several tracks. Judy Roderick died of diabetic complications in 1992. —*William Ashford*

Ain't Nothing but the Blues / 1963 / Columbia ✦✦✦
Roderick's first album, produced by Bobby Scott and featuring John Hammond Jr., on harmonica. Columbia seemed at a loss as to how to present this young woman who belted and moaned in the style and tradition of Bessie Smith and Memphis Minnie. Arrangements vary from large to intimate. A few jewels here, including inspired readings of "He was a Friend of Mine," "Brother Can You Spare a Dime," and Hoagy Carmichael's "Baltimore Oriole." —*William Ashford*

● **Woman Blue** / 1965 / Vanguard ✦✦✦✦✦
This album, recorded in 1965, was considered by many to be among the most stunning acoustic albums of its day. Of Midwestern origin, Roderick possessed a voice of maturity beyond her years and on this masterpiece, captured a haunting and haunted blues diary. The album mixes blues and folk classics, including "You Were on My Mind," prior to its release by We Five. *Woman Blue* was re-released on CD in 1995, with the ill-advised addition of several outtakes from the original sessions. This is a breathtaking document of a talent left virtually unknown. —*William Ashford*

Judy Roderick and the Forefears / 1984 / Oprea ✦✦
Judy's last recordings, in which the effects of her failing health on her vocals is painfully evident. Notable for its inclusion of several compositions written with lyricist Bill Ashford and not previously available, especially "Surprises," written originally as a country blues ode to Stephen Stills, but on this recording featuring keyboard work by Mac Rebennack and a Memphis-styled horn section. For serious fans only. —*William Ashford*

Mighty Mo Rodgers (Maurice Rodgers)

b. 1942, East Chicago, IN
Vocals, Songwriter / Contemporary Blues
Mighty Mo Rodgers (real name Maurice Rodgers) was born in Indiana where his father owned a club that featured blues performers. When Rodgers wasn't studying classical piano he was checking out the blues artists that played there. Growing up, Rodgers was deeply affected by the mid-'60s soul music from the Memphis-based Stax label. Using Stax as an influence, Rodgers started his first band while in high school called the Rocketeers. Upon entering Indiana State College, Rodgers fronted another band, the Maurice Rodgers Combo, playing Wurlitzer piano and incorporating originals with cover versions of popular songs from the era. He finally decided to quit college, move to L.A., and give music his full-time attention. There he played gigs and recorded with many blues and R&B legends; his organ can be heard on Brenton Wood's 1967 hit "Gimme Little Sign."

Throughout the years, Rodgers has not limited himself to performing. In 1973 he produced the album *Sonny and Terry* on A&M Records for Sonny Terry & Brownie McGhee. After growing tired of tedious session work, he continued to write songs and became a house songwriter for Motown and Chappel Publishing. Rodgers also continued to produce sessions for other artists and decided to go back to school where he received a degree in philosophy. In 1999 he released his first solo effort, *Blues Is My Wailin' Wall*, on Blue Thumb. The recording contained all original material, mixing his philosophical views with blues/soul musical roots. —*Al Campbell*

● **Blues Is My Wailin' Wall** / Oct. 5, 1999 / Blue Thumb ✦✦✦

Paul Rodgers

b. Dec. 17, 1949, Middlesborough, England
Vocals, Guitar / Hard Rock, Blues-Rock

In a career that now spans three decades, vocalist, guitarist, and songwriter Paul Rodgers and his various groups have sold in excess of 125 million records around the world. Best known for his expressive vocals on songs that have become rock & roll staples, like "All Right Now," "Feel Like Makin' Love," "Can't Get Enough," and "Rock 'n' Roll Fantasy," Rodgers has been cited by dozens of '70s and '80s-era rock groups and musicians as a major influence. U.S. groups like the Black Crowes and Guns N' Roses have cited Rodgers and his various groups—Free, Bad Company, the Firm, the Law—as an influence on their styles. As a vocalist and songwriter, Rodgers had great admiration and respect for the classic African-American blues and R&B vocalists. Rodgers credits his father for buying him a guitar in his youth, but he later taught himself bass and piano as well. He began writing songs when he was in his early teens, before he had mastered any instrument.

Rodgers began playing out in clubs around Middlesborough, in northern England, when he was 13, taking singers like Rod Stewart as his role models. Right after he left school, he set out for London in a van with a band called the Roadrunners. The van broke down en route, and while the other members hitchhiked back north, Rodgers went south to London. After a short time he returned home to his parents, who were supportive of his musical endeavors. But having seen the club scene in London, he became determined to go back and make his mark there.

Returning to London, he formed the blues band Brown Sugar, deciding to see how far he could go as a vocalist, songwriter and guitarist. In the mid- and late '60s, London was in the midst of a huge blues revival, and Rodgers had the opportunity to see Muddy Waters and dozens of other American blues musicians perform at London's Marquee Club and other blues and R&B venues. Seeing Waters live had a lasting effect on Rodgers, and his early experiments, Brown Sugar and Free, started out as blues bands. Rodgers was working with Brown Sugar when guitarist Paul Kossoff heard him sing. Kossoff was so impressed with Rodgers' voice, the two decided to create a new band, joined by Simon Kirke on drums and bassist Andy Fraser. After seeing them at the Nags Head Pub in Battersea, Britain's godfather of blues, Alexis Korner, suggested they call themselves Free. A song Rodgers co-wrote with Fraser, "All Right Now," hit number one in twenty territories around the world in 1970. The song remains a rock staple, having been entered into ASCAP's "One Million" airplay singles club. By the early '70s, Free were one of the biggest-selling British blues-rock groups; by the time the band dissolved in 1973, they had achieved an uncanny level of superstar success: they had sold more than 20 million albums around the world and had played more than 700 arena and festival concerts.

In 1973, Rodgers formed Bad Company, then a prototype "supergroup," with King Crimson bassist Boz Burrell, Mott the Hoople guitarist Mick Ralphs, and Free drummer Simon Kirke. But this time, Rodgers learned from the mistakes he'd made with Free; he was determined to have bandmates who shared his musical vision—the overnight success that Free experienced put undue pressures on the personalities in the band. Rodgers contacted Peter Grant, Led Zeppelin's notorious manager, who was fortuitously starting Swan Song Records, the group's vanity label. By the close of the '70s, Bad Company had recorded six multi-platinum albums, which spurred classic blues-rock and rock staples like "Can't Get Enough," "Feel Like Makin' Love," "Shooting Star," and "Rock 'n' Roll Fantasy." By the time Bad Company called it quits, they had played to over 10 million people around the world and sold 30 million albums.

Other highlights of Rodgers' career include a show-stopping version of Otis Redding's "Sittin' on the Dock of the Bay" at Atlantic Records' 40th anniversary party at Madison Square Garden in 1988, and his formation of a new group with Jimmy Page of Led Zeppelin, the Firm, in the mid-'80s. Following that band's two albums, Rodgers formed the Law with former Small Faces/Who drummer Kenny Jones.

Since the early '80s, Rodgers has also released a handful of solo albums. They include *Cut Loose* (1983) and *The Morning After the Night Before/Northwind* (1984), both for Atlantic Records. His 1990s output includes *Muddy Water Blues: A Tribute to Muddy Waters* (1993, Victory Records) and *The Hendrix Set*, a mini-CD released that same year. *Muddy Water Blues* was nominated for a Grammy and features guest performances by Slash, Richie Sambora of Bon Jovi, Jeff Beck, Steve Miller, Buddy Guy, and Pink Floyd's David Gilmour. More recently, Rodgers put together a backing band featuring guitarist Geoff Whitehorn, bassist Jaz Lochrie, and drummer Jim Copley, recording *Paul Rodgers Live* (1996) and *Paul Rodgers Now* (1997) for the New York-based Velvel Records. After a Bad Company reunion in 1999, Rodgers switched over to CMC International, issuing the album *Electric* in 2000. —*Richard Skelly*

Cut Loose / 1983 / Atlantic ✦✦✦

After the disappointing 1982 release *Rough Diamonds*, Bad Company split up and vocalist Paul Rodgers focused on his solo album *Cut Loose*. It's a "solo" album in every sense of the word; Rodgers wrote, produced, sang, and played every single note. Yep, besides highlighting his miraculous voice, *Cut Loose* features Rodgers playing guitar, keyboards, bass guitar, and drums. It's a competent release and it features some good songs, but one wonders how much better it could have been if he had interacted with other musicians. In a way, *Cut Loose* is almost like a demo tape. Sometimes individual songs lack dynamics because Rodgers bases them on repeating guitar or piano lines, and his bass playing is effective, but his drumming is rudimentary. "Fragile" is a decent, midtempo rock & roll song. "Cut Loose" has an upbeat, funky feel with a guitar riff that doubles Rodgers' vocals. "Rising Sun" is the most sophisticated and impressive song on the album; its fast, dramatic piano lines and biting guitar solo stand out. The breezy "Morning After the Night Before" is based on clever lyrics about life on the road. (It's an interesting companion to Bad Company's "Movin' On," which was written by guitarist Mick Ralphs.) The haunting arrangement on "Northwinds" is also noteworthy. The piano and organ parts add depth to Rodgers' gut-wrenching vocals. Two songs on *Cut Loose* have interesting histories. "Superstar Woman" is a re-recorded version of a previously unreleased Bad Company tune. (It was finally issued on 1999's *The 'Original' Bad Company Anthology*.)

Also, Rodgers and Led Zeppelin's Jimmy Page re-recorded "Live in Peace" for the Firm's 1986 album *Mean Business*. —*Bret Adams*

● **Muddy Water Blues: A Tribute to Muddy Waters** / 1993 / Victory ✦✦✦✦

Paul Rodgers' tribute to Muddy Waters is not a return to Waters electric Chicago blues, but a continuation of the blues-rock of Rodgers' old bands, Free and Bad Company. Taken on those terms, *Muddy Water Blues: A Tribute to Muddy Waters* works only when Rodgers is matched with a good blues-rock guitarist. Jeff Beck, Buddy Guy, and Gary Moore all play well, while Richie Sambora, Neal Schon, and Trevor Rabin all sound a bit lost; the rest, including David Gilmour and Brian May, fall somewhere in between. —*Stephen Thomas Erlewine*

The Hendrix Set / Nov. 2, 1993 / Victory Music ✦✦✦

Paul Rodgers and Company's *The Hendrix Set* is a five-song EP of Jimi Hendrix Experience covers recorded live at Bayfront Park in Miami, FL, on July 4, 1993. Joining the Free and Bad Company vocalist are Journey guitarist Neal Schon and bassist Todd Jensen and drummer Deen Castronovo. Schon played with Jensen and Castronovo in Hardline and with Castronovo in Bad English. *The Hendrix Set* is fairly enjoyable, but it's surprising that this vanity project—no matter how sincere—was released. In fact, it never even charted. Then again, Rodgers was honoring his influences at the time, hence the 1993 Muddy Waters' tribute *Muddy Water Blues*. The five songs here are "Purple Haze," "Stone Free," "Little Wing," "Manic Depression," and "Foxy Lady." Rodgers is strict with some vocal interpretations while much looser on others. Schon recreates Hendrix's guitar tone and riffs faithfully, but he does show off and shred regularly, too. The unsung key to recreating Hendrix's sound is Castronovo's sharp, tinny drum sound, which closely copies that of Jimi Hendrix Experience drummer Mitch Mitchell. The tempo of "Purple Haze" is a little too slow at times. "Stone Free" is the best track by far. Rodgers' singing is excellent and Schon, Jensen and Castronovo are solid. The best part occurs when the band turns the song into an uncredited medley by shifting briefly and smoothly into Hendrix's "Third Stone from the Sun" while Rodgers sings part of Cream's "I Feel Free." This practice is repeated on "Little Wing" when Rodgers includes a few lines from Hendrix's "Angel" at the end. Rodgers fans will likely appreciate *The Hendrix Set*. —*Bret Adams*

Now & Live / Jun. 17, 1997 / Velvel ✦✦✦

In a career dating back to 1968, *Now* was only Paul Rodgers' second solo album of original material, following 1983's *Cut Loose*. Of course, in that time he fronted Free, Bad Company, the Firm and the Law, and in the early '90s crafted tributes to Muddy Waters and Jimi Hendrix, so he wasn't exactly idle. *Now* was an album for Free and Bad Company fans, recreating those groups' guitar/bass/drums backing and bluesy hard rock sound. It has always been amazing that a singer as distinctive as Rodgers, whose gruff voice can be identified within seconds, has remained anonymous behind his group monikers. And it is doubly surprising since Rodgers has always performed the same kind of simple, driving rock. *Now* was more of the same: as a songwriter, Rodgers' lyrics rarely moved far from expressions of love and longing, and as a composer he never moved beyond a few basic chords. What mattered, of course, was that voice, and it was as powerful on *Now* as it had ever been. For good measure, the CD included a second bonus disc containing a 1995 live performance at which Rodgers performed Free and Bad Company favorites, an appropriate accompaniment to the essentially similar new material. —*William Ruhlmann*

Electric / Jun. 6, 2000 / CMC International ✦✦✦

If you didn't know that *Electric* was completed in 2000, you could easily assume that it was recorded back in the '70s. That's because this solo offering isn't much different from the recordings that Paul Rodgers made with Bad Company and Free during his youth. Instead of trying to be relevant to the alternative rock scene of 2000 like some veteran rockers have done, Rodgers excels by sticking with what he does best: '70s-type arena rock that is slick and bluesy at the same time. "Freedom," "Deep Blue," "Jasmine Flower," and other selections don't break any new ground for the British singer (who wrote and produced all of the material himself), and *Electric* will hardly be considered cutting-edge by 2000 standards. But Rodgers doesn't need to be innovative in the 21st century; arena rock is his forte, and on this CD, he sings it with a lot of feeling. Although *Electric* isn't quite in a class with Bad Company's *Straight Shooter* album of 1975 or Rodgers' best work with Free in the early '70s, it's a respectable, sincere effort that the rocker's hardcore fans will easily appreciate. —*Alex Henderson*

Rogers & Buffalo

Group / Acoustic Blues, Slide Guitar Blues

Slide guitarist/producer Roy Rogers and harmonica maestro Norton Buffalo teamed up for a one-off side project with surprisingly down-home results. —*Cub Koda*

● **R&B** / 1991 / Blind Pig ✦✦✦✦

R&B is straight out of the Sonny Terry & Brownie McGee book—a set of stripped-down acoustic blues. Roy Rogers and Norton Buffalo both play with surprising grit and unsurprising affection, making it a very pleasurable tribute. —*Thom Owens*

Travellin' Tracks / 1992 / Blind Pig ✦✦✦

Jimmy Rogers (James A. Lane)

b. Jun. 3, 1924, Ruleville, MS, **d.** Dec. 19, 1997
Guitar / Electric Chicago Blues, Chicago Blues

Guitarist Jimmy Rogers was the last living connection to the groundbreaking first Chicago band of Muddy Waters (informally dubbed the Headhunters for their penchant of dropping by other musicians' gigs and "cutting their heads" with a superior onstage performance). Instead of basking in worldwide veneration, he was merely a well-respected Chicago elder boasting a seminal '50s Chess Records catalog, both behind Waters and on his own.

Born James A. Lane (Rogers was his stepdad's surname), the guitarist grew up all over: Mississippi, Atlanta, West Memphis, Memphis, and St. Louis. Actually, Rogers started out on harp as a teenager. Big Bill Broonzy, Joe Willie Wilkins, and Robert Jr. Lockwood all influenced Rogers, the latter two when he passed through Helena. Rogers settled in Chicago during the early '40s and began playing professionally around 1946, gigging with Sonny Boy Williamson, Sunnyland Slim, and Broonzy.

Rogers was playing harp with guitarist Blue Smitty when Muddy Waters joined them. When Smitty split, Little Walter was welcomed into the configuration, Rogers switched over to second guitar, and the entire postwar Chicago blues genre felt the stylistic earthquake that directly followed. Rogers made his recorded debut as a leader in 1947 for the tiny Ora-Nelle logo, then saw his efforts for Regal and Apollo lay unissued.

Those labels' monumental errors in judgment were the gain of Leonard Chess, who recognized the comparatively smooth-voiced Rogers' potential as a blues star in his own right. (He first played with Muddy Waters on an Aristocrat 78 in 1949 and remained his indispensable rhythm guitarist on wax into 1955.) With Walter and bassist Big Crawford laying down support, Rogers' debut Chess single in 1950, "That's All Right," has earned standard status after countless covers, but his version still reigns supreme.

Rogers' artistic quality was remarkably high while at Chess. "The World Is in a Tangle," "Money, Marbles and Chalk," "Back Door Friend," "Left Me With a Broken Heart," "Act like You Love Me," and the 1954 rockers "Sloppy Drunk" and "Chicago Bound" are essential early-'50s Chicago blues.

In 1955, Rogers left Muddy Waters to venture out as a bandleader, cutting another gem, "You're the One," for Chess. He made his only appearance on Billboard's R&B charts in early 1957 with the driving "Walking by Myself," which boasted a stunning harp solo from Big Walter Horton (a last-second stand-in for no-show Good Rockin' Charles). The tune itself was an adaptation of a T-Bone Walker tune, "Why Not," that Rogers had played rhythm guitar on when Walker cut it for Atlantic.

By 1957, blues was losing favor at Chess, the label reaping the rewards of rock via Chuck Berry and Bo Diddley. Rogers' platters slowed to a trickle, though his 1959 Chess farewell, "Rock This House," ranked with his most exciting outings (Reggie Boyd's light-fingered guitar wasn't the least of its charms).

Rogers virtually retired from music for a time during the '60s, operating a West Side clothing shop that burned down in the aftermath of Dr. Martin Luther King Jr.'s tragic assassination. He returned to the studio in 1972 for Leon Russell's Shelter logo, cutting his first LP, *Gold Tailed Bird* (with help from the Aces and Freddie King). There were a few more fine albums—notably *Ludella*, a 1990 set for Antone's—but Rogers never fattened his discography nearly as much as some of his contemporaries have. Jimmy's son, Jimmy D. Lane, played rhythm guitar in his dad's band and fronts a combo of his own on the side. Rogers died December 19, 1997. At the time of his death, he was working on an all-star project featuring contributions from Eric Clapton, Taj Mahal, Robert Plant and Jimmy Page, and Mick Jagger and Keith Richards; upon its completion, the disc was issued posthumously in early 1999 under the title *Blues, Blues, Blues*. —*Bill Dahl*

Gold Tailed Bird / 1972 / Shelter ✦✦✦

Rogers' attempt to break through to a new, younger audience was less exciting than his Chess years but plausible nonetheless. —*Bill Dahl*

Sloppy Drunk / Dec. 8, 1973-Dec. 15, 1973 / Evidence ✦✦✦

Blues legend Jimmy Rogers had not worked steadily prior to cutting these early-'70s tracks since 1960. His return on this session's 16 tracks, originally recorded for Black and Blue and now reissued on CD by Evidence, was not a heralded one because there was not much mainstream attention paid to blues at the time. But Rogers' voice was in above-average shape; his sound, range, and tone were anguished and expressed with vigor and clarity. While Willie Mabon's tinkling piano chords and figures moved in and out of loping arrangements, Rogers played easy, penetrating fills, never trying for spectacular effects but nicely punctuating his leads. —*Ron Wynn*

That's All Right / 1974 / Black & Blue ✦✦

Living the Blues / 1976 / Vogue ✦✦

Bluemasters / 1976 / Chess ✦✦✦✦✦

This fine two-LP compilation of his early Chess sides deserves CD reissue soon. —*Bill Dahl*

★ **Chicago Bound** / 1976 / MCA/Chess ✦✦✦✦✦

Starkly printed in black and white with washed-out, grainy photographs, this is one heavy slab of blues by a player who is not as well-known as he should be. Guitarist Jimmy Rogers was usually overshadowed by the leaders he worked for, Muddy Waters particularly. He was also sometimes confused with the hillbilly singer Jimmie Rodgers, and although they might have sounded good together, they don't have anything in common. This reissue collection grabs 14 tracks done at various times in the mostly early '50s which involve practically a who's who of performers associated with the most intense and driving Chicago blues. This includes the aforementioned Waters, leaving behind his role as leader for a few numbers to add some stinging guitar parts. There is also a pair of harmonica players, each of whom could melt vinyl siding with their playing. These are the Walters, big and little, as in Big Walter Horton and Little Walter. Pianist Otis Spann, bassist Willie Dixon, and drummer Fred Below are also on hand, meaning the rhythm section action is first class. Blues listeners who have only skimmed the surface of the music may not have really discovered Rogers, as his reputation increased in the years after his death and he had nowhere near the following and status of Waters or even Little Walter. Some of the tracks here are numbers the musicians got together and played with Rogers at the end of what was probably an already grueling session by Waters. "Sloppy Drunk" is a killer track that joins the long list of great blues numbers concerning the inebriated, while "Walking by Myself" is a fine example of the kind of shuffling rhythm these players are so good at. The CD era was an opportunity to put together larger selections of Rogers' material, complete with outtakes and selections that are much rarer than the material here. If listeners' reactions to this album are as positive as they ought to be, they

can be assured the pickings will be equally tasty if they decide to go for more extensive documentation of this artist. —*Eugene Chadbourne*

Live / 1982 / JSP ✦✦

Feelin' Good / 1985 / Blind Pig ✦✦✦✦

This Blind Pig CD reissues material from 1983-1984. The legendary veteran Jimmy Rogers (taking most of the vocals and occasional guitar solos) is heard teamed up with the talented harmonica player Rod Piazza and his jumping group. The results are consistently exciting. Piazza's harmonica serves as a perfect foil to Rogers' voice, and the impressive backup band (which also features Honey Piazza on piano) clearly enjoys jamming on the basic blues changes. The many strong solos and the superior material make this an easily recommended set. —*Scott Yanow*

☆ **That's All Right** / 1989 / Charly ✦✦✦✦✦

Quite a few important items from Rogers' classic Chess catalog that aren't on *Chicago Bound* turn up on this 24-track British import (along with the prerequisite hits, natch), notably a torrid "Rock This House" (Reggie Boyd's mercurial guitar solos are stunning), the downcast "The World's in a Tangle," a rhumba-beat "My Baby Don't Love Me No More" with a tremendous Big Walter Horton harp solo, and the bizarre "My Last Meal." —*Bill Dahl*

Ludella / 1990 / Antone's ✦✦✦✦

One of the most enriching contemporary items in Rogers' growing album catalog. Combining studio tracks with live performances, the set trods heavily on the past with loving renditions of "Rock This House," "Ludella," "Sloppy Drunk," and "Chicago Bound." Kim Wilson proves a worthy harp disciple of Little Walter, while bassist Bob Stroger and drummer Ted Harvey lay down supple grooves behind the blues great. —*Bill Dahl*

Chicago's Jimmy Rogers Sings the Blues / 1990 / DCC ✦✦✦

Blue Bird / 1994 / Analogue Production Originals ✦✦✦✦

This was Jimmy Rogers' last "proper" Chicago blues album, and it deservedly won a W.C. Handy Award in 1995. There are no moonlighting rock stars here; they would come out in droves for Rogers' subsequent album *Blues Blues Blues*. And with the exception of the last track—which is basically pianist Johnnie Johnson showing off for eight minutes—Rogers sits squarely in the spotlight for the duration of *Blue Bird*. As expected, Rogers revisits a fair amount of his earlier repertoire ("Walking By Myself," "I Lost a Good Woman"), but he also digs up several original tunes that he had never gotten around to recording until now. Throw in a few Chicago standards ("Big Boss Man," "Rock Me," "Smokestack Lightning"), and you have a solid, laid-back, and tremendously satisfying album by one of the underrated masters. The backing band is a mix of Chicago blues brethren (Carey Bell on harp, Dave Myers on bass, Ted Harvey on drums) and family (Rogers' son Jimmy D. Lane on lead guitar), plus Johnson, who is perhaps a rock star by association since he played with Chuck Berry for 18 years. This one's a must-have. —*Ken Chang*

With Ronnie Earl and the Broadcasters / 1994 / Bullseye Blues ✦✦✦

Despite Earl's love and mastery of the '50s Chicago sound and Rogers' still-sharp talents, there's something about this live set that never really takes flight. Maybe it was just a matter of the two factions not being totally familiar with one another, but something's missing in the sparks department. —*Bill Dahl*

Complete Shelter Recordings: Chicago Blues Masters, Vol. 2 / Oct. 24, 1995 / Capitol ✦✦✦✦✦

Rogers reemerged after a long layoff with a 1972 album for Leon Russell's Shelter label called *Gold Tailed Bird*. It wasn't the equivalent of his immortal Chess stuff, but the Shelter sides, here in their entirety, are pretty decent themselves (and no wonder, with the Aces, Freddie King, and reliable Chicago pianist Bob Riedy all involved). A few extra numbers not on the original Shelter LP make this 18-song set even more solid. —*Bill Dahl*

Complete Chess Recordings (Chess 50th Anniversary) / Apr. 8, 1997 / Chess ✦✦✦✦

While the 1976 issue of *Chicago Bound*, the first collection of Jimmy Rogers' Chess material, has been rightly hailed as a definitive cornerstone in absorbing the history of early Chicago blues, sadly, that vinyl album has been out of print for a number of years with virtually nothing in the catalog to take its place. Until now. This two-CD (in a single-disc package) anthology collects up everything that appeared on *Chicago Bound*, a number of notable cuts from a two-vinyl-disc anthology that was barely released in the late '70s, and no less than ten unreleased alternate takes from a variety of sessions with one of them, "Ludella," emanating from his first solo session in 1950. The singing, playing, and songwriting is virtually a textbook for the early Chicago style, as the players involved include Muddy Waters, Little Walter, Otis Spann, Willie Dixon, and Big Walter Horton, with all but Horton and Dixon regular mainstays of Muddy's original band, the blueprint of the early electric band sound. While some novices will find a two-disc set perhaps more than they want to pop for, this is as good as '50s Chicago blues gets, and no collection should really be without this one. —*Cub Koda*

Blues Blues Blues / Oct. 27, 1998 / Atlantic ✦✦✦✦

Jimmy Rogers was very much a musician's musician—the kind of guitarist that earned accolades from contemporaries and successors alike, yet never wins a wide, mainstream audience. *Blues Blues Blues* was designed as the album that would find Rogers a larger audience, and as such, it has all the bells and whistles of a big-deal blues album. It has the classics ("Trouble No More," "Bright Lights, Big City," "Sweet Home Chicago," "Don't Start Me to Talkin'"), remakes of Rogers standards ("Ludella," "That's All Right"), cult covers (Muddy Waters' "Blow Wind Blow," which kicks off the album on just the right note) and an astounding number of guest appearances, including cameos from (get ready): Jimmy Page and Robert Plant, Keith Richards and Mick Jagger, Lowell Fulson, Johnnie

Johnson, Eric Clapton, Taj Mahal, Ted Harvey, Carey Bell, Stephen Stills, and Jeff Healey. That's a lot of star power—too much so, as a matter of fact, since they occasionally overwhelm Rogers himself. And it has to be said that Rogers' playing simply isn't as dynamic or overpowering as it once was. Nevertheless, when it's judged alongside other contemporary electric blues albums, *Blues Blues Blues* holds up very well. Like its peers, such as John Lee Hooker's Point Blank recordings, the record is slick and well-crafted—it may be blues-lite, but it's highly enjoyable. And it's likely that it would have broken Rogers' career wide open, if he had lived to see its release. Knowing that makes *Blues Blues Blues* a little bittersweet. Yes, it's enjoyable, but it would have been great to hear Rogers really tear it up on his final record. *—Stephen Thomas Erlewine*

Roy Rogers

b. Jul. 28, 1950, Redding, CA

Producer, Slide Guitar, Vocals, Guitar / Contemporary Blues, Slide Guitar Blues, Modern Electric Blues, Modern Acoustic Blues

A northern California-based blues guitarist, Roy Rogers works firmly out of a Delta blues acoustic style and is particularly good with a slide. A member of John Lee Hooker's '80s Coast to Coast Band, Rogers produced and played on Hooker's Grammy-winning album, *The Healer* and its follow-up, *Mr. Lucky*.

During the early '70s, Rogers played with a variety of Bay Area bar bands. In 1976, he and harpist David Burgin recorded *A Foot in the Door*, which was released on Waterhouse Records. For the next few years, he played in various bands before he formed his own, the Delta Rhythm Kings, in 1980. Two years later, John Lee Hooker asked Rogers to join his Coast to Coast Band and the guitarist accepted.

Rogers stayed with Hooker for four years, leaving in 1986. That same year, he released his debut album, *Chops Not Chaps*, on Blind Pig Records. The record was successful with blues audiences and was nominated for a W.C. Handy Award. In 1987, he released his second solo album, *Slidewinder*, which was followed two years later by *Blues on the Range*. In 1990, Rogers produced John Lee Hooker's Grammy-winning comeback album, *The Healer*. The following year, he produced Hooker's *Mr. Lucky*, which also won a Grammy.

In 1991, Roy Rogers recorded a duet album, *R&B*, with harmonica player Norton Buffalo. The following year, the duo released another record, *Travellin' Tracks*. Rogers' output lagged in the mid-'90s, but he worked steadily at the end of the decade, performing concerts across America and recording albums like 1996's *Rhythm & Groove* and 1998's *Pleasure and Pain*. He recorded an album in 2001 with Shana Morrison (Van Morrison's daughter) and released an instrumental album entitled *Slideways* in 2002. A duet album with Norton Buffalo appeared later that year called *Roots of Our Nature*. *—Stephen Thomas Erlewine*

Chops Not Chaps / Sep. 1986 / Blind Pig ✦✦✦

Roy Rogers' debut, *Chops Not Chaps*, is a fine blues-rock album, driven by his dynamite slide guitar. The album alternates between covers of blues classics and originals that are effective, but not particularly remarkable. Nevertheless, the quality of Rogers' performance makes this an impressive and memorable debut. *—Thom Owens*

● **Slidewinder** / 1988 / Blind Pig ✦✦✦✦✦

Slidewinder is one of Roy Rogers' best albums, a collection of smoking hot contemporary blues, ranging from jacked-up rocking boogie numbers and dirty Chicago blues to stripped-down acoustic numbers. It all works equally well, especially the two stellar duets with pianist Allen Toussaint. *—Thom Owens*

Blues on the Range / 1989 / Blind Pig ✦✦✦

Blues on the Range is a nice, but not particularly noteworthy, set of traditional blues. What makes the album worth a listen is Rogers' facility as a slide player—he can make his guitar sing. However, the quality of the songs and performances are slightly uneven, making it only of interest to diehard fans. *—Thom Owens*

R&B / 1991 / Blind Pig ✦✦

Slide of Hand / Jul. 27, 1993 / Liberty ✦✦✦

Slide Zone / 1994 / Capitol ✦✦✦✦

Roy Rogers is somewhat of a rarity in contemporary blues; he's not only a monstrous guitar player, but is also possessed of a distinctive singing voice. In addition, he differentiates himself from the Chicago-style hordes by concentrating primarily on Delta-influenced slide guitar. By no means simply a revivalist, however, he's managed to take the best of Son House and create a unique style that is much more than the sum of its influences. Often sounding like the swamp-bred offspring of Ry Cooder and the Allman Brothers, Rogers (along with bassist Steve Evans and drummer Mike Hyman) opens the album with a pair of furiously funky, syncopated stompers. From there, he explores myriad roots styles, moving from moody instrumental jazz to hyper-speed rockabilly to Béla Fleck banjo duets with equal facility. Like Duane Allman, Rogers uses the slide to play real melodies, not tired old Lightnin' Hopkins licks, and his versatility with the technique is nothing short of astonishing. Overall, though, his greatest strengths lie not in his chops nor in his commitment to authenticity, but in his sincerity; it's obvious in every note that the guy really loves this music, whether it's actually blues or not. Strangely, though (especially since he's a white boy from California), Roy Rogers often sounds more "bluesy" than contemporaries like Keb' Mo' and Alvin Youngblood Hart. *—Pemberton Roach*

Rhythm & Groove / Apr. 1996 / Pointblank ✦✦✦

Pleasure and Pain / Jun. 2, 1998 / Pointblank ✦✦✦

Caught between the blues and rock, *Pleasure and Pain* is an odd and appropriately titled effort from Roy Rogers. He's at his best when he's turning out modernized Delta blues, either acoustically or on electric, but this album moves a little too close to blues-rock, as on the awkward "You Can't Stop Now," which features Sammy Hagar on vocals. The tendency toward overdriven blues-rock and funky workouts hampers the album, but there's also some fine straight blues playing that makes the record worth a listen for longtime Rogers fans. *—Thom Owens*

Everybody's Angel / Dec. 23, 1999 / Roshan ✦✦

Slideways / Mar. 26, 2002 / Evidence ✦✦✦

Roots of Our Nature / Aug. 13, 2002 / Blind Pig ✦✦✦

In an intimate acoustic setting, Buffalo and Rogers present a set of original tunes whose flavor suggests roots much further back in time. Aside from a few tasteful string parts, *Roots* is all about crisp fingerpicked and slide guitar, Buffalo's earthy and expressive harmonica, and each artist's agreeably unpolished vocals. Their lyrics embrace traditional imagery, from saloon balladry to ramblin' songs. On "Trinity" the words sustain an especially rustic eloquence through multiple verses dedicated to visions of salvation. If retro affectation bothers you, it's best to imagine this session transpiring on some snowy night, within the glow of an iron stove at some crossroads general store. When heard on these terms, *Roots* can cast a spell to remember. *—Robert L. Doerschuk*

Walter Roland

b. 1900, Alabama

Piano / Prewar Country Blues, Boogie-Woogie, Piano Blues

Despite a relatively prolific recording career that yielded upwards of 40 solo sides in addition to a series of celebrated collaborations with vocalist Lucille Bogan, pianist/singer Walter Roland remains one of the blues' most elusive and mysterious figures. Likely born in or around Birmingham, AL, circa 1900, he first emerged on the city's blues circuit during the '20s, presumably running in the same circles as the equally enigmatic pianist Jabo Williams; a skilled, versatile pianist whose repertoire ran the gamut from slow, gut-wrenching blues to exuberant boogie-woogies, Roland was also a persuasive vocalist and even a fine guitarist. He went to New York City three times between 1933 and 1935 to record for ARC; during this same period he also accompanied Bogan (by now calling herself Bessie Jackson), additionally recording with Sonny Scott and Josh White. After 1935, however, Roland seems to have dropped off the face of the earth—his subsequent activities and ultimate fate remain unknown. *—Jason Ankeny*

● **Complete Recorded Works, Vol. 1 (1933)** / Jun. 2, 1994 / Document ✦✦✦✦✦

The 23 selections on this Document CD were all recorded during a four-day period. Walter Roland was a skillful pianist who was also an effective blues-based singer and even a fine guitarist. He is heard backing his vocals on solo performances (on piano or guitar), accompanying the vocals of Sonny Scott and on two joyous instrumentals ("Guitar Stomp" and "Railroad Stomp") as part of the Jolly Two, he holds his own on guitar duets with Scott. Lucille Bogan (who Roland regularly accompanied) pops up on two numbers where she comments (talking rather than singing) on the proceedings. Among the better selections on this enjoyable set of good-time music are "No Good Biddie," "Early This Morning," "Jookit Jookit," "Piano Stomp," "Whatcha Gonna Do," "Early This Morning," and the guitar duets. The second volume of Walter Roland recordings is worthwhile, too, but this is his definitive set. *—Scott Yanow*

Complete Recorded Works, Vol. 2 (1934–1935) / Jun. 2, 1994 / Document ✦✦✦✦

Unlike the first Walter Roland Document CD, there is a certain sameness to the 22 recordings (two previously unissued) on this second volume. Lucille Bogan makes comments on three numbers and Josh White (years before he became famous as a folksinger) plays background guitar on the last dozen numbers, but otherwise, the focus is completely on Roland. He sticks to piano this time (no departures on guitar), and all of the selections have his vocals and generally a similar medium-slow tempo. Although somewhat popular at the time, oddly enough, Walter Roland did not record again after 1935. The highlights of this program (which generally does hold one's interest) include "C.W.A. Blues," "Early in the Morning No. 2," "Bad Dream Blues," "I'm Gonna Shave You Dry," "S.O.L. Blues," and "Penniless Blues," but get *Vol. 1* first. *—Scott Yanow*

The Rolling Stones

f. Jan. 1963, London, England

Group / British Psychedelia, Album Rock, British Blues, Pop/Rock, Psychedelic, British Invasion, Hard Rock, Blues-Rock, Rock & Roll

By the time the Rolling Stones began calling themselves the World's Greatest Rock & Roll Band in the late '60s, they had already staked out an impressive claim on the title. As the self-consciously dangerous alternative to the bouncy Merseybeat of the Beatles in the British Invasion, the Stones had pioneered the gritty, hard-driving blues-based rock & roll that came to define hard rock. With his preening machismo and latent maliciousness, Mick Jagger became the prototypical rock frontman, tempering his macho showmanship with a detached, campy irony, while Keith Richards and Brian Jones wrote the blueprint for sinewy, interlocking rhythm guitars. Backed by the strong, yet subtly swinging rhythm section of bassist Bill Wyman and drummer Charlie Watts, the Stones became the breakout band of the British blues scene, eclipsing such contemporaries as the Animals and Them. Over the course of their career, the Stones never really abandoned blues, but as soon as they reached popularity in the U.K., they began experimenting musically, incorporating the British pop of contemporaries like the Beatles, Kinks, and Who into their sound. After a brief dalliance with psychedelia, the Stones re-emerged in the late '60s as a jaded, blues-soaked hard rock quintet. The Stones always flirted with the seedy side of rock & roll, but as the hippie dream began to break apart, they exposed and reveled in the new rock culture. It wasn't without difficulty, of course. Shortly after he was fired from the group, Jones was found dead in a swimming pool, while at a 1969 free concert at Altamont, a concertgoer was brutally killed during the Stones' show. But the Stones never stopped going. For the next 30 years, they continued to record and perform, and while their records weren't always blockbusters, they were never less than the most visible band of their era—certainly, none of their British peers continued to be as popular or productive as the Stones. And no band since has proven to have such a broad fan base or far-reaching popularity, and it is impossible to hear any of the groups that followed them without detecting some sort of influence, whether it was musical or aesthetic.

Throughout their career, Mick Jagger (vocals) and Keith Richards (guitar, vocals) remained at the core of the Rolling Stones. The pair initially met as children at Dartford Maypole County Primary School. They drifted apart over the next ten years, eventually making each other's acquaintance again in 1960, when they met through a mutual friend, Dick Taylor, who was attending Sidcup Art School with Richards. At the time, Jagger was studying at the London School of Economics and playing with Taylor in the blues band Little Boy Blue and the Blue Boys. Shortly afterward, Richards joined the band. Within a year, they had met Brian Jones (guitar, vocals), a Cheltenham native who had dropped out of school to play saxophone and clarinet. By the time he became a fixture on the British blues scene, Jones had already had a wild life. He ran away to Scandinavia when he was 16; by that time, he had already fathered two illegitimate children. He returned to Cheltenham after a few months, where he began playing with the Ramrods. Shortly afterward, he moved to London where he played in Alexis Korner's group, Blues Inc. Jones quickly decided he wanted to form his own group and advertised for members; among those he recruited was the heavyset blues pianist Ian Stewart.

As he played with his group, Jones also moonlighted under the name Elmo Jones at the Ealing Blues Club. At the pub, he became reacquainted with Blues Inc., which now featured drummer Charlie Watts, and, on occasion, cameos by Jagger and Richards. Jones became friends with Jagger and Richards, and they soon began playing together with Dick Taylor and Ian Stewart; during this time, Mick was elevated to the status of Blues Inc.'s lead singer. With the assistance of drummer Tony Chapman, the fledgling band recorded a demo tape. After the tape was rejected by EMI, Taylor left the band to attend the Royal College of Art; he would later form the Pretty Things. Before Taylor's departure, the group named themselves the Rolling Stones, borrowing the moniker from a Muddy Waters song.

The Rolling Stones gave their first performance at the Marquee Club in London on July 12, 1962. At the time, the group consisted of Jagger, Richards, Jones, pianist Ian Stewart, drummer Mick Avory, and Dick Taylor, who had briefly returned to the fold. Weeks after the concert, Taylor left again and was replaced by Bill Wyman, formerly of the Cliftons. Avory also left the group—he would later join the Kinks—and the Stones hired Tony Chapman, who proved to be unsatisfactory. After a few months of persuasion, the band recruited Charlie Watts, who had quit Blues Inc. to work at an advertising agency once the group's schedule became too hectic. By 1963, the band's lineup had been set, and the Stones began an eight-month residency at the Crawdaddy Club, which proved to substantially increase their fan base. It also attracted the attention of Andrew Loog Oldham, who became the Stones' manager, signing them from underneath Crawdaddy's Giorgio Gomelsky. Although Oldham didn't know much about music, he was gifted at promotion, and he latched upon the idea of fashioning the Stones as the bad-boy opposition to the clean-cut Beatles. At his insistence, the large yet meek Stewart was forced out of the group, since his appearance contrasted with the rest of the group. Stewart didn't disappear from the Stones; he became one of their key roadies and played on their albums and tours until his death in 1985.

With Oldham's help, the Rolling Stones signed with Decca Records, and that June, they released their debut single, a cover of Chuck Berry's "Come On." The single became a minor hit, reaching number 21, and the group supported it with appearances on festivals and package tours. At the end of the year, they released a version of Lennon-McCartney's "I Wanna Be Your Man" that soared into the Top 15. Early in 1964, they released a cover of Buddy Holly's "Not Fade Away," which shot to number three. "Not Fade Away" became their first American hit, reaching number 48 that spring. By that time, the Stones were notorious in their homeland. Considerably rougher and sexier than the Beatles, the Stones were the subject of numerous sensationalistic articles in the British press, culminating in a story about the band urinating in public. All of these stories cemented the Stones as a dangerous, rebellious band in the minds of the public, and had the effect of beginning a manufactured rivalry between them and the Beatles, which helped the group rocket to popularity in the U.S. In the spring of 1964, the Stones released their eponymous debut album, which was followed by "It's All Over Now," their first U.K. number one. That summer, they toured America to riotous crowds, recording the *Five By Five* EP at Chess Records in Chicago in the midst of the tour. By the time it was over, they had another number one U.K. single with Howlin' Wolf's "Little Red Rooster." Although the Stones had achieved massive popularity, Oldham decided to push Jagger and Richards into composing their own songs, since they—and his publishing company—would receive more money that away. In June of 1964, the group released their first original single, "Tell Me (You're Coming Back)," which became their first American Top 40 hit. Shortly afterward, a version of Irma Thomas' "Time Is on My Side" became their first U.S. Top Ten. It was followed by "The Last Time" in early 1965, a number one U.K. and Top Ten U.S. hit that began a virtually uninterrupted string of Jagger-Richards hit singles. Still, it wasn't until the group released "(I Can't Get No) Satisfaction" in the summer of 1965 that they were elevated to superstars. Driven by a fuzz-guitar riff designed to replicate the sound of a horn section, "Satisfaction" signaled that Jagger and Richards had come into their own as songwriters, breaking away from their blues roots and developing a signature style of big, bluesy riffs and wry, sardonic lyrics. It stayed at number one for four weeks and began a string of Top Ten singles that ran for the next two years, including such classics as "Get Off My Cloud," "19th Nervous Breakdown," "As Tears Go By," and "Have You Seen Your Mother, Baby, Standing in the Shadow?"

By 1966, the Stones had decided to respond to the Beatles' increasingly complex albums with their first album of all-original material, *Aftermath*. Due to Brian Jones' increasingly exotic musical tastes, the record boasted a wide range of influences, from the sitar-drenched "Paint It, Black" to the Eastern drones of "I'm Going Home." These eclectic influences continued to blossom on *Between the Buttons* (1967), the most pop-oriented album the group ever made. Ironically, the album's release was bookended by two of the most notorious incidents in the band's history. Before the record was released, the Stones performed the suggestive "Let's Spend the Night Together," the B-side to the medieval ballad "Ruby Tuesday," on *The Ed Sullivan Show*, which forced Jagger to alter the song's title to an incomprehensible mumble, or else face being banned. In February of 1967, Jagger and Richards were arrested for drug possession, and within three months, Jones was arrested on the same charge. All three were given suspended jail sentences, and the group backed away from the spotlight as the summer of love kicked into gear in 1967. Jagger, along with his then-girlfriend Marianne Faithfull, went with the Beatles to meet the Maharishi Mahesh Yogi; they were also prominent in the international broadcast of the Beatles' "All You Need Is Love." Appropriately, the Stones' next single, "Dandelion"/"We Love You," was a psychedelic pop effort, and it was followed by their response to *Sgt. Pepper, Their Satanic Majesties Request*, which was greeted with lukewarm reviews.

The Stones' infatuation with psychedelia was brief. By early 1968, they had fired Andrew Loog Oldham and hired Allen Klein as their manager. The move coincided with their return to driving rock & roll, which happened to coincide with Richards' discovery of open tunings, a move that gave the Stones their distinctively fat, powerful sound. The revitalized Stones were showcased on the malevolent single "Jumpin' Jack Flash," which climbed to number three in May 1968. Their next album, *Beggar's Banquet*, was finally released in the fall, after being delayed for five months due its controversial cover art of a dirty, graffiti-laden restroom. An edgy record filled with detours into straight blues and campy country, *Beggar's Banquet* was hailed as a masterpiece among the fledgling rock press. Although it was seen as a return to form, few realized that while it opened a new chapter of the Stones' history, it also was the closing of their time with Brian Jones. Throughout the recording of *Beggar's Banquet*, Jones was on the sidelines due to his deepening drug addiction and his resentment of the dominance of Jagger and Richards. Jones left the band on June 9, 1969, claiming to be suffering from artistic differences between himself and the rest of the band. On July 3, 1969—less than a month after his departure—Brian Jones was found dead in his swimming pool. The coroner ruled that it was "death by misadventure," yet his passing was the subject of countless rumors over the next two years.

By the time of his death, the Stones had already replaced Brian Jones with Mick Taylor, a former guitarist for John Mayall's Bluesbreakers. He wasn't featured on "Honky Tonk Women," a number one single released days after Jones' funeral, and he contributed only a handful of leads on their next album, *Let It Bleed*. Released in the fall of 1969, *Let It Bleed* was comprised of sessions with Jones and Taylor, yet it continued the direction of *Beggar's Banquet*, signaling that a new era in the Stones' career had begun, one marked by ragged music and an increasingly wasted sensibility. Following Jagger's filming of *Ned Kelly* in Australia during the first part of 1969, the group launched their first American tour in three years. Throughout the tour—the first where they were billed as the World's Greatest Rock & Roll Band—the group broke attendance records, but it was given a sour note when the group staged a free concert at Altamont Speedway. On the advice of the Grateful Dead, the Stones hired Hell's Angels as security, but that plan backfired tragically. The entire show was unorganized and in shambles, yet it turned tragic when the Angels killed a young black man, Meredith Hunter, during the Stones' performance. In the wake of the public outcry, the Stones again retreated from the spotlight and dropped "Sympathy for the Devil," which some critics ignorantly claimed incited the violence, from their set.

As the group entered hiatus, they released the live *Get Yer Ya-Ya's Out* in the fall of 1970. It was their last album for Decca/London, and they formed Rolling Stones Records, which became a subsidiary of Atlantic Records. During 1970, Jagger starred in Nicolas Roeg's cult film *Performance* and married Nicaraguan model Bianca Perez Morena de Macias, and the couple quickly entered high society. As Jagger was jet-setting, Richards was slumming, hanging out with country-rock pioneer Gram Parsons. Keith wound up having more musical influence on 1971's *Sticky Fingers*, the first album the Stones released though their new label. Following its release, the band retreated to France on tax exile, where they shared a house and recorded a double album, *Exile on Main St.* Upon its May 1972 release, *Exile on Main St.* was widely panned, but over time it came to be considered one of the group's defining moments.

Following *Exile*, the Stones began to splinter in two, as Jagger concentrated on being a celebrity and Richards sank into drug addiction. The band remained popular throughout the '70s, but their critical support waned. *Goats Head Soup*, released in 1973, reached number one, as did 1974's *It's Only Rock and Roll*, but neither record was particularly well-received. Taylor left the band after *It's Only Rock and Roll*, and the group recorded their next album as they auditioned new lead guitarists, including Jeff Beck. They finally settled on Ron Wood, former lead guitarist for the Faces and Rod Stewart, in 1976, the same year they released *Black and Blue*, which only featured Wood on a handful of cuts. During the mid- and late '70s, all the Stones pursued side projects, with both Wyman and Wood releasing solo albums with regularity. Richards was arrested in Canada in 1977 with his common-law wife Anita Pallenberg for heroin possession. After his arrest, he cleaned up and was given a suspended sentence the following year. The band reconvened in 1978 to record *Some Girls*, an energetic response to punk, new wave, and disco. The record and its first single, the thumping disco-rocker "Miss You," both reached number one, and the album restored the group's image. However, the group squandered that goodwill with the follow-up, *Emotional Rescue*, a number one record that nevertheless received lukewarm reviews upon its 1980 release. *Tattoo You*, released the following year, fared better both critically and commercially, as the singles "Start Me Up" and "Waiting on a Friend" helped the album spend nine weeks at number one. The Stones supported *Tattoo You* with an extensive stadium tour captured in Hal Ashby's movie *Let's Spend the Night Together* and the 1982 live album *Still Life*.

Tattoo You proved to be the last time the Stones completely dominated the charts and the stadiums. Although the group continued to sell out concerts in the '80s and '90s, their records didn't sell as well as previous efforts, partially because the albums suffered due to Jagger and Richards' notorious mid-'80s feud. Starting with 1983's *Undercover*, the duo conflicted about which way the band should go, with Jagger wanting the Stones to follow contemporary trends and Richards wanting them to stay true to their rock roots. As a result, *Undercover* was a mean-spirited, unfocused record that received relatively weak sales and mixed reviews. Released in 1986, *Dirty Work* suffered a worse fate, since Jagger was preoccupied with his fledgling solo career. Once Jagger decided that the Stones would not support *Dirty Work* with a tour, Richards decided to make his own solo record with

1988's *Talk Is Cheap*. Appearing a year after Jagger's failed second solo album, *Talk is Cheap* received good reviews and went gold, prompting Jagger and Richards to reunite late in 1988. The following year, the Stones released *Steel Wheels*, which was received with good reviews, but the record was overshadowed by its supporting tour, which grossed over $140 million dollars and broke many box office records. In 1991, the live album *Flashback*, which was culled from the *Steel Wheels* shows, was released.

Following the release of *Flashback*, Bill Wyman left the band; he published a memoir, *Stone Alone*, within a few years of leaving. The Stones didn't immediately replace Wyman, since they were all working on solo projects; this time, there was none of the animosity surrounding their mid-'80s projects. The group reconvened in 1994 with bassist Darryl Jones, who had previously played with Miles Davis and Sting, to record and release the Don Was-produced *Voodoo Lounge*. The album received the band's strongest reviews in years, and its accompanying tour was even more successful than the *Steel Wheels* tour. On top of being more successful than its predecessor, *Voodoo Lounge* also won the Stones their first Grammy for Best Rock Album. Upon the completion of the *Voodoo Lounge* tour, the Stones released the live, "unplugged" album *Stripped* in the fall of 1995. Similarly, after wrapping up their tour in support of 1997's *Bridges to Babylon*, the group issued yet another live set, *No Security*, the following year. *—Stephen Thomas Erlewine*

The Rolling Stones (England's Newest Hitmakers) / May 30, 1964 / ABKCO ✦✦✦✦✦

The group's debut album was the most uncompromisingly blues/R&B-oriented full-length recording they would ever release. Mostly occupied with covers, this was as hardcore as British R&B ever got; it's raw and ready. But the Stones succeeded in establishing themselves as creative interpreters, putting '50s and early '60s blues, rock, and soul classics (some quite obscure to white audiences) through a younger, more guitar-oriented filter. The record's highlighted by blistering versions of "Route 66," "Carol," the hypertempoed "I Just Want to Make Love to You," "I'm a King Bee," and "Walking the Dog." Their Bo Diddleyized version of Buddy Holly's "Not Fade Away" gave them their first British Top Ten hit (and their first small American one). The acoustic ballad "Tell Me" was Jagger-Richards' first good original tune, but the other group-penned originals were little more than rehashed jams of blues cliches, keeping this album from reaching truly classic status. *—Richie Unterberger*

☆ **12 × 5** / Oct. 17, 1964 / ABKCO ✦✦✦✦✦

The evolution from blues to rock accelerated with the Stones' second American LP. They turned soul into guitar rock for the hits "It's All Over Now" and "Time Is on My Side" (the latter of which was their first American Top Ten single). "2120 South Michigan Avenue" is a great instrumental blues-rock jam; "Around and Around" is one of their best Chuck Berry covers; and "If You Need Me" reflects an increasing contemporary soul influence. On the other hand, the group originals (except for the propulsive "Empty Heart") are weak and derivative, indicating that the band still had a way to go before they could truly challenge the Beatles' throne. *—Richie Unterberger*

☆ **The Rolling Stones Now!** / Apr. 1965 / ABKCO ✦✦✦✦✦

Although their third American album was patched together (in the usual British Invasion tradition) from a variety of sources, it's their best early R&B-oriented effort. Most of the Stones' early albums suffer from three or four very weak cuts; *Now!* is almost uniformly strong from start to finish, the emphasis being on some of their blackest material. The covers of "Down Home Girl," and Bo Diddley's vibrating "Mona," Otis Redding's "Pain in My Heart," and Barbara Lynn's "Oh Baby" are all among the group's best R&B interpretations. The best gem is "Little Red Rooster," a pure blues with wonderful slide guitar from Brian Jones (and a number one single in Britain, although it was only an album track in the U.S.). As songwriters, Jagger and Richards are still struggling, but they come up with one of their first winners (and an American Top 20 hit) with the yearning, soulful "Heart of Stone." *—Richie Unterberger*

Out of Our Heads [US] / Aug. 1965 / ABKCO ✦✦✦✦✦

In 1965, the Stones finally proved themselves capable of writing classic rock singles that mined their R&B/blues roots, but updated them into a more guitar-based, thoroughly contemporary context. The first enduring Jagger-Richards classics are here—"The Last Time," and its menacing, folky B-side "Play With Fire," and the riff-driven "Satisfaction," which made them superstars in the States and defined their sound and rebellious attitude better than any other single song. On the rest of the album, they largely opted for mid-'60s soul covers, Marvin Gaye's "Hitch Hike," Otis Redding's "Cry to Me," and Sam Cooke's "Good Times" being particular standouts. "I'm All Right" (based on a Bo Diddley sound) showed their 1965 sound at its rawest, and there are a couple of fun, though derivative, bluesy originals in "The Spider and the Fly" and "The Under Assistant West Coast Promotion Man." *—Richie Unterberger*

Out of Our Heads [UK] / Sep. 6, 1965 / ABKCO ✦✦✦✦✦

The usual assumption is that the British-issued Rolling Stones albums of the mid-'60s are, like the Beatles' British LPs of the same era, more accurate representations of the group and their work than their American equivalents; the latter were tailored to the U.S. market and usually had singles that had been recorded and released separately added to their programming. The reality, however, is that the group's British LPs were almost as much of a hodgepodge, but just devised differently. The U.K. version of *Out of Our Heads* actually came out later than its American counterpart by about a month and opens with the roaring, frenetic "She Said Yeah" rather than the soulful slowie "Mercy Mercy" (which follows it here). In place of "Satisfaction" and "The Last Time," listeners get "Oh Baby (We Got a Good Thing Going)" from five months earlier, "Heart of Stone" (which had already appeared in America on *The Rolling Stones Now!*), and "I'm Free" and "Talkin' 'Bout You," which would turn up in America on *December's Children*. To add to the confusion, the Gerard Mankowitz black-and-white cover shot (depicting the band looking as threatening as they ever would in this early phase of their history) used here would turn up in America three months later, also on the *December's Children* LP. The record is somewhat slapped together, but is superior to either of the American albums that it overlaps in balance. It's all good, solid, first-rate rock & roll and R&B, with a certain developing sophistication on songs like "I'm Free," and it flows better without any AM radio-oriented, riff-driven singles like "Satisfaction," "The Last Time," or "Get Off of My Cloud," or novelty numbers like "As Tears Go By" to break it up. Long out of print on LP and supplanted by its American version on CD, this album has turned up as a beautifully mastered and packaged expanded bootleg, complete with the original cover art. *—Bruce Eder*

December's Children (And Everybody's) / Dec. 1965 / ABKCO ✦✦✦✦✦

The last Stones album in which cover material accounted for 50 percent of the content was thrown together from a variety of singles, British LP tracks, outtakes, and a cut from an early 1964 U.K. EP. Haphazard assembly aside, much of it's great, including the huge hit "Get Off of My Cloud" and the controversial, string-laden acoustic ballad "As Tears Go By" (a Top Ten item in America). Raiding the R&B closet for the last time, they also offered a breathless run-through of Larry Williams' "She Said Yeah," a sultry Chuck Berry cover ("Talkin' About You"), and exciting live versions of "Route 66" and Hank Snow's "I'm Moving On." More importantly, Jagger-Richards' songwriting partnership had now developed to the extent that several non-A-side tracks were reasonably strong in their own right, such as "I'm Free" and "The Singer Not the Song." And the version of "You Better Move On" (which had been featured on a British EP at the beginning of 1964) was one of their best and most tender soul covers. *—Richie Unterberger*

Big Hits: High Tide and Green Grass / Mar. 1966 / ABKCO ✦✦✦✦✦

The first hits compilation of the Rolling Stones is still one of the most potent collections of singles that one can find. Listening to it in 1966 or today, one can understand how, almost prematurely for the '60s—as most of the material here dates from 1964 or 1965—the Stones set themselves up as the decade's most visible rock & roll rebels. The defiant, in-your-face fuzztone riff and sexually frustrated lyrics of "(I Can't Get No) Satisfaction" and the frenetic pounding punk anthem "Get Off of My Cloud" are highlights of a 12-song set that has no weak points, only peaks—the louder-than-life rhythm guitars on "It's All Over Now" and "The Last Time," the wailing R&B of "Time Is on My Side," the balladry, folk, and soul style of "As Tears Go By" and "Tell Me," and all of the rest make for a body of work that's still amazing to hear four decades after the fact. Appearing as it did in the late winter of 1966, this collection completely missed the group's drift into psychedelia, and it has since been supplanted by *Hot Rocks* and *More Hot Rocks*, but *Big Hits* is still the most concentrated dose of the early Stones at their most accessible that is to be had, short of simply playing their first five U.S. albums. The artwork and photography were pretty cool too, and the original LP had one of rock's early classic gatefold album designs. *—Bruce Eder*

☆ **Aftermath [UK]** / Apr. 15, 1966 / ABKCO ✦✦✦✦✦

The British version of *Aftermath* was released earlier than its American counterpart and had several differences beyond its cover design: it runs more than ten minutes longer, despite not having "Paint It Black" on it (singles were usually kept separate from LPs in England in those days), and it has four additional songs—"Mother's Little Helper," which was left off the U.S. album for release as a single; "Out of Time" in its full-length five-minute-36-second version, two minutes longer than the version of the song issued in America; "Take It or Leave It," which eventually turned up on *Flowers* in the U.S.; and "What to Do," which didn't surface in America until the release of *More Hot Rocks* more than six years later. Additionally, the song lineup is different, "Goin' Home" closing side one instead of side two. And the mixes used are different from the tracks that the two versions of the album do have in common—the U.K. album and CD used a much cleaner, quieter master that had a more discreet stereo sound, with wide separation in the two channels and the bass not centered, as it in the U.S. version. Thus, one gets a more vivid impression of the instruments. It's also louder, yet curiously, because of the cleaner sound, slightly less visceral in its overall impact, though the details in the playing revealed in the mixes may fascinate even casual listeners. It's still a great album, though the difference in song lineup makes it a different record; "Mother's Little Helper" is one of the more in-your-face drug songs of the period, as well as being a potent statement about middle-class hypocrisy and political inconsistency, and "Out of Time," "Take It Leave It" (which had been a hit for the Searchers), and "What to Do," if anything, add to the misogyny already on display in "Stupid Girl" and "Think," and "Out of Time" adds to the florid sound of the album's psychedelic component (and there's no good reason except for a plain oversight by the powers that be for the complete version of "Out of Time" never having been released in America). The British version of *Aftermath* (which was also released in mono on vinyl) has been available intermittently on CD since the late '80s as an import, and is worth tracking down. *—Bruce Eder*

☆ **Aftermath [US]** / Jun. 1966 / ABKCO ✦✦✦✦✦

The Rolling Stones finally delivered a set of all-original material with this LP, which also did much to define the group as the bad boys of rock & roll with their sneering attitude toward the world in general and the female sex in particular. The borderline misogyny could get a bit juvenile in tunes like "Stupid Girl." But on the other hand the group began incorporating the influences of psychedelia and Dylan into their material with classics like "Paint It Black," an eerily insistent number one hit graced by some of the best use of sitar (played by Brian Jones) on a rock record. Other classics included "Mother's Little Helper" (whose lyrics had extremely blatant and controversial drug references); Jones also added exotic accents with his vibes (on the jazzy "Under My Thumb") and dulcimer (the delicate Elizabethan ballad "Lady Jane"). Some of the material is fairly ho-hum, to be honest, as Jagger and Richards were still prone to inconsistent songwriting; "Goin' Home," a 11-minute blues jam, was remarkable more for its barrier-crashing length than its content. Look out for an obscure gem, however, in the brooding, meditative "I Am Waiting." *—Richie Unterberger*

Got Live if You Want It! / Nov. 4, 1966 / ABKCO ♦♦
A live document of the Brian Jones-era Stones sounds enticing, but the actual product is a letdown. The sound is lousy, and for that matter not all of it's live; a couple of old studio R&B covers were augmented by screaming fans that had obviously been overdubbed. Partially recorded at a 1966 Royal Albert Hall performance (where the audience rioted at the opening of the concert), the performances and singing are on the sloppy side (and sometimes alarmingly out of tune), the sound balance is atrocious, and several of the songs are taken at a let's-get-this-over-with-and-off-the-stage-before-we-get-torn-apart pace. It's a fun souvenir in its own way; just don't expect top-notch value, even factoring in the primitive state of live rock recording technology in 1966. *—Richie Unterberger*

☆ **Between the Buttons** / Jan. 1967 / ABKCO ♦♦♦♦♦
The Rolling Stones' 1967 recordings are a matter of some controversy; many critics felt that they were compromising their raw, rootsy power with trendy emulations of the Beatles, Kinks, Dylan, and psychedelic music. Approach this album with an open mind, though, and you'll find it to be one of their strongest, most eclectic LPs, with many fine songs that remain unknown to all but Stones devotees. The lyrics are getting better (if more savage), and the arrangements more creative, on brooding near-classics like "All Sold Out," "My Obsession," and "Yesterday's Papers." "She Smiled Sweetly" shows their hidden romantic side at its best, while "Connection" is one of the record's few slabs of conventionally driving rock. But the best tracks were the two songs that gave the group a double-sided number one in early 1967: the lustful "Let's Spend the Night Together" and the beautiful, melancholy "Ruby Tuesday," which is as melodic as anything Jagger and Richards would ever write. *—Richie Unterberger*

Flowers / Jun. 1967 / ABKCO ♦♦♦♦♦
Dismissed as a ripoff of sorts by some critics, as it took the patchwork bastardization of British releases for the American audience to extremes, gathering stray tracks from the U.K. versions of *Aftermath* and *Between the Buttons*, 1966-1967 singles (some of which had already been used on the U.S. editions of *Aftermath* and *Between the Buttons*), and a few outtakes. Judged solely by the music, though, it's rather great. "Lady Jane," "Ruby Tuesday," and "Let's Spend the Night Together" are all classics (although they had all been on an LP before); the 1966 single "Mother's Little Helper," a Top Ten hit, is also terrific; and "Have You Seen Your Mother, Baby, Standing in the Shadow?" making its first album appearance, is the early Stones at their most surrealistic and angst-ridden. A lot of the rest of the cuts rate among their most outstanding 1966-1967 work. "Out of Time" is hit-worthy in its own right (and in fact topped the British charts in an inferior cover by Chris Farlowe); "Back Street Girl," with its European waltz flavor, is one of *the* great underrated Stones songs. The same goes for the psychedelic Bo Diddley of "Please Go Home," and the acoustic, pensively sardonic "Sittin' on a Fence," with its strong Appalachian flavor. Almost every track is strong, so if you're serious about your Stones, don't pass this by just because a bunch of people slag it as an exploitative marketing trick (which it is). There's some outstanding material you can't get anywhere else, and the album as a whole plays very well from end to end. *—Richie Unterberger*

Their Satanic Majesties Request / Nov. 1967 / ABKCO ♦♦♦♦
Without a doubt, no Rolling Stones album—and, indeed, very few rock albums from any era—split critical opinion as much as the Rolling Stones' psychedelic outing. Many dismiss the record as sub-*Sgt. Pepper* posturing; others confess, if only in private, to a fascination with the album's inventive arrangements, which incorporated some African rhythms, mellotrons, and full orchestration. Never before or since did the Stones take so many chances in the studio. This writer, at least, feels that the record has been unfairly undervalued, partly because purists expect the Stones to constantly champion a blues 'n' raunch worldview. About half the material is very strong, particularly the glorious "She's a Rainbow," with its beautiful harmonies, piano, and strings; the riff-driven "Citadel"; the hazy, dream-like "In Another Land," Bill Wyman's debut writing (and singing) credit on a Stones release; and the majestically dark and doomy cosmic rocker "2000 Light Years from Home," with some of the creepiest synthesizer effects (devised by Brian Jones) ever to grace a rock record. The downfall of the album was caused by some weak songwriting on the lesser tracks, particularly the interminable psychedelic jam "Sing This All Together (See What Happens)." It's a much better record than most people give it credit for being, though, with a strong current of creeping uneasiness that undercuts the gaudy psychedelic flourishes. In 1968, the Stones would go back to the basics, and never wander down these paths again, making this all the more of a fascinating anomaly in the group's discography. *—Richie Unterberger*

☆ **Beggars Banquet** / Nov. 1968 / ABKCO ♦♦♦♦♦
The Stones forsook psychedelic experimentation to return to their blues roots on this celebrated album, which was immediately acclaimed as one of their landmark achievements. A strong acoustic Delta blues flavor colors much of the material, particularly "Salt of the Earth" and "No Expectations," which features some beautiful slide guitar work. Basic rock & roll was not forgotten, however: "Street Fighting Man," a reflection of the political turbulence of 1968, was one of their most innovative singles, and "Sympathy for the Devil," with its fire-dancing guitar licks, leering Jagger vocals, African rhythms, and explicitly satanic lyrics, was an image-defining epic. On "Stray Cat Blues," Jagger and crew began to explore the kind of decadent sexual sleaze that they would take to the point of self-parody by the mid-'70s. At the time, though, the approach was still fresh, and the lyrical bite of most of the material ensured *Beggars Banquet*'s place as one of the top blues-based rock records of all time. *—Richie Unterberger*

Through the Past, Darkly (Big Hits, Vol. 2) / Sep. 1969 / ABKCO ♦♦♦♦♦
This album was spawned by three coinciding events—the need to acknowledge the death of band co-founder Brian Jones (whose epitaph graces the inside cover) in July of 1969; the need to get "Honky Tonk Women," then a huge hit single, onto an LP; and to fill the ten-month gap since the release of *Beggars Banquet* and get an album with built-in appeal into stores ahead of the Stones' first American tour in three years. The fact that the Stones had amassed a sufficient number of hits since their last greatest-hits compilation in early 1966 (*Big Hits: High Tide and Green Grass*) made this a no-brainer, and its song lineup was as potent at the time as any compilation of hit singles by any artist. From the group's excursions into fey psychedelia ("Paint It Black," "Ruby Tuesday," "She's a Rainbow," "Dandelion"), space rock ("2000 Light Years from Home"), punk decadence ("Mother's Little Helper"), and back to straight-ahead rock & roll ("Jumpin' Jack Flash"), some of it with a topical edge ("Street Fighting Man"), it's all incredibly potent, though also redundant to the extent that "Ruby Tuesday" and "Let's Spend the Night Together" had previously appeared on two U.S. albums. The presence of "Honky Tonk Women" propelled it to gold record status upon release on both sides of the Atlantic, although the simultaneously released British version (long out of print, except as a bootleg CD) is different and more confusing, but also more diverse and rewarding musically than the American version. Both this album and *Big Hits: High Tide and Green Grass* have been supplanted by *Hot Rocks* and *More Hot Rocks*, but are still handy in their tight respective focuses. *—Bruce Eder*

☆ **Let It Bleed** / Nov. 28, 1969 / ABKCO ♦♦♦♦♦
Mostly recorded without Brian Jones—who died several months before its release (although he does play on two tracks) and was replaced by Mick Taylor (who also plays on just two songs)—this extends the rock & blues feel of *Beggar's Banquet* into slightly harder-rocking, more demonically sexual territory. The Stones were never as consistent on album as their main rivals, the Beatles, and *Let It Bleed* suffers from some rather perfunctory tracks, like "Monkey Man" and a countrified remake of the classic "Honky Tonk Woman" (here titled "Country Honk"). Yet some of the songs are among their very best, especially "Gimme Shelter," with its shimmering guitar lines and apocalyptic lyrics; the harmonica-driven "Midnight Rambler"; the druggy party ambience of the title track; and the stunning "You Can't Always Get What You Want," which was the Stones' "Hey Jude" of sorts, with its epic structure, horns, philosophical lyrics, and swelling choral vocals. "You Got the Silver" (Keith Richards' first lead vocal) and Robert Johnson's "Love in Vain," by contrast, were as close to the roots of acoustic down-home blues as the Stones ever got. *—Richie Unterberger*

Get Yer Ya-Ya's Out / Sep. 4, 1970 / ABKCO ♦♦♦♦♦
Recorded during their American tour in late 1969, and centered around live versions of material from the *Beggars Banquet-Let It Bleed* era. Often acclaimed as one of the top live rock albums of all time, its appeal has dimmed a little today. The live versions are reasonably different from the studio ones, but ultimately not as good, a notable exception being the long workout of "Midnight Rambler," with extended harmonica solos and the unforgettable section where the pace slows to a bump-and-grind crawl. Some Stones aficionados, in fact, prefer a bootleg from the same tour (*Liver Than You'll Ever Be*, to which this album was unleashed in response), or their amazing the-show-must-go-on performance in the jaws of hell at Altamont (preserved in the *Gimme Shelter* film). Fans who are unconcerned with picky comparisons such as these will still find *Ya-Ya's* an outstanding album, and it's certainly the Stones' best official live recording. *—Richie Unterberger*

☆ **Sticky Fingers** / Apr. 23, 1971 / Virgin ♦♦♦♦♦
Pieced together from outtakes and much-labored-over songs, *Sticky Fingers* manages to have a loose, ramshackle ambience that belies both its origins and the dark undercurrents of the songs. It's a weary, drug-laden album—well over half the songs explicitly mention drug use, while the others merely allude to it—that never fades away, but it barely keeps afloat. Apart from the classic opener, "Brown Sugar" (a gleeful tune about slavery, interracial sex, and lost virginity, not necessarily in that order), the long workout "Can't You Hear Me Knocking" and the mean-spirited "Bitch," *Sticky Fingers* is a slow, bluesy affair, with a few country touches thrown in for good measure. The laid-back tone of the album gives ample room for new lead guitarist Mick Taylor to stretch out, particularly on the extended coda of "Can't You Hear Me Knocking." But the key to the album isn't the instrumental interplay—although that is terrific—it's the utter weariness of the songs. "Wild Horses" is their first non-ironic stab at a country song, and it is a beautiful, heart-tugging masterpiece. Similarly, "I Got the Blues" is a ravished, late-night classic that ranks among their very best blues. "Sister Morphine" is a horrifying overdose tale, and "Moonlight Mile," with Paul Buckmaster's grandiose strings, is a perfect closure: sad, yearning, drug-addled, and beautiful. With its offhand mixture of decadence, roots music, and outright malevolence, *Sticky Fingers* set the tone for the rest of the decade for the Stones. *—Stephen Thomas Erlewine*

Jamming With Edward / Jan. 1972 / Rolling Stones ♦♦
Though many feel that the Stones were at their best when playing loose, sloppy rock & roll à la *Exile on Main Street*, with this 1972 release on Rolling Stones Records, the unrehearsed style of the album is more of a hindrance than a call to ragged glory. Not an official Rolling Stones release, the assembled band does contain three-fifths of the group (Jagger, Wyman, and Watts) along with session man extraordinaire Nicky Hopkins and guitarist Ry Cooder. The band stumbles through keyboard-dominated original numbers such as "Boudoir Stomp" and "Edward's Thrump Up," as well as more conventional cuts like a cover of Elmore James' "It Hurts Me Too." Yet, the songs never get beyond giving the listener the impression they were thrown together during a drunken night's rehearsals. In that sense the album is a bit of a letdown; though any Stones fan would surely clamor for lost material from the band's golden age, *Jamming With Edward* instead makes one wish it had never been released. *—Steve Kurutz*

● **Hot Rocks, 1964–1971** / Jan. 1972 / ABKCO ♦♦♦♦♦
This two-LP/two-CD set is both a lot more and a bit less than what it seems. It is seven years worth of mostly very high-charting, and all influential and important, songs,

leaving out some singles in favor of well-known album tracks and, in the process, giving an overview not just of the Rolling Stones' hits but of their evolving image. One hears them change from loud R&B-inspired rockers covering others' songs ("Time Is on My Side") into originators in their own right ("Satisfaction"); then into taste-makers and style-setters with a particularly decadent air ("Get Off of My Cloud," "19th Nervous Breakdown"); and finally into self-actualized rebel-poets ("Jumping Jack Flash," "Midnight Rambler") and Shaman-like symbols of chaos. On its initial release, *Hot Rocks* sold well, not only as a unique compilation but also as a panorama of the '60s. The only flaw was that it didn't give a good look at the Stones' full musical history, ignoring their early blues period and the psychedelic era. There are also some anomalies in *Hot Rocks'* history for the collector—the very first pressings included an outtake of "Brown Sugar" featuring Eric Clapton that was promptly replaced, and the original European CD version, issued as two separate discs on the Decca label, was also different from its American counterpart, featuring a version of "Satisfaction" mastered in stereo and putting the guitars on separate channels for the first time. Those musicologist concerns aside, this is still an exciting assembly of material. *—Bruce Eder*

☆ **Exile on Main St.** / May 12, 1972 / Virgin ♦♦♦♦♦

Greeted with decidedly mixed reviews upon its original release, *Exile on Main St.* has become generally regarded as the Rolling Stones' finest album. Part of the reason why the record was initially greeted with hesitant reviews is that it takes a while to assimilate. A sprawling, weary double album encompassing rock & roll, blues, soul, and country, *Exile* doesn't try anything new on the surface, but the substance is new. Taking the bleakness that underpinned *Let It Bleed* and *Sticky Fingers* to an extreme, *Exile* is a weary record, and not just lyrically. Jagger's vocals are buried in the mix, and the music is a series of dark, dense jams, with Keith Richards and Mick Taylor spinning off incredible riffs and solos. And the songs continue the breakthroughs of their three previous albums. No longer does their country sound forced or kitschy—it's lived-in and complex, just like the group's forays into soul and gospel. While the songs, including the masterpieces "Rocks Off," "Tumbling Dice," "Torn and Frayed," "Happy," "Let It Loose," and "Shine a Light," are all terrific, they blend together, with only certain lyrics and guitar lines emerging from the murk. It's the kind of record that's gripping on the very first listen, but each subsequent listen reveals something new. Few other albums, let alone double albums, have been so rich and masterful as *Exile on Main Street*, and it stands not only as one of the Stones' best records, but sets a remarkably high standard for all of hard rock. *—Stephen Thomas Erlewine*

● **More Hot Rocks (Big Hits and Fazed Cookies)** / Nov. 1972 / ABKCO ♦♦♦♦♦

Hot Rocks covers most of the monster hits from the Stones' first decade that remain in radio rotation in the '90s. *More Hot Rocks* goes for the somewhat smaller hits, some of the better album tracks, and a whole LP side worth of rarities that hadn't yet been available in the United States when this compilation was released in 1972. The material isn't as famous as what's on *Hot Rocks*, but the music is almost as excellent, including such vital cuts as "Not Fade Away," "It's All Over Now," "The Last Time," "Lady Jane," the psychedelic "Dandelion," "She's a Rainbow," "Have You Seen Your Mother, Baby, Standing in the Shadow?," "Out of Time," "Tell Me," and "We Love You." The eight rarities are pretty good as well, including their 1963 debut single "Come On," early R&B covers of "Fortune Teller" and "Bye Bye Johnnie," great slide guitar on Muddy Waters' "I Can't Be Satisfied," and the soulful 1966 U.K. B-side, "Long Long While." *—Richie Unterberger*

Goats Head Soup / Aug. 31, 1973 / Virgin ♦♦♦

Sliding out of perhaps the greatest winning streak in rock history, the Stones slipped into decadence and rock star excess with *Goats Head Soup*, their sequel to *Exile on Main St.* This is where the Stones image began to eclipse their accomplishments, as Mick ascended to jet-setting celebrity and Keith slowly sunk deeper into addiction, and it's possible hearing them moving in both directions on *Goats Head Soup*, at times in the same song. As Jagger plays the devil (or, dances with Mr. D, as he likes to say), the sex and sleaze quotient is increased, all of it underpinned by some genuinely affecting heartbreak, highlighted by "Angie." This may not be as downright funky, freaky, and fantastic as *Exile*, yet the extra layer of gloss brings out the enunciated lyrics, added strings, wah-wah guitars, explicit sex, and violence, making it all seem trippily decadent. If it doesn't seem like there's a surplus of classics here, all the songs work well, illustrating just how far they've traveled in their songcraft, as well as their exceptional talent as a band—they make this all sound really easy and darkly alluring, even when the sex 'n' satanism seems a little silly. To top it all of, they cap off this utterly excessive album with "Star Star," a nasty Chuck Berry rip that grooves on its own mean vulgarity—it's real title is "Starfucker," if you need any clarification, and even though they got nastier (the entirety of *Undercover*, for instance), they never again made something this dirty or nasty. And, it never feels more at home than it does at the end of this excessive record. *—Stephen Thomas Erlewine*

Bright Lights, Big City / 1973 / [Bootleg] ♦♦♦♦♦

As you'd expect, there are a ton of Rolling Stones bootlegs, but there isn't a great deal of essential material from the '60s to be found on them. The exceptions are these outtakes from 1963 and 1964, which have popped up under quite a few guises, but most frequently under the *Bright Lights, Big City* title. The five early-1963 demos were cut shortly before they signed with Decca, and capture the band at their bluesiest and blackest; when Brian Jones was being frozen out of the Stones in the late '60s, it's said that he would play these for listeners as examples of the purity of the group's original vision. With clear fidelity, the standards of these performances are well up to official release; "Baby What's Wrong," "Road Runner," and "I Want to Be Loved" are downright electrifying. The four 1964 cuts were recorded at Chess Studios, and again (with the possible exception of the jam "Stewed and Keefed") are well up to release quality, with fine, spare readings of "Hi-Heel Sneakers," Howlin' Wolf's "Down in the Bottom," and Big Bill Broonzy's "Tell Me Baby." Essential for serious fans. *—Richie Unterberger*

It's Only Rock and Roll / Oct. 18, 1974 / Virgin ♦♦♦

It's uneven, but at times *It's Only Rock and Roll* catches fire. The songs and performances are stronger than those on *Goats Head Soup*; the tossed-off numbers sound effortless, not careless. Throughout, the Stones wear their title as the World's Greatest Rock & Roll Band with a defiant smirk, which makes the bitter cynicism of "If You Can't Rock Me" and the title track all the more striking, and the reggae experimentation of "Luxury," the aching beauty of "Time Waits for No One," and the agreeable filler of "Dance Little Sister" and "Short and Curlies" all the more enjoyable. *—Stephen Thomas Erlewine*

Metamorphosis / Jun. 1975 / ABKCO ♦♦♦

Though it remains the only Rolling Stones outtakes collection album ever to be officially released, *Metamorphosis* is one of those albums that has been slighted by almost everyone who has touched it, a problem that lies in its genesis. While both the Stones and former manager Allen Klein agreed that some form of archive release was necessary, if only to stem the then-ongoing flow of bootlegs, they could not agree how to present it. Of the two, the band's own version of the album, compiled by Bill Wyman, probably came closest to the fan's ideal, cherrypicking the vaults for some of the more legendary outtakes and oddities for a bird's-eye view of the entire band's creative brilliance. Klein, on the other hand, chose to approach the issue from the songwriting point-of-view, focusing on the wealth of demos for songs that Jagger/Richards gave away (usually to artists being produced by Andrew Oldham) and which, therefore, frequently featured more session men than Rolling Stones. Both approaches had their virtues, but when Klein's version of the album became the one that got the green light, *of course* fans and collectors bemoaned the non-availability of the other. The fact is, if Wyman's selection had been released, then everyone would have been crying out for Klein's. Sometimes, you just can't win. So, rather than wring your hands over what you don't receive, you should celebrate what you do. A heavily orchestrated version of "Out of Time," with Jagger accompanying the backing track that would later give Chris Farlowe a U.K. number one hit, opens the show; a loose-limbed "Memo From Turner," recorded with Al Kooper, closes it. No complaints there, then. The real meat, however, lies in between times. During 1964-1965, Mick Jagger and Andrew Oldham headed a session team that also included the likes of arrangers Art Greenslade and Mike Leander, guitarist Jimmy Page, pianist Nicky Hopkins, bassist John Paul Jones, and many more, convened to cut demos for the plethora of songs then being churned out by Jagger and Keith Richards. Some would subsequently be redone by the Stones themselves; others, however, would be used as backing tracks for other artist's versions of the songs. *Metamorphosis* pulls a number of tracks from this latter grouping, and while "Each and Every Day of the Year" (covered by Bobby Jameson), "I'd Much Rather Be With the Boys" (the Toggery Five), "Some Things Just Stick in Your Mind" (Vashti), "Sleepy City" (the Mighty Avengers), and "We're Wasting Time" (Jimmy Tarbuck) may not be Stones performances per se, they are certainly Stones songs and, for the most part, as strong as any of the band originals included on the group's first four or five LPs. Elsewhere, the 1964 Chess studio outtake "Don't Lie to Me" is as fine a Chuck Berry cover as the Stones ever mustered, while "Family," the rocking "Jiving Sister Fanny," Bill Wyman's "Downtown Suzie," and a delightfully lackadaisical version of Stevie Wonder's "I Don't Know Why" are outtakes from two of the Stones' finest-ever albums, *Beggars Banquet* and *Let It Bleed*. All of which adds up to an impressive pedigree, whatever the circumstances behind the album, and whatever else could have been included on it. Indeed, if there are any criticisms to be made, it is that the album sleeve itself is singularly uninformative, and the contents are seriously jumbled. But those are its only sins. Everything else you've heard about it is simply wishful (or otherwise) thinking. *—Dave Thompson*

Black and Blue / Apr. 20, 1976 / Virgin ♦♦♦

The Stones recorded *Black and Blue* while auditioning Mick Taylor's replacement, so it's unfair to criticize it, really, for being longer on grooves and jams than songs, especially since that's what's good about it. Yes, the two songs that are undeniable highlights are "Memory Motel" and "Fool to Cry," the album's two ballads and, therefore, the two that had to be written and arranged, not knocked out in the studio; they're also the ones that don't quite make as much sense, though they still work in the context of the record. No, this is all about groove and sound, as the Stones work Wood into their fabric. And the remarkable thing is, apart from "Hand of Fate" and "Crazy Mama," there's little straight-ahead rock & roll here. They play with reggae extensively, funk and disco less so, making both sound like integral parts of the Stones' lifeblood. Apart from the ballads, there might not be many memorable tunes, but there are times that you listen to the Stones just to hear them play, and this is one of them. *—Stephen Thomas Erlewine*

Love You Live / Sep. 23, 1977 / Virgin ♦♦

Recorded on the supporting tour for 1976's *Black and Blue*, the double-album set *Love You Live* is an adequate live album, capturing the Stones' transition from a lean, lethal rock & roll band to accomplished showmen. As showmen, they aren't as compelling as they are when they're rockers, but the showbiz glitz of Mick Jagger's arena rock schtick remains thoroughly entertaining, even when it robs the music of its power. *—Stephen Thomas Erlewine*

☆ **Some Girls** / Jun. 9, 1978 / Virgin ♦♦♦♦♦

During the mid-'70s, the Rolling Stones remained massively popular, but their records suffered from Jagger's fascination with celebrity and Keith's worsening drug habit. By 1978, both punk and disco had swept the group off the front pages, and *Some Girls* was their fiery response to the younger generation. Opening with the disco-blues thump of

"Miss You," *Some Girls* is a tough, focused, and exciting record, full of more hooks and energy than any Stones record since *Exile on Main Street*. Even though the Stones make disco their own, they never quite take punk on their own ground. Instead, their rockers sound harder and nastier than they have in years. Using "Star Star" as a template, the Stones run through the seedy homosexual imagery of "When the Whip Comes Down," the bizarre, borderline-misogynistic vitriol of the title track, Keith's ultimate outlaw anthem, "Before They Make Me Run," and the decadent closer, "Shattered." In between, they deconstruct the Temptations' "(Just My) Imagination," unleash the devastatingly snide country parody "Far Away Eyes," and contribute "Beast of Burden," one of their very best ballads. *Some Girls* may not have the backstreet aggression of their '60s records, or the majestic, drugged-out murk of their early-'70s work, but its brand of glitzy, decadent hard rock still makes it a definitive Stones album. *—Stephen Thomas Erlewine*

Emotional Rescue / Jun. 23, 1980 / Virgin ✦✦✦
Coasting on the success of *Some Girls*, the Stones offered more of the same on *Emotional Rescue*. Comprised of leftovers from the previous album's sessions and hastily written new numbers, *Emotional Rescue* may consist mainly of filler, but it's expertly written and performed filler. The Stones toss off throwaways like the reggae-fueled, mail-order bride anthem "Send It to Me" or rockers like "Summer Romance" and "Where the Boys Go" with an authority that makes the record a guilty pleasure, even if it's clear that only two songs—the icy but sexy disco-rock of "Emotional Rescue" and the revamped Chuck Berry rocker "She's So Cold"—come close to being classic Stones. *—Stephen Thomas Erlewine*

Tattoo You / Aug. 30, 1981 / Virgin ✦✦✦✦✦
Like *Emotional Rescue* before it, *Tattoo You* was comprised primarily of leftovers, but unlike its predecessor, it never sounds that way. Instead, *Tattoo You* captures the Stones at their best as a professional stadium-rock band. Divided into a rock & roll side and a ballad side, the album delivers its share of thrills on the tight, dynamic first side. "Start Me Up" became the record's definitive Stonesy rocker, but the frenzied doo wop of "Hang Fire," the reggae jam of "Slave," the sleazy Chuck Berry rockers "Little T&A" and "Neighbours," and the hard blues of "Black Limousine" are all terrific. The ballad side suffers in comparison, especially since "Heaven" and "No Use in Crying" are faceless. But "Worried About You" and "Tops" are effortless, excellent ballads, and "Waiting on a Friend," with its Sonny Rollins sax solo, is an absolute masterpiece, with a moving lyric that captures Jagger in a shockingly reflective and affecting state of mind. "Waiting on a Friend" and the vigorous rock & roll of the first side make *Tattoo You* an essential latter-day Stones album, ranking just a few notches below *Some Girls*. *—Stephen Thomas Erlewine*

Still Life / Jun. 1, 1982 / Virgin ✦
Like *Love You Live* before it, *Still Life* showcases the Stones as pure entertainers, although the band adds enough rhythmic grit to keep the record from sinking into pure showbiz formula. Nevertheless, it isn't nearly enough grit to make it rock as hard as *Get Yer Ya-Ya's Out*. Or even *Love You Live*, depressingly enough. *—Stephen Thomas Erlewine*

Undercover / Nov. 7, 1983 / Virgin ✦✦✦
As their most ambitious album since *Some Girls*, *Undercover* is a weird, wild mix of hard rock, new wave pop, reggae, dub, and soul. Even with all the careening musical eclecticism, what distinguishes *Undercover* is its bleak, nihilistic attitude—it's teeming with sickness, with violence, kinky sex, and loathing dripping from almost every song. "Undercover of the Night" slams with echoing guitars and rubbery basslines, as Jagger gives a feverish litany of sex, corruption, and suicide. It set the tone for the rest of the album, whether it's the runaway nymphomaniac of "She Was Hot" or the ridiculous slasher imagery of "Too Much Blood." Only Keith's "Wanna Hold You" offers a reprieve from the carnage, and its relentless bloodletting makes the album a singularly fascinating listen. For some observers, that mixture was nearly too difficult to stomach, but for others, it's a fascinating record, particularly since much of its nastiness feels as if the Stones, and Jagger and Richards in particular, are running out of patience with each other. *—Stephen Thomas Erlewine*

Dirty Work / 1986 / Virgin ✦✦✦
Reuniting after three years and one solo album from Mick Jagger, the Rolling Stones attempted to settle their differences and craft a comeback with *Dirty Work*, but the tensions remained too great for the group. Designed as a return to their rock & roll roots after several years of vague dance experiments, *Dirty Work* is hampered by uneven songs and undistinguished performances, as well as a slick, lightly synthesized production that instantly dates the album to the mid-'80s. Jagger often sounds like he's saving his best work for his solo records, but a handful of songs have a spry, vigorous attack—"One Hit (To the Body)" is a classic, and "Winning Ugly" and "Had It With You" have a similar aggression. Still, most of *Dirty Work* sounds as forced as the cover of Bob & Earl's uptown soul obscurity "Harlem Shuffle," leaving the album as one of the group's most undistinguished efforts. *—Stephen Thomas Erlewine*

☆ **Singles Collection: The London Years** / 1989 / ABKCO ✦✦✦✦✦
The three-disc box set *Singles Collection: The London Years* contains every single the Rolling Stones released during the '60s, including both the A- and B-sides. It is the first Stones compilation that tries to be comprehensive and logical—for all their attributes, the two *Hot Rocks* sets and the two *Big Hits* collections didn't present the singles in chronological order. In essence, the previous compilations were excellent samplers, where *Singles Collection* tells most of the story (certain albums, like *Aftermath*, *Beggars Banquet*, and *Let It Bleed*, fill in the gaps left by the singles). The Rolling Stones made genuine albums—even their early R&B/blues albums were impeccably paced—but their singles had a power all their own, which is quite clearly illustrated by the *Singles Collection*. By presenting the singles in chronological order, the set takes on a relentless, exhilarating pace with each hit and neglected B-side piling on top of each other, adding a new dimension to the group; it has a power it wouldn't have had if it tried to sample from the albums. Although it cheats near the end, adding singles from the *Metamorphosis* outtakes collection and two singles from *Sticky Fingers*, this captures the essence of the '60s Stones as well as any compilation could. Casual fans might want to stick with the *Hot Rocks* sets, since they just have the hits, but for those who want a little bit more, the *Singles Collection* is absolutely essential. *—Stephen Thomas Erlewine*

Steel Wheels / Aug. 1989 / Virgin ✦✦✦
The Stones, or more accurately the relationship between Mick and Keith, imploded shortly after *Dirty Work*, resulting in Mick delivering a nearly unbearably mannered, ambitious solo effort that stiffed and Keith knocking out the greatest Stones album since *Tattoo You*, something that satisfied the cult but wasn't a hit. Clearly, they were worth more together than they were apart, so it was time for the reunion, and that's what *Steel Wheels* is—a self-styled reunion album. It often feels as if they sat down and decided exactly what their audience wanted from a Stones album, and they deliver a record that gives the people what they want, whether it's *Tattoo You*-styled rockers, ballads in the vein of "Fool to Cry," even a touch of old-fashioned experimentalism with "Continental Drift." Being professionals, in the business for over two-and-a-half decades, and being a band that always favored calculation, they wear all this well, even if this lacks the vigor and menace that fuels the best singles; after all, the rocking singles ("Sad Sad Sad," "Rock and a Hard Place," "Mixed Emotions") wind up being smoked by such throwaways as "Hold on to Your Hat." Even though it's just 12 songs, the record feels a little long, largely due to its lack of surprises and unabashed calculation (the jams are slicked up so much they don't have the visceral power of the jam record, *Black and Blue*). Still, the Stones sound good, and Mick and Keith both get off a killer ballad apiece with "Almost Hear You Sigh" and "Slipping Away," respectively. It doesn't make for a great Stones album, but it's not bad, and it feels like a comeback—which it was supposed to, after all. *—Stephen Thomas Erlewine*

Flashpoint / Apr. 1991 / Virgin ✦✦
The live follow-ups and a fond look back on 25 years of decadence. *—Bruce Eder*

Jump Back: The Best of the Rolling Stones 1971–1993 / Nov. 19, 1993 / Virgin ✦✦✦✦✦
Released in 1994 to coincide with the Stones' catalog moving to Virgin Records, as well as the accompanying remastering of their Rolling Stone Records catalog (1971's *Sticky Fingers* through 1989's *Steel Wheels*—actually 1991's *Flashpoint*, which is the last Rolling Stones Records release, but isn't featured here), *Jump Back* supplants *Rewind* as the best single-disc overview of the Stones' '70s and '80s recordings. The non-chronological order at times is a little irritating—bouncing between "Brown Sugar," "Harlem Shuffle," "It's Only Rock & Roll (But I Like It)," "Mixed Emotions," and "Angie" nearly causes whiplash—but nearly all the big songs from this period are included. Yes, "She Was Hot" isn't here, along with a couple other singles that didn't catch hold, but this has everything that the casual follower could want, which makes up for the fact that it could have been sequenced better (that's what home programming and burners are for anyway). *—Stephen Thomas Erlewine*

Voodoo Lounge / Jul. 19, 1994 / Virgin ✦✦✦
Funny that the much-touted "reunion/comeback" album *Steel Wheels* followed *Dirty Work* by just three years, while it took the Stones five years to turn out its sequel, *Voodoo Lounge*—a time frame that seems much more appropriate for a "comeback." To pile on the irony, *Voodoo Lounge* feels more like a return to form than its predecessor, even if it's every bit as calculated and Bill Wyman has flown the coup. With Don Was, a neo-classic rock producer that always attempts to reclaim his artist's original claim to greatness, helming the boards with the Glimmer Twins, the Stones strip their sound back to its spare, hard-rocking basics. The Stones act in kind, turning out a set of songs that are pretty traditionalist. There are no new twists or turns in either the rockers or ballads (apart maybe from the quiet menace of "Thru and Thru," later used to great effect on *The Sopranos*), even if they revive some of the English folk and acoustic country blues that was on *Beggars Banquet*. Still, this approach works, because they are turning out songs that may not be classics, but are first-rate examples of the value of craft. If this was released 10 years, even five years earlier, this would be a near-triumph of classicist rock, but since *Voodoo Lounge* came out in the CD age, it's padded out to 15 tracks, five of which could have been chopped to make the album much stronger. Instead, it runs on for nearly an hour, an ironically bloated length for an album whose greatest strengths are its lean, concentrated classic sound and songcraft. Still, it makes for a stronger record than its predecessor. *—Stephen Thomas Erlewine*

Stripped / Nov. 14, 1995 / Virgin ✦✦✦
Despite the odds, the Rolling Stones' *Stripped* held out great promise. *Voodoo Lounge* was an energized return to studio form for the Borg of rock & roll road shows. From that platform, the idea of taking it back to small clubs, live, lean and pared down without succumbing to the worn "unplugged" treadmill, seemed an inspired move. Patched together from an embroidery of tour rehearsals and live club dates in Paris and Amsterdam, the project was an extension of acoustic sets the group introduced on the North American leg of the *Voodoo Lounge* tour. The concept offered an invigorating opportunity to dust off some rough gems from the past that no longer felt at home on scoping stadium stages. Unfortunately, the cover photo depicting a lean, determined, leather-clad combo in spartan black and white proves to be misleading advertising. Within the brave packaging lies a listless, lethargic Dorian Gray bluff. Spongy keyboards gunk many of the tracks. The much-touted cover of Dylan's "Like a Rolling Stone" remains pointlessly devoted to the original. There are lazy, somnambulant versions of "I'm Free" and "Let It Bleed"; Keith

Richards' painfully intoned "Slipping Away"; the dozens of lost songs that any fan would chose to have renovated before "Angie." *—Roch Parisien*

Rolling Stones Rock and Roll Circus / Oct. 15, 1996 / ABKCO ♦♦♦

The most interesting archival release of the Rolling Stones since *More Hot Rocks*, 20 years ago, and the first issue of truly unreleased material by the Stones from this period. And the Stones have some competition from the Who, Taj Mahal, and John Lennon on the same release. Filmed and recorded on December 10-11, 1968, at a North London studio, *Rock and Roll Circus* has been, as much as the Beach Boys' *Smile*, "the one that got away" for most '60s music enthusiasts. The Jethro Tull sequence is the standard studio track, but the rest—except for the Stones' "Salt of the Earth"—is really live. The Who's portion has been out before, courtesy of various documentaries, but Taj Mahal playing some loud electric blues is new and great, the live Lennon rendition of "Yer Blues" is indispensable, and the Stones' set fills in lots of blanks in their history—"Jumpin' Jack Flash" in one of two live renditions it ever got with Brian Jones in the lineup, "Sympathy for the Devil" in an intense run-through, "Parachute Woman" as a lost live vehicle for the band, "You Can't Always Get What You Want" as a show-stopping rocker even without its extended ending (no Paul Buckmaster choir), and "No Expectations" as their first piece of great live blues since "Little Red Rooster." It's a must-own, period. *—Bruce Eder*

Bridges to Babylon / Sep. 23, 1997 / Virgin ♦♦♦

Voodoo Lounge confirmed that the Stones could age gracefully, but it never sounded modern; it sounded classicist. With its successor, *Bridges to Babylon*, Mick Jagger was determined to bring the Rolling Stones into the '90s, albeit tentatively, and hired hip collaborators like the Dust Brothers (Beck, Beastie Boys) and Danny Saber (Black Grape) to give the veteran group an edge on their explorations of drum loops and samples. Of course, the Stones are the Stones, and no production is going to erase that, but the group is smart enough—or Keith Richards is stubborn enough—to work within their limitations and to have producer Don Was act as executive producer. As a result, *Bridges to Babylon* sounds like the Stones without sounding tired. The band is tight and energetic, and there's just enough flair to the sultry "Anybody Seen My Baby?," the menacing "Gunface" and the low-key, sleazy "Might as Well Get Juiced" to make them sound contemporary. But the real key to the success of *Bridges to Babylon* is the solid, craftsmanlike songwriting. While there aren't any stunners on the album, nothing is bad, with rockers like "Flip the Switch" and "Low Down" sounding as convincing as ballads like "Already Over Me." And, as always, Keith contributes three winners—including the reggae workout "You Don't Have to Mean It" and the slow-burning "How Can I Stop"—that cap off another fine latter-day Stones record. *—Stephen Thomas Erlewine*

No Security / Nov. 3, 1998 / Virgin ♦♦♦

Another record, another tour, another live album chronicling the whole shebang. The Rolling Stones have followed this basic pattern since the early '80s—if Keith had been able to get Mick out on the road to support *Dirty Work*, there damn well would have been a live record in 1987—stepping up the production rate in the '90s, eventually winding their way to *No Security*, a document of the *Bridges of Babylon* tour of 1997-1998. Since the Stones (or at least Jagger) are sharp businessmen, they have given all three of their '90s live albums a hook, an angle for journalists and fans alike—*Flashpoint* was their return to form, *Stripped* was culled from unplugged and club dates, and *No Security* contains 11 songs that have never before appeared on a live Stones album. Of course, several of these date from *Voodoo Lounge* and *Bridges to Babylon* (five, to be exact), but they also dig out such great songs as "Gimme Shelter," "Respectable," "Sister Morphine," and "Memory Hotel," as well as reviving "The Last Time" and "Live With Me," which haven't been on a live record since *Got Live if You Want It!* and *Get Yer Ya-Ya's Out*, respectively. There are also guest spots from Taj Mahal and Dave Matthews. All of these things give some measure of distinction to *No Security* but they don't erase the feeling that this is more of a soundtrack to a spectacle than a musical event. Sure, the Stones are as accomplished as ever, the album is certainly enjoyable, but it just doesn't feel necessary. Which, again, doesn't make it any different than most Stones live records since *Love You Live*. *—Stephen Thomas Erlewine*

★ **Forty Licks** / Oct. 1, 2002 / Virgin ♦♦♦♦♦

Forty Licks, like Elvis' *Elvis 30 #1 Hits*, is a career-spanning compilation that wouldn't have happened without the unprecedented, blockbuster success of *Beatles 1*. Where Elvis' set is hurt by the simple fact that there are too many damn Elvis comps on the market, the Rolling Stones benefit greatly from the fact that there has not been any set that chronicles all their recordings from the '60s through the '90s. It also benefits that this is the concept behind the record—it's meant to be a journey through their biggest songs, not just the number one hits. Of course, the Stones couldn't have had a CD containing just their number ones that spanned one disc, much less two, because they never topped the charts that frequently. This is a liberating thing (compare it to Elvis', which got weighed down with the number ones, resulting in some subpar selections), since it opens the door for almost every Stones song of note to feature on this collection, along with four new songs (not great, but solid songs, all). Sure, there are many great Rolling Stones moments missing, and not just fan favorites *Beggars Banquet* or *Exile on Main St.*, either—"Play With Fire," "2000 Light Years from Home," "Tell Me," "Heart of Stone," "Doo Doo Doo Doo Doo (Heartbreaker)," "Lady Jane," "Time Is on My Side," "Waiting on a Friend," "I'm Free," and "We Love You" are all missing in action. The thing is, as the disc is playing, you don't miss any of them, and it feels like all the hits are here. At first, the non-chronological order seems to be a mistake, but both discs flow well, especially since they're roughly divided thematically (the first is devoted largely to the '60s, with the rest on the second). Yes, the Stones made great albums that should be in any serious rock collection, but if you just want a summary of their best moments, *Forty Licks* is it; it does its job as well as *Beatles 1* did. *—Stephen Thomas Erlewine*

BBC Sessions / [Bootleg] ♦♦♦

The Rolling Stones' BBC sessions haven't been accorded the same deluxe bootleg treatment as those of the Beatles, for two big reasons: They didn't record nearly as much for the Beeb as the Fab Four, and (unlike the Beatles) didn't record many tracks that they didn't release on record. Good-fidelity tapes exist of a few dozen of their mid-'60s BBC airshots, and fans will find them worth picking up. Heavy on R&B covers (the Stones, like the Beatles, didn't record for the BBC after 1965), the tracks, as is par for the course on radio sessions, don't better or usually even equal the studio renditions, but have an interesting rougher live feel. They did manage to let rip on a half-dozen or so unreleased covers, and these items are naturally the most interesting, especially their takes on "Memphis, Tennessee" and their incendiary "Roll Over Beethoven," which is perhaps even better than the well-known Beatle version. *—Richie Unterberger*

Out of Time / Monroe ♦♦♦♦

A great concept for an album that, no matter what Allen Klein might say, helps more people than it hurts: 16 songs assembled from the '60s B-sides, import-only singles, compilations, and soundtracks that have proven extremely hard to find in America. A few of the songs did finally show up on ABKCO's *Singles Collection*, but many remain unavailable. And some of these items are very good: a longer version of the smoking "2120 South Michigan Avenue" instrumental (only issued in Germany), the long, very different take of "Everybody Needs Somebody to Love" that was issued on their second British LP, "I've Been Loving You Too Long" minus the overdubbed screams on *Got Live if You Want It!*, the Italian version of "As Tears Go By," Jagger's "Memo from Turner" (from the *Performance* soundtrack), and two early songs that only showed up on the British version of *Metamorphosis*. "I Want to Be Loved" and "I Wanna Be Your Man" (which were officially reissued on *Singles Collection*) are among their best early tracks. Good sound, topped off with a superb picture sleeve of the Stones in drag in 1966, add up to an LP that is essential for serious Stones fans, and indeed better than many of their "official" albums. *—Richie Unterberger*

Tricky Fingers & Sticky Ringers / Luna ♦♦♦

"Alternate versions" of entire albums are somewhat in vogue by rock bootleggers, who compile entire CDs of alternate/live takes of songs from one specific full-length recording. This is one attempt at an alternate version of *Sticky Fingers*, and not bad, though not as successful as it may appear from a glance at the sleeve. There are indeed alternate studio takes of "Brown Sugar," "Wild Horses," "Sister Morphine," "You Gotta Move," and "Bitch." In fact, there are four different versions of "Brown Sugar" alone, including the famous one with a prominent slide guitar. The thing is, they really aren't *that* different; at a casual listen, they sound almost exactly like the album versions, sometimes amounting to nothing more drastic than different mixes. And it's uncertain whether the live versions of "Dead Flowers" and "Can't You Hear Me Knocking" actually come from 1969-1971, as the sleeve claims. A 14-minute performance of "Can't You Hear Me Knocking" sounds particularly enticing, but this fair-quality live recording (no source given) doesn't sound like it's from the *Sticky Fingers* period; indeed, it sounds suspiciously like it might be from a Jagger-less side project of Keith Richards or somebody. These reservations aside, hardcore Stones fans may find this worthwhile, with a 66-minute running time and the addition of a cover of Chuck Berry's "Let It Rock" (which was not included on *Sticky Fingers*). *—Richie Unterberger*

Roomful of Blues

f. 1967, Providence, RI

Group / Jump Blues, Modern Electric Blues, Swing

Over the course of its decades-long existence, Roomful of Blues effectively became a franchise unto itself, built more on a brand-name collective identity than on the voices of the myriad individual members who kept the band a smoothly humming machine. Describing Roomful of Blues that way, however, gives short shrift to the many accomplished musicians who have emerged from the band's ranks over the years: guitarists Duke Robillard and Ronnie Earl, organist Ron Levy, pianist Al Copley, singer Lou Ann Barton, vocalist/harmonica player Sugar Ray Norcia, and drummer Fran Christina (later of the Fabulous Thunderbirds), to name the most prominent. Plus, the band's horn section blossomed into a renowned freelancing unit, backing countless other artists both on stage and in the studio. They've evolved over the years, too; from a swinging jump blues revivalist group into expert blues historians with a handle on numerous regional variations: Texas, the West Coast, Chicago, New Orleans, Kansas City. Perhaps the best way to put it is that regardless of who was in the group, Roomful of Blues just kept going strong.

A nine-piece outfit for the majority of their existence, Roomful of Blues was founded in Westerly, RI, all the way back in 1967, by guitarist Duke Robillard and pianist Al Copley. Settling on drummer Fran Christina and bassist Larry Peduzzi, the group began playing around the local club and coffeehouse circuit, initially pursuing a contemporary blues-rock style. Robillard quickly rethought their direction when he discovered jump blues, and in 1970 he added a horn section featuring saxophonists Greg Piccolo (tenor) and Rich Lataille (alto/tenor), plus a more swinging drummer in John Rossi; baritone saxophonist Doug James joined up in 1971. After a couple of years honing their sound and achieving local popularity, Roomful of Blues started supporting established blues artists, and started what would become a 15-year residency at the Knickerbocker Cafe in Westerly. In 1974, they gigged with Count Basie, a professed admirer, and after a few more years of live work, songwriter Doc Pomus finally helped the band get a record deal with Island. Their self-titled debut was released in 1977, and they followed it up with 1979's *Let's Have a Party* for Antilles. Robillard subsequently left the group to pursue other projects, eventually finding considerable success as a solo artist.

Robillard's spot as guitarist and bandleader was taken by Ronnie Earl, and trombonist Porky Cohen was also added to flesh out the horn section. Meanwhile, female vocalist Lou Ann Barton spent a year with the group, and saxophonist Piccolo subsequently took over, making his vocal debut on 1981's *Hot Little Mama* (recorded for Blue Flame);

the same year, trumpeter Bob Enos joined the group, as did bassist Jimmy Wimpfheimer (who was replaced by Preston Hubbard in 1983). Roomful of Blues' reputation had been growing steadily in the blues world, and they soon attracted more mainstream notice by serving as a studio backing group for legends like Eddie "Cleanhead" Vinson (1982's *Eddie Cleanhead Vinson & Roomful of Blues*), Big Joe Turner (1983's *Blues Train*), and Earl King (1988's *Glazed*); all three albums in question earned Grammy nominations. Roomful of Blues hit the studios on their own as well, signing with Varrick and recording 1984's *Dressed Up to Get Messed Up*. Helped by good timing, the record raised the group's profile even further following the emergence of Stevie Ray Vaughan and the Fabulous Thunderbirds, and they were able to tour heavily behind it. Unfortunately, Piccolo needed throat surgery, and at first Keith Dunn filled his spot in concert; vocalist/harpist Curtis Salgado was brought in as a longer-term replacement, and fronted the group on 1987's *Live at Lupo's Heartbreak Hotel*; new organist Ron Levy also made his debut there, replacing Copley.

Unfortunately, Ronnie Earl left the group later that year, and while Roomful of Blues remained a popular touring attraction, it would be seven years before they would pull together and re-enter the recording studio (at least, on their own; they did back Pat Benatar on 1991's *True Love*). Predictably, several personnel shifts ensued: Salgado left when Piccolo's voice healed; trombonist Cohen was replaced by Carl Querfurth in 1988 (later serving as the group's producer as well); guitarist Chris Vachon joined in 1990; and new pianist Matt McCabe came on board in 1992. With a trail of busted record deals behind them, Roomful of Blues eventually bankrolled their own sessions and found a home for the result, *Dance All Night*, on Bullseye Blues in 1994. With Piccolo now departed, Ronnie Earl's longtime friend Sugar Ray Norcia handled vocals and harmonica, and stuck around for the subsequent Bullseye albums *Turn It On! Turn It Up!* (1995, nominated for a Grammy) and *Under One Roof* (1997). Following the latter, a mass exodus of personnel left Roomful of Blues down to just a core of drummer Rossi, guitarist Vachon, trumpeter Enos, and saxman Lataille (even the long-running horn team was broken up). The remaining members restored the band to a nine-piece fronted by new vocalist McKinley "Mac" Odom, and returned in 1998 with *There Goes the Neighborhood*. Prior to recording their next album, longtime stalwart Rossi finally retired from the band and was replaced by Chris Lemp on 2001's *Watch You When You Go*. Looking to return to a more traditional blues sound, in early 2002 the band replaced Odom with singer/harpist Mark DuFresne. *—Steve Huey*

Roomful of Blues / 1977 / Island ♦♦♦

● **Let's Have a Party** / Nov. 1979 / Mango ♦♦♦♦♦
Decent to good R&B-influenced jump and party blues. This group has always been great live; their albums have always been mixed affairs, and this was no different. *—Ron Wynn*

Hot Little Mama / 1981 / Varrick ♦♦♦♦
The third album by Roomful of Blues (which they originally put out on their own label; it was later reissued by Varrick) has plenty of exciting moments that should interest blues and jazz fans alike. The nine-piece group in 1980 featured Greg Piccolo on spirited vocals and romping tenor, trombonist Porky Cohen, and the up-and-coming guitarist Ronnie Earl (then known as Ronnie Earl Horvath) as the key soloists. Most of the music consists of blues at various tempos, but there are also a couple of blues ballads and a feature for Cohen on a fairly lengthy "Caravan." The music is accessible, jumping and creative within its genre. Well worth searching for. *—Scott Yanow*

Dressed Up to Get Messed Up / 1984 / Varrick ♦♦

Live at Lupo's Heartbreak Hotel / Nov. 1987 / Varrick ♦♦♦
Live at Lupo's Heartbreak Hotel is a fine, but unremarkable, set Roomful of Blues recorded in the late '80s. The source material—Fats Domino, Howlin' Wolf, etc.—is fine and there are good solos scattered throughout the album, but the entire record never quite catches fire. *—Thom Owens*

The First Album / Jul. 13, 1992 / Varrick ♦♦♦

Dance All Night / May 28, 1994 / Bullseye Blues ♦♦♦♦
This incarnation of Roomful of Blues includes vocalist and harmonica player Sugar Ray Norcia taking the singing spotlight, Matt McCabe now their pianist and Chris Vachon principal guitarist. This CD blends blues and R&B classics with a couple of originals; highlights include a fine reading of Smiley Lewis' "Lillie Mae," a remake of "Hey Now" originally done by Ray Charles and Norcia's fiery vocal and torrid harmonica solo on Little Walter Jacobs' "Up The Line." This is faithful to the classic tradition, but contains enough contemporary qualities to have a fresh and inviting sound. *—Ron Wynn*

Turn It On! Turn It Up! / Oct. 3, 1995 / Bullseye Blues ♦♦♦
Try to imagine for a moment if George Thorogood, Bill Haley, Glenn Miller, Louis Armstrong, B.B. King, Cab Calloway, and Count Basie all got together to record a CD. Got the picture in your mind? Well, then you probably are pretty close to knowing what *Turn It On! Turn It Up!* sounds like—a big band, rock & roll take on the blues. A ten-piece outfit, these guys really smoke this disc. They have created a style of music that at times feels like big band, at times old-time rock & roll, and at other times straight-ahead blues. Their awesome take on Count Basie's "I Left My Baby" alone makes this album worth having. You'll feel like you walked right into the Cotton Club with that one. At other times they rock out, feeling at one point like Stevie Ray Vaughan playing with a big band. The sound here is hard to pin down, but great to listen to. *—Gary Hill*

Under One Roof / Jan. 14, 1997 / Bullseye Blues ♦♦♦
At its best, Roomful of Blues is a throwback to the heated jump bands of the early '50s, which blended hard-driving swing with the extroverted emotions of early R&B. However, this particular release is different than expected. Listeners who hope to hear extended solos and riotous ensembles are sure to be disappointed, for much of the time Roomful of Blues sounds like an anonymous backup group put together specifically to accompany singer Sugar Ray Norcia. Sugar Ray is a versatile and talented singer, and his repertoire ranges from a Basie blues to tunes that are closer to rock, soul, and even country. If one comes to this CD without false expectations, the music is enjoyable on its own level, but from the jazz standpoint, the release is rather routine and not very significant. *—Scott Yanow*

Two Classic Albums / May 5, 1997 / 32 Jazz ♦♦♦♦

Roomful of Christmas / Sep. 9, 1997 / Bullseye Blues ♦♦♦
This Christmas platter adds another page to Roomful's voluminous releases for Rounder's Varrick and Bullseye Blues imprints. Their only holiday album is a unique collection of some of the greatest R&B Christmas tunes of all time, including Chuck Berry's "Run Rudolph Run," Fats Domino's "I Told Santa Claus" and Lloyd Glenn's "Christmas Celebration." Roomful also puts their distinctive touch on classics by Mel Torme ("The Christmas Song"), Nat King Cole ("Have Yourself a Merry Little Christmas"), Jesse Belvin ("I Want You With Me Christmas"), Lowell Fulson ("I Want to Spend Christmas With You") and swinging takes on "Let It Snow," the perennial "White Christmas" (done up New Orleans style) and a holiday slant to Count Basie's "Good Morning Blues." *—Cub Koda*

There Goes the Neighborhood / Aug. 18, 1998 / Bullseye Blues ♦♦
At the end of 1997, several members left the band, leaving their ranks decimated. But the remaining members brought in new blood, regrouped, opened up their musical outlook to start auditioning new material (rather than just covering old standards and obscure items), and 1998 saw the new Roomful of Blues hit the racks and the road. New vocalist Mac Odom brings along his "Backseat Blues" and turns in great versions of Duke-Peacock Records staples like "I Tried" and "I Smell Trouble," while guitarist Chris Vachon emerges from the Duke Robillard and Ronnie Earl shadows to contribute a pair of strong originals in "Blue Blue World" and "Just Like Dynamite." Strong versions of "The Comeback," "Lost Mind," and Duke Ellington's "Rocks in My Bed" and new material from Doyle Bramhall and the Cate Brothers complete the package. *—Cub Koda*

Swingin' & Jumpin' / Aug. 3, 1999 / 32 Jazz ♦♦♦♦
32 Jazz's *Swingin' & Jumpin'* is an excellent 12-track compilation of highlights from Roomful of Blues' early recordings, concentrating on their eponymous debut. *—Stephen Thomas Erlewine*

The Blues'll Make You Happy, Too / Oct. 31, 2000 / Rounder ♦♦♦♦♦
This is one of the first volumes in Rounder Records' *Rounder Heritage* series, which will celebrate the company's 30-year history with a line of 30 releases that dip into the label's deep catalog of blues, folk, and bluegrass recordings. *The Blues'll Make You Happy, Too!* compiles 14 tracks from various Roomful of Blues albums released over the past 20 years; the collection focuses on the '90s but includes tracks from as long ago as 1980, just after the departure of guitarist/leader Duke Robillard and his replacement by Ronnie Earl. At this point, the band took on more horns, and its style was subtly redefined. Although production values have changed since that period, the band's overall sound hasn't—the Roomful's winning combination of blues, soul, R&B and swing remains pretty much the same throughout the program. Singer Sugar Ray Norcia's original jump-blues composition from 1996 (the excellent "If You Know It") could have been written 30 years ago, and when the band covers Memphis Slim (with "The Comeback," featuring Mac Odom on vocals) or Duke Ellington (a fine, slinky interpretation of "Jeep's Blues," recorded in 1980), it's with the immediacy and energy of a band delivering its latest composition. This album is an excellent overview of an ensemble that has been making top-notch blues-based music for over 30 years and that shows no signs of slowing down. Highly recommended. *—Rick Anderson*

Watch You When You Go / Jun. 12, 2001 / Rounder ♦♦♦♦
This legendary blues-jam band is rolling past three decades now, and this fiery swinging collection is one of their most powerful and varied recordings ever. In addition to the "Tower of Power on speed" energies that have earned them various awards, critical accolades, and a devoted following, this collection boasts dashes of funk, soul, the inimitable saxman Rich Lataille, and the crisp guitar excitement of Chris Vachon. At the forefront is the raspy vocal believability of Mac Odom. It's always interesting how the best blues bands can make songs of despair sound so joyous, but Roomful of Blues also takes a few more wistful looks at romance. The feisty opener "Roll Me Over" is about finding ways to keep the dying flame from burning out completely; Vachon's wailing solo punctuates the energy the "protagonist" puts into the effort. "Love to Watch You When You Go" has a blast watching a lover strut out the door. The punchy rocker "The Salt of My Tears" is about the most cheerful song about loneliness you'll ever hear. "Your Love Was Never There" captures the classic Stax soul sound beautifully, while "Wait and See" has a little boogie-woogie element. The closer, "Where's Bubba?," is original but sounds like a sly cover of any sassy big-band number ever written. *—Jonathan Widran*

Doctor Ross (Isaiah Ross)

b. Oct. 21, 1925, Tunica, MS, **d.** May 28, 1993, Flint, MI
Vocals, Harmonica, Guitar / Detroit Blues, Juke Joint Blues, Modern Delta Blues, Delta Blues

A triple-threat guitarist, harp blower, and vocalist, Doctor Ross decided to fire his sidemen and carry on as a one-man band, a tradition that also includes Joe Hill Louis, Daddy Stovepipe, and Jesse Fuller. Ross' music did not depend on novelty effect, yet it had a distinctly recognizable sound, in part because he learned to play his own way and essentially played everything backwards. His guitar was tuned to open G (like John Lee Hooker and other Delta artists), but Ross played it left-handed and upside-down. He also played harmonica in a rack, but it was turned around with the low notes to the right. As an instrumentalist, Ross perfected the interplay between guitar and harmonica. Unlike other Delta artists who tune in G, Ross didn't use slide, preferring a series of banjo-like strummed riffs, a percussive approach reminiscent of Atlanta 12-string guitarist Barbecue Bob. A strong vocalist and excellent songwriter, Ross gained early experience playing Delta jukes and eventually landed radio shows in Clarksdale and Memphis, where he also recorded for Sam Phillips' Sun label.

At the peak of Ross' career, he quit Sun, concerned that his royalties were being used to promote Elvis Presley's recordings. Relocating in Michigan, he recorded for his own label and for several Detroit labels, while working for General Motors. Returning to music as a recording artist, he worked the festival circuit. Ross' music retained the spirit of his live radio and juke-joint work. The sides he recorded with a band for Sun produced his best material, including classics like "Chicago Breakdown" and "Boogie Disease." As Doctor Ross put it, "I'm kind of like the little boy from the West; I'm different from the rest." Different, yes, but very good. Ross died May 28, 1993, and was buried in Flint, MI. —*Barry Lee Pearson*

● **Boogie Disease** / 1954 / Arhoolie ✦✦✦✦✦
This one will make your teeth rattle. A veteran of the early '50s Sun Studio in Memphis, Ross became known as the "one-man band," a routine gleaned from his mentor Joe Hill Louis. He plays both fine harp (out of the Sonny Boy (John Lee) Williamson I mold) and exciting rhythm guitar characterized by churning, mesmerizing rhythms spiced by treble fills. These 22 infectious tracks are the good doctor's very first recordings, and they present him with rhythm section—a style that predates his "one-man band" days. —*Larry Hoffman*

One Man Band / 1965 / Takoma ✦✦✦
A selection of '60s recordings by Norman Dayron. —*Barry Lee Pearson*

Call the Doctor / Jun. 1965 / Testament ✦✦✦✦
If you're looking for one-man blues, this is one of the better efforts in that vein available. Ross is in fine form and strong voice on his first full-length album, sometimes pulling out as many stops as his limbs allow for all-out stompers, at other times just accompanying himself on harmonica. The tracks are largely adaptations of well-worn material like "Good Morning, Little Schoolgirl," "32-20," and "Going to the River"; the opening blast of "Cat Squirrel" is especially good. The one-man band approach gets a bit wearing over the course of 17 songs, though, unless you're a sucker for the style. The CD reissue adds the previously unissued bonus track "Jivin' Blues." —*Richie Unterberger*

I'd Rather Be an Old Woman's Baby / 1971 / Fortune ✦✦✦
A wild, chaotic session, featuring the title cut, "Good Things Come to My Remind," and the original version of "Cat Squirrel." —*Cub Koda*

Doctor Ross—The Harmonica Boss / 1972 / Fortune ✦✦✦✦✦
Known alternately as *Doctor Ross—The Harmonica Boss, I'd Rather Be an Old Woman's Baby Than a Young Woman's Slave*, or simply *The Harmonica Boss*, this combines earlier singles and album tracks recorded for Detroit's Fortune and Hi-Q imprints. Some of the tracks here—like the original version of "Cat Squirrel"—are cut in mono while the stereo sides emanate from a chaotic and rough and tumble session with the good Doctor being backed by a group known as the Disciples of Soul. This album differs greatly from his better one-man band sides, as everything on here finds Doctor Ross backed by a full band. He negotiates his way through some Sonny Boy Williamson material ("My Black Name Ringing," "Biscuit Baking Woman"), but it's the quirky originals like "I'd Rather Be an Old Woman's Baby Than a Young Woman's Slave" and "I Am Not Dead" (and the line about "arresting my baby, cause she smokin' that dope" in "Good Things Come to My Mind") that make this one well worth hunting down. —*Cub Koda*

His First Recordings / 1972 / Arhoolie ✦✦✦✦✦
His best material, originally recorded for the Sun label in the '50s. Outstanding Delta blues in the unique Dr. Ross guitar-and-harmonica style. —*Barry Lee Pearson*

I Want All My Friends to Know / Jan. 29, 1999 / JSP ✦✦✦

Laura Rucker

Vocals / Chicago Blues
When the popular blues radio show *Blues Before Sunrise* chose pianist and singer Laura Rucker as the subject of a Valentine's Day tribute, the host expressed wonder at the singer's credits with both the country blues artist Blind Blake and the jazzy, slick, experimental, and urban pianist Earl Hines. "Anyone who makes that stretch gets my attention," the show's host commented. But close examination of the discographical depository of evidence makes it seem more like Rucker and her peers on the blues scene were almost trying to avoid attention, releasing recording sessions under pseudonyms and sometimes aping each other's styles just to throw off spies from record company legal departments. Fans of classic female blues vocalists have listened to sides by Jane Lucas and Hannah May, exchanging nods and winks in the insider knowledge that it is really Laura Rucker, cleverly disguised on the labels by the typesetter. Yet this theory appears to be a blues urban legend. Was Jane Lucas, also known as Kansas City Kitty, really Mozell Alderson? Thankfully that is not our concern at present. Ruth Johnson, on the other hand was a pseudonym for Rucker. It gets worse. George Ramsey, who cut some vocal duets with Rucker, was actually Thomas A. Dorsey, better known as Georgia Tom. He also used the Ramsey identification when he cut vocal duets with Lucas, but that doesn't mean she was really Rucker. This game of who-am-I began in the recording studios in 1931, by which time was already a veteran of the Chicago club and recording scene. She had gigged with bandleader and trumpeter Big Ed Lewis on the Kansas City jazz scene in 1926. Her first sessions were in the last days of Paramount and resulted in four sides, including a duet with Georgia Tom Dorsey.

Another more intense spurt of releases came in the middle of that decade for Vocalion and Decca. Her 1935 version of "I'm Gonna Sit Right Down and Write Myself a Letter" was shelved at the time because it was felt to be too much an imitation of Fats Waller. One of her specialty numbers during this time was "Something's Wrong," with lyrics sure to offend gay activists: "If there's too much tenor in his talk, something's wrong." In 1939 she recorded for Bluebird as a vocalist with the Hines band, where her services at the keyboard were surely not needed. This is where her versatility becomes somewhat official, as record guides which label her as a blues singer on the earlier sides now refer to her as a jazz singer. Whatever it was, she worked regularly in clubs on the Chicago scene and

was known for her willingness to play and sing requests from popular songs of the day as well as her regal appearance. Her mainstay status on the Chicago club scene continued through the '40s. Vocalist supreme Peggy Lee has recalled hearing Rucker sing with drummer Baby Dodds and has credited Rucker with the source of her famous interpretation of Cole Porter's "Let's Do It" from Rucker. In 1949, the singer provided the legendary Chicago pianist Claude McLin with his recording debut, a collaboration that made about as big a ripple as a pebble tossed into Lake Superior. This session of ballads and blues numbers was done for Aristocrat, which eventually became the recording dynasty of the Chess brothers. As a result, the tracks of Rucker with the Claude McLin Combo have been released on various anthologies of this label. Rucker obviously did not let her fingers atrophy whilst working behind piano man Hines, and is credited with the swinging and fluent piano on these late-'40s sessions. There is indeed versatility in this artist, but perhaps not to the extent suggested by the association with both Blake and Hines. A better understanding of the relationship with the former man is immediate on the Austrian Wolf collection, entitled *Blind Blake: The Accompanist*. It was Blake that was able to adopt his style to the singer on what were the great blind blues guitarist's final recording sessions in 1931, not the other way around. —*Eugene Chadbourne*

Mason Ruffner

b. Fort Worth, TX
Vocals, Guitar / Rock & Roll, Memphis Blues
Working out of New Orleans for the past few years, Ruffner's style owes much to blues but has a slashing rock-tinged bent all its own. —*Cub Koda*

● **Gypsy Blood** / 1979 / CBS ✦✦✦✦✦
This CD, in places, just cranks it up and spits out a wall of undiluted rock & roll. Straight ahead, full speed ahead, and tell everything to get out of our way. "Gypsy Blood" and "Dancin' on Top of the World" are two cuts that really stand out in this vein. A couple of the tracks just seem to be languishing in a daze as if they've suffered a concussion, and can't decide which way to go. This CD is produced by Dave Edmunds, and when a lot of his work hits, it hits hard. However, when it misses it leaves you scratching your head wondering. The band is tight, just sometimes lacking that guiding hand. The hard-charging "Courage" alone makes this a worthwhile disc, and there is more than just that track to pick the listener up. —*Bob Gottlieb*

Mason Ruffner / 1979 / Epic ✦✦✦

Evolution / May 13, 1997 / Archer ✦✦✦

You Can't Win / Jul. 13, 1999 / Burnside ✦✦✦✦
There are 13 new songs on this disc and they range from some slow blues to his characteristic hard-driven Texas blues that he learned growing up in the Fort Worth. His main influences that you can hear are Jimmy Reed, Anson Funderburgh, and Stevie Ray Vaughan, though much of his vocal phrasing probably comes from the time he spent playing in Robert Ealey's band. His guitar playing is his strong point and he displays it well. From the tasteful slide work on "Mama's Girl" to the loping lines he uses on "Can't Stop Lovin' You," to the chuk chuk guitar of Back in the Alley" to the the hard-driving "Dee Blues." On this latter cut he lets his guitar soar and pound away at the restraints of the speakers, and spends his time really bending the wires to stretch any limits that remain. He makes excellent use of his horn players here, using them to augment his sound and make it fill up the room. A nod must be given at this point to Keith Sykes who co-produced the disc with Mason Ruffner for his contribution on that end. Its good to hear that rasp voice rubbing over the lyrics, but it is even better to hear the guitar-driven Texas blues of this man again. A dynamite performer if you get a chance to see him. —*Bob Gottlieb*

Bobby Rush (Emmit Ellis Jr.)

b. Nov. 10, 1940, Homer, LA
Vocals / Retro-Soul, Modern Electric Blues
The creator of a singular sound which he dubbed "folk-funk," multi-instrumentalist Bobby Rush was among the most colorful characters on the contemporary chitlin circuit, honing a unique style which brought together a cracked lyrical bent with elements of blues, soul, and funk. Born Emmit Ellis Jr., in Homer, LA, on November 10, 1940, he and his family relocated to Chicago in 1953, where he emerged on the West Side blues circuit of the '60s, fronting bands which included such notable alumni as Luther Allison and Freddie King. However, as Rush began to develop his own individual sound, he opted to forgo the blues market in favor of targeting the chitlin circuit, which offered a more receptive audience for his increasingly bawdy material; he notched his first hit in 1971 with his Galaxy label single "Chicken Heads," and later scored with "Bow-Legged Woman" for Jewel.

He appeared on a wide variety of labels as the decade progressed, culminating in the 1979 LP *Rush Hour*, produced by Kenny Gamble and Leon Huff for their Philadelphia International imprint. During the early '80s, Rush signed with the La Jam label, where he remained for a number of years; there his work became increasingly funky and deranged, with records like 1984's *Gotta Have Money* and 1985's *What's Good for the Goose Is Good for the Gander* often featuring material so suggestive he refused to re-create it live.

During the mid-'90s, Rush moved to Waldoxy, heralding a return to a soul-blues sound on LPs including 1995's *One Monkey Don't Stop No Show*, 1997's *Lovin' a Big Fat Woman*, and 2000's *Hoochie Man*. In April, 2001, his tour bus crashed, injuring several bandmembers and killing one, Latisha Brown. Rush was hospitalized for a short time, then returned home to recuperate. —*Jason Ankeny*

Rush Hour / 1979 / Philadelphia International ✦✦✦✦
Kenny Gamble and Leon Huff produced *Rush Hour*, Bobby Rush's belated full-length debut album, for the Philadelphia International label. By that time, their patented Philly soul sound was out of favor, and they wisely chose not to impose it on Rush. Nevertheless, the album is considerably slicker than any of his Ichiban albums. Oddly, this is hardly a problem, since Rush always favored soul more than blues and had a fondness for funk.

The only real flaw with the record is that the material is a bit uneven, but the quality of the performances carries it over rough spots and helps make the record one of the best in his catalog. *—Thom Owens*

Man Can Give / Oct. 17, 1990 / La Jam ♦♦♦

Handy Man / 1992 / Urgent! ♦♦♦

Like any of Bobby Rush's '90s recordings for Urgent! and Ichiban, *Handy Man* is a pretty good album that draws from Chicago blues and Southern soul equally. Rush gives some good performances which carry the album through some lame original songs and flat, synth-laden production, complete with robotic drum machines. Of course, this holds true for almost any of Rush's albums, which means you've got to take what you can get, and here you get a couple of good songs balanced by a lot of filler. And Rush fans should be used to that by now. *—Thom Owens*

● **Instant Replays: The Hits** / 1992 / Urgent! ♦♦♦♦♦

Instant Replays: The Hits is a good overview of Bobby Rush's '80s recordings for Urgent! and Ichiban, capturing all of the highlights from such funky, greasy blues albums as *Gotta Have Money* and *What's Good for the Goose is Good for the Gander*. *—Thom Owens*

One Monkey Don't Stop No Show / 1995 / Waldoxy ♦♦

Bobby Rush is a no-holds-barred showman, and his R-rated live shows are an unforgettable (if politically incorrect) experience. That makes it a pity that this recording (like many of his others) is so forgettable. He takes blues standards, adds a few lyric snippets of his own, and transforms their melodies into virtually identical funky vamps. This quickly gets uninteresting. The extensive use of synthesizers doesn't help. And claiming authorship of songs that are so obviously mere adaptations of others' is a dubious practice. *—Steve Hoffman*

She's a Good Un (It's Alright) / Dec. 5, 1995 / Ronn ♦♦♦

Sue / May 28, 1996 / La Jam ♦♦♦

Wearing It Out / Jun. 5, 1996 / La Jam ♦♦♦

It's Alright, Vol. 2 / May 7, 1997 / Ronn ♦♦♦

Lovin' a Big Fat Woman / May 27, 1997 / Waldoxy ♦♦♦

What's Good for the Goose Is Good for the Gander / Aug. 26, 1997 / La Jam ♦♦♦

Southern Soul / Sep. 8, 1998 / Cannonball ♦♦♦♦

Bobby Rush and Lynn White, the king and queen of the Southern soul and blues circuit, get a half dozen tracks apiece on this joint effort. Unfortunately, the duo does not team up on this disc, both sessions being produced separately by Willie Mitchell, but these are no leftover cuts by a long shot. Rush smokes and burns on "I Need a Bed Partner," "Funky Way to Treat Your Woman," and "Makin' a Decision (Can Be Hard)," while White is both sexy and assertive-sounding on tracks like "Get Your Lie Straight," "Down the Line," and "I Don't Want to Ever See Your Face Again." An excellent introduction to these modern day soul giants. *—Cub Koda*

The Best of Bobby Rush / Jun. 29, 1999 / La Jam ♦♦♦♦

Rush Hour Plus / Dec. 24, 1999 / West Side ♦♦♦♦♦

Hoochie Man / Apr. 25, 2000 / Waldoxy ♦♦♦

Otis Rush

b. Apr. 29, 1934, Philadelphia, MS

Vocals, Guitar / Electric Chicago Blues, Chicago Blues

Breaking into the R&B Top Ten his very first time out in 1956 with the startlingly intense slow blues "I Can't Quit You Baby," southpaw guitarist Otis Rush subsequently established himself as one of the premier bluesmen on the Chicago circuit. He remains so today.

Rush is often credited with being one of the architects of the West Side guitar style, along with Magic Sam and Buddy Guy. It's a nebulous honor, since Otis Rush played clubs on Chicago's South Side just as frequently during the sound's late-'50s incubation period. Nevertheless, his esteemed status as a prime Chicago innovator is eternally ensured by the ringing, vibrato-enhanced guitar work that remains his stock-in-trade and a tortured, super-intense vocal delivery that can force the hairs on the back of your neck upwards in silent salute.

If talent alone were the formula for widespread success, Rush would currently be Chicago's leading blues artist. But fate, luck, and the guitarist's own idiosyncrasies have conspired to hold him back on several occasions when opportunity was virtually begging to be accepted.

Rush came to Chicago in 1948, met Muddy Waters, and knew instantly what he wanted to do with the rest of his life. The omnipresent Willie Dixon caught Rush's act and signed him to Eli Toscano's Cobra Records in 1956. The frighteningly intense "I Can't Quit You Baby" was the maiden effort for both artist and label, streaking to number six on *Billboard*'s R&B chart.

His 1956-1958 Cobra legacy is a magnificent one, distinguished by the Dixon-produced minor-key masterpieces "Double Trouble" and "My Love Will Never Die," the nails-tough "Three Times a Fool" and "Keep on Loving Me Baby," and the rhumba-rocking classic "All Your Love (I Miss Loving)." Rush apparently dashed off the latter tune in the car en route to Cobra's West Roosevelt Road studios, where he would cut it with the nucleus of Ike Turner's combo.

After Cobra closed up shop, Rush's recording fortunes mostly floundered. He followed Dixon over to Chess in 1960, cutting another classic (the stunning "So Many Roads, So Many Trains") before moving on to Duke (one solitary single, 1962's "Homework"), Vanguard, and Cotillion (there he cut the underrated Mike Bloomfield-Nick Gravenites-produced 1969 album *Mourning in the Morning*, with yeoman help from the house rhythm section in Muscle Shoals).

Typical of Rush's horrendous luck was the unnerving saga of his *Right Place, Wrong Time* album. Laid down in 1971 for Capitol Records, the giant label inexplicably took a pass on the project despite its obvious excellence. It took another five years for the set to emerge on the tiny Bullfrog label, blunting Rush's momentum once again (the album is now available on Hightone).

An uneven but worthwhile 1975 set for Delmark, *Cold Day in Hell*, and a host of solid live albums that mostly sound very similar kept Rush's gilt-edged name in the marketplace to some extent during the '70s and '80s, a troubling period for the legendary southpaw.

In 1986, he walked out on an expensive session for Rooster Blues (Louis Myers, Lucky Peterson, and Casey Jones were among the assembled sidemen), complaining that his amplifier didn't sound right and thereby scuttling the entire project. Alligator picked up the rights to an album he had done overseas for Sonet originally called *Troubles, Troubles*. It turned out to be a prophetic title: Much to Rush's chagrin, the firm over-dubbed keyboardist Lucky Peterson and chopped out some masterful guitar work when it reissued the set as *Lost in the Blues* in 1991.

Finally, in 1994, the career of this Chicago blues legend began traveling in the right direction. *Ain't Enough Comin' In*, his first studio album in 16 years, was released on Mercury and ended up topping many blues critics' year-end lists. Produced spotlessly by John Porter with a skin-tight band, Rush roared a set of nothing but covers—but did them all his way, his blistering guitar consistently to the fore.

Once again, a series of personal problems threatened to end Rush's long-overdue return to national prominence before it got off the ground. But he's been in top-notch form recent years, fronting a tight band that's entirely sympathetic to the guitarist's sizzling approach. Rush signed with the House of Blues' fledgling record label, instantly granting that company a large dose of credibility and setting himself up for another career push when the album is completed. It still may not be too late for Otis Rush to assume his rightful throne as Chicago's blues king. *—Bill Dahl*

This One's a Good Un / 1968 / Blue Horizon ♦♦♦♦♦

Mourning in the Morning / Aug. 1969 / Atlantic ♦♦♦

Panned by many a critic upon its 1969 release, Otis Rush's trip to Muscle Shoals sounds pretty fine now (with the obvious exceptions of "My Old Lady" and "Me," which no amount of time will ever save). The house band (including Duane Allman and drummer Roger Hawkins) picks up on Rush's harrowing vibe and runs with it on the stunning "Gambler's Blues," a chomping "Feel So Bad," and a shimmering instrumental treatment of Aretha Franklin's "Baby I Love You." *—Bill Dahl*

Door to Door (With Albert King) / Jun. 1970 / MCA/Chess ♦♦♦♦♦

Although Albert King is pictured on the front cover and has the lion's share of tracks on this excellent compilation, six of the fourteen tracks come from Rush's shortlived tenure with the label and are some of his very best. Chronologically, these are his next recordings after the Cobra sides and they carry a lot of the emotional wallop of those tracks, albeit with much loftier production values with much of it recorded in early stereo. Oddly enough, some of the material ("All Your Love," "I'm Satisfied [Keep on Loving Me Baby]") were remakes—albeit great ones—of tunes that Cobra had already released as singles! But Rush's performance of "So Many Roads" (featuring one of the greatest slow blues guitar solos of all time) should not be missed at any cost. *—Cub Koda*

Blues Masters, Vol. 2 / 1972 / Blue Horizon ♦♦♦♦♦

1956-1958 Cobra classics. *—Bill Dahl*

Screamin' & Cryin' / Nov. 26, 1974 / Evidence ♦♦♦

Otis Rush's crunching guitar and vocals were never more emphatic than during the '70s when it seemed that he would actually find the pop attention and mass stardom he deserved. These mid-'70s tracks were originally cut for the Black and Blue label, with Rush playing grinding, relentless riffs and creating waves of sonic brilliance through creatively repeated motifs, jagged notes, and sustained lines and licks, while hollering, screaming, moaning, and wailing. Jimmy Dawkins, an outstanding lead artist in his own right, has also long been one of Chicago's great rhythm artists and shows it by adding plenty of tinkling, crackling figures and lines in the backgrounds. While not as consistently riveting as his live Evidence date, this one is also a valuable Rush document. *—Ron Wynn*

Cold Day in Hell / 1975 / Delmark ♦♦♦

Inconsistent but sometimes riveting 1975 studio set that hits some high highs (a crunchy "Cut You a Loose," the lickety-split jazzy instrumental "Motoring Along") right alongside some incredibly indulgent moments. But that's Otis—the transcendent instants are worth the hassle. *—Bill Dahl*

Right Place, Wrong Time / Feb. 1976 / Hightone ♦♦♦♦♦

This recording session was not released until five years after it was done. One can imagine the tapes practically smoldering in their cases, the music is so hot. Sorry, there is nothing "wrong" about this blues album at all. Otis Rush was a great blues expander, a man whose guitar playing was in every molecule pure blues. On his solos on this album he strips the idea of the blues down to very simple gestures (i.e., a bent string, but bent in such a subtle way that the seasoned blues listener will be surprised). As a performer he opens up the blues form with his chord progressions and use of horn sections, the latter instrumentation again added in a wonderfully spare manner, bringing to mind a master painter working certain parts of a canvas in order to bring in more light. Blues fans who get tired of the same old song structures, riff, and rhythms should be delighted with most of Rush's output, and this one is among his best. Sometimes all he does to make a song sound unlike any blues one has ever heard is just a small thing—a chord moving up when one expects it go down, for example. The production is particularly skilled, and the fact that Capitol Records turned this session down after originally producing it can only be reasonably accepted when combined with other decisions this label has made, such as turning down the Doors because singer Jim Morrison had "no charisma." This record doesn't mess around at all. The first track takes off like the man they fire out of a cannon at the end of a circus, a perceived climax swaggeringly representing just the beginning, after all. Some of the finest tracks are the ones that go longer than five minutes, allowing the players room to stretch. And that means more of Rush's great guitar playing, of course. For the final track he leaves the blues behind completely for a moving cover version of "Rainy Night in Georgia" by Tony Joe White. —*Eugene Chadbourne*

Lost in the Blues / Oct. 1977 / Alligator ♦♦♦

The powers-that-be at Alligator were subjected to a fair amount of criticism for taking a 1977 album of standards that Rush had cut in Sweden and overdubbing Lucky Peterson's keyboards to make the thing sound fuller and more contemporary. History, after all, should not be messed with. But it's still a reasonably successful enterprise, Rush imparting his own intense twist to "I Miss You So," "You Don't Have to Go," and "Little Red Rooster." —*Bill Dahl*

Live in Europe / Oct. 1977 / Evidence ♦♦♦♦

Recorded in France back in 1987, this ten-song set finds Otis backed by strong trio support throughout in a delightfully engaged performance. Though several live albums exist on him, seldom has his declamatory vocals and stinging left-handed upside down guitar style been so well documented. Rush puts forth solo after solo, each with its own unique set of twists and turns, making this a veritable textbook of what he does best. Inspired listening and highly recommended. —*Cub Koda*

Troubles Troubles / 1978 / Sonet ♦♦♦

Low-key collection of standards. —*Bill Dahl*

So Many Roads: Live in Concert [LP] / 1978 / Delmark ♦♦♦

There's a pile of Otis Rush live albums in the bins now, but this was the one that made everybody sit up and take notice and it's still his best. Recorded live outdoors in a Tokyo park in the Summer of 1975 with thousands of fans hanging on every note and word, Otis digs deep and delivers some of the most inspired singing and playing he's ever committed to magnetic tape. All the performances are of a nice, comfortable lenth with none of the interminable soloing that mars other Rush live sets. This is the one to have. —*Cub Koda*

Groaning the Blues / 1980 / Flyright ♦♦♦♦♦

This mixes gems and alternate takes previously issued on a limited edition Blue Horizon LP. The Rush Cobra material has been issued and reissued so much that you can get burned with the various titles and editions floating around. This is aimed more at the completists and Rush freaks than the general consumer. —*Ron Wynn*

Tops / 1985 / Blind Pig ♦♦♦

There are simply too many live albums by Rush on the market to keep track of anymore. This was one of the earlier entries, cut in 1985 with a West Coast combo following Rush pretty well. Since the same basic set list turns up on most every one of these things, there's not really a whole lot of difference between any of 'em (but go with Delmark's *So Many Roads* first). —*Bill Dahl*

☆ **Otis Rush, 1956–1958: His Cobra Recordings** / 1989 / Paula ♦♦♦♦♦

Otis Rush's debut recordings for the Cobra label are defining moments of Chicago blues. Seldom had a young Windy City artist recorded with this much harrowing emotion in both his singing and playing, simultaneously connecting with the best that Delta blues had to offer while plunging headlong into the electric future. These are the songs that continue to be the building blocks of his legend; "All Your Love," "Double Trouble," "I Can't Quit You, Baby," "Groaning the Blues," "It Takes Time," and "Checking on My Baby" are all singular masterpieces. This single disc collection features all sixteen Cobra sides issued as singles plus the bonus of four alternate takes, all presented here with the best sound to date. These are milestone recordings in the history of the blues and an essential part of anyone's collection. —*Cub Koda*

Ain't Enough Comin' In / 1994 / This Way Up ♦♦♦♦♦

With sympathetic production from John Porter, a great lineup of players who follow him every bluesy turn of the way and a dozen well chosen pieces of material, Rush wipes the unispired album slate clean with this one. Everything that makes Otis a unique master of his form is here to savor, from his passionate vocals to the shimmering finger vibrato he applies to the liquid tones of his Fender Stratocaster. While Rush has tackled some of this material on other outings, never has it been served up so passionately as it is here. Even the re-cut of his famous Duke 45 "Homework" burns with a new intensity that makes you believe that this is one opportunity that Rush—at least this time—refused to let go by the boards. —*Cub Koda*

This Way / 1994 / Mercury ♦♦♦♦♦

Otis Rush has never recorded or performed consistently. That's what makes this recent session so welcome; Rush gets first-rate production, engineering and material. There's only one original out of 12 cuts, but when he's putting his stamp on classics by Albert and B.B. King, Sam Cooke, Ray Charles and Percy Mayfield, it's hard to complain. Rush emphasizes uptempo, surging numbers rather than slow tunes, and there aren't many examples of his jagged, cutting solos, but Rush's vocals are among his most dynamic and arresting in many years. This is certainly his finest work since the '70s Bullfrog sessions. —*Ron Wynn*

So Many Roads: Live in Concert [CD] / Aug. 1, 1995 / Delmark ♦♦♦

The 1995 CD release of this title, complete with a bit more than an extra ten minutes of material, looks good on paper and received lots of praise. The original album release is among much live material by this artist that haunts the used-record pile, possibly because when blues fans begin culling through their collection, it is titles such as this that get the boot. Not that this is terrible or anything. Otis Rush is one of the finest blues guitarists, ever. He has made some records that are fantastic. On this one, he is in front of a huge live audience in Japan. The performance is reminiscent of some of the live albums by B.B. King. Backup is sparse in comparison, though. There are only drums and bass, plus second guitarist Jimmy Johnson, a capable player who is mixed pretty far to the background, sticking closely to chords or riff patterns. Blues purists will raise an eyebrow over the way the drummer and bassist play, ever mindful of the fact that Rush was a heavy guitarist who liked to stretch out and build intensity in his solos. His string-bending prowess never fails to surprise, and he also has other tricks for the fretboard, including feedback and ecstatic chording at the climax of an improvisation. Listeners familiar with the way bass and drums pursue a soloist in a fusion jazz band will have an inkling of the way bassist Sylvester Boines and drummer Tyrone Centuary attack the guitar happenings here. There are plenty of familiar gambits, such as suddenly doubling or even tripling the time at the turnaround, heavy-handed use of hi-hat splashes, and intense, synchronized accents that bring to mind the time the guy upstairs decided to demonstrate dance steps at three in the morning. "Crosscut Saw" is a version of this blues standard as if Rush had written it, every guitar lick delivered piping hot, fresh from the guitarist's bakery. It all adds up to showmanship and virtuosity, yes. What is missing is the really deep feeling of the blues. It just doesn't happen on this record. Deep as Rush's guitar burrows into one's soul, however, the listener might not even miss it. —*Eugene Chadbourne*

Any Place I'm Going / Aug. 11, 1998 / House of Blues ♦♦♦

This album on the House of Blues label is a bit smoother and more slickly produced (by Rush and famed Memphis producer Willie Mitchell) than Rush's classic, rough-edged Chess recordings, but there's still plenty here to like. With a solid horn section backing him on most cuts, Rush gets ample room to show off his razor-sharp guitar chops. And his distinctive, emotionally charged voice remains a true blues treasure. In addition to his own no-nonsense originals, Rush draws on some familiar tunes from classic soul and blues performers like Marvin Gaye, Sam Cooke, Nappy Brown, and Little Milton. —*Joel Roberts*

★ **Essential Collection: The Classic Cobra Recordings 1956–1958** / Sep. 19, 2000 / Varese Sarabande ♦♦♦♦♦

The title says it all. This *is* the essential Otis Rush, the singles recorded for Eli Toscano's Cobra label between 1956 and 1958. If Rush had never recorded another note, his legendary status would remain intact based solely on these recordings. Backed by players like Willie Dixon and Little Walter, it's Rush's impassioned vocals and stinging guitar lines that make "I Can't Quit You Baby," "All Your Love (I Miss Loving)," and "Double Trouble" the classics they are. In addition to the A- and B-sides of all eight singles released by Cobra, eight alternate takes are included, four more than the Paula edition of this material released in 1991. Along with a slightly better transfer from the original tapes, this is not only one of the best places to start for someone getting interested in the blues, but a vital part of any blues collection. Outstanding. —*Sean Westergaard*

Live at the Chicago Blues Festival / Intermedia ♦♦♦♦♦

Who knows where these live tracks were done, or when? If the sound wasn't so bad, they'd rate with his better concert efforts. It also includes latter-day Little Walter sides, which are less inspired. —*Bill Dahl*

Jimmy Rushing

b. Aug. 26, 1903, Oklahoma City, OK, **d.** Jun. 8, 1972, New York, NY

Vocals / Vocal Jazz, East Coast Blues, Jazz Blues, Jump Blues, Swing

He was known as "Mister Five-By-Five"—an affectionate reference to his height and girth—a blues shouter who defined and then transcended the form. The owner of a booming voice that radiated sheer joy in whatever material he sang, Jimmy Rushing could swing with anyone and dominate even the loudest of big bands. Rushing achieved his greatest fame in front of the Count Basie band from 1935 to 1950, yet unlike many band singers closely associated with one organization, he was able to carry on afterwards with a series of solo recordings that further enhanced his reputation as a first-class jazz singer.

Raised in a musical family, learning violin, piano and music theory in his youth, Rushing began performing in nightspots after a move to California in the mid-'20s. He joined Walter Page's Blue Devils in 1927, then toured with Bennie Moten from 1929 until the leader's death in 1935, going over to Basie when the latter picked up the pieces of the Moten band. The unquenchably swinging Basie rhythm section was a perfect match for Rushing, making their earliest showing together on a 1936 recording of "Boogie Woogie" that stamped not only Rushing's presence onto the national scene but also that of Lester Young. Rushing's recordings with Basie are scattered liberally throughout several reissues on Decca, Columbia and RCA. While with Basie, he also appeared in several film shorts and features.

After the Basie ensemble broke up in 1950, a victim of hard times for big bands, Rushing briefly retired, then formed his own septet. He started a series of solo albums for Vanguard in the mid-'50s, then turned in several distinguished recordings for Columbia in league with such luminaries as Dave Brubeck, Coleman Hawkins and Benny Goodman, the latter of whom he appeared with at the Brussels World's Fair in 1958 as immortalized in "Brussels Blues." He also recorded with Basie alumni such as Buck Clayton and Jo Jones, as well as with the Duke Ellington band on *Jazz Party.* He appeared on TV in *The Sound of Jazz* in 1957, was featured in Jon Hendricks' *The Evolution of the Blues*, and also had a singing and acting role in the 1969 film *The Learning Tree.* —*Richard S. Ginell*

Cat Meets Chick / Aug. 18, 1955-Aug. 23, 1955 / Columbia ♦♦♦

As the common format for LPs became 12" rather than 10" in the mid-'50s, record companies and artists struggled to come up with ideas for sustained musical performances lasting 30 to 45 minutes. In 1955, Columbia Records producer Irving Townsend put together a selection of pop songs with the singers Felicia Sanders, Peggy King, and Jerry Vale to come up with *Girl Meets Boy*, and he had a similar concept in the jazz realm for *Cat Meets Chick.* Borrowing Jimmy Rushing from Vanguard Records and hiring young Ada Moore, who had recently made her Broadway debut in the musical *House of Flowers*, he put them in front of an orchestra led by Buck Clayton and had them perform a series of songs in which the story line was that Clayton (through the medium of his trumpet) and Rushing were vying for Moore's attention. For example, Moore would say, "Buck, if I choose you, what are you gonna give me?," which would be a cue for Clayton to launch into "I Can't Give You Anything But Love." "Nothin' but love?" Moore would say, "Uh-huh, you got the wrong girl," after which Clayton would play "The Blues." The concept, of course, was just an excuse to have Rushing and Moore sing a bunch of old favorites before Clayton's band, and that was fine, especially because Moore, sporting a Sarah Vaughan-like alto, held her own against the great blues shouter. Of course, the ruling presence, even in his absence, was Count Basie, who had previously employed both Rushing and Clayton for extended periods. The music had much of the verve and swing of the Basie band, even without the leader being on the date. The story might be silly, but the music was not. —*William Ruhlmann*

The Jazz Odyssey of James Rushing, Esq. / Nov. 6, 1956–Nov. 7, 1956 / Columbia ✦✦✦✦
With four separate groups representing the distinct styles of jazz from New Orleans, Chicago, Kansas City, and New York, Jimmy Rushing sings a dozen favorites, revisiting staples from his repertoire like "Baby, Won't You Please Come Home" and "Rosetta," as well as classics he had recently discovered, such as W.C. Handy's "Careless Love." But the obvious high point is Rushing's first recording on piano, as he accompanies himself on his hilarious conversational narrative blues "Tricks Ain't Walkin' No More" (which he later reprised during a '60s appearance on Ralph Gleason's *Jazz Casual* TV series, though that performance wasn't released on video for the first time until 1995). The supporting cast is a strong one, including Buck Clayton, Vic Dickenson, Buddy Tate, Jo Jones, Milt Hinton, Hank Jones, Dicky Wells, and Budd Johnson, among others. —*Ken Dryden*

If This Ain't the Blues / 1958 / Vanguard ✦✦✦
Blues singer Jimmy Rushing put a flurry of classic LPs in the late '50s and early '60s, but the few CD reissues that have appeared have generally been in the form of compilations, rather than straight reissues of original sessions. It's a shame, because this original release—with all the similar material gathered and a priceless cover photo of Rushing resting on a drink case—is preferable to having to buy two separate CD anthologies to obtain all eight tracks heard on this album. Rushing is in great form, backed by fellow Count Basie alumni such as trumpeter Emmett Berry, trombonist Vic Dickenson, tenor saxophonist Buddy Tate, and drummer Jo Jones; the other musicians include bassist Aaron Bell, blues guitarist Roy Gaines, pianist Clarence Johnson, and the somewhat superfluous organist Marlowe Morris, who proves to be more of a distraction. The singer even sits out one track, "If This Ain't the Blues," to give his friends a chance to blow. The music, in spite of Morris' out of place electric organ, swings very well throughout the date, especially old favorites like "Dinah" and "Pennies from Heaven." Last reissued in 1982 on LP by King in Japan, it will be hard to locate in this format, but worth the effort. —*Ken Dryden*

Rushing Lullabies / Feb. 20, 1959–Jun. 19, 1959 / Sony ✦✦✦
Jimmy Rushing recorded several albums for Columbia during 1959-1960; although in his mid-fifties, he was still in peak form. This CD reissue (which has a previously unissued "The Road of Love") finds Rushing joined by both pianist Ray Bryant and organist Sir Charles Thompson, Buddy Tate on tenor, guitarist Skeeter Best, bassist Gene Ramey, and drummer Jo Jones. The combination works quite well, and Rushing, in addition to a few blues, puts his own stamp on such numbers as "'Deed I Do," "Pink Champagne," "I Cried For You," and even "Good Rockin' Tonight." Bryant and Tate in particular have strong solos (both are excellent on "I Can't Believe That You're in Love With Me"), and with Rushing in such good shape, this is an easily enjoyable mainstream swing session. —*Scott Yanow*

Jimmy Rushing and the Smith Girls / Jul. 7, 1960–Jul. 13, 1960 / Columbia ✦✦✦
Rushing does songs previously made famous by classic female blues singers. —*Ron Wynn*

Every Day I Have the Blues / Feb. 9, 1967–Feb. 10, 1967 / Impulse! ✦✦✦✦
It may have been relatively late in Jimmy Rushing's career when he recorded two albums for ABC/Bluesway (*Every Day I Have the Blues* and *Livin' the Blues*, both of which are reissued in full on this single CD), but he was still in prime singing voice. Joined by such friends as trombonist Dicky Wells, trumpeter Clark Terry, and tenor saxophonist Buddy Tate, Rushing shows that he was still relevant on such blues-based songs as "Berkeley Campus Blues," "Blues in the Dark," "I Left My Baby," "Sent for You Yesterday," and "We Remember Prez." Even with Oliver Nelson's arrangements on the first half and an electric rhythm section on the second, both Rushing and the musicians play off each other well, resulting in a swinging set. —*Scott Yanow*

Gee, Baby, Ain't I Good to You / Oct. 30, 1967 / Master Jazz ✦✦
This is a decent session that, considering the lineup, does not live up to its potential. At what was essentially a jazz party held in a recording studio, the musicians (trumpeter Buck Clayton, trombonist Dicky Wells, tenor saxophonist Julian Dash, pianist Sir Charles Thompson, bassist Gene Ramey, and drummer Jo Jones) are all veterans of the famous series of Buck Clayton jam sessions held in the '50s and, along with singer Jimmy Rushing, the majority are alumni of the Count Basie Orchestra. The problem is that their rendition of the blues and swing standards are often quite loose, there are a generous amount of missteps and, although Clayton is heroic under the circumstances (this was one of his final recordings before ill health caused his retirement), most of the musicians would have benefited from running through the songs an additional time. It's recommended only to completists. —*Scott Yanow*

Who Was It Sang That Song? / Oct. 30, 1967 / Master Jazz ✦✦✦
Recorded the same day as the music released on the Master Jazz album *Gee Baby, Ain't I Good to You*, this is the superior of the two recordings. This CD reissue not only has the original five songs from the LP, but also previously unreleased versions of "'Deed I Do," Sir Charles Thompson's "Almost Home," and "Moten Stomp." The classic swing singer Jimmy Rushing is joined by six veterans, including three fellow Basie-ites: trumpeter

Buck Clayton (near the end of his playing career), trombonist Dicky Wells, and drummer Jo Jones, plus Julian Dash on tenor, bassist Gene Ramey, and pianist Thompson. They jam enthusiastically, if predictably on loose versions of jazz standards including "Baby Won't You Please Come Home," a blues medley, and "All of Me." —*Scott Yanow*

Livin' the Blues / Oct. 1968 / Bluesway ✦✦✦
Jimmy Rushing enjoyed great success in applying the blues to jazz rhythms and in doing so he had the best those two genres could offer, soul and swing. On this 1968 session, one of the last recordings he made for the Bluesway label, he is joined by a combination of Count Basie alumni (with whom he enjoyed perhaps his greatest success), Dave Frishberg, and other jazz musicians who do not quite raise to the level of the former two groups. The play list is dotted with tunes that were part of the basic Rushing repertoire including his classic "Sent for You Yesterday (And Here You Come Today)." The list also includes two pieces by Connie Rushing. Basie trombonist Dicky Wells gets in some good drawn-out licks here. Similarly on the almost pure blues, another former Basie-ite, Buddy Tate, gets a couple of prolonged, mournful choruses. Not everything is down-in-the-dumps material. Wells' "We Remember Prez" gets a thorough workout featuring Frishberg's earthy piano, Bobby Bushnell's fender bass, Buddy Tate's honking tenor, and Wells again as Rushing sits this one out. Despite that this was one of the last recordings Rushing made before his death, he was still in the top of his form and could shout the blues with the best of them. This LP needs to be transferred to CD. —*Dave Nathan*

The You and Me That Used to Be / Oct. 1971 / Bluebird/RCA ✦✦✦✦✦
On this straight CD reissue of Jimmy Rushing's final recording sessions, the singer is in spirited form despite being little more than a year from his death. On the ten swing standards and a lone blues ("Fine and Mellow"), Rushing is joined by pianist Dave Frishberg (also responsible for the arrangements), bassist Milt Hinton, and drummer Mel Lewis, plus either Ray Nance on cornet and violin and tenor saxophonist Zoot Sims, or Budd Johnson (on soprano) and Al Cohn (on tenor). Touching renditions of "I Surrender Dear" and "More Than You Know" find Rushing backed only by Frishberg's very able piano. This recommended CD is proof that "Mr. Five by Five" (whose career spanned more than 40 years) went out on top. —*Scott Yanow*

● **The Essential Jimmy Rushing** / 1974 / Vanguard ✦✦✦✦✦
This single CD reissues an earlier Jimmy Rushing two-LP set, leaving off two cuts due to lack of space. Jimmy Rushing, who may very well have been the definitive male big band singer, sticks mostly to blues and Kansas City swing on the release and is backed by a variety of top swing all-stars, including most notably tenor saxophonist Buddy Tate, trumpeter Emmett Berry, and trombonists Lawrence Brown and Vic Dickenson. The sidemen receive plenty of space for concise solos, particularly pianists Pete Johnson and Sammy Price. The performances (plus the 11 other songs that are awaiting reissue someday) are among the most rewarding of Jimmy Rushing's post-Basie career and are full of joy and timeless swing. —*Scott Yanow*

Mr. Five by Five / Aug. 1981 / Columbia ✦✦✦
From 1956-1960, veteran swing/blues singer Jimmy Rushing recorded six albums for Columbia. Most of the sets have not yet been reissued on CD, so this two-LP sampler from 1981 (which inexcusably does not give the recording dates) is still worth picking up by listeners lucky enough to run across it. Rushing is featured in eight different settings on 30 selections, including with all-star groups featuring trumpeter Buck Clayton, tenors Coleman Hawkins and Buddy Tate, trombonist Dicky Wells, and pianist Ray Bryant. In addition, there are numbers with the Dave Brubeck Quartet, the Benny Goodman big band, and (on four previously unreleased songs) fellow singer Helen Humes and tenor saxophonist Ben Webster. Throughout the high-quality program, Rushing is heard in prime form, making one wonder why so much of this swinging material has not been brought back yet. —*Scott Yanow*

Bluesway Sessions / 1986 / Charly ✦✦✦✦
Singer Jimmy Rushing's two albums for Bluesway have been reissued in full on this British double-LP from 1986. Although recorded near the end of Rushing's life, he still sounds strong on the set of blues, ballads, and swinging material. The first album finds Rushing joined by the Oliver Nelson Orchestra (which includes flugelhornist Clark Terry and trombonist Dicky Wells), while the other has a septet that includes Wells, tenor saxophonist Buddy Tate, and pianist Dave Frishberg, plus a slightly funky studio rhythm section. Both combinations work well, and Rushing shows plenty of spirit throughout the performances (most of which have not yet been reissued on CD). —*Scott Yanow*

Rushing Lullabies: Little Jimmy Rushing and the Big Brass / Apr. 29, 1997 / Columbia ✦✦✦✦
Although named after a former LP, this CD actually contains the complete contents of two albums (the other one was called *Little Jimmy Rushing and the Big Brass*) plus a brief previously unreleased number. Known for his renditions of swing-oriented blues, but also quite effective on ballads and jumping standards, the great singer is featured with a big band (which has solo space for many musicians, including tenors Buddy Tate and Coleman Hawkins, trumpeter Buck Clayton, and trombonist Dicky Wells) and a sextet with Tate, organist Sir Charles Thompson, and pianist Ray Bryant. These were two of Rushing's better sets from the 1950s, and he is heard throughout the mostly veteran tunes in top form. Highlights include "I'm Coming Virginia," "Mister Five By Five," "When You're Smiling," "Good Rockin' Tonight," and "Russian Lullaby." —*Scott Yanow*

Five Feet of Soul / Jul. 28, 1998 / Collectables ✦✦✦
Collectable's *Five Feet of Soul* is a reissue of the original Colpix album, augmented by a couple of bonus tracks. Although Jimmy Rushing was past his prime at the time this was recorded, the album contains a number of greatly entertaining, jazzy jump blues tunes that is worth the time of any Count Basie or Rushing fan. —*Stephen Thomas Erlewine*

1930–1938 / Jan. 26, 1999 / Giants of Jazz ✦✦✦

1938–1945 / Jan. 26, 1999 / Giants of Jazz ✦✦✦

Oh Love / Jul. 7, 1999 / Vanguard ✦✦✦✦✦

Although Jimmy Rushing parted company with Count Basie in 1950, Basie's influence stayed with him right up until his death in 1972. Similarly, Basie didn't forget about Rushing either; the fact that Joe Williams, Basie's male vocalist from 1954-1961, was greatly influenced by Rushing certainly wasn't lost on the Count. Basie's influence is impossible to miss on *Oh Love*, a superb CD focusing on Rushing's John Hammond-produced work for Vanguard in the 1950s. Spanning 1955-1958, this collection of Kansas City swing, jump blues, and jazz/blues draws on three of the singer's old Vanguard LPs (*Listen to the Blues, If This Ain't the Blues*, and *Goin' to Chicago*), and finds him joined by such hard-swinging improvisers as tenor saxman Buddy Tate, trombonist Lawrence Brown, pianist Pete Johnson, and drummer Jo Jones (not to be confused with Philly Joe Jones). Rushing revisits many classics from his Basie years, including "Going to Chicago Blues," "Pennies From Heaven," "Gee Baby, Ain't I Good to You," and "Dinah," and he sings them with as much conviction as ever. These are essential recordings that have withstood the test of time quite nicely. —*Alex Henderson*

Every Day / Sep. 28, 1999 / Vanguard ✦✦✦✦✦

This CD compiles tracks from three separate LPs of the always swinging blues shouter Jimmy Rushing, produced by John Hammond in the 1950s. Most of the music comes from the best date, *Listen to the Blues*; highlights include a spirited "Evenin'," the classic "See See Rider" with a fine trumpet solo by Emmett Berry, and "Roll 'Em Pete," a popular boogie-woogie tune that finds the leader on the sidelines except for shouting encouragement. The three selections from *Listen to the Blues* are badly dated by the questionable

addition of organist Marlowe Morris, while only the oft-requested "Sent for You Yesterday" is included from the far superior album *Goin' to Chicago*. It's good to see some of this important music become available once again, though Rushing fans would have preferred intact reissues of the original albums. —*Ken Dryden*

Cat Meets Chick/The Jazz Odyssey of James Rushing, Esq. / May 7, 2002 / Collectables ✦✦✦✦✦

Jimmy Rushing's first two Columbia Records albums, recorded in 1955 and 1956 and originally released in 1956 and 1957, both have concepts behind them. *Cat Meets Chick* is actually co-billed to Ada Moore (who had just made her Broadway debut in *House of Flowers*) and trumpeter Buck Clayton, and it is "a story in jazz," the story being Rushing and Clayton's attempts to woo Moore in song. The plot is silly, but it's just an excuse to have Rushing, sometimes joined by the pleasant alto of Moore, fronting Clayton's Count Basie-style orchestra on some old favorites. *The Jazz Odyssey of James Rushing, Esq.* traces the development of jazz through four cities, each of which is represented by three songs: New Orleans, Kansas City, Chicago, and New York. Again, the concept is little more than a framing device, but producer Irving Townsend, using different musicians for each mini-set, does get the feel of jazz in each locale. Rushing, in his early fifties, may not have the voice he did when he was with Basie, but his performances are spirited and his first-ever piano accompaniment on his own "Tricks Ain't Walkin' No More" is a delight. The backup musicians, many of whom get solos, are a who's who of jazz greats, including Billy Butterfield, Urbie Green, Milt Hinton, Hank Jones, Jo Jones, Walter Page, and Zutty Singleton. With that kind of lineup, presenting the history of jazz (especially as it might sound played by Basie) isn't hard. These albums were long overdue for reissue, and putting them together on a discount-priced two-fer makes the release especially appealing. —*William Ruhlmann*

Saffire — The Uppity Blues Women

f. 1984, Virginia

Group / Folk-Blues, Modern Acoustic Blues

The ladies from Saffire at one point in the early '90s just considered themselves blues historians, but since their performing career has gotten launched on the festival circuit, they've become much more than that. All three have developed into talented songwriters. Since blues fans are always looking for fresh themes or new twists on old themes, this trio is a sought-after club and festival act. The core members of this Virginia-based group include pianist Ann Rabson (b. April 12, 1945) and Gaye Adegbalola (b. March 21, 1944), and while the trio was accompanied for a while by bassist Earlene Lewis, she has since left the group. Lewis was replaced by mandolinist Andra Faye McIntosh, also from the Washington, D.C./Virginia area. Rabson worked as a computer programmer and Adegbalola was an award-winning teacher before they gave up their day jobs to play blues full-time for a living.

Saffire has no shortage of fresh ideas. The group recorded seven albums for the Chicago-based Alligator Records label since 1990, and two of their more recent albums *Cleaning House* (1996) and *Old, New, Borrowed & Blue* (1994) showcase the trio's songwriting skills, although there are also a few covers, reinterpreted in their own distinctive way. These acoustic musicians inject a sense of humor into their songs and take it with them on stage. There is also a strong thread of feminism running through the band and their recorded output. The group's other albums for Alligator include their 1990 debut, *Saffire—The Uppity Blues Women* (1990), *Hot Flash* (1991), and *Broadcasting* (1992). Their prolific output as songwriters is matched only by their desire to tour, as they perform everywhere and anywhere, having already made several U.S., Canadian and European tours. In 1998 the trio released *Live and Uppity*, a rousing document of their crowd pleasing stage act. After a five year lay off since their last studio recording (during which time Rabson recorded two solo records), Saffire returned with another strong record, *Ain't Gonna Hush*, in 2001.

The group's fundamental appeal—to growing numbers of music fans who don't know much about blues—is their original songs and their ability to dig up and reinterpret old blues gems from the '20s and '30s. They specialize in songs made by the sassy original blues divas including Bessie Smith, Ma Rainey, Memphis Minnie, and Ida Cox. —*Richard Skelly*

The Middle Aged Blues / 1987 / Saffire ◆◆◆

Middle Aged Blues is Saffire's debut tape and the vocal trio has already developed a distinctive style. Although some listeners might find their material a bit too jokey, it's clear that the group is having fun with their material. They have respect for blues traditions, particularly classic female blues, but they don't merely regurgitate the same songs in the same fashion—Saffire makes them loose and fun, like you were eavesdropping on a party. *Middle Aged Blues* isn't as fully formed as their later albums for Alligator, but it still has plenty of good times. —*Thom Owens*

The Uppity Blues Women / 1990 / Alligator ◆◆◆

In 1984 three middle-aged women (guitarist Gaye Adegbalola, bassist Earlene Lewis and pianist Ann Rabson) came together to play blues as Saffire. Their 1990 Alligator CD is still Saffire's best all-around recording. Even overlooking the novelty of three women giving a female and middle-aged slant to the blues, this is a highly enjoyable and musical set. Assisted on three numbers by Mark Wenner's harmonica, Saffire plays spirited versions of such tunes as "Middle Aged Blues Boogie," "Even Yuppies Get the Blues," "Fess Up When You Mess Up," "I Almost Lost My Mind," and their theme "Wild Women Don't Have the Blues." Recommended. —*Scott Yanow*

● **Hot Flash** / 1991 / Alligator ◆◆◆◆

In many ways, *Hot Flash* is the definitive Saffire album. Racy and sassy—and to some tastes cutesy—the album is a fun, free-thinking update of classic female blues, performed with gusto and verve. The instrumentation is sparse—a piano, guitar, bass, harmonica, and kazoo provide the foundation of the music—but the focus of these songs is solely on the vocals, which are vigorous and humorous and if you share Saffire's sense of humor, it's a rollicking good time. —*Thom Owens*

Broadcasting / 1992 / Alligator ◆◆◆

Between *Hot Flash* and *Broadcasting*, Saffire lost a bassist, but added a mandolin, fiddler, an organist, and an electric guitarist, which gives *Broadcasting* a fuller, richer sound. Fortunately, that hasn't distracted attention from the bawdy, sassy vocals of Ann Rabson and Gaye Adegbalola, who still exhibit a raw, natural charisma. And the material—which ranges from fresh interpretations of warhorses from Louis Jordan and Hank Williams to clever originals—is all first-rate, helping make the album one of the group's best efforts. —*Thom Owens*

Old, New, Borrowed, & Blue / 1994 / Alligator ◆◆

Old, New, Borrowed, & Blue finds Saffire's sound bordering on the formulaic—songs like "Bitch With a Bad Attitude" and "There's Lighting in These Thunder Thighs" are simply

too cutesy and too predictable—but there is still plenty for their fans to treasure on the record. —*Thom Owens*

Cleaning House / May 21, 1996 / Alligator ◆◆◆

Another generally likable album from Saffire, *Cleaning House* contains plenty of the bold, sassy material (e.g., "Hungry Woman's Blues," "If Love Hurts, You're Not Doing It Right," "Tomorrow Ain't Promised") listeners have come to expect from the band that half seriously, half tongue-in-cheek, bills itself as the Uppity Blues Women. All three women take turns on lead vocals; Andra Faye McIntosh's singing is particularly enjoyable. The 17-song acoustic set includes five originals from band member Gaye Adegbalola, three originals from bandmate Ann Rabson, and a spirited variety of songs written by old-timers like Memphis Minnie and contemporary songsmiths like Rick Estrin. —*Steve Hoffman*

Live and Uppity / Mar. 10, 1998 / Alligator ◆◆◆◆

Saffire has been bringing their "uppity" brand of blues to stages from quite some time, and it was inevitable that a live album would rear its head sooner or later. But recording this one over a three-night stand at the Barns of Wolf Trap is a class-A affair all the way. With the ladies in top form, playing to an adoring audience cheering them on with every line, there's a symbiosis happening on this recording between audience and performers that seldom gets captured on a live album. There's no point in listing highlights simply because every track is a winner, and while the group's strong feminist stance is off-putting to some blues fans, none of them were in the audience on the nights these recordings were made, that's for sure. —*Cub Koda*

Ain't Gonna Hush / Jun. 5, 2001 / Alligator ◆◆◆◆

The first studio album in five years from the band finds them for the most part, having a rocking good time and placing an emphasis on the boogie-woogie end of the blues. Instrumentally and vocally they keep getting better and better, with pianist Ann Rabson a particular standout for her vibrant keyboard work. While they live up to their image of empowered, strong women, evident in "Ain't Gonna Hush," "It Takes a Mighty Good Man," and the lovely, if not very bluesy, "Unlove You," it's obvious from songs like "Let the Gin Do the Talking," "Prop Me Up Beside the Jukebox," and the almost bawdy "Footprints on the Ceiling" that they also enjoy a good time. In fact, these lighter songs, whether covers or band originals, are what works best, keeping the foot tapping and a smile on the face—"Coffee Flavored Kisses," with its elaborate doo wop backing vocal arrangement, is a prime example. When they turn more serious, the songs simply don't work as well. Gayle Adegbalola's "Blues for Sharon Bottoms" is heartfelt, and torn straight from the news, but it's musically and lyrically awkward, which detracts from the power it needs to hit home. And her "Happy Birthday to Me," which is probably meant to be tongue-in-cheek, ends up coming across as a hefty dose of self-pity. Those two aside, it's hard to find anything to criticize in this release, which has been far too long coming. As a trio they go from strength to strength, and even if their original focus has changed from vintage blues, they still do what they do very well indeed, and show that women of a certain age can have a home in the music. —*Chris Nickson*

Doug Sahm

b. Nov. 6, 1941, San Antonio, TX, d. Nov. 18, 1999, Taos, NM

Vocals, Leader, Violin, Songwriter, Guitar / Americana, Roots Rock, Tex-Mex, Country-Rock, Progressive Country, Blues-Rock, Rock & Roll

Guitarist, composer, arranger, and songwriter Doug Sahm was a knowledgeable music historian and veteran performer equally comfortable in a range of styles, including Texas blues, country, rock & roll, Western swing, and Cajun. Born November 6, 1941, in San Antonio, TX, he began his performing career at age nine when he was featured on a San Antonio area radio station, playing steel guitar. Sahm began recording for a procession of small labels (Harlem, Warrior, Renner and Personality), in 1955 with "A Real American Joe" under the name Little Doug Sahm. Three years later he was leading a group called the Pharoahs. Sahm recorded a series of singles for Texas-based record companies including "Crazy Daisy" (1959), "Sapphire" (1961), and "If You Ever Need Me" (1964). After being prompted in 1965 to assemble a group by producer Huey P. Meaux, Sahm asked his friends Augie Meyers (keyboards), Frank Morin (saxophone), Harvey Kagan (bass), and Johnny Perez (drums) if they would join him. Meaux gave the group the name the Sir Douglas Quintet. The group had some success on the radio with "The Rains Came," but Sahm later moved to California after the group broke up, where he formed the Honkey Blues Band. He reformed his Quintet in California and recorded a now-classic single, "Mendocino." The resulting album was a groundbreaking record in the then-emerging country-rock scene. The Sir Douglas Quintet followed *Mendocino* with *Together After Five*, another album that led them to a larger fan base.

But it was Atlantic Records producer Jerry Wexler who realized that country-rock sounds were coming into vogue (and there was no place in Nashville for people like

Sahm), so he signed both Sahm and Willie Nelson. One of his greatest albums, *Doug Sahm and Band*, (1973, Atlantic) was recorded in New York City with Bob Dylan, Dr. John, and accordionist Flaco Jimenez, and a resulting single, "Is Anybody Going to San Antone?" had some radio success. The Sir Douglas Quintet got back together again to record two more albums, *Wanted Very Much Alive* and *Back to the 'Dillo*.

Among Sahm's most essential blues records are *Hell of a Spell* (1980, reissued in 1999), a blues album dedicated to Guitar Slim, and his Grammy-nominated studio album for Antone's, *The Last Real Texas Blues Band*. For his other material, there are several good compilations, including *The Best of Doug Sahm* (Rhino). *SDQ '98* followed. Sahm died November 18, 1999; the posthumous *The Return of Wayne Douglas* appeared the following summer. *—Richard Skelly*

Rough Edges / 1973 / Mercury ✦✦

Doug Sahm and Band / Jan. 1973 / Atlantic ✦✦✦
Since major label Atlantic signed Doug Sahm as a solo artist and put him in a New York studio with top-flight producers Jerry Wexler and Arif Mardin and star sidemen like Bob Dylan, Dr. John, and David Bromberg (not to mention old stalwarts like Augie Meyers, Flaco Jimenez, and Martin Fierro), you might expect that the resulting album would be Sahm's big career move, a swing toward professionalism and the mainstream, and that's how it was perceived when it was released. Maybe that's why it also was dismissed when it didn't become a big hit. Trouble is, the record isn't slick at all—it sounds as loose as any of the Sir Douglas Quintet albums, if a little more country-oriented. But the album remains a Bob Dylan curio; Dylan's otherwise unavailable composition "Wallflower" is included, and he sings it and "Blues Stay Away from Me" with Sahm. *—William Ruhlmann*

Groover's Paradise / 1974 / Warner Brothers ✦✦✦✦
Anyone who finds hippies irritating might want to throw this record across the room—and that's a good review right there, since it has been long established via intense scientific study that music that somehow motivates people to throw records across the room is usually quite good. No exception to this rule here, as fans of Doug Sahm often choose this as a personal favorite, while it is also one of the better side projects of the Creedence Clearwater Revival rhythm section. If Sahm was writing the review himself in 1974, he would have no doubt described the whole thing as some kind of "trip"; after all, this expression is used three times alone on the back cover of this album, actually less than one might expect considering the stoned-out nature of the accompanying comics. These black-and-white illustrations by Kelly Fitzgerald are a great part of the record's enduring charm, but the music itself is deeper than the coolie hippie vibe. This is simply a great roots rock album, and like much of Sahm's work it is loaded with complex details as well as loving interplay between the musicians. These tracks indicate a mastery of many basic forms such as blues, rhythm & blues, norteño, country, and Cajun and the players always seem to be probing beyond this to find something new. Creedence Clearwater Revival drummer Doug Clifford produced as well as played, and did a superior job, irrigating the proceedings with a range of available Sahm streams like some kind of master gardener. The use of horns is excellent, not only providing plenty of punch in the arrangements but memorable effects such as the spooky baritone sax solo on "Just Groove Me." A large section of the sonic spread is always reserved for Sahm's lush guitar playing, including lots of rock, country, and blues licks, while bassist Stu Cook sometimes adds additional guitar, expertly mocking the patented hypnotic John Fogerty sound for an effect that is not unlike Sahm sitting in on a Creedence album. Of course, the range of that classic '60s and '70s rock group seems quite limited compared to Sahm, who whips off an expert version of the Tex-Mex instrumental "La Cacahueta," the only track here that he did not compose himself. The well-crafted yet daringly personal and unembarrassed songs include haunting country-influenced ballads such as "Her Dream Man Never Came," as well as really top-notch examples of good old rock & roll, the hilarious "For the Sake of Rock 'N' Roll" and the bewitchingly cooking "Devil Heart." The second side of the original vinyl is one of this artist's most perfect set of songs. The final track, "Catch Me in the Morning," is one of several on this album that benefits from a long, satisfying arrangement—hardly the kind of simple dirt that is often tossed off the shovel in the quest for roots rock. The band tends to move through these pieces with confidence, as if already expecting to have lost the attention of the simpletons in the crowd. At the same time, there are those listeners who will find it hard to believe a simple song, let alone such a magnum opus, could be created from the almost nonexistent message of this song. "Call me in the morning, I am too tired to talk right now," is just about all this song says, and it is one of the marvels of Sahm that he is able to parlay a near-operatic sense of importance into such a typical part of daily life. Giving him an instrumental credit for being a "dreamer"—nicely enough, it comes right after the credit for bajo sexto—is one of the most appropriate details, or "trips," on *Groover's Paradise*. *—Eugene Chadbourne*

Texas Rock for Country Rollers / 1976 / Edsel ✦✦✦
Upon original release, this album was credited to Sir Doug and the Texas Tornados. Little did anyone know how much confusion this might eventually create when years later Sahm formed a new band called the Texas Tornados with a nucleus of himself and several other musical legends from that state, only one of whom appears on this album, other than Sahm himself. That would be Augie Meyers, a regular sidekick of Sahm's from the Sir Douglas Quintet, so what is the reason that this isn't simply identified as a Sir Douglas Quintet album? Only the fact that there are at least six players present on the tracks, but funny, simple math never stopped Doug Sahm from doing anything sensible before. In terms of presentation, attitude, and musical direction, this is pretty much a Sir Douglas Quintet type affair, is definitely not a record by what would become the Texas Tornados, and includes at least three genuine classics such as the beautiful "Give Back the Key to My Heart," later to be redone by the band Uncle Tupelo. Good playing and better vibes abound but there is the feeling that somebody was asleep at the wheel, in that some of the best tracks simply fade out right in the middle of an important chorus. Why would a producer do this, unless there was some problem in the track that he couldn't stand to let anyone hear? An album most Sahm fans will want to own, and one in the could-have-been-a-contender category. *—Eugene Chadbourne*

Hell of a Spell / 1980 / Takoma ✦✦✦
This 1980 reissue is a hell of a disc. From the opening riffs this disc is crammed with Doug's typical rompin' and stompin' Texas blues/R&B mix. This also includes liberal dashes of the Tex-Mex and rockabilly he grew up cutting his teeth on. This is meant literally. Rudy "Tutti" Grayzell used to go to the school when Doug was 11, as legend goes, and pose as his uncle and pull the musical prodigy out of school to play some of the gigs that required some travel. This compilation is dedicated to one of his heroes, Eddie Jones, better known as Guitar Slim. He does one of his tunes on the disc, but it is the horns and overall sound and feel of the disc that bring back the memories of Jones. 6 of the 11 tunes were penned by Doug Sahm and they stand up as some of the best things he has done. He manages to take that voice of his and put all the ache and pain that things gone sour can evoke and guide you along with him down this road without ever getting sappy or maudlin. Listen to the tone and feel of "Hangin' on By a Thread" and the smooth shift to the Brook Benton heartbreak tune "I'll Take Care of You." He shifts gears with the precision of a Grand Prix driver. This disc shows off some of the remarkable range of Sahm's abilities and genius. This becomes clearer when you think of his work with Dylan, the Texas Tornadoes, and let's not forget the early rock hits, such as "Mendicino" and "She's About a Mover." This disc is the only one that comes to mind in which his long-time compadre, Augie Meyer, isn't helping with his familiar organ sound; instead Kelly Dunn is handling keyboards. Doug is Texas-bred, but his influences are as broad as the sky is big down there. Here he is concentrating on the blues, and he gets some exciting things down on the disc. *—Bob Gottlieb*

The Return of the Formerly Brothers / 1989 / Rykodisc ✦✦✦✦✦
Texan folk hero Sir Doug Sahm meets underrated guitarist Amos Garrett and ex-Blasters keyboardist Gene Taylor and they cook like an Austin barbecue. Originally released on Stony Plain Records in Canada in 1988, *The Return of the Formerly Brothers* was released in the U.S. by Rykodisc in 1989. *—Jeff Tamarkin*

Juke Box Music / 1989 / Antone's ✦✦✦✦✦
Supported by the Antone's house band, Doug Sahm runs through 15 R&B and doo wop classics for *Juke Box Music*. Oddly there's no Tex-Mex here, considering that Sahm is one of the defining figures of the genre, but that's just a minor complaint, since the music here is just terrific. There's a wonderful relaxed quality to the performances, and the song selection boasts a number of forgotten gems, resulting in a little treasure for fans of R&B and American roots music. *—Thom Owens*

● **The Best of Doug Sahm (1968–1975)** / 1991 / Rhino ✦✦✦✦✦
Doug Sham once sang, "You just can't live in Texas if you don't have a lot of soul," and, as a proud son of the Lone Star state, he seemed bent on proving that every time he stepped in front of a microphone. Whether he was playing roots rock, garage punk, blues, country, norteño, or (as was often the case) something that mixed up several of the above-mentioned ingredients, Doug Sahm always sounded like Doug Sahm—a little wild, a little loose, but always good company, and a guy with a whole lot of soul who knew a lot of musicians upon whom the same praise could be bestowed. Pulling together a single disc compilation that would make sense of the length and breadth of the artist's recording career (which spanned five decades) would be just about impossible (the licensing hassles involved with the many labels involved would probably scotch such a project anyway), but this disc, which boasts 22 songs recorded over the course of eight years, is a pretty good starter for anyone wanting to get to know Sahm's music. You get two almost-hits ("Mendocino" and "[Is Anybody Going To] San Antone"), a healthy portion of memorable album cuts, and even a few unreleased songs as Sir Doug and his pals (among them fellow future Texas Tornado Augie Meyers and Doug's pal Bob Dylan) swing through vintage blues, country weepers, rootsy hippie jams, and a few cuts that defy convenient description, all dominated by Sahm's warm, expressive drawl, distinctive guitar work, and the loose but emphatic sound he knew how to draw from a band. Put it this way—there's one guy in a million who could write and record a song called "You Never Get Too Big and You Sure Don't Get Too Heavy That You Don't Have to Stop and Pay Some Dues Sometime" and not sound like a fool. Doug Sahm was that man, and you get to hear him sing it on *The Best of Doug Sham*, along with 21 other equally cool tunes. *—Mark Deming*

The Last Real Texas Blues Band / 1994 / Discovery ✦✦✦
The Last Real Texas Blues Band is a typically eclectic and enjoyable record from Doug Sahm, but what makes it different than the rest of his catalog is focus. Where most of Sahm's albums are equally divided between the pedestrian and the genius, *The Last Real Texas Blues Band* is a nearly perfect roots record, boasting both a stellar set of songs and exciting, unpredictable performances that make it arguably his best record ever. *—Thom Owens*

The Best of Doug Sahm (1968–1975) / 1995 / Sequel ✦✦✦✦

S.D.Q. '98 / Oct. 20, 1998 / Watermelon ✦✦✦✦✦
Many fanatical music listeners feel an artist's greatest works are accomplished when they are young, and would thus go backward toward an early Sir Douglas Quintet record in order to capture the best of this legendary Texas artist. This release on an independent label hardly made a ripple in the late '90s, although musically there is enough here to create a tidal wave. Everything comes together beautifully in the proposed combination of tracks by Sahm and some of his old-time cohorts from both the quintet and the Texas Tornados and a collaboration with a younger bunch of dudes, namely the Gourds.

Highlights there are, galore. No Sahm record would be this good unless Augie Meyers was on hand, and the man gets lots of solo space on all his axes. Pedal steel guitar player Tommy Detamore has some nice moments on the country material, of which there is lots. Rhythm section partners from the past—such as bassist Speedy Sparks and the fine drummer Ernie Durawa—are around to give the tunes a solid feel. One of the great things about the CD is the way it suddenly takes on a whole new life as a historical, political project through the sequence of songs, starting with the wonderful Sahm-panned "Louis Riel," going through the hysterical version of "The Ballad of Davy Crockett," and winding up with "Sooner or Later." On a more romantic note, there is a new version of an older Sahm song, "Give Back the Key to My Heart," which is certainly welcome since the original recorded version had such an unfinished feel to it. "Goodbye San Francisco, Hello Amsterdam" is another Sahm classic and surely a song with the potential to become a favorite. There is also a rollicking rhythm & blues bonus track tossed in at the end for added fun. *—Eugene Chadbourne*

She's About a Mover: The Best of Crazy Cajun Recording / Oct. 26, 1999 / Edsel ♦♦♦♦
This differs from Music Club's package in that this set also includes tracks issued as Doug Sahm solo sides, giving us a time frame between 1964 and 1977 to hear Sahm's art unfold. Of course, the early SDQ sides are the big ticket here. Rough and raw, they include the two big hits "She's About a Mover" and "The Rains Came." Yet the solo sides that fill up the cracks here are also every bit as raw, sometimes disconcertingly so, like the bass and drums that lose track of each other in the middle of "Seguin" or the maracas that never quite catch up to the band track on "You've Got Your Good Thing Down." If you wondered what Huey P. Meaux had in the vault on Sahm, here's your chance to find out. *—Cub Koda*

San Antonio Rock: The Harlem Recordings 1957–1961 / Apr. 4, 2000 / Norton ♦♦♦♦
If you think Doug Sahm's career began with the Sir Douglas Quintet, guess again. This 18-track collection rounds up all of Sahm's early 45s and demos, as well as rarities with Doug playing sideman in various Texas combos, the majority of it issued on the Harlem label out of Fort Worth. It's raw Texas music, soaked in R&B and rock & roll, and Sahm goes through no less than seven different backing units on this set, not to mention his sideman work with Spot Barnett, Jimmy Dee, and Red Hilburn. Lots of alternate takes, great booklet with loads of information, all putting into historical perspective this missing chapter in the history of this modern Texas troubadour. *—Cub Koda*

The Return of Wayne Douglas / Jun. 20, 2000 / Tornado ♦♦♦♦
The Return of Wayne Douglas—the title comes from one of the aliases Doug Sahm used during country music gigs around Austin, TX—turned out to be Sahm's final studio album. It was recorded just before his heart gave out in a Taos, NM, motel room on November 18, 1999, but released posthumously in late 2000 by Tornado Records, a division of Birdman Recordings. Sahm's band—which includes fellow Texas Tornado organist Augie Meyers, Bill Kirchen (Commander Cody & the Lost Planet Airman) on guitar, Tommy Detamore (Moe Bandy, Ronnie Milsap) on steel guitar, Bobby Flores (Ray Price's Cherokee Cowboys) on fiddle, and son Shawn Sahm on background vocals—are the perfect support group, giving this "country as chicken-fried steak" material the stripped-down and soulful touch it requires. The album is almost an homage to the state of Texas. In addition to new songs like "I Can't Go Back to Austin" and "Cowboy Peyton Place"—his paean to an Austin that existed 25 years earlier—there are country-style arrangements of Sir Doug classics: "Dallas Alice" and the album's last track, "Texas Me," written in California during a bout of homesickness some 30 years earlier. "I wonder what happened to that man inside," Sahm moans in his gravel-hewn, throaty manner, "the real old Texas me." There are also two covers. Bob Dylan's "Love Minus Zero/No Limit" is sent up Sahm-style with great aplomb. Leon Payne's "They'll Never Take Her Love From Me" tells a little story about the time Sahm and his father paid a visit to Payne at the home of "Blind Balladeer'" in Bandera, TX. Sahm was reportedly surprised at how easily Payne seemed to be able to move around inside his house without stumbling over furniture. The liner notes by James "Big Boy" Medlin say it best: "Doug was a tornado. A true force of nature. I'll think of him every time I see a west Texas dust devil. Every time I drink a longneck. Every time I order a taco. Every time I see the skyline of Manhattan." Well, that's what they say. *—Bryan Thomas*

In the Beginning / Aug. 29, 2000 / Aim ♦♦♦
In the Beginning chronicles the earliest singles released by the late Texas renegade Doug Sahm. Recorded between 1958 and 1962, these 14 songs encompass Tex-Mex, R&B, doo wop, polka, and early rock & roll from Sahm's pre-Sir Douglas Quintet days on the Harlem, Cobra, and Renner labels. Rare regional singles "Crazy Daisy," "Why, Why, Why," "Slow Down," "Baby Tell Me," and "Just a Moment" are a few of the gems collected. *—Al Campbell*

Son of San Antonio: The Roots of Sir Douglas / Sep. 11, 2001 / Music Club ♦♦♦♦

Curtis Salgado

b. Feb. 4, 1954, Everett, WA

Vocals, Harmonica / Modern Electric Blues

While a longtime fixture of the Pacific Northwest blues community, singer/harpist Curtis Salgado ironically earned his greatest notoriety as the reputed inspiration behind John Belushi's character in *The Blues Brothers*. Born in Everett, WA, on February 4, 1954, he first emerged during the mid-'70s as the lead vocalist of the Robert Cray Band, making his recorded debut on the group's 1980 effort *Who's Been Talkin*; after leaving Cray in 1982, Salgado also fronted Roomful of Blues between 1984 and 1986. Upon forming his own band, the Stilettos, he signed to the JRS label to issue his 1991 solo debut, *Curtis Salgado and the Stilettos*; *More Than You Can Chew* followed in 1995, and two years later he resurfaced with *Hit It 'n' Quit It*, recorded with guitarist Terry Robb. *Wiggle Outta This* followed in 1999, and *Soul Activated* was issued in early 2001. *—Jason Ankeny*

● **Curtis Salgado and the Stilettos** / 1991 / JRS ♦♦♦♦♦
Curtis Salgado's first album, *Curtis Salgado and the Stilettos*, captures the vocalist at his very best, storming through a set of originals and covers that fall halfway between gritty Chicago blues and sweaty Stax soul. Salgado had long ago proven that he was a fine singer, but this proves he can do it on his own, without Robert Cray or Roomful of Blues—not only can he lead a band, but he can write fine songs in his own right. *—Thom Owens*

More Than You Can Chew / May 16, 1995 / Priority ♦♦♦♦

Hit It 'n' Quit It / Jun. 10, 1997 / Lucky ♦♦♦

Wiggle Outta This / Mar. 23, 1999 / Shanachie ♦♦♦
"Wiggle Outta This" features more of the gutsy harmonica playing and singing that have made Curtis Salgado a mainstay in the blues scene. Salgado's fourth solo album marks his debut for Shanachie Records, and includes ballads like "Why I Don't Care," the sexy, soulful "Cookie Dough" and "Sweet Jesus Buddha the Doctor." *—Heather Phares*

Soul Activated / Jan. 9, 2001 / Shanachie ♦♦♦
The album's title leaves no doubt as to its contents: *Soul Activated* is all about rockin' soul, classic R&B, and vocal throwbacks to the glory days of Sam & Dave, Otis Redding and the like. Salgado plunges headlong into a vocal potpourri, dishing out some very hip covers and adding four tunes of his own. The covers include the Hall & Oates/Paul Young hit "Everytime You Go Away," a funky rendering of Leon Russell's "I'd Rather Be Blind" (Freddie King), Jimmy Cliff's reggae smash "The Harder They Come," and a duet with Lou Ann Barton called "Hip Hip Baby" that features Jimmy Vaughan on guitar. Barton used to sing the tune with Stevie Ray Vaughan in her hometown of Austin (before SRV's tenure with Double Trouble). Salgado's originals extract powerful visuals, from the relaxed yet uplifting "Summertime Life" to the minor-key "Funny Man," a tale that tells a story most probably haven't heard before: one of losing the girl to a comedian. Salgado sings, "The funny man ain't funny when he takes your love from you." Ouch! "Lip Whippin' " is a traditional blues tune. It's a great harp instrumental that is arguably the best cut on the album, but it sounds ridiculously out of place sandwiched in between all the other "soul activated" tunes. Those are filled with cool phrasing, hot sweat, and a helluva voice. *—Ann Wickstrom*

The Sam Brothers

f. Louisiana

Group / Zydeco

The Sam Brothers—vocalist and bandleader Leon, lead guitarist Carl, bassist Glen, washboard player Calvin, and drummer Rodney—were among zydeco's most prominent family acts, making their initial splash while still in their teens and later becoming one of the most electrifying bands on the contemporary zydeco circuit. The Houston-based siblings took their earliest inspiration from their father Herbert Sam, himself a part-time accordionist who led his own five-piece zydeco band; as each of the brothers learned his respective instrument he then joined the group, and when Herbert retired from active duty the Sam Brothers—aka the Sam Brothers Five—were officially born. In 1979, the teens were discovered by Arhoolie Records producer Chris Strachwitz at the New Orleans Jazz and Heritage Festival; not only did Strachwitz organize a West Coast tour, but he also recorded their debut LP, the live *Sam Brothers Five. Cruisin' On* followed in 1981, after which the brothers spent the rest of the decade focusing on performing live; finally, in 1989 they returned to the studio to record *Zydeco Brotherhood*. *—Jason Ankeny*

● **Zydeco Brotherhood** / 1989 / Maison de Soul ♦♦♦♦
Not the most original of zydeco groups, the Sam Brothers still manage to jam a lot of energy into the covers they interpret. *—Jeff Hannusch*

Lafayette Zydeco / 1992 / Arhoolie ♦♦♦♦

Les Sampou

b. Nov. 4, 1962

Vocals / Folk-Blues, Singer/Songwriter

The young, up-and-coming Les Sampou may be a relative newcomer to the international folk/blues festival circuit, but she writes songs like she's been around forever. Her record deal came about relatively easily compared to the way a lot of blues and folksingers struggle in obscurity for years before being discovered.

The Boston-based Sampou released an album herself, *Sweet Perfume* (1994), before being signed to Flying Fish/Rounder Records in 1995. Although by that point she'd already made the rounds of coffeehouses and folk festivals around the Northeast, it wasn't until after the release of her debut, *Fall from Grace*, that she began to take on a national and international profile. Although it's easy to call her a contemporary blues singer, and she does play blues exceedingly well, there's a singer/songwriter side of her that comes out on her debut album in songs like "The Things I Should've Said" and "Home Again." Other tracks, like "Weather Vane" and "Fall from Grace," show her bluesier side.

Sampou did not get the music bug until she was in her early twenties, after seeing Ellen McIlwaine at a coffeehouse in Cambridge, MA. Shortly after that revelatory experience, Sampou began taking lessons, learning acoustic blues from Boston-based acoustic blues master Paul Rishell. After she began getting steady work in coffeehouses around the ultra-competitive Boston scene in the late '80s and early '90s, she made the break and quit her day job as a part-time editor to pursue her musical dreams. The initial result was a superb album, *Sweet Perfume*, her self-released 1994 debut. The follow-up, *Fall from Grace* (1996), is even better, and shows that Sampou is equally at home playing traditional blues, self-penned blues or self-penned ballads. Harmonica player Jerry Portnoy, a great songwriter himself, can be heard as well. A self-titled LP followed in 1999. *—Richard Skelly*

- **Fall from Grace** / 1996 / Flying Fish ✦✦✦

Though her lyric drives occasionally get in the way of the flow of the music, Les Sampou's stories are intelligent and cleverly told, and well-buoyed by the instrumental arrangements. Though Les sounds at times like a number of other musical muses—from Bonnie Raitt to Crystal Gayle—her voice and what she uses it to say are personal and individual. Musically, Sampou and her band are also quite talented and never let the music overpower the meaning. —*Matthew Robinson*

Les Sampou / May 11, 1999 / Flying Fish ✦✦✦

Sampou takes a left turn from her usual folk-blues sound to embrace a bit more of modern rock arrangements and guitar sounds to cushion the brutal reality of her often pointed lyrics. It all works magnificently; songs "Broken Pieces," "Hanging By a Thread," and "I Want You" all resonate with music and production every bit as fine as the songwriting they frame. Plenty of raw emotion and great sounds. —*Cub Koda*

Jumpin' Johnny Sansone

b. 1957, West Orange, NJ

Harmonica / Modern Electric Blues

Like his friend Sonny Landreth, harmonica player/accordionist Jumpin' Johnny Sansone takes his songwriting cues from the things he sees in his New Orleans home. Many of the songs on *Crescent City Moon*, his debut for Rounder's Bullseye Blues label, are inspired by the sights, sounds, and smells of the Crescent City.

Sansone left his native West Orange, NJ at 17 in 1975 to attend college in Colorado on a swimming scholarship. He began playing harmonica at age 13, also accompanying himself on guitar. "I was trying to be Jimmy Reed in our basement," he recalled in a 1997 interview. Sansone's father was a professional saxophonist who played with various jazz groups on the Newark, NJ, club scene.

Sansone lived in Colorado, Austin, Boston, and Chapel Hill, NC, before moving to New Orleans in 1990. The whole time, he led regional touring bands, most notably Jumpin' Johnny and the Blues Party. Sansone is no spring chicken when it comes to getting out on the road and supporting his independently released records. In 1987, Sansone and his former band, known as Jumpin' Johnny & the Blues Party, recorded an album *Where Y'at?* for the Kingsnake label of Sanford, FL. Jumpin' Johnny & the Blues Party also recorded and released *Mister Good Thing* for the Atlanta-based Ichiban label in 1991.

Sansone began playing accordion after attending Clifton Chenier's funeral, and Sansone said that some people assume he's a zydeco musician when they see him carrying it into a club.

Crescent City Moon (1997, Bullseye Blues) received rave reviews from around the country. The album fuses Chicago blues, swamp boogie, and lyrical images of New Orleans and the bayou country of southwest Louisiana. All of the songs on his debut album are his own, except his cover of Ted Hawkins' "Sweet Baby."

Sansone has won numerous awards in the Crescent City, including *Offbeat* magazine's annual "Best of the Beat" competition, where he won four awards after he released *Crescent City Moon* on his own label in 1996. Sansone won Song of the Year, Best Harmonica Player, Best Blues Band, and Best Blues Album of the Year.

Over the years, to get money together for various recording projects, Sansone has worked construction jobs. But with his deal with Rounder's Bullseye Blues subsidiary—which in addition to *Crescent City Moon* yielded 1999's *Watermelon Patch*—he should be able to take his artistry to the next level, touring nationally and internationally. —*Richard Skelly*

Mr. Good Thing / Mar. 1991 / King Snake ✦✦✦

- **Crescent City Moon** / 1997 / Bullseye Blues ✦✦✦✦✦

Sansone's second full-length album finds him stretching his creative wings, as a singer, multi-instrumentalist, and most importantly, as a songwriter. The Louisiana-bred Sansone has a much different spin on his music, embracing Cajun, New Orleans, Southern soul, Chicago, and Mississippi blues, with his nothing special but real solid accordion playing sharing equal space with his inventive harmonica work. Aside from a swamp-style cover of Ted Hawkins' "Sweet Baby" featuring Sonny Landreth on slide guitar, everything on this disc emanates from Sansone's pen and there's not a track aboard that's nothing less than interesting here. As Sansone changes gears from the soul classic of the future "Your Kind of Love" to the Slim Harpo-ish "Crawfish Walk" to the "kordeen" boogie romp of "Destination Unknown" to the eerie minor-key blues of the title track, this is an album with a lot of music to savour from an artist with a different slant to all things rootsy. Proof positive that it doesn't all have to be rehashes of Clifton Chenier or Little Walter. —*Cub Koda*

Watermelon Patch / Oct. 26, 1999 / Bullseye Blues ✦✦✦✦

Johnny Sansone is a bit of a jack of all trades: writing, singing, and playing masterful accordion, harmonica, and guitar. All of these tunes are originals, a similarly wide-ranging mix of Louisiana roots-rock, zydeco, and traditional blues. He enlisted some top-drawer New Orleans musicians for *Watermelon Patch*, including saxophonists from the Iguanas, organist Joe Krown (Clarence "Gatemouth" Brown), and pianist Jon Cleary (B.B. King, Bonnie Raitt, Taj Mahal); meanwhile, the rhythm section of bassist Dave Ranson and drummer Kenneth Blevins drove John Hiatt's *Slow Turning* album. Most of this release was cut live, in only one day. "Think of Me" is a rapid-fire, accordion-fueled zydeco tune with a nice guitar solo from Rick Olivarez. The title cut features some bluesy harp. "Look at Us Now" and "Loveline" showcase some nice horn playing, especially the accents from trumpet man Duke Heitger. Sansone pulls out the chromatic harp on "Pig's Feet & Tailmeat," "Stinkbait" and "Quagmire," the latter centered on a Latin-flavored jungle drum beat. "Stink Bait" is a tough, slow instrumental. "Civilized City" is pure 12-bar Chicago blues, and "Comin' for Sure" is another zydeco-flavored track, but this time Olivarez takes to the slide guitar. Sansone is originally from New Jersey and didn't settle in New Orleans until 1989, but you'd never know it from listening to *Watermelon Patch*. He clearly has found his geographical *and* musical home. —*Ann Wickstrom*

Santana

f. 1966, San Francisco, CA

Group / Latin Rock, Album Rock, Pop/Rock, Psychedelic, Fusion, Hard Rock, Blues-Rock

Santana is the primary exponent of Latin-tinged rock, particularly due to its combination of Latin percussion (congas, timbales, etc.) with bandleader Carlos Santana's distinctive, high-pitched lead guitar playing. The group was the last major act to emerge from the psychedelic San Francisco music scene of the '60s and it enjoyed massive success at the end of the decade and into the early '70s. The musical direction then changed to a more contemplative and jazzy style as the band's early personnel gradually departed, leaving the name in the hands of Carlos Santana, who guided the group to consistent commercial success over the next quarter-century. By the mid-'90s, Santana seemed spent as a commercial force on records, though the group continued to attract audiences for its concerts worldwide. But the band made a surprising and monumental comeback in 1999 with *Supernatural*, an album featuring many guest stars that became Santana's best-selling release and won a raft of Grammy Awards.

Mexican-native Carlos Santana (born July 20, 1947, in Autlan de Navarro, Mexico) moved to San Francisco in the early '60s, by which time he was already playing the guitar professionally. In 1966, he formed the Santana Blues Band with keyboard player and singer Gregg Rolie (born June 17, 1947, in Seattle, WA) and other musicians, the personnel changing frequently. The group was given its name due to a musicians union requirement that a single person be named a band's leader and it did not at first indicate that Carlos was in charge. Bass player David Brown (born February 15, 1947, in New York, NY) joined early on, as did Carlos' high-school friend, conga player Mike Carabello (born November 18, 1947, in San Francisco), though he did not stay long at first. By mid-1967, the band's lineup consisted of Carlos, Rolie, Brown, drummer Bob "Doc" Livingston, and percussionist Marcus Malone. The name was shortened simply to Santana and the group came to the attention of promoter Bill Graham, who gave it its debut at his Fillmore West theater on June 16, 1968. Santana was signed to Columbia Records, which sent producer David Rubinson to tape the band at a four-night stand at the Fillmore West December 19-22, 1968. The results were not released until almost 30 years later, when Columbia/Legacy issued *Live at the Fillmore 1968* in 1997.

Livingston and Malone left the lineup in 1969 and were replaced by Carabello and drummer Michael Shrieve (born July 6, 1949, in San Francisco), with a second percussionist, Jose "Chepito" Areas (born July 25, 1946, in Leon, Nicaragua) making Santana a sextet. The band recorded its self-titled debut album and began to tour nationally, making an important stop at the Woodstock festival on August 15, 1969. *Santana* was released the same month. It peaked in the Top Five, going on to remain in the charts over two years, sell over two million copies, and spawn the Top 40 single "Jingo" and the Top Ten single "Evil Ways." Santana's performance of "Soul Sacrifice" was a highlight of the documentary film *Woodstock* and its double-platinum soundtrack album, which appeared in 1970. The band's second album, *Abraxas*, was released in September 1970 and was even more successful than its first. It hit number one, remaining in the charts more than a year and a half and eventually selling over four million copies while spawning the Top Five hit "Black Magic Woman" and the Top Ten hit "Oye Como Va." By the end of the year, the group had added a seventh member, teenage guitarist Neal Schon (born February 27, 1954).

Santana's third album, *Santana III*, was performed by the seven band members, though several guest musicians were also mentioned in the credits, notably percussionist Coke Escovedo, who played on all the tracks. Released in September 1971, the album was another massive hit, reaching number one and eventually selling over two million copies while spawning the Top Ten hit "Everybody's Everything" and the Top 20 hit "No One to Depend On." But it marked the end of the Woodstock-era edition of Santana, which broke up at the end of the tour promoting it, with Carlos retaining rights to the band name.

Following a tour with Buddy Miles that resulted in a live duo album (*Carlos Santana & Buddy Miles! Live!*), Carlos reorganized Santana and recorded the fourth Santana band album, *Caravanserai*, on which each track featured individual musician credits. From the previous lineup, Rolie, Shrieve, Areas, and Schon appeared, alongside pianist Tom Coster, percussionist James Mingo Lewis, percussionist Armando Peraza, guitarist/bassist Douglas Rauch, and percussionist Rico Reyes, among others. (Rolie and Schon left to form Journey.) The album was released in September 1972; it peaked in the Top Five and was eventually certified platinum. It was nominated for a Grammy Award for Best Pop Instrumental Performance with Vocal Coloring.

Carlos, who had become a disciple of the guru Sri Chinmoy and adopted the name Devadip (meaning "the eye, the lamp, and the light of God"), next made a duo album with John McLaughlin, guitarist with the Mahavishnu Orchestra (*Love Devotion Surrender*). Meanwhile, the lineup of Santana continued to fluctuate. On *Welcome*, the band's fifth album, released in November 1973, it consisted of Carlos, Shrieve, Areas, Coster, Peraza, Rauch, keyboard player Richard Kermode, and singer Leon Thomas. The album went gold and peaked in the Top 20. In May 1974, *Lotus*, a live album featuring the same lineup, was released only in Japan. (It was issued in the U.S. in 1991.) Carlos continued to alternate side projects with Santana band albums, next recording a duo LP with John Coltrane's widow Alice Coltrane (*Illuminations*). Columbia decided to cash in on the band's diminishing popularity by releasing *Santana's Greatest Hits* in July 1974. The compilation peaked in the Top 20 and eventually went double platinum. The sixth new Santana album, *Borboletta*, followed in October. The band personnel for the LP featured Carlos, Shrieve, Areas, Coster, Peraza, a returning David Brown, saxophonist Jules Broussard, and singer Leon Patillo, plus guest stars Flora Purim, Airto Moreira, and Stanley Clarke. *Borboletta* peaked in the Top 20 and eventually went gold.

Carlos steered Santana back to a more commercial sound in the mid-'70s in an attempt to stop the eroding sales of the band's albums. He enlisted Santana's original producer, David Rubinson, to handle the next LP. The band was streamlined to a sextet consisting of himself, Coster, Peraza, Brown, drummer Ndugu Leon Chancler (Shrieve having departed to work with Stomu Yamashta), and singer Greg Walker. The result was *Amigos*, released in March 1976, which returned Santana to the Top Ten and went gold. The band was back only nine months later with another Rubinson production, *Festival*, for which Santana consisted of Carlos, Coster, returning members Jose "Chepito" Areas and Leon Patillo, drummer Gaylord Birch, percussionist Raul Rekow, and bass player Pablo Telez. This album peaked in the Top 40 and went gold. Never having issued a live album in the U.S., Santana made up for the lapse with *Moonflower*, released in October 1977, for which the band consisted of Carlos, Coster, Areas, Rekow, Telez, returning member Greg Walker, percussionist Pete Escovedo, drummer Graham Lear, and bass player David Margen. The album peaked in the Top Ten and eventually went platinum, its sales stimulated by the single release of a revival of the Zombies' "She's Not There" that peaked in the Top 20, Santana's first hit single in nearly six years.

Turning to producers Dennis Lambert and Brian Potter, Santana returned to the studio for *Inner Secrets*, released in October 1978. The revamped lineup this time was Carlos, Rekow, Walker, Lear, Margen, returning members Coke Escovedo and Armando Peraza, keyboard player Chris Rhyne, and guitarist/keyboard player Chris Solberg. The album was quickly certified gold, and a revival of the Classics IV hit "Stormy" made the Top 40, but *Inner Secrets* peaked disappointingly below the Top 20. Once again adopting his guru name of Devadip, Carlos issued his first real solo album (*Oneness/Silver Dreams—Golden Reality*) in February 1979. *Marathon*, the tenth Santana band studio album, followed in September, produced by Keith Olsen, the band here being Carlos, Rekow, Lear, Margen, Peraza, Solberg, singer Alex Ligertwood, and keyboard player Alan Pasqua. The album equaled the success of *Inner Secrets*, peaking outside the Top 20 but going gold, with "You Know That I Love You" becoming a Top 40 single. Again, Carlos followed in the winter with another solo effort (*The Swing of Delight*).

Santana (Carlos, Rekow, Lear, Margen, Peraza, Ligertwood, keyboard player Richard Baker, and percussionist Orestes Vilato) spent some extra time on its next release, not issuing *Zebop!* until March 1981, and the extra effort paid off. Paced by the Top 20 single "Winning," the album reached the Top Ten and went gold. The band lavished similar attention on *Shango*, which was released in August 1982. The same lineup as that on *Zebop!* was joined by original member Gregg Rolie, who also co-produced the album. A music video helped Santana enjoy its first Top Ten single in more than a decade with "Hold On," but that did not translate into increased sales for the album, which peaked in the Top 20 but became the band's first LP not to at least go gold. Carlos followed with another solo album (*Havana Moon*), but did not release a new Santana band album until February 1985 with *Beyond Appearances*, produced by Val Garay. By now the lineup consisted of Carlos, Rekow, Peraza, Ligertwood, Vilato, returning member Greg Walker, bass player Alphonso Johnson, keyboard player David Sancious, drummer Chester C. Thompson, and keyboard player Chester D. Thompson. "Say It Again," the album's single, reached the Top 40, but that was better than the LP did.

Santana staged a 20-year anniversary reunion concert in August 1986 featuring many past bandmembers. The February 1987 album *Freedom* marked the formal inclusion of Buddy Miles as a member of Santana, alongside Carlos, Rekow, Peraza, Vilato, Johnson, Chester D. Thompson, and returning members Tom Coster and Graham Lear. The album barely made the Top 100. Carlos followed in the fall with another solo album (*Blues for Salvador*), winning his first Grammy Award in the process (Best Rock Instrumental Performance for the title track). In 1988, he added Wayne Shorter to the band for a tour, then put together a reunion edition of Santana that featured Areas, Rolie, and Shrieve beside Johnson, Peraza, and Thompson. In October, Columbia celebrated the 20-year anniversary of the band's signing to the label with the retrospective *Viva Santana!* The next new Santana album was *Spirits Dancing in the Flesh*, released in June 1990, for which the band was Carlos, Peraza, Thompson, returning member Alex Ligertwood, drummer Walfredo Reyes, and bass player Benny Rietveld. A modest seller that made only the lower reaches of the Top 100, it marked the end of the band's 22-year tenure at Columbia Records.

In 1991, Santana signed to Polydor Records, which, in April 1992, released the band's 16th studio album, *Milagro*. The lineup was Carlos, Thompson, Ligertwood, Reyes, Rietveld, and percussionist Karl Perazzo. Polydor was not able to reverse the band's commercial decline, as the album became Santana's first new studio release not to reach the Top 100. The group followed in November 1993 with *Sacred Fire—Live in South America*, which featured Carlos, Thompson, Ligertwood, Reyes, Perazzo, singer Vorriece Cooper, bass player Myron Dove, and guitarist Jorge Santana, Carlos' brother. The album barely made the charts. In 1994, Carlos, Jorge, and their nephew Carlos Hernandez, released *Santana Brothers*, another marginal chart entry. The same year, Areas, Carabello, Rolie, and Shrieve formed a band called Abraxas and released the album *Abraxas Pool*, which did not chart.

Santana left Polydor and signed briefly to EMI before moving to Arista Records, run by Clive Davis, who had been president of Columbia during the band's heyday. Carlos and Davis put together *Supernatural*, which was stuffed with appearances by high-profile guest stars including Eagle-Eye Cherry, Wyclef Jean, Eric Clapton, Lauryn Hill, Rob Thomas of matchbox 20, Everlast, and Dave Matthews. Arista released the album in June 1999, followed by the single "Smooth" featuring Rob Thomas. Album and single hit number one and in 2000, a second single, "Maria Maria," also topped the charts. *Supernatural*'s sales exploded, taking it past ten million copies, and the album garnered 11 Grammy nominations. Santana won eight Grammys, for Record of the Year ("Smooth"), Album of the Year, Best Pop Performance by a Duo or Group with Vocal ("Maria Maria"), Best Pop Collaboration with Vocals ("Smooth"), Best Pop Instrumental Performance ("El Farol"), Best Rock Performance by a Duo or Group with Vocal ("Put Your Lights On"), Best Rock Instrumental Performance ("The Calling"), and Best Rock Album, and "Smooth" won the Grammy for Song of the Year for authors Rob Thomas and Itaal Shur. *—William Ruhlmann*

Santana / Aug. 1969 / Columbia/Legacy ✦✦✦✦✦
Released in 1969, the group's first album shot the group from local San Francisco band status to a worldwide forum. Included were the group's first hits ("Evil Ways" and "Soul Sacrifice") and others that combined Latin grooves with a rock sensibility. The newly remastered compact disc also adds three bonus tracks recorded live at Woodstock in 1969, "Savor," "Soul Sacrifice," and "Fried Neckbones." *—Cub Koda*

★ **Abraxas** / Sep. 1970 / Columbia/Legacy ✦✦✦✦✦
The San Francisco Bay Area rock scene of the late '60s was one that encouraged radical experimentation and discouraged the type of mindless conformity that's often plagued corporate rock. When one considers just how different Santana, Jefferson Airplane, Moby Grape, and the Grateful Dead sounded, it becomes obvious just how much it was encouraged. In the mid-'90s, an album as eclectic as *Abraxas* would be considered a marketing exec's worst nightmare. But at the dawn of the '70s, this unorthodox mix of rock, jazz, salsa, and blues proved quite successful. Whether adding rock elements to salsa king Tito Puente's "Oye Como Va," embracing instrumental jazz-rock on "Incident at Neshabur" and "Samba Pa Ti," or tackling moody blues-rock on Fleetwood Mac's "Black Magic Woman," the band keeps things unpredictable yet cohesive. Many of the Santana albums that came out in the '70s are worth acquiring, but for novices, *Abraxas* is an excellent place to start. [Columbia/Legacy's 1998 reissue of *Abraxas* featured three previously unreleased tracks—"Se a Cabo," "Toussaint L'Overture," "Black Magic Woman/Gypsy Queen"—which were all recorded live at the Royal Albert Hall on April 18, 1970.] *—Alex Henderson*

Santana III / Sep. 1971 / Columbia/Legacy ✦✦✦✦✦
The group's third album, simply titled *Santana* on its original September 1971 release, was the last work of the original Woodstock-era lineup. With hit singles and albums under its belt, the group became more experimental on its third go-round. This yielded some of their best work and another number one for the band. [The 1998 re-release also adds three bonus recorded live at the Fillmore West on July 4, 1971, bringing comparable on-stage versions of the album's "Batuka" and "Jungle Strut" along with the rocking "Gumbo."] *—Cub Koda*

Love Devotion Surrender / 1972 / Columbia ✦✦✦✦✦
Mahavishnu John McLaughlin and Devadip Carlos Santana came together under the influences of John Coltrane and Sri Chinmoy (the latter of whom McLaughlin would eventually renounce), cut their hair, and joined forces in probably the greatest guitar summit meeting of the jazz-rock era. Their rapport is obvious from the first track, Coltrane's "A Love Supreme"; both guitarists are on fire, flashing their stuff with extraordinary energy and remarkable arrhythmic placement of each note. From this point, the two fuse the high-octane virtuosity of the Mahavishnu Orchestra and Tony Williams' Lifetime (present are Billy Cobham and Jan Hammer—on drums!—from the former and Larry Young from the latter) with Santana's thundering Latin percussion team of Armando Peraza and James Mingo Lewis, without either element dominating. The music reaches an ecstatic peak on the lengthy jam "Let Us Go Into the House of the Lord" (based on the chords of Bobby Womack's "Breezin'"), where Santana's trademark ascending chromatic flurries give way to McLaughlin machine-gun volleys that make more coherent musical sense than anything he was recording with the first Mahavishnu group around this time. Whatever you may think of gurus and Indian religions, there must be something to it if the results of spiritual immersion are as spectacular and fulfilling as the music on this CD. *—Richard S. Ginell*

Carlos Santana & Buddy Miles! Live! / Jun. 1972 / Columbia ✦✦✦✦
From December 1971 to April 1972, Carlos Santana and several other members of Santana toured with drummer/vocalist Buddy Miles, a former member of the Electric Flag and Jimi Hendrix's Band of Gypsys. The resulting live album contained both Santana hits ("Evil Ways") and Buddy Miles hits ("Changes"), plus a 25-minute, side-long jam. It was not, perhaps, the live album Santana fans had been waiting for, but at this point in its career, the band could do no wrong. The album went into the Top Ten and sold a million copies. [Reissued on CD on September 6, 1994.] *—William Ruhlmann*

Caravanserai / Oct. 1972 / Columbia ✦✦✦✦✦
Drawing on rock, salsa, and jazz, Santana recorded one imaginative, unpredictable gem after another in the '70s. But *Caravanserai* is daring even by Santana's high standards. Carlos Santana was obviously very hip to jazz-fusion—something the innovative guitarist provides a generous dose of on the largely instrumental *Caravanserai*. Whether its approach is jazz-rock or simply rock, this album is consistently inspired and quite adventurous. Full of heartfelt, introspective guitar solos, it lacks the immediacy of *Santana* or *Abraxas*. Like the type of jazz that influenced it, this pearl (which marked the beginning of keyboardist/composer Tom Coster's highly benefical membership in the band) requires a number of listenings in order to be absorbed and fully appreciated. But make no mistake: This is one of Santana's finest accomplishments. *—Alex Henderson*

Welcome / Nov. 1973 / Columbia ✦✦✦
On the group's fifth album, "the New Santana Band," as it was called, was an octet. Musically, the album was something of a companion piece to Carlos Santana's duet album with John McLaughlin, *Love Devotion Surrender*, even including a song by that title and, like the earlier record, containing compositions by McLaughlin and John Coltrane. In addition to the jazz influences, there was also a new blues sound courtesy of Leon Thomas, a smooth-voiced singer in the Joe Williams tradition. The record was musically adventurous, but as Santana continued to diverge from its Latin rock roots, his popularity eroded. *—William Ruhlmann*

Lotus / May 1974 / Columbia ✦✦✦✦✦
Recorded in Japan in July 1973, this massive live album, originally on three LPs and now on two compact discs, was available outside the United States in 1974 but held back from domestic release until long into the CD age. It features the same "New Santana Band" that recorded *Welcome* and combines that group's jazz and spiritual influences with performances of earlier Latin rock favorites like "Oye Como Va." *—William Ruhlmann*

Greatest Hits / Jul. 1974 / Columbia ✦✦✦✦✦
This ten-song sampler presents the best of Santana, 1969-1971, the period of its greatest popularity. The hits include "Black Magic Woman," "Evil Ways," "Everybody's

Everything," and "Oye Como Va." But note that this is a bare minimum of prime Santana. Not only does the sampler choose from only Santana's first three albums, but it leaves out such seminal numbers as "Nobody to Depend On" and "Soul Sacrifice." Those looking for a more extensive overview should consider *Viva Santana!* *—William Ruhlmann*

Illuminations / Sep. 1974 / Columbia ✦✦

For his third duet album, Carlos Santana, who had been performing the works of John Coltrane, paired with Coltrane's widow, harpist/keyboardist Alice Coltrane, on this instrumental album. Side one includes several contemplative, string-filled numbers, while side two presents Santana's re-creation of John Coltrane's late free-jazz style in "Angel of Sunlight." Columbia Records could not have been pleased at Santana's determined drift into esoteric jazz: *Illuminations* was the first of the nine Santana-related albums so far released in the U.S. not to go gold. *—William Ruhlmann*

Borboletta / Oct. 1974 / Columbia ✦✦✦

Borboletta was the first new Santana band studio album in 11 months and the group's sixth overall. Once again, individual credits were listed for each song. The main problem was that the band seemed to be coasting; Carlos turned in the usual complement of high-pitched lead guitar work, and the percussionists pounded away, but the Santana sound had long since taken over from any individual composition, and the records were starting to sound alike. That, in turn, started to make them inessential; *Borboletta* spent less time in the charts than any previous Santana album. *—William Ruhlmann*

Amigos / Mar. 1976 / Columbia ✦✦✦✦✦

By the release of *Amigos*, the Santana band's seventh album, only Carlos Santana and David Brown remained from the band that conquered Woodstock, and only Carlos had been in the band continuously since. Meanwhile, the group had made some effort to arrest its commercial slide, hiring an outside producer, David Rubinson, and taking a tighter, more uptempo, and more vocal approach to its music. The overt jazz influences were replaced by strains of R&B/funk and Mexican folk music. The result was an album more dynamic than any since *Santana III* in 1971. "Let It Shine" (number 77), an R&B-tinged tune, became the group's first chart single in four years, and the album returned Santana to Top Ten status. *—William Ruhlmann*

Festival / Jan. 1977 / Columbia ✦✦✦

Santana's follow-up to its comeback album, *Amigos*, was another David Rubinson-produced effort that moved back toward more of a Latin-rock feel, although it retained an essentially pop focus—"The River" was the first real vocal ballad on a Santana album. If any doubt still existed that the group was no longer a band of equals but a platform for its lead guitarist, the current lineup dispelled that; Carlos Santana was now the only original member of the band left. Although the album went gold, the lack of a hit single hurt the album's commercial standing; its number 27 peak was the lowest yet for a Santana Band album. *—William Ruhlmann*

Moonflower / Oct. 1977 / Columbia ✦✦✦

Santana, which was renowned for its concert work dating back to Woodstock, did not release a live album in the U.S. until this one, and it's only partially live, with studio tracks added, notably a cover of the Zombies' "She's Not There" (number 27) that became Santana's first Top 40 hit in five years. The usual comings and goings in band membership had taken place since last time; the track listing was a good mixture of the old—"Black Magic Woman," "Soul Sacrifice"—and the recent, and with the added radio play of a hit single, *Moonflower* went Top Ten and sold a million copies, the first new Santana album to do that since 1972 and the last until *Supernatural* in 1999. *—William Ruhlmann*

Inner Secrets / Oct. 1978 / Columbia ✦✦

Since he had joined Santana in 1972, keyboard player Tom Coster had been Carlos Santana's right-hand man, playing, co-writing, co-producing, and generally taking the place of founding member Gregg Rolie. But Coster left the band in the spring of 1978, to be replaced by keyboardist/guitarist Chris Solberg and keyboardist Chris Rhyne. Despite the change, the band soldiered on, and with *Inner Secrets* they scored three chart singles: the disco-ish "One Chain (Don't Make No Prison)" (number 59), "Stormy" (number 32), and a cover of Buddy Holly's "Well All Right" (number 69), done in the Blind Faith arrangement. (There seems to be a Steve Winwood fixation here. The album also featured a cover of Traffic's "Dealer.") The singles kept the album on the charts longer than any Santana LP since 1971, but it was still a minor disappointment after *Moonflower*, and in retrospect seems like one of the band's more compromised efforts. *—William Ruhlmann*

Oneness: Silver Dreams—Golden Realities / Feb. 1979 / Columbia ✦✦✦

This is the first Carlos Santana solo album. It features members of the Santana band as backup, however, so the difference between a group effort and a solo work seems to be primarily in the musical approach, which is more esoteric and more varied than on a regular band album. The record is mostly instrumental and given over largely to contemplative ballads, although there is also, for example, in the song "Silver Dreams Golden Smiles," a traditional pop ballad sung by Saunders King. *—William Ruhlmann*

Marathon / Sep. 1979 / Columbia ✦✦

Marathon marked the addition of keyboard player Alan Pasqua and singer Greg Walker's replacement by singer/guitarist Alex Ligertwood in the Santana lineup. Otherwise, the album was notable for consisting entirely of band-written material, although those songs were in the established R&B/rock style evolved on albums like *Amigos*, *Festival*, and *Inner Secrets*. The formula seemed to be wearing thin by now, however, as, even with a Top 40 hit in "You Know That I Love You" (number 35), *Marathon* became the first Santana album to fall below the 500,000-sales mark necessary for gold record certification. (It has since made the mark.) *—William Ruhlmann*

The Swing of Delight / Aug. 1980 / Columbia ✦✦

For his second "solo" album, Carlos Santana used Miles Davis' famed '60s group—Herbie Hancock, Wayne Shorter, Ron Carter, and Tony Williams—plus members of the current Santana band, for a varied, jazz-oriented session that was one of his more pleasant excursions from the standard Santana sound. [Originally released as a double-LP, *The Swing of Delight* was reissued on a single CD.] *—William Ruhlmann*

Zebop! / Mar. 1981 / Columbia ✦✦✦

After teaming up with Herbie Hancock for the jazz-flavored *The Swing of Delight* album, Carlos Santana reentered the pop/rock realm with the rest of his band for 1981's *Zebop!*. He still managed to include a little bit of his famed Latino sound into a few of the tracks ("E Papa Re," "American Gypsy"), albeit only slightly, but *Zebop!*'s overall feel is that of commercial rock, with the guitar arriving at the forefront through most of the cuts. Santana does a marvelous job at covering Russ Ballard's "Winning," taking it to number 17 on the charts, while "The Sensitive Kind" is built around the same type of radio-friendly structure yet it stalled at number 56. *Zebop!*'s formula is simple, and all of the songs carry an appeal that is aimed at a wider and more marketable audience base, with "Changes," "Searchin," and "I Love You Much Too Much" coming through as efficient yet not overly extravagant rock & roll efforts. The album's adjustable rhythms and accommodating structures kept the band alive as the decade rolled over, peaking at number 33 in the U.K. but cracking the Top Ten in the United States, which eventually led to *Zebop!* going gold. Actually, "Winning" followed in the same footsteps as Santana's last couple of Top 40 singles in "You Know That I Love You" from 1980 and "Stormy" from 1979. *Shango*, the album that came after *Zebop!*, gave them another hit with "Hold On," sung by bandmember Alex Ligertwood. *—Mike DeGagne*

Shango / Aug. 1982 / Columbia ✦✦

Shango is notable for featuring the return, in the role of co-producer and co-songwriter, of original Santana keyboardist Gregg Rolie. The main producer, however, was Bill Szymczyk (James Gang, Eagles), who gave Santana an unusually sharp rock sound resulting in two more hit singles, "Hold On" (number 15) and "Nowhere to Run" (number 66), although the band once again slipped below Top Ten, gold-selling status, with the album peaking at only number 22, and even this was the highest Santana would get until *Supernatural* in 1999. *—William Ruhlmann*

Havana Moon / Apr. 1983 / Columbia ✦✦✦

The third Carlos Santana solo album marks a surprising turn toward '50s rock & roll and Tex-Mex, with covers such as Bo Diddley's "Who Do You Love" and Chuck Berry's title song. Produced by veteran R&B producers Jerry Wexler and Barry Beckett, the album features an eclectic mix of sidemen, including Booker T. Jones of Booker T & the MG's, Willie Nelson, and the Fabulous Thunderbirds. *Havana Moon* is a light effort, but it's one of Santana's most enjoyable albums, which may explain why it was also the best-selling Santana album outside the group releases in ten years. *—William Ruhlmann*

Beyond Appearances / Feb. 1985 / Columbia ✦✦

Seven months in the making, and appearing two and a half years after Santana's last album, *Beyond Appearances* was produced by Val ("Bette Davis Eyes") Garay in a hot '80s style replete with prominent synthesizers and drum machines. In the interim, the band had undergone changes, with Alphonso Johnson replacing David Margen on bass, Chester D. Thompson and David Sancious replacing Richard Baker on keyboards, Chester Cortez Thompson replacing Graham Lear on drums, and singer Greg Walker rejoining. Garay co-wrote "Say It Again" (number 46), Santana's final Hot 100 entry until "Smooth" in 1999 (a remake of Curtis Mayfield's "I'm The One Who Loves You" hit number 102), but this latest pop interpretation of the Santana sound did not endear it to fans, and, at a peak of number 50, *Beyond Appearances* was the lowest-charting Santana album yet. *—William Ruhlmann*

Freedom / Feb. 1987 / Columbia ✦✦✦

Freedom marked several reunions in the Santana band, which was now a nonet. In addition to Carlos, the band consisted of percussionists Armando Peraza, Orestes Vilato, and Raul Rekow; returning drummer Graham Lear; bassist Alphonso Johnson; returning keyboardist Tom Coster, keyboardist Chester D. Thompson, and, on lead vocals, Buddy Miles, who had made a duet album with Santana 15 years before. Credited as an "additional musician" was keyboard player Gregg Rolie, an original member. The music also marked a return from the hyper-pop sound of Val Garay on *Beyond Appearances* to a more traditional Santana Latin rock style. Thus, *Freedom* was a literal return to form, but, unfortunately, not to the quality of early Santana albums. And the group's commercial decline continued, with the LP getting to only number 95. *—William Ruhlmann*

Blues for Salvador / Oct. 1987 / Columbia ✦✦✦✦✦

On previous "solo" albums, Carlos Santana had made noticeable stylistic changes and worked with jazz, pop, and even country musicians. On this, his fourth Carlos Santana release, the line between a "solo" and a "group" project is blurred; this record is really a catchall of Santana band outtakes and stray tracks. For example, included are an instrumental version of "Deeper, Dig Deeper" from *Freedom* and an alternate take of "Hannibal" from *Zebop!*, as well as "Now That You Know" from the group's 1985 tour. Given the variety of material, the album is somewhat less focused than most Santana band albums, but there are individual tracks that are impressive, notably "Trane," which features Tony Williams on drums. *Blues for Salvador* won the Grammy Award for Best Rock Instrumental Performance. *—William Ruhlmann*

Viva Santana! / Oct. 1988 / Columbia ✦✦✦✦✦

Released in 1988, *Viva Santana!* is a generous 30-track overview of Santana's first 20 years of recording. Appropriately, it concentrates on the band's glory years of the late '60s and early '70s, when both Carlos Santana and his supporting musicians were on fire. There are several unreleased cuts, including live tracks included for hardcore fans, but

Viva Santana! is most useful as a thorough overview for curious listeners. —*Stephen Thomas Erlewine*

Spirits Dancing in the Flesh / Jun. 1990 / Columbia ♦♦♦

Following a 1989 20th-anniversary reunion tour to promote *Viva Santana!*, Carlos Santana reorganized the band as a sextet and recorded *Spirits Dancing in the Flesh*, Santana's 15th and final studio album for Columbia Records. It was an unusually eclectic collection, featuring songs by Curtis Mayfield ("Gypsy Woman"), the Isley Brothers ("Who's That Lady"), and Babatunde Olatunji ("Jin-Go-Lo-Ba"). For all those influences, it was more of a straightforward, guitar-heavy rock album than usual. Coming more than three years after Santana's last new album, *Freedom*, it sold to the band's core audience only, reaching number 85. —*William Ruhlmann*

Milagro / May 5, 1992 / Polydor ♦♦♦

Santana signed to Polydor in 1991 after 22 years with Columbia Records. Their label debut has a somewhat elegiac tone, beginning with a stage introduction by the late promoter Bill Graham and featuring an excerpt from a speech by Dr. Martin Luther King, Jr., solos taken from Miles Davis and John Coltrane, and music written by Bob Marley, Coltrane, and Gil Evans. Despite the presence of all these heroic ghosts, however, *Milagro* is only an average Santana release, familiar-sounding but undistinguished, and it failed to arrest the band's commercial slide, becoming the first new Santana studio album not to crack the Top 100. —*William Ruhlmann*

Sacred Fire—Santana Live in South America / Nov. 1993 / Polydor ♦♦

For its third live album, Santana introduced a new bass player, Myron Dove, and added guitarist Jorge Santana (Carlos Santana's brother) and singer Vorriece Cooper to bring the band up to nine members. Adopting the mantle of Bob Marley, the band played "Esperando," which borrowed Marley's characteristic audience chant. Much of the album, however, is given over to repeating Santana's earliest hits—"No One to Depend On," "Black Magic Woman," "Soul Sacrifice," etc.—which should please the band's new record label (it's always good to have versions of the hits in your catalog), but which make the album inessential for fans. *Sacred Fire* spent one week at number 181 in the charts, the worst performance ever for a Santana album. —*William Ruhlmann*

Dance of the Rainbow Serpent / Aug. 8, 1995 / Columbia/Legacy ♦♦♦

Guitarist Carlos Santana continues to record music, but when contemplating his body of work, it's difficult not to telescope to the "vintage" 1969-1975 period, from first albums *Santana* and *Abraxas* through to *Lotus*. *Dance of the Rainbow Serpent* offers a well-rounded, three-disc overview of his career, but its the sultry Latin rhythms and stinging guitar of the early years—captured on disc one, subtitled *Heart*—that prove most invigorating. The obvious hits like "Evil Ways" and "Black Magic Woman" are all included of course, although these are scorched by the speedy pyrotechnics of the likes of "Toussaint Overture" from *Lotus*. The second disc, mistitled *Soul*, covers material that is, to be kind, bland and overproduced. Without the Latin edge, there's nothing to distinguish the contents from a hundred other MOR performers. Third disc *Spirit* is more diverse and satisfying; delving into the funkier examples of his later work, plus sessions with John Lee Hooker (including hit "The Healer") and previously unreleased material (including a workout with Living Color's Vernon Reid). In all, plenty here to chew on for fans of Santana's fluid, spiritual style—with one of three discs left to gather. —*Roch Parisien*

Live at the Fillmore 1968 / Mar. 11, 1997 / Columbia/Legacy ♦♦♦♦

Two-CD package drawn from performances at the Fillmore West in December 1968, with an early lineup including Bob "Doc" Livingston on drums and Marcus Malone on congas (both of whom would be gone by the time the group recorded their official debut in 1969). The band sound only a bit more tentative here than they would in their Woodstock-era incarnation, running through several of the highlights of their first album ("Jingo," "Persuasion," "Soul Sacrifice," and "Treat"). More interesting to collectors will be the five songs that have not previously appeared on any Santana recording, including covers of songs by jazzmen Chico Hamilton and Willie Bobo and a half-hour original jam that concludes the set, "Freeway." The sound is excellent and the arrangements a bit more improv-oriented than what ended up on the early studio records. Its appeal isn't solely limited to committed fans; on its own terms it's a fine release, highlighted by some burning organ-guitar interplay in particular. —*Richie Unterberger*

● The Best of Santana / Mar. 31, 1998 / Columbia/Legacy ♦♦♦♦♦

The Best of Santana is a 16-track collection that greatly expands the scope of Santana's previous hits compilation, *Greatest Hits*. Drawing from the band's entire 30-year career, the disc contains such familiar items as "Evil Ways," "Jingo," "Black Magic Woman/Gypsy Queen," and "Oye Como Va," but it also has a number of longtime favorites of the band and fans. Furthermore, all the songs have been subjected to Super Bit remastering, resulting in the best sound ever. For some casual fans, *Greatest Hits* remains definitive, since it's a portrait of the band at its peak, but those wanting a career-spanning single-disc compilation will find that *The Best of Santana* suits their needs. —*Stephen Thomas Erlewine*

Supernatural / Jun. 15, 1999 / Arista ♦♦♦♦

Santana was still a respected rock veteran in 1999, but it had been years since he had a hit, even if he continued to fare well on the concert circuits. Clive Davis, the man who had signed Santana to Columbia in 1968, offered him the opportunity to set up shop at his label, Arista. In the tradition of comebacks and label debuts by veteran artists in the '90s, *Supernatural*, Santana's first effort for Arista, is designed as a star-studded event. At first listen, there doesn't seem to be a track that doesn't have a guest star, which brings up the primary problem with the album—despite several interesting or excellent moments, it never develops a consistent voice that holds the album together. The fault doesn't lay with the guest stars or even with Santana, who continues to turn in fine

performances. There's just a general directionless feeling to the record, enhanced by several songs that seem like excuses for jams, which, truth be told, isn't all that foreign on latter-day Santana records. Then again, the grooves often play better than the ploys for radio play, but that's not always the case, since Lauryn Hill's "Do You Like the Way" and the Dust Brothers-produced, Eagle-Eye Cherry-sung "Wishing It Was" are as captivating as the Eric Clapton duet, "The Calling." But that just confirms that *Supernatural* just doesn't have much of a direction, flipping between traditional Santana numbers and polished contemporary collaborations, with both extremes being equally likely to hit or miss. That doesn't quite constitute a triumph, but the peak moments of *Supernatural* are some of Santana's best music of the '90s, which does make it a successful comeback. —*Stephen Thomas Erlewine*

The Best of Santana, Vol. 2 / Nov. 21, 2000 / Columbia/Legacy ♦♦♦♦

These 14 tracks lean heavily on the earliest phase of Santana. Nine of them, in fact, were recorded prior to 1972, and just one postdates 1978. As 1969-1971 was Santana's most vital period, however, that's no cause for complaint, and indeed the later cuts really pale in comparison. For someone who wants a little more than a greatest hits collection but wants to stop after two volumes, this is good enough, with first-rate items like "Persuasion," "Se Acabo," and "Guajira." Nothing here is rare, and note that the versions of "Black Magic Woman" and "Europa" are live ones. —*Richie Unterberger*

Black Magic Woman / Apr. 16, 2002 / Collectables ♦♦♦

Black Magic Woman, the Santana title in Collectables Records' budget-priced *Priceless Collection* series, is, like other albums in the series, a reissue of an earlier budget album under a different title. In this case, that identical predecessor is *Between Good and Evil*. In fact, Collectables hasn't even bothered to change discs; open up the jewel box, and the CD itself still says *Between Good and Evil*. The compilation is intended for the casual fan of Santana. It includes the group's two biggest hit singles (up until 1999, anyway), "Evil Ways" and "Black Magic Woman," plus three other tracks from the massively popular first two Santana albums, "Soul Sacrifice" (the song the band performed in the *Woodstock* movie), "Persuasion," and "Samba Pa Ti." The other five tracks are taken from slightly later LPs: "Song of the Wind" from 1972's *Caravanserai*, "Practice What You Preach" from 1974's *Borboletta*, "Europa (Earth's Cry Heaven's Smile)" from 1976's *Amigos*, "Jugando" from 1977's *Festival*, and "I'll Be Waiting" from 1977's *Moonflower*. It's a highlights sampler rather than a hits or even a best-of collection, useful for the music fan who just wants a smattering of Santana, as long as it doesn't cost much. —*William Ruhlmann*

Booker T. Sapps

Harmonica / Harmonica Blues, Folk-Blues

To many people, the Booker T. Sapps might bring to mind a blackjack company run as a sideline by a funky rhythm & blues organist, or perhaps the name would mean nothing at all. To a blues harmonica player, it is the name of a mysterious figure who managed to get in the crosshairs of microphones and portable tape recording equipment being utilized by roving ethnomusicologists of the '30s and '40s, with possibly more accuracy than the hunting rifles of local residents. When a harmonica player says that Sapps was a classic straight blocker, again one might think the discussion has to do with thugs ready to commit mayhem, but this is pure harmonica talk. Sapps is an early blues harmonica player whose existence suggests the possible solving of technical mysteries connected to the fine art of making tiny metal reeds warble in and out of tune.

If the American blues scene is like a puzzle, like one of those 5,000 piece ones that nobody ever finishes, then Booker T. Sapps is the piece that someone finds stuck under the piano bench. He was recorded in the mid-'30s in the swampy state of Florida, accompanying singer and guitarist Roger Matthews. These field recordings were originally conducted by Alan Lomax, Zora Neale Hurston, and Mary Elizabeth Barnicle for the Library of Congress. The repertoire of the Matthews-Sapps duo was heavily laden with folk ballads and similar traditional material, as evidenced by their versions of "Frankie and Albert," "Fox and the Hounds," and "I'm a Pilgrim." Their style is a bit similar to the user-friendly coffeehouse blues of Sonny Terry & Brownie McGhee, but is even closer to the real down-home source of this style. "Blues as played outside the recording studio" was one critic's description of the sound of this duo, and it is a good one. "The Fox and the Hounds" is of course the showpiece for the harmonica and is a performance that would fit comfortably into an old-time country discography, that is as long as the gatekeepers were color blind.

Country blues and old-time players had one important thing in common: They were the "it" as far as musical entertainment at local events were concerned and Sapps' music comes firmly out of what would have been the traditional repertoire of a mid-'30s dance band of either color. It was certainly not an enterprise that provided the musician with a living, as is purely evidenced by the fact that the performers recording in Florida were all surviving as migrant workers at the time. The Florida recordings seem to have been Sapps' only time in front of a tape recorder, but it has had wide-reaching musical effects. No less a folk icon as Bob Dylan has expressed his enthusiasm for Booker T. Sapps, and he definitely wasn't discussing street weaponry. The weapon of choice for both Dylan and Sapps was the harmonica, used by both in an authentic country blues manner. If the latter artist was indeed an influence, then it can be said that the sound of Sapps is truly "Blowin' in the Wind." —*Eugene Chadbourne*

Eric Sardinas

Guitar / Blues-Rock, Modern Electric Blues

The term "blues-rock" brings with it a connotation of a blues artist "selling out" in order to make more money or a rock band blaring heavy riffs with a thinly veiled strain of blues. A worse offense is that many of these rock artists have little or no knowledge of the blues in its historical context or its mythological roots.

That is certainly not true in the case of Eric Sardinas. At six, his first love was Delta blues, as it "was the thrill of hearing one person playing the guitar and generating the energy of five—I loved the sheer strength and heart of a single player." Just as unusual was citing his first influences as Barbecue Bob, Charley Patton, and Bukka White, then Elmore James, Muddy Waters, and Big Bill Broonzy. He exclusively concentrates on slide guitar, employing his cherished Dobros, some that are customized to play by Edison's power. Sardinas listens to 78s, then couples these influences with modern sounds.

He moved around the country, landing in Los Angeles in 1990. Like the early blues folk, he played acoustic for a living on the street, then formed the Eric Sardinas Project (ESP) by hooking up with bassist Paul Loranger at a jam session. Loranger had the ideal sound that Sardinas wanted, a bassist who had exceptional playing ability on upright and electric and could work the upright in a blues-rock context. Two years later, drummer Scott Palacios joined them. It took ESP six years of experience of performing nearly 300 shows annually, playing from acoustic gigs in coffeehouses to sharing the bill with rock bands at Hollywood clubs. Musical-instrument companies sent them gigging at showcase concerts, which led the band to a gig as the opening act for a West Coast swing of a Johnny Winter's tour. Word got around, receiving the attention of Evidence Records. Blues discoverer Dick Shurman produced Sardinas' 1999 debut, *Treat Me Right.* In 2000, Sardinas released a three-song single spotlighting his burning take on J.B. Hutto's "Angel Face." *Devil's Train*, his second full-length album, followed in 2001 and featured more of Sardinas' trademark blues-rock. *—Char Ham*

● **Treat Me Right** / Feb. 23, 1999 / Evidence ✦✦✦

If you buy into all the hype and the look, then all your standard journalistic clichés about "a man playing like he was possessed" would certainly seem to apply in the case of this record. Sardinas has only one groove, and that's the one with the pedal put firmly to the metal. Playing electric Dobro gives his sound a raw, distorted edge right down to the wah-wah pedal that flirts with comparisons to George Thorogood and other ham-fisted slide rockers (he plays unamplified on his originals "Cherry Bomb," "Goin' to the River," and "Sweetwater Blues"), although Sardinas is a considerably more able player than Thorogood. Comparisons with Johnny Winter would also not be unfounded; he makes a guest appearance here on vocal and guitar on his "Tired of Tryin'." Hubert Sumlin is also brought aboard to reprise his original rhythm part of "Down In the Bottom," although he's totally swamped in the mix by Sardinas' over-the-top bombast, both vocally and instrumentally. Fans of the Stevie Ray Vaughan, Johnny Winter, and George Thorogood style of blues-rock will want to add this one to the collection. *—Cub Koda*

Devil's Train / Aug. 28, 2001 / Evidence ✦✦✦

Sardinas led a trio through a high-energy set of rocky roadhouse blues-rock on his second album. Given how tired the format sounds after being exploited by innumerable performers for many years, and also how much better the best of such practitioners are at the format, it's questionable whether another entry in this overcrowded field was unnecessary. Sardinas' skills as a technically accomplished, if somewhat bombastic and unimaginative, blues guitarist are undoubted. His hoarse, blustery vocals are another matter, as is the over-the-top macho posturing of his original songs. It's better when, as the cliché goes, he just shuts up and plays his guitar, as on the instrumental "Texola," or when he tones down the throaty strain of his vocals at least a little, as on the uncharacteristically laid-back closer, "8 Goin' South." Perhaps fans of George Thorogood looking for something in a more headbanging vein may dig this, but here's voting that Sardinas is more properly placed as a sideman than a frontman. He duets with Mississippi bluesman David "Honeyboy" Edwards, incidentally, on "Gambling Man Blues." *—Richie Unterberger*

Satan & Adam

f. 1986, Harlem, NY

Group / Electric Harmonica Blues, Modern Acoustic Blues

The blues duo of guitarist, singer, and songwriter Sterling Magee and harmonica player Adam Gussow have paid their dues. They began their career on the street. On the corner of Seventh Avenue and 125th Street, to be exact, and within a matter of weeks, they were drawing crowds to their corner, people pausing on their way home from work to stop and listen. For five years, nearly every afternoon that weather permitted, the pair would meet on the corner and Magee would set up his simple stool, drum kit, guitar, and amplifier. Using a combination of foot stomps, tambourines, hi-hat cymbals, and his guitar, Magee gives the duo a full sound.

Magee and Gussow specialize in funky, gritty, electric urban blues, and there are few groups or artists anywhere who sound anything remotely like them. Gussow's exquisite harmonica solos complement the driving, open-toned guitar playing of Magee, who prefers to be called Mr. Satan, and who frequently refers to Gussow in live performances as Mr. Gussow. Satan and Adam have redefined and shaped the sound of modern blues so much that their track, "I Want You" from their *Harlem Blues* debut is included on a Rhino Records release, *Modern Blues of the 1990s.*

Magee, born May 20, 1936, in Mississippi and raised in Florida, began his career playing piano in churches in both states. Since the early '80s, he's played on Harlem streets, but in the '60s he was a key session guitarist, playing on recordings by James Brown, King Curtis, George Benson and others. Adam Gussow, born April 3, 1958, and raised in Rockland County, NY, was a Princeton-educated harmonica player who had a little uptown apartment, and in passing Magee one day on the street in 1985, he asked if he could sit in on harmonica. That was the start of a musical and social relationship between the two that continues to this day.

The pair have recorded several critically acclaimed albums for the now-defunct Flying Fish label, and they include *Harlem Blues* (1991) and *Mother Mojo* (1993). Satan and Adam also performed in U2's *Rattle and Hum* movie. On their *Mother Mojo*, the group reinterprets and funkifies well-known songs like Herbie Hancock's "Watermelon Man" and Joe Turner's "Crawdad Hole." In 1996 the duo released *Living on the River.* Since then they have not recorded and play together only sporadically, as Satan moved out of Harlem to Lynchburg, VA. In 1998, Adam Gussow published a memoir, *Mister Satan's Apprentice*, telling of his years playing with Sterling Magee. *—Richard Skelly*

● **Harlem Blues** / 1991 / Flying Fish ✦✦✦✦✦

Harlem Blues sounds exactly like how Satan & Adam would sound playing on a street corner—it's raw and tough, with a surprisingly adventurous streak. Satan and Adam stick to a basic acoustic blues duo, but their rhythms and techniques occasionally stray into funkier, jazzier territory. And that sense of careening unpredictability is what makes *Harlem Blues* so entertaining—they might be playing blues in a traditional style, but the end result is anything but traditional. *—Thom Owens*

Mother Mojo / Jan. 1993 / Flying Fish ✦✦✦

Mother Mojo was an excellent follow-up to Satan & Adam's first-rate debut, *Harlem Blues.* The duo hasn't abandoned their minimalist guitar and harp blues, but there is a loose energy that keeps the music fresh and consistently engaging. *—Thom Owens*

Living on the River / Jun. 5, 1996 / Flying Fish ✦✦✦

Satan & Adam continue to mine the same two-man street-corner busker groove that has served them so well on this, their third album. The music is kept raw and alive in pursuing this, but on several tracks their sound is fleshed out with guest appearances from Ernie Colon on percussion, the Uptown Horns, and background singers appearing on their version of "Proud Mary." But despite the additions, their basic sound is every bit as unfettered as one would expect from these two blues anomalies. *—Cub Koda*

Savoy Brown

f. 1966, United Kingdom

Group / Blues-Rock, British Blues, Album Rock, Hard Rock, Arena Rock

Part of the late-'60s blues-rock movement, Britain's Savoy Brown never achieved as much success in their homeland as they did in America, where they promoted their albums with nonstop touring. The band was formed and led by guitarist Kim Simmonds, whose dominating personality has led to myriad personnel changes; the original lineup included singer Bruce Portius, keyboardist Bob Hall, guitarist Martin Stone, bassist Ray Chappell, and drummer Leo Manning. This lineup appeared on the band's 1967 debut, *Shake Down*, a collection of blues covers. Seeking a different approach, Simmonds dissolved the group and brought in guitarist "Lonesome" Dave Peverett, bassist Rivers Jobe, drummer Roger Earl, and singer Chris Youlden, who gave them a distinctive frontman with his vocal abilities, bowler hat, and monocle. With perhaps its strongest lineup, Savoy Brown quickly made a name for itself, now recording originals like "Train to Nowhere" as well. However, Youlden left the band in 1970 following *Raw Sienna*, and shortly thereafter, Peverett, Earl, and new bassist Tony Stevens departed to form Foghat, continuing the pattern of consistent membership turnover. Simmonds collected yet another lineup and began a hectic tour of America, showcasing the group's now-refined bluesy boogie-rock style, which dominated the rest of their albums. The group briefly broke up in 1973, but re-formed the following year and has continued to tour and record ever since. Simmonds has remained undeterred by a revolving-door membership and declining interest (no Savoy Brown album has charted in the U.S. since 1981's *Rock & Roll Warriors*). *—Steve Huey*

Getting to the Point / 1968 / Deram ✦✦✦

Getting to the Point marks the debut of a vastly different lineup, still led by Simmonds but now fronted by new vocalist Chris Youlden. The pair got off to a good start by writing or co-writing most of the album. The playing is solid blues revival, and though Youlden's vocals are often overly imitative of B.B. King and Muddy Waters, he has a confident voice and frontman persona. Originals like "Flood in Houston" and "Mr. Downchild" provide the highlights. *—Keith Farley*

Blue Matter / Mar. 1969 / Deram ✦✦✦✦✦

The third release by Kim Simmonds and company, but the first to feature the most memorable lineup of the group: Simmonds, "Lonesome" Dave Peverett, Tony "Tone" Stevens, Roger Earl, and charismatic singer Chris Youlden. This one serves up a nice mixture of blues covers and originals, with the first side devoted to studio cuts and the second a live club date recording. Certainly the standout track, indeed a signature song by the band, is the *tour de force* "Train to Nowhere," with its patient, insistent buildup and pounding train-whistle climax. Additionally, David Anstey's detailed, imaginative sleeve art further boosts this a notch above most other British blues efforts. *—Peter Kurtz*

A Step Further / Aug. 1969 / Deram ✦✦✦✦

With Kim Simmonds and Chris Youlden combining their talents in Savoy Brown's strongest configuration, 1969's *A Step Further* kept the band in the blues-rock spotlight after the release of their successful *Blue Matter* album. While *A Step Further* may not be as strong as the band's former release, all five tracks do a good job at maintaining their spirited blues shuffle. Plenty of horn work snuggles up to Simmonds' guitar playing and Youlden's singing is especially hearty on "Made Up My Mind" and "I'm Tired." The first four tracks are bona fide Brown movers, but they can't compete with the 20-plus minutes of "Savoy Brown Boogie," one of the group's best examples of their guitar playing prowess and a wonderful finale to the album. This lineup saw the release of *Raw Sienna* before "Lonesome" Dave Peverett stepped up to the microphone for *Looking In* upon the departure of Youlden, but the new arrangement was short-lived, as not long after three other members exited to form Foghat. As part of Savoy Brown's Chris Youlden days, *A Step Further* should be heard alongside *Getting to the Point*, *Blue Matter*, and *Raw Sienna*, as it's an integral part of the band's formative boogie blues years. *—Mike DeGagne*

Raw Sienna / Mar. 1970 / Deram ✦✦✦✦✦

This high watermark by the band finds them softening their rougher edges and stretching out into jazz territory, yet still retaining a blues foundation. There's not a bad cut here, with enough variety (bottleneck slide, acoustic guitar, horns, and strings) to warrant frequent late-night listenings. "A Hard Way to Go," "Needle and Spoon," and "Stay While the Night Is Young" are especially strong, as are two instrumental numbers. Unfortunately, leader Kim Simmonds lost his greatest asset when vocalist Chris Youlden quit for an ill-fated solo career after this recording. Youlden had one of the most distinctive voices in British blues, and Savoy would never fully recover from his exit. —*Peter Kurtz*

Looking In / Sep. 1970 / Deram ✦✦✦✦
Savoy Brown's blues-rock sound takes on a much more defined feel on 1970's *Looking In* and is one of this band's best efforts. Kim Simmonds is utterly bewildering on guitar, while "Lonesome" Dave Peverett does a fine job taking over lead singing duties from Chris Youlden who left halfway through the year. But it's the captivating arrangements and alluring ease of the music that makes this a superb listen. The pleading strain transformed through Simmonds' guitar on "Money Can't Save Your Soul" is mud-thick with raw blues, and the comfort of "Sunday Night" is extremely smooth and laid back. "Take It Easy" sounds like it could have been a B.B. King tune as it's doused with relaxed guitar fingering. The entire album is saturated with a simple, British blues sound but the pace and the marbled strands of bubbly instrumental perkiness fill it with life. Even the Yardbirds-flavored "Leaving Again" is appealing with its naïve hooks, capped off with a heart-stopping guitar solo. This album along with *Street Corner Talking* best exemplify Savoy Brown's tranquilizing style. —*Mike DeGagne*

Street Corner Talking / 1971 / Deram ✦✦✦✦
After 1970's *Looking In* album, Peverett, Roger Earl, and Tony Stevens left to form Foghat, leaving Kim Simmonds with yet another dilemma. But for Simmonds, things went a little smoother than he might have imagined, picking up piano player Paul Raymond, bassman Andy Silvester, and drummer Dave Bidwell, all from Chicken Shack. He also hired singer Dave Walker, who was the former frontman with the Idle Race, and together the new lineup recorded *Street Corner Talking*, one of Savoy Brown's finest moments. Gelling almost instantaneously, Walker's cozy yet fervent voice countered with Simmonds' strong, sturdy guitar playing, and an exuberant mixture of British blues and boogie rock prevailed. All of *Street Corner Talking*'s efforts are solid examples of the group's blues-rock power, from the slick cover of Willie Dixon's "Wang Dang Doodle" to the deep feel of "All I Can Do" to the subtle strength of "Tell Mama," Walker's best-sung tune. The album's blend of sultry guitar blues and upfront rock & roll flavor give it a multi-faceted appeal, with every musician contributing his talents uniformly, which is something that's rather difficult to achieve after there's been a wholesale change to the personnel. Although they stayed together for the *Hellbound Train* album, Silvester was replaced by Andy Pyle for 1972's *Lion's Share* release, and a year after that Walker left to join Fleetwood Mac. —*Mike DeGagne*

Hellbound Train / Feb. 1972 / Deram ✦✦✦
Comprising the same lineup as *Street Corner Talking*, Savoy Brown released *Hellbound Train* a year later. For this effort, Kim Simmonds' guitar theatrics are toned down a bit and the rest of the band seems to be a little less vivid and passionate with their music. The songs are still draped with Savoy Brown's sleek, bluesy feel, but the deep-rooted blues essence that so easily emerged from their last album doesn't rise as high throughout *Hellbound Train*'s tracks. The title cut is most definitely the strongest, with Dave Walker, Simmonds, and Paul Raymond sounding tighter than on any other song, and from a wider perspective, Andy Silvester's bass playing is easily *Hellbound*'s most complementing asset. On tracks like "Lost and Lonely Child," "Doin' Fine," and "If I Could See an End," the lifeblood of the band doesn't quite surge into the music as it did before, and the tracks become only average-sounding blues efforts. Because of Savoy Brown's depth of talent, this rather nonchalant approach doesn't make *Hellbound Train* a "bad" album by any means—it just fails to equal the potency of its predecessor. But there is a noticeable difference in the albums that followed this one, as the band and especially Simmonds himself was beginning to show signs of fatigue, and a significant decline in the group's overall sound was rapidly becoming apparent. —*Mike DeGagne*

Lion's Share / Oct. 1972 / Polygram ✦✦✦
"Shot in the Head," the slide guitar showcase that opens this solid set, became a staple of this veteran English band's live act. In his only full-time stint as singer for demanding bandleader Kim Simmonds, Dave Walker proves a serviceable, if unremarkable, successor to Chris Youlden. Besides their own tunes, the lads cover Howlin' Wolf and Little Walter. —*Mark Allan*

Jack the Toad / 1973 / Polygram ✦
Savoy Brown made the best of Dave Walker's departure for Fleetwood Mac by hiring Jack Lynton as their lead singer. While Lynton's voice can't match the warmth instilled by Walker's, he does do a competent job at melding with Kim Simmonds' guitar playing. His voice is sharp but not overly exciting, yet it still presents "Coming Down Your Way" with enough emotion to make it the album's standout track. The addition of Ron Berg on percussion and Stan Saltzman's saxophone are worthy instrumental extensions, helping to boost the album's energy level another notch. "Ride on Babe," "If I Want To," "Some People," and the title track are straight-sounding efforts, but they seem to lack the blues resilience of what the band is capable of. There's enough of Simmonds' talent to keep die-hard fans fascinated, yet the provocative blues-rock character that has evolved from Savoy Brown as a complete group has been slightly abandoned for the most part. Considering Savoy Brown's past tribulations that have played out in such a short time span, *Jack the Toad* can be labeled an adequate effort, but when paralleled to the quality of strut and swagger that Simmonds has administered with his members in the past, it may be regarded as a little less than that. —*Mike DeGagne*

Rock 'n' Roll Warriors / 1981 / Starburst ✦✦✦
Though Savoy Brown is primarily known as a blues band, *Rock 'n' Roll Warriors* says in the title what this is all about, as Kim Simmonds' aggregation obtained in vocalist Ralph Mormon a major component from the Joe Perry Project's first solo album, *Let the Music Do the Talking*, released the year before this. With producer Richie Wise, himself the lead singer of the heavy metal band Dust and co-producer of the first two albums from Kiss,

there is a decidedly different edge to this release on Capitol/Town House. The band-members look like they are the prototype for the 1984 film *Streets of Fire* on the cover, and though the three live tracks tacked onto the end of the LP on TKO Magnum's CD release has this group truer to its blues roots, the original ten studio tunes include some variety that Savoy Brown's followers may not have been accustomed to. Those bonus tracks, "Street Corner Talkin'," "I'm Tired," and "Hellbound Train," were recorded live at Denver's Rainbow Music Hall on June 27, 1981. They make a great reference point to hear how this version of the band tackled familiar territory, but original material like "Shot Down By Love" could easily have found itself on Joe Perry's disc and shows the bite producer Wise infused into this version of the group. This is the last Savoy Brown album to chart in the U.S., which is validation of its quality but still a shame, since the music here is vital enough to have jump-started SB's storied career. Mormon sounds comfortable and in control; that he had the opportunity to front bands featuring two guitar greats is something you can feel he embraced wholeheartedly. Michael Heatley's year 2000 liner notes to the CD reissue give some history and the Chinn/Chapman tune that hit for the U.K. band Smokie, "Lay Back in the Arms of Someone," is a real treat—pure pop that is wildly different from the band's minor '70s radio hit, "Tell Mama," or anything else here. The songs are mostly composed by Kim Simmonds, were recorded in North Hollywood, and shift from rock to blues to rock. Though viewed as an anomaly in the band's catalog, *Rock 'n' Roll Warriors* has gained credibility and much-deserved respect over the years. —*Joe Viglione*

● **The Savoy Brown Collection (Chronicles Series)** / Jul. 20, 1993 / Polygram ✦✦✦✦✦
With one of the smoothest and most compelling guitarists of the blues-rock style, Savoy Brown and the finger wizardry of Kim Simmonds unleashed some of the smoothest and most mesmerizing rock & roll of the '70s. Their ingenious blend of contented blues and hard-edged rock resulted in some wholesome yet somewhat bypassed guitar music. *The Savoy Brown Collection* is a two-disc compilation that takes their best tunes from 14 different albums and presents the listener with a sufficient amount of material that never becomes tiresome. Some of the meatier material comes from 1971's *Street Corner Talking*, like the ultra-smooth "I Can't Get Next to You" and Willie Dixon's "Wang Dang Doodle." Equally impressive is the haunting "Poor Girl" or the desperate guitar cry of "Leavin' Again," both from the sensational *Looking In* album. The real treasures are the lone tunes taken from some of their lesser-known albums. "I'm Tired," from *A Step Further*, emanates pathos through instrumentation, while "Stranger Blues" is a startling example of prime guitar manipulation. Early material from albums like *Shake Down* and *Blue Matter* have former lead singer Chris Youlden at the helm, who departed before the *Looking In* album, replaced by "Lonesome" Dave Peverett who later formed Foghat. Overshadowed by bands like the Yardbirds and Led Zeppelin, Savoy Brown didn't get the acclaim they actually deserved. Rightfully so, the words "Featuring Kim Simmonds" are underneath the title of this two-CD set, since his craftsmanship is truly the heart of this talented band. Everything that is even the least bit important from this group is strewn across this compilation. —*Mike DeGagne*

Live at the Record Plant / Mar. 3, 1998 / Archive ✦✦✦✦✦
The performance, recorded at the Record Plant for a radio broadcast, dates from 1975, when the band was at its peak promoting the *Wire Fire* album. The sound is hot, with Kim Simmonds taking some nice solos, and the band is in good form, covering "Tell Mama," "All I Can Do (Is Cry)," and Jimmy Reed's "You Don't Have to Go." It's all a little pale next to some of the acts that followed in the wake of Savoy Brown, but this tape is one of the best chances one has to hear the seminal group during the close of its original glory days. —*Bruce Eder*

20th Century Masters—The Millennium Collection: The Best of Savoy Brown / May 7, 2002 / Polydor ✦✦✦✦
Savoy Brown, the long-lived British blues-rock band, spent a decade signed to the British Decca label, which released their albums in America on the Parrot and London subsidiaries. The band's commercial heyday, a series of six modestly charting LPs, came early on, and this discount-priced compilation presents 11 highlights from that period, 1969-1972, including Savoy Brown's two minor chart singles: "I'm Tired" and "Tell Mama." Other than guitarist/founder Kim Simmonds, the band suffered frequent personnel changes, and even in this period of three years there was a complete turnover, starting with the "classic" lineup including singer Chris Youlden and guitarist "Lonesome" Dave Peverett and ending with another popular one featuring singer Dave Walker. The band's sound, however, remained much the same, driving blues-rock with screaming, lengthy guitar solos and forceful singing. This is not a comprehensive compilation of Savoy Brown on Decca by any means (for that, see 1993's *The Savoy Brown Collection*), but it does give a good sense of what the group sounded like at the top of their game. —*William Ruhlmann*

Ken Saydak

b. Chicago, IL

Piano, Organ / Modern Electric Chicago Blues, Piano Blues
A veteran sideman with Lonnie Brooks, Mighty Joe Young, Johnny Winter, and Dave Specter, pianist and singer/songwriter Ken Saydak stepped out for the first time with the 1999 album *Foolish Man* on Delmark. —*John Bush*

● **Foolish Man** / Mar. 9, 1999 / Delmark ✦✦✦
Ken Saydak's solo debut is an accomplished set of deep bluesy songs, and sees him flavoring his Chicago blues piano with hints of Cajun gumbo, honky tonk and swing. —*John Bush*

Love Without Trust / 2001 / Delmark ✦✦✦
Where the guitarless *Foolish Man* made Saydak's Otis Spann-influenced piano the axis around which everything else revolved, *Love Without Trust* places the veteran sideman

in the center of a full band. The more fleshed-out treatment gives him the flexibility to try new things—witness the grace with which he appropriates Bob Dylan's hard-driving blues shuffle "Watching the River Flow"—but it also seems to have instilled in him a tendency toward overly obvious arrangements. Interesting ideas are confounded by generic execution, resulting in songs that work better on paper than on disc. The title cut, for example, sets up an intriguing scenario of the sort not often explored in popular song, but ends up squandering it with female duet vocals that very predictably trade off with Saydak's own. To be fair, not every track is overpowered by that kind of calculated slickness; the jazzy, philosophical "Expressions of Tenderness" shows that Saydak is still one of the keenest observers of human nature in contemporary blues. And on its best cuts, like the witty original "Don't Blame the Messenger" and the incisive cover of Don Nix's "Everybody Wants to Go to Heaven," the album chugs along with confidence and uncommon conviction. In the end, *Love Without Trust* comes off as a solid but unadventurous sophomore effort for the gruff-voiced Saydak. *—Kenneth Bays*

Charlie Sayles

b. Jan. 4, 1948, Woburn, MA

Harmonica / Modern Electric Blues

Harmonica player Charlie Sayles is starting to carve out a hard-fought niche for himself in U.S. blues circles, thanks to some help from the London-based JSP Records. Although life hasn't been easy for Sayles, he seems to have come through the traumas OK. They started in his childhood, when he was shifted from his broken home to a long procession of foster homes. He ended up joining the Army in the late '60s and was promptly shipped to South Vietnam. His tour of duty ended in 1971, and he came back to Massachusetts for a time. Sayles picked up the blues harp while he was in Vietnam and made a slow adjustment back to civilized society upon his return from three years in the infantry. He discovered the music of Sonny Boy Williamson after he returned home and learned all he could from those recordings. Sayles began to make trips to New York City, Atlanta, St. Louis, and other cities, playing on the streets for tips from passersby in 1974 and for several years thereafter. He worked when he needed money as a day laborer. He hasn't had a real day job since then, patiently plying his craft in clubs, on street corners and more recently, at blues festivals.

What shows in Sayles' playing are the long periods of time he spent honing his craft on the streets and in subway stations. His approach as a solo artist was to get as full and bandlike a sound as he could with his harp. It appears to have paid off, because Sayles is unlike other harp players; his playing is full of extended phrasing and super-quick changes in register. Sayles uses the harmonica as a melodic device while coaxing sharp, almost percussive sounds from it. Sayles began to develop his songwriting voice in the mid-'70s as well.

Perhaps his first big break was being "discovered" by Ralph Rinzler, an organizer for the Smithsonian Festival of American Folklife. Rinzler paired Sayles up with Pete Seeger, and after a variety of festival appearances, Sayles ended up moving to Washington, D.C. By the early '80s, while living in Washington, Sayles had begun to form his first bands.

Sayles' first record, *Raw Harmonica Blues*, was issued in 1976, long before blues became fashionable, on the Dusty Road label. Sayles didn't record again for 15 years, when he got picked up by JSP Records. *I Got Something to Say* has some prominent guests on it, including Washington's most celebrated blues guitar player, Bobby Parker. Also performing on the record is guitarist Deborah Coleman. Sayles' JSP recordings are well worth seeking out, even at import prices, because of his original take on blues music. Sayles would be the first to tell you that he's not a straight-ahead Chicago blues player. He takes a much more mongrelized approach to the music, mixing in elements of New Orleans funk, Chicago blues, and rock & roll in his playing. *—Richard Skelly*

● **Night Ain't Right** / 1990 / JSP ✦✦✦✦

Charlie Sayles' *Night Ain't Right* is an impressive comeback, finding the harpist in prime form. The key to the record's success is the way Sayles twists conventions around, finding tastes of flourishes funk and jazz within the genre's boundaries. His willingness to play with the music is the reason why *Night Ain't Right* is a modern-day Chicago blues record worth exploring. *—Thom Owens*

I Got Something to Say / Oct. 3, 1995 / JSP ✦✦✦

On his second JSP release, Sayles artfully blends funky, gritty urban blues sounds with original, down-to-earth lyrics, successfully avoiding a lot of blues clichés. *—Richard Skelly*

Hip Guy / Mar. 21, 2000 / JSP ✦✦✦

Boz Scaggs (William Royce Scaggs)

b. Jun. 8, 1944, Canton, OH

Slide Guitar, Vocals, Guitar / Album Rock, Pop/Rock, Soft Rock, Blues-Rock

After first finding acclaim as a member of the Steve Miller Band, singer/songwriter Boz Scaggs went on to enjoy considerable solo success in the '70s. Born William Royce Scaggs in Ohio on June 8, 1944, he was raised in Oklahoma and Texas, and while attending prep school in Dallas met guitarist Steve Miller. After joining Miller's group the Marksmen as a vocalist in 1959, the pair later attended the University of Wisconsin together, playing in blues bands like the Ardells and the Fabulous Knight Trains.

In 1963 Scaggs returned to Dallas alone, fronting an R&B unit dubbed the Wigs; after relocating to England, the group promptly disbanded, and two of its members—John Andrews and Bob Arthur—soon formed Mother Earth. Scaggs remained in Europe, singing on street corners; in Sweden he recorded a failed solo LP, 1965's *Boz*, before returning to the U.S. two years later. Upon settling in San Francisco, he reunited with Miller, joining the fledgling Steve Miller Band; after recording two acclaimed albums with the group, *Children of the Future* and *Sailor*, Scaggs exited in 1968 to mount a solo career.

With the aid of *Rolling Stone* magazine publisher Jann Wenner, Scaggs secured a contract with Atlantic. Sporting a cameo from Duane Allman, 1968's soulful *Boz Scaggs* failed to find an audience despite winning critical favor; the track "Loan Me a Dime" later became the subject of a court battle when bluesman Fenton Robinson sued (successfully) for composer credit. After signing to Columbia, Scaggs teamed with producer Glyn Johns to record 1971's *Moments*, a skillful blend of rock and R&B which, like its predecessor, failed to make much of an impression on the charts.

Scaggs remained a critics' darling over the course of LPs like 1972's *My Time* and 1974's *Slow Dancer*, but he did not achieve a commercial breakthrough until 1976's *Silk Degrees*, which reached number two on the album charts while spawning the Top Three single "Lowdown," as well as the smash "Lido Shuffle." Released in 1977, *Down Two Then Left* was also a success, and 1980's *Middle Man* reached the Top Ten on the strength of the singles "Breakdown Dead Ahead" and "Jo Jo."

However, Scaggs spent much of the '80s in retirement, owning and operating the San Francisco nightclub Slim's and limiting his performances primarily to the club's annual black-tie New Year's Eve concerts. Finally, in 1988 he resurfaced with the album *Other Roads*, followed three years later by a tour with Donald Fagen's Rock and Soul Revue. The solo *Some Change* appeared in 1994, with *Come on Home* released in 1997. *—Jason Ankeny*

● **Boz Scaggs** / 1969 / Atlantic ✦✦✦✦✦

Produced by Jann Wenner and featuring crack accompaniment by the Muscle Shoals house band, Scaggs' solo debut is a near-masterwork, mingling the pathos and heartbreak of vintage honky tonk with the celebration and release of Southern soul. The highlights of the album also flaunt its diversity: "Loan Me a Dime," an extended blues dirge, which features some of Duane Allman's finest work, and "Waiting for a Train," Scaggs' marvelous revamping of Jimmie Rodgers' classic hobo song. *—John Floyd*

Moments / 1971 / Columbia ✦✦✦

"We Were Always Sweethearts" wasn't a huge hit single, but it was a good one, signaling that Boz Scaggs was a soul man of the first degree. *Moments* places him into a variety of settings, including soul, R&B, blues, country, and beautiful, string-drenched balladry. Side one of the LP is especially strong, the kind whose grooves were worn out by its listeners in the early '70s. The second half of the recording doesn't hold up as well, but the closer, "Can I Make It Last (Or Will It Just Be Over)," is a gorgeous, atmospheric instrumental that pulls at the heartstrings. Although Scaggs' big moment in the commercial spotlight was still a few years away, this recording provides many satisfying musical *Moments*. *—Jim Newsom*

Boz Scaggs & Band / Dec. 1971 / Columbia ✦✦✦✦

Although most listeners know Boz Scaggs primarily for his 1976 disco-era, multi-million seller *Silk Degrees*, he produced several excellent recordings in the years leading up to that breakthrough. *Boz Scaggs & Band* is the middle release of a three-disc spurt which Scaggs produced in a two-year period, between 1971 and 1972. Although it is weaker than *Moments* and *My Time* which bookend it, this album still has much to offer. Sounding at times like the original Average White Band, and at other times like a bunch of Nashville cats, Boz and his eight-piece group traverse a wide terrain with great facility and much soul. "Here to Stay" is particularly appealing, hinting at things to come, and "Flames of Love" is an extended piece of smoking funk. "Monkey Time" and "Why Why" also turn up the funk. This album is well worth checking out. *—Jim Newsom*

My Time / 1972 / Columbia ✦✦✦✦

Music critics of the early '70s kept predicting big things for Boz Scaggs, but his records of that period had trouble finding more than a cult audience. *My Time* continued with a mix similar to *Moments* from the previous year, with the opening "Dinah Flo," a great soul-drenched rocker that should have been a hit. In fact, the first three tracks present a powerful opening triumvirate which begs to be heard, with "Full-Lock Power Slide," an air guitarist's dream-come-true. Other high points are Scaggs' definitive cover of Allen Toussaint's "Freedom for the Stallion" and a take on Al Green's "Old Time Lovin'" that gives the original author a run for his money. Considering the success Van Morrison was having working the same territory, it's surprising that this album didn't achieve more in the commercial arena. Its blend of solid '60s soul and bluesy rock is very appealing. However, Boz Scaggs' time was still four years away. *My Time* is a rewarding listen nonetheless. *—Jim Newsom*

My Time: The Anthology (1969–1997) / Oct. 7, 1997 / Columbia/Legacy ✦✦✦✦

My Time: Anthology (1969-1997) is an excellent double-disc retrospective of Boz Scaggs' entire career, containing all of his hits, several key album tracks, and a handful of rarities designed to entice the hardcore collector. For any serious fan who wants a comprehensive overview of Scaggs' career, *My Time* is an ideal purchase. *—Thom Owens*

Buddy Scott (Kenneth Scott)

b. Jan. 9, 1935, Jackson, MS, **d.** Feb. 5, 1994, Chicago, IL

Vocals, Guitar / Electric Chicago Blues

Chicago guitarist Kenneth "Buddy" Scott hailed from an extended musical brood, to put it mildly. His brothers, singer Howard and guitarist Walter, are mainstays on the local scene; his son, guitarist Thomas "Hollywood" Scott, leads Tyrone Davis' Platinum Band, and even his grandmother Ida knew her way around a guitar—she played on the South side with the likes of Little Walter and Sonny Boy Williamson back in the '50s.

Buddy Scott left Mississippi for Chicago at age seven. Both his mom and local legend Reggie Boyd tutored him as a guitarist. Like several of his brothers, Buddy was a member of a local doo wop vocal group, the Masqueraders, during the early '60s, and recorded a few singles with his siblings as the Scott Brothers later in the decade. He was best known as leader of Scotty & the Rib Tips, who were staples of the South and West Side blues circuit; they were featured on Alligator's second batch of *Living Chicago Blues* anthologies in 1980.

By the time Scott caught his big major-label break with Verve in 1993 with his debut domestic album, *Bad Avenue*, it was too late for him to capitalize on his belated good fortune. The stomach cancer that had been gaining on him did him in shortly after its release. *—Bill Dahl*

● **Bad Avenue** / Oct. 19, 1993 / Verve ✦✦✦✦✦
Not the perfect vehicle for the late Chicago blues guitarist—it's a tad too slick, and some of the song choices fall into the realm of overworked cliche—but Scott's major-label debut album was a credible swan song, his enthusiastic vocals and clean guitar work ringing through well. —*Bill Dahl*

E.C. Scott

b. Oakland, CA
Vocals / Contemporary Blues, Vocal Pop, Soul-Blues
Modern blues singer E.C. Scott brings a funky '90s sensibility to her classic soul and gospel influences. Raised in Oakland, CA, Scott grew up listening to gospel singers like Shirley Caesar and Inez Andrews; as she grew older, she began to ignore her mother's restrictions on secular music and sampled the sounds of the rich soul music on her sisters' radio.

Scott was singing in nightclubs by the time she was 16, but her marriage soon put her career on hiatus. When her two children were old enough, Scott decided to resume her singing career with her family's blessing; she initially worked as a jazz stylist, but soon returned to the blues and R&B she knew well. Scott put together a backing band called Smoke and played the San Francisco club scene, becoming the house band at Slim's for a year and self-releasing the single "Just Dance" b/w "Let's Make It Real" in 1991. Scott built up her local fan base and performed at several blues festivals around the U.S. before signing to Blind Pig in 1994. Her debut album, *Come Get Your Love*, was released the following year; it was followed in 1998 by *Hard Act to Follow*. Two years later, Scott resurfaced with *Masterpiece*. —*Steve Huey*

Come Get Your Love / 1995 / Blind Pig ✦✦✦

● **Hard Act to Follow** / Jan. 2, 1998 / Blind Pig ✦✦✦✦
Soul singer extraordinaire E.C. Scott comes back from her 1995 debut with perhaps even a stronger album the second time at bat. Ten of the 11 tunes on here emanate from her prolific pen (the only cover is her interpretation of the Eurythmics' "Missionary Man"), and her earthy, engaging style is heard to great effect on the opener, "Steppin' Out on a Saturday Night," the bouncy shuffle "Don't Touch Me," the slow blues "Lyin' and Cheatin'," and the title track. Her time is impeccable, her phrasing straight and true, and every vocal on here is chock full of deep feeling; as a modern-day example of a soul-blues album, this one's about as good as the form gets. —*Cub Koda*

Masterpiece / May 2, 2000 / Blind Pig ✦✦✦
E.C. Scott has a voice that is perfect for the '60s soul/R&B-type songs that she performs. She has plenty of power, is in tune, is quite expressive, and shows an impressive amount of versatility. On the modestly titled *Masterpiece*, which is a bluish R&B set, the singer wrote or co-wrote all but one of the dozen songs. Scott stars throughout the program (including sometimes overdubbing her voice as a "choir"), is assisted by a fine cast of musicians, and on "Too Good to Keep to Myself" shows that she can excel as a pure blues singer too. Superior party music. —*Scott Yanow*

Irene Scruggs

b. Dec. 7, 1901, Mississippi
Vocals / Piedmont Blues, Prewar Country Blues
Blues singer Irene Scruggs was born somewhere in rural Mississippi, but blues anthropologists believe that she came up the river early on her life and was reportedly raised in St. Louis. That bustling town claims her as one of her own, and her career was certainly marked by the type of versatility and generous creativity that St. Louis is known for. Like Chuck Berry would decades later, Scruggs was part of a process wherein traditional rural musical roots blended into newly evolving urban styles. Like two cooks working out of the same spice cabinet, both artists wound up stirring country blues and swing jazz together. The great jazz pianist Mary Lou Williams recalls that Scruggs was already an established force on the St. Louis blues scene the first time Williams went there as a young member of a vaudeville revue. Furthermore, that revue felt it had to hire Scruggs, whose success in vaudeville apparently overshadowed her recording and nightclub career at times. "In St. Louis, our show picked up a young blues singer named Irene Scruggs," Williams said in an interview. "Irene had not long settled in St. Louis, and was starting out to become one of St. Louis' finest singers."

This apparently gave Scruggs the cache to get the treasured opportunity to collaborate with several of the bands King Oliver brought to St. Louis in the mid-'20s. Fans of classic jazz should enjoy all the nice playing of her voice off against superb instrumental talent such as clarinetist Albert Nicholas, trombonist Kid Ory, and of course Oliver himself on cornet. She was also well-suited for recording with the fascinating Blind Blake, whose impressive efforts as an accompanist to various singers are collected on the Wolf set *The Accompanist: 1926-1931*. Women who don't approve of their boyfriends playing the blues will develop a fondness for Scruggs' song "Itching Heel," that much is certain. In live shows, it was the setting for lively theatrical business between the singer and Blake, the blind guitarist responding to criticisms of his personality with wild blues licks. "He don't do nothing but play on his old guitar," Scruggs sings, "While I'm busting suds out in the white folks' yard."

Scruggs' earliest recordings were with pianist and bandleader Clarence Williams for OKeh in 1924. She began working with Oliver two years later, and cut a series of sides with the fine bluesman Lonnie Johnson in 1927, again for OKeh. She continued using St. Louis as her base when she formed her own band in the late '20s, gigging regularly at blues and jazz clubs. She recorded with Blake under the name of Chocolate Brown, and also used the alternative blues name of Dixie Nolan for several contract-breaking ventures. In the early '30s, she toured and recorded with Little Brother Montgomery, often stealing the shows with her guest spots.

Raunchy, sexy blues became one of her specialties, and this was not a subject she needed time getting used to, since it was one of the major concerns of every female blues recording artist from the prewar era. "Good Grindin'" and "Must Get Mine in Front" were just two example of the explicit sexual enthusiasm contained in her recordings, and it was no surprise that her material was included in *The Nasty Blues*, a collection of bawdy blues material and biographies published by Hal Leonard. By the '40s, Scruggs had joined the population of expatriate black performers living abroad, residing first in Paris with her daughter, the dancer Baby Leazar Scruggs. Later she moved to Germany, where she is thought to have died. In the '50s, she did several radio broadcasts for the British BBC. —*Eugene Chadbourne*

Son Seals (Frank Seals)

b. Aug. 13, 1942, Osceola, AR
Vocals, Drums, Guitar / Modern Electric Chicago Blues, Modern Electric Blues
It all started with a phone call from Wesley Race, who was at the Flamingo Club on Chicago's South Side, to Alligator Records owner Bruce Iglauer. Race was raving about a new find, a young guitarist named Son Seals. He held the phone in the direction of the bandstand, so Iglauer could get an on-site report. It didn't take long for Iglauer to scramble into action. Alligator issued Seals' 1973 eponymous debut album, which was followed by six more. When Alligator signed him up, his days fronting a band at the Flamingo Club and the Expressway Lounge were numbered. Seals' jagged, uncompromising guitar riffs and gruff vocals were showcased very effectively on that 1973 debut set, which contained his "Your Love Is Like a Cancer" and a raging instrumental called "Hot Sauce." *Midnight Son*, his 1976 encore, was by comparison a much slicker affair, with tight horns, funkier grooves, and a set list that included "Telephone Angel" and "On My Knees." Released in 1994, *Nothing but the Truth* sported some of the worst cover art in CD history but a stinging lineup of songs inside. —*Bill Dahl*

The Son Seals Blues Band / 1973 / Alligator ✦✦✦✦
The Chicago mainstay's debut album was a rough, gruff, no-nonsense affair typified by the decidedly unsentimental track "Your Love Is like a Cancer." Seals wasn't all that far removed from his southern roots at this point, and his slashing guitar work sports a strikingly raw feel on his originals "Look Now, Baby," "Cotton Picking Blues," and "Hot Sauce" (the latter a blistering instrumental that sounds a bit like the theme from *Batman* played sideways). —*Bill Dahl*

● **Midnight Son** / 1976 / Alligator ✦✦✦✦✦
A much more polished set than its predecessor, *Midnight Son* is a particularly effective effort with several numbers that remain in Seals' on-stage repertoire to this day—"Telephone Angel," "On My Knees," the jumping "Four Full Seasons of Love." The addition of a brisk horn section enhanced his staccato guitar attack and uncompromising vocals, rendering this his best set to date. —*Bill Dahl*

Live & Burning / 1978 / Alligator ✦✦✦✦
Lives up to its billing. Seals' smoking set, caught live at Chicago's long-gone (and definitely lamented) Wise Fools Pub, finds him attacking a sharp cross-section of material—Detroit Junior's deliberate "Call My Job," Elmore James' "I Can't Hold Out," his own "Help Me, Somebody"—with an outstanding band in tow—saxist A.C. Reed, guitarist Lacy Gibson, pianist Alberto Gianquinto, bassist Snapper Mitchum, and drummer Tony Gooden. —*Bill Dahl*

Chicago Fire / 1980 / Alligator ✦✦✦
Son Seals in an experimental mood, utilizing chord progressions that occasionally don't quite fit together seamlessly (but give him an A for trying to expand the idiom's boundaries). Less innovative but perhaps more accessible are his smoking covers of Albert King's "Nobody Wants a Loser" and Junior Parker's "Goodbye Little Girl." —*Bill Dahl*

Bad Axe / 1984 / Alligator ✦✦✦✦
One of Son Seals' finest collections, studded with vicious performances ranging from covers of Eddie Vinson's "Person to Person" and Little Sonny's "Going Home (Where Women Got Meat on Their Bones)" to his own "Can't Stand to See Her Cry" and swaggering "Cold Blood." Top-drawer Windy City studio musicians lay down skin-tight grooves throughout. —*Bill Dahl*

Living in the Danger Zone / 1991 / Alligator ✦✦✦
The guitarist keeps his string of consecutive fine releases alive with a studio-cut disc that sizzles with bandstand-level velocity (until its last cut, anyway). "Frigidaire Woman," "Woman in Black," and "Bad Axe" rate with the highlights; the self-pitying ballad closer "My Life" is the worst thing Seals has ever put on tape for Alligator. —*Bill Dahl*

Nothing But the Truth / 1994 / Alligator ✦✦✦✦
The grotesque cover illustration is an abomination, but the contents are right in the growling grizzly bear style that we've come to expect. Only four Seals-penned originals, but the R&B-laced "Life Is Hard" and "I'm Gonna Take It All Back" are quality efforts. So is his heartfelt tribute to Hound Dog Taylor, "Sadie." —*Bill Dahl*

Spontaneous Combustion / 1996 / Alligator ✦✦✦
Son Seals is a very powerful performer. While his vocals are full of passion, it is Seals' explosive guitar solos (egged on by two fine horn players who have some solo spots and a driving rhythm section) that are most notable. Recorded live at Buddy Guy's Legends in Chicago, Seals' interpretations of these spirited blues would certainly please the club owner. This enthusiastic set serves as a perfect introduction to the accessible and memorable blues of Son Seals. —*Scott Yanow*

Lettin' Go / Apr. 25, 2000 / Telarc ✦✦✦✦
After spending his entire recording career with Alligator, Son Seals' debut release on the Telarc Blues label is also the Chicago bluesman's first album of new material in almost six years. Although he lost part of his leg to diabetes in 1999, as somberly evidenced on the cover photo, little else has changed. Seals' gritty, booming vocals sound as authoritative as ever, and, if anything, the half decade between studio albums has added an even tougher quality to his traditionally gutsy singing. Working with the legendary Al Kooper on Hammond B-3 and top-notch musicians from Conan O'Brien's *Late Night* band gives Seals a firm, razor sharp backing on which to lay down his tough Chicago blues. The

four-piece horn section and Kooper work wonderfully together. Along with Seals' beefy vocal attack and his fat, stinging guitar tone, he turns in a solid, uncompromising set of primarily original tunes. The 70-minute album would be stronger if some of the weaker tracks like "Osceola Rock," little more than a bland rewrite of "Jailhouse Rock," were omitted. But the album-closing jam with Phish's Trey Anastasio on a remake of Seals' "Funky Bitch" is energized and electric, and with excursions into gospel, light funk, gritty country, Southern R&B, and even a sensitive ballad, the guitarist expands his palette while staying within the blues framework. All of which makes *Lettin' Go* a sturdy, hard-hitting, and above all welcome comeback album from one of the acknowledged greats of Chicago blues guitar. *—Hal Horowitz*

Deluxe Edition / Jan. 22, 2002 / Alligator ♦♦♦
Deluxe Edition collects 15 highlights from Son Seals' long association with Alligator Records that began in 1973. Seals' combination of gritty Chicago blues with horn-laden soul is well represented on classic tracks like "Your Love Is Like a Cancer," "Bad Axe," and "Landlord at My Door." While this is an excellent place for the Seals novice to begin, his live albums *Live & Burning* and *Spontaneous Combustion* are hard to beat. *—Al Campbell*

Marvin Sease

b. Feb. 16, 1946, South Carolina
Vocals / Retro-Soul, Modern Electric Blues
Despite a lack of attention from most print sources and other common avenues of publicity in the blues world, Marvin Sease has turned his smooth, X-rated ladies' man persona into a cottage industry complete with merchandising in the Deep South. Sease straddles the line between blues and gospel-drenched soul, much like fellow Southern singers Johnnie Taylor and Tyrone Davis, but his often racy lyrics and concert performances, coupled with the advantages of major-label distribution, have ensured Sease a strong following, particularly among female fans enamored of his signature song and breakthrough jukebox hit, the provocative, innuendo-laced "Candy Licker."

Born in Blackville, SC, Sease got his start by joining a gospel group in nearby Charleston called the Five Gospel Singers, and moved to New York at age 20, where he joined another gospel group called the Gospel Crowns. Preferring R&B, though, Sease put together a backing band (called Sease) featuring his three brothers. When this venture failed, Sease began singing to pre-recorded backing tracks at local dances and clubs, self-released several 45s, and eventually scored a regular gig at a Brooklyn nightspot called the Casablanca.

Gunning for greater success, Sease recorded a self-titled LP in 1986 featuring one of his most popular songs, "Ghetto Man," and began working the South's so-called chitlin' circuit of ghetto bars, rural juke joints, and blues festivals. While shopping the LP, released on his own Early label, to record stores, Sease stumbled upon a contact who eventually got him a deal with Polygram, which re-released the LP on London/Mercury in 1987 with the addition of the newly recorded, ten-minute track "Candy Licker." "Candy Licker" became an underground success on jukeboxes across the South; it was too explicit for radio airplay, but audiences—especially female ones—flocked to see Sease in concert.

Over the next ten years, Sease recorded a string of albums for London/Mercury (*Breakfast*, 1987; *The Real Deal*, 1989; *Show Me What You Got*, 1991) and the New York-based Jive (*The Housekeeper*, 1993; *Do You Need a Licker?*, 1994; *Please Take Me*, 1996) that sold consistently well, although none have yet matched the performance of *Marvin Sease*, which hit number 14 on *Billboard*'s R&B chart and number 114 on the pop chart. *The Bitch Git It All* (1997) and *Hoochie Momma* (1999) were issued before the '90s came to a close; *A Woman Would Rather Be Licked* was issued in early 2001. *—Steve Huey*

Marvin Sease / 1986 / London ♦♦♦♦
Marvin Sease hadn't quite perfected his vulgar soul on his eponymous debut album, but he certainly hinted at his new direction with the epic "Candy Licker." That final number pointed the way to the sex-drenched future, but the remainder of the album was relatively tame, as Sease just concentrated on sweaty Southern soul. He may not have found his gimmick, but he was nevertheless a good singer, and since it shies away from carnality, the album may actually be preferable to his later work for more conservative soul fans. *—Thom Owens*

Breakfast / Dec. 1987 / London ♦♦♦
For anyone who loves soul, listening to a Marvin Sease record is likely to be a frustrating experience. There's little questioning that he has a rich, soulful voice and can replicate the sweat-soaked, gritty sound of Stax soul or the bedroom crooning of Al Green at the drop of a hat. It's his subject matter, however, that may make blues and soul fans balk: Sease likes it dirty. Scratch that—he likes it *vulgar*, if "Condom on Your Tongue" and "I Ate You for My Breakfast" are any indication. That can be a problem for anyone with queasy stomachs, since Sease likes to belt out his dirty words, unless it's on the slow songs, where he murmurs his sweet, filthy nothings, presumably to get you in the mood. Musically, there's no way to fault *Breakfast*—it's first-rate retro-soul—but if you don't like nasty pillow talk, chances are the music isn't going to make this *Breakfast* digestible. *—Stephen Thomas Erlewine*

Tell Me Why / Jul. 31, 1989 / London ♦♦

The Real Deal / Sep. 15, 1989 / London ♦♦♦

Show Me What You Got / Oct. 8, 1991 / Mercury ♦♦
Marvin Sease generated a lot of noise on the Southern soul circuit in the late '80s with his albums, which combined a lowdown blues sensibility with some very adult (at times vulgar) sexual commentary. But things had pretty much run their creative course by the time this early-'90s LP was issued. Even fans on the dirt-floor circuit had heard Sease do this kind of material one time too many; he hadn't evolved, nor had the ballads and slower blues/soul cuts gotten any better. *—Ron Wynn*

The Housekeeper / Apr. 27, 1993 / Jive ♦♦♦

Do You Need a Licker / Oct. 25, 1994 / Jive ♦♦

Please Take Me / Apr. 16, 1996 / Jive ♦♦♦

● **The Best of Marvin Sease** / May 20, 1997 / Polygram ♦♦♦♦
The Best of Marvin Sease is the first comprehensive collection of Sease's best bawdy, funky '70s soul, culled from his four albums for Polygram. Among the 15 tracks are the notorious "Candy Licker" and a single that had never been available on an album prior to this collection. *—Stephen Thomas Erlewine*

The Bitch Git It All / Oct. 28, 1997 / Silvertone ♦♦♦♦
Another year, another Marvin Sease record. Throughout the years, Sease has stayed the same, turning out Southern soul in the classic sense, but spiking it with vulgar, raunchy lyrics. Despite its title, *The Bitch Git It All* isn't among his rudest work—there's still a bit of profanity, to be sure, but not on the level of his early albums, and that makes the record a bit more palatable for the timid. He still has a problem coming up with consistently compelling material, but *The Bitch Git It All* remains one of his stronger records. *—Thom Owens*

Hoochie Momma / Apr. 13, 1999 / Jive ♦♦♦

A Woman Would Rather Be Licked / Feb. 6, 2001 / Jive ♦♦♦♦
If you've heard one of his albums, you know Marvin Sease's schtick. He's not just a ribald loverman, he's really raunchy, delving into double and single entendres for his slow Southern soul grinds. You either dig it or you don't, but if you don't dig it, his 2001 album, *A Woman Would Rather Be Licked*, could change your mind. Yes, all the typical Sease schtick is in place, but his material and performances are more convincing than usual, and the vulgarity level is toned down slightly (however, the Parental Advisory sticker on the cover is still earned—although it's hard to imagine what kid would pick up this album). So, even if this doesn't deliver full-on, hardcore Sease, this is one of his most satisfying records, at least on a musical level. *—Stephen Thomas Erlewine*

Brother John Sellers

b. May 27, 1924, Clarksdale, MS, **d.** Mar. 27, 1999, New York, NY
Vocals, Guitar / Folk Revival, Folk-Blues
Singer/songwriter Brother John Sellers was known for his folksy mix of blues, jazz, and gospel. Born May 27, 1924, in Clarksdale, MS, Sellers performed in gospel tent shows. He grew up watching performances by such blues luminaries as Robert Johnson and Blind Lemon Jefferson. Sellers was discovered by gospel great Mahalia Jackson, and MS-born Johnson returned with the singer to Chicago. He performed with her as well as blues singer Big Bill Broonzy, with whom he did some recording in Europe. He recorded many gospel sides before turning to secular music. In 1954, Sellers recorded the LP, *Sings Blues and Folk Songs* for Vanguard Records. Another one of his albums was *Let Praise Arise* on Bird-wing, and Sellers appeared on Ella Jenkins' *A Long Time to Freedom.* After he returned from the European tour, Sellers became a part of the folk scene in New York's Greenwich Village. While there, he met choreographer Alvin Ailey and began a long collaboration with him, which included such dance pieces as "Revelations" and "Blues Suite." Sellers performed in the Broadway production of Langston Hughes' *Tambourines to Glory.* He also performed at lectures by Chicago writer Studs Terkel during the late '50s and early '60s. At the age of 74, Brother John Sellers died in Manhattan on March 27, 1999. *—Ed Hogan*

● **Sings Blues and Folk Songs** / 1954 / Vanguard ♦♦♦♦
A bit tame even by the standards of the folk revival, this showcased Sellers as a smooth and accomplished presenter of folk, blues, and a bit of jazz. The singer mixed original compositions with standards like "John Henry," "Down By the Riverside," and "Nobody Knows the Trouble I Have Seen" on a set that seemed conscientiously programmed to demonstrate his versatility. The blues and folk numbers were graced by harmonica from Sonny Terry; the less successful jazzy efforts had accompaniment from a combo featuring the original Count Basie rhythm section. *—Richie Unterberger*

Brother John Sellers / Sep. 8, 1954 / Vanguard ♦♦♦

The Sensational Nightingales

f. 1942
Group / Traditional Gospel, Southern Gospel, Black Gospel
The Sensational Nightingales were assembled in the '40s. In 1957 they appeared on the Gospel Train tour with The Clara Ward Singers and five other big-name gospel acts. Members included Julius Cheeks (lead), Carl Coates (bass), Joseph "Jo Jo" Wallace (tenor), Howard Carroll (baritone), and Paul Gwens (tenor). Their noted hit was "See How They Done My Lord." One of the earliest gospel quintets, they recorded and toured throughout the '90s. Many of their '50s and '60s sides (found on MCA reissues) feature the stunning vocals of Rev. Julius Cheeks. As with Archie Brownlee, Cheeks reaches an intensity that distorts the actual recordings, and his style has been heavily "borrowed" by Bobby "Blue" Bland, Wilson Pickett, and others. The later recordings by Charles Johnson are smoother and slicker, but still top-notch. *—Bil Carpenter & Billy C. Wirtz*

Songs of Praise / 1959 / Peacock ♦♦♦♦
The hardest-singing lead in gospel. Beautiful harmonies. *—Opal Louis Nations*

Glory, Glory / 1963 / Peacock ♦♦♦♦
More fine singing with soul and conviction at the helm. *—Opal Louis Nations*

It's Gonna Rain Again / 1975 / MCA Special Products ♦♦♦
Reissue of one of the quartet's best '70s Peacock albums. Featuring Charles Johnson. *—Opal Louis Nations*

Jesus Is Coming / 1976 / MCA ♦♦♦
Beautiful songs done up in country-hymn fashion by lead soloist Charles Johnson. ABC Paramount material. *—Opal Louis Nations*

● **The Best of the Sensational Nightingales** / 1978 / MCA ♦♦♦♦♦
Some of Rev. Julius Cheeks and the group's finest efforts on Peacock from the '50s. *—Opal Louis Nations*

Victory Is Mine / 1980 / Malaco ♦♦♦

• **Heart & Soul/You Know Not the Hour** / 1986 / Mobile Fidelity ✦✦✦✦✦
The CD remastering of these two early-'70s albums by this fine harmony quintet is well worth owning. *Heart & Soul* is taken from the better pre-Paramount days (1970-1971), and *You Know Not the Hour* presents the group in a later, more hymnal song setting, both with Charles Johnson on lead. *—Kip Lornell*

God Is Not Pleased / Mar. 24, 1998 / Malaco ✦✦✦✦
God Is Not Pleased is a fine latter-day effort from the Sensational Nightingales, who by this point feature a lineup of Jo Jo Wallace, Horace Thompson, and Richard Luster; this triumvirate also handled production duties. *—Steve Huey*

Wasted Years / Apr. 24, 2001 / Malaco ✦✦✦
Wasted Years is a great collection highlighting this legendary group's current sound. Longtime members Jo Jo Wallace and Horace Thompson carry on the tradition of quartet excellency. With remakes of some of the group's '70s hits, listeners are treated to a smooth listening experience with sparse instrumentation. While the majority of the selections are new compositions, the older selections garner the greatest attention. From the bass-driven "You Got to Do Something" to the classic "Christians, We Are the Ones," this project is a Bible-based tale through song. The instrumentation is minimized and vocal proficiency is given the utmost attention. *—Minister Donnie Addison*

Seven Foot Dilly & His Hot Pickles

Group / String Bands
The names of old-time string bands that recorded in the '20s and '30s tend to be pretty ridiculous, some of them made up by corny disc jockeys or promoters. This group may have the worst name of the bunch, based on both the surname and height of bandleader guitarist John Dilleshaw, a historical old-time guitar picker whose height was close enough to seven feet to suit the purposes of old-time band naming. The Pickles included hired guns from amongst the area's best fiddlers, including the one-handed Lowe Stokes, as well as novices such as Harry Kiker, who became interested in old-time music when Dilleshaw started courting his sister, Opal, as the shy guitarist would often bring his entire band along to assist with the romantic atmosphere. The leader was known for his driving, bluesy guitar playing, which along with the sound of the bowed bass and tenor banjo, played by the father and son team of Pink Lindsey, gave this group an absolutely distinctive sound. As is typical of the genre, a great deal of humor was interspersed with the music, and in the manner of Western swing bandleader Bob Wills, Dilleshaw (or Dilly) would sometimes talk right over the soloing or ensemble playing of the other musicians. Skits involving various members of the group were no doubt done in imitation of the widely popular Gid Tanner & the Skillet Lickers, which had also employed Stokes.

The group recorded in 1929 and 1930, and the tracks have all been reissued on a Document CD. The tracks include "Bad Lee Brown," perhaps an ancestor of Jim Croce's "Bad, Bad Leroy Brown," the rollicking "Bibb County Breakdown," the two-part "Fiddler's Tryout in Georgia" (a combination of music and theater), and the classic "Pickin' Off Peanuts."

A few sidemen from the group carried on with musical activity. Lindsey did a few sessions for Bluebird that featured Shorty, and possibly Dilleshaw as well, although nobody present can agree on this. Shorty also played tenor banjo on some recordings by fiddler John Carson. Kiker was the only player from this ensemble who survived into the year 2000, and at that time was still playing, mostly in his own kitchen, with an ex-violinist from the Atlanta Symphony. *—Eugene Chadbourne*

Charlie Sexton

b. Aug. 10, 1968, Austin, TX
Vocals, Guitar / New Wave, Singer/Songwriter, Blues-Rock
Despite his relative youthfulness, guitarist, singer, and songwriter Charlie Sexton has already had several phases to his career. Sexton, raised in Austin, TX, made his debut with *Pictures for Pleasure* in 1985 at age 16. He followed that up with a self-titled second album when he was 20. Because word of his reputation as a prodigy guitar player spread far and wide, he found himself an in-demand session player while still in his late teens, and he had the opportunity to record with Ron Wood, Keith Richards, and Bob Dylan.

His mother was just 16 when she gave birth to Charlie, and he and his mother moved to Austin when he was just four. His mother would get him out to clubs like the Armadillo World Headquarters and the Soap Creek Saloon. Places like the Split Rail and Antone's blues club became his classrooms. After living outside of Austin for a while with his mother, he moved back to Austin when he was 12, and the musicians around Austin, his heroes, people like Jimmie Vaughan and the late Stevie Ray Vaughan, Joe Ely and others, took him in and put him up until he could earn more of a living on his own.

From 1992 to 1994, he was a member of Austin's Arc Angels, along with Doyle Bramhall II, Tommy Shannon, and Chris "Whipper" Layton. That group recorded one self-titled album, released in 1992 on Geffen Records. By the time the Arc Angels decided to disband, Sexton was 24 years old and already pegged as a blues musician. But in fact, Sexton not only plays gutsy, fluid blues guitar, but also spirited rock & roll guitar.

In 1994 and 1995, he formed and recorded with his new group, the Charlie Sexton Sextet, and his debut for MCA Records, *Under the Wishing Tree*, was released in 1995. Sexton's album was well-received by the critics. *Under the Wishing Tree* presents Sexton in an array of musical genres, touching on Celtic-flavored rock, folk-rock, and blues. There is a lot of interplay between guitars, violins, cellos, Dobros, and mandolins on the recording, and Sexton's vocals ride high on top of the melodies. On his 1995 tour to support the album, he was accompanied by Susan Boelz, violin, Michael Ramos, organ, George Reiff, bass, and Rafael Gayol, drums.

As a songwriter, Sexton writes about what he knows, so Texas themes permeate his songs. He considers Bob Dylan his strongest songwriting influence, while he counts Austin legends Jimmie Vaughan and Stevie Ray Vaughan among his prime influences for guitar playing. His lyrics mix autobiographical experiences with images that are open to interpretation. More great things are in the offing for this young guitarist, singer, and songwriter. *—Richard Skelly*

• **Pictures for Pleasure** / 1985 / MCA ✦✦✦✦
Like many teenagers, Charlie Sexton lusted after rock stardom—the only difference was, he had a chance to pursue his dream. Sexton certainly looked like the part, with his high cheek bones and pompadour, but since he was living in the '80s instead of the '50s he worshipped, his producers decided to push him toward new wave for his debut album, *Pictures for Pleasure.* The teenaged guitarist had been bashing out blues and roots-rock around his native Austin, TX, but the market for that music was limited—hence the decision to layer the record with drum machines and synthesizers. Through sheer dumb luck, they came up with a classic MTV hit with the moody "Beat's So Lonely," where Sexton comes on like James Dean in Duran Duran clothing, crooning with Bryan Ferry's voice. There's nothing nearly as good on the remainder of *Pictures for Pleasure*, not only because the material is uneven, but because none of the other material benefits with the new wave treatment. That said, it's still a more interesting and entertaining record than many of Sexton's straitlaced latter-day blues efforts, where he often sounds just a bit too respectful.*—Stephen Thomas Erlewine*

Charlie Sexton / 1989 / MCA ✦✦✦✦
An about-face, with more emphasis on Sexton's guitar playing and Texas roots. *—Cub Koda*

Under the Wishing Tree / 1995 / MCA ✦✦✦✦
Jimi Hendrix circa 1968—swirling guitar leads, banging chords, and a chaotic, psychedelic sound. That's what "Neighborhood," the opening cut on Charlie Sexton's *Under the Wishing Tree*, calls to mind. Before the listener can get comfortable, the album switches gears with the whimsical, Celtic-flavored "Wishing Tree," slowing the pace down a notch and reining in a small bit of the previous song's musical anarchy without becoming the least bit dull. Fresh from the breakup of Austin supergroup Arc Angels, the critically acclaimed Texas guitar slinger formed the Charlie Sexton Sextet and recorded the most adventuresome album of his young career in 1985 with producer Malcolm Burn. Sexton's work on *Under the Wishing Tree* stands miles apart from the six-string pyrotechnics exhibited on "Living in a Dream" and other Arc Angels favorites. Assembling a band of relatively unknown but talented players—including keyboardist Michael Ramos, bassist George Reiff, and drummer Rafael Gayol—Sexton mixes raging blues riffs and big rock guitar with acoustic folk, New Orleans jazz, and Celtic influences on songs like "Spanish Words" and "Sunday Clothes." The 12-minute story song "Plain Bad Luck and Innocent Mistakes" is the album's centerpiece and defining moment, a tale as grand as the desert wasteland with Sexton pulling out the stops in a grandiose interplay of poetic lyrics and somber instrumentation. Collaborating with fellow Texas songwriters Tonio K, James McMurtry, and brother Will Sexton on *Under the Wishing Tree*, the younger Sexton's songwriting chops improved significantly from his earlier efforts. *Under the Wishing Tree* delivers on Sexton's long-promised potential, the album a portrait of a young artist caught in the throes of his growth pains, willing to experiment musically and lyrically in order to reach the next level of artistic maturity. Sexton would later gain further seasoning as a member of Bob Dylan's late-'90s touring band, adding his blazing guitar to the rock legend's acclaimed 2001 release *Love and Theft.* *—Rev. Keith A. Gordon*

Will Shade

b. Feb. 5, 1898, Memphis, TN, **d.** Sep. 18, 1966, Memphis, TN
Harmonica, Guitar / Prewar Country Blues, Acoustic Memphis Blues
Apparently almost as important a part of the Memphis scene as the Mississippi river, Will Shade was born near the end of the 19th century and was one of the founders of a particularly 20th century music combo, the Memphis Jug Band. The original lineup of this important group consisted of Shade on vocals, guitar, and harmonica, plus Ben Ramey, Will Weldon, and a man simply known as Roundhouse in some accounts and Lionhouse in others. Either way, he sounds like he would be an asset to any band when the going gets rough. Shade was also known as Son Brimmer, a nickname he had gotten from his grandmother, Annie Brimmer, who had raised him. The name stuck after it became apparent that bright sunlight bothered the lad; the brim of a hat kept the sun out. Perhaps the fear of sunlight was a warning of the musicians' lifestyle that was to come, complete with many a late night.

Shade first heard what would eventually be known as jug band music on records by a Louisville group called the Dixieland Jug Blowers in 1925. It was his vision that this kind of thing might go down smoothly in Memphis and it was he who had to convince the reluctant local musicians to make the appropriate changes. Lionhouse, for example, was coached to switch from blowing an empty whiskey bottle to a gallon jug by Shade, who apparently could hear the subtle difference in tone and pitch without it even having to be demonstrated, just like Stravinsky if he had led a jug band. Shade himself played guitar; harmonica; and a "bullfiddle," a standup bass concocted from a garbage can, a broom handle, and a string. Critics tend to say harmonica was his best instrument, perhaps just to be unpredictable. He did play harmonica in a pure country blues style that served as the foundation for the playing of later bluesmen such as Big Walter Horton and both of the Sonny Boy Williamson harmonica monsters, yet Shade's real importance was not as an instrumentalist, but as the foundation of the Memphis Jug Band group itself as its membership changed and then changed again and again over the years.

Vocalist and tenor guitarist Charlie Burse was one of the members who joined on in 1928, and he was still a happy playing partner of Shade's some 45 years later when the pair were lively participants on the fantastic *Beale St. Mess Around* album. Other members of the Memphis Jug Band at one time or another included Hattie Hart, Charlie Polk, Walter Horton, Memphis blues scene stalwart Furry Lewis, Memphis Minnie and her husband Kansas Joe McCoy, Dewey Corley, and Vol Stevens. It was Shade who kept track of all these players, lined up a quorum for a given gig, and ran all the business affairs. He seemed to know what he was doing in the latter department, the first Memphis musician to not only provide a full-time living for himself with his activities but to put a down payment on his own home as well.

The group was closely associated with the Beale Street scene and first signed with Victor in 1927. Until the mid-'30s, the group recorded regularly, producing some 60 sides and scoring great success with such classic songs as "Memphis Jug-Blues," "Sometimes I Think I Love You," "In the Jailhouse Now," and "Stealin'." Shade was personally responsible for some of the group's best material, either by adopting traditional material with his own touches or coming up with entirely new ditties. He made sure his copyright wound up on certain songs if at all possible, although not everyone agrees with the result. The jug band classic "Stealin'" is case in point; it is likely to appear with a Shade credit, but many blues scholars say this is a case of stealing "Stealin'." If he had heard the cover version of this song eventually done by British art rock band Uriah Heep, perhaps Shade would have left his name off the song after all. Shade's "Dirty Dozens" song routine was a good one for making straight-laced college blues fans blush with embarrassment. This was a pleasure the group had to wait until the '60s to enjoy, when a revival of classic folk music made the Memphis Jug Band and Shade regain their popularity. His death in 1966 ended the group, however, as they apparently needed his personality at the center in order to continue. *—Eugène Chadbourne*

Mem Shannon

b. Dec. 21, 1959, New Orleans, LA

Vocals / Retro-Soul, Modern Electric Blues, R&B

Guitarist, singer, and songwriter Mem Shannon is one of the Young Lions of blues who believes in expanding the parameters of the music. His two albums for Hannibal, *A Cab Driver's Blues* (his 1995 debut) and *2nd Blues Album* (1997), are both worth seeking out in record stores. Shannon brilliantly combines elements of funk, jazz, and rock & roll into his guitar playing, and his soulful vocals are not your run-of-the-mill stylings. In fact, most things about Shannon are exceptional: the way he write songs, the way he sings them, and the way he presents them. He's a rock & roll kid who played in a variety of cover bands in high school in his native New Orleans, but he always had a healthy appreciation for blues and gospel music.

Shannon was born in New Orleans and began playing clarinet at age 9. By the time he was 15, he was playing guitar, inspired by his father's blues record collection, but it wasn't until he saw B.B. King that he got serious about it and began practicing in earnest. He began playing in Top 40 and wedding bands around the Crescent City. His first band after high school, the Ebony Brothers Hot Band, played dances, parties and neighborhood bars. His second group, Free Enterprize, found work doing covers. However, his father passed away unexpectedly in 1981, and as the oldest son in a close-knit family, he began driving a cab to help the family pay bills. He also played guitar in the Dedicators, a gospel group, but there was no money whatsoever in that.

He put his music aside for awhile, but began playing again in 1990 after being encouraged to do so by Peter Carter, his old bassist from Free Enterprize. Shannon began working out lyrics and song ideas and working with Carter again. His songs were inspired partly by his life and experiences driving a cab. Regular club gigs followed at a few clubs in the French Quarter. In 1991, he spotted an ad in the local newspaper advertising a talent contest. Shannon & the Membership won the contest, ensuring them a spot at the New Orleans Jazz and Heritage Festival, plus $1,000 and a television commercial. Later in 1991, Shannon & the Membership went to the Long Beach Blues Festival's talent contest, but lost out in the finals and didn't get to play the festival.

After making a demo tape of his material, he got some interest from JSP, a London-based blues label, but an area producer offered his services to re-record some of the songs on Shannon's demo. The producer, Mark Bingham, brought Shannon's music to the attention of Joe Boyd of Hannibal Records in 1994. Boyd was impressed, and on Oct. 15, 1995, Shannon's debut, *A Cab Driver's Blues*, was released.

The album drew critical praise from far and wide, but it also got him an extraordinary amount of publicity. Because of the interesting nature of the recording, which includes snippets of conversation with passengers from his cab interspersed with the music, Shannon's story attracted the attention of producers at PBS-TV and CBS-TV's *Sunday Morning* and editors at *The New York Times*.

By April of 1996, at the annual New Orleans Jazz and Heritage Festival, Shannon announced from the stage that he was giving up his job as a cab driver to play blues full-time. He hasn't looked back and thanks to good booking agents and his own work ethic, he's already toured extensively around the U.S., Europe and Canada. Shannon is the first major new talent to come out of New Orleans in some time, and since thousands of foreigners visit New Orleans every spring for JazzFest, Shannon forged his reputation as an international touring musician easily.

Shannon's music isn't stuck in a jump-shuffle mode. He takes a broader view, incorporating elements of funk, jazz, swamp rock, and classic rock into the Membership's blues-based sound. The band funks it up with varying shuffle drum backbeats, throbbing basslines, a wailing saxophone, and feathery keyboard treatments. And there is room in Shannon's view of himself as a bluesman for political and social commentary in songs like "Wrong People in Charge," "Charity," and "Down Broke." *—Richard Skelly*

● **A Cab Driver's Blues** / Oct. 1995 / Hannibal ✦✦✦✦✦

Mem Shannon's first album, *A Cab Driver's Blues*, became a minor media sensation upon its 1995 release due to circumstance more than music. Shannon's story is fascinating—he's a New Orleans taxi driver who wanted to get out of the business and become a bluesman. That's basically what all the songs on the album are about, whether they're about the job ("5th Ward Horseman," "$17.00 Brunette"), domestic problems ("My Baby's Been Watching TV") or just life in general ("Food Drink and Music," "Ode to Benny Hill"). Shannon's songs have so much specificity and detail that they wind up being much more interesting than the average contemporary blues album. Also, his warm, laidback musical style is idiosyncratic and unpredictable. His delivery is friendly and conversational—he often sounds as if he's singing directly to the listener. And it's that special, intimate quality that makes *A Cab Driver's Blues* a truly unique and special contemporary blues record. *—Thom Owens*

2nd Blues Album / Apr. 29, 1997 / Hannibal ✦✦✦

Spend Some Time With Me / Feb. 16, 1999 / Shanachie ✦✦✦✦

Mem Shannon's Shanachie debut, *Spend Some Time With Me*, finds the ex-cab driver bluesman stretching his sound to the limit. Whether adding country flourishes on "A Certain Shade of Blue" or crafting danceable social commentary with "Who Are They?" and "Dirty Dishes," Shannon finds new ways to define and transcend the blues. "Don't Talk About My Mama" is a response to all the "yo' mama" jokes, while "The Last Time I Was Here (Millennium Blues)" traces the African-American experience, from slavery to the present, through reincarnation. An ambitious, enjoyable album, *Spend Some Time With Me* reveals growth and development in an already accomplished artist. *—Heather Phares*

Memphis in the Morning / May 8, 2001 / Shanachie ✦✦✦✦✦

Mem Shannon has come a long way from his days working as a cab driver. Six years after giving up his hack license, Shannon has four critically acclaimed albums under his belt. His fourth album, *Memphis in the Morning*, is his most polished effort to date. For *Memphis in the Morning*, Shannon collaborated with Dennis Walker, the Grammy-winning producer who has worked with artists such as Robert Cray. Shannon has evolved into an outstanding instrumentalist, mixing in blues with a little bit of funk à la the Meters. Shannon also brings a hearty sense of humor to his music, singing about traditional topics of heartbreak and loss as well as modern annoyances, as he does on the track "S.U.V." He also has a political edge, which comes through on his cover version of B.B. King's "Why I Sing the Blues," including new verses that attack the state of U.S. politics and education. After listening to *Memphis in the Morning*, it's easy to understand why Mem Shannon is considered one of the best modern bluesmen around. *—Jon Azpiri*

Preston Shannon

b. Olive Branch, MS

Vocals, Guitar / Soul-Blues, Contemporary Blues

Memphis-based guitarist, singer, and songwriter Preston Shannon delivers soul-filled vocals atop his burning, venom-tipped guitar chords. His voice is deep and guttural, and he's a veteran of hundreds of live club shows and recording sessions as a sideman. Shannon's specialty is a blend of Southern-fried soul and blues, and his albums and live shows—always with a horn section—are an eclectic mix of danceable, grooving tunes, and slow, soulful ballads.

Born in Olive Branch, MS, Shannon's family moved to Memphis when he was eight. Although his Pentecostal parents didn't initially accept his fascination with blues music, they eventually did when they saw how serious he was about pursuing the music for his livelihood. Shannon served as a member of a popular '70s bar band, Amnesty, and played in a succession of other Memphis-area bands while working by day for a hardware company. Finally, he decided to play music full time when he landed a spot in soul-blues belter Shirley Brown's band. It wasn't until 1991 that he put together his own band and began playing the clubs on Beale Street and other places. In the early '90s, he was discovered playing in a Beale Street blues club by producer/keyboardist Ron Levy, who brought Shannon's talents to the attention of executives at Rounder Records. Shortly afterwards, in 1994, his first widely distributed recording was issued on the label.

Shannon has recorded three albums for the Rounder Bullseye Blues subsidiary, *Break the Ice* (1994) *Midnight In Memphis* (1996), and *All in Time* (1999). All three albums more than adequately showcase his talents as a singer who can alternate between uptempo, gospel-inspired numbers and slower, soulful love songs and ballads. Shannon's guitar playing contains echoes of the Kings, Albert and B.B., T-Bone Walker, and some of the rhythmic sensibilities of Little Milton Campbell. For many years a homebody who couldn't be heard much outside the Memphis city limits, Shannon has done some road work in recent years, traveling to blues festivals around the U.S. *—Richard Skelly & Al Campbell*

Break the Ice / 1994 / Bullseye Blues ✦✦✦

Memphis guitarist Preston Shannon's debut as a bandleader, *Break the Ice* is a showcase not only for the singer/guitarist's considerable talents, but for his influences as well. Heavily influenced by the Kings, Albert and B.B., Shannon puts down a blazing version of the former's "Crosscut Saw," as well as covering two songs by Jimmy McCracklin (the songwriter who gave B.B. "The Thrill Is Gone"). Truly one of the strongest talents on the modern day Memphis blues scene, Shannon and his band do much to transcend their influences and add an original sound on the 12 songs collected here. *—Steve Kurutz*

● **Midnight in Memphis** / Apr. 1996 / Bullseye Blues ✦✦✦✦✦

King Curtis once recorded a groovy tune on which he described and demonstrated the recipe for "Memphis Soul Stew" ("a pound of fatback drums," "a half pint of horns," "a pinch of organ," etc.). *Midnight in Memphis* is like a Memphis *Blues* Stew seasoned with chunks of soul; it combines every tasty ingredient to be found in both the blues and soul cookbooks. Co-producers Ron Levy (an aficionado of the Memphis sound) and Willie Mitchell (one of the creators of that sound) work with guitarist/vocalist Shannon (a regular on the current Memphis scene) to create one of the strongest contemporary soul-blues albums of the decade. On cuts like the slow-burner "The Feeling Is Gone," the sexual epic "The Clock," and the knockout "Size 12 Shoes," Shannon's gritty vocals convey so much commitment and authority as to enthrall the listener, especially when the CD is played loud as it obviously was meant to be. Shannon hit the ground running on his debut album *Break the Ice*. On *Midnight in Memphis* he soars. *—Steve Hoffman*

All in Time / Feb. 2, 1999 / Bullseye Blues ✦✦✦✦

Memphis-based Beale Street regular Preston Shannon lays down a compelling blend of blues and soul on this outing. Recorded in Memphis and produced by Willie Mitchell, Shannon is backed by a crack staff of Memphis all-star session players, with bassist Leroy Hodges and songwriter session ace Thomas Bingham contributing mightily to the proceedings. Shannon has a rep as a people-pleasing live performer, so it's no surprise to hear him put his own spin to a club favorite like Prince's "Purple Rain," leaving the guitar pyrotechnics of the original on the back burner, investigating instead the soulful content of the song in a fine, stripped-down version. There are solid blues on board, too, in "Jail of Love" and "Welfare Woman." But he can lay down the soul groove on a tune like "That's the Way I Feel About Cha" and "Just Between Me and My Woman" with equal ability. In addition to his stellar and very soulful vocal chops, Shannon also delivers some fine B.B. King-approved stinging guitar fills throughout, particularly effectively on the closing instrumental, "Cold Beer Good Time." In another era, this album could have come out on Stax, and could stand nicely against Albert King albums of that time frame. As it is in the here and now, *All in Time* stands instead as a fine modern-day soul-blues album with a vintage pedigree a mile long. —*Cub Koda*

Omar Shariff (Dave Alexander)

b. Mar. 10, 1938
Vocals, Piano / Texas Blues
Texas blues singer and pianist Omar Shariff was born March 10, 1938; during the '60s he relocated to San Francisco, where in 1971 he recorded a pair of albums for the Arhoolie label under his given name Dave Alexander. Upon adopting his stage name he kept a low profile, and did not record for another two decades; *The Raven*, a collection made up of ten songs cut in 1991 and seven songs cut in 1972, marked his return to prominence. Shariff was nominated for a W.C. Handy Award in 1993. In 1996 small blues label Have Mercy released *Baddass* and followed it up with *Black Widow Spider* in 2000. Both records are stripped-down nasty blues: Song titles like "My Life Is a Nightmare" and "Seven Years of Torture" give the listener an idea where Shariff is coming from. His next album, *Anatomy of a Woman*, was a concept album about Shariff's favorite subject: women. Shariff remains an obscure artist, obscure but real and blues to the bone. Make sure you catch him if he comes to your town. —*Jason Ankeny & Tim Sendra*

● **The Raven** / 1972 / Arhoolie ✦✦✦✦✦
Omar Sharif returned from a two-decade recording layoff with *The Raven*, an impressive update of his native Texas blues style with elements of Latin and jazz. —*Jason Ankeny*

Baddass / Jan. 12, 1996 / Have Mercy ✦✦✦

Black Widow Spider / Jan. 1, 2000 / Have Mercy ✦✦✦

Eddie Shaw

b. Mar. 20, 1937, Stringtown, MS
Vocals, Saxophone / Electric Chicago Blues
When it comes to blues, Chicago's strictly a guitar and harmonica town. Saxophonists who make a living leading a blues band in the Windy City are scarce as hen's teeth. But Eddie Shaw has done precisely that ever since his longtime boss, Howlin' Wolf, died in 1976.

The powerfully constructed tenor saxist has rubbed elbows with an amazing array of luminaries over his 50-plus years in the business. By the time he was age 14, Shaw was jamming with Ike Turner's combo around Greenville, MS. At a gig in Itta Bena where Shaw sat in, Muddy Waters extended the young saxman an invitation he couldn't refuse: a steady job with Waters' unparalleled band in Chicago. After a few years, Shaw switched his on-stage allegiance to Waters' chief rival, the ferocious Howlin' Wolf, staying with him until the very end and eventually graduating to a featured role as Wolf's bandleader.

Eddie Shaw also shared a West Side bandstand or two along the way with Freddie King, Otis Rush, and Magic Sam. The saxist did a 1966 session with Sam that produced his first single, the down-in-the-alley instrumental "Blues for the West Side" (available on Delmark's *Sweet Home Chicago* anthology). Shaw also blew his heart out on Sam's 1968 Delmark encore LP, *Black Magic*.

Shaw's own recording career finally took off during the late '70s, with a standout appearance on Alligator's *Living Chicago Blues* anthologies in 1978, his own LPs for Simmons and Rooster Blues, and fine discs for Rooster Blues (*In the Land of the Crossroads*) and Austrian Wolf (*Home Alone*). Eddie Shaw, who once operated the hallowed 1815 Club on West Roosevelt Road (one of Wolf's favorite haunts), has sired a couple of high-profile sons: diminutive Eddie Jr., known as Vaan, plays lead guitar with Eddie's Wolf Gang and has cut a pair of his own albums for Wolf, while husky Stan Shaw is a prolific character actor in Hollywood. —*Bill Dahl*

Movin' and Groovin' Man / May 14, 1982 / Evidence ✦✦✦
Tenor saxophonist Eddie Shaw is a rarity in blues circles—a first-class instrumentalist who is not a guitarist or pianist. Shaw is a soulful, exuberant player whose lusty licks make a solid counterpoint to his rough-hewn vocals and narratives. While Shaw carries the majority of the load on this 10-cut date from 1982 previously recorded for Isabel (reissued on CD here by Evidence) it is guitarist Melvin Taylor who is the revelation as second soloist. Between his work with Lucky Peterson, his own CD, and his brisk, sizzling solos and accompaniment here, Taylor merits high praise as a workmanlike, flexible contributor. The others, with the exception of the great Eddie "Cleanhead" Vinson, are heady pros capably handling limited support duties. —*Ron Wynn*

King of the Road / Sep. 1986 / Rooster Blues ✦✦✦✦
A revealing compilation of the ballsy Chicago saxist's earlier work (1966-1984) that certainly deserves to be on CD but isn't yet. "Blues for the West Side" and "Lookin' Good," both with Magic Sam on guitar, are highlights of Shaw's entire career, while his vocal talents are well-served on "It's All Right," an amusing "I Don't Trust Nobody," and his touching tribute "Blues Men of Yesterday." —*Bill Dahl*

● **In the Land of the Crossroads** / 1992 / Rooster Blues ✦✦✦✦✦
The best contemporary Shaw offering, cut in his old Mississippi stomping grounds with his trusty combo, the Wolf Gang. Lots of lyrically unusual originals—"Dunkin' Donut Woman," "Wine Head Hole," and "She Didn't Tell Me Everything," for starters—and Shaw's usual diamond-hard horn lines and commanding vocals make this a standout selection. —*Bill Dahl*

Trail of Tears / 1994 / Wolf ✦✦✦✦✦

Home Alone / 1995 / Wolf ✦✦✦✦
Although it's pressed on an Austrian logo, Eddie Shaw's rollicking recent disc was waxed in his Chicago hometown with the Wolf Gang (son Vaan on guitar, longtime bassist Shorty Gilbert, and drummer Tim Taylor) summoning up solid support. Once again, Shaw tackles some interesting subjects—he fantasizes about "Blues in Paris," and decried being "Home Alone," and searches out an endorsement deal with "Motel Six" via his sprightly musical tribute to the budget chain. —*Bill Dahl*

The Blues Is Nothing but Good News! / 1996 / Wolf ✦✦✦

Can't Stop Now / Apr. 29, 1997 / Delmark ✦✦✦

Too Many Highways / May 4, 1999 / Wolf ✦✦✦

Robert Shaw

b. Aug. 9, 1908, Stafford, TX, **d.** May 18, 1985, Austin, TX
Vocals, Piano / Piano Blues, Boogie-Woogie
He didn't record much at all—a marvelous 1963 album for Almanac, reissued on Chris Strachwitz's Arhoolie label, remains his principal recorded legacy—but barrelhouse pianist Robert Shaw helped greatly to establish a distinctive regional style of pounding the 88s around Houston, Fort Worth, and Galveston during the '20s and '30s.

Those decades represented Shaw's playing heyday, when he forged a stunning barrelhouse style of his own in the bars, dance halls, and whorehouses along the route of the Santa Fe railroad. Shaw got around—in 1933, he had a radio program in Oklahoma City. But by the mid-'30s, Shaw relegated his playing to the back burner to open a grocery store. Mack McCormick coaxed him back into action in 1963 and the results as collected on Arhoolie were magnificent; "The Cows" was a piece of incredible complexity that would wilt anything less than a legitimate ivories master. Shaw continued to perform stateside and in Europe intermittently during the '70s, turning up unexpectedly in California in 1981 to help Strachwitz celebrate Arhoolie's 20th anniversary. —*Bill Dahl*

● **The Ma Grinder** / 1963 / Arhoolie ✦✦✦✦✦
Stunning solo Texas blues and barrelhouse piano by the late pianist. The most amazing material, produced by Mack McCormick in Austin, dates from 1963—the rhythmically and technically complex "The Cows" is a *tour de force*, and "The Ma Grinder" and "The Clinton" aren't far behind. Later numbers from 1973 and 1977 prove that Shaw's skills didn't degenerate with time. —*Bill Dahl*

Texas Barrelhouse Piano / Dec. 1980 / Arhoolie ✦✦✦✦

Robert Shaw 1971 Party Tape / Sep. 8, 2000 / Document ✦✦✦

Kenny Wayne Shepherd

b. Jun. 12, 1977, Shreveport, LA
Vocals, Guitar / Blues-Rock, Modern Electric Blues
Kenny Wayne Shepherd and his group exploded on the scene in the mid-'90s and garnered huge amounts of radio airplay on commercial radio, which historically has not been a solid home for blues and blues-rock music, with the exception of Stevie Ray Vaughan in the mid-'80s.

Shepherd was born June 12, 1977, in Shreveport, LA. The Shreveport native began playing at age seven, figuring out Muddy Waters licks from his father's record collection (he has never taken a formal lesson). At age 13, he was invited on-stage by New Orleans bluesman Brian Lee and held his own for several hours; thus proving himself, he decided on music as a career. He formed his own band, which featured lead vocalist Corey Sterling, gaining early exposure through club dates and, later, radio conventions. Shepherd's father/manager used his own contacts and pizzazz in the record business to help land his son a major-label record deal with Irving Azoff's Giant Records. *Ledbetter Heights*, his first album, was released two years later in 1995. *Ledbetter Heights* was an immediate hit, selling over 500,000 by early 1996. Most blues records never achieve that level of commercial success, much less ones released by artists who are still in their teens.

Although Shepherd—who has been influenced by (and has sometimes played with) guitarists Stevie Ray Vaughan, Albert King, Slash, Robert Cray, and Duane Allman—is definitely a performer who thrives in front of an audience, *Ledbetter Heights* is impressive for its range of styles: acoustic blues, rockin' blues, Texas blues, and Louisiana blues. The only style that he doesn't tackle is Chicago blues, owing to Shepherd's home base smack dab in the middle of the Texas triangle. Released in 1997, *Trouble Is* earned a Grammy nomination; *Live On* followed in 1999. —*Steve Huey & Richard Skelly*

● **Ledbetter Heights** / Oct. 1995 / Giant ✦✦✦✦
You would never guess from Kenny Wayne Shepherd's fiery playing that the guitarist is still only in his teens. On his debut, *Ledbetter Heights*, Shepherd burns through a set of rather generic blues-rock ravers that are made special by his exceptional technique. It may still be a while before he says something original, but he plays with style, energy, and dedication, which is more than enough for a debut album. —*Thom Owens*

Trouble Is / Oct. 7, 1997 / Revolution/Warner Brothers ✦✦✦
Instead of breaking from his high-energy, high-voltage blues-rock, Kenny Wayne Shepherd offers more of the same on his second album, *Trouble Is*. While the record lacks the surprise and impact of *Ledbetter Heights*, it's clear that Shepherd is growing as a guitarist, developing a cleaner, more nuanced technique. He still suffers from a lack of an original voice, plus a lack of strong material, but his growth as a guitarist compensates for what's missing. —*Thom Owens*

Live On / Oct. 12, 1999 / Giant ✦✦✦✦
Being a teenage blues guitar prodigy is a double-edged sword. Stunning technique brings attention, but also criticism that it's all style and no soul. This criticism has plagued Kenny Wayne Shepherd since his popular debut album, *Ledbetter Heights*, and it's warranted to a certain extent. It didn't help that Shepherd so strongly recalled Stevie Ray Vaughan. It also didn't help that some of his material was a little too slick, appealing as much to

album rock as to blues-rock audiences. By the time of his third album, 1999's *Live On*, he had begun to reconcile these two sides of his personality, but the best thing about the record is that it's tougher and stronger than its two predecessors. There's still a fair amount of crossover—a Hendrix cover and a cover of Fleetwood Mac's "Oh Well,"—but Shepherd not only seems to be developing a style of his own, the playing of his band has become grittier, or at least it's being captured better on record. Shepherd can still fall prey to excess, but not as often as he used to. He's figuring out how to restrain himself, and his music is all the better for it. *—Stephen Thomas Erlewine*

Lonnie Shields

b. Apr. 17, 1956, West Helena, AR

Vocals, Guitar / Contemporary Blues

Guitarist, singer and songwriter Lonnie Shields' *Portrait* (Rooster Blues) was praised by critics as one of the best debut albums of the year when it was released in 1992. Since then, the high praise from all corners of the world has continued for Shields' simple yet complex style of soulful, rhythmic blues.

Shields was brought up in a family where the church played a central role in daily life, and his gospel roots show through in everything he sings. He began playing soul and funk before discovering the Delta blues through his friend Sam Carr. Shields worked with Carr in the Unforgettable Blues Band and took as his other mentors local musicians like Frank Frost and Big Jack Johnson. Later, he discovered B.B. King, whom he considers his primary influence.

Shields formed his first group when he was 15. Called the Checkmates, they took their musical cues from the sounds of Earth, Wind and Fire and the Isley Brothers. After the band broke up, Shields gave up playing guitar for some time until he met drummer Sam Carr in Lula, MS. Carr was insistent that Shields learn to play authentic blues, and a short time later, he was out on the road with Carr, Frank Frost, and Big Jack Johnson.

After Shields played the King Biscuit Blues Festival in Helena, Arkansas in 1986, he was asked to record a single for the Rooster Blues label. This in turn led to his first album for Rooster Blues, released in 1993. The album got him noticed in the blues world and let to a broader touring base that included festival stops around the Northeast. Shields recorded and released *Tired of Waiting* (1996) and *Blues Is on Fire* (1997) for the London-based JSP record label. A second Rooster Blues album, *Midnight Delight*, was released in 2000. He continues to perform around the U.S., Europe, and Canada. *—Richard Skelly*

● **Portrait** / 1992 / Rooster Blues ♦♦♦♦♦

Lonnie Shields' debut album, *Portrait*, introduced an accomplished, talented bluesman, one that was equally capable of playing guitar with abandon and delivering a song with soul. Unlike many of his peers, he doesn't oversell a song, he caresses it with his voice, knowing when to bring it all back home. Supported by guitarist Jack Johnson, keyboardist Frank Frost, and drummer Sam Carr, he's able to pull off contemporary blues, laidback soul and funky grooves, resulting in a truly impressive and detailed *Portrait*. *—Thom Owens*

Tired of Waiting / Jun. 18, 1996 / JSP ♦♦♦♦

Blues Is on Fire / Sep. 23, 1997 / JSP ♦♦♦♦

Midnight Delight / Apr. 11, 2000 / Rooster Blues ♦♦♦

Johnny Shines

b. Apr. 26, 1915, Frayser, TN, **d.** Apr. 20, 1992, Tuscaloosa, AL

Vocals, Guitar / Slide Guitar Blues, Delta Blues, Electric Delta Blues, Electric Chicago Blues, Chicago Blues

Best known as a traveling companion of Robert Johnson, Johnny Shines' own contributions to the blues have often been unfairly shortchanged, simply because Johnson's own legend casts such a long shadow. In his early days, Shines was one of the top slide guitarists in Delta blues, with his own distinctive, energized style; one that may have echoed Johnson's spirit and influence, but was never a mere imitation. Shines eventually made his way north to Chicago, and made the transition to electrified urban blues with ease, helped in part by his robust, impassioned vocals. He was vastly under-recorded during his prime years, even quitting the music business for a time, but was rediscovered in the late '60s and recorded and toured steadily for quite some time. A 1980 stroke robbed him of some of his dexterity on guitar, but his voice remained a powerfully emotive instrument, and he performed up until his death in 1992.

John Ned Shines was born April 26, 1915, in Frayser, TN, and grew up in Memphis from the age of six. Part of a musical family, he learned guitar from his mother, and as a youth he played for tips on the streets of Memphis with several friends, inspired by the likes of Charley Patton, Blind Lemon Jefferson, Lonnie Johnson, and the young Howlin' Wolf. In 1932, he moved to Hughes, AR, to work as a sharecropper, keeping up his musical activities on the side; in 1935, he decided to try and make it as a professional musician. Shines had first met Robert Johnson in Memphis in 1934, and he began accompanying Johnson on his wanderings around the Southern juke-joint circuit, playing wherever they could find gigs; the two made their way as far north as Windsor, Ontario, where they appeared on a radio program. After around three years on the road together—which made Shines one of Johnson's most intimate associates, along with Johnson's stepson Robert Jr. Lockwood—the two split up in Arkansas in 1937, and never saw each other again before Johnson's death in 1938.

Shines continued to play around the South for a few years, and in 1941 decided to make his way north in hopes of finding work in Canada, and from there catching a boat to Africa. Instead, when he stopped in Chicago, his cousin immediately offered him a job in construction, and Shines wound up staying. He started making the rounds of the local blues club scene, and in 1946 he made his first-ever recordings; four tracks for Columbia that the label declined to release. In 1950, he resurfaced on Chess, cutting sides that were rarely released (and, when they were, often appeared under the name "Shoe Shine Johnny"). Meanwhile, Shines was finding work supporting other artists at live shows and recording sessions. From 1952-1953, he laid down some storming sides for the JOB label, which constitute some of his finest work ever (some featured Big Walter Horton on harmonica). They went underappreciated commercially, however, and Shines returned to his supporting roles. In 1958, fed up with the musicians' union over a financial dispute, Shines quit the music business, pawned all of his equipment, and made his living solely with the construction job he'd kept all the while.

Shines did, however, stay plugged into the local blues scene by working as a photographer at live events, selling photos to patrons as souvenirs. Eventually, he was sought out by blues historians, and talked into recording for Vanguard's now-classic *Chicago/The Blues/Today!* series; his appearance on the third volume in 1966 rejuvenated his career. Shines next cut sessions for Testament (1966's *Master of the Modern Blues, Vol. 1*, a couple with Big Walter Horton, and more) and Blue Horizon (1968's *Last Night's Dream*), which effectively introduced him to much of the listening public. The reception was much greater this time around, and Shines hit the road, first with Horton and Willie Dixon as the Chicago All-Stars, then leading his own band. In the meantime, his daughter died unexpectedly, leaving Shines to raise his grandchildren; concerned about bringing them up in an urban environment, he moved the whole family down to Tuscaloosa, AL.

During the early '70s, Shines recorded for Biograph and Advent, among others, and enjoyed one of his most acclaimed releases with 1975's more Delta-styled *Too Wet to Plow* (for Tomato). He also taught guitar locally in Tuscaloosa in between touring engagements. Despite his own generally high-quality work, Shines was a fascinating figure to many white blues fans simply because of the mythology surrounding Robert Johnson, and he was interviewed repeatedly about his experiences with Johnson to the exclusion of discussing his own music and contemporary career; which understandably frustrated him after a while. However, that didn't stop him from rediscovering his roots in acoustic Delta blues, or including many of Johnson's classic songs in his own repertoire; in fact, during the late '70s, Shines toured and recorded often with Robert Jr. Lockwood, a teaming that owed much to Johnson's legacy if ever there was one. Unfortunately, in 1980, Shines suffered a stroke that greatly affected his guitar playing, which would never return to its former glories. He was able to sing as effectively as before, though, and helped by some of his students, he continued to tour America and Europe. In the early '90s, Shines appeared in the documentary film *Searching for Robert Johnson*, and he also cut one last album with Snooky Pryor, 1991's *Back to the Country*, which won a W.C. Handy Award. Shines' health was failing, however, and he passed away on April 20, 1992, in a Tuscaloosa hospital. *—Steve Huey*

Master of the Modern Blues, Vol. 1 / 1966 / Testament ♦♦♦♦

Although this artist recorded here and there in the '40s and '50s, most of this material was never released or is as rare as a bona fide Mojo Hand. In terms of the blues listening audience, this mid-'60s Testament production was basically his recording debut, and it can be summarized as a grand entrance. Although in retrospect the music would end up not having all that much to do with Shines himself, who began to investigate acoustic blues in the following decade and would become much more known as a solo performer than the leader of an electric band such as this. The playing on this record is simply fascinating; in fact, it makes something of a good "how to" instruction for a budding blues band, although whether there are players around who can drum like Fred Below is questionable. The intelligent bassist is Lee Jackson, and not the guy from the Nice who had the Lee Jackson bass named after him. Completing the band are two absolute legends of Chicago blues, the pianist Otis Spann and harmonica player Big Walter Horton. These big names don't dominate the proceedings, however. There is a lot of material that is done with just drums and bass, or in the case of the mesmerizing "Tom Green's Farm," just bass and guitar. Stripped down to two instruments, the interplay involved in the blues playing here is wonderful, especially since the sound of Shines' electric guitar is so unusual and Jackson's technique is also not run-of-the-mill blues bass thumping. The bassist listens to Shines so carefully it might make the listener's heart stop, and the beautifully precise moments of musical mingling are the results of this concentration and not endless by-rote practice sessions. Group joy is reached by adding the drums of Below, almost providing yet another melodic accompaniment, as his snare drum playing is so tuneful. It is the sound of these three that dominates the album, so fans of Spann and Horton shouldn't expect too much of their heroes. The latter harmonica man did other recordings with Shines on which he is more prominently featured. It is Shines himself who is center stage, both as a vocalist and a guitarist. He excels in both areas, the singing providing moments of saloon-style jazz as well as loud, hollering blues shouting and a piercing, quivering vibrato that would probably have been good for calling in a mule that has wandered off. On guitar he uses space in an interesting manner, suddenly coming in to insert just the perfect bassline or hitting the high strings with the slide in a way that is excitingly harsh even in a style of playing known for its strong bite. On other tracks he tosses in bits of rhythm guitar magic, again jazzy, in a manner that predicts his later collaborations with Robert Jr. Lockwood. *—Eugene Chadbourne*

Last Night's Dream / 1968 / Warner Brothers ♦♦♦♦♦

It's no wonder that this album, cut in 1968 with British blues maven Mike Vernon at the helm, works so well. When you team a rejuvenated Shines with his longtime compadres Horton, Spann, bassist Willie Dixon, and drummer Clifton James, a little blues history was bound to be made. *—Bill Dahl*

☆ **Johnny Shines With Big Walter Horton** / Nov. 1969 / Testament ♦♦♦♦♦

Calling an album one the best in this particular genre, Chicago blues, is a pretty big move. There are plenty of masters of this particular form, and the success of several different record companies recording the genre over the years has assured no shortage of material. Something just comes together splendidly on these sessions that elevates this album well above the level of even some of the great Chicago sides of artists such as Muddy Waters. It might not exude the timeless gold dust of such records, but at the same time has a raw energy and breathless courage that goes well beyond anything the Chess label got on tape in its studios. The sound is also richly thick and loaded with midrange overtones. This benefits not only bass sounds but the presence of the drummers as well. Outrageous drum breaks are one byproduct, and the listener might even sense the ensemble somehow about to topple before everything comes together at the slightest chicken scratch of Johnny Shines' electric guitar. Bringing that subject up: in the late '60s, this artist had yet to start developing his acoustic country blues phase and was playing the electric as if a concrete pick had been welded to his hand. One can only imagine an uptight recording engineer fussing with this sound, trying get something slicker and more professional. Thankfully, the recording teams in charge of this blues masterpiece don't indulge in the quiver, shiver, and shake mentality and just let the sounds go down, including this Shines guitar sound, which is almost more like a living creature scratching at the insides of the speaker box like a misdirected rodent. We are approaching guitar heaven, but it vaults over the gates with the appearance of Luther Allison, whose meaty, juicy tone is the perfect contrast for Shines. This album collects tracks from two different recording sessions a few years apart. Allison is present for only one of the sessions, but the harmonica genius Big Walter Horton is on both dates, flooding the bandstand with chordal cascades and even bringing a frightening edge to some cuts with distorted vocalese. This is not only a great blues record, it is a great party blues record. *—Eugene Chadbourne*

Sitting on Top of the World / 1972 / Biograph ✦✦✦
This label specialized mostly in archival releases, but taped new sessions with Johnny Shines a couple of years after this blues artist's first solo acoustic recordings had come out. He's back at it again here in a set that should score solidly with anyone who likes the country blues sound of one guy playing an acoustic guitar and singing. The latter area is where Shines shines brighter than a lot of the sad and moaning competition, and it is a shame that he didn't get as much credit as a vocalist during his career as he deserved. In his last years, after a stroke had made it difficult to play guitar well, he was still able to get out as a show frontman with just his singing. It is strong and solid here, full of held vibrato notes peculated in the nasal passages and seamless shifting between singing and spoken passages, often within a line. His guitar playing is more aggressive than on the earlier acoustic recordings, with bass lines as hard as steel. While his country blues playing is often compared with his traveling buddy and mentor, Robert Johnson, there are tracks here that sound more like the work of Bukka White or Son House, including the demonic intensity that makes these artists so much fun to listen to. Muffled bass and rhythm patterns reveal a skill at pronunciating notes that is worthy of a killer funk bassist. Part of the fun of a Shines record is his versatility, too. "Glad Rags" is a performance that only he could come up with, full of slow and thoughtful guitar picking that also shows a knowledge of Buddy Guy and whatever else Shines might have heard over the radio in the '60s while working his construction jobs. This is a performance Jimi Hendrix would have been proud of if he had played it. The recorded sound on the guitar is a trifle lacking, be warned. It is the type of sound some engineers might refer to as "boxy," although with a right arm like this guy's, the sides of the box are bound to collapse, and they do. *—Eugene Chadbourne*

Blues Masters / 1972 / Blue Horizon ✦✦✦
On this eclectic and largely electric 1970 set, Shines is joined by an all-star West Coast band comprised of guitarist Phillip Walker, pianist Nat Dove, bassist Charles Jones, drummer Murl Downy, and sax player David II. The music dips into soul balladry ("Just a Little Tenderness") and Chicago boogie ("Give My Heart a Break"), and on a handful of tracks, including "Too Lazy," "Skull and Crossbones Blues," "Vallie Lee," and "Ramblin'," the band steps aside to allow Shines to go it alone. *—Jason Ankeny*

Johnny Shines / 1974 / Advent ✦✦✦
Johnny Shines made this good, if not great, LP for Advent during a period when he was going ignored despite still being in solid form. There are strong vocals, fine arrangements and guitar support, but the production and the songs are too inconsistent to label this a significant session. *—Ron Wynn*

Too Wet to Plow / 1975 / Labor ✦✦✦
Johnny Shines was far from predictable. Though he recorded his share of inspired electric dates, he had no problem turning around and delivering a stripped-down, all-acoustic Delta blues session like *Too Wet To Plow.* Recorded in Edmonton, Canada, in 1975 and reissued on CD by Concord Jazz's Blues Alliance label in 1996, *Too Wet to Plow* finds Shines in excellent form. His solid accompaniment includes harmonica player Sugar Blue and bassist Ron Rault, as well as guitarist/singer Louisiana Red (a superb bluesman who isn't nearly as well known as he should be), and Shines clearly has a strong rapport with them on "Red Sun," "Traveling Back Home," and other highly personal originals. Although Shines' own songs are dominant, one of the album's high points is an interpretation of Robert Johnson's "Hot Tamale." Highly recommended. *—Alex Henderson*

Johnny Shines / 1976 / Hightone ✦✦✦

Hey Ba-Ba-Re-Bop / 1978 / Rounder ✦✦✦✦✦
Delta blues vocalist, guitarist and composer Johnny Shines hadn't yet encountered the physical difficulties that made his final years so troubling when he recorded the 13 selections on this CD. He could still sing and moan with intensity and passion, hold a crowd hypnotized with his remembrances and asides, and play with a mix of fury and charm. While the menu includes oft-performed chestnuts "Sweet Home Chicago," "Terraplane Blues," and "Milk Cow Blues," there wasn't anything staid or predictable about the way Shines ripped through the lyrics and presented the music. If you missed it the first time around, grab this one immediately. *—Ron Wynn*

Dust My Broom / 1980 / Flyright ✦✦✦✦✦

Back to the Country / 1991 / Blind Pig ✦✦✦
Back to the Country finds Johnny Shines, accompanied by Snooky Pryor, running through a selection of standards, many of which they had played in their prime. At the time they made *Back to the Country*, they were well into old age, and had suffered some losses. Shines, in particular, was hit hard by the ravages of old age, suffering a stroke in the late '80s. As a result, Shines couldn't play guitar for this session, so producer John Nicholas and Kent Du Chane pick up the slack. This doesn't really hurt the music, but it's disheartening and awkward to listen to the album knowing that Shines isn't able to perform. That said, there are some nice moments on the record—Shines and Pryor have a nice rapport which shines through despite difficulties—but overall, it's hard not to view this as a nostalgia exercise. *—Thom Owens*

Traditional Delta Blues / 1991 / Biograph ✦✦✦✦✦

★ **Johnny Shines & Robert Lockwood** / 1991 / Paula ✦✦✦✦✦
Shines has half of this 20-track disc, the remainder being devoted to sides from the same era featuring Robert Jr. Lockwood. Recorded in 1952 and 1953 for the JOB label, this is Shines at his most primal, working with a drumless trio; Big Walter Horton plays harmonica on the 1953 sides. These tracks decidedly outshine the Lockwood efforts (also recorded for JOB in the early '50s), some of which only feature Robert as a sideman. *—Richie Unterberger*

Mr. Cover Shaker / 1992 / Biograph ✦✦✦

Masters of Modern Blues / 1994 / Testament ✦✦✦✦✦
After stepping away from the music business altogether for a while, Shines came back strong during the mid-'60s, recording far more prolifically than his first time around. This 1966 date is one of his best, spotlighting his booming pipes and sturdy guitar in front of an all-star Chicago crew: Big Walter Horton on harp, pianist Otis Spann, and drummer Fred Below. *—Bill Dahl*

Standing at the Crossroads / Apr. 18, 1995 / Testament ✦✦✦✦✦
This is one of several albums this artist made in the early '70s that stand as masterpieces of the acoustic country blues genre. Johnny Shines had begun recording in the mid-'60s, the albums done with electric guitar and full-combo backup, one of them reportedly cut after he hadn't picked up an instrument in years. It was as if he reinvented himself in the following decade, playing pristine and flawless acoustic slide guitar pieces complete with shuffling, stuttering, and stimulatingly complicated tempos. The message was that he had been a young sidekick to Robert Johnson and had absorbed everything. No deal had been made with the Devil, on the other hand. Shines was a steady, dependable, religious, and forthright chap who lived in Tuscaloosa, AL, and held down a steady job as a construction foreman. Mild-mannered and extremely intellectual, he let loose the reserve of emotion when doing a Delta blues number. The magic and heart were in his fingertips as well as in his voice, which sounds stupendous here. The emergence of the Johnson song canon into his repertoire, done with almost Baroque detail, was also something of a revelation. Some of Shines' earlier albums had featured songs that almost seemed made up on the spot. He was good at that, and was rumored to have played whole sets that were completely improvised when working the country juke joints of his home state, but on this album he showed what he could do when sinking his teeth into a bona fide blues classic. "Kind Hearted Woman" is the musical equivalent of an absolutely perfect chopped-barbecue sandwich with sauce the way they do it in Tuscaloosa, and obviously of much less offense to vegetarians when taken in this form. There were 11 perfect songs chosen by Pete Welding from his set of recording sessions for this project. Once again this great producer has come up with a blues release that is basically a required item for any good collection of this genre. *—Eugene Chadbourne*

Worried Blues Ain't Bad / May 21, 1996 / Blues Alliance ✦✦✦
It wasn't until 1996 (four years after Johnny Shines' death) that this rare 1974 session finally saw the light of day. The '60s had found the singer/guitarist successfully embracing electric blues some of the time and working with such Chicagoans as Otis Spann, Luther Allison and Big Walter Horton, but when he recorded what would become the CD *Worried Blues Ain't Bad*, it was back to an entirely acoustic Delta-blues approach. Though Shines had his own style, it's hard to miss Robert Johnson's influence on such heartfelt originals as "Went to the River to Drown," "Devil's Daughter," and "Down in Spirit." Minimalism is the rule here, and Shines' sidemen (Don Audet on harmonica, Richard Baker on second acoustic guitar, and Bob Derkach on upright bass) do their part to keep things personal and intimate. It's just unfortunate that this solid date went unreleased for 22 years. *—Alex Henderson*

1915–1992 / Jun. 18, 1998 / Wolf ✦✦

Evening Shuffle / Jun. 26, 2002 / West Side ✦✦✦✦✦

Shirley & Lee

f. 1951, New Orleans, LA, **db.** 1963
Group / New Orleans R&B, R&B
Shirley Goodman and Leonard Lee, born just ten days apart in 1936, scored three massive R&B hits before either one of them were both 20 years old: "Feel So Good," "Let the Good Times Roll," and "I Feel Good" were all written by the talented young couple.

They had one trait in common among their recordings; this New Orleans-based duo almost never sang in harmony, let alone together at all. Their contrasting male-female duet style was later influential on early ska and reggae productions from Jamaica. Shirley & Lee recorded extensively for Eddie Messner and Leo Messner's L.A.-based Aladdin label. The Messners—along with former NBC radio exec. Lew Chudd's Imperial Records and Art Rupe's Specialty—seemed to have a knack for signing talent straight out of the Crescent City.

Shirley & Lee's debut single, "I'm Gone," was written and produced by Dave Bartholomew, Imperial's writer/arranger/producer/A&R man and a major contributor to New Orleans-style R&B. (It was Bartholomew's production work with Fats Domino that utilized the talents of a great house band—pianist Allen Toussaint, bassist Frank Fields, drummer Earl Palmer, and saxophonists Lee Allen, Red Tyler, and Herb Hardesty—and elevated nearly everything he worked on to "legendary" status.) With their backing "I'm Gone" went on to become a major R&B hit in the fall of 1952.

Early in their careers, Shirley & Lee became known as "the Sweethearts of the Blues," a nickname given not for their personal relationship, but for their romantic sagas of their songs, which often bordered on telling a fictional soap opera story line about two lovers. Their fans would buy the singles simply to keep up with the continuing story of the two sweethearts. The story continued with the very next single, "Shirley Come Back to Me," a heartbreaker released in early 1953, followed by "Shirley's Back," later that year. This happy theme continued through the happy ending for the next single, "The Proposal" b/w "Two Happy People."

By the end of the year, Aladdin was reveling in success of the story of Shirley & Lee. Of course, the couple in the songs had already been apart and were now back together, so they had to shake things up with the next release, called "Lee Goofed," and followed that with "Confessin'" but by now the audience seemed to be tiring of the soap opera, so Shirley & Lee moved on to new lyrical subject matter.

Messner decided to try something new for the duo in May of 1955, issuing a medium-tempo rocker called "Feel So Good." The song featured full vocal group backup (reportedly by the Spiders) and did well, but it was the bluesy B-side, "You'd Be Thinking of Me," that put the duo back on the R&B hit charts. "Lee's Dream" also charted. In early 1956, Aladdin released the duo's slow blues ballad, "A Little Word," which received good airplay, but sales weren't spectacular. Trying to get back on track, Aladdin finally opted to issue a full-length album, *Let the Good Times Roll*, in December. It was reissued two years later on Score, Aladdin's budget label.

By the middle of 1957, Shirley & Lee were back on top, this time with the biggest hit in their careers. Goodman and Lee borrowed one of New Orleans' most familiar refrains and built a rocking tune around it called "Let the Good Times Roll." The recording was an instant smash and received substantial airplay, climbing up the charts in the process. It sold well-over one million copies and for more than 40 years has been a staple of oldies play lists. To date, there are over a hundred cover versions of the song, but most still prefer the original.

The pair stayed on Aladdin into 1959 before moving to Warwick, where they ended up re-recording "Let the Good Times Roll." Other tunes followed—"I Feel Good" and "The Flirt" among them—but like many acts, Shirley & Lee were never able to recapture the nationwide success of their biggest hit. After a few final singles in 1962-1963, this time for Imperial—Aladdin and Imperial continued their rivalry and tried to one-up each other until Aladdin was acquired by Imperial outright—the "Sweethearts of the Blues" decided to call it a day.

In 1974, Shirley Goodman reappeared on the R&B scene, this time paired with studio musicians—they called themselves Shirley and Company—for "Shame, Shame, Shame," released on the Vibration label. (The song also featured Jesus Alvarez supplying lead vocals). The disco-fied hit topped the R&B charts at number one that summer and peaked at number 12 on the pop charts. It was written by producer Sylvia Robinson, who had also been part of a successful '50s duo, Mickey & Sylvia, with Mickey Baker. Robinson also penned Goodman's less successful follow-up, "Cry, Cry, Cry." They issued one more single on Vibration, then dropped out of sight.

Leonard Lee passed away on October 23, 1976. *—Bryan Thomas*

Legendary Masters Series, Vol. 1 / Mar. 16, 1990 / EMI America ♦♦♦♦♦
The Sweethearts of the Blues were a ragged duo at best, with Shirley Goodman's intonation flying all over the place and Leonard Lee's droning baritone sounding unfazed no matter what was going on. But the duo also had a sound that was totally unique (if you've never heard them, then there's simply no one else that *sounds* like them) and produced one R&B hit after another, including the epochal "Let the Good Times Roll" and "I Feel So Good." This is a reissue of a reissue, Collectables' 1995 repackage of the original 1991 EMI Masters set on this New Orleans twosome, and it's a pip. If you dig New Orleans music, you gotta have this one for the collection. Weird, wild, and wonderful, just like the city it emanates from. *—Cub Koda*

The Legendary Master Series, Vol. 1 / 1995 / Collectables ♦♦♦♦♦
Shirley & Lee were responsible for a few enduring classics of New Orleans rock & roll, particularly "Let the Good Times Roll," which topped the R&B charts and crossed over to the pop Top 20 in 1956. Shirley Goodman's helium voice is simply unforgettable, and her partner, Leonard Lee, was a talented teenage songwriter. *The Legendary Master Series, Vol. 1* is a reissue of a deleted 1991 anthology, and contains all of the duo's Aladdin hits and more with extensive notes and annotation. Serious collectors may wish to seek out Bear Family's four-disc box set of Shirley & Lee's complete Aladdin recordings, but most buyers will be content with this excellent distillation. *—Greg Adams*

Sweethearts of the Blues / Mar. 18, 1997 / Bear Family ♦♦♦♦♦
Many folks only know New Orleans R&B through the teenage singing and songwriting duo of Shirley Goodman and Leonard Lee, who penned and recorded the definitive version of the most explosive party tune of all time (with the possible exception of "Great Balls of Fire" that came six years later), "Let the Good Times Roll." Given the fact that this box set is four CDs in length, anyone who believes that Shirley & Lee were mainly responsible for that smash hit alone have incomplete knowledge of the duo. Here are 113 performances that include all of their singles, outtakes, albums, and unreleased and rehearsal tracks, which serve not only as a chronology of the pair's contribution to the Crescent City's R&B tradition, but as a portrait of the studio scene and its players who were already changing musical history. This set has all the chapters of their "Sweethearts of the Blues" story on disc one and then gets deep into their scorching, risqué, utterly moving, and joyous R&B tracks. The "Sweethearts of the Blues" moniker was concocted by Aladdin, their label, as a way of getting regional fame based upon the success of their first single, "Sweethearts" and "I'm Gone." When they had the "Sweethearts" angle in place, Shirley & Lee began to write songs to match the chapters in a love affair. With "I'm Gone," the first chapter was written; next came "Shirley, Come Back to Me," which was followed by "Shirley's Back" (the alternate take of which is the better of the two), "So in Love," "The Time Has Come," "I Love You So," "The Proposal," and "Two Happy People," before Lee got sick of it and wrote "Lee Goofed." The folks in New Orleans and throughout the regional South followed the pair's antics on record and Aladdin's scheme worked. Shirley & Lee even had a stage routine to go with the songs! This set documents Shirley & Lee's regional successes and their gradual national buildup, which broke down popular culture's door nationwide with "Let the Good Times Roll." Finally, the appeal of the pair was noticed in terms of the raw excitement they provided. The record broke out of New Orleans like a rocket and didn't stop for years. DJs everywhere were playing the hell out of it until about 1960, four years after it was released! The pair's edgy, sharp voices enunciated perfectly above the crackling din of the Crescent City's finest musicians.

And that's the other part of the story—that many players, such as Dave Bartholomew (who first recorded them commercially), Earl Palmer, Alvin "Red" Tyler, Lee Allen, James Booker, Frank Fields, Herbert Hardesty, Wardell Quezergue, and many others played on dozens of these records. Bartholomew, Palmer, Tyler, and Allen appear on almost everything here! The cream of the crop in New Orleans backed these two singer/songwriters. And as a unit, the combination was unbeatable, as the Aladdin, Warwick, and Imperial sides all attest. Just check the deep horn section swing on "When I Saw You," or hear Allen check out of the stratosphere on "The Reason Why" and "Why Did I," or Booker's flailing arpeggios on "Honey Bee." When listening to this box, a foggy part of American musical history begins to reveal itself, the other side of the rock & roll coin that white American was obsessed with in Elvis, Jerry Lee Lewis, and fakes like Pat Boone and Frankie Avalon. This is the other side, a musically diverse and challenging catalog that drove black audiences wild all over America under the noises of white kids who would have flipped if they'd only had the opportunity to hear Shirley & Lee. New Orleans, being what it is, would probably have remained unchanged, but it might have gotten a different kind of attention for its musical wealth in the same way that Memphis did, where its musicians would be regarded as kings throughout the rest of the world—and not just among other musicians. But these are all big "ifs." Shirley & Lee created an atmosphere conducive to asking those kinds of questions while listening, but this collection does plenty more—for starters, it makes you get your damn shoes off, take your loved one in your arms, and begin to slip and shimmy all over the floor until.... There is no higher tribute for great R&B music than to inspire people to dance and to get busy, and this music certainly does that. *—Thom Jurek*

● **Let the Good Times Roll** / May 2, 2000 / Ace ♦♦♦♦♦
The track listing of this 30-song disc is based on the 1973 double-LP Shirley & Lee compilation in United Artists' *Legendary Masters* series, with "I Feel Good" substituted for "Do You Mean to Hurt Me So." Spanning their 1952-1959 work for Aladdin, it's comprehensive enough to serve as a best-of, particularly as it included the four songs that are by far their most famous cuts: "Let the Good Times Roll," "I'm Gone," "I Feel Good," and "Feel So Good." As the American best-of CD compilation *Legendary Masters* (issued first on EMI America, then on Collectables) has only 20 numbers, one might presume that this 30-track anthology has the edge. It doesn't make the *Legendary Masters* CD redundant, though, as *Legendary Masters* has seven songs that don't appear here. At any rate, *Let the Good Times Roll* will almost certainly be a sufficient overview of the duo's prime output for those who haven't picked up a Shirley & Lee greatest hits anthology yet. Truth to tell, for most listeners 30 Shirley & Lee songs is more than enough, as the accomplished, good-timey New Orleans R&B/rock groove gets pretty similar-sounding over the course of an hour-plus. One thing you could note is how the contrasting male-female duet style of Shirley & Lee was influential on early ska and reggae productions from Jamaica; listen to "Marry Me" for one instance in which Shirley & Lee themselves played calypso/Caribbean rhythms. It's also interesting to note that almost all of the material on this disc was self-penned, an impressive feat for teenage R&B singers of the '50s. *—Richie Unterberger*

J.D. Short

b. Feb. 26, 1902, Port Gibson, MS, **d.** Oct. 21, 1962, St. Louis, MO
Vocals, Harmonica / Prewar Country Blues, Acoustic Memphis Blues, Acoustic Blues
Gifted with a striking and almost immediately identifable vocal style characterized by an amazing vibrato, J.D. Short was also a very versatile musician. He played piano, saxophone, guitar, harmonica, clarinet, and drums. Growing up in the Mississippi Delta, Short learned guitar and piano. He was a frequent performer at house parties before he moved to St. Louis in the '20s. Short played with the Neckbones, Henry Spaulding, David "Honeyboy" Edwards, Douglas Williams, and Big Joe Williams from the '30s until the early '60s. He recorded for Vocalion, Delmark, Folkways, and Sonet. Short was in the 1963 documentary *The Blues*, but died before it was released. *—Ron Wynn*

Legacy of the Blues, Vol. 8 / 1962 / Sonet ♦♦♦

● **Stavin' Chain Blues** / Jul. 1965 / Delmark ♦♦♦♦♦
He could sing, wail, holler or moan traditional Delta blues with a lot of names that were much bigger. J.D. Short didn't make a lot of records, but the few he cut during the '30s should be heard over and over to truly appreciate their quality. *—Ron Wynn*

Siegel-Schwall Band

f. 1964, Chicago, IL, **db.** 1974
Group / Modern Electric Chicago Blues, Folk-Blues
Paul Butterfield and Elvin Bishop were not the only white dudes who formed a blues band in Chicago in the early '60s. Siegel and Jim Schwall formed the Siegel-Schwall Band in the mid-'60s in Chicago and worked as a duo playing blues clubs like Pepper's Lounge, where they were the house band. All of the great blues players would sit in—all the time. Corky Siegel played harp and electric Wurlizter piano, with an abbreviated drum set stashed under the piano; Jim Schwall played guitar and mandolin. Both sang.

Corky Siegel was born in Chicago on October 24, 1943; Jim Schwall was born on November 11, 1942, also in Chicago. Corky Siegel met Jim Schwall in 1964, when they were both music students at Roosevelt University—Schwall studying guitar, Siegel studying classical saxophone and playing in the University Jazz Big Band. Corky Siegel first became interested in the blues that same year. Schwall's background ran more to country and bluegrass. The Siegel-Schwall Band approach to music (and blues) was lighter than groups like Butterfield or Musselwhite, representing somewhat more of a fusion of blues and more country-oriented material. They seldom played at high volume, while stressing group cooperation and sharing the solo spotlight.

When the Butterfield band left their in gig at Big Johns on Chicago's North Side, it was the Siegel-Schwall Band that took their place. Signed by Vanguard scout Sam Charters in 1965, they released their first album in 1966, the first of five they would do with that label. Bass player Jack Dawson, formerly of the Prime Movers Blues Band joined the band in 1967.

In 1969 the band toured playing the Fillmore West, blues/folk festivals, and many club dates—one of several white blues bands that introduced the blues genre to millions of Americans during that era. They were, however, the first blues band to play with a full orchestra, performing "Three Pieces for Blues Band and Orchestra" in 1968 with the San Francisco Orchestra. The band signed later with RCA (Wooden Nickel) and produced five albums in the next several years. The band broke up in 1974.

In 1987, the band re-formed and produced a live album on Alligator, *The Siegel-Schwall Reunion Concert.* Jim Schwall is a university professor of music and lives in Madison, WI. Corky Siegel has been involved in many projects over the years that fuse classical music with blues, including his current group, Chamber Blues—a string quartet with a percussionist (tabla) and Siegel on piano and harmonica. And on rare occasions, the old band still gets together and performs. *—Michael Erlewine*

Siegel-Schwall Band / 1966 / Vanguard ✦✦✦

Their debut album is played a little too timidly to stand up to repeated listenings in today's noisy world, but their takes on Jimmy Reed's "Going to New York" and others are fascinating nonetheless. A different way of approaching any color blues, period. *—Cub Koda*

Say Siegel-Schwall / 1967 / Vanguard ✦✦✦✦

For all parties concerned, this was the group's breakthrough album. Corky Siegel's emotional harp work and foxy, sly (almost cutesy) vocals, coupled with a hot rhythm section and Jim Schwall's cardboard sounding acoustic with a pickup guitar work made this the one that connected big with White audiences. Some of it rocks, some of it boogies, some of it's downright creepy and eerie. Worth seeking out. *—Cub Koda*

Shake / 1968 / Vanguard ✦✦✦

Shake! was probably the group's second best album and certainly the one that came the closest to representing their live act. The major highlight is their take on Howlin' Wolf's "Shake for Me." Lots of fun and fireworks on this one, the sound of a band at the top of their game. *—Cub Koda*

Siegel-Schwall 70 / 1970 / Vanguard ✦✦✦

The group's fourth album, and their final one for Vanguard, showed them mildly progressing within the strictures of the blues format, although in large measure this was more of the same second-division white Chicago blues. There were some slight funk and soul influences in tunes like "Geronimo" and "Walk in My Mind," the latter of which has a psychedelic tinge both to the spacy lyrics and the wavering wordless vocal-harmonica effects heard at the end of the verses. The two live cuts, particularly "Angel Food Cake," captured their jittery take on the blues better than any of their Vanguard studio recordings. The most unusual offering, however, is "Song," which breaks out of the usual blues format with a gentle, hippyish rock ballad not far from the territory of the early work of Vanguard labelmates Country Joe & the Fish, complete with inventive electric piano. Far from being a failed departure, that cut's actually a highlight of this uneven set, which is weighed down by some pedestrian 12-bar blues. *—Richie Unterberger*

Siegel-Schwall Band / 1971 / Wounded Bird ✦✦✦

Sleepy Hollow / 1972 / Wounded Bird ✦✦✦

953 West / 1973 / Wounded Bird ✦✦✦

R.I.P. / 1974 / Wounded Bird ✦✦✦✦

Before the Siegel-Schwall Band decided to wrap things up, they released one more album, and it became one of their best. With their bountiful, down-on-the-farm blues sound led by Corky Siegel's harmonica, *R.I.P.* became an excellent sendoff for one of the most enjoyable groups ever to play this style of blues music. Most of the cuts belong to the band's favorite musicians and songwriters, but are wonderfully molded in the SSB's traditional style of rollicking piano riffs and greasy mandolin. "Take Out Some Insurance" kicks things off with a wallop, followed by a respectful cover of John Prine's "Pretty Good." Although the lyrics aren't exactly dead-on, the band's version of Little Richard's "I Can't Believe You Wanna Leave" fairs as one of the album's strongest tracks, and the background vocals on "Night Time's the Right Time" give the song its character as the band humorously tries to imitate a horn section. Little Walter's "Tell Me Mama" and Jimmy Reed's "You Don't Have to Go" are equally impressive, right down to Sheldon Plotkin's loosely knit percussion work, and the whistles and foot-stomping that fill the album's last track are proof that these guys weren't just another blues band. Every one of the Siegel-Schwall Band's albums have something to offer, but they really outdid themselves on *R.I.P.*, their farewell album. *—Mike DeGagne*

Three Pieces for Blues and Orchestra / 1973 / Polydor ✦✦

This is *not* an album—or a piece of music—to be neutral about. Collaborations between the high brow and the low down have always been dicey (anyone ever heard Albert King playing with a symphony orchestra?), but this one will definitely leave on one side of the debate or the other; either you'll hail it as the blues brought "uptown" or as an experiment gone terrible awry. *—Cub Koda*

Live Last Summer / 1974 / Wounded Bird ✦✦✦

The Best of Siegel Schwall / Dec. 1974 / Vanguard ✦✦✦✦

Vinyl best-of compilation that hits a few (but not all) of the high notes of their tenure with Vanguard Records. *—Cub Koda*

The Siegel-Schwall Reunion Concert / 1988 / Alligator ✦✦

The coziness the band always had on their good nights seems totally lost on this live radio broadcast. Proof positive that you can't go home again. File under "guess you had to be there." *—Cub Koda*

● **Where We Walked (1966–1970)** / 1991 / Vanguard ✦✦✦✦✦

A very nice, fairly thorough, compilation that supersedes the old vinyl collection on several levels; nice mastering, better notes, and nicer selection. For a basic introduction to their sound, this one's hard to beat. *—Cub Koda*

Wooden Nickel Years: 1971–1974 / May 18, 1999 / Varese Sarabande ✦✦✦✦

Subtitled "the Wooden Nickel years," these are the sides made between 1971 and 1973 for the RCA subsidiary. While the music the group made during this period was blues based, much of it can't really be called straight blues. But Siegel-Schwall always marched to the beat of a different drummer and just how different is collected up nicely here with everything from traditional blues ("Corrina," "Next to You," "Blues for a Lady," "[I Wish I Was on A] Country Road") to New Orleans funk ("Old Time Shimmy") to what can only be described as polka-blues ("Somethin's Wrong," "Sick to My Stomach") in the mix. Grab this one after you digest their earlier Vanguard sides for the full picture. *—Cub Koda*

The Complete Vanguard Recordings and More / Apr. 10, 2001 / Vanguard ✦✦✦

Is a three-CD set of the Siegel-Schwall Band—including all four of their Vanguard albums (spanning 1966-1970) in their entirety, along with six previously unissued cuts—too much to take at once? In a word, yes. If you're a blues-rock history nut, though—and there must be some such listeners out there—it is a handy collection that gathers every last shred of recorded evidence of their early years. In the Chicago-style '60s white blues sweepstakes, the group lagged way behind the Paul Butterfield Blues Band, an unavoidable reference point due to the similarity of approach and repertoire. Nor were they as good as Charlie Musselwhite or John Hammond, in part because of their vocal limitations, and also in part because of their lesser levels of virtuosity and imagination. They could, however, sometimes summon respectable raffish energy, particularly on the faster or more Bo Diddley-esque tunes, though the slow ones were usually pretty mundane. The highlights of this set are the moments when they do manage to break toward some more original territory, whether it's in the occasional use of mandolin, or the tentative psychedelic pop of the atypical "Song," from *Siegel-Schwall 70.* If you've heard the albums already, you'll be most interested in the half-dozen previously unreleased tracks, none of which are too great or different from most of their early work. These include two 1965 demos (one of them a cover of Howlin' Wolf's "Howlin' for My Darlin'"); two outtakes from their first Vanguard recording session in 1966; and two 1970 demos, the highlight of that pair being "Easy Rider," which has good slide work. The 12-page booklet, which contains some quotes from the band, is a plus; the absence of songwriter credits is a minus. *—Richie Unterberger*

Corky Siegel

b. Oct. 24, 1943, Chicago, IL

Vocals, Keyboards, Harmonica / Modern Electric Blues

The Siegel-Schwall Blues Band, with Corky Siegel, gained popularity when his band and Seiji Ozawa's Chicago Symphony Orchestra collaborated on William Russo's "Three Pieces for Blues Band and Orchestra" in 1968. The next year, he recorded with the New York Philharmonic. These projects led to Siegel's work for Alligator Records, *Corky Siegel's Chamber Blues.* It has been performed throughout America, at the Aspen Music Festival, Chicago's Orchestra Hall, and UCLA's Fine Arts Series. *—John Bush*

Corky Siegel / 1974 / Dharma ✦✦

● **Corky Siegel's Chamber Blues** / 1994 / Alligator ✦✦✦

Corky Siegel decided to return to solo recording in the early '90s, prompted by a few reunion concerts with his old partner, Jim Schwall. Instead of taking the easy way out and running through a few standards predictably, Siegel came up with his Chamber Blues project. As the title suggests, *Corky Siegel's Chamber Blues* fuses blues with classical music and blues. Specifically, it features a string quartet, Siegel on piano and harmonica, and a tabla player. It certainly sounds intriguing on paper, but it never quite gels, since it's always possible to visualize the scaffolding that supports the music. Still, Siegel proves himself to be more ambitious than the average blues musician, and more adventurous blues listeners may find this worth exploring at least once. *—Thom Owens*

Complementary Colors / Sep. 29, 1998 / Gadfly ✦✦✦

Solo Flight 1975–1980 / Sep. 14, 1999 / Gadfly ✦✦✦

Terrance Simien

b. Sep. 3, 1965, Eunice, LA

Vocals, Accordion / Zydeco

One of zydeco's most soulful vocalists and fieriest accordionists, Terrance Simien was also among the music's most pop-oriented artists, infusing his sound with elements of R&B, funk, gospel and reggae. Born September 3, 1965, in Eunice, LA, he first heard zydeco at local dances as a boy, but did not show any real interest in the music until it began growing in popularity during the early '80s. After learning the accordion and writing a handful of songs in collaboration with his brother Greg, Simien formed his first band; in the years to follow, he honed his chops in area zydeco clubs each weekend, working as a bricklayer during the day.

His big break arrived in 1984, when an appearance at the New Orleans World's Fair launched him to the attention of Paul Simon, with whom Simien recorded a cover of

Clifton Chenier's "You Used to Call Me." He also was tapped to appear in the feature film *The Big Easy*, writing and performing a song with star Dennis Quaid. With his band the Mallet Playboys, Simien made his full-length debut in 1990 with *Zydeco on the Bayou*; *There's Room for Us All* followed in 1993, and after a six-year recording hiatus he returned with *Positively Beadhead*. *—Jason Ankeny*

- **Zydeco on the Bayou** / 1990 / Restless ✦✦✦✦✦

A modern zydeco artist whose songs aren't yet in an essential category. More rock than zydeco, but lots of energy nonetheless. *—Ron Wynn & Jeff Hannusch*

There's Room for Us / Sep. 17, 1993 / Black Top ✦✦✦

Jam the Jazzfest [EP] / Apr. 7, 1998 / Tone-Cool ✦✦✦✦

Before the release of his third full-length album, Simien released this five-song EP. A tribute to his regular appearances at the New Orleans Jazz Fest, Terrance cooks up a potent groove on the title track. A medley of "Iko Iko/Brother John/Jambalaya" stretches out to almost seven minutes, followed by a great version of Dylan's "Baby Stop Crying." A great little zydeco instrumental, "Macque Choux," sets the stage for the closer, "May Your Music Live On," a tribute to John Delafose, one of Terrance's early influences. As always, the Mallet Playboys keep the groove steady and rocking throughout. As a stopping-off point between full length projects, this makes a wonderful appetizer. *—Cub Koda*

Positively Beadhead / May 4, 1999 / Tone-Cool ✦✦✦✦

A smooth and flowing disc that has many of the rough edges of his energy knocked off without diminishing that same energy. The passion is strong in his voice and there is a seasoned maturity that replaces the flaming rawness that reigned before. He is no longer the wild 20-something-year-old playing his accordion while doing black flips on stage, but he is presenting the songs (he wrote or co-wrote eight of the 12) in a total and much tighter fashion. This band has been with him for years and they are tight and playing better than ever, providing the support that allows him to take the chances he does. There also seems to be a real dedication to the family, happiness, and getting a handle on all of the twists and turns that life presents. Many of his songs seem to be reflections along these lines—from his beautiful love song "All Her Lovin'" to the thoughts and revelations expressed in "Grandma's House." Terrance Simien has always been more associated with a burst of sheer energy than playing with the subtleties of a song. *Positively Beadhead* is one of the finest zydeco discs to come down the pike in a long time, and it represents a giant step toward the bright future for this fine musician. *—Bob Gottlieb*

The Tribute Sessions / Jul. 10, 2001 / Aim ✦✦✦✦✦

This is honest and straight from the heart. Normally discs that have talking about the songs or the reasons for doing the songs will inspire many to pass over the spoken word. This is not the case here—it is partially Terrance's voice, his obvious love and veneration for these people, and the sincerity of these emotions that comes through (besides, some of these vignettes draw wonderful pictures). Most important is the material presented, and this is done with that energy and feeling for which this artist is known. He takes songs from those who have inspired and/or helped him, and are no longer living, and he does them in a way that is a tribute to the artist and the song. There are many surprises, some concerning the artists. Some concerning the songs he chooses by the artist may not be their best-known ones, however there is no surprise as to the quality of the music presented. He does such a fantastic job on Sam Cooke's "Rome Wasn't Built in a Day" that you may have trouble initially getting past it in on the disc, until you discover the gems following it. There is not a weak song here. This is that rare disc that transcends all genres of music and stands solid to repeated playing as it is music from the heart, and if anything only gets better and better. *—Bob Gottbieb*

Frankie Lee Sims

b. Apr. 30, 1917, New Orleans, LA, **d.** May 10, 1970, Dallas, TX

Vocals, Guitar / Juke Joint Blues, Electric Texas Blues

A traditionalist who was a staunch member of the Texas country blues movement of the late '40s and early '50s (along with the likes of his cousin Lightnin' Hopkins, Lil' Son Jackson, and Smokey Hogg), guitarist Frankie Lee Sims developed a twangy, ringing electric guitar style that was irresistible on fast numbers and stung hard on the downbeat stuff.

Sims picked up a guitar when he was 12 years old. By then, he had left his native New Orleans for Marshall, TX. After World War II ended, he played local dances and clubs around Dallas and crossed paths with T-Bone Walker. Sims cut his first 78s for Herb Rippa's Blue Bonnet Records in 1948 in Dallas, but didn't taste anything resembling regional success until 1953, when his bouncy "Lucy Mae Blues" did well in the South.

The guitarist recorded fairly prolifically for Los Angeles-based Specialty into 1954, then switched to Johnny Vincent's Ace label (and its Vin subsidiary) in 1957 to cut the mighty rockers "Walking With Frankie" and "She Likes to Boogie Real Low," both of which pounded harder than a ballpeen hammer.

Sims claimed to play guitar on King Curtis' 1962 instrumental hit "Soul Twist" for Bobby Robinson's Enjoy label, but that seems unlikely. It is assumed that he recorded for Robinson in late 1960 (the battered contents of three long-lost acetates emerged in 1985 on the British Krazy Kat label).

Sims mostly missed out on the folk-blues revival of the early '60s that his cousin Lightnin' Hopkins cashed in on handily. When he died at age 53 in Dallas of pneumonia, Sims was reportedly in trouble with the law due to a shooting incident and had been dogged by drinking problems. *—Bill Dahl*

- **Lucy Mae Blues** / 1970 / Specialty ✦✦✦✦

This collection of Sims' Specialty sides, primarily in a drums and electric guitar format, is pretty hard to beat. It combines all of the original singles, the extra tracks from his lone album plus unissued material and until further alternate takes come to light, the best overview of his tenure with the label. Some tracks are augmented with harmonica and/or string bass, but it's Frankie Lee's guitar and sly vocals that drive things along. Until his early Bluebonnet and later Ace material is cobbled together to complete the picture, this compilation is all you'll need. *—Cub Koda*

Henry "Son" Sims

b. Aug. 22, 1890, Anguilla, MS, **d.** Dec. 23, 1958, Memphis, TN

Fiddle / Delta Blues

Delta bluesman Henry "Son" Sims is best known as the fiddler who played with Charley Patton. Born in Anguilla, MS, in 1890, Sims was taught to play the violin by his grandfather, a former slave named Warren Scott. He eventually learned to play the mandolin, guitar, and piano, as well. Although he led a rural string band called the Mississippi Corn Shuckers for several years, the first recording that Sims did was with Patton, who asked him to come along to Wisconsin for a 1929 Paramount session. Sims also recorded under his own name on two separate occasions, during the Patton session when he cut four songs, including "Tell Me Man Blues," and several years later with guitarist and singer McKinley Morganfield (who later became known as Muddy Waters). *—Joslyn Layne*

Paul "Lil' Buck" Sinegal

b. Lafayette, LA

Guitar / Louisiana Blues, Zydeco

Paul "Lil' Buck" Sinegal is a true Louisiana guitarist in that he's played in several styles. He may be best known as a zydeco guitarist, having played and recorded with Clifton Chenier, Rockin' Dopsie, and Buckwheat Zydeco; he played on Paul Simon's *Graceland*. He also worked as a session guitarist for Excello on swamp blues by Slim Harpo and Lazy Lester, and has played straight blues and funk too. In the late '90s, Sinegal recorded a decent if non-trailblazing album for Allen Toussaint's NYNO label (on which Toussaint also played keyboards and produced) that gave a good idea of his wide-ranging abilities. *—Richie Unterberger*

- **Buck Starts Here** / Apr. 6, 1999 / NYNO ✦✦✦

In spite of Sinegal's zydeco credentials, this is a fairly straight blues album with faint or nonexistent traces of zydeco. Even the instrumental "Blues Into Zydeco" is more a hard-charging roadhouse number than something listeners would be likely to identify as a zydeco cut. Sinegal co-wrote much of the material with Allen Toussaint, and it has an easygoing feel that often incorporates rolling New Orleans funk and R&B rhythms, most obviously on Toussaint's "Line Dancer." Sinegal has a competent if undistinguished voice, plays well in a contemporary electric style that owes something to B.B. King, and throws in some instrumentals along the way. *—Richie Unterberger*

Hal "Cornbread" Singer

b. Oct. 8, 1919, Tulsa, OK

Sax (Tenor) / Jazz Blues, Jump Blues, Swing

Equally at home blowing scorching R&B or tasty jazz, Hal "Cornbread" Singer has played and recorded both over a career spanning more than half a century. Singer picked up his early experience as a hornman with various Southwestern territory bands, including the outfits of Ernie Fields, Lloyd Hunter, and Nat Towles. He made it to Kansas City in 1939, working with pianist Jay McShann (whose sax section also included Charlie Parker), before venturing to New York in 1941, and playing with Hot Lips Page, Earl Bostic, Don Byas, and Roy Eldridge (with whom he first recorded in 1944). After the close of the war, Singer signed on with Lucky Millinder's orchestra.

Singer had just fulfilled his life's ambition—a chair in Duke Ellington's prestigious reed section—in 1948, when a honking R&B instrumental called "Cornbread" that he'd recently waxed for Savoy as a leader began to take off. That presented a wrenching dilemma for the young saxist, but in the end, his decision to go out on his own paid off; "Cornbread" paced the R&B charts for four weeks and gave him his enduring nickname. Another of his Savoy instrumentals, "Beef Stew," also cracked the R&B lists.

Singer recorded rocking R&B workouts for Savoy into 1956 (the cuisine motif resulting in helpings of "Neck Bones," "Rice and Red Beans," and "Hot Bread"), working with sidemen including pianists Wynton Kelly and George Rhodes, guitarist Mickey Baker, bassist Walter Page, and drummer Panama Francis. One of his last dates for the firm produced the torrid "Rock 'n' Roll," which may have featured Singer as vocalist as well as saxist.

By the late '50s, Singer had abandoned rock & roll for a life as a jazz saxist. He recorded for Prestige in a more restrained manner in 1959, and stayed in that general groove. Singer relocated to Paris in 1965, winning over European audiences with his hearty blowing and engaging in quite a bit of session work with visiting blues and jazz luminaries. The old R&B fire flared up temporarily in 1990, when he cut *Royal Blue* for Black Top with boogie piano specialist Al Copley. *—Bill Dahl*

Blue Stompin' / Feb. 20, 1959 / Prestige/OJC ✦✦✦✦

This is a fun set of heated swing with early R&B overtones. The title cut is a real romp, with tenor saxophonist Hal Singer and trumpeter Charlie Shavers not only constructing exciting solos but riffing behind each other. With the exception of the standard "With a Song in My Heart," Singer and Shavers wrote the remainder of the repertoire, and with the assistance of a particularly strong rhythm section (pianist Ray Bryant, bassist Wendell Marshall and drummer Osie Johnson), there are many fine moments on this enjoyable set. Recommended. *—Scott Yanow*

Royal Blue / 1990 / Black Top ✦✦✦

There's no way that this collaboration between the veteran saxist and boogie piano specialist Al Copley could equal the searing power of Singer's late-'40s/early-'50s sides for Savoy; a few too many years had passed for Singer to play in the same searing fashion. But his jazzy riffs and Copley's keyboard antics are enjoyable enough in their own right. *—Bill Dahl*

- **Rent Party** / 1994 / Savoy ✦✦✦✦✦

Tenor saxophonist Hal Singer, who had a surprise hit with "Cornbread," which led to him leaving Duke Ellington's orchestra shortly after joining it (he had temporarily become more popular than Ellington), was a honker if not a screamer. His 16 R&B-ish sides that are reissued on this CD are full of spirited and joyfully repetitious tenor. Most of the chord changes are related to "Flying Home" or the blues, although Singer did sneak in a couple of ballads ("Indian Love Call" and "Easy Living"). Singer did not have any future hits that would quite equal "Cornbread" (a one-note blues that is the leadoff cut), but he remained a popular attraction on the R&B circuit for a decade. These jump sides (which also include such memorable numbers as "Hot Rod" and "Rock 'n' Roll") might be a bit lightweight compared to the bop music of the time, but they are quite fun. This is Hal Singer's definitive set. —*Scott Yanow*

T-Bone Singleton
b. New Orleans, LA
Guitar / Modern Electric Blues
Guitarist, singer, and songwriter T-Bone Singleton was born in New Orleans and grew up in Baton Rouge, where he still lives. In 1996, JSP Records of London released his debut recording, *Walkin' the Floor*, which represents some of his best songs over a ten-year period.

As a youth, T-Bone recalls seeing and hearing the old-style Southern swamp bluesmen like Silas Hogan and Guitar Kelly playing in local cafes, and musicians like Slim Harpo and Lightnin' Slim were also frequent performers in Baton Rouge juke joints. Singleton was raised on gospel and soul music and became interested in guitar after hearing his neighbor play, and he began playing a nylon-stringed acoustic guitar at 14. In high school, he worked nights with his father building cabinets, and it was on a job with his father that he got his first electric guitar and amplifier. Within months, he was playing guitar and bass in a gospel group and playing soul music with high school friends. Later, he began playing in clubs in north Baton Rouge until he was approached in the mid-'70s by Buddy Powell, who asked him to become the guitarist for his band, the Condors. The regional band toured the Gulf Coast for several years, playing blues, soul, and Top 20 hits until Powell quit to become musical director at Gloryland Baptist Church.

Singleton went on to become an ordained minister and has delivered numerous sermons since then, but he still has no full-time position as a pastor. Like many other bluesmen from the South, Singleton's style of blues guitar playing and singing is heavily gospel-oriented, and these days, he still plays local clubs in and around Baton Rouge and has made several appearances at the annual River City Blues Festival.

Walkin' the Floor is a small fraction of his output from the last ten years, and the ever-inventive songwriter and guitarist probably has another three albums worth of material ready to be recorded. Well-respected in Baton Rouge, Singleton's debut album was produced by blues guitarist and singer Larry Garner. —*Richard Skelly*

● **Walkin' the Floor** / Jun. 4, 1996 / JSP ✦✦✦

The Skunks
f. 1964, Milwaukee, WI
Group / Blues-Rock, Electric Chicago Blues
Guitarist Larry Lynne and keyboardist Rick Allen formed the Skunks in 1964, a short-lived band perhaps best known for recording a rare single for Chess Records with Sonny Boy Williamson, "Fanny Mae." Originally, Lynne led a Milwaukee-based band called the Bonnevilles. Allen joined the group when he was only 18, and the Bonnevilles toured the Midwest. Together, Lynne and Allen formed the Skunks in 1964 as somewhat of a gimmick. The members dyed their hair black and then added white stripes, making themselves resemble skunks. The gimmick didn't last long and the two went their respective ways, but the Skunks did manage to record a few singles in the Chicago area, including some work for Chess such as the rare Williamson single, "Fanny Mae." —*Jason Birchmeier*

Slo Leak
Group / Blues-Rock, Modern Electric Blues
Producer Danny Kortchmar (Billy Joel, Spin Doctors, Fabulous Thunderbirds), also a guitarist, decided to form his own blues band in the mid-'90s. Called Slo Leak, the band is composed of Kortchmar on guitar, ex-Paul Butterfield bassist Harvey Brooks, and vocalist/guitarist Charlie Karp.

For the purposes of their first album, *Slo Leak*, on Pure Records, out of Georgetown, CT, the trio used two drummers, Leroy Clouden and James Wormworth. Other musicians, most from the New York City area, include Steve Russell on harmonica, Rob Paparozzi on harmonica, Fred McFarlane on piano, and Chris Eminizer on tenor and baritone saxophones. Aside from working with Butterfield for many years, bassist Brooks also forged a reputation for his work with Bob Dylan and the Doors. Guitarist and vocalist Karp has recorded and toured with Buddy Miles, Aerosmith, Buster Poindexter, and Meatloaf.

The members of Slo Leak show some taste and knowledge of the idiom in the songs they cover, obscure gems like Willie Dixon's "I Cry for You," Lightnin' Hopkins' "Katie Mae," Bo Diddley's "You Don't Love Me," and Jimmy Liggins' "Drunk," but they do so in a '90s blues-rock fashion. The group's founders, Karp, Kortchmar, and Brooks, also throw in a few self-penned songs on their debut album. Unless this group is ready to tour, however, chances are their renown won't spread much beyond New York City and Westport, CT, where Kortchmar and much of the rest of the band are based. They returned in 1999 with *When the Clock Strikes 12*.—*Richard Skelly*

Slo Leak / Aug. 27, 1996 / Pure ✦✦✦

● **When the Clock Strikes 12** / 1999 / TVT ✦✦✦✦✦
With Danny Kortchmar on guitar and programming and Charlie Karp on guitar and vocals, this band moves roots music into the 21st century with a unique blend of nasty guitars, sampled everything, and attitude galore. The synthesis of the overdubs and samples on Jimmy Liggins' "Drunk" is worth the price of admission alone. Harvey Brooks makes an appearance on "When the Clock Strikes 12" and his own "The Man Who Gave Himself the Blues." Other big-ticket highlights include "If I Get Rich," "Big Bad Luck," and "Can't

Kill Me Twice," "Why," and "Stranger in Your Town." A whole new way to look at roots music for sure. —*Cub Koda*

Drink Small
b. Jan. 28, 1933, Bishopville, SC
Vocals, Guitar / Acoustic Blues, Soul-Blues, Electric Blues
The breadth of Drink Small's repertoire is fascinating in itself, but what's even more impressive is his depth as a performer in any of his chosen genres. His records may suddenly shift from a solo acoustic blues-guitar track to a smooth soul ballad with horns to who-knows-what, yet Small never seems to be caught out of place. He can be gruff and rough, clean and modern, or light and bouncy, altering his voice and guitar to suit the mood. Rated one of America's top gospel guitarists before he turned to blues in the late '50s, the South Carolina "Blues Doctor" for years had only one 45 on the market (Sharp, 1959). His discography has recently begun to grow considerably, finally revealing the extent of his songwriting and performing talents. —*Jim O'Neal*

I Know My Blues Are Different / 1976 / Southland ✦✦

● **The Blues Doctor** / 1990 / Ichiban ✦✦✦✦
Drink's own special blend of Delta, Chicago, and Carolina blues, it includes some band stuff, some solo stuff. Particularly wonderful is Drink's rich, gospel-influenced bass voice. A truly unique artist sharing his unique point of view, Drink includes a couple of saucy items ("Tittie Man" and "Baby, Leave His Panties Home") along with covers of "Little Red Rooster" and "Stormy Monday Blues." —*Niles J. Frantz*

Round Two / 1991 / Ichiban ✦✦✦
With more good stuff, it's much like the first. Highlights: the cautionary "D.U.I." and the funky "Don't Let Nobody Else." —*Niles J. Frantz*

Electric Blues Doctor Live / Mar. 1, 1994 / Mapleshade ✦✦✦

Bessie Smith
b. Apr. 15, 1894, Chattanooga, TN, **d.** Sep. 26, 1937, Clarksdale, MS
Vocals / Classic Jazz, Classic Female Blues
The first major blues and jazz singer on record and one of the most powerful of all time, Bessie Smith rightly earned the title of the "Empress of the Blues." Even on her first records in 1923, her passionate voice overcame the primitive recording quality of the day and still communicates easily to today's listeners (which is not true of any other singer from that early period). At a time when the blues were in and most vocalists (particularly vaudevillians) were being dubbed "blues singers," Bessie Smith simply had no competition.

Back in 1912, Bessie Smith sang in the same show as Ma Rainey, who took her under her wing and coached her. Although Rainey would achieve a measure of fame throughout her career, she was soon surpassed by her protégée. In 1920, Smith had her own show in Atlantic City and, in 1923, she moved to New York. She was soon signed by Columbia and her first recording (Alberta Hunter's "Downhearted Blues") made her famous. Bessie Smith worked and recorded steadily throughout the decade, using many top musicians as sidemen on sessions including Louis Armstrong, Joe Smith (her favorite cornetist), James P. Johnson, and Charlie Green. Her summer tent show Harlem Frolics was a big success during 1925-1927, and Mississippi Days in 1928 kept the momentum going.

However, by 1929 the blues were out of fashion and Bessie Smith's career was declining despite being at the peak of her powers (and still only 35). She appeared in *St. Louis Blues* that year (a low-budget movie short that contains the only footage of her), but her hit recording of "Nobody Knows You When You're Down and Out" predicted her leaner Depression years. Although she was dropped by Columbia in 1931 and made her final recordings on a four-song session in 1933, Bessie Smith kept on working. She played the Apollo in 1935 and substituted for Billie Holiday in the show *Stars Over Broadway*. The chances are very good that she would have made a comeback, starting with a Carnegie Hall appearance at John Hammond's upcoming From Spirituals to Swing concert, but she was killed in a car crash in Mississippi. Columbia has reissued all of her recordings, first in five two-LP sets and more recently on five two-CD box sets that also contain her five alternate takes, the soundtrack of *St. Louis Blues*, and an interview with her niece Ruby Smith the Empress of the Blues, based on her recordings, will never have to abdicate her throne. —*Scott Yanow*

☆ **The Collection** / 1989 / Columbia ✦✦✦✦✦
While there's no denying the importance and quality of Columbia/Legacy's *Complete Recordings* series, nine discs may seem a bit intimidating to the newcomer. *The Collection*, a mid-priced, 16-track collection that spans most of Smith's career, ultimately does a better service to the casual listener with a limited budget. This is probably the best introduction—undoubtedly many will seek out the more comprehensive packages afterward. —*Chris Woodstra*

☆ **The Complete Recordings, Vol. 1** / Apr. 9, 1991 / Columbia/Legacy ✦✦✦✦✦
In the '70s, Bessie Smith's recordings were reissued on five double LPs. Her CD reissue series also has five volumes (the first four are double-CD sets) with the main difference being that the final volume includes all of her rare alternate takes (which were bypassed on LP). The first set (which, as with all of the CD volumes, is housed in an oversize box that includes an informative booklet) contains her first 38 recordings. During this early era, Bessie Smith had no competitors on record and she was one of the few vocalists who could overcome the primitive recording techniques; her power really comes through. Her very first recording (Alberta Hunter's "Down Hearted Blues") was a big hit and is one of the highlights of this set along with "'Tain't Nobody's Bizness If I Do" (two decades before Billie Holiday), "Jail-House Blues," and "Ticket Agent, Ease Your Window Down." Smith's accompaniment is nothing that special (usually just a pianist and maybe a weak horn or two), but she dominates the music anyway, even on two vocal duets with her rival

Clara Smith. All of these volumes reward close listenings and are full of timeless recordings. *—Scott Yanow*

☆ **The Complete Recordings, Vol. 2 (1924–1925)** / Sep. 10, 1991 / Columbia/Legacy ✦✦✦✦✦

Bessie Smith, even on the evidence of her earliest recordings, well deserved the title "Empress of the Blues" for in the '20s there was no one in her league for emotional intensity, honest blues feeling, and power. The second of five volumes (the first four are two-CD sets) finds her accompaniment improving rapidly with such sympathetic sidemen as trombonist Charlie Green, cornetist Joe Smith, and clarinetist Buster Bailey often helping her out. However, they are overshadowed by Louis Armstrong, whose two sessions with Smith (nine songs in all) fall into the time period of this second set; particularly classic are their versions of "St. Louis Blues," "Careless Love Blues," and "I Ain't Goin' to Play Second Fiddle." Other gems on this essential set include "Cake Walkin' Babies from Home," "The Yellow Dog Blues," and "At the Christmas Ball." *—Scott Yanow*

The Complete Recordings, Vol. 3 / Sep. 22, 1992 / Columbia/Legacy ✦✦✦✦✦

On the third of five volumes (the first four are double-CD box sets) that reissue all of her recordings, the great Bessie Smith is greatly assisted on some of the 39 selections by a few of her favorite sidemen: cornetist Joe Smith, trombonist Charlie Green and clarinetist Buster Bailey. But the most important of her occasional musicians was pianist James P. Johnson who makes his first appearance in 1927 and can be heard on four duets with Bessie including the monumental "Back Water Blues." Other highlights of this highly recommended set (all five volumes are essential) include "After You've Gone," "Muddy Water," "There'll be a Hot Time in the Old Town Tonight," "Trombone Cholly," "Send Me to the 'Lectric Chair," and "Mean Old Bedbug Blues." The power and intensity of Bessie Smith's recordings should be considered required listening; even 70 years later they still communicate. *—Scott Yanow*

The Complete Recordings, Vol. 4 / Apr. 27, 1993 / Columbia/Legacy ✦✦✦✦✦

The fourth of five volumes (the first four are two-CD sets) that reissue all of Bessie Smith's recordings traces her career from a period when her popularity was at its height down to just six songs away from the halt of her recording career. But although her commercial fortunes might have slipped, Bessie Smith never declined and these later recordings are consistently powerful. The two-part "Empty Bed Blues" and "Nobody Knows You When You're Down and Out" (hers is the original version) are true classics and none of the other 40 songs (including the double entendre "Kitchen Man") are throwaways. With strong accompaniment during some performances by trombonist Charlie Green, guitarist Eddie Lang, Clarence Williams' band, and on ten songs (eight of which are duets) the masterful pianist James P. Johnson, this volume (as with the others) is quite essential. *—Scott Yanow*

The Complete Recordings, Vol. 5: The Final Chapter / Feb. 6, 1996 / Columbia/Legacy ✦✦✦✦✦

Bessie Smith cut 160 sides for the Columbia and OKeh labels between 1923 and 1933, and the four previous two-CD/cassette box sets of her complete recordings released in the '90s covered 154 of them, which introduces the question, what can a fifth two-CD/cassette box set contain in addition to the remaining six cuts? First, there are five previously unreleased alternate takes; second, there is the 15-minute low-fi soundtrack to the two-reel short *St. Louis Blues*, which constitutes the only film of Smith; and third, taking up all of the second CD/cassette, there are 72 minutes of interview tapes of Ruby Smith, Bessie Smith's niece, who traveled as part of her show. The box contains a "Parental Advisory—Explicit Lyrics" warning because of the nature of Ruby Smith's reminiscences. You won't learn much about Bessie Smith's music from her niece's remarks, but you will learn a lot about her sexual preferences. *—William Ruhlmann*

1923 / Nov. 19, 1996 / Classics ✦✦✦✦

This document of Smith's first year in the studio reveals a blues giant in full command of her talents. And while later dates—especially the epochal 1925 sessions with Louis Armstrong—offer more in the way of the era's horn-blowing royalty, these early sides nicely showcase Smith in the unadorned company of a variety of top pianists like Clarence Williams and Fletcher Henderson. The Empress of the Blues flexes her vocal muscle throughout, ranging from Broadway fare like "Baby Won't You Please Come Home" to the dark-hued rumblings of "Graveyard Dream Blues." She also revels in the provocative ambiguities of "Nobody in Town Can Bake a Sweet Jelly Roll" and puts her stamp on the future blues warhorse "'Tain't Nobody's Bizness if I Do." From the opening strain of her first best-seller, "Downhearted Blues," until the end of the disc, lovers of classic female blues will find plenty here to keep them enthralled. *—Stephen Cook*

1925–1927 / Nov. 19, 1996 / Classics ✦✦✦✦

The Empress of the Blues is heard here in all her prime from 1925-1927. While also touring the country in the Harlem Frolics tent show during this time, Smith laid down hundreds of tracks in New York studios. These 24 performances feature such jazz luminaries of the day as pianist Fletcher Henderson, trumpeter Joe Smith, trombonist Charlie Green, and clarinetist Buster Bailey (the latter three men all played in Henderson's groundbreaking band of the day). Also on hand are Gotham legend and pianist James P. Johnson and songwriter extraordinaire Clarence Williams (along with such '20s classics as "Royal Garden Blues," "Taint Nobody's Bizness if I Do," and "Everybody Loves My Baby," Williams penned a handful of the tracks covered here, including his collaboration with Fats Waller, "Just Squeeze Me"). Smith is powerful and in total command throughout, churning out her jazz-tinged blues on such standouts as "Backwater Blues," "The Gin House Blues," and "Hard Driving Papa." A must for all Smith devotees. *—Stephen Cook*

American Legends No. 14: Bessie Smith / 1996 / LaserLight ✦✦✦

Like other volumes in LaserLight's 20-album *American Legends* series, the Bessie Smith disc presents a miscellaneous collection of tracks with next-to-nothing in the way of annotation. Smith's catalog is controlled by Columbia Records, which seems to be the source for the 12 performances here, but they have been licensed from Rod McKuen's Stanyan Records and are attributed to "the collection of T. Richard Williams." In any case, such tracks as "'Tain't Nobody's Business" and "St. Louis Blues" are among Smith's classics, and at a $9.98 list price, it should be possible to obtain this album for much less than any of the Columbia/Legacy box sets. But for that you're only getting a taste of what is best experienced as a sumptuous meal. *—William Ruhlmann*

★ **The Essential Bessie Smith** / Aug. 27, 1997 / Columbia/Legacy ✦✦✦✦✦

Although there are a multitude of box sets chronicling Bessie's entire recorded career, this two-disc, 36-song set sweats it down to the bare essentials in quite an effective manner. Bessie could sing it all, from the lowdown moan of "St. Louis Blues" and "Nobody Knows You When You're Down and Out" to her torch treatment of the jazz standard "After You've Gone" to the downright salaciousness of "Need a Little Sugar in My Bowl." Covering a time span from her first recordings in 1923 to her final session in 1933, this is the perfect entry-level set to go with. Utilizing the latest in remastering technology, these recordings have never sounded quite this clear and full, and the selection—collecting her best-known sides and collaborations with jazz giants like Louis Armstrong, Coleman Hawkins, and Benny Goodman—is first-rate. If you've never experienced the genius of Bessie Smith, pick this one up and prepare yourself to be devastated. *—Cub Koda*

1929–1933 / Apr. 7, 1998 / Classics ✦✦✦✦

These 24 tracks represent the last phase of Bessie Smith's recording career. Over the course of ten years and 160 great songs, Smith had without a doubt earned her place as the Empress of the Blues. Unfortunately, until her passing in 1937, she spent most of her time on the show circuit. For fans hungry for a healthy dose of her legacy, though, generous discs such as this provide a chance to revel in the classic female blues singing queen's lusty power. As usual, Smith is helped out by the day's jazz royalty. Featured over the course of the cuts here—many penned by both Smith and pianist Clarence Williams—are such top soloists as Benny Goodman, Chu Berry, James P. Johnson, and Frankie Newton. Of course, Smith grabs most of the attention, especially on definitive sides like "Gimme a Pigfoot" and "Black Mountain Blues," not to mention the ribald gem "Need a Little Sugar in My Bowl." And as far as sound quality goes, this and many other of the discs in the Classics chronological series provide a viable alternative to Columbia's celebrated *Complete Recordings* line. *—Stephen Cook*

After You've Gone / Oct. 23, 2001 / Catfish ✦✦✦✦

When the Band sang "Bessie Smith" on *The Basement Tapes*, they eerily evoked the legend of the greatest classic blues singer. The depth of Bessie Smith's vocals, the myths that filled in her shadowy bio, and her early death combine to create a mythic figure. The 21 selections on *After You've Gone* find Smith once again battling no-good men, complaining about her empty bed, and trying to stay out of the jailhouse. After 70 years, "Downhearted Blues," "St. Louis Blues," and "Nobody Knows You When You're Down and Out" still sound superb, while the joyful ribaldry of "Empty Bed Blues, Pt. 1" and "Empty Bed Blues, Pt. 2," complete with coffee grinders and deep-sea divers, remains amusing. Smith sings a blues song like "T'Ain't Nobody's Bizness if I Do" from the point of view of a woman who's seen the world…and then some. In a few years, Billie Holiday, another singer with a bad case of the blues, would pick up the torch. The solo piano and jazz combos that accompany Smith on most of these recordings provide a nice backdrop for her vocals which, after all, are the main attraction. *After You've Gone* offers a nice introduction to the powerful, moving vocals of the Empress of the Blues. *—Ronnie D. Lankford Jr.*

Byther Smith

b. Apr. 17, 1933, Monticello, MS
Vocals, Guitar, Bass / Modern Electric Blues, Modern Electric Chicago Blues
Strictly judging from the lyrical sentiment of his recordings to this point, it might be wise not to make Chicago guitarist Byther Smith angry. Smitty's uncompromising songs are filled with threats of violence and ominous menace (the way blues used to be before the age of political correctness), sometimes to the point where his words don't even rhyme. They don't have to, either—you're transfixed by the sheer intensity of his music.

Smitty came to Chicago during the mid-'50s after spending time toiling on an Arizona cattle ranch. He picked up guitar tips from J.B. Lenoir (his first cousin), Robert Jr. Lockwood, and Hubert Sumlin, then began playing in the clubs during the early '60s. Theresa's Lounge was his main haunt for five years as he backed Junior Wells; he also played with the likes of Big Mama Thornton, George "Harmonica" Smith, and Otis Rush.

A couple of acclaimed singles for C.J. (the two-part "Give Me My White Robe") and BeBe ("Money Tree"/"So Unhappy") spread his name among aficionados, as did a 1983 album for Grits, *Tell Me How You Like It*. The rest of the country then began to appreciate Smitty, thanks to a pair of extremely solid albums on Bullseye Blues: 1991's *Housefire* (first out on Grits back in 1985) and *I'm a Mad Man* two years later. With two sets on Delmark and a stepped-up touring itinerary on the horizon, Smitty's really hit his stride. *—Bill Dahl*

Tell Me How Do You Like It / 1983 / Grits ✦✦✦✦✦

Fine guitar from this longtime Chicago bluesman, including four originals. *—Barry Lee Pearson*

Big Shot Smitty / Apr. 1986 / Mina ✦✦✦

Addressing the Nation With the Blues / 1989 / JSP ✦✦✦

Smith was so far outside the domestic blues loop that this Chicago-cut set only found release on a British logo, JSP. It was our loss—Smith is typically brusque and ominous, threatening to "Play the Blues on the Moon" and "Addressing the Nation With the Blues" as only he can. Nothing derivative about his lyrical muse—he's intense to the point of allowing his words not to rhyme to make his points, while his lead guitar work is inevitably to the point. —*Bill Dahl*

Housefire / 1991 / Bullseye Blues ✦✦✦
An unheralded gem that fell through the cracks during its initial issue in 1985 and definitely deserved its higher Bullseye Blues profile six years later. Except for a stinging cover of Detroit Junior's "Money Tree" that leads off, Smitty wrote the entire disc, and it's typically singular stuff: a paranoid "The Man Wants Me Dead," a promise to "Live on and Sing the Blues," all solidly backed by a sympathetic combo. —*Bill Dahl*

● **I'm a Mad Man** / 1993 / Bullseye Blues ✦✦✦✦✦
Smitty is unequivocally not mellowing with age. This set finds him physically threatening some poor slob in "Get Outta My Way" and generally living up to the beast of the title track. As his profile finally rises, Smith is receiving a little high-profile assistance—Ron Levy produced the set and handles keyboards, while the Memphis Horns add their punchy interjections wherever appropriate. —*Bill Dahl*

Mississippi Kid / 1996 / Delmark ✦✦✦

All Night Long / 1997 / Delmark ✦✦✦
Sporting a dozen Smith originals, *All Night Long* is also a showcase for his incendiary guitar skills. —*Jason Ankeny*

Smitty's Blues / Oct. 16, 2001 / Black & Tan ✦✦✦

Carrie Smith
b. Aug. 25, 1941, Fort Gaines, GA
Vocals / Blues Gospel, Jazz Blues
A blues belter in the classic tradition, Carrie Smith was born August 25, 1941, in Fort Gaines, GA. Despite making her debut at the 1957 Newport Jazz Festival while a member of a New Jersey church choir, she did not truly emerge on the jazz circuit until the early '70s, in the company of Big "Tiny" Little. In November of 1974, Smith's riveting performance as Bessie Smith (no relation) in Dick Hyman's Carnegie Hall production of *Satchmo Remembered* earned her fame throughout the international musical community. Soon, she began touring as a solo act, and in a short time began recording as well; still, despite subsequent performances in conjunction with the New York Jazz Repertory Orchestra, Tyree Glenn, and the World's Greatest Jazz Band, Smith remained little more than a cult figure in the U.S., proving better received in Europe.

While rooted firmly in the blues and gospel, she was a singer of considerable range and depth, as recordings like 1976's *Do Your Duty* and the following year's *When You're Down and Out* prove; despite never earning significant success, she remained an active figure both on stage and in the studio through the '90s. —*Jason Ankeny*

Do Your Duty / Jul. 26, 1976 / Classic Jazz ✦✦✦
Nice updated set of classic blues done in a strutting, assertive fashion by Carrie Smith. Smith, also a good singer in a jazzy vein, was among the few surviving female vocalists capable of doing authentic bawdy blues, and she shows how it's done throughout this date. —*Ron Wynn*

● **Confessin' the Blues** / Jul. 26, 1976-Jul. 19, 1977 / Evidence ✦✦✦✦✦
This CD reissues not only Carrie Smith's original hard-to-find *Black & Blue* LP, but six selections from two other sessions including three previously unissued alternate takes. Smith, who was coming into her own during this period, is in top form on a variety of vintage material ranging from Bessie Smith songs in the '20s to the '50s Ruth Brown hit "Mama He Treats Your Daughter Mean" and Big Bill Broonzy's "When I've Been Drinkin'." It is interesting to hear some of the altered lyrics, which have been changed to reflect a female rather than a male singing; "I Want a Little Boy" is the most obvious example. Most selections find Smith backed by a quartet that includes tenor saxophonist George Kelly and pianist Ram Ramirez, while a few of the added tracks have short spots for trumpeter Doc Cheatham and trombonist Vic Dickenson. This is one of the best Carrie Smith CDs currently available. —*Scott Yanow*

Fine and Mellow / Nov. 1976 / Audiophile ✦✦✦

Nobody Wants You / Apr. 23, 1977 / Black & Blue ✦✦✦
Smith, among the last surviving classic blues greats, shows how it's done on this set. She can sing bawdy, rocking tunes or turn slow and sentimental, and her voice hasn't lost its richness or impact over the years. —*Ron Wynn*

Carrie Smith / Oct. 1979 / West 54 ✦✦✦

Every Now and Then / Nov. 1993 / Silver Shadow ✦✦✦
This particular effort by singer Carrie Smith is more of an R&B date than a jazz session, despite the presence of such players as tenorman Houston Person, Jerome Richardson on reeds, and pianist James Williams (who alternates with Bross Townsend). Smith performs both jazz and R&B standards (this version of "Without a Song," despite what it says, is not the jazz tune) and infuses each interpretation with a strong dose of gospel and soul. Some of the performances are a bit trivial and obvious, with the background singers not adding much of value during their two appearances. An OK set, but of lesser interest to jazz listeners than some of Carrie Smith's earlier dates. —*Scott Yanow*

Gospel Time: The Definitive Black & Blue Sessions / Apr. 30, 2002 / Black & Blue ✦✦✦

Clara Smith
b. 1894, Spartanburg, SC, d. Feb. 2, 1935, Detroit, MI
Vocals / Classic Female Blues
One of the legendary unrelated Smith singers of the '20s, Clara Smith was never on Bessie's level or as significant as Mamie but she had something of her own to offer. She

began working on the theatre circuit and in vaudeville around 1910, learning her craft during the next 13 years while traveling throughout the South.

In 1923 Clara Smith came to New York and she recorded steadily for Columbia through 1932, cutting 122 songs often with the backing of top musicians (especially after 1925) including Louis Armstrong, Charlie Green, Joe Smith, Freddy Jenkins, and James P. Johnson (in 1929). Plus she recorded two vocal duets with Bessie Smith and four with Lonnie Johnson. She was billed as the "Queen of the Moaners," although Smith actually had a lighter and sweeter voice than her contemporaries and main competitors. She performed throughout the country (even appearing on the West Coast during 1924-1925) and in Harlem revues during her prime years. Clara Smith was active until shortly before her death in 1935 from heart failure at the age of 40. —*Scott Yanow*

Complete Recorded Works, Vol. 1 (1923-1924) / Nov. 21, 1995 / Document ✦✦✦✦✦
Complete Recorded Works, Vol. 2 (1924) / Nov. 21, 1995 / Document ✦✦✦✦✦
Complete Recorded Works, Vol. 3 (1925) / Nov. 21, 1995 / Document ✦✦✦✦✦
Complete Recorded Works, Vol. 4 (1926-1927) / Nov. 21, 1995 / Document ✦✦✦✦✦
Complete Recorded Works, Vol. 5 (1927-1929) / Nov. 21, 1995 / Document ✦✦✦✦✦
Complete Recorded Works, Vol. 6 (1930-1932) / Nov. 21, 1995 / Document ✦✦✦✦✦
● **Clara Smith: The Essential** / Aug. 7, 2001 / Classic Blues ✦✦✦✦✦

Funny Paper Smith (John T. Smith)
Vocals, Guitar / Prewar Blues, Acoustic Texas Blues
John T. "Funny Paper" Smith was a pioneering force behind the development of the Texas blues guitar style of the prewar era; in addition to honing a signature sound distinguished by intricate melody lines and simple, repetitive bass riffs, he was also a gifted composer, authoring songs of surprising narrative complexity. A contemporary of such legends as Blind Lemon Jefferson and Dennis "Little Hat" Jones, next to nothing concrete is known of John T. Smith's life; assumed to have been born in East Texas during the latter half of the 1880s, he was a minstrel who wandered about the panhandle region, performing at fairs, fish fries, dances, and other community events (often in the company of figures including Tom Shaw, Texas Alexander, and Bernice Edwards).

Smith settled down long enough to record some 22 songs between 1930 and 1931, among them his trademark number "Howling Wolf Blues, Pts. 1-2"; indeed, he claimed the alternate nickname "Howling Wolf" some two decades before it was appropriated by his more famous successor, Chester Burnett. (The true story behind Smith's more common nickname remains a matter of some debate—some blues archivists claim he was instead dubbed "Funny Papa," with the "Funny Paper" alias resulting only from record company error.) His career came to an abrupt end during the mid-'30s, when he was arrested for murdering a man over a gambling dispute; Smith was found guilty and imprisoned, and it is believed to have died in his cell circa 1940. —*Jason Ankeny*

● **The Howling Wolf (1930-1931)** / 1971 / Yazoo ✦✦✦✦✦
This is fine guitar-based Texas country blues by an artist completely unlike the later Howlin' Wolf. —*Mark A. Humphrey*

Complete Recorded Works (1930-1931) / 1991 / Document ✦✦✦✦
Document's *Complete Recorded Works (1930-1931)* offers an exhaustive overview of Funny Paper Smith's entire career, featuring all 22 sides he produced during the early '30s. Highlights are all over this disc, including the original "Howling Wolf Blues," "Tell It to the Judge," and the two-part "Seven Sisters Blues." However, there are also quite a few alternate takes, which will make it more of a chore to get through for casual listeners. The features that make it appealing to academics—long running time, exacting chronological sequencing, poor fidelity (all cuts are transferred from original acetates and 78s), and an exhaustive number of performances—will likely impair its overall listenability for most audiences. —*Thom Owens*

True Texas Blues / 1995 / Collectables ✦✦✦

George Harmonica Smith
b. Apr. 22, 1924, Helena, AR, d. Oct. 2, 1983, Los Angeles, CA
Vocals, Harmonica / Juke Joint Blues, Harmonica Blues, Electric Harmonica Blues, Electric Blues
George Smith was born on April 22, 1924, in Helena, AR, but was raised in Cairo, IL. At age four, Smith was already taking harp lessons from his mother, a guitar player and a somewhat stern taskmaster—it was a case of get it right or else. In his early teens, he started hoboing around the towns in the South and later joined Early Woods, a country band with Early Woods on fiddle and Curtis Gould on spoons. He also worked with a gospel group in Mississippi called the Jackson Jubilee Singers.

Smith moved to Rock Island, IL, in 1941 and played with a group that included Francis Clay on drums. There is evidence that he was one of the first to amplify his harp. While working at the Dixie Theater, he took an old 16mm cinema projector, extracted the amplifier/speaker, and began using this on the streets.

His influences include Larry Adler and later Little Walter. Smith would sometimes bill himself as Little Walter Jr. or Big Walter. He played in a number of bands including one with a young guitarist named Otis Rush and later went on the road with the Muddy Waters Band, after replacing Henry Strong.

In 1954, he was offered a permanent job at the Orchid Room in Kansas City where, early in 1955, Joe Bihari of Modern Records (on a scouting trip), heard Smith, and signed him to Modern. These recording sessions were released under the name Little George Smith, and included "Telephone Blues" and "Blues in the Dark." The records were a success.

Smith traveled with Little Willie John and Champion Jack Dupree on one of the Universal Attractions tours. While on the tour, he recorded with Champion Jack Dupree in November of 1955 in Cincinnati, producing "Sharp Harp" and "Overhead Blues." The tour ended in Los Angeles and Smith settled down—spending the rest of his life in that city.

In the late '50s he recorded for J&M, Lapel, Melker, and Caddy under the names Harmonica King or Little Walter Junior. He also worked with Big Mama Thornton on many shows.

In 1960, Smith met producer Nat McCoy, who owned the Sotoplay and Carolyn labels, with whom he recorded ten singles under the name of George Allen. In 1966, while Muddy Waters was on West Coast, he asked Smith to join him and they worked together for a while, recording for Spivey Records.

Smith's first album on World Pacific, *A Tribute to Little Walter*, was released in 1968. In 1969 Bob Thiele produced an excellent solo album of Smith on BluesWay, and later made use of Smith as a sideman for his Blues Times label, including sets with T-Bone Walker, and Harmonica Slim. Smith met Rod Piazza, a young white harp player and they formed the Southside Blues Band, later known as Bacon Fat.

In 1969, Smith signed with U.K. producer Mike Vernon, whose Blue Horizon label released the *No Time for Jive* album in 1970. Smith was less active in the '70s, appearing with Eddie Taylor and Big Mama Thornton. Around 1977, Smith became friends with William Clarke, and they began working together. Their working relationship and friendship continued until Smith died on October 2, 1983.

William Clarke, Smith's protégé, writes, "He had a technique on the chromatic harp where he would play two notes at once, but one octave apart. He would get an organ-type sound by doing this. George really knew how to make his notes count by not playing too much and taking his time by letting the music unfold easily. He could also swing like crazy and was a first-class entertainer. I have heard from a friend that they had seen George Smith in the '50s playing a club in Chicago, tap dancing around everybody's drinks on top of the bar while playing his harp."

"I have been with him in church and seen him play amplified harmonica by himself. This was very soulful. I have never heard George play a song the same way twice. He was very creative and played directly from his heart. He admired all great musicians but had his own sound and style. He was a true original. Mr. Smith would always give 100 percent on stage whether or not there were 1 or 1,000 people listening. This was his performing style, *always*."

"George Smith greatly admired harmonica player Larry Adler, and although Adler used the octave technique on the harp also, George really was the one that developed this to its full potential. Before Mr. Smith, nobody in blues had used this octave technique. An extremely kind and gentle man, George always went all out to help other harmonica players. Everybody liked George Smith. He played a huge role in advancing blues harmonica and should never be forgotten. You can hear the influence of George Smith in most everyone playing blues harmonica today, whether directly or indirectly. He also was a great blues singer. He had a huge baritone voice that conveyed great emotion and soulfulness."

Recommended Smith recordings include *Blowin' the Blues* (1960) on P-Vine, *A Tribute to Little Walter* (1968) on Liberty, *No Time for Jive* (1970) on Blue Horizon, *Of the Blues* (1973) reissued on Crosscut Records, and *Little George Smith* (1991) on Ace Records. *—Michael Erlewine*

A Tribute to Little Walter / 1968 / World Pacific ✦✦✦✦✦

The L.A. harp ace pays tribute to one of his peers and influences with a well-conceived set of Little Walter covers. *—Bill Dahl*

No Time for Jive / 1970 / Blue Horizon ✦✦✦

Laidback L.A. session from 1969 produced by Mike Vernon for his Blue Horizon label that's dominated by a mellow feel. There are a few upbeat items—"Before You Do Your Thing (You'd Better Think)" and "Soul Feet"—but mostly George sits back and blows with a relaxed ease. His sidemen include guitarists Pee Wee Crayton and Marshall Hooks, pianist J.D. Nicholson, and drummer Richard Innes. *—Bill Dahl*

Arkansas Trap / 1971 / Deram ✦✦

George Smith of the Blues / 1973 / BluesWay ✦✦✦

Blowing the Blues / 1979 / El Segundo ✦✦✦

These were culled from sessions from 1956 to 1966 and 1978, and originally recorded for local labels J&M, Sotoplay, Carolyn, and Hittin' Heavy. Although this material taps the depths of Smith's mastery, little care was done to digitally clean up these cuts. Just as shameful are that some of the personnel is unknown, as they serve up some tasty morsels. Al Bedorsian (later associated with Robert Lucas' Luke and the Locomotives) and William Clarke join on the 1978 session. Smith's gab for songwriting needs more notice, as "Rope This Twist," influenced by Chubby Checker's "Do the Twist," is more like a one-up on that popular favorite, going with complex instrumental layering, yet keeping a danceable feel. *—Char Ham*

Oopin' Doopin' Doopin' / 1991 / Ace ✦✦✦

● **Harmonica Ace: The Modern Masters** / 1993 / Flair ✦✦✦✦✦

Smith cut these sides for Joe Bihari of Modern Records shortly after he left the Muddy Waters Band in the early '50s. He is featured here with a rhythm section framed by horns arranged by the legendary and prolific Maxwell Davis. Smith's innate sense of drive and swing, coupled with his rich and diverse palette of texture and tone, truly place him in the very first rank of modern harp masters. This disc is aptly described by note-writer Ray Topping as "a lasting memorial to one of the last great harp players of the postwar blues scene." *—Larry Hoffman*

Now You Can Talk About Me / Sep. 29, 1998 / Blind Pig ✦✦✦✦✦

A collection of middle- and late-period Smith with the harmonica genius' '60s sides for the microscopic imprint Sotoplay sampled here with the first five cuts. The remainder of the album is the 1982 session for the Murray Brothers label with Rod Piazza behind the board that produced the *Boogie'n With George* album with the addition of the previously unreleased "Last Chance," and a powerful instrumental slow burner. Junior Watson shines on guitar on these tracks and Smith's tone is big, fat, rich and full of ideas galore on tunes like "Bad Start," "Astatic Stomp," "Sunbird," and the title track. But Smith's use of a chromatic will strike most blues mavens as something unique and out of the ordinary as he tackles such standards as "I Left My Heart In San Francisco" and "Peg O'My Heart" with considerable élan, imparting both with a bluesy feel that Jerry Murad and the Harmonicats could only envision. If you like great blues harmonica playing, you're going to *love* this one. Add Smith's name to the list of all-time greats near the top with this one. *—Cub Koda*

Huey "Piano" Smith

b. Jan. 26, 1934, New Orleans, LA

Songwriter, Piano / New Orleans R&B, R&B

Huey "Piano" Smith was an important part of the great New Orleans piano tradition, following in the footsteps of Professor Longhair and Fats Domino to take his place among the Crescent City's R&B elite. He was also one of R&B's great comedians, his best singles matching the Coasters for genial, good-time humor, although his taste often ran more towards nonsense lyrics. Smith's sound was too earthy to match the pop crossover appeal of Domino or the Coasters, which limited his exposure, and he couldn't match the latter's amazing consistency, lacking their reliable supply of material. But at the peak of his game, Smith epitomized New Orleans R&B at its most infectious and rollicking, as showcased on his classic signature tune "Rockin' Pneumonia and the Boogie Woogie Flu."

Huey Smith was born in New Orleans on January 2, 1934, and began playing the piano at age 15. At the dawn of the '50s, Smith backed New Orleans guitar legends Earl King and Guitar Slim, and quickly became a popular session pianist, playing on records by the cream of the New Orleans R&B scene: Smiley Lewis (the classic "I Hear You Knockin'"), Lloyd Price, and Little Richard. During the mid-'50s, Smith began leading his own band, the Clowns, which usually featured popular local blues singer and female impersonator Bobby Marchan on lead vocals. Smith & the Clowns signed with the Ace label and scored a breakout Top Five R&B hit in 1957 with "Rockin' Pneumonia and the Boogie Woogie Flu," which despite becoming a classic rock & roll standard didn't even make the pop Top 40, thanks to reticent white radio programmers. The following year, Smith scored his biggest hit with the double-sided smash "Don't You Just Know It"/"High Blood Pressure," which reached the pop Top Ten and the R&B Top Five. In 1959, Smith cut the original tune "Sea Cruise," and seeking pop radio airplay, Ace had white teenage R&B singer Frankie Ford overdub his own vocal onto Smith's backing track; the result became a nationwide hit.

Smith cut a few novelty numbers in an attempt to duplicate the success of "Rockin' Pneumonia," some even using the same type of illness joke ("Tu-Ber-Cu-Lucas and the Sinus Blues," for example). It didn't work, and Marchan left the Clowns after scoring a solo hit with "There Is Something on Your Mind" in 1960; he was replaced by female singer Gerri Hall and male vocalist Curley Moore. Smith switched briefly to the Imperial label, then returned to Ace for one last chart single in 1962, "Pop Eye." Smith spent part of the '60s recording for Instant and touring not only with the Clowns, but alternate groups the Hueys and the Pitter Pats as well. Unable to return to the charts, he eventually converted to the Jehovah's Witnesses and left the music industry permanently. *—Steve Huey*

Having a Good Time / 1959 / Edsel ✦✦✦✦✦

A straight-up reissue of Huey's debut album. No collection of leftovers here, this original 12 song collection featured the hits "Rockin' Pneumonia and the Boogie Woogie Flu," "High Blood Pressure," and "Don't You Just Know It" along with Crescent City favorites like "Little Liza Jane," "Don't You Know Yockomo," "Just A Lonely Clown," and Bobby Marchan's "Little Chickee Wah Wah." As a budget-priced collection, this one's hard to turn down. An essential building block for any New Orleans collection. *—Cub Koda*

'Twas the Night Before Christmas / 1962 / West Side ✦✦✦✦

One of the most unique Christmas holiday albums of all time, this was recorded in 1962, after Smith's small string of hits and the departure of lead singer/secret weapon Bobby Marchan from the ranks. But the band kept rockin' and the vocals are ably handled on this disc by Gerri Hall, "Scarface" John Williams and even Huey himself on the title cut. Six of the ten songs from the original album were written by Smith, and tracks like "Happy New Year," "Almost Time for Christmas" and "White Christmas Blues" closely mirror the melodies and arrangements for some of his better known hits like "We Like Birdland," "For Cryin' Out Loud," and "Little Liza Jane." Even old standbys like "Jingle Bells" and "Silent Night" get the Crescent City groove applied to them here. Adding guitar to the Clowns' regular sax- and piano-dominated New Orleans sound is Mac Rebennack, who also chimes in vocally on "Doing the Santa Claus." To bring the CD to a respectable length, the instrumental tracks to eight of the ten tracks are tagged on to the end and even as band track extras, these sound just fine. A disc of Christmas cheer, New Orleans style. *—Cub Koda*

Rock & Roll Revival / Jan. 1991 / Ace ✦✦✦✦✦

A terrific 16-track collection of Huey "Piano" Smith & the Clowns' biggest hits and best material, including "Rocking Pneumonia" and "Don't You Just Know It," plus a couple of fine previously unreleased tracks. *—Stephen Thomas Erlewine*

Having a Good Time With Huey "Piano" Smith & His Clowns / 1997 / West Side ✦✦✦✦✦

Next to Professor Longhair and Fats Domino, no one better typified the New Orleans piano style than the work of Huey "Piano" Smith. This 24-track, single-disc compilation is the first proposed installment of Huey & the Clowns' tenure with the Jackson, MS-based Ace label, home to his biggest hits. Kicking off with the first and second parts of his first hit, "Rockin' Pneumonia and the Boogie Woogie Flu" (although the second part used here seems one overdub away from the single version issued), more obscure but equally worthwhile items like "Little Liza Jane," "Just a Lonely Clown," "Would You Believe It (I Have a Cold)," and "She Got Low Down" sit comfortably next to the hits ("High Blood Pressure," "Don't You Just Know It," "Tu-Ber-Cu-Lucas and the Sinus Blues," "Don't You Know Yockomo," and "Pop-Eye"), making this volume a perfect introduction to the music of this Crescent City genius. Transfers are as crisp as you could ask for, and the packaging and liner notes are equally fine. —*Cub Koda*

● **This Is Huey Piano Smith** / Apr. 21, 1998 / Music Club ✦✦✦✦✦
For years, Huey "Piano" Smith lacked a comprehensive overview of his recording career, and no compilation ever appeared on CD in the United States. The budget-line label Music Club rectified that situation in 1998 with the release of *This is Huey Piano Smith*, an 18-track collection that features all of his hit singles for Ace plus several failed singles and New Orleans staples. Smith's hits and standards—"Rockin' Pneumonia and the Boogie Woogie Flu," "Don't You Just Know It," "High Blood Pressure," "Pop-Eye," the original version of "Sea Cruise," with his vocals instead of Frankie Ford's—are so good that it's an inevitable disappointment to find many of the songs here are blatant attempts to get back on the charts ("Tu-Ber-Cu-Lucas and the Sinus Blues," "Would You Believe It [I Have a Cold]"). These fall flat, as do a couple of the other cuts, but unfortunately, that's an accurate portrait of Smith's career—he had a handful of wonderful, essential songs and was a hell of a performer, but he wasn't a consistent hitmaker. Nevertheless, the strong stuff is so good—even essential—that this is still highly recommended for New Orleans R&B fans and R&B fans in general.—*Stephen Thomas Erlewine*

Havin' Fun With Huey "Piano" Smith: More of the Best / Mar. 3, 1999 / West Side ✦✦✦✦
The second part of Ace Records combing through their Huey "Piano" Smith vault, *More of the Best* includes 24 tracks of new-to-disc songs and unreleased recordings, with vocalists including Bobby Marchan and Curley Moore, as well as Smith himself. —*Keith Farley*

That'll Get It: Even More of the Best / Aug. 24, 1999 / West Side ✦✦✦✦
The third volume of West Side's retrospective into the music of Huey "Piano" Smith yields even more amazing treasures. It seems as if Huey never stopped recording and recording in every conceivable configuration it seems, as sideman, leader, songwriter, backing up young singing hopefuls, and beyond. With the advent of recording band tracks separately from vocals (the beginnings of stereo recording), label owner Johnny Vincent could take Huey's old tracks and try new vocals on them and in many cases that's what we have here. But also along the way are another brace of Ace and related label singles and album tracks that go just that further in making the case for Huey being one of the most influential and prolific of all New Orleans musicians. Not the place to start your Huey "Piano" Smith collection, but definitely not a bad place to end up. —*Cub Koda*

For Dancing / Sep. 28, 1999 / Edsel ✦✦✦

Mamie Smith

b. May 26, 1883, Cincinnati, OH, **d.** Aug. 16, 1946, New York, NY
Vocals / Classic Female Blues
Though technically not a blues performer, Mamie Smith notched her place in American music as the first black female singer to record a vocal blues. That record was "Crazy Blues" (recorded August 10, 1920), which sold a million copies in its first six months and made record labels aware of the huge potential market for "race records," thus paving the way for Bessie Smith (no relation) and other blues and jazz performers. An entertainer who sported a powerful, penetrating, feminine voice with belting vaudeville qualities, as opposed to blues inflections, Smith toured as a dancer with Tutt-Whitney's Smart Set Company in her early teens, and sang in Harlem clubs before World War I. Smith's pioneering recording session was an accident, since she was filling in for Sophie Tucker, but the success of the record made her wealthy.
    Soon thereafter, Smith began touring and recording with a band called the Jazz Hounds, which featured such jazz notables as Coleman Hawkins, Bubber Miley, Johnny Dunn, and more, and she toured with the bands of Andy Kirk and Fats Pichon in the '30s. She appeared in several films, including *Paradise in Harlem* late in her life (1939). She recorded several sides for OKeh during her heyday; one unissued take of "My Sportin' Man" is included on Columbia's *Roots N' Blues Retrospective 1925-1950* box set. In the '80s, all of her recordings were reissued on LP by the imported Document label. —*Richard S. Ginell*

● **Complete Recorded Works, Vol. 1** / 1995 / Document ✦✦✦✦✦
This first volume of a five-volume import set of her complete recordings features her earliest and best sides, including the classic "Crazy Blues." —*Cub Koda*

Complete Recorded Works, Vol. 2 (1921–1922) / 1995 / Document ✦✦✦✦

Complete Recorded Works, Vol. 3 / 1995 / Document ✦✦✦✦

Complete Recorded Works, Vol. 4 / 1995 / Document ✦✦✦✦

Pinetop Smith (Clarence Smith)

b. Jun. 11, 1904, Troy, AL, **d.** Mar. 15, 1929, Chicago, IL
Vocals, Piano / Boogie-Woogie, Piano Blues
One of the driving forces behind the advent of boogie-woogie piano, Clarence "Pinetop" Smith ranks among the most influential blues figures of the '20s. Born January 11, 1904, in Troy, AL, he was raised in nearby Birmingham; a self-taught player, he began performing at area house parties while in his mid-teens, and after relocating to Pittsburgh accompanied Ma Rainey and Butterbeans & Susie. On the advice of fellow pianist "Cow Cow" Davenport—himself a seminal figure in boogie-woogie's development—Smith relocated to Chicago in 1928, where he lived in the same apartment house as Meade "Lux" Lewis and Albert Ammons, conditions that resulted in frequent all-night jam sessions; there, he also made a name for himself on the city's house-rent party and club circuits.
    While boogie-woogie's exact origins are a mystery, Smith's energetic "Pine Top's Boogie Woogie" (cut during his first Vocalion label sessions in 1928) marked the first known use of the phrase on record, and its lyrics—a cry of "Hold it now/Stop/Boogie woogie!"—became the template for any number of subsequent piano tunes. Another

recording session followed in early 1929, but just weeks later, on March 15, Smith's bright career came to an abrupt halt when he was shot and killed by a stray bullet during a dancehall fracas; he was just 25 at the time of his death, leaving behind a legacy of only 11 recorded tracks. —*Jason Ankeny*

● **Pine Top Smith (With Jelly Roll Morton)** / 1950 / Brunswick ✦✦✦

Tab Smith (Talmadge Smith)

b. Jan. 11, 1909, Kingston, NC, **d.** Aug. 17, 1971, St. Louis, MO
Sax (Alto) / Jump Blues, Swing
Tab Smith's career can easily be divided into two. One of the finest altoists to emerge during the swing era, Smith became a popular attraction in the R&B world of the '50s due to his record "Because of You." After early experience playing in territory bands during the '30s, Tab Smith played and recorded with Lucky Millinder's Orchestra (1936-1938) and then freelanced with various swing all-stars in New York. He had opportunities to solo with Count Basie's band (1940-1942) before returning to Millinder (1942-1944), and took honors on a recording of "On the Sunny Side of the Street" with a stunning cadenza that followed statements by Coleman Hawkins, Don Byas, and Harry Carney.
    After leaving Millinder, Smith led his own sessions which became increasingly R&B-oriented (he never became involved with bop). His string of recordings for United in the '50s (which have been reissued by Delmark on CD) made him a fairly major name for a time even though he had a relatively mellow sound and avoided honking. In the early '60s Tab Smith retired to St. Louis and later became involved in selling real estate. —*Scott Yanow*

Joy at the Savoy / May 10, 1944-May 18, 1954 / Saxophonograph ✦✦✦
Stalwart '40s and '50s swing and honking sax cuts. —*Ron Wynn*

I Don't Want to Play in the Kitchen / May 10, 1944-1956 / Saxophonograph ✦✦✦✦✦
Tab Smith made his first solo recordings shortly after leaving Lucky Millinder's band, and they're collected on the fine *I Don't Want to Play in the Kitchen*. The material on the album features Smith running through a number of different bands and vocalists—including Trevor Bacon, Robbie Kirk, and Betty Mays—but, throughout it all, the distinguishing factor is his lovely saxophone, which sounds warm and appealing even on these swinging jump blues numbers. —*Leo Stanley*

● **Jump Time** / Aug. 28, 1951-Feb. 26, 1952 / Delmark ✦✦✦✦✦
Altoist Tab Smith, who first gained recognition with Count Basie's orchestra in the mid-'40s, became an unexpected R&B star in the early '50s, thanks in large part to his hit version of "Because of You." Between 1951-1957, Smith recorded 90 songs for the United Record Company, of which only 48 were issued. Delmark, in their CD reissue series, came out with all of the music in chronological order. This first release has the initial 20 (including the hit), and Tab Smith sounds fine on the sweet ballads, blues, and concise jump tunes. The backup crew includes trumpeter Sonny Cohn, tenor Leon Washington, and either Lavern Dillon or Teddy Brannon on piano. —*Scott Yanow*

Because of You / Aug. 28, 1951-1955 / Delmark ✦✦✦
This LP, which has a dozen of altoist Tab Smith's better recordings for the United label, has been superceded by Delmark's CD reissue series which will eventually include all 90 of Smith's sides. This best-of set does have more than its share of enjoyable ballads, blues, novelties and jump tunes from Smith, who had a big commercial hit in 1951 with "Because of You." Commercial but enjoyable music. —*Scott Yanow*

Ace High / Feb. 26, 1952-Apr. 23, 1953 / Delmark ✦✦✦✦
During 1951-1957, Tab Smith recorded extensively for the United label, and although he was initially popular (due to the hit record "Because of You"), nearly half of the 90 titles he cut went unissued. Delmark's second Tab Smith release has 20 selections, including five songs being released for the first time. Smith, a former swing stylist who was best known in the R&B market during the '50s, was not a honker like many others in the genre, and his mixture of relatively gentle stomps and ballads is appealing. The distinctive altoist (who takes four vocals) is often joined by Sonny Cohn (mistakenly listed as "Sammy Cohn") or Irving Woods on trumpet and Leon Washington or Charlie Wright on tenor, along with a rocking rhythm section, on four complete sessions from 1952-1953. Fun if not essential music. —*Scott Yanow*

Top 'n' Bottom / Nov. 17, 1953-Aug. 26, 1954 / Delmark ✦✦✦
The third CD volume of altoist Tab Smith's United recordings features 21 selections, 14 of which had never been released before. The music ranges from Johnny Hodges-type small-group stomping swing and R&B-ish jump sides to sentimental ballads and a few vocal numbers (featuring unidentified singers). Among the personnel are trumpeter Irving Woods, pianist Teddy Brannon, and drummer Walter Johnson. Accessible and fairly creative jazz, conservative for the early '50s but still quite enjoyable. —*Scott Yanow*

Red, Hot and Cool Blues / 195 / United ✦✦✦
Alto saxophonist Tab Smith, along with many other instrumentalists who got their starts in the swing era, decided against playing bop and instead helped forge a new style, one that merged swing arrangements with explosive, gospel-tinged vocals; the results were R&B. This album is a collection featuring vintage R&B and blues material, supported by Smith's surging saxophone. —*Ron Wynn*

Trixie Smith

b. 1895, Atlanta, GA, **d.** Sep. 21, 1943, New York, NY
Vocals / Classic Female Blues, Classic Jazz
One of the classic blues singers of the '20s (although unrelated to Bessie, Clara and Mamie), Trixie Smith had a distinctive voice and a pleasing style of her own. She studied at Selma University, moved to New York in 1915, and performed in vaudeville and on the TOBA circuit. Smith worked in New York's theaters during the '20s and '30s as an actress-singer and stayed active throughout her life. She recorded prolifically during

1922-1925 for Black Swan and Paramount with her best-known dates resulting in four songs in 1925 in which Louis Armstrong was in her backup group; other sidemen along the way included James P. Johnson, Phil Napoleon, and members of Fletcher Henderson's Orchestra.

Oddly enough, Smith did not record after 1925 until 1938 when she headed an all-star jazz group (which included Sidney Bechet, Charlie Shavers, and Sammy Price) on one session; in addition in 1939 she cut "No Good Man" with a band including Henry "Red" Allen and Barney Bigard. But by the time she passed away at the age of 48 in 1943, Trixie Smith was largely forgotten. *—Scott Yanow*

Complete Recorded Works, Vol. 1 (1922–1924) / Sep. 1921-Dec. 1924 / Document ♦♦♦♦

Part of the European Document label's giant prewar blues reissue series includes two Trixie Smith CDs that repackage all of her recordings. The second disc is the preferred acquisition, but *Vol. 1* is not without interest. The majority of Smith's recordings (particularly in the early days) were vaudeville and pop songs, but on the relatively rare occasions when she sang a lowdown blues, she fared quite well. The first volume starts out with four numbers that are dated either January or March 1922 here, but are probably from September and November 1921. Trixie Smith improved on records as time went on; her first few numbers have rather dated accompaniment. In fact, despite the presence of pianist James P. Johnson (who is well buried on two numbers), her musicians do not get very stimulating until after the first 20 of the 25 numbers. Most notable among the selections are "He May Be Your Man" (which has some familiar lyrics), "My Man Rocks Me" (a song that would be among Trixie's most famous), the heated "Ride Jockey Ride," and a couple of train songs ("Freight Train Blues" and "Choo Choo Blues"), which would become one of her specialties. This is historic music that set the stage for Trixie's later, generally superior performances. *—Scott Yanow*

● **Complete Recorded Works, Vol. 2 (1925–1939)** / Jan. 1925-Jun. 14, 1939 / Document ♦♦♦♦♦

Trixie Smith was a fine vaudeville-style singer who could also do a powerful job on the blues when called for. The second of two Document CDs that contain all of her recordings starts out with 13 selections from 1925. Smith is joined by her "Down Home Syncopators" (actually the Original Memphis Five) on the first two songs, "Everybody Loves My Baby" and "How Come You Do Me Like You Do." She is heard on two sets in which she is joined by a quintet that includes trombonist Charlie Green, clarinetist Buster Bailey and most notably Louis Armstrong, and is featured later in the year with several top Fletcher Henderson sidemen. On these dates, the more memorable selections include the masochistic "You've Got to Beat Me to Keep Me," "He Likes It Slow" and her classic train song "Railroad Blues." There are also two takes of "Messin' Around" from 1926 in which Trixie is heard as part of Jimmy Blythe's Ragamuffins, a band including clarinetist Johnny Dodds and the legendary cornetist Freddie Keppard. The final eight selections on this 23-cut CD are taken from Smith's May 26, 1938 session, with one number, "No Good Man," dating from the following year and finding her assisted by a band that includes trumpeter Henry "Red" Allen and clarinetist Barney Bigard. The 1938 set matches Trixie with the fiery young trumpeter Charlie Shavers, a restrained Sidney Bechet on soprano, and a four-piece rhythm section. Although she had not recorded in a dozen years, Trixie Smith is in prime form on such numbers as "Freight Train Blues," two versions of "My Daddy Rocks Me" and "He May Be Your Man (But He Comes to See Me Sometime)." Apparently an alcohol problem shortened both Smith's career and life, but one does not hear any decline during these excellent performances. Highly recommended, while the less essential *Vol. 1* is worth picking up too. *—Scott Yanow*

Whispering Smith (Moses Smith)

b. Jan. 25, 1932, Brookhaven, MS, **d.** Apr. 28, 1984, Baton Rouge, LA

Vocals, Harmonica / Swamp Blues

Harpist Whispering Smith made it in on the tail end of the swamp blues movement that swept the Baton Rouge region, working with Lightnin' Slim and Silas Hogan before making his own fine singles for Crowley, LA, producer J.D. Miller.

Alternating down-in-the-bayou entries such as "Mean Woman Blues" (not the Elvis Presley/Roy Orbison rocker), "I Tried So Hard," and "Don't Leave Me Baby" with the storming instrumentals "Live Jive" (also featuring the fleet guitar of Ulysses Williams) and "Hound Dog Twist," Smith was an excellent performer who arrived in Crowley just a trifle late, after the heyday of the swamp blues sound.

Excello decided to give swamp music another try in 1970 without Miller's expert supervision, inviting Smith back to cut an LP in Baton Rouge that just didn't live up to his former glory. *—Bill Dahl*

● **Over Easy** / 1971 / Excello ♦♦♦♦

Willie "The Lion" Smith

b. Nov. 25, 1897, Goshen, NY, **d.** Apr. 18, 1973, New York, NY

Piano / Classic Jazz, Stride, Piano Blues

Willie "The Lion" Smith in the '20s was considered one of the big three of stride piano (along with James P. Johnson and Fats Waller) even though he made almost no recordings until the mid-'30s. His mother was an organist and pianist, and Smith started playing piano when he was six. He earned a living playing piano as a teenager, gained his nickname "the Lion" for his heroism in World War I, and after his discharge he became one of the star attractions at Harlem's nightly rent parties.

Although he toured with Mamie Smith (and played piano on her pioneering 1920 blues record "Crazy Blues"), Smith mostly freelanced throughout his life. He was an influence on the young Duke Ellington (who would later write "Portrait of the Lion") and most younger New York-based pianists of the '20s and '30s. Although he was a braggart and (with his cigar and trademark derby hat) appeared to be a rough character, Smith was actually more colorful than menacing and a very sophisticated pianist with a light touch.

His recordings with his Cubs (starting in 1935) and particularly his 1939 piano solos for Commodore (highlighted by "Echoes of Spring") cemented his place in history. Because he remained very active into the early '70s (writing his memoirs *Music on My Mind* in 1965), for quite a few decades Willie "The Lion" Smith was considered a living link to the glory days of early jazz. *—Scott Yanow*

1925–1937 / Nov. 5, 1925-Sep. 15, 1937 / Classics ♦♦♦♦♦

Willie "The Lion" Smith, one of stride piano's Big Three of the '20s (along with James P. Johnson and Fats Waller), recorded a lot less than his two friends. In fact, with the exception of two selections apiece with the Gulf Coast Seven in 1925 (which features trombonist Jimmy Harrison and clarinetist Buster Bailey) and 1927's Georgia Strutters (starring singer Perry Bradford, Harrison, and cornetist Jabbo Smith), along with the rare and originally unreleased 1934 solo piano showcase "Finger Buster," this CD does not get started until 1935. Smith's Decca recordings of 1935 and 1937 were formerly quite obscure, showcasing his piano with three different versions of "His Cubs." The Lion is heard with a Clarence Williams-type quartet which includes cornetist Ed Allen and clarinetist Cecil Scott, matched up with trumpeter Dave Nelson and clarinetist Buster Bailey in a septet; and temporarily heading an early version of the John Kirby Sextet on a session dominated by drummer O'Neil Spencer's vocals. Highlights of this historic and enjoyable CD include "Santa Claus Blues," "Keep Your Temper," "Blues, Why Don't You Let Me Alone," and the earliest recording of the Lion's most famous composition, "Echo of Spring." *—Scott Yanow*

1937–1938 / Sep. 15, 1937-Nov. 30, 1938 / Classics ♦♦

The second Classics CD in their Willie "The Lion" Smith series is surprisingly weak. Of the 25 selections, 21 actually feature the dated organ of Milt Herth. Smith's presence in the trio (with drummer-vocalist O'Neil Spencer) fails to uplift the music (Herth's wheezing organ mostly drowns him out) although guitarist Teddy Bunn helps a bit on the last seven numbers. Easily the best selections on the CD are two songs performed by Willie "The Lion" Smith and His Cubs (a septet with trumpeter Frankie Newton and clarinetist Buster Bailey) and a pair of duets with drummer Spencer on Smith's own "Passionette" and "Morning Air." But the preceding and following volumes in this program are much more valuable. *—Scott Yanow*

The Original 14 Plus Two / Nov. 30, 1938+Jan. 10, 1939 / Commodore ♦♦♦♦♦

This 1981 LP, released through Columbia, has the highpoints of Willie "The Lion" Smith's career. On Jan. 10, 1939, he recorded 14 piano solos including eight of his own impressionistic compositions. These include such classics as "Echoes of Spring," "Passionette," "Morning Air" and the rambunctious "Finger Buster" and find the pianist at the top of his form. Also on this LP are his versions of six standards along with two numbers ("Three Keyboards" and "The Lion and the Lamb") from a slightly earlier session in which he plays with drummer George Wettling and fellow pianists Joe Bushkin and Jess Stacy. This is essential music which has fortunately been reissued on CD by the European Classics series. *—Scott Yanow*

★ **1938–1940** / Nov. 30, 1938-Feb. 17, 1940 / Classics ♦♦♦♦♦

This is the one Willie "the Lion" Smith CD to get. The bulk of the release features Smith on 14 piano solos from January 10, 1939, performing six standards and eight of his finest compositions. Although Smith (with his derby hat and cigar) could look quite tough, he was actually a sensitive player whose chord structures were very original and impressionistic. On such numbers as "Echoes of Spring" (his most famous work), "Passionette," "Rippling Waters," and "Morning Air," Smith was at his most expressive. In addition, this CD has a couple of collaborations with fellow pianists Joe Bushkin and Jess Stacy and a four-song 1940 swing/Dixieland 1940 session with an octet featuring trumpeter Sidney DeParis. Because of the classic piano solos, this memorable set is quite essential. *—Scott Yanow*

Willie "The Lion" Smith / Dec. 1, 1949-Dec. 24, 1949 / GNP ♦♦♦

On this album, Willie "The Lion" Smith is featured either as a piano soloist, in duets with drummer Wallace Bishop or in a quartet with Bishop, trumpeter Buck Clayton and clarinetist Claude Luter. Eight of the 12 selections were also included on a similarly titled Inner City LP although four were not. While the Inner City set is preferable (it has 16 cuts), the GNP LP will probably be a little easier to find. The Lion is in particularly fine form on "Relaxin'," "Contrary Motions," "Portrait of the Duke," and "La Madelon." *—Scott Yanow*

Willie the Lion Smith / Dec. 1, 1949-Jan. 29, 1950 / Inner City ♦♦♦♦

This out of print LP has some of the highlights of pianist Willie "The Lion" Smith's four recording sessions recorded in Paris for the Vogue label during 1949-1950. For the fine all-round showcase, the Lion is heard performing six originals in duet with drummer Wallace Bishop (including "Echoes of Spring," "Portrait of the Duke," and "Contrary Motion"), playing six romping piano solos (including his rendition of James P. Johnson's "Carolina Shout") and jamming three standards and a blues in a Dixieland quartet with trumpeter Buck Clayton, clarinetist Claude Luter, and drummer Bishop. The performances overlap with a similar GNP/Crescendo LP but this is the better buy, although both sets will be difficult to find. *—Scott Yanow*

The Lion of the Piano / 1951 / Commodore ♦♦♦

Echoes of Spring / Dec. 17, 1965 / Milan ♦♦♦

On this CD pianist Willie "The Lion" Smith is featured during a solo concert from France. The recording quality is just OK and Smith's performance (which combines his piano with a few unfortunate vocals and a little reminiscing) was typical for the period but his piano playing is generally pretty strong. He performs four of his originals (including "Echoes of Spring" and "Zig Zag"), a few standards, a James P. Johnson medley, a medley of songs associated with some of his favorite pianists, Chopin's "Polonaise," and even "La Marseillaise." Although not quite essential, there are enough colorful moments on this set to make the date recommended to Willie "The Lion" Smith collectors. *—Scott Yanow*

Pork and Beans / Nov. 8, 1966 / 1201 Music ✦✦✦✦
One of the last of the major stride pianists, Willie "The Lion" Smith pays tribute to some of his contemporaries during this solo studio set. Smith performs four numbers by Luckey Roberts, three by Eubie Blake, two apiece from Fats Waller and George Gershwin, and four veteran standards. Smith was in the last part of his musical prime and is still quite strong on this spirited and definitive late-period program, infusing his hot stride with impressionistic ideas. *—Scott Yanow*

Duets / Feb. 20, 1967 / Sackville ✦✦✦
To relieve the workload late in his career, Willie "The Lion" Smith often hired fellow pianist Don Ewell to join him for duets. On this Sackville session, Smith and Ewell romp on a variety of superior swing standards including "I've Found a New Baby," "I Would Do Anything for You," "Everybody Loves My Baby," and "You Took Advantage of Me." Although not as significant as other individual sets of Smith and Ewell, the combination works well, making this date easily recommended to fans of stride piano. *—Scott Yanow*

Music on My Mind / Dec. 1967 / Sunnyside ✦✦✦
Willie "The Lion" Smith was pretty busy for a 70-year-old man on November 8, 1966. After the veteran Harlem stride master performed at the Berlin Jazz Festival, he recorded an extended solo set, some of which was featured on the Black Lion release *Pork and Beans.* The remaining music, with only a slight overlap, is featured on this LP, which was issued only in Europe. Before an invited audience in the studio, with his wife Lady Jane at his side, Smith reminisces and introduces each tune as only he could, with the same flair that he played piano. He may have been a little past his prime at this point in his life, but he is still the consummate entertainer as he plays a medley of Luckey Roberts' works, including "Moonlight Cocktail," "Junk Man Rag," and "Pork and Beans." The program also includes a medley of Duke Ellington songs ("Rockin' in Rhythm," "Sophisticated Lady," and "Solitude"), Fats Waller's "Keepin' Out of Mischief Now," and a romping "Shine," during which Smith makes comments and even adds a spirited vocal to captivate his audience, which is evidently in the booth outside the studio since there is no audible response. He also plays his obscure but delightful "Oh You Devil" and closes with his well-known theme song, "Relaxin'." Long out of print, this hard to find LP will be coveted by fans of stride piano and especially Willie "The Lion" Smith, as relatively few of his recordings have been reissued on CD. *—Ken Dryden*

Memoirs of Willie "The Lion" Smith / Apr. 25, 1968-Apr. 28, 1968 / RCA ✦✦✦✦
This double LP is the equivalent of Jelly Roll Morton's *Library of Congress* recordings. The legendary Willie "The Lion" Smith reminisces about his colorful life, plays some piano and warbles out some vocals. Particularly interesting are his stories of the early days, his medleys of songs associated with Eubie Blake, James P. Johnson, Fats Waller and Duke Ellington, and his performances of eight of his own compositions, some of which are quite obscure. Not everything works and some of the talking rambles on a bit, but overall this is a fascinating historical document that has many interesting moments. *—Scott Yanow*

Relaxin' / 1970-1971 / Chiaroscuro ✦✦✦✦
For this Chiaroscuro LP (not yet reissued on CD), veteran stride pianist Willie "The Lion" Smith is heard in the studio in 1970 and live at a club in 1971, in both cases usually accompanied by drummer Dude Brown. The well-rounded program mostly sticks to veteran standards (including "I've Found a New Baby," "Nagasaki," and "Keeping Out of Mischief Now") plus "Chopin Variations" and three versions of "Relaxin'," which Smith was using as a theme song. This fine outing (one of the Lion's last) is worth searching for. *—Scott Yanow*

Willie the Lion and His Washington Cubs / Feb. 20, 1971 / Fat Cat Jazz ✦✦✦✦
Willie "The Lion" Smith passed away in 1973 but this live jam session set shows that two years before his death he still retained most of his power. Teamed up with Australian trumpeter Tony Newstead, clarinetist Tommy Gwaltney, bassist Van Perry, and drummer Skip Tomlinson, Smith runs through ten veteran warhorses and brings a great deal of joy to such songs as "Ain't She Sweet," "Louisiana," "Darktown Strutters' Ball" (which has one of Fat Cat McRee's two vocals), and "Love Is Just Around the Corner." This hard to find Fat Cat LP can easily be enjoyed by Dixieland and Willie "The Lion" Smith collectors. *—Scott Yanow*

Willie "The Lion" Smith & His Jazz All Stars / 1974 / Jazz Kings ✦✦✦
This Willie "the Lion" Smith LP first appeared in 1957 on Urania, and was reissued not long after his death in 1973 on the short-lived Jazz Kings label. Although Smith is billed as being solo on six selections, Pops Foster's bass, Sidney Gross' guitar, and Arthur Trappier's drums are generally audible accompanying him, with Smith is in good form. The remaining four tracks feature Smith in a Dixieland setting with trumpet Henry Goodwin, trombonist George Stevenson, and clarinetist and tenor saxophonist Cecil Scott joining him, along with the rhythm section. Highlights include Goodwin's spirited muted solo on "Fidgety Feet" and a raucous take of Lil Hardin Armstrong's "Struttin' With Some Barbecue." Although this isn't by far Smith's best date as a leader, the music is quite enjoyable and worth picking up. *—Ken Dryden*

Memorial, Vol. 1 / 1974 / Vogue ✦✦✦✦
Relatively few of stride piano master Willie "The Lion" Smith's LPs have been reissued on CD. This is the first volume of a two-record set recorded in Paris by the pianist, featuring eight duets with drummer Wallace Bishop and six solos. Smith is at the top of his game throughout both sessions, running through his well-known "Echoes of Spring" and the romping "Here Comes the Band," while his theme song, "Relaxin'," is heard in its entirety with an elaborate introduction. He responds to Duke Ellington's "Portrait of the Lion" with his own "Portrait of the Duke," during which he sings along and talks in a happy-go-lucky manner. The remaining tracks are from a solo session at the end of the year, including once popular standards like "Dardanella," excellent interpretations of two of James P. Johnson's most popular compositions ("Charleston" and "Carolina Shout"), and several more originals by Smith. This record will be extremely difficult to find, but it is well worth acquiring for fans of stride. *—Ken Dryden*

Memorial, Vol. 2 / 1974 / Vogue ✦✦✦✦
This second volume of Willie "The Lion" Smith's recordings for Vogue took place during his stay in Paris in 1949 and 1950. The first session adds trumpeter Buck Clayton and clarinetist Claude Luter, in addition to drummer Wallace Bishop; no bassist was needed because a stride pianist the caliber of Smith has no problems creating a solid bass line. Two takes of "At the Darktown Strutter's Ball" and Fats Waller's "Ain't Misbehavin'" feature spirited vocals by Smith and great solos by Smith, Clayton, and Luter. Clayton shines during "Nagasaki," but Smith rises to the occasion to direct the spotlight back to himself. Most of Smith's originals from the solo tracks are fairly obscure originals, except for his jaunty "Conversation on Park Avenue" and a rather intricate arrangement of "Sweet Sue." Like its companion Vogue LP, this record (last reissued in 1974, the year after Smith's death) will be difficult to find but worth the investment. *—Ken Dryden*

Lion Roars: His Greatest 1934–44 / Jun. 16, 1998 / ASV/Living Era ✦✦✦

1944–1949 / Jul. 2, 2002 / Classics ✦✦✦✦

Willie Mae Ford Smith

b. 1906, Rolling Fork, MS, **d.** Feb. 2, 1994, St. Louis, MO
Vocals / Traditional Gospel, Black Gospel
Considered the greatest of the "anointed singers"—artists who live according to the spirit, and who perform with the ultimate aim of saving souls—Willie Mae Ford Smith was among the most legendary gospel vocalists of her era; rarely recorded, her enormous reputation instead rested almost entirely on her incendiary live performances, where her dramatic, physical style inspired many of the finest soloists to follow in her wake. She was also the first to introduce the "song and sermonette," the act of delivering a lengthy sermon before, during or after a performance.

Smith was born in 1906 in Rolling Fork, MS, and raised in Memphis; one of 14 children, she was the daughter of a railroad brakeman who relocated the family to St. Louis in 1918. There her mother opened a restaurant, where Smith soon began working full-time, leaving school during the eighth grade; though raised as a devout Baptist, she sang everything from blues to reels as a child, but upon forming her family quartet the Ford Sisters, she turned solely to gospel.

Debuting at the National Baptist Convention in 1922, the Fords created a sensation with their performances of "Ezekiel Saw the Wheel" and "I'm in His Care." After her sisters married and quit the group, Smith mounted a solo career; a high soprano, she briefly flirted with pursuing classical music, but was so profoundly moved by Detroit's Madame Artelia Hutchins' performance at the 1926 Baptist Convention that she returned to gospel once and for all. Upon marrying a man who operated a general hauling business, Smith began touring to supplement their household income; with the exception of the legendary Sallie Martin, she was arguably the first gospel performer to tour relentlessly, conducting musical revivals in many of the cities she visited. In her travels Smith crossed paths with Thomas A. Dorsey, who in 1932 invited her to Chicago to help organize the National Convention of Gospel Choirs and Choruses. She later formed a St. Louis chapter, and was the longtime head of the soloists' bureau.

Smith's rendition of her own composition "If You Just Keep Still," delivered at the 1937 National Baptist Convention, set a new standard for solo singing; just as influential was her skill as an arranger, with her radical reinterpretations of chestnuts like "Jesus Loves Me," "Throw Out the Lifeline" and "What a Friend We Have in Jesus" galvanizing a new generation of singers to include the songs in their repertoires. As a teacher, Smith also mentored Brother Joe May, Myrtle Scott, Edna Gallmon Cooke, and Martha Bass. She joined the Church of God Apostolic in 1939, and immediately her music reflected the rhythm and energy of the sanctified church; still, she did not finally begin recording until the end of the following decade—with her protégé May enjoying massive success with her style, she saw no point in entering the studio. Only a handful of Smith recordings were issued in her own lifetime, and by the early '50s she had turned to evangelical work; still, she continued to remain a great inspiration, dying on February 2, 1994. *—Jason Ankeny*

● **Mother Smith & Her Children** / 1989 / Spirit Feel ✦✦✦✦
Willie Mae Ford Smith is one of the pivotal figures in gospel; born in 1904, she inspired innumerable younger vocalists. *Mother Smith & Her Children* collects sides by Smith and her spiritual descendents. Among them is Martha Bass, who joins with her own son David Peaston (later a gospel star in his own right) and daughter Fontella, the woman behind the secular hit "Rescue Me" (the best record Aretha Franklin never cut). Brother Joe May, once esteemed as the male Mahalia Jackson, takes the reins for three unreleased and undated performances, while five contributions from Edna Gallmon Cooke round out the collection. *—Jason Ankeny*

Willie Mae Ford Smith / Savoy ✦✦✦✦
Includes "I Must Tell Jesus" and "He Never Left Me Alone." *—Bil Carpenter*

Going on with the Spirit / Nashboro ✦✦✦
Of special note: "Give Me Wings" and "I've Got a Secret." *—Bil Carpenter*

Willie "Big Eyes" Smith

b. Jan. 19, 1936, Helena, AR
Drums / Contemporary Blues, Electric Chicago Blues
The longtime drummer with the Muddy Waters Band, bluesman Willie "Big Eyes" Smith was born in Helena, AR, on January 19, 1936; raised by his sharecropper grandparents,

as a child his neighbors included the likes of Robert Nighthawk and Pinetop Perkins. At 17 he traveled to Chicago to visit his mother and never returned home; instead, Smith taught himself harmonica and drums, and with harpist Clifton James and guitarist Bobby Lee Burns formed a blues trio.

Upon marrying his first wife in 1955, Smith agreed to retire from performing, but within a year he was backing Arthur "Big Boy" Spires; after a brief attempt at fronting his own band, he returned to his drum kit, joining Hudson Shower's Red Devil Trio. After a few lean years that forced him to go on welfare, Smith joined Waters in 1961 and remained with the blues giant until 1980, when he co-founded the Legendary Blues Band. His first solo recording, *Bag Full of Blues*, did not appear until 1995; *Nothin' but the Blues Y'All* followed four years later and *Blues from the Heart* was issued in fall 2000. *—Jason Ankeny*

● **Bag Full of Blues** / Nov. 1995 / Blind Pig ✦✦✦
The former Muddy Waters drummer Willie "Big Eyes" Smith turns in an enjoyable, but unremarkable, set of Chicago blues with *Bag Full of Blues*. Supported by Pinetop Perkins and Fabulous Thunderbirds harpist Kim Wilson, Smith runs through a set of midtempo blues, combining some competent originals with covers like "Baby Please Don't Go." There's not many solos—Wilson mainly shines, while guitarists James Wheeler, Nick Moss, and Gareth Best all contribute small, pithy leads—but the grooves are nice and relaxed. *Bag Full of Blues* may not be a jaw-dropper, but it does have some fine moments. *—Stephen Thomas Erlewine*

Nothin' but the Blues Y'All / Dec. 14, 1999 / Juke Joint ✦✦✦

Blues from the Heart / Nov. 14, 2000 / Juke Joint ✦✦✦

Chris Smither

b. Nov. 11, 1944, New Orleans, LA
Vocals, Guitar / Contemporary Folk, Singer/Songwriter, Modern Acoustic Blues, Folk-Blues

Like John Hammond and a handful of other musicians whose careers began in the '60s blues revival, guitarist, singer, and songwriter Chris Smither can take pride in the fact that he's been there since the beginning. Except for a few years when he was away from performing in the '70s, Smither has been a mainstay of the festival, coffeehouse, and club circuits around the U.S., Canada, and Europe since his performing career began in earnest in the coffeehouses in Boston in the spring of 1966.

Smither is best known for his great songs, items like "Love You Like a Man" and "I Feel the Same," both of which have been recorded by guitarist Bonnie Raitt. Raitt and Smither got started at about the same time in the coffeehouse scene around Boston, though Smither was born and raised in New Orleans, the son of university professors.

Smither's earliest awareness of blues and folk music came from his parents' record collection. In a 1992 interview, he recalled it included albums by Josh White, Susan Reed, and Burl Ives. After a short stint taking piano lessons, Smither switched to ukulele after discovering his mother's old instrument in a closet. The young Smither was passionately attached to the ukulele, and now, years later, it helps to explain the emotion and expertise behind his unique fingerpicking guitar style. Smither discovered blues music when he was 17 and heard a Lightnin' Hopkins album, *Blues in the Bottle*. The album was a major revelation to him and he subsequently spent weeks trying to figure out the intricate guitar parts he'd heard on that record. Smither moved to Boston after realizing he was a big fish in a small pond in the New Orleans folk/coffeehouse circuit of the mid-'60s. Also, acoustic blues pioneer Ric Von Schmidt had recommended Smither check out the Boston folk/blues scene.

Smither recorded his first couple of albums for the Poppy label in 1970 and 1972, *I'm a Stranger Too!* and *Don't It Drag On*. In 1972, Smither recorded a third album, *Honeysuckle Dog*, for United Artists, that was never released. On the sessions for that album, he was joined in the studio by his old friends Bonnie Raitt and Mac Rebennack, aka Dr. John. After a long bout with alcohol, Smither launched his recording career again in the late '80s, although he was performing through the whole time he wasn't sober.

His return to a proper recording career, due to a deal with Flying Fish Records, didn't happen again until 1991, when the label released *Another Way to Find You*, a folk-blues album. Smither did record for Adelphi label in 1984, *It Ain't Easy*, which has since been re-released on compact disc. Since then, he's more than proved his mettle as an enormously gifted songwriter, releasing albums of mostly his own compositions for the Flying Fish and Hightone labels. Smither's other albums include *Happier Blue* (1993, Flying Fish), and *Up on the Lowdown* (1995, Hightone Records).

Any of Smither's Flying Fish releases or his Hightone releases (including 1999's *Drive You Home Again* and 2000's *Live as I'll Ever Be*) are worthy of careful examination by guitarists and students of all schools of blues music. Smither is still to some extent anunheralded master of modern acoustic blues. Fortunately, his festival bookings in recent years elevated his profile to a higher level than he'd ever enjoyed previously. *—Richard Skelly*

I'm a Stranger Too! / 1970 / Tomato ✦✦✦

Don't Drag It On / 1972 / Tomato ✦✦✦

It Ain't Easy / 1984 / Genes ✦✦✦
Following two releases for Poppy Records in the early '70s, as well as a third recording that never saw the light of day, Chris Smither finally returned in 1984 with *It Ain't Easy*. Armed simply with guitar and voice, Smither delivers a dozen tunes (14 on the CD reissue) that embody the best tradition of blues and folk. Whether it's his originals, a standard like "Glory of Love," or material by the likes of Randy Newman, Chuck Berry, Mississippi John Hurt, and Howlin' Wolf, Smither infuses every track with the same timeless quality. Though he may, on occasion, choose rather standard folk, blues, and rock & roll fare ("Green Rocky Road," "Sittin' on Top of the World," "Maybelline") Smither never treats the songs as if they were museum pieces. In his hands, they're given a life and vitality they probably haven't seen in years. His masterful guitar work and dark, resonant baritone are ideally suited to the songs on *It Ain't Easy*. Like Mississippi John Hurt or Rev. Gary Davis, his playing is that perfect combination of simplicity and sophistication, discovering and filling harmonic voids without ever overstating or wasting a single note. There's not a false moment on the entire record. Highly recommended. *—Brett Hartenbach*

Another Way to Find You / 1991 / Hightone ✦✦✦✦✦
This captures folk-blues guitarist/singer/songwriter Smither playing live in the studio for a hand-picked audience over the Christmas holidays in 1989. Smither presents 17 songs of his own derivation and others, blasting it all out in a couple of sharp sets in the time-honored folk music club tradition. His guitar work is clean and well played, and his vocals attain a sense of engagement throughout. While his interpretations of tunes by Chuck Berry, Randy Newman, Elizabeth Cotten, Blind Willie McTell, Jimmy Reed, and others are fine, the true highlights come with the originals "Lonely Time," "Don't Drag It On," "A Song for Susan," "Lonesome Georgia Brown," "I Feel the Same" and the title track. *—Cub Koda*

● **Happier Blue** / 1993 / Hightone ✦✦✦✦✦
All the elements of Chris Smither's distinctive style are here: passionate vocals, his cool songs, and some covers. This is a NAIRD award winning album. *—Richard Meyer*

Up on the Lowdown / 1995 / Hightone ✦✦✦✦✦

Small Revelations / Jan. 14, 1997 / Hightone ✦✦✦

I'm a Stranger Too!/Don't Drag It On / Mar. 25, 1997 / Collectables ✦✦✦
Chris Smither's first two albums, *I'm a Stranger Too!* and *Don't Drag It On*, were combined on this single-CD reissue by Collectables. Although the sound and the packaging could be a little better, this still is a fine way for collectors to pick up these two records on disc. *—Stephen Thomas Erlewine*

Drive You Home Again / Mar. 16, 1999 / Hightone ✦✦✦✦
Veteran Texas singer/songwriter Chris Smither sounds a bit like a Tim Hardin for the '90s, so it's no surprise to come upon a cover of Hardin's "Don't Make Promises" halfway through this excellent album. Smither's gravelly, instantly recognizable voice is a perfect fit for his pensive, sharply honed lyrics and his blues- and folk-based music. Smither's 15 accompanists, who employ everything from sax to accordion to tuba, do a uniformly first-rate job with a varied program. Like Nick Drake and the Van Morrison of *Astral Weeks* days, Smither makes you feel as if you're in a dream. You may not want to wake up for a while. *—Jeff Burger*

Live as I'll Ever Be / Jul. 18, 2000 / Hightone ✦✦✦✦
Chris Smither's *Another Way to Find You* was the live album that chronicled his career up to 1991. *Live As I'll Ever Be* takes up where that one left off, featuring songs from the four albums he released in the '90s. It was recorded over several years—beginning in 1996—and captured performances in California, Virginia, Massachusetts, and Ireland. One mike recorded his large, unmistakable voice; the other was placed on the floor to pick up his steadily tapping and stomping feet. Many audience favorites were included, such as "I Am the Ride," "Slow Surprise," "Small Revelations," and "Up on the Lowdown." Two covers, Robert Johnson's "Dust My Broom" and Rolly Sally's "Killin' the Blues," were also recorded. There are entertaining song intros and bits of warm banter with the audience, too. Chris Smither is always at his best when he is performing live. In fact, he often says that he writes songs and records albums just so he can perform live, and not the other way around. *Live as I'll Ever Be* gives you a great front-row seat, any time you want it. *—Ann Wickstrom*

Little Smokey Smothers

b. Jan. 2, 1939, Tchula, MS
Vocals, Guitar / Electric Chicago Blues

Not to be confused with his late older brother Big Smokey, Albert "Little Smokey" Smothers began to transcend his journeyman status in 1993 with a superlative Dick Shurman-produced album for the Dutch Black Magic label, *Bossman! The Chicago Blues of Little Smokey Smothers*. The set happily reunited him with his ex-guitar pupil Elvin Bishop and his cousin, singer Lee Shot Williams.

Little Smokey rolled into Chicago during the mid-'50s, landing gigs with guitarist Arthur "Big Boy" Spires and pianist Lazy Bill Lucas and playing with Howlin' Wolf on the 1959 Chess session that produced "I've Been Abused" and "Mr. Airplane Man." Smothers fell in with young White harpist Paul Butterfield when the latter was just starting out in the early '60s and is still fondly recalled as a major influence by his buddy Bishop, who would go on to make history as Butterfield's slashing axeman after Smothers left the harpist's employ.

There was a time during the '70s when Little Smokey pretty much gave up music, but he slid back into playing gradually during the next decade with the Legendary Blues Band. Heart problems temporarily shelved Smothers for a spell not too long ago, but he's back in action now, releasing *That's My Partner* with Elvin Bishop in 2000 among other dates. *—Bill Dahl*

● **Bossman! The Chicago Blues of Little Smokey Smothers** / 1993 / Black Magic ✦✦✦✦✦
Sizzling and long-overdue debut album by the veteran Chicago bluesman, whose approach is considerably more contemporary than that of his late older brother. Producer Dick Shurman recruited vocalist Lee Shot Williams (Smokey's cousin) and Elvin Bishop (who Smokey tutored during the early '60s) for this project, a fine showcase for Smothers' hearty vocals and expressive guitar. *—Bill Dahl*

Otis Smokey Smothers

b. Mar. 21, 1929, Lexington, MS, **d.** Jul. 23, 1993, Chicago, IL
Vocals, Guitar / Electric Chicago Blues

The Chicago blues scene boasted its own pair of Smothers Brothers, but there was nothing particularly amusing about their tough brand of blues music. The older of the two by a decade, Otis "Big Smokey" Smothers was first to arrive in the Windy City from Mississippi in the mid-'40s. Howlin' Wolf liked the way he played enough to invite him into the Chess studios as his rhythm guitarist on several 1956-1957 sessions (songs included "Who's Been Talking," "Tell Me," "Going Back Home," and "I Asked for Water").

Federal Records found Smothers simple shuffle sound immensely appealing in 1960, recording 12 tracks by the good-natured bluesman with labelmate Freddie King handling lead guitar duties (King, Federal's parent logo, even issued a Smothers' LP that's worth a pretty penny today). A four-song 1962 session that included "Way Up in the Mountains of Kentucky" and an updated version of the Hank Ballard & the Midnighters' classic "Work With Me Annie" ("Twist With Me Annie") completed his Federal tenure.

Apart from a 1968 single for Gamma ("I Got My Eyes on You"), Smothers didn't make it back onto wax until 1986, when Red Beans Records, a small Chicago outfit run by pianist Erwin Helfer and guitarist Pete Crawford, brought him back to the record racks with an LP called *Got My Eyes on You* that showed his style hadn't changed a whit with the decades. Smokey Smothers was a beloved Chicago traditionalist until the very end. *—Bill Dahl*

● **Sings the Backporch Blues** / 1962 / Ace ✦✦✦✦✦

Lowdown Chicago blues album that's exceedingly rare on vinyl. Smothers was a master of the slow-grinding shuffle, and some tracks sport the presence of Freddie King on lead guitar. The 2002 Ace CD reissue adds nine alternate takes and four tracks from 1962-1963 singles. *—Bill Dahl*

Got My Eyes on You / 1986 / Red Beans ✦✦✦

Got My Eyes on You was a decent representation of his gutbucket sound, backing him with a crew of sympathetic young traditionalists who didn't update his basic shuffles a bit. *—Bill Dahl*

Second Time Around / Sep. 3, 1996 / Crosscut ✦✦✦

Chicago Blues, Vol. 1 / Jun. 17, 1998 / Wolf ✦✦✦

Drivin Blues / King ✦✦✦✦✦

Uncompromising Chicago blues. *—Bill Dahl*

James Solberg

b. Wisconsin

Guitar / Modern Electric Blues

Whenever Luther Allison toured the U.S. in the '90s, he was backed by the Jim Solberg Band. Solberg and Allison had a long, friendly working relationship that dated back to the early '70s, when Allison was living in Milwaukee.

Solberg, a talented guitarist, singer, and songwriter, frequently co-wrote with Allison, but since Luther spent a good portion of each year in Europe, touring out of his home in Paris, Solberg toured with his band under his own name when Allison was not around. In the late '90s, Solberg released several albums under his own name for the Atomic Theory label. The records drew high praise from critics, and well they should—Solberg was no spring chicken when it comes to playing blues and touring. He has broken many a guitar string and logged thousands of miles in his van since he started to get serious about the music in the late '60s.

Solberg was raised in Eau Claire and Milwaukee, WI, and worked in various psychedelic blues cover bands (fashionable in the late '60s) before moving to Vancouver, B.C., as a conscientious objector in 1968. After returning to the U.S. after the war, Solberg formed a band called Whirlhouse. That group didn't last very long, and in 1970, he toured with the Sam Lays Blues Band, which included Big Walter "Shakey" Horton, Eddie Taylor, and Johnny Young. In 1972, working with bassist Jon Paris, he formed a band called Dynamite Duck. Paris would later go on to accompany Johnny Winter as bassist for the next 14 years. Beginning in 1975, Solberg toured with Jimmy Reed and began his full time association with Allison. Solberg and his bands backed Allison from 1975 to 1979, pausing only to tour with John Lee Hooker, whom Solberg would rejoin for another tour in 1981. After Allison relocated permanently to Paris, Solberg worked with the Milwaukee group Short Stuff, a group led by harp player Jim Liban.

In the '80s, Solberg toured with Hooker, the Legendary Blues Band, the Nighthawks and Elvin Bishop, among others. In 1987 Solberg opened his own club, the Stone's Throw, in Eau Claire, Wisconsin.

After Allison signed to the Chicago-based Alligator Records in 1993, the Jim Solberg Band, in its then-incarnation, renewed its relationship with Allison, acting as his touring band on domestic dates and select overseas shows. Much of Allison's debut for Alligator, *Soul Fixin' Man* (1993), was co-written and arranged by Solberg. Solberg, a true blues veteran, was also heavily involved in the songwriting and arranging for Allison's two final albums for Alligator, *Blue Streak* (1996) and *Reckless* (1997). *L.A. Blues*, his first for the RUF label, followed in 1998, and two years later Solberg returned with *The Hand You're Dealt*.

By the very nature of his job as a sideman, it may take a while for the blues-buying public to realize that Solberg is a phenomenally talented songwriter, guitarist, and singer in his own right. Both *See That My Grave Is Kept Clean* and *One of These Days* are superb, highly recommended albums. *—Richard Skelly*

● **See That My Grave Is Kept Clean** / Aug. 1, 1995 / MP ✦✦✦✦

Jim Solberg's debut album *See That My Grave Is Kept Clean* is a storming collection of hard-driving electric blues. Before he had the chance to make this record, Solberg perfected his trade by working as a sideman. Those years slinging a guitar paid off in spades, as this record demonstrates. There's a maturity to his style, but there's also unbridled energy—the combination is, at times, irresistable. The songs may be a little uneven, but there's no denying that Solberg and his crack supporting band have made *See That My Grave Is Kept Clean* into something to remember. *—Thom Owens*

One of These Days / 1996 / Ruf ✦✦✦

If you owned a blues club and insisted that you would only book hardcore blues purists, you would miss out on a lot of talented people. That's because so many of the artists playing the blues circuit in the 21st century have other influences—perhaps rock, perhaps soul, perhaps jazz. All of those things have influenced James Solberg, who is essentially a bluesman but is far from a purist. Those who expect everything a bluesman records to have 12 bars are bound to find *One of These Days* disappointing, but more eclectic and broad-minded listeners will find a lot to admire about this German release, which finds the charming singer embracing everything from moody, Bobby "Blue" Bland-ish soul-blues ("One of These Days," "Everyday") to exuberant blues-rock ("One False Move," "Too Damn Much Lovin'"). Solberg's performance of "Do You Call That a Buddy?" recalls the blues-jazz of the '30s and '40s, and his own "Litehouse Keeper" is a Southern soul item that takes us back to a time when Otis Redding, Sam & Dave, Rufus Thomas, and Wilson Pickett were all over R&B radio. Overall, *One of These Days* is quite solid. The only disappointing track is a surprisingly lackluster version of Sir Mack Rice's "Cheaper to Keep Her," which was a major hit for the late soulster Johnnie Taylor (as opposed to bluesman Little Johnny Taylor) in the early '70s. Solberg should have soared on this track, but, for whatever reason, he drops the ball. Most of the time, however, *One of These Days* turns out to be a rewarding and welcome addition to Solberg's catalog. *—Alex Henderson*

L.A. Blues / May 5, 1998 / Ruf ✦✦✦

An album from Luther Allison's long-standing bandleader of the last several years. Released a few months after Allison's death, the album can be taken as a tribute album by Solberg of sorts to his old boss. Utilizing a strong, distorted tone throughout, Solberg keeps Luther's high-energy approach alive on a batch of shuffles ("Bubba's Boogie," "Must Be a Reason"), slow blues ("L.A. Blues," "Ballad of a Thin Man"), and uptempo rockers ("Wally World U.S.A.," "Rhumba Juice"). Midtempo shuffles abound in tracks like "A Closer Walk With Thee," "Robb's Souffle," and the closing "Happy Snails." The music on this record is heartfelt and inspired, a moving tribute. Fans of Allison's final work will say his memory is well served here. *—Cub Koda*

The Hand You're Dealt / May 2, 2000 / Ruf ✦✦✦

Soledad Brothers

f. 1998

Group / Garage Rock Revival, Indie Rock, Alternative Pop/Rock, Blues-Rock

The dark blues duo Soledad Brothers began in early 1998 after guitarist/vocalist Johnny Wirick, aka Johnny Walker, asked drummer Ben Smith, aka Ben Swank, if he wanted to play a show. Since then, they have recorded for Detroit's Italy Records and Bellingham, WA-based Estrus label. Wirick and Smith's partnership can be traced back to their days in the Toledo, OH, blues group Henry and June, which existed from 1994 until 1996. After that group broke up, Wirick continued playing with drummer Doug Walker in the two-piece blues outfit Johnny Walker. Before one of the band's shows in early 1998, Walker decided to leave the group. Looking for someone to fill in for the gig, Wirick turned to Smith, who agreed to play. Developing from what was supposed to be a one-off show, Wirick and Smith decided to continue as the Soledad Brothers.

After a few performances around the Toledo, OH and Detroit areas, Dave Buick, owner of the Detroit-based Italy Records, approached the Soledad Brothers about cutting a single. This turned out to be their first 7", released in late 1998. Around the same time as the release of the single, the national independent label Estrus began distributing some of Italy's catalog. Upon hearing the Soledad Brothers, Estrus signed the group in early 1999. With the label, the band recorded their second single, which was released late that year. Jack White, a member of the Detroit band White Stripes, produced the 7". White had known the Soledad Brothers since their first gig and was a labelmate of the group during their time with Italy. White also assisted the band for two years recording their self-titled debut. It was during those two years that the group opened a show at Pat's in Cleveland, OH, located in the famous Flats, for legendary MC5 manager John Sinclair. He enjoyed the Soledad Brothers so much that he invited them to be the backing group for his part of the performance. This led to a friendship with Sinclair that resulted in him writing the liner notes for the band's 2000 debut album. Their sophomore effort, 2002's *Steal Your Soul and Dare Your Spirit to Move*, added several new instruments, including a second guitar. *—Stephen Howell*

● **Soledad Brothers** / Jul. 18, 2000 / Estrus ✦✦✦✦

Guitarist/vocalist Johnny Walker presents a faux southern minister's drawl for much of the record, and while some of the tracks become repetitive ("Gospel According to John"), they are saved by Walker's Delta bluesman-derived style of fingerpicking between the bass and treble strings on his guitar. This helps to fill out the bass-less sound of the duo. Drummer Ben Swank keeps his playing straightforward for much of the record, adding fills only where they're needed ("Front St. Front," "Gimme Back My Wig"). Swank also knows where to add feeling and depth, such as on "The Weight of the World," where he only accents the first beat of every measure with his drums for the first half of the song until the tension builds and the full drum kit enters. Walker and Swank also manage to sound like a more threatening and haunting version of the "Play With Fire"-era Rolling Stones on tracks like "Mysterious Ways" and "Handle Song." This is a raw album that should be well liked by fans of the British Invasion and blues artists such as John Lee Hooker and David "Honeyboy" Edwards. *—Stephen Howell*

Steal Your Soul and Dare Your Spirit to Move / Mar. 19, 2002 / Estrus ✦✦✦

It has been the goal of countless bands to re-awaken the energy of *Exile on Main Street*-era Rolling Stones into some workable modern sound. Many have tried, but only a few have come close. Detroit's punk-blues upstarts Soledad Brothers have made a brisk career of just such imitation and prove that imitation is itself the sincerest form of irony. On *Steal Your Soul and Dare Your Spirit to Move* they make no apologies of their fascination with both British and American blues-rock, and imbue all the lifted riffs and self-serving sexual swagger with enough drunken abandon and reckless energy to almost convince you that they are picking up where the Stones themselves left off. The aptly named "Prodigal Stones Blues" cops the signature Stones riffs and tone of the period, and singer Johnny Walker even intones Mick Jagger's vocal quirks. On their own "32 Blues," where Walker belts oaths and shout-outs overtop fuzzy guitar and greasy saxophone, you are almost convinced that these guys are the real thing. A take on "R.L. Burnside's Michigan Line" reveals the group's more reckless side. He sings "I was raised in a trailer down by the tracks/Where I would lay and listen to the clackety-clack/That's where I got that hard-drivin' Soledad beat" on his confessional piece "Miracle Birth." Whether that is true or just a bunch of sycophantic blues imagery hardly matters. When Walker sings it, he believes it, and that just may be enough. *—John Duffy*

The Soul Stirrers

f. 1927, Trinity, Texas

Group / Traditional Gospel, Black Gospel, R&B, Soul

Indisputably among the premier gospel groups of the modern era, the Soul Stirrers pioneered the contemporary quartet sound. Pushing the music away from the traditional repertoire of jubilees and spirituals towards the visceral, deeply emotional hard gospel style so popular among postwar listeners, the group's innovative arrangements—they were the first quartet to add a second lead—and sexually charged presence irrevocably blurred the lines between religious and secular music while becoming a seminal influence on the development of rock & roll and soul, most notably by virtue of their connection to the legendary Sam Cooke. The Soul Stirrers' origins date back to 1926, where in the town of Trinity, TX, baritone Senior Roy H. Crain formed a quartet with a number of other teens with whom he attended church. After one of the group's early appearances, a member of the audience approached Crain to tell him how their performance had "stirred his soul," and from this chance compliment the Soul Stirrers were officially born.

The original group fell apart soon after, but Crain continued to pursue a singing career; upon relocating to Houston during the early '30s, he joined a group called the New Pleasant Green Singers on the condition that they change their name to the Soul Stirrers. So rechristened, this incarnation of the quartet made a 1936 field recording for Alan Lomax; as other members dropped out, Crain brought in replacements, finally arriving at the classic early lineup which also included bass Jesse Farley, baritone T.L. Bruster, second lead James Medlock and, most notably, lead R.H. Harris, whose high, crystalline voice remains the inspiration for virtually all great male quartet leads to follow since. After moving to Chicago, the Soul Stirrers began shifting away from the signature tight harmonies and compact songs of traditional gospel towards a harder style distinguished by shifting leads and performances elongated to increase their emotional potency; they also began performing new material from the pens of Thomas A. Dorsey, Kenneth Morris, and others.

Throughout the '40s, the Soul Stirrers' reputation grew; not only were they constantly on tour, but they booked most of the major gospel programs in the Chicago area—in their spare hours, they even operated their own cleaning business. When the grind got to be too much for Medlock, he retired from the road, and was replaced by onetime Golden Echo Paul Foster. In early 1950, the Soul Stirrers signed to the Specialty label, debuting with the single "By and By"; it was quickly followed by "I'm Still Living on Mother's Prayer" and "In That Awful Hour," both originals composed by Detroit's Reuben L.C. Henry. In total, the Soul Stirrers recorded over two dozen tracks for Specialty in 1950 before Harris quit the group that same year; many predicted a dire future, especially when it was announced that his replacement was a relatively unknown 20-year-old named Sam Cooke. When Cooke made his recording debut with the Soul Stirrers in 1951, however, any reservations were quickly dispelled—blessed with a gossamer voice even sweeter and more graceful than Harris', he would take the group to even greater heights than before.

The first Soul Stirrers 78 to feature Cooke, "Jesus Gave Me Water," was a major hit, and with his good looks the young singer made an instant impact with female audiences, in the process becoming the gospel circuit's first sex symbol. The group's popularity continued to soar, but as the Soul Stirrers entered their third decade, the daily grind began to wear on its members, and soon Bruster retired; he was replaced by baritone Bob King, who also doubled as a guitarist, becoming their first-ever steady instrumentalist. In 1954, the Soul Stirrers briefly added Julius Cheeks to their roster; after lending his raspy vocals to a recording of "All Right Now," however, contractual obligations forced him to exit almost as quickly as he arrived. In 1956, Cooke finally crossed over to the pop market, and was replaced by ex-Highway Q.C. Johnnie Taylor; while Taylor himself would also enjoy pop success in the years to follow, he failed to command the same devotion as his predecessor. Lineup changes continued regularly in the years to follow, but the Soul Stirrers forged on, with new, younger members keeping the group afloat into the '90s. *—Jason Ankeny*

☆ **Shine on Me** / 1950 / Specialty ✦✦✦✦✦

If you want to hear one of the most impassioned gospel performances ever recorded, just throw this disc in the player, and brace yourself. R.H. Harris was undoubtedly one of the great voices and stylists of the genre, and his performances on this disc go a long way to justifying the claim that he was the greatest of them all. Every track on here is a gem of beauty, tone, and commitment. But the kickoff track on this compilation, an alternate take of their two-part single, "By and By," is absolutely devastating in its use of shading, dynamics, and unrelenting fervor in getting its message across. The Soul Stirrers lock the groove down mightily, chiming up on those low seventh chords like 12 feet of concrete. Harris, as the old saying goes, sings his rear end off on this one, and, as transcendent moments go, this one is in a class all by itself. If the issued versions included here are slightly less subdued and don't quite hit as high a quotient on the fervor meter, so what?—we should be grateful enough that this performance has survived. If impassioned gospel is your thing, boy, are you gonna love this. *—Cub Koda*

Jesus Be a Fence Around Me / 1961 / S.A.R. ✦✦✦✦✦

Sweet soul in Cooke-ing tradition. *—Opal Louis Nations*

Gospel Pearls / 1962 / S.A.R. ✦✦✦✦✦

Strong lead work from Cooke, Harris, Jimmy Outler, and Leroy Crume. Also features the Gospel Paraders. *—Opal Louis Nations*

★ **The Soul Stirrers** / 1964 / Specialty ✦✦✦✦✦

Specialty's *Soul Stirrers* is a wonderful, definitive collection that contains the best moments from the seminal gospel group, including material recorded with all four lead vocalists—Sam Cooke, Johnnie Taylor, R.H. Harris, and Paul Foster. *—Leo Stanley*

☆ **The Original Soul Stirrers Featuring Sam Cooke** / 1964 / Specialty ✦✦✦✦✦

The split between the secular and spiritual in black music has not only caused controversy, but has been the springboard for some of the best gospel, R&B, soul, and even hip-hop records to come out in the last 50 years; Ray Charles, Sam Cooke, Little Richard, and Al Green certainly come to mind in relation to seemingly irreconcilable allegiances to God and the commercial spotlight. Cooke's own move into the soul music field (in fact, he practically created the style) certainly caused major problems for fans of his first group and gospel music's own vocal royalty, the Soul Stirrers; it was one thing to sing sexy in church, but to embrace rock & roll with songs like "Having a Party" and "Shake" was tantamount to blasphemy. This fine Soul Stirrers collection reveals what some of the fuss was about, as Cooke is featured on a handful of the group's innovative and highly expressive gospel hits. At times sharing the mike with second lead Paul Foster, Cooke soars with angelic soulfulness on hits like "Wonderful," "Touch the Hem of His Garment," and "I'm So Glad (Trouble Don't Last Always)." Beyond the cuts featuring Cooke, the record also spotlights the talents of Cooke's replacement and future soulster Johnnie Taylor as well as veteran group member R.H. Crain. There's also plenty of fine, post-Cooke material like "Feel Like My Time Ain't Long." Check this collection out before picking up Cooke's popular records and see why "soul music" has been a part of the church all along. *—Stephen Cook*

The Best of the Soul Stirrers / 1966 / Checker ✦✦✦✦✦

Little Willie Rogers wails in the Cooke tradition. Fine singing by all. *—Opal Louis Nations*

The Golden Gospel / 1967 / Checker ✦✦✦✦✦

Great moments. Successful pairing of choir with quartet. *—Opal Louis Nations*

The Thrilling Soul Stirrers in Concert (Live) / 1968 / Checker ✦✦✦✦✦

Vocal pyrotechnics by Willie Rogers and Martin Jacox in a live setting. *—Opal Louis Nations*

Gospel Music / 1969 / ✦✦✦✦✦

The most impressive and influential gospel quartet of the pre- and postwar era. Strong leads and perfect soul-inspired harmonies. '40s recordings. *—Opal Louis Nations*

The Gospel Soul of Sam Cooke & the Soul Stirrers, Vol. 2 / 1969 / Specialty ✦✦✦✦✦

The Gospel Soul of Sam Cooke & the Soul Stirrers, Vol. 2 is being promoted under Sam Cooke's name, but it's really the Stirrers' show with first-class titles like "Farther Along" and "I'm So Glad." Some of Cooke's greatest moments, ca. 1951-1955, with great second-lead support from Paul Foster Sr. Includes three previously unreleased cuts. *—Kip Lornell*

Going Back to the Lord Again / 1972 / Specialty ✦✦✦✦

The best of the Crume brothers set of the Soul Stirrers, featuring Richard Miles and Martin Jacox. *—Opal Louis Nations*

Resting Easy / 1984 / Chess ✦✦✦

Fine '60s gospel singing and soulful lead work by Little Willie Rogers. *—Opal Louis Nations*

A Tribute to Sam Cooke / 1984 / MCA/Chess ✦✦✦

Little Willie Rogers personalizes some of Cooke's finest songs on this '60s Chess reissue. *—Opal Louis Nations*

Heaven Is My Home / 1988 / Specialty ✦✦✦

The Soul Stirrers have been gospel's most honored and recognized vocal group since the '40s, when R.H. Harris made musical history by shifting the genre's focus from unison singing to improvisational theatrics and inter-group dynamics. The selections on this reissue cover a significant and too-often ignored aspect of the ensemble's history: the music of its other premier lead singers besides Harris and Sam Cooke. Paul Foster and Johnnie Taylor, the set's featured vocalists, weren't virtuosos like Harris or Cooke; they relied on timing, delivery, and fervor. *—Ron Wynn*

In the Beginning / 1991 / Ace ✦✦✦✦✦

Ace's *In the Beginning* is an excellent collection of recordings the Soul Stirrers made in the early '50s. The disc is augmented by several solo cuts from Sam Cooke, making it an excellent distillation of the essence of the group's stirring, extraordinary music. *—Leo Stanley*

Sam Cooke With the Soul Stirrers / 1992 / Specialty ✦✦✦

This 1992 reissue features previously unreleased material. Sam Cooke incorporated the styles of Archie Brownlee, R. H. Harris, and Julius Cheeks (along with his own natural abilities) to become, as many say, the best all-around gospel and R&B singer ever. This recording gives 25 reasons why people might say that. *—Billy C. Wirtz*

Jesus Gave Me Water / 1992 / Specialty ✦✦✦

Sam Cooke was only a tender 19 years of age when he was tapped to replace R.H. Harris as the lead singer of legendary gospel group the Soul Stirrers. Cooke's break came when Soul Stirrer baritone R.B. Robinson saw him perform with the Highway Q.C.'s and decided to take the young singer under his wing. Well, if this recording is any indication, Cooke was already the master and everyone else, students. Cooke gives a command performance running in and out of the Stirrers' characteristically solid backing. Never sounding better, he lends energy and sense of teenage desperation to this set of gospel classics and originals. Especially outstanding are the tracks "I'm on the Firing Line," "Jesus Will Lead Me to That Promised Land," and the brilliantly arranged "Jesus Paid the Debt." It wouldn't be until 1958 that Sam Cooke would break into the pop charts, but this record reveals he was a consummate performer. As a total unknown suddenly thrust into leading the most popular gospel group in America, Cooke breaks not a sweat. An excellent, though largely forgotten, record. —*Brian Whitener*

The Last Mile of the Way / 1994 / Specialty ◆◆◆

While the Soul Stirrers' catalog has been thoroughly documented on various Specialty reissues, the 28 tracks presented on this set show that even their secondary and/or alternate cuts were outstanding. They pioneered the use of a double lead, with Sam Cooke's wondrous tenor contrasted by several other superb vocalists from Paul Foster to Julius Cheeks. There's even one cut where guitarist Bob King takes a turn at the microphone and doesn't disgrace himself. Although many of these songs have been previously released, it's instructive to hear the discussions, fragments, and partial pieces that show the Soul Stirrers experimenting and perfecting the formula that made gospel history. —*Ron Wynn*

Heritage / Sep. 23, 1994 / Jewel ◆◆◆

Swing Time Gospel, Vol. 1 / Jul. 25, 1995 / Night Train ◆◆◆◆
Important release of '40s-'50s jubilee quartet material. Includes the Soul Stirrers. —*Opal Louis Nations*

Strength, Power and Love / 1996 / Jewel ◆◆◆
Strong singing, sweet and sanctified with plenty of melodic harmony. —*Opal Louis Nations*

Heritage, Vol. 2 / 1996 / Jewel ◆◆◆
Reworking of some of the group's earlier charts on Checker and Specialty. —*Opal Louis Nations*

Clarence Spady

b. Jul. 1, 1961, Paterson, NJ
Vocals / Modern Electric Blues, Soul-Blues
Blues guitarist, singer, and songwriter Clarence Spady has a bright future. Spady, born in Paterson, NJ, has been credited with taking the music in new and exciting directions, writing at times introspective, autobiographical blues lyrics attuned to contemporary life.

His debut for the Philadelphia-based Evidence Music, *Nature of the Beast*, received critical praise from all corners of the blues world, and he's signed to a multi-album deal with the label. (Spady recorded the album independently before executives at Evidence signed him.) Like diddley bow player Lonnie Pitchford, Spady was cited by *Living Blues* magazine as one of the "top 40 under 40" blues players to watch in the future.

Spady learned blues from his father, and played his first professional show while still in kindergarten, where he performed B.B. King and James Brown tunes for his classmates.

Raised in Scranton, PA, where he's still based, Spady would sit on his dad's lap and watch him play guitar until bedtime. Spady got his first guitar at age four; blues fever caught him early on, and he's never let it go. His first professional show came when he was six, playing with his father, older brother, aunt, and uncle at the Paterson Elks Club in New Jersey. Like any good bluesman, Spady was raised singing in church, which he attended every Sunday with his mother. Unlike other Southern bluesmen who were raised just a generation earlier, the blues were not forbidden in the Spady household; quite the contrary, they were encouraged, since his father and other relatives played the music.

Spady sang gospel music in church and took his cue from the secular music of the day played on the radio around New York City, including James Brown, the Isley Brothers, and Jimi Hendrix. He counts B.B. King and Albert Collins among his main blues mentors, and throughout his formative years, Spady played with various rock and gospel groups, honing his chops in the hope that one day he would lead his own blues band.

After he graduated from high school in 1979, Spady hit the road with regional groups and spent most of the '80s with the Greg Palmer Band, which opened for major touring acts like the Temptations, the Four Tops, and the Spinners. After getting off the road in 1987, Spady played lead guitar in several Scranton-area blues bands and also directed the Shiloh Baptist Church Choir. By the early '90s, Spady decided to lead his own band.

Much of the material on *Nature of the Beast* is drawn from his personal experience with drugs and his former relationships with women. Although he's long since dropped the drug habit he picked up in his years after high school, the experiences provided him with fodder for some of the songs on his debut.

Spady's multi-album deal with Evidence Music was formalized in February 1996, after the company agreed to remaster and repackage *Nature of the Beast*, the independently released album that got him radio airplay and allowed him to tour clubs and festivals up and down the East Coast.

Spady will be a force in the blues world for a long time to come, as he backs up great singing with stellar guitar playing and a creative muse for blues lyric writing that the world will find refreshing. —*Richard Skelly*

● **Nature of the Beast** / 1996 / Evidence ◆◆◆

Charlie Spand

Vocals, Piano / Piano Blues
Next to nothing is known about barrelhouse pianist Charlie Spand—the 33 scattered tracks that comprise his recorded legacy are virtually the only concrete proof that he even existed. Although his exact origins are unclear, his 1940 recording "Alabama Blues" contains references to his birth there; academics also offer his earlier performances of

"Mississippi Blues" and "Levee Camp Man" as strong evidence of a connection to the Delta. However, Spand first made a name for himself as a product of the fecund Detroit boogie-woogie scene of the '20s; between 1929 and 1931, he cut at least 25 tracks for the Paramount label, duetting with Blind Blake on a rendition of "Moanin' the Blues." His trail is next picked up in 1940, when he recorded eight final tracks in Chicago backed by Little Son Joe and Big Bill Broonzy; at that point, however, Spand seemingly vanished into thin air, and his subsequent activities both in and out of music remain a mystery. —*Jason Ankeny*

The Complete Paramounts (1929–1931) / 1992 / Document ◆◆◆◆◆
Document's *The Complete Paramounts (1929-1931)* is an invaluable Charlie Spand anthology, reissuing all of the pianist's early sides for Paramount. Classic performances include "Got to Have My Sweetbread," "Soon This Morning Blues," "Hastings Street," and his seminal duet with Blind (Arthur) Blake on "Moanin' the Blues." Still, it's not an exhilarating, start-to-finish listen—the long running time, chronological sequencing, and poor fidelity make it hard to digest. The more serious, intellectual blues listener will find all these factors to be positive, but enthusiasts and casual listeners will find that the collection is of marginal interest for those very reasons. —*Thom Owens*

● **Dreaming the Blues: The Best of Charlie Spand** / Jan. 8, 2002 / Yazoo ◆◆◆◆◆

Otis Spann

b. Mar. 21, 1930, Jackson, MS, d. Apr. 24, 1970, Chicago, IL
Vocals, Piano / Blues Revival, Piano Blues, Acoustic Blues, Electric Chicago Blues, Chicago Blues
An integral member of the nonpareil Muddy Waters band of the '50s and '60s, pianist Otis Spann took his sweet time in launching a full-fledged solo career. But his own discography is a satisfying one nonetheless, offering ample proof as to why so many aficionados considered him then and now as Chicago's leading postwar blues pianist.

Spann played on most of Waters classic Chess waxings between 1953 and 1969, his rippling 88s providing the drive on Waters' seminal 1960 live version of "Got My Mojo Working" (cut at the prestigious Newport Jazz Festival, where Spann dazzled the assembled throng with some sensational storming boogies).

The Mississippi native began playing piano by age eight, influenced by local ivories stalwart Friday Ford. At 14, he was playing in bands around Jackson, finding more inspiration in the 78s of Big Maceo Merriweather, who took the young pianist under his wing once Spann migrated to Chicago in 1946 or 1947.

Spann gigged on his own and with guitarist Morris Pejoe before hooking up with Waters in 1952. His first Chess date behind the Chicago icon the next year produced "Blow Wind Blow." Subsequent Waters' classics sporting Spann's ivories include "Hoochie Coochie Man," "I'm Ready," and "Just Make Love to Me."

Strangely, Chess somehow failed to recognize Spann's vocal abilities. His own Chess output was limited to a 1954 single, "It Must Have Been the Devil," that featured B.B. King on guitar, and sessions in 1956 and 1963 that remained in the can for decades. So Spann looked elsewhere, waxing a stunning album for Candid with guitarist Robert Jr. Lockwood in 1960, a largely solo outing for Storyville in 1963 that was cut in Copenhagen, a set for British Decca the following year that found him in the company of Waters and Eric Clapton, and a 1964 LP for Prestige where Spann shared vocal duties with bandmate James Cotton. Testament and Vanguard both recorded Spann as a leader in 1965.

The Blues Is Where It's At, Spann's enduring 1966 album for ABC-BluesWay, sounded like a live recording but was actually a studio date enlivened by a gaggle of enthusiastic onlookers who applauded every song (Waters, guitarist Sammy Lawhorn, and George "Harmonica" Smith were among the support crew on the date). A BluesWay encore, *The Bottom of the Blues*, followed in 1967 and featured Otis' wife, Lucille Spann, helping out on vocals.

Spann's last few years with Muddy Waters were memorable for their collaboration on the Chess set *Fathers and Sons*, but the pianist was clearly ready to launch a solo career, recording a set for Blue Horizon with British blues-rockers Fleetwood Mac that produced Spann's laid-back "Hungry Country Girl." He finally turned the piano chair in the Waters' band over to Pinetop Perkins in 1969, but fate didn't grant Spann long to achieve solo stardom. He was stricken with cancer and died in April of 1970. —*Bill Dahl*

Otis Spann Is the Blues / Aug. 1960 / Candid ◆◆◆◆◆
He may not have been *the* blues, but he was sure close to being *the blues pianist*. Spann provided wonderful, imaginative, tasty piano solos and better-than-average vocals, and was arguably the best player whose style was more restrained than animated. Not that he couldn't rock the house, but Spann's forte was making you think as well as making you dance. —*Ron Wynn*

☆ **Complete Candid Recordings—Otis Spann/Lightnin' Hopkins Sessions** / Aug. 23, 1960 / Mosaic ◆◆◆◆◆
With Robert Jr. Lockwood. Two classic Spann albums: *Otis Spann Is the Blues* and *Walkin' the Blues*. Early, potent Spann with flawless liner notes and a complete discography. Also included are the Candid sessions of Lightnin' Hopkins. —*Michael Erlewine*

The Blues Is Where It's At / 1966 / BGO ◆◆◆◆◆

Cracked Spanner Head / 1969 / Deram ◆◆◆

The Blues Never Die! / Oct. 1969 / Prestige/Original Blues Classics ◆◆◆◆◆
Boasting fellow Chicago blues dynamo James Cotton on both harmonica and lead vocals, *The Blues Never Die!* is one of Otis Spann's most inspired albums. When this session was recorded for Prestige's Bluesville subsidiary in 1964, Spann was still best known for playing acoustic piano in Muddy Waters' band. But *The Blues Never Die!* (which Fantasy reissued on CD in 1990 for its Original Blues Classics series) shows that he was as great a leader as he was a sideman. From Willie Dixon's "I'm Ready" (a Chess gem Spann had played numerous times with Waters) and Elmore James' "Dust My Broom" to Cotton's spirited "Feelin' Good" and Spann's dark-humored "Must Have Been the Devil," Spann

and Cotton enjoy a very strong rapport on this consistently rewarding date. —*Alex Henderson*

Cryin' Time / 1970 / Vanguard ✦✦✦
While the Muddy Waters sideman is best known for piano, his soulful organ steals the show on this late-'60s release. His singing is serviceable, helped by wife Lucille Spann on two cuts. Country Joe & the Fish co-founder Barry Melton plays lead guitar, with Luther "Guitar Junior" Johnson taking the second chair. —*Mark Allan*

Sweet Giant of the Blues / 1970 / Blues Time ✦✦✦
Sweet Giant of the Blues is a solid record. Seemingly more accidental than intentional, the production is clean and separated. Yet it has a roomy quality that highlights the superb musicianship on this record. The record starts out with a fast and furious version of "Got My Mojo Workin'." Spann's Delta-inspired voice shines over the group, which sounds very tight and much like the Chess session men. "Moon Blues" is a song highlighted with fuzz guitar leads and a '70s sound. The funky "I'm a Dues Payin' Man" is a refreshing change of pace on the album, while "Bird in a Cage" is soulful instrumental. Coming through as the standout track, "Bird in a Cage" reaffirms blues musicians as some of the best players in music. The track showcases Ray Charles-esque piano playing and blues saxophone—which takes away from the song by adding a '70s feel to the recording. Overall, this is a tight record by a man with one of the best voices in the blues. —*Zachary Curd*

★ **Walking the Blues** / 1972 / Candid ✦✦✦✦✦
Walking the Blues is arguably the finest record Otis Spann ever cut, boasting 11 cuts of astounding blues piano. On several numbers, Spann is supported by guitarist Robert Jr. Lockwood and their interaction is sympathetic, warm, and utterly inviting. Spann relies on originals here, from "Half Ain't Been Told" to "Walking the Blues," but he also throws in a few standards ("Goin' Down Slow," "My Home Is in the Delta") that help draw a fuller portrait of his musicianship. Most importantly, however, is the fact that *Walking the Blues* simply sounds great—it's some of the finest blues piano you'll ever hear. —*Thom Owens*

Blues Masters, Vol. 10 / 1991 / Storyville ✦✦✦

Blues of Otis Spann . . . Plus / 1993 / See for Miles ✦✦✦
A Mike Vernon-produced British album from 1964 that was one of Spann's first full-length dates as a leader. Nice band, too: Muddy Waters on guitar, bassist Ransom Knowling, and drummer Willie "Big Eyes" Smith, along with a young Eric Clapton playing on a couple of cuts. Spann plays a harpsichord on a few items; needless to say, they aren't the album's shining moments! —*Bill Dahl*

Otis Spann's Chicago Blues / 1994 / Testament ✦✦
Recorded in 1965 and 1966, these 15 tracks are divided between solo piano performances and pieces with a full band, with support from guitarist Johnny Young and members of the Muddy Waters Band. The variation in approach means that this isn't the most consistent Spann album, and the material and performances don't rank among his best either, although they're reasonably solid. Includes some of the rare tracks on which Spann played organ rather than piano. —*Richie Unterberger*

Down to Earth / 1995 / MCA ✦✦✦✦✦
Both of the great Chicago pianist's albums for ABC-BluesWay, characterized with rippling piano and ruminative vocals. Backed in style by his mates in the Muddy Waters band (including the man himself), Spann responds to a studio full of people on "Popcorn Man," "Steel Mill Blues," and "Nobody Knows Chicago like I Do." Spann's 1967 encore LP united him in the studio with wife Lucille for several vocals. —*Bill Dahl*

Live the Life / Jun. 10, 1997 / Testament ✦✦✦✦
This release includes 16 rare and previously unissued Otis Spann tracks recorded between 1964 and 1969. Featuring the blues piano genius in both a solo context and supporting a bevy of Chicago artists in a variety of settings, this plows through Pete Welding's old Testament tape vaults to uncover new treasures by the carload. Muddy Waters is listed on the front cover and, indeed, 12 of the 16 songs here are played in his company, most of it in the unusual role of backup musician to Spann. The compilation begins with five songs from a Dr. Martin Luther King, Jr., tribute concert in 1968 featuring Spann and Waters on acoustic guitar performing as an "unplugged" duo, including a heartfelt "Tribute to Martin Luther King" standing next to his own tribute to Big Maceo Merriweather, "Worried Life Blues." Next up are seven tracks from a late-'60s Muddy Waters concert, kicking off with Spann doing a rip-roaring "Kansas City" and a somber take of "Tin Pan Alley," and dueting later with Waters on a gospel-tinged "I Wanna Go Home." Spann's piano work in both of these live settings is nothing short of elegant and extraordinary, whether he's soloing, comping perfectly behind Waters' vocals, or directing the band with an all-knowing lick. Two solo tracks from 1965 ("Everything's Gonna Be Alright" and "What's on Your Worried Mind") are followed by two songs showcasing Spann as a session player behind Johnny Young and harmonica man Slim Willis. Perhaps not the most essential Otis Spann collection you'll ever hear, but one that nonetheless showcases his wide range of talents. —*Cub Koda*

The Best of the Vanguard Years / Jun. 22, 1999 / Vanguard ✦✦✦✦
Most of the 18 songs on this fine, if slightly lackluster, compilation come near the end of Spann's 15-year run with Muddy Waters, placing them in the mid- to late '60s. There's plenty of talent here and some of the songs are among the best of Spann's solo efforts, but too much of it seems overly polished compared with the raw, stellar session piano work he did with Waters a decade earlier. Still, a decent assessment of the blues great's final years. —*Michael Gallucci*

Last Call: Live at Boston Tea Party, April 2, 1970 / Aug. 8, 2000 / No Bones ✦✦✦
Essential primarily as a historical document, this album's tapes—recorded in 1970 only three weeks before the pianist's death from liver cancer—were thought to have been

destroyed until they were found in a warehouse in 1999. Otis Spann, the classic Chicago bluesman whose work is revered and studied by almost every blues pianist who followed in his wake, was so weak that he couldn't sing, and was clearly not at the top of his form for these shows. Spann's wife Lucille handles the vocals on the majority of the tracks, and her powerful singing seems to push Spann to perform with his classic restraint and style. Still, there's plenty of interest here. Spann's tinkling work on Big Joe Turner's "Chains of Love" shows that his chops were still sharp, even as he knew he was in death's final throws. Another Muddy Waters sideman, Luther "Snake" Johnson, handles the vocals and guitar duties on workmanlike but unspectacular covers of Muddy's "Long Distance Call" and "I Got My Mojo Working." But the instrumental workout on "Stomp With Spann" and the intro to "My Baby (Sweet As an Apple)," the latter with a vocal from Lucille so gritty and intense it's a wonder it didn't knock the frail pianist from his bench, best exhibit the subtle quality that made Spann's playing so magnificent. His inconspicuous but reliable backup band for these dates was also unusually understated. The sound, taken from 7" reel-to-reel tapes that had been in storage for almost 30 years, is remarkably clean and only the clunky mix—which isolates Lucille onto one side of the stereo, and the guitar played by this album's producer and label president Peter Malick onto the other—belies the age and raw qualities of the recording. Spann's playing remains classy, modest, yet flexible even during the final shows of his legendary life, making this a short but sweet reminder that the man lived the blues. A final track, "Blues for Otis," recorded in 1998, is a loving tribute from Malick to Spann and closes the disc out with a sweet, heartfelt coda. Undoubtedly not the place to start your Otis Spann collection, *Last Call* is still a remarkable album to own for any Chicago blues fan. It shows that the blues ran deep in this musician, and even in his last weeks on earth, his playing plumbed the depth of his soul. —*Hal Horowitz*

Speckled Red (Rufus G. Perryman)
b. Oct. 23, 1892, Monroe, LA, **d.** Jan. 2, 1973, St. Louis, MO
Piano, Organ / Jazz Blues, Piano Blues
Pianist Speckled Red (born Rufus Perryman) was born in Monroe, LA, but he made his reputation as part of the St. Louis and Memphis blues scenes of the '20s and '30s. Red was equally proficient in early jazz and boogie woogie—his style is similar to Roosevelt Sykes and Little Brother Montgomery.

Speckled Red was born in Louisiana, but he was raised in Hampton, GA, where he learned how to play his church's organ. In his early teens, his family—including his brother Willie Perryman, who is better known as Piano Red—moved to Atlanta, Georgia.

Throughout his childhood and adolescence he played piano and organ and by the time he was a teenager, he was playing house parties and juke joints. Red moved to Detroit in the mid-'20s and while he was there, he played various nightclubs and parties. After a few years in Detroit, he moved back south to Memphis. In 1929, he cut his first recording sessions. One song from these sessions, "The Dirty Dozens," was released on Brunswick and became a hit in late 1929. He recorded a sequel, "The Dirty Dozens, No. 2," the following year, but it failed to become a hit.

After Red's second set of sessions failed to sell, the pianist spent the next few years without a contract—he simply played local Memphis clubs. In 1938, he cut a few sides for Bluebird, but they were largely ignored.

In the early '40s, Speckled Red moved to St. Louis, where he played local clubs and bars for the next decade and a half. In 1954, he was rediscovered by a number of blues aficionados and record label owners. By 1956, he had recorded several songs for the Tone label and began a tour of America and Europe. In 1960, he made some recordings for Folkways. By this time, Red's increasing age was causing him to cut back the number of concerts he gave. For the rest of the '60s, he only performed occasionally. Speckled Red died in 1973. —*Stephen Thomas Erlewine & Michael G. Nastos*

Piano Blues / 197 / Storyville ✦✦✦✦✦

Blues Masters, Vol. 11 / 1991 / Storyville ✦✦✦

Complete Recorded Works 1929–1938 / Jun. 2, 1994 / Document ✦✦✦

● **Dirty Dozens** / 1996 / Delmark ✦✦✦✦✦
If you have trouble keeping track of the "Reds," Rufus G. Perryman was "Speckled Red," while William Lee Perryman was either "Piano Red" or "Doctor Feelgood." In addition, Speckled Red's style contained more rag and folk elements than Piano Red's, as this set reveals. But both Reds talked a lot of trash, and Speckled Red had a lighter barrelhouse approach than his younger brother. —*Ron Wynn*

Dave Specter
b. May 21, 1963, Chicago, IL
Vocals, Guitar / Modern Electric Blues, Modern Electric Chicago Blues
In a relatively short timeframe, Chicago guitarist Dave Specter has found his way onto the blues equivalent of the fast track. Just over a decade ago, the towering guitarist with the carefully coiffed hair first made his presence felt as a good-natured bouncer at B.L.U.E.S., a Windy City blues mecca. Now, he's got six acclaimed albums in the Delmark catalog, every one a satisfying, challenging mix of blues (Specter lists influences including T-Bone Walker, Pee Wee Crayton, Magic Sam, and Otis Rush) and jazz (Kenny Burrell is another of his main men).

The native of Chicago's northwest side didn't even grab a guitar until he was 18 years old, inspired by his harp-blowing older brother Howard. While working at Jazz Record Mart and in the shipping department at Delmark, he took guitar lessons from Sunnyland Slim's former guitarist Steve Freund. Once he gained some skills, Freund set him up with legendary drummer Sam Lay and Howlin Wolf's guitar player Hubert Sumlin for a tour. At this time he was also working at B.L.U.E.S., making valuable contacts on the job that led to sideman gigs with Johnny Littlejohn, Son Seals, and the Legendary Blues Band before he assembled his own outfit, the Bluebirds, in 1989.

Since Specter doesn't sing, he recruited deep-voiced crooner Barkin' Bill Smith as his first vocalist. The two shared the spotlight on Specter's alluring 1991 Delmark debut,

Bluebird Blues. After Smith departed, Specter latched on to another West Side veteran, Jesse Fortune, backing the singer on his 1993 Delmark set, *Fortune Tellin' Man.* Dazzling harpist Tad Robinson took over frontman duties for the Bluebirds' 1994 disc *Blueplicity* and *Live in Europe* the next year. California harpman Lynwood Slim became the band's resident singer when Robinson left.

Jazz is growing increasingly prominent in Specter's evolving guitar attack. He imported legendary jazz organist Brother Jack McDuff to provide a Hammond B-3 cushion for his 1996 Delmark project *Left Turn on Blue.* In 1998 he returned with a new singer, Lenny Lynn, and a new record for Delmark, *Blues Spoken Here.*

For 2000's *Speculatin'*, Spector did away with vocals and cut 13 instrumentals. Squeezing frequent European tours in between myriad local gigs, Specter wears his love for swinging blues tradition on his sleeve—and it fits him well. *—Bill Dahl*

Bluebird Blues / 1991 / Delmark ♦♦♦♦

There wasn't any musical generation gap between young Chicago guitarist Specter and his much older front man Barkin' Bill Smith. Specter's love for the electrified '50s styles of Magic Sam, T-Bone Walker, and B.B. King blended well with Smith's deep, almost crooning baritone pipes on what was the debut album for both men. Lots of breezy swing informs the retro-styled set. *—Bill Dahl*

● **Blueplicity** / 1994 / Delmark ♦♦♦♦♦

Sometimes conviction, charm and humor can be as important as performing proficiency. While there's little in the playing or singing of guitarist Dave Specter or vocalist/harmonica player Tad Robinson that you haven't heard before, they so obviously enjoy what they're doing and communicate it so well that you eventually overlook their familiar material and become engrossed in their performances. This disc has a gritty, rough-edged sound often missing from modern blues dates. The menu ranges from jazzy tunes to low-down wailers, soul-tinged pieces, and uptempo instrumentals. *—Ron Wynn*

Live in Europe / 1995 / Delmark ♦♦♦♦

Specter, his ultra-soulful singer/harpist of the time Tad Robinson, and his swinging Bluebirds ventured over to Germany on tour in 1994, cutting this fine set over two memorable evenings. Robinson, now on his own, was an exceptional match for Specter's concise, crisp guitar style; equally conversant in blues and soul, Robinson is also an exceptional songscribe who penned three of the disc's highlights ("On the Outside Looking In," "Sweet Serenity," "Dose of Reality"). More straight blues than on *Blueplicity*: "Little By Little," "Bad Boy," "Kidney Stew," Little Walter's "It's Too Late Brother." *—Bill Dahl*

Left Turn on Blue / 1996 / Delmark ♦♦♦

This was Specter's fifth album for Delmark Records. It saw the Chicago guitarist team up with singer/harpslinger Lynwood Slim (who wrote or co-wrote four of the songs) and organist Jack McDuff. A smooth and easy listen, *Left Turn on Blue* shuffles, swings, and bops at the juncture of blues and jazz. From the blues chestnut "Party Girl" to the Albert Collins' instrumental "Tremble" to the steady jazz groove of Slim's "Stop! Hold It," this is a very classy album. The horns are nicely done, and jazz buffs will particularly enjoy Specter's brief interjections of other tunes into the songs: "'Til the End of Time," "Unleavened Soul," and "Killer Jack." *—Ann Wickstrom*

Blues Spoken Here / Mar. 24, 1998 / Delmark ♦♦♦

Speculatin' / May 30, 2000 / Delmark ♦♦♦

This is an all-instrumental disc that is exclusively neither blues nor jazz, but a blend of each. It marked the first time the tasty Chicago guitarist recorded only instrumentals, but folks who were Specter fans before this one could probably feel it coming. Though he has worked with some delightful vocalists (Barkin' Bill Smith, Lenny Lynn, Tad Robinson, and Lynwood Slim) he has sprinkled a few instrumentals into previous albums, and the format clearly suits him perfectly. For the most part, Specter is accompanied here by his working band and gives Rob Waters plenty of room to roam on Hammond B-3. Nine tunes are originals (one by Waters), and covers include Dizzy Gillespie's "Birk's Works," the Meters' "Look-Ka Py Py," and "Hot Cha" (a Willie Woods tune that became a hit for Junior Walker). The band also swings on soul-jazz organist Charles Earland's "The Mighty Burner" (the flipside to Earland's "More Today Than Yesterday"). You won't find many covers of this one, save a 1970 recording by Clarence Wheeler and the Enforcers. "At Whit's End" is Specter's tribute to his late compadre and guitar pal, Bob Whitman. The minor-key cha-cha spotlights Specter's frugal, delicately paced guitar style and Waters' rapid B-3 runs. "Blues A-La-King," with phrasing similar to some of B.B. King's earlier work, is a "backward" shuffle that best demonstrates how tight this band is. Specter and Waters adopt a marvelously aloof, sassy mood and take off together on the opening phrases of "The Haleiwa Shuffle," named for the artist's favorite Oahu getaway. The only song that doesn't fall in line with the general feeling here is "Dark Hour Blues," a slow and grinding stomp in the key of E through J.L. Hooker/Lightnin' Hopkins territory that is tacked on to the end of the disc. Still, it's proof positive that Specter can do it all. *Speculatin'* has set the record straight: Blues instrumentals are not just for breakfast anymore! *—Ann Wickstrom*

Benny Spellman

b. Dec. 11, 1931, Pensacola, FL

Vocals / New Orleans R&B, R&B

New Orleans R&B vocalist. His deep bass voice booms through loud and clear on many early-'60s Allen Toussaint productions, but Benny Spellman enjoyed a major hit of his own in 1962, "Lipstick Traces (On a Cigarette)." Spellman spent some time with Huey "Piano" Smith & the Clowns before signing with Minit, where Toussaint utilized his deep pipes to full advantage as a backing vocalist behind Ernie K-Doe on "Mother-In-Law" and countless others. The Rolling Stones covered "Fortune Teller," the flip side of this hit. Spellman recorded through much of the '60s, his "Word Game" turning up on Atlantic in 1965, before he took a day gig as a beer salesman. *—Bill Dahl*

● **Fortune Teller** / 1988 / Collectables ♦♦♦♦♦

Infectious and influential early-'60s New Orleans R&B. Spellman's low-pitched vocals are perfectly produced by pianist Allen Toussaint. *—Bill Dahl*

Jeremy Spencer

b. Jul. 4, 1948, Lancashire, England

Vocals, Guitar / British Blues, Album Rock, Blues-Rock

An early member of Fleetwood Mac, slide guitarist Jeremy Spencer left behind a fine (if limited) musical legacy, but is perhaps better remembered for his sudden defection from the group to join a religious cult. Spencer was born in West Hartlepool, Lancashire, England, on July 4, 1948; he started taking piano lessons at age nine, switched to guitar at 15 to emulate his rock & roll idols, and the following year discovered Elmore James, who became his chief influence. In 1967, Spencer became the fourth member of the fledgling Fleetwood Mac, concentrating primarily on slide guitar but also doubling up on piano. He was a major component of the group's early blues-rock sound on albums like 1968's *Peter Green's Fleetwood Mac* and 1969's *English Rose.*

A gifted musical impressionist, Spencer's affectionate send-ups of early rock & roll styles and artists were sometimes incorporated into the group's live shows; in 1970, Spencer released a self-titled solo LP in that vein on Reprise, featuring parodies of rockabilly, teen idol ballads, surf, Elvis, psychedelia, and even Mac itself. That same year's *Kiln House* would prove to be the last Mac album Spencer played on, however.

In early 1971, hours before the Los Angeles gig on Mac's American tour, Spencer vanished without warning; five days later, police traced him to the headquarters of a Christian sect called the Children of God, which Spencer had apparently joined after being approached on the street. Always somewhat religious, Spencer later revealed that he'd been feeling spiritually unfulfilled in the wake of the group's success; nonetheless, his abrupt departure left the group in a lurch. Not only did they have to call upon the unstable Green (who'd left a year earlier) to complete the tour, but in Green's absence, Spencer had been the main link to Mac's blues-rock past, which sent them into an identity crisis that wouldn't be resolved for several years.

Meanwhile, Spencer re-emerged in 1973 with a new album, *Jeremy Spencer & the Children*, on CBS; influenced by psychedelia and folk-rock, it was wholly devoted to Spencer's newfound faith. In 1975, Spencer returned to London and formed a blues-rock group called Albatross, which featured other Children of God; in 1979, he released another solo album on Atlantic, titled *Flee.* Though Spencer remained silent on record, he continued to play music and tour, and devoted much of his time to charitable causes. As the millennium drew to a close, Spencer toured India three times (in 1995, 1998, and 2000), worked on material for an instrumental album, and remained an active member of the Family (as the Children of God were later called). *—Steve Huey*

Jeremy Spencer / 1970 / Reprise ♦♦♦

Spencer's rare solo debut is almost something of a 1970 Fleetwood Mac album that happens to feature Jeremy Spencer as lead vocalist and principal songwriter, since he's backed by Fleetwood Mac's own Danny Kirwan, John McVie, and Mick Fleetwood. (Peter Green appears on just one song, and then only on banjo.) If you think that gave Spencer the opportunity to fully indulge in aspects of Fleetwood Mac that only peeked through intermittently in the group's recordings and shows—namely, his love of formulaic slide blues and '50s oldies pastiches—that's pretty spot-on. Yet, even though he's not a terribly imaginative songwriter or powerful vocalist, even when posing as a loving satirist, there's still a sense of love and sincerity that comes through stronger here than it does on most similar vanity side projects. Rockabilly, Buddy Holly, doo wop, Bo Diddley, surf, Elvis Presley, and (of course) ham-handed British electric blues all come in for treatments mixing reverence and pisstake humor. "Mean Blues," actually, is funnier than the ridicule the blues-rock boom would have likely been given by outlets like the *National Lampoon* radio series, which is doubly impressive given that Spencer was very much part of the blues-rock boom he was poking in the eyes. Psychedelic hippie hard rock, too, is given a mockingly sophomoric, working-class filter with "Take a Look Around Mrs. Brown." The album's material might have been funnier live, naturally, but it's fairly funny and/or pleasing, and the styles are varied enough that it doesn't get tiresome. *—Richie Unterberger*

● **Jeremy Spencer & the Children** / 1973 / CBS ♦♦♦

This 1972 release by ex-Fleetwood Mac guitarist Jeremy Spencer with his religious group the Children is as consistently good as the work by other members of that venerable band: Danny Kirwan's 1979 effort *Hello There Big Boy,* Christine McVie's 1969 recordings re-released in 1976 as *The Legendary Christine Perfect Album*, Bob Welch's *Man Overboard* from 1980, and *In the Skies* by Peter Green. These enormous talents should have somehow been able to shuffle a new combination/working relationship, or subbed with the real deal when Mick Fleetwood put a tour together sans Lindsey Buckingham, Stevie Nicks, and McVie; listening to these amazing discs it becomes clear that the public needed the trademark in order to hear what's in these grooves—none of these albums garnering success on the same level as Fleetwood Mac. The album that may have suffered the worst fate is *Jeremy Spencer & the Children*—this elegant "psychedelic Christian music," which in itself is a paradox. Phil Ham and Spencer's guitar playing is superb, the instruments singing with melodies and fragrances that are at some points breathtaking. The record works better than the band live, containing power that didn't translate well in the downstairs of Boston's Kenmore Club in the early '70s. It shimmers from the vinyl decades later, "Beauty for Ashes" a sweeping and precise essay with folk guitars embellished by the electric guitarists' immaculate leads. Did the religious overtones stunt the potential popularity, or was the presentation a little too "out there" for the record-buying public to grasp? The cover has a figure of death surrounded by material goods: television, guitar, amplifer, a swank car, tons of "things." This is so much like a Jefferson Airplane doppelgänger that it is frightening—or amazing. Ham adds lead guitar, flute, and sitar, while it is Spencer on slide guitar, piano, and vocals. "War Horse" is powerful: "Another young man dead/But who gives a damn/Those generals on Wall Street/Got control of our land." Paul Kantner must have approved of this big-time, the song sounding like latter-day Airplane musically veering off into Jethro Tull territory. The album is a combination of British and American styles, but its psychedelic/folk leanings are the dominant sound, with remarkable harmonies and a pristine production, as well-crafted as it was badly marketed. It is an impressive work, and possibly the most forgotten solo recording from a member of Fleetwood Mac. —*Joe Viglione*

Flee / 1979 / Atlantic ✦✦✦
After leaving Fleetwood Mac to join a religious cult, Jeremy Spencer was not heard from until the late '70s, when he put together this release. Pleasingly lightweight, nothing here burns with the fire he had when he was a member of the Mac, but nothing grates on your nerves, either. —*James Chrispell*

Jon Spencer Blues Explosion

f. 1990, New York, NY
Group / Indie Rock, Alternative Pop/Rock, Blues-Rock
After a long and semi-successful tenure as leader of scuzz-rock heroes Pussy Galore, Jon Spencer took his anti-rock vision and hooked up with guitarist Judah Bauer and drummer Russell Simins to create the scuzz-blues trio the Jon Spencer Blues Explosion. Postmodern to the core, this is an ironic name; little of what this band plays resembles standard blues. There is, however, a blues feel to what they play, meaning that in many instances they appropriate aspects of the blues (very often clichés) and incorporate them into their anarchic, noisy sound. Not part of alternarock's commercial establishment, Spencer also managed to sharply divide critics who tended to see him as either inspired showman or mendacious con man (frankly, he's both). He did, however, gain popularity and critical respect throughout the '90s.

As with Royal Trux, the other band to emerge after the breakup of Pussy Galore, the Blues Explosion's earliest recordings are virtually incomprehensible (and impossible to find). The bass-less mix is awash in distorted guitars, precious little backbeat, and howled vocals. In its favor is the music's exciting, improvisatory feel; also true is that it's frequently incoherent and careless, and doesn't hold up well to repeated listenings. It was with the the Blues Explosion's 1992 self-titled release that the band began to write semi-coherent songs: Spencer adopted an imitation blues vocal style, and the band riffed wildly and crashed around him in a bluesy sort of way. It was mostly fun, but it also seemed like a bit of a put-on, and more than a little smug.

The Blues Explosion's "breakthrough" came (as it did for Royal Trux) when they began to sound like a '70s rock band. With the release of *Extra Width* in 1993, Spencer and company got some air time on MTV's alterna-rock show *120 Minutes* with the video for the song "Afro." The most noticeable change was the new emphasis on tight songs, funky backbeats, and loads of catchy riffs and hooks. As for Spencer, he was now singing like a grade-Z Elvis impersonator, but, in turn, lost some of the condescending attitude. Live, the band was (and remains) quite a show, generating the kind of sweat and excitement that became anathema to many punk and post-punk bands. *Orange*, which is even more accessible than *Extra Width*, netted the band even more fans upon its release in 1994; 1996's *Now I Got Worry* and 1998's *Acme* were also successful. Still, there is a compelling argument to be made that despite his hip credentials, Spencer is more style than substance. Love him or loathe him (and it's easy to do both), he's a force to be reckoned with. —*John Dougan*

Crypt Style / 1992 / 1+2 ✦✦✦✦
Jon Spencer Blues Explosion / Apr. 24, 1992 / Caroline ✦✦✦
Produced by underground rock's most notorious producer, Steve Albini, this is as close as you're going to get to the Blues Explosion's primal, industrial strength noise rock. From the cacophonous start of "Write a Song," it's clear that this is not going to be your average blues album. Still, it's contagious in a demented kind of way, and the sloppiness, intentional crudeness, and semicoherence are punk rock to the core (the furious, psychobilly track "Rachel"). Not recommended as a place to start with Spencer, and definitely not recommended to those who think they're going to hear Muddy Waters songs. —*John Dougan*

Extra Width / Nov. 1, 1993 / Matador ✦✦✦✦✦
Much more accessible than the aforementioned record, but in no way does its accessibility detract from the record's adventurousness. *Extra Width* is a crankin' piece of bluesoid ranting, with Spencer working up one hysterical performance after another. "Afro" is as funky as all get-out and sounds like an old Curtis Mayfield track. Similarly, "Soul Letter" is a hefty chunk of riff-muck, as is the noisy bliss of "Soul Typecast." The playing is energetic and unhinged, and Spencer drives the engine with his whoopin' and hollerin'. Plenty of noticeably '70s production techniques add to the atmosphere, contributing significantly to what may be Spencer's best record. —*John Dougan*

Orange / Oct. 1994 / Matador ✦✦✦✦
By this juncture, you either love Spencer enough to listen to every record, or you've heard plenty and are decidedly uninterested. Still, *Orange* mines the same territory as *Extra Width*, and that may not be enough. At times, even during *Orange*'s best tracks ("Bell Bottoms"), the thin, retro-'70s worshipping sounds phoned-in and lacking in real emotional commitment. But, as with a lot of junk-rock, sometimes it can be appreciated for simply being junk, and that's fine. But I'm willing to bet that Spencer's core fans like the idea of the blues more than the reality. In other words, they don't mind the pose, nor do they mind the façade. In Jon Spencer's world, image is everything. —*John Dougan*

Experimental Remixes / 1995 / Matador ✦✦✦
With *Experimental Remixes*, various indie rock, dance, and hip-hop luminaries step in to remix and rearrange a handful of Blues Explosion songs, and manage to create an interesting and enjoyable collection. Jon Spencer has long voiced his admiration for hip-hop, so it's no surprise that he would want to collaborate with some of the best samplers

and remixers in the business. Beck and the Beastie Boys' Mike D turn "Flavor" into a cut-and-paste workout, while Calvin Johnson's Dub Narcotic injects "Soul Typecast" with funk and menace. However, it's "Greyhound" that gets the best makeover, courtesy of Moby and the Wu-Tang Clan's Genius/GZA and Killah Priest. Moby's version is a screaming piece of techno-pop, with a brilliant guitar solo laid on top. This segues into Genius/GZA's starker version, in which nearly all of the instruments have dropped out, leaving only the rolling bass line and drums to contend with Killah Priest's rapping. *Experimental Remixes* is sure to appeal to both fans of the Blues Explosion and to fans of the artists featured throughout the album. —*Brandon Gentry*

● **Now I Got Worry** / Oct. 15, 1996 / Matador ✦✦✦✦✦
Where *Orange* had some awkward attempts at funk, *Now I Got Worry* is a raw bloozy workout, full of harsh guitars and barked vocals. The sound of the Blues Explosion is so fiery and alive that it overshadows Spencer's habit for campy posturing, and that's what keeps *Now I Got Worry* afloat. Once it's finished, it becomes hard not to second-guess Spencer's intentions, but the album is the closest the Blues Explosion has come to capturing their wild, intense live show on record. —*Stephen Thomas Erlewine*

Controversial Negro: Live in Tucson / 1997 / Toy's Factory ✦✦✦
Love them or hate them, the Jon Spencer Blues Explosion put on one hell of a show. *Controversial Negro*, originally a promo-only LP issued by the fine folks at Matador Records, has now been given the CD treatment, appearing as a Japanese import much to the joy of hungry fans unable to find a copy of the original limited edition pressing. The record is a document of one of the Blues Explosion's legendary live rock bonanzas, but in the end it is also a case of a "you had to be there" sort of event. Live, Spencer's wild antics—dancing, preaching, climbing things, and whatnot—come off like a fabulous circus gone awry. On record, the visual element is gone and all that remains is the group's playing, an aspect that, intentionally or not, tends to be pretty sloppy live. This is not to say that JSBX come off like a bad talent show contestant, but more that in the case of a rollicking good time the intricacies of the music often fall to the wayside. On the energetic opening "Get With It," the howling "Skunk," and a number of other tracks, the band rocks pretty forcefully, and though the actual recording is occasionally muddied up a bit due to the lack of any real low end, the songs for the most part are still highly entertaining. Even second guitarist Judah Bauer's turn in the spotlight on "Fuck Shit Up" comes across pretty convincingly, as the screamed lyrics take center stage instead of Spencer's outlandish physical behavior. *Controversial Negro* is the live record only JSBX could make; like their shows it contains a lot more rock than blues and plenty of noisy howls and bursts of feedback. It's still a far cry from the actual experience, but the record succeeds in transferring as much of the original event's ragged glory as the medium will allow. —*Peter J. D'Angelo*

Acme / Oct. 20, 1998 / Matador ✦✦✦
Part of the reason Jon Spencer Blues Explosion has been so distasteful to legions of blues purists is that Spencer cherishes not the mythology of the blues or the songcraft, but the actual *sound* of classic blues records—what's important is the feel and the grit of the performance. Often, that means that the Blues Explosion's records are better when they're playing than they are in memory, but there's no question that the trio has shrewdly crafted albums that pack real sonic force. They've also been sharp enough to subtly explore new territory with each album, and on *Acme*, pure sound matters more than ever. Like the Stones, the Blues Explosion never abandons their signature sound, even when they're branching into new territory. No matter how many electronic bleeps, hip-hop loops, or cut-and-paste arrangements rear their heads on *Acme*, or how many producers or remixers are employed, the primal, two-guitar racket remains at the center of Blues Explosion's sound. But the electronica and hip-hop flourishes aren't folly, either—they confirm Spencer's ultimate goal of sound over structure, force over sense. And while there are only a handful of songs to latch on to, the dynamic explosions of sound guarantee that *Acme* is a captivating listen, at least the first time through. Still, it doesn't quite live up to the standards of its three predecessors, not only because it lacks full-fledged songs (the other three were weak on those, anyway) but because it simply isn't as overwhelmingly visceral as other Blues Explosion excursions. While frequently exciting, the sonic experimentations sound cerebral instead of primal, and JSBX have always been better when they aimed straight for the gut, since that's when they came the closest to capturing the feel, if not the sound, of the classic blues records they've used as a blueprint. —*Stephen Thomas Erlewine*

Xtra Acme USA / Sep. 14, 1999 / Matador ✦✦✦✦
As its title implies, *Xtra Acme USA* is a collection of unused leftovers and remixes of selections culled from *Acme*'s recording sessions. However, unlike 1995's *Experimental Remixes* EP, this is more than a visitation of older songs via celebrity remixes. Rather, *Xtra Acme* holds its own as a complete album of new material that tastes great and is very filling. There's no doubt about it: Spencer's certainly got the flava he raves about. *Xtra Acme* is a furious storm of energy, a quality that characterizes the Blues Explosion's *Extra Width* and *Orange*, but one that doesn't readily rear its head on 1996's *Now I Got Worry* or 1998's *Acme*. *Xtra Acme* finds Spencer and company returning to a structureless pattern, mixing tempos and beats, using theremins and modulation boxes, and tossing humor up against lustful sexuality. Hip-hop beats and scratches and samples are part of the cocktail, but the record's strongest segments find Spencer, Bauer, and Simins digging for adrenaline, strutting across an imaginary stage with zesty blues-boogie riffs, and stopping for occasional pauses, thus allowing Spencer the time he needs to vent to the audience and scream instructions to his bandmates. For the first time since *Orange*, Spencer sounds like a man with unlimited confidence and possessed by a fervent desire to belt out momentous melodies. On a remix of "Blue Green Olga," Spencer's voice is so suave, he could fill Ben E. King's shoes and sing at a '50s prom. Conversely, the

full-throttle "Get Down Lover" has an ending that packs such a wallop, it punctures the skin. There are a few stale moments here and there, but *Xtra Acme* has such a wealth of pops, eruptions, reversals and hard-earned sweat that the listener won't notice. Those searching for definitive Blues Explosion, look no further than "Leave Me Alone So I Can Rock Again." Spencer's voice is plain and tight, and fights all temptations to scream. All the while, the band keeps kicking the music's pace up a notch, until it reaches a breaking point where a greasy harmonica wails like a car's radiator on a sultry day and Spencer unleashes his consummate screams—somehow, it urges us to shake, dance, boogie, go crazy. In other words, it screams "rock & roll!" *—Bob Gendron*

Plastic Fang / Apr. 9, 2002 / Matador ♦♦♦
The Jon Spencer Blues Explosion's funky wild blues on critical albums like *Orange* and *Now I Got Worry* defined the band as being in a league of its own. With an intoxicating and sexy vocal growl, Spencer united with bassist Judah Bauer and drummer Russell Simins to define raw rock & roll outside of grunge, post-grunge, and modern rock throughout the '90s. The bamboozled electronica mold of 1998's *Acme* album was sophisticatedly different, but the grit found in the band's previous work was a bit lax. The band might have known it as well; however, a change in direction was happening. The Jon Spencer Blues Explosion's eighth record, *Plastic Fang*, doesn't overlook anything this time, for the album exudes a new power. Spencer and his mates sought the expertise and slick work of musician/producer Steve Jordan, who brought brashness back to the front on *Plastic Fang*. "Sweet 'n' Sour" flourishes with a huge guitar blast, and Spencer's tangy cool vocal howl has never sounded better. "She Said" is comprised of typical swagger, but it's the Rolling Stones-like romp of "Mean Heart" that's truly killer. It's Spencer's best take on a ballad, too, and it's bittersweet, but he's not totally hung up on love. The explosive wail of "Down in the Beast" definitely says so and the chug-chug-chugga rawk of "Money Rock 'n' Roll" rollicks even harder. As a songwriter, Spencer is impressive, and the Blues Explosion's collaboration with Dr. John and Bernie Worrell on the seductive, bluesy, and brooding "Hold On" suggests that *Plastic Fang* isn't exactly focused on one particular sound. It's simple, and the depth behind the band's musicianship has expanded into something fiery once more. With Jordan's assistance, *Plastic Fang* sounds live and abrasive, and it's infectiously undeniable. *—MacKenzie Wilson*

The Spiders

f. 1953, **db.** 1957
Group / New Orleans R&B, R&B
A fine New Orleans vocal ensemble who started as a gospel group, the Spiders scored five Top Ten R&B hits for Imperial in 1954 and 1955. They were originally the Zion City Harmonizers in the '40s, and also did radio work as the Delta Southernaires in 1952 and 1953. Lead singer Hayward "Chuck" Carbo, Joe Maxon, Matthew West, Oliver Howard, and Leonard "Chick" Carbo and got their first hit with "I Didn't Want to Do It" in 1954. It was also their biggest, peaking at number three. They continued the string until the end of 1955. The Carbo brothers departed in 1956, moving on to solo careers. *—Ron Wynn*

● **The Imperial Sessions** / 1993 / Bear Family ♦♦♦♦♦
All of the Spiders' best songs are collected on this extensive double-disc set. *—AMG*

Addie "Sweet Peas" Spivey

b. Aug. 22, 1910, Houston, TX, **d.** 1943, Detroit, MI
Vocals / Classic Female Blues
This blues vocalist from the late '20s and '30s worked under the pseudonym of Sweet Peas, giving shop owners the option of filing her product amongst the frozen foods. With the classic blues style's emphasis on different types of food as a metaphor for sexual encounters, it only seems natural that a performer in the genre would provide herself with an edible name, although the practice hasn't spread much beyond Addie Spivey. She is often confused with her sister, the more famous Victoria Spivey; both grew up around music, as their father had his own string band. Sister Victoria's fatter discography of recordings under her own name was certainly enriched by her starting up one of the first musician-owned blues labels. Not so for Sweet Peas, whose few recordings and alternate takes are shrouded in obscurity, the backgrounds of some of her backup players unknown.

It is also worth mentioning the slight variations in the use of her pseudonym. She did her first recordings for Victor in 1929 as Sweet Peas, and of all her material this is often considered best due to classy backing by trumpeter Henry "Red" Allen. She recorded for Decca seven years later as Sweet Pease Spivey and cut for Bluebird as Sweet Peas Spivey the following year. Becoming the owner of this material, as her sister did, was hardly the case; in fact, these recordings seem to have entered the copyright zone known as "anything goes," resulting in her music being anthologized on blues compilations in several different countries. As a female blues performer, Addie Spivey is often in the good company of artists such as Sippie Wallace and Lizzie Miles on these sets.

Her obscurity also lends her certain status among would-be hipsters, such as a rock musician who, when asked to name some of his current listening faves for his own publicity hype, "admits little has impressed him aside from his Chet Baker, Lil Green, Addie Spivey, and Big Bill Broonzy records." If that hypothetical musician were so smart, he would have known to use the name she recorded under, in turn allowing him to run together several names into the quite appropriate "lil' green sweet peas." Oh well.

Victoria Spivey had another blues performing sister as well, Elton Spivey, who worked under the stage name of the Za Zu Girl, the "girl" probably there in case anyone got confused about the "Elton" part of her name. One would think that with Elton, Addie, and Victoria present and accounted for that life would be simple, but this is not the case. Further recordings by Addie Spivey and perhaps her sister Elton Spivey might be lurking, hidden under mysterious pseudonyms such as Jane Lucas and Hannah May. In the discussion amongst blues scholars over just who these latter two artists really are, some voice an opinion that it was Addie Spivey, although there are others who believe it was really Mozelle Alderson. Researchers agree that at one point singers recording under the names of Jane Lucas and Hannah May were actually the same person, with the same voice also responsible for some 1930 tracks under the name of Kansas City Kitty.

Digging into the CBS files for "dead artists," information on the Vocalion material acquired by the corporation indicates that this so-called Jane Lucas was a Spivey, but Victoria, not Addie; something that was denied vehemently by Victoria Spivey, who was usually more inclined to take credit for things than decline, no matter what her participation was. (Her grandest achievement was "discovering" Bob Dylan.) The same records indicate that the Hannah May that recorded on Vocalion right around the same time was "Victoria Spivey's sister," which might mean an additional credit for the Sweet Peas girl, although it requires scotching the theory of Hannah and Jane being the same person. Unless the Vocalion files are confused, and the tracks are both done by the same sister. But which one? One blues expert testifies: "aurally she sounds like the Za Zu Girl . . .," meaning perhaps Elton Spivey should get the credit.

The *Blues Who's Who* does very little to clear up this dilemma, claiming authoritatively that Hannah May was Addie Spivey. Other pundits have threatened to burn their copy of this tome in outrage, claiming that it was Victoria Spivey. One way of studying the dilemma is to hear them sing together, possible on the recording entitled "I Can't Last Long," which Victoria Spivey wrote and recorded in 1936, perhaps to describe her own participation in the ongoing debate about blueswomen's identities. The number was recorded under the name of Jane Lucas and the State Street Four with Sweet Peas coming in on the final verse. *—Eugene Chadbourne*

Victoria Spivey

b. Oct. 15, 1906, Houston, TX, **d.** Oct. 3, 1976, New York, NY
Vocals, Piano / Classic Female Blues, Acoustic Blues
Victoria Spivey was one of the more influential blues women simply because she was around long enough to influence legions of younger women and men who rediscovered blues music during the mid-'60s U.S. blues revival brought about by British blues bands as well as their American counterparts, like Paul Butterfield and Elvin Bishop. Spivey could do it all: she wrote songs, sang them well, and accompanied herself on piano and organ, and occasionally ukulele.

Spivey began her recording career at age 19 and came from the same rough-and-tumble clubs in Houston and Dallas that produced Sippie Wallace. In 1918, she left home to work as a pianist at the Lincoln Theater in Dallas. In the early '20s, she played in gambling parlors, gay hangouts and whorehouses in Galveston and Houston with Blind Lemon Jefferson. Among Spivey's many influences was Ida Cox, herself a sassy blues woman, and taking her cue from Cox, Spivey wrote and recorded tunes like "TB Blues," "Dope Head Blues" and "Organ Grinder Blues" in the '20s. Spivey's other influences included Robert Calvin, Sara Martin and Bessie Smith. Like so many other women blues singers who had their heyday in the '20s and '30s, Spivey wasn't afraid to sing sexually suggestive lyrics, and this turned out to be a blessing nearly 40 years later in the sexual revolution of the '60s and early '70s.

She recorded her first song, "Black Snake Blues," for the OKeh label in 1926, and then worked as a songwriter at a music publishing company in St. Louis in the late '20s. In the '30s, Spivey recorded for the Victor, Vocalion, Decca and OKeh labels, and moved to New York City, working as a featured performer in a number of African-American musical revues, including the "Hellzapoppin' Revue." In the '30s, she recorded and spent time on the road with Louis Armstrong's various bands. By the '50s, Spivey had left show business and sang only in church. But in forming her own Spivey Records label in 1962, she found new life in her old career. Her first release on her own label featured Bob Dylan as an accompanist. As the folk revival began to take hold in the early '60s, Spivey found herself an in-demand performer on the folk-blues festival circuit. She also performed frequently in nightclubs around New York City. Unlike others from her generation, Spivey continued her recording career until well into the '70s, performing at the Ann Arbor Blues and Jazz Festival in 1973 with Roosevelt Sykes. Throughout the '60s and '70s, she had an influence on musicians as varied as Dylan, Sparky Rucker, Ralph Rush, Carrie Smith, Edith Johnson, and Bonnie Raitt.

Spivey's many albums for Spivey and other labels include the excellent *Songs We Taught Your Mother* (1962), which also includes contributions from Alberta Hunter and Lucille Hegamin, *Idle Hours* (1961), *The Queen and Her Knights* (1965), and *The Victoria Spivey Recorded Legacy of the Blues* (1970).

In 1970, Spivey was awarded a "BMI Commendation of Excellence" from the music publishing organization for her long and outstanding contributions to many worlds of music. After entering Beekman Downtown Hospital with an internal hemorrhage, she died a short while later in 1976. Spivey is buried in Hempstead, NY. *—Richard Skelly*

☆ **Complete Recorded Works, Vol. 1 (1926–1927)** / 1926-1927 / Document ♦♦♦♦♦
The first of four Document CDs that contain all of singer Victoria Spivey's prewar recordings has her first 23 sides. Spivey made her initial reputation with her series of dark blues that were full of symbolism, such as her trademark "Black Snake Blues"—snakes and tuberculosis were common topics in her lyrics. Her first four selections were recorded in St. Louis from May 11-13, 1926 (she was 19 at the time), and then she relocated to New York. Spivey is heard backed by several ensembles led by pianist John Erby in August 1926 (including her first meetings with guitarist Lonnie Johnson) and on five pieces in October 1927 with Johnson and pianist Porter Grainger. By the time the latter sides were recorded, her style was becoming a little more lighthearted and softer but no less powerful. Among the highlights of this superior set are "Black Snake Blues," "Hoodoo Man Blues," "Spider Web Blues," "Got the Blues So Bad," "The Alligator Pond Went Dry," "T-B Blues," and "Garter Snake Blues." This is highly recommended, as are the other three CDs in this important series. *—Scott Yanow*

● **1926–1931** / 1926-1931 / Document ♦♦♦♦♦
Spivey is in marvelous form throughout. This album features the classics "Steady Grind," "Black Snake Blues," and "Blood Thirsty Blues." *—Cub Koda*

Recorded Legacy of the Blues / Apr. 27, 1927-Mar. 12, 1937 / Spivey ♦♦♦♦
Victoria Spivey started her own Spivey label in 1961, and ran it successfully for 15 years. This album is the only Spivey release to reissue some of her earlier vintage material. The 14 selections (which give discographical details, although they are not programmed in chronological order) feature the classic blues singer on sessions from 1927-1929, 1931 and 1936-1937 using such sidemen as guitarists Lonnie Johnson and Tampa Red and trumpeters Louis Armstrong (on "How Do You Do It That Way"), King Oliver, Henry "Red" Allen, and Lee Collins; some of the versions are rare alternate takes. Although it is a pity that all of Spivey's early recordings were not put out by her label, this is a valuable collection. *—Scott Yanow*

☆ **Complete Recorded Works, Vol. 2 (1927–1929)** / 1927-1929 / Document ♦♦♦♦♦
Victoria Spivey, who made her initial reputation with dark and somewhat scary blues lyrics, altered her style during the period covered by this second of four "complete" Document CDs. She is heard in a series of double entendre songs (usually issued in two parts) with singer/guitarist Lonnie Johnson, including "New Black Snake Blues," "Toothache Blues," "Furniture Man Blues," and "You Done Lost Your Good Thing Now." Also, Spivey is heard with an all-star group led by pianist Clarence Williams (including cornetist King Oliver and guitarist Eddie Lang) that unfortunately does not get much space to stretch out; on two classic performances ("Funny Feathers" and "How Do You Do It that Way") on which she is joined by Louis Armstrong's Savoy Ballroom Five (with pianist Gene Anderson in Earl Hines' place); and guesting on two versions apiece of those two same songs with Henry "Red" Allen's Octet (which was really Luis Russell's Orchestra). Spivey, who was a strong singer from the start, is featured throughout in peak form, showing that she could not only sing blues but good-time jazz of the era. *—Scott Yanow*

Complete Recorded Works, Vol. 3 (1929–1936) / 1929-1936 / Document ♦♦♦♦♦
Victoria Spivey's ability to evolve with the times and often reinvent her style can be heard throughout the third of four CDs in Document's reissuance of her prewar recordings. She is heard singing classic blues on four numbers with an all-star group drawn from Luis Russell's Orchestra (including trumpeter Henry "Red" Allen and trombonist J.C. Higginbotham) and on four other songs in which she is just backed by pianist Russell and guitarist Will Johnson. She investigates double entendre blues with the assistance of pianist/vocalist Porter Grainger and (for the two-part "Mama's Quittin' and Leavin'") with guitarist/singer J.T. "Funny Paper" Smith. For a 1931 date, Spivey does her take on hokum (particularly on "He Wants Too Much") with the help of pianist Georgia Tom Dorsey and guitarist Tampa Red. And on "Dreaming 'Bout My Man" she is backed by the pre-swing big band Hunter's Serenaders. This volume concludes by jumping ahead five years and featuring Spivey singing quite confidently with a first-rate Chicago-based swing band (including "Black Snake Swing"). Although not quite as essential as the first two volumes in this series, this set (and *Vol. 4*) is also easily recommended. *—Scott Yanow*

Complete Recorded Works, Vol. 4 (1936–1937) / 1936-1937 / Document ♦♦♦♦
Victoria Spivey is best remembered today for her recordings in the '20s and for her work with her Spivey label in the '60s, but she also made a fairly extensive series of records from 1936-1937. The final of her four Document CDs has all of the latter except for a few titles included on *Vol. 3*. The 22 cuts include ten previously unreleased performances. Spivey is joined by a variety of Chicago-based musicians on four of the five sessions: either Lee Collins (who gets carried away in spots) or Sheiks on trumpet; sometimes the erratic clarinetist Arnett Nelson; and a rhythm section with either Dorothy Scott, Black Bob, J.H. Shayne, Aletha Robinson, or Addie "Sweet Pease" Spivey on piano. (Big Bill Broonzy plays guitar on one session.) In addition, Spivey is heard on a New York date with five musicians who were with the Luis Russell Orchestra (which had become Louis Armstrong's backup group): pianist Russell, trumpeter Henry "Red" Allen, clarinetist Albert Nicholas, altoist Charlie Holmes, and bassist Pops Foster. Throughout, Spivey's voice is in fine form with the music ranging from good-time music to Chicago-style blues. Highlights include "Mr. Freddie Blues," "Trouble in Mind," "Detroit Moan," "I Ain't Gonna Let You See My Santa Claus," "One Hour Mama," and "Good Cabbage." Although not as essential as her earlier work, this CD is worth picking up. It seems strange that Spivey (who up to the late '30s managed to stay fairly up-to-date) did not hook up with a swinging big band; instead, she would not record again until 1961.*—Scott Yanow*

And Her Blues, Vol. 2 / Jun. 10, 1961-Jun. 4, 1972 / Spivey ♦♦♦
Victoria Spivey, a classic blues singer of the '20s, started her own label Spivey in 1961 and kept it going for 15 years. This LP, released posthumously, has three solo performances from 1961 (on which the singer plays either piano or ukulele), a trio rendition of "The Rising Sun" from 1962 with clarinetist Eddie Barefield, four numbers from 1972 in small combos and a loose three-song live performance from 1963 with a guitarist and a kazoo player. Although not essential, the music on this set is enjoyable and should be of interest to jazz historians. *—Scott Yanow*

Woman Blues! / Sep. 1961 / Bluesville/Original Blues Classics ♦♦♦♦
Shortly before she formed her own Spivey label, veteran classic blues singer Victoria Spivey made a fine duo album (reissued on CD in the Original Blues Classic series) with guitarist/vocalist Lonnie Johnson whom she had last recorded with back in 1929. Spivey, 55 at the time, is also heard playing piano, and she takes four of the ten selections as solo performances. All of the compositions are hers, including "Christmas Without Santa Claus," "I'm a Red Hot Mama," "Grow Old Together," and "I Got Men All Over This Town." Recommended as a strong example of Victoria Spivey's later work. *—Scott Yanow*

And Her Blues / Feb. 12, 1962 / Spivey ♦♦♦♦
Victoria Spivey's first full-length set for her Spivey label is one of her best. Joined by Eddie Barefield (on alto and clarinet) and drummer Pat Wilson, Spivey mostly plays piano, but also has two songs apiece on organ and ukelele. Her singing voice was still in fine form, and she performs a dozen of her own blues (most recently written at the time), including "Grant Spivey," "From Broadway to 7th Avenue," "Cool Papa," and "Buddy Tate." *—Scott Yanow*

A Basket of Blues / Feb. 21, 1962-Aug. 16, 1962 / Spivey ♦♦♦♦
This LP, the first release from the Spivey label, has quite a grab bag of performers. Victoria Spivey and Hannah Sylvester (her only recordings after 1923) take four vocals apiece, while Lucille Hegamin has three (the trio were all classic blues veterans of the '20s); the backup band includes tenor saxophonist Buddy Tate (who is featured on the lone instrumental "Swingin' Away"), Eddie Barefield on alto and clarinet, pianist Sadik Hakim, and (on one song) trumpeter Dick Vance. With the exception of the instrumental and the standard "He May Be Your Man," all of the music was composed by Victoria Spivey. An interesting if increasingly difficult-to-find blues set. *—Scott Yanow*

Three Kings and the Queen / Mar. 14, 1962-1963 / Spivey ♦♦♦
This sampler features pianist Roosevelt Sykes, guitarists Lonnie Johnson and Big Joe Williams, and pianist Victoria Spivey on four vocal selections apiece. With the exception of the closing "Thirteen Hours" (which has Spivey joining Sykes for a piano duet) and a pair of Joe Williams tracks (which utilize the then-unknown harmonica player Bob Dylan), all of the performances are unaccompanied. Although each of the blues greats have recorded more classic performances elsewhere, this obscure LP from the Spivey label has its colorful moments. *—Scott Yanow*

Spivey's Blues Parade / 1963-1965 / Spivey ♦♦♦
This LP is a grab bag of previously unreleased numbers recorded for the Spivey label and put together as a blues revue. There are many all-stars involved, plus fine supporting players including Sippie Wallace (heard on a remake of her hit "I'm a Mighty Tight Woman"), Sonny Boy Williamson, Lonnie Johnson, guitarists John Hammond, Benny Jefferson, and Johnny Shines, pianists Sunnyland Slim and Little Brother Montgomery, altoist Eddie Barefield, trumpeter Dick Vance, singers Pat Blackman, Carolina Rose, Nita Washington, Little Sonny Parker, and Delsey McKay, harmonica players Bill Dicey, Sugar Blue, and Walter "Shakey" Horton, comedian Billy Mitchell, and Victoria Spivey herself. Nothing essential occurs, but taken as a whole, it makes for an entertaining show. *—Scott Yanow*

The Queen and Her Knights / Apr. 12, 1965 / Spivey ♦♦♦
Victoria Spivey had an unlikely comeback in the '60s, emerging from a long period off the blues scene to record frequently and run her own successful Spivey label. Although known as a classic blues singer, she was flexible enough to record country blues too, and to hold her own in collaborations with other famous performers. This little-known LP features such immortal bluesmen as guitarist Lonnie Johnson, pianist Little Brother Montgomery, and pianist Memphis Slim, along with guest drummer Sonny Greer. Spivey takes most of the vocals, Montgomery has two, Johnson and Slim are featured on one selection apiece, and Spivey also has vocal duets with Slim ("I'm a Tigress") and Johnson ("Somebody's Got to Go"). Spirited if not quite essential music. *—Scott Yanow*

Victoria Spivey & the Easy Riders Jazz Band / 1990 / GHB ♦♦♦
Veteran blues singer Victoria Spivey teams up with trombonist Big Bill Bissonnette's Easy Riders Jazz Band for this successful and often-romping effort. Actually, Spivey is on just six songs, doing her best on such numbers as "Sister Kate," "See See Rider," "Careless Love," and "Mama's Gone Goodbye." The other seven selections are instrumentals recorded a year later, giving the erratic but spirited trumpeter Fred Vigorito, Bissonnette, and clarinetist Sammy Rimington an opportunity to dig into a variety of standards, including "Four or Five Times," "That Teasin' Rag" (which is the main strain of "The Original Dixieland One-Step"), and "Tin Roof Blues." Fans of New Orleans revival jazz will not mind the occasional missteps, for the spirit and drive of the music generally compensate during this fun set. *—Scott Yanow*

Grind It! / 1999 / Total Energy ♦♦♦
This CD features six tracks recorded with the electric band the Brooklyn Blues Busters in September 1973 at the Ann Arbor Blues & Jazz Festival. It's a little unusual to hear Spivey in this setting, backed by musicians that sound more like the Paul Butterfield group than the prewar "classic" urban blues accompaniment with which she is most associated. It's not a bad or uncomfortable combination, however, the set including her famous "Black Snake Blues" and "Detroit Moan." The band doesn't overplay, as sometimes happened in these situations, and Spivey's vocals are likable, though not especially powerful. While this is not among her most highly recommended or representative recordings to be sure, it is not an embarrassment. Spivey's six tracks occupy only half of this CD, the remainder of which is devoted to six songs by another early blues legend, pianist Roosevelt Sykes, also recorded at the 1973 Ann Arbor Blues & Jazz Festival. *—Richie Unterberger*

The Essential / May 1, 2001 / Classic Blues ♦♦♦

Spooky Tooth

f. 1967, **db.** 1974
Group / Prog-Rock/Art Rock, Hard Rock, Blues-Rock
Part of the early-'70s British hard rock scene, Spooky Tooth grew out of the bluesy VIPs and prog rock group Art and consisted of vocalist Mike Harrison, keyboardist/vocalist Gary Wright, guitarist Luther Grosvenor, bassist Greg Ridley, and drummer Mike Kellie. The group built a following through countless gigs and recorded its debut album, *It's All About*, in 1968. *Spooky Two* became their most successful album in the U.S.; afterwards, Ridley left to join Humble Pie and was replaced by Andy Leigh. Following 1970's *Ceremony*, Wright left to form Wonderwheel, while Grosvenor took the name Ariel Bender and joined Stealers Wheel and later Mott the Hoople. The addition of three members of Joe Cocker's Grease Band—Henry McCullough, Chris Stainton, and Alan Spenner—was not enough to keep the band afloat, and Spooky Tooth broke up after *The Last Puff* in 1970. A reunion in 1973 with Wright, Harrison, and future Foreigner guitarist Mick Jones produced several LPs, including the moderately successful *You Broke My Heart So I*

Busted Your Jaw, but personnel shifts and a lack of top-notch material ended the project in 1974. Wright went on to a successful solo career, scoring pop hits like "Dream Weaver," and Mike Kellie later joined the punk-pop Only Ones. *—Steve Huey*

It's All About / 1968 / Edsel ♦♦♦♦
This full-length debut from British blues-rockers Spooky Tooth has a tone similar to Traffic with its psychedelic take on the influential pop and soul music of the '60s. A few cover tunes including Janis Ian's "Society's Child" and the Nashville Teens' "Tobacco Road" are included, but original songs like the soulful ballad "It Hurts You So" and "Bubbles" (with its Beach Boys sensibility) are the real standouts. The cheery, psychedelic "It's All About a Roundabout" is the catchiest number by far. On this dreamy cut, vocalist/keyboardist Gary Wright demonstrates some sharp melodic and compositional instincts. Although Spooky Tooth eventually became better-known for their straightforward blues-rock, the trippy pop of *It's All About* counts as a career highlight for the group. Fans of late-'60s British rock are definitely advised to check out this impressive release. [*It's All About* was renamed *Tobacco Road* and released in the U.S. by A&M.] *—Vincent Jeffries*

● **Spooky Two** / 1969 / A&M ♦♦♦♦♦
Spooky Two is this British blues-rock band's *pièce de résistance*. All eight of the tracks compound free-styled rock and loose-fitting guitar playing that result in some fantastic raw music. With Gary Wright on keyboards and vocals and lead singer Mike Harrison behind the microphone, their smooth, relaxed tempos and riffs mirrored bands like Savoy Brown and, at times, even the Yardbirds. With some emphasis on keyboards, songs like "Lost in My Dream" and the nine-minute masterpiece "Evil Woman" present a cool, nonchalant air that grooves and slides along perfectly. "I've Got Enough Heartache" whines and grieves with some sharp bass playing from Greg Ridley, while "Better By You, Better By Me" is the catchiest of the songs, with it's clinging hooks and desperate-sounding chorus. The last song, "Hangman Hang My Shell on a Tree," is a splendid example of this group's ability to play off of one another, mixing soulful lyrics with downtrodden instrumentation to conjure up the perfect melancholia. Although the band lasted about seven years, their other albums never really contained the same passion or talented collaborating by each individual musician as *Spooky Two*. *—Mike DeGagne*

Ceremony / 1970 / Edsel ♦♦
This is unlike any other release by an English band normally rooted in the blues. Think of it as Spooky Tooth's version of *Concerto for Group and Orchestra* by Deep Purple. After two or three promising blues-based rock releases, one member of the band somehow convinces the others to go for a wildly ambitious, experimental concept album. Jon Lord persuaded Deep Purple to dive into the deep end, and Gary Wright got Spooky Tooth to welcome Frenchman Pierre Henry for this electronic mass. Wright left the band after *Ceremony* and Lord never had the same influence on Purple again as Ritchie Blackmore led them to heavy metal glory. *—Mark Allan*

The Last Puff / 1970 / A&M ♦♦♦♦♦
Perhaps "The Last Gasp" would have been a more apt title here. Spooky Tooth appeared to be on its last legs, and being propped up by member of the Grease Band, this record should have been merely one of those contract fulfillments, but it isn't. It's a good, solid effort that includes a burning cover of the Beatles' "I Am the Walrus." Unfortunately, Spooky Tooth didn't stay together to reap the rewards of this new combination of musicians. *—James Chrispell*

The Best of Spooky Tooth / 1976 / Island ♦♦♦
Four of the 13 tracks on Island's *The Best of Spooky Tooth* come from 1969's *Spooky Two* album, while the remaining tracks represent the band's less celebrated material. Spooky Tooth's mellow, easy blues-rock sound is experienced from the first track, a slick rendition of John D. Loudermilk's "Tobacco Road." Most of the band's peak material is included here, like "Better by You, Better by Me" and "Evil Woman." The dreamy, psychedelic-tinged "It's All About a Roundabout" is one of the album's best songs, proving the band could be adventurous at will. Much in the same manner is "As Long as the World Keeps Changing," with its hippie-like hallucinatory feel. Versions of the Beatles' "I Am the Walrus" and the Band's "The Weight" are covered peculiarly, but not terribly, chock full of Spooky Tooth's own laid-back formula. Missed is the greyish "Hangman Hang My Shell on a Tree" from *Spooky Two*, which would have made a nice addition to the set. Nevertheless, this best-of does present listeners with Spooky Tooth's most worthwhile songs. The band's unconventional sound and eased style is prevalent on each of the tracks offered here. *—Mike DeGagne*

The Best of Spooky Tooth: That Was Only Yesterday / Jul. 27, 1999 / A&M ♦♦♦♦

That Was Yesterday: Introduction / Dec. 12, 2000 / Island ♦♦♦♦

BBC Sessions / May 22, 2001 / Spitfire ♦♦♦

Houston Stackhouse

b. Sep. 28, 1910, Wesson, MS, **d.** Sep. 23, 1980, Houston, TX
Guitar, Vocals, Harmonica / Delta Blues
The mentor of Delta slide virtuoso Robert Nighthawk, Houston Stackhouse never achieved the same commercial or artistic success as his famed pupil, and remained little known outside of his native Mississippi. Born in the small town of Wesson on September 28, 1910, he was a devotee of Tommy Johnson, whose songs he frequently covered; neither an especially gifted singer nor guitarist, he was quickly surpassed by the young Nighthawk, although the student repaid his debts by backing Stackhouse on a series of sessions cut during the mid- to late '60s. Outside of the rare European tour, Stackhouse was primarily confined to playing Delta border towns throughout the majority of his career; he died in Houston, TX, in 1980. *—Jason Ankeny*

● **Cryin Won't Help You** / Nov. 4, 1994 / Genes ♦♦♦

Big Road Blues / Nov. 9, 1999 / Wolf ♦♦♦

The Staple Singers

f. 1951, Chicago, IL
Group / Traditional Gospel, Country-Soul, Southern Gospel, Black Gospel, Soul
The Staples story goes all the way back to Winona, MS, in 1915. It was then and there that patriarch Roebuck Staples entered the world. A contemporary and familiar of Charley Patton, Roebuck quickly became adept as a solo blues guitarist, entertaining at local dances and picnics. Gradually drawn to the church, by 1937 he was singing and playing guitar with a spiritual group based out of Drew, MS., the Golden Trumpets. Moving to Chicago four years later, he continued playing gospel music with the Windy City's Trumpet Jubilees. A decade later Pops Staples (as he had become known) presented two of his daughters, Cleotha and Mavis, and his one son, Pervis, in front of a church audience, and the Staple Singers were born.

The Staples recorded in an older, slightly archaic, deeply Southern spiritual style first for United and then for Vee-Jay. Pops and Mavis Staples shared lead vocal chores, with most records underpinned by Pops' heavily reverbed Mississippi cottonpatch guitar. In 1960 the Staples signed with Riverside, a label that specialized in jazz and folk. With Riverside and later Epic, the Staples attempted to move into the then-burgeoning white folk boom. Two Epic releases, "Why (Am I Treated So Bad)" and a cover of Stephen Stills' "For What It's Worth," briefly graced the pop charts in 1967.

In 1968 the Staples signed with Memphis-based Stax. The first two albums, *Soul Folk in Action* and *We'll Get Over*, were produced by Steve Cropper and backed by Booker T and the MG's. The Staples were now singing entirely contemporary "message" songs such as "Long Walk to D.C." and "When Will We Be Paid." In 1970 Pervis Staples left, and was replaced by sister Yvonne Staples. Even more significantly, Al Bell took over production chores. Bell took them down the road to Muscle Shoals, and things got decidedly funky.

Starting with "Heavy Makes You Happy (Sha-Na-Boom Boom)" and "I'll Take You There," the Staples counted 12 chart hits at Stax. When Stax encountered financial problems, Curtis Mayfield signed the Staples to his Curtom label and produced a number one hit in "Let's Do It Again." The Staples went on to continued chart success, albeit less spectacularly, with Warner, through 1979. One more album followed on 20th Century Fox in 1981.

After a three-year hiatus, they signed a two-album deal with Private I and hit the R&B charts five more times, once with an unlikely cover of Talking Heads' "Slippery People."

The Staple Singers found a new audience in 1994 when they teamed with Marty Stuart to perform "The Weight" on the *Rhythm, Country and Blues* LP for MCA. Sadly, Pops Staples passed away on December 19, 2000, shortly after suffering a concussion due to a fall in his home. *—Rob Bowman*

Uncloudy Day / 1959 / Vee-Jay ♦♦♦♦♦
Classic folk-rooted gospel from this mixed group. Stinging Delta guitar. Stunning harmonies. *—Opal Louis Nations*

The 25th Day of December / 1962 / Riverside ♦♦♦♦
The group's finest '60s collection. *—Opal Louis Nations*

Hammer and Nails / Oct. 1962 / Riverside ♦♦♦
Fine material, beautifully recorded and produced. *—Opal Louis Nations*

Freedom Highway / 1965 / Columbia ♦♦♦
Classic live in-church Epic recordings from the height of the civil rights movement of 1965. *—Opal Louis Nations*

Soul Folk in Action / 1968 / Stax ♦♦♦
This is one you are probably going to have to search out, but this gem is worth all the effort. First, take the stunning voices of the Staple Singers, with the closely blending harmonies that can only come from the years of a family singing together. Put in the crack vibrato guitar of Pops (he was a blues player early on), add in a top-notch rhythm section that play as close as it gets, and throw in the Memphis Horns. Then add some material that was just about custom-tailored for them, mixed and mastered by Steve Cropper, and you have the makings of a fantastic disc. Still, how many times have we seen all the right ingredients and been disappointed? Not this time. The only disappointment might come from the brevity of the disc; you just want it to continue. The power and majesty that these voices carry comes as close to heaven as can be felt here on earth. They are truly performers who give their all. There are few performers who could rival Otis Redding, and to try and do one of his songs while he was still alive was almost considered sacrilege, yet listen to what they do with "(Sittin' On) The Dock of the Bay." It is a completely different take, yet it loses absolutely nothing and in fact gains a new dimension with their controlled power. True, it probably helps that Steve Cropper, the co-writer of the song, is leading the backing band. Two of the highlights of an incredibly strong disc are "Slow Train," for its slow adept building of potency, and "The Weight." It is a vital testament to belief and love, and you will thank yourself for following a hunch. *—Bob Gottlieb*

Pray On / 1968 / Frank Music ♦♦♦♦♦
The Staple Singers recorded ten 78s over a four-year period for Chicago's Vee-Jay. These have been reissued countless times in various forms. The Charly CD is simply the most recent. For Vee-Jay, the Staples recorded a number of Pops Staples' originals as well as radical rearrangements of standards. Pops Staples and Mavis Staples shared the lead singing chores, with Pervis and Cleotha Staples moaning in the background. Superb gospel shouting. *—Rob Bowman*

Will the Circle Be Unbroken / 1969 / Buddah ♦♦♦
More fine singing plus live recordings. *—Opal Louis Nations*

We'll Get Over / 1970 / Stax ♦♦♦
Their second Stax release was similar to *Soul Folk in Action*. The album's highlight is Randall Stewart's "When Will We Be Paid?" *—Rob Bowman*

The Staple Swingers / 1971 / Stax ♦♦♦
The Staples' first album produced by Al Bell and recorded in Muscle Shoals hit the winning formula. Other changes saw Pervis Staples departing just before the album was

recorded and being replaced by sister Yvonne Staples. Everything was now in place for the Staples' golden years. Three songs, "Heavy Makes You Happy," "Love Is Plentiful," and "You've Got to Earn It," all charted. *—Rob Bowman*

Staple Singers Make You Happy / 1971 / Epic ✦✦

From Riverside, the Staples moved on to Columbia subsidiary Epic in 1964. With Epic, they delved further into the secular realm, hitting the pop charts twice with Pops Staples' plaintive "Why (Am I Treated So Bad)" and a cover of Stephen Stills' "For What It's Worth." Both are included on this two-disc anthology, as is a stunning side of live performance. Great stuff. *—Rob Bowman*

Be Altitude: Respect Yourself / 1972 / Stax ✦✦✦

The Staples' finest single album, containing three Top Ten R&B hits, "Respect Yourself," "I'll Take You There," and "This World." The first two also were pop Top 20s, "I'll Take You There" going all the way to number one. *—Rob Bowman*

Be What You Are / 1973 / Stax ✦✦✦

By the early '70s, despite a roster that included the Dramatics and Isaac Hayes, Stax Records was winding down. The Staple Singers, signed to the label in the late '60s, always provided hit singles and respected album efforts. Despite their gospel beginnings, the Staple Singers' biggest draws became Pops Staples' blues-based "devil's music" guitar and Mavis Staples' breathy and sexy vocals. Their 1972 album, *Be Altitude: Respect Yourself*, all but set the template for their subsequent work. *Be What You Are* in some respects is an often overly cautious follow-up. The first single, "If You're Ready (Come Go With Me)," comes off as a softer take on "I'll Take You There." While the implications of having a narrow lyrical scope did impede the group somewhat, *Be What You Are* has the group mining familiar terrain with minimal wear. Tracks like "Love Comes in All Colors," "Tellin' Lies," and the masterful "Touch a Hand, Make a Friend" are all strong and well-produced tracks in the group's rural yet urbane style. The effort's lone cover of Bill Withers' "Grandma's Hands," despite Mavis Staples' lead, comes up short due to the perfection of the Withers original. Mavis Staples also gets two solo efforts here, including Bettye Crutcher's tough "Drown Yourself" and the spare "Heaven." *Be What You Are* isn't as strong or innovative as its predecessor, but it is a cohesive album and a must-have for fans. *—Jason Elias*

City in the Sky / 1974 / Stax ✦✦✦

City in the Sky, the final LP that the Staple Singers made with Stax Records, features the same socially conscious lyrics and powerful singing that had become their trademark before the album's 1974 release. While the original recording didn't have the kind of explosive singles like "Respect Yourself" and "I'll Take You There" that helped them become legends of soul music, this is by no means a weak album. The opener "Back Road Into Town" seethes with energy and anger-tinged pride, while "Washington We're Watching You" combines that same message of anger and pride with organ and horn-driven funk. The Staple Singers return to the gospel style that had begun their musical career nearly 20 years before with "Who Made the Man,"—perhaps the strongest song on the album, alternating between gentle invectives by Pops Staples and powerful harmonic blasts by Mavis, Cleotha, and Yvonne. Overall, the album combines a classic Stax-influenced soul sound with a strong message, making it an essential part of the Staples Singers' catalog. [The 1996 CD reissue of *City in the Sky* features four bonus tracks, including "Oh La De Da" and live versions of "I Like the Things About You," "Respect Yourself," and "I'll Take You There."] *—Stacia Proefrock*

Let's Do It Again / 1975 / Spy ✦✦✦

As Stax neared bankruptcy, the Staples signed with Curtis Mayfield's Curtom label for this soundtrack album. The title track was a number one hit and "New Orleans" reached number 70, returning the Staples to the upper echelons of the charts for the last time. *—Rob Bowman*

Unlock Your Mind / 1978 / Warner Brothers ✦✦✦

Not one of their best, but it does feature two songs by singer/songwriter Paul Kelly, a cult favorite. Kelly should have gotten the Staples to sing more of his tunes because they sound better interpreting them than he does. Kelly's "God Can" and "Don't Burn Me," benefits from the singing and recording technique, Kelly's own recordings sounded like he cut them in a closet. The productions by Jerry Wexler and Barry Beckett are first class but the material is third rate. Other than the two Paul Kelly songs, "Leave It All Up to Love," and the percolating "Chica Boom," there's nothing else to get excited about. *—Andrew Hamilton*

Chronicle / 1979 / Stax ✦✦✦✦✦

Released in 1979, *Chronicle* remains a near-definitive overview of the Staple Singers' time at Stax Records, containing 12 tracks including such classic soul singles as "Heavy Makes You Happy (Sha-Na-Boom-Boom)," "You've Got to Earn It," "Touch a Hand (Make a Friend)," "If You're Ready (Come Go with Me)," "Be What You Are," "Respect Yourself," and "I'll Take You There." *—Stephen Thomas Erlewine*

Turning Point / 1984 / Epic/Legacy ✦✦✦✦

The last of the truly great gospel sides by this seminal family folk-gospel outfit. *—Opal Louis Nations*

★ **The Best of the Staple Singers** / Oct. 17, 1990 / Stax ✦✦✦✦✦

The best and most famous cuts from their glory years at Stax. Includes their massive hits "Respect Yourself" and "I'll Take You There"; less famous but similar gospel-funk fusions like "Touch a Hand (Make a Friend)" and "Heavy Makes You Happy (Sha-Na-Boom Boom)"; and less expected items like a cover of "(Sittin' On) The Dock of the Bay." It does not, however, have their 1975 number one single "Let's Do It Again," which they recorded just after cutting their ties to Stax. *—Richie Unterberger*

Great Day / Oct. 15, 1991 / Milestone ✦✦✦

This two-album Fantasy reissue is an anthology of the material the Staples recorded for Riverside between 1960 and 1963. For Riverside, the Staples recorded mostly gospel but the shouting was toned down a bit. A few modern-day "message" songs make their way into their repertoire as well, including Bob Dylan's "Masters of War." Not quite as cataclysmic as their Vee-Jay material but still essential. *—Rob Bowman*

Uncloudy Day/Will the Circle Be Unbroken / 1992 / Vee-Jay ✦✦✦✦✦

The Staple Singers brilliantly fused gospel, folk, blues, and soul into a cohesive, commercially potent sound in the '50s and '60s. They perfected this approach during their tenure at Vee-Jay, the first label that fully presented their harmonies and allowed the twangy, expert guitar licks of Roebuck "Pops" Staples to be heard in the group's mix. This single disc contains two pivotal Staples albums; *Uncloudy Day* includes such gospel favorites as "I Know I Got Religion" and "Let Me Ride," while *Will the Circle Be Unbroken* offers the splendid title track, plus masterpieces like "Pray On" and "Come Up in Glory." *—Ron Wynn*

Uncloudy Day / May 30, 1995 / Charly ✦✦✦✦✦

Classic Vee-Jay '50s sides with previously unreleased alternates. The very best Staples' recordings with Pops and Mavis on lead mike. *—Opal Louis Nations*

The Very Best of the Staple Singers, Vol. 1: Live / Mar. 3, 1998 / Collectables ✦✦✦

'50s Vee-Jay classics with Pops' Delta guitar and Mavis' deep, compelling vocals. *—Opal Louis Nations*

The Very Best of the Staple Singers, Vol. 2: On My Way to Heaven / Mar. 3, 1998 / Collectables ✦✦✦

The cream of the cream. Their choice Vee-Jay sides. *—Opal Louis Nations*

Greatest Hits / 1999 / Fantasy ✦✦✦✦✦

A reissue of some of the fine Riverside sides (ca. 1962-1964) produced by Orrin Keepnews. This package actually does contain many of their best-known selections (like "Hammer and Nails") and is a good value for the money. *—Kip Lornell*

Good News: The Collection / Jul. 31, 2001 / Music Club ✦✦

Soulful and intimate, this collection of the Staple Singers follows their musical career from their early spirituals to their later endeavors in country-influenced, guitar-driven gospel. Though the production of the individual tracks is at times very basic and rough-cut and there are few moments when the instrumentation exceeds four voices and a guitar, the Staple Singers sound the best in the most spare of technological conditions. Their ability to express indomitable spirituality in every note of this collection explains their large audiences in religious and secular communities alike. *—Nate Cavalieri*

Roebuck "Pops" Staples

b. Dec. 2, 1915, Winoma, MS, **d.** Dec. 19, 2000

Vocals, Guitar / Country-Soul, Soul

The patriarch of one of music's most successful families, Pops Staples worked with everyone from Robert Johnson to Curtis Mayfield. Roebuck Staples was born December 2, 1915, in Winona, MS, a close friend of Charley Patton, he also played not only with Johnson but also such legends as Son House and Robert Jr. Lockwood, becoming a top-notch blues guitarist in the process. Increasingly drawn to the church, he joined the gospel group the Golden Trumpets in 1937, and upon relocating to Chicago in 1941, he signed on with the Windy City's Trumpet Jubilees; by the following decade, Staples was regularly performing at services in the company of his daughters Mavis and Cleotha and son Pervis, and soon they began appearing professionally as the Staple Singers. While originally a gospel group, the family achieved their first commercial success with a more contemporary soul sound honed during the late '60s while signed to the Stax label; by the early '70s, the Staples even moved into funk, scoring a major pop hit with "I'll Take You There." After signing with Mayfield's Curtom label, they also found success with "Let's Do It Again." Pops Staples did not pursue a solo career prior to releasing 1992's *Peace to the Neighborhood*, which returned him to his blues and gospel roots. Its follow-up, 1994's *Father Father*, earned a Grammy for Best Contemporary Blues Album. Staples also appeared in several films, including 1998's *Wag the Dog*. Late in 2000, Staples suffered a concussion after a fall in his home; shortly thereafter, on December 19, he passed away at the age of 85. *—Jason Ankeny*

● **Peace to the Neighborhood** / 1992 / Pointblank ✦✦✦✦

Pops Staples puts a lot of younger performers to shame with his integrity-laden solo release *Peace to the Neighborhood*. The founder of The Staple Singers combines joyous soul and gospel with swampy funk and blues. Of course, it doesn't hurt to have the rest of the Staples and admirers Bonnie Raitt, Jackson Browne, and Ry Cooder along for the ride. Includes the streetwise, anti-drug-culture "Miss Cocaine." *—Roch Parisien*

Father Father / 1994 / Pointblank ✦✦✦

Pops Staples was 78 was when he recorded *Father Father*, which was only his second solo album. The patriarch of the Staples family was always a team player, and providing solo albums was something he didn't do until he was well into his seventies. Although *Father Father* won Staples a Grammy for Best Contemporary Blues Album, this isn't strictly a blues offering—true to form, *Father Father* is the work of an artist who had long had one foot in secular music and another in gospel. This CD, in fact, has as much to do with gospel and R&B as it does with the blues. Staples' secular side is heard on his cover of Sir Mac Rice's "Getting Too Big for Your Britches," but the singer's spirituality asserts itself on everything from "Glory Glory" and the traditional "Jesus Is Going to Make Up My Dying Bed" to a remake of the Impressions' civil rights anthem "People, Get Ready." To be sure, Staples' voice had declined considerably over the years—comparing his performances on this album to his work with the Staple Singers in the '60s and '70s, it becomes obvious just how much his voice had thinned out. Even so, Staples manages to deliver an enjoyable and meaningful album, but one that—despite its assets and Grammy-winning status—is less than essential. Not for the casual listener, *Father Father* is primarily for completists and die-hard fans. *—Alex Henderson*

Steampacket

f. 1962, **db.** 1965

Group / Mod, British Blues, British Invasion

Because their ranks included a future superstar, the Steampacket have received more attention than they really deserve. Featuring vocalists Rod Stewart, Long John Baldry, and Julie Driscoll, as well as organist Brian Auger, misleading reissues of the group's demos bill the act as "the first supergroup." That's simply not the case. They were an interesting conglomeration, and innovative in the respect of featuring several singers. But their true status is as a short-lived footnote, and not one that rates as a highlight of any of the principals' careers.

Though the Steampacket played gigs at small venues around London as early as 1962, the nucleus of the band formed in mid-1965, after the demise of Baldry's backing outfit, the Hoochie Coochie Men. Baldry envisioned a soul-type revue, each singer taking the material for which he or she was most suited. Management by Giorgio Gomelsky (who also handled the Yardbirds and several other interesting British groups) and a supporting slot on the Rolling Stones' summer 1965 British tour seemed to promise a bright future.

Their professional activities were complicated by the fact that Baldry and Stewart retained separate managers for their individual careers. Additionally, Baldry was already signed to United Artists as a solo act, thwarting Gomelsky's plans to record the band. This led to disputes between the different managers, and the Steampacket broke up before they managed to enter the studio.

Officially enter the studio, that is. Gomelsky did record some tapes with the band at a rehearsal at the famous Marquee club in London. These have been reissued numerous times since the '70s, and show the band to be a competent but hardly thrilling soul-rock outfit, anchored instrumentally by Auger's jazz blues organ. Stewart moved on to the Jeff Beck Group, the Faces, and solo stardom; Baldry moved into middle-of-the-road pop, landing some British hit singles in the late '60s. Auger had recorded as a backup musician on Baldry's mid-'60s solo records, and his Brian Auger Trinity group continued working with Julie Driscoll, reaching the U.K. Top Five in 1968 with "This Wheel's on Fire." *—Richie Unterberger*

• **The First Supergroup: Steampacket Featuring Rod Stewart** / 1992 / Charly ✦✦✦✦

Also packaged (with equal exploitation) as *The First Supergroup*, it's unfair to judge the Steampacket on the basis of these demos, which were never intended for release. Still, what exists is a fair but unremarkable vestige of a typical mid-'60s British club band, perhaps more soul-oriented than most, heavily reliant upon American covers. Their most distinguishing feature was Brian Auger's bubbly organ, whose style was indebted to American soul-jazz keyboardists like Ramsey Lewis and Jimmy Smith. Despite the title, Stewart only sings lead on one track, "Can I Get a Witness," which is available on Rod's *Storyteller* boxed set. The much inferior Baldry is heard much more often, and the program also includes some instrumental showcases for Auger. *—Richie Unterberger*

Corey Stevens

b. Centralia, IL

Vocals, Guitar / Singer/Songwriter, Country-Rock, Blues-Rock

Born and raised in Illinois, Corey Stevens was 11 years old when he first picked up a guitar. By 15 he was playing rhythm guitar and writing songs in bands. During college he studied music and eventually earned a degree. Upon graduation, a move to Los Angeles solidified the dreams Stevens had held in his heart since childhood. Paying his dues was like doing hard time, but a job teaching third grade made life a little easier and allowed Stevens to keep a band together and begin his first recording project. Spending ten years teaching was a positive experience that helped build character. Along the way, Corey met and married Linda, a voice and piano teacher. They had one child, a daughter who truly is the apple of her father's eye. An early comparison to the late Stevie Ray Vaughan was a mixed blessing that forced Stevens to push himself in order to make his own statement.

In 1995, with the expertise of producer/gunslinger Edward Tree, the first project was released. *Blue Drops of Rain*, originally released on Eureka Records, brought attention and opportunity to a man who had worked 14 years to get a break. The project also brought Corey to the attention of Discovery Records, which licensed *Blue Drops of Rain* and funded a second project. Chart action lasted from 1996 into 1997, when *Road to Zen*, also produced by Tree was released. A road warrior who continues to tour alone and with the likes of Lynyrd Skynyrd, Corey Stevens has distinguished himself as an artist of integrity and vision, issuing *Getaway* in early 2000. *—Jana Pendragon*

Blue Drops of Rain / 1995 / Eureka ✦✦✦✦✦

This first project by Corey Stevens is an energetic, witty combination of country, rock and blues. Stevens exhibits a talent for writing the kind of songs that appeal to a wide variety of listeners. Always poignant, Stevens can cover a tune and make it his own, as he does here with the R.G. Ford song "Crosscut Saw." He can also hold his own when tackling a Stevie Ray Vaughan number—his version of "Lenny" is graphic in its approach and delivery. As for his own tunes, "Gone Too Long," "Goin' Crazy," and the title cut all come across with panache. A most impressive first round for a man with the promise of a long career. *—Jana Pendragon*

• **The Road to Zen** / May 5, 1997 / Discovery ✦✦✦✦✦

Making a name for himself from live performances and a successful first release, being proclaimed the heir to Stevie Ray Vaughan, Stevens shows himself to be a more mature, evolved guitarist, writer, and performer. While not as raw as his freshman effort, *Blue Drops of Rain*, Stevens continues to build a rock-solid career. *Road to Zen* features more of Stevens' guitar style as well as a tighter production spearheaded by Edward Tree. A passionate performer, this comes through clearly. Especially effective is the Linda and Corey Stevens effort, "Only One for You," a tribute to their partnership; also good are "Lessons of Love," "Take It Back," and "Charles Bronson Vibe." With all cuts written by Stevens this time, he establishes himself as a talent to be reckoned with in several different arenas. *—Jana Pendragon*

Getaway / Jan. 25, 2000 / Eureka ✦✦✦

Greatest Hits / Aug. 14, 2001 / Eureka ✦✦✦✦

Arbee Stidham

b. Feb. 9, 1917, DeValls Bluff, AR

Vocals, Guitar / Electric Chicago Blues, R&B

An exciting and expressive jazz-influenced blues vocalist, Arbee Stidham also plays alto sax, guitar and harmonica. His father Luddie Stidham worked in Jimmie Lunceford's orchestra, while his uncle was a leader of the Memphis Jug Band. Stidham formed the Southern Syncopators and played various clubs in his native Arkansas in the '30s. He appeared on Little Rock radio station KARK and his band backed Bessie Smith on a Southern tour in 1930 and 1931. Stidham frequently performed in Little Rock and Memphis until he moved to Chicago in the '40s. Stidham recorded with Lucky Millinder's orchestra for Victor in the '40s. He did his own sessions for Victor, Sittin' In, Checker, Abco, Prestige/Bluesville, Mainstream, and Folkways in the '50s and '60s, and appeared in the film *The Bluesman* in 1973. Stidham also made many festival and club appearances nationwide and internationally. He did occasional blues lectures at Cleveland State University in the '70s. *—Ron Wynn*

• **Tired of Wandering** / 1961 / Bluesville/Original Blues Classics ✦✦✦✦

Over the years, the term R&B has been used to describe everything from the '50s doo wop of the Five Satins to the hip-hop-influenced urban contemporary of Erykah Badu and R. Kelly—in other words, a variety of African-American popular music with roots in the blues. Arbee Stidham was exactly the sort of singer who thrived in the R&B or "race" market after World War II; although essentially a bluesman, he wasn't a blues purist who embraced the 12-bar format 100 percent of the time. But his mixture of blues, jazz, and gospel made him quite popular among what were considered rhythm & blues audiences in the '40s and '50s. Recorded for Prestige's Bluesville label in 1960—eight years before Stidham's death—*Tired of Wandering* is among his finest albums. This session, which boasts King Curtis on tenor sax, doesn't cater to blues purists; while some of the tunes have 12 bars, others don't. Regardless, the feeling of the blues enriches everything on the CD; that is true whether Stidham is turning his attention to Big Joe Turner's "Last Goodbye Blues" or revisiting his 1948 hit, "My Heart Belongs to You." Equally triumphant is Brownie McGhee's "Pawn Shop," which is associated with Piedmont country blues but gets a big-city makeover from Stidham. Like Jimmy Witherspoon—someone he inspires comparisons to—Stidham demonstrates that the blues can be sophisticated, polished, and jazz-influenced without losing their grit. The big-voiced singer/guitarist was born in Arkansas, but Chicago was his adopted home—and the Windy City had a definite influence on his work. Anyone who has spent a lot of time savoring jazz-influenced bluesmen like Witherspoon and Percy Mayfield owes it to himself/herself to give *Tired of Wandering* a very close listen. *—Alex Henderson*

Time for Blues / 1972 / Mainstream ✦✦✦

The Blues of Arbee Stidham / 2001 / Bluesville/Original Blues Classics ✦✦✦✦

Stidham presented decent, straight-ahead postwar Chicago blues with some jazz flavors on this 1960 session, which included low-key saxophone by King Curtis. Stidham sings rather like a slightly more urbane Muddy Waters, holding his own on guitar with cleanly decorative licks that again have a touch of jazz. He wrote or co-wrote most of the tunes on the album, dotted with covers of the likes of Joe Turner and Brownie McGhee. For the most part he plays it midtempo or slow, only getting into brisk uptempo beats occasionally, as on "You Keep Me Yearning" and "Teenage Kiss." It's not a godsend, but it's solid material that proves that good Chicago electric blues from the era existed that had more of a blues-jazz crossover feel than the more well-known earthy performers from the time and place. And unlike much blues-jazz, it really is more blues than jazz, avoiding the politeness that takes hold of much such music. *—Richie Unterberger*

Frank Stokes

b. Jan. 1, 1888, Whitehaven, TN, **d.** Sep. 12, 1955, Memphis, TN

Vocals, Guitar / Prewar Country Blues, Acoustic Memphis Blues, Early American Blues

Frank Stokes and partner Dan Sane recorded as the Beale Street Sheiks, a Memphis answer to the musical Chatmon family string band, the Mississippi Sheiks. According to local tradition, Stokes was already playing the streets of Memphis by the turn of the century, about the same time the blues began to flourish. As a street artist, he needed a broad repertoire of songs and patter palatable to blacks and whites. A medicine show and house party favorite, Stokes was remembered as a consummate entertainer who drew on songs from the 19th and 20th centuries with equal facility. Solo or with Sane and sometimes fiddler Will Batts, Stokes recorded 38 sides for Paramount and Victor. These treasures include blues as well as older pieces: "Chicken You Can't Roost Too High for Me," "Mr. Crump Don't Like It," an outstanding version of "You Shall" (commonly known as "You Shall Be Free"), and "Hey Mourner," a traditional comic anticlerical piece. Stokes possessed a remarkable declamatory voice and was an adroit guitarist. His duets with Sane merit special attention because of their subtle interplay and propulsive rhythm. *—Barry Lee Pearson*

Creator of the Memphis Blues / 1990 / Yazoo ✦✦✦

The most prominent musicians in early country blues tended to emerge from the Mississippi Delta. This region's rich tradition has long overshadowed developments in states like Tennessee and Texas. However, for blues fans in Memphis during the late '20s, Frank Stokes was the king. Having spent time traveling as a minstrel entertainer, Stokes picked up medicine show tunes and popular songs to complement his conventional blues material. His verses read like a catalog of common themes and phrases that roamed the American South. While not a strong singer, Stokes was blessed with one of the music's most distinctive voices. He was the antithesis of "hard" Delta singers like Son House and Charley Patton. In comparison, Stokes seemed perpetually uncertain of himself. When he sings "Don't know what'n the world to do" on "Nehi Mama Blues," he is truly believable. Even on lighter material like "'Tain't Nobody's Bizness," an underlying worry is evident in his signature quiver. The effect begins to fade only on his most boisterous performances ("Beale Town Bound"). Concluding that Stokes was unstable, however, would be incorrect. "You Shall" and "Mr. Crump" are clearly meant to amuse. The blues itself, which is often construed as being autobiographical, typically served the function of entertainment. Stokes is perhaps best remembered for his guitar duet work with performance partner Dan Sane. Typical of the Memphis blues, their style was lighter than the Delta equivalent. The hard playing and prominent slide was replaced by more intricate and graceful fingerpicking. Sane meshed so well with Stokes that he became an extension of his own guitar. The two incorporated more guitar breaks than were conventional (especially on record) to showcase their interplay. Sane is active on "Take Me Back," animating the song with his sprightly fills and runs. He has a similar effect on "'Tain't Nobody's Bizness," expanding on Stokes' standard chord work. Yazoo maintains its usual standards of excellent song selection, the best possible sound reproduction, and informative liner notes. *Creator of the Memphis Blues* is the companion to the various-artists compilation. *Frank Stokes' Dream.* —*Nathan Bush*

The Beale Street Sheiks / 1990 / Document ✦✦✦✦
Forget the shaky sound and noise on some of the tracks, and the slightly sketchy notes, and the fact that some tracks on this supposedly "complete" collection are missing—these are Paramount recordings, and we're lucky to have what we do, as good as it does sound. What's here are 19 songs cut by Frank Stokes and Dan Sane between August of 1927 and March of 1929. Included are lyrics on numbers like "You Shall" (in two different versions, either one worth the price of the disc) that constitute historical artifacts, going back to the era of slavery; topical songs like "Mr. Crump Don't Like It," that tell of Memphis' life and death as a blues Mecca; and infectiously catchy pieces like the sly, witty, supposedly anti-prostitution pieces like "It's a Good Thing" (also in two different versions). At their best, which is most of this CD, they had an appeal that transcended the decades—the inter-weaving of the two guitars is about as tight as anything in blues, the rhythms are catchy, and the vocal phrasing by Stokes is delicious. —*Bruce Eder*

★ **The Frank Stokes Victor Recordings (1928–1929)** / 1990 / Document ✦✦✦✦✦
This 20-song compilation of Frank Stokes' late-'20s recordings for the Victor label is a more expansive version of the Stokes collection available on Yazoo Records, with very little overlap between the two. The sound is variable, as is usually the case with Document's releases, some songs sounding like they came from decent master sources and others purely of academic interest, in terms of the playback quality. What isn't variable is the quality of Stokes' playing, singing, and songwriting, which is filled with wry humor throughout, veiling a certain degree of pride and restlessness, and all manner of clever lyrical and musical conceits. This disc is well worth owning in tandem with CDs devoted to Stokes' work with the Mississippi Sheiks. —*Bruce Eder*

Victor Recordings: 1928–1929 / Oct. 4, 2000 / Document ✦✦✦✦

Storyville
f. 1994, Texas
Group / Contemporary Blues, Blues-Rock, Modern Electric Blues
Veterans from dozens of blues jam sessions and all-star backing bands, the members of Storyville—all native Texans—gelled at just such a jam, in 1994 at the Austin club known as Antone's. Bassist Tommy Shannon and drummer Chris Layton had played in Stevie Ray Vaughan's Double Trouble for ten years before the bluesman's death in 1990, and both moved on to the Arc Angels before meeting the other members of Storyville. Lead guitarist David Holt played on the Mavericks' debut album, and appeared with rhythm guitarist David Grissom in Joe Ely's backing band. Grissom had gained his early experience touring with John Mellencamp and the Allman Brothers. The only member of the band with less than ten sideman credits, vocalist Malford Milligan, sang with the Austin band Stick People before the formation of Storyville—named, of course, in honor of New Orleans' historic red-light district.

After several sessions to work out their bluesy soul/R&B, Storyville hopped into the recording studio and produced an album for November Records. Released the same year of the band's foundation, *The Bluest Eyes* won the band six awards at the 1995 Austin Music Awards, including Best Band and Best Single. The LP was rated highly in mainstream publications, and earned Storyville a major-label contract, with the Atlantic subsidiary Code Blue. Though the band released no new material during 1995, three more trophies at that year's Austin Music Awards were forthcoming. Second album *A Piece of Your Soul* was released in 1996, followed in 1998 by *Dog Years.* —*John Bush*

Bluest Eyes / 1994 / November ✦✦✦

● **Piece of Your Soul** / 1996 / Code Blue ✦✦✦✦✦
Storyville's second album, *Piece of Your Soul*, is a gritty Texas blues record, but it's delivered with enough rock & roll savvy to crossover into the mainstream. That's not to say that the group has watered-down the greasy roadhouse R&B that is their stock and trade—they simply inject it with a shot of feverish rock & roll energy, and that's what makes *Piece of Your Soul* a successful follow-up to the award-winning debut, *The Bluest Eyes.* —*Thom Owens*

Dog Years / Jun. 16, 1998 / Atlantic ✦✦✦
Storyville doesn't change their tune much on *Dog Years*, their first major label effort and third album overall. Granted, the album has a slicker sound than its predecessors, but at its core it remains a hard-rocking blend of Texas blues-rock and Southern rock. The primary pleasure of *Dog Years* is hearing the band play. David Grissom and Dave Holt may not be distinctive guitarists, but they're solid musicians, pushing the record in the right

direction. The songs themselves aren't particularly memorable, but there's enough energy in the hard rockers (the ballads fall a little flat) to make it an enjoyable contemporary Southern blues-rock record. —*Stephen Thomas Erlewine*

Angela Strehli
b. Nov. 22, 1945, Lubbock, TX
Vocals / Modern Electric Blues
Don't let her lack of albums fool you: Vocalist Angela Strehli is an immensely gifted singer and songwriter, a Texas blues historian, impresario, and fan. Born November 22, 1945, in Lubbock, TX, Strehli comes out of the same school of hippie folksingers that gave rise to some of Americana music's most gifted writers, people like Jimmie Dale Gilmore and her brother Al Strehli.

Raised in Lubbock and inspired by the mix of blues, country, and rock & roll she heard on West Texas early-'60s radio, she learned harmonica and played bass before becoming a full-time vocalist. Despite the fact that her recordings are scant, Strehli spends a good portion of each year performing live shows in Europe and around the U.S. and Canada.

You can hear Strehli, who's now based in San Francisco, in all her glory on *Soul Shake* (1987, Antone's Records), *Dreams Come True* with Lou Ann Barton and Marcia Ball (1990, Antone's Records), and *Blonde and Blue* (1993, Rounder Records). Of these, *Blonde and Blue* seems to best showcase her talents as a vocalist and writer of quality songs. Strehli, an avid student of the blues and a sharp blues historian, also helped build the Austin blues scene with club owner Clifford Antone and musicians like Kim Wilson and the Vaughan brothers; she resurfaced in 1998 with *Deja Blue.* —*Richard Skelly*

● **Soul Shake** / Nov. 1987 / Antone's ✦✦✦✦✦
Soul Shake is an excellent album that effectively captures Angela Strehli's gritting, hard-edged roadhouse blues. Not only is her singing gutsy and powerful, the band is tough and the songs are first-rate, making *Soul Shake* a welcome reminder of the power of straight-ahead Texas blues-rock. —*Thom Owens*

Blonde and Blue / 1993 / Rounder ✦✦✦✦
The danger for modern blues performers is turning into a parody of what you're allegedly celebrating or honoring. Vocalist Angela Strehli avoids that trap by simply being herself; her honesty and individuality make her cover of Major Lance's "Um, Um, Um, Um, Um" a legitimate treatment. Strehli's tough-talking persona was tailor-made for such songs as "Two Bit Texas Town" and "Go On," while she managed to register pain without pathos on "Can't Stop These Teardrops" and "I'm Just Your Fool." Only on Elmore James' "The Sun Is Shining" did she falter, more because Albert King has established a credible alternate vision of that number. But she makes up for that with the remarkable closing tune, "Going to That City." While she doesn't eclipse Sister O.M. Terrell's transcendent original, she comes as close as anyone possibly could to providing a treatment that's just as valid. —*Ron Wynn*

Deja Blue / Jul. 28, 1998 / A&M ✦✦✦

Percy Strother
b. Jul. 23, 1946, Vicksburg, MS
Vocals / Modern Electric Blues
For a sense of the blues at its most tangible, one needs to look no further than singer/guitarist Percy Strother, who triumphed over incredible tragedy to create music of genuine pain and sorrow. Born July 23, 1946, in Vicksburg, MS, he was still a child when his father died violently; his mother passed away shortly afterward, and rather than submitting to life in an orphanage, Strother simply took to the road. He drifted from job to job for a number of years, all the while fighting a battle with alcoholism; the blues turned his life around, however, and after sobering up he began teaching himself guitar, honing his chops in virtual anonymity before recording his debut LP, *A Good Woman Is Hard to Find*, in 1992. *The Highway Is My Home* followed in 1995, and in 1997 Strother returned with *It's My Time.* —*Jason Ankeny*

Highway Is My Home / May 30, 1995 / Black Magic ✦✦✦✦

A Good Woman Is Hard to Find / Apr. 16, 1996 / Blue Loon ✦✦✦

● **It's My Time** / Nov. 18, 1997 / JSP ✦✦✦✦
It's My Time may be Percy Strother's best record yet, capturing his explosive soul-blues in all of its raging intensity. Truth be told, Strother hasn't really ever given a bad performance on record, but the key to the album's success is that he has a set of terrific original songs which effectively showcase his raging, soulful roar and his blistering guitar. This is raw soul, with little of the slickness that distinguishes latter-day retro-soul—and that's why it's worth hearing. —*Thom Owens*

Home at Last / Oct. 16, 2001 / Black & Tan ✦✦✦

Studebaker John (John Grimaldi)
b. Nov. 5, 1952, Chicago, IL
Vocals, Harmonica / Modern Electric Chicago Blues
Taking his stage name from an automobile he once owned, Studebaker John Grimaldi was a product of the vibrant blues scene of Chicago's West Side. His father was himself an amateur musician, and as a youngster Grimaldi began playing the many instruments lying about the house. Becoming a fixture at the open-air flea markets in the Maxwell Street area—a venue for countless blues buskers—he began focusing on harmonica after catching performances from the likes of Little Walter and Sonny Boy Williamson; after taking in a Hound Dog Taylor club date, Grimaldi also turned to guitar. He formed the blues-rock band the Hawks during the early '70s as a showcase for his reedy vocals, primal harp sound, and blistering slide guitar skills, and in the years to follow also developed into a fine songwriter, while keeping his day job as a construction worker. Grimaldi began recording during the mid-'80s, issuing a live Netherlands set later re-released domestically as *Rockin' the Blues '85*. His next major release was 1994's *Too*

Tough, followed in 1995 by *Outside Lookin' In*. He maintained a prolific recording schedule in the years to come, issuing *Tremoluxe* in 1996 and *Time Will Tell* in 1997. —*Jason Ankeny*

Too Tough / 1994 / Blind Pig ✦✦✦✦

Rockin' the Blues '85 / 1994 / Double Trouble ✦✦✦

● **Outside Lookin' In** / 1995 / Blind Pig ✦✦✦✦✦
Outside Lookin' In finds Studebaker John perfecting his overdriven, propulsive Chicago blues. His originals may not always be memorable, but they're sturdy vehicles for his hard-driving harmonica and gutsy guitar. Studebaker hasn't changed his style at all—essentially, this is the same album he's delivered before, and he made several others like it afterward—but this is the one that features his best playing. —*Thom Owens*

Studebaker John & the Hawks / Mar. 26, 1996 / Blind Pig ✦✦✦

Tremoluxe / Apr. 1996 / Blind Pig ✦✦✦

Time Will Tell / Sep. 23, 1997 / Blind Pig ✦✦✦✦
Studebaker John, who dominates this release, has diverse talents in four areas: as a guitarist, harmonica soloist, singer and songwriter. His abilities on both guitar and harmonica are quite impressive, playing the very different instruments with equal intensity and passion. In contrast, John's singing is serviceable, and none of his dozen originals on his fourth Blind Pig release are destined to become standards. Overall, this bluesy, often high-powered set is a good showcase for his playing, although one would love to hear Studebaker John perform blues standards sometime. —*Scott Yanow*

Born to Win / 199 / Double Trouble ✦✦✦

Howl With the Wolf / Apr. 24, 2001 / Evidence ✦✦✦

Sugar Blue (James Whiting)
b. 1950, New York, NY
Harmonica / Contemporary Blues, Harmonica Blues, Electric Harmonica Blues, Modern Electric Blues
One of the foremost electric blues harpists of the modern era, Sugar Blue was born James Whiting in New York City in 1950. The son of a singer/dancer who regularly performed at the legendary Apollo Theater, he was given his first harmonica at the age of ten, and by his mid-teens had already performed in the company of Muddy Waters; in the early '70s he made his first recordings, sitting in on sessions by the likes of Johnny Shines and Louisiana Red. Sugar Blue relocated to Paris in 1976, where he was introduced to the Rolling Stones; he went on to play on the group's LPs *Some Girls*, *Emotional Rescue* and *Tattoo You*, lending his skills to such hits as "Miss You." He also played on jazz dates for Stan Getz and Paul Horn, and in 1979 cut the solo effort *Crossroads*. Upon returning to the U.S. in the mid-'80s, Sugar Blue settled in Chicago; after signing to Alligator, he cut *Blue Blazes* in 1994, followed a year later by *In Your Eyes*. —*Jason Ankeny*

Crossroads / 1980 / Blue Silver ✦✦✦

● **Blue Blazes** / Mar. 1994 / Alligator ✦✦✦✦
Harmonica player and vocalist Sugar Blue isn't a singer who doubles on harp; he's an extraordinary instrumentalist who's also a quality vocalist. Blue covers tunes by Willie Dixon, Muddy Waters, James Cotton and Sonny Boy Williamson classics, presents a decent, if disposable version of the Rolling Stones' "Miss You," and adds the good-natured original "Country Blues," co-written with his guitarist Motoaaki Makino. But it's those harmonica lines and phrases that make the CD. One of Alligator's best contemporary albums in a long time. —*Ron Wynn*

In Your Eyes / 1995 / Alligator ✦✦✦

Sugar Ray & the Bluetones
f. 1992, Orange County, CA
Group / Modern Electric Blues, Electric Harmonica Blues, Soul-Blues
East Coast based blues band fronted by singer/harmonica man Ray Norcia and featuring guitar work over the years by Ronnie Earl (Roomful of Blues, Ronnie Earl & the Broadcasters) and Kid Bangham (The Fabulous Thunderbirds). —*AMG*

Sugar Ray and the Bluetones / 1980 / Baron ✦✦✦

● **Knockout** / 1989 / Varrick ✦✦✦✦
A surprisingly tasteful and solidly swinging album, Sugar Ray is a powerhouse vocalist and a more-than-respectable harp player. There are some good songs, too, especially the slow blues "I'm Tortured." —*Niles J. Frantz*

Don't Stand in My Way / 1990 / Bullseye Blues ✦✦✦
There's more swagger and less swing; it's still quite good. —*Niles J. Frantz*

Rockin' Sugar Daddy / May 22, 2001 / Severn ✦✦✦
Kim Wilson-styled vocalist/harmonica player and songwriter Sugar Ray Norcia edges toward Fabulous Thunderbirds territory on his fourth album with his Bluetones band (and first after ending his nearly seven-year tenure with Roomful of Blues). Former T-Bird guitarist Kid Bangham is also on hand to further cement the connection, and with this album's stripped-down sound and tougher R&B approach, it's a ringer for a new release from Austin's favorite blues band. There are differences of course: Ray's band is less pounding and more subtle and swampy in their approach to blues and R&B. His harp work isn't as overdriven as Wilson's and his phrasing remains understated while distinctive in its grits-and-honey delivery, even on the album's most charging tracks. Still, anyone who is a fan of either the Fabulous Thunderbirds or Roomful's more rocking/bluesy side will certainly be attracted to this release. Covers from the catalogs of Slim Harpo ("I Got Love if You Want It"), Little Walter ("Off the Wall"), and Bobby "Blue" Bland (a sizzling, seven-minute "It's My Life, Baby") pepper the predominantly original tunes, which slot somewhere between slinky Texas and rugged Chicago blues infused with classic urban R&B. Ray, whose harp talents were underutilized in the horn-heavy Roomful, makes up for lost time by soloing

on almost every track, and Kid Bangham's guitar swings and stings without overshadowing the headliner's work. A deeply soulful and honest album whose understated attack and ensemble playing is more powerful than louder blues bands who substitute volume for passion. —*Hal Horowitz*

Hubert Sumlin
b. Nov. 16, 1931, Greenwood, MS
Vocals, Guitar / Electric Chicago Blues, Modern Electric Blues
Quiet and extremely unassuming off the bandstand, Hubert Sumlin played a style of guitar incendiary enough to stand tall beside the immortal Howlin' Wolf. The Wolf was Sumlin's imposing mentor for more than two decades, and it proved a mutually beneficial relationship; Sumlin's twisting, darting, unpredictable lead guitar constantly energized the Wolf's '60s Chess sides, even when the songs themselves (check out "Do the Do" or "Mama's Baby" for conclusive proof) were less than stellar.
Sumlin started out twanging the proverbial broom wire nailed to the wall before he got his mitts on a real guitar. He grew up near West Memphis, AR, briefly hooking up with another Young Lion with a rosy future, harpist James Cotton, before receiving a summons from the mighty Wolf to join him in Chicago in 1954.
Sumlin learned his craft nightly on the bandstand beside Wolf, his confidence growing as he graduated from rhythm guitar duties to lead. By the dawn of the '60s, Sumlin's slashing axe was a prominent component on the great majority of Wolf's waxings, including "Wang Dang Doodle," "Shake for Me," "Hidden Charms" (boasting perhaps Sumlin's greatest recorded solo), "Three Hundred Pounds of Joy," and "Killing Floor."
Although they had a somewhat tempestuous relationship, Sumlin remained loyal to Wolf until the big man's 1976 death. But there were a handful of solo sessions for Sumlin before that, beginning with a most unusual 1964 date in East Berlin that was produced by Horst Lippmann during a European tour under the auspices of the American Folk Blues Festival (the behind-the-Iron Curtain session also featured pianist Sunnyland Slim and bassist Willie Dixon).
Only in recent years has Sumlin allowed his vocal talents to shine. He's recorded solo sets for Black Top and Blind Pig that show him to be an understated but effective singer—and his guitar continues to communicate most forcefully. —*Bill Dahl*

Kings of Chicago Blues, Vol. 2 / Jan. 1971 / Vogue ✦✦✦

My Guitar & Me / Dec. 1975 / Evidence ✦✦
Sumlin's exceptionally low-key vocals and unexceptional backing by two-thirds of the Aces, pianist Willie Mabon, and rhythm guitarist Lonnie Brooks render this 1975 session pretty disposable overall. Sumlin cops plenty of solo space, but there's too little of the unrepdictable fire that greatly distinguished his work with Howlin' Wolf. —*Bill Dahl*

Groove / 1976 / Black & Blue ✦✦✦

Hubert Sumlin's Blues Party / Nov. 1987 / Black Top ✦✦✦
Sumlin still wasn't totally prepared for solo stardom by the time of this disc, relying on the hearty contributions of guitarist Ronnie Earl and soul-searing singer Mighty Sam McClain to get over. —*Bill Dahl*

Heart & Soul / 1989 / Blind Pig ✦✦✦✦
The veteran guitarist sounds more confident and expressive vocally here than on any other of his contemporary recordings. Backing by harpist James Cotton, along with Little Mike & the Tornadoes, is nicely understated, affording Sumlin just enough drive without drowning his easygoing vocals out (no small feat). —*Bill Dahl*

Healing Feeling / 1990 / Black Top ✦✦✦
An improvement over his previous Black Top disc, especially on Sumlin's two vocal showcases, "Come Back Little Girl" and "Honey Dumplins." James "Thunderbird" Davis is also on board in a guest role, though he has to share his mike time with the considerably less remarkable Darrell Nulisch, who dominates the vocals. —*Bill Dahl*

Blues Anytime! / 1994 / Evidence ✦✦✦✦
A remarkable 1964 session produced by Horst Lippmann behind the Iron Curtain in East Germany that found Sumlin trying for the first time on record to sing. He played both electric and acoustic axe on the historic date, sharing the singing with more experienced hands Willie Dixon and Sunnyland Slim (Clifton James is on drums). All three Chicago legends acquit themselves well. —*Bill Dahl*

Blues Guitar Boss / Oct. 31, 1994 / JSP ✦✦✦
The man who gave the guitar bite to Howlin' Wolf classics like "Wang Dang Doodle" and "Killing Floor" put together a set of originals almost as solid as his past work. —*Keith Farley*

● **I Know You** / 1998 / AcousTech ✦✦✦✦✦
This is arguably the first musically indispensable album that Hubert Sumlin has done since Howlin' Wolf died some 23 years before. That isn't to say that he hasn't done any good albums prior to this, just that *I Know You* has a degree of urgency, coupled with remarkable ease, that makes it a real delight. The result is a record that compares very favorably with Wolf's *London Sessions* record as a mix of old and new. Sumlin will never sound like Wolf as a singer, but he can't help sounding like him in every other way, since it was Wolf's guitar on practically every cut after 1954; but he does his best with a limited voice and a hot guitar to deliver some superb electric blues. Whether he's acknowledging Elmore James, Jimmy Reed, or John Lee Hooker, or paying tribute to Wolf himself ("How Many More Years," in a killer interpretation), Sumlin sounds like he's having great fun grinding and crunching away on his instrument. He even turns in a surprisingly strong vocal and guitar performance on a familiar piece of subdued blues, "That's Why I'm Gonna Leave You." There is a little dross here—Sumlin doesn't do all that well stepping into John Lee Hooker territory; but generally, *I Know You* is a record that should please any fan of the Wolf or Sumlin (or, for that matter, James or Reed), with two tracks, "I'm Not Your Clown" and "Smokestack" (based on guess which song), indispensable to fans of hot blues guitar. Playing with him are Sam Lay (drums) and

Carrie Bell (harp), with Jimmy D. Lane on second guitar and David Krull at the piano and organ. *—Bruce Eder*

Wake Up Call / Apr. 21, 1998 / Blues Planet ♦♦♦

Sunnyland Slim (Albert Luandrew)

b. Sep. 5, 1907, Vance, MS, **d.** Mar. 17, 1995, Chicago, IL

Vocals, Piano / Delta Blues, Piano Blues, Acoustic Blues, Electric Chicago Blues

Exhibiting truly amazing longevity that was commensurate with his powerful, imposing physical build, Sunnyland Slim's status as a beloved Chicago piano patriarch endured long after most of his peers had perished. For more than 50 years, the towering Sunnyland had rumbled the ivories around the Windy City, playing with virtually every local luminary imaginable and backing the great majority in the studio at one time or another.

He was born Albert Luandrew in Mississippi and received his early training on a pump organ. After entertaining at juke joints and movie houses in the Delta, Luandrew made Memphis his home base during the late '20s, playing along Beale Street and hanging out with the likes of Little Brother Montgomery and Ma Rainey.

He adopted his colorful stage name from the title of one of his best-known songs, the mournful "Sunnyland Train." (The downbeat piece immortalized the speed and deadly power of a St. Louis-to-Memphis locomotive that mowed down numerous people unfortunate enough to cross its tracks at the wrong instant.)

Slim moved to Chicago in 1939 and set up shop as an in-demand piano man, playing for a spell with John Lee "Sonny Boy" Williamson before waxing eight sides for RCA Victor in 1947 under the somewhat misleading handle of "Doctor Clayton's Buddy." If it hadn't been for the helpful Sunnyland, Muddy Waters may not have found his way onto Chess; it was at the pianist's 1947 session for Aristocrat that the Chess brothers made Waters' acquaintance.

Aristocrat (which issued his harrowing "Johnson Machine Gun") was but one of myriad labels that Sunnyland recorded for between 1948 and 1956: Hytone, Opera, Chance, Tempo-Tone, Mercury, Apollo, JOB, Regal, Vee-Jay (unissued), Blue Lake, Club 51, and Cobra all cut dates on Slim, whose vocals thundered with the same resonant authority as his 88s. In addition, his distinctive playing enlivened hundreds of sessions by other artists during the same time frame.

In 1960, Sunnyland Slim traveled to Englewood Cliffs, NJ, to cut his debut LP for Prestige's Bluesville subsidiary with King Curtis supplying diamond-hard tenor sax breaks on many cuts. The album, *Slim's Shout*, ranks as one of his finest, with definitive renditions of the pianist's "The Devil Is a Busy Man," "Shake It," "Brownskin Woman," and "It's You Baby."

Like a deep-rooted tree, Sunnyland Slim persevered despite the passing decades. For a time, he helmed his own label, Airway Records. As late as 1985, he made a fine set for the Red Beans logo, *Chicago Jump*, backed by the same crack combo that shared the stage with him every Sunday evening at a popular North side club called B.L.U.E.S. for some 12 years.

There were times when the pianist fell seriously ill, but he always defied the odds and returned to action, warbling his trademark Woody Woodpecker chortle and kicking off one more exultant slow blues as he had done for the previous half century. Finally, after a calamitous fall on the ice coming home from a gig led to numerous complications, -Sunnyland Slim finally died of kidney failure in 1995. He's sorely missed. *—Bill Dahl*

House Rent Party / 1949 / Delmark ♦♦♦♦♦

From deep in the vaults of Apollo Records comes this sensational collection of 1949 artifacts by the veteran pianist, along with sides by singer St. Louis Jimmy, young pianist Willie Mabon, and two unissued sides by guitarist Jimmy Rogers (including a pre-Chess rendition of his seminal "That's All Right"). Slim's mighty roar shines on "Brown Skin Woman," "I'm Just a Lonesome Man," and "Bad Times (Cost of Living)," all from the emerging heyday of the genre. *—Bill Dahl*

Sunnyland Slim / 1951-1955 / Flyright ♦♦♦♦♦

This vinyl compendium of the pianist's work as leader and sideman for the JOB label from 1951 to 1955 contains some of his hardiest sides. His vocal roar on the jumping "When I Was Young" and a lowdown "Worried About My Baby" and "Down Home Child" is exemplary, while the swinging instrumental "Bassology" verges on a Count Basie motif. Slim's 88s anchor sides by J.B. Lenoir, Johnny Shines, and drummer Alfred Wallace to complete the LP. *—Bill Dahl*

Midnight Jump / 1969 / BGO ♦♦♦♦♦

Slim cut this session in May 1968 in Chicago (with Mike Vernon producing) as a member of the Chicago Blues All Stars, an ad hoc touring group that consisted of Willie Dixon, Johnny Shines, Walter Horton, and Clifton James. With all that to recommend it, it's still a pretty workmanlike set—no real sparks of any kind, just competently played blues by five old veterans who could knock this stuff out in their sleep, and probably did. Not bad, necessarily, but not essential. *—Cub Koda*

● **Slim's Shout** / 1969 / Prestige/Original Blues Classics ♦♦♦♦♦

You wouldn't think that transporting one of Chicago's reigning piano patriarchs to Englewood Cliffs, NJ, would produce such a fine album, but this 1960 set cooks from beginning to end. His swinging New York rhythm section has no trouble following Slim's bedrock piano, and the estimable King Curtis peels off diamond-hard tenor sax solos in the great Texas tradition that also mesh seamlessly. Slim runs through his standards—"The Devil Is a Busy Man," "Shake It," "It's You Baby"—in gorgeous stereo, and two unissued bonus cuts (including another of his best-known tunes, "Everytime I Get to Drinking") make the CD reissue even more appealing. *—Bill Dahl*

Slim's Got His Thing Goin' on / 1969 / Sequel ♦♦♦

Legacy of the Blues / 1975 / Storyville ♦♦♦

Chicago Jump / Apr. 1986 / Evidence ♦♦♦♦

The last of Slim's great band-backed albums, cut with yeoman help from his longtime combo (guitarist Steve Freund and drummer Robert Covington share the vocals). At the heart of the matter are Slim's rolling 88s and still-commanding vocals, invested with experience beyond all comprehension. *—Bill Dahl*

Be Careful How You Vote / 1989 / Earwig ♦♦♦♦

This CD reissues a variety of recordings cut by the veteran blues pianist/vocalist Sunnyland Slim during 1981-1983 for his private label, Airway Records. In his mid-seventies at the time, Slim's energetic vocals and powerful piano playing belie his age. As is typical of the pioneer Chicago bluesman, he allocated plenty of solo space to his sidemen (who include Hubert Sumlin, Eddie Taylor, Lurrie Bell, or Magic Slim on guitar), although there was never any doubt about who was in control. The intelligent lyrics, high musicianship, mood variation (including two excellent instrumentals) and spirited playing make this a highly enjoyable and recommeded date despite the LP-length playing time. *—Scott Yanow*

Live in Europe / 1991 / Airway ♦♦♦

A labor of love project by Slim's longtime saxman Sam Burckhardt, who assembled this collection of informally taped performances from the pianist's Germany stopover on April 23, 1975. Burckhardt wasn't playing his horn that day; instead, he laid down a simple backbeat on drums and let Sunnyland do the rest. Sturdy versions of many of the pianist's signature numbers grace the disc. *—Bill Dahl*

Live at the D.C. Blues Society / 1995 / Mapleshade ♦♦♦

Sunnyland Slim's brand of weary blues, punctuated by rolling piano accents and boogie riffs, predates both the rise and fall of Delta blues and the emergence of its urban successor. Slim toured the South in the '20s, '30s, and early '40s, then left for Chicago and had been there ever since. This blend of Delta and urban sensibilities has been infused in his songs since he began recording and permeates the 14 selections (recorded in 1987) on CD *Live at the D.C. Blues Society.* Although long since past his vocal peak, Slim still spun a nifty yarn and mournful lament. *—Ron Wynn*

Sunnyland Train / 1995 / Evidence ♦♦♦

There are definite signs of Slim's increasing frailty on this solo outing from the '80s, but the majestic power of his aging frame comes through frequently nevertheless. *—Bill Dahl*

She Got a Thing Goin' On / Oct. 13, 1998 / Blind Pig ♦♦♦♦

A nice collection of sides recorded and produced by Sunnyland Slim for his Airways label in the mid-'70s. Although Slim fronts the various bands here for a few numbers, on this set he's in the main working as a sideman behind vocalists Zora Young, Big Time Sarah, and Bonnie Lee. The backup on these sides is superb, with Magic Slim & the Teardrops, Hubert Sumlin, Eddie Taylor, and Mack Simmons showing up in various lineups. Highlights include Zora Young's "Bus Station Blues," Big Time Sarah's "Big Time Operator," and Bonnie Lee's "Sad and Evil Woman." As an extra bonus, the set also includes two previously unissued tracks from the 1979 *Old Friends* sessions, with Sunnyland playing with Floyd Jones, Kansas City Red, and Honeyboy Edwards. *—Cub Koda*

Smile on My Face / Nov. 23, 1999 / Delmark ♦♦♦♦

One of the ten infamous Ralph Bass sessions from 1977, this teams Slim up with guitarist Lacy Gibson and the top-notch rhythm section of Willie Black and Fred Below for a loose and inspired session. The songs are tried and true staples from Sunnyland's songbook, and while Gibson sprays more modern licks, it's still the elder piano man who's the real star here. An extra bonus has guitarist Lee Jackson fronting the band on three tunes from the same session. A good one. *—Cub Koda*

Sunnyland Special: The Cobra & J.O.B. Recordings / Oct. 9, 2001 / West Side ♦♦♦♦♦

1947–1948 / Feb. 5, 2002 / Classics ♦♦♦♦

Super Chikan (James Louis Johnson)

b. Feb. 16, 1951, Darling, MS

Vocals, Guitar / Modern Delta Blues, Electric Delta Blues

Super Chikan, born James Louis Johnson, was one of the more acclaimed emerging blues performers of the late '90s. His small-combo, good-humored blues has a funky touch. As an instrumentalist, he's distinguished not so much by his style as his equipment: His "Chicantars" are constructed with flattened gas can bodies. Super Chikan worked as a cab driver, truck driver, and tractor driver until becoming a full-time musician in his forties, basing himself in Clarksdale, MS. *—Richie Unterberger*

● **Blues Come Home to Roost** / Mar. 11, 1997 / Rooster Blues ♦♦♦♦

As far as debuts go, the one from James "Super Chikan" Johnson is one of the most auspicious and accomplished of modern times. Recorded in Clarksdale, MS—about as close to a home as blues has—it covers the bases, from the sophisticated soulful swing of "Crystal Ball Eyes" to the funk of "Super Chikan Strut" and the Mississippi pride of "Down in the Delta" (albeit with a bayou rhythm). Unlike so many bluesmen, however, Super Chikan doesn't always take himself too seriously—he's not averse to crowing like a rooster, or throwing in a self-deprecatory chicken scratch on the guitar, or the overbearing mama of "Mama & the Chillen." In addition to being a very solid, occasionally inspired, writer (as on the soul "service" history of "Captain Love Juice"), he's a very decent vocalist, and a guitarist who tends to hide his light under a bushel, rarely unleashing his talents, which is a shame, because the ability is there. When he does get (semi-) properly serious, on the slow-jam "Bleeding from the Heart," he shows himself following classic footsteps, a Chicago wail tempered by a Delta heart that simply oozes the blues in every note and syllable. More than simply a novelty act, Super Chikan is part of the great lineage of American blues music, and proof that the blues is very much still alive and kicking—thankfully. *—Chris Nickson*

What You See / Jan. 25, 2000 / Fat Possum ♦♦♦

Is Super Chikan, aka James Johnson, a soul man or a blues man? And where's the line between the two anyway? On *What You See,* Chikan certainly blurs them: The title cut roars out of the blocks as if it has come straight from the funk store, a greasy wah-wah riff over some blues licks (although one of those licks sounds worryingly like the Stranglers' "Peaches") and an infectious backbeat. "Ain't Nobody" brings in some great horns, straight out of the Stax studio, while "El Camino" comes close to surf blues over a New Orleans second-line rhythm. In other words, Super Chikan isn't a big believer in boundaries, and he continues to cross them at will throughout the disc—which makes for some wonderful listening. "Okie Doak" is pure soul-blues, "Good Thing" could teach a lot of rockers how to approach the blues—it needs to be laid-back like this—and "You Said" gives it up on one of the funkiest bass lines ever to emerge. There's plenty of '60s and '70s influence running through this, like the playful 12-bar synthesizer line on "Willie Brown Jr.," which tends to distract from some fine blues guitar work from the man himself, stretching out a little and showing excellent taste and chops. "Big Boy Now" takes an archetypal blues riff, and while it doesn't add anything new, it does generate plenty of excitement, with the inevitable rooster crows (a Chikan trademark), and a humorous lyric about country music and yodeling. It all rounds out with "Fighting Cock," with a riff any bluesman would give his eye teeth for, not taken too seriously (another Chikan trademark), stripped-down to the point of falling apart, and a guaranteed good time for all. Soul to blues and back again, Chikan knows his way around the rootsy side of music. —*Chris Nickson*

Shoot That Thang / Jun. 12, 2001 / Rooster Blues ◆◆◆

A four-page cartoon, penned by excellent cartoon author Harvey Pekar, tells a capsule history of Super Chikan in the liner notes to this release. To be honest, it makes the guitarist/singer's music out to be more interesting than it really is. It's agreeable, laid-back, funky Mississippi blues, by a trio also including Dione Thomas on drums and Harvell Thomas on bass. Although Super Chikan plays ingeniously constructed guitars made from flattened gas cans, the sounds aren't much different from what you hear on many a juke-jointish blues record. Occasionally he gets some "Shaft"-like distorted effects, giving his fullest vent to them on the eight-minute title track. His lyrics are often wry and observational, as on "Mennonite Blues," and sometimes he interjects some spoken comments. That's all a good day's work, but not a notable twist or forward step in the blues' evolutionary path. —*Richie Unterberger*

Swamp Dogg (Jerry Williams)

b. Jul. 1942, Portsmouth, VA

Producer, Vocals, Keyboards, Piano / Blues-Rock, R&B, Soul

One of the great characters in rock and soul music is Jerry Williams, better known as the eccentric, idiosyncratic, and always entertaining Swamp Dogg (no relation to Snoop Doggy Dogg). A Virginia native, Williams invented his own legend by claiming that he had little proper schooling, only to wake up one day and find himself a musical genius (his words). Actually, Williams is very talented, and an early association with Jerry Wexler and Phil Walden led to him working for a number of years as a producer, engineer, and occasional songwriter with Atlantic in the '60s.

At decade's end, however, he decided that the time was right to unleash Swamp Dogg's singular view of the world on an unsuspecting public. The initial result was one of the most gloriously gonzo soul recordings of all time, *Total Destruction to Your Mind.* Along with living up to its title, it was a renegade chunk of not-quite-commercial music, with an unforgettable (though fuzzy) cover shot of the portly Dogg in his underwear. Although undeniably great, *Total Destruction to Your Mind* is one of the most obscure soul records ever made. That, however, has nothing to do with the music, which rocks in a way reminiscent of Solomon Burke or Wilson Pickett. The album's charm may have to do with Dogg's world view: part libertarian politics; part Zappa-style critiques of commerciality and capitalism; and part horny male, the latter defining for better and worse his view of women. Although he spent years working in the industry, Dogg was simply not the standard-issue soul type. And that was good.

Dogg continued to make records, albeit infrequently, after 1969, some good, a few great, and most all extremely difficult to find. With contemporary soul sounding increasingly mannered and sterile, Dogg's yelling, screaming, and general craziness is missed. Thankfully, he hasn't disappeared for good, although he only makes records when he feels like it. His release *Surfin' In Harlem* came out in 1991. And as is often the case with quirky "legends," what he's up to at any given time is the source of wild speculation. It would be wise to not count him out; just when you think this Dogg is down and out, he sneaks up and bites you. —*John Dougan*

Total Destruction to Your Mind / 1970 / Canyon ◆◆◆◆◆

The title track is a slam-bangin' chunk of rock and funk that's pushed by a great session band including guitarist Jesse Carr and drummer Johnny Sandlin, and is easily Dogg's finest moment on record. But the rest of this is great too, ranging from the consumer nightmare "Synthetic World" to the paternity blues of "Mama's Baby, Daddy's Maybe." Plus, Dogg is a great singer, and his dizzying range gets a workout on these songs. —*John Dougan*

Swamp Dogg (Rat On) / 1971 / Elektra ◆◆◆◆◆

The cover of this LP—Swamp Dogg riding a white rat, hands raised and fists clenched in triumph—lets you know that you're not in for any ol' R&B record, even before the needle hits the grooves. It's a satisfying continuation of the eclectic soul singer/songwriter mix of his debut. Vocally, Swamp Dogg sounds like a cross between General Johnson (of Chairmen of the Board) and Van Morrison; as a songwriter, he's his own man. With the exception of Sly Stone, no other soul men of the period were investigating controversial topics with such infectious musicality and good humor. He takes on promiscuity with unbridled frankness in cuts like "Predicament No. 2," and bemoans the eternal delay of American justice for minorities in "Remember I Said Tomorrow," and twists Irving Berlin's "God Bless America" into a protest song (and also, bizarrely, covers the Bee Gees' "Got to Get a Message to You"). None of this endeared him to industry insiders, and Swamp Dogg was dropped by Elektra after the album's release. It's long been out of

print, but in the U.K. Charly has reissued it on CD on a two-fer with *Total Destruction to Your Mind.* —*Richie Unterberger*

Cuffed, Collared and Tagged / 1972 / Edsel ◆◆◆◆◆

This UK import, part of a two-fer, features a great band with dynamite lyrics. —*Richard Pack*

Gag a Maggot / 1973 / Stonedogg ◆◆◆◆◆

Another great album title, another tiny label, another great record long forgotten. Not as consistently manic as *Destruction, Maggot* is as ferocious sounding and does have a good cover of Wilson Pickett's "In the Midnight Hour." Never one to let a love lyric go by without a sarcastic twist, Dogg's love song here is called "I Couldn't Pay for What I Got Last Night." —*John Dougan*

I'm Not Selling Out, I'm Buying In / 1981 / Takoma ◆◆◆◆◆

After years of keeping a low profile, Dogg emerged from out of nowhere with this fine record. Instead of streamlined hard soul, this record carries a rock & roll clout that keeps even its most banal moments ("Wine, Women and Rock 'n' Roll") from terminal tedium. Song title highlight: Dogg's duet with Esther Phillips, "The Love We Got Ain't Worth Two Dead Flies." Kind of says it all, doesn't it. —*John Dougan*

● **Total Destruction to Your Mind/Rat On** / 1991 / Charly ◆◆◆◆◆

These two early Swamp Dogg albums were unheralded landmarks of early '70s soul; Charly has now combined both of them onto a single-disc CD reissue. The liner notes seem to have been written by someone who speaks English as a third language, but that minor gripe aside, this probably contains the singer's most significant work. —*Richie Unterberger*

Surfin' in Harlem / Oct. 31, 1991 / Volt ◆◆

Come the '90s, Swamp Dogg's voice still sounds fine, and he's still singing about racism and promiscuity with some wit. He's still a soul inconoclast, and for some longtime fans, that in itself might be enough to recommend this album. It couldn't be classified among his better releases, though, chiefly because the updated soul backing is sort of leaden. "I've Never Been to Africa (And It's Your Fault)," however, was a strong contender for Song Title of the Month award. —*Richie Unterberger*

● **The Best of 25 Years of Swamp Dogg** / Mar. 5, 1996 / Pointblank ◆◆◆◆◆

The 18-track retrospective *Best of 25 Years of Swamp Dogg* collects many of the highlights from his scattershot career. Concentrating on his '80s output, the compilation doesn't provide a definitive portrait of the warped blues and soul man, but it does offer enough of his best material to make it an excellent introduction. —*Stephen Thomas Erlewine*

Swamp's Things: The Complete Calla Recordings 1966–1967 / May 2, 2000 / West Side ◆◆◆◆

A collection of Swamp Dogg's '60s Calla sides, making their first time on CD appearance with the bonus of a whole album's worth of new-to-CD '70s recordings. The first ten tracks were released as Jerry Williams or Little Jerry Williams while the remainder came out under the sobriquet of Swamp Dogg. Highlights include "Eat the Goose (Before the Goose Eats You)," "Call Me Nigger," "Paradoxical (No Bugles)," "Baby, Bunny, Sugar, Honey," "Philly Duck," and "Baby You're My Everything." A stellar collection of '60s and '70s soul-funk. —*Cub Koda*

Cuffed, Collared and Tagged/Doing a Party Tonite / Jun. 6, 2000 / West Side ◆◆◆◆◆

The Re-Invention of Swamp Dogg / Jun. 20, 2000 / S.D.E.G. ◆◆

Jerry "Swamp Dogg" Williams has written and produced some of rock's most imaginative novelty/tongue-in-cheek lyrics, but has never risen above cult status. He's almost as lyrically twisted as George Clinton and nearly as prolific, as he churns out CDs quicker than people can find out about them due to poor promotion and publicity. On this set, he shows versatility with tunes spanning from the Jamaican-ish "I Have Touched the Sky" to Southern soul via the wry "Ain't a Nineteen Year Old Got Nothing on You" to the jubilant gospel of "Jesus Is Alive in My Heart." While an ingenious lyricist, Swamp Dogg's melodies and arrangements are tired and formulaic, particularly in this package. The titles entice you to listen but, once you do, the freshness of topical subjects like "Artificial Insemination" stales fast if just about everything else is lacking. —*Andrew Hamilton*

The Swan Silvertones

f. 1938, Coalwood, WV

Group / Traditional Gospel, Southern Gospel, Black Gospel, R&B

The Swan Silvertones are a premier gospel group and one of the great music experiences awaiting anyone who has never heard them. If you are not a fan of gospel music or "religious" music of any kind, don't let that fact deter you from having this unique listening experience. This is pure music at the highest level.

The a cappella quartet Four Harmony Kings was created by tenor Claude Jeter in 1938 in Coalwood, WV, but the name was changed to the Swan Silvertones when they began a 15-minute radio show sponsored by the Swan Bakery Company on the Knoxville station WBIR in 1942. They developed a national reputation during their contract with King Records from 1946 to 1951, recording some 21 recordings (mostly in the jubilee gospel style) including "I Cried Holy" and "Go Ahead." They joined Specialty Records from 1951 to 1953, but issued only four singles (in a more contemporary, harder style) before they were dropped by that label. The early group had lead singers Jeter and Solomon Womack, tenors Robert Crenshaw and John Manson, baritone John H. Myles, and bass Henry K. Bossard.

They really came into their own when they signed and recorded with Vee-Jay and recorded with that label from 1956 through 1964. The smoother Vee-Jay sound is probably due to arranger Paul Owens, who joined the group in 1952. Influenced by jazz-vocal groups like the Four Freshmen and the Hi-Los, Owens smoothed out the sound and made it more contemporary, even progressive. Starting in 1956, the group began adding instruments to what had been up until then a purely vocal or a cappella sound. The excellent guitarist Linwood Hargrove added greatly to the emerging Vee-Jay sound and the additions (on recordings) of jazz sidemen Bob Cranshaw on bass and Walter Perkins—founding members of MJT +3—on drums completed the sound.

Perhaps their greatest hit was "Oh Mary Don't You Weep," released in 1959—an incredible listening experience. It is in this song that Claude Jeter intones the phrase "I'll be a bridge over deep water, if you trust in my name" that inspired Paul Simon to compose "Bridge Over Troubled Water" some years later. The Swan Silvertones had a great effect on many rock (Al Kooper) and country (Gary Stewart) artists. During their nine years at Vee-Jay, the main members of the group were tenor (and falsetto) Claude Jeter, baritone John H. Myles, tenor Paul Owens, and bass William Conner. Other singers who were in the group during that time were tenors Dewey Young, Robert Crutcher, and Louis Johnson. When Vee-Jay closed in 1965, the group moved to HOB records, where they did one last album before Claude Jeter left to record on his own and focus on his ministry. *—Michael Erlewine*

Heavenly Light / 1952 / Specialty ✦✦✦✦✦
The Swan Silvertones only recorded for Specialty Records from 1952 until 1955, and it's generally not considered a prime period in their tenure. But this set of newly released performances from the early '50s, most of which even the label lacks information about, show that they did turn in some top-flight outings during that period. Ten of the tracks were done live before hollering, celebrating audiences that weren't attending a concert, but participating in a spiritual renewal. The other eight are studio numbers, but they contain the same intensity and spark that make this a memorable Swan Silvertones document. *—Ron Wynn*

The Swan Silvertones / 1959 / Vee-Jay ✦✦✦✦
Here is perhaps the best of the Vee-Jay albums (12 tracks) of vintage Swan Silvertones. These tracks came from six sessions for Vee-Jay when the group was at its creative peak—perhaps the single best album they ever put out. It contains their hit "Oh Mary Don't You Weep," "How I Got Over," "My Rock," "The Lord's Prayer," "When Jesus Comes," and "Great Day in December"—all incredible music experiences. *—Michael Erlewine*

Singin' in My Soul / 1960 / Vee-Jay ✦✦✦✦✦
Here is one of the classic Vee-Jay albums (12 tracks) of vintage Swan Silvertones. These tracks came from six sessions for Vee-Jay when the group was at its creative peak. The album includes "End of My Journey," "Jesus Is Alright with Me," and their version of "Rock My Soul." *—Michael Erlewine*

Savior Pass Me Not / 1962 / Vee-Jay ✦✦✦✦
The Swans at the peak of perfection. *—Opal Louis Nations*

Blessed Assurance / 1963 / Vee-Jay ✦✦✦✦✦
Great singing. Well produced. Fine arrangements. *—Opal Louis Nations*

☆ **Let's Go to Church Together** / 1964 / Vee-Jay ✦✦✦✦
This is quintessential Swan Silvertones at their peak. Songs like "Love Lifted Me" and "I'll Be Satisfied" are among 12 songs from a single session in 1964 that have captured some of the finest work of this legendary group. This makes for deep satisfying listening. *—Michael Erlewine*

Glory Gospel / 1967 / HOB ✦✦✦✦
The last truly great Swans collection with Jeter at the helm. *—Opal Louis Nations*

Love Lifted Me / 1970 / Specialty ✦✦✦✦✦
Tight harmonies, soaring high tenor lead set against hard-sung preaching to create heightened effect. Circa 1951-1956. *—Opal Louis Nations*

My Rock / 1972 / Specialty ✦✦✦✦✦
More gospel in the spirit, circa 1952-1957. *—Opal Louis Nations*

Get Right With the Swan Silvertones / 1982 / Rhino ✦✦✦✦
A reissue of various '50s and '60s singles and album sides plus two unissued cuts. Lead vocal dynamics from Rev. Claude Jeter, Paul Owens, and Louis Johnson. This well-rounded and amply annotated cross-section deserves serious consideration. *—Kip Lornell*

My Rock/Love Lifted Me / 1991 / Specialty ✦✦✦✦✦
Some of the group's best hard-gospel harmonizing from the mid-'50s, most notably "How I Got Over" and "My Rock." The group's toughest sides, with firm conviction from lead soloists Solomon Womack, Rev. Bob Crenshaw, Dewey Young, and Paul Owens. *—Kip Lornell*

★ **The Swan Silvertones/Singin' in My Soul** / Oct. 1993 / Vee-Jay ✦✦✦✦✦
Here is one CD with two classic Vee-Jay albums (24 tracks) of vintage Swan Silvertones. The tracks from both albums came from six sessions for Vee-Jay, when the group was at its creative peak. The album *The Swan Silvertones* is perhaps the single best album they ever put out, containing 12 tunes including their hit "Oh Mary Don't You Weep," "How I Got Over," "My Rock," "The Lord's Prayer," "When Jesus Comes," and "Great Day in December." The music continues from the album *Singin' in My Soul*, featuring 12 more prime Vee-Jay cuts including "End of My Journey," "Jesus Is Alright With Me," and their version of "Rock My Soul." *—Michael Erlewine*

Do You Believe: The Very Best of the Swan Silvertones / Mar. 3, 1998 / Collectables ✦✦✦✦✦
All you want to hear of the Vee-Jay sides by Rev. Claude Jeter and the boys. *—Opal Louis Nations*

Hallelujah: A Collection of Their Finest Recordings / May 18, 1999 / Music Club ✦✦✦✦
This 15-track collection brings together both live and studio recordings made for the HOB label. Both of the famous leads with the group—the Rev. Claude Jeter and Louis Johnson—are featured on tracks like "Only Believe," "I Love the Lord," "Home in That Rock," "Call Him Up," "Jesus, I Love You," their two magnificent voices dueting on "Leaning on Jesus," "In My Heart," and "He's My Friend." The live tracks on here literally sweat with emotion and fervor. A nice set. *—Cub Koda*

☆ **Pray for Me/Let's Go to Church Together** / 2000 / Collectables ✦✦✦✦✦
The Swan Silvertones perfected their shimmering, explosive vocals while on Vee-Jay Records from 1956-1964. The elastic, dazzling falsetto of Rev. Claude Jeter, which was later adapted and reworked by Al Green, was contrasted by any number of powerful second lead singers within the group: Paul Owens, Louis Johnson, or Azell Monk. The songs on this disc, with one exception, cover the Silvertones' last great period and offer resounding harmonies, soaring leads, and remarkable music. The lead selection, "Sinners Crossroad," is actually the Silver Quintette, an Indiana group probably most famous for having on its roster two future soul stars in Roscoe Robinson and Joe Henderson. *—Ron Wynn*

The Swan Silvertones/Saviour Pass Me Not / Jul. 10, 2001 / Collectables ✦✦✦✦✦

Singing in My Soul / Up Front ✦✦✦✦
Great sessions of 1956-1957. *—Opal Louis Nations*

☆ **The Best of Swan Silvertones** / Chameleon ✦✦✦✦✦

Roosevelt Sykes

b. Jan. 31, 1906, Elmar, AR, d. Jul. 17, 1983, New Orleans, LA
Vocals, Piano / Acoustic Chicago Blues, Piano Blues, Acoustic Blues, St. Louis Blues
For those voicing the goofball opinion that blues is simply too depressing to embrace, sit 'em down and expose 'em to a heady dose of Roosevelt Sykes. If he doesn't change their minds, nothing will.

There was absolutely nothing downbeat about this roly-poly, effervescent pianist (nicknamed "Honeydripper" for his youthful prowess around the girls), whose lengthy career spanned the prewar and postwar eras with no interruption whatsoever. Sykes' romping boogies and hilariously risqué lyrics (his double entendre gems included "Dirty Mother for You," "Ice Cream Freezer," and "Peeping Tom") characterize his monumental contributions to the blues idiom—he was a pioneering piano-pounder responsible for the seminal pieces "44 Blues," "Driving Wheel," and "Night Time Is the Right Time."

Sykes began playing while growing up in Helena, AR. At age 15, he hit the road, developing his rowdy barrelhouse style around the blues-fertile St. Louis area. Sykes began recording in 1929 for OKeh and was signed to four different labels the next year under four different names (he was variously billed as Dobby Bragg, Willie Kelly, and Easy Papa Johnson)! Sykes joined Decca Records in 1935, where his popularity blossomed.

After relocating to Chicago, Sykes inked a pact with Bluebird in 1943 and recorded prolifically for the RCA subsidiary with his combo, the Honeydrippers, scoring a pair of R&B hits in 1945 (covers of Cecil Gant's "I Wonder" and Joe Liggins' "The Honeydripper"). The following year, he scored one more national chart item for the parent Victor logo, the low-down blues "Sunny Road." He also often toured and recorded with singer St. Louis Jimmy Oden, the originator of the classic "Going Down Slow."

In 1951, Sykes joined Chicago's United Records, cutting more fine sides over the next couple of years. A pair of Dave Bartholomew-produced 1955 dates for Imperial in New Orleans included a rollicking version of "Sweet Home Chicago" that presaged all the covers that would surface later on. A slew of albums for Bluesville, Folkways, Crown, and Delmark kept Sykes on the shelves during the '60s (a time when European tours began to take up quite a bit of the pianist's itinerary). He settled in New Orleans during the late '60s, where he remained a local treasure until his death.

Precious few pianists could boast the thundering boogie prowess of Roosevelt Sykes—and even fewer could chase away the blues with his blues as the rotund cigar-chomping 88s ace did. *—Bill Dahl*

Complete Recorded Works, Vol. 1 (1929–1930) / Jun. 14, 1929-Jun. 1, 1930 / Document ✦✦✦✦
This volume, the first in a seven-part series collecting all of Roosevelt Sykes' recordings between 1929 and 1942, begins with the classic "44 Blues" and includes 22 more sides from late 1929 and early 1930. Also including several duets with Mae Bell Miller and Bee Turner, it is essential for hardcore fans of blues piano. *—AMG*

★ **Roosevelt Sykes (1929–1941)** / Jun. 14, 1929-Apr. 3, 1941 / Story of the Blues ✦✦✦✦✦
A good sampling of some of Sykes' best tracks, it offers a perfect introduction to this seminal pianist. *—AMG*

Blues Man / Jun. 14, 1929-Dec. 1944 / Collector's Edition ✦✦✦
This is an 18-song cross section of Sykes' work (some originally released under the name Willie Kelly) cut between 1929 and 1944. Even on the early sides, cut under relatively primitive technical conditions, his rollicking good spirits are conveyed beautifully, both in his singing and his stomping piano style. Among his enduring classics, "44 Blues" is represented, along with his de facto signature tune "The Honey Dripper," but there's hardly a song among the other 16 that's not just as worthwhile, and this is a good introduction to Sykes' sound and music overall, especially at its budget price. What's more, the sound is good (veering toward excellent on some tracks, such as "She's in My Blood"), and even at the low retail price the producers have included recording dates on every cut. *—Bruce Eder*

The Country Blues Piano (1929–1932) / 1929-1932 / Yazoo ✦✦✦✦✦
Featured in this Arkansas-born pianist/songster in some of his best early outings. *—Mark A. Humphrey*

Complete Recorded Works, Vol. 2 (1930–1931) / 1930-1931 / Document ✦✦✦
Part of the most ambitious series of Roosevelt Sykes reissues ever undertaken, Document's *Complete Recorded Works, Vol. 2 (1930-1931)* features 24 tracks of prime blues piano, everything Sykes recorded during the year-long period between June of 1930 and June of 1931. Though there aren't as many classic tracks here as on other volumes, there are highlights: a remake of one of his more famous sides, this time called "Kelly's 44 Blues," and a couple of risqué titles ("Nasty but It's Clean," "Big Time Woman"). That's enough to make it of interest to completists and serious fans, though the long running time, chronological sequencing, and poor fidelity could make for difficult listening. *—Thom Owens*

1931–1941 / Apr. 1931-Apr. 30, 1941 / Wolf ✦✦✦✦

Complete Recorded Works, Vol. 3 (1931–1933) / Sep. 19, 1931-Dec. 11, 1933 / Document ✦✦✦
Document's *Complete Recorded Works, Vol. 3 (1932-1933)* continues its chronological overview of Roosevelt Sykes' early recordings. As on the previous volume, Sykes reworks his "44 Blues," hits a few highlights ("Sail on Black Sue," "Highway 61 Blues"), tries his hand at a double entendre or two, and invites a few guests. (Actually, most of the tracks are features for outside vocalists, including Emerson Houston, Clarence Emerson, "Stump" Johnson, and Carl Rafferty.) Also in common with most Document collections, the lengthy running time, chronological sequencing, and fair audio quality are enough to make it a bit off-putting for most listeners. *—Thom Owens*

Complete Recorded Works, Vol. 4 (1934–1936) / 1934-1936 / Document ✦✦✦
The fourth volume in Document's *Complete Recorded Works* covers Roosevelt Sykes' career from late 1934 to mid-1936, a period during which he introduced his signature tune "Honeydripper," along with "Soft and Mellow (Stella Blues)," the bawdy gem "Dirty Mother for You," and a few songs with vocalists Johnnie Strauss and Arthur McKay. Most of these highlights, though, are also available on the *Roosevelt Sykes (1929-1941)* compilation, so casual listeners shouldn't feel the need to spring for anything extra. *—Thom Owens*

Complete Recorded Works, Vol. 5 (1937–1939) / 1937-1939 / Document ✦✦✦
Document's *Complete Recorded Works, Vol. 5 (1937-1939)* offers an exhaustive overview of a two-year period from Roosevelt Sykes' career. During that era, Sykes first recorded a raft of classics: "Night Time Is the Right Time," "Drunken Gambler," "Mistake in Life," and the double (or single) entendre classics "Ice Cream Freezer," "Let Me Hang My Stockings in Your Christmas Tree," and "Somebody's Been Ridin' My Black Gal." The novelties are delicious fun, though only completists will be interested in this lengthy compilation of exactingly sequenced recordings. *—Thom Owens*

Complete Recorded Works, Vol. 6 (1939–1941) / Apr. 13, 1939-Feb. 27, 1941 / Document ✦✦✦✦
Pianist/singer Roosevelt Sykes is heard at his prime throughout these 25 selections, all of which are duets with drummer Big Sid Catlett. Sykes was always an expressive singer and a powerful pianist, at times sounding like two different performers who were nevertheless very much attuned to each other. With Catlett offering tasteful and swinging support, Sykes is particularly effective on "44 Blues," "New Mistake in Life," "I've Made a Change," "Unlucky 13 Blues," "Knock Me Out," and "47th Street Jive." Fans of '30s/'40s blues will want all of the Roosevelt Sykes discs in Document's valuable series. *—Scott Yanow*

Complete Recorded Works, Vol. 7 (1941–1944) / 1941-1944 / Document ✦✦✦
Roosevelt Sykes, one of the best prewar blues pianists, is heard on this chronological Document compilation from a nearly four-year period of his career. With support from drummer Big Sid Catlett, bassist Alfred Elkins, and guitarist Ted Summit, Sykes enthuses over a host of his original songs, along with a sprightly version of Fats Waller's "Honeysuckle Rose." Fans of piano blues will love this edition in Document's lengthy series of reissues, though beginners are advised to head first for the *Roosevelt Sykes (1929-1941)* compilation on Story of the Blues. *—Thom Owens*

1944–1950, Vol. 2: The Honey Dripper / 1944-1950 / EPM Musique ✦✦✦✦

Complete Recorded Works, Vol. 8 (1945–1947) / 1945-1947 / Document ✦✦✦

Complete Recorded Works, Vol. 9 (1947–1951) / 1947-1951 / Document ✦✦✦

Raining in My Heart / Jul. 12, 1951-Mar. 19, 1953 / Delmark ✦✦✦✦
This fine collection of Sykes' early-'50s sides for Chicago's United Records was reissued on Delmark in 2000. It contains some of the pianist's finest work with his jumping combo, the Honeydrippers (with unusual augmentation from violinist Remo Biondi on one 1952 date). "Toy Piano Blues" finds Sykes switching over to celeste, but "Too Hot to Handle," "Walking the Boogie," and "Fine and Brown" are in the customary Sykes mode. *—Bill Dahl*

Complete Recorded Works, Vol. 10 (1951–1957) / 1951-1957 / Document ✦✦✦

The Return of Roosevelt Sykes / Mar. 1, 1960+Mar. 2, 1960 / Bluesville/Original Blues Classics ✦✦✦✦
Sykes' lyrical images are as vivid and amusing as ever on this 1960 set, with titles like "Set the Meat Outdoors" and "Hangover" among its standouts. Other than drummer Jump Jackson, the quartet behind the pianist is pretty obscure, but they rock his boogies with a vengeance. Contains a nice remake of his classic "Drivin' Wheel." *—Bill Dahl*

The Honeydripper / Sep. 14, 1960 / Storyville ✦✦✦✦✦

Roosevelt Sykes Sings the Blues / 1962 / Diablo ✦✦✦
Despite the shoddiness of the recording, this album nevertheless impressively captured Sykes' rough-and-tumble boogie and blues prowess in a band setting. *—Bill Dahl*

Hard Drivin' Blues / Jan. 27, 1962-May 17, 1963 / Delmark ✦✦✦

Feel Like Blowing My Horn / Jan. 1966 / Delmark ✦✦✦✦✦
This loveable pianist and singer sustained a long recording and performing career, the last decades of which he was frequently heard as a soloist. Although this was an artistically defendable position and Sykes made the most of the solo context, he was quick to admit in interviews that he was most known as a bandleader in his romping, stomping days, and these were bands that featured horns and arrangements of a style somewhere between Kansas City and New Orleans. Producer Bob Koester gets kudos for bringing about a studio session for Sykes involving such a group later in his career. What a great combination of players is involved, including the brilliant guitarist Robert Jr. Lockwood, the crack rhythm section of Dave Myers and Fred Below, and two horn players whose affiliation with the bandleader goes back to the '30s and '40s. One of them, trumpeter King Kolax, is a name who frequently shows up in discographies of jazz great John Coltrane, who played in the Kolax band when he was a whippersnapper. These legendary players hardly sit on their laurels; they use the opportunity to lay down really beautiful music, the rocking and fun-loving spirit of Sykes looking down on all of it like some kind of barbecue munching holy spirit. One of the best recordings on the Delmark label, and that is saying a mouthful. *—Eugene Chadbourne*

Is Blue and Ribald / 1973 / Southland ✦✦✦
Somehow the esteemed Sykes charges through this low-rent production like a high-priced quarterback, scoring and then coming back around for the field goal. The independent blues label that released this was based out of Columbia, SC, and their production is on the cheap side, with flimsy vinyl, generic printing, and a recording sound that might make the listener imagine that the fellow with the microphone wasn't sure how close he was supposed to get. Sykes was allowed to re-record material he had already committed to posterity a few times already, as well as completely extemporize an instrumental inspired by a swipe through a deck of cards, which must be the boogie-woogie equivalent of a John Cage composition. He even picks up a guitar for the only time in his recorded career, and although the instrument sounds in need of repair and the song is wretched, he manages to pull off an impressive lead break, especially for a pianist. He seems to have been in a rowdy mood, which saves the day in terms of what have could have been a substandard album. After playing a filthier than usual "Dirty Mother for You," he follows up with an arrogant number entitled "Put Up or Shut Up," the type of material the artist does with glee. The only trick the label seems to have missed is promoting this as a filthy or sexy record. The title doesn't quite indicate how many numbers of this sort are on the record, and how much free rein Sykes is given. This certainly isn't the set he would play if there were little old ladies in the front row. Or maybe it would be! *—Eugene Chadbourne*

Grind It! / 1973 / Total Energy ✦✦✦
Six songs, recorded (in decent sound) in September 1973 at the Ann Arbor Blues & Jazz Festival. Sykes, then 66 years old, is in good form both musically and instrumentally; his set includes a version of his classic "Driving Wheel" and the standards "St. James Infirmary" and "Night Time Is the Right Time." Most of it is relaxed and laid-back, but he does crank up the tempo on "Run This Boogie," and milks the crude double entendre of "Dirty Mother for You" ("gonna be a jumping mother for you" and many such variations) for all it's worth. His singing is high-spirited, as are his boogie piano riffs. Sykes' tracks occupy only half of this CD—the remainder of which is devoted to six songs by another early blues legend, Victoria Spivey, also recorded at the 1973 Ann Arbor Blues & Jazz Festival. *—Richie Unterberger*

Music Is My Business / Sep. 17, 1975 / Blues Alliance ✦✦✦
The nonexistent fall had already shifted into winter weather when a Volkswagen packed with two record producers and two blues musicians pulled into Edmonton, Alberta, in the late '70s. They were looking to hook up with another pair of classic blues players, pianist Roosevelt Sykes and slide guitarist Johnny Shines, up north on a series of club and concert dates combining them in an evening of solo performances. The idea was to cut albums by Sykes and Shines, in combination with the younger blues players that were stuffed in the back of the car: none other than the intense Louisiana Red and a harmonica player who called himself Sugar Blue (at this point most likely to be heard on the streets of New York, but eventually to cut records with none other than the Rolling Stones). This album presents the pianist's side of what happened. The cranky Sykes had a particular loathing for harmonicas and barely let the Sugar out of the bowl, while the combination of the florid, technically adept New Orleans pianist with the raw Red was not always a good color match. When Red first enters here, he tries to provide lead guitar fills in the Buddy Guy style, but the sustained string choking always start to sound out of tune with at least a few of the many notes Sykes is hitting, seeing as the piano man doesn't really go for restrained comping. Sykes hears the problem and comes up with a tune called "Stop Stopping Me," effectively bringing forth the guitarist's talents by providing him with a more fixed harmonic base. Shines, in general, fares better blending his guitar with Sykes; not only is his style more relaxed, word was the two bluesmen has been arguing about the Bible all day and were making an effort to get along a little, which one can hear. A large chunk of the tracks are solo piano, which is of course something Sykes does with great flair and intoxicating élan. This is perhaps not an essential blues album, but the set of performances are well recorded and provide an entertaining document of what can happen in the studio when a gang of sharp blues players are assembled. *—Eugene Chadbourne*

Original Honeydripper / 1978 / Blind Pig ✦✦✦✦
This label can really be counted on to do a fine job on documenting an artist. For a recording of this artist in his later years, one can't really do better than this set, which captures Sykes live on-stage in a club, alone at the piano, as he usually was during this stage of his career. By then he was way beyond worrying about dancers like in the old days and was becoming more and more expansive on the keyboard, certainly bringing to mind Fats Waller and Art Tatum. And beyond that, listeners at that time who had heard even more modern pianists were convinced that Sykes was getting into their territory, too. Which he probably was, especially when the entry way was a number such as "Honeysuckle Rose" or "Please Don't Talk About Me," a regular set-ender and forum for some of his wildest playing. The tradeoff in a live set such as this, as opposed to Sykes in a studio, was that for an audience; he always trotted out a certain set of hardy favorites, and they are here, but he always reinvented them with the artistry of his piano playing. In the studio he would try to devise some catchy new numbers, and perhaps take one of the old favorites, change it slightly and then rename it. There is a touch of the latter skullduggery here. The solo version of "I'm a Nut," which had served so well as a band vehicle, is very nice to hear, and the Ray Charles cover is also perfect. *—Eugene Chadbourne*

Gold Mine: Live in Europe / 1992 / Delmark ✦✦✦
A solid 1966 solo set, cut during one of the effervescent piano pounder's frequent overseas jaunts and originally issued on Delmark as *In Europe*. A winning combination of

material ancient even back then ("44 Blues," the jaunty boogie "Boot That Thing") and fresh numbers. —*Bill Dahl*

Blues By Roosevelt "The Honey-Dripper" Sykes / 1995 / Smithsonian/Folkways ♦♦♦♦
Other than a cameo piano appearance by his producer (and peer) Memphis Slim on the appropriately titled "Memphis Slim Rock," this is a stellar solo outing by the prolific pianist from 1961. He belts out a booming "Sweet Old Chicago," takes a trip to Chicago's South side on "47th Street Jive," and indulges in a little ribald imagery for "The Sweet Root Man." —*Bill Dahl*

The Meek Roosevelt Sykes / Nov. 18, 1997 / Jewel ♦♦♦
Yes, the Jewel label. A fine example of a regional Louisiana outfit, with lots of offspring. This release, for example, is manufactured by Paula, a division of Sue. OK gals, whatever you say. The music of Roosevelt Sykes remains uniquely his own, no matter how many times he might have signed his name on the dotted line. As for *The Meek*, has there ever been a less appropriate album title? Whether singing or tickling the ivories, Sykes is about as meek as the breath of a wounded water buffalo. This set is typical of one of the man's solo piano outings from the '70s. It pretty well all fits into the blues mode, although he neighbors into the swing area from time to time, and when he does, shows off plenty of chops as well as ideas. "I Am in Love With a Lover" and "Dangerous Man" are from his lusty and bragging bags, while instrumentals such as "Roosevelt's Mood" and "Shaking the Boogie" are hard to fault, no matter how familiar some of the material is. "Safety Pin Blues" gathers together all the best aspects of his artist, the energetic fills and thumping beat backing up clever and witty lyrics. It seems to have been a pretty decent recording, but pressings and mastering jobs from this company can vary in quality. —*Eugene Chadbourne*

Boogie Honky Tonk / Oldie Blues ♦♦♦♦♦
Vinyl compilation of the pianist's 1944-1947 output for RCA with his jumping little combo, the Honeydrippers, all of it cut in Chicago. Backed by myriad swinging Windy City sidemen (saxists Leon Washington, J.T. Brown, and Bill Casimir; bassist Ransom Knowling; drummers Jump Jackson and Judge Riley), Sykes rips through "Peeping Tom," to the wonderfully titled "Flames of Jive," and his often-covered "Sunny Road" with ebullient charm. —*Bill Dahl*

T-Lou (Louis Joseph Eaglen)

b. Grand Coteau, LA
Vocals, Accordian / Zydeco
A leading light of the Los Angeles zydeco scene, singer and accordionist T-Lou was born Louis Joseph Eaglin in Grand Coteau, LA; the son of sharecroppers, he taught himself guitar at the age of 15 and later played bass in a high school R&B combo. Upon graduating high school, he relocated to Houston before settling in California; there T-Lou attended a Clifton Chenier concert and fell under zydeco's sway, soon learning accordion and forming the Los Angeles Zydeco Band. After issuing 1985's *T-Lou and His Los Angeles Zydeco Band*, he continued playing regularly along the West Coast in the years leading up to the release of 1993's *Super Hot. —Jason Ankeny*

T-Lou and His Los Angeles Zydeco Band / 1985 / Maison de Soul ◆◆◆◆
T-Lou and His Los Angeles Zydeco Band is a solid zydeco album and a very impressive debut from the accordionist. His L.A.-based band sound like they're natural-born Louisianans (granted, many of them are transplants), and the record rocks with true energy and spirit, even when the recording is a little too clean. — *Thom Owens*

● **Super Hot** / 1993 / Maison de Soul ◆◆◆◆◆
It took T-Lou a few years to follow-up his debut, but *Super Hot* makes it clear that the wait was worthwhile. It's nothing but straight-up, traditional zydeco, but the music is performed with so much energy, the result is simply intoxicating. T-Lou's nine original songs prove that he's a solid songwriter, and they give the record a solid foundation upon which he contributes a series of truly intoxicating performances that confirm his place as one of the best zydeco performers of the '90s. — *Thom Owens*

Blind Joe Taggart

Vocals, Guitar / Prewar Gospel Blues, Country Blues
If one ever ran into Blind Joe Taggart in a dark alley, the only possible protection would be to have Blind John Henry Arnold with you. According to the famous folksinger and blues artist Josh White, there was only one man on earth who was meaner than Taggart, and that was Arnold. White obviously knew what he was talking about, having been abused and kicked around by both men, as well as the even more famous Blind Lemon Jefferson. Back in the old days when blind blues virtuoso roamed the streets displaying their genius for coins, someone had to lead them around. White was perhaps the most famous of a class of ex-lead boys for blind blues singers, a form of apprenticeship that has disappeared from the modern blues scene along with performers of the class of Taggart and his ilk. Performers trying to survive in such a lifestyle can hardly be blamed for developing what can be best described as street-hardened personalities.

Taggart was a fairly typical itinerant performer of the '20s, and most of the available information on him was handed down in interviews from White, who first met him when he was known as Joel Taggart in Greenville, SC. White's description of the difference between the two tyrants has become famous. Arnold was "mean, honest mean." Taggart, on the other hand, was "tricky, nasty mean." Furthermore, he was not really blind, something that puts him in a subclass of blind blues musicians who actually had some vision available to them. Taggart had cataracts and could "see a little," according to White.

Of more importance than what Taggart could or couldn't see was the fact he was noticed in 1926. The Brunswick-Balke-Collender company from Chicago, which was beginning a series of record releases under the Vocalion label, was keenly aware that similar series of so-called "race" records were selling like hotcakes. Many types of performers were recorded during the '20s, and among these stacks of historic sides were this label's first ventures into recording singing evangelists, basically the gospel equivalent of country blues players. Near the end of that year, Taggart became the first full-time guitar evangelist to cut a side. The material he recorded was a happy meeting between his obvious versatility as a performer and the label's desire to try as many approaches as possible to the hitmaking destination. Taggart recorded several vocal duets with Emma Taggart, who was most likely his wife. Alternative takes that were released much later from these sessions helped create a further revision in the opinion of this artist held by blues scholars.

Not discovered by the mass blues audience during the folk revival of the '60s as was fellow meanie Blind Lemon Jefferson, Taggart basically had to wait for the CD-driven thoroughness of the Document label to fully illustrate the amount of ingenuity and inventiveness he brought to each of his performances. He also recorded duets with James Taggart, assumed to be his son. Like many busy blues artists, Taggart cut corners around recording contracts by recording under other names, including the pseudonyms Blind Joe Amos, Blind Jeremiah Taylor, Blind Tim Russell, and Blind Joe Donnel. Some of this activity was an attempt not to fool record labels but the Lord above, who it was assumed might not approve of Taggart playing the "devil's music" and could be tricked by a pseudonym. Taggart's music is sometimes considered to feature some of the oldest roots of

any country blues artist. This includes melodic and stylistic influences from the Civil War era, considered a time when black and white musicians were perhaps not as restricted in access to each other's musical traditions as they would become later. —*Eugene Chadbourne*

● **Complete Recorded Works, Vol. 1 (1926–1934)** / Jun. 2, 1994 / Document ◆◆◆◆

Complete Recorded Works, Vol. 2 (1929–1934) / Jun. 2, 1994 / Document ◆◆◆◆

Tail Dragger (James Yancy Jones)

b. 1940, Altheimer, AR
Group / Modern Electric Blues, Electric Chicago Blues
James Yancy Jones, aka Tail Dragger, was born in Altheimer, AR, in 1940. He was brought up by his grandparents and was influenced as a child by the electric Chicago blues of Muddy Waters, Sonny Boy Williamson, and especially Chester Burnett, the Howlin' Wolf. Jones was a Howlin' Wolf devotee, right down to his deep, gruff voice. After moving to Chicago in the '60s, he began playing with blues legends on the West and South Side. It was Howlin' Wolf that gave Jones the title "Tail Dragger" because of his habit of showing up late to gigs.

When Jones first appeared on the Chicago blues circuit he was known as "Crawlin' James." A number of local West and South Side blues artists, including Hubert Sumlin, Carey Bell, Eddie Shaw, Mack Simmons, and Willie Kent, got their start playing in Tail Dragger's bands. The difficult lifestyle that contribute to many blues lyrics caught up with Tail Dragger in 1993 when he shot and killed fellow bluesman Boston Blackie, supposedly over profits owed from a show. Jones spent 17 months in an Illinois jail. Following years of playing juke joints and releasing a handful of singles, his first full-length disc, *Crawlin' Kingsnake*, was released in 1996. Three years later he returned with *American People* on the legendary Chicago blues and jazz label Delmark. —*Al Campbell*

● **Crawlin' Kingsnake** / Jun. 11, 1996 / St. George ◆◆◆◆
The blues gets served up hard, heavy and raunchy on the debut album from this Chicago blues club legend. The 12 tracks here run the gamut from the modal "Don't Trust No Woman," six and a half minutes of a non-stop trance groove, to the nastiest version of "Baby Please Don't Go" you'll ever hear to the Jimmy Reed groove of "Cold Outdoors." With a straightforward, driving band featuring Studebaker John on harmonica, Rockin' Johnny Burgin on lead guitar, and Twist Turner on drums, a great song selection with seven of the 12 tunes emanating from the pens of either the Tail Dragger or producer George Paulus, and an uncluttered production, this is one modern-day blues album that captures the spirit of Chicago blues in its classic period, yet in the here and now. The cover of this CD announces that disc contains "one hour of hardcore juke joint blues." Believe it. —*Cub Koda*

American People / Mar. 9, 1999 / Delmark ◆◆◆
James Yancy Jones, aka the Tail Dragger, Arkansas born and Chicago based, shows no sign of slowing down. A Howlin' Wolf devotee, he even apes the Wolf's deep, gruff voice on occasion. But he has a distinctive, oak-solid voice of his own, singing and shouting his way through these 11 numbers, seven of which he wrote. Guitarists Rockin' Johnny Burgin, Johnny B. Moore, and Johnny Dawkins are on one cut, and harmonicists Billy Branch and Martin Lang, bassist Aron Burton, drummers Baldhead Pete and Rob Lorenz help out, all in tune with the Dragger's feverish notions. Primarily a pleader asking forgiveness for mean mistreating, he has the ultimate blues experience talking about love won and lost, wondering why and stating his case. Songs about "Bertha" and "Betty" are sweeter, clearly about women he's had, "You Gotta Go" is a typical 12-bar blues with tenor saxophonist Eddie Shaw's honking urging the woman out the door, and "Bought Me a New Home," another 12-bar, states "new house, new woman." At his most Wolfish, the Dragger's voice is lower-pitched and more pronounced for the nearly nine-minute endless vamp "My Woman Is Gone," Branch's searing harmonica and twin guitarists Moore and Rockin' Johnny with the rhythm section signifying the ramblin' juggernaut sound that was the Wolf. "My Head Is Bald" is king snake patient and delicious. A "Killin' Floor" type version of Wolf's "Ooh Baby" further examines the Dragger's hero worship of Wolf. There's also a fine take of Sonny Boy Williamson's quick stop and go "Don't Start Me to Talkin'" with Lang's fine harmonica exclamations, the deliberate Eddie Taylor evergreen "Bad Boy," and a nice cover of the Muddy Waters' classic "Long Distance Call," where the Dragger comes a bit out of his Wolfen shell. The title track is destined to be be a time capsule historical novelty, the Dragger singing about the Clinton-Lewinsky affair, taking the president's side, telling people "forgive him, let him do his job." A pretty fine pure blues recording from an underappreciated roots singer in the general scheme of things. Maybe he should cop more to the Wolf. We all could use it during these troubled days. Recommended. —*Michael G. Nastos*

Tampa Red (Hudson Whittaker)

b. Jan. 8, 1904, Smithville, GA, **d.** Mar. 19, 1981, Chicago, IL

Slide Guitar, Vocals, Leader, Kazoo, Piano, Guitar / Acoustic Chicago Blues, Electric Chicago Blues

Out of the dozens of fine slide guitarists who recorded blues, only a handful—Elmore James, Muddy Waters, and Robert Johnson, for example—left a clear imprint on tradition by creating a recognizable and widely imitated instrumental style. Tampa Red was another influential musical model. During his heyday in the '20s and '30s, he was billed as "The Guitar Wizard," and his stunning slide work on steel National or electric guitar shows why he earned the title. His 30-year recording career produced hundreds of sides: hokum, pop, and jive, but mostly blues (including classic compositions "Anna Lou Blues," "Black Angel Blues," "Crying Won't Help You," "It Hurts Me Too," and "Love Her with a Feeling"). Early in Red's career, he teamed up with pianist, songwriter, and latter-day gospel composer Georgia Tom (Rev. Thomas A. Dorsey), collaborating on double entendre classics like "Tight Like That."

Listeners who only know Tampa Red's hokum material are missing the deeper side of one of the mainstays of Chicago blues. His peers included Big Bill Broonzy, with whom he shared a special friendship. Members of Lester Melrose's musical mafia and drinking buddies, they once managed to sleep through both games of a Chicago White Sox double header. Eventually alcohol caught up with Red, and he blamed his latter-day health problems on an inability to refuse a drink.

During Red's prime, his musical venues ran the gamut of blues institutions: downhome jukes, the streets, the vaudeville theater circuit, and the Chicago club scene. Due to his polish and theater experience, he is often described as a city musician or urban artist in contrast to many of his more limited musical contemporaries. Furthermore, his house served as the blues community's rehearsal hall and an informal booking agency. According to the testimonies of Broonzy and Big Joe Williams, Red cared for other musicians by offering them a meal and a place to stay and generally easing their transition from country to city life.

Today's listener will enjoy Tampa Red's expressive vocals and perhaps be taken aback by his kazoo solos. His songwriting has stood the test of time, and any serious slide guitar student had better be familiar with Red's guitar wizardry. —*Barry Lee Pearson*

Tampa Red (1928–1942) / Dec. 11, 1928-Feb. 6, 1942 / Story of the Blues ♦♦♦♦♦
Tampa Red sang and played the guitar and kazoo with a joy and flair that made almost every tune he did instantly unforgettable. His early work has been reissued and repackaged so often that it's easy to get caught in the mire. These are marvelous cuts, matching him with various accompanists, including Georgia Tom (later Rev. Thomas A. Dorsey), and offering the best in double entendre, rags, topical, and novelty material. —*Ron Wynn*

Don't Tampa With the Blues / Nov. 1961 / Prestige/Bluesville ♦♦♦
The kazoo-toting bluesman wasn't as powerful a presence when he came back in 1960 to record this set in a solo setting as he was in his Bluebird heyday, but it's hard to resist these agreeable versions of "Let Me Play With Your Poodle," "Love Her With a Feeling," and "It's Tight Like That" nonetheless. —*Bill Dahl*

☆ **Bottleneck Guitar (1928–1937)** / 1974 / Yazoo ♦♦♦♦♦
Yazoo's *Bottleneck Guitar (1928-1937)* is a great collection of early recordings from slide guitarist Tampa Red. The 14-track collection has a number of classic solo cuts from Tampa—including "You Gotta Reap What You Sow" and "Seminole Blues"—plus duets with the likes of Georgia Tom and Ma Rainey, making it an excellent overview of his earliest sides. —*Thom Owens*

The Guitar Wizard / Oct. 1975 / Columbia/Legacy ♦♦♦♦♦
Some of the earliest work (1928-1934) by the slide guitar great, ranging from the irresistible hokum he served up with piano-playing partner Georgia Tom ("Dead Cats on the Line," "No Matter How She Done It") to the gorgeous "Black Angel Blues" (eventually known as "Sweet Little Angel") and the solo guitar masterpieces "Things 'Bout Comin' My Way" and "Denver Blues." —*Bill Dahl*

It's Tight Like That / 1976 / Blues Document ♦♦♦♦♦

Bawdy Blues / 1977 / Bluesville/Original Blues Classics ♦♦♦

Complete Recorded Works, Vol. 1 (1928–1929) / 1991 / Document ♦♦♦♦
The first volume in this long series covering Tampa Red's complete recordings from 1928 to 1934 includes the original "It's Tight Like That," "It's Red Hot," and a version of Leroy Carr's "How Long, How Long Blues." —*AMG*

Complete Recorded Works, Vol. 2 (1929) / 1991 / Document ♦♦♦
The second volume in Document's series of *Complete Recorded Works* covers barely six months in the career of Tampa Red, though the range of material is quite wide. The slide guitar legend recorded a few guitar solos, led the Hokum Boys through several songs, did two sides of gospel, and invited high-profile guests including Georgia Tom Dorsey, Frankie "Half Pint" Jaxon, and Lil Johnson. —*Thom Owens*

Complete Recorded Works, Vol. 3 (1929–1930) / 1991 / Document ♦♦♦
Document's *Complete Recorded Works, Vol. 3 (1929-1930)* wraps up a year in the life of Tampa Red, finding the Chicago bluesman recording a parade of blues, including "Chicago Moan Blues" and "Whiskey Drinkin' Blues." He also takes on several tracks of lighthearted hokum ("I Wonder Where My Easy Rider's Gone?," "Mama Don't Allow No Easy Riders Here"), along with the traditional standard "Corrine, Corrina." —*Thom Owens*

Complete Recorded Works, Vol. 4 (1930–1931) / 1991 / Document ♦♦♦
Volume four in the Document series of Tampa Red's *Complete Recorded Works* reissues two dozen sides originally recorded during late 1930 and most of 1931. During this period, he introduced two career classics ("Boogie Woogie Dance," "Things 'Bout Coming My Way"), did several versions of "You Rascal You," and took on boogie-woogie with a

pair of novelties. Still, only collectors and serious blues fans should feel the need to pursue this compilation, instead of the excellent *It Hurts Me Too* collection available on Indigo. —*Thom Owens*

Complete Recorded Works, Vol. 5 (1931–1934) / 1991 / Document ♦♦♦

Keep Jumping 1944–1952 / 1993 / Wolf ♦♦♦♦
The material on this 19-song compilation isn't quite ideal, covering what were the declining years not only of Red's recordings, but of the RCA-Victor's blues releases. On the other hand, the producers have drawn from among Red's best sides of this era, including "Midnight Boogie" and Midnight Blues" from 1950, both great and amazingly late works. This could be the ideal way to hear most of the stuff here, since Red otherwise cut a lot of second-rate work. The sound is also quite good, although there are no notes of any kind, just a sessionography. —*Bruce Eder*

Complete Recorded Works, Vol. 6 (1934–1935) / 1993 / Document ♦♦♦

Complete Recorded Works, Vol. 7 (1935–1936) / 1993 / Document ♦♦♦

Complete Recorded Works, Vol. 8 (1936–1937) / 1993 / Document ♦♦♦
For completists, specialists and academics, Document's *Complete Recorded Works, Vol. 8 (1936-1937)* is invaluable, offering an exhaustive overview of Tampa Red's early recordings. For less dedicated listeners, the disc is a mixed blessing. There are some absolutely wonderful, classic performances on the collection, but the long running time, exacting chronological sequencing, poor fidelity (all cuts are transferred from original acetates and 78s), and number of performances are hard to digest. The serious blues listener will find all these factors to be positive, but enthusiasts and casual listeners will find that the collection is of marginal interest for those very reasons. —*Thom Owens*

Complete Recorded Works, Vol. 9 (1937–1938) / 1993 / Document ♦♦♦♦

Complete Recorded Works, Vol. 10 (1938–1939) / 1993 / Document ♦♦♦
Over ten years into Tampa Red's career and ten discs into their voluminous, multi-decade-spanning series of *Complete Recorded Works*, Document continued as strong as ever. These 22 tracks, recorded from mid-1938 to late 1939, embrace blues, rhythm tunes, and an occasional novelty like "Booze Head Woman" or "I Got a Big Surprise for You." As on previous volumes, collectors and serious blues fans will have the most interest in this completist format; everything from poor fidelity to chronological sequencing and a lengthy running time will prevent casual listeners from enjoying the entire proceedings. —*Thom Owens*

Complete Recorded Works, Vol. 11 (1939–1940) / 1993 / Document ♦♦♦♦

Complete Recorded Works, Vol. 12 (1941–1945) / 1993 / Document ♦♦♦♦♦

Complete Recorded Works, Vol. 15 / 1993 / Document ♦♦♦

★ **It Hurts Me Too: The Essential Recordings of Tampa Red** / 1994 / Indigo ♦♦♦♦♦
A magnificent primer on the catalog of this prolific guitar/kazoo ace that spans 1928-1942. Opening with his immortal hokum duet with Georgia Tom, the bawdy "It's Tight Like That," the disc makes clear just how seminal Red's Chicago-cut output was—here are the original versions of "It Hurts Me Too," "Love With a Feeling," "Don't You Lie to Me," and the double entendre hoots "She Wants to Sell My Monkey" and "Let Me Play With Your Poodle." —*Bill Dahl*

Complete Recorded Works, Vol. 13 (1945–1947) / Jun. 2, 1994 / Document ♦♦♦♦

Complete Recorded Works, Vol. 14 (1949–1951) / Jun. 2, 1994 / Document ♦♦♦

The Complete Bluebird Recordings, Vol. 1: 1934–1936 / Feb. 24, 1997 / Bluebird/RCA ♦♦♦♦♦
The Complete Bluebird Recordings: 1934-1936 is a double-disc set containing 46 songs Tampa Red recorded for Bluebird in the mid-'30s, when he was one of the most popular and influential bluesmen in America. The length of the collection means that it's only of interest to serious blues fans and scholars, which is a shame, because there are many wonderful performances scattered throughout the set that demonstrate Tampa Red's mastery of the guitar and the blues song. —*Thom Owens*

The Complete Bluebird Recordings, Vol. 2: 1936–1938 / Feb. 24, 1997 / Bluebird/RCA ♦♦♦♦♦
By the mid-'30s, Tampa Red was a famous blues singer and guitarist, when he suddenly did an artistic about-face. The records Tampa Red made for the Bluebird label between 1936 and 1938 were certainly unlike anything he made before or after in his long recording career. His fabled guitar was relegated to the back burner, and he cut in two modes: first as a bandleader/vocalist fronting a small jazz-pop band, and secondly as a solo pianist/vocalist working the recently departed turf of Leroy Carr. All of these were cut at the same sessions, following a seamless thread except for a lone appearance of that patented slide guitar on two cuts from a 1937 date. Certainly not the place to start with Tampa, but an interesting sidebar for sure. Excellent notes by Jim O'Neal enhance the package. —*Cub Koda*

1928–1946 / Nov. 9, 1999 / Wolf ♦♦♦♦
This early compilation of Tampa's work both as soloist and sideman covers a good 20-year period, from his early hokum recordings with Georgia Tom and his jug band to his later sides for Bluebird. Highlights include his liquid slide guitar work behind Jenny Pope on "Whiskey Drinkin' Blues" and when he accompanies the Gospel Camp Meeting Singers on "Hold to His Hand" and "Come and Go to That Land." Unfortunately, the set also suffers from excessively noisy transfers, making some of these rarities much harder to listen to than need be. Some tracks fare better than others, and the set gets better as it moves on chronologically, but you may have to a-b this with other collections to get better-sounding versions of these seminal sides. —*Cub Koda*

The Essential / Mar. 6, 2001 / Classic Blues ♦♦♦
Tampa Red might well have been the most sophisticated of the early bluesmen; he was certainly the most urbane, and a number of his sides also offered some of the best sound

around at the time. Playing on a National guitar, he offered impeccable picking and wonderful slide guitar work. Early on he worked with pianist Georgia Tom, although their big hit from the late '20s, "It's Tight Like That," isn't included here—a serious omission, really, in any collection claiming to be essential. But this compilation tends to keep away from the double entendre side of Red's repertoire and concentrates instead on his more serious blues work, which is perhaps best, because songs like "Sweet Little Angel" and "Don't Deal With the Devil" perfectly represent Red's art. "You Got to Reap What You Sow" shows him solo and illustrates the real range of his ability—this was a man who could move though almost any kind of music convincingly—although he generally seemed more comfortable working with an accompanist, as with "Dead Cats on the Line," where Georgia Tom again backs him up. Whether this is the best collection to begin with is debatable—as is the question of whether all these really are essential. But as a treasure trove of blues history, it's worth delving into. *—Chris Nickson*

Tarbox Ramblers

Group / Blues Gospel, Americana, Old-Timey, String Bands, Country Blues
Bridging the racial gap between pre-World War II roots music, the Tarbox Ramblers draw equally upon early-20th century blues, hillbilly, and gospel. The Boston group's original sound, which emerges not only from tradition but from primal alt-rock energy, consists of leader/singer Michael Tarbox's open-tuned slide guitar, Johnny Sciascia's upright string bass, Daniel Kellar's fiddle, and Jon Cohan's tribalistic drums. Lighting up their hometown and abroad with their acclaimed live shows, the iconoclastic Tarbox Ramblers drew raves from *The New Yorker* and *The Washington Post*, among others. The group released its self-titled debut in early 2000 on Rounder Records. *—Erik Hage*

● **Tarbox Ramblers** / Mar. 21, 2000 / Rounder ♦♦♦♦
A longtime Boston club favorite, the Tarbox Ramblers show why on this very impressive debut. A true musical amalgam, the Ramblers play an intoxicating hybrid of pre-World War II black and white hillbilly songs, blues, and gospel music. Their instrumentation consists of fiddle, string bass, wildly thudding drums, and electric slide guitar played in open tuning, but that only begins to scratch the surface of the band's wonderfully eclectic sound and style. Singer/guitarist/leader Michael Tarbox's vocals are anguished and bluesy without ever once being mannered, gliding from hillbilly to ancient blues effortlessly. The band swing when the tune calls for it, and play like cavemen when needed; this is the type of record that'll make you get up and dance. If you're looking for a roots music album that's got something really different to offer, this is it. *—Cub Koda*

Tarheel Slim (Alden Bunn)

b. Sep. 24, 1924, Wilson, NC, **d.** Aug. 21, 1977, New York, NY [The Bronx]
Vocals, Guitar / Electric Blues, R&B
Talk about a versatile musician: Alden Bunn recorded in virtually every postwar musical genre imaginable. Lowdown blues, gospel, vocal group R&B, poppish duets, even rockabilly weren't outside the sphere of his musicianship.

Spirituals were Bunn's first love. While still in North Carolina during the early '40s, the guitarist worked with the Gospel Four and then the Selah Jubilee Singers, who recorded for Continental and Decca. Bunn and Thurman Ruth broke away in 1949 to form their own group, the Jubilators. During a single day in New York in 1950, they recorded for four labels under four different names!

One of those labels was Apollo, who convinced them to go secular. That's basically how the Larks, one of the seminal early R&B vocal groups whose mellifluous early-'50s Apollo platters rank with the era's best, came to be. Bunn sang lead on a few of their bluesier items ("Eyesight to the Blind," for one), as well as doing two sessions of his own for the firm in 1952 under the name of Allen Bunn. As Alden Bunn, he encored on Bobby Robinson's Red Robin logo the next year.

Bunn also sang with another R&B vocal group, the Wheels. And coupled with his future wife, Anna Sanford, Bunn recorded as the Lovers; "Darling It's Wonderful," their 1957 duet for Aladdin's Lamp subsidiary, was a substantial pop seller. (Ray Ellis did the arranging.)

Tarheel Slim made his official entrance in 1958 with his wife, now dubbed Little Ann, in a duet format for Robinson's Fire imprint ("It's Too Late," "Much Too Late"). Then old Tarheel came out of the gate like his pants were on fire with a pair of rockabilly raveups of his own, "Wilcat Tamer" and "No. 9 Train," with Jimmy Spruill on blazing lead guitar. After a few years off the scene, Tarheel Slim made a bit of a comeback during the early '70s, with an album for Pete Lowry's Trix logo that harked back to Bunn's Carolina blues heritage. It would prove his last. *—Bill Dahl*

No Time at All / Jun. 1977 / Trix ♦♦♦♦♦
Tarheel Slim made some great almost-black rockabilly records for Bobby Robinson in the early '60s, but these 1975 recordings for Pete Lowery's Trix label are loose, informal, and largely acoustic performances. The good news is that they're every bit as engaged as the earlier, rockier Fire sides, full of involved vocals and plucky guitar work that veers between single-note clusters and fleet fingerpicked runs. For all the rough hewness of these recordings, Slim's personality comes through in full force, which makes for one powerful blues album in the bargain. *—Cub Koda*

Number 9 Train / 1980 / Charly ♦♦♦

● **The Red Robin & Fire Years** / Apr. 20, 1990 / Collectables ♦♦♦♦♦
Slim was quite an eclectic soul during his '50s tenure with Bobby Robinson's Red Robin and Fire imprints (as this set conclusively shows). New York blues, pop/R&B duets with Little Ann, even blistering rockabilly-tinged outings ("Number 9 Train," and "Wildcat Tamer") were all well within the versatile guitarist's stylistic scope. *—Bill Dahl*

Golden Classics (With Little Ann) / 1993 / Collectables ♦♦♦♦♦
Tarheel Slim was one of a handful of blues artists signed to Bobby Robinson's Fire Records and its predecessor, Red Robin. Although he's mostly known on Fire for his R&B work with his wife "Little Ann," a surprising amount of the material on this 15-song collection is straight blues, including "Wildcat Tamer" and "Number 9 Train," stuff that he could have cut on acoustic guitar without a whole lot of difference around 1951. It was excellent commercial electric blues, with hard, crunchy electric guitar and a brisk beat. The two "Allen Bunn" tracks here, "My Kinda Woman" and "Too Much Competition," ashow a more sophisticated band sound, although they could also be remnants of Slim's early-'50s rural roots. It turned out, however, that Slim was as engaging an R&B singer as he was a guitarist and blues singer, so "Can't Stay Away" and the other duets here are a pretty compelling case for the switch that he made at the end of the '50s. Neither one was as compelling vocally as their duets were, although Ann starts to hit her stride solo on "You're Gonna Reap," awhere she starts moving into Arlene Smith territory. "It's a Sin" is also pleasing, reminiscent in its way of Buddy Holly's "True Love Ways." Some of the duets, such as "Much Too Late," are a little too bluesy, in retrospect, to have caught on with a wide audience, although it is a strong performance. Robinson was obviously ready to try anything, because it's followed by a straight near-pop ballad, "Anything for You." The collection ends with "Can't Stay Away from You," one of the more interesting and intense Bo Diddley-inspired songs of the period. There are no notes, and the sound quality fluctuates, although it is of a fairly high standard for its period. *—Bruce Eder*

Jimmie Tarlton

b. May 8, 1892, Chesterfield County, SC, **d.** Nov. 29, 1979
Slide Guitar, Vocals / Country Blues, Old-Timey
Jimmie Tarlton is best known for his partnership with Tom Darby, which lasted from the late '20s until the mid '30s. The two were never especially fond of each other, however, and although they both saw some activity in the '60s as part of the folk-blues revival, and Tarlton got to make a record, there was no impetus for continuing the partnership.

Tarlton's style was rooted in rural South Carolina, where he was born and raised. His father, a sometime farmer and sawmill worker, played a fretless banjo and his mother sang. At age six, Tarlton was playing banjo and French harp, and he later took up the guitar and learned to play bottleneck, using glass and a knife. In the '20s, he also discovered the Hawaiian guitar style. He played around the northeast and the Texas-Louisiana-Oklahoma region in the teens, and eventually made his way to California, playing at bars, cafes and in medicine shows.

Poor eyesight kept him out of World War I, and he made his living working at local cotton mills in South Carolina before becoming a telegraph worker. He began recording in 1927 in partnership with Tom Darby, but across his career, his performances included collaborations with Hank Williams, Jimmie Rodgers, the Delmore Brothers, and the Skillet Lickers, among numerous others. Although Darby and Tarlton had a substantial hit with "Cumberland Stockade Blues" and "Birmingham Jail," their contract only gave them a flat payment of $75 for the records, and there were no follow-up releases with any similar success. By the mid '40s, Tarlton had left the music business.

He was rediscovered in 1963, living in Phenix City, AL (a notorious locale in its own right, incidentally, as the sin capital of its county and a crime and corruption center whose story was chronicled in two separate feature films in the '50s), and became a renowned figure in the folk and folk-blues revival. Tarlton played some shows at the Ash Grove in Los Angeles, and made a record, but was too old by that time to pursue the opportunities in front of him.

Tarlton became one of a handful of figures—country fiddler Eck Robertson is another—who preserved a style of music-making that would otherwise have been lost and embellished it into something new and all his own. His music, as preserved on his solo sides recorded at his own home in the early '60s, incorporated by then the influences of Hawaiian guitar and ragtime, but beneath it all was a native South Carolina folk style that predated recorded music. *—Bruce Eder*

● **Steel Guitar Rag** / Oct. 13, 1998 / HMG ♦♦♦♦♦
Although they were recorded in the early to mid-'60s in association with Pete Welding, the 19 tracks here sound like music from another era. Tarlton sings in a pleasing baritone, with an uninflected style, without artifice—he sounds like the real version of what Bob Dylan has tried for in his country covers—and his fingers slide, strum, and glide over the fretboard, sounding like at least two guitars at once and a multitude of voices. The repertory is almost entirely traditional and arranged by Tarlton, who sounds like he's coming from a place at least 100 years before Jimmie Rodgers. Some of the tracks reveal the presence of an audience, others are the product of a studio, but the sound is generally first-rate, regardless of which. *—Bruce Eder*

Finis Tasby

b. 1940, Dallas, TX
Vocals / Soul-Blues, Contemporary Blues
Although he only recently recorded his first nationally distributed full-length album, Los Angeles-based singer and songwriter Finis Tasby is no spring chicken in the blues world. Tasby has been singing in the Los Angeles area for years, and for years before that in Dallas.

Tasby was born in Dallas, TX, in 1940. He formed a band called the Thunderbirds in Dallas in 1962. While working with the Thunderbirds, Tasby played bass and sang backup vocals behind legendary blues singer-songwriter Z.Z. Hill. Hill eventually secured a recording contract, as did Hill's replacement, Joe Simon. From the mid-'60s, Tasby led the band, delivering lead vocals and playing bass. When not touring under their own name, the Thunderbirds backed up the likes of Clarence Carter, Lowell Fulson, and Freddie King, touring regionally throughout Texas and Oklahoma.

In 1973, Tasby moved to Los Angeles and found a home in that city's blues clubs. He formed a new group in Los Angeles and had the chance to open for B.B. King, Percy Mayfield, and Big Mama Thornton.

Tasby recorded several singles in the '70s and '80s: "Get Drunk and Be Somebody," in 1978, and "Blues Mechanic," a 1985 release for Ace Records. Tasby also landed an acting role in the film *Sharkey's Machine* with Burt Reynolds, all the while playing regularly around L.A. blues clubs with his own Finis Tasby Band. Next, three of Tasby's songs from his Shanachie Records debut, *People Don't Care* (1995), were featured in the mid-'90s film *The Babysitter* (his singles are surely collectors' items). Accompanying Tasby on *People Don't Care* are some world-class talents: Lowell Fulson, Elvin Bishop, Mick Taylor, and Vernon Reid, who was formerly of the rock group Living Colour. While some tracks on the album are less appealing, urban contemporary pop-blues, other tracks reveal Tasby's authentic Texas blues roots.

Tasby, a prolific songwriter, has many more good albums in his notebooks. Let's hope circumstances allow him to record and tour a lot more outside of Los Angeles. —*Richard Skelly*

People Don't Care / 1995 / Shanachie ✦✦✦

Blues Mechanic / Aug. 1, 1995 / Ace ✦✦✦

● **Jump Children!** / Sep. 15, 1998 / Evidence ✦✦✦✦
Rocking, hopping, and socking—three active verbs that paint the picture of Tasby's vocals. They are extraordinary without being explosive. This was Lester Butler's last recordings before his untimely death, and showcases rarely his heard pure blues side. Butler marks the genius of playing straight from the gut. Producer Randy Chordkoff made a wise choice in guesting highly profiled guitarists Rick Holmstrom, Coco Montoya, and Kid Ramos, who are equally as skilled as team players. —*Char Ham*

Taste

f. 1966, Ireland, **db.** 1971
Group / Blues-Rock
Before becoming a solo star, Rory Gallagher fronted the blues-rock trio Taste, which experienced reasonable success in the U.K. in the late '60s and early '70s. Taste was molded very much on the model of Cream, adding some folk, pop, and jazz elements to a blues-rock base, and featuring a virtuosic guitarist. They weren't in the same league as Cream, particularly in the songwriting department, and were (like Cream) prone to occasional blues-rock bombast. But they weren't a bad band in their own right, exhibiting a lighter touch than most British blues boom outfits.

The focus of Taste was always upon Gallagher. In addition to playing accomplished and versatile lead guitar, he sang in a gentle but convincing fashion, and wrote the band's original material. Much of Taste's repertoire was more restrained and balanced than the territory Gallagher would explore on his '70s outings, which placed more emphasis upon him as guitar hero. Gallagher also played occasional saxophone and harmonica with the group.

Gallagher formed the first version of Taste in his native Ireland in 1966, with bassist Eric Kittringham and drummer Norman Damery. In May of 1968, he relocated to London and, still months shy of his 20th birthday, formed a new version of Taste with bassist Richard "Charlie" McCracken (who had played bass with Spencer Davis, though not at the peak of Davis' hit-making days) and drummer John Wilson (who had been a drummer with Them, likewise not during one of their well-known incarnations). Two studio albums followed in 1969 and 1970, the second of which made the British Top 20. Taste was still virtually unknown in the States when they broke up shortly afterwards, although a couple of live albums were released in the early '70s to keep some product on the shelves. —*Richie Unterberger*

Taste / 1969 / Polydor ✦✦✦

On the Boards / 1970 / Atco ✦✦✦✦
The second and final studio recording by Irish guitarist Rory Gallagher's neo-Cream trio reins in the playing to focus more on songwriting. The material is a virtual grab bag of blues-rock styles, moving from driving rockers ("What's Going On," "I'll Remember") and basic boogies ("Morning Sun," "If I Don't Sing I'll Cry") to a bottleneck blitz ("Eat My Words") and a pair of acoustic ballads. There's a pronounced jazzy tinge to his spiky guitar and never-again-heard alto sax on the slow blues of the title track and "It's Happened Before, It'll Happen Again," the latter giving the Richard McCracken-John Wilson rhythm section a chance to stretch out and swing fluidly. The lyrics, never a Gallagher strong suit, are pretty simplistic, but the chorus hooks do stick. It could all have added up to one big eclectic mess, but for the often one-dimensional, sometimes ham-fisted Gallagher, the laudable variety turns *On the Boards* into the high point of his recording career. —*Don Snowden*

● **The Best of Taste** / 1994 / Polydor ✦✦✦✦✦
A well-chosen 16-track retrospective, mostly drawn from the band's two studio albums. Not in the upper echelon of British blues, but not far from that level either, showing Rory Gallagher capable of a wider compositional and interpretive range than some listeners may recall. —*Richie Unterberger*

Baby Tate (Charles Henry Tate)

b. Jan. 28, 1916, Elberton, GA, **d.** Aug. 17, 1972, Columbia, SC
Vocals, Guitar / Piedmont Blues, Country Blues
In the course of his nearly 50-year career, guitarist Baby Tate recorded only a handful of sessions. The bulk of his life was spent as a sideman, playing with musicians like Blind Boy Fuller, Pink Anderson, and Peg Leg Sam.

Born Charles Henry Tate, he was born in Elberton, GA, but raised in Greenville, SC. When he was 14 years old, Tate taught himself how to play guitar. Shortly afterward, he began playing with Blind Boy Fuller, who taught Tate the fundamentals of blues guitar. When he was in his late teens, Baby began playing with Joe Walker and Roosevelt Brooks; the trio played clubs throughout the Greenville area.

In 1932, Tate stopped working with Walker and Brooks, hooking up with Carolina Blackbirds. The duo played a number of shows for the radio station WFBC. For most of the '30s, Baby played music as a hobby, performing at local parties, celebrations, and medicine shows.

Tate served in the U.S. Army in the late '30s and early '40s. While he was stationed in Europe, he played local taverns and dances. In 1942, he returned to Greenville, SC, where he earned a living doing odd jobs around the town. Tate picked up music again in 1946, setting out on the local blues club circuit. In 1950, he cut several sessions for the Atlanta-based Kapp label.

In the early '50s, Baby moved to Spartanburg, SC, where he performed both as a solo act and as a duo with Pink Anderson. Tate and Anderson performed as duo into the '70s. In 1962, Tate recorded his first album, *See What You Done*. The following year, he was featured in the documentary film, *The Blues*. For the rest of the decade, Baby Tate played various gigs, concerts, and festivals across America. With the assistance of harmonica player Peg Leg Sam, Baby Tate recorded another set of sessions in 1972. Later that year, Tate suffered a fatal heart attack. He died on August 17, 1972. —*Stephen Thomas Erlewine*

● **Blues of Baby Tate: See What You Done Done** / 1962 / Prestige/Original Blues Classics ✦✦✦
Recorded during the blues revival of the early '60s, *The Blues of Baby Tate: See What You Done Done* is a wonderful collection of country blues. Tate's teacher was Blind Boy Fuller, and his influence shines through on the album. That doesn't mean that *See What You Done Done* is simply a Fuller record, however—Tate has absorbed his influence and developed his own warm, rambling style that suits these traditional numbers perfectly. —*Thom Owens*

Tommy Tate

b. Sep. 29, 1944, Homestead, FL
Vocals (Background), Vocals / R&B, Soul, Southern Soul
Florida vocalist Tommy Tate is a consistent, if unspectacular, Southern soul wailer. He debuted on Rise in 1964, and continued recording for OKeh, Verve, and Big Ten before joining the Nightingales at Stax in 1970. He returned to the solo scene a couple of years later, recording for Koko. He had a Top 30 R&B single with "School of Love" in 1972, and it has been his only substantial hit. But Tate has kept plugging, working in Mississippi clubs and recording for Juana, Sundance, and other independents, including most recent release was *Love Me Now* for Ichiban's subsidiary label Urgent! in 1992. —*Ron Wynn*

● **Love Me Now** / Sep. 9, 1992 / Urgent! ✦✦✦
Tommy Tate tried his luck with the Urgent! label, an Atlanta-based company distributed by Ichiban. He had some nice, but dated material done in vintage '60s and '70s soul style. They attempted at times to update the framework with drum machines and other trappings, but wound up with another strictly regional item, although it's not that bad for fans of the genre. —*Ron Wynn*

Eddie Taylor

b. Jan. 29, 1923, Benoit, MS, **d.** Dec. 25, 1985, Chicago, IL
Vocals, Guitar / Electric Chicago Blues, Modern Electric Blues, R&B
When you're talking about the patented Jimmy Reed laconic shuffle sound, you're talking about Eddie Taylor just as much as Reed himself. Taylor was the glue that kept Reed's lowdown grooves from falling into serious disrepair. His rock-steady rhythm guitar powered the great majority of Reed's Vee-Jay sides during the '50s and early '60s, and he even found time to wax a few classic sides of his own for Vee-Jay during the mid-'50s.

Eddie Taylor was as versatile a blues guitarist as anyone could ever hope to encounter. His style was deeply rooted in Delta tradition, but he could snap off a modern funk-tinged groove just as convincingly as a straight shuffle. Taylor viewed Delta immortals Robert Johnson and Charley Patton as a lad, taking up the guitar himself in 1936 and teaching the basics of the instrument to his childhood pal Reed. After a stop in Memphis, he hit Chicago in 1949, falling in with harpist Snooky Pryor, guitarist Floyd Jones, and—you guessed it—his old homey Reed.

From Jimmy Reed's second Vee-Jay date in 1953 on, Eddie Taylor was right there to help Reed through the rough spots. Taylor's own Vee-Jay debut came in 1955 with the immortal "Bad Boy" (Reed returning the favor on harp). Taylor's second Vee-Jay single coupled two more classics, "Ride 'Em on Down" and "Big Town Playboy," and his last two platters for the firm, "You'll Always Have a Home" and "I'm Gonna Love You," were similarly inspired. But Taylor's records didn't sell in the quantities that Reed's did, so he was largely relegated to the role of sideman (he recorded behind John Lee Hooker, John Brim, Elmore James, Snooky Pryor, and many more during the '50s) until his 1972 set for Advent, *I Feel So Bad*, made it abundantly clear that this quiet, unassuming guitarist didn't have to play second fiddle to anyone. When he died in 1985, he left a void on the Chicago circuit that remains apparent even now. They just don't make 'em like Eddie Taylor anymore. —*Bill Dahl*

I Feel So Bad / 1972 / Hightone ✦✦✦✦
One of the Chicago guitarist's most satisfying contemporary albums, this 1972 set (first issued on Advent) was cut not in the Windy City, but in L.A. in 1972 with a combo featuring Phillip Walker on second guitar and George Smith on harp. Taylor was no strict traditionalist; he was as conversant with funk-tinged modern rhythms as with Delta-based styles—and he exhibits both sides of his musical personality on this one. —*Bill Dahl*

Ready for Eddie / 1972 / Big Bear ✦✦

Bad Boy a Long Way from Chicago / 1978 / P-Vine ✦✦✦

Big Town Playboy / 1981 / Charly ✦✦✦✦✦
Nice cuts from the sorely underrated Eddie Taylor, who found in death the respect and widespread praise he'd earned while alive. This contains some of his best songs and hottest playing. —*Ron Wynn*

Still Not Ready for Eddie / Jul. 1988 / Antone's ✦✦✦
Shows signs of the brilliance that we've long come to expect from the uncommonly versatile Taylor, but clearly not the equal of some of the other Taylor sets on the market. —*Bill Dahl*

☆ **Bad Boy** / 1993 / Charly ♦♦♦♦♦
The Delta-rooted mid-'50s Vee-Jay label classics by perennially underrated Chicago guitarist Eddie Taylor, who stepped out of Jimmy Reed's shadow long enough to leave behind "Bad Boy," "Big Town Playboy," "Ride 'Em on Down," the bouncy "I'm Gonna Love You," and several more brilliant sides. Fifteen songs in all, including five from 1964 that are scarcely less impressive than his previous stuff. *—Bill Dahl*

My Heart Is Bleeding / 1994 / Evidence ♦♦♦
Credible set from 1980 mostly cut in Chicago but first out on the German L+R logo. Taylor's in typically solid form, and his tough backing includes the marvelous Sunnyland Slim on piano and harpist Carey Bell. Taylor pays homage to his pal Jimmy Reed with a loping "Going to Virginia" and Muddy Waters on "Blow Wind Blow," but "Soul Brother" rides a chunky R&B groove that's a long way from Reed's rudimentary rhythms. The last five sides stem from a 1980 European tour (with Hubert Sumlin and Bell handling some of the vocals) and don't add much to the package. *—Bill Dahl*

Long Way from Home / Nov. 1995 / Blind Pig ♦♦♦
Okay effort from the venerable Chicago guitarist's later days that's not as essential as Taylor's prior recording activities. *—Bill Dahl*

★ **Ride 'Em on Down** / Charly ♦♦♦♦♦
An absolutely essential 24-track collection which alternates 12 of Taylor's classic Vee-Jay sides (including "Bad Boy," "Big Town Playboy," "Find My Baby," "Looking for Trouble," and the title track) with a dozen more early Jimmy Reed sides with Taylor in support. As a collection of Taylor's best solo sides, it's as complete as any on the market. As a sample of Taylor's impeccable backup work behind Reed—while containing no hits—it stands by itself as a very nice collection of rarities that shows both artists off to good advantage. As a document of early-'50s Chicago blues, it's a major brick in the wall. As seamless blues groove listening, consider it a must-have. *—Cub Koda*

Eva Taylor

b. Jan. 22, 1895, St. Louis, MO, **d.** Oct. 31, 1977, Mineola, NY
Vocals / Classic Jazz, Classic Female Blues
Blues singer Eva Taylor broke new ground as an African American vocalist during the early part of the 20th century. She was among the first whose talent was broadcast on radio programs of the day, and she held down her own program in the '20s for NBC. She began recording around 1922, first for Black Swan and eventually for other labels that included Columbia, OKeh, and Bluebird. Her work spanned popular music and jazz in addition to her blues work.

The Dixie Nightingale, as she was christened by Black Swan, was born in St. Louis, MO, in 1895 and began touring in revues before she turned three. Her vaudeville work took her all over the world, including stops throughout New Zealand, Australia, and Europe. She settled in New York by 1920. There she established herself as a performer in Harlem nightspots. Within a year she wed Clarence Williams, a producer and piano player. The newlyweds worked together on radio and recordings, as well as in the revue *Bottomland.*

The couple recorded together through 1930. Their legacy includes numbers made as the Blue Five in the mid-'20s, which included such luminaries as jazz clarinetist and saxophonist Sidney Bechet and trumpet virtuoso Louis Armstrong. Taylor stopped performing during the '40s, but she returned in the mid-'60s following her husband's death. Taylor's grandchild is Clarence Williams III, an actor whose work includes appearances on television in *Mod Squad* during the late '60s and the movies *Tales from the Hood* in 1995 and *The General's Daughter* in 1999. *—Linda Seida*

Complete Recorded Works, Vol. 1 (1922–1923) / Feb. 15, 1996 / Document ♦♦♦♦♦
Document's *Complete Recorded Works, Vol. 1 (1922-1923)* reissues the first 23 sides of Eva Taylor's solo career. Though there aren't as many classic performances as on other volumes, the disc does include tracks with several important sidemen: clarinet player Sidney Bechet, pianist Clarence Williams, and cornet player Johnny Dunn. That's enough to make it an important acquisition for collectors and serious blues or jazz fans, though casual listeners won't find as much of interest. *—Thom Owens*

• **Complete Recorded Works, Vol. 2 (1923–1927)** / Mar. 5, 1996 / Document ♦♦♦♦♦
Of the three "complete" Eva Taylor CDs put out by Document, this is the main one to get. Although the singer's activity as a leader on records went from very busy (23 titles during her first year) to more occasional (the 25 songs on this CD cover a four-year period), many of her finest recordings as a leader are on this volume. Among the highlights are "Jazzin' Babies Blues," which has Sidney Bechet on soprano; two interesting titles ("Old Fashioned Love" and "Open Your Heart") sung as vocal duets with Lawrence Lomax; "Ghost of the Blues"; a couple selections where Taylor and husband-singer Clarence Williams are accompanied only by cornetist Tom Morris and banjoist Buddy Christian; a jubilant version of "When the Red, Red Robin Comes Bob, Bob Bobbin' Along"; two numbers with the brilliant young cornetist Jabbo Smith featured in the backup group; and a couple of somber tributes to the late singer Florence Mills. Eva Taylor's most famous vocals were generally made under Clarence Williams' leadership, but it is very good to hear the mostly obscure items cut under her own name like this, complete and in chronological order. *—Scott Yanow*

Complete Recorded Works, Vol. 3 (1928–1932) / Apr. 9, 1996 / Document ♦♦♦♦
The third of three Document CDs that have all of singer Eva Taylor's recordings under her own name prior to 1967 contains a wide variety of material. Never strictly a blues singer, Taylor had the potential to go the route later traveled by Ethel Waters, but she chose to mostly record with her husband Clarence Williams' groups. Taylor's infrequent sessions as a leader always found her in good voice although during 1928-1929 the material could be erratic. Some of the selections on this 24-cut disc are fairly sappy ballads but there are also excellent versions of "Back in Your Own Backyard," "I'm Busy and You Can't Come In," two renditions apiece of "Have You Ever Felt That Way" and "West End Blues," plus "You Don't Understand." Among the more notable backup musicians are pianist Williams, cornetists Ed Allen and (on two songs) King Oliver, clarinetist Buster Bailey, the pioneer jazz flutist Albert Socarras, guitarist Eddie Lang, pianist James P. Johnson and (on two songs) a white dance orchestra that includes Leo McConville and Tommy Dorsey. Four of the numbers on this CD (their recording quality is a bit shaky) were previously unissued. After the final 1929 date, Taylor only had one more early date as a leader: two numbers in 1932 with "The Riffers," an intriguing vocal group that includes Lil Armstrong and Clarence Williams (whose piano provides the only accompaniment). *Vol. 2* is the Eva Taylor Document to get, but all three have their moments. *—Scott Yanow*

Edison Laterals 4 / 1997 / Diamond Cut ♦♦♦♦
Eva Taylor is best known for appearing on a lengthy series of recordings during the '20s and early '30s with her husband, pianist/composer/bandleader Clarence Williams. Taylor's sophisticated yet soulful sound was often a little reminiscent of Ethel Waters, and there was always an appealing sweetness to her singing, even when interpreting occasional double entendre songs. The formerly rare music on this very interesting CD puts the focus throughout on her voice. Unfortunately, the songs differ in order from the listing on the back cover (although they are all here), so a little more quality control should have taken place, but the performances are consistently delightful. Recorded originally for the Edison label, there are eight selections from three sessions in 1929, along with three alternate takes, and most excitingly, all but two numbers were previously unreleased. In most cases, Taylor is accompanied only by Williams' piano, although on two songs she is joined by a colorful six-piece band. Even if the lyrics of "In Our Cottage of Love" get a bit sticky, such tunes as "You Don't Understand," "Have You Ever Felt That Way," and "You Don't Understand" are strong enough to deserve revivals. In the middle of the CD (separating the main takes from the alternate versions) are some very interesting late-period examples of Eva Taylor. Recorded at a couple of private concerts, Taylor is heard in 1976 doing an ad-lib a cappella version of "Baby Won't You Please Come Home" (the verse plus two strong choruses), and in 1977 performing five songs while backed by an unidentified pianist (who does his best on an out-of-tune instrument). Eva Taylor shows that her voice was still in pretty good shape late in her life. Highly recommended to vintage jazz collectors. *—Scott Yanow*

Hound Dog Taylor (Theodore Roosevelt Taylor)

b. Apr. 12, 1915, Natchez, MS, **d.** Dec. 17, 1975, Chicago, IL
Slide Guitar, Vocals, Guitar / Slide Guitar Blues, Electric Chicago Blues, Modern Electric Blues
Alligator Records, Chicago's leading contemporary blues label, might never have been launched at all if not for the crashing, slashing slide guitar antics of Hound Dog Taylor. Bruce Iglauer, then an employee of Delmark Records, couldn't convince his boss, Bob Koester, of Taylor's potential, so Iglauer took matters into his own hands. In 1971, Alligator was born for the express purpose of releasing Hound Dog's debut album. We all know what transpired after that.

Named after President Theodore Roosevelt, Mississippi-native Taylor took up the guitar when he was 20 years old. He made a few appearances on Sonny Boy Williamson's fabled KFFA *King Biscuit Time* radio broadcasts out of Helena, AR, before coming to Chicago in 1942. It was another 15 years before Taylor made blues his full-time vocation, though. Taylor was a favorite on the South and West Sides during the late '50s and early '60s. It's generally accepted that Freddie King copped a good portion of his classic "Hide Away" from an instrumental he heard Taylor cranking out on the bandstand.

Taylor's pre-Alligator credits were light—only a 1960 single for Cadillac baby's Bea & Baby imprint ("Baby Is Coming Home"/"Take Five"), a 1962 45 for Carl Jones' Firma Records ("Christine"/"Alley Music"), and a 1967 effort for Checker ("Watch Out"/"Down Home") predated his output for Iglauer.

Taylor's relentlessly raucous band, the Houserockers, consisted of only two men, though their combined racket sounded like quite a few more. Second guitarist Brewer Phillips, who often supplied buzzing pseudo-bass lines on his guitar, had developed such an empathy with Taylor that their guitars intertwined with ESP-like force, while drummer Ted Harvey kept everything moving along at a brisk pace.

Their eponymous 1971 debut LP contained the typically rowdy "Give Me Back My Wig," while Taylor's first Alligator encore in 1973, *Natural Boogie,* boasted the hypnotic "Sadie" and a stomping "Roll Your Moneymaker." *Beware of the Dog,* a live set, vividly captured the good-time vibe that the perpetually beaming guitarist emanated, but Taylor didn't live to see its release—he died of cancer shortly before it hit the shelves.

Hound Dog Taylor was the obvious inspiration for Alligator's "Genuine Houserocking Music" motto, a credo Iglauer's firm still tries to live up to today. He wasn't the most accomplished of slide guitarists, but Hound Dog Taylor could definitely rock any house he played at. *—Bill Dahl*

★ **Hound Dog Taylor & the Houserockers** / 1971 / Alligator ♦♦♦♦♦
The first album and the perfect place to start. Wild, raucous, crazy music straight out of the South Side clubs. The incessant drive of Hound Dog's playing is best heard on "Give Me Back My Wig," "55th Street Boogie," and "Taylor's Rock," while the sound of Brewer Phillips' Telecaster on "Phillips' Theme" gives new meaning to the phrase "sheet metal tone." One of the greatest slide guitar albums of all time. *—Cub Koda*

Natural Boogie / 1973 / Alligator ♦♦♦♦♦
Hound Dog's second album was every bit as wild as the first, bringing with it a fatter sound and a wider range of emotions and music. A recut here of Hound Dog's first single, "Take Five," totally burns the original while the smoldering intensity of "See Me in the Evening" and "Sadie" take this album to places the first one never reached. *—Cub Koda*

Beware of the Dog / 1975 / Alligator ♦♦♦♦♦
This was Hound Dog's posthumous live album containing performances that are even steamier than the first two studio albums, if such a notion is possible. For low-down slow

blues, it's hard to beat the heartfelt closer "Freddie's Blues," and for surreal moments on wax, it's equally hard to beat the funkhouse turned looney-bin dementia of "Let's Get Funky" or the hopped-up hillbilly fever rendition of "Comin' Around the Mountain." *—Cub Koda*

Genuine Houserocking Music / 1982 / Alligator ✦✦✦
With Alligator label prexy Bruce Iglauer recording some 20 or 30 tracks over two nights everytime the band went into the studio, there were bound to be some really great tracks lurking in the vaults and these are it. Noteworthy for the great performance of Robert Johnson's "Crossroads," (previously only available as a Japanese 45) but also for the "rock & roll" inclusion of "What'd I Say" and Brewer Phillips' take on "Kansas City." No bottom of the barrel scrapings here. *—Cub Koda*

Have Some Fun / 1992 / Wolf ✦✦✦
More 1972 live recordings from Joe's Place. Different song selection, somewhat better fidelity. Confusingly for people who'll want to order this as an import, it's issued under the name "The Houserockers" with only Hound Dog's photo on the front! *—Cub Koda*

Live at Joe's Place / 1992 / New Rose ✦✦✦✦✦
Boston live recordings from 1972. They're drunk, they're out of tune, but the crowd goes nuts and the overall vibe cancels out any musical inconsistencies. Doesn't really add anything to the Alligator legacy, as it's extremely loose and chaotic, but it's great fun anyway. *—Cub Koda*

Freddie's Blues / May 20, 1994 / Wolf ✦✦✦
This is the third volume of live recordings from Joe's Place in Cambridge, MA, in 1972. Six of the 11 tunes here are instrumentals (four of them featuring the lead guitar of Brewer Phillips), and while Taylor & the Houserockers are generally in rare form here, some chaotic moments ("Let's Get Funky") do abound, but that's half the fun and charm of it all. *—Cub Koda*

Houserockin' Boogie / 1997 / JSP ✦✦✦
This second album of recordings from Florence's (Taylor & the Houserockers' regular Sunday afternoon everybody-can-sit-in gig) is just as crude and low fidelity as the first one. It also features the maddening (and disreputable) practice of retitling tunes so the record company can cop the publishing rights, a most odious business move. Future Houserocker Lefty Dizz is featured sitting in with the band (minus Taylor) on "Ships on the Ocean," although the credits do not list him at all. Probably the toughest to locate of all the semi-legal Hound Dog Taylor and although the perfect bookend companion to *Live At Florence's*, for die-hard completists only who are willing to hunt it down. *—Cub Koda*

Live at Florence's / 1997 / JSP ✦✦✦
This is the first Hound Dog Taylor material to be released without the approval of Alligator or the Taylor estate and the first whose origins are totally suspect; in short, one step away from being a bootleg, making its non-appearance on compact disc no small mystery. The fidelity is strictly cheap tape recorder on a table by the bandstand quality; one can hear people walking in front of the single microphone, the signal is full of extra distortion and occasional dropouts, and the editing on this album is nothing short of truly annoying. But if—as the old adage goes—the play is the thing, then *this* is the Hound Dog Taylor & the Houserockers album to avidly track down, as the band is absolutely in their home turf element, rocking the house down to the bricks and then some. There are only two vocals among the ten selections here and that actually aids the listenability of the record, as Hound Dog's vocals on "Rock Me" and Elmore James' "I Held My Baby Last Night" are completely reduced to audio mush between the low grade microphone he's singing into and the lo-fi recording itself. But the instrumentals cover a wide area, indeed. Some, like "Comin' Round the Mountain," "Let's Get Funky," and "Goodnight Boogie" are simply superior in their original Alligator versions. But storming takes on "You Can't Sit Down," the mistitled (to grab publishing credit) "Stompin'"—actually "Howlin' For My Darling"—and "Juke Joint Boogie" tip the scales into making this a tough-to-find piece that's well worth any effort it takes to acquire a copy. Not the place to start, and certainly for completists only, but some of the best and nastiest Hound Dog you'll ever hear. *—Cub Koda*

Deluxe Edition / Feb. 23, 1999 / Alligator ✦✦✦✦✦
This is the raw treble-infested blues espoused by Hound Dog Taylor. His trademark, no bass guitar to be found for miles around, and cheap Japanese guitars played through the even cheaper Sears Roebuck amps, blues with layers of distortion. Backed only by a second guitar, and a wild and tumultuous drummer, this six finger slide guitar master produced some of the wildest music to stretch out of the south side of Chicago. To help this sound achieve its maximum desired effect, tuning was not obligatory. This is the way he liked it. Raw Raw Raw. Sounds like the makings of a fine headache, and I guess for some it was. But to his legion of fans (me being one) this is the blues, as he saw it. This disc just doesn't stop and allow one to catch one's breath. It is part of a fantastic new series from Alligator. A series of artist retrospectives, *Deluxe Edition* is just what it claims to be, a remastered, remixed, and repackaged showcase of the best of the careers of these artists. Taylor is one of those rare blues men that wanted you up and dancing from the first notes to the very last squealing, snarling and bleeding notes of his distorted guitar faded down into an obscure ringing silence, that seemed to have its own corrupted distortion. The only complaint one can have of this disc is that he only recorded for an all too brief four years, but this disc culls some of the best of that much too brief career in the studio. As an added bonus on this disc, as well as displaying some of the best from his five albums, there are two previously unreleased tracks. One of these tracks is a live take of "Phillips' Theme," which lets Brewer Phillips show off his often overlooked skills as a guitarist. The world lost a wonderful performer when Hound Dog passed away, but we are much the richer for his having been here, in more ways than we knew. His wild and woolly blues was the energy force and excitement that caused Bruce Iglauer to start Alligator Records just to record the excitement he felt that night all these years ago in Florence's Lounge on the South Side. The sheer raw force that resided in this man that was released in his music is captured on this disc. It is one that should not be missed. *—Bob Gottlieb*

Jude Taylor

b. 1949, Grand Coteau, LA
Vocals, Accordion / Zydeco
A zydeco performer in the blues-based tradition of Clifton Chenier, Creole singer and accordionist Jude Taylor was born in Grand Coteau, LA, in 1949. After growing up singing in church and school choirs, he later fronted a number of blues combos before turning to zydeco after receiving an accordion as a gift from his brother-in-law; assembling a backing band dubbed the Burning Flames which included his sons "Curly" on drums and Errol on rub board, Taylor debuted in 1994 with the LP *The Best of Zydeco. Zydeco Bayou!* followed in 1997. *—Jason Ankeny*

● **The Best of Zydeco** / Dec. 14, 1994 / Mardi Gras ✦✦✦✦✦
The title of *The Best of Zydeco* makes it sound like a greatest-hits collection, but the record is actully Jude Taylor's debut effort. The accordionist has assembled a great band—including his sons Curly (drums) and Errol (rub board)—and leads them through rollicking zydeco and steamy slow blues. Occasionally, he flirts with soul and blues, such as on a cover of Clarence Carter's "Strokin'," but Taylor is at his best when he sticks to classic zydeco sounds. The inclusion of these storming, party-oriented tracks is how *The Best of Zydeco* nearly lives up to its name. *—Thom Owens*

Zydeco Bayou! / Jun. 3, 1997 / Mardi Gras ✦✦✦

Koko Taylor (Cora Walton)

b. Sep. 28, 1935, Memphis, TN
Vocals / Modern Electric Chicago Blues, Electric Chicago Blues, R&B
Accurately dubbed the "Queen of Chicago Blues" (and sometimes just the blues in general), Koko Taylor helped keep the tradition of big-voiced, brassy female blues belters alive, recasting the spirits of early legends like Bessie Smith, Ma Rainey, Big Mama Thornton, and Memphis Minnie for the modern age. Taylor's rough, raw vocals were perfect for the swaggering new electrified era of the blues, and her massive hit "Wang Dang Doodle" served notice that male dominance in the blues wasn't as exclusive as it seemed. After a productive initial stint on Chess, Taylor spent several decades on the prominent contemporary blues label Alligator, going on to win more W.C. Handy Awards than any other female performer in history, and establishing herself as far and away the greatest female blues singer of her time.

Koko Taylor was born Cora Walton on September 28, 1935, on a sharecropper's farm in Memphis, TN. Her mother died in 1939, and she and her siblings grew up helping their father in the fields; she got the nickname "Koko" because of her love of chocolate. Koko began singing gospel music in a local Baptist church; inspired by the music they heard on the radio, she and her siblings also played blues on makeshift instruments. In 1953, Koko married truck driver Robert "Pops" Taylor and moved with him to Chicago to look for work; settling on the South Side, Pops worked in a slaughterhouse and Koko got a job as a housemaid. The Taylors often played blues songs together at night, and frequented the bustling South Side blues clubs whenever they could; Pops encouraged Koko to sit in with some of the bands, and her singing—which reflected not only the classic female blues shouters, but contemporaries Muddy Waters and Howlin' Wolf—quickly made a name for her. In 1962, Taylor met legendary Chess Records songwriter/producer/bassist Willie Dixon, who was so impressed with her live performance that he took her under his wing. He produced her 1963 debut single "Honky Tonky" for the small USA label, then secured her a recording contract with Chess.

Taylor made her recording debut for Chess in 1964 and hit it big the following year with the Dixon-penned "Wang Dang Doodle," which sold over a million copies and hit number four on the R&B charts. It became her signature song forever after, and it was also the last Chess single to hit the R&B Top Ten. Demand for Taylor's live act skyrocketed, even though none of her follow-ups sold as well, and as the blues audience began to shift from black to white, the relatively new Taylor became one of the first Chicago blues artists to command a following on the city's white-dominated North Side. Eventually, she and her husband were able to quit their day jobs, and he served as her manager; she also put together a backing band called the Blues Machine. With the release of two albums—1969's *Koko Taylor*, which featured a number of her previous singles; and 1972's *Basic Soul*—Taylor's live gigs kept branching out further and further from Chicago, and when she played the 1972 Ann Arbor Blues & Jazz Festival, the resulting live album on Atlantic helped bring her to a more national audience.

By the early '70s, Chess Records was floundering financially, and eventually went under in 1975. Taylor signed with a then-young Chicago-based label called Alligator, which grew into one of America's most prominent blues labels over the years. Taylor debuted for Alligator in 1975 with *I Got What It Takes*, an acclaimed effort that garnered her first Grammy nomination. Her 1978 follow-up *The Earthshaker* featured several tunes that became staples of her live show, including "I'm a Woman" and "Hey Bartender," and her popularity on the blues circuit just kept growing in spite of the music's commercial decline. In 1980, she won the first of an incredible string of W.C. Handy Awards (for Best Contemporary Female Artist), and over the next two decades, she would capture at least one more almost every year (save for 1989, 1997, and 1998). *From the Heart of a Woman* was released in 1981, and in 1984, Taylor won her first Grammy thanks to her appearance on Atlantic's various-artists compilation *Blues Explosion*, which was named Best Traditional Blues Album. She followed that success with the guest-laden *Queen of the Blues* in 1985, which won her a couple extra Handy Awards for Vocalist of the Year and Entertainer of the Year (no "female" qualifier attached). In 1987, she released her first domestic live album, *Live in Chicago: An Audience With the Queen*.

Tragedy struck in 1988. Taylor broke her shoulder, collarbone, and several ribs in a van accident while on tour, and her husband went into cardiac arrest; although Pops survived for the time being, his health was never the same, and he passed away some months later. After recuperating, Taylor made a comeback at the annual Chicago Blues Festival, and in 1990 she issued *Jump for Joy*, as well as making a cameo appearance in the typically bizarre David Lynch film *Wild at Heart*. Taylor followed it in 1993 with the aptly titled *Force of Nature*, after which she took a seven-year hiatus from recording; during that time, she remarried and continued to tour extensively, maintaining the stature she'd achieved with her '80s work as the living Queen of the Blues. In 2000, she finally returned with a new album, *Royal Blue*, which featured a plethora of guest stars: B.B. King, Kenny Wayne Shepherd, Johnnie Johnson, and Keb' Mo'. —*Steve Huey*

Koko Taylor / 1969 / MCA/Chess ✦✦✦✦✦
Straight digital reissue of Taylor's debut Chess album from 1969. Produced by Willie Dixon (who can intermittently be heard as a duet partner), the set is one of the strongest representations of the belter's Chess days available, with her immortal smash "Wang Dang Doodle," and the chunky "Twenty-Nine Ways," "I'm a Little Mixed Up," and "Don't Mess with the Messer." Top-flight session musicians on Taylor's 1965-1969 output included guitarists Buddy Guy, Matt "Guitar" Murphy, and Johnny Shines, and saxman Gene "Daddy G" Barge. —*Bill Dahl*

Basic Soul / 1972 / Chess ✦✦✦

South Side Lady / Dec. 1, 1973 / Evidence ✦✦✦
Cut during the period when she was between Chess and Alligator, this 15-song selection, cut in a French studio and live in the Netherlands in 1973, is a potent set that finds her ably backed by the Aces, guitarist Jimmy Rogers, and pianist Willie Mabon. Lots of familiar titles—a live "Wang Dang Doodle," studio remakes of "I'm a Little Mixed Up" and "Twenty-Nine Ways"—and a few numbers that aren't usually associated with Chicago's undisputed blues queen. —*Bill Dahl*

Southside Baby / 1975 / Black & Blue ✦✦✦
Taylor's first Alligator album is as tough and uncompromising as any she's done for the firm. —*Bill Dahl*

I Got What It Takes / 1975 / Alligator ✦✦✦✦✦
The queen's first album for Alligator, and still one of her very best to date. A tasty combo sparked by guitarists Mighty Joe Young and Sammy Lawhorn and saxist Abb Locke provide sharp support as the clear-voiced Taylor belts Bobby Saxton's "Trying to Make a Living," and Magic Sam's "That's Why I'm Crying," her own "Honkey Tonkey" and "Voodoo Woman," and Ruth Brown's swinging "Mama, He Treats Your Daughter Mean." —*Bill Dahl*

Queen of the Blues / 1975 / Alligator ✦✦✦✦
Co-producer Bruce Iglauer anticipated a future trend by making this a set filled with cameos—but the presence of Lonnie Brooks, James Cotton, Albert Collins, and Son Seals is entirely warranted and the contributions of each work quite well in the context of the whole. Taylor's gritty "I Cried like a Baby" and a snazzy remake of Ann Peebles' "Come to Mama" are among the many highlights. —*Bill Dahl*

★ **What It Takes: The Chess Years** / 1977 / MCA/Chess ✦✦✦✦✦
With 18 tracks spanning 1964-1971, this compilation receives the nod over the shorter *Koko Taylor* (eight cuts double off anyway). Opening with her nails-tough "I Got What It Takes," the disc boasts "Wang Dang Doodle," several sides never before on album, and the strange previously unissued "Blue Prelude." Four 1971 tracks from Taylor's tough-to-find second Chess album, *Basic Soul*, are also aboard (including "Bills, Bills and More Bills" and her queenly version of "Let Me Love You Baby"). Producer Willie Dixon's guiding hand is apparent everywhere. —*Bill Dahl*

The Earthshaker / 1978 / Alligator ✦✦✦✦✦
Koko Taylor's Alligator encore harbored a number of tunes that still pepper her set list to this day—the grinding "I'm a Woman" and the party-down specials "Let the Good Times Roll" and "Hey Bartender." Her uncompromising slow blues "Please Don't Dog Me" and a sassy remake of Irma Thomas' "You Can Have My Husband" also stand out, as does the fine backing by guitarists Sammy Lawhorn and Johnny B. Moore, pianist Pinetop Perkins, and saxman Abb Locke. —*Bill Dahl*

From the Heart of a Woman / Jan. 1981 / Alligator ✦✦✦
Another very credible outing, though Taylor's not quite convincing on the jazzily swinging "Sure Had a Wonderful Time Last Night." Far more suited to her raspy growl are her own "It Took a Long Time," a funky "Something Strange Is Going On," and Etta James' moving soul ballad "I'd Rather Go Blind" (beautifully complemented by Criss Johnson's liquidic guitar). —*Bill Dahl*

An Audience With Koko Taylor / 1987 / Alligator ✦✦✦
Growling and lightly lacking in dynamics. —*Bill Dahl*

Live from Chicago / 1987 / Alligator ✦✦✦
Unfortunately, Koko Taylor's only domestic live album to date was cut with one of the lesser incarnations of her band, the Blues Machine, whose work could have displayed considerably more subtlety and swing than it does. Still, the set offers a vivid portrait of Chicago's blues queen in action, with faithful recitals of "Wang Dang Doodle," "I'm a Woman," and "Let the Good Times Roll." —*Bill Dahl*

Jump for Joy / 1990 / Alligator ✦✦✦
A slightly slicker Koko Taylor than we've generally been accustomed to, with nice horn arrangements by Gene Barge that farme the blues queen's growl effectively. A Taylor duet with Lonnie Brooks would normally be something to savor, but they're saddled here with an extremely corny "It's a Dirty Job" that's beneath both their statures. Taylor wrote four of thet disc's best numbers herself, including "Can't Let Go" and the title cut. —*Bill Dahl*

Love You Like a Woman / 1990 / Charly ✦✦✦✦✦
These 21 songs by Koko Taylor were produced and mostly written by Willie Dixon between 1964 and 1969, with Lafayette Leake, Buddy Guy, Robert Nighthawk (on some of

the earliest tracks), Johnny Shines, Clifton James, Big Walter Horton, and Dixon backing her up. The songs run the gamut from blues standards in the making ("Wang Dang Doodle") to topical subjects ("Separate or Integrate"), with Taylor in great voice throughout. Worth the price just for "I Love a Lover Like You." The notes are minimal, but it's difficult to argue about the sound quality or the content. —*Bruce Eder*

Wang Dang Doodle / Jul. 1, 1991 / Huub ✦✦✦

Force of Nature / 1993 / Alligator ✦✦✦✦
A solid contemporary blues album that ranges from Taylor's own "Spellbound" and "Put the Pot On," a rendition of Toussaint McCall's tender soul lament "Nothing Takes the Place of You," and a saucy revival of the old Ike & Tina Turner R&B gem "If I Can't Be First." Gene Barge once again penned the horn charts, Carey Bell contributes his usual harp mastery to Taylor's remake of Little Milton's "Mother Nature," and only Buddy Guy's over-the-top guitar histrionics on "Born Under a Bad Sign" grate. Long may the queen reign! —*Bill Dahl*

Royal Blue / Jun. 6, 2000 / Alligator ✦✦✦
Royal Blue is the first Alligator release from Koko Taylor since 1993's Grammy nominated *Force of Nature*. This is a mainly uptempo set with excellent support from several guest appearances by B.B. King, Johnnie Johnson, Ken Saydak, and Kenny Wayne Shepherd, who contributes some scorching guitar on the Melissa Ethridge-penned hit "Bring Me Some Water." Taylor not only co-produced this release but wrote four of the 12 tracks, including the acoustic "The Man Next Door." On this track, the combination of Koko's passionate voice with Keb' Mo's gritty Delta slide guitar makes you wish she would move further in this direction on future releases. *Royal Blue* proves Koko Taylor is still the undisputed Queen of the Blues. —*Al Campbell*

Deluxe Edition / Jan. 22, 2002 / Alligator ✦✦✦
While some fans may argue that Koko Taylor's Chess material is slightly superior, there is no denying the power of these Alligator sessions. *Deluxe Edition* collects 15 of her very best tracks from her Alligator releases since 1975. Some of the high points include the many guest spots from Buddy Guy, B.B. King, Pinetop Perkins, Mighty Joe Young, and Carey Bell. As a *Deluxe Edition* bonus, the unreleased track "Man Size Job" is included, making this collection hard to beat for both collectors and the novice. —*Al Campbell*

Little Johnny Taylor (Johnny Lamont Merrett)

b. Feb. 11, 1943, Gregory, AR, **d.** May 17, 2002, Conway, AR
Vocals / Soul-Blues, R&B, Soul

Some folks still get them mixed up, so let's get it straight from the outset. Little Johnny Taylor was best known for his scorching slow blues smashes "Part Time Love" (for Bay Area-based Galaxy Records in 1963) and 1971's "Everybody Knows About My Good Thing" for Ronn Records in Shreveport, LA. This Johnny Taylor was not the suave Sam Cooke protégé who blitzed the charts with "Who's Making Love" for Stax in 1968; that's Johnnie Taylor, who added to the confusion by covering "Part Time Love" for Stax. Another similarity between the two Taylors: Both hailed from strong gospel backgrounds.

Little Johnny came to Los Angeles in 1950 and did a stint with the Mighty Clouds of Joy before going secular. Influenced by Little Willie John, he debuted as an R&B artist with a pair of 45s for Hunter Hancock's Swingin' logo, but his career didn't soar until he inked a pact with Fantasy's Galaxy subsidiary in 1963 (where he benefited from crisp production by Cliff Goldsmith and Ray Shanklin's arrangements).

The gliding midtempo blues "You'll Need Another Favor," firmly in a Bobby "Blue" Bland mode, was Taylor's first chart item. He followed it up with the tortured R&B chart-topper "Part Time Love," which found him testifying in gospel-fired style over Arthur Wright's biting guitar and a grinding, horn-leavened downbeat groove. The singer also did fairly well with "Since I Found a New Love" in 1964 and "Zig Zag Lightning" in 1966.

Taylor's tenure at Stan Lewis' Ronn imprint elicited the slow blues smash "Everybody Knows About My Good Thing" in 1971 and a similar witty hit follow-up, "Open House at My House," the next year (both were covered later by Z.Z. Hill for Malaco). While at Ronn, Little Johnny cut some duets with yet another Taylor, this one named Ted (no, they weren't related either). Though he recorded only sparingly during the 1980s and '90s, he remained an active performer until his death in 2002. —*Bill Dahl*

Part Time Love / 1962 / Ronn ✦✦✦✦✦
Soulful Little Johnny Taylor's brand of shuffling R&B/Blues is exploited fully on this reissue of this debut album originally released on Galaxy Records in 1962. The grandiose horns are spectacular and impressive, and the lyrics express real-life, down-to-earth love dramas. A signifying blues guitar makes both draggers "Part Time Love" and "Found a New Love" totally mesmerizing. There's not a hint of mere filler among the ten tracks. "Junkie for Your Love," the harmonic "True Lovin'," "You're Gonna Need Another Favor," and "I Don't Want It All" each effectively portray the blues style that Taylor helped establish. —*Andrew Hamilton*

Little Johnny Taylor / 1963 / Galaxy ✦✦✦✦
Terrific brass-heavy charts by Roy Shanklin push Taylor's soulful pipes heavenward on this great LP that includes hit "Part Time Love." —*Bill Dahl*

Everybody Knows About My Good Thing / 1970 / Ronn ✦✦✦✦
A great simmering soul-blues album. Two R&B hits—"It's My Fault Darling" and the ironic two-part title cut, later revived by Z.Z. Hill—share microgroove space with eight more solid efforts, supervised by Miles Grayson (who co-wrote a good deal of the album). —*Bill Dahl*

Open House / 1973 / Ronn ✦✦✦
Another hot mixture of blues and soul. —*Bill Dahl*

The Super Taylors / 1974 / Ronn ✦✦✦
Now here'a a relic from Taylor's prolific early '70s Ronn tenure that also features soul-blue singer Ted Taylor. Although they weren't related (except by label), the "Super Taylors"

shared this album like long-lost brothers. Four duets find the two complementing one another most soulfully; otherwise, the album is comprised of solo sides by both (including Johnny Taylor's "Everybody Knows About My Good Thing"). *—Bill Dahl*

L.J.T. / 1979 / Ronn ✦✦✦

I Shoulda Been a Preacher / 1981 / Red Lightnin' ✦✦✦✦✦

Only his pastor knows that for sure, but this is one wailing collection. It contains the hottest gospel-tinged singles Little Johnny Taylor cut for Galaxy, and anyone turned off by the tepid material coming out for Ichiban should consult these before hopping off the bandwagon. *—Ron Wynn*

Stuck in the Mud / 1988 / Ichiban ✦✦✦

Ugly Man / 1989 / Ichiban ✦✦✦

Frankly, Taylor's voice isn't what it used to be, but this effort isn't without its merits. *—Bill Dahl*

● **Greatest Hits** / 1991 / Fantasy ✦✦✦✦✦

The gospel-tinged and decidedly soul-inflected 1963-1968 blues sides of Little Johnny Taylor on Galaxy Records benefitted from marvelous horn-powered arrangements by Ray Shanklin that brilliantly pushed Taylor's melismatic vocals. Naturally, the impassioned "Part Time Love" is included, along with the Bobby "Blue" Bland-tinged midtempo groover "You'll Need Another Favor," a delicious "Since I Found a New Love," and the blistering "You Win, I Lose." There are 17 tracks in all, many of them bolstered by Arthur Wright's stinging guitar. *—Bill Dahl*

Everybody Knows About My Good Thing/Open House / Apr. 10, 2001 / West Side ✦✦✦✦

L.J.T./Part Time Love / May 8, 2001 / West Side ✦✦✦

Melvin Taylor

b. Mar. 13, 1959, Jackson, MS

Guitar / Contemporary Blues, Modern Electric Chicago Blues, Modern Electric Blues

Chicago-based guitarist Melvin Taylor is a star in Europe, but it may take some time for U.S. audiences to catch on to just how phenomenally talented a bluesman he is. Part of the problem for Taylor may be his own natural eclecticism. He's equally adept playing jazz or blues, but in the last few years, he's forged a name for himself as a blues guitarist with a slew of releases for Evidence Music. Taylor may well be the most talented new guitarist to come along since Stevie Ray Vaughan.

Taylor was born in Mississippi but raised in Chicago after the family moved there in 1962. He learned guitar from his mother's brother, Uncle Floyd Vaughan, who jammed to tunes by Muddy Waters, Jimmy Reed and Howlin' Wolf with his buddies. By the time Taylor was 12, he was sitting in with his uncle and other grown-ups at those sessions. Almost entirely self-taught, the young Taylor learned slide playing, fingerpicking and flat-picking styles from his favorite recordings by B.B. King, Albert King, and Jimi Hendrix.

In his teens, Taylor joined the Transistors, a group managed by his future father-in-law, and they made their mark playing popular music of the '70s at talent shows and night clubs. After the Transistors broke up in the early '80s, Taylor again devoted his full attention to playing blues in the Windy City's West Side clubs. Shortly after, pianist Joe Willie "Pinetop" Perkins came looking for a guitarist for a string of European dates. Taylor joined the Legendary Blues Band for a year and made such an impact in Europe that several club and festival bookers wanted him back with his own group. Since the late '80s, he's been making regular tours of Europe, often backed by former members of the Transistors, where they opened for the likes of B.B. King, Buddy Guy, Santana, George Benson, and Canned Heat.

Aside from taking his musical inspiration from guitar heroes like Albert King, B.B. King, and Stevie Ray Vaughan, Taylor also became enamored with the jazz stylings of George Benson and Wes Montgomery, incorporating their styles into his playing.

Taylor's recordings include two he first recorded for a French label that have seen been reissued on the Pennsylvania-based Evidence Music: *Blues on the Run*, originally recorded in 1982, and 1984's *Melvin Taylor Plays the Blues for You*. Back in the U.S., Taylor continued to build a buzz around the strength of his marathon live shows at Rosa's Lounge and other venues in Chicago. Several small labels tried to sign Taylor, but they weren't successful. In 1995, Taylor was signed to Evidence Music and entered the studio with blues impresario John Snyder to record his debut for the label, *Melvin Taylor & the Slack Band*, which showcased his original songwriting. He returned in 1997 with his second U.S. album, *Dirty Pool*. Taylor's debut remains the Evidence label's best-selling release ever. Both records showcase Taylor's awe-inspiring guitar playing and original renderings of classic Chicago blues tunes. *Bang That Bell* followed in 2000, featuring racy cover art and a somewhat funk-influenced sound, but it was his teaming with Lucky Peterson and Mato Nanji on 2002's *Rendezvous With the Blues* that cemented his reputation as a mainstay in the American blues and roots rock scene. *—Richard Skelly*

Blues on the Run / Apr. 1982 / Evidence ✦✦✦✦

Melvin Taylor may run a little long at times on his *Blues on the Run*, but that gives him the opportunity to dazzle with the full scope of his chops. He can play Chicago blues as gritty as anyone, but he can also rock hard and has enough sensitivity for jazz. Hearing him run through all these styles is a little dizzying, however, especially since he doesn't know when to let a little space into the music. Nevertheless, the record functions as an effective showcase for his talents. *—Thom Owens*

Melvin Taylor Plays the Blues for You / Mar. 21, 1984 / Evidence ✦✦✦✦

Guitarist Melvin Taylor's fluid, smartly constructed solos and understated yet winning vocals are surprises on this 1984 nine-track set recorded for Isabel and recently reissued by Evidence on CD. Taylor is not a fancy or arresting singer but succeeds through his simple, effective delivery of lyrics, slight inflections, and vocal nuances. His guitar work is impressive, with skittering riffs, shifting runs, and dashing solos. Organist/pianist Lucky Peterson is an excellent second soloist, adding cute background phrases at times, then stepping forward and challenging or buttressing Taylor's playing with his own dazzling lines. *—Ron Wynn*

Melvin Taylor & the Slack Band / Oct. 17, 1995 / Evidence ✦✦✦✦

● **Dirty Pool** / Aug. 12, 1997 / Evidence ✦✦✦✦✦

Fans of Stevie Ray Vaughan will notice the title of this disc is that of a Vaughan song. Indeed, three selections from his songbook are covered here: "Too Sorry," "Telephone Song" and the title track. The impressive Melvin Taylor is an electric blues guitarist that will appeal to the fans of the legendary Texan for his skilled and precise playing along with smooth and expressive vocals. Taylor definitely is a continuation of the Chicago blues tradition that begot Luther Allison, Buddy Guy and Otis Rush. Taylor gives his version of Rush's "Right Place, Wrong Time" on this collection of nine covers. Taylor's lineup here is a trio—a reliable bass and drum rhythm section keeps up a steady bottom end for to showcase his ability to handle all vocals and guitar parts. Every track here is rife in the easy genius that marks a true master of the blues craft. *—Thomas Schulte*

Bang That Bell / Apr. 4, 2000 / Evidence ✦✦✦

Taylor continues to change with each new album, and *Bang That Bell* continues the forward look of 1997's *Dirty Pool*. Taylor is undoubtedly blues-oriented, but his music is also fueled by bursts of jazz, R&B, funk, and distorted wah-wah-inflected rock. While this will be off-putting to most blues diehards, Taylor forges his own path, and the result is an album with strong blues ties that doesn't fall into one comfortable roots bag or another. A strong effort, albeit one not suited to every blues fan's taste. *—Cub Koda*

Rendezvous With the Blues / Jun. 25, 2002 / Evidence ✦✦✦

Montana Taylor (Arthur Taylor)

b. 1903, Butte, MT, **d.** 1954

Vocals, Piano / Piano Blues

Listeners who have ducked the flying chairs in a typical Hollywood saloon scene of the Old West should have a pretty good idea what the atmosphere of such a place was like. The pianists who played music for the clientele of these venues became known as barrel house pianists, the style of music also called barrelhouse to perhaps associate it from its close relative boogie-woogie. The latter style at least suggests the merest hint of politeness, while in barrelhouse the overall idea is that all hell will be breaking loose, the music expected to compete with all manner of saloon noise, sometimes including rip-roaring fights. To be able to play "low-down" is the ultimate compliment for such a player, perhaps one of the clearest cases in music of what bandleader, composer, and musical scholar Col. Bruce Hampton has established as a cardinal rule of making good music: to go "lower."

Born Arthur Taylor, but of no relation to the stylish bebop drummer of the same name, Montana Taylor picked up his nickname as a tribute to his home; and perhaps it was above all an attempt to balance out the high altitude of Montana with the low attitude of Taylor the musician. He is considered the lowest of the low in terms of barrelhouse playing, with fans of boogie-woogie sometimes claiming that nobody could play the barrelhouse style with quite the authority of this artist. It can certainly be said without the slightest indecision that he is the finest blues pianist, and possibly even the best blues artist in general, from the state of Montana, since there hardly seem to be any others. Taylor himself seemed to be in a big hurry to get out of Montana as well, nicknames aside. He was raised in Indianapolis, where he learned piano around 1919. Coffeeshops, nightclubs, and rent parties were the gig possibilities, and he dove into this world with the fingers of both hands flying, moving on to Chicago where he cut two 78s for Vocalion in 1929. It can't be said to be a recording debut that went without a hitch, as one of the sides was rendered a dismal mess by a vocal outfit known as the Jazoo Boys. The pianist did everything he could to make up for this group's almost complete lack of talent, demonstrating a pounding, rhythmically invigorating style with traces of the melodic sweetness that later prompted comparisons between one of his solos and the *Midnight Sonata* of Beethoven.

Eventually, Taylor halted his piano playing, and the story is that he did it because he was discouraged by the absence of royalties. A glance at his discography confirms the fact that somebody along the way lost control of these recordings and whatever legal publishing copyright status they might have had. Like some of his contemporaries such as Cripple Clarence Lofton or Romeo Nelson, the Montana pianist would have been even more discouraged had he realized what would be the eventual disposition of his masterworks. These early recordings have basically been fair game for a variety of small-label enterprises, appearing on several dozen different piano anthologies originating in Austria, Japan, France, England, and the United States.

Located by jazz fans in 1946, Taylor created a new series of recordings in which he proved the recording hiatus had robbed of him of none of his instrumental abilities, either as a soloist or as an accompanist to Bertha Chippie Hill. He also had grown as a singer by the time of these later recordings, performing effectively on ballads such as the marvelous "I Can't Sleep." This comeback was apparently just as discouraging as his first run at a career had been, and Taylor dropped out of sight again, never to be found again. The quality of his performances has led to honors above and beyond that of almost setting a record for being ripped off. No more important a blues fan than the Rolling Stones' Bill Wyman picked a Taylor recording as one of the blues tracks that most influenced him to become a musician, part of Wyman's project for Biograph entitled *Blues Odyssey*. Classical piano composer David Matthews also created the short tribute piece "Montana Taylor's Blues." *—Eugene Chadbourne*

● **Montana Taylor and Freddie Shayne: Complete Recorded Works (1929–1946)** / 1991 / Document ✦✦✦✦

The Document collection *Montana Taylor and Freddie Shayne: Complete Recorded Works (1929-1946)* does fans of barrelhouse piano a favor by issuing the 17 tracks associated with Montana Taylor, from his recording debut in 1929 to his (all-too-brief) rediscovery in 1946. Taylor plays it low-down on highlights like "Detroit Rocks," "Whoop and Holler Stomp," and "Indiana Avenue Stomp," and Bertha "Chippie" Hill guests on three sides (most notably "Worried Jailhouse Blues"). If that wasn't enough, the label also tacked on six sides recorded by piano/accordion expert J.H. "Mr. Freddie" Shayne, which also includes a few vocals from Hill. *—Thom Owens*

Otis Taylor

b. 1948, Chicago, IL

Guitar, Banjo, Vocals / Electric Country Blues

Bluesman Otis Taylor never skirted tough subject matter in a career that took him from the Folklore Center in Denver to a brief stay in London, England, to retirement from music in 1977 to operate as a successful antiques broker and since 1995 back again to the blues.

Taylor's 2001 CD, *White African* (Northern Blues Music), featuring Kenny Passarelli (bass, keyboards) and Eddie Turner (lead guitar), became his most direct and personal statement about the experiences of African-Americans. He addressed the lynching of his great-grandfather and the murder of his uncle. Brutality became his concern in songs about a black man executed in the '30s for a murder he did not commit and about a father who could not afford doctor's bills and sat powerless watching his son die. Faith met Taylor's irony in his vision of Jesus as a mortal man who looked for ways to avoid his crucifixion and in his take on romantic infidelity among common men.

Taylor's first CD, *Blue-Eyed Monster*, and 1997's *When Negroes Walked the Earth* also cast an uneasy spell on the blues world. Part of Taylor's music could feel comfortable on the back roads of the Delta in the '20s and '30s. It came as no surprise when he interpreted Charley Patton's "Stone Pony" on a Shanachie Records' compilation, *Screamin' and Hollerin' the Blues: New Acoustic Recordings of Pre-War Blues Classics*, which also featured popular blues performers such as Alvin Youngblood Hart, John Hammond, Duke Robillard, and Corey Harris. At other times, Taylor's music was so uncompromisingly contemporary in its outlook on social injustices that he seemed more akin to South African poet and activist Stephen Biko.

Taylor was born in Chicago in 1948. After his uncle was murdered, his family moved to Denver for apparent safe haven. Taylor took an interest in blues and folk music at Denver's Folklore Center. After hearing Etta James sing "All I Wanna Do Is Make Love to You (Can't By Just Looking Under the Cover)," Taylor knew he liked the blues. He then went to the Folklore Center, where he heard the banjo and country blues and Mississippi John Hurt. He also liked Junior Wells and Muddy Waters and got into the folkie blues and Appalachian music. He learned to play guitar, banjo, and harmonica. Only several decades later did he begin to understand the ties of the blues and its instrumentation to the savannah of western Africa. By his mid-teens, he formed his first groups—the Butterscotch Fire Department Blues Band and later the Otis Taylor Blues Band. He briefly stayed in England in 1969 to pursue a record deal with Blue Horizon, but negotiations failed and he returned to the U.S. In the '70s, he took up mandolin. He decided to leave music behind in 1976 and started a successful career as an antiques broker. After much prodding from Passarelli, Taylor returned to music in 1995. He first played a benefit concert. Then he started to play again both solo and with his band in America and Europe. In the summer of 2000, he received a composition fellowship from the Sundance Institute in Park City, UT, and hobnobbed with film celebrities at the Sundance Film Festival. Taylor began participating in "Writing the Blues" in the Blues in the Schools program, sponsored by the National Blues Foundation, and he started writing and performing new songs in 2001. *—Robert Hicks*

When Negroes Walked the Earth / Jan. 1, 2000 / Shoelace Music ♦♦♦♦

Otis Taylor earned acclaim in 2001 when his *White African* release got picked up for national distribution, but this previous disc could just as easily have been the one to bring him into the spotlight: It was every bit as deep, ambitious, and listenable as *White African*. Listening to the independently issued *When Negroes Walked the Earth* reveals that Taylor was already one of the most fully developed voices in contemporary blues—an artist in the true sense of the word, intent on crafting his ideas into sharply realized songs and then into a full-fledged album. Everything seems purposeful; the skeletal arrangements lend emotional resonance to chilling songs like "500 Roses" and "12 String Mile," and the remarkable variety in Taylor's droning, single-chord structures rivals even that of John Lee Hooker. And lest anyone wonder whether a drumless trio can keep a groove, hearing album highlight "Cold at Midnight," driven to the brink of oblivion by bassist Kenny Passarelli's heartbeat pulse, should put all fears to rest. Taylor would return to many of the same lyrical themes later in his career—references to violence, death, and the paradoxes of African-American history are frequent—but *When Negroes Walked the Earth* covered these topics just as powerfully as his subsequent, more widely distributed work. *—Kenneth Bays*

● **White African** / Mar. 6, 2001 / Northern Blues ♦♦♦♦♦

Otis Taylor has a knack for interesting titles; *Blue-Eyed Monster* and *When Negros Walked the Earth* are among the CDs that the Denver bluesman recorded before *White African*. Taylor also has a knack for very dark and sobering themes—this 2001 release, in fact, is full of them. On *White African*, Taylor's subject matter ranges from lynching in the Deep South ("Saint Martha Blues") to homelessness ("Hungry People") to being unable to afford health care for a sick, dying child ("3 Days and 3 Nights"). And Taylor doesn't try to sugarcoat his often disturbing lyrics with happy melodies. Greatly influenced by John Lee Hooker, the very soulful Taylor often favors moody, dusky, haunting grooves. So *White African* is as dark musically as it is lyrically. Over the years, dark humor has played a major role in the blues—like country and hip-hop artists, bluesmen are known for finding a variety of humorous, clever ways to tell you how cruel and punishing life can be. But *White African* isn't dark humored; it's simply dark. This CD is also incredibly compelling, and it is enthusiastically recommended to those who don't expect lighthearted escapism from all of their music. *—Alex Henderson*

Respect the Dead / 2002 / Northern Blues ♦♦♦♦♦

Otis Taylor might well be the best and most inspired of contemporary bluesmen. His *White African* album was a masterpiece—which makes the task of following it doubly difficult. With *Respect the Dead*, however, he does a superb job—the man is still very much on a roll. Kicking off with the stark, banjo-led "Ten Million Slaves," the intensity level never dips. It doesn't matter whether he's basing a song around a single chord, as he does on "Hands on Your Stomach," or simply using voice and harmonica on "Baby So," there's a remarkable urgency about his singing and lyrics, never more so than with "Black Witch," a tale of the American South that goes right back to Africa—but the album returns and takes its tone to Mexico and racing for "Three Stripes on a Cadillac." The support, from Kenny Passarelli, Cassie Taylor, and atmospheric lead guitarist Eddie Turner, always serves to push the tension of the songs even higher. Taylor doesn't work within standard blues structures, and his lyrics stray far from the standard blues lines to encompass history and mythology. Where others seem content with the established limits, Taylor is pushing them further and further—and in doing so, he's making some of the most exciting music around. *—Chris Nickson*

Sam "The Man" Taylor

b. Jul. 12, 1916, Lexington, TN

Sax (Tenor) / Jazz Blues, Jump Blues, Soul-Jazz, Swing, R&B

A certified honking sax legend, Sam "The Man" Taylor's non-stop drive and power worked perfectly in swing, blues, and R&B sessions. He had a huge tone, perfect timing, and sense of drama, as well as relentless energy and spirit. Taylor began working with Scat Man Crothers and the Sunset Royal Orchestra in the late '30s. He played with Cootie Williams and Lucky Millinder in the early '40s, then worked six years with Cab Calloway. Taylor toured South America and the Caribbean during his tenure with Calloway. Then, Taylor became the saxophonist of choice for many R&B dates through the '50s, recording with Ray Charles, Buddy Johnson, Louis Jordan, and Big Joe Turner, among others. He also did sessions with Ella Fitzgerald and Sy Oliver. During the '60s, Taylor led his own bands and recorded in a quintet called the Blues Chasers. *—Ron Wynn*

Blue Mist / 1957 / MGM ♦♦♦♦

Jazz for Commuters / Oct. 15, 1958-Oct. 22, 1958 / Metro Jazz ♦♦♦

More Blue Mist / Jan. 1960 / MGM ♦♦♦♦

● **The Bad and the Beautiful** / Feb. 20, 1962 / Prestige ♦♦♦♦

Misty Mood / 1962-1963 / Decca ♦♦♦

It's a Blue World / 1962-1963 / Decca ♦♦♦

Swingsation / Nov. 9, 1999 / Verve ♦♦♦

Like fellow saxophone player Hal Singer, Sam "The Man" Taylor" moved easily between jazz and R&B (with early rock & roll overtones), although his rough, hard driving way with the horn usually finds him classified as an R&B icon. This bargain-priced album goes a long way to support the R&B labeling. Joined by another sax player who often found himself moving between jazz and R&B, baritone Haywood Henry, this album catches Taylor in three sessions he made for MGM Records in March of 1955 and November of 1956. In addition to Henry he is joined by other habitués of the R&B world like Lloyd Trotman on bass and Freddie Washington on piano. Among the tracks which show off Taylor's unique ways with the sax are "Ride, Sammy, Ride" where Taylor is urged on by the band shouting the title line, and a blues dripping "Sam's Blues." There's some yakety—yak à la Boots Randolph on "High Winds" which also features a rousing give and take between Taylor and Henry. With the exception of Henry and some occasional choruses by Freddie Washington, this album is pretty much Taylor's show. Little room is made for any of the other participants to solo. While this album is an excellent vehicle to show off the talents of a foremost R&B sax player, it also demonstrates that this sax style with its one-dimensional approach to the art of the sax wears thin very quickly. This is an interesting, but not a major reissue. However, it shows Taylor as he was before he started making romantic albums in the '60s like *The Bad and the Beautiful*. *—Dave Nathan*

Sam Taylor

Guitar, Vocals / New York Blues

Vocalist, guitarist, and songwriter Sam Taylor is the son of the saxophonist Sam "The Man" Taylor. The younger Taylor didn't really grow up with his father, though, as Sam Sr. left the family to find a better career in New York. Taylor's family eventually moved to Brooklyn, and the young Sam was influenced by his mother, who also came from a performing background in vaudeville shows. He began singing in church at age five and later trained to become a boxer. He eventually fought as a pro boxer for 86 bouts and then found a more peaceful pursuit with his guitar. But through it all, he kept up his gospel singing and songwriting efforts.

Taylor has been recording since 1959. His discography and sessionography credits include Atlantic, Colpix, Capitol, Roulette, Stax, and Road Show Records. As a songwriter, he's written songs recorded by Sam and Dave, Elvis Presley, Freddie King, Jackie Wilson, Jimmy Witherspoon, Esther Phillips, Brook Benton, the Beach Boys, Maxine Brown, and Joey Dee & the Starlighters. As a guitarist and singer, he's accompanied the likes of Otis Redding, the Isley Brothers, Albert Collins, T-Bone Walker, Tracy Nelson, and Mother Earth, Big Joe Turner and the Drifters.

Taylor recorded two albums for the Tucson-based Trope Records in 1995, *Desert Soul* and *Bluz Man*. On both his records for Trope, Taylor is accompanied by Heather "Lil Mama" Hardy on violin, Ed DeLucia on guitar, Mike Nordberg on bass, and Jerome Kimsey on drums. Taylor now resides in the Long Island area and was voted 2000 "Bluesman of the Year" by the New York and Long Island Blues Societies. *—Richard Skelly*

● **I Came from the Dirt** / Oct. 26, 1999 / Etherhaus ♦♦♦

Susan Tedeschi

b. Nov. 9, 1970, Boston, MA

Vocals, Guitar / Modern Electric Blues

Guitarist, singer, and songwriter Susan Tedeschi is part of the new generation of blues musicians looking for ways to keep the form exciting, vital and evolving. Tedeschi's live shows are by no means straight-ahead urban blues. Instead, she freely mixes classic R&B, blues and her own gospel and blues-flavored original songs into her sets. She's a young, sexy, sassy blues belter with musical sensibilities that belie her years.

Tedeschi began singing when she was four and was active in local choir and theater in Norwell, a southern suburb of Boston. She began singing at 13 with local bands and continued her music studies at Berklee, honing her guitar skills and also joining the Reverence Gospel Ensemble. She started the first incarnation of her blues band upon graduating in 1991, with vocalist/guitarist Adrienne Hayes, a fellow blues enthusiast whom she met at the House of Blues in Cambridge, Massachusetts. Bonnie Raitt, Janis Joplin, and Boston-area singer Toni Lynn Washington were Tedeschi's most important influences; in starting her band, in fact, she used Washington's backing band and hustled up gigs on nights when Washington and her band were not already booked. Since they began performing around Boston's fertile blues scene, Tedeschi and her band developed into a tightly knit, road-ready group, and have played several major blues festivals. Guitarist Sean Costello has since replaced original guitarist and co-vocalist Hayes, who left the group to pursue her own musical interests.

The Susan Tedeschi Band's first album, *Just Won't Burn*, was released on the Boston-based Tone-Cool Records in early 1998. The band for her debut on Tone-Cool includes guitarist Costello, bassist Jim Lamond and drummer Tom Hambridge; guitarist Hayes also contributes. *Just Won't Burn* is a powerful collection of originals, plus a sparkling cover of John Prine's "Angel From Montgomery." Tedeschi and band also do justice to a tune Ruth Brown popularized, "Mama, He Treats Your Daughter Mean," and Junior Wells' "Little By Little." *—Richard Skelly*

● **Just Won't Burn** / Feb. 10, 1998 / Tone-Cool ✦✦✦✦

The very idea of a lady slinging a guitar sets traditional blues fans swooning. But with the release of her debut, Susan Tedeschi slings, aims, and hits her target. What a talent! Singer, songwriter, player, performer, and more, the lady from Boston can do it all. Effective, she does justice to John Prine's classic "Angel From Montgomery" while making her own efforts known. Her tunes include "You Need to Be With Me," "Found Someone New" and the title cut. Leading her own band, she has what it takes to keep the boys in line while she wails away. Big Mama Thornton and Bessie Smith must be proud and B.B. King must be impressed, since she has opened for this blues master on several occasions. Just a little taste of things to come, *Just Won't Burn* blazes a trail that Tedeschi is pioneering for herself and younger women in the blues world. A brave heart with spunk and plenty of soul. *—Jana Pendragon*

Better Days / Dec. 15, 1998 / Oarfin ✦✦✦

Originally released in 1995, *Better Days* was re-released after the success of *Just Won't Burn* created a legion of blues fans wanting more of Susan Tedeschi. This record finds Tedeschi's guitar prowess and eminent vocals proliferating the musical landscape in the same manner of blues legends who have gone before her. The tracks "It Hurts Me Too" and "Ain't Nobody's Business" are classic slow, bluesy songs complete with emotional vocal wailings that are sure to bring the house down when performed in a live arena. She picks up the pace with "Locomotive" and "I Don't Want Nobody," showing off her six-string skills. While there is no question that Tedeschi is a true talent and a blues force to be reckoned with, the musical arrangements could be improved by using a less-formulaic blues structure and attempting to offer something more contemporary. She has proven herself worthy of sharing the stage with the masters; her next challenge should be to break away and create her own sound. *—Erik Crawford*

Johnnie "Geechie" Temple

b. Oct. 18, 1906, Canton, MS, **d.** Nov. 22, 1968, Jackson, MS

Vocals, Guitar, Bass / Prewar Blues, Delta Blues, Chicago Blues

Johnnie Temple is one of the great unsung heroes of the blues. A contemporary of Skip James, Son House, and other Delta legends, Temple was one of the very first to develop the now-standard bottom-string boogie bass figure, generally credited to Robert Johnson.

Born and raised in Mississippi, Temple learned to play guitar and mandolin as a child. By the time he was a teenager, he was playing house parties and various other local events. Temple moved to Chicago in the early '30s, where he quickly became part of the town's blues scene. Often, he performed with Charlie and Joe McCoy. In 1935, Temple began his recording, releasing "Louise Louise Blues" the following year on Decca Records.

Although he never achieved stardom, Temple's records—which were released on a variety of record labels—sold consistently throughout the late '30s and '40s. In the '50s, his recording career stopped, but he continued to perform, frequently with Big Walter Horton and Billy Boy Arnold. Once electrified postwar blues overtook acoustic blues in the mid-'50s, Temple left Chicago and moved to Mississippi. After he returned to his home state, he played clubs and juke joints around the Jackson area for a few years before he disappeared from the scene. Johnny Temple died in 1968. *—Cub Koda & Stephen Thomas Erlewine*

1935–1939 / 1935-1939 / Document ✦✦✦✦✦

A solid collection of Temple's earliest sides, including the killer "Lead Pencil Blues." *—Cub Koda*

● **Complete Recorded Works, Vol. 1** / 1994 / Document ✦✦✦✦✦

Temple's first recordings, beginning with the classic "Lead Pencil Blues" and three other songs (best of all, "Pig Boat Whistle") from his May 14, 1935, sessions for Vocalion. "Lead Pencil Blues" was the first known use on record of the "walking bass" (Temple called it "running bass") figure on the bottom string, which would become commonplace in blues in just a few years, popularized by Robert Johnson. Alas, these were also the most country-sounding records that Temple ever recorded—their lack of success convinced producers that Temple needed a more sophisticated sound, and all of his subsequent sessions, beginning 18 months later with "New Vicksburg Blues," feature a prominent piano sharing the spotlight with the guitar, and the latter instrument played by Charlie McCoy. It's all solid Chicago blues, "Louise Louise Blues," "Snapping Cat," and "So Lonely and So Blue" all being worth the price of the disc by themselves. Much of the later material, especially from the 1938 sessions backed by the Harlem Hamfats, is very smooth, commercial Chicago blues. Most of the sources are in better than decent condition, except for a very noisy "Beale Street Sheik," which can be forgiven as a previously unissued Vocalion side. *—Bruce Eder*

Complete Recorded Works, Vol. 2 (1938–1940) / 1994 / Document ✦✦✦✦✦

Another 23 sides, covering the years 1938 through 1940. The sound on these records is much more jazz than blues, especially in the guitar and clarinet playing, and it sold, "Big Leg Woman" being a major hit and "Mississippi Woman's Blues" repeating the same melody. By the end of the decade, Temple would be working with Lonnie Johnson, one of the jazziest of blues guitarists, and jazz legend clarinetist Buster Bailey, and doing his most mainstream popular music, in terms of sound. The raunchiness of his material was still pronounced and delightful, however, from "Big Leg Woman" and "Grinding Mill" (another musical metaphor for impotence) to "Jelly Roll Bert" (featuring some delightful guitar/voice call-and-response work between Temple and axman Teddy Bunn), "Mississippi Woman's Blues," and "Better Not Let My Good Gal Catch You Here"—it's all surprisingly sophisticated, however, especially with the echoey piano backup, and more evocative of a Chicago club than any roadhouse. Temple's guitar playing may have lacked the jazz inflections that his recording manager was looking for, but his voice was one of the best in blues, alternately mournful and leering, with a surprising amount of power and expressiveness. *—Bruce Eder*

Complete Recorded Works, Vol. 3 / May 1, 1995 / Document ✦✦✦

Ten Years After

f. 1967, Nottingham, England, **db.** 1974

Group / British Blues, Hard Rock, Blues-Rock

Ten Years After was a British blues-rock quartet consisting of Alvin Lee (b. Dec. 19, 1944), guitar and vocals; Chick Churchill (b. Jan. 2, 1949), keyboards; Leo Lyons (b. Nov. 30, 1944), bass; and Ric Lee (b. Oct. 20, 1945), drums. The group was formed in 1967 and signed to Decca in England. Its first album was not a success, but its second, the live *Undead* (1968) containing "I'm Going Home," a six-minute blues workout by the fleet-fingered Alvin hit the charts on both sides of the Atlantic. *Stonedhenge* (1969) hit the U.K. Top Ten in early 1969.

Ten Years After's U.S. breakthrough came as a result of its appearance at Woodstock, at which it played a nine-minute version of "I'm Going Home." Its next album, *Ssssh*, reached the U.S. Top 20, and *Cricklewood Green*, containing the hit single "Love Like a Man," reached number 14. *Watt* completed the group's Decca contract, after which it signed with Columbia and moved in a more mainstream pop direction, typified by the gold-selling 1971 album *A Space in Time* and its Top 40 single "I'd Love to Change the World." Subsequent efforts in that direction were less successful, however, and Ten Years After split up after the release of *Positive Vibrations* in 1974. They reunited in 1988 for concerts in Europe and recorded their first new album in 15 years, *About Time*, in 1989. *—William Ruhlmann*

Ten Years After / 1967 / Deram ✦✦✦

Undead / 1968 / Deram ✦✦✦

Recorded live in a small London club, *Undead* contains the original "I'm Going Home," the song which brought Ten Years After its first blush of popularity following the Woodstock festival and film in which it was featured. However, the real strength of this album is side one, which contains two extended jazz jams, "I May Be Wrong But I Won't Be Wrong Always" and Woody Herman's "Woodchopper's Ball," both of which spotlight guitarist Alvin Lee's amazing speed and technique. Side two is less interesting, with an extended slow blues typical of the time, a drum solo feature, and the rock & roll rave-up of "I'm Going Home." *—Jim Newsom*

Ssssh / 1969 / BGO ✦✦✦✦

This was Ten Years After's new release at the time of their incendiary performance at the Woodstock Festival in August 1969. As a result, it was their first hit album in the U.S., peaking at number 20 in September of that year. This recording is a primer of British blues-rock of the era, showcasing Alvin Lee's guitar pyrotechnics and the band's propulsive rhythm section. As with most of TYA's work, the lyrics were throwaways, but the music was hot. Featured is a lengthy cover of Sonny Boy Williamson's "Good Morning Little Schoolgirl," with reworked lyrics leaving little doubt what the singer had in mind for the title character. Also included was a 12-bar blues song with the ultimate generic blues title, "I Woke Up This Morning." *Ssssh* marked the beginning of the band's two-year run of popularity on the U.S. album charts and in the "underground" FM-radio scene. *—Jim Newsom*

Cricklewood Green / Apr. 1970 / Chrysalis ✦✦✦✦✦

Cricklewood Green provides the best example of Ten Years After's recorded sound. On this album, the band and engineer Andy Johns mix studio tricks and sound effects, blues-based song structures, a driving rhythm section, and Alvin Lee's signature lightning-fast guitar licks into a unified album that flows nicely from start to finish. *Cricklewood Green* opens with a pair of bluesy rockers, with "Working on the Road" propelled by a guitar and organ riff that holds the listener's attention through the use of tape manipulation as the song develops. "50,000 Miles Beneath My Brain" and "Love Like a Man" are classics of TYA's jam genre, with lyrically meaningless verses setting up extended guitar workouts that build in intensity, rhythmically and sonically. The latter was an FM-radio staple in the early '70s. "Year 3000 Blues" is a country romp sprinkled with Lee's silly sci-fi lyrics, while "Me and My Baby" concisely showcases the band's jazz licks better than any other TYA studio track, and features a tasty piano solo by Chick Churchill. It has a feel similar to the extended pieces on side one of the live album *Undead*. "Circles" is a hippie-ish acoustic guitar piece, while "As the Sun Still Burns Away" closes the album by building on another classic guitar-organ riff and more sci-fi sound effects. *—Jim Newsom*

Watt / Dec. 1970 / Chrysalis ♦♦♦
Watt had many of the same ingredients as its predecessor, *Cricklewood Green*, but wasn't nearly as well thought out. The band had obviously spent much time on the road, leaving little time for developing new material. Consequently, a cover of Chuck Berry's "Sweet Little Sixteen," recorded live at the Isle of Wight Festival, is included here, as is a short instrumental with the uninspired title "The Band With No Name." Other song titles like "I Say Yeah" and "My Baby Left Me" betray the lack of spark in Alvin Lee's songwriting. Nonetheless, his guitar work is fast and clean (though the licks are beginning to sound repetitive from album to album), and the band continues to cook in the manner exemplified best on *Cricklewood Green*. *—Jim Newsom*

A Space in Time / 1971 / BGO ♦♦♦♦
A Space in Time was Ten Years After's best-selling album. This was due primarily to the strength of "I'd Love to Change the World," the band's only hit single, and one of the most ubiquitous AM and FM radio cuts of the summer of 1971. TYA's first album for Columbia, *A Space in Time* has more of a pop-oriented feel than any of their previous releases had. The individual cuts are shorter, and Alvin Lee displays a broader instrumental palette than before. In fact, six of the disc's ten songs are built around acoustic guitar riffs. However, there are still a couple of barn-burning jams. The leadoff track, "One of These Days," is a particularly scorching workout, featuring extended harmonica and guitar solos. After the opener, however, the album settles back into a more relaxed mood than one would have expected from Ten Years After. Many of the cuts make effective use of dynamic shifts, and the guitar solos are generally more understated than on previous outings. The production on *A Space in Time* is crisp and clean, a sound quite different from the denseness of its predecessors. Though not as consistent as *Cricklewood Green*, *A Space in Time* has its share of sparkling moments. *—Jim Newsom*

Alvin Lee & Company / 1972 / Deram ♦♦
After Ten Years After found commercial success with a new record label, Columbia, and the hit single "I'd Love to Change the World," the band's former label released this collection of outtakes from earlier recording sessions. One listen shows why these tracks were not included on album releases at the time of their recording. *—Jim Newsom*

Rock & Roll Music to the World / 1972 / BGO ♦♦♦
Here, Ten Years After expanded on their boogie base and continued the hits. The title cut was the hit, and while they continued to groove along in the boogie atmosphere, things on *Rock & Roll Music to the World* sounded a bit too tame for the thundering hordes to chant along to at the time. "Turned Off T.V. Blues" showed just how tiring touring was getting for the band, and there wasn't much else here to bring out the beast to party with. A little too much of the same thing was starting to stunt this band's growth, except in their wallets. *—James Chrispell*

Recorded Live / 1973 / BGO ♦♦♦
This two-record set is OK, in small doses. Ten Years After were always rooted in the blues, and the highlights here, such as "Good Morning Little Schoolgirl" and "Slow Blues In C" show they hadn't changed. While this set is competent enough, there just isn't enough of the excitement you would expect coming from the band here. You could say that they could do no more and no less, and that proved to be the conundrum for Ten Years After. With *Recorded Live* they had become predictable, and there wasn't really anywhere left for them to go. *—James Chrispell*

Positive Vibrations / 1974 / Chrysalis ♦♦
There's not much happening here. By the time *Positive Vibrations* was released, Ten Years After had run out of gas. Leader Alvin Lee had already released two solo albums, *On the Road to Freedom* and *In Flight*, and the band was simply going through the motions on this album. The band broke up following its release. *—Jim Newsom*

Greatest Hits / 1977 / Deram ♦♦♦♦
The group's 1968-1970 best, including the hit "Love like a Man" and the Woodstock version of "I'm Going Home." *—William Ruhlmann*

Essential / 1991 / Chrysalis ♦♦♦♦♦
While it doesn't include all of their prime material, *Essential* features enough of their best songs to make it a fine introduction. *—AMG*

Ssssh/Cricklewood Green / Feb. 25, 1997 / Mobile Fidelity ♦♦♦♦♦
Mobile Fidelity reissued two of Ten Years After's best albums, 1969's *Ssssh* and 1970's *Cricklewood Green*, on one gold disc in 1997. These records are among the group's best and this is a good way to acquire them, but fans should know that this disc costs more than buying the two records separately. For audiophiles, this won't be a problem, since the remastered tapes will be worth the extra money, but less dedicated fans should be aware of the steep retail price of this disc. *—Stephen Thomas Erlewine*

Live at the Fillmore East 1970 / Aug. 14, 2001 / Chrysalis ♦♦♦♦
This superbly recorded double disc (the original engineer was Eddie Kramer, best-known for his work with Hendrix) captured over a weekend worth of dates in February 1970 at the venerable New York City venue catches the Brit boogie quartet at the peak of their powers. These shows were sandwiched between their triumphant Woodstock set and the release of *Cricklewood Green*, generally considered the band's best work. They find the group primed through years of roadwork, as well as obviously excited to be playing in front of an appreciative N.Y.C. crowd. Kicking off with one of Bill Graham's patented individual-member intros, the group winds their way through the ominous riff of "Love Like a Man." Mixing extended and rocking versions of blues standards—like Sonny Boy Williamson classics "Help Me" and "Good Morning Little Schoolgirl," as well as Willie Dixon's "Spoonful"—with two Chuck Berry covers and some nuggets from their own catalog, Ten Years After burns through this show with enormous energy and infectious enthusiasm. Alvin Lee and his flying fingers stay firmly in the spotlight, but the remastered sound is so immaculate you can finally appreciate the contributions of the other, generally overlooked TYA members: Chick Churchill on keyboards and especially Leo Lyons' fluid bass work, along with Ric Lee's jazzy drums. The songs shift into overdrive on the jams—the longest of which pushes "I Can't Keep from Crying Sometimes" to 20 minutes—and amazingly stay interesting for the majority of that time thanks to Lee's sense of flashy dynamics, as he quotes liberally from Hendrix and Cream licks. Detailed liner notes from drummer Lee describe the scene, not only in terms of Ten Years After, but also of the musical camaraderie of the time. Some of this is almost embarrassingly dated—the drum solo-laden "The Hobbit" is particularly guilty, as are the often-interminable guitar gymnastics—and the Chuck Berry numbers might have been live crowd-pleasers but don't add much to the originals. Still, this is the best Ten Years After concert album (of the three in the catalog), and proves just how vibrant these boogie boys could be when inspired by the crowd and each other on a perfect night. *—Hal Horowitz*

Very Best Ten Years After Album Ever / Nov. 6, 2001 / EMI ♦♦♦♦
Ten Years After was one of the premiere blues-rock bands of the '60s and '70s, making gritty rock in their uniquely British way for almost ten years. Tracks like "Me and My Baby" are fun, bouncy rockers that were paving the way for artists like Stevie Ray Vaughan. Although time has eroded some of the initial impact of Ten Years After, there are still some strong reminders. The hit single "Love Like a Man" is still a classic, charged with a hypnotic riff that winds throughout the song like a cobra. The ten-minute version of "I'm Going Home" from Woodstock is included in its entirety, as is the psychedelic blues epic "50,000 Miles Beneath My Brain." These longer tracks go to show how their style of improvisation still incorporated the hooks and riffs from the source song as the noodling traveled into space, a practice that would influence groups from Phish to the Flaming Lips. This may not be the most complete collection that could have been assembled, but this album has an ebb and flow about it that most greatest-hits collections cannot pull off. Fans of solid blues-based rock should give this a listen—this is a career worth dedicating a collection to. *—Bradley Torreano*

● **The Anthology 1967–1971** / Apr. 9, 2002 / Hip-O ♦♦♦♦♦
Since Ten Years After's albums weren't stand-alone classics, this double CD of their prime years is the best bet for those who like the band but don't want to sit through some pretty mediocre and monotonous stuff to get to the best bits. The 26 cuts are pretty well chosen, including naturally their most famed songs: "I'm Going Home" (the live Woodstock version), "I'd Love to Change the World," and the British hit "Love Like a Man." Even as it draws from the cream of their work, it can't quite make the argument for them as a major band, but it does show that they were a more versatile act than many would remember. There are some reasonable pop- and folk-rock-flavored songs from the pen of Alvin Lee; a fair amount of jazz influence from time to time, as on "Me and My Baby" and "Woman Trouble"; a song ("50,000 Miles Beneath My Brain") that borrows rather too liberally from the Rolling Stones, "Sympathy for My Devil"; and even a bit of Grateful Dead-like vocal harmony on "Hear Me Calling." There's still, of course, quite a bit of blues-rock, flash guitar, and boogie, which sound better when broken up by more subdued and varied cuts and also benefit from the wise decision not to include too many covers. It's also nice that the collection includes both sides of two 1968 singles, although those were released on LP in the early '70s as part of *Alvin Lee & Company*. *—Richie Unterberger*

Sonny Terry (Saunders Terrell)

b. Oct. 24, 1911, Greensboro, NC, **d.** Mar. 11, 1986, Mineola, NY

Vocals, Harmonica / Field Recordings, Blues Revival, East Coast Blues, Folk-Blues, Piedmont Blues, Prewar Country Blues, Country Blues, Harmonica Blues

Harmonica player Sonny Terry was one of the initial bluesmen who crossed over into areas not normally associated with the genre before he came along. Along with his partner, guitarist Brownie McGhee, Terry played on numerous folk recordings with the likes of Woody Guthrie, developed an acting career showcased on television and Broadway, and never compromised his unique high-pitched penetrating harmonica style called whoppin'.

Sonny Terry was born Saunders Terrell on October 24, 1911, in Greensboro, NC. He lost his sight by the time he was 16 in two separate accidents. His father played harmonica in local functions around town and taught Terry at an early age. Realizing his eyesight would keep him from pursuing a profession in farming, Terry decided instead to be a blues singer. He began traveling to nearby Raleigh and Durham, performing on street corners for tips. In 1934, he befriended the popular guitarist Blind Boy Fuller. Fuller convinced Terry to move to Durham, where the two immediately gained a strong local following. By 1937, they were offered an opportunity to go to New York and record for the Vocalion label. A year later, Terry would be back in New York taking part in John Hammond's legendary Spirituals to Swing concert, where he performed one of his memorable tunes, "Mountain Blues."

Upon returning to Durham, Terry continued playing regularly with Fuller and also met his future partner, guitarist Brownie McGhee, who would accompany Terry off and on for the next two decades. McGhee was initially sent to look after Terry by Blind Boy's manager, J.B. Long. Long figured McGhee might get a chance to play some of the same shows as Terry. A friendship developed between the two men and following Fuller's death in 1941, Terry and McGhee moved to New York. The change proved fruitful as they immediately found steady work, playing concerts both as a duo and solo. Terry became an in-demand session player who started showing up regularly on the records of folk luminaries including Leadbelly, Woody Guthrie, and Pete Seeger.

An acting role was also initiated at this time, in the long-running Broadway production of *Finian's Rainbow* in 1946. By the mid-'50s, Terry and McGhee began broadening their collective horizons and traveled extensively outside of New York. They released a multitude of recordings for labels like Folkways, Savoy, and Fantasy that crossed the boundaries of race, becoming well-known in folk and blues circles performing for black and white audiences. It was also in the mid-'50s that Terry and McGhee accepted roles on Broadway, joining the cast of *Cat on a Hot Tin Roof*, exposing them to an even broader audience. In the early '60s, the duo performed at numerous folk and blues festivals around the world, while Terry found time to work with singer Harry Belafonte and in television commercials. Terry was constantly traveling throughout the '70s, stopping only long enough to write his instructional book, *The Harp Styles of Sonny Terry*.

By the mid-'70s, the strain of being on the road developed into personal problems between McGhee and Terry. Unfortunately, they resigned their long partnership, divided by the bitterness of constant touring. Terry was still being discovered by a younger blues generation via the Johnny Winter-produced album *Whoppin'* for the Alligator label, featuring Winter and Willie Dixon. Winter had produced a comeback album for Muddy Waters (*Hard Again*) that helped rejuvenate his career, and he was attempting the same with Terry. By the '80s, Terry's age was catching up with him. He quit recording and only accepted sporadic live appearances. Terry passed away in 1986, the year he was inducted into the Blues Foundations Hall of Fame. *—Al Campbell*

Sonny's Story / 1960 / Bluesville/Original Blues Classics ♦♦♦

Sonny's Story is an excellent showcase for Sonny Terry's talents, which sometimes went unheralded because they largely were showcased in the shadow of Brownie McGhee. Here, Terry is largely playing solo acoustic, with J.C. Burris joining in for harmonica duets every so often; Stick McGhee and drummer Belton Evans also play on a few cuts. Unlike some solo acoustic blues albums, *Sonny's Story* is positively infectious. It's hard not to get caught up in Terry's shouts and boogies, and that's one major reason why this is among his best solo recordings. *—Thom Owens*

Sonny Is King / 1963 / Bluesville/Original Blues Classics ♦♦♦

Half of *Sonny Is King* is devoted to a rare session between Sonny Terry and Lightnin' Hopkins. The two guitarists are supported by bassist Leonard Gaskin and drummer Belton Evans, but the rhythm section fails to kick the pair into overdrive, and much of the music disappointingly meanders. Sometimes change is not a good thing. That's proven by the second side of the album, where Terry falls into the comfortable setting of duetting with Brownie McGhee. While these aren't among the duo's very best recordings, they are nonetheless enjoyable, suggesting that there's something to be said for the familiar. *—Thom Owens*

Whoopin' / 1984 / Alligator ♦♦♦

The textbook charge usually levelled against Alligator sessions are that they're sanitized. You couldn't lodge that one against this set with a straight face; if anything, somebody turned Sonny Terry loose. It didn't hurt that Johnny Winter was around on guitar and piano, playing gritty blues with a passion. It didn't help that Terry didn't put any amplified muscle behind his harmonica, however. Otherwise, this is a strong session. *—Ron Wynn*

★ **The Folkways Years, 1944–1963** / 1991 / Smithsonian/Folkways ♦♦♦♦♦

While he's best known as guitarist Brownie McGhee's longtime partner, harmonica ace and vocalist Sonny Terry made many excellent recordings as a solo act, and also recorded with Blind Boy Fuller and others. The 17 songs on this anthology include Terry playing with McGhee's brother Stick, Pete Seeger, and others, as well as several featuring Terry's biting harmonica and wry leads relating stories of failure, triumph, and resiliency, backed by McGhee's flickering but always audible guitar. The title is a bit misleading, since the earliest date for any session is 1946 (one number), and most are done between 1955 and 1959. *—Ron Wynn*

Sonny Terry / Oct. 21, 1991 / Collectables ♦♦♦♦♦

Harmonica player and vocalist Sonny Terry cut some stunning material for Gotham in the early '50s. Some of it was issued, and much of it wasn't. This is a healthy chunk of things that were and weren't released, with good remastering embellishing Terry's cutting vocals and splintering harmonica. *—Ron Wynn*

Sonny Terry / 1995 / Capitol ♦♦♦♦♦

Some of the whooping harmonicist's finest stuff as a bandleader, dating from his 1947-1950 Capitol Records tenure. Brownie McGhee handles the guitar on two sessions, his brother Stick on the other two, but Terry is front and center on all. Contains all 16 numbers Terry did for the major label, notably "Whoopin' the Blues," "Custard Pie Blues," and "Beer Garden Blues." *—Bill Dahl*

Whoopin' the Blues: The Capitol Recordings, 1947–1950 / Oct. 1995 / Capitol ♦♦♦

Complete Recordings 1938–1945 / Jan. 10, 1996 / Document ♦♦♦♦

Sonny Terry & His Mouth Harp / 1999 / Stinson ♦♦♦

This rare December 1953 session (reissued on CD in 1999) was unusual for Terry in that his guitar accompanist was not Brownie McGhee, but Alec Seward, who had previously recorded as Guitar Slim in a duo with "Fat Boy" Hayes, aka Jelly Belly. It's unusual only in the personnel, however. It sounds like typical Sonny Terry, as he works his way through original material, including standards like "John Henry" and other blues tunes like "In the Evening" (the song that would provide much of the basis for Robert Johnson's "Love in Vain"). You'd have to say that it's usually more interesting to hear Terry with his longtime partner McGhee than it is to hear him with Seward, but it's not *terribly* different. The trademark vocal and harmonica whoops and hollers are in gear and running throughout the album, sometimes to exhilarating effect, as on the rapid "The Fox Chase (aka "Hound Dog Holler"). His lyrics get uncommonly specific on "Goodbye Leadbelly," a tribute to the then-recently deceased folk-blues legend, composed by "writer unknown." The recording engineer on the session, incidentally, was a young Jac Holzman, who had just started Elektra Records. *—Richie Unterberger*

Complete Works in Chronological Order, Vol. 2: 1944–1949 / Jan. 25, 2000 / Document ♦♦♦♦

This second volume in the complete chronological recordings of Sonny Terry covers everything from 1944 to 1949, excepting his Capitol recordings from this period, which are collected in a separate package. Terry's joined by the likes of Woody Guthrie, Cisco Houston, Alec Seward, and others on a delightful brace of country blues and folk tunes, including an unissued version of "Rain Crow Bill," an alternate take of "Goin' Down Slow," and hot versions of "Silver Fox Chase," "Lost John," and "Pick a Bale of Cotton." Nice transfers, good notes, and a lot of great music. *—Cub Koda*

Sonny Terry & Brownie McGhee

f. 1941, **db.** 1975

Group / Folk-Blues, Piedmont Blues, Country Blues, Acoustic Blues

The joyous whoop that Sonny Terry naturally emitted between raucous harp blasts was as distinctive a signature sound as can possibly be imagined. Only a handful of blues harmonica players wielded as much of a lasting influence on the genre as did the sightless Terry (Buster Brown, for one, copied the whoop and all), who recorded some fine urban blues as a bandleader in addition to serving as guitarist Brownie McGhee's longtime duet partner.

Saunders Terrell's father was a folk-styled harmonica player who performed locally at dances, but blues wasn't part of his repertoire (he blew reels and jigs). Terry wasn't born blind—he lost sight in one eye when he was five, the other at age 18. That left him with extremely limited options for making any sort of feasible living, so he took to the streets armed with his trusty harmonicas. Terry soon joined forces with Piedmont pioneer Blind Boy Fuller, first recording with the guitarist in 1937 for Vocalion.

Terry's unique talents were given an extremely classy airing in 1938 when he was invited to perform at New York's Carnegie Hall at the fabled From Spirituals to Swing concert. He recorded for the Library of Congress that same year and cut his first commercial sides in 1940. Terry had met McGhee in 1939, and upon the death of Fuller, they joined forces, playing together on a 1941 McGhee date for OKeh and settling in New York as a duo in 1942. There they broke into the folk scene, working alongside Leadbelly, Josh White, and Woody Guthrie.

While Brownie McGhee was incredibly prolific in the studio during the mid-'40s, Terry was somewhat less so as a leader (perhaps most of his time was occupied by his prominent role in *Finian's Rainbow* on Broadway for approximately two years beginning in 1946). There were sides for Asch and Savoy in 1944 before three fine sessions for Capitol in 1947 (the first two featuring Stick McGhee rather than Brownie on guitar) and another in 1950.

Terry made some nice sides in an R&B mode for Jax, Jackson, Red Robin, RCA Victor, Groove, Harlem, Old Town, and Ember during the '50s, usually with Brownie close by on guitar. But it was the folk boom of the late '50s and early '60s that made Brownie and Sonny household names (at least among folk aficionados). They toured long and hard as a duo, cutting a horde of endearing acoustic duet LPs along the way, before scuttling their decades-long partnership amidst a fair amount of reported acrimony during the mid-'70s. *—Bill Dahl*

The 1958 London Sessions / 1958 / Collectables ♦♦♦♦

Brownie McGhee & Sonny Terry Sing / 1958 / Smithsonian/Folkways ♦♦♦♦♦

One of the duo's best acoustic folk-blues collaborations, originally issued in 1958. They convincingly run through a very enjoyable series of collaborations marked by affectionate interplay, with drummer Gene Moore adding rhythmic power. *—Bill Dahl*

The Bluesville Years, Vol. 5: Mr. Brownie & Mr. Sonny / Oct. 6, 1960-Apr. 1962 / Prestige ♦♦♦

The musical partnership of Brownie McGhee and Sonny Terry stood the test of time and quality wise hardly ever wavered below magnificent. This 17-track collection is culled from four excellent Bluesville vinyl albums from the early '60s and features numerous fine moments. Starting with five selections from Brownie's first solo album for the label, we find the duo augmented with the presence of Bennie Foster on second guitar with Brownie handling all the vocals. Sonny's solo sides emanate from two separate sessions, the first of which features Brownie's famous brother Stick ("Drinkin' Wine Spo-Dee-O-Dee") contributing guitar on three tracks which also include J.C. Burris on second harmonica behind Terry. The second 1960 session features Lightnin' Hopkins as a somewhat chaotic backup guitarist behind Sonny on two cuts. The compilation closes with seven romping, loosely played tracks from a live performance at the Philadelphia folk club, the Second Fret, in April of 1962. The oddball instrumentation on several tracks and the guest turns by Stick and Lightnin' makes this a Brownie and Sonny a cut above the usual and worth seeking out. *—Cub Koda*

Just a Closer Walk With Thee / Nov. 1960 / Fantasy/Original Blues Classics ♦♦♦

Here's Brownie and Sonny's gospel album, recorded in 1957 at Jenny Lind Hall in Oakland, California. Those used to hearing this duo stomp and hoot the blues will be surprised as they tackle material like "What a Beautiful City," "I Shall Not Be Moved," "If I Could Hear My Mother Pray," and Gary Davis' "Get Right Church" in their own inimitable style. But an even bigger surprise comes with the liner notes, penned by major league baseball player Orlando Cepeda! By far the most interesting of all the many recordings this twosome made during their time together. *—Cub Koda*

Sonny & Brownie at Sugar Hill / Dec. 1961 / Fantasy/Original Blues Classics ♦♦♦

Sonny & Brownie at Sugar Hill is a live album recorded at the famous San Franciscan nightclub. Both musicans were in fine form, with each getting a chance to sing some of their standards, including "Sweet Woman Blues," "Born to Live the Blues," "Baby, I

Knocked on Your Door," and "I Got a Little Girl." Their interplay is always a joy to hear, and while there are some better live shows available, this is thoroughly entertaining and worth the time of any of their fans. *—Thom Owens*

Guitar Highway / 1963 / Verve ♦♦♦

Brownie McGhee & Sonny Terry at the 2nd Fret / Mar. 1963 / Bluesville/Original Blues Classics ♦♦♦♦♦

Brownie McGhee and Sonny Terry were the ultimate blues duo; McGhee's stylized singing and light, flickering guitar was wonderfully contrasted by Terry's sweeping, whirling harmonica solos and intense, country-tinged singing. They were in great form during the 10 tunes featured on this live date, recently reissued on CD. Sometimes, as on "Custard Pie" or "Barking Bull Dog," they're funny; at other times, they were prophetic, chilling or moving. This is Piedmont blues at its best, and this disc's tremendous remastering provides a strong sonic framework. *—Ron Wynn*

Hometown Blues / 1969 / Mainstream ♦♦♦♦♦

Early-'50s sides catch this prolific duo at their best. *—Bill Dahl*

Sonny & Brownie / 1973 / A&M ♦♦♦♦♦

In a way, this is the veteran duo's version of *Fathers and Sons*, a meeting of old black bluesmen with young white admirers that Muddy Waters and Otis Spann cut with Mike Bloomfield and Paul Butterfield. John Mayall and John Hammond, Jr. are among the "youngsters" on this powerful statement that includes a definitive version of Randy Newman's wickedly subtle anti-slavery tune "Sail Away." Sonny Terry's trademark whoops are energizing. The repartee between him and Brownie McGhee might convince you they were fast friends if you didn't know otherwise. *—Mark Allan*

Po' Boys / 1994 / Drive Archive ♦♦♦

McGhee and Terry in their folkie mode again, most of the ten selections stemming from a 1960 LP for Vee-Jay. One of their anthems, "Walk On," receives a spirited reading, as do "Down By the Riverside" and "Trouble in Mind." *—Bill Dahl*

Blowin' the Fuses: Golden Classics / Aug. 30, 1994 / Collectables ♦♦♦

The 1958 London Sessions / Oct. 25, 1994 / Sequel ♦♦♦

Blowin' the Fuses / Apr. 1996 / Rykodisc/Tradition ♦♦♦♦

This mid-priced 12-track compilation album presents six performances from an early-'60s Sonny Terry & Brownie McGhee appearance at the Troubadour (the album cover says 1961, the liner notes 1962), two studio recordings from the same era, and four bonus tracks recorded in 1944 and featuring Terry with varying combinations of musicians including Woody Guthrie, Alec Seward, and Cisco Houston. The Terry and McGhee live material is excellent, with McGhee's vocals and guitar playing carrying the tunes, embellished by Terry's inventive harmonica and occasional harmony singing. The studio tracks are more off the cuff than the live ones, notably the six-minute title track, recorded during a studio blackout. *—William Ruhlmann*

Live at the New Penelope Cafe / Nov. 18, 1997 / Just a Memory ♦♦♦♦♦

It sometimes seems like there are about 90 live albums by Sonny Terry & Brownie McGhee, all from the '60s. This one, taped at a show in Montreal in 1967, stands out from the rest because the duo are in unusually lively form, and its having been recorded in a more raw than usual manner. As with other releases in this Canadian-taped series by Michael Nerenberg, it's possible that the duo weren't even thinking about the fact that they were being recorded, and so were less stiff and formal than they could sometimes sound playing in front of white collegiate audiences. The result is a record a bit louder and noisier, but also more exciting than most of their other live albums—the voices mesh together a bit rougher and more honestly than they do on some of their other live releases. The sound is clean mono, with the audience present but not overly obtrusive, and the repertory includes "Cornbread, Peas and Black Molasses," "Sportin' Life," "Easy Rider," "Pack It Up and Go," "Hooray Hooray (These Women Is Killing Me)," Champion Jack Dupree's "Under Your Hood," and a medley of stuff like the Broonzy/Segar "Key to the Highway" and Leroy Carr's "In the Evening." *—Bruce Eder*

Backwater Blues / Jun. 29, 1999 / Fantasy ♦♦♦♦♦

Songs of whiskey, women, and money—nothing was more important to the repertoire of this classic acoustic blues duo. Good relations on stage were not, but during this 18-tune club date at Sugar Hill in San Francisco, Terry and McGhee are in good spirits. The former's fingerpicking, good-time guitar strummin', and even-keeled singing, joined by Terry's frantic harmonica and frequent whoops and hollers were the epitome of this genre's style, and these two performing in their heyday. They do hits familiar to all like "One Bourbon, One Scotch, One Beer," "Key to the Highway," and "Careless Love," while changing up "Sittin' on Top of the World," making it "Climbin' on Top of the Hill." Advice songs include the poignant "My Father's Words," "(If You) Lose Your Money (Please Don't Lose Your Mind")", and "Walk On." There's also a lone instrumental, "Playing With the Blues"; the title track identified by Terry as "Backwater Rising"; and occasionally call-and-response vocalizing as on "Climbin'" or harmony singing on "You'd Better Mind." The clarity of the recording and the singing is pure as the driven snow, with no distortion or compression. It's the way this blues should be heard. Lee Hildebrand's episodic liner notes relating the strained relationship between Terry and McGhee, and the tale of Barbara Dane's involvement in the Sugar Hill club is as important a story as the songs the duo sing. The words and music prove a last will and testament accenting this posthumous release, a companion to the *Live at Sugar Hill* Original Blues Classic CD. It's a must buy for those who treasure this type of no-nonsense porch-style get-down blues. *—Michael G. Nastos*

● **Absolutely the Best** / Aug. 8, 2000 / Fuel 2000 ♦♦♦♦♦

Absolutely the Best collects 14 of the acclaimed country blues duo's most memorable performances, including "I'm a Stranger Here," "Down By the Riverside," "Drinkin' in the Blues," and "Blowin' the Fuses." Terry and McGhee are joined by Lightnin' Hopkins and Big Joe Williams on "Blues for Gamblers," "Early Mornin' Blues," and "Right on That Shore," and "Trouble in Mind," "I'm a Stranger Here," and "Po' Boys" are among the album's other highlights. While it's not quite as extensive a collection as *Complete Recorded Works, Vol. 1, Absolutely the Best* is an entertaining, thoughtfully chosen compilation of Terry and McGhee's beloved folk-blues. *—Heather Phares*

Jimmy Thackery

b. May 19, 1953, Pittsburgh, PA

Vocals, Guitar / Modern Electric Blues, Bar Band, Blues-Rock

Singer, songwriter, and guitar virtuoso Jimmy Thackery has carved an enviable niche for himself in the world of electric blues. Known for his gritty, blue-collar approach and marathon live shows, Thackery was for many years part of the Nighthawks, one of the hardest-working blues bar bands in North America; since the late '80s, he has been touring and recording under his own name, and has found widespread acceptance on the festival circuit. His hard-edged, tough-as-nails approach to guitar playing and his trio's driving rhythm section holds appeal for fans of both the straight-ahead blues of Muddy Waters and the roots-rock of Bruce Springsteen and Joe Grushecky. Like the Nighthawks and Grushecky's Houserockers, much of the material Thackery performs can safely be called blues or blues-rock. Hardcore blues like "It's My Own Fault" and popular blues-rock chestnuts like "Red House" from Jimi Hendrix are fair game for Thackery and his Drivers, who include Michael Patrick on bass and Mark Stutso on drums and vocals.

Born in Pittsburgh, Thackery was raised in Washington, D.C. In high school, he played in a band with Bonnie Raitt's brother, David, who exposed him to the music of Buddy Guy; Thackery saw both Guy and Jimi Hendrix perform in Washington, D.C. Thackery joined the Nighthawks in 1974, after being introduced to harmonica man Mark Wenner by fellow guitarist Bobby Radcliff, who was then based in D.C. Thackery recorded more than 20 albums with the Nighthawks and toured the U.S, Canada, Europe, and Japan. He left the band in 1987 and struck out on his own, needing a break from the Nighthawks' 300-nights-a-year tour schedule.

He formed a new band, Jimmy Thackery & the Assassins, and toured the East Coast heavily with that band until they split up in 1991. Since then Thackery has been leading a trio, Jimmy Thackery & the Drivers, and quickly forged a name for himself on the blues festival and club circuit through a prolific recording pace and a lot of roadwork. His albums for the San Francisco-based Blind Pig label include *Empty Arms Motel* (1992), *Sideways In Paradise* (Jimmy Thackery and John Mooney, 1993), *Trouble Man* (1994), *Wild Night Out!* (1995), *Drive to Survive* (1996), and *Switching Gears* (1998). Two years later, Thackery released *Sinner Street*. His 1998 album includes guest performances by Joe Louis Walker, Lonnie Brooks, Chubby Carrier, and Francine Reed, but any of Thackery's albums will delight fans of tough, heavy, driving guitar playing. For a taste of his thorough mastery of several styles, *Drive to Survive* touches on rockabilly, jazz, bebop, and surf music. Most of Thackery's albums include at least a few covers mixed in with his batch of self-penned songs. *—Richard Skelly*

● **Empty Arms Motel** / 1992 / Blind Pig ♦♦♦♦♦

Not a prolific composer, Thackery's strength lies in strong arrangements that make other people's material his own. He covers Stevie Ray Vaghan's "Rude Mood," and one suspects there will be comparisons made in this direction. His solos burn the motel down on Luther Johnson's "Lickin' Gravy," and he manages a more than credible job on Hendrix's "Red House." Of the two self-penned numbers, the title track is a convincing boogie driven by an ultra-cool, echoed, chicken-scratch guitar riff, while "Getting Tired of Waiting" offers a more traditional blues shuffle. *—Roch Parisien*

Sideways in Paradise / 1993 / Blind Pig ♦♦♦

A collection of acoustic delights recorded by Jimmy Thackery and John Mooney in 1985. Vintage blues and ragtime played by a pool in Jamaica. Guitars, mandocello, mandolins and guttural vocals are backed by native tree frogs (which sound a lot like crickets). *—Roch Parisien*

Trouble Man / 1994 / Blind Pig ♦♦♦

Trouble Man is a hard-driving blues-rock album, with more emphasis on the "rock" than Thackery's other releases. It slows down just long enough for the slightly dark "Lovin' You Right" and the jazzy "Anchor to a Drowning Man," arguably the best cut here. "Doin' 100" and the instrumental "Hang Up and Drive" have a strong Stevie Ray Vaughan sound. Thackery applies a steady yet lighthearted and uptempo pace to William Harris' "Bullfrog," which has also been covered by the likes of Dave Hole and John Hammond. The K.C. Douglas cover "Mercury Blues" has been recorded by everyone from Steve Miller to Alan Jackson (remember the "Crazy 'bout a Ford truck" commercials?), but this is one of the best versions you're likely to hear. The Albert Collins instrumental "Don't Lose Your Cool" is another highlight of *Trouble Man*; Thackery attacks the tune while remaining in total control of his instrument, as he always does. If you've seen him live, you can just envision his arms swinging wildly on this one. *Trouble Man* doesn't quite live up to the material on *Empty Arms Motel* or *Drive to Survive*, but you really can't go wrong with any Thackery release. *—Ann Wickstrom*

Wild Night Out! / 1995 / Blind Pig ♦♦♦

Drive to Survive / 1996 / Blind Pig ♦♦♦♦

Put your seat belt on before you "drive" this one. Thackery lets loose on both guitar and vocals here, with a solid, screaming set of originals and a handful of covers. Although it probably wasn't the intention, *Drive to Survive* quickly became synonymous with "Apache," the jungle drum-flavored surf instrumental that Thackery included simply because he "wanted to do a surf tune that no one had messed with." In reality, more than 20 artists had recorded the Ventures tune by the time *Drive to Survive* was released. Nonetheless, it served as a much-requested anthem of sorts in Thackery's live shows for years to come. "All About My Girl" is a Jimmy McGriff-meets-Albert Collins instrumental, and "Burford's Bop" is high-energy swing. Thackery delivers tough, gritty vocals on the JL Hooker/ZZ Top-style "You Got Work to Do." The bluesiest offering, "Rub on Up," features some serious guitar licks and has lyrics that could make just about anyone blush. The real gem on *Drive to Survive*, though, is the ballad "That's How I Feel." Drummer Mark Stutso handles the vocals, and both the song and the singing are superb. —*Ann Wickstrom*

Switching Gears / Jan. 2, 1998 / Blind Pig ✦✦✦
Guitarist-singer Jimmy Thackery's 1997 set stretches beyond the blues. A ferocious rockish guitarist with a vocal style that ranges from shouting to mellow, Thackery is easily the main star of his disc. However the other members of his Drivers are strong (Al Gamble on organ and piano, bassist Michael Patrick, and drummer Mark Stutso), and there are features for guest accordionist Chubby Carrier on "Take Me With You When You Go" (a zydeco romp) and singer Reba Russell ("Dancing on Broken Glass") plus a helpful appearance apiece by Lonnie Brooks and Joe Louis Walker. From blues to rock with touches of zydeco, country, pop and folk, Thackery constantly stretches himself and gives the music his best. —*Scott Yanow*

Sinner Street / Sep. 26, 2000 / Blind Pig ✦✦✦✦
On his eighth album, Jimmy Thackery churns out rugged, no-nonsense, authoritative rock, with a passion and commitment that seeps through every track. Thackery's grinding guitar and growling voice pound out each song as if he's playing for thousands of people. Produced once again by the experienced Jim Gaines who, through his work with Stevie Ray Vaughn, Albert Collins, Tommy Castro, and Santana, knows his way around a blues-rock record. The uncut Stonesy chug of "Never Enough" and "Lovin' My Money" is offset by the harder-edged funk of "Grab the Rafters" and the easier jazz shuffle of "Bad News." Saxist Jimmy Carpenter, new to the Thackery band, adds a soulful honk on the latter tune, gradually shifting the disc into more subtle territory. When the band starts wading into swampy waters like on the deep, dark groove of the album's instrumental title track, Carpenter provides a rough bed for the guitarist's poker-hot solo to nuzzle next to. Thackery's gruff and unremarkable voice remains his most limiting asset, and may be the reason his music hasn't crossed over like that of the more ostentatious Kenny Wayne Shepherd and Jonny Lang. But similar to most blues guitarists, the song is secondary to its presentation, and when Thackery unleashes his barely contained six-string fury, there are few who can compare. Considering the bluesman's arena is predominantly the live stage, *Sinner Street* is another extraordinarily strong entry into his catalog. Established blues-rock fans will naturally devour this whole, but the disc is as good a place as any for the novice to enjoy one of the more overlooked talents in the field. —*Hal Horowitz*

We Got It / May 28, 2002 / Telarc ✦✦✦✦
For his first album for Telarc, Jimmy Thackery—backed by his band, the Drivers—has come up with a near-tribute album to Eddie Hinton, covering eight of his songs on this 11-track set while offering three originals that illustrate the depth of his debt and love for the underappreciated singer/songwriter. Hinton was one of the leading white Southern soul singer/songwriters of the '70s, '80s, and '90s, and Thackery learned a lot from him—especially how R&B, blues, and rock could be seamlessly fused and that roots are as import as strong songwriting. Thackery turns up the volume a little bit more and rocks it hard, not just here but overall, but he can also convincingly deliver a slow-burner like "It's All Wrong but It's All Right," which is what makes *We Got It* so satisfying—not just as a testament to Hinton, but as a strong Thackery record. It's a great way to begin his association with Telarc. —*Stephen Thomas Erlewine*

Sister Rosetta Tharpe

b. Mar. 20, 1921, Cotton Plant, AR, **d.** Oct. 9, 1973, Philadelphia, PA
Vocals, Guitar / Jump Blues, Black Gospel, Blues Gospel, Classic Female Blues
Alongside Willie Mae Ford Smith, Sister Rosetta Tharpe is widely acclaimed among the greatest Sanctified gospel singers of her generation; a flamboyant performer whose music often flirted with the blues and swing, she was also one of the most controversial talents of her day, shocking purists with her leap into the secular market—by playing nightclubs and theatres, she not only pushed spiritual music into the mainstream, but in the process also helped pioneer the rise of pop-gospel. Tharpe was born March 20, 1921, in Cotton Plant, AR; the daughter of Katie Bell Nubin, a traveling missionary and shouter in the classic gospel tradition known throughout the circuit as "Mother Bell," she was a prodigy, mastering the guitar by the age of six. At the same time she attended Holiness conventions alongside her mother, performing renditions of songs including "The Day Is Past and Gone" and "I Looked Down the Line."

In time the family relocated to Chicago, where Tharpe began honing her unique style; blessed with a resonant vibrato, both her vocal phrasing and guitar style drew heavy inspiration from the blues, and she further aligned herself with the secular world with a sense of showmanship and glamour unique among the gospel performers of her era. Signing to Decca in 1938, Tharpe became a virtual overnight sensation; her first records, among them Rev. Thomas A. Dorsey's "Rock Me" and "This Train," were smash hits, and quickly she was performing in the company of mainstream superstars including Cab Calloway and Benny Goodman. She led an almost schizophrenic existence, remaining in the good graces of her core audience by recording material like "Precious Lord," "Beams of Heaven" and "End of My Journey" while also appealing to her growing white audience by performing rearranged, uptempo spirituals including "Didn't It Rain" and "Down by the Riverside."

During World War II, Tharpe was so popular that she was one of only two black gospel acts—the Golden Gate Quartet being the other—to record V-Discs for American soldiers overseas; she also toured the nation in the company of the Dixie Hummingbirds, among others. In 1944, she began recording with boogie-woogie pianist Sammy Price; their first collaboration, "Strange Things Happening Every Day," even cracked Billboard's race records Top Ten, a rare feat for a gospel act and one which she repeated several more times during the course of her career. In 1946 she teamed with the Newark-based Sanc-

tified shouter Madame Marie Knight, whose simple, unaffected vocals made her the perfect counterpoint for Tharpe's theatrics; the duo's first single, "Up Above My Head," was a huge hit, and over the next few years they played to tremendous crowds across the church circuit.

However, in the early '50s Tharpe and Knight cut a handful of straight blues sides; their fans were outraged, and although Knight soon made a permanent leap into secular music—to little success—Tharpe remained first and foremost a gospel artist, although her credibility and popularity were seriously damaged. Not only did her record sales drop off and her live engagements become fewer and farther between, but many purists took Tharpe's foray into the mainstream as a personal affront; the situation did not improve, and she spent over a year touring clubs in Europe, waiting for the controversy to die down. Tharpe's comeback was slow but steady, and by 1960 she had returned far enough into the audience's good graces to appear at the Apollo Theatre alongside the Caravans and James Cleveland. While not a household name like before, she continued touring even after suffering a major stroke in 1970, dying in Philadelphia on October 9, 1973. —*Jason Ankeny*

Gospel 1938–1943 / 1938-1943 / Frémeaux & Associés ✦✦✦✦

Sacred & Secular / 1941-1969 / Rosetta ✦✦✦✦✦
Sacred & Secular is a wonderful collection of 16 tracks that Sister Rosetta Tharpe recorded between 1941 and 1969. Although she recorded both sacred and secular material as the title indicates, this collection favors religious music. All the music here features Tharpe supported by a band, ranging from an orchestra conducted by Leroy Kirkland to small combos led by Lucky Millinder and Sam Price. While many critics and fans prefer Tharpe's solo performances—only one solo performance, a live cut from 1969, is present—these group sessions offer ample proof that Tharpe is compelling in nearly any setting. —*Thom Owens*

Sister Rosetta Tharpe/The Sam Price Trio / 1958 / Decca ✦✦✦✦✦
Fine singing and excellent blues-laden guitar playing; circa 1944-1949. —*Opal Louis Nations*

Live in 1960 / 1960 / Southland ✦✦✦
Sister Rosetta Tharpe was a talented jazz guitarist and vocalist who, although she spent most of her later years finding fame as a gospel singer, never turned her back on her jazz roots. On this 1991 CD taken from a previously unreleased European concert, Tharpe is heard solo, entertaining and uplifting the audience. Although there are a few more ballads than usual, the set has plenty of variety, lots of sincere feeling, and high levels of musicianship from the unique performer. Highlights include "He's Got the Whole World in His Hands," "Didn't It Rain," "The Gospel Train," and "Down by the Riverside." —*Scott Yanow*

Gospel Train, Vol. 2 / 1960 / Lection ✦✦✦
This was recorded later than the material on *Vol. 1*, some of Sister Rosetta's worst, most-overproduced recordings. —*Opal Louis Nations*

Live in Paris: 1964 / 1964 / French Concerts ✦✦✦
A nice, rather folk-like concert performance in front of an enthusiastic audience. —*Kip Lornell*

Live at the Hot Club de France / 1966 / Milan ✦✦✦
Live at the Hot Club de France was recorded in 1966. At first, Sister Rosetta Tharpe seems a little uneasy in front of the French audience, but she soon loosens up, tearing through a set of spiritual standards (plus a handful of originals). There isn't much guitar on the record, but Tharpe's impassioned voice makes this a concert worth hearing. —*Thom Owens*

Gospel Train / 1989 / Polygram ✦✦✦✦✦
Super collection of the gal's best Mercury sides, circa 1956. —*Opal Louis Nations*

Sincerely, Sister Rosetta Tharpe / 1992 / Rosetta ✦✦✦
Boasting such classic numbers as "Down by the Riverside," "Swing Low (Sweet Chariot)" and "Sometimes I Feel Like a Motherless Child," *Sincerely, Sister Rosetta Tharpe* is a collection of material the seminal gospel singer recorded in the '40s. Although it's not comprehensive, it's one of the best samplings of its kind in existence. —*Thom Owens*

★ **Complete Recorded Works, Vol. 1 (1938–1941)** / Feb. 20, 1996 / Document ✦✦✦✦
Sister Rosetta Tharpe was an exciting performer and one of the first singers to bring the power of gospel music into the secular world, predating Ray Charles and Aretha Franklin by quite a few years. Unlike those two, Tharpe's main loyalty remained religious music, although her acoustic guitar playing was jazz-oriented, and she spent 1941-1943 being featured regularly with Lucky Millinder's Orchestra before returning to work as a solo performer. This Document CD has Tharpe's first 26 recordings. The first 14 numbers are from her unaccompanied solo dates of 1938-1941, and despite the similar message of most of the selections, they do hold one's interest due to her exciting delivery. Highlights include her earliest versions of "Rock Me," "That's All," "The Lonesome Road," and "This Train." Next up are eight songs cut with Millinder's big band: five studio numbers (including "Trouble in Mind," "Rock Daniel," "Shout Sister Shout," and "That's All") and three selections taken from the soundtracks of their filmed "Soundies." The CD wraps up with four solo performances from December 1, 1941, including a spirited "Just a Closer Walk With Thee" and "Precious Lord Hold My Hand." This CD and *Vol. 2* (which finds the singer-guitarist finishing her Millinder period and resuming her solo career during 1943-1944) are highly recommended and contain most of the finest work of Sister Rosetta Tharpe's career. —*Scott Yanow*

Complete Recorded Works, Vol. 2 (1942–1944) / Feb. 20, 1996 / Document ✦✦✦✦
The second of two well-packed discs released on the Austrian reissue label Document, Sister Rosetta Tharpe's *Complete Recorded Works, Vol. 2* covers the years of 1942 to 1944, a period during which Tharpe was raising the ire of her religious audience by branching

out into a more secular era. Though in retrospect the sentiments of songs like "I Want a Tall Skinny Papa" seem tame, the outcry was similar to when Sam Cooke went pop in the late '50s: How dare the pop market take away our Sister? It stands to reason; Sister Rosetta Tharpe was gospel's most fiery voice and one of the finest guitarists in any style of her era. (The stabbing, rhythmic lead guitar underpinning these songs sounds like it was probably a huge influence on Chicago blues later that decade.) The passion and vitality of these performances is remarkable, as is the joy Tharpe clearly takes in the physicality of even her most pious recordings. Even for non-believers, this is rich, fulfilling music. The quality of these transfers on the rarer material can be a little rough, but not distractingly so. —*Stewart Mason*

Complete Recorded Works, Vol. 3 / Oct. 14, 1998 / Document ✦✦✦✦

Hans Theessink
b. Apr. 5, 1948, Enschede, Netherlands
Jew's-Harp, Violin, Mandolin, Harmonica, Guitar / Modern Electric Blues, Modern Delta Blues

Dutch blues guitarist, singer, and songwriter Hans Theessink carved a niche for himself in the U.S. market during the late '80s and early '90s. It's no easy task growing up in the Netherlands and teaching oneself the blues, but perhaps that's the reason Theessink's guitar stylings are so unique. Theessink became hooked on blues as a teenager listening to the radio, playing mandolin and guitar. His favorites became Big Bill Broonzy and Sonny Terry & Brownie McGhee, but later on he was exposed to a wider variety of influences. Theessink was 12 or 13 when he began playing guitar in earnest, and by his late teens he was playing in clubs and coffeehouses around Germany and the Netherlands.

Theessink began his recording career in 1970 for a variety of small labels in Netherlands and Germany, and continued perfecting his craft and honing his skills at clubs and festivals across Europe. Through the '70s, his eventual goal was to come to America to learn firsthand from the masters in the Mississippi Delta. It would be 1979 before Theessink would make it to America, and not surprisingly, his first stop was the Mississippi Delta. The trip proved fruitful, as he met and jammed with many Delta musicians, absorbing all he could from them and eventually incorporating their knowledge into his own style.

Theessink's U.S. albums include two albums for Flying Fish/Rounder Records, *Baby Wants to Boogie* (1987) and *Johnny and the Devil* (1989). His other domestically available albums for a variety of labels include *Call Me* (1992), *Live* (1993), *Hard Road Blues* (1995), and *Crazy Moon* (1997). —*Richard Skelly*

Next Morning at Sunrise / 1970 / Autogram ✦✦✦✦
Klasselotteriet / 1976 / Rillerod ✦✦✦
Slow and Easy / 1978 / Blue Bird ✦✦✦
Late Last Night / 1980 / Kettle ✦✦✦
Antoon Met 'n Bok / 1981 / Jama ✦✦✦
Cushioned for a Soft Ride Inside / 1982 / Autogram ✦✦✦
Titanic / 1983 / Extraplatte ✦✦✦
All Night Long / 1986 / Extraplatte ✦✦✦
● **Baby Wants to Boogie** / 1987 / Blue Groove ✦✦✦✦✦

Hans Theessink often gets the short end of the stick because he's a Dutch bluesman, which means he couldn't possibly be "legitimate" in the eyes of some critics. That's not really fair, since he's actually an imaginative, unpredictable guitarist. Granted, his albums can sound a little sterile, but that criticism can be applied to most contemporary blues albums. The main problem with his records is that they're interchangeable—all of them sound similar and all of them are about as strong as their predecessor. *Baby Wants to Boogie* isn't particularly different from his other albums, but it does have some good songs and solos, making it as good a place to learn about Theessink as any. —*Thom Owens*

Johnny and the Devil / 1989 / Blue Groove ✦✦✦
Call Me / 1992 / Deluge ✦✦✦
Live / 1993 / Minor Music ✦✦✦✦
Hard Road Blues / May 23, 1995 / Minor Music ✦✦✦✦
Journey On / Apr. 28, 1997 / Minor Music ✦✦✦✦✦

Taking his cues from the '70s output of Ry Cooder, there is nothing in the sound of the Dutch-born and raised Hans Theessink that would indicate he learned his craft from albums and not from being raised in the swamps of Mississippi. His dusky baritone, greasy slide licks, and soulful male backup singers (led by Cooder vet Terry Evans who turns in a stunning performance throughout) plant him firmly into the deep South. The gospel feel of the title track, along with its subtle shuffle beat and rousing yet mellifluous supporting vocalists, sounds as natural as if he spent his entire life soaking up the spirits of the bluesmen he obviously adores. When he and the elegant singers harmonize on "Set Me Free," with pedal steel crying and longtime cohort John Sass' tuba counterpointing the bass, you can almost feel the flies buzzing around your head as you sit beside the banks of the mighty Mississippi. The ghost of Robert Johnson haunts this graceful music, yet the feel is less of the raw Delta blues than of a shimmering, daydream inhabited by the spirits of the swamp. Similar to J.J. Cale, Theessink finds his soul hovering through the backwoods, and with his sympathetic band, he has created an album that is hypnotizing in its intensity. Jaunty covers of Willie Dixon's humorous "29 Ways," Rufus Thomas' classic "Walking the Dog," and Leadbelly's "Bourgeois Blues" all get similar treatment, as Theessink nudges these often-covered tunes into the marsh and mud, wrapping his voice around them and providing interpretations so unique and distinctive it seems he's rewritten the songs. An album-closing solo turn on Muddy Waters' "Feel Like Going Home" is a beautiful, sad coda, as the guitarist takes his time languidly unspooling the track, as

if he's playing at home alone. In fact, the entire disc sounds comfy and cozy, with Theessink secure in his talents and especially those of his remarkable band. This is an artist steeped in the blues, but like Ry Cooder, one who successfully interprets it in his own characteristic fashion, which is what makes *Journey On* so consistently engaging, on so many levels. —*Hal Horowitz*

Crazy Moon / May 27, 1997 / Ruf ✦✦✦

Them
f. 1963, Belfast, Northern Ireland, **db.** 1971, Belfast, Northern Ireland
Group / British Blues, British Invasion, Blues-Rock, Rock & Roll

Not strictly a British group, but packaged as part of the British Invasion, Them forged their hard-nosed R&B sound in Belfast, Ireland, moving to England in 1964 after landing a deal with Decca Records. The band's simmering sound was dominated by boiling organ riffs, lean guitars, and the tough vocals of lead singer Van Morrison, whose recordings with Them rank among the very best performances of the British Invasion. Morrison also wrote top-notch original material for the outfit, whose lineup changed numerous times over the course of their brief existence. As a hit-making act, their resumé was brief—"Here Comes the Night" and "Baby Please Don't Go" were Top Ten hits in England, "Mystic Eyes" and "Here Comes the Night" made the Top 40 in the U.S.—but their influence was considerable, reaching bands like the Doors, who Them played with during a residency in Los Angeles just before Van Morrison quit the band in 1966. Their most influential song of all, the classic three-chord stormer "Gloria," was actually a B-side, although the Shadows of Knight had a hit in the U.S. with a faithful, tamer cover version.

Morrison recalled his days with Them with some bitterness, noting that the heart of the original group was torn out by image-conscious record company politics, and that sessionmen (including Jimmy Page, who played a scorching solo on "Baby Please Don't Go") often replaced members on recordings. In addition to hits, Them released a couple of fine albums and several flop singles that mixed Morrison compositions with R&B and soul covers, as well as a few songs written for them by producers like Bert Berns (who penned "Here Comes the Night"). After Morrison left the group, Them splintered into the Belfast Gypsies, who released an album that (except for the vocals) approximated Them's early records, and a psychedelic outfit that kept the name Them, releasing four LPs with little resemblance to the tough sounds of their mid-'60s heyday. —*Richie Unterberger*

Them / 1965 / Decca ✦✦✦✦✦

The debut album by the group, also known as *The Angry Young Them*, and half its tracks make it a dead-on rival to the Stones' debut album. This reissue features the album's original British configuration ("Just a Little Bit," "I Gave My Love a Diamond," "Bright Lights, Big City," and "My Little Baby" are here; "One Two Brown Eyes" and "Here Comes the Night" are absent). "My Little Baby" was no huge loss, being a pale imitation of "Here Comes the Night," but the omitted "Just a Little Bit" features a Howlin' Wolf/"Spoonful"-style performance by Van Morrison that would have incinerated a lot of American teens. On the other hand, Morrison's soul-shouting performance on the deleted "I Gave My Love a Diamond," appropriated by Bert Berns from the public domain "Cherry Song," would have shocked any folkie familiar with the original. Morrison's "You Just Can't Win" isn't nearly as impressive, but even as a time-filler it isn't half bad. And then there's "Gloria," rock's ultimate '60s sex anthem, and one of the handful of white-authored songs that can just about hold its own against any blues standard you'd care to name. —*Bruce Eder*

Them Again / Apr. 1966 / Deram ✦✦✦

The group's second and, for all intents and purposes, last full album was recorded while Them was in a state of imminent collapse. To this day, nobody knows who played on the album, other than Van Morrison and bassist Alan Henderson, though it is probable that Jimmy Page was seldom very far away when Them was recording. The 16 songs here are a little less focused than the first LP. The material was cut under siege conditions, with a constantly shifting lineup and a grueling tour schedule; essentially, there was no "group" to provide focus to the sound, only Morrison's voice, so the material bounces from a surprisingly restrained "I Put a Spell on You" to the garage-punkoid "I Can Only Give You Everything." Folk-rock rears its head not only on the moody cover of Dylan's "It's All Over Now, Baby Blue" but also the Morrison-authored "My Lonely Sad Eyes," but the main thrust is soul, which Morrison oozes everywhere—while there's some filler, his is a voice that could easily have knocked Mick Jagger or Eric Burdon off their respective perches. —*Bruce Eder*

Backtrackin' / 1974 / London ✦✦✦

This collection of ten tracks from all phases of their career is haphazard, but the material is mostly excellent. Highlights include their blistering raveup of "Baby Please Don't Go" with Jimmy Page on guitar, a Top Ten hit in Britain; the angry cover of Paul Simon's "Richard Cory"; their breakneck version of Slim Harpo's "Don't Start Crying Now," which was their first single in 1964; the great obscure, bluesy Morrison-penned B-side, "All for Myself"; and the vicious cover of the R&B standard "Just a Little Bit." —*Richie Unterberger*

Story of Them / 1977 / London ✦✦✦

Another ragtag compilation of material that somehow hadn't found its way to an American album, this uneven but worthy collection is divided between R&B covers (Jimmy Reed's "Bright Lights, Big City" and Jimmy Witherspoon's "Times Gettin' Tougher Than Tough" are the best) and some good Morrison originals. Of those, the folk-tinged "Philosphy" and "Friday's Child" point to his more expressive solo work, and "The Story of Them" is a rambling, seven-and-a-half-minute autobiographical talking blues about the group's early days. —*Richie Unterberger*

● **Them Featuring Van Morrison** / 1987 / London ✦✦✦✦✦

Not to be confused with the identically titled Parrot Records release, which is a 20-track double-LP set, this is a 13-track single CD set and a U.S. reissue of the Decca U.K. LP from 1982. It would have been less confusing if they had called it *Them's Greatest Hits*, since it is primarily a singles compilation. But then, only four of Them's singles were hits, either in the U.K. or the U.S.—"Baby, Please Don't Go," "Gloria," "Here Comes the Night," and "Mystic Eyes," all included here. Also featured are such non-charting singles as "Don't Start Crying Now," "One More Time," "(It Won't Hurt) Half as Much," and "Richard Cory." This is not the ideal Them compilation, but this is the one that contains Them's most familiar material. *—William Ruhlmann*

The Story of Them Featuring Van Morrison / 1997 / Deram ✦✦✦✦✦

This long-overdue double CD collects all but one of the 50 songs (only "Mighty Like a Rose" is missing) the legendary British blues band left behind in the English Decca and American London vaults. The sound is a significant improvement over prior reissues—really loud, the way it was meant to be heard—with little touches like "The Story of Them Parts 1 and 2" linked together. It doesn't follow chronological order of release, but the order is entertaining, with alternate takes (stereo single mixes, American single edits, etc.) broken up between the two discs. It would have been nice to have had recording dates and personnel, but considering the fact that the band's lineup, apart from Morrison and bassist Alan Henderson, seemed to change every month, it's conceivable that any session information would be suspect. And one wishes for a coherent essay on the history of the band to go with the spread of photographs of the different lineups that are reprinted here. *—Bruce Eder*

Earl Thomas (Earl Thomas Bridgeman)

b. Aug. 29, 1960, Pikeville, TN

Bass / Piano Blues, Modern Electric Blues

Earl Thomas, a 22-year-old dental student, had never picked up a microphone in his life until he was nearly killed after losing his footing at the edge of a 50-foot ravine and slid all the way down, landing unconscious on a pile of broken glass and debris. Luckily, Thomas was only bruised, but not knowing the extent of the damage upon regaining consciousness, he reflected on his disappointment at not having pursued his dream of becoming a singer, and resolved to do just that if he survived. Nine years later, he recorded 1991's *Blue... Not Blues*, a record strongly influenced by his parents' love of blues and gospel music and his own affinity for '60s and '70s soul. His "I Sing the Blues" became a hit for Etta James, and he played European music festivals with such artists as Elvis Costello and B.B. King. His second album, *Extra Soul*, was released in 1994. *—Steve Huey*

● **Blue ... Not Blues** / 1991 / Bizarre/Straight ✦✦✦✦

Earl Thomas' debut album *Blue... Not Blues* blends the sensuality of Stax soul with the grittiness of modern electric blues. Given that Thomas didn't make this album until he had a particularly gruesome brush with death, it may seem a little churlish to point out that some of the songs are underdeveloped, but that's just a sign that it is indeed his debut. The real indication of his talent is the power of his voice and the way his best songs, such as "Nothing Left to Lose" and "The Way She Shakes That Thang," show that he has a knack for crafting memorable contemporary blues songs. That is what makes *Blue... Not Blues* a successful debut. *—Thom Owens*

Extra Soul / 1994 / Bizarre Planet ✦✦✦

Henry Thomas

b. 1874, Big Sandy, TX, **d.** 1930

Vocals, Songwriter, Guitar / Songster, Prewar Country Blues

Texas songster Henry Thomas remains a relative stranger who made some great recordings, then returned to obscurity. Evidence suggests he was an itinerant street musician, a musical hobo who rode the rails across Texas and possibly to the World Fairs in St. Louis and Chicago just before and after the turn of the century. Most agree he was the oldest African-American folk artist to produce a significant body of recordings. His projected 1874 birthdate would predate Charley Patton by a good 17 years. Like Patton and a handful of other musicians generally termed songsters (including John Hurt, Jim Jackson, Mance Lipscomb, Furry Lewis, and Leadbelly), Thomas' repertoire bridged the 19th and 20th centuries, providing a compelling glimpse into a wide range of African-American musical genres. The 23 songs he cut for Vocalion between 1927 and 1929 include a spiritual, ballads, reels, dance songs, and eight selections titled blues. Obviously dance music, his songs were geared to older dance styles shared by black and white audiences.

Thomas' sound, like his repertoire, is unique. He capoed his guitar high up the neck and strummed it in the manner of a banjo, favoring dance rhythm over complex fingerwork. On many of his pieces, he simultaneously played the quills or reed pipes, a common but seldom-recorded African-American folk instrument indigenous to Mississippi, Louisiana, and Texas. Combining the quills, a limited-range melody instrument, with his banjo-like strummed guitar produced one of the most memorable sounds in American folk music. For example, his lead-in on "Bull Doze Blues" still worked as a hook when recycled 40 years later by blues/rockers Canned Heat in their version of "Going Up the Country." "Ragtime Texas," as Thomas was known, provides a welcome inroad to 19th century dance music, but his music is neither obscure nor merely educational: it has a timeless quality—and while it may be an acquired taste, once you catch on to it, you're hooked. *—Barry Lee Pearson*

★ **Texas Worried Blues: Complete Recorded Works 1927–1929** / 1989 / Yazoo ✦✦✦✦✦

These recordings, dating between 1927 and 1929, are a unique body of work: work songs, minstrel numbers, rags, and what we now define as the blues, all offered in an unpretentious form that would have been every bit as compelling had Henry Thomas cut them this way 40 years later. Songs such as "Arkansas," "Fox and the Hounds" (featuring the reed pipes that Thomas also excelled at playing), and "Little Red Caboose" represent a brand of upbeat dance music associated with late-19th century entertainment, a tradition already largely lost or becoming lost when Thomas cut these numbers. Yet Thomas, who was already in his fifties when he recorded these tracks, sings and plays them with a beguiling ease and honesty, not to mention a dexterity on the guitar that makes him sound every bit as vital and urgent as Big Bill Broonzy or any of the other up and coming blues legends just starting out at the time these sides were laid down. The blues numbers, including "Shanty Blues," "Woodhouse Blues," "Honey, Won't You Allow Me One More Chance?," and "Bull Doze Blues" are compelling in their own right—they display musical and lyrical virtuosity and, in the latter two cases, offer a chance to hear the sources for classic works by Bob Dylan and Canned Heat, respectively. Luckily for historians, Henry Thomas recorded for Vocalion and not for one of the truly lost labels like Paramount, and all 23 surviving sides of his work sound very good on this CD. *—Bruce Eder*

Sings the Texas Blues / 1991 / Origin ✦✦✦✦✦

☆ **Ragtime Texas: 1927–1929** / Oct. 17, 2000 / Document ✦✦✦✦✦

Many versions of "John Henry" exist, but Henry Thomas' version, because of his use of reeds, is unique. The reeds have a light, radiant air that lifts this song to something joyous. Thomas was born in Texas in 1874 and didn't record his first sessions until he was in his early fifties. His music incorporated blues and patched together songs ("rags") that seemed to come from earlier traditions, including nine pieces on which he uses reeds. The use of them may point to an earlier African-American tradition that had nearly vanished by the time he was recording. These pieces represent the best songs on this collection, with standouts like "The Little Red Caboose" and "Bull-Doze Blues." The later song sounds very similar to Canned Heat's "Goin' Up the Country," including the reed solo that sets the song in motion. Songs like "Don't Ease Me In," would later be performed by the Grateful Dead and many others, while "Honey, Won't You Allow Me One More Chance?" is lyrically related to an early Bob Dylan song with almost the same title. The songs gathered here have been taken from five recording sessions between 1927 and 1929, and are ordered chronologically. The liner notes explain the origins of reeds/quills in African-American music, and help place Thomas in a historical context. The fidelity on certain cuts is scratchy, but his voice and instrumentation are still always discernable. This is a good collection of an early-Texas songster, especially valuable because of Thomas' unique use of reeds. *—Ronnie Lankford, Jr.*

Hociel Thomas

b. Jul. 10, 1904, Houston, TX, **d.** Aug. 22, 1952, Oakland, CA

Vocals, Piano / Piano Blues

Singer and pianist Hociel Thomas (married name "Tebo") was a member of the Houston, Texas-based Thomas family. Her father was George W. Thomas, who made the first boogie-woogie solo on records, "The Rocks," for OKeh in October, 1923. Hociel Thomas' nephew was pianist and bandleader Hersal Thomas, composer of the popular "Suitcase Blues." Hociel Thomas' aunt was blues legend Sippie Wallace. You might conclude that her fortune would have been easily made, given her royal family connections. On the contrary, her career was marked by unimaginable personal tragedies and her work is preserved on only 22 recordings, most of which are mainly remembered on account of the musicians who worked with her.

Hociel Thomas relocated from Houston, TX, at about the age of 12 to live with Sippie Wallace in New Orleans. There she made a living as a singer and pianist in the Storyville redlight district until it closed, then afterward worked private parties and the summer resorts, often in combination with Wallace. Wallace resettled in Chicago in 1923, and it is assumed that Hociel Thomas followed her there about a year later. Thomas made her first three records for Gennett in their Richmond, IN, studio on April 6, 1925, backed by a small band led by her nephew, Hersal Thomas. The following month, two more sides were made with Hociel and Hersal on piano for OKeh, and the tune "Worried Down With the Blues" was a small-scale hit, and OKeh asked for more.

For their next session, held on November 11, 1925, Hersal Thomas managed to bring in Louis Armstrong, recently returned from New York to Chicago, and reunited him with clarinetist Johnny Dodds, his old bandmate from King Oliver's Creole Jazz Band. Adding banjoist Johnny St. Cyr, the group resembled Louis Armstrong's pivotal group the Hot Five, and it should—the first Hot Five session was held the following day on November 12, adding Kid Ory and replacing Hersal Thomas with Lil Hardin Armstrong. Altogether "Louis Armstrong's Jazz Four" made six records backing up Hociel Thomas, and these are currently included along with the rest of Armstrong's "Hot" records on *The Complete Hot Five and Hot Seven Recordings* issued on Columbia/Legacy. Armstrong, as was his wont, returned the favor on February 24, 1926, by providing the obbligato on four more sides with the Thomases, and it was on these that Hociel Thomas was heard to her best advantage among her early recordings.

Hersal Thomas perished of food poisoning later in 1926; he was only 20 years old. This sad development was devastating to Hociel Thomas and Sippie Wallace, yet both attempted to move on with their careers. But while Sippie managed to keep things going, even after moving to Detroit and taking up work in sacred music, Hociel ultimately drifted away from music. She was discovered living in Oakland after World War II, and recorded seven more tunes, her last, for Circle Records with New Orleans trumpeter Mutt Carey (these were later reissued on Riverside and on American Music). They are the best recordings that Thomas made, and are the only ones on which she provides her own, fine piano accompaniment. "Tebo's Texas Boogie" is a great example of primordial Texas boogie-woogie, and the only example of her boogie piano playing left. Hociel Thomas is often cited as an annoyance in her early recordings with Armstrong, and admittedly she sounds weak on songs like "Sunshine Baby," which is played in a key that is too low-lying for her voice. Nothing in the Circle session suggests this problem; her singing throughout is rich and soulful, and suggests the presence of a master blues singer.

In the later '40s Hociel Thomas was not recorded again, but did continue to perform with Kid Ory's band in the San Francisco area. In 1948, Thomas got into a knockdown, drag-out fight with one of her sisters, during which Hociel was blinded and the sister was killed. After a lengthy incarceration and trial she was acquitted of manslaughter charges, but barely two years later, totally blind and badly overweight, Hociel Thomas died of heart disease at the age of 48. *—Uncle Dave Lewis*

● **1925–1928** / May 21, 1996 / Document ✦✦✦✦

Irma Thomas

b. Feb. 18, 1941, Ponchatoula, LA

Vocals / New Orleans R&B, Soul

Radiating an outgoing joy that's inevitably at the heart of her infectious vocal delivery, Irma Thomas has no rivals as the Soul Queen of New Orleans. Working at a Crescent City nightery as a waitress in 1959, Thomas sat in one night with Tommy Ridgley's band and made such a favorable impression that the veteran bandleader hustled her into the studio shortly thereafter to wax her first hit for the Ron label, the driving "Don't Mess with My Man." She joined forces with producer Allen Toussaint to make some of her most moving outings for Minit Records during the early '60s, notably "It's Raining," "Ruler of My Heart," and "Cry On," before venturing to the West Coast, where she cut both her biggest seller, the lushly produced "Wish Someone Would Care," and her best-known song, the original "Time Is on My Side"—and she's still bitter enough about the Rolling Stones' cover stealing her thunder to discourage requests for the tune.

The highly adaptable chanteuse also made some sizzling soul at Rich Hall's Muscle Shoals studio for Chess in the summer of 1967 before cooling off for a while during the '70s. But she came back, as radiant as ever—and for convincing proof, listen to her buoyant 1990 concert performance captured on Rounder's *Live! Simply the Best*. Now that's truth in packaging!

Irma Thomas finally fulfilled a lifelong ambition in 1993 by recording her first gospel release. *Walk Around Heaven* was as magnificently sung and emotionally convincing as any of her classic New Orleans soul cuts. Thomas followed the album in 1997 with *The Story of My Life*, which featured several songs written by Dan Penn. She continued this trend with 2000's *My Heart's in Memphis: The Songs of Dan Penn. —Bill Dahl*

Wish Someone Would Care / 1964 / Imperial ✦✦✦✦✦

Irma Thomas has been New Orleans' reigning soul queen since the early '60s, and this landmark album was her most stunning and complete session. It didn't make her a national star, but it showed vulnerability as captivating as lust, anger or pain. Thomas' voice seemed deliberately frail at times, but she made "Time Is on My Side" and "I Wish Someone Would Care," remarkable triumphs. There were many other fine songs, such as "I Need Your Love So Bad," "Please Send Me Someone to Love" and "Break-A-Way." It remains one of the greatest soul albums ever recorded. —*Ron Wynn*

Take a Look / 1968 / Imperial ✦✦✦

The songs from Irma Thomas' Imperial sessions are timeless and magnificent; they've also been constantly reissued and are available all over the place. That reduces the value of this anthology, one of two that were issued featuring her Imperial cuts. Every significant song from both of these releases has subsequently been compiled and issued on the EMI domestic CD package. —*Ron Wynn*

Hip Shakin' Mama / 1981 / Charly ✦✦✦

A popular title for an album, Ruby Andrews put out her own *Hip Shakin' Mama* collection in 1998. This is one of many Irma Thomas CDs on the market. The queen of New Orleans soul's fans have a bevy of CDs to choose from. It's a staggering list that grows every year. Charly cut to the chase with this ten-song package—and left out some big hits. But they did include morsels like "You Can Have My Husband"; Labelle's "Lady Marmalade"; "I Done Got Over It," which is as southern as grits and gravy; "Cry, Cry"; and "Ruler of My Heart." —*Andrew Hamilton*

Safe With Me / May 1981 / Paula ✦

Time Is on My Side / 1983 / Kent ✦✦✦✦✦

A solid 16-song compilation of material from the mid-'60s. Most of this is duplicated by the more extensive CD compilations of the same era on EMI and Razor & Tie. But it's not entirely superfluous; five of the songs don't appear on either of the other collections. Those tracks are worth hearing, particularly the gutsy soul-pop concoction "Baby Don't Look Down," one of Randy Newman's earliest compositions. —*Richie Unterberger*

The New Rules / 1986 / Rounder ✦✦✦

Irma Thomas balanced classic and contemporary sensibilities on this 1986 album. She did such songs as "Gonna Cry 'Til My Tears Run Dry" and "I Gave You Everything" from the '60s, and also did more recent tunes, such as the title track and a good remake of "The Wind Beneath My Wings (Hero)." In the 1980s, there was little interest at urban contemporary stations in older, more soulful artists, and thus this worthy session got almost no attention outside New Orleans and the South. However, Irma Thomas can still sing with authority and quality. —*Ron Wynn*

The Way I Feel / 1988 / Rounder ✦✦✦✦✦

Irma Thomas deserves hits and wider exposure more than almost any other R&B vocalist you could name. While the material on this album was uneven, she retained her credibility regardless. It took real guts to cover "Dancing in the Street" and "Baby I Love You," and even more talent not to be subsumed by their history. She's vibrant on "Old Records," hard-hitting on "You Don't Know Nothin' About Love," and poignant on "Sorry Wrong Number," "Sit Down and Cry," and "I'll Take Care of You." —*Ron Wynn*

Ruler of Hearts / 1989 / Charly ✦✦✦

Sides from her early-'60s Minit sessions. The most New Orleans R&B-influenced of Thomas' early work, it includes "Cry On," "It's Raining," and "Ruler of My Heart," as well as lesser-known but equally moving cuts like "Two Winters Long" and "It's Too Soon to Know." —*Richie Unterberger*

Something Good: Muscle Shoals / 1990 / Chess ✦✦✦✦✦

Thomas' brief liaison with Chess in 1967 saw her, like labelmates Laura Lee and Etta James, record in Muscle Shoals' Fame studios to tap into the southern/deep soul grooves that were one of the hottest tickets in soul music at the time. Commercially, these sessions (all recorded in June and July of '67) weren't a success. It's also fair to say that they don't rate as her finest work of the '60s; her early New Orleans sessions, along with her

pop/rock sides of the mid-'60s, featured both stronger material and more suitable accompaniment. That's hardly a knock, though; these were solid soul performances paced by Thomas' habitual excellent, committed vocals. But there's a bit of a generic Stax/Volt feel, and not much of the material (which features several compositions by Otis Redding and the Spooner Oldham-Dan Penn team) leaps out and grabs you. It's still worth finding if you're an Irma fan, with 14 tracks that include several Chess singles and nine songs recorded for an unreleased LP that were previously unavailable in the United States. —*Richie Unterberger*

Live! Simply the Best / 1991 / Rounder ✦✦✦✦✦

Irma Thomas has long been an institution in New Orleans-based R&B. This live CD is both a strong introduction to her powerful voice and a summation of her career up to 1990, mixing together remakes of some of her mid-'60s recordings with more current material. Cheered on by an enthusiastic crowd, Irma Thomas sounds inspired and in her prime for the consistently passionate set. Of the highlights, "Hip Shakin' Mama" is a humorous blues, "I Needed Somebody" is especially soulful (if overly repetitive near its conclusion), "It's Raining" is memorable and the "Second Line Medley" effectively mixes in a touch of Dixieland with R&B. An excellent introduction to the talented Irma Thomas. —*Scott Yanow*

★ **Time Is on My Side: The Best of Irma Thomas, Vol. 1** / Apr. 21, 1992 / EMI America ✦✦✦✦✦

Here are 23 sides representing the cream of Irma Thomas' brilliant Minit/Liberty years (1961-1966), when her reputation as "The Soul Queen of New Orleans" was built. Virtually all her best-known tunes are here—"Wish Someone Would Care," "Ruler of My Heart," "It's Raining," and "Time Is on My Side" (covered note-for-note by The Stones). Beautiful singing from one of the first ladies of soul music. Essential. —*Christine Ohlman*

True Believer / Jun. 1992 / Rounder ✦✦✦✦✦

Like her first two efforts for Rounder, *True Believer* is a stellar collection of contemporary soul performed in the classic '50s New Orleans tradition. The difference is in conception. *True Believer* focuses on heartbreak songs, and there is genuine anguish in Irma Thomas' voice, making new songs by the likes of Dan Penn, Dr. John, Tony Joe White, Allen Toussaint, and Doc Pomus sound like instant classics. Another excellent effort from a woman who has plenty to her credit. —*Thom Owens*

Walk Around Heaven: New Orleans Gospel Soul / Oct. 1993 / Rounder ✦✦✦

During R&B's glory years—the '50s, '60s and '70s—the African-American church provided one great singer after another. Church choirs served as a magnificent training ground for so many of the great soul shouters, and it clearly had a positive effect on Irma Thomas (arguably the greatest female soul singer to come out of New Orleans). At 52, Thomas celebrated her gospel heritage with this solid, heartfelt CD. Thomas' voice had held up quite well since the '60s, and she brings an impressive range and a seemingly endless supply of emotion to songs like "Where We'll Never Grow Old," "Ask What You Will," and "Careful Hands." *Walk Around Heaven* reminds us that as impressive as her contributions to secular soul have been, Thomas hasn't forgotten the church. —*Alex Henderson*

Sweet Soul Queen of New Orleans: The Irma Thomas Collection / Feb. 20, 1996 / Razor & Tie ✦✦✦✦

23-track collection of early and mid-'60s sides largely duplicates the material on EMI's *Time Is on My Side* collection, with some additions and subtractions. The EMI set has a very slight edge, though for most listeners either compilation will do the job. It's too bad somebody doesn't take the plunge and issue an 80-minute CD documenting this era; as it is, serious Irma fans will need to get each best-of, as each contains tracks not on the other. —*Richie Unterberger*

The Story of My Life / Feb. 11, 1997 / Rounder ✦✦✦✦

The Story of My Life stands out among latter-day Irma Thomas albums not only because she gives a consistently excellent performance, but because the record boasts three new songs from Dan Penn, who wrote some of the greatest soul songs of the '60s. While his new songs ("Hold Me While I Cry," "I Count the Teardrops," "I Won't Cry for You") aren't quite as strong as his best, they are nevertheless wonderful contemporary soul numbers, and they help make the record, the remainder of which is comprised of covers and slightly weaker new numbers, one of Thomas' best latter-day albums. —*Stephen Thomas Erlewine*

My Heart's in Memphis: The Songs of Dan Penn / Aug. 8, 2000 / Rounder ✦✦✦

Dan Penn is one of the great Southern soul songwriters, and Irma Thomas is one of the great soul singers, so devoting an entire album to Penn songs was a good idea. Actually, Penn didn't so much write the material as co-write it; he composed every track with one or more co-writers, with Thomas herself getting in on the act on a couple. Four of the 13 tunes are actually interpretations of songs that have been around for a long time (such as "I'm Your Puppet" and "Woman Left Lonely"), but otherwise they were done specifically for this album. So is the result godhead? No, though it's OK. Thomas sings very well—it's been pretty rare that she *hasn't* sung well, on anything—and has a good sense of staying within herself where a lot of singers would over-emote, as on "If You Want It, Come and Get It." Recorded in Memphis (noted frequent Penn associate Spooner Oldham plays keyboards on several cuts), there's a laid-back modern soul feel that gets too laid back at times and not fiery on enough occasions. It's respectable modern soul, slicker than purists would like, but not annoyingly so. The newly written songs are alright, but again not amazing. Thomas' vocals are the highlight, as they should be. —*Richie Unterberger*

If You Want It, Come and Get It / Apr. 10, 2001 / Rounder ✦✦✦✦✦

It's a crime that soul singer Irma Thomas isn't a household name. Her recordings for the Minit and Chess labels in the '60s and '70s remain classics of the genre, and one of her compositions, the torchy "Time Is on My Side," was a big hit for a young British band called the Rolling Stones. She took some time off to raise a family, but came back on the scene in the late '70s, and in 1984 she teamed up with producer Scott Billington to make a series of albums for the Rounder label. The songs collected here were all recorded between 1985 and 1999, and all but one were previously released on those earlier albums. Thomas' singing style and the playing of her various backing musicians is so consistent, though, that it's almost impossible to tell which tracks were recorded when; every one partakes of that joyful mix of New Orleans steam and chugging Memphis soul that has become her trademark. The songs are all classics—the Dan Penn composition "If You Want It, Come and Get It," Paul Kelly's "The New Rules," Doc Pomus and Dr. John's "I Never Fool Nobody but Me." And there's even a gospel tune, the exuberant "Yield Not to Temptation" (with backing vocals by Marcia Ball and Tracy Nelson). Any fan of soul music ought to own all of the albums from which this collection was taken, but this disc is a good place to start. *—Rick Anderson*

James "Son" Thomas

b. Oct. 14, 1926, Eden, MS, **d.** Jun. 26, 1993, Greenville, MS
Vocals, Guitar / Delta Blues
One of the last great traditional Delta blues musicians, James "Son" Thomas style conveyed the power, earnesty and integrity of masterful country artists like Arthur "Big Boy" Crudup. Thomas grew up on a farm in Mississippi and played in juke joints and barrelhouses before he began recording in the late '60s. He appeared in the films *Delta Blues Singer: James "Sonny Ford" Thomas* in 1970 and *Give My Poor Heart Ease: Mississippi Delta Bluesmen* in 1975, plus the short *Mississippi Delta Blues* in 1974. Thomas also made festival appearances in the '70s and '80s. He recorded for Transatlantic, Matchbox, Southern Folklore, and regional labels in the '60s, '70s, and '80s. *—Ron Wynn*

• **Son Thomas: Son Down on the Delta** / 1981 / Flying High ♦♦♦♦♦
Son Thomas: Son Down on the Delta is a very good live album recorded in Fort Worth, TX, in 1981. Thomas largely sticks to standards here, but the reason to listen to him is the subtle textures of his guitar and voice, which make these well-known songs come alive. *—Thom Owens*

Beefsteak Blues / Jun. 23, 1998 / Evidence ♦♦♦♦
Down-and-dirty blues don't get any downer or dirtier than James "Son" Thomas. A former sharecropper and grave digger (as well as an accomplished sculptor) who was shot by an ex-wife, Thomas, to put it mildly, lived the blues life he sang about. Eventually his hard road took him all the way to the White House, where he sang the blues for the Reagans (those noted blues lovers) in 1982. This Evidence collection of early-'80s performances features Thomas accompanying himself on acoustic and electric guitar on a set of blues standards associated with his Mississippi Delta mentors Elmore James, Arthur "Big Boy" Crudup, and Sonny Boy Williamson. Compare the two versions of "Catfish Blues" for an example of what "unexpurgated" really means. *—Joel Roberts*

Mississippi Delta Bluesman / Jul. 10, 2001 / Swingmaster ♦♦♦

Jesse Thomas

b. Feb. 3, 1911, Logansport, LA., **d.** 1995
Vocals, Guitar / Acoustic Texas Blues, Electric Texas Blues
The brother of Texas bluesman Willard "Ramblin'" Thomas, Jesse "Babyface" Thomas never had the success of his more famous sibling. He moved to Dallas in 1929, when Blind Lemon Jefferson and Lonnie Johnson were in their heyday, and tried to establish himself but found little success in recording despite work for numerous labels right up through the '40s. His early acoustic playing was heavily influenced by Lonnie Johnson and Blind Blake, but he later developed a style of his own. Unlike his older brother, Babyface Thomas was not a slide player. He also tended to write and sing about more upbeat and romantic subjects than Ramblin' Thomas. He favored a highly rhythmic and animated style on his instrument—he also lasted into the electric blues era, and he could make some brilliant amplified dance music—"Double Do Love You" could recall T-Bone Walker at his best, and anticipates the work of Chuck Berry by several years. During the '60s, after moving back to Shreveport, LA, he did some soul-styled recordings for his own label, which failed to find an audience. *—Bruce Eder*

Complete Recorded Works 1948–1958 / Jun. 2, 1994 / Document ♦♦♦

• **Dallas Blues Before 1950** / 1995 / Collectables ♦♦♦♦
Ramblin' Thomas is the better known artist on this 16 song collection, but Babyface Thomas has eight songs featured, recorded for the Houston-based Freedom label in 1949. His music is more upbeat and playful than that of Ramblin' Thomas, with no slide playing, but a very nimble technique. The strangest cut here is "Good Night," a distinctly non-blues romantic number that features a whistled, bird-like accompaniment on the break and a harmony accompaniment. "Same Old Stuff" boasts a rippling guitar part, and is clearly in a more modern Texas blues style, evoking images of T-Bone Walker, while "Double Do Love You" anticipates images of Chuck Berry (especially his "Guitar Boogie"), and two more tracks are in a big-band blues idiom, complete with saxes. There's lots more Babyface Thomas out there, making these eight songs a decent if unambitious introduction to his music. *—Bruce Eder*

Lookin' for That Woman / Feb. 1996 / Black Top ♦♦♦

Easy in the Apple / Jun. 6, 2000 / Fedora ♦♦♦

Blues Is a Feeling / 2001 / Delmark ♦♦♦
Although Jesse "Babyface" Thomas never received as much attention as he deserved to, the country bluesman continued to perform and record during the final years of his life. Thomas was 81 when he recorded *Blues Is a Feeling*, a 1992 session that wasn't actually released until 2001. This CD was recorded three years before his death, and it was also recorded during a visit to Chicago in June 1992 (when he was in town to perform at the Chicago Blues Festival). At 81, Thomas didn't have the vocal power he once did—his voice had grown frail, withered, and thin. But, despite those limitations, Thomas still had charisma, and he was still capable of providing a meaningful album. *Blue Is a Feeling* isn't in a class with his best work, although it is a decent effort that thrives on simplicity and rawness. Nothing elaborate is heard on this CD; the performances have a loose, informal quality, and the singer/acoustic guitarist's only accompaniment consists of fellow guitarist John Primer and acoustic pianist Jodie Christian. There are no drums or bass, which turns out to be a good thing, as Thomas is well served by minimalism. Those who are familiar with Christian's background will tell you that he is primarily a jazz improviser, not a blues artist. But he has no problem rising to the occasion on this CD. In fact, Christian fits right in because Thomas had a slightly jazz-influenced approach to country blues—that was one of the things he had in common with Lonnie Johnson. *Blue Is a Feeling* isn't among Thomas' essential releases, but it's a CD that his hardcore fans will enjoy. *—Alex Henderson*

Kid Thomas (Louis Thomas Watts)

b. Jun. 20, 1934, Sturgis, Mississippi, **d.** Apr. 12, 1970, Beverly Hills, California
Vocals, Harmonica / Harmonica Blues, Rock & Roll
Kid Thomas, aka Tommy Louis, aka Tommy Lewis, was and is one of the great unsung heroes of that crazy kind of music that skirts the fine line between blues and straight-out rock & roll. Though success constantly eluded him throughout his career, it wasn't for lack of talent. With a powerful voice that could emit banshee wails and Little Richard howls with consummate ease, and a harmonica style that, at his best ("Rockin' This Joint Tonight"), sounded like Little Walter powered by a vacuum cleaner, Kid Thomas was a man who knew how to rock the joint, indeed.

He was born Louis Thomas Watts on June 20, 1934, in Sturgis, MS. About seven years later, his parents, Virgie and VT, moved the family up to Chicago. By the time young Louis reached street-wise, teenage manhood, he was taking harmonica lessons from Little Willie Smith, one of the many peripheral bluesmen on the Chicago scene, in exchange for giving Smith lessons on the drums, the Kid's original instrument.

The late '40s and early '50s found him semi-gainfully employed blowing harp at Cadillac Babys and a dozen other clubs whose names are now lost to the mists of time. According to all accounts, he appears to have sat in with everybody at one time or another during the early to mid-'50s; Muddy Waters, Elmore James, and Bo Diddley all welcomed him on-stage on a regular basis, while Thomas found himself even deputizing for his harmonica hero Little Walter on the not-so-odd occasion when said hero was too drunk to make it up to the bandstand.

By 1955, Kid Thomas decided he needed to make a record to help promote his club appearances. Walking by the King-Federal distributors one day, he simply poked his head and announced that he'd like to record. As luck would have it, he was immediately introduced to Ralph Bass, then working for Syd Nathan's label conglomerate as an A&R man. Bass listened to Thomas spiel, then sent him off with instructions to put a band together and come back for a demo session. Deputizing Smith on drums, a guitarist only remembered as "James," and an unknown piano man, our hero headed back for the audition loaded down with tunes he had been working up on his gigs. In his only known interview, conducted in 1969 by Darryl Stolper, Thomas remembered that first session that led to his first record being issued: "The first few numbers didn't go over, so I started thinking about the (Howlin') Wolf, and I came up with 'Wolf Pack.' And 'The Spell' I got from Screamin' Jay Hawkins. Both of them were thought up on the spur of the moment, and Ralph Bass dug them." Rather than have Thomas come back in and do a formal session, Bass was so taken with the results of the Kid's ad-lib compositions, that the results were duly pressed up as Federal single 12298.

After several months of pounding the pavement trying to promote the single, Thomas came to face the cold, hard reality that having a record out and having a hit record out are two very different things. One day, while munching down on the $1.98 chicken special at a local Chicago diner, our hero struck up a conversation with a couple of guys who had just hitchhiked into town from Wichita, KS. After asking where the best live music was in town, Kid invited them down to a band rehearsal at Cadillac Babys. The two transients in question were duly blown away and pumped much wind up Thomas' skirt by telling him how well the show would go over in their home town. A few weeks later, the Kid received a letter from them, informing him they had him booked at a place called the Sportsman's Lounge. Thomas, possessing no transportation to make the trip, hit upon what someone with a million dollars worth of talent and no bankroll would conceive as a good idea…

"At that time, I was doing some light work for a minister, and he had a '49 Buick. I didn't have a car, so I waited until he was asleep and I told my guitarist to ease the car out,'cause if he woke up, he'd recognize me. So he starts up the car and bangs it into the car behind him, and the one in front. But he finally got it out, and we made it to Wichita." In a classic case of karma coming back with a vengeance, the Kid made it to Wichita, only to have his band immediately break up, and split to Tennessee in the heisted automobile! "When I got back (to Chicago), the minister asked me what happened to his car. I told him I hadn't any idea. He told me, 'Thats funny, 'cause it disappeared the same night you did'."

About a month later, Thomas tried the trip to Wichita again, this time with a new band and a newly decorated, but very beat-up, 1947 DeSoto station wagon with bald tires. After a treacherous ride through the Ozark Mountains, they made it to the gig and proceeded to set up. In an effort to class up the DeSoto into something resembling a touring band vehicle, the Kid had painted his name all over it. As the crowd began to swell on opening night, Thomas' drummer mentioned that everyone was stopping to look at the car on the way in. It seems that our hero had spelled his first name correctly, but left the "o" out of Thomas, thus rendering the pronunciation of it to something close to "Kid Thumbass!!" No wonder they were curious.

Botched self-promotion aside, Thomas found his new confines much to his liking. He ran into Hound Dog Taylor there (!), and the two Chicago expatriates played some dates together in early 1956. But after crowning his head with a pompadour processed hair-do that reached higher than most buildings in the city (check out the cover photo; izzat some hair or what?!?), the Kid was soon cashing in on the newly emerging rock & roll craze as an aces-up Little Richard impersonator. Thomas was good enough at it ("I had a big set of hair and some slick outfits") that some of the locals even mistook him for Little Richard, a mistake that would be rectified one afternoon when the Real Thing came to town: "I was in the lobby of the hotel where I was staying, and here's this little guy with a big set of hair like mine, and I'm looking at him and he's looking at me; I went over and said 'my name is Kid Thomas,' and he said 'my name is Little Richard, very pleased to meet you.' That night he came to watch me play and I did some B.B. King numbers that really knocked him out."

Thomas drifted about for the next three or four years, working the low-end of the Chicago club circuit, ocassionally landing a double booking with Magic Sam or Otis Rush. With no further recording prospects on hand, our hero headed out West, working a couple of clubs in Wichita again until 1958, when he pulled up stakes to Denver, before finally settling in Los Angeles sometime in late 1958 or the first part of 1959.

By the next year, Thomas hooked up with legendary record man George Mottola. Mottola, one of the great unsung heroes of the early days of rock & roll, was still working his regular gig as A&R man for Modern Records, producing acts like Jesse Belvin and writing hits like "Goodnight, My Love." But the Kid's powerhouse act apparently bowled him over. Studio time was duly booked, and Thomas, backed by a two guitars/drums/no bass combo, recorded the first version of the eerie slow blues howler "You Are an Angel," and what remains his finest moment, the utterly berserk "Rockin' This Joint Tonight." When Mottola became too busy to do anything with the record, he pointed the Kid in the direction of one Brad Atwood, who promptly took one-half writers credit and issued it on his TRC-Transcontinental label. But just as Thomas was all set to do some television appearances and start promoting the record, Atwood got into some unspecified problems and the label folded.

Another five years of club dates blew by before Kid Thomas entered a studio to record again. Now working under the name of Tommy Louis & the Rhythm Rockers, he recorded a pair of singles for the Los Angeles-based Muriel label. The first release, coupling "The Hurt Is On" with "I Love You So," got little to no airplay in California, but did some brisk business in the Southern states without any promotion behind it. The second single, combined the storming "Wail Baby Wail" with the shuffle stomp of "Lookie There." Though "Wail" was firmly in the Little Richard mold of "Rockin This Joint Tonight," and featured deranged guitar work courtesy of Thomas regular axeman Marshall Hooks, the record sank without a trace.

By the late '60s, our hero was working everything from low-rent beer joints to private parties (one of these finding him employed by Dean Martin!). While working one of his mainstays, the Cozy Lounge in South East Los Angeles, the owner of Cenco Records caught the act and signed him to the label. With Lloyd Glenn on piano and Joe Bennett from the Rhythm Rockers on guitar, Kid Thomas entered a recording studio for one last time and recorded a new version of "(You Are An) Angel" and an instrumental tip of the hat to his home neighborhood, "Willowbrook." By the time anybody knew about it in the blues community, the label was out of business.

By the time blues researcher Darryl Stolper tracked him down for an interview late in 1969, Thomas was sounding a lot more grizzled than his 35 years would lead you to believe: "I would love to go to England and do some records. It seems as if I have to work over there before I can be a hit over here, and I hear the people over there really dig the blues. Over here, someone will tell me I gotta do soul stuff . . . hell, I'm a blues singer, and my harp is my life, and my image or style isn't going to be changed for anybody. I'm Kid Thomas, the blues singer, like it or not."

Maybe so, but during the day it was Kid Thomas, the lawn mowin' man, who was paying most of the bills during these lean times. One afternoon, while pulling his van away from a lucrative Beverly Hills home he had just finished up, he ran over a young boy who had suddenly appeared out of nowhere. The boy died later that afternoon. A manslaughter indictment against Thomas was dropped because of insufficient evidence, but a few months later he was due back in court on charges of driving with a revoked license. Waiting for him outside the courthouse was the boy's father, who pulled out a gun and shot Kid Thomas dead. Since the man who died in that shooting incident was named Louis Thomas Watts, scarcely a word on Kid Thomas' death was heard in the blues community for quite some time.

The eight issued sides of Kid Thomas/Tommy Louis continued to show up piecemeal on various European compilations throughout the '70s, but a complete overview was finally issued in the '90s on El Diablo. Those who love great harmonica work and wild-ass singing would do well to investigate the good rockin' sounds and deep blues of Kid Thomas, a man who knew the value of crazy, rockin' music and a big set of hair. *—Cub Koda*

Here's My Story / 1991 / Wolf ♦♦♦♦

He may not be a household name, but a whole CD's worth of unissued Kid Thomas is something worth bringing to your attention. After all, it is a) scorching, chaotic, harmonica-driven, rockin' blues straight out of the '50s acetate mentality, chock-full of alternate-take heaven, and b) an undisputable fact that a joint purchase of this and the *Rockin' Harmonica Blues Men* CD will make you pretty much a Kid Thomas completist. Titles on this 16-tracker include four takes of "The Wolf Pack," and four takes (I count up five on the back, but the disc only plays four; make that a 15-song compilation—earth to quality control at Wolf) of "Beulah Come Back," two just-plain-nasty takes of "The Spell" (off an acetate that *skips* on the second take, for God's sake) the instrumental "Jivin' Mess," "Come in This House," "She's Fine," and the title track, an "I'm a Man"-style voodoo stomp that truly justifies the pompadour the Kid is sporting on the cover. *—Cub Koda*

● **Wail Baby Wail!** / 1993 / AVI-El Diablo ♦♦♦♦♦

The chronicling of the complete recorded works of Kid Thomas has been an ongoing affair, each compact disc reissue turning up more rare and unissued sides. This 1993 issue is the most complete of all the Kid Thomas packages available, bringing together all of his extant Federal recordings, including myriad alternate takes (all originally chronicled on Wolf's *Here's My Story* compilation) and all of the West Coast recordings made under different names that appeared on Wolf's *Rockin' Harmonica Men* collection, which Thomas shared with Jerry McCain. This surpasses both of those with the whopping addition of no less than 13 bonus tracks, most of them unissued demos and rehearsal tapes from various vintages. Unfortunately, none of these bonus tracks are listed anywhere on the package, and even the most avid Kid Thomas fan familiar with the preceding packages will still have trouble identifying which tracks are which, a curious oversight in a package so complete. *—Cub Koda*

Rockin' Harmonica Blues Man / Wolf ♦♦♦

Of all the amplified harmonica blues guys that transversed the audio highway back in the '50s and early '60s, two guys who truly deserve a bigger tip of the hat than they've received thus far are Kid Thomas and Jerry McCain. Thomas was a pompadoured, Little Richard-styled howler, short on subtleties and long on wind power. McCain made records for a variety of labels that constantly blurred the line between what was blues and what was rock & roll. This 21-track CD captures some of their best from a variety of sources. The Kid Thomas section kicks off with "Rockin This Joint Tonight," and one of the fastest, howlin'est, and downright ornery records ever made. Backed by nothing more than a guitarist and drummer bathed in a wash of tape echo, Thomas blows a 36-bar harmonica solo at breakneck tempo. If none of the other nine tracks included here match the intensity of this one—well, perhaps it's because nothing really could. The remaining 11 tracks by Jerry McCain come from homemade demo tapes circa 1955 that were originally released on White Label Records back in the early '80s as the *Choo Choo Rock* album, one of the great unsung records of all time. Their CD debut is made even more noteworthy with the use of better-sounding masters than the original vinyl version. Featuring grinding, distorted guitars, crashing drums, and lyrical texts concerning themselves with going crazy to rock & roll, rock & roll as salvation ("Rock & Roll Ball," "Geronimo's Rock"), and going crazy from outside worldly pressures ("Bell in My Heart," "It Must Be Love," and the pre-Excello "My Next Door Neighbors"), these 11 masterpieces answer the musical question: What would a rock & roll album by Little Walter have sounded like? Beyond essential. *—Cub Koda*

Ramblin' Thomas (Willard Thomas)

b. 1902, Logansport, LA, **d.** c. 1945, Memphis, TN

Vocals, Guitar / Acoustic Texas Blues, Prewar Country Blues

The rediscovery of bluesman Jesse "Babyface" Thomas in the '70s was the equivalent of a blues archivist's two-for-one sale. It turned out that the mysterious and up-til-then totally obscure '20s recording artist known as Ramblin' Thomas was the brother of Jesse Thomas, and the latter man was able to spill the beans on just who the rambling man with the fascinating guitar style really was. The Thomas clan, which also included the guitar picking older brother Joe L. Thomas, were sons of an old-time fiddler and were raised in Louisiana close to the Texas border. The boys got into playing guitar after looking with admiration at various models in a Sears catalog. Jesse Thomas has recalled that the mail-order guitar purchased by his brother, Willard "Rambling" Thomas, came equipped with a metal bar for playing slide; indicating the tremendous popularity of country blues at the time or the possibility that someone at Sears knew the guitar was headed into the arms of a Southern bluesman.

Thomas rambled, indeed he did. He was discovered by recording scouts playing in Dallas, but prior to that had performed in San Antonio and Oklahoma. His style also seemed influenced by the double threat of blues guitarist and pianist Lonnie Johnson, suggesting a possible St. Louis sojourn as well. Thomas played quite a bit in the key of E, making him harmonically quite a typical Delta bluesman. His picking style is curious, however, and even more interesting is his timing. His rhythmic variations suggest that his nickname might have been handed out by a musician attempting to accompany him, and not just relate to his geographical roaming. On some of his recordings for Paramount and Victor, such as "Ground Hog Blues," he plays it a little straighter, going for an imitation of then current hitmaker Tampa Red. The Document label is among several blues record companies that have released collections of Thomas' material, usually in the form of either a compilation or a collection of several artists; since Thomas' was apparently too busy rambling to record a full album's worth of material. Thomas reportedly died of unexplained circumstances in Memphis circa 1945. *—Eugene Chadbourne*

● **1928–1932** / 1928-1932 / Document ♦♦♦♦♦

Solid but thematically unvarying country blues from a fine practitioner. "Ramblin'" Thomas told great stories and backed himself just as nicely. *—Ron Wynn*

Ramblin' Mind Blues: Chicago Blues, 1928 / Biograph ♦♦♦♦

An album released during the initial blues craze of the '60s, this fine Biograph set is the musical equivalent of a set of snapshots of a mysterious and talented country blues artist on his way in and out of town. Paramount was the label that originally halted this character's rambling long enough to put a microphone in front of him, and what they got is a series of pretty intense performances. The material can seem too similar, an effect not enhanced by the gnawed and garbled sound from antique masters, but lines about women who "would make a tom cat heist its tail" and rhythmically substantial guitar picking are just two reasons why the collection will grow on a listener. There are also tracks such as "Jig Head Blues" and "Sawmill Moan" that are as evocative as the best country blues, each note quivering with a reality of time and place that could never be duplicated by even the most seasoned of revival country blues performers. *—Eugene Chadbourne*

Rockin' Tabby Thomas (Ernest Joseph Thomas)

b. Jan. 5, 1929, Baton Rouge, LA

Vocals, Piano, Guitar / Swamp Blues, Louisiana Blues

A solid Louisiana vocalist who plays both guitar and piano, "Rockin'" Tabby Thomas has been cutting stirring recordings since the mid-'50s. He's teamed often with harmonica players Whispering Smith and Lazy Lester, and has done several sessions for Maison de Soul and various labels owned by Jay Miller.

Thomas was born in Baton Rouge, LA, but he began his musical career in San Francisco, which is where he was stationed while he was in the army. After he completed his time in the service, Thomas stayed in San Francisco, playing shows and talent contests.

He happened to win a talent contest, which led to a record contract with Hollywood Records. Hollywood issued "Midnight Is Calling," which gained no attention, and the label dropped Thomas.

After the failure of "Midnight Is Calling," Tabby Thomas returned to Baton Rouge. He began playing local clubs with his supporting band the Mellow, Mellow Men. In 1953, the group recorded two songs—"Thinking Blues" and "Church Members Ball"—for the Delta label. After those songs didn't gain much attention, Thomas went through a number of record labels—including Feature, Rocko, and Zynn—before having a hit on Excello Records in 1962 with "Voodoo Party."

Thomas wasn't able to record a hit follow-up to "Voodoo Party" and by the end of the '60s, he retired from performing music. His retirement was short-lived—in 1970, he founded his own record label, Blue Beat. In addition to releasing Thomas' own recordings, Blue Beat spotlighted emerging Baton Rouge talent. Within a few years, the label was very successful and Thomas began his own blues club, Tabby's Blues Box and Heritage Hall. By the mid-'80s, the club was the most popular blues joint in Baton Rouge.

Although he had become a successful businessman in the late '70s, Thomas continued to perform and record. All of his efforts—from his recordings and concerts, to his label and nightclub—made Tabby Thomas the leading figure of Baton Rouge's blues scene for nearly three decades. Thomas was still active into the new millennium, although he wasn't performing as frequently as he had in the past. He was seriously injured in an automobile accident in Baton Rouge in October 2002. *—Ron Wynn & Stephen Thomas Erlewine*

Rockin' With the Blues / 1985 / Maison de Soul ♦♦♦

● **King of Swamp Blues** / 1988 / Maison de Soul ♦♦♦♦♦

Good, hard-rocking Louisiana blues with just a tinge of swamp from "Rockin'" Tabby Thomas. What he lacks in vocal range, he compensates for with exuberance. The backing band is no all-star unit, but they provide some solid grooves behind Thomas' surging leads. *—Ron Wynn*

Swamp Blues Man / Nov. 28, 1995 / Dejan ♦♦♦♦

Rufus Thomas

b. Mar. 26, 1917, Cayce, MS, **d.** Dec. 15, 2001, Memphis, TN

Vocals / Memphis Soul, Southern Soul, Electric Memphis Blues, Modern Electric Blues, R&B, Soul

Few of rock & roll's founding figures are as likable as Rufus Thomas. From the '40s onward, he has personified Memphis music; his small but witty cameo role in Jim Jarmusch's *Mystery Train*, a film which satirizes and enshrines the city's role in popular culture, was entirely appropriate. As a recording artist, he wasn't a major innovator, but he could always be depended upon for some good, silly, and/or outrageous fun with his soul dance tunes. He was one of the few rock or soul stars to reach his commercial and artistic peak in middle age, and was a crucial mentor to many important Memphis blues, rock, and soul musicians.

Thomas was already a professional entertainer in the mid-'30s, when he was a comedian with the Rabbit Foot Minstrels. He recorded music as early as 1941, but really made his mark on the Memphis music scene as a deejay on WDIA, one of the few black-owned stations of the era. He also ran talent shows on Memphis' famous Beale Street that helped showcase the emerging skills of such influential figures as B.B. King, Bobby "Blue" Bland, Junior Parker, Ike Turner, and Roscoe Gordon.

Thomas had his first success as a recording artist in 1953 with "Bear Cat," a funny answer record to Big Mama Thornton's "Hound Dog." It made number three on the R&B charts, giving Sun Records its first national hit, though some of the sweetness went out of the triumph after Sun owner Sam Phillips lost a lawsuit for plagiarizing the original Jerry Leiber/Mike Stoller tune. Thomas, strangely, would make only one other record for Sun, and recorded only sporadically throughout the rest of the '50s.

Thomas and his daughter Carla would become the first stars for the Stax label, for whom they recorded a duet in 1959, "'Cause I Love You" (when the company was still known as Satellite). In the '60s, Carla would become one of Stax's biggest stars. On his own, Rufus wasn't as successful as his daughter, but issued a steady stream of decent dance/novelty singles. These were not deep or emotional statements, or meant to be. Vaguely prefiguring elements of funk, the accent was on the stripped-down groove and Rufus' good-time vocals, which didn't take himself or anything seriously. The biggest by far was "Walking the Dog," which made the Top Ten in 1963, and was covered by the Rolling Stones on their first album.

Thomas hit his commercial peak in the early '70s, when "Do the Funky Chicken," "(Do the) Push and Pull," and "The Breakdown" all made the R&B Top Five. As the song titles themselves make clear, funk was now driving his sound rather than blues or soul. Thomas drew upon his vaudeville background to put them over on-stage with fancy footwork that displayed remarkable agility for a man well into his fifties. The collapse of the Stax label in the mid-'70s meant the end of his career, basically, as it did for many other artists with the company. In 2001, Rufus Thomas was inducted into the Blues Hall of Fame. Later that year, on December 15, he died at St. Francis Hospital in Memphis, TN. *—Richie Unterberger*

Walking the Dog / 1964 / Rhino ♦♦♦♦♦

One of the artists who defined Memphis soul and put Stax Records on the map, Rufus Thomas is known for liking his R&B hard-edged, gritty and earthy. That approach served him impressively well on his debut album *Walking the Dog*. In contrast to the sleeker, more elaborate production style favored by the Northern soulsters of Motown, Thomas rejects pop elements altogether and thrives on rawness on his hits "Walking the Dog" and "The Dog," as well as inspired versions of "Land of 1000 Dances" (which became a major hit for Wilson Pickett), Lee Dorsey's "Ya Ya," and John Lee Hooker's "Boom Boom." Thomas was in his mid-forties when these fun, infectious recordings were made, and he definitely lives up to his title "The World's Oldest Teenager" (a title later given to Dick Clark as well). Reissued on CD in the early '90s, *Walking the Dog* is an album Memphis soul aficionados shouldn't overlook. *—Alex Henderson*

May I Have Your Ticket Please / 1969 / Stax ♦♦♦

Rufus Thomas played it halfway between inspired lunacy and straight soul sanity, and was only partly successful here. Thomas hadn't yet found the formula for dance/novelty success, and didn't really have any strong singles on this release. His bluesy vocals were well done, but not enough to generate any action for the record. *—Ron Wynn*

Funky Chicken / Jun. 1969 / Stax ♦♦♦

Thomas' first album following Stax's break from Atlantic (and in fact his first since 1963) had "Do the Funky Chicken" at its centerpiece, so the emphasis upon good-humored dance tunes was unsurprising. There were some weird moments, particularly the down-and-bestial seven-minute update of "Sixty Minute Man" (on which Rufus sounds like he's singing in tongues), a remake of "Bear Cat," and a two-part version of "Old McDonald Had a Farm." Still, the slightly goofy uptempo arrangements can get a little tiresome, and as his best hits from the period are better than the album-only tracks, almost everyone should just stick with a compilation. The CD adds seven bonus tracks from 1968-1974 singles, which are OK but not essential; Eddie Floyd's "Funky Mississippi" (from 1968) is about the best. *—Richie Unterberger*

Do the Funky Chicken / 1970 / Stax ♦♦♦

Rufus Thomas would storm the soul charts in 1970, scoring three hits, two of them in the Top Ten. The title track and his number one smash "(Do The) Push and Pull" were identical—dance-based novelty tunes featuring Thomas' manic instructions and bluesy shouts backed by surging, horn-based soul and funk from the Stax band. It wasn't earth-shaking, just fun, brilliantly produced and arranged stuff. *—Ron Wynn*

Doing the Push and Pull Live at P.J.'s / 1971 / Stax ♦♦♦

One of only a couple of Rufus Thomas albums that actually cracked the pop charts, this featured live versions of "Do The Funky Chicken" and "(Do The) Push and Pull," plus warhorses like "The Preacher and the Bear" and "Night Time Is the Right Time." The label also stuck the recent number one hit "Walkin' the Dog" onto the album from its prior release, an unnecessary move and one that couldn't get it any more pop action than it enjoyed. *—Ron Wynn*

The Crown Prince of Dance / 1973 / Stax ♦♦♦♦♦

The "world's oldest teenager" was springy, sassy, and jubilant when he cut this date in the mid-'70s. Thomas, whose career goes back to the days of the Rabbit Foot Minstrels, made some brilliant novelty cuts for Stax in the '70s. He simply went into the studio and clowned, backed by the great Stax session pros. The results are comic gems, numbers that are purposefully lightweight and succeed without sounding sappy. *—Ron Wynn*

If There Were No Music / 1977 / Avid ♦♦♦

Rufus Thomas was on Avid when he issued this 1977 album, and the difference between this label and Stax was evident in the colorless backing, routine production, and general blandness of the tracks featured on the LP. Thomas tried to whip up some enthusiasm, and his rendition of the title cut came close to generating some attention for the album. But it was weighted down with too much disposable fodder, and not a single definitive dance or novelty classic to boot. *—Ron Wynn*

I Ain't Gettin' Older, I'm Gettin' Better / 1977 / Avid ♦♦

Rufus Thomas was right vocally, but otherwise this album didn't live up to the title. After years of inspired productions, arrangements, and compositions, Thomas didn't get similar treatment for his debut on the Avid label. They did a respectable job, but didn't get him any hits or inventive novelty tunes. Thomas eventually went from being a hit act to a nostalgia/oldies performer. *—Ron Wynn*

Rufus Thomas / 1980 / Gusto ♦♦♦

A low-budget collection of Rufus Thomas material inferior to material available on various Sun anthologies, Charly reissues, or any of the Stax sessions. It's to be avoided unless you're interested in only the most cursory overview and aren't fussy about sound quality or accuracy of information. *—Ron Wynn*

Jump Back / 1984 / Edsel ♦♦♦♦♦

The best compilation of his early Stax sides. The 16 tracks include "Walking the Dog," "The Dog," and some lesser-known songs in the same league, some of which ("Jump Back," "All Night Worker," "Sister's Got a Boyfriend," "Sophisticated Sissy") made the rounds via cover versions by both black and white artists. *—Richie Unterberger*

That Woman Is Poison! / 1988 / Alligator ♦♦♦

A masterful comeback album from a blues and soul veteran who was assumed to be ready for the retirement home. Rufus Thomas went back to the comic blues that had been his forte in the '50s, and the edge in his voice and defiance in his tone proclaimed that he wasn't finished yet. After years of taking heat from purists for not issuing enough "real" blues albums, Alligator didn't get nearly enough credit for being the only label to give Rufus Thomas a fair shot in the '80s. *—Ron Wynn*

Can't Get Away from This Dog / 1992 / Stax ♦♦♦

Can't Get Away from This Dog gathers 20 previously unreleased Rufus Thomas recordings from the Stax vaults. Stylistically, fans won't find any surprises—this is still hard-hitting, hard-driving Memphis soul—but they'll find a couple of hidden treasures, such as versions of "Wang Dang Doodle," "Reconsider Baby," and "Barefootin'," as well as alternates of "Walking the Dog," "Jump Back," and "Can Your Monkey Do the Dog?" Some of Thomas' original material is a little thin—there's only so many times you can work the word "dog" into a song title, after all—but this is a surprisingly successful collection of rarities that will not only satiate diehards, but will entertain casual fans as well. *—Stephen Thomas Erlewine*

Did You Head Me/Crown Prince of Dance / 1995 / Stax ♦♦♦

This pairs up two of Thomas' original Stax albums on one compact disc. The first ten tracks emanate from 1970 and 1971 sessions that produced the *Did You Heard Me?*

album, featuring the hits "Do the Push and Pull" and "Do the Funky Penguin." The follow-up, 1972's *Crown Prince of Dance*, wasn't as successful musically or sales-wise, but features plenty of Thomas' funky dancefloor rave-ups like "Funkiest Man Alive," "The Funky Bird," and a nice duet with daughter Carla Thomas on "Steal a Little." This would end up being Thomas' last album for the label before it went under, and it still holds up well. —*Cub Koda*

Rufus Thomas Live! / Oct. 1995 / Stax ✦✦

The Crown Prince of Memphis Soul, aka the Oldest Living Teenager, Rufus Thomas clowns, jokes, brags, and dances while singing five lengthy numbers. Rufus penned three songs, including the hits "Walking the Dog," and the 17-minute-long "Do the Funky Chicken"; the third, "Big Fine Hunk of a Woman," is a blues set off by a comedic rap. He turns Merle Haggard's classic "Today I Started Loving You Again," into a nearly 19-minute *tour de force*, and goes deep soul on "Somebody's Got to Go." If you never saw Rufus in person, then this remastered live taping is a good introduction to one of America's most beloved soul artists. —*Andrew Hamilton*

● **The Best of Rufus Thomas: Do the Funky Somethin'** / Apr. 1996 / Rhino ✦✦✦✦✦

Overdue career-spanning collection of his best material, centering around his Stax hits from the '60s and early '70s. The whole "dog" series of novelty dance songs from 1963-1964 is here, as well as the hit "Jump Back" and a clutch of Stax singles that weren't hits, but became pretty well-known anyway, like "Sister's Got a Boyfriend" and "Sophisticated Sissy." There are also the early-'70s funk dance hits "Do the Funky Chicken," "(Do The) Push and Pull," "The Breakdown," and "Do the Funky Penguin," a couple of '60s duets with his daughter Carla, and his 1953 blues single "Bear Cat (The Answer to Hound Dog)," the first hit on Sun Records. A few other compilations have gone into specific phases of his career in greater depth, but this is certainly the best overview of a man who offered some of the funkiest and funniest Memphis blues around. —*Richie Unterberger*

Swing Out With Rufus / May 18, 1999 / High Stacks ✦✦✦

These tracks sound like reissues—the Crown Prince of Dance's gruff baritone is unusually strong for a guy his age—but these are actually new recordings cut with many of the musicians and vocalists from Stax's heyday, including Mabon "Teenie" Hodges, Carla Thomas, and Michael Toles. This endearing set is blues-based with an ample helping of '50s R&B thrown in. As recordings go, it's a keeper; some highlights are Thomas' rendition of Ike Turner's R&B classic "Rocket 88," as well as some true-to-the-genre blues wails à la "Just Because I Leave, That Don't Mean I'm Gone" and energetic jumps like "Fool for You Mama." —*Andrew Hamilton*

Dave Thompson

b. 1971, Jackson, MS

Vocals, Guitar / Contemporary Blues, Modern Electric Blues

Dave Thompson has been playing blues guitar since age nine, with the encouragement and help of his musician father. A native of Mississippi, Thompson was playing in backing bands for local acts like the Greenville Letts by his early teens. Club owner and fellow bluesman Booba Barnes hooked up with Thompson when the latter was 15, and the two made the rounds on Mississippi's sometimes-violent club circuit. Thompson's first appearance on record was on David Malone's debut album for Fat Possum Records. (Malone is the son of bluesman Junior Kimbrough.) This gig gave Thompson a springboard for his own solo project, *Little Dave and Big Love*, which was released in 1995 and showcases Thompson's fiery playing. —*Steve Huey*

Little Dave and Big Love / 1995 / Fat Possum ✦✦✦

Robert Palmer's notes declaring Dave Thompson a "thoroughly original" bluesman "without a veneer of irony or posturing" sound downright ludicrous after actually listening to the music. While he insists that Thompson's songs are "[not] stylistically indebted to any obvious influence," one can clearly hear echoes of Stevie Ray Vaughan, especially on "Instrumental No. 7" and "You Took My Baby." Most of the tracks (save the funky "Standing Up on My Own") are conventional bar-blues jams, and as such are merely vehicles for Thompson's lead guitar work, which is by far the most enjoyable aspect of the album. Using a quarter as a pick, he produces a lockjaw tone that screams, cries, and slugs with the best of them, making one long for the days when a guitarist of his caliber recognized their limitations and opted to back up a gifted bandleader, instead of wasting their time with boring musicians, writing boring songs, and stifling their own success. —*Jim Smith*

● **C'mon Down to the Delta** / Apr. 30, 2002 / JSP ✦✦✦

Ron Thompson

b. Jul. 5, 1953, Oakland, CA

Vocals, Guitar / Modern Electric Blues, Blues-Rock

After honing his chops behind Little Joe Blue and John Lee Hooker, guitarist Ron Thompson went solo in 1980, forming his own blues/roots rock trio, the Resisters. *Just Like a Devil*, a 1990 release on pianist Mark Naftalin's Winner label, was culled from Thompson's appearances on Naftalin's *Blue Monday Party* radio program.

Born and raised in Oakland, CA, Thompson began playing guitar when he was 11, picking up slide guitar shortly afterward. When he was in his late teens, he was playing slide guitar with Little Joe Blue. For about five years, he worked in local Bay Area clubs, both as a solo artist and a supporting musician. In 1975, John Lee Hooker asked Thompson to join his backing band and the guitarist accepted. For the next three years, he played with Hooker, developing a national reputation.

Thompson left Hooker in 1978. Two years later, he formed his own band, the Resistors, and landed a contract with Takoma Records. Thompson's debut album, *Treat Her Like Gold*, appeared in 1983. Although he launched a solo career, Thompson continued to play with a number of other musicians, including Lowell Fulson, Etta James, and Big Mama Thornton. In 1987, his second album, *Resister Twister*, was released; it was followed

shortly afterward by *Just Like a Devil*. Thompson continued to perform during subsequent years, although he didn't record quite as frequently. —*Bill Dahl & Stephen Thomas Erlewine*

Treat Her Like Gold/No Bad Days / 1983 / Takoma ✦✦✦

● **Resister Twister** / 1987 / Blind Pig ✦✦✦✦✦

Resister Twister, the second album from Ron Thompson, is an enjoyable soul-blues collection that finds the slide guitarist at the peak of his form. There's not much original on the record, but Thompson plays very, very well, and the result is a fun contemporary blues recording. —*Thom Owens*

Just Like a Devil / 1990 / Winner ✦✦✦

Sonny Thompson

b. Aug. 22, 1923, Centreville, MS, d. Aug. 11, 1989, Chicago, IL

Conductor, Piano / Jump Blues, R&B

Bandleader and pianist Sonny Thompson was among the most prolific R&B instrumentalists of the late '40s and early '50s. Thompson began recording for Sultan in 1946, then did several sessions for Miracle, King, Federal, and Deluxe, while also backing vocalist Lula Reed from 1951 to 1961. Thompson scored two number one R&B hits for Miracle in 1948: "Long Gone, Pts. 1-2," and "Late Freight." He landed another Top Ten and two more Top 20 singles for Miracle in 1949, and then had three Top Ten hits for King in 1952. The biggest was "I'll Drown in My Tears," which reached number five. —*Ron Wynn*

Mellow Blues for the Late Hours / 1959 / King ✦✦✦

Jam Sonny Jam / Feb. 25, 1997 / Sequel ✦✦✦

● **EP Collection** / Dec. 14, 1999 / See for Miles ✦✦✦✦

Big Mama Thornton (Willie Mae Thornton)

b. Dec. 11, 1926, Montgomery, AL, d. Jul. 25, 1984, Los Angeles, CA

Vocals, Drums, Harmonica / Juke Joint Blues, Texas Blues, Electric Texas Blues, R&B

Willie Mae "Big Mama" Thornton only notched one national hit in her lifetime, but it was a true monster. "Hound Dog" held down the top slot on Billboard's R&B charts for seven long weeks in 1953. Alas, Elvis Presley's rocking 1956 cover was even bigger, effectively obscuring Thornton's chief claim to immortality.

That's a damned shame, because Thornton's menacing growl was indeed something special. The hefty belter first opened her pipes in church but soon embraced the blues. She toured with Sammy Green's Hot Harlem Revue during the '40s. Thornton was ensconced on the Houston circuit when Peacock Records boss Don Robey signed her in 1951. She debuted on Peacock with "Partnership Blues" that year, backed by trumpeter Joe Scott's band.

But it was her third Peacock date with Johnny Otis' band that proved the winner. With Pete Lewis laying down some truly nasty guitar behind her, Big Mama shouted "Hound Dog," a tune whose authorship remains a bone of contention to this day (both Otis and the team of Jerry Leiber and Mike Stoller claim responsibility), and soon hit the road a star.

But it was an isolated incident. Though Thornton cut some fine Peacock follow-ups—"I Smell a Rat," "Stop Hoppin' on Me," "The Fish," "Just Like a Dog"—through 1957, she never again reached the hit parade. Even Elvis was apparently unaware of her; he was handed "Hound Dog" by Freddie Bell, a Vegas lounge rocker. Early-'60s 45s for Irma, Bay-Tone, Kent, and Sotoplay did little to revive her sagging fortunes, but a series of dates for Arhoolie that included her first vinyl rendition of "Ball and Chain" in 1968 and two albums for Mercury in 1969-1970 put her back in circulation (Janis Joplin's overwrought but well-intentioned cover of "Ball and Chain" didn't hurt either). Along with her imposing vocals, Thornton began to emphasize her harmonica skills during the '60s.

Thornton was a tough cookie. She dressed like a man and took no guff from anyone, even as the pounds fell off her once-ample frame and she became downright scrawny during the last years of her life. Medical personnel found her lifeless body in an L.A. rooming house in 1984. —*Bill Dahl*

In Europe: Big Mama Thornton With Muddy Waters' Blues Band / 1965 / Arhoolie ✦✦✦✦✦

Live sessions with the Muddy Waters Blues Band. —*Barry Lee Pearson*

Big Mama Thorton in Europe / Sep. 1966 / Arhoolie ✦✦✦✦✦

Big Mama the Queen at Monterey / Dec. 1967 / MCA ✦✦✦✦✦

She's Back / 1968 / Back Beat ✦✦✦✦✦

Growling Texas blues; includes "Hound Dog." —*Bill Dahl*

Ball N' Chain / 1968 / Arhoolie ✦✦✦

Arhoolie's *Ball N' Chain* is a terrific collection of late-'60s recordings from Big Mama Thornton. Supported on various tracks by Lightnin' Hopkins and Larry Williams, Big Mama runs through such familiar items as "Hound Dog," "Sometimes I Have a Heartache," "Sweet Little Angel," "Little Red Rooster," "Wade in the Water," and "Ball and Chain," turning in generally powerful performances. By and large, these don't necessarily rival her classic '50s recordings, but they are worth investigating if you're looking for something more. —*Thom Owens*

Stronger Than Dirt / 1969 / Mercury ✦✦✦

The Way It Is / 1970 / Mercury ✦✦✦

Sassy Mama / 1975 / Vanguard ✦✦✦

Jail / 1975 / Vanguard ✦✦✦

It's ironic that blues great Big Mama Thornton is most famous for originating songs that later became associated with other singers. Her sole R&B hit, which never made the pop charts, became Elvis Presley's "Hound Dog" in most listeners' minds, just as surely as Otis Redding's "Respect" was universally credited to Aretha Franklin. It must have seemed like déjà vu when Thornton's "Ball and Chain" became known to most music lovers via

Janis Joplin's version with Big Brother & the Holding Company. Nevertheless, Thornton has rarely had trouble reclaiming these and other compositions once on-stage, and *Jail* vividly captures her gruff charm during a couple of mid-'70s gigs at two northwestern prisons. As a live album, *Jail* works largely because Thornton gives her musicians plenty of room to improvise, especially on six-minute versions of "Little Red Rooster" and "Ball and Chain." In her spoken introduction to "Ball and Chain," Thornton initially gives props to Janis Joplin, then reminds the audience, "I wrote this song." Having lost little of her commanding, masculine voice, Thornton becomes the talented leader of a gritty blues ensemble that features sustained jams from George "Harmonica" Smith and guitarists B. Huston and Steve Wachsman. Despite several lengthy numbers, the running time is less than 40 minutes, and there's not much between-song banter à la *Johnny Cash at Folsom Prison*. Listeners who are left wanting more Big Mama Thornton can invest in *The Complete Vanguard Recordings*, a triple-CD set that includes all of *Jail* and two albums from the same era: *Sassy Mama* and the previously unreleased *Big Mama Swings*. — *Vince Ripol*

The Original Hound Dog / 1990 / Ace ♦♦♦♦♦
This British import compilation of Peacock sides is a bit more comprehensive than the domestic *Hound Dog* anthology, including a few more tracks (22 in all, some previously unreleased). The MCA collection, more readily available for most North American consumers, should suffice for most listeners. If you come across this one first, though, it's certainly an equal or greater value, highlighted by "Hound Dog" and "I Smell a Rat." — *Richie Unterberger*

● **Hound Dog: The Peacock Recordings** / 1992 / MCA ♦♦♦♦♦
Let's face it, Big Mama Thornton will always be chiefly recalled for her growling 1952 reading of the classic "Hound Dog." But the other 17 sides on this collection of her 1952-1957 output for Don Robey's Peacock Records aren't exactly makeweight. Thornton's mighty roar was backed by the jumping combos of Johnny Otis and saxist Bill Harvey, producing additional gems in "My Man Called Me," "They Call Me Big Mama," "The Fish," and a duet with the ill-fated Johnny Ace, "Yes Baby." — *Bill Dahl*

The Rising Sun Collection / Sep. 25, 1994 / Just a Memory ♦♦♦
Rising Sun Collection features Big Mama on foreign soil with a good band behind her playing for the Euros in 1977. With Phil Guy and John Primer on guitar, and Johnny "Big Moose" Walker on piano, the band is truly kicking behind her as Willie Mae stretches out the tunes to a comfortable length. The tunes are old standards like "Spoonful," "Rock Me Baby," "Summertime," "Sweet Little Angel," and the inevitable "Ball and Chain," as well as the "Hound Dog-Walkin' the Dog" medley. As these kind of old tapes go, this is pretty inspired stuff and Big Mama is in good form throughout. — *Cub Koda*

The Complete Vanguard Recordings / Apr. 18, 2000 / Vanguard ♦♦♦♦♦
This wonderful three-disc set brings together everything Willie Mae Thornton recorded for the folk music label in the mid-'70s. It's comprised of her two released albums from 1975, *Jail* and *Sassy Mama*, and a complete unreleased album, *Big Mama Swings*. Thornton was still in good voice on these sessions and while not as powerful as her Peacock sides, the production is solid and these recordings make an excellent addition to her scant discography. — *Cub Koda*

Margaret Thornton
Vocals / Classic Female Blues
That the blues vocalist Margaret Thornton recorded only one song in her life is, unfortunately, a fact that is off by only half; the correct number is two, but in terms of quality impact, it might as well have been dozens. Her recordings of the tunes "Texas Bound Blues" and "Jockey Blues," cut in 1927 for the short-lived Black Patti label, are among the dozens of recordings of early female-blues artists rescued from obscurity by archivist producers such as Document's Johnny Parth. As a result, her efforts have been assured a place in recording history, indeed inspiring one critic to remark that such critics give a double meaning to the concept of CD "jewel cases."

Thornton's crown jewels were recorded in collaboration with pianist Blind James Beck, a performer even more obscure than the singer he accompanies, and even harder to hear due to the primitive recording equipment in use at this time. Nothing is known about her personal background, but the family name of Thornton was certainly acquired via the slave-holding, widespread Thornton dynasty that arrived on the American shores early on in the country's history via ships such as the Devon. While the most prolific Margaret Thornton is a romance novelist, and the most socially conscious Margaret Thornton a crusader in the battle against draconic drug laws, the blues singer is the one who inspires the most "might-have-been" thinking, such as this comment from an impressed blues critic who wanted more: "Anyone who could have as much fun with a song as she does with 'Jockey Blues' should've gotten more opportunity." Like many such recordings that have struck a resonant chord with blues fans, there are actually more compilation albums containing Thornton tracks than actual songs by the artist, normally one of the highlights of whatever collection they appear. — *Eugene Chadbourne*

George Thorogood
b. Dec. 24, 1950, Wilmington, DE
Slide Guitar, Vocals, Guitar / Slide Guitar Blues, Album Rock, Boogie Rock, Hard Rock, Blues-Rock
A blues-rock guitarist who draws his inspiration from Elmore James, Hound Dog Taylor, and Chuck Berry, George Thorogood never earned much respect from blues purists, but he became a popular favorite in the early '80s through repeated exposure on FM radio and the arena rock circuit. Thorogood's music was always loud, simple, and direct—his riffs and licks were taken straight out of '50s Chicago blues and rock & roll—but his formulaic approach helped him gain a rather large audience in the '80s, when his albums regularly went gold.

Originally, Thorogood was a minor-league baseball player, but decided to become a musician in 1970 after seeing John Paul Hammond in concert. Three years later, he assembled the Destroyers in his home state of Delaware; in addition to Thorogood, the band featured bassist Michael Lenn, second guitarist Ron Smith, and drummer Jeff Simon. Shortly after the group was formed, he moved them to Boston, where they became regulars on the blues club circuit. In 1974, they cut a batch of demos which were later released in 1979 as the *Better Than the Rest* album.

Within a year of recording the demos, the Destroyers were discovered by John Forward, who helped them secure a contract with Rounder Records. Before they made their first album, Lenn was replaced by Billy Blough. Thorogood & the Destroyers' eponymous debut was released in early 1977. The group's second album, *Move It on Over*, was released in 1978. The title track, a cover of Hank Williams' classic, was pulled as a single and it received heavy FM airplay, helping the album enter the American Top 40 and go gold. Its success led to MCA's release of *Better Than the Rest*, which the band disdained.

In 1980, Ron Smith left the band and the group added a saxophonist, Hank Carter, and released their third album, *More George Thorogood and the Destroyers*.

Following the release of *More George Thorogood*, the guitarist signed with EMI Records, releasing his major-label debut *Bad to the Bone* in 1982. The title track of the album became his first major crossover hit, thanks to MTV's saturation airplay of the song's video. The album went gold and spent nearly a full year on the charts. Thorogood's next three albums after *Bad to the Bone* all went gold. Between *Bad to the Bone* and Thorogood's next album, 1985's *Maverick*, the Destroyers added a second guitarist, Steve Chrismar.

By the beginning of the '90s, Thorogood's audience began to decrease. None of the albums he released went gold, even though the title track from 1993's *Haircut* was a number two album rock hit. Despite his declining record sales, Thorogood continued to tour blues and rock clubs and he usually drew large crowds; subsequent efforts include 1997's *Rockin' My Life Away*, 1999's *Half a Boy/Half a Man*, and *Live in 1999*. — *Stephen Thomas Erlewine*

George Thorogood and the Destroyers / 1977 / Rounder ♦♦♦♦♦
Contains Thorogood's crowd-pleasing rendition of John Lee Hooker's "One Bourbon, One Scotch, One Beer." Its basic approach—heavy on Thorogood's bluesy guitar playing—serves as the prototype for every Destroyers record that followed. — *William Ruhlmann*

Move It on Over / 1978 / Rounder ♦♦♦
In 1978, George Thorogood was just beginning to make some noise on the blues-rock circuit. This was his second album, and what's now almost a cliché then sounded fresh and vital. Thorogood's energy, rousing vocals and driving guitar playing came roaring through on inspired covers of Elmore James' "The Sky Is Crying," Bo Diddley's "Who Do You Love," and Chuck Berry's "It Wasn't Me." He even did a credible Piedmont blues on Brownie McGhee's "So Much Trouble." While Thorogood went on to make more commercially succesful albums, the spirit and innocence in his early releases has seldom been duplicated. This Rounder CD reissue returns him to a simpler, and in some ways superior, period. — *Ron Wynn*

More George Thorogood and the Destroyers / 1980 / Rounder ♦♦
George Thorogood was honing his focus and getting The Destroyers concept down pat on this 1980 album. He hadn't yet become so established and comfortable that his rocking blues licks and vocals were more show business than intensity and energy. Thorogood's playing and singing on such tracks as "House of Blue Lights," "Night Time," and "I'm Wanted" were earnest enough to make the treatments convincing, and retain interest. While this wasn't quite as memorable as his earlier dates, George Thorogood still had the hunger that fueled his breakout sessions. — *Ron Wynn*

Bad to the Bone / 1982 / BGO ♦♦♦♦♦
Though songs such as "Back to Wentzville" are credited to G. Thorogood, he'd be the first to admit that they are proudly derivative of Chuck Berry and his other mentors. The title track, another Thorogood copyright, has become ubiquitous in *Terminator 2* and the *Problem Child* movies and elsewhere, but it's still terrific. — *William Ruhlmann*

Maverick / 1985 / Rounder ♦♦♦
George Thorogood is forever consistent and *Maverick* is more of the blues/rock driving sound the journeyman guitarist is known for. John Lee Hooker's "Crawling King Snake" is what you expect from this crew while "Memphis, Tennessee" bursts at the seams with George's trademark slide and Hank Carter's saxophone. Recorded at the legendary Dimension Sound Studio in July of 1984 on the outskirts of Boston, the earthy sound catches all the band's primal energy from opener "Gear Jammer" to the wailing sax of "Long Gone." There are only four originals from Thorogood, the album chock full of Johnny Otis, Chuck Berry, Carl Perkins, John Lee Hooker and others. It is territory that the group has covered on pretty much every previous record, but it's done with the artistic passion that makes it real. The vocal on "What a Price" full of torment, it's a nice contrast to the rocking numbers. — *Joe Viglione*

Nadine / 1986 / MCA Special Products ♦♦♦
MCA Special Products' *Nadine* is a repackaging of the material that comprised *Better Than the Rest*, which itself was a compilation of unreleased demos that George Thorogood recorded for MCA in 1974. The recordings capture Thorogood's bull-headed boogie in its formative stages, and while he hadn't quite found the right tone, there are enough flashes of his future self to make it of interest to hardcore fans who have never heard this music. — *Stephen Thomas Erlewine*

Live / 1986 / EMI America ♦♦
This live release by George Thorogood & the Destroyers is a good representation of the live show of the band. However, it can be said that in places, the recording seems to fall a bit flat. One of the better sections of the disc, though, is the pairing of "I Drink Alone" with "One Bourbon, One Scotch, One Beer." That combo makes for a hard-drinking twosome of tracks, delivered in Thorogood's trademark take on retro blues and rock & roll.

Other highlights of the disc include the obligatory "Bad to the Bone," "Who Do You Love," "The Sky Is Crying," and "Bottom of the Sea." The saxophone on many of the arrangements really stands out and makes a big difference in the power of the pieces. The only other complaint on the album is that the liner notes really leave a lot to be desired. Still, for fans of Thorogood, and blues or rock & roll in general, this is a good, solid introduction to the live sound of the group. *—Gary Hill*

Born to Be Bad / 1988 / BGO ✦

Boogie People / Jan. 1991 / BGO ✦✦✦✦

George Thorogood can usually be counted on to deliver infectious, rowdy blues-rock, and *Boogie People* is no exception. Though not quite on a par with *Bad to the Bone*, this is an unpretentious party album with more than a few assets. The splendor of Chess Records had long been one of Thorogood's primary inspirations, so it shouldn't come as a major surprise that his versions of John Lee Hooker's "Mad Man Blues," Howlin' Wolf's "No Place to Go," and Muddy Waters' "Can't Be Satisfied" are as appealing as they are. The Delaware singer managed to offend the "Political Correctness Police" with "If You Don't Start Drinkin' (I'm Gonna Leave)," which finds a drunken man chastising his companion for choosing to remain sober. But they missed a key point: this song is an example of pure humor that, like so many blues songs before it, isn't meant to be taken all that seriously. *—Alex Henderson*

• **The Baddest of George Thorogood and the Destroyers** / Jul. 28, 1992 / EMI America ✦✦✦✦✦

The aptly titled *The Baddest of George Thorogood and the Destroyers* offers a dozen tracks that cleanse the church of rock & roll of all but its most basic elements: guitar, bass, drums, and a pile of Chuck Berry, Bo Diddley, and Rolling Stone licks. Delaware's George Thorogood has never quite captured his wildman live presence in the studio, but having all his best material gathered on one disc—including "Bad to the Bone," "Move It on Over," and "One Bourbon, One Scotch, One Beer"—makes for a great party. Steve Morse's liner notes are brief but, like the songs, get right to the point... cut to the bone, you might say. *—Roch Parisien*

Haircut / Jul. 27, 1993 / EMI ✦✦

You wouldn't expect any changes from George Thorogood, whose pile-driving rocking-blues and boogie have maintained their appeal despite the emergence of numerous similar-sounding ensembles. Thorogood's rough-hewn singing and always tantalizing playing are on target through the usual mix of originals and covers (this time including Bo Diddley and Willie Dixon). Besides the bonus of major label engineering and production, Thorogood's work has never lost its edge because he avoids becoming indulgent or a parody, and continues to sound genuinely interested in and a fan of the tunes he's doing. *—Ron Wynn*

Let's Work Together Live / 1995 / BGO ✦✦

George Thorogood hasn't changed his sound at all since his first live album, the aptly titled *Live*. That's not necessarily a bad thing—his beer-stained bare-bones boogie has always satisfied his fans and it is never lacking in energy, particularly when he is stoked by the enthusiasm of a live crowd. But that doesn't guarantee that *Let's Work Together Live* will be a successful, enjoyable record. Quite simply, that energy does not translate to tape very well, leaving *Let's Work Together* curiously unengaging and somewhat distant. There are good moments scattered throughout the record, but it never pulls together into a cohesive album. *—Stephen Thomas Erlewine*

Rockin' My Life Away / Mar. 25, 1997 / Capitol ✦✦

As the title says, George Thorogood has been rockin' his life away, churning out a series of heavy blues-rock records, all of them stylistically identical to each other. *Rockin' My Life Away* is no exception to the rule, and while it is marginally better than the tepid *Haircut*, it sounds so damned similar to all of his other records that even fans have to wonder what the point is anymore. There are some differences, most notably that the selection of material is more interesting than before—out of the ten covers, there are songs by John Hiatt ("The Usual"), Jerry Lee Lewis, Frank Zappa, and Chuck Willis—and while he's losing energy as he ages, it actually adds some subtlety to his music. Still, if *Rockin' My Life Away* is anything, it's bloozy boogie and it's predictable, and for longtime fans, the lack of spark may cancel out the strength of the material. *—Stephen Thomas Erlewine*

Half a Boy/Half a Man / Apr. 13, 1999 / CMC International ✦✦✦

Capitol/EMI finally dropped George Thorogood after 1997's *Rockin' My Life Away* stiffed, so where else was there for him to go than CMC International, the label that doesn't care if their artists keep remaking the same record for years on end? That's exactly where Thorogood and his Destroyers landed in 1998 and they released their first record for the label, *Half a Boy, Half a Man*, the following spring. Not surprisingly, there are no surprises anywhere on the album, unless you count the fact that it was a good idea for him to tackle Nick Lowe's great rocker "Half a Boy, Half a Man." No, the album serves up the blooze 'n' boogie that Thorogood fans love and his detractors have come to despise. The difference is, Terry Manning's production keeps things moving, resulting in his liveliest record in nearly a decade. Unfortunately, the album isn't blessed with the strong material that characterized *Rockin' My Life Away*, but that album didn't have the raw, visceral edge that this album does. And when it comes to rockin' blues, sometimes it's better to have better sound than better songs. *—Stephen Thomas Erlewine*

Live in 1999 / Nov. 23, 1999 / CMC International ✦✦✦

Recorded almost two months after the release of *Half a Boy/Half a Man*, his first album for CMC International, and released five months later, *Live in 1999* is what you'd expect from an artist who has spent over 20 years playing the same blooze 'n' boogie. That's right—a little more blooze 'n' boogie. Depending on your point of view, Thorogood has either kept it real or has recycled himself since the second song on his first album, but either way, *Live in 1999* offers no surprises in either camp. He keeps the same roadhouse grooves, the same thundering slide guitar, and the same songs ("Bad to the Bone," "Who Do You Love," "I Drink Alone," "Move It on Over," "Get a Haircut," and "One Bourbon, One Scotch, One Beer" all make another appearance). The only thing that's changed slightly is the banter—thanking Budweiser and the Fox Theater, saying there will be no violence or guns tonight, only love and rock & roll. The performances probably sounded fine in concert, where there's a palpable dynamic between the artist and audience, but on record, they're flat. Not necessarily unenjoyable, but certainly flat, with no real spark from the band nor any exceptional solos or singing. In other words, this album is a bit predictable. That might not bother indiscriminate hardcore fans—who, after all, haven't objected to hearing the same basic album for over two decades—but some discerning diehards may question why he does the same songs the same way year after year, especially when he has more than enough rarities or covers to choose from. The answer? The hits are crowd pleasers and the crowd wouldn't be happy if they didn't hear them. There's no rule, however, that a live album needs to be a replica of a concert (though those are occasionally nice), and given how the familiarity of the performances and material makes *Live in 1999* feel a little ordinary, perhaps Thorogood should take the opportunity with his next album to shake things up a little bit. Not that he would abandon blooze 'n' boogie—but it would be enough to hear blooze 'n' boogie through different songs. *—Stephen Thomas Erlewine*

Anthology / Aug. 29, 2000 / Capitol ✦✦✦✦

Just because this double CD practically triples the tracks of 1992's *The Baddest of George Thorogood and the Destroyers*, features better fidelity, more informative liner notes, songs recorded for four more albums, and a handful of rarities, doesn't make it the better collection. A little bit of Thorogood's meat and potatoes mix of Chuck Berry riffs, Elmore James slide guitar, and stripped-down Hound Dog Taylor house rocking goes an awfully long way, and a double-disc dose of similar sounding, non-stop rocking becomes mind-numbing over the course of more than two hours of in-your-face boogie. As you'd expect, all of the Delaware pile-driving guitarist's recorded highlights are here, including six concert recordings that catch the band in their natural habitat. Thorogood and his road-hardened crew will bring any crowd to a frenzy, but having to wade through what amounts to the same three chords, albeit ones played with dogged enthusiasm and robust fervor, for 30 tracks without the sweat, beer, and infectious energy of actually being there, makes for a tiring and repetitious experience. Although you have to admire the guy for sticking to his guns for three decades, the lack of ballads, or really any change-ups chosen for this set, presents a limited, one-sided picture of this rugged rocker. Thorogood's individual albums include the occasional country or novelty tune, and his versions of Frank Zappa's "Trouble Everyday," Nick Lowe's "Half a Boy, Half a Man," or the trucking classic "Six Days on the Road," none of which are found here, would have made for a far more listenable and somewhat more eclectic compilation. Rough, tough, and unfailingly intense, *Anthology* is just too much reelin' and rocking for all but the most die-hard fan. *—Hal Horowitz*

Allen Toussaint

b. Jan. 14, 1938, New Orleans, LA

Vocals, Keyboards, Piano / New Orleans R&B, R&B, Southern Soul, Soul

His inherently funky piano work heavily influenced by his Crescent City forefathers—Professor Longhair, Huey "Piano" Smith, and Fats Domino—and with a heavy dose of Ray Charles, a young visionary named Allen Toussaint almost singlehandedly fashioned a fresh, vital New Orleans R&B sound for the early '60s. Earning a vaunted reputation as a session pianist, Toussaint debuted on vinyl in 1958 with an obscure RCA album whimsically billed as "A. Tousan." When Joe Banashak inaugurated his Minit label in 1960, Toussaint joined the firm as A&R man and quickly proved himself the ultimate behind-the-scenes wizard on the New Orleans scene. During the early to mid-'60s, Toussaint tirelessly wrote, arranged, produced, and played on hits by Ernie K-Doe, Irma Thomas, Jessie Hill, Chris Kenner, Barbara George, Lee Dorsey, Benny Spellman, the Showmen, and many more, his rolling keyboards vital to the charm of virtually all of them.

After unleashing the Meters on the world, Toussaint finally began to step out as a front man in 1970, although his low-key vocals have never achieved quite the same level of success as his previous productions for others. His brilliant compositions have been covered by everyone from Herb Alpert & the Tijuana Brass to Robert Palmer and Bonnie Raitt. Allen Toussaint's stature as a New Orleans musical giant endures. *—Bill Dahl*

The Wild Sound of New Orleans / 1958 / Edsel ✦✦✦✦✦

His debut album, featuring a killer band, storming second-line instrumentals, and Toussaint's rolling 88s. *—Bill Dahl*

Toussaint / 1971 / Scepter ✦✦✦

New Orleans production and performing wizard Allen Toussaint launched his solo career with this early-'70s release. But for some strange reason, the same performer who's written and produced marvelous material for Irma Thomas, Lee Dorsey, Chocolate Milk, and General Johnson among others, was never able to score the same success working as a lead act. There was nothing on this album even in the same arena as his classic R&B tunes, and throughout Toussaint's run of solo releases, only the song "Southern Nights," which Glen Campbell made a hit, could be even mentioned in the same sentence with Toussaint classics like "Ride Your Pony" or "It Will Stand." *—Ron Wynn*

Southern Nights / 1975 / Reprise ✦✦✦✦✦

Motion / Aug. 1978 / WEA International ✦✦✦

A nicely produced, competently performed, but disappointing album by New Orleans giant Allen Toussaint. He seemed unable to find a groove or a sound, dabbling in pop, light R&B, rock, and mild funk, but never coming close to duplicating prior magical productions or compositions. This was perhaps Toussaint's least impressive material, and was especially surprising in light of the artistic success of his prior Warner Bros/Reprise album. *—Ron Wynn*

★ **Allen Toussaint Collection** / Apr. 30, 1991 / Reprise ♦♦♦♦♦
Allen Toussaint's contribution to New Orleans R&B is indelible and his presence can be felt throughout classic recordings from the late '50s, '60s, and beyond. His name, though, is the province of connoisseurs, those that peruse album jackets, looking for who wrote that great song, or wrote out that phenomenal arrangement. Many that know his name may not even know that he was a solo recording artist, partially because his discography is a little confusing, as he cut for little New Orleans record labels, then signed with Reprise, before returning to sporadic waxings for indies. Of all the albums and compilations that have poured onto the market, the best, by far, is Reprise's *The Allen Toussaint Collection*, even if it spotlights just a small portion of his career—namely, his '70s recordings for Reprise. True, this doesn't have all the great songs he's written, or records he's made, but it does provide an irresistible, comprehensive overview of his best albums. These aren't nearly as gritty as any of his productions of the '60s, lacking the earthiness of, say, Lee Dorsey or the down 'n' dirty grind of the Meters. Instead, it's elegant, *sexy* music—witness how "From a Whisper to a Scream" eases its way out of the speakers as the collection begins, seducing the listener, not hitting them in the gut. Even the funkiest moments here have style and are delivered subtly, which only makes them funkier, while putting such stylistic detours as the trippy "Southern Nights" into perspective. The individual albums Toussaint made for Reprise range from very good to excellent, yet this simply named collection eclipses them all, since it has all the best moments, expertly sequenced. It may be softer than his famous productions, but it's every bit as good and essential—in fact, it's one of the greatest "greatest hits" albums of '70s soul, funk, and R&B. —*Stephen Thomas Erlewine*

The Complete "Tousan" Sessions / 1992 / Bear Family ♦♦♦♦♦
Bear Family's *The Complete "Tousan" Sessions* compiles material Allen Toussaint recorded between 1958 and 1963—namely, a 1958 instrumental album for RCA called *The Wild Sounds of New Orleans by Tousan*, plus several very rare singles he recorded for the small label Seville. Though they were cut for different labels, the sound is basically the same: it's lively, jumping instrumentals, which effectively showcase Toussaint's remarkable skill at the piano. If you're looking just to hear him play, this is the best bet, since his piano is always at the forefront, whether he's vamping, strutting or tearing loose with nimble leads. As a listening experience, though, it can get a little samey; it's performed well, but there's not much variety in the style or approach, and only "Java," which Al Hirt later popularized, sticks out as a song. Still, it's an entirely pleasant listen and for serious collectors of New Orleans R&B it's worth seeking out, even if you don't play it that much, since it captures Toussaint in a relatively rare setting, pounding out jukehouse instrumentals. —*Stephen Thomas Erlewine*

Connected / May 7, 1996 / NYNO ♦♦♦♦♦
Allen Toussaint's name became synonymous with New Orleans music, even though he didn't seem to "do" the records his name was on as producer, arranger, or writer on records by artists such as Ernie K-Doe or Irma Thomas. This is his first studio album in at least a decade, and it is a very worthy effort of all self-penned songs that seem to be a mix of old and new (if not in age, at least in feel). He is supported by an extremely worthy cast of the finest New Orleans musicians. Funky material like "Funky Bars," "Ahya," and the rolling gait of "Oh My" stands next to much softer pieces that require a more versatile voice. There are times when his voice doesn't have that reaching pain, for instance, that Aaron Neville gave to "Wrong Number." On most cuts, his easy delivery is just what is called for, and his rollicking piano is always perfectly matched to the song. This is not a disc of memories, though it may bring up a few, it is fresh new funk and roll from the city where American music has always stretched to new levels. —*Bob Gottlieb*

A Taste of New Orleans / Mar. 9, 1999 / NYNO ♦♦♦
A 12-cut sampler of artists on Allen Toussaint's NYNO label, which is devoted to contemporary New Orleans music, and produced by Toussaint himself. All of these tracks are on single-artist NYNO albums, so it's more a promo for the company than a cohesive anthology. There's jazz from Amadee Castenell, gospel from Raymond Myles, reggae from Cool Riddims & Sista Teedy, updated old-time jazz from the New Birth Brass Band, and good ol' New Orleans R&B from Toussaint, James Andrews, and others. Toussaint is doing a noble service by recording New Orleans musicians, but this is not going to convince anyone that the city is headed for a new golden age. The traditional-style New Orleans cuts are pleasantly familiar and unexceptional, while others seem to be trying too hard to add contemporary pop seasoning to New Orleans music, as if figuring that it might somehow help them get played on the radio. —*Richie Unterberger*

Henry Townsend

b. Oct. 27, 1909, Shelby, MS
Vocals, Piano, Guitar / Country Blues, Piano Blues, St. Louis Blues
Influenced by Roosevelt Sykes and Lonnie Johnson, Henry Townsend was a commanding musician, adept on both piano and guitar. During the '20s and '30s, Townsend was one of the musicians who helped make St. Louis one of the blues centers of America. Townsend arrived in St. Louis when he was around ten years old, just before the '20s began. By the end of the '20s, he had landed a record contract with Columbia, cutting several sides of open-tuning slide guitar for the label. Two years later, he made some simliar recordings for Paramount. During this time, Townsend began playing the piano, learning the instrument by playing along with Roosevelt Sykes records. Within a few years, he was able to perform concerts with pianists like Walter Davis and Henry Brown.

During the '30s, Townsend was a popular session musician, performing with many of the era's most popular artists. By the late '30s, he had cut several tracks for Bluebird. Those were among the last recordings he ever made as a leader. During the '40s and '50s, Townsend continued to perform and record as a session musician, but he never made any solo records.

In 1960, he led a few sessions, but they didn't receive much attention. Toward the end of the '60s, Townsend became a staple on the blues and folk festivals in America, which led to a comeback. He cut a number of albums for Adelphi and he played shows throughout America. By the end of the '70s, he had switched from Adelphi to Nighthawk Records. Townsend had become an elder statesmen of St. Louis blues by the early '80s, recording albums for Wolf and Swingmaster and playing a handful of shows every year. *That's the Way I Do It*, a documentary about Townsend, appeared on public television in 1984. By the late '80s, Townsend was nearly retired, but he continued to play the occasional concert.—*Cub Koda & Stephen Thomas Erlewine*

Tired of Bein' Mistreated / 1962 / Bluesville ♦♦♦

Music Man / Dec. 1975 / Adelphi ♦♦♦♦♦
Several related factors come together here to make this a particularly wonderful blues album, something in the nature of a sleeper that may become a listener's favorite choice when it comes time for some blues. For one thing, there's the surprise factor in that this is not one of the "star" names in blues, due to the fact that Henry Townsend mostly recorded as a sideman, or under a bogus name such as St. Louis Jimmy. His is a top-quality blues voice and he is a sharp and accurate blues picker on both the electric and acoustic model, in the Lightnin' Hopkins and Skip James mode but with a harder edge. And he even throws in some decent blues piano, although the out-of-tune model he uses moves the whole thing into the rarified realm of microtonal blues. Over-familiarity can sometimes take the luster off a performance by a big-name artist, but that is guaranteed not to happen with Townsend because very few blues fans can say they have heard too much of him. Material was recorded over a five-year period, and the wandering and ever-changing sound quality also helps the album, as do the different instrumental combinations. The tandem guitar picking really sounds good, with that wooden back-porch quality that escaped most of the primitive recording machines in the old days, and couldn't possibly be recreated in a modern studio. One track worthy of special mention—they are all really good—is the vocal duet performance with Vernell Townsend, a song entitled "Why Do We Love Each Other?" This has a sound that really sticks with you. —*Eugene Chadbourne*

Mule / 1980 / Nighthawk ♦♦♦♦♦
Venerable St. Louis guitarist and pianist Henry Townsend mostly stuck to the keyboard on this outstanding session. It was forceful, wonderfully sung and alternately moving, impressive and inspiring. —*Ron Wynn*

● **Henry Townsend & Henry Spaulding** / 1986 / Wolf ♦♦♦♦♦
Wolf's *Henry Townsend & Henry Spaulding* isn't a collaboration—it's a collection that features the 13 known songs Townsend recorded beteen 1929 and 1937, plus the two songs Spaulding recorded in 1929. Spaulding's pair are fine country blues, but the true value in this disc is that it features the majority of Townsend's early work. He recorded four other songs during this era, but those are currently missing, which means this is the closest thing to a "complete" document of his earliest recordings. Most of his recordings find him alone with a guitar and these are wonderful, haunting country blues. A couple of other cuts are duets between Townsend and pianist Roosevelt Sykes, while on the remainder he plays with a small group featuring piano, harmonica, and guitar. These are great performances, and rank among the most underrated sides of their era. —*Thom Owens*

St. Louis Blues Ace / Jul. 11, 2000 / Swingmaster ♦♦♦
St. Louis bluesman Henry Townsend only released a handful of recordings from 1929 through 1981. *St. Louis Blues Ace* compiles material recorded in the '80s in St. Louis and the Netherlands. Switching between solo guitar and piano, Townsend composed all 15 titles, five of which had been released briefly on the Swingmaster label while the remaining ten are being issued for the first time. Townsend is one of the original early bluesman who remained true to his unique lyrical vision and has over the years showcased his musical ability alongside Big Joe Williams, Roosevelt Sykes, Robert Nighthawk, Sonny Boy Williamson, and Robert Johnson. —*Al Campbell*

Henry's Worry Blues / Nov. 14, 2000 / Catfish ♦♦♦

My Story / Oct. 9, 2001 / APO ♦♦♦♦

Tré

b. Grenada, MS
Vocals, Guitar / Modern Electric Blues
The son of bluesman L.V. Banks, the singer/guitarist known simply as Tré carried on the traditions of his father's music, recapturing the sound and feeling of '50s-era Chicago blues with accuracy and real affection. Born in Grenada, MS, he was raised on Chicago's South Side, initially playing rock and R&B; his musical allegiance moved to the blues while backing Banks between 1981 and 1987, during which time he honed a fluid, shimmering guitar style. Tré's solo debut, *Delivered for Glory—Reclaiming the Blues*, appeared in 1996; the follow-up, *Blues Knock'n Baby*—recorded with backing band the Blueknights—was released a year later. —*Jason Ankeny*

● **Delivered for Glory—Reclaiming the Blues** / Mar. 19, 1996 / JSP ♦♦♦♦
Delivered for Glory—Reclaiming the Blues is a promising debut from Tré, the son of L.V. Banks. There are some Banks' influences on the record, particularly in his guitar phrasing, but the record remains grounded in Chicago blues, with the occasional uptown flourish that distinguishes it from the pack of modern electric blues. He needs to grow as a songwriter, but he shows enough potential as a vocalist and guitarist to have *Delivered for Glory* be a strong debut. —*Thom Owens*

Blues Knock'n Baby / Jul. 1, 1997 / Wolf ♦♦♦

The Treniers

f. 1947
Group / Jump Blues, R&B
Featuring twin brothers Cliff and Claude Trenier, the Treniers helped link swing music to rock & roll with their brand of hot jump blues in the late '40s and early '50s. To the latter-day listener, their early-'50s singles sound closer to swing than rock; indeed, Cliff

and Claude had once sung with the Jimmie Lunceford Orchestra. The group did anticipate some crucial elements of rock & roll, though, with their solid, thumping beats, their squealing saxophone solos, and their song titles, such as "Rocking on Sunday Night," "Rockin' Is Our Business," and "It Rocks! It Rolls! It Swings!" The Treniers' brand of swing-cum-R&B was undoubtedly an influence on Bill Haley, who saw them when both acts were playing summer shows in Wildwood, NJ. They had work recorded for OKeh in the early '50s; by the middle of the decade, their sound was more R&B-oriented. Like many early R&B pioneers, they were unable to find success in the rock & roll era, though they appeared in a few of the first rock & roll films. —*Richie Unterberger*

● **They Rock! They Roll! They Swing!: The Best of the Treniers** / Feb. 28, 1995 / Epic/Legacy ✦✦✦✦✦
This 20-track compilation has all of their key early- and mid-'50s OKeh singles (only one of which, "Go! Go! Go!," was actually an R&B hit), five previously unreleased songs, and their 1953 version of Bill Haley's "Rock-A-Beatin' Boogie," which must rank as one of the first (if not the very first) covers of a white rock song by a black artist. —*Richie Unterberger*

Walter Trout

b. Mar. 6, 1951, Ocean City, NJ
Guitar / Blues-Rock, Modern Electric Blues
New Jersey-born blues-rocker Walter Trout spent decades as an ace sideman, playing guitar behind the likes of John Lee Hooker, Big Mama Thornton and Joe Tex; in 1981, he was also tapped to replace the late Bob Hite in Canned Heat, remaining with the venerable group through the middle of the decade. While filling in one night for an ailing John Mayall, Trout (also a Bluesbreaker for some five years) was spotted by a Danish concert promoter who agreed to finance a solo tour; assembling his own backing band, in 1990 he released his debut LP, *Life in the Jungle*, trailed a year later by *Prisoner of a Dream*. Albums including 1992's *Live (No More Fish Jokes)*, 1994's *Tellin' Stories*, and 1997's *Positively Beale Street* followed before Trout signed to A&M to release his self-titled major label debut in 1998; *Livin' Everyday* appeared the next year, trailed by *Live Trout: Recorded at the Tampa Blues Fest March 2000*. —*Jason Ankeny*

● **Life in the Jungle** / 1990 / Ruf ✦✦✦✦
Albums that combine live and studio tracks can, in some cases, be inconsistent. Some artists are so reliant on studio technology that they fall apart in a live setting; they sound stiff and awkward the minute they take the stage. And on the other hand, some artists are so fond of playing live that they become inhibited in the studio. But there is nothing inconsistent or uneven about Walter Trout's debut album, *Life in the Jungle*, a collection of live and studio recordings from 1989; on this release, the blues-rocker is as focused and inspired on-stage as he is in the studio. All of the tracks were recorded in Scandinavian countries; the live performances are from an appearance at the Midtfyn Festival in Denmark on July 2, 1989, while the studio material is from a session in Stockholm, Sweden, on June 21 and July 9 of that year. And in both settings, Trout really shines—the singer/guitarist has no problem going that extra mile on original tunes (including the title song and "Good Enough to Eat"), as well as passionate versions of Jimi Hendrix's "Red House," Buddy Guy's "She's out There Somewhere," and John Lee Hooker's "Serves Me Right to Suffer." On the latter, Trout shows his appreciation of Canned Heat without allowing his own personality to become obscured. *Life in the Jungle*, which the German Ruf label reissued on CD in 2002, is blues-rock the way it should be: tough, gritty, rugged, and heartfelt. Not all of Trout's releases are strong or as consistent as *Life in the Jungle*, but this is one Trout album that blues-rock enthusiasts will be happy to get their hands on. —*Alex Henderson*

Walter Trout / Jan. 27, 1998 / A&M ✦✦✦✦
Walter Trout's eponymous debut for Ruf frinds the former Canned Heat and John Mayall guitarist at the top of his game, tearing through a number of original contemporary blues songs. The songwriting occasionally is a little undistinguished, but Trout sounds dynamic throughout the album, capable of fiery leads and sensitive, lyrical solos. It was made for aficionados of blues guitar, and it won't disappoint anyone looking for that kind of record. —*Thom Owens*

Livin' Everyday / Jun. 8, 1999 / Ruf ✦✦✦✦
Blues-rocker Walter Trout struts his stuff on *Livin' Every Day*, the follow-up to his self-titled 1998 major-label debut. Overall, it's another fine outing for rabid blues guitar fans, full of gritty, gutsy playing and well-executed band support. Although songwriting isn't the album's primary focus, there are a number of tough survivor's tales here that resonate pretty well. On the other side of the coin, his balladry tries to be sincere yet leans toward sentimentality, which can dissipate the fire of the harder-rocking tracks. Still, *Livin' Every Day* is an entirely worthy effort by one of contemporary blues-rock's most underrated instrumentalists. —*Steve Huey*

Live Trout: Recorded at the Tampa Blues Fest March 2000 / Jun. 13, 2000 / Ruf ✦✦✦
No overdubs, no sweetening, in fact, no extra music to flesh out this relatively slim double disc (available at a single price) that clocks in at a combined total of only 96 minutes: Welcome to one full Walter Trout performance, complete with between song patter as well as every note—and there are a lot of them—the guitarist played at this March 2000 show. Filled with blistering, unrefined, and unadulterated blues-rock, Trout has been playing shows identical to this for years in Europe where he is a fairly major star. The accomplished guitar slinger unfailingly delivers the sizzling six-string goods, especially in concert with his gritty yet undistinguished voice and frenetic leads. On his second live album, but first easily available in the States, Trout pulls out all the stops, shifting from the stinging slow blues and soft-loud dynamics of "Finally Gotten Over You" and "The Reason I'm Gone" to the all-out grinding swamp of "Gotta Broken Heart" and the meat and potatoes Chuck Berry by way of Johnny Winter rock & roll of "Good Enough to Eat." Tough, roughshod, and passionate, Trout, who had gone without sleep for 24 hours before this

show, doesn't sound a bit fatigued. The liner notes state that this even adds an edge to this performance. A sideline into Bob Dylan's "I Shall Be Released" adds some much needed subtly and a bit of gospel flavor to the proceedings, but Trout works best when his lightening fingers, brawny sustain, and hot dog fret runs are given free reign. It's all sweaty, powerful, and uncompromising, but without a unique voice, either vocally or instrumentally, Trout remains a gifted, hard working, undoubtedly scintillating live performer without the idiosyncratic edge to pull away from a pack of equally talented blues rockers. —*Hal Horowitz*

Go the Distance / May 22, 2001 / Ruf ✦✦✦
One of the songs on *Go the Distance* that tells listeners a lot about Walter Trout is "I Don't Want My MTV," a humorous rock & roll number that finds the blues-rocker railing against MTV for—as he sees it—making image, looks, and physical appearance more important than the quality of the music itself. Trout even rewrites a line from Chuck Berry's "Roll Over Beethoven," singing, "Roll over, Martha Quinn, and tell Kurt Loder the news." The tune is a defining moment for Trout because it tells you a lot about him. "I Don't Want My MTV" expresses, without apology, Trout's impatience with slickness—and whether or not you share his opinion of MTV, it is his down-home earthiness that makes *Go the Distance* an honest blues-rock/roots rock outing. Trout's sincerity is one of his strongest assets, and it comes through on gritty offerings like "Message on the Doorway" and "Lookin' for the Promised Land." This CD isn't for blues purists, however; *Go the Distance* has as much to do with roots rock as it does with the blues. But regardless of whether or not a song has 12 bars, Trout brings the *feeling* of the blues to everything he does. *Go the Distance* falls short of remarkable, but it's a solid, enjoyable effort that succeeds because Trout is willing to be true to himself. —*Alex Henderson*

Robin Trower

b. Mar. 9, 1945, London, England
Guitar / Hard Rock, Blues-Rock
Guitarist Robin Trower began his career in a British R&B group called the Paramounts in 1963, which evolved into Procol Harum following a breakup. Trower left for a solo career in 1971 owing to a divergence of musical direction; while his former group was exploring its classical-rock leanings, Trower wanted to continue playing the Clapton- and Hendrix-influenced power-trio blues-rock that had inspired him. Trower's first project, the quartet Jude, went nowhere, and he took a year off to form a power trio with bassist Jimmy Dewar and drummer Reg Isadore. Trower's early work strongly recalled that of Jimi Hendrix, almost to the point of imitation, but constant touring established him as a new guitar hero and landed two gold Top Ten albums in 1974's *Bridge of Sighs* and 1975's *For Earth Below*. The latter LP featured ex-Sly & the Family Stone drummer Bill Lordan. Trower returned to his R&B roots for *In City Dreams* and *Caravan to Midnight*; in danger of losing his audience, Trower returned to rock on *Victims of the Fury*.

In 1981, Trower and Lordan formed BLT with ex-Cream bassist Jack Bruce, recording one album as a group and another credited to Bruce and Trower. The Robin Trower Band was re-formed in 1983, and has continued to record for several labels in spite of declining success and varying personnel. During the '90s and into the new millennium, Trower continued to tour and record, as well as produce records for other musicians. —*Steve Huey*

Twice Removed from Yesterday / 1973 / Chrysalis ✦✦✦✦
Robin Trower's debut solo album was the first evidence that the Fender Stratocaster sound of Jimi Hendrix could be effectively replicated and even refabricated. And like Hendrix, Trower had paid his dues as a more-or-less backup musician, his former band Procol Harum having emphasized stately organ and piano rather than guitar. After leaving his old group, Trower experimented with different musicians and ideas for several years, which paid off when he finally released *Twice Removed From Yesterday*, a record that displayed the characteristics that would make him a guitar hero and stadium attraction of the mid-'70s. He de-emphasized the Hendrix fuzz, feedback, and distortion, and let the reverb from his Strat become his dominant tonal device. He wasn't as flamboyant as Hendrix, as earthy as Eric Clapton, or as unpredictable as Jeff Beck, but he played cleanly, emphasizing singular, effective notes, and he brought a melodicism and creativity to the electric blues. His style is best suited for the slow, somber blues of songs like "Daydream" and "I Can't Wait Much Longer," where his solos are both carefully structured and melodic. The most intriguing tune on the album is the title track, a nugget of '70s-style psychedelic rock that showed Trower to be a pretty good songwriter. The best aspects of *Twice Removed* would come to full flowering on his next album, *Bridge of Sighs*, but this debut showed Trower to be an effective interpreter of the Hendrix sound, and not just what numerous others who came in his wake would prove to be: mere imitators. —*Peter Kurtz*

Bridge of Sighs / 1974 / Chrysalis ✦✦✦✦✦
Guitarist Robin Trower's watershed sophomore solo disc remains his most stunning, representative, and consistent collection of tunes. This 24-bit digitally remastered 25th anniversary reissue, which tacks on five live tracks adding nearly 25 minutes to the original playing time, actually improves upon the original. Mixing obvious Hendrix influences with blues and psychedelia, then adding the immensely soulful vocals of James Dewer, Robin Trower pushed the often limited boundaries of the power trio concept into refreshing new waters. The concept gels best in the first track, "Day of the Eagle," where the opening riff rocking morphs into the dreamy washes of gooey guitar chords that characterize the album's distinctive title track that follows. At his best, Trower's gauzy sheets of oozing, wistful sound and subtle use of wah-wah combine with Dewer's whisky-soaked soul-drenched vocals to take a song like the wistful ballad "In This Place" into orbit. "Too Rolling Stoned," another highlight and one of the most covered tracks from this album, adds throbbing, subtle funk to the mix, changing tempos midway to a slow, forceful amble on top of which Trower lays his quicksilver guitar. The live tracks, although similar to the album versions, prove that even without overdubs and the safety of the studio, Trower

and band easily convey the same feel, and add a slightly rougher edge, along with some low-key, crowd-pleasing flourishes. One of the few Trower albums without a weak cut, and in 2000, unfortunately one of the only ones still in print in the U.S., *Bridge of Sighs* holds up to repeated listenings as a timeless work, as well as the crown jewel in Robin Trower's extensive yet inconsistent catalog. *—Hal Horowitz*

For Earth Below / 1975 / Chrysalis ✦✦✦

For Earth Below, Trower's third solo album, is heavily induced with a blues-rock formula that withstands the duration of the eight tracks and arrantly displays his slick guitar mastery. His subtle yet dominant fusion of blues and hard rock styles not only inflicts character throughout each song, but also demonstrates how effective an instrument the guitar can become when the proper techniques are applied. Much like *Twice Removed from Yesterday* but not as diverse as *Bridge of Sighs,* this album has Trower sounding a tad more velvety around the edges, with the blues element sometimes governing the entire piece, an asset to the album's complete texture. The opening "Shame the Devil" and "A Tale Untold" best exemplify his distilled playing style, while a song like "Gonna Be More Suspicious" represents how focused a musician he really is, making each chord pour into the next so that the sound becomes totally viscous. James Dewar, who plays bass and sings vocals, contributes aptly to the low end of the music, filling in where needed, while drummer Bill Lordan helps out on percussion. Finishing off with the sultry but dimensioned aura of "For Earth Below," the album wraps up with a wholehearted satisfactory feel. The albums that followed *For Earth Below* began to stray slowly from being blues-influenced to a sound that contained a mainstream feel, with fragments of bright rock adding a sheen to his raw guitar repertoire. *—Mike DeGagne*

Long Misty Days / 1976 / Chrysalis ✦✦✦

A good mix of down-and-dirty blues, it also features Trower's ethereal ballads. *—Michael P. Dawson*

Live / 1976 / Chrysalis ✦✦✦✦✦

An excellent recording of a superb 1975 stadium show in Sweden, Robin Trower's *Live* album is a perfect snapshot of the guitar hero in his prime. The record also gives ample evidence of why the Robin Trower Band was one of the most successful live guitar rock acts of the '70s, highlighting not only Trower's virtuoso Stratocaster licks, but the soulful vocals of bassist James Dewar and the polyrhythmic drumming of Bill Lordan. The song selection here is top-notch, the most obvious treat being the perennial Trower classic "Too Rolling Stoned," to which Lordon (who replaced Reg Isadore, drummer on the studio version of the song) contributes a somewhat funkier flavor. The same treatment is given to a blistering take on "Little Bit of Sympathy," which contains moments that recall the legendarily telepathic interplay between Jimi Hendrix and Mitch Mitchell. It's a mystery why James Dewar isn't generally recognized as one of the finest blue-eyed soul singers of the '70s, as he is easily as talented and convincing as Paul Rogers or Joe Cocker. Here, he's in excellent form and his vocals on the slow-burning "I Can't Wait Much Longer" are spine-tingling. Although none of the performances stray too far from the songs' studio versions, that fact is part of what makes this album interesting. *Live* shows the Robin Trower Band to be a quintessential no-frills blues-rock band, capable of kicking serious ass no matter what the setting. *—Pemberton Roach*

In City Dreams / 1977 / Chrysalis ✦✦✦

In City Dreams marked a change in direction for Robin Trower. He played his axe just as sweetly as before, but he began to put more emphasis on song accessibility. Additionally, he brought in a funk-style bass player named Rustee Allen to give more punch to the rhythm. The album was a welcome change from the misty, murky blues of his earlier records, but the songs weren't strong enough to effectively displace what had made his name in the first place: potent guitar work. Several of the songs have a real "party" feel, such as the opener "Somebody's Calling" and the 12-bar blues of "Further on Up the Road," with its raucous background noise. "Bluebird" calls to mind "Little Wing" by Hendrix, but James Dewar's saccharine singing ultimately ruins the effect. The one song that successfully conveys the mood that Trower intended for this record is "Sweet Wine of Love," a midtempo tune about a wedding night celebration; it's straightforward and melodic, with a lilting, understated guitar solo. *—Peter Kurtz*

Caravan to Midnight / 1978 / Chrysalis ✦✦✦

It continues the funkier direction of *In City Dreams. —Michael P. Dawson*

Victims of the Fury / 1980 / Chrysalis ✦✦✦

B.L.T. / 1981 / Chrysalis ✦✦✦

It wasn't until the 1980 *Victims of the Fury* album, seven years into his solo career, that Robin Trower would employ former Procul Harum bandmate Keith Reid to provide lyrics (with Reid probably the only lyricist in history to get band status). Though this is officially a Robin Trower release entitled *B.L.T.,* the marquee giving Jack Bruce and Bill Lordan equal heading above the double-sized name of Robin Trower, the project is shouldered by all talents involved and inhibited by a dreadful cover photo of a white bread sandwich: bacon, lettuce and tomato with—if you look closely—raw bacon. All concerned would have been better off titling this a Jack Bruce/Robin Trower project with drummer Bill Lordan. The vocals are all the work of Bruce with the production by Trower, and a moment like "Won't Let You Down" is among the best for both the vocalist of Cream and the guitar player from Procol Harum. "Won't Let You Down" is subtle, stunning, and beautiful. It oozes out of the speakers with double-tracked Trower guitar work that sounds like he was listening to Hendrix's *Cry of Love* album again. And there's nothing wrong with that. "Into Money," "What It Is" (another song about money), and "No Island Lost" are interesting because they take the West, Bruce & Laing concept further into the realm of progressive rock, a place where all parties concerned feel very comfortable. For the Trower fans who couldn't get enough of him sounding like Hendrix, take the "Voodoo Chile" riffs of "No Island Lost" and add the highly commercial voice of Jack Bruce. The combination is appealing while the artists lift the melody of "Voodoo Chile" as well the guitar, making for some amazing and magnetic stuff. With the exception of "End Game" and "Won't Let You Down," the songs are all in the three-minute range for this artistic experiment which works so well. Where Peter Brown is to Jack Bruce what Dewer and Reid are to Trower (a rare Brown/Bruce/Trower composition would show up on the following disc, *Truce*), this is only the second album where Keith Reid gets to collaborate with his former bandmate in the eight years between Trower's solo debut and *B.L.T.* There would be more. The Trower/Reid combo makes perfect sense, especially since the lyricist is probably the only one in history who got band billing. The music these fellows weave is tremendous and becomes a distinctive work in the Jack Bruce catalog, combining his talents with colleagues who share his vision. The fluid sounds which make "Life on Earth" such an appealing opener for side two show that even on a title written solely by Bruce, the only one on the disc, it blends in perfectly with the material, mostly written by Trower and Reid. "Carmen" is absolutely haunting, and this is one of those beautiful discs that true fans have to seek out. Couple the terrible album cover of *B.L.T.* with the equally absurd marketing of West, Bruce & Laing's *Whatever Turns You On* and one gets the feeling that numerous record labels were trying their hardest to keep Jack Bruce's music as underground as possible. He deserves better, and *B.L.T.* is an experiment that, musically, is very successful and holds many revelations. A more compelling package is in order for the magic that's in these grooves. *—Joe Viglione*

Truce / 1982 / Chrysalis ✦✦

Back It Up / 1983 / Chrysalis ✦✦✦

After two albums with singer Jack Bruce, Robin Trower brought back original vocalist James Dewar for his 1983 release *Back It Up.* Longtime fans surely hoped for another *Bridge of Sighs,* but by this time the songwriting had been reduced to pedestrian hard rock, with only occasional flashes of the old cosmic brilliance. Both "The River" and "Benny Dancer" have some of the old edge, and the instrumental "Island" is one of the most beautiful songs Trower ever did. Unfortunately, however, this record was ignored by the old fans (many of whom were now busy starting families and toting briefcases), and it was hard for him to win over a new audience when haircut bands like Culture Club flooded both the radio and the latest media sensation—MTV. *—Peter Kurtz*

Beyond the Mist / 1985 / Passport ✦✦

This mostly live release recorded at London's Marquee club in 1985 is a rather dull effort, since Trower plays only seven tracks with plenty of his best material absent from the set. Sounding slightly murky and muddled, the five live tracks are short on Trower's guitar playing flair, and since he's not the most animated musician to begin with, these songs have an even harder time holding the least bit of attention. Some redemption is established with his signature "Bridge of Sighs" at the end of the album, as Trower reveals his talents with a semi-spirited arrangement of his most famous piece. The two studio tracks at the beginning of the album aren't ear catchers either, with "The Last Time" coming out on top because of its steam engine rhythm. Even with a solid tandem of studio musicians like Martin Clapson behind the kit and Dave Bronze on bass and backing vocals, Robin Trower's usual array of manipulated feedback, bent and twisted guitar chords, and flashy fret bending is kept to a bare minimum. This time around, his instrumental meandering comes up short on guitar nutriment and the album is bettered by any of his '70s studio material. *—Mike DeGagne*

Passion / 1987 / GNP Crescendo ✦✦

Guitarist Robin Trower enjoyed considerable success in the mid-'70s with his tasteful, Jimi Hendrix-inspired style of blues-rock. The Procol Harum veteran's popularity faded as the '80s progressed, but Trower generally stayed active. Released in 1987, *Passion* is interesting because it straddles '70s grittiness and '80s slickness. Trower and his band—lead vocalist Davey Pattison, bass guitarist/vocalist Dave Bronze, and drummer Pete Thompson—form a tight, efficient unit. The simple textures provided by guest keyboardists Robert A. Martin and Reg Webb give the songs extra depth. "Caroline" earned a bit of rock radio airplay, and justifiably so, thanks to its hooks and Trower's warm guitar solo; Pattison's singing is reliable, but his voice isn't quite as rich, deep and distinctive as that of James Dewar, Trower's best-known vocalist. "If Forever" is a clean, no-frills ballad, and Trower's guitar solo balances blues and pop. Both "Won't Even Think About You" and "Passion" are melodic hard rock. The soothing instrumental "Night" gives *Passion* an enjoyable change of pace. *—Bret Adams*

Take What You Need / 1988 / Atlantic ✦✦✦

No Stopping Anytime / 1989 / Chrysalis ✦✦✦✦✦

This is a compilation from Trower's two collaborations with Cream bassist Jack Bruce. *—Michael P. Dawson*

In the Line of Fire / 1990 / Atlantic ✦✦

● **Essential** / 1991 / Chrysalis ✦✦✦✦✦

Essential is a strong single-disc collection that features 16 highlights from Robin Trower's long career at Chrysalis, including such staples as "Too Rolling Stoned," plus several key album tracks. While such albums as *Bridge of Sighs* work as individual albums, this does a nice job of rounding up highlights from uneven records, making it a nice sampler both for casual fans and the curious.*—Stephen Thomas Erlewine*

Collection / Jun. 30, 1992 / Castle ✦✦✦✦

King Biscuit Flower Hour (In Concert) / Feb. 27, 1996 / King Biscuit ✦✦✦

Recorded on October 18, 1977, at the New Haven Coliseum in Connecticut, *King Biscuit Flower Hour* captures Robin Trower moving into a more R&B-driven phase of his career, although the heavy blues-rock of his smash *Bridge of Sighs* album is amply represented in addition to the newer material on *In City Dreams,* the album he was supporting at the time. For this performance, originally broadcast on the *King Biscuit Flower Hour* radio show, Trower's band features vocalist James Dewar, bassist Rusty Allen, and drummer Bill Lordan, formerly of Sly & the Family Stone. It's a versatile band, and in some ways, the live venue is an even better way to hear them than on their studio output. —*Steve Huey*

Twice Removed from Yesterday/Bridge of Sighs / 1997 / BGO ✦✦✦✦
Robin Trower's two best albums, *Twice Removed from Yesterday* and *Bridge of Sighs*, were combined on this single disc from Beat Goes On. —*Stephen Thomas Erlewine*

Live/For Earth Below / Apr. 8, 1997 / BGO ✦✦✦
Robin Trower's third album, 1975's *For Earth Below* is less consistent than the previous two but still contains much excellent material; the Beat Goes On label's reissue teams it with 1976's *Live*, a truly fine set recorded in Sweden. —*Michael P. Dawson*

Long Misty Days/In City Dreams / May 20, 1997 / BGO ✦✦✦
A good mix of down-and-dirty blues, 1976's *Long Misty Days* also features Trower's ethereal ballads. Its 1977 follow-up *In City Dreams*—also included on this two-fer—is slightly funkier than the previous albums, but still highlighted by a delicate ballad, "Bluebird" and the majestic title track. —*Michael P. Dawson*

Caravan to Midnight/Victims of the Fury / Jun. 24, 1997 / BGO ✦✦✦✦
Caravan to Midnight, first released in 1978, continues the funkier direction of the previous *In City Dreams*; the Beat Goes On label's reissue pairs the album with its 1980 follow-up, *Victims of the Fury*. —*Michael P. Dawson*

Go My Way / Jun. 6, 2000 / V-12 ✦✦✦✦
Robin Trower's first rock, as opposed to blues, studio album in five years, returns the guitarist to the fluid, Hendrix-infused trio sound of his salad days. While the songwriting isn't quite up to the quality of his '70s work, Trower's snaky, echoed, languid guitar and his powerful duo's sympathetic backing make this a welcome addition to his extensive catalog. While the smooth, soulful whisky-soaked vocals of original singer Jimmy Dewer are sorely missed (Trower, who handles some of the singing here, is at best adequate), the songs still shimmer with the uniquely silvery quality fans have come to expect from the guitarist. Tunes like "Into Dusk," "Run With the Wolves," and, especially, the nine-minute opening title track with their "Little Wing"-"Third Stone from the Sun" grooves, would have been right at home on *Bridge of Sighs*. The snappy midtempo rocker "Too Much Joy" shoehorns Trower's distinctive guitar solo into a three-minute pop tune, but the similarly inclined chunky "This Old World" doesn't rise above its blues-rock clichés. Trower excels on ballads and slightly funky, slowly simmering psychedelic rockers like "Take This River" where his lava lamp guitar flourishes intricately weave between the dreamy words and construct musical visions uniquely his own. Likely difficult to find because of its indie label release, *Go My Way* is a welcome return from Robin Trower. Those unfamiliar with his work are advised to first hunt down his '70s classics, but long-time fans will be delighted with this solid, uncompromising album. —*Hal Horowitz*

Derek Trucks

b. Jacksonville, FL
Slide Guitar / Blues-Rock, Slide Guitar Blues
Blues/blues-rock guitarist Derek Trucks is the nephew of longtime Allman Brothers drummer Butch Trucks. He displays a command of slide guitar styles that run the gamut from blues to classic R&B and early rock & roll to classic jazz. Although blues players like Buddy Guy, Elmore James, and Duane Allman have been a strong influence on Trucks' slide guitar playing, so have pre-'70s jazz players like Coltrane, Charlie Parker, and Sun Ra.

Trucks began playing guitar when he was nine, and shared stages and sat in with the likes of Buddy Guy and the Allman Brothers Band by the time he was 12. Trucks began his professional career playing with blues bands around his native Jacksonville, FL, and formed his own group in high school. Before the age of 20, Trucks shared stages and jammed with Bob Dylan, Joe Walsh, and Stephen Stills.

The Derek Trucks Band, which has members ranging in age from their twenties to their forties, released their self-titled debut album in 1997 on Landslide Records. *Out of the Madness* followed in late 1998. —*Richard Skelly*

● **Derek Trucks** / Oct. 7, 1997 / Landslide ✦✦✦✦✦
Derek Trucks began building his own legacy at the age of 12, playing scorching slide guitar that prompted many to hypothesize that he was the reincarnation of Duane Allman in the flesh. The nephew of Allman Brothers Band drummer Butch Trucks, Derek was virtually born into a show business family, but don't think for a minute that he doesn't create his own opportunity. Backed by a skin-tight rhythm section and complemented by a top-notch organist, the youthful guitarist blazes through new arrangements of jazz and blues classics. He turns the trumpet wizardry of Miles Davis into slide guitar magic, and his readings of a couple of Coltrane tunes pack a terrific punch. The band also contribute several of their own compositions, paving the way for a bright future as a group of tight-knit, talented musicians. A flawless recording. —*Michael B. Smith*

Out of the Madness / Oct. 20, 1998 / House of Blues ✦✦✦
Whereas guitar phenom Trucks' first album was of the improvisational sort to the highest degree, fusing Coltrane and Sun Ra to Hendrix, this second effort (his first for the House of Blues imprint) puts his playing and music more firmly in Southern American roots music territory. With guest shots from Warren Haynes ("Good Morning Little Schoolgirl," "Forty-Four," and "Death Letter"), Larry McCray ("Ain't That Lovin' You"), Matt Tutor (vocals on "Preachin' Blues" and "Alright"), and Jimmy Herring, there's more of a jam session feeling to this disc than that of a cohesive album. But Trucks also continues to blaze out with hot solos on the more rocking efforts aboard, like "Young Funk," "Kickin' Back," "Spillway," and the closing "Deltaraga." Even New Orleans funk beats come in for a look-see on "Look-ka Py-Py," a curious addition. All in all, a young artist still showing promise. —*Cub Koda*

Joyful Noise / 2002 / Columbia ✦✦✦✦
For his first solo project after replacing Dickie Betts in the Allman Brothers Band, 23-year-old Derek Trucks pushes the stylistic envelope even further than on his last diverse release. Prodding into Latin, Indian, and fusion jazz, this stylistically varied effort exudes enough blues and funky R&B to keep the Allman Brothers Band fan's attention while expanding their boundaries—sometimes radically—beyond what the typical Southern rock fan might expect or even tolerate. It's a brave and largely successful experiment, due in part to the vocals of his guest stars, since Trucks himself does not sing. Opening with the title track, a funky Meters-style bubbler that employs a gospel chorus to frame Trucks' searing slide work, it sounds like the guitarist is working within borders he established on his two previous albums. The laconic instrumental "So Close, So Far Away" sounds like a mid-"Whipping Post" jam, but the disc shifts into high gear with Otis Blackwell's "Home in Your Heart," one of two contributions from the amazing soulman Solomon Burke. He kicks up a Wilson Pickett-style storm on this funky rocker, which both he and Otis Redding recorded 30 years earlier. But gears then switch drastically as Rahat Fateh Ali Khan guests on a traditional Indian tune that gives Trucks' slide a chance to snake through the song, adding a slight blues edge to the tabla and eerie moaning vocals. Rubén Blades guests on a Santana-style workout on "Kam-ma-Lay," but after a scorching Susan Tedeschi appearance on a down-and-dirty version of James Brown's "Baby, You're Right," Trucks veers way off course into the John McLaughlin territory of "Lookout 31," one of the few tracks where Trucks doesn't play slide. It's an intense Mahavishnu Orchestra fusion piece that even swerves into dissonant, avant-garde waters. The instrumental ballad "Frisell" ends this wildly, sometimes disconcertingly eclectic album on a rueful, jazzy note. Trucks' playing is edgy, electric, and distinctive throughout, with his slide work not surprisingly reminiscent of Duane Allman at times. *Joyful Noise* is a powerful, uncompromising statement, if you can stay with it. Derek Trucks shows he is a remarkably talented young guitarist who refuses to be stylistically pigeonholed by the history of the legendary band he joined. —*Hal Horowitz*

The Trumpeteers

f. 1945, Baltimore, MD
Group / Traditional Gospel, Black Gospel
Influenced by the Golden Gate Quartet and led by the spectacular singing of Joe Johnson, this quartet hit the public's consciousness in the late '40s with "Milky White Way," which they recorded for Score Records. Other members included Raleigh Tunrage (tenor), Joseph Armstrong (baritone), and James Keels (bass). There were numerous personnel changes, and they changed their name to the CBS Trumpeteers during the mid-'50s to promote their CBS radio program. —*Bil Carpenter & Kip Lornell*

1948–1959 / 1948-1959 / ✦✦✦✦✦

★ **Milky White Way** / 1956 / Score ✦✦✦✦
One of the last great jubilee singing quartets. Score and Grant material. 1947-1954. —*Opal Louis Nations*

In Memory of Laura / 1970 / Jewel ✦✦✦✦✦
Very talented mixed family group. —*Opal Louis Nations*

The Mighty Number / 1970 / HSF ✦✦✦✦
The group's impressive comeback album. —*Opal Louis Nations*

Bessie Tucker

b. Texas
Vocals / Prewar Country Blues, Classic Female Blues, Acoustic Memphis Blues
Very little is known of the classic blues belter Bessie Tucker, a product of the folk and field holler vocal traditions of her native East Texas region. A woman whose petite frame belied the earthy power of her voice, her legend is largely founded on a bawdy 1928 Memphis session for the Victor label on which she was accompanied by pianist K.D. Johnson; the date yielded her best-known track, "Penitentiary" (sung in honor of an institution to which she was reportedly no stranger). A 1929 date followed, at which time Tucker disappeared from performing, apparently for good; no data exists on the later events of her life. —*Jason Ankeny*

★ **Complete Recorded Works (1928–1929)** / 1991 / Document ✦✦✦✦✦
Document's *Complete Recorded Works (1928-1929)* is an exhaustive overview of Bessie Tucker's known recordings, compiled from a pair of late-'20s sessions and including no less than seven alternate takes (each presented right next to the original). This reliance on exact sequencing, along with the poor fidelity and a large number of performances, are enough to make this of limited interest to casual listeners. Since this is the only Bessie Tucker collection in print, however, it's the best place to find classic recordings like "Penitentiary" and "Fryin' Pan Skillet Blues." —*Thom Owens*

Luther Tucker

b. Jan. 20, 1936, Memphis, TN, d. Jun. 18, 1993, Greenbrae, CA
Guitar / Electric Chicago Blues
Guitarist Luther Tucker was born on January 20, 1936, in Memphis, TN, but relocated to Chicago's South Side when Tucker was around seven years of age. His father, a carpenter, built Tucker his first guitar and his mother, who played boogie-woogie piano, introduced him to Big Bill Broonzy around that time. He went on to study guitar with Robert Jr. Lockwood, for whom he had the greatest admiration and respect. Tucker worked with Little Walter Jacobs for seven years and played on many of Walter's classic sides. He recorded with Otis Rush, Robben Ford, Sonny Boy Williamson, Jimmy Rogers, Snooky Pryor, Muddy Waters, John Lee Hooker, Elvin Bishop, and James Cotton.

In the mid-'60s, Tucker was featured in the James Cotton Blues Band and traveled with that band extensively. He relocated to Marin County, CA, in 1973 and formed the Luther Tucker Band. He played in clubs in the San Francisco Bay area until his death on June 18,

1993, in Greenbrae, CA. Luther Tucker, who was soft-spoken and even shy, was one of a handful of backup artists (the Four Aces/Jukes were others) who helped to create and shape the small combo sound of Chicago blues. Unfortunately, they seldom get much credit. Yet, as the history of Chicago blues gets written, there will be more and more time to discover the wonderful understated rhythmic guitar mastery of Luther Tucker. *—Michael Erlewine*

● **Sad Hours** / 1990 / Antone's ♦♦♦♦
This album is more of a memorial to late guitarist Tucker (who died in June 1993) than a solo debut (the tracks were recorded three years before his death). Still, it's a very nice, soulful slice of the funkier edge of blues, a good tribute, and showcases some nice guitar work. *—Steven McDonald*

Luther Tucker & the Ford Blues Band / May 22, 1995 / Blue Rock'it ♦♦♦

Tommy Tucker (Robert Higginbotham)

b. Mar. 5, 1933, Springfield, OH, **d.** Jan. 17, 1982, Newark, NJ
Vocals, Piano / Memphis Soul, R&B
When Tommy Tucker ordered his lady to "put on her hi-heel sneakers" in 1964, the whole world was listening, judging from the myriad covers and sequels that followed in its wake.

Robert Higginbotham (Tucker's legal handle) grew up in Springfield, getting his little fingers accustomed to the ivories by age seven. Tucker joined saxist Bobby Wood's band in the late '40s as its piano player. When vocal groups became the rage, the band switched gears and became the Cavaliers, a doo wop outfit that remained intact into the late '50s. Tucker put together his own combo after that to play bars in Dayton, his personnel including guitarist Weldon Young and bassist Brenda Jones.

The trio eventually relocated to Newark, NJ, setting Tucker up for his debut solo session in 1961 for Atco. "Rock and Roll Machine" was issued as by Tee Tucker and already exhibited the gritty, Ray Charles-inflected vocal delivery that Tucker later used to great advantage. His traveling companions did pretty well for themselves, too: renamed Dean & Jean, they hit big in 1963-1964 with the lighthearted duets "Tra La La La Suzy" and "Hey Jean, Hey Dean" for Rust Records.

Tommy Tucker fortuitously hooked up with Atlantic Records co-founder Herb Abramson, who was working as an independent R&B producer during the early '60s. Among their early collaborations was the lowdown Jimmy Reed-style shuffle "Hi-Heel Sneakers" (Dean Young was the nasty lead guitarist). Abramson leased it to Checker Records and watched it sail to the upper reaches of the pop charts in early 1964. A terrific Checker LP and a trip to Great Britain were among the immediate upshot for the organist.

R&B star Don Covay co-wrote Tucker's follow-up, "Long Tall Shorty," an amusing tune in a similar groove. It barely scraped the lower end of the charts, and Tucker never scored another hit. That didn't stop Abramson from trying, though—he produced Tucker singing a soulful "That's Life" in 1966 for his own Festival label, while "Alimony," another standout Checker 45, certainly deserved a better reception than it got in 1965.

Although the majority of his waxings were under Abramson's supervision, Tucker did travel to Chicago in 1966 to record with producer Willie Dixon in an effort to jump-start his fading career. "I'm Shorty" had Dixon contributing harmony vocals and Big Walter Horton on harp, but it didn't do the trick.

Abramson admirably stuck by his protégé, recording him anew for at least another decade, but most of the mixed results just gathered dust in his vaults. Tucker was still musically active when he died, a relatively young man, in 1982. *—Bill Dahl*

● **Hi Heel Sneakers** / 1964 / Checker ♦♦♦♦♦
A dozen of his best blues and soul outings for producer Herb Abramson, including the two hits, the grinding soul rockers "Just for a Day," "I Don't Want 'Cha" and "I Warned You About Him" (oodles of Ray Charles influence on all of 'em), and an absolutely stunning "Come Rain or Come Shine." The 1995 CD reissue adds eight bonus tracks from the mid-'60s that were not on the original LP, including the single "Alimony," effectively making it a Tommy Tucker best-of. *—Bill Dahl*

Mother Tucker / 1974 / Red Lightnin' ♦♦♦
Leftovers from deep in the Abramson archives. A precious few tracks—"Lean Greens," "Drunk"—possess the same gritty charm that invested Tucker's greatest hit, "Hi-Heel Sneakers" (here in longer, unedited form with Tucker's faltering organ solo intact). Most of the 16-song LP is comprised of demo tapes and other flotsam that doesn't present the keyboardist in the best light. *—Bill Dahl*

Hi Heel Sneakers / Dec. 12, 2000 / Chrisly ♦♦♦♦

Duke Tumatoe

Group / Contemporary Blues, Blues-Rock, Modern Electric Blues
Chicago-born Duke Tumatoe is a musician/showman who has retained a firm career by fusing gritty R&B, rock, blues, and funk injected with equal parts humor and gut level sincerity. Tumatoe was a founding member of what would become REO Speedwagon. His tenure with that band was short-lived, leaving in 1969 and forming Duke Tumatoe & the All-Star Frogs. For the next 13 years, they toured relentlessly playing throughout the Midwest on countless college campuses and bars. Because of this grueling tour schedule, the band managed to release two albums, *Red Pepper Hot* (1976) and *Back to Chicago* (1982).

In 1983, Tumatoe decided to slow down the pace and break up the Frogs. He immediately rebounded with the creation of the Power Trio who recorded *Duke's Up* for Blind Pig Records. Tumatoe took advantage of the more flexible schedule and formed his own record label, Sweetfinger Music. Over the next several years, Tumatoe released four discs on his label, *Dr. Duke* (1992), *Wild Animals* (1994), *Greatest Hits Plus* (1996), and the all-instrumental *Picks & Sticks* (1997). Throughout his illustrious career, Tumatoe opened for several legendary figures in blues and rock including Muddy Waters, Buddy Guy, B.B. King, George Thorogood, Fabulous Thunderbirds, and John Fogerty. Fogerty was so taken with Tumatoe's performance, he produced the critically acclaimed 1988 live album *I Like My Job* on Warner Bros. In 1999, Tumatoe signed with the J-Bird label, where he released *A Ejukatid Man* that same year. In 2001, Tumatoe had tongue firmly in cheek with the releases *Pompous & Overrated* and the raunchy seasonal disc *It's Christmas (Let's Have Sex)*. *—Al Campbell*

Naughty Child / 1980 / Blind Pig ♦♦♦♦
This is rock & roll steeped in the blues. *—AMG*

Back to Chicago / 1982 / Trouserworm Tunes ♦♦♦

Dukes Up / Apr. 1986 / Blind Pig ♦♦♦

● **I Like My Job!** / Jan. 1988 / Warner Brothers ♦♦♦♦
If you're seeking a joyous blast of Chicago blues, you need look no further. This album of energetic party music is the best-sounding album from Duke Tumatoe, thanks to the meticulous production of John Fogerty, who saw them in a bar and decided to produce their major-label debut. In fact, if it wasn't for Fogerty, they probably wouldn't have gotten on a major label; the following album, without Fogerty producing, was back on J-Bird. *I Like My Job!* crackles with energy from the opening notes of the cheerful "Get Loose." Recording live was a smart move, since the audience response to songs like "If I Hadn't Been High" and "More Love, More Money" makes both vastly better than any studio take. This is doubly true for the salacious "Tie You Up," as seductive a song about bondage play ever written—at least, up to the point where Tumatoe is raving about using garbanzo beans and croutons as sex toys. This inspired silliness holds from end to end and makes this a must-have album for anyone who likes their blues spiced with more than a dash of humor. *—Richard Foss*

A Ejukatid Man / Apr. 20, 1999 / J-Bird ♦♦♦

Pompous and Overrated / May 8, 2001 / J-Bird ♦♦♦

It's Christmas (Let's Have Sex) / Aug. 14, 2001 / J-Bird ♦♦♦
Duke Tumatoe offers his take on the holidays with *It's Christmas (Let's Have Sex)*. Filled with sexually charged takes on popular Christmas traditions, Tumatoe's humor is not for everyone. But those interested in a humorous album for the holidays might enjoy his juvenile comedy songs; just keep it away from children. *—Bradley Torreano*

Big Joe Turner

b. May 18, 1911, Kansas City, MO, **d.** Nov. 24, 1985, Inglewood, CA
Vocals / Jump Blues, Swing, Rock & Roll, R&B, Urban Blues
The premier blues shouter of the postwar era, Big Joe Turner's roar could rattle the very foundation of any gin joint he sang within—and that's without a microphone. Turner was a resilient figure in the history of blues—he effortlessly spanned boogie-woogie, jump blues, even the first wave of rock & roll, enjoying great success in each genre.

Turner, whose powerful physique certainly matched his vocal might, was a product of the swinging, wide-open Kansas City scene. Even in his teens, the big-boned Turner looked entirely mature enough to gain entry to various K.C. niteries. He ended up simultaneously tending bar and singing the blues before hooking up with boogie piano master Pete Johnson during the early '30s. Theirs was a partnership that would endure for 13 years.

The pair initially traveled to New York at John Hammond's behest in 1936. On December 23, 1938, they appeared on the fabled Spirituals to Swing concert at Carnegie Hall on a bill with Big Bill Broonzy, Sonny Terry, the Golden Gate Quartet, and Count Basie. Big Joe and Johnson performed "Low Down Dog" and "It's All Right, Baby" on the historic show, kicking off a boogie-woogie craze that landed them a long-running slot at the Cafe Society (along with piano giants Meade "Lux" Lewis and Albert Ammons).

As 1938 came to a close, Turner and Johnson waxed the thundering "Roll 'Em Pete" for Vocalion. It was a thrilling uptempo number anchored by Johnson's crashing 88s, and Turner would re-record it many times over the decades. Turner and Johnson waxed their seminal blues "Cherry Red" the next year for Vocalion with trumpeter Hot Lips Page and a full combo in support. In 1940, the massive shouter moved over to Decca and cut "Piney Brown Blues" with Johnson rippling the ivories. But not all of Turner's Decca sides teamed him with Johnson; Willie "The Lion" Smith accompanied him on the mournful "Careless Love," while Freddie Slack's Trio provided backing for "Rocks in My Bed" in 1941.

Turner ventured out to the West Coast during the war years, building quite a following while ensconced on the L.A. circuit. In 1945, he signed on with National Records and cut some fine small combo platters under Herb Abramson's supervision. Turner remained with National through 1947, belting an exuberant "My Gal's a Jockey" that became his first national R&B smash. Contracts didn't stop him from waxing an incredibly risqué two-part "Around the Clock" for the aptly named Stag imprint (as Big Vernon!) in 1947. There were also solid sessions for Aladdin that year that included a wild vocal duel with one of Turner's principal rivals, Wynonie Harris, on the ribald two-part "Battle of the Blues."

Few West Coast indie labels of the late '40s didn't boast at least one or two Turner titles in their catalogs. The shouter bounced from RPM to Down Beat/Swing Time to MGM (all those dates were anchored by Johnson's piano) to Texas-based Freedom (which moved some of their masters to Specialty) to Imperial in 1950 (his New Orleans backing crew there included a young Fats Domino on piano). But apart from the 1950 Freedom 78, "Still in the Dark," none of Big Joe's records were selling particularly well. When Atlantic Records bosses Abramson and Ahmet Ertegun fortuitously dropped by the Apollo Theater to check out Count Basie's band one day, they discovered that Turner had temporarily replaced Jimmy Rushing as the Basie band's front man, and he was having a tough go of it. Atlantic picked up his spirits by picking up his recording contract, and Big Joe Turner's heyday was about to commence.

At Turner's first Atlantic date in April of 1951, he imparted a gorgeously world-weary reading to the moving blues ballad "Chains of Love" (co-penned by Ertegun and pianist Harry Van Walls) that restored him to the uppermost reaches of the R&B charts. From there, the hits came in droves: "Chill Is On," "Sweet Sixteen" (yeah, the same downbeat blues B.B. King's usually associated with; Turner did it first), and "Don't You Cry" were all done in New York, and all hit big.

Big Joe Turner had no problem whatsoever adapting his prodigious pipes to whatever regional setting he was in. In 1953, he cut his first R&B chart-topper, the storming rocker "Honey Hush" (later covered by Johnny Burnette and Jerry Lee Lewis), in New Orleans, with trombonist Pluma Davis and tenor saxman Lee Allen in rip-roaring support. Before the year was through, he stopped off in Chicago to record with slide guitarist Elmore James' considerably rougher-edged combo and hit again with the salacious "T.V. Mama."

Prolific Atlantic house writer Jesse Stone was the source of Turner's biggest smash of all, "Shake, Rattle and Roll," which proved his second chart-topper in 1954. With the Atlantic braintrust reportedly chiming in on the chorus behind Turner's rumbling lead, the song sported enough pop possibilities to merit a considerably cleaned-up cover by Bill Haley & the Comets (and a subsequent version by Elvis Presley that came a lot closer to the original leering intent).

Suddenly, at the age of 43, Big Joe Turner was a rock star. His jumping follow-ups—"Well All Right," "Flip Flop and Fly," "Hide and Seek," "Morning, Noon and Night," "The Chicken and the Hawk"—all mined the same goodtime groove as "Shake, Rattle and Roll," with crisp backing from New York's top session aces and typically superb production by Ertegun and Jerry Wexler.

Turner turned up on a couple episodes of the groundbreaking TV program *Showtime at the Apollo* during the mid-'50s, commanding center stage with a joyous rendition of "Shake, Rattle and Roll" in front of saxman Paul "Hucklebuck" Williams' band. Nor was the silver screen immune to his considerable charms: Turner mimed a couple of numbers in the 1957 film *Shake Rattle & Rock* (Fats Domino and Mike "Mannix" Connors also starred in the flick).

Updating the prewar number "Corrine Corrina" was an inspired notion that provided Turner with another massive seller in 1956. But after the two-sided hit "Rock a While"/"Lipstick Powder and Paint" later that year, his Atlantic output swiftly faded from commercial acceptance. Atlantic's recording strategy wisely involved recording Turner in a jazzier setting for the adult-oriented album market; to that end, a Kansas City-styled set (with his former partner Johnson at the piano stool) was laid down in 1956 and remains a linchpin of his legacy.

Turner stayed on at Atlantic into 1959, but nobody bought his violin-enriched remake of "Chains of Love" (on the other hand, a revival of "Honey Hush" with King Curtis blowing a scorching sax break from the same session was a gem in its own right). The '60s didn't produce too much of lasting substance for the shouter—he actually cut an album with longtime admirer Haley and his latest batch of Comets in Mexico City in 1966!

But by the tail end of the decade, Big Joe Turner's essential contributions to blues history were beginning to receive proper recognition; he cut LPs for BluesWay and Blues Time. During the '70s and '80s, Turner recorded prolifically for Norman Granz's jazz-oriented Pablo label. These were super-relaxed impromptu sessions that often paired the allegedly illiterate shouter with various jazz luminaries in what amounted to loosely run jam sessions. Turner contentedly roared the familiar lyrics of one or another of his hits, then sat back while somebody took a lengthy solo. Other notable album projects included a 1983 collaboration with Roomful of Blues, *Blues Train*, for Muse. Although health problems and the size of his humongous frame forced him to sit down during his latter-day performances, Turner continued to tour until shortly before his death in 1985. They called him the Boss of the Blues, and the appellation was truly a fitting one: when Big Joe Turner shouted a lyric, you were definitely at his beck and call. *—Bill Dahl*

☆ **Big, Bad & Blue: The Big Joe Turner Anthology** / Dec. 30, 1938-Jan. 26, 1983 / Rhino ♦♦♦♦♦
This three-record anthology shows how Turner, without really ever changing his style, moved from strict Kansas City swing to pioneering rock & roll and back to basic jazzy blues. It contains 62 songs, everything from treasured hits to slow, sweltering ballads, strident uptempo wailers, moaning blues, novelty tunes, and fiery pieces with lyrics and sentiments that wouldn't make it in today's environment. A comprehensive, well-written, and lavishly prepared and illustrated booklet with numerous anecdotes and remembrances is the icing on a superb cake. *—Ron Wynn*

I've Been to Kansas City / Nov. 11, 1940-Jul. 17, 1941 / Decca ♦♦♦♦♦
This excellent 1990 CD reissues singer Big Joe Turner's first eight recordings for Decca and the six songs (plus two alternate takes) that he made with the remarkable pianist Art Tatum. Turner is joined by trumpeter Hot Lips Page and a top Kansas City group (including pianist Pete Johnson) for "Piney Brown Blues," has four surprisingly effective duets with the sophisticated pianist Willie "The Lion" Smith and is backed by pianist Sammy Price's trio for three of the four numbers that he recorded on July 17, 1941. The Tatum sides (highlighted by the classic "Wee Baby Blues" and "Corrine Corrina") also feature trumpeter Joe Thomas and (on two songs) clarinetist Edmond Hall prominent in the backup group. Just 29 and 30 during this time, Turner already sounded quite mature and powerful. *—Scott Yanow*

☆ **Complete 1940–1944** / Nov. 11, 1940-Nov. 13, 1944 / Official ♦♦♦♦♦
Big Joe Turner's 25 Decca recordings are all included on this excellent set. The music is consistently exciting and finds the blues singer in prime form. His accompaniment is quite varied and always colorful with such pianists as Art Tatum, Pete Johnson, Willie "The Lion" Smith (a perfect match), Sam Price, and the surprisingly effective Freddie Slack all getting their spots. Turner had a remarkably long and commercially successful career considering that he never changed his basic approach; he just never went out of style. *—Scott Yanow*

Every Day in the Week / Sep. 8, 1941-Apr. 13, 1967 / GRP/Decca ♦♦♦
Most of the material on this grab bag dates from early- and mid-'40s sessions for Decca. Rather muted and jazzy in feel, they're made more interesting or tedious, depending on your perspective, by the inclusion of many alternate takes (some previously unissued). As these are grouped together one after another, it can make tough listening for the general fan, although Turner completists will appreciate the attention to detail. Rounding out the collection are four 1963-1964 tracks which awkwardly update Turner's R&B with modern soul and pop touches, and a track from a 1967 BluesWay LP. *—Richie Unterberger*

1941–1946 / 1941-1946 / Classics ♦♦♦♦
The original blues shouter found a way to meld some of Jimmy Rushing's rambling jazz phrasing with the low-down tone he naturally bellowed out to Kansas City audiences—sometimes while behind the bar serving drinks. And before hitting the charts with several early rock & roll hits, Big Joe Turner did bedrock work with such fine stride and boogie-woogie pianists as Pete Johnson, Freddie Slack, and Willie "The Lion" Smith. On Classics' 1941-1946 chronological sampler of Turner's early prime, these and other luminaries of the after-hours fraternity sympathetically back Turner over the course of 22 gems. A good chunk of the material finds Turner ideally framed by just a piano trio, with highlights including "Nobody in Mind" (Sammy Price is at the keys for this cut), "Little Bittie Gal's Blues," and "Blues on Central Avenue." As the last title indicates, this and several other numbers were recorded during Turner's wartime stay in L.A., where many blues and R&B performers first made it big. Piano trios and geographical considerations aside, there are also fine cameos from tenor great Don Byas and trumpeter Frankie Newton to expand the sonic landscape. A fine collection for listeners wanting to check out Turner's early work before the Atlantic party that was "Shake, Rattle and Roll." *—Stephen Cook*

Have No Fear, Big Joe Turner Is Here / Feb. 2, 1945-Nov. 29, 1947 / Savoy ♦♦♦♦
Producer Herb Abramson's first encounters with Big Joe Turner weren't at Atlantic, but for the National logo, where Turner paused from 1945 to 1947 and cut the 26 swinging numbers on this collection. For once, the CD format limits the amount of selections rather than enlarging it; the original two-LP version of this package boasted a few more cuts. Pete Johnson returns to run the 88s on the first seven numbers (including a two-part cover of Saunders King's "S.K. Blues"), and familiar names like saxman Wild Bill Moore and drummer Red Saunders also turn up. "Sally Zu-Zazz," "I Got Love for Sale," and "My Gal's a Jockey" capture the peerless shouter at his ribald best. *—Bill Dahl*

Tell Me Pretty Baby / Nov. 1947-1949 / Arhoolie ♦♦♦♦
Lusty, romping jump blues and boogies from 1947-1949 that team Big Joe Turner with his longtime piano partner Pete Johnson and a coterie of solid L.A. sessioneers. The two dozen entries include party rockers like "Wine-O-Baby Boogie," "Christmas Date Boogie," "I Don't Dig It," and an incredibly raunchy two-part "Around the Clock Blues" (where Turner spends his time in a by-the-hour sexual tryst). *—Bill Dahl*

Rhythm & Blues Years / Apr. 17, 1951-Sep. 29, 1959 / Atlantic ♦♦♦♦♦
Picks up the rest of the '50s Atlantic Records motherlode. The Chicago-cut double entendre gem "TV Mama" (with Elmore James on guitar), the lighthearted rockers "Rock a While," "Morning Noon and Night," and "Lipstick, Powder and Paint," and a rip-snorting remake of Turner's classic "Roll 'Em Pete," here titled "(We're Gonna) Jump for Joy," that in its own way rivals the original (King Curtis' blistering sax solo doesn't hurt), are among the many highlights on the 28-song collection. *—Bill Dahl*

★ **Big Joe Turner's Greatest Hits** / Apr. 19, 1951-Jan. 22, 1958 / Atlantic Jazz ♦♦♦♦♦
The best single-disc collection available of Turner's seminal '50s Atlantic sides (21 sides in all). Most of the essential stuff is here—the world-weary blues ballads "Chains of Love" and "Sweet Sixteen"; the rockers "Shake, Rattle and Roll," "Flip Flop and Fly," and "Boogie Woogie Country Girl"; and a lusty "Well All Right" that rates with Turner's best jump blues outings ever. *—Bill Dahl*

★ **The Very Best of Big Joe Turner** / 1951-1959 / Rhino ♦♦♦♦♦
The Very Best of Big Joe Turner is an excellent 16-track collection that features his biggest hits from 1951-1959, including "Chains of Love," "Sweet Sixteen," "Honey Hush," "TV Mama," "Shake, Rattle and Roll," "Well All Right," "Flip Flop and Fly," "Hide and Seek," "The Chicken and the Hawk (Up, Up and Away)," "Boogie Woogie Country Girl," "Corrine Corrina," and "Midnight Special Train." All of his best-known songs in their hit versions are available on this concise, affordable disc, which makes for an ideal introduction to this legendary R&B vocalist. *—Stephen Thomas Erlewine*

☆ **The Boss of the Blues** / Mar. 6, 1956-Mar. 7, 1956 / Atlantic ♦♦♦♦♦
During an era when Big Joe Turner recordings were often surprise hits with rock & roll fans (particularly "Shake, Rattle and Roll"), he occasionally recorded no-nonsense blues-oriented jazz dates too. This reissue album matched Turner for one of the last times with the veteran boogie-woogie pianist Pete Johnson and also includes a variety of top swing players: trumpeter Joe Newman, trombonist Lawrence Brown, altoist Pete Brown, tenor saxophonist Frank Wess, guitarist Freddie Green, bassist Walter Page, and drummer Cliff Leeman. It is not surprising, considering the number of Basie-ites on the date, that the band often sounds like a Count Basie combo. Turner is in top form on remakes of some of his early tunes (including "Cherry Red," "Roll 'Em Pete," and "Wee Baby Blues"), a few traditional blues, and a couple of swing standards. This music should appeal to many listeners. *—Scott Yanow*

Big Joe Rides Again / Mar. 7, 1956-Sep. 10, 1959 / Atlantic ♦♦♦♦
With the exception of one selection ("Pennies from Heaven") left over from his 1956 record *The Boss of the Blue*, the music on this album was all recorded in September 1959. Veteran blues singer Big Joe Turner returns to his roots, belting out blues and early standards while accompanied by an octet arranged by Ernie Wilkins. Among the key sidemen are the great tenor Coleman Hawkins, trombonist Vic Dickenson, trumpeter Paul Ricard and altoist Jerome Richardson; and the highlights include "Nobody in Mind," "Rebecca," and "Don't You Make Me High." An excellent outing for Turner, whose boisterous style would be largely unchanged over his half-century career. *—Scott Yanow*

Rockin' the Blues / 1958 / Atlantic ♦♦♦
Swinging jump blues from the unparalleled shouter. *—Bill Dahl*

Joe Turner / 1958 / Atlantic ✦✦✦
Turner's classic rocking Atlantic catalog. *—Bill Dahl*

Singing the Blues / Dec. 1967 / Mobile Fidelity ✦✦✦
Big Joe Turner made relatively few recordings during 1960-1966 but things started to look up in 1967 when he began recording for BluesWay. His initial BluesWay set has been reissued as a Mobile Fidelity audiophile CD. Backed by some top studio players of the era (Buddy Lucas on tenor and harmonica along with a four-piece rhythm section), the 56-year old classic blues singer shows that he was still in prime form. Nothing too surprising occurs other than the fact that the ten songs are all Turner's originals. Best known are the two vintage hits "Roll 'Em Pete" and "Cherry Red," while some of the newer tunes are more forgettable although still delivered with spirit. *—Scott Yanow*

Bosses of the Blues, Vol. 1 / Aug. 18, 1969-Aug. 19, 1969 / Bluebird/RCA ✦✦✦✦
Two BluesWay albums recorded on consecutive days are reissued in full on this single CD. Big Joe Turner sings eight numbers while T-Bone Walker stretches out on seven; both mix together remakes of earlier hits with some newer material. While Turner is accompanied by an orchestra, Walker is joined by a crack studio group with some space allocated to the young tenor Tom Scott. Although not essential, this CD finds the two bluesmen in excellent form; pity that they did not record together. *—Scott Yanow*

His Greatest Recordings / 1971 / Atco ✦✦✦✦
Big Joe Turner is a great recording artist, and listeners should be encouraged to dig deeply into his discography, as if a plate of Kansas City-style barbecued turkey breast and sausage was placed in front of them. Vegetarians should feel free to substitute collard greens, kale, red cabbage, or whatever else suits them. Just the fact that he was called "big" isn't the reason to create such an image, since the nickname could have easily been applied to his voice, and not just his girth. But Turner was fond of sending thank-you letters to critics who wrote positive reviews about him, these notes invariably accompanied with a snapshot of the singer and his wife chowing down on a huge lunch. Once a critic has received one of these pictures, the image is forever planted and an appetite begins building as soon as the first strains of "Honey Hush" come out of the speakers. Hopefully, the listener's appetite for this artist will extend well beyond a greatest-hits package, yet this sampling of 14 songs is by itself musically faultless. "Hits" or not, these are also not tunes that have been played to death over the radio 30 or 40 years after they were recorded, so the overfamiliarity that mars some greatest-hits packages shouldn't be a problem here. Turner can be compared to one of the other early giants of rock & roll, Chuck Berry, in that both helped create the new genre by combining swing and R&B styles in the perfect proportion. Whereas Berry took a few pages from country & western with its clever, humorous, and down-to-earth lyrics, Turner preferred a harder edge. Some of these numbers literally stomp, but always still maintain a sense of swing. Hard rock and boogie bands have been attracted to numbers such as "Flip Flop and Fly" and the aforementioned "Honey Hush," yet anyone who has been stuck in a bar listening to such an outfit will immediately recognize what is missing: the swing.

Turner's "Shake, Rattle and Roll" has all three elements, and beyond such a simple description the essence of his music dictates the combination of a variety of rural and urban musical influences. The listener will hear the old country blues and the new R&B style—and running through it all is the solid Kansas City swing that gives the jazz from this town such a solid groove. Turner's vocals are just fantastic. It's rare to hear a rock & roll singer who can hit notes with the precision of an opera baritone, and this skill is combined with extreme charisma, a thick dollop of good humor literally built up from his years shouting blues numbers from behind the bar where he worked. An advantage of this particular greatest-hits package is the fact that these recordings are presented in all the glory of their original mono, while some other sets that are available have ghastly stereo versions. It is a gatefold album design, but with much wasted space. The long essay is fine, but on the opposing face there is nothing but an extremely ugly bit of graphics nonsense that already gets too much play on the back cover. More details about the original recordings would have been better, including a list of the session players. These anonymous musicians figure a great deal in the success of these tracks, despite the fact that Turner would have sounded good singing over an organ grinder and his monkey. Another oversight is the jacket identifying him as Joe Turner, flying completely in the face of one of the basic rules of the music business: Once an artist has been given the "big" prefix to his or her name, it should always be used. It's a shame this big guy is no longer around to respond with one of his thank-you notes. *—Eugene Chadbourne*

Texas Style / Apr. 26, 1971 / Evidence ✦✦✦
This somewhat obscure Black & Blue session (reissued by Evidence on CD) features the great blues singer Big Joe Turner a year before he hooked up with the Pablo label. Turner is backed by a particularly colorful and supportive trio comprised of pianist Milt Buckner (the master of block chords), bassist Slam Stewart (who takes a few of his trademark solos in which he sings along with his bowed bass) and veteran swing drummer Jo Jones. Turner was still in his prime at the time and, even if his material was not too adventurous, the music (which includes a few newer bluish originals plus such standbys as "Cherry Red" and "'Tain't Nobody's Bizness If I Do") is performed with enthusiasm and solid swing. *—Scott Yanow*

Flip, Flop & Fly / Apr. 17, 1972+Apr. 24, 1972 / Pablo/OJC ✦✦✦✦
Big Joe Turner's first of many recordings for Pablo was not initially released until 1989. In the spring of 1972, the 60-year-old blues singer toured Europe with the Count Basie Orchestra and this CD has music from two concerts. Turner's repertoire offered few surprises at that late date (he mostly performs remakes of earlier hits), but his interplay with the Basie big band makes this set somewhat special. Among the soloists heard from are tenors Eddie "Lockjaw" Davis and Jimmy Forrest, trumpeter Pete Minger, altoist Curtis Peagler, and trombonist Al Grey, along with Basie himself. Easily recommended to Big Joe Turner fans and a rare opportunity for him to be heard fronting a solid big band. *—Scott Yanow*

Life Ain't Easy / Jun. 3, 1974 / Pablo/OJC ✦✦✦
Big Joe Turner's Pablo recordings of 1974-1984 tended to be loose and sometimes a bit sloppy (with some overlong performances) but they were always full of spirit. On this particular CD, Turner's classic singing is matched with a mostly all-star crew including trumpeter Roy Eldridge, trombonist Al Grey, tenor saxophonist Lee Allen, bassist Ray Brown and drummer Earl Palmer (along with guitarist Thomas Gadson and Jimmy Robins on piano and organ). Turner performs Woody Guthrie's "So Long" and five of his recent originals; Eldridge and Grey's occasional competitive solos uplift the music. *—Scott Yanow*

The Trumpet Kings Meet Joe Turner / Sep. 19, 1974 / Pablo/OJC ✦✦✦✦
This album has a most unusual session. Veteran blues singer Joe Turner and his usual rhythm section of the mid-'70s (which includes guitarist Pee Wee Crayton) are joined by four notable trumpeters: Dizzy Gillespie, Roy Eldridge, Harry "Sweets" Edison and Clark Terry. On three blues (including the 15-minute "I Know You Love Me Baby") and "'Tain't Nobody's Bizness if I Do," the group stretches out with each of the trumpeters getting ample solo space. It is not a classic outing (a little more planning and better material might have helped) but it is colorful and unique enough to be easily recommended to straight-ahead jazz and blues fans. *—Scott Yanow*

Stormy Monday / Sep. 19, 1974-Jun. 22, 1978 / Pablo ✦✦✦
This 1991 CD contains six selections taken from Big Joe Turner's 1974-1978 Pablo sessions but never previously released. The veteran blues singer is joined by a variety of famous and obscure musicians with guitarist Pee Wee Crayton and pianist Lloyd Glenn appearing on the majority of the tracks. The most interesting selection, "Stormy Monday," is taken from a 1974 encounter with trumpeters Roy Eldridge, Dizzy Gillespie, Clark Terry, and Harry "Sweets" Edison. The first half of the ten-minute performance works well, with each of the trumpeters getting a solo, but then it rambles on aimlessly, demonstrating why the performance went unreleased. The other five numbers (which include one appearance by altoist Eddie "Cleanhead" Vinson) are more coherent and Turner sounds consistently strong. Overall this is a worthwhile set for Big Joe Turner fans. *—Scott Yanow*

Everyday I Have the Blues / Mar. 3, 1975 / Pablo/OJC ✦✦✦✦
This CD reissues one of Big Joe Turner's better Pablo releases. In 1975 Turner's voice was still strong and he had a compatible four-piece group that featured veteran guitarist Pee Wee Crayton. With guest Sonny Stitt contributing typically boppish solos on tenor and alto, Turner sings mostly familiar material (including "Stormy Monday," "Piney Brown," and "Shake, Rattle and Roll") plus his recent "Martin Luther King Southside." Recommended. *—Scott Yanow*

The Midnight Special / Mar. 27, 1976 / Pablo ✦✦✦✦
Big Joe Turner had the ability to turn every song into the blues. He displays that skill on this loose Pablo session (reissued on CD) during such nonblues songs as "I Left My Heart in San Francisco," "I'm Gonna Sit Right Down and Write Myself a Letter," "I Can't Give You Anything but Love," and "You're Driving Me Crazy." In addition to a four-piece rhythm section of obscure but compatible players, Turner is joined by trumpeter Jake Porter, Roy Brewster on baritone horn, and Curtis Kirk on harmonica. A slightly off-the-wall set that stands apart from most of Turner's Pablo dates. *—Scott Yanow*

Things That I Used to Do / Feb. 8, 1977 / Pablo/OJC ✦✦✦✦✦
This is one of Big Joe Turner's best albums of his last period. Turner is in fine form and joined by some superb blues and jazz musicians. Altoist Eddie "Cleanhead" Vinson (pity that he didn't have a vocal duet with Turner) and trumpeter Blue Mitchell get some solo space as does the veteran R&B tenor Wild Bill Moore, pianist Lloyd Glenn, and guitarist Gary Bell. Mitchell can be heard on many of the tunes setting hot ensemble riffs. There are some loose spots but the spirit is definitely there and Turner's voice can be heard still in its prime on such tunes as "Jelly Jelly Blues," "Shake It and Break It," and "St. Louis Blues." Fun music. *—Scott Yanow*

In the Evening / Oct. 1977 / Pablo/OJC ✦✦✦
Many of Big Joe Turner's Pablo recordings matched him with big names, but this workout finds him jubilant and in top form singing with some lesser-known musicians (altoist Bob Smith, Herman Bennett on second guitar, pianist J.D. Nicholson, bassist Winston McGregor, drummer Charles Randall, and the only "name" of the date, guitarist Pee Wee Crayton). The solos of Smith (who sounds like a mixture of Tab Smith and Johnny Hodges) and Crayton are consistently excellent, and Big Joe turns everything into blues, including such unlikely material as "Sweet Lorraine" and "Pennies from Heaven." This CD reissue gives listeners a good example of what it was like to catch the great blues singer during a club date with a pickup band. *—Scott Yanow*

Nobody in Mind / 1982 / Pablo/OJC ✦✦✦✦
Blues singer Big Joe Turner is in good form on this late-period session. In addition to his usual rhythm section (featuring guitarist Pee Wee Crayton), Turner is joined by two notable soloists: trumpeter Roy Eldridge (whose determination makes up for his occasional misses) and vibraphonist Milt Jackson. Other than "Red Sails in the Sunset" (which is largely turned into a blues), the music is fairly typical for Turner but the spirit and sincerity of the singer and his sidemen make this CD reissue worth picking up. *—Scott Yanow*

Blues Train / Jan. 26, 1983 / Muse ✦✦✦
Big Joe Turner was a bit past his prime at age 72, when he recorded this set, but he was clearly inspired by the opportunity to sing with Roomful of Blues. Turner stars on seven numbers (including "I Want a Little Girl," which has a piano solo by guest Dr. John), and there are also two instrumentals that let the impressive band stretch out. With the group featuring guitarist Ronnie Earl, Greg Piccolo on tenor, trumpeter Bob Enos, and

trombonist Porky Cohen, among others, Turner was ably supported, and his high spirits made the music well worth hearing. *—Scott Yanow*

Kansas City Here I Come / Feb. 1984 / Pablo/OJC ♦♦♦
Big Joe Turner's next-to-last recording is certainly listenable but not prime material. Turner's elocution became quite blurry in his later years with a lot of slurring of words and rather loose singing and yet his ability to express blues feeling and his sense of swing were unimpaired. Among the mostly obscure backup crew are tenor saxophonist Lee Allen, Jerry Jumonville on baritone and alto, and guitarist Terry Evans, but in general the playing is pretty anonymous. This CD, one of many Big Joe Turner releases currently available, is mostly for completists. *—Scott Yanow*

Patcha, Patcha All Night Long / Apr. 11, 1985 / Pablo/OJC ♦♦♦
This CD reissue, which is subtitled "Joe Turner Meets Jimmy Witherspoon," does not quite deliver on its promise. Turner (who would pass away within a year) and Witherspoon only actually meet up on the first two numbers and, other than some interplay on "Patcha, Patcha," the matchup generates few sparks. However the individual features (two songs apiece) are excellent, particularly Witherspoon's "You Got Me Runnin' " and Turner's "The Chicken and the Hawk." In addition there are many fine solos from altoist Red Holloway, Lee Allen on tenor, and guitarist Gary Bell. This is a worthwhile and obviously historic set, recommended as much to blues as jazz collectors. *—Scott Yanow*

☆ **Jumpin' With Joe: The Complete Aladdin & Imperial Recordings** / Jan. 11, 1994 / EMI America ♦♦♦♦♦
Big Joe Turner's remarkable recordings for Atlantic and Decca have been frequently reissued and evaluated. But his singles for other labels haven't gotten similar treatment, which makes this 18-cut single-disc anthology of Aladdin and Imperial material so welcome. These were recorded in the late '40s and early '50s and were closer to the Kansas City swing Turner had done earlier in his career; there was more emphasis on lyric interpretation, swing, and timing than sheer volume and volcanic, non-stop hollering. Although these songs aren't remembered as fondly as the landmark Atlantic numbers, they're just as important a part of Turner's legacy. *—Ron Wynn*

Have No Fear, Joe Turner Is Here / 1996 / Pablo/OJC ♦♦♦
Big Joe Turner really stretches out during this Pablo date (reissued on CD), singing only five songs: an 11-minute version of Woody Guthrie's "How Come My Dog Don't Bark," three basic originals, and "Rocks in My Bed." Sticking to the blues, Turner is joined by four horns (including altoist Bobby Smith), pianist Lloyd Glenn, and a rhythm section that includes guitarist Pee Wee Crayton (the most prominent soloist). The very spontaneous music has plenty of riffing from the horns and fine late-period shouting from Big Joe. *—Scott Yanow*

Shoutin' the Blues / Jan. 1, 1996 / Eclipse Music Group ♦
This budget collection features Turner doing stereo remakes of his biggest hits. As remakes go, these mixes are far too busy too be effective, but at least there are no wah-wah pedals or synths aboard. There are just too many titles in listed in too jumbled of an order to explain in this review, but every track from number four almost to the end is *not* what's printed on the tray card. Pass on this confusing mess and buy any of his Atlantic/Rhino packages instead. *—Cub Koda*

1947–1948 / Apr. 11, 2000 / Classics ♦♦♦
Big Joe Turner went through record companies like some people go through cigarettes, one after another, cutting sides for anybody who waved a dollar in his face. This installment of the Big Joe story focuses on an eight-month period that found him recording for National, Savoy, EmArcy, RPM, and Downbeat, usually in the company of longtime piano-playing partner Pete Johnson. A mixture of live and studio tracks, it's the usual blend of blues and boogie, with Big Joe hammering the notes flat by the sheer strength of his voice alone. Another excellent entry in this series. *—Cub Koda*

Joe Turner/Rockin' the Blues / Jun. 20, 2000 / Collectables ♦♦♦♦
This reissue from Collectables combines two classic Joe Turner Atlantic sides, *Joe Turner* and *Rockin' the Blues*, originally released in 1957 and 1958, respectively. It features 28 tracks, including a number of R&B staples that crossed over into the pop realm: "Shake Rattle & Roll," "Flip Flop & Fly," "Honey Hush," "Chains of Love," and more. This is a sure bet purchase and also sports the addition of the original LP track sequence that highlights jump blues cuts not often heard, which are just as enjoyable as the hits. *—Al Campbell*

Shoutin' the Blues / Nov. 14, 2000 / Catfish ♦♦♦♦
This is an excellent collection of Big Joe Turner's early blues sides from the '40s. Cut before Turner gained widespread fame scoring rock & roll hits for Atlantic, the 26 cuts here were recorded on both coasts while the singer notched up a slew of gigs nationwide. Working for several labels, including RPM, Aladdin, and MGM, Turner waxed immortal versions of such classic R&B and blues sides as "Corrine Corrina," "Nobody in Mind," and the Leroy Carr gem "How Long, How Long Blues." Turner also penned many of the songs here and collaborated with jump blues great Wynonie Harris on the raucous duet "Battle of the Blues." Besides Harris, Turner gets fine help from pianists Willie "The Lion" Smith, Freddie Slack, and his early cohort Pete Johnson. A stellar addition to the Turner catalog. *—Stephen Cook*

Ike Turner

b. Nov. 5, 1931, Clarksdale, MS
Producer, Vocals, Guitar (Electric), Songwriter, Piano, Guitar / Electric Memphis Blues, Soul-Blues, R&B, Soul
It is arguably true that Ike Turner would have never amounted to more than a footnote to rock history if he hadn't joined forces with Tina Turner in 1960. But as a solo artist, he's an important footnote. In 1951, he made a lasting contribution to music by playing piano on Jackie Brenston's "Rocket 88," which is often cited as one of the very first rock & roll records. That session was one of the first blues/R&B/rock & roll dates produced at Sun Studios in Memphis; Turner learned guitar shortly afterward, and backed up other R&B artists at Sun in the early '50s. Throughout the decade, the guitarist and piano player was a prolific session player, contributing to records by blues legends Elmore James, Howlin' Wolf, and Otis Rush.

Ike also backed a host of obscure R&B artists in his early years, occasionally issuing discs under his name. Not much of a singer, both his own records and the ones he contributed to and/or produced often showcased his stinging, bluesy licks, and the best of his solo outings tended to be his instrumentals. He continued to put out the occasional solo session and work with other artists after he hooked up with Tina, sometimes under the name Ike Turner's Kings of Rhythm. His career lurched along in obscurity after he broke up with Tina in the mid-'70s, though he has remained active. *—Richie Unterberger*

Trailblazer / 1957 / Charly ♦♦♦♦♦
During 1956 and early 1957, Ike Turner's Kings of Rhythm recorded for the Cincinnati-based Federal label—the group's personnel included Raymond Hill and Eddie Jones on tenor sax, Jackie Brenston on baritone sax, Annie Mae Wilson and Fred Sample on piano, Jessie Knight Jr. on bass, Eugene Washington on drums, and Turner on guitar, with vocalists including Brenston and Billy Gayles. This is some of the most solid material in Turner's output, with a rich, soulful sound, more polished than most of the group's output on Cobra. Some of the music is derivative—in seeking chart success, the group at various times sought to emulate the Coasters, Bill Justis, et al., but they almost always put their own spin on these numbers. Billy Gayles' impassioned vocals on "No Coming Back," Jackie Brenston's boisterous rendition of "The Mistreater," and the rest are all worth the price of admission, which is fairly low on this mid-priced import—but, surprisingly, some of the best stuff on here is by the Kings of Rhythm backing the vocal group the Gardenias ("Miserable," one of the best tracks among these 20, remained unreleased until 1991). And the real treat here is Turner's guitar pyrotechnics. He could strum along like most band guitarists, and occasionally did this, but he preferred to step out front and, having discovered the use of the tremelo arm on his guitar, he fairly tortures the instrument on several of these sides (check out the break on "No Comin' Back," and his accompaniment on "She Made My Blood Run Cold," itself an R&B track deserving of legendary status), and even gets a Hawaiian sound out of his instrument on "Trail Blazer." Fans of rock & roll guitar must own this record. *—Bruce Eder*

Ike Turner Rocks the Blues / 1963 / Crown ♦♦♦♦♦
Ike Turner's Kings of Rhythm, rocking the blues in 1954, with a 23-year-old Turner performing some astonishing guitar acrobatics only a couple of years after taking up the instrument, including the legendary "All the Blues, All the Time." The only pity is that this '50s material only exists on this incredibly expensive import from Japan, when it ought to be out at an affordable price over here. The late Lester Bangs called it "one of the greatest albums ever made, if not the absolute certifiable Greatest Guitar Album of All Time," and understandably so. *—Bruce Eder*

1958–1959 / May 13, 1993 / Paula ♦♦♦♦♦
Ever the hustler, Ike Turner found himself picking up some extra money on a road trip through Chicago recording for Cobra Records both as a bandleader and sideman. After contributing the sparkle to several Otis Rush classics (an alternate of one of them, "Keep on Loving Me Baby" is found here) and some early Buddy Guy sides, Turner also recorded a handful of sides, scant few of them seeing release until now. This CD collects them all up, including surviving alternate versions, and is a delightful fly on the wall invite to a '50s Chicago blues session. *—Cub Koda*

● **I Like Ike! The Best of Ike Turner** / Nov. 15, 1994 / Rhino ♦♦♦♦♦
These 18 songs spotlight Turner's work as a bandleader, guitarist, and solo artist from 1951 to 1972, concentrating heavily on his work in the '50s and early '60s. Leading off with Jackie Brenston's classic "Rocket 88," it includes rare singles featuring Turner by Dennis Binder, the Sly Fox, Willie King, and others, along with rare Turner solo recordings, some under the pseudonym Icky Renrut, and a 1958 45 with Tina, then known as Anna Mae Bullock, on backing vocals. These singers are usually journeymen, frankly, and the material is rather standard-issue R&B; better are the instrumentals, which give Ike a chance to really strut his distinctive tone. *—Richie Unterberger*

Rhythm Rockin' Blues / Nov. 1995 / Ace ♦♦♦
This is the definitive early Ike Turner collection, at least until someone comes out with a box that assembles *everything*. The 21 tracks here are mostly drawn from Turner's early-'50s sessions with the Kings of Rhythm at the Clarksdale studio, done under the auspices of the Bihari Brothers' Modern, RPM, and Flair labels. Apart from a few well-known numbers like the classic "Rocket 88," much of the material here isn't in other collections, nor has it been assembled in one place before—some of it has shown up on vinyl, but never together on CD. It consists of Turner working with the Kings of Rhythm, evolving his guitar and piano technique and pumping up the volume and beat on R&B, pushing it toward rock & roll. The highlight for completists is the medley "All the Blues, All the Time," on which Turner, newly confident on the guitar, goes through an extended instrumental medley of B.B. King, Elmore James, Muddy Waters, and John Lee Hooker material. Also included is some hard R&B-cum-rock & roll by the Kings of Rhythm fronted by J.W. Walker, Little Johnny Burton, Dennis Binder, Lonnie "The Cat," and Billy Gayles. The interesting thing is that "Rocket 88," for all of its renown, is just one of the good tracks here—"Early Times" by Dennis Binder could just as easily have caught the public's fancy with its beat. The sound is somewhat compressed on some of the early material (and, especially, the Johnny Wright/Ike Turner orchestra numbers, although Turner's guitar is real sharp on "The World Is Yours"), but generally it is equal or superior to any other digital incarnation of the individual tracks, and the notes are extremely thorough. *—Bruce Eder*

Ike's Instrumentals / 2000 / Ace ♦♦♦
Taken from a variety of sources, this collects 22 of Ike Turner's instrumentals from 1954-1965, none of them vocals, none of them recorded with Tina Turner, and all of

them highlighting his guitar work. Turner's really wild and uninhibited for much of this set, especially in his ferocious string-bending and use of the whammy bar. While the tunes themselves are mostly generic R&B with a touch of rock & roll, it's also fair to say that generic instrumental rock rarely sounds this good, mostly because Turner's guitar work is so much more inventive and passionate than the nominal songs to which they're tethered. About half of this consists of the tracks on his 1962 Sue album, *Dance With Ike & Tina Turner & Their Kings of Rhythm Band*, a good showcase for his crackling axework on a batch of mostly self-imposed wordless workouts. There are also a couple of numbers he cut in the late '50s under the pseudonym Icky Renrut; a 1965 single with brass that has a more soul-oriented arrangement than anything else here, albeit soul of a gutbucket kind; and a smattering of items dating back to his mid-'50s R&B days with Flair. There's also an odd nine-minute medley of instrumental blues covers, "All the Blues All the Time," which wound up on a 1963 Crown LP, *Rocks the Blues*. *—Richie Unterberger*

The Sun Sessions / Jun. 26, 2001 / Varese Sarabande ♦♦♦♦♦
The early recordings of Ike Turner & His Kings of Rhythm (also sometimes known as the Kings of Rhythm featuring Ike Turner) are scattered all over the map, mostly owing to the sheer number of labels for which they recorded from 1951 until 1958. Astonishingly, given their reputation, Turner's Sun Records sides have always been a lot tougher to get hold of than the stuff he did for the RPM and Federal labels, which are downright ubiquitous on CD. Varese has fixed that problem with this 19-song disc covering his work for Sam Phillips between 1951 and 1958, working in every idiom from mournful blues ballads such as "You Can't Be the One for Me" (featuring Tommy Hodge) and "When My Baby Left Me" (sung by Billy "The Kid" Emerson) to the bouncy jump blues of "Love Is a Gamble," featuring his then-girlfriend Bonnie Turner on vocals. A couple of instrumentals, "The Snuggle" and "Bourbon Street Jump," also make this worth hearing as a cross-section of the band's sound and output, and some of the sides also present Turner's guitar, up close and personal—indeed, the best track on the album is arguably "Ugly Woman," one of the funniest songs in Turner's output and one that shows off the bandleader/guitarist/singer Johnny O'Neal working on all cylinders in overdrive. Tommy Hodge is the most consistent singer here, though the disc is also worth hearing for Bonnie Turner's work—whatever their other attributes, Turner evidently did choose the women around him at least partly on the basis of their vocal skills. The sound is excellent and the annotation by Bill Dahl is thorough and very well detailed. *—Bruce Eder*

Ike & Tina Turner

f. 1959, **db.** 1976
Group / R&B, Soul
There was a time when the Ike & Tina Turner Revue was one of the hottest, most durable, and potentially most explosive of all R&B ensembles. Fronted by Tina, with one of the rawest, most sensual and impossibly dynamic voices in black music, the Ike and Tina Revue was an ensemble that dripped musical discipline while manifesting nearly unbearable tension, eventually giving way to wave upon wave of catharsis.

Their story is a long and convoluted one. Ike was born in 1931 in Clarksdale, MS; Tina was born Anna Mae Bullock in 1938 in Nutbush, TN. They met in 1959 in East St. Louis, where Ike's Kings of Rhythm were the reigning patriarchs of the local R&B scene. Up to that point, Ike had been a DJ on WROX in Clarksdale, a talent scout and producer for Modern Records (waxing sides for the likes of B.B. King, Rosco Gordon, Elmore James, and Junior Parker), and a recording artist, his Kings of Rhythm appearing in one guise or another on Chess, Modern, King, Cobra, Artistic, and Stevens. Their most famous record, "Rocket 88," appeared under the moniker "Jackie Brenston With His Delta Cats" in 1951. It played an integral part in jump-starting the rock & roll revolution.

Once Tina joined the Kings of Rhythm, life changed for all concerned. They recorded a demo of "A Fool in Love" in late 1959; by the autumn of 1960 the record was a number two R&B hit on Sue Records. "I Idolize You," "It's Gonna Work Out Fine," "Poor Fool," and "Tra La La La La" all quickly followed, giving the Revue five Top Ten R&B hits in two and a half years. All told, from 1960 to 1975 Ike & Tina Turner placed 25 records on the R&B charts for nine separate record companies. Their most successful pop recording was a reworking of Creedence Clearwater Revival's "Proud Mary" in 1971. *—Rob Bowman*

The Sound of Ike & Tina Turner / 1960 / Collectables ♦♦♦♦♦
Another early-'60s Ike & Tina Turner album, with Tina sounding tentative at times, and other times gaining confidence as the song progressed. They were far from a finished, polished act, especially in the studio. Tina was still determining how much power and sensuality she had in her voice and was developing her delivery and presentation, while Ike was honing the backdrop, and his band learning when to push and when to lay out behind Tina. *—Ron Wynn*

Dance With Ike & Tina Turner & Their Kings of Rhythm Band / 1962 / Sue ♦♦♦
Although the 14 tracks on this album are very typical early-'60s rock/R&B instrumentals in their tunes and arrangements, Ike Turner's guitar work is sparkling, lifting the LP out of the generic realm. All but one of the songs were written by Turner, and are mostly uptempo, dance-oriented workouts, probably intended to cash in on the twist craze, as titles like "Twist-a-Rod," "Trackdown Twist," "Potato Mash," and "Prancing" indicate. Ike Turner really squeezes the last drop of invention out of these run-of-the-mill backdrops, though, relentlessly bending notes, wangling the whammy bar, and letting loose with some unpredictable runs and aggressive chording. Tina Turner does not sing on the album (nor does anyone), despite what the title might lead you to believe, but it does include an instrumental version of the duo's big hit "It's Gonna Work Out Fine." All of the songs are included on the Ace CD reissue compilation *Ike's Instrumentals*, which collects an assortment of Ike Turner instrumentals spanning the mid-'50s to mid-'60s. *—Richie Unterberger*

Festival of Live Performances / 1962 / United ♦♦♦♦♦
A great album that needs to be reissued immediately. Early Ike & Tina Turner in concert, long before things became so formulaic that even the Turner dance routines and sexy costumes became predictable and tiring. They were still a hungry, eager, galvanizing band then, and even performed with energy and fire on mundane filler. If you ever spot this one, grab it immediately. *—Ron Wynn*

Don't Play Me Cheap / 1963 / Collectables ♦♦♦
An early-'60s album from the formative days of the Ike & Tina Turner Revue. They were still developing the formula, but would soon begin striking soul gold. In the meantime, Turner was operating as an R&B and soul diva, although she later said that she hated singing these tunes. In this instance, what she was doing was mostly second-level material, but her husky, powerful voice sounded convincing. *—Ron Wynn*

Dynamite / 1963 / Collectables ♦♦
The first of three Ike & Tina Turner albums issued in 1963 had its moments, but overall was rather listless from a material standpoint. There wasn't a standout track among the batch; only Turner's shattering vocals and some good funky backdrops by Ike Turner's band saved things from total disaster. *—Ron Wynn*

The Ike & Tina Turner Revue Live / 1965 / Kent ♦♦
Ike & Tina Turner had two live albums issued in 1965 that were virtually the same record; one spotlighted the show and the other the Revue, which was itself simply the act that did the show. Since they're both long gone anyway, it doesn't really matter, but it was just as sassy and uneven but compelling as its predecessor. *—Ron Wynn*

River Deep—Mountain High / 1966 / A&M ♦♦♦♦♦
These sessions, recorded in 1966, were produced by Phil Spector. Spector's production chops and Tina's voice were a match made in heaven. Tina possesses one of the strongest voices ever committed to wax; Spector envelops it in the grandest version of his Wall of Sound that he ever conceived. Besides the title track, Spector cut the Turners redoing their first three chart hits, "A Fool in Love," "I Idolize You," and "It's Gonna Work Out Fine." Although it's a sacrilege to say so, these versions are better than the originals. Finally, Turner's performance of the obscure Holland-Dozier-Holland ditty "A Love Like Yours" is another phenomenal highlight. *—Rob Bowman*

Live! The Ike & Tina Show, Vols. 1-2 / 1966 / One Way ♦♦♦♦
Ike & Tina Turner left behind more than one live album from the early '60s, but this double-LP/double-CD set is probably the best of them. Not only is the sound superb and the performance of the band spot-on, but Tina Turner is in exceptionally good voice, and the range of material—from R&B standards like "Hi Heel Sneakers" (done here as "Tight Pants") to country-pop songs such as "I Can't Stop Loving You"—is not only astounding but a brilliant showcase for the duo and their band; they even bring a subtle soulfulness amid the broader, more shouting pieces, to Sam Cooke's "Good Times" and the virtual Tina Turner solo piece "All I Could Do Was Cry." The CD reissue is so clean that it captures all of those nuances—but when the sax solo and the chorus come up on "Early in the Morning," it also sounds like your ear is down the bell of the instrument and the rest of you is lying in the lap of the Ikettes. The sound varies radically between some songs, as though the microphone setups were very different between the two concert venues used as sources for this release, and there's no attempt at making this seem like a complete show from one source, the silence between the songs breaking up the ambience. The set is as vital a document, however, as essential by itself as any compilation of the best of the duo's early work (and one wonders if there are any outtakes lying around the Warner Bros. holdings from Loma Records, which originally released this set). *—Bruce Eder*

Ike & Tina Turner's Greatest Hits / 1967 / Warner Brothers ♦♦♦
This CD reaches back in time to a year when America was poised on the threshold of so many political and social changes. That year was 1967, and one of the hottest acts in the music business was the Ike & Tina Turner Revue. The incredible voice and energy of Tina Turner, backed by her husband's band, the Kings of Rhythm, had turned the R&B world upside down with their electrifying shows. Their influence on the evolving genre of rock & roll was huge. This was soul music at its best. It burned hot with Tina Turner's sensual persona. Though largely overshadowed by his wife's stage presence, Ike Turner holds a place in rock & roll history, often credited with recording its first tune, "Rocket 88," in 1950. But it was in the '60s that the Ike & Tina Turner Revue ruled. This CD compiles some of the best songs recorded by the band, one of the top revenue groups of all time, with 25 hits on the charts in the tumultuous decade of the '60s. The recording includes the song that catapulted Ike and Tina Turner to fame in 1960: the chart-topping "Fool in Love." "Poor Fool," "It's Gonna Work Out Fine," and "Tra La La La La" are among the others. Perhaps the title of another work of the Turners describes the music best: "Too Hot to Hold." *—Rose of Sharon Witmer*

So Fine / 1968 / Special Music ♦♦♦
A late-'60s session, with Tina Turner wailing, moaning, and shouting over chunky, hard-driving funk. They didn't make much commercial noise with this one, but it was some of Turner's most soulful, bluesy singing, done strictly for the soul and R&B audience. The title cut actually scraped the lower regions of the soul charts, but otherwise it was strictly a fans' album. It's now long-deleted, but still worthy of mention. *—Ron Wynn*

Hunter / 1969 / Blue Thumb ♦♦♦
Released just a few years after the epochal Phil Spector-produced *River Deep Mountain High* and close to six years before their breakup, Ike & Tina Turner's *Hunter* often gets lost in the duo's long and stormy existence. And while the album certainly is not on the same plane as the Spector album or later work like *Workin' Together*, Hunter still boasts several fine blues workouts in the inimitably electrifying Ike and Tina mode. The Stax sound figures prominently here, with producer Bob Krasnow (Captain Beefheart)

keeping things nice and uncluttered to better frame Tina's intense vocal workouts. Maybe not the best first-disc choice, but still a worthwhile title for Ike and Tina fans. —*Stephen Cook*

Get It Together / 1969 / Pompeii ✦✦
An amazing eight Ike & Tina Turner albums came down the pike in 1969, on every label from A&B to Blue Thumb to Minit. The glut resulted in the ludicrous situation of Ike and Tina competing en masse against themselves. It also doomed the prospects of most of the albums before they were even out of the chute. Yet amazingly, half made the pop charts, although this wasn't one of them. It was a decent album of routine soul and R&B, sung with Turner's usual sizzling energy, but otherwise lacking in distinction. —*Ron Wynn*

Outta Season / 1969 / Blue Thumb ✦✦
One of eight albums that were issued in this landmark year; this one is among the lesser-known or noticed. It contained routine soul and R&B numbers sung with little variety or emotion by Turner, and produced and arranged with almost no variety or flair. It was more a collection of singles than an actual album, but was rushed out among the raft of Ike and Tina product that glutted the market. It has since been deleted, and deservedly so. —*Ron Wynn*

Ike and Tina Turner in Person / 1969 / Minit ✦✦✦
An interesting, although quite erratic, album from their wealth of late-'60s releases. The Revue was featured in various concert performances ranging from inspired to ragged and loose. Tina Turner was at her rampaging, husky best, and at times Ike Turner had the band whipped to a frenzy behind her. At other times they sounded completely unrehearsed and awkward, while Tina just kept plowing on ahead, undeterred by the chaos behind her. —*Ron Wynn*

Greatest Hits / Sep. 1969 / Curb ✦✦✦
There are numerous Ike & Tina Turner hits packages ranging over various periods and different labels. This anthology covers '60s cuts and has some familiar titles, but is haphazardly sequenced and mastered. The best single collection of their early material was issued by EMI in 1991. —*Ron Wynn*

Workin' Together / 1970 / One Way ✦✦✦✦✦
Released late in 1970, a few months after *Come Together*, their first album for Liberty Records, *Workin' Together* was the first genuine hit album Ike & Tina had in years; actually, it was their biggest ever, working its way into Billboard's Top 25 and spending 38 weeks on the charts. They never had a bigger hit (the closest was their Blue Thumb release, *Outta Season*, which peaked at number 91), and, in many ways, they didn't make a better album. After all, their classic '60s sides were just that—sides of a single, not an album. Even though it doesn't boast the sustained vision of such contemporaries as, say, Marvin Gaye and Al Green, *Workin' Together* feels like a proper album, where many of the buried album tracks are as strong as the singles. Like its predecessor, it relies a bit too much on contemporary covers, which isn't bad when it's the perennial "Proud Mary," since it deftly reinterprets the original, but readings of the Beatles' "Get Back" and "Let It Be," while not bad, are a little bit too pedestrian. Fortunately, they're entirely listenable and they're the only slow moments, outweighed by songs that crackle with style and passion. Nowhere is this truer than on the opening title track, a midtempo groover (written by Icky Renrut, Ike's brilliant inverted alias) powered by a soulful chorus and a guitar line that plays like a mutated version of Dylan's "I Want You" riff. Then, there's the terrific Stax/Volt stomper "(Long As I Can) Get You When I Want You," possibly the highlight on the record. Though they cut a couple of classics over the next few years, most notably "Nutbush City Limits," the duo never topped this, possibly the best proper album they ever cut. —*Stephen Thomas Erlewine*

16 Great Performances / 1971 / Collectables ✦✦
Ike & Tina Turner's tenure on the Blue Thumb label, like all their other label stays, was stormy, uneven, and occasionally productive. They only remained with the company a short time, but recorded enough material for two full albums. These were both cranked out in 1969, and this anthology supposedly features the best 16 cuts. It includes the odd single "The Hunter," and a good remake of Otis Redding's "I've Been Loving You Too Long," and the ahead-of-its-time "Bold Soul Sister." It has long since disappeared, but there are better presentations of Ike and Tina material available. —*Ron Wynn*

What You Hear Is What You Get / 1971 / EMI ✦✦✦
The duo were at their peak of popularity when this hour-long performance was recorded in New York on April 1, 1971. Of course Turner's volcanic stage presence can't be fully translated onto disc, and the set list goes heavy on predictable covers like "Sweet Soul Music," "Honky Tonk Women," "I've Been Loving You Too Long," "Respect," and a ten-minute-plus "Proud Mary." And the opening two numbers are sung not by Tina, but by the Ikettes. You'd be a real sourpuss, though, to let your rock critic microscope keep you from enjoying this smoky set. Tina drains every last bit of emotion from the material, especially on the bluesy "I Smell Trouble" and the drawn-out covers of "I've Been Loving You Too Long" and "Proud Mary," and the band offers a cookin' stew of R&B-soul-rock, paced by Ike's reverberating guitar. —*Richie Unterberger*

Feel Good / 1972 / United Artists ✦✦
Things were beginning to unravel with the Turners domestically, although they were still packing them in at various shows. But this album wasn't among their more inspired, as the formula was now wearing quite thin and Tina sounded less and less interested. The backing, arrangements, and production were equally uninspired, and everyone involved just punched the clock and ground this one out. —*Ron Wynn*

Let Me Touch Your Mind / 1973 / United Artists ✦✦
One of the final albums in the Ike & Tina Turner saga, and things had almost evaporated by this time. The Turners would score one more big hit with their next album, but it was evident that Tina had little interest in continuing to do soul and R&B ballads, and that

their domestic problems were causing professional havoc. Her voice hadn't lost its power or resilience, but she had absolutely no energy or conviction in her vocals. The band was now on cruise control, and the entire operation was near its end. —*Ron Wynn*

Nutbush City Limits / 1973 / United Artists ✦✦✦✦
The album that marked the end of the Ike & Tina Turner alliance, although it wasn't their last album. But the turmoil that they were undergoing off-stage would soon shatter their personal and professional union. They scored a major international hit with the title cut, and also told their life story, although it turned out that this tale was a fantasy. Here's one of the few Ike and Tina Turner albums that deserves to be back in print. —*Ron Wynn*

Golden Classics / Apr. 20, 1990 / Collectables ✦✦✦
The legend of Tina Turner begins with these recordings, made with then-hubby Ike Turner for Juggy Murray's Sue Records in the early '60s. They're crudely produced sides, and sometimes Tina is handed some downright flabby material by producer-songwriter Ike ("Tra La La La La" and "You Can't Blame Me" are weak in the extreme), but the formula also brought the duo their first hits in tracks like "A Fool in Love," "It's Gonna Work Out Fine" (with Ike's voice over played by Mickey "Guitar" Baker of Mickey and Sylvia fame), "I Idolize You," and "Poor Fool." Also aboard are alternate takes of "Poor Fool" and "I Idolize You." All in all, a solid collection of this duo's earliest sides. —*Cub Koda*

● **Proud Mary—The Best of Ike & Tina Turner** / Mar. 18, 1991 / EMI America ✦✦✦✦✦
Proud Mary—The Best of Ike & Tina Turner is a fine 23-track collection that looks at the Turners' career at the beginning and the end. Their early-'60s hits on Juggy Murray's Sue label are included, as are their early- and mid-'70s successes on Liberty and United Artists. The mid- and late-'60s recordings for Kent, Loma, Modern, Innis, Blue Thumb, and Minit are not here, unfortunately. Superior liner notes round out a fine package. —*Rob Bowman*

It's Gonna Work Out Fine / 1994 / Collectables ✦✦✦
Collectables features the vaunted A&M material of Ike & Tina Turner, including the outstanding title track from the *River Deep, Mountain High* set, whose commercial failure allegedly drove Phil Spector temporarily out of the business. It's decently mastered, but hold out if you can for the original; it's worth the effort. —*Ron Wynn*

Bold Soul Sister: The Best of the Blue Thumb Recordings / Jul. 15, 1997 / Hip-O ✦✦✦✦✦
Make no mistake about it, this 16-track collection culled from their two albums recorded for the Blue Thumb label in 1969 (*Outta Season* and *The Hunter*) is as much Ike's show as it is Tina's—truly the other half of the equation, the blues part of rhythm & blues. His stinging guitar matches Tina's voice lick for nasty lick, and the blues song choices ("Dust My Broom," "Three O'Clock Blues," "Please Love Me," "Five Long Years," "You Don't Love Me," "Mean Old World," "Rock Me Baby," "Honest I Do," "Reconsider Baby") were undoubtedly tunes he and the Kings of Rhythm knew in their sleep, playing them since they were new hits on the charts. These were the last truly pure R&B albums the two of them would ever make, and even the then-current stabs at R&B trends (the title track is little more than Ike's version of a James Brown groove with Tina babbling in true JB incomprehensibility in spots) shine brightly in the spotlight of hindsight. Subtitled *The Best of the Blue Thumb Recordings*, this makes a great document of what they must have sounded like in the clubs that dotted the landscape of the chitlin circuit way back when. —*Cub Koda*

The Kent Years / May 16, 2000 / Kent ✦✦✦✦
This compilation features 26 of the duo's 1964-1967 recordings (five previously unissued) for the Kent and Modern labels. Note, however, that this is just a partial retrospective of their mid-'60s work, since during this time the Turners were also releasing sides on several different other labels. It remains, though, a good sampling of their sound during this era, when their soul tracks still betrayed much of their blues/R&B roots, and before the arrangements had gotten as heavy and beefy as they would in the late '60s and early '70s. Tina Turner's vocals are unflaggingly enthusiastic and committed, if perhaps not as nuanced as they could be. What keeps this from the top rank of mid-'60s soul, however, is the largely average, occasionally below average material (mostly written by Ike Turner). It's often a collision of blues, chitlin circuit R&B, and brassy pop-soul that sounds a bit dashed off. There are some ace moments along the way, of course, like the infectious "I Can't Believe What You Say," the down-and-bluesy "Hurt Is All You Gave Me," and the swaggering soul-swing shuffle of "Chicken Shack." Ike Turner's twangy guitar seems underutilized for much of the set, and there's very little of the vocal sparring that would be such a big part of their act by the early '70s. Tina Turner goes into a big rap on the previously unissued "All I Could Do Was Cry" where she really overdoes the raspy breast-beating; Etta James' more famous version has a big edge. "Give Me Your Love" is minor-keyed blues/R&B that's not too far from Otis Rush territory; at the other extreme, "Makin' Plans Together" has gossamer strings typical of the New York pop-soul on the Scepter/Wand labels. —*Richie Unterberger*

Funkier Than a Mosquito's Tweeter / Jul. 2, 2002 / EMI ✦✦✦✦✦
Funkier Than a Mosquito's Tweeter is a 21-track collection culled from one of Ike & Tina's most prolific and creative periods. It is also a largely forgotten period because they had no hits. Between 1969 and 1972, Ike & Tina released eight records on two different labels: two for Blue Thumb and six for Liberty/UA. On this set they took four tracks from 1970's *Come Together*, five from 1971's *Nuff Said*, and three each from 1972's *Feel Good* and *Let Me Touch Your Mind*. Also thrown in are a single from 1969, an Ikettes song from 1972, and a solo Tina cut from 1974. Ike & Tina had been many things in their long career: R&B pioneers, blues belters, stars of a soul revue, and pop stars. After coming off a tour with the Rolling Stones in 1969, Ike decided that the band needed to rock. He set about creating a hard-rocking brand of funk overloaded with proto-punk attitude perfect for the post-Woodstock and Altamont comedown. Ike's guitar playing is meaner than ever; he

really attacks the strings on songs like "I Wanna Jump" and "The Chopper." Tina is at her snarling best throughout, cutting a wide path with her withering sneer and screaming emotion. It is especially fun on the title track to hear her reading the riot act to some jerk who is doing her dirt (although it is less fun when you realize she is talking about Ike and her life with him was a living hell at this point). Ike's production shows him to be on a creative high (and probably just high as well) as he builds walls of funk-nasty guitar riffs and grinding bass topped off with sleazy-sounding horns and all kinds of weird touches. He was getting into synthesizers at this time and he does strange things with them, like the wobbly drone that runs through "What You Don't See (Is Better Yet)" or the burbling tones on "Popcorn." Production-wise, the high point comes on "Up on the Roof," where he turns the Spector chestnut into a psychedelic soul tune not unlike the Temptations' "Ball of Confusion." Another highlight is Ike & Tina's version of Sly & the Family Stone's "I Wanna Take You Higher." They never rocked harder than this. Where Sly's original is an invitation, Ike & Tina make it sound like a command you don't dare disobey. The inclusion of Tina's "Whole Lotta Love" shows how important Ike's production was to their sound. The take on the Led Zeppelin track is pretty good, with Tina wailing away frantically as usual, but it lacks the rawness and sonic unpredictability that is Ike's trademark. The whole disc lives up to its title. It is no doubt funkier than a mosquito's tweeter and heavier than a mosquito's woofer too. If you are a fan of Ike & Tina, you need this disc. If you are a fan of raw and nasty funk-rock, you need this disc. If you are a fan of music, you need this disc. —*Tim Sendra*

Othar Turner

b. Jun. 2, 1907, Jackson, MS

Fife / Field Recordings, Country Blues

The last surviving master of the Mississippi back-country fife-and-drum tradition, veteran bluesman Othar Turner was born in 1907, spending his adult life as a sharecropper in the city of Como, an area several miles northeast of the Delta region which also gave rise to musicians including Fred McDowell, R.L. Burnside, and Junior Kimbrough. Beginning his performing career around 1923, Turner initially played the blues as well before picking up the thread of the fife and drum tradition, a primitive take on African-American hymns and songs which dates back to the northern Mississippi hill country culture of the 1800s; mastering the fife (a hollow, flute-like instrument typically manufactured from bamboo cane), he toiled in relative obscurity for six decades while leading the Rising Star Fife and Drum Band, a loose confederation of relatives, friends and neighbors that played primarily at picnics on his farm. (For a number of years, the group annually opened the Chicago Blues Festival as well.) With his contemporaries either deceased or infirmed, by the 1990s Turner was the final surviving link to fife and drum's roots; in 1998, his music was finally preserved on the album *Everybody Hollerin' Goat*, recorded between 1992 and 1997 by producer Luther Dickinson. A follow-up, *Senegal to Senatobia*, appeared in 2000. —*Jason Ankeny*

Everybody Hollerin' Goat / Jan. 20, 1998 / Birdman ✦✦✦

Credited to Othar Turner's Rising Star Fife and Drum Band, *Everybody Hollerin' Goat* is a collection of haunting, authentic Mississippi-born fife and drum blues from Turner, aged 90 at the time of recording this, his solo debut. A compilation of field recordings

and home recordings, it was assembled by Luther Dickinson, the son of the legendary Memphis producer Jim Dickinson. —*Jason Ankeny*

● **From Senegal to Senatobia** / Nov. 16, 1999 / Birdman ✦✦✦

Mississippi fife legend Turner is joined on this outing by a loose union of players billed as the Afrosippi All Stars. This makeshift band is comprised of members of Turner's family, visiting Senegalese musicians, a university percussion student/organizer, and slide guitarist/producer/North Mississippi All Star Luther Dickinson. Their sympathetic accompaniment on African percussion, kora, and bottleneck guitar give "Shimmy She Wobble," "Station Blues," and "Bounce Ball"—reprised from his recording debut, *Everybody Hollerin' Goat*—a depth lacking on his earlier versions. Traditional African drums exchange rhythms with marching-band snares and bass drums. Staccato kora melodies complement whining slide guitar riffs. And Turner's shrill, archaic fife floats freely over it all. The title track is the album's most distinctly African number, and probably the only track here easy on the listener's ears. The closing "Sunu" is five minutes of nothing but drums. This is hardly good-time music for casual blues listeners or weekend world music fans, but it's important music all the same, bridging, as it does, great distances between continents and traditions. —*Brian Beatty*

TV Slim (Oscar Wills)

b. Feb. 10, 1916, Houston, TX, **d.** Oct. 21, 1969, Klingman, AZ

Vocals, Guitar / Country Blues, Electric Blues, R&B

Oscar "TV Slim" Wills' hilarious tale of a sad sack named "Flat Foot Sam" briefly made him a bankable name in 1957. Sam's ongoing saga lasted longer than Slim's minute or two in the spotlight, but that didn't stop him from recording throughout the '60s.

Influenced by DeFord Bailey and both Sonny Boy Williamsons on harp and Guitar Slim on axe while living in Houston, Wills sold one of his early compositions, "Dolly Bee," to Don Robey for Junior Parker's use on Duke Records before getting the itch to record himself. To that end, he set up Speed Records, his own label and source for the great majority of his output over the next dozen years.

The first version of "Flat Foot Sam" came out on a tiny Shreveport logo, Cliff Records, in 1957. Local record man Stan Lewis, later the owner of Jewel/Paula Records, reportedly bestowed the colorful nickname of TV Slim on Wills; he was a skinny television repairman, so the handle fit perfectly.

"Flat Foot Sam" generated sufficient regional sales to merit reissue on Checker, but its ragged edges must have rankled someone at the Chicago label enough to convince Slim to recut it in much tighter form in New Orleans with the vaunted studio band at Cosimo's. This time, Robert "Barefootin'" Parker blew a strong sax solo, Chess A&R man Paul Gayten handled piano duties, and Charles "Hungry" Williams laid down a brisk second-line beat. It became Slim's biggest seller when unleashed on another Chess subsidiary, Argo Records.

Slim cut a torrent of 45s for Speed, Checker, Pzazz, USA, Timbre, Excell, and Ideel after that, chronicling the further adventures of his prime mealticket with "Flatfoot Sam Made a Bet," "Flat Foot Sam Met Jim Dandy," and "Flat Foot Sam No. 2." Albert Collins later covered Slim's Speed waxing of the surreal "Don't Reach Cross My Plate." Wills died in a car wreck outside Klingman, AZ, in 1969 en route home to Los Angeles after playing a date in Chicago. —*Bill Dahl*

The Vagabonds

f. 1927

Group / Traditional Pop

Billed during their heyday as "America's daffiest, laughiest swing quartet," the Vagabonds (Attilio Risso on accordion, Pete Peterson on stand-up bass and comedy guitarists Dominic Germano and Al Torriere) were comedians first and musicians second. There were seemingly a million groups like this after World War II working the taverns and nightclubs on both coasts; a couple of guitars, an accordion, and a stand-up bass, doing "special material," song parodies and comedy routines, usually to hide the woeful vocal deficiencies of the group itself. Not as corny or as rural in content or presentation as the Hoosier Hot Shots, or as manic as Spike Jones & His City Slickers or the Schnickelfritzers, the Vagabonds were just the kind of light comedy act that made great nightclub entertainment after World War II, and made comic relief appearances in several RKO movies during the same time period. —*Cub Koda*

● **The Original RKO & Unique Masters** / Apr. 8, 1997 / Varese Sarabande ✦✦✦✦✦
This, their lone album, originally issued on RKO's Unique subsidiary in the early '50s, comes to compact disc with ten tracks that closely replicate their successful nightclub act minus the visuals. With a blaring, brassy big band largely obscuring the inherent rhythm of the quartet, they provide unison glee club singing on most numbers ("Vagabonds Theme," "Pony Ride," "Salt"), sounding for all the world like a low-budget Broadway production number. Their takes on "I Wish I Could Shimmy Like My Sister Kate" and "Lazy River" feature bass player Pete Peterson doing scat vocals highly reminiscent of Louis Prima. Smooth group harmonies appear on "Wrong" and the atypical ballad "I Wonder, I Wonder, I Wonder," while the set closer—a rousing "minstrel" medley consisting of "Back in Your Own Back Yard," "I Want to Say Hello," "Rockabye Your Baby," and "Waitin' for the Robert E. Lee"—shows the group off to good comic effect. —*Cub Koda*

Vaughan Brothers

f. 1990

Group / Album Rock, Blues-Rock, Modern Electric Blues, Texas Blues

Sibling blues guitarists Jimmie Vaughan (born in 1951) and Stevie Ray Vaughan (1954-1990) were born and raised in Dallas, TX. Each began playing guitar during childhood, Stevie Ray inspired to take up the instrument by his older brother. Jimmie Vaughan played in various groups in Dallas and Austin before hooking up with singer/harmonica player Kim Wilson and forming the Fabulous Thunderbirds in 1974. The group was signed to Chrysalis Records, for which they made four albums, starting with a self-titled 1979 debut. The second and third of them, *What's the Word* (1980) and *Butt Rockin'* (1981), made the lower reaches of the charts, but the band was dropped by the label after the commercial failure of *T-Bird Rhythm* in the fall of 1982.

Meanwhile, Stevie Ray Vaughan had been playing around Texas, at first with Triple Threat featuring singer Lou Ann Barton, and then, after her departure, with drummer Chris Layton and newly recruited bassist Tommy Shannon as Stevie Ray Vaughan & Double Trouble. His appearance at the Montreux Jazz Festival in 1982 led to a recording contract with Epic Records and the release of his debut album, *Texas Flood*, a Top 40 hit, in 1983. He followed it with the even more successful *Couldn't Stand the Weather* (1984) and *Soul to Soul* (1985), each of which went gold within two years. (All three albums have since gone platinum.)

Stevie Ray Vaughan's success stimulated Epic's interest in his brother's band. The Epic subsidiary CBS Associated signed the Fabulous Thunderbirds and issued *Tuff Enuff* (1986), which spawned a Top Ten single in the title-track and itself made the Top 20, going gold within six months and eventually platinum. The same year, Stevie Ray Vaughan issued *Live Alive*, which eventually went platinum.

The careers of both brothers subsided soon after. Stevie Ray Vaughan went into rehab, while the Fabulous Thunderbirds' follow-ups to *Tuff Enuff*, *Hot Number* (1987) and *Powerful Stuff* (1989), did not match its commercial success. Jimmie Vaughan amicably parted from the band in June 1990. Stevie Ray Vaughan returned after more than two and a half years with *In Step* (1989), which became his biggest seller yet, eventually going double platinum. The brothers had long planned a duo project, and in 1990 they finally found time for it, recording *Family Style*. But the month before the album's scheduled release, Stevie Ray Vaughan was killed in a helicopter crash on August 27, 1990. The album appeared in September and it soared into the Top Ten, selling over a million copies.

Jimmie Vaughan helped oversee posthumous releases of his brother's recordings, such as the two-million-selling Top Ten hit *The Sky Is Crying* (1991). He launched his own solo career in the spring of 1994 with *Strange Pleasure*, released by Epic. —*William Ruhlmann*

● **Family Style** / Jan. 1990 / Epic ✦✦✦
With slick production from Nile Rodgers and employing neither guitarist's band (Double Trouble nor the Fabulous Thunderbirds), this is bluesy, but far from purist. Jimmie makes

his vocal debut on "White Boots" and "Good Texan," and the brothers blur the lines between their expected guitar styles—Stevie sometimes going for a less sustainy twang, Jimmie moving into Albert King territory. When standard blues is the order of the day (the slow intro "Brothers"), the key word is "standard"—bordering on run-of-the-mill. Instrumentals "D/FW" and "Hillbillies from Outer Space" fare better—offering ZZ Top crunch and Santo & Johnny steel, respectively. —*Dan Forte*

Jimmie Vaughan

b. Mar. 20, 1951, Dallas, TX

Vocals, Guitar / Modern Electric Texas Blues, Roots Rock, Blues-Rock, Modern Electric Blues

As a founding member of the Fabulous Thunderbirds, Jimmie Vaughan was one of the leading Austin, TX, guitarists of the late '70s and '80s, responsible for opening the national market up for gritty roadhouse blues and R&B. Influenced by guitarists like Freddie King, B.B. King, and Albert King, Vaughan developed a tough, lean sound that became one of the most recognizable sounds of '70s and '80s blues and blues-rock. For most of his career, Vaughan co-led the Fabulous Thunderbirds with vocalist Kim Wilson. It wasn't until 1994 that he launched a full-fledged solo career.

Born and raised in Dallas, TX, Jimmie Vaughan began playing guitar as a child. Initially, Vaughan was influenced by both blues and rock & roll. While he was in his teens, he played in a number of garage rock bands, none of which attained any success. At the age of 19, he left Dallas and moved to Austin. For his first few years in Austin, Vaughan played in a variety of blues bar bands. In 1972, he formed his own group, the Storm, which supported many touring blues musicians.

In 1974, Vaughan met a vocalist and harmonica player named Kim Wilson. Within a year, the pair had formed the Fabulous Thunderbirds along with bassist Keith Ferguson and drummer Mike Buck. For four years, the T-Birds played local Texas clubs, gaining a strong fan base. By the end of the decade, the group had signed a major label contract with Chrysalis Records and seemed bound for national stardom. However, none of their albums became hits and they were dropped by Chrysalis at the end of 1982.

At the same time the T-Birds were left without a recording contract, Jimmie's younger brother, Stevie Ray Vaughan, came storming upon the national scene with his debut album, *Texas Flood*. For the next few years, Stevie Ray dominated not only the Texan blues scene, but the entire American scene, while Jimmie and the Thunderbirds were struggling to survive. The T-Birds finally received a new major label contract in 1986 with Epic/Associated and their first album for the label, *Tuff Enuff*, was a surprise hit, selling over a million copies and spawning the Top Ten hit single.

The Fabulous Thunderbirds spent the rest of the '80s trying to replicate the success of *Tuff Enuff*, often pursuing slicker, more commercially oriented directions. By 1989, Jimmie Vaughan was frustrated by the group's musical direction and he left the band. Before launching a solo career, he recorded a duet album with his brother, Stevie Ray, *Family Style*. Following the completion of the record, Stevie Ray Vaughan died in a tragic helicopter crash in August of 1990. *Family Style* appeared just a few months later, in the fall of 1990.

After Stevie Ray's death, Jimmie took a couple of years off, in order to grieve and recoup. After a couple of years, he began playing the occasional concert. In 1994, he returned with his first solo album, *Strange Pleasures*, which received good reviews and sold respectably. Vaughan supported *Strange Pleasures* with a national tour. *Out There* followed in 1998. —*Stephen Thomas Erlewine*

● **Strange Pleasure** / 1995 / Epic ✦✦✦✦✦

Out There / Jun. 9, 1998 / Epic ✦✦✦
Jimmie Vaughan's second solo album, *Out There*, is quite similar to its predecessor, *Strange Pleasure*, delivering a familiar blend of Texas blues and roadhouse blues-rock. Of course, that isn't a problem. Ever since the Fabulous Thunderbirds, Vaughan has been at the forefront of Texas blues-rock, and while he's calmed down some with age, he remains a vital, classy guitarist—even on the weaker material, his tasteful solos are utterly engaging. It's too bad that his material doesn't always match his skills, but there's enough straight-ahead, enjoyable music here to make it worth a listen. —*Stephen Thomas Erlewine*

Do You Get the Blues? / Sep. 11, 2001 / Artemis ✦✦✦✦
If anyone deserves a crack at being "the next Stevie Ray Vaughan," it's his older brother Jimmie. Thankfully, he's not concerned with aping his sibling's gruff, guitar-heavy approach, as he's proved through his previous two solo albums. It's not that he doesn't have the chops to be an often spellbinding guitarist in his own right; his work with the Fabulous Thunderbirds proved that he could tear off hot licks with the best of them. But on his third solo album, Jimmie pulls even further away from his brother's sound, whipping up a scrumptious concoction of jazzy, often funky R&B and blues that's every bit as enticing in its own way as Stevie Ray's more bombastic approach was. Recorded in both Memphis and Texas and prominently featuring the amazing Bill Willis on Hammond B-3

(who doubles on bass pedals—leaving this as one of the few blues albums without an official bassist), Jimmie's more subtle approach leaves lots of spaces to nail a groove that gets deeper as the album progresses. Guests like James Cotton on harp and longtime associate singer Lou Ann Barton (who just about steals the show on the songs where she duets with Vaughan) inject extra spice, but the singer/guitarist has crafted a compelling slice of contemporary blues that blends traditional elements in a distinctive way. His own soloing stings in a less abrasive, more organic fashion, and his honest, lived-in vocals, while not technically accomplished, fit the tunes perfectly. Rootsy yet polished tracks like the R&B swamp of "Without You" and the Texas soul of Johnny "Guitar" Watson's "In the Middle of the Night" (featuring Stevie Ray's Double Trouble rhythm section) crackle with taut energy and low-down soul. By forging an individual musical style, Jimmie Vaughan not only avoids all Stevie Ray comparisons, but has produced a remarkable album that truly sounds like no one else. —*Hal Horowitz*

Stevie Ray Vaughan

b. Oct. 3, 1954, Dallas, TX, d. Aug. 27, 1990, East Troy, WI
Vocals, Guitar (Electric), Guitar / Album Rock, Modern Electric Texas Blues, Electric Texas Blues, Blues-Rock, Modern Electric Blues, Texas Blues
With his astonishingly accomplished guitar playing, Stevie Ray Vaughan ignited the blues revival of the '80s. Vaughan drew equally from bluesmen like Albert King, Otis Rush, and Muddy Waters and rock & roll players like Jimi Hendrix and Lonnie Mack, as well as the stray jazz guitarist like Kenny Burrell, developing a uniquely eclectic and fiery style that sounded like no other guitarist, regardless of genre. Vaughan bridged the gap between blues and rock like no other artist had since the late '60s. For the next seven years, Stevie Ray was the leading light in American blues, consistently selling out concerts while his albums regularly went gold. His tragic death in 1990 only emphasized his influence in blues and American rock & roll.

Born and raised in Dallas, Stevie Ray Vaughan began playing guitar as a child, inspired by older brother Jimmie. When he was in junior high school, he began playing in a number of garage bands, which occasionally landed gigs in local nightclubs. By the time he was 17, he had dropped out of high school to concentrate on playing music. Vaughan's first real band was the Cobras, who played clubs and bars in Austin during the mid-'70s. Following that group's demise, he formed Triple Threat in 1975. Triple Threat also featured bassist Jackie Newhouse, drummer Chris Layton, and vocalist Lou Ann Barton. After a few years of playing Texas bars and clubs, Barton left the band in 1978. The group decided to continue performing under the name Double Trouble, which was inspired by the Otis Rush song of the same name; Stevie Ray became the band's lead singer.

For the next few years, Stevie Ray Vaughan and Double Trouble played the Austin area, becoming one of the most popular bands in Texas. In 1982, the band played the Montreux Festival and their performance caught the attention of David Bowie and Jackson Browne. After Double Trouble's performance, Bowie asked Vaughan to play on his forthcoming album, while Browne offered the group free recording time at his Los Angeles studio, Downtown; both offers were accepted. Stevie Ray laid down the lead guitar tracks for what became Bowie's *Let's Dance* album in late 1982. Shortly afterward, John Hammond, Sr. landed Vaughan and Double Trouble a record contract with Epic and the band recorded their debut album in less than a week at Downtown.

Vaughan's debut album, *Texas Flood*, was released in the summer of 1983, a few months after Bowie's *Let's Dance* appeared. On its own, *Let's Dance* earned Vaughan quite a bit of attention, but *Texas Flood* was a blockbuster blues success, receiving positive reviews in both blues and rock publications, reaching number 38 on the charts, and crossing over to album rock radio stations. Bowie offered Vaughan the lead guitarist role for his 1983 stadium tour, but Stevie Ray turned him down, preferring to play with Double Trouble. Stevie Ray and Double Trouble set off on a successful tour and quickly recorded their second album, *Couldn't Stand the Weather*, which was released in May of 1984. The album was more successful than its predecessor, reaching number 31 on the charts; by the end of 1985, the album went gold. Double Trouble added keyboardist Reese Wynans in 1985, before they recorded their third album, *Soul to Soul*. The record was released in August, 1985 and was also quite successful, reaching number 34 on the charts.

Although his professional career was soaring, Vaughan was sinking deep into alcoholism and drug addiction. Despite his declining health, Stevie Ray continued to push himself, releasing the double live album *Live Alive* in October of 1986 and launching an extensive American tour in early 1987. Following the tour, Vaughan checked into a rehabilitation clinic. The guitarist's time in rehab was kept fairly quiet and for the next year, Stevie Ray and Double Trouble were fairly inactive. Vaughan performed a number of concerts in 1988, including a headlining gig at the New Orleans Jazz & Heritage Festival, and wrote his fourth album. The resulting record, *In Step*, appeared in June of 1989 and became his most successful album, peaking at number 33 on the charts, earning a Grammy for Best Contemporary Blues Recording, and going gold just over six months after its release.

In the spring of 1990, Stevie Ray recorded an album with his brother Jimmie, which was scheduled for release in the fall of the year. In the late summer of 1990, Vaughan and Double Trouble set out on an American headlining tour. On August 26, 1990, their East Troy, WI, gig concluded with an encore jam featuring guitaritsts Eric Clapton, Buddy Guy, Jimmie Vaughan, and Robert Cray. After the concert, Stevie Ray Vaughan boarded a helicopter bound for Chicago. Minutes after its 12:30 AM takeoff, the helicopter crashed, killing Vaughan and the other four passengers. Vaughan was only 35 years old.

Family Style, Stevie Ray's duet album with Jimmie Vaughan, appeared in October and entered the charts at number seven. *Family Style* began a series of posthumous releases that were as popular as the albums Stevie Ray released during his lifetime. *The Sky Is Crying*, a collection of studio outtakes compiled by Jimmie Vaughan, was released in October of 1991; it entered the charts at number ten and went platinum three months after its release. *In the Beginning*, a recording of a Double Trouble concert in 1980, was released in the fall of 1992 and the compilation *Greatest Hits* was released in 1995. In 1999, Vaughan's original albums were remastered and reissued, with *The Real Deal: Greatest Hits, Vol. 2* also appearing that year. The four-disc box *SRV*, which concentrated

heavily on outtakes, live performances, and rarities, was released in 2000. —*Stephen Thomas Erlewine*

★ **Texas Flood** / 1983 / Epic/Legacy ✦✦✦✦✦
It's hard to overestimate the impact Stevie Ray Vaughan's debut *Texas Flood* had upon its release in 1983. At that point, blues was no longer hip, the way it was in the '60s. *Texas Flood* changed all that, climbing into the Top 40 and spending over half a year on the charts, which was practically unheard of for a blues recording. Vaughan became a genuine star and, in doing so, sparked a revitalization of the blues. This was a monumental impact, but his critics claimed that, no matter how prodigious Vaughan's instrumental talents were, he didn't forge a distinctive voice; instead, he wore his influences on his sleeve, whether it was Albert King's pinched yet muscular soloing or Larry Davis' emotive singing. There's a certain element of truth in that, but that was sort of the point of *Texas Flood*. Vaughan didn't hide his influences, he celebrated them, pumping fresh blood into a familiar genre. When Vaughan and Double Trouble cut the album over the course of three days in 1982, he had already played his set lists countless times; he knew how to turn this material inside out or goose it up for maximum impact. The album is paced like a club show, kicking off with Vaughan's two best self-penned songs, "Love Struck Baby" and "Pride and Joy," then settling into a pair of covers, the slow-burning title track and an exciting reading of Howlin' Wolf's "Tell Me," before building to the climax of "Dirty Pool" and "I'm Crying." Vaughan caps the entire thing with "Lenny," a lyrical, jazzy tribute to his wife. It becomes clear that Vaughan's true achievement was finding something personal and emotional by fusing different elements of his idols. Sometimes the borrowing was overt, and other times subtle, but it all blended together into a style that recalled the past while seizing the excitement and essence of the present. —*Stephen Thomas Erlewine*

Couldn't Stand the Weather / 1984 / Epic/Legacy ✦✦✦✦
Stevie Ray Vaughan's second album, *Couldn't Stand the Weather*, pretty much did everything a second album should do: it confirmed that the acclaimed debut was no fluke, while matching, if not bettering, the sales of its predecessor, thereby cementing Vaughan's status as a giant of modern blues. So why does it feel like a letdown? Perhaps because it simply offers more of the same, all the while relying heavily on covers. Of the eight songs, half are covers, while two of his four originals are instrumentals—not necessarily a bad thing, but it gives the impression that Vaughan threw the album together in a rush, even if he didn't. Nevertheless, *Couldn't Stand the Weather* feels a bit like a holding pattern, since there's no elaboration on Double Trouble's core sound and no great strides forward, whether it's in Vaughan's songwriting or musicianship. Still, as holding patterns go, it's a pretty enjoyable one, since Vaughan and Double Trouble play spiritedly throughout the record. With its swaggering, stuttering riff, the title track ranks as one of Vaughan's classics, and thanks to a nuanced vocal, he makes W.C. Clark's "Cold Shot" his own. The instrumentals—the breakneck Lonnie Mack-styled "Scuttle Buttin'" and "Stang's Swang," another effective demonstration of Vaughan's jazz inclinations—work well, even if the original shuffle "Honey Bee" fails to make much of an impression and the cover of "Voodoo Chile (Slight Return)" is too reminiscent of Jimi Hendrix's original. So, there aren't many weaknesses on the record, aside from the suspicion that Vaughan didn't really push himself as hard as he could have, and the feeling that if he had, he would have come up with something a bit stronger. —*Stephen Thomas Erlewine*

Soul to Soul / 1985 / Epic/Legacy ✦✦✦
By adding two members to Double Trouble—keyboardist Reese Wynans and saxophonist Joe Sublett—Stevie Ray Vaughan indicated he wanted to add soul and R&B inflections to his basic blues sound, and *Soul to Soul* does exactly that. It's still a modern blues album, yet it has a wider sonic palette, finding Vaughan fusing a variety of blues, rock, and R&B styles. Most of this is done through covers—notably Hank Ballard's "Look at Little Sister," the exquisitely jazzy "Gone Home," and Doyle Bramhall's impassioned soul-blues "Change It"—but Vaughan's songwriting occasionally follows suit, as well. Even if only the tortured blues wailer "Ain't Gone 'N' Give Up on Love" entered his acknowledged canon, he throws in some delightful soul-funk touches on "Say What!," the instrumental wah-wah workout that kicks off the album, and the Curtis Mayfield-inspired closer "Life Without You" captures Vaughan at his best as a composer and performer. It's such a seductive number—such a full realization of his soul-blues ambitions—that the rest of the album pales in comparison. In fact, for all of its positive attributes, *Soul to Soul* winds up being less than the sum of its parts, and it's hard to pinpoint an exact reason why. Perhaps it was because Vaughan was on the verge of a horrible battle with substance abuse at the time of recording or perhaps it just has that unevenness inherent in transitional albums. Still, he has good taste in covers, his originals are sturdy, and there's not a bad performance here, so *Soul to Soul* winds up enjoyable in spite of its flaws, and it clearly points the way to his 1989 masterpiece, *In Step*. —*Stephen Thomas Erlewine*

Live Alive / Jul. 1986 / Epic ✦✦✦
Live Alive is a magnificent double-length showcase for Stevie Ray Vaughan's guitar playing, featuring a number of extended jams on a selection of most of the best material from Vaughan's first three albums, plus covers of "Willie the Wimp," "I'm Leaving You (Commit a Crime)," and Stevie Wonder's "Superstition." The album may not be exceptionally tight or concise, but then again, that's not the point. The renditions here sound less polished than the studio versions, with Vaughan's guitar tone bitingly down and dirty and his playing spontaneous and passionate. —*Steve Huey*

☆ **In Step** / Jun. 1989 / Epic/Legacy ✦✦✦✦✦
Stevie Ray Vaughan had always been a phenomenal guitarist, but prior to *In Step*, his songwriting was hit or miss. Even when he wrote a classic modern blues song, it was firmly within the genre's conventions; only on *Soul to Soul*'s exquisite soul-blues "Life Without You" did he attempt to stretch the boundaries of the form. As it turns out, that

was the keynote for *In Step*, an album where Vaughan found his own songwriting voice, blending blues, soul, and rock in unique ways, and writing with startling emotional honesty. Yes, there are a few covers, all well chosen, but the heart of the album rests in the songs he cowrote with Doyle Bramhall, the man who penned the *Soul to Soul* highlight "Change It." Bramhall proved to be an ideal collaborator for Vaughan; tunes like the terse "Tightrope" and the dense "Wall of Denial" feel so intensely personal, it's hard to believe that they weren't the product of just one man. Yet the lighter numbers—the dynamite boogie "The House Is Rockin'" and the breakneck blues of "Scratch-N-Sniff"—are just as effective as songs. Of course, he didn't need words to make effective music: "Travis Walk" is a blistering instrumental, complete with intricate fingerpicking reminiscent of the great country guitarist Merle Travis, while the shimmering "Riviera Paradise" is every bit as lyrical and lovely as his previous charmer, "Lenny." The magnificent thing about *In Step* is how it's fully realized, presenting every facet of Vaughan's musical personality, yet it still soars with a sense of discovery. It's a bittersweet triumph, given Vaughan's tragic death a little over a year after its release, yet it's a triumph all the same. *—Stephen Thomas Erlewine*

The Sky Is Crying / Nov. 5, 1991 / Epic ♦♦♦♦

The posthumously assembled ten-track outtakes collection *The Sky Is Crying* actually proves to be one of Vaughan's most consistent albums, rivaling *In Step* as the best outside of the *Greatest Hits* collection. These songs were recorded in sessions spanning from 1984's *Couldn't Stand the Weather* to 1989's *In Step* and were left off of the LPs for whatever reason (or, in the case of *Soul to Soul*'s "Empty Arms," a different version was used). What makes the record work is its eclectic diversity—Vaughan plays slide guitar on "Boot Hill" and acoustic on "Life By the Drop"; he smokes on the slow blues of "May I Have a Talk With You" and the title track just as much as on the uptempo Lonnie Mack cover "Wham"; and he shows the jazzy side of his playing on Hendrix's "Little Wing" and Kenny Burrell's "Chitlins Con Carne." But it's not just musical diversity that makes the record work, it's also Vaughan's emotional range. From the morbidly dark "Boot Hill" to the lilting "Little Wing" to the exuberant tributes to his influences—Lonnie Mack on "Wham" and Albert King on "The Sky Is Crying"—Vaughan makes the material resonate, and in light of his death, "The Sky Is Crying" and the touching survivor-story ballad "Life By the Drop" are two of the most moving moments in Vaughan's oeuvre. *—Steve Huey*

In the Beginning / Oct. 6, 1992 / Epic ♦♦

This 1980 live broadcast from Austin, TX, captures a young Stevie Vaughan (he had yet to become Stevie Ray) blasting the hometown crowd with a style that was already very well-formed. With Chris Layton on drums and bassist Jackie Newhouse (Tommy Shannon would join up a year later), his basic sound was already in place, albeit still in need of some polishing. Taken from the surviving two-track master, Vaughan's guitar is raw and in your face every note of the way. His takes on Freddie King's "In the Open" and the lengthy "Tin Pan Alley" are the real highlights here. Fans of this mercurial guitarist will want to add this one to the collection. *—Cub Koda*

Greatest Hits / Nov. 21, 1995 / Epic ♦♦♦♦♦

Stevie Ray Vaughan was a great guitarist, but he had trouble making consistent albums. *Greatest Hits* rectifies that problem by collecting all of his best-known tracks, from "Pride and Joy" to "Crossfire." Not only is it a terrific introduction, it's his most consistent album, demonstrating exactly why he was one of the most important guitarists of the '80s. *—Stephen Thomas Erlewine*

Live at Carnegie Hall / Jul. 29, 1997 / Epic ♦♦♦♦

Live at Carnegie Hall captures Stevie Ray Vaughan on the supporting tour for his second album, 1984's *Couldn't Stand the Weather*. The Carnegie Hall concert was a special show, since it was the only time Vaughan and Double Trouble added the brass section from Roomful of Blues to augment their sound; in addition, the concert featured guest appearences from Stevie's brother Jimmie and Dr. John. There might have been more musicians than usual on-stage, but Stevie Ray remains the center of attention, and he is in prime form here, tearing through a selection of his best-known songs which generally sound tougher in concert than they do in the studio. It's the best live Stevie Ray record yet released. *—Thom Owens*

The Real Deal: Greatest Hits, Vol. 2 / Mar. 23, 1999 / Epic/Legacy ♦♦♦♦

Stevie Ray Vaughan was one of a kind. Even his peers knew so. So many times, people like Eric Clapton and Buddy Guy have spoken publicly about Stevie Ray's gift, and it was a gift. His guitar leads would jet off into the stratosphere, return, reload and blast off again, time after time. *The Real Deal* is exactly what it says it is. This is a 16-song set that doesn't let up, not one time. Throughout classic Stevie Ray Vaughan tracks, like the full-speed-ahead instrumental "Scuttle Buttin'," "Love Struck Baby" and "Look at Little Sister," Stevie and the Double Trouble band consistently stand and deliver. Live tracks include the funky Stevie Wonder penned "Superstition," Vaughan favorite "Willie the Wimp," "Shake for Me," and the blues fire of "Leave My Girl Alone." It's Stevie Ray unleashed, live and without a net. One of the biggest crowd pleasers is included here, Stevie's retelling of the Jimi Hendrix standard, "Voodoo Chile (Slight Return)." Awesome. "Lenny" shows off Stevie's jazz influence with subtle phrasing that evokes memories of "Little Wing" or the coda on "Layla." No more perfect closer could have been chosen for this set than the solo acoustic number, "Life By the Drop." It's a touching tale of two old friends who become estranged, and then rekindle their old friendship. With *The Real Deal*, we are all in that same boat. Rekindling a friendship that never really died, but may have been forgotten by some for a while. The friendship we all have with the heart and soul of Stevie Ray Vaughan, his music. *—Michael B. Smith*

Blues at Sunrise / Apr. 4, 2000 / Epic/Legacy ♦♦♦

The concept behind *Blues at Sunrise* is a good one: collect ten of SRV's best slow blues numbers, primarily from the official studio albums but also a couple of unreleased cuts and rarities, and sequence them as if they were a lost studio album. It's a neat idea, especially when it's packaged in artwork that deliberately evokes memories of classic blues albums from the '60s (there's even a fake, faded record ring on the front and back covers), and it's hard to fault the music here. All the obvious selections are here—"Ain't Gone 'N' Give Up on Love," "The Things (That) I Used to Do," "Leave My Girl Alone." And the rarities are all worthwhile, including a live "Texas Flood" from the *Live at the El Macambo* video, a live duet with Johnny Copeland on "Tin Pan Alley" from 1985, an unreleased take of "The Sky Is Crying" from *Couldn't Stand the Weather*, and a duet with Albert King on "Blues at Sunrise" (also available on the Fantasy disc *In Session*). Still, some fans may complain, since this is the first posthumous release that feels as if it's trying to trick the hardcore into purchasing music they already have. That's a legitimate complaint, because there are only two songs that the hardcore won't have, and they very well may not want to sink down dollars for something that's just a reconfiguration of familiar tunes. But, as reconfigurations and repackagings go, *Blues at Sunrise* is strong and entertaining, working quite well as a mood piece. It may not be revelatory, but if you strip away your qualms and quibbles, it's enjoyable. *—Stephen Thomas Erlewine*

SRV / Nov. 21, 2000 / Epic/Legacy ♦♦♦♦

If you're gonna put out a box set that really offers something to the devoted fans of an artist—who are, after all, probably bound to have much or all of the artist's other records already if they're interesting in buying a box set to begin with—this four-CD package is the way to do it. It's not so much a best-of or career retrospective as a very generous pile of career-spanning material that will genuinely add a new dimension to the Stevie Ray Vaughan listener's library, as fully two-thirds of the 54 tracks were previously unreleased. In addition, of the songs that have been previously available, five of those are cuts on which Vaughan was a sideman or partner (for Johnny Copeland, Albert King, Lonnie Mack, A.C. Reed, and as part of the Vaughan Brothers), so the Vaughan collector might have missed those in the past. Each of the first three discs clock in at more than 75 minutes, progressing from 1977 to 1990 and emphasizing live material, from soundchecks and radio programs to arena-headlining gigs and three solo acoustic tunes (one of which was previously on *The Unplugged Collection, Vol. 1*) from a 1990 *MTV Unplugged* episode. As music, though, it's uneven. The earliest and leanest cuts are a valuable supplement to Vaughan's discography since he didn't have much opportunity to record until the early '80s. Yet sometimes these are too-long shuffles and boogies; his songwriting and singing is not nearly as impressive as his instrumental technique; and his occasional attempts to replicate Jimi Hendrix are inessential. A few familiar popular studio cuts like "Pride and Joy" and "Wall of Denial" are here, presumably to entertain the more casual Vaughan fans that need an extra push to spring for the box. More rabid Vaughan followers will likely be so overwhelmed by the quantity of unreleased items that they're unlikely to quibble about the presence of tracks they already own. The fourth disc is a DVD with five never-aired and never-issued performances from an episode of the television program *Austin City Limits*, recorded on October 10, 1989; the 72-page booklet of essays, appreciative quotes from several dozen peers, and more are other bonuses. *—Richie Unterberger*

Live at Montreux 1982 and 1985 / Nov. 20, 2001 / Epic/Legacy ♦♦♦♦

Epic/Legacy's 2001 archival release, *Live at Montreux 1982 and 1985*, is a godsend for his legions of diehards since it preserves one of his most legendary performances while teaming it with a performance that helps put the other in context. The historical performance, of course, is his appearance at the Montreux Blues & Jazz Festival in 1982. At the time he was just breaking into the business, and this performance had a large part in his success since it helped maintain the buzz started from his popularity in Texas. Here he plays a lot of covers, and the concentration is almost entirely on his solos, but that's why it works; he's in front of an audience that wants to hear that, and he's eager to prove himself, and the kinetic energy is positively electric. The 1985 performance is also pretty hot, with a lot of guitar, but it's clear that Vaughan is no longer as hungry and no longer has as much to prove. Consequently, it's a little more relaxed, even if it still follows the same basic template, with lots and lots of guitar, and it's good to hear, but if you're not already converted, it may seem a little samey toward the end. Still, this sounds great, is lovingly packaged, and, in terms of Vaughan's legacy, is very important—probably the most welcome posthumous release. *—Stephen Thomas Erlewine*

Maurice John Vaughn

b. Nov. 6, 1952, Chicago, IL

Vocals, Saxophone, Guitar / Modern Electric Chicago Blues, Soul-Blues, Funk

Maurice John Vaughn's 1984 debut set, *Generic Blues Album*, came packaged in a plain white jacket, its title unceremoniously stamped on its front like a package of no-brand rice on a grocer's shelf. It looked like the cleverest of publicity ploys, but in reality, it was a simple economic necessity—Vaughn's own Reecy label was operating on a shoestring.

Vaughn is no longer a blues unknown. With a challenging 1993 album on Alligator (*In the Shadow of the City*) melding blues, soul, funk, and other contemporary influences, he's grown into one of Chicago's most interesting and versatile younger blues artists. Fluent on both guitar and sax, Vaughn played both in sideman roles prior to stepping out on his own.

Sax came first. Vaughn grew up on Chicago's South Side, blowing his horn with various R&B groups and recording with the Chosen Few for Chi-Sound Records in 1976. When sax gigs grew scarce, Vaughn began to emphasize his guitar skills. Blues guitarist Phil Guy recruited him and his band for a 1979 Canadian tour, and the genre appealed to him. Vaughn later held down sideman spots with Luther Allison, Son Seals, Valerie Wellington, and A.C. Reed.

Alligator Records retained the no-frills packaging when it reissued *Generic Blues Album* after Vaughn sang "Nothing Left to Believe In" on the label's 1987 anthology *The New Bluebloods*. *In the Shadow of the City* came in 1993. Vaughn toured sporadically following the release, somtimes playing in schools for kids who had never heard the blues before. He left the road to work as an A&R man for Appaloosa Records, producing records by the likes of Maxine Carr and Shirley Johnson. He also did some session work playing on two albums by Detroit Junior. In 2001, he finally released his next album, *Dangerous Road.* Despite the cover art on his first LP, there's nothing generic at all about Maurice Vaughn's brand of soulful blues. *—Bill Dahl*

● **Generic Blues Album** / 1984 / Alligator ✦✦✦✦✦
Anything but generic, this is actually powerful, contemporary, funky Chicago blues. With excellent musicianship, Vaughn performs interesting songs focusing on the trials of modern urban life and work. Vaughn, a top session player, sings and plays guitar and sax. *—Niles J. Frantz*

In the Shadow of the City / 1993 / Alligator ✦✦✦✦
The Chicago guitarist/saxist spreads his stylistic wings considerably further than he did on his debut, embracing funk more fully than his first time around but offering enough tasty contemporary blues to keep everyone happy. The prolific triple threat (he's also an engaging singer) wrote all but three tracks himself (one of the covers is the shuffling "Small Town Baby"; its composer, veteran pianist Jimmy Walker, plays on the cut). *—Bill Dahl*

Dangerous Road / May 22, 2001 / Blue Suit ✦✦✦✦

Eddie "Cleanhead" Vinson

b. Dec. 18, 1917, Houston, TX, **d.** Jul. 2, 1988, Los Angeles, CA
Vocals, Sax (Alto) / New York Blues, Jump Blues, Bop, West Coast Blues, R&B
An advanced stylist on alto saxophone who vacillated throughout his career between jump blues and jazz, bald-pated Eddie "Cleanhead" Vinson (he lost his hair early on after a botched bout with a lye-based hair-straightener) also possessed a playfully distinctive vocal delivery that stood him in good stead with blues fans.

Vinson first picked up a horn while attending high school in Houston. During the late '30s, he was a member of an incredible horn section in Milton Larkin's orchestra, sitting next to Arnett Cobb and Illinois Jacquet. After exiting Larkin's employ in 1941, Vinson picked up a few vocal tricks while on tour with bluesman Big Bill Broonzy. Vinson joined the Cootie Williams Orchestra from 1942 to 1945. His vocals on trumpeter Williams' renditions of "Cherry Red" and "Somebody's Got to Go" were in large part responsible for their wartime hit status.

Vinson struck out on his own in 1945, forming his own large band, signing with Mercury, and enjoying a double-sided smash in 1947 with his romping R&B chart-topper "Old Maid Boogie" and the song that would prove his signature number, "Kidney Stew Blues" (both songs featured Vinson's instantly identifiable vocals). A 1949-1952 stint at King Records produced only one hit, the amusing sequel "Somebody Done Stole My Cherry Red," along with the classic blues "Person to Person" (later revived by another King artist, Little Willie John).

Vinson's jazz leanings were probably heightened during 1952-1953, when his band included a young John Coltrane. Somewhere along about here, Vinson wrote two Miles Davis classics, "Tune Up" and "Four." Vinson steadfastly kept one foot in the blues camp and the other in jazz, waxing jumping R&B for Mercury (in 1954) and Bethlehem (1957), jazz for Riverside in 1961 (with Cannonball Adderly), and blues for Blues Time and ABC-BluesWay. A 1969 set for Black & Blue, cut in France with pianist Jay McShann and tenor saxophonist Hal Singer, beautifully recounted Vinson's blues shouting heyday (it's available on Delmark as *Kidney Stew Is Fine*). A much later set for Muse teamed him with the sympathetic little big band approach of Rhode Island-based Roomful of Blues. Vinson toured the States and Europe frequently prior to his 1988 death of a heart attack. *—Bill Dahl*

● **Cherry Red Blues** / Aug. 10, 1949-Jul. 7, 1952 / King/Gusto ✦✦✦✦✦
Somehow, amidst all the CD reissues from the King Records vaults unleashed by Charly, Ace, Rhino, and King's current ownership, this versatile alto saxist has fallen through the cracks. Thus, this two-LP collection, boasting all but a handful of his jumping 1949-1952 outings for King, remains your best introduction to the Cleanheaded one's R&B output (along with the 1945-1947 sides he waxed for Mercury, which grace the seven-disc anthology *Blues, Boogie, & Bop: The 1940s Mercury Sessions*). *—Bill Dahl*

Eddie Cleanhead Vinson Sings / Sep. 1957 / Charly ✦✦✦✦✦
One of only two albums that altoist/singer Eddie "Cleanhead" Vinson led during 1956-1966, this infectious set finds him performing some of his best-known tunes. With assistance by a medium-size group that plays in a Count Basie groove (including such Basieites as trumpeter Joe Newman, trombonist Henry Coker, either Frank Foster or Paul Quinichette on tenor, and pianist Nat Pierce), Cleanhead makes such songs as "Kidney Stew," "Caldonia," "Cherry Red," "Is You Is or Is You Ain't My Baby," and "Hold It Right There" sound full of joy. This CD reissue adds three alternate takes that were originally recorded in stereo. A good sampling of the great Cleanhead. *—Scott Yanow*

Back in Town / Sep. 1957 / Bethlehem ✦✦✦
Although he had achieved a certain amount of popularity in the late '40s with his blues vocals and boppish alto, Eddie "Cleanhead" Vinson's Bethlehem album was one of only two recordings he made as a leader between 1956-1966. With arrangements by Ernie Wilkins, Manny Albam, and Harry Tubbs, and his sidemen including several members (past and present) of the Count Basie Orchestra, the blues-oriented music (which gives Vinson a chance to sing such material as "It Ain't Necessarily So," "Is You Is or Is You Ain't My Baby," and "Caledonia") is quite enjoyable and really rocks; pity that this record did not catch on. *—Scott Yanow*

Cleanhead & Cannonball / Sep. 19, 1961+Feb. 14, 1962 / Landmark ✦✦✦✦
During these two sessions, Eddie "Cleanhead" Vinson was joined by the Cannonball Adderley Quintet. Five of the ten selections were previously unissued altogether until this album came out in 1988. On Vinson's vocal numbers he is backed by altoist Cannonball Adderley, cornetist Nat Adderley, pianist Joe Zawinul, bassist Sam Jones, and drummer Louis Hayes. Unfortunately on the instrumentals and the one vocal tune ("Kidney Stew") in which he plays, Vinson is the only altoist as Cannonball sits out; it's a pity that the two very different stylists did not have a chance to trade off. Despite that missed opportunity, the music on this release is quite worthy with Cleanhead in top form on such numbers as "Person to Person," "Just a Dream," and the three instrumentals. *—Scott Yanow*

Kidney Stew Is Fine / Mar. 28, 1969 / Delmark ✦✦✦✦✦
Although its programming has been juggled a bit, and the CD has been given liner notes, this Delmark release is a straight reissue of the original LP. Clocking in at around 38 minutes, the relatively brief set is the only recording that exists of Vinson, pianist Jay McShann, and guitarist T-Bone Walker playing together; the sextet is rounded out by the fine tenor Hal Singer, bassist Jackie Sampson, and drummer Paul Gunther. Vinson, whether singing "Please Send Me Somebody to Love," "Just a Dream," and "Juice Head Baby" or taking boppish alto solos, is the main star throughout this album (originally on Black & Blue), a date that helped launch Vinson's commercial comeback. *—Scott Yanow*

You Can't Make Love Alone / Jun. 18, 1971 / Mega ✦✦✦
Eddie "Cleanhead" Vinson was in inspired form at the 1971 Montreux Jazz Festival. He stole the show when he sat in with Oliver Nelson's big band during their "Swiss Suite" and played a brilliant blues alto solo. The same day he recorded this Mega album but, due to its extreme brevity (under 24 minutes), perhaps this label should have changed its name to "Mini." Despite the low quantity, the quality of his performance (on which Vinson is joined by the guitars of Larry Coryell and Cornell Dupree, pianist Neal Creque, bassist Chuck Rainey, and drummer Pretty Purdie) makes this album still worth acquiring, although preferably at a budget price. Vinson takes "Straight No Chaser" as an instrumental and does a fine job of singing "Cleanhead Blues," "You Can't Make Love Alone," "I Had a Dream," and "Person to Person." *—Scott Yanow*

Jamming the Blues / Jul. 2, 1974 / Black Lion ✦✦✦✦
For this lesser-known outing (reissued on CD), the great altoist and blues singer Eddie "Cleanhead" Vinson is heard in fine form at the 1974 Montreux Jazz Festival. With fine support from a four-piece rhythm section that includes pianist Peter Wingfield and some solo space for tenor saxophonist Hal Singer, Vinson plays a few of his familiar but always welcome numbers ("Just A Dream," "Person to Person," and "Hold It Right There") plus "Laura" and some basic instrumental blues. An excellent outing from a performer who was claimed by both the jazz and blues worlds. *—Scott Yanow*

Kidney Stew / Apr. 17, 1976 / Black & Blue ✦✦✦✦
Eddie "Cleanhead" Vinson plays and sings his usual material in this meeting with Ted Easton's five-piece Dutch jazz band. The group is enthusiastic and Vinson, even though he had performed such material as "Kidney Stew," "Just a Dream," and "Somebody Sure Has Gotta Go" a countless number of times by 1976, was still able to come up with something fresh to say on this blues-oriented set. *—Scott Yanow*

The Clean Machine / Feb. 22, 1978 / Muse ✦✦✦✦
What makes this album different from many of Eddie "Cleanhead" Vinson's is that four of the seven selections are taken as instrumentals. Vinson's alto playing has long been underrated due to his popularity as a blues singer, so this release gives one the opportunity to hear his bop-influenced solos at greater length. With the assistance of a strong rhythm section led by pianist Lloyd Glenn and some contributions from trumpeter Jerry Rusch and Rashid Ali on tenor, Vinson is in excellent form throughout this enjoyable set. *—Scott Yanow*

Hold It Right There! / Aug. 25, 1978-Aug. 26, 1978 / Muse ✦✦✦✦✦
After years of neglect, Eddie "Cleanhead" Vinson was finally receiving long overdue recognition at the time of this live session—one of six albums recorded during a week at Sandy's Jazz Revival. Two of these albums featured tenors Arnett Cobb and Buddy Tate in lead roles. While Vinson has fine blues vocals on "Cherry Red" and "Hold It," it is his boppish alto solos on "Cherokee," "Now's the Time," and "Take the 'A' Train" (the latter also having spots for Cobb and Tate) that make this set recommended to blues and bop fans alike. *—Scott Yanow*

Live at Sandy's / Aug. 25, 1978-Aug. 26, 1978 / Muse ✦✦✦
Muse recorded six albums during one week at Sandy's Jazz Revival, a club in Beverly, MA; two of them (this one and *Hold It Right There*) feature the blues vocals and alto solos of Eddie "Cleanhead" Vinson. Some of the songs also have the tenors of Arnett Cobb and Buddy Tate in a supporting role but this album is largely Vinson's show. Backed by a superb rhythm section (pianist Ray Bryant, bassist George Duvivier, and drummer Alan Dawson), Vinson takes four fine vocals and plays many swinging alto solos including one on "Tune Up," a song he wrote that has been mistakenly credited to Miles Davis for decades. *—Scott Yanow*

I Want a Little Girl / Feb. 10, 1981 / Pablo/OJC ✦✦✦✦✦
Eddie "Cleanhead" Vinson, 64 at the time of this Pablo recording, is in superior form on the blues-oriented material. With Art Hillery (on piano and organ) and guitarist Cal Green leading the rhythm section, and trumpeter Martin Banks and the tenor of Rashid Ali offering contrasting solo voices, this is a particularly strong release. It is true that Vinson had sung such songs as "I Want a Little Girl," "Somebody's Got to Go," and "Stormy Monday" a countless number of times previously, but he still infuses these versions with enthusiasm and spirit, making this set a good example of Cleanhead's talents in his later years. *—Scott Yanow*

Eddie Cleanhead Vinson & Roomful of Blues / Jan. 27, 1982 / Muse ✦✦✦✦✦
If there were justice in the world, Eddie "Cleanhead" Vinson would have been able to tour with this type of group throughout much of his career. Roomful of Blues, a popular five-horn nonet, has rarely sounded more exciting than on this musical meeting with the

legendary singer/altoist. Vinson himself is exuberant on some of the selections, particularly "House of Joy," one of five instrumentals among the eight selections. Whether one calls it blues, bebop, or early R&B, this accessible music is very enjoyable and deserves to be more widely heard. Among the supporting players, tenor man Greg Piccolo, trumpeter Bob Enos, and guitarist Ronnie Earl (in one of his earliest recordings) win honors. —*Scott Yanow*

Cleanhead Blues: 1945–1947 / Oct. 12, 1999 / EPM Musique ✦✦✦✦

1945–1947 / Mar. 5, 2002 / Classics ✦✦✦✦

Mose Vinson

b. Aug. 7, 1917, Holly Springs, MS, **d.** Nov. 30, 2002, Memphis, TN
Vocals, Piano / Piano Blues
A Memphis piano institution for more than half a century, Mose Vinson recorded a handful of unreleased sides for Sun in 1953 (recently liberated by Bear Family) and did scattered session work for Sam Phillips as well.

Vinson began playing piano as a child in the Mississippi Delta, initially playing in his local church. By his teens, he had begun playing jazz and blues. In 1932, he moved to Memphis, TN, where he played local juke joints and parties throughout the '30s and '40s. In the early '50s, Sam Phillips had Vinson accompany a number of Sun Records blues artists, most notably Ike Cotton. During that time, Phillips also had Vinson cut some tracks, but they remained unreleased until the '80s.

For the next three decades, Vinson continued to perform at local Memphis clubs. However, he didn't play as frequently as he did in the previous two decades. In the early '80s, the Center for Southern Folklore hired Vinson to perform at special cultural festivals, as well as local schools. For the next two decades, he played concerts and educational and cultural festivals associated with the Center for Southern Folklore. Mose Vinson died in Memphis from diabetes on November 30, 2002. —*Bill Dahl & Stephen Thomas Erlewine*

● **Memphis Piano Blues Today** / 1990 / Wolf ✦✦✦✦✦
Memphis Piano Blues Today collects a number of latter-day recordings from Mose Vinson. Although he was past his prime, the pianist was still in good form and, since he recorded so infrequently as a leader, this is a valuable addition to any serious fan of piano blues and Memphis blues. —*Thom Owens*

Walter Vinson

b. Feb. 2, 1901, Bolton, MS, **d.** Apr. 22, 1975, Chicago, IL
Vocals, Violin, Guitar / Memphis Blues, Acoustic Memphis Blues
One half of the legendary Mississippi Sheiks, singer/guitarist Walter Vinson was also among the most noteworthy blues accompanists of his era. Born February 2, 1901, in Bolton, MS, Vinson (also known variously as Vincson and Vincent) began performing as a child, and during his teen years was a fixture at area parties and picnics. Even from the outset, however, he rarely if ever appeared as a solo act, seemingly much more at home in duets and trios; towards that end, during the '20s he worked with Charlie McCoy, Rubin Lacy, and Son Spand before forging his most pivotal and long-lasting union, with Lonnie Chatmon, in 1928. In addition to teaming with Chatmon in the Mississippi Sheiks, Vinson also recorded with him in the Mississippi Hot Footers, and even worked with Chatmon's brothers Bo and Harry. Upon the Sheiks' 1933 dissolution, Vinson recorded with various players in areas ranging from Jackson, MS, to New Orleans to finally Chicago; while an active club performer during the early '40s, by the middle of the decade he had begun a lengthy hiatus from music which continued through 1960, at which point he returned to both recording and festival appearances. Hardening of the arteries forced Vinson into retirement during the early '70s; he died in Chicago in 1975. —*Jason Ankeny*

● **Complete Recorded Works (1928–1941)** / 1991 / Document ✦✦✦✦
This Document collection reissues all of Walter Vinson's prewar recordings, including several of his accompaniment performances for Leroy Carter ("Black Widow Spider") and Mary Butler ("Mad Dog Blues"), as well as sideman roles for the Chatmon brothers from the Mississippi Sheiks and Charlie McCoy. Also included are career highlights "Overtime Blues" and "Losin' Blues," though the rest of this lengthy, exhaustive collection has material of lesser quality. —*Thom Owens*

Jimmy Vivino

b. Jan. 10, 1955, Paterson, NJ
Guitar / Modern Electric Blues
Guitarist, singer and songwriter Jimmy Vivino has enjoyed a high-visibility gig in recent years as part of the Max Weinberg Seven on TV's *Late Night With Conan O'Brien*. Vivino began his musical education on trumpet, an instrument his father Jerome also played; his earliest musical memories are of his father spinning Louis Armstrong and Roy Eldridge records at their home in Glen Rock, NJ. By the time he was in high school, he was playing lead trumpet and arranging for big bands.

After hearing producer/impresario Al Kooper play organ with Blood, Sweat & Tears, Vivino was inspired to begin teaching himself organ. He didn't begin playing guitar until 1978, studying with Joe Cinderella and jazz guitarist Jack Wilkins. Given his love for Louis Armstrong, he was naturally drawn to blues—in particular, the music of the Paul Butterfield Blues Band with guitarist Michael Bloomfield. In the late '70s and early '80s, he was able to meet Muddy Waters on several occasions through his friend Brian Bisesi, who was an auxiliary guitarist when Waters was passing through the New Jersey/New York area.

Allan Pepper, the owner of New York's Bottom Line nightclub, took an active interest in Vivino's career as a guitarist and arranger, and soon Vivino found himself working with musicians as varied as Phoebe Snow, Laura Nyro, Felix Cavaliere, and Dion. Vivino also played with Jules Shear and Steve Holly in a New York group called the Reckless Sleepers.

After Al Kooper asked Vivino to assemble a band for his New York performances, mostly at the Bottom Line, Vivino began accompanying him there, later recording with him on the Music Masters/BMG albums *Soul of a Man* and *Rekooperator*. Vivino later began playing with Chuck Berry pianist Johnnie Johnson in 1990, all the while honing his fingerpicking chops with John Sebastian's J-Band.

Since *Late Night With Conan O'Brien* began in 1992, Vivino has been an integral part of the Max Weinberg Seven. He'd known Weinberg from a regional R&B group, Killer Joe, which both were a part of. Although he has the benefit of a glamorous day job as part of the house band for O'Brien's show, he remains a humble student of the blues.

When Vivino finally had the chance to record his own album, it was not a moment too soon. Unlike a lot of more seasoned musicians, Vivino has always been ambitious, involving himself in a multitude of bands and projects, learning as much as could about various musical genres from the best available sources. Not surprisingly, Vivino decided to record his debut album the old-fashioned way. He and his band cut it in the space of two days, without rehearsing the material backwards and forwards. This contributes an air of spontaneity and a live feeling to *Do What, Now?* (Music Masters/BMG, 1997). He's joined by his musical heroes, Al Kooper (who produced the album) and bassist Harvey Brooks; guests on *Do What, Now?* include former Stevie Ray Vaughan keyboardist Reese Wynans, John Sebastian on harmonica, and Sam Bush on mandolin.

When he's not taping shows with O'Brien, Vivino can be found hanging out in New York's blues clubs at night, sometimes to sit in, other times to just sit and listen. —*Richard Skelly*

● **Do What, Now?** / Mar. 11, 1997 / Music Masters ✦✦✦

Albertina Walker

b. Aug. 29, 1929, Chicago, IL
Vocals / Traditional Gospel, Black Gospel

Born the youngest of nine children on August 29, 1929, in Chicago, IL, Albertina Walker grew up on the South Side and started singing as a child at Westpoint Baptist Church. A lot of great gospel artists used to come to her church: the Roberta Martin Singers, Sadie Durham, and Professor Fyre. She joined gospel groups, beginning with the Pete Williams Singers, the Willie Webb Singers, and the Robert Anderson Singers, before forming the Caravans in 1951. The original group also included Ora Lee Hopkins, Elyse Yancey, and Nellie Grace Daniels. Classic recordings for the States label between 1952 and 1954 were "Mary Don't You Weep," "Soldiers in the Army," "The Solid Rock," "The Lord I'll Keep Me Day By Day," "The Blood Will Never Lose Its Power," and "Blessed Assurance." The latter song was redone by Walker for the soundtrack of Steve Martin's movie *Leap of Faith*, in which she makes a brief cameo.

The Caravans are heralded as an unparalleled launching pad for future gospel superstars: Shirley Caesar, Inez Andrews, Bessie Griffin, Dorothy Norwood, Cassietta George, and James Cleveland were just a few of the ensemble's alumni who later went on to solo fame. In that tradition, the pioneering gospel singer started The Albertina Walker Foundation for the Creative Arts which provides scholarships to gospel musicians and singers. In 1955, they were signed to Savoy Records. Dance fans should take note that the Caravans, in 1966, included teenager and future disco diva Loleatta Holloway.

By 1956, the Caravans were among the most popular acts on the gospel music circuit due in part to their ethereal, amazing vocal interplay and strong alternating leads. Riding high in 1962, the Caravans signed to pioneering Chicago record label Vee-Jay to record the LP *Seek Ye the Lord*. Other hit albums with Vee-Jay include *Walk Around Heaven All Day* and *To Whom Shall I Turn*. The Caravans disbanded in the mid-'70s, though there were occasional reunion tours.

The '70s saw Walker re-signed with Savoy releasing such LPs as *Please Be Patient With Me* (her first Grammy-nominated album), *I Can Go to God in Prayer, Spread the Word*, and *I Won't Last a Day Without You*. By the '80s, Ms. Walker had moved to Word/Epic, recording *Let Jesus Come Into Your Heart*, *I Will Wait on You*, and *Joy Will Come in the Morning*. By this time, she had been nominated 11 times for the Grammy Award. In 1995, she won a Grammy Award for the Best Traditional Gospel Album, *Songs of the Church*. Also that year, she recorded an album with Phoebe Snow, Thelma Houston, CeCe Peniston, and Lois Walden as the Sisters of Glory, and released an album called *Good News in Hard Times* on LLF/Warner Bros. Records. The veteran's warm, venerable vocals graced Rev. Thomas A. Dorsey's "Precious Lord" and Dorothy Love Coates' "He's Right on Time." In 1997, she won a Dove Award for Traditional Gospel Album of the Year for the Grammy-nominated album, *Let's Go Back—Live in Chicago*. Released in summer 1997, *I'm Still Here* (BMG/Zomba/Verity) was a solid contribution to a catalog that includes over 40 albums. Some of the standout tracks are the title track, "Sanctify Me (I'm Available)," "Lord I Want to Thank You," and a jazzy orchestrated cover of "The Impossible Dream." As the 21st century began, Albertina Walker was guesting on albums by Kurt Carr, the Gospel Music Workshop of America, and the National Baptist Convention. —*Ed Hogan*

Tell the Angels / 1960 / Savoy ✦✦✦
Her 1960 debut, after the Caravans. —*Bil Carpenter*

● **God Is Love** / 1975 / Lection/Polygram ✦✦✦✦✦
God Is Love ranks among Albertina Walker's best recordings, capturing the gospel vocalist at her most moving and simply best. It may be a latter-day album from Walker, but her power and influence is readily apparent. —*Thom Owens*

The Best Is Yet to Come / 1988 / Savoy ✦✦✦

My Time Is Not Over / 1989 / Word ✦✦✦✦

You Believed in Me / 1991 / Benson ✦✦✦
This recent album includes "Working on a Building." —*Bil Carpenter*

Live / 1992 / Benson ✦✦✦
Albertina Walker's second album for Benson Records finds the former lead singer of the Caravans running through nine of her most popular songs—including "You've Been So Good," "That's the Way Heaven Will Be," "Watch Tower," "He Knows (Just How Much You Can Bear)," "My Best Friend," "I've Got a Feeling," "Day By Day" and "I Can Go to God in Prayer"—in concert. Supported by the Trinity All Nations Choir, Walker turns in a wonderful performance. Even cameos from Ralph Lofton, Derrick Lee and Darius Brooks can't take the spotlight away from Walker, who once again proves why she is considered one of the greatest singers in contemporary gospel. —*Thom Owens*

Albertina Walker Live / 1992 / A&M ✦✦✦
Good singing in the grand tradition. —*Opal Louis Nations*

Gospel Greats / Sep. 13, 1994 / Benson ✦✦✦

Freedom / 1996 / Jewel ✦✦✦✦✦
Good rousing material by this important aggregation. —*Opal Louis Nations*

Joe Louis Walker

b. Dec. 25, 1949, San Francisco, CA
Vocals, Guitar / Modern Electric Blues, Soul-Blues

Without a doubt one of the most exciting and innovative artists gracing contemporary blues, guitarist Joe Louis Walker has glowed like a shining blue beacon over the last decade. His 1986 debut album for HighTone, *Cold Is the Night*, announced his arrival in stunning fashion; his subsequent output on HighTone and Verve has only served to further establish Walker as one of the leading younger bluesmen on the scene. He traveled a circuitous route to get to where he is today. At age 14, he took up the guitar, playing blues (with an occasional foray into psychedelic rock) on the mushrooming San Francisco circuit. By 1975, Walker was burned out on blues and turned to God, singing for the next decade with a gospel group, the Spiritual Corinthians. When the Corinthians played the 1985 New Orleans Jazz & Heritage Festival, Walker was inspired to embrace his blues roots again. He assembled a band, the Boss Talkers, and wrote some stunning originals that ended up on *Cold Is the Night*. More acclaimed albums for HighTone—1988's *The Gift, Blue Soul* the next year, and two riveting sets cut live at Slim's in 1990—preceded a switch to the major Verve imprint and three more discs that were considerably more polished than their grittier HighTone counterparts. —*Bill Dahl*

Cold Is the Night / 1986 / HighTone ✦✦✦✦
The Bay Area blues guitarist's debut album sounds underproduced compared to what would soon follow—and that's no knock. Walker's gritty, expressive vocals and ringing, concise guitar work shine through loud and clear in front of his band, the Boss Talkers. Walker and his producers Dennis Walker and Bruce Bromberg wrote virtually the entire set, including the slashing "Cold Is the Night," "Don't Play Games," and "One Woman." —*Bill Dahl*

● **The Gift** / 1988 / HighTone ✦✦✦✦✦
Although it didn't enjoy the major label hype that his current output does, Walker's High-Tone encore just may be his finest album of all, filled with soulful vocal performances, bone-cutting guitar work, and tight backing from the Boss Talkers and the Memphis Horns. Honestly, you can't go wrong with any of Walker's remarkably consistent High-Tone discs—but give this one the slightest of edges over the rest. —*Bill Dahl*

Blue Soul / 1989 / HighTone ✦✦✦✦✦
Another winner sporting memorable songs ("T.L.C.," "Personal Baby," "City of Angels," "Prove Your Love"), sinuous grooves, and a whole lot of vicious guitar from one of the hottest relatively young bluesmen on the circuit. He goes it alone on the finale, "I'll Get to Heaven on My Own," sounding as conversant with the country blues tradition as he does with the contemporary stuff. —*Bill Dahl*

Live at Slim's, Vol. 1 / May 1991 / HighTone ✦✦✦✦
Walker was hot enough over the course of a two-day stand at Slim's in San Francisco to warrant the issue of two full albums from the dates. The first is a sizzling combination of past triumphs, new items, and covers of Clifton Chenier's "Hot Tamale Baby," Junior Wells' "Little By Little" (with Huey Lewis, no less, on harp), and a saucy duet with Angela Strehli on the old Fontella Bass/Bobby McClure rocker "Don't Mess Up a Good Thing." —*Bill Dahl*

Live at Slim's, Vol. 2 / Nov. 1992 / HighTone ✦✦✦✦
More from that searing Slim's engagement, including Joe Louis ripping through Ray Charles' "Don't You Know," Little Milton's "Love at First Sight," and Rosco Gordon's overworked "Just a Little Bit," along with his own gems. Huey Lewis turns up again as the harpist on Walker's version of Haskell Sadler's "747." —*Bill Dahl*

Blues Survivor / Oct. 19, 1993 / Verve ✦✦✦
By no means a bad album, Walker's major-label debut just wasn't quite as terrific as what directly preceded it. The studio atmosphere seems a bit slicker than before, and the songs are in several cases considerably longer than they need to be (generally in the five- to seven-minute range). A reworking of Howlin' Wolf's "Shake for Me" is the only familiar entry. —*Bill Dahl*

JLW / 1994 / Polygram ✦✦✦
Another overly polished effort that nevertheless packs a punch on many selections. Walker's songwriting is considerably less prominent, with only three self-penned tunes on the disc this time. Otis Blackwell's pulsating "On That Power Line" and the Don Gardner and Dee Dee Ford dustie "I Need Your Lovin'" receive spirited revivals, and there's an acoustic duet with James Cotton, "Going to Canada." —*Bill Dahl*

Blues of the Month Club / Sep. 12, 1995 / Verve ✦✦✦
This was Walker's weakest to date—strange, since he shares production credit this time with the legendary Steve Cropper. Once again, some songs drag on far after their logical

conclusions; also, Walker doesn't quite possess the pipes to effectively belt the old Jackie Brenston rouser "You've Got to Lose." The title track, with Cropper co-featured on guitar, is a clever piece of material, but overall, the slick production values strip some of the grit from Walker's incendiary attack. *—Bill Dahl*

Hello Everybody / Oct. 1995 / Verve ♦♦♦

Great Guitars / Apr. 8, 1997 / Polygram ♦♦♦
Joe Louis Walker is a powerful blues guitarist and singer whose versatility and musical courage are showcased throughout this frequently rousing set. Walker collaborates (and sometimes battles it out) with Bonnie Raitt, Ike Turner, Otis Rush, Buddy Guy, Matt "Guitar" Murphy, Taj Mahal, Robert Jr. Lockwood, and the Johnny Nocturne Horns on one song apiece, in addition to having three features of his own. Of the many highlights, "Low Down Dirty Blues" (which features Walker and Raitt jamming on slide guitars), the 1940s jump band feel of "Mile-Hi Club," the Walker-Guy guitar explosions on "Every Girl I See," the joyful encounter with Matt Murphy on "Nighttime," and Lockwood's appearance on "High Blood Pressure" are all quite memorable. This all-star gathering works quite well and is consistently memorable; all 11 selections are well worth hearing. *—Scott Yanow*

Preacher and the President / Aug. 25, 1998 / Verve ♦♦♦♦
San Francisco blues pilgrim Joe Louis Walker documents an eclectic career with a landmark album, assembling elements from his productive stabs at Delta and Chicago blues, slide acoustic and funk-rock, motor jazz and gospel. He even throws a taste of social commentary into the mix with the title cut of *Preacher and the President*, which is mostly a tribute to (and graduation from) his preferred (and stricter) urban-pulpit forms of late. Sure to be criticized by some as lacking in depth, Walker makes up for it in range, with viable demonstrations of influence by Buddy Guy, B.B. King, and old roommate Mike Bloomfield. Those in the need of a smidge of convincing should cut directly to the way-down "Uhhh!" and the reassuringly lustful "Yveline," since "Repay My Love" wouldn't offend a fan of easy listening, and the oddly colorless "I Ain't Messin' Around" speaks accurately of itself: it ain't. Too bad—Walker's restraint reminds many blues fans of the glossy filler of Robert Cray rather than the gritty business of Otis Rush or T-Bone Walker, all considered influences of Walker's. A sturdy example of the multiple flavors of the modern blues. *—Becky Byrkit*

Silvertone Blues / Oct. 5, 1999 / Verve ♦♦♦
Some critics tagged this the best blues release of 1999; others weren't nearly as kind. It's a beauty-is-in-the-ear-of-the-beholder situation. Blues "purists" who lament the fact that very few artists today are playing down-home, traditional blues will very much enjoy and appreciate this return to the roots. Fans of more contemporary styles might quickly grow tired of the intense, piercing vocals and upper-register slide guitar work. There are ten originals and two covers (Robert Nighthawk's "Crying Won't Help You" and Sunnyland Slim's "It's You Baby"). Most of the tunes are sparse, gritty duets with either James Cotton on harp, Alvin Youngblood Hart on guitar/vocals, or Kenny "Blues Boss" Wayne on piano. Walker sings and plays dobro on the only solo track "Talk to Me." If you long for a modern-day artist with the delivery of a Robert Johnson or a Howlin' Wolf and you like your blues pure and raw, *Silvertone Blues* is right up your alley. *—Ann Wickstrom*

In the Morning / Jul. 23, 2002 / Telarc ♦♦♦♦
Rootsier than Robert Cray, more soulful than Jimmie Vaughan, and boasting a gospel background similar to the great Sam Cooke, Joe Louis Walker is a contemporary soul/bluesman who flawlessly and effortlessly mixes his diverse influences. On his first album in three years (and Telarc label debut), Walker proves he's an artist capable of terse, searing guitar solos, as on the R&B "Do You Wanna' Be With Me?"; midtempo, jazzy soul such as "Leave that Girl Alone"; or rugged acoustic Delta blues like the appropriate album-closing "Strangers in Our House." Walker—who began his career playing religious music—not surprisingly proves himself a more than adequate soul/gospel vocalist in the Al Green vein on the spiritual "Where Jesus Leads." In fact, the Memphis groove is infused through much of this album, with Walker's simmering version of the Stones' "2120 South Michigan Avenue" sounding like a lost Booker T. & the MG's B-side. But he's at his strongest when plowing through gritty, Southern-styled swamp-rocking R&B, as on "Strange Love," the album's strongest track, where he shouts, growls, howls, and testifies like Wilson Pickett in his prime. Walker is in full control throughout, moaning and crooning in a honey-and-grits style that is immediately recognizable. Even when he plays it straight on "Joe's Jump," Walker sounds invigorated, whipping off piercing leads even in a timeworn shuffle style. The opening tracks, "You're Just About to Lose Your Crown" with its bubbling Latin percussion, and the easygoing groove of the title tune smoothly coalesce Walker's soul, blues, and gospel roots. One of the versatile musician's most consistently successful albums, this is convincing proof that Joe Louis Walker is one of the most overlooked and distinctive artists working in the soul/blues genre. *—Hal Horowitz*

Joe Walker

b. Dec. 13, 1944, Lafayette, LA
Vocals, Keyboards / Zydeco
With a signature sound bridging the gap between zydeco and Southern soul music, singer and multi-instumentalist Joe Walker was best known as an ace sideman prior to his rediscovery during the early 1990s. Born December 13, 1944, in Lafayette, LA, he played guitar in Rockin' Dopsie's band while still in his teens, later backing Rockin' Sidney on a number of singles cut for the Goldband label during the 1960s. Upon relocating to the Lake Charles area in 1967, Walker formed a band to back soul and blues artists like Tyrone Davis and Barbara Lynn as they passed through town; after a decade of regional success, however, the rise of disco brought an end to the combo's career. With a keyboard and drum machine in tow, Walker then turned to performing as a solo lounge act; during the blues revival of the mid-'80s he returned to the studio as a respected session man, leading to his discovery in 1991 by Cajun producer Lee Lavergne. His solo debut LP, *The Soulful Side of Zydeco*, appeared later that year, and was followed in quick succession by 1992's *Zydeco Fever* and 1993's *In the Dog House*. *—Jason Ankeny*

Zydeco Fever / 1992 / Zane ♦♦♦

● **In the Dog House** / 1993 / Zane ♦♦♦♦
In the Dog House illustrates that Joe Walker is a zydeco musician with true ambition and range. There are a number of rollicking zydeco cuts here, but he also injects soul into his style, plays a few striaght blues cuts and contributes a lovely, lilting waltz. It's a diverse array of sounds, but it all holds together because of his stellar musicianship. *In the Dog House* isn't your average party zydeco record, but it's worth the attention of any serious fan of the style who wants to hear a musician with a little imagination. *—Thom Owens*

Phillip Walker

b. Feb. 11, 1937, Welsh, LA
Vocals, Guitar / Louisiana Blues, Electric Texas Blues
Despite recording somewhat sparingly since debuting as a leader in 1959 on Elko Records with the storming rocker "Hello My Darling," Louisiana-born guitarist Phillip Walker enjoys a sterling reputation as a contemporary blues guitarist with a distinctive sound honed along the Gulf Coast during the 1950s.

A teenaged Walker picked up his early licks around Port Arthur, TX, from the likes of Clarence "Gatemouth" Brown, Long John Hunter, Lightnin' Hopkins, and Lonnie "Guitar Junior" Brooks. Zydeco king Clifton Chenier hired Walker in 1953 as his guitarist, a post he held for three and a half years.

In 1959, Walker moved to Los Angeles, waxing "Hello My Darling" for producer J.R. Fulbright (a song he's revived several times since, most effectively for the short-lived Playboy logo). Scattered 45s emerged during the '60s, but it wasn't until he joined forces with young producer Bruce Bromberg in 1969 that Walker began to get a studio foothold. Their impressive work together resulted in a 1973 album for Playboy (reissued by HighTone in 1989), *Bottom of the Top*, that remains Walker's finest to date.

Walker cut a fine follow-up set for Bromberg's Joliet label, *Someday You'll Have These Blues*, that showcased his tough Texas guitar style (it was later reissued by Alligator). Sets for Rounder and HighTone were high points of the 1980s for the guitarist, and 1994's *Big Blues from Texas* (reissued in 1999) continued his string of worthy material. His 1995 set for Black Top, *Working Girl Blues*, shows Walker at peak operating power, combining attractively contrasting tracks waxed in New Orleans and Los Angeles. *I Got a Sweet Tooth* followed in 1998, and displayed no letdown in quality or power. Walker got together with fellow blues legends Lonnie Brooks and Long John Hunter in 1999 to record *Lone Star Shootout* for Alligator. Walker is featured as lead vocalist on four tracks and backs the others on the rest of the record. In the fall of 2002, a live recording of a spring concert was released on M.C. Records. —Bill Dahl

● **The Bottom of the Top** / 1973 / HighTone ♦♦♦♦♦
There weren't many blues albums issued during the early '70s that hit harder than this one. First out on the short-lived Playboy logo, the set firmly established Walker as a blistering axeman sporting enduring Gulf Coast roots despite his adopted L.A. homebase. Of all the times he's cut the rocking "Hello My Darling," this is indeed the hottest, while his funky, horn-driven revival of Lester Williams' "I Can't Lose (With the Stuff I Lose)" and his own R&B-drenched "It's All in Your Mind" are irresistible. After-hours renditions of Sam Cooke's "Laughing and Clowning" and Long John Hunter's "Crazy Girl" are striking vehicles for Walker's twisting, turning guitar riffs and impassioned vocal delivery. *—Bill Dahl*

Someday You'll Have These Blues / 1977 / HighTone ♦♦♦
Recorded in 1975-1976 and initially out on the short-lived Joliet logo (later Alligator picked it up; it's now out on HighTone), this collection wasn't quite the masterpiece that its predecessor was ("Breakin' Up Somebody's Home" and "Part Time Love" were hardly inspired cover choices), but the set does have its moments—the uncompromising title track and "Beaumont Blues," to cite a couple. *—Bill Dahl*

Blues Show Live at Pit Inn / 1980 / Ypuiteru ♦♦

From L.A. to L.A. / 1982 / Rounder ♦♦♦
Walker's tunes from 1969, 1970, and 1976 sessions were produced by Bruce Bromberg and recorded with Lonesome Sundown. They're very nice. *—Niles J. Frantz*

Tough As I Want to Be / 1984 / Rounder ♦♦♦♦♦
Hotter and fiercer than other recordings, these originals and covers come from Lowell Fulson and Jimmy McCracklin. *—Niles J. Frantz*

Blues / 1988 / HighTone ♦♦♦
Contains a rich, reassuring reading of "Don't Be Afraid of the Dark," a tune generally associated with HighTone stablemate Robert Cray (Walker's version was reportedly waxed the day before Cray's), with the Memphis Horns adding extra punch. *—Bill Dahl*

Big Blues from Texas / 1994 / JSP ♦♦♦
This nice comeback set after a lengthy absence from the recording scene was cut in London under the direction of guitarist Otis Grand (who shares axe duties throughout). Why this Louisiana-born guitarist hasn't been recorded more heavily is a mystery; he seldom fails to connect, and this import is no exception to the rule. *—Bill Dahl*

Working Girl Blues / 1995 / Black Top ♦♦♦♦
Walker remains in fine form on this set, a mix of remakes of past triumphs ("Hello, My Darling," "Hey, Hey Baby's Gone") and fresh explorations. Two distinct bands were utilized—a New Orleans crew populated by bassist George Porter, Jr., and his funky cohorts, and an L.A. posse with more of a straight-up swinging feel. *—Bill Dahl*

I Got a Sweet Tooth / Jun. 23, 1998 / Black Top ♦♦♦♦
Phillip Walker takes his brand of Louisiana-via-Texas blues for a thoroughly contemporary ride on this release. With two hand-picked bands recording in New Orleans and Austin, TX, Walker's sensuous and languid vocals and his economical and taut guitar work both shine through brightly. There's only one original aboard, but Walker's interpretive skills are evident on a wide variety of material by Junior Parker and O.V. Wright. Highlights are bountiful, but his work is especially impressive on the low-down funky title track (shades of Lightnin' Hopkins, for sure) and its atmospheric kindred-spirit track, "Laughin' and Clownin'" (a slow blues that's anything *but* as jolly as the title implies). Strong, uncluttered production also plays a big role in making this disc such a delight on repeated listenings. *—Cub Koda*

Robert "Bilbo" Walker

b. Feb. 19, 1937, Clarksdale, MS
Vocals, Guitar / Modern Electric Blues
Befitting his life as an itinerant bluesman, the music of Robert "Bilbo" Walker reflected a wide range of geographical influences; Delta blues, Chicago blues, and even a hint of Bakersfield country all found their way into his eclectic sound. Born in Clarksdale, MS, on February 19, 1937, Walker took early inspiration from sources ranging from Chuck Berry to Muddy Waters to J.B. Lenoir; over the course of the decades to follow, he lived all across the continental U.S., eventually settling in Bakersfield, CA, to operate a cotton plantation. He did not pursue a full-time musical career until the mid-'90s, and cut his 1997 debut *Promised Land* at the age of 60. *—Jason Ankeny*

● **Promised Land** / 1997 / Rooster Blues ♦♦♦♦
Right from the opening call on "Goin' to the Train Station" to the last notes of "Berry Pickin'" (Roll over Chuck), you'll be kept pleasantly off balance and surprised. What disc can you think of where you are going to find Chuck Berry ("Promised Land") crossed with Merle Haggard ("The Wild Side of Life/It Wasn't God Who Made Honky Tonk Angels") backcrossed with Muddy Waters ("Still a Fool")? Stinging guitar licks in as many different styles as you can think of are always played through a blues disposition, with a verve and conviction not often heard recently. The gospel overtones on many of the cuts are strong; just listen to some of the subtle vocal inflections hiding in the background. No real weak cuts here and a good number of true gems. The downside of this disc is that it sometimes sounds like it was recorded in a tin can, with a poor mix, but even so, it's worth rooting around in the bins to find. *—Bob Gottlieb*

Rompin' & Stompin' / Apr. 14, 1998 / Fedora ♦♦♦

Rock the Night / Oct. 23, 2001 / Rooster Blues ♦♦♦♦

T-Bone Walker (Aaron Thibeaux Walker)

b. May 28, 1910, Linden, TX, **d.** Mar. 16, 1975, Los Angeles, CA
Vocals, Leader, Guitar (Electric), Songwriter, Guitar / Texas Blues, Electric Texas Blues
Modern electric blues guitar can be traced directly back to this Texas-born pioneer, who began amplifying his sumptuous lead lines for public consumption circa 1940 and thus initiated a revolution so total that its tremors are still being felt today.

Few major postwar blues guitarists come to mind that don't owe T-Bone Walker an unpayable debt of gratitude. B.B. King has long cited him as a primary influence, marveling at Walker's penchant for holding the body of his guitar outward while he played it. Clarence "Gatemouth" Brown, Pee Wee Crayton, Goree Carter, Pete Mayes, and a wealth of other prominent Texas-bred axemen came stylistically right out of Walker during the late '40s and early '50s. Walker's nephew, guitarist R.S. Rankin, went so far as to bill himself as T-Bone Walker, Jr. for a 1962 single on Dot, "Midnight Bells Are Ringing" (with his uncle's complete blessing, of course; the two had worked up a father-and-son-type act long before that).

Aaron Thibeaux Walker was a product of the primordial Dallas blues scene. His stepfather, Marco Washington, stroked the bass fiddle with the Dallas String Band, and T-Bone followed his stepdad's example by learning the rudiments of every stringed instrument he could lay his talented hands on. One notable visitor to the band's jam sessions was the legendary Blind Lemon Jefferson. During the early '20s, Walker led the sightless guitarist from bar to bar as the older man played for tips.

In 1929, Walker made his recording debut with a single 78 for Columbia, "Wichita Falls Blues"/"Trinity River Blues," billed as Oak Cliff T-Bone. Pianist Douglas Fernell was his musical partner for the disc. Walker was exposed to some pretty outstanding guitar talent during his formative years; besides Jefferson, Charlie Christian—who would totally transform the role of the guitar in jazz with his electrified riffs much as Walker would with blues—was one of his playing partners circa 1933.

T-Bone Walker split the Southwest for Los Angeles during the mid-'30s, earning his keep with saxist Big Jim Wynn's band with his feet rather than his hands as a dancer. Popular bandleader Les Hite hired Walker as his vocalist in 1939. Walker sang "T-Bone Blues" with the Hite aggregation for Varsity Records in 1940, but didn't play guitar on the outing. It was about then, though, that his fascination with electrifying his axe bore fruit; he played L.A. clubs with his daring new toy after assembling his own combo, engaging in acrobatic stage moves—splits, playing behind his back—to further enliven his show.

Capitol Records was a fledgling Hollywood concern in 1942, when Walker signed on and cut "Mean Old World" and "I Got a Break Baby" with boogie master Freddie Slack hammering the 88s. This was the first sign of the T-Bone Walker that blues guitar aficionados know and love, his fluid, elegant riffs and mellow, burnished vocals setting a standard that all future blues guitarists would measure themselves by.

Chicago's Rhumboogie Club served as Walker's home away from home during a good portion of the war years. He even cut a few sides for the joint's house label in 1945 under the direction of pianist Marl Young. But after a solitary session that same year for Old Swingmaster that soon made its way onto another newly established logo, Mercury, Walker signed with L.A.-based Black & White Records in 1946 and proceeded to amass a stunning legacy.

The immortal "Call It Stormy Monday (But Tuesday Is Just as Bad)" was the product of a 1947 Black & White date with Teddy Buckner on trumpet and invaluable pianist Lloyd Glenn in the backing quintet. Many of Walker's best sides were smoky after-hours blues, though an occasional uptempo entry—"T-Bone Jumps Again," a storming instrumental from the same date, for example—illustrated his nimble dexterity at faster speeds.

Walker recorded prolifically for Black & White until the close of 1947, waxing classics like the often-covered "T-Bone Shuffle" and "West Side Baby," though many of the sides came out on Capitol after the demise of Black & White. In 1950, Walker turned up on Imperial. His first date for the L.A. indie elicited the after-hours gem "Glamour Girl" and perhaps the penultimate jumping instrumental in his repertoire, "Strollin' With Bones" (Snake Sims' drum kit cracks like a whip behind Walker's impeccable licks).

Walker's 1950-1954 Imperial stint was studded with more classics: "The Hustle Is On," "Cold Cold Feeling," "Blue Mood," "Vida Lee" (named for his wife), "Party Girl," and, from a 1952 New Orleans jaunt, "Railroad Station Blues," which was produced by Dave Bartholomew. Atlantic was T-Bone Walker's next stop in 1955; his first date for them was an unlikely but successful collaboration with a crew of Chicago mainstays (harpist Junior Wells, guitarist Jimmy Rogers, and bassist Ransom Knowling among them). Rogers found the experience especially useful; he later adapted Walker's "Why Not" as his own Chess hit "Walking By Myself."

With a slightly more sympathetic L.A. band in staunch support, Walker cut two follow-up sessions for Atlantic in 1956-1957. The latter date produced some amazing instrumentals ("Two Bones and a Pick," "Blues Rock," "Shufflin' the Blues") that saw him duelling it out with his nephew R.S. Rankin and jazzman Barney Kessel (Walker emerged victorious in every case).

Unfortunately, the remainder of Walker's discography isn't of the same sterling quality for the most part. As it had with so many of his peers from the postwar R&B era, rock's rise had made Walker's classy style an anachronism (at least during much of the 1960s). He journeyed overseas on the first American Folk Blues Festival in 1962, starring on the Lippmann and Rau-promoted bill across Europe with Memphis Slim, Willie Dixon, and a host of other American luminaries. A 1964 45 for Modern and an obscure LP on Brunswick preceded a pair of BluesWay albums in 1967-1968 that restored this seminal pioneer to American record shelves.

European tours often beckoned. A 1968 visit to Paris resulted in one of his best latter-day albums, *I Want a Little Girl*, for Black & Blue (and later issued stateside on Delmark). With expatriate tenor saxophonist Hal "Cornbread" Singer and Chicago drummer S.P. Leary picking up Walker's jazz-tinged style brilliantly, the guitarist glided through a stellar set list.

Good Feelin', a 1970 release on Polydor, won a Grammy for the guitarist, though it doesn't rank with his best efforts. A five-song appearance on a 1973 set for Reprise, *Very Rare*, was also a disappointment. Persistent stomach woes and a 1974 stroke slowed Walker's career to a crawl, and he died in 1975.

No amount of written accolades can fully convey the monumental importance of what T-Bone Walker gave to the blues. He was the idiom's first true lead guitarist, and undeniably one of its very best. *—Bill Dahl*

☆ **T-Bone Blues** / 1959 / Atlantic ♦♦♦♦♦
The last truly indispensable disc of the great guitar hero's career, and perhaps the most innately satisfying of all—these mid-'50s recordings boast magnificent presence, with Walker's axe so crisp and clear it seems as though he's sitting right next to you as he delivers a luxurious remake of "Call It Stormy Monday." Atlantic took some chances with Bone, dispatching him to Chicago for a 1955 date with Junior Wells and Jimmy Rogers that produced "Why Not" and "Papa Ain't Salty." Even better were the 1956-1957 L.A. dates that produced the scalding instrumental "Two Bones and a Pick" (finding Walker duelling it out with nephew R.S. Rankin and jazzman Barney Kessel). *—Bill Dahl*

Sings the Blues / 1959 / Imperial ♦♦♦♦♦
These early-'50s Imperial sides find the Texas guitar pioneer in top form. *—Bill Dahl*

Singing the Blues / 1960 / Imperial ♦♦♦♦♦
More early-'50s gems. *—Bill Dahl*

I Get So Weary / 1961 / Imperial ♦♦♦♦♦
Still another LP of Walker's elegant guitar and smooth vocals. *—Bill Dahl*

Great Blues Vocals and Guitar / 1963 / Capitol ♦♦♦♦♦

I Want a Little Girl / 1967 / Delmark ♦♦♦
The first impression made here is surprisingly not from the master's guitar, but from his vocal, the song itself more of a doo wop ballad than a gutbucket blues. The only kind of T-Bone still savored by European blues fans since the mad cow disease scare barely plays guitar at all as the song begins to unfold, casually wrapping his lips around the lines like a saloon singer with a couple of shots under his belt. But when the instrumental section starts and he begins playing guitar, that's when the listener knows for sure this isn't a Johnny Hartman record. *I Want a Little Girl* was originally recorded in the late '60s for release on another label, and is in some ways like some of the sides Hartman created for Impulse with small combos backing him, sometimes even featuring guitarists, although never with the edge exhibited by Walker. That is not to say that the knives and swords brandished by the king of the Texas guitarists here are his sharpest and deadliest. The fact is, this is a relatively laid-back session to the point where the comparison to a smooth crooner such as Hartman becomes no joke, as the second side cuddles in with a version of "Gee Baby, Ain't I Good to You" that is probably more delightful than what Hartman himself might have made of the number. The band is tight yet laid-back and never pushy, with a tenor saxophonist and pianist who like to get adventurous in their solos, referencing various jazz points of departure. Tenorman Hal Singer serves something of a full-course meal on his "Feeling the Blues" break. The first musician one notices will inevitably be the drummer, S.P. Leary, whose ability to set the proper rhythmic tone as

well as control the group's dynamics is evident from the first moments of the title track. He plays superbly throughout the entire record. Bassist Jackie Samson works perfectly with both the drummer and the pianist, while the leader himself seems to assume the role of a kind benefactor. It is an image that might work at odds with the notion of a bandleader in sharp control of the happenings. T-Bone Walker is just that, however. The notion is enforced every time he lays down the law with the sudden entrance of chopped chordal patterns, or sets a new number up with a riff that will later become the essence of his guitar solo. The tone of his instrument itself has been better and fans of the guitarist may even rate parts of his work here as chopped steak in comparison with other T-Bones that have been served. —*Eugene Chadbourne*

The Legendary T-Bone Walker / 1967 / Brunswick ◆◆◆

Funky Town / 1969 / BGO ◆◆◆

Dirty Mistreater / 1973 / BluesWay ◆◆◆
A reissue of a 1973 BluesWay album, it shows T-Bone near the end. —*Hank Davis*

Classics of Modern Blues / Aug. 1975 / Blue Note ◆◆◆◆◆
A scholarly 17-track compilation, it has great photos and notes, and features selections from 1929 to 1953. For the serious collector. —*Hank Davis*

Original 1945–50 Performances / 1975 / EMI ◆◆◆◆◆
A deep look into T-Bone's roots, it features 12 classic performances, including the original "Stormy Monday Blues." —*Hank Davis*

Inventor of the Electric Guitar Blues / 1983 / Blue Boy/RBD ◆◆◆◆◆
Some formative and masterful recordings by Aaron T-Bone Walker, among the greatest pure vocalists in modern blues history. The find is a side with Walker playing 1929 country blues and sounding just as comfortable and exciting as he does on the 16 other 1940s and '50s numbers. —*Ron Wynn*

The Hustle Is On / 1990 / Sequel ◆◆◆◆◆
Nice CD compilation of Imperial material. —*Bill Dahl*

☆ **The Complete Recordings of T-Bone Walker 1940–1954** / Oct. 1990 / Mosaic ◆◆◆◆◆
A six-CD boxed set—an education in the lineage of urban blues. It appears that T-Bone Walker had a greater influence on urban blues players than any other single talent. His guitar, vocals, song selection, and sheer style live on today in nearly every blues performer. He is the master. —*Michael Erlewine*

Rare T-Bone / 1991 / Off-Beat ◆◆◆
A compilation of ten tracks, recorded late in Walker's career on albums for the BluesWay label. His vocal and instrumental power is undiminished on these solid sides, which are somewhat overlooked in comparison to his work in the '40s and '50s. Soul and funk touches update his sound without sounding contrived. As an overview of the BluesWay period, though, it's too skimpy, with sub-standard liner notes and track documentation. —*Richie Unterberger*

☆ **The Complete Imperial Recordings: 1950–1954** / 1991 / EMI America ◆◆◆◆◆
Another essential T-Bone Walker stake, this time a two-disc dish with 52 sensational tracks from his stint at Lew Chudd's Imperial Records. Whether waxing with his own jump blues unit in L.A. or Dave Bartholomew's hard-drivers in New Orleans, Walker always stayed true to his vision, and the proof was in the grooves: "Glamour Girl," "The Hustle Is On," "Tell Me What's the Reason," "High Society," "Cold, Cold Feeling," and the immaculate jumping instrumental "Strollin' With Bones" all date from this historic period of Walker's legacy. —*Bill Dahl*

☆ **Complete Capitol/Black & White Recordings** / 1995 / Capitol ◆◆◆◆◆
Three-CD, 75-track box of T-Bone Walker's recordings for the Capitol and Black & White labels in the 1940s. From a historical perspective, this is perhaps the most important phase of Walker's evolution. It was here where he perfected his electric guitar style, becoming an important influence on everyone from B.B. King down. It was also here where he acted as one of the key players in a small combo West Coast bands' transition from jazz to a more jump blues/R&B-oriented sound (though most of these sides retain a pretty strong jazz flavor). These sessions, which include the original version of his most famous tune ("Call It Stormy Monday"), have previously been chopped up into small morsels for reissue, or incorporated into the mammoth limited-edition Mosaic box set; this isolates them more conveniently. At the same time, it may be too extensive for some listeners, especially with the abundance of alternate takes (which are placed right after the official versions). Excellent liner notes, although the discographical information is surprisingly inconsistent. —*Richie Unterberger*

Cold Cold Feeling / Jun. 16, 1995 / Cema Special Markets ◆◆◆
Although there's nothing to indicate in the CD booklet—in fact there is no CD booklet, just a front cover that's blank inside—the cuts on this disc would seem to come from the early '50s and Walker's tenure with the Imperial label. Certainly three of these songs—the title track, "Strollin' With Bones" and "Party Girl"—are among his classics, with a vocal that really has the blues, and some precise electric guitar work—his trademark—that smokes without ever going over the top. However, all ten of the songs here are gems, and though Walker is the star of the proceedings, his instrumental work is very much a part of the ensemble, offering snaking lines and solos (plus some stirring rhythm work), but never hogging the spotlight at the expense of others. Like all of Walker's best work, this music feels like it should be heard at 1 a.m. in a smoky nightclub; it was simply a vibe that was part of him; even an uptempo track like "Party Girl" is nothing more than a shuffle. And when the horns come in, as they do on "I Get So Weary," it's like his wonderful "Stormy Monday Blues" all over again—and there's nothing wrong with that. At a little over 27 minutes this might not be the best value for your money around, but the music really does speak for itself. —*Chris Nickson*

Beginning 1929–1946 / Jul. 15, 1997 / EPM Musique ◆◆◆◆
One of the most important and original figures in blues, T-Bone Walker not only lit up the blues idiom with his one-of-a-kind guitar work, but he also helped set the stage for rock & roll via jump blues. Ranging from smoky ballads to swinging blues, Walker matched his scintillating picking with some slightly gruff yet smoothly urbane vocals. This fine collection brings together the country blues material he cut in 1929 as Oak Cliff T-Bone ("Trinity Rive Blues"), some early-'40s cuts on Capitol ("Mean Old World"), and his initial sides for the L.A. independent Black & White label ("Bobby Sox Blues"). The sessions often featured the great R&B pianist and bandleader Freddie Slack and a host of other top jump soloists, like tenor saxophonist Jack McVea. Despite the absence of any of Walker's stellar Imperial sides from the early '50s, this disc still works very nicely as an introduction for T-Bone Walker newcomers. —*Stephen Cook*

T-Bone Standard Time / Feb. 18, 1999 / Edsel ◆◆◆

American Blues Legend / Jul. 1, 1999 / Charly ◆◆◆
Here's a solid 20-track lineup of T-Bone's breakthrough recordings from 1942 to 1947 for the Black & White label. Here you'll hear the original versions of "Mean Old World," "Call It Stormy Monday," "T-Bone Shuffle," and "T-Bone Jumps Again." Throughout, Walker's patented guitar licks evoke all who came after him, principally B.B. King and Chuck Berry, who both adapted much of T-Bone's vocabulary to their respective styles. Not the definitive collection, but a good one to add to the collection, supported by great liner notes and good-sounding transfers. —*Cub Koda*

Back on the Scene: Texas, 1966 / Aug. 10, 1999 / Aim ◆◆◆
According to the liner notes—which offer a reasonable and lengthy biography of Walker, but only one paragraph about the music on this disc—these tracks, recorded in Texas in 1966, were released by Jet Stream as an album titled *Home Cooking*. Walker's post-'50s recordings don't get much attention, but these are pretty good tunes, with Walker in decent instrumental and vocal shape, offering some admirably slashing guitar licks. The recording fidelity isn't so hot, with a hollow, echoed quality, though actually that lends an atmospheric touch that's not displeasing. After all, at least it's not too slick. The sidemen aren't well-known (and, in fact, the drummer is listed as "unknown"), but they swing OK, even if they're on the raw side. This is a little more R&B/rock-tinged than Walker records from previous decades (occasionally an organ is heard), but he doesn't sound ill at ease with that approach. There's a good mixture of upbeat, rollicking numbers and slower, more morose ones (such as "Please Come Back to Me") less indebted to his jump blues roots. So it's not at all a bad addition to the library if you're a Walker fan, even if it's imperfect. —*Richie Unterberger*

Sings the Blues/Singing the Blues / Nov. 24, 1999 / BGO ◆◆◆◆
This contains straight-up reissues of two of T-Bone's Imperial albums, themselves merely collections of the original 78s. Everything on these 24 sides was recorded between 1950 and 1954—not as trailblazing a period as the one from 1946 to 1947 on Black & White, but still prime T-Bone by any yardstick. The majority of these sides were cut in Los Angeles, with the exception of the New Orleans-recorded "I'm Still in Love With You" and the Windy City cut of "Bye Bye Baby." Loads of great T-Bone guitar and a cool West Coast sound to most everything on here make this an important addition to anyone's blues collection. —*Cub Koda*

★ **The Very Best of T-Bone Walker** / Mar. 28, 2000 / Koch ◆◆◆◆◆
A classic collection of his best Black & White and Imperial recordings from a time frame between 1949 and 1954. T-Bone's in fine swinging and appropriately bluesy form on tracks like "T-Bone Shuffle," "T-Bone Jumps Again," "They Call It Stormy Monday," "Strollin' With Bones," and "The Hustle Is On." If you're only going to add one T-Bone Walker to your collection, this would be the one to get. File under essential blues recordings for sure. —*Cub Koda*

T-Bone Blues: The Essential Recordings / Jun. 13, 2000 / Indigo ◆◆◆◆
Another package of T-Bone's Black & White and early Capitol sides from 1942 to 1947 aboard. This features a generous 22 sides, starting with 1942's "I Got a Break" with Freddie Slack and finishing up with 1947's "Vacation Blues." In between are loads of that classic guitar and smooth vocals by one of the all-time greats of the blues, including "They Call It Stormy Monday" and "T-Bone Shuffle." Hard to say no to a package like this. —*Cub Koda*

★ **Blues Masters: The Very Best of T-Bone Walker** / Jun. 20, 2000 / Rhino ◆◆◆◆◆
A title as lofty as *The Very Best of T-Bone Walker* begs the question, "Does this CD really contain the seminal Texas bluesman's very best work?" And in fact, this 2000 release (which spans 1945-1957), *does* contain some of Walker's finest, most essential recordings of the '40s and '50s. It isn't the only collection focusing on Walker's recordings of that period—in 1995, for example, Capitol released the comprehensive three-CD set *The Complete Capitol/Black & White Recordings*. But if you need a more concise, single-disc collection of Walker's '40s and '50s classics, *Blues Masters: The Very Best of T-Bone Walker* would be an excellent choice. All of the material is superb—Walker's original 1947 version of "Call It Stormy Monday" (his most famous song) is included, and anyone with even a casual interest in the singer/guitarist's output also needs to hear gems like "The Hustle Is On" (1950), "Tell Me What's the Reason" (1953), "Bobby Sox Blues" (a number three R&B hit in 1946) and "West Side Baby" (which was recorded in 1947 and made it to number eight on R&B singles charts in 1948). This is primarily a blues collection, but it's a blues collection with a lot of jazz influence. Walker's love of jazz is evident on much of the material, whether he's providing uptempo jump blues and Texas shuffles or becoming an outright torch singer on "Evenin'" and "I'm Still in Love With You" (both from 1945). As rewarding as this CD is, it isn't the last word on Walker's recording career—for the serious blues collector, one Walker album could never be enough. But if you don't own

any Walker discs and are exploring his work for the first time, this collection is the most logical place to start. —*Alex Henderson*

1929–1946 / Oct. 2, 2001 / Classics ✦✦✦

Stormy Monday / Jul. 25, 2002 / BGO ✦✦✦✦

Sippie Wallace (Beulah Thomas)

b. Nov. 1, 1898, Houston, TX, **d.** Nov. 1, 1986, Detroit, MI

Vocals, Piano / Classic Female Blues, Piano Blues

A classic female blues singer from the '20s, Wallace kept performing and recording until her death. She was a major influence on a young Bonnie Raitt, who recorded several of Wallace's songs and performed live with her.

The daughter of a Baptist deacon, Sippie Wallace (born Beulah Thomas) was born and raised in Houston. As a child, she sang and played piano in church. Before she was in her teens, she began performing with her pianist brother Hersal Thomas. By the time she was in her mid-teens, she had left Houston to pursue a musical career, singing in a number of tent shows and earning a dedicated fan base. In 1915, she moved to New Orleans with Hersal. Two years later, she married Matt Wallace.

In 1923, Sippie, Hersal, and their older brother George moved to Chicago, where Sippie became part of the city's jazz scene. By the end of the year, she had earned a contract with OKeh Records. Her first two songs for the label, "Shorty George" and "Up the Country Blues," were hits and Sippie soon became a star. Throughout the '20s, she produced a series of singles that were nearly all hits. Wallace's OKeh recordings featured a number of celebrated jazz musicians, including Louis Armstrong, Eddie Heywood, King Oliver, and Clarence Williams; both Hersal and George Thomas performed on Sippie's records as well, in addition to supporting her at concerts. Between 1923 and 1927, she recorded over 40 songs for OKeh. Many of the songs that were Wallace originals or co-written by Sippie and her brothers.

In 1926, Hersal Thomas died of food poisoning, but Sippie Wallace continued to perform and record. Within a few years, however, she stopped performing regularly. After her contract with OKeh was finished in the late '20s, she moved to Detroit in 1929. In the early '30s, Wallace stopped recording, only performing the occasional gig. In 1936, both George Thomas and her husband Matt died. Following their deaths, Sippie joined the Leland Baptist Church in Detroit, where she was an organist and vocalist; she stayed with the church for the next 40 years.

Between 1936 and 1966, Sippie Wallace was inactive on the blues scene—she only performed a handful of concerts and cut a few records. In 1966, she was lured out of retirement by her friend Victoria Spivey, who convinced Sippie to join the thriving blues and folk festival circuit. Wallace not only joined the circuit, she began recording again. Her first new album was a collection of duets with Spivey, appropriately titled *Sippie Wallace and Victoria Spivey*, which was recorded in 1966; the album wasn't released until 1970. Also in 1966, Wallace recorded *Sippie Wallace Sings the Blues* for Storyville, which featured support from musicians like Little Brother Montgomery and Roosevelt Sykes. The album was quite popular, as were Sippie's festival performances.

In 1970, Sippie Wallace suffered a stroke, but she was able to continue recording and performing, although not as frequently as she had before. In 1982, Bonnie Raitt—who had longed claimed Sippie as a major influence—helped Wallace land a contract with Atlantic Records. Raitt produced the resulting album, *Sippie*, which was released in 1983. *Sippie* won the W.C. Handy Award for best blues album of the year and was nominated for a Grammy. The album turned out to be Sippie Wallace's last recording—she died in 1986, when she was 88 years old. —*Stephen Thomas Erlewine & Cub Koda*

★ **1923–1929** / Oct. 26, 1923-Feb. 7, 1929 / Document ✦✦✦✦✦

Document's *1923-1929* is an excellent 18-track collection of Sippie Wallace's first recordings. Many of her very best (and most notorious) songs, such as "I'm a Mighty Tight Woman," are included among these performances, most of which feature Wallace supported by a solitary piano; a few of the cuts have Wallace supported by a small jazz combo. Since Sippie Wallace's classic work has not been widely distributed, this is the best collection simply by default, but even if there were more discs available, *1923-1929* would still rank among the best compilations, since it has many of her best songs presented in the best fidelity possible. —*Thom Owens*

Complete Recorded Works, Vol. 1 (1923–1925) / 1923-1925 / Document ✦✦✦✦✦

Sippie Wallace was one of the great blues singers of the 1920s. Although she occasionally sang non-blues material on records, the blues was where her powerful voice sounded best. Document, on two CDs, has released all of her recordings prior to 1958. The first disc starts out with impressive performances on the hits "Up the Country Blues" and "Shorty George Blues," which find Sippie backed by Eddie Heywood Sr.'s fluid piano (one of his best records). Wallace is heard accompanied by Clarence Williams' more basic piano during 1924-1925 and with bands that include Louis Armstrong (very much in the background on two songs), Sidney Bechet, cornetist King Oliver (for three songs), other Williams associates of the period, plus her young brother, pianist Hersal Thomas. Among the more notable selections are "Mama's Gone, Goodbye," "Leavin' Me Daddy Is Hard to Do," "Baby, I Can't Use You No More," "Walkin' Talkin' Blues," "I'm So Glad I'm Brownskin," and "Devil Dance Blues." Although the second Document volume gets the edge (better recording quality and some exciting contributions by Louis Armstrong), the first CD is well worth getting too by vintage blues collectors. Most of these performances have been difficult to find for decades. —*Scott Yanow*

Complete Recorded Works, Vol. 2 (1925–1945) / 1925-1945 / Document ✦✦✦✦✦

The second half of blues singer Sippie Wallace's early career is fully chronicled on this Document CD, the second of two. All but the last four numbers were recorded from 1925-1927. Although the four tunes from the August 25, 1925, session have a cornball gaspipe clarinetist, this is more than compensated for by ten numbers that feature Louis Armstrong in 1926-1927. Satch does not get that much space to cut loose, but he clearly inspired Sippie, and vice versa. In addition, Wallace's younger brother, pianist Hersal Thomas, is heard on his last recordings before his early death, while cornetist Cicero Thomas fares well on two songs. Among the high points are "Murder's Gonna Be My Crime," "Suitcase Blues," "Special Delivery Blues" (which has some brief talking by Armstrong), the two earliest versions of Sippie's "I'm a Mighty Tight Woman" (including one from 1929 with clarinetist Johnny Dodds), and "The Flood Blues." Unfortunately, Sippie Wallace apparently lost the desire to record after Hersal Thomas' passing, and she only recorded four selections during the 1928-1957 period. There are two cuts here from 1929, plus a pair from 1945 that have the singer backed by a quintet that includes tenor saxophonist Artie Starks, pianist Albert Ammons and guitarist Lonnie Johnson. Highly recommended for blues collectors, as is the first volume. —*Scott Yanow*

★ **Sings the Blues** / Oct. 23, 1966 / Storyville ✦✦✦✦✦

Although Sippie Wallace had begun recording again in 1958 after a long absence (just two 1945 numbers were cut after 1929), she had only recorded a total of 11 selections (including three songs a week earlier in 1966) when she made this album, her definitive LP of her later years. Sixty-eight at the time, Sippie was still a powerful singer, as she shows here on such numbers as "Woman Be Wise," "Shorty George Blues," "I'm a Mighty Tight Woman," and "Up the Country Blues." On the latter song, Wallace accompanied herself on piano; otherwise she is backed by either Roosevelt Sykes or Little Brother Montgomery on piano. Other than a 1967 album for the forgotten Mountain Railroad label that also included Jim Kweskin's Jug Band and Otis Spann, her highly recommended Storyville outing was Sippie Wallace's only full-length set during this period. When she cut her next record in 1982, the singer was way past her prime. —*Scott Yanow*

Women Be Wise / Oct. 31, 1966 / Alligator ✦✦✦

Recorded on Halloween night, 1966, in Copenhagen, Denmark, this one of the few great "blues rediscovery" albums that comes by its reputation honestly. With Roosevelt Sykes and Little Brother Montgomery sharing the piano stool, Sippie clearly shows that the intervening years had, indeed, been kind to her, belting out one great tune after another. Listing highlights is superfluous, simply because every track's a gem. The no-frills production is warm and cozy enough to make you feel like you're hearing the world's greatest one-woman concert right in your living room. And you're glad you bought a ticket. —*Cub Koda*

Sippie / 1982 / Atlantic ✦✦✦

Sippie Wallace's first album in 15 years, and—other than two slightly later albums for the German Vagabond label with pianist Axel Zwingenberger—her final recording, finds the last surviving classic blues singer of the 1920s (along with Alberta Hunter who would pass away two years later) doing her best at the age of 83. Blues/pop star Bonnie Raitt had long loved Wallace's music and helped Sippie return to music after her 1970 stroke; she also influenced Atlantic to record the ancient blues veteran. Unfortunately, by 1982, Wallace's voice was considerably weaker than it had been in the 1920s or even in 1966 for a Storyville album. This date (which has been reissued on CD) has its historic value and charm, but is actually more highly recommended for the heated playing of Sippie's backup group, pianist Jim Dapogny's Chicago Jazz Band. The octet features superior stride piano from the leader and a strong front line consisting of cornetist Paul Klinger, trombonist Bob Smith, and Russ Whitman and Peter Ferran on reeds. Sippie Wallace revives some of her best-known 1920s numbers ("Woman Be Wise," "Up the Country Blues," "Mighty Tight Woman," and "Suitcase Blues") and performs a few vintage standards too. Still, get this CD for the musicians rather than for the spirited but fading singer. —*Scott Yanow*

Mighty Tight Woman / 1994 / Drive Archive ✦✦✦

Mighty Tight Woman from 1967 represents the unusual marriage of the classic blues era with the urban folk revival of the '60s, pitting a couple of blues legends with their improbable inheritors. The star of the album is Sippie Wallace, one of the original "red hot mamas" of the '20s and '30s vaudeville circuit, who cut her first record ("Up the Country") in 1923; rediscovered in 1965 and performing again, she is joined here by the Jim Kweskin Jug Band, with whom she also teamed up for a couple of live shows. The record attracted little attention, but it did manage to showcase the abilities and personality of the 69-year-old blueswoman, who surely enjoyed strutting her stuff with her young white hippie admirers; furthermore, four tracks boast first-rate accompaniment by Otis Spann, Muddy Waters' exemplary pianist. On these tracks, above all, Wallace seems wonderfully in her element. The Jug Band themselves have the good sense to remain on the sidelines for the most part (compared with their usual over-the-top exuberance), allowing the veteran Wallace to do her own thing, performing in classic blues style. The album's repertoire consists largely of Wallace's earlier tunes, including "Up the Country," "Special Delivery," and the title track; also included is her tribute to the modern-day Joe Lewis, Mohammed Ali. In the final cut—the jazz standard "Everybody Loves My Baby (But My Baby Don't Love Nobody But Me)"—Kweskin and company do join in full swing, offering a magnificent duet between kazoo and comb; the band also fares pretty well on "Separation Blues," in which vocalist Maria Muldaur lends a nice support to Wallace's refrain. All in all, *Mighty Tight Woman* is not a must-have on anyone's list, but it is probably much more overlooked than it deserves. The unlikely three-way collaboration shows a more serious and subtle side of Kweskin's Jug Band, and—most importantly—it provides a welcome new vehicle and audience for both Wallace and Spann, two legitimate blues masters. —*Burgin Mathews*

Mercy Dee Walton

b. Aug. 3, 1915, Waco, TX, **d.** Dec. 2, 1962, Stockton, CA

Vocals, Piano / West Coast Blues, Piano Blues

Mose Allison certainly recognized the uncommon brilliance of pianist Mercy Dee Walton. The young jazz-based Allison faithfully covered Walton's downtrodden "One Room

Country Shack" in 1957, four years after Walton had waxed the original for Los Angeles-based Specialty Records (his original was a huge R&B smash).

Walton was a Texas émigré, like so many other postwar California R&B pioneers, who had played piano around Waco from the age of 13 before hitting the coast in 1938. Once there, the pianist gigged up and down the length of the Golden State before debuting on record in 1949 with "Lonesome Cabin Blues" for the tiny Spire logo, which became a national R&B hit. Those sides were cut in Fresno, but Los Angeles hosted some of the pianist's best sessions for Imperial in 1950 and Specialty in 1952-1953.

Walton, who usually recorded under the handle of Mercy Dee, was a talented songsmith whose compositions ran the gamut from low-down blues to jumping R&B items. A half dozen tracks for the Bihari brothers' Flair imprint in 1955 included "Come Back Maybellene," a rocking sequel to Chuck Berry's then-current hit.

After a lengthy layoff, Walton returned to the studio in a big way in 1961, recording prolifically for Chris Strachwitz's Arhoolie label with his northern California compatriots: K.C. Douglas on guitar, harpist Sidney Maiden, and drummer Otis Cherry (some of this material ended up on Prestige's Bluesville subsidiary). It's very fortunate that Strachwitz took an interest in documenting Walton's versatility, for in December of 1962, the pianist died. *—Bill Dahl*

One Room Country Shack / 1952-1953 / Specialty ♦♦♦
A solid 24-track collection of Walton's Specialty sides. With the exception of his three issued singles, most everything on here is previously unreleased, filling in some major holes in the artist's discography. Both of his big hits, "Lonesome Cabin Blues" and the title track, are aboard, along with some interesting duets with female vocalists Lady Fox and the cryptically named Thelma. Walton was like a more countrified version of Percy Mayfield, with a strong sense of imagery to his writing and the ability to work in a number of styles. This collection of down-home piano blues showcases his legacy well. *—Cub Koda*

Troublesome Mind / 1961 / Arhoolie ♦♦♦♦
A fine 16-song selection from the California-based pianist's 1961 sessions for Chris Strachwitz's Arhoolie logo. A trio of sympathetic cohorts (harpist Sidney Maiden, guitarist K.C. Douglas, and drummer Otis Cherry) give the music a rough-edged barroom feel as Dee pounds out "After the Fight," "Call the Asylum," and a nice remake of his dour "One Room Country Shack." *—Bill Dahl*

Mercy Dee Walton & His Piano / 1961 / Arhoolie ♦♦♦

● **Pity and a Shame** / Aug. 1962 / Bluesville/Original Blues Classics ♦♦♦♦♦
Whether you know him as Mercy Dee Walton, Mercy Dee, or just plain Mercy, there was no doubt that he could write some incredible songs and spin some wonderful yarns. The playing wasn't bad either, and these early-'60s recordings are among his finest. *—Ron Wynn*

Danger Zone (1949–55) / Feb. 20, 1996 / RST ♦♦♦♦

Clara Ward

b. Aug. 21, 1924, Philadelphia, PA, **d.** Jan. 16, 1973, Los Angeles, CA
Vocals / Traditional Gospel, Black Gospel
Widely acclaimed among the greatest soloists in gospel history, Clara Ward was also the subject of much criticism from purists—with her backing group the Ward Singers, she pushed gospel out of the church and into the nightclubs, infusing the music with a shot of glitz and glamour the likes of which had never before been seen. Decked out in colorful gowns, towering wigs and dazzling jewelry, the Wards sang only the biggest pop-gospel hits, flamboyantly delivered for maximum commercial appeal; while many observers decried their clownish on-stage behavior as demeaning not only to the music but also to their African-American heritage, at their creative peak the group was a true phenomenon, combining superb soloists, exceptional material and innovative arrangements to leave an indelible mark on the generations of spiritual performers who followed.

Born in Philadelphia on August 21, 1924, Ward was unquestionably the driving creative force behind her group's success, but the business smarts belonged to her mother, Gertrude Mae Murphy Ward. The textbook stage mother, Gertude and her husband relocated to the Philadelphia area from a life of abject poverty in rural South Carolina; the family struggled throughout the Depression, but in 1931 she was struck by a vision which commanded her to begin a singing career. Forming a family group which included Clara and her sister Willa on piano, Gertrude quickly emerged among the most forceful promoters in all of gospel—a gifted vocalist in her own right, her truest talents were nonetheless of an entrepreneurial nature, and after a transcendent performance at the 1943 National Baptist Convention, the Ward Singers were one of the top attractions on the church circuit.

The Wards' success, however, did not come without a price—Clara, the star of the group, later admitted to constant frustrations with her life as a teen phenomenon, and although she loved gospel, it appears unlikely that she would have pursued a singing career if not for the constant pressure applied by her mother. By the late 1940s, the group had grown so successful that they added a pair of new members, Henrietta Waddy and Marion Williams, a Miami teen whose powerhouse voice became the Wards' trademark. With Williams installed as soloist, the Wards hit their creative peak, issuing such masterful hits as "Surely God Is Able" and "Packin' Up." For her part, Clara remained content to remain somewhat in the background, accompanying the group on piano while Williams stole the spotlight.

While her gorgeous alto was the centerpiece of hits like "How I Got Over," arguably Ward's greatest strength was as an arranger; "Surely," the group's biggest hit, even introduced a new waltz rhythm into the gospel lexicon. The Wards—who by now also included Frances Steadman and Kitty Parham—were also the first gospel group to employ the switch-lead style of the shouting quartets, always keeping at least four vocalists in their ranks at all times. The consenus pick as the best hymn singers in the business, the Wards also rejected the homespun choir robes of the past in favor of elaborate costumes—according to legend, on one occasion their infamous wigs grew so tall that they actually touched the ceiling. Throughout the 1950s, they were among gospel's elite, scoring more hits and making more money than any group before them.

During the early 1950s, the Wards began regularly touring with the Reverend C.L. Franklin of Detroit; the father of Aretha Franklin—herself an admitted disciple of Clara Ward—he was a gifted singer and preacher in his own right, and as his star rose the group's fame continued to grow. However, in 1958, Williams quit, and the bottom fell out—Parham and Steadman exited as well, all over their notoriously low salaries, and although new recruits including Thelma Jackson, Carrie Williams, and Jessie Tucker were quickly brought in, the Wards' popularity nosedived. By 1961, amid considerable hoopla, they moved to the club circuit, playing Las Vegas and even Disneyland all to the shock of gospel traditionalists; white audiences were intrigued, and the group continued touring throughout the 1960s, until Ward's declining health forced her into retirement. She died January 16, 1973. *—Jason Ankeny*

Surely God Is Able / 1955 / Savgos ♦♦♦

Lord Touch Me / 1956 / Savoy ♦♦♦♦♦
More passion and drive, circa 1953-1955. *—Opal Louis Nations*

That Old Landmark / 1958 / Savoy ♦♦♦♦♦
Some of the group's most memorable compositions. *—Opal Louis Nations*

Down By the Riverside (Live at the Town Hall, NY) / 1958 / Dot ♦♦♦♦♦
Gospel excitement with the group in full throttle, backed by lap steel guitar whiz Sammy Fein. *—Opal Louis Nations*

● **The Clara Ward Singers** / 1963 / Roulette ♦♦♦♦♦
The Clara Ward Singers contains 22 tracks the group recorded for Roulette Records in 1963. Although Ward had been a well-known vocalist for nearly 20 years at the time these songs were recorded, she had lost none of her power, and these are as energetic and representative as any she has ever recorded. The presence of a jumping slide guitarist is slightly surprising, but he gets into the spirit of things, helping propel these sessions to joyful new heights. Highly recommended. *—Leo Stanley*

Memorial Album / 1988 / Savoy ♦♦♦
Fine performances by the "core" group from the early 1950s. *—Opal Louis Nations*

The Best of the Ward Singers / 1990 / Savoy ♦♦♦♦

Meetin' Tonight! / 1994 / Vanguard ♦♦♦♦♦
A two-album reissue collection of some of this stellar group's most explosive moments. *—Opal Louis Nations*

The Very Greatest / 1995 / Nashboro ♦♦♦♦♦
Surprisingly fine material from this leading diva's later repertoire. Nashboro sides. *—Opal Louis Nations*

Take My Hand, Precious Lord / Jun. 4, 1996 / MCA Special Products ♦♦♦
MCA Special Products' *Take My Hand, Precious Lord* collects ten highlights from the recordings of Clara Ward, including "Swing Low, Sweet Chariot," "I Found the Keys to the Kingdom," "Only a Visit," "I'm Packin' Up," "Silver Wings," "You'll Never Walk Alone," and "When the Saints Go Marching In." It's unclear when these recordings were made, or how they were initially released, but the end result isn't designed for collectors—it's made for casual fans who will enjoy this as an affordable sampler. *—Stephen Thomas Erlewine*

Somebody Bigger Than You & I / May 11, 1999 / MCA ♦♦♦
As the woman who mentored Aretha Franklin and had, at one time or another, Della Reese, Marion Williams, and Sarah Vaughan in the ranks of her group, Clara Ward's place in gospel history is assured. To hear what makes her music so very special is right here on this ten-song budget collection that sweats her best down to her very best: "Swing Low Sweet Chariot," "When the Saints Go Marching In," "Joshua Fit the Battle," "Packing Up," "How Great Thou Art," and "Peace in the Valley." Ward has a low-down gospel moan that'll make the hairs on the back of your neck pop right out. Great stuff. *—Cub Koda*

The Gospel Soul of Clara Ward / Nashboro ♦♦♦♦♦

Robert Ward

b. Oct. 15, 1938, Luthersville, GA
Vocals, Guitar / Modern Electric Blues, Soul-Blues
Comeback tales don't come any more heartwarming (or unlikely) than Robert Ward's. Totally off the scene and thought by many aficionados to be dead, Ward's chance encounter with guitar-shop owner Dave Hussong in Dayton, OH, set off a rapid chain of events that culminated in Ward's 1990 debut album for Black Top, *Fear No Evil*, and a second chance at the brass ring.

Ward's first taste of stardom came as leader of the Ohio Untouchables (who later mutated into the Ohio Players long after Ward's departure) during the early '60s. Born into impoverished circumstances in rural Georgia, Ward had picked up his first guitar at age ten. Singles by Sister Rosetta Tharpe, B.B. King, and Muddy Waters left their mark on the youth. After a stint in the Army, Ward came home in 1959 and joined his first band, the Brassettes (who also included Roy Lee Johnson, soon to join Piano Red's band and croon "Mister Moonlight").

Tired of seeing little monetary reward for opening for the likes of James Brown and Piano Red with the Brassettes, Ward moved to Dayton, OH, in 1960. Inspired by hard-bitten FBI man Eliott Ness on TV's *The Untouchables*, Ward recruited bassist Levoy Fredrick and drummer Cornelius Johnson to form the first edition of the Ohio Untouchables. Ward's trademark vibrato-soaked guitar sound was the direct result of acquiring a Magnatone amplifier at a Dayton music store. Lonnie Mack was so entranced by the watery sound of Ward's amp that he bought a Magnatone as well; both still utilize the same trademark sound to this day.

Detroit producer Robert West signed the Untouchables to his LuPine logo in 1962. Ward's quirky touch was beautifully exhibited on the hard-bitten "I'm Tired," a chilling doo wop-tinged "Forgive Me Darling," and the exotic "Your Love Is Amazing" for Lupine.

In addition, the Untouchables backed Wilson Pickett and the Falcons on their gospel-charged 1962 smash "I Found a Love."

Ward and his band also briefly recorded for Detroit's Thelma Records, waxing the driving blues "Your Love Is Real" and a soul-sending "I'm Gonna Cry a River." Ward left the Untouchables in 1965 (to be replaced by Leroy "Sugarfoot" Bonner), stopping at Don Davis' Groove City label long enough to cut a super Detroit soul pairing, "Fear No Evil" (the original version) and "My Love Is Strictly Reserved for You," circa 1966-1967.

During the early '70s, Ward worked as a session guitarist at Motown, playing behind the Temptations and the Undisputed Truth (he was an old pal of Joe Harris, lead singer of the latter group). But when his wife died in 1977, Ward hit the skids. He moved back to Georgia, and served a year in jail at one point (ironically, one of his prison mates was singer Major Lance, whose career was at similarly low ebb).

In 1990, that auspicious encounter with Hussong started the ball rolling for Ward's return to action. Black Top boss Hammond Scott signed the guitarist and produced the amazing *Fear No Evil* and a credible 1993 follow-up, *Rhythm of the People*. The label then issued a third set, *Black Bottom*, that once again captured Ward's curiously mystical appeal. Living in tiny Dry Branch, GA, with his second wife Roberta, who contributed background vocals to his encore album, Ward resurfaced in 1997 with *Twiggs County Soul Man*, followed three years later by *New Role Soul*. *—Bill Dahl*

★ **Fear No Evil** / 1990 / Black Top ✦✦✦✦✦

One of the most amazing comeback stories of the modern blues era was ignited by this astonishing album. Robert Ward hadn't recorded as a leader in close to a quarter century, but his melismatic, almost mystical vocal quality and quirky, vibrato-enriched guitar sound utterly vital and electrifying as he revives some of his own obscure oldies ("Your Love Is Amazing," "Forgive Me Darling," "Strictly Reserved for You") and debuts a few new compositions for good measure. One of the classic blues/soul albums of the '90s. *—Bill Dahl*

Rhythm of the People / Apr. 1, 1993 / Black Top ✦✦✦

Disappointing sequel to Ward's magnificent first Black Top disc—his vocals don't sound nearly as hearty this time around, and a some of the songs just aren't up to par ("All Proud Races" is downright stupid). There's a taste of gospel in "What a Friend We Have in Jesus," Ward's own take on "I Found a Love," and a steamy remake of James Brown's "And I Do Just What I Want." *—Bill Dahl*

Hot Stuff / 1995 / Relic ✦✦✦✦✦

These are the first magnificent 1960s waxings of guitarist Robert Ward & the Ohio Untouchables for the tiny LuPine, Thelma, and Groove City logos; full of fiery soul, watery, vibrato-enhanced axe, and sinuous rhythms. Ward's piercing vocals on "I'm Tired," "Your Love Is Amazing," and "Fear No Evil" are mesmerizing. Also aboard are four classic cuts by the Wilson Pickett-led Falcons from 1962 with the Untouchables in support (the gospel-soaked "I Found a Love" was a legit smash, while Ward sears the strings on their "Let's Kiss and Make Up"). *—Bill Dahl*

Black Bottom / Oct. 17, 1995 / Black Top ✦✦✦✦

Now this is more like it. Ward is back in top form for his third Black Top outing, with better songs (most of them originals), skin-tight support from the Black Top house band, and plenty of that singularly gurgly guitar that inspired Lonnie Mack to follow Ward's lead and buy a Magnatone amp when he was starting out. *—Bill Dahl*

Twiggs County Soul Man / Feb. 4, 1997 / Black Top ✦✦✦

Ward's trembling, vibrating guitar sound is not as riveting as when he backed the Falcons on "I Found a Love" or recorded with the Ohio Untouchables in the early '60s. Like his guitar playing, his singing voice has mellowed, and there are too many unimaginative songs. A few are interesting, though. "Newborn Music" sounds like an old Major Lance recording—not surprising, given that Lance and Ward befriended each other while serving time together in a Georgia prison. The material ranges from R&B to whiskey blues ditties like "Something for Nothing." The Mideastern-sounding "White Fox" celebrates the irascible Ward's love of white women. He needs some new material, though. Many of his compositions rehash his older songs, both musically and lyrically—"I'm Tired of Wandering" was a line in "I'm Tired," an old Ohio Untouchables song. This recycling occurs on all of Ward's Black Top records, making you think you've heard it all before. *—Andrew Hamilton*

New Role Soul / May 30, 2000 / Delmark ✦✦✦✦

Less of a horn-drenched affair than his Black Top albums, *New Role Soul* presents Robert Ward in a smaller, looser setting that definitely works to his advantage. Instead of taking the usual let's-cut-come-oldies approach, the producers let Ward create on the fly, and the results easily rank up there with his 1990 comeback album *Fear No Evil*. For most of *New Role Soul* Ward is backed by just a three-piece rhythm section of bass, drums, and organ, leaving plenty of room for his testifying vocals and Magnatone-enhanced guitar. The two instrumentals here, "The Chicken Jerk" and "Chitlins Con Carne," are classy arrangements full of funky, fingerpicked guitar solos—like Albert Collins, Ward knew how to milk a guitar-organ combo to the last drop. Even more impressive is Ward's rhythm guitar playing, a virtual bottomless pit of cool grooves and subtle fills. (Power chords will never be the same after "Peace of Mind.") In the decade since *Fear No Evil*, Ward's vocals have lost some power, but that doesn't stop him from diving into tortured-soul territory, as he does on "Whatever I Receive" and "I'm So Proud to Have You for My Love." This is probably the most well-rounded album Ward has recorded. *—Ken Chang*

Baby Boy Warren (Robert Warren)

b. Aug. 13, 1919, Lake Providence, LA, **d.** Jul. 1, 1977, Detroit, MI

Vocals, Guitar / Electric Blues

The denizens of Detroit's postwar blues scene never really received their due (except for John Lee Hooker, of course). Robert "Baby Boy" Warren compiled a sterling discography from 1949 to 1954 for a variety of Motor City firms without ever managing to transcend his local status along Hastings Street.

After honing his blues guitar approach in Memphis (where he was raised), Warren came to Detroit in 1942 to work for General Motors and gig on the side. The fruits of his first recording session in 1949 with pianist Charley Mills supporting him came out on several different logos: Prize, Staff, Gotham, even King's Federal subsidiary. A second date in 1950 that found him backed by pianist Boogie Woogie Red was split between Staff and Sampson; Swing Time snagged "I Got Lucky"/"Let's Renew Our Love" and pressed it for West Coast consumption.

One of his most memorable sessions took place in 1954, when wizened harpist Sonny Boy Williamson came to Detroit and backed Warren on "Sanafee" and "Chuck-A-Luck," which found their way to Nashville's Excello label. Joe Von Battle's JVB imprint unleashed Warren's "Hello Stranger" and "Baby Boy Blues" from the same date. That same year, a single for powerful Chicago deejay Al Benson's Blue Lake Records coupled "Mattie Mae" and "Santa Fe."

The 1970s brought Baby Boy Warren a taste of European touring, though nothing substantial, before he passed away in 1977. *—Bill Dahl*

● **Baby Boy Warren** / BBW ✦✦✦✦✦

This may be a bootleg vinyl album (issued at various times with different covers ranging from a mocked-up newspaper headline to a grotesque, sloppy cartoon impressionistic rendering of the bluesman) taped off of old scratchy 78s, but it's the only place you're going to hear the recorded output of this marvelous Detroit bluesman. Recording for JVB, Excello, Drummond, Staff and Gotham, Warren's sense of song structure owes a strong debt to Robert Johnson and his lyrics are full of wry humor and mordant wit. As the leader of the first great band to emerge from the Detroit blues scene, the lineup of players on these sides include Boogie Woogie Red on piano, Calvin Frazier (another running buddy of Robert Johnson) on lead guitar, the self-describable Washboard Willie, and on four tracks, Sonny Boy Williamson, moonlighting away from the King Biscuit Boys. Highlights include "Not Welcome Anymore," "Baby Boy Blues," the stomping instrumental "Chuck-A-Luck," "Mattie Mae," "Hello Stranger" (a different version of "Mattie Mae" from a later session), and a driving take on Robert Johnson's "Stop Breaking Down." Next to the early work of John Lee Hooker and a stray anthology, this is Detroit blues at its finest. *—Cub Koda*

Washboard Sam (Robert Brown)

b. Jul. 15, 1910, Walnut Ridge, AR, **d.** Nov. 13, 1966, Chicago, IL

Washboard, Vocals / Prewar Country Blues, Acoustic Chicago Blues

A popular hokum blues artist, Washboard Sam recorded hundreds of records in the late '30s and '40s, usually with singer/guitarist Big Bill Broonzy. Out of all the washboard players of the era, Sam was the most popular, which was due not only to his to his washboard talent, but also his skills as a songwriter, as well as his strong voice. As an accompanist, Washboard Sam not only played with Broonzy, but also with bluesmen like Bukka White, Memphis Slim, Willie Lacey, and Jazz Gillum.

Washboard Sam (born Robert Brown) was the illegitimate son of Frank Broonzy, who also fathered Big Bill Broonzy. Sam was raised in Arkansas, working on a farm. He moved to Memphis in the early '20s to play the blues. While in Memphis, he met Sleepy John Estes and Hammie Nixon and the trio played street corners, collecting tips from passers-by. In 1932, Washboard Sam moved to Chicago. Initially he played for tips, but soon he began performing regularly with Big Bill Broonzy. Within a few years, Sam was supporting Broonzy on the guitarist's Bluebird recordings. Soon, he was supporting a number of different musicians on their recording sessions, including pianist Memphis Slim, bassist Ransom Knowling, and a handful of saxophone players, who all recorded for Bluebird.

In 1935, Washboard Sam began recording for both Bluebird and Vocalion Records, often supported by Big Bill Broonzy. Throughout the rest of the '30s and the '40s, Sam was one of the most popular Chicago bluesmen, selling numerous records and playing to packed audiences. After World War II, his audience began to shrink, largely because he had difficulty adapting to the new electric blues. In 1953, Washboard Sam recorded a session for Chess Records and then retired. In the early '60s, Willie Dixon and Memphis Slim tried to persuade Sam to return to the stage to capitalize on the blues revival. Initially, he refused, but in 1963 began perfoming concerts in clubs and coffeehouses in Chicago; he even played a handful of dates in Europe in early 1964.

Washboard Sam made his final recordings for the small Chicago-based label Spivey in 1964. The following year, his health quickly declined and he stopped recording and playing shows. In November of 1966, he died of heart disease. *—Stephen Thomas Erlewine & Cub Koda*

Blues Classics by Washboard Sam 1935–1941 / 1935-1941 / Blues Classics ✦✦✦✦✦

Blues Classics by Washboard Sam 1935-1941 is an excellent collection of 14 songs Sam recorded during those six years. Almost of his classic numbers—"Mama Don't Allow," "Back Door," "Low Down Woman," and "Digging My Potatoes" among them—are here in pretty good fidelity, making this a good single-disc overview for listeners who don't want to invest in Document's exhaustive multi-volume series of Washboard Sam's *Complete Recorded Works*. *—Thom Owens*

Washboard Sam (1935–1947) / Jan. 1991 / Story of the Blues ✦✦✦

Forget the washboard, which was almost more a prop than an instrument. Robert Brown was a captivating vocalist and an expert at working off his sidemen, and he coaxed creditable riffs out of that washboard, even if they all sounded the same. This is peak material, done when he was in excellent voice and hadn't yet gotten stagnant in his material or approach. *—Ron Wynn*

Rockin' My Blues Away / Feb. 1992 / RCA ✦✦✦✦✦

Washboard Sam recorded many selections as both a leader and as a sideman for Bluebird from 1936-1949. His citified country blues were a transition music between the Delta blues and early R&B while being quite likable in their own right. On this fine CD sampler, Sam's strong voice is greatly assisted by his half-brother Big Bill Broonzy's guitar. A certain sameness creeps in by the fifth song, but the party music (all from 1941-1942 except for one session from 1947) is quite accessible and enjoyable. —*Scott Yanow*

Complete Recorded Works, Vol. 1 (1935–1949) / Jun. 2, 1994 / Document ◆◆◆

Complete Recorded Works, Vol. 2 (1937–1938) / Jun. 2, 1994 / Document ◆◆◆◆
Washboard Sam's recordings are always fun to hear. The good-time music, which also includes occasional lowdown blues, is quite accessible and not all that far from swinging jazz. This CD has 23 selections from three record dates, with Sam (on vocals and washboard) joined by the primitive but effective clarinetist Arnett Nelson, pianist Black Bob, guitarist Big Bill Broonzy, and an occasional unknown bassist. Among the fun numbers are "I Drink Good Whiskey," "Want to Woogie Some More," "Somebody's Got to Go," and "My Woman's a Sender." —*Scott Yanow*

Complete Recorded Works, Vol. 3 (1938) / Jun. 2, 1994 / Document ◆◆◆◆
The recordings of Washboard Sam are consistently fun, emphasizing good-time music and swinging playing. The performances fall between blues and 1930s jazz. Even if there is a certain sameness to some of the records (Washboard Sam recorded a great deal), one never gets bored with the happy sounds. On *Vol. 3* in this seven-CD series, he is heard on three recording dates from 1938. The supporting cast often includes trumpeter Herb Morand, pianist Black Bob, and guitarist Big Bill Broonzy. George Barnes' electric guitar spots (which preceded Charlie Christian on record by a year) are a major asset on three of the songs from the first session. Fun music. —*Scott Yanow*

Complete Recorded Works, Vol. 4 (1939–1940) / Jun. 2, 1994 / Document ◆◆◆

Complete Recorded Works, Vol. 5 / Jun. 2, 1994 / Document ◆◆◆

Complete Recorded Works, Vol. 6 / Jun. 2, 1994 / Document ◆◆◆

Complete Recorded Works, Vol. 7 / Jun. 2, 1994 / Document ◆◆◆◆
Washboard Sam had a long and lengthy recording career and this volume zeroes in on the period of activity from July 1942 to October 1949. Recording in the company of Big Bill Broonzy, Roosevelt Sykes, Ransom Knowling, Willie Dixon, Bob Call, and Ernest "Big" Crawford, highlights include the unissued "Down South Woman Blues," "You Can't Make the Grade," "Soap and Water Blues," "No. 1 Drunkard," "Nothing in Rambling," and "Gamblin' Man." Sam tended to stick within a limited framework but the man had a groove, no two ways about it. —*Cub Koda*

● **Washboard Blues 1935–1941** / Feb. 18, 1997 / EPM Musique ◆◆◆◆◆
Washboard Blues 1935-1941 is an excellent overview of Washboard Sam's great tracks, containing all the highlights from his peak years. It's ideal for the curious, or listeners who don't want to dig as deep as Document's multi-volume *Complete Recorded Works* series. —*Thom Owens*

Washboard Sam: The Essential / Jun. 5, 2001 / Classic Blues ◆◆◆◆◆

Albert Washington

b. Aug. 17, 1935, Rome, GA, **d.** Oct. 23, 1998, Columbus, OH
Sax (Tenor), Clarinet / Soul, Soul-Blues
Singer and songwriter Albert Washington spent most of his career singing in the blues clubs around Cincinnati, Ohio and his home in Long Island, N.Y. Washington, who is blind, released two recordings for Iris Records in the 1990s, *Step It Up and Go* in 1993 and *A Brighter Day* in 1994.

One of four children of Jerry and Helen Washington, Albert's love of blues and gospel made itself known at a very early age. Washington remembers wanting to play his uncle's guitar at age five. At seven, he made his own guitar out of a gasoline can using rubber bands as strings. After losing his father at age nine, Washington got a job washing dishes after school to help his mother with the bills. After moving to Newport, Kentucky, with his family while in his teens, Washington was encouraged by his mother to continue his gospel singing, but not his blues singing. At 16, he joined the Gospelaires, then recording for Don Robey's Duke and Peacock labels out of Houston. A few years later, he formed his own gospel group, the Washington Singers.

In his late teens, Washington would sneak into blues clubs in nearby Cincinnati every chance he had, and there he was first exposed to the music of artists like Sam Cooke, Big Maybelle, Charles Brown, and Amos Milburn.

Washington cited B.B. King as most influential on his style of singing and guitar playing, which was heavily sprinkled with his gospel singing roots. Shortly after his mother died, he began singing blues as often as he could at the Vet's Inn in Cincinnati, where he worked with a house band for 16 years. In 1962, he recorded his first single for the Finch label in Cincinnati, and it was later released on the Bluestown label. His 1964 singles for the VLM label, including a song he wrote called "Haven't Got a Friend," got him noticed in England, and this in turn led to a deal with Fraternity Records in 1966. Lonnie Mack joined Washington on several singles for Fraternity recorded in 1969. In 1970, he recorded two singles for the Jewel label before finally recording his first LP for the Detroit-based Eastbound Records in 1972.

Because of complications from diabetes, Washington lost his sight, and his career fell into a trough from the mid-'70s to the early '90s.

But despite the crippling effects of diabetes and the tragedies that befell him over the course of his life, Washington remained an upbeat, positive figure.

In January, 1993, Long Island-based Iris Records released his first recording in two decades, *Step It Up and Go*. He began touring regionally again, and frequented clubs in Long Island. His 1994 follow-up album, *A Brighter Day*, was named one of the top three blues recordings of 1994 by France's Academie du Jazz. Washington continued to perform in blues clubs around Long Island prior to dying of complications from diabetes on October 23, 1998. —*Richard Skelly*

Step It Up and Go / 1993 / Iris ◆◆◆◆
Albert Washington's debut album *Step It Up and Go* is an impressive, soul-tinged collection of contemporary blues highlighted by Washington's powerful voice and knack for writing sturdy, memorable songs. Unlike some modern blues albums, *Step It Up and Go* has true grit to it, which brings true heart and soul to these songs and makes it a record well worth exploring. —*Thom Owens*

A Brighter Day / 1994 / Iris ◆◆◆

● **Blues & Soul Man** / Aug. 24, 1999 / Ace ◆◆◆◆◆
Washington may have been a journeyman at what he did, but he was at the very top of the journeyman class, and what he did—a hybrid of blues and soul—is not as overmined a genre as many blues styles are. That means that if you like blues-soul crossover, you will almost certainly like this compilation of late-'60s and early-'70s sides, which represent the peak of Washington as a recording artist. Most of these were done for Fraternity from 1967-1970, and show him comfortable in deep gospelly Southern soul grooves ("Doggin' Me Around"), quasi-Sam Cooke pop-soul ("A Woman Is a Funny Thing"), and party-tempo blues-soul hybrids that sometimes show a B.B. King influence. The material is more soul than blues; the blues bite is usually supplied by the sharp guitar licks (sometimes played by the great Lonnie Mack), the soul embellished by Washington's cheery, uplifting vocals. The exact tracks featuring Mack are not precisely identified, but his burning, slightly distorted tone is certainly on "Turn on the Bright Lights." Three of the 25 tracks were previously unissued, and in addition to the Fraternity material there are a couple of subsequent singles on Jewel from 1971 and 1973. —*Richie Unterberger*

Dinah Washington (Ruth Lee Jones)

b. Aug. 29, 1924, Tuscaloosa, AL, **d.** Dec. 14, 1963, Detroit, MI
Vocals / Vocal Jazz, Traditional Pop, Standards, Jump Blues, Ballads
Dinah Washington was at once one of the most beloved and controversial singers of the mid-20th century—beloved to her fans, devotees, and fellow singers; controversial to critics who still accuse her of selling out her art to commerce and bad taste. Her principal sin, apparently, was to cultivate a distinctive vocal style that was at home in all kinds of music, be it R&B, blues, jazz, middle-of-the-road pop—and she probably would have made a fine gospel or country singer had she the time. Hers was a gritty, salty, high-pitched voice, marked by absolute clarity of diction and clipped, bluesy phrasing. Dinah's personal life was turbulent, with seven marriages behind her, and her interpretations showed it, for she displayed a tough, totally unsentimental, yet still gripping hold on the universal subject of lost love. She has had a huge influence on R&B and jazz singers who have followed in her wake, notably Nancy Wilson, Esther Phillips, and Diane Schuur, and her music is abundantly available nowadays via the huge seven-volume series *The Complete Dinah Washington on Mercury*.

Born Ruth Lee Jones, she moved to Chicago at age three and was raised in a world of gospel, playing the piano and directing her church choir. At 15, after winning an amateur contest at the Regal Theatre, she began performing in nightclubs as a pianist and singer, opening at the Garrick Bar in 1942. Talent manager Joe Glaser heard her there and recommended her to Lionel Hampton, who asked her to join his band. Hampton says that it was he who gave Ruth Jones the name Dinah Washington, although other sources claim it was Glaser or the manager of the Garrick Bar. In any case, she stayed with Hampton from 1943 to 1946 and made her recording debut for Keynote at the end of 1943 in a blues session organized by Leonard Feather with a sextet drawn from the Hampton band. With Feather's "Evil Gal Blues" as her first hit, the records took off, and by the time she left Hampton to go solo, Washington was already an R&B headliner. Signing with the young Mercury label, Washington produced an enviable string of Top Ten hits on the R&B charts from 1948 to 1955, singing blues, standards, novelties, pop covers, even Hank Williams' "Cold, Cold Heart." She also recorded many straight jazz sessions with big bands and small combos, most memorably with Clifford Brown on *Dinah Jams* but also with Cannonball Adderley, Clark Terry, Ben Webster, Wynton Kelly, and the young Joe Zawinul (who was her regular accompanist for a couple of years).

In 1959, Washington made a sudden breakthrough into the mainstream pop market with "What a Diff'rence a Day Makes," a revival of a Dorsey Brothers hit set to a Latin American bolero tune. For the rest of her career, she would concentrate on singing ballads backed by lush orchestrations for Mercury and Roulette, a formula similar to that of another R&B-based singer at that time, Ray Charles, and one that drew plenty of fire from critics even though her basic vocal approach had not changed one iota. Although her later records could be as banal as any easy-listening dross of the period, there are gems to be found, like Billie Holiday's "Don't Explain," which has a beautiful, bluesy Ernie Wilkins chart conducted by Quincy Jones. Struggling with a weight problem, Washington died of an accidental overdose of diet pills mixed with alcohol at the tragically early age of 39, still in peak voice, still singing the blues in an L.A. club only two weeks before the end. —*Richard S. Ginell*

Slick Chick: R&B Years / Dec. 29, 1943-Nov. 17, 1954 / EmArcy ◆◆◆◆◆
This double LP has the cream of Dinah Washington's early recordings. She recorded extensively for Mercury and EmArcy and all of the performances are available on multi-disc sets but, for those listeners who want just a sampling of Dinah Washington at her best, this two-fer is the one to get. All 16 of her R&B hits from 1949-1954 are here plus her very first recording session (which is highlighted by the original version of "Evil Gal Blues") and seven other selections. Whether backed by the Gerald Wilson Orchestra, Tab Smith, Cootie Williams, an all-star unit headed by drummer Jimmy Cobb, or studio orchestras, she is in superb form. —*Scott Yanow*

Jazz Sides / Jun. 15, 1954-Jul. 6, 1958 / EmArcy ◆◆◆◆◆
This two-LP set has many of singer Dinah Washington's most exciting jazz performances. For the first album Washington is joined by such masterful players as trumpeter Clark

Terry, trombonist Jimmy Cleveland, and tenor man Paul Quinichette on a variety of Quincy Jones arrangements. Four other selections are from a particularly heated session with an explosive nonet propelled by Terry and tenor saxophonist Eddie "Lockjaw" Davis; "Bye Bye Blues" is really taken uptempo but somehow Washington still sounds under control. The final four numbers are from the 1958 Newport Jazz Festival (with solos from pianist Wynton Kelly and vibraphonist Terry Gibbs) and can be considered her final jazz sides before going strictly commercial. All of this valuable music has since been reissued on Mercury's *Complete* series. *—Scott Yanow*

Dinah Jams / Aug. 15, 1954 / EmArcy ♦♦♦♦♦

Recorded at the start of Dinah Washington's climb to fame, 1954's *Dinah Jams* was taped live in front of a studio audience in Los Angeles. While Washington is in top form throughout, effortlessly working her powerful, blues-based voice on both ballads and swingers, the cast of star soloists almost steals the show. In addition to drummer Max Roach, trumpeter Clifford Brown, and other members of Brown and Roach's band at the time—tenor saxophonist Harold Land, pianist Richie Powell, and bassist George Morrow—trumpeters Maynard Ferguson and Clark Terry, alto saxophonist Herb Geller, and pianist Junior Mance also contribute to the session. Along with extended jams like "Lover Come Back to Me," "You Go to My Head," and "I'll Remember April"—all including a round of solos—there are shorter ballad numbers such as "There Is No Greater Love" and "No More," the last of which features excellent muted, obbligato work by Brown. Other solo highlights include Land's fine tenor solo on "Darn That Dream" and Geller's alto statement on the disc's standout Washington vocal, "Crazy." And even though she's in the midst of these stellar soloists, Washington expertly works her supple voice throughout to remain the star attraction, even matching the insane, high-note solo blasts trumpeter Ferguson expectedly delivers. A fine disc. Newcomers, though, should start with more accessible and more vocal-centered Washington titles like *The Swingin' Miss D* or *The Fats Waller Songbook*, both of which feature top arrangements by Quincy Jones. *—Stephen Cook*

In the Land of Hi-Fi / Apr. 1956 / EmArcy ♦♦♦♦♦

As with most Dinah Washington records, *In the Land of Hi-Fi* includes an eclectic program of ballads and swingers, all of which become prime vehicles for the singer's dramatic, blues-tinged vocal stylings. Framed by Hal Mooney's mix of string-laden arrangements and big-band charts, Washington imparts both tenderness and passion to slow numbers like "I've Got a Crush on You" and "Say It Isn't So," while getting into some charged vocal buildups on swingers like "Our Love Is Here to Stay" and "If I Were a Bell." In addition to the gospel-imbued number "There'll Be a Jubilee," Latin-tinged cuts like the beautiful bolero-style "Let Me Love You" and the lounge mambo "Nothing Ever Changes My Love for You" provide nice contrast to this jazz and pop set. Topped off with fine contributions by alto saxophonist Cannonball Adderley and pianist Junior Mance, *In the Land of Hi-Fi* is yet another impressive set among the many fine EmArcy records Washington cut in the '50s. *—Stephen Cook*

Dinah! / 1956 / EmArcy ♦♦♦♦♦

One of many fine EmArcy titles Dinah Washington recorded in the '50s, *Dinah!* includes a very enjoyable mix of medium-tempo and after-hours vocal numbers. On a handful of cuts, Washington gets into the kind of smoldering and declamatory blues mode she excelled at, especially on "All of Me" and "There'll Be Some Changes Made." Showing her versatility, Washington also shines on relatively tame pop numbers, like the album's waltz-tempo version of "Look to the Rainbow" and an easy-strolling "Accent on Youth." Even here, her vocal power comes through, albeit with the blues phrasing mostly kept under wraps. On "A Cottage for Sale," Washington seems to harness all her vocal talents, creating a dazzling mix of jazz phrases, dramatic tonal shifts, and bluesy exclamations, all enveloped in a weary and melancholic tone befitting a breakup song. Besides this gem, other standout selections include "More Than You Know" and "Smoke Gets in Your Eyes." Hal Mooney provides solid, if not terribly provocative big-band and strings arrangements, with fine solos and obbligato passages coming from former Benny Goodman tenorman George Auld and West Coast jazz luminaries like trombonist Frank Rosolino and alto saxophonist Herb Geller. Washington's rhythm section at the time, pianist Wynton Kelly, bassist Keeter Betts, and drummer Jimmy Cobb, provides stellar rhythmic accompaniment throughout. A top Dinah Washington date, and a fine place to start for newcomers to the singer's catalog. *—Stephen Cook*

The Swingin' Miss D / 1956 / EmArcy ♦♦♦♦♦

Dinah Washington was accompanied by an orchestra organized and conducted by Quincy Jones on this 1957 album, and she was singing to arrangements mostly written by the young bandleader, swing charts of pop standards by the likes of Cole Porter, George Gershwin, and Duke Ellington. The result had much in common with the swing albums of Frank Sinatra in the same period, especially because Jones' arrangements were heavily influenced by Billy May and Nelson Riddle. Sinatra's records were regarded as "pop," of course, and Washington's, at least when released on the EmArcy subsidiary of Mercury Records, as "jazz," but her precise articulation and attention to lyrical meaning left little room for improvisation, and while Jones allowed for brief solos from a band that included Charlie Shavers, Clark Terry, Urbie Green, and Milt Hinton, the jazz categorization was actually arbitrary. Whatever musical genre you assign it to, however, this is an excellent Washington album. For the 1998 reissue, Verve has added seven bonus tracks recorded around the same time and with much the same personnel, though they were intended as singles and thus are inferior contemporary tunes. Often, however, Washington sounds more comfortable and enthusiastic on these pop and R&B songs than she does on the standards. *—William Ruhlmann*

The Best in Blues / 1957 / Mercury ♦♦♦

This 1997 CD is an expanded reissue of a reissue. The original 1957 record featured the great singer Dinah Washington on a variety of "greatest hits" dating back to 1943. The blues-oriented material included "Evil Gal Blues," "Trouble in Mind," "TV Is the Thing This Year," and "New Blowtop Blues" and was taken from five different sessions spanning a decade. The CD adds three songs and four alternate takes from the same dates; despite what it says on the liners, all of these tracks have been released previously. Despite a few multiple versions, this accessible music serves as a fine introduction to the spirited early style of Dinah Washington. *—Scott Yanow*

The Fats Waller Songbook / Oct. 1957 / EmArcy ♦♦♦♦♦

This is one of the finest, if not most obscure titles in the Verve/Emarcy *Songbook* series. Long out of print, 1957's *The Fats Waller Songbook* appropriately brings together Waller's vivacious songs and Dinah Washington's demonstrative vocal talents. The jazz diva effortlessly handles Waller classics like "Keeping out of Mischief Now," "Just Squeeze Me," and "Ain't Mibehavin'," while turning in particularly emotive renditions of "'Tain't Noboby's Bizness If I Do" (actually a Clarence Williams tune), and "Jitterbug Waltz" (this last cut featuring Washington's keen and signature blend of blues vocal power and streamlined diction). Adding nice variety to the already strong set, Washington's husband at the time, saxophonist Eddie Chamblee, joins the singer for playful duets on "Honeysuckle Rose" and "Everybody Loves My Baby" (ironically, the love sentiments of both songs were not to stick, as the couple called it quits after just a year of marriage). In addition to "Everybody Loves My Baby" and "'Tain't Noboby's Bizness If I Do," Washington covers other songs associated with Waller, but not penned by him, including "Christopher Columbus" and the highlight of the set, "Somebody's Rocking My Dreamboat." Topped off with solidly swinging charts by Ernie Wilkins and fine backing by an all-star band, the *The Fats Waller Songbook* registers as one of Dinah Washington's best and most enjoyable records. *—Stephen Cook*

Dinah Washington Sings Bessie Smith / Dec. 30, 1957-Jan. 20, 1958 / EmArcy ♦♦♦♦♦

Gifted with a strong, beautiful voice and very precise phrasing, Dinah Washington translated Bessie Smith's irrepressible spirit and flair even better than Billie Holiday, Smith's most famous devotee. For her tribute album, Washington avoided Smith's best-known songs ("'Tain't Nobody's Bizness If I Do," "Nobody Knows You When You're Down and Out," "Baby Won't You Please Come Home"). Instead, she wisely concentrated on the more defiant standards from "The Empress of the Blues," including "Send Me to the 'Lectric Chair," "Jailhouse Blues," and "You've Been a Good Ole Wagon." Washington sounds simply glorious, focused on alternating Smith's phrasing to emphasize her own gospel roots. The accompaniment, by Eddie Chamblee & His Orchestra, emphasizes the vaudeville and Dixieland sound of early-century blues, heavy on the slide trombone, growling trumpet, and skeletal, rickety percussion. Reissued several times (occasionally under the title *The Bessie Smith Songbook*), *Dinah Washington Sings Bessie Smith* charts a perfect balance between tribute and genuine artistic statement. A Verve master edition reissue added alternate takes of "Trombone Butter" and "Careless Love," plus three songs taken from a Newport performance later in 1958. *—John Bush*

The Bessie Smith Songbook / Dec. 30, 1957-Jan. 20, 1958 / EmArcy ♦♦♦

It was only natural that the "Queen of the Blues" should record songs associated with the "Empress of the Blues." The performances by the septet/octet do not sound like the 1920s and the purposely ricky-tick drumming is insulting, but Dinah Washington sounds quite at home on this music. "Trombone Butter" (featuring trombonist Quentin Jackson in Charlie Green's role), "You've Been a Good Ole Wagon," "After You've Gone," and "Back Water Blues" are high points as she overcomes the cornball arrangements. *—Scott Yanow*

What a Diff'rence a Day Makes! / Feb. 19, 1959-Aug. 1959 / Mercury ♦♦♦♦♦

Dinah Washington's career reached a turning point with this album. A very talented singer who could interpret jazz, blues, pop, novelties and religious songs with equal skill, Washington had an unexpected pop hit with her straightforward version of "What a Diff'rence a Day Makes." From then on she would only record with commercial studio orchestras and stick to middle-of-the-road pop music. This 1959 set is not as bad as what would follow, with such songs as "I Remember You," "I Thought About You," "Manhattan," and "A Sunday Kind of Love" all receiving tasteful melodic treatment (although no chances are taken) by Washington and an orchestra conducted and arranged by Belford Hendricks. *—Scott Yanow*

Unforgettable / Aug. 1959-Jan. 15, 1961 / Mercury ♦♦

After her hit of "What a Diff'rence a Day Makes" in 1959, Dinah Washington largely discarded her blues and jazz roots (at least on recordings) and played the role of a pop star. This CD (which has the original LP program of 12 songs joined by six others) finds Washington singing brief (mostly under three-minute) versions of standards in hopes of gaining another hit. The backing is strictly commercial and, although some may enjoy "This Bitter Earth," "The Song Is Ended," and "A Bad Case of the Blues," the music is consistently predictable and disappointingly forgettable. *—Scott Yanow*

Two of Us / 1960 / Polygram ♦♦♦

Wonderful duets between Brook Benton and Washington, plus solo cuts by both from 1960. *—Ron Wynn*

In Love / May 1962-Aug. 1962 / Roulette ♦♦

Dinah Washington's final four years of recordings (1959-1963) were purely commercial. Even her mannerisms and phrasing leaned closer to middle-of-the-road pop than to her roots in jazz and blues. For this so-so Roulette CD, Washington interprets standards and current pop tunes in very predictable fashion. Everything has the impression of being planned in advance and the accompanying orchestra (arranged by Don Costa) is quite anonymous. Pass on this and get Dinah Washington's earlier jazz sides instead. *—Scott Yanow*

Back to the Blues / Jul. 5, 1962-Nov. 29, 1962 / Roulette ♦♦♦♦♦

Prior to her 1959 hit "What a Diff'rence a Day Makes," nearly every Dinah Washington recording (no matter what the style) was of interest to jazz listeners. However, after her unexpected success on the pop charts, most of Washington's sessions for Mercury and Roulette during the last four years of her life were quite commercial, with string arrangements better suited to country singers and Dinah nearly parodying herself with exaggerated gestures. Fortunately, this 1997 CD reissue brings back an exception, a blues-oriented collection that features Washington returning to her roots, backed by a jazz-oriented big band (although with occasional strings and background voices); in addition to the original program, there are previously unreleased versions of "No One Man" and "Me and My Gin." Eddie Chamblee and Illinois Jacquet have some tenor solos, guitarist Billy Butler is heard from and the trumpet soloist is probably Joe Newman. In general, this is a more successful date than Dinah Washington's earlier investigation of Bessie Smith material, since the backup band is more sympathetic and the talented singer is heard in prime form. Dinah Washington clearly had a real feeling for this bluesy material. *—Scott Yanow*

The Best of Dinah Washington / 1962-1963 / Capitol ♦♦♦

Dinah '63 / 1963 / Roulette ♦♦
It is fairly easy to evaluate Dinah Washington's recordings. Before 1959 virtually everything she recorded (even when in a commercial setting) is worth acquiring but the opposite is true of the records from her final period (1959-1963). As a pop artist, Washington was better than many but only a shadow of what she had been. Her pre-planned emotions and exaggerated mannerisms on her Roulette recordings (of which *Dinah '63* was one of her last) get tiring very fast. *—Scott Yanow*

A Stranger on Earth / 1964 / Roulette ♦♦♦
A brilliant mid-'60s album that was exactly what Washington wanted to do: pop compositions and production, soulful delivery and performances. The title cut ranks among her most moving, and everything else reaffirmed her place among the greatest vocalists in any style. *—Ron Wynn*

Compact Jazz: Dinah Washington / 1987 / Verve ♦♦♦♦
Not quite as fine as Sarah Vaughan's *Compact Jazz* disc, this Verve roundup still nicely frames Dinah Washington's stay at the label with a fetching array of her best cuts from the '50s and early '60s. Taking in some of Washington's best-known pop songs ("What a Diff'rence a Day Makes"), the disc touches on her excellent Fats Waller ("Keepin' Out of Mischief Now") and Bessie Smith ("Backwater Blues") songbooks, while also including something from a fiery live date with Clifford Brown ("I've Got You Under My Skin"). And this is not to forget a handful of finely gauged readings of such perennials as "Smoke Gets in Your Eyes," "Easy Living," and "I Could Write a Book." Topped off with fine support by a bevy of top players, *Compact Jazz: Dinah Washington* makes for the ideal introductory disc. *—Stephen Cook*

Compact Jazz: Dinah Sings the Blues / 1987 / Verve ♦♦♦♦
Dinah Washington is one of the all-time great jazz singers, and she staked that claim with a whole lot of blues in her delivery. This roundup of blues-heavy sides from her Mercury heyday, then, is a welcome addition to an already impressive catalog. Cut during the '50s and early '60s, the 16 tracks include such usual suspects as "Trouble in Mind," "You Don't Know What Love Is," and Bessie Smith's classic "Backwater Blues." Nicely augmenting these fine renditions, Washington transforms pop numbers like "Since I Fell for You" and "Soft Winds" with some juke-joint heat. And with plenty more gems to be had and fine support from arranger Quincy Jones, tenor saxophonist Lucky Thompson, trombonist Jimmy Cleveland, drummer Max Roach, and many others, one can't lose gettin' real low-down with the swingin' (and bluesy) "Miss D." *—Stephen Cook*

★ **The Complete Dinah Washington on Mercury, Vol. 1 (1946–1949)** / 1987 / Mercury ♦♦♦♦♦
All of Dinah Washington's studio recordings from 1946-1961 have been reissued in definitive fashion by Polygram on seven three-CD sets. *Vol. 1* finds the youthful singer (who was 21 on the earliest sessions) evolving from a little-known but already talented singer to a best-selling R&B artist. Ranging from jazz and spirited blues to middle-of-the-road ballads, this set (as with the others in the *Complete* series) includes both gems and duds but fortunately the great majority fall into the former category. The backup groups include orchestras led by Gerald Wilson, Tab Smith, Cootie Williams, Chubby Jackson, and Teddy Stewart and there are a dozen strong numbers with just a rhythm section. The first five volumes in this series are highly recommended. *—Scott Yanow*

☆ **The Complete Dinah Washington on Mercury, Vol. 2 (1950–1952)** / 1987 / Mercury ♦♦♦♦♦
Dinah Washington was a best-selling artist on the R&B charts during this period but she was also a very versatile singer who could easily handle swinging jazz, schmaltzy ballads, blues, and novelties with equal skill. The second of these seven three-CD sets in Mercury's *Complete* program mostly finds Washington being accompanied by studio orchestras, although the Ravens join her on two numbers and drummer Jimmy Cobb heads a couple of jazz groups (including one with both Ben Webster and Wardell Gray on tenors). Not every selection is a classic but the quality level is quite high and the packaging is impeccable. Recommended. *—Scott Yanow*

☆ **The Complete Dinah Washington on Mercury, Vol. 3 (1952–1954)** / 1991 / Mercury ♦♦♦♦♦
Of the seven three-CD sets in Mercury's *Complete* series of Dinah Washington recordings, this is the most jazz-oriented one. The versatile singer participates in a very memorable jam session with an all-star group (featuring Clifford Brown, Maynard Ferguson, and Clark Terry on trumpets), meets up with Terry and tenor saxophonist Eddie "Lockjaw" Davis on another spontaneous date (highlighted by uptempo romps on "Bye Bye Blues" and "Blue Skies"), and has several classic collaborations with the warm Lester Young-ish tenor of Paul Quinichette. There are a few commercial sides with studio orchestras that are included (since they took place during the same period), but those are in the great minority on this essential volume. *—Scott Yanow*

☆ **The Complete Dinah Washington on Mercury, Vol. 4 (1954–1956)** / Jul. 1991 / Mercury ♦♦♦♦♦
The fourth of seven three-CD sets in Mercury's *Complete* series alternates between strong swinging jazz with the likes of trumpeter Clark Terry, tenor saxophonist Paul Quinichette, pianist Wynton Kelly, and altoist Cannonball Adderley, and middle-of-the-road pop performances with studio orchestras. The third volume is the strongest in this series but the first five sets all contain more than enough jazz to justify their purchase. *Vol. 4* really attests to Dinah Washington's versatility. *—Scott Yanow*

☆ **The Complete Dinah Washington on Mercury, Vol. 5 (1956–1958)** / Jul. 1991 / Mercury ♦♦♦♦♦
Mercury has given the great singer Dinah Washington the complete treatment with seven three-CD sets that contain all of her recordings during the 1946-1961 period, practically her entire career. *Vol. 5* is the final volume to be highly recommended, since it has her final jazz recordings. On many of these performances she is backed by orchestras led by Quincy Jones, Ernie Wilkins (including a tribute to Fats Waller), or Eddie Chamblee in arrangements that often leave room for short statements from some of the sidemen; one of the albums with Chamblee has a full set of songs associated with Bessie Smith. *Vol. 5* (which contains only a few commercial sides) concludes with her strong performance at the 1958 Newport Jazz Festival. *—Scott Yanow*

The Complete Dinah Washington on Mercury, Vol. 6 / Jul. 1991 / Mercury ♦♦
Up until 1959, Dinah Washington was able to excel in every musical setting that she found herself. A strong jazz/blues vocalist who had many R&B hits, Washington always sounded confident and soulful even when backed by insipid studio orchestras. However, after her Feb. 19, 1959 recording of "What a Diff'rence a Day Makes" became a major hit and she gained fame, Dinah Washington stuck to safely commercial pop music. Even when she was singing superior songs during the 1959-1963 period, Washington was always backed by large orchestras outfitted with extremely commercial charts better suited to country-pop stars. The sixth in Mercury's series of three-CD sets starts with the Feb. 19 session and covers 21 months in Dinah Washington's career. Most of the 73 performances are difficult to sit through. *—Scott Yanow*

The Complete Dinah Washington on Mercury, Vol. 7 (1961) / Jul. 1991 / Mercury ♦♦
The seventh and final volume in Mercury's *Complete* series of Dinah Washington's recordings has impeccable packaging and largely inferior music, at least from the jazz standpoint. After recording a surprising hit version of "What a Diff'rence a Day Makes" in 1959, the singer stuck exclusively to middle-of-the-road pop music with large string orchestras on her recordings. This three-CD set (which contains Washington's final 67 recordings for Mercury plus a recently discovered alternate take from 1947) is often difficult to sit through, for it totally lacks surprises, suspense, or spontaneity. For completists only, but get the first five volumes. *—Scott Yanow*

Wise Woman Blues / 1992 / Rosetta ♦♦♦♦
This Rosetta LP draws its material from three sources. Eight of the 15 recordings are from Dinah Washington's Apollo sessions of December 1945 (all of which are included on Delmark's CD). Six songs are taken from live performances with Lionel Hampton's orchestra during 1943-1945 and "Do Nothing Till You Hear from Me" is a real rarity with Washington backed by Duke Ellington's Orchestra in 1963. The extensive liner notes (which have ten pictures of the singer from various stages of her career) are a major plus. *—Scott Yanow*

Mellow Mama / 1992 / Delmark ♦♦♦♦♦
Dinah Washington's first solo recordings (with the exception of a session supervised by Lionel Hampton in 1943) are included on this Delmark repackaging of her Apollo sides. Recorded in Los Angeles during a three-day period, the 12 selections feature the singer with a swinging jazz combo that has tenor saxophonist Lucky Thompson, trumpeter Karl George, vibraphonist Milt Jackson, and bassist Charles Mingus among its eight members. The 21-year-old Washington was already quite distinctive at this early stage and easily handles the blues and jive material with color and humor. Recommended despite the brevity (34 minutes) of the CD. *—Scott Yanow*

The Essential Dinah Washington: The Great Songs / Dec. 11, 1992 / Verve ♦♦♦

First Issue: The Dinah Washington Story (The Original Recordings) / Jun. 22, 1993 / Polygram ♦♦♦♦♦
First Issue, which coincided with the United States Postal Service's issue of a stamp bearing the image of Dinah Washington, is a two-disc, 46-song anthology of her recordings for Keynote, Mercury, Verve, Wing, and EmArcy from 1943-1961. The set chronicles Washington's evolution from a strictly jazz and blues vocalist in the Bessie Smith tradition to an important crossover artist who could appeal equally to the pop audience. The collection is not entirely hit-oriented—although it rounds up her important R&B and pop singles, including the crossover hits "What a Diff'rence a Day Makes" and "Baby, You've Got What It Takes" (a duet with Brook Benton), there is also an early bluesy session with Lionel Hampton and a few notable album tracks that show the variety of material she handled. Some of her Top Ten R&B hits are omitted, but Washington was a prolific hit-maker beyond that which a two-disc set can contain. Washington recorded nearly 500 sides during the period covered by *First Issue*, and this generous survey is an excellent compromise for buyers wanting a thorough anthology but who are unwilling to commit to the expensive series of box sets that comprise *The Complete Dinah Washington on Mercury*. *—Greg Adams*

Verve Jazz Masters 19 / Apr. 19, 1994 / Verve ♦♦♦♦
Dinah Washington's *Verve Jazz Masters 19* may not be a definitive overview of her time at the label, but it's nevertheless a good 16-track sampler, containing excellent versions

of such songs as "What a Diff'rence a Day Makes," "Please Send Me Someone to Love," "Cold, Cold Heart," "This Can't Be Love," "A Foggy Day," "Pennies from Heaven," "Our Love Is Here to Stay," and "Unforgettable." *—Stephen Thomas Erlewine*

Blue Gardenia / Oct. 1995 / EmArcy ♦♦♦
Yet another sampling from the massive Dinah Washington Mercury catalog, this one shows off her tart, immaculately crisp voice in a pleasant, undemanding collection of love songs. You get a smattering of charted hits ("What a Diff'rence a Day Makes," "Teach Me Tonight," "Unforgettable," "Soft Winds"), some standards, lots of period strings, subdued big bands and jazz combos, and some choral backups—none of which fazes or alters the approach of this focused stylist. There is one track from the celebrated Brownie session, "There Is No Greater Love," but without any of the celebrated horns on hand. Obviously this is hardly an all-inclusive summary of Washington's diversified Mercury record shelf, yet it does make for good, relaxed listening. *—Richard S. Ginell*

Jazz Profile, Vol. 5 / Apr. 1, 1997 / Blue Note ♦♦♦
This set is a bit out of place in this collector's series, for it is really a gap-filler, mostly comprised of Dinah Washington recordings from her last two years that have not (with a few exceptions) been included in other CD reissues. Washington was at her best prior to 1959, but her later recordings are not without interest. Backed by an unidentified big band with occasional strings (why is no personnel given?), the music is superior to Dinah's later Mercury records and shows that she was still very much in her prime. Also obvious is how much of an influence she became on many black female singers who followed her. An excellent overview of her last period, recorded just prior to Washington's premature death, the 14 selections (highlighted by "The Blues Ain't Nothin'" and "I Wanna Be Around") are taken from six of her seven Roulette albums. *—Scott Yanow*

The Ultimate Dinah Washington / Nov. 4, 1997 / Verve ♦♦♦
Abbey Lincoln compiled *The Ultimate Dinah Washington*, a 16-track selection of her best-known songs that offers an excellent introduction to her Verve recordings. Although purists and collectors will have little use for this set, it suits the purposes of neophytes and curious listeners quite well. Among the highlights are "What a Diff'rence a Day Makes," "Back Water Blues," "Cry Me a River," "I Wanna Be Loved," "Cold, Cold Heart," "Harbor Lights," "You Don't Know What Love Is," "I Won't Cry Anymore," "Unforgettable" and "The Bitter Earth." *—Stephen Thomas Erlewine*

Live at Birdland 1962 / Dec. 30, 1997 / Baldwin Street Music ♦♦♦
Dinah Washington's career can easily be divided into two periods. Prior to 1959, she was one of jazz's great individualists, able to sing anything from standards to blues, R&B, pop and spirituals, and yet retain her own musical personality, always uplifting the material. After she had a surprise pop hit in 1959 with "What a Diff'rence a Day Makes," her recording career declined artistically, as she was continually backed by string sections on pop ballads in hopes of duplicating her commercial success. On some records before her accidental death in 1963, the Queen of the Blues almost sounded like a parody of herself. However, as this CD shows, Dinah Washington was much more interesting in person than on records during her last four years. She is backed on most of the selections by her regular trio of the period (pianist Joe Zawinul, a year before he joined Cannonball Adderley; bassist Jimmy Rowser, and drummer Al Jones); the last couple numbers find her joined by an organ combo. Washington shows that she was still in prime form this late in her career. Five of the 11 selections (all taken from radio broadcasts that originated from Birdland) are actually three-song medleys. Fortunately, her rhythm section was quite alert, for Dinah continually ties together ideas from different songs and switches tunes in odd places to humorous effect. She somehow combines "What a Diff'rence a Day Makes" with "I Thought About You" and "Makin' Whoopee"; another unlikely medley consists of "A Foggy Day," "Unforgettable," and "Baby Won't You Please Come Home." Since there are relatively few examples of Dinah Washington singing live this late in her career, and she still sounds so saucy here, this CD is easily recommended. *—Scott Yanow*

Verve Jazz Masters 40: Dinah Sings Standards / Apr. 25, 2000 / Verve ♦♦♦♦
Creating yet another series to justify reissuing material from its vaults, this Verve *Jazz Masters* entry raids albums Dinah Washington recorded for the Mercury label from 1952 through 1958. This is the second Dinah Washington compilation in this series. Although advertised as an album of standards, Washington avoids making these tunes come across as the romantic warhorses most of them are. Rather, her gospel-inspired voice conveys the song's message with a blues, funky tinge that always distinguished her from the rest of the crowd since she began her career at the age of 15. On these tracks, Washington is joined by the *crème de la crème* of jazz musicians who were part of the Mercury stable during these years. While some of the arrangements were not all that creative, Washington's inimitable style and the playing of her fellow musicians make up for any shortcomings. "I'll Remember April" is an 11-plus minute jam session spotlighting solos by Clifford Brown, Harold Land, Herb Geller, and Junior Mance (or Richie Powell). Washington swings hard on "They Didn't Believe Me" in front of a big band led by Quincy Jones and then goes sentimental on "You Go to My Head" before seguing into a second chorus behind a Latin beat. On the latter track Washington and the unknown group backing her is energized by the urging of a live audience. There's more Latin on "I've Got You Under My Skin," built around the trumpet trio of Clifford Brown, Clark Terry, and Maynard Ferguson. (The liner notes listing of personnel for this track are incorrect.) While the album has several excellent instrumental solos, none is better than Rick Henderson's extended alto sax work on "Blue Skies." There's a relaxed traditional jazz atmosphere underlying "All of Me," with Washington chatting away in the background during solos by vibist Terry Gibbs and trombonist Urbie Green. Whatever style or beat, each tune is delivered by Washington's instantly recognizable penetrating but tender voice, buttressed by her consistently precise enunciation. Over an hour long, this album is a worthy tribute to the one-of-a-kind vocal skills of Dinah Washington. *—Dave Nathan*

Ernestine Washington

b. Arkansas, **d.** Jul. 5, 1983, Brooklyn, NY
Vocals / Traditional Gospel, Black Gospel
Born in Arkansas, Sister Ernestine B. Washington grew up on the sanctified gospel of the '20s, singing primarily for her husband's church and denomination, Washington Temple C.O.G.I.C. Though inspired by the controlled Baptist style of the Roberta Martin Singers, she had a strident voice and was known to be a singing shouter in the mode of Mahalia Jackson. Her rare and most important recordings were executed from the late '40s through the '50s. *—Bil Carpenter*

● **In Washington Temple** / 1958 / Collector's Issue ♦♦♦♦♦
Sensational solos are supported rousingly by Brooklyn's Congregation of the Washington Temple C.O.G.I.C. Reissue of material recorded in 1958. *—Opal Louis Nations*

Complete Recorded Works (1943–48) / Sep. 10, 1996 / Document ♦♦♦♦
One of gospel's premier female soloists who recorded with both Bunk Johnson and the Dixie Hummingbirds. *—Opal Louis Nations*

Sister Ernestine Washington, Vol. 2 / Sep. 7, 2000 / Document ♦♦♦♦

Marco Washington

Bass / Acoustic Texas Blues, String Bands
Some musicians are best known as relatives of other more famous musicians, even if nobody can agree on exactly the nature of the relation. The Texas bassist Marco Washington is one such character, his main claim to fame being the fact that he was either the stepfather or the uncle of the great Texas bluesman T-Bone Walker, depending on which blues scholar has shimmied up the Washington family tree. The bassist took the young Walker under his guidance from the early '20s onward, introducing him not only to an earlier Texas legend, Blind Lemon Jefferson, but to the fascinating music of Washington's own group, the Dallas String Band. The latter group was so remarkable that Washington deserves to be better known for his involvement as a musician with this outfit, which cut nearly a dozen sides for Columbia in the late '20s. Washington's bass feel is quite catchy on these tracks, which feature the mandolin lead of Coley Jones as well as rhythm guitar partner Sam Harris.

The music of the Dallas String Band has been described alternately as pre-blues, proto-blues, primitive blues, and when all that fails, Texas country music. The group is a rare example of a black string band, although hardly only one has been sometimes reported. Washington and Harris also show up on some of the early recordings of blues harmonica master Sonny Boy Williamson. Cooperatively, all three members of the Dallas String Band came up with several tunes that have proved to be hits: the "Dallas Rag," "Hokum Blues," and "Chasin' Rainbows. Some of these titles have been reissued more than a dozen times on various compilations of historic blues or American music. *—Eugene Chadbourne*

Toni Lynn Washington

b. Dec. 6, 1936, Southern Pines, NC
Vocals / Modern Electric Blues
Boston-based blues singer Toni Lynn Washington recorded and released *Blues at Midnight* for the Tone-Cool subsidiary of Rounder Records in 1995. Washington is considered Boston's "Queen of the Blues," where she has a long and storied history on the club scene.

Raised in a procession of gospel choirs in Southern Pines, NC, Washington performed with classic R&B artists like Sam and Dave and Jackie Wilson throughout the South in her youth. Washington also made USO tours of the U.S. and Asia in the 1960s and recorded the Top 50 single "Dear Diary" for the New Orleans-based Conti label, then a subsidiary of Atlantic Records.

After two decades off the road and out of the recording studio, Washington returned to performing in 1992 with a ten-piece band. On her debut for Tone-Cool, *Blues at Midnight*, Washington comes across best as an interpreter: She tackles B.B. King's "Ask Me No Questions," Jimmy Reed's "Ain't That Loving You Baby," and a tune popularized by Jimmy Rushing and the Basie Orchestra and T-Bone Walker, "Evening."

It's My Turn Now followed in 1997, and in early 2000, Washington returned with *Good Things*. *—Richard Skelly*

Blue at Midnight / 1995 / Tone-Cool ♦♦♦

● **It's My Turn Now** / Oct. 7, 1997 / Tone-Cool ♦♦♦♦
Soul/R&B belter Toni Lynn Washington steps up to the plate and delivers an album full of great songs and solid performances on *It's My Turn Now*. With simple, straightforward production centered around her regular working band, including guitarist Tim Gearan, who writes three of the tunes on here, Washington belts her way through this 14-track collection with style and grace to spare. Highlights include "Just Around the Corner," "Paycheck in My Pocket," "You Can Stay, But the Noise Must Go," "Ain't Gonna Cry No More," and her own "I'm Leaving You." *—Cub Koda*

Good Things / Feb. 15, 2000 / Tone-Cool ♦♦♦♦
Toni Lynn Washington's third album on the Tone-Cool imprint is the epitome of cool. Toni Lynn has never been a Koko Taylor-style blues screamer, instead choosing to deliver her vocals in a smoother and jazzier style, and she has never sounded better. Producer Bobby Keyes sets Washington right into the heart of some fine musical arrangements, and the sound is blues at its best. "Good Things Come to Those Who Wait" opens the album with a soulful vocal, surrounded by layer upon layer of equally soulful horns. She delivers the lyrics with delicious cool. "You're Gonna Make Me Cry," which closes out this 12-song disc, combines elements of gospel and the blues for a soul-stirring performance that is

sure to please. The uptempo "Alright, Okay, You Win" sets the house to rocking, and Washington stays right in the groove. While she is known for her laid-back style, she proves that she can hold her own when the rhythm kicks into high gear. The Stax-style soul of "Looking at the Future" allows the singer to stretch even further, and she proves once again that she can handle any style of blues song. It is, however, on songs like the jazzy blues ballad "We Don't See Eye to Eye" that Washington's star truly shines the brightest. *—Michael B. Smith*

Tuts Washington

b. Jan. 24, 1907, New Orleans, LA, **d.** Aug. 5, 1984, New Orleans, LA

Piano / New Orleans Blues, Boogie-Woogie, Modern Electric Blues, Piano Blues

A longtime staple of the New Orleans blues and boogie-woogie community, pianist Isidore "Tuts" Washington was a primary influence on later Crescent City players spanning from Professor Longhair to Allen Toussaint to Fats Domino. Born January 24, 1907, he began teaching himself piano at the age of ten; inspired by the itinerant New Orleans musician Joseph Louis "Red" Cayou, Washington amassed a vast repertoire of songs by memorizing performances by area brass bands, then quickly returning home to develop his own renditions. Recognized as something of a prodigy, Washington—also known as "Papa Yellow"—was already the superior of most local barrelhouse pianists by his teen years, and he regularly sat in with prominent Dixieland and society bands; his style brought together an eclectic mix of ragtime, jazz and blues textures, and despite a general reliance on instrumentals, he was also known to pull the occasionally bawdy vocal number out of his bag of tricks.

Washington achieved his greatest success in the company of singer/guitarist Smiley Lewis, with whom he joined forces during the late 1940s; prior to the 1952 breakup, they cut for Imperial some of the landmark New Orleans R&B sides of the period, among them "Tee-Nah-Nah," "The Bells Are Ringing," and "Dirty People." However, for the most part, Washington considered recording of little consequence, content instead in his standing as the consensus choice as the French Quarter's champion pianist; as a result, he regularly rejected offers to cut solo sides, and in 1950 set out to conquer new territories, relocating to St. Louis to join the Tab Smith Orchestra. He was back in New Orleans by the end of the decade, signing on with the Clyde Kerr Orchestra and adding a new pop-oriented dimension to his playing for the sake of tourists. Finally, in 1983—at the age of 76—Washington consented to his first solo recordings, cutting *New Orleans Piano Professor* for Rounder; he died on August 5, 1984, during a performance at the New Orleans World's Fair. *—Jason Ankeny*

• **New Orleans Piano Professor** / Apr. 1984 / Rounder ♦♦♦♦♦

Venerable New Orleans pianist Tuts Washington didn't get many chances to record during his lifetime. This 1983 session, now available on CD, was his most extensive project, with 23 songs covering everything from spirituals to traditional jazz numbers, pop pieces, novelty tunes, blues, and country. Washington played them all in a seamless manner, displaying the mix of boogie-woogie and barrelhouse riffs, R&B, blues, and gospel elements, Afro-Latin and Caribbean rhythmic accents, and jazz phrasing and licks mastered through many decades of playing in bars and clubs. This was his chance in the spotlight, and Washington didn't waste it. *—Ron Wynn*

Walter "Wolfman" Washington

b. Dec. 21, 1943, New Orleans, LA

Vocals, Guitar / Soul-Blues, New Orleans Blues

Walter Washington became a local legend in the Black clubs of New Orleans in the '70s and '80s and worked his way up to national status with a series of well-received albums and appearances. His recording affiliations have likewise moved from local to national independent to major label. An innovative guitarist and fine singer who has also done some excellent work with vocalist Johnny Adams, Washington does not perform in the classic New Orleans R&B mold but incorporates soul, funk, jazz, and blues with fluency and power.

Washington was born and raised in New Orleans, where he performed in his mother's church choir as a child. As he grew older, he fell in love with blues and R&B and he learned how to play guitar. His first big break came in the form of a supporting role for vocalist Johnny Adams, working with the singer in the late '50s. In the early '60s, Washington became a member of Lee Dorsey's touring band; after that engagment was through, he worked with Irma Thomas.

In the mid-'60s, Washington formed his own group, the All Fools Band, and began headlining at local New Orleans clubs. By the early '70s, his popularity had grown enough to earn him a slot on a European package tour of New Orleans R&B acts. In the late '70s, he toured Europe on his own with his new band, the Roadmasters.

Washington began his recording career relatively late, cutting his first album in 1981. The record, *Rainin' in My Heart*, appeared on a small independent lable called Help Me; it was later re-released on Maison de Soul. Four years after his debut, Washington landed a contract with Rounder Records, releasing *Wolf Tracks* in 1986. The guitarist recorded two more albums for Rounder—*Out of the Dark* (1988) and *Wolf at the Door*—before moving to the major label, Point Blank/Charisma in 1991. Throughout the '90s, Washington continued to perform regularly, particularly in New Orleans clubs, and he recorded occasionally, yielding *Blue Moon Risin'* in 1999 and *On the Prowl* a year later. *—Jim O'Neal & Stephen Thomas Erlewine*

Wolf Tracks / 1986 / Rounder ♦♦♦

Guitarist/vocalist Walter "Wolfman" Washington didn't get his shot on a national label until his 1986 debut for Rounder. While the album wasn't flawless, he possessed a strong, often compelling voice and was a skilled guitarist who could play effectively in a blues, R&B or jazz mode. Washington turned in a competent cover of the Tyrone Davis hit "Can I Change My Mind," spun a good yarn on "You Got Me Worried" and sounded weary, forlorn and anguished on various cuts. Although his songs weren't exactly lyrical triumphs, they were earnestly performed, and Washington displayed more than enough talent to justify subsequent followups. *—Ron Wynn*

Out of the Dark / 1988 / Rounder ♦♦♦

Walter "Wolfman" Washington's second Rounder session mixed Crescent City R&B and jazz licks with contemporary and vintage songs and production. Washington's cover of "Ain't That Loving You," while not quite as dramatic as Bobby "Blue" Bland's, was still outstanding, while he was appropriately ironic and bemused on "You Can Stay but the Noise Must Go" and vividly soulful on "Save Your Love for Me" and "Steal Away." Only on "Feel So Bad," a questionable song at best, did he sound strained and unfocused. Washington's guitar playing was sharp, creative, and tasty without being self-indulgent. It wasn't the kind of glossy, trendy work that garners the pop spotlight, but Washington showed progress and fine skills. *—Ron Wynn*

Heatin' It Up / 1991 / Rounder ♦♦♦

Sada / 1991 / Pointblank ♦♦♦

Walter Washington's *Sada* is a blues album only in the loosest sense of the term—Washington draws from Southern soul and funk as much as Chicago blues. Even so, he and his band are accomplished professionals, capable of negotiating every twist and turn in the music. The uptempo numbers are fun, but the best part about the record are the ballads—Washington is a smooth, seductive singer and he makes all of his slow ones sound heartfelt and genuine. *—Thom Owens*

• **Wolf at the Door** / 1991 / Rounder ♦♦♦♦

Most of this CD from Walter "Wolfman" Washington puts the focus on his voice, which is reminiscent of a young Ray Charles. The horn arrangements look back toward 1960s Motown, and five of the six tracks fall squarely into the idiom of pre-disco R&B, with touches of funk and gospel. "Peepin'" is a bit of a surprise, a minor-toned instrumental with Tom Fitzpatrick's soprano in the lead and some nice George Benson-ish guitar by Washington. Even better are the last three tracks: the joyful blues "Tailspin," a minor blues ("At Night in the City"), and a bluesy ballad ("Don't Say Goodbye"). Wolfman Washington's versatility is quite impressive, making this a fairly memorable recording. *—Scott Yanow*

New Orleans Rhythm & Blues, Vol. 2 / Apr. 16, 1995 / Mardi Gras ♦♦♦

Funk Is in the House / Apr. 7, 1998 / Bullseye Blues ♦♦♦

Walter "Wolfman" Washington, who has an expressive and enthusiastic if not overly memorable voice, is virtually the entire show during this set which mixes together New Orleans funk and '60s soul with aspects of the blues. Although there are pieces by Jerry Butler, Ray Charles, and Gamble and Huff, most of the selections are Washington originals. Wolfman's backup group, the Roadmasters (a rhythm section with keyboardist Luca Fredericksen plus three guest horn players), is fine in support but fairly anonymous. So this set is primarily recommended to listeners who enjoy Washington's voice and the '60s soul style in general. *—Scott Yanow*

Blue Moon Risin' / Sep. 14, 1999 / Artelier ♦♦♦

On the Prowl / Mar. 7, 2000 / Rounder ♦♦♦♦

Ethel Waters (Ethel Howard)

b. Oct. 31, 1896, Chester, PA, **d.** Sep. 1, 1977, Chatsworth, CA

Vocals / Traditional Pop, Classic Jazz, Swing, Classic Female Blues

Ethel Waters had a long and varied career, and was one of the first true jazz singers to record. Defying racism with her talent and bravery, Waters became a stage and movie star in the 1930s and '40s without leaving the U.S. She grew up near Philadelphia and, unlike many of her contemporaries, developed a clear and easily understandable diction. Originally classified as a blues singer (and she could sing the blues almost on the level of a Bessie Smith), Waters' jazz-oriented recordings of 1921-1928 swung before that term was even coined. A star early on at theaters and nightclubs, Waters introduced such songs as "Dinah," "Am I Blue" (in a 1929 movie), and "Stormy Weather."

She made a smooth transition from jazz singer of the 1920s to a pop music star of the '30s, and she was a strong influence on many vocalists including Mildred Bailey, Lee Wiley, and Connee Boswell. Waters spent the latter half of the 1930s touring with a group headed by her husband, trumpeter Eddie Mallory, and appeared on Broadway (*Mamba's Daughter* in 1939) and in the 1943 film *Cabin in the Sky*; in the latter she introduced "Taking a Chance on Love," "Good for Nothing Joe," and the title cut. In later years Waters was seen in nonmusical dramatic roles, and after 1960 she mostly confined her performances to religious work for the evangelist Billy Graham. The European Classics label has reissued all of Ethel Waters' prime recordings and they still sound fresh and lively today. *—Scott Yanow*

1921–1923 / Mar. 21, 1921-Mar. 1923 / Classics ♦♦♦♦♦

Ethel Waters was one of the few singers from the early '20s whose early recordings are still quite listenable. This CD from the Classics label has her first 22 sides (many previously rare including five interesting instrumentals by Waters' band) and, although not on the same level as her performances from a few years later, the music is quite good for the time period. The sidemen are mostly obscure but include pianist Fletcher Henderson and cornetists Gus Aiken and Joe Smith with the highlights being "The New York Glide," "Down Home Blues," "There'll Be Some Changes Made," and "Midnight Blues." *—Scott Yanow*

Jazzin' Babies Blues, Vol. 2 (1921–1927) / Mar. 21, 1921-Oct. 14, 1927 / Biograph ♦♦♦

From the start of her career, Ethel Waters was one of the most accomplished jazz singers on record. This Biograph LP (the second of two) offers proof for it contains her very first session and, with one exception (a previously unissued version of "One Sweet Letter from You" from 1927), sticks to the 1921-1924 period. The recording quality is a bit primitive and the backup work (except for brief appearances by cornetists Joe Smith and

Tommy Ladnier) is forgettable, but Waters' smooth and appealing voice cuts through the years. *—Scott Yanow*

Oh Daddy, Vol. 1 (1921–1924) / May 1921-Apr. 1924 / Biograph ♦♦♦

Ethel Waters had a fairly long and very productive career as a singer and actress. This Biograph LP (the first of two) reissued for the first time many of her earliest recordings, 14 selections (all but one from 1921-1923). The backup work and recording quality are a bit primitive but Ethel Waters was already near the top of the field, one of the first jazz (as opposed to blues) singers to record. "Oh Daddy," "There'll Be Some Changes Made," "You Can't Do What My Last Man Did," and "Sweet Man" are highlights of this enjoyable set. *—Scott Yanow*

★ **An Introduction to Ethel Waters: Her Best Recordings 1921–1940** / Aug. 1921-Nov. 7, 1940 / Best of Jazz ♦♦♦♦♦

This comprehensive 70-and-a-half-minute, 22-track French disc presents the best recordings of Ethel Waters during her most popular and accomplished period as a recording artist, from the start of her recording career in 1921 to her Broadway triumph in the 1940 musical *Cabin in the Sky*. Drawing material from the Black Swan, Columbia, Brunswick, Decca, Bluebird, and Liberty Shop labels, the album includes Waters' major hits—"Dinah," "Am I Blue?," and "Stormy Weather"—as well as many of the songs she popularized, notably "Heat Wave." Waters transcends her usual categorization as a blues singer, assaying jazz material like "Sweet Georgia Brown" as well as classic pop by the likes of Jimmy McHugh, Irving Berlin, Harold Arlen, Cole Porter, Hoagy Carmichael, and Vernon Duke. The tracks sound like they have been mastered from records, and the earliest ones, from the acoustic era of recording, are primitive sounding. But Waters' projection and precise articulation overcome the sound limitations to confirm her influence on the singers who followed her. *—William Ruhlmann*

1923–1925 / 1923-Jul. 28, 1925 / Classics ♦♦♦♦♦

The European Classics label's Ethel Waters program completely wipes out all of the other Waters reissues for it reissues all of her recordings from her prime years in chronological order. Since the singer was very consistent, there are very few duds and many gems in these sets. This particular CD traces Ethel Waters during a two-year period; both the recording quality and her accompaniment greatly improve during this time; cornetist Joe Smith is a standout and pianist Fats Waller is present on "Pleasure Mad" and "Back-Bitin' Mamma." Highlights includes "You Can't Do What My Last Man Did," "Sweet Georgia Brown," "Go Back Where You Stayed Last Night," and "Sympathetic Dan." *—Scott Yanow*

Ethel Waters (1924–1928) / Mar. 1924-Aug. 23, 1928 / Wolf ♦♦♦♦♦

This LP from the Austrian Wolf label reissues 20 of Ethel Waters' rarer recordings from the 1924-1928 period. Although it has been succeeded by the Classics *Complete* series, this album filled a lot of gaps when it was released and was quite generous with 20 selections and nearly an hour of music. "Sympathetic Dan," "Home," "Take Your Black Bottom Outside," and "Do What You Did Last Night" are high points of the fine release. *—Scott Yanow*

Ethel Waters' Greatest Years / Apr. 29, 1925-Mar. 30, 1934 / Columbia ♦♦♦♦♦

When this two-LP set was originally released, it was the definitive Ethel Waters reissue although now it has been succeeded by Classics' more complete CD program. However this two-fer is still the best single package ever released of the singer. The first album (covering 1925-1928) focuses on her jazz years and has particularly strong contributions from cornetist Joe Smith and pianist James P. Johnson among others; "Sweet Georgia Brown," "Go Back Where You Stayed Last Night," "You Can't Do What My Last Man Did," "Sweet Man," "I've Found a New Baby," "Sugar," "Guess Who's in Town," and "My Handy Man" all qualify as classics. The second album mostly dates from 1929-1934 and finds Waters joined by studio orchestras on most tracks. The emphasis is on ballads and sweet melodies, but Waters still excels, particularly on "Waiting at the End of the Road," "Porgy," and "A Hundred Years from Today." This set is highly recommended to listeners who do not have the Classics CDs. *—Scott Yanow*

Am I Blue? / May 13, 1925+Sep. 22, 1939 / ASV/Living Era ♦♦♦

☆ **1925–1926** / Aug. 25, 1925-Jul. 29, 1926 / Classics ♦♦♦♦♦

This CD in the Classics Ethel Waters series contains plenty of gems, including "You Can't Do What My Last Man Did," the original version of "Dinah," "Shake That Thing," "I've Found a New Baby" (which has some memorable cornet playing from Joe Smith), "Sugar," and "Heebie Jeebies." On "Maybe Not at All," Waters does eerie imitations of both Bessie Smith and Clara Smith. She had few competitors as a jazz singer during this era, and the mostly intimate recordings (12 of the 23 tracks find her backed by just a pianist) feature Waters at her best. *—Scott Yanow*

Ethel Waters on Stage and Screen (1925–1940) / Oct. 20, 1925-Nov. 7, 1940 / Columbia ♦♦♦♦

The Columbia LP features Ethel Waters performing 16 songs that debuted in shows or movies. With the exception of "Dinah" (this 1925 version is the original one) and "I'm Coming Virginia," all of the music dates from the 1929-1940 era when Waters was better known as a musical comedy star than as a jazz singer. However, although the backing is generally a bit commercial, her performances of such numbers as "You're Lucky to Me," "Stormy Weather," "Taking a Chance on Love," and "Cabin in the Sky" are consistently memorable and definitive. *—Scott Yanow*

☆ **1926–1929** / Sep. 14, 1926-May 14, 1929 / Classics ♦♦♦♦♦

Few female jazz singers were on Ethel Waters' level during this period—just Bessie Smith and Annette Hanshaw, and all three were quite different from each other. Waters has rarely sounded better than on the four numbers in which she is backed rather forcefully by pianist James P. Johnson (particularly "Guess Who's in Town" and "Do What You Did Last Night"), but she is also in fine form on the other small-group sides. "I'm Coming Virginia," "Home," "Take Your Black Bottom Outside," "Someday Sweetheart," and "Am I Blue" (which she introduced) are among the many gems on this highly recommended entry in Classics' chronological series. *—Scott Yanow*

1929–1931 / Jun. 6, 1929-Jun. 16, 1931 / Classics ♦♦♦♦♦

During the period covered in this CD from Classics' *Complete* Ethel Waters series, the singer was quickly developing into a top musical comedy and Broadway star. Although her backup was not as jazz-oriented as previously (despite the presence of such players as clarinetist Benny Goodman, trombonist Tommy Dorsey, Jimmy Dorsey on clarinet and alto and trumpeter Manny Klein), Waters' renditions of many of these future standards are definitive, particularly "True Blue Lou," "Waiting at the End of the Road," "Porgy," "You're Lucky to Me," and "When Your Lover Has Gone." Superior jazz-oriented singing from one of the very best. *—Scott Yanow*

1931–1934 / Aug. 10, 1931-Sep. 5, 1934 / Classics ♦♦♦♦♦

Ethel Waters was one of the very few black performers who was able to keep working in music during the early years of the Depression; in fact her fame grew during the period covered by this excellent CD from Classics' *Complete* series. Among her backup musicians on these consistently excellent sides are violinist Joe Venuti, the Dorsey Brothers, trumpeter Bunny Berigan, trombonist Jack Teagarden, clarinetist Benny Goodman members of the Chick Webb big band and the entire Duke Ellington Orchestra (the latter on "I Can't Give You Anything but Love" and "Porgy"). High points include the Ellington tracks, "St. Louis Blues" (with the Cecil Mack Choir), the original version of "Stormy Weather," "A Hundred Years from Today," and a remake of "Dinah." Highly recommended, as are all of the Ethel Waters Classics discs. *—Scott Yanow*

1931–1940 / Aug. 10, 1931-Nov. 7, 1940 / Giants of Jazz ♦♦♦

1935–1940 / Oct. 16, 1935-Nov. 7, 1940 / Classics ♦♦♦♦

Classics does its usual stellar job in chronicling a five-year tenure of Ethel Waters, covering sides she made for Bluebird, Decca, and New York's Liberty Music Shop. It's an interesting mix of blues, pop, and jazz, with her inimitable style guiding it all. A few big jazz names like Tyree Glenn, Danny Barker, and Milt Hinton pop up in the various backing units, but ultimately, it's all Waters' show. *—Cub Koda*

Foremothers, Vol. 6 / Nov. 9, 1938-Aug. 15, 1939 / Rosetta ♦♦♦♦

This very attractive Rosetta LP (which has definitive liner notes and numerous pictures) includes all of singer Ethel Waters' 16 Bluebird recordings of 1938-1939. She is accompanied by two different bands led by her husband (trumpeter Eddie Mallory), with Benny Carter on alto and clarinet and trombonist Tyree Glenn (doubling on vibes) among the sidemen. Waters was not a major part of the swing era but her own career (on stage and in films) was booming around this period. Her voice is heard in its prime on a variety of period pieces which are highlighted by "Old Man Harlem," "Georgia on My Mind," "Jeepers Creepers," and "They Say." *—Scott Yanow*

Performing in Person Highlights from Her Illustrious Career / 1957 / Monmouth Evergreen ♦♦♦

Ethel Waters is heard at the twilight of her career during this live performance. Recorded a decade after her last studio recordings, this was the singer's final nonreligious album. Accompanied by pianist Reginald Beane, Waters revisits most of her hits ("Am I Blue," "Dinah" "Porgy," "Supper Time," "Stormy Weather," and a medley from "Cabin in the Sky") and shows that, even at this late stage, her voice was still quite expressive. This is an LP that her many fans will want to search for. *—Scott Yanow*

Muddy Waters (McKinley Morganfield)

b. Apr. 4, 1915, Rolling Fork, MS, **d.** Apr. 30, 1983, Westmont, IL

Slide Guitar, Vocals, Leader, Arranger, Guitar / Slide Guitar Blues, Blues Revival, Delta Blues, Electric Chicago Blues, Chicago Blues, Electric Blues

A postwar Chicago blues scene without the magnificent contributions of Muddy Waters is absolutely unimaginable. From the late '40s on, he eloquently defined the city's aggressive, swaggering, Delta-rooted sound with his declamatory vocals and piercing slide guitar attack. When he passed away in 1983, the Windy City would never quite recover. Like many of his contemporaries on the Chicago circuit, Waters was a product of the fertile Mississippi Delta. Born McKinley Morganfield in Rolling Fork, he grew up in nearby Clarksdale on Stovall's Plantation. His idol was the powerful Son House, a Delta patriarch whose flailing slide work and intimidating intensity Waters would emulate in his own fashion.

Musicologist Alan Lomax traveled through Stovall's in August of 1941 under the auspices of the Library of Congress, in search of new talent for purposes of field recording. With the discovery of Morganfield, Lomax must have immediately known he'd stumbled across someone very special.

Setting up his portable recording rig in the Delta bluesman's house, Lomax captured for Library of Congress posterity Waters' mesmerizing rendition of "I Be's Troubled," which became his first big seller when he recut it a few years later for the Chess brothers' Aristocrat logo as "I Can't Be Satisfied." Lomax returned the next summer to record his bottleneck-wielding find more extensively, also cutting sides by the Son Simms Four (a string band that Waters belonged to).

Waters was renowned for his blues-playing prowess across the Delta, but that was about it until 1943, when he left for the bright lights of Chicago. A tiff with "the bossman" apparently also had a little something to do with his relocation plans. By the mid-'40s, Waters' slide skills were becoming a recognized entity on Chicago's South Side, where he shared a stage or two with pianists Sunnyland Slim and Eddie Boyd and guitarist Blue Smitty. Producer Lester Melrose, who still had the local recording scene pretty much sewn up in 1946, accompanied Waters into the studio to wax a date for Columbia, but the urban nature of the sides didn't electrify anyone in the label's hierarchy and remained unissued for decades.

Sunnyland Slim played a large role in launching the career of Muddy Waters. The pianist invited him to provide accompaniment for his 1947 Aristocrat session that would produce "Johnson Machine Gun." One obstacle remained beforehand: Waters had a day gig delivering venetian blinds. But he wasn't about to let such a golden opportunity slip through his talented fingers. He informed his boss that a fictitious cousin had been murdered in an alley, so he needed a little time off to take care of business.

When Sunnyland was finished that auspicious day, Waters sang a pair of numbers, "Little Anna Mae" and "Gypsy Woman," that would become his own Aristocrat debut 78. They were rawer than the Columbia stuff, but not as inexorably down-home as "I Can't Be Satisfied" and its flip, "I Feel Like Going Home" (the latter was his first national R&B hit in 1948). With Big Crawford slapping the bass behind Waters' gruff growl and slashing slide, "I Can't Be Satisfied" was such a local sensation that even Muddy Waters himself had a hard time buying a copy down on Maxwell Street.

He assembled a band that was so tight and vicious on stage that they were informally known as the Headhunters; they'd come into a bar where a band was playing, ask to sit in, and then "cut the heads" off their competitors with their superior musicianship. Little Walter, of course, would single-handedly revolutionize the role of the harmonica within the Chicago blues hierarchy; Jimmy Rogers was an utterly dependable second guitarist, and Baby Face Leroy Foster could play both drums and guitar. On top of their instrumental skills, all four men could sing powerfully.

In 1951 Waters climbed the R&B charts no less than four times, beginning with "Louisiana Blues" and continuing through "Long Distance Call," "Honey Bee," and "Still a Fool." Although it didn't chart, his 1950 classic "Rollin' Stone" provided a certain young British combo with a rather enduring name. Leonard Chess himself provided the incredibly unsubtle bass-drum bombs on Waters' 1952 smash, "She Moves Me."

"Mad Love," his only chart bow in 1953, is noteworthy as the first hit to feature the rolling piano of Otis Spann, who would anchor the Waters aggregation for the next 16 years. By this time, Foster was long gone from the band, but Rogers remained, and Chess insisted that Walter—by then a popular act in his own right—make nearly every Waters session into 1958 (why break up a winning combination?). There was one downside to having such a peerless band; as the ensemble work got tighter and more urbanized, Waters' trademark slide guitar was largely absent on many of his Chess waxings.

Willie Dixon was playing an increasingly important role in Muddy Waters' success. In addition to slapping his upright bass on Waters' platters, the burly Dixon was writing one future bedrock standard after another for him: "I'm Your Hoochie Coochie Man," "Just Make Love to Me," and "I'm Ready," seminal performances all, and each blasted to the uppermost reaches of the R&B lists in 1954.

When labelmate Bo Diddley borrowed Waters' swaggering beat for his strutting "I'm a Man" in 1955, Muddy turned around and did him tit for tat by reworking the tune ever so slightly as "Mannish Boy" and enjoying his own hit. "Sugar Sweet," a piledriving rocker with Spann's 88s anchoring the proceedings, also did well that year. Three more R&B smashes came in 1956: "Trouble No More," "Forty Days and Forty Nights," and "Don't Go No Farther."

But rock & roll was quickly blunting the momentum of veteran blues aces like Waters; Chess was growing more attuned to the modern sounds of Chuck Berry, Bo Diddley, the Moonglows, and the Flamingos. Ironically, it was Muddy Waters that had sent Berry to Chess in the first place.

After that, there was only one more chart item, 1958's typically uncompromising (and metaphorically loaded) "Close to You." But Waters' Chess output was still of uniformly stellar quality, boasting gems like "Walking Thru the Park" (as close as he was likely to come to mining a rock & roll groove) and "She's Nineteen Years Old," among the first sides to feature James Cotton's harp instead of Little Walter's, in 1958. That was also the year that Muddy Waters and Spann made their first sojourn to England, where his electrified guitar horrified sedate Britishers accustomed to the folksy homilies of Big Bill Broonzy. Perhaps chagrined by the response, Waters paid tribute to Broonzy with a solid LP of his material in 1959.

Cotton was apparently the bandmember who first turned Muddy on to "Got My Mojo Working," originally cut by Ann Cole in New York. Waters' 1956 cover was pleasing enough but went nowhere on the charts. But when the band launched into a supercharged version of the same tune at the 1960 Newport Jazz Festival, Cotton and Spann put an entirely new groove to it, making it an instant classic (fortuitously, Chess was on hand to capture the festivities on tape).

As the 1960s dawned, Muddy Waters' Chess sides were sounding a trifle tired. Oh, the novelty thumper "Tiger in Your Tank" packed a reasonably high-octane wallop, but his adaptation of Junior Wells' "Messin' With the Kid" (as "Messin' With the Man") and a less-than-timely "Muddy Waters Twist" were a long way removed indeed from the mesmerizing Delta sizzle that Waters had purveyed a decade earlier.

Overdubbing his vocal over an instrumental track by guitarist Earl Hooker, Waters laid down an uncompromising "You Shook Me" in 1962 that was a step in the right direction. Drummer Casey Jones supplied some intriguing percussive effects on another 1962 workout, "You Need Love," which Led Zeppelin liked so much that they purloined it as their own creation later on.

In the wake of the folk-blues boom, Waters reverted to an acoustic format for a fine 1964 LP, *Folk Singer*, that found him receiving superb backing from guitarist Buddy Guy, Dixon on bass, and drummer Clifton James. In October, he ventured overseas again as part of the Lippmann and Rau-promoted American Folk Blues Festival, sharing the bill with Sonny Boy Williamson, Memphis Slim, Big Joe Williams, and Lonnie Johnson. The personnel of the Waters band was much more fluid during the 1960s, but he always whipped them into first-rate shape. Guitarists Pee Wee Madison, Luther "Snake Boy" Johnson, and Sammy Lawhorn, harpists George "Mojo" Buford and George Smith, bassists Jimmy Lee Morris and Calvin "Fuzz" Jones, and drummers Francis Clay and Willie "Big Eyes" Smith (along with Spann, of course) all passed through the ranks.

In 1964, Waters cut a two-sided gem for Chess, "The Same Thing"/"You Can't Lose What You Never Had," that boasted a distinct 1950s feel in its sparse, reflexive approach. Most of his subsequent Chess catalog, though, is fairly forgettable. Worst of all were two horrific attempts to make him a psychedelic icon. Released in 1968, *Electric Mud* forced Waters to ape his pupils via an unintentionally hilarious cover of the Stones' "Let's Spend the Night Together" (session guitarist Phil Upchurch still cringes at the mere mention of this album). *After the Rain* was no improvement the following year.

Partially salvaging this barren period in his discography was the *Fathers and Sons* project, also done in 1969 for Chess, which paired Muddy Waters and Spann with local youngbloods Paul Butterfield and Mike Bloomfield in a multi-generational celebration of legitimate Chicago blues.

After a period of steady touring worldwide but little standout recording activity, Waters' studio fortunes were resuscitated by another of his legion of disciples, guitarist Johnny Winter. Signed to Blue Sky, a Columbia subsidiary, Waters found himself during the making of the first LP, *Hard Again*—backed by pianist Pinetop Perkins, drummer Willie "Big Eyes" Smith, and guitarist Bob Margolin from his touring band, Cotton on harp, and Winter's slam-bang guitar, Waters roared like a lion who had just awoken from a long nap.

Three subsequent Blue Sky albums continued the heartwarming back-to-the basics campaign. In 1980, his entire combo split to form the Legendary Blues Band; needless to note, he didn't have much trouble assembling another one (new members included pianist Lovie Lee, guitarist John Primer, and harpist George "Mojo" Buford).

By the time of his death in 1983, Muddy Waters' exalted place in the history of blues (and 20th century popular music, for that matter) was eternally assured. The Chicago blues genre that he turned upside down during the years following World War II would never recover—and that's a debt we'll never be able to repay. *—Bill Dahl*

Muddy Waters Sings Big Bill Broonzy / 1960 / MCA/Chess ✦✦✦✦✦

Waters' tribute album to the man who gave him his start on the Chicago circuit, this stuff doesn't sound much like Broonzy so much as a virtual recasting of his songs into Muddy's electric Chicago style. Evidently The first time Waters and his band were recorded in stereo, the highlights include high-voltage takes on "When I Get to Drinkin'" and "The Mopper's Blues," with some really great harp from James Cotton as an added bonus. *—Cub Koda*

★ **At Newport** / 1960 / MCA/Chess ✦✦✦✦✦

For many back in the early '60s, this was their first exposure to live recorded blues, and it's still pretty damn impressive some 40-plus years down the line. Muddy, with a band featuring Otis Spann, James Cotton, and guitarist Pat Hare, lays it down tough and cool with a set that literally had 'em dancing in the aisles by the set closer, a rippling version of "Got My Mojo Working," reprised again in a short encore version. Kicking off the album with a version of "I've Got My Brand on You" that positively burns the relatively tame (in comparison) studio take, Waters heads full bore through impressive versions of "Hoochie Coochie Man," Big Bill Broonzy's "Feel So Good," and "Tiger in Your Tank." A great breakthrough moment in blues history, when the jazz audience opened its ears and embraced Chicago blues. This album was in print almost continuously on vinyl for 20-plus years, and MCA reissued it in a fair CD version in 1986. At least one enterprising European bootlegger issued their version in the early '90s, but the real edition of this album to get is the March 2001 remastering from MCA. Transferred in high-resolution digital audio, it brings up the bass overall and the details of just about every aspect of the playing, as well as moving Muddy's singing several layers forward in the mix, so that one gets a very vivid stage ambience, making the original CD seem very ragged. The reissue has been augmented by the presence of four studio sides cut by the same group a month prior to the concert—none hold a candle to the live material, but they do fill in a few holes in Muddy's U.S. discography. The new notes by Mary Katherine Aldin also give a much better picture of the background of the show and Muddy's performance (so where's the film of the performance that she mentions?). *—Cub Koda & Bruce Eder*

Folk Festival of the Blues / 1963 / MCA ✦✦✦✦✦

This is a compilation album that isn't, a live album that isn't (at least in a couple of spots), and a Muddy Waters album that isn't, if one counts the appearances by four other artists on it. But for all things it isn't, it is also just happens to be one of the greatest and certainly most underrated live blues album of all time, unbelievably crude, raw, and as real as it gets. Originally issued on Chess' Argo label during the height of the folk music blues revival (hence the goofy title), this was a record that was aimed at a white market who responded in kind. But anybody purchasing it thinking they were getting some nice acoustic coffeehouse blues were in for the reality-check shock of their lives. Recorded on July 26, 1963, at a WPOA live radio broadcast MCed by local Chicago disc jockey Big Bill Hill emanating from the Copacabana Club (hence when this was reissued in 1967, it was retitled *Blues from Big Bill's Copacabana*), this features Buddy Guy's band as the backup band for everybody, augmented by Muddy's right-hand man, pianist Otis Spann. Although Big Bill announces the presence of Little Walter and Sonny Boy Williamson on the album's intro, they're no-shows; the studio version of Williamson's "Bring It on Home" appears here with dubbed-on applause (along with the studio version of Guy's "Worried Blues," one of the two bits of audio chicanery here). Everything else is just amazingly raw, crude, and blistering, with some of the most electrifying Buddy Guy guitar ever committed to tape, droning saxes, thundering drums, and Otis Spann anchoring everything with consummate elegance, as nobody's bothered to check their tuning in the last half dozen drinks or more. The combination of performances of Guy, Howlin' Wolf, Willie Dixon, and Sonny Boy in tandem with Waters would certainly checklist this one into "various artists" category, but with half of the ten tracks here being fronted by Waters, it's clearly Muddy's show all the way. His performances of "I Got My Mojo Working," "She's 19 Years Old," "Clouds in My Heart," "Sitting and Thinking," and the vocal trio effort with Guy and Dixon on the show-opening "Wee Wee Baby" are nothing less than exemplary. No matter how you slice it or end up filing it, one would be very hard-pressed indeed to find a live blues album that captures the spirit and a moment in time the way this one does. Unavailable on compact disc as of press time, but worth tracking down in its vinyl incarnations at any cost. *—Cub Koda*

Folk Singer / Apr. 1964 / MCA/Chess ✦✦✦✦✦
Muddy's "unplugged" album was cut in September of 1963 and still sounds fresh and vital today. It was Muddy simply returning to his original style on a plain acoustic guitar in a well-tuned room with Willie Dixon on string bass, Clifton James on drums, and Buddy Guy on second acoustic guitar. The nine tracks are divvied up between full rhythm section treatments with Buddy and Muddy as a duo and the final track, "Feel Like Going Home," which Waters approaches solo. What makes this version of the album a worthwhile buy is the inclusion of five bonus tracks from his next two sessions: An April 1964 session brings us Willie Dixon's "The Same Thing" and Muddy's "You Can't Lose What You Never Had," while the October 1964 session features J.T. Brown on sax and clarinet on "Short Dress Woman" and "My John the Conqueror Root," as well as "Put Me in Your Lay Away," another strong side. *Folk Singer* offers both sides of Muddy from the early '60s. *—Cub Koda*

The Real Folk Blues / 1965 / MCA/Chess ✦✦✦✦✦
Once Chess discovered a white folk-blues audience ripe and ready to hear the real thing, they released a series of albums under the *Real Folk Blues* banner. This is one of the best entries in the series, a mixed bag of early Chess sides from 1949-1954, some of it hearkening back to Muddy's first recordings for Aristocrat with only Ernest "Big" Crawford on string bass in support with some wonderful full band sides rounding out the package to give everyone the big picture. A couple of highlights to pay special attention to are the cha cha/shuffle strut of the band charging through "Walkin' Thru the Park" and the "I'm a Man"-derived nastiness of "Mannish Boy." *—Cub Koda*

Brass and the Blues / 1967 / Chess ✦✦
Mid-'60s action from the Chicago blues king, who was apparently due for an updated sound in the eyes of the Chess braintrust. So they overdubbed a brass section on Waters' competent renderings of a variety of old standards that intrudes as often as it enhances. *—Bill Dahl*

More Real Folk Blues / 1967 / Chess ✦✦✦✦✦
The companion volume to the first Waters entry in the series is even more down-home than the first. Featuring another brace of early Chess sides from 1948-1952, this release features some essential tracks not found on *The Chess Box*. With the bludgeoning stomp of "She's Alright" featuring Elgin Evans' kickass drumming and the moody introspection of "My Life Is Ruined" to be counted up among the numerous highlights, this is a fine budget package that Muddy (and lovers of early Chicago blues) fans certainly shouldn't overlook. *—Cub Koda*

Electric Mud / 1968 / MCA/Chess ✦✦
In an attempt to make Muddy more sellable to his newly found white audience, Chess lumbered him with Hendrix-influenced psychedelic blues arrangements for *Electric Mud*. Commercially, actually, the results weren't bad; Marshall Chess claims it sold between 150,000 and 200,000 copies. Musically, it was as ill-advised as putting Dustin Hoffman into a *Star Wars* epic. Guitarists Pete Cosey and Phil Upchurch are very talented players, but Muddy's brand of down-home electric blues suffered greatly at the hands of extended fuzzy solos. Muddy and band overhaul classics like "I Just Want to Make Love to You" and "Hoochie Coochie Man," and do a ludicrous cover of "Let's Spend the Night Together"; wah-wah guitars and occasional wailing soprano sax bounce around like loose basketballs. It's a classically wrongheaded, crass update of the blues for a modern audience. The 1996 CD reissue adds interesting historical liner notes. *—Richie Unterberger*

Super Blues / Nov. 1968 / Chess ✦✦
This is the first of two super session albums that Chess produced in the late '60s. Time has been a bit kinder to this one, featuring Muddy, Bo Diddley, and Little Walter, than the one cut a year later with Howlin' Wolf standing in for Walter. It's loose and *extremely* sloppy, the time gets pushed around here and there and Little Walter's obviously in bad shape, his voice rusted to a croak and trying to blow with a collapsed lung. But there are moments where Bo's heavily tremoloed guitar sounds just fine and the band kicks it in a few spots and Muddy seems to be genuinely enjoying himself. Granted, these moments are few and way too far between, but at least nobody's playing a wah-wah pedal on here. *—Cub Koda*

Fathers and Sons / 1969 / MCA/Chess ✦✦✦
The resurgence of Chicago-based blues in the mid- to late '60s came with an entirely new breed of icons to bear the torch. Among them were the decidedly electric Paul Butterfield Blues Band. Joining Muddy Waters (guitar/vocals) and Otis Spann (piano) on the aptly titled *Fathers and Sons* are three Butterfield Blues Band alumni: Michael Bloomfield (guitar), Sam Lay (drums), and leader Paul Butterfield (guitar). Further augmenting the personnel is Booker T. and the MG's Donald "Duck" Dunn (bass) and Buddy Miles (drums)—who cameos during the live "Got My Mojo Workin'" finale. This all-star cast helps reclaim some of Waters' fire, which had been summarily doused on his previous outing *Electric Mud*—a tasteless pseudo-psychedelic disaster. The poorly executed scheme had been designed to introduce Waters' music to a younger and mostly white audience. In essence, *Fathers and Sons* is able to accomplish with musical integrity what *Electric Mud* couldn't through gimmickry. Additionally, the incorporation of the younger-generation blues men solidified Waters' stature as one of the preeminent forces in Chicago blues to a decidedly fresh and underdeveloped audience. The disc is split between studio sides cut on April 21-23 and a half-hour live set. This performance, during the Super Cosmic Joy-Scout Jamboree, was documented on the evening following the final day of studio recording. The event was held at Auditorium Theater in (where else?) Chicago. Simplifying the process is *Fathers and Sons* set list, which consists of exclusively vintage Waters material. "Mean Disposition" and "Standin' Round Cryin'" drip with Bloomfield and Butterfield's nasty languid electric funk and feature Waters' determined and energized vocals. On the uptempo blues-rockers "Walking Thru the Park" and "Sugar Sweet," the nimble and lyrical guitar passages meld the distance between Waters and the electric blues of Cream and Led Zeppelin. The 2001 remastered CD edition includes four additional studio sides issued here for the first time: "Country Boy," "I Love the Life I Live (I Live the Life I Love)," "Oh Yeah," and "I Feel So Good." Without question, the highlight of *Fathers and Sons* is the live performances which are incessantly fueled by the explosive nature of the musicians on-stage as well as the audience. "Long Distance Call" and the two-part "Got My Mojo Working" are the finest pieces on the album. They likewise rate among the most complementary marriages of Chicago R&B with rock & roll. Of Muddy Waters' later recordings, it certainly got no better than the summit meeting heard on *Fathers and Sons*. Fans of Waters' true and natural showmanship, as well as enthusiasts of blues-based rock & roll will find plenty to revisit. *—Lindsay Planer*

Sail On / 1969 / Wolf ✦✦✦✦
Classic hits. *—Bill Dahl*

After the Rain / 1969 / Chess ✦
Another psychedelic mess. *—Bill Dahl*

They Call Me Muddy Waters / 1970 / MCA/Chess ✦✦✦
Upon its original 1970 release, this was a Grammy winner for Best Ethnic/Traditional Recording. A quarter of a century later, it seems like an interesting, but diffuse, collection of Muddy Waters tracks, running chronologically from 1951 up to 1967. Excepting the title track and a couple others, there's nothing really indispensable here. A good one to add to the collection after you've picked up on a half dozen others. *—Cub Koda*

Goin' Home: Live in Paris 1970 / 1970 / New Rose ✦✦✦
Goin' Home: Live in Paris 1970 finds Muddy supported by his longtime backing band—guitarists Pee Wee Madison and Sam Lawhorn, pianist Pinetop Perkins, bassist Calvin Jones, and drummer Willie "Big Eyes" Smith—as well as harpist Carey Bell on several tracks. Waters performed many of his familiar numbers—"Honey Bee," "Trouble No More," "Hoochie Coochie Man," "Mojo Workin'"—in front of a small French crowd, and while the performances aren't crackling with energy, they have a nice, relaxed, and friendly vibe that makes the album worth checking out. *—Thom Owens*

The London Muddy Waters Sessions / 1971 / MCA/Chess ✦✦
If you like hearing '70s British rock stars attempting to jam with one of the originators of the form, then you'll probably like the results from this tepid 1971 session. Only the late Irish guitarist Rory Gallagher seems to be interacting with the old master here (and guitarist Sammy Lawhorn), while Stevie Winwood, Georgie Fame, and Mitch Mitchell seem to be totally lost. *—Cub Koda*

A.K.A. McKinley Morganfield / 1971 / Chess ✦✦✦✦✦
The real title of this was actually *A.K.A. Muddy Waters*, with the name McKinley Morganfield in the bigger typeface reserved for the artist's name. Of course, this created confusion in some quarters, with the result that consumers were sometimes unable to find this set in the Muddy Waters bin. And of course they would be looking for it, since at the time it was one of the best retrospectives of his material available. Every conceivable classic by Waters is present here, in an intelligently edited presentation that flows through a dozen years of the great bluesman's career. The trip starts with a solo, pure Delta blues sound in 1948, but by 1960 a sophisticated, swinging Chicago blues combo style had been established for several years, with Waters an acknowledged master. The title/artist boondoggle didn't faze Chess; the company simply figured out other ways to repackage this material and all the other Muddy Waters in the archive, which it has continued doing over and over and over. This collection was done in the "two-fer" gatefold package that was popular at the time, and followed a period when most of the Chess catalog had long since been unavailable except in a few cutout bins. There are several nice full-face shots of Waters, and the liner notes aren't bad, but one can't say this is a set that is loaded with information. The sidemen credits are not printed clearly anywhere, for example. Combined with the photographic snub, this is not a good way to establish the band ambience that is such an important part of Waters' work, let alone alert the unsophisticated listener to the presence of so many great players on board. The sound is great, though. The analog mastering is the required oven for cooking this kind of bread, while this particular production sticks with mono whenever no stereo was present on the original. *—Eugene Chadbourne*

Can't Get No Grindin' / 1973 / Chess ✦✦✦
After eight or nine years of pleasing reissues offset with idiotic experiments (the *Super Blues* sessions and the two psychedelic albums *Electric Mud* and *After the Rain*), Muddy returned to form with a new band on this 1973 outing. Sounding positively encumbered and armed with a pretty great batch of tunes, this was his finest album in a quite a few years. *—Cub Koda*

London Revisited / 1974 / Chess ✦✦
As mediocre as its predecessor. *—Bill Dahl*

Muddy & the Wolf / 1974 / MCA/Chess ✦✦✦
The title is a bit of a ringer, since this isn't a collaborative effort in any way, shape or form. This contains a half dozen live Waters tracks with Mike Bloomfield, Paul Butterfield, and Otis Spann culled from the *Father and Sons* sessions and also features tracks by Howlin' Wolf from his London sessions with Eric Clapton and Ringo Starr. File under "just OK." *—Cub Koda*

Woodstock Album / 1975 / MCA/Chess ✦✦✦✦
Of all the post-*Fathers and Sons* attempts at updating Muddy's sound in collaboration with younger white musicians, this album worked best because they let Muddy be

himself, producing music that compared favorably to his concerts of the period, which were wonderful. His final album for Chess (recorded at Levon Helm's Woodstock studio, not in Chicago), with Helm and fellow Band-member Garth Hudson teaming up with Muddy's touring band, it was a rocking (in the bluesy sense) soulful swansong to the label where he got his start. Muddy covers some songs he knew back when (including Louis Jordan's "Caldonia" and "Let the Good Times Roll"), plays some slide, and generally has a great time on this Grammy-winning album. This record got lost in the shuffle between the collapse of Chess Records and the revival of Muddy's career under the auspices of Johnny Winter, and was forgotten until 1995. The CD contains one previously unreleased number, "Fox Squirrel." *—Bruce Eder*

☆ **The Best of Muddy Waters** / 1975 / MCA/Chess ✦✦✦✦✦
The profile of Muddy Waters on the front of this album is a classic bit of color portrait photography. The bluesman seems to be staring up at something, a glazed look of wonder in his eyes. What could it be? Perhaps a vision of all the different "best-of" sets and repackagings of his material that would happen in the future. In the end, it comes down to "That Same Thing" that Waters used to sing about, although he was talking about something else. The material this artist cut for Chess during this period is nothing short of a blues revelation. There has never been anything quite like it, before or after, and when one has heard Muddy Waters from this period, one has simply heard the best blues has to offer. This collection was the first "best-of" Chess created, obviously mindful that what they had on their hands was nothing less than a tray of gold. The earliest pieces, such as "Louisiana Blues," are just marvelous, the country blues slide guitar augmented just so slightly by string bass, the harmonica of Little Walter, and the barest trace of percussion. Rhythmically, these performances are flawless and drenched with the feel as if they were slabs of chicken that had spent the day simmering in a jerk sauce. From there, one hears the classic Chicago blues combo sound emerging, which it does with great glory on tracks such as "Standing Around Crying." Yet with all the more extensive material that has been released of this artist since the late '50s, it is hard to conceive of why a consumer looking for Waters would settle for this collection. It is not a question of "less is more," as there is great consistency to the Waters discography from this period; listeners who enjoy this material will want more, more, more. *—Eugene Chadbourne*

Live at Jazz Jamboree '76 / 1976 / Poljazz ✦✦✦
Released on the small Poljazz label, *Live at Jazz Jamboree '76* is a minor but valuable addition to the live Muddy Waters catalog. Recorded at the Palace of Culture and Sciences in Warsaw, Poland, the 14-track album finds Muddy in good form. Part of the reason the concert works is that his supporting band is excellent, boasting such musicians as pianist Pinetop Perkins, harpist Jerry Portnoy, and guitarists Luther "Guitar Junior" Johnson and Bob Margolin. They give Waters enthusiastic support, bringing the music alive. Even better, the set list isn't entirely predictable, so you can hear Muddy and the band work out on such numbers as "Screamin' and Cryin'," "Blow Wind Blow," "Howlin' Wolf," and "Caldonia," which makes this an interesting disc for hardcore fans. *—Thom Owens*

☆ **Hard Again** / May 1977 / Blue Sky ✦✦✦✦✦
After a string of mediocre albums throughout most of the 1970s, Muddy Waters hooked up with Johnny Winter for 1977's *Hard Again*, a startling comeback and a gritty demonstration of the master's powers. Fronting a band that includes such luminaries as James Cotton and Pinetop Perkins, Waters is not only at the top of his game, but is having the time of his life while he's at it. The bits of studio chatter that close "Mannish Boy" and open "Bus Driver" show him to be relaxed and obviously excited about the proceedings. Part of this has to be because the record sounds so good. Winter has gone for an extremely bare production style, clearly aiming to capture Waters in conversation with a band in what sounds like a single studio room. This means that sometimes the songs threaten to explode in chaos as two or three musicians begin soloing simultaneously. Such messiness is actually perfect in keeping with the raw nature of this music; you simply couldn't have it any other way. There is something so incredibly gratifying about hearing Waters shout out for different soloists, about the band missing hits or messing with the tempos. Hey this isn't pop music, it's the blues, and a little dirt never hurt anybody. The unsung star of this session is drummer Willie "Big Eyes" Smith, whose deep grooves make this record come alive. The five-minute, one-chord "Mannish Boy" wouldn't be nearly as compelling as it is if it weren't for Smith's colossal pocket. Great blues from one of the dominant voices of the genre. *—Daniel Gioffre*

I'm Ready / Jun. 1978 / Chess ✦✦✦✦
Another fine latter-day effort. *—Bill Dahl*

King Bee / 1981 / Blue Sky ✦✦✦
This 1981 recording found Waters being produced by rocker Johnny Winter, who had brought Muddy back to form on the *Hard Again* album. Winter was smart enough to surround the great one with musicians who knew his music intimately—regular band members like Calvin Jones, Willie "Big Eyes" Smith, Luther "Guitar Junior" Johnson, and Bob Margolin dot the lineup—and Johnny keeps his own excesses in check on a nice brace of tunes. While most of the tunes here are recuts of older Chess material, Muddy's versions of Slim Harpo's title track and his own "Champagne & Reefer" are worth checking out. Not the place to start a Muddy Waters collection, but a good one to add to the collection after you've absorbed the classics on Chess. *—Cub Koda*

Rolling Stone / 1982 / Chess ✦✦✦✦✦
This 14-song quasi-best-of anthology appeared during a murky period in which the Chess catalog was briefly owned by the Sugar Hill label. Thus it was only available for a short time, and all of the material has since appeared on other compilations. If you happen upon it and just want some of Muddy Waters' best stuff, though, it's not bad at all, featuring prime late-'40s and '50s cuts like "I Just Want to Make Love to You," "Long Distance Call," "Tiger in Your Tank," and "Walking Thru the Park." *—Richie Unterberger*

Hoochie Coochie Man / 1983 / LRC ✦✦✦✦
The source for this 1964 live performance appears to be Lippmann and Rau, the sponsors of Europe's American Folk Blues Festival. Considering that Chess Records never recorded Muddy's live set during this era, this disc is priceless. Otis Spann is at the piano, George Smith plays sax, Sammy Lawhorn is the second guitarist, and Francis Clay and Luther "Guitar Junior" Johnson are the rhythm section. The dozen songs include "Country Boy," "Baby Please Don't Go," "Sweet Little Angel," and "Rock Me Baby." The show is loose and lively, the band incredibly tight (especially Johnson and Clay on bass and drums), including a delightfully sly, teasing performance on "Hoochie Coochie Man," a rip-roaring "Sittin' and Thinkin'," and surging, volcanic renditions of "Long Distance Call," "She's Nineteen Years Old," and "County Jail." The sound is generally excellent as well, making this an indispensable part of any serious blues collection, and doubly so for Muddy's fans. *—Bruce Eder*

Rare & Unissued / 1984 / MCA/Chess ✦✦✦✦✦
Compiler Dick Shurman rummaged around in the voluminous Chess vaults long enough to emerge with this sterling 14-song collection of unissued and rare sides, most of them dating from Waters' 1947-1954 heyday. "Little Anna Mae," "Feel Like Going Home," and "You're Gonna Miss Me" spotlight his stark Delta roots; "Stuff You Gotta Watch," "Smokestack Lightnin'," and "Born Lover" boast fuller Waters bands of immense power and drive. *—Bill Dahl*

Sings Big Bill Broonzy/Folk Singer / 1986 / MCA/Chess ✦✦✦✦✦
The original version of this two-LPs-on-one-CD release was done by MCA in 1986. Beat Goes On's 1998 remastering runs circles around the MCA version for sound, and also outclasses, ever so slightly, Mobile Fidelity's Ultradisc edition of *Folk Singer*. The *Sings Big Bill* album is the main beneficiary, songs like "Tell Me Baby" finally leaping out at you with the kind of impact that Muddy's work was supposed to have—now you can hear what the Rolling Stones must have when they decided to cover this number, not the washed out resonances of the earlier reissues, vinyl and CD alike. The drums and bass are infinitely brighter and sharper, and heavier, and Muddy's singing is close, so much so that the older CD pales. New notes are provided along with a reprint of the original jacket copy, and while there's no session information, these do provide insights into the thinking behind the two albums and Muddy's approach to them, as well as the surprisingly mixed critical reaction to each at the time. One anomaly is that the songs from *Folk Singer* are present in their reverse side order, with the B-side numbers from the LP preceding those from A-side. The BGO mastering on those is also slightly punchier and brighter than the Mobile Fidelity version, though it is the *Sings Big Bill* numbers that are far and away the most altered for the better. *—Bruce Eder*

Trouble No More/Singles (1955–1959) / 1989 / MCA/Chess ✦✦✦✦✦
This is an excellent compilation of some of Muddy Waters' singles that are less frequently anthologized, all of them dating from the late '50s. Some of these were surprisingly hard to acquire in *any* form until this appeared: the original version of "Got My Mojo Working," for instance, as well as some of his higher-profile tracks, like "Rock Me," "Trouble No More," "Close to You," and "Don't Go No Further." All of these tracks appear on the *Chess Box*, so if you have that one, you don't need this one. But if you don't, you do. *—Richie Unterberger & Cub Koda*

☆ **The Chess Box** / 1989 / MCA/Chess ✦✦✦✦✦
The Chess Box does not contain all the great music Muddy Waters made. His talent and legacy is too large to be captured in a mere three discs, even one that spans from 1947 to 1972. This means, of course, that his legendary plantation recordings with Alan Lomax are not here, nor is his dynamic late '70s comeback, *Hard Again*. But, truth be told, it doesn't feel like they're missing, since Muddy's legend was built on the music that he made for Chess, and much of the greatest of that is here. Few box sets have chronicled an artist's best work as effectively as this; even the handful of rare, previously unreleased recordings sit perfectly next to the essential singles (this is particularly true of alternate takes of *Fathers and Songs* material). Sure, there are great Chess sides that aren't here, but those are great sides that the serious listener and aficionado need to seek out. For everybody else, this is a monumental chronicle of Muddy at his best, illustrating his influence while providing rich, endlessly fascinating music. *—Stephen Thomas Erlewine*

First Recording Sessions 1941–1946 / 1992 / Document ✦✦✦
The landmark sides that comprise Muddy Waters' *First Recording Sessions* trace the early evolution of one of the blues' most enduring greats, offering invaluable insight into the primal influences which helped shape his musical identity. The profound influence of Waters' idol Son House is most indelibly etched into these early sides, with the bottleneck guitar sound on the first cuts "Country Blues" and "I Be's Troubled"—both recorded by Alan Lomax in 1941—a prime example of the Mississippi blues style of the period. When Lomax returned a year later, he recorded Waters in a string band also including violinist Son Simms, guitarist Percy Thomas, and mandolinist Louis Ford; among the tracks they cut is "Take a Walk With Me," in all likelihood inspired by Robert Jr. Lockwood. By the final group of songs, dating from 1946, Waters was in Chicago, and here his guitar style began to move toward his future trademark sound, which is most in evidence on the classic closer, the two-part "Rollin' and Tumblin'." *—Jason Ankeny*

The Complete Muddy Waters 1947–1967 / 1992 / Charly ✦✦✦✦✦
No, this mammoth nine-disc compilation—205 tracks in all—isn't actually complete, since alternate takes have since turned up of a couple of items. Further, the sound quality is decidedly spotty, and Charly's legal right to put Chess material on the market at all has long been in question. But this is the only place CD enthusiasts are currently

going to find more than a few indispensable 1950s sides that MCA hasn't gotten around to releasing quite yet. And the final disc holds some enlightening alternate takes (including a whopping eight runthroughs of "Woman Wanted" and nine versions of "Read Way Back") that may never see domestic light of day. For aficionados only, make no mistake! *—Bill Dahl*

Blues Sky / Jun. 16, 1992 / Columbia/Legacy ♦♦♦♦♦
This is a nice collection paring down the best of the material Waters recorded for the Blue Sky label between 1976 to 1980. With Johnny Winter in the producer's chair, the backings are sympathetic and the songs are great (some of them remakes of earlier Chess material): These are the tracks that garnered three consecutive Grammy Awards (for Best Ethnic or Traditional Recording) for Waters. And that can't be *all* bad. Not the place to start by any means, but definitely worth a listen or two.*—Cub Koda*

Live in 1958 / 1993 / MW ♦♦♦
In the fall of 1958, Muddy Waters came to England to perform for the first time. With his regular pianist Otis Spann along for the ride and backed by the jazzy, horn-dominated Chris Barber Band, Muddy's declamatory vocals and electric slide guitar (set at Chicago blues tavern levels) proved to be too much reality for purist British audiences to handle. He immediately toned down his approach to appease the straight-laced Brits, and what survives here is the complete concert from the following night at the Manchester Free Trade Hall, dubbed from the only existing acetate. *—Cub Koda*

☆ **The Complete Plantation Recordings** / Jun. 8, 1993 / MCA/Chess ♦♦♦♦♦
At long last, Muddy's historic 1941-1942 Library of Congress field recordings are all collected in one place, with the best fidelity that's been heard thus far. Waters performs solo pieces (you can hear his slide rattling against the fretboard in spots) and band pieces with the Son Simms Four, "Rosalie" being a virtual blueprint for his later Chicago style. Of particular note are the inclusion of several interview segments with Muddy from that embryonic period and a photo of Muddy playing on the porch of his cabin, dressed up and looking sharper than any Mississippi sharecropper on Stovall's plantation you could possibly imagine. This much more than just an important historical document; this is some really fine music imbued with a sense of place and time and loads of ambience. *—Cub Koda*

One More Mile / 1994 / MCA/Chess ♦♦♦♦♦
A double CD of 41 tracks, none of which are found on *The Chess Box.* With only three exceptions, none of them have ever been available on an American album before, and quite a few were never previously released anywhere. During most of his stay at Chess, Muddy's output was remarkably prolific and consistent. If you are interested enough in him to own more than one of his albums, you'll like what you hear on this collection, which matches or nearly matches the standards of his best work. Lots of rarities spanning the late '40s to the early '70s, with some special points of interest: the original 1955 version of "I Want to Be Loved," covered by the Rolling Stones on the B-side of their very first single, finally makes its first appearance on an American album, and the final 11 songs are from a previously unreleased 1972 Swiss radio broadcast, showcasing Muddy in a drummerless trio. *—Richie Unterberger*

Collaboration / 1995 / Rhino ♦♦
This is the same package as one earlier released in England. It's Muddy with Otis Spann, playing England's Manchester Free Trade Hall in 1958 with the Chris Barber Jazz Band backing them. The Tomato version adds "Long Distance Call" and "Baby Please Don't Go" to the original ten-song lineup; overall, the sound is still rough, taken from the original—and existing—acetate. Muddy's guitar was deliberately turned down for this concert, making him nigh to inaudible, but he's in fine voice and Spann fills in all the missing holes nicely. Not essential, but an interesting sidebar to his recorded legacy. *—Cub Koda*

Muddy Waters at Newport/Muddy Waters Live / 1996 / BGO ♦♦♦
Muddy Waters' classic *Muddy Waters at Newport* album is combined with the passable 1977 record *Muddy Waters Live* on this single-disc Beat Goes On reissue. The packaging and sound quality on this disc are first-rate, but the juxtaposition of the two records isn't particularly wise, since the Newport album dwarfs the 1977 album in terms of excitement, energy, and overall quality. *—Stephen Thomas Erlewine*

Muddy Waters in Concert / 1996 / One Way ♦♦♦♦
This is a later concert performance by Muddy, from sometime in the mid-'70s to judge by the repertory ("Garbage Man," "Corrine Corrina," "Caldonia," and "Screamin' and Cryin'" in addition to "Hoochie Coochie Man," "Got My Mojo Working," "Howlin' Wolf," etc.). There are no credits or dates mentioned, but that's not really important. The performance and recording are both excellent—the sound is bigger and busier, as well as somewhat more elegant, than Muddy's mid-'60s work, and the repertory is different from both his official Chess and Columbia live albums, so it's a must-own. This same performance previously appeared in a fairly widely distributed CD from Classic Sound Inc., and either is acceptable. *—Bruce Eder*

★ **His Best: 1947 to 1955** / 1997 / MCA/Chess ♦♦♦♦♦
This entry into MCA's Chess 50th Anniversary Collection now officially takes the place of *The Best of Muddy Waters* as an essential first purchase in building a Muddy Waters collection, as the original 12-song collection has been forced out of print with the issuance of this 20-tracker. All 12 songs that comprise the budget priced *The Best of Muddy Waters* are aboard, with eight more essential goodies from his first great period of creativity, including great early ones like "Rollin' and Tumblin'," "Train Fare Blues," and "I Feel like Going Home." The one ringer that keeps this collection from being *The Best of Muddy*-plus is an alternate take of "Hoochie Coochie Man" in place of the original issued master, a production error of the highest order. It's a radically different sounding one, too, with some surprisingly sloppy unthought-out harp work from Little Walter (at one point he simply stops playing), but with a far more intense vocal from Muddy than the issued version. But it is the issued version which by rights *should* have been the one heard here, as this *is* supposed to be a true best-of compilation. That niggling point aside, this collection (part of a two-volume best-of retrospective, the second covering the years 1956 to 1964) sports far superior sound and excellent liner notes, and will now take pride of place as the essential first purchase toward building the perfect Muddy Waters collection. *—Cub Koda*

Muddy Waters & Friends / 1997 / Just a Memory ♦♦♦
These 11 songs were cut by Muddy at an informal session in a Montreal hotel room on Oct. 18, 1967, recorded by Michael Nerenberg. The tape is sort of the companion to the *Folk Singer* album that he'd cut a few years earlier—Muddy is joined on acoustic guitar and vocals by Otis Spann, Sam Lawhorn, George "Mojo" Buford, and Luther Johnson. The sound is rough, and there's a certain amount of talk and ambient noise, especially on "Little Anna Mae." Other songs include "My Home Is in the Delta," "Take a Little Walk," "Crazy About You Baby," and "Mean Disposition," all done with Muddy in good form—this was when he was in his fifties, and before the car accident and subsequent health problems that slowed him down, and given the fact that Chess didn't record Muddy for an official live album until a few years after this, *Muddy Waters & Friends* partly fills a gap in his history. Still, this isn't a definitive recording, because Muddy and company were winging the sound, and had no inkling that what they were taping would ever be heard publicly. *—Bruce Eder*

Paris 1972 / Mar. 4, 1997 / Pablo ♦♦♦
This concert in Paris (part of Norman Granz's latter-day Jazz at the Philharmonic master holdings) emanates from a better-than-decent-quality board tape complete with maddening fader moves keying up the wrong instrument in spots—most notably two choruses of Waters' rhythm guitar unintentionally drowning out everyone, plodding along while Louis Myers solos on "Blow Wind Blow"—and missing the first part of several guitar solos and intros by Muddy. But even with every song in the same maddening key of G natural, this 1972 concert nonetheless catches Muddy in good '70s form, presiding over the proceedings in typical dignified bearing. With an all-star lineup of Pinetop Perkins on piano, Mojo Buford on harmonica, Calvin Jones on bass, and Willie Smith on drums (along with the aforementioned Myers substituting for Sammy Lawhorn on guitar), the music presented here is rock-solid, even if the key never varies. Things catch fire early on, with the band laying back when Muddy does (a fairly desultory reading of "Hoochie Coochie Man" that never really gets going) and getting hotter when he gets the itch, as he does on "County Jail," "Honey Bee," and "Lovin' Man," all boasting stinging slide solos. An interesting bonus are full-band treatments of "Rollin' and Tumblin'" and Robert Johnson's "Walking Blues." There's nothing on here that's going to make you trade in your copy of *Muddy Waters at Newport*, but as a document of latter-day Waters (especially in light of all the samey, uninspired live discs from this period that have come out), this is some pretty great stuff. *—Cub Koda*

☆ **His Best: 1956–1964** / May 20, 1997 / MCA/Chess ♦♦♦♦♦
The first eight tracks of this 20-track collection date from 1956: "All Aboard," and featuring both James Cotton and Little Walter on twin harmonicas, "Forty Days and Forty Nights," "Just to Be With You," "Don't Go No Farther," "Diamonds at Your Feet," "I Love the Life I Live," "Rock Me," and the studio version of "I Got My Mojo Working." By now, Waters was a rhythm & blues star, as far removed from the Clarksdale plantation he grew up on as you could get. He also had developed the modern-day blues band lineup and by this time had his running like a well-oiled machine. Little Walter (by now a star in his own right) was still on call for studio dates and if not, Big Walter Horton, Otis Spann, and Jimmy Rogers were still in the lineup. By 1958's "She's Nineteen Years Old," Muddy had built up his second great band with James Cotton, Pat Hare, and Luther Tucker on guitars and Francis Clay on drums, the unit he would take to Newport in 1960. It's this unit that contributes so mightily to "Walkin' Thru the Park," "She's Into Something," and Big Bill Broonzy's "I Feel So Good." Two of Muddy's most influential tracks, "You Shook Me" and "You Need Love" (the blueprint for Led Zeppelin's "Whole Lotta Love"), curiously feature Earl Hooker on slide guitar, along with A.C. Reed and John "Big Moose" Walker, the core of the Age-Profile label's house band. A pair of tracks from his now-celebrated *Folk Singer* album with Buddy Guy and Willie Dixon ("My Home Is in the Delta" and "Good Morning Little Schoolgirl") offset the collection's final selections, Willie Dixon's "The Same Thing" and Muddy's classic "You Can't Lose What You Ain't Never Had," a perfect closer for this essential collection. *—Cub Koda*

King of the Electric Blues / Oct. 7, 1997 / Epic/Legacy ♦♦♦
The first 20-bit remastering of any of Muddy's late career work for Johnny Winter's Blue Sky label is of considerable interest. The fact that, in the wake of the earlier *Blues Sky* best-of disc, there's enough material to do another 60-minute-plus collection, also speaks well for this catalog. The clarity of the Super Bit Mapping audio brings out a sharpness in these recordings that the original vinyl and CD issues barely hinted at. The stuff is finally mastered at the volume it always should have been (this is a potential lease-breaker) and more than justifies the purchase. The music isn't as viscerally exciting as Muddy's work for Chess—he's slower, starts at a lower energy level, and takes his time building up intensity, but the climaxes are majestic. The playing is also as solid as ever, and Muddy still had a considerable amount to say musically. *Blues Sky* still has the edge for songs, although the producers here have wisely included Muddy's covers of songs that he liked by Sonny Boy Williamson, Arthur "Big Boy" Crudup, and Big Joe Williams, in addition to some of his own tunes. *—Bruce Eder*

Live Recordings 1965–1973 / Jan. 12, 1999 / Wolf ♦♦♦
These are ten tracks of Waters pretty much on top of his game, with the bulk of them coming from 1965–1968 and featuring Pinetop Perkins, Carey Bell, and Sammy Lawhorn

in support. Three tracks from 1973 may sport better fidelity than the scratchier-sounding mid-'60s stuff, but every track's a gem no matter how you slice it. *—Cub Koda*

The Real Folk Blues/More Real Folk Blues / Mar. 10, 1999 / BGO ♦♦♦♦♦
Waters' *The Real Folk Blues* and *More Real Folk Blues*, combined here onto one CD, were not exactly random collections of tracks—the quality was too consistently high for them to just have been picked out of a hat. Still, it was a pretty arbitrary grouping of items that he recorded between 1947 and 1964. In fact, they hail from throughout his whole stint at Chess, virtually; at the time these albums were first issued, though, all of the material on *More Real Folk Blues* was from the late '40s and early '50s. They didn't exactly concentrate on his most well-known songs, but they didn't entirely neglect them either, including "Mannish Boy," "Walking Thru the Park," "The Same Thing," "Rollin' & Tumblin', Pt. 1," "She's Alright," and "Honey Bee," amongst somewhat more obscure selections. So ultimately, this disc's usefulness depends on your fussiness as a collector—if it's the only Waters you ever pick up, you'll still have a good idea of his greatness, and if you don't mind getting some tracks you might already have on more avowedly best-of sets, you'll probably hear some stuff you don't already have in your collection. On the basis of the music alone, it's fine material, representing his hardest-rocking electric blues ("Mannish Boy," "Walking Thru the Park"), his most rural down-home sides (particularly the earliest sides, on which his only accompanist is bassist Ernest "Big" Crawford), and more idiosyncratic cuts like "The Same Thing," with Willie Dixon's captivatingly out-of-tune bass. Incidentally, just to make matters confusing, Waters *did* record a folk-oriented album in the mid-'60s, but it's not one of the two records included here—it's his entirely separate *Folk Singer* album, from 1964. *—Richie Unterberger*

Best of Muddy Waters: 20th Century Masters / Mar. 23, 1999 / MCA ♦♦♦
Like any record company worth their salt, MCA knows a good gimmick when they see it, and when the millennium came around...well, the *20th Century Masters—The Millennium Collection* wasn't too far behind. Supposedly, the millennium is a momentous occasion, but it's hard to feel that way when it's used as another excuse to turn out a budget-line series. But apart from the presumptuous title, *20th Century Masters—The Millennium Collection* turns out to be a very good budget-line series. True, it's impossible for any of these brief collections to be definitive, but they're nevertheless solid samplers that don't feature a bad song in the bunch. For example, take Muddy Waters' *20th Century* volume—it's an irresistible 12-song summary of his Chess recordings. There may be several noteworthy songs missing, but many of his best-known songs for the label are here, including "I Just Want to Make Love to You," "Long Distance Call," "I'm Your Hoochie Coochie Man," "Honey Bee," "I'm Ready," "Trouble No More," "Mannish Boy," "Rock Me," "Forty Days and Forty Nights," and "Got My Mojo Working." Serious fans will want something more extensive, but this is an excellent introduction for neophytes and a great sampler for casual fans, considering its length and price. That doesn't erase the ridiculousness of the series title, but the silliness is excusable when the music and the collections are good. *—Stephen Thomas Erlewine*

The Lost Tapes / Jun. 22, 1999 / Blind Pig ♦♦♦
It's been a while since we've seen any unreleased material from Muddy. You've heard all of this before, but the clarity of the sound, and the fact that Muddy seems in pretty good spirits, playing with a crack band, makes this an essential addition to any blues lovers collection, and a must buy for Muddy devotees. It is also an enhanced CD that can be run on Windows systems; unfortunately Macintosh owners are out of luck. The band is really a great one with pianist Pinetop Perkins, guitarists Pee Wee Madison and Sammy Lawhorn, George "Harmonica" Smith, bassist Calvin Jones, and drummer Willie "Big Eyes" Smith. They push Muddy in a mostly mellow framework. The first seven cuts were recorded at the University of Washington, and comprise faves like "Honey Bee," "Hoochie Coochie Man," "Walkin' Thru the Park," "Trouble No More," "Just to Be With You," and a lengthy spoken intro by Mud prior to the ten-minute "She's Nineteen Years Old." Tracks are banded for radio airplay, and everything is so very well recorded. The final four cuts were recorded at the University of Oregon: "Long Distance Call," "Mannish Boy," "Crawlin' Kingsnake," and the cookin' "Got My Mojo Workin'." Muddy's signature mellow but insistent persona shines, the band is ultra-tight, Pinetop and Smith lay it out time after ever lovin' time, and Muddy's slide work gets some overdue play. Don't hesitate on this one thinking it's outtakes or damaged, substandard goods. It's not by a long shot; in fact, it might be the best live Mud ever released, and an important audio document from perhaps the greatest bluesman of them all. *—Michael G. Nastos*

In Concert / Nov. 9, 1999 / Prestige Jazz ♦♦♦
An undated and unspecified location Muddy concert (though judging from the set it's probably from the early '80s because of the inclusion of "Garbage Man"), reasonably well recorded with a hot band behind him, his Fender Telecaster stinging with each slide of the string. Although the backing musicians are uncredited, they provide exciting support as well as a top-notch version of "Floyd's Guitar Blues." There is some distortion in the recording, but a largely hot concert by the Mudman and crew make this one a keeper. *—Cub Koda*

Mojo: The Best of Muddy Waters Live! 1971–1976 / May 23, 2000 / Music Club ♦♦♦
This compilation was assembled from three live performances, two in the Northwest in 1971, and one in Switzerland in April 1976. There are already several live Muddy Waters albums available, including some recorded during this era. Not only that, the 74-minute program does not exactly offer much in the way of surprising repertoire: "Rollin' and Tumblin'," "Hoochie Coochie Man," "Walking Thru the Park," "Mannish Boy," and "Got My Mojo Working" are all available in superior live and/or studio versions, sometimes several times over. So is this an essential addition to your Waters collection? Probably not. However, if you can't drink enough of those Muddy Waters, it's respectable enough. The sound quality is good, and the atmosphere a little more electric and driving than that on *Paris 1972*, to give one example of another live disc from the period. The 1971 band was quite full, with Sammy Lawhorn and Pee Wee Madison on guitar, George "Harmonica" Smith on harmonica, and Pinetop Perkins on piano; the 1976 band, with the same rhythm section but new members on guitar and harmonica, were pretty good as well. If you're looking for particular points of interest, Waters and the band really stretch things out on a ten-minute "She's Nineteen Years Old"; Luther "Guitar Junior" Johnson, and not Waters, takes the lead vocal on "Dust My Broom"; and "Mannish Boy" has an unusual minor-note flavor. *—Richie Unterberger*

☆ **Rollin' Stone: The Golden Anniversary Collection** / Jun. 27, 2000 / MCA/Chess ♦♦♦♦♦
Like the Bear Family sets that include every available recording of an artist, this two-disc collection finally presents every known track Muddy Waters recorded for the Aristocrat and Chess labels from 1947 to 1952. Since Waters was such a vital architect of the Chicago blues sound, it's an indispensable historical and educational document, as well as a wonderful listening experience. The mono sound, remastered in 2000, is clean, crisp, and remarkably vibrant considering the age of these masters, and the liner notes, pictures, and track documentation in the 16-page booklet are enlightening, professional, and complete. Brought to Aristocrat's attention by Sunnyland Slim who accompanies Waters on the earliest sides here, Muddy quickly established himself as an important and talented artist in his own right. Even the first recordings from 1947 show the guitarist/vocalist/songwriter as confident, mature, and, above all, driven, with his songs focused and tightly constructed. The majority of the tracks on disc one feature Waters with accompaniment from only bassist Earnest "Big" Crawford and prove what an astonishingly inventive slide guitarist Muddy was, even at this fresh-faced stage in his career. Little Walter adds his distinctive harp to increase the band to a trio, but percussion doesn't appear until about three-quarters through this album when Leonard Chess beats a rudimentary bass drum on four songs recorded in July 1951. Although many of Waters' signature tunes, including "Got My Mojo Workin'," "Hootchie Cootchie Man," and "I'm Ready" were recorded after the five years covered on these discs, this set is not for completists only. The bluesman's work here is as vital as on those hits, and even the most obscure tracks trace the formation of the Chicago sound that revolutionized blues and even pop music. Muddy's version of "All Night Long" was a blueprint for B.B. King's "Rock Me Baby" and classics like "Honey Bee," "Rollin' and Tumblin'," and "I Can't Be Satisfied" are essential to any blues collection. Those unfamiliar with Muddy Waters' work should still start with the crucial three-disc *Chess Box*, but this double album shouldn't be far behind. Not just an essential historical record of an artist and genre, these are some of the most seminal and inspired blues performances ever recorded. *—Hal Horowitz*

★ **The Anthology: 1947–1972** / Aug. 28, 2001 / MCA/Chess ♦♦♦♦♦
There have been countless collections of Muddy Waters' classic Chess material released over the years, but Chess began to whittle down the domestic catalog toward the late '90s. The triple-disc Chess box remained in print, but they added two single-disc collections that each covered a specific period in Waters' career at Chess. Then, in 2001, MCA/Chess released *The Anthology*, a double-disc set that essentially contained much of those two single-disc collections, with several extra tracks, remastering, and new liner notes. This still didn't correct the lack of a concise, single-disc overview with all the hits—something that Muddy, Chuck Berry, and Howlin' Wolf all desperately need—but if you're going to be buying two discs to get the full Muddy Waters story, you should get this instead of two separate discs, since it's simply easier. Besides, this, even if it does contain a bunch of familiar material, nevertheless contains some of the greatest music of the 20th century, and if you're not going to get the box but still want a comprehensive Muddy set, this is it. *—Stephen Thomas Erlewine*

Johnny "Guitar" Watson

b. Feb. 3, 1935, Houston, TX, **d.** May 17, 1996, Yokohama, Japan
Vocals, Guitar / Modern Electric Texas Blues, Electric Texas Blues, Soul-Blues, R&B, Funk
"Reinvention" could just as easily have been Johnny "Guitar" Watson's middle name. The multi-talented performer parlayed his stunning guitar skills into a vaunted reputation as one of the hottest blues axemen on the West Coast during the 1950s. But that admirable trait wasn't paying the bills as the 1970s rolled in. So he totally changed his image to that of a pimp-styled funkster, enjoying more popularity than ever before for his down-and-dirty R&B smashes "A Real Mother for Ya" and "Superman Lover."

Watson's roots resided within the fertile blues scene of Houston. As a teen, he played with fellow Texas future greats Albert Collins and Johnny Copeland. But he left Houston for Los Angeles when he was only 15 years old. Back then, Watson's main instrument was piano; that's what he played with Chuck Higgins' band when the saxist cut "Motorhead Baby" for Combo in 1952 (Watson also handled vocal duties).

He was listed as Young John Watson when he signed with Federal in 1953. His first sides for the King subsidiary found him still tinkling the ivories, but by 1954, when he dreamed up the absolutely astonishing instrumental "Space Guitar," the youth (he was two days short of his 17th birthday!) had switched over to guitar. "Space Guitar" ranks with the greatest achievements of its era—Watson's blistering rapid-fire attack, done without the aid of a pick, presages futuristic effects that rock guitarists still hadn't mastered another 15 years down the line.

Watson moved over to the Bihari brothers' RPM label in 1955 and waxed some of the toughest upbeat blues of their time frame (usually under saxist Maxwell Davis' supervision). "Hot Little Mama," "Too Tired," and "Oh Baby" scorched the strings with their blazing attack; "Someone Cares for Me" was a churchy Ray Charles-styled slow-dragger; and "Three Hours Past Midnight" cut bone-deep with its outrageous guitar work and laid-back vocal (Watson's cool phrasing as a singer was scarcely less distinctive than his playing). He scored his first hit in 1955 for RPM with a note-perfect cover of New Orleanian Earl King's two-chord swamp ballad "Those Lonely Lonely Nights."

Though he cut a demo version of the tune while at RPM, Watson's first released version of "Gangster of Love" emerged in 1957 on Keen. Singles for Class ("One Kiss"), Goth, Arvee (the rocking introduction "Johnny Guitar"), and Escort preceded a hookup with Johnny Otis at King during the early '60s. He recut "Gangster" for King, reaching a few more listeners this time, and dented the R&B charts again in 1962 with his impassioned, violin-enriched blues ballad "Cuttin' In."

Never content to remain in one stylistic bag for long, Watson landed at Chess just long enough to cut a jazz album in 1964 that placed him back behind the 88s. Along with longtime pal Larry Williams, Watson rocked England in 1965 (their dynamic repartee was captured for posterity by British Decca). Their partnership lasted stateside through several singles and an LP for OKeh; among their achievements as a duo was the first vocal hit on "Mercy, Mercy, Mercy" in 1967 (predating the Buckinghams by a few months).

Little had been heard of this musical chameleon before he returned decked out in funk threads during the mid-'70s. He hit with "I Don't Want to Be a Lone Ranger" for Fantasy before putting together an incredible run at DJM Records paced by "A Real Mother for Ya" in 1977 and an updated "Gangster of Love" the next year.

After a typically clever "Strike on Computers" nicked the R&B lists in 1984, Watson again seemed to fall off the planet. But counting this remarkable performer out was always a mistake. *Bow Wow*, his 1994 album for Al Bell's Bellmark logo, returned him to prominence and earned a Grammy nomination for best contemporary blues album, even though its contents were pure old-school funk. Sadly, in the midst of a truly heartwarming comeback campaign, Watson passed away while touring Japan in 1996. *—Bill Dahl*

Gangster of Love / 1958 / King ✦✦✦✦✦
The innovative guitar wizard when he was young and wearing his Texas blues roots prominently on his sleeve. Watson spent two stints at King/Federal, both of them sampled here: his 1953-1954 output includes the incomparable "Space Guitar," and a sizzling "Half Pint of Whiskey," and a woozy "Gettin' Drunk." The 1961-1963 King stuff is headed by the definitive version of "Gangster of Love," the searing soul-tinged "Cuttin' In," and a chunky "Broke and Lonely." *—Bill Dahl*

Johnny Guitar Watson / 1963 / King ✦✦✦✦✦
Fine collection of guitarist's innovative 1950s and '60s stuff. *—Bill Dahl*

Larry Williams Show With Johnny Guitar Watson / 1965 / Decca ✦✦✦
An exciting pairing tears up Britain. *—Bill Dahl*

The Blues Soul of Johnny Guitar Watson / 1964 / MCA/Chess ✦✦✦
This 1964 album, later reissued under the title of *I Cried for You*, displays an entirely different facet of the multi-talented R&B star's musical personality. Here he's an accomplished jazz pianist in a trio setting, giving old standards like "Witchcraft" and "Misty" his own vocal twist. Lowell Fulson's "Reconsider Baby" is the only blues number on the LP. *—Bill Dahl*

In the Fats Bag / 1967 / OKeh ✦✦✦
Another piano set. *—Bill Dahl*

Two for the Price of One / 1967 / OKeh ✦✦✦
Watson and Williams sing rockin' soul. *—Bill Dahl*

Listen / 1973 / Fantasy ✦✦✦
When Johnny "Guitar" Watson recorded *Listen* for Fantasy in 1973, he was three years away from the major comeback he would enjoy with 1976's *Ain't That a Bitch*. The singer/guitarist still had some very devoted fans, who remembered him for his blues output of the 1950s. But Watson was going after young R&B audiences in 1973, which is why *Listen* is a soul/funk album and not a blues album. You won't find another "Gangster of Love" or "Hot Little Mama" on *Listen*, an LP that was produced and arranged by Watson himself and makes it clear that he was paying close attention to what black radio (or "soul radio," as it was called) was playing at the time. Black radio, of course, was playing very few 12-bar blues numbers in the early 1970s; nonetheless, R&B still had plenty of blues feeling, and Watson knew that soul and funk (just like rock) were very much an outgrowth of the blues. So he sounds quite comfortable on soul items like "You're the Sweetest Thing I've Ever Had," "It's All About You," and the sentimental "You Stole My Heart." However, *Listen* isn't a great record—decent, but not great and not in a class with subsequent DJM gems like *Ain't That a Bitch* and 1977's *A Real Mother for Ya*. This LP, although likable, is only recommended to serious Watson collectors. *—Alex Henderson*

The Gangster Is Back / 1975 / Red Lightnin' ✦✦
The Digital reissue of an old Red Lightnin' bootleg covering Watson's 1950s output that was revered back in the pre-CD era but sounds very rough now. One thing in its favor: the disc sports Watson's otherwise digitally unavailable 1957 version of "Gangster of Love" for Keen. *—Bill Dahl*

I Don't Want to Be a Lone Ranger / 1975 / Fantasy ✦✦✦
It isn't easy to reinvent yourself when you're in your late thirties, but Johnny "Guitar" Watson was among the artists who was able to pull it off. In the 1950s, the singer/-guitarist became well known in the blues world for classics like "Gangster of Love" and "Hot Little Mama"; some blues fans would have been happy if he had remained a blues singer for the rest of his life. But in the 1970s, Watson was determined to change with the times and appeal to young R&B audiences. So he reinvented himself as a funk-soul artist, and that stylistic makeover paid off in a major way when 1976's *Ain't That a Bitch* went through the roof commercially. Released in 1975, *I Don't Want to Be a Lone Ranger* isn't in a class with *Ain't That a Bitch* or 1977's *A Real Mother for Ya*, but it's still a decent record. Although Watson turned 40 in 1975, this LP (which was his last album for Fantasy) is hardly the work of someone who was stuck in the past. Enjoyable soul items like "It's Way Too Late," "Tripping," and "You Make My Heart Want to Sing" are definitely relevant to what young soul audiences were demanding in 1975—and they weren't demanding the type of 12-bar blues recordings that put Watson on the map back in the 1950s. *I Don't Want to Be a Lone Ranger* falls short of essential, but it's a respectable effort that's worth hearing if you're among Watson's hardcore fans. *—Alex Henderson*

Ain't That a Bitch / 1976 / Collectables ✦✦✦✦
Coming out of Houston's fertile blues scene with Albert Collins and Johnny Copeland, Johnny "Guitar" Watson tread the same route to fame that his peers did in the latter half of the '50s and for most of the '60s. Unlike Collins and Copeland, though, Watson found his biggest success as a funkster in the '70s. And lest one thinks of an aging blues legend embarrassing himself aping the innovations of George Clinton and Sly Stone, Watson found a singular groove by slicking up his already urbane blues style with lots of tasty horn arrangements, plenty of fat bass lines, and wah-wah-issue guitar licks. The latter element, of course, was to be expected from a virtuoso such as Watson. And whether reeling off one of his subtle solos or blending in with the band, the reborn blues star was never less than compelling. *Ain't That a Bitch*, from 1976, heralded Watson's new funk era with plenty of guitar treats and one of the best batch of songs he ever cooked up. The variety here is stunning, ranging from the calypso-based blues swinger "I Need It" to the quiet storm soul ballad "Since I Met You Baby." In between, Watson goes wide-screen with the comic book funk of "Superman Lover" and eases into an after-hours mood on the organ-driven jazz and blues gem "I Want to Ta Ta You Baby." Besides the fine Watson roundups on the Rhino and Charly labels, *Ain't That a Bitch* works beautifully as a first-disc choice for newcomers, especially those who want to hear the '70s funk material. *—Stephen Cook*

A Real Mother for Ya / Jan. 1977 / Collectables ✦✦✦
Obviously, the storming funk workout that gives this 1977 gold album its title is the album's principal draw (it's been covered countless times, but never duplicated). As was his wont by this time, the multitalented Watson plays everything except drums and horns. *—Bill Dahl*

Funk Beyond the Call of Duty / Feb. 1977 / Collectables ✦✦✦
Less consistent than its immediate predecessors but still a reasonably good funky time, as Johnny Guitar once again displays his streetwise humor on "It's About the Dollar Bill" and "Barn Door" on the 1977 set. *—Bill Dahl*

Hot Little Mama / 1978 / Big Town ✦
Avoid these '50s RPM sides with overdubbed modern instrumentation. *—Bill Dahl*

Gettin' Down With Johnny "Guitar" Watson / 1978 / Cadet ✦✦
That same Chess jazz piano set again. *—Bill Dahl*

Love Jones / 1980 / Collectables ✦✦✦✦
From 1974 through 1980, Johnny "Guitar" Watson was on a tear no one, including George Clinton or Bootsy Collins, could equal. While the P-Funk machine began to run out of steam by 1978—with the exception of the Brides of Funkenstein—Watson kept churning out the weird, kinky funk well into the era of Rick James. *Love Jones*, his last fine record for quite a while, had all the trademarks in place: the choppy, heavily reverbed and wah-wahed guitar that had made Watson a blues sensation, the sci-fi keyboards, the handclap that Nile Rodgers and Bernard Edwards ripped off for Chic, the expandable horn section that intertwined with the guitar riffs, and the punched up basic basslines that kept the funk a simple but ultimately moving thing. It's true that some of the crazy lyrics that graced *Ain't That a Bitch* had given way to chanted clichés by this time, but it hardly mattered since Watson was making music for discos and clubs, and not for radio play any longer. He got hip to the fact that if you wanted to break a record you had to get a club DJ to play the hell out of it. Here, the standouts are "Booty Ooty," the truly weird and wonderful "Goin' Up in Smoke," "Telephone Bill," and the hilarious—and extremely funky—"Lone Ranger." This may have been the last real winner in Watson's catalog for a long time, but there is plenty of magic still present in these grooves. *—Thom Jurek*

The Very Best of Johnny Guitar Watson / 1981 / DJM ✦✦✦✦
Culled from the fine run of bluesy funk sides Watson cut between 1976-1980, DJM's *The Very Best of Johnny Guitar Watson* doesn't really qualify as a complete hits package—"Superman Love" and "Tarzan" are missing, for starters—but sports an attractive mix of solid tracks all the same. Featuring plenty of Watson's P-Funk-inspired grooves and inflation-era commentary, the 14 tracks include such highlights as "Ain't That a Bitch," "Lover Jones," "A Real Mother for Ya," and "I Need It." Equally heavy on the funk, but a bit off the quality radar, more obscure album tracks like "Booty Ooty," "Mother-In-Law," and "Miss Frisco" still come through with an abundance of Watson's irresistible guitar licks and wry vocals. Also adding to the fine stock here are progressive funk sides like "What the Hell Is This" (reminiscent of P-Funk experiments like "Hydraulic Pump"), the after-hours blues ballad "I Want to Ta-Ta You Baby," and the gospel-tinged "Strung Out"—and that's not to mention the incredible arrangements and seamless blend of styles Watson pulls off. Even without all the hits, this DJM package is quality all the way. *—Stephen Cook*

I Heard That / 1985 / Charly ✦✦✦✦✦
King-Federal sides from the 1950s and '60s, including the amazing "Space Guitar." *—Bill Dahl*

3 Hours Past Midnight / 1986 / Flair ✦✦✦✦
Watson's mid-'50s catalog for the Bihari brothers' Flair logo is unassailable with searing rockers like "Oh Baby," "Hot Little Mama," and "Ruben" and the blistering slow blues title cut. Unfortunately, this 16-song collection utilizes inferior alternate takes on several of the most important titles. On the positive side, it contains both sides of his rare 1959 single for Class, "One Kiss"/"The Bear." *—Bill Dahl*

Gonna Hit That Highway: The Complete RPM Recordings / 1992 / P-Vine ✦✦✦✦✦
No omissions with this two-disc Japanese set—not only are the official versions of all of Watson's vicious RPM sides here, so are a plethora of alternate takes and extreme rarities (including a demo version of "Gangster of Love" as "Love Bandit"). Could be tough to locate, but for anyone seriously into this brilliant guitarist's early blues output, absolutely essential! *—Bill Dahl*

Listen/I Don't Want to Be Alone, Stranger / 1992 / Fantasy ✦✦✦✦
Watson's first two funk-slanted albums, combined conveniently on one disc. *Listen* dates from 1973, *I Don't Want to Be Alone* from two years later, and both are very together funk outings with a heady dose of modern blues at their core. *—Bill Dahl*

Bow Wow / 1994 / Bellmark ✦✦
No matter how you felt about changes that Johnny "Guitar" Watson made during his long career, he always tried to keep current and go with the funky flow. *Bow Wow* finds Watson treading on disco, funk, and early rap territory. Even though Watson produced, wrote, and arranged these sessions, it often sounds as if someone else should have been in control to help keep up the energy. Most of this material would have been more effective if a funkmeister like George Clinton could have been at the production helm, found some better material, and completely pushed Watson to simply have fun as an innovator and elder statesman to an up and coming generation primed for the kind of mischief unfortunately missing from *Bow Wow*. *—Al Campbell*

Giant / 1994 / Collectables ✦✦✦
Disco rhythms rear their repetitive head on much of this 1978 set, making it a whole lot less likable than Watson's earlier DJM albums. But his updated "Gangster of Love" packs a killer groove and sports some nice, very concise blues guitar work by the man. *—Bill Dahl*

Hot Just Like TNT / 1996 / Ace ✦✦✦✦✦
This generous serving of 28 tracks focuses on Watson's mid-'50s recordings (both released and unissued) for RPM, throwing in some songs by singers Devonia Williams, Jeannie Barnes, and Cordella de Milo (on whose songs he was accompanist); a couple of 1957-1958 singles for Keen; and some previously unavailable tracks he recorded for Johnny Otis, probably dating from the late '50s and early '60s. This is worthwhile for fans of Watson in particular as well as fans of the R&B-blues crossover sound of the '50s in general. It's a patchy set, however, in which Watson and his associates try on several different styles for size, but not always with memorable success. Watson's stinging guitar is satisfying on cuts like "Hot Little Mama," and one can tell that it was probably played at a volume that challenged the limitations of 1950s engineering technology; but his playing is sometimes less to the fore in the arrangement than is desirable. For the most part, the material is adequate but not exciting. Sometimes it follows the lead of Watson's avowed hero Ray Charles, while other times it is shaded with doo wop and New Orleans R&B. On the Keen tracks he ventures into Larry Willliams-styled rock; on "Gangster of Love" (one of the standouts on the disc), he accomplishes swinging and boasting first-person-narrative blues. The tunes certainly aren't as impressive as the instrumental skills of Watson and the RPM/Modern house bands overseen by Maxwell Davis. Among the tracks, one will find the 1956 single "Three Hours Past Midnight"—a slow blues that, according to the liner notes, the teenaged Frank Zappa considered "his number one record which had a big influence on his own guitar playing." *—Richie Unterberger*

● **The Very Best of Johnny "Guitar" Watson: In Loving Memory** / Nov. 5, 1996 / Collectables ✦✦✦✦✦
Watson had been in the business for over 20 years before he began to amass a large following and achieved gold albums with his first two efforts for DJM. Despite the sad title, *The Very Best of Johnny "Guitar" Watson: In Loving Memory* is a great overview of his 1976 to 1980 work. He quietly started on his hit-making path on Fantasy with 1975's "I Don't Want to Be Lone Ranger." This set ignores that work but offers a healthy sampling from his commercial peak. By 1976 Watson had his sound down pat, his great "band" was essentially him on keyboards, guitar, and bass with drummer Emery Thomas and a three-piece horn section augmenting the patently laid-back sound. The great "Ain't That Bitch" found his caustic yet smooth style refined to perfection. His biggest hit, "A Real Mother for Ya," has great melodic changes and proved that as a "bluesman" Watson had more in common vocally with Leroy "Sugarfoot" Bonner and Mick Jagger, than, say, Bobby "Blue" Bland. "Tarzan," despite the silly title, has Watson doing great work on electric piano and, of course, the guitar. Shortly after, the tracks "Love That Will Not Die" and "What the Hell Is This?" well-addressed the disco and dance concerns; this effort proves that Watson did run out of ideas. The ballad "Love Jones" is a dispiriting rewrite of the Emotions' "Don't Ask My Neighbors." The laugh-proof "Telephone Bill" is an embarrassing stab at rap with an inane premise. The best work here proves that Watson was one of the more influential artists and is still enjoyable to listen to. *—Jason Elias*

★ **The Very Best of Johnny Guitar Watson** / Apr. 20, 1999 / Rhino ✦✦✦✦✦
Johnny "Guitar" Watson was a blues/R&B/funk pioneer, both in sound and music, and this 18-track collection zeroes in on his bluesiest and earliest sides. Watson was a true multi-talent and this set shows it off to great advantage while still staying firmly in the blues mode throughout; he was a blazing boogie-woogie pianist (check him out on the earlier version with Chuck Higgins of "Motorhead Baby"), a futuristic guitarist who influenced Bo Diddley and Ike Turner in the instrument-as-noisemaker department (1954's "Space Guitar"), a soulful singer who was both uptown and as gutbucket as you could possibly ask for (1962's "That's the Chance You've Got to Take" and 1955's "Three Hours Past Midnight," which also sports one mean and spare guitar solo), and an artist who understood low-down blues and bebop jazz and came up with his own melding of it. Watson is the lost genius of the blues and this set is a long overdue tribute to a true pioneer visionary. *—Cub Koda*

Gangster of Love / Nov. 28, 2000 / Collectables ✦✦✦✦

You Need It: Anthology / Aug. 20, 2002 / Castle ✦✦✦✦

The Essential Johnny Guitar Watson / Aug. 27, 2002 / Fuel 2000 ✦✦✦✦✦

Junior Watson

Vocals, Guitar / West Coast Blues
Despite playing the role of perrenial sideman, often in fine bands that left much to be desired in the visibility department, Mike "Junior" Watson was, and is, one of the most influential blues guitarists of his generation. In fact, following Robben Ford's defection into fusion, Watson was rivaled only by Hollywood Fats as king of the hill in California and only by Jimmie Vaughan anywhere else. While he and Vaughan have radically different approaches, Watson's arch-top-cheapo-through-reverb-tank sound has much in common with Hollywood Fats', as does his ability to nail seemingly every traditional electric blues style. But whereas Fats was a master of mimickry, Watson has a spontaneous, original bent laced with his oddball sense of humor.

After starting out with harpist Gary Smith in northern California in the early '70s, he teamed with Rod Piazza's Mighty Flyers (née Flying Sauce Band) for 11 years, where he was instrumental in injecting the Chicago-styled blues band (and countless others in its wake) with ample doses of swing, culling licks from guitarists Bill Jennings, Tiny Grimes, and Billy Butler. Along the way he gigged with Charlie Musselwhite, Jimmy Rogers, Luther Tucker, and others, eventually joining the '80s edition of Canned Heat, with whom he continued to tour until the late '90s. *—Dan Forte*

● **Long Overdue** / Jan. 24, 1994 / Black Top ✦✦✦✦✦
Giving jump blues and early R&B a kick in its baggy pants, Watson's aptly titled solo debut revealed what only guitarists (the more conscientious of them) had known for more than a decade: Here is a six-stringer of rare talent, with the unique ability to play authentically *and* spontaneously—all-too-often contradictory paths in the late '70s blues revival. The best and most fitting compliment one could give a Watson solo is that it makes you laugh; this is blues of the rent party variety and Watson never lapses into the maudlin. Along with singers Brenda Burns and Lynwood Slim (on harp as well), Watson favors us with half a dozen surprisingly confident vocals. In fact, the only criticism is that his voice is sometimes too low in the mix. *—Dan Forte*

Noble "Thin Man" Watts

b. Feb. 17, 1926, DeLand, FL
Sax (Tenor), Saxophone / East Coast Blues, R&B, Jump Blues, Jazz Blues
The 1950s R&B scene was rife with fire-breathing tenor sax honkers. Noble "Thin Man" Watts was one of the most incendiary. Watts enrolled at Florida A&M University in 1942 (his mates in the school marching band included future jazz luminaries Nat and Cannonball Adderley). The Griffin Brothers, one of Dot Records' top R&B acts (obviously, this was before the days when Randy Wood's label provided safe haven for the hopelessly pale likes of Pat Boone and Gale Storm) hired young Noble Watts after he got out of college. Watts joined baritone saxist Paul "Hucklebuck" Williams in 1952, recording with him for Jax and taking sax solos behind Dinah Washington, Amos Milburn, and Ruth Brown on the groundbreaking mid-'50s TV program *Showtime at the Apollo* (Williams led the house band for the Willie Bryant-hosted extravaganza). Later, there was a stint with Lionel Hampton.

Watts' own discography commenced in 1954 with a tasty coupling for DeLuxe ("Mashing Potatoes"/"Pig Ears and Rice"). A 1956 single for Vee-Jay with Williams' band ("South Shore Drive") came just prior to Watts' salad days on the New York-based Baton label. With his band, the Rhythm Sparks, in support, Watts wailed "Easy Going," "Blast Off," "Shakin'," "Flap Jack," and quite a few more searing instrumentals for Baton from 1957 to 1959, the biggest of all being "Hard Times (The Slop)," which propelled the saxist onto the pop charts in December of 1957. Guitar twanger Duane Eddy must have dug what he heard—he covered the grinding shuffle for Jamie a few years later. That wasn't Noble Watts' only connection to rock & roll—he played behind Jerry Lee Lewis, Buddy Holly, Chuck Berry, the Everly Brothers, and many more on various late-'50s package tours.

Boxer Sugar Ray Robinson managed Watts during the late '50s and early '60s, recruiting the saxist to lead the house band at the pugilist's Harlem lounge. Things got thin for the Thin Man during the '60s (45s for Sir, Cub, Enjoy, Peanut, Jell, Clamike, and Brunswick came and went without much notice) and '70s, but he mounted a comeback bid in 1987 with a fresh album, *Return of the Thin Man*, for Bob Greenlee's King Snake logo (later picked up by Alligator). *King of the Boogie Sax* followed in 1993 for Ichiban's Wild Dog imprint. Watts continues to work as a session saxist when he's not pursuing his own interests. *—Bill Dahl*

● **Return of the Thin Man** / 1987 / Alligator ✦✦✦✦
After taking several years off, Noble Watts returned in 1987 with *Return of the Thin Man*. Instead of following through on his storming, honking '50s and '60s R&B, Watts decided to take things in a different direction, toning things down a bit and concentrating on mellow grooves. There are a couple of uptempo workouts, of course, but the songs that make a lasting impression on *Return of the Thin Man* are the slower, conversational pieces that are warm, relaxed, and friendly. It's the sound of an aging master who has found strength in maturity and isn't afraid to celebrate that fact. *—Thom Owens*

Noble & Nat / 1990 / King Snake ✦✦✦✦
Watts and Nat Adderley. *—Niles J. Frantz*

King of The Boogie Sax / 1993 / Wild Dog ✦✦✦
A less inspired follow-up to Watts' previous outings for King Snake. *—Bill Dahl*

Carl Weathersby

b. Feb. 24, 1953, Jackson, MS

Guitar / Electric Chicago Blues, Soul-Blues

Vocalist, songwriter, and guitarist Carl Weathersby is a soul-blues crooner in the classic Chicago tradition. Best known for his work with Billy Branch and Sons of the Blues, Weathersby's first album, 1996's *Don't Lay Your Blues on Me*, was hailed as genuine, state-of-the-art Chicago blues for the '90s. Weathersby released his second album, *Looking Out My Window*, in 1997, and the raves continued; the song "The Blues Follow Me Around," which Weathersby first recorded with Branch, was nominated for a W.C. Handy Award.

Born in Jackson, MS, Weathersby was eight when his family moved to East Chicago, IN. He spent his summers back home with relatives in Mississippi. Weathersby grew up immersed in blues music and has many family links to the blues, R&B and Motown legacies: He's related to the late Leonard "Baby Doo" Caston, Willie Dixon's pianist in the Big Three Trio, a popular Chicago group in the early 1950s; Weathersby's cousin is Leonard Caston, Jr., a member of the Chicago soul group the Radiants, who had a 1965 Chess Records hit with "Voice Your Choice"; singer G.C. Cameron from the Motown group the Spinners is another cousin. Additionally, a neighbor was a cousin of Hound Dog Taylor, and Weathersby's father was friendly with Albert King. One day while Weathersby was practicing King's licks from a 45 rpm recording of "Crosscut Saw," his father and King overheard him. King encouraged the boy, who hadn't realized his identity until then, and eventually hired him as a rhythm guitarist for short road trips in 1979, 1980, and 1982.

Before becoming a full-time musician with Branch's Sons of the Blues, Weathersby worked in a steel mill, as a police officer, and as a prison guard. He also spent time in Vietnam serving in the Army from 1971 to 1977. His life experiences in all four occupations are rich fodder for his songwriting, which is as fresh, original, and life-affirming as one is likely to find from any other contemporary blues player.

Weathersby spent 14 years, from 1982 to 1996, with harmonica player Branch's Sons of the Blues before he decided to have a go at leading a band under his own name. For his Evidence albums, Weathersby is accompanied by two great New Orleans musicians, who add just the right touches of funk to the band's sound: David Torkanowsky on piano and keyboards and Herman Ernest III on drums, the latter a key element in Dr. John's quartet, the Lower 911. Weathersby's first album, *Don't Lay Your Blues on Me*, won nominations in the 1996 *Living Blues* Critics' Awards for Best New Blues Album, Best Blues Album, and Best Debut Album. Weathersby was also nominated for a 1997 W.C. Handy Blues Award for Best New Blues Artist. Subsequent outings include 1998's *Restless Feeling* and 2000's *Come to Papa. —Richard Skelly*

● **Don't Lay Your Blues on Me** / 1996 / Evidence ✦✦✦✦✦

Weathersby's debut CD as a session leader is a satisfactory set of contemporary guitar-driven blues. Weathersby plays in an Albert King style, typically bending and sustaining each note for all it's worth. Although his career is not associated with New Orleans, he recorded this album there with ace Crescent City sidemen Lee Zeno on bass, Herman Ernest III on drums, and Dave Torkanowsky on keyboards. They lay down a solid foundation that really cooks. —*Steve Hoffman*

Looking Out My Window / Aug. 26, 1997 / Evidence ✦✦✦✦

Although *Looking Out My Window* doesn't quite reach the same heights as Carl Weathersby's debut, *Don't Lay Your Blues on Me*, that's merely a relative judgment—the album remains an engaging piece of modern blues. Weathersby draws from both the Delta and Chicago traditions, creating a nice fusion. Occasionally, his playing is a little too flashy—if he reigned himself in, he would wind up saying more—but there's enough excitement in the band's interaction to make this a satisfying second effort. —*Thom Owens*

Restless Feeling / Sep. 29, 1998 / Evidence ✦✦✦

Come to Papa / Jun. 20, 2000 / Evidence ✦✦

Come to Papa is the fourth Evidence release from blues guitarist Carl Weathersby. While still retaining a blues edge, there is an undeniable Memphis Stax/soul influence that permeates these sessions, especially realized on the title track featuring guest vocalist Ann Peebles. Weathersby also tackles covers of Albert King's "Floodin' in California" and Charles Brown on "Drifting Blues." With plenty of spirited assistance from the Memphis Horns and Hammond B-3 organ and piano soul from Lucky Peterson, this could prove to be the release that gains Weathersby a wider audience. —*Al Campbell*

Curley Weaver

b. Mar. 26, 1906, Covington, GA, **d.** Sep. 20, 1962, Almon, GA

Vocals, Guitar, Guitar (Acoustic) / Piedmont Blues, Prewar Country Blues, Country Blues

Curley Weaver, who was known for much of his life as "the Georgia Guitar Wizard," is only just beginning to be appreciated as one of the best players ever to pick up a six-string instrument. Although he recorded a fair number of sides on his own during the 1920s and '30s, Weaver was most commonly heard in performances and recordings in association with his better known colleagues Blind Willie McTell (with whom he worked from the 1930s until the early '50s), Barbecue Bob, and Buddy Moss. Weaver was born in Newton County, GA, in Covington, and was raised on a cotton farm. His mother, Savannah "Dip" Weaver, encouraged him to sing from a very early age and also taught him to play the guitar, beginning when he was ten years old. Savannah "Dip" Weaver was a renowned guitarist in her own right around Newton County, and also taught guitar legends Barbecue Bob and his brother, Charlie Lincoln, to play the instrument when they were children. Her musical interests lay in gospel but, as in the case of Hicks and Lincoln, her son gravitated in the opposite direction, toward the blues. Curley Weaver learned to play slide guitar from two legendary (and, alas, never recorded) local bluesmen, Nehemiah Smith and Blind Buddy Keith. He showed extraordinary aptitude and, at age 19, teamed up with harmonica player Eddie Mapp, and moved to Atlanta. There he hooked up with Barbecue Bob and Charlie Lincoln, who

quickly showed their younger friend the ins-and-outs of life, busking on Decatur Street, the heart of Atlanta's black entertainment district, with its bars, restaurants, clubs, and theaters.

The association between the three guitarists was to prove providential. Barbecue Bob emerged as a local star first and, as a consequence, was also the first to go into the recording studio for the Columbia Records label in 1927—his first releases sold well, and he, in turn, arranged for his brother and Curley Weaver to make their debuts in the studio the following year. Weaver paid his first visit to the recording studio in Atlanta on October 26, 1928, laying down two tracks, "Sweet Petunia" and "No No Blues." Weaver's debut led to more recording work, both as a solo act and in the company of Eddie Mapp, as well as Barbecue Bob. It was also through the recording studio, appearing as the Georgia Cotton Pickers in association with Barbecue Bob, that Weaver first made the acquaintance of Buddy Moss, a 16-year-old harmonica player who learned guitar from Weaver and Bob and later emerged as a major star on the instrument himself. The two were to work together throughout the decade.

Although many of Weaver's recording sessions in the 1930s were in New York, he kept his home base in Atlanta for his entire life, and it was while playing at clubs, parties, dances, picnics, and even on streetcorners in the early part of the decade that he struck up the most important professional relationship of his life, with Blind Willie McTell. A renowned 12-string guitarist, McTell had begun his recording career in 1927, and was a local legend around Atlanta. The two played and recorded together for 20 years or more, and comprised one of the most important and celebrated East Coast blues teams in history. Weaver's most renowned recordings were done in association either with McTell or Moss, the latter under the guise of the Georgia Browns, during the mid-'30s. His playing, either on its own or in association with either McTell or Moss, was nothing less than dazzling. It wasn't possible for Weaver to sustain his brilliance, though not for lack of his ability or trying. The mid-'30s were a trying time for most blues players. The boom years of the late teens and very early '30s had seen lots of opportunities to perform and record. The Great Depression destroyed much of the marketplace that had led to these successes, and sales by the mid-'30s had, for most bluesmen dried up considerably from their former levels, and most labels cut back on the chances they were offering to record.

For Weaver, the decade was an even more bitter period. Barbecue Bob had died of pneumonia at the beginning of the 1930s. Eddie Mapp was killed, and Buddy Moss ended up in prison at age 21 on a five-year stretch that halted his career, essentially permanently. Weaver continued playing with McTell across the South, but the onset of World War II saw even a lot of this activity dry up. He continued to play around Atlanta, and in 1950 cut an album's worth of material with McTell for the Regal label. He continued playing whenever he could, and was reunited with Buddy Moss in a trio that performed in northern Georgia but never recorded. Weaver's performing career was brought to a halt only by the failure of his eyesight. He passed away three years later, in 1962, remembered around Atlanta and by serious blues enthusiasts elsewhere, but largely unheralded during the blues revival of which he'd just missed being a part.

Curley Weaver was, by virtue of his virtuosity and the associations that he kept throughout his life and career, a guitarist's guitarist, a virtuoso among a small coterie of Atlanta-based guitar wizards. He never had the renown of Blind Willie McTell, but he was Willie's equal and match in just about every conceivable respect as a player and singer, his six-string being perfectly mated to Willie's 12-string. When he was playing or recording with McTell, Buddy Moss, or Barbecue Bob, the results were the blues equivalent of what rock people later would've called a "super session" except that, as a listen to the surviving records reveals, the results were more natural and overpowering—these guys genuinely liked each other, and loved playing together, and it shows beyond the virtuosity of the music, in the warmth and elegance of the playing and the sound. —*Bruce Eder*

★ **Georgia Guitar Wizard (1928–1935)** / 1987 / Story of the Blues ✦✦✦✦

Why Atlanta blues guitarist and vocalist Curley Weaver is so obscure when cohorts Blind Willie McTell and Buddy Moss are so well-known is one of those why-ask-why deals. Weaver was an outstanding player and convincing singer, and this collection nicely outlines his attributes. McTell and Moss appear here in accompanying roles. —*Ron Wynn*

☆ **Complete Studio Recordings** / 1990 / Document ✦✦✦✦

Weaver's complete recordings, taking into account all of the sessions for Moss, McTell, et al. where he played guitar, would comprise a lot more than the 19 tracks here, but that's no reason not to spring for this slightly more expensive collection, which doesn't entirely overlap with the Story of the Blues disc. —*Bruce Eder*

Curley Weaver: 1933–1935 / Sep. 8, 2000 / Document ✦✦✦✦

Sylvester Weaver

b. Jul. 25, 1897, Louisville, KY, **d.** Apr. 4, 1960, Louisville, KY

Vocals, Arranger, Guitar / Piedmont Blues, Prewar Country Blues

Sylvester Weaver was a versatile guitarist of Louisville origin who made the first solo recordings of blues guitar playing. Information is lacking on Weaver's early years, though it is not unreasonable to assume that during this time he may have had some connection to the Louisville Jug Bands led by Earl MacDonald and Clifford Hayes. Sylvester Weaver first turns up in New York in 1923, where on October 23 of that year he accompanied vaudeville blues singer Sara Martin on two numbers, "Longing for Daddy Blues" and "I've Got to Go and Leave My Daddy Behind," for OKeh. Two weeks later, Weaver cut his first pair of solo recordings, "Guitar Blues" and "Guitar Rag," for the same concern.

The Sara Martin selections represented the first time on records that a popular female singer had been backed up solely by guitar, and were an immediate success. Weaver would be assigned to cut 25 more selections accompanying Martin in the years through 1927. As to the fate of Weaver's own first recorded solos, they were equally well received and would prove massively influential in the country market. "Guitar Rag" was later reinvented by Bob Wills into "Steel Guitar Rag" and became a country standard. Through the end of 1927, when Weaver decided to retire from music altogether, he recorded a total of 26 solo sides, and on some of the later ones Weaver was joined by another guitarist, Walter Beasley. In addition to his own solo selections, Weaver made four recordings in accompaniment to Beasley.

All of the issued records were avidly snapped up by customers in the rural mail-order market, and both the Weaver solo items and the Weaver and Beasley records were well-known to string band musicians in the American South and West. Sylvester Weaver's work lies stylistically between blues and country music, and he had considerable impact on both musical fronts; among his recorded solos he made both a banjo record and several solos which make use of a bottleneck style slide (probably a pocket knife in Weaver's case). Although four of Weaver's pieces, including the banjo solo, were rejected by OKeh, all but one of these have been recovered and issued since.

After his heady days in New York had ended, Sylvester Weaver returned to Louisville and entered another line of work. Weaver was almost totally forgotten by the time he died in 1960. One player who still recalled Weaver was Lonnie Johnson, who remembered him as a good player, outstanding songwriter, and somebody who deserved a great deal more credit for his efforts than he would ever receive in his lifetime. In 1992 the Kentucky Blues Society raised enough funds to place a headstone on the grave of Sylvester Weaver, and this same organization presents its Sylvester Weaver Award annually to "those who have dedicated their lives to presenting, preserving, and perpetuating the blues." *—Uncle Dave Lewis*

- **Smoketown Strut** / 1923 / Agram ✦✦✦✦
  Weaver's earliest and best sides, including "Guitar Rag." The sound is horrible in spots, but every note of the music is great. *—Cub Koda*

Complete Recorded Works, Vol. 1 (1923–1927) / 2000 / Document ✦✦✦✦

Complete Recorded Works, Vol. 2 (1927) / 2000 / Document ✦✦✦✦

Bill "Boogie Bill" Webb

b. Mar. 24, 1924, Jackson, MS, **d.** Aug. 22, 1990, New Orleans, LA

Vocals, Guitar / Louisiana Blues, Electric Country Blues, New Orleans R&B

Although he lived in New Orleans most of his life, and none other than Fats Domino brought him to Imperial Records for his recording debut in 1953, Boogie Bill Webb was never much a part of the New Orleans R&B scene. Webb's music grew out of the Jackson area country blues tradition of Tommy Johnson and others, and he retained a down-home, idiosyncratic approach to a wide range of material from C&W to R&B and traditional jazz. Beginning in 1966, Webb recorded occasionally for folklorists and field researchers, finally recording his first full album in 1989 with funding from the Louisiana Endowment for the Humanities. Album producer Ben Sandmel, who also played drums with Webb for five years, described Boogie Bill's approach as "quirky, often anarchic," but it is appealing in its very unpredictability, humor, and warmth. *—Jim O'Neal*

- **Drinkin' & Stinkin'** / 1989 / Flying Fish ✦✦✦✦
  Boogie Bill had cut a few stray sides for Imperial back in the early 1950s that surfaced on vinyl in the '70s on a couple of blues compilations, but this is his only full-length album. Produced by journalist and Hackberry Rambler drummer Ben Sandmel (who thumps the tubs and scrubs the washboard on this), Webb was in fine and totally idiosyncratic form on this. The tunes range from re-creations of his early sides ("Bill's Boogie Woogie"), tunes learned from Leadbelly ("Red Cross Store"), Lowell Fulson ("Black Night"), and Tommy Johnson (a heartfelt tribute version of "Canned Heat"), originals that have deep roots in vaudeville ("You Can't Tell My Business After Dark" and the slow blues title track), black oral tradition "toasts" ("Paul Jones and Little Virginia Dare"), and a ballad, "Love Me Cause I Love My Baby So," that is so structurally odd in its meter that it almost qualifies as abstract art. As if this wasn't wide-ranging enough, Webb closes the album with his version of King Curtis' "Soul Serenade," showing that his singular disregard for time isn't just restricted to older blues forms. Few blues albums are as much fun as this, or stamped with the full force of an artist's personality. *—Cub Koda*

Jitterbug Webb

b. Sep. 28, 1941, San Antonio, TX, **d.** Nov. 1997, San Antonio, TX

Guitar / Texas Blues, Electric Texas Blues, Soul-Blues

What ho, another great Texas bluesman? The largest state has produced quite a few great players in this genre, and fans of Jitterbug Webb can only hope that one day he will receive the recognition and status of T-Bone Walker or Johnny Winter. After all, neither of these stellar Texas blues guitar giants can claim that they backed up the Monkees. Born William or "Willie," he picked up the nickname of "Jitterbug" quite early in the game because he happened to be one of those babies who learns to walk early and how to jump around only a few days later. Since he never seemed to sit still, his mother and grandmother discovered music as a kind of distraction, or hopefully even an aural sedative. His mother played piano, mostly gospel, but also some down-home blues. One of Webb's earliest memories was, at six, listening to his mother playing 78s by the classic blues artist Peetie Wheatstraw. She encouraged the young Jitterbug to take trumpet and guitar lessons, beginning at the age of nine.

The church featured heavily in his upbringing, and he sang in the youth choir in San Antonio. But like his mom, he had antennae out and ready for the so-called music of the devil: jazz and blues. As a teenager in the early '50s, he went to many concerts such as the Jazz at the Philharmonic extravaganzas and gigs featuring the smooth singer Arthur Prysock, the one and only Louis Armstrong, R&B pioneer Louis Jordan, and others. Radio was also an important factor, introducing him to artists such as the blues shouter Big Joe Turner, as well as essential recording artists of the day such as Clyde McPhatter, Johnny Ace, and of course guitarist T-Bone Walker, who seems to have had the same relationship with the Texas blues scene that Moses had with the Ten Commandments. Groundwork was being laid for a musical career via going to gigs, but the next important part of this foundation was personal contact with real working musicians. When he was still a child, Jitterbug had a neighbor who was a landlord, and one of his tenants was none other than Big Walter "Thunderbird" Price, at that point in the midst of an extended San Antonio residency. Jitterbug had ambitions to become this man's guitarist, and even secured an audition although it is not known for sure whether Price was aware that the pimply picker was all of 13 years old. At any rate, he didn't cut the audition, although it was only a year later when Webb actually became a professional musician. Ironically, it would take 40 years for him to be reunited with the man who had turned him down, when Webb and Price headlined a blues festival in San Antonio in 1994.

Webb formed his own band at 14, optimistically naming it the Five Stars. These original members, hardly stars of any sort but worth mentioning for historical purposes, were Walter Johnson on sax and keyboards, Billy Wilson on tenor sax, Mack Wilson on trombone but later switching to drums, Robert Boyd on drums, and McCarly Luke on alto sax and vocals. The group did become popular around the San Antonio area in the late '50s, playing clubs, dancehalls, and military bases. In 1956, the band went to Houston and recorded two numbers for the Duke/Peacock label. "I cannot remember the names of the tunes," Webb admitted in what perhaps was a senior moment in an extended interview, but the recordings never saw the light of day, whatever they were. Had the tracks been released, it might have established Webb as one of the youngest blues artists to ever record, give or take a Shuggie Otis. Tenor sax player Jimmy Johnson, who would later record on many sessions for the Motown label, was a major influence on Webb at the time, teaching him just about everything he would ever learn about jazz, which he managed to incorporate into his blues playing.

Webb headed west in 1958 with fellow bluesman and friend Ricky Aguary to see what they could get happening on the West Coast. A band developed, Ricky Aguary & the Keys, whose success could be judged by how often the members wound up sleeping on the beach. Not exactly thrilled with these accommodations at the age of 17, Webb limped back home grabbed a gig with the local band Charlie & the Jives. It turned out to be a good time to be in the Alamo city, as the '60s music scene began exploding with blend of R&B, Southern soul, and Tex-Mex. Local artists Webb performed with during this period included Cora Woods, Freddy Fender, Doug Sahm, Johnny Olen, Augie Meyers, Rocky Morales, and Charlie Alvarado. With the latter artist, Webb recorded for the Harlem label in the early '60s. This was the Charlie & the Jives band that had kept Webb from being washed off like driftwood while he tried to get a good night's sleep. The San Antonio audience demanded versatility. Musicians couldn't just get by on being funky, they also had to whip off conjuntos, boleros, or polkas. Bands had to know all the new rock & roll hits as well. Jitterbug re-formed the Five Stars band and began touring farther afield, as far north as Illinois and south as Louisiana.

During the course of these road tours, Webb encountered the equally roaming bandleader Ike Turner several times, and eventually Webb would be hired on the spot after being asked to sit in with Turner's band at a nightclub in the steaming south central district of Los Angeles in 1966. Turner's Kings of Rhythm band also included tenor saxophonist Clifford Solomon, keyboardist Ernest Lane, trumpeter Gabriel Flemings, and baritone saxophonist Johnny Williams, as well as Webb, Turner, and last but hardly least, the dynamite singer Tina Turner. Webb's chores would change from lead to rhythm guitar during the course of the show as the various performers made their star entrances. Webb also recorded with Ike Turner during this time at the leader's studio in California. Webb finally left the revue over money worries, despite the fact that the hit "River Deep, Mountain High" was flowing on the radio and peaking on the charts. It was back to his home ground of making music, good old San Antonio. He took up right where he had left off on that local scene, and in 1968 he got a call from several ex-members of Turner's band who were performing in Houston under the name of Sam & the Good-Timers. Sam was bassist and vocalist Sam Rhodes. Webb again tried the West Coast, this time doing better than a blanket of sand by meeting up with the R&B bandleader and legend Johnny Otis. He also began recording regularly in Los Angeles, cutting sides with bluesmen Lowell Fulson and Charles Brown for Savoy. Under the direction of Maxwell Davis, Webb and his sidemen became a house band for this label, which recorded much classic jazz, blues, and R&B material. Webb also recorded with gospel singer Charles May, also for Savoy.

Meanwhile Webb's band was burning the midnight candle at all the local nightclubs, playing gigs, and rubbing shoulders with artists such as soul singer and songwriter Percy Mayfield and rock legend Little Richard. According to the latter artist, who was also an early employer of Jimi Hendrix, Webb was the "funkiest guitar player in the world." Richard offered Webb a job in his band several times, but it was always turned down as the guitarist preferred being the bandleader himself. It was during one of the Good-Timers' nightclub residencies that the band came to the attention of the prefabricated rock group the Monkees, who went to hear Webb and his cohorts almost every night for two weeks before inviting the band on a Monkees' tour. In 1970, following a month of rehearsals, the bands began their combined tour, the Good-Timers also playing their own opening set on an itinerary that took Webb farther away from Texas than he had ever been before, including countries such as France and Tunisia. Prestigious television work also came along, including *The Tonight Show*, *The Joey Bishop Show*, and an episode of *Music Scene* with host David Steinberg that was coincidentally the last live show that the famous comedian Groucho Marx would be featured on. Out of the past came contact Johnny Otis, who hired Webb to play guitar on a tour with himself, Joe Turner, and Eddie "Cleanhead" Vinson.

It was the ill health of his father that brought Webb back to San Antonio after several more fruitful years on the West Coast. As a musician in the '80s, he became more of a weekend warrior and formed several business ventures in order to survive. He took the idea of an alternative to the music business very seriously, studying both real estate and financial management. He wound opening his own bar, dry cleaner, and liquor store, none of which satisfied or eliminated his love of music, although it might have been convenient for getting drunk and/or doing the laundry. Webb recalled that during this period in his life he constantly had music going through his head, and "finally just submitted to the calling..." He formed the Super Crew in 1987, mixing together both youngsters and veterans of the Texas music scene, including Albert Gotson on bass, Robert Benitez on tenor sax, Chip Skaggs on trombone, Al Garcia on drums, and James Morales on trumpet. The music Webb was hearing in his head must have been predominantly tunes of his own invention, because from the late '80s on he began composing prolifically. His most famous song is entitled "That's the Way Life Is." Webb was nominated and crowned the "Blues King" during a 1994 San Antonio city festival, receiving a special proclamation from the mayor, but more importantly sharing billing with another blues king, B.B. King. A few years later, Webb contracted cancer. *—Eugene Chadbourne*

Katie Webster (Kathryn Jewel Thorne)

b. Jan. 11, 1936, Houston, TX, **d.** Sep. 5, 1999, League City, TX

Vocals, Piano, Harmonica, Organ / Swamp Blues, Louisiana Blues, New Orleans Blues, R&B

A piano-pounding institution on the southern Louisiana swamp blues scene during the late '50s and early '60s, Katie Webster later grabbed a long-deserved share of national recognition with a series of well-received Alligator albums.

Poor Kathryn Thorne had to deal with deeply religious parents who did everything in their power to stop their daughter from playing R&B. But the rocking sounds of Fats Domino and Little Richard were simply too persuasive. Local guitarist Ashton Savoy took her under his wing, sharing her 1958 debut 45 for the Kry logo ("Baby Baby").

Webster rapidly became an invaluable studio sessioneer for Louisiana producers J.D. Miller in Crowley and Eddie Shuler in Lake Charles. She played on sides by Guitar Junior (Lonnie Brooks), Clarence Garlow, Jimmy Wilson, Lazy Lester, and Phil Phillips (her gently rolling 88s powered his hit "Sea of Love").

The young pianist also waxed some terrific sides of her own for Miller from 1959 to 1961 for his Rocko, Action, and Spot labels (where she introduced a dance called "The Katie Lee"). Webster led her own band, the Uptighters, at the same time she was spending her days in the studio. In 1964, she guested with Otis Redding's band at the Bamboo Club in Lake Charles and so impressed the charismatic Redding that he absconded with her. For the next three years, Webster served as his opening act!

The 1970s were pretty much a lost decade for Katie Webster as she took care of her ailing parents in Oakland, CA. But in 1982 a European tour beckoned, and she journeyed overseas for the first of many such jaunts. The Alligator connection commenced in 1988 with some high-profile help: Bonnie Raitt, Robert Cray, and Kim Wilson all made guest appearances on *The Swamp Boogie Queen*. The lovably extroverted boogie pianist encored with *Two-Fisted Mama!* and *No Foolin'* before suffering a stroke. She died on September 5, 1999, at the age of 63. *—Bill Dahl*

You Know That's Right / Apr. 1985 / Arhoolie ♦♦♦

I Know That's Right / 1987 / Arhoolie ♦♦♦

I Know That's Right is an OK step in the venerable boogie pianist's comeback bid, but the mediocre band backing she receives on most cuts doesn't add much to the swampy brew. *—Bill Dahl*

The Swamp Boogie Queen / 1988 / Alligator ♦♦♦♦

Lovable Katie Webster had some high-profile help for this impressive comeback album—Bonnie Raitt shares the vocal on "Somebody's on Your Case" and plays guitar on "On the Run"; Kim Wilson duets with Webster for a cover of Johnnie Taylor's "Who's Making Love" (a track that Robert Cray contributes crisp guitar to). Throughout, Webster's vocals are throatier than they used to be (she soulfully covers one-time mentor Otis Redding's "Fa-Fa-Fa-Fa-Fa [Sad Song]" and "Try a Little Tenderness"), while her driving left hand still lays down some powerhouse boogie rhythms. *—Bill Dahl*

Two-Fisted Mama! / 1990 / Alligator ♦♦♦♦

Another impressive showcase for Katie Webster's rollicking 88s and earthy vocals. Other than the Memphis Horns, no special guests this time—just Webster and her tight trio (anchored by guitarist Vasti Jackson). *—Bill Dahl*

Katie Webster / 1991 / Paula ♦♦♦♦♦

Webster is at her full bayou-bred boogie-blues best here, when she was the queen of south Louisiana's swamp sessioneers. Webster's own late-'50s/early-'60s output for producer J.D. Miller was no less captivating; her self-named dance number "The Katie Lee" and "Mama Don't Allow" that uproots the Gary U.S. Bonds party vibe to New Orleans are two of the best items on the 20-track disc. There's also her blues-drenched "No Bread, No Meat" and a nice version of "Sea of Love" (Webster added the gently rolling piano to Phil Phillips' original hit). *—Bill Dahl*

No Foolin'! / 1991 / Alligator ♦♦♦

Katie Webster is a powerful singer who can really belt out the blues, but perhaps her greatest skill is her two-handed piano solos. On this CD she is featured on a fairly wide range of material within the idiom including a zydeco-flavored blues, a sincere blues ballad ("It's Mighty Hard"), a couple of Motown-ish soul numbers, a rock & roll-ish "Those Lonely Lonely Nights" (on which she shares vocals with Lonnie Brooks), and, best of all, a variety of basic blues. Although she also contributes some atmospheric chordal organ, it is Katie Webster's piano playing that gives her music its most distinctive personality. A fun set. *—Scott Yanow*

● **Deluxe Edition** / Feb. 23, 1999 / Alligator ♦♦♦♦♦

Katie Webster plays barrelhouse boogie-woogie, New Orleans R&B, Gulf Coast swamp pop, deep bayou blues, and Southern gospel-flavored soul like nobody's business; her 35 years of professional piano work has appeared on at least 500 singles, including the original version of "Sea of Love," and countless albums. Music critics and fans around the world acknowledge her as the premier female blues piano player anywhere. Alligator Records' *Deluxe Edition* collects 15 of her very best tracks from her three albums since 1988, and there isn't a filler track to be found. Webster never once failed to deliver on her sassy and sensuous blend of barrelhouse boogie-woogie. Some of the high points of *Deluxe Edition* include several duets—"Love Deluxe" with Vasti Jackson and the classic "Who's Making Love," which finds Kim Wilson (the Fabulous Thunderbirds) and bluesman Robert Cray jamming with the Boogie Queen. Wilson also accompanies Bonnie Raitt and Webster to wail "On the Run." Other standout tracks include her remake of "Sea of Love" and the non-vegetarian "A Little Meat on the Side." "The Love You Save" and "Two Fisted Mama" are sure to go down in the music history books as prime examples of Webster's swamp boogie styles. But perhaps the best cuts of the 15 are the blues-rich vocals and sax of "Try a Little Tenderness," a sure winner, and "Never Let Me Go," a torch-bearing ballad. Alligator's *Deluxe Editions* are just that—the best songs by the best artists in their catalog. And Katie Webster ranks right there at the top of that rich list. *—Michael B. Smith*

Weepin' Willie (William Lorenzo Robinson)

b. Jul. 6, 1926, Atlanta, GA

Vocals / Modern Electric Blues

Known as "Boston's Elder Statesman of the Blues," vocalist Weepin' Willie decided on a music career after getting hooked on the polished, urban blues style pioneered by the likes of B.B. King, Bobby "Blue" Bland, and Joe Williams. Remarkably, it took Willie 50 years of working the clubs as an MC and singer before he got his first record deal (with APO) in 1998. The resulting album, *At Last, on Time*, was co-produced by Mighty Sam McClain and its release garnered Willie some belated recognition for his hard-earned life as a bluesman.

Born William Lorenzo Robinson in Atlanta, GA, in 1926, Willie grew up as a field worker drifting from farm to farm along the East Coast. After finishing a three-year stint in the army in 1948, Willie moved to Trenton, NJ, where he began MCing jazz and R&B gigs under the name Willie the Weeper. Over the next decade he warmed up the stage for a long line of entertainers passing through Trenton, including B.B. King, Lloyd Price, Titus Turner, and Bill Doggett. At the same time, Willie also discovered his own talent as a singer and he began fronting a blues combo led by saxophonist Jimmy Taylor.

In 1959, Willie moved to Boston and changed his stage name to Weepin' Willie. Through the '60s he found steady work as an MC, including a regular gig opening for R&B singer Tommy Hunt. When Hunt decided to move to England, Willie stayed behind and joined forces with bassist Buddy Johnson to form the Buddy Johnson/Weepin' Willie All-Star Band, which lasted until Johnson's death in 1998. Willie subsequently took over the band, which then became known as Weepin' Willie and the All-Star Blues Band. Notable All-Star alumni include sax players Gordon "Sax" Beadle (of the Duke Robillard Band), Lynwood Cooke (of Luther "Guitar Junior" Johnson's Magic Rockers, and Emmett Simmons (a former James Brown sideman who has performed with Willie on and off since 1964).

Prior to 1999's *At Last, on Time*, Willie had only recorded once, cutting "Can't Go Wrong Woman" for the 1991 Tone-Cool compilation *Boston Blues Blast, Vol. 1*. *—Ken Chang*

● **At Last, on Time** / May 2, 2000 / APO ♦♦♦

Weepin' Willie's long-awaited debut album (he was 72 when he recorded it) finally got made thanks to the efforts of Mighty Sam McClain, who co-produced the session, wrote or co-wrote five of the songs, and sang on three. Although Willie waited 50 years to record this album, *At Last, on Time* certainly doesn't sound like it was 50 years in the making; McClain rather hastily steers Willie's sound in more of a soul/R&B direction, which seems to have left Willie relying on the arrangements instead of his usual blues instincts. Still, Willie manages to find his stride here, especially on the slow blues numbers "Dirty Old Man," "They Call Me Weepin' Willie," and "Can't Go Wrong Woman," the latter featuring Jimmy D. Lane on lead guitar. The other special guest on this album is Susan Tedeschi, whose overpowering vocal histrionics, unfortunately, tend to clash with Willie's subtler, dapper style of singing; furthermore, when McClain chimes in on "Glory Train" and "Let the Good Times Roll," Willie's voice all but gets lost in the threesome. Perhaps Willie didn't get as much room to stretch out as he would have liked, but his performance on *At Last, on Time* nonetheless comes off as pretty solid. *—Ken Chang*

Mike Welch

b. Boston, MA

Guitar, Vocals, Producer / Modern Electric Blues

Mike Welch is a Boston-area blues guitarist, vocalist, and songwriter who has released several albums on the Rounder Tone-Cool subsidiary. The fact that he's so good and so young part of the reason why they call him "Monster." Welch got his name from actor/comedian/Blues Brother Dan Aykroyd, although the moniker was dropped following his second album.

Welch's releases for Tone-Cool, which essentially launched his career as an international touring act, include a 1996 release, *These Blues Are Mine*, and his 1997 album, *Axe to Grind*. He returned in 1998 with *Catch Me*.

He began his blues education with his father's record collection, and he picked up the guitar at age eight and tried to emulate the sounds he heard from recordings by Magic Sam, Earl Hooker, and B.B. King. Welch also studied the rock & roll and blues-rock records of the Beatles and the Rolling Stones, but after hearing more of Albert King and other blues guitarists, he found his calling in life.

When he was 11, his parents began driving him to blues jams around Boston. In the clubs, Welch learned from some of the greats of that scene, including Ronnie Earl and Luther "Guitar Junior" Johnson. Welch was invited to play at the opening of the first House of Blues club in Cambridge, MA, in 1992. After co-owner Aykroyd heard him, his nickname changed from "Little Mikey" to "Monster Mike."

A few months later, Welch began working with George Lewis, who ran the blues jams at House of Blues, to put together the Monster Mike Welch Band. Welch is accompanied on his records by Lewis on guitar, Jon Ross on bass, and Warren Grant on drums. Welch's biting, stinging Albert King-style guitar playing has better-than-average backing from these three on his Tone-Cool releases.

The crop of original songs he wrote on his first albums for Tone-Cool demonstrate his prowess as a crafty blues songwriter. Welch has a bright future. All indications are that Welch, who got a flood of publicity because of his age and was even quoted in *People* magazine ("being an adolescent is more than enough blues for anyone to handle"), should go on to a lengthy and varied career as a bluesman. *—Richard Skelly*

- **These Blues Are Mine** / 1996 / Tone-Cool ♦♦♦♦

He was only 16 years old at the time of release, but you wouldn't know it from the way he plays guitar—this kid has the chops some seasoned professionals dream of, and has gained a lot of respect for them. The big problem comes when he opens his mouth to sing—he does a creditable job of trying to nail down that rough blues vocal tone, but he more often than not sounds just like a kid trying to get to a grown-up voice. Meanwhile, his band is well-worn and the songwriting is definitely up to par. *—Steven McDonald*

Axe to Grind / Feb. 11, 1997 / Tone-Cool ♦♦♦

Catch Me / Jun. 9, 1998 / Tone-Cool ♦♦♦♦

In the kid-blues sweepstakes, "Monster" Mike Welch was one of the first on the scene and one who quickly got lost in the shuffle. This probably had more to do with his non-Hanson-like looks (à la Kenny Wayne Shepherd and Jonny Lang) than his actual talent on his instrument, never a real consideration in these matters. Therefore in a move to distance himself from the pack and grab a little credibility in the bargain, his third album finds him dropping the teenybopper "Monster Mike" tag, growing a beard, and scowling into the camera whenever possible. Musically, this time around shows little growth since his previous two outings. Welch dials in every SRV-approved sound from his Stratocaster and his playing is still highly derivative, offering note-for-note guitar runs from everyone from Magic Sam to Albert Collins to B.B. King. To his credit, however, Welch sounds less like a Stevie Ray "Vaughnabee" than Kenny Wayne Shepherd does, and if his vocals are wispy-kid embarrassing on tunes like "Catch Me" and "My Love Belongs to You," he never tries to strangle his voice to attain Jonny Lang's phony blues rasp. But nobody can deny that Welch can play his rear end off; if all blues album were ever meant to be was one big hot lick festival, then this one would rank as an all-time great. *—Cub Koda*

Casey Bill Weldon

b. Jul. 10, 1909, Pine Bluff, AR

Vocals, Guitar (Steel) / Prewar Country Blues, Country Blues, Acoustic Blues, Jug Band

Among the premier "Hawaiian" guitarists, Casey Bill Weldon's voicings, fluidity, and tunings were creative and imaginative, as were his arrangements. He was married to Memphis Minnie in the '20s, and they made some superb recordings together in the late '20s. Weldon played in medicine shows before beginning his recording career in 1927 for Victor. There were later dates for Champion, Vocalion, and Bluebird. Weldon recorded and played with the Memphis Jug Band, Charlie Burse and the Picaninny Jug Band, and the Brown Bombers of Swing. He moved to the West Coast in the '40s and purportedly recorded for several soundtracks. Weldon moved to Detroit and left the music world in the '60s. *—Ron Wynn*

- **Bottleneck Guitar Trendsetters of the 1930s** / 1992 / Yazoo ♦♦♦♦

Outstanding bottleneck guitar and above-average singing from Casey Bill Weldon, one of the least publicized but tremendous prewar stylists. *—Ron Wynn*

Complete Recorded Works, Vol. 1 (1935–1936) / Jun. 2, 1994 / Document ♦♦♦♦

Nearly nothing is known about Casey Bill Weldon, a fine blues performer who recorded 100 titles under his own name. He is believed to have recorded with the Memphis Jug Band in 1927 (when he led his first sessions) and then nothing was heard from him until 1935, when he re-emerged as a steel guitarist and vocalist, recording for Vocalion and Bluebird. Three CDs from Document have all of Weldon's post-1934 recordings. The music ranges from low-down blues to good-time romps with Weldon usually joined by Peetie Wheatstraw (whose vocal style influenced him) or Black Bob on piano and sometimes Bill Settles on bass. One four-song session is with a version of the Washboard Rhythm Kings that has clarinetist Arnett Nelson, Tampa Red on kazoo and/or guitar, and Washboard Sam on washboard, in addition to Weldon. Among the 25 numbers on this CD are "What's the Matter With My Milk Cow," "My Stove Won't Work," "Howlin' Dog Blues," "Somebody Changed the Lock on That Door," and "Let Me Be Your Butcher." Blues collectors will want to explore Casey Bill Weldon's music. *—Scott Yanow*

Complete Recorded Works, Vol. 2 (1936–1937) / Jun. 2, 1994 / Document ♦♦♦♦

Singer and steel guitarist Casey Bill Weldon may be obscure today, but he recorded enough material in a three-year period to fill up three CDs. *Vol. 2* has five unissued performances (four of which are alternate takes) among the 25 performances. Various selections have Weldon joined by pianist Black Bob, Tampa Red or Big Bill Broonzy on guitars, Charlie McCoy on mandolin, and clarinetist Arnett Nelson. Weldon is best remembered for his composition "We Gonna Move to the Outskirts of Town," and the original version of that future standard is a highlight of this disc, along with such numbers as "I'se Just a Bad Luck Man," "Streamline Woman," "I Believe I'll Make a Change," and the good-time "Oh, Red." *—Scott Yanow*

Complete Recorded Works, Vol. 3 (1937–1938) / Jun. 2, 1994 / Document ♦♦♦

Guitar Swing / Apr. 30, 2002 / Catfish ♦♦♦

Valerie Wellington (Valerie Eileen Hall)

b. Nov. 14, 1959, Chicago, IL, **d.** Jan. 2, 1993, Maywood, IL

Vocals / Modern Electric Chicago Blues

Valerie Wellington took the Chicago blues scene by surprise in 1982, perhaps not forgoing her classical training as an opera singer as much as using it to enhance her work in the blues. As a blueswoman she fit right in, not only becoming a regular in the blues clubs but also compiling an impressive theatrical resumé for her portrayals of Ma Rainey and Bessie Smith—women who, like opera singers, learned to project their voices without microphones. The influence of Koko Taylor was also evident in Wellington's blues approach, which combined classic vaudeville-era blues with hard-driving Chicago sounds. Her power-packed voice was heard on only a few record releases but was featured frequently in TV and radio commercials. Valerie Wellington was only 33 years old when she died of a brain aneurysm. *—Jim O'Neal*

- **Million Dollar $ecret** / Oct. 1984 / Flying Fish ♦♦♦♦♦

Wellington is a powerful yet subtle vocalist, backed by some of the best Chicago blues players, including Sunnyland Slim, Billy Branch, Casey Jones, and Magic Slim & the Teardrops. The CD reissue contains two bonus tracks. *—Niles J. Frantz*

Life in the Big City / 1991 / GBW ♦♦

Want to hear the late Chicago belter warble "Trouble in Mind" in Japanese? That's the strongest track on her last disc, but much of the set is pretty mundane. *—Bill Dahl*

Junior Wells (Amos Blackmore)

b. Dec. 9, 1934, Memphis, TN, **d.** Jan. 15, 1998

Vocals, Leader, Harmonica / Blues Revival, Modern Electric Chicago Blues, Electric Harmonica Blues, Electric Chicago Blues

He was one bad dude, strutting across the stage like a harp-toting gangster, mesmerizing the crowd with his tough-guy antics and rib-sticking Chicago blues attack. Amazingly, Junior Wells kept at precisely this sort of thing for over 40 years—he was an active performer from the dawn of the 1950s to his death in the late '90s.

Born in Memphis, Wells learned his earliest harp licks from another future legend, Little Junior Parker, before he came to Chicago at age 12. In 1950, the teenager passed an impromptu audition for guitarists Louis and David Myers at a house party on the South Side, and the Deuces were born. When drummer Fred Below came aboard, they changed their name to the Aces.

Little Walter left Muddy Waters in 1952 (in the wake of his hit instrumental, "Juke"), and Wells jumped ship to take his place with Waters. That didn't stop the Aces (who joined forces with Little Walter) from backing Wells on his initial sessions for States Records, though—his debut date produced some seminal Chicago blues efforts, including his first reading of "Hoodoo Man," a rollicking "Cut That Out," and the blazing instrumentals "Eagle Rock" and "Junior's Wail."

More fireworks ensued the next year when he encored for States with a mournful "So All Alone" and the jumping "Lawdy! Lawdy!" (Muddy Waters moonlighted on guitar for the session). Already Wells was exhibiting his tempestuous side—he was allegedly AWOL from the Army at the time.

In 1957, Wells hooked up with producer Mel London, who owned the Chief and Profile logos. The association resulted in many of Wells' most enduring sides, including "I Could Cry" and the rock & rolling "Lovey Dovey Lovely One" in 1957; the grinding national R&B hit "Little by Little" (with Willie Dixon providing vocal harmony) in 1959, and the R&B-laced classic "Messin' with the Kid" in 1960 (sporting Earl Hooker's immaculate guitar work). Wells' harp was de-emphasized during this period on record in favor of his animated vocals.

With Bob Koester producing, the harpist cut an all-time classic LP for Delmark in 1965. *Hoodoo Man Blues* vividly captured the feel of a typical Wells set at Theresa's Lounge, even though it was cut in a studio. With Buddy Guy (initially billed as "Friendly Chap" due to his contract with Chess) providing concise lead guitar, Wells laid down definitive versions of "Snatch It Back and Hold It," "You Don't Love Me," and "Chittlin' Con Carne."

The harpist made his second appearance on the national R&B lists in 1968 with a funky James Brown-tinged piece, "You're Tuff Enough," for Mercury's feisty Blue Rock logo. Wells had been working in this bag for some time, alarming the purists but delighting R&B fans; his brass-powered 1966 single for Bright Star, "Up in Heah," had previously made a lot of local noise.

After a fine mid-'70s set for Delmark (*On Tap*), little was heard from Wells on vinyl for an extended spell, though he continued to enjoy massive appeal at home (Theresa's was his principal haunt for many a moon) and abroad (whether on his own or in partnership with Guy; they opened for the Rolling Stones on one memorable tour and cut an inconsistent but interesting album for Atco in the early '70s).

Toward the end of his career, Wells just didn't seem to be into recording anymore; a pair of sets for Telarc in the early '90s were major disappointments, but his last studio session, 1997's *Come on in This House*, found him on the rebound and the critics noticed—the album won the W.C. Handy Blues Award for Traditional Blues Album in 1997. Even when he came up short in the studio, Wells remained a potent live attraction, cutting a familiar swaggering figure, commanding the attention of everyone in the room with one menacing yelp or a punctuating blast from his amplified harmonica. He continued performing until he was diagnosed with lymphatic cancer in the summer of 1997. That fall, he suffered a heart attack while undergoing treatment, sending him into a coma. Wells stayed in the coma until he passed away on January 15, 1998. A handful of compilations were released shortly after his death, as was the film *Blues Brothers 2000*, which featured a cameo by Wells. *—Bill Dahl*

★ **Hoodoo Man Blues** / 1965 / Delmark ♦♦♦♦♦

One of the truly classic blues albums of the 1960s, and one of the first to fully document the smoky ambience of a night at a West Side nightspot in the superior acoustics of a recording studio. Wells just set up with his usual cohorts—guitarist Buddy Guy (billed as "Friendly Chap" on first vinyl pressings), bassist Jack Myers, and drummer Billy Warren—and proceeded to blow up a storm, bringing an immediacy to "Snatch It Back and Hold It," "You Don't Love Me," "Chitlin Con Carne," and the rest that is absolutely mesmerizing. *—Bill Dahl*

It's My Life, Baby! / 1966 / Vanguard ♦♦♦

Partly live from Pepper's Lounge in Chicago, with Buddy Guy and Freddy Below. Junior's first Vanguard album. *—Barry Lee Pearson*

Coming at You / 1968 / Vanguard ♦♦♦

You're Tuff Enough / 1968 / Mercury ♦♦♦♦

Another period of the veteran Chicago harp man's career that awaits CD documentation—and one of the most exciting. Wells' late-'60s output for Bright Star and Mercury's Blue Rock subsidiary frequently found him mining funky James Brown grooves (with a bluesy base, of course) to great effect—"Up in Heah" and his national smash "You're Tuff Enough" are marvelous examples of his refusal to bend to purists' wishes (though there's a glorious version of Bobby "Blue" Bland's blues-soaked "You're the One" that benefits handily from Sammy Lawhorn's delicate guitar work). *—Bill Dahl*

Comin' at You / 1968 / Vanguard ♦♦♦

Another eminently solid outing by the legendary harpist that captures his trademark barroom bravado in a studio setting. The band is quite tight—Buddy Guy and Lefty Dizz are the guitarists, Douglas Fagan plays sax, and Clark Terry, believe it or not, occupies a third of the trumpet section—and the set list is dominated by oldies from both Sonny Boys, Willie Dixon, and John D. Loudermilk (Junior invests his "Tobacco Road" with a lights-out toughness that the Nashville Teens could never even imagine). *—Bill Dahl*

Live at the Golden Bear / Dec. 1969 / Mercury ♦♦♦

The swaggering harpman took his act on the road to Huntington Beach, CA, to do this live set with his touring quartet of the moment. Virtually nothing but blues and soul standards that show his wide stylistic range—alongside tunes by Muddy Waters, both Sonny Boys, and the Wolf resides an impassioned reading of James Brown's "Please, Please, Please." *—Bill Dahl*

South Side Blues Jam / 1970 / Delmark ♦♦♦

An enjoyable but less electrifying follow-up to *Hoodoo Man Blues*, cut in 1969-1970—looser, with longer songs that afford more room to stretch out instrumentally but don't quite equal the stunning precision of what came before. Buddy Guy returns on guitar; Otis Spann is the pianist, and Fred Below keeps superb time. *—Bill Dahl*

Buddy Guy & Junior Wells Play the Blues / 1972 / Rhino ♦♦♦

Buddy Guy and Junior Wells seldom made more effective records than this celebrated album (reissued on CD in 1992). There were none of the erratic vocals, questionable song selection or rambling solos that sometimes plagued their live shows. Wells was sizzling and aggressive as lead vocalist, Guy's solos were controlled and disciplined, yet strikingly effective in uptempo and ballad situations, while saxophonist A.C. Reed provided soulful and shattering fills and solos behind the vocalists and during the interludes. They were helped by assorted rock luminaries from Eric Clapton, J. Geils, and Magic Dick to Dr. John. This deserves a place among the other tremendous items in the Rhino/Atlantic *Blues Masters* series. *—Ron Wynn*

In My Younger Days / 1972 / Red Lightnin' ♦♦

Although not an essential release by this fine blues harmonica frontman, there are some tracks on this collection of early recordings that are outstanding. Blues harmonica players will want the set just for the instrumental track "Junior's Wail," which is beautiful harp playing to be sure. Heard as a contrast to the later Wells period where he went overboard into the realm of soul jive, the completely straightforward blues on this collection is downright refreshing, although some of the 1953 pieces are done with so much more respect than personality that Wells comes across almost like a choirboy. By 1957, he was beginning to dig his own potatoes; the terrific "Cha Cha in Blues" is a preview of the type of fine music that would make the Delmark *Hoodoo Man Blues* so classic, yet this is delightfully more over the top, featuring Eugene Lounge (what a name) on heavily reverberated drums, including a really loud cowbell. While on the subject of reverb, the guitar of Syl Johnson motorizes into the Chuck Berry lane on "Lovey Dovey Lovely One," but also gets into aggressive single string picking as well. When Earl Hooker stops in to fill out the band on the rest of the album it is the equivalent of a blessing from above, as Wells works particularly well when he has an inventive guitar foil. The nifty instrumental "Universal Rock" gives Hooker a bit of a loud, boisterous showcase while also sporting the sax work of Gerry Gibson. The final track, "I Need a Car," even includes vibraphone, which might explain why a harmonica player would need a car, to help the vibraphone player get around. *—Eugene Chadbourne*

On Tap / Mar. 1975 / Delmark ♦♦♦

Underrated mid-'70s collection boasting a contemporary, funky edge driven by guitarists Phil Guy and Sammy Lawhorn, keyboardist Johnny "Big Moose" Walker, and saxman A.C. Reed. Especially potent is the crackling "The Train I Ride," a kissin' cousin to Little Junior Parker's "Mystery Train." *—Bill Dahl*

Blues Hit Big Town / 1977 / Delmark ♦♦♦♦♦

This 1998 CD reissue of Wells' debut recordings for the States label adds four previously unheard tracks along with the original 13-track vinyl lineup. Wells' legacy begins with these landmark sides, featuring Elmore James, Muddy Waters, Johnny Jones, Otis Spann, Willie Dixon, and the Aces in the lineup at various points. Whether it's a slow one like his original take on "Hoodoo Man" or a jump number like "Cut That Out," the grooves are classic Chicago and a mile deep. Most telling are the acoustic duets with Louis Myers recorded between the 1953 and 1954 studio sessions and the fine instrumentals like "Junior's Wail" and "Eagle Rock." Although at the start of a long career, it's obvious that Junior Wells was already a young man with a style all his own, ready to make blues history. File under essential. *—Cub Koda*

Pleading the Blues / Oct. 31, 1979 / Evidence ♦♦♦

Recorded on Halloween night in 1979, this pairs up Wells and Guy in a fashion that hasn't been heard since *Hoodoo Man Blues*, their first, and best collaboration. Solid backing by the Philip Guy band (Buddy's brother) makes this album a rare treat. *—Cub Koda*

Drinkin' TNT 'n Smokin' Dynamite / Jun. 1982 / Blind Pig ♦♦♦

Live at Montreux, featuring Junior and Buddy. *—Bill Dahl*

Harp Attack! / 1990 / Alligator ♦♦♦♦

Along with his Windy City peers James Cotton, Carey Bell, and Billy Branch, Wells trades harp solos and vocals on this raucous meeting of the minds. Junior's front and center on a fine rendition of Sonny Boy Williamson's "Keep Your Hands Out of My Pockets" and the tailor-made "Somebody Changed the Lock" and "Broke and Hungry," obviously relishing the camaraderie between himself and his fellow harmonica giants. *—Bill Dahl*

Alone & Acoustic / 1991 / Alligator ♦♦♦

☆ **1957–1966** / 1991 / Paula ♦♦♦♦♦

The indispensable sides for Mel London's Profile, Chief, and Age labels (and a few for USA Records that directly followed). Backed by a modern-sounding crew that included immaculate guitarist Earl Hooker, saxist A.C. Reed, and keyboardist Johnny "Big Moose" Walker. Wells enjoyed a considerable R&B hit with the grinding "Little By Little," glides atop a churning rhythm groove on the original "Messin' With the Kid," rocks "Lovey Dovey Lovely One" and the hokey-but-fun "I Need Me a Car," and blows some husky amplified harmonica on "Cha Cha Cha in Blue" and "Calling All Blues." *—Bill Dahl*

Undisputed Godfather of the Blues / Dec. 1992 / GBW ♦♦♦

About half is a decent Junior Wells album. The other half's mired in hopelessly overdone standards that we've heard a few too many times before—but every once in a while, he exhibits signs of the old fire. *—Bill Dahl*

Better Off With the Blues / Jun. 1993 / Telarc ♦♦

A remarkably mundane effort that leaves one with the impression that Wells didn't care a whole lot about making this disc. Even the presence of Buddy Guy, Lucky Peterson, and bassist Johnny B. Gayden can't save the overly slick set, where Wells waxes one more "Messin' With the Kid," and a dire reading of the country-soul standby "Today I Started Loving You Again," and a way-too-long title track. *—Bill Dahl*

Everybody's Gettin' Some / Mar. 28, 1995 / Telarc ♦♦

Makes his prior Telarc offering look like a masterpiece by comparison. A passel of superfluous guest stars—Bonnie Raitt, Carlos Santana, Sonny Landreth—unite to produce the most worthless Wells album ever down in Louisiana rather than in Wells' Chicago stomping grounds. Why he wanted to remake songs from the songbooks of WAR and Bill Withers is a mystery better left for future generations to ponder. *—Bill Dahl*

Come on in This House / Feb. 1997 / Telarc ♦♦♦♦♦

Junior Wells' penchant for clowning around sometimes conflicts with his craftsmanship, but he's all business on *Come on in This House*, his most unadulterated blues record since his highly acclaimed *Hoodoo Man Blues* of more than 30 years vintage. This is what has come to be known as an "unplugged" session—that is, predominately, although not exclusively, acoustic instrumentation. Producer John Snyder's concept was threefold: (1) to team Wells with some of the era's top younger traditional blues guitarists—Corey Harris, Alvin Youngblood Hart, Sonny Landreth, Bob Margolin, and John Mooney, (2) to have those musicians, in various combinations, accompany Wells on a variety of slide guitars, and (3) to concentrate on vintage Chicago and Delta blues from the repertoires of Rice Miller, Little Walter, Tampa Red, Arthur "Big Boy" Crudup, and Wells himself. The result is a virtual slide guitar mini-fest and a demonstration of the timeless appeal of classic blues done well. Wells' vocals are deep and manly; his harp playing is high-pitched, like a child's pleading. A surprising highlight is the only contemporary tune on the disc, Tracy Chapman's "Give Me One Reason." New Orleans drummer Herman Ernest III, who appears on 11 of the 14 cuts, does a masterful job laying down understated rhythmic grooves. *—Steve Hoffman*

Live at Buddy Guy's Legends / Jun. 24, 1997 / Telarc ♦♦♦

Backed by a funk-minded, James Brown-influenced band, Junior Wells is in good form on these live recordings from Buddy Guy's Legends in Chicago. Wells (who was 61 when this CD was recorded) really comes alive in front of a live audience, and he's certainly in a very extroverted mood on such familiar material as "Hoodoo Man," "Little By Little" and his signature tune, "Messin' With the Kid." Wells has been one of Brown's most ardent admirers for a long time, and he frequently shows his love of the Godfather's soul/funk innovations without letting us forget that he's a bluesman first and foremost. Although this CD doesn't offer a lot of surprises, it's an invigorating documentation of the energy and passion Wells brings to the stage. *—Alex Henderson*

Keep on Steppin': The Best of Junior Wells / Feb. 24, 1998 / Telarc ♦♦♦

The title's a bit of a ringer here; this is actually what Telarc considers the best tracks Wells recorded for their label between 1993 and 1997. Taken from his last four albums before his untimely death in early 1998, Wells won a fair amount of trophies with this quartet of albums, and while the material isn't anything that's going to make a hardline fan want to toss out their copies of *Hoodoo Man Blues*, the music and production are exemplary on every track. Guest appearances proliferate on every number and the work from Sonny Landreth, John Mooney, Derek Trucks, Lucky Peterson, Corey Harris, Bob Margolin, and Carlos Santana keep these tunes on firmly contemporary footing. *—Cub Koda*

Best of the Vanguard Years / Mar. 10, 1998 / Vanguard ♦♦♦♦

Best of the Vanguard Years collects Junior Wells' material from the *Chicago! The Blues! Today!* various-artists series, live and studio tracks from the albums *It's My Life, Baby!* and *Comin' at You*, and a smattering of rare and/or unreleased cuts. As a Wells retrospective, it's irredeemably incomplete, covering as it does his output for only one label, but the fine-quality material does make it an engaging listen, and it may be a good way for some collectors to plug holes in their Wells discographies. *—Steve Huey*

Calling All Blues / Nov. 14, 2000 / Fuel 2000 ✦✦✦✦✦

Following his recorded debut as a leader for States Records, Junior Wells signed with Mel London, producing a number of sides for the producer's Chief and Profile imprints. Perhaps best-known for his spectacular harmonica playing, this period, documented on *Calling All Blues*, saw Wells emerging as an outstanding vocalist as well. A consummate performer with a firm grasp of the range of emotions the music can produce, Wells wrings every drop of feeling out of the lyrics. The singer growls, shouts, howls, moans across these 24 tracks including two versions of his great "I Could Cry" and other classics like "Little By Little," "Cha-Cha-Cha in Blue," and "Lovey Dovey Lovey One." While it has a great deal of overlap with the collections from Paula Records, *Calling All Blues* remains a fine introduction with no glaring omissions. The bulk of the compositions come from three sources: his employer, London; the "poet of the blues," Willie Dixon; and Wells himself. While the recording quality may be shaky at times, it's to be expected and in fact only adds to the feeling of authenticity emanating from the music. It's like stepping inside a hot, sweaty room for a forbidden peek at a late-night jam session. Wells and company imbue the material with such intensity, it can almost be overwhelming at times. For the most part, the singer leaves his harp alone, but the handful of harmonica moments are memorable. On the instrumental title track, he lays into his instrument, battling for space amongst piercing guitar and piano leads. Only when the music is tempered by the more popular forms of rock & roll and R&B on songs like "I'll Get You Too," "One Day (Every Goodbye Ain't Gone)," and "I Need a Car" does it begin to lose its potency. Leading up to the sessions that produced Wells' classic 1966 album *Hoodoo Man Blues*, this is electric blues at its fiery best. —*Nathan Bush*

Live Around the World: The Best of Junior Wells / Jan. 29, 2002 / Columbia/Legacy ✦✦✦

Culled from various live recordings Junior Wells made in his final year or so, *Live Around the World: The Best of Junior Wells* is *not* a "best-of." Instead, it intends to present the legendary Chicago bluesman in a late-career renaissance—or, as Donald E. Wilcock says in his affectionate liner notes, "This album is not the last gasps of a dying legend." To a certain extent that's true, because Wells does not sound tired, weary, or disengaged. He turns in spirited, energetic performances throughout and his harp playing remains a marvel, never following expected routes, always melodic and invigorating. That doesn't mean the album *itself* is invigorating, something that is a worthy bookend to *Hoodoo Man Blues*, since it suffers from the problem that plagues so many contemporary blues albums—clean, precise production with perfectly separated instruments, plus the band's tendency to veer into funk vamps instead of dirty grooves. Even if Wells sounds good, the music as a whole feels too polished for its own good, which is really not the way Chicago blues should sound. That said, this is certainly no worse than the average contemporary blues album and in many ways, even better, thanks to Wells. He was a powerhouse right until the very end, and if you just listen to him play, *Live Around the World* does seem like a fitting epilogue to his career, although it's hard not to wish that this were a collection of greasy, intimate club dates instead of slick concert dates in Osaka and Paris. Perhaps then the band would have sounded as alive as Wells. —*Stephen Thomas Erlewine*

Wet Willie

f. 1970, Mobile, AL, db. 1980
Group / Boogie Rock, Southern Rock, Blues-Rock

Wet Willie was, after the Allman Brothers Band and Lynyrd Skynyrd, the hardest-rocking of the Southern bands to come to national attention in the early '70s. For seven years, from 1971 until 1978, they produced an enviable array of albums awash in good-time music, rollicking high-energy blues-rock, and white Southern soul, and for their trouble they racked up just one Top Ten hit ("Keep on Smilin'") and a lot of admirers. In contrast to the Allman Brothers Band, whose jumping-off point was really Cream and who based their music on long jams, Wet Willie were closer in spirit to Booker T. & the MG's and perhaps the Mar-Keys, of Stax/Volt fame, much more steeped in sweaty, good-time R&B than the blues-rock of the Allmans or the country-rock of the Marshall Tucker Band. Think of what Lynyrd Skynyrd might have sounded like with but one lead guitar on a white chitlin circuit, if such a thing had existed.

The band, originally called Fox, got together in Mobile, AL, behind the powerful vocals and distinctive sax of Jimmy Hall, with Jimmy's brother Jack on bass and banjo, Ricky Hirsch on lead and slide guitars and mandolin (as well as writing a lot of the songs), Lewis Ross on the skins, and John Anthony (later succeeded by Michael Duke) playing the keyboards. They counted the Rolling Stones and the Animals among their influences, but their sound was closer in spirit to early Otis Redding or Little Richard in his prime—which made the move to Macon, GA, in early 1970 a natural one, the town being Richard Penniman's onetime home, as well as the headquarters of Capricorn Records, the company run by Otis' onetime manager, Phil Walden. Wet Willie auditioned for Capricorn that summer and were at work on their debut album by the fall of that same year.

Despite sharing the same label as the Allmans and the Marshall Tucker Band, Wet Willie wasn't like either of those groups. They jammed, but usually not for stretches of more than ten or 12 minutes, and they weren't laid-back Southerners. Rather, Wet Willie played an intense, very vocal-oriented brand of white Southern soul. Indeed, they were probably the only white group that one could imagine doing a song such as, say, "Papa Was a Rolling Stone," and not embarrassing themselves in the process.

Their first two albums were released with barely a ripple, and their third, a live concert document called *Drippin' Wet*, was the first to scrape the lower reaches of the Top 200 albums. The group's third studio release, *Keep on Smilin'*, finally gave them a hit with the title track, a peculiar piece of reggae-flavored Southern rock, and yielded a handful of other popular tracks including "Leona." The addition of the female backing group the Williettes only opened the group's sound out further with a gospel and soul sensibility. *Dixie Rock* and *The Wetter the Better* followed in short order. The band issued one final album on Capricorn in 1977, which was followed, perhaps too closely, by *Wet Willie's*

Greatest Hits (Capricorn by that time had run into severe financial problems and was releasing anything that looked like it might sell).

The band jumped to Epic Records in 1978 with a whole new lineup—only Jimmy Hall and Michael Duke from the earlier incarnation turned up on *Manorisms*. Neither this record nor its follow-up, *Which One's Willie*, could do much to change public taste, which had moved on past even the Allman Brothers and the Marshall Tucker Band—forget about Wet Willie. The group finally broke up in 1980 after nearly a decade of great records and even better shows. —*Bruce Eder*

Wet Willie / 1971 / Capricorn ✦✦✦

It has an atrocious title and an atrocious album cover, but Wet Willie's eponymous debut is a good slice of Southern rock. The band occasionally stretches out a bit, getting into bluesy improvised sections, but their main talent is for laid-back Southern grooves. The album is a little uneven, but "Shame, Shame, Shame," "Dirty Leg," and "Have a Good Time" illustrate their potential. —*Stephen Thomas Erlewine*

Wet Willie II / 1972 / Capricorn ✦✦✦

Continuing from their first album, *Wet Willie II* finds this Southern band charging ahead in the boogie stakes while attempting to establish themselves as a harder-edged companion to the Allman Brothers. Half the tunes are covers and the other half are self-written, but there is a continuity to this album that makes the listener just groove. While the highlight is Wet Willie's version of Otis Redding's "Shout Bamalama," the group is putting forth more of their own identity than on their first disc. Good, raucous fun, *Wet Willie 11* is another fine product from those good ol' Southern boys who like their grits and their rock & roll. —*James Chrispell*

Drippin' Wet / 1973 / Capricorn ✦✦✦✦

This is the album to start with on Wet Willie, and their real best-of, a surging, forceful concert recording of white Southern soul and blues-rock at its best. The band holds its own alongside outfits like the Allman Brothers—no, this isn't the kind of history-making set that *At Fillmore East* by the latter band constituted, but it is a great show presenting this group and its members at their very best. The playing is hard and muscular, the singing rich and expressive, and they have serious fun with numbers like "Red Hot Chicken" (stretched to ten minutes) and do a nice, laid-back "Macon Hambone Blues," surrounded by crunchy renditions of pieces like "Airport." What's more, they switch effortlessly from a lean, guitar-centered blues-rock to a much funkier, sax-driven sound—maybe it was that diversity that prevented Wet Willie from really breaking big outside of the Southeast. The vibes they were picking up from the audience on New Year's Eve at the Warehouse in New Orleans make this a compelling concert document. —*Bruce Eder*

Keep on Smilin' / 1974 / Capricorn ✦✦✦✦

The definitive Wet Willie studio album, bluesier than a lot of their other work, and much of it also somewhat more laid-back. Beginning with "Country Side of Life," the band sounds tight, tuned, and in top form. Their playing is clean and crisp, and the vocals exude a bold confidence. The hit title track is a compelling reggae-country meld that's one of the more interesting and long-wearing country-rock hits of its period. It's surrounded by gospel-flavored material and also one of the neater Stax-influenced tracks ever put down by a white band, "Soul Sister," which is also a great showcase for the Williettes. Other highlights include the acoustic country ballad "Alabama," a major change of pace for this band with some clever lyrical conceits, the ultra-funky "Soul Jones" (which manages to work in a quote from the Allman Brothers), and the soulful rocker "Lucy Was in Trouble," which became a key part of the group's concert sets. The only drawback is that the group didn't quite have enough material to cover a whole album here, and also is a little too loose compared with their live performances, as on *Drippin' Wet*. The 1998 Capricorn remastering has an especially full sound, improving significantly on the original LP. —*Bruce Eder*

Dixie Rock / 1975 / Capricorn ✦✦✦

The follow-up to Wet Willie's breakthrough benchmark release, *Keep on Smilin'*, didn't match its predecessor in sales, and began a commercial decline from which they never recovered. But although there's nothing as catchy as the previous album's title track, *Dixie Rock* is a worthy successor and another excellent yet underrated entry in the band's catalog. With their picture dominating the back cover, backing singers the Williettes (Ella Avery and Donna Hall) receive featured treatment, and their contribution adds substantial gospel flavor to the group's approach. Avery's duet with frontman Jimmy Hall on "Mama Don't Raise No Fools" is one of the disc's highlights, and the stripped-down version of Albert Brumly's "He Set Me Free" could have come directly off a traditional spiritual album. But "Leona" (a minor hit single), is pure greasy Southern singalong funk and rock that, along with the title cut, slots into Willie's established sound. The R&B-drenched "It's Gonna Stop Rainin' Soon," featuring sublime slide work from Ricky Hirsch and Jimmy Hall's mournful harp along with the deep Delta blues of "Jailhouse Moan," help make this one of the band's most cohesive works, although it takes a few spins for their charms to be appreciated. Those who enjoy Wet Willie's gritty Southern soul will find lots to like on this low-key, predominantly hitless gem, which, as of 2002, had been taken out of print after being digitally remastered and reissued in 1999. —*Hal Horowitz*

The Wetter the Better / 1976 / Capricorn ✦✦✦

Though they had a hit with "Keep on Smilin'," Wet Willie has long since been forgotten, and yet they were among the original Capricorn Southern boogie bands of the day. The sound was based around dueling and slide guitars, rolling pianos and organs, harmony vocals, and lots of jamming, but this album, their sixth, stands out for another reason: its completely inappropriate cover photo of a glistening woman's torso, from nipple to crotch, holding a popsicle. You've seen it in the $1 bins for ages, and it's a wonder it was reissued at all. Among the bluesy Southern rock songs is a jam with a funky beat and horns, "Baby Fat"; it could pass for the disco of the era and sounds like something KC & the Sunshine Band would do. The easy soul of "Everybody's Stoned" would be great for a time capsule. Forget this one, though it's certainly plausible that enjoyment on a sentimental level could be obtained by some folk out there. *—Denise Sullivan*

Left Coast Live / 1977 / Capricorn ♦♦♦♦♦

Originally released in 1977, the second live album from these funky, soulful Southerners was reissued in 1999 with five extra cuts, adding a whopping 30 minutes to the original vinyl record's limited playing time. With a completely different track listing than 1973's excellent *Drippin' Wet*, *Left Coast Live* captures all that was memorable about Wet Willie. They tear through soul standards, like Jimmy Reed's "Shame, Shame, Shame," Little Milton's "Grits Ain't Groceries," and a shimmering 13-minute slow blues version of Billy Eckstein's "Jelly Jelly" (featuring guest guitarist Toy Caldwell on loan from the Marshall Tucker Band), with obvious passion for not only the songs, but for performing them in front of an enthusiastic audience like the one fortunate to be at this 1976 second set at L.A.'s Roxy club. Lead vocal, sax, and harmonica man Jimmy Hall is in solid form as he hoots, hollers, shouts, moans, and blows like the soul men he obviously idolizes and the band, now tightened through almost a decade of playing one-night stands, chugs along like a fine-tuned engine pumped with high octane gas. Pianist Mike Duke pounds the ivories with religious fervor and guitarist Ricky Hersh plays with barely controlled passion throughout. Featuring touches of gospel on "Ring You Up," Sly Stone-styled funk with "Baby Fat," and Southern-fried R&B on their show-stopping 12-minute version of "Lucy Was in Trouble," it's evident how overlooked this group was as one of the most eclectic, soulful, and talented bands to emerge from the glutted '70s Southern rock circuit. Oddly, the album's least impressive moment is a rote rendition of their biggest hit, "Keep on Smiling," played without the energy injected into the rest of the show. Wet Willie lost the majority of its original members and direction after this final, contract-fulfilling Capricorn release, but *Left Coast Live* remains a compelling and often exhilarating document of a gifted band in their prime. *—Hal Horowitz*

Manorisms / 1978 / Epic ♦♦♦♦♦

Which One's Willie / 1979 / Epic ♦♦

● **The Best of Wet Willie** / Jul. 26, 1994 / Polygram ♦♦♦♦♦

It may be more expensive than *Wet Willie's Greatest Hits*, but *The Best of Wet Willie* runs circles around the earlier compilation, and it's worth the extra six bucks. Running well over an hour and comprising many of their strongest studio cuts (plus an 11-minute live version of "Lucy Was in Trouble"), this is a good-time rock album par excellence, with liberal dollops of soul, blues, boogie, and country thrown in. The notes are slightly soft in the information side, but other than that one reservation, this disc and the live *Drippin' Wet* are the two discs by this band that belong in any serious collection of modern Southern rock. *—Bruce Eder*

Peetie Wheatstraw (William Bunch)

b. Dec. 21, 1902, Ripley, TN, **d.** Dec. 21, 1941, East St. Louis, IL

Vocals, Piano / Prewar Country Blues, Piano Blues, St. Louis Blues

Peetie Wheatstraw was the name adopted by singer William Bunch, taking it from black American folklore. According to author Ralph Ellison, who made use of the Wheatstraw legend to model characters in his novels *Invisible Man* and *Juneteenth*, "Peetie Wheatstraw" was the evil half of a twin personality whose challenge was invoked at the start of a pool game. He was "the Devil's Son-In-Law" or "the High Sheriff of Hell," in search of his other half, the "Lord God Stingerroy" to shoot him a game. Nothing is known of the early life of William Bunch, other than that he was born in Ripley, TN, and raised in Cotton Plant, AR. In 1929, he arrived in East St. Louis, already using the name Peetie Wheatstraw. Allegedly, as Wheatstraw, Bunch was also spreading the rumor that he had been to the "crossroads" and had sold his soul to the Prince of Darkness in exchange for success as a musician.

Without regard for the validity of Wheatstraw's claims, this self-promotion paid off in short order. Peetie Wheatstraw soon became a popular performer in East St. Louis and his fame quickly spread to Chicago. At a time when most record companies were cutting their entire blues rosters in order to survive the depression, Peetie Wheatstraw suddenly became a hot item. Wheatstraw began his recording career singing vocal duets with the unknown "Neckbones" (possibly J.D. Short) for ARC on September 13, 1930, and continued recording on his own into the early part of 1931. After an isolated session for Bluebird in September 1931, Wheatstraw returned to ARC, and then moved to Decca in 1934, where the bulk of his best recordings were made. Peetie Wheatstraw recorded in every year of the 1930s save 1933, ultimately producing 175 sides in all with only one rejection, an enormous total for a blues artist in the prewar period. This figure does not include recordings made by Wheatstraw sitting in on records made by his frequent partner, Kokomo Arnold, or ones made with Amos Easton, aka Bumble Bee Slim.

In the only known photograph of Peetie Wheatstraw, he is shown holding a guitar; curious, as he was a primarily a piano player, although he may have played his own guitar on a couple of recording dates. On his records Wheatstraw usually required a guitarist to play with him, and had many excellent ones to choose from, including Kokomo Arnold, Lonnie Johnson, Charlie Jordan, Charlie McCoy, and Teddy Bunn, in addition to pianist Champion Jack Dupree. On some of his last dates, Peetie Wheatstraw recorded within a jazz-inspired framework, collaborating with Lil Hardin Armstrong and trumpeter Jonah Jones. His true strength was not so much in terms of instrumental ability as it was his singing and the varied lyrical content of his songs, which dealt with topics such as loose women, alcohol, supernaturalism, gambling, suicide, and murder. Robert Johnson cribbed so many lyrical ideas from the work of Peetie Wheatstraw that it's not even worth going into specific examples of that derivation here.

The sheer size of Peetie Wheatstraw's recorded output has worked against his reputation. Some blues experts have expressed the opinion that Wheatstraw's recordings are limited stylistically, lack variety, and tend towards repetition. One hallmark of his style was the use of pet phrases for purposes of punctuation, most typically "Oh, well, well" in third verses of songs. On the contrary, it would seem that anyone who was thinking of formalizing aspects of blues songwriting in the 1930s would be hailed a harbinger of things to come, rather than blamed for a lack of imagination. In the later '30s, Peetie Wheatstraw's recording sessions were being held once every two or three months and consisted of six to eight songs per date, so he had to develop formulas in order to keep his content fresh. That Wheatstraw did so successfully was something that affected nearly blues musician within hearing distance of one of his records. He was overwhelmingly popular throughout the 1930s, and he is credited in some quarters with being the artist who carried the blues from its lowly status as rural "devil's music" into the cities where, in time, it would grow, thrive, and change to suit the needs of a new urban audience.

Peetie Wheatstraw would not personally live to witness these future changes. Since his death, researchers have probed arduously in an attempt get at more information about him, interviewing his acquaintances and reviewing civic records. But even more than 60 years after his death, practically nothing substantive is known about him or his life, despite his ambitious recording schedule and tremendous popularity. For someone cultivating the legend of a deal with the devil, Wheatstraw's death was eerily appropriate—celebrating his 39th birthday, Wheatstraw and some friends decided to drive to the local market to pick up some liquor, and on their way out they tried to beat a railroad train that was coming down the tracks at full speed. Needless to say, they didn't make it. *—Uncle Dave Lewis*

Complete Works, Vol. 1 / May 1, 1995 / Document ♦♦♦

Complete Works, Vol. 2 / May 1, 1995 / Document ♦♦♦

Complete Works, Vol. 3 / May 1, 1995 / Document ♦♦♦

Complete Works, Vol. 4 / May 1, 1995 / Document ♦♦♦

Complete Works, Vol. 5 / May 1, 1995 / Document ♦♦♦

Complete Works, Vol. 6 / May 1, 1995 / Document ♦♦♦

Complete Works, Vol. 7 / May 1, 1995 / Document ♦♦♦

The Blues / 1997 / Frémeaux & Associés ♦♦♦♦

This 36-song double-CD collection from France is the most comprehensive collection of Wheatstraw's music available, covering a significant spread of his music from 1931 until 1941 and his moves from St. Louis to Chicago and New York. The self-proclaimed "Devil's Son-In-Law" is represented by the song of that name and its B-side, "Peetie Wheatstraw," on the opening two tracks—the mastering is very clean, sufficient to give Charlie McCoy's guitar a hearing. Wheatstraw's own guitar—seldom recorded—is heard as a rhythm instrument surrounded by trumpet and violin on the jazzy "Throw Me in the Alley," from 1934. Some of the later recordings on disc two, dating from 1939 on, also feature blues/jazz crossover legend Lonnie Johnson on guitar and jazz trumpet man Jonah Jones. The sound is surprisingly good throughout, the notes are, alas, only partly in English, but the $20 price is just right. *—Bruce Eder*

● **The Devil's Son-In-Law** / Blues Document ♦♦♦♦♦

Blues Document's *The Devil's Son-In-Law* (not to be confused with Best of Blues' similarly titled effort) is a strong overview of Peetie Wheatstraw's recordings between 1930 and 1941, containing a total of 20 tracks. The collection does a nice job of balancing his piano, guitar, and vocal efforts, containing such signature tracks as "Ooh Well, Well," "Meat Cutter Blues," "Beggar Man Blues," and "I Want Some Sea Food." *—Stephen Thomas Erlewine*

James Wheeler

b. Aug. 28, 1937, Albany, GA

Guitar, Vocals / Modern Electric Blues, Modern Electric Chicago Blues

Blues guitarist James Wheeler was born in Albany, GA, on August 28, 1937. His earliest musical influences were the big bands of the time, especially Glenn Miller, Duke Ellington, and his first idol, Louis Jordan. Following his older brother Golden, Wheeler moved to Chicago in 1956. Golden had started playing harmonica in the clubs, becoming friends with many blues musicians, including Little Walter. It was after the move to Chicago that James Wheeler picked up the guitar and started jamming with local musicians.

Wheeler's first big break came when he played guitar with Billy Boy Arnold, which lead to the formation of the Jaguars in 1963, backing up B.B. King, Millie Jackson, O.V. Wright, and Otis Clay. Clay was so impressed with Wheeler's playing that after the Jaguars broke up in 1972 he asked Wheeler to put together his touring band, which lasted three years. Following a brief tour with the Impressions, Wheeler took a non-music day job, picking up weekend gigs here and there for the next decade. In 1986, Wheeler received a call from Otis Rush asking him to play a weekend gig that turned full-time, lasting until 1993.

After recording and touring stints with Mississippi Heat, Magic Slim, and Willie Kent, he released his much anticipated solo recording, *Ready*, in 1998 on Delmark Records. Featuring ten original tracks plus three covers, his band featured brother Big Golden Wheeler on harmonica and pianist Ken Saydak. Following a hectic tour schedule through Europe and South America, Wheeler's second release, *Can't Take It*, followed in 2000, again, on the Delmark label. *Can't Take It* spotlights all original compositions by Wheeler, fronting the same band, with the exception of Ron Sorin replacing Big Golden on harp. *—Al Campbell*

Ready / Mar. 24, 1998 / Delmark ♦♦♦

● **Can't Take It** / May 30, 2000 / Delmark ♦♦♦

Can't Take It is the second Delmark release from Chicago blues guitarist James Wheeler, who is backed by pianist Ken Saydak, guitarist Billy Flynn (heard on the right channel), bassist Bob Stroger, drummer Marty Binder, and harp player Ron Sorin taking the place of James' brother Golden Big Wheeler on this session. Wheeler's guitar playing is consistently flashy through this set, while other bright moments include Flynn's twangy solo on the dirty blues "You Make It Hard Baby" and Saydak's funky organ playing on the lazy shuffle "Goin to the Station." Wheeler isn't the strongest vocalist around but he gets his message across on tracks like "This Can't Be Happening to Me," "My Baby's Gone," and "I Can't Take It." —*Al Campbell*

Whistler & His Jug Band

f. 1915, Louisville, KY

Group / Jug Band, Acoustic Blues

Whistler & His Jug Band was a long-lasting and popular group that recorded for several labels from the mid-'20s through the early '30s, and influenced many of the jug bands that followed. The group was formed in 1915 in Louisville, KY, by guitarist, vocalist and whistler Buford Threlkeld, and went through occasional lineup changes over the years, but fiddler Jess Ferguson and banjo player Willie Black were steady members of Whistler & His Jug Band for over a decade. The jazz-influenced jug band first entered the recording studios in September 1924 when they traveled to Richmond, IN, to cut several sides for the Gennett label. These included "Chicago Flip," "Jail House Blues," and "I'm a Jazz Baby," as well as songs that went unissued, such as "The Vampire Woman."

The second recording trip for Whistler & His Jug Band took them to St. Louis in April 1927. On this trip, the jug band recorded ten songs for OKeh, including "Low Down Blues," "The Vamps of 28," and "Pig Meat Blues." The jug player during this session was 13-year-old Rudolph Thompson, who was still with the group by the time of their next recording session in June 1931. This time, the band got to record in their hometown of Louisville. "Hold That Tiger" and "Foldin' Bed" are some of the songs that they recorded for Victor during this session. —*Joslyn Layne*

The White Stripes

f. 1997, Detroit, MI

Group / Garage Rock Revival, Indie Rock, Blues-Rock

Detroit minimalist rock duo (specifically, southwest Detroit minimalist rock duo) the White Stripes—Jack White, guitar and vocals, Meg White, drums—formed in 1997 (Bastille Day, to be precise) with the idea of making simple rock & roll music. From the red and white peppermint candy motif of their debut singles, self-titled album, and stage show to their on-the-surface rudimentary style, they succeeded wildly and immediately with that mission. Their first recordings were a mix of garage rock, blues, and the occasional show tune. In frontman Jack (a former drummer for Detroit country outfit Goober & the Peas), the White Stripes have a formidable songwriter, guitar player, and vocalist capable of both morphing between styles and changing the musical styles themselves; ranging from the folk blues of Blind Willie McTell to soaring Kinks-esque pop and narrative pop tunes worthy of Cole Porter and into deepest Captain Beefheart territory within the span of 15 minutes is not an uncommon listening experience with either the White Stripes live show or on record. In drummer Meg, the White Stripes have a minimalist percussionist who seems to sense intuitively exactly when to not play. The White Stripes are grounded in punk and blues, but the undercurrent to all of their work has been the aforementioned striving for simplicity, a love of American folk music, and a careful approach to intriguing, emotional, and evocative lyrics not found anywhere else in modern punk or garage rock (or amongst postmodern "blues" practitioners such as Jon Spencer, for that matter).

While they may have sprung from the Detroit rock scene (and they remain regular fixtures on the Detroit club circuit with Jack producing or working with many Detroit-area bands), the White Stripes quickly gained a national following after two successive tours with indie rockers Pavement and Sleater-Kinney in 1999 and 2000. The White Stripes released their second LP, *De Stijl*, in 2000 and it further spread the group's reputation. They followed its release with successful tours of Japan and Australia and entered the Memphis studio of renowned producer Doug Easley for 2001's *White Blood Cells*. The album was a critical smash and the White Stripes soon found themselves, along with the Strokes and the Hives, at the forefront of the new wave of rock & roll bands poised to take over the world. The band certainly did their best to achieve world domination, appearing on *Late Night With David Letterman*, being written about in *Time*, *The New Yorker*, and *Entertainment Weekly*, playing the MTV Movie Awards, and having their video for "Fell in Love With a Girl" in heavy rotation on MTV. They also made the tough decision to jump to a major label; *White Blood Cells* was reissued on V2 in January of 2002 and their first two records followed suit in June. The White Stripes truly became big-time rock stars when their "Fell in Love With a Girl" clip was nominated for four MTV Video Awards, including Best Video of the Year (alongside Eminem and *NSYNC!), Breakthrough Video, Best Special Effects in a Video, and Best Editing in a Video. Not bad for a brother and sister from southwest Detroit. —*Chris Handyside*

The White Stripes / Jun. 15, 1999 / Sympathy for the Record Industry ✦✦✦✦

Minimal to the point of sounding monumental, this Detroit guitar-drums-voice duo makes the most of its aesthetic choices and the spaces between riffage and the big beat. In fact, the White Stripes sound like arena rock as hand-crafted in the attic. Singer/guitarist Jack White's voice is a singular, evocative combination of punk, metal, blues, and backwoods while his guitar work is grand and banging with just enough lyrical touches of slide and subtle solo work to let you know he means to use the metal-blues riff collisions just so. Drummer Meg White balances out the fretwork and the fretting with methodical, spare, and booming cymbal, bass drum, and snare cracks. In a word, economy (and that goes for both of the players). The Whites' choice of covers is inspired, too. J. White's voice is equally suited to the task of tackling both the desperation of Robert Johnson's "Stop Breakin' Down" and the loneliness of Bob Dylan's "One More Cup of Coffee." Neither are equal to the originals, but they take a distinctive, haunting spin around

the turntable nevertheless. All D.I.Y. punk-country blues-metal singer/songwriting duos should sound this good. —*Chris Handyside*

De Stijl / Jun. 20, 2000 / Sympathy for the Record Industry ✦✦✦✦✦

Despite their reputation as garage rock revivalists, the White Stripes display an impressive range of styles on their second album, *De Stijl*, which is Dutch for "the style." Perhaps the album's diversity—which incorporates elements of bubblegum, cabaret, blues, and classic rock—shouldn't come as a surprise from a band that dedicates its album to bluesman Blind Willie McTell and Dutch artist Gerrit Rietveld. Nevertheless, it's refreshing to hear the band go from the Tommy James-style pop of "You're Pretty Good Looking" to the garage-y stomp of "Hello Operator" in a one-two punch. It's even more impressive that the theatrical, piano-driven ballad "Apple Blossom" and a cover of Son House's "Death Letter" go so well together on the same album. Jack White's understated production work and versatile guitar playing and vocals also stand out on the languid, fuzzy "Sister, Do You Know My Name?" as well as insistent rockers like "Little Bird" and "Why Can't You Be Nicer to Me?" As distinctive as it is diverse, *De Stijl* blends the Stripes' arty leanings with enough rock muscle to back up the band's ambitions. —*Heather Phares*

● **White Blood Cells** / Jul. 3, 2001 / Sympathy for the Record Industry ✦✦✦✦✦

Despite the seemingly instant attention surrounding them—glowing write-ups in glossy magazines like *Rolling Stone* and *Mojo*, guest lists boasting names like Kate Hudson and Chris Robinson, and appearances on national TV—the White Stripes have stayed true to the approach that brought them this success in the first place. *White Blood Cells*, Jack and Meg White's third effort for Sympathy for the Record Industry, wraps their powerful, deceptively simple style around meditations on fame, love, and betrayal. As produced by Doug Easley, it sounds exactly how an underground sensation's breakthrough album should: bigger and tighter than their earlier material, but not so polished that it will scare away longtime fans. Admittedly, *White Blood Cells* lacks some of the White Stripes' blues influence and urgency, but it perfects the pop skills the duo honed on *De Stijl* and expands on them. The country-tinged "Hotel Yorba" and immediate, crazed garage pop of "Fell in Love With a Girl" define the album's immediacy, along with the folky, McCartney-esque "We're Going to Be Friends," a charming, schooldays love song that's among Jack White's finest work. However, White's growth as a songwriter shines through on virtually every track, from the cocky opener "Dead Leaves and the Dirty Ground" to vicious indictments like "The Union Forever" and "I Think I Smell a Rat." "Same Boy You've Always Known" and "Offend in Every Way" are two more quintessential tracks, offering up more of the group's stomping riffs and rhythms and us-against-the-world attitude. Few garage rock groups would name one of their most driving numbers "I'm Finding It Harder to Be a Gentleman," and fewer still would pen lyrics like "I'm so tired of acting tough/I'm gonna do what I please/Let's get married," but it's precisely this mix of strength and sweetness, among other contrasts, that makes the White Stripes so intriguing. Likewise, *White Blood Cells*' ability to surprise old fans and win over new ones makes it the Stripes' finest work to date. —*Heather Phares*

Artie "Blues Boy" White

b. Apr. 16, 1937, Vicksburg, MS

Vocals / Soul-Blues, Soul, Chicago Blues

Very few Chicago blues artists were able to pierce the R&B charts during the 1970s, when interest in the genre was at rock-bottom. But smooth-voiced Artie "Blues Boy" White managed the rare feat with his 1977 single for Altee, "Leanin' Tree."

Gospel was White's initial musical pursuit. He sang with a spiritual aggregation, the Harps of David, at the age of 11 prior to coming to Chicago in 1956. More church singing was in store for White with the Full Gospel Wonders. The singer claims that he was lured into singing the devil's music by a well-heeled gent who drove up to an unsuspecting White in a flashy Cadillac and promised him $10,000 to record some blues songs!

White's '70s singles for PM and Gamma stiffed, but with the advent of "Leanin' Tree," White was able to command a nice asking price on the Chicago circuit (and still does). For a while, White tried his hand at running a blues club, Bootsy's Lounge. But performing and recording won out; White waxed a terrific debut LP in 1985 for Shreveport-based Ronn Records called *Blues Boy*.

White signed with Ichiban in 1987 and waxed six fine sets in the soul-blues vein (enough to merit a best-of CD in 1991, which made seven), utilizing Chicago songwriter Bob Jones (the composer of "Leanin' Tree") and labelmate Travis Haddix as chief sources of material. On 1989's *Thangs Got to Change*, White enjoyed the presence of Little Milton Campbell, one of his prime influences, on lead guitar. A move to the Waldoxy label resulted in 1994's *Different Shades of Blue*, 1997's *Home Tonight*, and 1999's *Can We Get Together*. White was still going strong in 2002 with a new record, *Can't Get Enough*, and a new label, Gold Circle. —*Bill Dahl*

Blues Boy / 1985 / Ronn ✦✦✦✦

Blues Boy's first album, dating back to the mid-'80s, also ranks as one of his most soulfully satisfying, thanks to the contemporary grooves of a Chicago outfit called Amuzement Park and White's smoky, Little Milton-influenced vocal delivery. He delivers a fine remake of his own modern blues "Leaning Tree" and Little Beaver's "Jimmie" and adapts Aretha Franklin's "Chain of Fools" to his own rich vocal range. —*Bill Dahl*

Nothing Takes the Place of You / 1987 / Ichiban ✦✦✦

Artie White's Ichiban debut is typically confident and soulful. Along with standards by Toussaint McCall and Willie Nelson, White does a solid job on a sheaf of original material and Z.Z. Hill's anguished "I Need Someone." —*Bill Dahl*

Where It's At / 1989 / Ichiban ✦✦✦

Sam Cooke, Clarence Carter, and Al Green receive the cover treatment this time, but White and his usual cohorts (writers Bob Jones and Travis Haddix, in addition to the singer himself) penned the majority of the fine blues-soul set. A fine band helps, too: guitarists Criss Johnson and Pete Allen and a six-piece horn section led by Willie Henderson frame White's husky vocals beautifully. *—Bill Dahl*

Thangs Got to Change / 1989 / Ichiban ✦✦✦
Little Milton Campbell—one of Artie White's principal influences and advisors—wrote a good portion of this typically solid soul-blues collection, and White covers numbers by Lowell Fulson, Brook Benton, and B.B. King for flavor. *—Bill Dahl*

Tired of Sneaking Around / 1990 / Ichiban ✦✦✦✦✦
White is a B.B. King-sounding singer, with an original overall sound, who makes great records with big-band feel. There are lots of horns and stuff. *—Niles J. Frantz*

Dark End of the Street / 1991 / Ichiban ✦✦✦✦
Whether it's blues, soul, or something midway between the two, White does a fine job throughout this disc. Travis Haddix, once White's Ichiban labelmate, contributes three nice tunes, Bob Jones a couple more, and White dips into past triumphs by B.B. King, Ike Turner, James Carr, and Little Milton for the rest. *—Bill Dahl*

● **The Best of Artie White** / 1991 / Ichiban ✦✦✦✦✦
A well-selected 12-song overview of White's prolific tenure at Ichiban. His delivery, pitched somewhere between blues and soul, is equally effective on the contemporary blues-based items "Hattie Mae" and "Jodie" and the soul-slanted "Dark End of the Street" (though he can't give James Carr a run for his money in the intensity department) and Toussaint McCall's tender "Nothing Takes the Place of You." *—Bill Dahl*

Hit & Run / 1992 / Ichiban ✦✦✦✦
Without a great deal of fanfare, Artie White released a steady stream of quality contemporary releases on Ichiban, each straddling the sometimes imperceptible fence between blues and deep soul. This one's no exception—backed by a Chicago combo called Masheen Co., White delivers originals penned by Travis Haddix, Bob Jones (the title cut), and himself in assured, smooth style. *—Bill Dahl*

Different Shades of Blue / 1994 / Waldoxy ✦✦✦

Home Tonight / Feb. 25, 1997 / Waldoxy ✦✦✦✦✦

Can We Get Together / Jun. 1, 1999 / Waldoxy ✦✦✦

Can't Get Enough / Feb. 19, 2002 / Achilltown ✦✦✦

American Roots: Blues / Aug. 20, 2002 / Ichiban ✦✦✦

Bukka White (Booker T. Washington White)

b. Nov. 12, 1906, Houston, MS, **d.** Feb. 26, 1977, Memphis, TN
Slide Guitar, Vocals, Piano, Harmonica, Guitar / Slide Guitar Blues, Prewar Gospel Blues, Delta Blues, Prewar Country Blues

Bukka White (true name: Booker T. Washington White) was born in Houstin, MS (not Houston, TX), in 1906 (not any date between 1902-1905 or 1907-1909, as is variously reported). He got his initial start in music learning fiddle tunes from his father. Guitar instruction soon followed, but White's grandmother objected to anyone playing "that Devil music" in the household; nonetheless, his father eventually bought him a guitar. When Bukka White was 14 he spent some time with an uncle in Clarksdale, MS, and passed himself off as a 21-year-old, using his guitar playing as a way to attract women. Somewhere along the line, White came in contact with Delta blues legend Charley Patton, who no doubt was able to give Bukka White instruction on how to improve his skills in both areas of endeavor. In addition to music, White pursued careers in sports, playing in Negro Leagues baseball and, for a time, taking up boxing.

In 1930 Bukka White met furniture salesman Ralph Limbo, who was also a talent scout for Victor. White traveled to Memphis where he made his first recordings, singing a mixture of blues and gospel material under the name of Washington White. Victor only saw fit to release four of the 14 songs Bukka White recorded that day. As the Depression set in, opportunity to record didn't knock again for Bukka White until 1937, when Big Bill Broonzy asked him to come to Chicago and record for Lester Melrose. By this time, Bukka White had gotten into some trouble—he later claimed he and a friend had been "ambushed" by a man along a highway, and White shot the man in the thigh in self defense. While awaiting trial, White jumped bail and headed for Chicago, making two sides before being apprehended and sent back to Mississippi to do a three-year stretch at Parchman Farm. While he was serving time, White's record "Shake 'Em on Down" became a hit.

Bukka White proved a model prisoner, popular with inmates and prison guards alike and earning the nickname "Barrelhouse." It was as "Washington Barrelhouse White" that White recorded two numbers for John and Alan Lomax at Parchman Farm in 1939. After earning his release in 1940, he returned to Chicago with 12 newly minted songs to record for Lester Melrose. These became the backbone of his lifelong repertoire, and the Melrose session today is regarded as the pinnacle of Bukka White's achievements on record. Among the songs he recorded on that occasion were "Parchman Farm Blues" (not to be confused with "Parchman Farm" written by Mose Allison and covered by John Mayall's Bluesbreakers and Blue Cheer, among others), "Good Gin Blues," "Bukka's Jitterbug Swing," "Aberdeen, Mississippi Blues," and "Fixin' to Die Blues," all timeless classics of the Delta blues. Then, Bukka disappeared—not into the depths of some Mississippi Delta mystery, but into factory work in Memphis during World War II.

Bob Dylan recorded "Fixin' to Die Blues" on his 1961 debut Columbia album, and at the time no one in the music business knew who Bukka White was—most figured a fellow who'd written a song like "Fixin' to Die" had to be dead already. Two California-based blues enthusiasts, John Fahey and Ed Denson, were more skeptical about this assumption, and in 1963 addressed a letter to "Bukka White (Old Blues Singer), c/o General Delivery, Aberdeen, Mississippi." By chance, one of White's relatives was working in the Post Office in Aberdeen, and forwarded the letter to White in Memphis.

Things moved quickly from the time Bukka White met up with Fahey and Denson; by the end of 1963 Bukka White was already recording on contract with Chris Strachwitz and Arhoolie. White wrote a new song celebrating his good fortune entitled "1963 Isn't 1962 Blues" and swiftly recorded three albums of material for Strachwitz which the latter entitled *Sky Songs*, referring to White's habit of "reaching up and pulling songs out of the sky." Nonetheless, even White knew he couldn't get away with making up all his material regularly in performance, so he also studied his 78s and relearned all the songs he'd written for Lester Melrose. Although Bukka White was practically the same age as other survivors of the Delta and Memphis blues scenes of the 1920s and '30s, he didn't look like someone who belonged in a nursing home. White was a sharp dresser, in the prime of health, was a compelling entertainer and raconteur, and clearly enjoyed being the center of attention. He thrived on the folk festival and coffeehouse circuit of the 1960s.

By the '70s, however, Bukka White couldn't help getting a little bored with his celebrity status as an acoustic bluesman. White's tastes had grown with the times, and he would have loved to have played an electric guitar and fronted a band, as his old acquaintance Chester Burnett, aka Howlin' Wolf, and Bukka's own cousin, B. B. King, had been already doing successfully for years. But he only needed to look at what happened to his friend Bob Dylan's career for a lesson on what happens to folk blues artists who try to "go electric." So, Bukka White stayed on the festival circuit to the end of his days, beating the hell out of his National steel guitar, and sometimes his monologues would go on a little long, and sometimes his playing was a little more willfully eccentric than at others. Patrons would wait patiently to hear Bukka play "Parchman Farm Blues," although some of them were under the mistaken impression that they had paid their money to hear an artist who had originated a number that Eric Clapton made famous.

Blues purists will tell you that nothing Bukka White recorded after 1940 is ultimately worth listening to. This isn't accurate, or fair. White was an incredibly compelling performer who gave up of more of himself in his work than many artists in any musical discipline. The *Sky Songs* albums for Arhoolie are an eminently rewarding document of Bukka's charm and candor, particularly in the long monologue "Mixed Water." "Big Daddy," recorded in 1974 for Arnold S. Caplin's Biograph label, likewise is a classic of its kind and should not be neglected. *—Uncle Dave Lewis*

Sky Songs, Vol. 1 / 1965 / Arhoolie ✦✦✦
If records were rated for being unique alone, this series of two volumes on Arhoolie would be prizewinners. Amongst the many available recordings of American country blues, there is absolutely nothing that the *Sky Songs* could be compared to, something some blues listeners might be thankful for. The concept of a producer taking an artist and refining his statements into a polished, professionally acceptable version of a finished product is turned around completely on its ear here. That this kind of approach might be the enemy of the eccentric such as White is a given, but to allow him to do exactly what he wanted for as long as he wanted over the course of four sides may not have been a good alternative. As a result, these records could perhaps figure into the *Guinness Book of World Records* as containing the longest country blues numbers on record, such as the 13-minute and counting "Sugar Hill," the piano track on this volume. White is of course much more effective and exciting to listen to when he plays his steel guitar, and many blues fans might go much further than that simple statement and insist that the blues in general is better in little morsels rather than extended epics. Of course, the history of the genre on recordings begins with abbreviated performances, because it was impossible to cut more than three minutes at once. But skip ahead 50 years and even the electrified blues styles contain long tracks only in the case of extended jams of some kind, the longest one of all being some two hours of "Refried Boogie" plopped onto four sides by Canned Heat. Compared to that, the performances here are mere burps in the sands of time. The listener may still find it tedious making it through these tracks no matter what instrument White is playing or how friendly his vocals sound.

It isn't a situation without hope, mind you. "My Baby" is an example of a good result that can came from this lack of editing. White builds the song's intensity surely and slowly, verse upon verse of detail backboned by an insistent riff that literally brings chills to the spine while he sings about this very image. It doesn't hurt that as the verses progress, he gets into some narrative action that would fit right into *The Evil Dead*. As is the case with incredibly long movies and plays, a psychic adjustment can be made and the most monotonous tracks such as "Sugar Hill" can become some kind of a metaphysical experience, including the piano solo that he plays almost identically at least four times. Who's counting? Perhaps the fellow who faded out the track. Some of the tracks fade in as well, as if they were captured in the middle of their creation. This was the whole idea, as the artist coined the term *Sky Songs* to describe the idea of ditties coming to him as if they were falling into his mind from up above. The concept of musicians receiving inspiration from the universe at large is of course something even the elite such as Karlheinz Stockhausen lay claim to, so there is no need to dismiss White's inspiration offhand. Whether country blues artists missed an opportunity for greatness by not recording similarly long performances is not something anyone will ever be able to judge, as these recordings remain the lone examples of a country blues imagination allowed to run wild. Inexplicably, timings are provided for two of the tracks and not the others; perhaps the guy with the stopwatch kept dozing off on the job. *—Eugene Chadbourne*

Sky Songs, Vol. 2 / 1965 / Arhoolie ✦✦✦
There are two volumes in this series, but one could make a guess that twice as many boxes of this second volume are sitting on the warehouse shelf, unwanted. That's because eventually word got out that one side of the second volume consisted of a long monologue entitled "Mixed Water," basically the story of how Bukka White got a bunch of people drunk via trickery. If one were to purchase only one *Sky Songs* volume, some would give the nod to the first in the series, since it is all music. The term "music," however, is vague enough to apply to that album's nearly 14 minutes of piano playing. The second volume of *Sky Songs* features a higher overall proportion of this artist's

wonderful slide steel guitar music, and less piano. As for "Mixed Water," it is a curiosity piece. If recordings such as this had more of an audience, it would be a real boon for journalists, many of whom have stacks of recordings such as this, done for interview sessions and featuring musicians raving about this and that. Over the years, "Mixed Water" sometimes showed up on college radio programs, even getting the montage treatment from the late-'80s crowd of taping weirdos. The length of the pieces would encourage even a sane listener to want to fiddle along, but this was the whole idea of this series and makes it totally unique in the history of country blues recording. White indulged in stream of consciousness improvised songcrafting for these recordings, and was encouraged to go on to his heart's content. The monologue may have been the result of him running out of musical ideas—his steamroller ran magnificently in only two gears, apparently—or producer Chris Strachwitz may have felt that this material had enough historical importance to merit the gobble of so much vinyl. Bukka White fans will find a handful of recordings available that present the artist in the confines of a more structured setting, which as disappointing as it is to admit, was actually the way to go with this guy. These records will in turn make the newly fanatic White supremacy converts covet the *Sky Songs* just because the idea of them will sound so appealing. In the end, the idea is better than the reality, but it sure would be nice if there were recordings like this of other country blues greats. —*Eugene Chadbourne*

☆ **Legacy of the Blues** / 1969 / Sonet ✦✦✦✦✦
A CD reissue of the recordings that led to Bukka White's rediscovery, made by Ed Denson and John Fahey at a Memphis rooming house in 1963, nearly a quarter century after his last recordings. White is in astonishingly good form, as both a singer and guitarist—his rendition of "Baby Please Don't Go" is closer to what one by Howlin' Wolf might have sounded like, with an almost palpable fury and desperation, and none of the cultured smoothness of the familiar versions by Big Joe Williams or Muddy Waters. "Aberdeen Mississippi Blues," "New Orleans Streamline," "Parchman Farm Blues," and "Shake 'Em on Down" have an almost preternatural power, and White gets his one acoustic guitar to make sounds one would expect should require two or three. Of almost equal importance, he reminisces about Charley Patton for several minutes. Denson and Fahey caught this blues master at the right time, just the right moment, rising to the sudden occasion to make a new record, spontaneous and unplanned, and got something about as valuable as any of Alan Lomax's field recordings of the 1940s. —*Bruce Eder*

Mississippi Blues / 1969 / Aim ✦✦✦✦
In the true Takoma style of obscurity, there is not much information on this recording. Most of the back cover is taken up with a catalog listing, while the front cover photo is of a dried-up muddy riverbed, which actually looks like a blow-up of a small section of this artist's face. Bukka White is a name known to blues lovers since he was one of the group of early Delta blues recording artists that were rediscovered in the '60s. This album is one of the new recordings he made during this latter period. It is appropriate that White recorded a monologue at one point entitled "Mixed Water" for another label, because blues listeners tend to be mixed about this artist's output. The final analysis is usually in his favor, as he has a tremendously appealing voice, and while not a guitar virtuoso, he certainly creates an authentic Delta blues sound and keeps three or four rhythms that blues bar bands would die for. Sometimes listeners just expect too much from the man, such as a more extensive repertoire of styles or a more forceful guitar attack. Slide guitar and dobro playing have gone so far to the front and center in various types of music that some listeners are just used to hearing it that way, and won't comprehend why White's licks are sometimes simply chiming way in the background, like angels heard from a distance. Despite a lack of intensity—he just sounds tired some of the time—there are several classic performances on this recording. What is identified as "Parchman Farm" was actually recorded under the title of "Where Can I Change My Clothes" in the '40s for Vocalion. While he also recorded another song entitled "Parchman Farm" as well, neither is the blues song of this name that has become a standard. The incorrectly titled performance of "Where Can I Change My Clothes" here is brilliant, as is his intense "Army Blues." His "Baby Please Don't Go" and "Shake 'Em on Down" both display his unforced, calm method of delivery, the main point of focus being the twists and turns taken by his magnificently rich vocal as the guitar plays a very straightforward accompaniment. The distinctive plunk of the steel guitar or dobro is present here throughout; listeners that find this sound appealing will be in heaven, daydreaming of guitars with pictures of palm trees on their backs. The track consisting of stories about blues legend Charley Patton spoon-feeding him small amounts of whisky is amusing, but brings the side to a dead halt. —*Eugene Chadbourne*

Parchman Farm / 1970 / Columbia ✦✦✦✦✦
The artist's face fills the front cover, with a look of quiet and desperation. Sure, he looks like he has the blues, but furthermore, he seems to be secretly begging the listener not to judge this release as his best. That's because the recordings included here date from the late '30s and early '40s, while the photography of the artist is all from the '60s, when he was rediscovered and began performing again for the blues and folk revival audience. A man of pride, White surely wanted to feel that he was doing his best work artistically in the present, not back in his younger days. Records certainly sounded better in the '60s than they did decades earlier, and some blues fans will prefer the later recordings of this artist just because of the lack of surface noise, as well as the more fully developed recorded sound of his characteristic national steel resophonic guitar. White tried very hard in his later years and made some excellent new recordings, but he was often at a loss to fulfill expectations, especially in front of live audiences. He didn't seem to have enough different variations on his song material, went off on too many weird tangents, and sometimes seemed to be in a rotten mood, which certainly seems to be a strange thing for anyone to complain about when it comes to the blues genre. Out of sympathy for this elder statesman of the Delta blues, several of whose songs provide a

textbook example of the style, one wants to pick a later recording as his best, but too many chips fall on the side of these old Vocalion sides, which, despite some surface mess, have been remastered beautifully. The tracks in which White is accompanied by Washboard Sam are really fantastic, representing some of the best country blues one can find, rhythmically snappy and melodically clear. In terms of the musical styles that White employed, they are all here: The basis for every single song he ever recorded, if not the song itself, is included among these 14 tracks. "Where Can I Change My Clothes," one of the best songs about prison, is included along with White's unique version of "Parchman Farm." The former song was one he re-recorded in the '60s, releasing it under the latter title: Neither song is the same as the "Parchman Farm" blues standard that was later satirized by Mose Allison and obliterated by Blue Cheer. One of the great things about White's style is his vocals. His pronunciation and accent are fascinating. Take the way he pronounces the title of "district attorney" in the song of the same name. As well, he could be the only blues singer to deliver the following couplet and make it sound like it actually rhymes: "Doctor, put that temperature gauge under my tongue/And tell me, all I need is my baby's lovin' arms." The use of photographs of White as an old man to accompany music he recorded when he was young may not be completely inappropriate, but it is a bit misleading. The lengthy liner notes are superb. —*Eugene Chadbourne*

☆ **The Complete Sessions 1930–1940** / 1976 / Travelin' Man ✦✦✦✦✦
Travelin' Man's *Complete Sessions 1930-1940* is a strong, 20-track collection of Bukka White's earliest recordings. Although the sound is a little raw, the music itself has lost none of its power over the years. Many of his greatest songs—"Shake 'Em on Down," "Pinebluff, Arkansas," "Parchman Farm Blues," "Fixin' to Die," "New Frisco Train," and "I Am in the Heavenly Way"—are here in arguably their best versions. This is a valuable disc, but it may be difficult to find. In that case, Columbia/Legacy's *The Complete Bukka White* may be a good substitute, since it contains 14 of this disc's 20 tracks. —*Thom Owens*

Aberdeen Mississippi Blues / 1976 / Travelin' Man ✦✦✦
Aberdeen Mississippi Blues collects some of the sessions he cut in 1937 for Vocalion. Although the music is superb, it is available in better collections. —*Thom Owens*

Three Shades of Blues / 1989 / Biograph ✦✦✦
Three Shades of Blues comprises a selection of tracks cut by Bukka White, Skip James, and Blind Willie McTell, all recorded during different eras. James' tracks were made in 1964, the first he cut since 1931. James fares the worst—he sounds unsure of himself and several of the songs are painful to listen to. The five White tracks were recorded in 1974, after he was released from prison; while his voice does sound worn, they're fascinating historical items. McTell's recordings are taken from the last commercial sessions he made in 1949, and they're more than historical curiosities—he sounds as haunted and powerful as he ever has. —*Thom Owens*

Legacy of the Blues, Vol. 1 / 1991 / GNP Crescendo ✦✦✦

Shake 'Em on Down / 1993 / New Rose ✦✦✦✦✦
This fine collection supplants *Parchman Farm* as the definitive set spotlighting Bukka White's Vocalion country blues recordings. —*Ron Wynn*

★ **The Complete Bukka White** / 1994 / Columbia/Legacy ✦✦✦✦✦
Here it is all in one place, all 14 of Bukka White's legendary Vocalion recordings. Kicking off with his lone 1937 single of "Pinebluff, Arkansas" and "Shake 'Em on Down," the set continues with the marathon 12-song session from 1940 that produced such classics as "Sleepy Man Blues," "Parchman Farm Blues," "Fixin' to Die Blues," and "Bukka's Jitterbug Swing." This is personal blues, hitting on a number of subjects usually too stark for blues lyrics, but all on open-wound display here. Powerful stuff, indeed. —*Cub Koda*

1963 Isn't 1962 / 1994 / Genes ✦✦✦
Bukka White was "rediscovered"—alive and well, despite rumors that he'd died a violent death sometime after his last official recording session in 1940—by blues enthusiasts John Fahey and Ed Denson. These live tapes, made late that year by Fahey and Denson, were among the first tangible results of that rediscovery. This older cousin to B.B. King still had all of his stuff—he was only in his mid-fifties, and unlike a lot of older bluesmen who were well past their primes for the '60s blues revival, he could still play and sing up a storm. Indeed, he was playing faster and more precisely in 1963 than he was in 1940, and his slide work shimmers and glistens throughout this CD, and the voice is superb as well. Opening with "Streamline Special," he goes through a dazzling display of repertory, sounding like two or three players at once as he works the strings, playing lead and rhythm simultaneously on his acoustic guitar, in pieces running anywhere from a minute and a half to eight minutes or more. King has admitted trying to re-create White's sound in his own electric playing, but these tapes show just how much of a losing battle that was, against this acoustic guitar virtuoso. —*Bruce Eder*

Big Daddy Mississippi Blues / Sep. 3, 1996 / Biograph ✦✦✦
Bukka White proves the staying power of the traditional blues style with his 1973 sessions. Riding the folk-blues popularity wave in the '60s, these early-'70s recordings find the storyteller/singer still in his prime. Bukka White conjures up in the studio the essence of the revival sound: a man, a guitar, and an authentic delivery. Recorded just a few years before Bukka White's 1977 death, this album of White solos with guitar reaches back into the catalog that made even a large figure in the pre-World War II blues. Among these songs is "Sic 'Em Dogs," which, like most of the tracks, features the ex-boxer percussively playing with the force on his guitar that made him switch from wooden-body guitars to the more durable steel-bodied models. The production is clear vocally, through somewhat thin in the guitar area, and the accompanying notes are detailed. —*Tom Schulte*

Georgia White

b. Mar. 9, 1903, Sandersville, GA, **d.** 1980
Vocals / Classic Female Blues, Piano Blues, Dirty Blues
Barrelhouse blues vocalist Georgia White recorded mildly risqué blues songs from the mid-'30s through the early '40s, including "I'll Keep Sitting on It," "Take Me for a Buggy Ride," "Mama Knows What Papa Wants When Papa's Feeling Blue," and "Hot Nuts." She reportedly moved to Chicago in the 1920s and began working as a singer in the nightclubs during the late '20s. Georgia White first recorded in May 1930 for the Vocalion label with Jimmie Noone's Apex Club Orchestra when she sang just one song, "When You're Smiling, the Whole World Smiles With You." White didn't return to the studios until 1935, but recorded regularly from then on through the early '40s for the Decca label. In 1935, she also recorded a couple of songs, including "Your Worries Ain't Like Mine," under the alias Georgia Lawson. From her first sessions until the late '30s, White was accompanied by pianist Richard Jones. The late '30s found White accompanied by blues guitarist Lonnie Johnson. In the late '40s, Georgia White formed an all-women band. She also worked with Big Bill Broonzy from 1949-1950, and returned to singing in the clubs during the 1950s. Georgia White's last known public performance was in 1959, after which she retired from the music business. *—Joslyn Layne*

● **Trouble in Mind 1935–1941** / 1995 / Blues Collection ♦♦♦♦♦

Complete Recorded Works, Vol. 1 (1930–1936) / Feb. 15, 1996 / Document ♦♦♦♦
Document's *Complete Recorded Works, Vol. 1 (1930-1936)* reissues all of Georgia White's 24 recordings from the first five years of her career, including highlights like "You Done Lost Your Good Thing Now," "Dupree Blues," and the double entendre classic "Get 'Em From the Peanut Man (Hot Nuts)." Less-dedicated listeners will find this disc a mixed blessing, though, with the long running time and poor fidelity combining to make it of only marginal interest. *—Thom Owens*

Complete Recorded Works, Vol. 2 (1936–37) / Mar. 5, 1996 / Document ♦♦♦♦

Complete Recorded Works, Vol. 3 (1937–39) / Apr. 9, 1996 / Document ♦♦♦♦

Complete Recorded Works, Vol. 4 (1939–41) / Apr. 9, 1996 / Document ♦♦♦♦

Josh White

b. Feb. 11, 1914, Greensboro, NC, **d.** Sep. 5, 1969, Manhasset, NY
Vocals, Guitar / Prewar Gospel Blues, Blues Revival, Folk Revival, Folk-Blues, Piedmont Blues, Songster, Political Folk
Most blues enthusiasts think of Josh White as a folk revival artist. It's true that the second half of his music career found him based in New York playing to the coffeehouse and cabaret set and hanging out with Burl Ives, Woody Guthrie, and fellow transplanted blues artists Sonny Terry and Brownie McGhee. When he played in Chicago in the 1960s, his shirt was unbuttoned to his waist à la Harry Belafonte and his repertoire consisted of folk revival standards such as "Scarlet Ribbons." He was a show business personality—a star renowned for his sexual magnetism and his dramatic vocal presentations. What many people don't know is that Josh White was a major figure in the Piedmont blues tradition.

The first part of his career saw him as apprentice and lead boy to some of the greatest blues and religious artists ever, including Willie Walker, Blind Blake, Blind Joe Taggart (with whom he recorded), and allegedly even Blind Lemon Jefferson. On his own, he recorded both blues and religious songs, including a classic version of "Blood Red River." A fine guitar technician with an appealing voice, he became progressively more sophisticated in his presentation. Like many other Carolinians and Virginians who moved north to urban areas, he took up city ways, remaining a fine musician if no longer a down-home artist. Like several other canny blues players, he used his roots music to broaden and enhance his life experience, and his talent was such that he could choose the musical idiom that was most lucrative at the time. *—Barry Lee Pearson*

Josh White 1933–1944 / May 5, 1994 / Best of Blues ♦♦♦♦♦

Complete Recorded Works, Vol. 1 (1929–1933) / Jun. 2, 1994 / Document ♦♦♦♦
Josh White, who became famous in the 1940s as an accessible and highly intelligent folksinger, began his career as a blues-oriented vocalist and guitarist. *Vol. 1* of his complete early recordings starts with a couple instrumental jams from 1929 with the Carver Boys (a quartet consisting of harmonica and three guitars). The remainder of this CD is from 1932-1933, with White heard on some easy-to-take religious songs and as a blues performer. These 24 recordings are all solo numbers other than two selections that have an unknown pianist added. White's voice is strong, and his guitar playing is quite fluent. Among the better numbers are "Black and Evil Blues," "Things About Coming My Way," "Double Crossing Woman," and "Lay Some Flowers on My Grave." This set is particularly recommended to blues collectors who were not aware of Josh White's musical beginnings. *—Scott Yanow*

Complete Recorded Works, Vol. 2 (1933–1935) / Jun. 2, 1994 / Document ♦♦♦♦
The second of three Josh White CDs that document the folk singer's early period features him both as a gospel performer (known as "The Singing Christian") and as a blues singer (billed as "Pinewood Tom"). White's guitar playing was quite fluent during this period and he sounds quite authentic in these different idioms. The first two sessions feature him solo and then other selections have Walter Roland, Leroy Carr, or Clarence Williams on piano, with two songs adding Scrapper Blackwell on second guitar. Among the better selections are "Welfare Blues," "I Believe I'll Make a Change," "Evil Man Blues," "Black Gal," "Milk Cow Blues," and "Homeless and Hungry Blues." *—Scott Yanow*

Complete Recorded Works, Vol. 3 (1935–1940) / Jun. 2, 1994 / Document ♦♦♦♦
The third of three Document CDs that cover Josh White's early years has 16 selections from 1935-1936 and eight from 1940. In between those periods, White suffered a serious injury to a hand that forced him out of music temporarily. The earlier numbers feature him either as "The Singing Christian" or as a blues singer under the name of "Pinewood Tom." Those duets (with either pianist Walter Roland or guitarist Buddy Moss) are excellent including such numbers as "Jet Black Woman," "Got a Key to the Kingdom," and "No More Ball and Chain." The later eight numbers have White accompanied by bassist Wilson Meyers and, on "Careless Love" and "Milk Cow Blues," the great clarinetist Sidney Bechet. Listeners who think of Josh White as primarily an urban folksinger, will find these performances, and those are the preceding two Document CDs, to be quite intriguing. *—Scott Yanow*

Roots of the Blues / Sep. 27, 1994 / Legacy ♦♦♦♦♦

Sings the Blues / 1995 / Collectables ♦♦♦

Complete Recorded Works, Vol. 4 (1940–41) / Nov. 30, 1995 / Document ♦♦♦♦

★ **The Legendary Josh White** / 1996 / Collector's Edition ♦♦♦♦♦
This release highlights 18 songs cut by Josh White during the early '60s. Accompanied by his solo acoustic guitar and a string bass, he goes through a range of songs, from his concert favorite "One Meat Ball" to more generic traditional numbers such as the guitar virtuoso showcase "Prison Bound." White also performs contemporary pieces with which he is associated, including the Earl Robinson and Allen Lewis song "House I Live In" (which became much more famous in the hands of Frank Sinatra), jazz pieces like "Miss Otis Regrets," and even his version of "Waltzing Matilda," which in its tempo and accents is perhaps the most stylized rendition ever heard. The material shows off White's range to exceptionally good advantage, and this is as fine a representation of the music that made him famous in the 1960s as any single CD collection currently available. *—Bruce Eder*

● **Blues Singer 1932–1936** / Feb. 6, 1996 / Columbia/Legacy ♦♦♦♦♦
The suave and debonair blues sex symbol in his earliest and purest period, when the Piedmont influence was at its peak in his playing. This is strong stuff, eons away from the collegiate crowd-pleasing folkie stuff he engaged in during the '60s: "Milk Cow Blues," "Lazy Black Snake Blues," and "Silicosis Is Killin' Me" are acoustic solo blues of a consistently high quality, and there are a few religious tunes thrown in to spotlight the other side of White's early recording activities. *—Bill Dahl*

Complete Recorded Works, Vol. 5 (1944) / Jan. 2, 1998 / Document ♦♦♦

Complete Recorded Works, Vol. 6 (1944–1945) / Jan. 2, 1998 / Document ♦♦♦

Free & Equal Blues / Mar. 17, 1998 / Smithsonian/Folkways ♦♦♦♦♦
Fine 26-song compilation of material recorded by folklorist Moe Asch in the 1940s, at a time when White was beginning to reach an urban, educated audience with his mixture of blues, folk, and pop styles. What comes across particularly strong in this set is his versatility and all-around appeal; he handles topical songs about discrimination and war, spirituals, covers of blues by Leroy Carr and Victoria Spivey, folk ballads, and theatrical pieces, even extending to a cover of Cole Porter's "Miss Otis Regrets." "One Meat Ball" provided some of the musical inspiration for the classic Merle Travis tune "Sixteen Tons"; "Freedom Road" had lyrics by poet Langston Hughes. Because he was less earthy and not as Southern-sounding as Leadbelly and Big Bill Broonzy, White has been accorded less critical respect, but this anthology shows him to be one of the unquestioned linchpins of the first stirrings of the folk revival. Includes copious notes by White biographer Elijah Wald. *—Richie Unterberger*

Remaining Titles: 1941–1947 / Oct. 12, 1999 / Document ♦♦♦

Lavelle White

b. Jul. 3, 1929, Amite, LA
Vocals / Soul-Blues, Electric Texas Blues
Texas-based vocalist and songwriter "Miss" Lavelle White has a significant discography of singles, most dating back to the 1950s and '60s, but she only released her first full-length album, *Miss Lavelle*, on the Austin, TX-based Antone's label in 1994. To say the album had been a long time coming would be the understatement of the year, for White's talents as a songwriter and singer were well-known in 1950s Houston, where she recorded several singles for the Duke/Peacock labels. In the late '50s, her labelmates included Bobby "Blue" Bland, B.B. King, and Junior Parker. *Miss Lavelle* was White's first recording of any kind, in fact, in 30 years. The fact that it's a gorgeous album helped White play some large blues festivals across the U.S., Canada, and Europe, but for a number of years when she had no record deal, White continued to entertain club crowds with her singing in Chicago, Texas, Louisiana, and Florida.

White's first big break as a vocalist came about with something she wrote for herself, "If I Could Be With You," and a procession of other singles followed for the Duke/Peacock label, including "Just Look at You Fool," "Stop These Teardrops," and "The Tide of Love." Unlike many other blues singers, White didn't get started recording until she was 25, thanks to fellow Houstonian Johnny "Clyde" Copeland, who brought White to Duke/Peacock owner Don Robey's attention.

White began writing poems and songs when she was 12, she said in a 1994 interview. "Hardships in life made me start to write," she explained, "and the first record I cut was with a gospel group, 'Precious Lord, Lead Me On.'" When she was 16, White moved to Houston and fell into the city's burgeoning blues club scene with Clarence Hollimon, who now records with his wife Carol Fran for the Rounder label.

Today, long after she got her humble start in the blues clubs in Houston, White sings as well as she ever did, and though she's had time off from the road over the years, she's never stopped singing or writing songs. She released her first album, *Miss Lavelle*, in 1994. It was followed three years later by *It Haven't Been Easy*. *—Richard Skelly*

● **Miss Lavelle** / May 28, 1994 / Antone's ♦♦♦♦
More than 30 years after she got her humble start in the blues clubs in Houston, Lavelle White was singing as well as she ever did, and though she's had time off from the road over the years, she never stopped singing or writing songs. All of this is apparent with one listen to *Miss Lavelle*. The dignified manner in which White conducts herself on-stage, dressed in flashy outfits and walking about confidently, is something that was

instilled in her from an early age. This respect for the stage, or stage presence, that is apparent when Miss Lavelle White performs is something the younger generation of blues players (and many rock & rollers) seem to lack. *—Richard Skelly*

It Haven't Been Easy / Jan. 14, 1997 / Discovery ♦♦♦

Barrence Whitfield (Barry White)

Vocals / Rock & Roll, R&B

A Boston-based singer of what one might refer to as "traditional" R&B (i.e., '50s- and '60s-style), Whitfield is the owner of one incredible pair of lungs and limitless energy and enthusiasm for his music. A soul screamer in the spirit of Little Richard, Wilson Pickett, Solomon Burke, and early Don Covay, Whitfield & the Savages, though never breaking big nationally, are a great cult act, a triumph of substance over style, with a bunch of terrific records to boot.

Whitfield (real name Barry White, no joke!) came to Boston from New Jersey in the late '70s to attend Boston University. Prior to college, he'd spent time singing in an assortment of ill-fated hard rock, disco, and even progressive rock bands, never really singing the soul music he grew up loving. His move to Boston was a way of putting (at least temporarily) his musical past behind him. He had no intention of starting another band; his focus was on college. That was until he fell in with a bunch of Boston musicians led by ex-Lyres guitarist Peter Greenberg, who shared Barry's love of raging soul and R&B. After hearing Barry sing, Greenberg was convinced they'd found the best voice in the city and Barrence Whitfield & the Savages were born. For a while, they were the toast of the town, and without a doubt one of the best live acts in Boston. It was a hopeful sign too—an African-American man working with a bunch of white guys in a city not known for its racial hospitality. After some dues-paying at college frat-house parties, the Savages were ready for the local club scene, and they tore it up. Whitfield was a dervish on-stage, working himself into such a frenzy of screaming and running around that he would occasionally black out. The band, especially Greenberg and drummer Howie Ferguson, were raucous and rough, in high gear from the moment they hit the stage.

Their debut LP was released to much acclaim (some of it national) in 1984, but the Savages' brand of old R&B, and the fact that they relied almost exclusively on covers, didn't help them get beyond their status as enthusiastic archivists. By the time the third album was released, the Savages had been replaced by a whole new band, and while the mania remained intact, there was a concerted effort for smoother soul songs designed to show off Barry's voice. While America was being apathetic to the Savages, England was going wild for them. BBC disc jockey Andy Kershaw fell in love with the band, taped a gig in Boston for air in Britain, and brought the Savages over for a tour. Among their English fans were Robert Plant (who showed up at some gigs) and Elvis Costello, who was supposedly writing a song for them.

Unfortunately, English success didn't translate back into big sales in America, and the band soldiered on with a few more personnel changes, but remained a cult act, touring in their strongholds and releasing fewer and fewer records. Today, the Savages live and Barry is busy with them and as a solo act, even trying his hand at country music. But for a brief moment, they set the world on fire, and there were few bands better. *—John Dougan*

Barrence Whitfield and the Savages / 1984 / Rounder ♦♦♦

It clocks in at under 30 minutes, so these days it qualifies as an EP, but the Savages' debut record is a scorcher. A 100-mph rave-up from the moment Barry screams his way through Don Covay's "Bip Bop Bip" to the go-for-broke "Ship Sails at Six." Peter Greenberg's garage grunge guitar sounds great propelling these tracks, and the whole thing just screeches party. *—John Dougan*

Dig Yourself / 1985 / Rounder ♦♦♦

Better produced than their debut, *Dig Yourself* picks up where the mania of the first album left off. Again, Barry sounds great, as does the band, ripping it up with a wild-eyed exuberance that you could go months without hearing these days. Contains one of the best favorite Savages tracks, "Juicy Fruit." Caveat emptor: This was recorded in the vinyl era and is only 30 minutes long. *—John Dougan*

● **Ow! Ow! Ow!** / 1987 / Rounder ♦♦♦♦♦

This was the first record with the "New" Savages, and the turn is to more original material. Guitarist Milton Reder's "Madhouse" is a wonderful fit for Barry's voice, as is sax player David Scholl's "I Don't Dig Your Noise." But the payoff is the Reder-penned "Girl from Outer Space," which Barry sings in a falsetto scream that is dazzling (he even riffs on Sun Ra at the end of the song). What makes this the strongest Whitfield/Savages album is its variety, and the fact that Barry's voice is strong and versatile enough to bring more nuance and emotion to the material. Why this wasn't a big hit for them one will never know; it's a fine, fine record. *—John Dougan*

Call of the Wild / 1987 / Demon/Rounder Europa ♦♦♦

Live Emulsified / 1989 / Rounder ♦♦

Hearing a Barrence Whitfield and the Savages gig is fun; being at one can be transforming. So, this live record is a good example of the muss 'n' fuss these guys could kick out on-stage, but it lacks the physicality of being there and feeling the band's almost brute strength. Still, it's lot of fun, and you can hear Barry let go. *—John Dougan*

Let's Lose It / 1990 / Stony Plain ♦♦♦♦♦

More personality in each song—better playing, better sound. *—Robert Gordon*

Hillbilly Voodoo / 1993 / East Side Digital ♦♦♦♦

It's appropriate that soul singer Barrence Whitfield has his mouth wide open and folkie Tom Russell has his closed in the cover photos of both this album and its follow-up, *Cowboy Mambo.* Throughout each disk, Whitfield holds the spotlight; Russell joins in the fun and also contributes some songs, but his main role seems to be as producer and fan: he clearly loves Whitfield's music and seems determined to help popularize it. And no wonder—Whitfield's music is terrific stuff. If you had to slap a label on him, it would be country-soul singer, but he's soaked up far too many influences and turned them into something far too special for that tag to do him justice. The material—alternately playful and emotional—is uniformly first-rate, with highlights including Lucinda Williams' "I Just Want to See You So Bad," and Bob Dylan's "Blind Willie McTell," Van Morrison's "Cleaning Windows," Jesse Winchester's "Mississippi, You're on My Mind," and Russell's own "The Cuban Sandwich." *—Jeff Burger*

Cowboy Mambo / 1993 / East Side Digital ♦♦♦♦♦

Fans of *Hillbilly Voodoo,* the fine first collaboration between country-soul singer Barrence Whitfield and folkie Tom Russell, will not be disappointed by this follow-up. Once again, Russell skillfully handles production chores, and once again, he leaves the spotlight to Whitfield, who turns in a dozen high-spirited, live-in-the-studio-sounding performances. The inspired program of tunes taps writers ranging from the Band's Robbie Robertson ("Daniel and the Sacred Harp") to Nashville outlaws like Steve Earle ("The Devil's Right Hand") and Gram Parsons ("Brass Buttons"). There are also several contributions from Russell, including the title cut and the affecting "Home Before Dark." *—Jeff Burger*

Ritual of the Savages / Jul. 4, 1995 / Ocean Music ♦♦♦♦

If you think that cult acts become bitter as they get older and release records that are pale copies of their (albeit fleeting) glory days, that ain't the case with the Savages. *Ritual of the Savages* may not be as totally berserk as, say, *Dig Yourself,* but Barry and band still make fine records, alternately energetic and soulful; their repertoire has expanded, and Milton Reder's writing chops (e.g., "Got Your Love Right Here" and "House of Love") have become a valuable asset to the sound. Since the late '80s, the Savages have had a relationship with Ben Vaughn, and his presence and songwriting contributions have helped them continue to refine their sound without loosing the sense of manic energy that made their earlier releases so important. Now a decade-plus on, Barrence Whitfield and the Savages are clearly no the same band they were in 1984, but they're still a fine band; spin "Wiggy Waggy Woo" and you'll see. *—John Dougan*

Chris Whitley

b. Aug. 31, 1960, Houston, TX

Slide Guitar, Vocals, Guitar / Americana, Roots Rock, Singer/Songwriter, Blues-Rock

Chris Whitley is a Texas-based singer-songwriter who initially began his career as a bluesy roots-rocker, but as his career progressed, he moved deeper into rock & roll and alternative rock. Though Whitley's albums usually received positive reviews, they rarely sold, and his tendency to rework his sound prevented him from developing a sizable cult following among singer-songwriter fans.

As a child, Whitley moved frequently through the Southeast, eventually moving with his mother to Mexico after his parents divorced when he was 11; they later settled in a log cabin in Vermont. At the age of 15, he began playing guitar, inspired by Creedence Clearwater Revival, Johnny Winter, and Jimi Hendrix, eventually learning how to play slide guitar. He quit high school a year before graduation, moving to New York City, where he busked on the streets. One of his performances was witnessed by a listener who ran a travel agency, and decided that Whitley would be a success in Belgium and offered to send him to Europe. With nothing to lose, Whitley accepted the offer.

Once in Belgium, Whitley recorded a series of albums that flip-flopped between blues, rock, and funk. The records made him a minor success in Belgium, but he decided to return to New York anyway in 1990. He happened to meet producer Daniel Lanois later that year. Impressed by Whitley's songs, Lanois helped set up a deal with Columbia Records for the songwriter, and produced his first album. Released in the spring of 1991, Whitley's U.S. debut *Living With the Law* was an atmospheric set of blues and folk-rock that received glowing reviews and earned him a slot opening for Tom Petty & the Heartbreakers.

Though *Living With the Law* seemed to position Chris Whitley for a breakthrough into a cult audience, he waited four years to deliver his second record, *Din of Ecstasy.* An attempt to connect with the hard-edged mainstream alternative rock audience that developed in the years following the release of *Living With the Law,* the grunge-flavored *Din of Ecstasy*—which was released on Columbia's recently developed "alternative" subsidiary, WORK—received mixed reviews and alienated his roots rock audience without winning him new fans. Two years later, Whitley released *Terra Incognita,* which combined elements of his first two records. *Dirt Floor* followed on the Messenger label in 1998, restoring Whitley to a level of critical acclaim that rivaled his early work. *Live at Martyrs'* followed in the spring of 2000, and just a few months later, the spare studio effort *Perfect Day* appeared on the Valley imprint. *Rocket House* (2001) expanded on more soulful grooves, and boasted eclectic collaborations with Bruce Hornsby, Blondie Chaplin, and Dave Matthews. It was also his first for Matthews' own imprint, ATO Records. *—Stephen Thomas Erlewine*

● **Living With the Law** / Dec. 5, 1991 / Columbia ♦♦♦♦♦

Chris Whitley's 1991 debut, *Living With the Law,* was recorded in Daniel Lanois' New Orleans mansion and was produced by Malcolm Burn. The sublimely dark, creepy, and possessed collection sounds completely out of place for the era of slick pop/rock like Milli Vanilli. The tortured album is rich with old-style sounds, from slide-guitars to pedal steel. (Lanois contributes some on the album.) *Living With the Law* has a full, ambient feel that transports the listener into the recording. Whitley humbly (and falsely) claims, at the beginning of the record, that "God knows it's all been done." But these 12 songs attempt an original look at a honest style and passionate mood that is lacking in much of rock music. Whitley sings of drug abuse, alienation, failure, and loneliness with a Delta blues flavor. Standout tracks include "Phone Call from Leavenworth," "Big Sky Country," and "Dirt Radio." Those who liked Whitley's *Dirt Floor* must own *Living With the Law* if they don't already. It is more of a full-band sound, but similar in tone and feel. An exceptional and mesmerizing debut, one with the potential to inspire all who hear it. (This release is also fascinating for those who enjoy *Rocket House*. Influences on the 2001 album can be heard throughout *Living With the Law*, released a decade earlier.) An album Robert Johnson may have recorded, were he still alive. —*JT Griffith*

Din of Ecstasy / 1995 / Work ✦✦
On his second album, Whitley abandons the atmospheric acoustic blues-rock of his debut for a hard-hitting, grungy guitar attack. Appropriately, the songs are all about losers and hard times—it's a dark, bleak album, twisting through its songs with a grim determination. The problem is, it doesn't always work. Whitley's lyrics are still rooted in the folk-blues storytelling tradition, while his music follows the rules of contemporary hard rock, complete with start-stop dynamics and thick layers of distortion. However, he can't write riffs that equal the best of Nirvana, Pearl Jam, and Soundgarden, nor does he have melodies to rival theirs. His music works best a lyrical level and the musical approach on *Din of Ecstasy* obscures his lyrics, making the record a muddled affair. —*Stephen Thomas Erlewine*

Terra Incognita / Feb. 18, 1997 / Work ✦✦✦
On *Terra Incognita*, Chris Whitley incorporates the grunge flourishes of *Din of Ecstasy* into the roots rock foundations of his debut, *Living With the Law*. Instead of relying on processed distorted guitars, Whitley uses noise as texture, which helps his songs breathe. While the musical direction of *Terra Incognita* is considerably more focused than its confused predecessor, Whitley's songwriting remains uneven. Though he has written a better, more diverse record than before, he has yet to produce a set of songs that demonstrate the depth and variety of *Living With the Law*. Too often, he relies on clichés or simplistic ideas, like the single "Automatic," but when he digs a little deeper, his songs still resonate deeply, which means *Terra Incognita* is a partial, not a full, comeback. —*Stephen Thomas Erlewine*

Dirt Floor / Mar. 17, 1998 / Messenger ✦✦✦✦
This is the most consistent and accessible disc of Chris Whitley's off-and-on recording career. The album is just Whitley singing and accompanying himself on banjo, guitar, and foot stomp. It has a simple and wonderfully stripped-down sound that fits perfectly with the morose yet tumultuous mood of the songs, establishing a strong atmosphere that is almost as important to the work as the mood in a '40s film noir. This is an exceedingly short work, only 27-plus minutes, yet it really shouldn't be much longer. If you were expecting *Big Sky Country* in sound, you will be both happy and disappointed: happy because there is the same stripped-down, nasal singing and story-songs, and disappointed because there is not as much dobro, nor a band helping him flesh out the tunes. He does an excellent job on the small amount of material here, yet it does not develop into anything due to the lack of time; at the same time, the tone is so very angst-ridden that the short length may work in its favor. There are no liner notes or comments for this disc. What is here is excellent in its own right and stands up as some of his best work; one just wonders if maybe another song or two might have made it a stronger work. —*Bob Gottlieb*

Chris Whitley Live at Martyrs' / May 16, 2000 / Messenger ✦✦✦✦
Just a man and his guitar: That's all *Live at Martyrs'* is. Yet it is perhaps the best way to hear Chris Whitley, separated from the studio trappings that had a tendency to obscure and hinder his otherwise gutsy folk-blues on previous recordings, and planted precisely in the element that helped earn him his name in singer/songwriter and critical circles. That is part of what makes the album such a welcome addition to the cult musician's mixed catalog. Recorded in Chicago over a few nights in 1999, *Live* captures all the things that make Whitley's music so enticing: heated passion, raw intensity, and an indescribable urge toward both the sacred and profane. It is, in fact, a logical extension from both his outstanding debut album and his previous effort, *Dirt Floor*, the two most lauded releases of his career. Stripped of commercial production and all other confusing affectations, the recording allows his wonderful songs and torrid delivery to take center stage. It might be instructive to note that half the set list comes from the first two studio albums, with only three deriving from the third and fourth albums. His second and third albums received only lukewarm reviews, but the songs from those efforts are given revelatory readings that far surpass the original incarnations, almost sounding like entirely new songs. The two new songs that are included prove strong additions to Whitley's songbook, while his cover of Kraftwerk's "The Model" is virtually unrecognizable and like nothing else in his canon. His guitar picking on the song is almost banjo style, and he sings with a smooth croon instead of his normal cavorting vocals. In general, though, even as spare as the recording is, it is highly atmospheric. Whitley's electrified guitar can sound like warped metal ("Dirt Floor") or like sepia-toned, foot-stomping country blues, and on the new "Home Is Where You Get Across" his playing is strikingly close to the phenomenal picking skills of Leo Kottke. Much of the music is blues-based, and certain songs still roll around in the mud and get rather grungy, but surprisingly, in this naked setting, the songs take on a folk-like dimension (albeit overdriven folk) with progressive songwriters from the '60s such as Tim Hardin and Tim Buckley (or, for a more contemporary comparison, Jeff Buckley) frequently springing to mind. It is soulful stuff and gets at the essence of what makes Chris Whitley such a thrilling musician when he is "on": electrifying instrumental abilities and shadowy, dark-edge story-songs that dig into your skin and unravel you layer by layer. Although it is top-heavy on the first two albums, *Live at Martyrs'* is possibly the best end-to-end effort in his early catalog. —*Stanton Swihart*

Perfect Day / Jul. 25, 2000 / Valley ✦✦✦
After issuing the spare, entirely solo *Live at Martyrs'* in early 2000, Chris Whitley returned to the studio with drummer Billy Martin and bassist Chris Wood (of Medeski, Martin & Wood fame) to cut the similarly low-key, all covers album *Perfect Day*. It's a mix of blues

standards and rock songs with a poetic bent (writers like Dylan, Reed, and Morrison) all given hauntingly minimalistic treatments. Whitley's guitar work is subdued and spacious, as are Martin and Wood's constantly shifting backing rhythms. The cover photo of a haggard-looking Whitley sets the tone for his performances: he sounds committed but weary, which gives these renditions a darkly compelling power. "Spoonful," in particular, often seems on the verge of falling apart, as Whitley's guitar slashes almost randomly over the rhythm section's syncopations. But—perhaps like the singer himself—it somehow holds together in the face of desperation, which is a handy way to sum up the album's impact as a whole. —*Steve Huey*

Rocket House / Jun. 5, 2001 / ATO ✦✦✦✦
Anyone who has the balls to combine turntable scratching and trip-hop beats with banjo playing on the same song—and make it work—as Chris Whitley does on the Middle Eastern-tinged "To Joy (Revolution of the Innocents)" deserves a collective bow-down to. This unorthodox, textured, and electronic-oriented album opener to Whitley's seventh studio effort, *Rocket House*, sets the stage for one of the best collections to drop in 2001. Whitley's husky, soulful voice smoothly roams through throaty lows and lofty falsettos in a single sweep and is captivating, to say the least. Meanwhile, all things synthesizer and programming—keyboards, synth guitars, synth bass, electronic "abstractions" (according to the liner notes), jaw harp, drum machines, samples, and others—coupled with "traditional" instruments—guitars, drums, bass, and piano—and some pretty avant-garde arrangements further launch *Rocket House* right into the sky. There is plenty to recommend on this impressive collection. "Say Goodbye" is an earnest and moving blues-rock number—accented with turntable scratching and contemporary sound effects—marked by Whitley's visceral vocal delivery and a haunting piano. Elsewhere, the title track is entirely infectious and mesmerizing. A simple breakbeat drives organic guitar parts and hypnotic vibe and piano lines. The song ends with a series of instrumental repetitions, which inspires a lingering effect. Some artists unsuccessfully try to do this—repetition—and their songs sound painfully boring. But this is not the case with Whitley; "Rocket House," with each closing verse that pulses on, captivates listeners even more; you're still "in" the song way after it's done. "Serve You," in its haunting simplicity, is one of the most seductive songs ever recorded. Whitley's husky voice is layered over moody, dark tones, strategically random (!) synth chords, and a lone rim-shot line. The chorus, "Some day I will serve you/some day," co-sung with daughter Trixie Whitley, repeats throughout, and the effect is simply hypnotic. This song—much like the rest of the album—is like a drug, mind-altering. An impressive roster of musicians—producer Tony Mangurian, DJ Logic, Dave Matthews, and Bruce Hornsby—guest on *Rocket House*. For the uninitiated—and if you are, you should change this status immediately—Whitley's voice is reminiscent of Jeff Healy, Joe Cocker, and Shawn Mullins in its bluesy soul style. *Rocket House* is an out-of-body experience, and that just doesn't happen too often these days. Get this album and prepare for takeoff to a place that is like no other. —*Liana Jonas*

Long Way Around: An Anthology 1991–2001 / Sep. 3, 2002 / Columbia/Legacy ✦✦✦✦✦

Johnny Wicks' Swinging Ozarks

f. Louisville, KY
Group / Jump Blues, R&B
An unbelievably obscure outfit from Louisville, KY, who cut one session for Chicago's United Records in 1952, Johnny Wicks' Swinging Ozarks were partially rescued from historical oblivion by Delmark boss Bob Koester, who bucked the commercial odds by issuing an LP of their United material. Wicks played bass; Preacher Stephens blew tuba and sang. —*Bill Dahl*

The Wild Tchoupitoulas

f. New Orleans, LA
Group / New Orleans R&B, Zydeco, Creole
The Wild Tchoupitoulas—Spy Boy (Amos Landry), Trail Chief (Booker Washington), Big Chief Jolly (George Landry), Flag Boy (Carl Christmas), the Third Chief (Thomas Jackson), and Second Chief (Norman Bell)—are a Mardi Gras ceremonial parade group and "black Indian tribe" based in New Orleans. George Landry is an uncle to the Neville brothers. *The Wild Tchoupitoulas* is their only album. —*William Ruhlmann*

★ **The Wild Tchoupitoulas** / 1976 / Mango ✦✦✦✦✦
The Wild Tchoupitoulas—a group of Mardi Gras Indians headed by George "Big Chief Jolly" Landry—only released one album, but that one record caused a sensation upon its initial 1976 release. It was one of the first records of the album-rock generation that captured the heady gumbo of New Orleans R&B and funk. Landry may have fronted the Wild Tchoupitoulas, but the key to the record's success was his nephews, Charles and Cyril Neville, who headed the rhythm section. They drafted in their brothers, Art and Aaron, to harmonize, and thereby unwittingly gave birth to the band that became the Neville Brothers. Still, the fact that *The Wild Tchoupitoulas* ranks among the great New Orleans albums isn't because of the Nevilles themselves, but the way the Tchoupitoulas lock into an extraordinary hybrid that marries several indigenous New Orleans musics, with swampy, dirty funk taking its place in the forefront. There are only eight songs, and they are all strung together, as if they're variations on the same themes and rhythms. That's a compliment, by the way, since the organic, flowing groove is the key to the album's success. —*Stephen Thomas Erlewine*

Joe Willie Wilkins

b. Jan. 7, 1923, Davenport, MS, d. 1981, Memphis, TN
Guitar, Vocals / Memphis Blues
Rebellion against his parents was certainly not part of the scenario with this bluesman, who was mostly known as a sideman, but was a major influence as a guitarist all the

same. He was born in the heart of the Mississippi Delta and his father was the bluesman Papa Frank Wilkins, a friend of the great country bluesman Charley Patton. Joe Willie Wilkins was already picking pretty good blues guitar at an early age, after also learning both harmonica and accordion. He picked up the nickname of "the Walkin' Seeburg," a reference to the brand name of a popular jukebox in the '30s, for his knack at learning songs, resulting in a unique ability to perform almost any request. In the early '40s, he replaced Robert Jr. Lockwood in the band of the hard-driving harmonica champion Sonny Boy Williamson, a gig that required an ability to play the type of jazzy phrases, chords, and runs that the leader favored in his arrangements. The guitarist can be heard on a good number of recordings by Williamson, as well as on sides by artists such as Willie Love and Big Joe Williams, playing bass with the latter master of blues eccentricity. Along with fellow guitarist Houston Stackhouse, Wilkins performed with Williamson on the famous KKFA *Mother's Best Flour Hour* radio show out of Helena, AR; if blues fans were all bakers, this would be the most popular brand of flour in the world. Whatever effect the music did have on flour sales, it certainly turned heads of musicians. According to no less an expert than Muddy Waters, Wilkins was the first guitarist he heard in Mississippi who was playing single-string patterns without using a slide. The dropping of the slide was an essential stylistic trademark of the new postwar electric blues guitar playing. Waters has been quoted praising Wilkins highly: "The man is great, the man is stone great. For blues, like I say, he's the best." B.B. King must have also thought so; he took lessons from Wilkins in the late '40s, and some blues fans feel there is a little bit of this elder statesman in every riff B.B. King plays.

Spinoff bands also evolved from the membership of Williamson's bands. In 1950, Wilkins formed the Three Aces with Willie Nix and Love, although "the Three Willies" would have been a more obvious name. This group broadcast over KWEM in 1950, attracting the attention of producer Sam Phillips, leading to Wilkins' tenure as house guitarist for Phillips' Sun Records at its Memphis studio. The guitarist also backed many artists recording for Trumpet in Jackson, MS. He recorded as a sideman with most great '50s bluesmen, including Arthur "Big Boy" Crudup, Roosevelt Sykes, Big Walter Horton, Little Walter Jacobs, Mose Vinson, Memphis Al Williams, Joe Hill Louis, Elmore James, and Floyd Jones. Some of the guitarist's wildest playing can be heard on the Sykes track entitled "Sputnick"; the guitar solo has almost a rockabilly sound.Wilkins toured a great deal in the South, spent many hours in Chicago recording studios, but always wound up returning home to his adopted home of Memphis. His relationship with Stackhouse continued through the years out of their mutual base in this city. Wilkins was Stackhouse's landlord, a relationship which did not prevent them from performing together frequently in the city's blues festival and the traveling Memphis Blues Caravan, a Sonny Boy Williamson tribute band. One can assume the repertoire did not include the famous blues "House Rent Boogie," with lyrics boasting: "You ain't gettin' no back rent! You ain't gettin' no front rent either!"

Wilkins was so dedicated to performing that he continued touring even after undergoing a colostomy in the late '70s. Although some biographers list his death as occurring in 1979, his final performances were an East Coast tour in 1981, and he died in the week following these engagements. This artist's original songs include "Hard Headed Woman" and "It's Too Bad." There is a biographical essay on him in the book entitled *Goin' Back to Sweet Memphis: Conversations With the Blues* by Fred J. Hay. *—Eugene Chadbourne*

Robert Wilkins

b. Jan. 16, 1896, Hernando, MS, **d.** May 26, 1987, Memphis, TN

Vocals, Guitar / Prewar Country Blues, Acoustic Memphis Blues, Vaudeville Blues, Minstrel, Prewar Gospel Blues

It is quite obvious to anyone with functioning ears that Mick Jagger and Keith Richards had heard the late-'20s song entitled "That's No Way to Get Along" by the Reverend Robert Wilkins, because the Rolling Stones album track "Prodigal Son" is a direct copy, at least to the point in the road where the imitation of Wilkins' guitar style hits a technical roadblock. Yet the early pressings of the Stones' cover listed the writers as Jagger and Richards, a deception that was only corrected following legal action. According to the Stones, the mistake was inadvertent and happened because the original artwork for the *Beggars Banquet* album had to be redone. Because a publisher connected with the original Vocalion label had nabbed the actual collecting rights to the song, this unfortunately did not result in a financial windfall for Wilkins. And although he took great advantage of the '60s roots music revival and performed both concerts and new recordings in the absolute prime of his musical power, there is no way that every pimply high school kid who sat around listening to the Stones' "Prodigal Son" actually was lucky enough to get a taste of the real thing.

A mix of Afro-American and Cherokee Indian, Wilkins hailed from De Soto County, MS, famous stomping grounds for Delta blues. His later fight with the powerful Rolling Stones probably didn't seem like much of a hassle compared to what he went through growing up. His father was kicked out of the state due to bootlegging activities. His mother made a better choice with her second husband, the fine guitarist Tim Oliver, who taught his new stepson plenty. Other country blues musicians would come by the house to jam, the source of further musical knowledge hanging in the air. By the time he was 15, Wilkins was performing and making money at dances and parties. He relocated to Memphis with his mother when he was in his early twenties, this simple geographical movement north having the expected effect of an equal mix of the Delta blues and Memphis styles. He stayed in Memphis, mingling with many of the great blues talents who passed through, including Charley Patton and Furry Lewis. He taught Memphis Minnie a good deal of her guitar style. Wilkins' early performing life included touring with small vaudeville and minstrel shows. In 1928, he met Ralph Peer of the Victor label and was invited to cut four songs. One result of these releases was Wilkins being invited to perform on a one-hour radio program, making him apparently the first black artist to make a live radio appearance in Memphis.

Vocalion, a main rival in the "race" records business, dispatched a microphone-toting field unit about a year later, doing the competition better by recording eight new Wilkins songs as the Roaring Twenties roared out. These sessions produced the aforementioned "That's No Way to Get Along," which he himself had no qualms about retitling "Prodigal Son" on his own new versions of the song recorded in the '60s. The song's status as a hit gave him particular license as its creator to push it heavily during his later career revival and a ten-minute version recorded for the Piedmont album *Memphis Gospel Singer* is one of the rare masterpieces of extended blues. His first batch of recording activity continued in 1935, when he recorded five more blues songs, backed this time by a second guitarist and a wonderful spoons player. During this year, his philosophy of life went through a radical switch, the catalyst being the casual violence and sleazy atmosphere of one of the typical house party gigs that he played. Apparently, it was enough to make him believe this music really was an instrument of Satan. He joined the Church of God in Christ and became a minister with a speciality in healing and herbal remedies, his wares ranging from gospel to gingko.

Although it seemed like a radical change in lifestyle, the actual musical effects were almost nil. He went on playing guitar exactly the same way, but just stuck to a repertoire of gospel numbers. Often the meat of an old guitar arrangement would be re-cooked with a different broth. The sexy "My Baby" was changed into the devout "My Lord," for example. His efforts in this style hold up well in comparison to the monsters of gospel blues such as Blind Willie Johnson or Blind Joe Taggart, and Wilkins also has the light-fingered steel-string charm of Reverend Gary Davis or Mississippi John Hurt. The continuing guitar workout as a minister meant his chops were in plenty fine shape when he was "rediscovered" in the '60s. A better description would be to say he was lured from the churches back out into the secular concert world. Of all the blues musicians unearthed during this period—some of whom looked like they had literally been pulled out of the ground—Wilkins was one of the easiest to find. Based on a rumor that Wilkins had been corresponding with an elderly British blues collector, which he actually hadn't, another blues enthusiast checked the Memphis phone book and found Wilkins' name right there. Hmm, if only finding Blind Joe Death could be so easy. Wilkins performed recorded plenty of gospel material along with the blues, including cutting a full album devoted to sacred songs. The grandson of this great bluesman wrote a biography of Wilkins, entitled *To Profit a Man*, which was published in Memphis by Museum Publishing in 1995. *—Eugene Chadbourne*

Memphis Blues 1928–1935 / 1928-1935 / Document ♦♦♦♦♦

Document's *Memphis Blues 1928-1935* contains the 14 Robert Wilkins sides that are currently in circulation, augmented with cuts by a pair of country bluesmen, Tom Dickinson and Allen Shaw. Since Wilkins' recordings are also available on Yazoo's *Original Rolling Stone*, which is easier to find than this disc, *Memphis Blues 1928-1935* isn't a necessary purchase for Wilkins fans, unless they're serious country blues fans who want the cuts by Dickinson and Shaw, as well. *—Thom Owens*

☆ **Memphis Gospel Singer** / Jul. 1964 / Piedmont ♦♦♦♦♦

Of the handful of blues artists who were rediscovered and recorded anew in the '60s, this particular fellow was the least prolific, but perhaps the most consistent. In the course of only a few recording opportunities, he completely captured the intensity of his recording output of the late '20s and '30s as well as that of any of his contemporaries, and he did it all effortlessly. On some of the tracks, it is just a matter of setting a mood or keeping the rhythm consistently engaging as he strums his guitar. Playing the guitar flat on his lap, he gets a slightly different sound from some of the same licks that other country blues or slide players come up with, but also works in his own non-slide fingerpicking, including extremely intelligent use of the ringing overtones that can be created by doubling up bass notes. Most blues listeners found out about Wilkins because the Rolling Stones somehow thought they could get away with completely ripping off his song "Prodigal Son." Early pressings of their cover version can be identified by the fact that it is credited to Mick Jagger and Keith Richards as songwriters, a scam that was corrected later due to legal action. Many blues artists had trouble squaring up such treachery, but perhaps Wilkins had God on his side: He was devoutly religious, devoting each of the songs on this set to a gospel theme. Listeners who may feel unholy should not let this scare them off, as it is solid blues playing all the way and in fact even branches out into other areas of acoustic playing. The long instrumental section of "Thank You, Jesus," with its ringing chords and interesting repeating patterns, is something John Fahey would have been proud of playing. The ten-minute version of "Prodigal Son" is the centerpiece of the set, one of the few examples of an extended country blues performance and one of the best. Although this is the album's longest track, others are stretched out to nearly five minutes, Wilkins never flagging in his momentum or involvement with each piece. His interpretation of "Just a Closer Walk With Thee" is extremely beautiful. The album benefits from an extremely clear and vivid recorded sound. *—Eugene Chadbourne*

Remember Me / 1971 / Genes ♦♦♦

Although he left the world of blues for gospel, Rev. Robert Wilkins never abandoned his guitar or toned down his brillant instrumental tendencies; he simply took his rampaging playing style and used it in the service of the Lord. While he wasn't in peak form for this newly discovered and released 1971 concert, he was far from second-rate. He performed 13 cuts and sang with passion, power and conviction. Robert Palmer's liner notes outline Wilkins' contributions and style. *—Ron Wynn*

★ **The Original Rolling Stone** / 1980 / Yazoo ♦♦♦♦♦

Yazoo's *Original Rolling Stone* is a wonderful disc containing 14 of the 17 sides Robert Wilkins recorded before the war. Wilkins was one of the great country blues artists, and these songs—including "Rollin' Stone," "That's No Way to Get Along," "Jailhouse Blues" and "I'll Go with Her"—became legendary, not only because the songs were terrific (which they are) but also because the performances are intense and haunting. *The Original Rolling Stone* features these songs in the best fidelity possible, along with some fairly good liner notes, making this the best package of his most influential recordings. *—Thom Owens*

Alanda Williams

Vocals / Modern Electric Blues

Alanda Williams is one of the Young Lions on the Dallas/Fort Worth Texas blues scene. The vocalist continues the tradition of beer joint blues set down by people like Robert Ealey and U.P. Wilson.

Williams began playing drums at age five, inspired by James Brown's drummer. When he was 16, Williams met Brown's drummer in Memphis and had the chance to play with him on stage, and that made a lasting impression on the young Williams, who had already begun singing at age 12 at the Baptist church in Pace. Williams' grandfather was the choir director, and he encouraged the young man to sing, even though he was already obsessed with playing drums and a little guitar.

Williams credits his influences as people like Brown, the Temptations, Marvin Gaye, and Curtis Mayfield. After joining a gospel group, the Sons of the South, at age 14, he sang gospel for another six years, recording one album with the group. At 20, he got a music scholarship to Coahoma Junior College and Jackson State College and received formal training there. In 1968, Williams moved to Philadelphia, where he started a soul group, For Love, which opened for the Platters, the Drifters, and other touring vocal groups. After meeting Charlie Brown from the Coasters, who liked Williams' singing, he joined the group and toured extensively.

Between 1970 and 1991, Williams toured the world with the Coasters, eventually settling in Fort Worth in 1991. He formed his own group, the Soul Kings, and began performing around Fort Worth and Dallas clubs. The Soul Kings can be heard backing up guitarist U.P. Wilson on his first recording for JSP Records, and it was his relationship with Wilson that led Williams to his own contract with the label. In 1997, JSP Records released *Kid Dynamite*, Williams' debut album under his own name. On *Kid Dynamite*, Williams is accompanied by some of the Dallas/Fort Worth scene's brightest stars: Tone Sommer, Andrew Junior Boy Jones, Ty Grimes, and Joe Rios. *—Richard Skelly*

● **Kid Dynamite** / Apr. 8, 1997 / JSP ♦♦♦

It Don't Get No Better / Jul. 28, 2000 / Genes ♦♦♦

Andre Williams

b. Nov. 1, 1936, Chicago, IL

Vocals, Guitar / Detroit Blues, R&B, Soul

Multi-talented Zeffrey "Andre" Williams has worn many musical hats during his long career: recording artist, songwriter, producer, road manager, etc. The "Father of Rap" was born November 1, 1936, in Chicago, and was raised in a housing project by his mother who died when Andre was six years old. Thereafter, Andre's aunties raised the precocious lad who had already become quite the character. The R&B legend is best known for co-writing and producing "Twine Time," for Alvin Cash & the Crawlers, "Shake a Tailfeather," by the Five Du-Tones, and a greasy solo recording "Bacon Fat," where Andre talked over a funky, crude rhythm.

A slick, street-smart Dapper Dan, music was one of Andre's hustles, he ventured to Detroit in his late teens and befriended Jack and Devora Brown, the owners of Fortune Records. He started singing with the Don Juans, a group in which the Brown's titled their 45s according to whom the lead singer of the side was, something Gwen Gordy and Billy Davis later did with the Voicemasters. At Fortune, Andre became adept at putting songs together, to date he has more than 230 compositions registered with Broadcast Music Incorporated.

In 1956, Fortune issued seven singles by Andre Williams, all but two with co-billing with the Don Juans: "Going Down to Tia Juana," "It's All Over," "Bacon Fat," "Mean Jean," "Jail Bait," "The Greasy Chicken," and "Country Girl." "Bacon Fat," and "Jail Bait" were solo shots; the former got a boost from Epic Records, who took over the distribution when the demand got too great for Fortune to handle. Fortune also released "Ooh Ooh Those Eyes" by Don Lake & the Don Juans, and two by Joe Weaver (pianist) & the Don Juans, "Baby I Love You" and "Baby Child," in 1956. Little Eddie & the Don Juans recorded the first Don Juans' record on Fortune, "This Is a Miracle" b/w "Calypso Beat," in 1955. Andre later sang with the Five Dollars who released records on Fortune from 1956 to 1957, and were billed as Andre Williams & the Five Dollars on a 1960 release.

During his Fortune stint, Andre kept busy playing the popular clubs in Detroit, and other locales, including the Flamingo Club in Memphis, TN. His biggest solo hit, "Bacon Fat," occurred during a drive to Memphis' Flamingo Club. When he got back to Detroit he persuaded Devora Brown to book a session. Fortune's recording studio was in the back room of a record shop the Browns owned. "Bacon Fat" was Andre's third single for Fortune; he didn't even have the lyrics written, but hurried and did so on a napkin while Ms. Brown busied herself setting up the studio mikes. Thank God for DJ Frantic Eddie Durham, who observed the session; he was the only one down with what was going on. Everyone else, including Joe Weaver, thought Andre was wasting time and money with this talk-singing. Andre and Ernie proved them wrong when "Bacon Fat" took off, becoming (with "The Wind," by Nolan Strong & Diablos) Fortune's most popular record.

Andre starting talking instead of singing because he knew he couldn't compete vocally with Nolan Strong, Clyde McPhatter, Little Willie John, Jackie Wilson, and others. He created a new style that was later adapted by Harvey Fuqua ("Any Way You Wanna"), Jerry-O, Shorty Long, Bootsy Collins, and others.

After Fortune, Andre languished with Berry Gordy and Motown from 1961 to 1965. He signed as an artist, producer, and writer; his only 45, "Rosa Lee" b/w "Shoo Ooo," was scheduled for release on Gordy's short-lived Miracle label, but never was. Gina Parks, a friend from the Don Juans, enjoyed a couple more solo releases on Motown's labels, but none scored. Andre co-wrote Little Stevie Wonder's first record, "Thank You for Loving Me," "Oh Little Boy What You Do to Me," the flip of Mary Wells' "My Guy," an early Eddie Holland single "It Cleopatra Took a Chance," and "Mo Jo Hanah," recorded first by Henry Lumpkin, then Marvin Gaye; outside of Motown it's been remade by Tami Lynn, the Ideals, the Neville Brothers, and others.

His relationship with Berry Gordy was one of mutual respect but stormy; he never conformed to Berry's way of doing things, and the four years he spent at Motown weren't consecutive months. When Williams got under Berry's skin, Berry fired him; Andre would leave for a few months and produce a hit with someone for another label, and Berry would invite him back. Andre was still associating with Motown when he masterminded "Shake a Tail Feather" for the Five DuTones and "Twine Time" for Alvin Cash & the Crawlers for the late George Leaner's Onederful Records in Chicago. Williams cut a lot of tracks for the Contours; by his estimate, he supervised at least two albums worth of material for the wild, raucous, dancing group, but few were released. During this time, Andre co-wrote "Girls Are Getting Prettier," a non-hit for Edwin Starr on Ric Tic Records. At one point, Andre was Edwin's road manager.

By 1965 he left Motown for good, signing with Chicago's Chess Records, and had a string of R&B releases including "The Stroke," "Girdle Up," "Humpin' Bumpin' & Thumpin," and "Cadillac Jack." His legend grew, a nefarious character but a good entertainer, Andre wore lavender suits and continued to entertain crowds at bucket-of-blood type establishments. He produced and wrote for more acts then he remembers, including "The Funky Judge" by Bull & the Matadors on Toddlin' Town Records. A 18-month stint with Ike Turner led to Andre's hitting rock bottom; after the experience he returned to Chicago a full-blown street junkie, was on the verge of self-destruction for years.

His biggest period as an artist was around 1960, when Fortune released the LP *Jail Bait*. He contributed to many sessions, including Parliament, Jesse James, Funkadelic, the Red Hot Chili Peppers, the Spinners, Trey Lewd (George Clinton's son), and Amos Milburn. He produced tracks for Mary Wells when she left Motown for 20th Century Fox Records.

Andre now lives in Queens, NY, and is back active in the business of music. He performs at much better venues then he did during his "Jail Bait" years, and still dazzles audiences with his swagger and loud pimp-ish wardrobe. He's released more albums in the last few years than he did the first 40 years of his career, including *Silky* on In the Red, *Fat Back & Corn Liquor* on St. George, and *Directly from the Streets* on SDE Records. *The Black Godfather* followed in the spring of 2000. *—Andrew Hamilton*

● **Jail Bait** / 1960 / Fortune ♦♦♦♦♦

Good (though not complete) overview of Andre's Fortune period. *—Cub Koda*

Bacon Fat / 1986 / Fortune ♦♦♦♦

Silky / Feb. 10, 1998 / In the Red ♦♦♦

After spending most of the '80s and '90s out of music and living on the streets thanks to a severe drug problem, Andre Williams cleaned himself up and cut a new album in 1996, in which he dusted off some of the classic tunes he cut for Fortune Records in the '50s and '60s. But Williams dove head first into the present day with 1998's *Silky*. Working with Mick Collins and Dan Kroha (formerly of the Gories, now respectively recording with the Dirtbombs and the Demolition Doll Rods), Williams merged his wild and greasy R&B style with Collins and Kroha's noise-spattered, stripped-down, roots-punk assault, and the results are flat-out nuts. On "Agile, Mobile, and Hostile," "I Wanna Be Your Favorite Pair of Pajamas," and "Looking Down at You Looking Up at Me," Williams sounds like the world's most spectacularly dirty old man as a squadron of Detroit alt-rock all-stars kick up a wall of rockin' din behind him, and the two side-closers, "Bring Me Back My Car Unstripped" and "Everybody Knew," are *Twilight Zone* psychodramas so bizarre they defy conventional description. Vintage soul purists will doubtless be horrified by *Silky*, but anyone wanting to hear the wildest man in '50s R&B getting even wilder 40 years on ought to give *Silky* a spin at their next stag party or parole hearing. *—Mark Deming*

Red Dirt / 1999 / Bloodshot ♦♦♦♦

Sure, it's sloppy and it sags in the middle, but the jumping snarl of "She's a Bag of Potato Chips" alone warrants the purchase of this disc. Williams mines the darker, funkier side of the country ethos, tossing out a truly creepy stalker ballad, "I Can Tell," with such twanging covers as "Pardon Me (I've Got Someone to Kill)" and "Psycho." Backing by the Sadies is first-rate, and if you get enough beers in you even the weaker spots start to sound right pretty. *—Tim Sheridan*

● **Rib Tips & Pig Snoots: Rare & Unreleased Au-Go-Go Soul, 1965–1971** / 2000 / Soul-Tay-Shus ♦♦♦♦

The sound of a soulful, leering swagger. That's what you want in an Andre Williams record, and *Rib Tips & Pig Snoots* delivers the mother lode. This collection of rare and unreleased soul from small labels, covering 1965-1971, finds Williams moving and grooving, showing and proving. Known for his greasy rhythm & blues of the 1950s, Williams had already scored hits in the early '60s writing and producing for Alvin Cash & the Crawlers ("Twine Time") and the Five Du-Tones ("Shake a Tail Feather"). *Rib Tips & Pig Snoots* finds Williams complementing his grooves with the occasional flute or string arrangement, all to a positive effect. "Pearl Time" and "Do It," among other vocal numbers, show that Williams still had his game uptight, working the ladies and starting new dance steps at the same time. A strong, long-overdue collection that showcases Williams at the top of his game as a performer and producer. *—Kurt Edwards*

The Black Godfather / May 2, 2000 / In the Red ♦♦♦

After recording one of the sleaziest albums of recent memory, 1998's *Silky*, what was Andre Williams supposed to do for an encore? Well, with *The Black Godfather*, Mr. Rhythm brings sleaze rock to new heights (or depths, depending on how you look at it). On *Silky*, producer and general co-conspirator Mick Collins (of the Gories and the Dirtbombs) rounded up an impressive team of Detroit-area grit-rock all-stars to back up Williams, but for *The Black Godfather*, Collins and Williams went nationwide, with the Jon Spencer Blues Explosion, the Compulsive Gamblers (formerly the Oblivions), the Cheater Slicks, and the Countdowns all kicking up a fuss as Williams wails on "Whip That Booty," "Nasty Women" "I Hate Cha," and "The Dealer, the Peeler, and the Stealer." While *Silky* sounded somewhat more unified, *The Black Godfather* rocks a good bit harder, and while the previous album featured the occasional moment of (relatively) subtle calm, this time out Williams is firing on all cylinders at once and sounding as nasty as he wants to be.

The Black Godfather is loud, it's wild, and my, but it's in poor taste; if that sounds like a bad thing to you, you're best off leaving this be, but if that description sounds like fun, pick this up and have a party as Andre Williams shows you how to Sling That Thing. Points added for the cover, a hilariously accurate parody of a typical No Limit Records package. *—Mark Deming*

Fat Back & Corn Liquor / Jun. 23, 2000 / St. George ♦♦♦
Andre Williams, the man who was rappin' three decades before they had a name for it, is back after a much too long sabbatical, with the kind of comeback album that would do any R&B legend proud. With a tight little band and the El Dorados providing crackerjack support, producer George Paulus has managed to restoke some of the fires that burned so brightly on a spate of brilliant, creative singles for Fortune and Checker in the '50s and '60s. The big plus here is that Williams can still deliver that deadpan badass turn of the phrase better than anybody. Although I personally find the recuts here of his old Fortune classics like "Jail Bait" ill-advised (to quote Rocky, the Flying Squirrel, "That trick never works!"), there's just so much great stuff on this biscuit that it's a minor niggling point at best. By far and away, my favorite track on here is one simply titled "Gin." Recalling one of his legendary Fortune sides, "Please Pass the Biscuits," without Xeroxing it, this is four minutes plus of Williams at his nutzo best. A winner. *—Cub Koda*

Bait & Switch / Jun. 12, 2001 / Norton ♦♦♦♦
Another irreverent, punkish set from the king of sleaze rock, *Bait and Switch* contains almost no surprises for fans of Andre Williams' predictably wild and raucous R&B. Backed by a garage band featuring the aggressive guitar of Matt Verta-Ray and the greasy, growling tenor sax of Lonnie Youngblood, Williams belts his tales of double-standard misogyny with the same enthusiasm as his early singles back in the 1950s. Fans of music that denigrates women will find "Sling It, Bang It and Give It Cab Fare Home" appealing, but Williams also goes far enough to balance the tables with the hilarious "Put That Skillet Away" (his lover is not cooking with it, but threatening to beat him). Long-lost brother to the late Screamin' Jay Hawkins or thug rapper born 40 years too early, Williams is still a treasure of the American rock underground. *—John Duffy*

Big Joe Williams

b. Oct. 16, 1903, Crawford, MS, **d.** Dec. 17, 1982, Macon, MS
Vocals, Songwriter, Guitar / Blues Revival, Delta Blues, Prewar Country Blues, Electric Delta Blues, Acoustic Blues

Big Joe Williams may have been the most cantankerous human being who ever walked the earth with guitar in hand. At the same time, he was an incredible blues musician: a gifted songwriter, a powerhouse vocalist, and an exceptional idiosyncratic guitarist. Despite his deserved reputation as a fighter (documented in Michael Bloomfield's bizarre booklet *Me and Big Joe*), artists who knew him well treated him as a respected elder statesman. Even so, they may not have chosen to play with him, because—as with other older Delta artists if you played with him you played by his rules.

As protégé David "Honeyboy" Edwards described him, Williams in his early Delta days was a walking musician who played work camps, jukes, store porches, streets, and alleys from New Orleans to Chicago. He recorded through five decades for Vocalion, OKeh, Paramount, Bluebird, Prestige, Delmark, and many others. According to Charlie Musselwhite, he and Big Joe kicked off the blues revival in Chicago in the '60s.

When playing at Mike Bloomfield's "blues night" at the Fickle Pickle, Williams was playing an electric nine-string guitar through a small ramshackle amp with a pie plate nailed to it and a beer can dangling against that. When he played, everything rattled but Big Joe himself. The total effect of this incredible apparatus produced the most buzzing, sizzling, African-sounding music anyone was ever likely to hear.

Anyone who wants to learn Delta blues must one day come to grips with the idea that the guitar is a drum as well as a melody-producing instrument. A continuous, African-derived musical tradition emphasizing percussive techniques on stringed instruments from the banjo to the guitar can be heard in the music of Delta stalwarts Charley Patton, Fred McDowell, and Bukka White. Each employed decidedly percussive techniques, beating on his box, knocking on the neck, snapping the strings, or adding buzzing or sizzling effects to augment the instrument's percussive potential. However, Big Joe Williams, more than any other major recording artist, embodied the concept of guitar-as-drum, bashing out an incredible series of riffs on his G-tuned nine-string for over 60 years. *—Barry Lee Pearson*

Piney Woods Blues / 1958 / Delmark ♦♦♦
Fine Delmark cuts from the late-'50s rediscovery phase of Big Joe's career. *—Barry Lee Pearson*

Nine String Guitar Blues / 1961 / Collectables ♦♦♦♦♦
The title says it all—Big Joe Williams plays a custom-made nine-string guitar, which sounds like no other instrument in existence. That alone would give his stripped-down acoustic Delta blues a new spin, but he brings so much grit and passion to his performances, they would have sounded fresh and vital anyway. *—Thom Owens*

Blues on Highway 49 / 1961 / Delmark ♦♦♦
One of Big Joe Williams' better releases, *Blues on Highway 49* is a tense, gritty set of roadhouse blues. Williams' stinging playing and singing brings out the best in such songs as "Tia Juana Blues" and "45 Blues"—he shows exactly how Delta blues could be updated. *—Thom Owens*

Tough Times / 1960 / Arhoolie ♦♦♦♦
There is some argument about exactly when this record hit the streets, but back then it would have cost only a nickel to get the Arhoolie catalog mailed to you. Big Joe Williams is a timeless kind of bluesman, the sort of artist that sounds completely like his own man rather than aspiring toward the muddled, sound-alike mainstream. There is nothing mainstream about this guy at all. He doesn't even play a normal guitar, having pieced together some kind of nine-string creation that has the best aspects of both the six- and 12-string models, ringing like chimes in the high end. The cover of this album has one of the best pictures of this instrument that has been published. Down low, Big Joe might be the originator of many bass string licks that are attributed to funk bassists, although in other cases he is simply imitating big band bass players and doing it well. There is another style of bass line playing he does that sounds like he is boxing with the instrument, displayed prominently on the rollicking "Shake Your Boogie." He is also one of the great shouting blues vocalists, loud enough to cut through a bank of machine guns and friendly sounding on top of that. One really wants to understand everything he says in order for him to fully communicate, but another aspect of his vocal style is that he sounds like he is still partially chewing his dinner, making full comprehension of the lyrics pretty hard. His wife sings on one track and is even harder to understand than he is. *—Eugene Chadbourne*

Walking Blues / Oct. 1961 / Fantasy ♦♦♦

Blues for 9 Strings / Mar. 1963 / Bluesville ♦♦♦

Back to the Country / 1964 / Testament ♦♦♦♦
Fellow Mississippians Jimmy Brown on fiddle and Willie Lee Harris on harmonica augment Big Joe's down-home Delta blues from the blues revival of the '70s. *—Barry Lee Pearson*

Big Joe Williams at Folk City / 1964 / Prestige/Bluesville ♦♦♦
Cut at Gerdes Folk City in New York on February 26, 1962, this record shows Big Joe Williams in top late-era form, enjoying himself before an audience of mostly white college kids and beats. He plays his signature nine-string guitar, accompanying himself on kazoo, which basically works (even subbing for what would have been a fuzz-tone guitar on "Bugle Blues"), although the kazoo was never meant to be captured in digital sound. The material includes Tommy McClennan's "Bottle Up and Go" and 11 traditional songs, including the intense "Trouble Take Me to My Grave" (his version of a song more familiar in Muddy Waters' version as "I Can't Be Satisfied"), "Mink Coat Blues," and "Burned Child Is Scared of Fire," all done in lively fashion with daunting fingerpicking. Williams left behind several folk club recordings from the early '60s, and they make a good contrast to the vast body of studio recordings from the same era. He was evidently at his best playing directly to an audience. *—Bruce Eder*

Early Recordings 1935–41 / 1965 / Mamlish ♦♦♦♦
This blues legend and guitar wizard's best initial Bluebird recordings, including the best versions of "49 Highway" and "Baby Please Don't Go" from 1935. *—Barry Lee Pearson*

Stavin' Chain Blues / 1966 / Delmark ♦♦♦♦
A CD reissue of 1958 recordings, it includes four previously unreleased tracks. This is raw but beautiful country blues, featuring the otherworldly sound of Big Joe's nine-string guitar. *—Niles J. Frantz*

Classic Delta Blues / 1966 / Milestone/Original Blues Classics ♦♦♦
Classic Delta Blues collects 12 cuts Big Joe Williams cut in 1964. For these recordings, he played a standard six-string guitars instead of hauling out his custom nine-string and the effects are pleasant, but not revelatory. *—Thom Owens*

Live at Folk City / 1968 / Bluesville ♦♦

Hand Me Down My Old Walking Stick / Oct. 1969 / Sequel ♦♦♦
This disc is drawn from tapes made solo by Big Joe Williams in October of 1968, in London for Liberty Records, using his usual jerry-rigged nine-string guitar with a pickup. The resulting session, a mix of numbers improvised on the spot and established part of his repertory (including the obligatory "Baby Please Don't Go"), was one of the recordings that Williams was most pleased with, among the many records that he cut during this era. The material mostly shows him creating spontaneously (including a distinctly bluesy "She'll Be Comin' Round the Mountain"), and recreating old songs in a new mode. "Baby Please Don't Go" resembles none of his many other renditions of the piece, or any of the various covers done by white rock and blues performers, with far more animated and intricate playing throughout, Williams making bold, slashing attacks on his instrument. "Everybody's Gonna Miss Me When I'm Gone" is more mellow and brooding, and closer in spirit to some of his more reflective acoustic blues performances—but the amplification adds a piercing level of intensity to his slide playing. The balances are a little haywire at times (the engineers don't seem to have found their way properly until "Buffalo," a track on which his rhythm playing is most prominent), thanks to the radical changes in timbre and volume in Williams' playing, but the record is still mesmerizing. *—Bruce Eder*

Big Joe Williams & Sonny Boy Williamson / 1969 / Blues Classics ♦♦♦♦♦
This is one of the great team-ups of artists from the country blues fields. Not only do these two performers work well together, they both play blues with such great intensity that fans of the genre will be drawn to their efforts like the proverbial flies on manure. These recordings are fantastic examples of country blues becoming urbanized with use of drums and bass backup, although it must be said that primitive recording sometimes relegates these instruments to a distant background thumping. The reality is that Sonny Boy and Big Joe hardly need a rhythm section at all, so mightily do they put forth their grooves. It is a sign of a great blues album when a done-to-death standard comes across as if one had never heard it before, and such is the case with the delightful, slightly laid-back version of "Baby, Please Don't Go." Harmonica fans should note this is the first of the Sonny Boys, i.e., John Lee Williamson. There is some confusion over when the initial vinyl release of this came out, but it is later than some of the Arhoolie Big Joe albums, because by now the cost of sending for a catalog had climbed from a nickel to a quarter. *—Eugene Chadbourne*

Big Joe Williams / 1975 / Storyville ♦♦♦

Malvina My Sweet Woman (M) / 1988 / Oldie Blues ♦♦♦♦♦

- **Shake Your Boogie** / 1990 / Arhoolie ✦✦✦✦✦
Arhoolie reissued two of Big Joe Williams' seminal rediscovery albums on one disc in 1990. The first, 1960's *Tough Times*, ranks among his best; the second, 1969's *Thinking of What They Did*, isn't as strong, but the two albums provide an excellent introduction to this Delta bluesman. *—Stephen Thomas Erlewine*

Delta Blues: 1951 / 1991 / Trumpet ✦✦✦✦✦
Although the early '50s were not a great time for Delta blues musicians, there remained some proficient players performing in this vein throughout the South. The three presented on this new collection of classic Trumpet recordings include Big Joe Williams, known for his nine-string guitar and robust singing, Luther Huff, a good, if derivative vocalist/guitarist, and the spry pianist and vocalist Willie Love, an exuberant performer whose Three Aces band at various times contained Elmore James and Little Milton. This anthology includes 18 selections that show the link between older, traditional blues and the urban, electric sounds that emerged as the idiom's dominant form later in the decade. *—Ron Wynn*

- **Complete Recorded Works, Vol. 1 (1935–1941)** / 1991 / Document ✦✦✦✦✦
Document's *Complete Recorded Works, Vol. 1 (1935-1941)* is an invaluable collection of Big Joe Williams' late-'30s and early-'40s recordings. Most of the best performances of Williams' career are here ("Baby Please Don't Go," "Somebody's Been Borrowing That Stuff," "Crawlin' King Snake," "Little Leg Woman," "Stack of Dollars," "Highway 49"), with support from figures including Sonny Boy Williamson and Henry Townsend. *—Thom Owens*

Complete Recorded Works, Vol. 2 (1945–1949) / 1991 / Document ✦✦✦
The second volume in Document's *Complete Recorded Works* series compiles 19 tracks recorded by Big Joe Williams during the latter half of the '40s and adds a pair of 1935 sides featuring the nine-string bluesman with Chasey Collins. Williams revisited earlier territory during this period, and though his redos of "Baby Please Don't Go" and "Stack of Dollars" don't pack the punch of the originals, they're still highlights here. *—Thom Owens*

Mississippi's Big Joe Williams and His Nine-String Guitar / 1995 / Smithsonian/Folkways ✦✦✦✦
Those who've never heard Big Joe Williams might be genuinely surprised at just how outstanding a musician he was, being tremendously accomplished on his self-made nine-string guitar and with vocals as expressive and forceful as Muddy Waters. Beautifully remastered, this collection finds Williams' talents at their peak with a fine variation of raw country blues like "Whistling Pines" and "Kings Highway Blues," and more strongly uptempo tracks like "Somebody's Been Fooling No. 1" and "King Bisquit Stomp No. 2." None of the 13 tracks disappoint, as this ranks among the strongest releases in the Big Joe Williams' catalog. *—Matt Fink*

Have Mercy! / Apr. 1996 / Tradition ✦✦✦

These Are My Blues / Jun. 9, 1998 / Testament ✦✦✦✦
This previously unissued 17-track collection finds Big Joe Williams performing live in concert at Rockford College in Rockford, Illinois. Williams is in fine form throughout, hollering the blues with his typical no-holds-barred approach, singing and playing with passion and zest. He tackles many of his standard pieces here ("Baby Please Don't Go," "Highway 49," "Mellow Peaches") and puts his own spin on blues standards like "Rock Me Mama," "Good Morning Little Schoolgirl," John Lee Hooker's "Boogie Chillen," and Jimmy Rogers' "Sloppy Drunk." There is new material; his tribute to President Kennedy, "A Man Amongst Men" and his "'56 Plymouth" are equally as fine as the more standard fare aboard. What is *truly* unique on here is the sound of Williams' nine-string guitar. Here it's highly amplified with the tremolo unit turned all the way up in intensity, creating an other-worldly effect, at times sounding like two guitars shimmering in tandem and at others, sounding like a cross between Pops Staples and Bo Diddley. Recorded by blues-researching trailblazer Pete Welding, this is one great addition to Williams' latter-day discography. *—Cub Koda*

No More Whiskey / Jun. 23, 1998 / Evidence ✦✦✦
It's to the credit of Evidence Records in the United States for releasing *No More Whiskey*, originally released on the L and R label in Germany. The unique percussive Delta blues of Big Joe Williams is captured from sessions recorded in 1973, 1977, 1978, and 1980. The 16 tracks feature Williams on dobro, six-string guitar, and his patented nine-string guitar. While the majority of the disc is mainly Big Joe Williams solos, it also includes Lydia Carter contributing vocals on "Somebody's Been Borrowin' That Heavy Stuff o' Mine," "Jesus Gonna Make Up My Dyin' Bed," and "When I Lay My Burden Down," and Cooper Terry's harmonica on "Texas Blues." All tracks were recorded in Crawford, MS, except "Don't Your House Look Lonesome" and "Texas Blues," which were recorded in Berlin. *—Al Campbell*

Going Back to Crawford / May 18, 1999 / Arhoolie ✦✦✦
Although Williams takes lead vocals on eight of the 26 songs on this disc, and plays his distinctive guitar throughout, it's billed to Big Joe Williams and Friends since the majority of the tracks feature other Mississippi singers on vocals. Williams was trying to bring other singers from his region to the attention of folklorist/Arhoolie owner Chris Strachwitz; most of this CD was recorded by Strachwitz in May 1971 in Crawford, MS, although seven songs were done at a Mississippi radio station a few months earlier. Because of Williams' oft-secondary role, it would have to be considered a secondary item in the Williams catalog, but it's still pretty solid Mississippi country blues. The performances are pretty tight and focused, and the guitar work good, especially the slide. None of the other singers—Austen Pete (who also plays second guitar behind Williams), John "Shortstuff" Macon (who plays what's listed on the sleeve as "rattling" guitar), Glover Lee Connor, and Amelia Johnson—are as arresting as Williams, but none are bad. The fidelity on the Strachwitz-recorded material is good; the quality of the material done at the radio station is less clear, but not hard to listen to. Williams recorded "Baby Please Don't Go" several times, but the one here is certainly good and a highlight of the disc. *—Richie Unterberger*

Big Joe Williams and Friends / Mar. 14, 2000 / Cleopatra ✦✦✦✦✦
Here's what *should* be listed under "various artists," as it's a real hodgepodge of great stuff. What we have are seven of Big Joe's eight Trumpet recordings, along with four tracks by Luther Huff, a pair from Arthur "Big Boy" Crudup that were originally issued under the pseudonym Elmer James, and the stray recording of Bobo Thomas' "Catfish Blues," which was originally issued as the B-side to Elmore James' "Dust My Broom." The Crudup sides (featuring Sonny Boy Williamson on harp) and Huff tracks have a particular bite to them that's very exciting. A greatlittle chunk of raw Mississippi blues that belongs in everybody's blues collection. *—Cub Koda*

Absolutely the Best / Sep. 11, 2001 / Fuel 2000 ✦✦✦✦

Baby Please Don't Go / Wolf ✦✦✦✦
Here are 70 minutes of Big Joe Williams' recordings in the prime of his life, from 1935 through 1947, and in surprisingly good sound. Along with the *original* recording of "Baby Please Don't Go," and other highlights include "Little Leg Woman" and "49 Highway Blues" (with Henry "Too Tight Henry" Townsend on second guitar), his 1941 recordings of "Crawling King Snake," and "Throw a Boogie Woogie." The notes are sketchy but the session information is fair. Some of the material here was available paired off with Sonny Boy Williamson material on RCA's *Throw a Boogie Woogie*. *—Bruce Eder*

Brooks Williams

b. Nov. 10, 1958 / Statesboro, GA
Vocals, Guitar / Contemporary Singer/Songwriter, Contemporary Folk
Folk-blues guitarist and singer Brooks Williams is as adept playing traditional blues as he is singing his own contemporary folk songs. His voice has been endlessly compared to James Taylor's, and yet his unique renderings of self-penned and blues classics on guitar make him an original.

Based in western Massachusetts for most of the 1990s, Williams was born in Statesboro, GA, and lived in other small towns in Georgia, Alabama, and Mississippi while growing up. In his youth, he heard a lot of gospel and roadhouse blues, but after he discovered rock & roll, he forgot about blues until one day in 1987, when he opened for blues/folk diva Rory Block at a club in upstate New York. Block inspired Williams to rediscover the acoustic blues he knew in his youth, and he began teaching himself songs by Robert Johnson, Muddy Waters, and Little Walter Jacobs.

Williams began to draw more of his performing persona from classic blues, and while working the folk circuit, opening up for crafty songwriters like Cheryl Wheeler, Bill Morrissey, and John Hiatt, he also began to develop his own skills as a songwriter. Since then, Williams' live shows have become an artful mix of classic acoustic blues, original blues songs, and self-penned contemporary folk songs. His development as a songwriter has been speedy, and he's got a slew of albums to prove it—*Back to Mercy* (1992), *Inland Sailor* (1994), *Knife Edge* (1995), and *7 Sisters* (1997), all for the Green Linnet label—as well as 1989's *Red Guitar Plays Blue*, 1990's *North from Statesboro*, and 1991's *How the Night-Time Sings* on his own Red Guitar Blue Music label. *—Richard Skelly*

- **North from Statesboro** / 1990 / Red Guitar ✦✦✦✦✦
Brooks Williams' debut album, *North from Statesboro*, falls halfway between the mellow folk-pop of James Taylor and the relaxed, respectful folk-blues of such contemporaries as Rory Block. Williams devotes his album to original songs, including instrumentals and musical adaptations of Robert Frost poems ("Acquainted With the Night"). Occasionally, he gets a little too wordy for his own good, but that doesn't prevent *North from Statesboro* from being an engaging collection of quietly lovely folk-blues. *—Thom Owens*

How the Night-Time Sings / 1991 / Red Guitar ✦✦✦✦✦
"Jubilee" is a joyous lush song, and "Hard Love" is also excellent. *—Richard Meyer*

Back to Mercy / 1992 / Green Linnet ✦✦✦
Back to Mercy has more ambitious production but it always serves to support his strong singing. Here are songs of hope and human renewal. *—Richard Meyer*

Inland Sailor / 1994 / Green Linnet ✦✦✦
Brooks Williams has delivered another collection of expressive original songs about romance and the underlying spiritual nature of life. As we have come to expect, it is distinguished by exceptional guitar work and his carefully articulated vocals. For the sake of guitarists among his audience, Williams has noted the tuning and capo positions he uses for each song. *—Richard Meyer*

Knife Edge / 1995 / Green Linnet ✦✦✦
Knife Edge displays Brooks Williams' colorful palette of musical influences—not just American and British folk, but Delta and electric Chicago blues, Hawaiian slack-key guitar, and even calypso on occasion. *—Steve Huey*

7 Sisters / Aug. 12, 1997 / Green Linnet ✦✦✦✦

Little Lion / Jan. 25, 2000 / Signature ✦✦✦✦
Brooks Williams is primarily known as a singer/songwriter with a strong cult following on the acoustic circuit. But his guitar playing has also won him considerable attention, and on this album it's the guitar that takes center stage. Playing alone and with the accompaniment of second guitarist John Daniel, Williams delivers a set of originals and well-chosen covers, the latter including a bossa nova arrangement of the "Ode to Joy" chorale from Beethoven's "Ninth Symphony," an acoustic version of Hot Tuna's "Water Song," and a rollicking rendition of "54-46 (Was My Number)" by Toots & the Maytals. Williams is one of those rare guitarists whose virtuosity falls gently on the ear; listening to his mournful bottleneck slide playing on "Goodbye Walker Percy" or the intricate syncopations of his kora-inspired "Lizard Logic," you won't often find yourself

wondering how on earth anyone could play that stuff—instead, you'll just be surprised and moved by his melodic inventiveness and by his sweet clarity of tone. Not to mention his sense of humor; it's not every day you hear a bossa nova arrangement of the "Ode to Joy." (Somewhere Herbert von Karajan is rolling in his grave, and that's just fine.) —*Rick Anderson*

Dead Sea Cafe / Feb. 13, 2001 / Silent Planet ✦✦✦✦

While a number of singer/songwriters never have hits per se, they nonetheless create a number of memorable songs over the course of their career. *Dead Sea Cafe* collects a dozen songs and a couple instrumentals by guitarist/songwriter Brooks Williams, from 1988's "Mystery" to 2000's "Happy All the Time." Williams' warm vocals and skilled guitar work make him a double threat to other singer/songwriters. The rolling guitar kickoff at the beginning of "Seven Sisters" renders it immediately likable, while the tasteful slide guitar of the "Wanderer's Song" combines the best of the Mississippi Delta with a more modern sensibility. Williams utilizes a number of guitar tunings to give each song/instrumental a rich, acoustic sound. Arrangements of "Late Night Train" and "Island Sailor" add touches of organ and drums, but the sound remains, primarily, acoustic. Lyrically, Williams has a penchant for poetic and, occasionally, unusual phrases. "Caves of Missouri" begins with "strange light at sunset, minutes from night/nuclear-red horizon nearly blinds me with half-light." Clearly a dark story is about to unfold. On the instrumental front, the groovy "When the Dentist Dreams" is filled with lovely cascades and a bouncy clean sound. "Before Coffee" begins like a Bach harpsichord piece, only to dip into a bluesy romp that pays homage to Django Reinhardt. So, whether one enjoys good songwriting or apt fingerpicking, *Dead Sea Cafe* offers a fine introduction to the work of Brooks Williams. —*Ronnie D. Lankford, Jr.*

Skiffle-Bop / Apr. 10, 2001 / Signature ✦✦✦✦

Brooks Williams is a man blessed with multiple talents: He's a songwriter, a singer, and a heck of a guitar player. In 2000 he released *Little Lion*, a nice collection of instrumental work, and the wonderfully titled *Dead Sea Cafe*, a collection of personal favorites. Now *Skiffle-Bop* finds him confidently singing and playing his way through 11 tunes. "Restless" begins as a slow spiritual, only to turn into a funky song of professed love. In an interesting twist, the need for meaning or purpose isn't centered on a higher being in "Restless," but on being with the person one should be with. "Mountain" invites one to experience real life by rolling up one's sleeves and becoming involved. Talking or thinking about life in the abstract, he suggests, is just another useless sermon. Williams' vocals are smooth and pleasant, and may remind one of David Wilcox or of Carly Simon's ex-husband (whom he's probably tired of being compared to). On the guitar front, there are several standouts. "Ring Bell" is a bluesy piece with a little Latin texture that features intriguing percussion (cowbells?) by Scott Kessel, while "Zoe" gathers its inspiration from Eastern Europe. "Liberation Waltz" and a short, untitled hidden track include—shocking though it may be—electric guitar. Luckily, though, the electric guitar has nylon strings and Williams' approach remains low-key. It might have been nice to have the printed lyrics to allow the listener to linger on the words, and the CD photo—two rather lifeless looking dogs—fails to inspire. But these are minor complaints. *Skiffle-Bop* has caught Williams in the act of doing what he does best: merging acoustic guitar wizardry with the singer/songwriter tradition. Guitar lovers and contemporary folkies will like this one. —*Ronnie Lankford, Jr.*

Jody Williams

b. Feb. 3, 1935, Mobile, AL

Vocals, Guitar / Electric Chicago Blues

Retired from the Chicago blues business for decades and now back again and sounding as good as ever, Jody Williams' stinging lead guitar work is still stirringly felt every time someone punches up Billy Boy Arnold's "I Was Fooled," Bo Diddley's "Who Do You Love," Otis Spann's "Five Spot," or Williams' eerie minor-key instrumental masterpiece, "Lucky Lou."

Born in Alabama, Joseph Leon Williams moved to Chicago at age six. He grew up alongside Bo Diddley, the two trading licks as kids and playing for real by 1951. By the mid-'50s, Williams was ensconced as a Chicago session guitarist of high stature, but he began to grow disenchanted when the signature lick he created for newcomer Billy Stewart's Argo waxing of "Billy's Blues" was appropriated by Mickey Baker for the Mickey & Sylvia smash "Love Is Strange." Baker apparently caught Williams playing the riff in Washington, D.C., at the Howard Theatre. When the legal smoke had cleared, Bo Diddley's wife owned the writing credit for "Love Is Strange" and Jody Williams had zipola for monetary compensation.

Williams made his recording debut (singing as well as playing) as a leader for powerhouse DJ Al Benson's Blue Lake imprint in 1955: "Looking for My Baby" was credited to Little Papa Joe. That alias pattern held in 1957, when Argo unleashed "Lucky Lou" and its sumptuous slow blues vocal flip "You May" as by Little Joe Lee (quite a band here—saxists Harold Ashby and Red Holloway, keyboardist Lafayette Leake, and bassist Willie Dixon). In 1960, Herald Records labeled him Sugar Boy Williams on "Little Girl." Outings for Nike, Jive, Smash, and Yulando during the 1960s rounded out Williams' slim discography.

Jody Williams dropped out of the blues game and went to work at Xerox as a technical engineer. He retired in 1994 and began to think about getting back into music. In 1999 at the urging of producer Dick Shurman, he went to a blues club for the first time in many, many years to see his old friend Robert Jr. Lockwood. Soon after Williams broke out some old tapes he made in 1964, liked what he heard so much that it brought tears to his eyes and decided to recapture the sound he created back when he was a top session man. After playing some gigs in 2000 and 2001, Williams and Dick Shurman went into the studio to cut his first solo album. *Return of a Legend* was issued in 2002, garnering rave reviews and sparking newfound interest in one of the unsung heroes of the blues guitar. —*Bill Dahl*

Leading Brand / 1977 / Red Lightnin' ✦✦✦✦

A bootleg LP, very welcome nevertheless in its day, spotlighting two of Chicago's most advanced blues pickers of the '50s and early '60s. Earl Hooker's brilliant stuff for producer Mel London dominates, but the last six sides showcase Jody Williams' taut, ringing guitar lines (especially on 1957's West Side-styled minor-key "Lucky Lou") and smooth vocals on "You May" and "Looking for My Baby." —*Bill Dahl*

Return of a Legend / Feb. 2002 / Evidence ✦✦✦✦

The boastful title is no exaggeration; this is a welcome return for the classic Chicago blues sideman, who, primarily because of the misfortune of his music being exploited by other musicians, took a self-imposed retirement for nearly 30 years. It's especially rewarding since Williams—whose work you hear on early Howlin' Wolf, Otis Spann, Bo Diddley, and Billy Boy Arnold (who guests here) sides—hadn't played a lick during that time, keeping his guitar stashed under his bed. He sounds like he never put the instrument away on this album, the first cohesive disc under his own name ever. Aided by comparative youngsters Tinsley Ellis, Ronnie Baker Brooks, and Rusty Zinn, along with a 21-year-old Sean Costello, Williams holds the spotlight like the pro his is. Though well into his sixties when this was recorded in 2001, he sounds remarkably vibrant, completely confident, and totally in his element. Whether reprising past glories like the magnificent instrumental "Moanin' for Molasses" along with Costello (who had revived the tune as the title track to his third release) or "Lucky Lou," which most blues fans will immediately recognize as the opening to Otis Rush's "All Your Love" (but was nicked from Williams), or writing new originals like the slow blues of "She Found a Fool and Bumped His Head," the guitarist sounds like he's thrilled to be recording again. That enthusiasm infects the band and pervades this album with a glow all too seldom felt when bluesmen attempt comebacks, especially after laying low as long as Williams has. Between his clean, jazzy yet direct blues style, the remarkably sympathetic band, and wonderfully understated production from Dick Shurman (the man heavily credited with enticing Williams back from obscurity), there are no missteps on this return. It's a tasteful showcase for one of the blues' lesser-known yet classic stars, and will hopefully be the beginning of a new lease on life for Jody Williams. —*Hal Horowitz*

Joe Williams (Joseph Goreed)

b. Dec. 12, 1918, Cordele, GA, **d.** Mar. 29, 1999, Las Vegas, NV

Vocals / Vocal Jazz, Traditional Pop, Standards, Swing

Joe Williams was the last great big-band singer, a smooth baritone who graced the rejuvenated Count Basie Orchestra during the 1950s and captivated audiences well into the '90s. Born in Georgia, he moved to Chicago with his grandmother at the age of three. Reunited with his mother, she taught him to play the piano and took him to the symphony. Though tuberculosis slowed him while a teenager, Williams began performing at social events and formed his own gospel vocal quartet, the Jubilee Boys.

By the end of the '30s he had made the transition to the Chicago club scene, and appeared with orchestras led by Jimmie Noone and Les Hite during the late '30s. He sang with Coleman Hawkins and Lionel Hampton during the early '40s, and toured with Andy Kirk & His Clouds of Joy during the mid-'40s (making his first recording with that band). Still, lingering illness kept him sidelined from active touring, and he worked as a theater doorman and door-to-door cosmetics salesman before his first minor hit for Checker, 1952's "Every Day (I Have the Blues)."

Finally, at the age of 35, he got his big break when in 1954 he was hired as the male vocalist for Count Basie's Orchestra. He soon helped audiences forget the absence of Basie's longtime vocalist, Jimmy Rushing. Indeed, he did more than just pull his own weight during the '50s; he became a major star in his own right and helped revive the lagging fortunes of the Basie band. His first (and best) LP, *Count Basie Swings—Joe Williams Sings*, appeared in 1955, containing definitive versions of "Every Day (I Have the Blues)" (already his signature song) and "Alright, Okay, You Win." "Every Day" hit number two on the R&B charts, and sparked another LP—1957's *The Greatest! Count Basie Swings, Joe Williams Sings Standards*—spotlighting Williams' command of the traditional pop repertory. Even while performing and touring the world with Basie during the late '50s, Williams made his solo-billed debut LP for Regent in 1956, and followed it with a trio of albums for Roulette.

Despite an inevitable parting from Basie in 1961, Joe Williams stayed close to the fold, working in a small group led by Basieite Harry "Sweets" Edison, then formed his own quartet in 1962. For his RCA debut, 1963's *Jump for Joy*, the lineup included jazz greats Thad Jones, Clark Terry, Snooky Young, Kenny Burrell, Oliver Nelson, Urbie Green, and Phil Woods. He recorded two more albums during the year—*At Newport '63* and *Me and the Blues*—and hit another peak in 1966 with an LP for Blue Note, *Presenting Joe Williams and the Thad Jones/Mel Lewis Orchestra*. Though he toured consistently during the 1970s, his recordings fell off until a pair of mid-'80s LPs for Delos, *Nothin' but the Blues* and *I Just Wanna Sing*. After the former won a Grammy Award for Best Jazz Vocal Performance, he landed a recurring role on the popular television series *The Cosby Show* and signed a contract for Verve.

Live appearances at Vine St. resulted in material for his first two Verve albums, *Every Night: Live at Vine St.* and *Ballad and Blues Master*. Still in extraordinarily fine voice, Williams recorded two more albums for Verve and toured constantly during the '90s. He appeared again with Count Basie's Orchestra (led by Frank Foster), released several albums through Telarc, and remained one of the most talented jazz vocalists in the world right up until his death in 1999. —*John Bush*

Everyday I Have the Blues / 1951-Sep. 28, 1953 / Savoy ✦✦✦✦

From the Roulette catalog, this superior Joe Williams/Count Basie collaboration finds the singer concentrating on the blues with consistently excellent results. In addition to a remake of the title cut, Williams is heard at his best on the classic "Going to Chicago" and such numbers as "Just a Dream," "Cherry Red," and "Good Mornin' Blues." This LP is well worth searching for. —*Scott Yanow*

● **Every Day: The Best of the Verve Years** / May 17, 1955-Jun. 25, 1990 / Verve ◆◆◆◆◆
In effect, this double-disc set, released in anticipation of Joe Williams' 75th birthday, is two compilation albums in one. The first CD, containing material recorded between 1955 and 1957, presents the artist singing with Count Basie and His Orchestra at the start of Williams' national career, when he and Basie scored a major R&B hit with the title song and made albums like *Count Basie Swings—Joe Williams Sings*, *One O'Clock Jump*, and *The Greatest! Count Basie Swings/Joe Williams Sings Standards*. Along with *The Count Basie Band and the Dizzy Gillespie Band at Newport*, these provide most of the selections included, among them memorable Williams performances such as "Teach Me Tonight," "I'm Beginning to See the Light," and "The Comeback." The second CD chronicles Williams' return to Verve Records in the years 1987 to 1990, for such albums as *Every Night* and *Ballad and Blues Master*, both of which were recorded live May 7-8, 1987, at the Vine St. Bar and Grill in Hollywood. So, we have the (relatively) young Williams and a much older Williams toward the end of his career. In both cases, however, he displays considerable dexterity in his blues-tinged jazz singing, and he gets tremendous support from his instrumentalists. The 30-year gap from one disc to another prevents this from being a definitive look at his career, but for the periods covered the anthology is well-chosen. —*William Ruhlmann*

A Night at Count Basie's / Oct. 22, 1955 / Vanguard ◆◆◆
This is *not* a Count Basie album, although thanks to its title, there's a good chance that you'll find it in the Count Basie bin in your record store. But the bandleader/keyboard legend doesn't play any music here; rather, it's a live performance at his bar on 132nd St. and Seventh Ave. in New York's Harlem, with Basie as host and master of ceremonies, announcer, and even tending bar. This may possibly have been, as claimed, the first authorized commercial recording ever done from a neighborhood bar (complete with the sounds of telephones, cash registers, etc., in the distant background), and the results are priceless. Williams is the featured musician and sounds just great on the slow, moody blues "More Than One for My Baby." The band—Emmett Berry on trumpet, Marlowe Morris on the organ, Bobby Donaldson at the drums, Vic Dickenson on trombone, Bobby Henderson at the piano, and Aaron Bell on bass—is very tight, and Berry's, Morris', and Henderson's instrumental voices are beautifully articulated. Marlowe and Henderson turn in a stunning performance together, both keyboards out in front, on "Too Marvelous for Words," which they stretch out in a long, languid jam into "Sent for You Yesterday" with Williams back in front. The group also has a great time reworking Duke Ellington's "Perdido" and stretches "Canadian Sunset" into a soaring ten-minute finale. The sound is remarkably clean and sharp, which makes the fact that the band was incredibly "on" that night even more appreciated. A must-own CD for any fan of Williams and of small-group jazz of this era. —*Bruce Eder*

The Best of Joe Williams: The Roulette, Solid State & Blue Note Years / Oct. 11, 1957+Oct. 12, 1957 / Blue Note ◆◆◆◆◆
The Best of Joe Williams: The Roulette, Solid State & Blue Note Years is an excellent sampler of Williams' work for Roulette and Solid State, providing a terrific overview of Williams' early records. Most of these 18 tracks feature Williams with the Count Basie Orchestra; there are also several cuts with Jimmy Jones, Harry "Sweets" Edison, Horace Ott, Jimmy Mundy, the Thad Jones/Mel Lewis Orchestra and Lambert, Hendricks and Ross. For anyone wondering why Williams is considered one of the great blues and big-band vocalists, this offers a reason why. —*Stephen Thomas Erlewine*

A Man Ain't Supposed to Cry / 1958 / Label M. ◆◆◆◆
Out of print for nearly 25 years, Label M has reissued Joe Williams' *A Man Ain't Supposed to Cry* just in time for those that have been yearning for true jazz vocals from a velvety balladeer. Williams' vocals speak legions about the state of jazz vocals in the '50s when this CD was originally released on Roulette Records. The baritone sings 12 classic standards including "I'll Never Smile Again," "Where Are You?," "What's New?," and closes with the title track. These songs were radio hits of Williams' day, and with heartbreaking numbers like "I'm Through With Love," his sincerity had many believing in his sentiment. This is classic Joe Williams and is an excellent addition to your collection of great jazz vocalists. —*Paula Edelstein*

Together/Have a Good Time / Jan. 31, 1961-Jul. 1961 / Roulette ◆◆◆◆
When singer Joe Williams left Count Basie's orchestra to go out on his own in early 1961, at first he co-led a group with veteran trumpeter Harry "Sweets" Edison. Their two joint recordings for Roulette have been reissued in full on this single CD. The *Together* set matches Williams and Edison with tenor saxophonist Jimmy Foster and a four-piece rhythm section that includes pianist Sir Charles Thompson. Among the highlights of the dozen standards are "I Don't Know Why," "Aren't You Glad You're You," and "Lover Come Back to Me." *Have a Good Time* has 11 songs performed by a mostly unidentified larger group arranged by Ernie Wilkins, including fine versions of "Sometimes I'm Happy," "Old Folks," "September in the Rain," and "Moonlight in Vermont." Throughout the sets, Joe Williams did his best to de-emphasize the blues (he wanted to be known as a well-rounded singer), instead choosing to uplift and personalize standards. Excellent music. —*Scott Yanow*

A Swingin' Night at Birdland / 1962 / Blue Note ◆◆◆◆
In 1961, after six years as one of the main attractions of Count Basie's orchestra, Williams (with Basie's blessing) went out on his own. One of his first sessions was this live recording, cut at Birdland with a strong quintet that featured trumpeter Harry "Sweets" Edison and Jimmy Forrest on tenor. Williams mostly sings standards and ballads, but also tosses in a few of his popular blues (including "Well Alright, Okay, You Win" and "Goin' to Chicago") during a well-rounded and thoroughly enjoyable set. —*Scott Yanow*

Jump for Joy / 1963 / RCA ◆◆◆◆
Here the classic singer is backed by a big band (and in some cases a smaller group from the orchestra) arranged by Oliver Nelson and Jimmy Jones. Doing his best to escape

from the stereotype of being strictly a blues singer, Williams performs both superior standards and obscurities on the spirited LP. Highlights include "Wrap Your Troubles in Dreams," "It's a Wonderful World," "Just A-Sittin' and A-Rockin'" and "Jump for Joy." Worth searching for. —*Scott Yanow*

At Newport '63 / 1963 / RCA ◆◆◆
The second LP Joe Williams released on RCA was this live set recorded at 1963's Newport Jazz Festival. The recording had actually been in the works for a year; Williams' energetic performance at the previous year's festivities was what got him his contract with George Avakian and the RCA label, and the two agreed that same night to record one studio LP (*Jump for Joy*) before releasing his next Newport performance as his second album. With an amazing lineup (Clark Terry and Howard McGhee on trumpets, Coleman Hawkins and Zoot Sims on tenor saxes), Williams took listeners through a 12-song journey comprising urbane rhythm tunes ("Gravy Waltz," "Roll 'Em Pete," "Some of This 'n' Some of That") and a few blues ballads ("Come Back, Baby," "Wayfaring Stranger"), plus his pair of inimitable standards "Every Day (I Have the Blues)" and "In the Evenin' (When the Sun Goes Down)." The statement in the liner notes describing "the entire program that rocked the 1963 Newport Jazz Festival" is overstating the case, but Williams displays all of his talents—a subtle blend of blues singer, band singer, and rhythm singer—and proves himself quite the triple threat in the process. [Once combined on a Collectables CD with *Jump for Joy*, *At Newport '63* was reissued by Bluebird in 2002, with studio and live versions of the three songs—"Gravy Waltz," "Medley," and "Some of This 'n' Some of That"—re-recorded in the studio after the live versions were deemed unusable.] —*John Bush*

At Newport '63/Jump for Joy / 1963 / Collectables ◆◆◆◆
This Collectables single-disc collects two very good albums Joe Williams recorded for RCA from the early '60s. While the presentation of this collection could have been better—the packaging looks a little cheap and the sound isn't all it could have been—both of these records are quite good and this is a good way to collect both records on disc, even if RCA has reissued these albums as better-sounding single discs. —*Stephen Thomas Erlewine*

Me and the Blues / 1964 / RCA ◆◆◆◆◆

Then and Now / Apr. 29, 1965-Nov. 23, 1983 / Sea Breeze ◆◆◆◆◆
This lesser-known but excellent Joe Williams reissue features the classic singer on a pair of sessions recorded 18 years apart. The earlier date was cut live with Williams joined by pianist Mike Melvoin, bassist Jim Hughart and drummer Bill Goodwin. The latter session, made in the studio, once again has Melvoin and Hughart but this time with drummer Nick Ceroli and tenor saxophonist Pete Christlieb. Despite the passing of so many years, Joe Williams sounds pretty identical on both dates. His style had not changed, his voice really had not aged yet and he sounds quite happy to be performing with the rhythm section. Highlights include "I'll Follow You," "I Wanna Go Where You Go," "Close Enough for Love," and Eubie Blake's "I'd Give a Dollar for a Dime." Well worth searching for by fans of Joe Williams, many of whom probably do not know of this album's existence! —*Scott Yanow*

☆ **Presenting Joe Williams and the Thad Jones/Mel Lewis Jazz Orchestra** / Sep. 30, 1966 / Solid State ◆◆◆◆◆
This CD reissues one of Joe Williams' finest recordings. Accompanied by the Thad Jones/Mel Lewis Orchestra, the singer is heard at the peak of his powers. The big band primarily functions as an ensemble (Snooky Young gets off some good blasts on "Nobody Knows the Way I Feel This Morning"), but the inventive Thad Jones arrangements ensure that his illustrious sidemen have plenty to play. Many of the selections (half of which have been in the singer's repertoire ever since) are given definitive treatment on this set (particularly a humorous "Evil Man Blues," "Gee Baby, Ain't I Good to You," and "Smack Dab in the Middle"), and Williams scats at his best on "It Don't Mean a Thing." Get this one. —*Scott Yanow*

Live in Vegas / 1971 / Monad ◆◆◆◆
This previously unreleased set features Joe Williams at a late-night performance in Las Vegas. Very well-recorded, the music offers few surprises but finds the singer in prime form. Although the Count Basie Orchestra backs him on most selections, the personnel is not listed, there are no significant solos and Basie himself is probably not on most of the tracks. The breezy liner notes say that "John Young, pianist extraordinaire" sat in during "Midnight Medley" (four ballads and "Thou Swell") and "Going to Chicago"; is this the Chicago-based player of the early '60s? Highlights include an animated "Nobody Loves You When You're Down and Out" (during which Williams really tells a story with the words), "Going to Chicago" (on this version he sings all of the famous big-band riffs along with his regular vocal) and the joyous "Smack Dab in the Middle." This is an excellent recording, easily recommended to Joe Williams fans. —*Scott Yanow*

The Heart and Soul of Joe Williams and George Shearing / Mar. 1, 1971-Mar. 2, 1971 / Koch ◆◆◆◆
By the time this record first appeared in 1971 on George Shearing's short-lived Sheba label, jazz was in the doldrums due to the preponderance of rock on radio and in record stores. Shearing formed his own label in an attempt to control his own destiny, and singer Joe Williams was one of the first people he asked to appear on with him. The two veterans are joined by bassist Andy Simpkins and drummer Stix Hooper for a collection of ballads (both familiar and obscure) that feature either "heart" and/or "soul" in their titles. They work very well together due to their love of great melodies and their ability to build upon them. The surprise opener is "Heart and Soul," a fairly simple Hoagy Carmichael-Frank Loesser ditty that is often the first piece would-be pianists learn on their own; Shearing's easygoing yet swinging arrangement removes its typically monotonous character. Even though Rodgers & Hart's lovely "My Heart Stood Still" is barely over two minutes, the enchanting duo rendition by Williams and Shearing not only restores the often

omitted verse but proves that less can be more. The out-of-tempo interpretation of "Young at Heart" and rather playful take of "I Let a Song Go Out of My Heart" are very refreshing. The lesser-known tunes are hardly lesser quality. Jimmy van Heusen and Johnny Burke penned the gorgeous yet unjustly forgotten "Humpty Dumpty Heart," while Alec Wilder's "Sleep My Heart" is another long lost treasure. Out of print since the label's demise in 1973, this 2001 reissue will be readily welcomed by fans of Joe Williams and George Shearing. —*Ken Dryden*

Joe Williams Live / Aug. 7, 1973 / Fantasy/Original Jazz Classics ✦✦✦✦
Williams meets the Cannonball Adderley Septet on this rather interesting session. The expanded rhythm section (which includes keyboardist George Duke and both acoustic bassist Walter Booker and the electric bass of Carol Kaye) gives funky accompaniment to Williams, while altoist Cannonball and cornetist Nat have some solo space. Actually, the singer easily steals the show on a searing version of "Goin' to Chicago Blues," his own "Who She Do," and a few unusual songs, including Duke Ellington's "Heritage." —*Scott Yanow*

Dave Pell's Prez Conference / 1979 / GNP Crescendo ✦✦✦✦✦
Dave Pell's Prez Conference was to Lester Young what Supersax is to Charlie Parker. Pell's short-lived group featured harmonized Lester Young solos recreated by three tenors and a baritone; their matchup with singer Joe Williams is quite enjoyable. Since Young was in Count Basie's orchestra when Jimmy Rushing was the vocalist, Joe Williams has a rare opportunity to give his own interpretation to Rushing and Billie Holiday classics like "I May Be Wrong," "You Can Depend on Me," "If Dreams Come True," and "Easy Living." A delightful and swinging date. —*Scott Yanow*

Nothin' but the Blues / 1983 / Delos ✦✦✦✦
Sticking to blues, Joe Williams is in prime form on this special session. His backup crew includes such all-stars as tenor saxophonist Red Holloway, organist Brother Jack McDuff, and (on alto and one lone vocal) the great Eddie "Cleanhead" Vinson. The many blues standards are familiar but these versions are lively and fresh. —*Scott Yanow*

I Just Wanna Sing / 1985 / Delos ✦✦✦✦
For this session, Joe Williams is backed by such master jazzmen as trumpeter Thad Jones, the contrasting tenors of Eddie "Lockjaw" Davis and Benny Golson, and guitarist John Collins. The material varies from the dated humor of "It's Not Easy Being White" to classic versions of "Until I Met You" and "I Got It Bad." Joe Williams is in prime form, and this is one of his better sessions from his later years. —*Scott Yanow*

Ballad and Blues Master / May 7, 1987-May 8, 1987 / Verve ✦✦✦✦
Taken from the same sessions that had previously resulted in *Every Night*, the identical adjectives apply. Joe Williams was in superior form for this live date, putting a lot of feeling into such songs as "You Can Depend on Me," "When Sunny Gets Blue," and "Dinner for One Please, James." A closing blues medley is particularly enjoyable and the backup by a quartet that includes pianist Norman Simmons and guitarist Henry Johnson is tasteful and swinging. —*Scott Yanow*

Every Night: Live at Vine St. / May 7, 1987-May 8, 1987 / Verve ✦✦✦✦✦
The focus is entirely on Joe Williams (who is backed by a standard four-piece rhythm section) during this live session from Vine Street. Then 69, Williams had not lost a thing and his voice has rarely sounded stronger. This version of "Every Day (I Have the Blues)" is transformed into Miles Davis' "All Blues"; Williams revives Eubie Blake's "A Dollar for a Dime" and sounds wonderful on such songs as "Too Marvelous for Words," "I Want a Little Girl," and "Roll 'Em Pete." This is the best of Joe Williams' records from the '80s. —*Scott Yanow*

The Overwhelmin' / 1988 / Bluebird/RCA ✦✦✦✦✦
A CD sampler taken from five former LPs, this fine CD features Joe Williams doing three songs from Duke Ellington's play *Jump for Joy*, five numbers at the 1963 Newport Jazz Festival (during which he is joined by trumpeters Clark Terry and Howard McGhee, and tenor greats Coleman Hawkins, Zoot Sims, and Ben Webster), four blues numbers backed by an all-star jazz group, and five ballads in front of an orchestra. Although it would be preferable to have each of the five original albums intact, this superb collection features Joe Williams on a wide variety of material, and he is heard close to his peak throughout. —*Scott Yanow*

In Good Company / Jan. 19, 1989-Jan. 21, 1989 / Verve ✦✦✦✦
A bit of a grab bag, this CD finds Joe Williams joined by Supersax on two numbers, doing a pair of vocal duets with Marlena Shaw ("Is You Is or Is You Ain't My Baby" is excellent), teaming up with vocalist/pianist Shirley Horn for two ballads, and being joined by the Norman Simmons Quartet for the remainder. Sticking mostly to standards, Joe Williams shows that at 70 he still had the magic. —*Scott Yanow*

That Holiday Feeling / 1990 / Verve ✦✦✦
One of the better Christmas jazz sets, Joe Williams is heard in quartets and quintets with pianist Norman Simmons, in several tender duets with pianist Ellis Larkins, and backed by a horn section on a few tracks. It is nice to hear Williams' versions of such tunes as "Winter Wonderland," "Silent Night," and "The Christmas Song," but it's his interpretation of Thad Jones' "A Child Is Born" that takes honors. —*Scott Yanow*

Live at Orchestra Hall, Detroit / 1993 / Telarc ✦✦✦✦
Joe Williams is so closely associated with the Count Basie Orchestra that it is difficult to believe that this Telarc CD was his first recording with jazz's great institution in over 30 years. Williams (in generally fine form despite an occasionally raspy voice) performs a well-rounded set of blues, ballads, and standards with the Frank Foster-led Basie orchestra, combining some of his older hits with a few newer songs such as Grady Tate's "A Little at a Time" and "My Baby Upsets Me." Foster's sidemen are mostly heard in an ensemble role with all of the instrumental solos being rather brief; there is little interaction with

the vocalist. That fault aside, this is one of Joe Williams' better recordings of the past decade. —*Scott Yanow*

Here's to Life / 1994 / Telarc ✦✦
Joe Williams loves the string arrangements of Robert Farnon and the sappy ballad "Here's to Life," but in truth the charts border on Muzak and the slow tempos on this Telarc CD have little variety. Reminiscent a bit of Nat King Cole's string sessions of the 1950s with Gordon Jenkins, there is little jazz content to this set. Williams is in particularly strong form, interpreting the ballads in dramatic and sensitive fashion, but, despite his charm, this is one of his lesser recordings. —*Scott Yanow*

Feel the Spirit / Sep. 20, 1994-Sep. 23, 1994 / Telarc ✦✦✦
Joe Williams had been wanting to record an album of spirituals since 1957 and this is it. The veteran singer gives a blues feeling and swing to the traditional pieces which range from the rollicking title cut to "Go Down Moses," "I Couldn't Hear Nobody Pray," and "The Lord's Prayer." He is assisted by Marlena Shaw (a particularly effective partner on three of the numbers) and a five-piece chorus on four other songs. The backing usually features Patrice Rushen getting organ sounds out of her synthesizer. Despite the one-message content, the music has more variety than one might expect and Joe Williams acquits himself very well on this sincere and heartfelt effort. —*Scott Yanow*

Me and the Blues/The Song Is You / Oct. 21, 1997 / Collectables ✦✦✦
This Collectables single-disc collects two very good albums Joe Williams recorded for RCA from the early '60s. While the presentation of this collection could have been better—the packaging looks a little cheap and the sound isn't all it could have been—both of these records are quite good and this is a good way to collect both records on disc, even if RCA has reissued these albums as better-sounding single discs. —*Stephen Thomas Erlewine*

Me and the Blues [Bonus Tracks] / Aug. 10, 1999 / RCA ✦✦✦✦
This recording features singer Joe Williams backed by a studio orchestra headed and arranged by Jimmy Jones. Williams mostly sticks to blues-oriented material but there is a surprising amount of mood variation on the dozen selections along with short solos by trumpeters Thad Jones and Clark Terry, altoist Phil Woods and Seldon Powell on tenor; Ben Webster has a guest spot on "Rocks in My Bed." Williams, heard at the peak of his powers, is at his best on "Me and the Blues," "Rocks in My Bed," "Work Song," and "Kansas City." —*Scott Yanow*

Ultimate Joe Williams / Sep. 28, 1999 / Verve ✦✦✦✦
Verve's *Ultimate* series unveils a new concept in the hackneyed concept of greatest-hits collections: instead of compilation producers, these albums feature tracks selected by figures who either worked with or were influenced by the artists themselves. The results are much more than your average best-of compilations; they're closer to treatises on the immense influence those artists exerted on generations to come, documenting exactly why they were special and deserve to be remembered. For vocalist Kevin Mahogany, the major figure in male jazz vocals during the '90s, the natural choice is none other than Joe Williams, the epitome of graceful swing. The collection begins with two versions of Williams' most popular song—"Every Day I Have the Blues"—recorded 30 years apart (Williams recorded only one full-length album released on Verve during the '50s, then returned to the label during the late '80s). Most of the rest of the songs are from Williams' later career at Verve, sophisticated swing selections like "How Deep Is the Ocean?," "Embraceable You," "I'm Beginning to See the Light," and "Sometimes I'm Happy." Williams himself participated in another volume of the *Ultimate* series by selecting songs for the Ella Fitzgerald compilation. —*John Bush*

Juanita Williams

Vocals / Contemporary Blues
Although Juanita Williams may seem like a new face on the blues scene, one listen to her brilliant debut album on the Big Mo label, *Introducing Juanita Williams*, and you realize this woman is a pro. In fact, she spent 20 years as lead vocalist for the Airmen of Note, a prestigious Air Force Big Band originally founded by Glenn Miller. Williams began singing in the church, but her secular influences eventually stole her heart, and they included singers like Etta James and Aretha Franklin. However, Williams' voice, passion, and energy are completely unique. —*Richard Skelly*

● **Introducing Juanita Williams** / 1994 / Big Mo ✦✦✦✦
The comparisons to Aretha Franklin are inevitable, but Juanita Williams' voice and passion are her own. Her debut, *Introducing Juanita Williams*, features a wide-ranging sample of modern and classic blues tunes, everything from Ike & Tina Turner's "Crazy About You Baby" to Freddie King's "That Will Never Do" and Bobby "Blue" Bland's "Two Steps from the Blues." Anybody who has doubts about the future of women blues vocalists should pick up Williams' impressive debut. —*Richard Skelly*

It's Who I Am / May 4, 1999 / HQ ✦✦✦

Larry Williams

b. May 10, 1935, New Orleans, LA, **d.** Jan. 7, 1980, Los Angeles, CA
Vocals, Saxophone, Keyboards, Songwriter, Piano / Pop-Soul, Rock & Roll, R&B, Soul
A rough, rowdy rock & roll singer, Larry Williams had several hits in the late '50s, several of which—"Bony Maronie," "Dizzy, Miss Lizzy," "Short Fat Fannie," "Bad Boy," "She Said Yeah"—became genuine rock & roll classics and were recorded by British Invasion groups; John Lennon, in particular, was a fan of Williams, recording several of his songs over the course of his career.

As a child in New Orleans, Williams learned how to play piano. When he was a teenager, he and his family moved to Oakland, CA, where he joined a local R&B group called the Lemon Drops. In 1954, when he was 19 years old, Williams went back to New Orleans for a visit. During his trip, he met Lloyd Price, who was recording for Specialty

Records. Price hired the teenager as his valet and introduced him to Robert "Bumps" Blackwell, the label's house producer. Soon, the label's owner, Art Rupe, signed Williams to a solo recording contract.

Just after Specialty signed Larry Williams, Specialty lost Little Richard, who had been their biggest star and guaranteed hitmaker. Little Richard decided to abandon rock & roll for the ministry shortly after Williams cut his first single, a cover of Price's "Just Because," with Richard's backing band; "Just Because" peaked at number 11 on the R&B charts in the spring of 1957. After Richard left the label, the label put all of its energy into making Williams a star, giving him an image makeover and a set of material—ranging from hard R&B, rock & roll, to ballads—that were quite similar to Richard's hits.

Williams' first post-Little Richard single was the raucous "Short Fat Fannie," which shot to number one on the R&B charts and number five on the pop charts in the summer of 1957. It was followed in the fall by "Bony Maronie," which hit number four on the R&B charts and number 14 on the pop charts. Williams wasn't able to maintain that momentum, however. "You Bug Me, Baby" and "Dizzy Miss Lizzy," his next two singles, missed the R&B charts but became minor pop hits in late 1957 and early 1958. Despite the relative failure of these singles, Williams' records became popular import items in Britain; the Beatles would cover both sides of the "Dizzy Miss Lizzy" single (the B-side was "Slow Down") in the mid-'60s. However, Williams' commercial fortunes in America continued to decline, despite Specialty's release of a constant stream of singles and one full-length album.

In 1959, Williams was arrested for selling narcotics, which caused Specialty to drop him from the record label. He drifted through a number of labels in the early '60s, recording songs for Chess, Mercury, Island, and Decca. By the mid-'60s, he had hooked up with Johnny "Guitar" Watson and the duo cut several sides for OKeh Records in the mid- and late '60s, including the Top 40 R&B hits "Mercy, Mercy, Mercy" (spring 1967) and "Nobody," which was recorded with Kaleidoscope (early 1968). Williams also became a house producer for OKeh Records in 1966, although very few of his productions became hits.

Between 1968 and and 1978, Williams was inactive, recording nothing and performing very little. In 1978, he released a funk album, *That's Larry Williams*, for Fantasy Records that sold poorly and received bad reviews. In 1980, Larry Williams was found dead in his Los Angeles home; he died of a gunshot wound to his head. The medical examiners called the death a suicide, but rumors persisted for years after his death that he was murdered because of his involvement in drugs, crime, and—allegedly—prostitution.

A compilation of Larry Williams' biggest hits and best-known songs entitled *Bad Boy* was released on Specialty Records in 1989. *—Stephen Thomas Erlewine*

Here's Larry Williams / 1959 / Specialty ✦✦✦✦✦
One of the great R&B long-players of the '50s, *Here's Larry Williams* collects nearly all of the Los Angeles-based singer/songwriter's key work ("Bad Boy" and 1967's "Mercy, Mercy, Mercy" are the only truly essential tracks missing), and a bunch of smokin' obscurities besides. Listening to these tracks, it's clear why John Lennon was such a huge Larry Williams fan; his rough-and-ready no-bull voice is elastic enough to move from a Little Richard trill to a Ray Charles growl, and songs like "Dizzy Miss Lizzy" and "Short Fat Fannie" are raucous enough to be punk rock nearly a full two decades before the concept was even in existence. Of the lesser-known tracks, the giddy Buddy Holly-meets-Richard Berry "You Bug Me, Baby" and the salacious "Little School Girl," featuring a good and greasy sax solo, are the highlights; on the downside, "Ting A Ling" is as slight and tossed-off as its title, and the intrusive female chorus that sounds like it made the wrong turn from the Rosemary Clooney session down the hall is just plain awful. *—Stewart Mason*

Larry Williams Show with Johnny Guitar Watson / 1965 / Edsel ✦✦✦

Unreleased Larry Williams / 1986 / Specialty ✦✦✦
This deeper look into the obscure and alternate takes of Williams' work is mostly for collectors. *—Hank Davis*

★ **Bad Boy** / Apr. 6, 1992 / Specialty ✦✦✦✦✦
Bad Boy compiles 23 tracks Larry Williams recorded between 1957 and 1958. The core of the collection are his hit singles—"Bony Maronie," "She Said Yeah," "Lawdy Miss Clawdy," "Just Because," "Dizzy Miss Lizzy," "Short Fat Fannie," "Bad Boy," "Slow Down"—many of which became standards. *—Stephen Thomas Erlewine*

Bad Boy of Rock n' Roll / Feb. 19, 1999 / Ace ✦✦✦✦✦
Essential late '50s R&B by one of rock's most nefarious characters. Specialty Records released Williams from his contract in 1959 after he was sent to prison for drug dealing. The singer/pianist expired from a gunshot in 1980 that was rumored a hit but ruled self-inflicted. Bad career choice aside, Williams uncorks with unbridled fury on his classic musical caricatures: "Short Fat Fannie," "Bony Maronie," "Dizzy Miss Lizzy," and 21 others. He recorded these in New Orleans with some of the city's finest young musicians–Art Neville (piano), Leo Morris, aka Idris Muhammad (drums), and Lee Allen (tenor sax). Early, raw R&B at its best. *—Andrew Hamilton*

Lee "Shot" Williams

b. May 21, 1938, Lexington, MS
Vocals / Retro-Soul, Soul-Blues
Vocalist Lee "Shot" Williams sings a style of Southern soul-blues in keeping with the tradition of vocalists like Bobby "Blue" Bland, Johnnie Taylor, and Albert King. He got the nickname "Shot" from his mother at a young age, owing to his fondness for wearing suits and dressing up as a "big shot."

Williams grew up with guitar player Little Smokey Smothers and knew his older brother, Big Smokey Smothers. Williams' stepsister, Arlean Brown, was surrounded by a family of musicians, and the Brown brothers gave Williams his first introduction to blues performing via the juke joints of the Delta.

Williams moved to Detroit in 1954 and to Chicago in 1958. He rejoined Little Smokey Smothers there and got to know other paragons of Chicago blues, including Magic Sam (McGhee) and Howlin' Wolf. Williams began singing with Smokey's band in 1960 and a few years later joined Magic Sam's band as a vocalist.

In 1962, Williams recorded his first singles for Chicago's Foxy label, "Hello Baby" and "I'm Trying." He recorded a series of singles for other labels, including King/Federal, Palos, Gamma, Shama, and Tchula. His 1964 recording "Welcome to the Club" was a hit in Chicago, so much so that it was later covered by guitarist/singer Little Milton Campbell for Checker Records in 1965. Another regional hit, "I Like Your Style," came out in 1969 and was later covered by Junior Parker. (Williams remade the single in 1993.)

After joining up with guitarist Earl Hooker, he had his first experience on the road as part of a touring band in the mid-'60s, playing around the South. Williams also served tenures with Little Milton and Bobby "Blue" Bland.

His first album under his own name, *Country Disco*, was released on the Roots label in 1977. In the 1980s, Williams moved back to Memphis, where he had spent many of his earlier years, knowing there would still be an audience for his brand of soul-blues. He released an album on cassette and recorded for a Japanese label in 1992. Later that year, his guest vocals on his cousin's album prompted the Black Magic label to look into recording Williams with his own band. The result, *Cold Shot*, was released in 1995, demonstrating Williams' gospel-inflected, powerful vocals in the proper setting. Williams is accompanied by a seasoned team of studio musicians, including former Albert Collins bassist Johnny B. Gayden, Ronnie Earl organist Tony Zamagni, saxist Charles Kimble, and trumpeter Mike Barber of the Chicago Playboy Horns. The album was voted best blues album of 1995 in a poll conducted by the magazine *Living Blues*. On *Cold Shot*, Williams interprets familiar covers by Gladys Knight, "Neither One of Us," and Wilson Pickett's "Don't Let the Green Grass Fool You."

His debut for the Memphis-based Ecko Records, *Hot Shot*, was released in 1996; *She Made a Freak Out of Me* followed in early 2000; *Somebody's After My Freak* appeared in early 2001. Williams made an appearance at the 1994 Chicago Blues Festival, and while it boosted his visibility, he continues to perform mostly in clubs around the U.S. *—Richard Skelly*

Cold Shot / 1995 / Black Magic ✦✦✦
Competent modern soul-blues with a friendly, non-threatening tone, augmented by a three-man brass section, the Chicago Playboy Horns. *—Richie Unterberger*

● **Hot Shot** / Oct. 15, 1996 / Ecko ✦✦✦✦
Hot Shot may be the best record Lee "Shot" Williams has yet released, due both to the quality of the performances and songwriting. He has re-recorded many of his older singles for the album, giving them appropriately greasy, energetic performances. Unfortunately, the production is a little too polished to make *Hot Shot* really sound like a rockin' juke joint, but there's no discounting the passion in Williams' performances. *—Thom Owens*

She Made a Freak Out of Me / Feb. 29, 2000 / Ecko ✦✦✦

Somebody's After My Freak / Mar. 27, 2001 / Ecko ✦✦✦

Lester Williams

b. Jun. 24, 1920, Groveton, TX, **d.** Nov. 13, 1990, Houston, TX
Vocals, Guitar, Bass / R&B, Electric Texas Blues
Though little known outside of the Houston blues circuit where he made his home for several decades, vocalist/guitarist Lester Williams was a local phenomenon during the early '50s whose success even led to an appearance at Carnegie Hall. Born in Groveton, TX, on June 24, 1920, he grew up infatuated with the sound of T-Bone Walker, whose style Williams consciously emulated; after serving in World War II, he formed his own combo, and in 1949 signed on with the Houston-based Macy's Records. The label's then-stockboy, Steve Poncio, produced Williams' debut single, "Winter Time Blues"; it became a regional hit, although subsequent efforts were less successful. However, by 1951 Poncio owned and operated his own distributorship, United Distributors, and through various channels struck up a business relationship with Specialty Records owner Art Rupe; as a result, Williams joined the Specialty stable, and with Poncio again behind the boards scored his biggest hit in 1952 with "I Can't Lose With the Stuff I Use," a track later covered by B.B. King. The song was another regional smash, and was sufficiently popular on a national basis to land the singer on a February 1953 Carnegie Hall bill that also included Dinah Washington, Billy Eckstine, and Nat King Cole. Williams' follow-ups failed to catch on, however, and by 1954 he was regularly performing on Houston station KLVL and touring throughout the South. He later recorded on Duke before one final date for Imperial in 1956; in the years to follow he remained a staple of the Houston club circuit, touring Europe four years prior to his death on November 13, 1990. *—Jason Ankeny*

● **I Can't Lose With the Stuff I Use** / 1993 / Specialty ✦✦✦✦✦
Singer/guitarist Lester Williams wasn't an innovative player or a top-flight vocalist; still, he made good, occasionally great music that was enjoyable and reflective of a prime blues/R&B period. Williams' one moment in the spotlight came via the hit "I Can't Lose With the Stuff I Use," a great single that had wit, stinging guitar licks, stomping rhythms, and his finest vocal. It was later covered by B.B. King, and the song helped Williams get a Carnegie Hall gig. That song leads off this 25-track disc covering Lester Williams' tunes from 1952 and 1953. There's little here that's new, but plenty that's worth hearing. *—Ron Wynn*

The Godfather of Blues / 1993 / Collectables ✦✦✦

Texas Troubadour / 1995 / Ace ✦✦✦✦

Marion Williams

b. Aug. 29, 1927, Miami, FL, **d.** Jul. 2, 1994, Philadelphia, PA
Vocals, Keyboards / Traditional Gospel, Black Gospel
With an amazing grace, a powerful yet lyrical voice, and unmatched improvisational skills Marion Williams punctuated her sanctified shouting with gut-wrenching growls, low moans, joyful whoops, and soaring, angelic falsettos that made her one of the most

influential singers in gospel music. In her heyday she was hailed by some critics as one the greatest singers in the U.S.

Williams was born in a Miami ghetto, the daughter of a West Indian butcher and a South Carolina laundry woman. When not working, her father would give music lessons, while her devout mother introduced to her to religion. Williams' own love of gospel music began in childhood, and she would sing and listen to it at every opportunity. One of her older brothers frequently played blues and jazz on the family jukebox; although gospel was Williams' main interest, her music is infused with elements of those jukebox tunes, as well as the calypso music played throughout her neighborhood. When she was nine, her father died, and at age 14, Williams quit school to work all day in the laundry beside her mother. Later the responsibility for supporting the family fell totally on Williams' young shoulders when her mother lost both legs due to diabetes. Still her interest in sanctified gospel continued, and on weekends she sang in church programs and on street corners. She was particularly inspired by the Smith Jubilee Singers (her favorites) and the Kings of Harmony; influential soloists included such women as Mary Johnson Davis and particularly Sister Rosetta Tharpe. Williams' extraordinary singing attracted considerable attention, but though attempts were made to steer her into everything from opera to the blues, she was determined to spread the gospel and by 1946 was known as the best gospel soloist in Miami.

While at a Clara Ward & the Ward Singers program, Williams was called up to sing. Impressed, Clara and Gertrude Ward invited the young singer to join their nationally known group. The following year, she joined the Wards and remained with them for the next eleven years as their star attraction. Her natural sparkle and enthusiasm in performance earned her the nickname "Miss Personality." She made her recording debut singing "How Far Am I from Canaan" with the Ward Singers in 1948 for Savoy; it was the Rev. W. Herbert Brewster-penned "Surely God Is Able" that made Williams and the Ward Singers stars. During their dynamic performances, it was not uncommon for audience members to fall out in frenzied ecstasy, something Williams encouraged by getting right down into the audience, sashaying about and shouting at the top of her lungs, occasionally sitting demurely upon listeners' laps, and even literally trying to pack up the earthly goods of audience members during her renditions of her second big hit, "Packin' Up." She put so much into her performances with the Ward Singers that in time she began suffering "nervous spells" in which she would yell just to express the remaining energy generated by singing those high notes. Williams and a few others from the group left in 1958 to form Stars of Faith.

The Stars of Faith got off to a rocky start, as they lacked many of the things that made the Wards great, including Gertrude's ability to manage, Clara's driving vision, and Brewster's exquisite songs. It did not help that Williams was not putting the energy into singing she did with the Wards. She frequently allowed other group members to do the shouting and avoided the vocal extremes that characterized her earlier work. The lull continued until 1961, when she again found Jesus and approached music with renewed vigor. She and the Stars got major exposure when they appeared in the off-Broadway production *Black Nativity* and began touring North America and Europe. Williams left the group in 1965 to launch a solo career. Returning to Europe, she appeared in an unsuccessful show until her mother's death caused her to go back to Miami. It was at her mother's funeral that she became committed, bringing back her old fire to her new career. Starting at Yale, Williams began a long series of college campus tours that gave her the opportunity to thrill audiences in North America, Europe (where she also appeared at jazz festivals), Africa, and the Caribbean with stirring renditions of such great songs as "Jesus Is All" and her biggest solo hit, the reflective "Standing Here Wondering Which Way to Go."

Though she died in 1994, Marion Williams' influence upon contemporary music continues to be felt. Back in the '50s, her unique singing style, that inimitable hollering and whooping, inspired artists such as Little Richard and the Isley Brothers to emulate her. *—Sandra Brennan*

Somebody Bigger Than You and I / 1958 / Relic ✦✦✦
Her first album after leaving the Ward Singers. Recorded in 1958, it includes "I Can't Forget." *—Bil Carpenter*

O Holy Night / 1959 / Savoy ✦✦✦
A Christmas album with the Stars of Faith. *—Bil Carpenter*

Standing Here Wondering Which Way to Go / 1971 / Atlantic ✦✦✦✦✦

The New Message / Jan. 1971 / Atlantic ✦✦✦✦✦
Some of the late gospel diva's finest moments. *—Opal Louis Nations*

Blessed Assurance / 1974 / Atlantic ✦✦✦✦
This glimpse into the power and joyous release of a black revivalist church is the kind of "testifying" for which Ray Charles and Sam Cooke were years earlier chastised for introducing to popular music. Recorded live in her Philadelphia church 20 years before her death, this sensational gospel shouter uses tremendous range and emotional commitment to hold her own against a small combo and a 41-member choir. Until the end of the album, the preaching does not interfere with the music. You don't have to be black or even Christian to appreciate the rollicking Jessy Dixon-penned "These Old Burdens" or the showstopping "Jesus Jesus," clocking in at almost ten minutes long and written by Marion Williams herself. *—Mark Allan*

Surely God Is Able / 1989 / Spirit Feel ✦✦✦✦✦
A very strong soloist who reworked classic gospel material from the '30s and '40s into a wonderful 1989 album. *—Kip Lornell*

Back to the Cross / Oct. 25, 1990 / Light ✦✦✦✦

★ **Strong Again** / 1991 / Spirit Feel ✦✦✦✦✦
An eclectic though satisfying 20-cut album by this major singer, her most impressive solo set in years. Sparse accompaniment; mainly traditional material. Excellent. *—Kip Lornell*

If You Ever Needed the Lord Before / Jul. 28, 1992 / Columbia/Legacy ✦✦✦✦
Stunning sides by this glorious gospel diva and ex-Ward singer. *—Opal Louis Nations*

Can't Keep It to Myself / 1993 / Shanachie ✦✦✦✦✦
Marion Williams has a majesty in her voice, a power in her delivery, and a compelling, dynamic quality that underscores her vocals. This disc features 22 awesome performances recorded with minimal, sympathetic accompaniment and little production support—just mostly Williams' smashing, note-bending, soaring vocals. She flies on slow, bluesy numbers, testifies and shouts on originals like "Ride in the Clouds" and "I'll Never Return No More," and turns old standards such as Roberta Martin's "God's Amazing Grace" and Rev. Thomas A. Dorsey's "Live the Life I Sing About in My Song" into gripping, fresh reaffirmations of her own faith. *—Ron Wynn*

☆ **My Soul Looks Back: The Genius of Marion Williams 1962–1992** / 1994 / Shanachie ✦✦✦✦✦
My Soul Looks Back: The Genius of Marion Williams 1962-1992 is an outstanding 25-track portrait of the legendary gospel singer in all of her glory. Listening to early sides like "Packin' Up" and "Surely God Is Able," it's easy to understand her influence on the likes of Little Richard and Aretha Franklin. These powerful songs are primal blasts of energy with all the cathartic transcendence more commonly attributed to rock & roll. Closer to R&B than any of her contemporaries, Williams also flirts playfully with the blues on cuts like "Dead Cat on the Line" and "It's Your Time Now but My Time After Awhile," and even dabbles in country on a cover of Roy Acuff's "The Great Speckled Bird." Whatever the setting, however, her voice is a marvel of improvisatory brilliance, her soprano never less than devastating. This is gospel at its finest. *—Jason Ankeny*

God & Me / Jan. 27, 1994 / Vee-Jay ✦✦✦✦✦

Born to Sing the Gospel / 1995 / Shanachie ✦✦✦✦
Born to Sing the Gospel returns Marion Williams to her home church, Philadelphia's B.M. Oakley Memorial Church of God in Christ; the material is engagingly varied, spanning from the bluesy original "Sometimes I Ring Up Heaven" to the traditional title track to the medley of the classics "Christ Is All" and "Jesus Is All." Though in fine form throughout, Williams hits her peak on "Death in the Morning," her delivery charged with all of the raw power of a field recording. [Shanachie's CD reissue appends five tracks not included on the original LP.] *—Jason Ankeny*

This Too Shall Pass / Sep. 12, 1995 / Nashboro ✦✦✦✦
Ten-song celebrations by one of the world's greatest gospel singers. Nashboro sides. *—Opal Louis Nations*

Through Many Dangers / Sep. 24, 1996 / Shanachie ✦✦✦✦

Gospel Soul of Marion Williams / Mar. 23, 1999 / Shanachie ✦✦✦✦

Paul "Hucklebuck" Williams

b. Jul. 15, 1915, Lewisburg, TN, **d.** Sep. 14, 2002, New York, NY
Vocals, Sax (Baritone), Sax (Alto), Composer / R&B, Jump Blues
Saxophonist and bandleader Paul Williams scored one of the first big hits of the R&B era in 1949 with "The Hucklebuck," an adaption of Charlie Parker's "Now's the Time." The song topped the R&B charts for 14 weeks in 1949, and was one of three Top Ten and five other Top 20 R&B instrumental hits that Williams scored for Savoy in 1948 and 1949.

He played with Clarence Dorsey in 1946 and then made his recording debut with King Porter in 1947 for Paradise before forming his own band late that year. Saxophonists Noble "Thin Man" Watts and Wild Bill Moore, trumpeter Phil Guilbeau, and vocalists Danny Cobb, Jimmy Brown, Joan Shaw, and Connie Allen were among Williams' band members. He was later part of Atlantic Records' house band in the '60s and directed the Lloyd Price and James Brown orchestras until 1964. After leaving the music business temporarily, Williams opened a booking agency in New York in 1968. Other Top Ten hits were "35-30" in 1948 and "Walkin' Around" in 1949. *—Ron Wynn*

● **The Hucklebuck** / Dec. 1948-Dec. 17, 1956 / Saxophonograph ✦✦✦

Robert Pete Williams

b. Mar. 14, 1914, Zachary, LA, **d.** Dec. 31, 1980, Rosedale, LA
Vocals, Guitar / Blues Revival, Country Blues, Acoustic Louisiana Blues
Discovered in the Louisiana State Penitentiary, Robert Pete Williams became one of the great blues discoveries during the folk boom of the early '60s. His disregard for conventional patterns, tunings, and structures kept him from a wider audience, but his music remains one of the great, intense treats of the blues.

Williams was born in Zachary, LA, the son of sharecropping parents. While he was a child, he worked the fields with his family; he never attended school. Williams didn't begin playing blues until his late teens, when he made himself a guitar out of a cigar box. Playing his homemade guitar, Williams began performing at local parties, dances, and fish fries at night while he worked during the day. Even though he was constantly working, he never made quite enough money to support his family, which caused considerable tension between him and his wife—according to legend, she burned his guitar one night in a fit of anger.

Despite all of the domestic tension, Williams continued to play throughout the Baton Rouge area, performing at dances and juke joints. In 1956, he shot and killed a man in a local club. Williams claimed the act was in self-defense, but he was convicted of murder and sentenced to life in prison. He was sent to Angola prison, where he served for two years before being discovered by ethnomusicologists Dr. Harry Oster and Richard Allen. The pair recorded Williams performing several of his own songs, which were all about life in prison. Impressed with the guitarist's talents, Oster and Allen pleaded for a pardon for Williams. The pardon was granted in 1959, after he had served a total of three and a half years. For the first five years after he left prison, Williams could only perform in Lousiana, but his recordings—which appeared on Folk-Lyric, Arhoolie, and Prestige, among other labels—were popular and he received positive word of mouth reviews.

In 1964, Williams played his first concert outside of Louisiana—it was a set at the legendary Newport Folk Festival. Williams' performance was enthusiastically received and he began touring the United States, often playing shows with Mississippi

Fred McDowell. For the remainder of the '60s and most of the '70s, Robert Pete Williams constantly played concerts and festivals across America, as well a handful of dates in Europe. Along the way, he recorded for a handful of small independent labels, including Fontana and Storyville. Williams slowed down his work schedule in the late '70s, largely due to his old age and declining health. The guitarist died on December 31, 1980, at the age of 66. —*Cub Koda & Stephen Thomas Erlewine*

★ **Angola Prisoner's Blues** / Mar. 1961 / Arhoolie ✦✦✦✦✦
Not enough great things to say about this one, one of the finest field recordings ever done anywhere. If Robert Pete's "Prisoner's Talking Blues" doesn't move you, check your heart into your refrigerator's freezer section. —*Cub Koda*

Free Again / Nov. 1961 / Prestige/Original Blues Classics ✦✦✦✦
In 1959, blues singer/guitarist Robert Pete Williams was residing in Angola prison, serving a life sentence for a murder he claimed he committed in self-defense, when he was discovered by blues researchers Harry Oster and Richard Allen. Immediately struck by the power of Williams' blues, the pair commenced the recordings that would appear on the collections *Robert Pete Williams, Vol. 1 & 2* (including the stunning "Prisoner's Talking Blues"). Subsequent efforts by Oster and Allen led to Williams' release. No longer surrounded by the bars of Angola, the singer found himself trapped instead by the strict rules and regulations of his harsh parole. Thus on *Free Again*, the singer walks the streets like a stranger with death on his mind. "You know I walk along and talk to myself," he declares in "Death Blues," remembering his confinement. "Sometimes I have a mind to leave this place/But they say, you know you're doing time." In "A Thousand Miles from Nowhere," Williams finds himself alone on the streets of a "one horse town." Settling down for the night, he sings with a "tombstone for my pillow and the fairground for my bed." Sitting on the roadside in "Thumbing a Ride," he finds that the cars just pass him by as if he didn't exist. Despite the constant, restless movement of Williams' guitar lines, these recordings have a stillness to them, as if the reverberation of his blunt, heavy attack might be the only sound for miles around. Intimately recorded by Oster himself, these ten solo guitar and vocal performances represent some of the finest of Williams' career and some of the best the blues has to offer. —*Nathan Bush*

Louisiana Blues / 1967 / Takoma ✦✦✦✦✦
Great blues artists need not be virtuoso musicians of the sort proudly paraded around by genres such as jazz and classical music. When expression and emotion are the main requirements—and *real* expression and emotion, not just professional stage dramatics—then playing one million notes per minute or having the most perfect sound on earth becomes much less important. But this is all a way of building up to the opinion that Robert Pete Williams is indeed a virtuoso, making him one of the most exciting country blues musicians to ever record as well as one of the most musically interesting. Again, it isn't a matter of playing a lot of notes, but how he plays them. Within a single passage he will sometimes employ three or four brilliantly subtle techniques—for example, a run played with the strings slightly muted followed by a clever punching of the rhythm with a single staccato chord. He creates passages of notes in which each one is played with a slightly different feel, an intricate and difficult accomplishment that few blues artists even think about, let alone do. He also rarely repeats himself, does fascinating things with the harmonic structure, and in each song evolves a relationship between guitar and voice that is stunning. On his "I'm Going Down Slow," for example, his blues lines utilize syncopation and offbeat accents that are more commonly associated with the blues inventions of jazz giants such as Charlie Parker, not country blues artists who are thought of as more primitive in their concept. Is that notion ever wrong! "Ugly," also known as "Grown So Ugly," is one of the most powerful songs ever from the country blues tradition. It is also easily this artist's most famous number due to a cool, but eventually inferior, cover version by Captain Beefheart, one of the few times the Captain took on something he couldn't quite handle. The only real quibble with this set, and it is very small, is the missed opportunity for a good album cover. Someone at this label had strange notions of design when Takoma's handful of blues releases came out. The small photo of the artist on the back cover with his scribbled signature would have been a much better choice if enlarged to fill the front cover than the awful artwork that is featured. Whatever. Put a paper bag over it, but just listen to it. —*Eugene Chadbourne*

Legacy of the Blues, Vol. 9 / 1973 / GNP ✦✦✦✦✦

Rural (With Snooks Eaglin) / 1973 / Fantasy ✦✦✦✦✦
Not only does Snooks Eaglin prove a fine partner for Robert Pete Williams, but his vocals and playing have seldom been more disciplined and exciting. —*Ron Wynn*

Those Prison Blues / 1981 / Arhoolie ✦✦✦
It is an interesting type of blindfold test to play these recordings of this artist that were made when he was in prison serving a life sentence for murder, then compare them with tracks he cut after being released, supposedly for his great abilities as a blues improviser. The question might be, how would life in the prison environment affect the musical output of a performer such as this, and can a listener tell the difference between the blues of a prisoner and a free man? There are several tracks here in which the perfunctory nature of the performances simply do not compare with the majesty of later recordings Robert Pete Williams made when breathing free air again. Perhaps this is why some of these tracks were not released the first time around. However, the flaws described are not consistently true about this entire set of prison performances, and neither is the dimensionless recording sound that the listener is initially greeted with, the strings flapping as if tuning up would have brought on the guards. Things pick up with "Texas Blues," in which the guitarist's fingers seem to be flying over the strings, picking out notes the way a bird might nip at a seed on the ground. The guitar sound becomes transformed on "Louise," emphasizing middle tones in a way that reaches into the gut. At this

juncture, one might be willing to admit the obvious intensity of a prison performance when it represents a human's only possible emotional outlet, but from the sound of this man's blues, this remained pretty much the case long after he was released from the slammer. Although some of these tracks are brilliant, there are more consistent collections available by this artist, as well as ones that are more generous with playing time. —*Eugene Chadbourne*

Blues Masters / 1991 / Storyville ✦✦✦

I'm as Blue as a Man Can Be / 1994 / Arhoolie ✦✦✦
Robert Pete Williams' music had the striking lyricism and highly individualized sound of the great Delta blues masters, but it was made well after the heyday of that style. Williams improvised considerably in his performances, using the blues' language but varying his approach. These songs were mostly recorded at the Angola State Penitentiary. While Williams sings mournful, anguished blues with spectacular impact, he also can turn around and do more joyous fare effectively. His vigorous accompaniment, especially on six-string guitar, is just as creative and stunning as his vocals. This 15-cut disc, which has five bonus cuts, is most welcome. —*Ron Wynn*

When a Man Takes the Blues / 1994 / Arhoolie ✦✦✦
This second volume of Robert Pete Williams material released on CD for the first time was recorded in Louisiana in 1959, shortly after Williams was paroled from Angola by Governor Earl Long. The cuts recorded during this time reflect both his appreciation for being out of jail and his understanding that he was still not completely free. The searing "All Night Long," "I Got the Blues So Bad," and "This Train Is Heaven Bound" are punctuated by equally gripping guitar accompaniment on either six- or 12-string. There's also material recorded later in his career in Berkeley. The three cuts from 1970 show Williams in a more reflective mode, though no less powerful. These are two of nine previously unissued cuts comprising the majority of the disc. —*Ron Wynn*

Robert Pete Williams / Sep. 11, 2001 / Fat Possum ✦✦✦✦

Homesick James Williamson

b. 1910, Somerville, TN
Slide Guitar, Vocals, Guitar / Slide Guitar Blues, Electric Chicago Blues
His correct age may remain in doubt (he's claimed he was born as early as 1905), but the slashing slide guitar skills of Homesick James Williamson have never been in question. Many of his most satisfying recordings have placed him in a solo setting, where his timing eccentricities don't disrupt the proceedings (though he's made some fine band-backed waxings as well).
Williamson was playing guitar at age ten and soon ran away from his Tennessee home to play at fish fries and dances. His travels took the guitarist through Mississippi and North Carolina during the 1920s, where he crossed paths with Yank Rachell, Sleepy John Estes, Blind Boy Fuller, and Big Joe Williams.
Settling in Chicago during the 1930s, Williamson played local clubs and recorded for RCA Victor in 1937. The miles and gigs had added up before Williamson made some of his finest sides in 1952-1953 for Art Sheridan's Chance Records (including the classic "Homesick" that gave him his enduring stage name).
James also worked extensively as a sideman, backing harp great Sonny Boy Williamson in 1945 at a Chicago gin joint called the Purple Cat and during the 1950s with his cousin, slide master Elmore James (to whom Homesick is stylistically indebted). He also recorded with James during the 1950s. Homesick's own output included crashing 45s for Colt and USA in 1962, a fine 1964 album for Prestige, and four tracks on a Vanguard anthology in 1965.
Williamson has continued recording and touring; he's done recent albums for Appaloosa, Earwig, and Fedora. No matter what his current chronological age, there's nothing over the hill about the blues of Homesick James Williamson. —*Bill Dahl*

● **Blues on the South Side** / 1964 / Prestige/Original Blues Classics ✦✦✦✦
Probably the best album the slide guitarist ever laid down (originally for Prestige in 1964). His stylistic similarities to his cousin, the great Elmore James, are obvious, but Homesick deviates repeatedly from the form. Tough as nails with a bottleneck, he goes for the jugular on "Goin' Down Swingin'," "Johnny Mae," and "Gotta Move," supported by pianist Lafayette Leake, guitarist Eddie Taylor, and drummer Clifton James. —*Bill Dahl*

Homesick James Williamson & Snooky Pryor / 1973 / Caroline ✦✦✦

Ain't Sick No More / 1973 / BluesWay ✦✦✦

Goin' Back Home / Jun. 1977 / 32 Jazz ✦✦✦
Originally recorded for Pete Lowry's Trix label back in 1974 and 1975, here's Homesick's acoustic album. While his timing (or lack of it) is still firmly in place, it somehow makes these tracks work all the better, keeping a loose time and making the tunes come alive. His voice is unbelievably strong and engaged on the tracks, and as Homesick James sessions go, this is one of his very best. Highly recommended. —*Cub Koda*

Goin' Back in the Times / 1994 / Earwig ✦✦✦
A credible, reflective return to the slide guitar veteran's country blues days. —*Bill Dahl*

Juanita / Mar. 18, 1997 / Appaloosa ✦✦✦

Chicago Slide Guitar Legend / 1998 / Official ✦✦✦✦✦
This 26-track overview brings together the early and impossibly rare tracks James recorded for imprints like Chance, Colt, USA, and others, from his earliest efforts in 1952 into the mid-'60s before signing with Prestige and producing the *Blues on the South Side* album for them. The first 15 tracks are culled from his 1952 and 1953 sessions for Chance Records (including an alternate take of his first single, "Lonesome Old Train"), and some great harp work from Big Walter Horton on the instrumental "Williamson Shuffle." Along with the surviving Chance material are stray singles for USA (an uptown version of "Crossroads" featuring a droning sax section), Colt ("Set a Date"), U.K. Decca ("Got to

Move"), Spivey ("Can't Hold Out") and a pair of sides shared with Sunnyland Slim ("Sunnyland/Homesick Special"). There are no real session dates or personnel information on here, and only scant liner notes only giving introductory information; the set also leaves off both sides of his 1960 Atomic H single and thus can't be a complete overview. But the music is just as fine as you could possibly ask for, Grade A Chicago blues chock full of raw slide guitar and Homesick's grainy vocals, making this the best overview of this artist's early work available on compact disc. *—Cub Koda*

The Last of the Broomdusters / Apr. 14, 1998 / Fedora ♦♦♦

Sonny Boy Williamson [I] (John Lee Williamson)

b. Mar. 30, 1914, Jackson, TN, **d.** Jun. 1, 1948, Chicago, IL

Vocals, Harmonica / Harmonica Blues, Acoustic Chicago Blues, Chicago Blues

Easily the most important harmonica player of the prewar era, John Lee Williamson almost single-handedly made the humble mouth organ a worthy lead instrument for blues bands—leading the way for the amazing innovations of Little Walter and a platoon of others to follow. If not for his tragic murder in 1948 while on his way home from a Chicago gin mill, Williamson would doubtless have been right there alongside them, exploring new and exciting directions.

It can safely be noted that Williamson made the most of his limited time on the planet. Already a harp virtuoso in his teens, the first Sonny Boy (Rice Miller would adopt the same moniker down in the Delta) learned from Hammie Nixon and Noah Lewis and rambled with Sleepy John Estes and Yank Rachell before settling in Chicago in 1934.

Williamson's extreme versatility and consistent ingenuity won him a Bluebird recording contract in 1937. Under the direction of the ubiquitous Lester Melrose, Sonny Boy Williamson recorded prolifically for Victor both as a leader and behind others in the vast Melrose stable (including Robert Lee McCoy and Big Joe Williams, who in turn played on some of Williamson's sides).

Williamson commenced his sensational recording career with a resounding bang. His first vocal offering on Bluebird was the seminal "Good Morning School Girl," covered countless times across the decades. That same auspicious date also produced "Sugar Mama Blues" and "Blue Bird Blues," both of them every bit as classic in their own right.

The next year brought more gems, including "Decoration Blues" and "Whiskey Headed Woman Blues." The output of 1939 included "T.B. Blues" and "Tell Me Baby," while Williamson cut "My Little Machine" and "Jivin' the Blues" in 1940. Jimmy Rogers apparently took note of Williamson's "Sloppy Drunk Blues," cut with pianist Blind John Davis and bassist Ransom Knowling in 1941; Rogers adapted the tune in storming fashion for Chess in 1954. The motherlode of 1941 also included "Ground Hog Blues" and "My Black Name," while the popular "Stop Breaking Down" (1945) found the harpist backed by guitarist Tampa Red and pianist Big Maceo Merriweather.

Sonny Boy cut more than 120 sides in all for RCA from 1937 to 1947, many of them turning up in the postwar repertoires of various Chicago blues giants. His call-and-response style of alternating vocal passages with pungent harmonica blasts was a development of mammoth proportions that would be adopted across-the-board by virtually every blues harpist to follow in his wake.

But Sonny Boy Williamson wouldn't live to reap any appreciable rewards from his inventions. He died at the age of 34, while at the zenith of his popularity (his romping "Shake That Boogie" was a national R&B hit in 1947 on Victor), from a violent bludgeoning about the head that occurred during a strong-arm robbery on the South Side. "Better Cut That Out," another storming rocker later appropriated by Junior Wells, became a posthumous hit for Williamson in late 1948. It was the very last song he had committed to posterity. Wells was only one young harpist to display his enduring allegiance; a teenaged Billy Boy Arnold had recently summoned up the nerve to knock on his idol's door to ask for lessons. The accommodating Sonny Boy Williamson was only too happy to oblige, a kindness Arnold has never forgotten (nor does he fail to pay tribute to his eternal main man every chance he gets). Such is the lasting legacy of the blues' first great harmonicist. *—Bill Dahl*

Bluebird Blues / 1970 / RCA ♦♦♦

Throw a Boogie Woogie (With Big Joe Williams) / Apr. 1990 / RCA ♦♦♦♦♦

Eight indispensable Bluebird sides dating from 1937-1938—right at the very beginning of his reign as king of the blues harpists—that display precisely why Williamson was such a revered innovator (and continues to be even now). Highlights include his classic "Good Morning School Girl" and "Sugar Mama Blues." He shares the disc with itinerant rambler Big Joe Williams, whose eight 1937-1941 selections include six featuring Sonny Boy playing harp behind the nine-string guitarist. *—Bill Dahl*

Complete Recorded Works, Vol. 1 (1937–1938) / 1991 / Document ♦♦♦♦♦

Complete Recorded Works, Vol. 2 (1938–1939) / 1991 / Document ♦♦♦♦♦

Document's *Complete Recorded Works, Vol. 2 (1938-1939)* picks up where the first volume left off, reissuing 24 tracks from the 13-month period of June 1938 to July 1939. Unfortunately, there weren't as many classic performances during this era, leaving this the odd one out from the many volumes in this set. Serious blues fans will still find much of interest here, including versions of "Susie-Q" and "You've Been Foolin' Round Town," plus a second stab at his classic "Sugar Mama Blues." *—Thom Owens*

Complete Recorded Works, Vol. 3 (1939–1941) / 1991 / Document ♦♦♦♦♦

The third volume in Document's impressive five-part series of Sonny Boy Williamson collections includes a raft of great sides recorded between July 1939 and April 1941. Beginning with Williamson's classic "T.B. Blues," *Complete Recorded Works, Vol. 3 (1939-1941)* cycles through two dozen great performances, including "Tell Me, Baby," "My Little Machine," and "Jivin' the Blues," with accompaniment from a trio of strong sidemen: Big Bill Broonzy, Walter Davis, and Blind John Davis. Casual listeners may not find this as immediately interesting as a career-spanning compilation like *Sugar Mama*, but there's plenty of interest for nearly any level of fan. *—Thom Owens*

Complete Recorded Works, Vol. 4 (1941–1945) / 1991 / Document ♦♦♦♦♦

Complete Recorded Works, Vol. 5 (1945–1947) / 1991 / Document ♦♦♦♦♦

★ **Sugar Mama** / 1995 / Indigo ♦♦♦♦♦

A well-researched 24-track compendium of the first Sonny Boy Williamson's massively influential Bluebird catalog that spans 1937-1942. Besides being such an innovator on the mouth organ, Williamson's songs themselves have stood the test of time strikingly—"Good Morning School Girl," "Blue Bird Blues," "Decoration Blues," "Sloppy Drunk Blues," and many more on the collection are recognized classics. *—Bill Dahl*

Sonny Boy Williamson, Vol. 1 (1937–1939) / Feb. 20, 1996 / Blues Collection ♦♦♦♦♦

This artist was perhaps the most significant pioneer of the city-styled, horn-oriented blues harp—a style brought to perfection by Little Walter. Williamson adapted the country-styled, chordal-rhythmic technique that he learned from Noah Lewis and Hammie Nixon to suit the demands of the evolving urban blues styles. These 24 tracks include Sonny Boy's first six records cut in 1937 and sport an imposing list of sidemen: Robert Nighthawk, Big Joe Williams, Henry Townsend, Walter Davis, Yank Rachell, Big Bill Broonzy, and Speckled Red. This is a definitive collection. *—Larry Hoffman*

The Bluebird Recordings 1937–1938 / Jan. 28, 1997 / Bluebird/RCA ♦♦♦♦

This 24-track overview of the blues harp master's brief tenure with the Bluebird label includes "Good Morning School Girl," probably Williamson's best known work thanks to subsequent covers by Howlin' Wolf and the Grateful Dead. *—Jason Ankeny*

The Bluebird Recordings 1938 / Apr. 29, 1997 / Bluebird/RCA ♦♦♦♦

Picking up where *Bluebird Recordings 1937-1938* left off, *Bluebird Recordings 1938* features the remaining 18 tracks that Sonny Boy Williamson recorded for the label in 1938. These are the recordings that established Williamson's career, and several of his classics, including "Deep Down in the Ground," as well as several duets with Speckled Red are included here. *—Thom Owens*

Sonny Boy Williamson [II] (Aleck Ford Miller)

b. Dec. 5, 1899, Glendora, MS, **d.** May 25, 1965, Helena, AR

Vocals, Leader, Songwriter, Harmonica / Delta Blues, Harmonica Blues, Electric Chicago Blues, Chicago Blues, Electric Harmonica Blues

Sonny Boy Williamson was, in many ways, the ultimate blues legend. By the time of his death in 1965, he had been around long enough to have played with Robert Johnson at the start of his career and Eric Clapton, Jimmy Page, and Robbie Robertson at the end of it. In between, he drank a lot of whiskey, hoboed around the country, had a successful radio show for 15 years, toured Europe to great acclaim, and simply wrote, played and sang some of the greatest blues ever etched into black phonograph records. His delivery was sly, evil, and world-weary, while his harp-playing was full of short, rhythmic bursts one minute and powerful, impassioned blowing the next. His songs were chock-full of mordant wit, with largely autobiographical lyrics that hold up to the scrutiny of the printed page. Though he took his namesake from another well-known harmonica player, no one really sounded like him.

A moody, bitter, and suspicious man, no one wove such a confusing web of misinformation as this Sonny Boy Williamson. Even his birth date (stated as December 5, 1899 in most reference books, but some sources claim his birth may have been in either 1897 or 1910) and real name (Aleck or Alex or Willie "Rice"—which may or may not be a nickname—Miller or Ford) cannot be verified with absolute certainty. Of his childhood days in Mississippi, absolutely nothing is known. What *is* known is that by the mid-'30s, he was traveling the Delta working under the alias of Little Boy Blue. With blues legends like Robert Johnson, Robert Nighthawk, Robert Jr. Lockwood, and Elmore James as interchangeable playing partners, he worked the juke joints, fish fries, country suppers, and ballgames of the era. By the early '40s, he was the star of KFFA's *King Biscuit Time*, the first live blues radio show to hit the American airwaves. As one of the major ruses to occur in blues history, his sponsor—the Interstate Grocery Company—felt they could push more sacks of their King Biscuit Flour with Miller posing as Chicago harmonica star John Lee "Sonny Boy" Williamson. In today's everybody-knows-everything video age, it's hard to think that such an idea would work, much less prosper. After all, the real Sonny Boy was a national recording star, and Miller's vocal and harmonica style was in no way derivative of him. But Williamson had no desire to tour in the South, so prosper it did, and when John Lee was murdered in Chicago, Miller became—in his own words—"the original Sonny Boy." Among his fellow musicians, he was usually still referred to as Rice Miller, but to the rest of the world he did, indeed, become *the* Sonny Boy Williamson.

The show was an immediate hit, prompting IGC to introduce Sonny Boy Corn Meal, complete with a likeness of Williamson on the front of the package. With all this local success, however, Sonny Boy was not particularly eager to record. Though he often claimed in his twilight years that he had recorded in the '30s, no evidence of that appears to have existed. Lillian McMurray, the owner of Trumpet Records in Jackson, MS, had literally tracked him down to a boarding house in nearby Belzoni and enticed him to record for her. The music Sonny Boy made for her between 1951 to 1954 shows him in peak form, his vocal, instrumental, and songwriting skills honed to perfection. Williamson struck paydirt on his first Trumpet release, "Eyesight to the Blind," and though the later production on his Chess records would make the Trumpet sides seem woefully under-recorded by comparison, they nonetheless stand today as classic performances, capturing juke-joint music in one of its finest hours.

Another major contribution to the history of the blues occurred when Sonny Boy brought *King Biscuit Time* guest star Elmore James into the studio for a session. With Williamson blowing harp, a drummer keeping time, and the tape machine running surreptitiously, Elmore recorded the first version of what would become his signature tune, Robert Johnson's "Dust My Broom." By this time Sonny Boy had divorced his first wife (who also happened to be the Howlin' Wolf's sister) and married Mattie Gordon. This would prove to be the longest and most enduring relationship of his life outside of music, with Mattie putting up with the man's rambling ways, and living a life of general rootlessness in the bargain. On two different occasions Sonny Boy moved to Detroit, taking up residence in the Baby Boy Warren band for brief periods, and contributed earth-shattering solos on Warren sides for Blue Lake and Excello in 1954.

By early 1955, after leasing a single to Johnny Vincent's Ace label, McMurray had sold Williamson's contract to Buster Williams in Memphis, who in turn sold it to Leonard Chess in Chicago. All the pieces were finally tumbling into place, and Sonny Boy finally had a reason to take up permanent residence north of the Mason-Dixon line; he now was officially a Chess recording artist. His first session for Chess took place on August 12, 1955, and the single pulled from it, "Don't Start Me to Talkin'," started doing brisk business on the R&B charts. By his second session for the label, he was reunited with longtime musical partner Robert Jr. Lockwood. Lockwood—who had been one of the original King Biscuit Boys—had become de facto house guitarist for Chess, as well as moonlighting for other Chicago labels. With Lockwood's combination of Robert Johnson rhythms and jazz chord embellishments, Williamson's harp and parched vocals sounded fresher than ever and Lockwood's contributions to the success of Sonny Boy's Chess recordings cannot be overestimated.

For a national recording artist, Williamson had a remarkable penchant for pulling a disappearing act for months at a time. Sometimes, when Chicago bookings got too lean, he would head back to Arkansas, fronting the *King Biscuit* radio show for brief periods. But in 1963 he was headed to Europe for the first time, as part of the American Folk Blues Festival. The folk music boom was in full swing and Europeans were bringing over blues artists, both in and past their prime, to face wildly appreciative white audiences for the first time. Sonny Boy unleashed his bag of tricks and stole the show every night. He loved Europe and stayed behind in Britain when the tour headed home. He started working the teenage beat club circuit, touring and recording with the Yardbirds and Eric Burdon's band, whom he always referred to as "de Mammimals." On the folk blues tours, Sonny Boy would be very dignified and laid-back. But in the beat club setting, with young white bands playing on 11 behind him, he'd pull out every juke-joint trick he used with the King Biscuit Entertainers and drive the kids nuts. "Help Me" became a surprise hit in Britain and across Europe. Now in his mid-sixties (or possibly older), Williamson was truly appreciative of all the attention, and contemplated moving to Europe permanently. But after getting a harlequin, two-tone, city gentleman's suit (complete with bowler hat, rolled umbrella, and attaché case full of harmonicas) made up for himself, he headed back to the States—and the Chess studios—for some final sessions. When he returned to England in 1964, it was as a conquering hero. One of his final recordings, with Jimmy Page on guitar, was entitled "I'm Trying to Make London My Home."

In 1965, he headed home, back to Mississippi one last time, and took over the *King Biscuit* show again. Still wearing his custom-made suit, he regaled the locals with stories of his travels across Europe. Some were impressed; others who had known him for years felt he could have just as well substituted the name "Mars" for Europe in explaining his exploits, so used were they to Sonny Boy's tall tales. But after hoboing his way around the United States for 30-odd years, and playing to appreciative audiences throughout Europe, Sonny Boy had a perfectly good reason for returning to the Delta; he had come home to die. He would enlist the help of old friends like Houston Stackhouse and Peck Curtis to take him around to all the back-road spots he had seen as a boy, sometimes paying his respects to old friends, other days just whiling away an afternoon on the banks of a river fishing.

When Ronnie Hawkins' ex-bandmates, the Hawks, were playing in the area, they made a special point of seeking out Sonny Boy and spent an entire evening backing him up in a juke joint. All through the night, Williamson kept spitting into a coffee can beside him. When Robbie Robertson got up to leave the bandstand during a break, he noticed the can was filled with blood. On May 25, 1965, Curtis and Stackhouse were waiting at the KFFA studios for Sonny Boy to do the daily *King Biscuit* broadcast. When Williamson didn't show, Curtis left the station and headed to the rooming house where Sonny Boy was staying, only to find him lying in bed, dead of an apparent heart attack. He was buried in the Whitfield Cemetery in Tutwiler, MS, and his funeral was well-attended. As Houston Stackhouse said, "He was well thought of through that country." He was elected to the Blues Foundation Hall of Fame in 1980. *—Cub Koda*

Down and Out Blues / 1959 / MCA/Chess ✦✦✦✦✦
Retaining photographer Don Bronstein's cover shot of a disheveled bum lying on the sidewalk (some former Chess artist, perhaps?) Sonny Boy Williamson's original 1959 album made it to digital reissue but has now been supplanted by MCA's exhaustive *The Essential Sonny Boy Williamson.* Still, for a budget price, there are a dozen unforgettable tracks: "Don't Start Me to Talkin'," and his Checker debut; "All My Love in Vain," "Wake Up Baby," "99," "Cross My Heart," "Let Me Explain," and "The Key (To Your Door)." *—Bill Dahl*

Help Me / 1964 / Chess ✦✦✦✦✦

In Memorium / 1965 / Chess ✦✦

The Real Folk Blues / 1965 / MCA/Chess ✦✦✦✦✦
Part of Chess' long line of introductory blues compilations, Sonny Boy Williamson's *Real Folk Blues* keeps up the high standard with another solid batch of classic Chicago blues. Mostly taken from his last years in the first half of the '60s, the 12 cuts here represent some of the best of Williamson's juke joint and dancefloor-friendly mix. Helping out this fine harp player are such Chicago royalty as Willie Dixon, Robert Jr. Lockwood, Fred Below, and Otis Spann. Also available as a two-fer with his *More Real Folk Blues* LP. *—Stephen Cook*

Sonny Boy Williamson & the Yardbirds / 1966 / Mercury ✦✦

More Real Folk Blues / Sep. 1967 / Chess ✦✦✦✦✦
More good early-'60s Chess Recordings from Sonny Boy Williamson. "Help Me," "Bye Bye Bird," and "Nine Below Zero" have been covered by numerous blues and rock acts. Most of the songs, however, show up on the *Essential* best-of collection. *—Richie Unterberger*

One Way Out / 1968 / MCA/Chess ✦✦✦✦✦
Although lacking the hilarious slice-of-life studio banter that makes its companion album *Bummer Road* so priceless, this is certainly a collection of terrific Chicago blues tracks as only Sonny Boy Williamson could do it. Like the Tennessee harmonica player with whom he shared a stage name, this Sonny Boy's music comes from the country blues tradition, fair and square. The way he plays harmonica is straight out of the country, with only a slight trace of the kind of microphone and amplifier distortion that the slightly younger Little Walter would exploit. Even the way these two harmonica men solo is quite different. Williamson can and does give individual notes detailed attention, creating a sound that could make a listener think the instrument responsible must be the size of a car, not something small enough to be tucked into a shirt pocket. But he often does it in such a rhythmically supportive way that instead of a chorus of harmonica soloing with band background, the result sounds more like a coordinated ensemble statement. This instrumental emphasis combines with his love of subtly shuffling, comfortable medium tempos and the sympathetic sound of his voice to create a style of blues that can approach the warm and fuzzy feeling of a good cup of hot chocolate. The instrumentalists involved all deserve much credit for the final blend. Is it Muddy Waters, or Jimmy Rogers, who picks the guitar riffs out on "Good Evening Everybody"? The sound of the instrument is unforgettably quaint, like someone playing on a 15-dollar guitar. Drummer Fred Below raises the roof on almost every track he appears, at times going over the top. The hilariously named "This Is My Apartment" has wonderfully recorded drums, including a robust tom tom sound, while the leader's harp improvisations and the guitar playing of Luther Tucker and Robert Jr. Lockwood sometimes even takes off in different directions, the result forecasting the sound of Ornette Coleman's electric groups. The same instrumental lineup makes the album's title track a classic of stinging whammy bar guitar mixed with thick, gloppy harmonica. "Like Wolf" is another one in which the drums are slathered with enough reverb to camouflage a small restaurant, while Williamson's vocal is an uncanny imitation of Howlin' Wolf. Bassist Willie Dixon may be doubling up his line with one of the guitarists on this one—the sound of the bass seems higher than usual. Like many of the this leader's band arrangements, it is just plain amazing. Country blues or not, the sounds of the city influenced this music in just the right way. The Chicago recording scene of the '50s was a hotbed of interplay between musicians who took part in jazz and blues sessions or gigs without batting an eye at the supposed difference. The sway of jazz rhythms is not the only influence that impacts the sound of these recordings. There is also a vivid use of space and dimension, the individual instruments each given a giant amount of room and responsibility. Lockwood Jr. takes particular advantage, developing interesting tones as he fits the guitar into the picture with a constant ear for attention-grabbing moments. *—Eugene Chadbourne*

Bummer Road / 1969 / MCA/Chess ✦✦✦✦✦
This album by the Rice Miller fellow who called himself Sonny Boy Williamson—in other words, the Mississippi harmonica player rather than the Tennessee harmonica player—may have been one of the best volumes in the grim-looking series of single-album reissues and collections Chess put out before switching to double-album sets. Those who enjoy both blues and the film noir style will enjoy the graphic design of these albums, which often sported singularly unattractive photography of the artists. The grainy, out-of-focus picture of Williamson that fills this front cover is no exception; in fact, in a way, it established the rule. It isn't that he looks mean, he just looks like he could care less. Such a look of indifference has perhaps never before been captured by the camera. It could easily have been taken during some of the discussion that occurs between the artist and his producers during the recording of a song called "Little Village." It was the reissue producer's decision to put an entire 11 minutes of takes, re-takes, and related arguing on the first side of this collection, complete with a severe warning that the proceedings are not suitable for airplay. Blues fans rushed to this track immediately, and were not disappointed in the slice of recording-studio life that is revealed here. Far better than Frank Zappa's secretly recorded band discussions and arguments, this is one of the best examples of enlarging the scope of a musical track by adding auxiliary material that wasn't originally meant for release. Bless T.T. Swan for compiling this series, and giving us this view of the "Little Village," such a profound moment that an all-star rock band eventually named itself after the track. There's lots of other great stuff here as well; really, every track is a burner. Robert Jr. Lockwood is here on lead guitar, playing from the heart in his style of that era, not as jazzy as what would come later but hardly just a bunch of stock blues licks. "Temperature 110" is fantastic, a totally believable sizzler. "Santa Claus Blues" is many listeners' favorite Sonny Boy Williamson track, after which one can never rummage through a room looking for hidden booty without hearing harmonica riffs in the background. Other great tracks include "Open Road" and "This Old Life." Quite a bit of this material was released for the first time in this set, certainly one the blues fans will want to sail off to that desert island with. *—Eugene Chadbourne*

This Is My Story / 1972 / Chess ✦✦✦✦✦
If collected together, the recording output of both harmonica players who called themselves Sonny Boy Williamson that was available by the year 2002 would surely fill a large-size home freezer. Yet there was a time, circa the '60s, when the only available recording by Sonny Boy Williamson was the one he did with the Yardbirds, which was apparently not even mastered at the right speed because the record company was afraid an old black man's low voice would frighten teenagers. Chess finally came to the rescue with two absolutely superb single-album releases decorated in particularly grimy black and white, and then had no problem coming up with even more artillery when double-album reissue sets became the fad. *This Is My Story* managed not to repeat any of the tracks from the previous albums, meaning the holder of all was in possession of a first-class collection of work by the artist, and that means great Chicago blues with some of the best harmonica playing this genre has to offer. (An alternate version of "One Way Out" is featured on the album of the same name; other than that, are no duplications of titles at all.) Much like Little Walter, his peer and adversary, this Sonny Boy had a sharp, cynical

sense of humor and a knack for arranging little philosophies into snappy, cooking blues numbers. "Fattenin' Frogs for Snakes" is a life lesson all in itself, while "My Younger Days," "The Goat," and "Down Child" are equally profound. The way the melody is sung on the latter number is really beautiful. Several of these performances are absolute blues classics, such as "Help Me." Only one song isn't credited to Williamson, which is quite impressive. Equally impressive are the man's bandleading skills in terms of laying down the law rhythmically. Players getting into blues rhythm sections will need to check these sides out: This is how it is done. The liner notes inside the gatefold are up to the usual Pete Welding standard of excellence, but a clear listing of the players, track by track, was apparently not considered an essential thing. That's a shame; the blues musicianship on these tracks is so wonderful that listeners will want to shout the players' names out the window. *—Eugene Chadbourne*

Sonny Boy Williamson / 1976 / Chess ♦♦♦♦♦
A good two-LP, 28-song anthology of Williamson's best Chess material. All but a half dozen of these cuts appear on the more extensive *Essential* CD. *—Richie Unterberger*

The Original / 1976 / Blues Classics ♦♦♦♦
Life is confusing for everyone, but for blues fans, it must really be worse. Where else can one find two artists playing the same instrument, using the same name? Part of being accepted into the elite echelon of blues scholars, is, of course, being able to recognize and explain the differences between the two Sonny Boy Williamson harp blowers, but the Blues Classics label must have decided things weren't complicated enough by issuing a set by the Sonny Boy most commonly known as the second of the bunch under the title of *The Original.* Blues listeners may become bewildered when they realize that the same label has issued a series of recordings by the other Sonny Boy, also known as John Lee Williamson, with very similar packaging. Another blues label has also issued a set by that Sonny Boy with the same title as this one, *The Original.* Looking closely at the photo on the front of this, one can clearly see the unmistakable sourpuss of Rice Miller, the so-called second Sonny Boy Williamson. The recording sound on these vintage tracks is just as muddy as all the confusion that has just been described, but, delightfully, this is a case where the sound quality augments the music wonderfully. This Sonny Boy was a master at getting bands to pump out stomping rhythms, the effect of which is intensified by the primitive recording sound in which only small parts of the drum set break through the band sound, sometimes the bass drum or a tom, sometimes a crisp snare. There is also pumping blues piano, and some very early electric guitar playing. One can strain one's eyes reading the liner notes by Paul Oliver, set in the same type used for the classified ads, but one will still not really know for sure if the circa 1951 recordings that were the first ones for this artist are the ones that are featured here. Presuming this is the case, perhaps "the original" is meant to refer to the recordings. At any case, these tracks predate the material this artist cut a bit later during a long period of action with the Chicago Chess label. The same excited spirit, drive, and lyrical cleverness are all there, however, especially on standout tracks such as the famous "Eyesight to the Blind" and the intense "Nine Below Zero." Those that believe the power of the blues was diluted by fancy recording studios and digital sound should really enjoy this. *—Eugene Chadbourne*

Chess Masters / 1981 / Chess ♦♦♦♦♦

☆ **King Biscuit Time** / 1989 / Arhoolie ♦♦♦♦♦
Sonny Boy's early Trumpet sides, 1951. The original "Eyesight to the Blind," "Nine Below Zero," and "Mighty Long Time" are Sonny Boy at his very best. Added bonuses include Williamson backing Elmore James on his original recording of "Dust My Broom" and a live KFFA broadcast from 1965. *—Cub Koda*

Clownin' With the World / 1989 / Trumpet ♦♦♦♦♦
This batch of mostly unreleased Trumpet blues cuts from the early '50s offers some sizzling, if sometimes uneven, material by Sonny Boy Williamson (Rice Miller) and Willie Love. Each gets eight numbers, with Williamson's being recorded both in Houston and Jackson, MS, while Love did all of his in Jackson. Williamson's ripping, searing harmonica and craggy vocals were then becoming popular, while Love's equally decisive singing and wild, carefree tunes were also attracting big audiences. This is undiluted, frequently chaotic, and always enjoyable music. *—Ron Wynn*

Keep It to Ourselves / 1990 / Analogue ♦♦♦♦
An intimate 1963 collection of Sonny Boy Williamson in solo and duet (with guitarist Matt "Guitar" Murphy) formats; on three tracks, pianist Memphis Slim hops aboard. This delightful addendum to Williamson's electric output of the same era was cut in Denmark and first issued on Storyville. *—Bill Dahl*

The Chess Years / 1991 / Charly ♦♦♦♦♦
This import multi-disc boxed set of Williamson's Chess sides (1955-1964) is a definitive overview. *—Cub Koda*

☆ **The Essential Sonny Boy Williamson** / Jun. 8, 1993 / MCA/Chess ♦♦♦♦♦
A two-disc compilation offering 45 of the wizened harmonica genius' best efforts for the Chess brothers, this is the best domestic Williamson package you'll find. Not everything you might want, but pretty close to it: "Don't Start Me to Talkin'," "Let Me Explain," "The Key (To Your Door)" (an alternate take), "Bring It on Home," "Help Me," "One Way Out," "Your Funeral and My Trial," and plenty more. With Robert Jr. Lockwood and Luther Tucker peeling off sizzling guitar riffs behind him, Williamson always had a trick or two up his sleeve until the end. *—Bill Dahl*

Goin' in Your Direction / 1994 / Alligator ♦♦♦♦♦
Alligator continues its Trumpet reissue series with an excellent 15-cut anthology covering early Rice Miller (Sonny Boy Williamson) material, some of it also including guitarist Arthur "Big Boy" Crudup and guitarist Bobo "Slim" Thomas. Miller was honing the uncanny technique that made him a harmonica legend, playing long overtones, spitting lines, droning and angular phrases that are now part of blues lore. His voice was gaining strength and stature, and he repeatedly demonstrated the kind of vocal character and instrumental acumen later immortalized on his Chess sessions. Alligator has found a genuine treasure chest with this series. *—Ron Wynn*

Trumpet Masters, Vol. 5: From the Bottom / 1994 / Collectables ♦♦♦♦♦
As you would expect, Sonny Boy Williamson's Trumpet sides were rough, raspy, and combative, punctuated by biting harmonica and accented by his piercing vocals. This CD cleans up the sound a bit, but not enough to rob it of its energy or grit. *—Ron Wynn*

In Europe With Clapton, Dixon and Spann / 1995 / Evidence ♦♦♦
More highlights from Sonny Boy Williamson's overseas travels, in a wide variety of settings—during the 1963 and 1964 American Folk Blues Festivals with old friends like Willie Dixon, Sunnyland Slim, Hubert Sumlin and Matt "Guitar" Murphy behind him, and for nine tracks, with the Yardbirds in support. The latter combination works pretty well—Clapton and company offer reverent, laid-back rhythms that seldom intrude and often mesh nicely. *—Bill Dahl*

★ **His Best** / May 20, 1997 / MCA/Chess ♦♦♦♦♦
While some hardliners will point to his early '50s Trumpet recordings as his most undiluted work, Sonny Boy's tenure at Chess Records was his longest and most successful and therefore deserves first look for the novice coming to this remarkable bluesman at ground level. This 20-track collection takes 17 tracks from the excellent two-disc *Essential Sonny Boy Williamson* collection and adds "Sad to Be Alone," "My Younger Days," and an alternate session-second version of "One Way Out" with Buddy Guy on guitar (yes, *this* is the version that the Allman Brothers used as the blueprint for their cover version) to the final mix. This is another entry into MCA's Chess *50th Anniversary* series and the digital transfers here are exemplary, making this an automatic audio upgrade for those who already have this material in their collection. Because his output for the label was of such a uniformly high quality, virtually everything Williamson put down on tape at the Chess studios could make a final cut on any best of package you'd want to put together on the man. So bemoaning the absence of any track here would be minor critical carping, especially in light of the other Sonny Boy Chess packages still in print. But if you're only going to own *one* of them and your wallet tends to shy away from two-disc anthologies, this makes an excellent first purchase. *—Cub Koda*

U.K. Blues / Jul. 24, 2001 / Fuel 2000 ♦♦♦
Recorded over two nights with the Yardbirds in December 1963, and then two weeks later with the Animals, the historical live recordings offer a rare glimpse into one of the main catalysts behind the British blues explosion of the early '60s. Notable not just for the quality of the recording but the backing bands behind the blues legend, the songs show a man not past his prime but fortunate enough to have it finally exposed to a wider audience. "The River Rhine," which sounds slightly similar to the Champs' hit "Tequila," doesn't lose its stamina, while the harmonica work carries most of the album. Apparently changing the prearranged set list, some of the numbers consist mainly of Williamson on harmonica, but Eric Clapton can be heard on "Take It Easy Baby." Although "Western Arizona" and "My Little Cabin" are boogie- and blues-riddled high points, the second half of the album is more energized. Culminating with Eric Burdon on "Nobody but You," the quality is only surpassed by the significance of this momentous event between teacher and students. *—Jason MacNeil*

The Real Folk Blues/More Real Folk Blues / Mar. 12, 2002 / MCA/Chess ♦♦♦♦♦
Like other entries in the Chess *Real Folk Blues* series, Sonny Boy Williamson's *The Real Folk Blues* and *More Real Folk Blues* (here combined onto one CD) were not really folk, and not really regular albums. Rather, they were somewhat arbitrarily chosen compilations, titled to appeal to the crowd that had gotten turned onto the blues during the 1960s folk revival. In Williamson's case, all 24 tracks were done between 1960 and 1964, save "Dissatisfied," which dates from 1957. Because the standard of the electric blues on this disc is very good, whether on the smaller-combo workouts or ones that add organ or saxes, one hates to discuss it dispassionately in terms of whether it's really necessary or advisable to fit into your collection. But the presence of other comprehensive Williamson anthologies on the market, and the lack of any real coherent theme to this particular grouping of songs, makes that necessary. If you have the one-disc *His Best* CD, this doesn't make a bad supplement; it does repeat eight songs from *His Best*, it's true, but it has 16 songs that are not on that collection. Conversely, if you have the more extensive two-CD *Essential* anthology, you'll find only eight songs here that aren't on *Essential*, which means rather short value. At any rate, this does have several of his best and most familiar songs: "One Way Out," "Bye Bye Bird," "Help Me," "Nine Below Zero," and "Down Child." The eight songs that don't show up on either *His Best* or *Essential* are worth having, whether you get them here or on another disc, the highlights of those being "Got to Move" (with cool gospel organ), the bouncy "Peach Tree," and the novelty rap "The Hunt," which sounds like an attempt to match the success of Bo Diddley's similarly constructed "Say Man." *—Richie Unterberger*

Willie & the Poor Boys

f. 1984

Group / Rock & Roll, R&B, Blues-Rock, British Blues

With Mick Jagger and Keith Richards bickering back and forth in the press during the mid-'80s (leading many to assume that the Stones were kaput), bassist Bill Wyman decided to fill up his newly acquired spare time by forming an all-star band, Willie & the Poor Boys. The group's roots lay in the series of high-profile 1983 ARMS (Action for Research into Multiple Sclerosis) concerts, which led to several of the tour's participants taking it a step further and laying down some tracks in the studio. Included in this stellar lineup were Wyman's Stones-mates Ron Wood and Charlie Watts, as well as Jimmy

Page, Mel Collins, Andy Fairweather-Low, Kenny Jones, and Ringo Starr, among others, while Wyman also served as the album's producer. The resulting 1985 self-titled album was a pleasant enough set of 12 rock & roll/R&B standards (including "Baby Please Don't Go," which a promo video was filmed for), but certainly not anything musically earth-shattering. A self-titled home video was also issued the same year as the album, but little was heard from the group subsequently, leading many to believe that Willie & the Poor Boys was a one-off side project. Yet in 1994 (a few years after Wyman retired from the Stones), Willie & the Poor Boys reappeared once more, with the 12-track *Tear It Up: Live*. — *Greg Prato*

● **Willie and the Poor Boys** / 1985 / Mercury ✦✦✦

Tear It Up: Live / 1994 / Blind Pig ✦✦✦

Chick Willis (Robert Willis)

b. Sep. 29, 1934, Cabiness, GA

Vocals, Guitar / Modern Electric Blues, Soul-Blues, R&B, Dirty Blues

Cousin to the late blues ballad singer Chuck Willis, Robert "Chick" Willis is primarily beloved for his ribald, dirty dozens-based rocker "Stoop Down Baby." The guitarist cut his original version in 1972 for tiny La Val Records of Kalamazoo, MI, selling a ton of 45s for the jukebox market only (the tune's lyrics were way too raunchy for airplay).

Willis left the military in 1954, hiring on as valet and chauffeur to cousin Chuck, then riding high with his many R&B hits for OKeh Records. At that point, Chick's primary role on the show was as a singer (he made his own vinyl debut in 1956 with a single, "You're Mine," for Lee Rupe's Ebb Records after winning a talent contest at Atlanta's Magnolia Ballroom), but he picked up the guitar while on the road with his cousin (Chick cites Guitar Slim as his main man in that department).

When Chuck died of stomach problems in 1958, Willis soldiered on, pausing in Chicago to work as a sideman with slide guitar great Elmore James. A few obscure 45s ("Twistin' in the Hospital Ward," cut for Alto in 1962, sounds promising) preceded the advent of "Stoop Down Baby," which Willis has freshened up for countless sequels ever since (he developed the song by teasing passersby with his ribald rhymes while working in a carnival variety show).

Risqué material has remained a staple of Willis' output in recent years. He cut several albums for Ichiban, notably 1988's *Now*, *Footprints in My Bed* in 1990, and *Back to the Blues* in 1991. — *Bill Dahl*

● **Stoop Down Baby . . . Let Your Daddy See** / 1972 / Collectables ✦✦✦✦✦

Here's the signifyin' original "Stoop Down Baby" in its long, unexpurgated version as issued on the tiny La Val label in 1972. "Mother Fuyer" travels the same salacious route, but Chick Willis has a serious side too—a pair of Guitar Slim covers spotlight Willis' stinging guitar and sturdy singing. — *Bill Dahl*

Now / 1988 / Ichiban ✦✦

Willis updates his biggest seller with a "Stoop Down '88," and there's a leering "I Want to Play With Your Poodle" and "I Want a Big Fat Woman" for those who like their blues blue. — *Bill Dahl*

Footprints in My Bed / 1990 / Ichiban ✦✦✦✦

One of the few real blues LPs to post a warning about explicit lyrics, though it seems pretty tame in these rap-hardened times. Nevertheless, "Jack You Up," "Nuts for Sale," and "Big Red Caboose" are firmly in the best risqué Willis tradition—and very well produced and played to boot. — *Bill Dahl*

Back to the Blues / 1991 / Ichiban ✦✦✦

Willis takes things a little more seriously than usual, concentrating largely on covers of material by Percy Mayfield, Howlin' Wolf, Clarence Carter, and Guitar Slim. His own contributions include "I Ain't Jivin' Baby" and "Bow-Legged Woman" (he couldn't resist the raunchy stuff entirely!). — *Bill Dahl*

Holdin' Hands With the Blues / 1992 / Ichiban ✦✦

Thanks to a weak selection of songs and an indifferent production, *Holdin' Hands With the Blues* is one of Chick Willis' lesser efforts. Occasionally, he works up a nice lascivious snarl and spits out a couple of good solos, but for the most part, the record falls into predictable, uninspiring, dirty-minded shuffles and boogies. — *Thom Owens*

Nasty Chick / 1992 / Ichiban ✦✦✦

I Got a Big Fat Woman / 1994 / Ichiban ✦✦

Blue Class Blues / Sep. 8, 1998 / Paula ✦✦✦

From the Heart and Soul / Mar. 20, 2001 / Rock House ✦✦✦

Chuck Willis (Harold Willis)

b. Jan. 31, 1928, Atlanta, GA, d. Apr. 10, 1958, Atlanta, GA

Vocals / R&B

There were two distinct sides to Chuck Willis. In addition to being a convincing blues shouter, the Atlanta-born Willis harbored a vulnerable blues balladeer side. In addition, he was a masterful songwriter who penned some of the most distinctive R&B numbers of the 1950s. We can't grant him principal credit for his 1957 smash adaptation of "C.C. Rider," an irresistible update of a classic folk-blues, but Willis did write such gems as "I Feel So Bad" (later covered by Elvis Presley, Little Milton, and Otis Rush), the anguished ballads "Don't Deceive Me (Please Don't Go)" and "It's Too Late" (the latter attracting covers by Buddy Holly, Charlie Rich, and Otis Redding), and his swan song, "Hang Up My Rock and Roll Shoes."

Harold Willis (he adopted Chuck as a stage handle) received his early training singing at YMCA-sponsored "Teenage Canteens" in Atlanta and fronting the combos of local bandleaders Roy Mays and Red McAllister. Powerful DJ Zenas "Daddy" Sears took an interest in the young vocalist's career, hooking him up with Columbia Records in 1951. After a solitary single for the major firm, Willis was shuttled over to its recently reactivated OKeh R&B subsidiary.

In 1952, he crashed the national R&B lists for OKeh with a typically plaintive ballad, "My Story," swiftly encoring on the hit parade with a gentle cover of Fats Domino's "Goin' to the River" and his own "Don't Deceive Me" the next year and "You're Still My Baby" and the surging Latin-beat "I Feel So Bad" in 1954. Willis also penned a heart-tugging chart-topper for Ruth Brown that year, "Oh What a Dream."

Willis moved over to Atlantic Records in 1956 and immediately enjoyed another round of hits with "It's Too Late" and "Juanita." Atlantic strove mightily to cross Willis over into pop territory, inserting an exotic steel guitar at one session and chirpy choirs on several more. The strategy eventually worked when his 1957 revival of the ancient "C.C. Rider" proved the perfect number to do the "Stroll" to; *American Bandstand* gave the track a big push, and Willis had his first R&B number one hit as well as a huge pop seller (Gene "Daddy G" Barge's magnificent sax solo likely aided its ascent).

Barge returned for Willis' similar follow-up, "Betty and Dupree," which also did well for him. But the turban-wearing crooner's time was growing short—he had long suffered from ulcers prior to his 1958 death from peritonitis. Much has been made of the ironic title of his last hit, the touching "What Am I Living For," but it was no more a clue to his impending demise than its flip, the joyous "Hang Up My Rock and Roll Shoes." Both tracks became massive hits upon the singer's death, and his posthumous roll continued with "My Life" and a powerful "Keep A-Drivin'" later that year.

Willis' cousin, Robert "Chick" Willis, who began his career as a backup singer for Chuck, remains active nationally. — *Bill Dahl*

My Story / 1980 / Columbia ✦✦✦

Not as exhaustive as Legacy's subsequent look at Willis' early- to mid-'50s hitmaking stint at OKeh, but this 14-tracker still gets the job done with the smooth ballads "Going to the River," "Don't Deceive Me," and "My Story" and Willis' surging, Latin-tempoed original "I Feel So Bad." — *Bill Dahl*

Let's Jump Tonight! The Best of Chuck Willis: 1951–1956 / 1994 / Epic/Legacy ✦✦✦✦✦

Before his brief turn as a rock & roll star with Atlantic, Willis cut a lot of material for OKeh in much more of an R&B/jump blues vein. This 26-cut collection includes all of his early- and mid-'50s R&B hits—"My Story," "Goin' to the River," "Don't Deceive Me," "You're Still My Baby," and his most famous number from this period, "I Feel So Bad" (revived by Elvis Presley, among others). The influence of Joe Turner, Charles Brown, early Lloyd Price, and similar performers is strongly felt; Willis could shout competently, but was much better on the emotional R&B ballads. Not as strong or distinctive as his Atlantic material, this includes several cuts that were previously unreleased or previously unavailable in the U.S. — *Richie Unterberger*

★ **Stroll On: The Chuck Willis Collection** / Oct. 19, 1994 / Razor & Tie ✦✦✦✦✦

All 25 of the versatile Atlanta-bred singer's Atlantic Records sides, presented beautifully (every R&B reissue on CD should be packaged so well, with plenty of brilliant stereo). Willis really hit his stride at Atlantic, doing the Stroll with his easygoing "C.C. Rider" and "Betty and Dupree" (both boasting darting sax breaks from Gene "Daddy G" Barge), baring his tender soul on a devotional "What Am I Living For," and taking R&B into fresh directions with a jumping "Kansas City Woman," the relentless "Keep A-Drivin'," and a buoyant "Hang Up My Rock and Roll Shoes." — *Bill Dahl*

I Remember Chuck Willis/The King of the Stroll / Nov. 13, 2001 / Collectables ✦✦✦

This reissue from Collectables combines two classic Chuck Willis albums: one for OKeh and the other from Atlantic. These are *I Remember Chuck Wills* and *King of the Stroll*, released in 1963 and 1958, respectively. The disc features 25 tracks, including a number of jump blues, early R&B, and tender, yearning ballads. This is a sure-bet purchase and also sports the addition of the original LP track sequence that highlights obscure cuts that are just as enjoyable as the hits. — *Al Campbell*

Michelle Willson

b. Jan. 5, 1958, Massachusetts

Vocals / Jump Blues, Retro Swing, R&B

A gifted swing and jump blues vocalist, Michelle Willson—a native of the Boston area—began singing as a teenager, often fronting bands quixotically named after nonexistent members (for example, Mimi Jones and Alex Clayton). As a solo performer, she organized a well-received tribute to her singing idols Dinah Washington and Ruth Brown, then joined the band Evil Gal; again working solo in 1994, Willson issued her debut LP, *Evil Gal Blues*, followed in 1996 by *So Emotional*. *Wake Up Call* marked her first release in the new millennium. — *Jason Ankeny*

Evil Gal Blues / 1994 / Bullseye Blues ✦✦✦

The liner notes to this record proclaim that Michelle Willson will take over the crown, worn for many years by Dinah Washington, as the next queen of the blues. While that may be a bit of an overstatement, Willson does have great vocal ability, which she shows off here on her debut. Backed by the jump blues band Evil Gal, Willson shows her range by smoking through songs associated with her idols (Washington and Ruth Brown), such as "Voodoo Voodoo" and "I Know How to Do It," then doing a complete turnaround and giving beautiful readings of such classics as "At Last" and "Cry Me a River." She may not have reached the dizzying heights of her great influences, but with this fine debut, Willson is well on her way. — *Steve Kurutz*

● **So Emotional** / 1996 / Bullseye Blues ✦✦✦✦

Michelle Willson is a shouting blues singer with plenty of sass who is quite assertive and not shy about talking about her desires and feelings, some of which are fairly obvious. This CD is full of extroverted singing with fine backup from a '50s style jump blues group that plays in the vein of Roomful of Blues. There are a liberal amount of tenor and guitar solos and some of the music really cooks. Highlights include "Better Left Unsaid" (whose lyrics change direction in a surprising way), the double entendre "Long John Blues" (the usual tale about visiting a dentist), a rare remake of Bobby Troup's "The Girl Can't Help It" (from the Jayne Mansfield movie of the same name) and the jubilant

"Strange Things Are Happening Everyday." There is plenty of fun goodtime music on this often-rollicking and easily recommended set from the thus far underrated Michelle Willson. *—Scott Yanow*

Tryin' to Make a Little Love / Jan. 12, 1999 / Bullseye Blues ♦♦♦♦
For her third album, *Tryin' to Make a Little Love*, Boston's Michelle Willson traveled to New Orleans, worked with producer Scott Billington and embraced a variety of material. Her singing was still brassy, sassy, and full of attitude, and she could still handle the type of invigorating '40s/early '50s jump blues for which she was known. But this isn't an album that neatly fits into any one category. Though retailers placed *Tryin' to Make a Little Love* in the blues bins, this isn't strictly a blues outing. Willson brings her passion to the jump blues of Dolly Cooper's "Ay La Bas," the Latin jazz of "Corazon de Hielo," and the Southern-style soul of "I Would Rather Do Without It." Also, her emotion can be heard on "Shifting Sand" (a Willson original), "Life Rolls On," and "Responsibility" (a Dr. John/Doc Pomus composition). Before this album came out, the singers Willson was most often compared to included Dinah Washington, Ruth Brown, and Big Maybelle—and they're still valid comparisons; this time Etta James' name can be added to that list. While it doesn't hurt to name Willson's influences, it's important to point out that she's quite recognizable herself—*Tryin' to Make a Little Love* is the work of a singer who shouldn't be pigeonholed. *—Alex Henderson*

Wake Up Call / Aug. 7, 2001 / Bullseye Blues ♦♦♦♦
Songstress Michelle Willson tears it up on her jazz-infused blues set *Wake Up Call*. The album is rife with dancing organs, bouncing drums, a sizzling saxophone, and the robust vocal stylings of Willson. The album opener and title track is an entirely funky affair. Willson's voice struts over a groovin' rhythm, bass clarinet accents, and soulful Hammond B3 organ trills. It is impossible to not be moved by this performer. With her lush, sultry, and robust voice, Willson can get a rise out of a stone statue. The smoking blues-rock anthem "Just Like a Dog (Barking Up the Wrong Tree)" is among the disc's many shining moments and boasts a siren of a saxophone line and Willson, again, cutting it up. Five of the 13 tracks are originals by Willson—she generally performs music by other songwriters and artists—and they fit right in with the disc's funky jazz-blues. "Set You Free," one of Willson's own, snaps, crackles, and pops as the singer says good riddance to a deadbeat lover. What a bouncin' good time this recording is. Just try to sit still while listening—it won't happen. Willson's singing is like a strong cup of Joe—it beelines right to the gut and jolts the system. If there ever was a wake-up call, this worthy album would be it. *—Liana Jonas*

Charles Wilson

b. Jan. 27, 1957, Chicago, IL
Vocals / Modern Electric Blues, Soul-Blues, Southern Soul
Charles Wilson was raised in Chicago, and started singing early, as a teenager he sang in Chicago area nightclubs but was too young to have a beer. R&B/blues singer Little Milton ("We're Gonna Make It") is his uncle, but his break came when he got the opportunity to go on the road with Bobby Rush. He later opened for Z.Z. Hill, Otis Clay, Tyrone Davis, and Bobby "Blue" Bland. Wilson waxed his first single in 1964, but "Trying to Make a Wrong Thing Right" didn't do much; his next effort "You Cut Off My Love Supply," wasn't a smash either but it established Wilson as a blues player of note. He drifted into Southern soul when he cut his first album, *Blues in the Key of C* on Ichiban Records in Atlanta, GA, which increased his bookings in the South, the Midwest, and overseas. He now records for Ecko Records and has cut four tight blues collections to date: *It's Sweet on the Backstreet* in 1995, *Love Seat* in 1998, *It Ain't the Size* in 1999, *Mr. Freak* in 2000. Wilson also released *Why?* in 1997 for the Traction label and *Songs from the Vault* in 2001 on his own Wilson imprint. Still looking for that increasingly unlikely monster crossover, Wilson has built a firm foundation, and has displayed remarkable staying power when you consider he's been performing in public since he was seven. *—Andrew Hamilton*

Blues in the Key of C / 1991 / Ichiban ♦♦♦
Not to be confused with Charles Wilson of the Gap Band, this Charles Wilson is an obscure but talented blues/soul man who doesn't always sound like a man. In fact, he often sounds like a woman—although a woman with a fairly deep voice. *Blues in the Key of C*, which employs Little Milton on guitar, gives the impression that Wilson has spent a lot of time listening to great female singers like Esther Phillips. Although this CD ended up in the blues bins, most of the material is R&B rather than actual 12-bar blues. Wilson is at his best on "Selfish Lover," "Is It Over," and "Who's It Going to Me," all of which recall the soul music of the 1970s and show us how convincing a singer he can be. Less memorable is the urban contemporary-ish "Love Supply." Unfortunately, much of the album suffers from weak production. Underproduced can be a healthy thing when you're going for earthy, down-home blues, but the low-budget approach becomes a liability when you're using synthesizers, sequencers, and drum machines as much as Wilson does on *Blues*. In that case, it doesn't sound underproduced—it sounds *poorly* produced. "Love Supply," in fact, sounds like an urban contemporary demo. But for all its flaws, *Blues* generally isn't a bad album. Most of the songs are decent, and the disc's shortcomings don't erase the fact that Wilson is capable of greatness. *—Alex Henderson*

It's Sweet on the Backstreet / 1995 / Ecko ♦♦♦

● **Why?** / Aug. 12, 1997 / Traction ♦♦♦♦

Love Seat / Aug. 11, 1998 / Ecko ♦♦♦

It Ain't the Size / Jul. 13, 1999 / Ecko ♦♦♦

Mr. Freak / Sep. 12, 2000 / Ecko ♦♦♦
Despite the strong lyrical content and the E-for-explicit sticker, *Mr. Freak* is as lighthearted at times as Wilson's affable *Def Comedy Jam* looks. You expect to hear a standup routine instead of the warm, robust soul singing you get. Every one of the ten songs has merit; not a dud in the bunch. The title track's boastful lyrics are softened by a jubilant beat and a singalong *Sesame Street*- styled chorus; "Lets Stomp" is a groovin' party song about drinkin' whiskey, eatin' chicken wings, and dancin' till dusk; a James Brown scream initiates the scandalous "Hoochie Booty," where Wilson describes the type of booty he likes—a hoochie booty. He gives an open invitation to married women encouraging infidelity on "I'll Be Your Lover," and he's love-struck on the romantic "I'm So Glad," which is perfect for slow dragging. *—Andrew Hamilton*

Songs from the Vault / Feb. 27, 2001 / Wilson ♦♦♦

Goin' Jookin' / Jul. 31, 2001 / Ecko ♦♦♦

You Got to Pay to Play / Jul. 16, 2002 / Wilson ♦♦♦

Edith Wilson (Edith Goodall)

b. Sep. 2, 1896, Louisville, KY, **d.** Mar. 30, 1981, Chicago, IL
Vocals / Classic Female Blues, Vaudeville Blues
Edith Wilson belongs to that first group of African-American women referred to as vaudeville or cabaret blues singers who in the early '20s followed Mamie Smith into the recording studios. Wilson's recording career started with Columbia in 1921 with accompaniments provided by trumpeter Johnny Dunn's Jazz Hounds.

She was born Edith Goodall to a middle-class black family in Louisville, KY, on September 2, 1896. Her birth date is often stated as ten years later, but this was due to vanity. Her ancestors included an American Vice President, John C. Breckenridge, and a woman who was the model for the Liza character in Harriet Beecher Stowe's novel *Uncle Tom's Cabin*.

Edith Wilson entered show business in 1919 at the Park Theater in Louisville. Shortly afterwards she joined blues singer Lena Wilson and her pianist brother Danny when they performed in Louisville. Edith and Danny Wilson were married and the three formed an act. They opened in Baltimore to success and played locations on the East Coast. When they encountered talent scout Perry Bradford in New York, who had brought Mamie Smith to OKeh Records, Edith Wilson was introduced to Columbia Records, where she was paired with Johnny Dunn's Jazz Hounds for a series of 17 recordings made in 1921 and 1922. Edith Wilson would make few recordings in subsequent years until she made her comeback in the 1970s.

While working at the Club Alabam in New York in 1924, Edith Wilson was caught up in a dispute between the Fletcher Henderson Orchestra and the club managers. They wanted tenor saxophonist Coleman Hawkins to appear on stage with Edith Wilson. Hawkins was perfectly willing to oblige but asked for extra compensation, which was refused. Edith Wilson once recalled, "I was to come out on-stage carrying Hawk's saxophone and sing a song called "Nobody's Used It Since You've Been Gone" and then I'd give him back his horn and he'd play." It's not certain if this incident led to the Henderson band's departure from the Club Alabam right away, but soon the orchestra was hired by the Roseland Ballroom.

Edith Wilson never really was a blues singer in the sense of Bessie Smith or Ma Rainey. Her career would be spent performing on theater stages and in nightclubs. She became a major star in the New York black entertainment world. She was a member, with the famous Florence Mills, of "Lew Leslie's Plantation Review" at the Lafayette Theater in Harlem. In the mid- to late '20s, Edith Wilson was in England, where she would establish herself as an international star. She would return to England many times over the course of following decades. Later, in New York, Edith Wilson appeared in the famous revue *Hot Chocolates*, where she introduced the Fats Waller/Andy Razaf tune "What Did I Do to Be So Black and Blue." Louis Armstrong also appeared on the show with Fats Waller and Wilson; the three were billed as "The Thousand Pounds of Harmony." Edith Wilson would appear with all the greatest names in black show business of the day, including Bill Robinson, Duke Ellington, Alberta Hunter, Cab Calloway, Noble Sissle, and many others.

Edith Wilson was also a recognized actress, appearing in non-singing roles on radio shows like *Amos and Andy* and in the Humphrey Bogart/Lauren Bacall classic film *To Have and Have Not*. She was also active in early network television. Around 1950, Edith Wilson assumed the character of Aunt Jemima, promoting the pancake mix for the Quaker Oats Company. Some criticized Wilson for playing a black stereotype, but she refused to be intimidated and was proud of what she considered the aura of dignity she brought to the character.

Edith Wilson retired from show business in 1963 to work as an executive secretary with the Negro Actors Guild and to involve herself with other charitable, religious, and literary activities. She returned from retirement in 1973, performing and recording with various artists such as Eubie Blake, Little Brother Montgomery, and Terry Waldo's Gutbucket Syncopators. Edith Wilson's last appearance was at the Newport Jazz Festival in 1980. *—Frank Powers*

● **He May Be Your Man (But He Comes to See Me Sometimes)** / Jul. 5, 1973-Apr. 16, 1975 / Delmark ♦♦♦♦
A classic blues singer from the 1920s, Edith Wilson had not recorded since 1930 when she made this excellent set for Delmark, which was reissued on CD in 1993. Wilson had been active in the interim as a singer and actress and as "Aunt Jemina" during the 1950s up until 1965. Although her voice had naturally deepened, Wilson's basic style was unchanged, and at 69 she still sounded pretty strong on this collection of blues-related material. Her two overlapping backup groups had three horns (including trombonist Preston Jackson and usually Franz Jackson on clarinet and tenor), pianist Little Brother Montgomery, guitarist/banjoist Ikey Robinson, and a rhythm section. Among the songs that Wilson revives are "Mistreatin' Blues," "He May Be Your Man," "My Handy Man Ain't Handy Anymore," and "Put a Little Love In Everything You Do." She would recorded one further album (for Wolverine) in 1974 and a couple isolated tracks in 1976 before her death in 1981. Recommended. *—Scott Yanow*

Edith & Lena Wilson, Vol. 2 / Sep. 7, 2000 / Document ♦♦♦♦

Hop Wilson (Harding Wilson)

b. Apr. 27, 1927, Grapeland, TX, **d.** Aug. 27, 1975, Houston, TX

Slide Guitar, Vocals, Guitar / Slide Guitar Blues, Acoustic Texas Blues, Electric Texas Blues

Slide guitar blues with an Elmore James flavor played on an eight-string table (non-pedal) steel guitar was the trademarked sound of Houston blues legend Hop Wilson. Strictly a local phenomenon, Wilson recorded fitfully and hated touring. Though he also played fine down-home blues on conventional electric guitar and was a powerful singer as well, it is Wilson's unique slide stylings that remain a signature influence on Johnny Winter and Jimmie Vaughan, to name a few.

Wilson learned how to play guitar and harmonica as a child. By the time he was 18, he received his first steel guitar and began playing it at local Houston juke joints and clubs. His musical career was interrupted when he served in World War II. After his discharge from the Army, he decided to pursue a serious career as a blues musician, performing with Ivory Semien's group in the late '50s. Wilson and Semien recorded a number of sides for Goldband Records in 1957.

Hop Wilson didn't lead his own sessions until 1960, when he signed with the Ivory record label. Wilson only recorded for the label for two years—his final sessions were in 1961. After 1961, Wilson concentrated on playing local Houston clubs and bars. He continued to perform in Houston until his death in 1975. *—Cub Koda & Stephen Thomas Erlewine*

Blues With Friends / 1986 / Goldband ♦♦♦

These are the original trio sides with King Ivory Lee Semiens on drums and "Ice Water" Jones on string bass. Unfortunately some of the tracks on this vinyl issue have electric bass and/or piano overdubbed to make them stereo recordings. *—Cub Koda*

● **Steel Guitar Flash!** / 1988 / Ace ♦♦♦♦♦

Although the majority of the recordings collected here already show up on Bullseye Blues' 1993, *Houston Ghetto Blues*, this is the one to get. The main reason for this is the inclusion of all the known extant tracks cut in the '50s for the Lake Charles, LA, Goldband label, where Wilson's versions of "Chicken Stuff" and "Rockin' in the Coconut Top" became tri-state biggies, giving him his 15 seconds of fame and influencing the likes of a young Johnny Winter and other young Texan slide-slingers in the process. With his drummer/sometimes-vocalist King Ivory Lee Semien banging the daylights out of a set that sounds like Salvation Army rejects (check out the floor-tom intro on the Goldband version of "Rockin' in the Coconut Top"), a string bass played by the ubiquitous "Ice Water" Jones, and a crackling, wires sticking out of it steel guitar going to places Elmore James could only think of after watching a bad sci-fi movie, Hop Wilson's dour singing delivery combined with his wild-ass playing becomes a whole genre of blues in and of itself and one well worth investigating. With a full generous 29 tracks aboard (including Wilson and the boys backing up Fenton Robinson and Larry Davis on newly discovered cuts) covering all the Goldband, Trey, and Ivory takes known to exist, this is now *the* definitive Hop Wilson collection and reason enough to start haunting the blues import bins to track it down. Programming tip: For full frontal assault, program up tracks 13 and 25-29 first and prepare yourself for something really special. There was only one Hop Wilson and here's where you check in to get his message. *—Cub Koda*

Rockin' Blues Party / 1989 / Charly ♦♦♦♦

A vinyl abum with a full side of Hop Wilson, featuring alternate (and superior) takes of all the classic Goldband sides. Import. *—Cub Koda*

Houston Ghetto Blues / Nov. 1993 / Bullseye Blues ♦♦♦♦

This collects 18 later early-'60s sides for the Houston-based Ivory label, owned by fellow bandmate and drummer King Ivory Lee Semien. Not really the place to start, as the Goldband sides are vastly superior. *—Cub Koda*

Kim Wilson

b. Jan. 6, 1951, Detroit, MI

Vocals, Harmonica / Modern Electric Texas Blues, Harmonica Blues, Electric Harmonica Blues, Electric Texas Blues

Harmonica player, songwriter, and singer Kim Wilson is as much a student and historian of classic blues as he is one of the U.S.'s top harmonica players. Simply put, Wilson has taste; when he enters the recording studio, he has a clear vision of what he wants his next record to sound like. Aside from all this, he's also an extremely hard worker and a major road hog, spending upwards of 200 nights a year on the road, playing festivals and clubs throughout the U.S., Canada, and Europe with his own Kim Wilson Band and leading the Fabulous Thunderbirds.

Although he's long been known as the charismatic frontman for the Fabulous Thunderbirds, Wilson's solo albums—which feature bands of his own choosing for different tracks—is where the genius in his work shows through most clearly. Born January 6, 1951, in Detroit, Wilson grew up in California. His parents were singers who would sing popular standards on the radio, and while Wilson took trombone and guitar lessons, he didn't discover blues until he was a senior in high school. Wilson's father later worked for General Motors and raised his family in Goleta, CA, he recalled in a 1994 interview in his adopted hometown of Austin.

"We weren't rich, but we were alright," he recalled. Wilson dropped out of college and began playing blues full-time in 1970. Wilson had a rented room and lived the hippie existence, getting his harmonica chops together by playing with traveling blues musicians like Eddie Taylor. Even though Wilson had only switched to harmonica in his senior year in high school, his progress on the instrument was rapid and every bit as all-consuming as his blues record-buying habit. Charlie Musselwhite, John Lee Hooker, and Sonny Rhodes were among the other Bay Area musicians Wilson befriended and worked with in clubs. But Wilson didn't meet his biggest mentor until after he moved to Austin in the mid-'70s.

"Muddy Waters was my biggest mentor. He really made my reputation for me, and that was a fantastic time of my life, being associated with that man," he recalled of his early days with the Fabulous Thunderbirds in Austin. There, at the Antone's blues nightclub, Wilson and his Thunderbirds would back up whoever came into town, and it didn't take long for the band to realize they had Waters' blessing.

As a songwriter, Wilson takes his cue from the long-forgotten names like Tampa Red, Roosevelt Sykes, and Lonnie Johnson. His 1993 solo album, *Tigerman*, for the Austin-based Antone's label, features just three of his own tunes. Being the student of the blues that he is, Wilson was understandably hesitant to record too many of his own tunes when he'd already had a vision in his head of how he was going to rework classics like Joe Hill Louis' "Tiger Man," the album's title track. He followed up his debut with the equally brilliant *That's Life* (1994), also for Antone's, and again this recording contains just three self-penned songs.

Wilson's solo albums are solid productions, highly recommended for harmonica students and fans of classic Texas blues and rhythm & blues. Meanwhile, Wilson's career has taken boosts from a major-label deal with Private Music/BMG for the Fabulous Thunderbirds and from his frequent concert appearances with Bonnie Raitt. *—Richard Skelly*

Tigerman / 1993 / Antone's ♦♦♦

Tigerman, the first solo effort from the Fabulous Thunderbirds' frontman, Kim Wilson, is an uneven album, hampered by the uncertainness of Wilson and his band. They run through a standard set of blues-rock, plus Texas- and Chicago-style shuffles and boogies, but they never really let loose. Consequently, there are pleasant, enjoyable spots on the album, but never anything truly memorable. *—Thom Owens*

● **That's Life** / 1994 / Discovery ♦♦♦♦

On *That's Life*, Kim Wilson's second solo album, the vocalist/harpist hits on the right formula of Texas roadhouse blues and gritty blues-rock, turning out a uniformly satisfying album. Some of the original songs are a little weak, but the performances are convincing and enjoyable, even if they don't offer a new spin on Texas blues-rock. *—Thom Owens*

My Blues / Nov. 4, 1997 / Blue Collar ♦♦♦

Since the last Fabulous Thunderbirds album didn't feature any of the current band members except founder Kim Wilson, one may fairly ask what the difference is these days between a T-Birds record and a Wilson solo disc. The answer, at least on the basis of this one, seems to be that, while the T-Birds sessions find Wilson coming up with mostly original material in a blues-rock mode, his solo work consists mostly of covers in a straight electric blues mode. Here Wilson evokes such heroes as Muddy Waters, Sonny Boy Williamson, and, especially, Little Walter in three live-to-tape sessions cut in the fall of 1996 with a band led by pianist Fred Kaplan and bassist Larry Taylor. Junior Watson and Rusty Zinn alternate on guitar, while some tracks instead feature a two-man horn section of Scott Steen on trumpet and Tom Fabre on tenor saxophone. They acquit themselves well, though as with all such ventures, the obvious question for the record buyer is, why not listen to the originals instead? *—William Ruhlmann*

Smokey Wilson (Robert Lee Wilson)

b. Jul. 11, 1936, Glen Allen, MS

Vocals, Guitar / Electric Blues, Juke Joint Blues

When Los Angeles-based guitarist Smokey Wilson really got serious about setting a full-fledged career as a bluesman in motion, it didn't take him long to astound the aficionados with an incendiary 1993 set for Bullseye Blues, *Smoke n' Fire*, that conjured up echoes of the Mississippi Delta of his youth.

Robert Lee Wilson lived and played the blues with Roosevelt "Booba" Barnes, Big Jack Johnson, Frank Frost, and other Mississippi stalwarts before relocating to L.A. in 1970 when he was 35 years old. But instead of grabbing for the gold as a touring entity, he opened the Pioneer Club in Watts, leading the house band and nobly booking the very best in blues talent (all-star attractions at the fabled joint included Joe Turner, Percy Mayfield, Pee Wee Crayton, Albert Collins, and plenty more).

Wilson recorded sparingly at first, his LPs for Big Town not doing the man justice. A 1983 set for Murray Brothers (reissued on Blind Pig) with harpist Rod Piazza and Hollywood Fats on rhythm guitar may have been the turning point; clearly, he was gearing up to leave his Mississippi mark on Southern California blues.

Smoke n' Fire and its 1995 encore, *The Real Deal* (a title now used for three contemporary blues albums in a year's time: John Primer and Buddy Guy have also claimed it), nominate Smokey Wilson as one of the hottest late-bloomers in the blues business. *—Bill Dahl*

With the William Clarke Band / 1990 / Black Magic ♦♦♦♦

This is a reissue, originally released 1990, issued posthumously in the memory of harmonica virtuoso William Clarke, who plays prominently along with his band. Both frequently performed together at Wilson's Pioneer Club and their close friendship is reflected in the musical interaction of Wilson's Mississippi roots mixed with Clarke's hard-blowin' harp attack. Wilson described his life best in "Tell Me What Do You See" with the words, "I've been all around the world/And blues is all I know to play." Other greats hop along for the ride, including keyboardist Fred Kaplan, and Mighty Flyers' alumni Junior Watson and Alex Schultz. It's no accident that Wilson has some of Howlin' Wolf's vocal mannerisms on the song named after the Wolf himself. The story is that Wolf "willed" his voice to Wilson during one of Wolf's shows. *—Char Ham*

● **Smoke n' Fire** / 1993 / Bullseye Blues ♦♦♦♦♦

Transplanted Mississippian Smokey Wilson has made plenty of records, but usually for poorly distributed regional labels. So although he is far from a newcomer, he might as well be a fledgling rookie to the average listener. The songs, aside from the lyrically commendable but awkward "Don't Burn Down L.A.," are primarily his own urgent expositions on love, life's unfairness, and pain. His playing blends slamming fills, chunky riffs, and sonic barrages mixed with expert uses of distortion, bent notes, and flashy chords. This is the kind of no-nonsense set that has earned Rounder/Bullseye its exemplary reputation. *—Ron Wynn*

The Real Deal / 1995 / Bullseye Blues ♦♦♦♦

More steady-burning blues sparked by Wilson's unyielding guitar work and mean vocals. One difference—he goes the unplugged route on solo versions of Muddy Waters' "Feel like Going Home" and his own "Son of a ... Blues Player." Elsewhere, it's electric juke-joint nirvana, Wilson cutting close to the bone on "Rat Takin' Your Cheese," "I Wanna Do It to You Baby," and "House in Hollywood." *—Bill Dahl*

88th Street Blues / Nov. 1995 / Blind Pig ♦♦♦

The barbed-wire vocals and slashing guitar of Mississippi-bred Smokey Wilson blend well with harpist Rod Piazza and company on this 1983 set first out on Murray Brothers Records. Not quite as stunning as his more recent work for Bullseye Blues, but definitely has some incendiary moments. *—Bill Dahl*

The Man from Mars / 1997 / Bullseye Blues ♦♦♦

This West Coast-based guitarist shines brilliantly on his third album for Bullseye Blues. While some of his earlier locally produced efforts have been uneven affairs, here kudos must go forth to producer and keyboard sideman Ron Levy. Levy keeps Wilson's guitar tone at sting and bite level ten and his vocals right up front and toasty, surrounding him with a solid rhythm section and spare horn stabs. Eight of the 12 songs here are from Smokey's prolific pen, including "You Don't Drink What I Drink," the title track, "Too Drunk to Drive," "Don't Tangle With Me," and "Black Widow," winners all. A quartet of covers (Magic Sam's "Easy Baby," Elmore James' "Something Inside of Me," and a pair of Howlin' Wolf tunes, "Louise" and "44 Blues," with the latter featuring a guest turn from James Harman) rounds out this excellent session. Those who can't get enough of nasty, stinging lead guitar lines would do well to investigate this album. *—Cub Koda*

More Blues from the South Side / Jul. 25, 2000 / South Side ♦♦♦

U.P. Wilson

b. Sep. 4, 1935, Shreveport, LA

Vocals, Guitar / Electric Texas Blues, Modern Electric Blues

Fort Worth-based guitarist, singer, and songwriter U.P. Wilson plays a startlingly refreshing style of deep Southern soul-blues that is gospel-inflected and rural, yet urban. His very rhythmic guitar playing is showcased on three albums for JSP Records, and it appears that after years of being known as a regional performer around Texas, Wilson is ready to take his show on the road. Wilson has recorded three albums for the London-based JSP Records—*Boogie Boy! The Texas Guitar Tornado Returns* in 1994, *This Is U.P. Wilson* (1995), and *Whirlwind*, a 1996 release. Wilson also has two early-'90s recordings for the small Texas labels Red Lightnin' and Double Trouble.

Raised in West Dallas, Wilson learned his craft in the rough-and-tumble beer joints around the South and West Sides of the city, taking his cues from the likes of ZuZu Bollin, Cat Man Fleming, Frankie Lee Sims, Mercy Baby, and Nappy "Chin" Evans. Wilson moved from Dallas to Fort Worth and formed a band called the Boogie Chillun with drummer and vocalist Robert Ealey. Later, he worked with Cornell Dupree before Dupree left to become a favorite session guitarist.

By the late '70s, Wilson and Ealey were frequenting a Fort Worth club called the New Bluebird, where they were attracting ever-growing legions of true Texas blues fans. Wilson began recording locally in 1987 and touring again around Texas. Since the mid-'90s release of his JSP albums, Wilson and his band have toured regionally around the South, pleasing audiences with his inventiveness, clever songwriting, great arrangements, and sheer originality. He returned in 1999 with *On My Way*. *—Richard Skelly*

Wild Texas Guitar / 1989 / Double Trouble ♦♦♦♦♦

U.P. Wilson With Paul Orta & the Kingpins / 1990 / Red Lightnin' ♦♦♦

● **Attack of the Atomic Guitar** / 1992 / Red Lightnin' ♦♦♦♦♦

This slashing live CD by the underrecorded veteran Texas guitarist includes harpist Paul Orta and The Kingpins providing support. *—Bill Dahl*

Boogie Boy! The Texas Guitar Tornado Returns / 1994 / JSP ♦♦♦♦

This Is U.P. Wilson / 1995 / JSP ♦♦♦

Texas Blues Party, Vol. 1 / 1995 / Wolf ♦♦♦

Whirlwind / 1996 / JSP ♦♦♦

Good Bad Blues / May 19, 1998 / JSP ♦♦♦

The Best of Texas Blues Guitar Tornado / Sep. 29, 1998 / JSP ♦♦♦♦

Wilson's four JSP CDs are excerpted here with one cut added from Texas Blues Guitar Summit. It's a mix of down-home electric blues, 12-bar shuffles and boogies, cool West Coast swing, and funk. His guitar playing is simple like J.B. Hutto and John Lee Hooker, and he favors a staccato picking style and an exciting sound. His songs rework familiar themes, and his voice, while unconvincing in falsetto, is good otherwise. The guitar solos are unidentified. Someone sounds like the explosive Albert Collins on a couple of cuts. The bands are very tight, with some horns. Great JSP sound. *—Sigmund Finman*

Edgar Winter

b. Dec. 28, 1946, Beaumont, TX

Vocals, Saxophone, Keyboards / Album Rock, Boogie Rock, Hard Rock, Blues-Rock

Although he's often skirted the edges of blues music, at base, saxophonist, keyboardist, and composer Edgar Winter is a blues musician. Raised in Beaumont, TX, the younger brother of ukulele player and guitarist Johnny Winter, Edgar Winter has always pushed himself in new directions, synthesizing the rock, blues and jazz melodies he hears in his head. As a consequence, his fan base may not be what it could have been, had he made a conscious effort—like his brother Johnny—to stay in a blues-rock mold over the years. He's one musician who's never been afraid to venture into multiple musical arenas, often times, within the space of one album, as in his debut, *Entrance* (1970).

Edgar Winter, the second son of John and Edwina Winter, was born December 28, 1946, in Beaumont, TX, and much of the credit for Edgar and Johnny's early musical awareness must go to the brothers' parents, who have been a constant source of encouragement throughout their respective musical careers. The boys' father sang in a barbershop quartet, and in their church choir, and played saxophone in a jazz group. Edgar and Johnny, who's three years older, began performing together as teens, playing local watering holes like Tom's Fish Camp before they were old enough to drink. The pair's early R&B and blues groups included Johnny & the Jammers, the Crystaliers, and the Black Plague.

In high school, Edgar became fascinated with the saxophone stylings of Julian "Cannonball" Adderley and Hank Crawford, and he began playing alto sax in earnest. As a preteen, he had played ukulele, like his older brother. But by the time he was of college age, Edgar had become competent on keyboards, bass, guitar, and drums.

Edgar was signed to Epic Records in 1970 after performing on his brother's *Second Winter* album. He recorded *Entrance*, his debut, which featured himself on most of the instruments. After radio success accompanying his brother on *Johnny Winter And*, he formed a large horn ensemble called White Trash. Although it was a short-lived group that broke up in mid-1972, Winter assembled another group to record two more albums for Epic Records, Edgar Winter's *White Trash* and *Roadwork*. Winter's single, "Keep Playing That Rock 'n' Roll," reached number 70 on the U.S. rock radio charts, and the album *Roadwork* hit number 23 on the album charts. By the summer of 1972, through constant touring (and a ready willingness to do interviews, unlike his older brother), Winter formed the Edgar Winter Group in the summer of 1972. In January 1973, Epic released *They Only Come Out at Night*, produced by guitarist Rick Derringer, which reached number three in the U.S. This album had Winter's most famous song, "Frankenstein," which reached number one in the U.S. in May of 1973. Later that year, "Free Ride," from the same album, reached number 14. Although he's never matched that kind of commercial radio success again, Winter has continued to tour and record at a prolific pace. He relocated from New York City to Beverly Hills in 1989 to pursue movie score work, which he's had some success with, most notably with a slightly reworked version of "Frankenstein" for the movie *Wayne's World II*.

Although his early-'70s albums like *Entrance*, *Edgar Winter's White Trash*, *They Only Come Out at Night*, and *Shock Treatment* are bluesier affairs than some of his later albums, there are blues tunes like "Big City Woman" on one of his 1990s releases, *Not a Kid Anymore* (1994), on the Intersound label, and 1999's *Winter Blues* was almost wholly devoted to the idiom. A good introduction to Winter for those who weren't around in the early '70s is *The Edgar Winter Collection* (1993) on Rhino Records. *—Richard Skelly*

Entrance / Nov. 1970 / Epic ♦♦♦♦♦

Edgar Winter came out of the chute kicking with this remarkable record filled with jazz, blues, and a little old-fashioned rock & roll. The record follows an established theme throughout its first side, stringing the songs together without breaks, highlighted by dreamy keyboard and sax work, plus Winter's smooth vocalizations. But jazz isn't the only thing Edgar brings to the party. His first recorded version of the old J.P. Loudermilk tune "Tobacco Road" has a few nice punches in it (although the live version with White Trash a few years later would prove the definitive one). "Jimmy's Gospel" plays on his early church influences, while "Jump Right Out" is the predecessor of half a dozen "jump up and dance" numbers Winter would pepper his records with in years to come. *—Michael B. Smith*

Edgar Winter's White Trash / 1971 / Epic ♦♦♦♦♦

Perhaps one of his best-loved albums, *Edgar Winter's White Trash* combined funk, blues, R&B, and rock & roll to create one of the freshest sounds of the early '70s. Touching on gospel with "Fly Away" and "Save the Planet," Winter and his band cover all the bases, climbing into the lower end of the Top 40 with "Keep Playin' That Rock and Roll." Winter's hauntingly beautiful "Dying to Live," featuring some of his best piano work, serves as a valid anti-war statement, written at the height of the Vietnam era, and the remainder of the record is filled with genuine rock and roll/boogie-woogie/blues that will keep your head bobbing and your toes tapping. *—Michael B. Smith*

Roadwork / 1972 / Epic ♦♦♦♦♦

The live follow-up to 1971's *Edgar Winter's White Trash* finds the group running through a handful of the tunes from their debut album, as well as rocking things up a bit with "Still Alive and Well" (a track later recorded by Edgar's brother Johnny) and "Back in the U.S.A." One of the most immortal lines for any live rock album has to be "People keep askin' me—where's your brother?" The introduction of guest artist Johnny Winter by his brother Edgar sets the stage for a rousing rendition of Rick Derringer's "Rock and Roll Hootchie Koo." The extended version of blues classic "Tobacco Road" is one of the finest moments on this album, which is itself a classic. *—Michael B. Smith*

They Only Come Out at Night / 1972 / Epic ♦♦♦♦♦

While this album will forever be remembered for spawning the huge hit singles "Frankenstein" and "Free Ride," there's plenty more to appreciate on this stellar release. From "the other" single, "Hangin' Around," to the pretty melodies of "Round and Around" and "Autumn," the set collects ten outstanding cuts, played with fervor by Edgar Winter, Chuck Ruff, Dan Hartman, Randy Jo Hobbs, and Ronnie Montrose, along with guest artist/producer Rick Derringer. The "party" feel of "We All Had a Real Good Time" and the singalong "Alta Mira" only add to this already red-hot mix, making *They Only Come Out at Night* the album Edgar Winter will always be remembered for. *—Michael B. Smith*

Shock Treatment / 1974 / Epic ♦♦

With this release, Edgar Winter was faced with the question that haunts many a superstar following a highly successful album—how can he outdo himself? While *Shock Treatment* falls short of outdoing himself, it still manages to rock pretty righteously. Beginning with this album's answer to their previous "Hangin' Around," "Some Kinda Animal," the band moves into the excellent blues torcher "Easy Street," which is painted with highlights from the substantial saxophone talent of Winter, not to mention some of his finest singing. Like *They Only Come Out at Night*, this recording includes a pair of haunting ballads, "Maybe Someday You'll Call My Name" and "Someone Take My Heart Away." "Queen of My Dreams," along with "River's Risin'," showcase the Edgar Winter Group doing what they do best—rocking out with passion and lots of drums and guitar. Not as good as their previous album, but still a winner in its own right. *—Michael B. Smith*

The Edgar Winter Group With Rick Derringer / 1975 / Blue Sky ✦✦✦
After his excellent showings with *Edgar Winter's White Trash* and the orbit-escaping success of *They Only Come Out at Night*, *The Edgar Winter Group With Rick Derringer* comes as a bit of a letdown. While there are at least a couple of outstanding tracks here, namely "Diamond Eyes" and "Paradise," the remainder of the album just doesn't meet Winter's self-imposed standards. *—Michael B. Smith*

Jasmine Nightdreams / 1975 / Blue Sky ✦✦✦✦✦
Not since his debut, *Entrance*, had Edgar Winter appeared in a solo capacity. This time out, he reverts to his heavy jazz and gospel influences to produce an album that merits much more attention than what it ultimately received. Winter is decidedly laid-back on tracks such as "Hello Mellow Feelin'" and "Tell Me in a Whisper," which serve as the finest of the nine tracks here. Winter puts on his party hat once again with the rocking "Out of Control," the final track on a pretty nice little rock & roll document. *—Michael B. Smith*

Entrance/Edgar Winter's White Trash / 1976 / Epic ✦✦✦
Epic reissued Edgar Winter's first two albums, *Entrance* and *Edgar Winter's White Trash*, as a double-LP/single cassette in the late '70s. For casual listeners, this may not be a bad way to purchase these records, but the packaging and sound on the tape are subpar. Most fans, even casual ones, will be better served by the original vinyl editions or subsequent CD reissues. *—Stephen Thomas Erlewine*

Together—Live / 1976 / Blue Sky ✦✦✦✦✦
Individually, Edgar Winter and his brother Johnny Winter are powerful artists, but combined, they are virtually unstoppable. In this live set, the brothers are just having the time of their lives, digging deep into their bag of favorites, and pulling out smoking renditions of the Sam & Dave classic "Soul Man" and the Righteous Brothers' "You've Lost That Lovin' Feeling." The history of rock & roll continues with Little Richard's "Tutti Frutti" and "Good Golly Miss Molly" and Chuck Berry's "Reelin' and Rockin'." The Winters go Detroit on Mitch Ryder's "Jenny Take a Ride," and pay homage to the king, Elvis Presley, with "Blue Suede Shoes" and "Jailhouse Rock." From start to finish, Edgar and Johnny are having a rockin' & rollin' good time, and that happiness channels over to the listener. *—Michael B. Smith*

Recycled / 1977 / Blue Sky ✦✦✦
The much-anticipated reunion of Edgar Winter's White Trash brings the powerhouse vocalist Jerry LaCroix back to the forefront, allowing Edgar Winter to put more of his energy into the keyboards, saxophones, and percussion. While *Recycled* is by no means any competition for their 1971 debut album or their subsequent live release, *Roadwork*, it still houses a few punches that will catch you with your guard down if you aren't careful. Extreme musicianship dominates, but a few classic covers might have helped endear this release to its listeners. After all, that was the key to the original success. *—Michael B. Smith*

Edgar Winter Album / 1979 / Blue Sky ✦✦✦
Edgar Winter reworks one of his best old songs, "Dying to Live," and dishes up a handful of new tunes to round out a fairly good album. "It Took Your Love" and "Forever in Love" highlight the record, which, although it doesn't measure up to his prior efforts, still manages to put forth some good vibes. *—Michael B. Smith*

Standing on Rock / 1981 / Blue Sky ✦✦
Edgar Winter delves into a newfound fascination with sci-fi, and the resulting two albums are the end product. A confusing mixed bag of lyrics, this sounds unlike anything Winter has produced before. Considering his immense body of excellent work, from White Trash to the Edgar Winter Group, *Standing on Rock* comes across as something of a disappointment. That is, until *Mission Earth* came along in 1986. While there are a few good moments on *Standing on Rock*, its successor doesn't fare nearly as well. Thankfully, Edgar got back on track later in his career, and the "sci-fi" years became nothing more than a bad memory. *—Michael B. Smith*

Mission Earth / 1986 / Rhino ✦
The hands-down choice as the golden turkey of Edgar Winter's career, *Mission Earth* builds on the theme he began establishing with several of the tracks on *Standing on Rock*. An admirable attempt at a sci-fi space-rock opera, the LP fails to blend the music with the theme, making for an almost unlistenable release. In years to come, Winter's sidetrack to neverland would disappear, and he would start making more of the good old rock & roll hootchie koo everyone loved in the early days of his career. *—Michael B. Smith*

● **Collection** / 1986 / Rhino ✦✦✦✦✦
Much more than the usual greatest-hits package, *Collection* is a well thought-out compilation of the very best tracks of Edgar Winter's career. Obviously, his radio hits are here. "Frankenstein," "Free Ride," and "Hangin' Around" were all staples of mid-'70s AM radio. But Rhino Records doesn't kick this set off with any of the "hits," choosing to rock things up with a track from *Edgar Winter's White Trash*, "Give It Everything You've Got," before moving into the mellow blues of "Easy Street," highlighted by Winter's jazzy saxophone work. Also included are the excellent anti-war ballad "Dying to Live" and the melodic and catchy "Diamond Eyes" and "Round and Around." All in all, this is a definitive buffet of Edgar Winter, but don't let that stop you from sampling the original platters. *—Michael B. Smith*

Not a Kid Anymore / Jun. 14, 1994 / Intersound ✦✦✦✦✦
Gone is the obsession with outer space themes, and back is the rock & roll/rhythm & blues that Edgar Winter does so well. *Not a Kid Anymore* reunites Winter with his old White Trash bandmate Jerry LaCroix, and the resulting mix of musicianship and vocal prowess make for an excellent album. Choice cuts include "Way Down South," "Big City Woman," and the remake of his solid-gold 1973 classic "Frankenstein." *—Michael B. Smith*

The Real Deal / 1996 / Intersound ✦✦✦✦✦
It's like a comeback album from a star that never really went away, as Edgar Winter plays host to musicians ranging from Leon Russell to Jermaine Jackson, Ronnie Montrose, Jeff "Skunk" Baxter, and perennial sidekick Rick Derringer. Even Edgar's brother Johnny Winter shows up to play. "Hoochie Koo" kicks off the record, a rocking number that includes vocal solos from Russell, brother Johnny, and others. The mellow "Sanctuary" is quite nice, and "The Real Deal" is a real kicker. This is one of Winter's best albums in quite some time. *—Michael B. Smith*

Live in Japan / Oct. 27, 1998 / Gold Castle ✦✦
Aside from the fact that Rick Derringer seems to have lost the biggest part of his voice prior to this recording, the album serves as a rocking documentation of Winter in Japan, where he is revered as a star of the highest magnitude. And why not? After all, it was Edgar Winter who led that powerhouse rock & roll band called White Trash in the early '70s. Here, he re-creates the sound of that band with "Fly Away" and "Keep Playing That Rock and Roll." And who can forget "Frankenstein" and "Free Ride," both played live here. Rick Derringer pulls out one from his *All American Boy* release, "Teenage Love Affair," and walks through his earliest hit with the McCoys, "Hang on Sloopy." Not the best live work Edgar Winter has ever commited to magnetic tape, but certainly worth the price of admission. *—Michael B. Smith*

Winter Blues / Jun. 15, 1999 / Pyramid/Rhino ✦✦✦
Through steady work, Edgar Winter kept himself visible throughout the '90s, culminating with a pair of solid efforts for Intersound. Those appeared under the radar of popular consciousness, known only to hard rock and blues-rock fans. For the general public, Winter re-entered consciousness through a series of television commercials—usually, they just featured his songs, but he was the star in a clever Miller campaign that suggested Winter and George Hamilton were twins—along with a prominent song in the political satire *Wag the Dog*. All of this led to a contract with Pyramid Records and *Winter Blues*, his first large-scale, heavily promoted release in nearly 20 years. As is customary for any comeback release, *Winter Blues* is flush with cameos, but this time around, they make sense—brother Johnny, Rick Derringer, and Leon Russell have been longtime colleagues of Edgar, while Dr. John and (surprisingly) Eddie Money fit in quite nicely. Their presence is welcome, since Winter has never been the strongest of frontmen and they never take away from his guitar playing, which remains the best reason to hear *Winter Blues*. Anyone who paid attention to his Intersound releases would have realized that Winter has been cutting good, solid records in the '90s and this is no different, but anyone who hasn't followed him will be surprised how consistent this is. Really, there's nothing new here, since it's in the vein of his electrified blues and hard rock of the '70s, but it's done well and performed with conviction, resulting in an album that may not reach the heights of his classics, but certainly is among his most enjoyable and consistent works. In other words, it will please both the hardcore fans and listeners in the process of (re)discovering Winter. *—Stephen Thomas Erlewine*

The Best of Edgar Winter / May 7, 2002 / Epic/Legacy ✦✦✦
While some might argue that one reasonably well-compiled Edgar Winter best-of is enough, Sony Legacy follows Rhino's 1986 *Collection* with this 2002 edition, which only shares six tracks with its predecessor. With liner notes and involvement from Winter, this might be a little closer to what he would like to be remembered by, and since all of his best work was recorded for Epic, there are no cross-licensing issues complicating matters. But that doesn't mean it's better. There are some major differences; Rhino chose the 17-minute live "Tobacco Road" from *Roadwork*, while this sticks with the shorter studio version from the *Entrance* album. *The Best of Edgar Winter* also nabs two other tunes from that debut, which Winter is clearly proud of according to his album notes. But neither the title track nor the jazzy seven-minute "Fire and Ice" gels with the rockin' gospel of White Trash or the pop/rock of *They Only Come Out at Night*, making the sequencing rough going. The cheesy disco of "It's Your Life to Live" has not aged well and its inclusion here is puzzling, especially when nothing from the relatively well-received *Shock Treatment* album is included. "Rock and Roll Revival" seems forced and stiff, yet picking "Harlem Shuffle" from Edgar and Johnny Winter's only joint album, *Together*, is a smart addition. Oddly, neither disc selected Edgar Winter's live version of "Rock & Roll, Hoochie Koo," a perplexing omission. Since this new compilation doesn't improve on Rhino's, its appearance is difficult to understand. While the sound quality might be slightly crisper due to technological improvements over the years, there's no other reason to choose this over the previous version, which, as of its appearance in 2002, was still in print and track for track is a more enjoyable listen. *—Hal Horowitz*

Johnny Winter

b. Feb. 23, 1944, Beaumont, TX

Slide Guitar, Vocals, Harmonica, Guitar / Slide Guitar Blues, Album Rock, Modern Electric Texas Blues, Boogie Rock, Arena Rock, Hard Rock, Blues-Rock, Modern Electric Blues

Blues guitarist Winter became a major star in the late '60s and early '70s. Since that time he's confirmed his reputation in the blues by working with Muddy Waters and continuing to play in the style, despite musical fashion. Born in Beaumont, TX, Winter formed his first band at 14 with his brother Edgar in Beaumont, and spent his youth in recording studios cutting regional singles and in bars playing the blues.

His discovery on a national level came via an article in *Rolling Stone* in 1968, which led to a management contract with New York club owner Steve Paul and a record deal with Columbia. His debut album (there are numerous albums of juvenilia), *Johnny*

Winter, reached the charts in 1969. Starting out with a trio, Winter later formed a band with former members of the McCoys, including second guitarist Rick Derringer. It was called Johnny Winter And. He achieved a sales peak in 1971 with the gold-selling *Live Johnny Winter And.* He returned in 1973 with *Still Alive and Well,* his highest-charting album. His albums became more overtly blues-oriented in the late '70s and he also produced several albums for Muddy Waters.

In the '80s he switched to the blues label Alligator for three albums, and has since recorded for the labels MCA and Pointblank/Virgin. *Back in Beaumont* was released in 2000. —*William Ruhlmann*

Johnny Winter / 1969 / Columbia ✦✦✦✦✦
Winter's debut album for Columbia was also arguably his bluesiest and best. Straight out of Texas with a hot trio, Winter made blues-rock music for the angels, tearing up a cheap Fender guitar with total abandon on tracks like "I'm Yours and I'm Hers," "Leland Mississippi Blues," and perhaps the slow blues moment to die for on this set, B.B. King's "Be Careful With a Fool." Winter's playing and vocals have yet to become mannered or clichéd on this session, and if you've ever wondered what the fuss is all about, here's the best place to check out his true legacy. —*Cub Koda*

The Progressive Blues Experiment / 1969 / Razor & Tie ✦✦✦
Although his early Columbia albums brought him worldwide stardom, it was this modest little album (first released on Imperial before the Columbia sides) that first brought Johnny Winter to the attention of guitarheads in America. It's also Winter at the beginning of a long career, playing the blues as if his life depends on it, without applying a glimmer of rock commercialism. The standard classic repertoire here includes "Rollin' & Tumblin'," "Got Love If You Want It," "44," "It's My Own Fault," and "Help Me," with Winter mixing it up with his original Texas trio of Red Turner on drums and Tommy Shannon (later of Stevie Ray Vaughan's Double Trouble) on bass. A true classic. —*Cub Koda*

● **Second Winter** / 1969 / Columbia ✦✦✦✦✦
Johnny's second Columbia album shows an artist in transition. He's still obviously a Texas bluesman, recording in the same trio format that he left Dallas with. But his music is moving toward the more rock & roll sounds he would go on to create. The opener, "Memory Pain," moves him into psychedelic blues-rock territory, while old-time rockers like "Johnny B. Goode," "Miss Ann," and "Slippin' and Slidin'" provide him with familiar landscapes on which to spray his patented licks. His reworking of Dylan's "Highway 61 Revisited" is the high spot of the record, a career-defining track that's still a major component of his modern-day set list. This was originally released back in the day as a three-sided vinyl double album, by the way. —*Cub Koda*

Johnny Winter And / 1970 / DCC ✦✦✦✦✦
Winter puts together a new band and takes on the assistance of Rick Derringer, who coproduces and provides such great songs as "Rock & Roll, Hoochie Koo." —*William Ruhlmann*

Live Johnny Winter And / 1971 / Columbia ✦✦✦
Winter and his new band turn out hard-rock versions of "Jumpin' Jack Flash," "Johnny B. Goode," and other rock & roll favorites. —*William Ruhlmann*

Still Alive and Well / 1973 / Columbia ✦✦✦
Still Alive and Well proved to the record-buying public that Johnny Winter was both. This is a truly enjoyable album, chock-full of great tunes played well. Johnny's version of the Rolling Stones' "Silver Train" shows us the potential this song has and what the Stones failed to capture. Everything here is good, so get it and dig in. —*James Chrispell*

Saints & Sinners / 1974 / Columbia ✦✦✦
Johnny Winter's sixth Columbia album was also his second since his comeback from drug addiction. Its predecessor, *Still Alive and Well,* had been his highest charting effort. *Saints & Sinners* was just as energetically played, but its mixture of material, including 1950s rock & roll oldies like Chuck Berry's "Thirty Days," Larry Williams' "Bony Maronie," and Leiber & Stoller's "Riot in Cell Block No. 9," recent covers like the Rolling Stones' "Stray Cat Blues," and a couple of originals, was more eclectic than inspired. (Van Morrison completists should note that the album also contains Winter's cover of Morrison's "Feedback on Highway 101," a typical bluesy groove song that Morrison recorded for his 1973 *Hardnose the Highway* album but dropped. Winter's is the only released recording of the song.) Abetted by the members of the old Johnny Winter And band, Rick Derringer, Randy Hobbs, and Richard Hughes, plus his brother Edgar and Dan Hartman, Winter produced forceful hard rock focused on his searing lead guitar runs and rough-edged voice. It was the less-impressive choice of material that kept this collection from matching its predecessor. [Originally released in February 1974, *Saints & Sinners* was reissued on February 27, 1996, with the previously unreleased song "Dirty," a Winter original, added. The slide guitar-and-flute track is not consistent with the rest of the album, but it is interesting to hear. Wonder who played the flute?] —*William Ruhlmann*

John Dawson Winter III / 1974 / Blue Sky ✦✦

Captured Live! / 1976 / Blue Sky ✦✦✦

Together—Live / 1976 / Blue Sky ✦✦✦✦✦
Individually, Edgar Winter and his brother Johnny Winter are powerful artists, but combined, they are virtually unstoppable. On this live set, the brothers are just having the time of their lives, digging deep into their bag of favorites and pulling out smoking renditions of the Sam & Dave classic "Soul Man" and the Righteous Brothers' "You've Lost That Lovin' Feeling." The history of rock & roll continues with Little Richard's "Tutti Frutti" and "Good Golly Miss Molly" and Chuck Berry's "Reelin' and Rockin'." The Winters go Detroit on Mitch Ryder's "Jenny Take a Ride" and pay homage to the King, Elvis Presley, with "Blue Suede Shoes" and "Jailhouse Rock." From start to finish, Edgar and Johnny are having a rockin' and rollin' good time, and that happiness channels over to the listener. —*Michael B. Smith*

Nothin' but the Blues / 1977 / Blue Sky ✦✦✦✦
After a long period making rock records, Winter fronts the Muddy Waters band (with Waters singing) on this Chicago blues workout. He sounds happier than ever before. —*William Ruhlmann*

White Hot & Blue / 1978 / Blue Sky ✦✦✦✦✦

Raisin' Cain / 1980 / Blue Sky ✦✦✦

Guitar Slinger / 1984 / Alligator ✦✦✦✦
The first of three blues albums recorded after a four-year studio hiatus finds Winter as fleet-fingered as before and sounding more vocally involved than in some of the later Columbia material. —*William Ruhlmann*

Serious Business / 1985 / Alligator ✦✦

Third Degree / 1986 / Alligator ✦✦✦

The Winter of '88 / 1988 / Voyager ✦✦

Birds Can't Row Boats / 1988 / Relix ✦✦✦✦
Aside from "Ice Cube" (a 1959 instrumental), these tracks date from 1965-1968. Many are previously unissued or only available on rare 45s. Those accustomed to his more famous recordings are in for a jolt, as this shows Johnny in several unexpected settings: grinding Texas psych-punk, the British Invasion-cum-folk-rock garage single "Gone for Bad," blue-eyed R&B/soul, an Everly Brothers cover, a *Highway 61*-era Dylan imitation, and even a shit-kickin' C&W tune. There are also some straight, predominantly acoustic blues numbers. —*Richie Unterberger*

A Lone Star Kind of Day / 1990 / Relix ✦✦✦

Let Me In / Aug. 1991 / Pointblank ✦✦✦✦
Let Me In is a star-studded all-blues set from Johnny Winter, featuring cameos from Dr. John, Albert Collins, and several others. Though the set focuses on blues material, Winters can never leave his rock roots behind—the sheer volume and pile-driving energy of his performances ensures that. For most of the record, his enthusiasm is contagious, but there are a couple of bland, generic exercises that fail to work up a head of steam. But there is a lovely acoustic number called "Blue Mood," which shows Winter trying to stretch a bit by playing jazzy licks. It's a refreshing change of pace. —*Thom Owens*

Scorchin' Blues / Jun. 16, 1992 / Epic/Legacy ✦✦✦
Scorchin' Blues marries tracks from Johnny Winter's early Columbia albums—including the classic National steel-driven "Dallas" from his 1969 debut—with material from his return-to-roots Blue Sky period in the late '70s. The aggressive playing and raunchy vocals will appeal to both blues and rock fans, and Ben Sandmel crams an authoritative biography into seven pages, complete with interesting Winter quotes. The one downside: a miserly ten tracks spread over only 45 minutes of playing time. —*Roch Parisien*

Collection / Jun. 30, 1992 / Castle ✦✦✦

Hey, Where's Your Brother? / Jul. 1992 / Pointblank ✦✦✦
On the classic 1972 live album *Roadwork,* Edgar Winter immortalized the words, when introducing brother Johnny: "Everybody asks me ... where's your brother?" It's a question that fans have besieged both Winters with for over two decades, and now Johnny gets a chance to return the tribute with his latest. Edgar does in fact guest on the sessions, blowing sax and tinkling keys on a few tracks, and dueting with big bro on a superb, seasonal rendition of "Please Come Home for Christmas." —*Roch Parisien*

A Rock n' Roll Collection / 1994 / Columbia/Legacy ✦✦✦✦✦
A two-CD survey of Winter's recordings for Columbia between 1969 and 1979, the era of his greatest commercial success. This collects many of his most popular tracks, though it doesn't do much to argue a case for artistic diversity. Includes two otherwise unavailable songs: an alternate take of "30 Days," and a previously unreleased 1973 cover of Robert Johnson's "Come on in My Kitchen." —*Richie Unterberger*

Blues to the Bone / Aug. 29, 1995 / Relix ✦✦
This previously unissued 1967 session teams up Winter with local Dallas bluesman Calvin "Loudmouth" Johnson on 13 loose blues jams. Johnson's timing is erratic as all get out and Winter fills in wherever possible while the band fumbles through the changes, including the most obvious ones, mucking up even the instrumental passages. Despite the promise implied by the package, it's easy to see why this session stayed unissued all this time, as it's a disjointed mess that's very hard to listen to. If you're a blues or Johnny Winter fan, pass this one right by. —*Cub Koda*

Relix's Best of the Blues, Vol. 2 / Apr. 15, 1997 / Relix ✦✦✦

White Hot Blues / Oct. 7, 1997 / Columbia/Legacy ✦✦✦
Slowly over the years, perhaps through sheer survival, if nothing else, Johnny Winter has finally forged a reputation as a real bluesman rather than a flashy guitar player with a built-in genetic gimmick to sell himself with. That his blues has always been rock & roll and his rock & roll has always been blues is no better highlighted than on this 16-track collection. The raw rock of "Highway 61 Revisited" and the live version of "Johnny B. Goode" sit just fine next to the burner "Be Careful With a Fool," perhaps Winter's finest slow blues performance. The performances span his tenure with Columbia from 1969 to 1980, with the other highlights including "Too Much Seconal," "New York, New York," "Leland Mississippi Blues," and "The Crawl." This may just very well be some of the best blues-rock guitar your money can buy. —*Cub Koda*

Livin' in the Blues / 1997 / Sundazed ✦✦✦

Ease My Pain / 1997 / Sundazed ✦✦✦

Live in NYC '97 / Mar. 10, 1998 / Virgin ✦✦✦✦
Johnny Winter assembled *Live in NYC '97* with assistance of his fan club, drawing all of the recordings from an April 1997 performance at the Bottom Line. Produced by Winter's

longtime colleague Dick Shurman, the record doesn't follow the predictable pattern of a live album—instead of hits, it offers fan favorites and covers, which makes for a much more interesting listen. Throughout the album, Winter simply rips, tearing through all five songs with blistering energy. This is the live album hardcore fans have been wanting for years, and it doesn't fail to deliver on its promise. *—Stephen Thomas Erlewine*

Deluxe Edition / Jan. 30, 2001 / Alligator ♦♦♦♦♦
Johnny Winter joined Chicago's Alligator Records in 1984 after a four-year recording hiatus. Following 12 generally spotty albums and 11 years associated with Columbia, either on their label or his own Blue Sky imprint (which they distributed), Winter was itching to get back to the sparse, house-rocking, rough Texas blues on which he made his name, and forego the flashy rock & roll—often just substandard rock—that dominated many of his patchy albums, especially toward the end of the Columbia association. Alligator doubtlessly was thrilled to have him aboard their roster, as it supplied them with their first full-fledged superstar. His three albums for the label were released in three consecutive years: *Guitar Slinger, Serious Business*, and *Third Degree* were slam-bang affairs that provided an ideal forum for Winter's gritty voice and edgy, quicksilver guitar firepower. This 14-track compilation of these years rounds up the best of those releases and is a testament to the albino bluesman's substantial talents musically and as an interpreter of other artists' material. He sounds positively enthusiastic throughout, whooping and hollering like it's his first time in the studio, and when he whips out his nasty slide on "Murdering Blues," J.B. Lenoir's "Mojo Boogie," and his own "Good Time Woman" (one of the few Winter originals from the Alligator discs, as well as his lone writing credit on this collection), the searing intensity of his tone practically rips through the speakers. You can tell he's having a stone blast on the slow blues numbers like Eddie Boyd and Willie Dixon's "Third Degree" (in which Winter exclaims in the song's first 20 seconds, "I like it!"), and on the previously unreleased version of "Nothing but the Devil" (which includes a blistering James Cotton harp solo). Winter does a bit of fast country blues on "Broke and Lonely" and pulls out his National steel on Memphis Willie B.'s "Bad Girl Blues," but generally these cuts find the guitarist in fine boogie form. The collection closes with *Guitar Slinger*'s "Kiss Tomorrow Goodbye," a smoking slice of '50s R&B that proved all too prophetic; he was to release only two more studio albums of original material through 2001. Johnny Winter's subsequent work in the '90s was sporadically energized, seldom matching the ground-rumbling yet uncluttered approach he favored during these crucial years. *—Hal Horowitz*

Lone Star Shootout / Nov. 6, 2001 / Fuel 2000 ♦♦♦

● **The Best of Johnny Winter** / Jan. 29, 2002 / Columbia/Legacy ♦♦♦♦♦
Columbia/Legacy's 2002 release *The Best of Johnny Winter* concentrates solely on the guitarist's early recordings for Columbia, which are often (and deservedly) considered his best work. Nearly all of the 16 selections here were recorded between 1969 and 1971—there's a stray cut from 1973, plus two cuts from 1979, dating from his time on Blue Sky—and all of them showcase Winter at his best, not just as a fiery blues-rock guitarist, but as a bandleader. While there are a few items that may be relatively rare here, there is no unreleased material, just selections from Winter at his prime, and this collection does a very good job of summarizing that peak succinctly and enjoyably. *—Stephen Thomas Erlewine*

Jimmy Witherspoon

b. Aug. 8, 1923, Gurdon, AR, **d.** Sep. 18, 1997, Los Angeles, CA
Vocals / Jazz Blues, Jump Blues, Urban Blues
One of the great blues singers of the post-World War II period, Jimmy Witherspoon was also versatile enough to fit comfortably into the jazz world. Witherspoon was born on August 8, 1923, in Gurdon, AR. As a child, he sang in a church choir, and made his debut recordings with Jay McShann for Philo and Mercury in 1945 and 1946. His own first recordings, using McShann's band, resulted in a number one R&B hit in 1949 with "Ain't Nobody's Business Pts. 1-2" on Supreme Records. Live performances of "No Rollin' Blues" and "Big Fine Girl" provided 'Spoon with two more hits in 1950.

The mid-'50s were a lean time, with his style of shouting blues temporarily out of fashion; singles were tried for Federal, Chess, Atco, Vee-Jay, and others, with little success. Witherspoon's album *Live at the Monterey Jazz Festival* (HiFi Jazz) from 1959 lifted him back into the limelight. Partnerships with Ben Webster or Groove Holmes were recorded, and he toured Europe in 1961 with Buck Clayton, performing overseas many more times in the decades to follow; some memorable music resulted, but Witherspoon's best 1960s album is *Evening Blues* (Prestige), which features T-Bone Walker on guitar and Clifford Scott on saxophone. As the '70s began, Witherspoon decided to take a short break from live performances, settled in Los Angeles, took a job as a DJ and continued making records. In 1971 Witherspoon teamed up with former Animals vocalist Eric Burdon for the album *Guilty*. Unfortunately, it sold poorly. By 1973 his short retirement from live performances was over.

Witherspoon was ready to get back on the road and assembled an amazing band featuring a young Robben Ford on lead guitar. Those live shows had received positive reviews, rejuvanting Witherspoon's move toward a definite rock/soul sound. He traveled to London in 1974 to record *Love Is a Five Letter Word* with British blues producer Mike Vernon. Vernon had produced critically acclaimed British blues albums by John Mayall, Fleetwood Mac, and Ten Years After. By the early '80s, Witherspoon was diagnosed with throat cancer. Although he remained active and was a popular concert attraction, the effect of the disease on his vocals was obvious. Jimmy Witherspoon passed away on September 18, 1997, at the age of 74. *—Bob Porter, Scott Yanow, & Al Campbell*

Jimmy Witherspoon & Jay McShann / Nov. 15, 1947-1949 / 1201 Music ♦♦♦♦
Although Jimmy Witherspoon gets first billing on this CD reissue, he actually only has vocals on 11 of the 24 selections and is just present on three of the seven sessions; high points include two versions of his signature song "Ain't Nobody's Business." Pianist Jay McShann is the real leader of these Los Angeles recordings and the brand of music he performs mixes together swing, blues, slight touches of bebop, and early R&B. Most of the songs are basic originals and there are spirited solos from many lesser-known horn players; only the young trumpeter Art Farmer, his brother bassist Addison Farmer, and the popular studio tenor saxophonist Maxwell Davis are still remembered. In addition to Witherspoon (who is in excellent early form), Lois Booker, Maxine Reed, and Crown Prince Waterford also take vocals. An easily recommended set of rarities from the later period of Kansas City jazz. *—Scott Yanow*

Ain't Nobody's Business / May 9, 1949-1950 / Jazz Hour ♦♦♦♦♦
It is unfortunate that the recording dates and personnel are not given on this budget CD, for the performances (although not always that well-recorded) are excellent. Singer Jimmy Witherspoon is heard near the beginning of his career. Five songs (the third through the seventh) are taken from a Pasadena, CA, concert on May 9, 1949. Backed by pianist Gene Gilbeaux's quartet (with Donald Hill featured on alto), Witherspoon is in extroverted form entertaining the enthusiastic crowd; on "New Orleans Woman," a few unidentified horns honk away to the audience's enjoyment. Of the other five songs, two are from 1950 ("I Done Found Out" and "Fickle Woman") and have Witherspoon backed by a nonet including pianist Jay McShann and tenor saxophonist Maxwell Davis. "Good Jumpin'" is with the Buddy Floyd sextet in 1948, and two others are not listed in discographies. But details aside, the enjoyable music straddles the boundary between blues, early R&B, and jazz. *—Scott Yanow*

Spoon So Easy: The Chess Years / Jun. 10, 1954-Aug. 15, 1956 / MCA/Chess ♦♦♦
By the mid-'50s, it seemed that Jimmy Witherspoon's brand of Kansas City blues was going permanently out of style; Big Joe Turner was starting to turn toward rock & roll, and many of the older singers were no longer recording. Witherspoon, who was only in his early thirties, was flexible enough to fit into different situations, so the Chess label (best known for its intense Chicago blues) took a chance on him. This CD contains most of Witherspoon's records for the Chess and Checker labels: five that were issued and nine that remained in the vaults until the release of this CD in 1990. Unfortunately, Witherspoon did not have any hits during this era (his comeback would not really get going until his appearance at the 1959 Monterey Jazz Festival) but fortunately, these records did survive. 'Spoon is actually heard in good form, and even if the personnel is mostly unidentified, he received suitable backup. Since all but three of Witherspoon's Chess recordings are on this CD (which clocks in around 39 minutes), one does wonder why it was not decided to make this a "complete" set. *—Scott Yanow*

Goin' to Kansas City Blues / Dec. 4, 1957-Dec. 5, 1957 / RCA ♦♦♦♦
A reunion of sorts with McShann, with whom Witherspoon had sung for four years in the late '40s. A relaxed, swinging set that bisects jazz and blues, it holds no great surprises, but 'Spoon fans will find this an enjoyable and accomplished record. About half of the material was penned by McShann or Witherspoon, including a remake of "Confessin' the Blues," and "Blue Monday Blues," Jimmy's adaptation of "Kansas City Blues." *—Richie Unterberger*

Singin' the Blues / 1959 / Blue Note ♦♦♦♦♦
Jimmy Witherspoon is heard in superior form throughout the two Pacific Jazz sessions included on this 1998 CD reissue. With fine backup and short solos from either Harry "Sweets" Edison (in top form) or Gerald Wilson on trumpet, both Teddy Edwards and Jimmy Allen on tenors, Henry McDode or Hampton Hawes on piano, rhythm guitarist Herman Mitchell, bassist Jimmy Hamilton, and drummer Jimmy Miller, 'Spoon digs into such numbers as "When I've Been Drinkin'," "Then the Lights Go Out," "There's Good Rockin' Tonight," and a remake of his big hit, "Ain't Nobody's Business." The closing "Midnight Blues" is an instrumental, giving the band a chance to stretch out a bit. Recommended. *—Scott Yanow*

★ **The 'Spoon Concerts** / Oct. 2, 1959+Dec. 2, 1959 / Fantasy ♦♦♦♦♦
This single CD (which reissues all of the music from an earlier two-LP set) includes the high point of singer Jimmy Witherspoon's career. On October 2, 1959, he appeared at the Monterey Jazz Festival and created such a sensation that it caused his career to go through a renaissance. Heard at the peak of his powers, Witherspoon holds his own with a mighty group of veterans (trumpeter Roy Eldridge, both Ben Webster and Coleman Hawkins on tenors, clarinetist Woody Herman, pianist Earl Hines, bassist Vernon Alley, and drummer Mel Lewis). Although the five-song set only lasted 25 minutes, Witherspoon's performance was the hit of the festival. The other half of this CD features Witherspoon romping through ten mostly traditional blues songs two months later with Webster, baritonist Gerry Mulligan, pianist Jimmy Rowles, bassist Leroy Vinnegar, and drummer Mel Lewis; the performance is equally exciting. Highly recommended, this CD is the one truly essential Jimmy Witherspoon release. *—Scott Yanow*

Jazz Legacy: Olympia Concert / Apr. 22, 1961 / Inner City ♦♦♦♦
Recorded in Paris when he was touring with a group dominated by Count Basie alumni, this concert features singer Jimmy Witherspoon in prime form. His repertoire was fairly typical (highlighted by "See See Rider," "Roll 'Em Pete," and his biggest hit "Ain't Nobody's Business"), but Witherspoon pours so much enthusiasm and soul into the music that he sounds as if he had recently discovered the songs. This sadly out of print LP also features some short solos and excellent support from 'Spoon's sidemen: trumpeters Buck Clayton and Emmett Berry, trombonist Dicky Wells, altoist Earl Warren, tenor saxophonist Buddy Tate, pianist Sir Charles Thompson, bassist Gene Ramey, and drummer Oliver Jackson. Fortunately, the band appeared on television in Europe and a Shanachie video (readily available) has been released of the Buck Clayton All-Stars. *—Scott Yanow*

Roots (Jazzlore, Vol. 34) / May 23, 1962 / Atlantic ♦♦♦♦♦
This album features singer Jimmy Witherspoon in a perfect setting, interpreting older blues and Kansas City swing standards while accompanied by a fine two-horn sextet. Witherspoon's friend, tenor saxophonist Ben Webster, has plenty of solos, as does

trumpeter Gerald Wilson (in one of his last recordings as an active player). Witherspoon sounds quite inspired on such songs as "I'd Rather Drink Muddy Water," "Confessin' the Blues," "Nobody Knows You When You're Down and Out," and "Cherry Red." *—Scott Yanow*

Baby Baby Baby / Mar. 6, 1963 / Bluesville/Original Blues Classics ♦♦♦
Veteran singer Jimmy Witherspoon is in good voice on this CD reissue, performing a dozen two- to four-minute songs that include such blues standards as Duke Ellington's "Rocks in My Bed," "Bad Bad Whiskey," "One Scotch, One Bourbon, One Beer," and "It's a Lonesome Old World." He is joined by a quintet featuring altoist Leo Wright and guitarist Kenny Burrell on the first eight numbers and a background septet (with trumpeter Bobby Bryant and Arthur Wright on harmonica) for the remainder of the set. The music is enjoyable if not classic, and should please Witherspoon's many fans. *—Scott Yanow*

Evenin' Blues / Aug. 15, 1963 / Prestige/Original Blues Classics ♦♦♦♦
A good, relaxed (but not laid-back) session, and one of his bluesier ones, with organ, Clifford Scott (who played on Bill Doggett's "Honky Tonk") on sax, and T-Bone Walker on guitar. Nothing too adventurous about the song selection, including well-traveled items like "Good Rockin' Tonight" and "Kansas City," but Witherspoon sings them with ingratiating soul, reaching his peaks on his cover of "Don't Let Go" (perhaps better than the hit version by Roy Hamilton) and the late-night ambience of the title track. The CD reissue adds previously unissued alternate takes of four of the songs. *—Richie Unterberger*

Blues Around the Clock / Nov. 5, 1963 / Prestige/Original Blues Classics ♦♦♦
Veteran singer Jimmy Witherspoon (who bridges the gap between jazz and blues) mostly sticks to the latter on this spirited set. His backup group (organist Paul Griffin, guitarist Lord Westbrook, bassist Leonard Gaskin, and drummer Herbie Lovelle) is fine in support, but the spotlight is almost entirely on Witherspoon throughout these ten concise performances, only one of which exceeds four minutes. Highlights include "No Rollin' Blues," "S.K. Blues," and "Around the Clock." Witherspoon is in fine voice and, even if nothing all that memorable occurs, the music is enjoyable. *—Scott Yanow*

Some of My Best Friends Are the Blues / Jul. 15, 1964 / Prestige/Original Blues Classics ♦♦♦
Jimmy Witherspoon is accompanied by a large orchestra arranged by Benny Golson for a set emphasizing slow tempos (even on "And the Angels Sing" and "Who's Sorry Now"), ballads, and blues. Nothing all that memorable occurs, but the singer is in strong voice, and his fans will want to pick up this interesting CD reissue. *—Scott Yanow*

Blue Spoon / Jul. 20, 1964 / Prestige ♦♦♦
Blue Spoon was one of Witherspoon's jazzier sessions, still retaining his characteristic jazz-blues blend, but lighter on the soul, pop, and shouting R&B elements of some of his other releases. The jazzy flavor was guaranteed by his backup quartet of Kenny Burrell on guitar, Eddie Kahn on bass, Gildo Mahones on piano, and Roy Haynes on drums. Dominated by ballads, it's on the mellow side, with a pleasant yet unadventurous selection of covers. These include Cecil Gant's "I Wonder," "Nobody Knows You When You're Down and Out," "It's All in the Game," and "Baby Please Don't Go" (here retitled "Back to New Orleans," with the writing credits given to Brownie McGhee and Sonny Terry). Kenny Burrell contributed one composition, "Blues in the Morning." The album was combined with a quite different 1965 session, *Spoon in London*, on a 2001 single-CD reissue. *—Richie Unterberger*

Spoon in London / 1965 / Prestige ♦♦♦♦
Spoon in London is an uncharacteristic entry in the Witherspoon catalog. Recorded in London in June 1965, there's a definite soul-pop slant to the production, with backup women singers that wouldn't have been out of place at a Ray Charles session; brassy, bright arrangements; and lean blues-rock guitar backup that leads one to suspect that an ace U.K. session man like Jimmy Page or Big Jim Sullivan might have been responsible (the personnel, unfortunately, is not documented). The orchestra was arranged and conducted by Benny Golson, and there's a definite sense of trying to cross Witherspoon's habitual classy soul-jazz over into the soul and rock markets. Purists, of course, will probably be offended, but, in fact, this deviation from the usual format makes this one of Witherspoon's more interesting and, yes, fun releases. He's more than up to the task of broaching this territory, sounding rather like a cross between Ray Charles and Brook Benton at times (yet closer to Benton). Tracks like "Free Spirits" swing in a more traditionally jazz manner; "Room for Everybody" has a singalong country-folk feel; and "Two Hearts Are Better Than One" is decorated by odd Dixieland touches. The album was combined with a quite different 1964 session, *Blue Spoon*, on a 2001 single-CD reissue. *—Richie Unterberger*

Blues for Easy Livers / 1965-1966 / Prestige/Original Blues Classics ♦♦♦
Despite the title, this actually leans considerably further to the jazz side of Witherspoon's muse than the blues one, with backing by Pepper Adams on baritone sax, Roger Kellaway on piano, Bill Watrous on trombone, Richard Davis on bass, and Mel Lewis on drums. The songs, too, are much more in the jazz/pop vein than the blues/jazz one, heavy on standards by the likes of Johnny Mercer, the Gershwins, and Ellington. Witherspoon's one of the masters of closing-time bluesy jazz, and he doesn't let anyone down on that account on this relaxed (but not sleepy) session. *—Richie Unterberger*

Hey Mr. Landlord / 1965 / Route 66 ♦♦♦♦♦
This satisfying collection covers the early part of the great blues singer's career from his mid-'40s, Philo and Mercury days through his tenures at Modern and Chess in the early '50s. The 17 rare cuts have been nicely remastered and feature Witherspoon backed by the Jay McShann Band and other, unknown personnel on blues, jazz, and jump blues cuts. Being equally at home in all these idioms, Witherspoon is commanding on everything from ballads like "Strange Woman Blues" to the gospel revival novelty "Practice What You Preach." He also eats up the big-band swing number "Geneva Blues" and makes decent work of rock & roll cuts like "My Girl Ivy." Witherspoon is at his best, though, on driving blues swingers like "Big Daddy," "Why Do I Love You Like I Do," and "Daddy Pinocchio." A fine collection that complements both his other early collections and the comeback recordings he made for Prestige in the early '60s. *—Stephen Cook*

Jazz Heritage: Jimmy's Blues / Sep. 15, 1969 / MCA ♦♦♦
This out of print MCA album from 1983 reissued a fairly obscure session from singer Jimmy Witherspoon. Backed by a Los Angeles rhythm section that includes pianist Charles Brown (who unfortunately does not sing on this date) along with tenor saxophonist Red Holloway (who is not included in the personnel listing), Witherspoon sticks mostly to blues with tunes by Brownie McGhee, Art Hillery (who plays organ on one song), Buddy Scott, and four of his own originals (including "You Can't Do a Thing When You're Drunk" and "Pillar to Post"). This set (originally titled *Huhh*) was cut for the BluesWay label. *—Scott Yanow*

Love Is a Five Letter Word / Feb. 1974 / Rhino ♦♦
Jimmy Witherspoon traveled to London to record *Love Is a Five Letter Word* with producer Mike Vernon in 1974, and the pair came up with a surprise—a glossy album that owed as much to pop and contemporary soul as it did to the blues. In fact, there's not much on *Love Is a Five Letter Word* that sounds like true, gutbucket blues—it all sounds processed and stylized, as if he were reaching for a hit. Some of the results work, but Witherspoon's true essence is buried by the slick groove, steel guitars, and electric sitars. For anyone but completists, *Love is a Five Letter Word* isn't particularly worth exploring. *—Stephen Thomas Erlewine*

Spoonful / 1975 / Avenue Jazz ♦♦
Spoonful finds Jimmy Witherspoon stretching out a bit, exploring soul and funk rhythms rather heavily. In fact, many fans of his jazz and blues recordings will find that this concentrates too much on the rhythm, to the detriment of the songs and performances. Consquently, *Spoonful* doesn't rank much more than an interesting experiment. *—Thom Owens*

Live / 1976 / MCA ♦♦♦
Jimmy Witherspoon sticks exclusively to the blues during this Los Angeles club date from 1976. Guitarist Robben Ford's fiery Chicago blues playing is consistently exciting and imaginative, often stealing the show from 'Spoon. This CD can easily be enjoyed by fans of both blues and swinging jazz. *—Scott Yanow*

Jimmy Witherspoon With Panama Francis & the Savoy Sultans Sings the Blues / May 25, 1980 / Muse ♦♦♦♦♦
The Savoy Sultans, as revived by drummer Panama Francis, was one of the hottest small-group swing bands of the late '70s/early '80s. Singer Jimmy Witherspoon fits right in with the group, emphasizing the Kansas City swing and blues side of his repertoire. With the Sultans (a nonet also including trumpeters Francis Williams and Irv Stokes, tenor man George Kelly, and pianist Red Richards) inspiring him, Witherspoon revives some of the most memorable songs associated with Jimmy Rushing, including "Sent for You Yesterday," "I Want a Little Girl," and "Boogie Woogie." This highly recommended set is one of Jimmy Witherspoon's best from his later years. *—Scott Yanow*

Spoon's Life / Oct. 27, 1980 / Evidence ♦♦♦
Pair the K.C. shouter with a Chicago band and the results from this 1980 set aren't half bad. *—Bill Dahl*

Patcha, Patcha, All Night Long / Apr. 11, 1985 / Pablo ♦♦♦
This wouldn't find a place in the cutting edge of either Big Joe Turner or Witherspoon's catalog, but it's a decent enough 1985 session of Kansas City-type blues/jazz. Saxophonists Red Holloway and Lee Allen are the featured players in a band that bisects the swing and jump blues idioms, Witherspoon acquitting himself better than Turner (the latter of whom died later that year). *—Richie Unterberger*

Midnight Lady Called the Blues / Jan. 14, 1986 / Muse ♦♦♦♦
Singer Jimmy Witherspoon was starting to show his age by 1986, but he is in pretty strong form on these seven selections co-composed by Dr. John and Doc Pomus. With altoist Hank Crawford (who also wrote some of the arrangements) and tenor saxophonist David "Fathead" Newman contributing plenty of solos while pianist Dr. John leads the rhythm section, the spirited set has more than its share of interesting and exciting moments despite the obscurity of the material. *—Scott Yanow*

Rockin' L.A. / Oct. 24, 1988-Oct. 25, 1988 / Fantasy ♦♦♦♦
This CD finds Jimmy Witherspoon at age 65 on one of his last fairly strong records before his voice began to really shrink and fade. 'Spoon, assisted on this live set by tenor saxophonist Teddy Edwards, pianist Gerald Wiggins, bassist John Clayton, and drummer Paul Humphrey, revives some of his hits, performs a pair of medleys and emphasizes swinging blues and ballads. Highlights include "Sweet Lotus Blossom" (a standard whose authorship should not have been credited to Witherspoon), "Stormy Monday," and "I Want a Little Girl." Easily recommended to Jimmy Witherspoon fans. *—Scott Yanow*

Jay's Blues / 1991 / Charly ♦♦♦♦♦
Jays Blues is a fine collection of early-'50s jump blues sides that Jimmy Witherspoon cut for Federal Records. This 23-track collection offers a good retrospective of one of Witherspoon's most neglected—and admittedly uneven—periods. *—Thom Owens*

☆ **Blowin' in from Kansas City** / 1993 / Flair ♦♦♦♦♦
These 20 tunes pair the great Mr.Witherspoon with the finest jazz, jump, and blues talents around. Jay McShann, Maxwell Davis, Tiny Webb, and Chuck Norris are only a few of the first-rate sessionmen and arrangers who grace the tracks of this essential CD. A special mention must be made of tenor sax legend Ben Webster, whose solo on "I'm Going

Around in Circles" is simply magnificent. This is quintessential Kansas City blues. Of all the shouters, Witherspoon is perhaps the greatest singer. *—Larry Hoffman*

Live at the Mint / Nov. 18, 1994-Nov. 19, 1994 / Private Music ✦✦✦

Beloved old blues shouter Jimmy Witherspoon had a party thrown for him twice a year by guitarist Robben Ford at L.A.'s quintessential blues club, the Mint. Although throat cancer intensified the already ultra-raspy quality of Mr. Witherspoon's voice, he never failed to deliver a textured show with surprises and genuine radiance. Backed by the Robben Ford Band, we hear a reunion of Yellowjackets keyboardist Russ Ferrante, Blue Line's drummer Tom Brechtleinm, and bassline driver Roscoe Beck, with significant enthusiastic contributions by the club's intimate audience. Witherspoon presents songs ("Ain't Nobody's Business," "Goin' to Chicago") that are in fact identified with a West Coast blend of Kansas City, New Orleans, and Chicago influence; although he enjoyed moderate success within all those musical regions, he developed much of his "shouting" style touring Europe and stationed himself, for the latter decade of his life, in Los Angeles. At some moments there's a scratched-up, old-recording feel, probably due to the quality of his voice and the nature of venue-recordings at large. But you can't miss a note of how slow he goes down on "Goin' Down Slow," and there should surely be a dance named after "Big Boss Man." Recorded three years before Jimmy succumbed to cancer in L.A., although that did not curtail continuing tribute parties at the Mint. A fine blues document. *—Becky Byrkit*

'Spoon & Groove / Apr. 1996 / Tradition ✦✦✦

This was originally released as *Groovin' & Spoonin'* on Olympic. It's a decent if unremarkable set of blues-jazz, heavier on the blues, with organist Groove Holmes being Witherspoon's most important sideman on this date (which also features tenor saxophonist Teddy Edwards). Several of the numbers are shopworn standards like "Take This Hammer," "Key to the Highway," "Please Send Me Someone to Love," and "Since I Fell for You," though everything's performed with taste. If you're looking for Witherspoon blues-jazz with an organ groove, the 1963 album *Evenin' Blues* (1963) is more highly recommended, though *'Spoon & Groove* has no serious flaws. *—Richie Unterberger*

Jimmy Witherspoon With the Duke Robillard Band / 2000 / Stony Plain ✦✦✦

The material on this album was recorded in concert shortly before Jimmy Witherspoon's death at age 74, and it appears that this was his last recording. The significance of that fact cuts both ways on this attractive but sometimes frustrating album. On the one hand, fans will welcome it as a last document of Witherspoon's undeniable talent and presence. On the other hand, it's hard to overlook the fact that by this point he was no longer at the peak of his powers. Although he tries gamely to generate the energy of his past work—and occasionally succeeds, as on the electrifying "I'll Always Be in Love With You"—for the most part his voice is phlegmy and weak, his intonation approximate at best. Duke Robillard works well with Witherspoon, goosing his band to a level of energy intended to invigorate the aging singer without overpowering him, and delivering sharp and witty solos that keep things lively and interesting. There is also a fine cameo appearance by the British blues singer Long John Baldry, whose presence also seems to give Witherspoon a shot in the arm. Overall, though, this is an album that will appeal primarily to die-hard fans of the singer and to Robillard completists. *—Rick Anderson*

Bluespoon/Spoon in London / 2001 / Prestige/Original Blues Classics ✦✦✦

This CD combines two chronologically close, but stylistically different, LPs onto a single-disc reissue.

Jazz Casual: Jimmyin' the Blues / Feb. 27, 2001 / Koch ✦✦✦

Drawing from the legendary television series produced by journalist Ralph Gleason, this recording collects aural tracks from two shows broadcast in 1962. The first features blues singer Jimmy Witherspoon backed by a highly compatible small jazz group, with the legendary Ben Webster on tenor sax and Vince Guaraldi on piano. The second broadcast highlights vocalist Jimmy Rushing accompanying himself on piano. As with other recordings in this series, there are relaxed yet probing interviews by Gleason that give fascinating insights into the music and the performers. Some of the tracks are slightly truncated to fit the format but, as with all of Gleason's productions, there is a serious professional commitment that was seldom seen on television at the time. Webster is in fine form, and is clearly one of the highlights on the disc, easily acclimating himself to Witherspoon's style. Neither Witherspoon nor Rushing breaks any new ground, but instead each offers representative samplings, with Witherspoon singing signature tunes such as "Ain't Nobody's Business" and "I'm Gonna Move to the Outskirts of Town," and Rushing serving up lots of traditional blues, plus his infamous version of the perennial favorite "Tricks Ain't Walkin' No More." Rarely did commercial television reach the artistic heights to which Gleason brought it, and this recording represents some of the best episodes from the series. *—Steven Loewy*

Mitch Woods

b. Apr. 3, 1951, Brooklyn, NY

Vocals, Piano / Boogie-Woogie, Jump Blues

Dubbing his swinging approach "rock-a-boogie," pianist Mitch Woods & His Rocket 88's have revived the jump blues approach of the '40s and '50s on three Blind Pig albums.

Originally from Brooklyn, NY, Mitch Woods moved to San Francisco in 1970. While he was growing up in Brooklyn, he studied both jazz and classical music, but when he relocated to the Bay Area, he primarily played jump blues and R&B. San Franciscan guitarist HiTide Harris introduced Woods to the joyous jive of Louis Jordan, and the pianist's musical tastes were transformed. Between 1970 and 1980, Woods performed as a solo artist, gigging at a number of local clubs. In 1980, he formed the Rocket 88s—which featured Harris on guitar—and four years later, the band released their debut album, *Steady Date*, on Blind Pig. The album led to concerts at national blues clubs and festivals, as well as several European dates in 1987.

In 1988, Woods & His Rocket 88's released their second album, *Mr. Boogie's Back in Town*, and embarked on another round of shows in America, Canada, and Europe. Three years later, their third album, *Solid Gold Cadillac*, appeared. Woods & His Rocket 88's continued to tour and perform in the '90s, releasing their fourth album, *Shakin' the Shack*, in 1993. *Jump for Joy* was issued in early 2001. *—Bill Dahl & Stephen Thomas Erlewine*

Steady Date With Mitch Woods & His Rocket 88's / 1984 / Blind Pig ✦✦

Mr. Boogie's Back in Town / 1988 / Blind Pig ✦✦✦

Jump blues and boogie with a rockabilly edge. *—Niles J. Frantz*

● **Solid Gold Cadillac** / 1991 / Blind Pig ✦✦✦✦✦

With West Coast jump blues and boogie-woogie piano. this is tasty, if not particularly original. Charlie Musselwhite guests on harp. *—Niles J. Frantz*

Shakin' the Shack / 1993 / Blind Pig ✦✦

Woods—a boogie-woogie pianist of first order—is rooted in good-timey rock, with interesting tangents into the Louisiana bayou ("Zydeco Boogie") and New Orleans Mardi Gras ("Hattie Queen"). "Boogie" is the operative word here, with the lead track, "Honkin', Shoutin', Pumpin', Poundin'," accurately setting the tone. *—Roch Parisien*

Keeper of the Flame / Oct. 29, 1996 / Lightyear ✦✦✦

Jump for Joy / Feb. 13, 2001 / Blind Pig ✦✦✦✦

This is swing revival, boogie-woogie, jump, big band, and the blues all rolled into one satisfying serving. This album, *Jump for Joy*, recorded by Mitch Woods & His Rocket 88's, is hip-rolling, feet-moving joy for the ears. In fact, the title is a name the artist felt fit the style of music he was offering here, and fans have agreed with him. Longtime singer/songwriter and pianist Mitch Woods brought not only his band, the Rocket 88's, in on this recording, but also a number of other musicians, including saxophonists Danny Bittker, Michael Peloquin, and Jeff Ervin, trumpeters Tim Hyland and Mike Whitwell, and trombonist Mike Rinta. They actually finished this album three years before it was finally released to the public. This album is probably one of the best works Woods has put together in a while, if not the best altogether. Some of the good-time groove numbers you can sample on this album are "Swingin' at the Savoy," "Jive Mr. Boogie," "Golden Gate Jump," "Easy Street," and "Straight Eight." *—Charlotte Dillon*

Big John Wrencher

b. Feb. 12, 1923, Sunflower, MS, **d.** Jul. 15, 1977, Clarksdale, MS

Vocals, Harmonica / Harmonica Blues, Electric Chicago Blues

The Maxwell Street open-air market was a seven- to ten-block area in Chicago that from the 1920s to the mid-'60s played host to various blues musicians—both professional and amateur—who performed right on the street for tips from passersby. Most of them who started their careers there (like Little Walter, Earl Hooker, Hound Dog Taylor, and others) moved up to the more comfortable confines of club work. But one who stayed and became a most recognizable fixture of the area was a marvelous harmonica player and singer named One-Arm or Big John Wrencher.

Wrencher was born in Sunflower County, MS, in 1924 on a plantation. His youthful interest in music—particularly the harmonica—kept him on the move as a traveling musician, playing throughout Tennessee and neighboring Arkansas from the late '40s to the early '50s. In 1958, Big John lost his left arm in a car crash in Memphis. By the early '60s, he had moved north to Chicago and quickly became a regular fixture on Maxwell Street, always working on Sundays from ten in the morning to nearly three in the afternoon virtually nonstop, as Sundays were the big payday for most busking musicians working the area.

Although cupping both harmonica and bulky microphone in one hand (which he also sang through), Wrencher's physical challenge seemingly did little to alter the hugeness of his sound or the slurring attack he brought to the instrument. Usually backed by nothing more than an electric guitar and a drummer, Big John's sound and style was country juke joint blues brought to the city and amplified to the maximum. A flamboyant showman, he'd put on quite a show for the people on the street, moving and dancing constantly while the cigar box was passed around for tips. By all accounts, no one was ever disappointed by the show or the music.

But despite his enormous playing and performing talents, the discography on Wrencher, unfortunately, remains woefully thin. He appears to have played on a session with Detroit bluesman Baby Boy Warren in the '50s, but this tape appears to be lost to the ravages of time. His first official recordings surfaced on a pair of Testament albums from the '60s, featuring Big John in a sideman role behind slide legend Robert Nighthawk. His only full album of material surfaced in the early '70s on the Barrelhouse label. Producer George Paulus also used him as a backing musician behind the slide guitarist, but these sides laid unissued until showing up piecemeal on various compilations.

After years of vacillating between his regular Maxwell Street gig and a few appearances on European blues festivals, Wrencher decided to go back to Mississippi to visit family and old friends in July of 1977. While swapping stories of his travels with some buddies at bluesman Wade Walton's barber shop in Clarksdale, he suddenly dropped dead from a heart attack at the age of 54. As a heartfelt (and somewhat surreal) memorial to his old pal, Big John's final bottle of whiskey is permanently ensconced on a shelf at Walton's barbershop.*—Cub Koda*

Big John's Boogie / 1974 / Big Bear ✦✦✦

● **Maxwell Street Alley Blues** / 1978 / Barrelhouse ✦✦✦✦✦

While most blues albums bear romantic-sounding titles like the one used here, this is the real deal. Wrencher's one-armed amplified harp playing is perfectly supported by the lone guitar of Little Buddy Scott and the bare-bones basic drumming of Playboy Vinson. Listing titles is superfluous, since the feel and the ambience are the important things. But blues albums seldom capture that elusive quality the way it is here, and that's the secret of its charm. Superlative in every regard, this is a great album by a very under-recorded artist. *—Cub Koda*

Billy Wright

b. May 21, 1932, Atlanta, GA, **d.** Oct. 27, 1991, Atlanta, GA

Vocals, Fiddle / Jump Blues, R&B, Soul-Blues

A prime influence on Little Richard during his formative years, "Prince of the Blues" Billy Wright's hearty shouting delivery was an Atlanta staple during the postwar years. Wright was a regular at Atlanta's 81 Theatre as a youth, soaking up the vaudevillians before graduating to singing and dancing status there himself. Saxist Paul "Hucklebuck" Williams caught Wright's act when they shared a bill with Charles Brown and Wynonie Harris at Atlanta's Auditorium, recommending the teenaged singer to Savoy Records boss Herman Lubinsky.

Wright's 1949 Savoy debut, "Blues for My Baby," shot up to number three on *Billboard*'s R&B charts, and its flip, "You Satisfy," did almost as well. Two more of Wright's Savoy 78s, "Stacked Deck" and "Hey Little Girl," were also Top Ten R&B entries in 1951. The flamboyant Wright set his pal Little Richard up with powerful WGST DJ Zenas "Daddy" Sears, who scored the newcomer his first contract with RCA in 1951. It's no knock on Richard to note that his early sides sound very much like Billy Wright.

Wright recorded steadily for Savoy through 1954, the great majority of his sessions held in his hometown with hot local players (saxist Fred Jackson and guitarist Wesley Jackson were often recruited). After he left Savoy, Wright's recording fortunes plummeted—a 1955 date for Don Robey's Peacock diskery in Houston and sessions for Fire (unissued) and Carrollton in 1959 ended his discography. Wright later MCed shows in Atlanta, remaining active until a stroke in the mid-'70s slowed him down. —*Bill Dahl*

Stacked Deck / 1980 / Route 66 ◆◆◆◆

The title track was a major R&B hit for Wright in 1951, and there are 13 more gems by the animated blues shouter on this import piece of vinyl. Everything's from the Savoy vaults except for an ultra-rare Wright cover of Billy Ward & the Dominoes' "Do Something for Me" that was cut live at Atlanta's Harlem Theatre in 1952. —*Bill Dahl*

Goin' Down Slow (Blues, Soul & Early R 'n' R, Vol. 14) / 1984 / Savoy ◆◆◆◆◆

Crying and pleading the blues, Wright's early-'50s Savoy output was very influential. —*Bill Dahl*

● Billy Wright / 1994 / Savoy Jazz ◆◆◆◆◆

Here are 15 of the Atlanta jump blues shouter's very best outings for Savoy, spanning 1949-1954. Wright's pleading style, a large influence indeed on a developing Little Richard, is irresistibly spotlighted on "After Awhile," "I Remember," and the romping "Billy's Boogie Blues." —*Bill Dahl*

Hey Baby, Don't You Want a Man Like Me? / 1995 / Ace ◆◆◆

Jimmy Yancey

b. 1894, Chicago, IL, **d.** Sep. 17, 1951, Chicago, IL
Piano / Boogie-Woogie, Piano Blues
One of the seminal boogie-woogie pianists, Yancey was active in and around Chicago playing house parties and clubs from 1915, yet he remained unrecorded until May 1939, when he recorded "The Fives" and "Jimmy's Stuff" for a small label. Soon after, he became the first boogie-woogie pianist to record an album of solos, for Victor. By then, Yancey's work around Chicago had already influenced such younger and better-known pianists as Meade "Lux" Lewis, Pinetop Smith, and Albert Ammons.

Yancey played vaudeville as a tap dancer and singer from the age of six. He settled in Chicago in 1915, where he began composing songs and playing music at informal gatherings. In 1925, he became groundskeeper at Comiskey Park, home of the Chicago White Sox baseball team. Yancey was a musician's musician, remaining mostly unknown and unheard outside of Chicago until 1936, when Lewis recorded one of his tunes, "Yancey Special." Three years later, producer Dan Qualey became the first to record Yancey for his new Solo Art label. After the Victor recordings, Yancey went on to record for OKeh and Bluebird. In later years, Yancey performed with his wife, blues singer Estella "Mama" Yancey; they appeared together at Carnegie Hall in 1948.

Yancey was not as technically flashy as some of his disciples, but he was an expressive, earthy player with a flexible left hand that introduced an air of unpredictability into his bass lines. His playing had a notable peculiarity: Although he wrote and performed compositions in a variety of keys, he ended every tune in E flat. He was also an undistinguished blues singer, accompanying himself on piano. Although Yancey attained a measure of fame for his music late in life, he never quit his day job, remaining with the White Sox until just before his death. —*Chris Kelsey*

In the Beginning / May 4, 1939 / Solo Art ✦✦✦✦✦
This LP has 12 of the 17 selections that pianist Jimmy Yancey cut during his first recording session. All of the music (plus the missing titles) have been reissued in full on CD by Document but this album has the advantage of also having Rudi Blesh's extensive and informative liner notes. Yancey's subtle boogie-woogie style is heard in prime form on solo performances originally cut for Solo Art. —*Scott Yanow*

The Yancey-Lofton Sessions, Vol. 1 / Dec. 1943 / Storyville ✦✦✦✦
The music on this LP (which has been reissued on CD by Document) is timeless. The first of two volumes is comprised of three of the only four piano solos made by the obscure ragtime-oriented Alonzo Yancey (Jimmy's older brother), seven by the lyrical Jimmy Yancey (including "Death Letter Blues" which has a rare vocal), and six from the erratic but exciting Cripple Clarence Lofton. All three pianists are heard in prime form and contrast each other very well. Easily recommended to jazz, blues, and boogie-woogie collectors who do not already have the Document CDs. —*Scott Yanow*

The Yancey-Lofton Sessions, Vol. 2 / Dec. 1943 / Storyville ✦✦✦✦
This is the second of two LPs reissuing the 1943 recordings of pianists Jimmy and Alonzo Yancey and Cripple Clarence Lofton. Alonzo Yancey (Jimmy's older brother) only recorded four numbers in his life; three are on *Vol. 1* while his "Ecstatic Rag" is a highlight on this album. In addition there are nine numbers from Jimmy Yancey (including two that have vocals by Mama Yancey) and four from Lofton. Overall, the music is quite enjoyable and unique in its own way; all of it has since been reissued on CD. —*Scott Yanow*

Jimmy & Mama Yancey: Chicago Piano, Vol. 1 / Jul. 18, 1951 / Atlantic ✦✦✦✦
Jimmy Yancey was one of the pioneer boogie-woogie pianists, but unlike many of the other pacesetters, he had a gentle and thoughtful style that also crossed over into the blues. This Atlantic CD, a straight reissue of the 1972 LP, contains Yancey's final recordings, cut just eight weeks before his death from diabetes. The pianist is in fine form on these introspective and often emotional performances which, with the exception of Meade "Lux" Lewis' "Yancey Special" and the traditional "Make Me a Pallet on the Floor," are comprised entirely of Yancey's originals. His wife, Mama Yancey, takes five memorable vocals on this memorable set of classic blues. —*Scott Yanow*

☆ **Complete Recorded Works, Vol. 1 (1939–1940)** / 1991 / Document ✦✦✦✦✦
The first of three Document CDs that reissue all of pianist Jimmy Yancey's recordings (other than his final Atlantic session) is filled with classic performances. Yancey, a subtle boogie-woogie/blues pianist who was a major influence and inspiration on the better-known players of the 1930s, is featured on his first two solo sessions, including "The Fives," "La Salle Street Breakdown," "South Side Stuff," "Yancey's Getaway," "Yancey Stomp," and "State Street Special." Highly recommended as are the two following volumes in this valuable Document series. —*Scott Yanow*

☆ **Complete Recorded Works, Vol. 2 (1940–1943)** / 1991 / Document ✦✦✦✦✦
On the second of three CDs that trace virtually his entire recording career, pianist Jimmy Yancey is showcased on a variety of solo tracks. Two numbers from February 1940 are highlighted by the classic "Bear Trap Blues." There are a couple of numbers made for the tiny Art Center Jazz Gems label, a four-song (plus two alternate takes) definitive set cut for Bluebird (which includes "Death Letter Blues" and "Yancey's Bugle Call"), and nine songs (five previously unissued) from 1943; on one version of "How Long Blues," Mama Yancey sings while Jimmy switches to the spooky-sounding harmonium. This set also has Jimmy Yancey's only four recorded vocals, which are quite effective even though his voice is limited. All three volumes in this series are highly recommended collections of music by this subtle pianist, who made expert use of space and ended every tune in E flat. —*Scott Yanow*

★ **Complete Recorded Works, Vol. 3 (1939–1950)** / 1991 / Document ✦✦✦✦✦
The third of three CDs tracing the recording career of the unique boogie-woogie pianist Jimmy Yancey, whose subtlety could often result in some dramatic music, completes his December 1943 session and also has his December 23, 1950 solo set; his final recordings from July 1951 are available on an Atlantic release. The 1943 titles, three of which were previously unreleased, include two with Mama Yancey's vocals (Jimmy switches to harmonium on one) and are highlighted by "White Sox Stomp," "Yancey Special," and two versions of "Make Me a Pallet on the Floor." After the six fine titles from 1950, this CD finishes off with the only four numbers that Jimmy's older brother, the more ragtime-oriented Alonzo Yancey, ever recorded. Although his style was different, on "Ecstatic Rag" Alonzo does sound a bit like Jimmy. All three of these Document CDs, plus the Atlantic set, are highly recommended and preferable to the piecemeal domestic Bluebird reissues. —*Scott Yanow*

Recorded at Yancey's Apartment / Jan. 2, 1998 / Document ✦✦✦

Mama Yancey (Estella Harris)

b. Jan. 1, 1896, Cairo, IL, **d.** Apr. 19, 1986, Chicago, IL
Vocals / Classic Female Blues
The other half of the blues team led by pioneering boogie-woogie pianist Jimmy Yancey, Estella "Mama" Yancey was a talented vocalist known for her warm sense of humor and great command of the stage. In her childhood, Estella Harris sang in church choirs and learned guitar. Jimmy Yancey, who had traveled the U.S. and Europe as a vaudeville dancer, married Estella in 1917, when she was 21. Yancey often sang with her husband at informal gatherings, house rent parties, and clubs in the 1930s and '40s in Chicago. Because Jimmy Yancey was not that good a blues singer, but was a great boogie-woogie/blues piano player, Estella recorded frequently with her husband.

Yancey sang with her husband in 1948 at Carnegie Hall, and this performance in turn led to Jimmy Yancey's last recording with Mama, *Pure Blues*, in 1951 for a fledgling Atlantic Records. Jimmy Yancey died a few months later from a stroke brought on by complications from diabetes, but Estella continued to perform and record. One of the best examples of her soulful, expressive vocals can be found on an album for Atlantic, *Jimmy & Mama Yancey: Chicago Piano, Vol. 1*.

Mama Yancey's recordings with other pianists include *South Side Blues* for the Riverside label (1961), some records with Art Hodes for Verve in 1965, and *Maybe I'll Cry* with Erwin Helfer for the Red Beans label in 1983, at age 87. Yancey died in 1986. —*Richard Skelly*

Mama Yancey Sings / 1965 / Smithsonian/Folkways ✦✦✦

● **Blues** / Jan. 1966 / Verve ✦✦✦✦
Blues, Mama Yancey's 1966 effort for Verve Records, finds the esteemed pianist maturing quite gracefully, turning a nicely understated collection of standards and originals. Throughout it all, her boogie-woogie piano sounds rich and friendly, offering a nice introduction to her groundbreaking work. —*Thom Owens*

Maybe I'll Cry / 1983 / Evidence ✦✦✦✦

The Yardbirds

f. 1963, Surrey, England, **db.** Jul. 1968, London, England
Group / British Psychedelia, British Blues, Psychedelic, British Invasion, Blues-Rock, Rock & Roll
The Yardbirds are mostly known to the casual rock fan as the starting point for three of the greatest British rock guitarists—Eric Clapton, Jeff Beck, and Jimmy Page. Undoubtedly these three figures did much to shape the group's sound, but throughout their career, the Yardbirds were very much a unit, albeit a rather unstable one. And they were truly one of the great rock bands—one whose contributions went far beyond the scope of their half dozen or so mid-'60s hits ("For Your Love," "Heart Full of Soul," "Shapes of Things," "I'm a Man," "Over Under Sideways Down," "Happenings Ten Years Time Ago"). Not content to limit themselves to the R&B and blues covers they concentrated upon initially, they quickly branched out into moody, increasingly experimental pop/rock. The innovations of Clapton, Beck, and Page redefined the role of the guitar in rock music, breaking immense ground in the use of feedback, distortion, and amplification with finesse and

breathtaking virtuosity. With the arguable exception of the Byrds, they did more than any other outfit to pioneer psychedelia, with an eclectic, risk-taking approach that laid the groundwork for much of the hard rock and progressive rock from the late '60s to the present.

No one could have predicted the band's metamorphosis from their humble beginnings in the early '60s in the London suburbs as the Metropolis Blues Quartet. By 1963, they were calling themselves the Yardbirds, with a lineup featuring Keith Relf (vocals), Paul Samwell-Smith (bass), Chris Dreja (rhythm guitar), Jim McCarty (drums), and Anthony "Top" Topham (lead guitar). The 16-year-old Topham was only to last for a very short time, pressured to leave by his family. His replacement was an art college classmate of Relf's, Eric Clapton, nicknamed "Slowhand."

The Yardbirds quickly made a name for themselves in London's rapidly exploding R&B circuit, taking over the Rolling Stones' residency at the famed Crawdaddy club. The band took a similar guitar-based, frenetic approach to classic blues/R&B as the Stones, and for their first few years they were managed by Giorgio Gomelsky, a colorful figure who had acted as a mentor and informal manager for the Rolling Stones in that band's early days.

The Yardbirds made their first recordings as a backup band for Chicago blues great Sonny Boy Williamson, and little of their future greatness is evident in these sides, in which they were still developing their basic chops. (Some tapes of these live shows were issued after the group had become international stars; the material has been reissued ad infinitum since then.) But they really didn't find their footing until 1964, when they stretched out from straight R&B rehash into extended, frantic guitar-harmonica instrumental passages. Calling these ad hoc jams "rave ups," the Yardbirds were basically making the blues their own by applying a fiercer, heavily amplified electric base. Taking some cues from improvisational jazz by inserting their own impassioned solos, they would turn their source material inside out and sideways, heightening the restless tension by building the tempo and heated exchange of instrumental riffs to a feverish climax, adroitly cooling off and switching to a lower gear just at the point where the energy seemed uncontrollable. The live 1964 album *Five Live Yardbirds* is the best document of their early years, consisting entirely of reckless interpretations of U.S. R&B/blues numbers, and displaying the increasing confidence and imagination of Clapton's guitar work.

As much they might have preferred to stay close to the American blues and R&B that had inspired them (at least at first), the Yardbirds made efforts to crack the pop market from the beginning. A couple of fine studio singles of R&B covers were recorded with Clapton that gave the band's sound a slight polish without sacrificing its power. The commercial impact was modest in the U.K. and nonexistent in the States, however, and the group decided to change direction radically on their third single. Turning away from their blues roots entirely, "For Your Love" was penned by British pop/rock songwriter Graham Gouldman, and introduced many of the traits that would characterize the Yardbirds' work over the next two years. The melodies were strange (by pop standards) combinations of minor chords; the tempos slowed, speeded up, or ground to a halt unpredictably; the harmonies were droning, almost Gregorian; the arrangements were, by the standards of the time, downright weird, though retaining enough pop appeal to generate chart action. "For Your Love" featured a harpsichord, bongos, and a menacing Keith Relf vocal; it would reach number two in Britain, and number six in the States.

For all its brilliance, "For Your Love" precipitated a major crisis in the band. Eric Clapton wanted to stick close to the blues, and for that matter didn't like "For Your Love," barely playing on the record. Shortly afterwards, around the beginning of 1965, he left the band, opting to join John Mayall's Bluesbreakers a bit later in order to keep playing blues guitar. Clapton's spot was first offered to Jimmy Page, then one of the hottest session players in Britain; Page turned it down, figuring he could make a lot more money by staying where he was. He did, however, recommend another guitarist, Jeff Beck, then playing with an obscure band called the Tridents, as well as having worked a few sessions himself.

While Beck's stint with the band lasted only about 18 months, in this period he did more to influence the sound of '60s rock guitar than anyone except Jimi Hendrix. Clapton saw the group's decision to record adventurous pop like "For Your Love" as a sellout of their purist blues ethic. Beck, on the other hand, saw such material as a challenge that offered room for unprecedented experimentation. Not that he wasn't a capable R&B player as well—on tracks like "The Train Kept A-Rollin'" and "I'm Not Talking," he coaxed a sinister sustain from his instrument by bending the notes and using fuzz and other types of distorted amplification. The Middle Eastern influence extended to his work on all of their material, including his first single with the band, "Heart Full of Soul," which (like "For Your Love") was written by Gouldman. After initial attempts to record the song with a sitar had failed, Beck saved the day by emulating the instrument's exotic twang with fuzz riffs of his own. It became their second transatlantic Top Ten hit; the similar "Evil-Hearted You," again penned by Gouldman, gave them another big British hit later in 1965.

The chief criticism that could be levied against the band at this point was their shortage of quality original material, a gap addressed by "Still I'm Sad," a haunting group composition based around a Gregorian chant and Beck's sinewy, wicked guitar riffs. In the United States, it was coupled with "I'm a Man," a rehaul of the Bo Diddley classic that built to an almost avant-garde climax, Beck scraping the strings of the guitar for a purely percussive effect; it became a Top 20 hit in the United States in early 1966. Beck's guitar pyrotechnics came to fruition with "Shapes of Things," which (along with the Byrds' "Eight Miles High") can justifiably be classified as the first psychedelic rock classic. The group had already moved into social comment with a superb album track, "Mr. You're a Better Man Than I"; on "Shapes of Things" they did so more succinctly, with Beck's explosively warped solo and feedback propelling the single near the U.S. Top Ten. At this point the group were as innovative as any in rock & roll, building their resumé with the similar hit follow-up to "Shapes of Things," "Over Under Sideways Down."

But the Yardbirds could not claim to be nearly as consistent as peers like the Beatles, Rolling Stones, and Kinks. Their first (and, in fact, only) studio album comprised entirely of original material was 1966's *Roger the Engineer*, and highlighted the group's erratic quality, bouncing between derivative blues rockers and numbers incorporating monks-of-doom chants, Oriental dance rhythms, and good old guitar rave ups, sometimes in the same track. Its highlights, however, were truly thrilling; even when the experiments weren't wholly successful, they served as proof that the band were second to none in their appetite for taking risks previously unheard of within rock.

Yet at the same time, the group's cohesiveness began to unravel when bassist Samwell-Smith—who had shouldered most of the production responsibilities as well—left the band in mid-1966. Jimmy Page, by this time fed up with session work, eagerly joined on bass. It quickly became apparent that Page had more to offer, and the group unexpectedly reorganized, Dreja switching from rhythm guitar to bass, and Page assuming dual lead guitar duties with Beck.

It was a dream lineup that was, like the best dreams, too good to be true, or at least to last long. Only one single was recorded with the Beck/Page lineup, "Happenings Ten Years Time Ago," which—with its astral guitar leads, muffled explosions, eerie harmonies, and enigmatic lyrics—was psychedelia at its pinnacle. But not at its most commercial—in comparison with previous Yardbirds singles, it fared poorly on the charts, reaching only number 30 in the States. Around this time, the group (Page and Beck in tow) made a memorable appearance in Michaelangelo Antonioni's film classic *Blow Up*, playing a reworked version of "The Train Kept A-Rollin'" (retitled "Stroll On"). But in late 1966, Beck—who had become increasingly unreliable, not turning up for some shows and suffering from nervous exhaustion—left the band, emerging the following year as the leader of the Jeff Beck Group.

The remaining Yardbirds were determined to continue as a quartet, but in hindsight it was Beck's departure that began to burn out a band that had already survived the loss of a couple important original members. Also to blame was their mysterious failure to summon original material on the order of their classic 1965-1966 tracks. More to blame than anyone, however, was Mickey Most (Donovan, Herman's Hermits, Lulu, the Animals), who assumed the producer's chair in 1967, and matched the group with inappropriately lightweight pop tunes. The band's unbridled experimentalism would simmer in isolated moments on some B-sides and album tracks, like "Puzzles," the psychedelic UFO instrumental "Glimpses," and the acoustic "White Summer," which would serve as a blueprint for Page's acoustic excursions with Led Zeppelin. "Little Games," "Ha Ha Said the Clown," and "Ten Little Indians" were all low-charting singles for the group in 1967, but were travesties compared to the magnificence of their previous hits, trading in fury and invention for sappy singlong pop. The 1967 *Little Games* album (issued in the U.S. only) was little better, suffering from both hasty, anemic production and weak material.

The Yardbirds continued to be an exciting concert act, concentrating most of their energies upon the United States, having been virtually left for dead in their native Britain. The B-side of their final single, the Page-penned "Think About It," was the best track of the entire Jimmy Page era, showing they were still capable of delivering intriguing, energic psychedelia. It was too little too late—the group were truly on the wane by 1968, as an artistic rift developed within the ranks. To overgeneralize somewhat, Relf and McCarty wanted to pursue more acoustic, melodic music; Page especially wanted to rock hard and loud. A live album was recorded in New York in early 1968, but scrapped; overdubbed with unbelievably cheesy crowd noises, it was briefly released in 1971 after Page had become a superstar in Led Zeppelin, but was withdrawn in a matter of days (it has since been issued on CD). By this time the group was going through the motions, leaving Page holding the bag after a final show in mid-1968. Relf and McCarty formed the first incarnation of Renaissance. Page fulfilled existing contracts by assembling a "New Yardbirds" that, as many know, would soon change their name to Led Zeppelin.

It took years for the rock community to truly comprehend the Yardbirds' significance; younger listeners were led to the recordings in search of the roots of Clapton, Beck, and Page, each of whom had become a superstar by the end of the 1960s. Their wonderful catalog, however, has been subject to more exploitation than any other group of the '60s; dozens, if not hundreds, of cheesy packages of early material are generated throughout the world on a seemingly monthly basis. Fortunately, the best of the reissues cited below (on Rhino, Sony, Edsel and EMI) are packaged with great intelligence, enabling both collectors and new listeners to acquire all of their classic output with a minimum of fuss and repetition. *—Richie Unterberger*

Five Live Yardbirds / Dec. 1964 / Repertoire ♦♦♦♦♦

Five Live Yardbirds was the first important—indeed, essential—live album to come out of the 1960s British rock & roll boom. In terms of the performance captured and the recording quality, it was also the best such live record of the entire middle of the decade. Cut at a Marquee Club show in 1964 , *Five Live Yardbirds* was a popular album, especially once Eric Clapton's fame began to spread after leaving the band. Although the album didn't appear officially in the United States until its CD release by Rhino in the late '80s, four of its tracks—"Smokestack Lightning," "Respectable," "I'm a Man," and "Here 'Tis"—made up one side of their classic U.S. album *Having a Rave Up*, and the British EMI LP became a very popular import during the early '70s as a showcase for both the band and the playing of Eric Clapton. That album had astonishingly good sound, which was not the case with any of the reissues that followed, on vinyl or CD—even Rhino's compact disc suffered from blurry textures and noise, though it was an improvement over any release since the original EMI LP. The 1999 Repertoire Records reissue is the first CD that matches the clarity and sharpness of the original LP, and along with that improvement, their original concert has been very sensibly expanded with a half-dozen live cuts from roughly the same period, recorded at the Crawdaddy Club. Among them is a killer live version of the Billy Boy Arnold classic "I Wish You Would." There's also a pair of live tracks from German television in 1967—"I'm a Man" and "Shapes of Things"; the two, in a flash, make up for what they lack in perfect fidelity. *—Bruce Eder*

For Your Love / 1965 / Repertoire ♦♦♦

Back in 1965, this album seemed like a real mess, which was understandable, because *For Your Love* wasn't a "real" album, in the sense that the Yardbirds ever assembled an LP of that name or content. Rather, it was the response of their American label, Epic Records, to the band's achieving a number six single with the title track, with manager Giorgio Gomelsky selecting the cuts. The quasi-progressive "For Your Love," dominated by guest artist Brian Auger's harpsichord, is juxtaposed with hard-rocking blues-based numbers, almost all of which featured departed lead guitarist Eric Clapton (who is mentioned nowhere on the LP), with current lead guitarist Jeff Beck on just three tracks. The Clapton cuts, although primitive next to the material he was soon to cut with John Mayall, have an intensity that's still riveting to hear four decades later, and was some of the best blues-based rock & roll of its era. The three Beck sides show where the band was really heading, beyond the immediate success of "For Your Love"—"I'm Not Talking" and "I Ain't Done Wrong" were hard, loud, blazing showcases for Beck's concise blues playing, while "My Girl Sloopy" was the first extended jam to emerge on record from a band on the British blues scene; the source material isn't ideal, but Beck and company make their point in an era where bands were seldom allowed to go more than four minutes on even an album track—these boys could play and make it count. The 13 bonus tracks are mostly blues-rock and are mostly scintillating, and the Repertoire CD has the best sound that any of this music has ever displayed. *—Bruce Eder*

Having a Rave Up / Nov. 1965 / Repertoire ✦✦✦✦✦

In its original U.S. vinyl release, this album, comprised of several singles and B-sides plus excerpts off of *Five Live Yardbirds*, was one of the best LPs of the entire British Invasion, ranking on a par with the greatest mid-'60s work of the Beatles and the Rolling Stones; it was also just a step away from being a Yardbirds best-of as well. The contents have reappeared numerous times in many different configurations, but no collection has ever outdone the sheer compactness and high quality of *Having a Rave Up*. One major problem since the 1960s, as with all of the Yardbirds material owned by Charly Records, has been the sound—for years, Charly only had substandard master materials to offer. That situation improved significantly in the mid- to late '90s, and Repertoire Records is working from sources that are the cleanest and most impressive to have surfaced on these tracks during the CD era; one suspects that there might still be room for improvement, but not nearly as much as was previously the case—a quick comparison of tracks between this and the contents of *Train Kept A-Rollin'* reveals somewhat superior sound here. The Repertoire reissue also adds 11 songs that cut across the group's history: principally outtakes from later in their careers and some odd studio sides from much earlier, plus the B-side "New York City Blues" (a rewrite of "Five Long Years"), the single "Shapes of Things, and their featured number from the Antonioni movie *Blow Up*, the "Train Kept A-Rollin'" rewrite "Stroll On," featuring Jeff Beck and Jimmy Page in the lineup. There are new notes by Chris Welch that, although structured somewhat haphazardly, give a good account of the history of the varied (and overall stunning) contents of this CD. *—Bruce Eder*

Sonny Boy Williamson & the Yardbirds / 1966 / Repertoire ✦✦

An exploitative album, released in 1966 shortly after the Yardbirds had their first American hits. This is a live show from late 1963, on which Chicago blues great Sonny Boy Williamson is backed by an extremely green Yardbirds. Yes, Eric Clapton is on here; no, he doesn't play well, managing some thin, extremely tentative solos that find him stumbling occasionally. It's really not that bad, though, as Sonny Boy himself sings well. But it should really be treated as a Sonny Boy Williamson release that happens to have a soon-to-be-famous-but-still-embryonic band in the background, in the manner of the sides the Beatles cut in Hamburg supporting Tony Sheridan. Seven bonus tracks are included on the Repertoire reissue. *—Richie Unterberger*

Roger the Engineer / Jul. 15, 1966 / Edsel ✦✦✦✦✦

Once Jeff Beck joined the Yardbirds, the group began to explore uncharted territory, expanding their blues-rock into wild sonic permutations of psychedelia, Indian music, and avant-garde white noise. Each subsequent single displayed a new direction, one that expanded on the ideas of the previous single, so it would seem that *Roger the Engineer*—Beck's first full album with the group and the band's first album of all original material—would have offered them the opportunity to fully explore their adventurous inclinations. Despite a handful of brilliant moments, *Roger the Engineer* falls short of expectations, partially because the band is reluctant to leave their blues roots behind and partially because they simply can't write a consistent set of songs. At their best on *Roger*, the Yardbirds strike a kinetic balance of blues-rock form and explosive psychedelia ("Lost Woman," "Over Under Sideways Down," "The Nazz Are Blue," "He's Always There," "Psycho Daisies") but they can also bog down in silly Eastern drones (although "Happenings Ten Years Time Ago" is a classic piece of menacing psychedelia) or blues tradition ("Jeff's Boogie" is a pointless guitar workout that doesn't even showcase Beck at his most imaginative). The result is an unfocused record that careens between the great and the merely adequate, but the Yardbirds always had a problem with consistency—none of their early albums had the impact of the singles, and *Roger the Engineer* suffers from the same problem. Nevertheless, it is the Yardbirds' best individual studio album, offering some of their very best psychedelia, even if it doesn't rank among the great albums of its era. *—Stephen Thomas Erlewine*

Over Under Sideways Down / Aug. 8, 1966 / Repertoire ✦✦✦✦✦

Over Under Sideways Down is American version of *The Yardbirds* (aka *Roger the Engineer*), with a cool cover photo but also stripped of "The Nazz Are Blue" and "Rack My Mind," which means that two of the harder rocking blues tracks are absent, along with some superb Jeff Beck guitar playing and a good Keith Relf performance. Add an extra star for the mono version of this album, which differs markedly from its stereo counterpart, and from the mono and stereo British editions—the mono *Over Under Sideways Down* featured versions of "Hot House of Omagararshid" and "Lost Woman" with lead guitar parts that are different (or, in the case of "Hot House," missing) from the stereo versions, and longer versions of "He's Always There," "Turn Into Earth," and "I Can't Make Your Way." Those longer, superior mono cuts have surfaced on post-1997 CD issues of the album. *—Bruce Eder*

Little Games / 1967 / EMI ✦✦✦✦

If almost any group other than the Yardbirds had released *Little Games*, it would be considered a prime late-'60s artifact, instead of a mild disappointment. Not that it's a bad album—it just lacks the polish of the group's other LPs. The Yardbirds' blues roots and progressive tendencies clashed with the pop/rock preferences of their record company-mandated producer, Mickie Most, resulting in a hastily done and uneven LP. The two best cuts were "White Summer" and "Drinking Muddy Water," excellent showcases for the experimental and bluesy sides of the band; both, curiously, were also virtually thefts, "White Summer" lifted from Davy Graham's arrangement of "She Moved Thro' the Fair" and "Drinking Muddy Water" a rewrite of Muddy Waters' "Rollin' and Tumblin'." The best of the rest included "Only the Black Rose," a strangely beautiful, moody acoustic psychedelic piece; "Stealing Stealing," an unusual (for this band) pre-World War II-style acoustic blues; and "Smile on Me," a hard, bluesy number that could have come from any part of the group's history. The attempt at a catchy rocker, "No Excess Baggage," however, needed more work; the power-chord laden "Tinker Tailor Soldier Sailor" sounded more like the Who than the Yardbirds, though it did introduce Jimmy Page's violin bow discourses on the guitar; and "Little Soldier Boy" was a silly pop-psychedelic piece more appropriate to the Monkees than the Yardbirds. *Little Games* was reissued in vastly expanded form in 1992. *—Bruce Eder*

Live Yardbirds Featuring Jimmy Page / 1971 / Moreland Street ✦✦✦✦✦

Arguably the most famous lost live album in history, *Live Yardbirds Featuring Jimmy Page*, cut at the Anderson Theater in New York on March 30, 1968, has been issued twice on vinyl legitimately (only to be suppressed by legal action) and innumerable times since as a bootleg. In August 2000, Mooreland Street Records put out the first authorized CD edition of the performance, and it is a complete revelation. The original master tape has been improved significantly; the absence of vinyl noise is an obvious plus, but the sheer impact of the instruments is also startling, given that the show was taped by a producer who had never recorded a rock band before, on equipment that was ten years out of date. The producers have expanded this reissue with help from a separate reference tape, an audience recording that preserved the complete unedited show; it's somewhat lo-fi, but it captures material edited from the finished master, and it allows for the restoration of little nuances. Page's guitar (which goes out of tune several times) is the dominant instrument, alternately crunchy and lyrical, but always loud and dexterous; the roughness of Keith Relf's singing is also more apparent, but his shortcomings don't really hurt the music. The performance also reveals just how far out in front of the psychedelic pack the Yardbirds were by the spring of 1968; Page had pushed the envelope about as far as he could, in terms of high-velocity guitar pyrotechnics. Ironically, this album isn't quite as strong as the contemporary *Truth* album by Jeff Beck, mostly because the Yardbirds were still juggling three sounds: the group's progressive pop/rock past, the psychedelia of 1968, and a harder, more advanced blues-based sound. It's clear that they had few places left to go with the first two; "Dazed and Confused," by contrast, represented something new, a slow blues as dark, forbidding, and intense as anything that the band had ever cut—it showed where Page, if not this band, was heading. *—Bruce Eder*

Golden Eggs / 1975 / Berkeley ✦✦✦

One of the first widely circulated bootlegs of a non-superstar (but hugely important) act, this did collectors quite a service at the time, assembling 17 of the Yardbirds' rarest tracks—from non-LP singles, soundtracks, and rare LPs—onto one disc. The passage of time and the digital age, though, has made this virtually useless: most of the tracks show up on the Sony and EMI CD reissues. The only true rarities to be found here now are the two songs that comprised the rare 1966 solo single by Keith Relf, "Mr. Zero"/"Knowing," which are odd bits of baroquely produced folk-pop not at all like the Yardbirds' own records. Beware of cheap-quality reproductions of the original (always fair game in the bootleg business), on which some tracks lack a stereo channel from the original recordings. *—Richie Unterberger*

More Golden Eggs / 1975 / Trademark of Quality ✦✦✦

This sequel to *Golden Eggs* actually offers much more of value to the collector than the original installment. Although some of this (like the 1966 B-side "Psycho Daisies") finally became easily available on reissues, most of this has not. And this includes some pretty interesting stuff—live TV broadcasts with Jeff Beck from the mid-'60s, the super-rare and super-moody second Keith Relf solo single "Shapes in My Mind" (two versions!), a pre-Yardbirds Jimmy Page solo single, and downright weird Europop bubblegum numbers that the group (actually Relf with session men) recorded for an Italian single. There's also an actual lengthy interview with Keith Relf on a printed insert; if you're lucky, the copy you hunt down will have this intact. Pricey and hard to find, but worth the search for Yardbird fanatics. *—Richie Unterberger*

Last Rave-Up in L.A. / 1979 / Glimpses ✦

A three-record set of the Yardbirds with Jimmy Page, recorded live in May and June of 1968, may sound real enticing, especially given the general scarcity of material that Page recorded with the band. But you should think real hard before forking over for it. The sound quality is abysmal, obviously recorded by a single mike somewhere not too close to the stage; you can barely hear the vocals and the instruments. Nor are the performances that great; the band sounds ragged though not quite dispirited. If the fidelity on these performances had been acceptable, there would have been some interesting, extremely extended versions of standbys like "I'm a Man," "I Wish You Would," and "White Summer" to be heard, along with the pre-Led Zep incarnation of "Dazed and Confused," finding the band improvising and jamming to a degree not allowable in the studio. *—Richie Unterberger*

★ **Greatest Hits, Vol. 1: 1964–1966** / 1986 / Rhino ✦✦✦✦✦

Greatest Hits, Vol. 1: 1964-1966 falls short of being a truly definitive compilation, stopping shortly after Jeff Beck joined the group and thereby leaving off anything from *Roger the Engineer* on. Still, as a collection of early singles, plus highlights from *Five Live Yardbirds*, this is first-rate, containing their tough blues-rock ravers and their first forays into psychedelia. *—Stephen Thomas Erlewine*

On Air / 1991 / Band of Joy ♦♦♦

Like most of the major British Invasion bands, the Yardbirds recorded many sessions for the BBC during their heyday. *On Air* contains 27 of these, recorded between 1965 and 1968; 21 of them feature Jeff Beck, the rest Jimmy Page (Eric Clapton is not featured on any). The BBC sessions offered listeners the opportunity to hear groups in a relatively live setting with relatively good sound quality, and that's basically what you get here. Most of their major hits—"For Your Love," "Heart Full of Soul," "Shapes of Things," "Over Under Sideways Down," "Still I'm Sad"—are included. By and large, these versions don't differ enormously from the studio cuts, with slightly different arrangements and guitar solos. One could argue, of course, that with a band so responsible for pushing rock guitar to the stratosphere, different guitar solos are a tasty discovery. And they are interesting, but they don't outdo the stellar studio renditions. Of most interest, if not highest quality, are a few covers never waxed by the group on their official releases: "Dust My Blues," "The Sun Is Shining," Garnett Mimms' "My Baby," and Dylan's "Most Likely You'll Go Your Way." On cuts like "I'm Not Talking" and "Too Much Monkey Business," Beck's pyrotechnics are truly breathtaking. But generally this release is more for Yardbirds fans than novices. *—Richie Unterberger*

Vol. 1: Smokestack Lightning / Oct. 1, 1991 / Columbia ♦♦♦♦

This two-CD set was part of the first serious attempt to assemble the early Yardbirds material in a coherent form, mastered from decent sources. As the first Yardbirds release to come from Columbia Records' offices (by then part of Sony Music) in more than a decade, it was also the first CD set to be made from something resembling master tape sources on at least some of the tracks—up to that point, most of the CDs (apart from Rhino's somewhat limited *Greatest Hits, Vol. 1*), had come from vinyl sources and other less than optimum masters. The results were respectable in their time, although since then further research and digging in vaults has yielded superior sources, available from Charly Records directly in their four-CD Yardbirds box and, even better and more recently, from Repertoire Records' expanded reissues of the original Yardbirds albums. The emphasis on this volume is on the chart hits, coupled with the early blues-based recordings, both live and in the studio, making this a good starter set for anyone just discovering the group and its reputation, as well as anyone seeking insights into Eric Clapton's earliest official studio sides or his work on-stage circa 1963-1964. The material featuring Jeff Beck, which is essentially all of the charted songs represented here apart from "For Your Love," is also very impressive, and focuses on his surprisingly advanced technique from very early on as Clapton's successor. *—Bruce Eder*

Vol. 2: Blues, Backtracks and Shapes of Things / Oct. 1, 1991 / Columbia ♦♦♦♦

The second volume of Sony Music Special Products' attempt to make coherent sense of the early Yardbirds catalog is just about a match for the first. This material had been circulating in one form or another since the early '80s, mostly in very substandard versions on vinyl and CD, which this set and its *Vol. 1: Smokestack Lightning* companion sought to correct. Concentrating on the 1965-vintage studio material, this double-CD set is a celebration of Jeff Beck's early tenure with the group, including outtakes of their classic singles ("Heart Full of Soul" played with a sitar, etc.) and working versions of songs that later turned up on *The Yardbirds* (aka *Roger the Engineer*), coupled with one groundbreaking single ("Shapes of Things") and a Jimmy Page-era cut ("Stroll On"), both mastered from what were then the best sources used for a CD. *—Bruce Eder*

The Little Games Sessions & More / Aug. 25, 1992 / EMI America ♦♦♦

This two-CD set assembles the complete *Little Games* album and all of the usable rehearsals, unmixed backing tracks, and alternate takes associated with it in one place, along with a few Yardbirds-related holdings in the EMI vaults. For a variety of reasons (not all the fault of the band), *Little Games* was the Yardbirds' least successful album, but it was also their only full-length studio recording featuring guitarist Jimmy Page, who seems to have hung back here in exerting his musical inclinations, in keeping with the desires of producer Mickie Most's quest for a pop/rock tone to the album. The odd B-sides, outtakes, alternate takes, and bonus tracks reveal a high level of virtuosity that Most failed to exploit—the unanthologized B-sides "Puzzles" and "Think About It," the acoustic version of "White Summer," and the punchier mono mixes of "Little Games" and "Drinking Muddy Water" are superior to much on the finished album; other tracks like the instrumental backing track for "Tinker, Tailor, Soldier, Sailor" and an alternate version of "Glimpses" merely fill in holes for Page completists. Keith Relf and Jim McCarty's post-Yardbirds acoustic duo, Together, which evolved into the original Renaissance, is also represented on three tracks, doing the brand of folkish soft rock that they favored, even as Page had moved on to setting the rock music world on fire with Led Zeppelin. Fans of the Yardbirds, and anyone who could appreciate the original album, will prefer this pricier alternative for the bonus tracks, Led Zeppelin fans will love large parts of this set, and British psychedelic enthusiasts will consider it essential. *—Bruce Eder*

BBC Radio Sessions / Jun. 30, 1993 / Dutch East ♦♦♦

A cut-down single-CD, 26-song version of the British *Where the Action Is* double set, with duplicate Jeff Beck/Jimmy Page tracks eliminated and notes by *Trouser Press'* Ira Robbins aimed specifically at an American audience, with few recollections about early/mid-'60s musical and cultural life in England and more analysis. Otherwise identical, but about $10 cheaper for nine fewer songs, although the Dylan cover is included here. *—Bruce Eder*

Live Saga 63–67 / 1994 / Import ♦♦♦

An import compilation of borderline legality, combining some oft-rehashed live releases with some much rarer live '60s performances. The most important tracks by far are the first eight, taken from a Swedish show in 1967, with Jimmy Page on guitar. These cuts, more than almost anything the Page lineup recorded in the studio, comprise the best evidence of how well Jimmy and the group could play at their best, when they were unencumbered by unsympathetic producers and material. The sound quality is very good, and the performances are good to excellent, including reprises of several of their biggest hits, the otherwise unavailable Dylan cover "Most Likely You Go Your Way (And I'll Go Mine)," and an extended psychedelic version of "I'm a Man" with violin-guitar bowing by Page. Other rarities on the disc—four songs from Germany in 1967 (with Page), one from France in 1965 (with Beck)—are OK, but more in the hardcore collector category. The CD is filled out by six songs from *Five Live Yardbirds* (which has been reissued zillions of times) and a live 1963 version of "Honey in Your Hips." *—Richie Unterberger*

Little Games [Expanded] / Nov. 12, 1996 / EMI ♦♦♦

A curious release that basically condenses the 1992 *Little Games Sessions & More* 32-track double CD into a 26-song, single-disc package. Six of the less essential cuts from the expanded version were dropped, with all of the group's principal 1967-1968 material (from the *Little Games* LP and a few non-LP singles) remaining, along with a few alternates and outtakes. You don't lose that much in the transition, but it's annoying because anybody who bothers to track down this stuff in the first place is probably a collector who would prefer the double CD with everything, rather than a slightly abridged version. *—Richie Unterberger*

Live at the BBC / 1997 / Warner Archives ♦♦♦♦

The Yardbirds recorded several live sessions for the BBC between 1965 and 1968, following Eric Clapton's departure from the band. These recordings have previously been released on bootlegs and small independent labels but Warner Archives' *The Yardbirds BBC Sessions* marks the first big-budget, official release of the material. The disc contains 26 tracks—20 featuring Jeff Beck, six featuring Jimmy Page—which is slightly less than some editions of this same material, but that won't matter to anyone but completists since the gist is the same: The Yardbirds were a tough live band that essentially re-created its studio recordings on the BBC stage. There are slight differences in the guitar solos but the songs are so short, neither Beck nor Page have the opportunity to completely tear loose. Nevertheless, hardcore Yardbirds fans will relish the few rarities here, which mainly are covers the band never recorded in the studio: "Dust My Broom," "Most Likely You Go Your Way (And I'll Go Mine)," "My Baby," and "The Sun is Shining." *—Stephen Thomas Erlewine*

Where the Action Is / 1997 / BBC ♦♦♦

An astonishingly fine, generally high-quality live-in-the-studio anthology, covering the Jeff Beck and Jimmy Page periods in the band's history. Buying it should be a no-brainer for any real Yardbirds fan, as it matches any of the hours of Beatles outtakes and BBC sessions issued in the 1990s in both importance and vitality. The double-CD set consists of 35 live BBC and Stockholm radio performances that are more than sufficiently different from the group's studio sides to justify the purchase, all in superb sound with a healthy, robust volume and presence, except for the typical anemic bass of the period. Disc one is the BBC material, 27 songs performed with Jeff Beck and Jimmy Page on guitars, covering "I Ain't Got You" through to "Little Games," "Goodnight Sweet Josephine," "My Baby," and "Think About It"—no Eric Clapton-era tapes have survived. These raw, single-take renditions showcase the sheer dexterity and power of this band better than any studio sides. The Jimmy Page material shows the fissures in the band, with less sense of a tightly knit group and more of four guys who just happen to be together, rather like the Beatles' *White Album* sessions. The Stockholm tracks on disc two have more hiss but also better-recorded bass and drums, and feature a nicely raw cover of Dylan's "Most Likely You'll Go Your Way (And I'll Go Mine)," one of many outside songs (Velvet Underground tracks included) that the group did in concert but never put on their records. The notes feature an in-depth interview with Jim McCarty and Chris Dreja in which they recall the early and mid-'60s, the recording procedure at the BBC, the stresses within the group, and, curiously, the virtues of the bootleg *Last Rave-Up in L.A.* *—Bruce Eder*

Cumular Limit / Oct. 24, 2000 / Pilot ♦♦♦♦

This is an uneven but generally pleasing compilation of Yardbirds material. The highlight is a series of four-tracks off German television from March of 1967, a point when the band, with Jimmy Page on lead guitar, was immersed in psychedelia. Among the tracks played live is "Happenings Ten Years Time Ago," perhaps the culmination of the group's psychedelic period and otherwise under-represented in their concert output; Page does a good job of replicating the single's double lead guitar sound, including the stripped-down break. "Over Under Sideways Down," "Shapes of Things," and "I'm a Man," all of which are represented on the group's official live album, are all well recorded, and "I'm a Man" (perhaps the most ubiquitous song in the group's output, with three official versions) comes off well, apart from the closing credit announcement in German that intrudes over the finale, but the other cuts reveal just how sloppy the band could be in their media appearances; on the plus side, Keith Relf is in much better voice here than he is on the official Anderson Theater live album from a year later. The major part of disc one is a set of alternate takes of late-era tracks of which "White Summer" and "Tinker Tailor Soldier Sailor" are the strongest numbers. What sounds like a work-in-progress version of "Ten Little Indians" featuring the guitar up close and personal (and projecting some ornate feedback) may please Jimmy Page completists (who will also devour the tracks "You Stood My Love" and its accompanying unreleased cuts, "Avron Knows"; they aren't much as songs (though they're better than much of what is on *Little Games*), but they do offer Page playing some aggressive and appealing leads, while "Spanish Blood" has him playing gorgeous Spanish guitar. A live version of "I'm Confused" from France in March of 1968 comes off much better than the official Anderson Theater version from later the same month. The second disc is a CD-ROM containing the video version of the four German television songs on disc one; it has amazingly high quality and is enjoyable as one of the few fairly lengthy extant glimpses of the group playing to an audience. *—Bruce Eder*

★ **Ultimate!** / Jul. 17, 2001 / Rhino ♦♦♦♦♦

It had to happen sometime, and after about 30 years of piecemeal Yardbirds compilations, here it is: a lengthy best-of anthology that manages to cross-license material from the Clapton, Beck, and Page eras. The result is a two-CD, 52-song anthology that includes all of their big hits, most of their outstanding albums tracks and non-hit singles, and a few rarities. If you're looking for one Yardbirds compilation, either as a starter or a summary, this is it. Previous anthologies almost always had to be divided in early 1966 after the "Shapes of Things" single for licensing reasons, but finally you can hear early blues-derived Clapton sides, 1965 initial British Invasion hit singles, "Shapes of Things," "Over Under Sideways Down," "Happenings Ten Years Time Ago," and the (comparatively slight) highlights of the 1967-1968 Page lineup all in one place. As quite minor quibbles, one could argue that some of the album tracks that were passed over—like "Respectable," "Ever Since the World Began," and "Glimpses"—would have been better choices than some of the cuts that did make it. A few relatively obscure items are included—the late 1963 recording "Boom Boom"/"Honey in Your Hips," the 1965 B-side "Steeled Blues," the 1966 B-side "Psycho Daises," the *Blow-Up* soundtrack item "Stroll On," the weird Italian pop single "Questa Volta"/"Pafff... Bum," and particularly the three pop-folky 1966 songs from Keith Relf's solo singles. Some of those lesser rarities are at cross-purposes with the overall tone of a set largely selected on the basis of quality, rather than collectability. Still, with fine liner notes and packaging, overall it gives the music of one of the greatest rock bands the respectful, high-class presentation it deserves. *—Richie Unterberger*

Yardbirds Story: 1963–66 / May 28, 2002 / Charly ♦♦♦♦

Johnny Young

b. Jan. 1, 1918, Vicksburg, MS, **d.** Apr. 18, 1974, Chicago, IL

Vocals, Mandolin, Guitar / Electric Chicago Blues, Blues Revival, Chicago Blues

Although the mandolin is not an instrument commonly associated with Chicago blues, it has been used by Chicago-based string bands or on Chicago-made recordings by artists such as Carl Martin, Charles and Joe McCoy, and Yank Rachell. However, the only artist to use it successfully in the later electric blues format was Mississippi-born bluesman Johnny Young. An important figure in blues history, Young loved the rough-and-tumble string band tradition of the Delta, a style that readily coexisted with blues.

Young's initial 1947 Chicago classic, "Money Taking Women," exhibits the same exuberant down-home sound, fusing blues with the older country breakdown traditions. The string-band ensemble sound suited street performance as well, whether in Memphis or in Chicago's open-air Maxwell Street Market, where Young and his cronies were brought in off the streets to record. Over the years, Young's mandolin activity declined as Chicago's African-American blues audience demanded a more modern and urban sound. Since Young was also a skilled guitarist and a fine vocalist, he easily weathered the transition.

During the late '60s, an emerging white blues revival audience proved eager for Young's mandolin styling. Unlike Yank Rachell, whose mandolin playing retained an older string band feel, Young's style was firmly grounded in a more contemporary postwar blues idiom, and he interacted well with other electric blues artists. Through his life, he had worked with the major figures of blues history, including Sonny Boy Williamson, Muddy Waters, Big Walter Horton, and Otis Spann. He was, he insisted, born to be a musician. When interviewed shortly before he died, he told how he had struggled all his life trying to make it in the music business. An emotional man, he hoped he would live long enough to make enough money to buy a house. He never made it. *—Barry Lee Pearson*

Johnny Young and His Chicago Blues Band / 1966 / Arhoolie ♦♦♦

James Cotton nearly blew the roof off on harmonica, and Otis Spann added some wonderful rumbling piano. Johnny Young's spirited guitar, vocals, and occasional mandolin provided the final elements for a superb mid-'60s date. *—Ron Wynn*

Chicago/The Blues/Today!, Vol. 3 / 1967 / Vanguard ♦♦♦♦♦

● **Chicago Blues** / 1968 / Arhoolie ♦♦♦♦♦

This is an excellent '60s recording by the down-home urban singer, guitarist, and mandolinist, accompanied by Otis Spann on piano and James Cotton and Big Walter Horton on harmonicas. *—Mark A. Humphrey*

Fat Mandolin / 1970 / Blue Horizon ♦♦♦

Blues Master No. 9 / 1972 / Blue Horizon ♦♦♦

I Can't Keep My Foot from Jumping / 1973 / BluesWay ♦♦

Johnny Young and His Friends / 1994 / Testament ♦♦♦

Recorded in informal settings between 1962 and 1966, this presents Young with various configurations, with major Chicago blues talents like Otis Spann, Robert Nighthawk, Little Walter, and Big Walter Horton lending a hand at different points (Young also plays solo on a couple of numbers). Only three cuts feature drums, so this is usually at the midpoint between Delta blues and the electric Chicago sound; Young usually plays guitar, but also brings out his mandolin for a couple of songs. Warm performances, though not especially noteworthy. The CD reissue adds four previously unreleased bonus cuts. *—Richie Unterberger*

Mighty Joe Young

b. Sep. 23, 1927, Shreveport, LA, **d.** Mar. 27, 1999, Chicago, IL

Vocals, Guitar / Electric Chicago Blues, Chicago Blues

There was a time during the late '70s and early '80s when Mighty Joe Young was one of the leading blues guitarists on Chicago's budding North Side blues circuit. The Louisiana native got his start not in the Windy City, but in Milwaukee, where he was raised. He earned a reputation as a reliable guitarist on Chicago's West Side with Joe Little & His Heart Breakers during the mid-'50s, later changing his on-stage allegiance to harpist Billy Boy Arnold. Young recorded with Arnold for Prestige and Testament during the '60s and backed Jimmy Rogers for Chess in 1958.

After abortive attempts to inaugurate a solo career with Jiffy Records in Louisiana in 1955 and Chicago's Atomic-H label three years later, Young hit his stride in 1961 with the sizzling "Why Baby"/"Empty Arms" for Bobby Robinson's Fire label. Young gigged as Otis Rush's rhythm guitarist from 1960 to 1963 and cut a series of excellent Chicago blues 45s for a variety of firms: "I Want a Love," "Voo Doo Dust," and "Something's Wrong" for Webcor during the mid-'60s; "Something's Wrong" for Webcor in 1966; "Sweet Kisses" and "Henpecked" on Celtex and "Hard Times (Follow Me)" for USA (all 1967); and "Guitar Star" for Jacklyn in 1969. Young even guested on Bill "Hoss" Allen's groundbreaking 1966 syndicated R&B TV program *The Beat* in Dallas. Late-'60s session work included dates with Tyrone Davis and Jimmy Dawkins.

Delmark issued Young's solo album debut, *Blues With a Touch of Soul*, in 1971, but a pair of mid-'70s LPs for Ovation (1974's *Chicken Heads* and an eponymous set in 1976) showcased the guitarist's blues-soul synthesis far more effectively. Young's main local haunt during the '70s and early '80s was Wise Fools Pub, where he packed 'em in nightly (with Freddie King's brother, Benny Turner, on bass).

In 1986 Joe began work on a self-financed recording that would finally allow him to have complete artistic control. At this time he also discovered surgery was needed on a pinched nerve in his neck. Following the operation, complications arose that affected his ability to play guitar. As part of physical therapy he continued to work on the album sporadically until *Mighty Man* was finally released in 1997. Unfortunately health problems continued to plague Mighty Joe and he passed away on March 25, 1999, in Chicago. He was 71. *—Bill Dahl & Al Campbell*

Blues With a Touch of Soul / 1971 / Delmark ♦♦

A soporific album debut for the Chicago guitarist—only seven songs, many of them way too long (10:40 of "Somebody Loan Me a Dime" being the worst offender), which sport little of the excitement of Young's '60s 45s for a variety of local firms. Young doesn't sound like he was prepared for the opportunity, and the stiff two-piece horn section doesn't help either. *—Bill Dahl*

Legacy of the Blues, Vol. 4 / 1972 / GNP Crescendo ♦♦♦

Chicken Heads / 1974 / Ovation ♦♦♦♦

One of Mighty Joe Young's best efforts (and one that's not out on CD), an up-to-the-minute effort that combines soul and blues most effectively. Predominantly original material that suits his booming vocals and stinging guitar well. Nice band, too: Bassist Louis Satterfield, drummer Ira Gates, and keyboardist Floyd Morris were all veterans of the '60s soul session scene. *—Bill Dahl*

● **Mighty Joe Young** / 1976 / Ovation ♦♦♦♦♦

Another out of print collection that's the crown jewel in Young's album discography. Many of Young's finest originals—"Need a Friend," "Takes Money," "Take My Advice (She Likes the Blues and Barbecue)"—reside in their most memorable recorded forms on this worthwhile LP. *—Bill Dahl*

Bluesy Josephine / Nov. 28, 1976 / Evidence ♦♦♦

Not exactly the most incendiary outing that Chicago guitarist Mighty Joe Young has ever cut. This 1976 album was cut in France for Black & Blue with a handful of Chicago stalwarts, but the excitement that Young routinely summoned up back home is in short supply as he walks through "Sweet Home Chicago" and "Five Long Years." Young's own "Takes Money" and "Need a Friend" are a definite improvement on those shopworn standards, but with only seven lengthy selections ("Teasing the Blues" runs 10:27), there isn't a lot to choose from. *—Bill Dahl*

Live at the Wise Fools / 1990 / Quicksilver ♦♦

For much of the 1970s and '80s, guitarist Mighty Joe Young "owned" Chicago's cozy Wise Fools Pub—at least musically speaking. He was the club's top draw, but this live disc, caught at the late and still-lamented Wise Fools, finds him sticking to the tiredest of warhorses. "Stormy Monday," "Turning Point," "That's All Right," and "I Can't Quit You Baby" may have wowed the home folks, but they don't hold up all that well when transferred to the digital format. Young's quartet features Freddie King's brother, Benny Turner, on bass, and Lafayette Leake on piano. *—Bill Dahl*

Mighty Man / May 5, 1997 / Blind Pig ♦♦♦♦

Young embarked on this album in early 1986, financing it himself, determined to finally complete a project his way. But surgery and the subsequent rehabilitation time needed to repair a pinched nerve in his neck (making him unable to play guitar) shelved the project for many years. Young continued writing and recording, however, and with the help of musicians, friends, family, and Blind Pig's Jerry Del Giudice, the project reached completion a decade later. Guitarist Will Crosby handles all the solo work here (Young plays on the three tracks that were completed before his accident), and the majority of tracks feature his son on rhythm guitar. With co-producer Willie Henderson and Gene "Daddy G" Barge doing the horn charts, Leo Davis on keyboards, and the rhythm section of veterans Bernard Reed and B.J. Jones, the resulting mixture is, in Young's words, "a different sound." Those familiar with his spate of 45s for Webcor, Atomic H, U.S.A., and Celtex from the mid-'60s will recognize the direct link these sides have to classic period Chicago-style soul-blues. Tracks like "Turning Point," "Got My Mind on My Woman," "Got a Hold on Me," and the ballad "Bring It On" are soul music deluxe with strong blues roots, and if his fiery guitar work had been silenced, the 70-year-old bluesman continued to look forward with this release. Billy Branch makes a guest appearance on "Wishy Washy Woman," perhaps the most straight-ahead thing on here. *—Cub Koda*

● **Mighty Joe Young** / 2002 / Blind Pig ♦♦♦♦♦

Blind Pig's 2002 release *Mighty Joe Young* is a compilation that picks from Mighty Joe Young's Ovation releases *Chicken Heads* (1974) and *Mighty Joe Young* (1976). These are generally considered to be among Young's best work, yet they have been out of print for years and never have appeared on CD. Thankfully, this collection picks the 12 best tracks from these records, bringing back into circulation the work that showcases Young at his best. While it would have been nice to have these two albums in their entirety in their original running order, the music is so good and so rare, it's nice just to have it out officially, since this is the place to go to hear him at his best. — *Stephen Thomas Erlewine*

Zora Young

b. Jan. 21, 1948, West Point, MS
Vocals / Modern Electric Chicago Blues, Soul-Blues, Blues Gospel

Despite the prominent presence of celebrated blues artist Howlin' Wolf in her family tree, singer Zora Young grew up singing not blues, but gospel. Even when the Mississippi native shook off her roots at the age of seven to relocate with family to Chicago, she attended the Greater Harvest Baptist Church and continued to sing gospel. It wasn't until later that she switched over to R&B, and evolved into a powerhouse blues vocalist with three decades of experience behind her. She has performed with a long list of artists, including Junior Wells, Jimmy Dawkins, Bobby Rush, Buddy Guy, Professor Eddie Lusk, Albert King, and B.B. King. Her recording credits include collaborations with Willie Dixon, Sunnyland Slim, Mississippi Heat, Paul deLay, and Maurice John Vaughn, among others. Her own recordings as a solo artist include releases from the labels Deluge, Black Lightning, and Delmark. Young has also performed on both television and stage. She is a veteran of more than 30 tours of Europe, and she has been a featured performer three times at the Chicago Blues Festival. She has performed throughout North America, and on stages in Italy, Germany, Belgium, Sweden, France, Switzerland, and Greece, as well as Austria, Taipei, and Turkey. — *Linda Seida*

● **Travelin' Light** / Sep. 1991 / Deluge ✦✦✦✦

An absolutely dynamite debut from this growly and sultry blues belter. With the focus on Young's brassy original material, this is one modern blues album that's a winner all the way. — *Cub Koda*

Learned My Lesson / 2000 / Delmark ✦✦✦

All the songs played in Chicago blues clubs don't necessarily have 12 bars. Many of Chicago's blues singers are also R&B and/or rock singers, and Zora Young is a prime example. Based in Chi-Town but originally from Mississippi, the expressive singer provides an enjoyable, if derivative, blues/soul/rock mix on her 2000 date *Learned My Lesson*. Young is far from a blues purist—while "My Man's an Undertaker" and Young originals like the humorous "Pity Party" are straight-up urban blues, she confidently detours into soul and rock territory on "Girl Friend" (another Young original) and sweaty performances of Ike & Tina Turner's "Nutbush City Limits" and Chuck Berry's "Living in the U.S.A." Meanwhile, Young draws heavily on her gospel background on a passionate version of Percy Mayfield's "Please Send Me Someone to Love." No one will accuse Young of being an innovator; drawing on such influences as Koko Taylor and Etta James, she is quite derivative. But a CD doesn't have to be groundbreaking to be likable, and *Learned My Lesson* is a CD that's easy to like. — *Alex Henderson*

Z

Tony Z (Tony Zamagni)
b. Boston, MA
Organ / Jazz Blues, Modern Electric Blues, Soul-Blues

Hammond B-3 blues organist Tony Z was long a fixture on the New England blues club circuit, and for two years as part of Boston-area guitarist Ronnie Earl's touring band, the Broadcasters.

Born and raised in Boston, Tony Zamagni began playing organ at St. Patrick's School in Roxbury. He cut his musical teeth with the Boston band Combat Zone and then went on to play with the Platters for the next ten years. He spent most of the latter part of the 1980s trying to organize his own touring band (no small feat) and working as a session player in Miami for TK Records, where he recorded an LP with the group Miami. After meeting Ronnie Earl through a mutual friend, trumpeter Bob Enos, Zamagni teamed up with the guitarist and joined his road band, the Broadcasters, from 1989 to 1991.

In 1991, Zamagni moved to Chicago, where he worked for three years with guitarist Larry McCray and found work as a session musician on albums by Son Seals, Saffire, Little Smokey Smothers, and Lee "Shot" Williams. Zamagni's debut album, *Get Down With the Blues*, was released on Rounder's Tone-Cool subsidiary in 1995. The outing is first-class, self-produced in Chicago's Streeterville Studios with some stellar backing musicians: former Roomful of Blues guitarist Duke Robillard, drummer Bernard "Pretty" Purdie, saxophonist Houston Person, harmonica master Sugar Blue, and former Albert Collins band bassist Johnny B. Gayden. Buddy Guy was so impressed by *Get Down With the Blues* that he hired Tony Z to tour with him. In 1998 Tony Z released his second record for Tone-Cool, *Kiss My Blues*. The record featured another all-star cast, including Cornell Dupree on guitar, Bernard "Pretty" Purdie on drums again, Chuck Rainey on bass, Lenny Pickett on sax, and Kim Wilson blowing harp on two tracks. Since then he has toured with Buddy Guy and on his own, continuing to spread his unique take on the B-3 sound—*Richard Skelly*

Get Down With the Blues / 1995 / Tone-Cool ✦✦✦

● **Kiss My Blues** / Jan. 13, 1998 / Tone-Cool ✦✦✦✦

Keyboardist Tony Z uses the Hammond B-3 organ blues sound and style to paint a new tapestry of music on this disc. The groove on this album is immensely fortified by the formidable presence of Cornell Dupree on guitar, Bernard Purdie on drums, and Chuck Rainey on bass as the rhythm section. But instead of aping the tunes and styles of B-3 masters like Jimmy Smith, Jimmy McGriff, or Groove Holmes, Tony comes to the plate with a batch of his own songs for this album. With Lenny Pickett emoting soulfully on saxophone and a two-song guest turn from Kim Wilson on harmonica, this session goes into realms previously uncharted by your Hammond B-3 practitioner, retro or otherwise. Highlights include "Voodootize Me Baby," "All Alone," "You Ain't Who You Think You Are," and "Communicate." —*Cub Koda*

Zephyr
f. 1968, Denver, CO
Group / Psychedelic, Hard Rock, Blues-Rock, Album Rock

This late-'60s Denver group is most notable as the starting point for guitarist Tommy Bolin, who was still in his teens when they recorded their first album in 1969. A rather routine slab of bluesy, heavy rock, it made the Top 50. Aside from Bolin's extended hard rock riffing, it prominently featured the lead vocals of Candy Givens, who affected a blues-wailing pose along the lines of Janis Joplin. But she didn't have the full throat or guts to back it up, ending up closer to also-ran female psychedelic singers like Lydia Pense (of Cold Blood). Zephyr recorded one more album before Bolin left for stints with James Gang, Deep Purple, and a solo career; the group carried on with little success throughout the 1970s. —*Richie Unterberger*

Zephyr / 1969 / One Way ✦✦✦✦

The band's debut finds Bolin already developed as a skilled player, but his playing, and the largely group-penned material, lacks strength or subtlety. The most distinctive trait of the band at this point, in fact, is the somewhat histrionic singing of lead vocalist Candy Givens. —*Richie Unterberger*

Going Back to Colorado / 1971 / Warner Brothers ✦✦✦

The second and last Zephyr LP to feature wunderkind guitarist Tommy Bolin, *Going Back to Colorado* is a '70s rock sleeper, popular only among obsessive Bolin fans. Singer Candy Givens refines her Joplinesque delivery on the 1971 Warner Brothers release, but fails to define a sound of her own. Hippy-drippy moments like those on "Miss Libertine" come off as a little naïve, and the entire recording lacks a unique vision. When Bolin rips it up on tracks like "See My People Come Together," all the revolutionary clichés become tolerable. Unfortunately, most of this album's material is tired, and Givens' delivery is too derivative. Bolin has his share of shining moments, but they are not quite in keeping with his band's "free love" aesthetic, and ultimately the choice licks are wasted on *Going Back to Colorado*. Fans of the guitarist should still snatch this record up when they can, if for no other reason than to chart Bolin's musical development. —*Vincent Jeffries*

● **Sunset Ride** / May 1972 / One Way ✦✦✦✦

There are two kinds of Zephyr fans; those who think the band died when Tommy Bolin left, and those who know it didn't. This second and final album for Warner featured Boulder, CO, guitar slinger Jock Bartley in place of Tommy Bolin, the replacement of Bobby Berge and John Faris, and one of the few known recorded appearances of Bobby Notkoff, other than his work with Neil Young, for whom he created the heart-wrenching violin break on "Running Dry." Without Bolin, the band took a decided turn toward jazz. This is a stunning album, featuring unknown classics like "Moving Too Fast," "Chasing Clouds," and "Winter Always Finds Me." Lead singer Candy Givens passed away some years ago, and this album is perhaps her most passionate legacy. Reissued on CD by the One Way label in 2000. —*William Ashford*

Zephyr Live / May 13, 1997 / Tommy Bolin Archives ✦✦✦

Rusty Zinn
b. Apr. 3, 1970, Long Beach, CA
Guitar / Modern Electric Blues

A young, red-haired guitarist with a monster tone and technique that belies his relatively young years, Rusty Zinn grew up in the Santa Cruz mountains in northern California. He was introduced to classic R&B through his mother's collection of 45 singles, which included rare discs from Fats Domino and Elvis Presley. While in his teens, his brother brought home recordings by Muddy Waters and Howlin' Wolf, and these proved to be a revelation for the young blues aficionado. He would empty his pockets regularly to purchase blues recordings and became fascinated by the guitar stylings of Robert Jr. Lockwood, Eddie Taylor, Luther Tucker, and Jimmy Rogers. These records prompted him to begin playing guitar at 17.

He had some background in music, having played drums when he was younger, but he enjoyed another crystallizing moment when he saw Luther Tucker perform with Jimmy Rogers at a local club. He credits the nightclub showcase with changing his life, and he sought out all the recordings he could find with Luther Tucker as a sideman, which included records by Little Walter Jacobs, Muddy Waters, Sonny Boy Williamson and James Cotton. A year later, when Zinn again went to see his idol, Tucker invited him onstage. Tucker took the young Zinn under his wing and shared guitar techniques with him. Meanwhile, Zinn was working with several northern California blues bands in the late '80s, and he was often tapped to back touring musicians like Snooky Pryor and Rogers.

After joining Mark Hummel's band, Zinn honed his craft through hundreds of shows and thousands of miles. One of the shows with Hummel's band was at the San Francisco Blues Festival, where Zinn was introduced to harp player Kim Wilson. Wilson invited Zinn to come to Austin's Arlyn Studios to play on his 1993 album *Tigerman*, for the Antone's label. Wilson soon put together a band that included Zinn on guitar, ex-Canned Heat bass player Larry Taylor, and former Blaster "Blue" Gene Taylor on keyboards. Zinn toured around with Wilson and his band, surprising Wilson with the dexterity of his playing at such a young age (he was then in his early twenties).

In early 1996, Wilson approached Black Top Records executives about recording Zinn, and fortunately, they agreed with him.

Zinn's debut for the Crescent City-based Black Top Records, *Sittin' and Waitin'*, was released in 1996. Naturally, he's accompanied by his friend and mentor Kim Wilson throughout his first album, who also served as producer. *Confessin'* followed three years later, with *The Chill* surfacing in fall 2000. —*Richard Skelly*

● **Sittin' & Waitin'** / Jun. 18, 1996 / Black Top ✦✦✦✦

Confessin' / Jan. 26, 1999 / Black Top ✦✦✦✦

This is a long-awaited release by a promising guitarist. Rusty Zinn carries more weight than the guitar-slinger epithet tells. He is an exceptional songwriter, as the five tunes he wrote or co-wrote on this disc will show. Plus, he is a singer and is exceptionally good at handling other people's material. Give a listen to the treatment he gives to Robert Nighthawk's "Someday"; he makes it his own song without messing up the writer's intentions. A very large plus is that the material he is doing isn't the Chicago sound that is so popular with a lot of young guitarists. He is using Austin, TX, as his base and has quite a bit of the Texas countrified blues influence in his music. This is music that at times strays into the West Texas bluesy countrified sound of Bob Wills & His Texas Playboys. It is definitely a more laid-back and rural sound that leaves room for each of the players in the two bands he uses to great advantage here, to give short but effective solos. It is more ensemble and group effort than individual flash. Both groups are equally tight and able to go with the song; one has just a little more of a citified sound while still avoiding that Chicago guitar-driven emphasis. He uses his bandmates very well; look at the room he gives Jimmy Pugh to stretch out on organ in "Confessin' About My Baby." Or maybe you'd prefer the space Little Charlie Baty fills taking over the lead guitar and solos on "Someday." If you have any doubts about his roots, just listen to what he does by himself on the Rick Estrin tune "Come Get These Blues Up Off Me." This is a another top-notch disc of interesting blues on the Black Top label that you'll want to get your hands on. *—Bob Gottlieb*

The Chill / Sep. 12, 2000 / Alligator ♦♦♦

Zinn's talent as a guitarist cannot be denied. But his brand of Texas blues is flat and unimaginative, sounding too much like Stevie Ray Vaughn too often. Ultimately, tunes like "Just Like a Fish" and "Fallin' Rain" just don't have enough unique personality to set Zinn apart from a crowded field of guitar slingers. *—Tim Sheridan*

Zydeco Force

f. 1988, Opelousas, LA

Group / Zydeco

Originally formed in the spirit of the rural, old-time zydeco style, over time the Opelousas, LA-based group Zydeco Force began moving toward a funkier, more bass-driven sound reflecting a wide range of influences. Upon debuting in 1988, Zydeco Force comprised bandleader Bobby "Mann" Robinson, vocalist/accordionist Jeffery Broussard (the son of Lawtell Playboys frontman Delton Broussard), his brothers Hebert on rub board and Shelton on guitar, and drummer Raymond Thomas. Quickly their propulsive sound caught on with dancehall audiences throughout Louisiana and East Texas, and in 1990 they released their self-titled debut LP, followed a year later by *The Sun's Going Down*. After issuing 1992's *Shaggy Dog Two-Step*, Zydeco Force returned in 1994 with *The Zydeco Push*, with the title track spawning a lambada-like dance craze among fans. *It's La La Time* followed in 1995. *—Jason Ankeny*

Shaggy Dog Two-Step / 1992 / Maison de Soul ♦♦♦♦

● **The Zydeco Push** / 1994 / Maison de Soul ♦♦♦♦

Zydeco Force are caught between trying to extend their popularity with pop covers and then verifying their credentials doing Clifton Chenier's "I'm on the Wonder" and Lightnin' Hopkins' "12-String Boogie." As a result, an air of confusion reigns, and they seldom sound either comfortable or creditable. *—Ron Wynn*

It's La La Time / Apr. 11, 1995 / Flat Town ♦♦♦

You Mean the World to Me / Oct. 9, 2001 / Maison de Soul ♦♦♦

Zydeco Hurricanes

f. Louisiana

Group / Zydeco

The Zydeco Hurricanes were led by guitarist Selwyn Cooper, a noted sideman who toured with such renowned figures as Clifton Chenier, Buckwheat Zydeco, Rockin' Dopsie, and Fernest Arceneaux. Additionally including bassist Alonzo Johnson, Jr. (himself a Chenier alum as well) and former Buckwheat Zydeco drummer Nathaniel Jolivette, as well as two newcomers—vocalist/accordionist John Wilson and washboard player Adam Robinson—the Zydeco Hurricanes made their debut in 1995 with *Louisiana Zydeco!* *—Jason Ankeny*

● **Louisiana Zydeco!** / Mar. 28, 1995 / Mardi Gras ♦♦♦♦

ZZ Top

f. 1970, Houston, TX

Group / Album Rock, Boogie Rock, Arena Rock, Southern Rock, Hard Rock, Blues-Rock

This sturdy American blues-rock trio from Texas consists of Billy Gibbons (guitar), Dusty Hill (bass), and Frank Beard (drums). They were formed in 1970 in and around Houston from rival bands the Moving Sidewalks (Gibbons) and the American Blues (Hill and Beard). Their first two albums reflected the strong blues roots and Texas humor of the band. Their third album (*Tres Hombres*) gained them national attention with the hit "La Grange," a signature riff tune to this day, based on John Lee Hooker's "Boogie Chillen." Their success continued unabated throughout the '70s, culminating with the year-and-a-half-long Worldwide Texas Tour.

Exhausted from the overwhelming workload, they took a three-year break, then switched labels and returned to form with *Deguello* and *El Loco*, both harbingers of what was to come. By their next album, *Eliminator*, and its worldwide smash follow-up, *Afterburner*, they had successfully harnessed the potential of synthesizers to their patented grungy blues-groove, giving their material a more contemporary edge while retaining their patented Texas style. Now sporting long beards, golf hats, and boiler suits, they met the emerging video age head-on, reducing their "message" to simple iconography. Becoming even more popular in the long run, they moved with the times while simultaneously bucking every trend that crossed their path.

As genuine roots musicians, they have few peers; Gibbons is one of America's finest blues guitarists working in the arena rock idiom—both influenced by the originators of the form and British blues-rock guitarists like Peter Green—while Hill and Beard provide the ultimate rhythm section support. The only rock & roll group that's out there with its original members still aboard after three decades (an anniversary celebrated on 1999's *XXX*), ZZ Top's music is always instantly recognizable, eminently powerful, profoundly soulful, and 100 percent American in derivation. They have continued to support the blues through various means, perhaps the most visible when they were given a piece of wood from Muddy Waters' shack in Clarksdale, MS. The group members had it made into a guitar, dubbed the "Muddywood," then sent it out on tour to raise money for the Delta Blues Museum. ZZ Top's support and link to the blues remains as rock-solid as the music they play. *—Cub Koda*

ZZ Top's First Album / 1970 / Warner Brothers ♦♦♦

ZZ Top's First Album may not be perfectly polished, but it does establish their sound, attitude, and quirks. Simply put, it's a dirty little blues-rock record, filled with fuzzy guitars, barrelhouse rhythms, dirty jokes, and Texan slang. They have a good, ballsy sound that hits at gut level, and if the record's not entirely satisfying, it's because they're still learning how to craft records—which means that they're still learning pacing as much as they're learning how to assemble a set of indelible material. Too much of this record glides by on its sound, without offering any true substance, but the tracks that really work—"(Somebody Else Been) Shaking Your Tree," "Backdoor Love Affair," "Brown Sugar," and "Goin' Down to Mexico," among them—show that ZZ Top was that lil' ol' blues band from Texas from their very first record on. *—Stephen Thomas Erlewine*

Rio Grande Mud / 1972 / Warner Brothers ♦♦♦

With their second album, *Rio Grande Mud*, ZZ Top uses the sound they sketched out on their debut as a blueprint, yet tweak it in slight but important ways. The first is heavier, more powerful sound, turning the boogie guitars into a locomotive force. There are slight production flares that date this as a 1972 record, but for the most part, this is a straight-ahead, dirty blues-rock difference. Essentially like the first album, then. That's where the second difference comes in—they have a much better set of songs this time around, highlighted by the swaggering shuffle "Just Got Paid," the pile-driving boogie "Bar-B-Q," the slide guitar workout "Apologies to Pearly," and two Dusty Hill-sung numbers, "Francine" and "Chevrolet." There are still a couple of tracks that don't quite gel and their fuzz-blues still can sound a little one-dimensional at times, but *Rio Grande Mud* is the first flowering of ZZ Top as a great, down 'n' dirty blooze-rock band. *—Stephen Thomas Erlewine*

Tres Hombres / 1973 / Warner Brothers ♦♦♦♦♦

Tres Hombres is the record that brought ZZ Top their first Top Ten record, making them stars in the process. It couldn't have happened to a better record. ZZ Top finally got their low-down, cheerfully sleazy blooze 'n' boogie right on this, their third album. As their sound gelled, producer Bill Ham discovered how to record the trio so simply that they sound indestructible, and the group brought the best set of songs they'd ever have to the table. On the surface, there's nothing really special about the record, since it is just a driving blues-rock album from a Texas bar band, but that's what's special about it. It has a filthy groove and an infectious feel, thanks to Billy Gibbons' growling guitars and the steady propulsion of Dusty Hill and Frank Beard's rhythm section. They get the blend of bluesy shuffles, gut-bucket rocking, and off-beat humor just right. ZZ Top's very identity comes from this earthy sound and songs as utterly infectious as "Waitin' for the Bus," "Jesus Just Left Chicago," "Move Me on Down the Line," and the John Lee Hooker boogie "La Grange." In a sense, they kept trying to remake this record from this point on—what is *Eliminator* if not *Tres Hombres* with sequencers and synthesizers?—but they never got it better than they did here. *—Stephen Thomas Erlewine*

Fandango / 1975 / Warner Brothers ♦♦♦

Blessed with their first full-fledged hit album, ZZ Top followed it up with *Fandango*, a record split between a side of live tracks and a side of new studio cuts. In a way, this might have made sense, since they were a kickass live band, and they do sound good here, but it's hard not to see this as a bit of a wasted opportunity in retrospect. Why? Because the studio side is a worthy successor to the all-fine *Tres Hombres*, driven by "Tush" and "Heard It on the X," two of their greatest songs that build on that album by consolidating their sound and amplifying their humor. If they had sustained this energy and quality throughout a full studio album, it would have been their greatest, but instead the mood is broken by the live cuts. Now, these are really good live cuts—and "Backdoor Medley" and "Jailhouse Rock" were fine interpretations, making familiar songs sound utterly comfortable in their signature sound—and *Fandango* remains one of their better albums, but it's hard not to think that it could have been even better. *—Stephen Thomas Erlewine*

Tejas / 1976 / Warner Brothers ♦♦

ZZ Top was riding high in the mid-'70s on the strength of *Tres Hombres* and *Fandango*, but they were starting to run out of steam by 1976's *Tejas*. Its predecessor was padded with a live side, but even if it was close to padding, it was still enjoyable. *Tejas*, despite sounding pretty good, is just forgettable. It has the patented, propulsive ZZ boogie, but none of the songs are particularly memorable, even if the whole thing sounds pretty good as it's playing. ZZ Top and their label, London, must have noticed this too, since even though the album went gold, they followed it months later with *The Best of ZZ Top*, which contained none of the songs from this album. *—Stephen Thomas Erlewine*

● **The Best of ZZ Top** / 1977 / Warner Brothers ♦♦♦♦♦

ZZ Top closed out their tenure with London Records in 1977 with *The Best of ZZ Top*, a basic but terrific ten-song retrospective of highlights from their first five albums (well, four, actually, since the underwhelming *Tejas* is ignored). There are no surprises here, just album rock favorites, which means it does draw heavily on *Tres Hombres* (four songs, total), adds *Fandango*'s "Tush," "Blue Jean Blues," and "Heard It on the X" for good measure, then rounds it out with two songs from *Rio Grande Mud* and a selection from the debut. Yeah, there are a couple good album tracks missing, but as a ten-song summary of their early years, this can't be beat. *—Stephen Thomas Erlewine*

Deguello / 1979 / Warner Brothers ♦♦♦♦♦

ZZ Top returned after an extended layoff in late 1979 with *Deguello*, their best album since 1973's *Tres Hombres*. During their time off, ZZ Top didn't change much—hell, their sound never really changed during their entire career—but it did harden, in a way. The grooves became harder, sleeker, and their off-kilter sensibility and humor began to dominate, as "Cheap Sunglasses" and "Fool for Your Stockings" illustrate. Ironically, this, their wildest album lyrically, doesn't have the unhinged rawness of their early blooze rockers, but the streamlined production makes it feel sleazier all the same, since its slickness lets the perversity slide forth. And, let us not forget, the trio is in fine shape here, knocking out a great set of rockers and sounding stylish all the time. Undoubtedly one of their strong suits. *—Stephen Thomas Erlewine*

El Loco / 1981 / Warner Brothers ♦♦♦

El Loco follows through on the streamlined, jet-engine boogie-rock of *Deguello*, but kicking all the ingredients up a notch. That means that the grooves are getting a little slicker, while the jokes are getting a little sillier, a little raunchier. The double entendres on "Tube Snake Boogie" and "Pearl Necklace" are barely disguised, while much of the record plays as flat-out goofy party rock. Not necessarily a bad thing, but much of it is a little too obvious to be totally winning. Still, the most telling thing about *El Loco* may be the rhythm of "Pearl Necklace," its biggest single and best song, which clearly points the way to the new wave blues-rock of *Eliminator*. —*Stephen Thomas Erlewine*

Eliminator / 1983 / Warner Brothers ♦♦♦♦♦

ZZ Top had reached the top of the charts before, but that didn't make their sudden popularity in 1983 any more predictable. It wasn't that they were just popular—they were *hip*, for God's sake, since they were one of the only AOR favorites to figure out to harness the stylish, synthesized grooves of new wave, and then figure out how to sell it on MTV. Of course, it helped that they had songs that deserved to be hits. With "Gimme All Your Lovin'," "Sharp Dressed Man," and "Legs," they had their greatest set of singles since the heady days of *Tres Hombres*, and the songs that surrounded them weren't bad either—they would have been singles on *El Loco*, as a matter of fact. The songs alone would have made *Eliminator* one of ZZ Top's three greatest albums, but their embrace of synths and sequencers made it a blockbuster hit, since it was the sound of the times. Years later, the sound of the times winds up sounding a bit stiff. It's still an excellent ZZ Top album, one of their best, yet it sounds like a mechanized ZZ Top thanks to the unflaggingly accurate grooves. Then again, that's part of the album's charm—this is new wave blues-rock, glossed up for the video, looking as good as the omnipresent convertible on the cover and sounding as irresistible as Reaganomics. Not the sort the old-school fans or blues-rock purists will love, but ZZ Top never sounded as much like a band of its time as they did here. —*Stephen Thomas Erlewine*

Afterburner / 1985 / Warner Brothers ♦♦♦

Well, if you just had your biggest hit ever, you'd probably try to replicate it, too. And if you were called visionary because you played your blues to a slightly sequenced beat, you'd probably be tempted to turn on the drum-machine and graft on synthesizers, too, since it'll all signal how futuristic you are. While you're at it, you might as well visualize how space age this all is by turning your signature car into a space shuttle. From this viewpoint, *Afterburner* makes perfect sense—ZZ Top are just giving the people *more* of what they want. Problem is, no matter how much you dress 'em up, they're still ZZ Top, they're still that li'l ol' blues band from Texas, and blues-rock just doesn't have a kick when it's synthesized, even if ZZ Top's grooves always bordered on robotic. So, *Afterburner*, their most synthetic album, will not please most ZZ Top fans, even if it did go platinum several times over. That's just a sign of the times, when even hard rock bands had to sound as slick as synth-pop, complete with clanging DX-7s and cavernous drums. As an artifact of that time, *Afterburner* is pretty good—never has a hard rock album sounded so artificial, nor has a blues-rock album sounded so devoid of blues. Apart from the chugging "Sleeping Bag," not even the singles sound like ZZ Top: the terrific post-new wave rocker "Stages" is the poppiest thing they ever cut, the ballad "Rough Boy" is far removed from slow blues, and the full-fledged synth-blooze of "Velcro Fly" is a true mind-bender. Above all, *Afterburner* is merely an album of its time—the only record ZZ Top could have made in 1985, and it remains forever tied to that year. —*Stephen Thomas Erlewine*

Recycler / 1990 / Warner Brothers ♦♦

The continuation of *Eliminator*'s synthesized blues-boogie made sense on *Afterburner*, since it arrived two years after its predecessor. ZZ Top's choice to pursue that direction on *Recycler* is puzzling, since a full five years separates this from *Afterburner*. It's not just that they continue to follow this path, it's that they embalm it, creating a record that may be marginally ballsier than its predecessor, but lacking the sense of goofy fun and warped ambition that made *Afterburner* fascinating. Here, there's just a steady, relentless beat (Frank Beard is still chained to the sequencer, as he has been for a decade), topped off by processed guitars turning out licks that fall short of being true riffs. Put it this way, apart from "Doubleback," a continuation of the arena pop of "Stages," the other number that really works here is "My Head's in Mississippi," the closest they've come to the greasy boogie of "La Grange" since *Deguello*. When it arrives halfway through *Recycler*, it not only sounds refreshing, it puts the rest of the album in perspective, showing how tired the once-bracing synth-blooze-boogie has become. And the worst thing about it all, it doesn't seem like the band realizes how uncomfortably ironic the title of *Recycler* is. —*Stephen Thomas Erlewine*

Greatest Hits / Apr. 14, 1992 / Warner Brothers ♦♦♦♦♦

This isn't a perfect roundup of ZZ Top's superstar years of the '80s, but it comes pretty close. It dips back into the '70s for "Pearl Necklace" and "La Grange," with a couple of selections from the post-peak '90s, but this does offer the MTV-era basics: "Gimme All Your Lovin'," "Sharp Dressed Man," "Rough Boy," "Tush," "My Head's in Mississippi," "Doubleback," "Cheap Sunglasses," "Sleeping Bag." What slows this record down are some new cuts and album tracks that don't deserve to be here, along with a remix, not the original version, of "Legs." Still, that may just be quibbling for some listeners, since the basics are all here, making this a good complement to the '70s-focused *The Best of ZZ Top* (although it would be nice if a definitive disc, with all the hits, would appear on the market). —*Stephen Thomas Erlewine*

Antenna / Jan. 18, 1994 / RCA ♦♦♦

Like precious few bands from the '70s whose best work is mummified daily thanks to classic rock radio, ZZ Top just keeps rolling on into the next decade. There's much to love here, from the downright nasty stomp of "Fuzzbox Voodoo," the powerhouse slow blues of "Cover Your Rig," the bass-pumping looniness of "Girl in a T-Shirt," to the slow grind of "Breakaway." While Billy Gibbons' guitar tones on this album are highly reminiscent of *Tres Hombres* (an early high-water mark for the band), the high production sheen from their '80s albums remains intact. But Gibbons hasn't played with this much over-the-top abandon since their pre-beard 'n' babes days, and that's what separates this album from the three that came before it. —*Cub Koda*

One Foot in the Blues / Nov. 22, 1994 / Warner Brothers ♦♦

Before they sweated their image down to beards, babes, and hot rods, ZZ Top were a down 'n' dirty blues-rock trio with a bona fide hot guitar player in Billy Gibbons. On this 14-track offering, Warner goes back through the back ZZ catalog and cobbles together an interesting collection of the Texas trio's bluesier sides that originally appeared on their earliest albums. Highlights include "Brown Sugar," "A Fool for Your Stockings," "My Head's in Mississippi," "Apologies to Pearly," and Gibbons' storming stringwork on "Bar-B-Q." —*Cub Koda*

Rhythmeen / Sep. 17, 1996 / RCA ♦♦♦

ZZ Top's long-awaited return to the blues finally arrived in 1996, well over a decade after they abandoned their simple three-chord boogie for a synth and drum machine-driven three-chord boogie. Like *Antenna* before it, *Rhythmeen* is stripped of all the synthesizers that characterized the group's albums since *Eliminator* but the key difference between the two albums is how *Rhythmeen* goes for the gut, not the gloss. It's a record that is steeped in the blues and garage rock, one that pounds out its riffs with sweat and feeling. Though ZZ Top sounds reinvigorated, playing with a salacious abandon they haven't displayed since the '70s, they simply haven't come up with enough interesting songs and riffs to make it a true return to form. For dedicated fans, it's a welcome return to their classic "La Grange" sound, but anyone with a just a passing interest in the band will wonder where the hooks went. —*Stephen Thomas Erlewine*

XXX / Sep. 28, 1999 / RCA ♦♦

Theoretically, aging wouldn't be that difficult of a trick for ZZ Top to pull off, since the little ol' band from Texas is thoroughly grounded in the blues, an ageless music that can sound equally good from the young and old alike. So why does ZZ Top sound so stiff and useless on *XXX*, a record celebrating their 30th anniversary? Part of it could be that the songwriting is decidedly weak, but a band as seasoned as ZZ Top should be able to make third-rate material at least listenable. The real problem is that the band long ago sacrificed organic rhythms for a steady synthesized pulse. They suggested this even before 1983's *Eliminator*, but that record was a bizarre, unpredictable masterstroke; after all, nobody would have predicted that a blend of Texas blues-rock and new wave drum machines would work, let alone flourish. The problem was, the massive success of *Eliminator* made ZZ Top reluctant to abandon that sound; on every album since, they retained the steady click track, even as they stripped away the synthesizers. Each album of the '90s suffered because of this, but *XXX* really reveals the extent of the damage, possibly because it should have been a celebratory release, possibly because it ends with four tracks that were recorded live but sound as processed as the eight studio cuts that precede them. There is no grit or sensuality to the music, no propulsion in the rhythm, and no joy to the playing; even when the band stretches out, they feel tightly wound. Ironically, ZZ Top doesn't follow the advice they offer in "Fearless Boogie": They're too scared of sounding organic to really let loose and boogie, or play the blues like the accomplished veterans they are. —*Stephen Thomas Erlewine*

Various Artists

15 Down Home Gospel Classics / Jan. 20, 1998 / Arhoolie ✦✦✦✦
Arhoolie, as is made plain in this 15-song sampler of their gospel catalog, does not favor slick modern spiritual music. (Or, as they say straight-up in the brief liner note, "The selections on this disc…are not by trendy, popular massed choirs.") Much of this is in fact gospel-blues: spiritually oriented numbers by major bluesmen Big Joe Williams, Mance Lipscomb, Robert Pete Williams, Jesse Fuller (a nice slide guitar treatment of "Amazing Grace"), and Mississippi Fred McDowell, as well as more contemporary steel guitar-flavored gospel by Aubrey Ghent. The arrangements are sparse (sometimes acoustic) and the vocals are soulful, not just by the aforementioned acts, but also by such relative unknowns as the Campbell Brothers, who work more in a contemporary electric vein. It's not being heretical to say that there's more passion and musical quality on this compilation than there is on innumerable glossily produced gospel recordings by feel-good ensembles with higher profiles. By the way, the track by steel guitarist Black Ace, "Farther Along," was previously unissued on CD. —*Richie Unterberger*

1942–45: The R&B Hits / Nov. 5, 1997 / Indigo ✦✦✦✦
Yet another excellent collection from British blues and R&B label Indigo, *1942-45: The R&B Hits* chronicles the heady period when small and big band swing morphed into jump blues in major cities across the U.S. Including 44 cuts spread over two discs, the mix takes in most of the major players, including Louis Jordan, Lucky Millinder, Wynonie Harris, Joe Turner, Jimmy Rushing, the Count Basie band, and Jimmy Liggins. Also on hand are such smoothies as Nat King Cole, Ivory Joe Hunter, and Helen Humes. And the party rolls on, as mighty contributions are heard from vintage blues picker Tampa Red, R&B-hewn jazz diva Dinah Washington, rock & roll forefather Arthur "Big Boy" Crudup (they're all forerunners, for that matter), and vibraphone master Lionel Hampton. Crucial cuts abound and the joint just keeps getting hotter. —*Stephen Cook*

20 to Life: Prison Blues—Songs from the Angola State Penitentiary / Nov. 13, 2001 / Fuel 2000 ✦✦✦
A date of significant historic value, these field recordings took place in Angola State Penitentiary featuring solo performances usually accompanied by six- or 12-string guitar. There is even a full-band performance featuring Cyprien Huston & the Cool Cats. *20 to Life* adds an interesting twist to most prison recordings from the same time period. Those tunes, sung on the chain gang, tended to be call and response, usually featuring the human voice as the lone instrument. These laments are of a more lyrically personal statement with a haunting nature. The musicianship is intricate in its simplicity. Another fine reissue from the Fuel 2000 label. —*Al Campbell*

20th Century Blues [Catfish] / Apr. 18, 2000 / Catfish ✦✦✦
This four-disc box set is a veritable treasure chest of early prewar blues with a cut-off point somewhere in the early '50s. The first disc features seminal tracks from the dawn of the music by Bessie Smith ("Weeping Willow Blues"), Blind Blake ("West Coast Blues number two"), Barbecue Bob ("Barbecue Blues"), Blind Lemon Jefferson ("One Dime Blues," Tommy Johnson ("Cool Drink of Water Blues"), and Ma Rainey ("See See Rider Blues"). Disc two features sides by Charley Patton, Son House, Big Bill Broonzy, Memphis Minnie, and Charley Patton. The third disc features classics by Bo Carter, Robert Johnson, Blind Boy Fuller, and Black Ace, while the final volume finally showcases a few postwar performances from Louis Jordan, Muddy Waters, Pee Wee Crayton, John Lee Hooker (the original "Boogie Chillen"), and B.B. King. Each of the four discs in the set pack a generous 25 tracks apiece and the transfers are reasonably decent, taking into consideration the rarity of many of the materials at hand. —*Cub Koda*

40th Anniversary Blues / 1993 / Delmark ✦✦✦
Delmark's jazz anthology deserves praise despite the fundamental problems inherent within the sampler concept; the same holds true for its blues collection. This is a good 19-cut retrospective item containing exceptional cuts by Robert Jr. Lockwood, Otis Rush, J.B. Hutto, Roosevelt Sykes and Magic Sam, plus nice ones from Jimmy Johnson, Arthur "Big Boy" Crudup, Yank Rachell and Big Joe Williams. But no Eddie "Cleanhead" Vinson? —*Ron Wynn*

Absolutely the Best of the Blues, Vol. 2 / Jul. 18, 2000 / Varese ✦✦✦✦
Fuel 2000's *Absolutely the Best of the Blues, Vol. 2* collects 14 remastered classics from Otis Spann, Big Bill Broonzy, Peppermint Harris, Lightnin' Hopkins, and other blues greats. Buddy Guy's "This Is the End," Sunnyland Slim's "Highway 61," Mississippi John Hurt's "Make Me a Pallet on Your Floor," and Big Joe Turner's "Nighttime Is the Right Time" are among the highlights of the set, which features previously unreleased performances and extensive liner notes. While it may not entirely live up to its title, *Absolutely the Best of the Blues, Vol. 2* is another solid compilation of blues standards. —*Heather Phares*

Ace Blues Masters, Vol. 1: Sing My Blues Tonight / Apr. 7, 1998 / Westside ✦✦✦
This first volume in Westside's exploration of the blues treasures from the original Jackson, MS-based Ace label yields a treasure trove of unreleased gems. Only five of the

25 selections have seen release before, either on original Ace 45s or on album. Culled from various sessions, these tracks feature tracks from Floyd Dixon, H-Bomb Ferguson, Amos Milburn, and Charles Brown. An extra bonus is that all of the tracks here by Floyd Dixon and the majority of those by Charles Brown reveal crude, but effective, stereo recordings from the late '50s, a treat for the ears, combining the old sound in a new format. This compilation is simply a jump blues aficionado's dream. —*Cub Koda*

Ace Blues Masters, Vol. 2: 4th & Beale and Further South / Jun. 9, 1998 / Westside ✦✦✦✦✦
This second volume of blues recordings from the vaults of the Jackson, MS-based Ace label yields several tracks to make this a compilation well worth revisiting again and again. It kicks off with six songs from a 1954 unissued session on Memphis musician Joe Hill Louis, with Joe Hill trimming his one-man-band approach down to singing and playing guitar while a three-piece combo beefs up the ensemble sound. Also on board are four songs from Arthur "Big Boy" Crudup's 1952 session for the label. Two of these tracks ("My Baby Boogies All the Time" and "I Wonder") saw issuance as a single on Ace, while an atmospheric "Mean Old World" later came out on a Japanese album. The real motherlode on this compilation, however, is the nine tracks that comprise Texas guitarist's Frankie Lee Sims' entire output for the label, including a spirited "What Will Lucy Do?," his big hit "Walkin' With Frankie" and the previously unissued "How Long." Closing out the collection on a very high note are the two singles one on Ace, the other on Ric by drummer/vocalist Julius "Mercy Baby" Mullins. His steaming shuffle "Marked Deck" features one of the longest verses in 12-bar blues history, a whopping 28-bar count that leaves the musicians lunging for the second change in two different spots. Obscure, wonderful music that deserves a place on compact disc and in most anyone's blues collection. —*Cub Koda*

Ace Blues Masters, Vol. 3: Tuff Enuff / Oct. 13, 1998 / Westside ✦✦✦✦
The third entry in Westside's chronicling of the Ace blues masters lurking in Johnny Vincent's vaults yields yet another treasure trove of goodies from this Jackson, MS-based label. Kicking off with Joe Dyson's ultra-rare jump classic "Looped," this 24-track compilation also includes the label's first-ever release, Al Collins' "I Got the Blues for You," as well as true rarities and other classics from Lightnin' Slim ("Bad Feeling Blues" and "Lightnin' Slim's Boogie"), Jerry McCain ("Steady" and "She's Tough"), and Sammy Myers ("Sleeping in the Ground" and "My Love Is Here to Stay"). The first recordings from Buddy Guy are aboard ("The Way You Been Treating Me," "Baby Don't You Wanna Come Home"), along with rare sides from Schoolboy Cleve, Jesse Allen, and Guitar Reed, and unissued items from Kenzie Moore and the mysterious Little Cameron and Frankie Fair. The usual strong quotient of New Orleans piano-dominated blues sides are here, but there's also a large number of down-home items peppering the mix to satisfy backwoods fans as well. —*Cub Koda*

Adios Amigo: A Tribute to Arthur Alexander / 1994 / Razor & Tie ✦✦✦✦
Among musicians, Arthur Alexander was always considered one of the greatest R&B songwriters. Both the Beatles and the Rolling Stones covered his songs, "Anna (Go to Him)" and "You Better Move On" respectively, early in their careers. But they weren't the only ones—throughout the years, his work was rich source material for many blues, soul, rock, and country artists. He may have earned the recognition of his peers, but he remained relatively unknown to the general public, right up to his death in 1993. In order to raise his profile, Razor & Tie released *Adios Amigo: A Tribute to Arthur Alexander* in 1994, assembling a stellar and diverse lineup to record new versions of his songs. The diversity and the fresh arrangements illustrate the depth of Alexander's songs and how well they lent themselves to new readings. Like any tribute album, *Adios Amigo* is uneven, with a few tracks falling flat, but the best moments—Elvis Costello's "Sally Sue Brown," Robert Plant's "If It's Really Got to Be This Way," Chuck Jackson's "You Better Move On," Frank Black's "Old John Amos," John Prine's "Lonely Just Like Me," Gary U.S. Bonds' "Genie in the Jug," Graham Parker's "Every Day I Have to Cry" and Nick Lowe's "In the Middle of It All"—are affectionate salutes to a departed master, and they're damn enjoyable in their own right as well. —*Stephen Thomas Erlewine*

Ain't No Funk Like N.O. Funk / Aug. 18, 1998 / Bullseye Blues ✦✦✦✦
Funk has been an ongoing tradition in New Orleans music since the days of the Meters and further back than that if you really want to split musical hairs. This 12-song collection brings several of today's best Crescent City funk outfits including a pair of tracks each from Galactic ("Welcome to New Orleans" and "Something's Wrong With This Picture"), All That ("Back to Broke" and "Wolf's Remedy"), and Walter "Wolfman" Washington ("Funk Is in the House" and "Funkyard"). Other highlights include "Earle" by the Brides of Jesus, "Funky Fourth Dimension" by Iris May Tango, "The White Shadow" by the New World Funk Ensemble, "Johnny" by Smilin' Myron, "Reply" by the New Orleans Nightcrawlers, "House That Jack Built" by Davell Crawford, and "Sugar Shack" by Flavor. A solid collection of the 1998 scene. —*Cub Koda*

Alabama: Black Country Dance Bands—Complete Recorded Works (1924–1949) / Jun. 2, 1994 / Document ✦✦✦✦✦
Document's *Alabama: Black Country Dance Bands (1924-1949)* collects the recorded work of Mississippi Sarah and Daddy Stovepipe, Bogus Blind Ben Covington, and the Mobile Strugglers, together constituting a mixed bag of primarily vaudeville and dance-oriented pieces. While Daddy Stovepipe's four recordings for the Gennett label, made in 1924 and 1927, are relatively uninteresting and characterized by bad sound quality. His later eight sides with wife Mississippi Sarah are among the best jug band breakdowns on record, encompassing themes from *the Bible* to the Depression in consistently magnificent style. In "Burleskin' Blues" and the glorious "The Spasm," Sarah and Stovepipe are at their liveliest, funniest, and raunchiest, swapping insults and threats, Stovepipe rapping his rhymes against the pounding rhythm of his wife's jug, and Sarah wailing her blues to her husband's screaming harmonica. Bogus Blind Ben Covington ("Bogus" because he wasn't actually blind) was probably a pseudonym for Ben Curry, a banjo player and medicine show entertainer whose repertoire consisted of such comic pieces as "I Heard the Voice of a Pork Chop." His performances are typically less captivating than those of Mississippi Sarah and Daddy Stovepipe, but are at times very amusing and always valuable as provocative glimpses into the songster tradition. The two tracks by the Mobile Strugglers, recorded over ten years after the last pieces by either Covington or Stovepipe, conclude the collection with an unusually gritty string-band style. Though the sound quality is extremely poor on a few of the recordings in this set, and some of the performances mediocre or redundant, the duets by Mississippi Sarah and Daddy Stovepipe and the six minutes of the Mobile Strugglers represent some of the most thrilling sounds to come out of the period, or out of the state, whose contributions to early blues and country music are generally overlooked. Recommended, if only for the lead vocal and mandolin/violin backup on the Strugglers' "Fattenin' Frogs," or for Mississippi Sarah's spoken protest that "I've got too many men to have any sense." *—Burgin Mathews*

Alabama Blues: 1927–1931 / Yazoo ✦✦✦
Along with Austria's Document, blues reissue label Yazoo has done a great deal to reassemble the faded history of American country blues music. While they have received great acclaim for anthologies of blues greats like Charley Patton, Skip James, and Blind Willie Johnson, they've also compiled the work of a number of more mysterious figures. Enter *Alabama Blues: 1927-1931*. The collection focuses on the output of two largely unknown players: Clifford Gibson, a guitar player who spent a great deal of time in the St. Louis area, even backing Jimmie Rodgers on recordings for Victor, and the even more obscure Edward Thompson. The set is fleshed out with sides from harmonica wizard Jay Bird Coleman (perhaps the biggest name here), George "Bullet" Williams, Marshall Owens, and Barefoot Bill. Gibson's recordings are most notable for some fine guitar playing, his mediocre vocal abilities failing to distinguish him from many of his contemporaries. Edwards has a stronger vocal presence, almost overshadowing his rough but competent lines. Of the bluesmen who join them on this disc, Williams stands out with "The Escaped Convict," an otherworldly piece that combines fierce harp playing with vocal hollering. At the time they were made, these recordings were nothing less than bids by the musicians for wider fame outside their local circles. Unbeknownst to them, however, they were also bids for a place in musical history; a place Yazoo has reserved for them. While this music is not the recommended introduction to the genre, it will no doubt be a revelation for country blues collectors. *—Nathan Bush*

Alive Down South / Jul. 29, 1997 / White Clay ✦✦✦
The musical history of Macon, GA, is undeniably rooted in the R&B, Southern rock and blues that exploded from the region in the late '60s and early '70s. *Alive Down South* features previously unreleased live recordings from some of Southern rock's most influential and popular artists—the Allman Brothers Band, Wet Willie, Stillwater, the Dixie Dregs, Sea Level, and Elvin Bishop. The cuts on this disc were remastered and sequenced to sound like one continuous concert, making the music showcased here bold, robust, and definitely alive, like its title implies. Stillwater is captured live at the "Rebel Jam" in Atlanta in 1978 doing "Out on a Limb" and "Mind-Bender," followed by the Dixie Dregs from the same venue contributing "Take It Off the Top" and their musical tribute to the home of their label (Capricorn), "Macon Bacon." Elvin Bishop is featured on two of his good-natured tunes from an unspecified date, "Stealin' Watermelons" and "Goin' Fishin'." One of the earliest acts to sign with Capricorn, Wet Willie, is represented by a pair of tunes (Little Willie John's and Little Milton's "Grits Ain't Groceries" and "Everything That Cha Do") recorded at the Roxy in Los Angeles in 1976. Sea Level, the offshoot project including the rhythm section from the Allman Brothers Band, are also captured live at the Roxy with "Take Out Some Insurance" and "Tidal Wave," a song from their first album. Following this is the Allman Brothers Band at the Nassau Coliseum in 1976 with "Statesboro Blues" (featuring a rough-as-a-cob vocal from Gregg Allman) and an uptempo version of "One Way Out" to which the crowd responds quite audibly. The disc closes out with a jam between Sea Level and the Dixie Dregs ("Hot 'Lanta Jam") that really shines as Chuck Leavell tags it with a beautiful coda, incorporating "Little Martha," the Duane Allman and Dickey Betts acoustic tune that closes the *Eat a Peach* album. For lovers of classic Southern rock, this disc provides a treasure trove of performances. *—Cub Koda*

All Night Long They Play the Blues / 1992 / Specialty ✦✦✦✦✦
This excellent soul-blues '60s anthology comes from the Galaxy label vaults. *—Bill Dahl*

Alley Special / Oct. 21, 1991 / Collectables ✦✦✦✦✦
These are blues of various styles and consistently high quality, released on the Gotham and 20th Century labels, with three previously unreleased cuts. Raw, early electric blues from the late '40s and early '50s. Includes Muddy Waters' first commercial recording. *—Niles J. Frantz*

The Alligator Records Christmas Collection / 1992 / Alligator ✦✦✦
This entertaining CD serves a dual purpose, introducing listeners to many of the blues artists who have recorded for Alligator and giving consumers a rare Christmas blues record. The performers include Koko Taylor, Kenny Neal, Lil' Ed & the Blues Imperials, Katie Webster (on a rollicking "Deck the Halls With Boogie Woogie"), William Clarke, Tinsley Ellis, Charles Brown ("Boogie Woogie Santa Claus"), Son Seals, Lonnie Brooks, Little Charlie & the Nightcats, Elvin Bishop, Saffire, Clarence "Gatemouth" Brown, and Charlie Musselwhite. With the exception of Bishop's "The Little Drummer Boy" and Musselwhite's "Silent Night," all of the selections are originals by the artists. Although the musicians all play in the same general genre, this set has enough variety (and good feelings) to hold one's interest throughout. *—Scott Yanow*

The Alligator Records 20th Anniversary Tour / 1993 / Alligator ✦✦✦
Recorded on live on Alligator Records' 20th Anniversary Tour, this double disc set is a showcase for the label's artists. Featuring an array of their most popular acts—Koko Taylor, Lonnie Brooks, Lil' Ed & the Blues Imperials, Elvin Bishop—the record doesn't deliver any surprises, yet these performances are frequently more exciting than the studio versions. *—Stephen Thomas Erlewine*

The Alligator Records 25th Anniversary Collection / Mar. 1996 / Alligator ✦✦✦✦✦
This is a specially priced, two-CDs-for-the-price-of-one photocube set, loaded with great stuff from Charlie Musselwhite, Koko Taylor, Lonnie Brooks, Johnny Winter, Billy Boy Arnold, Lonnie Mack, and a host of others who've trotted their wares on the label over the years. Besides giving the novice one great introduction to the label (as the music runs from traditional to modern), the big bonus here is a treasure trove of previously unissued tracks from Roy Buchanan (a chaotic version of Link Wray's "Jack the Ripper"), Floyd Dixon (a recut of his Blues Brothers-approved hit "Hey Bartender"), Albert Collins and Johnny Copeland in a marvelous outtake from the *Showdown!* album ("Something to Remember You By") and the band that started it all, Hound Dog Taylor & the HouseRockers, with a crazed version of Elmore James' "Look on Yonder's Wall," as sloppy as it is cool. Very good stuff and at these prices, a bargain and then some. *—Cub Koda*

Alternate Blues / Mar. 10, 1980 / Original Jazz Classics ✦✦✦
This CD is a straight reissue of a Pablo LP. Norman Granz teamed together the very distinctive trumpeters Dizzy Gillespie, Freddie Hubbard, and Clark Terry with pianist Oscar Peterson, guitarist Joe Pass, bassist Ray Brown and drummer Bobby Durham for a "Trumpet Summit." This particular release features (with one exception) unissued material from the session. There are four versions of a slow blues (only the fourth was released before), all of which have very different solos from the three trumpeters. In addition they interact on "Wrap Your Troubles in Dreams" and share the spotlight on a three-song ballad medley; Hubbard's "Here's That Rainy Day" is hard to beat. This release is not quite essential but fans of the trumpeters will want to pick it up. *—Scott Yanow*

American Folk Blues Festival: 1962–1965 / Dec. 1995 / Evidence ✦✦✦✦✦
From 1962 until 1971, the American Folk Blues Festival was responsible for bringing dozens of the most celebrated American blues artists to audiences from England to Poland. For many of the musicians, these were the largest audiences they'd ever played to, and the first (and often only) decent money they ever made. This five-CD set captures the vital early years of the festival more fully than any prior issues, with previously unreleased bonus tracks (some of which overlaps). The 1962 volume was recorded live in Hamburg, and has no extra tracks, but the material is so vital and robust that this volume, featuring Memphis Slim, John Lee Hooker, T-Bone Walker, and Sonny Terry & Brownie McGhee, never needed it. The 1963 disc, recorded live in Bremen, opens with three previously unreleased live Memphis Slim cuts, and follows these with a previously unissued Muddy Waters solo acoustic guitar piece and three more never-issued numbers featuring Muddy backed by Dixon, Otis Spann, and Matt "Guitar" Murphy. The three Sonny Boy Williamson bonus tracks were very late in the day and constitute some of the very last songs left behind by the increasingly ailing harp legend. The 1964 volume is a little less enhanced, with two songs by Willie Dixon and one song each by Sonny Boy Williamson, Sleepy John Estes and Hammie Nixon, and Sugar Pie DeSanto. The 1965 volume was always the odd one in this series; as a studio recording rather than a concert document, it lacks the vibrancy of the earlier volumes, but its eight bonus tracks do include some interesting moments by Buddy Guy, Big Mama Thornton, John Lee Hooker, and Big Walter Horton. The sound quality is good, but given the time that's passed, a full set of notes might have been nice. *—Bruce Eder*

American Folk Blues Festival '62–'65: Highlights / Jun. 10, 1997 / Evidence ✦✦✦
Taken from the Five CD set, American Folk Blues Festival: 1962-1965, these 17 tracks have been deemed the highlights. It's hard to argue with that assessment especially when it includes legends like Mississippi Fred McDowell, Howlin' Wolf, Muddy Waters, Memphis Slim, Sonny Boy Williamson, Buddy Guy, and T-Bone Walker. Any serious collector will want the full five-disc set, but these highlights are the perfect place for the curious blues novice to start. *—Al Campbell*

Angola Prisoners' Blues / 1959 / Arhoolie ✦✦✦
In the 1950s, Harry Oster made several recordings of African-American inmates at the penitentiary in Angola, Louisiana. These sessions are primarily remembered for the discovery of Robert Pete Williams, but Oster also found several other acoustic blues performers of merit. Several of them are featured on this 20-track, 80-minute CD (which includes three tracks by Williams). Although these singers had hard daily lives, and went through hard times before they were jailed, this is hardly a downer record. It's largely first-class acoustic blues with a relaxed (if sometimes sad) dignity. The lyrics are sometimes related to prison life, as in Robert Pete Williams' minor-keyed "Prisoner's Talking Blues" and Guitar Welch's "Electric Chair Blues." Yet much of the material is

simply the usual songs of struggle and hope common to the blues, mixed in with some a cappella, spiritual-flavored cuts by female prisoners, and one male vocal group performance clearly derived from doo-wop. Guitar blues is the predominant style, though, and country blues fans will find much to enjoy here, whether they're interested in the folklore aspect or not. Thirteen of the tracks on the CD version were previously unreleased. *—Richie Unterberger*

Ann Arbor Blues & Jazz Festival, Vol. 3 / Mar. 19, 1996 / Schoolkids ✦✦✦✦

There were three Ann Arbor Blues & Jazz Festivals held during 1972-1974 (succeeding the Ann Arbor Blues Festivals of 1969-1970) and several CDs have brought back highpoints from the 1973 event. Although pianist Roosevelt Sykes and singer Victoria Spivey (who share this CD) probably seemed ancient to the young and enthusiastic college audience (they were 67 at the time), they were still in their musical prime in the early '70s. Pianist-vocalist Sykes runs through his usual repertoire during a spirited solo set with the highlights including "Night Time Is the Right Time," "St. James Infirmary," and his double entendre "Dirty Mother for You" (which really excites the crowd). Spivey, a classic blues singer from the 1920s, is heard with an electric blues band which features prominent guitar and harmonica in the ensembles. She basically performs in an unchanged style from her earlier days, revisiting "Black Snake Blues" (which was from her debut recording session in 1926), "Detroit Moan" and Clarence Williams' "Organ Grinder Blues." Although neither of the short sets contain any real surprises, the spirit and joy of the veteran blues performers (plus the historic nature of their performances) makes this CD well worth picking up. *—Scott Yanow*

Ann Arbor Blues & Jazz Festival, Vol. 4 / Mar. 19, 1996 / Schoolkids ✦✦✦✦

The entries in Schoolkids' *Ann Arbor Blues & Jazz Festival* series have been a dodgy affair thus far; some volumes hit the bullseye while others distinctly fall into that "guess you had to be there" category. To be fair, not *all* of the performances are worth documenting, some of them suffering from obtrusive, loud funk bands cluttering up everything, and Schoolkids has problems assigning proper song titles and credits. And yes, these should all come with historical importance/audio disclaimers; even if these are multi-track mobile unit masters, there's still that fluctuating mix that comes from the old late-'60s/early-'70s mentality of taking a hit off a joint while simultaneously pushing a fader on a recording console. OK, that's the bad part, now on to the good stuff. If low-down gutbucket juke joint blues floats your boat, then the nine selections by the King Biscuit Boys is just the thing you've been waiting to hear. The King Biscuit Boys were a floating personnel of gentlemen who all worked the famous radio show back in the '50s. At this stage of the game they were fronted by Houston Stackhouse and Joe Willie Wilkins on guitars and Sonny Blake on harmonica with jake-legged "what are we doing here" support from the truly clueless Melvin Lee on bass and Homer Jackson on drums. But Joe Willie, Stack, and Sonny are just too real, too down-home to be worried about *anything* except flat laying it out, so if *they* aren't paying any attention, then why should we? There's goof-ups galore, like the bass player taking a chorus and a half to figure the song *isn't* in the key he thinks it's in ("Me and the Devil"), the *whole band* trying to figure what key Joe Willie's in on "It's Too Bad." Yeah, if it's perfection you're after, you came to the wrong address, but the stuff is just so potent and utterly charming, it sets all malfunctions squarely in the file "take the hairy with the smooth" file. You want to hear some blues, check this out. Scary.

The Walter Horton set brings back a flood of positive memories for this writer; Hey, I was there, I *saw* this set as it went down and it was a killer. Volume and fader fluctations aside, Horton was having the time of his life and Johnny Nicholas on guitar, Fran Christina on drums, and Sarah Brown on bass from Nicholas' band, the Boogie Brothers, were following Big Walter's every crazy musical move without ever letting go of the groove, no small feat, believe me. If you're even a little bit of a blues harp aficionado, put this one in your CD player and prepare to be astounded. Big Walter Horton on an inspired night with a good backup unit and a fresh harp was a musical force to be reckoned with. The man could blow, oh Lord, how the man could blow. *—Cub Koda*

Anthology of the Blues: Detroit Blues—Archive Series, Vol. 6 / Kent ✦✦✦

This album collects a few performances each by four different bluesmen, the most famous of whom is John Lee Hooker. Two of the others are players who were also associated with "the Hook," Eddie Kirkland and Eddie Burns. The fourth performer is Sylvester Cotton, about whom very little is known. The album's packaging is overblown, hinting at something much more grandiose than what is here. A cover shot of two cute black kids has about as much to do with the music as the listener's last haircut, while two photos of John Lee Hooker—the same shot, actually, in mini and maxi sizings—and no pictures of anyone else seems hack. It gets worse. No one takes credit for the ugly gray-and-white line drawing inside the gatefold; it portrays not only a bluesman strumming his guitar, but prostitutes, several couples embracing, a robber with a knife, a man reading a newspaper with the word "War" visible in the headline, and a boxer dog. There also seems to be some liquid all over the ground. Wow. Hooker fans need not embark on a quest in order to own this record, as there is plenty of this bluesman's material available elsewhere. The four tracks here offer his remarkable vocals and a guitar sound that will literally throttle the speakers. What really makes this album of interest to collectors would be the Kirkland tracks. This terrific player has gone in and out of the spotlight over the years, and hearing some of his earlier material is a treat, even if it is just a squibbly little pair of tracks. Eddie Burns played some mighty fine harmonica on Hooker sides from this period, but when it came time to make his own recordings, he switched to guitar. His material has a nice, rhythmic feel, but not particularly thrilling lyrics. The Burns songs pale alongside the tracks by Sylvester Cotton, one of which is titled "I Tried" and is an apology in advance to listeners who might not approve of what he has done in the recording studio. *—Eugene Chadbourne*

Antone's—Bringing You the Best in Blues / 1989 / Antone's ✦✦✦✦✦

A sampler of artists on this Austin, TX, label, it includes a variety of Texas blues and R&B, originally released 1987-1990. Featured are Otis Rush, Angela Strehli, Doug Sahm, Matt "Guitar" Murphy, and several others. *—Niles J. Frantz*

Antone's 10th Anniversary Anthology, Vol. 1 / 1986 / Antone's ✦✦✦✦✦

Chicago blues living legends were recorded live at a popular Austin, TX, club in July 1985. Included is Buddy Guy, Jimmy Rogers, Eddie Taylor, James Cotton, Snooky Pryor, Otis Rush, Albert Collins, and more. The CD has three bonus cuts. Good sound and very good performances. *—Niles J. Frantz*

Antone's 10th Anniversary Anthology, Vol. 2 / 1991 / Antone's ✦✦✦✦✦

This very consistent live package was cut at the Austin club. It includes incendiary tracks by Buddy Guy and Matt "Guitar" Murphy. *—Bill Dahl*

Antone's 20th Anniversary / Jul. 29, 1996 / Discovery ✦✦✦

Antone's 20th Anniversary is a double-disc set that celebrates the legendary Texas club and it rich musical legacy. Over the course of the set, some of the biggest and best names of not only Texas blues, but American blues contribute positively ripping live tracks—it's always a joy to hear the likes of Buddy Guy, James Cotton, Kim Wilson, and Doug Sahm, and each of these artists, among many others, turn in first-rate contributions on this set. For a strong encapsulation of the American blues/blues-rock scene of the '70s, '80s, and '90s, *Antone's 20th Anniversary* delivers the goods. *—Thom Owens*

Arhoolie's American Masters, Vol. 1: 15 Down Home Country Blues Classics / 1996 / Arhoolie ✦✦✦

The origins of the blues can be found in the grooves of this fine budget-priced sampler, which includes performances from Mississippi Fred McDowell ("Frisco Line"), the Black Ace ("Drink On, Little Girl"), Bukka White ("Columbus Mississippi Blues"), and Big Joe Williams ("Brother James"). *—Jason Ankeny*

Arhoolie's American Masters, Vol. 2: 15 Down Home Urban Blues Classics / 1996 / Arhoolie ✦✦✦

A fine introduction to the form, *15 DownHome Urban Blues Classics* features recordings from Sonny Boy Williamson ("Pontiac Blues"), Big Mama Thornton ("Big Mama's Bumble Bee"), Charlie Musselwhite ("Up and Down the Avenue"), and Katie Webster ("I Know That's Right"). *—Jason Ankeny*

Arhoolie's American Masters, Vol. 8: 15 Piano Blues & Boogie Classics / Feb. 25, 1997 / Arhoolie ✦✦✦✦

For *Vol. 8* of its *American Masters* budget series, Arhoolie tackles the "blues piano" theme, with a crushing emphasis on the boogie-woogie styles of various Chicago, Kansas City, Texas, Louisiana, and Delta players. The pacing of this album does get predictable after a while (fast boogie, slow blues, fast boogie, slow blues...), but there's so much stylistic diversity here that the formula never gets tiresome. Producer Chris Strachwitz wisely avoids instrumental overkill (the trademark of most blues piano anthologies) by including several outstanding vocal performances by the likes of Mercy Dee Walton, Omar Sharriff, Johnny Young (who duets with Otis Spann), and Clifton Chenier (backed by Elmore Nixon). But in the end, the speed demons get to flaunt plenty of their pounding instrumental fare—the main culprits being Pete Johnson, Big Joe Duskin, Katie Webster, and Lafayette Leake. This is a no-frills package (no liner notes whatsoever and minimal track info), but the music is without a doubt spectacular. *—Ken Chang*

The Aristocrat of the Blues: The Best of Aristocrat Records / Aug. 26, 1997 / MCA ✦✦✦✦✦

The 51 songs here represent some of the highlights from the vaults of Aristocrat, the precursor to the Chess label—but to get the rarities by St. Louis Jimmy, Forest City Joe, Little Johnny Jones, and Robert Nighthawk, listeners should be prepared to buy 25 Muddy Waters songs they likely already own. Actually, despite that drawback, this collection is fascinating for the perspective it gives to the history of Chess Records and the development of Chicago blues between 1947 and 1950. The earliest tracks are '40s big-band-influenced R&B: the Five Blazes, featuring pianist/singer/songwriter Ernie Harper; the ominous "Ice Man Blues" and the raunchy "Fishin' Pole" by Tom Archia, fronting a sax-dominated outfit with Jo Jo Adams and Sheba Griffin on vocals, respectively; "Boogie Woogie Blues" by Clarence Samuels; and "Bilbo Is Dead" by Andrew Tibbs. The Chess sound as we've come to know it arrives with Sunnyland Slim, and the guitar blues that Chess became famous for doesn't show up until the Muddy Waters tracks "Gypsy Woman," "Little Anna Mae," etc. Muddy is nearly omnipresent, represented by 25 songs of his own here, and playing on many of the others. Of the rest, Robert Nighthawk, a one-time mentor to Muddy, has six songs represented here, while Forest City Joe has one ("Memory of Sonny Boy"). Forrest Sykes has one song, a rip-roaring piano instrumental, and St. Louis Jimmy Oden gets two. The quality throughout is crisp, sharp, finely detailed, and loud, with each song remastered in 20-bit high-definition sound, making them superior to any other CD package of this material. Given the familiarity of the Muddy songs, however, it might have been wiser to just do a three-CD Aristocrat box with a broader cross-section of the label's output. *—Bruce Eder*

Atlantic Blues: Chicago / 1986 / Atlantic ✦✦✦✦

Chess is arguably the first label for blues, but behemoth Atlantic has enough of the stuff—albeit a bit past its prime—to still warrant a multi-disc box. This separately sold part of that package takes in some of the giants from the Illinois epicenter of urban blues. Two of the best, Howlin' Wolf and Muddy Waters, as well as latter-day Windy City queen Koko Taylor, are featured on cuts taped live at the 1972 Ann Arbor Blues Festival. Back in the studio, the mighty tandem of Buddy Guy and Junior Wells mixes it up with Dr. John and Eric Clapton, while Southern blues scion Duane Allman contributes fine slide work to a couple of top-notch Otis Rush performances. Freddie King's three numbers, featuring honking sax star King Curtis and the arrangements of soul great Donny Hathaway, take the prize, though. Not a good primer, maybe, but a solid blues roundup all the same. —*Stephen Cook*

Atlantic Blues: Piano / 1986 / Atlantic ✦✦✦✦

Sampling treats from such blues hotbeds as Chicago, Kansas City, and New Orleans, this single disc from Atlantic's blues box spotlights the men at the ivories with 23 good-to-excellent sides. Giving due respect to the boogie-woogie heyday of the '30s and '40s, the collection includes four 1972 sides by Jimmy Yancey (cut just prior to his death) and three early-'50s numbers by Meade "Lux" Lewis. Another fine tinkler, Champion Jack Dupree, reveals the rougher side of the boogie craze with some fine, latter-day barrelhouse gems off of his universally lauded *Blues from the Gutter* album. And not to forget Kansas City and the Crescent City, the disc also includes a true classic by Big Joe Turner and Pete Johnson ("Roll 'Em Pete"), a few solid sides by big-band veteran and onetime Charlie Parker employer Jay McShann, and a genre-defining bayou classic compliments of Professor Longhair ("Tipitina"). With an intriguing 1953 demo by Ray Charles and an early-'70s funk rambler from Dr. John ("Junco Partner") to top things off, *Atlantic Blues: Piano* makes for a quality session by the stereo. —*Stephen Cook*

Atlantic Blues [Box] / 1986 / Atlantic ✦✦✦✦✦

At the time of its release, this 83-song collection was one of the bolder efforts by a major label at doing a proper survey of major blues categories. The material ranges from old-style big-band jump blues to the leaner, louder guitar sounds of the '60s and '70s, and isn't limited to artists who cut for Atlantic—the producers had to license in a certain amount, especially where Chicago blues was concerned. Overall, they've done a good job as far as the sheer variety of performers, but trying to summarize any of these areas—blues vocalists, Chicago blues, guitar blues, or piano blues—with only 20 tracks on a single CD each is an exercise in futility. It is a place to start if one has the money, however, showing some of the strong points of a lot of key artists, and the sound was also good for its time. This is also a good chance for the neophyte to hear tracks by certain performers—like Jay McShann and Meade "Lux" Lewis—who aren't otherwise represented on easy-to-find major label releases. However, there are other releases on the market now (especially Rhino's blues retrospective series) that can make the same claims and are more thorough and ambitious in scope. Additionally, anyone with a little knowledge and the $60 or so that this box can cost might better spend it on some of the more recent compilations devoted to the top artists on this box's roster, like Muddy Waters or Howlin' Wolf. Those, plus some of the other Chess reissues from MCA, will tell one a lot more about Chicago blues than the one or two tracks by each that show up in this set. —*Bruce Eder*

Atlantic Blues: Guitar / 1986 / Atlantic ✦✦✦✦

Ranging from the country blues stylings of Blind Willie McTell to modern-day pyrotechnics by Stevie Ray Vaughan, this edition of the *Atlantic Blues* series spotlights some of the fine blues pickers to grace many a 20th century stage and stereo. These aren't necessarily all classic performances, but most of the music is of the highest quality. The mix includes cuts by such marquee names as B.B. King and John Lee Hooker, as well as more obscure fare from the likes of Texas Johnny Brown and Cornell Dupree. And for a bit of soul, there's even a clutch of songs by Albert King and Ike & Tina Turner. A fine blues party soundtrack. —*Stephen Cook*

Atlantic Blues: Vocalists / 1986 / Atlantic ✦✦✦✦

Atlantic continues to trawl through its blues vaults on this generous set featuring many of the music's outstanding and often overlooked vocalists. Taking in some rarities and many updated classics, the 28-track mix includes excellent sides by longtime label star Ruth Brown, vintage blues chanteuse Sippie Wallace, urban blues pioneer Leroy Carr, and the "Poet of the Blues," Percy Mayfield. And while a few other marquee names appear, the bulk is comprised of highlights from such relatively obscure singers as Pearl Woods, Wesley Wilson (doing his version of the Bessie Smith perennial "Give Me a Pigfoot [And a Bottle of Beer]"), and Lou Willie Turner. In the spotlight or not, though, this wide-ranging collection makes for a fine stretch by the stereo. —*Stephen Cook*

Avalon Blues: A Tribute to the Music of Mississippi John Hurt / Jun. 12, 2001 / Vanguard ✦✦✦✦

If you assemble a bunch of above-average artists to pay tribute to a major artist, is the result an above-average tribute record? Not always, but in this case it is. Organized and executive-produced by Peter Case, this contains covers of the Mississippi bluesman's songs by more than a dozen medium-big and very-big names from the folk and rock worlds, including Beck, Taj Mahal, Bruce Cockburn, Lucinda Williams, Steve Earle (dueting with Justin Earle), Ben Harper, Peter Case & Dave Alvin (performing together), Geoff Muldaur, Gillian Welch, and John Hiatt. It's more a folk-rock-blues crossover album than a Delta blues one, which is fine: tribute albums shouldn't be re-creations of the originals, and whether or not it was the intention, it will expose some of John Hurt's songs to fans who identify themselves primarily as folk or rock listeners. And not many of these songs *are* very well-known, with the exception of "Candy Man" (done by Steve & Justin Earle) and "Stagolee" (sung by Beck). The arrangements are low-key and respectful, the best ones being Ben Harper's "Sliding Delta" (which is one of the bluesiest performances) and Victoria Williams' "Since I've Laid My Burden Down," which has very eccentric banjo sounds. —*Richie Unterberger*

Baby Let's Burn: Blues from Baton Rouge / 1992 / Flyright ✦✦✦

A thoroughly delicious slice of down home Louisiana blues (21 tracks in all) by some of the lesser-known artists who recorded for the Excello label. The seven tracks by Jimmy Reed sound-alike Jimmy Anderson are choice listening, while "I Don't Know Why" by the mysterious Boogie Jake is as low-down as it gets. —*Cub Koda*

Back Against the Wall: The Texas Country / 1992 / Collectables ✦✦

Very uneven; a few vintage gems alternate with truly mediocre contemporary sides. —*Bill Dahl*

Back Alley Blues, Vol. 2 / RHC ✦✦✦

A collection of raw '50s blues sides recorded for various small imprints. As the legality of this issue is raised when one hears the took-it-off-a-scratchy-record quality of this collection, all audio concerns take a back seat once you actually sample the rarities at hand, because this is blistering '50s postwar blues at its best. "Rhythm Rockin' Boogie" by John Lee Henley, Baby Face Leroy's "Rollin' & Tumblin', Pt. 2," the original "Cat Squirrel" by Doctor Ross, "Sweet Black Angel" by Earl Hooker, Otis Spann's "Five Spot," Eddie Taylor's "Find Me a Baby," "The Wolf Pack" by Kid Thomas, "Keep Your Arms Around Me" by Joe Hill Louis, "Bad Feeling Blues" by Lightnin' Slim, Robert Nighthawk's "Maggie Campbell," "Dim Lights" by J.B. Hutto, "Rough Treatment" by Little Hudson, and "Johnnie Mae" by Homesick James are just a few of the many highlights on this 24-tracker. While the material is all must-have stuff for any blues fan, the transfers are so poorly done that it almost negates the usefulness of this package. —*Cub Koda*

Backwood Blues 1926–1935 / Jan. 10, 1996 / Document ✦✦✦

Backwood Blues 1926-1935 contains a selection of material from the early country blues singers. The best-known name is Bo Weavil Jackson, who has the best cuts on this 18-track collection; Bobby Grant, King Solomon Hill, and Lane Hardin are the other singers here. While the Jackson cuts are uniformly interesting, much of the music here is only appealing to specialists and academics. For anyone else, the exacting chronological sequencing, poor fidelity (everything was transferred from acetates and 78s), and uneven performances make this collection of marginal interest. —*Thom Owens*

Bad, Bad Whiskey (The Galaxy Masters) / 1994 / Specialty ✦✦✦✦✦

A subsidiary of Fantasy, the Galaxy label recorded a diverse assortment of soul and R&B in the 1960s and early '70s. This is a 26-track compilation of highlights from the company's output, covering 1962 to 1972. Landing the occasional minor R&B chart hit, Galaxy couldn't be said to have an especially distinctive label sound, though their efforts were on the whole bluesier than much soul of the era. But this is still a decent grab bag of odds and ends from soul's vintage period, with obscure sides by well-known performers like Betty Everett, Little Johnny Taylor, Lenny Williams, Charles Brown, Johnny "Guitar" Watson, Merl Saunders, and a host of unknowns. Especially good are the three sides by Rodger Collins, whose 1966 single "She's Looking Good" (which leads off the CD) was one of the better regional soul hits of the '60s, and was covered by Wilson Pickett for a Top 20 smash a couple of years later. —*Richie Unterberger*

'Bama Bound: Alabama Blues Connection / May 28, 1996 / Collectables ✦✦✦

The first two-thirds of *Bama Bound: Alabama Blues Connection* is made up of raw and gritty country blues. Artists like Clifford Gibson (whose four songs feature his keening voice and solid sense of melody) and Jaybird Coleman sing accompanied only by a lone guitar and maybe a harmonica. A particular highlight here is Bullet Williams' keening "Touch Me Light, Mama; the moment when Williams and the harmonica player both lose their minds and go off into strange yodeling harmonics is worth the price of admission. Also making the CD worthwhile are the five tracks by the very cool Cow Cow Davenport that make up the remainder of the disc. Davenport is more citified and features light and breezy piano playing. His winking vocal style and comic timing make songs like "Alabama Mistreater" and "We Gonna Rub It" a delightful listening experience. If you buy this CD, the very next thing you'll want to do is track down more Cow Cow Davenport. —*Tim Sendra*

Barbecue Blues / Jun. 23, 1998 / House of Blues/A&M ✦✦✦

Barbecue Blues relies on a cutesy concept—it contains nothing but blues and R&B songs about food, barbecues, and appetites—but it works surprsingly well, mainly because most of the featured artists are excellent. Surprisingly, the compilers decided to bypass modern electric blues for classic female blues, jump blues, classic R&B, and country blues. It's a gambit that works, because it gives the album a distinctive identity. There are a couple of weak cuts, to be sure—that's usually the case with various-artists compilations—but the majority of the songs here are excellent and the disc itself is a great choice for a party—or a barbecue, for that matter. Among the featured artists are Professor Longhair ("Red Beans"), Big Twist & the Mellow Fellows ("Too Much Barbecue"), Andre Williams ("Pass the Biscuits"), the Big Three Trio ("Appetite Blues"), Bessie Smith ("Gimme a Pigfoot and a Bottle of Beer"), John Brim ("Ice Cream Man"), Louis Jordan ("Saturday Night Fish Fry"), and, of course, Barbecue Bob ("Barbecue Blues"). —*Stephen Thomas Erlewine*

Barrelhouse Women, Vol. 1 (1925–1930) / Nov. 21, 1995 / Document ✦✦✦✦

Five long-forgotten female singers from the mid- to late '20s have their complete output reissued on this CD. Evelyn Brickey and Katherine Adkins only recorded two songs apiece, both accompanied by a pianist; Adkins plays piano for herself on "Did She Fall or Was She Pushed." Bertha Ross (who may have been Lucille Bogan) made it to records under that name for four songs, with backing by pianist Vance Patterson and (on one song) Jaybird Coleman on harmonica. The bulk of this disc features Frances Wallace and/or Clara Burston. Burston is heard on nine numbers, including two on which she is accompanied by Wallace's piano and the two-part "Frankie and Clara," which teams the duo as a vocal duet. In addition, Wallace is featured on four numbers of her own. None of the five singers were destined for great fame (or necessarily deserving of it), but their recordings should interest collectors of 1920s blues. —*Scott Yanow*

Barrelhouse Women, Vol. 2 (1924–1928) / Mar. 18, 1997 / Document ✦✦✦✦

Barrelhouse Women, Vol. 2 (1924-1928) contains an abundance of cuts from the obscure female blues singers Sodarisa Miller, Alice Pearson, Mattie Dorsey, and Star Page. Miller has 15 tracks, Pearson has five, Dorsey has four, and Page has two. For specialists, this is interesting material, but for anyone else, the approach of the collection is too academic to be of interest. —*Stephen Thomas Erlewine*

Battle of the Blues, Vol. 1 / 1959 / King ◆◆◆◆
This first volume of King's *Battle of the Blues* series features two of the label's biggest acts: Roy Brown and Wynonie Harris. Having already made their names in the late '40s as premier blues shouters on the R&B and jump blues circuit, both singers migrated to the Cincinnati independent label and reached even loftier chart heights. Brown takes up the first side with seven sides of his animated and gospel-fired vocals, including the classic "Boogie at Midnight." For his part, Harris indulges his rougher-hewn vocal cords for an update of his big smash, the Brown-penned "Good Rockin' Tonight," and one of his all-time King highlights, "Bloodshot Eyes." For some whiskey-soaked R&B nostalgia, this fine collection is hard to beat. —*Stephen Cook*

Battle of the Blues, Vol. 2 / 1959 / King ◆◆◆◆
The second round of King's *Battle of the Blues* series features another healthy dose of tracks by Roy Brown and Wynonie Harris. And while more academically minded fans will want to first check out the wealth of earlier classics these two singers cut in the '40s, this roundup of '50s material will still provide a fine introduction to both of these giants. Again, Brown kicks things off with a side of his smooth yet powerful uptown blues; showing a deft pen, he sticks to a set of top-notch originals. Harris might not have written much of his own material, but he does show why his was one of the most incendiary and impassioned voices around, especially on the confessional "Drinking Blues." A perfect accouterment to your next after-hours shindig. —*Stephen Cook*

Battle of the Blues, Vol. 4 / 1959 / King ◆◆◆
Eddie "Cleanhead" Vinson joins the *Battle of the Blues* party this time around with some honking tenor saxophone and his own brand of blues shouting. And while Vinson is given a good share of vocals here, his King label compatriots Roy Brown and Wynonie Harris make good on their earlier showcases with another dose of high-end jump blues vocals as well. No real jousting here, just 12 solid R&B scorchers and slow-burners. —*Stephen Cook*

Beale St. Mess Around / 1975 / Rounder ◆◆◆◆◆
A collection of recordings by veterans of the once-frantic Memphis blues and jug band scene, *Beale St. Mess Around* at first seems more comfortable and relaxed than an overwhelming masterpiece. And that makes sense, because while the city of Memphis is just up the river apiece from the birthplace of the intense Mississippi Delta blues style, the city had its own perspective on the blues. This includes loose medium tempos with a touch of swing, suited to jug band music as well as blues. Guitars tend to be strummed or fingerpicked in solid rhythmic patterns, with gentler use of slides or bottlenecks, if any at all. Rowdy, enthusiastic accompaniment on instruments such as harmonica, washtub bass, kazoo, or simple foot stomping is encouraged. Some blues fans consider it more of a good-time music than a deep blues experience. Deep listening to this record, however, results in an ever-growing appreciation of just how special this particular album is. It really does stand out from many other albums of acoustic blues that are available, especially when it comes to compilation collections.

Most of the tracks here come from a recording session undertaken by producers George Mitchell and Roger Brown in the early '60s, while selected studio cuts from sessions a few years later provide a perfect contrast. From the description in the liner notes, the earlier recording trip was something like getting an old gang of pals together. This feeling is completely captured in the ensuing recordings, with plenty of good-humored looseness. It is this element that makes this record so special. When it comes to old-time blues performers, one can't really judge to what effect the pressured and sterile atmosphere of the modern recording studio hampered their ability to make relaxed music. Gathered together in someone's apartment with "some Golden Harvest sherry" and a few good microphones, on the other hand, and it's easy to imagine the potential for greatness. Some aspects of this recording will either horrify audio purists or tantalize them completely. Certain instruments leap out for a note or beat or three, predating this kind of activity in rap and DJ music by decades. More important, an ambience of a room with other people sitting in it is immediately established and never lost, not even when there is only one artist performing unaccompanied.

Furry Lewis is the most famous performer, a man whose blues contains a rarefied essence of both the Memphis Beale Street scene and Delta slide blues. He is really amazingly versatile, able to deliver his own variation of the "Spanish Flangdang" called "U.S. Waltz," complete with skillfully executed harmonics, a drum imitation on the soundboard, and astute historical narration. There are, of course, a variety of full albums of Lewis available, but this disc contains one of his greatest performances, "Hello, Judge." This is a masterpiece of blues guitar, including a startling technique where Lewis snaps the strings while also playing them with a slide. Will Shade, aka Son Brimmer, pops up all over the place, dueting with Lewis, as well as the incredibly funky singer Catherine Porter, and participating in several trio pieces. The founder of the original Memphis Jug Band, Shade had lost none of his spark by the '60s. He sure has a punchy guitar sound, the intro to the latter number sounding like someone is plunging a garden trowel into the soundhole of a Gibson. He also does an excellent job playing harmonica on the performance of "Muscle Shoal Blues" by Lewis. Dewey Corley plays a mean kazoo on "I'm Going Home," while "Jump on Down" reveals the little-known Earl Bell to be a ringer. His guitar sound is snappy and dry, as if old leaves had been left on the fretboard. —*Eugene Chadbourne*

The Beauty of the Blues / 1991 / Columbia/Legacy ◆◆◆◆◆
This is a beautiful 18-track collection from a sampling of Columbia/Legacy's *Roots n' Blues* series. The recordings, from 1929-1947, include a wide variety of traditional blues

and blues-related styles. Excellent sound, with music from Robert Johnson, Big Bill Broonzy, and others. —*Niles J. Frantz*

Before the Blues, Vol. 1: The Early American Black Music Scene / 1996 / Yazoo ◆◆◆◆
Although the blues is the most renowned form of early 20th century African-American music (other than jazz), it didn't dominate rural black music to the extent that many listeners often assume. Black and white folk musics mingled extensively before the advent of recorded technology, and black musicians often performed gospel, religious hymns, folk ballads, and fiddle tunes as well as what we now recognize as the blues. This compilation does a good job of illustrating the diverse ancestry of African-American music with 23 rare sides from the 1920s and 1930s, when records and mass media had yet to fully introduce elements that would standardize musical genres and approaches to some degree. Some of these performers would indeed become classified as blues artists (Mississippi John Hurt, Robert Wilkins, Henry Thomas). But most of these tracks are not explicitly rooted in blues forms, examples being B.F. Shelton's banjo ballad interpretation of "Pretty Polly," Taylor's Kentucky Boys' fiddle breakdown version of "Forked Deer," or the Seventh Day Adventist Choir's "On Jordan's Stormy Banks We Stand." Remastered from old 78s, this may be of more educational than entertainment value to most modern listeners, but it's well done, with extensive liner notes explaining the various forms of black music preserved on the disc. —*Richie Unterberger*

Before the Blues, Vol. 2: The Early American Black Music Scene / 1996 / Yazoo ◆◆◆◆
The title of this compilation, *Before the Blues*, may be a deceiving one, particularly as it comes from Yazoo Records, a label that specializes in the earliest music of the genre. While the performances here date back to the first commercial recordings (made during the mid-'20s), the blues, as a musical form, was probably born a good 20 years earlier, at the turn of the century. Maintaining a looser format than many of their compilations, *Before the Blues* follows the music from the juke joint on a Saturday night to church the next morning. Included are tracks from some of the most popular musicians of the period (Charley Patton, Blind Lemon Jefferson, the Memphis Jug Band, and Frank Stokes), as well as curios from little-known performers. At one end of the spectrum, there is the raw, earthy mountain music of Frank Jenkins' "Roving Cowboy," the violin and vocal performance that closes the collection. At the other is Tommy McClennan's "Deep Sea Blues," the song Muddy Waters and Jimi Hendrix (among many others) would record as "Catfish Blues." Though his performance is loose, McClennan's guitar sounds ripe for urban electrification. In the process of migrating to the city, the music witnessed the extinction of rural string combos like the Memphis Jug Band. "K.C. Moan" is an example of the type of material they recorded before the pressure to adapt brought jazz influences into their music. By the 1940s, the commercial heyday of this music had come and gone. Never again would companies seek out recordings like "Cold Morning Shout" (an otherworldly blend of fiddle, banjo, and guitar by the Southside Trio) or the deep gospel of slide guitar master Blind Willie Johnson. Thanks to Yazoo, the music has been preserved with the best possible fidelity. As always, songs have been arranged according to listenability. Boundaries of style and chronology are ignored, with the gaps filled in by extensive liner notes. —*Nathan Bush*

Before the Blues, Vol. 3: The Early American Black Music Scene / 1996 / Yazoo ◆◆◆◆◆
This final volume in an indispensable series collects work by better-known artists like Memphis Minnie and Mississippi John Hurt as well as more obscure geniuses like Henry Thomas and Texas Alexander. What stands out is the amazingly consistent level of quality of the recordings. While some preservation efforts such as this might fill spaces with padding, all the music here is heartbreakingly beautiful. —*Tim Sheridan*

Berkeley Blues Festival / 1966 / Arhoolie ◆◆◆◆
Now available as an expanded CD with several bonus tracks, Arhoolie's *Berkeley Blues Festival* showcases the talents of Mance Lipscomb, Clifton Chenier, and Lightnin' Hopkins, all of whom found an expanded audience through Arhoolie head Chris Strachwitz. The three future legends were recorded at the 1966 Berkeley Blues Festival, playing a mix of originals and covers. Bookended by guitarist Lipscomb's solo acoustic set and Hopkins' electric guitar musings, Chenier and drummer Francis Clay take the prize for a spirited stretch of prime zydeco and Louisiana boogie. A very enjoyable way to check out three roots legends in fine form. —*Stephen Cook*

The Best Blues Album in the World Ever / Feb. 29, 2000 / Virgin ◆◆
Hardly. What *is* on this two-disc set is a real hodgepodge of new and old tracks by a variety of artists ranging from soul shouters and blues-rockers to the true originators. Disc one gets off to a sluggish start with tracks from Johnny Winter, the Boneshakers, Colin James, Larry McCray, the Kinsey Report, John Hammond, Duke Robillard, and Terry Evans, but picks up a bit with entries from Elmore James, Lowell Fulson, B.B. King, and Albert Collins. The second disc is better, with classics from Muddy Waters, Little Walter, Koko Taylor, Howlin' Wolf, Chuck Berry, John Lee Hooker, Albert King, and Lightnin' Hopkins paving the way, with only entries from Gary Moore, Jon Cleary, Johnny Winter, J.J. Cale, and John Mayall dropping the quality. Although heavily advertised on TV, this is a long, long way from being an ultimate blues collection. —*Cub Koda*

The Best of Candlelite Records, Vol. 3 / 1994 / Juke Box Treasures ◆◆◆
Another installment of obscure doo wop singles from Wayne Stierle, this time featuring the El Domingos, the Original Sonics, the Sensation Owls (their track taken from a live '50s gospel radio broadcast), and the Delacardos. But the true winner here is the out of tune, surreal ballad "Empty Hours" by the Melodees, which must be heard to be believed. —*Cub Koda*

The Best of Chess Blues, Vol. 1 / 1988 / MCA ◆◆◆◆
Yet another of many Chess starter discs, *The Best of Chess Blues, Vol. 1* offers a slim but strong mix of classic Chicago blues from the late '40s through the '50s. Including several

key electric blues cuts and plenty seeds from which both early rock & roll and the bluesier side of the British Invasion took inspiration, the 14 tracks touch on both the legendary (Muddy Waters' "Rolling Stone" and Lowell Fulson's "Reconsider Baby") and dark-horse gems (Robert Nighthawk's "Black Angel Blues" and J.B. Lenoir's "Eisenhower Blues"). And in between? Well, just several more milestones by the likes of Little Walter, Howlin' Wolf, and Sonny Boy Williamson, among others. A great way to get to know the blues. *—Stephen Cook*

The Best of Chess Blues, Vol. 2 / 1988 / MCA ✦✦✦✦✦

A dozen classic blues performances from the bursting-at-the-seams riches of the Chess vaults. A pair each from Howlin' Wolf ("Back Door Man" and "Little Red Rooster") and Sonny Boy Williamson ("Your Funeral and My Trial" and "Bring It on Home") are rounded out with equally stellar cuts from Muddy Waters, Koko Taylor, Little Milton, Etta James, John Lee Hooker, Otis Rush, and Elmore James. Together, they amounts to a pretty garden variety song selection, but if you *don't* have any, or most, of these tracks, it's well worth picking up. *—Cub Koda*

The Best of Duke-Peacock Blues / 1992 / MCA ✦✦✦✦✦

An interesting collection of sides from this seminal Texas label. Highlights includes tracks by Bobby "Blue" Bland ("Stormy Monday," "Turn on Your Love Light"), Otis Rush ("Homework"), Junior Parker "Driving Wheel"), and Larry Davis' original version of "Texas Flood," made popular to a new audience by Stevie Ray Vaughan. *—Cub Koda*

The Best of Excello Records / 1995 / Excello ✦✦✦✦✦

Although several overviews of the Excello label exist (including Rhino's two-volume set), this single-disc thumbnail collection may be the most digestible and therefore the best of the bunch. With a generous 30 tracks on a single disc to recommend it for openers, this collection tries to hit virtually all popular strains that the label dabbled in, from big city blues to doo wop to rockabilly to rhythm & blues to its best known swamp blues offerings. With hits aboard like Slim Harpo's "Raining in My Heart" and "Baby, Scratch My Back," the Gladiolas' original version of "Little Darlin'," Lillian Offitt's "Miss You So," the Marigolds' "Rollin' Stone," and Guitar Gable's "Congo Mombo," this collection delves far further into collectors' favorites, including "Hey! Baby" by rockabilly Al Ferrier, "Wild Cherry" by Leroy Washington, "Now That She's Gone" by the King Crooners, and the original version of "This Should Go on Forever" by Guitar Gable. The blues quotient inherent in the label's output is also well represented with the inclusion of "Rooster Blues" by Lightnin' Slim, "Baby Let's Play House" by Arthur Gunter, "My Next Door Neighbor" by Jerry McCain, "My Home Is a Prison" by Lonesome Sundown, and "I Hear You Knockin'" by Lazy Lester. All in all, a collection that's hard to beat, especially if your budget doesn't extend to multi-disc retrospectives. *—Cub Koda*

The Best of Fat Possum / 1997 / Fat Possum ✦✦✦✦✦

These 11 songs live up to what the title promises and then some—from R.L. Burnside's pumping, surging opening cut, "Georgia Woman," and Junior Kimbrough's more reflective and subtle "Meet Me in the City" to Cadell Davis' more elegantly textured workouts ("Cadell's Boogie," etc.), the sounds are down and dirty, but highly varied, in keeping with this modern blues label's distinctive output. Dave Thompson, Paul Jones, and the Jelly Roll Kings are also here. *—Bruce Eder*

The Best of King & Federal R&B Instrumentals: Honky Tonk / 2000 / Ace ✦✦✦

With Bill Doggett and Freddie King alone, the King/Federal labels had two of the most popular and significant instrumental R&B/rock hitmakers of the 1950s and early '60s. Both are represented by their most popular instrumental tracks (four by Doggett, three by King) here. But this compilation, assembling 24 instrumentals from 1948-1964, also demonstrates that King/Federal was quite active in the instrumental R&B field beyond its work with those two artists. In many of the 24 cuts (particularly the earliest ones), the label mined R&B/jazz crossover sounds with a smoky barroom flavor. Giving the sleeve a casual glance, most would assume that the material for the most part flopped upon release, but actually a few of these were big (if virtually forgotten) R&B hits, like Todd Rhodes' "Blues for the Red Boy" (from 1948), Earl Bostic's effervescent "Flamingo" (from 1951), and Sonny Thompson's shuffling "Long Gone" (1948), a groundbreaker in that it not only sat atop the R&B charts for a long time but also made the pop Top 30. Beyond that, things do get rather generic, even though there are some relatively big names like Mickey Baker and King Curtis (heard backing Washboard Bill) and future James Brown sideman Jimmy Nolen (who shines on blues guitar on the 1956 single "After Hours"/"Strollin' With Nolen"). There's no denying, however, that Doggett's massive and classic "Honky Tonk" (parts one and two are both here) and King's snazzy blues guitar instrumentals are easily the most worthwhile items on board. There is, however, one other great cut: Johnny "Guitar" Watson's astonishingly futuristic 1954 workout "Space Guitar" (released under the billing Young John Watson), one of the great relatively obscure classics of the mid-'50s. *—Richie Unterberger*

The Best of the Blues / 1988 / Pair ✦✦✦

This disc (subtitled "A Summit Meeting") isn't exactly the "best of the blues" by any means, but it is a fine—though edited—live concert, from Lincoln Center's Philharmonic (now Avery Fisher) Hall in June of 1973. Big Mama Thornton is in excellent form, doing "Little Red Rooster" and "Ball and Chain," Eddie "Cleanhead" Vinson is represented by "Back Door Blues," "Hold It Right There," "Kidney Stew," and "They Call Me Mr. Cleanhead," and Arthur "Big Boy" Crudup sings "That's All Right." But the big treat is Muddy Waters, in one of his first appearances after the car crash that nearly took his life, doing "Long Distance Call," "Where's My Woman Been," "and "Got My Mojo Workin'." The sound is excellent, and the performances are all very strong. Serious fans, however, should be aware that a European double-CD set exists, which includes four more songs off the original double album. But as a mid-priced release that is easily available, this isn't bad. *—Bruce Eder*

Biddle Street Barrelhousin' / 2000 / Delmark ✦✦✦

The majority of these recordings from St. Louis-based blues pianists have never been issued. They represent a fading slice of American music that was barely documented, so this is more of an historical issue. Speckled Red, Henry Brown, James Crutchfield, James "Stump" Johnson, and Lawrence Henry are the participants, and each has his own style. Speckled Red gets the most play on seven of the 19 tracks, bookending and appearing in the middle of the program. Red is perhaps the most talented of the lot, but also is clearly undisciplined. He's sloppy and rushed, tossing extra measures on "Oh Red"; he also talks about a man in Detroit who taught him "Dad's Blues," echoes a Roosevelt Sykes vocal style during "Goin' Down Slow," gets raspy on "Milk Cow Blues," is gruffly outrageous on "Black Gal," goes wack on "All on Account of You," and is more controlled for the boogie instrumental "Wilkins Street Stomp." Crutchfield is the star of this set, with six tracks. He uses a slow tempo with frantic improv and serene, soulful singing on "Levee Blues," scats lightly in bebop fashion with a drummer on brushes for "Blow North Wind," does a classic take of the classic "How Long Blues," and sings "that's alright, I'm wondering who's lovin' my baby tonight" during "Ora-Nellie Blues." Crutchfield is a softie at heart, represented on the tender and delicate "Black Gal," and can be deliberate with intense chords for the slow, carefree, dee-dee-dee vocalized "Pearly Mae Blues." Brown gets two shots: the straight 12-bar, half-instrumental/half-talking "21st Street Stomp," and the talkin' trash boogie blues "Goin' Down to Becky Thatcher." Brown does the classics "St. Louis" and "Memphis Blues"—the former a rousing barrelhouse take with original lyrics about his women and the Red Sox and Cardinals baseball teams, and the latter a ragtime blues with chiming chords. "Stump" is the anomalous key here, one who never really wanted to record. He does a short instrumental titled "Snitcher's Blues" (would have loved to hear a lyric on this one) and a patient "Blues for Lindy." The recording quality is acceptable, not great, and the information about recording dates and backup musicians is nonexistent; regardless, this is a potent reminder that this tradition has roots other than New Orleans, Chicago, or in the deep South. St. Louis was a hotbed, and here's the proof. *—Michael G. Nastos*

Big Road Blues: The Real Thing from Mississippi / 1992 / Collectables ✦✦✦

Another uneven Collectables collection, it has some rough but atmospheric (and totally obscure) early-'50s material mixed with later efforts by Houston Stackhouse. *—Bill Dahl*

Black Top Blues Vocal Dynamite! / Nov. 1995 / Black Top ✦✦✦

This is a great sampler of Black Top's underrated vault of blues, soul, and R&B, and it's hardly limited to vocalists as the cheesy title (and cover art) might suggest. (In fact, behind all the singing is a stack of instrumental dynamite, courtesy of the Tri-Sax-ual Soul Champs, harp blowers James Harman and Sam Myers, and guitarists Earl King, Phillip Walker, Robert Ward, and Mike Morgan.) With the exception of Kim Wilson's overwrought cover of "So Many Roads," everything on this compilation delivers, from straight-ahead blues to soul ballads to funky New Orleans grooves. Fans looking for warhorse blues standards won't find them here; most of these songs are relatively new originals that go well beyond the boundaries of 12-bar blues. Be patient with this one: It clocks in at a whopping 73 minutes, and three of the best performances come at the very end—The Crawl's "I Should've Done Better," Carol Fran's "I'll Never Be Free," and Snooks Eaglin's "Nine Pound Steel." *—Ken Chang*

Black Top Blues-A-Rama, Vol. 7: Live at Tipitinas / 1993 / Black Top ✦✦✦

Robert Ward makes his live recording debut on this simmering 1992 *Blues-A-Rama* set. Also aboard are bluesy zydeco expert Lynn August and three numbers by Carol Fran and Clarence Hollimon. *—Bill Dahl*

Blind Pig Records: 20th Anniversary Collection / Apr. 22, 1997 / Blind Pig ✦✦✦

San Francisco's Blind Pig Records celebrates their 20th anniversary with this two-disc, 36-track collection featuring over two hours' worth of highlights from their many releases with a few unreleased bonus tracks to spice up the mix. Originally started as a sideline to a blues club in Ann Arbor, MI, with an ear toward documenting the local scene and blues artists who played there regularly, Blind Pig has grown to record new artists like Debbie Davies, Joanna Connor, Tommy Castro, Jimmy Thackery, and Sarah Brown while more traditional bluesmen like Otis Rush, Snooky Pryor, Big Walter Horton, James Cotton, and Jimmy Rogers have all stopped in at various points and recorded an album or two for the label. Although the label already has one retrospective available (*The Blind Pig Sampler*), this one brings matters more up to date, including tracks from Coco Montoya ("Monkey See, Monkey Do"), Chubby Carrier ("Wastin' Time"), Sarah Brown ("Bad Thing"), and Studebaker John & the Hawks ("Two Time Boogie"), and sides from the aforementioned Thackery, Connor, Davies, and Castro. The traditional side of things is shored up by tracks from James Cotton ("Take Me Back"), Johnny Shines ("Blues Come From Texas"), Snooky Pryor ("Crazy 'Bout My Baby"), Otis Rush ("Right Place, Wrong Time"), and John Lee Hooker's version of "Terraplane Blues," taken from his guest appearance on a Roy Rogers album. Four previously unissued bonus tracks courtesy of Big Walter Horton ("If I Get Lucky"), Roosevelt Sykes ("I Wonder"), Pinetop Perkins ("Worried Life Blues"), and Henry Gray ("Cold Chills") make this collection another must-have. With sides from artists as diverse as soul singers Otis Clay and E.C. Scott to Preacher Boy and the Gospel Hummingbirds aboard, this double-disc set reaffirms the label's commitment to releasing brand-name blues and roots music. Blind Pig has released a multitude of great music in their many years as a label, and here's where you can pick up on some of the best of it. *—Cub Koda*

Blow It 'Till You Like It: Memphis Harmonica 1951–1954 / 1990 / Sun ✦✦✦✦✦

More blues and R&B harmonica is included on this generous 24-track import sampler. *—Hank Davis*

Blow'n the Blues: Best of the Great Harp Players / 2000 / Vanguard ✦✦✦✦✦

Subtitled "Best of the Great Harp Players," this pulls tracks from various Vanguard releases from the 1960s. Kicking off with five tracks from Junior Wells and five more from James Cotton, the set moves to pick up performances of Big Walter Horton behind Johnny Shines and a duet with a very young Charlie Musselwhite. Musselwhite has four tracks as solo artist, followed by two from the Siegel-Schwall Band. But the true highlight is a live at the 1965 Newport Folk Festival recording of the original Paul Butterfield Blues Band. With Mike Bloomfield on slide guitar, Butterfield tears into a version of Little Walter's "Blues With a Feeling" that would challenge his studio recording of the tune until Sam Lay inadvertently short circuits the tune a chorus too early, leaving Butterfield and the band scrambling for the ending—a great moment. A classic compilation, especially if you don't already have these tracks on other sets. —*Cub Koda*

Blue Flames: Sun Blues Collection / 1990 / Rhino ✦✦✦✦✦

If you are curious how the blues helped shape rock & roll, then get this collection of Sun Records' Memphis blues recordings. Stars of Sam Phillips' label and early rock icons Elvis, Jerry Lee Lewis, and Carl Perkins all sighted the influence of many of the performers here, and Elvis even covered one of the songs included on this disc ("Mystery Train" by Little Junior's Blue Flames). A more oblique tie-in to "The King" comes from Rufus Thomas' "Bear Cat," the answer song to Big Mama Thornton's original version of "Hound Dog." Other high-profile cuts include Jackie Brenston's "Rocket 88" (considered by many to be the first rock & roll song) and Roscoe Gordon's "I Found a New Love," as well as numbers by one-time Memphis DJ B.B. King ("B.B. Blues") and one-time Memphis resident Howlin' Wolf ("My Baby Walked Off"). Along the lines of Wolf's electric, Chicago blues sound, there's also James Cotton's "Cotton Crop Blues," Joe Hill Louis' "When I Am Gone (Treat Me Mean and Evil)," and Pat Hare's apparently true-to-life number "I'm Gonna Murder My Baby." And with the inclusion of Doctor Ross' "Terra Mae" and Sleepy John Estes' "Runnin' Around," country blues also gets its due. The set is rounded out by fine instrumentals from Jimmy & Walter and Johnny London, aka Alto Wizard, and with an excellent gospel number by the Southern Jubilee Singers. This is an exceptional collection, one that is essential listening for fans of early rock & roll and the blues. —*Stephen Cook*

Blue Girls, Vol. 1: 1924–1930 / Mar. 18, 1997 / Document ✦✦✦

Blue Girls, Vol. 1 (1924-1930) contains a selection of material from the obscure female blues singers Edna Johnson, Sadie James, Helen Beasley, Coletha Simpson, Julia Johnson, and Alura Mack. For specialists and academics, there is some interesting music here, but for anyone else, the exacting chronological sequencing, poor fidelity, and uneven performances make this collection of marginal interest. —*Thom Owens*

Blue Girls, Vol. 2: 1928–1930 / Mar. 18, 1997 / Document ✦✦✦

Blue Girls, Vol. 2 (1928-1930) contains a selection of material from the obscure female blues singers Katherine McDavid, Margaret Thornton, Mozelle Alderson, Issie Ringgold, and Mary Dixon. For specialists and academics, there is some interesting music here, but for anyone else, the exacting chronological sequencing, poor fidelity, and uneven performances make this collection of marginal interest. —*Thom Owens*

The Blue Horizon Story, Vol. 1: 1965–1970 / 1997 / Columbia ✦✦✦

While Blue Horizon gained its reputation as the home of great British blues (early Peter Green-era Fleetwood Mac, Chicken Shack, and others), its spiritual home was in America, and it released far more American artists than most people realize, beginning with its first disc—99 copies (for tax reasons) of a Hubert Sumlin single. That largely set the tone for the first five years of the label admirably covered in this three-CD set. Label head Mike Vernon was a blues lover and he released the music he loved, often licensing a track and sometimes signing and developing artists, as he did with his British stable, most especially Fleetwood Mac, born after Green left employer John Mayall (who also released two cuts on Blue Horizon, both with another former Bluesbreaker, Eric Clapton, and both, thankfully, here). Mac hit the big time with "Albatross," which definitely wasn't a blues, but their Chicago-influenced grit is apparent elsewhere, especially on "Temperature Is Rising (98.8F)," recorded with the legendary Otis Spann in the Windy City. But the label could easily move from the raw Delta sound of Bukka White to the electrifying slide of Hound Dog Taylor without it seeming unreasonable, while bringing on British artists like Duster Bennett, Jo Ann Kelly, and T.S. McPhee (who'd go on to head the Groundhogs) along the way. At best this can only be a taster, but it makes for a magnificent smorgasbord, not only of the real blues, but also of its very gritty and always authentic (at least on this label) British counterpart. —*Chris Nickson*

Blue Ladies / Mar. 7, 1921-Oct. 28, 1925 / Memphis Archives ✦✦✦✦

This collector's item CD has 18 selections from early classic blues singers. In addition to Bessie Smith, Mamie Smith, Clara Smith, Ida Cox, Trixie Smith, Ma Rainey, and Ethel Waters, a variety of lesser-known vocalists are represented: Edith Wilson, Clementine Smith, Sara Martin, Maggie Jones, Margaret Johnson, Rosa Henderson, Lucille Hegamin, Dora Carr, Mary Stafford, Viola McCoy, and Ethel Ridley. The majority of the selections were formerly rare (including Mary Stafford's "I'm Gonna Jazz My Way Straight Through Paradise"), and the sidemen include Johnny Dunn, Coleman Hawkins, Charlie Green, Louis Metcalf, Tommy Ladnier, Cow Cow Davenport, Joe Smith, and even Louis Armstrong, making this a CD worth picking up by 1920s collectors. —*Scott Yanow*

Blue Yule: Christmas Blues and R&B Classics / 1991 / Rhino ✦✦✦✦✦

A stellar 18-song compilation with most tracks not duplicated on other in-print collections. Treasures abound here: rare tracks from John Lee Hooker and Lightnin' Hopkins, Hop Wilson's original "Merry Christmas, Darling" (covered by the Fabulous Thunderbirds on *An Austin Rhythm & Blues Christmas*), Louis Jordan's last recording ("Santa Claus, Santa Claus," [1968]), and more. —*Dennis MacDonald*

The Blues: 1923 to 1933 / Jan. 31, 1923-Jul. 7, 1933 / ABC ✦✦✦

Engineer Robert Parker has the ability to turn music from the 1920s and '30s into stereo, or at least what sounds like a modern recording on a technological level. This particular set has him working his magic on 16 blues-oriented recordings from the 1923-1933 period. The music is excellent but the programming is fairly random (not in chronological order); classics alternate with obscurities and there is no logical "plot" to the set. Included is one selection apiece from Ida Cox, Cleo Gibson, Rosa Henderson, Frances Hereford ("Midnight Mama" with Jelly Roll Morton), the Memphis Jug Band, Ma Rainey, Issie Ringgold, country pioneer Jimmie Rodgers ("Blue Yodel No. 9" with Louis Armstrong helping out), Bessie Smith ("Nobody Knows You When You're Down and Out"), Mamie Smith, Victoria Spivey, Eva Taylor, Ethel Waters, Margaret Webster, Margaret Whitmire, and Lena Wilson (1923's "He Used to Be Your Man"). Excellent music, but the programming could be much more logical. —*Scott Yanow*

Blues Across America: The Detroit Scene / Jul. 1, 1997 / Cannonball ✦✦✦✦

Produced by Ron Levy, this entry in Cannonball's *Blues Across America* series focuses on the once-again burgeoning blues scene in the Motor City. The set kicks off with three tracks from Johnnie Bassett, former guitarist for Joe Weaver's Blue Notes. Here his big-bodied jazz guitar stylings meld perfectly with his regular working band, the Blues Insurgents, on a quartet of excellent tunes that led to his full-length albums for the label. Next up are the Butler Twins, mainstays on the local scene. Their harmonica and guitar work is a throwback to the 1950s style of Detroit blues, rough and crude, reminiscent of Baby Boy Warren's best sides. Chanteuse Alberta Adams, a longtime fixture on the scene, closes things out with four wonderful sides using a core band that revolves around Johnnie Bassett. With this entry in this important series, it's obvious that Detroit blues is alive, well, and thriving. —*Cub Koda*

Blues Across America: The Dallas Scene / Oct. 14, 1997 / Cannonball ✦✦✦

These new recordings produced by former Rounder/Bullseye Blues session whiz Ron Levy are part of a projected series highlighting regional blues scenes. This volume features three of the more unsung, but interesting, bluesmen of Dallas, TX. From the sheet-metal tone of Henry Qualls' guitar work ("Squirrel Sandwich," "Elmo Boogie") to the citified sound of pianist Big Al Dupree ("Waitin' on My Rider") to the B.B. King-inspired style of Charles Young and "Jr. Boy" Jones (featuring a six-minute B.B./Little Joe Blue medley), this collection gives an idea of the marvelous cross section of blues still alive in the Dallas area. —*Cub Koda*

Blues Across America: The Chicago Scene / Jan. 20, 1998 / Cannonball ✦✦✦

Blues Across America: The Chicago Scene assembles tracks from performers including Robert Plunkett, Emery Williams, Jr., and Little Arthur Duncan. While the material ranges from superb to mediocre, the collection is nevertheless a good introduction to the contemporary Windy City blues community. —*Jason Ankeny*

Blues Across America: The Nashville Scene / Apr. 27, 1999 / Cannonball ✦✦✦

Produced by songwriter/guitar wizard Fred James, this entry in Cannonball's *Blues Across America* series focuses on the bluesy and R&B side of Music City, U.S.A. The set kicks off with three tracks from Al Garner, former drummer behind Larry Birdsong, Gene Allison, and others. Here Garner steps forward as a lead singer with his band, the Roadrunners, and the results are outstanding and smooth as can be on numbers like "Rhythm Rockin' Blues" and Leiber & Stoller's "Yeah Yeah Yeah." Johnny Jones, former member of the Jimmy Beck Orchestra ("Pipe Dreams"), is up next with three excellent numbers co-written by James, all of them featuring Jones' stinging lead guitar work and laid-back vocals. Vocalist Charles "Wigg" Walker is next, getting soulful on James' "Even the Sky Is Blue" and the driving "99,000 Watts of Soul Power." Closing things out is Clifford Curry (best known for his hit "She Shot a Hole in My Soul") with three self-penned originals, all of them featuring James' tasty guitar with a guest appearance by Sam Lay on drums on "Welfare Blues." All in all, another excellent entry in this important series. —*Cub Koda*

Blues and Gospel from the Bandera, Laredo & Jerico Road Labels of Chicago / 2001 / Ace ✦✦✦

You can tell from the title alone that this isn't the kind of release likely to feature heavily in major chain discount ads, but rather one targeted toward the specialist collector. The Bandera label was one of many recording blues in Chicago in the late '50s and early '60s; Laredo and Jerico Road were Bandera subsidiaries, Jerico Road specializing in gospel. This anthology is split between electric blues (17 tracks) and gospel (ten tracks), and none of the artists achieved widespread recognition. Sometimes these compilations serve as little more than to suck up generic rarities for the convenience of collectors, but this one is on a higher level. Dusty Brown, Jimmie Lee Robinson, Grover Pruitt, and Bobby Davis all play decent classic '50s-style Chicago electric blues, pretty well produced (and boasting good fidelity on this reissue CD). But it also retains the raw edge that attracts so many listeners to blues from this time and place. No one would have been that surprised if Dusty Brown's four tracks were identified as vault finds from the Cobra and Chess labels. Jimmie Lee Robinson's "All My Life" was covered by John Mayall, and his seven tunes are pretty versatile for a little-known bluesman, getting into Johnny Cash rockabilly-influenced sounds on "Cry Over Me" and taking a slight R&B/early soul flavor on some other sides. Grover Pruitt's 1959 single "Mean Train" also has an interesting rockabilly residue, and Bobby Davis' four songs have a good-time mixture of blues and New Orleans R&B. The gospel tunes by the Norfleet Brothers, the Space Spiritual Singers, the Faithful Wanderers, and Elder Samuel Patterson are not as interesting as the blues material, but have a well-produced (yet not slick) R&B-blues-informed feel. It's a collection worth investigating by blues fans who want to dig into some obscure stuff that's just notable for its obscurity. —*Richie Unterberger*

Blues as Big as Texas, Vol. 1 / 1991 / Collectables ♦♦♦♦♦
These previously unreleased Texas blues were digitally remastered from the original tapes. The various artists recorded between 1958 and 1971 in Houston (one cut in Beaumont, TX) include Johnny Copeland, Clarence "Gatemouth" Brown, Percy Mayfield, and more. It's a good and varied set. *—Niles J. Frantz*

Blues at Newport / 1959 / Vanguard ♦♦♦
Blues at Newport offers fine performances by Mississippi John Hurt, Skip James, Rev. Gary Davis, Robert Wilkins, and others recorded live at the Newport Folk Festival from 1959 to 1964. *—Mark A. Humphrey*

The Blues Box / Jun. 21, 1994 / LaserLight ♦♦♦
Here are five discs, originally issued separately on the label, boxed up together as sort of a "deluxe" budget set. All of the material is licensed from the Delmark label and, as such, it is all top-notch, with classic performances throughout. *Chicago Blues Bash* features tracks from Junior Wells, Big Joe Williams, J.B. Hutto, and Jimmy Johnson, while *Windy City Blues* features tracks from Robert Jr. Lockwood, Otis Rush, Mighty Joe Young, and Roosevelt Sykes. Early sides from Robert Nighthawk and Little Walter show up on *Blues Legends*, whereas *Chicago Blues Masters* spotlights the work of Magic Sam, Carey Bell, Junior Wells, Arthur "Big Boy" Crudup, and Big Walter Horton. The final disc, *Midnight Blues*, features more tracks from Little Walter, Junior Wells, Louis Myers, Luther Allison, and Dave Specter. A lot of great blues for only pennies a serving. *—Cub Koda*

The Blues Came Down from Memphis / 1988 / Charly ♦♦♦♦♦
Nice overview of Sun Records' early-'50s blues recordings on a single-disc CD, primarily sticking to an issued singles format. Perfect place to start. *—Cub Koda*

Blues Classics / Jul. 29, 1996 / MCA ♦♦♦
Blues Classics is a three-disc box set that attempts to tell the history of the blues over the course of its 72 tracks. In a way, it does offer a good sampler. Drawing from tracks recorded between 1927 and 1969, many major artists are featured: Muddy Waters, Howlin' Wolf, Roosevelt Sykes, B.B. King, Lonnie Johnson, Lightnin' Hopkins, Bobby "Blue" Bland, Etta James, and John Lee Hooker are all featured, among many others. The catch is, several very, very important figures didn't make the cut—there's no Robert Johnson, Charley Patton, Magic Sam, etc.—even if it is probably because of legal rights. Furthermore, the selected tracks aren't always the best choices. Neverthless, *Blues Classics* does contain a lot of excellent performances and, in its own way, offers a good introduction to genre for neophytes, even if it is bound to frustrate collectors. *—Stephen Thomas Erlewine*

Blues Complete / Jan. 1, 1999 / Westside ♦♦♦
An enigmatic title, but one that refers to this gathering up of the complete recordings of Ralph Willis for Jubilee, Lonnie Johnson on Rama, and Johnny "Big Moose" Walker's unissued session for End. Willis' 1950-1951 sessions show a strong tie to his Piedmont background with Brownie McGhee on second guitar. Johnson's sessions for Rama in 1956 show an artist in the twilight of his career, playing it safe and easy, turning in some decidedly non-blues items like "Vaya Con Dios" and "Will You Remember," the latter a rewrite of his hit ballad, "Tomorrow Night." The session with Big Moose Walker and Jump Jackson features plenty of breakdowns, off-color studio chitchat, and solid playing by the carload on tunes like "Footrace to a Resting Place," "Wrong Doin' Woman," and "One Eyed Woman." Not the most vital blues recordings to own, but an interesting batch nonetheless. *—Cub Koda*

Blues Deluxe / 1989 / Alligator ♦♦♦♦♦
A 1989 reissue, this budget CD (only 39 minutes long) was recorded live at the 1980 Chicagofest. Included are Muddy Waters, Koko Taylor, Willie Dixon, and three others. *—Niles J. Frantz*

Blues Dimension / 1969 / Decca ♦♦♦♦♦
This is a very good collection of in-concert recordings from Stevie Ray Vaughan, Sugar Blue, and more. *—Niles J. Frantz*

Blues Fest: Modern Blues of the '70s / Oct. 24, 1995 / Rhino ♦♦♦
Historically, this is where the blues first started rearing its head, reaching a larger—and whiter—audience and eventually going more mainstream than the music ever had. Artists as diverse as B.B. King, Ann Peebles, Bobby Rush, the Allman Brothers Band, the Fabulous Thunderbirds, Koko Taylor, Chick Willis, and Hound Dog Taylor all have a voice in this excellent collection, every one of them sign pointers for the change that took place in the following decade. Excellent liner notes from Bill Dahl make this a modern-day compilation worth picking up. *—Cub Koda*

Blues Fest: Modern Blues of the '90s / Oct. 24, 1995 / Rhino ♦♦♦
By the 1990s, the face of blues had changed immensely and this 18-track collection attempts to chronicle those changes. While old-timers like Buddy Guy, Charles Brown, and Etta James were still making new, groundbreaking music, second-liners like Billy Boy Arnold, Smokey Wilson, Willie Kent, and R.L. Burnside had moved up through the ranks to take their place in the blues firmament. Equally explosive tracks from new names like William Clarke, Rod Piazza, Larry McCray, Lucky Peterson, and John Primer make this a modern-day compilation well worth investigating. *—Cub Koda*

Blues for a Rotten Afternoon / 2000 / Telarc ♦♦♦
From the "ain't nothin' more authentic" dirge of Luther "Guitar Junior" Johnson's "So Mean to Me" to the barrelhouse cluckin' of Marty Grebb's "Hen House," this blatant copy of Joel Dorn's *Jazz For* series combines true tales of loss with rather peppy pleas for love, wealth, and the other anti-ingredients of the blues. In true blues, everything gets lost, prompting Junior Wells to ask the somewhat musical question "Why Are People Like That" (a bluesy companion to Dylan's "Rainy Day Women"). While John Primer's "Brutal Hearted Woman" might be the culprit, Son Seals tells listeners that it can be the love itself that has the breakdown. In those cases where the problem is not your woman (which is actually the desired aim in Sugar Ray Norcia's blues-hearted "Life Will Be Better"), another common culprit is money (which is the titular theme of Debbie Davies' contribution). In the modern blues age, that can also mean a case of "Credit Card Blues," which Terry Evans diagnoses with insightful and cautionary humor. In the worst case scenario, love and money can combine for even more tragic results, as in Sam Lay's "Somebody's Gotta Do It." Though you may not want to admit it, there are times when the loss is your own darn fault, as in Kenny Neal's Cocker-esque "Killed the Goose That Laid the Golden Egg." Other times, the loss is not intentional, but still ends up being your fault, as in Lady Bianca's Motown-worthy heart-burner "How Do I Tell My Little Sister?" No matter what causes the pain, sometimes the only answer seems to be diving into a sea of drink, as Willie Dixon prepares to do in "If the Sea Was Whiskey." Other times, there isn't anything to do but sing the blues. Though the repertoire and cast of characters on this label sampler is impressive, nobody puts it together better than Maria Muldaur, whose aching "Misery and the Blues" sums it all up in more than name. *—Matthew S. Robinson*

Blues from "Big Bill's Copacabana" Live / Oct. 17, 1990 / Chess ♦♦♦♦♦
Classic 1963 Chicago blues. *—Bill Dahl*

Blues from the Montreux Jazz Festival / 1991 / Malaco ♦♦♦♦♦
Recorded at the Montreux Jazz Festival in Switzerland, during the Malaco Records European Tour in 1989, it features Bobby "Blue" Bland, Denise LaSalle, Johnnie Taylor, and Mosley & Johnson. Anything LaSalle was doing at the time is worth listening to, and it's nice to have a snapshot of her in-concert style. *—Niles J. Frantz*

Blues Goin' Down / Red Pelican ♦♦♦
This 18-track vinyl compilation brings together some truly great and very obscure early-'50s blues classics together on one disc. John Lee Henley's "Rhythm Rockin' Boogie" (which features Robert Jr. Lockwood on guitar, who spends most of the track trying to keep Henley from breaking meter) kicks things off, followed by J.B. Hutto's storming "Combination Boogie" and "Price of Love," the latter being originally unissued in the '50s and taken here from the lone surviving acetate. Jimmy Reed sideman Eddie Taylor brings three excellent performances ("Find Me a Baby," "Stroll Out West" and "I'm Looking for Somebody") to the side, which closes with three tracks from Sun harmonica legend Doctor Ross ("Call the Doctor," "Doctor Ross Boogie" and "32-20 Blues"), all three taken from his late-'50s tenure with Detroit's Fortune Records. The second half of the album is equally potent, featuring stellar sides from Jody Williams ("You May"), Little George Smith ("Oopin' Doopin' Doopin," "Blues Stay Away," "Blues in the Dark," "Telephone Blues"), Big Boy Spires ("About to Lose My Mind," "Which One Do I Love"), James Stewart ("Sweet Woman"), and James Walton & His Blues Kings ("Leaving Blues"). The fidelity on this compilation of dubious legality is spotty throughout (all of it taken from fairly beat-up vinyl transfers), but the ultra rarity of these sides make this a safe bet not to be seeing the compact disc light of day anytime in the near future, even in piecemeal form. *—Cub Koda*

Blues Guitar Blasters / 1987 / Ace ♦♦♦♦♦
This album is a decent, but rather unfocused, compilation of outstanding electric blues guitarists from the '50s and '60s, including selections from B.B. King, Albert King, Elmore James, John Lee Hooker, Pee Wee Crayton, Guitar Slim, and less-discussed masters like Jimmy Nolen (spelled "Jimmy Nolan" here) and Lafayette Thomas. The tracks and artists aren't linked by the same label, the same decade, or anything except outstanding guitar skills. They're not even all rare or uncommon: B.B. King's "Early in the Morning," Elmore James' "Dust My Blues," and Guitar Slim's "The Things That I Used to Do" are all well-known classics that are easy to pick up elsewhere. What might excite blues collectors are some of the lesser-heard items, such as the previously unissued "After Hours," a picked instrumental by Jimmy Nolen, who would become an important sideman to James Brown in the early funk era with his chicken scratch guitar. Perhaps this reflects a bias on the part of the compiler, but (on Nolen's selection and others) this disc generally favors the more cleanly picked and articulated, urbane blues than the looser and more wildly imaginative forms. There are exceptions to that, though, as on Lafayette Thomas' sudden stuttering flight up the strings on "Jumpin' in the Heart of Town" and Ike Turner's previously unissued "Twistin' the Strings." Original dates and labels are not supplied in the track listings—very unusual for Ace—although some are revealed in the liner notes. *—Richie Unterberger*

Blues Guitar Greats / 1996 / Delmark ♦♦♦
This 17-track collection runs from 1961 to 1995, a good 30-plus years of the label's existence. As such, it covers just about every strain of blues guitar that has ever appeared on Delmark. With standout tracks from Big Joe Williams, Magic Sam (an unreleased live track from 1968), Luther Allison, J.B. Hutto, Robert Jr. Lockwood, Junior Wells with Buddy Guy, Lonnie Brooks, and Lurrie Bell, this is a really nice overview of Chicago blues guitar-oriented recordings covering a good three decades of important music. Highly recommended. *—Cub Koda*

Blues Guitar Summit / Jan. 12, 1993 / Charly ♦♦♦
The short-lived American TV series *Chicago Blues Jam* provides this collection's audio tracks, taken from the stage at Buddy Guy's Legends in Chicago. As such, many of the tunes fade in mid-flight, as if you walked into a club and rounded the corner. Once there, the performances are raw and heartfelt, with stage-worthy turns from Magic Slim & the Teardrops, Son Seals, and Lonnie Brooks. Sounding exactly what a hot night in a blues bar should sound like, this gives you three headlining acts for the price of one—a pretty good deal, warts and all. *—Cub Koda*

Blues Hangover / 1995 / Excello ♦♦♦♦
This two-disc, 43-track collection collects up a treasure trove of rare and unissued performances from the vaults of Excello Records. All but one of the 17 tracks collected on the first disc were produced by Jay Miller in his Crowley, LA, studio, home of Excello's unmistakable "swamp blues" sound. The first ten tracks are by Jimmy Anderson, who impersonates the vocal and harmonica style of Jimmy Reed so pervasively, it's downright eerie. Three tracks from Whispering Smith, a stray Lightnin' Slim cut, and both sides of the mysterious Blue Charlie single are aboard, as well as rare singles from the equally mysterious Ole Sonny Boy, Little Al (Gunter), and Little Sonny. But the true find here are the first time release of 15 tracks from a 1966 audition tape by one Early Drane. For all intents and purposes, this appears to be the same "Earl Draines" who recorded for the label as part of the Blues Rockers ("Calling All Cows") in the mid-'50s. But these remarkable tapes are the man alone in his living room, singing and playing a quirky collection of original material, blues, and gospel covers that careen from brilliant to downright loony. Add to this lineup four tracks by Detroit bluesman Baby Boy Warren (featuring Sonny Boy Williamson on harmonica) and two early-'60s stereo swingers by the little-known James Stewart and you've got an Excello rarities packages that's pretty hard to beat. *—AMG*

Blues in the Mississippi Night / Jul. 13, 1991 / Rykodisc ♦♦♦♦♦
This pioneering, documentary-style recording was produced by Alan Lomax and laid unissued for decades after its 1946 recording due to its frank discussion of racism by Big Bill Broonzy, Sonny Boy Williamson, and Memphis Slim. *—Bill Dahl*

Blues Is Killin' Me / 1991 / Paula/Flyright ♦♦♦♦♦
This is a 20-track, rock-solid collection of classic blues sides from Chicago's JOB label, primarily focusing on both sides of original issue 78s by Floyd Jones, Memphis Minnie, Baby Face Leroy, and Little Hudson's Red Devil Trio, with a few unissued surprises rounding out the already excellent package. *—Cub Koda*

☆ **Blues Masters, Vol. 1: Urban Blues** / 1992 / Rhino ♦♦♦♦♦
While more horn-driven and less guitar reliant than other forms of blues, the urban style nonetheless provides its own spectacular highlights, some of the best of which are right here. The first volume in this 15 volume series features classic performances by Eddie "Cleanhead" Vinson, Dinah Washington, T-Bone Walker, Charles Brown, Joe Turner, and Jimmy Witherspoon. Where the blues meets the jazz and heads uptown for a party. *—Cub Koda*

☆ **Blues Masters, Vol. 2: Postwar Chicago Blues** / 1992 / Rhino ♦♦♦♦♦
An excellent 18-track compendium of all the major movers and shakers who helped shape the Chicago blues scene in the '50s. Everyone is well represented here, and major stars like Muddy Waters and Howlin' Wolf stand next to behind-the-scenes geniuses like Earl Hooker and Jody Williams for an interesting, and accurate, blend. *—Cub Koda*

☆ **Blues Masters, Vol. 3: Texas Blues** / 1992 / Rhino ♦♦♦♦♦
The best that the Lone Star State had to offer over a 60-year period is right here, from Blind Lemon Jefferson's "Match Box Blues" (1927) to Stevie Ray Vaughan's live version of "Flood Down in Texas (Texas Flood)" from 1986. This compilation also features great sides by the Fabulous Thunderbirds, Lightnin' Hopkins, T-Bone Walker, and Albert Collins. As a introduction to the Texas blues style, this is a pretty darn good one. *—Cub Koda*

★ **Blues Masters, Vol. 4: Harmonica Classics** / 1992 / Rhino ♦♦♦♦♦
This typically ace installment of the *Blues Masters* series has examples *par excellence* from most of the major electric blues harmonica geniuses, including Little Walter, Junior Wells, Sonny Boy Williamson, James Cotton, Paul Butterfield, Billy Boy Arnold, Lazy Lester, and Jimmy Reed. And while there are a few expected classics here (Little Walter's "Juke," Sonny Boy Williamson's "Help Me," Junior Wells' "Messin' With the Kid," Slim Harpo's "I Got Love If You Want It"), there are numerous delightful obscurities, like Jerry McCain's "Steady," Walter Horton's "Easy" (credited to "Jimmy & Walter"), and Snooky Pryor's "Boogie Twist." Charlie Musselwhite's 11-minute adaptation of the jazz tune "Christo Redemptor" is superb and challenges conventional ideas of what should and shouldn't be done with blues harmonica. *—Richie Unterberger*

☆ **Blues Masters, Vol. 5: Jump Blues Classics** / 1992 / Rhino ♦♦♦♦♦
Jump blues, of course, was crucial to the birth of R&B and rock & roll. More important, the infectious swing, grit, and humor were great in themselves. *Jump Blues Classics* collects 18 tracks from the golden days of the genre in the late '40s and '50s. Most of the pioneers of the style are here—Joe Turner, Wynonie Harris, Roy Brown, Ruth Brown, Roy Milton, Big Jay McNeely, and others, even Louis Prima. The collection includes several cuts that were revived to become rock & roll classics, including "The Train Kept A-Rollin'" (Tiny Bradshaw), "Shake, Rattle and Roll" (Joe Turner), "Good Rockin' Tonight" (Wynonie Harris), "Hound Dog" (Big Mama Thornton), and the little-known original, pre-Muddy Waters version of "Got My Mojo Working" (Ann Cole). This is, of course, just the surface of a genre that was hugely successful in its time, producing hundreds of memorable recordings. This well-annotated anthology is a good starting point and a good representative sampling for those who only want the cream of the crop in their collection. *—Richie Unterberger*

★ **Blues Masters, Vol. 6: Blues Originals** / 1993 / Rhino ♦♦♦♦♦
It's unfortunate, but it's true: The original versions of many blues classics aren't nearly as well-known as their hit covers by (usually white) rock groups. That's not to say that some of these covers aren't great as well, but it's both educational and enjoyable to hear them from the source's mouth. *Blues Originals* contains 18 original versions of classics that went on to reach a wide audience via covers by the Stones, Yardbirds, Elvis, Led Zeppelin, the Doors, and others. The Chess stable of Howlin' Wolf, Muddy Waters, Bo Diddley, Little Walter, and Sonny Boy Williamson is represented here, of course, along with standards by Elmore James, Otis Rush, Robert Johnson, Slim Harpo, and Jimmy Reed. Mixed in with great and fairly available performances like Bo Diddley's "I'm a Man" and Howlin' Wolf's "Back Door Man" are some quite obscure and collectable delights. Arthur "Big Boy" Crudup's original version of "That's All Right," covered by Elvis Presley for his first single, has been surprisingly hard to find over the years; ditto for Muddy Waters' "You Need Love," which formed the blueprint for Led Zeppelin's "Whole Lotta Love." Even most Yardbirds fanatics are unaware that the prototype for "Lost Woman" was taken from (and retitled from) an obscure Snooky Pryor single, "Someone to Love Me." And even many Chicago blues fanatics will be surprised to find the original version of "Got My Mojo Working," which was not recorded by Muddy Waters, but little-known jump blues singer Ann Cole. A fine collection, mixing together famous standards and obscure gems with thorough liner notes. *—Richie Unterberger*

Blues Masters, Vol. 7: Blues Revival / 1993 / Rhino ♦♦♦♦♦
It's hard to believe from the vantage point of a period when blues songs are used for network television commercials, but it wasn't so long ago that the blues was, though hardly in danger of extinction, certainly limited to a pretty specialized audience. The blues revival of the early '60s brought the music back into the spotlight through its prominence at major folk festivals and college concerts, the rediscovery of lost legends like Skip James and Mississippi John Hurt, and the efforts of several musicians and record labels to popularize the work of the form's originators. *Blues Revival* covers a lot of these bases. This 17-track collection includes some of the biggest hit blues singles of the '60s (by Jimmy Reed, John Lee Hooker, Slim Harpo, and B.B. King), '60s recordings by acoustic Delta blues giants like Mississippi Fred McDowell and Son House, hot electric Chicago blues by Junior Wells and Muddy Waters, and white, rock-oriented revivalists like Paul Butterfield, John Mayall, and Canned Heat. Seasoned collectors won't find anything too obscure here, but it's a handy primer to some of the best blues recorded during an era in which the idiom reestablished itself as a vital and living form. *—Richie Unterberger*

Blues Masters, Vol. 8: Mississippi Delta Blues / 1993 / Rhino ♦♦♦
The title for this volume is a bit of a misnomer. While there is easily half a compilation's worth of authentic acoustic material here (including classics by Tommy Johnson, Charley Patton, Willie Brown, and Robert Johnson), the inclusion of tracks by B.B. and Albert King and recorded in Chicago sides by Howlin' Wolf, Elmore James, and Robert Nighthawk do much to blur the distinctiveness of this package. *—Cub Koda*

Blues Masters, Vol. 9: Postmodern Blues / 1993 / Rhino ♦♦♦♦♦
A wonderful compendium of artists and styles illustrating the coming of blues into the mainstream. This volume features representative tracks by B.B. King, Albert Collins, Albert King, George Thorogood, Stevie Ray Vaughan, Johnny Winter, and the Fabulous Thunderbirds. The modern sound at its best, and most diverse. *—Cub Koda*

Blues Masters, Vol. 10: Blues Roots / 1993 / Rhino ♦♦♦
Expertly compiled, annotated, and in most cases recorded by pioneering blues researcher Samuel Charters, this volume explores all areas of the blues' origins. Featuring devastating recordings of prison work hands, native African music to Texas prison songs, this is as hardcore a collection as you're likely to find, yet still very accessible to the average fan. *—Cub Koda*

☆ **Blues Masters, Vol. 11: Classic Blues Women** / 1993 / Rhino ♦♦♦♦♦
Although it is now a male-dominated field, the earliest to record and have success in the blues field were women. This volume not only collects up many of the great recordings by these women (Mamie, Trixie, and Bessie Smith, Billie Holiday, Sippie Wallace, Ma Rainey), but also holds the distinction in the series of being one of the few that offers multiple selections by some of these artists. Highly recommended. *—Cub Koda*

☆ **Blues Masters, Vol. 12: Memphis Blues** / 1993 / Rhino ♦♦♦♦♦
Running the blues history of America's craziest city from early offerings by Cannon's Jug Stompers and the Memphis Jug Band to early Sun recordings from the '50s by Junior Parker, Rufus Thomas, and Joe Hill Louis, this is undoubtedly one of the best compiled volumes in the series. *—Cub Koda*

Blues Masters, Vol. 13: New York City Blues / 1993 / Rhino ♦♦♦♦♦
While other volumes in the series showcase the down-home aspects of the music, this one highlights the big-band sound. Great sides by Lionel Hampton ("Hamp's Boogie Woogie"), Duke Ellington, Buddy Johnson, Count Basie, Sam "The Man" Taylor ("Oo-Wee"), and Lucky Millinder showcase a side to the music that is seldom heard. *—Cub Koda*

★ **Blues Masters, Vol. 14: More Jump Blues** / 1993 / Rhino ♦♦♦♦♦
Just as essential as the previous Rhino jump blues collection (the fifth volume of the *Blues Masters* series), this has classics by Floyd Dixon ("Hey Bartender"), Joe Liggins ("Pink Champagne"), Joe Turner, Wynonie Harris, Ruth Brown, Big Maybelle, and Louis Jordan. It also takes some chances by presenting cuts by performers not strictly identified with the style, like Louis Prima, Bobby Charles (the original version of Bill Haley's "See You Later Alligator"), Little Richard, and Faye Adams, whose rousing "I'll Be True" is a touchstone of early R&B. *—Richie Unterberger*

Blues Masters, Vol. 15: Slide Guitar Classics / 1993 / Rhino ♦♦♦♦♦
This volume in the series features seminal and classic tracks from Elmore James ("Dust My Broom"), Muddy Waters ("Honey Bee"), and Hound Dog Taylor to modern-day disciples like Johnny Winter and Ry Cooder. Blind Willie Johnson's "Dark Was the Night, Cold Was the Ground" is worth the price of admission alone. *—Cub Koda*

☆ **Blues Masters, Vol. 16: More Harmonica Classics** / Jul. 14, 1998 / Rhino ♦♦♦♦♦
With such a wealth of great harmonica blues out there, and with such an outstanding track record on Rhino's part in general when it comes to historical compilations, it's no

surprise that their second anthology of harmonica blues is just as good as the first. There are fine cuts by many big guns here, including Little Walter, both Sonny Boy Williamsons, James Cotton, Jimmy Reed, Junior Wells, Paul Butterfield, Slim Harpo, and Sonny Terry (whose hard-rocking, electric "Hootin' Blues No. 2," from a 1956 RCA single, is a highlight). The less-obvious choices make this a pleasure for mid-level blues fans looking for something they haven't heard before as well as more familiar material: Papa Lightfoot's "Jump the Boogie" is great early raw electric blues with vocals that sound as if the mike was covered with sandpaper, and Doctor Ross' "Come Back Baby" is one of the most primordial blues recorded at Sun. —*Richie Unterberger*

Blues Masters, Vol. 17: More Postmodern Blues / Jul. 14, 1998 / Rhino ✦✦✦✦✦

Putting together a compilation of "postmodern" (post-1970) blues is a challenge because the classics of the era are not as commonly agreed upon as they are for previous decades, and because the form has been more static than it was in the earlier days of the blues' evolution. It's not as good as Rhino's previous *Postmodern Blues* compilation (issued as the ninth volume of the *Blues Masters* series), but it still has a good alternation of good cuts by major figures (the Allman Brothers, Albert King, B.B. King, James Cotton, Little Milton, Robert Cray, Koko Taylor, Albert Collins), solid journeyman types (Johnny Copeland, Joe Louis Walker, Luther Allison, Johnny Adams), and the occasional name that still isn't widely known to the general audience (W.C. Clark, Larry Garner). Soul-blues-funk-rock fusion is often characteristic of the selections, but there is is a nod to acoustic traditions by Keb' Mo'. —*Richie Unterberger*

☆ Blues Masters, Vol. 18: More Slide Guitar Classics / Jul. 14, 1998 / Rhino ✦✦✦✦✦

Rhino's second slide guitar anthology leads off with a couple of dyed-in-the-wool classics with Muddy Waters' "I Can't Be Satisfied" and Elmore James' "The Sky Is Crying." But the emphasis on this 18-track disc is much more on little-heard delights that might come as surprises even to knowledgeable blues fans. Earl Hooker's "Wah Wah Blues" shows him playing around with the wah wah pedal to great effect in late 1968; Boyd Gilmore's 1952 single "All My Dreams" has great raw soloing from Elmore James (spliced in from James' "Please Find My Baby" single); Chuck Berry's "Blues for Hawaiians" reveals a little-noted aspect of his playing; and Eddie "One String" Jones' "John Henry" is a primitive one-string blues that takes the slide back to its diddley bow origins. There's also the strange rockabilly-blues hybrid "Rocking in the Coconut Top" by Hop Wilson, with weird background noises that sound like balloons being rubbed. There are also plenty of quality selections by bigger names like Blind Willie Johnson, J.B. Hutto, Robert Jr. Lockwood, Son House, Tampa Red, and Johnny Winter, with the expected expert liner notes by Cub Koda. —*Richie Unterberger*

Blues Next: The New Generation / Feb. 24, 1998 / Simitar ✦✦✦

This budget-priced 11-track compilation highlights selections from contemporary blues artists and blues-rockers in a wide range of styles that holds together nicely. Pulling together selections all recorded in the 1990s, this features modern-day blues rockers like Monster Mike Welch ("Axe to Grind"), Tinsley Ellis ("To the Devil for a Dime"), Chris Duarte ("My Way Down"), Corey Stevens, and Tommy Castro ("This Soul Is Mine"), pitted against more traditionally minded or rootsier players like Bernard Allison, Lucky Peterson, Coco Montoya ("Same Dog"), and Smokin' Joe Kubek ("Can't See for Lovin'"). Transfers are clear and crisp, and fans of modern-day blues who like a lot of guitar solos to go with it will love this one. —*Cub Koda*

Blues on the Charts 1948 to 1972 / AMC ✦✦✦✦

This six-CD set serves as a promotional sampler for the vast holdings of the Arc Music publishing catalog, the lion's share of which constitutes the large amount of blues classics that were released on the Chess and Vee-Jay labels. And true to form, the set is loaded with R&B chart material going back to 1948 with Memphis Slim's "Messin' Around," bringing classics to the mix from Howlin' Wolf ("How Many More Years," "Moanin' at Midnight," "Rockin' Daddy," "Forty-Four," "Killing Floor," "Smokestack Lightnin'," "May I Have a Talk With You"), Little Walter ("Juke," "Off the Wall," "Sad Hours," "Blues With a Feeling," "Last Night," "You're So Fine"), Bo Diddley ("Who Do You Love," "I'm a Man," "Diddley Daddy," "Bo Diddley," "Mona," "Hey! Bo Diddley"), Chuck Berry ("Brown Eyed Handsome Man," "Go Go Go," "Come On," "You Never Can Tell," "No Particular Place to Go," "The Promised Land"), Muddy Waters ("Sugar Sweet," "Forty Days and Forty Nights," "She's Into Something," "Good Morning Little Schoolgirl," "Bird Nest on the Ground"), and Jimmy Reed ("You Got Me Dizzy," "Ain't That Lovin' You Baby," "Honest I Do," "The Sun Is Shining," "Baby, What You Want Me to Do," "Bright Lights, Big City"). Certainly doo wop classics abound with the Spaniels' "Baby, It's You" and "Goodnight, Sweetheart, Goodnight," the El Dorados' "I'll Be Forever Loving You" and "At My Front Door," the Flamingos' "I'll Be Home," the Tune Weavers' "Happy Happy Birthday Baby," the Moonglows' "Ten Commandments of Love" and "See Saw," Lee Andrews & the Hearts' "Long Lonely Nights" and "Teardrops," the Dells' "Stay in My Corner," Danny & the Juniors' "At the Hop" and "Rock'n'Roll Is Here to Stay," and the Students' "I'm So Young" all contributing heavily. But just as Arc's holdings reach far afield, so does the licensing in this mammoth set, ranging from the original 1951 Trumpet recordings of Elmore James' "Dust My Broom" and Sonny Boy Williamson's "Eyesight to the Blind" to Johnny Hodges' "Castle Rock" to Aaron Neville's "Tell It Like It Is" to the Beach Boys' "Surfin' U.S.A." (actually Chuck Berry's "Sweet Little Sixteen"), to the last track on disc six, the Allman Brothers' rendition of Willie Dixon's "One Way Out." With a brace of marvelous one-offs aboard (Otis Redding's "Pain in My Heart," the Sensations' "Let Me In," Pigmeat Markham's "Here Comes the Judge," Phil Upchurch's "You Can't Sit Down," Dee Clark's "Raindrops," Dale Hawkins' "Susie-Q"), it's hard to believe you could cram 150 tunes on six discs and not find a single boring cut anywhere. But believe it, for the length and depth of this collection is overwhelming, but immensely listenable, and this is well worth

hunting down as it will make a wonderful and hefty addition to anyone's blues/R&B collection. —*Cub Koda*

Blues on the High Seas, King Snake Live! / Jul. 21, 1998 / King Snake ✦✦✦✦

Recorded live on a blues cruise ship, this is the label's first live album, featuring several of the label's mainstays, Ace Moreland, Junior Markham, Sonny Rhodes, Noble Watts, and Floyd Miles, backed by the Midnight Creepers, the house band. Kenny Neal puts in a guest shot with Sonny Rhodes, the two of them trading lap steel licks on Jimmy Rogers' "You're the One." With the presence of a full horn section on most cuts and the enthusiastic interaction of the players involved, there was an awful lot of energy pouring off that stage when the tapes were rolling, and it's all here to savor. An inspired session that weds blues and blues-rock players together quite successfully. —*Cub Koda*

Blues Piano Orgy / 1972 / Delmark ✦✦✦✦

Thanks in part to the luridly alluring title and the enthusiastically informative liner notes by Bob Koester, this solid collection was many a young musician's introduction to the men who pioneered blues piano in the first half of the 20th century. Roosevelt Sykes is the best-represented artist here, and his leering vocals are hard to resist: After hearing the ribald metaphor of "Dresser Drawers," you'll never view furniture quite the same way again. His "Kickin' Motor Scooter" is truly a marvel of smiling euphemism, with the song devoted to boasts of how he's "A dangerous motor scooter...A tricky motor scooter!" Other artists, while not always as inventive lyrically, show a wide range of piano styles, from the bouncing syncopated jazz of "Stendahl Stomp" to the trickling upper registers and restrained bass coaxed by Curtis Jones from a battered old piano in "Tin Pan Alley Blues No. 2." Not every track is unaccompanied piano, though. "Every Time I Get to Drinking," a blues dirge to the bottle, revolves around the elastic pull of an upright bass. The closing instrumental, Otis Spann's "Three-in-One Blues," features ominous bass chords wracked by a scattershot backing of drums. Despite being essentially a glorified soundcheck, and by far the least-structured piece on the album, it's also the most primally satisfying. —*Paul Collins*

Blues Power: Songs of Eric Clapton / Jun. 22, 1999 / House of Blues ✦✦✦

Although *Blues Power: Songs of Eric Clapton* contains a couple versions of blues standards recorded at one time or another by Clapton, it's mostly devoted to covers of Clapton compositions by blues veterans and relative newcomers alike (i.e., either influences on Clapton or artists who have been influenced by him). The performances are generally spot-on, but that's to be expected from an artist roster that includes Koko Taylor, Pinetop Perkins, Otis Rush, Bo Diddley, Buddy Guy, Larry McCray, and Eric Gales, among others. —*Steve Huey*

The Blues Project / 1964 / Elektra ✦✦

Not to be confused with the *group* the Blues Project (although future Blues Project guitarist Danny Kalb is one of the artists), this is an anthology of white mid-'60s folk-blues, just before folk-rock turned everything around and made such excursions largely passé. It's not what you would want to hold up as ammunition when trying to prove that white boys really *can* play the blues. Most of these guys were important in exposing the blues to white folk audiences; John Koerner and Dave Ray were part of Koerner, Ray & Glover, Kalb as mentioned became central to the actual Blues Project, Geoff Muldaur was a well-known jug band revivalist, and Mark Spoelstra and Eric Von Schmidt both had peripheral connections with Bob Dylan's early career. (John Sebastian, though he is not featured as a soloist, is credited as one of the "assisting musicians.") Although the fingerpicking is OK, the vocals are tepid and callow. Only Dave Van Ronk's two tracks betray a man who can feel, live, and therefore sing the blues in his distinctive growl. The LP is musically insignificant, though of interest for the rare appearances by some of its better-known musicians. —*Richie Unterberger*

Blues Routes: Heroes & Tricksters / Jul. 20, 1999 / Smithsonian/Folkways ✦✦✦

This blues compilation features 17 live performances drawn from 1990-1995 recordings that were done for the *Folk Masters* series distributed by Public Radio International; all of these were recorded at either the Barns of Wolf Trap or Carnegie Hall. There's a lot of variety and numerous styles represented: work songs, folksy songsters, modern electric blues (Joe Louis Walker does an eight-minute "Bluesifyin"), Delta-styled blues (Robert Jr. Lockwood), piano jazz-blues, and more. It's adventurous enough to go off into some detours that aren't strictly blues, but certainly blues-related, as in the zydeco by Boozoo Chavis, the a cappella vocals of the Georgia Sea Island Singers, the jazz violin of Claude Williams, and the New Orleans trad jazz of Don Vappie & the Creole Jazz Serenaders. Many of the performers were quite elderly when they made their contributions, and while it's great that there is a venue for these guardians of tradition, much of the disc is overly polite in execution. When the White Cloud Hunters Mardi Gras Indians come on with their unbridled chants on "Sew, Sew, Sew," the energy and daring really pick up. The go-go music of Rapper Dee, C.J., and Five Gallons of Fun's "My Mind Has No Color/Doing It the Go-Go Way," with percussion performed largely on paint buckets and other found objects, is another ambitious detour worth applauding. —*Richie Unterberger*

The Blues Scene / 1999 / Deram ✦✦✦✦

Contrary to historical impressions, England's Decca Records did have a connection to blues beyond the Rolling Stones, as the 25 songs on this CD illustrate. The Stones, in fact, are absent from this disc, owing to contractual restrictions, but John Mayall is present on five of the cuts (one with Eric Clapton, the others mostly with Peter Green), as are British blues founding father Alexis Korner (very well-represented on "Night Time Is the Right Time") and veteran keyboard player and bandleader Zoot Money. A lot of what's here is electric blues-rock, beginning with the Peter Green guitar showcase "Curly," cut by Green, John McVie, and Aynsley Dunbar—Green and Mayall's band are downright ubiquitous on this disc, along with most of the other blues-rock outfits signed by producer Mike Vernon, but there are a surprising number of authentic American blues people as well: Eddie

Boyd ("Key to the Highway," "Blue Coat Man," "Dust My Broom"), Otis Spann ("Pretty Girls Everywhere"), Curtis Jones ("Roll Me Over"), Mae Mercer ("Sweet Little Angel"), and Champion Jack Dupree ("Barrel House Woman," "Third Degree"). The old-timers outclass most of the white British bluesmen surrounding them and raise the value on this collection, Curtis Jones' "Roll Me Over" being worth about a third of the price of this disc by itself. Keef Hartley's presence can be debated as a virtue, but generally the blues-rock sides are well-chosen: "Train to Nowhere" is one of the best songs in Savoy Brown's output; similarly, "Steppin' Out" is one of the best Clapton/Bluesbreakers cuts, and "Strut Around" is a good Graham Bond Organization dance number. Additionally, the producers have reached out to such one-off vault items as "Long Night," an instrumental duet featuring John Mayall and a musician billed as "Steve Anglo," who was none other than Steve Winwood testing the waters beyond the boundaries of the Spencer Davis Group; that track and "Goin' Down Slow," as performed on acoustic guitar and sung by Davy Graham, justify the rest of the cost of this disc, by themselves. The sound is excellent and the notes are very thorough, and most of the 25 tracks here have simply not been widely available on CD before. *—Bruce Eder*

The Blues White Album / Jan. 22, 2002 / Telarc ♦♦♦

Telarc stretches their label tribute series concept practically to the breaking point when they attempt to breathe blues life into the Beatles' sprawling masterwork. George Benson and Booker T. & the MG's tried similar treatments of *Abbey Road*, but the *White Album*, with its wildly diverse styles, hasn't been ripe for reinterpretation, especially in a blues mode. Although it's ultimately disappointing, this does have enough moments to appeal to fans of the participating artists and the genre. Whittling down the original double album's 30 tracks to a more manageable ten still doesn't explain why such naturally bluesy rockers like "Savoy Truffle," "Birthday," and "Back in the USSR" were ignored in favor of the bouncy pop of "Ob-la-di, Ob-la-da" and "Don't Pass Me By." Both fall flat here, with Maria Muldaur sounding completely lost on the former, and bass-playing sessionman T-Bone Wolk's unconvincingly wimpy vocals on the latter. Chris Duarte takes the title of "I'm So Tired" too much too heart as he practically sleepwalks though a mumbling, shambling version of the druggy tune that sounds like a demo bolstered by a snazzy guitar solo. Anders Osborne comes up empty-handed while attempting to inject R&B into the twisting "Happiness Is a Warm Gun," but the song's winding, disjointed melody and free-form lyrics don't translate well to a blues interpretation. Even "Yer Blues," the most obvious cover, comes up short of its potential, as Lucky Peterson seems like a caricature of himself, working too hard to put it across as slow Chicago blues. Peterson shares guitar and vocals with Louisiana's Kenny Neal and Tab Benoit (at the time of this disc's issue, all three were not-so-coincidentally signed to Telarc, as were most of the other artists involved) on a rocking "Revolution" that comes closest to achieving this album's intention. Joe Louis Walker expands "While My Guitar Gently Weeps" to twice its original length, effectively digging into the guts of the tune in a stirring, near-wrenching performance. Similarly, the always-classy Charlie Musselwhite transforms "Dear Prudence" into an eight-minute instrumental epic, complete with crying harp and Colin Linden's sympathetic slide guitar. That, along with an acoustic "Blackbird," which takes McCartney's simple love song down to the Delta in an imaginative and moving unplugged version by Linden, shows the potential of this undertaking. It doesn't all gel, but the highlights show promise for future projects to be more successful. *—Hal Horowitz*

The Blues: A Smithsonian Collection of Classic Blues Singers / 1993 / Smithsonian Collection ♦♦♦♦♦

While *any* collection professing to be a definitive overview of a genre usually falls short of the mark, it's hard to find fault with this excellently researched and compiled four-disc set from the Smithsonian Collection. Running the recorded history of the music chronologically, the first disc explores the early sides by guitarists like Blind Lemon Jefferson, Barbecue Bob, Blind Willie Johnson, and Tommy Johnson, and classic blues singers like Bessie Smith, Ma Rainey, and Sippie Wallace. Volume two rounds up sides from Leroy Carr, Mississippi John Hurt, Charley Patton, Memphis Minnie, Son House, and Big Joe Williams, as well as off-the-beaten-track delights from the Memphis Jug Band and the Mississippi Sheiks. The third volume continues in the history of Delta blues with classic entries from Robert Johnson and Bukka White, moving into the Bluebird beat, ending up with the first recordings from John Lee Hooker and Lightnin' Hopkins. The final disc is a veritable feast of Chicago blues with classic sides galore from Muddy Waters, Junior Wells, Elmore James, Howlin' Wolf, Otis Rush, and Jimmy Reed, finishing with more contemporary offerings from Ray Charles, Latimore, and a retro style closer from Cephas & Wiggins. The transfers on the really vintage sides are as good as any you're likely to come across, and the song selection throughout is impeccable. Add a sumptuous booklet chock-full of photos and an abundance of historical facts, all well-annotated by W.K. McNeil, and you've got a box set for the ages. Very, very well done. *—Cub Koda*

The Blues, Vol. 1 / 1990 / Chess/MCA ♦♦♦♦

Even though Chess should be releasing collections with more than just over 30 minutes of music on them, this thin blues roundup from the legendary Chicago label's vaults still works well enough as a sampler of vintage electric blues. Recorded between 1952 and 1960, the 12 tracks spotlight such legends as Muddy Waters, Howlin' Wolf, Little Walter, Buddy Guy, John Lee Hooker, and Sonny Boy Williamson. Most of the numbers are classics, including Waters' "Hoochie Coochie Man," Wolf's "Smokestack Lightning," and Walter's "Juke." The inclusion of Lowell Fulson's perennial "Reconsider Baby," Chuck Berry's "Worried Life Blues," and Jimmy Witherspoon's "When the Lights Go Out" does come as a surprising but welcome addition to a basic overview such as this. In addition to being floored by Buddy Guy's manic, high-voltage performance on "First Time I Met the Blues," fans will be pleased to hear legendary Chicago blues sidemen like Otis Spann, Willie Dixon, Jimmy Rogers, Fred Below, and Hubert Sumlin filling the support roles. A fine yet slim blues collection that's best purchased for a discount price. *—Stephen Cook*

The Blues, Vol. 2 / 1987 / Chess/MCA ♦♦♦♦♦

Only Chess Records could issue a blues compilation so laden with standards without even venturing beyond its own vault. This no-frills 1963 collection (later reissued by MCA) celebrates every blues powerhouse Chess ever had—including Chuck Berry, Muddy Waters, Howlin' Wolf, Bo Diddley, and Little Walter—and packs into 31 minutes what feels like a motherlode of rock & roll roots. Countless reissuings of this material over the years have perhaps rendered *The Blues, Vol. 2* a cheap relic in the current blues market; MCA, after all, gave the Chess catalog a celebrity facelift with the advent of the *Chess 50th Anniversary Collection* series in 1997. (Blues listeners who demand extensive documentation with their CD purchases are advised to go there.) But if you can ferret out a copy of *The Blues, Vol. 2*—check the vinyl bins, the discount bins, and the public libraries—it's certainly worth the effort, if nothing else than to realize that the blues don't need fancy packaging to keep you riveted. *—Ken Chang*

The Blues, Vol. 3 / Jul. 1965 / Chess/MCA ♦♦♦♦

Squarely taking in some prime Chess real estate, the third edition of the *Blues* series mostly spotlights such royalty as Muddy Waters, John Lee Hooker, Howlin' Wolf, and Sonny Boy Williamson. Thankfully, there's the relatively obscure likes of Washboard Sam, Jimmy Rogers, and Jimmy Witherspoon to enjoy as well. So, whether you prefer some horns-aplenty R&B touches (Little Milton) or raw juke joint harp playing (Little Walter), you will certainly appreciate this somewhat slim yet solid compilation. *—Stephen Cook*

The Blues, Vol. 4 / Jul. 6, 1989 / Chess/MCA ♦♦♦♦

More classic Chess blues. *—Bill Dahl*

The Blues, Vol. 5 / Aug. 27, 1990 / Chess/MCA ♦♦♦♦

Continuing in the format of earlier volumes, the fifth installment in Chess' *Blues* series offers up 12 more cuts of prime '50s blues. Chicago heavy hitters like Muddy Waters, Little Walter, and Sonny Boy Williamson are included, along with the likes of Memphis Minnie, Percy Mayfield, and Lowell Fulson. There are also fine tracks by more obscure singers like Houston, TX, native Jimmy Nelson and longtime Chessman Eddie Boyd. John Lee Hooker's here too, hitting a solo groove with his guitar and inimitable boogie stomp. All the tracks, save for just two, come from the first half of the '50s and feature all-star sideman like bassist Willie Dixon, guitarist Willie Johnson, and drummer Fred Below. While not part of the Chicago studio clique but notable all the same, Ike Turner and Lloyd Glenn avail themselves impressively on the sides by Howlin' Wolf (in his early Memphis days) and Fulson, respectively. One may pine for more generous blues collections than this, but there's no denying *The Blues, Vol. 5* works just fine as a budget-level introduction to the fertile sounds of '50s blues. *—Stephen Cook*

The Blues, Vol. 6 / Sep. 10, 1991 / Chess/MCA ♦♦♦♦♦

Going beyond the slim selection and hits-biased format of previous volumes, Chess delivers with this 16-track collection of blues rarities from the '50s. And where label mainstays like Muddy Waters and Howlin' Wolf dominated earlier discs, this go 'round features a balanced mix heavy on the obscure likes of Rocky Fuller and Blue Smitty; others, like Floyd Jones, Percy Mayfield, and Lowell Fulson, nicely fill the middle ground in between the Chicago masters and the more countrified singers. This is especially true of Mayfield, whose urbane and swinging style was removed in many ways from both Fuller's back-porch simplicity and Waters' fulsome sexual innuendo. Other low-profile highlights come courtesy of the Little Walter-inspired guitarist John Brim and singers Alberta Adams and Willie Mabon. Chipping in on the A-list side of things, stars like Walter, Memphis Minnie, and Sonny Boy Williamson turn in a fine mix of master takes and alternate cuts. Taking in Delta ramblings, city grit, and R&B's after-hours sophistication, this disc of rarities qualifies as the one volume in the *Blues* series that aficionados will not want to miss. *—Stephen Cook*

Bluesiana Hot Sauce / 1993 / Shanachie ♦♦♦

Joe Ferry brought Art Blakey, David Newman, and Dr. John together for the concept album *Bluesiana Triangle* in 1989. This later project, conceived as a tribute to the prior Bluesiana records, again links jazz, R&B, and rock players doing both pop and improvisational material, with the funds again going to the homeless. The assembled cast included trombonist Ray Anderson, harmonica ace Toots Thielemans at his bluesiest on "Brickyard Blues," and soulful tenor from Mike Brecker. Living Colour drummer Will Calhoun was once more funky and in the groove, contributing a solid vocal on "Ruby's Flowers," his own composition. This group does an admirable job of saluting the original cast while also making its own effective statement. *—Ron Wynn*

The Bluesville Years, Vol. 1: Big Blues Honks and Wails / 1995 / Prestige ♦♦♦♦

For almost a decade Bluesville operated as a subsidiary label to the indie jazz pioneer Prestige Records. With a chaotic catalog, they issued everything from barrelhouse piano players working with hipster jazz combos to semi-pro street singers to tons of Lightnin' Hopkins albums. What we have here are the beginnings of the modern blues album as we know it. The Bluesville label captured that awkward moment in time where the blues first lost its commercial restraints and started making music of a different power and a nice cross section of it is here on all four of these volumes. There's a decidedly acoustic air to everything here, even the wilder Chicago sides. If you've been brought up on a steady blues album diet of electric guitars and heavy drumming, some of this will sound almost quaint by comparison, but it's well worth a listen. The first entry in the series, *Big Blues Honks and Wails* features tracks by piano giants Sunnyland Slim and Roosevelt Sykes and uptown blues belters Mildred Anderson, Jimmy Witherspoon, and Al Smith paired with small, jazz-oriented combos with sax legends King Curtis, Eddie "Lockjaw" Davis, and Clifford Scott honkin' away. *—Cub Koda*

The Bluesville Years, Vol. 2: Feelin' Down on the South Side / 1995 / Prestige ✦✦✦✦
Feelin' Down on the South Side culls the best of the albums that were cut in Chicago with top-flight selections by Billy Boy Arnold, Homesick James, Otis Spann, and James Cotton. Cotton's "One More Mile to Go" with its voodoo backup chorus from the Muddy Waters band is downright bone-chilling and eerie. *—Cub Koda*

The Bluesville Years, Vol. 3: Beale Street Get-Down / 1995 / Prestige ✦✦✦✦
This third volume in Prestige's *Bluesville* series brings together sides that were recorded in Memphis and New York City and produced by Sam Charters, and that originally appeared on six different vinyl albums. The set of Furry Lewis tracks and the session with Memphis Willie B. were both recorded at the Sun studios in Memphis, while the Memphis Slim cuts emanate from a New York session. All three sets were recorded in 1961. Lewis is in top-notch form, as is Memphis Willie B., both accompanying themselves on guitar. Slim's tracks are solo as well, as he moves between piano and organ on a batch of originals and a nice take on Leroy Carr's "Mean Mistreatin' Mama." This series distills a lot of so-so albums down to their very best tracks. A terrific bargain. *—Cub Koda*

The Bluesville Years, Vol. 4: In the Key of Blues / 1995 / Prestige ✦✦✦✦
The final volume features an all-piano fest with boogies and blues from Mercy Dee Walton, Little Brother Montgomery, Curtis Jones, and still more from Roosevelt Sykes and Memphis Slim. *—Cub Koda*

The Bluesville Years, Vol. 6: Blues Sweet Carolina Blues / Oct. 6, 1960-Nov. 25, 1965 / Prestige ✦✦✦✦✦
If the blues has a "kinder, gentler" side, one could make a strong case for the Piedmont-Carolina style with its immaculately fingerpicked guitar and casual vocals. This volume is subtitled *Blues Sweet Carolina Blues* and these 1960s "discovery-rediscovery" recordings make for a nice cross section of the various strains within the genre. Pink Anderson, his "blues mentor" Baby Tate, Larry Johnson, Reverend Gary Davis (heard to good advantage on two instrumentals), and the ubiquitous Brownie McGhee and Sonny Terry all weigh in with choice selections, culled from a half dozen original Bluesville vinyl albums. Light, delicate, airy, and reflective, this is some very special music, a sound in blues seldom heard these days. *—Cub Koda*

The Bluesville Years, Vol. 7: Blues Blue, Blues White / Oct. 1, 1996 / Prestige ✦✦✦✦✦
A 21-track compilation of white folk-blues from the early and mid-'60s, originally recorded for Prestige. Some of the top talents of that mini-genre are represented here, including Dave Van Ronk, Tom Rush, Geoff Muldaur, Tracy Nelson, Eric Von Schmidt, and Danny Kalb. This kind of white acoustic blues revivalism has fallen out of favor since the '60s, but it certainly played its role in bringing the blues to a wider audience. The performances are respectful and occasionally stirring. If you want just a mild dose instead of entire albums by the above artists, this is a good pickup. *—Richie Unterberger*

The Bluesville Years, Vol. 8: Roll Over, Ms. Beethoven / Oct. 1, 1996 / Prestige ✦✦✦✦
Since classic female blues singer compilations usually consist of dubs of scratchy 78s, this collection of the best selections from three 1961 Bluesville albums (and one of them a compilation at that) is a welcome one, indeed. On *Roll Over, Ms. Beethoven*, the accent is on sassy, assertive vocals and lyrics, with strong 1920s-style jazz band support on most tracks. Lucille Hegamin's four tracks feature the two-fisted piano work of Willie "The Lion" Smith, while the four tracks by Alberta Hunter feature hot support from jazz legends J.C. Higginbotham, Buster Bailey, and Zutty Singleton. The bulk of this compilation turns the spotlight on Victoria Spivey, showcasing four tracks with the same combo that blew so beautifully behind Hunter; it then ups the ante with five songs with Lonnie Johnson, four of them performed as duets with Spivey on piano. This is an excellent entry into an already fine series. *—Cub Koda*

The Bluesville Years, Vol. 9: Down the Country Way / Sep. 29, 1998 / Prestige ✦✦✦✦
Subtitled *Down the Country Way*, this 20-track collection cherry-picks the best stuff from ten different Prestige-Bluesville albums that were originally issued during the first blues revival between 1960 and 1962. The song selection is impeccable, and with each artist getting a two-song entry, the set holds together remarkably well. Highlights include Smoky Babe ("Hottest Brand Goin'"), Robert Pete Williams ("Free Again"), Wade Walton ("Rock Me, Mama"), J.T. Adams and Shirley Griffith ("Match Box Blues"), Big Joe Williams ("Coal and Iceman Blues"), Pete Franklin ("Black Gal"), Scrapper Blackwell ("Blues Before Sunrise"), and Blind Willie McTell ("Broke Down Engine Blues"). Another added bonus is the inclusion of Tampa Red's impossibly rare Atlantic single, "Dark and Stormy Night," originally issued under the pseudonym of Barrelhouse Sammy. *—Cub Koda*

The Bluesville Years, Vol. 10: Country Roads, Country Days / Sep. 29, 1998 / Prestige ✦✦✦✦
Subtitled *Country Roads, Country Days*, this 21-track collection cherry-picks the best stuff from 11 different Prestige-Bluesville albums that were originally issued during the first blues revival between 1960 and 1962. The song selection is wide and varied within the confines of the genre, and with each artist getting a two-song entry (with the one-song exception of St. Louis Jimmy's "Goin' Down Slow"), the set has a feel quite similar to a small blues recital from the mid-'60s. Highlights include K.C. Douglas ("Wake Up, Working Woman"), Alec Seward ("Evil Woman Blues"), Doug Quattlebaum ("You Is One Black Rat"), Scrapper Blackwell and Brooks Berry ("Blues and Trouble"), Jesse Fuller ("Key to the Highway"), Snooks Eaglin ("That's All Right"), Henry Townsend ("I Asked Her If She Loved Me"), Shakey Jake ("Jake's Cha Cha"), and Arbee Stidham ("You Can't Live in This World By Yourself"). A nice combination of acoustic and mild electric performances. *—Cub Koda*

The Bluesville Years, Vol. 11: Blues Is a Heart's Sorrow / Apr. 11, 2000 / Prestige ✦✦✦
As the title all but announces, this is a compilation of tunes devoted to the more disappointing and mournful side of the blues experience, all recorded for the Bluesville and Prestige labels between 1959 and 1963. In the blues genre, of course, you don't have to look very far to assemble a collection of sorrowful tunes. However, the 20-song compilation, largely comprised of well-known names such as Roosevelt Sykes, Sunnyland Slim, Jimmy Witherspoon, Lightnin' Hopkins, Willie Dixon, and Lonnie Johnson, isn't all that much of a downer. For the most part it's urban blues with a light blues-jazz crossover feel, as epitomized by the Witherspoon cuts, one of which even features Kenny Burrell on guitar. Eddie "Lockjaw" Davis and Shirley Scott are on hand for Mildred Anderson's "I'm Gettin' Long Alright," with its exaggerated crying vocal noises. If you want something more down-home, there's Hopkins trading riffs with Sonny Terry on "Last Night Blues" (though even that has drums and bass), and Henry Townsend. Yet this might be better described as after-hours blues, often with somewhat downbeat lyrics and moods, but certainly classy, with an anguish that is more polished than raw. It's a rather patchy way to catch up on the Prestige-Bluesville catalog. But as most people don't want to accumulate a complete set of those LPs, this is a decent, though not great, overview of a slice of its discography. *—Richie Unterberger*

The Bluesville Years, Vol. 12: Jump, Jumpin' the Blues / Apr. 11, 2000 / Prestige ✦✦✦
The title might lead you to believe that you're going to hear a jump blues collection, but many listeners wouldn't find that categorization strictly accurate. It would be better to say that these 22 songs, all recorded for Bluesville and Prestige between 1959 and 1964, concentrate more on the upbeat, uptempo face of the blues experience, rather than the more downbeat aspects that have more visibility in popular culture. (In fact, they're given more visibility on compilations such as this one's direct predecessor, *The Bluesville Years Vol. 11: Blues Is a Heart's Sorrow.*) Most of the names here are mid- to upper-level blues icons—Otis Spann and James Cotton (playing together), Sonny Terry, Lightnin' Hopkins, Memphis Slim, Willie Dixon, Billy Boy Arnold, Roosevelt Sykes, and Jimmy Witherspoon—though rather more obscure performers like K.C. Douglas, Homesick James, and Mildred Anderson are here too. Both rural and urban styles are represented, but urban styles are more in evidence. Sometimes, the blues is not just urban but urbane, with a jazzy feel on cuts by Little Brother Montgomery, Witherspoon, and Anderson (the last of whom has a band including tenor saxophonist Eddie "Lockjaw" Davis and organist Shirley Scott). A more hard-hitting brand of brash electric blues, however, is on board via cuts by Arnold, Homesick James, Spann, and Cotton. The Spann-Cotton duet on "Lightnin'" (with Muddy Waters on guitar) is the high spot of the disc, although the recording quality isn't so hot. Like all of the volumes in this series, this is a decent sampler of the Prestige-Bluesville catalog, though too loose in its thematic and musical groupings to rate among the better blues compilations. *—Richie Unterberger*

Boogie Blues: Women Sing & Play / Mar. 1930-Oct. 31, 1961 / Rosetta ✦✦✦
All 16 performances on this LP are boogie-blues and put the spotlight on female singers and/or pianists. There is a wide variety of material ranging from a Lil Armstrong piano solo from the soundtrack of the TV show *Chicago & That Jazz* in 1961 to Memphis Minnie, Ella Fitzgerald ("Cow Cow Boogie"), and Dorothy Donegan in 1942. Other performers include Georgia White, Helen Humes, Lucille Bogan, Hazel Scott, Merline Johnson, Sweet Georgia Brown, Gladys Bentley, Christine Chatman, Hadda Brooks, Myrtle Jenkins, Sister Rosetta Tharpe, and Mary Lou Williams. As usual with Rosetta's albums, this obvious labor of love has informative liner notes, colorful pictures, and many rare recordings that have not yet been reissued on CD. *—Scott Yanow*

Boogie Woogie Blues / Sep. 1922-Apr. 1927 / Biograph ✦✦✦
Biograph has come out with many releases of piano rolls through the years. This CD has some by Cow Cow Davenport, James P. Johnson, Clarence Williams, Jimmy Blythe, Hersal Thomas, Lemuel Fowler, and two totally forgotten names: Everett Robbins and Clarence Johnson. As is usual with piano rolls, the rhythms are inflexible and the touch a bit unnatural so it may take listeners a while to get used to these performances. The emphasis is more on blues than on boogie-woogie but in general the music is fine for this idiom, although not as lively as real piano solos. *—Scott Yanow*

Boogie Woogie Masters / 1992 / Charly ✦✦✦
Without inner liner notes, and not much in the way of remastering from the original 78s, this compilation succeeds by sheer virtue of the fine material on it. Launching off with a joyful rendition of Cow Cow Davenport's signature tune "Cow Cow Blues" and the hectoring "State Street Jive," there's not a bad track to be found on here. The highlights of the rest of the album, as in many of the best barrelhouse tunes, have the feel of a hooch-swilling good time; the emphasis is on rollicking solo piano, though several full-band pieces are included. "Pine Top's Boogie Woogie," with Pinetop Smith's devilish exhortations to "stop!" and then "mess around!," is always a joy to hear. And while songs like "Dearborn Street Breakdown" and "No. 29" are buried by a thick layer of sonic crud, even the most jaded child of the digital era can't help bopping around to "Boogie Woogie Stomp," an Albert Ammons band tune that can still leap to life and dance. *—Paul Collins*

Booze & the Blues / Feb. 6, 1996 / Columbia/Legacy ✦✦✦
Booze & the Blues is a thoroughly entertaining collection of 22 prewar blues songs about wine, drinking, whiskey, and blues. It's a gimmicky excuse for a collection, but it works, not only because the songs and performances are good, but because the tracks all have a similar spirit. Among the highlights are tracks by Memphis Minnie, Mississippi Sheiks, Robert Hicks, the Memphis Jug Band, Amos Easton, Lucille Bogan, Peetie Wheatstraw, and Joshua White. *—Stephen Thomas Erlewine*

Broke Down: Blues About Automobiles / 1992 / Collectables ✦✦✦
The title tells it like it is: *Broke Down: Blues About Automobiles* contains 14 songs about cars. From the stripped-down acoustic sound of Billy Bizor and Tommy Lee Thompson to the big city blues of Texas Pete Mayne and Clarence Green to the rock-influenced sounds of Johnny Winter and Steven Owens, the songs cover a wide range of blues styles. The

songs that really stand out are Jerry McCain with a message to young girls with "Stay Out of Those Automobiles," Peppermint Harris' last wish for a "Cadillac Funeral," and Willie Love's "Little Car Blues," which really isn't about cars at all. The wide range of blues styles can be a bit off-putting, and purists will absolutely hate about a third of this record, but the casual fan will find this to be a fun record. *—Tim Sendra*

Can't Keep from Crying: Topical Blues on the Death of President Kennedy / 1994 / Testament ♦♦♦

In the wake of John Kennedy's assassination, Pete Welding recorded over a dozen acoustic blues tributes to the late president for this compilation in late 1963 and early 1964. Big Joe Williams, Otis Spann, and Johnny Young are the only widely recognized names on the disc, which also features performers like Mary Ross, Fannie Brewer, and Jimmy Brown. It's hard to be critical about a project devoted to such an emotional and devastating event, but this doesn't hold up too well as more than a slice of history. However heartfelt these pieces may have been, the compositions are not outstanding, and it's wearying to hear more than a dozen topical blues on *any* subject all in a row. The CD reissue adds previously unreleased tracks by Johnny Young and Avery Brady. *—Richie Unterberger*

Chapter VII: All Men Are Liars / Aug. 25, 1998 / Epitaph ♦♦♦

For fans who got turned on to R.L. Burnside thanks to *The Sopranos*, this compilation perhaps represents the next logical step toward embracing the postmodern juke joint sound of the Fat Possum label. *Chapter VII: All Men Are Liars* goes where no blues compilation has ever dared to go, blurring the lines between Delta blues and, yes, punk. (Fat Possum would outdo this feat with *New Beats from the Delta*, which straddled the blues/hip-hop fence). Featuring some of the crunchiest guitar riffs imaginable, *Chapter VII* is a quick 41-minute romp that invites Mississippi blues legends (Burnside, Junior Kimbrough) and their garage band progeny (20 Miles, Bob Log III, the Neckbones) to the same mosh pit. The results range from one-chord, John Lee Hooker-style boogies to pure headbanger material—and somehow, it all gels together. Less blues intensive than its sister compilation *Not the Same Old Blues Crap, Chapter VII* is also louder, cruder, and much more fun. *—Ken Chang*

☆ **Chess Blues** / 1992 / Chess ♦♦♦♦♦

A superlative four-CD box set, featuring important tracks by all the main stars of the label (Muddy Waters, Howlin' Wolf, Little Walter, Sonny Boy Williamson), as well as much previously unreleased material. A well-done retrospective of Chicago blues in its heyday, as recorded by America's greatest blues label, Chess. *—Cub Koda*

Chess Blues Classics: 1947 to 1956 / 1997 / Chess ♦♦♦♦♦

Part of a two-volume set as part of MCA's Chess 50th anniversary collection, this offers a 16-track thumbnail sketch of the sounds that made the label the tops in the blues field. Beginning with two Aristocrat sides (the label's original moniker) from 1948 and 1949 featuring Muddy Waters ("I Can't Be Satisfied") and Little Johnny Jones ("Big Town Playboy" with Muddy on backup guitar), the collection rolls through its treasures chronologically, virtually cherry-picking the hits from the innumerable classics stored in the Chess vaults. With Jimmy Rogers' "That's All Right," Eddie Boyd's "Twenty-Four Hours," John Lee Hooker's "Sugar Mama," Lowell Fulson's "Reconsider Baby" and J.B. Lenoir's "Eisenhower Blues" providing nice changes of pace from the big hits of Muddy, Howlin' Wolf, Sonny Boy Williamson, and Little Walter aboard, this is by no means a lightweight collection. As a greatest-hits package, perhaps one could easily nitpick over what *isn't* on here, while also just as easily dismissing their inclusion as another repackaging of the same old stuff. But as a simple-to-digest primer of some of the best the label had to offer during its first landmark decade in business, this compilation hits the bullseye in a big way. A perfect one to stick in a multi-disc CD player, hit shuffle play, and prepare to be continually pleased. *—Cub Koda*

Chess Blues Classics: 1957 to 1967 / 1997 / Chess ♦♦♦♦♦

This second volume of a two-volume entry in MCA's Chess 50th anniversary reissue series chronicles the second decade of blues classics produced by the landmark company. Although Chess' big four (Muddy Waters, Howlin' Wolf, Little Walter, and Sonny Boy Williamson) are all finely represented, influential sides by Elmore James ("Madison Blues"), Otis Rush ("So Many Roads, So Many Trains"), and John Lee Hooker (his monochord boogie treatment of Amos Milburn's "One Bourbon, One Scotch, One Beer") pepper the mix as well. As Chess moved into the soul market, so it was that latter-day blues sides by Little Milton, Koko Taylor, and Etta James took on a more pronounced R&B edge, and it is these sides that close this compilation in a near-perfect bookend fashion. Extra special highlight: Etta James' nitro reading of Jimmy Reed's "Baby, What You Want Me to Do," recorded live in 1964. *—Cub Koda*

Chess Blues Guitar: Two Decades of Killer Fretwork, 1949–1969 / Jan. 13, 1998 / MCA ♦♦♦♦♦

This 45-song, two-disc collection is subtitled "Two Decades of Killer Fretwork," and never was a set so aptly described. Chess Records was the home to seemingly every hot guitar player in the Chicago area, and many of them make their appearance here. Besides the usual label guitar hotshots (Muddy Waters, Jimmy Rogers, Chuck Berry, Bo Diddley, Buddy Guy, Lowell Fulson, Earl Hooker, Otis Rush, Robert Nighthawk, Little Milton), space is given to sideman work from legends like Hubert Sumlin and Robert Jr. Lockwood and great one-offs by lesser-known artists like Jody Williams, Danny Overbea, Eddie Burns, Joe Hill Louis, Morris Pejoe, Lafayette Thomas, and others. It seems as if everyone recorded for Chess at one time or another, also explaining the inclusion of tracks by John Lee Hooker, Albert King, Clarence "Gatemouth" Brown, Lonnie Brooks, Hound Dog Taylor, and Elmore James. If electric blues guitar's your thing, then look no further than this fine two-disc compilation. *—Cub Koda*

Chess Blues Piano Greats / Jun. 17, 1997 / MCA ♦♦♦♦♦

Back before the electric guitar became the primary focal instrument of the blues, two-fisted piano players dominated the genre, and record companies flocked to record them. Chess Records was no exception, and this two-disc, 45-track anthology shines the spotlight on four of the best who ever sat on the piano stool at the Chess studios. The first disc begins with 20 tracks from Eddie Boyd (eight of them previously unissued in the U.S.), full of introspective reflection and the darkest of moods. Kicking off with one of his big hits, "24 Hours," and the dourness of Boyd's work reaches epic proportions on tunes like "I Began to Sing the Blues," "Third Degree," and "Blues for Baby," the latter featuring stellar jazz guitar runs and chordal work from Robert Jr. Lockwood. Even on uptempo numbers like "Hard Time Getting Started," "Nothing but Trouble," and "Just a Fool," the somber nature of Boyd's delivery cuts through everything, underscoring the bouncier lilt of these tracks with a much darker cast. Finishing out the disc are four tracks from Otis Spann, comprising the A- and B-sides of his lone 1954 single for the label ("It Must Have Been the Devil" and the instrumental "Five Spot," both sides featuring a rare maverick uncredited appearance by B.B. King on a Chess record) and two sides from a 1956 session that stayed unreleased for several decades, both featuring shattering harp work from Big Walter Horton. The second disc collects 18 sides from Willie Mabon (three sides previously unreleased), including his big hits "I Don't Know," "I'm Mad," "Poison Ivy" and Willie Dixon's "The Seventh Son." Mabon was much more an R&B novelty entertainer than a hard bluesman (think Cripple Clarence Lofton as opposed to Big Maceo Merriweather), but his more down-home side comes up for air on "Willie's Blues," pitting solid piano work against Dixieland trumpet growls. The anthology finishes out with three tracks from Chess session stalwart Lafayette Leake, who backed everyone from Chuck Berry to Howlin' Wolf and yet remains Chess Records' true mystery man. Lafayette was most elusive when it came time to record under his own name, but a stray instrumental from 1957 ("Slow Leake") stands alongside two live tracks recorded in Montreux, Switzerland in 1972 as his meager frontman legacy for the label. Although there's no Sunnyland or Memphis Slim aboard (two other Chess piano greats equally worthy of a separate anthology), this is a fine collection that is most deserving of an encore. *—Cub Koda*

The Chess Story: 1947–1975 / Feb. 2000 / MCA International ♦♦♦♦♦

First the good news, which is really good: the sound on this 340-song set is about as good as one ever fantasized it could be, and that means it runs circles around any prior reissues; from the earliest Aristocrat sides right up through Muddy Waters' "Going Down to Main Street," it doesn't get any better than this set. The clarity pays a lot of bonuses, beginning with the impression that it gives of various artists' instrumental prowess. In sharp contrast to the past efforts in this direction by MCA, however, the producers of this set have not emasculated the sound in the course of cleaning it up. When the rock & roll era dawns at Chess as depicted on disc five, the sound is nice and dirty, just really sharp. The contents of the set are largely "limited"—if that's the word for any 340-song collection—to Chess' blues, R&B, rock & roll, and soul output, although Ramsey Lewis gets a nod, as does comedian Pigmeat Markham. What's more, the care lavished on the songs is virtually universal—there was time spent getting all of it right. One wishes that the same could be said for one of the featured bonuses on this set, the CD-ROM that comprises the 15th disc. First, there are the skimpy film clips, misspellings ("Arether Franklin"), and incorrect dates. There also would have been enough room to put a complete Chess discography on the CD-ROM, rather than just the MCA reissues of Chess' material. The CDs themselves are conveniently assembled in three fold-out volumes in a slipcase, but identifying individual tracks and artists means constantly referring back to the booklets glued into those volumes; additionally, it would've been nice to have had a sessionography on the songs, or at least the release dates, or even release years. *—Bruce Eder*

Chicago Ain't Nothin' but a Blues Band / 1972 / Delmark ♦♦♦♦♦

Solid collection of sides from Chicago's Atomic H label with JoJo Williams, J.T. Brown, and Eddy Clearwater's earliest recordings being among the highlights. *—AMG*

Chicago Blues After Midnight 1952–1957 / Delta Swing ♦♦♦

Most of the artists on this anthology are fairly well known, even if the selected material is more than a little bit obscure. Beginning with J.B. Hutto, his "Price of Love" was one of two tracks from his 1954 Chance session that never made it to a single, this being pulled from a lone surviving acetate. Also from the originally unissued file is Jimmy Reed's "State Street Boogie," an instrumental featuring the same unidentified Chicago symphony violin player who added so much sparkle to Jimmy's "Odds and Ends" and a fine pair of tracks from Eddie Taylor, "Stroll Out West" and "Find Me a Baby." Grace Brim, the drumming wife of John Brim, contributes "Hospitality Blues" and "Man Around My Door," while Baby Face Leroy is featured with both sides of his 1952 JOB single, "Pet Rabbit" and "Louella." Howlin' Wolf is the ringer of this Chicago anthology with his "Sweet Woman" and "Dorothy Mae," both actually recorded in Memphis. The collection is rounded off with a pair of tracks each from Tampa Red ("Please Mr. Doctor" and "I Should Have Loved Her More"), Curtis Jones ("Flamin' Blues" and "Upside Down Blues"), and L.C. McKinley ("Rosalie Blues" and "Pains in My Heart"), making this collection some of the rarest of the classic Chicago sound and a fine cross section of the musical activity in Chicago in this formative period. *—Cub Koda*

Chicago Blues Anthology / 1984 / Chess ♦♦♦♦♦

A wonderful 24-cut set of raw, early Chicago blues from the Chess label, Delta blues influences are evident in the work of Johnny Shines, Robert Nighthawk, and Floyd Jones. A more modern, urban style is shown by Buddy Guy and Otis Rush on this worthwhile collection. *—Niles J. Frantz*

Chicago Blues from Federal Records / May 11, 1999 / Ace ♦♦♦♦♦

Although the Federal label (a subsidiary of King) wasn't a huge force in electric blues in the late '50s and early '60s, it did make some interesting, quality Chicago blues sides,

22 of which are collected here. Kid Thomas leads off with eight tracks, including the fine 1957 single "Wolf Pack"/"The Spell," which sound like Chess '50s blues heavily influenced by Howlin' Wolf, and crossed with a smidgen of Screamin' Jay Hawkins. The other six Thomas tunes were previously unissued, and are decent outings that, again, could have fit in well with the Chess label with the shrill, full sound, Thomas' accomplished harmonica playing (reminiscent of Little Walter), and the slight echo on the production. Next are four early-'60s singles by Smokey Smothers, which sound a few years behind the times in their basic electric blues arrangements, but are certainly fine performances, particularly "I've Been Drinking Muddy Water," which contains some excellent guitar licks by Freddie King. Pianist Willie Mabon weighs in with four 1957 efforts, only two of which were issued, although they're solid numbers with soulful vocals. Bobby King, the most obscure artist on the anthology, is represented by four 1961-1964 tracks that are quality early blues-soul, although unfortunately (considering his last name) they sometimes show a heavy B.B. King influence; "W-A-S-T-E-D" was co-written by Pat Vegas, later of Redbone. Eddie Clearwater wraps it up with his 1962 single "Real Good Time"/"Hey Bernardine," which is about as close a facsimile of Chuck Berry in the "You Never Can Tell" era as you're likely to hear. *—Richie Unterberger*

Chicago Blues Harmonicas / 1990 / Paula/Flyright ♦♦♦♦♦
The four remaining JOB sides by Snooky Pryor ("Boogy Fool," "Raisin' Sand," "Cryin' Shame," and "Eighty Nine Ten") are to be found here on this compilation, with Snooky also found in support on two tracks from a 1949 Baby Face Leroy session. With the other 13 tracks including John Lee Henley's "Rhythm Rockin' Boogie," Walter Horton's "Have a Good Time," and rare but notable sides by Sonny Boy Williamson, Little Willie Foster, and Louis Myers And the Aces, this is a harmonica rarities package that's pretty tough to beat. *—Cub Koda*

Chicago Blues Masters, Vol. 3 / Jun. 3, 1997 / Capitol ♦♦♦
Chicago Blues Masters, Vol. 3 is an odd collection, featuring 14 tracks from Shakey Jake, ten cuts from James Cotton (including his inexplicable cover of Todd Rundgren's "Kiddy Boy"), and 14 cuts from George Harmonica Smith. There's enough from each artist to constitute a full collection, but these songs are all thrown together without much rhyme or reason. Furthermore, the recordings are latter-day efforts, all of which are interesting, but not necessarily among their best work. Consequently, it's primarily of interest to hardcore fans and collectors—the kind of listener who will sift through the mediocre recordings to find the good stuff. *—Stephen Thomas Erlewine*

Chicago Blues Meeting: Snake in My Bedroom / Oct. 1995 / Drive ♦♦♦
This is an interesting little set made up of two sessions (held in 1983 and 1986) that combined Chicago blues players with Scandinavian blues musicians. The Chicago players included S.P. Leary, Bob Stroger, and Sunnyland Slim. While the concept is a noble one, it's an overwrought exercise full of guitar playing that imitates Otis Rush and Albert Collins, harmonica playing that mimics Lazy Lester and Little Walter, and over the top vocals from the Scandinavian blues musicians that need every bit of echo lavished on them. *—Cub Koda*

Chicago Blues of the 1950's / May 20, 1997 / Paula ♦♦♦
This compilation gathers some of the seldom-anthologized blues rarities of the era as originally issued on the Cobra, JOB, ABCO, and Chief labels in Chicago. Kicking off with both sides of Guitar Shorty's Cobra single ("Irma Lee" and "You Don't Treat Me Right"), the first half delves into the Cobra catalog to bring tracks by Lee Jackson, Clarence Jolly, Sunnyland Slim, and an alternate take of Magic Sam's "Easy Baby" to the mix. Following this is a major dip into the JOB vaults, bringing an unreleased Moody Jones ("Why Should I Worry") and ten tracks from John and Grace Brim, including five previously unissued sides. Completing this treasure trove of rarities is the inclusion of both sides of Morris Pejoe's single for Cobra's ABCO subsidiary, "Screaming and Crying" and "Maybe Blues," and Lillian Offitt's "Will My Man Be Home Tonight," featuring excellent slide guitar work from Earl Hooker. *—Cub Koda*

Chicago Blues of the 1960's / May 20, 1997 / Paula ♦♦♦
This 22-track collection brings together many of the rare singles from the seldom-anthologized USA label from Chicago. The only exceptions to this are the inclusion of a TV Slim track ("You Can't Love Me") from the Speed label, Lillian Offitt's "Oh Mama" from Chief, and Harold Burrage's Cobra recording of "I Cry for You." Kicking off with Homesick James' interpretation of "Crossroads," the compilation also features equally stellar tracks from J.B. Lenoir ("I Feel So Good"), Koko Taylor ("Honky Tonky" and "Like Heaven to Me," her first single), Detroit Junior ("Call My Job"), Jesse Fortune, Fenton Robinson ("Say You're Leavin'"), Big Moose Walker, Mighty Joe Young, Andrew Brown, and five tracks from Willie Mabon. The other side of Chicago's heyday away from the Chess studios. *—Cub Koda*

Chicago Blues: Rockin' After Midnight / Jul. 28, 1998 / St. George ♦♦♦♦
Anyone who thinks the old, raw Chicago style of blues is dead and buried in the grooves of old 78s should be directed straight to the tracks that make up this 1998 compilation. Kicking off with nearly six minutes of Tail Dragger singing Elmore James' "Done Somebody Wrong" as if he were channeling Muddy Waters, here are an even-dozen hardcore, play-for-keeps blues sides featuring folks as committed to making real-deal music as you can ask for. The St. George houseband players of Studebaker John Grimaldi on harp and slide guitar and Twist Turner on drums keep things grounded and grooving on three-quarters of the tracks they work on together. Grimaldi ends up appearing on all 12 tracks assembled, also turning in a stellar version of Frank Frost's "My Back Scratcher," with members of the Yardbirds and Pretty Things in the backing group. Highlights bounce off this disc everywhere the laser beam hits, but particularly fine are the late, great Big Mojo Elem's take on Willie Dixon's "Live the Life I Love," Little Mack Simmons' "Nine Below Zero," El Dorado slow blowing their way through Elmore's "Mean Mistreatin' Mama," Andre Williams' ode to the weed on "Smoke Daddy Johnson," and the mysterious Chicago Slim's completely garbled "Low Down Dirty Woman." Not only are Chicago blues alive and well, but from the sound of this compilation, a little bit crazy, too—perhaps an even better sign. *—Cub Koda*

Chicago Blues: The Chance Era / Feb. 18, 1998 / Charly ♦♦♦♦♦
The opening two or three cuts on this 50-song, 140-minute compilation sound ominously rough and ragged, and I'm not talking about the music, but the sources. But then the quality rights itself, and the rest is above-average quality early Chicago blues. Chance Records was never as big as Chess, though they shared a few artists like John Lee Hooker (as John L. Booker) and Sunnyland Slim (as Delta Joe) in common, but it managed to get its share of worthwhile blues and R&B records out during its four years of active life. John Lee Hooker opens disc one with a pair of wildly chaotic, raw blues tracks, "Miss Lorraine" and "I Love to Boogie," that were probably recorded in the back of a local record store. A single side by Little Walter dating from 1947, originally cut for Ora Nelle Records and issued by Chance as "Ora Nelle Blues," is another primordial treasure contained on this CD, and the surface noise of these early sides can be forgiven under the circumstances. Arthur "Big Boy" Spires stood to be Chance's answer to Muddy Waters, based on "Some Day Little Darling" and "My Baby Left Me," but the big surprise on these sides is Lazy Bill Lucas, an Arkansas-born bluesman, who attacks his songs (especially "I Had a Dream") with bristling aggressiveness at the piano and the microphone, ably backed by Louis Myers in a searing set of guitar workouts. J.B. Hutto cut only six commercial sides for Chance before vanishing into the relative obscurity of club performances in Chicago, and then re-emerging on the folk-blues revival scene courtesy of Vanguard Records a decade later. The six sides here are worth their weight in gold—loud, defiant blues that manage to be both raw in sound and smooth in execution, with a crunchy yet dexterous guitar sound and wonderfully expressive vocals—check out "Lovin' You," maybe the best piece of blues ever cut in Chicago that didn't come from Chess. The 14 cuts by Homesick James (John Williamson Henderson) here represent more of this man's music than almost anyone has heard in 45 years—he also appears to have been the first artist to actually record for Chance. And lo and behold, Tampa Red also shows up—sans guitar, alas—as Jimmy Eager, doing a trio of cuts that outclass much of the rest of his late-career output; cut in 1953, they mark the tail end of Red's commercial career as a full-time bluesman, and one only wishes that he, and not Vee-Jay Records alumnus L.C. McKinley, were playing the guitar on those cuts, but he was signed to Victor, and they were even less amused than companies like Chess about label-hopping by their artists. *—Bruce Eder*

Chicago Boogie: 1947 / 1983 / St. George ♦♦♦♦♦
All the earliest Maxwell Street acetate recordings from the short-lived Ora Nelle label, featuring the earliest sides of Little Walter, Jimmy Rogers, Johnny Young, and Othum Brown. Delta bluesman Johnny Temple's "Olds 98 Blues," done Robert Johnson-style with an electric guitar, is a particular standout. *—Cub Koda*

Chicago Boss Guitars / 1991 / Paula ♦♦♦♦♦
Otis Rush shares this compilation with Buddy Guy's early Artistic sides and five alternate takes from Magic Sam. The nine Cobra alternates by Rush are raw and even awkward in spots when compared to the issued versions, but chock-full of emotional intensity. If you're a Cobra Records alternate take freak, here's the mother lode. *—Cub Koda*

Chicago Piano (1929–1936) / Jun. 2, 1994 / Document ♦♦♦♦
All of the music recorded under the names of singer John Oscar and vocalist/pianists Eddie Miller and George Noble are reissued on this enjoyable blues-oriented CD. Oscar (who is accompanied by either an unknown pianist or Miller) proves to be a fine singer on his six selections from 1929-1934 although virtually nothing is known about him; "Mama Don't Allow No Easy Riders Here" is a highlight. Eddie Miller (no relation to the tenor saxophonist of the same name) is heard on eight solo performances (including three versions of "I'd Rather Drink Muddy Water") and two duets (under the name of Eddie Morgan) with guitarist Big Bill Broonzy; two songs have vocals by Billie McKenzie. George Noble, who is heard solo on eight songs from 1935, has no real connection with Oscar or Miller but does a fine job on "New Milk Cow Blues," "If You Lose Your Good Gal, Don't Mess With Mine," and "T.B. Blues." As with most of the hundreds of Document releases, this set is a delight for serious blues collectors. *—Scott Yanow*

Chicago South Side, 1927–31 / May 1926-Mar. 1932 / Historical ♦♦♦♦♦
Although the music on this sampler does not contain complete sessions, this LP is well worth searching for. The performances are quite spirited, featuring music from J.C. Cobb's Grains of Corn, Roy Palmer's Alabama Rascals, Jimmy Wade's Dixielanders, Jimmy Bertrand's Washboard Wizards, Harry Dial's Blusicians, and Jimmie Noone. Among the star soloists are cornetist Punch Miller, Junie Cobb on reeds, clarinetist Darnell Howard and Johnny Dodds, the great trombonist Roy Palmer, Louis Armstrong (on two of the Bertrand performances), and pianists Jimmy Blythe and Earl Hines. These performances are consistently joyful and essential to 1920s collectors in one form or another. *—Scott Yanow*

Chicago South Side, Vol. 2: 1927–29 / Jul. 20, 1927-Jul. 27, 1931 / Historical ♦♦♦♦♦
This consistently enjoyable LP has a variety of performances recorded in Chicago during 1927-1931. The songs in this collection are not reissued as complete sessions but what is here is often quite memorable: three numbers from Jimmy Noone, two apiece by Tiny Parham, the Dixie Rhythm Kings, the Chicago Footwarmers, the State Street Ramblers, and Jimmy Blythe with the Washboard Wizards, and one song from Willie Hightower. With the sidemen including pianists Earl Hines and Jimmy Blythe, cornetists Punch Miller and Natty Dominique, and the great clarinetist Johnny Dodds, the music is often quite special and always spirited. *—Scott Yanow*

★ **Chicago/The Blues/Today!** / Aug. 24, 1999 / Vanguard ✦✦✦✦✦
Vanguard's 1999 release of *Chicago/The Blues/Today!* combines the three volumes of the legendary series, which were originally all available separately, into one stand-alone triple-disc set. Apart from the cardboard gatefold packaging and some new liner notes from Ed Ward, there isn't much here to interest collectors, but anyone who has yet to pick up these landmark albums—or who have yet to replace their vinyl copies—should consider this set, since it offers all the classic music at a reasonable price. The only drawback is the packaging, which forces the discs into cardboard sleeves, but that's a small price to pay for music this good. *—Stephen Thomas Erlewine*

☆ **Chicago/The Blues/Today! Vol. 1** / Oct. 1966 / Vanguard ✦✦✦✦✦
The first volume in the groundbreaking, definitive series *Chicago/The Blues/Today!* contains selections from J.B. Hutto, Junior Wells, and Otis Spann. All three contribute stellar performances, but for Hutto it's truly the place to start, because it doesn't get much better than this; "Too Much Alcohol," "Please Help," "Going Ahead," and "That's the Truth" are all classics, and Hutto is in perfect form throughout, with swinging support from the Turner's Blue Lounge version of the Hawks, bass-rhythm guitarist Herman Hassell and former Bo Diddley drummer Frank Kirkland. Sound is crystal clear. *—Cub Koda*

● **Chicago/The Blues/Today! Vol. 2** / 1967 / Vanguard ✦✦✦✦✦
After his tenure at Chess, Otis Rush signed with Duke Records in Houston, who only released one 45 during his entire five year stay at the label. This Vanguard session from 1966 was his first in several years and finds him in exemplary form. Backed by a tough little club band, Otis' guitar tone is crystal clear and well focused, while his singing is simply superb. With two excellent instrumentals aboard ("Rock" is Otis' version of Earl Hooker's "Universal Rock"), the other big ticket highlight is the version of "I Can't Quit You, Baby" that Led Zeppelin would later copy note for note on their first album. This is part of a three-volume series and also features excellent tracks by James Cotton ("Cotton Crop Blues" and a wild version of "Rocket 88") and Homesick James. *—Cub Koda*

★ **Chicago/The Blues/Today! Vol. 3** / 1967 / Vanguard ✦✦✦✦✦
This is one of the all-time great blues series ever recorded. Aside from the classic Chess albums (Muddy Waters, Little Walter, Howlin' Wolf, etc.), there is no better introduction to Chicago-style blues than this three-volume set. Each one is incredible. This third album contains the Johnny Shines Blues Band, Johnny Young's South Side Blues Band, and Big Walter Horton's Blues Harp Band with Memphis Charlie Musselwhite. Here are the original Chicago artists who have grown up and played together for most of their lives, so the musical time is spacious—wide open. This is South Side Chicago blues with a trace of country at its best. Big Walter Horton plays some of the best harmonica of his career on this album. Listening to Horton on backup and solo harp is an education. This album is definitive. *—Michael Erlewine*

Cincinnati Blues (1928–1936) / 1990 / Story of the Blues ✦✦✦
So little is known of the performers on this CD (most of whom are unidentified) that it is believed the featured vocalists Kid Cole, Bob Coleman, and Walter Coleman (who double on guitars) might all be the same person! He is thought to have been based in Cincinnati (particularly since one of the groups that he recorded with is called the Cincinnati Jug Band), although the music (from 1928-1929 and 1936) was actually recorded in Chicago and Richmond, IN. The 15 selections are the complete output of this mysterious figure, of whom nothing is known. Coleman is heard with the jug band (which includes harmonica, two jugs, washboard, and a second guitarist) on four numbers, playing unaccompanied on "Sing Song Blues," joined by a second guitarist, and backed by the equally mysterious pianist Jesse James. The music is fine for the period and is recommended to blues and jug band collectors. *—Scott Yanow*

Clownin' With the World / 1989 / Acoustic Archives ✦✦✦✦✦
A wonderful CD from the vaults of Trumpet Records. Features unissued Sonny Boy Williamson sides and great tracks by his piano playin' buddy, Willie Love. *—AMG*

The Cobra Records Story / Apr. 26, 1993 / Capricorn ✦✦✦✦✦
This double-disc set featuring over 50 tracks from the vaults of Eli Toscano's Cobra Records also includes the half-dozen or so most important tracks recorded by Ike Turner's Kings of Rhythm between 1958 and 1959, plus other artists' sides that they played on. *—Bruce Eder*

The Collectables Blues Collection, Vol. 1 / Feb. 2, 1990 / Collectables ✦✦✦✦
As blues collections go, this Collectables compilation holds its own quite nicely. And while many of these are not the classic versions, the majority of the sides here are still top-notch. Representing a cross section of labels, the 16 tracks include hit material by Muddy Waters ("Hoochie Coochie Man"), John Lee Hooker ("Boogie Chillen"), and Jimmy Reed ("Bright Lights, Big City" and "Big Boss Man"). And don't fret, these recordings were made in the prime blues decades of the '40s, '50s, and '60s—no worries here about dreary, latter-day remakes by overzealous producers. The quality sides roll on with meaty performances by Lightnin' Hopkins, Elmore James, Champion Jack Dupree, and Sonny Terry, not to mention quality contributions by R&B and jazz greats Thelma Cooper and Jimmy Rushing. A fine accompaniment for your next after-hours blues party. *—Stephen Cook*

Cool Playing Blues Chicago Style / 1989 / Relic ✦✦✦✦✦
The 15 songs on this compilation were left behind by Parrot Records' Al Benson, all cut during the mid-'50s. The music could have passed muster at Parrot's better-known Chicago rival Chess—Jody Williams may have been Parrot's answer to Muddy Waters (Willie Dixon is even playing the bass), although his style was closer to an amalgam of B.B. King and T-Bone Walker. In addition to some established sides, this CD features one outtake, "Groan My Blues Away," his only known workout on slide guitar. Guitarist L.C. McKinley ("All Alone Blues"—worth it for the guitar-sax duet on the break) and pianist Curtis Jones are also featured in numbers cut under their respective names, and St. Louis Jimmy Oden has two tracks represented here, backed by the Red Saunders Band, including a sultry version of his classic "Goin' Down Slow." This and "Murder in the First Degree" are among the very last sides Oden is known to have recorded. Three obscure tracks by John T. "Nature Boy" Brown, a saxman and singer, close this extraordinary collection of little-known Chicago blues, which should impress any fan of Chess or Cobra Records (indeed, Parrot had a stronger roster than Cobra, based on what we hear here). The sound quality is generally very good, the only significant surface noise from a non-tape source coming up on the Oden sides, which still sound clean and very listenable. *—Bruce Eder*

Copulatin' Blues / Apr. 29, 1929-Feb. 5, 1940 / Stash ✦✦✦
The Stash label began in 1976 with a dozen or so LPs that featured subject matter from the 1930s that was considered risqué for the period. In the case of this album, the 16 selections all have to do with sex; several cuts were previously unreleased and few had very wide circulation. Such top jazz and blues artists as Sidney Bechet, Lil Johnson, Bessie Smith ("Do Your Duty" and "I Need a Little Sugar in My Bowl"), the Harlem Hamfats, Merline Johnson, Tampa Red, Grant & Wilson, Jelly Roll Morton ("Winin' Boy"), and Lucille Bogan (an absolutely filthy "Shave 'Em Dry") are heard from. Some of this music has been reissued by Stash through its subsidiary Jass on CD but not in the same format. *—Scott Yanow*

Copulatin' Blues, Vol. 2 / Jan. 26, 1929-1955 / Stash ✦✦✦
This collection contains a truthful warning and description: "A Party Record for Adults—Screen Before Airplay." It is doubtful if more than a couple of these 15 selections could be played on the radio, even now. Mostly dating from the 1930s, the risqué performances include several (including a very profane "parody" by the Clovers in the 1950s) that were previously unissued. Best are "The Duck's Yas Yas" by Eddie Johnson & His Crackerjacks, "It Feels So Good" by the Hokum Boys, and the classic "Pussy" by Harry Roy's Bat Club Boys. *—Scott Yanow*

Country Blues Bottleneck Guitar Classics: 1926–1937 / 1972 / Yazoo ✦✦✦✦
Originating with the homemade, single-string instruments created by musicians from Mississippi and neighboring states, the slide style of guitar playing was particularly effective when applied to the developing blues. Employing open tunings, guitarists could gracefully blur notes for a quality not unlike the human voice. Consisting almost entirely of solo vocal/guitar numbers, *Country Blues Bottleneck Guitar Classics: 1926-1937* excels in its portrait of the instrument's range in the hands of players like Barbecue Bob, Bukka White, King Solomon Hill, and Robert Johnson. Only four of Hill's six 78 sides had seen the light of day at the time of this release. On the basis of "Whoopee Blues" (and the superior "Gone Dead Train," not included), this is a sad fact. The performance is a killer both for the brilliance of Hill's penetrating falsetto and for his adept slide work. Bukka White's debut, "The Panama Limited," with its spoken verses (accompanied by train-like vamp) and sung choruses (mimicked by wonderfully distilled slide lines), sets the stage for many of his subsequent recordings. A further highlight is provided by the exceptional husband and wife team of Kansas Joe McCoy and Memphis Minnie on the biting slide performance "My Wash Woman's Gone." *Country Blues Bottleneck Guitar Classics* is of course only one version of the story: Its selection, while excellent, doesn't provide the slide guitar primer one might expect. There are, for example, no selections by either Kokomo Arnold or Casey Bill Weldon. Rather, the collection feels like a Yazoo sampler that focuses on slide material. A minor qualm as the artists contained here are, for the most part, all formidable players, and almost every performance stands as a classic example of the style. *—Nathan Bush*

Country Blues Collector's Items (1930–1941) / Feb. 15, 1996 / Document ✦✦✦
Despite its uneven fidelity, *Country Blues Collector's Items (1930-1941)* is a fascinating collection of early country blues from the likes of Tommy Griffin, One Arm Slim, and Frank Edwards. There are some gems on this extensive collection, but the academic approach of the collection means that the disc will appeal primarily to specialists and academics. *—Thom Owens*

Country Gospel (1946–1953) / May 1, 1995 / Document ✦✦✦
Fine historical recordings by the Two Gospel Keys and Sister O.M. Terrell. *—Opal Louis Nations*

Cryin' in the Morning: An Anthology of Post-War Blues / 1979 / Muse ✦✦✦
Some of the actual performances on this collection would deserve a higher rating, and they get it when found in other collections, including the complete albums that have been released by some of the artists featured here. This compilation chooses "post-war blues" as its thematic subject, hiding the real program, which is to present tracks recorded by the Regal label under the auspices of producer Fred Mendelsohn. As such there are good tracks, and some blues names of Mt. Rushmore stature, including John Lee Hooker and Blind Willie McTell, the latter artist cheating on a recording contract and hiding out with the name of Pig 'n' Whistle Red. There are also artists of great obscurity, such as Blind Billy Tate and Dennis McMillan. The tracks are tossed together like a blues college radio show that has been shrunken down to a half an hour and shoved into a blender. Sure, it is difficult to string together a bunch of sides that have nothing in common other than the label they were recorded for, but a little bit of concentration on someone's part and a more effective sequencing could have been created. The liner notes maintain a flat tone, describing Hooker as "out of meter vocal and lack of rhyme" but basically getting the message across that in the postwar era, country blues were being replaced by a new electric version of the music, much of which represents the early formative stages of rock & roll. Players became more conscious of using the recording studio, including creating sound effects or boosting the power of an instrument or player through mixing techniques. These trends are more than just hinted at on some of these tracks, while others are still in the older solo acoustic styles. With the vast amount of blues material available,

it is hard to find this album particularly significant. Its entire existence is mostly due to the fact that the Muse label attempted to create as large a catalog as possible as quickly as it could. *—Eugene Chadbourne*

Dallas Alley Drag: Piano Blues, Rags & Stomps / May 9, 2000 / Yazoo ♦♦♦♦
A collection of Texas piano sides recorded in the '20s, this set documents the earliest recordings in that style. Forged in Dallas' "Deep Ellum" district, players like Whistlin' Alex Moore, Texas Billy Day, Billiken Johnson, and Bessie Tucker forged the style heard on these sides along with names from obscurity like Bobby Cadillac, Jack Ranger, Ida Mae Mack, and Hattie Hudson. Pulled from extremely rare 78s, the sound is rough in spots, but the music's worth every pop, click, and scratch that goes with it. *—Cub Koda*

Deep Blue: 25 Years of Blues on Rounder Records / Sep. 12, 1995 / Rounder ♦♦♦
Over the course of two CDs, *Deep Blue—25 Years of Blues on Rounder Records* rounds up the highlights of Rounder's blues catalog, including tracks from Professor Longhair, Clarence "Gatemouth" Brown, Lowell Fulson, Robert Nighthawk, Champion Jack Dupree, Luther "Guitar Junior" Johnson, Ronnie Earl, and Smokin' Joe Kubek, among many others. It's a fairly consistent collection, giving a good representation of the record label's catalog. *—Stephen Thomas Erlewine*

Deep in the Soul of Texas / 1991 / Collectables ♦♦♦♦♦
Texas soul from the '60s and '70s includes some previously unissued material. *—Niles J. Frantz*

Deep in the Soul of Texas, Vol. 2 / Nov. 30, 1992 / Collectables ♦♦♦♦♦
More one-star obscurities. *—Bill Dahl*

Deep South Blues / Mar. 23, 1999 / Hangar 18 ♦♦♦
Those who believe that the newer, cruder recording of Mississippi bluesmen playing distorted electric guitars is some newly recorded phenomenon should grab this collection and get straight. In it, they'll find 15 superb homemade performances, all of them put down for posterity in the early '80s, proof that the scene was being documented early and excellently. Kicking off with two dynamite sides from Junior Kimbrough, the set moves on with riveting performances from Jessie Mae Hemphill, R.L. Burnside & the Sound Machine, Hezekiah & the Houserockers, Raymond Hill, Hammie Nixon, Waynell Jones, and Ranie Burnette. This is riveting stuff—not for the casual blues fan. *—Cub Koda*

Delta Blues: 1951 / 1990 / Acoustic Archives ♦♦♦♦♦
A great compilation from the Jackson, MS-based Trumpet Records. Features early-'50s sides by Big Joe Williams, wonderful acoustic duets by the Huff Brothers, and the last recordings of original King Biscuit Boy Willie Love. A wonderful document. *—AMG*

Destination GB Blues / Apr. 21, 1998 / Music Club ♦♦♦
A good solid hour of British blues playing and singing aboard here, with stellar contributions from some big names and some others who deserve a wider hearing. Among the highlights are Duster Bennett with Peter Green conjuring up some tasty fills on "Trying So Hard to Forget," Alan Price turning in a nice revisit of "House of the Rising Sun," Chris Farlowe's "Out of Time," Blodwyn Pig's "Long Black Veil," Chicken Shack's "I'd Rather Go Blind," and Dave Kelly's "Let's Talk It Over." The other side of early Clapton, Mayall, Fleetwood Mac, etc. *—Cub Koda*

Detroit Blues: Early 1950's / Blues Classics ♦♦♦♦♦
These 15 tracks are tough, raw-edged, primitive urban blues from the Motor City. Kicking off with four sides from Baby Boy Warren ("Sanafee," "Baby Boy Blues," "Mattie Mae," and the instrumental "Chicken"), three of them feature the harmonica talents of Sonny Boy Williamson, Washboard Willie, Boogie Woogie Red on piano, and former Robert Johnson running buddy Calvin Frazier on lead guitar, making this combo the Detroit equivalent of the original Muddy Waters band. Doctor Ross' Fortune recording of "Thirty Two Twenty" along with Bobo Jenkins' "Baby Don't You Want to Go" and "10 Below Zero" gives a glimpse of that label's bare-bones production techniques, while Eddie Kirkland's "No Shoes," Big Maceo's "Big City Blues," and L.C. Green's "Remember Way Back" mirror the gritty sound that emerged from Detroit's ghettos in the early '50s. John Lee Hooker is also aboard with the original "House Rent Boogie," providing a semi-comedic foil for the Detroit Count's hilarious two-part "Hastings Street Opera," One String Sam's eerie "I Need $100," and the set closer, "Alabama Bus" by Brother Will Hairston, featuring Washboard Willie well to the fore. Much cruder than the more polished sound of Chicago blues, this compilation highlights some of the very best that emerged from this early, embryonic period. *—Cub Koda & Bill Dahl*

Dig These Blues: The Legendary Dig Masters / 1992 / Ace ♦♦♦♦♦
Johnny Otis produced these hot R&B sides for his Dig label during the mid-'50s. *—Bill Dahl*

Don't Leave Me Here: The Blues of Texas, Arkansas and Louisiana 1927–1932 / Aug. 12, 1991 / Yazoo ♦♦♦♦♦
Don't Leave Me Here is a 14-track country blues collection of recordings from 1927-1932. This contains a variety of traditional acoustic blues styles from the Gulf Coast area. Highlights include King Solomon Hill and Little Hat Jones. *—Niles J. Frantz*

Double Crossing Blues / May 12, 1998 / A&M ♦♦♦
This compilation, made up of duets between various all-star blues artists, is an interesting idea that unfortunately doesn't deliver. The blues' most famous partnerships (Buddy Guy & Junior Wells, Shirley & Lee, Sonny Terry & Brownie McGhee) are represented, along with a slew of one-off singles pairing Ella Fitzgerald with Louis Jordan, Big Mama Thornton with Johnny Ace, and others. It works well on a conceptual level, but drastic jumps between styles and sound quality make it come off as more of an odd duck than a good idea. Most of these songs are cool, but do they really play well back to back? *—Jim Smith*

Down & Out: The Sad Soul of the Black South / 1998 / Trikont ♦♦♦♦♦
This volume in Trikont's wonderfully eclectic, well-researched American music series should have been called "Dogged Again, the Dirty Blue Soul of the Deep South." Never has a collection of obscure, raging heartbreak songs like these been issued. These are "done wrong" songs, but they have an edge missing in so much of the period's R&B and blues. These songs believe in a love so pure, it can only be consummated by murder, suicide, or an act of divine intervention, such is its emotional intensity. Even where the protagonist begs, such as Johnny Copeland on "Down on Bended Knees," there is a rage in his hurt, an anger barely hidden in the cage of his heart. And then there's the suicidal—literally—"Dead" by Ede Robin, who sings, "And then there's me along, with a razor in my hand/ I remove my watchband." There's a B-3 blazing in the background and Illinois Jacquet blasting out the blues on his tenor before Robin comes back in, begging her lover not to do her "like that." When her spoken vocal whispers out at the end of the tune, we know how it ends. There is just so much bad-assed material here, almost all of it B-sides, discarded tracks, or singles played only on jukeboxes in the bars south of the Mason-Dixon Line. Shouters like Virgil Griffin come out and beg the Lord to abate his loneliness that has reached the pitch of anger. Only a power higher than himself can relieve his fear and misery. Elsewhere, Bill Brandon, Ella Brown, Betty Lavette, James Kelly Duhon, Ella Washington, Geater Adams, Juke Boy Bonner, Percy Mayfield, and even Gashead—with his underground classic "Why Do You Treat Me Like a Tramp"—weigh in with tales of domestic problems, and the attempt to survive them. Perhaps nowhere is the desire to transcend these circumstances more evident than O.V. Wright's "Everybody Knows (The River Song)," where he sings, "God, I'm so sad and so scared/I want to go to heaven/But I'm scared to fly." When Joe Medwick follows this will, a gospel blues called "I Cried" with a chorus answering his testimony, trying to hold him up the whole record comes undone, it spills rivers of tears and rage and pain into the listener's space; it would be overwhelming were it not for the powerful groove and roll of the rhythms and arrangements. This is deep soul as it hasn't been presented in a long, long while, if ever. Unadorned, raw, immediate, *Down & Out* tells a truth so simple and all-encompassing it will be unfathomable to many. *—Thom Jurek*

Down Home Harp / Jun. 23, 1998 / Testament ♦♦♦♦
A companion volume to Testament's *Down Home Slide* compilation, this brings together 21 previously unreleased tracks from that label's vaults and a reprise of "Billy Boy's Jump" by Billy Boy Arnold from the original album *Goin' to Chicago.* There's a real nice blend of styles, and even with big guns aboard like Big Walter Horton and Little Walter playing with Johnny Young and Robert Nighthawk, this is no mere amplified Chicago honkfest. The country side of things is represented in a right primitive way by Willie Lee Harris and Coot Vinson, with Doctor Ross, Driftin' Slim, and James "Bat" Robinson holding up the one-man band side of the equation. And a can't-miss highlight is the harmonica Slim Willis Quartet taking the pop standard "Canadian Sunset" for a low-down blues ride. Selections from Big John Wrencher, George Robertson, John Lee Henley, and Andrew Cauthen round out this superlative little collection. Not just another harmonica compilation, there are great performances in enough divergent styles to make this a wonderful harmonica introductory primer disc for anyone who wants to investigate both city and country styles. *—Cub Koda*

Down Home Slide / May 19, 1998 / Testament ♦♦♦♦
Although slide guitar compilations at times seem to proliferate like kudzu, this particular collection has much to recommend adding it to the collection. For openers, there's the inclusion of three previously unreleased live performances from Robert Nighthawk. Playing in a 1964 Chicago concert accompanied by Johnny Young on guitar and mandolin, and Little Walter on acoustic harmonica (a rarity), Nighthawk turns in stellar readings of Jimmy Rogers' "That's All Right" (a number he apparently never recorded anywhere else), Little Walter's "Everything's Gonna Be Alright" (set to a "Dust My Broom" arrangement), and his standard "Anna Lee," all in highly relaxed versions that add much to his meager discography. Other highlights include a track of Eddie Taylor making a rare appearance on slide with Nighthawk's "Jackson Town," four tracks by Big Joe Williams, two from Mississippi Fred McDowell, a Johnny Littlejohn instrumental with Jimmy Rogers on rhythm guitar ("Slidin'"), and Homesick James guesting behind vocalist George Coleman on "Mad and Evil." Selections from David "Honeyboy" Edwards, Arthur Weston, Blind Connie Williams, John Henry Barbee, Elijah Brown, and Johnny Shines complete this excellent collection. *—Cub Koda*

Down in Black Bottom: Lowdown Barrelhouse Piano / Apr. 20, 1999 / Yazoo ♦♦♦♦
In addition to their indispensable compilations devoted to the bluesmen and women of the '20s and '30s, Yazoo has delivered a number of excellent, topical country blues sets as well. Though not always as essential as the single-artist discs, they are nonetheless valuable on both musical and historical terms. Released simultaneously with the label's bawdy *Barrelhouse Mamas* collection, *Down in Black Bottom* is a similar collection of early piano blues, with the focus once again being on small combos. Possibly due to the fact that pianists were so often thrust into the role of accompanist, few of these artists made significant names for themselves on record. There is a handful of exceptions, of course. Little Brother Montgomery was an exceptionally gifted pianist who, before moving to Chicago during the '40s, absorbed the rich and varied piano traditions that surrounded him in the Jackson, MS, area. Tampa Red remained a popular performer long after his move to the Windy City, where the hokum material he favored went over well with Chicago audiences. Names like Sammy Brown, Sylvester Palmer, and Parish Turner, however, remain more mysterious. Most of the musicians on this compilation who managed to achieve popularity did so through their piano skills rather than their singing. This was good-time music for the most part and, as a result, these signers weren't the most exceptional of blues versifiers either. Oftentimes the lyrics rely on the sort of stock

phrases that nearly every bluesman acquired as a matter of course. Though the blues on this disc hardly represent the most emotionally compelling of Yazoo's extensive catalog, the set will certainly appeal to enthusiasts of the style, as well as blues fans in search of a less demanding introduction to the early recordings. —*Nathan Bush*

Down the Dirt Road: The Songs of Charley Patton / Aug. 28, 2001 / Telarc ✦✦✦✦
Coordinated by acoustic Delta guitarist Steve James (who also penned the liner notes and appears on two tracks), this is a respectful but refreshingly not-always-reverent tribute to the undisputed king of the Delta blues. Although there are only 12 tracks and some of Patton's defining tunes—like "Screamin' and Hollerin' the Blues" and "A Spoonful Blues"—are MIA, these performances capture the spirit of Patton and show how his legacy extends to contemporary blues musicians. There really isn't a bad or misguided track here (unusual for tribute discs), a situation helped by the quality and pedigree of the musicians involved, who seek to maintain the rawness of Patton's blues. Certainly keeping the predominantly unplugged music stripped to just guitar or harmonica (in the case of Snooky Pryor's amazing "Pony Blues," which finds the classic bluesman sounding as inspired as ever), or both (as Annie Raines and Paul Rishell's take on Patton's spiritual "I Shall Not Be Moved"), maintains the focus. Delta-based artists such as Corey Harris and Dave Van Ronk turn in fine if unsurprising performances. But the unexpected addition of Brit pub rocker Graham Parker works surprisingly well, as his gritty voice (although not necessarily rudimentary guitar) does justice to "Poor Me." Harpist Charlie Musselwhite sticks to guitar for an ominous yet sweet "Pea Vine Blues," but it's Joe Louis Walker's incendiary seven-and-a-half-minute version of "Sugar Mama" and the closing medley of "Down the Dirt Road Blues"/"When Your Way Gets Dark," sung with a sexy, knockout approach by the album's only female vocalist, Colleen Sexton, clocking in at nearly ten minutes, that are the album's highlights. They open up these songs, leaving room for improvisation that expands the concepts but stays true to Patton's originals. One of the most successful albums of this type, this is an excellent (and well-recorded) introduction to the music of one of the touchstones of the blues. —*Hal Horowitz*

Drop Down Mama / 1970 / Chess ✦✦✦✦✦
This collection features Robert Nighthawk's early sides for Chess back when they were still called Aristocrat, including the original "Sweet Black Angel" (which later became a hit for B.B. King as "Sweet Little Angel") and "Anna Lee," two of his very best. Even with minimal band support on these sides, Nighthawk's voice and slide guitar resonate like an orchestra. This wonderful compilation also features seminal tracks by Johnny Shines ("So Glad I Found You"), Floyd Jones ("Dark Road"), Arthur "Big Boy" Spires ("One of These Days"), and David "Honeyboy" Edwards doing the title track with a full band. Truly a compilation that should be residing in everyone's collection. —*Cub Koda*

Drove from Home Blues / 1988 / Flyright ✦✦✦✦✦
This is an interesting collection of tunes recorded by artists who are virtually unknown. The music is excellent, finding its niche in the stylish, pre-rockabilly/R&B world—a reflection of the work being done in the late '40s and early '50s by artists such as Arthur "Big Boy" Crudup, Lightnin' Hopkins, Tommy McClennan, and Blind Boy Fuller. The music of Wright Holmes, for example, is cast in a Lightnin' Hopkins' mold, but his imaginative guitar style is very wild and unconventional. In addition, harpist Sonny Boy Johnson emerges from the John Lee "Sonny Boy" Williamson school. Also present is Muddy Waters' very first commercial recording. —*Larry Hoffman*

☆ **Duke-Peacock's Greatest Hits** / 1992 / MCA ✦✦✦✦✦
Don Robey, something of an infamous figure even in the rough-and-tumble world of '50s R&B labels, owned one of the first successful black-owned labels in the country, and his output was rich and varied. *Duke-Peacock's Greatest Hits* offers a revealing overview of his operation, beginning with major hits by two of the company's humongous female belters, Big Mama Thornton's "Hound Dog" and Marie Adams' "I'm Gonna Play the Honky Tonks." Johnny Ace, Bobby "Blue" Bland, and Junior Parker are represented by a few of their biggest hits, but it's the relatively unknown "Pack Fair and Square" by San Antonio pianist Big Walter Price that wields a knockout punch. Vocal groups aren't forgotten, with sides by Norman Fox & the Rob Roys and the El Torros, and a foray into rockabilly is recalled by the Original Casuals' "So Tough." —*Bill Dahl*

☆ **The Earliest Negro Vocal Quartets (1894–1928)** / 1991 / Document ✦✦✦✦✦
A treasure trove for archivists, *The Earliest Negro Vocal Quartets (1894–1928)* compiles 23 impossibly rare recordings spotlighting the African-American four-part harmony singing style that predated both jazz and the blues. The real treat here is the lone surviving recording by the Standard Quintette, 1894's "Keep Movin'"; a cylinder cut for Columbia, it is in fact the only black music recording of its time to survive into the 20th century, and as a piece of history alone it's invaluable. The first-ever commercial recordings by a black group, cut in 1902 by the Dinwiddle Colored Quartet, are included as well, as are tracks by the Apollo Male Quartette and Polk Miller & His Old South Quartette. Understandably, the music here is buried under considerable surface noise; casual listeners may wish to pass, but for historians the release of *The Earliest Negro Vocal Quartets (1894-1928)* is a major event. —*Jason Ankeny*

East Coast Blues in the Thirties (1934–1939) / 1990 / Story of the Blues ✦✦✦✦
Four long-forgotten singer/guitarists have all of their recordings reissued on this interesting CD. Bob Campbell is heard on four numbers, Tampa Kid (who does his best to emulate Tampa Red) and Poor Bill (who might be William White) are heard on two songs apiece, and Sam Montgomery made it into the studio enough to cut eight sides. Other than Montgomery (who is joined by a second guitarist on four of his eight selections), all of the performances are unaccompanied solos with vocals. The music is surprisingly good considering that virtually nothing is known about the four performers. Serious blues

collectors will want this music, which hints at the great musical treasures that were never—or just barely—documented. —*Scott Yanow*

East Coast Blues: 1926–1935 / Sep. 30, 1991 / Yazoo ✦✦✦✦
A fine assortment from Carl Martin, Willie Walker, William Moore, Blind Blake, Bayless Rose, and other East Coast guitarists. There are several very traditional blues like "Black Dog Blues" and "Crow Jane," plus lots of good ragtime guitar. For serious guitar players and Piedmont blues fans. —*Barry Lee Pearson*

The Essential Blues / 1995 / House of Blues ✦✦✦
Essential Blues is an attempt to trace the evolution of the music from the Mississippi Delta to Chicago and other modern, urban cities. It does a fairly good job in providing a brief history, but the main strength of the collection simply comes from the music. Featuring cuts from Lightnin' Hopkins, Howlin' Wolf, B.B. King, Slim Harpo, Junior Parker, Elmore James, Albert Collins, and many, many others, it's a quick and effective way to sample a variety of different blues styles. For neophytes, *Essential Blues* does offer a splendid introduction to the genre. —*Stephen Thomas Erlewine*

Essential Blues, Vol. 3 / Jun. 22, 1999 / House of Blues ✦✦✦✦✦
A two-disc set of blues recordings that makes the "essential" in the title a very arguable point indeed, unless you consider Junior Wells doing the Rolling Stones' "Satisfaction" and Taj Mahal doing "Honky Tonk Women" must-haves for the collection. The rest of the set features notable contributions from Muddy Waters, Magic Sam, Jimmy Reed, Lightnin' Hopkins, Professor Longhair, John Lee Hooker, Jimmy Rogers, Sonny Boy Williamson, Little Walter, T-Bone Walker, and Bobby "Blue" Bland. There are also less essential contributions from Robert Cray, Charles Brown, Johnny Adams, Otis Rush, and others that tip the scales in the opposite direction. This isn't a *bad* collection, necessarily, but there are overall far better collections out there to spend your money on. —*Cub Koda*

Evidence Blues Sampler / Oct. 1, 1992 / Evidence ✦✦✦
Evidence's blues reissue campaign has been exhaustive and diverse in its artistic and stylistic range, something that is reflected in this 15-cut sampler culled from various sessions. There is vintage material from John Lee Hooker, J.B. Hutto, and the tandem of Junior Wells and Buddy Guy, plus classic R&B by Louis Jordan and Big Joe Turner and contemporary blues by Magic Slim, Lonnie Brooks, and Luther "Guitar Junior" Johnson. You can also hear Otis Rush and Luther Allison at their best or Pinetop Perkins offering prototypical boogie-woogie and rumbling piano licks. —*Ron Wynn*

Excello Blues: House Rockin' & Hip Shakin' / Nov. 4, 1997 / Hip-O ✦✦✦
This 16-track collection rounds up the usual favorites (Slim Harpo's "I'm a King Bee," Arthur Gunter's "Baby Let's Play House," Lazy Lester's "Sugar Coated Love," Lightnin' Slim's "Rooster Blues") along with others less often anthologized like Jerry McCain's "My Next Door Neighbor" and "That's What They Want," Leroy Washington's "Wild Cherry," Jimmy Anderson's "Naggin'," Whispering Smith's "I Tried So Hard," and the alternate take of Lazy Lester's "I'm a Lover, Not a Fighter." A solid mid-line collection that makes a perfect introduction into the blues side of this legendary label. —*Cub Koda*

Excello Harmonica Blues Variety / 1994 / Excello ✦✦✦✦
This is a 39-track, double-CD package collecting up various stray cuts in the Excello vaults by artists who didn't leave enough tracks behind to justify having compilations under their own names. The highlights include multiple tracks by Jimmy Reed sound-alike Jimmy Anderson, Lightnin' Slim sideman Lazy Lester, and Jerry McCain & His Upstarts. Add to this stray singles by Baby Boy Warren (with Sonny Boy Williamson), Little Sonny, Whispering Smith, and the obscure Ole Sonny Boy and you have a package that fills up the holes in your Excello collection quite nicely. Over half of the tracks are dubbed from disc, but the music's fine just the same. —*Cub Koda*

The Excello Story, Vol. 1: 1952–1955 / Feb. 9, 1999 / Hip-O ✦✦✦✦
Here are 20 sides from the earliest years of Excello, the Nashville-based label best known for Southern-style blues and R&B, though it also recorded some country and gospel. All of these styles are present on this compilation, which may make it an uneven listen for those whose interests don't encompass each of the genres. The quality, however, is good, including a number of rarities that don't make it onto many anthologies. Arthur Gunter's original version of "Baby Let's Play House," an R&B hit before it was covered by Elvis Presley the following year, is the most famous cut by far; the only other one to be a big hit was Kid King's Combo's "Banana Split," a New Orleans-styled instrumental that made the R&B Top Ten in 1953. A number of the other blues/R&B crossovers here are delights, including the Charlie Dowell Orchestra's jump blues "Wail Daddy"; Del Thorne's jiving "Down South in Birmingham," which sounds familiar enough to be a hit, although it wasn't; the Blues Rockers' "Calling All Cows," which sounds like a bluesier variation of the famous New Orleans tune "Iko Iko"; and the Leap Frogs' "Dirty Britches," with Arthur Gunter on guitar, which like Gunter's "Baby Let's Play House" sounds pretty close to rock & roll. Beyond the blues/R&B realm, there's updated jugband-style blues from the Dixie Doodlers, pretty hot honky-tonk by Rat Batts on "Stealin' Sugar," and early uptempo doo wop on the Peacheroos' "Be Bop Baby." —*Richie Unterberger*

The Excello Story, Vol. 2: 1955–1957 / Feb. 9, 1999 / Hip-O ✦✦✦✦
The end of the period covered on the second installment of this Excello retrospective saw the label start to record the Louisiana swamp blues artists for whom it is most famed: Slim Harpo, Lazy Lester, Lightnin' Slim, Lonesome Sundown. While each of those artists is represented here by a cut or two (including Harpo's classic "I'm a King Bee"), much of it's devoted to more urban mid-'50s blues/R&B crossover, most of it recorded in Nashville. A couple of these were big hits: The Marigolds' "Rollin' Stone" made the R&B Top Ten in 1955 (and was covered for a pop hit by the Fontane Sisters), while Louis Brooks made number two R&B that same year with "It's Love Baby (24 Hours a Day)" (covered with success by Ruth Brown). Jerry McCain does raw, early electric blues with "Courtin' in a

Cadillac," Guitar Gable does blues with a Mardi Gras rhythm on "Congo Mambo," a young Johnny Copeland plays "chicken licking" guitar on Clarence Samuels' "Chicken Hearted Woman," and there are a couple of low-down blues by Little Al (Arthur Gunter's brother). There's also some rockabilly by Johnny Jano, whose "Havin' a Whole Lot of Fun" is attractively over the top, and Al Ferrier, whose "Hey! Baby" is a transparent derivation of "Baby Let's Play House." Like the first volume of this fine series, it's a good collection of a variety of sounds on the cusp of becoming rock & roll, though by this point the line was sometimes being crossed into bona fide early rock. *—Richie Unterberger*

The Excello Story, Vol. 3: 1957–1961 / Apr. 6, 1999 / Hip-O ♦♦♦♦
Excello was hitting its prime as a good R&B, blues and rock label in this era. This has swamp blues by Slim Harpo (just one song, but that's OK as he's well represented by single-artist anthologies), Lightnin' Slim, Lonesome Sundown, and Lazy Lester, who's represented by the great "I Hear You Knockin'" and the original version of "I'm a Lover, Not a Fighter" (covered by the Kinks in the '60s). There's more than Louisiana blues, though. For doo wop, there's the Gladiolas' original version of "Little Darlin'" (covered for a big pop hit by the Diamonds), and the one-shot smash "Oh Julie" by the Crescendos. Carol Fran's "Emmitt Lee" is top-notch, early New Orleans soul that will find favor with any Irma Thomas fan, so close is the arrangement to the sound of Thomas' early records. The sound strays closer to straight rock & roll with Lattimore Brown's "Somebody's Gonna Miss Me" and two early sides by swamp pop legend Warren Storm. *—Richie Unterberger*

The Excello Story, Vol. 4: 1961–1975 / Apr. 6, 1999 / Hip-O ♦♦♦
Just from the large chronological span of the final volume of this series, it's obvious that Excello's momentum started to peter out in its later years. Still, over half of this is fine, rock-solid blues that saw the label keep the flame of raw & funky blues with a soul/R&B influence alive better than almost any other company did in the '60s. There are good cuts by Excello, swamp blues stalwarts Slim Harpo (his hits "Baby, Scratch My Back" and "Tip on In"), Lonesome Sundown, Lightnin' Slim, and Silas Hogan, but also some decent tracks by less famed bluesmen like Tabby Thomas, Little Sonny and Charles Sheffield (whose "It's Your Voodoo Working" has a snaky modern New Orleans feel). The last 40 percent of the compilation is given over to more modern-sounding soul from the '60s and the first half of the '70s, and this isn't nearly as enjoyable, the last few selections in particularly boasting a generic "sweet soul" feel. It's obvious Tiny Watkins is trying to emulate the feel of Percy Sledge's early material with "Soldier's Sad Story," one of the better soul songs here. *—Richie Unterberger*

Fathers & Sons / Sep. 1982 / Chess ♦♦♦♦♦
Put blues legends Muddy Waters and Otis Spann together in a recording studio with young upstarts such as Paul Butterfield, Mike Bloomfield, Buddy Miles, amongst others, and hope that the magic will flow. On *Fathers and Sons* it does, and then some. Originally a two-record set now pared down to one CD, *Fathers and Sons* displays the love that these musicians shared for the blues and the care they put into getting that feeling down on tape. Standout cuts include "Can't Lose What You Ain't Never Had," "I'm Ready," and "Standing 'Round Cryin'," which Eric Clapton covered in 1994. The live concert is loose and funky with everyone getting in their licks, especially Muddy Waters, who shines throughout. A fine touchstone for anyone looking into Chicago blues and generally good music. *—James Chrispell*

Female Blues Singers, Vol. 1: A/B (1924–1932) / Mar. 18, 1997 / Document ♦♦♦♦
This is the first of 14 CDs that the Austrian Document label has put out that includes the complete output of obscure classic blues singers from the 1920s/early '30s. In most cases, the vocalists recorded only a handful of sides, so these performances have eluded previous reissue programs. *Vol. 1* has eight numbers by Ora Alexander (the high point of the disc), a lone number by Louise Anderson, four tunes featuring Mildred Austin, six from Baby Bonnie (Ernestine Bomburyero), and four by Eloise Bennett. James P. Johnson might be the pianist on a few of the Ora Alexander numbers while cornetist Wingy Carpenter helps out on the Baby Bonnie selections. This is a very valuable series that classic blues collectors will certainly want to acquire. *—Scott Yanow*

Female Blues Singers, Vol. 2: B (1920–1928) / Mar. 18, 1997 / Document ♦♦♦♦
This intriguing CD has the complete work of Baby Benbow (two sides), Glory Bernard (four songs), Flo Bert (six tunes and an alternate), Mary Bradford (five songs), Florence Bristol (just one selection), and Lil and Will Brown (four numbers by the team of Ivy Smith and Cow Cow Davenport). Flo Bert, whose lone session was in December 1920, was among the very first of the vaudevillian blues singers to record, and it seems strange that she did not have an encore. Florence Bristol is quite a mystery figure, and her only recording ("How Come You Do Me Like You Do") has her backed by altoist Otto Hardwick and pianist Duke Ellington in November 1924. In addition to two numbers from 1928, Mary Bradford is heard on three selections with the 1923 Bennie Moten Orchestra. Overall, these rarities are quite listenable and sometimes rather fascinating. *—Scott Yanow*

Female Blues Singers, Vol. 3: B/C (1923–1928) / Mar. 18, 1997 / Document ♦♦♦♦
Vol. 3 in this 14-CD series has the complete recordings of Marie Bradley, Kitty Brown, Josephine Byrd, and Alice Carter. Bradley, who was best-known for her moaning and falsetto singing (particularly on two versions of "Down Home Moan"), is the most interesting of the four vocalists although apparently Josephine Byrd (who only recorded two numbers in her career) was well-known in theatres in the Midwest during the 1920s. Among the sidemen (most of whom are unidentified) who are heard from on this interesting CD are pianists Will Ezell, Freddie Longshaw, and possibly Tiny Parham. *—Scott Yanow*

Female Blues Singers, Vol. 4: C (1921–1930) / Mar. 18, 1997 / Document ♦♦♦♦
Seven long-forgotten classic blues singers are featured on this CD, which has their total output. Alice Leslie Carter is heard on 11 dated but often charming performances from 1921, in which she is backed by a combo led by pianist James P. Johnson, including the debut vocal recording of "Aunt Hagar's Children Blues." Josephine Carter fares OK on four numbers, while Margaret Carter's two numbers in 1926 ("I Want Plenty Grease in My Frying Pan" and "Come Get Me, Papa, Before I Faint") are excellent, making one wish that she had recorded again. Alta Cates' lone title (the ironically titled "Never Again") is forgettable while Juanita Stinette Chappelle's only solo side (she normally recorded as a team with her husband) is fine. Finishing off this set are two numbers apiece from Alice Clinton (who is probably actress Nina Mae McKinney under a pseudonym) in 1928 and the fine low-down blues singer Anna Belle Coleman, who would have been considered out-of-date in 1930. *—Scott Yanow*

Female Blues Singers, Vol. 5: C/D/E (1921–1928) / Mar. 18, 1997 / Document ♦♦♦♦
Vol. 5 in this 14-CD series has all of the recordings by Ruth Coleman (other than one number released elsewhere of her with Jimmy O'Bryant), Henryette Davis, Madlyn Davis (other than her 1928 recordings with Tampa Red), Louise De Vant (other than her session with Perry Bradford), Jessie Derrick, Dorothy Dodd, and Maureen Englin. Most of these performances are quite interesting, with highlights including Ruth Coleman's "Original Charleston Strut," Henryette Davis' charming but dated "Jazzaphobia Blues," Jessie Derrick's interaction with Harvey Brooks' Quality Four and the singing overall of Madlyn Davis and Dorothy Dodd. Also of interest is Maureen Englin's lone selection, "Foolin' Me," since it includes Sidney Bechet on soprano sax. *—Scott Yanow*

Female Blues Singers, Vol. 6: E/F/G (1922–1928) / Mar. 18, 1997 / Document ♦♦♦♦
A wide variety of obscure singers have their entire and brief recording careers reissued on this CD, the sixth of 14 discs in this fascinating series. Included are two songs apiece by Dorothy Everetts, Madam Hurd Fairfax (who was really a semi-opera singer performing spirituals), Georgie Gorham, and Betty Gray, four songs by Miss Frankie (including two numbers in which she is backed by pianist Eubie Blake), three by Hattie Garland, six from Lillian Goodner (these are among the better selections including two numbers that have background work from cornetist Bubber Miley), three by Ruby Gowdy, and a lone performance by Cry Baby Godfrey. Styles range from vaudevillian to low-down blues, and, in general, the rarely heard performances hold one's interest. *—Scott Yanow*

Female Blues Singers, Vol. 7: G/H (1922–1929) / Mar. 18, 1997 / Document ♦♦♦♦
For this intriguing CD in the 14-disc Document series, the complete recordings of Fannie May Goosby (11 selections), Christina Gray, Ruth Green, Sadie Green, and Katherine Handy (all two numbers apiece) are reissued, along with obscurities left out of other sets by Marie Gristner and Helen Gross. Goosby, a singer from Atlanta, had a particularly bluesy style, and she fares well on her recordings from 1923 and 1928. The other vocalists vary in quality, though it is interesting to hear W.C. Handy's daughter singing his "Loveless Love." Fans of early female classic blues singers will want all of the rarities included in this series. *—Scott Yanow*

Female Blues Singers, Vol. 8: H1 (1923–1928) / Mar. 18, 1997 / Document ♦♦♦♦
Included on this CD are all of the recordings by Josie Harley (a couple forgettable numbers), Lillian Harris (six songs plus three alternate takes), Sister Harris (eight numbers), and Clara Herring (just two songs), plus a couple of previously unreleased test pressings by Alma Henderson (with backing from guitarist Lonnie Johnson and pianist DeLoise Searcy). Both Lillian Harris and Sister Harris (who is backed on "Sugar Blues" by the Original Memphis Five) are excellent, but it is Clara Herring (whose two songs hint at Bessie Smith) who is the biggest surprise; whatever happened to her? Recommended, as are all 14 CDs in this series of true rarities. *—Scott Yanow*

Female Blues Singers, Vol. 9: H2 (1923–1930) / Mar. 18, 1997 / Document ♦♦♦♦
The complete recordings of three singers, plus the early sessions of Edmonia Henderson, are on *Vol. 9* of this 14-CD series. Henderson, whose 1925-1927 dates are available elsewhere, is heard on her first nine selections (from 1923-1924) and shows that she was an excellent vaudevillian classic blues singer. She is joined on some numbers by Lovie Austin's Blues Serenaders (with cornetist Tommy Ladnier and, on "Jelly Roll Blues," clarinetist Johnny Dodds). The completely obscure Lena Henry is OK on six numbers from 1924, Lethia Hill is excellent on her only recording ("Old North State Blues"), being clearly inspired by cornetist Bubber Miley, and Mattie Hite is heard on six numbers from 1923-1924 (some with Fletcher Henderson and Coleman Hawkins) a final pair from 1930 with pianist Cliff Jackson. Interesting historic music. *—Scott Yanow*

Female Blues Singers, Vol. 10: H/I/J (1923–1929) / Mar. 18, 1997 / Document ♦♦♦♦
This is one of the strongest sets in this 14-CD series. The disc has all of the recordings released under the names of classic blues singers Nellie Hite, Jane Howard, Bertha Idaho, Mary Jackson, Sadie Jackson, Zaidee Jackson, and Elnora Johnson, along with two of the four selections led by Caroline Johnson. Some of these names are pseudonyms, with Nellie Hite actually being Mattie Hite (whose other work was reissued on *Vol. 9*), Jane Howard probably being the same person as Miss Frankie (who is otherwise covered in *Vol. 6*), Zaidee and Sadie Jackson most likely being the same singer, and Elnora Johnson possibly being another name for Alberta Hunter! In general, the music is of pretty high quality, particularly the four enjoyable numbers by Bertha Idaho (a Bessie Smith-type singer who should have gained fame and a much more extensive recording career). Sidemen along the way include cornetists Tom Morris and Ed Allen, pianists Clarence Williams and Fletcher Henderson, Perry Bradford's Jazz Phools, and (on the two Sadie Jackson numbers) the great James P. Johnson. Recommended. *—Scott Yanow*

Female Blues Singers, Vol. 11: J/L (1921–1931) / Mar. 18, 1997 / Document ♦♦♦♦
Vol. 11 of this 14-CD series that includes the complete recordings of quite a few obscure classic blues singers of the '20s is a varied affair. Four of the vocalists (Flo Johnson, Ruth Johnson, Josephine Jones, and Eliza Christmas Lee) only cut two songs apiece and one can understand, listening to these rare performances, why there were no encores! Better is Genevieve Jordan (whose only recording went unissued until now), Florence Lowery's

four selections, and the 11 performances by Mandy Lee, whose name might have been used for two different singers! The backup groups are often unidentified (lost to history) but pianist Casino Simpson does what he can to uplift Ruth Johnson's two numbers, and Ladd's Black Aces (with cornetist Phil Napoleon) are on the first five Mandy Lee numbers. Intriguing music, well worth hearing by fans of 1920s blues-oriented singers, despite being a bit erratic. —*Scott Yanow*

Female Blues Singers, Vol. 12: M/O/P/Q/R (1922–1935) / Mar. 18, 1997 / Document ✦✦✦✦

There are some particularly interesting performances on this intriguing CD. Hattie McDaniels (the black movie actress of the '30s and '40s) is heard singing a pair of blues in 1926 with backup from Lovie Austin's Blues Serenaders. Anna Meyers is assisted in 1922 by the Original Memphis Five, Kathryn Perry in 1935 sings "Body and Soul" while joined by her husband Earl Hines' orchestra, Teddy Peters has King Oliver or Johnny Dodds in her backup bands, and Evelyn Preer's "If You Can't Hold the Man You Love" finds her backed by a Duke Ellington small group in 1927. In addition, there are performances by Helene Manley, Anna Oliver, Dolly Perkins, Nettie Potter, Sis Quander, and Nina Reeves. With the exception of McDaniels (who had a few of her performances released on other Document sets), this valuable CD has the complete output of each of these singers. —*Scott Yanow*

Female Blues Singers, Vol. 13: R/S (1921–1931) / Mar. 18, 1997 / Document ✦✦✦✦

This CD has two songs apiece by a pair of obscure singers (Nettie Robinson and Laura Rucker) and the complete output of a couple early-'20s stage performers: Gertrude Saunders and Mary Stafford. Saunder's semi-operatic style is often unintentionally humorous, particularly on "I'm Craving for That Kind of Love." Mary Stafford (heard on 14 numbers, all but the final two from 1921) was an excellent singer as can be heard on early versions of such songs as "Royal Garden Blues," "Strut Miss Lizzie," and "Arkansas Blues." Stafford's singing is the main reason to acquire *Vol. 13* in this 14-CD series. —*Scott Yanow*

Female Blues Singers, Vol. 14: S/T/U/W/Y (1923–1932) / Mar. 18, 1997 / Document ✦✦✦✦

The final volume in this 14-CD series has all of the recordings by Helen Savage, Clementine Smith, Edna Taylor, Georgia Taylor, Kitty Waters, Florence White, Gussie Williams, and Margaret Williams, plus most of the performances by Billie Wilson and Billie Young. Despite the obscurity of most of these singers, the performances are mostly of strong interest. Helen Savage is joined by the Dixie Syncopators (including clarinetist Omer Simeon) in Chicago, Clementine Smith has the assistance on some numbers of Louis Metcalf & the Kansas City Five, Edna Taylor (who only cut two songs) is backed by a duo with cornetist Tommy Ladnier, and Georgia Taylor's one recording is "Jackass Blues" with King Oliver. In addition, there is a completely unknown singer for one cut, most of the other vocalists have a solid pianist behind them, and Billie Young (who is heard on two alternate takes) is accompanied by Jelly Roll Morton. A strong ending to this fascinating reissue series. —*Scott Yanow*

Female Chicago Blues: Complete Works (1936–1947) / Feb. 15, 1995 / Document ✦✦✦✦

Four blues singers of whom very little is known are featured on this CD. Billie McKenzie sings in a friendly and mildly sexy double-entendre style during her ten numbers, Clara Morris' only four selections (she is assisted by pianist Blind John Davis and guitarist Lonnie Johnson), and the only three that Trixie Butler cut (accompanied by pianist Black Bob) that are worth hearing. Best known is Merline Johnson (known as the "Yas Yas Girl") who recorded around 95 numbers in her career. Her final recordings (six from 1941 and the previously unissued "Bad Whiskey Blues" from 1947) are among the better selections on this interesting reissue. Prewar blues collectors will be interested in this set. —*Scott Yanow*

Female Country Blues, Vol. 1: "The Twenties" (1924 to 1928) / Jul. 1, 1992 / Story of the Blues ✦✦✦

All of the recordings by five female classic blues/country blues singers from the '20s are included on this 18-song CD. The music, leased in the early '90s by the Da Music label from Document, has since been reissued by Document too. Virtually nothing is known of the vocalists, three of whom (Anna Lee Chisholm, Virginia Childs, and Cora Perkins) recorded only two songs apiece. Eva Parker fared a bit better with six numbers, while Lulu Jackson (who accompanies herself on guitar) made eight. Many of the sidemen are unknown, but Lonnie Johnson (on violin) helps out Cora Perkins. None of the music is essential, but early blues collectors will find some of the performances to be quite interesting. —*Scott Yanow*

The Fifties: Juke Joint Blues / 1987 / Capitol ✦✦✦✦✦

This is a valuable look at some of the toughest Delta and West Coast blues sides issued by Modern Records in the 1950s. —*Bill Dahl*

The First Take Is the Deepest / Jun. 9, 1998 / Westside ✦✦✦

Ace Records label owner Johnny Vincent did a lot of his recording at the dawn of the multi-track era. He would cut backing tracks and have the vocals added later. But in plowing through the vaults, compilers have found many live-with-the-band vocals as the session players were learning the song, and these early takes have a spontaneous quality that's largely missing from the issued versions. This compilation is supposedly the first of many in this series, bringing these warm-up takes to light for the first time. While 14 of the songs collected here are early or first takes of songs that were issued on either Ace or its subsidiary Vin, the remaining ten tunes are totally unissued in *any* form and making their debut appearance here. Featuring tracks from Joe Tex, Bobby Marchan, Huey "Piano" Smith, Little Booker, Chuck Carbo, Earl King, and others, here's a compilation with a twist that makes for some fine listening. —*Cub Koda*

Flashbacks, Vol. 3: Copulation Blues 1926–1940: Hot & Sexy / 2000 / Trikont ✦✦✦✦

There have been numerous collections that boast the title *Copulation Blues* or *Copulatin' Blues*, but none of them holds a torch to this Trikont compilation that features 25 bawdy tales of well, you know, doin' it. If you slap this slab on the stack at a bash, things will get moist and steamy very quickly. The dancers will be grinding a little more slowly, the corners will fill up nice and cozy, and the bushes outside will be crawling with anxious, agitated lovers. The platter opens with Alberta Hunter's lament for sex by telling her suitor that it doesn't matter if she's black or white because in the dark you can't tell anyway. It's all a slippery slope from there, to say the least. But aside from the topical concerns of the disc, it's the quality of the tracks that sets it apart, from the better-known jams of the sort (Louise Bogan's "Shave 'Em Dry," Clarence Williams' "Organ Grinder Blues," Victoria Spivey's "Black Snake Blues," Mae West's "A Guy What Takes His Time," etc.). But there are other lesser-known blues, R&B, and pop classics as well that are sparkling in their spirited excellence, such as Buddy Burton and Irene Sanders' "Electric Man," Bea Foote's "Try and Get It," Art Fowler's "No Wonder She's a Blushing Bride," and Halfpint Jaxon with Tampa Red doing "My Daddy Rocks Me (With One Steady Roll)." And this is just to list a few. There's over an hour of sweltering hokum blues and risqué rhythms on this set guaranteed to make the most serious person on earth laugh and the most amorous person on earth blush. What could you ask for in a "roots" music collection? Take a cold shower—or don't—after spinning this wondrous blast form the past. Now these folks know what the word "raunchy" meant; Eminem, Nelly, Kid Rock, Missy Elliot, please take note. —*Thom Jurek*

Folk Festival of the Blues / 1963 / MCA ✦✦✦✦✦

This is a compilation album that isn't, a live album that isn't (at least in a couple of spots), and a Muddy Waters album that isn't, if one counts the appearances by four other artists on it. But for all things it isn't, it is also just happens to be one of the greatest and certainly most underrated live blues album of all time, unbelievably crude, raw, and as real as it gets. Originally issued on Chess' Argo label during the height of the folk music blues revival (hence the goofy title), this was a record that was aimed at a white market who responded in kind. But anybody purchasing it thinking they were getting some nice acoustic coffeehouse blues were in for the reality-check shock of their lives. Recorded on July 26, 1963, at a WPOA live radio broadcast MCed by local Chicago disc jockey Big Bill Hill emanating from the Copacabana Club (hence when this was reissued in 1967, it was retitled *Blues from Big Bill's Copacabana*), this features Buddy Guy's band as the backup band for everybody, augmented by Muddy's right-hand man, pianist Otis Spann. Although Big Bill announces the presence of Little Walter and Sonny Boy Williamson on the album's intro, they're no-shows; the studio version of Williamson's "Bring It on Home" appears here with dubbed-on applause (along with the studio version of Guy's "Worried Blues," one of the two bits of audio chicanery here). Everything else is just amazingly raw, crude, and blistering, with some of the most electrifying Buddy Guy guitar ever committed to tape, droning saxes, thundering drums, and Otis Spann anchoring everything with consummate elegance, as nobody's bothered to check their tuning in the last half dozen drinks or more. The combination of performances of Guy, Howlin' Wolf, Willie Dixon, and Sonny Boy in tandem with Waters would certainly checklist this one into "various artists" category, but with half of the ten tracks here being fronted by Waters, it's clearly Muddy's show all the way. His performances of "I Got My Mojo Working," "She's 19 Years Old," "Clouds in My Heart," "Sitting and Thinking," and the vocal trio effort with Guy and Dixon on the show-opening "Wee Wee Baby" are nothing less than exemplary. No matter how you slice it or end up filing it, one would be very hard-pressed indeed to find a live blues album that captures the spirit and a moment in time the way this one does. Unavailable on compact disc as of press time, but worth tracking down in its vinyl incarnations at any cost. —*Cub Koda*

Free at Last: Gospel Quartets from Stax Records' Chalice Label / May 5, 1997 / Specialty ✦✦✦✦

Stax Records launched a gospel subsidiary called Chalice during the mid-'60s that, although short-lived, recorded some remarkable quartets from Memphis and surrounding areas. This 24-track compilation gathers up some ultra-rare selections from that label's archives, including such then-topical songs as the Dixie Nightingales' "The Assassination" (a harrowing lament for President John F. Kennedy) and the Jubilee Hummingbirds' "Our Freedom Song," about Dr. Martin Luther King's receipt of the Nobel Peace Prize. What is especially appealing is the crack instrumental support behind these various quartets being provided by Steve Cropper, Al Jackson, Jr., Isaac Hayes, and other Stax R&B session stalwarts. Selections from the Stars of Virginia and the Pattersonaires complete the package. This compilation was previously released by Ace Records (U.K.) as *Disturb My Soul: Gospel from Stax Records' Chalice Label.* —*Cub Koda*

Frett'n the Blues: Best of the Great Blues Guitarists / Jan. 25, 2000 / Vanguard ✦✦✦✦

In the '60s, lovers of electric blues had a lot to choose from—not only the Chicago blues, but also the electric blues of Texas, Louisiana, Detroit, and Memphis. Vanguard's electric blues output of the '60s is the main focus of this 2000 compilation, which spans 1965-1968 and spotlights some of the guitar playing singers who recorded for the label. Vanguard was no stranger to acoustic country blues—one of the CD's highlights, in fact, is Texas native Lightnin' Hopkins performing "Baby, Please Don't Go" at the Newport Folk Festival—but for the most part, *Frett'n the Blues* concerns itself with electric Northern blues. Chicago-based artists dominate the CD, and the vitality of Chicago's blues scene of the '60s is illustrated by such delights as Buddy Guy performing "Sweet Little Angel" and "One Room Country Shack," Homesick James tackling "Dust My Broom," and Otis Rush embracing "It's a Mean Old World." Muddy Waters, meanwhile, is in fine form on three Newport Folk Festival performances, including "She's Nineteen Years Old" and "I Can't Be Satisfied." And the unique John Lee Hooker, one of the non-Chicagoans on this

CD, gives an enjoyable, if too brief, performance on "I Can't Quit You, Baby." *Frett'n the Blues* is far from the last word on blues singers/guitarists in the '60s; nonetheless, it paints a generally impressive picture of Vanguard's contributions to the electric Northern blues during that decade. *—Alex Henderson*

From Hell to Gone and Back: Texas Blues / Jul. 9, 2002 / Vanguard ♦♦♦♦
From Hell to Gone and Back: Texas Blues seems like an apt expression for a collection of blues songs from Mance Lipscomb, Lightnin' Hopkins, Big Mama Thornton, Pee Wee Crayton, and Lee Roy Parnell. A mixture of live and studio, issued and unissued tracks, the material stretches from the Newport Folk Festival in 1964 to the four walls of a recording facility in 2001. While the connection between these artists, and the eras they recorded in, may seem disparate on the surface, each has been baptized in the deep waters of Texas blues. Lipscomb kicks off the album with fine acoustic work on three originals, "Freddie," "So Different Blues," and "God Moves on the Water." His quiet vocals and tasteful slide prepare the way for Hopkins' more modern sound. Hopkins is in fine form on "Baby Please Don't Go" and "Shake That Thing," spinning out sharp guitar lines to bolster his idiosyncratic vocal delivery. Unreleased versions of "Mojo Hand" and "Where Can I Find My Baby" also appear here. The highlight of this collection arrives at exactly the midpoint, with Big Mama Thornton offering live takes of "Ball and Chain," "Hound Dog," and "Rock Me Baby." Recorded live at two different prisons, the material is boosted by a bluesy, rocking band, featuring electric guitar, piano, and sax. A seven-minute version of "Ball and Chain" will remind anyone who doesn't already know where Janis Joplin got part of her inspiration. Both Crayton and Parnell also deliver fine sets, bringing the album to a close on a rousing note. At nearly 75 minutes, *From Hell to Gone and Back* is a fine collection of classic and contemporary Texas blues artists. *—Ronnie D. Lankford, Jr.*

Full Spectrum Blues / Jul. 16, 1996 / Star Sounds ♦♦♦
A four-disc set split into four distinct approaches to the blues. Disc one is entitled "Rural Blues" and features tracks by Charley Patton, Son House, Papa Charlie Jackson, Blind Blake, Blind Lemon Jefferson, Blind Willie Johnson, Blind Boy Fuller and Sonny Terry, and Robert Johnson. The second disc is entitled "Piano Blues & Boogie Woogie" and spotlights classics from Little Brother Montgomery, Pinetop Smith, Cripple Clarence Lofton, Leroy Carr and Scrapper Blackwell, Jimmy Yancey, Meade "Lux" Lewis, Peetie Wheatstraw, Memphis Slim, Big Maceo Merriweather, Pete Johnson, and Albert Ammons. Next up is "Classic Blues & Vaudeville" with old-time turns from Ma Rainey, Bessie Smith, Mamie Smith, Clara Smith, Sippie Wallace, Coot Grant and Sox Wilson, Butterbeans & Susie, Victoria Spivey, Alberta Hunter, Ida Cox, and Lizzie Miles. Rounding out the collection is "Urban Blues," a bit of a misnomer as the tracks only take us up to the 1940s with tunes by Washboard Sam, Tampa Red, Memphis Minnie, Big Bill Broonzy, Big Joe Turner, Sonny Boy Williamson, Jimmy Rushing, and Billie Holiday rounding out this largely exemplary collection. A small but informative booklet accompanies the discs and the transfers of much of the material are clean with decent sound considering the sources. *—Cub Koda*

Genuine Houserockin' Music, Vol. 1 / 1986 / Alligator ♦♦♦♦♦
These virtually interchangeable samplers of good-time, high-energy, modern R&B were produced by Chicago's Alligator label. Lonnie Brooks, Lonnie Mack, Koko Taylor, Fenton Robinson, Albert Collins, and others are included. Slick and well-produced. *—Hank Davis*

Genuine Houserockin' Music, Vol. 2 / 1987 / Alligator ♦♦♦
If not a definitive blues recording, this 16-track collection delivers on the promise of its title. James Cotton, Johnny Winter, Buddy Guy, Lonnie Mack, and the inestimable Professor Longhair rock the house like the veterans they are. The respected label also showcases relative newcomers, including Robert Cray and Little Charlie & the Nightcats, to show that blues has a future as well as a rich past. *—Mark Allan*

Genuine Houserockin' Music, Vol. 3 / 1988 / Alligator ♦♦♦

Genuine Houserockin' Music, Vol. 4 / Aug. 30, 1990 / Alligator ♦♦♦

Georgia Blues / Rounder ♦♦♦♦
Blues fans, loyal as they might be to classic superstar historic figures such as Blind Lemon Jefferson, will always enjoy being exposed to lesser-known artists who are still creating the old-time country blues despite whatever might pass for musical progress all around them. From this point of view this collection is indispensable. It presents tracks by a slew of Georgia-based artists, none of whom have large discographies. Some of the pieces are absolutely unique, such as the nearly atonal fiddle and vocal track "You Can't Play Me Down" by George Hollis, the ending of which practically collapses in what sounds like a horde of invading children. Other tracks follow the well-known country blues trails, meaning a solo performance with vocal and guitar and sometimes harmonica, the rhythms lively, and the licks simple but effective. "16 Snow White Horses" is an intense performance by Bud White that brings to mind the best of both Mississippi Fred McDowell and Lightnin' Hopkins. Like the latter man, White does not use a bottleneck or slide, but instead snaps out melodic blues riffs that are funky enough to empower a Rolling Stones record, and probably have considering these old goats' habit of swiping such material. Other tracks do feature slide playing, as well as intricate fingerpicking, falsetto vocalizing, and just about any country blues approach one could imagine. By the time these tracks were recorded in the '70s, the notion of regional blues styles meant something much different then it did in the early days of recording technology. The artists featured here have had the benefit of both exposure to their own family and regional traditions and to whatever they might have heard on radio or record players as well. "I Wanna Love You" features harmonica player and singer Bruce Upshaw laying down a chromatic harmonica groove that is straight out of Little Walter and Chicago, not the rural country blues. But instead of a full-band backing, he has only simple guitar accompaniment from Albert Yarbrough. The effect is unique and memorable. "Old Hen Cackle" is from the fascinating fife and drum band tradition, a style with even more direct links to African music than even the blues is supposed to have, represented here by the Georgia Fife and Drum Band.

Although obviously nothing can replace the classic country blues recordings of the '20s and '30s, there is something to be said for hearing this type of music when it is recorded well. The results when a blues scholar such as George Mitchell roams the countryside with a fairly decent portable tape recorder are relaxed and intimate enough to be an acceptable compromise for blues purists who might not like hearing the music presented with too much high-tech glitz. Speaking of Mitchell, it is curious that he gets his name set in a typeface at least ten times the size of any of the performing artists, with this oversize credit printed on both the front and back cover. This colossal display of ego is only slightly forgiven for the brilliance of the opening paragraph the liner notes: "In Georgia, it is said that a man who wants to learn to play guitar should take his box to the cemetery at night, sit on a grave, and throw sticks over his shoulder." Apparently a lot of unnecessary money is getting in the hands of guitar teachers who must be trying to suppress valuable tips such as this. The real stars of the set are, of course, the performers themselves. It is unclear how much material Mitchell had to work with when assembling this in the end, but he did a brilliant job of selection and sequencing; the listening experience is much smoother and unified than many compilations can ever hope to be. *—Eugene Chadbourne*

Georgia Blues (1928–1933) / Jun. 2, 1994 / Document ♦♦♦♦
The Atlanta blues scene of the '20s was among the most fertile in all the South, with a steady stream of rural musicians converging on the city hoping to gain exposure playing the local club circuit, with any luck rising to perform at Decatur Street's famed 81 Theatre; *Georgia Blues 1928-1933* assembles sides from some of the era's most prominent artists, among them Curley Weaver, Fred McMullen, and harpist Eddie Mapp. Far and away the best known of the featured artists, Weaver is captured at the dawn of his career; on his first sides, among them "No No Blues," he sounds remarkably like fellow Atlanta bluesmen the Hicks Brothers. The little-known McMullen is the wild card here, a slide guitarist also noted for his picking finesse; of his seven tracks, the best is "DeKalb Chain Gang," a cut so vividly harrowing it seems undoubtedly autobiographical. *—Jason Ankeny*

Georgia String Bands (1928–1930) / 1992 / Story of the Blues ♦♦♦
All 17 selections on this CD (music leased from the Austrian Document label) were recorded in Atlanta during 1928-1930. The string bands usually feature banjo and guitar with occasional violin and plenty of vocals. This disc has the complete output from the team of Pink Anderson and Simmie Dooley (four selections), Henry Williams and Eddie Anthony (two songs), Lonnie Coleman (also just two numbers), Macon Ed and Tampa Joe (eight selections), and the lone side (which was previously unreleased) by Brothers Wright and Williams (who may actually have been Macon Ed and Tampa Joe under a pseudonym). The music is mostly good-time with occasional low-down blues and plenty of spirit. Nothing essential, but overall these performances give one a good flavor of what blues and country music sounded like in Atlanta in the late '20s. *—Scott Yanow*

Goin' Back to Memphis / 1976 / Bopcat ♦♦♦
Fans of the real-deal, raw rockabilly sound will love this 16-track collection of Memphis-based artists, with half of the tracks being original Sun recordings. Of the eight selections recorded at Sam Phillips' studio at 706 Union Avenue, only one failed to see a release on his Sun label, the countryish call-and-response number "Daisy Bread Boogie." "Michigan's Singing Cowboy," Earl Peterson, is listed as the artist on "Daisy Bread Boogie," but despite the vocal similarity, this is in actuality Memphis radio personality Gene Steele doing the lead vocal chores. Tommy Blake's "Lordy Hoody," featuring the mercurial guitar work of Carl Adams, is here, along with Onie Wheeler's country bopper "Jump Right Out of This Jukebox." Country crossover artist Ernie Chaffin and Memphis bandleader Slim Rhodes are both aboard with two cuts each. Chaffin's "I'm Lonesome" and "Lonesome for My Baby" both feature great steel guitar from Pee Wee Maddux, while Rhodes' "Do What I Do" and "Take and Give" are strong rockabilly efforts with Sandy Brooks doing the Elvis lead vocal chores. The final Sun selection, Hardrock Gunter's "Jukebox Help Me Find My Baby" was actually recorded at a radio station in Wheeling, WV. Two tracks from Carl Perkins, "Big Taxes" and "It Started," were recorded in Nashville in the early '60s, but retain the small-group charm that marked his Sun sides. Perkins also appears in the supporting role of songwriter/guitarist on Randy Lee's Nashville recording of "Tell Me." Another Nashville effort comes from Sun producer Jack Clement with "The Edge of Town." Other Sun alumni contributing (but recording elsewhere in Memphis) are Billy Riley with the instrumental "Memphis Blues," Glenn Honeycutt with the bouncy shuffle "Right Gal, Right Place, Right Time," and Gene Simmons' bluesy title track. The high-dollar collector's item here is one side of Malcolm Yelvington's ultra-rare Meteor single (as "Mac and Jake With the Esquire Trio"), "A Gal Named Joe," recorded between his two Sun singles and a true rarity today. An interesting collection of rarities for the serious Memphis music fan. *—Cub Koda*

Goin' Down to Louisiana / Oct. 9, 2001 / Ace ♦♦♦♦
The Goldband label recorded a decent share of down-home Louisiana blues between the mid-'50s and mid-'60s, with 30 such outings from the period collected onto this CD. It didn't have any Louisiana masters on the order of Slim Harpo, but the material on this disc still makes for acceptable genre fare. While about a third of it appeared on the 1965 Storyville LP *The Louisiana Blues*, the rest of it did not; ten tracks were previously unissued, and some of the others didn't surface until they appeared on compilations in the 1990s. Certainly the best-known of these cuts are the ones by Juke Boy Bonner, who made effectively moody, grungy electric blues, usually with sluggish rhythms on the ten selections here. The collection also includes material by Ashton Savoy, Al Smith, Tal Miller, Hop Wilson, and Big Chenier that's not as interesting as Bonner's offerings, but has its

moments. Most often their electric blues, like Bonner's, has a swampy feel, with Al Smith putting much more vibrato on his voice than most bluesmen do. Hop Wilson gets a great wiggly steel sound on "That Wouldn't Satisfy," and his boogie "Chicken Stuff" is a previously unissued alternate take. Big Chenier, incidentally, is not a pseudonym for Clifton Chenier, although he was Clifton Chenier's uncle. His sound is not zydeco, but a cross between R&B and blues, with just a touch of zydeco influence (most notably on "Come on Little Girl," on which he plays fiddle). *—Richie Unterberger*

Golden Age Gospel Choirs / Dec. 24, 1997 / Specialty ♦♦♦♦
This entry into Specialty's *Legends of Gospel* series brings together 23 selections from four groundbreaking gospel choirs. The Back Home Choir of Newark, NJ, clocks in with ten performances from 1962 with "Climbing High Mountains," "He Knows How Much We Can Bear," and "Without God I Can Do Nothing" being particular standouts. Next up is the Pentecostal Choir of Detroit with two rousing selections, "Prayer Wheel Turning Over" and "How Glad I Am." The Helen Robinson Youth Choir from Chicago contributes three tracks from a previously unreleased 1959 session for Specialty, including "Sit Down Children," "Working on the Building," and "Run and Help Us Tell." Closing out the set is a 1954 Choir album session from the Voices of Victory. Intended to simulate an actual church service, their set starts with an invocation and ends with a benediction, with the strong musical highlights "I'm So Glad Jesus Lifted Me," "Lord, Lord, Lord," "The Angels Keep Watching," and "Blessed Assurance" sandwiched in between. Once again compiling material from the Specialty and Tru-Sound labels, this brings together some great gospel performances culled from two different decades. *—Cub Koda*

Golden Age Gospel Quartets, Vol. 1 (1947–1954) / Dec. 24, 1997 / Specialty ♦♦♦♦
The accent is on harmony in this collection of 26 tracks from the gospel side of the Specialty Records vaults. The bulk of the selections here are previously unissued and in the main feature a cappella performances. Besides worthy entries from the Pilgrim Travelers ("The Old Rugged Cross"), the Soul Stirrers ("By and By"), the Swan Silvertones ("I'm Coming Home"), and the Five Blind Boys of Alabama ("Marching Up to Zion"), this disc also boasts equally fine performances from lesser-known groups like the Paramount Singers ("He Means So Much to Me"), the Southern Harmonizers ("What Are They Doing In Heaven Today?"), the Golden Echoes ("Since I Laid My Burden Down"), the Detroiters ("Let Jesus Lead You"), the Chosen Gospel Singers ("Leaning on the Lord"), and the West Coast Jubilees ("Since Jesus Came Into My Heart"). Recorded between 1947 and 1954, the set runs in roughly chronological order to better spotlight the change in gospel singing from a cappella to full rhythm section backing during this time period. A remarkable set of recordings. *—Cub Koda*

Golden Age Gospel Quartets, Vol. 2 (1954–1963) / Dec. 24, 1997 / Specialty ♦♦♦♦
The second volume of gospel quartet music in Specialty's *Legends of Gospel* series is best seen as a companion volume to its predecessor, picking up right where the first volume left off. Starting with sides from 1954, it furthers chronicles important performances from the Specialty Records vaults of the Soul Stirrers ("He'll Make a Way," "Be With Me Jesus"), the Chosen Gospel Singers ("The Lifeboat Is Coming," "What a Wonderful Sight"), the Pilgrim Travelers ("Straight Street," "Did You Stop to Pray This Morning?"), and the Original Five Blind Boys of Alabama ("Broken Heart of Mine," "Goodbye Mother"). But also aboard are early-'60s sides recorded for the New York-based Tru-Sound and Battle labels by the Gate City Singers ("Peace in the Valley"), the Capitol City Stars ("Friends Talk About Me"), the Clefs of Calvary ("Troubles of This World"), and the Gable-Airs ("Travelin' Shoes"). An important chunk of gospel history to savor. *—Cub Koda*

Gonna Head for Home / Flyright ♦♦♦♦♦
A nice compendium of rare and unissued Excello sides by lesser-known names (Boogie Jake, Mr. Calhoun, Silas Hogan, and Jimmy Anderson) who recorded for the label. Excellent Louisiana swamp blues, crude and low-down. *—AMG*

Good Time Blues: Harmonicas, Kazoos, Washboards & Cow-Bells / 1991 / Columbia/Legacy ♦♦♦♦
This CD sampler largely lives up to its name. Subtitled "Harmonicas, Kazoos, Washboards & Cow-Bells," the collection consists of good-time blues performed by an assortment of artists. Many of the bands feature washboards, but a kazoo only pops up on one song. Actually, it is the harmonica players (particularly Will Shade, Buddy Moss, Robert Lee McCoy, and Sonny Terry) who generally take solo honors. A certain sameness emerges by the fifth or sixth song, but taken in small doses, this often exuberant music is enjoyable. There are selections by the Mississippi Jook Band, the Memphis Jug Band, Son Becky, Charlie Burse's Memphis Mudcats, the Georgia Browns, the Georgia Cotton Pickers, Big Joe & His Washboard Band, Buddy Moss, Memphis Slim, Sonny Terry/Jordan Webb, and Bernice Edwards; four of the selections were previously unreleased. *—Scott Yanow*

☆ **Gospel Warriors: 50 Years of Female Gospel Classics** / 1990 / Spirit Feel ♦♦♦♦♦
Spanning a half century of classic performances, *Gospel Warriors* assembles 16 tracks from some of the church circuit's most renowned female soloists, among them Marion Williams, Bessie Griffin and Sister Rosetta Tharpe. While each vocalist is clearly a singular talent, listening to their music side by side offers real insight into their common gifts for improvisation; all are in total command of melody, tone, and lyric, transcending their material to enjoy an unparalleled sense of creative freedom. An ideal introduction for new gospel listeners, the collection's highlights include Tharpe's "Just a Closer Walk With Thee," Williams' "It's Getting Late in the Evening," and Clara Ward's "Precious Lord." *—Jason Ankeny*

Got My Mojo Working / 1991 / Flyright ♦♦♦♦♦
Collection of blues sides recorded for New York's Baton label in the mid- to late '50s, featuring Chris Kenner's first recording and Ann Cole's original, pre-Muddy Waters version performance of the title track. *—Cub Koda*

The Great 1955 Shrine Concert / 1993 / Specialty ♦♦♦♦
The power and splendor that was gospel in the '50s radiates throughout the performances on *The Great 1955 Shrine Concert.* The Pilgrim Travelers, with twin powerhouse leads Kylo Turner and Keith Barber, get things started in fiery fashion, followed by the dynamic Caravans, whose roster at that time included Albertina Walker and Rev. James Cleveland, who doubled as a pianist. Also on the bill were Brother Joe May, justifying his "Thunderbolt of the Midwest" nickname, the Soul Stirrers with Sam Cooke still in the fold, and the Original Gospel Harmonettes concluding the proceedings with a flourish. Anyone who attended certainly felt the spirit, as will anyone who listens to this magnificent 14-song set. *—Ron Wynn*

Great Blues Guitarists: String Dazzlers / Aug. 1991 / Columbia/Legacy ♦♦♦♦
Ten excellent blues guitarists are heard on 20 selections dating from 1924-1940 on this enjoyable CD reissue from the Columbia/Legacy series. Included are Sylvester Weaver (the first blues guitarist to record an unaccompanied solo), the team of Lonnie Johnson and Eddie Lang (who are heard on a pair of duets and with singer Texas Alexander), the influential Big Bill Broonzy (superb on "How You Want It Done?"), the always passionate Blind Willie Johnson, Blind Willie McTell, Casey Bill Weldon, Blind Lemon Jefferson ("Black Snake Moan"), Joshua White, and Tampa Red. Three previously unheard selections are included on this fine overview but completists will probably prefer to skip over the set in favor of the more comprehensive Document CDs. *—Scott Yanow*

☆ **The Great Bluesmen at Newport** / 1976 / Vanguard ♦♦♦♦♦
This two-LP, single-CD compilation offers up 21 songs recorded live between 1959 and 1965 at the Newport Folk Festival. This is a killer selection of cuts by rediscovered '30s blues legends, many rising to the occasion to perform in front of thousands of people at once. A lot of comebacks and late-in-life careers were sparked by the performances captured on this CD, which is essential listening for anyone who cares about the blues. Robert Pete Williams, playing his first concert outside Louisiana gave a performance so powerful, energetic, and dexterous, that he built a new career while still a relatively young man at the age of 40. Everyone who has heard Son House's album on Columbia and wondered if they were missing something might better look to the performance on this CD. With Mance Lipscomb accompanying him, the legendary slide player provides a good look at what his playing and singing were like in his prime. Mississippi John Hurt, who made some great records during this era, was at his best working in front of an audience, and had done so in Mississippi for decades. He gives a devastatingly nimble performance on this concert disc, both in his singing and playing. Similarly, Skip James launched a whole new career for himself with his performance on "Hard Time Killing Floor Blues" and "Illinois Blues." Willie Doss appears to have gotten not too much further than his Newport performances, fine though they were, but the Rev. Gary Davis and Mississippi Fred McDowell both reignited their commercial careers with the work heard here. Rounding out the set are contributions from Sonny Terry & Brownie McGhee, John Lee Hooker, and Lightnin' Hopkins, working musicians for decades up to that time, who were simply playing very big outdoor gigs. *—Bruce Eder*

☆ **The Great Gospel Men** / 1995 / Shanachie ♦♦♦♦♦
A wide range of magnificent vocals are displayed on *The Great Gospel Men*, a 27-song anthology. Some names such as Brother Joe May, Rev. James Cleveland, and Prof. Alex Bradford are familiar even to non-gospel fans; others, like the intense Robert Anderson, Professor J. Earle Hines, Norsalus McKissick, Robert Bradley, and R.L. Knowles are known only to the hardcore, and even they probably haven't heard many songs by any one artist. This collection alternates nicely between slow and fast pieces, giving each artist a chance to demonstrate his skills. *—Ron Wynn*

☆ **The Great Gospel Women** / 1993 / Shanachie ♦♦♦♦♦
Like its male counterpoint, this anthology spotlights contributions from both famous stars (Mahalia Jackson, Marion Williams, Dorothy Love Coates, and Sister Rosetta Tharpe) and obscure figures (Mary Johnson Davis, Jessie Mae Renfro, Lucy Smith, and Goldia Haynes, among others), presenting a hefty 31 selections. While some might quibble that celebrated stars Jackson and Williams get six tracks apiece, it's hard to argue with the greatness of what's presented by them. Others who give head-turning performances include Frances Steadman, Roberta Martin, and Clara Ward. *—Ron Wynn*

Great Gospel Women, Vol. 2 / 1995 / Shanachie ♦♦♦♦♦
The Great Gospel Women, Vol. 2 is a worthy follow-up to the first edition of the series; wisely refusing to mess with a good thing, producer Anthony Heilbut holds over most of the same artists from before, dipping into the well for more classic material from soloists including Mahalia Jackson, Marion Williams, Clara Ward, and Sister Rosetta Tharpe. While the overall quality is somewhat diluted this time out, in its favor the disc offers two more tracks than its predecessor, as well as choice cuts from performers making their series debut, among them Bessie Griffin, Ernestine B. Washington, Edna Gallmon Cooke, Imogene Green, and Myrtle Scott. An excellent companion piece. *—Jason Ankeny*

The Great Harp Players (1927–1936) / 1992 / Document ♦♦♦♦
Although one may think of the blues harp beginning with Little Walter, the first Sonny Boy Williamson, or Sonny Terry, a variety of harmonica players did record in the '20s. Some of their recordings were technical displays that featured them imitating everything from animals to trains, while other players were more blues-oriented. This valuable CD has two selections from the guitar/harmonica team of William Francis and Richard Sowell; Ollis Martin's "Police and High Sheriff Come Ridin' Down"; six pieces by Eli Watson (including "El Watson's Fox Chase"); two cuts apiece by Palmer McAbee, Ellis Williams, Alfred Lewis, and the team of Smith & Harper (which is the only music on this CD recorded after 1930); plus four songs/displays from Blues Birdhead (including "Get Up Off That Jazzophone") and George "Bullet" Williams (highlighted by "Frisco Leaving Birmingham" and "The Escaped Convict"). Fascinating music. *—Scott Yanow*

Greatest Blues Legends / 1994 / MCA Special Products ♦♦♦
Although some may argue whether they're the "greatest" blues artists or not, there's little arguing that all ten featured artists on *Greatest Blues Legends* are legendary to some extent or another. Problem is, not all of the songs here illustrate why these greats are legendary—thankfully, the Rolling Stones named themselves after a Muddy Waters song other than "Funky Butt." Sadly, "Funky Butt" is the featured Muddy here, even though MCA Special Products presumably could have chosen anything from Waters' prodigious recordings for Chess. That problem also plagues the selection by T-Bone Walker, who is represented by "Goin' to Funky Town," of all things. The Jimmy Reed ("Heartaches & Troubles"), B.B. King ("Ask Me No Questions"), and Buddy Guy ("Stone Crazy") inclusions aren't nearly as bad, but they're nevertheless not the first songs you think of when you hear their names. The remainder of *Greatest Blues Legends* is considerably more reasonable—Koko Taylor's "Wang Dang Doodle," Little Milton's "We're Gonna Make It," Elmore James' "Call It Stormy Monday," and Howlin' Wolf's "How Many More Years" are all classics—and that is what makes it an acceptable, entertaining budget-price compilation, despite all of its flaws. *—Stephen Thomas Erlewine*

Greatest Gospel Gems / 1991 / Specialty ♦♦♦♦♦
An excellent 24-song sampling of '50s and '60s sacred testifying from the vaults of Specialty Records, it includes essential cuts from Dorothy Love Coates, the Swan Silvertones, and Sam Cooke with the Soul Stirrers. *—John Floyd*

Greatest Gospel Gems, Vol. 1 / Oct. 17, 1990 / Specialty ♦♦♦♦♦
Heart-stopping gospel by the Soul Stirrers, Robert Anderson, the Gospel Harmonettes, etc. *—Opal Louis Nations*

Greatest Gospel Gems, Vol. 2 / Oct. 17, 1990 / Specialty ♦♦♦♦♦
More gospel greats by Prof. Alex Bradford, Brother Joe May, Rev. James Cleveland, and more. *—Opal Louis Nations*

• **The Greatest in Country Blues (1929–1956), Vol. 1** / Jan. 1, 1992 / Story of the Blues ♦♦♦♦♦
Story of the Blues provides an excellent introductions to acoustic country blues with its three-volume *Greatest in Country Blues* series. While it collects most of the major figures as well as the obscure and their finest performances, there are a certain number of odd omissions such as Rev. Gary Davis and Robert Nighthawk that prevent it from being the definitive country blues set. Nevertheless, each of the three volumes is an invaluable reference as well as an interesting listen for both the specialist and the novice. *—Chris Woodstra*

• **The Greatest in Country Blues (1929–1956), Vol. 3** / Sep. 1, 1992 / Story of the Blues ♦♦♦♦♦
Anyone interested in a survey of early blues will be thrilled with having any of these three historical volumes, suited to both novice and connoisseur alike. Each provides a dazzling, panoramic survey of artists both famous and obscure and covers every region known to have nurtured the music. *Vol. 2* features Skip James' "Devil Got My Woman," Robert Johnson's "Preaching' Blues," and Kokomo Arnold's "Paddlin' Madeline Blues." From Texas Alexander there is a version of "Levee Camp Moan Blues" which is made timeless by the incomparable guitar of Lonnie Johnson. Great instrumentals like Palmer McAbee's "Railroad Piece" and the Dallas String Band's "Dallas Rag" add spice, and there are also first-rate entries by more obscure giants like King Solomon Hill, George "Bullet" Williams, "Hi" Henry Brown, and Blind Joe Taggart. *—Larry Hoffman*

Grinder Man Blues: Masters of Blues Piano / 1990 / RCA ♦♦♦♦♦
Six tracks each come from Little Brother Montgomery (1935-1936), Memphis Slim (1940-1941), and Big Maceo Merriweather (1941-1945). With piano blues and boogie-woogie, it's wonderful listening from beginning to end. *—Niles J. Frantz*

Guitar Player Presents: Legends of Guitar: Electric Blues, Vol. 1 / Rhino ♦♦♦
Excellent 18-track CD compilation featuring definitive sides by Muddy Waters, Otis Rush, Hound Dog Taylor, Albert King, Eddie Taylor, and many more. *—Cub Koda*

Guitar Player Presents: Legends of Guitar: Electric Blues, Vol. 2 / Rhino ♦♦♦♦
This second volume in the blues part of this series rounds up 18 hot examples of string-bending power. Kicking off with Joe Hill Louis' amazing work on Rufus Thomas' "Bear Cat (The Answer to Hound Dog)," the set also includes hot moments from B.B. King, Michael Bloomfield (with the Electric Flag), Freddie King, Magic Sam, Buddy Guy with Junior Wells, Albert Collins, and both Eric Clapton and Peter Green with John Mayall. Heading up the old-school entries are John Lee Hooker, Houston Boines, Muddy Waters, Lowell Fulson, Frankie Lee Sims, Snooks Eaglin, and Willie Johnson backing Howlin' Wolf. A solid set of classic moments on guitar. *—Cub Koda*

Guitar Wizards: 1926–1935 / Feb. 19, 1992 / Yazoo ♦♦♦
Guitar Wizards: 1926-1935 showcases some of the finest six-string players who resided in the Carolinas and along the Atlantic coast during the period. While it has consistently been afforded less significance than its Mississippi and Memphis counterparts, the area has one of the oldest blues traditions. Still, its recorded legacy remains small in comparison. Many of the musicians here had to make their way to larger cities for recording opportunities. The most successful was Blind Blake, a highly popular and influential recording artist with ties to both Chicago and the coast. An average singer and versifier, Blake's reputation rests almost entirely on his stunning guitar technique. He makes four appearances on *Guitar Wizards*, the most impressive of which is the dazzling "Guitar Chimes Blues." Blake sounds completely relaxed, taking the time to pause to repeat a chord or figure or spin graceful, syncopated lines. Also included is a tasteful stroll through the songster standard "You're Gonna Quit Me Blues" and an example of his ragtime style on "Wabash Rag." By contrast, there's a sense of recklessness in the brisk picking of Sam Butler. His lines seem to jump ahead of the vocal, then wait for it to catch up. The results are thrilling on performances like "Jefferson County Blues" and "Some Scream High Yellow." Tampa Red (whose technique won him the "Guitar Wizard" tag) plays in a forceful style, with clear, punctuating notes being broken by his characteristic, crying slide interjections. Unfortunately, all the Blind Blake selections are also available on *The Best of Blind Blake*: a foundational set for any country blues collection. While it's nearly impossible to disregard any Yazoo compilation as insignificant, *Guitar Wizards* (despite its high quality) is only necessary for more serious collectors. *—Nathan Bush*

Gulf Coast Blues / 1990 / Black Top ♦♦♦♦♦
These contemporary Texas and Louisiana blues come from four artists deserving wider attention. Carol Fran, Joe "Guitar" Hughes, and Grady Gaines each contribute two cuts, with four from Teddy Reynolds. Fran and Reynolds are the highlights, and they deserve their own full releases. *—Niles J. Frantz*

Hand Me Down Blues Chicago Style / 1990 / Relic ♦♦♦♦♦
This is one of the finest 1950s Chicago Blues compilations in existence, taken from the vaults of Parrot-Blue Lake Records. Unissued sides and rare singles create an incredible ambience here. Essential listening. *—Cub Koda*

Hard Rock Cafe: Modern Blues / Oct. 27, 1998 / Rhino ♦♦♦
DJs at Hard Rock Cafes all over the planet throw parties every night of the week. Thus music must be selected that is at once familiar, occasionally classic, always excellent, and dancefloor friendly. Ironically, this surefire craftsmanship produces little better than a homogenized sampling that reads like a competent AM-radio playlist on the Hard Rock Cafe's *Modern Blues*. Are Cream's "Crossroads," Bonnie Raitt's "Runaway," and the Allman Brothers' "Ain't Wastin' Time No More" really "modern blues"? Less arguable selections are certainly John Mayall & the Bluesbreakers' spirited "The Super-Natural" and Albert Collins' killer "Ice Pick." But even the sun in the solar system of the blues, B.B. King's "The Thrill Is Gone," has been so thinned out by exhaustive airplay that it's hard to really hear it any more. The Hard Rock's attempts to create meaningful musical documents include previous compilations *Heavy Metal* and *Surf*, as well as the reasonably decent-selling *Party Classics*, which this dance franchise seems most authorized to produce. The cafe's lunch-menu aesthetic is probably not best suited for hardcore epicures of the blues. *—Becky Byrkit*

• **Hard Times Come Again No More, Vol. 1** / Aug. 18, 1998 / Yazoo ♦♦♦♦♦
Another fine Yazoo collection of vintage American recordings of the '20s and '30s. The theme here of first-hand hardship experience makes for some amazing music, whether by white or black artists. The buoyant "Down on Penny's Farm" is beautifully offset by Blind Alfred Reed's baleful complaint "How Can a Poor Man Stand," complete with fragile fiddle work and loping guitar work. And that's just the first two tracks. It's amazing stuff: part oral history, part entertainment, and all priceless, though both volumes together may make for more hard times than you want to experience. *—Tim Sheridan*

• **Hard Times Come Again No More, Vol. 2** / Aug. 18, 1998 / Yazoo ♦♦♦♦♦
With the unlikely sound of a kazoo, the Allen Brothers kick off this fine volume of hard-time blues collected from the '20s and '30s. More tongue-in-cheek than its predecessor, this volume is not all moaning and weeping. Uncle Dave Macon and Sam McGhee create a joyful sound with dueling banjos on "Wreck of the Tennessee Gravey Train" and Earl Johnson & His Dixie Entertainers are hilarious on "I'm Satisfied." The disc proves some things never change: You have to laugh sometimes to keep from crying. *—Tim Sheridan*

Harlem Rock n' Blues, Vol. 3 / Oct. 22, 1991 / Collectables ♦♦♦
Material that either influenced or reflected evolutionary trends in blues and R&B. *—Ron Wynn*

Harmonica Blues / 1991 / Yazoo ♦♦♦♦
It is perhaps a testament to the harmonica's status in music that even its finest practitioners remain relatively obscure. Compiling a disc of harp players, as Yazoo has done here, isn't going to turn up a bunch of familiar names. As an early document of an instrument that remained essential to the blues well after it became an electric medium, however, *Harmonica Blues* is excellent. The instrument served numerous roles during the '20s and '30s (the period covered here), showing up in dance music, solo showcases, and blues, on street corners and in juke joints. An example of the instrument's novelty appeal is as good a place to start as any. Though Freeman Stowers' recorded conventional blues, he also relished in comic fare like "Railroad Blues." Bidding his woman farewell as she steps aboard a train, Stowers builds to a blistering pace in his steam engine imitation. The harmonica's ability to bend notes and produce vibrato made it particularly expressive when applied to blues. Its dynamic range and unique timbre meant that it could cut through an acoustic ensemble in a manner similar to a violin or slide guitar. Harp men step into the spotlight for particularly spectacular solos on the otherwise tepid blues of "I Want You by My Side" and "My Driving Wheel." Both DeFord Bailey and Jaybird Coleman, the two players to gain some degree of fame during their prime, are represented by a cut each. Bailey, a popular performer on Nashville's *Grand Ole Opry*, displays his unparalleled technique on "Davidson County Blues," while Coleman proves that he was an exceptional vocalist as well on "Man Trouble Blues." Together, the artists gathered on *Harmonica Blues* represent the precursors to the great harp players of the electric era like Little Walter, Junior Wells, and Sonny Boy Williamson. *—Nathan Bush*

Harmonica Blues Kings / 1986 / Delmark ♦♦♦♦♦
Featuring a side each of Big Walter Horton and Alfred "Blues King" Harris in primarily supporting roles behind various vocalists from the vaults of United/States Records, 1954. Raw, lively, harmonica and another missing piece of the early Chicago blues puzzle. *—AMG*

Harmonica Masters / 1996 / Yazoo ♦♦♦♦
Continuing the label's exploration deep into the early vernacular music of the U.S., Yazoo Records devotes this compilation to some of the finest harmonica players of the '20s and '30s. *Harmonica Masters* features performances by harp greats like DeFord Bailey, Noah Lewis, Jed Davenport, Jaybird Coleman, and 19 others. The smallest and therefore most portable of instruments, the harmonica took a place not unlike that of the violin in blues and jug band combos. As the musicians here demonstrate, it can also be a fine solo instrument. In the hands of an expert, the harmonic and melodic musical elements mesh so perfectly, it can sound as if they are occurring at the same time. In fact, they are being swapped at such a pace that the absence of neither is very noticeable at any given time. Alfred Lewis' fine playing is overshadowed only by his otherworldly falsetto on "Mississippi Swamp Moan." It takes on such a bizarre quality that it sounds more like an instrument than a voice and is matched beautifully with responsive harp lines. At the opposite extreme, "Touch Me Light Mama" is a wonderfully raw blues piece featuring George "Bullet" Williams' earthy baritone. Whatever Williams and his accompanist lack in technique, they make up for in the visceral quality of their unguarded performance. Gwen Foster's "Wilks County Blues" is an astonishing, vibrato-laden showcase of the musician's harmonica powers, reaching the upper registers of the instrument. On "Chickasaw Special," Noah Lewis expertly imitates the sounds of a train—an example of a performance style probably introduced by Williams McCoy. From novelty to dance music to deep blues, from accompanist to soloist, *Harmonica Masters* demonstrates the fascinating tonal and musical possibilities of this underacknowledged instrument. *—Nathan Bush*

Harp Attack! / 1991 / Alligator ♦♦♦♦♦
This 11-track CD spotlights four Chicago harmonica players—Carey Bell, Billy Branch, James Cotton, and Junior Wells—in new recordings. All have played with Muddy Waters or Willie Dixon's Chicago Blues All-Stars (or both). This is solid electric-band-style Chicago blues. *—Niles J. Frantz*

Harp Blowers (1925–1936) / Jun. 2, 1994 / Document ♦♦♦♦♦
This is a rather fascinating CD that features music from some of the earliest harmonica players on record. The forgotten John Henry Howard sounds fine on his only recordings (four songs from 1925 in which he sings and plays both harmonica and guitar) and also here are the only three cuts by George Clarke, a harmonica player from 1936. However the real reason to acquire this disc is for the performances of DeFord Bailey and D.H. "Bert" Bilbro. Bailey was a star on the *Grand Ole Opry* during 1925-1940, a virtuoso solo harmonica player who could imitate trains, barnyard animals, and all types of sounds. He recorded just 11 selections in his career despite his fame, all dating from 1927-1928; among the more impressive cuts are "Old Hen Cackle," "The Alcoholic Blues," and "Fox Chase." Bilbro is more obscure but on Bailey's level, as he shows during the remarkable "C. & N.W. Blues," in which he does a close re-creation of a train. An essential acquisition for vintage blues collectors. *—Scott Yanow*

☆ **Harp Blues** / Feb. 26, 1999 / Ace ♦♦♦♦♦
This 25-track collection brings together some of the most inspiring blues harp performances on record. With the exception of Sonny Boy Williamson's "Bring Me Another Half a Pint" (better known as Jimmy Rogers' "Sloppy Drunk" and originally penned even earlier by Lucille Bogan) from 1948, everything on here was recorded in the '50s to the late '60s at the height of the electric blues boom. Representative and sometimes definitive performances from Big Walter Horton ("Easy," "Need My Baby," and the solo on Jimmy Rogers' "Walkin' By Myself"), Little Walter ("Roller Coaster"), Jimmy Reed ("Found Love"), Snooky Pryor ("Boogie Twist"), Sonny Boy Williamson ("99"), Jerry McCain (the rare, alternate take of "Steady"), and Little Junior Parker ("Sweet Home Chicago") pepper this set. But the rarities from Eddie Hope (the raucous "A Fool No More"), Little Willie Foster ("Little Girl"), Papa Lightfoot (an explosive transfer of "Wine, Women, Whiskey"), Howlin' Wolf ("Howlin' Wolf Boogie"), Sammy Myers ("Sleeping in the Ground"), and Joe Hill Louis ("Western Union Man") are every bit as potent as the bigger names aboard. Great selections from Doctor Ross, Billy Boy Arnold, Frank Frost, James Cotton, Junior Wells, George Smith, Shy Guy Douglas and the mysterious Cousin Leroy complete the collection. *—Cub Koda*

Harps, Jugs, Washboards & Kazoos: 1926–1940 / Jun. 1926-Oct. 10, 1940 / RST ♦♦♦♦
Included on this fun CD from the Austrian RST label are all of the recordings done by the Five Harmaniacs (which date from 1926-1927), the Salty Dog Four (from 1930-1931 and also known as the Red Devils), the Scorpion Washboard Band (1933), and Rhythm Willie & His Gang (1940). While Rhythm Willie's group is an acoustic blues quartet led by a harmonica player, Scorpion has a kazoo and washboard (along with more conventional instruments), the Salty Dog Four uses kazoo, violin, and sometimes mandolin and the Harmaniacs have harmonica, kazoo, and washboard. The good-time music overall falls between jazz and blues and is difficult to resist, particularly tunes such as "Sadie Green, The Vamp of New Orleans," "Coney Island Washboard," "What Did Romie-O Juliet (When He Climbed Her Balcony)," and "Bedroom Stomp." *—Scott Yanow*

Hellhound on My Trail: Songs of Robert Johnson / 2001 / Telarc ♦♦♦
Not the first compilation of bluesmen (and one woman) interpreting the limited but radically influential work of Robert Johnson, and almost certainly not the last, this 2001 entry is one of the more substantial efforts in the lineage. Instead of refashioning these classics in unique arrangements, the compilers have stripped the artists and songs down to their unplugged roots. Most perform solo or with another musician. Drums are all but nonexistent, and a sublime organ augments another, but the rest wend their way with the basics of guitar, voice, and harp, as well as a touch of Pinetop Perkins' tinkling piano. What results is an honest, unpretentious, and often thrilling tribute to Johnson by an eclectic array of young and established blues journeymen. As for the old-timers, you don't get any more authentic than Robert Jr. Lockwood and David "Honeyboy" Edwards, both of whom actually played with the legendary Johnson, and their presence instills a legitimate authenticity to the project. Edwards sounds weak but inspired on "Traveling Riverside Blues," and Chicago harp master Carey Bell adds sizzle to Lockwood Jr.'s "Steady Rollin' Man." Muddy Waters' sidemen Bob Margolin and Pinetop Perkins alternate on vocals for two sparkling tracks, and the always dependable Taj Mahal takes on the daunting "Crossroads" with typical aplomb. The album's most radical pairing is guitarist/vocalist Eric Gales, who plays with subtle Hammond B-3 organ accompaniment, offering a changeup from the traditional approach. Susan Tedeschi, the disc's only woman, howls with righteous passion as Derek Trucks turns in a rare unplugged performance on one of two versions of "Walking Blues." Only pop/rocker Robert Palmer seems out of place on the roster, but his version of "Milkcow's Calf Blues" is remarkably faithful to the original and free of the flashy glitz that mars his own work. He even overdubs himself on low-key tuba, adding a distinctive perspective to the track. Elsewhere Joe Louis Walker, Alvin "Youngblood" Hart, and Lucky Peterson represent the youngsters. All acquit themselves with grace and intensity on an album that consistently remains true to the spirit of this most classic of blues music. Few tributes are this honestly constructed and pay respect so gracefully to one of the blues' most beloved and cherished catalogs. *—Hal Horowitz*

Hokum Blues (1924–1929) / Nov. 21, 1995 / Document ♦♦♦♦
Although this CD is titled *Hokum Blues*, all but two of the eight groups actually predate hokum (which came of age in the fall of 1928), although all have some aspects of the good-time music. The performances are quite obscure, with two titles apiece by Ukulele Bob Williams, the Two of Spades, Louise Ross, Feathers and Frogs, and Swan & Lee (the only recordings by any of these performers). In addition, there are four songs apiece from Ki Ki Johnson and the team of Danny Small and Ukulele Mays, plus seven numbers (including two instrumentals) by the Pebbles. Listening to this early acoustic music, the performances both look forward to hokum and even swing in spots, while hinting strongly at its early roots in string music and minstrel shows. Collectors will want this one. *—Scott Yanow*

Hound Dog Taylor: A Tribute / 1998 / Alligator ♦♦♦♦
In many respects, you could call Hound Dog Taylor a cult artist. Respected by bluesmen and critics alike, he built a small, devoted following across America simply by constantly touring. There were no hits and very few covers of his songs, but his rowdy concerts and incendiary records on Alligator convinced any who heard him. In the process, he put Alligator Records on the blues map, so it only makes sense that the label return the favor with *Hound Dog Taylor: A Tribute*, one of the few blues tributes that really works. Taylor's wild, careening slide guitar became one of the more influential sounds in contemporary blues, as evidenced by this quality-packed record. Out of the 14 tracks, only George Thorogood's thuggish, sluggish "I Just Can't Make It" falls flat, but the quality of the remaining cuts is so high that it's forgivable. Luther Allison's "Give Me Back My Wig" rocks, Gov't Mule's "Gonna Send You Back to Georgia" is tough, Vernon Reid and Alvin "Youngblood" Hart do a nice acoustic reading of "It's Alright," Steady Rollin' Bob Margolin turns "See Me in the Evening" into an appealing, straightforward blues-rocker, and Cub Koda tears through "Take Five" with the help of Hound Dog's backing band, the Houserockers. Moments like these are what elevates this tribute album above the average. *—Stephen Thomas Erlewine*

House of Blues: Essential Chicago Blues / May 20, 1997 / A&M ♦♦♦
"Essential" is a subjective word, but this two-disc set certainly contains some pretty great blues performances sandwiched in between the just passable ones. On the plus side, there are classics aboard from Bo Diddley, Otis Rush, Little Walter, Hound Dog Taylor, Muddy Waters (the rarer alternate take of "Hoochie Coochie Man"), J.B. Lenoir, Buddy Guy, Willie Mabon, Sonny Boy Williamson, Junior Wells, Howlin' Wolf, Jimmy Reed, J.B. Hutto, Eddie Taylor, Earl Hooker, and Big John Wrencher. On the debit side, there are re-cuts by Otis Spann, Willie Dixon, Billy Boy Arnold, Hubert Sumlin, and so-so tracks from Son Seals, Carey Bell, Pinetop Perkins, Eddy Clearwater, Eddie C. Campbell, Jimmy Dawkins, John Primer, James Cotton, and Koko Taylor. This is a pretty good little collection if you can overlook about half of it. *—Cub Koda*

House Rockin' & Hip Shakin', Vol. 2: Louisiana Hoodoo Party / Jun. 16, 1998 / Hip-O ♦♦♦♦
Subtitled "Louisiana Hoodoo Party," this second volume of Excello blues recordings collects 16 great ones with some obscurities making their first CD appearance. In addition to holdover artists from *Vol. 1* (Slim Harpo with "Blues Hangover" and "Baby, Scratch My Back," Lightnin' Slim with "You Know You're So Fine," and Lazy Lester with "Lester Stomp"), there's great stuff aboard from Jimmy Anderson, Silas Hogan, Lonesome Sundown, and Tabby Thomas with the title track. Other highlights rounding out the collection include Guitar Gable's "Congo Mombo," Charles Sheffield's "It's Your Voo-Doo Working," Earl Gaines & His Hi-Toppers' "It's Love Pretty Baby (24 Hours a Day)," a three-song set from brothers Arthur Gunter and Little Al Gunter, and Kid King's Combo with Good Rockin' Sam Beasley's "Now Listen Baby," the blueprint for Little Walter's "Everything's Gonna Be Alright." *—Cub Koda*

House Rockin' & Hip Shakin', Vol. 3: Killer Swamp Blues / Aug. 11, 1998 / Hip-O ♦♦♦
This third volume of Excello Records treasures rounds up some obvious big names from the label's catalog of blues stars (Slim Harpo, Lightnin' Slim, Lazy Lester, Lonesome Sundown, Arthur Gunter, etc.) along with marvelous one-shots like the Fat Man (reported to be Sunnyland Slim), Robert Garrett, Leroy Washington, and the mysterious Blue Charlie. The song selection is superb, pairing up obscure tracks with big names (Lightnin' Slim's "The Strangest Feelin'" contains the strangest guitar sound) and definitive selections for the lesser lights aboard, Jimmy Reed sound-alike Jimmy Anderson turning in a Grade A version of Slim Harpo's "I'm a King Bee" along the way. Three not-to-be-missed

highlights are Guitar Gable's original version of the swamp pop classic "This Could Go on Forever"; Clarence Samuels' "Chicken Hearted Baby," with barnyard guitar from Johnny Copeland (his very first session); and the correct 45 single version of Lazy Lester's "I'm a Lover, Not a Fighter," making its first appearance on CD after years of the alternate take being issued instead. Perhaps the strongest volume in the series to date. *—Cub Koda*

House Rockin' & Hip Shakin', Vol. 4: Bayou Blues Harp / Oct. 20, 1998 / Hip-O ✦✦✦✦
Hip-O's fourth volume of rarities from the Excello catalog shines the light on the harmonica heroes who proliferated on the label back in the '50s and early '60s. Lazy Lester shows up on four tracks, featured as a leader on "If You Think You've Lost Me," "Ponderosa Stomp," and "I Told My Little Woman," and backing Lightnin' Slim on "Wintertime Blues." Slim Harpo's two instrumentals "Buzzin'" and "Snoopin' Around" are on board, along with a pair from Jerry McCain, "Trying to Please" and "Things Ain't Right." In the rarities department, the inclusion of Baby Boy Warren's "Santa Fe" and "Bring Me My Machine Gun" (with Sonny Boy Williamson on harp) along with both sides of Little Sonny's Excello single ("Love Shock" and "I'll Love You Baby") and the impossibly rare "You Better Change" by the mysterious Ole Sonny Boy raise the ante in that sweepstakes. Lightnin' Slim with Schoolboy Cleve's "I'm Him," Jimmy Anderson's "Frankie & Johnny," Vincent Monroe's "If I Had My Life to Live Over," Silas Hogan's "Lonesome La La" (featuring Sylvester Buckley), and a pair from Whispering Smith complete the collection. *—Cub Koda*

House Rockin' Blues / 1995 / Ace ✦✦✦✦
Compilations of vintage Chess material seem to be plentiful these days, but this excellent collection of strictly uptempo material should not be passed by at any cost. With a healthy 27 tracks aboard, the highlights are numerous with the label's stars and second stringers like Howlin' Wolf, J.B. Lenoir, John Brim, Billy Boy Arnold, Bo Diddley, Willie Mabon, Elmore James, and Otis Rush all present and accounted for. But rather than opt for the same tracks that have been around the block time and again, true obscurities like the anonymous Little Luther's "The Twirl," G.L. Crockett's "Look Out Mabel," the previously unissued Robert Nighthawk with Buddy Guy shuffle "Someday," "Tired of Crying Over You" by Morris Pejoe, and "He Knows the Rules" by Jimmy McCracklin pepper the mix to keep the collectors happy as well. If the boogie side of the Chess cannonade is your particular cup of coffee, this collection is the one you'll keep going back to time and again. Great! *—Cub Koda*

How Blue Can You Get? Great Blues Vocals in the Jazz Tradition / Jun. 29, 1938-Nov. 20, 1963 / Bluebird ✦✦✦✦✦
On record, the marriage of blues and jazz singing goes back as far as Mamie Smith's song "Crazy Blues." In addition to being the first known vocal performance on wax by a black woman, the record also launched a craze for classic blues recordings by Bessie Smith, Ma Rainey, Sippie Wallace, and others. These urbane vocalists may have taken many cues from the Southern world of blues and gospel, but having migrated north they also incorporated the jazz of New York and Chicago clubs into their performance (Louis Armstrong and other star jazz soloists of the day regularly accompanied these powerful singers). And from those auspicious beginnings, the blues has always had a place in the jazz world, whether in the direct form heard on many of the sides here or in the more fractured sense evident in the bebop, hard bop, and free jazz to come later. And as is made clear on *How Blue Can You Get?*, a more straightforward approach certainly doesn't mean a lack of variety. This expansive set ambles from country blues legend Leadbelly's "Good Morning Blues" to swing veteran Hot Lips Page's "Just Another Woman." In between, the marriage is taken to supreme heights by Louis Armstrong, played hot and cool by the great '30s jazz vocalist Mildred Bailey, and given over to the comical theatrics of Fats Waller. And while the blues shouter tradition is well represented here by one of the greatest, Jimmy Rushing, its more urbane and Bing Crosby-styled incarnation of the '40s and '50s is taken up by Billy Eckstine and Joe Williams (all three of these singers cut records with that greatest of blues and jazz bandleaders, Count Basie). In addition to two low-profile cuts that steal the show—Wingy Manone's "Corrina Corrina" and Johnny Valentine's "How Blue Can You Get"—we hear the blues' next triumph in Little Richard's proto-rock & roll cut "Taxi Blues." A history lesson on vinyl and a very enjoyable one at that. *—Stephen Cook*

How Can I Keep from Singing, Vol. 1 / 1996 / Yazoo ✦✦✦✦
Another of Yazoo Records' wonderful themed compilations, *How Can I Keep from Singing* is a collection of sacred music from the '20s and '30s. It provides an indispensable series of portraits that sheds light on how people from the period celebrated their religion in song. Beyond historical significance, every performance here is an enjoyable listening experience, and there are many highlights. Jay Bird Coleman delivers a fantastic harmonica duet with Ollis Martin on "I'm Gonna Cross the River of Jordan." Their performance is raw and seems to lie outside of the confines of the church, much closer to the earth. The music seems to jump out of the recording. "He's Got Better Things for You" by the Memphis Sanctified Singers is equally exciting and is sung so beautifully that it could win the church new converts. "He's got the holy ghost and the fire," the singer advertises. This is religious music, but she isn't above making the song a showcase for her unique style as she growls her way through the chorus. On "Woke Up This Morning," Roosevelt Graves and Brother create a joyful syncopation with two voices, guitar, and some basic percussion. Typically, Yazoo gives no thought to musical or racial segregation. Thus, the heavily stylized voice of Rev. H.B. Jackson is backed by the authentic gospel sounds of Rev. E.D. Campbell and Congregation. Uncle Dave Macon (a white, vaudeville-influenced performer), who delivers a humorous, spoken introduction on "Walking in Sunlight," is followed by the unique tradition of sacred harp singing on a performance by the Middle Georgia Singing Convention. Slim Ducket and Pig Norwood's wonderful, subdued reading of "I Want to Go Where Jesus Is," which seems to bear the mark of a blues (secular) performer, is up against Rev. J.O. Hanes. The group's "The Great Transaction's Done," with its inclusion of a sermon, attempts to re-create the environment of a church meeting on record. By making faith the only requirement, Yazoo has brought together a range of performers, styles, and voices to gather and congregate, resulting in a blend that's all too rare. *—Nathan Bush*

How Can I Keep from Singing, Vol. 2 / 1996 / Yazoo ✦✦✦✦
As with its predecessor, *How Can I Keep from Singing, Vol. 2* combines a mere handful of well-known performers from the golden age of American folk music with a number of more mysterious names. In the place of obvious choices like Rev. Gary Davis and Blind Willie Johnson, for example, we find Shands Superior Jubilee Singers and Ridgel's Fountain Citians. After all, both Davis and Johnson have full-length Yazoo collections devoted to their music. What *How Can I Keep from Singing* does so well, then, is to convey the scope of religious song (on record) during the '20s and '30s. Placing bluesman Sam Collins' gorgeous "I Want to Be Like Jesus in My Heart" between the sacred harp singers of "Weeping Mary" and Morris Family's "He Rose Unknown" proves how much apparently disparate musicians had in common, even if the sound of their music seemed so far apart. Even secular performers join in. Sacred music certainly wasn't prominent in the repertoire of Cliff Carlisle, but that hardly concerns Yazoo. The guitarist and his quartet give a spirited reading of the popular "Shine on Me." The sound of the Golden Jubilee Quartet on "Job" seems to predate everything from the sacred style adopted by bluegrass singers in the '40s to the rockabilly panache of the '50s. Elsewhere, Washington Philips finds comfort on "Jesus Is My Friend," Shands Superior Jubilee Singers describe appropriate attire for heaven on "Silver Slippers," and the genteel voices of the Copperhill Male Quartet sound chilling delivering the title of "There Is a Fountain Filled With Blood." In bringing together these artists, Yazoo creates a religious community on *How Can I Keep from Singing.* Though the musicians themselves might not have recognized it as such, on record it seems very real indeed. *—Nathan Bush*

I Can't Be Satisfied: Early American Women Blues Singers, Vol. 1: Country / Apr. 22, 1997 / Yazoo ✦✦✦✦✦
Required listening, *I Can't Be Satisfied, Vol. 1* is the "Country" volume in a two-part series of early American blueswomen (*Vol. 2* is the "Town" volume). It is an absolutely essential compilation of early country blueswomen, many of whom appear on virtually no other recordings. This definitive archival collection of underdocumented, classic blueswomen and the better-known bluesmen who performed with them includes such artists as Ruby Glaze backed by husband Blind Willie McTell and Hattie Hart, who performs here with the Memphis Jug Band. Also heard are the only two available tracks by the intense Bertha Lee (Charley Patton's wife during the last years of his life), "Yellow Bee" and "Mind Reader Blues." The sound quality of these '20s recordings varies from mild surface noise to the intense hiss of Geeshie Wiley's "Eagles on a Half," but some listeners will find that the power and rarity of this music outweighs such aesthetic inconveniences. If you want to hear incredible, tough women sing country blues, get this. *—Joslyn Layne*

If It Ain't a Hit . . . / Zu-Zazz ✦✦✦✦✦
X-rated blues is the theme here, with selections ranging from totally raunchy to mildly titillating with great listening and a full dollop of humor throughout. Features under-the-counter performances by Jackie Wilson, LaVern Baker, Chick Willis, the Clovers, and the Fred Wolff Combo. Blues with a nudge and a wink to it. *—Cub Koda*

In the Pocket: A Taste of Blues Harmonica / Jul. 23, 2002 / Telarc ✦✦✦
It's nearly impossible to think of any traditional blues band without one of their members blowing on a harmonica. This collection of great mouth organ players begins with Ronnie Earl performing "Mighty Fine Boogie," a song living up to its name. James Cotton's harmonica begins to take a more prominent role as the song progresses, but it's only near the end that he begins to shine. Cotton also duels with Billy Branch during a rendition of Tommy Dorsey's "T.D.'s Boogie Woogie." "Knocking at Your Door" has a slower tempo to it, allowing for Matthew Skoller to showcase his talents. It works particularly well against John Primer's guitar solo. One of the stronger performances is Annie Raines during "Rock Me Baby," a track where she does a lot by simply doing less harmonica work. It resembles an early Rolling Stones cover of "Little Red Rooster" in some parts. One of the timeless qualities of any blues harmonica is the emotion it tends to emit despite its lack of size or amplification. "I'm a Steady Rollin' Man" demonstrates this perfectly as Carey Bell does a fine performance over Robert Jr. Lockwood's vocals. Equally interesting is Kenny Neal performing "Bring It on Home," using his harmonica to accentuate the song while his guitar maintains a steady rhythm. Junior Wells has a style all his own with the jazz and swing feeling of "The Goat." Taken from his *Come on in This House* album, it possesses one of the catchier and more infectious beats on the album. The last third of the album features more extended blues numbers, including Raful Neal's rendition of "Starlight Diamond." It's a song that has a deliberate and leisurely pace to it, but tends to drag near its ending. The earthy and gut-wrenching feeling coming from Snooky Pryor's voice and mouth organ during "Pony Blues" is hair-raising at some points, which is another shining moment. Ending the compilation is an "all-star" assortment contributing to "Harp to Harp." Featuring James Cotton, Sugar Ray Norcia, Billy Branch, and Charlie Musselwhite, it is a proper finish despite having a rather lengthy and bland beginning. *—Scott Yanow*

Independent Women's Blues, Vol. 1: Mean Mothers / Rosetta ✦✦✦
Independent Women's Blues is an excellent four-disc series of early blues and jazz recordings by women—all come highly recommended for not only the abundance of rarities but also for the quality of the music. *Vol. 1,* subtitled *Mean Mothers*, includes selections from Billie Holiday, Ida Cox, and Bessie Brown. *—Chris Woodstra*

Independent Women's Blues, Vol. 2: Big Mamas / Apr. 1925-1953 / Rosetta ✦✦✦
Despite the title of this LP, many of the 16 blues and jazz singers heard here were not necessarily "big" physically but women in control of their situations, at least on these

records. There is one song apiece from Ethel Waters, Edith Johnson, Viola McCoy, Hattie McDaniel (the same person as the actress), Issie Ringgold, Gussie Williams, Clara Smith, Ida Cox, Julia Lee, Susie Edwards, Martha Copeland, Ora Alexander, Rosa Henderson, Bea Foote, Billie Holiday, and Ella Johnson, and the majority are still quite rare. All of the Rosetta releases are worth searching for and this attractive album is no exception. *—Scott Yanow*

Independent Women's Blues, Vol. 3: Super Sisters / Apr. 9, 1927-May 3, 1955 / Rosetta ♦♦♦

The third of four LPs issued by Rosetta in its *Independent Women's Blues* series has 16 blues and jazz recordings, one apiece from Ida Cox, Bertha Idaho, Helen Humes (in 1927), Sara Martin, Mildred Bailey, Sweet Peas Spivey, Lil Johnson, Trixie Smith, Susie Edwards, Lucille Bogan, Cleo Gibson, Martha Copeland, Edith Johnson, Albennie Jones, Lizzie Miles, and Ella Fitzgerald. Many of these valuable performances are still quite rare and have not yet been reissued on CD. *—Scott Yanow*

Independent Women's Blues, Vol. 4: Sweet Petunias / Jun. 20, 1929-Jun. 5, 1956 / Rosetta ♦♦♦

There is a wide variety of vocals on this Rosetta LP which, with one exception (O'Neil Spencer's "Sweet Patootie" with Sidney Bechet), features female singers. Such fine vocalists as June Richmond, Annisteen Allen, Mary Dixon, Etta Jones ("The Richest Guy in the Graveyard"), Monette Moore, Mae West, Stella Johnson, Ella Johnson, Bea Foote, Chippie Hill, Victoria Spivey, the Bandanna Girls, Betty Hall Jones, Helen Humes, and Big Mama Thornton perform one song apiece. Most of the recordings are rare and this appealing set, *Vol. 4* of Rosetta's *Independent Women's Blues* series, is easily recommended. *—Scott Yanow*

Jackson Blues: 1928–1938 / Jul. 1, 1991 / Yazoo ♦♦♦♦

The blues tradition in Mississippi is probably the richest the genre has produced. Giving birth to Charley Patton and Robert Johnson alone would be enough to ensure the state's legacy, but it hardly stops there. Yazoo Records has turned up enough material for three compilations devoted to Mississippi blues. That's impressive considering the recorded output of many of these artists is so small. The most prolific performer on *Jackson Blues: 1928-1938*, Tommy Johnson, recorded merely a dozen 78 sides. *Jackson Blues* gives the listener a good idea of the sort of musical interbreeding that occurred regularly in any given region. Songs, lyrics, and techniques were acquired from traveling performers and commercial recordings. They would then make the rounds of a small community, finding their way into each musician's unique style. Both Willie "Poor Boy" Lofton's "Dark Road Blues" and the Mississippi Sheiks' "Stop & Listen Blues," for example, are based on Tommy Johnson's popular "Big Road Blues," yet they are miles apart. Lofton rushes through the song, delivering hard, fast, repetitious runs that sound as if they are struggling to keep up with the singing. The performance is energized, but stiff. "Stop & Listen," on the other hand, sounds completely relaxed, even when singer Walter Vinson seems to increase the tempo, singing against his hot, syncopated guitar lines. Johnson is featured here on three sides, including the excellent "Bye Bye Blues," a typically fine guitar and vocal performance with Charlie McCoy. An exceptional accompanist on both guitar and mandolin, McCoy recorded some outstanding duets with musicians from the Jackson area. His collaborators include Ishman Bracey, Bo Chatmon, the Mississippi Sheiks, and brother Joe McCoy (as Big Joe & the Mississippi Mudder). While some of the musicians here have full-length CDs devoted to their work, Yazoo collections like *Jackson Blues* also provide a home for lesser-known artists with little recorded legacy of which to speak. Not as essential as Charley Patton's *Founder of the Delta Blues* or *Masters of the Delta Blues: The Friends of Charlie Patton, Jackson Blues* remains a superb collection that allows for a more complete picture of the Mississippi blues tradition. *—Nathan Bush*

Jazzin' the Blues, Vol. 1 (1929–1937) / Nov. 30, 1995 / Document ♦♦♦♦

The music on this intriguing CD can be considered jazzy blues or blues-oriented jazz. The 24 performances are all quite obscure, featuring singer David Cross with Thomas' Devils, the Scare Crow (Willie Owens), Ike Smith & His Chicago Boys, Connie McLean's Rhythm Boys, and the Four Southerners (a group patterned after the Mills Brothers). The better-known sidemen include clarinetist Arnett Nelson, banjoist Ikey Robinson, bassist Bill Johnson, and cornetist Punch Miller; with the exception of the Connie McLean date (cut in New York), all of the music was recorded in either Chicago or Richmond, IN. Although not classic, the performances (from 1929-1930 and 1935-1937) are mostly quite fun and should interest vintage blues, trad jazz, and small-group swing collectors. *—Scott Yanow*

Jazzvisions: Jump the Blues Away / Oct. 4, 1989 / Polygram ♦♦♦♦

Nothing if not eclectic, the *Jazzvisions* series veers completely away from jazz on its blues installment. The idiom is blues-rock, the headliner is the once and future Eagles star Joe Walsh, and his co-partners are electric bluesman Albert Collins and the indestructible singer Etta James. Within that idiom, though, this is a strong program captained by experts in the arts of blues licks and working the crowd. Collins is terse and stinging on guitar, full of bent-note soul; James is right in her element, laying on the double entendres, whipping up the audience in her experienced manner; and Walsh, aside from the inevitable "Rocky Mountain Way," does well in the blues guitar idiom, even giving a tip of the cap to Collins, "Thanks for all the licks!" The backup band roars in the traditional journeyman electric blues-rock form, with strong piano and organ work and pumping drums. At its best, especially when Collins and James are on, this concert at the indoor Wiltern Theatre has much of the celebratory flavor of a jumping outdoor blues festival. *—Richard S. Ginell*

Jewel Spotlights the Blues, Vol. 1 / 1994 / Jewel ♦♦

Jewel Records was founded by Stan Lewis in 1963, and the company became something of a life raft for artists whose contracts with older companies had ended—thus, Willie Dixon, Frank Frost, Lightnin' Hopkins, Lowell Fulson, Big Joe Turner, and other internationally known names brushed up against more localized talent such as the Carter Brothers and a mysterious figure named Big Mac. This disc is the first in a series of releases highlighting Lewis' blues recordings, which tended toward extroverted electric blues. All of the artists are in good form, if not at the top of their game, including Fulson who sings with a graceful soulfulness, while Turner provides the kind of lean, big-band-based R&B on which he built his reputation, slimmed down slightly for '60s sensibilities. The strangest track here is "Rough Dried Woman, Pts. 1-2," featuring Hubert Sumlin on guitar and Big Mac on vocals. Mac, whoever he was, obviously thought he was Howlin' Wolf, even though his voice lacked the depth and power of Wolf's pipes. He tries hard, however, and Sumlin pitches in with a flashy, crunchy performance behind him (and is featured throughout the instrumental second half in one of his best recorded performances). Also, be warned that Kenny Wayne Shepherd, then 16 years old, redubbed the guitar part on Willie Dixon's "Sex Appeal"—that kid knows his blues, even if his playing is a little flashier than would've been the case circa 1960-whatever, and Dixon gives one of his more charismatic vocal performances. The sound needs no apologies, nor does the series, which is first-rate and starts off really well with this disc. *—Bruce Eder*

Jewel Spotlights the Blues, Vol. 2 / 1994 / Jewel ♦♦♦♦

The second volume in Jewel Records' blues retrospective features Buster Benton, Buddy Guy, Otis Rush, Lightnin' Hopkins, Willie Dixon, Magic Sam, John Lee Hooker, Lowell Fulson, Earl Hooker, Ike Turner, and Little Joe Blue. Dixon was also the producer on Benton's sessions and wrote "Spider in My Stew" for the latter. The best thing on here, worth the price of the disc, is Lightnin' Hopkins' "Mr. Charlie," with its extraordinary spoken word introduction, and Ike Turner's "Matchbox" isn't far behind. Willie Dixon's "New Way of Lovin'" is a great showcase for the composer's vocal prowess, and an even better one for the guitar skills of then 16-year-old Kenny Wayne Shepherd, whose playing is dubbed onto the original recording, though one wishes that Dixon's voice were a little bit more upfront in the mix. Otherwise, the sound is state-of-the-art, and the only thing one could wish for that isn't here would be actual recording or release dates. *—Bruce Eder*

☆ **Jubilation! Vol. 1: Black Gospel** / Jan. 1992 / Rhino ♦♦♦♦♦

Jubilation! Vol. 1 offers a first-rate introduction and overview of the key players in black gospel, including stellar performances by Mahalia Jackson, the Soul Stirrers, the Swan Silvertones, Shirley Caesar, Aretha Franklin with James Cleveland, and many other wonderful artists. *—Thom Owens*

☆ **Jubilation! Vol. 2: More Black Gospel** / Feb. 1992 / Rhino ♦♦♦♦♦

Like the title says, there's more of the same as the first volume, including the Staple Singers, the Original Gospel Harmonettes, Prof. Alex Bradford, the Harmonizing Four, Sam Cooke with the Soul Stirrers, and more. *—AMG*

Jubilation! Vol. 3: Country Gospel / Mar. 1992 / Rhino ♦♦♦♦♦

While the first two volumes in the series spotlighted the history of African-American gospel, this volume peeks over the other side of the fence and sheds the light on six decades' worth of country gospel performances. It's all top-notch, too, with Hank Williams' "I Saw the Light" spearheading an 18-track collection that includes classics from Kitty Wells, Roy Acuff, Bill Monroe, Patsy Cline, Johnny Cash, the Carter Family, the Louvin Brothers, Webb Pierce, and Martha Carson. That gospel is a long-running tradition in country is exemplified by the inclusion of tracks from modern stars like Ricky Skaggs and Tony Rice, Doyle Lawson and Quicksilver, the Nitty Gritty Dirt Band, and old guard performers like Buck Owens, George Jones and Tammy Wynette, and Ernest Tubb. A delightful set. *—Cub Koda*

Jubilee Jezebels, Vol. 2 / Jul. 8, 1997 / Sequel ♦♦♦

The second volume in this fine series brings together some of the finest female rhythm & blues and pop performers who recorded for Jerry Blaine's Jubilee, Josie, or Port labels between 1952 and 1964. The bulk of the material comes from the early to mid-'50s, prime years for Blaine's labels with only five of the 25 tracks emanating from 1964. The transfers sound bright and sharp, even on the tunes that were dubbed from disc. Several of the performers reappear from the initial volume with Edna McGriff represented by three tracks, six tracks by Little Sylvia (who would later become Sylvia of Mickey & Sylvia, of "Love Is Strange" fame), and two tracks each from Gloria Mann, Gloria Alleyne, Patti Jerome, Fay Simmons, Carol Fran, and Big Maybelle, plus single track entries from Fay Simmons ("I Can See Through You"), Ann Marie ("Runaround"), Viola Watkins ("Paint a Sky for Me," which features the Crows on backup vocals), the Enchanters ("Today Is Your Birthday"), and a 1957 cut by Della Reese, a bluesy reading of the old standard "I Cried for You." As the booklet states, this compilation makes a really great all-female R&B review. *—Cub Koda*

• **Juke Joint Jump: A Boogie Woogie Celebration** / Nov. 2, 1931-Jul. 7, 1961 / Columbia/Legacy ♦♦♦♦♦

While some purists would like to compartmentalize boogie-woogie into a nice, neat box as strictly a form of piano blues, this 18-track collection clearly demonstrates that the form lends itself to a wide variety of treatments. Tracks like "Baby Boogie Woogie" by country picker Curley Weaver, "Boogie Woogie" by Delta cum Detroit bluesman Calvin Frazier, and jazz visionary Art Tatum's "Tatum Pole Boogie" do much to support that claim, as does the inclusion of tracks from Red Saunders, Adrian Rollini, and Harry James. Much of the material reprised here comes from one of the very first Columbia 78 rpm "albums," a collection of boogie-woogie classics produced by John Hammond, the man who brought the music into national vogue in the late '30s by simply letting giants like Albert Ammons, Meade "Lux" Lewis, Pete Johnson, and Big Joe Turner do their thing. As a musical flavor of the month, boogie-woogie lasted long enough into the '40s to have its rhythms incorporated into Tin Pan Alley fodder, but its influence lasted much longer than that. And here are 18 perfect examples of its timeless appeal, minus the commercial affectations. *—Cub Koda*

Juke Joint Saturday Night: Classic Piano Blues, Rags & Stomps / May 9, 2000 / Yazoo ✦✦✦✦

Capable of producing music at a sufficient volume, the piano was a widely popular instrument in African-American entertainment spots across the south in the '20s and '30s. Like the guitar, its ability to combine harmony and melody simultaneously also made it very versatile for both solo performance and group accompaniment. *Juke Joint Saturday Night* collects 23 of the sort of piano "blues, rags, and stomps" one might have heard at a weekend hot spot during the early part of the 20th century. Kicking off with a pair of dazzling piano instrumentals from "Jabo" Williams, the compilation highlights barrelhouse players Louis Johnson, James Wiggins, Little Brother Montgomery, Skip James, and many more. Best known for his inimitable guitar pieces, James had an equally unique approach to the piano. "22-20 Blues" demonstrates his wild, animated attack. The song is answered immediately with James Wiggins' "Forty-Four Blues." Also included is the tamer but no less accomplished "If You Haven't Any Hay," featuring James' call-and-response piano work and a shuffle rhythm provided by his feet. The Mississippi bluesman acquired the melody for his "Special Rider Blues" from Little Brother Montgomery, in exchange for teaching the latter "Vicksburg Blues." A showcase for his milky vibrato and punctuated with unusual bass runs, "Vicksburg" would become Montgomery's most popular number. Another prominent presence on *Juke Joint*, Louise Johnson, first recorded at a session arranged by Charley Patton. Johnson's vibrant and bawdy "On the Wall" was apparently representative of her fast-living reputation. By the late '30s, jazz and other urban music styles began eclipsing country blues in popularity. While the brass and woodwind instruments began replacing acoustic guitars, the piano managed to survive. Musicians like Roosevelt Sykes (heard here on "3-6 and 9") bridged the gap between the older blues and the developing jazz, spanning both during his successful career. Like many Yazoo releases, *Juke Joint* offers a portrait of a style in one of its purest forms, before times and tastes forced it to change. —*Nathan Bush*

Jumpin' Jive: Jump Blues Essentials / Mar. 9, 1999 / Hip-O ✦✦✦

As mid-priced compilations go, this disc delivers a lot of value—not only state-of-the-art masters (so the trumpets and saxes sound like their bells are right in the room with you, and the vocals are up close and personal), but a creative selection, crossing between the bluesier side of the big-band era (Lionel Hampton's "Hey Ba-Ba-Re-Bop") through the work of Big Jay McNeely ("The Deacon's Hop") to Roy Brown ("Boogie at Midnight"), and to the place where jump blues spawned rock & roll (Jackie Brenston's "Rocket 88"). Not that all of this material isn't available elsewhere (though some of it, such as Margie Day's "Little Red Rooster" and Louis Prima's "Robin Hood/Oh Babe," aren't all that ubiquitous), but it's handy and the notes by Peter Grendysa are above average in depth and range for a compilation like this. —*Bruce Eder*

Jumpin' Like Mad: Cool Cats & Hip Chicks / Jun. 3, 1997 / Capitol ✦✦✦

This highly enjoyable two-CD set is comprised of 51 selections by over 40 different groups. Very much a sampler of the Capitol and Aladdin catalogs, the music emphasizes midtempo and rollicking blues, with an occasional slower piece tossed in for variety. In addition to such hits as "Cow Cow Boogie," "Jumpin' With Symphony Sid," and "He's a Real Gone Guy," there are also previously unreleased selections from Ella Mae Morse, Johnny Mercer, Harry "The Hipster" Gibson, and Gene Ammons. The performers range from jazz players to those more closely associated with blues and early R&B; among the participants are Jesse Price, Kay Starr, T-Bone Walker, the King Cole Trio, the Cootie Williams Orchestra, Big Jay McNeely, and Louis Jordan, plus many others. Fun party music. —*Scott Yanow*

Kansas City Blues (1924–1929) / Jun. 2, 1994 / Document ✦✦✦

This collection presents the complete recordings of Lottie Kimbrough and Winston Holmes, delving into the Kansas City music scene of the '20s. Kimbrough, who dominates this collection, was an excellent performer of the blues, and her two duets with Holmes integrate the yodels and sound effects of the latter performer into her readings of classic blues; their union of country yodel and bluesy moan, backed by the sophisticated, driving guitar playing of Miles Pruitt, reflects a stylistic and collaborative creativity indicative of Kansas City's musical community. Also joining Kimbrough on two tracks is her singing and kazoo-playing brother Sylvester; unfortunately, heavy surface noise hinders the enjoyment of their duets, but Sylvester emerges as a masterful performer in his own right on two later pieces, in which he delivers wicked, almost effeminate blues against the piano of Paul Banks. Holmes himself is a crucial presence throughout the selections here; as well as a performer, he was a successful promoter and managed much of Kimbrough's career. His duets with guitarist Charlie Turner are primarily novelty pieces, including the unusual two-part "The Death of Holmes' Mule," a parody of religious services and hymns in which Turner's slide guitar imitates a preacher and congregation. The underdog of this album, meanwhile, is Miles Pruitt, whose solid guitar work accompanied Kimbrough throughout her career and provided an excellent complement to her vocal style. Despite the immense talent represented on this collection, its comprehensiveness and the poor sound quality of a number of the recordings should deter most casual listeners; as with all mixed bags, though, there are a number of undeniable and irresistible gems couched in the performances of these very dynamic Kansas City figures. —*Burgin Mathews*

● **Kansas City Blues 1944–1949** / Jun. 3, 1997 / Capitol ✦✦✦✦✦

This wonderful three-CD set, released in 1997, has 73 consistently exciting—and mostly formerly rare—performances from Kansas City-based players, released complete and in chronological order. Pianist Jay McShann, vocalist/pianist Julia Lee, pianist/singer Buster Moten, blues singer Walter Brown, saxophonist Tommy Douglas, and vocalist Tiny Kennedy are the leaders of the overlapping groups, and although the sidemen are mostly obscure (other than tenor man Ben Webster, who is on two dates), they show plenty of

talent and color. The styles range from urban blues and Julia Lee's sly double-entendre songs to heated instrumentals that hint strongly at early R&B. Very enjoyable and accessible music quite suitable both for parties and for close listening. —*Scott Yanow*

Keep It Rollin': The Blues Piano Collection / Feb. 13, 2001 / Rounder ✦✦✦✦

Probably the most amazing thing about this record is how fresh the music sounds. In a genre that at best has been recycling its sounds for over 50 years, it's exciting to hear that indeed, there is a lot of blues piano music being made that is vibrant, individual, and yes, living. While this album has its share of "dum da dum da dum" repetition, what is simply stunning are the tracks that expose a rainbow of individualistic expression—no small accomplishment on an instrument and a genre most would consider fairly rigid. Of special note are the mean ramblings of James Booker, the furious virtuosity of Davell Crawford, and the near brilliant, jazzy explorations of Willie Tee. Also revelatory are the tracks by Charles Brown, a musician who refuses to be filed in some musical museum. This stuff is good, real good. One can only wonder why these men aren't bigger stars than they are. If you want to know what's been happening in blues piano for the last 20 years, this is where you start. —*Rob Ferrier*

Keys to the Crescent City / 1991 / Rounder ✦✦✦

The revelation on this CD anthology spotlighting three New Orleans greats and one West Coast blues legend (Charles Brown) was the late Willie Tee. Tee, who died in 1993, was known for his soulful vocals and skillful writing, but was undervalued as a pianist. He demonstrated with his voicings and solos on "Can It Be Done" and "In the Beginning" that he also merited attention as a keyboard stylist. Charles Brown turned in his customary polished, first-rate vocal and instrumental job on his three tunes, while Eddie Bo's singing exceeded his piano playing and Art Neville demonstrated again why he should do more recording outside the arenas of the Neville Brothers and the Meters. —*Ron Wynn*

King Biscuit Blues: The Helena Blues Legacy / 1996 / Blue Sun ✦✦✦✦

Compiled by the producers of the King Biscuit Blues Festival, *King Biscuit Blues* is a wonderful collection of both well-known and obscure tunes by bluesmen rooted in the Delta tradition—including several alumni of the original *King Biscuit Time* radio show. Naturally, a couple Trumpet label recordings turn up here (Rice Miller's "Too Close Together" and Elmore James' ubiquitous "Dust My Broom"), but the rest of the album is drawn from a variety of contexts, from Robert Nighthawk's 1952 session with United to James Cotton live at Antone's in 1987. A lot of this material is blatant Chicago-style blues, but the point is that most of these guys can be traced back to Helena, AR, during some point in their careers. There's also the nice bonus of getting to hear previously unreleased tracks by both David "Honeyboy" Edwards (a solo reading of "61 Highway") and an unlikely trio of Sunnyland Slim, Johnny Shines, and Big Joe Williams ("Evening Sun" and "Roll and Tumble Blues"). —*Ken Chang*

Ladies Sing the Blues / 1992 / ASV/Living Era ✦✦✦

Living Era's *Ladies Sing the Blues* compiles performances from some of the most popular female blues singers from the '30s and '40s. Lizzie Miles, Ida Cox, Marnie Smith, and Una Mae Carlisle are some of the artists included here, and performances like Bessie Smith's "Empty Bed Blues, Pts. 1-2," Ma Rainey's "Booze & Blues," Billie Holliday's "Long Gone Blues," and Ada Brown's "Evil Mama Blues" showcase the sultry, world-weary, and often humorous stylings of these pioneering blueswomen. —*Heather Phares*

Ladies Sing the Blues: Roots of Rock 'n' Roll, Vol. 5 / 1979 / Savoy ✦✦✦✦

Savoy bundled this two-LP set into its massive *Roots of Rock 'N' Roll* series, designating it as *Vol. 5*. The album has been reissued on CD by Savoy, but with ten fewer tracks than on the original two-LP album. All tracks were recorded in the New York City area. Thus, these are East Coast blues, horns rather than guitar being the major instruments of choice. That accounts for the presence of well-known jazz artists among the sidemen. Some of the singers went on to bigger things. Linda Hopkins found steady work on the musical stage, having a leading role in such shows as *Show Train*, where she portrayed Bessie Smith. Some of the performers recorded under their stage names. Little Esther, born Esther Phillips, who made her name singing with Johnny Otis, is heavily represented with her nasal twang; she made many albums. Miss Rhapsody, Viola Wells, shows an allegiance to the style and delivery of Ethel Waters. Big Maybelle, aka Maybelle Smith, is one of the more awesome performers on this set. Possessing a powerful voice, she attacks each of the cuts with abandon, but an abandon that she completely controls. She is backed by such prominent jazz personages as Frank Rehack, Sahib Shihab, and Jerome Richardson. Albinia Jones was able to command the presence of top-rank jazz performers on her albums. With her on this compilation are jazz greats Don Byas and Dizzy Gillespie. Over the years, Savoy was never reluctant to issue collections from many of its better albums, and this one is no exception. It includes its major blues artists with some of their major recordings. Blues and jazz fans alike will be thoroughly entertained by the performances on this set. One unexpected outcome of the release of this compilation is that Albinia Jones, thought to have died in obscurity, was found to be alive and well in the Bronx, NY. —*Dave Nathan*

Led Astray / Connoisseur Collection ✦✦✦

An interesting collection that helps debunk the long-standing myth of Led Zeppelin's songwriting "originality" by serving up 16 songs that were appropriated by Page and Plant on their way to the Rock & Roll Hall of Fame. These original versions bring home the goods from Muddy Waters ("You Need Love"), Blind Willie Johnson ("Jesus Make Up My Dyin' Bed"), Robert Johnson ("Traveling Riverside Blues"), Sonny Boy Williamson ("Bring It on Home"), Willie Dixon ("I Can't Quit You Baby"), Bukka White ("Shake 'Em on Down"), Memphis Minnie ("When the Levee Breaks"), and Howlin' Wolf ("How Many More Years"), as well as folk offerings from Joan Baez and Bert Jansch. This disc should be required listening for all metal heads. A fascinating and illuminating collection. —*Cub Koda*

Legends of the Blues, Vol. 1 / Feb. 1991 / Columbia/Legacy ✦✦✦✦✦
This CD serves as a perfect introduction to prewar blues for the novice since it contains fine examples of the music of 20 blues artists: Bessie Smith, Blind Lemon Jefferson, Mississippi John Hurt, Blind Willie Johnson, Bo Carter, Blind Willie McTell, Lonnie Johnson, Charley Patton, Leroy Carr, Josh White, Leadbelly, Peetie Wheatstraw, Robert Johnson, Blind Boy Fuller, Big Bill Broonzy, Memphis Minnie, Bukka White, Muddy Waters, Big Joe Williams, and Son House. Four selections are from the '20s, Son House's "Death Letter" is from 1965 and otherwise the music dates from 1931-1947. The who's who roster includes practically every early great (Tampa Red is missing but Washboard Sam and the first Sonny Boy Williamson appear as sidemen) and, with nine previously unreleased selections (both alternate takes and "new" performances), this CD is an essential purchase for both beginners and veteran collectors alike. —*Scott Yanow*

Legends of the Blues, Vol. 2 / Sep. 10, 1991 / Columbia/Legacy ✦✦✦✦
As with the first volume in the series Columbia/Legacy blues series, this CD has one selection apiece from 20 important blues artists, including many previously unissued (at least on Columbia) songs and alternate takes. The fact that 13 of the tracks are at best quite unfamiliar should make the set (in the absence of more "complete" collections) of interest to even veteran fans and well worth acquiring as an introduction for beginners. The music ranges from intimate country blues to hokum, from early efforts by T-Bone Walker, Roosevelt Sykes, and Champion Jack Dupree to prime Tampa Red, Lucille Bogan, and Charlie Spand; there are also selections from Texas Alexander, Robert Hicks, Curly Weaver, Bessie Jackson, Walter Roland, Bumble Bee Slim, Buddy Moss, Robert Wilkins, Lil Johnson, Casey Bill Weldon, Victoria Spivey, Curtis Jones, Merline Johnson, Bill "Jazz" Gillum, and Brownie McGhee. —*Scott Yanow*

Live! At the 1966 Berkeley Blues Festival / 1966 / Arhoolie ✦✦✦
Recorded live on KAL radio in Berkeley, CA, on April 15, 1966, this presents roughly equal shares of material from Mance Lipscomb, Clifton Chenier, and Lightnin' Hopkins, performing at the 1966 Berkeley Blues Festival. The sound is not state-of-the-art, but decent considering the vintage. The material is not going to surprise anyone familiar with the artists, which is good news if you're in love with their music and want typical excerpts of their sets, but bad news if you think you might have enough of them and you're considering whether to investigate further. Lipscomb does good-natured, rhythmic country blues, both of his own composition and otherwise, covering "When the Saints Go Marching In," "I Ain't Got Nobody," and "The Sinking of the Titanic," which has slide guitar and is perhaps the most interesting of his songs on the CD. Chenier's performance might be of the greatest historical interest of the three artists on this disc, since it was his first appearance before a "a mostly young, white, relatively sophisticated concert audience," as Chris Strachwitz writes in the liner notes. It's just him, his accordion, and drummer Francis Clay, mostly on original tunes, as well as zydeco arrangements of Slim Harpo's "Baby Scratch My Back" and Ray Charles' "What'd I Say?" Clay also plays drums as the sole other musician on Lightnin' Hopkins' portion which, with its electric guitar, has a nice, mild electric R&B-rock feel. Should you already have Lipscomb, Chenier, and/or Hopkins albums, this couldn't be considered an essential addition to your library. For the casual listener, though, it might not be a bad pickup. There's variety in the sets (especially as Lipscomb and Hopkins' blues sections are broken up by Chenier's zydeco one), none of the three go on so long that you get tired of any individual performer, and there are 74 minutes of music. Half of this was previously available on Arhoolie LP 1030, but 11 of the 23 songs on the CD were previously unreleased. —*Richie Unterberger*

Living Chicago Blues, Vol. 1 / 1978 / Alligator ✦✦✦✦✦
Arguably the best entry in this pioneering anthology series, this features excellent sides by guitarist Jimmy Johnson and saxophonist Eddie Shaw. —*Bill Dahl*

Living Chicago Blues, Vol. 2 / 1978 / Alligator ✦✦✦
This set is almost as incendiary as *Vol. 1*, thanks to four sides each from Magic Slim, Lonnie Brooks, and Pinetop Perkins. —*Bill Dahl*

Living Chicago Blues, Vol. 3 / 1980 / Alligator ✦✦✦
Laconic saxman A. C. Reed and crisp guitarist Lacy Gibson are standouts. —*Bill Dahl*

Living Chicago Blues, Vol. 4 / 1980 / Alligator ✦✦✦
Not quite as strong, although witty pianist Detroit Junior and guitarist Andrew Brown contribute strong tracks. —*Bill Dahl*

Living Chicago Blues, Vol. 5 / Oct. 17, 1990 / Alligator ✦✦✦✦
Living Chicago Blues, Vol. 6 / Oct. 17, 1990 / Alligator ✦✦✦

Living Country Blues: An Anthology / Sep. 28, 1999 / Evidence ✦✦✦✦✦
A three-disc set of recordings produced by music researcher Axel Kuestner and recording engineer Siegfried A. Christmann in 1980. This is one of the last of an exhaustive batch of field recordings made in the 20th century by Christmann. The music is pulled from 14 vinyl LPs issued originally on the L+R label in Germany, and features artists who often never recorded again after these sessions, along with better-known but still peripheral names like Son Thomas, Boogie Bill Webb, Cephas & Wiggins, Hammie Nixon, CeDell Davis, Eddie Cusic, and the late Lonnie Pitchford. The music is uniformly excellent throughout the 60 tracks presented, the sounds varying from acoustic to electric, almost always in a solo setting and literally brimming with raw energy. From broom scrapings to fife and one-string electric guitar playing to more conventional guitar work, there is a phenomenal cross section of styles and some wonderful listening in the four hours of music collected here. A solid recommendation. —*Cub Koda*

Lonesome Road Blues: 15 Years in the Mississippi Delta, 1926–1941 / Yazoo ✦✦✦✦✦
Tommy Johnson's influence is again here on *Lonesome Road Blues: 15 Years in the Mississippi Delta*, which includes other fine prewar Delta blues. —*Mark A. Humphrey*

Long Gone Daddies / Jul. 31, 2000 / Ace ✦✦✦
What unifies this motley assortment of non-hit '50s singles, mostly rockabilly in style, although there are a few R&B cuts tossed in? All were done for the Modern group of labels. Modern and its subsidiaries were much more known for early West Coast blues, R&B, and black vocal group sounds than they were for straight rock & roll. This fair but unexceptional sampler illustrates why that was the case: The singers were imitators, not innovators. Ploughing through the generous allotment of 32 cuts, there's the sense that Modern was throwing a lot of stuff against the studio wall to see what might come of attempts to ride the rock & roll craze (it *was* thought of as a craze back then, remember), though of course there were many other labels doing the same thing. It's certainly not lacking in energy, and some cuts stick out way above the others, such as Clarence Garlow's hot 1953 R&B-verging-on-rock single "Route 90"/"Crawfishin'," and Lee Denson's "High School Hop," soaked with an inordinate bucket of reverb even by rockabilly standards. Don Cole (with "Snake Eyed Mama") and Danny Flores (with "You Are My Sunshine") must have been wearing out the grooves on their Jerry Lee Lewis singles before their sessions, so blatant are the attempts to recapture that atmosphere; Artie Wilson's "Jerry Jerry" is an even more obvious cop of the Little Richard/Larry Williams train. So what might catch the attention of the thorough early rock collector here? Well, Mercy Dee's "Come Back, Maybellene" is a half-decent 1955 "answer" record to Chuck Berry's "Maybellene"; Long Tall Marvin (now *there's* a hip *nom de plume*), actually Marvin Phillips of Marvin and Johnny, does a super-jittery Little Richard impersonation on "Have Mercy, Miss Percy"; and Jessie James' "Red Hot Rockin' Blues" is about the most convincing rockabilly song on the disc, with some really twistin' 'n' growlin' vocals, a cool manic guitar solo, and blasting saxophones. Incidentally, half a dozen of these tracks, including three demos by Jesse James, were previously unreleased. —*Richie Unterberger*

Long Gone Daddy / Oct. 22, 1991 / Collectables ✦✦✦✦✦
This is the kind of rare country and Western swing material that might be too obscure even for Bear Family to touch—the 14 songs here include several previously unissued tracks, and all are drawn from the archive of Ivin Ballen's Gotham Records, dating from the early '50s. The range of styles is considerable, from Jimmie Rodgers country blues to Hank Williams-type honky tonk, with some Western swing as well, but lurking in the background is the spectre of rock & roll—not that any of these tracks exactly rock out, but it's easy to hear how quite a few of them could with a few changes in tempo. Lou Graham seems to have been influenced by both Rodgers and Williams, to judge from the style of his two solo numbers, "Two-Timin' Blues" and "Long Gone Daddy," and also is represented by a couple of cuts here backed by Bill Haley's Saddlemen before they'd hit it big as Bill Haley & His Comets. Sammy Bland & His Carolina Radio Boys perform a smooth, swing-style "I Just Heard the News," while "Our Shotgun Wedding Day" by the Howlington Brothers with the Tennessee Haymakers is a fun little novelty number that veers into bluegrass just a bit. Bob Dean & His Hi-Way Wanderers offer the earliest and most primitive track here, "I'll Take Her from the Valley," dating from 1947 and using a considerable portion of "Red River Valley" for its structure. Mustard & Gravy's "Be Bop Boogie" features a catchy litany of country dances in its lyrics, and a great beat to hear them by—the duo was actually Frank Rice and Ernest L. Stokes, and was a comedy act, yet they were also better than decent musicians, if the evidence of the gently rolling piano and even the effective kazoo sound can be believed. Sleepy McDaniel & His Radio Playboys' "Roadside Rag" is a steel-guitar driven dance instrumental with some serious fiddle playing, apparently by Buck Ryan, and with a few changes in tempo, might've made it as a quasi-rock & roll number in the mid-'50s. The sound is astonishingly good considering the age and the neglect to which several of these tracks have been subjected, and this is a nice little musical snapshot of what local and regional country music was like, just as R&B was starting to mix with it elsewhere and transform it into rock & roll. —*Bruce Eder*

Louisiana Gumbo / Jan. 25, 2000 / Putumayo ✦✦✦
The folks at Putumayo got it right on this one. The easiest trap to fall into when putting together a Louisiana compilation is to go for the tourist stuff—the Dixieland jazz, the second-line horn bands, or zydeco. There's nothing the matter with any of those traditions, but they're so obvious. What this compilation focuses on is New Orleans R&B, a tradition as rich as the others but not unique to the area and therefore not typically marketed aggressively by chambers of commerce and travel agencies. *Louisiana Gumbo* starts off strong, with Charles Sheffield's "It's Your Voodoo Working" and the even better "Door Poppin'" by Carol Fran and Clarence Hollimon—and then it gets even better. The late pianist James Booker is at his best on the spicy "African Gumbo" (the secret ingredient of which is the legendary drummer John Boudreaux), and there are equally fine contributions from Johnny Adams, Clifton Chenier (OK, they did include some zydeco), and, especially, Percy Mayfield, whose strange but brilliant "Festis Believe in Justice" is the album's highlight track. Highly recommended. —*Rick Anderson*

Louisiana Scrapbook / 1987 / Rykodisc ✦✦✦
Contemporary Louisiana sounds were presented on this 18-track compilation, culled from various albums. While veteran stylists like Irma Thomas, Tuts Washington, and Johnny Adams were included, the disc contained cuts by other acts not so readily identified with the state (Marcia Ball) and sorely neglected artists (Phillip Walker, James Booker, Lonesome Sundown), as well as then-emerging stars (The Dirty Dozen Brass Band, Beausoleil) and both zydeco (Buckwheat Zydeco) and Cajun performers (D.L. Menard, Jo-El Sonnier). —*Ron Wynn*

Low Blows: An Anthology of Chicago Harmonica Blues / 1994 / Rooster ✦✦✦✦✦
This is a scattershot compilation of great, early-'70s recordings by Chicago's better-known (Walter Horton, Carey Bell) and lesser-known (Big John Wrencher, Good Rockin' Charles Edwards) harmonica men. Another missing chapter in blues history. —*Cub Koda*

Male Blues of the Twenties, Vol. 2 / Dec. 3, 1997 / Document ♦♦♦♦
With the exception of some vocal duets and a few sessions that are available elsewhere, the complete output of five blues-oriented performers from the '20s are on this CD. Jesse Crump, best known as Ida Cox's husband and accompanist, is heard on a pair of previously unreleased piano solos from 1923 ("Mr. Crump Rag" and "Golden West Blues"), which make one wish that he had recorded extensively. J. Churchill (backed by pianist Lovie Austin), Charles Anderson, and Mike Jackson sing two numbers apiece, while Tom Delaney (a composer whose songs include "Jazz Me Blues") is heard on his only session, which resulted in four songs from 1925. The final dozen numbers feature "New Orleans" Willie Jackson (a lesser-known competitor of Papa Charlie Jackson), who fares well on his sessions from 1926-1928, including two songs that include guitarist Eddie Lang in the backing duo. This is another valuable Document blues release that vintage collectors will want. *—Scott Yanow*

☆ **Mama Let Me Lay It on You (1926–1936)** / Apr. 8, 1991 / Yazoo ♦♦♦♦♦
A fine collection of East Coast blues, including vintage Josh White, Pink Anderson, and guitarists Blind Blake and Willie Walker. *—Barry Lee Pearson*

Masters of Modern Blues / 1994 / Testament ♦♦♦
This compilation of sides culled from three different sessions featuring Robert Nighthawk, Johnny Young, and Houston Stackhouse mark the first official recordings of Big John Wrencher. Although he's relegated to a sideman role here behind Nighthawk and Young, he appears on nine of the 18 tracks on this excellent collection. While the addition of a drummer would have placed the Nighthawk-Young-Wrencher trio in a less deliberate folk-blues setting, the music (which also includes Nighthawk's last session from 1967, playing bass behind Delta blues legend Houston Stackhouse with King Biscuit Boy drummer Peck Curtis) is just about as superb as one can expect from mid-'60s collector-oriented recordings and helps to flesh out Wrencher's meager discography. *—Cub Koda*

● **Masters of Modern Blues** / 1995 / Testament ♦♦♦♦♦
This was originally released in the late '60s as part of a Chicago blues series of albums on the old Testament label. With an all-star lineup of Big Walter Horton on harmonica, Johnny Young on rhythm guitar, and Fred Below on drums, this murkily recorded album (which sounds much better on CD) nonetheless literally brims with energy. "Lulubelle's Here" and "Blues Stay Away from Me" is just J.B. Hutto at his most intense. A good album to listen to during a thunderstorm. *—Cub Koda*

Masters of the Delta Blues: The Friends of Charlie Patton / 1991 / Yazoo ♦♦♦♦♦
As the most popular blues craftsman of the Mississippi Delta, Charley Patton had a resounding influence on many of the musicians who passed through the region during the '20s and '30s. Following his initial session for Paramount in 1929, he recommended both Son House and Willie Brown, as well as his mistress Louise Johnson and common-law wife Bertha Lee, to legendary talent scout H.C. Speir for recordings of their own. Furthermore, casual acquaintances like Tommy Johnson, Ishmon Bracey, and Kid Bailey acquired Patton themes, adopting them to suit their own style and playing ability, emerging with a handful of country blues classics in the process. *Masters of the Delta Blues: The Friends of Charley Patton* focuses on Patton's role as musical disseminator, gathering sides from all the above mentioned artists, along with a pair of recordings by admirer Bukka White. Patton's legacy is unquestionable, but the works of his contemporaries are hardly examples of second-rate imitation. Though Brown made recordings for the Library of Congress during the '40s, his commercial output was extremely limited—an unfortunate fact, given the quality of his "Future Blues." Joining Brown, Patton, and Louise Johnson for a session at Paramount in the '30s, Son House cut a handful of the finest sides of his career. Though his music would retain an undeniable power into the '60s, he arguably never topped the likes of "Walking Blues," "My Black Mama," "Dry Spell Blues," and "Preachin' the Blues," four explosions of raw Delta blues. Also exceptional are Kid Bailey's "Rowdy Blues," Tommy Johnson's "Button Up Shoes" and "Maggie Campbell Blues," and Bukka White's "I Am in the Heavenly Way." Possibly the finest topical country blues compilation in Yazoo's catalog, *Masters of the Delta Blues* is also essential listening for anyone with more than a casual interest in the genre. *—Nathan Bush*

Matchbox Days / Mar. 25, 1997 / Big Beat ♦♦♦
The late-'60s British blues boom was dominated by electric blues-rock blues bands, yet there was also an active acoustic blues scene, though it made considerably less commercial impact. Record-wise, much of the activity centered around the Matchbox label, on which the bulk of the music on this 22-track compilation was originally released. Jo-Ann Kelly and Dave Kelly are the only names that might be remotely familiar to American listeners. There are also cuts by Wizz Jones, the Panama Limited Jug Band, Mike Cooper, and Ian Anderson (the Ian Anderson who now runs *Folk Roots* magazine, not the Ian Anderson from Jethro Tull), and others. White British blues sometimes takes quite a critical beating, but despite the fact that the guitar playing here is considerably more impressive than the singing, this is a perfectly respectable, very listenable compilation of an underappreciated facet of the British blues boom. The performances are sharp and committed, and there's a reasonable amount of variety, from the straight Delta blues derivations through the imaginative jug band revivalism of the Panama Limited Jug Band. Maybe you don't need many British '60s acoustic blues albums in your collection, but if you only want one, this would be a good choice. *—Richie Unterberger*

Mean Mothers/Independent Womens Blues, Vol. 1 / Jan. 1981 / Rosetta ♦♦♦♦♦
One of the best (and maybe the only) reissue label for classic female blues of the '20s-'50s, Rosetta Reitz's Rosetta Records has over the years released a wealth of compilations and single-artist records covering the work of both the famous (Bessie Smith, Dinah Washington) and the relatively obscure (Arizona Dranes, Lil Green). This early compilation features some of the best yet least known of the lady blues singers on tracks cut between 1926-1949. Save for fine cuts by Billie Holiday and Lil Armstrong, the rest here by the likes of Bertha Idaho, Martha Copeland, Harlem Hannah, and Mary Dixon probably have not surfaced since the original release dates. The mix, though, is very fresh all the same, with a bevy of powerful blues singing, several accounts of strong women and the no-good men that cross their paths, and some top-notch jazz accompaniment by Louis Armstrong, Chu Berry, James P. Johnson, and others. A fine spin on the decks for the historically minded blues lover. *—Stephen Cook*

☆ **Mean Old World: The Blues from 1940 to 1994** / 1996 / Smithsonian Institution Press ♦♦♦♦♦
A four-CD, 80-song box set that, in line with similar Smithsonian productions, outlines the history of blues spanning over 50 years, with cuts by major performers who represent its stylistic evolution. The set is stuffed with classics by the likes of Muddy Waters, Louis Jordan, T-Bone Walker, Little Walter, Big Mama Thornton, Howlin' Wolf, Elmore James, B.B. King, and Buddy Guy, with plenty of slightly lesser-known artists like Lil' Son Jackson, Billy Branch, Big Maybelle, J.B. Lenoir, Doctor Clayton, and Junior Kimbrough. The selections are a tad conservative (if very good), and it's likely that serious blues fans will have a good share of the tracks in their collections already. The set also concentrates much more heavily on 1940-1970 material (which takes up about 75 percent of the contents) than blues from the 25 years from 1970 onward. If your interest falls somewhere between casual fan and dedicated collector, though, it's a good survey of major blues performers and genres, with an excellent historical overview and notes about each performer in the accompanying 92-page booklet. *—Richie Unterberger*

Memphis Harp & Jug Blowers (1927–1939) / 1992 / Document ♦♦♦
During the '20s and early '30s, the harmonica and the jug permeated Memphis music, emerging in blues and hokum material, as well as in some religious performances by sanctified musicians. This set documents the presence of one or both of these instruments in the careers of a handful of Memphis secular musicians, most notably the multi-talented and highly distinctive Jed Davenport. Davenport transforms the standard "How Long How Long Blues" into a brilliant harmonica solo, which builds steadily into a harp-choking frenzy, the instrument seemingly sucked inside out in characteristic Davenport fashion. As well as a soloist, Davenport was the leader of the Beale Street Jug Band, whose six recorded songs are also included here. On most selections, the group unimaginatively provides quiet and disappointing backing to Davenport's playing; their "Beale Street Breakdown," however, is a classic, stomping instrumental in which jug, fiddle, and mandolin descend into a frantic, masterful madness alongside Davenport's screeching harmonica. The group again demonstrates its full capabilities in "You Ought to Move Out of Town," engaging jug and harmonica in a lively call-and-response coupled with infectious vocals. Another minor Memphis legend, Minnie Wallace delivers four low-down hokum blues to the accompaniment of her Night Hawks, a loose ensemble featuring the Memphis Jug Band's Will Shade on harmonica. Little Buddy Doyle concludes the set with a solid string of blues, backed by an unidentified harmonica player. For serious followers of the Memphis legends or of early harmonica styles, this album is a welcome collection with a few standout tracks; like many of Document's excellent compilations, however, its focus is too specialized for the average listener, and beginners would be better off first pursuing the Memphis Jug Band, Cannon's Jug Stompers, or Yazoo's more generalized *Memphis Masters* collection. *—Burgin Mathews*

Memphis Masters: Early American Blues Classics / 1994 / Yazoo ♦♦♦
A companion to Yazoo's excellent *Mississippi Masters* collection, this time focusing on Memphis artists recorded between 1927 to 1934. The tracks collected here offer up a musical ambience that accurately depicts time and place with classic selections from acknowledged area kingpins Frank Stokes, Furry Lewis, Gus Cannon's Jug Stompers, Memphis Minnie, Joe McCoy, and Jack Kelly. Like its companion volume, this 20 track compilation is mastered direct from extremely rare old 78s—in some cases, the only copies known to exist—and the sound varies wildly from track to track. But the music is so great and of such major historical significance, the 78 surface noise that remains only seems to add to the charm and romance of it all. *—Cub Koda*

Merry Christmas Baby / 1988 / King ♦♦♦♦
The original issue of this classic was subtitled *Intimate Christmas Music for Lovers*, and with five of the dozen tracks featuring the smoothest of the smooth vocalists, Charles Brown, that subtitle is appropriate. Other King artists represented here are bluesmen Lowell Fulson and Jimmy Witherspoon, and Lloyd Glenn on "Sleigh Ride" doing a swinging piano workout. Mabel Scott's original jumping "Boogie-Woogie Santa Claus" can be found here. *—Dennis MacDonald*

Messing With the Blues / Sep. 2000 / Ace ♦♦♦♦
Atlantic did not record a great deal of blues records, focusing even on its outset on more urban music that could be more comfortably classified as R&B (and later rock and soul). It did its share of worthwhile, though not classic, blues from the late '40s to the early '60s, and 25 examples are collected on this CD. Overall, the Atlantic blues sound, as heard here anyway, was usually smoother and more polished than that of more blues-oriented big indie labels like Chess and Modern. Of the famous figures on this anthology, Ray Charles is represented by three early cuts, the standout being "Losing Hand," with its unusual (for blues) minor jazz-tinged melody. T-Bone Walker is heard on a couple of OK 1955 singles; Jack Dupree does slightly jazz piano blues on two songs from a 1958 LP. John Lee Hooker's two characteristically biting, scabrous 1953 tracks were actually waxed for De Luxe in 1953, though the masters were later bought by Atlantic. Joe Turner's sole cut is his 1954 Top Ten hit "TV Mama," which featured guitar by Elmore James. James also plays guitar on the five sides by his pianist, Little Johnny Jones, who does acceptable journeyman Chicago blues. The other performers who fill out the disc—Tiny Grimes, Frank Culley, Jimmy Earle, Lucky Davis, Chuck Norris (no, *not* the famous actor), Jimmy

Griffin, Odelle Turner, and Hal Paige—do passable songs only of note to collectors, though Larry Dale does a nice 1961 cover of the standard "Drinkin' Wine Spo-Dee-O-Dee." —*Richie Unterberger*

Mississippi Blues / Kent ◆◆◆◆
This album provides a rare and fascinating insight into one of the most important but least recorded eras of the blues; that of the music played in the juke joints of the Mississippi Delta region during the late '40s and early '50s. The recordings on this album are the result of a field trip made in late 1951 and early 1952 by Joe and Jules Bihari of Modern Records, looking for releasable sides for their bevy of labels. This anthology features four tracks each from Boyd Gilmore ("Take a Little Walk With Me," "If That's Your Gal," "Just an Army Boy," and "All In My Dreams," the last featuring a dubbed-in solo taken from an Elmore James record), the almost incomprehensible at times Houston Boines ("Superintendent Blues," "Monkey Motion," "Going Home," and "Relation Blues"), and guitarist Charlie Booker ("Moonrise Blues," "Rabbit Blues," "No Riding Blues," and "Charlie's Boogie Woogie," which later became the theme for an impressionistic animated cartoon). Gilmore—a cousin to Elmore James—utilizes strong guitar work (his solo on "Take a Little Walk With Me" is the sound of the Delta in embryo), while Boine's garbled vocals nonetheless show a real flair for song lyrics, with "Monkey Motion" utilizing the deathless line, "She's got a face like Mary and hair just like the Lord." The recording quality and performances contained on this disc are crude and rough, both evoking a sound and period that has long since vanished from modern blues recordings. Still missing in action on CD, this 12-track vinyl album nonetheless contains some explosive performances well worth tracking down. —*Cub Koda*

Mississippi Delta Blues Jam in Memphis, Vol. 1 / Arhoolie ◆◆◆◆
Arhoolie label chief Chris Strachwitz was in the right place at the right time, capturing this marvelous set of studio performances from artists appearing at the 1969 Memphis Blues Festival. Kicking off with spirited fife and drum work from Napoleon Strickland with the Como Drum Band, the set also includes turns from Mississippi Fred McDowell (both solo and with harmonica man Johnny Woods), Memphis Piano Red, Otha Turner, Furry Lewis, and the mysterious deaf-mute guitar team of R.L. Watson & Josiah Jones. There are some really great performances here, all well-recorded. A marvelous document. —*Cub Koda*

Mississippi Delta Blues Jam in Memphis, Vol. 2 / 1993 / Arhoolie ◆◆◆
The more satisfying of the pair, cut in 1967-1968. Some of R.L. Burnside's best solo work, impressive country blues by Joe Callicott (along with sides of his 1930 78) and four items by guitarist Houston Stockhouse and his combo. —*Bill Dahl*

Mississippi Delta Blues, Vol. 1: Blow My Blues Away / 1994 / Arhoolie ◆◆◆◆
George Mitchell still recorded several vibrant, distinctive Delta blues performances here. The artists he chronicled ranged from such legendary greats as Robert Nighthawk, Johnny Woods, and Mississippi Fred McDowell to obscure but exciting performers such as Napoleon Strickland, Peck Curtis, and Do-Boy Diamond. Their songs were quite simple; many were reworked tunes they had heard and/or played all their lives. They performed with no fanfare, sophisticated support to cover flaws, or pretension. The songs were about heartbreak, anguish, disappointment, and indignation, and sometimes about getting drunk, sexual potency, or whatever else came to mind. There are 12 unreleased cuts among these 23 numbers, and the mastering and notes provide an added bonus to this nice set. —*Ron Wynn*

☆ **Mississippi Girls (1928–1931)** / Sep. 1991 / Story of the Blues ◆◆◆◆◆
This is an important collection, because it helps fill the gap in the recorded history of blueswomen who played and sang outside of the well-known sphere of the "classic singers" such as Ma Rainey and Bessie Smith. The highlights here are the two recordings of Mattie Delaney, a wonderful singer/guitarist about whom almost nothing is known. Fine also are the more rough-hewn offerings of Rosie Mae Moore who is accompanied by talented veterans Charlie McCoy and Ishmon Bracey. Although the Geechie Wiley/Elvie Thomas duets are marred by a scratchy background, they also are well worth hearing. —*Larry Hoffman*

Mississippi Masters: Early American Blues Classics 1927–1935 / 1994 / Yazoo ◆◆◆◆◆
This is a well-organized, smartly chosen 20-track compilation of some of the lesser-known early Mississippi blues artists. Garfield Akers is about the most famous, which tells you right there how obscure most of these names—King Solomon Hill, Otto Virgial, Mattie Delaney, Joe Callicott, Blind Joe Reynolds, John D. Fox, and others—are to the general listening public. It's quality material, however, and not in a drastically different league than the most renowned classics by singers like Tommy Johnson and Son House. The guitar playing and singing are emotional and inventive throughout, but standouts include Mattie Delaney, Elvie Thomas, and Geeshie Wiley, some of the relatively few guitar-playing Delta blueswomen who recorded; Wiley's minor-key, doomy "Last Kind Words" is particularly affecting. —*Richie Unterberger*

Mississippi String Bands and Associates (1928–1931): Complete Recorded Works / 1991 / Document ◆◆◆◆
The music on this enjoyable CD of rarities features overlapping groups that recorded in Atlanta in 1928, Jackson, MS, in 1930, and Chicago during several sessions in 1931. All of the recordings released under the names of singer Alec Johnson, the Mississippi Mud Steppers, the Mississippi Blacksnakes, and Sam Hill From Louisville are here. Such notables as guitarist/violinist Bo Carter, Charlie McCoy on mandolin, guitarist Joe McCoy, and guitarist/singer Walter Vincson are prominent in supporting roles and it is interesting to hear these future blues stars this early in their careers. Blues historians will want this valuable set. —*Scott Yanow*

Mississippi-Memphis-Chicago Blues / Mar. 2, 1999 / Nostalgia ◆◆◆◆
A nice, solid collection of country blues recorded between 1930 and 1941. Kicking off with Big Joe Williams' "Baby, Please Don't Go" and winding up with Blind Willie and Kate McTell's "Dying Gambler," this 20-track set features classics from Robert Johnson, Big Bill Broonzy, Tampa Red, Muddy Waters, Robert Jr. Lockwood, T-Bone Walker, Memphis Minnie, and Sister Rosetta Tharpe. Although some of the transfers are a bit noisy, the music's as fine as it gets. A good one to add to the collection. —*Cub Koda*

Mister Charlie's Blues: 1926–1938 / Oct. 9, 1992 / Yazoo ◆◆◆◆◆
A fascinating exploration of blues-drenched, prewar hillbilly recordings includes the great fingerpicked guitar of Sam McGee. —*Mark A. Humphrey*

Modern Blues Legends / Jan. 16, 1996 / ORC ◆◆◆
Modern Blues Legends is a solid collection of some of the most popular blues-rock artists of the late '80s and '90s. Featuring favorites like Johnny Winter, Robben Ford, Buddy Guy, Danny Gatton, and the Fabulous Thunderbirds, the album might lean to heavily on rock influences—Big Head Todd & the Monsters and Paul Rodgers contribute tracks, after all—but the music is fine and the disc does give a good feeling of the era. —*Stephen Thomas Erlewine*

● **Modern Chicago Blues** / Aug. 1965 / Testament ◆◆◆◆◆
Producer Pete Welding made many recordings for Testament in the early and mid-'60s at the start of the blues revival, and this is a grab bag of 21 tracks he recorded in Chicago between 1962 and 1966. This isn't postwar Chicago blues as many listeners picture the form. Only four of the cuts have drums, and not all of them are electric; it's more like a document of country blues getting citified, rather than the full electric Chicago band sound. The actual music—mixing performances by well-known figures like Robert Nighthawk and Big Walter Horton with unknowns like Wilbert Jenkins and John Lee Granderson—is respectable, but won't excite many listeners other than hardcore devotees. Some nice moments on the way, though, like Maxwell Street Jimmy's fine variation of John Lee Hooker's "Dimples," and the roll and tumble sound of Johnny Young (the only musician here to use a drummer). The CD reissue adds five previously unreleased tracks. —*Richie Unterberger*

Mojo Workin': Blues for the Next Generation / Oct. 7, 1997 / Sony ◆◆◆
This is a 16-track sampler from various entries in Columbia's *Mojo Workin'* series, which gets pared down to a one-big-hit-per-artist format, starting with Robert Johnson's "Cross Road Blues" and Memphis Minnie's "When the Levee Breaks" and finishing up with Stevie Ray Vaughan's "Texas Flood" and Keb' Mo's "Am I Wrong." The stopping-off points in between include entries from Muddy Waters ("The Blues Had a Baby and They Named It Rock'n'Roll"), Blind Boy Fuller ("Rag Mama Rag"), Blind Willie McTell ("Southern Can Is Mine"), Blind Willie Johnson ("Motherless Children"), and Bessie Smith ("It Makes My Love Come Down"), along with more modern tracks from Taj Mahal ("Last Fair Deal Gone Down"), the Electric Flag ("Killing Floor"), and Johnny Winter ("Johnny B. Goode"). Perhaps not so surprisingly, this mixing of time frames, styles, and divergent approaches to the blues makes for some fine listening, as well as making this a nice entry-level disc. —*Cub Koda*

Mojo Workin': The Best of Ace Blues / 1995 / Ace ◆◆◆◆
This 20-track collection puts together essential tracks by some of the biggest names in the genre. Elmore James, John Lee Hooker, Smokey Hogg, B.B. King, Slim Harpo, Albert King, Lowell Fulson, Lonesome Sundown, Howlin' Wolf, Johnny "Guitar" Watson, Arthur Gunter, Lazy Lester, Pee Wee Crayton, Ike Turner, and Lazy Lester are all represented by at least one track apiece and in, most cases, some of their representative work. A pretty great primer that not only serves as something of a greatest-hits package for the novice, but just plain great listening for the hardliners as well. —*Cub Koda*

Mountain Blues / County ◆◆◆
Here's a compilation that can't be faulted for false advertising. It promises blues, it delivers blues. Hey, the cover is even colored blue. The fact that it is on County and the title mentions "mountain" are strong clues of what sort of blues these are. No, it is not a Leslie West and Mountain blues jam collection. These are all performers from the Appalachian mountains, and the material is a mishmash of vintage stuff from the '20s and '30s and more recent cuts. All but two of the tracks have "blues" in the title. None of the songs are actually blues about mountains, not even "Johnson City Blues," which might pass since this is an important Tennessee town in the mountains. Chances are good that all the performers were somewhere in the mountains, maybe even looking at mountains when they recorded these numbers. This label could and did assemble many such compilations, drawing from the overflowing archive of tapes at its disposal. No doubt about it at all, many great old-timey and early country artists have simply great material available on this label. One could create a superior selection of this type of music simply by wandering through the company's warehouse blindfolded, grabbing titles at random. There are 12 tracks here, which isn't exactly a generous serving considering that all are quite short. The dozen artists represented are all totally historic old-timey music geniuses, and a string of so many brilliant performances in a row would be hard to find even on a Harry Smith anthology. The label seems to have the attitude that the listener will either know everything they want to about these artists, or won't care. The performers are treated like riff-raff, identified once on the track list and that's it. There is no information about the songs besides this whatsoever, County feeling it is more important to hog half the back cover with a catalog excerpt advertising other such productions. It is all a bit casual and ad hoc, and conceivably might not be the way someone interested in this type of music would like to see it presented. After all, there are labels that use compilations as a way of creating as much information about a topic as possible and not just simply whipping up another dish of leftovers. At the same time, it is not impossible to conceive of an audience for old-timey music collected by theme, even as general as this. The split is about even

between solo performances and string bands, the latter material the most striking. *—Eugene Chadbourne*

Mucho Mojo: Best of Fat Possum / Jan. 28, 1997 / Capricorn ✦✦✦✦
Mucho Mojo collects new and previously released tracks from the Jelly Roll Kings, R.L. Burnside, CeDell Davis, Paul "Wine" Jones, Junior Kimbrough, and Dave Thompson. *—Jason Ankeny*

My Rough and Rowdy Ways, Vol. 1 / Oct. 20, 1998 / Yazoo ✦✦✦✦
A disc of classic recordings is a rarity, but that's exactly what this is. Some of the performers are well-known people, like Clarence Ashley, Dock Boggs, Uncle Dave Macon, and Tommy Johnson. Others, like the Haywood County Ramblers, are far from household names, but that doesn't mean their songs are lesser creations. These ballads of bad men, hellraisers, violence, and drinking are the stuff of legends, like "Frankie" by the Dykes Magic City Trio, a version of "Frankie and Johnny" by a group reminiscent of the Carter Family. It's interesting that the performers on these songs from the '20s and '30s are both black and white, and the music sounds remarkably similar—a clear indication that prejudice didn't extend everywhere at the time, and that music was colorblind. From a time when American rural song was still a strong musical force—before Tin Pan Alley and commercialization had changed everything—"Little Sadie" and "Viola Lee Blues" come across the years with complete crispness, while the banjo style of Dock Boggs can be heard as an influence on so many who followed. But these pieces also come from the cusp, when urban culture was about to take over, and songs like the Allen Brothers' "Prisoner's Dream" would be replaced by other tunes. In fact, the one piece here that offers any kind of continuity is a version of "Stack-O-Lee" from the Fruit Jar Guzzlers, although their version seems hopelessly naïve and country compared to others that would come later. This is, as it's meant to be, a collection that's very much of its place and time. But since they both represent a crossroad, it's a great place and perfect time in the development of American music. *—Chris Nickson*

My Rough and Rowdy Ways, Vol. 2 / Oct. 20, 1998 / Yazoo ✦✦✦
Here are 23 songs from the '30s about badmen and hell-raisers, by artists ranging from legends like Uncle Dave Macon, Mississippi John Hurt, and Big Bill Broonzy, obscure music pioneers like George Reneau and groups like the Haywood County Ramblers. The mix of white country and black blues artists is one of the better in this series, the music meshing together to form a kind of audio panorama of story-songs dealing with life on the far side of law and order—"Otto Wood the Bandit" by the Carolina Buddies, aka Odel Smith (fiddle) and Norman Woodlief (guitar), segues into Mississippi John Hurt's "Frankie," followed by Uncle Dave Macon's rip-roaring banjo workout "Railroadin' and Gambin'" (anyone seeking a track that defines Macon's "claw-hammer" style of banjo playing need look no further than this cut). Among the too-little-heard bluesmen featured here are Waylon "Sloppy" Henry ("Canned Heat Blues"), and Joshua "Peg Leg" Howell ("Skin Game Blues"), who also plays on Henry's cut, and Robert Wilkins, whose "Old Jim Canan's" features a superb guitar duet between the singer and Little Son Joe, later the husband of Memphis Minnie. Country highlights include Georgia-based fiddle wildman Earl Johnson ("Nobody's Business") and George Reneau's "Jesse James," which features singing by future star crooner Gene Austin. Yazoo has done a generally good job of remastering these cuts, so the sound on most of it (David Miller's "That Bad Man Stackolee" and Uncle Dave Macon's "Late Last Night When Willie Come Home" are the big exceptions) holds together at a decent volume without any excessive artificial processing or distracting noise. The only drawback is the booklet, which is extremely confusing, since it refers extensively to artists and material on *Vol. 1* of this collection, a separate CD. *—Bruce Eder*

Nasty Blues / 1989 / Ichiban ✦✦✦
These are rather pedestrian outings that try to re-create the "party blues" of artists like Bo Carter and Blind Boy Fuller, with a more contemporary, Southern R&B sound. If you want this, get the older stuff. You won't be sorry. *—Niles J. Frantz*

Nasty Blues, Vol. 2 / 1990 / Ichiban ✦✦✦

Negro Blues and Hollers / 1962 / Rounder ✦✦✦
These 12 tracks were collected in a joint project by the Library of Congress and Fisk University in 1941 and 1942, concentrating on Mississippi country blues as well as the field hollers and spirituals that were the blues' direct ancestors. A couple of these performers are actually pretty well-known; Son House has three cuts and contributes to the "Camp Hollers" selection, while David "Honeyboy" Edwards does a version of "Worried Life Blues." The acoustic blues are OK but not among the greatest vintage Delta stuff available, and the fidelity is muffled, though not as raunchy as what you'll get on remastered 78s from the Depression era. There are actually only two a cappella hollers on the disc, and there are also a couple of spirituals by congregations that serve as examples of the oft-overlooked influence of gospel on the blues. *—Richie Unterberger*

New Bluebloods / 1987 / Alligator ✦✦✦✦✦
An attempt to document "the next generation of Chicago blues," this is generally a very exciting and successful collection, including The Kinsey Report, Lil' Ed and the Blues Imperials, Valerie Wellington, and several more. *—Niles J. Frantz*

New Blues Hits / Jun. 24, 1997 / Bullseye Blues ✦✦✦
This 18-track sampler from Bullseye Blues runs through a spate of 1996-1997 vintage releases to cobble together a nice selection from some of the label's better-known artists. Kicking off with the Persuasions' "Life Is Like a Ballgame" (in keeping with the baseball cover art motif), selected highlights from Smokin' Joe Kubek ("Can't See for Lookin'"), Magic Dick & Jay Geils & Bluestime ("Hot Leftover No. 1" and "Hot Leftover No. 3"), Eddy Clearwater ("Mean Case of the Blues"), Ruth Brown and Johnny Adams ("I Don't Know"), Jumpin' Johnny Sansone ("The Talkin' Is Over [The Walkin' Has Begun]"), and Pat Boyack & the Prowlers ("Longwailin'") make this a cut above your garden-variety independent blues label sampler. *—Cub Koda*

New Millennium Blues Party / Oct. 17, 2000 / Rhino ✦✦✦
Rhino's *New Millennium Blues Party* might as well be titled Blues' Greatest Hits. Its 20 tracks cover some of the most popular blues songs of (mostly) the latter half of the 20th century, and correspondingly, there's an enormously wide range of styles and approaches, from Chicago grit to slick blues-pop. Even though the variety does keep things interesting, it's also kind of jarring to jump from Robert Cray to Susan Tedeschi to Muddy Waters to George Thorogood to Jonny Lang, one right after the other. It does help, though, that the collection is packed with classic blues singles: Muddy Waters' "Mannish Boy," Howlin' Wolf's "Smokestack Lightning," Albert King's "Born Under a Bad Sign," B.B. King's "The Thrill Is Gone," and John Lee Hooker's "Boom Boom." There are a couple of odd artist/song matchups—"Johnny B. Goode" performed by Johnny Winter?—but overall, for a basic, hit-laden blues primer, you could do a lot worse than *New Millennium Blues Party*. *—Steve Huey*

New Orleans Blues: Troubles Troubles / 1988 / Rounder ✦✦✦✦✦
New Orleans blues tunes with traces of jazz, soul, and Afro-Latin tinged R&B are featured on this 14-track anthology. The CD includes performances by several either underrated (Edgar Blanchard, Jerry Morris) or obscure (Eddie Lang, Mercy Baby) acts. They're mostly period pieces from the late '50s and early '60s that range from stomping instrumental workouts to wailing testimonials, heartache numbers, novelty tunes, and songs reflecting the influence of Little Richard or Larry Williams. Eddie Lang gets the most space (five tunes) and displays a good sound and energized tone. Blanchard & the Gondoliers and Morris with Clarence Garlow's Orchestra provide driving musical punch. There's nothing fantastic or earth-shaking here, but much that's entertaining and instructive. *—Ron Wynn*

New Orleans Jazz & Heritage Festival, 1976 / 1976 / Rhino ✦✦✦
This wonderful set of live recordings may have a few flaws audio-wise here and there, but there's something in the excitement of the proceedings captured here that nullifies all of that. For sheer class, it's hard to beat Irma Thomas' or Allen Toussaint's turns with the crowd, just as it's impossible to ignore the loose and jagged performances of legends like Lightnin' Hopkins and Professor Longhair, perhaps the centerpieces of this unheralded work of genius. The real thing in front of the hometown crowd, this is one modern-day live album with some spirit to it. *—Cub Koda*

Newport Folk Festival: Best of the Blues 1959–1968 / Apr. 10, 2001 / Vanguard ✦✦✦✦✦
Newport Folk Festival: Best of the Blues 1959-1968 presents live performances from many of the top blues players of the era. From Skip James to Mance Lipscomb to Memphis Slim, these musicians play mostly acoustic blues before an appreciative audience. From the first disc, Mississippi John Hurt's six-song set is a standout. Piedmont fingerpicking and resonant vocals highlight "Sliding Delta," "Candy Man," and "Pallet on Your Floor." Muddy Waters delivers fine versions of "Walkin' Blues" and "I Can't Be Satisfied," but his acoustic guitar lacks the rude punch that usually flavors his blues. Still, these songs make for interesting comparison to his electric work. Disc two finds Rev. Gary Davis belting out "Samson & Delilah" and "I Won't Be Back No More." Sonny Terry & Brownie McGhee offer a rousing set, including a previously unreleased version of "Drink Muddy Water." Their spunky "Key to the Highway" proves once again that the blues can sometimes be joyful, while "My Baby Done Changed the Lock on the Door" reminds one to keep an eye on one's girl and best friend. Lightnin' Hopkins brings an urban touch along with—shocking though it may be—an electric guitar. Always laid-back and relaxed, there is something timeless about his performance of "The Woman I'm Loving, She's Taking My Appetite" and "Baby Please Don't Go." Like John Lee Hooker, his timing and approach are all his own. Many players like Son House had been brought back from obscurity thanks to the folk revival, so the historical value of this music cannot be overstated. With nearly three hours of music and a live audience, it is also the next best thing to having been at Newport during these exciting years. These discs are highly recommended to anyone with even a passing interest in acoustic blues. *—Ronnie Lankford, Jr.*

News & the Blues: Telling It Like It Is / Feb. 1991 / Columbia ✦✦✦✦
Like any form of popular music, the blues has reflected the social conditions of the times, sometimes quite explicitly. *News & the Blues* offers 20 songs from the Columbia vaults from between 1927 and 1947. The Depression is reflected often, as expected, but there are also songs about natrual disasters, public figures like Joe Louis, World War II, and even the atomic bomb. Memphis Minnie and Bill Gaither even take the step of recording specific tributes to other blues singers (Ma Rainey and Leroy Carr respectively). Many of the performers are well-known—Bessie Smith, Mississippi John Hurt, Big Bill Broonzy, Charley Patton, Memphis Minnie, Bukka White—and several others are unknown to any but blues scholars (Jack Kelly, Homer Harris, Alfred Fields). Like several of Columbia's anthologies that are loosely grouped under a theme, you don't necessarily have to have a keen interest in the album concept to appreciate the music, which is an above-average gathering of early blues tracks of various styles. *—Richie Unterberger*

Not the Same Old Blues Crap / Feb. 24, 1998 / Epitaph ✦✦✦
A sampler from the Fat Possum label that, as the title announces, really isn't the same old blues crap. Fat Possum made its name as a home for raw '90s juke-joint blues, and a lot of that is here in the cuts by Junior Kimbrough, R.L. Burnside, T-Model Ford, and the Jelly Roll Kings. It's straight-up electric guitar blues where the groove and spontaneous rhythms are more important than chord changes and tight song construction, which can be both a blessing and a curse; the Jelly Roll Kings add some nice texture to the form with whirling organ. You also get some almost punkish blues-rock from 20 Miles and the Neckbones, who sound a little like a bluesy Cramps on "Crack Whore Blues." *—Richie Unterberger*

Not the Same Old Blues Crap, Vol. 2 / Jun. 19, 2001 / Fat Possum ♦♦♦♦
It worked the first time around, so why not a second offering of *Not the Same Old Blues Crap*? For *Vol. 2*, Fat Possum has patched together another riveting collection of hypnotic boogies, wailing guitars, and Mississippi moans—but lo and behold, there's also a tender side to this album that may surprise both fans and critics of the label. While listeners can still expect to find plenty of electric juke-joint swagger courtesy of R.L. Burnside, Paul "Wine" Jones, and T-Model Ford, a good half of the songs here are statements of subtlety, with Scott Dunbar's falsetto-laden "Easy Rider" (reissued from his 1972 Ahura Mazda LP *From Lake Mary*) and King Ernest's soul ballad rendering of Tom Waits' "House Where Nobody Lives" leading the way. Fat Possum puts a fat spotlight on its deep lineup of solo performers—Robert Belfour, Asie Payton, Junior Kimbrough, Dunbar, and Burnside all take relaxed turns inhabiting the role of the lone bluesman, who has perhaps never sounded so alive since the prewar era. But the jewel of this compilation is actually a duet shared by Kimbrough and rockabilly guitarist Charlie Feathers: the lighthearted "I Feel Good Again," which was originally cut in 1969. It's an uncharacteristic but charming blues that marries Feathers' precise, flat-picked strumming with Kimbrough's loping vocals and lead guitar runs. There's absolutely nothing like it—just like Fat Possum, of course. *—Ken Chang*

Oakland Blues / Arhoolie ♦♦♦♦♦
As Lee Hildebrand states in his liner notes, Oakland blues—unlike the slicker L.A. blues—was a sophisticated yet rootsy version of the Southern and Chicago styles. Most of the players came from Louisiana and Texas to work in the shipyards of the Bay Area, which had no blues tradition of its own prior to World War II. This Arhoolie compilation of 1948-1957 material spotlights some of those top Oakland bluesmen, many of whom show the influence of the city's most famous blues resident, Oklahoma-native Lowell Fulson. From K.C. Douglas' countrified "Mercury Boogie" (later cut by David Lindley as "Mercury Blues") to Jim Wilson's slow-burning "Blues at Sundown," the mix offers a consistently fine selection of electric and acoustic delights. And whether you are excited about such billboard names as Jimmy McCracklin and Weldon "Juke Boy" Bonner or the obscure likes of pianist Mercy Dee or guitarist Johnny Fuller, this album makes for a very enjoyable primer on one of the blues' most overlooked hotbeds. *—Stephen Cook*

Old Town Blues, Vol. 1: Downtown Sides / 1993 / Ace ♦♦♦
This has 22 blues tracks recorded in the '50s for New York's Old Town label, most of which were unissued at the time. The core of this anthology is the 11 songs by Sonny Terry & Brownie McGhee, who do electrified city blues with an audible influence from Chicago performers like Bo Diddley and Jimmy Reed. It's not the style they're most renowned for, perhaps, but the results are pretty good. The rest of the CD is a hodgepodge of miscellany, including decent raw electric blues from James Wayne, fairly anonymous sides by Little Willie and Bob Gaddy, and a couple of rare Willie Dixon items from an unissued acetate of demos. *—Richie Unterberger*

Old Town Blues, Vol. 2: The Uptown Sides / 1994 / Ace ♦♦
A grab bag of blues sides with a strong R&B influence, recorded for New York's Old Town label between the mid-'50s and mid-'60s. This is aimed squarely at the blues collector/completist: there's nothing especially inept about these sides, but nothing especially captivating either. Nor is there a strong stylistic or instrumental thread connecting the tracks. It's period stuff, by obscure artists like Hal Paige, Ursula Reed, Lester Young (*not* the jazz great!), Larry Dale, and Sam Baker; Wild Bill Moore and Buddy and Ella Johnson, represented by some of their least-known work, are the most recognizable of the bunch. *—Richie Unterberger*

Old Town Country Blues / Jan. 25, 2000 / Collectables ♦♦♦♦
Old Town isn't a label most folks think of when classic blues recordings come to mind. But for a brief period in the '50s, this R&B-oriented label released some pretty potent discs, and the best are collected here. Featuring wild performances by Sonny Terry and Brownie McGhee (who cover ten of the 25 tracks aboard), the set also includes super-rare sides from Willie Dixon, James Wayne, Little Willie, and Bob Gaddy. New York blues isn't all that well documented, so this set is a most welcome addition to blues history. *—Cub Koda*

On the Road Again / Muskadine ♦♦♦♦♦
This 15-track anthology was one of the first to take a detailed look at the early history of postwar Chicago blues, collecting several of the truly important sides. Floyd Jones' title cut (who also handles the vocalizing chores on Snooky and Moody's "Keep What You Got") and Delta Joe's—most say Sunnyland Slim—"Roll, Tumble and Slip" sets up the stage for five sides featuring the earliest recordings of Little Walter. In addition to his 1947 debut recording for Ora-Nelle, "I Just Keep Lovin' Her," we're treated to a brace of 1950 Parkway sides, including "Bad Acting Woman" and "Moonshine Blues," along with two sides of Walter in support of Othum Brown ("Ora Nelle Blues") and Baby Face Leroy Foster on "Red Headed Woman." Equally as potent are two selections each from Johnny Shines ("Evening Sun" and "Brutal Hearted Woman," both featuring shattering harp work from Big Walter Horton) and John Brim ("Humming Blues" and "Trouble In the Morning") and finishing up with three tracks from J.B. Hutto & His Hawks' 1954 session for Chance Records ("Pet Cream Man," "Lovin' You" and "Now She's Gone"), featuring strong support from Porkchop Hines on washboard, George Mayweather on harmonica, and the ubiquitous Joe Custom on second guitar. *—Cub Koda*

Original American Folk Blues Festival / 1962 / Polygram ♦♦♦♦♦
This was recorded live in a studio in Hamburg, Germany, in October 1962. It includes artists involved with that year's American Folk Blues Festival tour, with generally relaxed and reflective performances. The artists include T-Bone Walker, Sonny Terry, and John Lee Hooker. *—Cub Koda*

Original Blues Classics / Apr. 16, 1995 / Original Blues Classics ♦♦♦
This 15-track compilation serves as a fine sampler of the OBC label. Included are "Trouble in Mind" (King Curtis), "I've Got Mine" (Pink Anderson), "The Dyin' Crapshooter's Blues" (Blind Willie McTell), and "Say No to the Devil" (Rev. Gary Davis). *—Roundup Newsletter*

Original Blues Classics, Vol. 1 / 1990 / Fantasy ♦♦♦♦♦
This budget-price, seven-cut, cassette-only release for non-record store retail outlets (such as drug stores) features blues and soul by Albert King, Etta James, Lightnin' Hopkins plus four more. It's not for real blues fans. *—Niles J. Frantz*

Original Memphis Blues Brothers / 2000 / Ace ♦♦♦
This originally came out as a 1989 LP on Ace; look, however, for the expanded 2000 Ace CD, as it increases the number of tracks from 15 to 26 with the addition of material by B.B. King, Ike Turner, and Rosco Gordon. All of the songs were recorded in Memphis in the early '50s by the Bihari brothers, and much of it released on 45s on their Modern, RPM, and Meteor labels, though some of it wasn't issued for decades. This was two or three years before the ascendancy of Memphis rockabilly, and blues/R&B crossover ruled the roost in the city. The CD is thus a rough snapshot of local electric blues just as it began to be recorded often, with some of the earliest sides by Bobby "Blue" Bland, Junior Parker, Johnny Ace, and the aforementioned King, Turner, and Gordon, as well as the nearly unknown Earl Forest. In comparison to the somewhat more famous early Memphis electric blues released in the early- to mid-'50s on Sun, this is a little more sluggish, and more tilted toward barroom piano styles. The songwriting, too, is not as sharp and electric as the best Sun stuff. All that taken into consideration, this is still a noteworthy supplement to those Sun recordings, as a document of the sound of Memphis electric blues—and, by extension, rock & roll—in its infancy. The band plays some serious havoc with timekeeping on Parker's chaotic "You're My Angel," which sounds like a drunken afterhours jam; Bland is well on his way to establishing his foggy urban blues delivery on his two singles. Forest is a typical but unremarkable period bluesman; Ace is represented by just one performance, the 1953 ballad "Midnight Hours Journey"; and Turner turns in relatively rare (and competent) vocal performances on his 1952 single. B.B. King's catalog from this period is actually pretty well represented by reissues, so collectors will be interested to note that the four numbers here are alternate takes of his first two 78 singles for RPM, from 1950. *—Richie Unterberger*

Out of the Blue / 1985 / Rykodisc ♦♦♦♦
A 17-cut sampler of some of Rounder's blues and blues-related releases of the period, it features "straight" blues from J.B. Hutto, Phillip Walker, and Johnny Copeland; blues-rock from the Nighthawks and George Thorogood; soulful blues from Johnny Adams and Ted Hawkins; pus cuts from Buckwheat Zydeco, piano-great James Booker, John Hammond, Solomon Burke, and several more. The Adams, Walker, and Copeland cuts are particularly nice, as is one entry from Marcia Ball and the Legendary Blues Band. *—Niles J. Frantz*

Paint It Blue: Songs of the Rolling Stones / Oct. 14, 1997 / A&M ♦♦♦
The idea behind *Paint It Blue: Songs of the Rolling Stones* is such a simple, appealing one that it's a wonder that the record wasn't made before 1997. The Stones never made any secret of their debt to the blues, so it makes sense that their songs would sound good when performed by blues and R&B artists. That's the idea behind *Paint It Blue*—contemporary blues and R&B artists sing some of the band's bluesiest songs. While some may quibble that the idea is a little too cute, the performances by Luther Allison ("You Can't Always Get What You Want"), Junior Wells ("[I Can't Get No] Satisfaction"), Taj Mahal ("Honky Tonk Women"), Clarence "Gatemouth" Brown ("Ventilator Blues"), the Holmes Brothers ("Beast of Burden"), and Bobby Womack ("It's All Over Now"), among many others, are hard to argue with. It's a rock-solid record that confirms what great songwriters Mick Jagger and Keith Richards are. *—Stephen Thomas Erlewine*

Piano Blues Rarities 1933–1937 / Mar. 1991 / Story of the Blues ♦♦♦
There are certainly no household names to be found on this somewhat obscure release from the Da Music label; the music was leased from Document and essentially duplicates an LP on CD. Included are the complete recordings of four pianist/singers (Whistlin' Rufus, Earl Thomas, Ben Abney, and Curtis Henry) plus two songs by singer/guitar Red Nelson that were left out of some other reissue series. The 20 selections (four apiece from Rufus, Thomas, and Henry, six by Abney, and the pair of Nelson sides) are fairly typical of the mid-'30s blues scene, covering both urban (Chicago) and rural (Charlotte, NC) styles. Although none of this music is essential, it does fill in some gaps and hints at the great treasures that can be found in the vintage blues world once one gets beyond the major names. *—Scott Yanow*

Piano Blues, Vol. 1: 1927–1936 / Jun. 2, 1994 / Document ♦♦♦♦
Eight different pianists plus singer Pigmeat Terry have their complete output reissued on this valuable CD. None of the pianists became famous, but they generally all are quite talented. Each of them also sings, with the exception of Jim Clarke, whose only recording ("Fat Fanny Stomp") has him leading listeners through a dance routine. Bert Mays is featured on six numbers; Jesse James (who allegedly was given a brief reprieve from prison in order to record his session) is heard on four songs; Pigmeat Terry, Joe Dean, and Blind Clyde Church cut two numbers apiece; and Dan Stewart, Jim Clarke, and Judson Brown only had one song documented. James "Bat" Robinson is heard on three cuts from 1931 and two extended numbers from 1956 to conclude this rewarding and intriguing CD. *—Scott Yanow*

Piano Blues, Vol. 2: 1927–1956 / Jun. 2, 1994 / Document ♦♦♦♦
Seven different pianists and/or singers have their complete output released on this collector's CD. Well, at least five do since Jesse Clayton (heard on two numbers) is possibly Doctor Clayton and the previously unissued "Throw Me Down" features an unknown pianist who may be guitarist Skip James on his second instrument. Also included is

singer I.C. Prigett (who is backed by pianist Clarence T. Walker), vocalist Willie Jones (on two songs), seven selections by singer-pianist Barrelhouse Buck McFarland, eight by pianist-singer Charles Segar (including four excellent piano solos), and two piano solos, by Doug Suggs from 1956 (his only recordings although he was really based in the '30s). There are enough bright moments along the way to make this intriguing set easily recommended to vintage blues collectors. *—Scott Yanow*

Piano Blues, Vol. 4: 1923–1928 / Aug. 1, 1995 / Document ♦♦♦♦
There are many rarities on this 25-song CD, which has the complete output (except for two Keghouse numbers with Lonnie Johnson, and one by Stovepipe Johnson with Jimmie Noone) by 11 different performers from the '20s. Q. Roscoe Snowden is excellent on two piano solos from 1923, Tiny Franklin is accompanied by pianist George W. Thomas on four numbers, the completely obscure Ray Logan, Hermes Zimmerman, Lucius Hardy, and Keghouse are heard on two songs apiece, and Skeet Brown and Yodeling Kid Brown are featured on a lone title. In addition, Sugar Underwood shows off some impressive technique on two piano solos cut in Savannah, GA, in 1927, Stovepipe Johnson sings three songs accompanied by pianist Georgia Tom Dorsey, and Jack Erby (best known for his duets with Lonnie Johnson) has four features. This wide-ranging yet unified set should be of great interest to both early blues and early jazz collectors. *—Scott Yanow*

Piano Blues, Vol. 5: 1929–1936 / Aug. 1, 1995 / Document ♦♦♦♦
A variety of different blues-oriented vocalists and singers are featured on this continually intriguing CD. The emphasis is on obscure performers, most of whom have their complete small output reissued on this disc. Dating from 1929-1932, there are two titles apiece by vocalist-pianist Bill Pearson, Guy Smith (who may be John Erby), the vocal duo of George Allison and Willie White, and singers Monroe Walker and Andy Chatman. None (except Erby) received second chances to return to the studios. In addition, there are four songs featuring singer Carrie Edwards (the great stride pianist Cliff Jackson is on two of them), pianist-vocalist George Ramsey (who is possibly Georgia Tom Dorsey) is heard in three different settings (including backing singers Peggy Walker and Mae Belle Lee), and, from 1936, Sophisticated Jimmy La Rue sings three songs that fit into the general style. Blues collectors will want this set, and the other releases in this miniseries. *—Scott Yanow*

Piano Blues, Vol. 1: The Twenties (1923–1930) / Jan. 1992 / Story of the Blues ♦♦♦
In the early '90s, the Da Music label leased albums from the Austrian Document company, reissuing the programs originally on LPs on their CDs, giving them new liner notes. Much of this vintage blues music has since been reissued in a different form by Document, so one has to pick and choose to see which CDs are worth picking up. This particular CD has Clay Custer's historic and haunting "The Rocks," a 1923 recording that is the first piano record utilizing a boogie-woogie bass; the pianist is actually George W. Thomas. In addition, there are all of the recordings by pianist Q. Roscoe Snowden and singers L.C. Prigett, Willie Jones, Jack Ranger, Blind Clyde Church, Jesse Clayton, and the team of George Allison and Willie White. The music is both historic and largely enjoyable. *—Scott Yanow*

Piano Blues, Vol. 2: The Thirties (1930–1936) / Jan. 1992 / Story of the Blues ♦♦♦
Much of this music, which was leased in the early '90s by Da Music from the Document label, has since been reissued by Document in more comprehensive sets. However, these performances, which emphasize blues pianists (even if most of the leaders are actually singers) are mostly well worth hearing in any format. Included on this CD are the complete (and rather slim) output of Judson Brown, Pigmeat Terry, Harry "Freddie" Shayne, Jesse James, Frank Busby, and James Carter; all of them only led one two-song session apiece, aside from James (who recorded four songs) and Brown (who only made a single side). In addition, there are four numbers by singer Bob Robinson's Bob-Cats and one number by Albert Clemens, who is probably Cripple Clarence Lofton. There are quite a few interesting and rare performances on this CD, which is becoming pretty scarce itself. *—Scott Yanow*

Piano Blues, Vol. 2: 1927–1932 / Magpie ♦♦♦♦♦

Planet Blues: The World of Blues-Rock / 1993 / Rhythm Safari ♦♦♦
There are so many blues anthologies and samplers currently available that most, if not all, of the music contained here can be found elsewhere. The disc succeeds in its objective—to show the links between urban blues and modern rock. Indeed, songs like Eric Clapton's "Tribute to Elmore" or Canned Heat's "Dimple" are literally electric blues done by rockers. Likewise, the Bo Diddley, Howlin' Wolf, and Muddy Waters numbers were blueprints fully studied and absorbed by the entire first wave of British invaders. These are fun tracks and worth having, whether you get them here or somewhere else. *—Ron Wynn*

Play My Juke Box: East Coast Blues (1943–1954) / Nov. 28, 1995 / Flyright ♦♦♦♦♦
Bruce Bastin's English Flyright label—only one of the magnificent tributaries of his Interstate Music Company—has consistently demonstrated a union of fine scholarship and great music. This collection of mostly little-known East Coast blues artists is no exception. There are seven tracks of singer/guitarists, four harp/guitar duets, four piano/guitar pairings, two guitar duos, and one arresting cut featuring three harps plus vocal. Artists such as Skoodle-Dum-Doo & Sheffield, Boy Green, Robert Lee Westmoreland, Marilyn Scott, and Sonny Jones serve up a startling reminder of all the amazing talent that has gone unrecognized over the years. *—Larry Hoffman*

Pot, Spoon, Pipe and Jug / May 19, 1924-Dec. 1975 / Stash ♦♦♦
The Stash label made its original reputation by releasing around a dozen LPs filled with mostly little-known vintage recordings of jazz and blues artists discussing (often in veiled ways) drugs and sex. This album sticks to the former and is (with two exceptions) from the 1927-1941 period. Highlights include a test-pressing version of Cab Calloway's classic "Kickin' the Gong Around," Cab's famous "Reefer Man," Stuff Smith's humorous "You'se a Viper," Lil Green's "Knockin' Myself Out," and Blue Lu Barker's "Don't You Make Me High." *—Scott Yanow*

Prime Chops: Blind Pig Sampler, Vol. 2 / 1993 / Blind Pig ♦♦♦
Plenty of choice blues, roots rock, gospel, and zydeco. You can sample 19 tracks from the Blind Pig catalog at a budget price here, including Jimmy Thackery and The Drivers, Joanna Connor, Roy Rogers, Little Mike & the Tornadoes, and more. *—Roch Parisien*

Pure Blues / Apr. 17, 2001 / UTV ♦♦♦♦♦
The "pure" in the Pure series initially suggested the unadulterated, soothing dulcet tones of new age in the *Pure Moods* discs, but as the series took off, Universal Music realized they had a real marketable brand name here, so they decided to use it for different genres. The one thing that all the collections shared was that they were exceptional collections that summarized the genre remarkably well. *Pure Blues*, one of the latter-day installments, is actually one of the very best of the series, and it's one of the best general blues overviews available, especially for the rock fan that wants to dabble in the genre. This is because Universal's catalog runs deep and contains not just the Chess label, but also such labels as Duke, Peacock, Cadet, and ABC, plus they have the licensing muscle to pull in key tracks from other majors. That means Howlin' Wolf, Muddy Waters, Freddy King, Jimmy Reed, John Lee Hooker, Albert King, Koko Taylor, Etta James, Bobby "Blue" Bland, B.B. King, Luther Allison, Buddy Guy, and Robert Cray are all here, all represented by some of their finest songs. If there is any problem here, it's when the record tilts toward modern blues-rock, but while Jonny Lang, Kenny Wayne Shepherd, and Susan Tedeschi don't quite fit alongside these blues titans, the selections from the Allman Brothers, Stevie Ray Vaughan (a relatively rare live version of "Flood Down in Texas [aka Texas Flood]" from an Atlantic album, *Blues Explosion*, from 1986), and a duet by Eric Clapton and Duane Allman on "Mean Old World" fit right in with the rest of the record. There's really nothing unexpected here, and if you have a large blues collection, there's not much reason to pick this up, but as a sampler, this is first-rate. *—Stephen Thomas Erlewine*

Putumayo Presents: Mississippi Blues / Feb. 12, 2002 / Putumayo ♦♦♦
More than Chicago, its electric home, or Detroit and Memphis, where it morphed into modern soul, Mississippi is the blues. But, like every musical form, the blues have evolved since the days Charley Patton lived on Dockery's Plantation and played house dances and juke joints around Clarksdale. And that very evolution is going to make any collection called *Mississippi Blues* problematic. To many, Mississippi is associated with the acoustic Delta blues. To a younger generation, it's the raw electric artists of Mississippi hill country who appear on the Fat Possum label (and who are essentially unrepresented here). To be fair, the compilers do their best in a thankless job. From the early generation listeners get Memphis Minnie, Memphis Slim, and Mississippi John Hurt (notably a cut from his '60s rediscovery). Slightly later come Arthur "Big Boy" Crudup—one of Elvis Presley's inspirations, with his big, laid-back voice—some relatively early Ike & Tina Turner, John Lee Hooker (an odd choice; although his roots were in Clarksdale, his work didn't begin until he was up north in Detroit), and the wonderful Bobby "Blue" Bland, with a take on the classic "St. James Infirmary." There is one young inclusion, happily, in the rising Chris Thomas King. But where's Muddy Waters, whose first work was recorded down in the Delta in the early '40s? Where are Robert Johnson and Charley Patton, whose styles epitomize and define early blues? Where's Junior Kimbrough or R.L. Burnside? This is a fair collection which tries to bill itself as "a musical journey down the Mississippi River," but from conception it never stood a chance of being remotely complete in just 11 tracks. *—Chris Nickson*

Ragtime Blues Guitar (1927–1930) / Mar. 24, 1994 / Document ♦♦♦♦
The emphasis is on inventive blues/ragtime guitarists on this CD. First there is a previously unreleased alternate take of Blind Blake playing the instrumental "Dry Bone Shuffle." Then there is the complete output of singer/guitarist Bill Moore (eight songs), the team of Tarter and Gay (two selections by the guitarists with Stephen Tarter singing), six cuts by guitarist George "Chicken" Wilson and harmonica/washboard player Jimmy "Skeeter" Hinton, four solo numbers (two of which are instrumentals) by guitarist/singer Bayless Ross, and three performances from singer/guitarist Willie Walker (including two of the "South Carolina Rag"). The obscurity of these performers should not keep vintage blues fans away, for the music is quite enjoyable in addition to being formerly very rare. *—Scott Yanow*

Rare Blues / 1980 / Takoma ♦♦♦♦
These recordings capture what compiler-producer Norman Dayron called an undocumented phenomenon: acoustic blues players who couldn't get gigs in an electrified Chicago scene. Nothing changed until hotshots like the late harpist Paul Butterfield and guitarist Michael Bloomfield—both of whom appear—began helping the people they'd so fervently admired, jump-starting a whole new scene. Made between 1963 and 1965, these tapes attest to the undiluted power of solo performance with a piano, acoustic guitar, or even harmonica, as Dr. Isaiah Ross shows on a blistering "Good Morning Little School-girl" (recorded in a large but acoustically perfect university hall, as Dayron notes). Maxwell Street Jimmy, the Rev. Robert Wilkins, and Big Joe Williams get two songs apiece, which ensures a more focused listening experience. The album illustrates the tremendous variety among traditional artists like Wilkins, well-known for his earthy gospel-blues style, or deft pianists like Little Brother Montgomery and the legendary Sunnyland Slim. The colorfully monikered Maxwell Street Jimmy breathes vigor into the oft-covered "Two Trains Running." (He's also the featured artist on the cover, which shows him as a short-order cook, complete with grease-spattered apron.) Dayron's liner notes place all the performers' selections and contributions in perspective, which should prove helpful for listeners not familiar with the genre. As compilations go, this release is a good primer on traditional acoustic blues. *—Ralph Heibutzki*

Rare Chicago Blues / May 1, 1993 / Bullseye Blues ♦♦♦
Recorded between 1962 and 1968 by Norman Dayron, *Rare Chicago Blues* is an enthralling collection of rare blues from artists like Otis Spann, Little Brother Montgomery, Big Joe Williams, Robert Pete Williams, as well as several others. Captured live in clubs and on the street, these tracks give a good taste of what real, gritty urban blues sounded like in the '60s and is worthwhile for true blues aficionados. *—Stephen Thomas Erlewine*

Rare Country Blues / Jun. 2, 1994 / Document ♦♦♦
This is an enjoyable trip into the lesser-known recesses of pre-World War II blues, covering artists who didn't record enough to justify separate CDs of their own. Opening with a pair of tracks by Virginia-born Seth Richard, including his kazoo-highlighted signature tune "Skoodeldum-Doo," it leads us to four extraordinarily dexterous solo guitar, songster-type numbers by Memphis-based, Texas-born Charlie Kyle, to the sole known song by the mystery-shrouded guitarist/singer "Freezone." Most of this material is fairly primitive, having been recorded in the late '20s, but the sound is anything but—Document has given us a pretty clean account of most of the early stuff, a match for any company's reissues of material from this era; only Freezone's side (from Paramount, of course) is somewhat substandard. Willie Harris' four numbers may have been done in Chicago, and feature a prominent piano (likely played by Charles Avery), but his style shows off his Mississippi roots, especially the slide playing. Leola Manning's six songs present religious lyrics in a blues setting, sung in a style resembling Memphis Minnie's, and anticipating the kind of hybrid performing that bluesmen-turned-ministers Gary Davis and others turned toward in the '60s. Jazzbo Tommy Settlers' eight songs, dating from 1937, are the most acquired taste here—the first four are Paramount titles and suffer from abysmal sound, coupled with the fact that they are dominated by the kazoo, while the second four, issued by ARC, are of significantly better quality and feature a full band, with piano and guitar. The latter are the choice parts of Settlers' output. *—Bruce Eder*

Rare Jazz & Blues Piano (1927–1937) / Nov. 30, 1995 / Document ♦♦♦
Despite the title of this CD, the emphasis in the music is more on the male vaudeville singers who are featured than their accompanying pianists. There are four songs apiece featuring singers "Talking" Billy Anderson and Scottie Nesbitt, and Billy Mitchell sings six good-time, mildly risqué numbers, including "Two Old Maids," "Looking for a Cherry," and "A Hole in One." Oliver Brown From New Orleans accompanies himself on piano for two numbers, and the vocal duo of Whistling Bob Howe and Frankie Griggs perform "The Coldest Stuff in Town" and "The Hottest Stuff in Town." Best known is singer/pianist Lil "Diamonds" Hardaway, who sings six duets with Old Ced Odom. Obviously none of this music is essential, but there are some fun and surprising moments along the way, making this a worthwhile acquisition by '20s collectors. *—Scott Yanow*

Raunchy Business: Hot Nuts & Lollypops / Aug. 1991 / Columbia/Legacy ♦♦♦♦
This sex-based set of early blues-oriented recordings has 19 double-entendre songs and a humorous (and quite profane) "alternate" version of Lucille Bogan's "Shave 'Em Dry" that still could not be played on the radio. Among the performers are Lil Johnson, Lonnie Johnson, Barrel House Annie, Bo Carter, and Buddy Moss. With titles such as "Sam the Hot Dog Man," "The Best Jockey in Town," "If It Don't Fit, Don't Force It," "Banana in Your Fruit Basket," and "You Got to Give Me Some of It," the subject matter is easy to figure out. *—Scott Yanow*

RCA Victor Blues & Rhythm Revue / Dec. 1987 / RCA ♦♦♦♦♦
A great 25-cut cross-section of Nipper's R&B activities 1940-1959, the set includes everyone from Count Basie to Little Richard to the Dew Droppers to the Isley Brothers. *—Bill Dahl*

The Real Blues Brothers / 1987 / DCC ♦♦♦♦♦
This is a nice Vee-Jay collection with representative cuts from Pee Wee Crayton, John Lee Hooker, Jimmy Reed, Lightnin' Hopkins, Billy Boy Arnold, Memphis Slim, and a stray track from Sonny Terry & Brownie McGhee. The big ticket for collectors on this one, however, is the inexplicable bonus of a previously unissued Eddie Taylor number, "Leave This Neighborhood," reason enough for hardcore fans to want to add this one to the collection. *—Cub Koda*

Red River Blues / Aug. 24, 1999 / Ace ♦♦♦
Recorded between the mid-'50s and mid-'60s, most of this electric blues and R&B was laid down at Mira Smith's studio in Shreveport, LA, appearing on tiny labels like Ram, Jo, Clif, Speed, and Red River; a dozen of the tracks were previously unreleased. It's pretty tenuous grounds for a compilation, and it should be pointed out that Smith also recorded some other styles in her studio that are not represented here; also, the disc is filled out by five cuts done elsewhere in Shreveport by Jesse Thomas in the early '60s. Nonetheless, it's a pretty fair collection of early electric Louisiana blues, TV Slim the only name likely to evince even faint recognition from most collectors. Yes, there are four cuts by Sonny Boy Williamson, but this not John Lee Williamson ("Sonny Boy I") or Rice Miller ("Sonny Boy II"); it is, hilariously, Jeff "Sonny Boy" Williamson, yet another harmonica-playing guy using the name. He's actually one of the better performers here, although his music is derivative, with flashes of Fats Domino and Bo Diddley here and there. New Orleans R&B, indeed, is a substantial influence on several of the cuts, and the swampy Excello-released blues of Slim Harpo and the like can also be heard from time to time. TV Slim, by contrast, does primitively recorded (even by mid-'50s standards) blues-boogie on his 1955 Speed single, as well as the original version of the rockabilly blues "Flat Foot Sam" (later recut for Chess in New Orleans). Talk about lo-fi: Chico Chism's "Romp & Stomp" instrumental sounds like it was recorded from the opposite end of a school hall. Jesse Thomas finishes things off with some pretty classy, urbane blues, which sound a little like early B.B. King. *—Richie Unterberger*

Rediscovered Blues / Jun. 20, 1995 / Capitol ♦♦♦♦
This two-CD set captures four blues giants in several classic studio dates. The first six tracks are spirited performances in a jam session that includes guitarists Lightnin' Hopkins, Brownie McGhee, and Big Joe Williams, plus Sonny Terry on harmonica. The humorous vocal exchanges on the laid-back "Ain't Nothin' Like Whiskey" and the upbeat "Wimmin from Coast to Coast" are riotous, and the crisp lines of the acoustic guitars are timeless. McGhee and Terry made many fine duo recordings together, but the dozen tracks included from a 1959 session are among their best. Their vocals complement one another very well on "Lose Your Money," while "Louise" showcases Terry's emotional harmonica against McGhee's strong vocal and driving guitar. The last 16 tracks featuring Big Joe Williams don't measure up to the rest of the package. Accompanied by an unidentified bassist and drummer in a 1968 studio session, the sound is surprisingly distorted due to sloppy engineering and poor microphone placement. Even so, Williams manages to perform decent, if poorly recorded, versions of "Pearly Mae" and "Toledo to Buffalo." This collectible set should be considered essential by blues fans. *—Ken Dryden*

Reefer Madness / Feb. 8, 1924-1944 / Stash ♦♦♦
By the time Stash came out with this LP, its 20th release, one would think that the label had run out of vintage drug and sex songs to reissue. However the quality of these performances is still pretty high and, although some of the musicians were quiet obscure, there are also selections from Cow Cow Davenport, Buck Washington, Louis Armstrong (1928's "Muggles"), Mills Blue Rhythm Band, Mezz Mezzrow, Fats Waller, and Django Reinhardt. This collection is not essential but remains quite fun. *—Scott Yanow*

Reefer Songs: Original Jazz & Blues Vocals / Jun. 17, 1932-Nov. 2, 1945 / Stash ♦♦♦♦♦
This LP was the very first release by the Stash label and, as with its first dozen or so collections, it features vintage material that deals with illicit subject matter. Many of the best marijuana and drug-based recordings are on this set, including Stuff Smith's "Here Comes the Man With the Jive" (which features some hot Jonah Jones trumpet), Trixie Smith's "Jack I'm Mellow," Barney Bigard's "Sweet Marijuana Brown" (which has Art Tatum on piano), Andy Kirk's "All the Jive Is Gone," and Harry "The Hipster" Gibson's classic "Who Put the Benzedrine in Mrs. Murphy's Ovaltine?" Other performers include Cab Calloway, Benny Goodman, Buster Bailey, Sidney Bechet, the Harlem Hamfats, Chick Webb, and Clarence Williams. Some of this material has since been reissued on CD but the original set is still the best. *—Scott Yanow*

Rhythm & Blues: 50's Blues & R&B / Mar. 3, 1999 / Westside ♦♦♦
The companion volume to Westside's delving into the vaults of Rhythm Records shines the spotlight on the bluesier side of the label's output. Kicking off with ten tracks by Little Willie Littlefield, the set also features vintage tracks from Roy Hawkins (the writer and original artist of B.B. King's "The Thrill Is Gone"), Sugar Pie DeSanto, Charles Walker, Roland Mitchell, and the cryptically named Paliya & Alvin. None of this falls under the category of hard blues, but it's all solidly played stuff with a distinct West Coast edge to it. One of the early West Coast R&B labels that deserves a wider hearing. *—Cub Koda*

Riot in Blues / Oct. 25, 1990 / Mobile Fidelity ♦♦♦♦♦
Excellent Lightnin' Hopkins, Sonny Terry, Brownie McGhee, James Wayne, and early Ray Charles scat singing. Partially field-recorded by Bob Shad in the early '50s. The best cuts include "Wayne's Junco Partner" and "Hopkins' Buck Dance Boogie." *—Barry Lee Pearson*

Risky Blues (R&B) / 1971 / King ♦♦♦♦♦
An old King LP boasting ribald early-'50s jump blues by Wynonie Harris, Bull Moose Jackson, etc. *—Bill Dahl*

Rolling Stone Presents: Blues / Feb. 5, 2002 / Rhino ♦♦
It's hard not to look at the ten songs that comprise *Rolling Stone Presents: Blues* and think that this is the reason why so many blues fans are disenchanted with the state of contemporary blues. This is what most modern listeners think of when they think of the blues—slick, stylized blues-rock, played either by veterans of the British Invasion or hippie chicks or boozy blooze bands or young virtuosos only interested in soloing. Apart from two classic cuts from Albert King and John Lee Hooker (actually, the latter isn't particularly well-known, it just dates from the '50s), that's what's here—a lot of glossy, bluesy arena rock. There are some good cuts here—the aforementioned King and Hook, plus Robert Cray's "Phone Booth," an early Fleetwood Mac cover of "Shake Your Moneymaker," Clapton's "Blues Before Sunrise" from 1994, the Fabulous Thunderbirds' sleek "Tuff Enuff"—but it's misleading to call this the blues, and the sad fact is many listeners (especially new converts to *Rolling Stone* magazine) do believe this is real blues, and it's unfortunate this disc perpetuates that falsehood. Especially since it contains "Bad to the Bone." *—Stephen Thomas Erlewine*

Rooster Blues Records: 1980–2000 Sampler / Apr. 11, 2000 / Rooster Blues ♦♦♦♦
Since 1980, Rooster Blues Records has released a slow but heartening trickle of solid, tough, uncompromising blues albums. Founded by a quartet of blues critics that included *Living Blues* founding editors Jim O'Neal and Amy van Singel, Rooster Blues was sold to Bottled MaJic Music in 1999, and this generous 19-track sampler serves as both a retrospective of the vaults as well as an introduction to the label's relative newcomers, such as D.C. Bellamy, Super Chikan, and "Philadelphia" Jerry Ricks. No other current blues label bridges the Chicago and Delta traditions better than Rooster, which has been swimming in indie credibility from the outset; rather than forge a "house" sound based on a few well-known blues artists, the label's operators hunted down the more obscure, under-recorded musicians who they felt deserved another shot in the studio. The results, as this compilation shows, were eclectic and often spectacular, ranging from the Delta blues finesse of Lonnie Pitchford to the juke joint strut of Roosevelt "Booba" Barnes to the West Side guitar antics of Eddy Clearwater. While the album's title suggests that all the songs were cut

over a 20-year interval, two of the tracks—Good Rockin' Charles' "Eyesight to the Blind" and Eddie C. Campbell's "King of the Jungle"—are actually pre-1980 recordings that were originally issued on Mr. Blues, a label that Rooster Blues acquired in 1981. For a single CD, you can't beat the amount of talent packed into this one. Rock stars didn't worship any of these players, but they are every bit as important to the blues as a Buddy Guy or Howlin' Wolf. *—Ken Chang*

Roots n' Blues: The Retrospective 1925–1950 / Jun. 30, 1992 / Columbia/Legacy ♦♦♦♦♦

Roots n' Blues: The Retrospective presents five hours of music over four discs, covering the traditional recordings made by Columbia Records and its associated labels from 1925 to 1950. As an all-inclusive survey of American roots music, this set is an invaluable library piece and a good reference, but where this collection really stands out is in its presentation. The collection does a better service than the more academic studies by including a variety of styles, including early string band recordings, spirituals, jug bands, blues, and Cajun and country music, mixing the better-known artists with the more obscure; in the end, the diversity makes for good listening as well as a good learning experience. *—Chris Woodstra*

The Roots of Rap: Classic Recordings from the 1920's and 30's / 1996 / Yazoo ♦♦♦♦

This ambitious and thought-provoking project turns to early black-and-white, religious, and secular traditions for antecedents to modern rap styles. Drawing from the commercial recordings of the '20s and '30s, *The Roots of Rap* provides a broad sampling of rural voices straddling the lines of speech and song against the rhythms of piano, banjo, and guitar. The roots of rap, this collection argues, existed in early black work songs and in the Southern pulpit; in the performances of singing street evangelists; and in black vocal traditions such as the "dozens." Early forms of rap emerged in the vaudeville routines of minstrel and medicine shows, arising also in the country humor and talking blues of many rural white performers. To illustrate its thesis, the album draws from some of the greatest performers of the period, including Blind Willie Johnson, Seven Foot Dilly, Butterbeans & Susie, and Memphis Minnie, whose extraordinarily funky "Frankie Jean" closes the set. Like the best of Yazoo's projects, this effort is carefully and intelligently constructed, as well as consistently entertaining. *—Burgin Mathews*

Roots of Rhythm & Blues: A Tribute to the Robert Johnson Era / Sep. 1, 1992 / Columbia/Legacy ♦♦♦♦♦

This live program featured some of the late legend's old partners—David "Honeyboy" Edwards, Johnny Shines, Robert Jr. Lockwood—and some of his contemporary successors such as Lionel Pitchford and Cephas & Wiggins paying heartfelt tribute. *—Bill Dahl*

☆ **Roots of Robert Johnson** / 1990 / Yazoo ♦♦♦♦♦

Robert Johnson's small body of recordings have become almost larger than life. Many novice listeners probably think the Delta blues began and ended with him. This 14-song collection traces the origins of Johnson's music, uncovering the roots of his tormented, anguished lyrics, and the origins of his wildly influential guitar style. Some of the finest songs by luminaries like Skip James, Charley Patton, Son House, Kokomo Arnold, and Lonnie Johnson are included. It's not only of use for Johnson archivists but for anyone interested in the greatest prewar Delta blues. *—Bruce Boyd Raeburn*

The Roots of Taj Mahal / Apr. 18, 2000 / Catfish ♦♦♦♦♦

An interesting concept to say the least, here's an exemplary collection of blues tunes all covered by Taj Mahal at one point or another. But here's the original versions of classics by Robert Johnson, Blind Willie Johnson, Blind Willie McTell, Leadbelly, Sleepy John Estes, Son House, Washboard Sam, Sonny Boy Williamson, and Blind Boy Fuller and they sound every bit as fine—if not infinitely superior—as Taj's later covers. If you want to know where it all really came from, here's a perfect starting point, and one hell of a blues collection bargain. *—Cub Koda*

Roots of the Blues / 1977 / New World ♦♦♦

This fine concept recording by Alan Lomax compares an American and a Senegalese (Africa) holler. It also includes elements of work songs, black string bands, church music, and other styles that fed into the blues before moving on to early blues styles themselves. The rarity of most of the cuts would make this a gem, even without Lomax's analysis. *—David L. Mayers*

The Rose Grew Round the Briar, Vol. 1: Early American Rural Love Songs / Jun. 17, 1997 / Yazoo ♦♦♦♦♦

Despite its "Early American Rural Love Songs" subtitle, Yazoo's *The Rose Grew Round the Briar* features at least as many false-hearted lovers and broken relationships as requited love affairs and happy romance. Indeed, the emotional power of so many of these recordings stems from entwined themes of love and death, illustrated by the ballad metaphor of the rose and the briar. The selections by Clarence Ashley and Dock Boggs are as stark depictions of forsaken, shaken, and demented lovers as the best pieces in those men's repertoires. Especially haunting are the eerie harmonies of the lesser-known Shortbuckle Roark & Family on "I Truly Understand That You Love Another Man"; subsequent covers of this song by the New Lost City Ramblers or Jerry Garcia & David Grisman have never been able to recapture the tone of the original. Another often-imitated recording included here is Grayson & Whitter's "Little Maggie With a Dram Glass in Her Hand," later translated into a bluegrass standard by the Stanley Brothers. While this collection delves deeply and unflinchingly into the darkest and lonesomest hollers of human relationships, love here is not exclusively somber or violent; it figures also, with equal emotion, into a smaller handful of breakdown pieces, and emerges with a warm beauty in Bascom Lamar Lunsford's "Lula Walls." Though white "country" performers dominate the compilation, there are a handful of blues performances by Blind Willie McTell, Cannon's Jug Stompers, Leroy Carr, and others, which nicely widen the scope and power of the project. In addition to showcasing some of the great talents of the '20s and '30s, this collection masterfully presents love in the tradition that 19th century Southern ballads and early-20th century blues characteristically cast it: as harsh, terrifying, deadly, beautiful, and profoundly real. *The Rose Grew Round the Briar* is consequently one of Yazoo's most effective collections and belongs in almost any collection. *—Burgin Mathews*

The Rose Grew Round the Briar, Vol. 2: Early American Rural Love Songs / Jun. 17, 1997 / Yazoo ♦♦♦♦♦

The folks at Yazoo have outdone themselves in two genres with this collection of love songs. This is a mixed blues and country release, except that it goes back to a point in the '20s and '30s when blues and country weren't always easy to distinguish from each other, so they fit together just fine. Solo bluesmen and white banjo pickers and fiddlers alternate—St. Louis-based bluesman Clifford Gibson deftly picks "Old Time Rider," followed by a rollicking duet of white Virginia fiddler B.F. Grayson and guitarist Henry Whitter whooping it up on "Handsome Molly," and a journey with a westward tilt, for Ephraim Woody & the Henpecked Husbands doing "Last Gold Dollar," and then a coarser, rougher solo blues lament ("Built Right on the Ground") from Teddy Darby. Among the major luminaries featured are Canadian cowboy singer Wilf Carter, aka Montana Slim, doing "You Are My Sunshine" and Lonnie Johnson, who turns up twice, playing piano (while Jelly Roll Anderson plays slide) behind Katherine Baker, the only woman privileged to appear here, whose mournful "My Man Left Me" leaves one asking for more, and then back on guitar with his brother James for the brooding, lusty "Baby Won't You Please Come Home." For guitar enthusiasts, the revelation of this album may be the work of Louis Lasky, an almost primordial Chicago bluesman, whose percussive guitar style and topical references make him unique for his era. The sound, except for Dock Boggs' "Lost Love," is generally very good, and the notes are nicely detailed. *—Bruce Eder*

The Rough Guide to Delta Blues / Jun. 4, 2002 / World Music Network ♦♦♦♦♦

A fantastic compilation that really does span the length of Mississippi Delta blues, from the early days of the Mississippi Sheiks and Charley Patton (with the classic "High Water Everywhere Pt. 1") through to the modern but equally rooted sounds of Asie Payton, R.L. Burnside, and the late Junior Kimbrough. And it's every bit as thorough in between, with all the big names (Robert Johnson [of course], Skip James, Son House, Muddy Waters, and many more) and some who are not so widely known, like Louise Johnson and Bo Carter. And it's not just the selection of artists that's astonishingly good and complete, but also the tracks picked, which have plenty of classics, as well as a real range of experience of the Delta blues. More than any other record that's attempted to convey the depth and breadth of the style, this succeeds in stunning fashion. It's the perfect primer to the roots of the blues as they stand, and while the tracks aren't arranged in any kind of chronological order, the feel that crosses time is consistent. This is absolute magic. *—Chris Nickson*

Ruff Stuff: Roots of Texas Blues Guitar / 1993 / Catfish ♦♦♦♦

This collection of Texas blues, 16 songs cut during the mid-'60s, features Mance Lipscomb and a brace of lesser-known Texas bluesmen born between 1895 and 1907 and, thus, heirs and successors to the likes of Blind Lemon Jefferson and other renowned Texas bluesmen of the '20s and '30s. Strangely, the notes refer to this collection as representing the "heart's blood of [those] anonymous Texas bluesmen who labored by day and played by night," but Lipscomb, at least, is far from anonymous today, mostly thanks to Arhoolie Records' recordings. What is sad is that the rest of the players here are genuinely obscure, but were clearly the equals of Lipscomb or any of his even more celebrated peers from Texas. Babe Stovall (whose nimble-fingered six-plus minute "Worried Blues" is a highlight of the album), Willie Minifee, Nathaniel "Bill" Barnes, T.J. Jackson, *et al.* all deserved better. The playing is mostly solo acoustic, although "Corrina Corrina" gets a solo electric treatment, as a sort of fragmentary instrumental. Other familiar songs given fresh renditions include "Jay Bird Blues" and "Jack O' Diamonds." And just for the record, there's little "ruff" here except the wonderfully spontaneous singing—the playing is as articulate and unselfconsciously beautiful as any acoustic blues you'll ever hear. *—Bruce Eder*

Rural Blues, Vol. 3 / Dec. 15, 1999 / BGO ♦♦♦♦

Originally issued on vinyl in the '70s, this set is even better on CD, featuring a treasure trove of rare and previously unissued sides from the vast EMI vaults. Big-ticket highlights include the Papa Lightfoot sides ("Jump the Boogie" is a major revelation), Boogie Bill Webb's chaotic "Boogie," and J.D. Edwards' "Playboy Blues" and "Hobo," both featuring massively distorted lead guitar work from Hop Wilson. Tracks from Lowell Fulson, Roosevelt Sykes, Manny Nichols, Country Jim Bledsoe, and Little Son Jackson complete this wonderful set. *—Cub Koda*

Sacred Steel Guitar / Jan. 21, 1997 / Arhoolie ♦♦♦♦

This is one amazing collection. Subtitled "Traditional Sacred African-American Steel Guitar Music in Florida," this multi-artist chronicling of this seldom-heard genre is a musical and emotional delight. The electric lap steel guitar has been the instrument of choice in both the Jewel Dominion and Keith Dominions (both African-American Holiness-Pentecostal churches) since the late '30s, replacing the traditional church organist. This collection showcases the pioneering work of five of its best known and most influential sacred steel practitioners: Willie Eason, Sonny Treadway, Glenn Lee, Henry Nelson, and his son, Aubrey Ghent. Their individual approaches to this style range from crude blues-based slides and slurs (blues table steel master Hop Wilson is called to mind more than once here) to highly technical flourishes bordering on country pedal steel sounds, with all of it played with a sincerity and spirit indigenous to the music, which is nothing short of heartfelt and energetic. Split evenly between instrumentals and the instrument interfacing with the congregation and choir at live religious services, the music runs the gamut from still and beautiful (Sonny Treadway's instrumentals) to the wild and abandoned playing of Aubrey Ghent. This is 75 minutes of music that will appeal to blues and gospel and even retro-minded rock & roll fans willing to take the time to explore this fascinating genre. —*Cub Koda*

St. Louis Blues (1929–1935) / Sep. 30, 1991 / Yazoo ✦✦✦
More fine prewar blues. —*Mark A. Humphrey*

Screaming Saxophones: Have a Ball / Swingtime ✦✦✦
Most of the tenor saxophonists do not actually scream on this LP, but there are plenty of honks, squeals, and roars during a variety of early R&B-ish performances. Such colorful players as Joe Houston, Charlie Singleton, Joe Thomas (one of his songs is called "Tearing Hair"), Morris Lane, Paul Bascomb, Bumps Myers, and baritonist Leo Parker are heard at their most exuberant. Accessible and frequently exciting music. —*Scott Yanow*

Shake Your Wicked Knees, Vol. 3: The Piano Blues / 1977 / Magpie ✦✦✦✦
This excellent collection is subtitled "Vocalion 1928-30," and that this label was able to record more than a dozen different and good blues and boogie-woogie pianists in the Chicago area over that time period means the Windy City's fabled long-winded music scene kept the company busy. The Vocalion archive has of course provided the raw material for many a blues compilation and reissue, so consumers may also find a later collection that shares the enticing command to *Shake Your Wicked Knees*, while featuring some of this material along with other selections by these artists and other members of the Vocalion stable. There are wonderful pianists here who will make amateurs feel as if their arms and hands were made out of pressboard. The titles themselves promise a good time, and deliver as well: "Fat Fanny Stomp" by Jim Clarke, "Head Rag Hop" by Romeo Nelson, and "Texas Shout" by Cow Cow Davenport are among the titles that are not nearly as exuberant as the music they identify. Other songs start with pronouncements of earthshaking importance—"I'm So Glad I'm Twenty-One Years Old Today," says Joe Dean From Bowling Green—and then takes the listener through the usual morbid blues thought process while the players manipulate the keys as if sorting through a basket of nuts. Most of the material is performed with solo piano, although there are a couple of tracks in which Tampa Red plays accompaniment or takes the lead with the fine piano work of Bill O'Bryant backing him up. The liner notes are unusually enjoyable. While texts such as this are normally the domain of gushing praise, with negative comments normally left for reviews, this particular album really smashes that mold. Listeners are informed that the final track, "Whoop and Holler Stomp" by Montana Taylor & the Jazoo Boys, has been sequenced in this way so that the listener can simply turn the record off and not suffer what writer Francis Smith indicates is a track that was only included for the quality of Taylor's playing. As for the Jazoo Boys, Smith describes the group as "abominable" and "wretched clowns," whose music is "inept and tuneless chanting." Bad music fanatics, the line forms to the rear. —*Eugene Chadbourne*

The Shouters / Savoy ✦✦✦
This two-LP collection features '40s and '50s jump blues from Gatemouth Moore, H-Bomb Ferguson, Eddie Mack, and Nappy Brown, whose scorching rockers are among the highlights of the set. —*Bill Dahl*

Shoutin', Swingin' & Makin' Love / Apr. 9, 1991 / MCA ✦✦✦✦✦
Chess Records has never been known for producing much in the way of big-band shouters or jump blues practitioners, but this compilation shows that the label at least dabbled in it from time to time. The Wynonie Harris date with Buddy Guy on guitar stems from 1964 and appears to be his final session. The Jimmy Rushing sides come from a 1953 date for Parrot Records, which Chess later took over. The Jimmy Witherspoon sides find him exploring the Willie Dixon catalog on "I Can Make It With You" and "Everything but You" while the Al Hibbler sides are master purchases from the Sunrise label, originally cut between 1947 and 1949. The remaining two sides feature an unknown vocalist (possibly Chick Young) with Tab Smith & His Orchestra, originally cut in 1951 for the Premium label, yet another master acquisition. —*Cub Koda*

Sinners and Saints (1926–1931) / Document ✦✦✦✦✦
Document's *Sinners and Saints (1926-1931)* presents the complete recorded works of nine artists and groups, whose combined repertoires and performance styles serve as a brief but fascinating lesson in the history of black music, expanding common conceptions of the musical continuum that created the blues. The CD presents minstrel and medicine show material, religious songs, two work songs, a few so-called "blues," and a bad man blues ballad, exhibiting a wide scope of black musical traditions dating back to the 19th century and still in circulation during the '20s and '30s. The performers not only represent a variety of genres, but demonstrate highly individualized styles that reflect their own personal aesthetics as much as any traditional form. The tones of their offerings range from the bizarre and the mirthful to the plaintive and deeply spiritual; the total effect of the album is hilarious, dark, and genuinely moving. Of the artists collected here, only Pink Anderson would record again after the '30s, producing three albums with his "rediscovery" in the '60s. Most of the performers on this compilation recorded two sides apiece, appearing in a studio for only one day of their lives; Freeman Stowers and the Pink Anderson-Simmie Dooley team have four tracks each, and the miraculous Nugrape Twins are blessed with six. Stowers performs two harmonica blues numbers, infusing one with a knockout, if grating, impersonation of a train, shrieking underneath the strains of his harp to simulate the roaring locomotive's whistle. In two other tracks, he abandons the instrument altogether for vocal imitations of animals, creating a surreal listening experience that is both terrifying and uproarious. If some of his impersonations, including a hog and a wildcat, are dead on the money, others of the inhabitants of his "Sunrise on the Farm" seem to have sprung out of the sideshows of hell. Taken together, Stowers' menagerie probably comprises some of the strangest six minutes ever recorded commercially.

"Beans" Hambone, accompanied by guitarist El Morrow, continues the surrealism of Stowers' "Sunrise" with an eerie comic song called "Beans," plunked out on an unusual

homemade guitar whose notes hypnotically punctuate the half-sung and half-spoken tale, in which a doctor writes prescriptions for beans, Biblical figures have gardens and arks full of beans, the singer dies from eating beans and is buried in beans, and his funeral is "preached...in beans, beans, beans." The six tracks by the Nugrape Twins (Matthew and Mark) are full of youthful energy, whether the twins are singing about the pleasures of heaven or of Nugrape Soda, or, at their most sublime, combining the two ("Way down yonder in the promised land, a-run and tell your mama, here's the Nugrape Man"). "I Got Your Ice Cold Nugrape" is their masterpiece, a simultaneous hymn and jingle that advertises the soda as a cure for any earthly or spiritual ailment; like all of their songs, it pits the two rural voices against a concert piano in a unique synthesis of styles. The twins are succeeded by the New Orleans songster Blind Roger Hays, whose two songs constitute the spiritual climax of the album. Hays' singing and playing are deceptively simple, reflecting a depth of emotion that transforms the sentimentality of his lyrics and tunes into deeply inspiring and soul-shaking work. Following Hays' "I Must Be Blind, I Cannot See" (a beautiful statement with a melody lifted from "Home Sweet Home"), the album concludes with the duets of Anderson and Dooley, whose quick fingerwork, raucous kazoo, and spirited vocals maintain the exuberance if not the spirituality of Hays' performances.

The performers assembled here recorded their few minutes of fame with a rich intensity, packing years and decades of experience—and ultimately disappearing—into the narrow circumference of a 78 record. Each artist in this well-crafted set presents his own model of rejuvenation and deliverance, whether grounded in the promise of heaven; the sound of a passenger train; the flavor of an ice-cold Nugrape; or the pleasures of stronger drink, sex, and dance—of "tipping out tonight" and "strutting his stuff." With brief notes by blues writer Paul Oliver, the album is as entertaining and educational as the best of Document's CDs. It is doubly commendable for illustrating the breadth of traditions captured on "race records," while also showcasing the talents of the lesser-known patron saints of the business. Highly recommended. —*Burgin Mathews*

Sissy Man Blues: Straight & Gay Blues / 1989 / Vintage Jazz ✦✦✦
Sexuality remains arguably America's most controversial subject, even more than race, religion, or politics. That will explain why many of the songs spotlighted on this 25-cut anthology haven't gotten widespread exposure. Not even an idiom like jazz, reputed for its loose, liberal nature, is free from homophobic strains, so it stands to reason that not everyone would want to hear such works as the title cut or "Freakish Man Blues" by George Hannah and Meade "Lux" Lewis. There are some numbers that are simply double-entendre pieces rather than gay treatises, but their inclusion doesn't detract from the eye-opening nature of such songs as "Two Old Maids in a Folding Bed" or "Fairy Blues." —*Ron Wynn*

Sizzling the Blues / Mar. 5, 1927-Dec. 15, 1929 / Frog ✦✦✦✦✦
Relatively little music was recorded in New Orleans during the '20s and what does exist was due to "field trips" taken by staff members of Victor, Columbia, Brunswick, and OKeh. This valuable CD (released by a small British label) features a set by Louis Dumaine's Jazzola Eight, both instrumentally and backing singers Genevieve Davis and Ann Cook. In addition, there are excellent overlapping groups headed by pianist Johnnie Miller and drummer Monk Hazel that feature trumpeter Sharkey Bonano and clarinetist Sidney Arodin and are inspired a bit by the New Orleans Rhythm Kings. However the main reason to pick up this disc is to acquire the four songs (plus two alternate takes) performed by the Jones-Collins Astoria Hot Eight, a legendary band featuring trumpeter Lee Collins in 1920 that ranks with the hottest groups of the period. This CD is easily recommended to fans of '20s jazz. —*Scott Yanow*

Slide Guitar Blues / Nov. 7, 1995 / Priority ✦✦✦
Slide Guitar Blues overlooks some major slide players, such as Hound Dog Taylor, J.B. Hutto, Muddy Waters, Earl Hooker, Robert Nighthawk, Bonnie Raitt, Ry Cooder, and Duane Allman, but it nevertheless is a good sampler of slide blues. There are a few classics from the likes of Elmore James and Homesick James, but for the most part the collection concentrates on modern electric blues, both for better and for worse. For better because it offers a taste of such players as Johnny Winter, Sonny Landreth, Larry Burton, and Bleu Jackson. For worse because it doesn't draw an accurate portrait of the genre's great instrumentalists. Nevertheless, the disc offers a lot of good music and for some curious listeners, it may spark interest in slide guitar. —*Stephen Thomas Erlewine*

Slide Guitar Gospel (1944–1964) / May 1, 1995 / Document ✦✦✦✦✦
This features striking fretwork by Rev. Utah Smith and the great Rev. Lonnie Farris. —*Opal Louis Nations*

The Slide Guitar: Bottles, Knives & Steel, Vol. 1 / Feb. 1991 / Columbia/Legacy ✦✦✦✦✦
This CD is a hodgepodge sampling of blues records featuring mostly prewar slide guitarists ranging from the simplicity of Barbecue Bob (who was much better known as a pianist) and Sylvester Weaver to the sophistication of Blind Willie McTell (backing Ruth Willis on "Experience Blues") and Tampa Red. Among the highlights are Blind Willie Johnson's wordless "Dark Was the Night" and Tampa Red's good-time "You Can't Get That Stuff No More," and also featured are Charley Patton, Blind Boy Fuller, Leadbelly, Casey Bill Weldon, Buddy Woods, Robert Johnson, Bukka White, Sister O.M. Terrell, and Son House. With the exception of two later cuts, all of the music (which includes a pair of previously unreleased selections) dates from 1927-1940. An interesting if not quite essential sampler. —*Scott Yanow*

The Slide Guitar: Bottles, Knives & Steel, Vol. 2 / Feb. 1991 / Columbia ✦✦✦
This is another excellent volume of various styles of blues slide guitar from Columbia's *Roots n' Blues* series. —*AMG*

Slidin' . . . Some Slide / 1948-1993 / Rounder ✦✦✦
Rounder's recent anthology of vintage and modern slide guitar playing is neither a disposable batch of recent hits nor merely a showcase for guitar freaks; it is a wonderful collection documenting the way bottleneck and slide styles have evolved. The sampler contains classics from Muddy Waters, Elmore James, Earl Hooker, J.B. Hutto, Hop Wilson, and Hound Dog Taylor that are either transcendent or delightful. They have also chosen songs from contemporary acts that demonstrate real craft and appreciation for the style; George Thorogood's nearly eight-minute workout on "Delaware Slide" and Sonny Landreth's "Zydeco Shuffle" are grinding, stunning treatments. This is one sampler with real musical and historical value. *—Ron Wynn*

Smackin' That Wax: the Kangaroo Records Story . . . / Nov. 30, 1992 / Collectables ✦✦✦✦✦
Obscure but solid '50s and '60s Texas blues and R&B, it includes a very early Albert Collins single. *—Bill Dahl*

The Songs of Willie Dixon / Aug. 24, 1999 / Telarc ✦✦✦
The Songs of Willie Dixon finds a number of mostly contemporary blues practitioners paying tribute to the legendary composer/bassist. Of course, it isn't difficult to pick quality material out of Dixon's catalog, so the collection will sink or swim with the performances. And, for the most part, they're pretty good, with some interesting, modern recastings of the original arrangements. Although there are some misfires, it isn't for lack of commitment, falling more into the valiant-attempt category; plus, the vast majority of the songs are successful. Some of the highlights are provided by Clarence "Gatemouth" Brown, Tab Benoit, Kenny Neal, Eddie Shaw, and Deborah Coleman. *—Steve Huey*

The Songster Tradition: Complete Works (1927–1935) / 1991 / Document ✦✦✦✦
Part of Document's very extensive reissuance of virtually all the prewar blues recordings, this CD has the complete works of six different songsters. The word "songster" is meant to describe a performer who was mostly self-sufficient, spending his life performing music (much of which predated blues) in the South for whoever wanted to hear him. Included on this CD of rarities are Papa Harvey Hull and Long Cleve Reed's Down Home Boys for six selections, Big Boy Cleveland's only two numbers (one on guitar and the other on an odd flute called the quill), guitarist/singer Eli Framer during his only two selections, Louie Lasky from 1935 (a couple of blues and a fine previously unreleased rendition of "Caroline"), the religious-oriented and rhythmic William and Versey Smith (they have four songs), and Luke Jordan. Jordan, the best known of these musicians, steals the show on six selections (plus two "new" alternate takes), which include "Church Bells Blues," "Pick Poor Robin Clean," and "Cocaine Blues." All of the singers are at a decent level and made the most of their only opportunities to be documented. Well worth exploring by vintage American music collectors. *—Scott Yanow*

Sorry but I Can't Take You: Women's Railroad Blues / Jan. 1981 / Rosetta ✦✦✦✦✦
Hats off to Rosetta Reitz for putting together an incredible catalog of women's classic blues on her Rosetta label. Besides filling a glaring gap in the blues record bins, the label's various compilations and single-artist discs feature both well-known and obscure female blues singers, bringing to life a black woman's take on a world defined in many ways by the great migration of Southern blacks to northern cities like Chicago and New York (mainly to escape draconian Jim Crow laws and find better paying jobs). Primarily covering the '20s and '30s, this fine collection in the label's *Women's Heritage* series chronicles the plight of women left behind as thousands of husbands "rode the blinds" north. While these New York and Chicago-recorded sides reveal that many of the singers here had some means to make the train fares, most Southern black women were too poor to come up with the money or not generally willing to risk death jumping a freight. Beautifully illustrating the split between the obvious attraction to railroad lore and the anguish of denial, the narrative of Clara Smith's "Freight Train Blues" switches from an impressionistic chronicle of boxcars and brakemen to the harsh reality of a woman crying alone back home when her man beats the blues by catching a train. And while most of the songs here, including Trixie Smith's "Choo Choo Blues" and Blue Lou Barker's "He Caught That B&O," mirror similar sentiments, one also hears Martha Copeland's chronicle of a Southern woman's desire to escape the chill of the north and return to Alabama and her man, as well as Sister Rosetta Tharpe's mythical casting of the train as a means to heaven. Beyond sociological concerns, this collection contains some of the most enjoyable blues on record, taking in the work of stars like Bessie Smith and Sippie Wallace along with tracks by less well-known, but equally impressive, singers like Nora Lee King and Bessie Jackson. The album's cast of jazz musicians (the standard support for these and other classic blues divas) is superb as well, and includes Louis Armstrong, Sidney Bechet, Don Redman, Henry "Red" Allen, and Dizzy Gillespie. From voice to horn and gruff to sweet, this essential collection reveals a rich world of blues expression often overlooked. *—Stephen Cook*

The Soul of Chicago / 1993 / Shanachie ✦✦✦✦
Distinguished gospel music critic, author, producer, and label executive Anthony Heilbut has provided many wonderful anthologies. For this one, he has taken 11 surviving artists from the golden age and recorded them in a traditional setting with their familiar spare backings (mostly piano, guitar and organ). The results are both impressive and memorable; Robert Anderson, Delois Barrett Campbell, Rev. Samuel Patterson, Gladys Beamon Gregory, and the Gay Sisters, among others, don't just sound good, but almost as fabulous as they did in their heyday. They have the spirit just as if they were performing and recording all the time, yet many of them have not sung regularly in decades. The quality of this masterful session blows most contemporary gospel out of the water. *—Ron Wynn*

The Soul of Texas Blues Women: Good 'Ol Texas 60s Soul and Blues / 1991 / Collectables ✦✦✦
This very interesting although uneven collection includes female blues and soul vocalists recorded between 1961 and 1970. *—Niles J. Frantz*

● **The Sound of the Delta** / Jun. 1966 / Testament ✦✦✦✦✦
Blues scholar Pete Welding assembled these 19 recordings—most solo, all acoustic, most prominently featuring guitar and vocal—between 1963 and 1965, just as the blues revival was gathering steam. This isn't the best Delta blues compilation, as an introduction or a general sampler. If you can't get enough of the stuff, though, it certainly stands up well. Big Joe Williams and Fred McDowell are the only well-known performers, but the others—obscure names like Arthur Weston and the delightfully raw-voiced Ruby McCoy—are generally in the same league. It's well-recorded, and contains a reasonable variety of styles. The CD reissue adds bonus tracks by Williams and Avery Brady that were not included on the original version. *—Richie Unterberger*

☆ **Sounds of the South** / Jul. 20, 1993 / Atlantic ✦✦✦✦✦
This compilation gathers some of the finest of musicologist Alan Lomax's field recordings together on four CDs. What is preserved are examples of American music not broadly documented: field hollers and folk tales, prison work songs and hardcore banjo breakdowns. This is an important collection that offers rewards for every kind of music lover. *—Tim Sheridan*

Southern Journey, Vol. 3: 61 Highway Mississippi / Apr. 22, 1997 / Rounder ✦✦✦✦✦
Here are 24 tracks from Alan Lomax's 1959 blues recordings in Mississippi, five previously unreleased. Fred McDowell (who has five songs) is the "star," you might say, of these sessions; he would go on to establish a successful performing and recording career, and is the only name recognizable to most listeners. This is an effective document, however, of the different strands of country blues and their roots. It includes not just rural Delta guitar blues, but also field hollers, spirituals, prison songs, fife-and-drum tunes, and Sid Hemphill's quills. Lomax would later note that when he revisited the area 20 years later, most of these forms had all but disappeared from view. This disc is a good reminder of how blues developed from several African-American Southern folk traditions whose influence has sometimes been underestimated. *—Richie Unterberger*

Southern Rhythm 'n' Rock: The Best of Excello Records, Vol. 2 / Rhino ✦✦✦
Southern Rhythm 'n' Rock: The Best of Excello Records, Vol. 2 is the second volume of the Excello Records collection, with its companion *Sound of the Swamp*. This volume rounds up some wild and woolly R&B obscurities. *—John Floyd*

St. Louis Country Blues, 1929–1937 / Jan. 10, 1996 / Document ✦✦✦✦✦
Three superior country blues vocalists/guitarists have all of their recordings as leaders reissued on this CD, with the exception of a few undiscovered titles and Henry Townsend's postwar sessions. Nothing much is known about Henry Spaulding, who just cut two titles in 1929, but his solo performances are excellent and haunting. Jaydee Short led three solo sessions during 1930-1933 (one under the pseudonym of Joe Stone) and is another mystery figure. Townsend, who is heard on 15 performances from 1929-1937 (with support here and there by guitarists Clifford Gibson and Robert Lee McCoy, Sonny Boy Williamson on harmonica, and pianist Roosevelt Sykes), is a legendary blues pioneer. Although all three of the leaders were based in St. Louis, their recordings were actually made in Chicago, Louisville, Aurora (IL), Grafton (WI), and New York City. Vintage blues collectors will definitely want this set. *—Scott Yanow*

The Stax Blues Brothers / 1970 / Stax ✦✦✦✦✦
Although Stax is always thought of as a soul label, there was some blues recordings of merit that emanated from the label, with Albert King spearheading the charge. This 12-track set rounds up some of the more notable suspects. King is on here three times, with his own "Cold Sweat" and "Drownin' on Dry Land" and in a trio setting with Steve Cropper and Pops Staple on "Tupelo." There's also a pair each from Jimmy McCracklin and Johnnie Taylor, and representative tracks from Pops Staples, Little Milton, John Lee Hooker, Little Sonny, and the mysterious Mighty Joe Hicks. An interesting, seldom-explored side of this well-known label. *—Cub Koda*

Stax Blues Masters: Blue Monday / Jul. 1, 1991 / Stax ✦✦✦
Stax was never *really* a blues label in the strictest sense of the term, but with artists like Albert King, Little Sonny, Freddie Robinson, and Little Milton, they at least had a presence in the field. This 11-track budget set features tunes from all four of these artists, offering a nice sampling of the blues filtered through the Memphis Stax/Volt sound. *—Cub Koda*

Stax: Superblues, Vol. 2: All-Time Classic Blues Hits / 1991 / Stax ✦✦✦✦✦
More soul and R&B influences are heard on this volume than the first, though it's not a detriment. The 18 tracks include prize items by Guitar Slim, Lloyd Price, Lowell Fulson, Elmore James, and Sonny Boy Williamson, with some bluesy Southern soul by O.V. Wright and Johnnie Taylor. It also has some little-anthologized gems, most notably Gene Allison's "You Can Make It if You Try" (covered by the Rolling Stones on their first album) and Jimmy Hughes' magnificent bluesy soul ballad, "Steal Away." *—Richie Unterberger*

Stax: Superblues, Vol. 3: All-Time Classic Blues Hits / 1995 / Stax ✦✦✦✦✦
What all these vintage blues recordings are doing under the Stax banner is a mystery, but just be thankful that they're here because they amount to a well-chosen batch of obscure classics. There are a lot of tunes aboard that simply don't make the rounds on these type of compilations usually; it's a real joy to hear unknown delights like Frankie Lee Sims' "Lucy Mae Blues," Billy Boy Arnold's "I Wish You Would," Jimmy Reed's rare "I Found My Baby," Eddie Taylor's "Big Town Playboy," Guitar Gable's "Irene," and Larry Birdsong's "Pleadin' for Love." Another surprise bonus is the production foul-up on Little Walter's "Last Night," inserting the alternate take for the hit version. Tracks from Elmore James,

Jimmy Liggins, Camille Howard, Piano Red, Mercy Dee Walton, Larry Davis, Joe Morris with Laurie Tate, Ted Taylor, Little Johnny Taylor, and Little Milton round out the set. *—Cub Koda*

Steeped in the Blues Tradition / Apr. 1996 / Rykodisc ♦♦♦
Steeped in the Blues Tradition is a notable budget compilation of pre- and postwar acoustic blues—a much more varied sampler of Tradition's blues catalog than the three-CD set *Best of Blues Tradition, Vol. 1.* While there might seem to be a lot of overly familiar blues fare here ("See See Rider," "Good Morning Little Schoolgirl," "Baby Please Don't Go"), when it's played by the likes of Lightnin' Hopkins, Mississippi Fred McDowell, and Big Bill Broonzy, it's as good as original. Compilation producer Anton Glovsky makes sure to include a handful of celebrated blues revival moments, such as performances by Hopkins, Sonny Terry, Brownie McGhee, and Big Joe Williams at the Ash Grove in the early '60s, as well as the jaw-dropping 1960 studio session that united this fantastic foursome on "Blues for Gamblers" (aka "Three Aces on the Bottom of the Deal"). Meanwhile, the prewar material pays homage to Leadbelly, Josh White, and Blind Lemon Jefferson. Overall, the only letdown—and a minor one at that—is that Lightnin' Hopkins' introduction to "Big Car Blues" was brutally edited down for no apparent reason. (For the full story of how his black Cadillac got stolen, check out the version on *Blues Hoot.*) *—Ken Chang*

Still on Target: The First Five Years / 1995 / Pointblank ♦♦♦
Still on Target: First Five Years chronicles the beginnings of Pointblank Records, one of the most popular blues record labels of the early '90s. Pointblank's roster includes veterans like Albert Collins, Isaac Hayes, and Johnny Winter, as well as newer artists like Terrell, Duke Robillard, and the Kinsey Report. All of those artists, and a handful of others, contribute a track to *Still on Target*, making it an effective introduction to the label, as well as a good representation of the state of the genre in the early '90s. *—Stephen Thomas Erlewine*

Stone Rock Blues / 1994 / Chess ♦♦♦
"The original recordings of songs covered by the Rolling Stones" is understandably heavy on the blues, R&B, and early rock & roll chestnuts they gleaned from Chess Records. Chuck Berry and Muddy Waters are, unsurprisingly, the most heavily represented artists here; seven Chuck tunes, five by Muddy (one of which, "Rollin' Stone," wasn't actually recorded by the Stones, but is included because it inspired their name). This 18-song collection is filled out by a couple of Bo Diddley tracks, Howlin' Wolf's "Little Red Rooster," and three songs outside of Chess' black music axis: Dale Hawkins' rockabilly classic "Suzie Q," Buddy Holly's "Not Fade Away" (which of course relied heavily on the Bo Diddley beat), and Arthur Alexander's early soul ballad "You Better Move On." What this collection doesn't have are the early soul classics by Otis Redding, Sam Cooke, Wilson Pickett, Marvin Gaye, and more obscure singers like Barbara Lynn and Gene Allison that formed another vital component of their early cover material. It's missing a few stray tracks by Slim Harpo, Rufus Thomas, Hank Snow, Larry Williams, and others that were covered by the Stones on their early albums. And it doesn't have Berry's "Let It Rock," which was available (albeit briefly) on a British maxi-single in the early '70s. But Chuck, Muddy, and Bo were their greatest influences, when you get down to it, and this is a handy basic primer of the blueprints for the Stones' early repertoire, with decent liner notes. *—Richie Unterberger*

★ **Storefront & Streetcorner Gospel (1927–1929)** / Jun. 2, 1994 / Document ♦♦♦♦♦
Assembling the complete recorded works of A.C. & Blind Mamie Forehand, Washington Phillips, and Luther Magby, *Storefront & Streetcorner Gospel (1927-1929)* offers a fascinating glimpse into the kind of spiritual music commonly heard throughout the urban areas of the south during the last years of the pre-Depression era. The common thread among these performers is their choice of unusual accompaniment—the Dallas-based Phillips is backed by the dolceola, an ethereal variant of the dulcimer, while the Forehands employ antique cymbals and Magby uses a harmonium; little or nothing is known about the various artists, yet their music still packs a punch all these decades later. *—Jason Ankeny*

The Story of the Blues / Jan. 1, 1995 / Columbia ♦♦♦
When writer and blues scholar Paul Oliver first came along, the genre he specialized in was something of a mystery to the music audience. Young listeners hearing the Rolling Stones do an old Delta blues number on the group's very first record usually thought this was some kind of original concept, not a tribute to a great African-American art form which at that point had been languishing in obscurity. The growing popularity and staying power that has accompanied the blues into the millennium has of course brought with it enormous amounts of additional research and the release of old and new blues material on what can only be considered a massive scale. The work of Oliver has certainly lost much of what used to make it exclusive. Fans no longer have to turn to his productions or books out of desperation. This double-album set may have been one of the best blues compilations available at one point, but that was only because that particular bin was almost completely empty. With so much other material subsequently available, consumers are free to look at this set with a sneer forming on their lips that may rival that of Mick Jagger. Of course there is nothing wrong with any of the 32 tracks that are included; it is all perfectly good music and some of it is downright brilliant. The rating above, then, is for the music performances. Judged purely as a historical document, this set has severe problems and should be rated much lower. The problem was that Oliver had come to his own conclusions about blues history and used whatever tracks he had access to contractually to try to shore up these points. For the most part, the seasoned blues listener would see this set not as a thorough history but as a collection of country blues tracks, although there are short excursions into the area of classic female blues singers such as Bessie Smith and a slight nod toward the electric urban blues sound. Oliver himself was much less fond of the latter development in blues than he was the work of solo acoustic artists, which, combined with problems licensing material, makes his urban blues section more like a trip to the suburbs. There is no Muddy Waters, for example, just a track with some of his backup players.

Trouble starts immediately with the very first piece on the album, an untitled performance recorded in Ghana in 1964. That the blues "came from Africa" was always one of this writer's preoccupations. Nobody will argue that the ancestors of the people who played the blues came from Africa, or that close study of African music will result in finding the occasional track with something of a bluesy sound, especially if one hunts for mystical connections to the one-chord grooves of John Lee Hooker. Yet in terms of really understanding different forms of music, the reality is that the incredibly diverse world of African music and American blues are extremely different things. The aspects the two music worlds have in common are components of musical style and construction that occur with equal regularity in many other kinds of music. There are sections of Mozart that use what can be considered blues chord progressions, any one of which could have replaced this African track as "proof" that the blues came from Austria. No, this track is included just the way it would be in a hack college music course, so it looks like someone has done some research. One track of African music doesn't prove or contribute anything positive to the musical flow of the tracks. Presenting a performance that was recorded in the mid-'60s as evidence of influence over music from the '20s is also ridiculous, unless one is plotting a science fiction film. An unaccompanied field holler would have made more historical sense. As the actual performances of blues begin with a 1928 cut by Mississippi John Hurt, the listener is presented for the next three sides with an extended series of country blues performances, with a dollop of classic jazz and blues in the center. Each side has a different theme. The third side is entitled "The '30s: Urban and Rural Blues," but doesn't have a single track that would be considered urban blues by any stretch of the imagination. Memphis Minnie, performing in duo with guitarist Little Son Joe, is the only thing that even comes close. As is typical with Oliver's sloppy documentation, it wasn't even recorded in the '30s. Most of the tracks on this side would fit just as easily on the first side, which is called "The Origin of the Blues." In fact, many blues fans would put the work of artists such as Bukka White and Robert Johnson, classified here as "urban and rural blues," as much closer to African music than the playing of Mississippi John Hurt, whose fingerpicking tunes sometimes don't even use blues progressions.

The tracks on the final side are identified as "World War II and After," but as Walter Mondale said to Ronald Reagan, "Here we go again." Two of these eight tracks were recorded well before World War II and are among the three songs here that once again are country blues and nothing more. Presenting artists such as Blind Boy Fuller and Sonny Terry as representing some kind of postwar modern blues sound is ludicrous. The Big Joe Williams track—and Oliver misidentifies him as Joe Williams, creating confusion with the Count Basie ballad singer and defying the unwritten law of using an artist's "Big" nickname at all times—is an excellent example of country blues developing into urban blues with the addition of a light drum sound. Instead, Oliver chooses it as an example of a modern blues sound, which it is not. The three tracks from the '60s that close out the set are fine music, but add to the confusion. Why nothing from the '50s, a heyday of urban blues recordings? One assumes this was a problem of licenses, but a writer attempting a historical overview could have at least mentioned such hassles. The final track is a late-'60s recording by Johnny Shines, and Oliver completely misses the train in his prediction that this artist, newly rediscovered and back in the studio as a result of the '60s resurgence in blues interest, would wind up mostly playing for the amusement of his friends. Oliver is like a shopkeeper who comes to work in the morning and finds the contents of his business have been turned upside down. He frantically tries to clean up, but the place is still a mess when the doors open. Nonetheless, the material here is fine, some is downright classic, and all will make enjoyable listening no matter what order it is presented in. Unless one wants to reach a state of confusion about blues history, skipping the liner notes and ignoring the subheadings and other so-called "information" is advised. Changing the programming so that it is at least chronological and replacing the African piece with another blues track would be big improvements. *—Eugene Chadbourne*

Straight and Gay / Dec. 10, 1924-Jun. 30, 1941 / Stash ♦♦♦
The Stash label had, by the release of this LP in 1979, almost totally exhuasted its collection of vintage recordings dealing with the subject matters of drug and sex. However with titles such as "Anybody Here Want to Try My Cabbage" (featuring singer Maggie Jones accompanied by Louis Armstrong), "Take Your Hand Off It," "Sissy Man," and "Two Old Maids in a Folding Bed," there were obviously still a few fiery titles left to be reissued. Highlights include Sippie Wallace's famous "I'm a Mighty Tight Woman" and Victoria Spivey's initial recording "Black Snake Blues"; the other important performers are Lonnie Johnson, Lil Johnson, Washboard Sam, Mae Glover, Blanche Calloway, the Hokum Boys, Papa Charlie Jackson, Josh White, Ma Rainey (with Doc Cheatham on soprano in 1926), Monette Moore, Blind Willie McTell, and Lucille Bogan. *—Scott Yanow*

Streetwalking Blues / Dec. 9, 1924-1956 / Stash ♦♦♦
One of many Stash LPs that reissued vintage recordings dealing with sexual topics, this album has performances by many fine blues and jazz singers including Memphis Minnie, Maggie Jones ("Good Time Flat Blues" with Louis Armstrong), Virginia Liston, Lil Johnson, Sam Theard, Billie Pierce (from 1956), Clarence Williams, Lonnie Johnson (1941's "Crowin' Rooster Blues"), Georgia White, Ma Rainey, Clara Smith, Irene Scruggs, Bertha "Chippie" Hill and Lucille Bogan. With titles such as "I've Got What It Takes," "I'm in the Racket," "Kitchen Mechanic Blues," and "Shave 'Em Dry," one gets the idea what this album is about pretty quickly. Most of these formerly rare performances (some of which have been reissued by Stash on their Jass subsidiary) are quite enjoyable. *—Scott Yanow*

String Bands (1926–1929) / Jun. 2, 1994 / Document ♦♦♦♦
String Bands (1926-1929) has a few remarkable tracks: the hilarious, warbling vocals on the Kansas City Blues Strummers' "Broken Bed Blues" and a very rare cello solo on the

Old Pal Smoke Shop Four's "Black Cat Blues" will single-handedly justify the purchase for some enthusiasts. The album is most recommended, however, for the light it sheds on the intersecting traditions of black-and-white rural musical styles in the early age of recording. Andrew and Jim Baxter, a fiddle-guitar duo from Georgia, demonstrate equal virtuosity at blues and country dance styles and are, deservedly, the best-known performers on the disc; Nap Hayes and Matthew Prater fuse Scott Joplin's ragtime with more traditional, country styles on their mandolin-guitar duets. Most interestingly, the compilation includes two racially integrated groups, a phenomenon otherwise absent in the '20s recording industry: fiddler Andrew Baxter joins the otherwise all-white Georgia Yellowhammers on "G Blues," and Jim Booker, another black fiddler, joins Taylor's Kentucky Boys for four standard dance pieces, including "Soldier's Joy" and "Grey Eagle." The four tracks by the Alabama Sheiks that conclude the album—recorded, despite the title of this collection, in 1931—are fair duets by another guitar-fiddle duo obviously influenced by the great Mississippi Sheiks, whose "Sittin' on Top of the World" they imitate reasonably well. Although not highly recommended for casual listeners, this collection will be of great interest to many and provides a welcomed expansion of modern understandings of string band music. *—Burgin Mathews*

String Ragtime: To Do This You Got to Know How / 1974 / Yazoo ✦✦✦✦
In 1974, the Yazoo label put out this superb compilation, apparently in an attempt to be viewed as something other than just a pure country blues label. The theme here was "ragtime," but as the character known as "promotion director" in the liner notes' mock interview puts it, "Look, it's all just semantics." Yes, the word "ragtime" is in practically every title, but the overall impression left by this collection of 14 tracks by different artists is of an overwhelming mix of styles in which the only common factors are extreme creativity, technical prowess, and the use of stringed instruments. Even in the latter regard it is an unusual collection, as it includes one of the only recordings of ragtime ever made on the harp, Robert Maxwell's "Spaghetti Rag." There is also "Sweet Georgia Brown" played Hawaiian style on slide ukuleles, a track by influential old-time string band leader John Dilleshaw, a performance of "Russian Rag" by Dave Appolon that utilizes a quote from Rachmaninoff, a mandolin arrangement based on some Scott Joplin themes—and a whole lot more. This is an album that simply bubbles over with ideas and inspiration. The themes the artists start with are difficult enough, yet on practically every track the actual performances go way beyond even that, turning the challenging music into personal statements ranging from hilariously kooky to extremely moving. An excellent job has been done on the selection and sequencing—it can truly be said that there are no flabby moments. Only Lonnie Johnson, who contributes a stunning performance of the album's title track, is a performer whose name is fairly well-known in blues circles. The listener will no doubt be inspired into trying to locate other material by these somewhat more obscure performers—not always an easy task, but worthwhile. Yazoo could have provided more information about these artists, not only for further research but for the sake of enjoying the album itself. The bogus conversation that takes up the entire back cover does include a few snippets of information about the performers, but is also packed with in-jokes and asides that only people who work for the company would probably enjoy, as well as some truly stupid remarks. "It's not as old-fashioned as you think," the promotion director says about this music and the Yazoo line in general, "We have the far-out cartoonist Robert Crumb on our sister label... doing the same kind of material." Crumb would be the first to describe this music as old-fashioned; in fact, with him that was the whole point—escaping the noxious reality of modern music. For the sake of this nonsense, instrumental and writing credits were apparently sacrificed. *—Eugene Chadbourne*

Sun Records Harmonica Classics / 1990 / Rounder ✦✦✦✦✦
Brilliant compilation of Blues sides cut at the Sun studios in the early '50s, featuring indispensable tracks by Big Walter Horton ("Easy" being one of the greatest harmonica instrumentals of all time), Joe Hill Louis, and Doctor Ross. *—Cub Koda*

Sun Records: 25 Blues Classics / Aug. 28, 2001 / Varese ✦✦✦✦✦
While it inevitably shares certain material with Rhino's similarly themed 1990 *Blue Flames: Sun Blues Collection*, this 2001 edition on Varese presents a generous 25 tracks (compared with Rhino's relatively meager 18) and digs deeper into the Sun vaults for its material. Since only five tunes are duplicated from the earlier release, it actually makes a perfect companion piece, as this chooses different songs from some of the same artists, as well as uncovers a few true obscurities. As most roots music fans know, Memphis and Sun Studios in particular were a hotbed of blues, as well as the birthing place for rock & roll as we know it. B.B. King, Howlin' Wolf, Little Milton, James Cotton, and Little Junior Parker all began their careers there. This music influenced nascent rockers like Elvis, Charlie Rich, and Jerry Lee Lewis to incorporate the bluesmen's sounds, and even songs, into their own repertoires. The collection skips over both Wolf and King (whose tracks are easily available elsewhere) in favor of many rarities, some making their debut appearance on CD. Four tracks from Pinetop Perkins, Joe Hill Louis, Earl Hooker (the first version of his "The Hucklebuck"), and Guitar Red are previously unreleased. The majority of the selections date from 1953-1955, with two from 1952, one from 1956, and one (Frank Frost's classic "Jelly Roll King") from 1962. The remastering is clean and crisp throughout, and although the sound is naturally a little thin, the music is so full of life and excitement that you ignore the sonics and just get lost in the groove. Less Delta and more upbeat than most traditional blues, this is music for dancing and partying. Predating John Lee Hooker's work, Doctor Ross' "Boogie Disease," and Little Junior Parker's "Feelin' Good" are virtual blueprints for what would later be associated with Hooker's trademarked sound. Lost artists like Eddie Snow and Guitar Red and a long forgotten track from Mr. Red Hot, Billy "The Kid" Emerson, are unearthed, but everything here is of remarkable quality. Even when the songs are simple retreads of blues themes, the artists inject so much enthusiasm into their performances that they become near classics. Six pages of liner notes from Bill Dahl help fill in the blanks and provide fascinating background material giving a detailed look into some of these relatively obscure tracks. It's not the final word on Sun's blues catalog, but this was the best single-disc exploration of this vital period in American music as of 2001, and is an essential addition to any blues lover's collection. *—Hal Horowitz*

Sun Records: The Blues Years / Charly ✦✦✦✦✦
A gigantic nine-record box with a 44-page booklet, this comes the closest to documenting the wide breadth of blues recordings done by Sam Phillips at the Sun studios in Memphis during the early '50s. A landmark achievement. *—Cub Koda*

Sweet Home Chicago / Nov. 1988 / Delmark ✦✦✦✦✦
This features solid '60s sides by Magic Sam, Eddie Shaw, Luther Allison, and Louis Myers. *—Bill Dahl*

Talkin' Trash / 1990 / Greasy ✦✦✦
Here is a very obscure R&B compilation with great irreverent jump and jivey blues from 1954-1963. The title cut is worth the price, but check out "Your Wire's Been Tapped" and "Roll Dem Bones." *—Richard Meyer*

A Taste of the Blues, Vol. 1 / Apr. 1993 / Vee-Jay ✦✦✦✦
After his tenure at Chess Records, J.B. Lenoir made a handful of 45s for a variety of smaller Chicago labels, and this 25-track compilation of largely obscure sides from the Vee-Jay vaults is where you go to find one of them. Although the singular reason for its listing here is the inclusion of the A-side of Lenoir's lone Vee-Jay single (the rocking "Do What I Say"), there are plenty of other classic tracks aboard by Elmore James ("The 12 Year Old Boy" and his original version of "It Hurts Me Too"), Jimmy Reed ("Boogie in the Dark"), Billy Boy Arnold ("Don't Stay Out All Night"), Eddie Taylor ("Bad Boy"), John Lee Hooker ("Tupelo"), and the highly unheralded Morris Pejoe ("Hurt My Feelings"). The Lenoir track, a thinly disguised version of Ray Charles' "What'd I Say," is a rockin' lost gem. *—Cub Koda*

A Taste of the Blues, Vol. 2 / Oct. 1993 / Vee-Jay ✦✦✦✦
A 26-track compilation of more obscure and rare Vee-Jay sides, this time featuring a previously unissued Snooky Pryor track, "You Tried to Ruin Me." Also includes tracks from Elmore James, Eddie Taylor, Pee Wee Crayton, plus the added bonus of the first time CD issue of Jimmy Reed's "I'm Gonna Ruin You." *—Cub Koda*

Tell Mama: Screamin' Soul Sisters / 1987 / Rhino ✦✦✦✦
Vociferous sounds from some dynamic soul sisters including two blasts from Aretha Franklin: a smoldering rendition of Sam Cooke's "You Send Me" and a remake of Walter Jackson's "Lee Cross." Ko Ko Taylor's "Wang Dang Doodle" is amazing, the blues singer's sandpaper-coarse vocal could startle a mummy. Jackie Members did the original take on "Hypnotized," she wrote the song with hubby Bobby Poindexter and his brother Richard, but producer George Kerr erased her effort and recorded Linda Jones on the track; Jones took the admission to new heights with a gut-wrenching delivery backed by Members and the Poindexters. Etta James wears her heart on her sleeve on "Tell Mama"; and the track of Fontella Bass' "Rescue Me" could use a cold shower, the musicians sounding like they're on fire. It could have stood alone, Bass' vocal was overkill. Powerful expressions by Shirley Ellis, Patti Drew, Ike & Tina Turner, Gloria Jones, Lorraine Ellison, Barbara George, Maxine Brown, and the Sweet Inspirations complete an explosive package. *—Andrew Hamilton*

Testament Records Sampler / 1995 / Testament ✦✦✦
This covers the story of the late Pete Welding's Testament blues label (now being brought to compact disc via Hightone Records), inspired by Delmark Records and driven by a desire just to get great blues recordings onto the market. This story is told both in this 23-track CD sampler and in the liner notes by Welding, who explains that he didn't care, when he started the label, whether or not it was commercially successful—his job paid well enough. Testament proceeded to release a stream of amazing blues and R&B albums over the years, ranging from an anthology of Southern black fife and drum bands all the way to roaring electric blues that'll set fire to the hair in your ears. This sampler is 72 minutes of amazing selections from 23 different albums, and if you're a blues fan unfamiliar with Testament's CD releases, it may very well present a danger to your bank account. The sampler itself is priced cheaply enough to present a temptation, and you should let yourself be tempted. *—Steven McDonald*

Texas Blues / 1992 / Arhoolie ✦✦✦✦✦
This excellent collection features eight little-known blues artists who recorded for Bill Quinn's Gold Star label in Houston. There are 27 tracks in all—split unequally between acoustic guitar/vocal (16) and piano/vocal (11). Lil' Son Jackson is perhaps the best known, and his ten tracks are all good, rocking acoustic blues. There are also tunes by L.C. Williams, a polished and imaginative guitarist, and one magnificent track by the obscure Buddy Chiles. *—Larry Hoffman*

Texas Blues Guitar (1929–1935) / 1987 / Story of the Blues ✦✦✦✦
This CD features music from a pair of blues vocalist/guitarists from the '30s who had unusual nicknames: Little Hat Jones and "Funny Paper" Smith (who was also known as the Howling Wolf, 15 years before the more famous Howlin' Wolf came to prominence). Jones' only ten recordings are on this set and are all unaccompanied performances, although a female vocalist helps out a little on "Little Hat Blues." Jones was an excellent guitarist but just appeared on three sessions in San Antonio, TX, during 1929-1930. Smith made more recordings than the ten included on this CD (they were put out on a Yazoo LP and later all of the music was combined on a Document disc). He is also heard on unaccompanied performances (including "Howling Wolf Blues, Nos. 3-4"), other than two songs in which he backs singer/pianist Bernice Edwards. Although this disc has been superceded by the much more extensive Document reissue program, the music is quite rewarding and these two underrated performers deserve more recognition. *—Scott Yanow*

Texas Blues Guitar Summit / Mar. 10, 1998 / JSP ♦♦♦
This 13-track anthology brings together new recordings from five distinctly different Texas blues players. U.P. Wilson from the Dallas/Fort Worth area is the biggest name here and his work on "That's Your Woman, but She Comes to See Me" and the instrumental "Chankety Chunk," and with Bobby Gilmore on "I Just Can't Help It," makes for some of the finest moments on this disc, full of wild skitterings up and down the guitar neck, with strong vocals in support. Henry Qualls is traditional to the point of being "backwoods," and his "Rosie Mae" and "Party Tonight" feature plenty of his ragged vocals and a sense of timing normally associated with folk-blues performers. Bobby Gilmore shines on his solo offerings, "Strange Bed" and "I Can't Be This Way No More," while Andrew "Junior Boy" Jones' slashing guitar work on "Stinky Dink" and "Fast Woman" makes them tracks that belong in the highlights file. Another Dallas/Forth Worth native, J.B. Wynne also heats things up on "All Alone Blues," "Dynamite," and "Are You Sticking With Me Baby," a fine close to this sampling of Texas guitar heroes on the road less frequently traveled. *—Cub Koda*

Texas Country Blues 1948–1951 / 1994 / Flyright ♦♦♦♦
Another entry in Flyright's ongoing quest to present the rare and the wonderful, this collects up some impossibly hard to find Texas 78s originally released on short lived, dime-sized labels like Talent, Freedom, Nucraft, ARC, Bluebonnet, and the colorfully named Oklahoma Tornado! David "Honeyboy" Edwards and Frankie Lee Sims are the only "big names" aboard, but the remainder of the tracks featuring Rattlesnake Cooper, James Tisdom, Andrew Thomas, Willie Lane, Monister Parker, Leroy "Country" Johnson, and others clearly illustrate how big the looming presence (both commercially and artistically) of Lightnin' Hopkins already was at this early stage of the game. *—Cub Koda*

Texas Guitar Greats / Aug. 30, 1994 / Collectables ♦♦
A throwaway collection of Texas blues-rock guitarists recorded between 1962 and 1988 in less than stellar circumstances. All of these are either clumsy attempts to update the artist's sound (Juke Boy Bonner, Freddie King), throwaway tracks of artists who can really play (Clarence Green, Clarence "Gatemouth" Brown, Johnny Copeland), or endless wanking that goes nowhere (Ted Hawley, Chris Holzhaus, Rockola). Since there's no rhyme or reason to this collection, there's no reason you should get stuck with it either. *—Cub Koda*

Texas Guitar Killers / Oct. 24, 1995 / Capitol ♦♦♦
Part of Capitol's ongoing development of its vaults, this two-disc set was produced by the late Pete Welding. The 39 cuts feature T-Bone Walker, Clarence "Gatemouth" Brown, Lowell Fulson, Lightnin' Hopkins, Smokey Hogg and Pee-Wee Crayton, with sides drawn from their stints with Imperial and Aladdin. While the intent is to represent Texas blues artists from those labels (with recordings from 1945 to 1953), the result is a fascinating conglomeration of styles that have a bit less to do with guitar than the album title would lead one to believe. Still, it's a fine compilation, wonderfully produced, marvelously annotated, and a lot of fun to listen to—T-Bone Walker, particularly, was a fine jazz vocalist, as well as a brilliant guitar player whose on-stage antics provided the model for Chuck Berry. *—Steven McDonald*

☆ **Texas Music, Vol. 1: Postwar Blues Combos** / 1994 / Rhino ♦♦♦♦♦
Texas blues is harder to define and pigeonhole than, say, Chicago electric blues, or Mississippi Delta country blues. In general terms, the Texas blues of the immediate postwar era often featured hard-driving, jazzy guitar lines, a jump blues influence, occasional brass, and a generally lighter, sunnier attitude than its more famous Chicago cousin. This is a fine 18-song survey of Texas blues from the late '40s to the early '70s, including both giants (T-Bone Walker, Bobby "Blue" Bland, Freddie King, Albert Collins) and names that are known only to blues collectors (Frankie Lee Sims, Goree Carter, Zuzu Bollin). Some of the selections, even by some of the more well-known names, are damned rare; there are mighty hard-to-find '50s singles by Collins, Clarence "Gatemouth" Brown, and Johnny Copeland (as well as one very well-known single, Ivory Joe Hunter's "Since I Met You Baby"). There are a good variety of styles here, encompassing both bluesy ballads and boogies; the thrilling instrumental string-benders by Clarence Green, Albert Collins, and T-Bone Walker may be the highlights. Whatever your preference, it's a fine survey/introduction to vintage Texas electric blues, and it's a good bet that even listeners with big blues collections won't have a lot of the rarities here. *—Richie Unterberger*

• **Texas Piano Blues (1929–1948)** / May 1, 1991 / Story of the Blues ♦♦♦♦♦
This is a good collection of piano-accompanied vocals sporting bluesmen who worked the lumber camps and oil fields of rural Texas, as well as the red-light districts of cities like Galveston and Houston. Big Boy Knox shows a strong city influence in his decorative right-hand work, as does Robert Cooper, whose playing points to the influence of Fats Waller. Joe Pullem is on board with his hit, "Black Gal," which is perhaps overstated by three takes and a variation. The vocals are good, however, and the piano playing is uniformly excellent. Stylistically, this music falls somewhere between ragtime, blues, and vaudeville. *—Larry Hoffman*

Texas Piano, Vol. 1: 1923–1935 / May 1, 1995 / Document ♦♦♦♦♦
There are several very valuable performances on this CD from two of blues singer Sippie Wallace's brothers and a woman who was raised by the Thomas family. In February 1923, pianist George W. Thomas (under the name of Clay Custer) recorded the first boogie-woogie performance, "The Rocks," a rather eerie original. That selection and Thomas' two 1929 selections (which have him singing too) lead off this disc. Hersal Thomas was a talented pianist, who unfortunately died quite young. His complete output is on this CD, other than his recordings with Louis Armstrong. He is heard on his only two piano solos ("Suitcase Blues" and "Hersal Blues") plus five numbers backing the singing of his niece Hociel Thomas (George Thomas' daughter). Moanin' Bernice Edwards recorded 16 selections during four sessions in 1928 and 1935, all of which are included. Most of these selections are solos in which she sings and play piano, or duets with a guitarist. Edwards, who is completely obscure, is an excellent low-down blues singer who deserved to be better known. Overall, this CD is highly recommended; "The Rocks" belongs in every blues collection. *—Scott Yanow*

Texas Piano, Vol. 2: 1927–1938 / May 1, 1995 / Document ♦♦♦♦
One of the joys of the Document label (which is in the process of reissuing virtually every prewar blues recording) are the sets that feature completely obscure artists. Virtually nothing is known of the four bandleaders who are featured on this CD, yet the music (recorded in Dallas or San Antonio) is largely excellent. Four songs from sessions in 1927-1928 feature singer Billiken Johnson either with Fred Adams or Neal Roberts in vocal duets. Willie Tyson and Roberts are the pianists. Texas Bill Day sings (and most likely plays piano) on six selections during his two sessions of 1929, two of which have Johnson joining in on kazoo. Jack Ranger sings three songs during his lone recording date in 1929. Finally, there are 11 numbers (one previously unissued) from 1937-1938 by Kitty Gray & Her Wampus Cats. Gray was an excellent pianist and singer, and her music straddles the boundaries between blues, swing, and Western swing, yet her life and what she did after 1938 are completely unknown. Recommended to serious blues collectors. *—Scott Yanow*

Texas Sax Greats / Nov. 30, 1992 / Collectables ♦♦♦♦♦
Slightly inconsistent but rewarding R&B sax compilation; Big Sambo, Link Davis, and Henry Hayes provide best moments. *—Bill Dahl*

Them Dirty Blues / 1989 / Jass ♦♦♦♦
The thin line between provocative and obscene, suggestive and disgusting, gets examined and stretched throughout the 50 tracks presented on the 1989 two-disc set *Them Dirty Blues*. Many of these songs could be deemed sexist using a modern measuring stick; on the other hand, many are also quite funny, language notwithstanding. They are reflective of a time when audiences were willing to accept songs with either overt carnal themes or with an implicit, yet rather pronounced, sexuality. *—Ron Wynn*

Times Ain't Like They Used to Be, Vol. 1 / Apr. 22, 1997 / Yazoo ♦♦♦♦♦
These are 23 rare 78s from the '20s and '30s, chosen to illustrate the wide range of "early American rural music" that made its way onto disc in the early days of the recording industry. This will not get nearly as much press as Harry Smith's *Anthology of American Folk Music* box, yet it's on par with that ballyhooed re-release as an overview of the roots of American roots music, so to speak. Styles vary from country blues and fiddle hoedowns to banjo music and jug bands. The Memphis Jug Band is the only name here that might be familiar to more than the most well-versed folk historians. Highlights include J.P. Nestor and Norman Edmonds' "Train on the Island," a frenetic string band gallop; the Four Wanderers' eerie gospel tune, "The Fault's in Me"; and Ken Maynard's "Fannie Moore," a direct predecessor of country music in its vocal phrasing. *—Richie Unterberger*

Times Ain't Like They Used to Be, Vol. 2 / Apr. 22, 1997 / Yazoo ♦♦♦♦♦
Like *Vol. 1*, this presents 23 examples of early American rural music, mastered from rare 78s of the '20s and '30s. And like *Vol. 1*, the names here will challenge the expertise of all but the most fanatical collector; only Uncle Dave Macon, Cannon's Jug Stompers, Henry Thomas, and maybe Blind Alfred Reed will be familiar. It's a valuable sampler of non-urban sounds as captured in the early days of the recording industry, when primitive technology and marketing naïveté ensured that the music was virtually unadulterated. Fiddles, banjos, and plaintive, spirited vocals abound. Bobby Leecan's jug band romp "Washboard Cut Out" is the most exuberant track; Rev. D.C. Rice's gospel number "Lord Keep Me With a Mind" starts off in a more somber mood, but soon evolves into a jubilant New Orleans-styled arrangement. *—Richie Unterberger*

Tomato Delta Blues Package / 1994 / Tomato/Rhino ♦♦♦♦
Tomato Delta Blues gathers 16 of the label's best-known performers, including Howlin' Wolf, Lightnin' Slim, John Lee Hooker, and Brownie McGhee. While a fair amount of the collection isn't technically Delta blues, the songs that are, such as Arthur "Big Boy" Crudup's "That's All Right," Mississippi John Hurt's "Talking Casey," and Johnny Shines' "Trouble's All I See" are some of the genre's finest examples. Though the compilation strays a bit beyond the confines of its title, it still manages to collect strong contributions from Lightnin' Hopkins, Sonny Terry, Little Walter, Leadbelly, and Otis Rush. While it would've been nice to see artists like Robert Johnson, Son House, Charley Patton, or Tommy Johnson included here, *Tomato Delta Blues* does a fair job of offering a sample of Delta blues, as well as other blues styles. *—Heather Phares*

Too Late, Too Late Blues, Vol. 1 / Jan. 10, 1996 / Document ♦♦♦
This CD initiated a logical series for the Document label. The company's goal of reissuing every single prewar recording has resulted in hundreds of valuable CDs being reissued. Inevitably, there were new discoveries of music after the fact, so this series consists of previously unreleased titles, alternate takes, and discoveries. *Vol. 1* has selections from Blind Blake ("Early Morning Blues"), Blind Lemon Jefferson ("Lock Step Blues" and "Hangman's Blues"), George "Bullet" Williams, Bessie Tucker, the Memphis Jug Band, Willie Baker, Rev. D.C. Rice, Charlie Spand, Robert Peeples, Charley Patton (an alternate of "I Shall Not Be Moved"), Big Bill Broonzy, Frank Brasswell, Memphis Minnie, the team of Kansas City Kitty & Georgia Tom Dorsey, Bo Carter, Joe McCoy, Kokomo Arnold (a test pressing of his famous "Milk Cow Blues"), Little Buddy Doyle, and Lonnie Johnson. More general blues collectors should explore the more obvious releases first, but specialists will find these 26 performances (and those in later CDs included in this series) to be quite fascinating. *—Scott Yanow*

Too Late, Too Late Blues, Vol. 3 / Oct. 25, 1994 / Document ♦♦♦
The third volume in this rewarding series has 26 isolated recordings that for one reason or another were left out of Document's "complete" collections of early blues. Three songs were previously unreleased while quite a few others are alternate takes or new

discoveries. Although not for the general collector, early blues fanatics and completists will find much to enjoy here. Featured on *Vol. 3* are Buddy Boy Hawkins, Side Wheel Sally Duffie, the Memphis Jug Band, Lottie Kimbrough, Jim Jackson, William Harris, Blind Lemon Jefferson ("Big Night Blues"), Charley Patton ("I Shall Not Be Moved"), the Mississippi Sheiks, Memphis Minnie, Curly Weaver, Tampa Red, Josh White, Leadbelly ("My Baby Quit Me"), Casey Bill Weldon, Ida Parham, the Two Gospel Keys, and a privately recorded 45 by Jesse Thomas that was cut sometime in the mid-'60s; most of the other music on this CD dates from 1927-1940. *—Scott Yanow*

Too Late, Too Late Blues, Vol. 4 / Sep. 8, 2000 / Document ♦♦♦
Vol. 4 in this valuable series has a variety of selections discovered too late to be included in various "complete" reissues of top early blues artists. Actually the first two performances are in a different category altogether. Way back in 1892, American artist Louis Vasnier was recorded relating and singing "Brudder Rasmus," but unfortunately the recording quality of the cylinder is so bad that it is impossible to hear what he is saying/singing. Next up is a much more rewarding and charming guitar duo from 1915 of "Southern Blues," which really fits more into Hawaiian-style music than blues. Otherwise, this disc has music from the 1925-1937 period, with selections from Papa Charlie Jackson, Blind Lemon Jefferson, Ida May Mack, Georgia Tom Dorsey, Big Bill Broonzy, Louise Johnson, Sweet Papa Tadpole, the team of Eddie Chafer and Oscar Woods, Blind Willie McTell (two previously unreleased cuts from 1933), Peetie Wheatstraw, Sam Montgomery, Casey Bill Weldon, and Andrew Hogg. After its rough start, *Vol. 4* contains quite a bit of interesting music. *—Scott Yanow*

Too Late, Too Late Blues, Vol. 5 / Feb. 15, 1996 / Document ♦♦♦
As is the case with each of the CDs in this series, *Vol. 5* of *Too Late, Too Late* has valuable alternate takes, newly discovered titles, and unissued material. Quite a few major names are represented, with ten of the 24 selections being released for the first time, including a pair of instrumentals from 1927 by the duo of guitarist Lonnie Johnson and pianist Jimmy Blythe. Also featured are Sister Morgan, Cow Cow Davenport (playing a piano solo on take B of "Cow Cow Blues"), Elizabeth Johnson, Leroy Carr ("Box Car Blues"), Frank Stokes, Henry Townsend, Blind Willie McTell, John Bray, Leadbelly, Sonny Terry, James "Jack of All Trades" McCain, Montana Taylor (1946), Big Maceo Merriweather (1952), Scrapper Blackwell (1959), and Rev. Lonnie Farris (playing steel guitar in 1964). *—Scott Yanow*

Too Late, Too Late Blues, Vol. 6 / Sep. 10, 1996 / Document ♦♦♦
Newly discovered titles, alternate takes, and previously unreleased material fill in *Vol. 6* in this very valuable collectors' blues series. Issued in chronological order as usual, the 25 selections on the CD (which include some religious pieces in addition to blues and a few instrumentals) contain performances by Emma E. Beacham, Billy & Mary Mack, Rev. J.M. Gates, Laura Smith, the team of Dessa Foster & Howling Smith, Three Stripped Gears (a string trio), the Memphis Night Hawks ("Beedle Um Bum"), Jack Kelly's South Memphis Jug Band, Elder Lightfoot Solomon Michaux, Josh White, Peetie Wheatstraw, Curtis Jones, One Arm Slim, Charlie Burse's Memphis Mudcats, Leadbelly, and the Nashville Washboard Band. Intriguing music, easily recommended to early blues collectors. *—Scott Yanow*

Too Late, Too Late Blues, Vol. 7 / Dec. 3, 1997 / Document ♦♦♦
Vol. 7 in this series of rarities (which includes alternate takes and 13 formerly unissued performances) has music that blues collectors will certainly consider valuable. There are a couple odd sermons from Deacon Mose, and then performances from Alice Pearson, Clifford Hayes' Louisville Stompers, Lonnie Johnson, Casey Bill Weldon (an entire session), and Southern Sons. There are also four unissued numbers from Big Bill Broonzy from 1945-1947, two real obscurities from Alberta Hunter in 1946, three songs from Merline Johnson's final recording date, two songs from Roosevelt Sykes, and three numbers by Alonzo Scales. Quite a variety of mostly rewarding music. *—Scott Yanow*

The Traveling Record Man: Historic Down South Recording Trips / Aug. 28, 2001 / Ace ♦♦♦
The bulky title of this disc was sparked by its documentation of recordings assembled by Joe Bihari of Modern Records on scouting trips through the South for talent between 1948 and 1953. (Starting in 1952, the young Ike Turner also worked for Modern in this capacity.) Just two of the names on this 24-track anthology are famous: Howlin' Wolf, represented by an audition acetate of "Riding in the Moonlight" (first issued in 1991), and Elmore James, whose two cuts appeared on an Ace box set in 1993. Some other names—like Smokey Hogg, Lil' Son Jackson, and Joe Hill Louis—will catch the eyes of in-the-know blues experts, but for the most part even those with extensive blues collections will be mostly or totally unfamiliar with most of the artists. This is raw, Southern, just-post-World War II blues, caught in its transition from its rural roots to something more electric and citified. Certainly it's rawer than much commercially released blues of the time, and in fact about half of it was either previously unissued, or not first issued until many years later on other specialist collections. It's not that unhoned, though, and there's decent variety within the genre, from rollicking piano blues and juke-joint harmonica-driven numbers to mournful slow tunes that sound barely off the farm. Actually Arkansas Johnny Todd's "I'll Be Glad When You're Dead, You Rascal You" sounds like it's still on the farm. But at the other extreme, Sunny Blair's "Please Send My Baby Back Home" (aka "Step Back Baby") is as well-produced and full-sounding as many a 1953 full-band electric Chicago blues single. This is not for everyone, certainly, but as a reflection of the sounds being unearthed as labels brought musicians from out-of-the-way Southern locales into the commercial world, it has considerable value. And the music is solid, if not as gripping as the best records in these styles. The fidelity is imperfect, as many of the tracks were taken from acetates or 78s, but has been cleaned up considerably by modern technology. *—Richie Unterberger*

A Tribute to Howlin' Wolf / May 26, 1998 / Telarc ♦♦♦
Unlike most tribute albums, Telarc's *A Tribute to Howlin' Wolf* plays it pretty close to the vest, rounding up members of Wolf's backing band—including guitarist Hubert Sumlin, pianist Henry Gray and drummer Sam Lay—to support the musicians paying tribute. As a result, the album has a more coherent sound than most tribute records, but that doesn't mean that it's a perfect record. *A Tribute to Howlin' Wolf* suffers from uneven performances, just like any other tribute, but there are enough strong moments to pull the weak spots and poor Howlin' Wolf impressions. Artists as eclectic as Taj Mahal, Christine Ohlman, Cub Koda, Ronnie Hawkins, and Lucinda Williams deliver spirited performances, capturing the sound and spirit of classic Wolf recordings. It may be a little hit-or-miss, but it packs enough of a wallop to be a genuine tribute to one of the mightiest bluesmen. *—Stephen Thomas Erlewine*

A Tribute to Magic Sam / Apr. 29, 1997 / Evidence ♦♦♦
This tribute to Magic Sam Maghett assembles three separate bands, two of which are fronted by musicians who played with the legendary Chicago blues guitarist in the '50s and '60s. The disc encompasses songs either written by or associated with the West Side Soul of Magic Sam. Highlights include Magic Slim (christened with that moniker by Magic Sam) & the Teardrops' version of "All Your Love," saxophonist Eddie Shaw & the Wolf Gang doing "Riding High," and J.W. Williams & the Chi-Town Hustlers' "Love Me With a Feeling." Even though bassist Williams was a bit young to have actually played with Sam, his West Side influence is obvious. While many blues tribute releases are better in concept than execution, this one delivers. And who knows, maybe someone who has never heard the original Magic Sam releases will be turned on enough by this tribute to check out the originals. Wouldn't that be the ultimate tribute! *—Al Campbell*

A Tribute to Muddy Waters: King of the Blues / Jun. 1, 1999 / Hybrid ♦♦♦
A Tribute to Muddy Waters: King of the Blues is the soundtrack to the PBS television special of the same name. The bulk of the show and the soundtrack is devoted to a tribute concert held at the Kennedy Center on October 11, 1997. As as typical with any Kennedy Center concert, the show was filled with American music legends, and even if the featured artists may occasionally seem a little odd—Phoebe Snow may be a great singer, but she's never truly been associated with the blues—they all turn in solid performances. Problem is, they're undone a little bit by the bookend contributions from Muddy himself. "Trouble No More" and "Got My Mojo Workin'" are undisputed classics and they hammer home the fact that even if other musicians can deliver enjoyable versions of Waters' songs, nobody can sing them like Muddy himself. Still, selections from Keb' Mo' ("I Can't Be Satisfied"), Koko Taylor ("Long Distance Call"), Charlie Musselwhite ("I Got a Rich Man's Woman"), John Hiatt ("The Same Thing"), Robert Jr. Lockwood ("Mean Red Spider"), and (especially) Peter Wolf ("Rollin' & Tumblin," plus the affectionate liner notes), make this worthwhile for Muddy devotees wanting to hear a loving new spin on classic tunes. *—Stephen Thomas Erlewine*

A Tribute to Stevie Ray Vaughan / Aug. 7, 1996 / Epic ♦♦♦♦
Unlike most tribute albums from the '90s, *A Tribute to Stevie Ray Vaughan* isn't a lifeless collection of piecemeal studio performances—it's a fiery, living tribute, which is only fitting for a guitarist who shone intensely and brightly during his brief life. Recorded live in Stevie Ray's hometown of Austin, TX, the album features many of Vaughan's idols, friends, and admirers ripping through his most famous numbers. Many of these musicians—including his brother Jimmie, Eric Clapton, Robert Cray, and Buddy Guy—played with Stevie the night he died, which makes the record all the more poignant; also on hand are superstars like B.B. King, Bonnie Raitt, Dr. John, and Art Neville. Although the memory and occasion remain bittersweet, the music on the album is simply teeming with life—everybody plays their heart out. Best of all are the collective jams at the end and the two new songs, "Six Strings Down" and "SRV Blues," which were written in Vaughan's memory. In short, it's what a tribute should be—a celebration of life, not death. *—Thom Owens*

Tuesday's Just as Bad / Nov. 17, 1994 / K-Tel ♦♦♦
Companion volume to K-Tel's *Best of the Blues*, this one features ten more indispensable cuts from Muddy Waters, Howlin' Wolf, Elmore James, B.B. King, and others. Great listening even if you already have the songs on other compilations. *—Cub Koda*

Up Jumped the Blues / 1996 / Music Club ♦♦♦
This 18-track budget-priced compilation features an uptempo collection of tracks from the vaults of the British JSP firm, who long have recorded visiting American blues artists with varying results. The highlights this time are numerous and the quality stays high—as all compilations should be—but several are worthy of special mention. Phillip Walker with Otis Grand do a nice opening turn with "Don't Leave Me Baby," and Carey Bell checks in with a live rendition of Little Walter's "Leaving in the Morning (I Got to Go)" as well as a nice duet with son Lurrie on "The Gladys Shuffle," and Buddy Guy is rockin' with "Girl You're Nice and Clean." Little Willie Littlefield checks in with some two-fisted piano boogie on "(Sit Right Down And) Cry Over You," U.P. Wilson contributes a nice instrumental in "Half Step" and a scorching shuffle with "Need the Need," Johnny "Big Moose" Walker takes it back home with "Rambling Woman," Guitar Shorty contributes two tracks with Otis Grand, and Hubert Sumlin's vocal on "Look Don't Touch" is both mellow and affecting. This compilation also includes tracks by Charlie Sayles, Phil Guy, Johnny Mars, Larry Garner, Byther Smith, Tre', and Tutu Jones. With a 77-minute running time and excellent liner notes from Bill Dahl, this is one blues compilation that's a solid value for the money. *—Cub Koda*

Vintage Toledo Blues 1950–1980 / TRH ♦♦♦
Blues fans don't normally think of Toledo, OH, as a haven for blues artists or recordings, but this independently produced disc collects some fairly astonishing recordings, both issued and unissued, that originated in that town or feature artists who plied their wares

in the Toledo area. The only big name here is Calvin Frazier, a guitarist whose chief claim to fame was being a running buddy to Robert Johnson and lead guitarist in the Baby Boy Warren band in nearby Detroit. Although his "Rock House" features patented Delta lines pushed through heavy amplification, his other three tracks here (including his playing behind vocalist Barbara Brown on "I Need Love") show him playing in an astonishing approximation of T-Bone Walker's style. Other highlights feature three sides from Little Walter Jr. taken from a previously unissued session for Detroit's J.V.B. Records in 1954, three sides by Eddie Carson, and two late entries ('70s and '80s vintage) from the Griswold brothers. Just when you think you had heard it all in rare recordings, a compilation like this proves that there are more gems to be unearthed. *—Cub Koda*

Violin, Sing the Blues for Me: African-American Fiddlers 1926–1949 / Aug. 24, 1999 / Old Hat ✦✦✦✦✦

As Marshall Wyatt's thorough liner notes explain in the accompanying 32-page booklet, the violin had a more prominent role in early blues than has often been supposed. Violins were far more apt to be played than guitars in the 19th century, and even when blues began to be recorded in the '20s, violins were still often used in blues songs, although they weren't as apt to be featured on disc as the guitar and other instruments were. This 24-track compilation (with only one cut dating from after 1935) includes some fairly recognizable blues names like Peg Leg Howell, Howard Armstrong, Cow Cow Davenport, the Mississippi Sheiks, the Memphis Jug Band, Charley Patton (accompanying Henry Sims), and Big Joe Williams (a 1935 version of his signature tune "Baby Please Don't Go"), although many of the performers are far more obscure. The material tends toward the more good-timey and folky side of the rural blues tradition; the violins can get into a hoedown kick, as on Peg Leg Howell's "Beaver Slide Rag," or get into a rapid ragtime mode, as on Louie Bluie and Ted Bogan's "Ted's Stomp." Because of the chronological span and wide roster of artists represented, it's a good overview of violin-informed early blues, a subgenre that hasn't gotten a whole of attention. Check out Frank Stoke's "Right Now Blues" to get your head spun around when you hear a lyric that was repeated in Chuck Berry's classic "Reelin' and Rockin'." *—Richie Unterberger*

The Voice of the Blues: Bottleneck Guitar Masterpieces / Dec. 1976 / Yazoo ✦✦✦✦

Musically this a great batch of stuff, the equivalent of tuning in somebody's really fantastic rootsy radio show. It is also a bit like 14 strangers, some of who have nothing in common, accidentally meeting in a random location and deciding they all get along just fine together. Anyone with a bit of intelligence might begin nitpicking about the philosophy of how this album has been compiled. There is obvious indecision about whether the focus is blues or bottleneck guitar. Or a third interpretation is that this is supposed to be a collection of masterpieces. By putting *The Voice of the Blues* out front in the title, an immediate blues emphasis is established. That is awkward for some of the material that is included here, including ragtime, old-time country, and Hawaiian. What everything does have in common is the bottleneck guitar, but this may have become a peg to hang the collection of tracks on simply because it is so popular amongst blues listeners, continually being discovered with much enthusiasm by each new generation. Because masterpiece or not, each track has a different degree of involvement with the bottleneck, sometimes major and sometimes minor. "Ground Hog Blues" by Rambling Thomas is for sure a bottleneck blues, with the sound of the quavering slide licks totally dominating the proceedings. "Decatur Street 81" by the Georgia Browns is something of an instrumental masterpiece, but the bottleneck is there only as a hard-working member of the trio, adding simple and carefully worked-out parts to the overall sound. This track could have just as easily been folded into a compilation of hot harmonica music.

If this is taken as some kind of overview of bottleneck guitar techniques, it is haphazard and incomplete. Most of the music is from the '20s and '30s, yet there is also one track from the '50s, and it is a gospel guitar number at that. Is this on the album just because it was lying around, or because it was the only bottleneck guitar masterpiece recorded in the '50s? The answer is surely no to the latter question, but it is great to have Sister O.M. Terrell on hand anyway, playing a wrist-cracking, jumping National steel style that brings to mind Mississippi Fred McDowell a few years prior to puberty. This track combined with the excellent Irene Scruggs track on the flip side provides an extra attraction within this collection of songs. Material by female country blues artists is rare, and listeners will certainly be interested in hearing more by both gals. The second side does have a slight problem in the overwhelming quality of one particular track, Roy Smeck's "Laughing Rag." This is guitar playing of such outrageous virtuosity that the songs before and after would limp off with their heads between their hands if they were able to assume human form. The worst hit is the track immediately before, because despite the lack of much interesting slide work other than a bit of mild chording, it is hyped as "one of the rare ragtime works ever attempted by a bottleneck guitarist." Uh, what is it that Roy Smeck is doing, then? Hint: It is called "Laughing Rag." Sam Butler kicks off the side with another fine example of the kind of playing consumers who think this is all going to be slide blues are probably looking for. These same listeners should still enjoy the cornpone "She's a Hum Dum Dinger From Dingersville" by Jimmie Davis, as it has an especially sweet bottleneck guitar part to it and a tempo change to boot. The conclusion is a version of "When the Saints Go Marchin' In" by Blind Willie Davis that works beautifully. *—Eugene Chadbourne*

★ **Wade in the Water, Vol. 1: African American Spirituals—The Concert Tradition** / May 1, 1994 / Smithsonian/Folkways ✦✦✦✦✦

☆ **Wade in the Water, Vol. 2: African American Congregational Singing—19th Century Roots** / May 1, 1994 / Smithsonian/Folkways ✦✦✦✦✦

Wade in the Water, Vol. 2: African American Congregational Singing offers a glimpse into the long history of black congregational vocals and worshiping practices, a tradition dating back centuries which once accounted for much of the oral transmission passed from generation to generation. Fascinatingly, the songs are never rehearsed—singers learn while they perform; while organized gospel choirs have since become more widely recognized, the congregational style still thrives, with six of the modern era's most stirring representatives—among them the McIntosh County Shouters, the Seniorlites, and the Rev. C.J. Johnson & Family—featured on this disc. *—Jason Ankeny*

☆ **Wade in the Water, Vol. 3: African American Gospel—The Pioneering Composers** / 1994 / Smithsonian/Folkways ✦✦✦✦✦

Wade in the Water, Vol. 3: African American Gospel focuses on six of the pioneering composers of the genre—Rev. Charles Albert Tindley, Lucie Eddie (Elizabeth) Campbell, Rev. William Herbert Brewster, Roberta Martin, Kenneth Morris, and the incomparable Thomas A. Dorsey. Recorded between 1992 and 1993, the disc features new renditions of such perennials as "Just a Closer Walk With Thee," "Precious Lord," "How I Got Over," and "We'll Understand It Better By and By." *—Jason Ankeny*

Wade in the Water, Vol. 4: African American Community Gospel / 1994 / Smithsonian/Folkways ✦✦✦✦✦

The final release in the series, *Wade in the Water, Vol. 4: African American Community Gospel*, focuses on the sacred music of two vastly different areas of the U.S.—Washington D.C. and rural Alabama—to illustrate the differences brought about by local perspective. The eight Alabama tracks run the gamut from newly arranged renditions of traditional favorites to popular hits to original compositions; all are in the quartet style, which remains the primary gospel vehicle throughout the state—group anniversary celebrations are even regularly held, with other quartets traveling from miles around to perform in their peers' honor. In D.C., the trend is toward performances connected with the worship services of the urban church community; again, however, the scope is vast, including traditional styles, processional praise songs and a contemporary reading of "Peace in the Valley." *—Jason Ankeny*

Wade in the Water: African American Sacred Music Traditions / 1996 / Smithsonian/Folkways ✦✦✦✦

This four-disc set, drawn from the musical examples to Bernice Johnson Reagon's outstanding National Public Radio series on African-American gospel music, deals respectively with the concert tradition in spiritual singing, the 19th century roots of African-American congregational singing, the pioneering composers, and community gospel. As ballet music lacks a dimension without the dance, the CDs lack a dimension without the powerful mind tying the whole thing together. And to have included some of the non-African-American roots Professor Reagon illustrated in the programs would also have made this more than just another fine gospel set. But "just another fine gospel set" is pretty fine in its own right. *—John Storm Roberts, Original Music*

Wake Up Dead Man: Black Convict Worksongs from Texas Prisons / 1994 / Rounder ✦✦✦✦✦

Warrior on the Battlefield: A Capella Trail Blazers—1920s–1940s / Oct. 21, 1997 / Rounder ✦✦✦✦

Here are 25 performances by African-American gospel quartets of the South, recorded between 1927 and 1942. The Silver Leaf Quartette of Norfolk and the Golden Gate Quartet get the most airtime (six and five tracks respectively), though there's also space for less familiar names like the Davis Bible Singers and the T.C.I. Womens Four. This documents Black gospel music in its transition from barbershop quartets to more polished forms, and while the sound quality isn't as dynamic as what you'll find on contemporary releases, the performances are generally much less showy. *—Richie Unterberger*

We Love You Bobby: A Tribute to Bobby Bland / 1992 / Collectables ✦✦✦

There's not much Bland influence on many of them, but these mostly '60s Texas R&B sides are soulful nonetheless. *—Bill Dahl*

Weed: A Rare Batch / Oct. 1928-Nov. 1947 / Stash ✦✦✦

As is usual with most of Stash's earliest releases, much of the music on this LP refers in one way or another to drugs in its lyrics but these jazz and blues performances from the swing era are most notable for the fine playing by a wide variety of artists. There is one selection apiece from Chick Webb (Ella Fitzgerald singing "When I Get Low I Get High"), Tampa Red, Oscar's Chicago Swingers, Carl Martin, the Harlem Hamfats, Julia Lee, Sammy Price, Cootie Williams (a hot version of "Ol' Man River"), Adrian Rollini, Lorraine Walton, Yack Taylor ("Knockin' Myself Out"), Blue Steele, and Lucille Bogan ("Pot Hound Blues"). Many of these selections have yet to be reissued on CD. *—Scott Yanow*

White Country Blues, 1926–1938: A Lighter Shade of Blue / 1993 / Columbia/Legacy ✦✦✦✦

White Country Blues, 1926-1938: A Lighter Shade of Blue is an excellent and revealing 48-track double-disc collection culled from the Columbia, American, and OKeh vaults. All of the material on this double-disc set was recorded by country artists that drew heavily from the blues, whether it was incorporating the genre into their own compositions or covering blues and hokum songs. Though there are several stars, such as Roy Acuff, many of the performers on *White Country Blues* are obscure, especially for listeners whose knowledge of country music stops at Hank Williams. That is one of the many reasons why *White Country Blues* is invaluable. It's a thoughtfully compiled and thorough historical reissue that presents a wealth of rare, fascinating material. While it might not always be an easy listen, it's remains an essential purchase for any comprehensive country collection. *—Thom Owens*

White Men Can't Jump but They Can Sing the Hell Out of Rock & Roll and Soul / Jul. 16, 1996 / Ace ✦✦✦

Music lovers will enjoy this 20-song collection by Southern soul and rock & roll singers associated with Louisiana's Ace recording family. "Just a Dream" and "Venus in Blue Jeans" by Jimmy Clanton capture the essence of adolescent romance. Dr. John presents a more adult point of view on "Storm Warning" and "Tears, Tears, and More Tears," done with Chuck Carbo. There are also memorable performances from Frankie Ford ("Sea Cruise") plus deeper items by Bobby Hood ("Three People (Sleeping in My Bed)"), Jimmy Elledge ("Reconsider Me"), and Johnny Fairchild ("I Was A Fool"), and more. —*Andrew Hamilton*

Whole Lotta Blues: Legends of Texas Blues / Jan. 15, 1999 / Eclipse Music Group ♦♦♦

Not a single Vaughan brother to be found here, but this anthology of Texas blues still packs a lot of punch. While not as comprehensive as, say, the *Blues Masters Vol. 3: Texas Blues* compilation on Rhino, Eclipse's *Legends of Texas Blues* generally covers all the bases for this kind of reissue: a few must-have classics ("One Room Country Shack," "Lucy Mae Blues"); a few titular tunes that fall in line with the theme (Larry Davis' "Angels in Houston," Floyd Dixon's "Dallas Blues"); and a few obscure gems to round out the album (Lou Ann Barton's rocking cover of "Shake Your Hips" almost steals the show). As expected, this is mostly an axe-slinging affair dominated by the likes of Albert Collins, T-Bone Walker, Freddie King, Johnny Copeland, and Johnny Winter, although the producers justly added to the mix some choice piano blues by Amos Milburn, Robert Shaw, and Mercy Dee Walton. Veteran electric blues and boogie-woogie fanatics already have most of these songs in their collections, but for newbies, this is a pretty good deal. —*Ken Chang*

Wild About My Lovin': Beale Street Blues 1928–30 / Aug. 13, 1991 / RCA ♦♦♦♦♦

Superb, eclectic music from Depression-era Memphis, remastered from the original source recordings. The material on *Wild About My Lovin'* is drawn from singers Frank Stokes and Jim Jackson and from a pair of the era's most popular jug bands, (Gus) Cannon's Jug Stompers and the Memphis Jug Band, whose "Stealin'" (included here) was later recorded by Bob Dylan. —*Jason Ankeny*

Windy City Blues—The Transition: 1935 to 1953 / Jul. 10, 1992 / Nighthawk ♦♦♦♦♦

Subtitled "The Transition: 1935 to 1953," this 12-track collection documents primarily the work of Southern-born blues artists who emigrated to Chicago before World War II, but whose careers endured into the postwar era. Starting with Aaron "Pinetop" Sparks' 1935 recording of the blues classic "Every Day (I Have the Blues)," the collection runs in chronological order, featuring several selections from the "Bluebird beat" period of Chicago blues. The State Street Boys' "Sweet to Mama" is an all-star aggregation featuring Big Bill Broonzy, violinist Carl Martin, pianist Black Bob, and Jazz Gillum on harmonica. Another Bluebird alumnus, Washboard Sam, is aboard with "Easy Ridin' Mama," recorded in 1937. Sonny Boy Williamson is aboard with two tracks, "Sunnyland" and "My Little Cornelius," both from 1938. Robert Lee McCoy is featured on the 1937 recording that gave him his signature piece, "Prowlin' Nighthawk." Robert Jr. Lockwood is documented with two of his earliest sides from 1941 ("Black Spider Blues" and "I'm Gonna Train My Baby") and a pair from a decade later, "Dust My Broom" and "Gonna Dig Myself a Hole." A late 1951 Tampa Red side, "Green and Lucky Blues," is also a standout, along with a 1953 Johnny Shines track ("Please Don't"), finding him in an unusual band setting with Elmore James' saxman J.T. Brown and Sunnyland Slim on piano. Two tracks each from Guitar Pete Franklin and Tony Hollins round out this excellent collection. —*Cub Koda*

Women of Gospel's Golden Age, Vol. 1 / 1994 / Specialty ♦♦♦♦♦

Although women have been at the forefront of gospel innovation since the beginning, the domination of male quartets may have fooled some into thinking they weren't that important. Anyone holding that mistaken impression will surely know better after hearing the 28 remarkable cuts on this valuable anthology. New Orleans' wondrous Bessie Griffin, whose vibrant, dazzling voice was overlooked due to Mahalia Jackson, gets the spotlight with six amazing numbers. She's not alone there, however; everyone from

the famous Clara Ward Singers and Dorothy Love Coates to the lesser-known Sallie Martin Singers sounds fantastic. —*Ron Wynn*

Women of the Blues / Feb. 1967 / Victor ♦♦♦

Is there any uglier record cover in existence than this one? Nobody would want to be the judge in that type of contest. What with a lineup of eight female blues recording artists from the '20s and '30s, there must have been some sort of photography that would have looked better than the atrocious design the label wound up with. Perhaps the notion was that any consumer who would go to the trouble to seek out recordings by lesser-known blues vocalists wouldn't care if the sides came wrapped in old newsprint (which would have looked better, mind you). One of these artists continued her recording career well past the release of this compilation in the ensuing decades, and as a result, she can be regarded as the most famous singer of this bunch. What makes her recordings from 1927 doubly rewarding is that her lone backup comes from Fats Waller seated behind a pipe organ, an image with more potential for adventure than Buck Rogers at the controls of his rocketship. The Waller dementia seemed to go up a notch further at the odd points in his career when he got near pipe organs. These two duets are so astounding that they threaten to drown out the memory of anything else on this album. Nonetheless, there is some musical competition as several of the studio bands assembled for these sessions contain hot players. A threesome of New Orleans guys creates magic behind Sippie Wallace, namely clarinetist Johnny Dodds, trombonist Honore Dutrey, and Natty Dominique on cornet. The Monette Moore songs contain some early playing from the sharp trumpeter Rex Stewart, while the Victoria Spivey tracks bring together a roomful of classic jazz soloists such as Henry "Red" Allen on trumpet, J.C. Higginbotham on trombone, and Albert Nicholas on clarinet. The classic female blues style always veered toward the jazzier side of the highway, which makes the performances by Margaret Johnson particularly special. She is backed by piano, guitar, and harmonica, representing a typical country blues backup for this era, which is complemented by her raunchy vocal style. Both her performances are good, but "Dead Drunk Blues" is a real winner, as well as yet another addition to the long list of fine blues recordings on the subject of being totally inebriated. Lizzie Miles has one of the better voices of this bunch, but the material she is provided with by Andy Razaf is about as trite as it gets. —*Eugene Chadbourne*

Yonder Come the Blues / 2001 / Document ♦♦♦♦

Yonder Come the Blues has a duel life: It serves as a companion disc to the book of the same name and as a thoughtful guide to the birth of the genre now called the blues. Compiler Paul Oliver has carefully chosen the tracks. This disc moves briskly from the early syncopations of fife player Othar Turner to the adoption of blues by the North Carolina Ramblers to the waxings of African-American bluesman Blind Willie Johnson. This collection does a better job than most of introducing acoustic blues because of its inclusion of earlier forms of the genre. The first two tracks, "Agbekor" and "Ring Dance," were recorded in Ghana and represent the propulsive rhythms that African slaves brought to America. Thyam Sy Griots plays a halam five-string chordophone on "Halam Improvisation," which sounds sort of like George Harrison playing the blues on a sitar. As the disc moves into its second stage, the listener is treated to Tom Darby and Jimmie Tarlton's "Sweet Sara Blues" and interestingly, Bob Wills & His Texas Playboys' "Brain Cloudy Blues." Finally, selections by Blind Lemon Jefferson and Big Bill Broonzy show the blues settling into a more recognizable form, while Pinetop Burks offers an early version of boogie-woogie. In time, acoustic guitars and pianos replaced fiddles and fifes, and many forgot that there were, indeed, other ways to play the blues. *Yonder Come the Blues* educates the listener by offering a generous and enjoyable collection that effectively traces the roots of a genre. —*Ronnie D. Lankford, Jr.*

Essays

The Roots of the Blues

The origins of the blues—a form that really didn't have a name until the early 20th century, although it had surely been around for some time before then—are impossible to pin down with any degree of certainty. There's the convenient thesis that the blues were imported to North America when African slaves were shipped to the continent in the centuries preceding the Civil War. Much of the blues is undeniably African in origin, but in fact there were many other influences that shaped the music as well. It's also reasonably certain that the blues did not take a recognizable shape until African-Americans were a large, established part of the population of the American South.

Formulating the origins of the blues is a much more difficult task than, say, describing the birth of rock & roll. For one thing, there are no tapes or recordings available to trace and document the sounds as they coalesced prior to 1900. The standard historical record of written and oral accounts, too, is much sketchier than it is for comparatively recent genres. Offering postulations and generalizations in a short overview such as this, really, is just asking for trouble—there are plenty of blues and folklore scholars that will challenge whatever point of view is espoused, often armed with considerable evidence. This piece will simply identify some of the likely sources. Readers interested in investigating the topic in greater depth will find many book-length studies of the subject in libraries and bookstores with a large selection.

The African roots of the blues are undeniable, particularly in the griots of western Africa. The griots functioned as sorts of musical storytellers for their communities, no doubt singing about subjects like romance, family, famine, ruling governments, and struggle that are commonplace in blues music—and, indeed, folk/popular music as a whole. They often used stringed instruments that bore some resemblance to ones that became prevalent in blues. When Ali Farka Toure of Senegal reached an international audience in the '80s and '90s, he was frequently described as "the African John Lee Hooker"; it's possible that his work is also an illustration of the close ties between the blues and some strains of African music.

Blues music, however, most likely didn't approach anything resembling its 20th century form until slavery was instituted in the American South. The mere fact that the slaves came from many different regions and spoke many different languages, for one thing, would have worked against the retention of the music of their homeland as they began working together. Subsequent generations lost the tongues or their mothers and fathers, by necessity adopting English, the language of their overlords.

The brutal and inhumane conditions of slavery, from some viewpoints, may have seemed to make it unlikely that any forms of artistic expression could develop and thrive. In some respects, however, slavery fostered such musical communication, simply as a means of making life bearable. Work songs and field hollers, some of the most oft-discussed precursors to the blues, were chanted and sung as the slaves worked or endured their punishment. They were also a means of telling stories, passing the endless hours of toil, or simply venting emotion that was impossible to express in more confined or closely supervised circumstances. The call-and-response quality of some blues music (and much gospel) may have derived in part from such singing; the blues' concentration upon earthy, day-to-day realities and struggles may have some of its roots in these styles as well.

The history of American popular music is often one of black and white styles meeting and mixing. As wide as the racial divide was in slavery days, the music of American blacks inevitably absorbed a lot of white flavor, from European, Southern folk, and Appalachian influences. In their limited contact with whites, blacks were also exposed to piano and string instruments that would figure strongly in their own music. By the time blues began to be recorded in the early 1920s, guitars and pianos were the most frequent instruments of choice among blues artists.

There was also the considerable influence of the church. Gospel music afforded the African-American community opportunities to sing with committed fervor. The harmonies and solo vocal styles associated with vocal music have left a strong imprint on black music to this day, including the blues. Relatively recent releases like Mississippi Fred McDowell's recordings of spirituals in the '60s demonstrate how strong the ties can be between down-home blues and gospel; Rev. Gary Davis was another acoustic bluesman known for performing a lot of gospel material.

The extraordinary power of the rural blues recorded in the '20s and '30s have sometimes left the impression that deep blues dominated the music of Southern black communities. The repertoire of black musicians from the Deep South was much more diverse than many people realize. Blues music was often only one element of their repertoire; some singers who only recorded blues music were likely able to play pop, country, and ragtime tunes as well in live performance, as the circumstances of the occasion demanded. Some of these musicians performed as part of traveling minstrel, vaudeville, and medicine shows; occasionally ones who toured with such concerns in the early 20th

century would survive to make recordings in the early days of the LP, such as Pink Anderson. Ragtime styles also made their way onto blues records, not only via pianists but guitarists such as Rev. Gary Davis.

Jug bands and the all-around entertainers that have been dubbed "songsters" are sometimes also thought of as precursors to the blues, although many such musicians were actually contemporaries of the early blues artists, and recorded often in the '20s and '30s. Jug bands like the Mississippi Sheiks and those of Gus Cannon used instruments not associated with the blues these days, such as the washboard, kazoo, and fiddle. They also frequently espoused a good-time air, in contrast to the more melancholic tone of deep rural guitar blues. They were still a vital part of the African-American popular music of the South in the '30s, although afterwards their styles were deemed hokey and passé, a relic of the minstrel tradition.

The wide repertoire of Southern black music lived on in blues performers that have come to be called the "songsters," who are examined in greater depth in a separate piece. They could play blues, certainly, but also folk tunes, country songs, pop, ragtime, and spirituals. Some of the oldest bluesmen who made it onto record, such as pan pipe-quill player Henry Thomas (famous for "Bull Doze Blues," which Canned Heat turned into "Going Up the Country"), were songsters. The eclecticism of the songsters lived on in some performers who became popular during the '60s blues revival, such as Mance Lipscomb and Mississippi John Hurt. Leadbelly and Josh White could be called "songsters" of sort, although they were more commonly categorized as folksingers, or blues/folksingers.

The blues, or forms closely tied to the blues, had likely existed for some time, and in various blends of the previously described styles, before its famous "discovery," at least in terms of verified historical accounts, by W.C. Handy, who recalled hearing something resembling the blues as early as 1892. The incident that has been enshrined in popular legend, however, occurred in Tutwiler, MS, in 1903, as Handy, a black bandleader of a minstrel orchestra, was waiting for a train. In his autobiography, *Father of the Blues*, he recalls listening to the guitarist that began to play:

"The singer repeated the line three times, accompanying himself on the guitar with the weirdest music I had ever heard. The tune stayed in my mind. When the singer paused, I leaned over and asked him what the words meant. He rolled his eyes, showing a trace of mild amusement. Perhaps I should have known, but he didn't mind explaining. At Morehead, the eastbound and westbound met and crossed the north and southbound trains four times a day…."

"He was simply singing…as he waited. This was not unusual. Southern Negroes sang about everything. Trains, steamboats, steam whistles, sledge hammers, fast women, mean bosses, stubborn mules—all became subjects for their songs. They accompany themselves on anything from which they can extract a musical sound or rhythmical effect, anything from a harmonica to a washboard."

Despite his title "Father of the Blues," Handy did not invent the blues. He was responsible for popularizing them by copyrighting and publishing blues compositions. "Memphis Blues," published in 1912, was the first one; "St. Louis Blues," which followed in 1914, was his most successful, and indeed one of the most popular tunes of any kind in the 20th century, performed and recorded by numerous jazz, blues, and pop artists. Handy published/wrote other numbers in the same vein, such as "Yellow Dog Blues" and "Beale Street Blues" (named after the main thoroughfare of the black community in Memphis).

"St. Louis Blues" can sound more like jazz than blues to contemporary listeners, perhaps reflecting the fact that Handy was steeped not the blues but in brass bands, which may have shaped his arrangements. The same can be said of the first popular blues recordings of the '20s, mostly performed by women with jazz accompanists, who sang such pop- and jazz-influenced "blues" compositions as those devised by Handy. Arguably, these records reflected a more urban and pop-oriented sensibility than what you would have heard from the mouths of the proto-blues and early blues performers of the South.

Those early blues songs and singles, however, were responsible to some degree for codifying certain blues trademarks. The blues is too volatile a form to ever be standardized, but much of it is typified by a 12-bar structure and three-line verses that follow what is called an AAB rhyming scheme. These are the traits, more than any other, that have endured in much (perhaps most) acoustic and modern electric blues, live or recorded, to this day.

Modern mass communications—the phonograph record and radio—began to unify the blues stylistically, exposing listeners and musicians to sounds, similar and different, from other regions. The inherent demands of a two- or three-minute 78 rpm single also necessitated a brevity and conciseness, forcing musicians to cut down the length of their songs, and perhaps to adopt certain standard methods (like the 12-bar structure and AAB scheme) to present their music commercially. The similar structure of many blues songs may have even been matters of convenience or imitation in many cases.

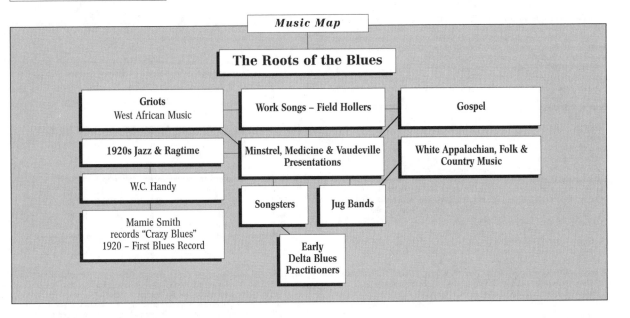

Music Map

The Roots of the Blues

Griots West African Music	**Work Songs – Field Hollers**	**Gospel**
1920s Jazz & Ragtime	**Minstrel, Medicine & Vaudeville Presentations**	**White Appalachian, Folk & Country Music**
W.C. Handy	**Songsters**	**Jug Bands**
Mamie Smith records "Crazy Blues" 1920 – First Blues Record	**Early Delta Blues Practitioners**	

What's certain is that after the phenomenal success of Mamie Smith's "Crazy Blues" (the first blues record) in 1920, and many other women singers performing in a similar vein over the next few years, the record industry—then in its infancy—was eager to record blues artists of all kinds, with a particular eye toward what was then called the "race" (i.e., African-American) market. This led to labels scouring several regions for talent, particularly the South, where most blues performers were based. Here they encountered the guitarists who sang deep country blues, as well as songsters and jug bands. Blues was off and running as an established part of the music industry, with an ever-widening repertoire of songs and styles that has endured to this day as one of the most popular and important forms of American music.

Six Recommended Albums:
Various Artists, *Blues Masters, Vol. 10: Blues Roots* (Rhino)
Various Artists, *Afro-American Spirituals, Work Songs and Ballads* (Library of Congress)
Various Artists, *Negro Work Songs and Calls* (Library of Congress)
Various Artists, *The Sounds of the South* (Atlantic)
Eddie "One-String" Jones, *One String Blues* (Gazell)
Ali Farka Toure, *The Source* (Hannibal)

—*Richie Unterberger*

Jug Bands

Jug bands may be only a footnote in the birth of the blues. Some may dispute whether they belong in the mainstream of blues history at all, finding them more convenient to categorize as old-time folk music. The relatively few recordings that blues influenced jug bands made in the '20s and '30s, at the very least, give us valuable insight into the roots of the blues, at a time when it had not solidified into guitar-based music that usually adhered to 12-bar structures. It also yields its share of high-spirited tunes in the bargain.

Some historians have speculated that at the turn of the century, jug band-type outfits were more common in the Southern African-American community than performers playing what we would now call the blues. The instrumentation and arrangements of the jug bands were often an outgrowth of the minstrel/vaudeville/traveling medicine shows that toured the South. String bands were a feature of many of these outfits, and the emphasis was on good-time entertainment, not the hard times and weighty expression that many associate with the blues.

A great deal of the charm of the jug bands was due to the homemade, almost improvised nature of the instruments. There were kazoos, washboards, washtubs, spoons, and all manner of percussion produced by items more commonly associated with work tools or playthings, like jugs, but also pipes, pans, and more. Even the relatively conventional instruments, like the fiddles and guitars, were sometimes made from scrap materials, like cigar boxes.

Elaborates Francis Davis in *The History of the Blues*, "Jug bands differed in size and instrumentation, though they invariably included either a harmonica or a kazoo as a lead melodic voice, a variety of string instruments, and at least one band member providing a bass line by blowing rhythmically across the top of a jug—a poor man's tuba, as it were. Like the rural fife-and drum bands of which we have regrettably few recorded examples, jug bands can be heard as a missing link between the blues and the music of West Africa...."

"Along with the washboard bands in which a simple laundry device was transformed into a percussion instrument, the jug bands were a tribute to the ingenuity shown by impoverished rural blacks in expressing themselves musically on whatever they found at

hand. For that matter, [early jug band leader Gus] Cannon fashioned his first banjo out of a bread pan and a broom handle. And there are obvious parallels to be drawn between the use of such homemade or 'nonmusical' instruments then and similar practices in hip-hop, most notably 'scratching.'"

Many of the jug bands that were active in the early 1900s didn't have professional aspirations; many of the ones that did doubtless were undiscovered by record companies. Like the barrelhouse blues pianists of the early 1900s, their representation on record is fairly scant, and certainly not fully documented for listeners of future decades who wish to get a relatively complete picture of the style. And many of the ones that did get to record only issued a single or two before vanishing into oblivion, only accessible today via obscure compilations aimed at a very small and specialized collector market.

Of the jug bands that managed to record in the '20s and '30s, more noteworthy ones emerged from Memphis than anywhere else. The most influential were the ones led by Gus Cannon, much of whose repertoire was grounded in a definite blues base. The most

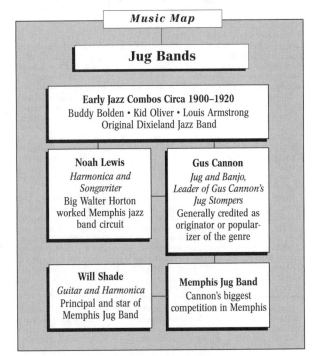

Music Map

Jug Bands

Early Jazz Combos Circa 1900–1920
Buddy Bolden • Kid Oliver • Louis Armstrong
Original Dixieland Jazz Band

Noah Lewis *Harmonica and Songwriter* Big Walter Horton worked Memphis jazz band circuit	**Gus Cannon** *Jug and Banjo, Leader of Gus Cannon's Jug Stompers* Generally credited as originator or popularizer of the genre
Will Shade *Guitar and Harmonica* Principal and star of Memphis Jug Band	**Memphis Jug Band** Cannon's biggest competition in Memphis

celebrated of Cannon's local rivals was the Memphis Jug Band; unlike many of the jug bands, they recorded prolifically, helping ensure that their reputation would outlive their lifespan. Individual stars within these bands were harmonica player Noah Lewis (an associate of Cannon's) and guitarist-harmonica player Will Shade, the most prominent member of the Memphis Jug Band.

Even at the time that Cannon and the Memphis Jug Band were recording, the jug band style was being threatened on several fronts. Country blues was evolving into a far more guitar-oriented form that put the emphasis on solo vocals; African-American bands were turning increasingly to swing and big band jazz. The jug bands may have reminded some African-Americans of a minstrel and blackface tradition that they were eager to evolve from, or even forget. The Depression meant a severe cutback on commercial blues recordings of all kinds, and the jug bands were hit especially hard; very few commercial jug band recordings were made after the '30s, and by the subsequent decade, the genre had pretty much vanished as a commercial consideration anyway.

Long after the prime of the Memphis jug bands, however, the influence of the music would linger. The Rooftop Singers, one of the more commercial ensembles of the early '60s folk revival, took Gus Cannon's "Walk Right In" to the top of the pop charts in 1963. The folk revival also spun off a small jug band revival of its own, the most successful act being Jim Kweskin & His Jug Band, featuring Maria and Geoff Muldaur (although the group's repertoire was not limited to the blues). And the Grateful Dead, who dug very deeply into the blues backlog for some of their covers, included Cannon's "Viola Lee Blues" on their first album.

Five Recommended Albums:
Gus Cannon's Jug Stompers, *The Complete Recordings* (Yazoo)
The Memphis Jug Band, *Memphis Jug Band* (Yazoo)
Various Artists, *The Jug & Washboard Bands, Vol. 1 (1924-31)* (RST Blues Documents)
Various Artists, *The Jug, Jook & Washboard Bands* (Blues Classics)
Jim Kweskin & His Jug Band, *Greatest Hits* (Vanguard)

—*Richie Unterberger*

Delta Blues

No other style of the blues has exerted such a grip on the popular imagination as the one associated with the Mississippi Delta. The image of the wracked bluesman hunched over his acoustic guitar, exorcising the demons from the depths of his soul, his rhythmic force often accentuated by thrilling slide guitar—this is a caricature that originated from Delta blues. Like any caricature, it's prone to over-generalizations that tend to obscure the considerable stylistic range of the form, and the eccentricities to be found in the repertoire of its major exponents. But there's no doubt that Delta blues epitomizes the music at its most emotional and expressive.

The history of Delta blues is inseparable from the African-American culture of the region itself. The Delta refers to the northwestern part of the state, where the fertile soil gave rise to many plantations. These were owned by whites and worked mostly by blacks, who often harvested the land as sharecroppers. The conditions for sharecroppers may have been better than those they endured in slavery, but not by a great deal. Backbreaking labor and low wages were the norm, as well as racial intolerance and segregation.

No amount of romanticization can obscure the grinding poverty of the everyday lives of the plantation workers. But the conditions of the Delta were conducive to the development of a sort of indigenous music. Huge numbers of African-Americans were working and living together in close promixity, exchanging the music and folk traditions they had developed and experienced over generations. In many instances, they were too poor to travel even moderate distances (and in any case didn't have the spare time to do so), intensifying the ferment of musical elements that gave birth to a distinctive style.

As hard as the plantation work was, there was still time for entertainment, in both informal settings and weekend parties. Musicians were in demand for these events, and would often circulate among different plantations. The solo guitarist was a natural fit for these situations; full bands would have found spontaneous ensemble traveling more difficult, both logistically and economically. In comparison to many other instruments, the guitar was relatively inexpensive and more portable. These factors may have accounted for the predominance of the solo guitarist in Mississippi Delta blues (not to mention country blues as a whole). Delta blues was certainly one of the first forms of the music, if not the first, to emphasize the guitar, an association that of course characterizes much blues music to the present day.

Robert Palmer, a Delta blues authority as both a critic and a record producer (and author of a book-length study of the subject, *Deep Blues*), explains in his liner notes to *Blues Masters Vol. 8: Mississippi Delta Blues* that "Delta blues is a dialogue between the overt and the hidden. The music's apparent simplicity—basic verse forms, little or no harmonic content, melodies with as few as three principal pitches—is superficial. Apparently straightforward rhythmic drive often proves, on careful listening, to be the by-product of a mercurial interplay between polyrhythms, layered in complex relationships. The music's supreme rhythmic masters—Charley Patton, Robert Johnson—kept several rhythms going simultaneously, like a juggler with balls in the air or like the most gifted modern jazz drummers. Sometimes the music seems to lie behind the beat and rush just ahead of it at the same time...."

"The simplest way to characterize the music's origin is as a turn-of-the-century innovation, accommodating the vocal traditions of work songs and field hollers to the expressive capabilities of a newly popular stringed instrument, the guitar. Older black ballads and dance songs, preaching and church singing, the rhythms of folk drumming, and the ring shout of 'holy dance' fed into the new music as well. But the richly

---

Music Map

Delta Blues

Charley Patton
First great star of the Delta blues

Son House • Willie Brown	Johnny Shines
Tommy Johnson	Eddie Taylor
Tommy McClennan	Muddy Waters
Ishman Bracey	Robert Nighthawk
Robert Johnson	John Lee Hooker
Skip James	Howlin' Wolf
Bukka White	Elmore James
Mississippi John Hurt	Mississippi Fred McDowell

---

ornamented, powerfully projected singing style associated with the field holler was dominant, which is hardly surprising; the Delta is more or less one big cotton field."

The man usually recognized as the first exponent of the Delta blues is Charley Patton. Most blues scholars, and indeed many general fans, are now well aware that Patton didn't invent the Delta blues; he was simply one of the first to record it, and was adept at absorbing many of the regional elements that were in the air. As David Evans writes in *The Blackwell Guide to the Blues*, "In Patton's blues, and indeed in his spirituals, ballads, and ragtime tunes, may be found fully formed all the essential characteristics of the Deep South blues style—the gruff impassioned voice suggesting the influence of country preaching and gospel singing style (which he displayed on his religious recordings), the percussive guitar technique, the bending of strings and use of slide style, the driving rhythms and repeated riffs, the traditional lyric formulas, and the simple harmonic structures."

"Patton, however, also displays one highly individual characteristic: he sings about his own experiences and events he observed—frequently ones outside the realm of the usual man-woman relationships in the blues—always shaping his lyrics from a highly personal point of view."

Indeed, the Delta blues as a whole were often more personal, earthy, and downcast than much popular music, reflecting the struggles and bitter realities of Southern blacks in the early '20s, as well as the basic details of rural life.

Other Mississippi bluesmen were already recording in the late '20s. The most important of these was probably Tommy Johnson, a contemporary of Patton's who knew and learned much from the guitarist; Ishman Bracey, who was an associate of Johnson's for a long time, also did a good deal of recording in the era. Much of the activity in this scene centered around the plantation of Will Dockery, where Patton and Johnson would often play, influencing such Dockery residents as the young Howlin' Wolf. The success of Patton's recordings in the race market led labels to issue 78s by other Delta bluesmen, the most notable of which was Son House, another musician who knew Patton well.

The most individual and eccentric of the Delta bluesmen, Skip James, was in a sense not a Delta bluesman at all. James was based in the tiny Mississippi hill town of Bentonia, whose isolation may have contributed to the development of his musical idiosyncrasies. His minor guitar tunings and strange, often falsetto vocals are very unusual for the country blues genre. It's the dark, anguished power of his compositions, though, that may hold the most enduring appeal for listeners throughout the ages.

The devastating effects of the Depression on the music industry meant that Delta bluesmen were rarely afforded the opportunity to record after the '30s. Hence the abrupt end of the recording careers of singers like James, House, and others in the early '30s, not to be resumed until their rediscovery several decades later (if they were still alive, or could still be found). Many others, doubtlessly, never had the chance to record at all, due either to the lack of opportunity within the record business, or the simple luck of the draw when companies scouted for talent.

But the most legendary Delta bluesman of all, Robert Johnson, didn't do any of his recording until 1936. Several books and film productions have been based around his life, much of which is based on legend, as the basic facts of his life (many of which were garnered from acquaintances and traveling companions, such as guitarist Johnny Shines) are surrounded by considerable mystery and confusion. The apocryphal story of how he sold his soul to the devil at the crossroads (a prominent image in Southern black music and culture) provided the basis for one of his most famous songs, and indeed for an entire Hollywood movie.

What we have for real, however, are the 29 songs he recorded in two sessions in 1936 and 1937. In addition to synthesizing much of what was best about the Delta blues, Johnson's songwriting, vocals, and instrumental skills also brought the music closer to a more modern sensibility, particularly in the haunted, agonized individuality of his songs. Famed talent scout and record producer John Hammond was trying to get in touch with Johnson to participate in the pivotal *Spirituals to Swing* concert at New York's Carnegie Hall in 1938, but the guitarist was impossible to locate. Shortly afterwards, it was discovered that he had died in August 1938, another incident that is shrouded in mystery, though many believe that he was poisoned.

Another Delta great who didn't make his best recordings until well after the early '30s was Bukka White. White, yet another guitarist who had met and been influenced by Charley Patton, actually made his recording debut in 1930 as a religious singer. His best music, however, dates from a 1940 session in Chicago. White's rhythmic guitar approach, tough lyrical attitude (he was fresh from a stint in Mississippi's notorious Parchman Farm), and accompaniment from Washboard Sam gave his music a hard-driving force. Combined with the fact that the fidelity on these sides is somewhat better than the more primitive recordings of the late '20s and '30s, this makes White's brand of Delta blues more accessible to many contemporary listeners than much of what was recorded a decade or so earlier.

The Delta blues, of course, didn't die just because it wasn't being recorded often. In the early '40s, Muddy Waters was recorded for the Library of Congress by folklorist Alan Lomax, playing in an acoustic Delta style. Just a few years later, Waters would be bringing Delta blues into the electric age after moving to Chicago, using some of the same sources for songs, and playing guitar in a similar (but amplified) style. He was merely the most famous of the musicians who did so; others included Johnny Shines, Robert Nighthawk, John Lee Hooker, Howlin' Wolf, and Elmore James.

The Delta bluesmen that had never electrified, and never recorded after the '30s, had seemingly vanished into the corridors of time. Until the early '60s, that is, when young enthusiasts, fired by a revival of interest in the blues, determined to trace and track down survivors from the era. They found a lot more than they could have hoped for, both in the way of living embodiments of old blues traditions, and actual blues singers from the Delta who were known only as names on rare 78s.

Skip James, Son House, and Bukka White were all rediscovered in this fashion, and launched new recording and performing careers based around the folk circuit and the LP market. There were also discoveries of elderly guitarists who had never recorded in the first place, some of whom also began professional careers, Mississippi Fred McDowell being the most successful. All of them played to far greater audiences in their old age than they had in their prime, often touring internationally, providing one of the music industry's too-rare tales of cosmic justice.

Many listeners who have never heard bona fide Delta blues have been exposed to it indirectly via rock covers, particularly Cream's versions of Robert Johnson's "Cross Road Blues" (retitled "Crossroads") and Skip James' "I'm So Glad." The Rolling Stones did Robert Johnson's "Love in Vain" and Mississippi Fred McDowell's "I've Got to Move," and explored the Delta blues style with considerable success on albums like *Beggars Banquet* and *Let It Bleed* in the late '60s. Bonnie Raitt toured with McDowell in his final years, and openly credited him as a major influence. Canned Heat and Captain Beefheart were two of the most prominent rock acts of the late '60s that delved into the Delta for much of their inspiration.

The surprise success of Robert Johnson's box set, which sold several hundred thousand copies in the early '90s, supplied proof that the original article will continue to enthrall audiences. This in turn greased the wheels for the reissue of many other compilations of early Delta blues, helping to ensure that the sound—which can still be heard as a living music in pockets of the actual Delta—will not be forgotten by subsequent generations.

Ten Recommended Albums:
Various Artists, *Blues Masters Vol. 8: Mississippi Delta Blues* (Rhino)
Robert Johnson, *The Complete Recordings* (CBS)
Skip James, *The Complete Early Recordings* (Yazoo)
Various Artists, *Roots of Robert Johnson* (Yazoo)
Charley Patton, *Founder of the Delta Blues* (Yazoo)
Tommy Johnson, *Complete Recorded Works* (Document)
Bukka White, *The Complete Bukka White* (Columbia)
Muddy Waters, *The Complete Plantation Recordings* (MCA)
Son House, *Delta Blues: The Original Library of Congress Sessions from Field
   Recordings 1941-42* (Biograph)
Mississippi Fred McDowell, *Mississippi Delta Blues* (Arhoolie)

          —Richie Unterberger

Piedmont Blues

Although Mississippi Delta blues may be the most renowned style of early acoustic blues, guitar-based forms of acoustic blues also thrived elsewhere. One of the most fertile regions was the Piedmont, the southeastern area of the United States stretching from Richmond, Virginia to Atlanta, Georgia. It encompasses music made both in the Appalachian foothills and big cities. Atlanta, base of Blind Willie McTell, Barbecue Bob, and others, was the most active urban center of southeastern blues (early Atlanta blues, it should be noted, is sometimes associated by authorities with the Piedmont style, but sometimes not specifically affiliated with it, or simply grouped in with southeastern regional sounds as a whole).

Styles could vary considerably within this region, but often they were distinguished from other blues recorded in the '20s and '30s by a more rhythmic base, and an emphasis on fingerpicking style of guitar playing. As Barry Lee Pearson explained in a previous *All Music Guide* edition, "The Piedmont guitar style employs a complex fingerpicking style in which a regular, alternating-thumb bass pattern supports a melody on treble strings. The guitar style is highly syncopated and connnects closely with an earlier string-band tradition incorporating ragtime, blues, and country dance songs. It's excellent party music with a full, rock-solid sound."

The relatively large numbers of blind guitarists from this region that recorded—Blind Blake, Blind Boy Fuller, and Blind Willie McTell being the most famous—is less surprising

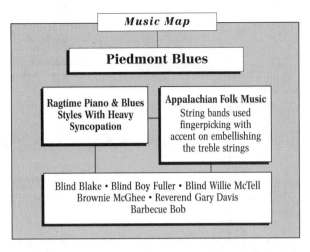

┌─────────────────────────────────┐
│ **Music Map** │
└─────────────────────────────────┘

Piedmont Blues

| Ragtime Piano & Blues Styles With Heavy Syncopation | Appalachian Folk Music String bands used fingerpicking with accent on embellishing the treble strings |

Blind Blake • Blind Boy Fuller • Blind Willie McTell
Brownie McGhee • Reverend Gary Davis
Barbecue Bob

when considering the daunting career prospects facing blind African-Americans of the era. Certainly they wouldn't be able to work at most of the jobs available to Southern blacks at the time, most of which involved skilled and unskilled manual labor. The limited social services available to blacks made the prospect of useful education unlikely. Playing for money in urban neighborhoods, if one had the skills to entertain and the wherewithal to survive on the streets, was actually one of the better options.

Several of the Piedmont bluesmen were instrumental virtuosos whose versatility could encompass other styles as well; Blind Willie McTell proved himself a master of the 12-string guitar, a relatively uncommon instrument in country blues. Ragtime styles were a particularly significant influence, much more so than they were in the Delta. The tone tended to be lighter than Delta blues as well, though as songwriters the Piedmont players were certainly capable of serious reflection.

Ruminating further on the distinction between Delta and Southeastern styles in *The History of the Blues*, Francis Davis speculates that the region's economy was "more diverse than that of Mississippi, and this contributed to a greater diversity of musical styles...there were fewer restrictions on black mobility than in either Mississippi or Texas, and consequently, a greater degree of interplay between black and white musicians. The songs of such Atlantic Seaboard fingerpickers as Blind Blake, Blind Willie McTell, and Blind Boy Fuller were more geniunely songlike than their contemporaries in the Delta and the Southwest. These guitarists were relative sophisticates, with an intuitive grasp of passing chords offsetting a rhythmic conception anchored in older ragtime and minstrel songs."

Plenty of Piedmont blues was recorded in the late '20s and early '30s. But as in other pockets of the blues market, the Depression—and then the onset of World War II—meant that recording activity of blues singers from the area came to a virtual halt. The style didn't die, but it was rarely documented on record from the mid-'30s onwards. Blind Boy Fuller died in 1941, and Blind Blake vanished; Willie McTell did some more recording for both the Library of Congress and commercial labels, though by the end of World War II, his style was appreciated more widely by folklorists than the commercial audience.

The blues revival of the '60s paid much more attention to Delta blues than Southeastern styles, but the Piedmont influence was felt in the successful, lengthy careers of Rev. Gary Davis and the duo of Sonny Terry & Brownie McGhee, all of whom were extremely popular with folk audiences. Performers of subsequent eras have also continued to dip into the repertoire of the Piedmont school, the most prominent example being the Allman Brothers' blues-rock adaptation of McTell's "Statesboro Blues."

Eight Recommended Albums:
Blind Willie McTell, *The Definitive Blind Willie McTell* (Columbia)
Blind Blake, *Ragtime Guitar's Foremost Fingerpicker* (Yazoo)
Blind Boy Fuller, *Blind Boy Fuller* (Document)
Barbecue Bob, *Chocolate to the Bone* (Yazoo)
Brownie McGhee, *Complete Brownie McGhee* (Columbia/Legacy)
Reverend Gary Davis, *1935-49* (Yazoo)
Various Artists, *East Coast Blues, 1926-1935* (Yazoo)
Various Artists, *The Georgia Blues, 1927-33* (Yazoo)

          —Richie Unterberger

Lester Melrose & Early Chicago Blues

Downhome Delta blues didn't mutate into Chicago electric blues overnight when Muddy Waters arrived on his train from Clarksdale, MS, in 1943. Even before Muddy had set foot in the city, Chicago had a thriving urban blues scene that did much to link country and urban styles. Much of the best blues to come out of the region in the '30s and '40s was recorded by one man, producer and A&R director Lester Melrose.

Today, with a record industry overstuffed with artists, producers, and corporate decision-makers from top to bottom, it's hard to imagine one person wielding as much influence as Melrose did at his peak. Two of the biggest labels in the world—Columbia and Victor—relied upon Melrose to develop much of the blues talent on its roster. (Victor

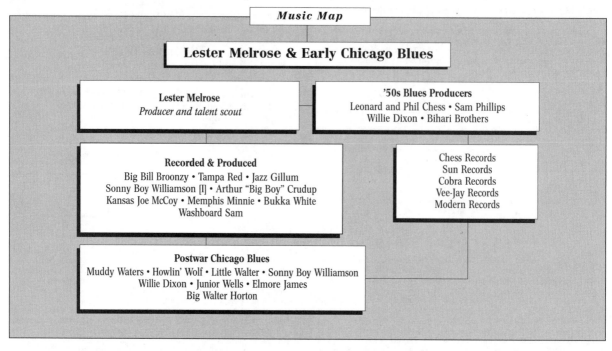

placed these blues artists on a subsidiary, Bluebird.) The musicians who Melrose assembled read like a who's who of early blues, including Big Bill Broonzy, Tampa Red, Memphis Minnie, Sonny Boy Williamson, Big Joe Williams, Bukka White, Washboard Sam, and Arthur "Big Boy" Crudup.

Many of Melrose's artists came from rural backgrounds; you couldn't get much deeper into the Delta than Bukka White, whom Melrose recorded shortly after his release from a sentence at the notorious Parchman Farm. Melrose's chief contribution to modernizing the blues was to establish a sound with full band arrangements. With ensemble playing, a rhythm section, and even some electricity, these clearly prefigured the Chicago electric blues sound that would begin to explode in the late '40s.

Comments Robert Palmer in *Deep Blues*, "Melrose's artists had down-home backgrounds: Tampa Red, a top-selling blues star since the late '20s, was from Georgia; John Lee 'Sonny Boy' Williamson, who was largely responsible for transforming the harmonica from an accompanying instrument into a major solo voice, was from Jackson, Tennessee, just north of Memphis; Washboard Sam was from Arkansas; Big Bill Broonzy was a Mississippian by birth. But in the interests of holding onto their increasingly urbanized audience and pleasing Melrose, who was interested both in record sales and in lucrative publishing royalties, they recorded several kinds of material, including jazz and novelty numbers, and began to favor band backing."

"During the mid-'30s the bands tended to be small—guitar and piano, sometimes a clarinet, a washboard, a string bass. But by the time Muddy arrived in Chicago, the 'Bluebird Beat,' as it has been called, was frequently carried by bass and drums. The music was a mixture of older black blues and vaudeville styles and material with the newer swing rhythms. Some of the records even featured popular black jazzmen."

Melrose was the sort of all-around entrepreneur that was much more common in the early days of the music business. He was not just a producer in the sense of overseeing sessions, but also a talent scout and a song publisher. His involvement in the actual music, however, was substantial. He established a consistent sound for his productions by often using his artists to play on each other's records (often they would rehearse at Tampa Red's house). Washboard Sam, for instance, was often used to supply a percussive beat, even if (as on Bukka White's material) he was the sole accompanist. In this sense, too, Melrose helped establish prototypes for "house bands" that gave important labels like Chess an identifiable sound and led listeners to expect a certain artistic quality from a company's roster, rather than just a bunch of artists that all happened to play blues.

It didn't hurt, of course, that the musicians themselves were about as talented as any group that consistently worked for the same operation. For starters, there was the greatest early blues harmonica player in the first Sonny Boy Williamson (not to be confused with the other great Sonny Boy Williamson, Rice Miller, who would record for Chess later on); the best early woman blues singer/guitarist, Memphis Minnie; and Big Bill Broonzy, one of the most prolific songwriters of the pre-World War II era. He also did his part to push country blues into something approaching rock & roll by recording Arthur "Big Boy" Crudup, whose "That's All Right Mama" was covered by Elvis Presley in 1954 for his first single.

Elvis would also turn in covers of Crudup's "My Baby Left Me" and "So Glad You're Mine" for two of his most exciting mid-'50s recordings. By that time, Melrose had been left in the dust by the rawer, louder, and far more electric Chicago blues sound that had

been developed at Chess Records and elsewhere in the late '40s and early '50s. Ironically, Melrose had been the first to record Muddy Waters, at a 1946 session, but Muddy really didn't find his voice in the studio until a couple of years later with Chess.

Melrose's assocation with Columbia and Victor had far reaching consequences that ensured the preservation of his work for future generations, in ways that no one could have foreseen back in the '30s and '40s, when blues was recorded strictly for the "race" market. These powerful labels were still powerful players in the record industry 50 years later, when the compact disc began to take over from vinyl, and when the blues audience had expanded to include many black and white collectors and enthusiasts. In the '90s, much of the classic work that Melrose recorded had been reissued on CD. As a consequence it's far more widely available—and widely respected—than it's ever been before.

Seven Recommended Albums:
Big Bill Broonzy, *Good Time Tonight* (CBS)
Memphis Minnie, *Hoodoo Lady (1933-37)* (CBS)
Tampa Red, *Guitar Wizard* (RCA)
Washboard Sam, *Rockin' My Blues Away* (RCA)
Bukka White, *The Complete Bukka White* (Columbia)
Sonny Boy Williamson I, *Throw a Boogie Woogie (With Big Joe Williams)* (RCA)
Arthur "Big Boy" Crudup, *That's Allright Mama* (RCA)

—Richie Unterberger

Classic Female Blues Singers

The image of the blues as a man hunched over his acoustic guitar in the Mississippi Delta—or, alternately, hunched over his electric axe or harmonica as he moans into a microphone at a sweaty club—is so ingrained in the collective consciousness that it comes as a shock to many to learn that the first blues stars were women. Indeed, women dominated the recorded blues field in the '20s, the first decade in which a market for blues records existed. Except for the very most famous of these singers, these pioneers are largely forgotten today, having been retroactively surpassed in popularity by some Southern bluesmen who only recorded a precious handful of sides in the '20s and '30s. But these women were the performers who first took blues to a national audience.

The popularity of the early blueswomen was intimately tied to the birth of the recording industry itself. There were many kinds of nascent blues on the rise in the early 20th century—Delta guitarists, yes, but also songsters, jug bands, and dance bands that employed elements of jazz, blues, and pop. And there was the vaudeville stage circuit, which frequently featured women singers. Presenting productions that toured widely, the musicians involved couldn't helped but be exposed to blues forms, if they hadn't been already.

It so happened that female-sung blues, with a prominent vaudeville-jazz-pop flavor, was the first kind of blues to be recorded for the popular audience. There are many possible reasons for this. Perhaps the record companies felt that other styles of blues were too raw to market. Or they may have been largely unaware of more rural and Southern blues styles. The female vaudevillian blues singers had a jazzier and more urban sound that commercial companies may have been more likely to encounter and stamp with approval.

What's far more certain is that "Crazy Blues," recorded by Mamie Smith in 1920, was the first commercial recording of what came to be recognized as the blues. By the standards of the day, the record was a phenomenal success, selling 75,000 copies within the first month—in an era, it must be remembered, when much of the U.S. population, and an even higher percentage of the U.S. African-American population, didn't own a record player. It set off an immediate storm of records in the same vein, by Smith and numerous other women.

But to today's listener, "Crazy Blues" hardly sounds like a blues at all. It sounds more like vaudeville, with a bit of the blues creeping into the edges of the vocal delivery and the song structure. The more judgmental might find that it resembles the music found in contemporary Broadway productions that offer a nostalgic facsimile of pre-Depression black theater. The song has to be taken in the context of its era, however. It was the first time anything with some allegiance to the blues form had been recorded—and the industry quickly found that such productions were being bought not just by blacks, but by all Americans.

Mamie Smith's success opened the floodgates for numerous blueswomen to record in the '20s, often on the OKeh and Paramount labels. Ida Cox, Sippie Wallace, Victoria Spivey, Lucille Bogan, Ethel Waters, and Alberta Hunter are some of the most famous; there were many others. The best of them were Ma Rainey and Bessie Smith, both of whom had rawer, more emotional qualities that gives their recordings a feel more akin to what later listeners expect of the blues.

Today, the early recordings by the "classic" female blues singers, as they have sometimes been labeled, sound as much or more like jazz as blues. The vocalists were usually accompanied by small jazz combos, often featuring piano, cornet, and other horn instruments. The guitar, the instrument associated with the blues more than any other, was frequently absent, and usually secondary when it was used. Lots of early jazz stars, in fact, can be heard on the early blueswomen's records, including Louis Armstrong, King Oliver, Duke Ellington, and Coleman Hawkins.

Yet the music is identifiable as blues, primarily via the vocal phrasing and the widespread use of the 12-bar song structures that are among the blues' most immediate trademarks. And it was not a form that thrived in isolation from the other styles of blues that were emerging throughout America. As top blues scholar Samuel Charters writes in his liner notes to *Blues Masters Vol. 11: Classic Blues Women*, "Even the men living in the South and playing the blues for themselves and their neighbors learned many of their songs from the records that made their way down to local music stores or came through the post office from the mail-order blues companies in Chicago. If they didn't learn the songs themselves, they learned the form and the style of what the record companies thought of as the blues."

"So when the companies sent scouts to find new artists in the South, what they found were the same three or four ways of putting blues verses together. After the sweeping success of the first recordings by women blues artists, the 12-bar harmonic form on the records had become so ubiquitous that even the Delta players who only fingered a single chord on their guitars managed to suggest all the usual chord changes with their singing."

The blues could also be heard in the singers' frank discussions of topics like sex, infidelity, and money and drink problems, often with a palpable hurt. These were offered with a female perspective that has never been as widespread in the blues since, as the music came to be dominated by male performers after the Depression. Listeners from all eras can cut through the often scratchy recordings to find the seeds of the blues, and much modern pop music, in their depiction of hard times, and the struggle and endurance necessary to survive them. It's not all bleakness—the celebratory tunes could have a frank bawdiness, particularly when dealing with sexual double entendres, that would probably generate warning stickers if they were being purchased by today's teenagers.

The onset of the Depression meant hard times for the record business, as it did for every other industry. The craze for female blues singers, which may have already peaked in the mid-'20s, was over, and not just because of artistic trends. Record labels in general were recording less sides. And they weren't eager to devote a lot of resources to the "race" market, populated as it was by the poorest Americans. These African-American listeners would have even less purchasing power in the '30s, as the Depression lowered their already low standard of living.

But it wasn't just economic factors that heralded the demise of the classic women blues singers. Urban African-American music was becoming more uptempo and elaborate. The swing and big band sound came to fruition in the '30s, making the staider accompaniment common to many '20s female blues recordings sound tame in comparison. And the vaudeville/theatrical circuit that supported the singers was crumbling, threatening their livelihood just years after they enjoyed positively unimaginable wealth (by the standards of African-Americans of the '20s). Many were unable to make records or, after a few years, even perform; the tale of Mamie Smith, who died penniless in 1946, is unfortunately not unique. Bessie Smith and Ma Rainey would themselves be dead by 1940.

It may be that many of the women who would have been blues singers had they started in the '20s ended up as jazz ones. Jazz as a whole proved much more fruitful for women singers fronting a band than blues would in the ensuing decades. Billie Holiday, acclaimed by many as one of the finest singers of any kind in the 20th century, certainly owed a great deal to the female blues vocalists of the '20s. Several of her earlier sides in particular could just as well be classified as blues as jazz. The blues feel remained prominent in many if not most of the major female jazz singers, from Dinah Washington to Cassandra Wilson.

The original female blues stars of the '20s didn't always disappear entirely. Alberta Hunter, for instance, if anything became more popular after the '20s, and made an unexpectedly successful comeback as a senior citizen in the '70s and '80s, after about 25 years of retirement. Ethel Waters expanded into jazz, and then into movies, getting an Academy Award nomination for Best Supporting Actress for a 1949 film. Victoria Spivey,

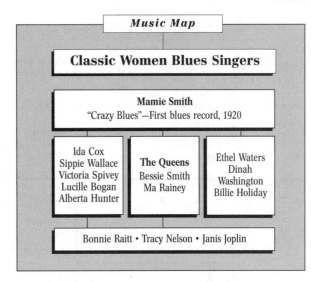

Music Map

Classic Women Blues Singers

Mamie Smith
"Crazy Blues"—First blues record, 1920

| Ida Cox Sippie Wallace Victoria Spivey Lucille Bogan Alberta Hunter | **The Queens** Bessie Smith Ma Rainey | Ethel Waters Dinah Washington Billie Holiday |

Bonnie Raitt • Tracy Nelson • Janis Joplin

returning to active recording in the '60s, started her own label; Bob Dylan made his first appearance on an official recording for the company, playing harmonica on a Big Joe Williams session.

The blues revival of the '60s, however, largely passed the classic female blues singers by, though Sippie Wallace did record an album with the Jim Kweskin Jug Band. The vocalists were a considerable influence on pioneering '60s rock singers Janis Joplin and Tracy Nelson (who recorded an entire album of Ma Rainey and Bessie Smith songs in her folkie days), thereby influencing rock performers who had never heard the originals. In any case, the styles that the early women blues singers brought to record had by then infiltrated all of blues, rock, soul, and pop, to be heard in almost everyone from Aretha Franklin on down.

Ten Recommended Albums:
Various Artists, *Blues Masters, Vol. 11: Classic Blues Women* (Rhino)
Bessie Smith, *The Collection* (CBS)
Ma Rainey, *Ma Rainey* (Milestone)
Sippie Wallace, *1923-29* (Alligator)
Victoria Spivey, *1926-31* (Document)
Mamie Smith, *In Chronological Order, Vol. 1* (Document)
Lucille Bogan, *1923-35* (Story of Blues)
Alberta Hunter, *Young Alberta Hunter* (Vintage Jazz)
Ethel Waters, *Jazzin' Babies' Blues, 1921-1927* (Biograph)
Various Artists, *Women's Railroad Blues: Sorry But I Can't Take You* (Rosetta)
—*Richie Unterberger*

Jump Blues

The currents of jazz and blues may have run closer together in the '40s than they did in any other decade. One of the biggest offshoots of this cross-breeding was jump blues, a form that thrived in the late '40s and early '50s in particular. With its rhythmic swing, boisterous vocalists, and oft-lighthearted songs about partying, drinking, and jiving, it hasn't lent itself as extensively to critical analysis as styles like rural Delta guitarists or electric Chicago blues. During the decade or so when it thrived, however, it laid much of the groundwork for what became known as rhythm & blues, and thus by extension rock & roll.

The roots of jump blues, like many popular styles that became widespread in the middle of the 20th century, can be traced to larger trends of social modernization. In the '40s, the large big bands of the '30s scaled back into smaller combos, partially because of economic considerations (particularly during World War II) that made supporting a large ensemble difficult. There were still plenty of African-American patrons for dance halls, however, who wanted a sound that was both danceable and loud. This led many swing bands to place a greater emphasis on honking saxophones and hard-driving vocalists who could be heard over the din, often categorized after the event as "honkers and shouters."

There were many notable forerunners of the jump blues sound to be heard in the jazz community of the '30s. Pianists like Meade "Lux" Lewis, Albert Ammons, and Jimmy Yancey devised boogie-woogie patterns; singers like Slim Gaillard and Cab Calloway sang hipster lyrics (sometimes dubbed "jive") with links to both blues and pop traditions. The midwestern cities of Kansas City and St. Louis acted as incubators for the jump blues scene, with their heritage of hot swing bands with vocalists that were open to the influence of the blues.

As Peter Grendysa writes in his liner notes to Rhino's *Blues Masters, Vol. 5: Jump Blues Classics*, "The antiphonal (call-and-response) characteristic of African music so evident in country blues and gospel was adapted by jump blues, often with the voice of the saxophone played against the vocalist, who shouted rather than sang the lyrics. The saxophone was

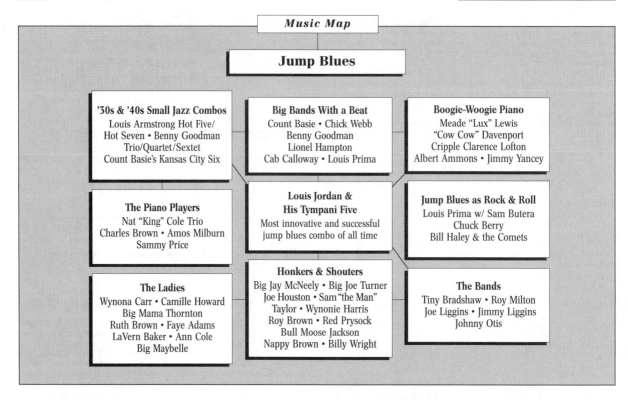

Music Map

Jump Blues

'30s & '40s Small Jazz Combos
Louis Armstrong Hot Five/
Hot Seven • Benny Goodman
Trio/Quartet/Sextet
Count Basie's Kansas City Six

Big Bands With a Beat
Count Basie • Chick Webb
Benny Goodman
Lionel Hampton
Cab Calloway • Louis Prima

Boogie-Woogie Piano
Meade "Lux" Lewis
"Cow Cow" Davenport
Cripple Clarence Lofton
Albert Ammons • Jimmy Yancey

The Piano Players
Nat "King" Cole Trio
Charles Brown • Amos Milburn
Sammy Price

**Louis Jordan &
His Tympani Five**
Most innovative and successful
jump blues combo of all time

Jump Blues as Rock & Roll
Louis Prima w/ Sam Butera
Chuck Berry
Bill Haley & the Comets

The Ladies
Wynona Carr • Camille Howard
Big Mama Thornton
Ruth Brown • Faye Adams
LaVern Baker • Ann Cole
Big Maybelle

Honkers & Shouters
Big Jay McNeely • Big Joe Turner
Joe Houston • Sam "the Man"
Taylor • Wynonie Harris
Roy Brown • Red Prysock
Bull Moose Jackson
Nappy Brown • Billy Wright

The Bands
Tiny Bradshaw • Roy Milton
Joe Liggins • Jimmy Liggins
Johnny Otis

played wth athletic power and exuberance; the saxman squeezing out honks, bleats, and squeals to the delight of the crowds and the dismay of traditional jazz fans. Strong backbeats were provided by the drummer's snares and rim shots on the second and fourth beats of every bar and reinforced by the bass player marking every beat."

Some of the first performers to sing in a readily identifiable "jump blues" style were very grounded in the jazz world. Big Joe Turner, one of the few performers to bridge the jazz, R&B, and rock & roll eras, had been singing jazz since the late '30s, even appearing at the famed *Spirituals to Swing* concert in 1938 at New York's Carnegie Hall. Turner may be more responsible than anyone else for founding the "shouting" school of R&B singing, emphasizing smooth but commanding vocal presence. Based (like Turner) in Kansas City, bandleader Jay McShann may be most famous for cultivating the talents of the young Charlie Parker, but he also did his part to create jump blues by employing Walter Brown, another of the earliest shouters.

The most influential architect of jump blues, however—indeed, one of the more significant figures in 20th century American music—was alto saxophonist and singer Louis Jordan. After serving in Chick Webb's band in the '30s, he formed his own outfit, the Tympany Five. In the mid- and late '40s, he ran off an astonishing series of R&B hits that set much of the tone for the jump blues genre, especially the fast, danceable rhythms and the joking, novelty-tinged lyrics—traits that did not pass unnoticed by Chuck Berry. Jordan was also a rock & roll forefather in that he was one of the first R&B performers to make significant inroads into the pop and white audiences.

Jump blues really began exploding commercially after World War II, as America got set to relax and party after years of contributing to the war effort, as jazz headed off in directions less conducive to dancing, and as large numbers of African-Americans moved from the country to the city, taking some of the country blues tradition with them. The West Coast, particularly Los Angeles, was a hotbed of jump blues/proto-R&B. There was a large black community (many recent arrivals), and large numbers of small-combo bands looking to survive the transition from big bands to earthier small ones. And there were new independent labels cropping up—Specialty, Modern, Aladdin, Swingtime—that saw a niche for black popular music that was being ignored by the majors.

Los Angeles in particular was a breeding ground for the saxophonists that would become known as the honkers—musicians who got a grainy, squealing tone and summon frenetic bursts of notes on the uptempo tunes. They were often great showmen in concert as well, playing on their backs sometimes to whip the crowds into more frenzy. Illinois Jacquet had set a model of sorts for the style on his classic soloing on Lionel Hampton's huge hit "Flying Home" and his work on the live Norman Granz-produced *Jazz at the Philharmonic* recordings, introducing a few elements that would become widespread in R&B and rock & roll. Big Jay McNeely, Joe Houston, and Chuck Higgins were some of the most noteworthy saxophonists of the style, sometimes doing without vocals entirely, the sheer bravado of their solos being enough to build their studio tracks around.

The West Coast favored an urbane brand of jump blues that owed much to jazz. Electric guitar pioneer T-Bone Walker is usually thought of as a bluesman, but certainly his

'40s recordings—which are usually pegged as his best and most influential—incorporated a lot from jazz and jump blues. Though not a bluesman per se, Nat King Cole in his early days would approach a jump blues mood, and traces of his suave charm can be found in many '40s jump blues sides.

Several West Coast bandleaders had a lot of success in the late '40s with a sort of polished grit. On Specialty Records alone, there was Joe Liggins, his brother Jimmy, and Roy Milton. Milton, though only a hazily remembered figure, was a huge star in his day, landing well over a dozen singles in the R&B Top Ten in the late '40s and early '50s. His pianist, Camille Howard, was a notable recording artist in his own right, and a premier example of a jazz-boogie performer who seemed to have gotten dragged into the R&B world more by happenstance and the forces of historical change than anything else. Johnny Otis would organize a lot of L.A. talent as a bandleader, vocalist, talent scout, promoter, label owner, and general all-around champion of the scene.

The boogie-woogie-derived structure of much jump blues lent itself well to pianists, and several of the best jump blues singers also excelled at the keyboards. Prominent among them was Amos Milburn, who could handle both Charles Brown-ish ballads and rowdy songs about drinking, and Floyd Dixon, famous as the originator of "Hey Bartender," served to the masses decades later via the Blues Brothers. For those who liked their jump blues a bit rougher, there were the pre-eminent shouters, Roy Brown and Wynonie Harris. Both of them had big R&B hits with "Good Rockin' Tonight," and both were influences upon Elvis Presley, who would make the tune his second Sun single. Jump blues also had more room for female participation than many other blues subgenres, with Camille Howard and Wynona Carr both scoring substantial successes for Specialty, and R&B-based singers like Big Maybelle and Big Mama Thornton recording singles heavily indebted to the style.

There were an enormous number of jump blues records cut between 1945 and 1955, and a brief survey of some of the most famous pianists, bandleaders, saxophonists, shouters, and women singers still leaves out a great many names that are treasured by blues and R&B fans. Just to scratch the surface, you could mention shouter Nappy Brown, Tiny Bradshaw (who did the original version of "The Train Kept A-Rollin'"), Red Prysock, Bull Moose Jackson, the pre-Atlantic recordings of Ray Charles, and Billy Wright (the last of whom was Little Richard's chief early inspiration). The Savoy label alone recorded enough singers, briefly and extensively, to generate numerous various artist compilations.

Yet by the mid-'50s, the jump blues style was definitely on the wane. It was a story that has repeated itself numerous times throughout the history of pop—a whole school of stylists, seemingly at its peak, was swept aside by a horde of younger and rawer upstarts. It wasn't just a few Elvis Presleys and Little Richards, though—it was the whole tidal wave of rock & roll.

Certainly the dividing line between jump blues and R&B is a very fine one. A transitional figure like Jackie Brenston, for instance, could fall into either camp. Early sides by Atlantic R&B artists like Ruth Brown and LaVern Baker sometimes owed a lot to jump blues and the same could be said of early rock instrumentalists like Bill Doggett. And

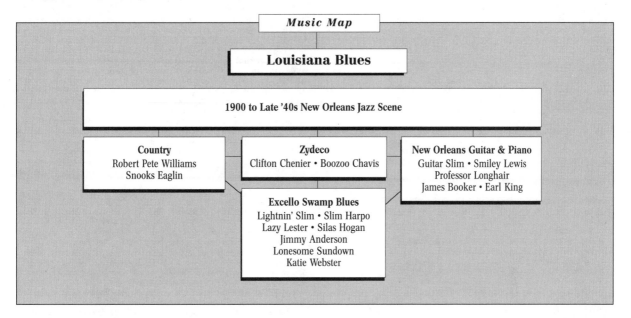

Music Map

Louisiana Blues

1900 to Late '40s New Orleans Jazz Scene

Country
Robert Pete Williams
Snooks Eaglin

Zydeco
Clifton Chenier • Boozoo Chavis

New Orleans Guitar & Piano
Guitar Slim • Smiley Lewis
Professor Longhair
James Booker • Earl King

Excello Swamp Blues
Lightnin' Slim • Slim Harpo
Lazy Lester • Silas Hogan
Jimmy Anderson
Lonesome Sundown
Katie Webster

many early doo-wop sides have a lot of jump blues in them—listen to Drifters tracks like "Fools Fall in Love" or "Such a Night" for the evidence. But the hard fact was that R&B, and its close relation rock & roll, had dropped much of the jazz and boogie woogie so prominent in jump blues. The most raucous sounds of its saxophones were retained, but there was progressively more emphasis on electric guitars, group vocals, and younger performers with a greater appeal to teenagers.

By 1956, most of the jump blues stars were scuffling for survival. Some adapted to the rock & roll era with some success, most notably Joe Turner and Johnny Otis; others tried to adapt to rock & roll trends unsuccessfully, like Roy Brown and even Louis Jordan. There were a few, like Turner and Jimmy Witherspoon, who could slide back into the jazz world if they wished, having never strayed far from it in the first place. Sometimes an old star would surface unexpectedly like Amos Milburn, who had a surprise tenure with Motown in the early '60s.

Unless you're a devoted collector or scholar, it can seem as though most jump blues greats have vanished into a black hole of history. Perhaps that's because the form bridged blues, jazz, R&B, and pop, without quite fitting into any of the forms comfortably. Another factor is the general absence of hot guitar solos, a general touchstone for most modern fans connecting with older forms of blues.

Jump blues, however, is blues at its most fun—a call to arms not to bewail tribulations or reflect upon the abyss, but to let loose, wail, and party. In the bargain, it was probably the most important foundation for what became known in the '50s as R&B, and gave us much of the rhythm and humor that we take for granted in contemporary rock, blues, and soul.

12 Recommended Albums:
Various Artists, *Blues Masters Vol. 5: Jump Blues Classics* (Rhino)
Various Artists, *Blues Masters Vol. 14: More Jump Blues* (Rhino)
Big Joe Turner, *Big, Bad & Blue: The Joe Turner Anthology* (Rhino)
Louis Jordan, *The Best of Louis Jordan* (MCA)
Roy Milton, *Roy Milton & His Solid Senders* (Specialty)
T-Bone Walker, *The Complete Capitol Black & White Recordings* (Capitol)
Amos Milburn, *Down the Road Apiece: The Best of Amos Milburn* (EMI)
Joe Houston, *Cornbread and Cabbage Greens* (Specialty)
Floyd Dixon, *Marshall Texas is My Home* (Specialty)
Roy Brown, *Good Rocking Tonight: The Best of Roy Brown* (Rhino)
Wynonie Harris, *Bloodshot Eyes: The Best of Wynonie Harris* (Rhino)
Various Artists, *The Original Johnny Otis Show* (Savoy)

—Richie Unterberger

Louisiana Blues

Long hailed as the birthplace of jazz, and a crucible of all kinds of roots sounds, New Orleans has influenced the course of American music as much as any other city. It does not, however, loom as large in the history of the blues as one might expect. Certainly regions like Chicago, Memphis, and the Mississippi Delta have produced many more performers of note; each of those areas also has a far more distinctive blues style. New Orleans is much more the champion of old-school jazz and funky rhythm & blues. But the city, and the Louisiana state, have made some estimable contributions to the history of blues, even if these are somewhat harder to finger and pigeonhole than many others.

As Robert Palmer muses in *Deep Blues*, "It seems strange that New Orleans, the metropolis at the mouth of the Mississippi River, didn't attract more Delta bluesmen. Rice Miller and Elmore James performed there frequently during the '40s, playing in the

streets before they gradutaed to club engagements, and other Mississippi bluesmen paid occasional visits. But New Orleans had its own indigenous brand of blues, a jazz-oriented style that had more to do with Texas and Kansas City music than with the Delta and often made use of the Afro-Caribbean rhythm patterns that have survived in the city's folklore since the celebrated slave gatherings that took place in Congo Square."

Not that deep blues was totally unknown in the region. Whatever vestiges of country blues may have remained in the area after World War II can be heard, at least in part, on *Bloodstains on the Wall: Country Blues from Specialty*, a compilation of performances recorded by the L.A.-based label in New Orleans. And some of the most traditional styles of Louisiana blues may have been preserved on sessions by Robert Pete Williams, who was recorded by folklorist Harry Oster in the Louisiana State Penitentiary in the late '50s (Williams went on to make other records as well after his release from prison).

The most significant urban blues to originate from the city, however, was recorded in 1953 by Guitar Slim, who originally hailed from the Delta. "The Things That I Used to Do," one of the biggest R&B hits of 1954, was Slim's definitive statement, as much gospel/R&B as blues, with the spiritual, funky feel that characterizes much New Orleans music. It's been speculated that the bandleader on the session, a young Ray Charles, was inspired to try a similar fusion of the gospel and secular on his own records as a result of the record's enormous success. The blues factor of Guitar Slim's equation, though, was unmistakable in his electric guitar work, which by the standards of the time was unimaginably hard and fuzzy.

Most New Orleans R&B of the '50s could not be comfortably classified as blues, as Guitar Slim was. With its funky rhythms and pop/jazz influences, it looked forward to rock & roll (or indeed was rock & roll) and soul music much more than it looked to blues roots. The line between blues and R&B can get thin, of course, as it does with jump blues; many if not most of the great New Orleans R&B/rock performers had a bluesy feel. None of this should obscure the fact that whatever it's called, it's a mammoth body of great music, available on numerous reissues.

Some Crescent City artists were bluesier than others, though, one of the most famous being pianist Professor Longhair, a beloved figure who symbolizes New Orleans music to many listeners. A similar but more obscure figure is James Booker, who like Longhair had a career renaissance in the '70s and '80s. For guitarists, you could check out Snooks Eaglin, who, in the songster tradition, led simultaneous careers as a commercial New Orleans R&B artist (for Imperial) and an acoustic blues/folk singer (for Prestige, Arhoolie, and other labels). Imperial was also responsible for recording some West Coast blues artists in New Orleans with hopes of reviving their flagging careers, including Roy Brown and Pee Wee Crayton. New Orleans guitar blues was kept alive through the '60s by Earl King, who flavored his touch with rock and soul, a combination appreciated by Jimi Hendrix, who covered King's "Come On."

A more distinctive Louisiana blues sound, that of "swamp" blues, was produced elsewhere in the state by Baton Rouge artists Slim Harpo, Lightnin' Slim, Silas Hogan, Lonesome Sundown, and Lazy Lester. All of them recorded under the direction of Crowley, LA, producer Jay Miller, producing a unique blues sound and style characterized by lazy beats, relaxed vocals, doom-laden reverberant production, trebly guitar work, odd percussion effects, and wailing harmonica. Slim Harpo was the greatest of these figures, and his compelling combinations of snaky guitar riffs and raw harmonica blasts were a huge influence on several British Invasion bands. Indeed, he spun a virtual catalog of material that would be covered by U.K. groups, including "I'm a King Bee" and "Shake Your Hips" (the Rolling Stones), "Got Love If You Want It" (the Kinks and Yardbirds), "Don't Start Crying Now" (Them), and "Raining in My Heart" (the Pretty Things); Slim himself made a well-deserved entry into the Top 20 in 1966 with "Baby Scratch My Back." Although not from Louisiana originally, pianist Katie Webster also made her mark on swamp blues, as a session musician for Jay Miller and a sporadic recording artist on her own.

New Orleans is a famed melting pot of sounds and cultures, and one of its most distinctive regional musics, zydeco, certainly owes a visible debt to the blues. Performers such as Clifton Chenier, Boozoo Chavis, and Rockin' Dopsie are in the main beyond the scope of this book, as they draw from Cajun, pop, R&B, and folk sources more than blues to devise their rhythmic brew. The best of them are certainly worth checking out, however, as an interesting branch of the roots music tree with definite ties to the blues in the phrasing and some of the rhythms and songs.

Although blues does not have as extensive a tradition in New Orleans as it does in some other cities, it's better positioned to thrive in the area these days than in most other parts of the country, simply because the region has an extensive support system for locally performed roots music. That's true at both the club/jukejoint level and internationally renowned festivals; the annual New Orleans Jazz & Blues Festival features carloads of blues performers from all over (in addition to numerous other jazz, R&B, and rock acts). Family connections to the music seemed to have endured better in Louisiana than some other regions, and performers like Guitar Slim, Jr., Kenny Neal (son of Raful), and Chris Thomas (son of Tabby) have all kept the blues flame burning with recent recordings.

14 Recommended Albums:

Various Artists, *Bloodstains on the Wall: Country Blues from Specialty* (Specialty)
Robert Pete Williams, *Those Prison Blues* (Arhoolie)
Guitar Slim, *Sufferin' Mind* (Specialty)
Professor Longhair, *Fess: Professor Longhair Anthology* (Rhino)
Slim Harpo, *Hip Shakin': The Excello Collection* (Rhino)
Snooks Eaglin, *The Complete Imperial Recordings* (Capitol)
Lightnin' Slim, *Rooster Blues* (Excello)
Lazy Lester, *I Hear You Knockin'* (Excello)
Lonesome Sundown, *I'm A Mojo Man* (Excello)
Silas Hogan, *Trouble* (Excello)
Katie Webster, *Katie Webster* (Paula)
Clifton Chenier, *Zydeco Dynamite: The Clifton Chenier Anthology* (Rhino)
Various Artists, *Alligator Stomp, Vols. 1-3* (Rhino)
Various Artists, *Crescent City Soul: The Sound of New Orleans 1947-1974* (EMI)

—Richie Unterberger

Harmonica Blues

Perhaps there is something special about free reeds (harmonica, accordion, concertina) that appeals to the human ear and soul—the sounds made when air rushes over a metal reed. The blues harp can have an intensity that reaches right past any personality barriers and grabs at the feelings like few instruments can. The plaintive wail of an acoustic harp (harmonica) and the powerful intensity of amplified harmonica are important sounds that are featured in the blues tradition.

Since the blues became amplified and electrified, the harmonica has been a staple for many bands—not as ubiquitous as the guitar, perhaps, but more the rule than the exception. The instrument has often served a horn-like function in the blues combo (giving rise to its nickname as the "Mississippi saxophone"), producing the sorts of full-bodied, grainy sounds that are nigh impossible to manufacture from string instruments.

Prior to World War II, the harmonica was not as prominent an instrument in live or recorded blues, and certainly very secondary in comparison to guitars and pianos. To get a facsimile of horn-like fullness, early blues recordings were apt to use other instruments; the kazoo was often employed on the records of jug bands (although Noah Lewis' work with Cannon's Jug Stompers are some of the earliest—and finest—recorded examples of blues harmonica on disc), and pan quill pipes were sometimes used, a famous example being Henry Thomas' "Bull Doze Blues" (which was remade into a pop hit by Canned Heat in the late '60s as "Going Up the Country"). The mysterious George "Bullet" Williams appears to be one of the first harmonica players to be recorded in the '20s before disappearing into the mists of time. DeFord Bailey was an extremely popular harmonica virtuoso in the '20s and '30s via his frequent appearances on the *Grand Old Opry,* though he was not solely a blues player, performing country and folk tunes as well. Sonny Terry may have been the most notable country blues harmonica man, later finding favor with the blues/folk crossover audience, both in his longstanding partnership with guitarist Brownie McGhee and his work as accompanist to artists like Leadbelly.

The man who did the most to popularize the instrument as well as linking country and urban blues together was undoubtedly John Lee "Sonny Boy" Williamson, now forever listed in the history books as Sonny Boy Williamson [I]. His use of "choked" notes and wah-wah hand effects, coupled with great songwriting and swinging vocals, made him the first great star of the instrument. His influence spread through the blues community like wildfire, spawning a raft of acolytes and making him literally one of the godfathers of the postwar Chicago scene. His recordings from the '30s and '40s popularized songs that would resurface in the repertoires of major Chicago blues stars like Junior Wells and Muddy Waters. His stabbing death in 1948 robbed the blues of one of its true original voices.

The reason for the numerical appendage to John Lee's name can be directly traced to a bit of chicanery involving a Mississippi blues harp genius named Rice Miller. Traversing the South in the '30s and '40s as Little Boy Blue, Miller worked with Robert Johnson, a young Howlin' Wolf, and myriad others, living the hard life of an itinerant bluesman. When the Interstate Grocers Association decided to broadcast him live on the *King Biscuit Time* radio show on KFFA from Helena, AR, they decided to change his name into something more recognizable to blues listeners. After Williamson's senseless death (who never toured the South, but whose records were nonetheless enormously popular), Miller became "the original" Sonny Boy Williamson; blues reference works now differentiate between the two men by referring to Miller as Sonny Boy Williamson [II]. Sonny Boy [II] (actually older than John Lee by about 15 years) did a lot to popularize harmonica blues with his broadcasts in the '40s and early '50s with his first recordings for the Trumpet label, the popularity of both eventually luring him North to Chicago where he became one of the shining jewels in the Chess Records blues crown.

But with the rise of the electric sound on the Chicago blues scene, the man who really changed it all was Little Walter, who is still acknowledged as the top virtuoso of blues harmonica. Walter Jacobs occupies a position in the history of the blues harmonica comparable to Charlie Parker's in the history of the jazz saxophone, or Jimi Hendrix's in the history of rock guitar. It was Walter, more than anyone else, who was responsible for establishing the basic vocabulary of the instrument, especially as it's used in electric blues bands.

A professional musician from about the time he entered his teenage years, Walter's arrival in Chicago in the late '40s found him playing for tips on Maxwell Street in the then popular style of Sonny Boy I. By the early '50s however, all of that changed, with Walter being one of the first to start amplifying his harp. Armed with a cheap microphone, cupping his hands over it to create incredible amounts of distortion through his amplifier, and taking rhythmic cues from jump blues and jazz, Little Walter popularized the sound most people associate with amplified blues harp. The volume and power increased when he began to record in the studio, first as a part of Muddy Waters' band on a brace of influential sides, and then (after his 1952 hit "Juke") as a solo artist. Walter also used several different kinds of harmonica to increase his sonic range, often alternating between a standard harp and a more complex chromatic one (sometimes in midsong) that gave him a greater variety of tones and note choices.

In the original edition of *The Rolling Stone Record Guide,* John Swenson summed up Walter's mammoth significance well: "Every harmonica player after Little Walter has in some way been influenced by his style, especially rock players, from John Mayall to Magic Dick of the J. Geils Band. Jacobs was able to take hard bop melodic ideas from contemporary saxophonists and match them to a simpler but more forceful blues rhythm with heavily emphasized guitar parts, suggesting a further link between bop-era jazz players and rock & roll. The Little Walter harmonica style thus transposed saxophone ideas into terms compatible with and influential on guitars." Not to be overlooked are his considerable talents as a songwriter, singer, and sideman, all of which helped make him one of the true greats of early electric Chicago blues.

Not as well-known as Little Walter was, no overview of blues harmonica greats could be considered complete without an equal nod to the "other Walter," the magnificent Big Walter Horton. Playing from the time he was a mere child, Horton was a fixture on the Memphis music scene, playing with everyone from semi-pro jug bands to the earliest electric combos. Several reports have Horton actually blowing amplified harp in the late '40s and the younger Jacobs learned much from the older musician when the two met up in Chicago in the early '50s. Capable of blowing with a sweet lyricism one moment and astonishing power the next, his style owed no stylistic debt to anyone and he could play both unamplified and electric styles with ease. The effect of Big Walter's harp is always soothing, slowing and opening up the time and the mind.

Most of the great Chicago electric blues harmonica players served at one time or another in the band of Muddy Waters. Little Walter, James Cotton, Junior Wells, the wonderful George "Harmonica" Smith, and Walter Horton all played and recorded with him in the '50s and early '60s. Cotton and Wells especially were successful in establishing careers as bandleaders in the '60s, playing in styles which effectively drew from contemporary rock and soul influences. Each of them were only a little younger than Little Walter, but the king of the blues harmonica went into a sad decline in the '60s that saw increasingly sporadic and unimpressive recordings before his death, at the age of 37, in 1968 in a street fight.

The harmonica was a more established presence in the blues of Chicago than anywhere else, and the city was home to several other notable players. Billy Boy Arnold cut some great singles for Vee-Jay records in the '50s, and also made important contributions to rock & roll as a sideman on some of Bo Diddley's early records. Some Chicago blues greats who were not really identified primarily as harmonica players could use the instrument effectively, like Jimmy Reed and Howlin' Wolf. Compilations like *Sun Records Harmonica Classics,* which features '50s blues recorded in Memphis, serve notice that not all harmonica blues of note originated from Chicago and the country blues sounds of Joe Hill Louis and the one-man band of Doctor Ross offer a decided change of pace from the more pervasive Windy City sounds. Another stylistic strain also worth investigating is the swamp blues sound from Louisiana with Slim Harpo and Lazy Lester being its two best-known exponents.

As Chicago blues was an enormous influence upon R&B-oriented British Invasion bands, it's no surprise that many U.K. rock groups of the '60s featured members (usually the lead vocalists) who were reasonably proficient on the instrument. It's not often noted, but singers like Mick Jagger, Keith Relf (of the Yardbirds), John Mayall, Van Morrison, and Paul Jones (of Manfred Mann) could blow with bluesy soul when appropriate, although none of them apparently thought of amplifying their instruments, imparting a decided wheeziness to most of their recorded performances. As the British Invasion turned into blues-rock and progressive rock, the instrument was used with less frequency, but could still be whipped out with impressive effect, as Mick Jagger demonstrated on "Midnight Rambler."

Music Map

Blues Harp (Harmonica): A Short History

Acoustic Beginnings (Chordal Harp)
Early acoustic harp included training whistle, vaudeville, ragtime, jazz

Memphis Jug Bands
Will Shade
Gus Cannon's Jug Stompers With Noah Lewis

Folk/Blues Players
DeFord Bailey (Grand Old Opry Radio) • Sonny Terry

Sonny Boy Williamson [I]
Major influence in the transition from chordal harp to its use as a melodic-line-oriented, lead instrument

Down-Home Electric
Jimmy Reed • "Dr." Isaiah Ross

Sonny Boy Williamson [II] (Rice Miller)
An original blues giant with a unique sound, and a touch of country never far away

Rhythm & Blues
Slim Harpo • Raful Neal • Lazy Lester

Urban Harps
Buster Brown • Mofo Buford • Frank Frost
George "Harmonica" Smith

Muddy Waters Blues Band
Muddy Waters was the Miles Davis of the blues. Almost every major harp player worked in his band, even Junior Wells and Big Walter Horton. Yet it was Little Walter who set the tone for what became the high-powered Chicago blues sound.

Big Walter Horton
Perhaps the most beautiful of all harp players

Little Walter
High-intensity Chicago harp at its best

Junior Wells
Outstanding funky blues

James Cotton
The last of Muddy's great players

Great Later Harp Players

Charlie Musselwhite • Jerry Portnoy • Paul Butterfield • William Clarke • Billy Branch • Phil Wiggins
Carey Bell • James Harman • Gary Primich • Rod Piazza • King Biscuit Boy • Paul Delay

As further proof that good blues has no color, some of the best American harmonica blues players of recent years have been White. Paul Butterfield and Charlie Musselwhite—both of whom rose through the Chicago club scene in the '60s and came by their blues honestly learning first hand from their idols—certainly had technique and feeling to match the best of them, whether playing straight Chicago blues or (in Butterfield's case) blues-rock. Notable white virtuosos of more recent years include Kim Wilson of the Fabulous Thunderbirds, Rod Piazza, the aforementioned Magic Dick, Paul deLay, and William Clarke—possibly the most inventive and original harmonica player out there before his untimely death in 1996.

Harmonica-playing bandleaders may not be as prominent as they were in the Chicago of the '50s and '60s, but harmonica is still very much part of the standard contemporary blues scene. Many of the masters, like James Cotton, are still around and very active, for one thing; with his national album deals, Billy Boy Arnold may be more well-known now (at least outside of Chicago) than he was when he was recording in the '50s. A 1991 blowout super-session of sorts (between Junior Wells, James Cotton, Carey Bell, and Billy Branch) demonstrated the enduring appeal of harmonica showcases. And two of the most noted modern acoustic blues acts, Satan & Adam and Cephas & Wiggins, prominently feature the instrument. And for all those who are inspired to take the instrument up to their lips and try to make a sound with it, there's always the chance that another blues master is a-borning. The history of blues harmonica is still being written.

16 Recommended Albums:
Various Artists, *Blues Masters, Vol. 4: Harmonica Classics* (Rhino)
Sonny Terry, *The Folkways Years, 1944-63* (Smithsonian/Rounder)
Sonny Boy Williamson [I], *Throw a Boogie Woogie* (RCA)

Music Map

Memphis Blues

W.C. Handy
Wrote "Memphis Blues" in 1912

Jug Bands & Street Musicians	**Memphis in the Late '40s/Early '50s**	**Sun Rockabilly/Memphis R&B 1954-1968**
Furry Lewis • Frank Stokes Gus Cannon • Robert Wilkins Memphis Willie Borum Noah Lewis • Will Shade Joe McCoy • Memphis Minnie Jack Kelly • Big Walter Horton	Joe Hill Louis • B.B. King Rufus Thomas • Big Walter Horton • Hot Shot Love Jimmy De Berry • Howlin' Wolf Bobby "Blue" Bland Junior Parker • Pat Hare Johnny Ace • Willie Johnson Sammy Lewis • Little Milton	Elvis Presley • Carl Perkins Jerry Lee Lewis • Albert King Stax Records **Memphis Soul Scene** Booker T. & the MG's Willie Mitchell Bill Black Combo

Little Walter, *Essential* (Chess)
Little Walter, *Blues With a Feeling* (Chess)
Sonny Boy Williamson [II], *King Bisuit Time* (Arhoolie)
Sonny Boy Williamson [II], *Essential* (Chess)
Big Walter Horton, *Chicago-The Blues-Today! Volume 3* (Vanguard)
Big Walter Horton, *The Soul of Blues Harmonica* (Chess)
Junior Wells, *Hoodoo Man Blues* (Delmark)
William Clarke, *Blowin' Like Hell* (Alligator)
Various Artists, *Sun Records Harmonica Classics* (Rounder)
James Cotton, *Best of the Verve Years* (Verve)
The Paul Butterfield Blues Band, *Paul Butterfield Blues Band* (Elektra)
Charlie Musselwhite, *Ace of Harps* (Alligator)
Junior Wells, James Cotton, Carey Bell, and Billy Branch, *Harp Attack!* (Alligator)
—Cub Koda & Richie Unterberger

Memphis Blues

A visit to Memphis' Beale Street these days is like walking through a museum or movie set. Clubs, stores, and even (yes) museums still do business, but more as an homage to the past than as a part of a vibrant present. For decades, however, Memphis was known as "the Main Street of Negro America," a drag where black business thrived during the day, and entertainment/nightlife during the dark.

Music, naturally, was a big part of that scene, and although the blues wasn't the only game in that part of town, it was a big part for several decades. As early as 1912, the community had an anthem, "Memphis Blues," penned by W.C. Handy. In the years prior to World War II, it was home to a diverse mixture of blues performers, from jug bands to Delta guitarists. In the early '50s, it was the most important crucible of the electric blues bar Chicago. Memphis blues has also played a huge role in the evolution of American popular music via its influence on the early rockabilly music and '60s soul empire for which Memphis is also renowned.

As one of the major urban centers of the South, Memphis had attracted a large African-American population for a long time before the blues became widely known. Though it wasn't far north enough for many blacks, who went on to Northern cities (especially Chicago) for more racial tolerance and economic opportunity, Memphis was as far as many newcomers to the urban experience got. Even those who eventually went on to Chicago and other cities would frequently stop in Memphis on the way, whether to live for a few years or for only a bit.

W.C. Handy, one of the key forefathers of the blues, based himself and his band in Memphis in 1909. Handy's form of dance music was more blues-influenced than actual blues and in the 20th century Memphis was as well known or more for its jazz musicians (Jimmie Lunceford being one of the most famous) than its blues. To this day, Memphis harbors so many different types of roots music that its regional styles are difficult to categorize, and such was the case with Memphis blues prior to World War II. It was always around, but not nearly as identifiable as, for example, the Delta blues so abundant to the south in Mississippi. The city was noted as the home of several blues jugbands (the Memphis Jug Band and Gus Cannon's group being some of the most famous), as well as a few fine blues guitarists, such as Furry Lewis and Robert Wilkins. Blues was often available at the park off Beale Street that now bears Handy's name, as local and itinerant musicians would often play for tips or anyone who was interested.

It was with the postwar amplification of the blues, however, that Memphis really began to leave its mark. Society itself was becoming more urban, higher-paced, and

electrified, and two of the important figures in Memphis blues made much of their initial impact not as musicians, but as radio announcers on WDIA (the first radio station in the U.S. to employ an all-black format, although it was white-owned). One was guitarist B.B. King, who used his experience at WDIA to perfect his diction and absorb the influence of gospel and early R&B music. With his 1951 number one R&B hit "Three O'Clock Blues," King launched a hugely successful and influential career that was vital to the urbanization of the blues, and by extension blues' eventual entry into mainstream American culture.

The other important WDIA DJ was Rufus Thomas, all around entertainment personality who, more than just about any other living legend, epitomizes Memphis music. Before working for WDIA, Thomas had met King when he emceed amateur night shows at the Palace Theater on Beale Street. At that time Thomas may have been more of a general R&B scenester than a professional musician. But it was as a singer that he would play a vital role in Sun Records, the label that would do more to spread the influence of Memphis blues than any other.

Sun was run by Sam Phillips, a young man with a genuine feel and appreciation for the forms of black popular music in the region. The company is most famous, of course, for launching the career of Elvis Presley, as well as several other rockabilly stars (Carl Perkins, Johnny Cash, Jerry Lee Lewis). When it began operations in the early '50s, however, it recorded mostly black artists and the sounds were those of blues/R&B, rockabilly not having been invented yet. (The history of Sun is examined more fully in a separate sidebar.)

The Memphis Recording Service, as Sun was originally named, at first leased sides to other labels. Early records by B.B. King, Howlin' Wolf, Roscoe Gordon, and others were handled by labels like Chess and RPM. Jackie Brenston's "Rocket 88" (actually Ike Turner & His Kings of Rhythm), from 1951, is often cited as one of the first rock & roll records. With the Howlin' Wolf sides in particular, Phillips developed the harshly amplified, spare sound that would be characteristic of the Memphis blues he recorded during this period, which was somewhat rawer and more countrified than its Chicago cousin.

Phillips began putting his blues sides out on his label, Sun, rather than leasing them. Sun's first national R&B hit was Rufus Thomas' "Bear Cat," an answer record to Big Mama Thornton's "Hound Dog." Thomas himself, ironically, only recorded one more single for the label (though he would become a soul star in the '60s and '70s at Stax). There was plenty of other talent around, and during the first half of the '50s Sun recorded seminal sides by Junior Parker, Big Walter Horton, James Cotton, Little Milton, and Rosco Gordon, as well obscurities by the likes of Pat Hare, Joe Hill Louis, D.A. Hunt and Doctor Ross that would attain legendary status among collectors and scholars decades later.

The rise and fall of Memphis electric blues in this period is heavily intertwined with developments at Sun Records. In 1954, he began recording Elvis Presley, a 19-year-old who had done his share of hanging out on Beale Street, checking out the blues singers and buying his clothes at Lansky's, a Beale Street store that catered to many local blacks. It's almost redundant to point this out now, but Elvis was the single most important figure in the birth of rockabilly, which blended country and western with blues, R&B, and elements of gospel and pop. The Memphis blues singers had done much to foster this combination, especially given that Phillips developed much of his studio acumen by overseeing their sessions. Indeed, Elvis covered Junior Parker's biggest hit, "Mystery Train," for his last Sun single, and one of his greatest performances on record.

Phillips turned his focus to the white country and rockabilly artists on his roster, especially after selling Presley's contract to RCA in late 1955, which gave him the capital to properly promote Perkins, Cash, Lewis, et al.

The truth, of course, is more complicated than that. If he had made blues/R&B his only priority, Phillips would have been an admirable idealist, perhaps. He also would have been waging a futile fight against inevitable historical forces. The biggest of these was rock & roll, of course, black and white, which in 1956 overran the recording industry. Even within blues, though, there was the magnet of Chicago, with its monolithic blues scene and its most powerful label, Chess.

Even if rockabilly had not intervened, the Memphis community had already begun to lose its most promising musicians to other cities. Howlin' Wolf, perhaps the greatest of the blues talents to enter the Memphis Recording Service, was signed by Chess, and moved to Chicago, well before Presley's advent. James Cotton (who joined Muddy Waters' band before becoming a star on his own) and guitarist Pat Hare (who also played with Waters for a while) also relocated to Chicago. Even Sonny Boy Williamson, a musician just across the Mississippi River (in Helena, AR) with some ties to the Memphis scene, would not truly make his mark until recording for Chess in Chicago. The city guaranteed blues performers more work, more musicians to choose from, and, should they be picked up by local labels, more effective national promotion.

It may also be that some of the blues artists in Memphis were in embryonic states of artistic development that could not be fully nurtured by the metropolis. Junior Parker and Little Milton, for instance, really hit their commercial stride as soul/blues artists in the '60s (and Little Milton would record for the Memphis-based Stax label, among others). B.B. King, another bluesman with prominent R&B and soul influences, became in the '60s a national figure who recorded in various distant cities, cultivating a sound that was too broad in scope to be pigeonholed as part of a regional movement. Ike Turner (never really identified with the Memphis scene) would move his base of operations to St. Louis, and move into rock and soul with his wife Tina.

Memphis blues didn't die, of course; it was too deeply embedded in the city's music scene to do so. But the focus of the city's African-American popular music production in the '60s and '70s was very much soul, specifically at Stax and Hi Records. Stax usually had some blues/soul hybrids on its roster, achieving a good deal of success with Albert King, who worked with Booker T. & the MG's on many of his records. The demise of Stax in the mid-'70s, however, meant lean times for black music as a whole in the city.

Blues is still heard and recorded in Memphis these days, even if it has a somewhat folkloric bent. Renowned blues scholar and author David Evans marshalled some fine down-home blues for the High Water label, most notably by guitarist Jessie Mae Hemphill. B.B. King owns a club on Beale Street, although he hasn't lived in Memphis for ages. And though it's more of a tourist attraction than a happening area, Beale Street and vicinity offers several places of homage for the serious blues fan, including the Center for Southern Folklore, a good if seriously undervisited blues museum; the famous Schwab's variety store (serving the community since 1976); the Memphis Music Museum; Handy Park; and, a mile or two away, Sun Studios, which remains open for tours.

Ten Recommended Albums:
Memphis Jug Band, *Memphis Jug Band* (Yazoo)
Various Artists, *Ten Years in Memphis, 1927-1937* (Yazoo)
Various Artists, *A Sun Blues Collection* (Rhino)
Various Artists, *Blues Masters, Vol. 12: Memphis Blues* (Rhino)
B.B. King, *The Best of B.B. King, Vol. 1* (Flair)
Howlin' Wolf, *Rides Again* (Flair)
Junior Parker, *James Cotton & Pat Hare, Mystery Train* (Rounder)
Albert King, *Born Under a Bad Sign* (Mobile Fidelity)
Various Artists, *Memphis Masters* (Yazoo)
Various Artists, *The Blues Came Down From Memphis* (Charly)

—Richie Unterberger

Piano Blues

The piano hasn't occupied as prominent a place in the blues as the guitar; in terms of blues virtuosos of recent decades, there may even be more harmonica players than keyboard specialists. The piano will certainly always have a place in the blues combo for both its rhythmic and melodic qualities, despite the hysterical predictions of some observers that the synthesizer will soon make it obsolete. Many of blues' finest singers and songwriters have been piano players; blues piano has also played a big part in influencing the directions of jazz, rock, and soul music.

Blues piano styles have much of their origins in the rough and tumble barrelhouses and railroad/lumber camps of the late 1800s and early 1900s. Here pianists had to develop a rhythmic, aggressive sound to be heard above the crowd, and to keep pace with the rowdy atmosphere. It's no accident that some of the early blues piano greats are noted for a "barrelhouse" style.

In some respects, early piano players may have been at a disadvantage when competing with guitarists and other instrumentalists. The acoustic guitar (or, say, the harmonica) is extremely portable, a big plus for musicians working the road in the days when private automobile travel was a lot less common. It might not have been as much as a drawback as one may think, though. Most settlements had entertainment establishments with house pianos; if residents or travelers could prove their skills, they were often welcome to have at it.

There's little question that considerably more blues guitarists were recorded than blues pianists in the early days of the phonograph. Blues scholars justifiably bewail the loss of important chapters in blues history because of the preferences of the companies responsible for recording blues in the '20s and '30s. Many pianists hardly recorded at all, and are now only represented on obscure import blues compilations. Many, no doubt, never had the opportunity to record at all.

Blues pianists, however, began to be recorded shortly after the first appearance of the blues itself on record. Some of the most significant early ones were Cow Cow Davenport, Roosevelt Sykes, and Clarence "Pinetop" Smith. Smith's "Pine Top's Boogie Woogie," from 1929, is generally credited as introducing the term "boogie-woogie" into widespread use.

The boogie-woogie piano style is characterized by a 12-bar blues structure and constantly repeating rhythmic patterns of the left hand, while the right hand plays the melodies and improvisations. It quickly caught on not just in blues, but in popular music as a whole; millions of people who couldn't tell you diddley squat about Robert Johnson know exactly what a boogie-woogie is. Boogie-woogie patterns would become a foundation of jazz in the '30s and '40s, jump blues in the '40s and '50s, and early R&B/rock & roll in the '50s.

Records by blues pianists in the '30s, however, didn't necessarily showcase their instrumental skills. As Mike Rowe notes in *The Blackwell Guide to the Blues*, "There had been a subtle change in the market for piano blues. Those pianists, such as Leroy Carr, Walter Davis, and even Roosevelt Sykes, who had lasted out the Depression were popular for their songs and singing; that they played piano was incidental. While the sawmill pianists played for dancers and had to survive on pianistic prowess, the blues pianist of the urban '30s had to achieve success as a singer or songwriter. Piano blues had been taken out of the lumber camps and whorehouses and into the homes of an increasingly sophisticated urban audience.

"This accent on the content of the song meant that pianists had little encouragement to stretch themselves, and Davis or Peetie Wheatstraw, for example, could make recording after recording using the same introduction and tempo, which tended to mask their abilities as pianists. Boogie-woogie had become integrated into blues accompaniments, and ragtime was all but eliminated. There was a smoother, more regular sound to the '30s piano blues, and although a few field trips by Bluebird, Decca, and ARC preserved some regional styles, and the iconoclastic Texas piano in particular, it was the cities such as Chicago and St. Louis that provided the bulk of the artists."

Key figures in the urbanization of blues piano—really, in the urbanization of the blues as a whole—would include Big Maceo Merriweather, Champion Jack Dupree, Sunnyland Slim, and Jimmy Yancey. Boogie-woogie was certainly a big element in swing and big band jazz, and several blues-based boogie-woogie pianists, such as Meade "Lux" Lewis, Albert Ammons, and Pete Johnson, fed into the jazz tributary with work that straddled the line between the two genres. A Carnegie Hall appearance in 1938 featuring all three of the aforementioned boogie-woogie specialists did much to popularize and legitimize the style.

When the blues started to electrify in Chicago and elsewhere during the '40s and '50s, the guitar and harmonica assumed more prominence than the piano. This wasn't true on the West Coast, however, were jump blues reigned supreme between the mid-'40s and mid-'50s. Jump blues' blend of blues and jazz ingredients made it a natural for pianists, and some of jump blues' greatest performers were keyboardist/singers. Amos Milburn, Floyd Dixon, and Camille Howard were some of the best; their achievements are described in greater depth in the jump blues essay. Several other West Coast blues pianists made their mark with a more ballad-inclined, gospel-influenced R&B style, including Charles Brown, Percy Mayfield, Cecil Gant (a great boogie-woogie player as well), and, on his earliest sides, Ray Charles. The blues/jazz piano connection would be kept alive, to a much subtler degree, via the work of blues-and boogie-influenced soul/jazz organists/pianists of the '60s and '70s, such as Jimmy Smith, Big John Patton, and Jimmy McGriff.

There was still room for a piano in the classic-style Chicago electric blues lineup, as Otis Spann proved during his lengthy stint with Muddy Waters. It took a while for Spann to emerge from Waters' shadow, but recordings on his own established him as a worthy artist in his own right, and perhaps the finest of the post-World War II piano players. Other players of note on the Chicago blues scene were Memphis Slim, Little Johnny Jones (whose two fisted work as a member of Elmore James' Broomdusters made the absence of a rhythm guitar in that band totally unnoticeable), Roosevelt Sykes, Eddie Boyd, Willie Mabon, and Johnnie Johnson, who's probably more famous for his contributions to rock & roll, as the pianist featured on many of Chuck Berry's classic sides.

Piano players as stars or singers, rather than side musicians, have been much thinner on the ground in the last few decades than they were 50-60 years ago. Louisiana was something of a pocket of blues and blues-influenced pianists; Professor Longhair, James Booker, and Katie Webster (all of whom have ties of varying strength to the region) developed some of the funkiest and most idiosyncratic styles to be found in the whole blues piano idiom. Memphis Slim and Pinetop Perkins, among others, kept old-school blues piano styles alive with frequent touring well past the '60s. Keyboards are still a staple of many a blues band, and will probably remain so. But the day may have passed when piano players exerted as fundamental an influence on the direction of the blues as they did in the heyday of boogie-woogie and barrelhouse.

16 Recommended Albums:
Cow Cow Davenport, *Alabama Strut* (Magpie)
Roosevelt Sykes, *Roosevelt Sykes (1929-41)* (Story of Blues)
Leroy Carr, *Naptown Blues* (Yazoo)
Albert Ammons, *King of Boogie Woogie (1939-1949)* (Blues Classics)
Meade Lux Lewis, *Complete Blue Note Recordings* (Mosaic)
Jimmy Yancey, *Vol. 1 (1939-40)* (Document)
Big Maceo, *King of Chicago Blues Piano, Vol. 1 & 2* (Arhoolie)
Amos Milburn, *Down the Road Apiece: The Best of Amos Milburn* (EMI)
Floyd Dixon, *Marshall Texas Is My Home* (Specialty)
Camille Howard, *Vol. 1: Rock Me Daddy* (Specialty)
Cecil Gant, *Rock the Boogie* (Krazy Kat)

Piano Blues Stylists by Region

St. Louis
Lee Green • Roosevelt Sykes
Peetie Wheatstraw
Henry Townsend • Walter Roland
Walter Davis

Indianapolis
Leroy Carr

Memphis & The Delta
Little Brother Montgomery
Sunnyland Slim
Booker T. Laury • Memphis Slim
Jab Jones • Piano Red
Mose Vinson

Kansas City
Jay McShann • Count Basie
Pete Johnson

Chicago
Willie Mabon • Otis Spann
Detroit Junior • Henry Gray
Eddie Boyd • Art Hodes

California
Charles Brown • Amos Milburn
Percy Mayfield

New Orleans
Cousin Joe • Archibald
Smiley Lewis • Jack Dupree
Professor Longhair • Fats Domino

Other Major Players
Speckled Red • Ray Charles

Texas
Alex Moore • Dr. Hepcat
Rob Cooper • Dave Alexander
Sammy Price

Sunnyland Slim, *Sunnyland Slim* (Flyright)
Otis Spann, *Otis Spann Is the Blues* (Candid)
Professor Longhair, *Fess: Professor Longhair Anthology* (Rhino)
James Booker, *New Orleans Piano Wizard: Live!* (Rounder)
Memphis Slim, *Rockin' the Blues* (Charly)

—Richie Unterberger

Songsters

The blues was such a young form when it first started to be recorded that not all of its early stars would have identified themselves as "blues" artists. Nor, indeed, were all of them blues artists all of the time. For many African-American singers and musicians, blues was just part of their repertoire. They were also able and willing to play country tunes, spirituals, popular standards, ragtime, jug band, folk songs, and more.

These are the artists labeled by researchers as "songsters." The songsters haven't fared nearly as well as, say, the acoustic guitarists of the Mississippi Delta in the annals of blues history. They often espouse a homey, sunny, good-timey air that is at odds with the serious, forceful image of the blues that many expect and retain. To listeners accustomed to contemporary blues, rock, and pop, their arrangements and delivery can sound quaintly old-fashioned. Yet the best of the songsters made important contributions to blues history, worth recognizing even by those who much prefer their blues deep and down-home.

It's no accident that some of the most notable songsters were the very oldest blues singers to record; their material would naturally tend to be older in origin, and less shaped by the blues trends of the early 20th century. One of the most famous, and probably the oldest, was Henry Thomas (born 1874). Only about a third of his two dozen sides were titled as blues; he also cut ballads, reels, and dance songs, often using the pan quill pipes, an unconventional instrument rarely heard today. He achieved a good deal of posthumous fame when his "Bull Doze Blues" was adapted by Canned Heat for their hit "Going Up the Country" in the late '60s. Bob Dylan included a song that Thomas had recorded, "Honey, Just Allow Me One More Chance," on his second LP (*Freewheelin' Bob Dylan*, 1963); the original liner notes explain that the tune "was first heard by Dylan from a recording by a now-dead Texas blues singer. Dylan can only remember that his first name was Henry."

One of the most frequently discussed songsters, Frank Stokes, betrayed the considerable influence of traveling medicine shows in which he participated. As a member of a cast that had to entertain lots of people in different regions, Stokes and similar songsters could have been expected to develop a wide range of material. Pink Anderson, another veteran of medicine shows, survived into the era of the long-playing record, and his '50s and '60s recordings offer better fidelity for those that find the primitive audio of the '20s too hard to handle.

Mississippi John Hurt was another guitarist with songster leanings who survived into the folk revival. Hurt recorded some stellar material in the late '20s, and then a number of LPs after his rediscovery in the early '60s. His early 78s are more esteemed by blues collectors than his latter efforts, but again you get the choice between better fidelity and performances that are closer to the source of the songster milieu, whatever your preference may be. Quite a few will want to hear Hurt in both contexts; his good-natured,

gospel-influenced singing and accomplished fingerpicking makes his work more accessible to contemporary listeners than any of the original "songsters."

The songster tradition lived on to a large degree in the work of subsequent singers who held strong appeal for both the blues and folk audiences. They've been usually classified as folk or folk/blues singers rather than songsters for this reason, and also because their work has less of an air of all-around entertainment than Stokes, Thomas, harmonica player DeFord Bailey (who was a regular on the Grand Ole Opry in the '20s and '30s), or '20s songsters like Peg Leg Howell.

The most famous of these blues/folk crossover artists was Leadbelly, discovered by John Lomax in a Louisiana prison in 1933. With his huge repertoire, stellar vocal and instrumental skills, and extremely colorful life, Leadbelly qualifies as one of the giants of 20th century American music, worth learning about even by music fans who've never heard any of his records. The eclectic approach of Leadbelly enabled him circulate easily in a New York-based community of folkies that also included Woody Guthrie and the duo of Brownie McGhee and Sonny Terry, two other performers who were also comfortable with both blues and folk.

Also treading the line between blues and folk was Josh White, who in his youth had recorded spirituals under his own name and blues under a pseudonym, along with the virtually forgotten Brother John Sellers. There was always a home for White on the folk circuit, and after the rediscovery of Hurt, Furry Lewis, and Mance Lipscomb (the latter of whom had never previously recorded) around 1960, acoustic blues legends also tapped into the folk constituency to get a second wind on their professional careers. Hurt, Lipscomb, and White were certainly not "songsters" in the classic sense, but their versatility owed quite a bit to the songster tradition, enabling them to bring the blues sensibility to many listeners who may have never been introduced to it otherwise.

11 Recommended Albums:
Henry Thomas, *Texas Worried Blues* (Yazoo)
Frank Stokes, *The Memphis Blues* (Yazoo)
Mississippi John Hurt, *1928 Sessions* (Yazoo)
Mississippi John Hurt, *The Immortal* (Vanguard)
Peg Leg Howell, *1928-29* (Matchbox)
Peg Leg Howell, *The Legendary Peg Leg Howell* (Testament)
Leadbelly, *King of the 12-String Guitar* (CBS)
Leadbelly, *Midnight Special* (Rounder)
Pink Anderson, *Ballad & Folksinger, Vol. 3* (Prestige/Bluesville)
Josh White, *Legendary Josh White* (MCA)
Mance Lipscomb, *Texas Sharecropper & Songster* (Arhoolie)

—Richie Unterberger

West Coast Blues

West Coast blues—it's undeniably a phrase with less instant hipster credibility than, say, Chicago blues or Delta blues. The cities of Los Angeles and San Francisco simply don't embody the hard times associated with the blues origins in the South, or the hothouse conditions that gave rise to much classic electric blues in the North. As the stereotype would have it, life is mellower, the pace slower, the living easier, and the weather sunnier on the West Coast—not the kinds of conditions which have, in the minds of many

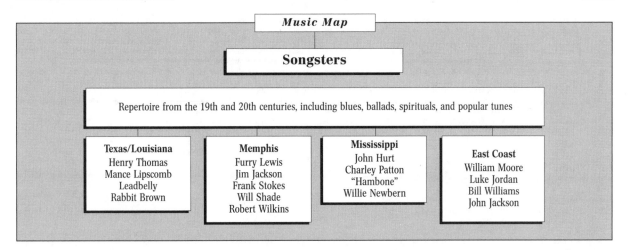

Music Map

Songsters

Repertoire from the 19th and 20th centuries, including blues, ballads, spirituals, and popular tunes

Texas/Louisiana	**Memphis**	**Mississippi**	**East Coast**
Henry Thomas	Furry Lewis	John Hurt	William Moore
Mance Lipscomb	Jim Jackson	Charley Patton	Luke Jordan
Leadbelly	Frank Stokes	"Hambone"	Bill Williams
Rabbit Brown	Will Shade	Willie Newbern	John Jackson
	Robert Wilkins		

listeners, been conducive to breeding the best kinds of blues music. The West Coast, however, has been home to many leading blues performers, although it may not have developed as identifiable a sound as some other regions.

When we talk about West Coast blues, we're really talking about California blues, most of which was centered around the Los Angeles and the San Francisco Bay areas. There's not much of a prewar Californian blues tradition, which must be at least partially attributable to the fact that the African-American communities there weren't nearly as large in the beginning of the 20th century. The black population of the state, however, would swell in the '40s, as the westward migration enhanced by the need for immense manpower to work in the U.S. defense industry during World War II. These new arrivals needed entertainment, of course, and the local jazz and blues club scene heated up quickly.

The towering figure of West Coast blues may be guitarist T-Bone Walker, a relocated Texan who had made his first recordings in the late '20s. Walker was a crucial figure in the electrification and urbanization of the blues, probably doing more to popularize the use of electric guitar in the form than anyone else. Much of his material had a distinct jazzy jump blues feel, an influence that would characterize much of the most influential blues to emerge from California in the '40s and '50s.

Many of the most popular blues performers to base themselves in California during the '40s and '50s were originally from Texas, perhaps accounting from some of the earthiest qualities of West Coast blues. Besides Walker, there was Pee Wee Crayton (a guitarist who modeled his style after T-Bone's), Charles Brown, Lowell Fulson, Joe Houston, Amos Milburn, Johnny "Guitar" Watson, and (after the mid-'50s) Big Mama Thornton. At times it seemed as though Texas was the true breeding ground of West Coast blues—Los Angeles just happened to be where it was refined and recorded.

There was an obvious reason, however, why so much blues was recorded in Los Angeles, as it was the city where many of the independent labels specializing in blues and R&B originated in the '40s. Specialty, Imperial, Aladdin, and the umbrella of labels run by the Bihari brothers (RPM/Modern/Kent/Flair/Crown) were the most famous of these. Their importance cannot be overestimated, for the simple reason that they were determined to record and distribute blues music that the big major companies were uninterested in, or not even aware of in the first place.

The history of early West Coast blues is heavily intertwined with that of jump blues, the snappy, rhythmic hybrid of jazz and blues that reigned supreme over much of the R&B world in the late '40s and early '50s. That history is covered in greater depth in a separate essay. For now, it should be noted that many of the greatest jump blues musicians were based in California, be they acrobatic saxophonists (Big Jay McNeely, Joe Houston), pianist/vocalists (Amos Milburn, Floyd Dixon, Camille Howard, Little Willie Littlefield), guitarists (Walker, Crayton), or bandleaders like Roy Milton.

A flipside of the uptempo jump bluesters were the singers who specialized in piano ballads that also drew from gospel and the pop-jazz of Nat King Cole. Charles Brown and Percy Mayfield were the most prominent of these vocalists; Ray Charles, based in Seattle at the outset of his career but recording for the Los Angeles based Swingtime label, also did quite a bit of recording in this vein before devising a more personal style. Today, these figures are all recognized as forefathers of soul music, making it a matter of good-natured debate as to whether they should be classified as blues or just plain R&B.

The R&B/blues line also gets thin when discussing the career of Johnny Otis, the bandleader who did as much as anyone to build the Los Angeles R&B community. Otis made plenty of blues/R&B hybrid recordings on his own, but he arguably made greater contributions as a promoter and organizer of live shows, DJ, producer, and general champion of talent. He did much to further the careers of Little Esther and Etta James, two singers who, again, are better classified as R&B singers than blues ones, though their allegiance to blues styles is certainly visible.

Urbane forms of blues may have dominated the early postwar Californian scene, but there was room for grittier performers as well, such as the aforementioned Pee Wee Crayton, and Johnny "Guitar" Watson, whose futuristic style has been rightly cited as an

influence on Jimi Hendrix. Nor was it confined solely to Los Angeles. San Francisco and Oakland were home to a small but notable blues scene, the most prominent spokesman being Jimmy McCracklin, who had a crossover rock & roll Top Ten hit in 1958 with "The Walk." Pee Wee Crayton was also based in San Francisco when he emerged, although he made his most important recordings in Los Angeles.

Blues, as it did throughout the rest of the country, fell on leaner times in California in the '60s, as rock, surf, and soul dominated the industry. Los Angeles' increasingly central position within the recording industry may have, if anything, decreased the presence of the blues within the city itself. Rock and pop musicians of all kinds were flocking to L.A. studios, and the big and small companies—more of whom were based in L.A. now than anywhere else—wanted to come up with successes in these fields, not the blues, which were considered passe by many, and had certainly long passed its commercial peak.

Tireless keepers of the flame such as Johnny Otis and his son Shuggie, however, ensured that the blues community continued to function, even if at a somewhat subterranean level. As there has been everywhere since the '60s, interest in the blues among the White audience on the West Coast has become much more commonplace. San Francisco and Los Angeles are each home to some of the biggest and most successful blues festivals in the world, and each have a decent number of venues for both local and visiting blues artists.

Some of the most notable blues performers of recent times have come from California, even if there's not much that can be pigeonholed as especially "regional" about their sound. Johnny Heartsman, who had been active since the '50s, really made his true impact with nationwide audiences in the '80s and '90s, remaining a versatile performer until his death in December of 1996. From San Francisco, Joe Louis Walker remains one of the most

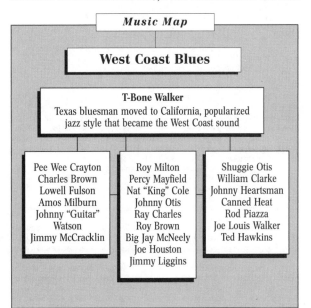

Music Map

West Coast Blues

T-Bone Walker
Texas bluesman moved to California, popularized jazz style that became the West Coast sound

Pee Wee Crayton	Roy Milton	Shuggie Otis
Charles Brown	Percy Mayfield	William Clarke
Lowell Fulson	Nat "King" Cole	Johnny Heartsman
Amos Milburn	Johnny Otis	Canned Heat
Johnny "Guitar"	Ray Charles	Rod Piazza
Watson	Roy Brown	Joe Louis Walker
Jimmy McCracklin	Big Jay McNeely	Ted Hawkins
	Joe Houston	
	Jimmy Liggins	

successful bluesmen of recent times, noted for his effective incorporation of rock and gospel influences into his material. Walker established himself as a recording artist on the San Francisco Bay Area-based Hightone label, one of the top contemporary roots music companies in the United States, before moving on to the Verve label in the mid-'90s.

Southern California has been home to many white blues bands as well, producing two noted harmonica virtuosos in Rod Piazza and the late William Clarke (and, way back in the '60s, one of the most successful American blues-rock groups, Canned Heat). And throughout the '80s, you could walk down the tourist-congested boardwalk of Venice Beach in Los Angeles and find Ted Hawkins playing for change for passersby. A repository of acoustic folk/blues in the urban madness that now suffuses the L.A. area, Hawkins achieved recognition as one of the top practitioners of contemporary acoustic blues before his premature death in the mid-'90s—giving California, perhaps, the acoustic blues roots it never really had.

15 Recommended Albums:

T-Bone Walker, *The Complete Capitol/Black & White Recordings* (Capitol)
T-Bone Walker, *The Complete Imperial Recordings* (EMI)
Pee Wee Crayton, *Rocking Down on Central Avenue* (Ace)
Amos Milburn, *Down the Road Apiece: The Best of Amos Milburn* (EMI)
Floyd Dixon, *Marshall Texas Is My Home* (Specialty)
Roy Milton, *Roy Milton and His Solid Senders* (Specialty)
Percy Mayfield, *Poet of the Blues* (Specialty)
Charles Brown, *Dritin' Blues: The Best of Charles Brown* (EMI)
Johnny "Guitar" Watson, *Three Hours Past Midnight* (Flair)
Lowell Fulson, *San Francisco Blues* (Black Lion)
Johnny Otis, *The Johnny Otis Show* (Savoy)
Jimmy McCracklin, *Everybody Rock: Let's Do It! The Best of Jimmy McCracklin* (Domino)
Johnny Heartsman, *The Touch* (Alligator)
Joe Louis Walker, *The Gift* (Hightone)
Ted Hawkins, *Happy Hour* (Rounder)

—Richie Unterberger

Chicago Blues

Probably no strain of blues has a more universally recognized form, feel and sound than Chicago blues. Chicago is where the music became amplified and had the big beat put to it and like Muddy Waters said, the blues had a baby and they named it rock'n'roll. As a simple point of reference, it's the music that most sounds like '50s rhythm and blues/rock & roll, its first notable offspring; when you hear a TV commercial with blues in it, it's usually the Chicago style they're playing. It's the sound of amplified harmonicas, electric slide guitars, big boogie piano and a rhythm section that just won't quit, with fierce, declamatory vocals booming over the top of it. It's the genius of Muddy Waters, Howlin' Wolf, Elmore James, and Little Walter knocking an urban audience on their collective ears at some smoky, noisy South Side tavern, then transmitting that signal to the world. It's the infectious boogie of Hound Dog Taylor, John Brim, Jimmy Reed, Joe Carter mining similar turf while Robert Nighthawk and Big John Wrencher lay it down with rough and tumble combos Sunday mornings at the Maxwell Street open-air market. And it's the up to date, gospel inspired vocals and B.B. King single note style of Otis Rush, Magic Sam, and Buddy Guy meshing with it all. Though there's much primitive beauty to be found in this strain of the music, there's nothing subtle about it; its rough edge ambience is the sound of the Delta, coming to terms with the various elements of city life and plugging in and going electric to keep pace with a changing world. Chicago blues was the first style to reach a mass audience and, with the passage of time, the first to reach a world wide audience as well. When the average Joe thinks of the blues, one of two musical sounds pop into their brain pan; one is the sound of Delta blues, usually slide-played on an acoustic guitar. The other, if it's played through an amplifier, is almost always Chicago blues.

Although the Windy City had a burgeoning blues scene before World War II (see separate essay on Lester Melrose and Early Chicago Blues), a number of elements combined after the war to put the modern Chicago scene into motion.

First, there was the societal aftermath of World War II to deal with. Blacks, after serving their country and seeing how the rest of the world was, came back home, packed up their few belongings and headed north to greener pastures, better-paying jobs, and the promise of a better life. It was a simple case of "how ya keep 'em down on the farm;" once blacks had left the oppressive life of Southern plantation life behind and "had seen the world," the prospect of toiling in a meat-packing plant in Chicago looked a whole lot more upscale than standing behind a mule somewhere in Mississippi.

And so they headed north. This influx of new migrants all finding new jobs and housing also infused Chicago with a lot of capital to be had and spent in these flush postwar times. The rise of the independent recording label after shellac rationing (and the development of space-age plastics) also had a lot to do with the development of the sound as well. New record labels that dealt exclusively with blues for a black market started to proliferate after 1950. Chess and its myriad subsidiaries and Vee-Jay had the lion's share of the market, but medium to tiny imprints like Ora-Nelle (an offshoot of the Maxwell Street Radio Repair Shop), JOB, Tempo Tone, Parkway, Cool, Atomic H, Cobra, Chance, Opera, United, States, Blue Lake, Parrot, C.J., and others all helped to bring the music to a wider audience.

Up to this point, Sonny Boy Williamson, Big Bill Broonzy, and Tampa Red were the three acknowledged kingpins of the local scene, but their hegemony was soon to be challenged and eventually relinquished to the new breed. The new migrants wanted to be citified and upscale, but still had strong down-home roots that needed to be tended to. The jazzier jump blues offerings in the city were fine, but newly arrived southerners wanted something a little more gritty, packed with a little more realism and a lot more emotional wallop. One day a train dropped a young slide guitarist from Mississippi into the city and soon the new audience had the sound and the style that suited their needs, urban, rural, and emotionally. Muddy Waters had come to Chicago and the sound of Chicago blues as we know it was about to be born.

Waters worked the house party circuit at first, driving truck by day and playing his music wherever he had the chance. He fell in with a loose group of players which included guitarists Baby Face Leroy Foster, Blue Smitty, and Jimmy Rogers. Muddy had tried to plug into the Melrose style recording scene three years after arriving, but a one-off recording session issued on Columbia under an assumed name did the singer little good. The sound was urban, but it wasn't his style, the sound that captivated his listeners at house rent parties along the South Side.

Muddy noticed two things about playing in Chicago. One, he needed amplification if he was going to be heard over the noisy din in your neighborhood tavern. He needed an electric guitar and an amplifier to go with it and he needed to turn both of them full blast if he was going to make an impression. Secondly, he needed a band; not a band with trumpets and saxophones in it, but a modern version of the kind of string band he worked in around Clarksdale, MS. It stands as a testament to Muddy Waters' genius that he created the blueprint for the first modern electric blues band and honed that design into a modern, lustrous musical sheen. There had certainly been blues combos in the city previous to Waters' arrival, but none sounded like this.

Muddy's first band was euphemistically called the Headhunters because of their competitive nature of blowing any band off the stage they came in contact with and usually taking their gig from them in the bargain. Although Muddy was having hits on Chess with just his guitar and a string bass in support, in a live situation it was a different matter entirely. Baby Face Leroy Foster was soon replaced by Elgar Edmonds, aka Elgin Evans, on drums, Jimmy Rogers wove complex second guitar patterns into the mix and in due time, Otis Spann would bring his beautiful piano stylings to the combo, following Muddy's every move. But it was with the addition of harmonica genius Little Walter where the face of the Chicago blues sound began to change. If Muddy and Jimmy's guitars were amplified and cranked up, Walter got his own microphone and amplifier and responded in kind. Though others played electric before him (Big Walter Horton among them), it was Little Walter who virtually defined the role and sound of amplified harmonica as it sat in this new band context. His honking, defiant tone, full of distortion and hand-controlled compression wedded to swooping saxophone-styled licks, became the sound for every aspiring combo and harmonica player to go after. By the time Walter left Muddy to form his own band, the Jukes (named after his hit instrumental), his sound was so pervasive that club owners would only hire combos that had a harmonica player working in that style. Bands would do without a drummer if need be, but the message was clear; one had to have that harp in order to work.

Soon there were newly amplified bands springing up everywhere and coming from everywhere, as the word was soon out that Chicago was quickly becoming the new promised land of the blues. The competition was fierce and tough, with lesser bands like Bo Diddley's Langley Avenue Jivecats or Earl Hooker working for tips on Maxwell Street, while others squeezed onto postage stamp sized stages just trying to establish their reputations. Among these were future blues legends in the making Big Walter Horton, Johnny Shines, J.B. Lenoir, Snooky Pryor, Jimmy Reed, John Brim, Billy Boy Arnold, and J.B. Hutto. Muddy Waters' first challenge to his newly acquired crown as king of the circuit came from Memphis bluesman Howlin' Wolf. Wolf had just signed a contract with Chess Records and had a hit on the R&B charts to go with it. He came into town, looking for work and by all accounts, Muddy was most helpful in getting him started. But what started as professional courtesy soon blossomed into a bitter, intense rivalry between the two bandleaders that lasted until Wolf's death in 1976. They'd steal sidemen from each other, compete with each other over who would record Willie Dixon's best material and when booked on the same bill together, would pull every trick possible to try and outdo each other onstage.

The preponderance here on the club scene in Chicago is pivotal in understanding how the music developed. For all their business acumen and commercial expertise, Chess and every other Chicago label that was recording this music was doing it because it was popular music in the black community. This was an untapped market that was tired of being spoon fed Billy Eckstine and Nat King Cole records and wanted to sent back home and a three minute 78 of it just might hit the spot. Just like every other honest trend or development in American music, it simply happened; the people responded, and somebody was smart enough to record it and sell it.

But by the mid-'50s—as one bluesman put it—"the beat had changed." The blues did have a baby and they did name it rock & roll. Suddenly everyone from Big Joe Turner to Bo Diddley were being lumped in with Elvis and Bill Haley and a hundred vocal groups named after birds or automobiles. The black audience started to turn away from blues to the new music and suddenly the local scene needed a fresh transfusion of new blood. Over on the West Side, younger musicians were totally enamored of the B.B. King style of playing and singing and began to incorporate both into a new Chicago blues hybrid. Working with a pair of saxes, a bass player and a drummer, most West Side combos were scaled down approximations of B.B.'s big band. When the group couldn't afford the sax section, the guitarists started throwing in heavy jazz chord like fills to flesh out the sound. Suddenly Otis Rush, Buddy Guy, and Magic Sam were on equal footing with the established heavies and even Howlin' Wolf and Elmore James started regularly recording and playing with saxophones. As rhythm and blues started getting a harder edged sound as it moved into soul music territory by the mid-'60s, the blues started keeping its ear to the ground and its beat focused on the dancefloor. While the three primary grooves up till now had been a slow blues, a boogie shuffle, and a "cut shuffle" (like

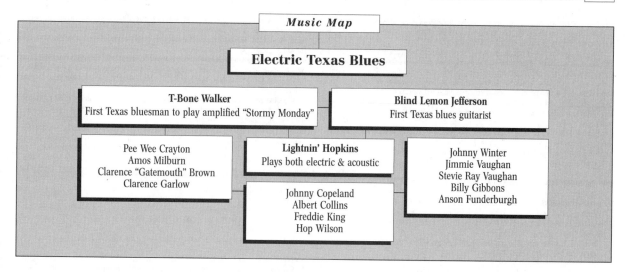

Music Map

Electric Texas Blues

T-Bone Walker
First Texas bluesman to play amplified "Stormy Monday"

Blind Lemon Jefferson
First Texas blues guitarist

Pee Wee Crayton
Amos Milburn
Clarence "Gatemouth" Brown
Clarence Garlow

Lightnin' Hopkins
Plays both electric & acoustic

Johnny Winter
Jimmie Vaughan
Stevie Ray Vaughan
Billy Gibbons
Anson Funderburgh

Johnny Copeland
Albert Collins
Freddie King
Hop Wilson

Muddy's "Got My Mojo Working"), suddenly it was OK to put a blues to a rock groove, sometimes with quite satisfying results. One of the first to mine this turf was harmonica ace Junior Wells. Wells' first hit, "Messing With the Kid," was blues with a driving beat and a great guitar riff, signaling that once again, the blues had reinvented itself to keep with the crowd. Working in tandem with Buddy Guy at Pepper's Lounge, the duo worked like a downscale miniature blues 'n' soul show, combining funky beats with the most down-in-the-alley blues imaginable. By the mid-'60s, Chicago produced its first racially mixed combo with the birth of the highly influential Paul Butterfield Blues Band, featuring the high-voltage guitar work of Michael Bloomfield and members from Howlin' Wolf's rhythm section. The permutations that have come since then and flourish in the current-day Chicago club scene echo those last two developments of the Chicago style. The beats and basslines may get funkier in approach, the guitars might be playing in a more modern style, sometimes even approaching rock pyrotechnics, in some cases. But every time a harmonica player cups his instrument around a cheap microphone or a crowd calls out for a slow one, the structure may change, but every musician and patron doffs their symbolic hats in appreciation to Muddy Waters and the beginnings of the Chicago blues, still very much alive and well today.

12 Recommended Albums:
Muddy Waters, *The Best Of Muddy Waters* (MCA-Chess)
Little Walter, *The Best Of Little Walter* (MCA-Chess)
Jimmy Reed, *Speak The Lyrics To Me, Mama Reed* (Vee-Jay)
Howlin' Wolf, *Howlin' Wolf/Moanin' In The Moonlight* (MCA-Chess)
Various Artists, *Chicago/The Blues/Today!, Volumes 1-3* (Vanguard)
Junior Wells, *Hoodoo Man Blues* (Delmark)
Otis Rush, *1956-1958* (Paula)
Elmore James, *The Best Of Elmore James—The Early Years* (Ace)
Hound Dog Taylor, *Hound Dog Taylor & the Houserockers* (Alligator)
Various Artists, *Blues Masters, Vol. 2: Postwar Chicago* (Rhino)
Paul Butterfield, *Paul Butterfield Blues Band* (Elektra)
Magic Sam, *West Side Soul* (Delmark)

—*Cub Koda*

Electric Texas Blues

The sound of Texas electric blues is difficult to define in general terms, not least because the sheer size of the state has given rise to several diverse sub-branches. Almost all blues fans can agree that they like the Texas sound; very few can actually agree what it is. What's more, it's a matter of some debate whether some major performers should be considered as Texas blues artists at all, since musicians like Freddie King, Bobby "Blue" Bland, T-Bone Walker, and Amos Milburn were only based there during part of their careers, often making their most influential recordings elsewhere. Saying that Texas blues has a distinctively earthy quotient won't do, either: What kind of blues worthy of the name isn't earthy?

In general terms, however, it can be said that Texas blues is a somewhat more variable animal than, say, Chicago blues, or Memphis blues. A country feel is often detectable, and it's more open to outside R&B influences. Bold touches of brass are frequent, yet the guitar, usually played with dazzling single string virtuosity, is king; the harmonica, in comparison to Chicago, is much more secondary. There's also a sense of joyous showmanship that often comes across on the records, which frequently have a small-club feel, even if they've been recorded in state-of-the-art studios.

Texas does have an estimable history of acoustic country blues talent. Blind Lemon Jefferson may be the most famous of the early Texas blues singers; Lightnin' Hopkins (who played in both acoustic and electric styles, aside from John Lee Hooker, may have made more records than any blues artist; Mance Lipscomb was a notable footnote to the early '60s blues revival, as one of the relatively few elderly bluesmen that emerged during

that era who hadn't actually made any records before being "rediscovered." For the purposes of this piece, however, we'll focus on Texas blues after the advent of the electric guitar.

One Texan would be the figure more responsible for electrifying the blues than any other. T-Bone Walker, born in 1910 in Texas, had in fact relocated to Los Angeles by the time he made his most influential sides in the '40s. Owing much to jazz as well as urban R&B, these were some of the first, if not the very first, blues sides that employed clean, horn-like single-string soloing in a style that came to be identified with much modern electric blues, from B.B. King on down. As John Morthland explains in the liner notes to *Texas Music, Vol. 1: Postwar Blues Combos,* "After feeling out the possibilities created by electricity, he began phrasing saxlike lines that exploited the guitar's new tonal capabilities and changed it from a rhythm to a lead instrument. Adapting rhythmic and harmonic ideas from jazz, T-Bone would hold his guitar sideways against his chest... and drag his pick across the strings for a fat, clean sound that he'd break up with grinding downstrokes."

The Texas-L.A. connection was so well-traveled in the '40s that it bore some resemblance to the railroad that seemingly shuttled nonstop between the Mississippi Delta and Chicago. Besides Walker, native Texans Amos Milburn, Pee Wee Crayton (a T-Bone Walker disciple), Charles Brown, Percy Mayfield, and Lowell Fulson all launched their careers after moving to California and hooking up with the independent R&B labels sprouting in Los Angeles.

Texas itself wasn't entirely bereft of recording opportunities, the most prominent R&B label, Duke/Peacock, being based in Houston. Duke/Peacock owner Don Robey was legendary for his iron hand, running his operation with a parsimonious, intimidating attitude that would result in hosts of anecdotes surfacing several decades later. Even today, some musicians are reluctant to discuss his rumored gangster-like tactics, and somewhat less so to note his practice of assigning songwriting credits and royalties to himself with reckless abandon.

Nevertheless, Duke/Peacock did record some excellent blues in the '50s by artists like Big Mama Thornton, Junior Parker, and Bobby "Blue" Bland. The latter two singers are not from Texas, but Bland in particular has come to represent the sort of blues/R&B/soul hybrids that are important facets of Texas blues, even if they were developed primarily in Texas studios, rather than within the Texas blues scene itself. Bland's extensive association with Duke/Peacock, which lasted throughout the '60s as well as the '50s, is usually rated as the finest blues/soul of all time, notable for its gospel vocal influence and blaring horn charts as well as its blues elements.

Bland's brassy soul blues may have been Texas' most successful blues export on record, but in practice, the guitar remained king. Clarence "Gatemouth" Brown, Johnny Copeland, and Albert Collins all began recording guitar-heavy material on Texas labels in the '50s, although Collins and Copeland wouldn't really achieve top-level national blues stardom for another two or three decades. Like most noted Texas electric blues guitarists, they were top showmen as well; the late Collins often using a guitar lead of 100 feet or so to enable him to wander around the audience while he played.

Freddie King is the most famous Texas blues guitarist to emerge during this era, though again it's almost arbitrary as to whether he should be classified as a Texas bluesman or not. He was born in Texas, but moved to Chicago as a teenager, and recorded his prime work for the Cincinnati-based King label. However you might classify his statehood, he was certainly one of the most important electric blues guitarists of his time, producing an authoritative, distorted tone that was a big influence on Eric Clapton in particular. He was also eager to incorporate R&B and soul influences into his repertoire, and was comfortable as both a vocal and instrumental artist, scoring his biggest hit with the instrumental "Hide Away" in 1961. Fans of Texas blues-indeed, blues fans of all kinds—should look for a video compilation of his mid-'60s performances on the Dallas-based R&B/soul television show, *The Beat,* which includes some guitar sparring with Clarence

"Gatemouth" Brown (who led the house band). Although slide guitar wasn't heard much in Texas blues, Hop Wilson's idiosyncratic work on a non-pedal steel guitar in the '50s is a sound no lover of blues can afford to miss.

With its constant interchange between black and white styles, it's not surprising that Texas developed a healthy white blues-rock scene in the late '60s and '70s. Johnny Winter was the most well known of its early practitioners, playing in both traditional styles and more Southern rock-influenced ones; his brother Edgar also had some national success, though with a far more rock-oriented sound. The late Texan Stevie Ray Vaughan is probably the most famous blues-rocker of recent times, and was indeed the primary torch-bearer for the whole modern day blues-rock genre prior to his unexpected death in 1990.

Texas will likely continue to supply a stream of blues talent due to its oft-thriving club scene, particularly in Austin, TX. The world is now well aware of the many talented white blues bands to emerge from the area, the best and most recognizable of those being the Fabulous Thunderbirds, which were founded by Stevie Ray Vaughan's brother Jimmie. The presence of one of the world's leading blues clubs, Antone's, in the city bodes well for ongoing development of regional blues talent.

Ten Recommended Albums:

Various Artists, *Blues Masters Series Vol. 3: Texas Blues* (Rhino)
Various Artist, *Texas Music, Vol. 1: Postwar Blues Combos* (Rhino)
T-Bone Walker, *The Complete Black & White Recordings* (Capitol)
Bobby "Blue" Bland, *I Pity the Fool* (MCA)
Clarence "Gatemouth" Brown, *The Original Peacock Recordings* (MCA)
Albert Collins, *Ice Pickin'* (Alligator)
Hop Wilson, *Steel Guitar Flash!* (Ace)
Freddie King, *Hide Away: The Best of Freddie King* (Rhino)
Johnny Winter, *Johnny Winter* (Columbia)
Stevie Ray Vaughan, *Greatest Hits* (Epic)

—Richie Unterberger

Blues Slide Guitar

The swooping, stinging sound of the slide guitar is one of the most striking and popular characteristics of the blues. It's also one of the sounds that most audibly links its rural traditions with its urban ones, and its acoustic styles with the electric age. Some guitarists, like Elmore James and his acolytes Hound Dog Taylor and J.B. Hutto, have more or less built their entire style around it; many others brandish their command of the slide at least occasionally.

The origins of the use of the slide guitar in the blues—like many topics concerning the origins of the blues as a whole—are subject to varying historical interpretations. Some assert that the style didn't become widespread until it became popular in Hawaii in the 1890s, spreading to the mainland by the turn of the 20th century. Joseph Kekuku has been credited with popularizing the concept of fretting guitar strings with objects rather than fingers, and the influence of the slide guitar as it was played in Hawaii became influential in pop music as a whole, not just within the blues.

On the other hand, in *Deep Blues*, Robert Palmer writes that "the slide technique was originally associated with an African instrument that has been reported from time to time in the American South, the single-stringed musical bow. One-stringed instruments played with sliders seem to have survived principally among black children, who would nail a length of broom wire to a wall and play it with a rock or pill bottle slider.

"The appearance of black slide guitarists in the early 1900s has often been linked to the popularization of a similar technique by Hawaiian guitarists, but slide guitar wasn't native to Hawaii; it was introduced there between 1893 and 1895, reputedly by a schoolboy, Joseph Kekuku. It did not spread from Hawaii to the mainland until 1900, when it was popularized by Frank Ferera, and by that time black guitarists in Mississippi were already fretting their instruments with knives or the broken-off necks of bottles."

The instrument that Palmer refers to is sometimes called the diddley bow, and is perhaps more common than he infers in this passage. A lot of the children who played with the diddley bow as a household toy became guitar players who adapted the technique to a proper instrument. And some of those musicians became professional, taking the rudiments of the technique with them even when they moved from the barn to the city. One of the most fascinating blues albums of all time was recorded by Eddie "One-String" Jones in 1960, then a homeless man on Los Angeles' Skid Row, who played a piece of wire on a two-by-four board with a whiskey flask. His album, *One String Blues*, may be the closest modern listeners can get to hearing the square root of the blues. Another interesting variation to this home made instrument can be heard on a handful of mid-'50s recordings on the Specialty label by Willie Joe Duncan playing a larger electric version of the diddley bow called the Unitar. Whatever the case, there can be no doubt that the slide guitar caught on quickly with blues musicians. Its keening wail emulated in some respects the moans and cries of the human voice, and was a great medium for conveying the intense emotions of the songs, whether joyful or sorrowful. It also did not demand a lot in the way of hi-tech equipment: pocket knives and a thimble-shaped piece of metal were adaptable for the purpose. One of the most popular vehicles for playing slide was a bottleneck that was shaped over flame; hence the term for "bottleneck" guitar, which is slide guitar as produced by such a device.

In his liner notes to *Blues Masters, Vol. 15: Slide Guitar Classics*, Cub Koda further distinguishes the style from its possible Hawaiian origins: "The major difference came largely in how the instrument was held. Hawaiian guitar was played with the instrument lying flat on the player's lap; this style was adapted by Whites to form the steel-guitar sound in country music."

"But by and large…black blues musicians replaced the steel bar with a bottleneck or metal tube fitted to one finger and simply continued to play the guitar in the standard Spanish position. Although the slide produced the same whiny effects that the bar did for Hawaiian guitarists, it was used more for lead fills, an extension of the singer's voice, allowing the instrument to be fretted for somewhat conventional chording when not in use. By the time examples of this type of playing started appearing on phonograph records in the late '20s, the banjo's days as a popular blues instrument were numbered; slide guitar was in."

The slide guitar is often associated with Delta blues, although its use was in fact widespread throughout the music. Delta bluesmen, however, may have been more responsible than any others for midwifing the style's transition from acoustic to electric music. Charley Patton, the first great star of Mississippi blues, left several excellent recorded examples behind, utilizing the slide to answer his own vocal lines. His contemporaries Son House and Bukka White took the style and sound content one step further with their allegiance to the metal bodied National guitar, which produced a loud, astrigent sound built more on sheer volume than subtlety. The Nationals and Dobro models were the true link between acoustic and electric guitars. They were called "ampliphonic" guitars in early catalogs and Delta players quickly adapted to them for two basic reasons: 1) they were loud enough to be heard over the din in a juke joint, and 2) they could be used to bash an adversary senseless with seemingly little damage to the instrument itself. Certainly Robert Johnson—an artist who had an absolute mastery of all guitar styles—is probably the best known Delta slide practioner, with his work on classics like "Crossroads Blues" and "Come on in My Kitchen" standing tall as the epitome of taste, tone, and feeling that modern-day artists working in the genre still aspire to. There was Muddy Waters, influenced by both Son House and Robert Nighthawk, who electrified the blues in Chicago. His 1948 "I Can't Be Satisfied"/"Feel Like Going Home" single, repeatedly referred to as a defining moment of early electric blues, utilized prominent slide guitar. Robert Nighthawk, who started recording in the '30s on acoustic and later went electric, was also a prime mover and shaker on the instrument. Playing in standard guitar tuning (most slide players tune their instrument to an open chord, usually pitched to E or G), Nighthawk's touch and tone were the smoothest and creamiest. Though largely a forgotten figure today, Nighthawk taught his style to Waters and Chicago's most versatile blues guitarist, Earl Hooker, and his influence extended all the way to Southern rocker Duane Allman.

One guitarist went as far as to make the electric slide guitar his defining trademark. Even listeners who aren't blues fans can identify the classic riff that Elmore James used on "Dust My Broom," the song that probably embodies the electric slide guitar sound more than any other. James' strongest suit, his unsurpassed mastery of the electric slide idiom fused with extreme volume and a unrelenting attack which he put to use on numerous recordings in the '50s and early '60s, is still the most prevalent style of slide guitar playing being heard today. He spawned a raft of Chicago acolytes who adapted his raw sound and style to their own needs, among them Hound Dog Taylor, Joe Carter, and J.B. Hutto. Elmore James had a particularly strong influence on British guitarists of the '60s. Brian Jones, whose slide work graced a handful of early Rolling Stones sides, worked on the British beat club circuit as Elmo(re) Lewis and Jeremy Spencer of Fleetwood Mac—the biggest band of the late-'60s British blues boom besides John Mayall's Bluesbreakers—worshiped James' approach and his immersion in Elmore's style approached the level of re-created art. To the larger record-buying public, James was immortalized in a spoken aside on the Beatles' "For You Blue," a George Harrison composition that prominently featured slide in the Elmore style.

Many blues-rock guitarists picked up the slide style, like Jeff Beck and Mike Bloomfield; though it didn't dominate their playing, they could summon the technique when called for. The best American blues-rock slide guitarist was certainly Duane Allman, who put the sound in the spotlight on Allman Brothers staples like their update of Blind Willie McTell's "Statesboro Blues." Duane's style evolved from the combination of Elmore's distorted tone and Earl Hooker's elegant standard-tuning flourishes wedded to the extreme volume from Marshall stack amplification. Another modern master of the slide idiom was Ry Cooder, who did not limit its application to the blues or blues-rock, using it for his diverse explorations of many kinds of roots music, as well as in his voluminous soundtrack work. And certainly no dissertation of modern slide styles could leave out George Thorogood and Bonnie Raitt, both of whom have gone on to great success in the rock field. Raitt, who toiled for years on the blues circuit before her breakthrough, is one of the finest slide players going, being prominently influenced (and personally instructed) by her mentors, Mississippi Fred McDowell and Son House. Thorogood's hamfisted approach took Hound Dog Taylor's bare-bones raucous style and reduced it even further, if such a notion was possible.

Today, the slide guitar continues to have a standard place in the repertoire of many blues performers, whether as an integral component or an occasional spotlight. Like the blues itself, its frequent use in mainstream settings like film soundtracks (by Cooder and others) means that blues slide guitar is no longer thought of as something exotic, but as part of the vernacular of American music.

Eight Recommended Albums:

Various Artists, *Blues Masters, Vol. 15: Slide Guitar Classics* (Rhino)
Various Artists, *Slide Guitar—Bottle Knives & Steel, Vol. 1 & 2* (CBS)
Various Artists, *Bottleneck Guitar Masterpieces* (Yazoo)
Robert Johnson, *King of the Delta Blues Singers* (CBS)
Elmore James, *The Sky is Crying* (Rhino)
Hound Dog Taylor, *Hound Dog Taylor & the Houserockers* (Alligator)
Eddie "One-String" Jones, *One String Blues* (Gazell)
Robert Nighthawk, *Live on Maxwell Street* (Rounder)

—Richie Unterberger

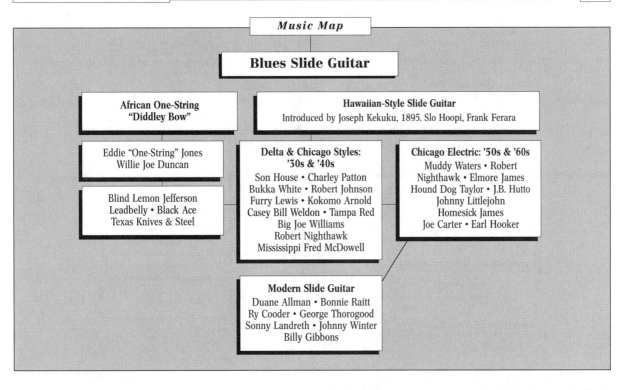

Music Map

Blues Slide Guitar

African One-String "Diddley Bow"

Hawaiian-Style Slide Guitar
Introduced by Joseph Kekuku, 1895. Slo Hoopi, Frank Ferara

Eddie "One-String" Jones
Willie Joe Duncan

Delta & Chicago Styles: '30s & '40s
Son House • Charley Patton
Bukka White • Robert Johnson
Furry Lewis • Kokomo Arnold
Casey Bill Weldon • Tampa Red
Big Joe Williams
Robert Nighthawk
Mississippi Fred McDowell

Chicago Electric: '50s & '60s
Muddy Waters • Robert
Nighthawk • Elmore James
Hound Dog Taylor • J.B. Hutto
Johnny Littlejohn
Homesick James
Joe Carter • Earl Hooker

Blind Lemon Jefferson
Leadbelly • Black Ace
Texas Knives & Steel

Modern Slide Guitar
Duane Allman • Bonnie Raitt
Ry Cooder • George Thorogood
Sonny Landreth • Johnny Winter
Billy Gibbons

Jazz/Blues Crossover

The blues and jazz both draw from a wellspring of similar roots in African-American popular music and culture. The paths of each genre have diverged widely since the beginning of the 1900s, but before 1950, the styles were often deeply intertwined with each other. It's a marriage that will endure to some degree as long as blues and jazz are around; even today, contemporary jazz acts throw in plenty of bluesy quotes, and many musicians boast service in both jazz bands and R&B/blues outfits. Many festivals spotlight both blues and jazz artists, the most famous of them being the annual New Orleans Jazz & Blues festival. Not many current artists, however, could be said to straddle the blues/jazz fence to such an extent that they could be classified as members of either camp.

The distinctions were much blurrier in the early 1900s, when both blues and jazz had yet to fully form their identities. The influence of ragtime music and barrelhouse piano styles were strong formative elements of each. W.C. Handy, the "Father of the Blues," led brass bands whose instrumentation and arrangements were likely more akin to jazz. The first artists to record the blues were women singers, but these were the blues more in song structure and vocal phrasing than in the jazz/pop arrangements, which employed jazz greats such as Louis Armstrong and Coleman Hawkins. (The significance of the classic female blues singers is detailed in a separate piece.) Much later, in the '50s, traditional jazz bandleader Chris Barber would play a key role in exposing the blues in his native Britain by featuring bluesmen as part of his shows, often imported from the States.

The most active period of cross-fertilization between blues and jazz may have been the '30s and '40s, when swing and big-band styles were at their peak, and when the blues was moving toward a fuller and more citified sound. Jazz was still often played in dance halls, and needed some singers and song structures to help maintain its accessibility. Blues was moving toward a more sophisticated sound that would soon encompass full bands and electricity. Each form had much to learn from the other.

Several of the early big bands featured vocalists that not only borrowed from the blues in their songs and phrasing, but in turn influenced the evolution of other bluesmen. Jimmy Rushing, in his work with Count Basie, may have been the first notable blues-based singer to front a big band with a precursor to the "shouting" style. This was developed to its fullest shortly afterwards by singers with Kansas City-based swing bands, including Big Joe Turner, Jimmy Witherspoon, and Walter Brown.

Brown and Witherspoon both sang with the band of pianist Jay McShann, the bandleader with whom Charlie Parker first recorded. McShann is one of the artists most likely to be found in either the blues or jazz section of fine record stores; Turner and Witherspoon, throughout their career, moved with ease between the jazz and R&B worlds, sometimes changing their focus to fit the requirements of the gig or the record date. Eddie "Cleanhead" Vinson, who doubled on vocals and saxophone, was another performer who would be hard to tie to either style; he could not only sing the blues, but could play bop jazz as well, and led a band including John Coltrane in the late '40s, long before Coltrane made his mark on the jazz world.

Besides the "shouters," the main tributary of blues feeding into jazz was found in the boogie-woogie pianists of the late '30s and early '40s. Taking some cues from blues styles that had been developed in barrelhouses, Albert Ammons, Pete Johnson, and Meade "Lux" Lewis were the most instrumental figures in introducing boogie-woogie to jazz. The famed *Spirituals to Swing* concerts in New York City's Carnegie Hall in the late '30s found the marriage between the idioms at their peak, featuring pioneers like Ammons, Johnson, Lewis, and Turner on the same stage; Robert Johnson, interestingly, was also planned to be included in the events, but had died before he could be contacted.

Jazz greats would often use bluesy riffs and signatures in their work; the Rhino collection *Blues Masters, Vol. 13: New York City Blues* contains some good illustrations. The wild sax solo of Illinois Jacquet in Lionel Hampton's "Flying Home" rates as a leading forerunner of R&B, particularly the "honking" style of sax associated with the form. The shouters, honkers, and boogie-woogie would coalesce in the '40s into jump blues, which in some senses was the ultimate jazz-blues fusion. As pioneered by Louis Jordan, Roy Milton, and many others starting in the mid-'40s (again, detailed in a separate piece), jump blues took the above factors and added a raw power and playful pop elements (particularly in the vocals) to the equation, while maintaining a rhythmic base and instrumentation quite close to swing jazz in some ways.

Jump blues wasn't solely composed of the above elements. The introduction of the electric guitar had far-reaching effects on pop music that nobody could have guessed in 1940, when a jazzman, Charlie Christian, established himself as the first virtuoso of the instrument. Christian can't be considered a blues/jazz artist (though examples of bluesy playing can be heard in his scant body of recorded work), but there's no question that he was a huge influence on the jump blues guitarists, particularly T-Bone Walker, one of the key figures of both jump blues and West Coast blues. Walker's single-string solos owed so much to jazz, as played by Christian on guitar and other jazzers on other instruments, that a case can be made for classifying Walker as a blues/jazzman as well, though his songs and roots were very much in the blues camp.

On the whole, the end of the jump blues phenomenon spelled an end to the intense interchange between blues and jazz. Jazz was evolving into bebop and beyond; jump blues fed into R&B and rock & roll. Chuck Berry's "Maybellene" may owe a little to jazz, for example, but the distance between Chuck Berry and, say, a mid-'50s jazz artist like Clifford Brown is a lot further than the distance between Louis Jordan and Lionel Hampton. Jazz bands were less oriented toward the dance halls now, and less apt to employ singers for that purpose, although some (such as Joe Williams, not to be confused with Big Joe Williams the country blues singer) kept the flame of old-school Jimmy Rushing-type vocals alive.

It's interesting to note, though, that quite a few major jazzmen were schooled in blues/R&B bands, or recorded sessions with them to help pay the rent, from Coltrane and Coleman on down. There was some movement in the other direction as well; guitarist Mickey Baker originally had his heart set on being a jazz musician, but instead became one of the best blues influenced rock & roll guitarists of all time—partly, again, as a result of being repeatedly called upon to play R&B sessions. Earl Bostic, who played in Lionel Hampton's band in the '40s, found his true calling as an R&B saxophonist. Two respected

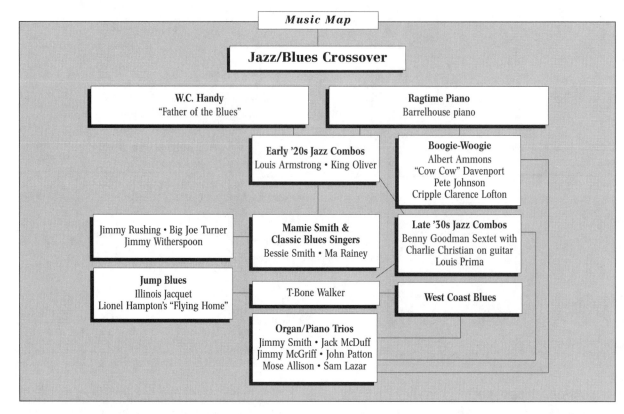

Music Map

Jazz/Blues Crossover

W.C. Handy
"Father of the Blues"

Ragtime Piano
Barrelhouse piano

Early '20s Jazz Combos
Louis Armstrong • King Oliver

Boogie-Woogie
Albert Ammons
"Cow Cow" Davenport
Pete Johnson
Cripple Clarence Lofton

Jimmy Rushing • Big Joe Turner
Jimmy Witherspoon

**Mamie Smith &
Classic Blues Singers**
Bessie Smith • Ma Rainey

Late '30s Jazz Combos
Benny Goodman Sextet with
Charlie Christian on guitar
Louis Prima

Jump Blues
Illinois Jacquet
Lionel Hampton's "Flying Home"

T-Bone Walker

West Coast Blues

Organ/Piano Trios
Jimmy Smith • Jack McDuff
Jimmy McGriff • John Patton
Mose Allison • Sam Lazar

jazz players, saxophonists David "Fathead" Newman and Hank Crawford, had bluesy leanings that would come in handy when they worked as sidemen on some of Ray Charles' bluesiest recordings. But even here, the relationship between blues and jazz grows increasingly tangential.

The blues-jazz link had another fling in the '60s, albeit in a somewhat distant form, in the work of several keyboardists. Organists Jack McDuff, Jimmy McGriff, Jimmy Smith, and John Patton, nowadays recognized as pioneers of "soul-jazz," often drew upon blues styles and material; one of Smith's biggest set pieces, for instance, was a cover of "I've Got My Mojo Working." Jazz pianist/vocalist Mose Allison (who began recording in the late '50s) had a distinctive bluesy hipster style, both on originals like "Young Man's Blues" and "Parchman Farm," and covers of songs by Willie Dixon and Sonny Boy Williamson; he'd prove to be an unexpected influence on British artists like the Who, the Yardbirds, and John Mayall, all of whom covered Allison songs. In Britain itself, Georgie Fame took up a blues/jazz style similar to Allison's, though with much more of a pop/R&B base.

15 Recommended Albums:
Various Artists, *Blues Masters, Vol. 11: Classic Blues Women* (Rhino)
Various Artists, *Blues Masters, Vol. 13: New York City Blues* (Rhino)
Jimmy Rushing, *The Essential Jimmy Rushing* (Vanguard)
Big Joe Turner, *Complete 1940-1944* (Official)
Jimmy Witherspoon & Jay McShann, *Jimmy Witherspoon & Jay McShann* (DA)
Albert Ammons, *King of Boogie (1939-1949)* (Blues Classics)
Meade "Lux" Lewis, *1939-1954* (Story of Blues)
Various Artists, *Blues Masters, Vol. 5: Jump Blues Classics* (Rhino)
Various Artists, *Blues Masters, Vol. 14: More Jump Blues* (Rhino)
Louis Jordan, *The Best of Louis Jordan* (MCA)
T-Bone Walker, *The Complete Capitol/Black & White Recordings* (Capitol)
Mose Allison, *Greatest Hits* (Prestige)
Ray Charles, *Blues & Jazz* (Rhino)
Various Artists, *Blue Funk: The History of the Hammond Organ* (Blue Note)
Eddie "Cleanhead" Vinson, *And Roomful of Blues* (Muse)

—*Richie Unterberger*

Soul-Blues

The blues is sometimes stereotyped as a purist sort of music that strays little from its conventions. While it's true that it's more static than some other styles, it's never been immune from outside trends. The classic female blues singers of the '20s drew heavily from vaudevillian pop; blues electric guitar pioneer T-Bone Walker had a lot of jazz on his mind; the jump blues greats took from jazz and R&B in almost equal measures. Also soul music has exerted a substantial influence upon the blues since the 1960s.

Some more skeptical blues fans may assert that many blues artists put some soul in their music as a matter of professional survival. The broader, more likely truth is that blues performers of the late 20th century and into the 21st century cannot help but reflect some of the musical and social climate of their time. Soul music was one of the primary voices of African-American culture in the '60s and '70s. Much more often than not, performers schooled in the blues added soul flavor not just to adapt, but because they genuinely loved and were inspired by soul music.

Soul-blues has been with us since soul music itself began to form as a distinct entity in the early '60s; precursors of soul music like Percy Mayfield and Charles Brown had already mixed R&B, gospel, and blues a good decade or more prior to that. The first, and maybe the best, of the soul-blues singers is Bobby "Blue" Bland. Bobby actually began recording in the early '50s, and always had a strong R&B flavor from the git-go. He truly reached his stride, however, in the '60s, when he recorded an extraordinarily lengthy series of fine singles that incorporated horn charts and the sort of gospel-inflected vocals common to most great soul singers. Many of these weren't confined to the specialist blues markets, but were genuine big R&B hits, occasionally making the pop charts as well. Line up a few listeners against a wall, play them Bland's greatest hits, and ask them whether to classify the results as blues or soul; you'll probably end up with something close to a 50-50 split, or at the least with a lot of people who can't make up their minds.

Bland is an unusual textbook example of a virtually equal blues/soul hybrid. One of his chief inspirations, B.B. King, has never been thought of as a soul man, but has often had a prominent gospel and soul feel to his work. This was particularly true in the late '60s, when he frequently employed a large horn section, and for a while enlisted the services of arranger Johnny Pate, who had contributed to classic Chicago soul records by the likes of Major Lance and the Impressions. Two other Kings, Freddie and (especially) Albert, maintained some presence on the R&B charts with their blends of fierce blues guitar and contemporary soul-leaning material.

Horns were key ingredients in updating '50s blues, or '50s R&B/blues, for the '60s audiences. By extension, they also enabled some performers to maintain a foothold on the R&B charts, while the more guitar-harmonica-oriented "classic" combos were confined to more specialized audiences and a lower level of the club circuit. Junior Parker, Little Milton, and Lowell Fulson (famous for "Tramp")—all of whom had roots in pre-'60s blues and R&B—were some of the most successful of them. Some of the more purist-minded blues collectors much prefer these singers' earlier work, finding their later soul/blues too smooth and urban, although in all cases these artists found their greatest popular success with their soul-conscious tunes.

Not all veterans in the '50s were as successful with this strategy. Amos Milburn, for instance, recorded an odd album for Motown in the early '60s that rounded off his jump blues with typical early-'60s Motown production values. Although the results actually weren't that bad, it was an instant collector's item (and, predictably enough, reissued on

CD with bonus cuts in the mid-'90s). It's not too well known that Motown occasionally tried to do similar things with a few other blues artists in the early '60s, as can be heard on the *Motown's Blue Evolution* compilation.

There were also a number of hardcore blues acts who simply added a dollop of soul to the proceedings without diminishing their basic power or substantially altering the focus of their guitar/bass/drums lineup. Major Chicago blues stars Junior Wells, Buddy Guy, and Magic Sam all made some of their best recordings in the '60s; all of them added a bit of inventive soul sophistication in their songwriting and arrangements without sounding forced. Check out Wells' vocal mannerisms on much of his 1965 classic, *Hoodoo Man Blues* (also featuring Buddy Guy), which betrays a definite James Brown influence.

Speaking of J.B., it wasn't unknown (although not very common either) for established soul singers to delve into the blues occasionally. Brown did this more often than most, though mostly limiting his blues excursions to album tracks. Nothing could hide the fact that he was far more talented and innovative as an R&B/soul/funk pioneer than a straight blues singer, but the double CD *Messin' With the Blues* compiles his most blues-oriented material; it's not so bad, and there's a lot more of it than you would guess.

In *The Blackwell Guide to Blues*, Jeff Hannusch defines soul-blues as "singers that have a gospel background and who bring an urgent 'churchy' approach to their music." Such performers usually fall on the soul side of the soul-blues hybrid. Artists such as Otis Clay, Little Johnny Taylor, and O.V. Wright are apt to strike many listeners not so much as blues singers, but as soul singers with a bluesy feel. Whether you classify them within the rubric of the blues or not, there's no doubt that the aforementioned vocalists enjoy a lot of appeal among both blues and soul fans (who, of course, are often one and the same).

Soul-blues as an artistic force diminished, naturally, when soul music itself began to be superseded by disco in the mid-'70s, and then by rap and urban contemporary in the '80s and '90s, among the black audience. The Malaco label was sort of stronghold for "old-school" soul-blues, releasing efforts in the style of Z.Z. Hill, Denise LaSalle, and Latimore, as well as recording veterans who had fallen out of favor with mainstream audiences, such as Johnnie Taylor, Bobby "Blue" Bland, and Little Milton. Some of the Malaco titles proved surprisingly popular with a black audience supposedly only concerned with less traditional styles. Hill's *Down Home* in particular was a popular success that exceeded all expectations.

More often than not, though, Malaco product was much more soul than blues. Many listeners who aren't concerned with critical distinctions would even be unlikely to classify is as soul-blues at all, but merely as rootsy soul. Popular blues and soul were so thin on the ground in the early half of the '80s that one sometimes got the feeling that critics were championing the Malaco sound not on its merit, but because it was utilizing some of the proper approved ingredients, and there were so few other releases of the sort attracting any attention outside of the specialized/collector audiences.

Soul-blues as a label is applied to few current releases, but that may be because soul itself has been permanently absorbed into the fabric of contemporary blues. Many if not most of today's top electric blues performers—Robert Cray, Joe Louis Walker, Koko Taylor, and Jimmy Johnson (brother of soul singer Syl Johnson)—to name a few—put a lot of soul flourishes into their songwriting, arrangements, and vocal delivery. The late Ted Hawkins also showed how soul could figure in contemporary acoustic blues. A rap-hip-hop/blues fusion, however, doesn't seem imminent, although white alternative rockers like Beck, G. Love, and Bobby Sichran have given it a try.   —*Richie Unterberger*

Blues Rediscoveries

When blues enthusiasts pawed through their collection of rare 78s in the '50s, performers like Robert Johnson, Bukka White, and Skip James were little more than names on a label. There was little if any historical information that documented how these singers lived, where they came from, how they came to be recorded (however briefly), or how they felt about their life and art. Looking at the records and imagining who the performers may have been seemed as futile as trying to touch a ghost; in many cases, it was uncertain whether these singers, few of whom had recorded after the early '40s, were still alive or not.

A few of these collectors and enthusiasts became determined to tackle the challenge of chasing down these ghosts, dead or alive. Sam Charters' *The Country Blues* (published

in 1959), and other scholarly studies that treated the blues as an art form worthy of serious respect, ignited a hunger for more information about its originators. Listening to the records (which, in the late '50s, were themselves hard to come by) wasn't enough; surely these men and women had stories to tell, and, if they were still alive and healthy, more songs to sing. Both folklorists and general enthusiasts, such as Mack McCormick, David Evans, Chris Strachwitz, Alan Lomax, John Fahey, and Ed Denson, were dedicated enough to start to comb the American South for living embodiments of the blues tradition. What they found was more than they could have possibly hoped existed.

By the mid-'60s, Bukka White, Skip James, Son House, Mississippi John Hurt, and Furry Lewis had all been relocated. They had not willfully vanished into obscurity, or deliberately retired from music. Their recording careers had come to an end, often under premature circumstances. In most instances they continued to play music, for live audiences, for their families, or simply for themselves. However, in the absence of opportunities to record in the studio, or to play for large audiences in an African-American community that was increasingly less interested in rural blues, they had turned to other sources of livelihood, unaware of the increasing appeal of their music to white audiences.

Finding these legends of the past often amounted to efforts bordering on private detective work. Skip James and Son House, it has been reported, were rediscovered on the exact same day in 1964, though in widely differing circumstances; James was ill in Tunica County Hospital in Mississippi, while House wasn't in the South at all, having relocated to upstate New York about 20 years previously. John Fahey found Bukka White by writing a letter to "Bukka White, Old Blues Singer, c/o General Delivery, Aberdeen, Mississippi" (a town that happened to be mentioned in one of White's songs); a relative of White's who worked for the post office chanced upon the correspondence, who helped direct Fahey to Memphis, where White had been living since the early '40s.

No doubt a good film lies in the haphazard and semi-comic circumstances of these searches. In his novel *Nighthawk Blues*, Peter Guralnick tells of three obsessive blues collectors who, after years of passionate correspondence, decide to meet face to face and embark upon a search of the South for one of their heroes, only to find that they can't stand each other. Guralnick also tells the true story, in his essay collection *Feel Like Going Home*, of the extreme difficulty in finding a bluesman who had already been rediscovered (Robert Pete Williams), as he navigates the Louisiana backroads with few clues or landmarks to guide him. Then there were the adjustments that some of the performers had to make as they readied themselves for new audiences. Dick Waterman, who located House in Buffalo and managed the guitarist, told the following story in Francis Davis' *History of the Blues*:

"A month or so later, we brought Son to Cambridge, Massachusetts, to get him ready for the Newport Folk Festival [and introduced him to] Al Wilson, who later moved to Los Angeles and was a founding member of the group Canned Heat. Al played open-tuning bottleneck and could play all the styles. He could play Bukka White, Son House, Charley Patton, and Blind Lemon Jefferson—he could really play. And he sat down with Son, knee to knee, guitar to guitar, and said, 'OK, this is the figure that in 1930, you called "My Black Mama",' and played it for him. And Son said, 'Yeah, yeah, that's me, that's me. I played that.'"

"And then Al said, 'Now about a dozen years later, when Mr. Lomax came around, you changed the name to 'My Black Woman,' and you did it this way.' He showed him. And Son would say, 'Yeah, yeah. I got my recollection now, I got my recollection now.' And he would start to play, and the two of them played together. Then, Al reminded him of how he changed tunings, and played his own 'Pony Blues' for him. There would not have been a rediscovery of Son House in the 1960s without Al Wilson. Really. Al Wilson taught Son House how to play Son House."

In many (but not all) cases, the actual skills of the performers were barely diminished, or undiminished. Since their "retirements," an LP market had developed for country blues, as well as a college/festival-oriented folk circuit that was eager to hear the music performed live. James, White, House, Hurt, and others resumed their careers with considerable success, with assistance from committed managers like Dick Waterman and sympathetic record labels like Vanguard.

Some purists held that the best work of these resuscitated legends were their original 78s, recorded in the artists' relative youth, in the '20s and '30s. Contemporary albums, they contended, were pale shadows of the glory of the vintage singles. For the most part, though, those who bought the LPs disagreed, finding them powerful statements on their own terms. There were also the considerations that: 1) in the '60s, before vintage blues reissue compilations were common, many listeners didn't have the patience to relocate the rare original singles; and 2) even if they could hear the originals, non-fanatics often much preferred the clear sound of modern studios to the scratchy and hissy original 78s. Certainly James, Hurt, and White made some good records in the '60s, and proved to be engaging and passionate live acts.

Another welcome effect of the search for old blues legends was the discovery (as opposed to rediscovery) of elderly talents that had never recorded before. Folklorist Alan Lomax included Mississippi Fred McDowell on his landmark box set of the late '50s, *The Sounds of the South*, which documented all sorts of American folk styles. McDowell went on to a lengthy and successful career that found him recording several albums, touring with Bonnie Raitt, and having one of songs, "You Got to Move," covered by the Rolling Stones on *Sticky Fingers*. Mance Lipscomb, a songster-type guitarist from Texas, released several well-received albums on Arhoolie. Robert Pete Williams was, like Leadbelly 25 years before him, discovered in the late '50s behind bars at a Louisiana penitentiary. Folklorist Harry Oster recorded him and helped arranged for his pardon, and Williams, one of the most idiosyncratic country bluesmen, went on to record more material and tour.

The '60s, and in some cases the '70s, found many of the rediscovered blues singers touring internationally, where they were sometimes filmed by organizations such as the BBC. Sometimes their compositions were covered by major rock groups, such as James' "I'm So Glad," giving those performers some measure of comfortable financial compensation for their work. In addition to generating some fine music, the blues revival enabled these originators to live out their later years with dignity, giving them the widespread acclaim they had often been denied in their younger years—an appropriate closure that any fan of the blues could appreciate.

Nine Recommended Albums:
Various Artists, *Great Bluesmen at Newport* (Vanguard)
Skip James, *Skip James Today!* (Vanguard)
Mississippi John Hurt, *The Immortal* (Vanguard)
Son House, *Father of the Delta Blues: The Complete 1965 Sessions* (CBS)
Bukka White, *Big Daddy* (Biograph)
Robert Pete Williams, *Angola Prisoner's Blues* (Arhoolie)
Mississippi Fred McDowell, *Mississippi Delta Blues* (Arhoolie)
Mance Lipscomb, *Texas Sharecropper & Songster* (Arhoolie)
Peg Leg Howell, *The Legendary Peg Leg Howell* (Testament)

—Richie Unterberger

British Blues

The very term British blues is an anomaly. By rights, it shouldn't even exist. After all, Great Britain coming into the 20th century had no blues tradition, or any basis for it. Blues in Britain was an American import, much the same as rock & roll, but predating it by a few years.

During the early '50s, the first American blues artists had made brief sojourns to England and found the environment fertile. The bookings were good, the money better than they could get in America, and there was enthusiasm from a small but dedicated audience.

Big Bill Broonzy was the first American bluesman of any note to appear in England. He got to make his first of many recordings for France's Vogue label on that first visit to Europe, and was back a year later for another tour and more recording for Vogue.

Ironically, Broonzy did not play the material that he was most closely associated with in America on these tours. He was, of course, one of Chicago's top bluesmen, but the British weren't looking for authentic Chicago blues, but for something much more rudimentary. They perceived American blues as a brand of folk music, and for these appearances in England Broonzy adopted a deliberately archaic country blues persona, doing material that he had never really played before. He played acoustic guitar, and performed folk songs on these tours, interspersing country blues with protest material that were perceived by British audiences as merely another strain of topical blues.

Broonzy returned again in 1955 and cut several sides for Pye Records; the producer for these sessions was future British pop recording impressario Joe Meek. Among those recordings, available on CD under the title *Big Bill Broonzy: The 1955 London Sessions*, are a handful of those topical songs, most notably the poignant "When Do I Get to Be Called a Man."

The man responsible for bringing Broonzy to England was Chris Barber, leader of a jazz band that included a small group dedicated to American blues. Guitarist Alexis Korner and blues harpist Cyril Davies formed the core of Barber's blues unit, performing a set during the band's shows that proved especially popular with a small but vocal part of Barber's audience.

Meanwhile, Barber continued to book American performers, who kept coming over and finding the atmosphere and the money very much to their liking. But it was Muddy Waters' visit to England in 1958 that provided the real flashpoint for British blues, as well as showing how far the English audiences had to go in their understanding of the genre.

Muddy went on-stage in England for the first time backed by Otis Spann and members of Barber's band, playing an electric solid-body Fender guitar. This was a shock to British audiences, especially the folk purists and jazz aficionados who made up most of the crowd that night—authentic American blues as the British understood it had nothing to do with electric guitar. More striking still, Muddy had his instrument turned up to his usual Chicago-scale decibel level. If the sight of the amplified guitar startled the audience, the slashing tone that it generated caused outrage and a near panic among the purists. Muddy's performances on the 1958 tour were greeted with ecstatic press coverage and unbridled enthusiasm by concertgoers, after the initial "shock" of his first performance wore off. His concerts had attracted thousands of fans from all over England who had only heard of him, including many younger blues enthusiasts who were only just beginning to discover the music that Korner and Davies had been playing all along.

By this time, Korner and Davies had split with Barber and after Muddy's tour, they chose to plug in themselves. From 1958 on, they began playing electric blues with a new, inspired urgency. The band was called Blues Incorporated, and featured, at various times, Art Wood (elder brother of Ron Wood) on vocals, Graham Bond, Long John Baldry, Charlie Watts, Jack Bruce, and Ginger Baker. Basically anyone with talent and the right instrument could sit in, and those that did in the early period of the band's existence included Mick Jagger and Brian Jones.

By 1962, Blues Incorporated had been given a residency at the Marquee Club in London, and it was here that the band recorded their first album—and the first blues long-player ever made in England—for Britain's Decca Records. *R&B from the Marquee*, was recorded live by producer/impressario Jack Good (best remembered for creating the American television series *Shindig*) after hours at the club.

But by the time it was released, Korner and Davies had split up over Korner's desire to add horns—which Davies abhored—to the group's lineup. Davies formed the Cyril Davies All-Stars, a very promising group. The band got to record a handful of singles when Davies was stricken with leukemia and died early in 1964. Korner kept Blues Incorporated going in different incarnations through 1966, but by that time the main thrust of British blues had passed him by.

From the days of its residency at the Marquee, the original Blues Incorporated served as a catalyst for the formation of numerous bands that would lay claim to dominance of British blues. John Mayall's Bluesbreakers featuring Eric Clapton, the original Fleetwood Mac with Peter Green, and Cream could all trace their roots back to Blues Incorporated.

But it was the Rolling Stones who dominated the pack. From 1963 onward the Rolling Stones were the definitive British blues band, although after their chart-topping success with a cover of Willie Dixon's "Little Red Rooster," the blues would serve more as a source of inspiration than songs for the group's most visible work.

Meanwhile, American blues had become big business in England and throughout Europe. Beginning in 1962, with the first American Folk-Blues Festival organized by German blues enthusiast Horst Lippmann, dozens of American blues stars—including Muddy Waters, Howlin' Wolf, and Sonny Boy Williamson—had begun making annual or semi-annual treks to Europe, appearing throughout Europe. These tours were extremely lucrative for the performers, and the fees were many times what these men and women could have expected to make in a week of working in American blues clubs. Some of the players, such as Eddie Boyd and Champion Jack Dupree, ultimately made their homes in Europe in the wake of their performing experience. The American and younger British enthusiasts also got to work together on occasion; Sonny Boy Williamson recorded with both the Yardbirds and the Animals, and also toured backed by both of those bands and the original R&B-based Moody Blues.

The Rolling Stones manifested their love of American blues in a slightly different fashion, covering songs by Willie Dixon and Muddy Waters on their singles and albums, and insisting that Howlin' Wolf be their featured guest for their debut appearance on *Shindig* in America. The sight of the Stones genuflecting before the 6'4", 250-pound Howlin' Wolf (making his first appearance on American network television) revealed as much about the groups' origins and tastes as their own records of the era did, and more about the roots of British rock than any routinely vacuous interviews of the period.

Although there were a handful of British blues pianists and harpists, the dominant instrument was the guitar. Muddy Waters marveled at the array of axemen he encountered in England, many of whom impressed him with their technical skills, although he doubted that England could produce a truly effective blues singer. Eric Burdon and Mick Jagger came the closest in the vocal department, but among guitarists, the list was virtually endless, beginning with Eric Clapton, Keith Richards, Jeff Beck, and Brian Jones, and ending later in the decade with Jimmy Page, Mick Taylor, and Peter Green.

The Rolling Stones' success made it possible for their manager, Andrew "Loog" Oldham, to form his own independent label, Immediate Records, which became a vehicle for many lesser known blues-based outfits and performers, including Fleetwood Mac, Santa Barbara Machine Head (whose members later formed the core of the original Deep Purple), Savoy Brown, T.S. McPhee, Jo Ann Kelly, and Dave Kelly. Jimmy Page, Jeff Beck, and Eric Clapton also recorded a large handful of instrumental tracks that later turned up on Immediate, to the distress and embarrassment of all concerned.

By 1966, the British blues boom had become an explosion as electric British blues began to dominate the entire field. Cream, Fleetwood Mac, the Yardbirds, Ten Years After, and, later on, Led Zeppelin—dominated by the sounds of guitarists Eric Clapton, Peter Green, Jeremy Spencer, Jeff Beck, Alvin Lee, and Jimmy Page—came to define British blues, and by the end of the '60s, British blues had become a part of mainstream rock on both sides of the Atlantic. Absorbed by the British in the '50s and very early '60s, the blues as they played it was carried back across to America by bands like the Stones and the Animals, and re-absorbed by the Americans, in the guise of the Allman Brothers and other Southern rock bands of the era like ZZ Top.

15 Recomended Albums:
The Animals, *The Complete Animals* (EMI)
Blues Incorporated, *R&B From the Marquee* (Mobile Fidelity)
Duster Bennett, *Justa Duster* (Blue Horizon)
Cream, *Fresh Cream* (Polydor)
John Mayall's Bluesbreakers, *Featuring Eric Clapton* (Polygram)
John Mayall, *London Blues (1964-1969)* (Polygram)

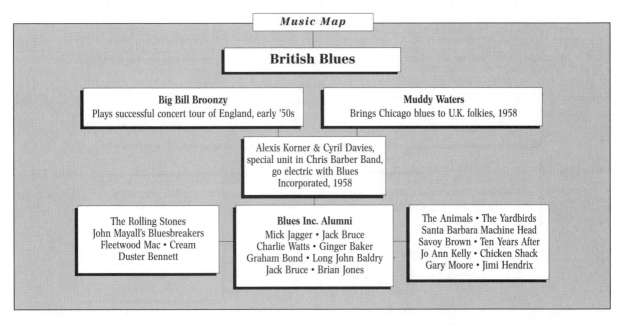

Music Map

British Blues

Big Bill Broonzy
Plays successful concert tour of England, early '50s

Muddy Waters
Brings Chicago blues to U.K. folkies, 1958

Alexis Korner & Cyril Davies,
special unit in Chris Barber Band,
go electric with Blues
Incorporated, 1958

The Rolling Stones
John Mayall's Bluesbreakers
Fleetwood Mac • Cream
Duster Bennett

Blues Inc. Alumni
Mick Jagger • Jack Bruce
Charlie Watts • Ginger Baker
Graham Bond • Long John Baldry
Jack Bruce • Brian Jones

The Animals • The Yardbirds
Santa Barbara Machine Head
Savoy Brown • Ten Years After
Jo Ann Kelly • Chicken Shack
Gary Moore • Jimi Hendrix

Rolling Stones, *Rolling Stones (England's Newest Hitmakers)* (ABKCO)
Rolling Stones, *Rolling Stones Now!* (ABKCO)
Rolling Stones, *12 × 5* (ABKCO)
The Yardbirds, *Five Live Yardbirds* (Rhino)
The Yardbirds, *Smokestack Lightning* (Sony Music)
Fleetwood Mac, *Black Magic Woman* (Epic)
Various Artists, *Anthology of British Blues, Vols. 1-2* (Immediate)
Various Artists, *Dealing With the Devil* (Sony Music)
Various Artists, *Stroll On* (Sony Music)

—Bruce Eder

Blues-Rock

The blues and rock & roll are often divided by the thinnest of margins. Blues, more than any other musical style, influenced the birth of rock & roll, and the amplified electric blues of Chicago, Memphis, and other cities during the '50s was separated from the new music only by its more traditional chord patterns, cruder production values, and narrower market. The term "blues-rock" came into being only around the mid-'60s, when white musicians infused electric blues with somewhat louder guitars and flashy images that helped the music make inroads into the white rock audience.

Many of the early blues-rockers were British musicians who had been schooled by Alexis Korner. Helping to organize the first overseas tours by many major American bluesmen, Korner—as well as his former boss Chris Barber, and his early collaborator Cyril Davies—was more responsible than any other musician for introducing the blues to Britain. More important, he acted as a mentor to many younger musicians who would form the R&B-oriented wing of the British Invasion, including Jack Bruce, members of Manfred Mann, Eric Clapton, and, most significantly, the Rolling Stones, whose lead vocalist, Mick Jagger, sang with Korner before the Stones were firmly established. (The evolution of British blues is discussed in more depth in a separate piece.)

The Rolling Stones featured a wealth of blues in their early repertoire. They and other British groups like the Yardbirds and Animals brought a faster and brasher flavor to traditional numbers. They would quickly branch out from 12-bar blues to R&B, soul, and finally, original material of a much more rock-oriented nature, without ever losing sight of their blues roots. Several British acts, however, were more steadfast in their devotion to traditional blues, sacrificing commercial success for purism. These included the Graham Bond Organization (who featured future Cream members Jack Bruce and Ginger Baker) and, most significantly, John Mayall's Bluesbreakers. In early 1965, Mayall's group provided a refuge for Eric Clapton, who left the Yardbirds on the eve of international success in protest to their forays into pop/rock. His sole album with Mayall, *Bluesbreakers With Eric Clapton (1966)*, was an unexpected Top Ten hit in the U.K. Clapton's lightning-fast and fluid leads were vastly influential, both on fellow musicians and in introducing tough electric blues to a wider audience.

While Clapton would rapidly depart the Bluesbreakers to form Cream (who took blues-rock to more amplified and psychedelic levels), Mayall continued to be Britain's foremost exponent of blues-rock, as a bandleader of innumerable Bluesbreakers lineups. Many musicians of note were schooled by Mayall, the most prominent being Clapton's successors, Peter Green and future Rolling Stone Mick Taylor. Like Clapton, Green left Mayall after just one album, forming the first incarnation of Fleetwood Mac with a couple members of Mayall's rhythm section, John McVie and Mick Fleetwood.

Under Green's helm, Fleetwood Mac were the finest British blues-rock act of the late '60s. They invested electric Chicago blues with zest and humor, but their own material—featuring Green's icy guitar tone (praised by no less a master than B.B. King), rich vocals, and personal, often somber lyrics—was more impressive, and extremely successful in Britain, where they racked up several hit albums and singles. As a bandleader of rotating lineups featuring budding guitar geniuses, Chicago harmonica player Paul Butterfield was Mayall's American counterpart; the two even recorded a rare EP together in the late '60s. The Paul Butterfield Blues Band's first pair of albums featured the sterling guitar duo of Michael Bloomfield and Elvin Bishop, as well as members of Howlin' Wolf's band in the rhythm section. Willing to tackle soul, jazz, and even psychedelic jams in addition to Chicago blues, they were the first American blues-rock band, and the best.

While blues rock was less of a commercial or artistic force in the U.S. than the U.K., several other American blues rockers of note emerged in the '60s. Canned Heat were probably the most successful, reaching the Top 20 with "On the Road Again" and an electric update of an obscure rural blues number, "Going Up the Country." Steve Miller played mostly blues, with Barry Goldberg and as the leader of his own band, in his early days before tuning into the psychedelic ethos of his adopted base of San Francisco. The Electric Flag, featuring Michael Bloomfield, mixed blues-rock with psychedelic music and tentative outings into an early version of jazz-rock. Captain Beefheart was briefly a white counterpart to Howlin' Wolf before heading off on a furious avant-garde tangent, though his growling vocals always seemed to maintain an unfathomable link to the Delta.

In New York, Bob Dylan used Bloomfield on much of his *Highway 61 Revisited* album, and teamed with the Butterfield Band for his enormously controversial electric appearance at the 1965 Newport Folk Festival. John Hammond, Jr. recorded blues rock in the mid-'60s with future members of the Band, and Dion cut some overlooked blues-rock sides after being exposed to classic blues by the legendary Columbia A&R man John Hammond, Sr. The Blues Project, led by Al Kooper, often reworked blues songs with rock arrangements, although their musical vision was too eclectic to be pigeonholed as blues rock.

The influence of the first generation of blues-rockers is evident in the early recordings of Jimi Hendrix, and indeed Jimi would always feature a strong element of the blues in his material. Albert King and B.B. King couldn't be called blues rockers by any stretch of the imagination, but their late-'60s material betrays contemporary influences from the worlds of rock and soul that found them leaning more in that direction. Early hard rock bands like Led Zeppelin, Free, and the Jeff Beck Group played a great deal of blues, though not enough for purists to consider them actual blues acts.

The blues-rock form became more pedestrian and boogie-oriented as the '60s came to a close. From Britain, Ten Years After, Savoy Brown, the Climax Blues Band, Rory Gallagher, Chicken Shack, Juicy Lucy, the Groundhogs, and Foghat all achieved some success. In the U.S., blues-rock was the cornerstone of the Allman Brothers' innovative early-'70s recordings (which in turned spawned the blues-influenced school of Southern rock), and Johnny Winter had success with a much more traditional approach.

Roy Buchanan, once billed (for a public television special) as "the best unknown guitarist in the world," had turned down an opportunity to join the Rolling Stones before concentrating on a solo career. Buchanan's vocals weren't strong enough to front a band, and thus his records were primarily instrumental showcases, although he did hire singers for his band. The same approach had been used by a couple of other brilliant guitarists with similar vocal liabilities, Jeff Beck and Harvey Mandel. Mandel, like Beck, was too eclectic to be categorized as a blues-rocker, but was often grounded in blues forms, and was a member of Canned Heat for a time.

Blues-Rock

Originators

Muddy Waters • Howlin' Wolf • Chuck Berry • Sonny Boy Williamson • Bo Diddley • Little Walter
Elmore James • Jimmy Reed • Robert Johnson • Willie Dixon • B.B. King • Albert King/Freddie King

The U.S.A.

The Paul Butterfield Blues Band
Blues Project • Bob Dylan
John Hammond Jr.
The Allman Brothers Band
Johnny Winter • Canned Heat
Steve Miller • Roy Buchanan

The Present

Stevie Ray Vaughan
The Fabulous Thunderbirds
Kenny Wayne Shepherd
Gary Moore • Chris Duarte
ZZ Top • George Thorogood
Robert Cray

The U.K.

Alexis Korner • Cyril Davies
Blues Incorporated
The Rolling Stones
John Mayall's Bluesbreakers
Cream • Ten Years After • Foghat
Savoy Brown • Rory Gallagher
Juicy Lucy • Chicken Shack
Climax Blues Band
Fleetwood Mac • The Yardbirds
The Animals

Another guitarist who was more of an instrumentalist/composer than a singer, and who was associated with Captain Beefheart and the Rolling Stones, was Ry Cooder, whose palette is really way too diverse to fall within blues-rock. Some would classify another associate of Cooder's, Taj Mahal, as a blues-rocker, but an equal or greater number would simply see Mahal as a modern-day bluesman, albeit one with rock influences (especially in the mid-'60s, when he played with Cooder in an L.A. folk-rock-blues group, the Rising Sons).

While blues-rock hasn't been a major commercial force since the late '60s, the style has spawned some hugely successful acts, like ZZ Top and Foghat, as well as influencing all hard rock since the late '60s to some degree. Those who kept the faith tended to concentrate on the more limited market of independent labels and small clubs, with the demand for party and boogie bands in small venues being a constant. Hence the appellation "bar band," one that serves as both a badge of honor and a putdown, depending upon the context and the tastes of the listener.

In general terms, second- and third-generation blues-rock bands have tended to prioritize instrumental virtuosity (unkinder souls would say instrumental flash) over vocal prowess. Guitarists Pat Travers and George Thorogood (noted for his crude, but effective, slide work) would fall in this category, as would Stevie Ray Vaughan in the '80s, although his more tasteful excursions would find favor with both critics and popular audiences. Vaughan was based in Austin, TX, a constant hotbed of blues-rock acts, due to its thriving roots music scene and club circuit. The Fabulous Thunderbirds were easily the best—and most influential—of the blues-influenced outfits to emerge from that community. The success of '90s artists like Kenny Wayne Shepherd, Chris Duarte, and British guitarist Gary Moore shows that the audience for blues-rock is far from dead. Many guitarists, like Jeff Healey, Sonny Landreth, and Tinsley Ellis, enjoy a large and steady live following belied by their relatively modest record sales, as do original blues-rock vets like Johnny Winter. And, of course, some blues-influenced singer/guitarists are huge superstars, the biggest being Eric Clapton (who returned to pure blues on 1994's *From the Cradle*) and Bonnie Raitt (an accomplished slide blues guitarist who was more rooted in traditional blues styles when she began recording in the early '70s). Some black blues bands have absorbed large influences from the rock world; the Robert Cray Band is the most well-known of these, and there are others, such as Michael Hill's Blues Mob. And it is a cliché, but it is often true, that many white listeners would be unaware of black blues performers if they hadn't been led to them through the work of white blues-rock bands.

20 Recommended Albums:
John Mayall, *Breakers With Eric Clapton* (Deram)
John Mayall, *London Blues (1964-1969)* (PolyGram)
The Paul Butterfield Blues Band, *The Paul Butterfield Blues Band* (Elektra)
The Paul Butterfield Blues Band, *East-West* (Elektra)
Fleetwood Mac, *Black Magic Woman* (Epic)
Jimi Hendrix, *Blues* (MCA)
The Graham Bond Organization, *The Sound of '65* (Edsel)
Captain Beefheart, *Legendary A&M Sessions* (A&M)
Canned Heat, *Best of Canned Heat* (EMI)
Cream, *Fresh Cream* (Polydor)
John Hammond, Jr., *So Many Roads* (Vanguard)
The Allman Brothers Band, *At Fillmore East* (Polydor)
Duffy Power, *Mary Open the Door* (Demon/Edsel)
Johnny Winter, *A Rock N' Roll Collection* (Columbia/Legacy)
Roy Buchanan, *Sweet Dreams: The Anthology* (Polydor)

Bonnie Raitt, *Bonnie Raitt* (Warner Bros.)
George Thorogood, *The Baddest of George Thorogood & the Destroyers* (EMI)
Stevie Ray Vaughan, *Greatest Hits* (Epic)
The Fabulous Thunderbirds, *The Essential* (Chrysalis)
Eric Clapton, *From the Cradle* (Reprise)

—Richie Unterberger

Modern Acoustic Blues

Modern acoustic blues isn't exactly a dying art, but it's certainly one that's bound to take a back seat to modern electric blues, perhaps forever. The new millennium is here, after all, and electricity has been a staple of blues music for over 50 years. Today's blues performers have never known a world in which electric modern conveniences, and electric instruments, were not commonplace items. Being men and women of their time, most blues musicians are eager to make their mark with an electric sound, not an acoustic one. But there will always be a room for the intimate and stark qualities associated with acoustic instruments, and modern blues has had its share of interesting unplugged moments.

Electric bluesmen had made conscious decisions to go unplugged for suitable occasions, especially when the folk circuit opened up to blues artists. John Lee Hooker in particular had simultaneous careers going for the electric R&B market, and for the LP-oriented acoustic audience. To this day, he has an equal command of the electric and acoustic idioms. Snooks Eaglin and Lightnin' Hopkins were other important bluesmen who could alternate between the two worlds with grace. Labels like Arhoolie, Prestige, and Testament recorded plenty of acoustic blues in the '60s, though these in the main reached back to a pre-World War II sensibility; one-man-band Dr. Isaiah Ross' *Call the Doctor* outing on Testament is certainly worth hearing as an example of how full band arrangements can be emulated by one multi-instrumentalist.

One of the most overlooked and important pioneers of modern acoustic blues was J.B. Lenoir, who made his original mark as a second-tier electric Chicago blues guitarist in the '50s. In the '60s, Lenoir found his greatest appreciation via European tours, and deliberately turned toward solo acoustic guitar arrangements. Lenoir recorded two acoustic albums, issued in Europe only, in the mid-'60s (with some minimal percussion from Fred Below and occasional backup vocal by Willie Dixon) that are notable not just for his full, rich guitar and vocals, but for their groundbreaking subject matter.

Lenoir had already revealed an unusually political bent in the '50s on "Eisenhower Blues" and "Korea Blues." On the *Alabama Blues* and *Down in Mississippi* albums, he tackled the issues of civil rights, segregation, and Vietnam directly, as well as recording more celebratory songs that suggested African rhythmic and melodic roots. (*The Rolling Stone Record Guide* once called him the Samuel Fuller of the blues, in acknowledgement of his social realism.) Lenoir, who died in 1967, is still an obscure figure, although he deeply impressed John Mayall, who recorded a song in his honor, and arranged for a posthumous compilation of some of his acoustic work.

Some of the most effective modern acoustic blues stylists had their roots in the blues/folk revival of the '60s. Dave Van Ronk and Koerner, Ray & Glover were among the earliest ones, but the best blues guitarists to emerge from this scene were John Hammond and Rory Block. Hammond, inspired by the work of early bluesmen like Son House and Robert Johnson, has sometimes offered capable electric work as well; Block is a more acoustic-oriented performer, and also covers a great deal of material by the likes of

Music Map

Modern Acoustic Blues

Originators	The '60s & '70s	Recent Years
Leadbelly • Blind Lemon Jefferson • Charley Patton Son House • Robert Johnson Robert Pete Williams John Lee Hooker • Jesse Fuller Doctor Ross • Lightnin' Hopkins J.B. Lenoir • Brownie McGhee Sonny Terry Mississippi Fred McDowell	Koerner • Ray & Glover Dave Van Ronk John Hammond Jr. • Taj Mahal Ry Cooder • John Mayall Duster Bennett • Jo Ann Kelly	Bonnie Raitt • John Cephas & Phil Wiggins • Ted Hawkins Lonnie Pitchford • Rory Block Corey Harris • Saffire

Tommy Johnson and Charley Patton. It may that their principal contributions are as instrumentalists rather than singers/composers, but they've done a lot to preserve the traditions of deep acoustic blues.

The British blues boom of the late '60s gave rise to a few acoustic interpreters, most of whom are known, like Jo Ann Kelly, are known only as names on obscure import compilations. The most entertaining of the lot was probably Duster Bennett, who was once described as "England's answer to Jesse Fuller" for his remarkable one-man band performances. In the late '60s John Mayall, never one to be satisfied with his personnel for too long, determined to explore an acoustic format while retaining a full band; *The Turning Point* (1969) was a very successful effort in this vein, both commercially and artistically.

For audiences with a rock orientation, the most accessible of the modern acoustic blues performers may be Taj Mahal, who's been making albums since the late '60s. Mahal is a master of Delta-ish acoustic blues, but is also an eclectic, blending the blues sensibility with some rock and roots music influences, including calypso and reggae. That may make him too much of an eclectic to be classified as a blues performer, at least in the eyes of some listeners, but it also ensures that his work holds greater interest for listeners who want something a little more ambitious than modern interpretations/updates of classic styles. An occasional associate of Taj's, Ry Cooder, could also be placed into this category. Cooder's plate is more diverse than Mahal's, and actually may be as diverse as anybody's, but often has a blues base. It's his soundtrack work, to the surprise of some, that often holds his bluesiest efforts.

Modern acoustic blues acts don't necessarily have to be solo performers. The duo act of John Cephas & Phil Wiggins have updated the Piedmont guitar-harmonica stylings of Sonny Terry & Brownie McGhee, occasionally nodding to gospel and R&B influences. Satan & Adam have had some success with a similar lineup, and Saffire, an all-woman trio, put a spin on things by mixing original material with covers of material by classic women blues singers like Bessie Smith and Ma Rainey.

Some of the press championed Ted Hawkins as the great acoustic blues hope of the '90s. Hawkins was "discovered" playing for tourists on the Venice Beach boardwalk in Los Angeles, and got much of his initial acclaim in England, rather than the U.S. The acoustic guitarist owed a lot to soul music as well, his sweet vocals sometimes generating comparisons to Sam Cooke. After some albums for independent labels, Hawkins was discovered (again) by the major Geffen label, and may have been poised for a breakthrough to a wider audience before his unexpected death in the mid-'90s. His death, however, didn't mean the death of acoustic blues; younger performers are making inroads, most notably Corey Harris, whose well-received music was noted for its African influence and its committed interpretation of Delta blues styles.

12 Recommended Albums:
John Lee Hooker, *The Country Blues of John Lee Hooker* (Riverside)
Lightnin' Hopkins, *Lightnin' Hopkins* (Smithsonian/Rounder)
Dr. Isaiah Ross, *Call the Doctor* (Testament)
J.B. Lenoir, *Down in Mississippi* (L&R)
John Hammond, *Live* (Vanguard)
Rory Block, *High Heeled Blues* (Rounder)
Taj Mahal, *Taj Mahal* (CBS)
Ry Cooder, *Music By Ry Cooder* (Reprise)
John Mayall, *The Turning Point* (Deram)
John Cephas & Phil Wiggins, *Dog Days of August* (Flying Fish)
Ted Hawkins, *The Next Hundred Years* (DGC)
Corey Harris, *Between Night and Day* (Alligator)

—*Richie Unterberger*

Modern Electric Blues

Ask a roomful of blues fans to appraise the state of contemporary electric blues, and you'll end up with almost as many opinions as there are people. In some senses, the blues has never been in better shape. Lots of major cities have clubs that feature the blues regularly, and the specialized market that attends to blues recordings is fairly healthy, though rarely cracking the pop charts. The blues has effectively penetrated the American mainstream via television specials, omnipresent use in films and commercials, and frequent representation at major music festivals.

Many blues fans, however, also fret that the music isn't as good as it used to be, or at least isn't evolving in satisfactory directions. Every form of music will have its share of naysayers that bewail the passing of the good old days; it's human nature to find the grass greener on the other side of the fence. It's also hard to gain perspective on an era when you're right in the middle of it. But the blues, like everything else at the beginning of the 21st century, is in a state of postmodernism that can make it difficult to identify trends or major developments.

The period that "contemporary electric blues" refers to varies from analyst to analyst; more out of convenience than anything else, it can be demarcated as the decades following the "blues revival" of the '60s. The survival of the blues itself, though oft-shaky, would never again be questioned. The challenge facing new and old artists alike would be to build upon the enormous body of classic work produced between 1920 and 1970 without either sounding repetitious, or abandoning the fundamental structures of the music. Looking back over the last couple of decades, we can at least zero in on a few widespread developments: the absorption of rock and soul influences, the proliferation of white blues or blues-rock bands, and the longevity/endurance of living legends who made their first recordings before the '70s.

Rock and soul had already started to infiltrate hardcore electric blues in the '60s, in the work of Junior Wells, Buddy Guy, Magic Sam, Albert King, Freddie King, Bobby "Blue" Bland, and B.B. King, to name just a few. There was also the frequent blues influence to be found in the work of Jimi Hendrix, who could at some points have been considered something of an avant-garde bluesman. Electric blues combos of recent decades have continued to reflect the rock and soul scene, as heard in the fierce, lengthy guitar solos, the occasional funk-influenced rhythms, and the brass sections that are often used to punch things up on stage and in the studio. Some old-school Chicago electric blues players did emerge into the spotlight in the '70s, such as Fenton Robinson, Luther Allison, and Son Seals (who themselves were not ignorant of soul music). But much new talent boasted an increasing appetite for music that was somewhat less grounded in electric blues conventions, though retaining an urban polish.

Purists who dismiss the rock and soul-inflected blues artists of recent years as sellouts are overlooking the fact that in order for the blues to survive as a living tradition, it cannot exist in a vacuum. From its inception, the blues has always responded to developments in popular music as a whole: the use of the guitar and piano in American folk and gospel, the percussive rhythms of jazz, the lyrics of Tin Pan Alley, and the widespread use of amplification and electric instruments all helped shape the evolution of the blues in the first half of the 20th century.

The blues artists that began to record in the '70s and '80s were also men and women of their time, listening not only to blues, but also to rock, pop, soul, and psychedelia. The result has been admixtures of the above elements, found in the funky, guitar-based sound of the Kinsey family, the soulish electric blues of Jimmy Johnson (brother of soul singer Syl Johnson), the African-leaning beats of some of Johnny Copeland's material, the soul-rock-blues fusion of Joe Louis Walker (who drew upon his extensive tenure on the gospel circuit), the horns that pepper some of Koko Taylor's records, or even the classical operatic training of the late Valerie Wellington. The most successful "crossover" efforts in these veins, by far, have been waxed by Robert Cray, whose modernized sound appeals to rock and pop audiences. His *Strong Persuader*, from 1986, became an unexpected pop hit, and he is one of the few blues performers of any era to dent the Top 40 of the pop album charts.

Those who like their soul-blues more down-home, and less oriented toward guitar showmanship, could look to offerings from the Malaco label, which gave a second lease on life to veterans like Z.Z. Hill, Bobby "Blue" Bland, Denise LaSalle, and Johnnie Taylor. These records generally enjoyed a more predominantly Black audience than those by electric guitar-oriented bands, finding a niche among soul fans who felt disenfranchised by the move

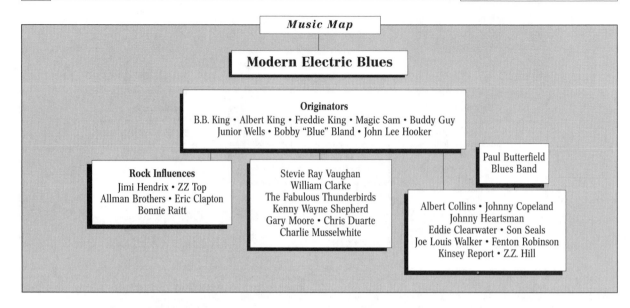

Music Map

Modern Electric Blues

Originators
B.B. King • Albert King • Freddie King • Magic Sam • Buddy Guy
Junior Wells • Bobby "Blue" Bland • John Lee Hooker

Rock Influences
Jimi Hendrix • ZZ Top
Allman Brothers • Eric Clapton
Bonnie Raitt

Stevie Ray Vaughan
William Clarke
The Fabulous Thunderbirds
Kenny Wayne Shepherd
Gary Moore • Chris Duarte
Charlie Musselwhite

Paul Butterfield
Blues Band

Albert Collins • Johnny Copeland
Johnny Heartsman
Eddie Clearwater • Son Seals
Joe Louis Walker • Fenton Robinson
Kinsey Report • Z.Z. Hill

towards disco and rap music in R&B. For these listeners, Z.Z. Hill's *Down Home* album of the early '80s was just as pivotal a release as Robert Cray's *Strong Persuader*, demonstrating that earthy contemporary blues could achieve a measure of commercial success.

In recent years the torch for the limited contemporary soul-blues market has been picked up by the Atlanta-based Ichiban label. And a whole strain of music with strong ties to the blues, zydeco, whose exposure had primarily been limited to Louisiana, reached an all-time high of popularity in the '80s and '90s. Also providing a rawer alternative to slicker electric guitar sounds was the Fat Possum label, which gave deep South juke-joint veterans like Junior Kimbrough and R.L. Burnside their first national exposure.

The role of white musicians in the blues is a minefield of controversy in some quarters, as anyone who has read the letters section of *Living Blues* magazine over the last few years could tell you. The blues-rock explosion of the late '60s may have peaked with acts like Cream, Jimi Hendrix, and the Allman Brothers, but the number of bands performing and recording in the style has remained pretty high. They rarely scale the pop charts anymore (acts like Stevie Ray Vaughan and the Fabulous Thunderbirds being the exception), but work frequently in urban clubs, and record often for independent labels. And some rock stars, like Bonnie Raitt and Eric Clapton, keep elements of the blues at the top of the charts and throughout the airwaves, although they don't limit themselves to blues material exclusively.

By and large, the white blues bands of recent times place a greater emphasis on instrumental virtuosity than other factors. Many of them have also been called "bar bands," a designation that can carry positive or negative connotations, depending upon your taste. The most frequent criticism leveled at the performers is a lack of soul in the vocals, a lack of songwriting imagination, and a certain generic, shallow flashiness that sometimes gives way to overlong solos that play much better in a sweaty club than on a compact disc.

The market is overcrowded with generic white blues band records (as it is with many other kinds of music, black and white), but that shouldn't disguise the emergence of some genuine blues talents in recent decades. Texan Stevie Ray Vaughan was hailed as the Great White Hope in the blues field until his premature, accidental death in 1990, although he will most likely be remembered primarily as a guitarist rather than a singer. California was a breeding ground for modern harmonica virtuosos, including William Clarke, Rod Piazza, and Charlie Musselwhite (the last of whom had moved to the state after starting in Chicago in the '60s). John Hammond, since the '60s, has been a living repository of sorts for most acoustic and electric blues guitar styles. The Fabulous Thunderbirds, featuring Jimmy Vaughan (brother of Stevie Ray) and Kim Wilson, were the best exponent of blues as you might experience it in a Texas club.

Blues, like jazz and folk, gives its performers a much longer lease on life than rock, rap, or pop. Blues acts do not so much reach a several-year peak and burn out, as they do reach that peak and maintain it, decade after decade. One of the pleasures of seeing B.B. King, Junior Wells, or Buddy Guy, is the knowledge that they'll sound about every bit as good now as they did 20 or 30 years ago. Such veterans have formed sturdy pillars of the modern electric blues scene simply by continuing to be themselves; Buddy Guy, for instance, seems to just get more and more popular, making inroads into the mainstream with his recent albums. And the late John Lee Hooker reached his commercial peak as a senior citizen with his CD *The Healer*, and started to show up on the list of Grammy nominations after only about 40 years as a top bluesman.

In some cases the later records of the blues vets don't match the best of their classic work, often due to a lack of good new material or ill-conceived production, but the performers can usually be counted upon to deliver the goods live. To enhance the appeal of middle-aged and elderly blues artists, labels sometimes flavor their new releases with high-profile appearances by rock and pop stars. Hooker's '90s albums are prime

examples of studio recordings that are jammed with celebrity cameos. It's an approach that doesn't wash well with many blues fans, but it does have the effect (as the Blues Brothers did in the late '70s) of leading lots of listeners with no blues schooling to the source, which can't be a bad thing.

The general ever-widening acceptance of the blues has also helped some performers break into a national audience after years or even decades of regional concentration and sporadic recording. Albert Collins, Johnny Copeland, and Johnny Heartsman are prominent examples of major bluesmen who began making records in the '50s and '60s, but are thought of as modern electric bluesmen who didn't make their true impact until the '70s and '80s. All of them proved extremely adaptable to the rock and soul influences that had infiltrated the music; fortunately the blues is willing to embrace artists who come into their musical prime in middle age, rather than dismiss them as non-contenders after a certain point in their youth.

If much contemporary blues has an easygoing, cheery air, that could be indicative of the whole form's emergence from the collector underground and African-American neighborhoods into the everyday fabric of life. Black America has changed a great deal since the early 1900s as well, and this too is reflected in the lyrical and musical values of today's electric blues stars. For those who find the music's use at sporting events and television commercials gratuitously exploitative, there's plenty of the authentic thing to be found with just a little effort.

20 Recommended Albums:
Various Artists, *Blues Masters, Vol. 9: Postmodern Blues* (Rhino)
Various Artists, *Blues Fest: Modern Blues of the '70s* (Rhino)
Various Artists, *Blues Fest: Modern Blues of the '80s* (Rhino)
Various Artists, *Blues Fest: Modern Blues of the '90s* (Rhino)
Son Seals, *The Son Seals Blues Band* (Alligator)
Robert Cray, *Strong Persuader* (Mercury)
Z.Z. Hill, *Down Home* (Malaco)
The Kinsey Report, *Edge of the City* (Alligator)
Valerie Wellington, *Million Dollar Secret* (Flying Fish)
Joe Louis Walker, *The Gift* (Hightone)
Eric Clapton, *From the Cradle* (Reprise)
John Lee Hooker, *The Healer* (Chameleon)
Stevie Ray Vaughan, *Greatest Hits* (Epic)
The Fabulous Thunderbirds, *The Essential Fabulous Thunderbirds Collection* (Epic)
Albert Collins, *Ice Pickin'* (Alligator)
Johnny Copeland, *Bringin' It All Back Home* (Rounder)
Junior Kimbrough, *All Night Long* (Fat Possum)
R.L. Burnside, *Too Bad Jim* (Fat Possum)
Fenton Robinson, *I Hear Some Blues Downstairs* (Alligator)
Buddy Guy, *Damn Right, I've Got the Blues* (Silvertone)

—*Richie Unterberger*

Independent Labels: The 1940s & 1950s

In many respects, 1945 was an incredibly scary time to be in America. World War II finally finished, and the country prepared to adjust from a wartime economy to a peacetime one that would need to reintegrate millions of returning veterans. The atomic bomb cast a cloud over the future of the planet; the rise of communism in the Soviet Union and Eastern Europe was sowing seeds of fear and paranoia. Many wanted to do nothing more

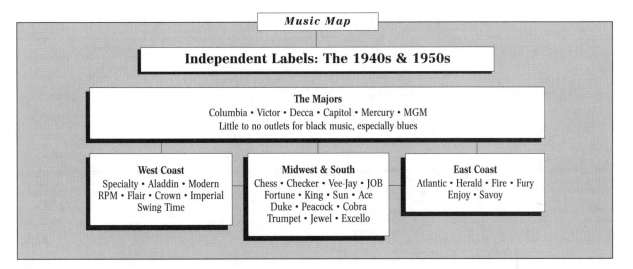

than resume life as normal, but the fact was that changing geopolitics, new technology, and developing mass media meant that life could never be the same.

But at the same time, life had never been more exciting. The U.S. had finally recovered from the effects of the Depression, and those who had survived the war with their families and health intact were ready to relax and, to a degree, party. Music was needed, and with the end of wartime rationing of certain materials, the record industry could resume full-scale operations after years of manufacturing restrictions. It was in this uncertain yet intoxicating climate that a boomlet of independent labels helped lay the foundation for the recording and distribution of postwar blues music.

Historically, the music business has always been dominated by about a half-dozen "major" labels. Their names and initials change according to corporate transactions and mergers, but in the middle of the '40s they were Columbia, Victor, Decca, Capitol, Mercury, and MGM. Ever since the blues began to be recorded, the major labels had paid some attention to the music, often placing the artists on subsidiary companies that were geared toward the "race" (i.e., black) audience. Hence the appearance of so many CD reissues of ancient blues on huge labels like Sony and BMG.

An independent label formed in the '40s faced enormous obstacles in competing against the majors, but also had enormous opportunities. Blues, R&B, and hillbilly artists were still recording for big companies in the '40s, but not in great numbers; the labels focused their energies on pop music that was oriented towards white Americans. This, naturally, left a vacuum in the marketplace, and several million disenfranchised listeners. Blues, R&B, and country were exploding as live, regional phenomenons, but weren't adequately represented on record. Demand necessitates supply, and numerous independent labels emerged to fill the gap.

There were no rule books for the new upstarts to adhere to, and one imagines that day-to-day life for these fledgling operations was both nerve-wracking and tremendously exciting. They didn't have the funds, state-of-the-art studios, or massive distribution networks that gave the Columbias of the world such huge advantages. All of them had to do things the hard way, driving from town to town to push their latest singles from the trunks of their cars, collect payments from shaky distributors and retailers, and chat up the local DJs in hopes of getting their releases on the air. What they usually had, above all, were ears to the ground: a real feel for what the communities of minority audiences—blacks, Southern whites, and teenagers—were listening to, on the regional radio stations (itself an exploding phenomenon of the time), the jukeboxes, and the dance halls. This was true whether the label owners were black or, as they were in many cases, white, sometimes being minorities of sorts themselves with Jewish and/or immigrant backgrounds.

Out of this crazy-quilt milieu came the labels so near and dear to the hearts of millions of blues, rock, and R&B fans: Chess, Sun, Specialty, Aladdin, Modern, King, Atlantic, Imperial, Vee-Jay, Duke/Peacock, and others. None of them focused on the blues exclusively; indeed, few of them even focused on black music exclusively. All of them, however, wanted in on the R&B market, to varying degrees. And thus it was that most of the best blues artists of the '40s and '50s recorded for these labels.

As far as establishing a label or "house" sound, Chess and Sun were probably the most distinctive of these operations, and their histories are outlined in separate pieces. While other prominent indies of the period may not have developed a production style as immediately distinctive, several made especially noteworthy contributions to blues and R&B history, and usually made a mark on rock & roll as well. In the mid-'40s, several companies sprouted up in Los Angeles, where the record and entertainment industry (which was then centered in New York) was truly beginning to establish roots. These labels also did a great deal to develop styles of blues/R&B that became identified with the West Coast, particularly jump blues.

One of the most important L.A. operations was Specialty, founded in 1945 by Art Rupe; that same year, it had one of the first truly monster independent R&B hits, Roy Milton's "R.M. Blues." Milton was one of the label's biggest stars, scoring nearly 20 R&B hits in a jump blues style; Camille Howard (Milton's pianist), Jimmy Liggins, Joe Liggins, and Floyd Dixon also had hits for the label, employing the boogie-woogie pianos and honking saxes that were early R&B staples. Specialty was also one of the first companies to scout the burgeoning New Orleans R&B scene, recording hugely influential hits in the early half of the '50s by Lloyd Price and Guitar Slim.

Specialty was not solely devoted to R&B; it had an extensive gospel line as well, the jewel in the crown being the Soul Stirrers, who featured the young Sam Cooke. They also landed one of the biggest original rock & roll stars, Little Richard, and also had some success in the rock field with Larry Williams and Don & Dewey. Yet by the late '50s, Specialty was winding down its activities; Art Rupe was finding lucrative economic opportunities outside of the record business. It's also been suggested that he was discouraged by the success of Sam Cooke, who became a huge pop star after Rupe, frightened of tampering with the gospel singer's track record, refused to release secular material by Cooke on Specialty, giving both Cooke and producer Bumps Blackwell their walking papers in the bargain. Numerous well-packaged Specialty reissues have appeared on the market since the label sold its catalog to Fantasy in 1990.

Aladdin, also formed in L.A. in 1945, was a virtual storehouse of West Coast jump blues/R&B pianists, recording Amos Milburn, Floyd Dixon, and Charles Brown. The "honking" element of West Coast jump blues was provided by saxophonist Big Jay McNeely. In the mid-'50s, like some other labels, they got a cut of the New Orleans R&B/rock scene with the vocal duo of Shirley & Lee.

Modern, yet another L.A. company formed in 1945 (by the Bihari brothers), also had some tentacles into the West Coast blues/R&B scene, with a roster including Floyd Dixon (who recorded for several labels during his prime), Etta James, and saxophonist Joe Houston. In comparison with Aladdin and Specialty, however, they had a greater taste for guitar-focused, grittier blues, releasing sides by Jimmy McCracklin, Johnny "Guitar" Watson, and Pee Wee Crayton. They were also aggressive in scouting talent outside of their region, distributing some of the first nationally popular recordings by blues legends John Lee Hooker, B.B. King, and Elmore James, all of whom were based east of the Mississippi. In the '50s, they formed active subsidiary labels, RPM and Flair; when times became leaner, however, they focused on budget LP compilations for another of their subsidiaries, the Crown label.

A final L.A. giant was Imperial, founded in the late '40s. Although it made significant contributions to West Coast blues by recording guitarists T-Bone Walker and Jimmy McCracklin, it will be mainly remembered for its forays into New Orleans R&B. No other label based outside of New Orleans (and maybe none within New Orleans) had as much success with Crescent City music, principally with Fats Domino, who spun out a never-ending series of hits for about a decade. Dave Bartholomew was an instrumental factor in many of Imperial's New Orleans hits as a producer and arranger, for Domino and others; the label also recorded some blues-oriented singers in New Orleans, like Roy Brown, Pee Wee Crayton, and Snooks Eaglin, in attempts to give them a commercial direction more in line with rock & roll's burgeoning popularity. The label's days as a major power came to end with its sale to Liberty in 1963, when Domino's never-ending chart success had finally ceased, and the company's biggest star, Rick Nelson, had been lured away to a major label.

Chicago blues was considerably rawer and more guitar-based than the kind usually issued by the West Coast labels, and Chess, though the giant in the field, wasn't the only game in town. Vee-Jay, also based in the Windy City, had two of the most commercially successful bluesmen of the era, Jimmy Reed and John Lee Hooker (it should be noted that Hooker recorded for quite a few labels in his early career, often for several simultaneously, and occasionally under pseudonyms). Lesser-known but great sides were also recorded for Vee-Jay by harmonica player/singer Billy Boy Arnold, and Eddie Taylor, who was Jimmy Reed's guitarist. In the early '60s, it had huge successes in the pop market with early recordings by the Four Seasons and the Beatles, but went belly-up in the mid-'60s.

A Chicago R&B label that flamed briefly and brightly was Cobra, which lured Chess bassist/arranger/songwriter Willie Dixon away for a brief time in the late '50s. If for nothing else, the label gained a niche in blues history for waxing classic early sides by Otis Rush that rate among the best and most chilling electric blues ever recorded. Magic Sam also recorded notable early sides for the label, although he wouldn't truly reach his peak until the '60s.

King, based in Cincinnati, was one of the most versatile independent labels of the time: R&B may have been its bread and butter, but it also made a great deal of key hillbilly records. But it certainly had an impressive roster of both blues shouters (Wynonie Harris, Bull Moose Jackson, Eddie "Cleanhead" Vinson) and instrumental-oriented honkers (Big Jay McNeely, organist Bill Doggett, Tiny Bradshaw, Earl Bostic, and others). In the '60s it also had claim to one of the decade's most commercially successful blues guitarists, Freddie King. By that time, though, it was heavily reliant upon the empire of soul brother number one, James Brown. King was sold to Polydor in the early '70s; in recent years compilations of important King R&B/blues artists have appeared on Rhino.

A major outpost of Southern blues was Duke/Peacock, founded by legendary micromanager Don Robey in Houston. In addition to recording Big Mama Thornton and Texan guitarists like Clarence "Gatemouth" Brown, Duke did its part to point the way for soul by recording two of the leading soul-bluesmen, Bobby "Blue" Bland and Junior Parker. The label seemed comfortable with both guitar-focused material and sophisticated horn arrangements that played off the gospel-influenced vocals of Bland in particular.

Excello, though founded in Nashville, really made its mark on blues history through its Louisiana-based artists, including Slim Harpo, Lightnin' Slim, and Lazy Lester. These are the singers who, aided by producer Jay Miller, were the key exponents of "swamp blues." By lending the musicians sympathetic production and the freedom to more or less be themselves, Miller was one of several producers who cultivated a characteristic sound, Sam Phillips (at Sun) and Leonard Chess (at Chess) being two of the most notable others.

New York is not noted as a groundswell of down-home blues, and it may be that the key contribution of Atlantic was in tilling the field for R&B, rock & roll, and soul, rather than developing straight blues. The company can't be overlooked, however, due to its crucial role in midwifing blues-derived R&B into more urbanized forms with a greater appeal to a younger audience. Joe Turner, Ray Charles, Stick McGhee, Chuck Willis, Ruth Brown, and LaVern Baker were just some of the most prominent players with Atlantic contracts. And the label did record some straight-up blues, even if much of it tended to be with artists that made their most significant music for other operations.

A smaller notable independent based in New York City was Bobby Robinson's Fire label, with the active Fury and Enjoy subsidiaries. Robinson recorded some of the rawest guitar blues of the era, including some of Elmore James' best work. Buster Brown's "Fannie Mae" was one of the most undiluted blues records ever to make the Top 40. And Fire was also responsible for Wilbert Harrison's number one hit "Kansas City," which may be the ultimate example of shuffle blues transposed into rock & roll, one of the key ingredients being Jimmy Spruill's scintillating guitar solo.

This roundup, it should be noted, has only encompassed some of the most active independent companies that recorded blues music between 1945 and 1960. Others made significant contributions, such as Savoy, which recorded a good deal of jump blues by Johnny Otis and others, and Trumpet, which released some primeval Southern blues in the early '50s by Sonny Boy Williamson and others. In the '90s, Capricorn Records dedicated a series of box sets to such labels, including ones for Cobra, Fire/Fury, Jewel/Paula, and Swingtime. Charlie Gillett's *The Sound of the City*, a history of rock & roll's first two decades, does an excellent job of detailing the many influential independent early rock and R&B labels, and is recommended further reading.

There were numerous tiny companies that released regional singles in small quantities; some lasted for only one or two 45s. Many of these can now only be enjoyed on small-run import reissues (if they even made it that far). But their deep obscurity, and the relatively raw production values employed on some of them, doesn't mean that they can't be just as enjoyable as sides produced on the "big" indies.

Independent rock and R&B labels, by and large, were reducing their blues rosters by the dawn of the '60s. This was not necessarily, as some might charge, a reflection of lack of interest in the blues by the label owners, or ingratitude towards the artists that had helped put them on the map in the first place. The independents, it must be remembered, were not PBS; they were commercial enterprises that needed chart hits and cash flow. In focusing their energies elsewhere, they were usually responding to trends in the overall marketplace, most notably the increasing success of rock & roll. And a lot of the biggest independents didn't even survive the competition of the era, going under or selling their catalog to other companies; Atlantic, which is still thriving today, is more the exception than the rule.

R&B itself was loosening its ties to the blues, and looking forward to soul music. Some artists, like Bobby "Blue" Bland, Little Milton, Albert King, and Freddie King, were well-suited for adapting to the new era; unfortunately, most of the blues stars of the '40s and '50s blues stars were left out in the cold. It should be noted that a lot of indies didn't give up on the blues completely; Motown, the most successful of the whole lot, made little-noticed recordings with Amos Milburn and Earl King in the '60s. But the commercial momentum of American pop had shifted away from blues and hardcore R&B, leaving the blues in the hands of a devoted but more specialized audience.

And the needs of that audience would be addressed from the '60s onwards by independent companies. These, however, were independent companies that were not as concerned with commercial chart success as satisfying the tastes of a niche market that included increasingly younger, more affluent, and white listeners. The prime medium would not be the 45 single, but the long-playing record and, much later, the compact disc. The stories of those independents—Arhoolie, Delmark, Alligator, Fat Possum, and others—is told in a separate sidebar. The legacy of the earlier generation of independents is readily available for today's audience, however, on a plethora of CD reissues, several of which provided thematically linked (and sometimes, truth to tell, haphazard) overviews of the labels' valuable contributions to American music.

Five Recommended Albums:
Various Artists, *Chess Blues* (Chess)
Various Artists, *A Sun Blues Collection* (Rhino)
Various Artists, *The Specialty Story* (Specialty)
Various Artists, *Atlantic Blues Box* (Atlantic)
Various Artists, *The Cobra Records Story* (Capricorn)

—Richie Unterberger

Sun Records — The Blues Years

In the late '40s, Memphis, TN, was still very much a segregated city. The many boundaries that separated black and white social life also separated the musical communities, despite the cracks starting to force open via radio stations like WDIA and WHBQ, which broadcast blues and R&B to young listeners in the region like Elvis Presley. Recognizing the genius of several blues performers in the Memphis region, there was one man, Sam Phillips, who became determined to record the music and bring it wider recognition.

As a radio engineer, Phillips had already gained technical expertise and appreciation for a wide variety of black and white popular music. Recording and distributing it was a huge challenge, as it was for many other independent regional labels of the time that handled R&B or hillbilly records for minority audiences. Explained Phillips to Robert Palmer in *Deep Blues*, "I thought it was vital music...and although my first love was radio, my second was the freedom we tried to give the people, black and white, to express their very complex personalities, personalities these people didn't know existed in the fifties. I just hope I was a part of giving the influence to the people to be free in their expression."

How much of Phillips' operation was artistic altruism, and how much the hopes of a businessman seeing a gap in the existing market, continues to be a matter of some historical debate. There's no question, though, that Phillips was the man for recording blues in Memphis as the '50s dawned. Initially he focused not on pressing discs on his own label, but recording local sides at his Memphis Recording Service studio that would be leased to labels that were not in Memphis itself. Phillips was fortunate to be situated in a city that was a hotbed of blues talent, and he quickly arranged for recordings by B.B. King, Howlin' Wolf, Jackie Brenston, Roscoe Gordon, and others to be leased to the Modern and Chess labels.

"I opened the Memphis Recording Service," elaborated Phillips in *Good Rockin' Tonight* (by Colin Escott with Martin Hawkins), "with the intention of recording singers and musicians from Memphis and the locality who I felt had something that people should be able to hear. I'm talking about blues—both the country style and the rhythm style—and also about gospel or spiritual music and about white country music. I always felt that the people who played this type of music had not been given the opportunity to reach an audience. I feel strongly that a lot of the blues was a real true story. Unadulterated life as it was.

"My aim was to try and record the blues and other music I liked and to prove whether I was right or wrong about this music. I knew or I felt I knew, that there was a bigger audience for blues than just the black man of the mid-South. There were city markets to be reached, and I knew that whites listened to blues surreptitiously."

Any characteristic sound that could be attached to Phillips' blues productions resulted not so much from what he brought to the sessions, but what he didn't do. He was astute enough to realize that the singers and musicians had a power that would have been diminished by extraneous production or a conscious softening of rough edges. Thus he concentrated on getting the best performances from his artists without coaxing them into changing their styles, and obtaining takes that were sufficiently commercial for release without losing their spontaneity.

He was also clever enough to capitalize upon accidents that could have been categorized as mistakes, as when Ike Turner's band (featuring vocalist-saxophonist Jackie Brenston) arrived at the studio with a damaged guitar speaker. Other producers might have canceled the session until the speaker could be fixed, but Phillips and the musicians found they liked the distorted guitar sound it produced. It would end up featuring prominently on Brenston's big hit, "Rocket 88," which is repeatedly referred to by historians as one of the first rock & roll records.

By 1952 Phillips, realizing that companies were going to start beating him to the punch by recording regional artists directly instead of leasing his masters, started the Sun label. (He had released a record by Joe Hill Louis in 1950 on the Phillips imprint.) The next few years found Sun releasing a few dozen blues/R&B sides that, although not nearly as great in quantity as those of Chess to the north, were nearly on the same level in terms of quality and historical influence. "Bear Cat," Rufus Thomas' answer record to Big Mama Thornton's "Hound Dog," was Sun's first big national R&B hit, although some of the sweetness went out of that triumph when a lawsuit from the "Hound Dog" publishers wiped out its profits.

Never releasing too much material by any one blues artist (although the vaults and subsequent reissues have yielded tons of unissued sides), Sun did have some further success in the R&B market with items like Junior Parker's "Feelin' Good." Parker's follow-up, "Mystery Train," didn't do as well, although it became one of the core classics of Memphis music, particularly after it was covered a couple of years later on the fifth and final single of a fellow Sun artist, Elvis Presley.

By that time, the focus of Sun Records had tilted almost entirely towards the white artists on its roster. Phillips had never stuck to recording black musicians exclusively

Sun Records—The Blues Years

Sam Phillips
Formed Memphis Recording Service in 1950 and Sun Records in 1952

1950–1952 Records & Leases to Chess, 4 Star & Modern	1952–1954 Sun Records Begins	1954–1959 Sun: Rockabilly & Country
Howlin' Wolf	Big Walter Horton	Elvis Presley
B.B. King	Jimmy De Berry	Johnny Cash
Joe Hill Louis	Little Milton	Jerry Lee Lewis
Big Walter Horton	Doctor Ross	Roy Orbison
Dr. Ross	Joe Hill Louis	Billy Riley
Jackie Brenston	James Cotton	Warren Smith
Rosco Gordon	Pat Hare	Sonny Burgess
Rufus Thomas	Frank Frost	Ray Harris
Harmonica Frank Floyd	Earl Hooker	Jack Earls
Ike Turner & the Kings of Rhythm	Charlie Booker	Charlie Feathers
	Billy "The Kid" Emerson	Carl Perkins
	Rosco Gordon	The Miller Sisters
	D.A. Hunt	Charlie Rich
	Mose Vinson	Ernie Chaffin
	Big Memphis Marainey	Barbara Pittman
	Rufus Thomas	

(although he issued almost nothing but blues records in the early days of the label), and the fortuitous discovery of Elvis in 1954 had resulted in the birth of rockabilly with Presley's first single, "That's All Right Mama." Elvis, of course, took much of his inspiration from the blues, both in vocal delivery and his choice of early cover material. By 1955, it became apparent that Elvis was Sun's ticket to much greater commercial success than anything they could achieve in blues/R&B, although the singles with Parker, Little Milton, James Cotton, and obscure artists like Doctor Ross, Frank Frost, Billy "The Kid" Emerson, and future Muddy Waters band guitarist Pat Hare seemed to augur well for continued success in the blues field.

Sun's subsequent move into rock & roll has been criticized by some, including Rufus Thomas, but a quick look at the release schedule shows that Phillips was issuing blues singles alongside hillbilly records and the emerging rockabilly sound. Indeed, Phillips was recording Frank Frost for his Phillips International label in the '60s, after most of his big stars had left for greener pastures.

Also in *Good Rockin' Tonight*, Phillips himself rejoins, "Keep in mind that there were a number of very good R&B labels. The base wasn't broad enough because of racial prejudice. It wasn't broad enough to get the amount of commercial play and general acceptance overall—not just in the South. So I knew what I had to do to broaden the base of acceptance."

Phillips achieved that by focusing on white country, and later, rockabilly artists, especially after he sold Presley's contract to RCA in late 1955 for $35,000, the bulk of which went back into his desperately cash-starved label. In retrospect, it seems he had little choice in the matter. Distributors were paying him on the sales of Presley singles with blues returns by the carload and labels like Duke, RPM, and Chess were swiftly decimating his blues artist roster. The Bihari brothers (who owned the Crown, RPM, Modern, and Flair labels) actually started their Meteor label in Memphis with the expressed purpose of putting Phillips out of business. With the capital from the Presley sale, he was able to promote and distribute his remaining roster much more effectively. Carl Perkins, Johnny Cash, Jerry Lee Lewis, and Charlie Rich all became stars in the late '50s as Sun artists.

Whether Phillips could have done this with black blues artists is doubtful. The sheer rawness of the Sun blues sides—both in the performances and the spartan production—still makes them difficult to listen to today and made them even tougher to program on radio back then. As a businessman with a tiny two-person operation, Phillips was torn between the music he loved and what would sell and reach a wider audience. Also, by the time of the twin national breakthrough of Presley and Carl Perkins' *Blue Suede Shoes,* blues was by and large a spent commercial force in the black community, with doo-wop groups and R&B singers now dominating the charts. Thus it was that many of Phillips' blues artists had their greatest commercial success on other labels. One could reasonably argue that Presley, Perkins, Cash, and Lewis reached their artistic peak at Sun. But one

could not say the same for B.B. King, Howlin' Wolf, Junior Parker, Little Milton, Big Walter Horton, and Rufus Thomas, all of whom truly found their calling with other concerns, often in much more of a blues/soul vein in the '60s, or even (in Thomas' case) as a straight soul singer with few overt ties to the blues at all.

As such, the relatively slim oeuvre of Sun blues recordings is more of a vault for the embryonic talents of major blues performers than their very best work. Which is not to suggest that what was preserved wasn't very good, far from it. The Chess brothers, for all their business acumen and "feel" for the music, could never have produced sides with the stark, lonesome feel of Big Walter Horton's "Easy" or the violent agression contained in James Cotton's "Cotton Crop Blues." And in the broader sense, few labels have done as much to weave the blues into mainstream American culture as Sun, both by giving major bluesmen their first opportunity to record and reach audiences beyond the region, and by exposing it (albeit indirectly) to the American masses via its incorporation into the rockabilly of Presley, Perkins, et al.

Seven Recommended Albums:
Various Artists, *A Sun Blues Collection* (Rhino)
Various Artists, *Sun Records: The Blues Years, 1950-1956* (Charly)
Junior Parker, James Cotton, & Pat Hare, *Mystery Train* (Rhino)
Howlin' Wolf, *Rides Again* (Flair/Virgin)
B.B. King, *The Memphis Masters* (Ace)
Various Artists, *Sun Records Harmonica Classics* (Rounder)
Joe Hill Louis, *The Be-Bop Boy* (Bear Family)

—Richie Unterberger

Chess Records

Some may argue that the history of blues is one of musicians, regions, and movements rather than something so business-oriented as a record label. Chess Records, however, is not just some record label. It's a sound in itself—a sound which, for many, epitomizes the best of Chicago blues, and maybe even the best electric blues has to offer. Through the recordings of Muddy Waters, Little Walter, Howlin' Wolf, and many other talents great and small, the Chicago-based label and its subsidiaries (Checker and Argo, later renamed Cadet) did an enormous amount to amplify the blues, record some of its greatest talents, and bring the form into the modern era.

These are achievements that few could have foreseen when the label was founded by Leonard and Phil Chess in the '40s. The brothers had come to the U.S. from Poland in the late '20s. In 1947 Leonard Chess was a nightclub owner in Chicago, entering the record business by buying into the local Aristocrat label. Aristocrat was not a blues label at its outset, recording pop and jazz. Its Chicago base, however, was in close proximity to more blues talent than any other Northern city, with more musicians relocating from the South all the time.

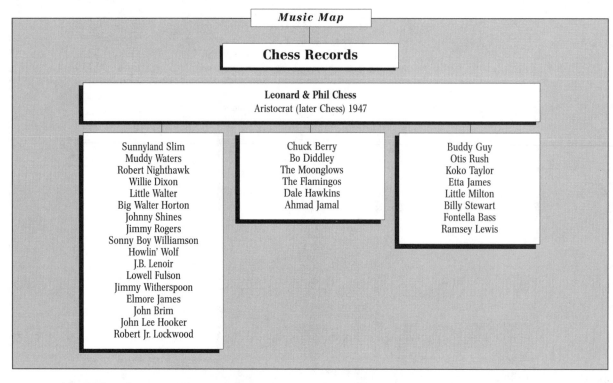

In the late '40s, Chicago blues—in its raw, amplified state—had yet to be captured on record in all its primal immediacy. Aristocrat had skirted around the blues with jazz-blues sorts of outings by the likes of Andrew Tibbs, and employed guitarist Muddy Waters as a sideman on a 1947 single by pianist Sunnyland Slim. But it would be Muddy's own efforts, starting with 1948's "I Can't Be Satisfied"/"I Feel Like Going Home," that truly began to urbanize and electrify the sound of the Delta. The Chess brothers became progressively more active in the blues field, and by 1950 they had taken over the Aristocrat label entirely, changing its name to Chess.

Although Waters was already starting to use a full band in his club appearances, Chess at first went easy on all-out amplification in the recording studio, preferring not to tamper with the stripped accompaniment that proven so successful on Muddy's first big hit. Early classics were recorded with Waters accompanied by no one except Big Crawford on bass ("I Can't Be Satisfied") and sometimes just with Muddy and his electric guitar ("Rollin' Stone"). Other musicians like Little Walter (harmonica) and Jimmy Rogers (guitar) started to come in as well, not only on Muddy's singles, but on those of some other Chess artists. By the early '50s, the addition of drums made the switch to electric blues complete, providing in the process the prototype for the guitars-bass-drums-harmonica lineup that would serve as the "classic" model for both electric blues and rock & roll.

Chess blues singles quickly developed an identifiable sound. A haunting and spacious echo was created by, according to Peter Guralnick's *Feel Like Going Home*, "rigging a loudspeaker and a microphone at both ends of a sewer pipe" and "a primitive system of tape delay." The voices and instruments often sounded slightly overamplified and recorded at levels that frequently intruded into the red zone. This resulted in recordings that preserved the focused punch of the small blues combo while maximizing its sonic power. Particularly in the early days, consistency was assured by using many of the same musicians (who often released records of their own as well) to play on Chess sessions, forming a sort of floating house band. "Session men" like Little Walter, Willie Dixon, and Jimmy Rogers are well-known, of course; more obscure are performers like drummer Fred Below, whose swinging backbeat did much to establish the bedrock of both electric blues and rock & roll.

While Phil Chess focused on the business end of the label, his brother Leonard concentrated on the studio. Historians have sometimes hinted that he was capturing magic more by accident than design. It's true that a Jewish Polish immigrant may not have been as attuned to the nuances of Delta-cum-Chicago blues as the musicians, but Chess deserves considerable credit for crafting the sound that appeared on the grooves. Leonard Chess apparently had a genuine knack for getting the best out of his performers in the studio and refining their material into product that was both commercial and artistic. On more than one memorable occasion, dissatisfied with the drum sound he was getting, he played the bass drum himself.

Leonard Chess' principal *aide-de-camp* was house bassist Willie Dixon. Dixon worked countless sessions in the '50s and '60s, though he briefly left Chess in the late '50s to work for the Chicago-based rival Cobra label. It's as a songwriter, however, that Dixon will be most remembered, penning numerous classics for Waters, Little Walter, Howlin' Wolf, and

many other artists in the Chess stable. Chess expanded its roster rapidly in the early half of the '50s, as electric Chicago blues became a major presence on the R&B charts. On swings through other regions to distribute and promote their records, the Chess brothers would check out and sometimes sign talent. They would also lease material cut elsewhere, the most famous example being their distribution of several crucial sides cut by Sam Phillips in Sun Studios in Memphis. After a bitter rivalry with the Bihari brothers (who Phillips was also leasing material to) Chess would place the most promising of the Sun recorded artists, Howlin' Wolf, on its own label.

There was plenty of home-grown talent in Chicago, of course. From within Muddy Waters' own band, Little Walter became a solo star, and Jimmy Rogers and pianist Otis Spann also had solid recording careers without nearly as much commercial success. The four W's—Waters, Walter, Wolf, and Sonny Boy Williamson—would become Chess' most durable blues artists. J.B. Lenoir, Lowell Fulson, and Willie Mabon, although not as iconic, also recorded a good deal of material for the label.

Chess' lengthy associations with Waters, Walter, Wolf, and Williamson were in fact more the exception than the rule. Throughout the '50s, it seemed like the label gave most major electric blues performers a trial at one time or another, although it wouldn't stick with them for very long. Thus it was that a who's who of modern blues passed through the Chess pipeline at one point or another. Elmore James, Otis Rush, John Lee Hooker, Johnny Shines, Robert Nighthawk, Billy Boy Arnold, Buddy Guy, and Memphis Minnie are not principally known for their Chess recordings, but all of them recorded or released product for the company, often in enough quantity to generate their own reissue LPs years later.

The wealth of Chess reissue LPs can give the understandable impression that the label was recording a bottomless well of classic blues throughout the '50s. However, Chess was never exclusively a blues concern, and in fact experienced its greatest commercial success with the rock & roll artists Chuck Berry and Bo Diddley. The success of Berry in particular, and the diminished presence of electric blues on the R&B charts in the second half of the '50s, meant that Chess began to put more effort into its non-blues product. That didn't just mean guitar rockers like Berry—Chess also recorded a good deal of R&B, doo-wop (Flamingos, Moonglows), and jazz (Ahmad Jamal), and even handled Dale Hawkins' great rockabilly recordings.

In the '60s, blues occupied an increasingly less central position within the company. Blues itself was not the music of choice for many African-American listeners anymore, having been overtaken by rock & roll, R&B, and then modern soul music. Little Walter was in a steep artistic decline, exacerbated by health and personal problems; Sonny Boy Williamson died in the mid-'60s; Muddy Waters, who had begun to tour England and Europe, was now broadening into the LP market, albums such as Muddy Waters *Folk Singer* being packaged for the white folk music crowd.

Chess' greatest commercial successes in the '60s were not in the blues field, but in soul (with Etta James, Billy Stewart, and Fontella Bass) and soul-jazz (Ramsey Lewis). At this time the old guard rock & rollers, Berry and Diddley, were finding their share of the marketplace shrinking due to changing trends. This sales decline, ironically, coincided with a period in which Chess Records was beginning to retroactively attain legendary status among some young white enthusiasts, particularly musicians in British Invasion bands. The Rolling Stones, who put a ton of Chess recordings into their early repertoire, paid homage to the label by recording at Chess Studios in 1964, in the midst of their first American tour.

Chess did not give up on their original stars, or the blues—Howlin' Wolf, for instance, recorded some of his greatest material in the '60s, and Koko Taylor established herself as one of the premier blueswomen. At times, however, it seemed to be making desperate attempts to make its blues artists sound more contemporary by adding rock and soul influences. Misbegotten albums such as Waters' *Brass and the Blues* (with overdubbed horns on some tracks), "supersession" albums pairing different bandleaders, psychedelic-influenced records with Waters (*Electric Mud*) and Howlin' Wolf (*This Is Howlin' Wolf's New Album, He Doesn't Like It*) all backfired artistically and commercially. Most of them have stayed mercifully unreissued in the digital age.

After Leonard Chess died in 1969, the company was sold to GRT, and control of the label passed to his son, Marshall. Chess in the '70s was a sad echo of its glory days, and Marshall Chess and Phil Chess would soon leave the company (Marshall to head up the Rolling Stones' new label), which wound down its activities as an ongoing concern. That left a huge back catalog, coveted by collectors (and just plain fans) the world over.

Despite the almost inexhaustible supply of great blues material, the Chess reissue program of the past two decades has been erratic until recently. A couple of domestic series, ranging from thorough double-LP retrospectives to interesting packages of obscure performers like John Brim, were halted or went out of print as the Chess catalog changed ownership. For a time, it was owned by the Sugar Hill label (most famous for its early rap productions); the Sugar Hill series, too, soon came to a stop. For a while, Chess reissues were easier to acquire as imports than they were in the land of their origin, the U.S. What's more, serious collectors, to their frustration, found many rare and unreleased tracks appearing on various European and Japanese compilations while remaining unavailable in the U.S.

Ownership of the catalog passed to MCA, with plans for comprehensive reissue programs remaining vague and unrealized. Happily, this unpleasant situation was remedied in the CD age, with Chess/MCA embarking upon a series of comprehensive reissues that restored almost all of the catalog to availability, including much of the rare and out of print material that had only surfaced on imports or bootlegs as well as material that had never surfaced.

The intentions and achievements of the Chess brothers have remained the subject of mixed scrutiny. They do, however, deserve an enormous amount of credit for recognizing the best in electric blues talent, distributing it, and translating it into recorded music that will endure for ages.

15 Recommended Albums (All on Chess Records):
Various Artists, *Chess Blues Box*
Muddy Waters, *The Chess Box*
Howlin' Wolf, *The Chess Box*
Little Walter, *The Essential*
Sonny Boy Williamson, *The Essential*
Muddy Waters, *One More Mile*
Howlin' Wolf, *Ain't Gonna Be Your Dog*
Little Walter, *Blues With a Feeling*
Jimmy Rogers, *Chicago Bound*
J.B. Lenoir, *Natural Man*
Buddy Guy, *The Complete Chess Studio Sessions*
Koko Taylor, *What It Takes: The Chess Years*
Willie Dixon, *The Chess Box*
Otis Rush/Albert King, *Door to Door*
Elmore James, *Whose Muddy Shoes*

—Richie Unterberger

Independent Blues Labels: The 1960s to the Present

While major labels continue to record a few major performers, such as Robert Cray and Buddy Guy, the overwhelming majority of contemporary blues music is to be found on independent companies—that is, labels that are not owned or distributed by the large corporations of Sony, BMG, CEMA, PGD, UNI, or WEA. Outfits such as Arhoolie, Delmark, Vanguard, Testament, Alligator, Hightone, and Fat Possum have played a huge role in both recording the best blues of the past few decades, and of preserving the best of past and living blues traditions. The relatively small commercial market for blues in recent times has virtually ensured that these operations are run by proprietors who are enthusiasts first, and businesspeople somewhere behind that—and their priorities are usually reflected in the quality of the music they release.

In the '40s and '50s, the blues enjoyed a much higher profile in the charts, carving out a sizable chunk of the R&B market. Independent labels like Chess, Sun, Vee-Jay, and Specialty were responsible for recording the greatest blues music of the era, often fostering production techniques that helped shape and advance the music itself. (The histories of these independents are detailed in other essays in this book.) But by the end of the '50s, blues had lost much of its audience share to the onslaught of R&B and rock and roll; it would lose more in the '60s with the British Invasion, Motown, folk-rock, psychedelia, soul, and other tremors revolutionizing the world of popular music. Those independents that had recorded blues, if they survived into the '60s, usually cut back or eliminated their blues rosters, focusing their energies on rock, soul, and pop.

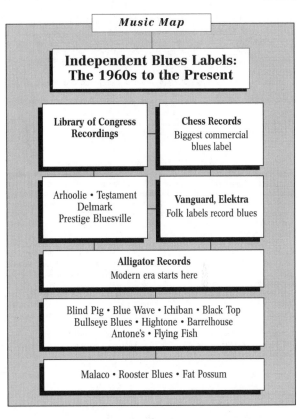

Music Map

Independent Blues Labels: The 1960s to the Present

Library of Congress Recordings

Chess Records
Biggest commercial blues label

Arhoolie • Testament Delmark Prestige Bluesville

Vanguard, Elektra
Folk labels record blues

Alligator Records
Modern era starts here

Blind Pig • Blue Wave • Ichiban • Black Top Bullseye Blues • Hightone • Barrelhouse Antone's • Flying Fish

Malaco • Rooster Blues • Fat Possum

The decline of the blues as a commercial force, however, coincided with a couple of developments that would create an opening for entirely different kinds of independents. The late '40s saw the introduction of the long-playing record, which in turn harvested more diverse sorts of productions than had been available on singles. The '50s brought the stirrings of a folk/blues "revival" that widened the audience for blues music from its African-American base into an increasingly white and young listenership, often to found in colleges and coffeehouses. Some of these fans were dedicated enough to write books on the subject, track down surviving blues legends, and make recordings of their own.

Some of the first modern blues independents took a somewhat folkloric approach to their releases, especially in the beginning. The **Prestige/Riverside/Bluesville** family, in addition to recording first-generation country bluesmen like Pink Anderson, arranged for John Lee Hooker and Snooks Eaglin to record acoustic (or at least solo) material for albums, although Hooker and Eaglin maintained simultaneous electric, full-band recording careers for the R&B market. Once the blues revival was really in gear in the '60s, **Testament** produced recordings of obscure country blues singers like Jack Owens, and also arranged for overlooked electric Chicago bluesmen like Johnny Shines to get some quality studio time. It even issued a whole album of topical songs about John F. Kennedy shortly after the president was assassinated.

Arhoolie, founded by German immigrant Chris Strachwitz, took a sort of field recording approach to some of its best releases. Driving around Texas and the South, as several blues scholars of the time did in hopes of encountering legends past and present, Strachwitz also took time to record some of the more interesting musicians with whom he crossed paths. His first release, Mance Lipscomb's *Texas Songster* (1960), initially pressed in a quantity of only 250 copies, is still in print. Lipscomb, like some of Arhoolie's other finds—Robert Pete Williams (actually recorded by Harry Oster in 1959 and 1960) was the most famous—had never recorded before. But the label also cut sessions, under pretty basic conditions, with performers who already had something of a reputation, such as Lightnin' Hopkins.

Arhoolie didn't limit itself to newly recorded sessions, arranging (to this day) for reissues of vintage material by Hopkins, Sonny Boy Williamson, and far more obscure performers such as Black Ace. They also don't limit themselves to blues, covering roots/folk styles of all kinds—there are more cajun albums than blues ones in their catalog, which also includes quite a bit of world, country, and Tejano music. Arhoolie maintains a busy release schedule and large back catalog; they also founded the leading roots music mail-order service, *Down Home Music*, which has been sold to different ownership.

By traveling to the source and recording their artists without adornment, Arhoolie was in some senses following the path of folklorists like the Lomaxes, who had recorded legends like Leadbelly, Muddy Waters, and Son House for the Library of Congress. Arhoolie releases, as well as similar ones by some other labels, differed from the Library of Congress and Folkways catalogs, however, in crucial respects. Sure, they aimed to preserve important elements of the blues tradition that were overlooked, or maybe even in danger of extinction. However, their albums were primarily produced not for academic archives, but for general listening pleasure. Commercial considerations were not paramount, but if the releases could help the musicians make a living, and generate enough profit to keep the label owners above water (and able to record more blues/roots music), so much the better.

At the outset of the blues revival, the new blues independents usually focused on acoustic recordings. This might have reflected the influence of the folk crowd buying many of the records, and the precedents set by folkloric field recordings of previous times. The electric blues was somehow felt by some to be more authentic, less sullied by the dirty waters of mass production. Electric blues continued to thrive, though, and by the mid-'60s it was obvious that the same people buying Rolling Stones and Paul Butterfield albums would also be willing to take a crack at LPs by living Chicago blues legends.

The Chicago-based **Delmark** label was instrumental in translating the energy of contemporary electric blues onto LP for the '60s market. Delmark owner Bob Koester had been recording acoustic blues since the '50s, when he worked with musicians like Sleepy John Estes and Big Joe Williams. In the late '50s, he moved to Chicago, where he operated the Jazz Record Mart retail store. The store was a meeting ground for many key musicians and supporters of the blues scene; employees who worked at the Jazz Record Mart at one time include guitarist Mike Bloomfield, harmonica player Charlie Musselwhite, the founders of *Living Blues* magazine, and some future label owners, including Bruce Iglauer (who now runs Alligator Records).

"The Jazz Record Mart was like a bridge between the blues world on the South and West Sides and the growing world of white international blues fans who hung out at the Jazz Record Mart, who came here to find out about gigs, musicians," Iglauer told the *Chicago Tribune* in 1993. "There were little signs, pieces of paper taped to the walls about various gigs at ghetto taverns."

"It was an incredible flow of musicians through there because it was one of the few ways that they could get a break. There weren't a lot of companies recording Chicago blues at that time, so musicians came to hang out at the Jazz Record Mart in hopes of attracting Bob's attention."

That's because Koester ran Delmark Records, which, like Arhoolie, did not limit itself to the blues, also releasing many fine and influential jazz albums by the likes of Sun Ra and the Art Ensemble of Chicago. He caught the lightning of Chicago electric club blues on record with his 1965 release by Junior Wells, *Hoodoo Man Blues.* As Koester claimed in the sleeve notes, "It is damn near the first LP by a Chicago blues band. Chess and a few other labels had reissued 45s by Muddy Waters, Sonny Boy Williamson, Howling Wolf, Jimmy Reed, Elmore James, etc. but virtually no one had tried to capture the Chicago blues sound free of the limitations of jukebox/airplay promotion."

Like some of the best blues producers, Koester realized that a less-is-more approach emphasizing spontaneity would make his artists comfortable and yield the best results in the studio. As Wells recalled in the same *Chicago Tribune* article, "When I did 'Hoodoo Man' for a guy a long time ago on a 78, he took it over to the radio station and asked them to play it. They threw it on the floor and broke it, stomped it. When I started recording for Bob, he wanted me to do the 'Hoodoo Man' and I really wasn't interested in doing it because of the disappointment from what happened to me when I was much younger. He kept talking to me about it, so I tried it and I'm proud of the record now…Bob was the type of person, he just made everything so easy, you couldn't help but to get something good from it. He just let you go with it."

Hoodoo Man Blues also featured Buddy Guy on guitar (early pressings of the album credited the guitar work to the transparent pseudonym of "Friendly Chap"). *Hoodoo Man Blues* eventually passed the 50,000 mark in sales, an astronomical number for an independent blues album. It remains the best seller in the Delmark catalog, but the label would also record quite a few other important titles, most notably by Magic Sam, J.B. Hutto, Jimmy Dawkins, and Luther Allison. Koester's label and store are still going strong today, though Koester himself is semi-retired.

Other labels made some important recordings of '60s electric blues for the LP market. **Vanguard**, which had already recorded significant acoustic '60s blues in the studio and at the Newport Folk Festivals, produced the excellent three-volume *The Blues Today!* series, featuring tracks by Wells, Big Walter Horton, J.B. Hutto, Otis Spann, Otis Rush, Johnny Shines, James Cotton, and others. **Verve** (which was distributed by MGM) recorded LPs with Cotton that also crossed over to the rock audience to some extent. The label that would truly take electric Chicago blues to the end of the century, however, was the one founded by Bruce Iglauer, Alligator.

Iglauer was inspired to found Alligator, as he writes in the liner notes to the label's 25th anniversary collection, "by the music that I heard in the little clubs on the South and West Sides in the black neighborhoods, where the city's (and the world's) greatest blues bands made music for their local fans. The blues clubs had been the heart of Chicago's Black music scene for over 30 years before I arrived there as a 'blues pilgrim' back in 1970. These weren't show lounges or theaters, but corner bars and taverns, often in grimly depressed neighborhoods, that put a chain across the doorway on weekends and charged 50 cents or a dollar to hear some of the most intense, fiery, and deeply emotional music you can imagine."

For a long time, Alligator was a one-man show, run by Iglauer out of his apartment. Important releases by artists like Son Seals, Fenton Robinson, and Hound Dog Taylor put Alligator on the map, but the label didn't really become a major force until its multi-volume *Living Chicago Blues* series of the late '70s and early '80s, exposing major overlooked talents such as Jimmy Johnson. Over five years later, the similar *New Bluebloods* anthology did the same for another generation of Chicago blues, including tracks by the Kinsey Report, Lil' Ed & the Blues Imperials, and Valerie Wellington.

Today Alligator's staff has swelled to 19 full-time employees, and there's over 200 albums in the catalog. Plenty of Chicago artists continue to record for the label, but Alligator has made a determined effort to seek talent from outside the region in recent years, including some Louisiana swamp blues performers. Uptempo Chicago-style blues is Alligator's most distinguishing trademark, but the roster has become fairly diverse, including white blues-rockers like Lonnie Mack, Johnny Winter, and Elvin Bishop, roots music gadfly Delbert McClinton, and acoustic artists Cephas & Wiggins, Saffire, and Corey Harris. It's also given several old-school veterans who were unable to pick up a contract for years a new lease on life, such as harmonica player Billy Boy Arnold. It also reissued long-unavailable recordings of primeval blues from the '50s from the Trumpet label.

Despite selling only about 10,000-25,000 copies of the average title, Alligator dominates the contemporary indie blues market; sometimes it seems that every other blues Grammy goes to the Alligator label. There are several other companies dedicated to the work of contemporary electric blues bands, including Blind Pig, Black Top, Bullseye Blues, and Antone's. There also continue to be roots/folk labels that issue occasional blues albums, such as Ichiban, Hightone, and Flying Fish.

Not every post-1960 blues label limited its aims to the collector audience. The most successful of these may have been **Malaco**, which in the minds of some fans is as much a soul/R&B label as a blues one. Its roster included soul stars fallen on leaner times, such as Johnnie Taylor and Bobby "Blue" Bland, as well as some younger acts. While much of their catalog appealed to the blues audience, it undoubtedly aimed for, and got, many listeners who hungered for some contemporary Southern soul-styled music in the absence of such recordings in the disco/dance/rap dominated R&B charts. Z.Z. Hill's *Down Home Blues* (1982) was an unexpected commercial success, proving that not all independent blues albums had to be confined to a smaller listenership.

For those who found Malaco's brand of Southern blues/soul too slick, alternatives arose in the early '90s that were rawer and more down-home than they probably could have imagined. The Mississippi-based **Fat Possum** label was founded in the early '90s by two *Living Blues* contributors in their twenties, Matthew Johnson and Peter Lee. Dissatisfied with what they perceived as the unwarranted slickness of many contemporary blues recordings, they headed out to their own back yard for something different, cruising the juke joints and country stores of rural Mississippi, where a fierce and untamed brand of electric blues was played for the locals. The result was recordings by artists like R.L. Burnside and Junior Kimbrough that got some of the most positive critical attention of any '90s blues releases.

Johnson told the Boston *Phoenix* that he and Lee decided to form Fat Possum "after hearing so many slick albums that sound nothing like what you hear on a Saturday night in Mississippi. We're trying to get a quality that's different from most of the other blues records you hear today. I find most of the blues records coming out just unlistenable. What is primitive to most people, we would consider slick. We prefer what [music critic and producer] Bob Palmer calls 'guerrilla recording,' just going out into the bars and juke joints and letting the tape roll."

It's tempting to think of Fat Possum's proprietors as updated variations of the blues revivalists of the '60s, who searched the Southern back roads for living exponents of deep acoustic blues, overlooked and forgotten by the modern world. A difference, of course, is that these are electric musicians, playing not on their porches, but in centers of day-to-day community life. Their relative isolation from the urban world has resulted in a certain primitive quality—replete with odd tunings and unsteady time meters—that seems unaffected by the slicker qualities of contemporary music. Artists like CeDell Davis, who plays an irregularly tuned guitar with a table knife, are, if not representative of a dying breed, at the very least unique. The earthy quality of the Fat Possum releases is maintained by a pared-to-the-bone recording budget. Most albums are recorded in a day or two, in facilities like Jimmy's Auto Care in Oxford, MS; the total budget for a full-length recording is unlikely to exceed $4,000.

Despite the critical acclaim that's rung through higher echelons like *The New York Times*, Fat Possum's sales haven't exactly torn the roof off the juke joint. After their first release (R.L. Burnside's *Bad Luck City*) moved a mere 713 units, it considered folding. But the partners found an investor in John Herrmann, who plays keyboards for the Southern rock group Widespread Panic. Widespread Panic's label, Capricorn, began distributing Fat Possum. The involvement of rock/blues scholar Robert Palmer in several releases as producer also helped raise the label's profile. Unfortunately, Fat Possum and Capricorn became involved in litigation, which caused recording to stop and album releases to be postponed. Following an out-of-court settlement, Fat Possum signed a distribution deal with Epitaph, a Los Angeles punk label that Johnson feels is more attuned to the Fat Possum sensibility.

Living Blues magazine founder Jim O'Neal's Mississippi-based Rooster Blues label makes similar albums. His activities, ironically, led him to a bona fide modern-day blues rediscovery of harmonica player Willie Cobb, who wrote the standard "You Don't Love Me." He refutes the notion that Rooster Blues and Fat Possum are comparable to archivists of an earlier era, bringing independent blues labels full circle to the folkloric activities of the late '50s and early '60s.

"The very little [recording] that was done over the past three decades or so was mostly folklorists or Europeans doing some kind of field recording," he told *Billboard.* "The contemporary blues here—the blues you were hearing in the juke joints—wasn't getting recorded. There's a void to be filled. There's still a lot of great talent. It's the birthplace of the blues, and it's still giving birth to a lot of great artists."

Concurred Fat Possum's Matthew Johnson in the Boston *Phoenix*, "We're not some kind of purists making field recordings. This is rockin' stuff; this music gets people moving. The stuff that purists go for is just garbage to me. Especially the acoustic records. Nobody plays acoustic guitar anymore except rich white people. Down here, a musician's got the juke box to compete with. The guys in Mississippi are the first to chuck their acoustic guitars when they bring back some good festival money."

Ten Recommended Albums:
Mance Lipscomb, *Texas Songster* (Arhoolie)
Dr. Isaiah Ross, *Call the Doctor* (Testament)
Various Artists, *Great Bluesmen at Newport* (Vanguard)
Junior Wells, *Hoodoo Man Blues* (Delmark)
Magic Sam, *West Side Soul* (Delmark)
Various Artists, *Chicago: The Blues Today! Vol. 1-3* (Vanguard)
Various Artists, *Living Chicago Blues Vols. 1-4* (Alligator)
Various Artists, *New Bluebloods* (Alligator)
Various Artists, *25th Anniversary Collection* (Alligator)
R.L. Burnside, *Bad Luck City* (Fat Possum)

—Richie Unterberger

Beginner's Guide and History — How to Listen to the Blues

We live in a miraculous age where music is concerned. In virtually any area of music, at any given moment, there is a wider selection of recordings available today than at any time in the past. This sounds like a wonderful thing—except when you look at an area of music that you know nothing about and wonder, where do I start?

Even more to the point, where historical musical forms are involved, if you really want to understand a particular form of music, it helps to know something about the people that made it and how they and their audience understood their music.

This should be pretty straightforward, with blues as with any other form of music—start by finding an accessible introduction to the music (such as the German Romantic repertory in classical, the Beatles in British rock, etc.), listen to the leaders in that part of the field, absorb the music and read what the liner notes and maybe a few reference books have to say, and take it from there.

But blues—especially historic blues, which, for our purposes, is almost anything recorded before 1960, when the white population began discovering the music—is fundamentally different from most other popular music that you're likely to find on album or compact disc. The differences lie in the way the music originated, the purpose it served, the way it was recorded, how it was released, and the manner in which it was intended to be heard.

For starters, the legacy of the blues is richer than casual listeners realize. But until recently, it was also among the most poorly documented.

For the rock listener, in particular, absorbing the blues on its own terms means going back to a period in which very little was standard in the recording or the music business, and even less so in the dire poverty of the Deep South. In those days, even the instruments weren't always standard. For one thing, it is highly probable that the blues as it came to be known to us in the '20s and '30s originally derived from banjo music, not guitar, and a few banjo players (or players of banjo-type instruments) did record during the '20s, and that is a blues sound that is utterly different (and quite wonderful) from what most of us would recognize today. But even the guitars weren't always "standard"—Big Joe Williams was renowned for his nine-string guitar, essentially a six-string modified so that the uppermost strings were doubled like a 12-string; Papa Charlie Jackson, the first male blues singer to record, used a six-string instrument with a banjo-type body, which created very unusual resonances; Leadbelly became best known for his 12-string "Stella" guitar (and six- and 12-string Stellas were extremely popular in the south during the '20s), yet his first commercial recordings for the American Record Company in New York were done almost entirely with a six-string instrument.

Even the one guitar most commonly associated with country blues, the steel-bodied National Dobro guitar with built in resonator cones (which created a sound remarkably like an electric guitar), is almost forgotten today outside the ranks of blues enthusiasts. You can see John Fogerty holding what looks like one on the cover of Creedence Clearwater Revival's *Green River* album, and Mark Knopfler of Dire Straights uses one—John Lennon also makes excellent use of one on his protest song "John Sinclair" off of *Sometime in New York City*.

Moreover, appreciating the blues today means forgetting a lot of our notions about how to listen to music.

For starters, anyone listening to blues on a CD or long-playing record should bear in mind that until 1956, there was no such thing as a blues "album."

In fact, for most blues listeners from 1920 until well into the late '50s, buying a dozen or more songs by a favorite artist at any one time would have been impossible. Records, especially blues records, just didn't get released or distributed that way. In fact, in the '30s, if you owned five records by the same blues artist, you were an unusually resourceful fan, and—depending upon the label they were done for—if those records were all in good shape and fully playable, you were a downright miracle worker.

Singers and Songs, Not Albums

For starters, the long-playing album didn't even come into existence until 1948. Until then, all records were released on fragile, heavy 78-rpm shellac discs holding up to three and a half minutes of music on a side. Before that, there were "albums"—big, photo album-like bound collections of 78s—but they were reserved for classical music and the very biggest pop stars.

The long-playing album, from its inception until around 1960, was a format reserved for classical and jazz, and better pop music, along with some of the bigger country & western artists of the day. Blues was confined to the realm of 45-rpm singles and 78-rpm discs (which, contrary to popular belief, continued to be produced until the end of the '50s).

The work of a handful of blues artists—Leadbelly, Pink Anderson, and Piano Red the best known among them—was released on album, but these were the exceptions that proved the rule. Leadbelly's following was confined to an almost exclusively to white folk music enthusiasts, who bought albums rather than 45s (and Folkways Records never did try to compete in the commercial 45-rpm market). Pink Anderson recorded for Bluesville, an offshoot of Prestige Records that, similarly, was cultivating a relatively sophisticated jazz audience, also attuned to the long-playing format. And Piano Red, on the RCA-offshoot label Groove Records, released an album made up on one side of a live performance from Atlanta's Magnolia Ballroom in March of 1955, and on the other of his previously released singles.

Red's work, however, was unique among commercial blues artists. Most blues records were aimed at an audience of poorer rural and urban blacks, with a smattering of poor whites. Neither group bought many long-playing records—they couldn't afford them, and some of the really poor had never upgraded from 78-rpm players, which helped keep that format marginally viable right into the end of the '50s.

The very first "album" by Muddy Waters, the biggest star on the roster of Chess Records, and the closest thing to a universal star that the blues had, didn't appear until 1958, 11 years after he'd started with Chess. And that album, *The Best of Muddy Waters*, was a collection of existing singles dating from 1948 through 1955, not new songs.

The few blues albums released in the '50s consisted of existing singles or, less often, concert performances. Muddy wouldn't do his first album of new recordings, *Muddy Waters Sings Big Bill Broonzy*, until two years later, in 1960—and that was made up of songs by his one-time mentor. He wouldn't get to do an album of new songs of his own until *Brass and the Blues* in 1967, two decades after he first started with Chess, and only nine years before his last album for the label. Muddy's Chess stablemate Howlin' Wolf didn't do his first album of new songs, *Back Door Wolf*, until 1971, just four years before he died. All of his album releases up to then were collections of singles or re-recordings of his best known songs. And B.B. King's first two albums, *Singin' the Blues* and *The Blues*, collections of existing singles, didn't get released by his original label, Crown Records, until after he'd signed to another company. His first real album, *Live at the Regal*, wouldn't appear until 1965, some 16 years after his first recordings, and his first studio album wouldn't follow that until two years later.

And blues artists such as Charley Patton, Robert Johnson, Blind Blake, Blind Lemon Jefferson, and Barbecue Bob, all of whom died before World War II, never even conceived of commercial releases of their music numbering more than two songs at a time. This is important, because most of us—especially rock listeners—have learned to listen to albums as a whole, ten or more songs at a time that are presumably on a disc together for a reason.

This is exactly the assumption one has to avoid in listening to the early output of Muddy Waters or B.B. King, most of Howlin' Wolf, and all of Charley Patton, Robert Johnson, or any of their contemporaries. It means "unlearning" everything that we've been taught about listening to albums since at least 1964-1967, the years that the Beatles, the Beach Boys, the Rolling Stones, and Bob Dylan established the album as an art form for most of us.

Blues Roots

Individual songs, not albums, were the focus of a traditional bluesman's recording career, and singles were usually released many months apart, so that audiences discovered their music over a period of years, not hours. When we listen today, it's easy to forget that a pre-World War II performer such as Papa Charlie Jackson developed his style and repertory in the recording studio during a period of over ten years, not the two hours it might take us to go through his entire record legacy, and that he knew and played hundreds of songs. Longer lived artists like Blind Willie McTell or Bukka White recorded four or six songs at a time, over 20 years or more; and Tampa Red laid down over 300 songs, four at a time, from 1927 until 1953, before he was ever asked to do a whole album's worth of songs at one time. Big Bill Broonzy got to record as many as 24 songs a year at the height of his career—Broonzy worked at that pace during the late '30s. But those songs were conceived separately, and heard two at a time by the public.

The songs that listeners today associate together by these artists are only established that way because some record producer chose to stick them on the same collection, years or decades after they were made. In that sense, while they are convenient, the album and the CD distort the origins and purposes of original blues songs. They're merely the wrapping in which the songs are packaged, and should never be mistaken for a coherent statement.

In order to understand the changes that had taken place in the blues leading up to the first blues albums, it's necessary to go back to its beginnings. The blues as an identifiable musical genre first appeared just after the turn-of-the-century, although it didn't begin to emerge as a genre with commercial possibilities in the middle of the next decade, in the music of W.C. Handy. There were musicians—mostly working minstrel shows, medicine shows, and carnivals, or playing the black hamlets of the Deep South—who played blues as part of their repertory, along with ragtime, novelty songs, and all other manner of repertory.

The blues was peculiar, as music born of despair, which had the effect of making people happy. Gospel and spirituals had similar social roots, but worked differently, focused as they were on matters of redemption, damnation, and one's place in the cosmos—blues was earthier, and frequently raunchier. Moreover, the blues had the effect—in detailing a source of distress (frequently romantic in nature)—of making the listener feel better; not uplifted, not "saved," but better, and always happier.

This was why Willie Dixon, perhaps the most renowned blues songwriter of the middle 20th century, always took exception to those people (especially black listeners) who rejected the blues for being too sad or depressing. Quite the contrary, Dixon insisted, "The blues is happy music!"

And it's true—if you listen to any good country blues from the '20s or early '30s, or electric blues from the late '60s, it's almost impossible not to feel happy listening to the play of the words, the interweaving of the instrument and the voice, and the overall effect of the song. It's as though the song becomes the receptacle, psychically speaking, for whatever might be troubling the listener, or the composer.

Earlier in the 20th century, this was no mystery to anyone. Almost as soon as record companies began recognizing a black clientele that was worth serving, they recognized the blues as good-time music. Strangely enough, it was among female singers that the blues first emerged on record, and in a surprisingly upbeat form.

Mamie Smith (1883-1946) introduced the term "blues" to the popular music culture in 1920, with her release of "Crazy Blues" on the OKeh label. Her early releases sold 75,000 copies a month, a massive figure for the era, and OKeh followed this up with more records using the name and primordial sound of the blues, and soon other record companies moved to capitalize on OKeh's success. By the summer of 1920 Lucille Hegamin was recorded on Arto, followed soon after by Lillyn Brown on Emerson and Alberta Hunter for the Black Swan label.

All of these records were designated "race records," a safe and relatively polite way of referring to their oriented toward black listeners. OKeh started the designation—the company had recorded a lot of what, today, would be considered ethnic and popular music from every country that might have had a significant number of listeners in the U.S., but had hesitated over what to call music for black listeners, until they came up with the "race records" designation, which stuck for the industry until the late '40s.

Stylistically, the earliest generally accepted blues record, however, was Bessie Smith's "Down Hearted Blues," released early in 1923. There were male blues singers recorded during this period, including guitarist Sylvester Weaver and singer/guitarist Ed Andrews, who cut a track called "Barrelhouse Blues" in 1924, but it was Papa Charlie Jackson (c. 1885-1938) with "Papa's Lawdy Lawdy Blues" and "Airy Man Blues" (aka "Hairy Man Blues"), who really opened the whole era of blues recording with a pair of hit records. Not long after, Uncle Gus Cannon, aka "Banjo Joe" (1885-1979), leader of Cannon's Jug Stompers—whose music provided the Grateful Dead with the sources of several of their songs—made his debut on record.

Jackson's recordings date from 1924 on the Paramount label, a subsidiary of the Wisconsin Chair Company that was based in New York, but also recorded in Chicago. Other major companies active in blues during the '20s and early '30s, in addition to OKeh, included Victor, Vocalion, and ARC (American Record Company). Blues recording in those days was often an informal affair, especially in rural settings—a company representative might come to a city such as Atlanta, posting notices about the auditions and where and when they were taking place, usually a local hotel; or they might pass through a town or hamlet to hear the local talent, and perhaps set up at a general store to listen to anyone who responded. (Note: This kind of scene was reenacted, loosely, in only one minor piece of American popular culture—the 1962 *Andy Griffith Show* episode "Mayberry on Record," depicts a record company talent scout showing up in Mayberry to audition and record local folk music talent, which, incidentally, included the bluegrass group the Kentucky Colonels.)

The best bluesmen from this era frequently had repertories numbering in the hundreds of songs, and usually at least a handful that were guaranteed crowd-pleasers. If a bluesman had at least one that seemed promising, he had a shot at getting it recorded; many musicians never got past their first two-song session, or perhaps eight or a dozen songs over three sessions. Others, like Big Bill Broonzy and Tampa Red, worked for 25 years writing and recording hundreds of songs, enough to fill a dozen CDs each.

Those who passed muster and seemed reliable were usually signed up on the spot. Recording was a haphazard process—microphones were crude, the fidelity sometimes doubtful, and recording tape didn't exist. The recording process in those days involved cutting a hot wax lacquer at 78 rpm, on a portable machine (that might weigh hundreds of pounds). There was no such thing as "playback," which would ruin the lacquer—a recording couldn't be checked for errors until a pressing was prepared, as much as a month later, so it was up to the musician and the producer, faced with limited time and money, to recognize whether a song was captured at its best.

Occasionally, some really lucky and ambitious producers might even get a pair of blues legends together in those days, with historic results—thus, Papa Charlie Jackson and Blind Arthur Blake, two of the greatest guitar players of the first half of the 20th century, cut a couple of sides together as "Papa Charlie and Blind Blake Talk About It, Pts. 1-2"; and Jackson cut duets with Hattie McDaniel of "Dentist Chair Blues, Pts. 1-2," decades before McDaniel won her Oscar for *Gone With the Wind*. And most of the first Sonny Boy Williamson's early recordings featured backup by Robert Lee McCollum, aka Robert Nighthawk, and Big Joe Williams, as well as blues mandolin star Yank Rachel.

It's also easy to forget the limitations under which these blues recordings were made. All recording was done and released on 78-rpm discs, which had a maximum running time of slightly over three minutes on a side. For blues players, this often meant abridging their performance of a work in order to fit it onto a record. A song that might last six or seven minutes as normally performed by the artist would be nothing but a shadow of itself on record—Leadbelly, for one, was constantly struggling to abbreviate his songs to fit them onto record, until his first session (among the very last of his career) captured on recording tape in 1948. Every so often, a song might prove sufficiently compelling that the producer would divide it in two and devote both sides of a record to it—Furry Lewis' epic "Casey Jones," one of the greatest blues records ever made, cut for Victor in the late '20s, is one of the greatest examples of this adaptation, but also a very rare occurrence.

The business arrangements behind these early recordings were "informal" by modern standards. According to the recollections of some participants, the fees, such as they were, could be as little as $50 to $100 and a supply of gin or bourbon for an afternoon's recording session that might yield four or six songs. Royalties, even if they were part of a contract, which would have been extraordinary, seem seldom to have been paid, and even if

a musician were interested in formally copyrighting an original song, there was virtually no way in those days to collect royalties on its sales. (One notable exception was Big Joe Williams, who had the foresight to copyright "Baby Please Don't Go," which kept him well provided for after it became a rock and blues standard in the '60s.)

The business of selling records was very different then. Record stores existed, but they were really music stores that carried sheet music and even piano rolls in the early days, as well as 78-rpm platters. Records were less important than sheet music, and most of what the biggest of these stores stocked was classical music and Tin Pan Alley-type popular music, and jazz. If blues records were carried at all, it was only in stores in neighborhoods—such as New York's Harlem and Chicago's South Side—that had large numbers of customers for them. And that was only in the biggest cities.

Elsewhere, and especially in the Deep South, there were no "record stores." Records were sold through general stores, furniture shops, and other completely unrelated businesses, usually by the same places that sold phonographs. Distribution was uneven, and within the same state a record might be available in one county, but not another.

Still, against this backdrop, several records by Blind Lemon Jefferson (1897-1929) easily sold as many as 500,000 to a million copies during the late '20s, a phenomenal number (and he saw precious little good for it—Jefferson froze to death on a Chicago street during the winter of 1929-1930). Indeed, on at least a handful of Blind Lemon Jefferson's songs, the sales were so high that the lacquer master wore out from overuse in pressing copies, and the singer had to re-record those songs again. Additionally, for all of its relative isolation in the poorer rural south or the ghettos of northern cities, the blues audience of the '20s was sophisticated enough to be expected to respond to advertisements emphasizing such matters as electrical recording, which Paramount began pushing with its advent in 1925. (Note: Electrical recording, which is to say recording through an electronic microphone which could amplify sound, as opposed to an acoustic recording horn.)

Paramount Records, in particular, had some dubious means of ensuring that its records sold in even greater numbers than their musical qualities alone dictated. The company's pressings of 78-rpm shellac discs, which were noisy and prone to wear under the best of circumstances, were unusually scratchy and pressed so cheaply that they would begin to wear out after as few as a half-dozen plays.

This ensured that listeners would have to repurchase Paramount releases that they liked. But it also meant that clean copies of most Paramount discs are all but impossible to obtain today, and that many modern, digital transfers of Paramount artists such as Charley Patton, Papa Charlie Jackson, and Blind Lemon Jefferson all require major noise reduction to be made listenable. This has blighted some of the most dedicated efforts at reissuing the complete work of numerous Paramount artists, including Blind Lemon Jefferson, Papa Charlie Jackson, the Beale Street Sheiks, aka Frank Stokes and Dan Sane, and Charley Patton (1887-1934)—even the best digital cleanup work can only accomplish so much. Added to the fact that the fragility of shellac discs, and the fact that relatively few people took the history of blues very seriously until the '50s, and the rarity of these discs becomes obvious. Paramount wasn't the only company guilty of these lapses in quality, but given the quality of the artists on its roster, the deficiencies become quite vexing.

Spearheaded by Blind Lemon Jefferson's success, blues records sold in ever increasing numbers during the late '20s, and producers and talent scouts fanned out across the South looking for talent that could emulate that success. Alas, all of this came to a halt with the Great Depression. This economic upheaval fell even more heavily on the rural South than it did elsewhere in the country, and by the early '30s, Paramount Records had gone out of business; before the end of the '30s, the American Record Company would be taken over by Columbia Records; and OKeh would also become part of Columbia. And very few talent scouts for the commercial record labels would make the trip across the Mason-Dixon Line much after 1931.

The disappearance of the scouts limited the chances for any new local talent being discovered, and coincided with several other events that slowed any recording activity involving the blues. The insolvency of recording companies such as Paramount, coupled with their exploitative business practices when they were in business, left many blues artists distrustful of the recording process. Some of the best players who were still alive at the end of the '30s realized that, as successful as their records might have been, they were going to see precious little in the way of monetary reward—some consciously despaired of ever being anything but poor, while others continued to record and play, realizing that this was probably a better life than anything else that might come their way.

Evolution: The '40s

Some acoustic country blues artists such as Blind Willie McTell and Curley Weaver continued to record into the late '30s, but changes were coming that cast doubt on the future of this brand of blues, mostly involving the black population of the South.

The Depression wiped out many of the jobs that poorer blacks in the South had relied upon for survival in years past. The black migration north had already started during the teens, and during the '20s cities like Chicago and New York had viable black communities, and were already the sites of many blues recordings. The Depression simply made the migration more of a necessity.

And as the black populations in Chicago, New York, and other northern cities gradually surged, the audience for the blues changed. A new, more sophisticated brand of blues, akin to big-band jazz, began to manifest itself alongside acoustic country blues. By the middle of the '30s, rural acoustic blues was on the decline, along with the economic situation of its audience.

The record companies happened to find this form of smooth, urban blues easier to absorb into their catalogs and their recording schedules—"blues," such as it was in the late '30s and early '40s, became an offshoot of the remnants of the swing orchestras, and sounded a lot like jazz except that the voices still had a rough, down-home quality and the lyrics tended to be raunchier; in fact, some of what was out there uncannily anticipated rock & roll by a decade or more. The result was that artists such as Tampa Red and Big Bill Broonzy, who had started their careers as solo acoustic performers, were suddenly leading groups of six players or more, and sounding very "un-country." The development of the electric guitar, which first turned up in blues on the records of T-Bone Walker (1910-1975)—who was just as respected by jazz audiences as he was among blues listeners—hastened this development as the '40s began.

The producer who was probably most responsible for helping to push this sound was Lester Melrose, who'd started with the Vocalion label in the early '30s and moved through several labels. During the early '40s he was closely associated with Victor, where he was responsible for signing many of the acts on the Bluebird label—indeed, he was called the mastermind of the "Bluebird beat," having devised the notion of establishing a rotating group of six players at a time, who would perform on each other's records. This ensured a high level of quality in the work that he recorded, but also—according to many critics of the sound—a sameness in many Melrose-produced records, especially when he would have his artists record each other's material. Of course, you really only notice this today, when listening to the records side by side.

Melrose's way of doing business, however, would, today, likely be considered just short of criminal. He usually signed up artists such as Arthur "Big Boy" Crudup directly under contract himself, paying them flat fees for their recordings while he held onto the recording contract with the label, which allowed him to collect any royalties himself. He also took the song copyrights himself as well, where there was original material involved—this is why originals such as Tampa Red's "Love With a Feeling" turned up on recordings by Merline Johnson, Sonny Jones, and Tommy McClellan, all Melrose artists. He kept his artists busy and money coming into them, in lieu of royalties, by using them as session musicians on each other's records. In other words, he became a one-man musical "company town"—an artist who said something about the business arrangements on his own records might well lose the income from the session work.

The recordings that Melrose produced were so successful, that he became a major influence even among companies competing with Victor, as they sought to emulate his work. Putting together this kind of small-band blues was not only a good way of smoothing out the music's roughest edges, but also gave labels and producers the chance to use some of the swing bands held over from the early '40s. By the mid-'40s, however, a lassitude had entered the music, as well as a high degree of predictability. Sales had begun declining as the market became saturated. And as it turned out, this kind of blues wasn't what the listeners wanted, either.

The major record companies, especially Victor and Columbia (which had absorbed the American Record Company and the OKeh label), responded by cutting back on the number of blues signings and blues sessions among their remaining artists. Tampa Red, who'd been with Victor since the mid-'30s and had often recorded as many as 26 songs a year, was only going into the studio once or twice a year by the end of the '40s, and only laying down a handful of songs. By the end of the decade, neither label was doing much with the blues anymore. One irony of this situation came in 1951 when Piano Red, aka Willie Perryman, newly signed to RCA, became the first blues artist in the label's history to reach the pop charts, and became one of the label's top-selling artists for a time with "Red's Boogie," "Rockin' With Red," "Right String but the Wrong Yo Yo," and "Layin' the Boogie."

Still, the major labels were in something of disarray when it came to blues, as well as R&B. The independent labels were closer to the public that bought the music, and it would show in the years from 1946 through the end of the '50s.

But the '40s, despite the commercial burnout of the blues, had seen a little order come to the business of the blues.

Royalty payments to the artists were still inadequate, when they did occur, but the concept of royalties was at least now understood, even if producers took steps to keep them to a minimum. Arthur "Big Boy" Crudup, signed to Victor's Bluebird label by Lester Melrose, didn't learn until far too late that his contract took away his publishing royalties he might've been entitled to, and left him with virtually nothing in the way of artists royalties, despite the substantial success of his records during the '40s. Even after he was rediscovered during the '60s and began to be paid something close to what his music and performances were worth, he despaired, telling one listener, "I was born poor, I've lived poor, and I know I'm gonna die poor."

So, one might ask, if that were the case, then why record, or keep making music?

One answer might be because the music still mattered, and still brought pleasure on some visceral level to men like Crudup, Blind Willie McTell, Buddy Moss, and Skip James, men who knew they'd been cheated and exploited, and probably robbed of any chance any of them had for a life of relative ease.

Yet they kept playing the blues, possibly because it was the blues—and if Willie Dixon was right, then the blues only sound sad, but make you happy. And "happiness" could refer to the satisfaction of holding crowds spellbound, of doing something with music that told people that these men had passed this way with something to say, and about the way life had treated them; that the money was coming too little, and probably too late to really matter, but people, black or white, were still listening. Additionally, some of these musicians simply loved the music, and kept at it even though they knew they were being cheated—"Right String but the Wrong Yo Yo" was a hit at least three different times for Piano Red, but he never saw any money for his success as a recording artist; on the other hand, he never minded the money he received as author of the song through the years.

The situation for songwriters didn't get much better, but the means for making it better in the future was put in place in 1939 with the founding of Broadcast Music Incorporated (BMI), a performing rights organization that could oversee the collecting of songwriters' royalties. Until then, the only such organization had been ASCAP, the American Society of Composers, Authors, and Producers. For decades, ASCAP had seen to it that its member songwriters were paid for the sales and broadcasts of their work. But ASCAP was run like an exclusive club, and deliberately limited its membership to the more "respectable" sides of composition: Broadway, Tin Pan Alley, classical, and the more sophisticated jazz. It was virtually impossible for anyone writing blues to become a member.

BMI was created to represent everyone creating worthwhile songs who wasn't represented by ASCAP, including country & western, hillbilly, jazz, and blues songwriters. Competition between the two was ferocious, so much so that a war initially broke out between them, which resulted in the disappearance of all ASCAP songs from the airwaves during the early '40s. Even afterward, with a truce more or less in place and BMI established and accepted, ASCAP remained restricted in membership, and it was considered the more upscale of the two organizations for many years. (Note: It was because of this prejudice that BMI, which had lagged behind ASCAP in both membership and revenues, suddenly came to challenge the older rival during the mid- and late '50s, as rock & roll, an offspring of country & western and blues, suddenly came to dominate the airwaves and record sales; most rock & roll songwriters were members of BMI. This resulted in attacks on BMI by people who hated rock & roll, for supposedly foisting this "low quality" music off on the public, rather than the good music controlled by ASCAP.)

With the creation of BMI, an organization at last existed to represent the blues songwriter. It didn't do a lot of good at first, as producers driven by greed simply got their artists to sign away their publishing, and the publishers themselves sometimes worked in collusion with the record companies to cheat the songwriter, but at least the mechanism to do something about making money from songwriting was there.

Certain artists did concern themselves sufficiently over songwriting to secure rights that would serve them and their families well in the future. Among the first was Leadbelly, aka Hudie Ledbetter. "Discovered" by folksong collector John Lomax and his son Alan on a Louisiana prison farm, Leadbelly was released from prison with help from Lomax and given a chance to record commercially.

Probably thanks to his contact with John Lomax, Leadbelly was among the first bluesmen to comprehend and take an interest in the business side of songwriting. Not that Lomax was entirely benevolent in showing any of this to Leadbelly—in the course of trying to secure a career and stardom for his discovery, Lomax simply registered numerous Leadbelly songs for copyright in both his name and Leadbelly's, thus ensuring himself a piece of the royalties that might result. As a result, the singer/guitarist arrived in New York knowing a bit more about that side of the business of songwriting than most of his contemporaries, and while he didn't live long enough to benefit from this knowledge, his widow did see some publishing money that made a difference in her life.

Big Bill Broonzy was another performer/songwriter who was aware of the importance of copyrights but never had a real chance to secure or protect his work. But the man who probably did the most to remind his fellow musicians, as well as listeners, of the importance of the blues songwriter and to establish some security for himself and other members of his generation, was Willie Dixon.

A natural, spontaneous composer who'd been writing songs since before he was a teenager—and who'd often sold them outright to various local bands when he was in his teens—Dixon in the early '40s had a sense of the importance of song copyrights. Although he would end up signing up with Arc Music, the publishing arm of Chess Records, as part of his relationship with Chess, he never lost sight of the songs he'd written. With help from an aggressive manager in the '70s, when the 28-year renewals on many of his '40s songs were coming due, Dixon did reclaim ownership and the financial rewards from many of his best songs. Dixon became the first—or, more properly, the oldest—songwriter in the blues field to see a significant amount of money from his work writing blues songs.

Postwar Blues: The Modern Era

Even as the major labels withdrew from the blues, there were businessmen who believed that there was still a market for blues, if only they could figure out what kind of sound would see. The most notable were Phil and Leonard Chess in Chicago, Sam Phillips in Memphis, and Saul, Jules, and Joe Bihari in Los Angeles. All three labels were on the look out for talent, and on at least one occasion, engaged in a three-way tug-of-war for the work of Chester "Howlin' Wolf" Burnett.

Chess Records is the label most familiar to the largest number of people, partly because of the sheer number of blues stars and superstars on its roster, and the label's later successful entry into rock & roll with the music of Chuck Berry and Bo Diddley, and into jazz through the work of Ramsey Lewis. Chess started after World War II, initially under the name Aristocrat, and at first the records that the label made were very much in a mid-'40s, big-band blues style, not much different from the majors, and also what founders Leonard and Phil Chess were booking in the club they owned.

Blues in Chicago had been dominated by various personalities since the '30s. At that time, from the very end of the '20s until the end of the '30s, Tampa Red had been the major figure in Chicago blues as a bandleader, guitarist, singer, and composer. By most accounts, Red's apartment was a mecca, meeting place, and hangout for all manner of musicians at all hours of the day or night, with Red's wife happily serving anyone who happened to be present. Later on, from the late '30s until the end of the '40s, Big Bill Broonzy had been the major figure in Chicago blues.

Both Red and Broonzy did most their recordings in their prime for Victor's Bluebird label—Tampa Red turned up as a sessionman in some Chess recordings, and Big Bill Broonzy cut a few sides for the label in the early '50s alongside his cousin, Washboard Sam. But it was their successor, as the major bandleader/guitarist/singer/songwriter, who gave shape to the familiar Chess Records sound: Muddy Waters.

A transplanted Delta bluesman, McKinley Morganfield, aka Muddy Waters, began recording for Chess in 1947. He had previously recorded a single for Columbia, and before that had been captured on a field recording in the Mississippi Delta by John and Alan

Lomax (Muddy was the only bluesman so introduced to recording to make it to the top of the commercial blues world, bridging both worlds) before coming to Chess, with the help of Sunnyland Slim, as a sessionman on one of Slim's records. Soon after, Muddy Waters was making his own records. His mix of powerful guttural vocals and electric guitar was based on Mississippi Delta blues, and a direct offshoot of the kind of acoustic country blues that Robert Johnson had been playing before the war, only louder and more aggressive.

What's more, it sold. Chess Records suddenly discovered a market for this new brand of raw, surging electric blues, completely different from the kind of commercial, dance-band-type blues that had been dominant in Chicago for ten years. Soon they were recording major blues stars of the next generation like Little Walter Jacobs, Howlin' Wolf, and Sonny Boy Williamson, and, later on, gifted players and singers like Jimmy Rogers, Buddy Guy, and Koko Taylor. Early in its history, Chess also gave an opportunity for older blues stars such as Robert Nighthawk to lay down some sides, one of which, "Sweet Black Angel," marked the Chess recording debut of Willie Dixon on bass.

The Bihari brothers on their various labels, including Modern, RPM, and Crown, never had quite as coherent an operation as Chess, but they had their share of stars, including B.B. King, Elmore James, and (briefly) Howlin' Wolf. Their operations lacked some of the unity of Chess, and they were also more ambitious in the way that they tried to sell their records, especially as time went on—after B.B. King left Crown in 1960, not only did the Biharis assemble two excellent albums of some of his most popular songs, but they also redubbed some of his singles, remastering them with added brass instruments to create a stereo effect.

Sam Phillips' Sun Records is best known as the label that discovered Elvis Presley (and for which Presley cut his best music, in many peoples' opinions) and as the early home of Johnny Cash, Jerry Lee Lewis, Carl Perkins, and Roy Orbison, but Phillips also cut lots of important blues. Phillips founded Memphis Recording Services in 1950, the first modern studio in Memphis, and cut any number of songs by local blues and R&B artists, which he would license to labels in different parts of the country—primarily Chess in Chicago and Modern or RPM, owned by the Biharis, in Los Angeles. To this day, Phillips considers Chester "Howlin' Wolf" Burnett to be his greatest discovery, and always felt that if Wolf had stayed with him, he could have made him as big a rock & roll star as Little Richard. As it was, Wolf cut his first sides for Phillips before the Memphis producer lost his new star, first to the Biharis and then to Chess, as part of a very complicated set of artist trades and contract disputes. Wolf's very first record, "Moanin' at Midnight," opened with a sound—crossing feedback and a basso moan from the six-foot-four Wolf—that nobody, in or out of the blues, had before, and he never stopped surprising people over the next 23 years. Other important artists recorded by Phillips included singer Jackie Brenston and guitarist Ike Turner—who, as part of the same band, recorded "Rocket 88," often referred to as the first "rock & roll" record, in 1951—and, at the end of the '50s, when Sun was established as a label, guitarist/singer Frank Frost.

Other labels that contributed in major ways to the history of postwar blues included Los Angeles-based Imperial Records, which recorded Texas bluesmen T-Bone Walker and Li'l Son Jackson, among others—Walker's playing on his sides for Imperial were a direct inspiration to Chuck Berry who, in turn, would become a star at Chess; Mississippi-based Trumpet Records, which gave Sonny Boy Williamson II and (briefly) Elmore James their starts; and Chicago's Cobra Records which, from 1956 until its demise in 1958, tried to rival Chess Records. Not only did Cobra have Otis Rush—who'd been rejected by Chess because he sounded too much like Muddy Waters—but Cobra was the first label to sign Buddy Guy after he arrived in Chicago, and they also had guitarist Magic Sam and Ike Turner's, Kings of Rhythm; and the label scored a major coup in 1956 when it acquired the services of veteran Chess Records producer, arranger, songwriter, and bassist Willie Dixon.

Imperial's commitment to the blues didn't outlast the '50s, and none of the smaller labels lasted too long. Trumpet was out of business by the early '50s, which proved fortuitous for Chess when Sonny Boy (Rice Miller) Williamson's contract ended up there, and Cobra closed its doors in 1958, after only two years of operation. Nor was either of them very well or widely distributed—Cobra's output didn't get true national distribution until the 1993 release of the Capricorn Records boxed set devoted to the label, some 33 years after the company ceased to exist. Nor did the Biharis or Sun continue as going concerns much past the early '60s. But they all became, along with Chess, the basis upon which modern blues recording was founded.

These labels found success during the late '40s and early and mid-'50s, selling blues singles to what they thought was mostly a black audience. What they didn't recognize, however, was that among their listeners, especially from the early- to mid-'50s on, was a tiny group of younger whites, who tuned in to black radio stations and occasionally bought the records, and even attended the concerts. "We don't play for white people," B.B. King said in 1957, adding, "Of course, a few whites come to hear us on one-night stands."

None of the labels, and even fewer of the artists, were quite certain of what to do about this tiny but growing phenomenon. After all, nobody could say what method could be used to reach the white audience without alienating the already substantial black audience for the blues. Moreover, these were all small, independent labels—even Chess, the most successful of the bunch, remained a family-run operation until the end of the 1960s—their resources were limited. When the long-playing record came along in 1948, producers in most fields did something about it immediately. Classical music was the obvious primary beneficiary, as listeners would no longer have to put symphonies on collections of six or more shellac 78s—the classical labels scrambled to make new recordings, but also transferred many 78-era performances to LP. Eventually, the jazz labels caught up, as players and producers saw the potential of being able to do works running up to 15 to 20 minutes in length without breaks. Popular music came along, exploiting both equally new 45-rpm disc as the basic format for songs, and the LP as the medium for collections of songs.

But the blues was different. Its audience was much poorer—78-rpm players were still common until late in the '50s—than the pop or classical listenership, and there just was no perceived demand for long-playing records. Moreover, there was not yet a sense of history of the blues in place, the way there was with classical and jazz—blues was put out to make money, and its past didn't yet matter in the way that classical and even jazz's past did to their respective listeners or the companies trading in them.

This meant that a lot of blues that had been recorded before the war, especially country blues from the '30s, was neglected—those masters meant nothing, and a lot of them were lost with the demise in the mid-'30s of labels like Paramount; even masters from the vaults of labels that had been absorbed by the majors, such as ARC and Vocalion, were often missing. The companies that were active in blues were all postwar-founded operations, without access to prewar blues.

The birth of rock & roll during 1954-1956 diverted some of the potential white interest from the blues proper. By the same token, rhythm & blues began to draw younger black listeners away from the likes of Muddy Waters and Howlin' Wolf in growing numbers. Thus, at the end of the '50s, doing business with the blues had become a lot more difficult.

There was some hope, however, from an unexpected quarter. A somewhat older group of white listeners—mostly of college age, who had little patience or need for songs of teenage angst—was increasingly fascinated by the blues. They were beginning to attract notice from the Chess or the Bihari brothers (although to his credit, Sam Phillips at Sun was convinced they were there from the early '50s onward), but nobody was sure how many of them there were, or how to reach them. And they didn't seem remotely capable of making up for the black listeners being lost to the blues.

The change came at the end of the '50s, and it happened in stages. Records by Muddy and the Wolf were selling well, and B.B. King had a big enough audience to attract the attention of numerous major labels once his contract with the Biharis had run out. In 1958, Muddy Waters was booked to play England for the first time, and was utterly astonished by the reception that he received, as tens of thousands of fans who'd only heard on record or of him from across the ocean cheered him at his concerts, and listened with rapt attention to every note he sang and played. Then, a year later, came Muddy's appearance at the Newport Folk Festival—now it was many thousands of Americans, the largest single audience that Muddy had ever played to in person, and almost all of them white, cheering wildly over his set. The resulting live album became a steady seller in the Chess catalog for over 30 years.

By then it was clear that the audience for the blues was bigger than anyone had previously thought, but reaching that audience was also going to be more complicated than anyone had guessed. The white listeners enjoyed modern Chicago bluesmen like Muddy Waters and Howlin' Wolf, and started attending B.B. King concerts in droves, but a lot of them also wanted to hear really old time bluesmen like Skip James, Mississippi John Hurt, and, perhaps most of all, Furry Lewis, who'd re-emerged after 30 years out of the recording business with an album, and a good one at that, and went on to a film career.

The situation was all as confusing as it was encouraging, especially with the black audience changing at the same time—older fans still listened to Muddy Waters and Howlin' Wolf, but younger blacks were turning toward more sophisticated and modern urban sounds, and political sounds. To them, musicians like Muddy, the Wolf, and Furry Lewis, and all of the acoustic blues players who were rediscovered during the early '60s were reminders of a time and a history that they wanted nothing to do with. And the rise of the civil rights movement, and the Black Power movement, seemed to make the blues irrelevant.

Already, in an effort to make his records sound more sophisticated and soulful—and less down-home and "country"—Muddy Waters had ceased playing guitar on his studio recordings after 1955. This was especially ironic, as Waters, one of the great guitar players in postwar Chicago, didn't have his instrument on hand when he recorded his very first original studio album, *Muddy Waters Sings Big Bill Broonzy*, and had to wait until his 1963 album *Folk Singer* to turn up with his axe (actually, an acoustic guitar on that record) on a studio album.

Chess and Cobra always needed good songs, and Willie Dixon had a proven knack for writing clever songs that seemed to catch the public's ear. In the '60s, this would be proven out geometrically, as his songs ended up in the repertories of white artists ranging from Peter, Paul & Mary to the Cream. From the mid-'50s onward, his songwriting abilities were increasingly pressed into service on behalf of Muddy, the Wolf, and anyone else who would record his work.

Sometimes, the players themselves were confused by all of this activity and the demands being placed on them. Muddy Waters had been playing electric blues since arriving in Chicago in the mid-'40s, and knew that no black audience to which he'd played since would sit still for him playing an acoustic country blues set. Even he'd come to consider such a sound hokey and out-of-date. But when Muddy toured England for the first time in 1958, for dates that paid him more money than most any individual shows he'd ever played before, he was forced to turn down his electric guitar because British audiences were utterly unprepared for Chicago-style electric blues.

But when Muddy next visited England four years later with his acoustic guitar in hand, he found that all of the blues being played there was now electric. And, yet, in 1963, when it was time to do another new album, Chess Records, in an effort to cash in on the folk music revival that was in full swing, had him pick up his acoustic guitar and record his *Folk Singer* album, his first acoustic tracks since the 1941 field recordings that John and Alan Lomax had made of him back in the Delta. After that it was back to electric blues for his singles, with Sammy Lawhorn and Pee Wee Madison on guitar, and the full electric Muddy, Brass, and the Blues album.

Muddy's Chess stablemate Howlin' Wolf, by contrast, seemed oblivious to the demands of these contradictory audiences and demands. A giant of a man, with a unique voice and special talents on the harmonica (which he'd learned from Rice Miller, aka Sonny Boy

Williamson [II]), and guitar, he went on playing the same kind of sets from the late '50s until his retirement in the '70s. Indeed, even after songs of his such as "Smokestack Lightning" and "Sitting on Top of the World" became staples of white rock bands, he never specially programmed them into his sets, even when he played a gig before a white collegiate crowd. Thus, contrary to what some blues guides say about the Wolf's 1971 concert album *Live and Cookin'* (At Alice's Revisited), is a not a late career cash-in effort, but an honest representation of his concert work during the final years of his life (and it's still a powerful record, especially with the CD bonus tracks). But when Chess Records tried to get the Wolf to re-record his music in a psychedelic style, on *The New Howlin' Wolf Album*, imposing a sound on him that wasn't his own and forcing him to pander, that was a disaster from the get-go, with Wolf himself publicly describing the record as "dogshit."

Between 1960 and 1963, Muddy Waters released three albums counting his *Best Of* collection, three more than he'd had out in his first 13 years with Chess Records. B.B. King's audience had gradually expanded to include white listeners during the late '50s and early '60s. The Biharis' Crown label (which reportedly sold their LPs for as little as $1.99 each) released two collections of his singles during 1960, and ABC-Paramount issued an LP on King in 1963, but the first album of his to achieve real crossover success was *Live at the Regal* in 1965. There was a certain irony in this, as *Live at the Regal* was one of the last opportunities to capture a blues show like that, in front of a rousing black audience, but the album served as a magnet for white audience once they discovered King (primarily through his crossover hit "The Thrill Is Gone," as well as a series of crossover engagements, most notably in Vegas playing the lounge to headliner Frank Sinatra, who had to give his personal approval for the gig). Even more than Muddy Waters, King was one of the top blues artists of the '60s, and became a major draw for white listeners increasingly fascinated by blues as one of the main sources for rock music.

By the mid-'60s, blues was a big business and album sessions were a fairly routine matter for most performers, even rediscovered stars from the prewar era such as Bukka White, Mississippi John Hurt, Skip James and Arthur "Big Boy" Crudup, who had left the music business decades earlier. The Rolling Stones visited Chess Records in Chicago, and cut some the best music of their careers at those 1964 sessions (the product of which, including "It's All Over Now," "Mona," "I Just Can't Be Satisfied," and "Confessin' the Blues," can be found spread among several of their early London albums, compilation records, and assorted bootlegs).

All of this coincided with a change in the nature of the blues audience—whites gradually became the mainstay of the blues, while younger blacks came to avoid it. In keeping with this change, it was far more likely that a Muddy Waters or a Howlin' Wolf would make the Top 100 album charts, selling their music to college students, than that they would ever hit the R&B charts again after the first half of the decade.

Most of the record labels appreciated the changes, but were at a loss as to how to sustain it. They tried everything—B.B. King released albums with psychedelic artwork, and Muddy Waters was made to sound like B.B. King on *Brass and the Blues*. Muddy and Howlin' Wolf each were given the full psychedelic treatment on a Chess offshoot label called Cadet/Concept (run by Leonard Chess' son Marshall). But despite these efforts, Leonard Chess was also slow to understand the changes taking place in the white audience of the period. He ignored the talents of figures such as Buddy Guy, who was playing in a flashy lead guitar style quite unlike Muddy Waters but which was in perfect sync with the work of Jimi Hendrix, Michael Bloomfield, and other guitarists whose work college kids were devouring, until after Guy was signed to another label. By contrast, Columbia Records and Capitol Records, neither of which had done much with rock & roll, much less blues during the '50s, began recording such blues figures as Son House, Bukka White, Willie Dixon, and Mississippi Fred McDowell in their authentic, established styles. In the case of Son House, it had been so many years since he'd played, that he had to be reacquainted with his own style by none other than Alan Wilson, the blues scholar and future co-founder of Canned Heat.

The artists themselves profited to varying degrees from all of this. The concert fees paid to Muddy, the Wolf, B.B. King, Lightnin' Hopkins, Albert King, and other blues stars rose considerably, not only when they started playing in Europe (where $2000 a show was routine—not much, but easily ten times what many of these men got playing clubs in America) but also the college circuit in America. For some of the survivors of the first half of the century, the sudden surge in demand and money was hard to take—Mississippi John Hurt, who had never even aspired to a performing career in the '20s but suddenly found himself playing before thousands of appreciative fans in the '60s, wasn't even sure how to deal with fees of $1500 a show. Most took it in stride and made the most of this late-in-the-day success, and a few, like Hurt and Furry Lewis, who'd achieved fame 40 years late, even made important recordings.

By now, royalties were expected to be paid, though this was problematic—Piano Red, for one, recalled that his recording activity for OKeh came to a near-standstill after 1962 when the company failed to pay him any royalties against the sales of his hit "Mr. Moonlight," despite its having sold over 300,000 copies. A few artists, Willie Dixon and Chuck Berry most notable among them, began bringing in attorneys and accountants to verify that they were seeing the money they were entitled to. Songwriting, in particular, became bigger than ever, especially when superstar white bands like the Rolling Stones and the Cream began covering this repertory—it took time, but eventually Muddy Waters and Willie Dixon achieved financial security based on their song copyrights, which proved as valuable as any of their own recordings.

The Post-Boom Years

By the end of the '60s, the blues was big business, though not necessarily for bluesmen or blues labels. Rock music had adopted its songs, and even its nuances, in the guise of bands such as the Rolling Stones, Cream, and the Yardbirds-cum-Led Zeppelin. They reaped millions of sales and tickets sold, while most established blues players and their

record labels were caught in a bind, losing their black audience and ignored by most of the millions of whites who would buy a Cream or a Led Zeppelin album.

Apart from the folk-based labels such as Vanguard—which, apart from Buddy Guy, mostly recorded rediscovered '20s and '30s bluesmen such as Skip James and Mississippi John Hurt—few record companies during the late '60s had much of a commitment to the blues. Part of the problem lay in the rising cost of studio time and recording; when costs were low, there had been less risk, but by the end of the '60s the risks, except where established stars like Muddy Waters and Howlin' Wolf were concerned, were much higher and the blues seemed an unattractive prospect to most producers.

B.B. King and Albert King, as recognized authentic blues stars, benefited to some degree, and played places like the Fillmore East and West, and recorded albums there. John Lee Hooker also began attracting a larger white audience, mostly by virtue of the illusion that he was one of the authentic originators of the blues—Hooker, born in 1917, always looked older than he was, and delivered his songs in a manner far more guttural than Muddy Waters, sounding to white kids like he must've been playing in the Delta at the turn of the century; his association with the white blues band Canned Heat didn't hurt, either. A few rural bluesmen still saw some recording activity—Capitol Records chose to record an electric album by Mississippi Fred McDowell in 1969, almost in time to capitalize on the Rolling Stones' recording of his song "You Got to Move." But it was mostly small labels such as Biograph that were recording the blues, most of it acoustic.

Of all the major blues labels active in the postwar period, only Chess Records was still active at the end of the '60s, but the label had missed many opportunities to expand its audience. Despite his prescience in signing Chuck Berry and Bo Diddley at the outset of the rock & roll era, Leonard Chess was usually a couple of years behind a trend—the Muddy Waters *Folk Singer* album, for example, would've been more appropriate and successful in 1961, not 1963; and he'd missed the chance to push some of Muddy's and the Wolf's records in the late '50s as rock & roll, and to actively push them in the mid-'60s to a white audience, when their sound and songs were being covered by the likes of the Rolling Stones. Instead, he'd allowed time to go by, and then permitted his son Marshall to try and reshape Muddy and the Wolf's songs in psychedelic form, and in a series of "super blues" jam albums that didn't represent the original records or the performers very well.

But whatever his faults, Leonard Chess had been the driving force behind the company, and his death from a heart attack in 1969 left no valid reason for the company to continue, except as a conduit for the still superb releases of its remaining roster, including Muddy, the Wolf, and Chuck Berry. Muddy's singles ceased to have much importance after the mid-'60s (indeed, Chess Records never had another R&B chart hit after Koko Taylor's 1966 single "Wang Dang Doodle"), but he continued recording great albums for Chess right up to and including *The Muddy Waters Woodstock Album* in 1975. Wolf didn't get to do his first real album of new material until 1971, with *Back Door Wolf*, but it was a brilliant piece of work when it finally appeared.

Meanwhile, over at ABC-Paramount, B.B. King was just about the only veteran postwar bluesman who managed to hold onto a major part of his black fandom even as he added hundreds of thousands of white fans. His sales skyrocketed, and his music became ever more accomplished—but it also lost some of its freshness and spontaneity as he started to come up with concepts (some would say "gimmicks") that added new wrinkles to his music. In 1996, at age 70, he has sold his name to a group of blues clubs (including a very successful one in Memphis), among other marketing strategies that Muddy Waters and Howlin' Wolf could only dream of, been honored by the Kennedy Center, and played at the Atlanta Olympics, and a ten-foot tall statue of him (with his beloved guitar Lucille) stands in Memphis, right next to one of Elvis Presley, and he has recorded with the likes of U2. But these calculated concept recordings are more for purposes of making money than musical statements.

Even artists whom fame and fortune had passed by began to get major exposure. Producer/scholar Norman Dayron, who was responsible for one of Muddy Waters' most successful blues/rock fusion releases, *Fathers and Sons*, made a tape of Robert Nighthawk playing live at Chicago's Maxwell Street Market—a legendary blues venue going back at least to the '20s—that became Nighthawk's most acclaimed album. Similarly, Arthur "Big Boy" Crudup, after languishing in obscurity for many years, began getting decently paid concert work and some new recordings out toward the end of his life, even playing the Newport Festival alongside Muddy Waters and Big Mama Thornton (by that time the Newport Festival was held at Lincoln Center, thus leaving behind a live recording of Crudup doing "That's All Right" from Avery Fisher Hall, no less)—not enough to make up for what he'd been cheated out of, but enough to make people remember who he was and how he'd been cheated.

Blues records were available in profusion during the '70s and '80s, but to truly appreciate even the most straightforward of them, one had to look closely. The musical and historical treasures on these compilation records are as precious as they are unexpected. Muddy Waters' *Rare and Unissued*, for example, issued the year after his death and consisting of late-'40s/early-'50s sides, contains a track entitled "Last Time I Fool Around with You," which features some stunning interplay between the two guitars. A look at the session credits reveals this song as a seemingly one-time-only meeting of Muddy Waters with that star Chicago bluesman of the previous generation, Tampa Red. Other tracks on other reissues show off Muddy's early work with Little Walter Jacobs, while some '60s reissues show Muddy playing with Buddy Guy, the man who became the closest thing to a successor that he had. But appreciating these recordings properly on CD means taking in many of them one song at a time, and thinking of them in the context of the time in which they were done, not how they're assembled for us.

By the '70s, the blues was an entrenched part of the popular music landscape—Led Zeppelin, the Rolling Stones, the Allman Brothers, Eric Clapton, Ten Years After, the

Marshall Tucker Band, Lynyrd Skynyrd, and a dozen other arena bands and their legions of imitators played it and sang it, and even the Doors covered Wolf's repertory. A few, like Clapton and the Stones, tried to give something back to originators like Muddy Waters by booking them onto tours with them. And Johnny Winter even gave Muddy a whole second career on his Blue Sky label, with a series of acclaimed albums in the late '70s that solidified his reputation with a new generation.

At the same time, such specialty blues labels as Yazoo and Arhoolie began making available for the first time the work of country blues artists of previous generations. Yazoo, in particular, was good at retrieving the best-known surviving 78s on people like Charley Patton and, decades after it should have been done, getting their work out on LP for the first time, while Arhoolie specialized in recording the work of surviving country bluesmen—Li'l Son Jackson, Mance Lipscomb, and dozens of other rural players who'd been forgotten got to make their first records in years, or decades, or ever (and, in some cases, their best records) for these and other labels.

Over in Europe—where American blues (along with jazz and rock) is treated with the respect that only classical music receives in America—there was even more reissue activity. Not only was the public interest established, but this activity was helped by the fact that copyright laws in Europe rendered much pre-World War II American blues public domain. The Austrian-based Document Records, Wolf Records, and RST Records have availed themselves of the collections of hardcore fans and produced some stunning blues reissues, including the complete studio outputs of Leadbelly, Tampa Red from 1927 through 1953 (on 13 CDs on Document), Scrapper Blackwell, Papa Charlie Jackson, Frank Stokes and Dan Sane, Furry Lewis, Curley Weaver, and dozens of others. Moreover, RST and Document Records' approaches tend to focus on each song individually, placing it in a valid historical context in relation to the other recordings by the same artist.

It was only in the late '80s and '90s that the major labels began issuing their historic blues. Sony Music, as successor to Columbia Records as well as the OKeh and ARC labels, began releasing indispensable blues collections as part of its legacy series, devoted to such figures as Blind Willie McTell, Leadbelly, Lonnie Johnson, and Tampa Red's early work, among many others. And MCA has done an admirable job with the Chess label, which it now owns, reissuing virtually every major release in the label's history. On the other hand, RCA/BMG, after a promising start with reissues of the work of Arthur Crudup and Leadbelly, virtually abandoned blues reissues in the early '90s, leaving it to European reissue and pirate labels to mine this vein of gold.

The whole business of reissues can be confusing in and of itself, especially where an artist recorded over decades or generations. Big Joe Williams, for example, recorded from the late '20s into the late '60s, and the sheer range of his material and its multiple rerecordings (he wrote "Baby Please Don't Go" and redid it many times during his career) could make any listener dizzy—the Wolf Records label from Austria has issued a surprisingly good collection of his 1920s/early-'30s material, however. Most of Muddy Waters' material is on the Chess label, reissued through MCA, except for his very last recordings from the final years of his career, which are on Columbia or Sony Legacy—but there is also Muddy Waters material (including his first recording of "Rollin' and Tumblin'") from the end of the '40s on the Delmark label, which you won't hear much about in notes from the other labels. Howlin' Wolf spent the years 1954 through 1974 with Chess Records, but before that he recorded for Sun and Modern Records, and although the Sun material was supposed to move with him to Chess, the Bear Family label from Germany unearthed two CDs' worth of priceless Howlin' Wolf outtakes from Sun Records, and Flair/Virgin reissued his Modern Records sides. It all overlaps to some extent, but it's all worth owning if you like the Wolf. Leadbelly is another artist represented by a massive number of seemingly overlapping CDs—the Smithsonian/Folkways releases, and the two Columbia discs are the most representative of his work, although the RCA reissue of his work with the Golden Gate Quartet is a fascinating addendum, and the fourth volume of Document Records' complete Leadbelly series contains his last commercial recordings.

The range of exploration in 1996 is extraordinary—it is possible to take a song like Willie Dixon's "Down in the Bottom," as recorded by the Rolling Stones at Chess Studios in 1964 (and featured on a very common bootleg), and compare it with Howlin' Wolf's 1961 recording of the same song. But it is also possible to go back to the sources for Dixon's song, including Buddy Moss' "Hey Lawdy Mama" and Blind Boy Fuller's "Boots and Shoes," from the mid-'30s. Or take a song like Willie Dixon's "Spoonful" as recorded by the Cream and trace it back through Wolf's original recording to Papa Charlie Jackson's 1925 original, "All I Want Is a Spoonful." Or start out with the song "Matchbox" by the Beatles, as written by Carl Perkins, go back to Perkins' own recording from the 1958, and then back to Leadbelly's recordings of "Packing Trunk Blues" and "Match Box Blues," which were Perkins' source, back to Blind Lemon Jefferson's "Match Box Blues," where Leadbelly learned it.

More likely, however, today's listener will know the Allman Brothers' version of "Statesboro Blues," and not Blind Willie McTell's original. How much the fans of the Allmans, Zeppelin, or Lynyrd Skynyrd, or any of the others know and understand what they're listening to is debatable. They hear a cool-sounding Jimmy Page guitar solo, but do they recognize the song or the riff as having come from a Willie Dixon song, or a Muddy Waters record? (Note: Zeppelin, in particular, has a chronic problem of being sued for plagiarism by everyone from Willie Dixon to the publisher of the late Ritchie Valens.) And do they even know (or care) that a man like Mance Lipscomb, who at age 70 could dazzle the ear and the eye with his fingers on a fretboard, was ever alive? Scholars and serious listeners could take comfort in the fact that the records were there to be found, even if few Led Zeppelin fans knew anything about the blues.

Muddy, with help from Johnny Winter and Eric Clapton and the Stones, got the word out until his death in 1983. Willie Dixon was left as the major veteran ambassador for the blues, playing in front of audiences (including presidents, judges, and senators) almost until his death in 1992 and reminding people of the blues' origins and history all along.

Today, the legacy of most of the postwar blues stars lies in their recordings. Prior to his death in 2001, John Lee Hooker remained active through much of the '90s, recording regularly with the likes of superstar rockers like Keith Richards. A few others, like B.B. King and Buddy Guy, have major followings and continue to record regularly and make money with their records as well as their concerts, and others, ex-Chess musicians like Hubert Sumlin (Howlin' Wolf's best-known lead guitarist), have ongoing careers.

The music is out there on CD, more of it than was ever available at one time before, and more shows up every day. The secret is to try and discover it the way that the men and women who made it meant it to be heard: Not as a body of songs, but with each song and, perhaps, its B-side companion, as a work unto itself, with moments—a duet between two guitar legends like Muddy Waters and Tampa Red, or two giants out of the mysterious and undocumented pre-World War II like Blind Arthur Blake and Papa Charlie Jackson playing and singing together on a set of scratchy 78s, or Howlin' Wolf spontaneously creating a new blues sound in Memphis—that should all be savored.

—Bruce Eder

The Blues as Folklore

The onslaught of the Depression in the '30s spelled the end of the recording careers for many blues artists, as well as nipping many others in the bud before they had even had a chance to begin. Between the mid-'30s and mid-'50s, country blues was sporadically documented on record. The commercial record companies of the time had turned their attention elsewhere; wide interest in the blues' roots, from national and/or white audiences, wouldn't gain momentum until the seeds of the blues/folk revival were planted in the late '50s.

Our archive of country blues style from this era—and indeed, our knowledge of traditional blues as a whole—would be much the poorer, if not for the pioneering efforts of a few dedicated folklorists. The institution most responsible for preserving this work was the Library of Congress, which arranged for important field recordings for use in their collection. While the tone and packaging of these performances could tend toward the scholarly and museum-like, more often they resulted in music that, unfettered by commercial considerations of sales and image, gave us a glimpse of authentic blues and folk.

By far, the most important of these archivists were John A. Lomax and his son Alan. The senior Lomax, a colorful figure worthy of a book of his own, had been collecting songs since his teenage years in the Southwest. After education at Harvard, he continued his field work on a more formal basis. As early as 1907, he made cylinder recordings of cowboy songs, which are the first folk songs in English to be recorded by an American. In 1910 he published a collection, *Cowboy Songs and Other Frontier Ballads*, one of the most famous works of its sort.

In the early '30s, however, Lomax was struggling to make a living at his chosen profession. It was with great enthusiasm that he became curator of the Library of Congress' Archive of Folk Song. The Archive had been established in 1928, but under Lomax's efforts it would truly fulfill its mission of recording and preserving important American folk music. In these endeavors, he was greatly aided by his son, Alan, who was still a teenager when the Lomaxes set out to collect songs for John's *American Folk Songs and Ballads* project in 1933. The work would also involve a lot of recording, with what was then considered state-of-the-art portable equipment (which still weighed a good 315 pounds).

The Lomaxes had only been on the road for a little over a month when they hit more paydirt than they could have ever expected. They did some of their recordings in prison, figuring that long-time inmates were more apt to preserve traditional styles in the absence of contact from the outside world. July 1933 found them at Louisiana's Angola Penitentiary, where they discovered 12-string guitarist and singer Leadbelly, one of the major figures in 20th century American music. In addition to being a galvanizing performer, Leadbelly was also a walking encyclopedia of American folk song, his repertoire encompassing blues, folk, spirituals, and more.

As Charles Wolfe and Kip Lornell observe in *The Life & Legend of Leadbelly*, "The recordings by Leadbelly made by the Lomaxes had historical significance beyond the fact that they were the first ones of a man who would become a major figure in American music. The whole idea of using a phonograph to preserve authentic folk music was still fairly new. Most of John Lomax's peers were involved in collecting songs the classic way: taking both words and melody down by hand, asking the singer to perform the song over and over until the collector had 'caught' it on paper...."

"John Lomax sensed at once the limitations of this kind of method, especially when getting songs from African-American singers, whose quarter tones, blue notes, and complex timing often frustrated white musicians trying to transcribe them with European notation systems. The whole concept of field recording was, in 1933 and still today, radically different from the popular notion of recording. Field recordings are not intended as commercial products, but as attempts at cultural preservation. There is no profit motive, nor any desire to make the singer a 'star.' As have hundreds of folk song collectors after him, John Lomax had to persuade his singers to perform, to explain to them why their songs wree important, and to convince the various authorities—the wardens, the trustees, the bureaucrats—that this was serious, worthwhile work. He faced the moral problem of how to safeguard the records and the rights of the singers—a problem he solved in this instance by donating the discs to the Library of Congress."

"He had to overcome the technical problems involved in recording outside a studio; one always hoped for quiet, with no doors slamming or alarms going off, but it was always a risk. His new state-of-the-art recording machine sported a new microphone

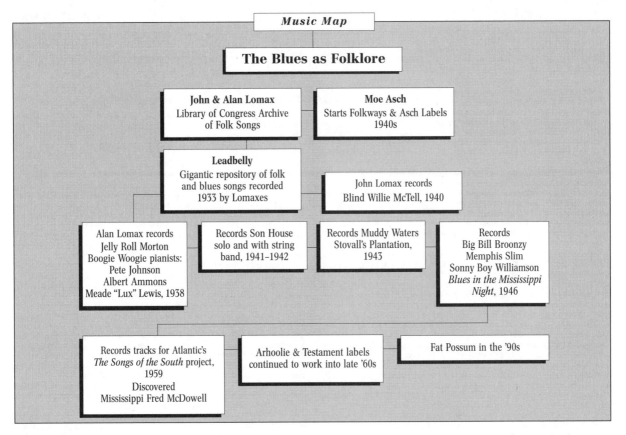

Music Map

The Blues as Folklore

John & Alan Lomax
Library of Congress Archive of Folk Songs

Moe Asch
Starts Folkways & Asch Labels 1940s

Leadbelly
Gigantic repository of folk and blues songs recorded 1933 by Lomaxes

John Lomax records Blind Willie McTell, 1940

Alan Lomax records Jelly Roll Morton Boogie Woogie pianists: Pete Johnson Albert Ammons Meade "Lux" Lewis, 1938

Records Son House solo and with string band, 1941–1942

Records Muddy Waters Stovall's Plantation, 1943

Records Big Bill Broonzy Memphis Slim Sonny Boy Williamson *Blues in the Mississippi Night*, 1946

Records tracks for Atlantic's *The Songs of the South* project, 1959 Discovered Mississippi Fred McDowell

Arhoolie & Testament labels continued to work into late '60s

Fat Possum in the '90s

---

designed by NBC, but there were no wind baffles to help reduce the noise when recording outside. Lomax learned how to balance sound, where to place microphones, how to work echoes and walls, and soon was a skilled recordist."

Leadbelly was released from prison shortly afterwards, becoming an assistant/chauffeur of sorts to Lomax. Their stormy relationship would dissolve amidst some acrimony within a few years, but not before Leadbelly had started a successful professional career, introducing many folk and blues classics to the public before his death in 1949. His Library of Congress recordings, eventually numbering over 200 songs, constitute much of his most important recorded work.

John and Alan Lomax didn't record only blues, or even focus on the blues. They recorded all sorts of folk music, from many different regions, including Cajun music, narratives of ex-slaves, and songs from California labor camps. By the late-'30s, John Lomax, already into his sixties, was less active in the field than Alan, who also recorded jazz, preserving a dozen albums' worth of Jelly Roll Morton singing and talking. Alan also recorded pianists Albert Ammons, Meade "Lux" Lewis, and Pete Johnson for the Library of Congress around the time of the famous *Spirituals to Swing* concert (which took place in New York City's Carnegie Hall in 1938). All three of those pianists, though really part of jazz, made their imprint on blues history by helping to popularize the boogie-woogie style. The elder Lomax was not retired, and in 1940 made a significant contribution to the blues library by recording Blind Willie McTell.

Alan undertook his most important blues sessions on behalf of the Library of Congress in the early '40s, as part of a project documenting black music in Coahoma County, MS. On these trips he found Muddy Waters and Son House, whose recordings were summaries of Delta blues styles past and present. House (who, apparently unbeknownst to Lomax, had already recorded a few commercial sides) would soon move to New York State, not to be rediscovered until the '60s blues revival. Waters, who recorded for Lomax as an acoustic guitarist, would take Delta blues into the future after moving to Chicago in 1943. Lomax also made interesting deep blues recordings in 1946 with Big Bill Broonzy, Sonny Boy Williamson, and Memphis Slim that also included, as many of the Library of Congress recordings do, conversation with the participants; this was issued by Rykodisc in the '90s as *Blues in the Mississippi Night*.

Alan Lomax, as stated previously, was not a blues specialist. He devoted the next five decades to championing folk music of all sorts. His late '50s recordings of styles associated with the American South, available on Atlantic's *The Songs of the South* box set, resulted in the discovery of Mississippi Fred McDowell (who had never previously recorded), who became one of the most popular acoustic performers of the '60s blues revival. He was a director of the Newport Folk Festival, and his staunch love of traditional styles led to some notoriety when he expressed resistance to the introduction of electric

instruments into festival events in the mid-'60s. Much of his life is recounted in his 1993 book, *The Land Where the Blues Began.*

The Library of Congress was not the sole organization dedicated to preserving traditional blues on record. Moe Asch's Folkways label, which began operations in the '40s, recorded a mammoth body of folk music of all sorts, which naturally included some blues. Leadbelly, Brownie McGhee, and Sonny Terry were some of the most prominent blues artists who did some recordings for the Folkways label. Before his death, Asch sold the Folkways catalog to the Smithsonian, which is currently engaged in an ongoing series of CD reissues of important Folkways sessions.

Some of the early albums arising from the '60s blues revival were folkloric in bent, inasmuch as they documented living exponents of rural traditions. There was Robert Pete Williams, for instance, discovered (like Leadbelly) at Angola Penitentiary in the late '50s. The Arhoolie label presented many blues and folk artists au naturel, coming up with a major find in Texas songster Mance Lipscomb. Testament Records issued titles by Jack Owens, Mississippi Fred McDowell, and others. Yet these recordings differed from the Library of Congress and Folkways sessions in that they were less geared toward, well, the library, and more for the general listener. They were not just concerned with documenting obscure and threatened styles, but in presenting material that could be enjoyed on its own terms, and prove modestly profitable in a small commercial niche market.

That doesn't mean that the Library of Congress recordings need to remained stored in the library. The performers the Lomaxes and others recorded may not have been playing for the general consumer, but they often gave their all. To an extent that the folklorists may not have realized, their work can serve purposes that are entertaining and inspirational, as well as educational.

11 Recommended Albums:
Leadbelly, *Midnight Special* (Rounder)
Leadbelly, *Leadbelly Sings Folk Songs* (Smithsonian/Folkways)
Various Artists, *Afro-American Blues and Game Songs* (Library of Congress)
Various Artists, *Negro Blues and Hollers* (Library of Congress)
Various Artists, *Negro Work Songs and Calls* (Library of Congress)
Muddy Waters, *The Complete Plantation Recordings* (MCA-Chess)
Son House, *Delta Blues: The Original Library of Congress Recordings, 1941-42* (Biograph)
Blind Willie McTell, *Complete Library of Congress Recordings (1940)* (Document)
Various Artists, *Brownie McGhee & Sonny Terry Sing* (Smithsonian/Folkways)
Various Artists, *Blues in the Mississippi Night* (Rykodisc)
Robert Pete Williams, *Angola Prisoner's Blues* (Arhoolie)

         —Richie Unterberger

The Blues Revival

Any retrospective of the '60s blues revival begs a rhetorical question: How could the blues be revived when it wasn't dead? Yes, in some respects, the blues scene was struggling in the late '50s. The blues' presence on the R&B charts had been diminished by rock & roll, doo-wop, and pure R&B recordings that were pointing the way for soul music. Country blues was rarely recorded; many of its greatest heroes had vanished into obscurity or died.

Yet the blues had never come close to dying. In urban centers, especially Chicago, electric blues legends continued to perform and record regularly, though they may have peaked in terms of vinyl sales. Hit blues singles on the R&B and even pop charts were not unknown; Jimmy Reed and John Lee Hooker had some of their biggest hits around 1960. Although the commercial market for acoustic blues was virtually nonexistent, many performers continued to play the music in Mississippi, Memphis, Texas, and elsewhere, either professionally, for their family or friends, or (in relatively rare cases) behind prison bars.

The "blues revival" really does not refer to the rebirth of the music, but an awakening of wider interest in the blues, particularly among younger white listeners. During its first few decades, blues recordings had been primarily marketed to black consumers, and primarily played live to black audiences. Blues performers that made a big impression with white listeners often had a good measure of crossover folk appeal, such as Leadbelly and Josh White. Names like Robert Johnson, Bukka White, and Charley Patton were virtually unknown; electric blues stars like Muddy Waters and Elmore James were not as totally obscure, but still little recognized within the white audience.

But in the late '50s and early '60s, young whites were starting to trace American roots music backwards from rock & roll, through to its sources in blues and folk. Often they were college-educated and relatively affluent, with affiliations in both the countercultural and academic communities. Some have taken a sociological perspective and mused that these listeners were rebelling against their comfortable, conformist upbringings, or hungering for an authenticity that they had been denied. The simpler explanation is that the blues was too good a thing to be kept a secret: larger and larger groups of Americans were responding to the power and magic of the music, especially after the "blues revival" made it easier to discover, hear, and see.

A small band of enthusiasts—their curiosity piqued by the great recordings they had been able to locate, and the little information that was available to them—began to undertake serious record collecting, documentation, and recording of the blues. Writers like Samuel Charters and Paul Oliver did a lot to get the ball rolling by publishing studies of the evolution of the blues that were both serious and accessible. Folklorists like Alan Lomax (who had been recording blues and folk for many years), and just plain fans like Chris Strachwitz and guitar virtuoso John Fahey, tracked down or discovered downhome blues singers for recording purposes. Often these champions of the blues would double as writers, record producers, promoters, and managers, fueled by their consuming love of the music.

Initially the blues revival was acoustic in tone. This may have been the result of purists who felt that the authenticity of the music was smothered by electric amplification that pulled it from its populist roots (a theory that doesn't hold up well in light of the fact that millions of working-class African-Americans were listening to electric blues regularly). It could have also been a side effect of the coffeehouse/college circuit that promoted most blues shows for the white/college audience in the early '60s, which emphasized acoustic performers, not electric ones. Many of the white singers on the early '60s folk scene would include blues material in their sets, most notably Dave Van Ronk, Bob Dylan, and the trio of Koerner, Ray & Glover.

The blues revival was aided and abetted by the development of the LP market. In 1960, those blues artists who recorded for an almost exclusively black/R&B audience concentrated almost solely upon 45-rpm singles. To address the whiter and more affluent market, they would focus upon long-playing records. In some cases, blues singers would maintain separate, simultaneous careers for the different markets, such as Snooks Eaglin, who recorded New Orleans R&B for Imperial and as the blues/folk street singer Blind Snooks Eaglin for Prestige. John Lee Hooker had R&B hits with a full electric band, like "Boom Boom," at the same time he was recording acoustic LPs; the liner notes to some of his early albums seem almost apologetic about his electric recordings, as if to infer that his acoustic albums were more authentic.

Several labels addressed the widening white audience for blues, including Arhoolie, Testament, and the Prestige/Riverside/Bluesville family. Often they brought original bluesmen of the '20s and '30s back to the studio after several decades of professional retirement, or even found some elderly acoustic blues singers who had never received the opportunities to record in the first place (phenomenons examined in more depth in a separate essay). Large festivals booked these artists and made live recordings of the events, the most notable of these being the Newport Folk Festival. And blues performers began to cross the Atlantic in large numbers for European tours, which both exposed the music on a whole new international scale, and gave the performers themselves a sense of just how much they were treasured, by an audience they hadn't quite expected to reach.

The initial impetus of the blues revival largely ignored contemporary electric performers, but the purist ethic couldn't survive for long. In England at least, the die had been cast back in 1958, when Muddy Waters first toured Britain. American bluesmen had already been touring the country earlier in the '50s, with assistance from British jazz and blues musicians like Chris Barber and Alexis Korner. Apparently British audiences conceived of the blues as a primarily acoustic medium as well, and were astounded when Waters showed up with an electric guitar. That proved too loud and brash for some British

listeners and critics, who might have saved themselves the shock if they had just listened to a few of Muddy's records, virtually all of which were Chicago electric blues.

Recalled Waters in James Rooney's *Bossmen*, "When I first went to England in '58 I didn't have no idea what was going on. I was touring with Chris Barber—a dixieland band. They thought I was a Big Bill Broonzy—which I wasn't. I had my amplifier and [pianist Otis] Spann and I was going to do a Chicago thing; we opened up in Leeds, England. I was definitely too loud for them then. The next morning we were in the headlines of the paper—'Screaming Guitar and Howling Piano.' That was when they were into the folk thing before the Rolling Stones."

When he made his next British tour in 1962, the tide had shifted. "I went back—took my acoustic with me—and everybody's hollering—'Where's your amplifier?' I said, 'When I was here before they didn't like my stuff.' But those English groups had picked up on my stuff and went wild with it. I said, 'I never know what's going on.' A bunch of those young kids came around. They could play. They'd pick up my guitar and fool with it. Then the Rolling Stones came out named after my song, you know, and recorded 'Just Make Love to Me' and the next I knew they were out there. And that's how people in the States really got to know who Muddy Waters was."

Young musicians like the Rolling Stones were making their own brand of rhythm & blues, inspired by artists like Muddy Waters; Mick Jagger and Keith Richard had discovered their mutual interest in the music, in fact, when Keith spotted Mick carrying a Chess Records album in a train. They and other early British Invasion bands like the Yardbirds, Animals, Them, and the Kinks covered many blues and R&B songs on their early records, evolving a form of rock & roll with heavy roots in the sources. Young British and American listeners were bound to be curious about the songs' original performers and writers, leading them back to the bluesmen and blueswomen themselves, many of whom were still in their primes.

Some purists have accused such bands of exploiting the music for their own ends, watering it down for a white teenage audience to achieve a commercial success that wouldn't have been possible with the real deal. It's an argument that doesn't wash for a lot of people. These groups were genuinely exciting and original, and quickly evolved from covering import records into writing their own material. Bands like the Beatles, Stones, and John Mayall's Bluesbreakers never made a secret of their influences, often taking time to publically praise and acknowledge their inspirations, and refusing to pretend that they were the first to be playing such music; Jagger once famously commented in an interview, "What's the point in listening to us doing 'I'm a King Bee' when you can hear Slim Harpo do it?" The Rolling Stones went as far as to record at Chess Studios during their first tour, and to have Howlin' Wolf perform with them on television in the mid-'60s.

By the mid-'60s, America was beginning to develop its own white blues-rockers, particularly in Chicago. Paul Butterfield led the best of these bands, which also included guitarists Michael Bloomfield and Elvin Bishop, as well as a black rhythm section of veterans from the Chicago blues/R&B scene. Also gigging in Chicago were harmonica player Charlie Musselwhite and (for a time) Steve Miller. In southern California, one of the leading collectors of rare blues records, Bob Hite, helped form one of the most successful blues-rock bands of the late '60s, Canned Heat.

The blues-rock acts are discussed in a separate piece; their importance to the blues revival was helping to focus attention not just on acoustic bluesmen, but on black electric blues bands and guitarists, many of whom had only been active for a decade or less, hardly qualifying for "revival." This also meant that such electric performers could now take a crack at the LP market, particularly if their 45 chart action wasn't so hot. Chess had already tried to sell Muddy Waters to the blues revival crowd with an album entitled *Folk Singer*, which actually wasn't much different from his prime electric material.

The Delmark label was one of the first to take the plunge into electric blues albums, with Junior Wells and Magic Sam. Wells' *Hoodoo Man Blues* (1965) is sometimes referred to as the first electric blues session conceived of as an album rather than a collection of tracks, and made no attempt to dilute the power or lower the volume for white listeners. Verve did the same with James Cotton, and Vanguard's excellent *The Blues Today!* series did much to present the blues as a living, thriving, often electric medium, not one that had to be presented as a sort of living museum piece in order to qualify for approval.

The albums in turn helped performers like Wells, Albert King, B.B. King, and Buddy Guy break into a whole new circuit that could find them sharing the bill with white rock bands, and playing to larger audiences that could include as many or more whites as blacks. Nor did their festival appearances have to be at folk events, which sometimes weren't eager to book electric acts; festivals devoted to blues, or giving equal weight to blues and jazz, began to appear, such as the Ann Arbor Blues Festival. Both enterprising small independents and large major labels belatedly became aware of the thousands of classic blues sides that were unavailable, leading to blues reissues programs that continue to expand to this day.

By the end of the '60s, blues was not a dominant force on the commercial market, but nobody was checking for vital signs either—many of its greatest musicians were performing to bigger audiences, and making better livelihoods, than they ever had. Since then, there's more or less constant talk of the blues making a comeback, or surging in popularity—but never talk of the blues dying. The blues, it seems, will never die—and never need to be "revived" again.

Ten Recommended Albums:

Various Artists, *Blues Masters, Vol. 7: Blues Revival* (Rhino)
Various Artists, *Blues at Newport: Newport Folk Festival 1959-64* (Vanguard)
Various Artists, *Chicago: The Blues Today! Vols. 1-3* (Vanguard)
Robert Pete Williams, *Angola Prisoner's Blues* (Arhoolie)
John Lee Hooker, *The Country Blues of John Lee Hooker* (Prestige)

Music Map

Blues Revival

Old-Time Bluesmen Play for White Audiences as Part of Folk Music Revival, 1960s	Electric Originators (Who Reach White Audiences)	White Guys Plug In (Early to Mid-'60s)
Son House • Skip James Mississippi John Hurt Lightnin' Hopkins John Lee Hooker	Muddy Waters • Howlin' Wolf Sonny Boy Williamson Albert King • B.B. King Freddie King • Slim Harpo Lightnin' Slim • Buddy Guy	Paul Butterfield Blues Band John Mayall's Bluesbreakers The Rolling Stones The Animals • The Yardbirds

Mance Lipscomb, *Texas Sharecropper & Songster* (Arhoolie)
Muddy Waters, *Folk Singer* (Chess)
The Rolling Stones, *The Rolling Stones (England's Newest Hitmakers)* (ABKCO)
The Paul Butterfield Blues Band, *The Paul Butterfield Blues Again* (Elektra)
John Mayall, *Bluesbreakers With Eric Clapton* (PolyGram)

—Richie Unterberger

The Blues Box Set

Some would say that the blues was never meant to be an elite kind of thing, displayed on the mantelpiece like some kind of trophy. With the widespread popularity of the box set in the '90s, though, that's what it sometimes becomes. The proliferation of box sets could be taken as an indication of the respect that classic rock, pop, and blues now generates in our culture (and marketplace). Not everyone, however, is certain that box sets are fulfilling their mission of offering the biggest bang for the buck.

Box sets have been a part of the music business for decades, although they were initially much more apt to be employed for classical recordings, or special projects like scholarly ethnomusicology documentaries. For the pop and rock audience, occasional box sets were produced (often in limited press runs) for artists with unusually devoted followings, like the Beatles, Elvis, and Brian Eno. This started to change in the mid-'80s, when a five-record live Bruce Springsteen box became a best seller. Around the same time, a Bob Dylan box set, *Biograph*, entered the Top 40, which probably helped convince labels that there was a viable market for multi-disc archival retrospectives.

Biograph also set a model of sorts for box set packages: some classic hits, some key album cuts, some rarities, and some previously unreleased material, as well as a lavish booklet. It took a while for this new strategy to trickle down to the blues world. After all, a very small percentage of record owners of any kind ever even buy box sets; an even smaller number buy them on anything approaching a regular basis. And, as we all know too well, the blues represents a very small share of the overall demographic that consumes music.

On the other hand, blues fans, at the risk of generalizing, take their music more seriously than the average Joe. Import companies such as Charly and Bear Family had realized this even before the mid-'80s, producing occasional box sets aimed squarely at the collector. And when they decided to go the box set route, they really went to town, often tracking down every item available, and raiding the vault for unreleased treasures and alternate takes.

When American companies began to issue blues boxes, they were considerably more selective, which is a mixed blessing. Many listeners, to be honest, lack the interest or patience to wade through every last B-side, or to hear successive alternate takes of a same song in a row. Box sets could be regarded as a selective weeding of an artist's oeuvre, in which only the very cream of the crop is bundled into a nifty package.

The Chess label in particular tapped into the market with enthusiasm, giving Muddy Waters, Howlin' Wolf, Willie Dixon, Chuck Berry, and Bo Diddley the box set treatment. There were also various artist box sets covering Chess material as a whole, an approach also employed by Specialty (which is now owned by Fantasy). Capricorn dug into the vaults of some somewhat obscure labels, such as Fire/Fury, Swingtime, Jewel/Paula, and Cobra. And the Robert Johnson box set (which was actually only two discs) was the surprise success story of the decade, selling several hundred thousand copies.

Not a great many blues heroes command a large enough following to make domestic box sets a viable proposition. Accordingly, plenty of two-disc packages are produced, sometimes in slip-cases, that fall just shy of bona fide "box" status. With the CD affording room for as much as 80 minutes a disc, however, such anthologies actually cram in as much music as would have fit on three or four average-length vinyl LPs. Chess, Legacy, and Rhino have been particularly active in establishing lines of double CDs; Capitol's blues series sometimes does this as well, and occasionally fits in three CDs to a standard-sized package, as they did with T-Bone Walker and John Lee Hooker.

Are there box sets out there that serve as introductions to the blues as a whole, or important blues styles? Not as many as you might think. Licensing hurdles, for one thing, are formidable obstacles to assembling material from many different labels in one

place; even if they can be overcome, labels may find that complicated process not worth the bother or the expense. Thus it is that most various artist boxes tend to be material from the same label. The Smithsonian has put together a couple of all-purpose-type introductions to the blues, although listeners with a reasonably sizable blues collection may find little there that they don't already own. The 15-volume *Blues Masters* series on Rhino is really the best project of that sort ever attempted, but it isn't available in the box form, except for a package containing the first five volumes. A box that had all 15 might be a desirable thing, but would certainly cost in the neighborhood of $200 or more.

In the event, however, a lot of boxes don't exactly turn out to be the last word. Labels often can't resist adding some hard-to-find tracks: B-sides, unreleased outtakes, live cuts, and the like. The presence of such material is usually quite welcome. The problem is that the collectors who covet such morsels almost inevitably own the bulk of the famous material on the box set already, sometimes several times over. And the more general fan, who's buying the box mostly for the "hits," doesn't really care about the unreleased material, or finds it something of a distraction from the main menu.

All of which leads the collector to pose some pretty tough, but merited, questions. Who is the typical box set—with its mixture of hits, rarities, and album cuts—really satisfying? The casual fan will be more likely to pick up a greatest hits collection, or one or two albums, and leave it at that. The completist isn't satisfied either; it's rare that a box will doggedly cover everything that an artist has released during a certain time period, or for a certain label. For that, the big league collector will still favor those obscure import companies that do the job right.

Listeners who are serious fans of an artist, but not unduly concerned with fancy packaging or remastering, find themselves caught in the middle. Enticed by rare and unreleased cuts that appear on almost every one of these sets—but rarely make up the majority of the content—they often find themselves paying quite a few dollars for the five to 15 cuts from a multi-disc box that they really want, and repurchasing quite a bit of music that they already have in their collections, and had no intention of buying again. And it's rare that a record company will accomodate these discerning listeners by issuing a separate collection that only contains the sought-after rarities. You could say that box sets give you access to more blues music than ever before—but at a higher price.

—Richie Unterberger

Blues Reissues

Taxes, global warming, geopolitical strife, overpopulation, pollution, invasion of privacy by super-sophisticated technologies…ah, but living in the '90s did have its small pleasures. One advantage that won't make as many headlines as the above calamaties is the increasing ease of collecting vintage blues music. It is no exaggeration to say that, on the whole, it's much easier to collect blues recordings of the '20s, or blues recordings of the '50s, now than it was when the music was first released. Not everything's been reissued, of course, but today's blues collector is offered (some would say confronted) with a dazzling variety of options that would have been unimaginable even 20 years ago. Dozens of companies in the U.S. and abroad offer an extensive line of blues reissues of all styles; some labels specialize in nothing but the blues.

Part of the reason that the blues needed to be "revived" in the '60s was that the music itself was so hard to come by on record. There's a bit of romance attached to the old days, when being a blues collector was akin to being a member of a secret society. Finding original blues 78s by the likes of Son House and Blind Lemon Jefferson involved searching through thrift stores, garage sales, warehouses, old radio station libraries, or canvassing neighborhoods in which the residents were likely to own the singles (and part with them for a monetary sum). Finding old singles of just a few years back by electric Chicago bluesmen was no easy task either. Some of the most active blues collectors became celebrities themselves, such as Bob Hite (who helped form Canned Heat), acoustic guitarist John Fahey, and Barry Hansen, who gained fame as syndicated radio personality Dr. Demento.

Getting there is sometimes half the fun in record collecting, and no doubt there was an element of excitement involved in diving into a dumpster on the edge of town that's missing these days when we drive down to the local mini-mall. Most blues fans, though, cannot spare the time for such pursuits, chained to more mundane realities like jobs and families. Nor, frankly, do most of us want to spend weekends (or weeks) on end in search of the original recordings. For the most part, you can't beat blues reissues for convenience, in terms of both time and money saved.

Ever since the LP was introduced, there have been various-artists and single-artist blues compilations. Many (if not most) Chess Records albums of the '50s and '60s were essentially compilations of singles, offering handy primers for those born too late to get the original 45s, or those who simply wanted the best of them in one place. But overall, the reissue programs of big and small labels in the '50s and '60s were sporadic, perhaps because they didn't always have an idea of how large the potential audience was, or to whom it should be marketed. Robert Johnson's vastly influential *King of the Delta Blues Singers* LP, for instance, appeared in the early '60s on Columbia as a roots-of-jazz sort of title.

The true impetus for comprehensive blues reissues programs came from unexpected sources. British and European blues fans had long been remarkably enthusiastic collectors, dating back to the early '60s, when English kids like Mick Jagger would actually mail-order Chess albums direct from the company itself in Chicago. In the '70s, British and European labels began to license and reissue vintage rock and blues in quantities that had been considered, for whatever reason, unrealistic in the land of the blues' origin, the U.S.

Charly was the initial leader of the field, given a leg up on the competition with its pipeline to the vast Sun catalog. They were soon joined by companies like Ace, Bear Family, Beat Goes On, Flyright, Document, and others. Often the releases were packaged and thoroughly annotated with a love and scholarship that had been conspicuously absent from many American productions of the type. There were even box sets, as well as previously unissued material that had never seen the light of day in the U.S.

This led to a frustrating situation for the many American consumers who wanted such albums. Most of the imports could be found with a little effort, in large stores or, failing that, specialty mail-order houses. The irony of needing to buy imports of such fundamentally American records was not lost on consumers or retailers, who shook their heads in half-disbelief at the necessity of needing to buy records from Europe or even Japan, usually at high prices, because U.S. labels wouldn't release the music. Due to some cumbersome legalities, at times American consumers found themselves unable to purchase material that was easily available to Japanese or European consumers, but could not be legally imported into the States.

The U.S., it should be noted, was not totally inactive in the blues reissue arena. Rhino, the leading American reissue company, produced occasional classy packages for artists like Slim Harpo; Arhoolie arranged for the re-release of some very obscure blues of all kinds. Yazoo was (and remains) incredibly active in the field of pre-World War II music, to the point where if any country or old-time blues packages were produced in the States, it seemed like a better-than-even bet that it would bear the Yazoo imprint.

Labels like Yazoo, Document, and Matchbox deserve a Red Badge of Courage of sorts for diving so deep into a field that will never yield big commercial returns. The companies are catering to the very specialized collector to offer music that is both out of fashion, and unable to compete with other reissues in terms of sound quality. Much of the material on their albums is remastered from existing copies of old 78s in dedicated archivists' collections, the source tapes (if there were any to begin with) having long vanished. This means that many modern day listeners are simply unable to put up with the relatively primitive audio and the remaining scratches and hisses, although modern CD technology has paved the way for some surprisingly clear transfers.

Beginning in the late '80s, the explosion of CD technology (which has rendered new vinyl releases all but obsolete) has led to a corresponding explosion in the reissue market. The logic behind this is quirky, but basically it seems as though many labels realized that many listeners were interesting in "upgrading" their scratchy vinyl records with CDs of the same material. American labels in particular also realized that many consumers were interested in buying albums and compilations of artists whose work had lingered out of print for quite some time.

Thus they began reissuing their own back catalog in addition to licensing it, eventually creating entire subsidiaries like Legacy and Capitol Blues for that purpose. Relative to new artists, the production, royalty, and promotion costs on reissues were minimal. Many of these reissues added the further enticements of additional bonus tracks (sometimes unreleased, sometimes from rare non-LP singles), remastering and remixing, and scholarly liner notes. For artists with wide appeal, these factors were often combined into box sets (see separate essay).

The watershed event that led to the windfall of blues reissues is easy to pinpoint. In 1990, Columbia/Legacy released a double-CD box set of Robert Johnson recordings that, to the shock of everyone, sold about half a million copies. Here was undeniable proof that blues fans would support quality reissues in force, even old ones with relatively raunchy fidelity. Very few blues reissues could approach such sales figures—Robert Johnson, after all, has been mythologized to death, and praised to the heavens by numerous rock stars like Eric Clapton and Keith Richard. But it probably did serve as evidence that old blues reissues stood a very good chance of accumulating a modest profit, or at least breaking even.

Columbia/Legacy itself embarked on a lengthy series of reissues that continues to the present, including some names that remain pretty obscure to pop audiences (Bukka White, Blind Willie Johnson, Blind Boy Fuller), and thematic anthologies devoted to the slide guitar and topical blues. The label also released no less than five Bessie Smith compilations as the kind of series that had historically only been undertaken by small foreign companies.

Another welcome development of the CD age has been the reactivation of most of the Chess catalog. MCA, indeed, produced several box sets for the greatest blues stars, as well as entire boxes showcasing the output of what was probably the greatest blues label of all time. Capricorn, which had experienced its greatest success as the home of the Allman Brothers, arranged for box sets spotlighting the contributions of smaller but significant labels to the blues, such as Fire/Fury, Jewel/Paula, Cobra, and Swingtime.

There's no question that CD technology has done much to increase the availability of vintage blues music. Whether it's the best format to hear the music, however, remains a hot matter of debate among fans and critics, despite the clarity of sound that can be achieved with state-of-the-art transfers from tape and vinyl.

Rock and R&B historian Charlie Gilliett, for instance, writes in *The Sound of the City* that "although compilations on CD provide a convenient way for the armchair listener to hear music from another ear, it's important to bear in mind that not all of them manage to recapture the true experience of how the music sounded at the time. The deep and wide grooves of 78 rpm singles generated a big, warm sound which progressively disappeared with each successive format—45 rpm singles, 33 rpm albums, and digitally mastered CDs all tended to favor higher frequencies, at the expense of the 'bottom end.' Played through the huge speakers of jukeboxes, 78s delivered a massive sound which can only be vaguely approximated by CDs on a domestic hi-fi or portable system. Owners of Elvis' 78 rpm singles on Sun justifiably believe that no other format has come close to reproducing their impact. It may help to turn up the bass on your amp, but you'll never quite get there."

"When 45 rpm singles became the standard format for pop music, and the focus of mastering engineers shifted from jukeboxes to radio, it became common practice to vari-speed tapes to raise the tempo, add compression to make records seem louder, and boost treble frequencies to enable them to cut through on poor quality transistor radios. Sometimes records which sounded terrific on the radio could be hard to bear on a good home system, where their harsh, brittle power seemed inappropriate. So now, when mastering compilations of these old records, engineers have to strike a balance between acknowledging their original function while seeking to meet a new generation's expectations of a clean, clear sound from CDs. In general, there's a tendency for most recordings to sound more 'polite' on CD, and sometimes it can be hard to understand why some tracks were ever regarded as being exciting. There's no absolute rule-sometimes the CD version delivers a presence and warmth that had never been caught on vinyl; but often, CDs fail to recapture the hard-to-describe 'earthy' qualities present on the microgroove pressings."

Should you have a lot of money and time, a large network of collector-oriented stores, magazines, and swap meets still exists that caters to the vinyl collector, even if the market is small potatoes compared to the billions of units shifted at most retail outlets. But even recent CD blues reissues can be hard to find at the store, particularly if you don't live in a big metropolis. For that purpose, there are several mail-order companies that have large catalogs of blues and other roots music, two of the most prominent being Down Home Music and Midnight Records.

For those who want to dive into the world of blues reissues with gusto, but don't know quite where to start, one series can be recommended above all others. Rhino's 18-volume *Blues Masters* provides well-chosen and well-annotated overviews of the most important major blues styles, including Mississippi Delta blues, slide guitar, jump blues, Memphis blues, blues roots, classic blues women, Texas blues, harmonica blues, and Chicago blues. As the cliché goes, it's both informative and enjoyable, for the novice and the well-traveled blues fan alike. The series can serve both as a basic collection of classic blues, and as a port of entry that will help listeners discover their favorite styles and performers.

—Richie Unterberger

The Blues on Film

While there's a fair amount of blues on film from the past and present, blues fans have a less bountiful selection of goodies to choose from than rock and jazz lovers. The blues, having usually lurked at the commercial margins, has gotten less media exposure than some other forms of popular music. That means less cameras whirring at both television studios and live festivals; it also means less serious documentaries about the subject.

But the number of blues film clips may surprise you. In the early days of the music business, movie studios occasionally filmed musical shorts (called "soundies" for a time) that would run in theaters, as sort of Stone Age precursors to MTV. One of the first of these was a short film starring Bessie Smith that was built around her performance of the theme song, "St. Louis Blues." The blues revival of the '60s found many of the rediscovered acoustic bluesmen being filmed for the first time, at folk festivals, by folklorists, or by television companies such as the BBC and PBS. As the blues assumes its rightful place as a pillar of American culture, there will no doubt be more and more historical documentaries of the music.

A trip to the video store (or, for that matter, a large music retail store) often yields a decent selection of blues videos to choose from, especially if you live in an urban area or university town. Those without access to these resources can still, for a larger cash outlay, order the videos themselves via roots music mail-order services such as Down Home Music. There are already so many blues videos that a comprehensive rundown is impossible to complete in a few paragraphs. Here we'll simply point readers to some of the best sources.

The two companies with the largest blues video catalogs are Vestapol and Yazoo. Vestapol's line is oriented toward the guitar player, with entire collections of clips for country blues guitar, Texas blues, and bottleneck guitar. Contrary to the impression you might get from a catalog listing, these are not instructional videos, but actual footage of the bluesmen and blueswomen themselves in performance. The appeal is not limited to guitar players (though they can certainly find much to admire); it's geared toward general blues fans, giving them a chance to watch their heroes in action.

There is an unavoidably inconsistent quality about the compilations, due to the varying nature of the sources. A sterling color clip from the BBC lies shoulder-to-shoulder, for instance, with grainy black-and-white footage in somebody's rundown kitchen (which can have an admitted charm all its own). The performances can vary as well; the elderly blues rediscoveries of the '60s can play as well as they did in their prime or, due to failing health, turn in performances that may have been best withheld from circulation, even given the rarity of clips in the field.

But this shouldn't dissuade blues enthusiasts from picking up Vestapol compilations, which are assembled with care. Each one is selected to ensure a diversity of content, and includes detailed liner notes about the musicians and the clips. Certainly the best of them are riveting; a trance-like John Lee Hooker playing solo, for instance, or a Swedish TV clip of Josh White suavely sticking a cigarette behind his ear as he plays. There are also entire compilations devoted to the work of major figures like Hooker, Albert King, and Freddie King. The Freddie King compilation *The Beat!!* is especially sweet, gathering about a dozen vintage color live film clips from a Texas-based R&B/soul TV show of the mid-'60s. (Vestapol also has several videos of jazz guitar players available.)

Yazoo is a name that most blues collectors associate with reissues of ancient country blues from the '20s and '30s. Their video line is more diverse than one might expect; indeed, it almost has to be, as there are few blues clips from the '20s and '30s of the kind of performers that Yazoo favors. The accent is still on country blues, with entire videos devoted to Furry Lewis, Son House, Big Joe Williams, and Mississippi Fred McDowell. More modern performers, however, are not ignored; there are also anthologies for Muddy Waters, John Lee Hooker, and Lightnin' Hopkins.

If you're still looking for more vintage film clips after exhausting the Vestapol and Yazoo catalog, you might want to try Rhino's two *Blues Masters* volumes. Companion pieces of sorts to the excellent 18-volume CD series of the same name, this unavoidably comes up short quantity-wise when stacked against the discs. But does offer footage of some of the greats, including Leadbelly, Muddy Waters, Buddy Guy, B.B. King, and less expected figures like Mamie Smith, Roy Milton, and Jimmy Rushing. There is also BMG's similar *Bluesland*, affiliated with a blues history book of the same name.

Considering that only two photos of Robert Johnson have ever been circulated (and that was only after years of searching), it's ironic that there is now a video based around his work, *Search for Robert Johnson* (SMV). As the title implies, this is not so much a standard documentary (no footage, after all, exists) as a look into his environment, sources, and the few recollections we have been granted by his associates, narrated by John Hammond. Another video that delves into Mississippi deep blues is titled, logically enough, *Deep Blues*. Although critic Robert Palmer authored an excellent book by the name in the early '80s, and is also involved in the video, this is not really a companion piece, but a look at Mississippi blues as it was played in the early '90s. Accompanied by, of all people, ex-Eurythmic Dave Stewart, Palmer spotlights the kind of contemporary, electric juke joint Delta performers that have surfaced on the Fat Possum label, including Junior Kimbrough and R.L. Burnside.

For modern blues, there are occasional releases of concerts by big names such as B.B. King and Buddy Guy, plus a mid-'90s PBS history of the blues, although the subject merits more than the three parts that the series allotted to it.

The milieu of the blues has yet to translate convincingly into fictional feature-length film treatments, despite the abundant fascinating source material. Maybe that's for the best; *Crossroads*, a mid-'80s Hollywood movie based around some aspects of the Robert Johnson legend, enraged purists even as it helped point some listeners who had been unaware of Mississippi Delta blues to the authentic thing. That film was scored by Ry Cooder, who has ensured that elements of traditional acoustic blues are conveyed to millions via his prolific soundtrack work. One movie worth keeping an eye out for that does not deal with the blues specifically, but does project aspects of the Southern black experience that the blues details, is *Sounder*, with a soundtrack by Taj Mahal (who also has a small role in the film).

—Richie Unterberger

Focus on the Blues Harmonica

The harmonica has secured an enduring place in American music and a very special and central place in the blues.

Its history, as related in *A Brief History of the Harmonica*, distributed by the Hohner Company, and in *America's Harp*, an article by Michael Licht, is as follows. The harmonica, or mouth harp, is one of the family of free-reed instruments—those which create a tone by the vibration of reeds which do not strike the frame to which they are attached. This free-reed concept led to the development of the Sheng (sublime voice), said to be invented in 3,000 BC by the Chinese empress Nyn-Kwa, and brought by a traveler to Western Europe in the 17th century. The Sheng is the earliest expression of the principle later applied to such instruments as the concertina and harmonica.

The prototype of the instrument in its present state was invented in 1821 by Christian Friedrich Ludwig Buschmann, a 16-year-old German clockmaker who put 15 pitch pipes together, and called it a "mund-eaoline" (mouth-harp). Another clockmaker, Christian Messner, learned how to make the instruments and sold them on the side to other clockmakers.

In 1857, at 24 years of age, Matthias Hohner bought one and decided to produce it commercially, making 650 of them the first year.

He was made the mayor of his home town of Trossingen which soon became the harmonica capital of the world. In 1932 his sons founded the State Music College of Trossingen, where harmonica, accordion, piano, and violin are still taught today. This school has graduated 3,000 harmonica players certified to teach the instrument.

Sometime before the outbreak of the Civil War, Hohner sent a few harmonicas to cousins who had emigrated to the United States, and they found the instrument to be extremely popular there. During the Civil War, many soldiers on both sides had one, and along with peddlers and immigrants, helped spread the instrument throughout the country.

By the end of the century, America was purchasing more than half of the ten million instruments being manufactured in Germany every year. The Marine Band harmonica, still widely popular today, was introduced in 1896 when it sold for 50 cents. The harmonica was well on its way to becoming the most popular instrument in America's history.

The first steps towards blues stylings on the harmonica must have resulted from attempts at what the 19th century classical musician might have termed "programmatic music"—that is, music that attempted to paint a sound-picture. The unique sound potential of the harmonica enabled the more clever players to imitate many of the sounds that surrounded them everyday.

Trains, for example, have inspired musicians of all eras. Arthur Honneger, the Swiss composer, created an orchestral train in his Pacific 231, while Duke Ellington created one for his orchestra in the "Happy Go Lucky Local." "The Orange Blossom Special" is a standard showcase tune for country fiddlers and banjo pickers, while "Honky Tonk Train Blues" by Meade "Lux" Lewis remains one of the most famous of all boogie-woogie piano compositions. Singer/guitarist Bukka White got on track with his famous Panama Limited, which he performed in a bottleneck style.

In the hands of a master, however, the harmonica creates the most vivid portrait of all, due to its capacities for tone-bending and chordal rhythm. Some of the first recorded and best examples available on record are Palmer McAbee's "Railroad Piece," Freeman Stowers' "Railroad Blues" and DeFord Bailey's "Dixie Flyer Blues." Of the many Library of Congress field recordings of train tunes, examples by Ace Johnson and Richard Amerson are extraordinary. Countless numbers of harmonica players must have been expert at imitating trains, but the vast majority of them were never recorded either by folklorists or commercial record companies.

Trains were not the only subjects of these folk tone-poems, however. There were "mama blues," in which the harmonica imitated a baby calling out "mama" or "I want my mama"; " fox chases" that depicted these ritualistic events step-by-step, complete with vocal yelps and descriptive interjections; vignettes of escaped convicts being hunted down by the dogs, as well as pure barnyard scenes with animal sounds of all varieties fill the harmonica repertory—some with uncanny realism.

The connection between this rural impressionism and the origin of what we recognize as blues-harp style lies in the way in the instrument is constructed and played. The ten-hole diatonic harmonica, the most common of the blues harmonicas, produces a major chord in the key of the harmonica when the holes are blown, and a dominant ninth chord in that same key when the holes are drawn. And, to put it simply, the lower part of the instrument is easier to manipulate when drawn, the upper when blown. That is, when each of the four lowest holes is drawn in a deflected manner, the tone bends and the pitch slides lower; and, when each of the highest four holes is blown in a deflected manner the pitch will also slide lower.

In addition to this, the players discovered that although each harmonica was pitched in a specific key, wherein the tonic or central pitch was located on the number one hole blow, it could be used effectively for other keys by using a different sound hole—blow or draw—as the tonic. Each key created a very different effect or mode that could be used for the purpose of varying the color. These alternative playing modes have become known as positions, of which there are four: straight harp or first position (C harp plays in the key of C); cross-harp or second position (C harp plays in key of G); third position (C Harp plays in key of D); and fourth position (C Harp plays in key of E). Other positions are used—but far less frequently.

Because the players found the lowest registers to be the most expressive, especially for the purposes of mimicry, they found themselves favoring the lowest holes drawn; especially number two, which became the central tone, or tonic. This meant that they were blowing their C Harp in the key of G—a perfect fifth higher than the actual key of the harp. This position produced cross-harp style, or second position.

First position, also known as straight-harp, consists of playing in the actual key of the harmonica, where the lowest hole (number one) when blown becomes tonic, and we play the C harp in the key of C. In this position the expressive high register is exploited. The most well-known master of this position is Jimmy Reed. Straight harp is also used by harmonica players to improvise over ragtime changes and for more folk-style melodies. That familiar, low, wailing sound, however, is an almost certain indication of cross-harp style.

Third position is achieved by making the lowest or first hole draw the tonic or central pitch; the C harp is played in the key of D. Little Walter is a master of third position and used it for a number of his instrumentals. The hallmark of third position is a very unusual and jazzy minor 13th chord with added 11th that is produced when the holes are drawn. This sound is unforgettable.

Most rarely, a fourth position can be achieved by making the number two hole blow the tonic; that is, playing our C harp in the key of E.

To the beginner this must be confusing, as it must have been for the first players who discovered these positions as well as for their guitar or piano-playing partners. There is a great example on record of a guitar and harmonica seemingly trying to get into the same key, as the guitar player was playing in the actual key of the harp while the harp player was playing in second position. Not until the very end of the tune were they finally in the same key ("Just It," *Harmonicas Unlimited*).

Harmonica players of classical and jazz music, however, obtain different keys and foreign tones to the key by using a chromatic harmonica rather than a diatonic one. A chromatic harp has a button on the side that when pushed raises the pitch of every blown or drawn tone one half-step. Larry Adler and John Sebastian Sr. are two modern-day classic masters, while Toots Thielemans is probably the greatest jazz and pop player well-known today. Blues players use the chromatic mostly in second or third position, in the same manner as the diatonic, to achieve a deep chordal timbre impossible to get on the smaller diatonic model. Bending is tougher, though, on the more sturdy chromatic type. Blues artists have been known to use two or more harps on the same tune—and, conversely, to use the same key harp for tunes pitched in different keys. Obviously, the players' talent, taste, and creativity are tested here.

The harmonica was for many reasons a very natural choice for Southern African-Americans in the developmental stages of the blues. It was small, inexpensive, durable, portable, and easy for the beginner to approach. Musically, it provided a modern and convenient substitute for the quills, an instrument made of three bound pieces of cane; and it was cheaper and easier to play than the violin—whose place in blues the harmonica usurped. In addition, it had the ability to mimic everything from the human voice to trains, animals, and whistling, as well as the Cajun concertina, and the sophisticated stylings of the jazz-aged clarinet and cornet.

One could get a tremendous variety of tone color, attack, vibrato, tremelo, and glissando, not to mention effects made by manipulating the hand used to cup the harmonica. Moreover, it provided three definite registers, was equally expressive chordally and melodically, and covered the entire dynamic range from a whisper to a shout—quite an arsenal for the size and money.

There must have been an enormous number of African-Americans playing the harmonica by the turn of the 20th century, but not until 1924 do we get our first harmonica blues on record. Johnny Watson, known as Daddy Stovepipe, recorded "Sundown Blues" that year—demonstrating a sort of melodic/folky sound using straight or first position harp for fills and solos around his vocals. If various written accounts are true of this amazing performer, born in 1867, we find him touring with the Rabbit Foot Minstrels in the early 1900s, playing for tips in Mexico during the Depression, with zydeco bands in Texas by the end of the '30s, and on Chicago's Maxwell Street from the early '40s until his death in 1963.

Among the very finest players who recorded in or before 1930 were Robert Cooksey, Chuck Darling, and Blues Birdhead. Cooksey was a master of the vaudeville sound which he executed in a unique, virtuosic style. He recorded often with his partner Bobby Leecan through the '20s and '30s. Chuck Darling was a ragtime virtuoso whose complex lines wove effortlessly through all registers. James Simons, known also as Blues Birdhead or Harmonica Tim, is perhaps the best example of how the diatonic harp functioned as a jazz instrument in the early days of that music. His phrasing and timbre are a cross between those of Louis Armstrong and Johnny Dodds vintage 1928. It is amazing to hear such an advanced jazz concept executed perfectly on this instrument, and one wonders how it could be that this master recorded only once.

The very first wailing, cross-harp style player to record solo seems to have been the Alabaman Jaybird Coleman, who made some 20 sides between 1927 and 1930. In his style we hear vestiges of the field holler and work song which were building blocks of the blues; and, through his music, we get an unadulterated and impassioned sense of the meaning of the blues in the South during the '20s. Jaybird entertained the troops during World War I, after which he toured the South with Big Joe Williams as part of the Rabbit Foot Minstrels show. He also toured with the Birmingham Jug Band, but seems to have spent a great deal of his time playing locally in the Birmingham/Bessemer, AL, region until he moved to West Memphis in 1949, the year before his death. Jaybird brought his unmistakable style to a large number of major Southern cities, inspiring and influencing many of the harp players of his era. It is perhaps one of blues' greatest ironies that he was managed in 1929 by the Ku Klux Klan.

The seeds of the modern day blues harp that reached fruition in the golden era of mid-'50s Chicago were sown in the American musical mecca of Memphis, TN. That city, which has played such a crucial role in almost every genre of indigenous American music, boasted the simultaneous presences of Noah Lewis, Jaybird Coleman, Will Shade, Jed Davenport, Hammie Nixon, John Lee "Sonny Boy" Williamson, and Big Walter Horton, all—off and on—between the years of 1925 and 1930. It must have been a boiling pot of musical ideas as these musicians, some of them not more than children at the time, played on the streets, in Handy Park, in clubs, with jug and jazz bands, and as solo attractions.

As reported in *Memphis Blues and Jug Bands*, by Bengt Olsson, jug bands probably started in Louisville and were active there from around 1915. By the early '30s there were at least six bands in Memphis. The two standout examples were the Memphis Jug Band with Will Shade on harp, and Gus Cannon's Jug Stompers with Noah Lewis on harp.

Noah Lewis was discovered in Ripley, TN, by guitar and banjo player Gus Cannon, and it said that his harmonica playing was unparalleled at the time. As many masters of the day, he was able to play two harps at one time—one with his nose. His style is unique and could be said to represent a consummation of the early chordal-melodic technique being practiced in the South for many years. His playing displays a wealth of ideas, always executed to perfection. His recordings show him to be equally at home as part of a duo, a larger ensemble, or as a solo. Unfortunately, no recordings seem to be available by the older musicians from whom he learned.

Will Shade before founding the Memphis Jug Band in 1925, played with Furry Lewis and various Medicine shows. After touring with the Memphis Jug Band he joined the Ma Rainey show in Indiana in 1931, and later recorded under his own name in Chicago as well as with Little Buddy Doyle. Probably his most memorable tune is "Jug Band Waltz," which he recorded with the Memphis Jug Band in 1928. His unique style is in the same general mold as Noah Lewis but his tone is darker and often he is more melodic.

Jed Davenport, on the other hand, had a distinctively wilder sound than his two contemporaries, often using a "flutter-tongue" technique that lent a metallic edge to his lines. Being flashy and dynamic, he was among the most exciting players of his time. He also recorded with Memphis Minnie and with some local Memphis jazz bands in the early '30s, and played on the streets of Memphis off and on through the '60s. There can be no doubt that these three players represented the models of excellence for all aspiring bluesmen fortunate enough to have heard them.

If we were to search for one talent that linked this wonderful chordal-melodic style to the horn-style pioneered in the 1930s, we might find Hammie Nixon who actually learned from Noah Lewis and taught John Lee "Sonny Boy" Williamson.

Hammie Nixon was the perfect musical counterpart for the traditional blues guitarist/singer. He had a great talent for filling the sound while never covering it. Perhaps this expertise defeated a possible career as a leader, for he was always the sideman. He became known for his work with Little Buddy Doyle, Son Bonds, Yank Rachell, and especially with Sleepy John Estes with whom he shared a partnership lasting over 50 years. It could be that Hammie recognized his niche, as did others, and that his career was perfectly suited to his talent. He had a unique sense of how to blow lines behind the singer's verses as sort of an obbligato trumpet, spinning a fragile, contrapuntal web that surrounded and enhanced the overall sound.

Before Nixon joined Sleepy John Estes, Noah Lewis was Estes' partner, and Nixon learned much by hearing and watching the master at work. Through the '20s and '30s, he practiced his trade on the streets and at parties and picnics, finding just the right riff or chordal touch to complement each song. According to David Evans (notes to Nixon's *Tappin' That Thing* LP released on High Water in the mid-'80s), Nixon played often in Brownsville, TN, a town that boasted a rich musical life for the blues musician throughout the '30s.

There was much work available for a good player, and many travelled there to take advantage of the opportunities—among them Rice Miller (Sonny Boy Williamson [II]), Big Joe Williams, and John Lee Williamson (Sonny Boy Williamson [I]). It was perhaps in Brownsville that the next link of the chain was forged, as John Lee Williamson absorbed the style of Hammie Nixon leaning more heavily on the melodic side, discarding much of the chordal work, and redoing this rural mix into a concept which he was to pioneer in Chicago in just a few years—a concept that was to shape the blues harp style into what it is a half century later.

It is necessary to digress at this point to consider the work of two very special and exceptional virtuosi: DeFord Bailey and his disciple, Sonny Terry.

Although there were many fine harp players active between the wars, the most influential and widely known was unquestionably DeFord Bailey, the Harmonica Wizard. As told by Bengt Olsson in his May-June 1975 *Living Blues* article, "The Grand Ole Opry's DeFord Bailey," Bailey's story is as unique as any in all of music. In spite of his color, he was a featured performer in the Grand Ole Opry, playing in 48 out of 52 Opry broadcasts—twice as many as any other performer. Between 1925 and 1941, Bailey was heard every Saturday night playing virtuosic train tunes, blues, and all sorts of harmonica showcase instrumentals, inspiring players around the country—white and black. Although there was more than just a touch of the backwoods influence in DeFord's playing (he was self-taught and learned as a child by imitating all of the animal and train sounds that he knew), his style was polished to the point of utter perfection—each original tune unique, each a gem. In addition to his astounding appearances on the Opry, Bailey was also the focus of the first major recording project in Nashville, TN and, during the years 1927-1928, he recorded 11 tunes that were to set the standard for harmonica display pieces in recorded American blues.

Sonny Terry was 11 years younger than DeFord Bailey and was one of his unnumberable admirers. Using the fox chases, train tunes, and original blues instrumentals as models, the younger player formed a basis for a personal style that would become world famous.

He began as a young child playing buck dances in his native Georgia, and then moved to the streets of North Carolina. He later toured as solist with Doc Bizell's Medicine Show before teaming with Blind Boy Fuller in 1934. His career breakthrough occurred when the great American producer John Hammond engaged him in New York City to participate in the From Spirituals to Swing concert in 1938 at Carnegie Hall.

In 1939 he met Brownie McGhee and there began one of the most famous musical partnerships in all of blues or, for that matter, all of American music. During the next 45 years, Sonny Terry & Brownie McGhee played concerts, clubs, and festivals. They appeared on radio, television, and motion pictures, making countless recordings together with other players, and as solo performers.

Sonny Terry was a tremendously influential player of brilliance whose career and talent could rival almost any other player in the history of blues. He was the finest exponent of the rural, chordal-rhythmic style characterized by whoops and hollers and driving chordal work. The vocal and harp work are so closely knit that one can hardly tell where one starts and the other takes over. He commands a wide variety of tone color and vibrato and an impeccable sense of timing—all of which combine to make his work instantly indentifiable and among the very best examples of this style of blues harp.

Prior to 1925, players were learning primarily by imitating the sounds of their surroundings, from older musicians who played in their area, by the instrumental styles heard on recorings, and from the music heard in the traveling shows such as the Rabbit Foot Minstrels.

However, when DeFord Bailey began his radio career in Nashville, he initiated an entirely new channel through which musicians would be influenced. James Cotton remembers, for example, that Rice Miller (Sonny Boy Williamson [II]) would talk of hearing

DeFord Bailey on the radio. In the early '50s in Memphis, Cotton was able to hear blues on radio from noon until well into the night. And, in fact, he first became seriously interested in the harmonica after hearing Sonny Boy Williamson [II] on KFFA radio in the mid-'40s.

These beginnings of blues on radio, along with the dissemination of race records featuring contemporary harp styles, and the subsequent invention of the jukebox—all in conjunction with the snowballing effects of the first great migration of African-Americans to the north, (as detailed by Mike Rowe in his *Chicago Blues: The City and the Music*), created an environment conducive to the assimilation of all existing styles of blues harp. The stage was set for the next plateau of growth for the instrument, as it soon would be participating in equal terms with the more urban piano and guitar stylings—and, later, with the full rhythm sections of the bands of the northern cities—especially Chicago.

Perhaps the finest Southern harp player to become an integral part of the modern professional Chicago blues scene was William "Jazz" Gillum, who traveled from Greenwood, MS, to Chicago in 1923, beginning an active career that was to last until his death in 1966. He recorded more than 100 tunes on the Bluebird and Victor labels between 1934 and 1950, using some of the finest sidemen in Chicago including Big Bill Broonzy, Blind John Davis and Ransom Knowling.

Gillum was at his best in a folksy or ragtime situation when he used the high end of the harmonica in first position (straight harp). Although he was not in the same class as Blues Birdhead or Chuck Darling he was a respectable singer and player who, nonetheless, enjoyed great success.

Gillum's influence, or lack of it, on the younger players, must be evaluated against the backdrop of the Chicago blues world of the '20s and '30s. The Jazz Age placed blues in a collateral position; and, as a result, jazzmen playing in the contemporary ragtime vein were often engaged for blues sessions. The great Ma Rainey for example, recorded with Tampa Red on some occasions and with jazz bands on others. As with many instrumentalists of the day, these classic blues singers can properly be regarded as belonging to either genre.

Players such as the legendary guitarist/singer Blind Blake found Chicago jazz to be a natural extension of their syncopated East Coast style. Blake often recorded with jazz horn players and singers; and, although it is brilliant work, it is not strictly blues. A real dichotomy of style exists in the work of guitarist/singer/pianist Lonnie Johnson who was perhaps the only bluesman who could hold his own with the greatest jazzman of the day, Louis Armstrong, while still functioning as a bluesman on other occasions. Some other startling combinations were down-home Mississippi bluesmen Ishman Bracey and Tommy Johnson, both of whom were recorded with clarinetist Ernest "Kid" Michall of the Nehi Boys.

Because the vast marjoity of bluesmen lacked either the skill or inclination to play in the demanding contemporary jazz style, some resorted to a sort of comic—or hokum—style—replete with nonsense lyrics, kazoos (sometimes called jazzhorns), washboards, and catchy choruses occurring over the same repetitive set of ragtime chord changes. They sounded like jug bands minus jug and soul, and their function was simply to entertain. Although a few exceptionally talented artists such as Tampa Red were able to transcend this limited style, most, including Jazz Gillum were not. His limitations were most obvious when he played in a "down-home" style using second position (cross-harp), and he seems to have had very little effect—if any—on the subsequent blues harp players in Chicago.

This entertainment-oriented strain of early urban blues in Chicago is documented excellently in Mike Rowe's aforementioned classic. He points out that "the urban blues were altogether more sophisticated—lighter in texture with the emotional power turned down and the beat turned up." And that, "It was probably a reaction to the trauma of the Depression years that the emphasis was more on entertainment." In addition, he describes a scene controlled almost entirely by Lester Rose, a white businessman who recorded almost every bluesman of note in Chicago. Big Bill Broonzy, Tampa Red, Jazz Gillum, Big Joe Williams, Memphis Minnie, Lonnie Johnson, and John Lee "Sonny Boy" Williamson, among others, formed a remarkable reservoir of talent used over and over again in various combinations throughout the '30s and '40s on the Bluebird label as fodder for innumerable blues hits based on the proven "formula." Although this is a one-sided look at the entrepreneur, it paints a vivid portrait of the same old sound issuing from Chicago during these years.

In spite of the application of this assembly-line production technique, certain talents were of such magnitude that they seemed to jump out of their prescribed setting. One such talent was John Lee "Sonny Boy" Williamson from Jackson, TN—the father of the modern blues harp style. John Lee Williamson's role in the evolution of the style can be compared to that of jazz pianist Earl Hines who is credited with developing the "trumpet-style" right hand; or later, to pianist Bud Powell who expressed the bop style concepts of Charlie Parker and Dizzy Gillespie through his right-hand work. Like these two great pianists, Williamson created a strongly melodic potential for an instrument bound mostly to a chordal or subordinate role. He transformed the harp into a dynamic lead voice.

Williamson, the original Sonny Boy, played straight and cross-harp styles, ragtime-type tunes, and straight blues—all with enormous conviction and great style. His vocals were equally impressive, employing expressive vibrato and changing timbre. He used formula-like fills and cadence figures to frame his lines, and switched freely from a chordally dominated style to a predominantly single-note style—with all possible graduations between these two stylistic poles. He used sustained tones, short repeated notes and five-six note motives with great intelligence and care and might well have been the first harp player to construct solos consistently in this manner.

One truly amazing characteristic of Williamson's music is that in it, one hears not only the past (shades of Noah Lewis and Hammie Nixon are always present), but also the

future. One hears some of the architecture of Little Walter the vocal and instrumental phrasing of the second Sonny Boy (Rice Miller), and the tone of Big Walter Horton—all virtually implied by the older musician's vocal and instrumental innovations. In addition, Williamson was the first of a long and distinguished modern line of accomplished singer/ harp players who performed their own tunes.

He began his recording career in Chicago in 1937 with a series of records that featured him fronting his own group and performing as a sideman with Big Joe Williams. He was enormously popular and successful but, tragically, was murdered one night in 1948 while walking home from a performance at the Plantation Club in Chicago. His career must be regarded as one of the most significant phases in the development of blues harp style.

Certain contemporary factors converged to exert a tremendous influence on blues music during the '40s. Perhaps the most significant of these was the so-called Petrillo Ban of 1942. Because James C. Petrillo, president of the Musicians Union, saw recordings and juke boxes as dire threats to the livelihood of musicians, he banned all union members from recording. "This and the strict rationing of shellac" (used for record production), recounts Paul Oliver in his *The Story of the Blues*, "effectively stopped the recording of blues." This two-year ban served to take blues out of the studio and into the clubs and streets where it was infused with new life.

In addition, another peak migration period of blacks to the north was creating a bigger audience for blues; and a grassroots talent-search by the new independent label owners in Chicago was providing encouragement and work for the younger players.

From the mid-'40s there collected in Chicago a nucleus of harp players whose work, based at least partially on that of John Lee Williamson constituted a new style that gained more and more definition as the strictures of the Melrose empire loosened and independent record labels began to appear. Maxwell Street served as the perfect breeding ground for these avant-gardists who jammed there regularly, exchanging ideas and strutting their stuff. In addition, the South Side was dotted with small clubs that seemed to unite the black community, serving as both a sweet reminder of the good side of what many of them had left behind, as well as a musical signpost towards the future. Although the lines of development that these Chicago-based artists were pursuing were very different from the directions being taken by the players based in the South, Junior Wells refuses to think of it as a "city style." Wells is quoted as saying: "We had a country sound, but we also were getting into a different type thing. I wouldn't call it a city-type thing, I would just say we had learned some new riffs to put into the thing and it was more of an uptempo sound. We were listening to different type records."

It was in Chicago that the Brownsville, Helena, and Memphis styles coalesced into what is now regarded as the modern blues harp style and sound. So definitive are its markings, so powerful its effect, that almost one half a century later, it has changed hardly at all. Perhaps there is no reason for it to change. Of the many fine harp players practicing today it would be difficult to find many who did not get the basis of their style from players who were fully mature in the '50s.

Snooky Pryor, born in Lambert, MS, moved permanently to Chicago in 1945, and was one of the first of these pioneers to record the new postwar Chicago sound. At his best, he is magnificent, displaying a perfect balance of chordal and melodic style. Using a tenor-range sound, he is capable of contrasting a beautifully smooth tone with a rough-edged complement. From a stylistic/historical point of view, one hears in his work the infuence of all the major players of the day. He was greatly influenced by his favorite player Rice Miller (Sonny Boy Williamson [II]) whom he heard on KFFA radio, as well as by the original Sonny Boy, John Lee Williamson, with whom he sat in regularly. An astonishing track, "Boogie," reveals the note-for-note opening motif of "Juke," the masterpiece recorded by Little Walter in 1952. We will perhaps never know who first developed this classic line, or if, in fact, it was a cliché used by many harp players at the time. Snooky is in great form at the time of this writing—still playing in the style he helped create in the late '40s.

"I had admired the original Sonny Boy, Rice Miller, Big Walter...but when I met Little Walter, then it was an entirely different thing to me. Walter was the best—to me—that I had heard. The different things that he could do on the harmonica was an entirely different thing from what everyone else was doing. John Lee had the blues-type thing—Walter had the blues, but he had that uptempo stuff also...it was the execution that he was getting out of the harmonica." This Junior Wells quotation echoes that of Louis Myers, Walter's guitar player of many years: "All of them cats come along and try to play after John Lee died—but Little Walter was more important than all those cats. He was the best after John Lee....was none of them as good as Walter...and none of them that have come after [are as good]. He was the best in Chicago...the baddest." Lester Davenport, a veteran harp player on the Chicago scene since 1944 who recorded with Bo Diddley, says: "I would say that Little Walter was the greatest and most influential that ever played."

Marion "Little Walter" Jacobs was born in Louisiana in 1930. At 12 he was working the small clubs and streets of New Orleans, at 14 he played on the second Sonny Boy Williamson's *King of Biscuit Time* on KFFA, at 15 he was in East St. Louis, IL, and St. Louis, MO—and, at 16 he was in Chicago on Maxwell Street. In 1947 he recorded for Ora-Nelle records and a year later was with Muddy Waters. During the next few years he toured and recorded with the Muddy Waters band and frequently recorded as a sideman with others. His breakthrough occurred with "Juke," recorded for the Checker label in 1952. As soon as he realized that he had a hit, he left Waters' band to pursue a solo career, backed by the Aces, a band that was at the time fronted by Junior Wells. The band consisted of Louis Myers on guitar, his brother Dave Myers on bass, and Fred Below on drums—arguably the finest band that ever played. Walter's reputation grew throughout the country as well as England and Europe. He was recognized by some of the superstar rock groups of the '60s and recorded as late as 1968, the year he died a violent death.

Little Walter is considered by many peers, harp-playing disciples, blues scholars, and serious fans to be the greatest blues harp player who ever lived. A great musician, songwriter, harmonica player, bandleader—a genius. And, as many productive geniuses, his influences were many and varied. David "Honeyboy" Edwards recalls Walter speaking of the profound effect on him by the musicians he heard in Louisiana as a child. Walter's third-position work, in fact, sounds sometimes like a Cajun concertina. Big Walter spoke of how he taught Walter in Memphis (Edwards introduced them in the '40s). Louis Myers remembers Walter hanging around John Lee Williamson—and how the older player took him under his wing. "John Lee liked Walter because he was young. He was a kid trying to learn," recalls Myers (who remembers this well because Robert Myers, Louis' brother, was playing gigs with John Lee Williamson at this time). On the other hand, Mike Rowe, in his *Chicago Blues: The City and the Music*, tells of Walter playing "all kinds of music" (probably waltzes, pop tunes, and polkas) "until he came under the influence of Big Bill Broonzy and Tampa Red." In addition, Willie Cobbs, Honeyboy Edwards and Junior Wells all relate stories of Walter learning licks from the jazz horn players of the day—especially Louis Jordan and Bull Moose Jackson. Given the broad range of his style and the marked originality of his concept, it is entirely believable that Walter absorbed all of these influences—that he was learning from everything musical that appealed to him—and that he was capable of assimilating all of this into an original style.

In considering Walter's style, one must admire how masterfully he was able to use every existing technique of blues harp-playing, and how easily he was able to shape each of them to his own expressive purpose. He used a rainbow of tone color and sometimes exploited that one facet for a solo ("Mean Old World"). His chordal work is fascinating, especially during his beautiful excursions into the dark choral regions of the chromatic harp or 12-hole diatonic, particulary in third position. ("Lights Out"). His "bent" tones are extremely effective, because he was capable both of controlled glissandi (slidings) at any speed ("Blue Midnight") or of merely jumping to the bent tone with perfect intonation at any point in the phrase. His trills, bent or natural, were executed at varying speeds; his numerous types of vibrato, his shifts of tone color, his Monk-ish gift for playing slightly off the beat (the introduction to "I Don't Play"), his jazz-oriented phrasing and overall concept (even Sonny Rollins would have been proud of inserting "A Tisket A Tasket" and then sequencing it in the very next phrase as Walter did in "Crazy Legs")—all of these techniques would have amounted to merely great virtuosity in the hands of a lesser artists. In addition, as a composer and soloist, perhaps Walter's greatest gift was his ability to perfectly balance his lines. He was always the master architect—creating original designs of consummate symmetry.

Walter was equally as creative and virtuosic in a supportive role, never disturbing the solo lines or integrity of the tune. Of the many songs he recorded as a sideman in the Muddy Waters band, "Forty Days and Forty Nights" and "I'm Ready" serve as fine examples of Walter's extraordinary talent in this capacity. In addition to making great tunes even greater, he was also able to make very ordinary ones such as Muddy's "Young Fashioned Ways" positively jump out of their grooves with his use of cross-rhythms and jazzy off-the-beat accents. Clearly, he was not challenged by Muddy's material then, and in fact, was not touring with him at the time—only recording with him at Chess' request.

Among Walter's many contributions to blues music in general, and to harmonica playing specifically, one must acknowledge as paramount his elevating the amplified harp style to state-of-the-art status. One hears the gradual development in style from the acoustic work in "Louisiana Blues" to the modern amplified masterpiece, "Juke." There are various accounts of John Lee Williamson, Rice Miller, Snooky Pryor, Big Walter Horton, and Little Walter being the first to cup the harp against a microphone, thereby completely altering the timbral attack and over-all playing style. One might conclude that this technique was a natural and gradual result of trying to be heard over a rhythm section that grew bigger and louder from the late '40s on.

Like T-Bone Walker and Charlie Parker, Walter redefined for all time the role of his instrument and set standards of excellence that will perhaps never be surpassed.

While the blues was being revolutionized in the Northern cities, a complementary strain was being nurtured and developed by players who remained active in the South throughout the '40s and '50s. The central figure of this activity—Rice Miller, aka Sonny Boy Williamson [II]—was perhaps every bit as great and influential as Walter in his own way.

As enigmatic as any character in the blues pantheon, Rice Miller would not divulge his real name or date of birth, although Paul Oliver in his notes to the 1989 Arhoolie CD *King Biscuit Time* fixes his birthplace as Glendora, MS, and the year as either 1894 or 1899. (Research of government documents by *Living Blues* suggests that Sonny Boy Williamson was born in 1910. This information was also confirmed by Williamson's surviving relatives.)

Sonny Boy Williamson's musical achievement is sometimes overshadowed by the enormous humanity, sense of humor, and personality that pervades his work. One of the greatest blues lyricists who ever lived, he recorded relatively few instrumentals and gave equal time to both his highly expressive vocals and his harp blowing, using both of these talents to underscore the humor, irony, and pathos that infuse his musical poems.

It is important to note that Sonny Boy Williamson was a born entertainer, and that his style was honed for the live, improvisational playing of the juke joints and, starting regulary in 1941, the live radio broadcasts from KFFA in Helena, AR. He was 40 years old when he made his first records for the Trumpet label in Jackson, MS. Although there are some gems such as "Mighty Long Time," some of these early recordings are perhaps too loose to qualify as classics. When he began recording with Chess in Chicago, the change in both producers and sidemen helped to tighten the arrangements and make the tunes more memorable. Talents such as Robert Jr. Lockwood, Otis Spann, Lafayette Leake, and Fred Below helped Williamson turn out lasting works—Chicago classics such as "Help Me," "Trust My Baby," "Nine Below Zero," "Cross My Heart," and many others.

Although he may have lifted the basics of his style from his namesake at some time or another, Rice Miller represents a wholly original style that is the modern epitome of the "down-home blues." He lacks none of the technique that other more "modern" players had. His use of vibrato, sustained tones, trills, glissandi, and varying timbral shades, his sense of symmetry, and his impeccable timing were uniquely developed for his personal, expressive needs. If Walter was abstract perfection, Sonny Boy Williamson was pure natural exuberance.

Rice Miller had many admirers who were greatly influenced by his style. In addition, though, he had a few who were his actual pupils, learning techniques directly from him. Among the first and most famous of these was Chester Burnett known as the Howlin' Wolf. Williamson and Wolf teamed up and toured the jukes of Tennessee, Arkansas, and Mississippi. Wolf was in no way the virtuosic harp-blower that his teacher was, although he was truly a great bluesman. His playing—expressive and dynamic—was used to create fills and solos around his imposing vocals, and add even more punch and character to his now-classic original tunes.

While Little Walter was in Chicago presiding over the new urban developments and Sonny Boy Williamson was in Arkansas bringing the rural style in to the '50s, there was a very important group of players ruling by committee in Memphis, TN. Once again, this city was to serve as a focal point for the development of the blues in general and of the harp in specific. Howlin' Wolf, both Walters, both Sonny Boys, Jed Davenport, Jaybird Coleman, Sammy Lewis, Junior Parker, James Cotton—all of this talent was in and around Memphis at some time during the late '40s and early '50s. Appearing on radio, in clubs, and on the streets and parks, some of these players were to begin their recording career there under the direction of Sam Phillips. Two very influential players who seemed to be always on the move between Chicago, Memphis, and points south were Big Walter Horton and Forrest City Joe Pugh.

"Big Walter was always in and out—a hard person to keep up with... always on the move," relates Junior Wells. Walter Horton was associated with almost all of the great blues scenes since he reputedly recorded as a child with the Memphis Jug Band in 1927. He claimed to have toured with the Ma Rainey Show in Indiana as well as with various bands in the South before settling for a brief time in Memphis in 1935. In 1940 he was on Chicago's Maxwell Street, and seemed to move between there and Memphis off and on from the '40s to the '60s, playing and recording with many of the great bluesmen of the day, including Muddy Waters, Jimmy Rogers, Robert Nighthawk, Howlin' Wolf, and Johnny Shines.

Although he never achieved much fame or fortune for his work, certain masterpieces such as "Easy," "Little Walter's Boogie," "Cotton Patch Hotfoot," and "Walkin' By Myself" (recorded as sideman with the Jimmy Rogers band) assure him a place among the very best players in history.

Sometimes called Mr. Tone, Big Walter played with as rich and deep a color as anyone. He also used various types and speeds of vibrato, trills, and glissandi that he employed with great imagination and flair. His playing bears the shades of Hammie Nixon, Will Shade, and even Jed Davenport; yet he delivers his sculptured lines with such swing that one finds believable his claim to have taught Little Walter.

If Walter Horton's output is uneven in quality it is because his career was interrupted by various bouts with sickness. In addition, he seemed to be teamed often with incompetent or unprepared sidemen and producers who ruined more than just a few of his best efforts. Big Walter who represents a middle ground between the downhome and uptempo styles, was an exceptionally gifted and personal player, who had an enormous influence on postwar blues harp style.

The enigmatic Forrest City Joe Pugh seems to have been a man of many parts. From his recordings, he seems little more than an expert imitator of John Lee Williamson yet, Junior Wells remembers that he had a far deeper tone than the first Sonny Boy: "I thought Forrest City Joe was great—but he didn't make it. I admired everything he did because he had such a deep, deep tone. He had a really, really deep tone... and notin' and shakin' the harp." James Cotton used to hear Forrest City play piano while playing harp on a rack, and added that "Forrest City was a boogie-woogie man. First time Big Walter ever heard boogie on the harp was from Forrest City Joe. He was his own man... independent. He had his own style and he infuenced me quite a bit. During the late '40s and early '50s, I used to love to hear him play—he used to tell us about Chicago 'cause he'd been there and back. He was very, very good." Lester Davenport says: "He was great... I'd put him in the same category as Big Walter. He did a lot of things with the harmonica that other players didn't do. I only remember hearing him outside, playing by himself on the street—never in a club." It is very unfortunate that Joe Pugh died at age 34.

Jimmy Reed began his harp-playing career in the early '50s, recording as a sideman with John Brim, John Lee Hooker, and Eddie Taylor. Often these early recordings showcase his cross-harp style; however, he became a superstar due to his high-end playing in first position over the lay-back shuffle rhythms and fine second guitar work provided by his childhood friend and longtime partner, Eddie Taylor.

Although many of his harp-blowing peers in Chicago did not recognize him as a major talent at first, he was an enormous influence in Louisiana, where he affected the work of an entire school of young players such as Silas Hogan, Lazy Lester, Louisiana Red, and the future star Slim Harpo. Reed continued to tour until his death in 1976.

Two brilliant musicians, James Cotton and Junior Wells, were born within a year of each other, and their careers intertwined for more than 50 years prior to Wells' death in 1998. Originally extremely derivative, their styles evolved and became highly personal.

Cotton began imitating trains on the harmonica at age six. Three years later he ran away from home to learn from Rice Miller whom he heard on KFFA radio. A few years later he had taken over Williamson's band when the older master had gone to Jackson, MS, to record. Cotton recorded with Howlin' Wolf in 1952, and two years later recorded the classic Cotton Crop Blues for Sun Records in Memphis. When he joined Muddy Waters' band after 1955, he was forced to play in a more urban style in order to fill the shoes of Walter, Junior, and George Smith—all of whom had preceded him. Since then he has toured and recorded with his own groups, being one of the few authentic bluesmen still working full-time and one of the greatest harp players alive.

Junior Wells was influenced by all the major players of the day and, in fact, recorded tributes to Rice Miller and Little Walter. His debt to John Lee Williamson is obvious in his recording of a number of the original Sonny Boy tunes, including "Hoodoo Man Blues" and "Cut That Out."

However, Wells was mostly influenced by Little Walter's "uptempo" sound, and remembered being taken to meet him one day in the late '40s when Walter and Waters were playing the Ebony Lounge. Walter let Junior sit in and use his microphone and amplifier. Afterwards, Walter asked him if he played the saxophone. Junior said "Nah" and Walter said "Good, you'll be alright—you got the same ideas about doin' things that I have." About five years later, Wells was to replace Walter in Muddy Waters' band, before going out on his own. Wells' country feel was tempered a great deal by the swing style pioneered by Walter, leaving him with a very dynamic and individual approach to the instrument. Wells' 1998 death leaves Cotton probably the greatest authentic player still alive and working.

Sources:

February, 1991: quotations from James Cotton, Lester Davenport, Honeyboy Edwards, Louis Myers, and Junior Wells taken from personal interviews with the author.

T.M.W. Dixon and J. Godrich, *Blues and Gospel Records 1902-1943*

David Evans, notes to *Tappin' That Thing, High Water* LP1003

Sheldon Harris, *Blues Who's Who*

Mike Leadbitter and Neil Slaven, *Blues Records 1943 to 179, Vol. 1*

Michael Licht, "Harmonica Magic: Virtuoso Display in American Folk Music," *Ethnomusicology, Vol. XXIV, No. 2*, May 1980

Paul Oliver, *The Story of the Blues*

Bengt Olsson, *Memphis Blues*

"The Grand Ole Opry's DeFord Bailey," *Living Blues*, May-June 1975, No. 21

Mike Rowe, Chicago Blues: *The City and the Music.*

—Larry Hoffmann

The History of Gospel Music

Gospel praise singing—a combination of joyous spontaneity and earnest supplication—has been around since the dawn of Christianity; although prevalent through the Old World for centuries, it did not take root in the United States until some time in the 19th century, although small numbers of slaves and slaveholders worshiped together as far back as 1734. The first published New England collection of hymns were those of Isaac Watts in 1907's *Hymns and Spiritual Songs*. Philip Bliss' publication *Gospel Songs* appeared in 1876 during a period of intense Christian revival: While pulpit-bashing sermons were being preached all over urban North America, Pentecostal black communities of the "Holiness" and "Sanctified" movements multiplied.

The black ghettos nurtured small independent churches like the Atlanta Highway sect and Chicago's Widow's Mite Holiness Church, where African-Americans found the freedom to enjoy long-established traditions of improvisation in sermon, prayer, music, and holiness dance. The continual dialogue and "lining-out" between pastor and flock were formalized in musical patterns of call-and-response. Surviving descriptions and line drawings give a glimpse of the worship at that time, but the informality of this oral form produced no written music, and no concerts were given for fear of change and dilution.

In the early 1870s, George L. White and pianist Ella Sheppard formed the original Fisk Jubilee Singers at Fisk University in Nashville. The basic premise was to demonstrate the potential usefulness of black religious singing in conditions of newfound, post-emancipation freedom, elevating the material from folk-liturgy to popular music. The Fisk Singers toured to raise funds for the university, and within a year similar aggregations or choirs had sprung up all over the country. Tours of the U.S. and Europe captured the imaginations of largely Caucasian audiences, and spirituals were written, the best collection of which was gathered by James Weldon and J. Rosamond Johnson and first published by Viking in 1925 as *American Negro Spirituals.*

Spirituals have inspired musicians the world over and have been re-absorbed time and again by African-American gospel singers. They were at first adapted from plantation songs, but gradually became formalized, with lyrical arrangement the norm. The music evolved into the expression of the community, a celebration of life in the context of a theology with a strong social and political dimension. As the Azusa Street Revival and the

Birth of Pentecostalism came about in California at the turn of the 20th century, nightly revival meetings were held to save sinners—choirs were hired, "altar calls" were enacted, "mourners' benches" were provided, and African-Americans became saved, sanctified, and filled with the Holy Ghost. Not only was "speaking in tongues" encouraged, but inter-racial membership was deemed necessary, and the music produced by the revival reflected African-American religious concerns and heightened sensibilities.

A second attempt to secularize gospel music by taking it out of a church-worship situation and placing it in the modern mainstream came about in the '20s. The main proponent was Thomas A. Dorsey, the son of an itinerant black Georgian preacher. In spite of a church upbringing and a blues singing career billed as "Georgia Tom," Dorsey reaffirmed his beliefs in Christian music through both personal tragedy and his love for the recorded works of the Rev. A.W. Nix, an extrovert singer and preacher. Dorsey took the simple blues format and adapted it for use in the church (the reverse of what later evolved into popular rhythm & blues music during the '50s; he wrote, published, performed, and encouraged an art form that later became known as "gospel music."

Dorsey capitalized on his earlier commercial experience and became the first gospel artist to market to a vast audience. He founded his own publishing company, printed great numbers of his own gospel songbooks, charged admission to religious concerts, and formed in the early '30s the first major female gospel quartet, the Roberta Martin Singers. He also discovered and promoted a new generation of singers, including Mahalia Jackson (who during the Great Depression traveled with one of the first important gospel quartets, Prince Johnson and the Johnson Singers). After initial misgivings, churches absorbed this new gospel music and found a place for it along with the older, traditional forms of worship. The preacher usually opened the service with a sermon, followed by gospel singing.

Of the seminal professional gospel quartets that had sprung up between the two World Wars, the Golden Gate Quartet is perhaps the best remembered and certainly the most revered and imitated. The Gates started out as a barbershop quartet in Berkeley, VA, in 1930, their repertoire including adaptations from Negro spirituals. Buddies A. C. "Eddie" Griffin (tenor) and Robert "Peg" Ford (bass), along with two high-school students from Norfolk, Willie Johnson (baritone) and Henry Owens (tenor), formed the original group, and the outfit grew so popular that out-of-town engagements multiplied. As both Griffin and Ford had local commitments, singers free of travel restrictions had to be found as replacements, so in 1935-1936, 16-year-old basso Orlandus Wilson and tenor/guitarist William (Bill) "Highpockets" Langford (Landford) stepped in.

With the growth of sell-out live appearances, the Golden Gate Quartet soon found itself a regular weekly radio show singing jubilee over WBT in Charlotte, NC. By 1937, the boys were being syndicated over NCB airwaves through local affiliates. The group signed with Victor that same year, and sessions were conducted from the Charlotte Hotel. With both records and nationwide radio exposure, the Gates made legions of fans and inspired many a quartet to come up after them. Only the Fairfield Four on WLAC in Nashville were able to exert as much influence, but that was five years down the line.

Jubilee singing by 1952 was fast becoming a thing of the past, but the Trumpeteers stuck to their winning formula of close rhythmic harmony, special vocal effects and infectious repetition. The presence of a booming basso, call and response, and alternating pitch take us into a more climactic form of quartet. Hard gospel was now replacing the lighter crooning style of the previous decades with an altogether more extravagant delivery, especially from lead and swing lead voices. Theatrical elements like knee drops, thigh slaps, and screaming falsetto ornamentation came to the fore. Quartets such as the Sensational Nightingales, Dixie Hummingbirds, Soul Stirrers, and Harmonizing Four arose to glory.

The beginnings of a real crossover came in the mid-'50s when solo artists like Ray Charles, James Brown, and Nappy Brown began to epitomize gospel with a secular, sometimes erotic lyric. Both James and Nappy Brown had begun their careers in gospel quartets. This was also true of many secular vocal groups. The Royal Sons Quartet became the "5" Royales and the Delta Southernaires became the Spiders, to mention just a few. Many black solo artists, in particular those who waxed for major independent labels like Atlantic, Chess, and later Motown, came from gospel backgrounds.

The '60s saw the growth of a soul-based, high singing gospel quartet movement with proponents like the Violinaires, Gospelaires, and Mighty Clouds, whose secular counterparts could be found in the Falcons, Impressions, and Incredibles. Since then, the paths of religious and secular black music have become more closely woven together, with gospel itself now drawing most of its input from commercial trends. The '70s saw the growth of choirs, and choirs into mass choirs, whose voices today seem to almost drown out the few remaining professional soldiers still scraping a living on the quartet circuit.

—Opal Louis Nations

Music Map

Gospel

Roots

Gospel praise singing's beginnings coincided with the dawn of Christianity,
and it was prevalent throughout the Old World in the centuries to follow.

• 1734: Slaves and slaveholders in the U.S. worshiped together for the first time.
• 19th century: Gospel took root in the U.S. First adapted from plantation songs, hymns gradually became
formalized, with lyrical arrangement the norm. The music evolved into the expression of the community,
a celebration of life in the context of a theology with a strong social and political dimension.
• 1876: Philip Bliss' *Gospel Songs* was published during a period of intense Christian revival.
• 1907: Isaac Watts' *Hymns and Spiritual Songs* was published.

Fisk Jubilee Singers

Founded in early 1870s in Nashville, the Fisk Jubilee Singers were created to demonstrate the
importance of black religious singing in the wake of the Emancipation Proclamation, and
in the process, elevated the material from folk-liturgy to popular music. The group's tours proved
profoundly influential–within a year similar choirs had sprung up across the U.S., their
live performances captured the imagination of white audiences, and spirituals were written.

Rev. Thomas A. Dorsey

The key figure behind the push to secularize gospel by pushing it out of the context of worship services
and into the contemporary mainstream of the '20s, Dorsey took the simple blues refrain and
adapted it for use in church; he wrote, published, performed, and encouraged an art form that
later became known as "gospel music." The first gospel artist to market to a vast audience, he founded
his own publishing company, printed his own gospel songbooks, charged admission to religious concerts,
and in the early '30s formed the first major female gospel quartet, the Roberta Martin Singers.
He also discovered and promoted a new generation of singers, including Mahalia Jackson.

The Rise of the Quartet Style

In the era between the two World Wars, the quartet style became gospel's predominant means of musical expression. Of the period's seminal professional quartets, the Golden Gate Quartet is perhaps the best remembered and certainly the most revered and imitated–with both
records and nationwide radio exposure, they made legions of fans across the country, and inspired many a quartet to come up after them.
Other key acts:
The Fairfield Four • The Soul Stirrers • The Dixie Hummingbirds • The Sensational Nightingales • The Harmonizing Four

Hard Gospel

By 1952, the jubilee sound of years past was quickly vanishing,
as the crooning style of previous decades gave way to hard
gospel, typified by the presence of a booming basso, call and
response, and alternating pitch. In addition to an altogether
more extravagant delivery, especially from lead and swing
lead voices, theatrical elements like knee drops, thigh slaps,
and screaming falsetto ornamentation came to the fore.

Crossover

During the mid-'50s, solo pop artists like James Brown
began infusing gospel with secular, sometimes erotic lyrics.
Many other solo performers and groups originating in
gospel found great success as pop acts–for example,
the Royal Sons Quartet became the "5" Royales,
and the Delta Southernaires became the Spiders.

The Modern Era

The '60s saw the growth of a soul-based, high-singing gospel quartet movement with proponents like the
Violinaires, the Gospelaires, and the Mighty Clouds of Joy, whose secular counterparts could be found in
the Falcons and the Impressions. Since then, the paths of religious and secular black music became
more closely woven together, with gospel itself now drawing most of its input from commercial
trends. The '70s saw the growth of choirs, and eventually choirs into mass choirs.

Index

More *ALL MUSIC GUIDES* from BACKBEAT BOOKS

All Music Guide
Fourth Edition

"The most useful single volume your money can buy." *–Mojo*

From rock to rap, country to reggae, avant-garde jazz to folk—and all the sounds in between—this is the definitive record guide, offering expert advice for every style of music. With over 20,000 album reviews, 4,000 artist biographies, educational essays, and "music maps", this is the one essential guide for music lovers.
Softcover, 1,491 pages, 8 charts, ISBN 0-87930-627-0, $34.95

All Music Guide to Jazz
Fourth Edition

"An indispensable resource for any jazz record collector." –Los Angeles Times

This entertaining, easy-to-use reference reviews and rates more than 20,000 top recordings by over 1,700 musicians in all jazz styles and eras—from New Orleans jazz to swing, bebop, cool, hard bop, Latin jazz, fusion, and beyond. Fully updated to cover the latest new releases, plus notable reissues and compilations.
Softcover, 1488 pages, 52 charts, ISBN 0-87930-717-X, $32.95

All Music Guide to Rock
Third Edition

"Best rock guide of the year." *– The Seattle Times*

Get the ultimate guide to the artists and recordings that really rock. Reflecting the ever-evolving world of rock, pop, and soul, this book reviews 12,000 albums by 2,000 performers—everything from rockabilly to British Invasion, Motown, folk-rock, psychedelic rock, funk, punk, R&B, hip-hop, and more.
Softcover, 1,399 pages, 29 charts, ISBN 0-87930-653-X, $29.95

All Music Guide to Country

"A definite must for any serious music collector." *–Country Song Roundup*

This is the comprehensive guide to the entire spectrum of country music—from the Grand Ole Opry to the sounds of today's Nashville superstars. Designed for devoted fans and newcomers alike, this book covers 5,500 cream-of-the-crop recordings by 1,000 top country artists.
Softcover, 611 pages, 14 charts, ISBN 0-87930-475-8, $22.95

All Music Guide to Electronica

"Has a true sense of what electronica really is . . . an informative format with zero elitist, you-should-know-by-now attitude." *–Rolling Stone*

Discover the most electrifying recordings with the irresistible rhythm of house, the engulfing pulse of techno, and the lush twirl of trance, and more. You get 5,000 album reviews, 1,200 artist bios, historical essays and "music maps," online resources, and more.
Softcover, 688 pages, 12 charts, ISBN 0-87930-628-9, $24.95

AVAILABLE AT FINE BOOK AND MUSIC STORES EVERYWHERE, OR CONTACT:

Backbeat Books • 6600 Silacci Way • Gilroy, CA 95020 USA • **Phone Toll Free: (866) 222-5232**
Fax: (408) 848-5784 • E-mail: backbeat@rushorder.com • Web: www.backbeatbooks.com